Holt McDougal Algebra 1 Features [illegible]uicklist

	SEE PAGE(S)
PROVEN INSTRUCTIONAL DESIGN	
• Consistent lesson format of **Example, Solution, Check It Out** provides a logical instructional approach.	77–78
• Step-by-step examples and color-coded explanations help students become independent learners.	92–95
• Know-it Notes indicate key concepts for students to remember and correspond to entries in the students' **Know-it Notebook**.	86
• Exercises matched to examples mean no homework surprises!	96
COMPREHENSIVE DIFFERENTIATED INSTRUCTION	
• Reaching All Learners includes strategies for adapting the material for all types of learners.	TE 121
• English Language Learners identifies strategies particularly effective with this group of students.	TE 85
• Algebra Labs allow students to explore math concepts through manipulatives.	150–151
• Technology Labs assist students in the use of graphing calculators, spreadsheets, and dynamic geometry software.	91
• Reteach, Practice, Challenge, Reading Strategies, and Problem Solving reduced images make selecting worksheets quick and easy.	TE 88–89
• Teaching Tips provide suggestions for addressing various learning styles.	TE 101
• Additional Examples offer more classroom review for struggling students.	TE 134
• Assignment Guide recommends homework assignments based on student ability.	TE 123
• Power Presentations are editable PowerPoint® presentations for every lesson as well as extra examples and quizzes.	TE 126
BUILT-IN ASSESSMENT AND INTERVENTION	
• Are You Ready? at the beginning of each chapter assesses students' prerequisite skills.	73
• Ready to Go On? diagnoses students' skill development within the chapter.	119
• Check It Out and Try This questions enable students to check their understanding after every example and activity.	120, 150
• Questioning Strategies aid on-the-spot intervention with questions crafted to assess student comprehension.	TE 121
• Common Error Alert helps teachers anticipate potential pitfalls for students.	TE 145
• Alternative Assessment provides options to monitor student progress.	TE 126
• Chapter Test assesses students' mastery of concepts and skills.	158

READING AND WRITING MATH FOR [illegible]	
• Reading and Writing Math helps students [illegible] communication skills as they master math conc[illegible].	
• Reading Connection recommends math-themed literature that ties into chapter content.	TE 75
• Reading Math and Writing Math hints appear throughout each chapter to help students use the language of math.	77, 102
• Write About It exercises require students to explain a math concept or procedure.	105
• Journal suggestions encourage students to write about math.	TE 90
• Think and Discuss questions in every lesson extend and enrich student knowledge.	135
• Graphic Organizers in every lesson help students organize and remember key information.	141
• Glossary contains definitions and illustrations of key mathematical terms in English and Spanish.	G1–G42
ENGAGING CONNECTIONS AND APPLICATIONS	
• Links spark student interest by giving them the opportunity to apply math skills to other disciplines and the real world.	81, 88, 105
• Connecting Algebra to Geometry provides review and application of previously learned geometry concepts.	83, 104
• Career Path relates math concepts to the real world.	106
• Real-World Connection uses real-world scenarios to develop higher-order thinking.	164–165
INTEGRATED TEST PREP	
• Countdown to Testing prepares students for state tests with daily practice questions.	T4–T27
• Test Prep exercises provide daily practice in standardized test format.	126
• Test Prep Doctor addresses specific test-taking strategies related to the lesson.	TE 143
• Multi-Step Test Prep uses real-world scenarios to develop higher order thinking skills.	125, 148
• Test Tackler targets specific test-taking strategies to help students become savvy test-takers.	160–161
• College Entrance Exam Practice provides practice for college entrance exams such as the SAT and ACT.	159
• Standardized Test Prep provides cumulative assessment in standardized test format.	162–163
STUDENT SUPPORT	
• Study Guide: Preview prepares students for concepts in the chapter and connects the concepts to the real world.	74
• Student to Student shares advice from other students on how to approach the math in the lesson.	78
• Homework Help Online provides stepped-out solutions and additional practice for students as they work independently. (go.hrw.com Homework Help Online KEYWORD: MA7 2-5)	109
• Study Guide: Review highlights lesson vocabulary and key skills and offers additional examples and practice exercises.	154–157

TEACHER'S EDITION

Algebra 1

Edward B. Burger
David J. Chard
Paul A. Kennedy
Steven J. Leinwand
Freddie L. Renfro
Tom W. Roby
Bert K. Waits

HOLT McDOUGAL

 HOUGHTON MIFFLIN HARCOURT

Algebra 1 Contents in Brief

Printed in the United States of America

ISBN-13 978-0-030-99577-4

ISBN-10 0-030-99577-9

2 3 4 5 6 7 8 9 10 0868 18 17 16 15 14 13 12 11 10 4500262633

Cover photo: © James L. Amos/Corbis

ALGEBRA 1 TEACHER'S EDITION

Contents in Brief

Chapter Teacher Material

Student Handbook

REVIEWERS

John Bakelaar
Assistant Principal
Whitten Middle School
Jackson, MS

Jennifer Bauer
Mathematics Instructional Leader
East Haven High School
East Haven, CT

Doug Becker
Mathematics Teacher
Gaylord High School
Gaylord, MI

Joe Brady
Mathematics Department Chair
Ensworth High School
Nashville, TN

Sharon Butler
Adjunct Faculty
Montgomery College of The Woodlands
Spring, TX

Kathy Dean Davis
Mathematics Department Chair, retired
Bowling Green Junior High
Bowling Green, KY

Maureen "Willie" DiLaura
Middle School Math Specialist, retired
Lockerman Middle School
Denton, MD

Arlane Frederick
Curriculum & Learning Specialist in Mathematics, retired
Kenmore-Town of Tonawanda UFSD
Buffalo, NY

Marieta W. Harris
Mathematics Specialist
Memphis, TN

Connie Johnsen
Mathematics Teacher
Harker Heights High School
Harker Heights, TX

Mary Jones
Mathematics Supervisor/Teacher
Grand Rapids Public Schools
Grand Rapids, MI

Lendy Jones
Algebra Teacher
Liberty Hill Middle School
Killeen, TX

Mary Joy
Algebra Teacher
Mayfield High School
Las Cruces, NM

Vilma Martinez
Algebra Teacher
Nikki Rowe High School
McAllen, TX

Mende Mays
Algebra Teacher
Crockett Junior High
Odessa, TX

Rebecca Newburn
Lead Math Teacher
Davidson Middle School
San Rafael, CA

Vicki Petty
Mathematics Teacher
Central Middle School
Murfreesboro, TN

Susan Pippen
Mathematics Department Chair
Hinsdale South High School
Darien, IL

Elaine Rafferty
Mathematics Learning Specialist
Charleston County SD
Charleston, SC

Susan Rash
Manager of Secondary Curriculum
Red Clay CSD
Wilmington, DE

John Remensky
Mathematics Department Chair
South Park High School
South Park, PA

Raymond Seymour
Mathematics Department Head, retired
Kirby Middle School
San Antonio, TX

Jennifer J. Southers
Mathematics Teacher
Hillcrest High School
Simpsonville, SC

Jill Springer
Mathematics Teacher
Henderson County High School
Henderson, KY

Dr. Katherine Staltare
Mathematics Consultant & Graduate Level Course Developer
NYSUT, Effective Teaching Program
New York State

Pam Walker
Curriculum Teacher Specialist
Nacogdoches ISD
Nacogdoches, TX

Larry Ward
Mathematics Supervisor, retired
Carrollton-Farmers Branch ISD
Carrollton, TX

Carmen Whitman
Director, Mathematics for All Consulting
Pflugerville, TX

Contributing Authors

Carmen Whitman
Pflugerville, TX

Linda Antinone
Fort Worth, TX

Field Test Participants

Len Zigment
Mesa Ridge High School
Colorado Springs, CO

Vicky Petty
Central Middle School
Murfreesboro, TN

John Bakelaar
Peebles Middle School
Jackson, MS

Carey Carter
Alvarado High School
Alvarado, TX

Preparing for Standardized Tests

Holt McDougal Algebra 1 provides many opportunities for you to prepare for standardized tests.

Test Prep Exercises

Use the Test Prep Exercises for daily practice of standardized test questions in various formats.

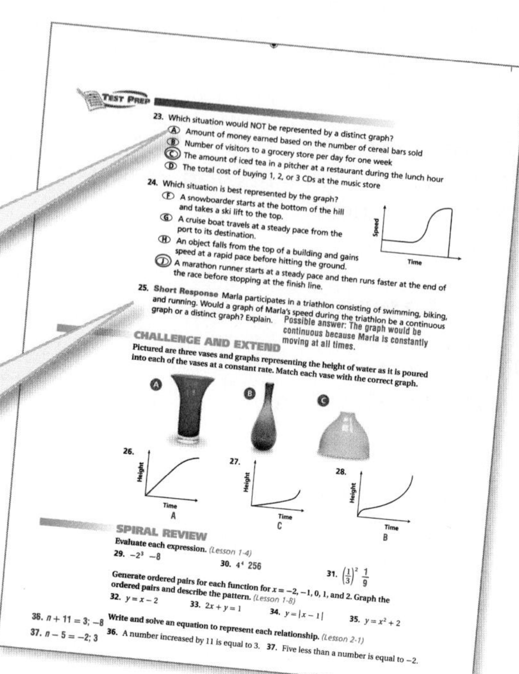

TEST PREP

23. Which situation would NOT be represented by a distinct graph?
    - (A) Amount of money earned based on the number of cereal bars sold
    - (B) Number of visitors to a grocery store per day for one week
    - (C) The amount of iced tea in a pitcher at a restaurant during the lunch hour
    - (D) The total cost of buying 1, 2, or 3 CDs at the music store
24. Which situation is best represented by the graph?
    - (F) A snowboarder starts at the bottom of the hill and takes a ski lift to the top.
    - (G) A cruise boat travels at a steady pace from the port to its destination.
    - (H) An object falls from the top of a building and gains speed at a rapid pace before hitting the ground.
    - (J) A marathon runner starts at a steady pace and then runs faster at the end of the race before stopping at the finish line.
25. **Short Response** Maria participates in a triathlon consisting of swimming, biking, and running. Would a graph of Maria's speed during the triathlon be a continuous graph or a distinct graph? Explain. Possible answer: The graph would be continuous because Maria is constantly moving at all times.

CHALLENGE AND EXTEND

Pictured are three vases and graphs representing the height of water as it is poured into each of the vases at a constant rate. Match each vase with the correct graph.

26. A
27. C
28. B

SPIRAL REVIEW

Evaluate each expression. *(Lesson 1-4)*

29. -2^3 -8
30. 4^4 256
31. $\left(\frac{1}{3}\right)^2$ $\frac{1}{9}$

Generate ordered pairs for each function for $x = -2, -1, 0, 1,$ and 2. Graph the ordered pairs and describe the pattern. *(Lesson 1-8)*

32. $y = x - 2$
33. $2x + y = 1$
34. $y = |x - 1|$
35. $y = x^2 + 2$

Write and solve an equation to represent each relationship. *(Lesson 2-1)*

36. A number increased by 11 is equal to 3. $n + 11 = 3; -8$
37. Five less than a number is equal to -2. $n - 5 = -2; 3$

Multiple Choice—choose your answer.

Gridded Response—write your answer in a grid and fill in the corresponding bubbles.

Short Response—write open-ended responses that are scored with a 2-point rubric.

Extended Response—write open-ended responses that are scored with a 4-point rubric.

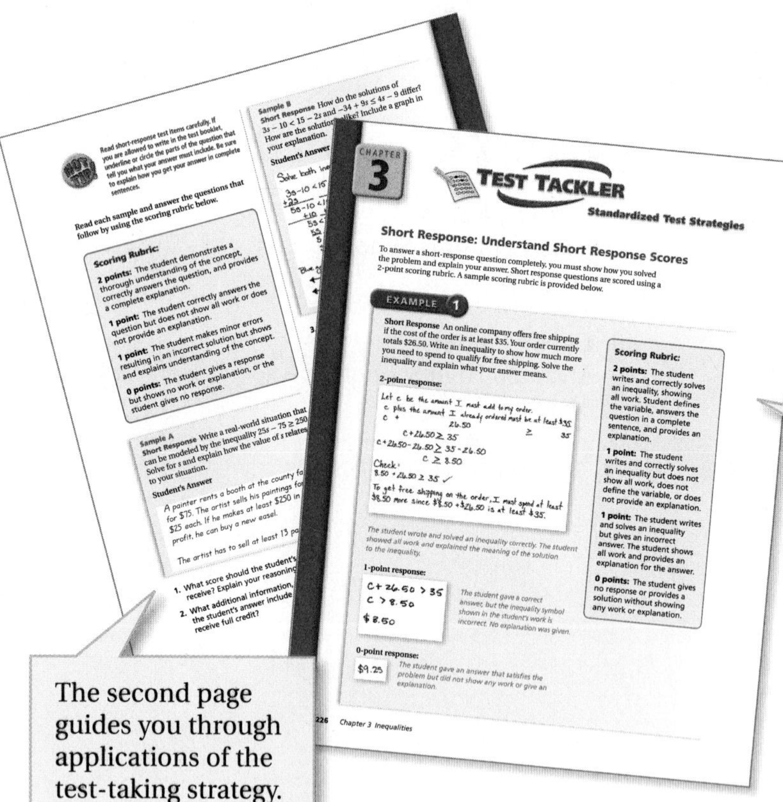

CHAPTER 3

TEST TACKLER

Standardized Test Strategies

Short Response: Understand Short Response Scores

To answer a short-response question completely, you must show how you solved the problem and explain your answer. Short response questions are scored using a 2-point scoring rubric. A sample scoring rubric is provided below.

EXAMPLE 1

Short Response An online company offers free shipping if the cost of the order is at least \$35. Your order currently totals \$26.50. Write an inequality to show how much more you need to spend to qualify for free shipping. Solve the inequality and explain what your answer means.

Scoring Rubric:

2 points: The student writes and correctly solves an inequality, showing all work. Student defines the variable, answers the question in a complete sentence, and provides an explanation.

1 point: The student writes and correctly solves an inequality but does not show all work, does not define the variable, or does not provide an explanation.

1 point: The student writes and solves an inequality but gives an incorrect answer. The student shows all work and provides an explanation for the answer.

0 points: The student gives no response or provides a solution without showing any work or explanation.

2-point response:

The student wrote and solved an inequality correctly. The student showed all work and explained the meaning of the solution to the inequality.

1-point response:

The student gave a correct answer, but the inequality symbol shown in the student's work is incorrect. No explanation was given.

0-point response:

The student gave an answer that satisfies the problem but did not show any work or give an explanation.

226 Chapter 3 Inequalities

Test Tackler

Use the Test Tackler to become familiar with and practice test-taking strategies.

The first page of this feature explains and shows an example of a test-taking strategy.

The second page guides you through applications of the test-taking strategy.

Standardized Test Prep

Use the Standardized Test Prep to apply test-taking strategies.

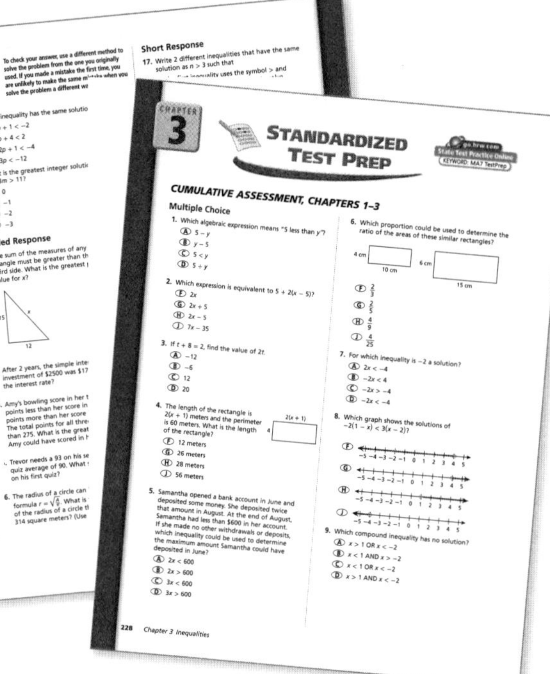

The Hot Tip provides test-taking tips to help you succeed on your tests.

These pages include practice with multiple choice, gridded response, short response, and extended response test items.

Countdown to Testing

Use the Countdown to Testing to practice for your state test every day.

There are 24 pages of practice for your state test. Each page is designed to be used in a week so that all practice will be completed before your state test is given.

Each week's page has five practice test items, one for each day of the week.

Test-Taking Tips

- Get plenty of sleep the night before the test. A rested mind thinks more clearly and you won't feel like falling asleep while taking the test.
- Draw a figure when one is not provided with the problem. If a figure is given, write any details from the problem on the figure.
- Read each problem carefully. As you finish each problem, read it again to make sure your answer is reasonable.
- Review the formula sheet that will be supplied with the test. Make sure you know when to use each formula.
- First answer problems that you know how to solve. If you do not know how to solve a problem, skip it and come back to it when you have finished the others.
- Use other test-taking strategies that can be found throughout this book, such as working backward and eliminating answer choices.

COUNTDOWN TO TESTING

Each problem on the *Countdown to Testing* is correlated to the 8th grade NAEP Assessment Standards and the 12th grade NAEP Assessment Standards. These correlations are shown at the bottom of each page.

WEEK 1

DAY 1

Which expression always represents an odd number when n is a natural number?

Ⓐ $n^2 + 1$
Ⓑ $2n + 1$ (circled)
Ⓒ n^2
Ⓓ $n + 1$

DAY 2

Cell phone bills are based on a flat monthly fee and the number of minutes used. In the equation $c = 0.07m + 29.99$, what does the variable m represent?

Ⓕ The number of months billed
Ⓖ The total amount of the bill
Ⓗ The number of minutes used (circled)
Ⓙ The phone number

DAY 3

Which equation best describes the relationship between the number of astudents and the number of tables in the cafeteria?

Students (n)	Tables (t)
720	18
600	15
960	24

Ⓐ $n = 40t$ (circled)   Ⓒ $t = 40n$
Ⓑ $n = 35t + 90$ Ⓓ $n = 45t - 90$

DAY 4

Which expression represents the verbal phrase "the sum of three times a number and five"?

Ⓕ $3(n + 5)$
Ⓖ $3 + n \cdot 5$
Ⓗ $3n + 5$ (circled)
Ⓙ $3 + (n + 5)$

DAY 5

What is the next term in the pattern?

$-3, 6, -12, 24, \_\_\_, \ldots$

Ⓐ 30
Ⓑ 36
Ⓒ −32
Ⓓ −48 (circled)

Day	NAEP Standards Grade 8	NAEP Standards Grade 12
1	Number Properties and Operations – Properties of number and operations: 8.1.5.a	Number Properties and Operations – Number Sense: 12.1.1.d
2	Algebra – Equations and inequalities: 8.5.4.c	Algebra – Equations and inequalities: 12.5.4.c
3	Algebra – Variables, expressions, and operations: 8.5.3.b	Algebra – Variables, expressions, and operations: 12.5.3.b
4	Algebra – Algebraic representations: 8.5.2.a	Algebra – Variables, expressions, and operations: 12.5.3.b
5	Algebra – Patterns, relations, and functions: 8.5.1.a	Algebra – Patterns, relations, and functions: 12.5.1.a

Countdown to Testing WEEK 2

DAY 1

What is the next term in the pattern?

$$-1, \frac{1}{2}, -\frac{1}{4}, \frac{1}{8}, \_\_\_, \ldots$$

(A) $-\frac{1}{16}$ (circled)

(B) $-\frac{1}{10}$

(C) $\frac{1}{10}$

(D) $\frac{1}{16}$

DAY 2

Which expression is equivalent to $2(3x - 4) - 8x + 3$?

(F) $2x + 11$

(G) $-2x - 5$ (circled)

(H) $2x - 5$

(J) $-2x - 11$

DAY 3

Based on the table, which inequality correctly shows the relationship between x and y?

x	2	3	5	6
y	−3	−8	−10	−9

(A) $x > -y$

(B) $2x < -y$

(C) $x < -y$ (circled)

(D) $2x > -y$

DAY 4

The sum of three consecutive even numbers is 42. The sum can be represented by the equation $n + (n + 2) + (n + 4) = 42$. What does n represent?

(F) The greatest number

(G) The average of the numbers

(H) The middle number

(J) The least number (circled)

DAY 5

A job advertisement states that the position pays $12 an hour. Which equation represents the relationship between the salary s and the number of hours h worked?

(A) $s = 12 + h$

(B) $s = 12h$ (circled)

(C) $h = 12s$

(D) $h = 12 + s$

Day	NAEP Standards Grade 8	NAEP Standards Grade 12
1	Algebra – Patterns, relations, and functions: 8.5.1.a	Algebra – Patterns, relations, and functions: 12.5.1.a
2	Algebra – Variables, expressions, and operations: 8.5.3.c	Algebra – Variables, expressions, and operations: 12.5.3.d
3	Algebra – Algebraic representations: 8.5.2.b	Algebra – Algebraic representations: 12.5.2.b
4	Algebra – Variables, expressions, and operations: 8.5.3.b	Algebra – Variables, expressions, and operations: 12.5.3.b
5	Algebra – Variables, expressions, and operations: 8.5.3.b	Algebra – Algebraic representations: 12.5.2.b

Countdown to Testing WEEK 3

DAY 1

Which expression is equivalent to 2^3?

(A) $2 \cdot 3$
(B) $3 + 3$
(C) $2 + 2 + 2$
(D) $2 \cdot 2 \cdot 2$

DAY 2

Which number is not a solution of $-7y + 19 < 75$?

(F) 13
(G) 0
(H) −2
(J) −8

DAY 3

Lydia received a gift card for $25.00 worth of smoothies from the Smoothie Spot. If the cost of each smoothie is $3.25, which table best describes *b*, the balance remaining on the gift card after she buys *n* smoothies?

(A)

n	*b*
1	$21.75
3	$15.25
4	$12.00
7	$2.25

(C)

n	*b*
1	$21.75
2	$18.50
5	$15.25
7	$12.00

(B)

n	*b*
2	$18.50
4	$12.00
6	$6.50
8	$0

(D)

n	*b*
2	$18.50
3	$15.25
5	$7.75
6	$4.50

DAY 4

The band is trying to raise money to take a field trip to the Rock and Roll Hall of Fame. They decide to sell sweatshirts. The equation for the amount of money *a* that they will make for selling *t* sweatshirts is $a = 22t - 350$. In order to make at least $2100, how many sweatshirts do the band members need to sell?

(F) 112
(G) 111
(H) 80
(J) 79

DAY 5

What is the solution to the equation $8x - 10 = 54$?

(A) 5.5
(B) 6.75
(C) 8
(D) 12

Day	NAEP Standards Grade 8	NAEP Standards Grade 12
1	Algebra – Variables, expressions, and operations: 8.5.3.c	Algebra – Variables, expressions, and operations: 12.5.3.d
2	Algebra – Equations and inequalities: 8.5.4.a	Algebra – Equations and inequalities: 12.5.4.a
3	Algebra – Algebraic representations: 8.5.2.b	Algebra – Algebraic representations: 12.5.2.b
4	Algebra – Equations and inequalities: 8.5.4.a	Algebra – Equations and inequalities: 12.5.4.a
5	Algebra – Equations and inequalities: 8.5.4.a	Algebra – Equations and inequalities: 12.5.4.a

Countdown to Testing WEEK 4

DAY 1

Which expression is equivalent to $2x(3x + 5) - x^2 + 8$?

Ⓐ $-x^2 + 6x + 18$

Ⓑ $5x^2 + 10x + 8$

Ⓒ $10x + 14$

Ⓓ $-x^2 + 16x + 8$

DAY 2

What is the value of $3x^2 - 5x + 2$ when $x = -4$?

Ⓕ −66

Ⓖ −26

Ⓗ 30

Ⓙ 70

DAY 3

Which graph matches the values from the table?

x	−3	−1	2	4
y	6	2	−4	−8

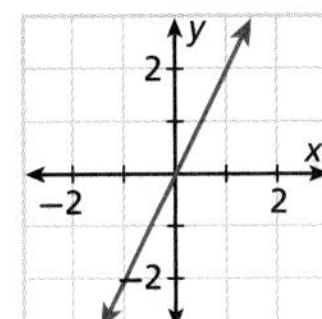

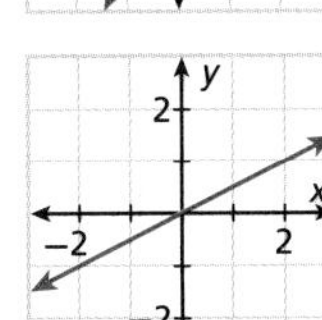

Ⓒ
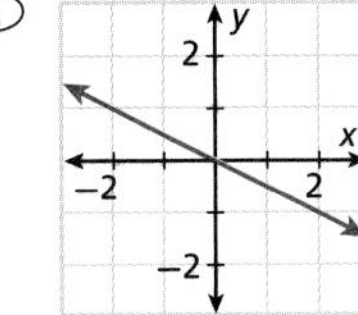

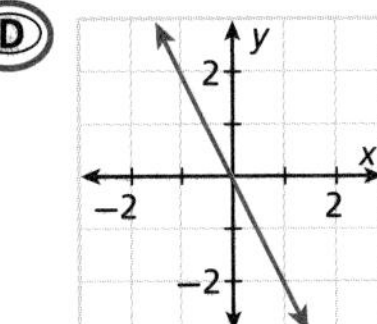

DAY 4

A rectangle has a length of 8 m and a width of 3 m. If a similar rectangle has a length of 22 m, what is its width?

Ⓕ 58.67 m

Ⓖ 17 m

Ⓗ 8.25 m

Ⓙ 9 m

DAY 5

Simplify the algebraic expression $4(x + 5) - 2(x + 5)$.

Ⓐ $2x + 10$

Ⓑ $2x + 30$

Ⓒ $6x + 30$

Ⓓ $-8x^2 - 200$

Day	NAEP Standards Grade 8	NAEP Standards Grade 12
1	Algebra – Variables, expressions, and operations: 8.5.3.c	Algebra – Variables, expressions, and operations: 12.5.3.d
2	Algebra – Variables, expressions, and operations: 8.5.3.c	Algebra – Variables, expressions, and operations: 12.5.3.c
3	Algebra – Algebraic representations: 8.5.2.a	Algebra – Algebraic representations: 12.5.2.a
4	Number Properties and Operations – Ratios and proportional reasoning: 8.1.4.c	Number Properties and Operations – Ratios and proportional reasoning: 12.1.4.c
5	Algebra – Variables, expressions, and operations: 8.5.3.c	Algebra – Variables, expressions, and operations: 12.5.3.c

Countdown to Testing WEEK 5

DAY 1

Which description of the relationship between x and y best represents the table below?

x	9	0	−6	1
y	3	0	−2	$\frac{1}{3}$

Ⓐ The value of y is three times the value of x.
Ⓑ The value of x is three more than the value of y.
Ⓒ The value of x is three less than the value of y.
Ⓓ The value of x is three times the value of y.

DAY 2

Claire's father is 6 years more than 3 times her age. If her dad is 39 years old, how old is Claire?

Ⓕ 15 years old
Ⓖ 11 years old
Ⓗ 7 years old
Ⓙ 6 years old

DAY 3

Which expression represents the phrase "four times the sum of a number and 2"?

Ⓐ $4n + 2$
Ⓑ $4(2n)$
Ⓒ $4(n + 2)$
Ⓓ $4 \cdot n + 2$

DAY 4

What is the solution to $-8x - 3 = -4x + 5$?

Ⓕ −4
Ⓖ −2
Ⓗ 2
Ⓙ 4

DAY 5

The cheerleaders are selling tickets to a pasta dinner to raise money for new competition outfits. They plan to charge $6 per person, and their total expenses for dinner are $135. Which value for the number of tickets sold would result in the cheerleaders not making a profit?

Ⓐ 46
Ⓑ 45
Ⓒ 23
Ⓓ 22

Day	NAEP Standards Grade 8	NAEP Standards Grade 12
1	Algebra – Algebraic representations: 8.5.2.a	Algebra – Algebraic representations: 12.5.2.b
2	Number Properties and Operations – Number operations: 8.1.3.g	Number Properties and Operations – Number operations: 12.1.3.g
3	Algebra – Variables, expressions, and operations: 8.5.3.b	Algebra – Variables, expressions, and operations: 12.5.3.b
4	Algebra – Equations and inequalities: 8.5.4.a	Algebra – Equations and inequalities: 12.5.4.a
5	Algebra – Equations and inequalities: 8.5.4.a	Algebra – Equations and inequalities: 12.5.4.a

Countdown to Testing WEEK 6

DAY 1

Which equation matches the data in the table?

x	3	1	−2	6
y	2	4	7	−1

(A) $y = -x + 5$
(B) $y = 2x - 1$
(C) $y = x + 3$
(D) $y = -3x + 11$

DAY 2

The drama club charges $3 admission to the one-act play festival. Their expenses are $115. In order for the club to make exactly $110 after expenses, how many people must attend the festival?

(F) 39
(G) 75
(H) 114
(J) 152

DAY 3

Melissa's brother is 6 years less than twice her age. The sum of her age and her brother's age is 27. Which equation best shows this information?

(A) $x + (6 - 2x) = 27$
(B) $x + (2x - 6) = 27$
(C) $2x - 6 = 27$
(D) $x = 2x - 6$

DAY 4

A rectangle has a length of 5 inches and a width of 3 inches. If a similar rectangle has a width of 15 inches, what is its length?

(F) 5 inches
(G) 9 inches
(H) 15 inches
(J) 25 inches

DAY 5

A bus company sells an annual bus pass for $8.50, and then charges a rider $0.25 per ride. Using the equation $c = 0.25b + 8.5$, how much will it cost for someone to ride the bus 38 times?

(A) $118.00
(B) $20.00
(C) $18.00
(D) $9.50

Day	NAEP Standards Grade 8	NAEP Standards Grade 12
1	Algebra – Algebraic representations: 8.5.2.a	Algebra – Algebraic representations: 12.5.2.a
2	Algebra – Equations and inequalities: 8.5.4.a	Algebra – Equations and inequalities: 12.5.4.a
3	Algebra – Variables, expressions, and operations: 8.5.3.b	Algebra – Variables, expressions, and operations: 12.5.3.b
4	Geometry – Transformation of shapes and preservation of properties: 8.3.2.e	Geometry – Transformation of shapes and preservation of properties: 12.3.2.e
5	Algebra – Equations and inequalities: 8.5.4.c	Algebra – Equations and inequalities: 12.5.4.a

Countdown to Testing WEEK 7

DAY 1

Daniel's recipe for 24 cookies calls for $2\frac{1}{2}$ cups of flour. How much flour will Daniel need to make 60 cookies?

Ⓐ 1 cup

Ⓑ $6\frac{1}{4}$ cups

Ⓒ $6\frac{1}{2}$ cups

Ⓓ $7\frac{1}{2}$ cups

DAY 2

What is the value of $2x^2 + 3x - 5$ when $x = -2$?

Ⓕ −7

Ⓖ −3

Ⓗ 5

Ⓙ 9

DAY 3

Which graph shows a line where each value of y is three more than half of x?

Ⓐ
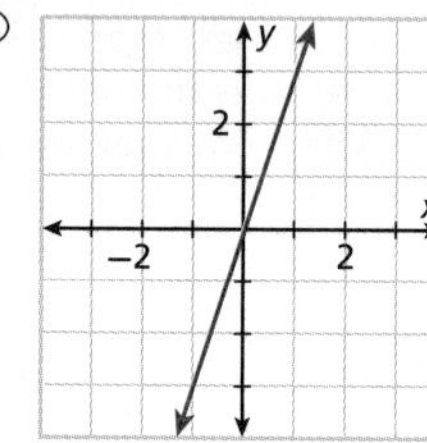

Ⓒ
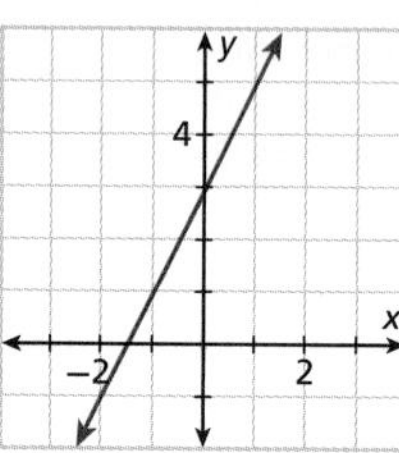

Ⓑ
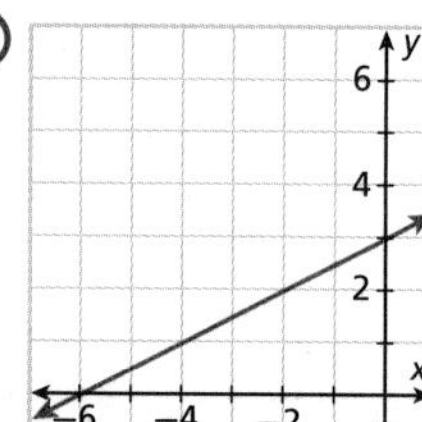

Ⓓ
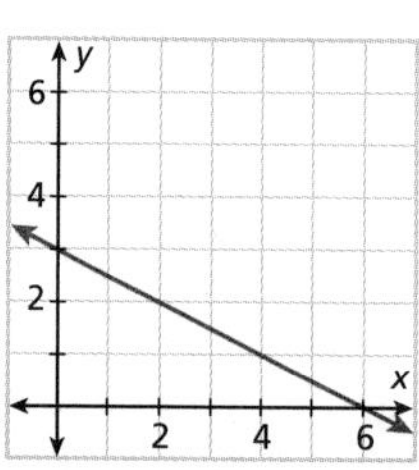

DAY 4

What is the solution to $2x + 8 < 3x - 4$?

Ⓕ $x < 12$

Ⓖ $x > \frac{12}{5}$

Ⓗ $x > 12$

Ⓙ $x < \frac{12}{5}$

DAY 5

Simplify the expression $3(5x - 8) + 2(4x - 1)$.

Ⓐ $23x + 26$

Ⓑ $23x + 22$

Ⓒ $23x - 22$

Ⓓ $23x - 26$

Day	NAEP Standards Grade 8	NAEP Standards Grade 12
1	Number Properties and Operations – Ratios and proportional reasoning: 8.1.4.c	Number Properties and Operations – Ratios and proportional reasoning: 12.1.4.c
2	Algebra – Variables, expressions, and operations: 8.5.3.c	Algebra – Variables, expressions, and operations: 12.5.3.c
3	Algebra – Algebraic representations: 8.5.2.a	Algebra – Algebraic representations: 12.5.2.a
4	Algebra – Equations and inequalities: 8.5.4.a	Algebra – Equations and inequalities: 12.5.4.a
5	Algebra – Variables, expressions, and operations: 8.5.3.c	Algebra – Variables, expressions, and operations: 12.5.3.c

Countdown to Testing WEEK 8

DAY 1

A swimming pool charges an annual \$75 membership fee, and it costs \$1.50 each time a member brings a guest. Which equation shows the yearly cost y in terms of the number of guests g?

Ⓐ $y = 75g + 1.5$

Ⓑ $y = -1.5g + 75$

Ⓒ $y = 1.5g + 75$

Ⓓ $y = 1.5g + 75g$

DAY 2

On a certain standardized test, the equation $s = 9q + 218$ is used to determine a student's score. In this equation, s is the score and q is the number of questions answered correctly. If the maximum score on the test is 650, how many questions are on the test?

Ⓕ 96 questions

Ⓖ 72 questions

Ⓗ 48 questions

Ⓙ 24 questions

DAY 3

If you belong to Lowell's Gym and plan to work out 82 times in a year, what is your total cost for the year?

Lowell's Gym	
Membership fee	\$75
Workout fee (per visit)	\$2

Ⓐ \$89 Ⓑ \$157 Ⓒ \$164 Ⓓ \$239

DAY 4

A publishing company must ship boxes of a particular book to bookstores around the country. The boxes used for shipping can hold a maximum of 35 pounds. If the company wants to ship at least 10 books per box, what is the maximum weight of a book that can be put in the box?

Ⓕ 3 pounds

Ⓖ $3\frac{1}{2}$ pounds

Ⓗ 4 pounds

Ⓙ 25 pounds

DAY 5

Which verbal description does not match the function $f(x) = -\frac{1}{3}x - 5$?

Ⓐ The function value is the difference between x times $-\frac{1}{3}$ and 5.

Ⓑ The function value is 5 less than the product of x and $-\frac{1}{3}$.

Ⓒ The function value is $-\frac{1}{3}$ of x subtracted from 5.

Ⓓ The function value is $-\frac{1}{3}$ of x decreased by 5.

Day	NAEP Standards Grade 8	NAEP Standards Grade 12
1	Algebra – Variables, expressions, and operations: 8.5.3.b	Algebra – Variables, expressions, and operations: 12.5.3.b
2	Algebra – Equations and inequalities: 8.5.4.a	Algebra – Equations and inequalities: 12.5.4.a
3	Number Properties and Operations – Number operations: 8.1.3.g	Number Properties and Operations – Number operations: 12.1.3.g
4	Number Properties and Operations – Number operations: 8.1.3.g	Number Properties and Operations – Number operations: 12.1.3.g
5	Algebra – Algebraic representations: 8.5.2.a	Algebra – Algebraic representations: 12.5.2.a

Countdown to Testing WEEK 9

DAY 1

Brian calculates the charge for each lawn he mows by using the function $f(t) = 10t + 5.5$, where t is the number of hours spent mowing the lawn. He always works for at least one full hour. Which statement cannot be inferred from this information?

Ⓐ Brian's hourly rate is $10.

Ⓑ Brian includes a charge of $5.50 for all lawns.

Ⓒ Brian uses $5.50 worth of gas for each job.

Ⓓ The minimum that Brian will make for each lawn is $15.50.

DAY 2

Which of the following relationships has a negative correlation?

Ⓕ A person's height and weight

Ⓖ The number of minutes spent studying and a test grade

Ⓗ The outside temperature and the number of layers of clothes a person wears

Ⓙ The number of years a person spent in school and the person's salary

DAY 3

The graph shows the value of a car over a period of years. Which of the following statements cannot be concluded from the graph?

Ⓐ The car started at a value of approximately $8400.

Ⓑ The car's value depreciates more quickly at the beginning, and then less quickly as time goes on.

Ⓒ The car is worth approximately $3000 when it is 5 years old.

Ⓓ The car should be sold before its worth drops below $2000.

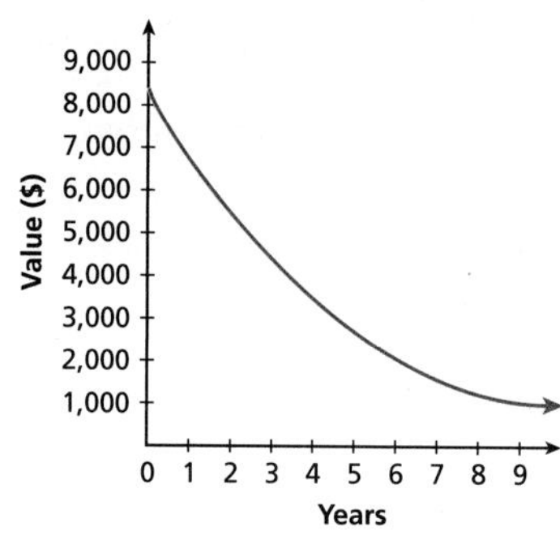

DAY 4

Which function best matches the table?

x	−3	0	3	6
y	2	4	6	8

Ⓕ $y = -\frac{2}{3}x$

Ⓖ $y = 2x + 4$

Ⓗ $y = \frac{2}{3}x + 4$

Ⓙ $y = \frac{1}{3}x + 3$

DAY 5

To change from degrees Celsius to degrees Fahrenheit, you can use the equation $f = \frac{9}{5}c + 32$. If the temperature is at least 55 degrees Fahrenheit, what inequality can you use to find the temperature in Celsius?

Ⓐ $55 \geq \frac{9}{5}c + 32$

Ⓑ $f \geq \frac{9}{5} \cdot 55 + 32$

Ⓒ $55 \leq \frac{9}{5}c + 32$

Ⓓ $f \leq \frac{9}{5} \cdot 55 + 32$

Day	NAEP Standards Grade 8	NAEP Standards Grade 12
1	Algebra – Equations and inequalities: 8.5.4.a	Algebra – Equations and inequalities: 12.5.4.a
2	Data Analysis and Probability – Data representation: 8.4.1.a	Data Analysis and Probability – Data representation: 12.4.2.h
3	Data Analysis and Probability – Data representation: 8.4.1.a	Data Analysis and Probability – Data representation: 12.4.1.a
4	Algebra – Algebraic representations: 8.5.2.a	Algebra – Algebraic representations: 12.5.2.a
5	Algebra – Variables, expressions, and operations: 8.5.3.b	Algebra – Variables, expressions, and operations: 12.5.3.b

Countdown to Testing

Countdown to Testing WEEK 10

DAY 1

A function relating two quantities is $f(x) = \frac{1}{5}x + 6$. What will always be true based on this function?

Ⓐ $f(x)$ will be less than x.

Ⓑ If x is positive, then $f(x)$ will be positive.

Ⓒ If x is negative, then $f(x)$ will be negative.

Ⓓ $f(x)$ will be greater than x.

DAY 2

In the equation $p = -40q + 163$, which relationship between p and q is true?

Ⓕ You cannot determine the relationship based on this information.

Ⓖ q is dependent on p.

Ⓗ p and q are independent of each other.

Ⓙ p is dependent on q.

DAY 3

What is the equation of the line shown?

Ⓐ $y = 2x$

Ⓑ $y = -2x$

Ⓒ $y = \frac{1}{2}x$

Ⓓ $y = -\frac{1}{2}x$

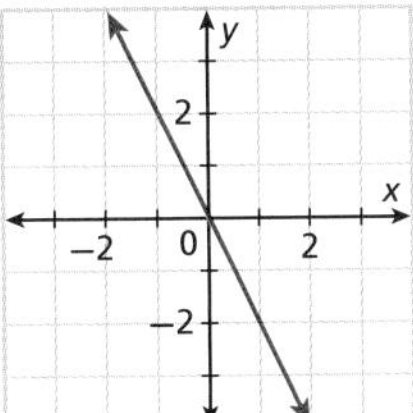

DAY 4

What is the solution to $-8x - 3 \geq -4x + 5$?

Ⓕ $x \leq -2$

Ⓖ $x \geq 2$

Ⓗ $x \leq 2$

Ⓙ $x \geq -2$

DAY 5

The sum of three consecutive integers is 54. What is the greatest of the three integers?

Ⓐ 17

Ⓑ 18

Ⓒ 19

Ⓓ 20

Day	NAEP Standards Grade 8	NAEP Standards Grade 12
1	Algebra – Algebraic representations: 8.5.2.b	Algebra – Algebraic representations: 12.5.2.b
2	Algebra – Algebraic representations: 8.5.2.b	Algebra – Algebraic representations: 12.5.2.b
3	Algebra – Algebraic representations: 8.5.2.a	Algebra – Algebraic representations: 12.5.2.a
4	Algebra – Equations and inequalities: 8.5.4.a	Algebra – Equations and inequalities: 12.5.4.a
5	Number Properties and Operations – Number operations: 8.1.3.g	Number Properties and Operations – Number operations: 12.1.3.g

Countdown to Testing WEEK 11

DAY 1

Darian has a picture that is 4 inches wide and 6 inches long. He wants to enlarge the picture so that it has a width of 18 inches. What is the length of the enlarged picture?

(A) 27 inches
(B) 24 inches
(C) 20 inches
(D) 12 inches

DAY 2

At a computer repair shop, the function $f(t) = 40t + 35$ is used to calculate fees, where t is the number of hours technicians spend working on the computer. If you pay $315 to get your computer repaired, how long did the technician work on repairing your computer?

(F) 8.75 hours
(G) 7.875 hours
(H) 7.5 hours
(J) 7 hours

DAY 3

The scatter plot shows the relationship between the size of a diamond in Carats and its retail price. What is the approximate retail price of a 0.30 Carat diamond?

(A) $400
(B) $600
(C) $800
(D) $1000

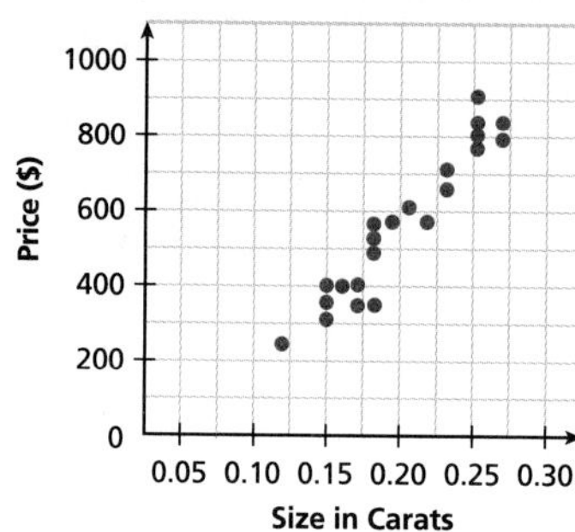

DAY 4

What is the next term in the pattern?

50, 10, 2, $\frac{2}{5}$, ___, ...

(F) $\frac{1}{25}$
(G) $\frac{2}{25}$
(H) $\frac{2}{10}$
(J) $\frac{1}{5}$

DAY 5

Which expression is equivalent to $5x - 35$?

(A) $5(x - 35)$
(B) $5(x - 7)$
(C) $5(x + 35)$
(D) $5(x + 7)$

Day	NAEP Standards Grade 8	NAEP Standards Grade 12
1	Number Properties and Operations – Ratios and proportional reasoning: 8.1.4.c	Number Properties and Operations – Ratios and proportional reasoning: 12.1.4.c
2	Algebra – Equations and inequalities: 8.5.4.a	Algebra – Equations and inequalities: 12.5.4.a
3	Data Analysis and Probability – Data representation: 8.4.1.c	Data Analysis and Probability – Characteristics of data sets: 12.4.2.g
4	Algebra – Patterns, relations and functions: 8.5.1.a	Algebra – Patterns, relations, and functions: 12.5.1.a
5	Algebra – Variables, expressions, and operations: 8.5.3.c	Algebra – Variables, expressions, and operations: 12.5.3.d

Countdown to Testing WEEK 12

COUNTDOWN TO TESTING

DAY 1

Based on the information in the table, what is the relationship between the weight of the object and its volume?

Weight (lb)	2	5	8	12
Volume (in^3)	0.5	1.25	2	3

Ⓐ The weight is 1.5 more than the volume.

Ⓑ The volume is 4 times the weight.

Ⓒ The weight is 4 times the volume.

Ⓓ The volume is 6 less than the weight.

DAY 2

What is the range of the function shown in the table?

x	1	3	5	8
$f(x)$	2	−2	0	2

Ⓕ {1, 3, 5, 8}

Ⓖ {4}

Ⓗ {−2, 0, 2}

Ⓙ {7}

DAY 3

Which graph shows a linear function?

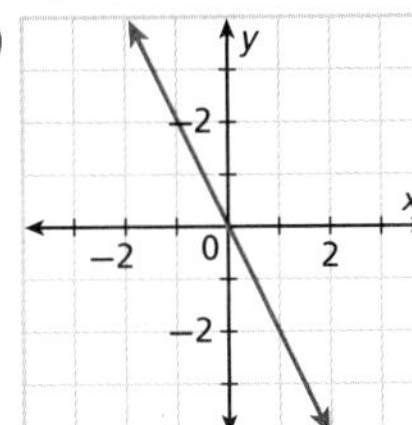

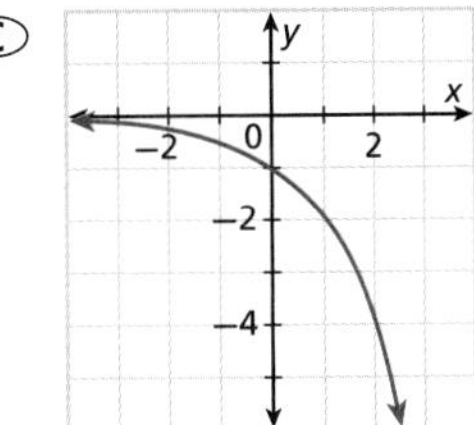

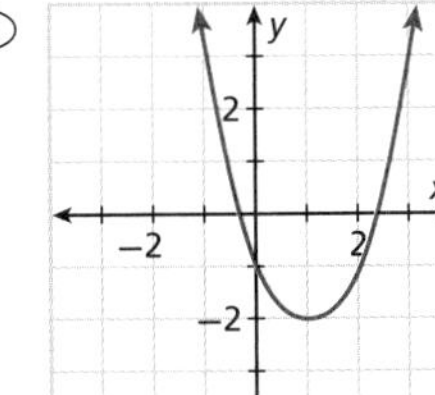

Ⓓ
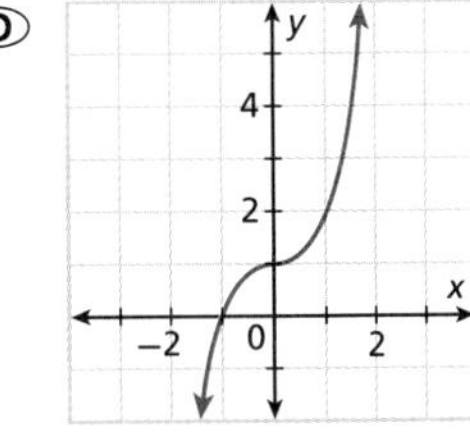

DAY 4

What is the solution to the equation $6(x - 9) = -12x + 36$?

Ⓕ $x = 5$

Ⓖ $x = 2.5$

Ⓗ $x = -1$

Ⓙ $x = -5$

DAY 5

Simplify the algebraic expression $5x - 2(4x - 3) + 7$.

Ⓐ $-3x + 1$

Ⓑ $13x + 13$

Ⓒ $-3x + 13$

Ⓓ $3x + 1$

Day	NAEP Standards Grade 8	NAEP Standards Grade 12
1	Algebra – Algebraic representations: 8.5.2.a	Algebra – Algebraic representations: 12.5.2.b
2	Algebra – Algebraic representations: 8.5.2.b	Algebra – Patterns, relations, and functions: 12.5.1.g
3	Algebra – Patterns, relations, and functions: 8.5.1.e	Algebra – Patterns, relations, and functions: 12.5.1.h
4	Algebra – Equations and inequalities: 8.5.4.a	Algebra – Equations and inequalities: 12.5.4.a
5	Algebra – Variables, expressions, and operations: 8.5.3.c	Algebra – Variables, expressions, and operations: 12.5.3.c

Countdown to Testing WEEK 13

DAY 1

The slope of a line is $-\frac{1}{4}$, and the y-intercept is –3. What is the equation of the line?

(A) $x + y = -3$

(B) $y = -\frac{1}{4}x + 1$

(C) $y = -\frac{1}{4}x - 3$

(D) $x - 4y = -3$

DAY 2

A taxi company charges a \$2.50 fee per ride plus an additional \$2.10 per mile traveled. If the taxi fee increases to \$2.75, which characteristic of this function would change?

(F) The slope

(G) The x-intercept

(H) The y-intercept

(J) There would be no changes

DAY 3

Which description of the relationship between x and y best matches the graph below?

(A) The value of y is 3 times the value of x.

(B) The value of x is 2 more than the value of y.

(C) The value of x is 2 less than the value of y.

(D) The value of x is 3 times the value of y.

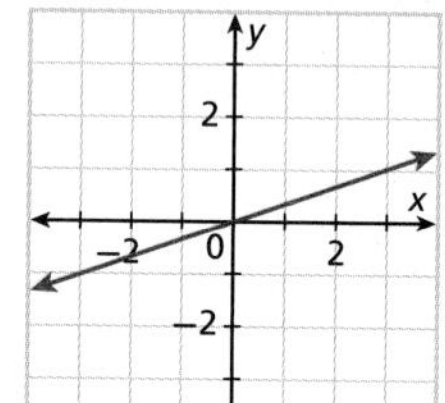

DAY 4

In which relationship are the two quantities independent of one another?

(F) The amount of tax paid for an item and the price of the item

(G) The number of snacks bought from a snack machine and the amount of money in the machine

(H) The number of hours worked at \$6.50 per hour and the amount of money earned

(J) The age of a person and the number of televisions in his or her home

DAY 5

The linear function $f(x) = 3x + 15$ models the cost of renting x movies over the course of a year from a certain store. What range restrictions will there be if you graph this function?

(A) $f(x) \geq 0$

(B) $f(x) \geq 15$

(C) $f(x) > 0$

(D) $0 \leq f(x) \leq 15$

Day	NAEP Standards Grade 8	NAEP Standards Grade 12
1	Algebra – Equations and inequalities: 8.5.4.d	Algebra – Patterns, relations, and functions: 12.5.1.a
2	Algebra – Algebraic representations: 8.5.2.b	Algebra – Algebraic representations: 12.5.2.d
3	Algebra – Algebraic representations: 8.5.2.a	Algebra – Algebraic representations: 12.5.2.a
4	Algebra – Algebraic representations: 8.5.2.b	Algebra – Algebraic representations: 12.5.2.b
5	Algebra – Algebraic representations: 8.5.2.b	Algebra – Patterns, relations, and functions: 12.5.1.g

Countdown to Testing WEEK 14

DAY 1

Which function matches the data in the table?

x	−3	2	5
$f(x)$	15	0	15

Ⓐ $f(x) = -3x + 6$

Ⓑ $f(x) = -5x$

Ⓒ $f(x) = x^2 - 2x$

Ⓓ $f(x) = 3x^2 - 12$

DAY 2

A consultant charges her clients for her services based on an equation relating the total bill $f(h)$ to the number of hours worked h. The best interpretation of this function $f(h) = 125h + 150$ is:

Ⓕ She charges \$150 per hour plus a \$125 flat fee.

Ⓖ She charges \$125 per hour plus a \$150 flat fee.

Ⓗ She charges \$275 per hour.

Ⓙ Her hourly charges vary from \$125 to \$150 depending on the job.

DAY 3

Which situation best fits the graph below?

Ⓐ The height of a candle if it is lit, blown out, lit again, and blown out again

Ⓑ The distance a car drives if it is driven a while, stops at a light, driven again, then stopped

Ⓒ The amount of water in a tub if the faucet is turned on, turned off, turned on again, and then turned off again

Ⓓ The altitude of a person who hikes up a mountain, then stops for a snack, continues up the mountain, and then rests at the top.

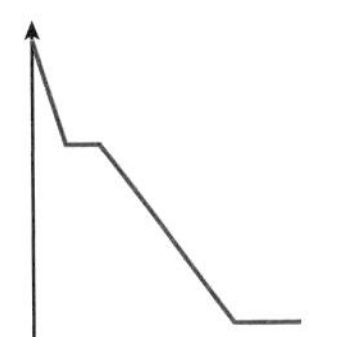

DAY 4

What is the range of the function $f(x) = 2x + 3$?

Ⓕ All real numbers

Ⓖ $f(x) \geq 3$

Ⓗ $f(x) \geq 0$

Ⓙ $f(x) \geq -3$

DAY 5

At Terry's TVs, profit is calculated using the equation $p = 0.4c - 125$, where p is the profit and c is the wholesale cost. If the company makes a profit of \$375 on one TV, what is the wholesale cost of the TV?

Ⓐ \$25

Ⓑ \$937.50

Ⓒ \$1250

Ⓓ \$1062.50

Day	NAEP Standards Grade 8	NAEP Standards Grade 12
1	Algebra – Algebraic representations: 8.5.2.a	Algebra – Algebraic representations: 12.5.2.a
2	Algebra – Algebraic representations: 8.5.2.a	Algebra – Algebraic representations: 12.5.2.a
3	Algebra – Algebraic representations: 8.5.2.b	Algebra – Algebraic representations: 12.5.2.b
4	Data Analysis and Probability – Characteristics of data sets: 8.4.2.a	Algebra – Patterns, relations, and functions: 12.5.1.g
5	Algebra – Equations and inequalities: 8.5.4.a	Algebra – Equations and inequalities: 12.5.4.a

COUNTDOWN TO TESTING

Countdown to Testing WEEK 15

DAY 1

Which graph shows a linear function?

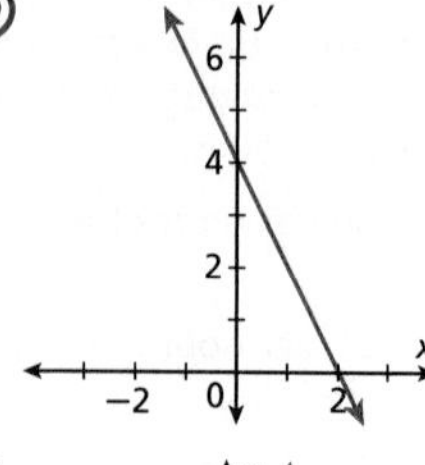

Ⓒ

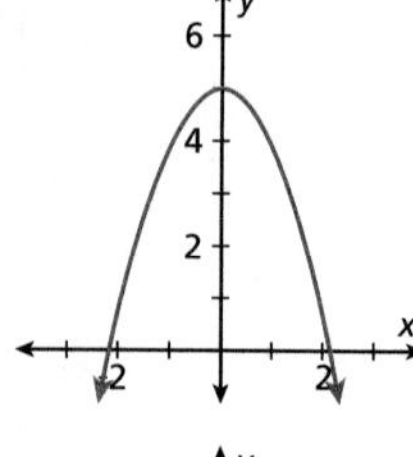

Ⓑ

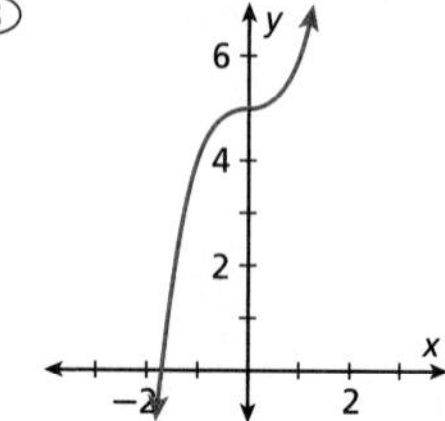

Ⓓ

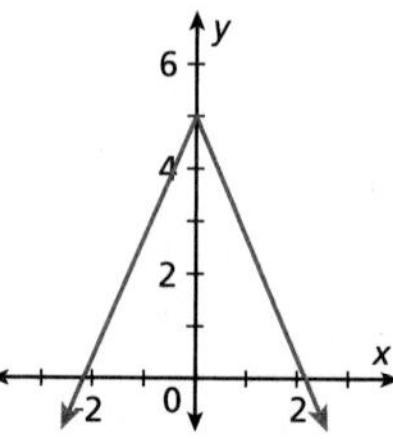

DAY 2

The relationship between which two quantities can be represented by a linear function?

Ⓕ The volume of a cube and its side length

Ⓖ The perimeter of a rectangle and its area

Ⓗ The perimeter of an equilateral triangle and its side length (circled)

Ⓙ The area of a square and its side length

DAY 3

Which equation represents a linear function with a slope of $\frac{2}{3}$?

Ⓐ $y = \frac{3}{2}x$

Ⓑ $y = \frac{2}{3}x + 4$ (circled)

Ⓒ $y = x + \frac{2}{3}$

Ⓓ $y = \frac{2}{3}$

DAY 4

What are the *x*- and *y*-intercepts of $y = \frac{2}{5}x - 2$?

Ⓕ *x*-intercept: –2; *y*-intercept: 5

Ⓖ *x*-intercept: $\frac{2}{5}$; *y*-intercept: –2

Ⓗ *x*-intercept: 0; *y*-intercept: –2

Ⓙ *x*-intercept: 5; *y*-intercept: –2 (circled)

DAY 5

A system of equations is set up to determine how many pounds of hazelnut coffee and how many pounds of Colombian coffee were mixed together to make a blend. The total mixture was 20 pounds of coffee. Which of the following is not a possible solution to the system?

Ⓐ (7, 13) Ⓒ (11, 9)

Ⓑ (32, –12) (circled) Ⓓ (1, 19)

Day	NAEP Standards Grade 8	NAEP Standards Grade 12
1	Algebra – Patterns, relations, and functions: 8.5.1.e	Algebra – Patterns, relations, and functions: 12.5.1.e
2	Algebra – Algebraic representations: 8.5.2.b	Algebra – Algebraic representations: 12.5.2.g
3	Algebra – Equations and inequalities: 8.5.4.d	Algebra – Patterns, relations, and functions: 12.5.1.e
4	Algebra – Equations and inequalities: 8.5.4.d	Algebra – Patterns, relations, and functions: 12.5.1.e
5	Algebra – Equations and inequalities: 8.5.4a	Algebra – Equations and inequalities: 12.5.4.g

Countdown to Testing WEEK 16

COUNTDOWN TO TESTING

DAY 1

If a graph shows the relationship between the amount of sand in the top of an hourglass y over time x, what quantity does the x-intercept represent?

(A) The amount of sand that is in the top of the hourglass originally

(B) The speed at which the sand passes to the bottom of the hourglass

(C) The height of the hourglass

(D) The amount of time it takes for all of the sand to pass to the bottom of the hourglass

DAY 2

Which equation represents a line parallel to the one shown?

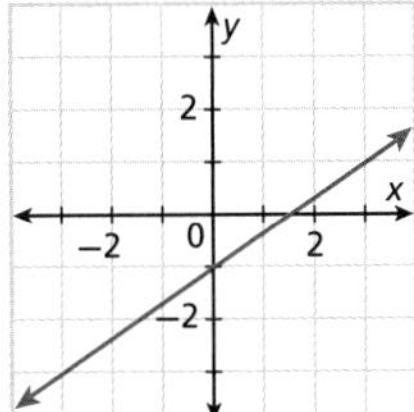

(F) $y = \frac{3}{2}x + 1$

(H) $y = \frac{2}{3}x + 1$

(G) $y = -\frac{3}{2}x - 1$

(J) $y = -\frac{2}{3}x$

DAY 3

Which situation best describes the graph shown if the x-axis represents time passed?

(A) The speed of a car as it accelerates

(B) The distance away from the finish as a person runs up a hill and then proceeds to run at a constant speed

(C) The amount of fuel remaining in a car's gas tank as the car travels at a constant speed

(D) The height of a baseball thrown upward and then rolled down a driveway

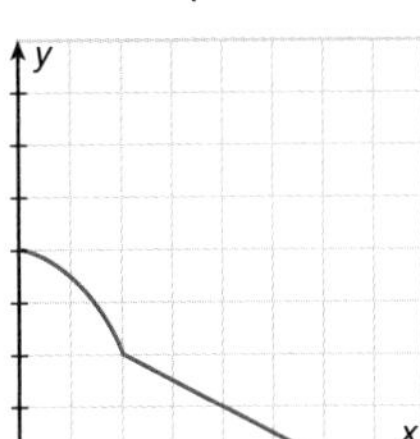

DAY 4

Your school is selling candles to raise money. If profit y is related to the number of items sold x, what are reasonable restrictions on the domain?

(F) $y \geq 0$

(G) No restrictions

(H) $x \geq 0$

(J) $0 \leq y \leq 2000$

DAY 5

What is the solution to the system of equations graphed below?

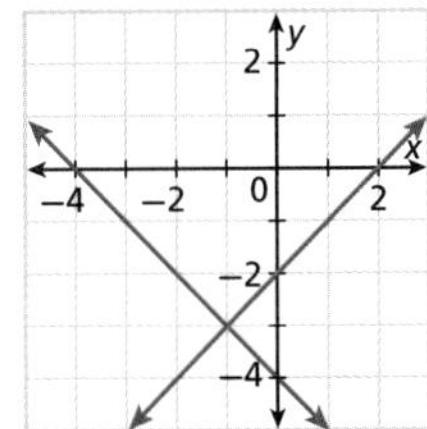

(A) $(-1, 3)$

(C) $(-3, -1)$

(B) $(-1, -3)$

(D) $(3, -1)$

Day	NAEP Standards Grade 8	NAEP Standards Grade 12
1	Algebra – Algebraic representations: 8.5.2.b	Algebra – Algebraic representations: 12.5.2.b
2	Algebra – Variables, expressions, and operations: 8.5.3.b	Algebra – Equations and inequalities: 12.5.4.c
3	Algebra – Algebraic representations: 8.5.2.b	Algebra – Algebraic representations: 12.5.2.b
4	Algebra – Algebraic representations: 8.5.2.b	Algebra – Patterns, relations, and functions: 12.5.1.g
5	Algebra – Equations and inequalities: 8.5.4.a	Algebra – Equations and inequalities: 12.5.4.g

Countdown to Testing WEEK 17

DAY 1

A store manager increases the wholesale cost of an item by 35%. Which statement best represents the functional relationship between the wholesale cost of the item and the markup on the item?

(A) The markup is dependent on the wholesale cost.

(B) The wholesale cost is dependent on the markup.

(C) The markup and the wholesale cost are independent of each other.

(D) The relationship cannot be determined.

DAY 2

Which situation can best be represented by a linear function?

(F) The distance that an airplane is away from the airport as it comes in for a landing and time

(G) The distance traveled by a car moving at a constant speed and time

(H) The number of apples on a tree and the number of trees in the orchard

(J) The height from the ground of a person riding a roller coaster and time

DAY 3

The scatter plot shows the percent of households that own a car versus the household income. What is a reasonable estimate for the percent of households that own a car if the household income is $50,000?

(A) 50%

(B) 65%

(C) 77%

(D) 85%

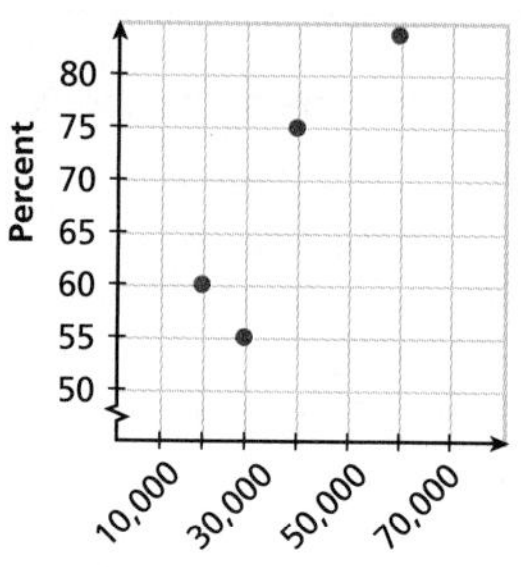

DAY 4

What is the slope of the line with equation $3x - 5y = 12$?

(F) -3

(G) $-\frac{3}{5}$

(H) $\frac{3}{5}$

(J) 3

DAY 5

Joy and a friend start a business. What linear function relates the total income and each partner's share of the profit based on the data in the table?

Total Income (t)	Profit Share (p)
$350.00	$50.00
$425.00	$87.50
$500.00	$125.00

(A) $p = \frac{1}{2}t - 125$

(B) $p = \frac{1}{4}t - 37.5$

(C) $p = t - 300$

(D) $p = \frac{1}{7}t$

Day	NAEP Standards Grade 8	NAEP Standards Grade 12
1	Algebra – Algebraic representations: 8.5.2.b	Algebra – Algebraic representations: 12.5.2.b
2	Algebra – Patterns, relations, and functions: 8.5.1.e	Algebra – Algebraic representations: 12.5.2.g
3	Data Analysis and Probability – Data representation: 8.4.1.a	Data Analysis and Probability – Characteristics of data sets: 12.4.2.g
4	Algebra – Equations and inequalities: 8.5.4.d	Algebra – Patterns, relations, and functions: 12.5.1.e
5	Algebra – Variables, expressions, and operations: 8.5.3.b	Algebra – Variables, expressions, and operations: 12.5.3.b

Countdown to Testing WEEK 18

DAY 1

What is the range of the function $f(x) = 2x^2 + 1$ if the domain is $\{-2, 0, 3\}$?

Ⓐ $\{1, 9, 19\}$ (circled)
Ⓑ $\{0, 8, 18\}$
Ⓒ $\{-9, 1, 19\}$
Ⓓ $\{-2, 0, 3\}$

DAY 2

Which function has a y-intercept of -2 and a graph whose slope is $\frac{5}{4}$?

Ⓕ $5x + 4y = 2$
Ⓖ $y = \frac{5}{4}x + 2$
Ⓗ $y = -\frac{5}{4}x + 2$
Ⓙ $y = \frac{5}{4}x - 2$ (circled)

DAY 3

The graph shows the relationship between a person's height and mass. Which of the following statements would be an invalid conclusion for this data?

Ⓐ The graph shows data for 20 people.
Ⓑ A person who is tall is likely to have a higher mass.
Ⓒ Two participants had a mass of 50 kg.
Ⓓ A person who has a low mass has a fast metabolism. (circled)

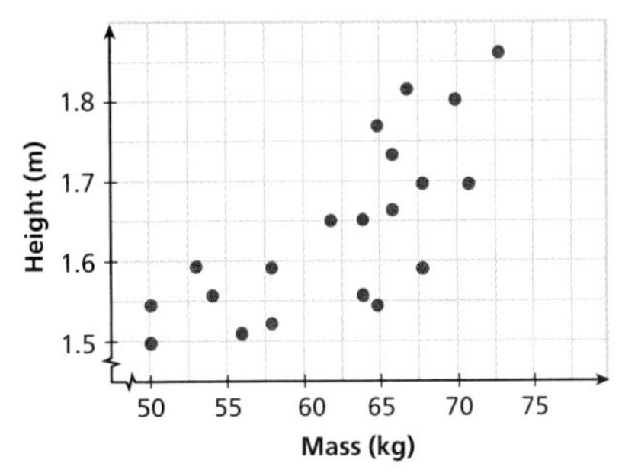

DAY 4

Which of the following cannot be represented by a linear function?

Ⓕ The amount of water w coming out of a dripping faucet over m minutes
Ⓖ The height h of a person over t years (circled)
Ⓗ The gross sales s made from the sale of c CDs priced at $14 each
Ⓙ The amount of sales tax on a purchase of d dollars if the rate is 6%

DAY 5

The graph shows the distance that a person is from home while driving at a constant speed. What quantity is represented by the y-intercept?

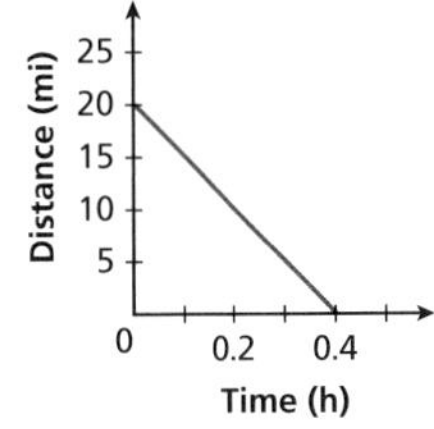

Ⓐ The speed at which the person is driving
Ⓑ The distance from home at the start (circled)
Ⓒ The amount of time it takes to get home
Ⓓ The distance from home at the end

Day	NAEP Standards Grade 8	NAEP Standards Grade 12
1	Algebra – Algebraic representations: 8.5.2.b	Algebra – Patterns, relations, and functions: 12.5.1.g
2	Algebra – Variables, expressions, and operations: 8.5.3.b	Algebra – Variables, expressions, and operations: 12.5.3.b
3	Data Analysis and Probability – Data representation: 8.4.1.a	Data Analysis and Probability – Characteristics of data sets: 12.4.2.g
4	Algebra – Patterns, relations, and functions: 8.5.1.e	Algebra – Algebraic representations: 12.5.2.g
5	Algebra – Algebraic representations: 8.5.2.b	Algebra – Algebraic representations: 12.5.2.b

Countdown to Testing — WEEK 19

DAY 1

Assuming that the graph below has the same x- and y-scale, which is the best estimate for the solution to the system?

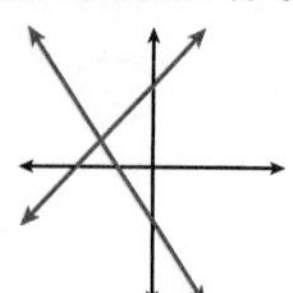

Ⓐ (−5, 10)
(B) (−4, 2) [circled]
Ⓒ (3, −6)
Ⓓ (8, −4)

DAY 2

What is the y-intercept of the function whose graph has a slope of $-\frac{1}{3}$ and passes through the point (−6, 4)?

Ⓕ 6
(G) 2 [circled]
Ⓗ −2
Ⓙ −6

DAY 3

Which graph shows a function from the family $f(x) = x^2$?

Ⓐ

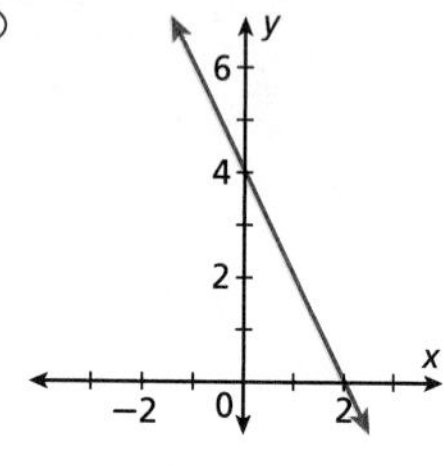

(C) [circled]

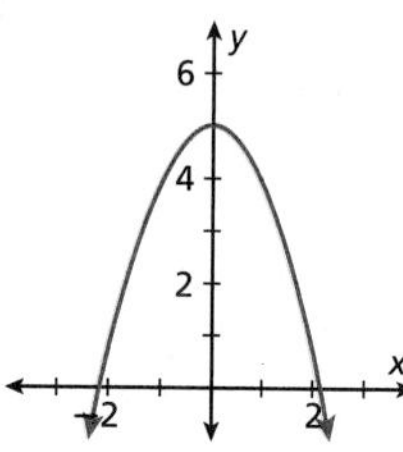

Ⓑ

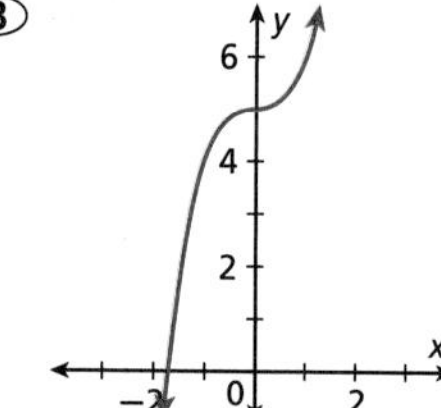

Ⓓ

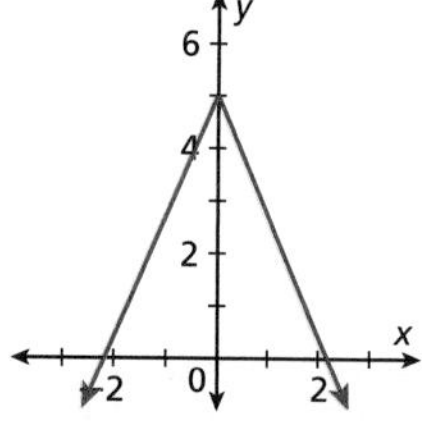

DAY 4

Miguel earns a 15% commission on his sales in addition to a salary of $500 a week. His earnings can be modeled by the equation $p = 0.15s + 500$. What restrictions on the values of p and s best fit this situation?

Ⓕ $p \geq 0$, s can be any value.
Ⓖ $s \geq 0$, p can be any value.
Ⓗ $s \geq 500$, $p \geq 0$
(J) $s \geq 0$, $p \geq 500$ [circled]

DAY 5

If $f(x) = \frac{1}{2}x$, what best describes the relationship between x and $f(x)$?

Ⓐ As the value of x increases by 1, the value of $f(x)$ will increase by 2.
Ⓑ As the value of x increases by 1, the value of $f(x)$ will remain the same.
(C) As the value of x increases by 1, the value of $f(x)$ will increase by $\frac{1}{2}$. [circled]
Ⓓ The value of x will not affect the value of $f(x)$.

Day	NAEP Standards Grade 8	NAEP Standards Grade 12
1	Data Analysis and Probability – Data representation: 8.4.1.c	Algebra – Equations and inequalities: 12.5.4.g
2	Algebra – Equations and inequalities: 8.5.4.d	Algebra – Patterns, relations, and functions: 12.5.1.e
3	Algebra – Patterns, relations, and functions: 8.5.1.e	Algebra – Patterns, relations, and functions: 12.5.1.h
4	Number Properties and Operations – Estimation: 8.1.2.c	Algebra – Equations and inequalities: 12.5.4.c
5	Algebra – Algebraic representations: 8.5.2.b	Algebra – Algebraic representations: 12.5.2.b

Countdown to Testing WEEK 20

DAY 1

On Saturday, Suzie's Pretzel Stand sells a total of 12 items. Suzie charges $3 for a pretzel and $2 for a milkshake. If she took in $32 on Saturday, which system of equations can be used to determine how many pretzels and how many milkshakes were sold?

Ⓐ $\begin{cases} 3x + 2y = 12 \\ x + y = 32 \end{cases}$

Ⓑ $\begin{cases} 3x - 2y = 32 \\ x + y = 12 \end{cases}$

Ⓒ $\begin{cases} 3x - 2y = 12 \\ x + y = 32 \end{cases}$

Ⓓ $\begin{cases} x + y = 12 \\ 3x + 2y = 32 \end{cases}$

DAY 2

What is the slope of the line shown?

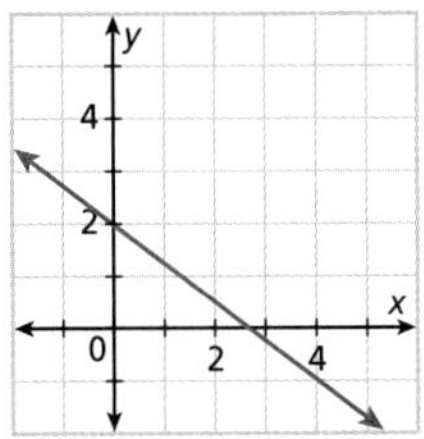

Ⓕ $-\frac{4}{3}$

Ⓖ $-\frac{3}{4}$

Ⓗ $\frac{3}{4}$

Ⓙ $\frac{4}{3}$

DAY 3

If the *x*-intercept of the function graphed below were to stay the same and the slope of the line decreased, what impact would that have on the *y*-intercept?

Ⓐ The *y*-intercept will decrease.

Ⓑ The *y*-intercept will remain the same.

Ⓒ The *y*-intercept will increase.

Ⓓ The *y*-intercept will double.

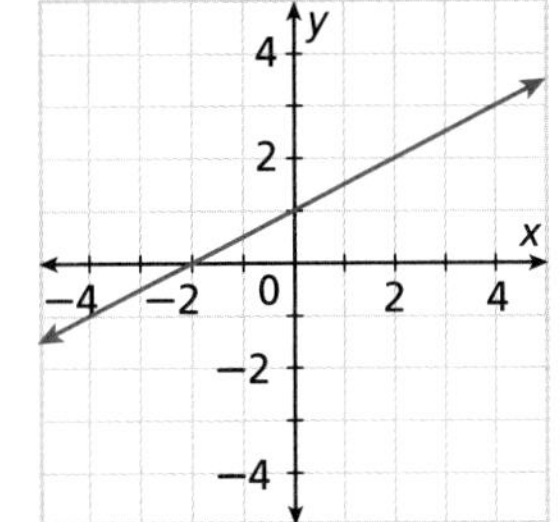

DAY 4

A system of equations is set up to determine the number of nickels and the number of quarters that Elissa has. Which ordered pair does not represent a valid solution to this system?

Ⓕ (0, 15)

Ⓖ (12, −5)

Ⓗ (31, 4)

Ⓙ (7, 0)

DAY 5

A gym membership costs $25 a month plus $3 per visit. This is modeled by the function $c = 3v + 25$, where *c* is the cost per month and *v* is the number of visits. If the slope of this function's graph were to increase, what would that mean about the prices that the gym charges?

Ⓐ The gym raised its monthly fee.

Ⓑ The gym lowered the cost per visit.

Ⓒ The gym raised the cost per visit.

Ⓓ The gym lowered its monthly fee.

Day	NAEP Standards Grade 8	NAEP Standards Grade 12
1	Algebra – Variables, expressions, and operations: 8.5.3.b	Algebra – Variables, expressions, and operations: 12.5.3.b
2	Algebra – Equations and inequalities: 8.5.4.d	Algebra – Patterns, relations, and functions: 12.5.1.e
3	Algebra – Algebraic representations: 8.5.2.b	Algebra – Algebraic representations: 12.5.2.b
4	Algebra – Equations and inequalities: 8.5.4.a	Algebra – Equations and inequalities: 12.5.4.g
5	Algebra – Patterns, relations, and functions: 8.5.1.f	Algebra – Algebraic representations: 12.5.2.b

Countdown to Testing WEEK 21

DAY 1

Which of the functions, when graphed, will result in the most narrow parabola?

(A) $y = 5x^2$

(B) $y = \frac{1}{5}x^2$

(C) $y = x^2$

(D) $y = \frac{1}{2}x^2$

DAY 2

How do the graphs of the functions $f(x) = x^2 - 5$ and $g(x) = x^2 + 4$ relate to each other?

(F) The graph of $f(x)$ is 9 units to the left of the graph of $g(x)$.

(G) The graph of $f(x)$ is 1 unit below the graph of $g(x)$.

(H) The graph of $f(x)$ is 9 units below the graph of $g(x)$.

(J) The graph of $f(x)$ is 1 unit to the left of the graph of $g(x)$.

DAY 3

The graph shows the proposed balance in Jake's bank account if Jake saves an average of $15 a week. Which statement would not be true if the slope of the line were to increase?

(A) Jake is saving more money per week.

(B) Jake started with more money in his bank account.

(C) It will take less time for Jake's bank balance to reach $120.

(D) After 6 weeks Jake will have more than $90 in his bank account.

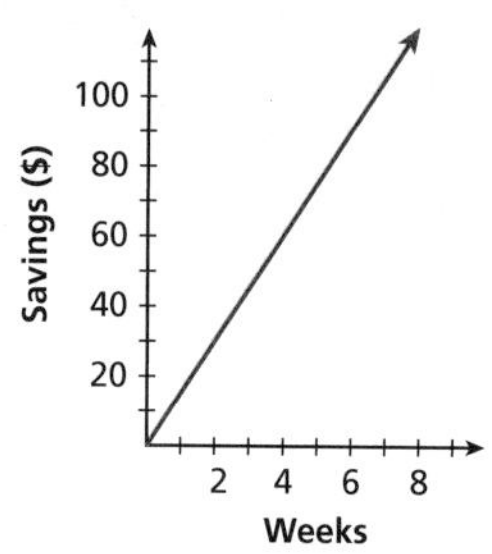

DAY 4

What are the roots of the function $f(x) = (2x - 1)(x + 5)$?

(F) $\frac{1}{2}$ and -5

(G) -1 and 5

(H) 1 and -5

(J) $-\frac{1}{2}$ and 5

DAY 5

For a typical shot in basketball, the ball's height in feet will be a function of time in seconds, modeled by an equation such as $h = -16t^2 + 25t + 6$. Which inequality shows the restrictions that should be put on the domain of this function?

(A) $t \leq 0$

(B) $h \leq 0$

(C) $h \geq 0$

(D) $t \geq 0$

Day	NAEP Standards Grade 8	NAEP Standards Grade 12
1	Algebra – Patterns, relations, and functions: 8.5.1.e	Algebra – Algebraic representations: 12.5.2.f
2	Algebra – Algebraic representations: 8.5.2.g	Algebra – Algebraic representations: 12.5.2.d
3	Algebra – Patterns, relations, and functions: 8.5.1.f	Algebra – Algebraic representations: 12.5.2.d
4	Algebra – Variables, expressions, and operations: 8.5.3.c	Algebra – Patterns, relations, and functions: 12.5.1.e
5	Algebra – Variables, expressions, and operations: 8.5.3.b	Algebra – Patterns, relations, and functions: 12.5.1.g

Countdown to Testing WEEK 22

DAY 1

What are the roots of the graphed function?

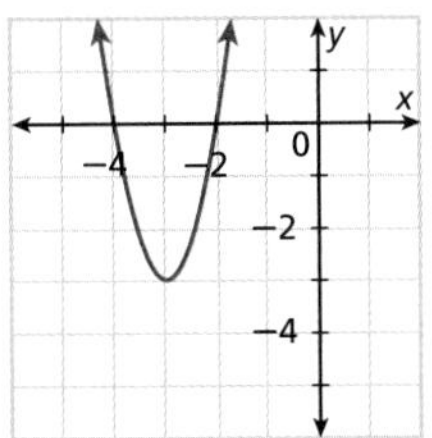

Ⓐ 2 and 4
Ⓑ −2 and −4
Ⓒ −2 and 4
Ⓓ 2 and −4

DAY 2

What is the range of the function shown?

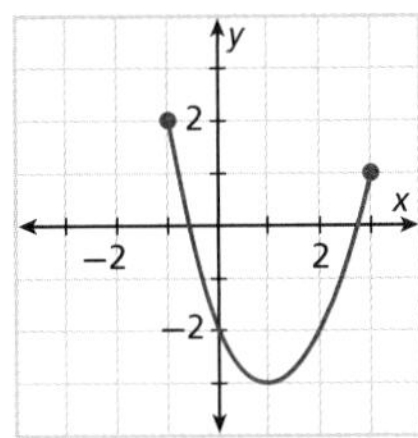

Ⓕ $-2 < y < 3$
Ⓖ $-3 < y \leq 2$
Ⓗ $-3 \leq y \leq 2$
Ⓙ $-2 \leq y \leq 3$

DAY 3

The graph shows the height of a baseball from the time it is thrown until the time it hits the ground. What value is not shown on the graph?

Ⓐ The amount of time that the ball was in the air
Ⓑ The height at which the ball started
Ⓒ The maximum height that the ball reached
Ⓓ The speed at which the ball was thrown

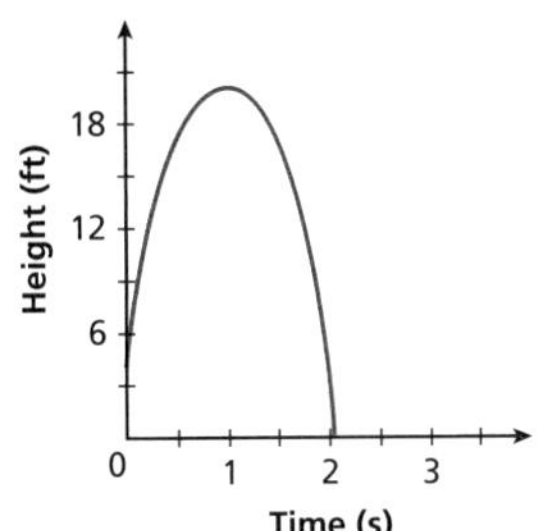

DAY 4

What are the solution(s) of the equation $x^2 - 10x - 24 = 0$?

Ⓕ $x = -4, 6$
Ⓖ $x = 2, -12$
Ⓗ $x = -2, 12$
Ⓙ $x = 4, -6$

DAY 5

What is the solution to the system of equations?

$$\begin{cases} 3x - 4y = 19 \\ y = 2x - 11 \end{cases}$$

Ⓐ (5, −1)
Ⓑ (−5, −21)
Ⓒ (5, 1)
Ⓓ (−5, −8.5)

Day	NAEP Standards Grade 8	NAEP Standards Grade 12
1	Algebra – Variables, expressions, and operations: 8.5.3.c	Algebra – Equations and inequalities: 12.5.4.a
2	Algebra – Algebraic representations: 8.5.2.b	Algebra – Patterns, relations, and functions: 12.5.1.g
3	Data Analysis and Probability – Data representation: 8.4.1.a	Algebra – Equations and inequalities: 12.5.4.c
4	Algebra – Equations and inequalities: 8.5.4.a	Algebra – Equations and inequalities: 12.5.4.a
5	Algebra – Equations and inequalities: 8.5.4.a	Algebra – Equations and inequalities: 12.5.4.g

Countdown to Testing — WEEK 23

DAY 1

Which graph shows a function $y = ax^2$ when $a > 1$?

Ⓐ 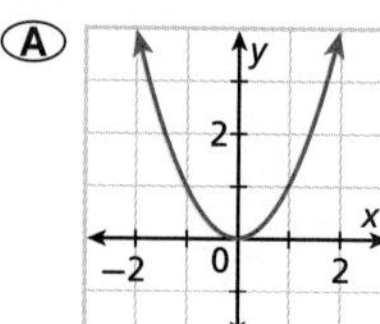

Ⓒ 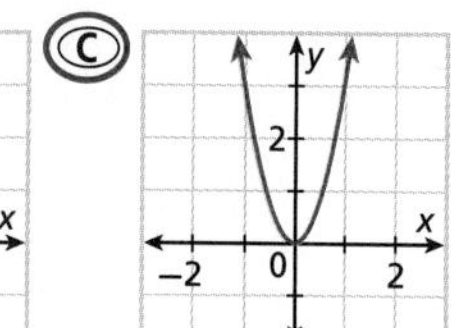

Ⓑ 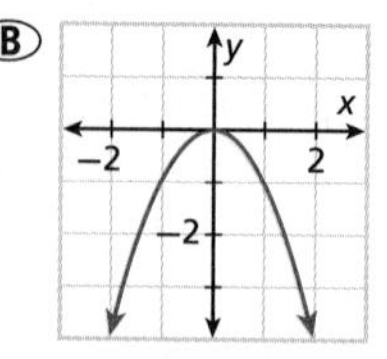

Ⓓ 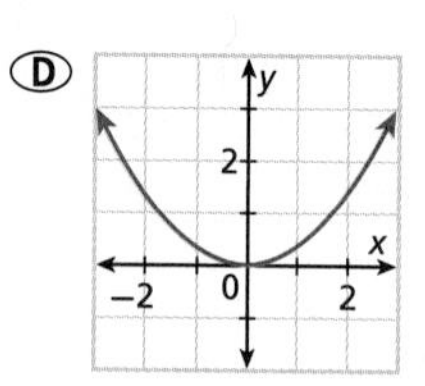

DAY 2

Which best describes the difference between the graphs of $f(x) = x^2$ and $g(x) = x^2 - 3$?

Ⓕ The graph of $g(x)$ is translated 3 units up from the graph of $f(x)$.

Ⓖ The graph of $g(x)$ is translated 3 units left from the graph of $f(x)$.

Ⓗ The graph of $g(x)$ is translated 3 units right from the graph of $f(x)$.

Ⓙ The graph of $g(x)$ is translated 3 units down from the graph of $f(x)$.

DAY 3

The graph shows the height of water coming out of a fountain over time. How many seconds pass before the water reaches the ground?

Ⓐ 0

Ⓑ 2

Ⓒ 4

Ⓓ 18

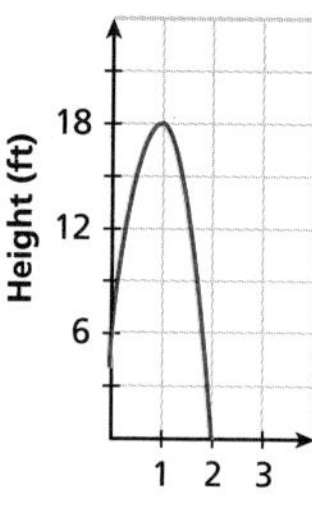

DAY 4

What is one solution to the equation $2x^2 + 7x + 3 = 0$?

Ⓕ $x = 3$

Ⓖ $x = \frac{1}{2}$

Ⓗ $x = -\frac{1}{2}$

Ⓙ $x = -1$

DAY 5

What is the solution to the system of equations $4x + 2y = -8$ and $x - 2y = 13$?

Ⓐ (25, 6)

Ⓑ (1, 6)

Ⓒ (−1, −6)

Ⓓ (1, −6)

Day	NAEP Standards Grade 8	NAEP Standards Grade 12
1	Algebra – Patterns, relations, and functions: 8.5.1.e	Algebra – Patterns, relations, and functions: 12.5.1.h
2	Algebra – Algebraic representations: 8.5.2.b	Algebra – Algebraic representations: 12.5.2.d
3	Data Analysis and Probability – Data representation: 8.4.1.a	Algebra – Equations and inequalities: 12.5.4.c
4	Algebra – Equations and inequalities: 8.5.4.a	Algebra – Equations and inequalities: 12.5.4.a
5	Algebra – Equations and inequalities: 8.5.4.a	Algebra – Equations and inequalities: 12.5.4.g

Countdown to Testing WEEK 24

DAY 1

Which is the parent function of the graph shown?

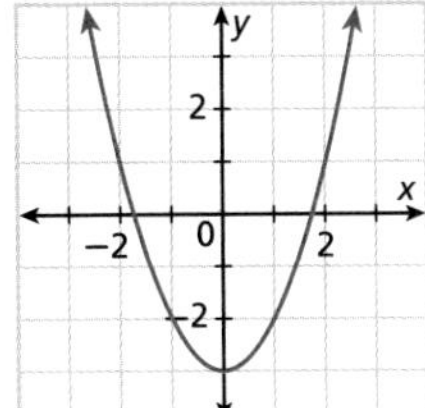

Ⓐ $y = x$
Ⓑ $y = |x|$
Ⓒ $y = x^2$
Ⓓ $y = x^3$

DAY 2

What is the x-intercept of the function shown?

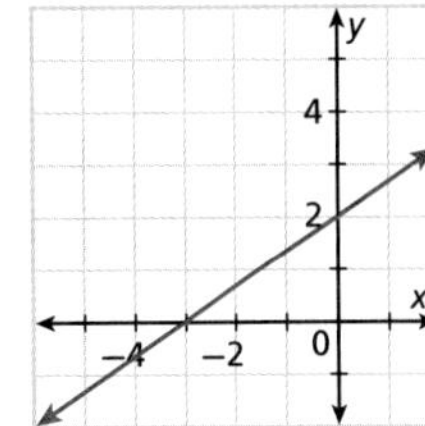

Ⓕ $x = -3$
Ⓖ $x = -2$
Ⓗ $x = 2$
Ⓙ $x = 3$

DAY 3

Which situation cannot be described by a linear function?

Ⓐ The amount of commission earned on a sale if the commission rate is 12%
Ⓑ The area of a square given its side length
Ⓒ The cost of renting a car if the charge is $25 plus $0.15 per mile
Ⓓ The amount paid for babysitting h hours if you charge $8.25 per hour

DAY 4

What is the equation of the line that passes through the points (−4, 2) and (−8, 8)?

Ⓕ $y = -\frac{3}{2}x - 4$
Ⓖ $y = -\frac{3}{2}x - 20$
Ⓗ $y = -\frac{3}{2}x - 8$
Ⓙ $y = -\frac{3}{2}x + 4$

DAY 5

What is the slope of the line given the equation $3x - 4y = -8$?

Ⓐ $m = 3$
Ⓑ $m = 2$
Ⓒ $m = \frac{3}{4}$
Ⓓ $m = -3$

Day	NAEP Standards Grade 8	NAEP Standards Grade 12
1	Algebra – Patterns, relations, and functions: 8.5.1.e	Algebra – Patterns, relations, and functions: 12.5.1.h
2	Algebra – Equations and inequalities: 8.5.4.d	Algebra – Algebraic representations: 12.5.2.c
3	Algebra – Patterns, relations, and functions: 8.5.1.e	Algebra – Algebraic representations: 12.5.2.g
4	Algebra – Variables, expressions, and operations: 8.5.3.b	Algebra – Variables, expressions, and operations: 12.5.3.b
5	Algebra – Equations and inequalities: 8.5.4.d	Algebra – Patterns, relations, and functions: 12.5.1.e

You can count on **Holt McDougal Algebra 1** for...

1 Built-in Assessment and Intervention.
Prescribe the resources your students need when they need them in order to lead your students to success.

2 Comprehensive Differentiated Instruction.
Ensure all students have the opportunity to succeed with strategies designed to reach students of all learning styles and skill levels.

3 Success on High-Stakes Tests.
Prepare students for success on test day with standards-based test preparation that's embedded into daily lessons.

4 Integrated Technology That Enhances Learning.
Motivate your students to excel and manage your classroom with maximum effectiveness using Holt McDougal technology.

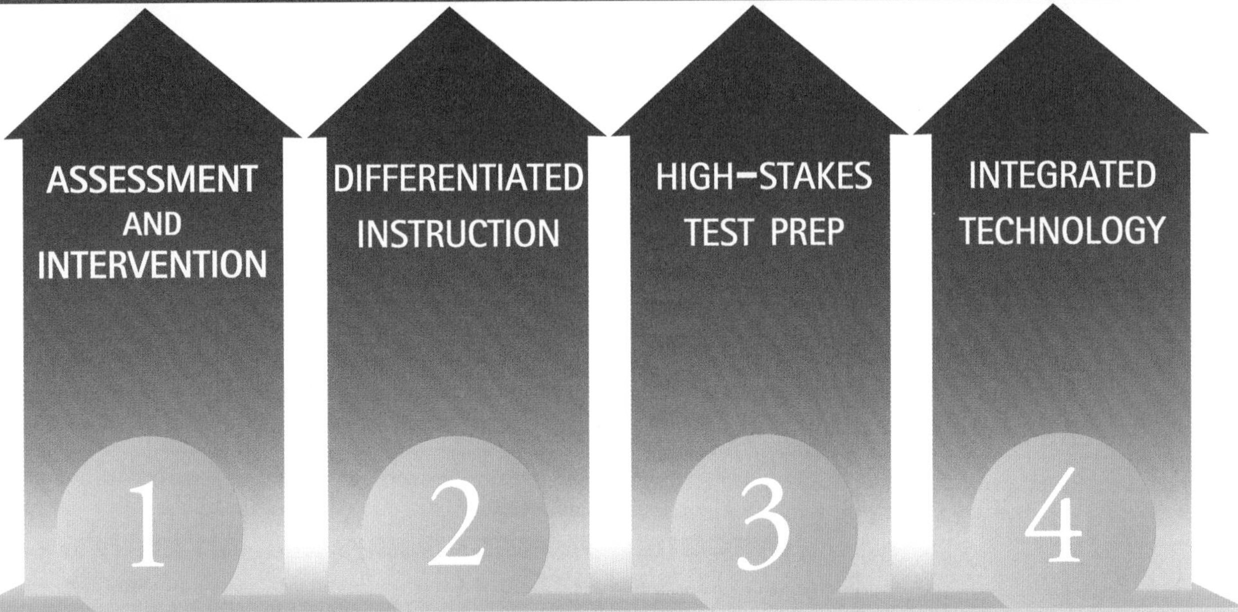

Built for Student Success... from the Ground Up

Every student is unique with individual strengths and weaknesses. Starting with **Holt McDougal Mathematics** for middle school through **Holt McDougal Algebra 1, Geometry,** and **Algebra 2,** this series provides the instruction and resources you need to reach and teach every one of your students. Weather it's an alternative approach to a lesson, a modification for a visual learner, or extra practice with basic skills, **Holt McDougal** has what you need to help all of your students succeed.

> *"Deep and abstract ideas are challenging to all, but the **challenge** should be a pleasurable one that students want to conquer."*
>
> **– Dr. Edward B. Burger, Holt author**

Program Highlights

Built-in Assessment and Intervention...

You need to know how well your students understand the lesson BEFORE they take the test. With **Holt McDougal Algebra 1**, informal and formal assessment options are given at every stage within the chapter. Response to Intervention (RtI) resources allow you to reteach or review material without simply sending students back to previous lessons in the book.

Assess Prior Knowledge

to make sure all students start the chapter on solid footing

- **Intervene** with alternate teaching strategies and basic skills review in *Are You Ready? Intervention and Enrichment*

Formative Assessment

to diagnose skill development within the chapter

- **Intervene** with *Ready to Go On?, Lesson Tutorial Videos, Homework Help Online*, and more

Summative Assessment

to allow students to demonstrate their mastery of the concepts

- **Intervene** with *Reteach* and *Lesson Tutorial Videos*

OPTIONS • RESOURCE OPTIONS • RESOURCE OPTIONS • RESOURCE OPTIONS

ONGOING ASSESSMENT and INTERVENTION

		DIAGNOSE	PRESCRIBE
Assess Prior Knowledge	**Before Chapter 2**	Diagnose readiness for the chapter. **Are You Ready?** SE p. 73	Prescribe intervention. ***Are You Ready? Intervention***
Formative Assessment	**Before Every Lesson**	Diagnose readiness for the lesson. **Warm Up** TE	Prescribe intervention. **Reteach** CRB
	During Every Lesson	Diagnose understanding of lesson concepts. **Check It Out!** SE **Questioning Strategies** TE **Think and Discuss** SE **Write About It** SE **Journal** TE	Prescribe intervention. **Reading Strategies** CRB ***Success for Every Learner*** ***Lesson Tutorial Videos***
	After Every Lesson	Diagnose mastery of lesson concepts. **Lesson Quiz** TE **Test Prep** SE ***Test and Practice Generator***	Prescribe intervention. **Reteach** CRB **Test Prep Doctor** TE ***Homework Help Online***
	Before Chapter 2 Testing	Diagnose mastery of concepts in chapter. **Ready to Go On?** SE pp. 119, 153 **Multi-Step Test Prep** SE pp. 118, 152 **Section Quizzes** AR ***Test and Practice Generator***	Prescribe intervention. ***Ready to Go On? Intervention*** **Scaffolding Questions** TE pp. 118, 152 **Reteach** CRB ***Lesson Tutorial Videos***
	Before High Stakes Testing	Diagnose mastery of benchmark concepts. **College Entrance Exam Practice** SE p. 159 **Standardized Test Prep** SE pp. 162–163	Prescribe intervention. ***College Entrance Exam Practice***
Summative Assessment	**After Chapter 2**	Check mastery of chapter concepts. **Multiple-Choice Tests (Forms A, B, C)** **Free-Response Tests (Forms A, B, C)** **Performance Assessment** AR **Cumulative Test** AR ***Test and Practice Generator***	Prescribe intervention. **Reteach** CRB ***Lesson Tutorial Videos***

KEY: **SE** = *Student Edition* **TE** = *Teacher's Edition* **CRB** = *Chapter Resource Book* **AR** = *Assessment Resources* Available online Available on CD- or DVD-ROM **72B**

Program Highlights

...using Data-Driven Instruction

When students are struggling, they don't want to keep re-reading the same lesson in the hope that eventually it will make sense. They need to try a new approach to the lesson. This is the core of the assessment and intervention system in **Holt McDougal Algebra 1**.

Are You Ready? Intervention and Enrichment

RtI Tier 2

Diagnose mastery of *prerequisite skills* and prescribe intervention

- Strengthens weaknesses with direct instruction, conceptual models, and scaffolded practice
- Enriches every chapter with critical thinking activities
- Available in print, on CD-ROM, and online

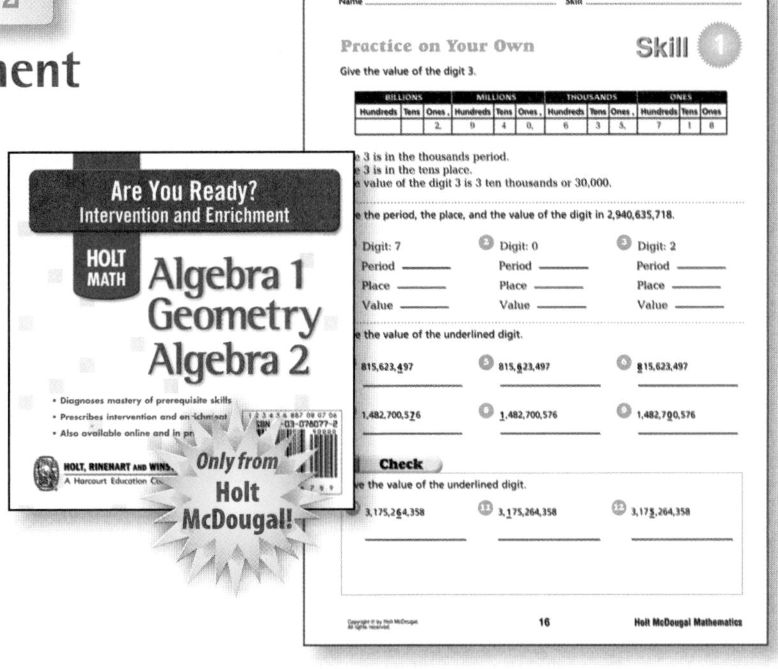

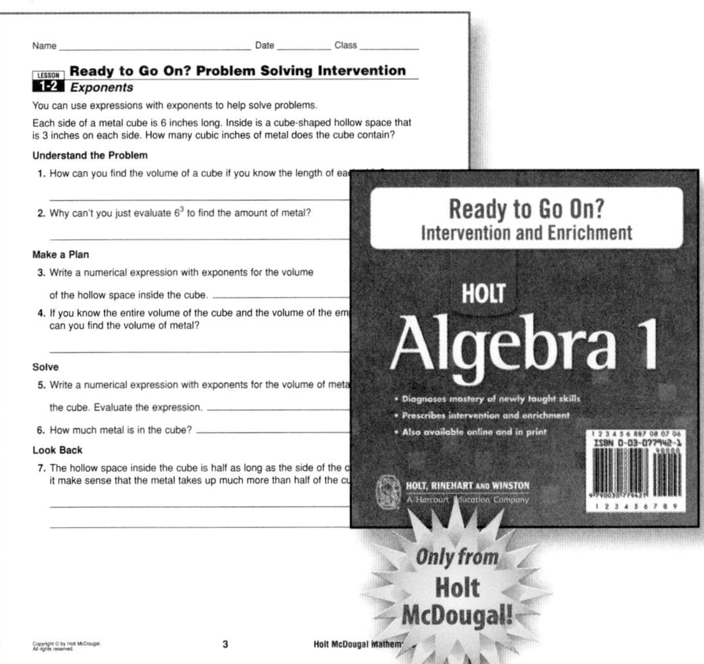

Ready to Go On? Intervention and Enrichment

RtI Tier 2

Diagnose mastery of *newly taught skills* and prescribe intervention

- Addresses deficiencies with alternative instruction and practice
- Checks progress with post-tests
- Available in print, on CD-ROM, and online

> *"Closing the gap in academic achievement occurs when the teacher responds to the learner's needs with flexible strategies and ongoing assessment."*
>
> — Freddie L. Renfro, Holt McDougal author

Program Highlights

Differentiated Instruction... 2

Holt McDougal Algebra 1 provides you with a multitude of instructional resources for Universal Access. The program also provides data resources for early intervention and monitoring as prescribed in Response to Intervention (RtI).

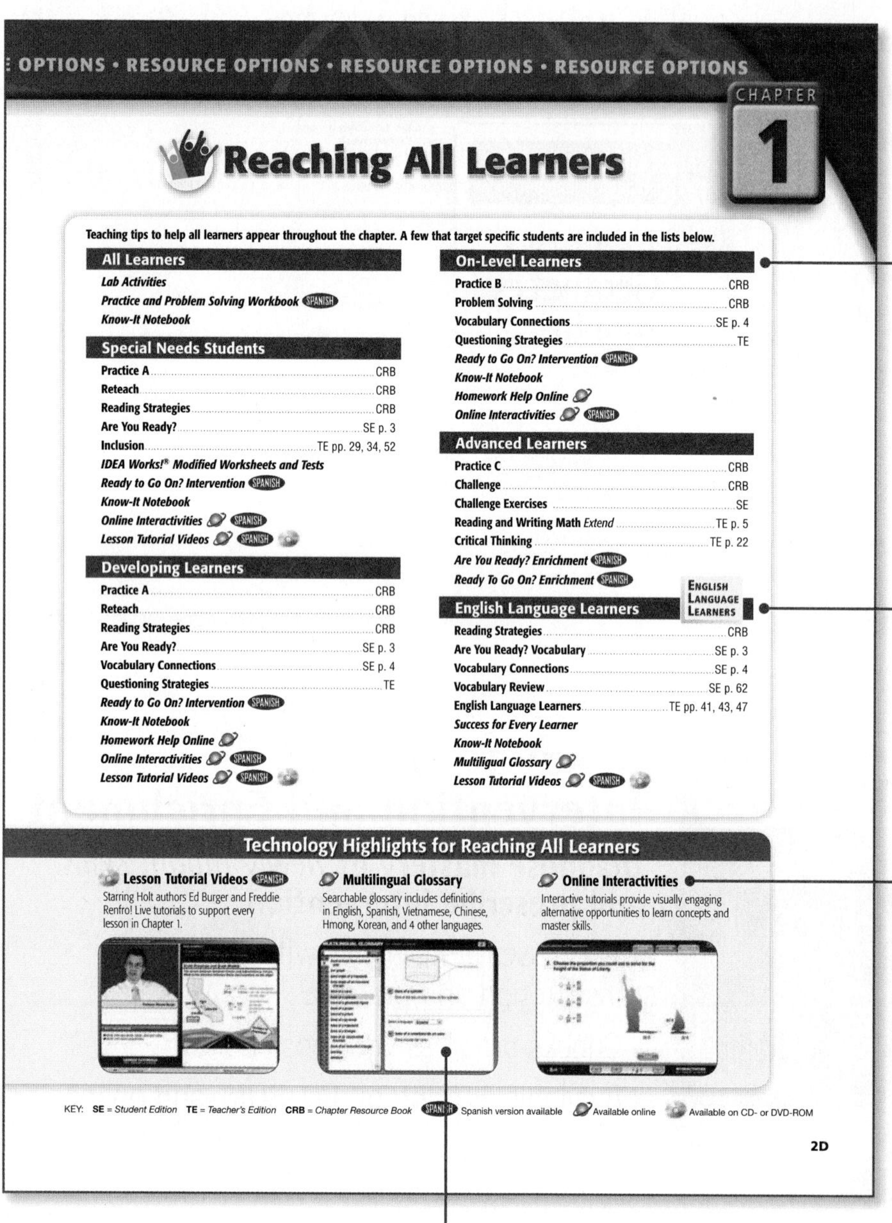

OPTIONS • RESOURCE OPTIONS • RESOURCE OPTIONS • RESOURCE OPTIONS

CHAPTER 1

Reaching All Learners

Teaching tips to help all learners appear throughout the chapter. A few that target specific students are included in the lists below.

All Learners
- *Lab Activities*
- *Practice and Problem Solving Workbook* SPANISH
- *Know-It Notebook*

Special Needs Students
- Practice A .... CRB
- Reteach .... CRB
- Reading Strategies .... CRB
- Are You Ready? .... SE p. 3
- Inclusion .... TE pp. 29, 34, 52
- *IDEA Works!® Modified Worksheets and Tests*
- *Ready to Go On? Intervention* SPANISH
- *Know-It Notebook*
- *Online Interactivities* SPANISH
- *Lesson Tutorial Videos* SPANISH

Developing Learners
- Practice A .... CRB
- Reteach .... CRB
- Reading Strategies .... CRB
- Are You Ready? .... SE p. 3
- Vocabulary Connections .... SE p. 4
- Questioning Strategies .... TE
- *Ready to Go On? Intervention* SPANISH
- *Know-It Notebook*
- *Homework Help Online*
- *Online Interactivities* SPANISH
- *Lesson Tutorial Videos* SPANISH

On-Level Learners
- Practice B .... CRB
- Problem Solving .... CRB
- Vocabulary Connections .... SE p. 4
- Questioning Strategies .... TE
- *Ready to Go On? Intervention* SPANISH
- *Know-It Notebook*
- *Homework Help Online*
- *Online Interactivities* SPANISH

Advanced Learners
- Practice C .... CRB
- Challenge .... CRB
- Challenge Exercises .... SE
- Reading and Writing Math *Extend* .... TE p. 5
- Critical Thinking .... TE p. 22
- *Are You Ready? Enrichment* SPANISH
- *Ready To Go On? Enrichment* SPANISH

English Language Learners (ENGLISH LANGUAGE LEARNERS)
- Reading Strategies .... CRB
- Are You Ready? Vocabulary .... SE p. 3
- Vocabulary Connections .... SE p. 4
- Vocabulary Review .... SE p. 62
- English Language Learners .... TE pp. 41, 43, 47
- *Success for Every Learner*
- *Know-It Notebook*
- *Multilingual Glossary*
- *Lesson Tutorial Videos* SPANISH

Technology Highlights for Reaching All Learners

Lesson Tutorial Videos SPANISH
Starring Holt authors Ed Burger and Freddie Renfro! Live tutorials to support every lesson in Chapter 1.

Multilingual Glossary
Searchable glossary includes definitions in English, Spanish, Vietnamese, Chinese, Hmong, Korean, and 4 other languages.

Online Interactivities
Interactive tutorials provide visually engaging alternative opportunities to learn concepts and master skills.

KEY: SE = *Student Edition* TE = *Teacher's Edition* CRB = *Chapter Resource Book* SPANISH Spanish version available; Available online; Available on CD- or DVD-ROM

2D

Special Needs, Developing, On-Level, and Advanced Learners

- Identifies features within the Teacher's Edition that target various skill levels
- Lists resources appropriate for different skill levels including 7 levels of lesson worksheets

English Language Learners

- Provides extensive support for English language learners
- Identifies appropriate reading strategies and vocabulary development

Online Interactivities

- Contains interactive tutorials with audio
- Features interactive exploration and practice items

Multilingual Glossary

- Includes an illustrated glossary in 13 languages
- Features English and Spanish audio

...to Reach All Learners

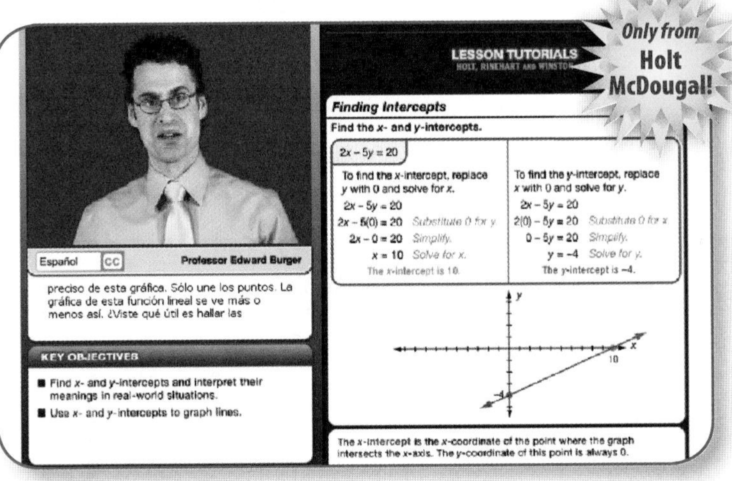

Lesson Tutorial Videos DVD-ROM

RtI Tiers 1,2

Illustrate every example using 382 videos

- Reaches visual and auditory learners
- Provides an at-home tutor for students who need to see the explanation again
- Includes Spanish subtitles
- Also available online

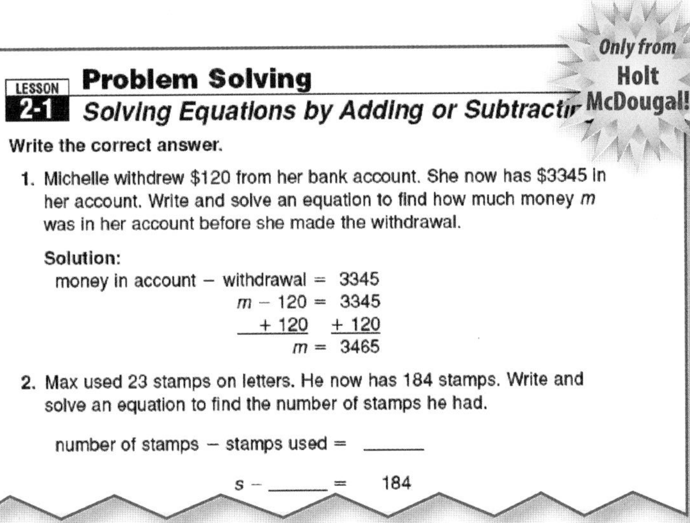

Only from Holt McDougal!

LESSON 2-1 **Problem Solving**

Solving Equations by Adding or Subtracting

Write the correct answer.

1. Michelle withdrew $120 from her bank account. She now has $3345 in her account. Write and solve an equation to find how much money m was in her account before she made the withdrawal.

   Solution:

   money in account − withdrawal = 3345

   $m - 120 = 3345$

   $+120 \quad +120$

   $m = 3465$

2. Max used 23 stamps on letters. He now has 184 stamps. Write and solve an equation to find the number of stamps he had.

   number of stamps − stamps used = ______

   s − ______ = 184

IDEA Works!® Modified Worksheets and Tests

RtI Tier 2

Offers adapted formats for students with special needs

- Provides modified practice and problem solving for every lesson
- Features modified tests and quizzes and vocabulary flash cards for every chapter
- Provides customization options through editable worksheets and tests

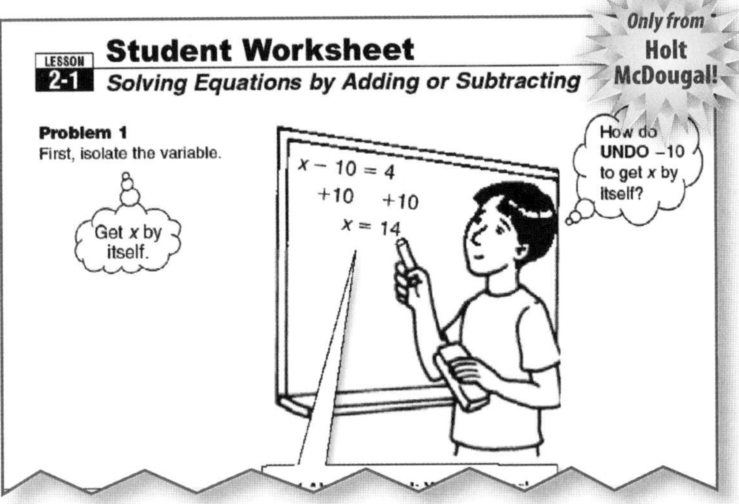

Only from Holt McDougal!

LESSON 2-1 **Student Worksheet**

Solving Equations by Adding or Subtracting

Problem 1

First, isolate the variable.

Success for Every Learner

RtI Tier 2

Ideal for developing, visual, and English Language Learners

- Explains lesson concepts with fewer words and more visuals
- Suggests alternate teaching strategies for English Language Learners

"*Key to* **effective instructional design** *is differentiated levels of support or scaffolding to support student learning when and where they need it.*" — **Dr. David J. Chard, Holt author**

Standards Mastery...

Integrated test prep means no surprises on test day. **Holt McDougal Algebra 1** includes lesson and cumulative review in standardized test format throughout every lesson and chapter to develop student confidence in test-taking skills without taking time away from core content.

Countdown to Testing

- Provides 120 days of test prep items to be used as daily warm-up exercises
- Items are located in the front of the Student Edition for easy access
- Teacher's Edition provides a correlation of the items to the NAEP standards

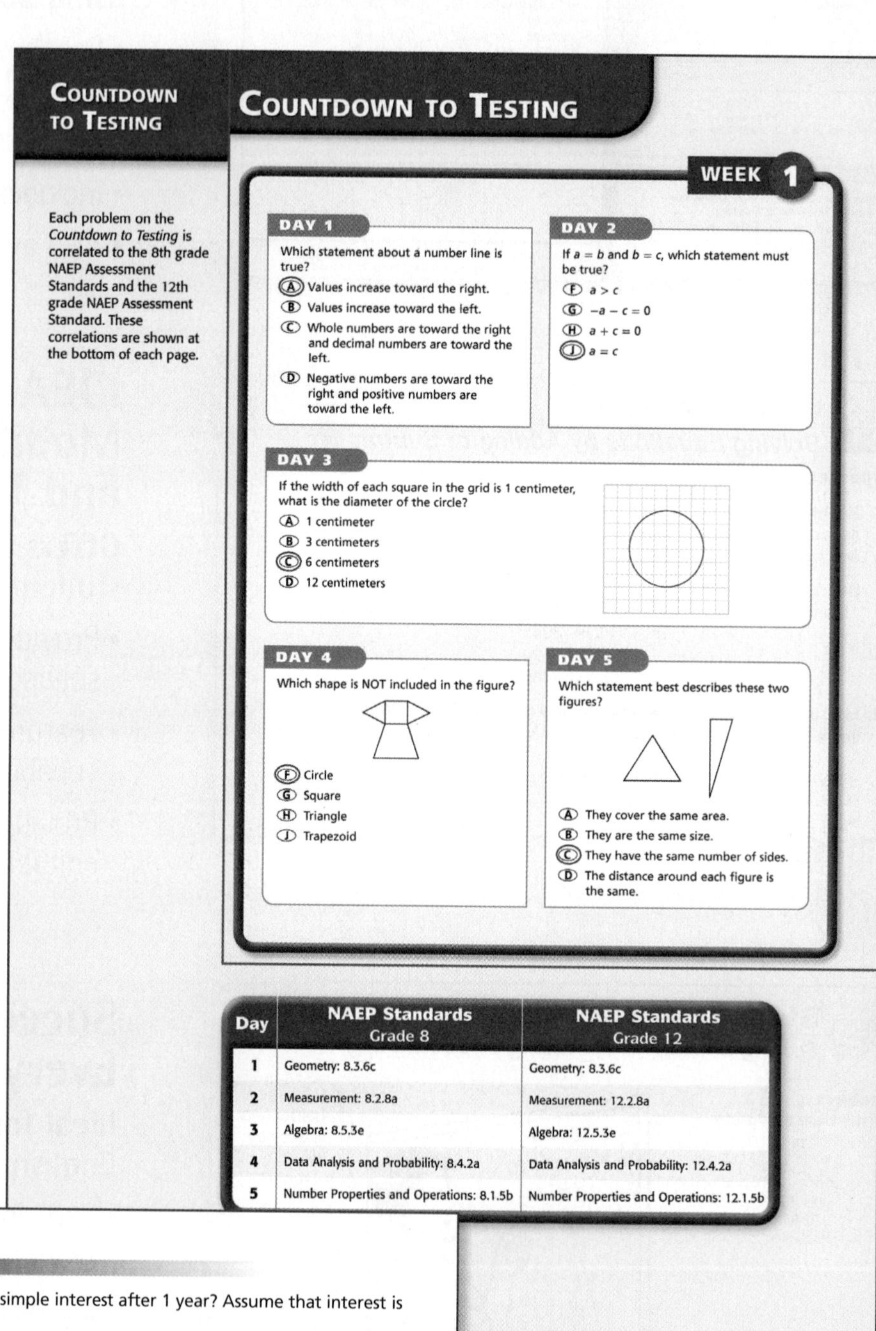

Countdown to Testing

Each problem on the *Countdown to Testing* is correlated to the 8th grade NAEP Assessment Standards and the 12th grade NAEP Assessment Standard. These correlations are shown at the bottom of each page.

COUNTDOWN TO TESTING

WEEK 1

DAY 1

Which statement about a number line is true?

(A) Values increase toward the right.
(B) Values increase toward the left.
(C) Whole numbers are toward the right and decimal numbers are toward the left.
(D) Negative numbers are toward the right and positive numbers are toward the left.

DAY 2

If $a = b$ and $b = c$, which statement must be true?

(F) $a > c$
(G) $-a - c = 0$
(H) $a + c = 0$
(J) $a = c$

DAY 3

If the width of each square in the grid is 1 centimeter, what is the diameter of the circle?

(A) 1 centimeter
(B) 3 centimeters
(C) 6 centimeters
(D) 12 centimeters

DAY 4

Which shape is NOT included in the figure?

(F) Circle
(G) Square
(H) Triangle
(J) Trapezoid

DAY 5

Which statement best describes these two figures?

(A) They cover the same area.
(B) They are the same size.
(C) They have the same number of sides.
(D) The distance around each figure is the same.

Day	NAEP Standards Grade 8	NAEP Standards Grade 12
1	Geometry: 8.3.6c	Geometry: 8.3.6c
2	Measurement: 8.2.8a	Measurement: 12.2.8a
3	Algebra: 8.5.3e	Algebra: 12.5.3e
4	Data Analysis and Probability: 8.4.2a	Data Analysis and Probability: 12.4.2a
5	Number Properties and Operations: 8.1.5b	Number Properties and Operations: 12.1.5b

Test Prep

- Provides daily practice of new and previously taught skills
- Uses various standardized test formats

TEST PREP

27. Which account earns the most simple interest after 1 year? Assume that interest is paid annually.
    (A) \$5000 at 8% per year
    (B) \$10,000 at 4% per year
    (C) \$8000 at 4.8% per year
    (D) \$4000 at 10.2% per year

28. Craig earns \$200 per week plus 8% commission on sales. Joan earns \$150 per week plus 12% commission on sales. Last week, both had sales of \$1500. Who earned more money?
    (F) Craig earned more than Joan.
    (G) Joan earned more than Craig.
    (H) Both earned the same amount.
    (J) Cannot be determined

29. **Short Response** If 2% of a number is 300, what is 6% of the number? Explain how you got your answer.

...and Test Preparation

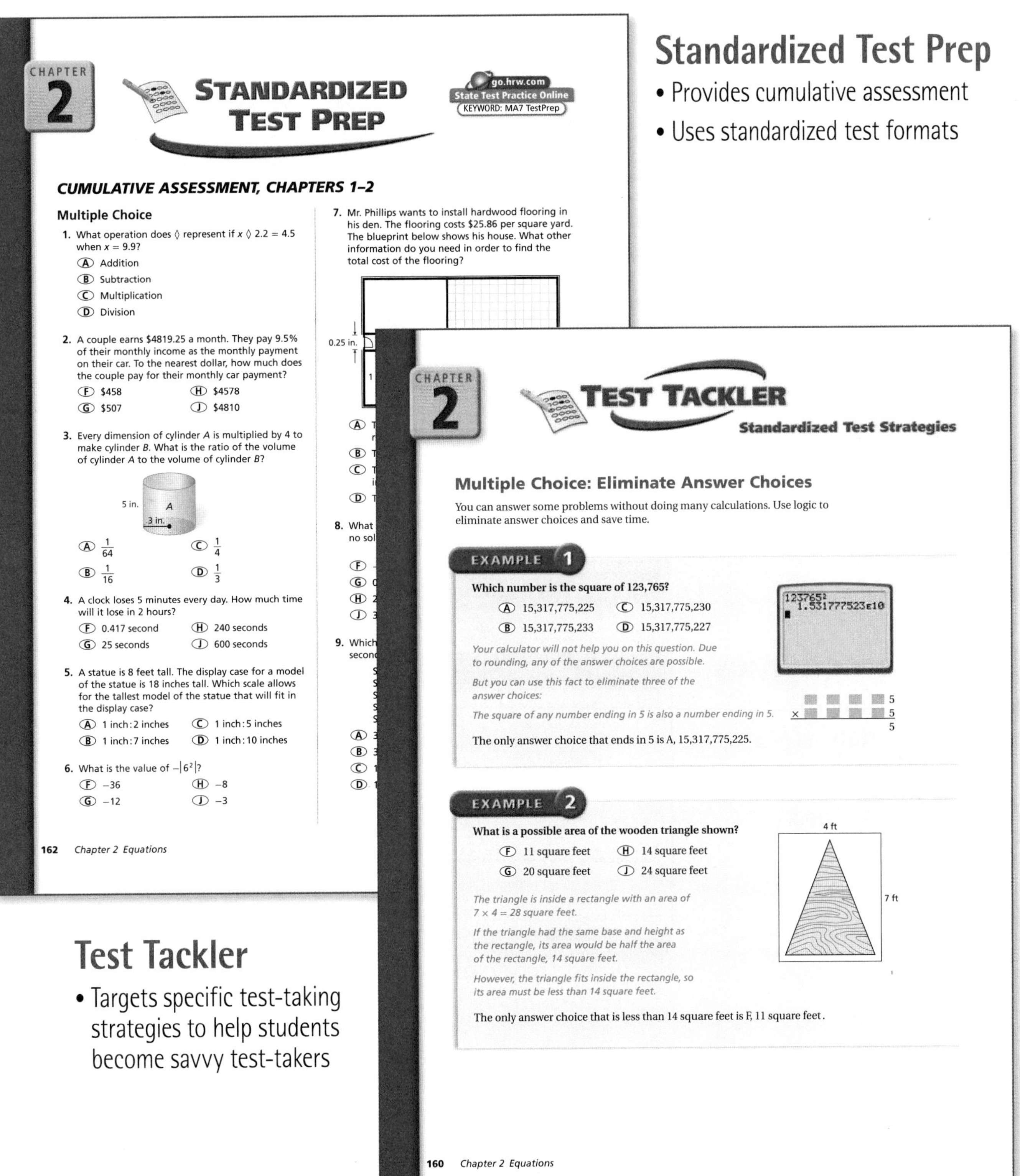

CHAPTER 2

STANDARDIZED TEST PREP

go.hrw.com
State Test Practice Online
KEYWORD: MA7 TestPrep

CUMULATIVE ASSESSMENT, CHAPTERS 1–2

Multiple Choice

1. What operation does ◊ represent if x ◊ 2.2 = 4.5 when x = 9.9?
   Ⓐ Addition
   Ⓑ Subtraction
   Ⓒ Multiplication
   Ⓓ Division

2. A couple earns $4819.25 a month. They pay 9.5% of their monthly income as the monthly payment on their car. To the nearest dollar, how much does the couple pay for their monthly car payment?
   Ⓕ $458 Ⓗ $4578
   Ⓖ $507 Ⓙ $4810

3. Every dimension of cylinder *A* is multiplied by 4 to make cylinder *B*. What is the ratio of the volume of cylinder *A* to the volume of cylinder *B*?
   5 in. A 3 in.
   Ⓐ $\frac{1}{64}$ Ⓒ $\frac{1}{4}$
   Ⓑ $\frac{1}{16}$ Ⓓ $\frac{1}{3}$

4. A clock loses 5 minutes every day. How much time will it lose in 2 hours?
   Ⓕ 0.417 second Ⓗ 240 seconds
   Ⓖ 25 seconds Ⓙ 600 seconds

5. A statue is 8 feet tall. The display case for a model of the statue is 18 inches tall. Which scale allows for the tallest model of the statue that will fit in the display case?
   Ⓐ 1 inch:2 inches Ⓒ 1 inch:5 inches
   Ⓑ 1 inch:7 inches Ⓓ 1 inch:10 inches

6. What is the value of $-|6^2|$?
   Ⓕ −36 Ⓗ −8
   Ⓖ −12 Ⓙ −3

7. Mr. Phillips wants to install hardwood flooring in his den. The flooring costs $25.86 per square yard. The blueprint below shows his house. What other information do you need in order to find the total cost of the flooring?
   0.25 in.

8. What ... no sol...

9. Which ... secon...

162 Chapter 2 Equations

CHAPTER 2

TEST TACKLER
Standardized Test Strategies

Multiple Choice: Eliminate Answer Choices

You can answer some problems without doing many calculations. Use logic to eliminate answer choices and save time.

EXAMPLE 1

Which number is the square of 123,765?
Ⓐ 15,317,775,225 Ⓒ 15,317,775,230
Ⓑ 15,317,775,233 Ⓓ 15,317,775,227

123765²
1.531777523E10

Your calculator will not help you on this question. Due to rounding, any of the answer choices are possible.

But you can use this fact to eliminate three of the answer choices:

The square of any number ending in 5 is also a number ending in 5.

5
× 5
5

The only answer choice that ends in 5 is A, 15,317,775,225.

EXAMPLE 2

What is a possible area of the wooden triangle shown?
Ⓕ 11 square feet Ⓗ 14 square feet
Ⓖ 20 square feet Ⓙ 24 square feet

4 ft
7 ft

The triangle is inside a rectangle with an area of 7 × 4 = 28 square feet.

If the triangle had the same base and height as the rectangle, its area would be half the area of the rectangle, 14 square feet.

However, the triangle fits inside the rectangle, so its area must be less than 14 square feet.

The only answer choice that is less than 14 square feet is F, 11 square feet.

160 Chapter 2 Equations

Standardized Test Prep

- Provides cumulative assessment
- Uses standardized test formats

Test Tackler

- Targets specific test-taking strategies to help students become savvy test-takers

“Assessment should enhance mathematics learning. What we assess and how we assess it communicates what we value.”

– Steven J. Leinwand, Holt McDougal author

Integrated Technology that Motivates Students...

4

Program Highlights

Lesson Tutorial Videos DVD-ROM

Illustrates every example using 382 videos

- Provides personal take-home tutor
- Keeps students learning when a substitute teacher is necessary
- Helps absent students learn concepts
- Also available online

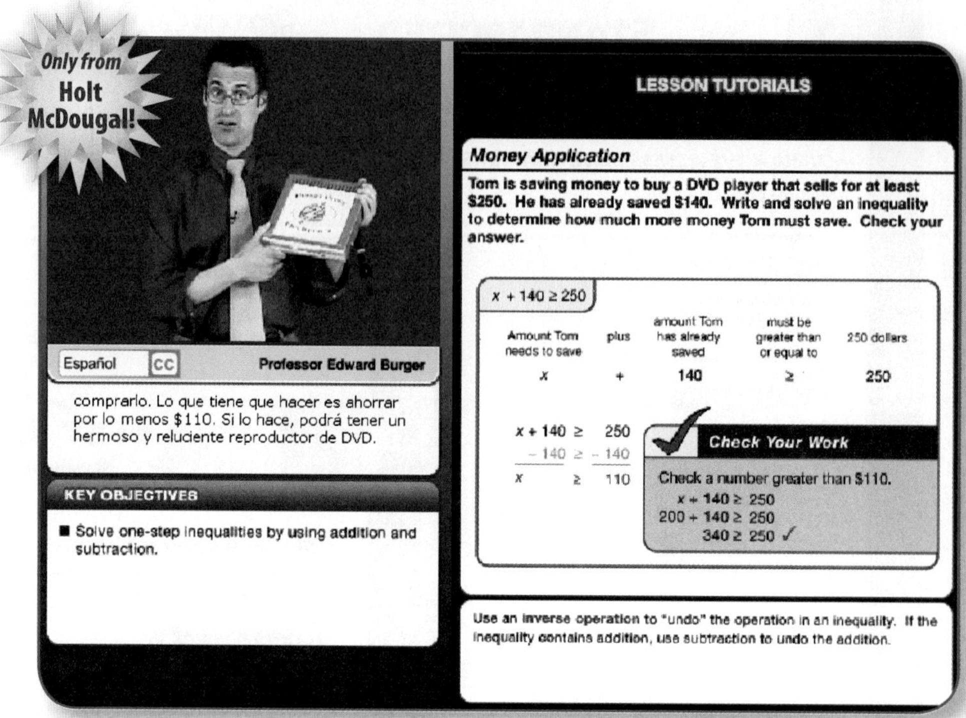

Online Interactivities

Engages students with interactive tutorials

- Visually engages students
- Provides at-home support with online examples
- Spanish audio available
- Found online

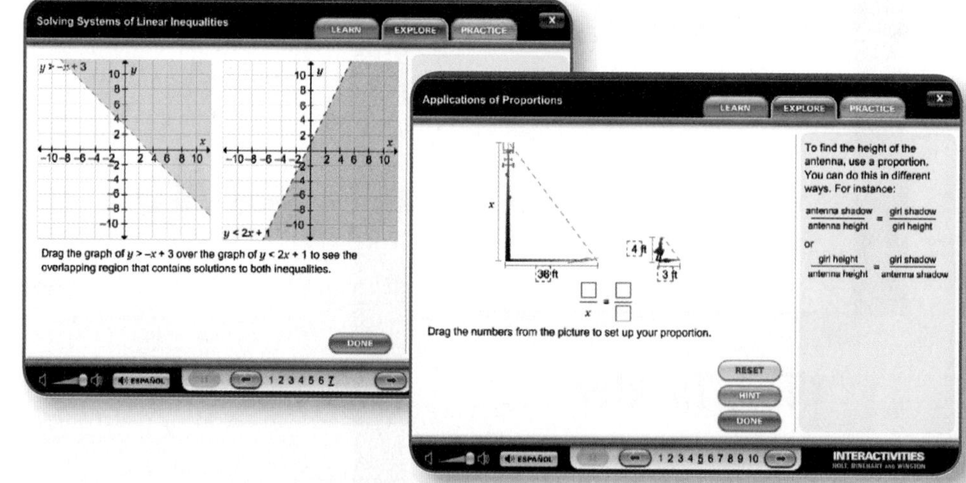

Homework Help Online

Provides interactive homework help

- Includes access to *Lesson Tutorial Videos* and *Online Interactivities*
- Provides interactive practice similar to lesson exercises
- Contains stepped-out solutions and hints for selected lesson exercises

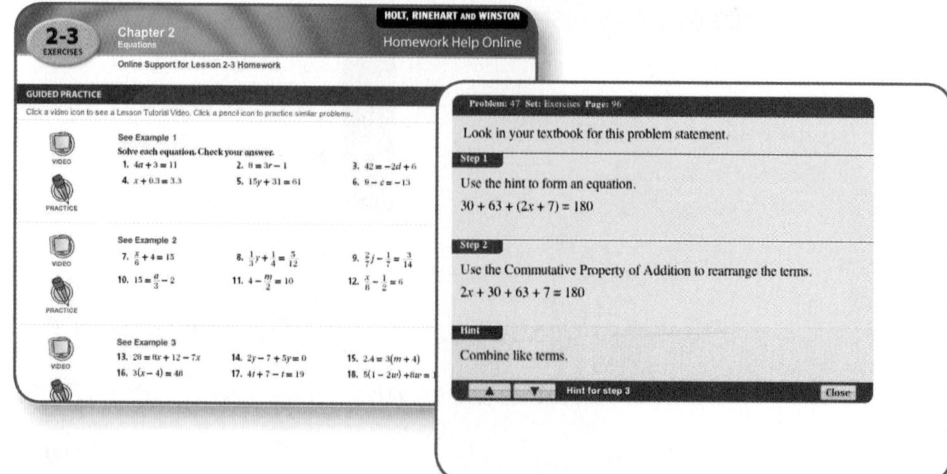

...Enhances Instruction...

Interactive Answers and Solutions CD-ROM

Create customized answer keys that contain only what you need

- Project the answers to only the exercises you assigned
- Make customized answer transparencies
- Display the complete solution for any exercise at the click of a mouse!

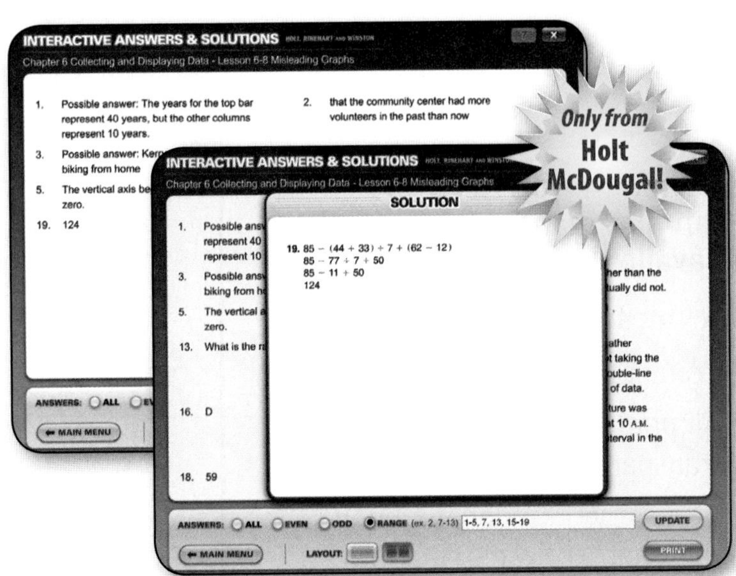

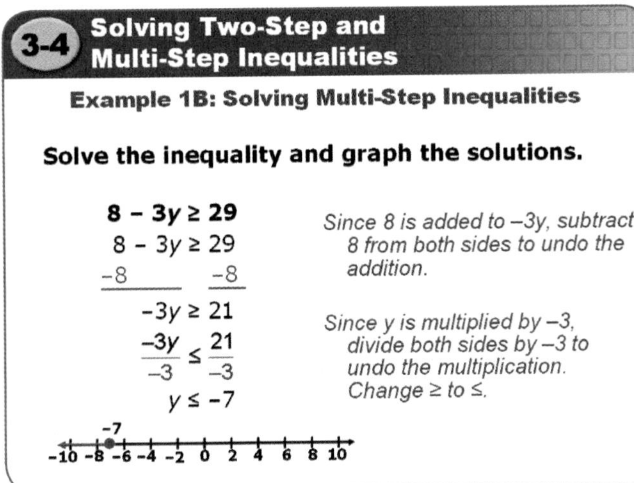

Power Presentations CD-ROM

Enlivens instruction through Power Point® presentations

- Includes Warm-Ups, Lesson Quizzes, and complete stepped-out lesson presentations
- Customizable to match your teaching style
- Found with the Teacher One-Stop™

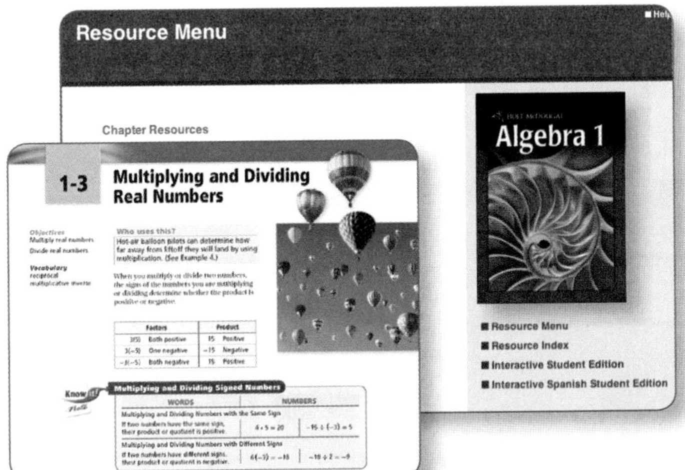

Student One Stop™ CD-ROM

Provides resources for students who may not have Internet access

- Contains entire Student Edition and all workbooks
- Includes both *Are You Ready? Intervention and Enrichment*, and *Ready to Go On? Intervention and Enrichment*

> "Technology, when used appropriately, can **improve students' mathematical understanding** and problem-solving skills."
>
> — Dr. Bert K. Waits, Holt author

Program Highlights

...Simplifies Planning and...

Teacher One Stop™ DVD-ROM

Everything you need to plan and manage lessons is available in one place

Includes:

- Complete Teacher's Edition
- All print resources and transparencies
- Editable worksheets found in the Chapter Resource Books
- Customizable lesson plans
- Calendar Planner
- PuzzleView
- MindPoint® Quiz Show
- Resources for TI Technology
- ExamView® Assessment Suite
- Editable Power Point® Presentations

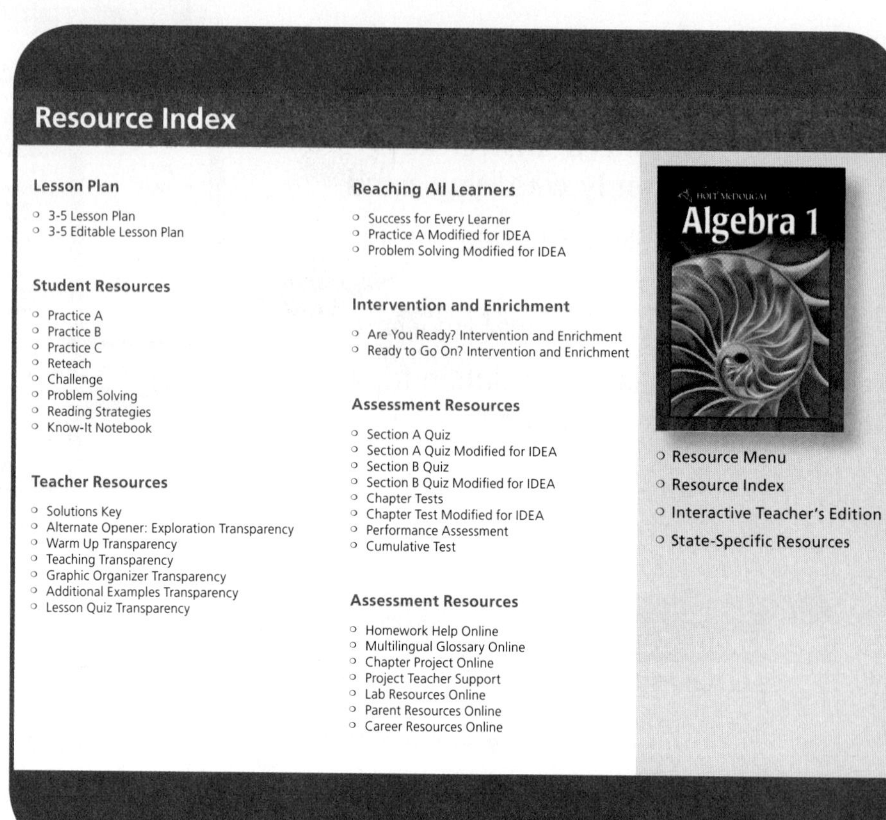

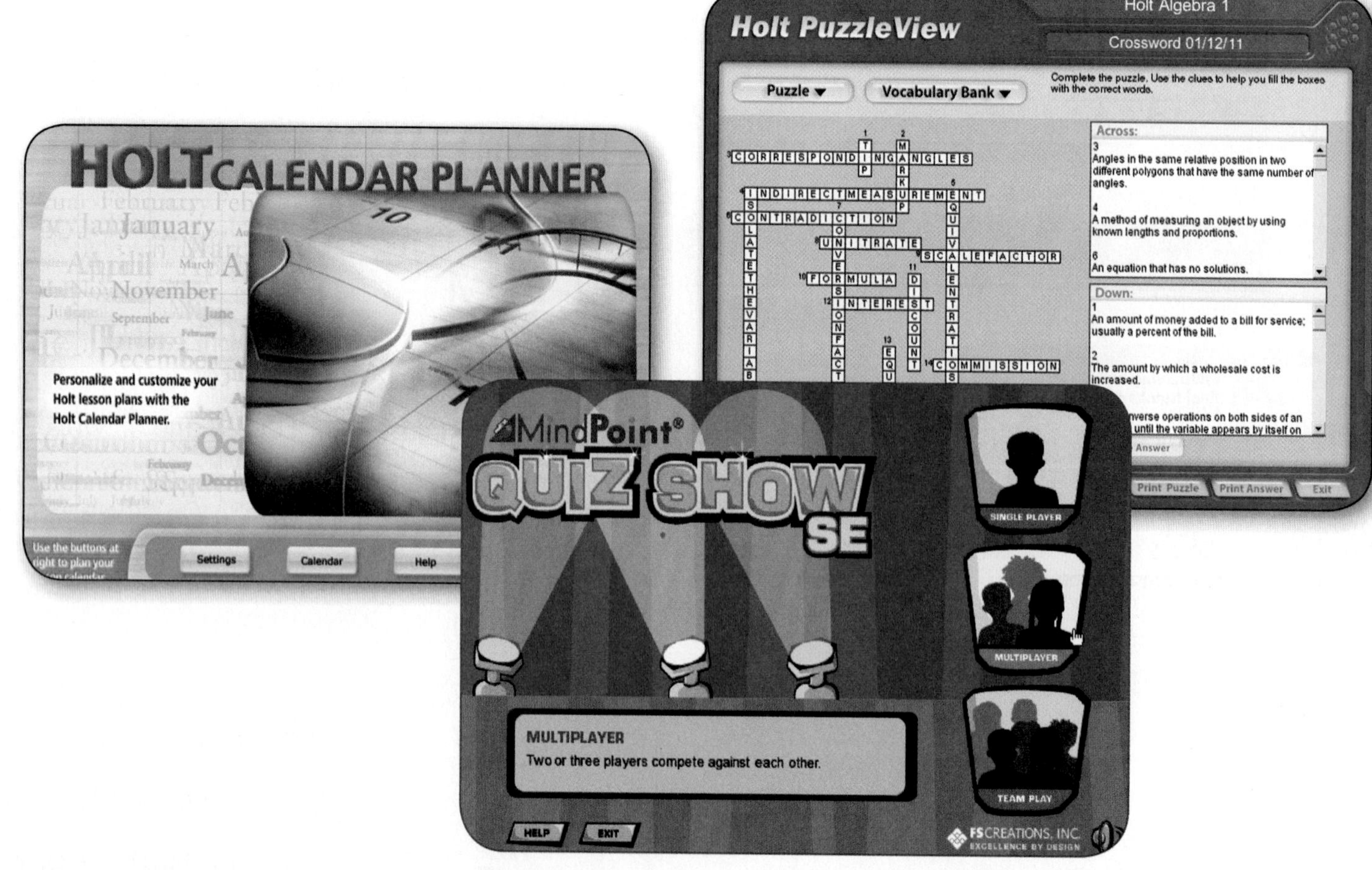

...Makes Online Resources Accessible

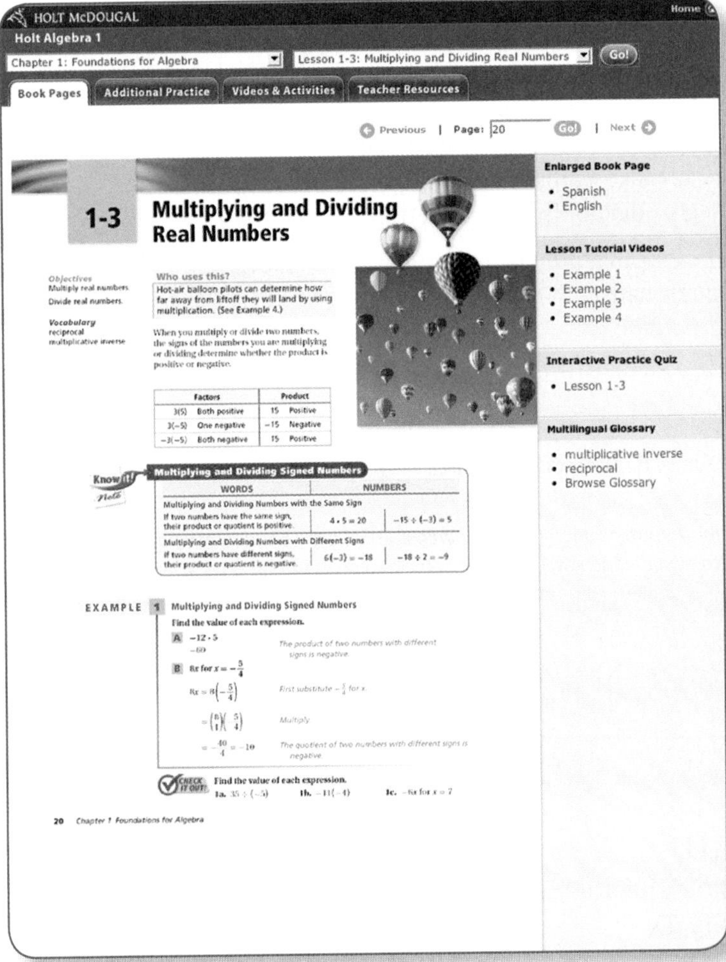

Online Edition

Go home empty-handed and work online

For teacher:

- Editable lesson plans and worksheets
- Lesson transparencies
- PowerPoint® presentations
- Leveled practice worksheets for every lesson
- *IDEA Works!* modified worksheets, quizzes, and tests for special needs students
- *Are You Ready?* and *Ready to Go On? Intervention and Enrichment*
- *Success for Every Learner* teaching strategies and worksheets

For students:

- Entire Student Edition
- Lesson Tutorial Videos
- Online Interactivities
- Homework Help Online
- Extra practice
- Interactive quizzes and tests
- All workbooks
- Graphing calculator
- Virtual manipulatives
- Parent resources

and much more...

Online Assessment

Automatically scores online assessments and prescribes and assigns intervention

- Analyze mastery by topic or standard
- Generate a variety of reports
- Seamlessly integrate content with the **ExamView® Assessment Suite**

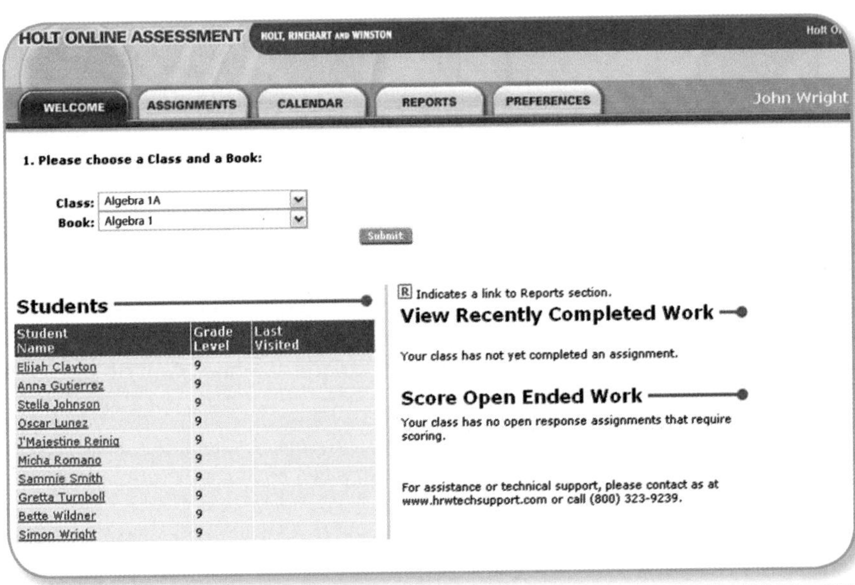

Program Highlights

Edward B. Burger, Ph.D.
Professor of Mathematics and Chair | Williams College, MA

Student Engagement

"Learning should be fun. Deep and abstract ideas are challenging to all, but the challenge should be a pleasurable one that students want to conquer. Thus we offer levity throughout the *Holt McDougal* series– jokes for the teachers to share with their students and entertaining antics on the accompanying videos, mixing mathematical insights with laughs. There is no better student than the student who wants to learn. In this program we worked hard to make learning fun so students enjoy the journey and, as a result, attain a deeper understanding of the mathematics they explore.

The mathematics is developed in a meaningful manner with student readers in mind. Questions such as "What would resonate with real middle school students today?" were asked at every stage of the writing."

SUPPORTING RESEARCH

Ames, R., & Ames, C. (Eds.). (1984). *Research on motivation in education: Vol. 1. Student motivation.* New York: Academic Press.

Brewster, Cori, and Jennifer Fager. (2000). Increasing Student Engagement and Motivation: From Time-on-Task to Homework. Portland, Ore.: Northwest Regional Educational Laboratory.

David J. Chard, Ph.D.
Leon Simmons Dean, School of Education and Human Development, Southern Methodist University, TX

Reaching All Learners

"*Holt McDougal Math* is designed to assist teachers in helping all their students to learn conceptual knowledge, skills, and strategies essential to understanding sophisticated mathematics.

This program was designed with instructional features that represent a coherent pedagogical approach to mathematics instruction. Each lesson begins with carefully wrought examples of all of the skills, concepts, and strategies addressed. Key to any instructional program is sufficient scaffolding to support student learning. This ensures that all students are able to understand and solve increasingly complex problems."

SUPPORTING RESEARCH

Bransford, J. D., Brown, A. L., & Cocking, R. R. (Eds.). (2000). *How people learn: Brain, mind, experience, and school.* Washington, DC: National Research Council.

Gersten, R., Chard, D. J., Baker, S., et al. (2005). A meta-analysis of research on mathematics instruction for students with learning disabilities. Signal Hill, CA: Instructional Research Group.

Paul A. Kennedy, Ph.D.
Professor, Department of Mathematics | Colorado State University, CO

Algebraic Thinking

"When students enter the middle grades, they are beginning the preparation for the transition to more advanced mathematical topics such as algebra and geometry while enhancing their basic arithmetic knowledge. It is crucial that they develop abstract reasoning as well as symbolic manipulation skills.

In the *Holt McDougal Math* series, content is carefully developed using methods aligned with standard best practices. The idea of "doing and undoing" is developed early in the program and carried thought the series. Additionally students need to see the relationships between the math they are learning and real-world scenarios."

SUPPORTING RESEARCH

Vygotsky, L.S. (1978). *Mind and society: The development of higher mental processes.* Cambridge, MA: Harvard University Press.

Driscoll, Mark J. (1997). *Fostering algebraic thinking.* Portsmouth, NH.; Heinemann.

Steven J. Leinwand
Principal Research Annalyst, American Institutes for Research | Washington, DC

Assessing Student Understanding

"As the mathematics curriculum has broadened to encompass communicating and conceptualizing, problem solving and reasoning, so too must our traditional view of assessment broaden. To reflect today's curriculum and more accurately determine students' progress, assessment should be an integral part of the teaching and learning process. Questioning strategies, such as those found in the *Holt McDougal Math* series, can be integral to daily assessment, along with lesson quizzes.

Additionally, assessment should provide opportunities for students to evaluate, reflect upon, and improve their work. The Are You Ready? feature allows students to determine if they have the skills to complete the chapter successfully. And more importantly Ready to Go On? provided understanding the material and to work several times in a chapter to improve their work before the Chapter Test (rather then after)."

SUPPORTING RESEARCH

NCTM Assessment Standards Working Groups (1995). *Assessment Standards for School Mathematics. National Council of Teachers of Mathematics. Reston, VA.*

National Research Council (1989). *Everybody Counts. Washington, DC; National Academy Press.*

Freddie L. Renfro
Former Director of Mathematics Instruction K–12 | Texas City Independent School District, TX

Differentiated Instruction

"Imagine a classroom where diversity in learning is the norm, and the teacher responds to the learners' needs with flexible strategies, open dialogue, and ongoing assessment.

Every child is unique. Finding ways to tailor instruction to meet individual student needs in the classroom can be a manageable task with the right support. In the *Holt McDougal Math* series, we promote differentiated instruction by including activities that address a variety of learning styles: discovery learning, the use of concrete examples, and student interaction, to name a few.

The Teacher's Edition offers suggestions for differentiated assessment as well so that students have the opportunity to demonstrate their understanding in a manner that reflects their learning style."

SUPPORTING RESEARCH

Tomlinson, C. (1999). *The differentiated classroom: Responding to the needs of all learners.* Alexandria, VA: Association for Supervision and Curriculum Development.

Willis, S. and Mann, Larry. (2000). *Differentiating instruction.* Alexandria, VA: Association for Supervision and Curriculum Development.

Tom Roby, Ph. D.
Associate Professor and Director of Quantitative Learning Center | University of Connecticut, CT

Intervention

"The middle grades mark a key transition for students, from basic arithmetical knowledge to the more abstract topics of algebra and geometry. Students need to understand the fundamental properties of numbers, not just the procedures of arithmetic, in order to become comfortable when numbers are replaced by variables. This transition from the concrete to the abstract can be facilitated by using manipulatives and pictures, as is done systematically in the *Holt McDougal Math* series .

The program is carefully designed so that topics fit together naturally. Just addressing each topic is not enough, since students can easily find themselves memorizing many specific individual procedures without ever seeing the bigger picture. Ensuring that the mathematics are not only accurate, but also coherent within the grade and well articulated from one grade to the next, is key to helping students succeed at this level and in those to come."

SUPPORTING RESEARCH

All National Research Council. (2001). *Adding it up: Helping Children learn mathematics.* J. Kilpatriack, J.. Swafford, and B. Findell (Eds.) Mathematics Learning Study Committee, Center for Education, Division of Behavioral and Social Sciences and Education: Washington, CD: National Academy Press. **Wu, H. H. (2001)** *How to prepare students for algebra.* American Educator 25 (2): 10-17.

Bert K. Waits, Ph.D.
Professor Emeritus of Mathematics | The Ohio State University, OH

Technology to Enhance Learning

"Research has demonstrated that technology, when used appropriately, can improve students' mathematical understanding and problem-solving skills. Similarly, technological tools can help teachers challenge students to use and understand mathematics in real-world scenarios.

The *Holt McDougal Math* series presents a balanced approach to learning. We stress that students must utilize all available tools, including mental and paper-and- pencil skills and technology, in the mathematics-learning process. This series uses technology not as an end in itself, but rather as a means for understanding and application. Current research supports this use of computer software including spreadsheets, dynamic geometry software, and graphing calculators."

SUPPORTING RESEARCH

Graham, A.T., & J.O.J. Thomas. (2000). Building a versatile understanding of algebraic variables with a graphic calculator. *Educational Studies in Mathematics*, 41 (3), 265-282.

Hallar, Jeannie C., & Karen Norwood. (1999). The effects of a graphing-approach intermediate algebra curriculum on students' understanding of function. *Journal for Research in Mathematics Education*, 30 (2), 220-226.

Holt McDougal Algebra 1 Program Components

Student Edition

Student One Stop™ CD-ROM

Premier Online Edition

Teacher's Edition

Assessment and Intervention

Are You Ready? Intervention and Enrichment

Assessment Resources

Ready to Go On? Intervention and Enrichment

Differentiated Instruction

Alternate Openers: Explorations Transparencies

Chapter Resources

IDEA Works!® Modified Worksheets and Tests

Lab Activities

Lesson Tutorial Videos DVD-ROM and Online

Manipulatives Kit

Multilingual Glossary

Premier Online Edition

Student One Stop™ CD-ROM

Success for Every Learner

Workbooks

Know-It Notebook™
and Teacher's Guide

Practice and Problem Solving Workbook
and Teacher's Guide

Spanish Resources

Spanish Student Edition

Are You Ready? Intervention and Enrichment

Assessment Resources

Practice and Problem Solving Workbook

Lesson Tutorial Videos with
Spanish closed captioning

Ready to Go On? Intervention and Enrichment

Integrated Technology

Are You Ready? Intervention and Enrichment
CD-ROM and online

Homework Help Online

Interactive Answers and Solutions CD-ROM

Interactivities Online

Lesson Tutorial Videos DVD-ROM and Online

Premier Online Edition

Ready to Go On? Intervention and Enrichment
CD-ROM and Online

Student One Stop™ CD-ROM

Teacher One Stop™ DVD-ROM

Additional Teaching Resources

Lesson Plans

Solutions Key

Teacher's Manipulatives Kit

To preview all Holt McDougal Algebra 1 products, go to hmhschool.com/virtualsampling/

Foundations for Algebra

Tools for Success

CHAPTER 2

Equations

go.hrw.com
Online Resources
KEYWORD: MA11 TOC

Inequalities

Tools for Success

CHAPTER 4

Functions

go.hrw.com
Online Resources
KEYWORD: MA11 TOC

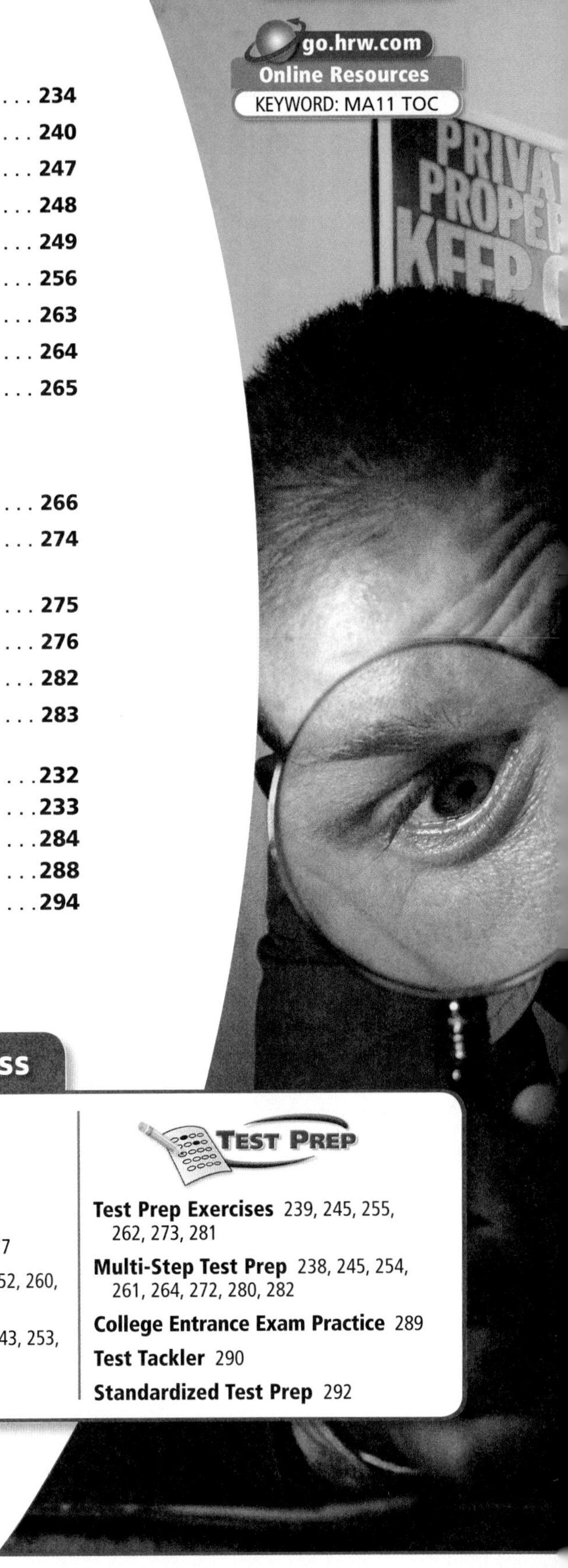

Tools for Success

Linear Functions

Tools for Success

Systems of Equations and Inequalities

CHAPTER 6

go.hrw.com
Online Resources
KEYWORD: MA11 TOC

Tools for Success

Exponents and Polynomials

Tools for Success

CHAPTER 8

Factoring Polynomials

go.hrw.com
Online Resources
KEYWORD: MA11 TOC

Tools for Success

Quadratic Functions and Equations

Tools for Success

CHAPTER 10

Data Analysis and Probability

go.hrw.com
Online Resources
KEYWORD: MA11 TOC

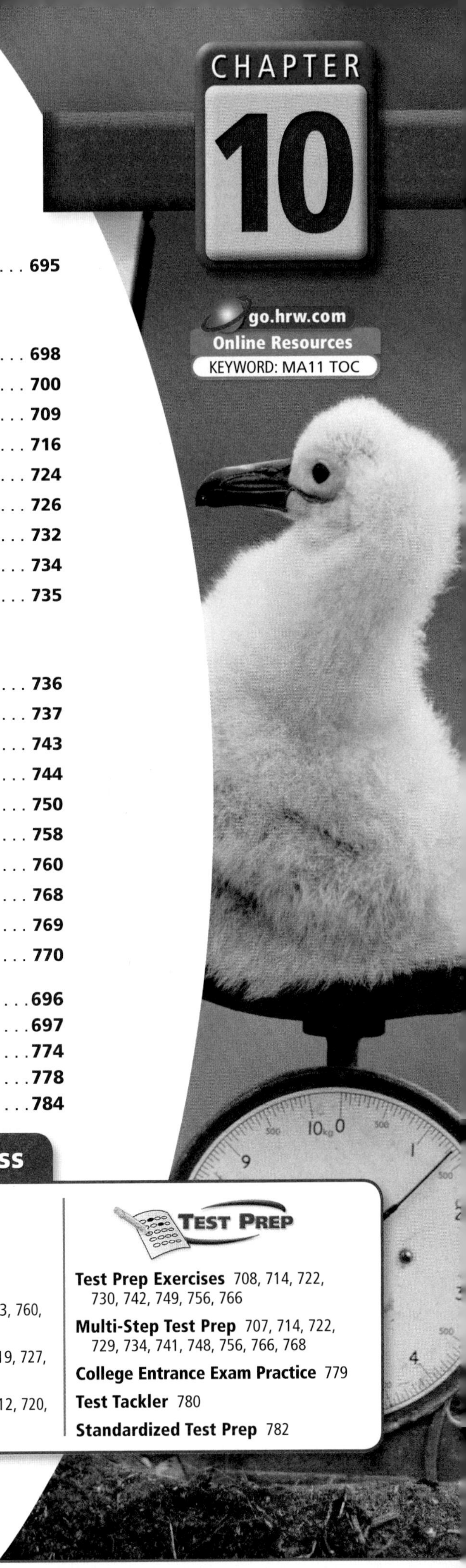

Tools for Success

Exponential and Radical Functions

Tools for Success

CHAPTER 12

Rational Functions and Equations

go.hrw.com
Online Resources
KEYWORD: MA11 TOC

Tools for Success

WHO USES MATHEMATICS?

The Career Path features are a set of interviews with young adults who are either preparing for or just beginning in different career fields. These people share what math courses they studied in high school, how math is used in their field, and what options the future holds. Also, many exercises throughout the book highlight the different skills used in various career fields.

Career Path

go.hrw.com
Career Resources Online
KEYWORD: MA7 Career

Career Applications

CULINARY ARTS *p. 202*

If you enjoy preparing food, you might be interested in a culinary arts program. Besides cooking, you can also learn business skills, like how to start and run your own catering business. See page 202 to find out what math courses will help prepare you for this career.

DATA MINING *p. 358*

Read the Career Path on page 358 to learn what courses a data mining major may take and what careers are available in this field. For example, do you like to keep track of sports statistics? If so, a background in data mining can help you find work with a professional sports team.

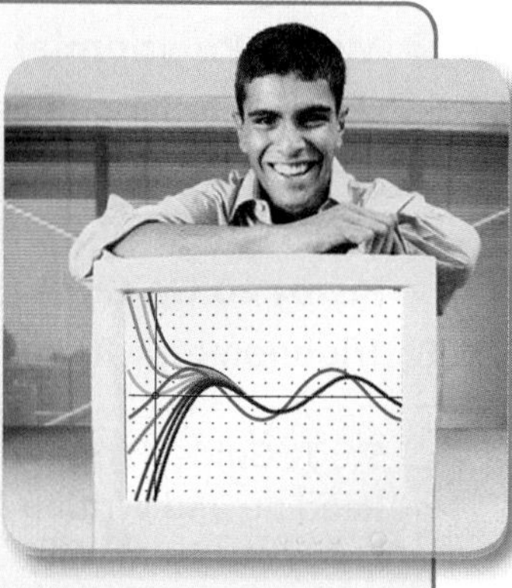

BIOSTATISTICS *p. 767*

The Career Path on page 767 describes the education and experience needed to be a successful biostatistician. One important job biostatisticians do is research and test medications to ensure that they are both effective and safe for human use.

Why Learn Mathematics?

Links to interesting topics may accompany real-world applications in the examples or exercises. For a complete list of all applications in *Holt McDougal Algebra 1*, see page IN1 in the Index.

LINK

Number Theory

Fibonacci numbers occur frequently throughout nature. The number of petals on many flowers are numbers of the Fibonacci sequence. Two petals on a flower are rare but 3, 5, and even 34 petals are common.

Find the given term of each arithmetic sequence.

34. 2.5, 8.5, 14.5, 20.5, ...; 30th term

35. 189.6, 172.3, 155, 137.7, ...; 18th term

36. $\frac{1}{4}, \frac{3}{4}, \frac{5}{4}, \frac{7}{4}, \ldots$; 15th term

37. $\frac{2}{3}, \frac{11}{12}, \frac{7}{6}, \frac{17}{12}, \ldots$; 25th term

38. **Number Theory** The sequence 1, 1, 2, 3, 5, 8, 13, ... is a famous sequence called the Fibonacci sequence. After the first two terms, each term is the sum of the previous two terms.

a. Write the first 10 terms of the Fibonacci sequence. Is the Fibonacci sequence arithmetic? Explain.

b. Notice that the third term is divisible by 2. Are the 6th and 9th terms also divisible by 2? What conclusion can you draw about every third term? Why is this true?

c. Can you find any other patterns? (*Hint:* Look at every 4th and 5th term.)

39. **Entertainment** Seats in a concert hall are arranged in the pattern shown.

a. The numbers of seats in the rows form an arithmetic sequence. Write a rule for the arithmetic sequence.

b. How many seats are in the 15th row?

LINKS

Real-World

LINK

Biology

When bleeding occurs, platelets (which appear green in the image above) help to form a clot to reduce blood loss. Calcium and vitamin K are also necessary for clot formation.

LINK

Engineering

This arched bridge spans a river near the city of Yokote in northwestern Japan.

LINK

Travel

Building began on the Tower of Pisa, located in Pisa, Italy, in 1173. The tower started leaning after the third story was added. At the fifth story, attempts were made to correct the leaning. The tower was finally complete in 1350.

Focus on Problem Solving

The Problem-Solving Plan

To be a good problem solver you need a good problem-solving plan. Using a problem-solving plan along with a problem-solving strategy helps you organize your work and correctly solve the problem. The plan used in this book is outlined below.

UNDERSTAND the Problem

- **What are you asked to find?** Make sure you understand exactly what the problem is asking. Restate the problem in your own words.
- **What information is given in the problem?** List every piece of information the problem gives you.
- **Is all the information relevant?** Sometimes problems have extra information that is not needed to solve the problem. Try to determine what is and is not needed. This helps you stay organized when you are making a plan.
- **Were you given enough information to solve the problem?** Sometimes there simply is not enough information to solve the problem. List what else you need to know to solve the problem.

Make a PLAN

- **What problem-solving strategy or strategies can you use to help you solve the problem?** Think about strategies you have used in the past to solve problems. Would any of them be helpful in solving this problem?
- **Create a step-by-step plan of how you will solve the problem.** Write out your plan in words to help you get a clearer idea of how to solve the problem mathematically.

SOLVE

- **Use your plan to solve the problem.** Translate your plan from words to math. Show each step in your solution and write your answer in a complete sentence.

LOOK BACK

- **Did you completely answer the question that was asked?** Be sure you answered the question that was asked and that your answer is complete.
- **Is your answer reasonable?** Your answer should make sense.
- **Could you have used a different strategy to solve the problem?** Solving the problem again with a different strategy is a good way to check your answer.
- **Did you learn anything that could help you solve similar problems in the future?** You may want to take notes about this kind of problem and the strategy you used to solve it.

Using the Problem-Solving Plan

The feeder at an animal shelter needs 125 pounds of food to feed the rescued dogs for a month. A local grocery store is having a special—buy two 10-pound bags of dog food and get a 3.5-pound bag free. What is the fewest number of 10-pound bags the feeder can buy to have enough dog food for the month?

UNDERSTAND the Problem

List the important information in the problem.

At least 125 pounds of dog food are needed for one month.
If the feeder buys two 10-pound bags of dog food, she gets a 3.5-pound bag free.
What is the problem asking you to find?

The fewest number of 10-pound bags the feeder needs to buy to have 125 pounds of dog food.

Make a PLAN

Choose a strategy.

You can **make a table** to organize the number of bags purchased, the number of pounds in those bags, the number of free pounds, and the total number of pounds. Make a table and work out one column at a time until there are at least 125 pounds of food.

SOLVE

Use the strategy.

For every even number of bags, increase the number of free pounds by 3.5.

Number of Bags	1	2	3	4	5	6	7	8	9	10	11
Pounds	10	20	30	40	50	60	70	80	90	100	110
Free Pounds	0	3.5	3.5	7	7	10.5	10.5	14	14	17.5	17.5
Total Pounds	10	23.5	33.5	47	57	70.5	80.5	94	104	117.5	127.5

The fewest number of bags the feeder must buy is 11.

LOOK BACK

Check your answer.

Multiply the number of bags purchased by the weight of each bag. This is the number of pounds paid for: $11 \times 10 = 110$.

Then divide the number of bags purchased by 2, and multiply the whole number result by 3.5. This is the number of free pounds received because of the special: $11 \div 2 = 5.5$, $5 \times 3.5 = 17.5$.
Add the pounds: $110 + 17.5 = 127.5$.
The feeder only needs 125 pounds, so this is enough.

How to Study Algebra 1

This book has many features designed to help you learn and study effectively. Becoming familiar with these features will prepare you for greater success on your exams.

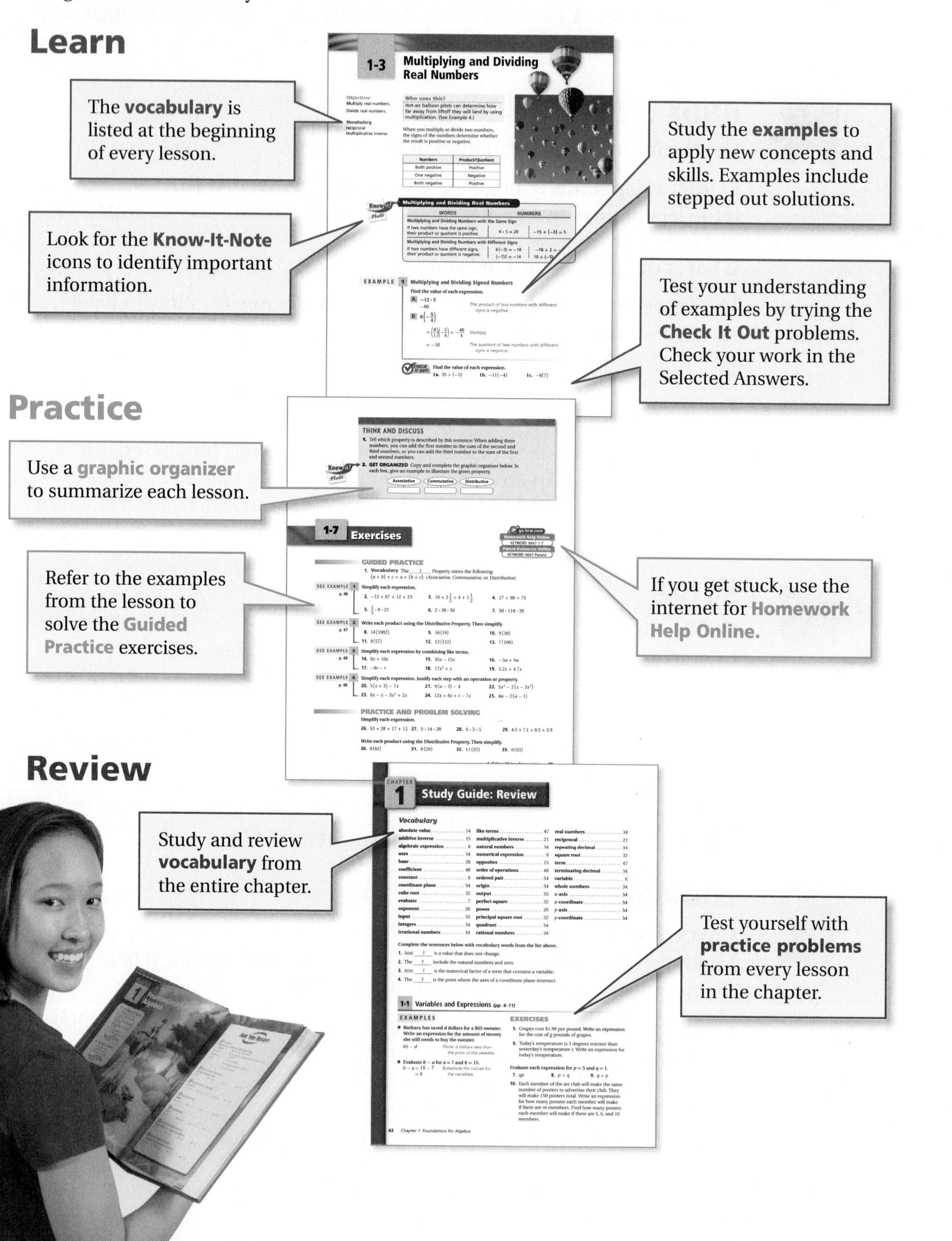

Scavenger Hunt

Use this scavenger hunt to discover a few of the many tools in ***Holt McDougal Algebra 1*** that you can use to become an independent learner. On a separate sheet of paper, write the answers to each question below. Within each answer, one letter will be in a yellow box. After you have answered every question, identify the letters that would be in yellow boxes and rearrange them to reveal the answer to the question at the bottom of the page.

1. What is the first **Vocabulary** term in the Study Guide: Preview for Chapter 2?

   EQUATION

2. What keyword should you enter for **Homework Help** for Lesson 6-3?

   MA76-3

3. In Lesson 7-3, what is **Example 1** teaching you to find?

   PRODUCTS OF POWERS

4. What are you asked to give an example of in the **Know-It Note** on page 563?

   TRINOMIAL

5. What college major is listed for the **Career Path** on page 567?

   ENVIRONMENTAL SCIENCES

6. To what school subject is **Exercise 44** on page 470 linked?

   CHEMISTRY

7. In the **Study Guide: Review** for Chapter 10, what sport do Questions 4 and 5 refer to?

   SOCCER

8. In Chapter 5's **Test Tackler**, what multiple choice strategy is described?

   RECOGNIZE DISTRACTERS

FACT!

Algebra was used to build what ancient structures?

PYRAMIDS

Scavenger Hunt **xxiii**

Foundations for Algebra

Section 1A
The Language of Algebra

- 1-1 **Variables and Expressions**
- 1-1 **Technology Lab** Create a Table to Evaluate Expressions
- 1-2 **Adding and Subtracting Real Numbers**
- 1-3 **Multiplying and Dividing Real Numbers**
- 1-4 **Powers and Exponents**
- 1-5 **Roots and Real Numbers**

Section 1B
Tools of Algebra

- 1-6 **Order of Operations**
- 1-7 **Simplifying Expressions**
- **Connecting Algebra to Geometry** Perimeter
- 1-8 **Introduction to Functions**

Pacing Guide for 45-Minute Classes

Teacher One Stop™ Calendar Planner®

Chapter 1

Countdown Weeks 1, 2

DAY 1	DAY 2	DAY 3	DAY 4	DAY 5
1-1 Lesson	1-1 Technology Lab 1-2 Lesson	1-2 Lesson 1-3 Lesson	1-3 Lesson 1-4 Lesson	1-4 Lesson 1-5 Lesson
DAY 6	**DAY 7**	**DAY 8**	**DAY 9**	**DAY 10**
1-5 Lesson Multi-Step Test Prep	Ready to Go On? 1-6 Lesson	1-6 Lesson 1-7 Lesson	1-7 Lesson Connecting Algebra to Geometry	1-8 Lesson
DAY 11	**DAY 12**	**DAY 13**		
Multi-Step Test Prep Ready to Go On?	Chapter 1 Review	Chapter 1 Test		

Pacing Guide for 90-Minute Classes

Teacher One Stop™ Calendar Planner®

Chapter 1

DAY 1	DAY 2	DAY 3	DAY 4	DAY 5
1-1 Lesson 1-1 Technology Lab 1-2 Lesson	1-2 Lesson 1-3 Lesson	1-4 Lesson 1-5 Lesson Multi-Step Test Prep Ready to Go On?	1-6 Lesson 1-7 Lesson Connecting Algebra to Geometry	1-8 Lesson Multi-Step Test Prep Ready to Go On?
DAY 6				
Chapter 1 Review Chapter 1 Test				

ONGOING ASSESSMENT and INTERVENTION

	DIAGNOSE	PRESCRIBE
Assess Prior Knowledge	**Before Chapter 1**	
	Diagnose readiness for the chapter.	Prescribe intervention.
	Are You Ready? SE p. 3	***Are You Ready? Intervention***
Formative Assessment	**Before Every Lesson**	
	Diagnose readiness for the lesson.	Prescribe intervention.
	Warm Up TE	**Reteach** CRB
	During Every Lesson	
	Diagnose understanding of lesson concepts.	Prescribe intervention.
	Check It Out! SE	**Reading Strategies** CRB
	Questioning Strategies TE	***Success for Every Learner***
	Think and Discuss SE	***Lesson Tutorial Videos***
	Write About It SE	
	Journal TE	
	After Every Lesson	
	Diagnose mastery of lesson concepts.	Prescribe intervention.
	Lesson Quiz TE	**Reteach** CRB
	Test Prep SE	**Test Prep Doctor** TE
	Test and Practice Generator	***Homework Help Online***
	Before Chapter 1 Testing	
	Diagnose mastery of concepts in chapter.	Prescribe intervention.
	Ready to Go On? SE pp. 39, 61	***Ready to Go On? Intervention***
	Multi-Step Test Prep SE pp. 38, 60	**Scaffolding Questions** TE pp. 38, 60
	Section Quizzes AR	**Reteach** CRB
	Test and Practice Generator	***Lesson Tutorial Videos***
	 **Before High Stakes Testing**	
	Diagnose mastery of benchmark concepts.	Prescribe intervention.
	College Entrance Exam Practice SE p. 67	***College Entrance Exam Practice***
	Standardized Test Prep SE pp. 70–71	
Summative Assessment	**After Chapter 1**	
	Check mastery of chapter concepts.	Prescribe intervention.
	Multiple-Choice Tests (Forms A, B, C)	**Reteach** CRB
	Free-Response Tests (Forms A, B, C)	***Lesson Tutorial Videos***
	Performance Assessment AR	
	Cumulative Test AR	
	Test and Practice Generator	

KEY: **SE** = *Student Edition* **TE** = *Teacher's Edition* **CRB** = *Chapter Resource Book* **AR** = *Assessment Resources*  Available online Available on CD- or DVD-ROM

CHAPTER 1

Lesson Resources

Before the Lesson

Prepare ***Teacher One Stop*** SPANISH 
- Editable lesson plans
- Calendar Planner
- Easy access to all chapter resources

Lesson Transparencies
- Teacher Tools

Teach the Lesson

Introduce ***Alternate Openers: Explorations***

Lesson Transparencies
- Warm Up
- Problem of the Day

Teach ***Lesson Transparencies***
- Teaching Transparencies

Know-It Notebook™
- Vocabulary
- Key Concepts

Power Presentations 

Lesson Tutorial Videos SPANISH 

Interactive Online Edition
- Lesson Activities
- Lesson Tutorial Videos

Lab Activities

Lab Resources Online

Online Interactivities SPANISH 

TechKeys

Practice the Lesson

Practice ***Chapter Resources***
- Practice A, B, C

Practice and Problem Solving Workbook SPANISH

IDEA Works!® Modified Worksheets and Tests

ExamView Test and Practice Generator SPANISH 

Homework Help Online

Online Interactivities SPANISH

Interactive Online Edition
- Homework Help

Apply ***Chapter Resources***
- Problem Solving SPANISH

Practice and Problem Solving Workbook SPANISH

Interactive Online Edition
- Chapter Project

Project Teacher Support

After the Lesson

Reteach ***Chapter Resources***
- Reteach
- Reading Strategies ELL

Success for Every Learner

Review ***Interactive Answers and Solutions***

Solutions Key

Know-It Notebook™
- Big Ideas
- Chapter Review

Extend ***Chapter Resources***
- Challenge

Technology Highlights for the Teacher

Power Presentations

Dynamic presentations to engage students. Complete PowerPoint® presentations for every lesson in Chapter 1.

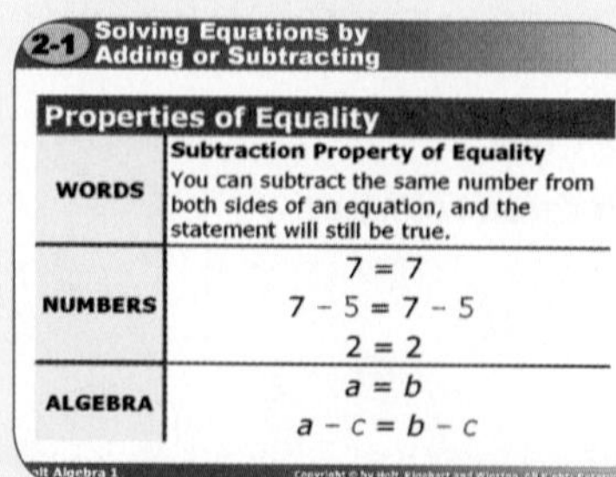

2-1 Solving Equations by Adding or Subtracting

Properties of Equality

	Subtraction Property of Equality
WORDS	You can subtract the same number from both sides of an equation, and the statement will still be true.
NUMBERS	$7 = 7$ $7 - 5 = 7 - 5$ $2 = 2$
ALGEBRA	$a = b$ $a - c = b - c$

Teacher One Stop SPANISH

Easy access to Chapter 1 resources and assessments. Includes lesson planning, test generation, and puzzle creation software.

Premier Online Edition SPANISH

Chapter 1 includes Tutorial Videos, Lesson Activities, Lesson Quizzes, Homework Help, and Chapter Project.

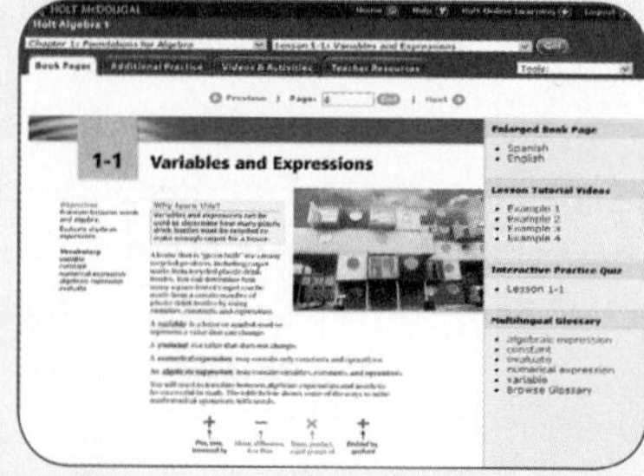

KEY: **SE** = *Student Edition* **TE** = *Teacher's Edition*  English Language Learners 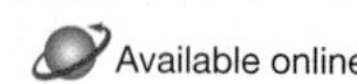 Spanish version available Available online  Available on CD- or DVD-ROM

Reaching All Learners

Teaching tips to help all learners appear throughout the chapter. A few that target specific students are included in the lists below.

All Learners

Lab Activities
Practice and Problem Solving Workbook SPANISH
Know-It Notebook

Special Needs Students

Practice A	CRB
Reteach	CRB
Reading Strategies	CRB
Are You Ready?	SE p. 3
Inclusion	TE pp. 29, 34, 52

IDEA Works!® Modified Worksheets and Tests
Ready to Go On? Intervention SPANISH
Know-It Notebook
Online Interactivities SPANISH
Lesson Tutorial Videos 

Developing Learners

Practice A	CRB
Reteach	CRB
Reading Strategies	CRB
Are You Ready?	SE p. 3
Vocabulary Connections	SE p. 4
Questioning Strategies	TE

Ready to Go On? Intervention SPANISH
Know-It Notebook
Homework Help Online
Online Interactivities SPANISH
Lesson Tutorial Videos 

On-Level Learners

Practice B	CRB
Problem Solving	CRB
Vocabulary Connections	SE p. 4
Questioning Strategies	TE

Ready to Go On? Intervention SPANISH
Know-It Notebook
Homework Help Online
Online Interactivities SPANISH

Advanced Learners

Practice C	CRB
Challenge	CRB
Challenge Exercises	SE
Reading and Writing Math *Extend*	TE p. 5
Critical Thinking	TE p. 22

Are You Ready? Enrichment SPANISH
Ready To Go On? Enrichment SPANISH

English Language Learners

ENGLISH LANGUAGE LEARNERS

Reading Strategies	CRB
Are You Ready? Vocabulary	SE p. 3
Vocabulary Connections	SE p. 4
Vocabulary Review	SE p. 62
English Language Learners	TE pp. 41, 43, 47

Success for Every Learner
Know-It Notebook
Multilingual Glossary
Lesson Tutorial Videos 

Technology Highlights for Reaching All Learners

Lesson Tutorial Videos SPANISH

Starring Holt authors Ed Burger and Freddie Renfro! Live tutorials to support every lesson in Chapter 1.

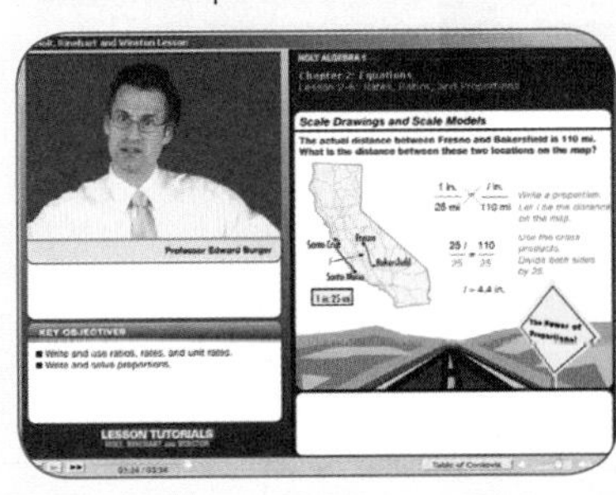

Multilingual Glossary

Searchable glossary includes definitions in English, Spanish, Vietnamese, Chinese, Hmong, Korean, and 4 other languages.

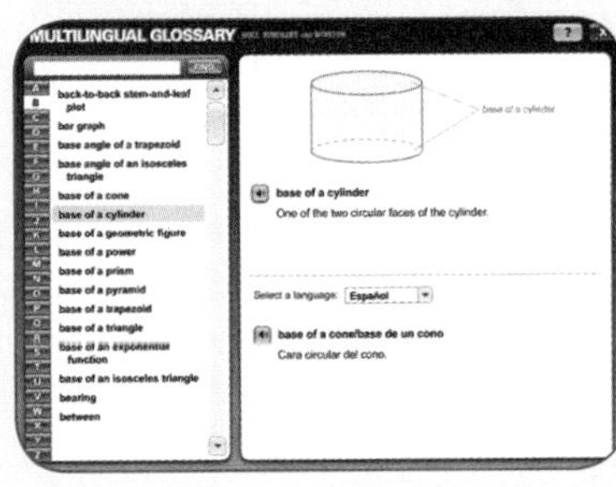

Online Interactivities

Interactive tutorials provide visually engaging alternative opportunities to learn concepts and master skills.

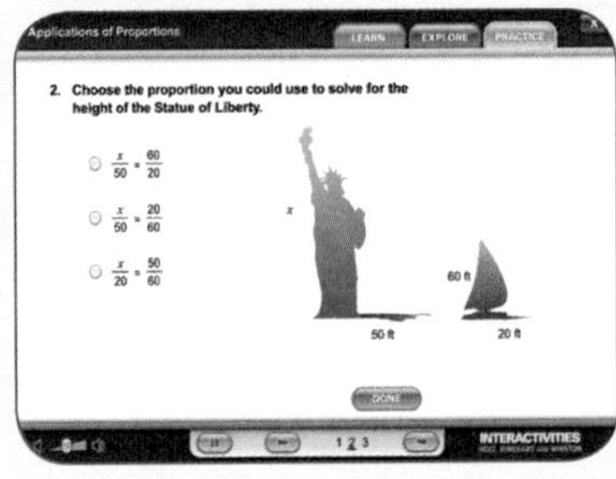

KEY: **SE** = *Student Edition* **TE** = *Teacher's Edition* **CRB** = *Chapter Resource Book*  Spanish version available · Available online · Available on CD- or DVD-ROM

CHAPTER 1

Ongoing Assessment

Assessing Prior Knowledge

Determine whether students have the prerequisite concepts and skills for success in Chapter 1.

Are You Ready? SPANISH .... SE p. 3
Warm Up .... TE

Test Preparation

Provide review and practice for Chapter 1 and standardized tests.

Multi-Step Test Prep .... SE pp. 38, 60
Study Guide: Review .... SE pp. 62–65
Test Tackler .... SE pp. 68–69
Standardized Test Prep .... SE pp. 70–71
College Entrance Exam Practice .... SE p. 67
Countdown to Testing .... SE pp. C4-C27
IDEA Works!® Modified Worksheets and Tests

Alternative Assessment

Assess students' understanding of Chapter 1 concepts and combined problem-solving skills.

Chapter 1 Project .... SE p. 2
Alternative Assessment .... TE
Performance Assessment SPANISH .... AR
Portfolio Assessment SPANISH .... AR

Lesson Assessment

Provide formative assessment for each lesson of Chapter 1.

Questioning Strategies .... TE
Think and Discuss .... SE
Check It Out! Exercises .... SE
Write About It .... SE
Journal .... TE
Lesson Quiz .... TE
Alternative Assessment .... TE
IDEA Works!® Modified Worksheets and Tests

Weekly Assessment

Provide formative assessment for each section of Chapter 1.

Multi-Step Test Prep .... SE pp. 38, 60
Ready to Go On? SPANISH .... SE pp. 39, 61
Section Quizzes SPANISH .... AR
Test and Practice Generator SPANISH .... *Teacher One Stop*

Chapter Assessment

Provide summative assessment of Chapter 1 mastery.

Chapter 1 Test .... SE p. 66
Chapter Test (Levels A, B, C) SPANISH .... AR
• Multiple Choice • Free Response
Cumulative Test SPANISH .... AR
Test and Practice Generator SPANISH .... *Teacher One Stop*
IDEA Works!® Modified Worksheets and Tests

Technology Highlights for Assessment

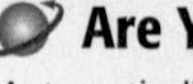

Are You Ready? SPANISH

Automatically assess readiness and prescribe intervention for Chapter 1 prerequisite skills.

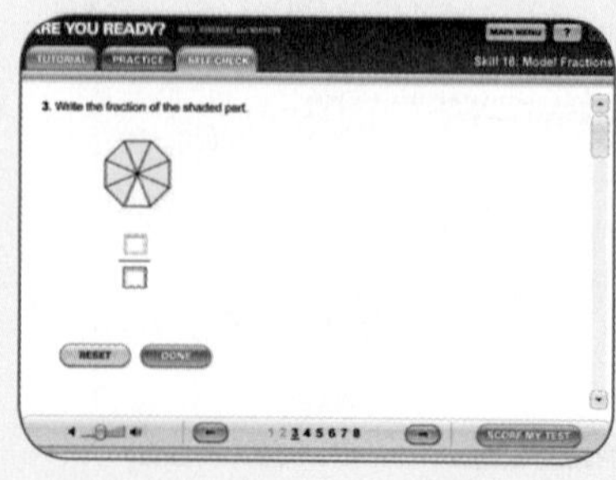

Ready to Go On?

Automatically assess understanding of and prescribe intervention for Sections 1A and 1B.

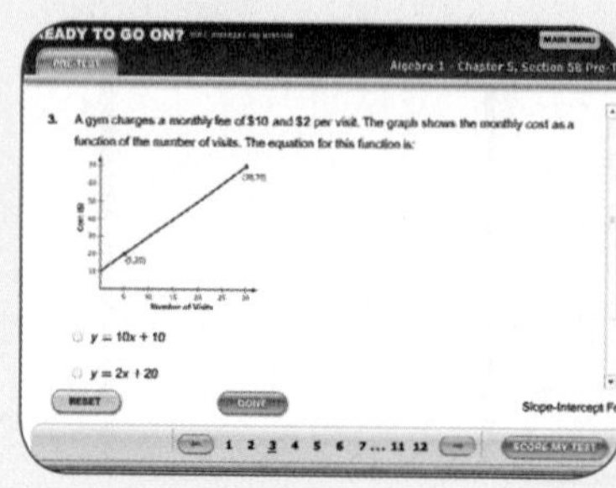

Test and Practice Generator SPANISH

Use Chapter 1 problem banks to create assessments and worksheets to print out or deliver online. Includes dynamic problems.

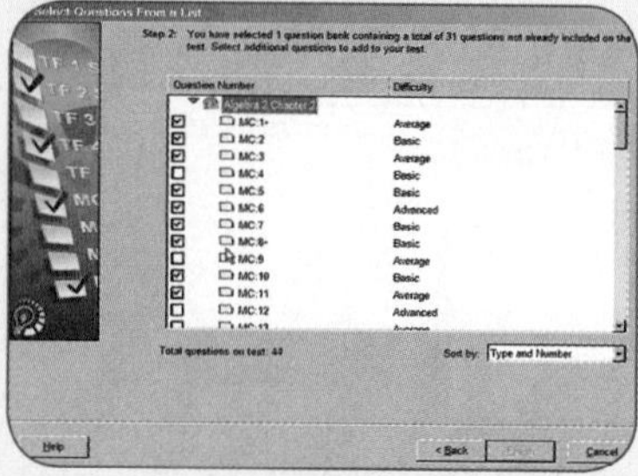

KEY: **SE** = *Student Edition* **TE** = *Teacher's Edition* **AR** = *Assessment Resources* SPANISH Spanish version available  Available online  Available on CD- or DVD-ROM

Formal Assessment

Three levels (A, B, C) of multiple-choice and free-response chapter tests, along with a performance assessment, are available in the *Assessment Resources.*

A Chapter 1 Test

C Chapter 1 Test

MULTIPLE CHOICE

B Chapter 1 Test

Select the best answer.

1. A principal spent \$1560 on c calculators for her school. Which expression shows the cost of one calculator?
   A $c + 1560$ C $1560c$
   B $1560 - c$ D $\frac{1560}{c}$
2. Which is a correct verbal expression for $8n$?
   F n more than 8
   G the quotient of 8 and n
   H the product of 8 and n
   J 8 increased by n
3. Evaluate $m + n$ for $m = 9$ and $n = 7$.
   A 2 C 63
   B 16 D 97
4. Add $-8 + -27$.
   F -35 H 19
   G -19 J 35
5. Subtract $16.5 - 40$.
   A -24.5 C 23.5
   B -23.5 D 24.5
6. Subtract $-10 - (-6)$.
   F -16 H 4
   G -4 J 16
7. Multiply $-1(-14)$.
   A -15 C 14
   B -14 D 15
8. Divide $-5 \div 30$.
   F -6 H $\frac{1}{6}$
   G $-\frac{1}{6}$ J 6
9. Divide $-\frac{3}{4} \div \frac{1}{4}$.
   A $-\frac{16}{3}$ C $-\frac{1}{3}$
   B -3 D $-\frac{3}{16}$
10. The room service manager of a hotel ordered 2100 bars of soap. The shipment was sent in 25 cases. How many bars of soap were in each case?
    F 40 H 84
    G 62 J 96
11. Simplify $\left(\frac{3}{4}\right)^3$.
    A $\frac{27}{64}$ C $\frac{9}{12}$
    B $\frac{9}{16}$ D $\frac{27}{16}$
12. Simplify -1^3.
    F -3 H 1
    G -1 J 3
13. Find $\sqrt{\frac{36}{100}}$.
    A $\frac{6}{50}$ C $\frac{6}{10}$
    B $\frac{18}{50}$ D $\frac{18}{10}$
14. Which of the following numbers is an integer?
    F -4 H $\frac{1}{2}$
    G $0.\overline{3}$ J $\sqrt{5}$
15. Which is NOT a rational number?
    A 0 C $\sqrt{12}$
    B $\frac{1}{9}$ D 17

B Chapter 1 Test (continued)

16. A square window has an area of 64 square feet. How long is one side of the window?
    F 6 feet H 14 feet
    G 8 feet J 16 feet
17. Simplify $(5 + 4 \cdot 2) - 3 \cdot 2^3$.
    A -203 C -6
    B -11 D 80
18. Simplify $\frac{-2 \cdot (3 + 9)}{8 \div 2 - 1}$.
    F -8 H 1
    G -3 J 6
19. Evaluate $4(6 - x)^3$ for $x = 2$.
    A 48 C 256
    B 64 D 4096
20. Which algebraic expression represents "the sum of the square of x and 5"?
    F $x^2 + 5$ H $x + 5^2$
    G $(x + 5)^2$ J $x^2 + 5^2$
21. Which algebraic expression represents "n squared less than 4"?
    A $(4 - n)^2$ C $n^2 - 4$
    B $(n - 4)^2$ D $4 - n^2$
22. The expression $6s^2$ can be used to find the surface area of a cube whose side length is s. Find the surface area of a cube whose side length is 7.25 inches.
    F 87 in² H 315.375 in²
    G 261 in² J 1892.25 in²
23. Simplify $3\frac{1}{3} - 7 + 10\frac{2}{3}$.
    A 6 C 7
    B $6\frac{1}{3}$ D $7\frac{2}{3}$
24. Simplify $3a + 6a - 5b$.
    F $4a$ H $9a - 5b$
    G $4ab$ J $9a^2 - 5b$
25. Simplify $-5(p + 8) + p$.
    A $-44p$ C $-4p + 8$
    B $36p$ D $-4p - 40$

Use this coordinate plane for questions 26 and 27.

26. What are the coordinates of point A?
    F $(-4, -3)$ H $(-3, -4)$
    G $(-3, 4)$ J $(4, -3)$
27. In which quadrant does point B lie?
    A Quadrant I C Quadrant III
    B Quadrant II D Quadrant IV
28. Generate and graph ordered pairs for $y = \left|\frac{1}{2}x\right|$.
    Which best describes the pattern formed?
    F a horizontal line
    G a vertical line
    H a V shape
    J a U shape

A Chapter 1 Test

C Chapter 1 Test

FREE RESPONSE

B Chapter 1 Test

1. Raquel bought p pencils. Write an expression to show the total cost of the pencils if each pencil cost \$0.75.
2. Write two verbal expressions for $b + 30$.
3. Evaluate $p - q$ for $p = 11$ and $q = 8$.

Add or subtract.

4. $-50 + 17$
5. $-4\frac{1}{3} + \left(-5\frac{1}{3}\right)$
6. $2 - (-7)$

Multiply or divide.

7. $16(-2)$
8. $-42 \div -6$
9. $\frac{4}{5} \div \left(-\frac{2}{5}\right)$
10. A typist can type 45 words per minute. At this rate, how many words can she type in half an hour?

Simplify each expression.

11. $(-7)^2$
12. $\left(-\frac{1}{5}\right)^4$
13. Find $-\sqrt{\frac{1}{36}}$.

Classify each real number. Write all classifications that apply.

14. $\frac{1}{5}$
15. 1
16. A dance floor is shaped like a square with an area of 196 square feet. Find the length of one side of the dance floor.

B Chapter 1 Test (continued)

Simplify each expression.

17. $\frac{(6 - 8)^2}{56 \div 4 \cdot 2}$
18. $(1 + 2^3) + 75 \div 25 + 5$
19. Evaluate $32 - x^2 + 2$ for $x = 2$.

Translate each word phrase into an algebraic expression.

20. 15 less than the square root of x
21. the product of 3 and the absolute value of n
22. The expression $2lw + 2wh + 2lh$ can be used to find the surface area of a rectangular prism, where l is the length, w is the width, and h is the height of the prism. A rectangular prism has a length of 8 inches, a width of 3 inches, and a height of 5 inches. Find the surface area of the prism.

Simplify each expression.

23. $45 \cdot 30 \cdot \frac{1}{9}$
24. $19t^2 - 14t + 6t + t^2$
25. $4(x + y) - 3y$

Use this coordinate plane for questions 26 and 27.

26. What are the coordinates of point A?
27. In which quadrant does point B lie?
28. Generate ordered pairs for the function $y = \left(\frac{1}{2}x\right)^2$ using $x = -4, -2, 0, 2,$ and 4.
    Graph the ordered pairs and describe the pattern.

PERFORMANCE ASSESSMENT

Chapter 1 Test

Purpose
This performance task assesses the student's understanding of ordered pairs in the coordinate plane and evaluating algebraic expressions.

Time
30–45 minutes

Grouping
Groups of four

Preparation Hints
Ask whether any students have created flip-books or computer animation. If any parents or other members of the community work in graphic arts, you could invite them to talk about computer graphics in their careers.

Overview
Students use algebraic expressions as rules to animate a figure about a plane. They also learn what effect a rule will have on a point.

Introduce the Task
Explain that animation uses a series of frames to make a figure appear to move. In each frame, the figure is drawn in a new position; when the frames are viewed quickly one after another, the figure appears to move smoothly through the series of positions.

Performance Indicators
____ Identifies the coordinates of the original figure.
____ Evaluates expressions to create new coordinates.
____ Plots new coordinates to create a repositioned figure.
____ Understands rules for moving figures right, left, up or down.
____ Writes new expressions to create the desired motion.

Scoring Rubric
Level 4: All members *collectively* understand and solve *all* of the problems.
Level 3: All members *collectively* understand and solve *some* of the problems.
Level 2: Each member *individually* understands and solves *all* of the problems.
Level 1: Each member *individually* understands and solves *some* of the problems.

Chapter 1 Test (continued)

In computer animation, figures are drawn on a plane called a *window* that is divided into points called *pixels*. The location of each pixel is described by an ordered pair (x, y).

At right, a dog is drawn by connecting nine pixels. The dog will be animated by evaluating rules that tell how to move each pixel.

Example:
Rule: $(x, y) \to (x + 4, y - 3)$
Original pixel: (10, 10)
$(10, 10) \to (10 + 4, 10 - 3)$
New pixel: (14, 7)

1. Write the coordinates of the nine original pixels.
2. Divide these rules among the members of your group. Use your rule to find and plot nine new pixels. Connect the pixels to show the dog in its new position.
   Rule 1: $(x, y) \to (x + 6, y)$ **Rule 3:** $(x, y) \to (x, y + 5)$
   Rule 2: $(x, y) \to (x - 3, y)$ **Rule 4:** $(x, y) \to (x, y - 2)$
3. As a group, discuss how each dog has moved in relation to the original dog. Describe the direction of the move and how far the dog moved.
   Rule 1: moved
   Rule 2: moved
   Rule 3: moved
   Rule 4: moved
4. Write rules that would make the dog move as described.
   a. Move the dog up 10 pixels.
   b. Move the dog left 8 pixels.
   c. Move the dog right 4 pixels *and* down 7 pixels.

Teacher One Stop™ 
Test & Practice Generator

Create and customize Chapter 1 Tests. Instantly generate multiple test versions, answer keys, and Spanish versions of test items.

Modified chapter tests that address special learning needs are available in *IDEA Works!*® *Modified Worksheets and Tests.*

CHAPTER 1

SECTION 1A

The Language of Algebra

On page 38, students write and evaluate algebraic expressions to describe the pressure exerted on a diver underwater, as well as the diver's speed of descent and depth.

Exercises designed to prepare students for success on the Multi-Step Test Prep can be found in each lesson.

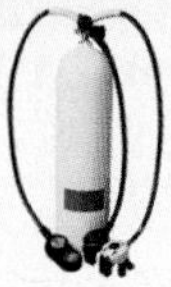

SECTION 1B

The Tools of Algebra

On page 60, students use algebraic properties and functions to determine the cost of supplies needed to decorate a room.

Exercises designed to prepare students for success on the Multi-Step Test Prep can be found in each lesson.

Interactivities Online ▶

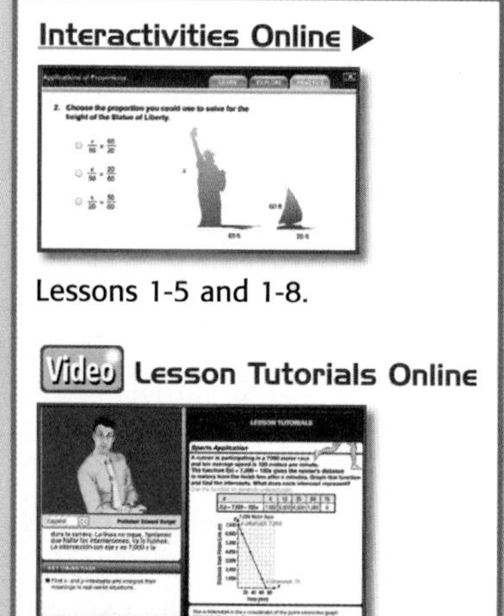

Lessons 1-5 and 1-8.

Video Lesson Tutorials Online

Lesson Tutorial Videos are available for EVERY example.

CHAPTER 1

Foundations for Algebra

Chapter Focus

- Solve problems with real numbers.
- Make connections between verbal and algebraic representations.

Discovering the *"Magic"*

You can use the operations and properties in this chapter to complete a magic square.

go.hrw.com
Chapter Project Online
KEYWORD: MA7 ChProj

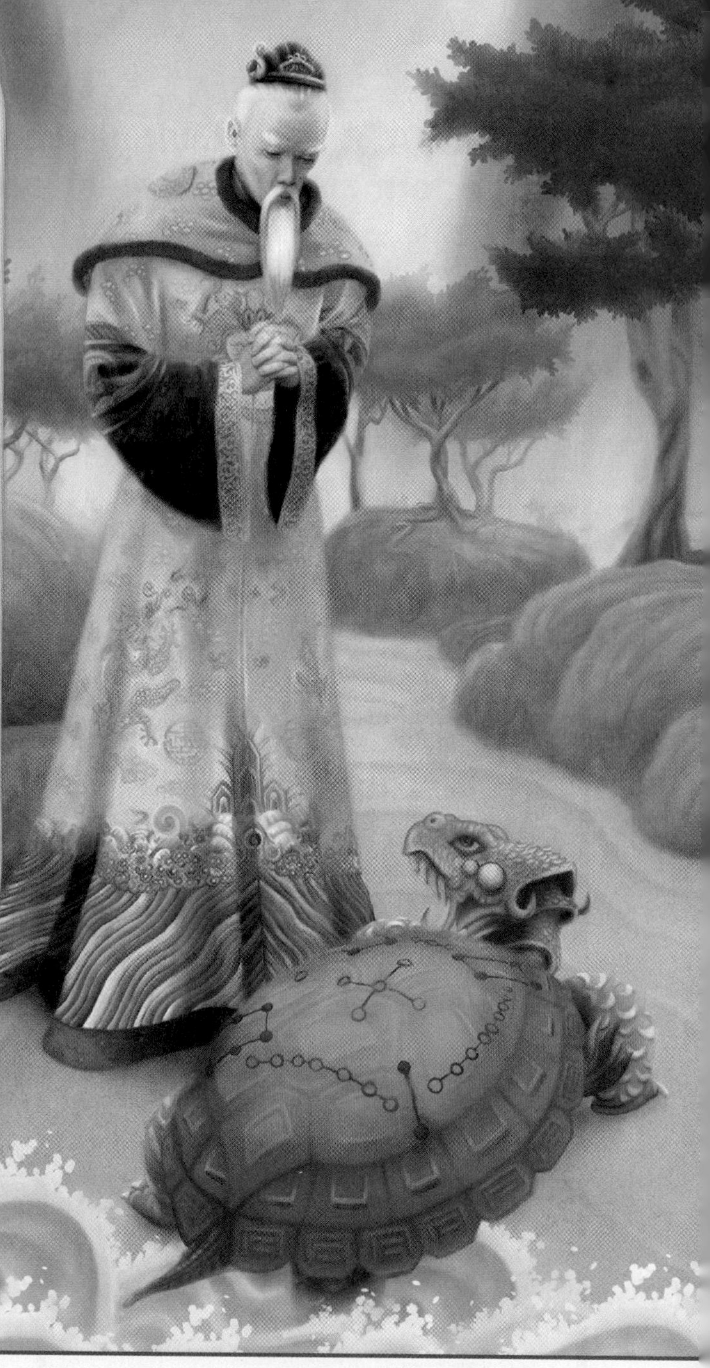

2 Chapter 1

Discovering the "Magic"

About the Project

The ancient Chinese legend of Lo Shu tells about a 3 x 3 magic square found on a turtle's back. In the Chapter Project, students explore 3 x 3 magic squares and the "magic" behind them.

Project Resources

All project resources for teachers and students are provided online.

ARE YOU READY?

Vocabulary

Match each term on the left with a definition on the right.

1. difference **E**
2. factor **B**
3. perimeter **A**
4. area **D**

A. the distance around a figure
B. a number that is multiplied by another number to form a product
C. a result of division
D. the number of square units a figure covers
E. a result of subtraction

Whole Number Operations

Add, subtract, multiply, or divide.

5. $23 + 6$ **29** 6. $156 \div 12$ **13** 7. 18×96 **1728** 8. $85 - 62$ **23**

Add and Subtract Decimals

Add or subtract.

9. $2.18 + 6.9$ **9.08** 10. $0.32 - 0.18$ **0.14** 11. $29.34 + 0.27$ **29.61** 12. $4 - 1.82$ **2.18**

Multiply Decimals

Multiply.

13. 0.7×0.6 **0.42** 14. 2.5×0.1 **0.25** 15. 1.5×1.5 **2.25** 16. 3.04×0.12 **0.3648**

Divide Decimals

Divide.

17. $6.15 \div 3$ **2.05** 18. $8.64 \div 2$ **4.32** 19. $7.2 \div 0.4$ **18** 20. $92.7 \div 0.3$ **309**

Multiply and Divide Fractions

Multiply or divide. Give your answer in simplest form.

21. $\frac{3}{5} \times \frac{1}{2}$ $\mathbf{\frac{3}{10}}$ 22. $\frac{2}{3} \div \frac{1}{6}$ **4** 23. $\frac{7}{8} \times \frac{4}{7}$ $\mathbf{\frac{1}{2}}$ 24. $4 \div \frac{2}{3}$ **6**

Add and Subtract Fractions

Add or subtract. Give your answer in simplest form.

25. $\frac{2}{5} + \frac{2}{5}$ $\mathbf{\frac{4}{5}}$ 26. $\frac{3}{8} - \frac{1}{8}$ $\mathbf{\frac{1}{4}}$ 27. $\frac{1}{2} + \frac{1}{4}$ $\mathbf{\frac{3}{4}}$ 28. $\frac{2}{3} - \frac{4}{9}$ $\mathbf{\frac{2}{9}}$

CHAPTER 1

ARE YOU READY?

Organizer

Objective: Assess students' understanding of prerequisite skills.

Assessing Prior Knowledge

INTERVENTION 

Diagnose and Prescribe

Use this page to determine whether intervention is necessary or whether enrichment is appropriate.

Resources

 ***Are You Ready? Intervention and Enrichment*** **Worksheets**

 ***Are You Ready?*** **CD-ROM**

 ***Are You Ready?*** **Online**

my.hrw.com

ARE YOU READY?
Diagnose and Prescribe

NO INTERVENE

Prerequisite Skill	*Are You Ready? Intervention,* Chapter 1 — Worksheets	CD-ROM	Online
Whole Number Operations	Skill 43	Activity 43	Diagnose and Prescribe Online
Add and Subtract Decimals	Skill 44	Activity 44	
Multiply Decimals	Skill 45	Activity 45	
Divide Decimals	Skill 46	Activity 46	
Multiply and Divide Fractions	Skill 47	Activity 47	
Add and Subtract Fractions	Skill 48	Activity 48	

YES ENRICH

***Are You Ready? Enrichment,* Chapter 1**

Worksheets

CD-ROM

Online

CHAPTER 1 Study Guide: Preview

Organizer

Objective: Help students organize the new concepts they will learn in Chapter 1.

Online Edition
Multilingual Glossary

Resources

Teacher One Stop™
PuzzleView

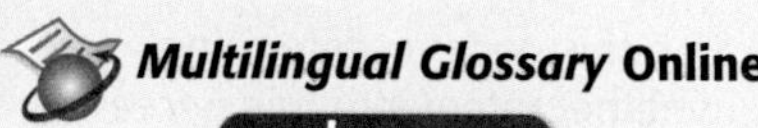
Multilingual Glossary **Online**
go.hrw.com
KEYWORD: MA7 Glossary

Possible answers to *Vocabulary Connections*

1. *Vary* means "to change." Something that is constant does not change, so *constant* has the opposite meaning of *variable*.
2. Something that reverses addition or does the opposite of addition
3. An irrational number is any number that is not rational.
4. The origin is the place at which you begin when graphing on a coordinate plane.

CHAPTER 1 Study Guide: Preview

Where You've Been

Previously, you

- learned words related to mathematical operations.
- identified numbers on a real number line.
- performed operations on whole numbers, decimals, and fractions.
- plotted points in the coordinate plane.

In This Chapter

You will study

- how to evaluate and simplify expressions.
- properties of the real number system.
- the order of operations.
- patterns formed by points plotted in the coordinate plane.

Where You're Going

You can use the skills in this chapter

- to form a solid foundation for the rest of this algebra course.
- in other classes, such as Biology, History, and Physics.
- to determine final costs, stock values, and profit.

Key Vocabulary/Vocabulario

additive inverse	inverso aditivo
coefficient	coeficiente
constant	constante
coordinate plane	plano cartesiano
irrational numbers	números irracionales
like terms	términos semejantes
origin	origen
rational numbers	números racionales
variable	variable

Vocabulary Connections

To become familiar with some of the vocabulary terms in the chapter, consider the following. You may refer to the chapter, the glossary, or a dictionary if you like.

1. The word **variable** comes from the word *vary*. What does *vary* mean? Which of the key vocabulary terms above has the opposite meaning?
2. Another word for *inverse* is *reverse*. The word *additive* relates to the operation of addition. What do you think an **additive inverse** is?
3. The prefix *ir-* means "not." What relationship do you think **rational numbers** and **irrational numbers** may have?
4. To *originate* means "to begin at." What do you think the **origin** of a coordinate plane is?

Reading Strategy: Use Your Book for Success

Understanding how your textbook is organized will help you locate and use helpful information.

Pay attention to the **margin notes.** Know-It Note icons point out key information. Writing Math notes, Helpful Hints, and Caution notes help you understand concepts and avoid common mistakes.

Writing Math

These expressions mean "2 times y":
$2y$ $2(y)$

Helpful Hint

A replacement set a set of numbers t can be substitute

Caution!

In the expression -5^2, 5 is the base because the nega

The **Glossary** is found in the back of your textbook. Use it as a resource when you need the definition of an unfamiliar word or property.

The **Index** is located at the end of your textbook. Use it to locate the page where a particular concept is taught.

The **Problem-Solving Handbook** is found in the back of your textbook. These pages review strategies that can help you solve real-world problems.

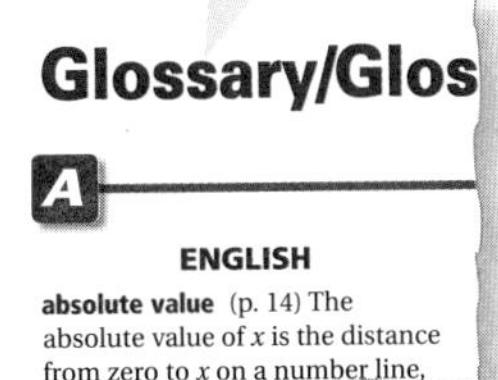

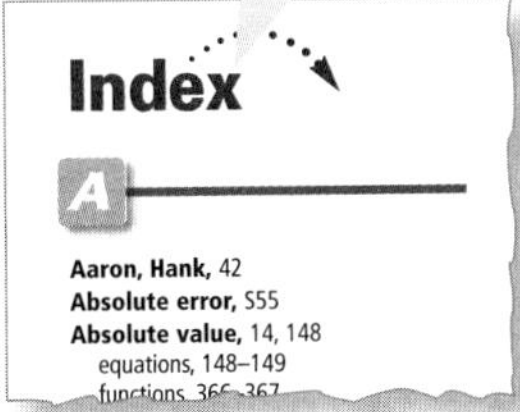

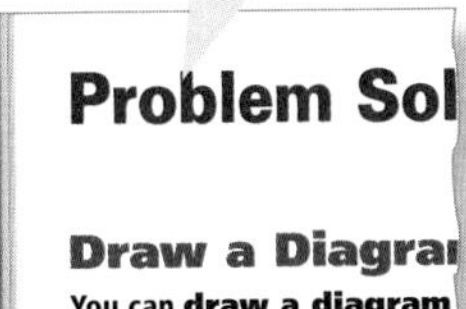

Use your textbook for the following problems.

1. Use the index to find the page where each term is defined: *algebraic expression, like terms, ordered pair, real numbers.*
2. What mnemonic device is taught in a Helpful Hint in Lesson 1-6, Order of Operations?
3. Use the glossary to find the definition of each term: *additive inverse, constant, perfect square, reciprocal.*

Reading and Writing Math

CHAPTER 1

Organizer

Objective: Help students apply strategies to understand and retain key concepts.

Reading Strategy: Use Your Book for Success

Discuss When students know the components of their book, and how to use them, they discover how to become independent learners.

Extend As students ask questions throughout Chapter 1, when appropriate, ask where they might find the answer in their book. Then have them look there.

Answers to *Try This*

1. algebraic expression: 6; like terms: 47; ordered pair: 54; real numbers: 14
2. Please Excuse My Dear Aunt Sally
3. additive inverse: the opposite of a number; constant: a value that does not change; perfect square: a number whose positive square root is a whole number; reciprocal: for a real number $a \neq 0$, the reciprocal of a is $\frac{1}{a}$.

Reading Connection

Of Men and Numbers
by Jane Muir

The author provides illuminating portraits of 12 of history's greatest mathematicians. Ancient Greek mathematics, the topic of Chapter 1 and the forerunner of algebra, will be of special interest to students as they begin their own study of the subject.

Activity After students have studied sets, have them read and report on Georg Cantor's surprising discovery about sets that have infinitely many elements, such as the set of all integers. Cantor discovered that some infinite sets are larger than others.

SECTION **1A**

The Language of Algebra

One-Minute Section Planner

Lesson	Lab Resources	Materials
Lesson 1-1 Variables and Expressions • Translate between words and algebra. • Evaluate algebraic expressions. ☑ SAT-10 ☐ NAEP ☑ ACT ☑ SAT ☐ SAT Subject Tests		**Optional** highlighters
1-1 Technology Lab Create a Table to Evaluate Expressions • Use a table to evaluate algebraic expressions. ☑ SAT-10 ☐ NAEP ☐ ACT ☐ SAT ☐ SAT Subject Tests	***Technology Lab Activities*** 1-1 Lab Recording Sheet	**Required** graphing calculator, spreadsheet program
Lesson 1-2 Adding and Subtracting Real Numbers • Add real numbers. • Subtract real numbers. ☑ SAT-10 ☐ NAEP ☑ ACT ☑ SAT ☐ SAT Subject Tests	***Algebra Lab Activities*** 1-2 Algebra Lab ***Technology Lab Activities*** 1-2 Technology Lab	**Optional** integer chips (MK)
Lesson 1-3 Multiplying and Dividing Real Numbers • Multiply real numbers. • Divide real numbers. ☑ SAT-10 ☐ NAEP ☑ ACT ☑ SAT ☐ SAT Subject Tests		**Optional** index cards
Lesson 1-4 Powers and Exponents • Evaluate expressions containing exponents. ☑ SAT-10 ☐ NAEP ☑ ACT ☑ SAT ☑ SAT Subject Tests		
Lesson 1-5 Roots and Real Numbers • Evaluate expressions containing roots. • Classify numbers within the real number system. ☑ SAT-10 ☐ NAEP ☑ ACT ☑ SAT ☑ SAT Subject Tests	***Algebra Lab Activities*** 1-5 Algebra Lab	

Note: If NAEP is checked, the content is tested on either the Grade 8 or the Grade 12 NAEP assessment.

MK = *Manipulatives Kit*

THE TRANSITION TO ALGEBRA

Lesson 1-1

The transition from arithmetic to algebra is a transition from the concrete to the abstract. An essential element of this transition, and one that sometimes causes difficulties for students, is the use of variables.

A *variable,* such as the symbol x, stands for a number. It is important to recognize, however, that variables are used in a variety of settings. For example, the expression $3x$ gives the cost of buying x gallons of gasoline at \$3 per gallon. The expression may be evaluated for any value of x greater than or equal to zero. Variables are used in this way in Lesson 1-1.

Later, students will solve equations such as $3x = 27$. Here, students must understand that the variable stands for a specific number and that solving the equation means finding the replacement value for x that makes the equation true. By way of contrast, the equation $4(x + 5) = 4x + 20$ states a mathematical identity. In this case, there is nothing to "solve"—the statement is true for all real values of x. It is advisable to point out and discuss these different uses of variables as they arise.

OPERATIONS WITH REAL NUMBERS

Lessons 1-2, 1-3, 1-4

In algebra, students are expected to work with real numbers, and, in particular, to perform arithmetic operations on integers. It is important to understand the underlying logic of integer arithmetic and be able to use patterns to develop generalizations about the operations.

For example, for any integer a, the *opposite* of a, $-a$, is the unique integer that satisfies $a + (-a) = 0$. This gives a basis for understanding addition with negative numbers. Using the Commutative and Associative Properties shows that $(2 + 3) + [(-2) + (-3)] = 2 + (-2) + 3 + (-3) = 0 + 0 = 0$. Therefore, $(-2) + (-3) = -(2 + 3)$. In other words, $(-2) + (-3) = -5$.

Patterns can be used to understand integer arithmetic. To see that the product of a positive integer and a negative integer is negative, students can extend the following pattern.

$$\begin{aligned} 3(3) &= 9 \\ 2(3) &= 6 \\ 1(3) &= 3 \\ 0(3) &= 0 \\ -1(3) &= -3 \\ -2(3) &= -6 \end{aligned}$$

-3 -3 -3

Continue the pattern of subtracting 3 at each stage to find the product when multiplying by a negative number.

When presenting division, emphasize that division by 0 is undefined. This is because $\frac{a}{b} = c$ means that $a = bc$ (this is the definition of division). For $\frac{a}{0}$, there is no value of c that makes $a = 0 \cdot c$ when $a \neq 0$. When $a = 0$, we have $\frac{0}{0}$, which is *indeterminate.* To see why, notice that $a \cdot 0 = 0$ for all values of a. Were it possible to define $\frac{0}{0}$, this would mean that $\frac{0}{0} = a$ for all values of a. That is, $\frac{0}{0} = 1$, $\frac{0}{0} = 2$, $\frac{0}{0} = 3.71$, and so on. There is no unique way to define $\frac{0}{0}$ that is consistent with the definition of division.

RATIONAL AND IRRATIONAL NUMBERS

Lesson 1-5

When we express a rational number as a decimal, we usually say it is a repeating decimal or a terminating decimal. However, it can be said that *all* rational numbers are repeating decimals since, for example, $8 = 8.00000...$. We can also write 8 as 7.99999... as shown below:

Let $x = 7.99999....$ Then $10x = 79.99999...$ and

$$\begin{aligned} 10x &= 79.99999... \\ -\ x &\quad -\ 7.99999... \\ 9x &= 72 \\ \frac{9x}{9} &= \frac{72}{9} \\ x &= 8 \end{aligned}$$

It is interesting to note that repeating decimals are base dependent. In base 10, the fraction $\frac{1}{3}$ is given by the repeating decimal 0.33333..., but in base 3 the fraction is given by simply 0.1.

1-1 Organizer

Pacing: Traditional 1 day
Block $\frac{1}{2}$ day

Objectives: Translate between words and algebra.

Evaluate algebraic expressions.

Online Edition
Tutorial Videos

Countdown Week 1

Power Presentations with PowerPoint®

Warm Up

Add or subtract.

1. $6 + 104$ 110 **2.** $12 + 1.9$ 13.9

3. $23 - 8$ 15 **4.** $\frac{1}{2} + \frac{1}{5}$ $\frac{7}{10}$

Multiply or divide.

5. $324 \div 18$ 18 **6.** $\frac{1}{4}(24)$ 6

7. $13.5(10)$ 135 **8.** $18.2 \div 2$ 9.1

Also available on transparency

Math Fact !!

The Rhind papyrus, an ancient Egyptian scroll, was written around 1832 B.C.E. It contains algebra problems and gives conclusive evidence that algebra was used in the building of the Egyptian pyramids.

State Resources

1-1 Variables and Expressions

Objectives
Translate between words and algebra.

Evaluate algebraic expressions.

Vocabulary
variable
constant
numerical expression
algebraic expression
evaluate

Why learn this?
Variables and expressions can be used to determine how many plastic drink bottles must be recycled to make enough carpet for a house.

Container City, in East London, UK, is a development of buildings made from recycled shipping containers.

A home that is "green built" uses many recycled products, including carpet made from recycled plastic drink bottles. You can determine how many square feet of carpet can be made from a certain number of plastic drink bottles by using *variables, constants,* and *expressions.*

A **variable** is a letter or symbol used to represent a value that can change.

A **constant** is a value that does not change.

A **numerical expression** may contain only constants and/or operations.

An **algebraic expression** may contain variables, constants, and/or operations.

You will need to translate between algebraic expressions and words to be successful in math. The diagram below shows some of the ways to write mathematical operations with words.

These expressions all mean "2 times y":

$2y$	$2(y)$
$2 \cdot y$	$(2)(y)$
$2 \times y$	$(2)y$

EXAMPLE 1 Translating from Algebraic Symbols to Words

Give two ways to write each algebraic expression in words.

A $x + 3$
the sum of x and 3
x increased by 3

B $m - 7$
the difference of m and 7
7 less than m

C $2 \cdot y$
2 times y
the product of 2 and y

D $k \div 5$
k divided by 5
the quotient of k and 5

CHECK IT OUT! **Give two ways to write each algebraic expression in words.**

1a. $4 - n$ **1b.** $\frac{t}{5}$ **1c.** $9 + q$ **1d.** $3(h)$

1 Introduce

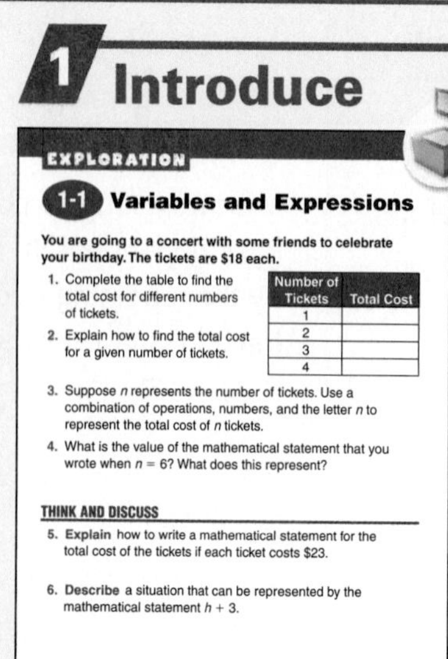

EXPLORATION

1-1 Variables and Expressions

You are going to a concert with some friends to celebrate your birthday. The tickets are $18 each.

1. Complete the table to find the total cost for different numbers of tickets.
2. Explain how to find the total cost for a given number of tickets.

Number of Tickets	Total Cost
1	
2	
3	
4	

3. Suppose n represents the number of tickets. Use a combination of operations, numbers, and the letter n to represent the total cost of n tickets.
4. What is the value of the mathematical statement that you wrote when $n = 6$? What does this represent?

THINK AND DISCUSS

5. **Explain** how to write a mathematical statement for the total cost of the tickets if each ticket costs $23.
6. **Describe** a situation that can be represented by the mathematical statement $h + 3$.

Motivate

Have students write a shopping list while you call out the items to them. Name the items quickly enough that the students have time to write down abbreviations for them, but not the entire words.

Point out to students that they probably used abbreviations or symbols to represent the words on the shopping list. Today they will learn how algebra can represent words and phrases by using variables, constants, and operation symbols.

Explorations and answers are provided in *Alternate Openers: Explorations Transparencies.*

To translate words into algebraic expressions, look for words that indicate the action that is taking place.

Add	Subtract	Multiply	Divide
↑	↑	↑	↑
Put together, combine	Find how much more or less	Put together equal groups	Separate into equal groups

EXAMPLE 2 Translating from Words to Algebraic Symbols

A **Eve reads 25 pages per hour. Write an expression for the number of pages she reads in h hours.**

h represents the number of hours that Eve reads.

$25 \cdot h$ or $25h$ *Think: h groups of 25 pages.*

B **Sam is 2 years younger than Sue, who is y years old. Write an expression for Sam's age.**

y represents Sue's age.

$y - 2$ *Think: "younger than" means "less than."*

C **William runs a mile in 12 minutes. Write an expression for the number of miles that William runs in m minutes.**

m represents the total time William runs.

$\frac{m}{12}$ *Think: How many groups of 12 are in m?*

2a. Lou drives at 65 mi/h. Write an expression for the number of miles that Lou drives in t hours. **$65t$**

2b. Miriam is 5 cm taller than her sister, who is m cm tall. Write an expression for Miriam's height in centimeters. **$m + 5$**

2c. Elaine earns $32 per day. Write an expression for the amount that she earns in d days. **$32d$**

To **evaluate** an expression is to find its value. To evaluate an algebraic expression, substitute numbers for the variables in the expression and then simplify the expression.

EXAMPLE 3 Evaluating Algebraic Expressions

Evaluate each expression for $x = 8$, $y = 5$, and $z = 4$.

A $x + y$

$x + y = 8 + 5$ *Substitute 8 for x and 5 for y.*

$= 13$ *Simplify.*

B $\frac{x}{z}$

$\frac{x}{z} = \frac{8}{4}$ *Substitute 8 for x and 4 for z.*

$= 2$ *Simplify.*

Evaluate each expression for $m = 3$, $n = 2$, and $p = 9$.

3a. mn **6** **3b.** $p - n$ **7** **3c.** $p \div m$ **3**

Power Presentations with PowerPoint®

Additional Examples

Example 1

Give two ways to write each algebraic expression in words.

Possible answers given.

A. $9 + r$ the sum of 9 and r; 9 increased by r

B. $q - 3$ the difference of q and 3; 3 less than q

C. $7m$ the product of m and 7; m times 7

D. $j \div 6$ the quotient of j and 6; j divided by 6

Example 2

A. John types 62 words per minute. Write an expression for the number of words he types in m minutes. $62m$

B. Roberto is 4 years older than Emily, who is y years old. Write an expression for Roberto's age. $y + 4$

C. Joey earns $5 for each car he washes. Write an expression for the number of cars Joey must wash to earn d dollars. $\frac{d}{5}$

Example 3

Evaluate each expression for $a = 4$, $b = 7$, and $c = 2$.

A. $b - c$ 5 **B.** ac 8

INTERVENTION

Questioning Strategies

EXAMPLE 1

- What words are indicated by each operation symbol?

EXAMPLE 2

- What clues tell you which operation to use?

EXAMPLE 3

- Explain why the value of an algebraic expression is numeric.

Answers to *Check It Out!*

Possible answers given.

1a. 4 decreased by n; n less than 4

1b. the quotient of t and 5; t divided by 5

1c. the sum of 9 and q; q added to 9

1d. the product of 3 and h; 3 times h

2 Teach

Guided Instruction

Before introducing variables and expressions, review elementary problems such as $2 + \square = 7$ and $\frac{10}{\square} = 2$. Tell students that in algebra, the box is replaced by a letter. Be sure students understand that the letter represents a number.

Visual When students translate words into algebraic expressions, encourage them to copy the word phrases and to use a highlighter to call attention to key words.

Reaching All Learners

Through Graphic Organizers

Copy the following table on the board and have students write real-world situations that might be modeled by each expression.

$100 - p$	$\frac{30}{x}$	$b - 1$	$\frac{m}{2}$	$6h$	$14 + s$

Power Presentations with PowerPoint®

Additional Examples

Example 4

Approximately eighty-five 20-ounce plastic bottles must be recycled to produce the fiberfill for a sleeping bag.

A. Write an expression for the number of bottles needed to make *s* sleeping bags. 85*s*

B. Find the number of bottles needed to make 20, 50, and 325 sleeping bags. 1700; 4250; 27,625

INTERVENTION

Questioning Strategies

EXAMPLE 4

- How do you think the letter for the variable was chosen?
- Why is multiplication used in the expression?

EXAMPLE 4 Recycling Application

Approximately fourteen 20-ounce plastic drink bottles must be recycled to produce 1 square foot of carpet.

a. Write an expression for the number of bottles needed to make *c* square feet of carpet.

The expression 14*c* models the number of bottles needed to make *c* square feet of carpet.

b. Find the number of bottles needed to make 40, 120, and 224 square feet of carpet.

Evaluate 14*c* for *c* = 40, 120, and 224.

c	14*c*
40	14(40) = 560
120	14(120) = 1680
224	14(224) = 3136

To make 40 ft^2 of carpet, 560 bottles are needed.
To make 120 ft^2 of carpet, 1680 bottles are needed.
To make 224 ft^2 of carpet, 3136 bottles are needed.

Helpful Hint

A *replacement set* is a set of numbers that can be substituted for a variable. The replacement set in Example 4 is {40, 120, 224}.

4. To make one sweater, sixty-three 20-ounce plastic drink bottles must be recycled.

a. Write an expression for the number of bottles needed to make *s* sweaters. **63*s***

b. Find the number of bottles needed to make 12, 25, and 50 sweaters. **756 bottles; 1575 bottles; 3150 bottles**

THINK AND DISCUSS

1. Write two ways to suggest each of the following, using words or phrases: addition, subtraction, multiplication, division.

2. Explain the difference between a numerical expression and an algebraic expression.

3. GET ORGANIZED Copy and complete the graphic organizer. Next to each operation, write a word phrase in the left box and its corresponding algebraic expression in the right box.

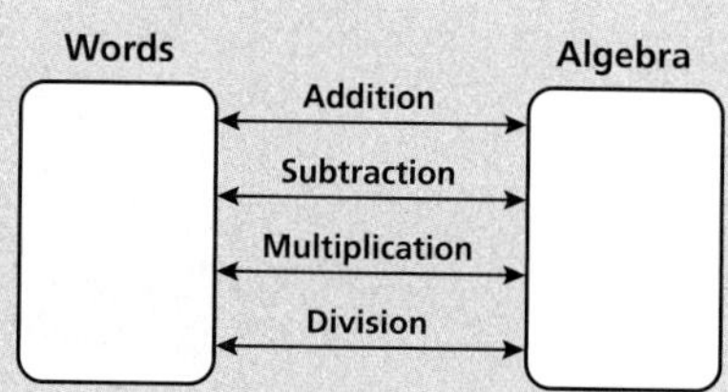

3 Close

Summarize

Have students list key words for each operation. Possible answers: addition–*add, sum*; subtraction–*minus, difference*; multiplication–*times, product*; division–*divided by, quotient* Have students explain the difference between a variable and a constant. A variable is a value that can change. A constant is a value that does not change.

ONGOING ASSESSMENT and INTERVENTION

***Diagnose Before* the Lesson**
1-1 Warm Up, TE p. 6

***Monitor During* the Lesson**
Check It Out! Exercises, SE pp. 6–8
Questioning Strategies, TE pp. 7–8

***Assess After* the Lesson**
1-1 Lesson Quiz, TE p. 11
Alternative Assessment, TE p. 11

Answers to *Think and Discuss*

Possible answers:

1. addition–*increased by, sum of*; subtraction–*decreased by, difference of*; multiplication–*multiplied by, product of*; division–*divided by, quotient of*
2. Both types of expressions may contain numbers and operations. Algebraic expressions may also contain variables.
3. See p. A2.

1-1 Exercises

go.hrw.com
Homework Help Online
KEYWORD: MA7 1-1
Parent Resources Online
KEYWORD: MA7 Parent

GUIDED PRACTICE

1. **Vocabulary** A(n) ___?___ is a value that can change. (*algebraic expression, constant,* or *variable*) **variable**

SEE EXAMPLE 1 p. 6

Give two ways to write each algebraic expression in words.

2. $n - 5$ **5 less than n; n decreased by 5**
3. $\frac{f}{3}$ **the quotient of f and 3; f divided by 3**
4. $c + 15$ **15; the sum of c and 15; c increased by 15**
5. $9 - y$ **9 decreased by y; y less than 9**
6. $\frac{x}{12}$
7. $t + 12$
8. $8x$
9. $x - 3$

SEE EXAMPLE 2 p. 7

10. George drives at 45 mi/h. Write an expression for the number of miles George travels in h hours. **$45h$**
11. The length of a rectangle is 4 units greater than its width w. Write an expression for the length of the rectangle. **$w + 4$**

SEE EXAMPLE 3 p. 7

Evaluate each expression for $a = 3$, $b = 4$, and $c = 2$.

12. $a - c$ **1**
13. ab **12**
14. $b \div c$ **2**
15. ac **6**

SEE EXAMPLE 4 p. 8

16. Brianna practices the piano 30 minutes each day.
    a. Write an expression for the number of hours she practices in d days. **$0.5d$**
    b. Find the number of hours Brianna practices in 2, 4, and 10 days. **1; 2; 5**

PRACTICE AND PROBLEM SOLVING

Independent Practice

For Exercises	See Example
17–24	1
25–26	2
27–30	3
31	4

Extra Practice
Skills Practice p. S4
Application Practice p. S28

Give two ways to write each algebraic expression in words.

17. $5p$
18. $4 - y$
19. $3 + x$
20. $3y$
21. $-3s$
22. $r \div 5$
23. $14 - t$
24. $x + 0.5$

25. Friday's temperature was 20° warmer than Monday's temperature t. Write an expression for Friday's temperature. **$t + 20$**
26. Ann sleeps 8 hours per night. Write an expression for the number of hours Ann sleeps in n nights. **$8n$**

Evaluate each expression for $r = 6$, $s = 5$, and $t = 3$.

27. $r - s$ **1**
28. $s + t$ **8**
29. $r \div t$ **2**
30. sr **30**

31. Jim is paid for overtime when he works more than 40 hours per week.
    a. Write an expression for the number of hours he works overtime when he works h hours. **$h - 40$**
    b. Find the number of hours Jim works overtime when he works 40, 44, 48, and 52 hours. **0; 4; 8; 12**

32. **Write About It** Write a paragraph that explains to another student how to evaluate an expression. **To evaluate an expression is to find its value. To do this, substitute values for the variables and perform all the indicated operations.**

Write an algebraic expression for each verbal expression. Then write a real-world situation that could be modeled by the expression.

33. the product of 2 and x
34. b less than 17
35. 10 more than y

1-1 Exercises

Assignment Guide

Assign *Guided Practice* exercises as necessary.

If you finished Examples **1–2**
Basic 17–26, 41–43
Average 17–26, 40–43
Advanced 17–26, 40–43

If you finished Examples **1–4**
Basic 17–31, 33, 34, 36–38, 40–43, 48–50, 55–64
Average 17–35, 36–40 even, 44, 48–51, 55–64
Advanced 18–26 even, 27–36, 39, 40, 44–64

Homework Quick Check
Quickly check key concepts.
Exercises: 18, 24, 26, 28, 31, 40

Answers

6–9. Possible answers given.

6. one-twelfth x; the quotient of x and 12

7. the sum of t and 12; t increased by 12

8. the product of 8 and x; 8 groups of x

9. x decreased by 3; the difference of x and 3

17–24, 33–35. See p. A12.

State Resources

go.hrw.com
State Resources Online
KEYWORD: MA7 Resources

Teacher to Teacher

I like to use the Think and Discuss questions from the previous lesson as a warm-up activity to begin the next class. It helps students refresh their memory of the concepts just learned and practiced. The Think and Discuss questions often begin very useful class discussions and allow students to learn from their peers.

John Bakelaar
Jackson, MS

Exercise 36 involves using algebraic expressions to describe the pressure on a diver's body at different depths. The exercise prepares students for the Multi-Step Test Prep on page 38.

Geometry In **Exercise 37,** students must write an expression for the area of a rectangle. Remind students that the area of a rectangle is its length times its width.

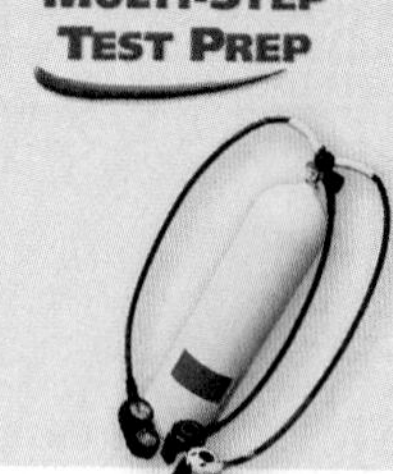

36. This problem will prepare you for the Multi-Step Test Prep on page 38.

The air around you puts pressure on your body equal to 14.7 pounds per square inch (psi). When you are underwater, the water exerts additional pressure on your body. For each foot you are below the surface of the water, the pressure increases by 0.445 psi.

a. What does 14.7 represent in the expression $14.7 + 0.445d$? **air pressure**

b. What does d represent in the expression? **depth below the water in feet**

c. What is the total pressure exerted on a person's body when $d = 8$ ft? **18.26 psi**

37. Geometry The length of a rectangle is 9 inches. Write an expression for the area of the rectangle if the width is w inches. Find the area of the rectangle when the width is 1, 8, 9, and 11 inches. **$9w$; 9 in^2; 72 in^2; 81 in^2; 99 in^2**

38. Geometry The perimeter of any rectangle is the sum of its lengths and widths. The area of any rectangle is the length ℓ times the width w.

a. Write an expression for the perimeter of a rectangle. **$2\ell + 2w$**

b. Find the perimeter of the rectangle shown. **44 cm**

c. Write an expression for the area of a rectangle. **ℓw**

d. Find the area of the rectangle shown. **112 cm^2**

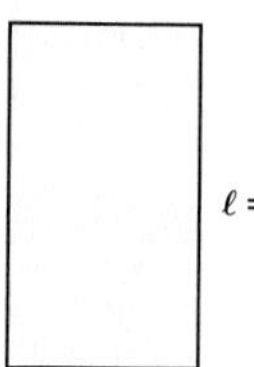

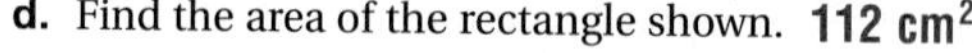

Complete each table. Evaluate the expression for each value of x.

39.

x	$x + 12$
1	**13**
2	**14**
3	**15**
4	**16**

40.

x	$10x$
1	**10**
5	**50**
10	**100**
15	**150**

41.

x	$x \div 2$
12	**6**
20	**10**
26	**13**
30	**15**

LINK

Astronomy

A crater on Canada's Devon Island is geologically similar to the surface of Mars. However, the temperature on Devon Island is about 37 °F in summer, and the average summer temperature on Mars is –85 °F.

42. Astronomy An object's weight on Mars can be found by multiplying 0.38 by the object's weight on Earth. **$0.38p$**

a. An object weighs p pounds on Earth. Write an expression for its weight on Mars.

b. Dana weighs 120 pounds, and her bicycle weighs 44 pounds. How much would Dana and her bicycle together weigh on Mars? **62.32 lb**

43. Meteorology Use the bar graph to write an expression for the average annual precipitation in New York, New York.

a. The average annual precipitation in New York is m inches more than the average annual precipitation in Houston, Texas. **$47.84 + m$**

b. The average annual precipitation in New York is s inches less than the average annual precipitation in Miami, Florida. **$58.53 - s$**

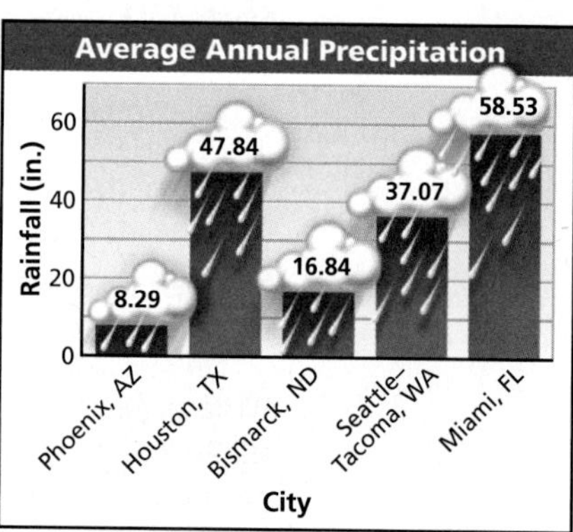

1-1 PRACTICE A
1-1 PRACTICE C
1-1 PRACTICE B

Give two ways to write each algebraic expression in words.

1. $15 - b$
   the difference of 15 and b
   b less than 15
2. $\frac{x}{16}$
   the quotient of x and 16
   x divided by 16
3. $x + 9$
   the sum of x and 9
   9 more than x
4. $(2)(t)$
   the product of 2 and t
   2 times t
5. $z - 7$
   the difference of z and 7
   7 less than z
6. $4y$
   the product of 4 and y
   4 times y
7. Sophie's math class has 6 fewer boys than girls, and there are g girls. Write an expression for the number of boys. **$g - 6$**
8. A computer printer can print 10 pages per minute. Write an expression for the number of pages the printer can print in m minutes. **$10m$**

Evaluate each expression for $r = 8$, $s = 2$, and $t = 5$.

9. st **10**
10. $r \div s$ **4**
11. $s + t$ **7**
12. $r - t$ **3**
13. $r \cdot s$ **16**
14. $t - s$ **3**
15. Paula always withdraws 20 dollars more than she needs from the bank.
    a. Write an expression for the amount of money Paula withdraws if she needs d dollars. **$d + 20$**
    b. Find the amount of money Paula withdraws if she needs 20, 60, and 75 dollars. **40 dollars; 80 dollars; 95 dollars**

1-1 READING STRATEGIES

To translate between phrases and algebraic expressions, you must connect words with symbols. Look at the examples in the table below.

Operations	Words	Symbols
Addition	"sum of 3 and n" "n more than 3" "3 plus n"	$3 + n$
Subtraction	"difference of 3 and n" "n less than 3" "3 minus n"	$3 - n$
Multiplication	"product of 3 and n" "3 times n" "3 groups of n"	$3n$ $3 \cdot n$ $3 \times n$ $3(n)$
Division	"quotient of 3 and n" "3 divided by n" "3 separated into n groups"	$3 \div n$ $\frac{3}{n}$

Solve each problem.

1. Write "10 times the value of y" in symbols in three different ways.
   Possible answers: $10y$, $10 \cdot y$, and $10(y)$
2. Write "$k \div 6$" in words in two different ways.
   Possible answers: k divided by 6, the quotient of k and 6
3. Write "4 less than b" in symbols. **$b - 4$**
4. Write "b less than 4" in symbols. **$4 - b$**

Translate each word phrase into an algebraic expression.

5. Craig types 20 words per minute. Write an expression for the number of words Craig types in m minutes. **$20m$**
6. Jeana is 58 inches tall. Her sister Janelle is t inches taller. Write an expression for Janelle's height. **$58 + t$**

1-1 RETEACH

To translate words into algebraic expressions, find words like these that tell you the operation.

+	–	•	÷
add	subtract	multiply	divide
sum	difference	product	quotient
more	less	times	split
increased	decreased	per	ratio

Kenny owns v video games. Stan owns 7 more video games than Kenny. Write an expression for the number of video games Stan owns.

v represents the number of video games Kenny owns.

$v + 7$ *Think: The word "more" indicates addition.*

Order does not matter for addition. The expression $7 + v$ is also correct.

Jenny is 12 years younger than Candy. Write an expression for Jenny's age if Candy is c years old.

c represents Candy's age.

The word "younger" means "less," which indicates subtraction.

$c - 12$ *Think: Candy is older, so subtract 12 from her age.*

Order does matter for subtraction. The expression $12 - c$ is incorrect.

1. Jared can type 35 words per minute. Write an expression for the number of words he can type in m minutes. **$35m$**
2. Mr. O'Brien's commute to work is 0.5 hour less than Miss Santos's commute. Write an expression for the length of Mr. O'Brien's commute if Miss Santos's commute is h hours. **$h - 0.5$**
3. Mrs. Knighten bought a box of c cookies and split them evenly between the 25 students in her classroom. Write an expression for the number of cookies each student received. **$c \div 25$**
4. Enrique collected 152 recyclable bottles, and Latasha collected b recyclable bottles. Write an expression for the number of bottles they collected altogether. **$152 + b$**
5. Tammy's current rent is r dollars. Next month it will be reduced by \$50. Write an expression for next month's rent in dollars. **$r - 50$**

44. Critical Thinking Compare algebraic expressions and numerical expressions. Give examples of each. **Both algebraic and numerical expressions contain numbers and operations, but algebraic expressions also contain variables.**

Write an algebraic expression for each verbal expression. Then evaluate the algebraic expression for the given values of x.

	Verbal	Algebraic	$x = 12$	$x = 14$
	x reduced by 5	$x - 5$	$12 - 5 = 7$	$14 - 5 = 9$
45.	7 more than x	$x + 7$	19	21
46.	The quotient of x and 2	$\frac{x}{2}$	6	7
47.	The sum of x and 3	$x + 3$	15	17

TEST PREP

48. Claire has had her driver's license for 3 years. Bill has had his license for b fewer years than Claire. Which expression can be used to show the number of years Bill has had his driver's license?

(A) $3 + b$ (B) $b + 3$ **(C)** $3 - b$ (D) $b - 3$

49. Which expression represents x?

(F) $12 - 5$ (H) $12(5)$
(G) $12 + 5$ (J) $12 \div 5$

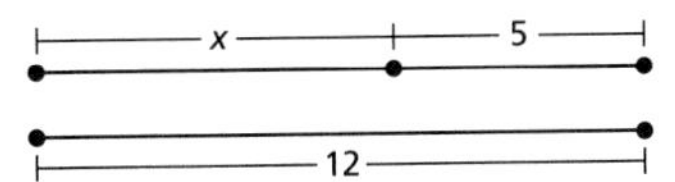

50. Which situation is best modeled by the expression $25 - x$?

(A) George places x more video games on a shelf with 25 games.
(B) Sarah has driven x miles of a 25-mile trip.
(C) Amelia paid 25 dollars of an x dollar lunch that she shared with Ariel.
(D) Jorge has 25 boxes full of x baseball cards each.

CHALLENGE AND EXTEND

Evaluate each expression for the given values of the variables.

51. $2ab$; $a = 6$, $b = 3$ **36** 52. $2x + y$; $x = 4$, $y = 5$ **13** 53. $3x \div 6y$; $x = 6$, $y = 3$ **1**

54. **Multi-Step** An Internet service provider charges \$9.95/month for the first 20 hours and \$0.50 for each additional hour. Write an expression representing the charges for h hours of use in one month when h is more than 20 hours. What is the charge for 35 hours? **$9.95 + 0.50(h - 20)$; \$17.45**

SPIRAL REVIEW

The sum of the angle measures in a triangle is 180°. Find the measure of the third angle given the other two angle measures. *(Previous course)*

55. 45° and 90° **45°** 56. 120° and 20° **40°** 57. 30° and 60° **90°**

Write an equivalent fraction for each percent. *(Previous course)*

58. 25% $\frac{1}{4}$ 59. 50% $\frac{1}{2}$ 60. 75% $\frac{3}{4}$ 61. 100% **1**

Find a pattern and use it to give the next three numbers. *(Previous course)*

62. 4, 12, 20, 28, … 63. 3, 9, 27, 81, 243, … 64. 2, 3, 5, 8, 12, …

62. Add 8 to the previous term; 36, 44, 52.

63. Multiply the previous term by 3; 729, 2187, 6561.

64. Add 1 to the previous term, then add 2, and then add 3, and so on; 17, 23, 30.

TEST PREP DOCTOR For **Exercise 50,** students may recognize choices **B** and **C** as indicating subtraction. Show students that since 25 is written first in the expression, 25 is the full amount being considered. In **C,** \$25 is only part of the cost of lunch, but in **B,** 25 miles is the whole trip, so **B** is the answer.

Journal

Have students describe some things in their lives that change, and then relate them to the algebraic definition of "variable."

ALTERNATIVE ASSESSMENT

Instruct students to look through newspapers and magazines to find real-world situations that can be described using words that indicate mathematical operations. Then have them write how they would model each situation with an algebraic expression.

Power Presentations with PowerPoint®

1-1 Lesson Quiz

Give two ways to write each algebraic expression in words.

1, 2. Possible answers given.

1. $j - 3$ the difference of j and 3; 3 less than j

2. $4p$ 4 times p; the product of 4 and p

3. Mark is 5 years older than Juan, who is y years old. Write an expression for Mark's age. $y + 5$

Evaluate each expression for $c = 6$, $d = 5$, and $e = 10$.

4. $\frac{d}{e}$ $\frac{1}{2}$ **5.** $c + d$ 11

Shemika practices basketball for 2 hours each day.

6. Write an expression for the number of hours she practices in d days. $2d$

7. Find the number of hours she practices in 5, 12, and 20 days. 10 hours; 24 hours; 40 hours

Also available on transparency

1-1 PROBLEM SOLVING

Write the correct answer.

1. For her book club, Sharon reads for 45 minutes each day. Write an expression for the number of hours she reads in d days.
   45d
2. The minimum wage in 2003 was \$5.15. This was w more than the minimum wage in 1996. Write an expression for the minimum wage in 1996.
   $5.15 - w$
3. According to the 2000 census, the number of people per square mile in Florida was about 216 more than the number of people per square mile in Texas. Write an expression for the number of people per square mile in Florida if there were t people per square mile in Texas.
   $216 + t$
4. The cost of a party is \$550. The price per person depends on how many people attend the party. Write an expression for the price per person if p people attend the party. Then find the price per person if 25, 50, and 55 people attend the party.
   $\frac{550}{p}$
   \$22, \$11, \$10

Use the table below to answer questions 5–6, which shows the years five states entered the Union. Select the best answer.

State	Year Entered into Union
Florida	1845
Indiana	1816
Pennsylvania	1787
Texas	1845
West Virginia	1863

5. North Carolina entered the Union x years after Pennsylvania. Which expression shows the year North Carolina entered the Union?
   A $1845 + x$ **C** $1787 + x$
   B $1845 - x$ D $1787 - x$
6. The expression $f - 26$ represents the year Alabama entered the Union, where f is the year Florida entered. In which year did Alabama enter the Union?
   F 1819 H 1837
   G 1826 J 1871
7. The number of states that entered the Union in 1889 was half the number of states s that entered in 1788. Which expression shows the number of states that entered the Union in 1889?
   A $2s$ C $s + 2$
   B $s \div 2$ D $2 - s$

1-1 CHALLENGE

A cell phone company is offering two different monthly plans. Each plan charges a monthly fee and then an additional cost per minute.

Plan A	\$40 fee	45 cents per minute
Plan B	\$70 fee	35 cents per minute

The mathematical expression for Plan A which represents the charges for the monthly fee plus the charge per minute m for one month is:

$$40 + 0.45(m)$$

1. Write the expression which represents the charges for the monthly fee plus the charge per minute m for Plan B for one month. **$70 + 0.35(m)$**

Use the expressions above to complete the chart.

Number of Minutes	Expression for Plan A	Cost of Plan A	Expression for Plan B	Cost for Plan B
100	$40 + 0.45(100)$	\$85	$70 + 0.35(100)$	\$105
200	$40 + 0.45(200)$	\$130	$70 + 0.35(200)$	\$140
300	$40 + 0.45(300)$	\$175	$70 + 0.35(300)$	\$175
400	$40 + 0.45(400)$	\$220	$70 + 0.35(400)$	\$210
500	$40 + 0.45(500)$	\$265	$70 + 0.35(500)$	\$245

2. Which plan is less expensive for 200 minutes or less each month? **Plan A**
3. Which plan is less expensive for 400 minutes or more each month? **Plan B**
4. Suppose a friend asks you which of the two plans is less expensive. How would you respond?
   Possible answer: It depends on the number of minutes used. Plan A is cheaper if you use less than 300 minutes each month. Plan B is cheaper if you use more than 300 minutes each month. If you use exactly 300 minutes each month, the plans cost the same.

Organizer

Use with Lesson 1-1

Pacing:
Traditional $\frac{1}{2}$ day
Block $\frac{1}{4}$ day

Objective: Use a table to evaluate algebraic expressions.

Materials: graphing calculator, spreadsheet program

Online Edition
TechKeys

Countdown Week 1

Resources

Technology Lab Activities
1-1 Lab Recording Sheet

Teach

Discuss

Viewing a table of values can help students see a pattern. When using technology to create a table, use an asterisk (*) for multiplication, a forward slash (/) for division, and a caret (^) for exponentiation.

State Resources

go.hrw.com
State Resources Online
KEYWORD: MA7 Resources

1-1

Create a Table to Evaluate Expressions

You can use a graphing calculator to quickly evaluate expressions for many values of the variable.

Use with Lesson 1-1

go.hrw.com
Lab Resources Online
KEYWORD: MA7 Lab1

Activity 1

Evaluate $2x + 7$ for $x = 25, 125, 225, 325$, and 425.

1. Press **Y=** and enter **2X+7** for **Y1**.

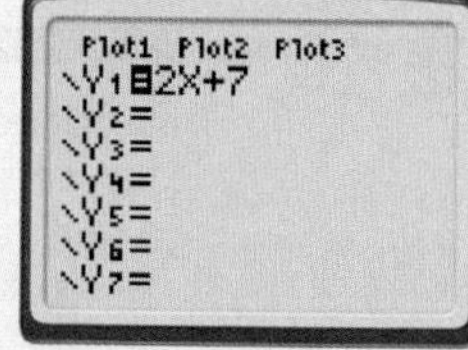

2. Determine a pattern for the values of x.
The x-values start with 25 and increase by 100.

3. Press **2nd** **WINDOW** (TBLSET) to view the *Table Setup* window.
Enter **25** as the starting value in **TblStart=**.
Enter **100** as the amount by which x changes in **ΔTbl=**.

4. Press **2nd** **GRAPH** (TABLE) to create a table of values.
The first column shows values of x starting with 25 and increasing by 100.
The second column shows values of the expression $2x + 7$ when x is equal to the value in the first column.
You can use the arrow keys to view the table when x is greater than 625.

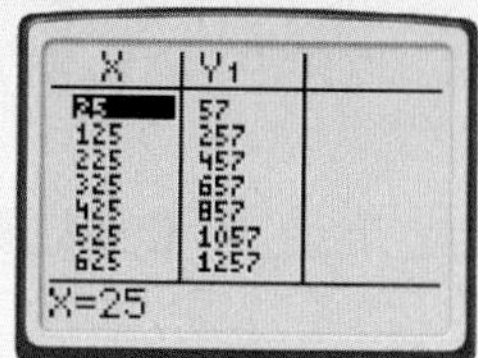

Try This

1. Use the table feature of a graphing calculator to evaluate $5x - 7$ for $x = 4, 6, 8, 10$, and 12. **13; 23; 33; 43; 53**
   a. What value did you enter in **TblStart=**? **4**
   b. What value did you enter in **ΔTbl=**? **2**
2. Use the table feature of a graphing calculator to evaluate $3x + 4$ for $x = -5, -1, 3$, 7, and 11. **−11; 1; 13; 25; 37**
   a. What value did you enter in **TblStart=**? **−5**
   b. What value did you enter in **ΔTbl=**? **4**

You can also use a spreadsheet program to evaluate expressions.

Activity 2

Evaluate $2x + 7$ for $x = 3, 5, 7, 9,$ and 11.

1. In the first column, enter the values 3, 5, 7, 9, and 11.

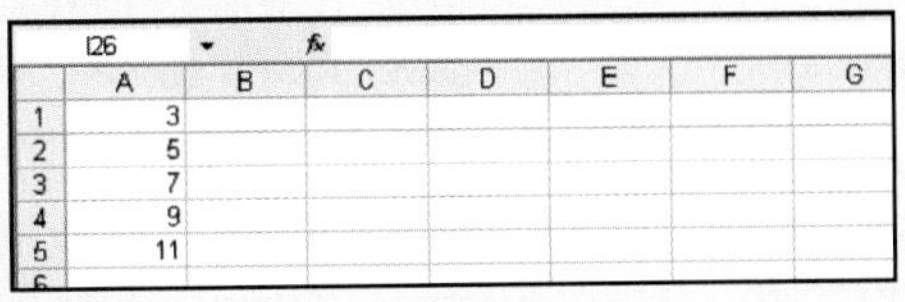

I26 ▾ fx

	A	B	C	D	E	F	G
1	3						
2	5						
3	7						
4	9						
5	11						

2. Enter the expression in cell B1.

   To do this, type the following:
   = 2 * A1 + 7

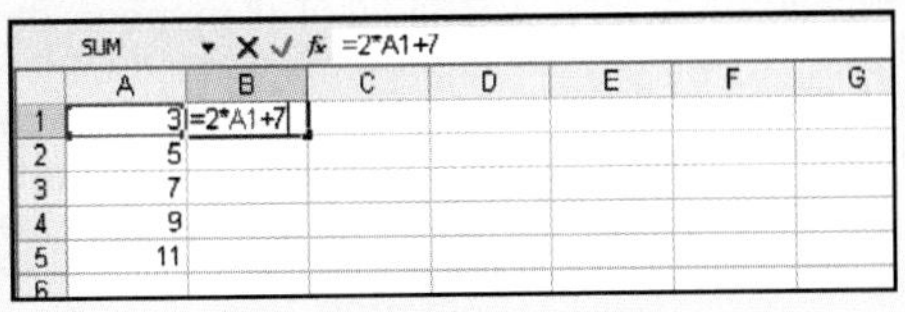

SUM ▾ X ✓ fx =2*A1+7

	A	B	C	D	E	F	G
1	3	=2*A1+7					
2	5						
3	7						
4	9						
5	11						

3. Press Enter.

   The value of $2x + 7$ when $x = 3$ appears in cell B1.

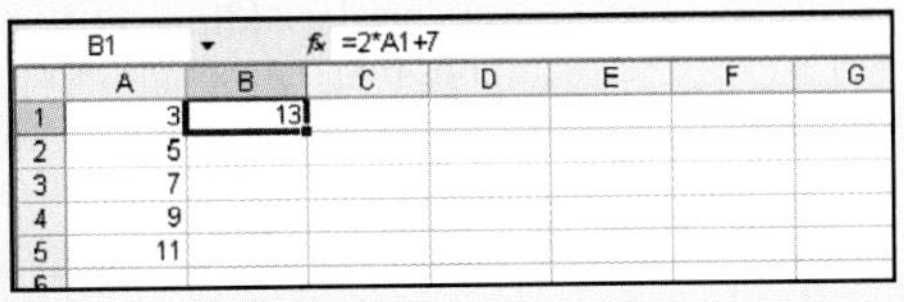

B1 ▾ fx =2*A1+7

	A	B	C	D	E	F	G
1	3	13					
2	5						
3	7						
4	9						
5	11						

4. Copy the formula into cells B2, B3, B4, and B5.

   Use the mouse to click on the lower right corner of cell B1. Hold down the mouse button and drag the cursor through cell B5.

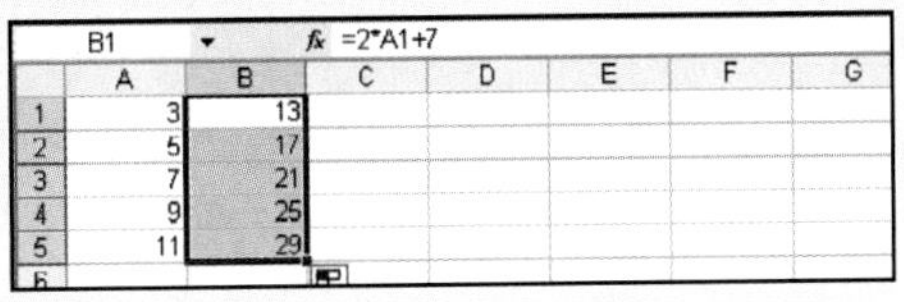

   For each row in column B, the number that is substituted for x is the value in the same row of column A.

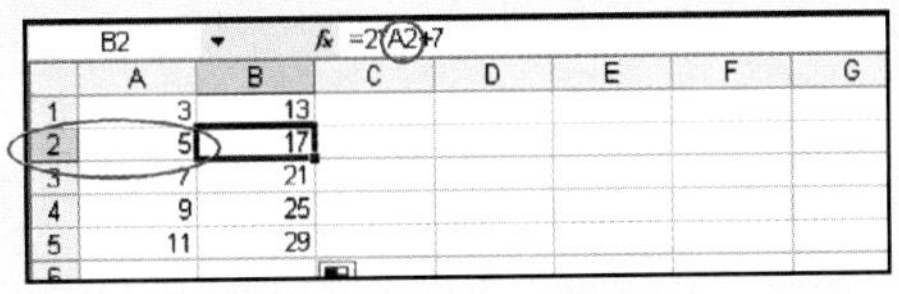

   You can continue the table by entering more values in column A and copying the formula from B1 into more cells in column B.

B1 ▾ fx =2*A1+7

	A	B	C	D	E	F	G
1	3	13					
2	5	17					
3	7	21					
4	9	25					
5	11	29					

B2 ▾ fx =2*A2+7

	A	B	C	D	E	F	G
1	3	13					
2	5	17					
3	7	21					
4	9	25					
5	11	29					

Try This

3. Use a spreadsheet program to evaluate $-2x + 9$ for $x = -5, -2, 1, 4,$ and 7. **19; 13; 7; 1; –5**
   a. What values did you enter in column A? **–5; –2; 1; 4; 7**
   b. What did you type in cell B1? **= –2*A1 + 9**
4. Use a spreadsheet program to evaluate $7x - 10$ for $x = 2, 7, 12, 17,$ and 22. **4; 39; 74; 109; 144**
   a. What values did you enter in column A? **2; 7; 12; 17; 22**
   b. What did you type in cell B1? **= 7*A1 – 10**

Close

Key Concept

The table feature of a graphing calculator or a spreadsheet can be used to evaluate an expression for many values of the variable(s) at one time.

Assessment

Journal Have students explain how to use a graphing calculator and a spreadsheet program to evaluate expressions.

1-1 Technology Lab **13**

1-2 Organizer

Pacing: Traditional 1 day
Block $\frac{1}{2}$ day

Objectives: Add real numbers.
Subtract real numbers.

Algebra Lab
In *Algebra Lab Activities*

Technology Lab
In *Technology Lab Activities*

Online Edition
Tutorial Videos

Countdown Week 1

Power Presentations with PowerPoint®

Warm Up

Simplify.

1. $|-3|$ 3 **2.** $-|4|$ -4

Write an improper fraction to represent each mixed number.

3. $4\frac{2}{3}$ $\frac{14}{3}$ **4.** $7\frac{6}{7}$ $\frac{55}{7}$

Write a mixed number to represent each improper fraction.

5. $\frac{12}{5}$ $2\frac{2}{5}$ **6.** $\frac{24}{9}$ $2\frac{2}{3}$

Also available on transparency

Math Humor

Student 1: How will we ever use negative numbers in the real world?

Student 2: You haven't seen my bank balance!

1-2 Adding and Subtracting Real Numbers

Objectives
Add real numbers.

Subtract real numbers.

Vocabulary
real numbers
absolute value
opposites
additive inverse

Why learn this?
The total length of a penguin's dive can be determined by adding real numbers. (See Example 4.)

The set of all numbers that can be represented on a number line are called **real numbers**. You can use a number line to model addition and subtraction of real numbers.

Addition
To model addition of a positive number, move right. To model addition of a negative number, move left.

Subtraction
To model subtraction of a positive number, move left.
To model subtraction of a negative number, move right.

EXAMPLE 1 Adding and Subtracting Numbers on a Number Line

Add or subtract using a number line.

A $-3 + 6$

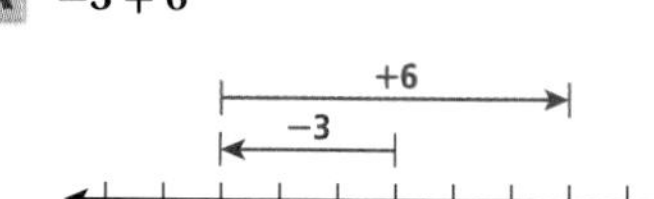

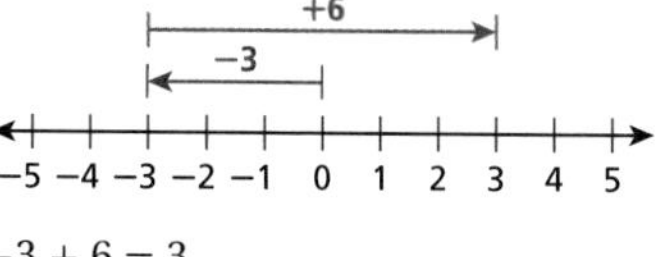

Start at 0. Move left to −3.

To add 6, move right 6 units.

$-3 + 6 = 3$

B $-2 - (-9)$

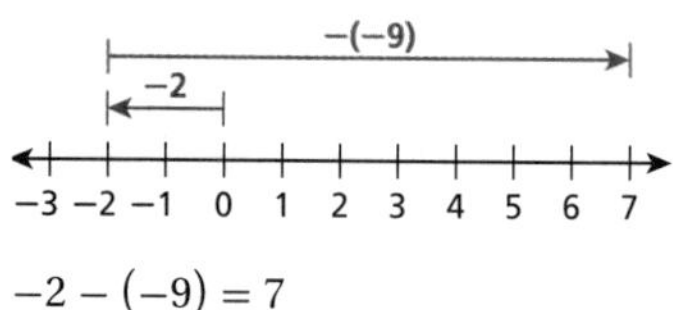

Start at 0. Move left to −2.

To subtract −9, move right 9 units.

$-2 - (-9) = 7$

CHECK IT OUT! Add or subtract using a number line.

1a. $-3 + 7$ **4** **1b.** $-3 - 7$ **−10** **1c.** $-5 - (-6.5)$ **1.5**

The **absolute value** of a number is its distance from zero on a number line. The absolute value of 5 is written as $|5|$.

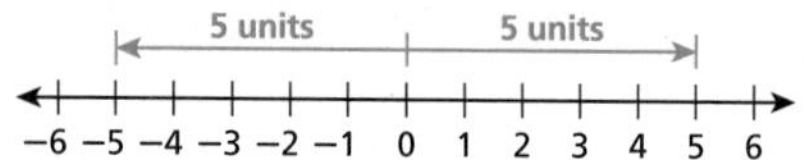

$|5| = 5$

$|-5| = 5$

State Resources

1 Introduce

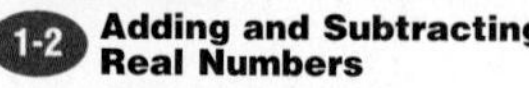

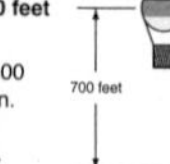

EXPLORATION

1-2 Adding and Subtracting Real Numbers

A hot-air balloon flies at an altitude of 700 feet above the ground.

1. A passenger in the balloon sees a kite 500 feet below. Draw a picture of the situation. How far is the kite above the ground?
2. The passenger sees a bird flying 50 feet above the balloon. Draw a picture of the situation. How far is the bird above the ground?
3. The balloon flies over a lake. The passenger spots a marker that is 20 feet below the surface of the lake. Draw a picture of the situation. What is the distance from the balloon to the marker?

THINK AND DISCUSS

4. **Explain** how you can use subtraction to find the distance from the balloon to the marker in the lake.
5. **Describe** a situation based on the hot-air balloon that can be modeled by the subtraction problem 700 − 60 = 640.

Motivate

Ask how many students have ever owed money to someone. Pose the following situation: "You borrow \$10 from a friend and spend it. Then you earn \$25 by mowing the lawn. How much money will you have after you pay back your friend?" \$15 Point out that not all of the money you earned for mowing the lawn is really yours. Owing money is like having a negative balance. You must add the \$25 you earned to your −\$10 balance.

Explorations and answers are provided in *Alternate Openers: Explorations Transparencies.*

Adding Real Numbers

WORDS	NUMBERS	
Adding Numbers with the Same Sign Add the absolute values and use the sign of the numbers.	$3 + 6$ 9	$-2 + (-9)$ -11
Adding Numbers with Different Signs Subtract the absolute values and use the sign of the number with the greater absolute value.	$-8 + 12$ 4	$3 + (-15)$ -12

EXAMPLE 2 Adding Real Numbers

Add.

A $-3 + (-16)$
$(3 + 16 = 19)$ *Same signs: add the absolute values.*
-19 *Both numbers are negative, so the sum is negative.*

B $-13 + 7$
$(13 - 7 = 6)$ *Different signs: subtract the absolute values.*
-6 *Use the sign of the number with the greater absolute value.*

C $6.2 + (-4.9)$
$(6.2 - 4.9 = 1.3)$ *Different signs: subtract the absolute values.*
1.3 *Use the sign of the number with the greater absolute value.*

Add.

2a. $-5 + (-7)$ **−12** **2b.** $-13.5 + (-22.3)$ **−35.8** **2c.** $52 + (-68)$ **−16**

Two numbers are **opposites** if their sum is 0. A number and its opposite are **additive inverses** and are the same distance from zero. They have the same absolute value.

Helpful Hint

Because adding 0 to a number does not change the number's value, 0 is called the *additive identity*. Two numbers are additive inverses if their sum is the additive identity.

Inverse Property of Addition

WORDS	NUMBERS	ALGEBRA
The sum of a real number and its opposite is 0.	$6 + (-6) = (-6) + 6 = 0$	For any real number a, $a + (-a) = (-a) + a = 0$

To subtract signed numbers, you can use additive inverses. Subtracting a number is the same as adding the opposite of the number.

Subtracting Real Numbers

WORDS	NUMBERS	ALGEBRA
To subtract a number, add its opposite. Then follow the rules for adding signed numbers.	$3 - 8 = 3 + (-8)$ $= -5$	$a - b = a + (-b)$

COMMON ERROR ALERT

Students may incorrectly calculate $-14 - (-12)$, getting -26 as the answer, because there are so many negative signs. Remind students to first write any subtraction as adding the opposite. Then the expression can be written as $-14 + 12$.

Power Presentations with PowerPoint®

Additional Examples

Example 1

Add or subtract using a number line.

A. $-4 + (-7)$ -11

B. $3 - (-6)$ 9

Example 2

Add.

A. $-\frac{3}{4} + \frac{1}{4}$ $-\frac{1}{2}$

B. $-6 + (-2)$ -8

INTERVENTION
Questioning Strategies

EXAMPLE 1

- What would happen if you used a number line to add the numbers in reverse order?
- What would happen if you used a number line to subtract the numbers in reverse order?

EXAMPLE 2

- How could a number line be used to perform addition?

2 Teach

Guided Instruction

Show students how to add and subtract on a number line. Use the results from the number line to develop the rules for adding and subtracting real numbers. Emphasize that subtracting is the same as adding the opposite.

Reaching All Learners
Through Concrete Manipulatives

Provide students with integer chips of two different colors. One color represents +1, and the other color represents −1. Show students that one chip of each color forms a zero pair. Use these chips to model addition of positive and negative numbers. Integer chips can be found in the Manipulatives Kit (MK).

Power Presentations with PowerPoint®

Additional Examples

Example 3

Subtract.

A. $-6.7 - 4.1$ $\quad -10.8$

B. $5 - (-4)$ $\quad 9$

C. $-2\frac{3}{5} - 2\frac{7}{10}$ $\quad -5\frac{3}{10}$

Example 4

An iceberg extends 75 feet above the sea. The bottom of the iceberg is at an elevation of −247 feet. What is the height of the iceberg?
322 feet

INTERVENTION
Questioning Strategies

EXAMPLE 3

- What is the first step in finding the value of an expression that contains subtraction and signed numbers?

EXAMPLE 4

- What does it mean for something to be at a negative elevation?
- What is another way to solve this problem?

Science Link A glacier is a large mass of ice moving across land. An iceberg is a piece of a glacier that has broken off into the sea.

EXAMPLE 3 Subtracting Real Numbers

Subtract.

A $7 - 10$

$7 - 10 = 7 + (-10)$ — *To subtract 10, add −10.*

$(10 - 7 = 3)$ — *Different signs: subtract absolute values.*

-3 — *Use the sign of the number with the greater absolute value.*

B $-3 - (-12)$

$-3 - (-12) = -3 + 12$ — *To subtract −12, add 12.*

$(12 - 3 = 9)$ — *Different signs: subtract absolute values.*

9 — *Use the sign of the number with the greater absolute value.*

C $-\frac{1}{8} - \frac{3}{8}$

$-\frac{1}{8} - \frac{3}{8} = -\frac{1}{8} + \left(-\frac{3}{8}\right)$ — *To subtract $\frac{3}{8}$, add $-\frac{3}{8}$.*

$\left(\frac{1}{8} + \frac{3}{8} = \frac{4}{8} = \frac{1}{2}\right)$ — *Same signs: add absolute values.*

$-\frac{1}{2}$ — *Both numbers are negative, so the sum is negative.*

D $22.5 - (-4)$

$22.5 - (-4) = 22.5 + 4$ — *To subtract −4, add 4.*

$(22.5 + 4 = 26.5)$ — *Same signs: add absolute values.*

26.5 — *Both numbers are positive, so the sum is positive.*

Helpful Hint

On many scientific and graphing calculators, there is one button to express the opposite of a number and a different button to express subtraction.

CHECK IT OUT! Subtract.

3a. $13 - 21$ **−8** **3b.** $\frac{1}{2} - \left(-3\frac{1}{2}\right)$ **4** **3c.** $-14 - (-12)$ **−2**

EXAMPLE 4 *Biology Application*

An emperor penguin stands on an iceberg that extends 10 feet above the water. Then the penguin dives to an elevation of −67 feet to catch a fish. What is the total length of the penguin's dive?

elevation of iceberg	minus	elevation of fish
10	−	−67

$10 - (-67) = 10 + 67$ — *To subtract −67, add 67.*

$= 77$ — *Same signs: add absolute values.*

The total length of the penguin's dive is 77 feet.

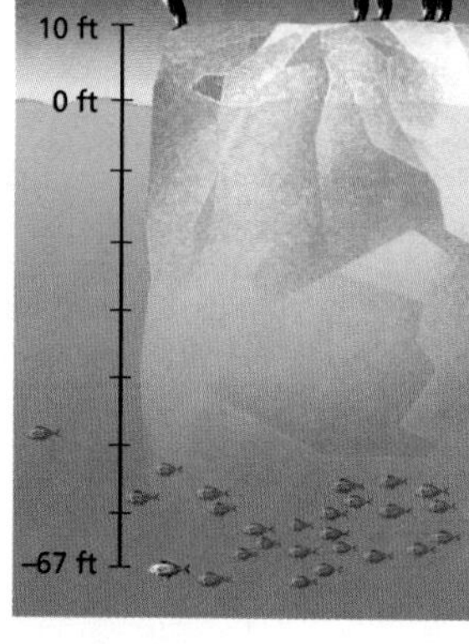

CHECK IT OUT! **4. What if...?** The tallest known iceberg in the North Atlantic rose 550 feet above the ocean's surface. How many feet would it be from the top of the tallest iceberg to the wreckage of the *Titanic*, which is at an elevation of −12,468 feet? **13,018 ft**

3 Close

Summarize

Review the rules for adding and subtracting real numbers on page 15. Have students explain the phrase "add the opposite."
Possible answer: To add the opposite means to rewrite a subtraction expression as addition by changing the minus to a plus and writing the additive inverse of the second number.

ONGOING ASSESSMENT and INTERVENTION

***Diagnose Before* the Lesson**
1-2 Warm Up, TE p. 14

***Monitor During* the Lesson**
Check It Out! Exercises, SE pp. 14–16
Questioning Strategies, TE pp. 15–16

***Assess After* the Lesson**
1-2 Lesson Quiz, TE p. 19
Alternative Assessment, TE p. 19

THINK AND DISCUSS

1. The difference of −7 and −5 is −2. Explain why the difference is greater than −7.
2. **GET ORGANIZED** Copy and complete the graphic organizer. For each pair of points, tell whether the sum and the difference of the first point and the second point are positive or negative.

Points	Sum	Difference
A, B		
B, A		
C, B		
D, A		

Answers to *Think and Discuss*

Possible answers:

1. Subtracting a negative number is the same as adding a positive number. This means you move right on the number line, making the sum greater than the first number.
2. See p. A2.

1-2 Exercises

go.hrw.com
Homework Help Online
KEYWORD: MA11 1-2
Parent Resources Online
KEYWORD: MA7 Parent

GUIDED PRACTICE

1. **Vocabulary** The sum of a number and its ___?___ is always zero. (*opposite* or *absolute value*) **opposite**

SEE EXAMPLE 1 p. 14

Add or subtract using a number line.

2. $-4 + 7$ **3**
3. $-3.5 - 5$ **−8.5**
4. $5.6 - 9.2$ **−3.6**
5. $3 - \left(-6\frac{1}{4}\right)$ $\mathbf{9\frac{1}{4}}$

SEE EXAMPLE 2 p. 15

Add.

6. $91 + (-11)$ **80**
7. $4\frac{3}{4} + \left(-3\frac{3}{4}\right)$ **1**
8. $15.6 + (-17.9)$ **−2.3**
9. $-\frac{1}{16} + \frac{5}{8}$ $\mathbf{\frac{9}{16}}$

SEE EXAMPLE 3 p. 16

Subtract.

10. $23 - 36$ **−13**
11. $4.3 - 8.4$ **−4.1**
12. $1\frac{1}{5} - 2\frac{4}{5}$ $\mathbf{-1\frac{3}{5}}$
13. $\frac{7}{10} - \left(-\frac{2}{5}\right)$ $\mathbf{1\frac{1}{10}}$

SEE EXAMPLE 4 p. 16

14. **Economics** The Dow Jones Industrial Average (DJIA) reports the average prices of stocks for 30 companies. Use the table to determine the total decrease in the DJIA for the two days. **−616.34**

DJIA 1987	
Friday, Oct. 16	−108.35
Monday, Oct. 19	−507.99

PRACTICE AND PROBLEM SOLVING

Independent Practice

For Exercises	See Example
15–18	1
19–22	2
23–26	3
27	4

Extra Practice
Skills Practice p. S4
Application Practice p. S28

Add or subtract using a number line.

15. $-2 + 6$ **4**
16. $6 + (-2)$ **4**
17. $\frac{1}{4} - 12$ $\mathbf{-11\frac{3}{4}}$
18. $-\frac{2}{5} + 6$ $\mathbf{5\frac{3}{5}}$

Add.

19. $-18 + (-12)$ **−30**
20. $-2.3 + 3.5$ **1.2**
21. $-15 + 29$ **14**
22. $-4.8 + (-5.4)$ **−10.2**

Subtract.

23. $12 - 22$ **−10**
24. $-\frac{3}{4} - \left(-\frac{1}{4}\right)$ $\mathbf{-\frac{1}{2}}$
25. $38 - 24.6$ **13.4**
26. $\frac{2}{3} - \left(-\frac{1}{2}\right)$ $\mathbf{1\frac{1}{6}}$

27. **Meteorology** A meteorologist reported that the day's high temperature was 17 °F and the low temperature was −6 °F. What was the difference between the day's high and low temperatures? **23 °F**

1-2 Exercises

Assignment Guide

Assign *Guided Practice* exercises as necessary.

If you finished Examples **1–2**
Basic 15–22, 28–31
Average 15–22, 28, 30, 57, 58
Advanced 15–22, 57–60

If you finished Examples **1–4**
Basic 15–39, 40–46 even, 47, 51–56, 64–70
Average 15–27, 32–38 even, 40–60, 64–70
Advanced 15–27, 32–46 even, 47–50, 52–70

Homework Quick Check
Quickly check key concepts.
Exercises: 16, 18, 22, 23, 40, 43

State Resources

go.hrw.com
State Resources Online
KEYWORD: MA7 Resources

Exercise 52 involves applying the subtraction of real numbers to diving. This exercise prepares students for the Multi-Step Test Prep on page 38.

Answers

48. Possible answer: The number represented by $-2 + n$ is always 2 units left of n on a number line.

49. Possible answer: When b is positive, $-b + (-b)$ represents the sum of two negative numbers, which is always negative.

50. Possible answer: If $x < -1$, then $x + 1$ is negative. If $x = -1$, then $x + 1$ equals 0. If $x > -1$, then $x + 1$ is positive.

52a. 1650 ft

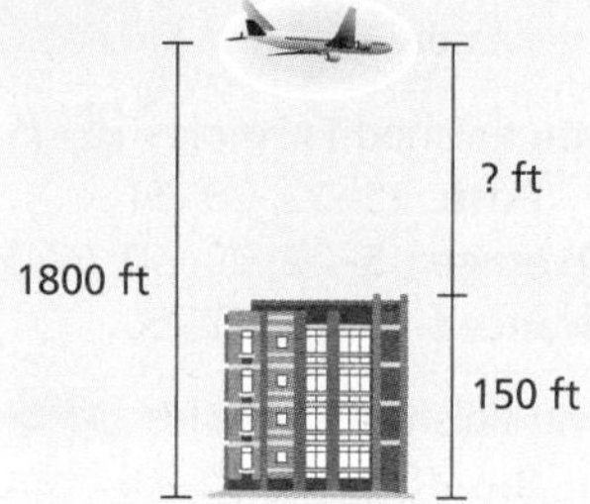

b. 1880 ft

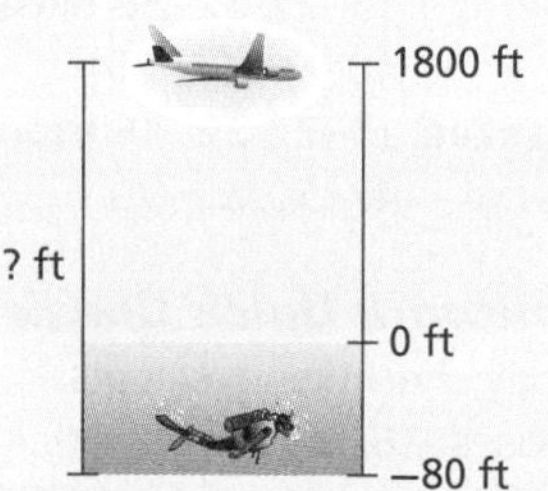

c. 1880 ft; because subtracting a negative number is the same as adding a positive number

Evaluate the expression $n + (-5)$ for each value of n.

28. $n = 312$ **307**
29. $n = 5.75$ **0.75**
30. $n = -\frac{7}{12}$ $\mathbf{-5\frac{7}{12}}$
31. $n = -7\frac{2}{5}$ $\mathbf{-12\frac{2}{5}}$

Add or subtract.

32. $-8 - 3$ **−11**
33. $-9 + (-3)$ **−12**
34. $16 - (-16)$ **32**
35. $100 - 63$ **37**
36. $5.2 - 2.5$ **2.7**
37. $-4.7 - (-4.7)$ **0**
38. $\frac{2}{5} - \frac{7}{8}$ $\mathbf{-\frac{19}{40}}$
39. $\frac{2}{5} - \frac{3}{10}$ $\mathbf{\frac{1}{10}}$

40. **Business** A restaurant manager lost \$415 in business during the month of January. Business picked up in February, and he ended that month with a profit of \$1580.
    a. What was the manager's profit after January and February? **\$1165**
    b. **What if...?** The restaurant lost \$245 in business during the month of March. What was the manager's profit after January, February, and March? **\$920**

Compare. Write <, >, or =.

41. $-4 - (-6)$ **>** $-7 - 3$
42. $|-51|$ **>** $|0|$
43. $3 - (-3)$ **>** $0 - (-3)$
44. $-3 - 8$ **=** $-22 + 11$
45. $|-10 + 5|$ **<** $|-15|$
46. $9 + (-8)$ **=** $-12 + 13$

47. **Travel** Death Valley National Park is located in California. Use the table to determine the difference in elevation between the highest and lowest locations. **11,331 ft**

Death Valley National Park	
Location	**Elevation (ft)**
Badwater	−282
Emigrant Pass	5,318
Furnace Creek Airport	−210
Telescope Peak	11,049

Critical Thinking Tell whether each statement is sometimes, always, or never true. Explain.

48. The value of the expression $-2 + n$ is less than the value of n. **always**

49. When b is positive, the expression $-b + (-b)$ is equal to 0. **never**

50. When x is negative, the value of the expression $x + 1$ is negative. **sometimes**

51. **///ERROR ANALYSIS///** Which is incorrect? Explain the error.

A; the opposite of −8 should have been added.

Ⓐ
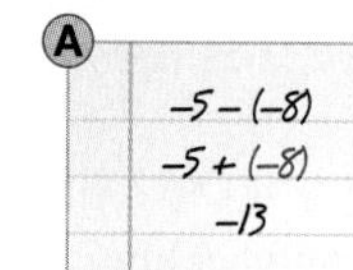

Ⓑ
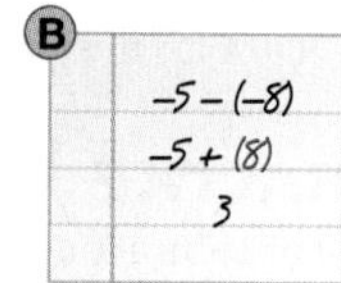

MULTI-STEP TEST PREP

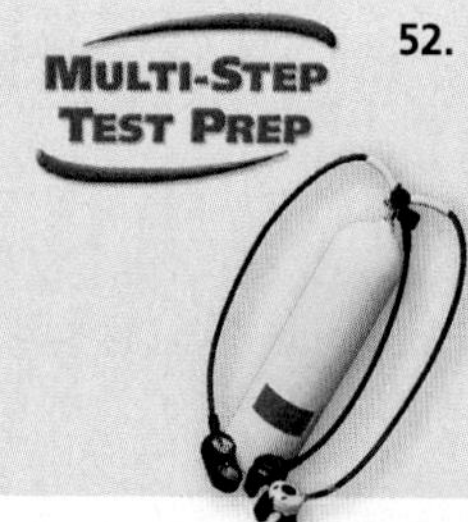

52. This problem will prepare you for the Multi-Step Test Prep on page 38.
    a. A plane flies at a height of 1800 feet directly over a 150-foot-tall building. How far above the building is the plane? Draw a diagram to explain your answer.
    b. The same plane then flies directly over a diver who is 80 feet below the surface of the water. How far is the plane above the diver? Draw a diagram to explain your answer.
    c. Subtract the diver's altitude of −80 feet from the plane's altitude of 1800 feet. Explain why this distance is greater than 1800 feet.

1-2 PRACTICE A

1-2 PRACTICE C

1-2 PRACTICE B

Add or subtract using a number line.

1. −6 + (−8) **−14**
2. 2 − (−8) **10**
3. 10 + (−4) = **6**
4. −2 − (−6) **4**
5. −7 + 7 **0**
6. −0.25 − 4 **−4.25**

Add.

7. −5 + 23 **18**
8. −15 + (−9) **−24**
9. 24.6 + (−45.5) **−20.9**
10. $-\frac{3}{8} + 5$ $\mathbf{4\frac{5}{8}}$
11. $a + (-14)$ for $a = 16$ **2**
12. $-3.3 + x$ for $x = -9.1$ **−12.4**

Subtract.

13. −35 − (−80) **45**
14. 12 − (−16) **28**
15. 8.3 − 10.7 **−2.4**
16. $-\frac{2}{3} - 5\frac{1}{3}$ **−6**
17. $15 - t$ for $t = -22$ **37**
18. $z - 3.5$ for $z = 1$ **−2.5**

19. The record high temperature for Asheville, North Carolina was 99°F. The record low was −17°F. What is the difference between these two temperatures? **116°F**

20. The balance in Mr. Sanchez's bank account was \$293.74. He accidentally wrote a check for \$300. What is his balance now? **−\$6.26**

Evaluate the expression 18 − *n* for each value of *n*.

21. $n = -13$ **31**
22. $n = 8.55$ **9.45**
23. $n = 20\frac{1}{5}$ $\mathbf{-2\frac{1}{5}}$

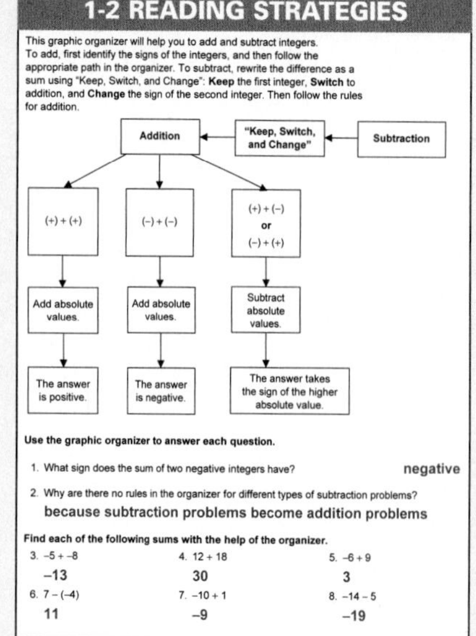
1-2 READING STRATEGIES

This graphic organizer will help you to add and subtract integers. To add, first identify the signs of the integers, and then follow the appropriate path in the organizer. To subtract, rewrite the difference as a sum using "Keep, Switch, and Change": **Keep** the first integer, **Switch** to addition, and **Change** the sign of the second integer. Then follow the rules for addition.

Use the graphic organizer to answer each question.

1. What sign does the sum of two negative integers have? **negative**
2. Why are there no rules in the organizer for different types of subtraction problems? **because subtraction problems become addition problems**

Find each of the following sums with the help of the organizer.

3. −5 + −8 **−13**
4. 12 + 18 **30**
5. −6 + 9 **3**
6. 7 − (−4) **11**
7. −10 + 1 **−9**
8. −14 − 5 **−19**

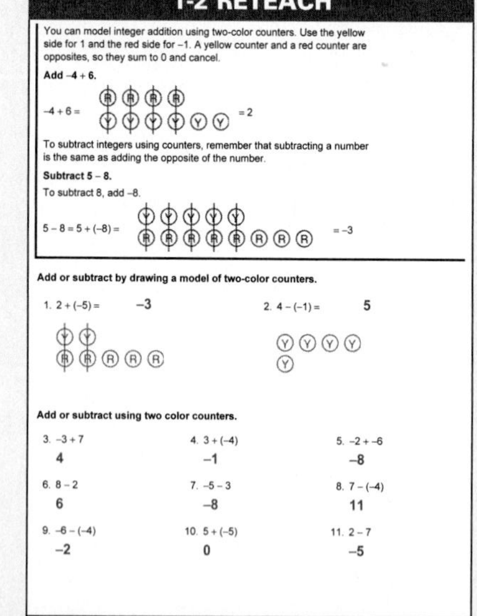
1-2 RETEACH

You can model integer addition using two-color counters. Use the yellow side for 1 and the red side for −1. A yellow counter and a red counter are opposites, so they sum to 0 and cancel.

Add −4 + 6.

−4 + 6 = Ⓡ Ⓡ Ⓡ Ⓡ / Ⓨ Ⓨ Ⓨ Ⓨ Ⓨ Ⓨ = 2

To subtract integers using counters, remember that subtracting a number is the same as adding the opposite of the number.

Subtract 5 − 8.

To subtract 8, add −8.

5 − 8 = 5 + (−8) = Ⓨ Ⓨ Ⓨ Ⓨ Ⓨ / Ⓡ Ⓡ Ⓡ Ⓡ Ⓡ Ⓡ Ⓡ Ⓡ = −3

Add or subtract by drawing a model of two-color counters.

1. 2 + (−5) = **−3**
2. 4 − (−1) = **5**

Add or subtract using two color counters.

3. −3 + 7 **4**
4. 3 + (−4) **−1**
5. −2 + −6 **−8**
6. 8 − 2 **6**
7. −5 − 3 **−8**
8. 7 − (−4) **11**
9. −6 − (−4) **−2**
10. 5 + (−5) **0**
11. 2 − 7 **−5**

53. **Write About It** Explain why addition and subtraction are called inverse operations. Use the following examples in your explanation:

$8 + (-2) = 8 - 2 \qquad 8 - (-2) = 8 + 2$

TEST PREP

54. Which expression is equivalent to $|-3 + 5|$?

   Ⓐ $-3 - 5$ Ⓑ $-3 + 5$ Ⓒ $3 - 5$ Ⓓ $3 + 5$

55. At midnight, the temperature was −12 °F. By noon, the temperature had risen 25 °F. During the afternoon, it fell 10 °F and fell another 3 °F by midnight. What was the temperature at midnight?

   Ⓕ 0 °F   Ⓖ 3 °F   Ⓗ 12 °F   Ⓙ 24 °F

56. The table shows the amounts Mr. Espinosa spent on lunch each day one week. What is the total amount Mr. Espinosa spent for lunch this week?

Day	Monday	Tuesday	Wednesday	Thursday	Friday
Amount ($)	5.40	4.16	7.07	5.40	9.52

   Ⓐ $21.83   Ⓑ $22.03   Ⓒ $31.55   Ⓓ $36.95

CHALLENGE AND EXTEND

Simplify each expression.

57. $-1\frac{1}{5} + (-7.8)$ **−9**

58. $-\frac{1}{5} + 2.1$ **1.9**

59. $9.75 + \left(-7\frac{3}{4}\right)$ **2**

60. $-2\frac{3}{10} + 8.5$ **6.2**

For each pattern shown below, describe a possible rule for finding the next term. Then use your rule to write the next 3 terms.

61. 14, 10, 6, 2, ... **Subtract 4; −2, −6, −10.**

62. $-2, -\frac{8}{5}, -\frac{6}{5}, -\frac{4}{5}, \ldots$ **Add $\frac{2}{5}$; $-\frac{2}{5}$, 0, $\frac{2}{5}$.**

63. **Geography** Sam visited two volcanoes, Cotapaxi and Sangay, and two caves, Sistema Huautla and Sistema Cheve. Cotapaxi, in Ecuador, has an elevation of 19,347 ft. Sangay, also in Ecuador, has an elevation of 17,159 ft. The main entrance of Sistema Huautla, in Mexico, has an elevation of 5051 ft. The main entrance of Sistema Cheve, also in Mexico, has an elevation of 9085 ft. What is the average elevation of these places? **12,660.5 ft**

SPIRAL REVIEW

Write each number as a terminating or repeating decimal. *(Previous course)*

64. $\frac{3}{16}$ **0.1875**

65. $\frac{2}{9}$ **$0.\overline{2}$**

66. $\frac{15}{12}$ **1.25**

67. $\frac{4}{11}$ **$0.\overline{36}$**

Divide each polygon into triangles to find the sum of its angle measures. (*Hint:* Remember that the sum of the angle measures in a triangle is 180°.) *(Previous course)*

68.  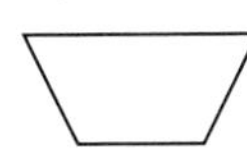 **360°**

69. 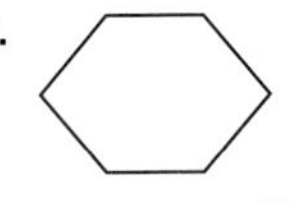 **720°**

70. 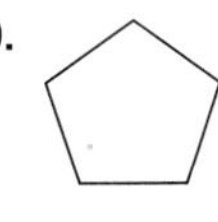 **540°**

TEST PREP DOCTOR For **Exercise 55,** students who chose **H** may have begun at 0° instead of −12°; students who chose **J** may have begun at +12°.

For **Exercise 56,** students should estimate the answer by rounding to the nearest dollar before looking at the answer choices. Choice **C** seems to be the correct one. Students can check this answer by working the problem.

Answers

53. Possible answer: The first example shows that adding the opposite of 2 and subtracting 2 are equal. The second example shows that subtracting the opposite of 2 and adding 2 are equal. After adding two numbers, you can get back to the first number by subtracting the second number.

Journal

Have students explain how they could teach a student who is absent from class to add and subtract real numbers. Have them include at least one example of each operation.

ALTERNATIVE ASSESSMENT

Have students create and solve two real-world problems involving some negative numbers. One problem should involve addition, and the other should involve subtraction.

Power Presentations with PowerPoint®

1-2 Lesson Quiz

Add or subtract using a number line.

1. $-2 + 9$ 7

2. $-5 - (-3)$ −2

Add or subtract.

3. $-23 + 42$ 19

4. $4.5 - (-3.7)$ 8.2

5. $-2\frac{2}{3} + \left(-\frac{5}{6}\right)$ $-3\frac{1}{2}$

6. The temperature at 6:00 A.M. was −23 °F. At 3:00 P.M., it was 18 °F. Find the difference in the temperatures.   41 °F

Also available on transparency

1-2 PROBLEM SOLVING

Write the correct answer.

1. The Pacific Ocean has an average depth of 12,925 feet, while the Atlantic Ocean has an average depth of 11,730 feet. Find the difference in average depths.

   1195 feet

2. A kite flies 74 feet above the ground. The person flying the kite is 5 feet 6 inches tall. How far above the person is the kite?

   68 feet 6 inches

3. Stock in ABC Company fell 12.67 points on Monday and 31.51 points on Tuesday. Determine the total change in the stock for the two days.

   −44.18 points

4. Muriel scored 30 points lower on her first practice SAT test than she did on her PSAT. She scored 20 points better on her second practice SAT test than she did on her first practice SAT test. How does her second practice SAT test score compare with her PSAT test score?

   10 points lower

Use the table below to answer questions 5–7, which shows some of the world's most extreme elevations. A negative number means the location is *below* sea level. Select the best answer.

Location	Elevation (ft)
Mount Everest	29,028
Aconcagua	22,834
Mount McKinley	20,320
Mariana Trench	−35,840
Puerto Rico Trench	−28,232
Java Trench	−23,376

5. Find the difference in elevation between the Puerto Rico Trench and the Java Trench.

   A 4856 ft   C 51,608 ft
   B 7608 ft   D 59,216 ft

6. Find the difference in elevation between the highest and lowest locations.

   F 64,868 ft   H 6812 ft
   G 52,404 ft   J 5652 ft

7. Denver is called the "Mile High City" because it is approximately 5280 feet above sea level. How much higher in elevation is Denver than the Mariana Trench?

   A 30,560 ft   C 35,840 ft
   B 34,308 ft   **D** 41,120 ft

1-2 CHALLENGE

The music club wanted to have a party at the end of the school year. Their advisor stated that if they had over $100 at the end of the school year, they would have a party.

The club's financial transactions for the second half of the school year are shown below. A balance of $500 was carried over from the first half of the school year.

A deposit indicates that a positive amount was added. A withdrawal indicates that a negative amount was added.

Complete the chart to help you answer the questions below.

Transaction Date	Type of Transaction	Amount	Math Expression	Balance
				$500
1/4	Deposit	$50	$500 + $50	$550
1/12	Withdrawal	$100	$500 + (−$100)	$450
1/18	Withdrawal	$25	$450 + (−$25)	$425
1/26	Withdrawal	$200	$425 + (−$200)	$225
2/10	Deposit	$50	$225 + $50	$275
3/8	Deposit	$50	$275 + $50	$325
3/23	Withdrawal	$350	$325 + (−$350)	−$25
4/6	Deposit	$75	−$25 + $75	$50
4/22	Withdrawal	$25	$50 + (−$25)	$25
5/11	Deposit	$100	$25 + $100	$125
5/17	Withdrawal	$200	$125 + (−$200)	−$75
6/7	Deposit	$225	−$75 + $225	$150

1. Did the balance ever go above $600? If so, on what date(s) did this occur?

   no

2. Did the balance ever go below $0? If so, on what date(s) did this occur?

   yes; 3/23 and 5/17

3. What was the ending balance? **$150**

4. Did the music club get to have a party? **yes**

1-3 Organizer

Pacing: Traditional 1 day
Block $\frac{1}{2}$ day

Objectives: Multiply real numbers.

Divide real numbers.

Online Edition
Tutorial Videos

Countdown Week 1

Power Presentations with PowerPoint®

Warm Up

Multiply or divide.

1. $6(7)$ 42
2. $\frac{1}{2}\left(\frac{3}{4}\right)$ $\frac{3}{8}$
3. $42 \div 7$ 6
4. $\frac{60}{15}$ 4
5. Write $\frac{16}{5}$ as a mixed number. $3\frac{1}{5}$
6. Write $4\frac{3}{8}$ as an improper fraction. $\frac{35}{8}$

Also available on transparency

Astrologer: Hey, what's your sign?
Confused math student: Negative?

State Resources

go.hrw.com
State Resources Online
KEYWORD: MA7 Resources

1-3 Multiplying and Dividing Real Numbers

Objectives
Multiply real numbers.

Divide real numbers.

Vocabulary
reciprocal
multiplicative inverse

Who uses this?
Hot-air balloon pilots can determine how far away from liftoff they will land by using multiplication. (See Example 4.)

When you multiply or divide two numbers, the signs of the numbers determine whether the result is positive or negative.

Numbers	Product/Quotient
Both positive	Positive
One negative	Negative
Both negative	Positive

Know it! Note

Multiplying and Dividing Real Numbers

WORDS	NUMBERS	
Multiplying and Dividing Numbers with the Same Sign		
If two numbers have the same sign, their product or quotient is positive.	$4 \cdot 5 = 20$	$-15 \div (-3) = 5$
Multiplying and Dividing Numbers with Different Signs		
If two numbers have different signs, their product or quotient is negative.	$6(-3) = -18$ $(-7)2 = -14$	$-18 \div 2 = -9$ $10 \div (-5) = -2$

EXAMPLE 1 Multiplying and Dividing Signed Numbers

Find the value of each expression.

A $-12 \cdot 5$

-60 *The product of two numbers with different signs is negative.*

B $8\left(-\frac{5}{4}\right)$

$= \left(\frac{8}{1}\right)\left(-\frac{5}{4}\right) = -\frac{40}{4}$ *Multiply.*

$= -10$ *The quotient of two numbers with different signs is negative.*

CHECK IT OUT! Find the value of each expression.

1a. $35 \div (-5)$ **−7** **1b.** $-11(-4)$ **44** **1c.** $-6(7)$ **−42**

1 Introduce

EXPLORATION
1-3 Multiplying and Dividing Real Numbers

Use a calculator to find each product or quotient.

1. a. $4 \div 5$
   b. $60\left(\frac{7}{3}\right)$
   c. 23.45×3.4
2. a. $-2 \cdot 53$
   b. $-2.5 \div 0.8$
   c. $7.5 \times (-4.1)$
3. a. $-555 \div (-5)$
   b. $-3.2(-7.53)$
   c. $-1500 \times (-0.4)$
4. What patterns do you notice about the signs of the answers?

THINK AND DISCUSS

5. **Explain** when the product or quotient of two real numbers is positive. When is the product or quotient negative?
6. **Discuss** whether the product of five negative numbers is positive or negative. Explain your reasoning.

Motivate

Pose the following situation: You are buying a car by paying $300 per month for 48 months. How much will you pay in all? $14,400 What operation did you use to get your answer? multiplication Suppose you pay a total of $15,000 for a car by making equal monthly payments for 60 months. What is the monthly payment? $250 What operation did you use to get your answer? division

Explorations and answers are provided in *Alternate Openers: Explorations Transparencies.*

> **Helpful Hint**
>
> Because multiplying by 1 does not change a number's value, 1 is the *multiplicative identity*. Two numbers are multiplicative inverses if their product is the multiplicative identity.

Two numbers are **reciprocals** if their product is 1. A number and its reciprocal are called **multiplicative inverses** .

Inverse Property of Multiplication

WORDS	NUMBERS	ALGEBRA
The product of a nonzero real number and its reciprocal is 1.	$4 \cdot \frac{1}{4} = \frac{1}{4} \cdot 4 = 1$ $-3 \cdot \left(-\frac{1}{3}\right) = -\frac{1}{3} \cdot (-3) = 1$	For any real number a $(a \neq 0)$, $a \cdot \frac{1}{a} = \frac{1}{a} \cdot a = 1$

To divide by a number, you can multiply by its multiplicative inverse.

EXAMPLE 2 Dividing with Fractions

> **Helpful Hint**
>
> You can write the reciprocal of a number by switching the numerator and denominator. A number written without a denominator has a denominator of 1.

Divide.

A $-\frac{4}{5} \div \left(-\frac{8}{15}\right)$

$-\frac{4}{5} \div \left(-\frac{8}{15}\right) = -\frac{4}{5}\left(-\frac{15}{8}\right)$ *To divide by $-\frac{8}{15}$, multiply by $-\frac{15}{8}$.*

$= \frac{(-4)(-15)}{5(8)}$ *Multiply the numerators and multiply the denominators.*

$= \frac{60}{40} = \frac{3}{2}$ *$-\frac{4}{5}$ and $-\frac{8}{15}$ have the same sign, so the quotient is positive.*

B $-4 \div 9\frac{1}{4}$

$-4 \div 9\frac{1}{4} = -\frac{4}{1} \div \frac{37}{4}$ *Write 4 as a fraction with a denominator of 1. Write $9\frac{1}{4}$ as an improper fraction.*

$= -\frac{4}{1} \cdot \frac{4}{37}$ *To divide by $\frac{37}{4}$, multiply by $\frac{4}{37}$.*

$= -\frac{4(4)}{1(37)} = -\frac{16}{37}$ *-4 and $9\frac{1}{4}$ have different signs, so the quotient is negative.*

Divide.

2a. $-\frac{3}{4} \div (-9)$ $\frac{1}{12}$ **2b.** $\frac{3}{10} \div \left(-\frac{6}{5}\right)$ $-\frac{1}{4}$ **2c.** $-\frac{5}{6} \div 1\frac{2}{3}$ $-\frac{1}{2}$

The number 0 has special properties for multiplication and division.

Properties of Zero

WORDS	NUMBERS		ALGEBRA	
Multiplication by Zero The product of any number and 0 is 0.	$\frac{1}{3} \cdot 0 = 0$	$0(-17) = 0$	$a \cdot 0 = 0$	$0 \cdot a = 0$
Zero Divided by a Number The quotient of 0 and any nonzero number is 0.	$\frac{0}{6} = 0$	$0 \div \frac{2}{3} = 0$	$\frac{0}{a} = 0$	$(a \neq 0)$
Division by Zero Division by 0 is undefined.	$12 \div 0$ ✗	$\frac{-5}{0}$ ✗	$a \div 0$ ✗	$\frac{a}{0}$ ✗

> **COMMON ERROR ALERT**
>
> Some students may think the fraction $-\frac{4}{5}$ can be rewritten as $\frac{-4}{-5}$. Remind them that a negative in both the numerator and the denominator results in a positive fraction because it indicates a negative number divided by a negative number. The fraction $-\frac{4}{5}$ can be rewritten as $\frac{-4}{5}$ or $\frac{4}{-5}$.

Power Presentations with PowerPoint®

Additional Examples

Example 1

Find the value of each expression.

A. $\frac{1}{2}(-10)$ -5

B. $\frac{-48}{-4}$ 12

C. $-3\left(\frac{2}{3}\right)$ -2

Example 2

Divide.

A. $-\frac{1}{2} \div \left(-\frac{5}{6}\right)$ $\frac{3}{5}$

B. $\frac{8}{9} \div \left(-2\frac{2}{3}\right)$ $-\frac{1}{3}$

INTERVENTION

Questioning Strategies

EXAMPLE 1

- What is the sign of the product of two negative numbers?

EXAMPLE 2

- Does every number have a reciprocal? Explain.

Communicating Math Ask "How many 3's are in 12?" 4 "What division problem shows this?" $12 \div 3 = 4$ Now ask students to explain how they know that $\frac{1}{2} \div \frac{1}{2} = 1$. There is one $\frac{1}{2}$ in $\frac{1}{2}$. Also, any nonzero number divided by itself is 1.

2 Teach

Guided Instruction

Before multiplying and dividing real numbers, review mixed numbers, improper fractions, and reciprocals. Then discuss the rules for multiplying and dividing signed numbers, as well as the properties of zero. Emphasize the difference between $\frac{0}{a}$ and $\frac{a}{0}$ for $a \neq 0$. $\left(\frac{0}{a} = 0\text{, and } \frac{a}{0} \text{ is undefined.}\right)$ This will be important later when finding the slopes of lines.

Reaching All Learners

Through Cooperative Learing

Pair students and give each student two index cards, one with a plus sign and one with a minus sign. The students take turns placing one of their cards on the table. If the product of two numbers with the chosen signs is positive, student A receives a point, and if the product is negative, student B receives a point. The cards are then picked up, and play continues. Play to a set number of points.

Optional: Play with three cards.

Power Presentations with PowerPoint®

Additional Examples

Example 3

Multiply or divide if possible.

A. $\frac{0}{15}$ 0

B. $-22 \div 0$ undefined

C. $-8.45(0)$ 0

Example 4

The speed of a hot air balloon is $3\frac{3}{4}$ mi/h. It travels in a straight line parallel to the ground for $1\frac{1}{3}$ hours before landing. How many miles away from the liftoff site will the balloon land? 5 miles

INTERVENTION

Questioning Strategies

EXAMPLE 3

- Why does $\frac{0}{4} = 0$?

EXAMPLE 4

- Why does the problem state that the hot air balloon travels in a straight line?

Teaching Tip

Critical Thinking

To understand why $\frac{2.04}{0}$ is undefined, have students think of what number times zero would equal 2.04. There is no such number, so the expression is undefined.

EXAMPLE 3 Multiplying and Dividing with Zero

Multiply or divide if possible.

A $0 \div 16.568$ — *Zero is divided by a nonzero number.*

0 — *The quotient of zero and any nonzero number is 0.*

B $63\frac{7}{8} \div 0$ — *A number is divided by zero.*

undefined — *Division by zero is undefined.*

C $1 \cdot 0$ — *A number is multiplied by zero.*

0 — *The product of any number and 0 is 0.*

Multiply or divide if possible.

3a. $0 \div \left(-8\frac{1}{6}\right)$ **0** **3b.** $2.04 \div 0$ **undefined** **3c.** $(-12{,}350)(0)$ **0**

EXAMPLE 4 *Recreation Application*

A hot-air balloon is taken for a 2.5-hour trip. The wind speed (and the speed of the balloon) is 4.75 mi/h. The balloon travels in a straight line parallel to the ground. How many miles away from the liftoff site will the balloon land?

Find the distance traveled at a rate of 4.75 mi/h for 2.5 hours. To find distance, multiply rate by time.

rate	times	time
4.75	•	2.5

$4.75 \cdot 2.5$

11.875

The hot-air balloon will land 11.875 miles from the liftoff site.

4. What if...? On another hot-air balloon trip, the wind speed is 5.25 mi/h. The trip is planned for 1.5 hours. The balloon travels in a straight line parallel to the ground. How many miles away from the liftoff site will the balloon land? **7.875 mi**

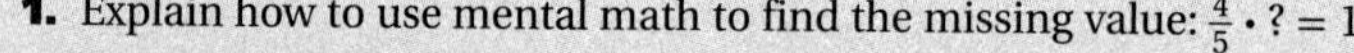

THINK AND DISCUSS

1. Explain how to use mental math to find the missing value: $\frac{4}{5} \cdot ? = 1$.

2. GET ORGANIZED Copy and complete the graphic organizer. In each blank, write "pos" or "neg" to indicate positive or negative.

Multiplying and Dividing Numbers	
Multiplication	**Division**
pos × ▒ = pos	pos ÷ ▒ = pos
pos × ▒ = neg	pos ÷ ▒ = neg
neg × ▒ = neg	neg ÷ ▒ = neg
neg × ▒ = pos	neg ÷ ▒ = pos

3 Close

Summarize

Review the rules for multiplying and dividing positive and negative numbers on page 20. Remind students that the number of negative factors in an expression determines the sign of the answer.

ONGOING ASSESSMENT and INTERVENTION

*Diagnose **Before** the Lesson*
1-3 Warm Up, TE p. 20

*Monitor **During** the Lesson*
Check It Out! Exercises, SE pp. 20–22
Questioning Strategies, TE pp. 21–22

*Assess **After** the Lesson*
1-3 Lesson Quiz, TE p. 25
Alternative Assessment, TE p. 25

Answers to *Think and Discuss*

1. A number multiplied by its reciprocal is 1. The reciprocal of $\frac{4}{5}$ is $\frac{5}{4}$.
2. See p. A2.

1-3 Exercises

go.hrw.com
Homework Help Online
KEYWORD: MA11 1-3
Parent Resources Online
KEYWORD: MA7 Parent

GUIDED PRACTICE

1. **Vocabulary** How do you find the *reciprocal* of $\frac{1}{2}$? **Switch the numerator and denominator. The reciprocal of $\frac{1}{2}$ is $\frac{2}{1}$, or 2.**

SEE EXAMPLE 1 p. 20

Find the value of each expression.

2. $-72 \div (-9)$ **8**
3. $11(-11)$ **−121**
4. $-7.2 \div 3.6$ **−2**

SEE EXAMPLE 2 p. 21

Divide.

5. $5 \div \frac{5}{7}$ **7**
6. $\frac{4}{5} \div \left(-\frac{7}{5}\right)$ **$-\frac{4}{7}$**
7. $-\frac{2}{3} \div \left(-\frac{1}{3}\right)$ **−2**
8. $-\frac{16}{25} \div \left(-\frac{4}{5}\right)$ **$\frac{4}{5}$**

SEE EXAMPLE 3 p. 22

Multiply or divide if possible.

9. $3.8 \div 0$ **undefined**
10. $0(-27)$ **0**
11. $0 \div \frac{2}{3}$ **0**
12. $\frac{7}{8} \div 0$ **undefined**

SEE EXAMPLE 4 p. 22

13. **Entertainment** It is estimated that 7 million people saw off-Broadway shows in 2002. Assume that the average price of a ticket was \$30. How much money was spent on tickets for off-Broadway shows in 2002? **about \$210 million**

PRACTICE AND PROBLEM SOLVING

Independent Practice

For Exercises	See Example
14–16	1
17–20	2
21–24	3
25	4

Extra Practice

Skills Practice p. S4
Application Practice p. S28

Find the value of each expression.

14. $-30 \div (-6)$ **5**
15. $8(-4)$ **−32**
16. $-25(-12)$ **300**

Divide.

17. $-\frac{3}{20} \div \left(-\frac{1}{6}\right)$ **$\frac{9}{10}$**
18. $\frac{3}{14} \div \frac{15}{28}$ **$\frac{2}{5}$**
19. $-4\frac{1}{2} \div 1\frac{1}{2}$ **−3**
20. $2\frac{3}{4} \div \left(-1\frac{1}{2}\right)$ **$-\frac{11}{6}$**

Multiply or divide if possible.

21. $0 \cdot 15$ **0**
22. $-0.25 \div 0$ **undefined**
23. $0 \div 1$ **0**
24. $\frac{0}{1} \div 3$ **0**

25. **Weather** A cold front changes the temperature by −3 °F each day. If the temperature started at 0 °F, what will the temperature be after 5 days? **−15 °F**

Multiply or divide.

26. $21 \div (-3)$ **−7**
27. $-100 \div 25$ **−4**
28. $-6 \div (-14)$ **$\frac{3}{7}$**
29. $-6.2(10)$ **−62**
30. $\frac{1}{2} \div \frac{1}{2}$ **1**
31. $-3.75(-5)$ **18.75**
32. $-12\frac{1}{2}(-3)$ **$\frac{75}{2}$**
33. $17\left(\frac{1}{17}\right)$ **1**

34. **Critical Thinking** What positive number is the same as its reciprocal? **1**

Evaluate each expression for $a = 4$, $b = -3$, and $c = -\frac{1}{2}$.

35. ab **−12**
36. $a \div c$ **−8**
37. bc **$\frac{3}{2}$**
38. $c \div a$ **$-\frac{1}{8}$**

Let p represent a positive number, n represent a negative number, and z represent zero. Tell whether each expression is positive, negative, zero, or undefined.

39. pn **negative**
40. pnz **zero**
41. $\frac{n}{p}$ **negative**
42. $-pz$ **zero**
43. $-\frac{p}{n}$ **positive**
44. $-(pn)$ **positive**
45. $\frac{pn}{z}$ **undefined**
46. $\frac{z}{n}$ **zero**

1-3 Exercises

Assignment Guide

Assign *Guided Practice* exercises as necessary.

If you finished Examples **1–2**
- **Basic** 14–20, 26–33, 35–38
- **Average** 14–20, 35–46, 76–78
- **Advanced** 14–20, 35–38, 43–46, 64–67, 76–81

If you finished Examples **1–4**
- **Basic** 14–33, 35–54, 60–62, 71–75, 90–96
- **Average** 14–25, 34–67, 71–78, 90–96
- **Advanced** 14–25, 34, 43–56, 63–70, 72–96

Homework Quick Check
Quickly check key concepts.
Exercises: 16, 18, 24, 25, 40, 48

Teaching Tip

Reading Math Help students see that the parentheses in **Exercise 2** are used to enclose a negative number. The parentheses in **Exercise 3** are used to indicate multiplication.

State Resources

Kinesthetic To help students understand **Exercise 63,** write a series of signs on the board. Students must stand when the sign of the resulting product is positive, and they must sit when the sign of the product is negative. Keep writing additional signs so that students change positions often.

For example:

+ +	(Students stand)
+ + −	sit
+ + − +	sit
+ + − + −	stand

If sitting and standing is not possible, thumbs up and thumbs down can be used.

Exercise 72 involves using the formula for rate. This exercise prepares students for the Multi-Step Test Prep on page 38.

Answers

63c. The product of two negative numbers is positive. The product of a positive number and a negative number is negative.

d. No; it does not matter how many times you multiply by a positive number, the sign does not change.

68–70. For explanations, see p. A12.

71. The product of two negative numbers is positive. You know that the product is positive and one factor is negative, so the second factor must also be negative.

Evaluate the expression $y \div \frac{3}{4}$ for each value of y.

47. $y = \frac{3}{4}$ **1**
48. $y = -\frac{9}{16}$ $\mathbf{-\frac{3}{4}}$
49. $y = \frac{3}{8}$ $\mathbf{\frac{1}{2}}$
50. $y = -2\frac{1}{4}$ **−3**

Evaluate the expression $\frac{1}{2} \div m$ for each value of m.

51. $m = -\frac{5}{2}$ $\mathbf{-\frac{1}{5}}$
52. $m = \frac{7}{8}$ $\mathbf{\frac{4}{7}}$
53. $m = \frac{4}{9}$ $\mathbf{\frac{9}{8}}$
54. $m = -5$ $\mathbf{-\frac{1}{10}}$

LINK

Diving

Florida is home to more than 300 freshwater springs, some of which are explored by cave divers.

55. **Education** Benjamin must have 120 credit hours of instruction to receive his college degree. Benjamin wants to graduate in 8 semesters without attending summer sessions. How many credit hours must Benjamin take on average each semester to graduate in 8 semesters? **15 h per semester**

56. **Diving** An underwater exploration team is swimming at a depth of −20 feet. Then they dive to an underwater cave that is at 7 times this depth. What is the depth of the underwater cave? **−140 ft**

Multiply or divide. Then compare using <, >, or =.

57. $10\left(-\frac{1}{2}\right)$ **<** $20 \div 4$
58. $16 \div (-2)$ **<** $-2(-4)$
59. $-2\frac{2}{3} \div 3$ **>** $5(-2.4)$
60. $20 \div 4$ **>** $\frac{3}{4} \div \left(-\frac{1}{2}\right)$
61. $2.1(-3.4)$ **=** $-3.4(2.1)$
62. $0\left(-\frac{3}{5}\right)$ **<** $\frac{1}{2} \div \frac{1}{2}$

63. **Critical Thinking** There is a relationship between the number of negative factors and the sign of the product.
   a. What is the sign of the product of an even number of negative factors? **positive**
   b. What is the sign of the product of an odd number of negative factors? **negative**
   c. Explain why the number of negative factors affects the sign of the product.
   d. Does the number of positive factors affect the sign of the product? Explain.

Write each division expression as a multiplication expression.

64. $12 \div (-3)$ $\mathbf{12\left(-\frac{1}{3}\right)}$
65. $75 \div 15$ $\mathbf{75\left(\frac{1}{15}\right)}$
66. $\frac{80}{-8}$ $\mathbf{80\left(-\frac{1}{8}\right)}$
67. $\frac{-121}{11}$ $\mathbf{-121\left(\frac{1}{11}\right)}$

Determine whether each statement is sometimes, always, or never true. Explain.

68. When t is negative, the expression $\frac{t}{10}$ is negative. **always**
69. When n is positive, the expression $-6n$ is positive. **never**
70. The value of the expression $4c$ is greater than the value of c. **sometimes**

71. **Write About It** The product of two factors is positive. One of the factors is negative. Explain how you can determine the sign of the second factor.

72b.

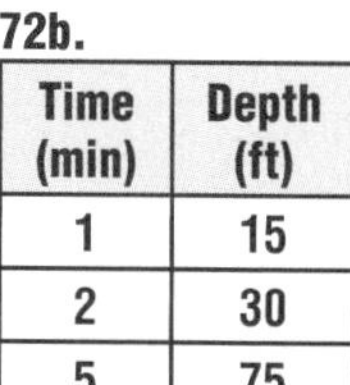

Time (min)	Depth (ft)
1	15
2	30
5	75

Multi-Step Test Prep

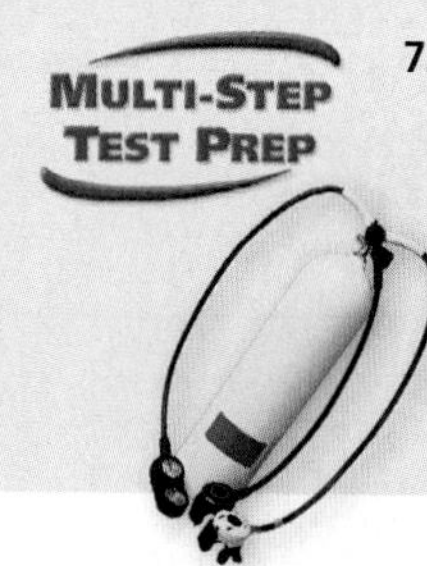

72. This problem will prepare you for the Multi-Step Test Prep on page 38.
   a. You swam 20 feet in 5 seconds. Use the formula $r = \frac{d}{t}$ to determine how fast you were swimming. **4 ft/s**
   b. A diver descended at a rate of 15 feet per minute. Make a table to show the diver's depth after 1, 2, and 5 minutes.
   c. Show two ways to find how far the diver descended in 5 minutes. Remember that multiplication is repeated addition. **5 • 15 = 75**
   15 + 15 + 15 + 15 + 15 = 75

1-3 PRACTICE A
1-3 PRACTICE C
1-3 PRACTICE B

Find the value of each expression.

1. −24 ÷ −8 **3**
2. 24(−5) **−120**
3. −96 ÷ 3 **−32**
4. −6(20) **−120**
5. $-7p$ for $p = -15$ **105**
6. $t \div (-1.5)$ for $t = 6$ **−4**

Divide.

7. $-\frac{8}{9} \div \frac{2}{3}$ $\mathbf{-\frac{4}{3} = -1\frac{1}{3}}$
8. $-12 \div \left(-\frac{6}{25}\right)$ **50**
9. $2\frac{1}{4} \div \left(-5\frac{1}{3}\right)$ $\mathbf{-\frac{27}{64}}$

Multiply or divide.

10. 0 • 4.75 **0**
11. 0 ÷ 10 **0**
12. $-\frac{1}{3} \div 0$ **undefined**
13. When Brianna's first CD sold a million copies, her record label gave her a $5000 bonus. She split the money evenly between herself, her agent, her producer, and her stylist. How much money did each person receive? **$1250**
14. (0.3)(−1.8) **−0.54**
15. $\frac{2}{5}\left(-\frac{5}{2}\right)$ **−1**
16. −15 ÷ (−6) $\mathbf{\frac{5}{2} = 2\frac{1}{2}}$

Evaluate each expression for $x = 16$, $y = -4$, and $z = -2$.

17. $y \div x$ $\mathbf{-\frac{1}{4}}$
18. $x \cdot y$ **−64**
19. xz **−32**
20. $z \div y$ $\mathbf{\frac{1}{2}}$
21. $(y)(z)$ **8**
22. $y \div z$ **2**
23. $x \div z$ **−8**
24. $x \div y$ **−4**
25. $z \div x$ $\mathbf{-\frac{1}{8}}$

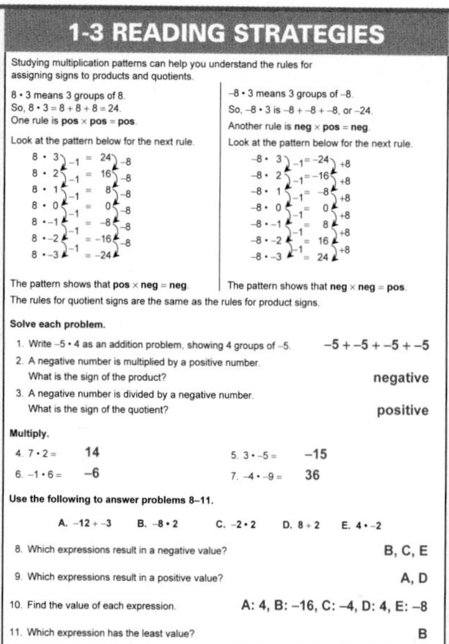

1-3 READING STRATEGIES

Studying multiplication patterns can help you understand the rules for assigning signs to products and quotients.

8 • 3 means 3 groups of 8.
So, 8 • 3 = 8 + 8 + 8 = 24.
One rule is **pos × pos = pos**.

Look at the pattern below for the next rule.

8 • 3 = 24
8 • 2 = 16
8 • 1 = 8
8 • 0 = 0
8 • −1 = −8
8 • −2 = −16
8 • −3 = −24
(each step: −1 in the factor, −8 in the product)

The pattern shows that **pos × neg = neg**.

−8 • 3 means 3 groups of −8.
So, −8 • 3 is −8 + −8 + −8, or −24.
Another rule is **neg × pos = neg**.

Look at the pattern below for the next rule.

−8 • 3 = −24
−8 • 2 = −16
−8 • 1 = −8
−8 • 0 = 0
−8 • −1 = 8
−8 • −2 = 16
−8 • −3 = 24
(each step: −1 in the factor, +8 in the product)

The pattern shows that **neg × neg = pos**.

The rules for quotient signs are the same as the rules for product signs.

Solve each problem.

1. Write −5 • 4 as an addition problem, showing 4 groups of −5. **−5 + −5 + −5 + −5**
2. A negative number is multiplied by a positive number. What is the sign of the product? **negative**
3. A negative number is divided by a negative number. What is the sign of the quotient? **positive**

Multiply.

4. 7 • 2 = **14**
5. 3 • −5 = **−15**
6. −1 • 6 = **−6**
7. −4 • −9 = **36**

Use the following to answer problems 8–11.

A. −12 ÷ −3 B. −8 • 2 C. −2 • 2 D. 8 ÷ 2 E. 4 • −2

8. Which expressions result in a negative value? **B, C, E**
9. Which expressions result in a positive value? **A, D**
10. Find the value of each expression. **A: 4, B: −16, C: −4, D: 4, E: −8**
11. Which expression has the least value? **B**

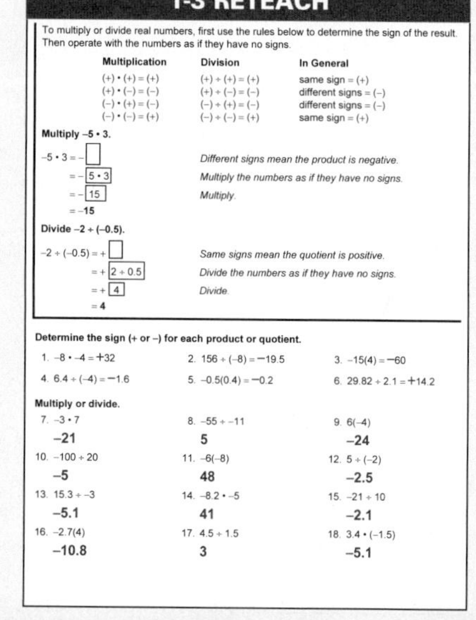

1-3 RETEACH

To multiply or divide real numbers, first use the rules below to determine the sign of the result. Then operate with the numbers as if they have no signs.

Multiplication	Division	In General
(+) • (+) = (+)	(+) ÷ (+) = (+)	same sign = (+)
(+) • (−) = (−)	(+) ÷ (−) = (−)	different signs = (−)
(−) • (+) = (−)	(−) ÷ (+) = (−)	different signs = (−)
(−) • (−) = (+)	(−) ÷ (−) = (+)	same sign = (+)

Multiply −5 • 3.

−5 • 3 = −☐ *Different signs mean the product is negative.*
= −[5 • 3] *Multiply the numbers as if they have no signs.*
= −[15] *Multiply.*
= **−15**

Divide −2 ÷ (−0.5).

−2 ÷ (−0.5) = +☐ *Same signs mean the quotient is positive.*
= +[2 ÷ 0.5] *Divide the numbers as if they have no signs.*
= +[4] *Divide.*
= **4**

Determine the sign (+ or −) for each product or quotient.

1. −8 • −4 = **+**32
2. 156 ÷ (−8) = **−**19.5
3. −15(4) = **−**60
4. 6.4 ÷ (−4) = **−**1.6
5. −0.5(0.4) = **−**0.2
6. 29.82 ÷ 2.1 = **+**14.2

Multiply or divide.

7. −3 • 7 **−21**
8. −55 ÷ −11 **5**
9. 6(−4) **−24**
10. −100 ÷ 20 **−5**
11. −6(−8) **48**
12. 5 ÷ (−2) **−2.5**
13. 15.3 ÷ −3 **−5.1**
14. −8.2 • −5 **41**
15. −21 ÷ 10 **−2.1**
16. −2.7(4) **−10.8**
17. 4.5 ÷ 1.5 **3**
18. 3.4 • (−1.5) **−5.1**

TEST PREP

75. Clarinets: 1 half note = $\frac{1}{2}$ whole note; 8 half notes = 4 whole notes; find the number of quarter notes that have the same length as 4 whole notes; $4 \div \frac{1}{4} = 16$; the flutes play 16 quarter notes.

73. A recipe for lemonade calls for $1\frac{1}{2}$ cups of lemon juice per batch. Berto estimates that he can get about $\frac{1}{4}$ cup of lemon juice from each lemon that he squeezes. Lemons cost $0.45 each. What is the approximate amount Berto will need to spend on lemons to make a batch of lemonade?

   Ⓐ $0.70   Ⓑ $1.70   **Ⓒ $2.70**   Ⓓ $3.70

74. Robyn is buying carpet for her bedroom floor, which is a 15-foot-by-12-foot rectangle. If carpeting costs $1.25 per square foot, how much will it cost Robyn to carpet her bedroom?

   Ⓕ $68   Ⓖ $144   Ⓗ $180   **Ⓙ $225**

75. **Short Response** In music notation, a half note is played $\frac{1}{2}$ the length of a whole note. A quarter note is played $\frac{1}{4}$ the length of a whole note. In a piece of music, the clarinets play 8 half notes. In the same length of time, the flutes play x quarter notes. Determine how many quarter notes the flutes play. Explain your method.

CHALLENGE AND EXTEND

Find the value of each expression.

76. $(-2)(-2)(-2)$ **−8**
77. $\frac{5}{7} \cdot \frac{5}{7}$ **$\frac{25}{49}$**
78. $5\left(-\frac{4}{5}\right)\left(-\frac{3}{4}\right)$ **3**
79. $\left|-\frac{1}{4}\right| \cdot |20|$ **5**
80. $5 \cdot 4 \cdot 3 \cdot 2 \cdot 1$ **120**
81. $\left|-\frac{2}{5}\right| \cdot \left|\frac{5}{2}\right|$ **1**
82. $\frac{1}{2} \cdot \frac{2}{3} \cdot \frac{3}{4} \cdot \frac{4}{5}$ **$\frac{1}{5}$**
83. $\left(-\frac{3}{4}\right)\left(-\frac{3}{4}\right)\left(-\frac{3}{4}\right)$ **$\frac{-27}{64}$**
84. $|(-4)(-4)(-4)|$ **64**

86. Multiply by −3; $\frac{9}{7}, \frac{-27}{7}, \frac{81}{7}$.

87. The numbers are alternating positive and negative multiples of 5; 30, −35, 40.

88. Multiply by 0.5; 0.03125, 0.015625, 0.0078125.

For each pattern shown below, describe a possible rule for finding the next term. Then use your rule to write the next 3 terms. **Possible answers are given.**

85. $-1, 2, -4, 8, \ldots$ **Multiply by −2; −16, 32, −64.**
86. $\frac{1}{63}, -\frac{1}{21}, \frac{1}{7}, -\frac{3}{7}, \ldots$
87. $-5, 10, -15, 20, -25, \ldots$
88. $0.5, 0.25, 0.125, 0.0625, \ldots$
89. A cleaning service charges $49.00 to clean a one-bedroom apartment. If the work takes longer than 2 hours, the service charges $18.00 for each additional hour. What would be the total cost for a job that took 4 hours to complete? **$85**

SPIRAL REVIEW

Find the surface area of each rectangular prism. *(Previous course)*

90. 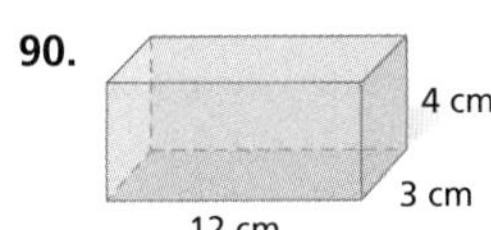

192 cm²

91. 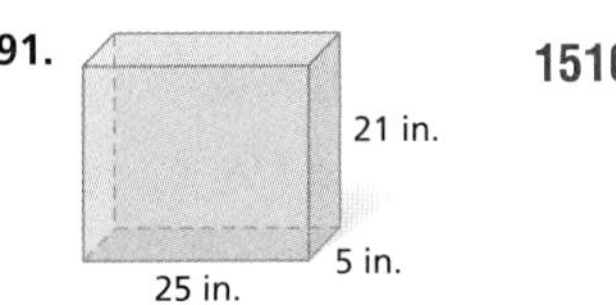

1510 in²

92. A prepaid phone card has a credit of 200 minutes. Write an expression for the number of minutes left on the card after t minutes have been used. *(Lesson 1-1)* **$200 - t$**

Compare. Write <, >, or =. *(Lesson 1-2)*

93. $-12 + 7$ **<** $10 + (-5)$
94. $|-14|$ **>** -2
95. $|-7 + 11|$ **=** $|-4|$
96. $-20 + (-35)$ **=** $-35 - 20$

COMMON ERROR ALERT

Students may fail to read the entire question on standardized tests. In **Exercise 74,** some students will find an area of 180 ft², and will immediately mark choice **H.** Remind students to reread the question to determine if additional calculations are required.

TEST PREP DOCTOR + If students have difficulty with **Exercise 73,** point out that the problem has two steps. The first step is to determine the number of lemons needed. The second step is to determine the cost of this number of lemons.

Journal

Write a word problem that uses the expression $7(-25)$. Then solve your word problem.

ALTERNATIVE ASSESSMENT

Have students write the two rules for multiplying and dividing signed numbers and an equation for each rule. One equation must contain a fraction. Next have students write a fraction that equals zero and a fraction that is undefined.

Power Presentations with PowerPoint®

1-3 Lesson Quiz

Find the value of each expression.

1. $\frac{35}{-7}$ −5
2. $2(-6)$ −12

Multiply or divide if possible.

3. $-3 \div 1\frac{3}{4}$ $-\frac{12}{7}$
4. $-2\frac{1}{3}(0)$ 0
5. $-\frac{3}{4} \div 0$ undefined
6. A cyclist traveled on a straight road for $1\frac{1}{4}$ hours at a speed of 12 mi/h. How many miles did the cyclist travel?
   15 miles

Also available on transparency 

1-3 PROBLEM SOLVING

Write the correct answer.

1. Jane's grade point average changed by −0.16 points each term. How much did her grade point average change after 4 terms?
   −0.64 points
2. Isari's recipe for strawberry smoothies requires $\frac{1}{2}$ cup of sliced strawberries per smoothie. How many smoothies can she make using 8 cups of strawberries?
   16 smoothies
3. The value of an investor's stock changed by $-1\frac{3}{4}$ points last week. This week, the value changed by 3 times as much. How much did the value of the investor's stock change this week?
   $-5\frac{1}{4}$ points
4. Jogging on pavement burns 13 calories per minute. Jogging on grass burns 1.07 times as many calories per minute. How many calories would you burn by jogging on grass for 5 minutes? (Round your answer to the nearest tenth.)
   69.6 calories

Use the table below for exercises 5–8, which shows the cost of three different types of season tickets during the Dallas Cowboys 2005 season. Select the best answer.

2005 Season Tickets	
Seat Location	Cost
Upper Level Sideline	$730
Upper Level Corner	$620
Upper Level Far Corner	$490

5. How much money was spent on Upper Level Sideline season tickets in 2005 if 2500 fans bought Upper Level Sideline season tickets?
   A $1,315,000   C $1,757,500
   B $1,550,000   **D** $1,825,000
6. Tom and his two brothers gave their father two Upper Level Far Corner season tickets as a gift. If the brothers shared the cost equally, how much did each one pay towards the gift?
   F $163   **H** $327
   G $245   J $980
7. If sales of Upper Level Corner season tickets totaled $1,116,000, how many Upper Level Corner season ticket holders were there?
   A 1529   C 2278
   B 1800   D 6919
8. Four friends bought a pair of Upper Level Sideline season tickets. If they shared the cost equally, how much did each pay?
   F $122.50   H $310
   G $182.50   **J** $365

1-3 CHALLENGE

For puzzles 1 and 2, draw a path from the Start box to the Finish box, multiplying by each number along the way, to find a product equal to the goal number.

Moves must be vertical or horizontal only, and the path cannot cross itself. An example is shown at right. The path is correct because 2 • 1 • −3 • −2 • 1 • 2 • −2 = −48.

Goal: Product of −48

3	−2	1
1	−3	2
2 Start	4	−2 Finish

1. Goal: Product of −8

−1	−1	2
2 Start	2	−1
−1	−2	−1 Finish

2. Goal: Product of 120

1	3	−2
−2	4	−1
−5 Start	−3	2 Finish

For puzzles 3 and 4, draw a path from the Start box to the Finish box, dividing by each number along the way, to find a quotient equal to the goal number. Moves must be vertical or horizontal only, and the path cannot cross itself.

3. Goal: Quotient of 1

−4	3	−2
−24 Start	3	2
1	2	−2 Finish

4. Goal: Quotient of −3

−36 Start	2	−3
3	−2	−3
4	2	−1 Finish

1-4 Organizer

Pacing: Traditional 1 day
Block $\frac{1}{2}$ day

Objective: Simplify expressions containing exponents.

Online Edition
Tutorial Videos

Countdown Week 1

Power Presentations with PowerPoint®

Warm Up

Simplify.

1. $2(2)$ 4
2. $(-2)(-2)$ 4
3. $(-2)(-2)(-2)$ -8
4. $3(3)(3)$ 27
5. $\left(-\frac{2}{3}\right)\left(-\frac{2}{3}\right)$ $\frac{4}{9}$

Also available on transparency

Math Fact !!!

A *googol* is 1 followed by 100 zeros. It can be expressed as a power of 10, as 10^{100}.

State Resources

go.hrw.com
State Resources Online
KEYWORD: MA7 Resources

1-4 Powers and Exponents

Objective
Simplify expressions containing exponents.

Vocabulary
power
base
exponent

Who uses this?
Biologists use exponents to model the growth patterns of living organisms.

When bacteria divide, their number increases exponentially. This means that the number of bacteria is multiplied by the same factor each time the bacteria divide. Instead of writing repeated multiplication to express a product, you can use a power.

A **power** is an expression written with an *exponent* and a *base* or the value of such an expression. 3^2 is an example of a power.

The base, 3, is the number that is used as a factor. →  ← The exponent, 2, tells how many times the base, 3, is used as a factor.

When a number is raised to the second power, we usually say it is "squared." The area of a *square* is $s \cdot s = s^2$, where s is the side length.

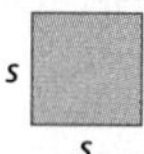

When a number is raised to the third power, we usually say it is "cubed." The volume of a *cube* is $s \cdot s \cdot s = s^3$, where s is the side length.

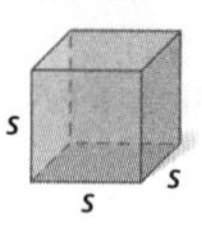

EXAMPLE 1 Writing Powers for Geometric Models

Write the power represented by each geometric model.

A 

3^2

There are 3 rows of 3 dots. 3×3
The factor 3 is used 2 times.

B 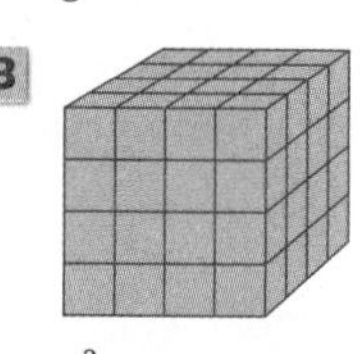

4^3

The figure is 4 cubes long, 4 cubes wide, and 4 cubes tall. $4 \times 4 \times 4$
The factor 4 is used 3 times.

CHECK IT OUT! **Write the power represented by each geometric model.**

1a. 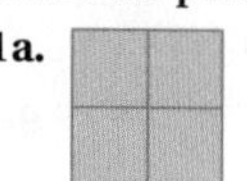 2^2

1b. 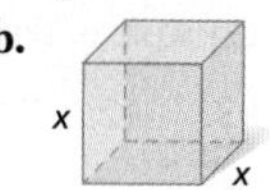 x^3

1 Introduce

EXPLORATION

Powers and Exponents

Powers are used to represent repeated multiplication. For example, the expression 8^3 means $8 \times 8 \times 8$.

1. This square has a length and width of 4 inches. The number of one-inch squares needed to fill the region is 4×4. Write this using powers.
2. A square has a length and width of 6 inches. How many one-inch squares are needed to fill the region? Write your answer using powers.
3. A cube has a length, width, and height of 4 inches. How many cubes that are 1 inch on each side are needed to fill this cube? Write your answer using powers.
4. Some expressions with powers cannot be modeled using a geometric model. Use multiplication to explain what $(-2)^5$ means. Then evaluate the expression.

THINK AND DISCUSS

5. **Explain** why $(-210)^4$ must be positive.
6. **Describe** what you think is meant by the expression 3^1.

Motivate

Review the idea of repeated addition with students. Ask students to write an example of repeated addition, such as $7 + 7 + 7 + 7 + 7$. Show how to write repeated addition as multiplication, $5(7)$. Now have students write an example of repeated multiplication, such as $4 \times 4 \times 4 \times 4 \times 4 \times 4$. Tell students that they will learn how to write repeated multiplication in this lesson.

Explorations and answers are provided in *Alternate Openers: Explorations Transparencies.*

There are no easy geometric models for numbers raised to exponents greater than 3, but you can still write them using repeated multiplication or a base and exponent.

Reading Exponents			
Words	**Multiplication**	**Power**	**Value**
3 to the first power	3	3^1	3
3 to the second power, or 3 squared	$3 \cdot 3$	3^2	9
3 to the third power, or 3 cubed	$3 \cdot 3 \cdot 3$	3^3	27
3 to the fourth power	$3 \cdot 3 \cdot 3 \cdot 3$	3^4	81
3 to the fifth power	$3 \cdot 3 \cdot 3 \cdot 3 \cdot 3$	3^5	243

EXAMPLE 2 Evaluating Powers

Simplify each expression.

A $(-2)^3$

$(-2)(-2)(-2)$ *Use −2 as a factor 3 times.*

-8

B -5^2

$-1 \cdot 5 \cdot 5$ *Think of a negative sign in front of a power as multiplying by −1. Find the product of −1 and two 5's.*

$-1 \cdot 25$

-25

C $\left(\frac{2}{3}\right)^2$

$\frac{2}{3} \cdot \frac{2}{3}$ *Use $\frac{2}{3}$ as a factor 2 times.*

$\frac{2}{3} \cdot \frac{2}{3} = \frac{4}{9}$

Caution!

In the expression -5^2, 5 is the base because the negative sign is not in parentheses.
In the expression $(-2)^3$, −2 is the base because of the parentheses.

CHECK IT OUT! Simplify each expression.

2a. $(-5)^3$ **−125** **2b.** -6^2 **−36** **2c.** $\left(\frac{3}{4}\right)^3$ $\mathbf{\frac{27}{64}}$

EXAMPLE 3 Writing Powers

Write each number as a power of the given base.

A 8; base 2

$2 \cdot 2 \cdot 2$ *The product of three 2's is 8.*

2^3

B −125; base −5

$(-5)(-5)(-5)$ *The product of three −5's is −125.*

$(-5)^3$

CHECK IT OUT! Write each number as a power of the given base.

3a. 64; base 8 $\mathbf{8^2}$ **3b.** −27; base −3 $\mathbf{(-3)^3}$

COMMON ERROR ALERT

Students may multiply the exponent by the base, especially when the base is 1. Encourage them to write the power as repeated multiplication.

$1^5 = 1 \cdot 1 \cdot 1 \cdot 1 \cdot 1 = 1$

$2^3 = 2 \cdot 2 \cdot 2 = 8$

Power Presentations with PowerPoint®

Additional Examples

Example 1

Write the power represented by each geometric model.

A. 5^3

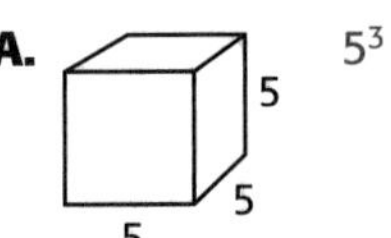

B. 6^2

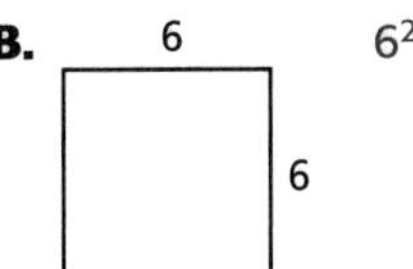

Example 2

Simplify each expression.

A. $(-6)^3$ -216

B. -10^2 -100

C. $\left(\frac{2}{9}\right)^2$ $\frac{4}{81}$

Example 3

Write each number as a power of the given base.

A. 64; base 8 8^2

B. 81; base −3 $(-3)^4$

2 Teach

Guided Instruction

Before writing expressions as powers, review multiplication of signed numbers, including fractions and decimals. Review the rules for products with an even and odd number of negative factors. Next have students write expressions as powers, such as $4 \times 4 \times 4 = 4^3$. Then have students simplify the expressions.

Reaching All Learners

Through Number Sense

Have students create a table of the common powers listed below. Have them include the value of each power. Suggest to students that they should be able to recall the value of each power.

$2^2, 2^3, 2^4, 2^5, 3^2, 3^3, 4^2, 4^3, 5^2, 5^3, 6^2, 7^2, 8^2, 9^2$

INTERVENTION

Questioning Strategies

EXAMPLE 1

- What multiplication expression does each model show?

EXAMPLE 2

- When is a negative sign part of the base?

EXAMPLE 3

- How can you determine what exponent to use with the base that is given?

Power Presentations with PowerPoint®

Additional Examples

Example 4

In case of a school closing, the PTA president calls 3 families. Each of these families calls 3 other families, and so on. How many families are called in the 4th round of calls? 81

INTERVENTION

Questioning Strategies

EXAMPLE 4

- Why do you use the same base to write expressions for the number in each stage of the problem?
- What does the exponent in each expression correspond to?

EXAMPLE 4 ***Problem-Solving Application***

A certain bacterium splits into 2 bacteria every hour. There is 1 bacterium on a slide. If each bacterium on the slide splits once per hour, how many bacteria will be on the slide after 6 hours?

1 Understand the Problem

The **answer** will be the number of bacteria on the slide after 6 hours.
List the **important information:**

- There is 1 bacterium on a slide that divides into 2 bacteria.
- Each bacterium then divides into 2 more bacteria.

2 Make a Plan

Draw a diagram to show the number of bacteria after each hour.

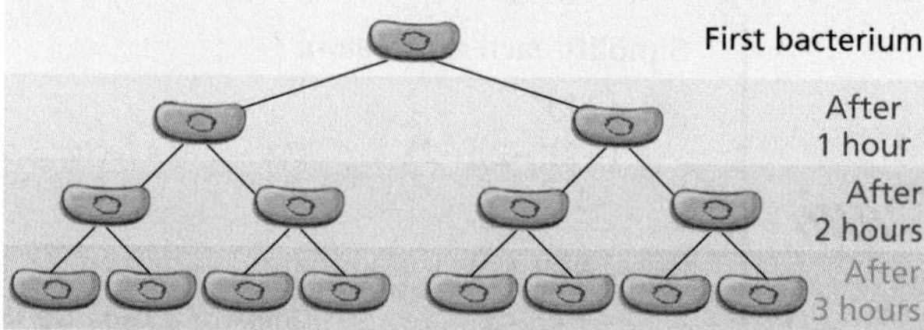

3 Solve

Notice that after each hour, the number of bacteria is a power of 2.

After 1 hour: $1 \cdot 2 = 2$ or 2^1 bacteria on the slide
After 2 hours: $2 \cdot 2 = 4$ or 2^2 bacteria on the slide
After 3 hours: $4 \cdot 2 = 8$ or 2^3 bacteria on the slide
So, after the 6th hour, there will be 2^6 bacteria.
$2^6 = 2 \cdot 2 \cdot 2 \cdot 2 \cdot 2 \cdot 2 = 64$ *Multiply six 2's.*
After 6 hours, there will be 64 bacteria on the slide.

4 Look Back

The numbers quickly become too large for a diagram, but a diagram helps you recognize a pattern. Then you can write the numbers as powers of 2.

4. **What if...?** How many bacteria will be on the slide after 8 hours? $2^8 = 256$

THINK AND DISCUSS

1. Express 8^3 in words two ways.

2. **GET ORGANIZED** Copy and complete the graphic organizer. In each box, give an example and tell whether the expression is positive or negative.

	Even Exponent	Odd Exponent
Positive Base		
Negative Base		

3 Close

Summarize

Make sure students recognize the differences between 3^2, 2^3, and $2 \cdot 3$. Explain that 3^2 means to multiply 3 times 3; 2^3 means to multiply 2 times 2 times 2; and $2 \cdot 3$ means to multiply 2 times 3. Review how to determine whether a negative sign is part of the base.

ONGOING ASSESSMENT and INTERVENTION

***Diagnose Before* the Lesson**
1-4 Warm Up, TE p. 26

***Monitor During* the Lesson**
Check It Out! Exercises, SE pp. 26–28
Questioning Strategies, TE pp. 27–28

***Assess After* the Lesson**
1-4 Lesson Quiz, TE p. 31
Alternative Assessment, TE p. 31

Answers to *Think and Discuss*

1. eight cubed; eight raised to the third power
2. See p. A2.

go.hrw.com
Homework Help Online
KEYWORD: MA7 1-4
Parent Resources Online
KEYWORD: MA7 Parent

GUIDED PRACTICE

1. **Vocabulary** What does the *exponent* in the expression 5^6 tell you? **the number of times to use the base as a factor**

SEE EXAMPLE 1 p. 26

Write the power represented by each geometric model.

2.  • • • • / • • • • / • • • • / • • • • 4^2

3. 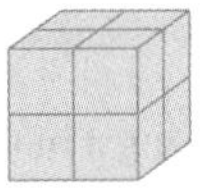 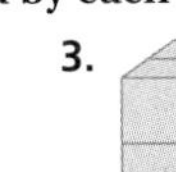 2^3

4. (square with sides 9 and 9) 9^2

SEE EXAMPLE 2 p. 27

Simplify each expression.

5. 7^2 **49**
6. $(-2)^4$ **16**
7. $(-2)^5$ **−32**
8. $-\left(\frac{1}{2}\right)^4$ $-\frac{1}{16}$

SEE EXAMPLE 3 p. 27

Write each number as a power of the given base.

9. 81; base 9 9^2
10. 100,000; base 10 10^5
11. −64; base −4 $(-4)^3$
12. 10; base 10 10^1
13. 81; base 3 3^4
14. 36; base −6 $(-6)^2$

SEE EXAMPLE 4 p. 28

15. **Technology** Jan wants to predict the number of hits she will get on her Web page. Her Web page received 3 hits during the first week it was posted. If the number of hits triples every week, how many hits will the Web page receive during the 5th week? $3^5 = 243$

PRACTICE AND PROBLEM SOLVING

Independent Practice

For Exercises	See Example
16–18	1
19–22	2
23–28	3
29	4

Extra Practice
Skills Practice p. S4
Application Practice p. S28

Write the power represented by each geometric model.

16.  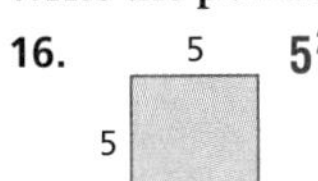 5^2

17. 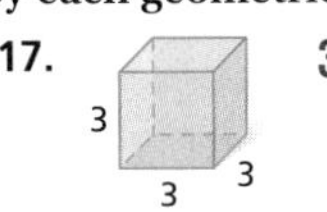 3^3

18. 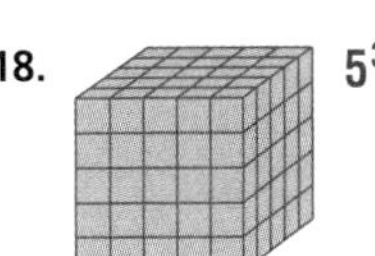 5^3

Simplify each expression.

19. 3^3 **27**
20. $(-4)^2$ **16**
21. -4^2 **−16**
22. $\left(-\frac{3}{5}\right)^2$ $\frac{9}{25}$

Write each number as a power of the given base.

23. 49; base 7 7^2
24. 1000; base 10 10^3
25. −8; base −2 $(-2)^3$
26. 1,000,000; base 10 10^6
27. 64; base 4 4^3
28. 343; base 7 7^3

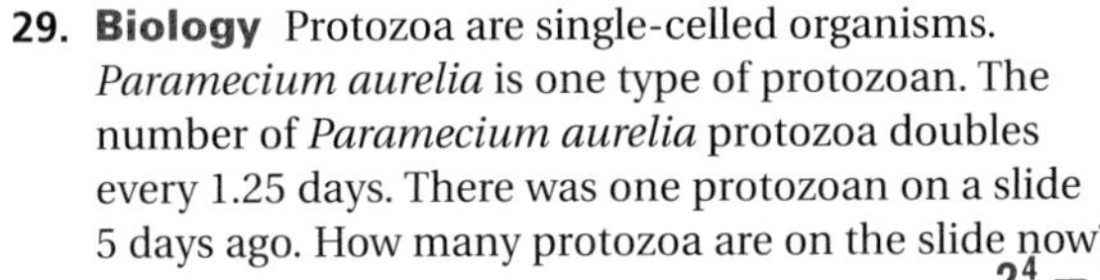

29. **Biology** Protozoa are single-celled organisms. *Paramecium aurelia* is one type of protozoan. The number of *Paramecium aurelia* protozoa doubles every 1.25 days. There was one protozoan on a slide 5 days ago. How many protozoa are on the slide now? $2^4 = 16$

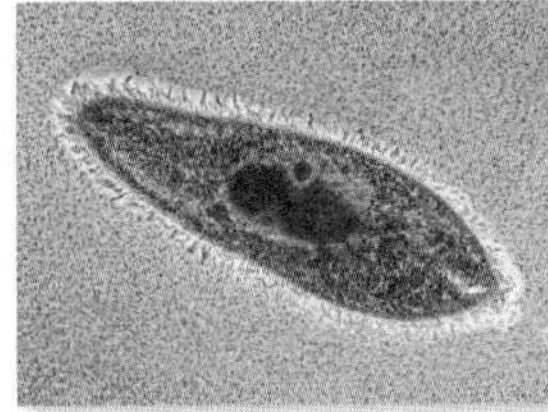

30. **Write About It** A classmate says that any number raised to an even power is positive. Give examples to explain whether your classmate is correct.

Compare. Write <, >, or =.

31. $3^2 < 3^3$
32. $5^2 < 2^5$
33. $4^2 = 2^4$
34. $1^9 = 1^4$
35. $-2^3 = (-2)^3$
36. $-3^2 < (-3)^2$
37. $10^2 > 2^6$
38. $2^2 = 4^1$

1-4 Exercises

Assignment Guide

Assign *Guided Practice* exercises as necessary.

If you finished Examples **1–2**
Basic 16–22, 31–39, 43–46
Average 16–22, 31–42, 44, 60–63
Advanced 16–22, 39–46, 48–53, 60–63

If you finished Examples **1–4**
Basic 16–29, 31–47, 54–59, 64, 66–70, 76–86
Average 16–30, 39–60, 64–73, 76–86
Advanced 16–30, 39–86

Homework Quick Check
Quickly check key concepts.
Exercises: 16, 20, 24, 29, 39, 44

Teaching Tip

Inclusion In **Exercise 29,** students may have difficulty determining how many times the protozoa double. Suggest to students that they make a chart like the one below:

1 division	1.25 days
2 divisions	2.5 days
⋮	⋮

Answers

30. Any number other than zero raised to an even power is positive. Zero raised to any power other than zero is zero.

State Resources

go.hrw.com
State Resources Online
KEYWORD: MA7 Resources

Teaching Tip

Geometry The figures in **Exercise 47** are squares, so the area can be found using the formula $A = s^2$.

Challenge advanced students to find the area of the yellow region by also using the formula for the area of a triangle, $A = \frac{1}{2}bh$.

MULTI-STEP TEST PREP **Exercise 66** involves converting units to work with the relationships between pressure, force, and area. This exercise prepares students for the Multi-Step Test Prep on page 38.

Answers

39. $2 \cdot 2 \cdot 2 = 8$
40. $1 \cdot 1 \cdot 1 \cdot 1 \cdot 1 \cdot 1 \cdot 1 = 1$
41. $(-4)(-4)(-4) = -64$
42. $-(4 \cdot 4 \cdot 4) = -64$
43. $(-1)(-1)(-1) = -1$
44. $(-1)(-1)(-1)(-1) = 1$
45. $\left(\frac{1}{3}\right)\left(\frac{1}{3}\right)\left(\frac{1}{3}\right) = \frac{1}{27}$
46. $-(2.2 \cdot 2.2) = -4.84$

64c. If the coin is fair, about half the tosses should result in heads and half should result in tails. Becky's score is increasing by a greater factor each time the coin lands tails up, so she will probably win.

66a. $\frac{1}{2}$ psi

b. $\frac{4}{9}$ psi

Write each expression as repeated multiplication. Then simplify the expression.

39. 2^3 40. 1^7 41. $(-4)^3$ 42. -4^3
43. $(-1)^3$ 44. $(-1)^4$ 45. $\left(\frac{1}{3}\right)^3$ 46. -2.2^2

47. **Geometry** The diagram shows an ornamental tile design.
 a. What is the area of the whole tile? **36 in^2**
 b. What is the area of the white square? **9 in^2**
 c. What is the area of the two shaded regions? **27 in^2**

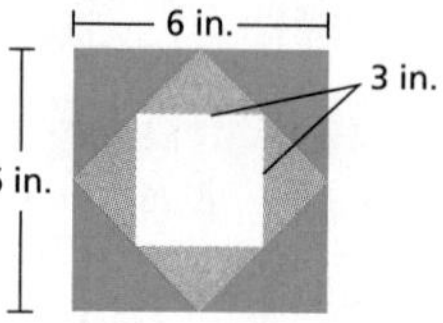

Write each expression using a base and an exponent.

48. $3 \cdot 3 \cdot 3 \cdot 3$ **3^4** 49. $6 \cdot 6$ **6^2** 50. $8 \cdot 8 \cdot 8 \cdot 8 \cdot 8$ **8^5**
51. $(-1)(-1)(-1)(-1)$ **$(-1)^4$** 52. $(-7)(-7)(-7)$ **$(-7)^3$** 53. $\left(\frac{1}{9}\right)\left(\frac{1}{9}\right)\left(\frac{1}{9}\right)$ **$\left(\frac{1}{9}\right)^3$**

54. **Art** A painting is made of 3 concentric squares. The side length of the largest square is 24 cm. What is the area of the painting? **576 cm^2**

55. **Estimation** A box is shaped like a cube with edges 22.7 centimeters long. What is the approximate volume of the box? **between 8000 cm^3 and 15,625 cm^3**

Write the exponent that makes each equation true.

56. $2^{■} = 4$ **2** 57. $4^{■} = 16$ **2** 58. $(-2)^{■} = 16$ **4** 59. $5^{■} = 625$ **4**
60. $-2^{■} = -8$ **3** 61. $10^{■} = 100$ **2** 62. $5^{■} = 125$ **3** 63. $3^{■} = 81$ **4**

64. **Entertainment** Mark and Becky play a coin toss game. Both start with one point. Every time the coin comes up heads, Mark doubles his score. Every time the coin comes up tails, Becky triples her score. The results of their game so far are shown in the table.
 a. What is Mark's score? **$2^5 = 32$**
 b. What is Becky's score? **$3^3 = 27$**
 c. **What if...?** If they toss the coin 50 more times, who do you think will win? Why?

Coin Toss Results

Heads	Tails
✓	✓
✓	✓
✓	✓
✓	
✓	

65. **Critical Thinking** The number of zeros in powers of 10 follow a pattern.
 a. Simplify each of the following: 10^2, 10^3, 10^4. **100, 1000, 10,000**
 b. Explain what relationship you see between the exponent of a power of 10 and the number of zeros in the answer. **The exponent is the same as the number of zeros in the answer.**

MULTI-STEP TEST PREP

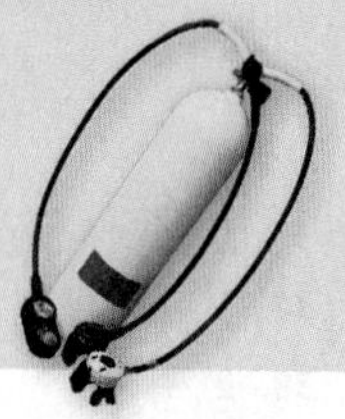

66. This problem will prepare you for the Multi-Step Test Prep on page 38.
The formula $p = \frac{F}{A}$ shows that pressure p is the amount of force F exerted over an area A in square units.
 a. A 50-pound bag of flour sits on a block and exerts a force over an area of 100 in^2. What is the pressure exerted on the block by the bag of flour?
 b. A weight exerts 64 pounds on each square foot of a diver's body. What force is exerted on each square *inch* of the diver's body? (*Hint:* Determine how many square inches are in one square foot.)

1-4 PRACTICE A
1-4 PRACTICE C
1-4 PRACTICE B

Write the power represented by each geometric model.

1. 5^3 2. 7^2 3. 3^3

Evaluate each expression.

4. 2^4 **16** 5. $(-3)^3$ **−27** 6. $\left(\frac{2}{5}\right)^2$ **$\frac{4}{25}$**
7. 3^5 **243** 8. $(-10)^4$ **10,000** 9. $\left(\frac{3}{4}\right)^2$ **$\frac{9}{16}$**

Write each number as a power of the given base.

10. 16; base 2 **2^4** 11. 1,000,000; base 10 **10^6** 12. −216; base −6 **$(-6)^3$**
13. 2401; base 7 **7^4** 14. 256; base −4 **$(-4)^4$** 15. $\frac{8}{27}$; base $\frac{2}{3}$ **$\left(\frac{2}{3}\right)^3$**

16. Anna needed to let everyone in the music club know the time of its next meeting. She called two people and asked each of them to call two other people, and so on. If each phone call takes one minute, how many phone calls were made during the fifth minute?
$2^5 = 32$

1-4 READING STRATEGIES

Examine the Venn diagram below for similarities and differences between the power expression 4^3 and the multiplication expression $4 \cdot 3$.

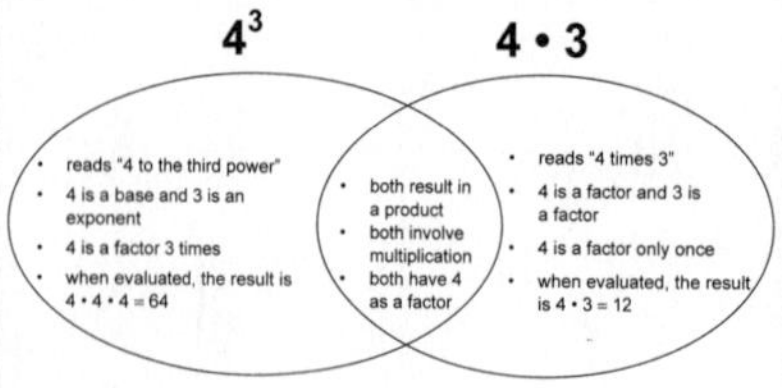

Answer the following with the help of the Venn diagram.

1. The expression 3^8 reads "3 to the **eighth** power."
2. Write the expression that represents "5 to the sixth power." **5^6**
3. In the expression 7^4, 7 is the **base** and 4 is the **exponent**.
4. In the expression 6^4, how many times is 6 used as a factor? **4 times**
5. The expression 2^6 **is not** (is/is not) equal in value to the expression $2 \cdot 6$.
6. When evaluated, which expression results in a value of 10, 2^5 or $2 \cdot 5$? **$2 \cdot 5$**
7. When evaluated, which expression results in a value of 1, 1^3 or $1 \cdot 3$? **1^3**

Evaluate each expression.

8. 9^2 **81** 9. 2^4 **16** 10. 1^5 **1**

1-4 RETEACH

A **power** is an expression that represents repeated multiplication of a factor. The factor is the **base**, and the number of times it is used as a factor is the **exponent**. Pay attention to parentheses, which tell you how much of the expression the exponent influences.

Power	Base	Exponent	Expanded Form
5^4	5	4	$5 \cdot 5 \cdot 5 \cdot 5$
-5^4	5	4	$-(5 \cdot 5 \cdot 5 \cdot 5)$
$(-5)^4$	−5	4	$(-5) \cdot (-5) \cdot (-5) \cdot (-5)$

To evaluate a power, perform the repeated multiplication.

Evaluate $\left(-\frac{4}{5}\right)^3$.

There are parentheses, so the exponent influences the negative *and* the fraction.

$\left(-\frac{4}{5}\right)^3 = \left(-\frac{4}{5}\right)\left(-\frac{4}{5}\right)\left(-\frac{4}{5}\right)$

$= \left(+\frac{16}{25}\right)\left(-\frac{4}{5}\right)$ *Multiply two of the factors. A negative times a negative is positive.*

$= -\frac{64}{125}$ *Multiply again. A positive times a negative is negative.*

Write the expanded form of each power.

1. 7^6 **$7 \cdot 7 \cdot 7 \cdot 7 \cdot 7 \cdot 7$** 2. $(-3)^2$ **$(-3) \cdot (-3)$**
3. $\frac{1}{2}^7$ **$\frac{1}{2} \cdot \frac{1}{2} \cdot \frac{1}{2} \cdot \frac{1}{2} \cdot \frac{1}{2} \cdot \frac{1}{2} \cdot \frac{1}{2}$** 4. -6^5 **$-(6 \cdot 6 \cdot 6 \cdot 6 \cdot 6)$**

Evaluate each expression.

5. 3^5 **243** 6. -2^4 **−16** 7. $\left(-\frac{2}{9}\right)^2$ **$\frac{4}{81}$**
8. $(-2)^3$ 9. 1^8 10. 0^2

TEST PREP

67. Which of the following is equal to 9^2?
Ⓐ $9 \cdot 2$ Ⓑ 27 **Ⓒ 3^4** Ⓓ -9^2

68. Which expression represents the same value as the product $(-16)(-16)(-16)(-16)$?
Ⓕ $(-16)4$ **Ⓖ $(-16)^4$** Ⓗ -16^4 Ⓙ $-(16 \cdot 4)$

69. A number raised to the third power is negative. What is true about the number?
Ⓐ The number is positive. Ⓒ The number is even.
Ⓑ The number is negative. Ⓓ The number is odd.

70. A pattern exists as a result of raising −1 to consecutive whole numbers. Which is the best representation of the value of −1 raised to the 100th power?

$(-1)^n$	$(-1)^1$	$(-1)^2$	$(-1)^3$	$(-1)^4$	$(-1)^5$	$(-1)^6$
Value	−1	1	−1	1	−1	1

Ⓕ -1^{100} Ⓖ −1 **Ⓗ 1** Ⓙ 0

CHALLENGE AND EXTEND

Simplify each expression.

71. $(2^2)(2^2)(2^2)$ **64** 72. $(2^3)(2^3)(2^3)$ **512** 73. $(-4^2)(-4^2)(-4^2)(-4^2)$ **65,536**

74. **Design** The diagram shows the layout of a pool and the surrounding path. The path is 2.5 feet wide.
a. What is the total area of the pool and path? **900 ft^2**
b. What is the area of the pool? **625 ft^2**
c. What is the area of the path? **275 ft^2**
d. One bag of pebbles covers 10 square feet. How many bags of pebbles are needed to cover the path? **28 bags**

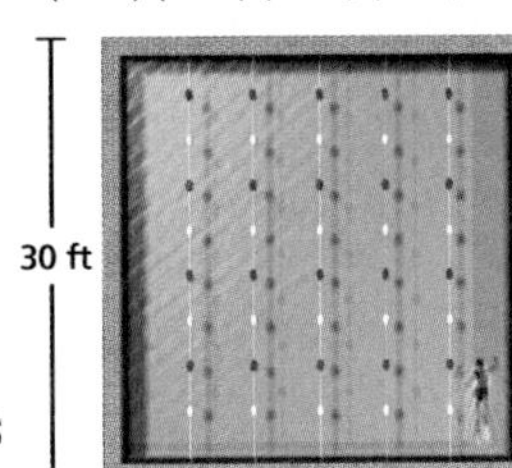

75. Exponents and powers have special properties.
a. Write both 4^2 and 4^3 as a product of 4's. **$4 \cdot 4$; $4 \cdot 4 \cdot 4$**
b. Write the product of the two expressions from part **a.** Write this product as a power of 4. **$4 \cdot 4 \cdot 4 \cdot 4 \cdot 4 = 4^5$**

c. **Write About It** Add the exponents in the expressions 4^2 and 4^3. Describe any relationship you see between your answer to part **b** and the sum of the exponents. **$2 + 3 = 5$; the sum of the exponents in 4^2 and 4^3 is the exponent in the product 4^5.**

SPIRAL REVIEW

Find the mean of each data set by dividing the sum of the data by the number of items in the data set. *(Previous course)*

76. 7, 7, 8, 8 **7.5** 77. 1, 3, 5, 7, 9 **5** 78. 10, 9, 9, 12, 12 **10.4**

Give two ways to write each algebraic expression in words. *(Lesson 1-1)*

79. $5 - x$ 80. $6n$ 81. $c \div d$ 82. $a + b$

79. 5 minus x; x less than 5

80. 6 times n; the product of 6 and n

81. c divided by d; the quotient of c and d

82. the sum of a and b; b more than a

Multiply or divide if possible. *(Lesson 1-3)*

83. $\frac{4}{5} \div \frac{8}{25}$ **$\frac{5}{2}$** 84. $0 \div \frac{6}{7}$ **0** 85. $-20(-14)$ **280** 86. $\frac{1}{2}\left(-\frac{4}{5}\right)$ **$-\frac{2}{5}$**

COMMON ERROR ALERT

In **Exercise 64,** students may multiply the number of heads by 2 and the number of tails by 3. Encourage students to write each score in a list as it is doubled or tripled from the previous score.

TEST PREP DOCTOR In **Exercise 67,** students may not recognize that powers with different bases and exponents may have the same value. Suggest that students first simplify the expressions given in choices **A, C,** and **D.**

Journal

Explain why the value of a power is not always greater than its base. Use examples in your explanation.

ALTERNATIVE ASSESSMENT

Have students write and simplify each of the following: a power containing a positive base with an odd exponent; a power containing a negative base with an odd exponent; a power containing a positive base with an even exponent; and a power containing a negative base with an even exponent.

Power Presentations with PowerPoint®

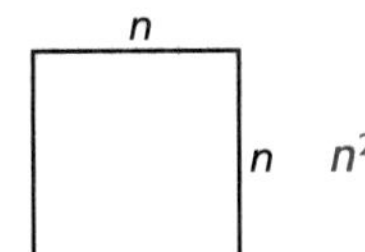

1-4 Lesson Quiz

1. Write the power represented by the geometric model. n^2

Simplify each expression.

2. $\left(-\frac{1}{8}\right)^3$ $-\frac{1}{512}$ 3. -6^3 −216

4. 6^3 216 5. $(-2)^6$ 64

Write each number as a power of the given base.

6. 343; base 7 7^3

7. 10,000; base 10 10^4

Also available on transparency

1-4 PROBLEM SOLVING

Write the correct answer.

1. The population of a certain bacteria doubles in size every 3 hours. If a population begins with one bacterium, how many will there be after one day?
$2^8 = 256$ bacteria

2. The top of Julie's nightstand has the shape of a circle with diameter 14 inches. Find the area of the top of Julie's nightstand. (Recall that the area of a circle can be approximated by squaring the length of its radius and then multiplying by 3.14.)
153.86 in^2

3. The population of Bridgeville triples every decade. If its population in 2000 was 25,000, how many people will be living in Bridgeville in 2030?
$25{,}000 \times 3^3 = 675{,}000$

4. The number of subscribers to a popular new magazine quadruples every month. If there were initially 500 subscribers, how many subscribers will there be after six months?
$500 \times 4^6 = 2{,}048{,}000$

A square photograph measuring 8 inches by 8 inches is positioned within a 1-inch wide picture frame as shown below. Select the best answer.

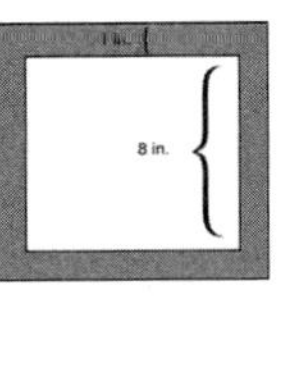

5. What is the area of the photograph alone?
A 16 in^2 C 49 in^2
B 32 in^2 **D 64 in^2**

6. What is the combined area of the photograph and frame?
F 64 in^2 **H 100 in^2**
G 81 in^2 J 144 in^2

7. What is the area of the frame alone?
A 8 in^2 **C 36 in^2**
B 17 in^2 D 49 in^2

8. If the 1-inch wide frame is replaced with a 2-inch wide frame, how much more wall space will be needed to hang the framed photograph?
F 19 in^2 H 102 in^2
G 44 in^2 J 144 in^2

1-4 CHALLENGE

Inflation occurs when the value of money decreases compared to the amount of goods that money can buy. As inflation increases, more money is needed to buy the same item.

The formula for determining the new cost of an item after inflation is:

new price = ab^x,

where a = original price, b = (1 + inflation rate), and x = number of years.

The price of a computer game is $50. Four percent inflation causes prices to rise 4% each year. Study and complete the chart below to determine the new price after each year of 4% inflation. Round final answers to the nearest hundredth.

Year	ab^x	New price
0	$50(1+0.04)^0$ $50(1.04)^0$ 50(1)	\$50.00
1	$50(1+0.04)^1$ $50(1.04)^1$ 50(1.04)	\$52.00
2	$50(1+0.04)^2$ $50(1.04)^2$ 50(1.0816)	\$54.08
3	$50(1+0.04)^3$ $50(1.04)^3$ 50(1.124864)	\$56.24
4	$50(1+0.04)^4$ $50(1.04)^4$ 50(1.16985856)	\$58.49

Year	ab^x	New price
5	$50(1+0.04)^5$ $50(1.04)^5$ 50(1.216652902)	\$60.83
6	$50(1+0.04)^6$ $50(1.04)^6$ 50(1.265319019)	\$63.27
7	$50(1+0.04)^7$ $50(1.04)^7$ 50(1.315931779)	\$65.80
8	$50(1+0.04)^8$ $50(1.04)^8$ 50(1.36856905)	\$68.43
9	$50(1+0.04)^9$ $50(1.04)^9$ 50(1.423311812)	\$71.17

1. What is the first year the new price rises to \$65 or more? **year 7**
2. What is the difference in price from Year 0 to Year 1? **\$2.00**
3. What is the difference in price from Year 8 to Year 9? **\$2.74**
4. If the inflation rate were 6%, what would be the first year the price of the game rises to \$65 or more? **5 years**
5. Find the lowest percent inflation rate (to the nearest whole number) at which the game price would reach \$100 or more in only 5 years. **15%**

1-5 Organizer

Pacing: Traditional 1 day
Block $\frac{1}{2}$ day

Objectives: Simplify expressions containing roots.

Classify numbers within the real number system.

Algebra Lab
In *Algebra Lab Activities*

Online Edition
Tutorial Videos, Interactivity

Countdown Week 2

Power Presentations with PowerPoint®

Warm Up

Simplify each expression.

1. 6^2 36 **2.** 11^2 121

3. $(-9)(-9)$ 81 **4.** $\left(\frac{5}{6}\right)\left(\frac{5}{6}\right)$ $\frac{25}{36}$

Write each fraction as a decimal.

5. $\frac{2}{5}$ 0.4 **6.** $\frac{5}{9}$ $0.\overline{5}$

7. $5\frac{3}{8}$ 5.375 **8.** $-1\frac{5}{6}$ $-1.8\overline{3}$

Also available on transparency

Teacher: What kind of roots does a "geom-e-tree" have?

Student: Square roots!

State Resources

State Resources Online
KEYWORD: MA7 Resources

1-5 Roots and Real Numbers

Objectives
Simplify expressions containing roots.

Classify numbers within the real number system.

Vocabulary
square root
principal square root
perfect square
cube root
natural numbers
whole numbers
integers
rational numbers
terminating decimal
repeating decimal
irrational numbers

Why learn this?
Square roots can be used to find the side length of a square garden when you know its area. (See Example 3.)

A number that is multiplied by itself to form a product is a **square root** of that product. The radical symbol $\sqrt{\ }$ is used to represent square roots. For nonnegative numbers, the operations of squaring and finding a square root are inverse operations. In other words, for $x \geq 0$, $\sqrt{x} \cdot \sqrt{x} = x$.

Positive real numbers have two square roots. The **principal square root** of a number is the positive square root and is represented by $\sqrt{\ }$. A negative square root is represented by $-\sqrt{\ }$. The symbol $\pm\sqrt{\ }$ is used to represent both square roots.

$$4 \cdot 4 = 4^2 = 16 \longrightarrow \sqrt{16} = 4 \longleftarrow \text{Positive square root of 16}$$

$$(-4)(-4) = (-4)^2 = 16 \rightarrow -\sqrt{16} = -4 \leftarrow \text{Negative square root of 16}$$

A **perfect square** is a number whose positive square root is a whole number. Some examples of perfect squares are shown in the table.

0	1	4	9	16	25	36	49	64	81	100
0^2	1^2	2^2	3^2	4^2	5^2	6^2	7^2	8^2	9^2	10^2

A number that is raised to the third power to form a product is a **cube root** of that product. The symbol $\sqrt[3]{\ }$ indicates a cube root. Since $2^3 = 8$, $\sqrt[3]{8} = 2$. Similarly, the symbol $\sqrt[4]{\ }$ indicates a fourth root: $2^4 = 16$, so $\sqrt[4]{16} = 2$.

EXAMPLE 1 Finding Roots

Find each root.

A $\sqrt{49}$

$\sqrt{49} = \sqrt{7^2}$ *Think: What number squared equals 49?*
$= 7$

B $-\sqrt{36}$

$-\sqrt{36} = -\sqrt{6^2}$ *Think: What number squared equals 36?*
$= -6$

C $\sqrt[3]{-125}$

$\sqrt[3]{-125} = \sqrt[3]{(-5^3)}$ *Think: What number cubed equals −125?*
$= -5$ $(-5)(-5)(-5) = 25(-5) = -125$

Writing Math
The small number to the left of the root is the *index*. In a square root, the index is understood to be 2. In other words, $\sqrt{\ }$ is the same as $\sqrt[2]{\ }$.

Find each root.

1a. $\sqrt{4}$ 2 **1b.** $-\sqrt{25}$ −5 **1c.** $\sqrt[4]{81}$ 3

1 Introduce

EXPLORATION

1-5 Roots and Real Numbers

Explore what happens when you square a set of numbers and then reverse the process.

1. Complete the table by squaring each number. One example has been filled in for you.

Number, n	1	2	3	4	5	6	7	8	9
Square of Number, n^2			9						

2. You can use the symbol $\sqrt{\ }$ to reverse the process. For example, $\sqrt{9} = 3$. Write additional mathematical statements using this symbol and the values in your table.

THINK AND DISCUSS

3. **Explain** how you can write a new mathematical statement if you are given that fact that $17^2 = 289$.
4. **Describe** how you can find the value of $\sqrt{121}$.

Motivate

Tell students that you are going to carpet a square room that has an area of 65 square feet. Before you cut the carpet, you need to find the length of the sides. Ask students what must be true about the sides of a square room. Then ask if they think the length of the sides is greater or less than 8 feet.

Explorations and answers are provided in *Alternate Openers: Explorations Transparencies.*

EXAMPLE  Finding Roots of Fractions

Find $\sqrt{\frac{1}{4}}$.

$\sqrt{\frac{1}{4}} = \sqrt{\left(\frac{1}{2}\right)^2}$ *Think: What number squared equals $\frac{1}{4}$?*

$\sqrt{\frac{1}{4}} = \frac{1}{2}$

CHECK IT OUT! Find each root.

2a. $\sqrt{\frac{4}{9}}$ **$\frac{2}{3}$** 2b. $\sqrt[3]{\frac{1}{8}}$ **$\frac{1}{2}$** 2c. $-\sqrt{\frac{4}{49}}$ **$-\frac{2}{7}$**

Square roots of numbers that are not perfect squares, such as 15, are not whole numbers. A calculator can approximate the value of $\sqrt{15}$ as 3.872983346… Without a calculator, you can use the square roots of perfect squares to help estimate the square roots of other numbers.

EXAMPLE  *Gardening Application*

Nancy wants to plant a square garden of wildflowers. She has enough wildflower seeds to cover 19 ft^2. Estimate to the nearest tenth the side length of a square with an area of 19 ft^2.

Since the area of the square is 19 ft^2, then each side of the square is $\sqrt{19}$ ft. 19 is not a perfect square, so find the two consecutive perfect squares that 19 is between: 16 and 25. $\sqrt{19}$ is between $\sqrt{16}$ and $\sqrt{25}$, or 4 and 5. Refine the estimate.

4.3:	$4.3^2 = 18.49$	too low	*$\sqrt{19}$ is greater than 4.3.*
4.4:	$4.4^2 = 19.36$	too high	*$\sqrt{19}$ is less than 4.4.*
4.35:	$4.35^2 = 18.9225$	too low	*$\sqrt{19}$ is greater than 4.35.*

Since 4.35 is too low and 4.4 is too high, $\sqrt{19}$ is between 4.35 and 4.4. Rounded to the nearest tenth, $\sqrt{19} \approx 4.4$.

The side length of the plot is $\sqrt{19} \approx 4.4$ ft.

Writing Math

The symbol ≈ means "is approximately equal to."

CHECK IT OUT! 3. Estimate to the nearest tenth the side length of a cube with a volume of 26 ft^3. **3.0 ft**

Real numbers can be classified according to their characteristics.

Natural numbers are the counting numbers: 1, 2, 3, …

Whole numbers are the natural numbers and zero: 0, 1, 2, 3, …

Integers are the whole numbers and their opposites: …, −3, −2, −1, 0, 1, 2, 3, …

Rational numbers are numbers that can be expressed in the form $\frac{a}{b}$, where a and b are both integers and $b \neq 0$. When expressed as a decimal, a rational number is either a *terminating decimal* or a *repeating decimal*.

- A **terminating decimal** has a finite number of digits after the decimal point (for example, 1.25, 2.75, and 4.0).
- A **repeating decimal** has a block of one or more digits after the decimal point that repeat continuously (where all digits are not zeros).

Writing Math

To show that one or more digits repeat continuously, write a bar over those digits.

$1.333333333... = 1.\overline{3}$

$2.14141414... = 2.\overline{14}$

Power Presentations with PowerPoint®

Additional Examples

Example 1

Find each root.

A. $\sqrt{81}$ 9 **B.** $-\sqrt{25}$ −5

C. $\sqrt[3]{-216}$ −6

Example 2

Find each root.

A. $\sqrt{\frac{49}{9}}$ $\frac{7}{3}$ **B.** $\sqrt[3]{\frac{8}{125}}$ $\frac{2}{5}$

C. $-\sqrt{\frac{4}{25}}$ $-\frac{2}{5}$

Example 2

As part of her art project, Shonda will need to make a paper square covered in glitter. Her tube of glitter covers 13 in^2. Estimate to the nearest tenth the side length of a square with an area of 13 in^2. ≈3.6 in.

INTERVENTION

Questioning Strategies

EXAMPLE 1

- What is the difference between and $-\sqrt{36}$ and $\sqrt{-36}$?
- What are some examples of integers that are not perfect squares?

EXAMPLE 2

- How are the numerators in the answers related to the numerators in the problems? What about the denominators?

EXAMPLE 3

- How can you choose two consecutive whole numbers that the square root of a non-perfect square falls between?

2 Teach

Guided Instruction

Review squaring and cubing numbers before finding square roots and cube roots. When presenting square roots, show why (within the real numbers) there cannot be a negative number under the radical symbol. Ask students to think of a number that when multiplied by itself equals a negative number. Point out how this differs from cube roots, in which there can be a negative number under the radical symbol because a negative number cubed equals a negative number.

Reaching All Learners

Through Graphic Organizers

Prior to class, prepare a list of rational and irrational numbers, including repeating decimals, terminating decimals, and the square roots of non-perfect squares. In class, have students discuss where to place each of the numbers in the following table.

Rational Numbers		Irrational Numbers
Terminating Decimals	**Repeating Decimals**	

Teaching Tip **Reading Math** Have students read the problem in **Example 3.** Then ask them to identify the information in the problem that will be essential in finding the solution.

Teaching Tip **Technology** Students can verify their answers in **Example 3** by using a calculator to find the roots. Be sure to emphasize that the calculator's answer, even though it has several decimal places, is still only an approximation.

Power Presentations with PowerPoint®

Additional Examples

Example 4

Write all classifications that apply to each number.

A. −32 rational number, integer, terminating decimal

B. $-\sqrt{14}$ irrational number

Inclusion When teaching the definition of terminating decimal, be sure students know the meaning and pronunciation of *finite*. Some students may be familiar with the concept of infinity. If so, you can point out that *infinite* is the opposite of *finite*.

INTERVENTION 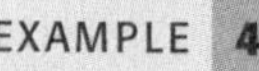

Questioning Strategies

EXAMPLE 4

- How can you recognize repeating decimals and terminating decimals?
- If you know that a number is a natural number, what other classifications automatically apply to that number?
- Which classifications do not include negative numbers?

Irrational numbers are all real numbers that are not rational. They cannot be expressed in the form $\frac{a}{b}$ where a and b are both integers and $b \neq 0$. They are neither terminating decimals nor repeating decimals. For example:

0.10100100010000100000... *After the decimal point, this number contains 1 followed by one 0, and then 1 followed by two 0's, and then 1 followed by three 0's, and so on.*

This decimal neither terminates nor repeats, so it is an irrational number.

If a whole number is not a perfect square, then its square root is irrational. For example, 2 is not a perfect square, and $\sqrt{2}$ is irrational.

The real numbers are made up of all rational and irrational numbers.

Reading Math

Note the symbols for the sets of numbers.
ℝ: real numbers
ℚ: rational numbers
ℤ: integers
𝕎: whole numbers
ℕ: natural numbers

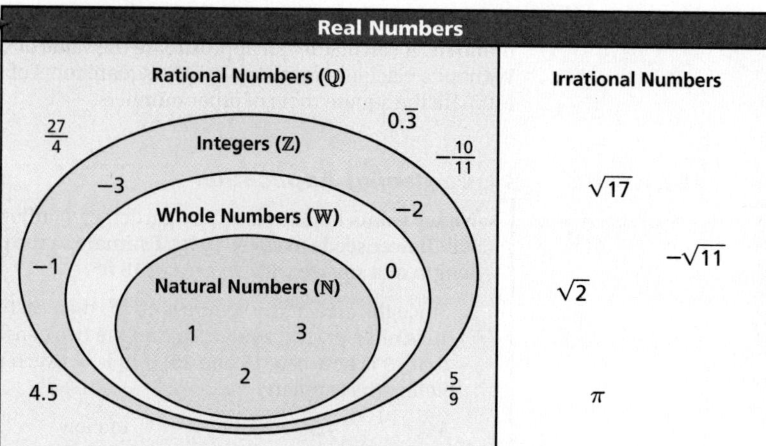

EXAMPLE 4 **Classifying Real Numbers**

Write all classifications that apply to each real number.

A $\frac{8}{9}$

$\frac{8}{9}$ *is in the form* $\frac{a}{b}$, *where a and b are integers and b ≠ 0.*

$8 \div 9 = 0.8888...$

$= 0.\overline{8}$ $\frac{8}{9}$ *can be written as a repeating decimal.*

rational, repeating decimal

B 18

$18 = \frac{18}{1}$ *18 can be written in the form* $\frac{a}{b}$.

$18 = 18.0$ *18 can be written as a terminating decimal.*

rational, terminating decimal, integer, whole, natural

C $\sqrt{20}$

irrational *20 is not a perfect square, so* $\sqrt{20}$ *is irrational.*

CHECK IT OUT! **Write all classifications that apply to each real number.**

4a. $7\frac{4}{9}$ **ℚ, rep. dec.**

4b. −12 **ℚ, term. dec., ℤ**

4c. $\sqrt{10}$ **irr.**

4d. $\sqrt{100}$ **ℕ, 𝕎, ℤ, ℚ, term. dec.**

3 Close

Summarize

Link the finding of square roots to the different subsets of the real numbers by asking students to think of a number whose square root is

- an integer
- a rational number, but not an integer
- an irrational number

ONGOING ASSESSMENT and INTERVENTION 

***Diagnose Before* the Lesson**
1-5 Warm Up, TE p. 32

***Monitor During* the Lesson**
Check It Out! Exercises, SE pp. 32–34
Questioning Strategies, TE pp. 33–34

***Assess After* the Lesson**
1-5 Lesson Quiz, TE p. 37
Alternative Assessment, TE p. 37

THINK AND DISCUSS

1. Write $\frac{2}{3}$ and $\frac{3}{5}$ as decimals. Identify what number classifications the two numbers share and how their classifications are different.
2. **GET ORGANIZED** Copy the graphic organizer and use the flowchart to classify each of the given numbers. Write each number in the box with the most specific classification that applies. 4, $\sqrt{25}$, 0, $\frac{1}{3}$, −15, −2.25, $\frac{1}{4}$, $\sqrt{21}$, 2^4, $(-1)^2$

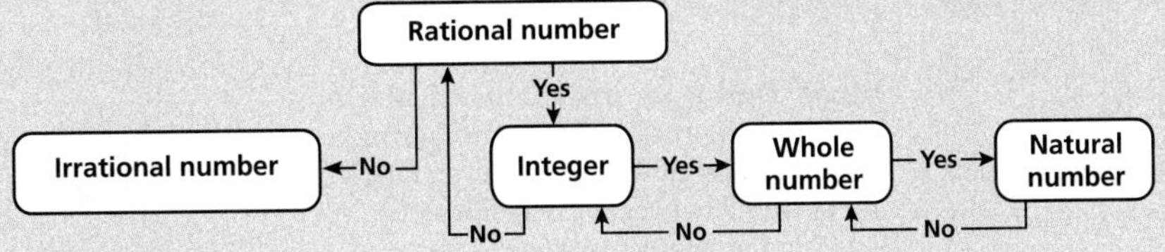

1-5 Exercises

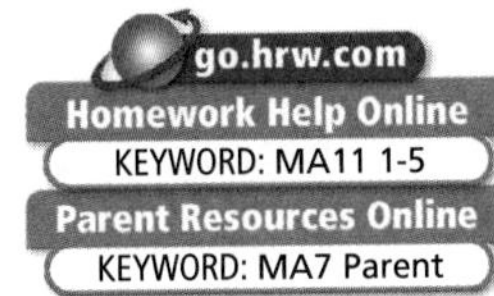

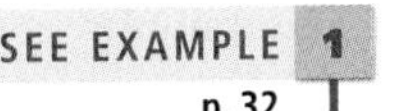

GUIDED PRACTICE

1. **Vocabulary** Give an example of a *square root* that is not a *rational number.* **Possible answer: $\sqrt{3}$**

Find each root.

SEE EXAMPLE 1 p. 32

2. $\sqrt{64}$ **8**
3. $-\sqrt{225}$ **−15**
4. $\sqrt[3]{-64}$ **−4**
5. $\sqrt[4]{625}$ **5**
6. $\sqrt{81}$ **9**
7. $-\sqrt[3]{27}$ **−3**
8. $-\sqrt[3]{-27}$ **3**
9. $-\sqrt{16}$ **−4**

SEE EXAMPLE 2 p. 33

10. $\sqrt{\frac{1}{16}}$ $\mathbf{\frac{1}{4}}$
11. $\sqrt[3]{\frac{8}{27}}$ $\mathbf{\frac{2}{3}}$
12. $-\sqrt{\frac{1}{9}}$ $\mathbf{-\frac{1}{3}}$
13. $\sqrt{\frac{9}{64}}$ $\mathbf{\frac{3}{8}}$
14. $\sqrt{\frac{1}{36}}$ $\mathbf{\frac{1}{6}}$
15. $\sqrt[3]{\frac{1}{64}}$ $\mathbf{\frac{1}{4}}$
16. $-\sqrt{\frac{4}{81}}$ $\mathbf{-\frac{2}{9}}$
17. $\sqrt[3]{-\frac{1}{125}}$ $\mathbf{-\frac{1}{5}}$

SEE EXAMPLE 3 p. 33

18. A contractor is told that a potential client's kitchen floor is in the shape of a square. The area of the floor is 45 ft^2. Estimate to the nearest tenth the side length of the floor. **about 6.7 ft**

SEE EXAMPLE 4 p. 34

Write all classifications that apply to each real number.

19. −27 **ℚ, term. dec., ℤ**
20. $\frac{1}{6}$ **ℚ, rep. dec.**
21. $\sqrt{33}$ **irr.**
22. −6.8 **ℚ, term. dec.**

PRACTICE AND PROBLEM SOLVING

Find each root.

23. $\sqrt{121}$ **11**
24. $\sqrt[3]{-1000}$ **−10**
25. $-\sqrt{100}$ **−10**
26. $\sqrt[4]{256}$ **4**
27. $\sqrt{\frac{1}{25}}$ $\mathbf{\frac{1}{5}}$
28. $\sqrt[4]{\frac{1}{16}}$ $\mathbf{\frac{1}{2}}$
29. $\sqrt[3]{-\frac{1}{8}}$ $\mathbf{-\frac{1}{2}}$
30. $-\sqrt{\frac{25}{36}}$ $\mathbf{-\frac{5}{6}}$
31. An artist makes glass paperweights in the shape of a cube. He uses 68 cm^3 of glass to make each paperweight. Estimate to the nearest tenth the side length of a paperweight. **4.1 cm**

Answers to *Think and Discuss*

1. $\frac{2}{3} = 0.\overline{6}$; $\frac{3}{5} = 0.6$; both numbers are rational. $\frac{2}{3}$ is a repeating decimal; $\frac{3}{5}$ is a terminating decimal.
2. See p. A2.

1-5 Exercises

Assignment Guide

Assign *Guided Practice* exercises as necessary.

If you finished Examples **1–2**

Basic	23–30, 36–40, 56
Average	23–30, 36–40, 56
Advanced	23–30, 36–40, 52, 57–64

If you finished Examples **1–4**

Basic	23–44, 51–56, 66–75
Average	23–60, 66–75
Advanced	23–41 odd, 42–75

Homework Quick Check
Quickly check key concepts.
Exercises: 26, 30, 31, 32, 36, 38

Teaching Tip **Reading Math** Students may need practice reading roots. If so, ask them to read some of the exercises aloud. For example, **Exercise 2** reads "the square root of 64." **Exercise 4** is "the cube root of −64" and **Exercise 5** is "the fourth root of 625."

State Resources

go.hrw.com
State Resources Online
KEYWORD: MA7 Resources

Exercise 50 involves using the Pythagorean Theorem to determine the distance of a diver from a boat. This exercise prepares students for the Multi-Step Test Prep on page 38.

Answers

41. 45; $\mathbb{Q}$, term. dec., $\mathbb{Z}$, $\mathbb{W}$, $\mathbb{N}$
42. $38.\overline{740}$; $\mathbb{Q}$, rep. dec.
43. 34.625; $\mathbb{Q}$, term. dec.
44. $47.\overline{1}$; $\mathbb{Q}$, rep. dec.
49. Possible answer: No; a pos. number has only one cube root because a neg. number cubed results in a neg. number. A pos. number has two fourth roots because a neg. number raised to the fourth power results in a pos. number.

Independent Practice	
For Exercises	See Example
23–26	1
27–30	2
31	3
32–35	4

Extra Practice
Skills Practice p. S5
Application Practice p. S28

33. $\mathbb{Q}$, term. dec., $\mathbb{Z}$, $\mathbb{W}$, $\mathbb{N}$

34. $\mathbb{Q}$, term. dec., $\mathbb{Z}$

Write all classifications that apply to each real number.

32. $\frac{5}{12}$ **$\mathbb{Q}$, rep. dec.** 33. $\sqrt{49}$ 34. -3 35. $\sqrt{18}$ **irr.**

36. **Geometry** The cube root of the volume of a cube gives the length of one side of the cube.
   a. Find the side length of the cube shown. **7 cm**
   b. Find the area of each face of the cube. **49 cm²**

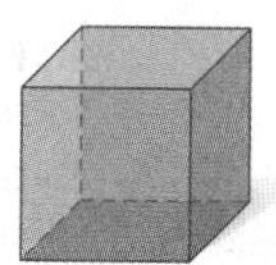

Compare. Write <, >, or =.

37. $8 \;\blacksquare\; \sqrt{63}$ **>** 38. $\sqrt{88} \;\blacksquare\; 9$ **>** 39. $6 \;\blacksquare\; \sqrt{40}$ **<** 40. $\sqrt{\frac{9}{25}} \;\blacksquare\; 0.61$ **<**

Travel During a cross-country road trip, Madeline recorded the distance between several major cities and the time it took her to travel between those cities. Find Madeline's average speed for each leg of the trip and classify that number.

Madeline's Cross-Country Road Trip

		Distance (mi)	Time (h)	Speed (mi/h)	Classification
41.	Portland, ME, to Memphis, TN	1485	33	■	■
42.	Memphis, TN, to Denver, CO	1046	27	■	■
43.	Denver, CO, to Boise, ID	831	24	■	■
44.	Boise, ID, to Portland, OR	424	9	■	■

Determine whether each statement is sometimes, always, or never true. If it is sometimes true, give one example that makes the statement true and one example that makes it false. If it is always true, explain. If it is never true, rewrite the statement so that it is always true.

45. Mixed numbers are rational numbers. **Always; mixed numbers can be written as improper fractions.**
46. The decimal form of an irrational number is a repeating decimal.
47. A terminating decimal is a rational number.
48. A negative number is irrational. **Sometimes; $-\sqrt{2}$ is irrational, but -6.2 is rational.**
49. **Critical Thinking** A positive number has two square roots, one that is positive and one that is negative. Is the same thing true for the cube root of a positive number? What about the fourth root of a positive number? Explain.

46. Never; the dec. form of an irrational number is a nonterminating, nonrepeating decimal.

47. Always; every term. dec. can be written as a fraction whose denom. is a power of 10.

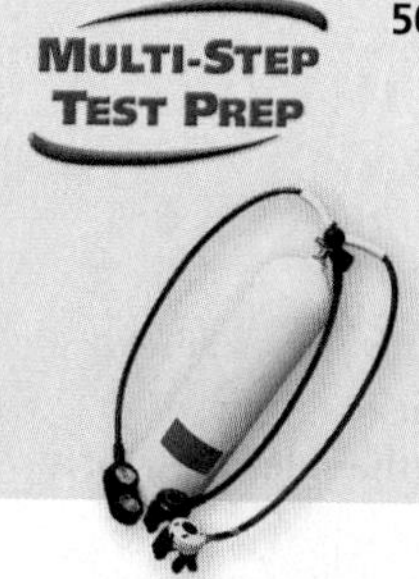

50. This problem will prepare you for the Multi-Step Test Prep on page 38.
   The equation $a^2 + b^2 = c^2$ relates the lengths of the sides of a right triangle. Sides a and b make the right angle of the triangle.
   a. What is the value of c^2 when $a = 5$ and $b = 12$? Determine the square root of c^2 to find the value of c. **169; 13**
   b. A diver is a horizontal distance of 50 feet from a boat and 120 feet beneath the surface of the water. What distance will the diver swim if he swims diagonally to the boat? **130 ft**

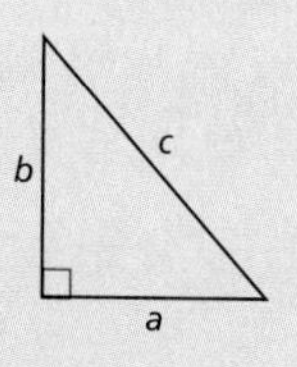

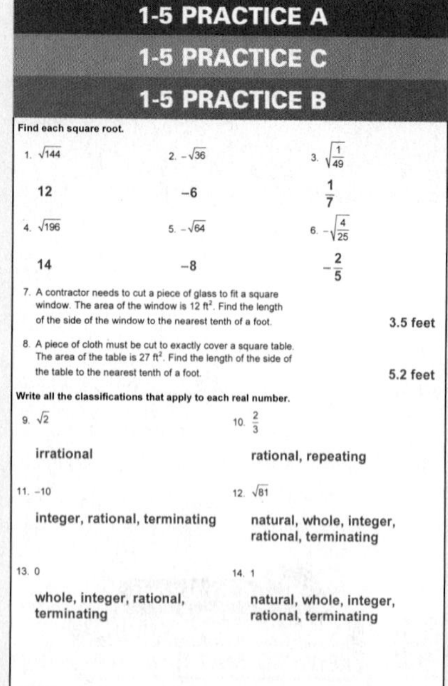

1-5 PRACTICE A
1-5 PRACTICE C
1-5 PRACTICE B

Find each square root.

1. $\sqrt{144}$ **12** 2. $-\sqrt{36}$ **−6** 3. $\sqrt{\frac{1}{49}}$ **$\frac{1}{7}$**
4. $\sqrt{196}$ **14** 5. $-\sqrt{64}$ **−8** 6. $-\sqrt{\frac{4}{25}}$ **$-\frac{2}{5}$**
7. A contractor needs to cut a piece of glass to fit a square window. The area of the window is 12 ft². Find the length of the side of the window to the nearest tenth of a foot. **3.5 feet**
8. A piece of cloth must be cut to exactly cover a square table. The area of the table is 27 ft². Find the length of the side of the table to the nearest tenth of a foot. **5.2 feet**

Write all the classifications that apply to each real number.

9. $\sqrt{2}$ **irrational** 10. $\frac{2}{3}$ **rational, repeating**
11. −10 **integer, rational, terminating** 12. $\sqrt{81}$ **natural, whole, integer, rational, terminating**
13. 0 **whole, integer, rational, terminating** 14. 1 **natural, whole, integer, rational, terminating**

1-5 READING STRATEGIES

The flow chart below can help you understand the relationships among different subsets of the real numbers.

- **Real Numbers**: 2.7, −4, 0, 8, $\frac{2}{3}$, $\sqrt{5}$
  - **Rational**: 2.7, −4, 0, 8, $\frac{2}{3}$
    - **Terminating Decimal**: 2.7, −4, 0, 8
      - **Integer**: −4, 0, 8
        - **Whole**: 0, 8
          - **Natural**: 8
    - **Repeating Decimal**: $\frac{2}{3} = 0.\overline{6}$
  - **Irrational**: $\sqrt{5}$

Answer true or false for each statement.

1. Real numbers are either rational or irrational. **true**
2. An irrational number can be a repeating decimal. **false**
3. Whole numbers include negative numbers. **false**
4. The number 12 is an integer. **true**
5. The only integer not included in the natural numbers is 0. **false**
6. Irrational numbers are not real numbers. **false**
7. The fraction $\frac{1}{2}$ can be written as a terminating decimal. **true**
8. All integers are rational numbers. **true**

1-5 RETEACH

The **square root** of a number is the positive factor that you would square to get that number.

the square root of 9 is 3 because 3 squared is 9

$\sqrt{9} = 3$ because $3^2 = 3 \cdot 3 = 9$

A negative square root is the negative factor that you would square to get the number.

the negative square root of 25 is −5 because −5 squared is 25

$-\sqrt{25} = -5$ because $(-5)^2 = (-5)(-5) = 25$

To evaluate a square root, think in reverse. Ask yourself, "What number do I square?"

Find $-\sqrt{36}$.

$(-6)^2 = (-6)(-6) = 36$ *Think: What negative factor do you square to get 36?*

$-\sqrt{36} = -6$

Find $\sqrt{\frac{4}{81}}$.

Think about the numerator and denominator separately.

$2^2 = 4$ *Think: What number do I square to get 4?*

$9^2 = 81$ *Think: What number do I square to get 81?*

$\left(\frac{2}{9}\right)^2 = \left(\frac{2}{9}\right)\left(\frac{2}{9}\right) = \frac{4}{81}$ *Combine the numerator and denominator to form a positive factor.*

$\sqrt{\frac{4}{81}} = \frac{2}{9}$

1. Complete this table of squares.

1^2	2^2	3^2	4^2	5^2	6^2	7^2	8^2	9^2	10^2	11^2	12^2	13^2
1	4	9	16	25	36	**49**	**64**	**81**	**100**	**121**	**144**	**169**

2. Complete this table of square roots.

$\sqrt{1}$	$\sqrt{4}$	$\sqrt{9}$	$\sqrt{16}$	$\sqrt{25}$	$\sqrt{36}$	$\sqrt{49}$	$\sqrt{64}$	$\sqrt{81}$	$\sqrt{100}$	$\sqrt{121}$	$\sqrt{144}$	$\sqrt{169}$
1	2	3	4	5	6	7	8	9	10	11	12	13

Find each square root.

3. $\sqrt{121}$ **11** 4. $-\sqrt{64}$ **−8** 5. $\sqrt{256}$ **16**
6. $-\sqrt{400}$ **−20** 7. $\sqrt{\frac{1}{169}}$ **$\frac{1}{13}$** 8. $-\sqrt{\frac{25}{144}}$ **$-\frac{5}{12}$**

51. **Entertainment** In a board game, players place different-colored stones on a grid. Each player tries to make rows of 5 or more stones in their color while preventing their opponent(s) from doing the same. The square game board has 324 squares on it. How many squares are on each side of the board? **18**

52. **Write About It** Explain why you cannot take the square root of a negative number but you can take the cube root of a negative number.

52. Possible answer: There is no number that when squared results in a neg. number, but when you cube a neg. number, the result is a neg. number.

TEST PREP

53. Which point on the number line is closest to $-\sqrt[3]{36}$?

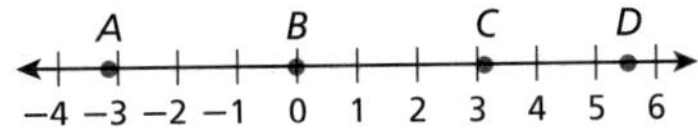

(A) *A* (circled) (B) *B* (C) *C* (D) *D*

54. What is the area of the figure at right?

(F) 24 cm^2 (circled) (H) 104 cm^2
(G) 52 cm^2 (J) 576 cm^2

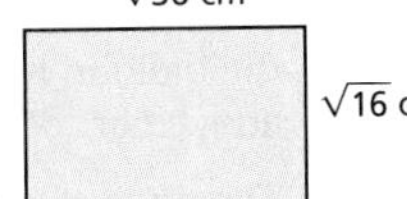
$\sqrt{36}$ cm
$\sqrt{16}$ cm

55. Which number is irrational?

(A) $-\sqrt{9}$ (B) 4.0005
(C) $2.\overline{17}$ (D) $\sqrt{40}$ (circled)

56. The square root of 175 is between which two whole numbers?

(F) 11 and 12 (G) 12 and 13 (H) 13 and 14 (circled) (J) 14 and 15

CHALLENGE AND EXTEND

Find each root.

57. $\sqrt{0.81}$ **0.9** 58. $\sqrt{0.25}$ **0.5** 59. $\sqrt[3]{-0.001}$ **−0.1** 60. $\sqrt{2.25}$ **1.5**

Evaluate each expression for $a = 9$ and $b = 7$.

61. $\sqrt{a+b}$ **4** 62. $b\sqrt{a} - a$ **12** 63. $\sqrt[4]{b+a+ab}$ **65** 64. $\sqrt{ab+1}$ **8**

65. The *Density Property of Real Numbers* states that between any two real numbers, there is another real number.
   a. Does the set of integers have this property? Explain.
   b. Use the Density Property to write a convincing argument that there are infinitely many real numbers between 0 and 1.

65a. No; possible answer: there are no integers between 1 and 2.

65b. Possible answer: Between 0 and 1, there is another real number *r*. Between 0 and *r*, there is another real number *q*. Between 0 and *q*, there is another real number *s*, and so on. Therefore, there must be infinitely many real numbers between 0 and 1.

SPIRAL REVIEW

Add or subtract. *(Lesson 1-2)*

66. $-14 + (-16)$ **−30** 67. $-\frac{1}{4} - \left(-\frac{3}{4}\right)$ $\mathbf{\frac{1}{2}}$ 68. $25 - 17.6$ **7.4**

Multiply or divide. *(Lesson 1-3)*

69. $\frac{1}{8} \div \left(-\frac{2}{3}\right)$ $\mathbf{-\frac{3}{16}}$ 70. $(-2.5)(-8)$ **20** 71. $-\frac{21}{6}$ **−3.5**

Simplify each expression. *(Lesson 1-4)*

72. -3^4 **−81** 73. $\left(-\frac{2}{5}\right)^3$ $\mathbf{-\frac{8}{125}}$ 74. 14^2 **196** 75. 4^3 **64**

COMMON ERROR ALERT

In **Exercises 57–60,** students may place the decimal point incorrectly. The square root of a decimal number will have half as many digits after the decimal point as the number under the radical.

$$\sqrt{1.5129} = 1.23$$

4 decimal places   2 decimal places

Students can check their answer by squaring it; they should get the number under the radical symbol.

TEST PREP DOCTOR If students answered **J** for **Exercise 54,** they may have multiplied 36 by 16. Tell students to simplify the numbers in the diagram before finding the area.

Journal

Have students explain how to estimate the square root of a number that is not a perfect square.

ALTERNATIVE ASSESSMENT

Have students write and solve their own word problems involving the dimensions of a square. Then have them define and give examples of rational numbers and irrational numbers.

Power Presentations with PowerPoint®

1-5 Lesson Quiz

Find each root.

1. $\sqrt{9}$ 3 2. $-\sqrt{\frac{1}{81}}$ $-\frac{1}{9}$

3. $\sqrt[3]{125}$ 5 4. $\sqrt[4]{1}$ 1

5. The area of a square piece of cloth is 68 in^2. Estimate to the nearest tenth the side length of the cloth. ≈ 8.2 in.

Write all classifications that apply to each real number.

6. $-3.\overline{89}$ rational, repeating decimal

7. $\sqrt{500}$ irrational

Also available on transparency

1-5 PROBLEM SOLVING

1. Jack is building a square pen for his dog. If he wants the area of the pen to be 121 square feet, how long should he make each side of the pen?

   11 ft

2. Danny needs a square-shaped picture to cover a hole in his wall. It has to cover at least 441 square inches of wall space. What is the smallest side length the picture can have?

   21 in.

3. The Statue of Liberty, which sits on Liberty Island in New York Harbor, is $151\frac{1}{12}$ feet high, from base to torch. Write all classifications that apply to $151\frac{1}{12}$: natural, whole, integer, rational, terminating decimal, repeating decimal, and irrational.

   rational number; repeating decimal

4. A square note card has an area of 5 in^2. Estimate the length of the side to the nearest tenth. Then write all classifications that apply to the actual side length: natural, whole, integer, rational, terminating decimal, repeating decimal, and irrational.

   2.2; irrational

Use the table below to answer questions 5–7. The table shows the area of four sizes of square-shaped pizzas sold at Town Pizza. Complete the table by finding the length of each side of the four pizzas. Round to the nearest tenth if needed. Select the best answer.

Pizza Size	Area (in^2)	Side length (in.)
Small	100	10
Medium	200	14.1
Large	420.25	20.5
Extra Large	576	24

5. What is the length of each side of an extra large pizza?
   A 24 in. C 26 in.
   B 25 in. D 36 in.

6. Which of the following classifications applies to the length of each side of a large pizza?
   F natural H integer
   G whole **J** rational

7. Which of the following is NOT a classification for the length of each side of a small pizza?
   A whole C rational
   B irrational D integer

1-5 CHALLENGE

A farmer wishes to raise alpacas. The alpaca is related to the llama and is best known for its fleece. Alpacas can be prey for dogs, wolves and coyotes, so it is important to build a fence around any alpaca farm.

The farmer currently owns a plot of land in the shape of a square. He knows that the land measures 532,900 square feet. To give the alpacas more room to graze, he buys an adjacent plot of land, which is in the shape of a right triangle. Both plots of land are shown below.

532,900 ft^2
a ft
c ft
x ft
b ft

The side labeled *b* ft has a length of 700 feet greater than the side labeled *x* ft. The farmer needs to determine the perimeter so he can build a fence.

Complete the steps below to find how much fencing the farmer needs.

1. Find the value of *x*. **730**
2. Find the value of *a*. **730**
3. Find the value of *b*. **1430**

The equation $a^2 + b^2 = c^2$ relates the lengths of the sides of a right triangle.

4. Find the value of a^2. **532,900**
5. Find the value of b^2. **2,044,900**
6. Find the value of $a^2 + b^2$. **2,577,800** (This is c^2.)
7. Find the value of *c*. Round to the nearest whole number. **1606**
8. Find the perimeter of the land. **5226 ft**
9. How much fencing does the farmer need? **5226 ft**

SECTION 1A MULTI-STEP TEST PREP

Organizer

Objective: Assess students' ability to apply concepts and skills in Lesson 1-1 through Lesson 1-5 in a real-world format.

 Online Edition

Resources

Algebra I Assessments
www.mathtekstoolkit.org

Problem	Text Reference
1	Lesson 1-1
2	Lesson 1-2
3	Lesson 1-3
4	Lesson 1-4
5	Lesson 1-5

Answers

1. See p. A12.
4. 6350.37 lb/ft^2; 44.09 psi; the pressure at 66 feet in the table is 44.1 psi, which is approximately the same as 44.09 psi.

State Resources

CHAPTER 1

MULTI-STEP TEST PREP

SECTION 1A

The Language of Algebra

Under Pressure Atmospheric pressure is 14.7 pounds per square inch (psi). Underwater, the water exerts additional pressure. The total pressure on a diver underwater is the atmospheric pressure plus the water pressure.

1. As a diver moves downward in the water, the water pressure increases by 14.7 psi for approximately every 33 ft of water. Make a table to show the total pressure on a diver at 0, 33, 66, and 99 ft below the surface of the water. At what depth would the total pressure equal 73.5 psi? Explain your method.
2. A diver is 40 ft below the surface of the water when a hot-air balloon flies over her. The hot-air balloon is 849 ft above the surface of the water. Draw a diagram and write an expression to find the distance between the diver and the balloon when the balloon is directly above her. **$849 + 40 = 889$ ft**

3. The diver swam 62.5 ft in 5 minutes. How fast was she swimming? What total distance will she have traveled after an additional 4 minutes if she maintains this same speed? **12.5 ft/min; 112.5 ft**
4. The total pressure on each square foot of the diver's body is given by the expression $2116.8 + 64.145d$, where d is the depth in feet. At a depth of 66 ft, what is the total pressure on each square foot of her body? What is the total pressure on each square *inch* of her body at this depth? How does your answer compare to your results for part **a?**
5. The diver realizes that she has drifted horizontally about 30 ft from the boat she left. She is at a depth of 40 ft from the surface. What is the diver's diagonal distance from the boat? **50 ft**

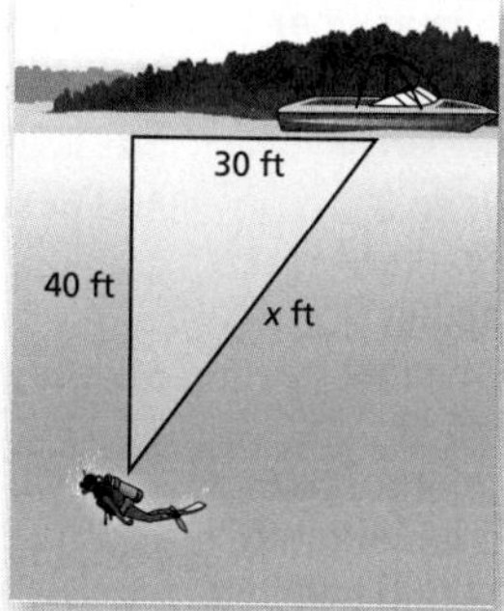

INTERVENTION

Scaffolding Questions

1. How do you decide which values to put in each column of the table? The values for depth are given, and they determine the values for pressure, so depth is in the 1st column, and pressure is in the 2nd column.
2. Can a distance be negative? No.
3. What is speed? a ratio of distance and time How can speed help you find a distance that is traveled? Use the formula $d = rt$.
4. How can you determine the number of square inches in a square foot? divide by 12^2
5. What type of triangle models the distance between the diver and her boat? a right triangle What formula can be used to find this distance? the Pythagorean Theorem

Extension

If the diver in Problem 5 swims at a speed of 10 ft/s, how long will it take her to reach the boat? 5 s

SECTION 1A

Quiz for Lessons 1-1 Through 1-5

1-1 Variables and Expressions

Give two ways to write each algebraic expression in words.

1. $4 + n$
2. $m - 9$
3. $\frac{g}{2}$
4. $4z$
5. Bob earns \$15 per hour. Write an expression for the amount of money he earns in h hours. **$15h$**
6. A soccer practice is 90 minutes long. Write an expression for the number of minutes left after m minutes have elapsed. **$90 - m$**

Evaluate each expression for $x = 3$, $y = 6$, and $z = 2$.

7. $y \div z$ **3**
8. xy **18**
9. $x + y$ **9**
10. $x - z$ **1**

1-2 Adding and Subtracting Real Numbers

Add or subtract.

11. $81 + (-15)$ **66**
12. $27 - 32$ **−5**
13. $2 - \left(-1\frac{1}{4}\right)$ **$3\frac{1}{4}$**
14. $-7 + (-14)$ **−21**
15. Brandon's bank statement shows a balance of −\$45.00. What will the balance be after Brandon deposits \$70.00? **\$25.00**

1-3 Multiplying and Dividing Real Numbers

Find the value of each expression if possible.

16. $9(-9)$ **−81**
17. $6 \div \frac{3}{5}$ **10**
18. $9.6 \div 0$ **undefined**
19. $\left(-\frac{1}{2}\right)\left(-\frac{1}{2}\right)$ **$\frac{1}{4}$**
20. Simon drove for $2\frac{1}{2}$ hours to get from his house to the beach. Simon averaged 55 miles per hour on the trip. What is the distance from Simon's house to the beach? **137.5 mi**

1-4 Powers and Exponents

Simplify each expression.

21. $(-3)^2$ **9**
22. -3^2 **−9**
23. $\left(-\frac{2}{3}\right)^3$ **$-\frac{8}{27}$**
24. $\left(-\frac{1}{2}\right)^5$ **$-\frac{1}{32}$**
25. The number of bytes in a kilobyte is 2 to the 10th power. Express this number in two ways. **2^{10}; 1024**

1-5 Roots and Real Numbers

Find each root.

26. $\sqrt{225}$ **15**
27. $-\sqrt{49}$ **−7**
28. $\sqrt[3]{8}$ **2**
29. $\sqrt{\frac{16}{25}}$ **$\frac{4}{5}$**
30. Mindy is building a patio that is in the shape of a square. The patio will cover 56 square yards. Find the length of a side of the patio to the nearest tenth of a yard. **7.5 yd**

Write all classifications that apply to each real number.

31. $\frac{1}{11}$
32. $\sqrt{12}$
33. $\sqrt{400}$
34. -6

31. $\mathbb{Q}$, repeating decimal
32. irrational number
33. $\mathbb{Q}$, terminating decimal, $\mathbb{Z}$, $\mathbb{W}$, $\mathbb{N}$
34. $\mathbb{Q}$, terminating decimal, $\mathbb{Z}$

READY TO GO ON? SECTION 1A

Organizer

Objective: Assess students' mastery of concepts and skills in Lessons 1-1 through 1-5.

Resources

Assessment Resources
Section 1A Quiz

Teacher One Stop™
Test & Practice Generator

INTERVENTION

Resources

***Ready to Go On? Intervention and Enrichment* Worksheets**

***Ready to Go On?* CD-ROM**

***Ready to Go On?* Online**

my.hrw.com

Answers

1–4. Possible answers given.

1. the sum of 4 and n; 4 increased by n
2. the difference of m and 9; 9 less than m
3. g divided by 2; the quotient of g and 2
4. 4 times z; the product of 4 and z

READY TO GO ON? Diagnose and Prescribe

Ready to Go On? Intervention	*Ready to Go On? Intervention*, Section 1A: Worksheets	CD-ROM	Online
Lesson 1-1	1-1 Intervention	Activity 1-1	Diagnose and Prescribe Online
Lesson 1-2	1-2 Intervention	Activity 1-2	
Lesson 1-3	1-3 Intervention	Activity 1-3	
Lesson 1-4	1-4 Intervention	Activity 1-4	
Lesson 1-5	1-5 Intervention	Activity 1-5	

***Ready to Go On? Enrichment*, Section 1A**

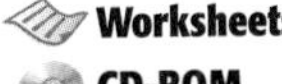
Worksheets
CD-ROM
Online

SECTION **1B**

The Tools of Algebra

One-Minute Section Planner

Lesson	Lab Resources	Materials
Lesson 1-6 Order of Operations • Use the order of operations to simplify expressions. ☑ SAT-10 ☐ NAEP ☑ ACT ☐ SAT ☐ SAT Subject Tests		
Lesson 1-7 Simplifying Expressions • Use the Commutative, Associative, and Distributive Properties to simplify expressions. • Combine like terms. ☑ SAT-10 ☐ NAEP ☑ ACT ☑ SAT ☐ SAT Subject Tests		**Optional** graphing calculator
Lesson 1-8 Introduction to Functions • Graph ordered pairs in the coordinate plane. • Graph functions from ordered pairs. ☑ SAT-10 ☐ NAEP ☑ ACT ☑ SAT ☐ SAT Subject Tests		**Optional** coordinate plane transparency

Note: If NAEP is checked, the content is tested on either the Grade 8 or Grade 12 NAEP assessment.

MK = *Manipulatives Kit*

Math Background

ORDER OF OPERATIONS

Lesson 1-6

The order of operations is part of the grammatical structure of mathematical language. It provides an agreed-upon sequence of steps for evaluating numerical and algebraic expressions. Note that although the order of operations establishes a unique value for the expression $25 - 18 - 3$ (namely, 4), it may be preferable to write such expressions using parentheses, $(25 - 18) - 3$, to avoid any possible confusion.

PROPERTIES

Lesson 1-7

Students may have been introduced to properties of addition and multiplication, such as the Commutative, Associative, and Distributive Properties, as early as the elementary grades. At that time, students may have wondered why an "obvious fact" such as $3 \times 4 = 4 \times 3$ requires the complicated name *Commutative Property of Multiplication.*

In algebra, these properties have a key role as part of the underlying logical system that makes it possible to simplify expressions and solve equations. Consider the steps in simplifying the expression $2(x + 3) + x$.

1. $2(x + 3) + x$
2. $= (2x + 6) + x$
3. $= 2x + (6 + x)$
4. $= 2x + (x + 6)$
5. $= (2x + x) + 6$
6. $= 3x + 6$

Although several of these steps would most likely be eliminated in a typical classroom presentation, the details motivate the need for *general* versions of the Commutative, Associative, and Distributive Properties. One can easily verify a specific case of the Distributive Property, such as $4(5 + 1) = 4 \cdot 5 + 4 \cdot 1$, by using simple arithmetic. However, to go from Step 1 to Step 2 in the above process, one must know that $2(x + 3) = 2x + 6$ for any arbitrary value of x. This is precisely what the Distributive Property states: $a(b + c) = ab + ac$ for all real values of a, b, and c. Similarly, Steps 3 and 4 illustrate applications of the Associative and Commutative Properties, respectively.

THE COORDINATE PLANE

Lesson 1-8

A number line is a straight line that extends indefinitely in both directions. One point on the line is labeled 0. Every other point can be located on the number line based on its distance from 0.

The two-dimensional analogue of a number line is the coordinate plane. The coordinate plane is created by the perpendicular intersection of a vertical number line and a horizontal number line. The number lines intersect at the point labeled 0 on both lines. This point of intersection is called the origin of the coordinate plane.

Points can be located on the coordinate plane by using ordered pairs of the form (x, y), where x indicates the horizontal directed distance from the origin and y indicates the vertical directed distance from the origin. Note that two pieces of information are needed to name a point on the plane, namely an x-coordinate and a y-coordinate. This makes sense because the plane is two-dimensional. In contrast, only one piece of information–a single real number–is needed to locate a point on a one-dimensional number line.

FUNCTIONS

Lesson 1-8

Functions are one of the fundamental ideas of algebra and a concept that students will investigate again and again in future mathematics courses. A *function* is a pairing of two quantities so that each input value corresponds to exactly one output value.

Functions are often compared to a machine that takes an input value and returns an output value. For example, consider a machine that takes the input values in the table and returns the corresponding outputs.

Input	4	5	12	53
Output	7	8	15	56

Based on the data in the table, a rule for the machine is "take the input value and add 3 to get the output value." By convention, input values are usually represented by the variable x, and output values are usually represented by the variable y. The function may be written as the equation $y = x + 3$.

1-6 Organizer

Pacing: Traditional 1 day
Block $\frac{1}{2}$ day

Objective: Use the order of operations to simplify expressions.

Online Edition
Tutorial Videos

Countdown Week 2

Power Presentations with PowerPoint®

Warm Up

Simplify.

1. 4^2 16 **2.** $|5 - 16|$ 11

3. -2^3 −8 **4.** $|3 - 7|$ 4

Translate each word phrase into a numerical or algebraic expression.

5. the product of 8 and 6 8×6

6. the difference of 10*y* and 4 $10y - 4$

Simplify each fraction.

7. $\frac{16}{2}$ 8 **8.** $\frac{8}{56}$ $\frac{1}{7}$

Also available on transparency

Math Humor

Q: Why are the parentheses wearing blue ribbons?

A: Because they always come first

1-6 Order of Operations

Objective
Use the order of operations to simplify expressions.

Vocabulary
order of operations

Who uses this?
Sports statisticians use the order of operations to calculate data. (See Example 5.)

A baseball player must run to first, second, and third bases before running back to home plate. In math, some tasks must be done in a certain order.

When a numerical or algebraic expression contains more than one operation symbol, the **order of operations** tells you which operation to perform first.

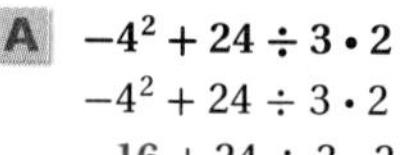

Order of Operations	
First:	Perform operations inside grouping symbols.
Second:	Simplify powers and roots.
Third:	Perform multiplication and division from left to right.
Fourth:	Perform addition and subtraction from left to right.

Grouping symbols include parentheses ( ), brackets [ ], and braces { }. If an expression contains more than one set of grouping symbols, simplify the expression inside the innermost set first. Follow the order of operations within that set of grouping symbols and then work outward.

EXAMPLE 1 Simplifying Numerical Expressions

Simplify each expression.

A $-4^2 + 24 \div 3 \cdot 2$

$-4^2 + 24 \div 3 \cdot 2$ *There are no grouping symbols.*
$-16 + 24 \div 3 \cdot 2$ *Simplify powers. The exponent applies only to the 4.*
$-16 + 8 \cdot 2$ *Divide.*
$-16 + 16$ *Multiply.*
0 *Add.*

B $4[25 - (5 - 2)^2]$

$4[25 - (5 - 2)^2]$ *There are two sets of grouping symbols.*
$4[25 - 3^2]$ *Perform the operation in the innermost set.*
$4[25 - 9]$ *Simplify powers within the brackets.*
$4 \cdot 16$ *Subtract within the brackets.*
64 *Multiply.*

Helpful Hint
The first letters of these words can help you remember the order of operations.

Please	Parentheses
Excuse	Exponents
My	Multiply/
Dear	Divide
Aunt	Add/
Sally	Subtract

CHECK IT OUT! Simplify each expression.

1a. $8 \div \frac{1}{2} \cdot 3$ **48** **1b.** $5.4 - 3^2 + 6.2$ **2.6** **1c.** $-20 \div [-2(4+1)]$ **2**

State Resources

go.hrw.com
State Resources Online
KEYWORD: MA7 Resources

1 Introduce

EXPLORATION

1-6 Order of Operations

You will need a graphing calculator for this Exploration.

1. Enter -4^2 on your calculator as shown. Then press [ENTER]. What is the result?
2. Now enter $(-4)^2$ on your calculator. What is the result this time?
3. How are the expressions -4^2 and $(-4)^2$ different?
4. Find the value of the following expression without using a calculator: $3^2 - 2 \cdot 4 + 5$. Compare your answer with those of other students. Did everyone get the same results?
5. Now find the value of $3^2 - 2 \cdot 4 + 5$ by entering the expression on your calculator as shown. How does the calculator's answer compare to your answer and those of your classmates?

THINK AND DISCUSS

6. Explain why everyone must agree on the order in which operations are performed when simplifying an expression.

Motivate

Write $15 - 5 + 3^2$ on the board. Ask students to simplify the expression and share their answers. If any students get different answers, discuss why a standard order of operations is important. If everyone gets the correct answer, change the expression to $(15 - 5 + 3)^2$ or $15 - (5 + 3)^2$ and use this as a basis for discussing how grouping symbols can affect the order of operations.

Explorations and answers are provided in *Alternate Openers: Explorations Transparencies.*

EXAMPLE 2 Evaluating Algebraic Expressions

Evaluate each expression for the given value of x.

A $21 - x + 2 \cdot 5$ for $x = 7$

$21 - x + 2 \cdot 5$	
$21 - 7 + 2 \cdot 5$	*First substitute 7 for x.*
$21 - 7 + 10$	*Multiply.*
$14 + 10$	*Subtract.*
24	*Add.*

B $5^2(30 - x)$ for $x = 24$

$5^2(30 - x)$	
$5^2(30 - 24)$	*First substitute 24 for x.*
$5^2(6)$	*Perform the operation inside the parentheses.*
$25(6)$	*Simplify powers.*
150	*Multiply.*

Evaluate each expression for the given value of x.

2a. $14 + x^2 \div 4$ for $x = 2$ **15** **2b.** $(x \cdot 2^2) \div (2 + 6)$ for $x = 6$ **3**

Fraction bars, radical symbols, and absolute-value symbols can also be used as grouping symbols. Remember that a fraction bar indicates division.

EXAMPLE 3 Simplifying Expressions with Other Grouping Symbols

Simplify each expression.

A $\dfrac{-22 - 2^2}{5 - 3}$

$\dfrac{(-22 - 2^2)}{(5 - 3)}$	*The fraction bar acts as a grouping symbol. Simplify the numerator and the denominator before dividing.*
$\dfrac{-22 - 4}{5 - 3}$	*Simplify the power in the numerator.*
$\dfrac{-26}{5 - 3}$	*Subtract to simplify the numerator.*
$\dfrac{-26}{2}$	*Subtract to simplify the denominator.*
-13	*Divide.*

B $|10 - 5^2| \div 5$

$|10 - 5^2| \div 5$	*The absolute-value symbols act as grouping symbols.*
$|10 - 25| \div 5$	*Simplify the power.*
$|-15| \div 5$	*Subtract within the absolute-value symbols.*
$15 \div 5$	*Write the absolute value of −15.*
3	*Divide.*

Helpful Hint

You may need to add grouping symbols to simplify expressions when using a scientific or graphing calculator. To simplify $\frac{2+3}{5-4}$ with a calculator, enter $(2 + 3) \div (5 - 4)$.

CHECK IT OUT! Simplify each expression.

3a. $\dfrac{5 + 2(-8)}{(-2)^3 - 3}$ **1** **3b.** $|4 - 7|^2 \div (-3)$ **−3** **3c.** $3\sqrt{50 - 1}$ **21**

COMMON ERROR ALERT

Students may always perform multiplication before division, or addition before subtraction. Tell students to write division as multiplication by the reciprocal, and subtraction as addition of the opposite. Then perform all multiplication from left to right or all addition from left to right.

Power Presentations with PowerPoint®

Additional Examples

Example 1

Simplify each expression.

A. $15 - 2 \cdot 3 + 1$ 10

B. $12 - 3^2 + 10 \div 2$ 8

C. $2.4 + 4[3^2 - 2(3 - 1.5)]$ 26.4

Example 2

Evaluate each expression for the given value of x.

A. $10 - x \cdot 6$ for $x = 3$ −8

B. $4^2(x + 3)$ for $x = -2$ 16

Example 3

Simplify each expression.

A. $\dfrac{2(-4) + 22}{4^2 - 9}$ 2

B. $3|4^2 + 8 \div 2|$ 60

INTERVENTION

Questioning Strategies

EXAMPLES 1–2

- How do you know which operation to perform first?

EXAMPLE 3

- What are two purposes of the fraction bar?

Reading Math Show how some symbols have more than one purpose. Parentheses can indicate multiplication and/or act as grouping symbols. The fraction bar is a grouping symbol and also can indicate division. The absolute-value bars are grouping symbols and indicate that the value will be nonnegative.

2 Teach

ENGLISH LANGUAGE LEARNERS

Guided Instruction

Before starting the lesson, review the rules for adding, subtracting, multiplying, and dividing real numbers. Suggest that students refer to the chart on page 40 when they are working the Check It Out problems.

Multiple Representations For **Example 3,** have students write the expressions in a calculator-ready format. This may mean adding parentheses to the expression.

Reaching All Learners

Through Cognitive Strategies

Have students think of a different mnemonic device to help them remember the order of operations. They could create a new catchphrase for PEMDAS, such as "Perfect Equations Might Delight Algebra Students."

Power Presentations with PowerPoint®

Additional Examples

Example 4

Translate each word phrase into a numerical or algebraic expression.

A. the sum of the quotient of 12 and −3 and the square root of 25 $\frac{12}{-3} + \sqrt{25}$

B. the difference of y and the product of 4 and $\frac{y}{2}$ $y - \left(4 \cdot \frac{y}{2}\right)$

Example 5

A shop offers gift-wrapping services at three price levels. The amount of money collected for wrapping gifts on a given day can be found using the expression $2B + 4S + 7D$. On Friday the shop wrapped 10 Basic packages B, 6 Super packages S, and 5 Deluxe packages D. Use the expression to find the amount of money collected for gift-wrapping on Friday. $79

INTERVENTION
Questioning Strategies

EXAMPLE 4

- How do you know when to use a grouping symbol?

EXAMPLE 5

- Why is it unreasonable to substitute negative values for the variables?

You may need to use grouping symbols when translating from words to numerical or algebraic expressions. Remember that operations inside grouping symbols are performed first.

EXAMPLE 4 Translating from Words to Math

Remember!

Look for words that imply mathematical operations.

difference → subtract
sum → add
product → multiply
quotient → divide

Translate each word phrase into a numerical or algebraic expression.

A **one half times the difference of −5 and 3**

$\frac{1}{2}(-5 - 3)$ *Use parentheses so that the difference is evaluated first.*

B **the square root of the quotient of −12 and n**

$\sqrt{\frac{-12}{n}}$ *Show the square root of a quotient.*

4. Translate the word phrase into a numerical or algebraic expression: the product of 6.2 and the sum of 9.4 and 8. **6.2(9.4 + 8)**

EXAMPLE 5 *Sports Application*

Hank Aaron's last season in the Major Leagues was in 1976. A player's total number of bases can be found using the expression $S + 2D + 3T + 4H$. Use the table to find Hank Aaron's total bases for 1976.

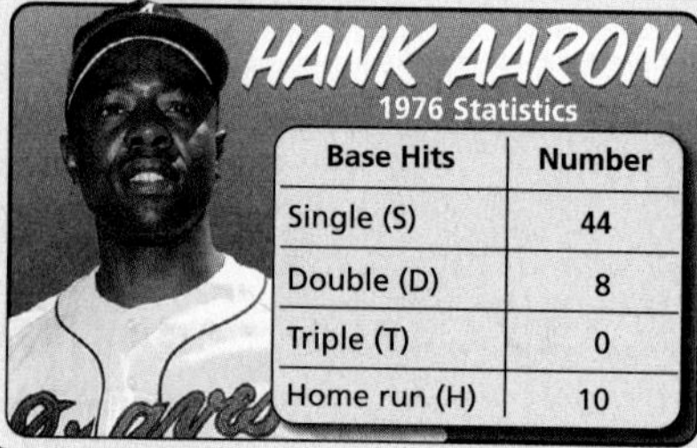

HANK AARON
1976 Statistics

Base Hits	Number
Single (S)	44
Double (D)	8
Triple (T)	0
Home run (H)	10

$S + 2D + 3T + 4H$

$44 + 2(8) + 3(0) + 4(10)$ *First substitute values for each variable.*

$44 + 16 + 0 + 40$ *Multiply.*

$60 + 0 + 40$ *Add from left to right.*

100 *Add.*

Hank Aaron's total number of bases for 1976 was 100.

5. Another formula for a player's total number of bases is Hits + $D + 2T + 3H$. Use this expression to find Hank Aaron's total bases for 1959, when he had 223 hits, 46 doubles, 7 triples, and 39 home runs. **400**

THINK AND DISCUSS

1. Explain whether you always perform addition before subtraction when simplifying a numerical or algebraic expression.

2. **GET ORGANIZED** Copy and complete the graphic organizer. In each box, show how grouping symbols can be placed so that the expression is equal to the number shown.

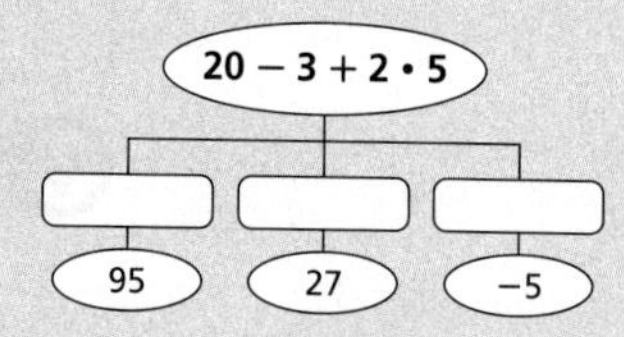

3 Close

Summarize

Review the order of operations. List all the possible grouping symbols, including fraction bars and the symbols for absolute value and square root. Emphasize that knowing and following the order of operations is necessary to the study of algebra and every other advanced math field.

ONGOING ASSESSMENT and INTERVENTION

***Diagnose Before* the Lesson**
1-6 Warm Up, TE p. 40

***Monitor During* the Lesson**
Check It Out! Exercises, SE pp. 40–42
Questioning Strategies, TE pp. 41–42

***Assess After* the Lesson**
1-6 Lesson Quiz, TE p. 45
Alternative Assessment, TE p. 45

Answers to *Think and Discuss*

1. Not always; subtraction should be performed before addition if it comes before addition from left to right or if it is within grouping symbols.
2. See p. A2.

1-6 Exercises

go.hrw.com
Homework Help Online
KEYWORD: MA7 1-6
Parent Resources Online
KEYWORD: MA7 Parent

GUIDED PRACTICE

1. **Vocabulary** Explain why the *order of operations* is necessary for simplifying numerical expressions. **Using the order of operations makes sure that everyone gets the same value for an expression.**

SEE EXAMPLE 1 p. 40

Simplify each expression.

2. $5 - 12 \div (-2)$ **11**
3. $30 - 5 \cdot 3$ **15**
4. $50 - 6 + 8$ **52**
5. $12 \div (-4)(3)$ **−9**
6. $(5 - 8)(3 - 9)$ **18**
7. $16 + [5 - (3 + 2^2)]$ **14**

SEE EXAMPLE 2 p. 41

Evaluate each expression for the given value of the variable.

8. $5 + 2x - 9$ for $x = 4$ **4**
9. $30 \div 2 - d$ for $d = 14$ **1**
10. $51 - 91 + g$ for $g = 20$ **−20**
11. $2(3 + n)$ for $n = 4$ **14**
12. $4(b - 4)^2$ for $b = 5$ **4**
13. $12 + [20(5 - k)]$ for $k = 1$ **92**

SEE EXAMPLE 3 p. 41

Simplify each expression.

14. $24 \div |4 - 10|$ **4**
15. $4.5 - \sqrt{2(4.5)}$ **1.5**
16. $5(2) + 16 \div |-4|$ **14**
17. $\frac{0 - 24}{6 + 2}$ **−3**
18. $\frac{2 + 3(6)}{2^2}$ **5**
19. $-44 \div \sqrt{12 \div 3}$ **−22**

SEE EXAMPLE 4 p. 42

Translate each word phrase into a numerical or algebraic expression.

20. 5 times the absolute value of the sum of s and -2 **$5|s + (-2)|$**
21. the product of 12 and the sum of -2 and 6 **$12(-2 + 6)$**
22. 14 divided by the sum of 52 and -3 **$\frac{14}{52 + (-3)}$**

SEE EXAMPLE 5 p. 42

23. **Geometry** The surface area of a cylinder can be found using the expression $2\pi r(h + r)$. Find the surface area of the cylinder shown. (Use 3.14 for π and give your final answer rounded to the nearest tenth.) **188.4 ft²**

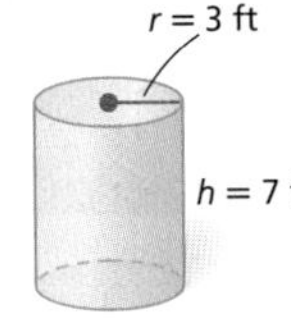

PRACTICE AND PROBLEM SOLVING

Independent Practice

For Exercises	See Example
24–32	1
33–41	2
42–49	3
50–53	4
54	5

Extra Practice
Skills Practice p. S5
Application Practice p. S28

Simplify each expression.

24. $3 + 4(-5)$ **−17**
25. $20 - 4 + 5 - 2$ **19**
26. $41 + 12 \div 2$ **47**
27. $3(-9) + (-2)(-6)$ **−15**
28. $10^2 \div (10 - 20)$ **−10**
29. $(6 + 2 \cdot 3) \div (9 - 7)^2$ **3**
30. $-9 - (-18) + 6$ **15**
31. $15 \div (2 - 5)$ **−5**
32. $5(1 - 2) - (3 - 2)$ **−6**

Evaluate each expression for the given value of the variable.

33. $-6(3 - p)$ for $p = 7$ **24**
34. $5 + (r + 2)^2$ for $r = 4$ **41**
35. $13 - [3 + (j - 12)]$ for $j = 5$ **17**
36. $(-4 - a)^2$ for $a = -3$ **1**
37. $7 - (21 - h)^2$ for $h = 25$ **−9**
38. $10 + [8 \div (q - 3)]$ for $q = 2$ **2**
39. $(4r - 2) + 7$ for $r = 3$ **17**
40. $-2(11b - 3)$ for $b = 5$ **−104**
41. $7x(3 + 2x)$ for $x = -1$ **−7**

Simplify each expression.

42. $-4|2.5 - 6|$ **−14**
43. $\frac{8 - 8}{2 - 1}$ **0**
44. $\frac{3 + |8 - 10|}{2}$ **$\frac{5}{2}$**
45. $\sqrt{3^2 - 5} \div 8$ **$\frac{1}{4}$**
46. $\frac{-18 - 36}{-9}$ **6**
47. $\frac{6|5 - 7|}{14 - 2}$ **1**
48. $\sqrt{5^2 - 4^2}$ **3**
49. $(-6 + 24) \div |-3|$ **6**

1-6 Exercises

Assignment Guide

Assign *Guided Practice* exercises as necessary.

If you finished Examples **1–2**
Basic 24–41, 55
Average 24–41, 55, 66
Advanced 24–32 even, 33–41 55–59, 62–64

If you finished Examples **1–5**
Basic 24–55, 60, 65, 66, 68–70, 78–88
Average 24–56, 58, 60, 61, 65–73, 78–88
Advanced 24–40 even, 42–88

Homework Quick Check
Quickly check key concepts.
Exercises: 28, 36, 42, 50, 54, 55

Visual For exercises like **Exercises 20–22,** suggest that students copy the word phrases onto their paper and then circle each phrase of the form "the ______ of *x* and *y*." Then they should write the appropriate mathematical symbol over the word for the operation. For example:

English Language Learners

one-half (the sum of 5 and −4) [+ written over "sum"]

State Resources

go.hrw.com
State Resources Online
KEYWORD: MA7 Resources

Exercise 65 involves using the formula for the surface area of a prism. This exercise prepares students for the Multi-Step Test Prep on page 60.

Answers

61. Parentheses are not needed, because the order of operations tells you to do multiplication before addition.

65b. Each pair of opposite faces are the same size, so to find the surface area of the prism, multiply the areas of the top, front, and side by 2, and then add the 3 products.

c. They should be equal because the expression in part b is another way of adding all 6 faces of the prism.

Translate each word phrase into a numerical or an algebraic expression.

50. the product of 7 and the sum of 2 and d **$7(2 + d)$**
51. the difference of 3 and the quotient of 2 and 5 **$3 - \frac{2}{5}$**
52. the square root of the sum of 5 and −4 **$\sqrt{5 + (-4)}$**
53. the difference of 8 and the absolute value of the product of 3 and 5 **$8 - |3 \cdot 5|$**

54. **Geometry** The perimeter of a rectangle can be found using the expression $2(\ell + w)$. Find the perimeter of the rectangle shown. **24 in.**

$w = 4$ in.

$\ell = 8$ in.

55. Simplify each expression.
    a. $50 + 10 \div 2$ **55**
    b. $50 \cdot 10 - 2$ **498**
    c. $50 \cdot 10 \div 2$ **250**
    d. $50 \div 10 \cdot 2$ **10**
    e. $50 - 10 \cdot 2$ **30**
    f. $50 + 10 \cdot 2$ **70**

Translate each word phrase into a numerical or algebraic expression.

56. the difference of 8 and the product of 4 and n **$8 - 4n$**
57. 2 times the sum of 9 and the opposite of x **$2[9 + (-x)]$**
58. two-thirds of the difference of −2 and 8 **$\frac{2}{3}(-2 - 8)$**
59. the square root of 7 divided by the product of 3 and 10 **$\frac{\sqrt{7}}{3 \cdot 10}$**

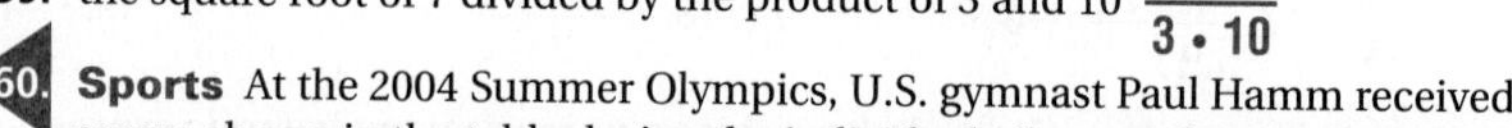

LINK Sports

In 2004, Paul Hamm became the first American to win a gold medal in the men's all-around gymnastics competition at the Olympics. He won by a margin of 0.012 point.

60. **Sports** At the 2004 Summer Olympics, U.S. gymnast Paul Hamm received the scores shown in the table during the individual all-around competition.

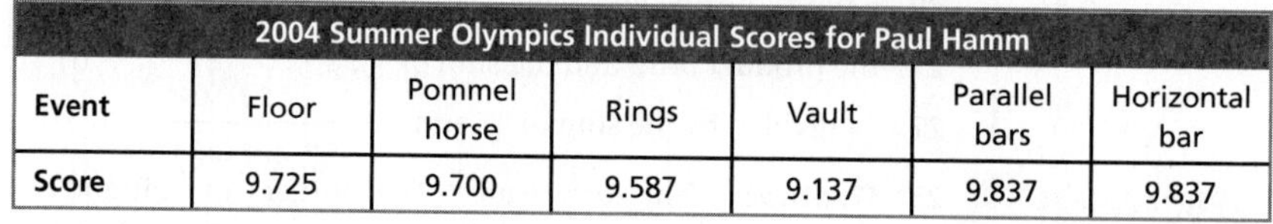

2004 Summer Olympics Individual Scores for Paul Hamm

Event	Floor	Pommel horse	Rings	Vault	Parallel bars	Horizontal bar
Score	9.725	9.700	9.587	9.137	9.837	9.837

a. Write a numerical expression to show the average of Hamm's scores. (*Hint:* The average of a set of values is the sum of the values divided by the number of values.) **$\frac{57.823}{6}$**

b. Simplify the expression to find Hamm's average score to the nearest thousandth. **9.637**

61. **Critical Thinking** Are parentheses required when translating the word phrase "the sum of 8 and the product of 3 and 2" into a numerical phrase? Explain.

Translate each word phrase into a numerical expression. Then simplify.

62. the sum of 8 and the product of −3 and 5 **$8 + (-3 \cdot 5) = -7$**
63. the difference of the product of 3 and 5 and the product of 6 and 2 **$3 \cdot 5 - 6 \cdot 2 = 3$**
64. the product of $\frac{2}{3}$ and the absolute value of the difference of 3 and −12 **$\frac{2}{3}|3 - (-12)| = 10$**

65. This problem will prepare you for the Multi-Step Test Prep on page 60.
    a. Find the area of each face of the prism. Find the sum of these areas to find the total surface area of the prism. **94 in²**
    b. The total surface area of a prism is described by the expression $2(\ell w) + 2(\ell h) + 2(wh)$. Explain how this expression relates to the sum you found in part **a**.
    c. Use the expression above to find the total surface area of the prism. Explain why your answers to parts **a** and **c** should be equal.

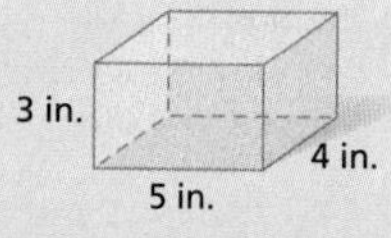

1-6 PRACTICE A
1-6 PRACTICE C
1-6 PRACTICE B

Simplify each expression.

1. $18 - 12 + 4^2$ **22**
2. $5 \cdot 3 + 2(4)$ **23**
3. $-2[7 + 6(3 - 5)]$ **10**
4. $-7 - (2^4 \div 8)$ **−9**
5. $-6 \cdot 3 + |-3(-4 + 2^3)|$ **−6**
6. $\frac{-16 + 4}{2(\sqrt{13 - 4})}$ **−2**

Evaluate each expression for the given value of the variable.

7. $3 - y^2 + 7$ for $y = 5$ **−15**
8. $-3(x + 12 \cdot 2)$ for $x = -8$ **−48**
9. $(m + 6) \div (2 - 5)$ for $m = 9$ **−5**
10. $-5t + 12 - \frac{1}{2}t$ for $t = -10$ **67**

Translate each word phrase into a numerical or algebraic expression.

11. the product of 6 and the sum of 3 and 20 **$6(3 + 20)$**
12. the absolute value of the difference of m and −15 **$|m - (-15)|$**
13. the quotient of −18 and the sum of −2 and d **$\frac{-18}{-2 + d}$**

Degrees Fahrenheit F can be converted to degrees Celsius C using the expression $\frac{5}{9}(F - 32)$. Degrees Celsius can be converted to degrees Fahrenheit using the expression $\frac{9}{5}C + 32$.

14. The hottest recorded day in Florida history was 109°F, which occurred on June 29, 1931 in Monticello. Convert this temperature to degrees Celsius. Round your answer to the nearest tenth of a degree. **42.8°C**
15. The coldest recorded day in Florida history was about −18.9°C, which occurred on February 13, 1899 in the city of Tallahassee. Convert this temperature to degrees Fahrenheit. Round your answer to the nearest tenth of a degree. **−2.0°F**

1-6 READING STRATEGIES

You can remember the correct order of operations by using the mnemonic **P**lease **E**xcuse **M**y **D**ear **A**unt **S**ally. The first letter of each word in the phrase represents an operation, as shown below.

1. **P**arentheses — **P**lease
2. **E**xponents — **E**xcuse
3. **M**ultiplication — **M**y
   Division — **D**ear
4. **A**ddition — **A**unt
   Subtraction — **S**ally

Notice the order used in the example below.
$6^2 \div (7 - 4) + 8 \cdot 2$
$6^2 \div 3 + 8 \cdot 2$ *Parentheses*
$36 \div 3 + 8 \cdot 2$ *Exponents*
$12 + 16$ *Multiplication and Division left to right*
28 *Addition and Subtraction left to right*

Make up your own mnemonic for remembering the order of operations. It can be funny, serious, creative, or personal. Just make sure it's something that YOU will remember.

P ____________________
E ____________________
M ____________________
D ____________________
A ____________________
S ____________________

Use your mnemonic to simplify the following expressions.

1. $15 - 4 + 2^3$ **19**
2. $6 - (12 + 9) \div 3$ **−1**
3. $-5(3 + 7^2 - 44)$ **−40**
4. $2[8 - (4 + 1)]$ **6**
5. $4^2[4(3^3 - 1 \cdot 2]$ **1600**
6. $\frac{-5 - 13}{-3^2}$ **2**

1-6 RETEACH

When an expression contains more than one operation, the operations must be performed in a certain order.

I. Evaluate powers (exponents).
II. Perform multiplication and division in order from left to right.
III. Perform addition and subtraction in order from left to right.

Simplify $4^2 + 7 - 2 \cdot 5 + 3$.

$4^2 + 7 - 2 \cdot 5 + 3$ *Identify powers.*
$16 + 7 - 2 \cdot 5 + 3$ *Evaluate 4^2.*
$16 + 7 - 2 \cdot 5 + 3$ *Identify multiplication and division.*
$16 + 7 - 10 + 3$ *Evaluate $2 \cdot 5$.*
$23 - 10 + 3$ *Start at the left and perform each addition and subtraction in order.*
$13 + 3$
16

Fill in the blanks to simplify each expression.

1. $3 + 5 \cdot 4 - 2$; $3 + 20 - 2$; $23 - 2$; **21**
2. $20 - 4^2 + 3$; $20 - 16 + 3$; $4 + 3$; **7**
3. $6 + 12 \div 4 - 8$; $6 + 3 - 8$; $9 - 8$; **1**

Simplify each expression.

4. $6 \div 2 \cdot 4 - 3$ **9**
5. $18 \div 3^2 - 5 + 2$ **−1**
6. $3 + 5 \cdot 3 - 8 \div 2$ **14**
7. $3 + 3 \div 3 + 3$ **7**
8. $7^2 + 4^2 \cdot 3$ **97**
9. $6 + 10 \div 2 \cdot 5 - 1$ **30**

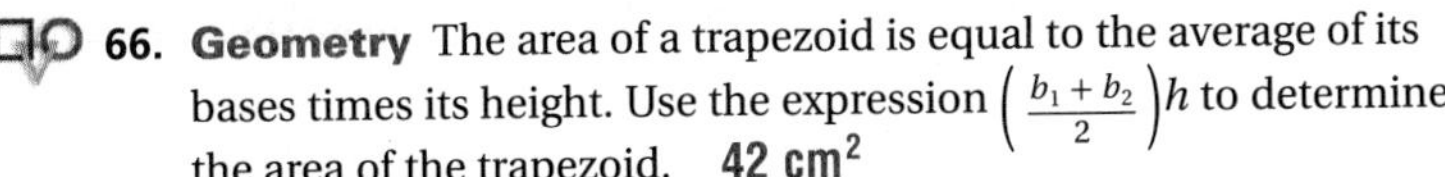

66. **Geometry** The area of a trapezoid is equal to the average of its bases times its height. Use the expression $\left(\frac{b_1 + b_2}{2}\right)h$ to determine the area of the trapezoid. **42 cm²**

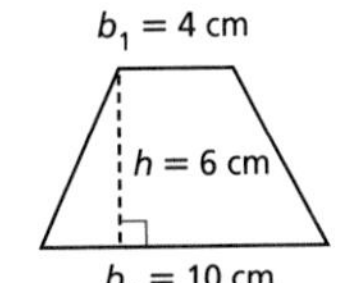

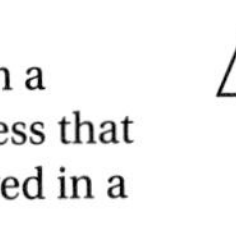

67. **Write About It** Many everyday processes must be done in a certain order to be completed successfully. Describe a process that requires several steps, and tell why the steps must be followed in a certain order.

TEST PREP

68. Cara's family rented a car for their 3-day vacation to the Grand Canyon. They paid $29.00 per day and $0.12 for each mile driven. Which expression represents Cara's family's cost to rent the car for 3 days and drive 318 miles?

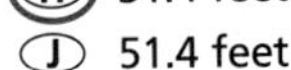

Ⓐ 29 + 0.12(318) | **Ⓒ 29(3) + 0.12(318)**
Ⓑ 29 + 3 + 0.12 + 318 | Ⓓ 3[9 + 0.12(318)]

69. The perimeter of the Norman window shown is approximated by the expression 2(3 + 8) + 3.14(3). Which is the closest approximation of the perimeter of the window?

Ⓕ 23.4 feet | **Ⓗ 31.4 feet**
Ⓖ 28.4 feet | Ⓙ 51.4 feet

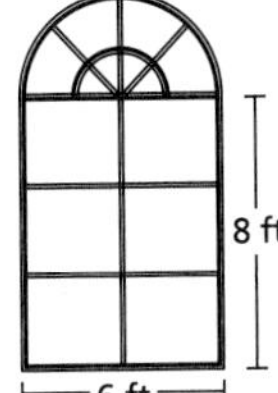

70. **Gridded Response** Simplify $\sqrt{\frac{54 - (-2)(5)}{20 - 4^2}}$. **4**

CHALLENGE AND EXTEND

Simplify each expression.

71. $\frac{3 + 9 \cdot 2}{2 - 3^2}$ **−3** 72. $\left[(-6 \cdot 4) \div (-6) \cdot 4\right]^2$ **256** 73. $\sqrt{\frac{8 + 10^2}{13 + (-10)}}$ **6**

74. Use the numbers 2, 4, 5, and 8 to write an expression that has a value of 5. You may use any operations, and you must use each of the numbers at least once.

74. Possible answer: 2 • 4 + 5 − 8

75. Use the numbers 2, 5, 6, and 9 to write an expression that has a value of 1. You may use any operations, and you must use each of the numbers at least once.

75. Possible answer: 2(9 − 6) − 5

76. If the value of $(\otimes + 5)^2$ is 81, what is the value of $(\otimes + 5)^2 + 1$? **82**

77. If the value of $(\otimes + 1)^2 - 3$ is 22, what is the value of $(\otimes + 1)^2 - 5$? **20**

SPIRAL REVIEW

Identify each angle as acute, right, obtuse, or straight. *(Previous course)*

78. 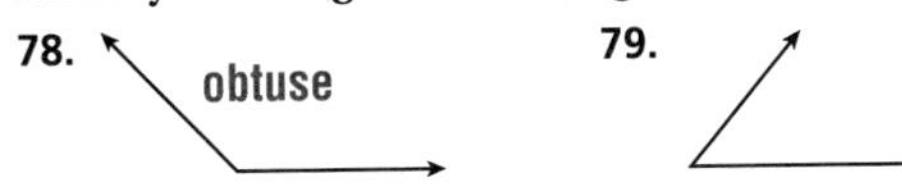 **obtuse** 79. 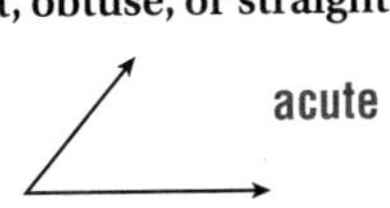 **acute** 80. 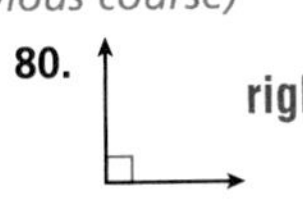 **right**

Add or subtract. *(Lesson 1-2)*

81. 51 − (−49) **100** 82. $-5 + \left(-1\frac{1}{3}\right)$ **$-6\frac{1}{3}$** 83. −3 + (−8) **−11** 84. 2.9 − 5.3 **−2.4**

Find each square root. *(Lesson 1-5)*

85. $\sqrt{64}$ **8** 86. $\sqrt{324}$ **18** 87. $\sqrt{\frac{36}{49}}$ **$\frac{6}{7}$** 88. $-\sqrt{121}$ **−11**

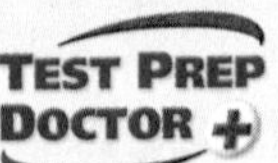

TEST PREP DOCTOR In **Exercise 70,** students can eliminate answer choices **F** and **J** by estimating the perimeter of the window.

Answers

67. Possible answer: To make a sandwich, you need to get out the ingredients, put the ingredients on either slice of bread, and then put the two slices together. You would not want to put the second slice of bread on top before putting the ingredients in the middle.

Journal

Have students describe what might happen if there were no standard order of operations. Require them to include formulas used in science or geometry.

ALTERNATIVE ASSESSMENT

Have students write a problem that includes at least three of the following: parentheses, exponents, multiplication, division, addition, and subtraction. Have them explain their step-by-step solution to the problem.

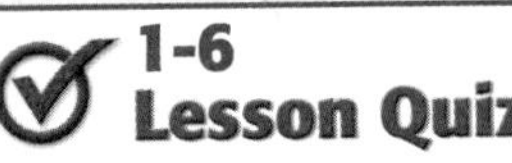

Power Presentations with PowerPoint®

1-6 Lesson Quiz

Simplify each expression.

1. $2[5 \div (-6 - 4)]$ −1
2. $\frac{5^2 - (5 + 4)}{|4 - 8|}$ 4
3. $5 \times 8 - 4 + 16 \div 2^2$ 40

Translate each word phrase into a numerical or algebraic expression.

4. 3 times the sum of −5 and n $3(-5 + n)$
5. the quotient of the difference of 34 and 9 and the square root of 25 $\frac{34 - 9}{\sqrt{25}}$
6. The volume of a storage box can be found using the expression $\ell w(w + 2)$. Find the volume of the box if $\ell = 3$ feet and $w = 2$ feet. 24 cubic feet

Also available on transparency

1-6 PROBLEM SOLVING

Write the correct answer.

1. A can of soup is in the shape of a cylinder with radius 3.8 cm and height 11 cm. What is the surface area of the can to the nearest tenth? Use 3.14 for π. (Hint: The expression $2\pi r^2 + 2\pi rh$ represents the surface area of a cylinder, where r is the radius and h is the height.)

$r = 3.8$ cm, $h = 11$ cm, Soup

353.2 cm²

2. One Boston household used the following amounts of electricity to run its heating system during the winter.

Month	Kilowatt-Hours Used
December	1500
January	1463
February	2260

Write an expression that can be used to find the average number of kilowatt hours used. Then simplify the expression.

Possible answer:
(1500 + 1463 + 2260) ÷ 3
1741

3. In a polygon with n sides, the sum of the measures of the interior angles is $180(n - 2)°$. What is the sum of the measures of the interior angles of a hexagon?

720°

4. In a regular polygon with n sides, the measure of each interior angle is $\frac{180(n-2)°}{n}$. What is the measure of an interior angle of an octagon?

135°

Select the best answer.

5. Anthony had 10 packages of markers. Each package contained 8 markers. He gave his 3 best friends 2 packages each. Which expression shows how many markers he kept for himself?
   A 10 • 8 − 10 • 3 • 2
   B 8(10 − 3 • 2)
   C 10 • 8 − 3 • 2
   D 8(10 + 3 • 2)

6. The area of the wall hanging below can be approximated by simplifying $14^2 + \frac{1}{2} \cdot 14 \cdot 8 + \frac{1}{2}(3.14)(7^2)$.

8 in.
14 in.

Which is closest to the area of the wall hanging?
   F 160.93 sq in. **H 328.93 sq in.**
   G 273.98 sq in. J 372.78 sq in.

7. Each month, Mrs. Li pays her phone company $28 for phone service, and $0.07 per minute for long distance calls. Which expression represents her bill for a month in which long distance calls totaled 4 hours?
   A 4[28 + 60(0.07)]
   B 28 + 4(60)(0.07)
   C 28 + 0.07 + 4
   D 28 + 0.07(4)

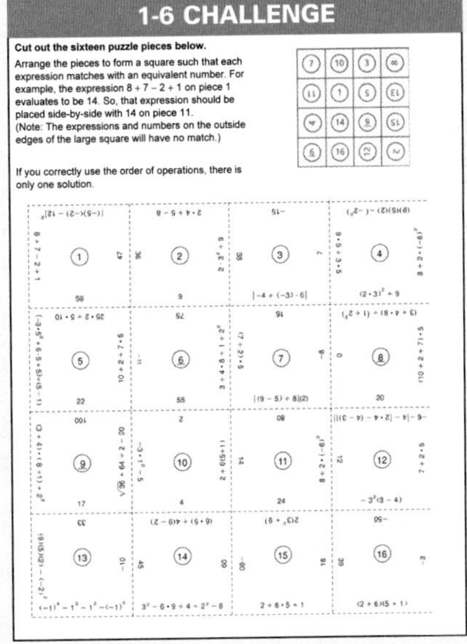

1-6 CHALLENGE

Cut out the sixteen puzzle pieces below.

Arrange the pieces to form a square such that each expression matches with an equivalent number. For example, the expression 8 + 7 − 2 + 1 on piece 1 evaluates to be 14. So, that expression should be placed side-by-side with 14 on piece 11. (Note: The expressions and numbers on the outside edges of the large square will have no match.)

If you correctly use the order of operations, there is only one solution.

1-7 Organizer

Pacing: Traditional 1 day
Block $\frac{1}{2}$ day

Objectives: Use the Commutative, Associative, and Distributive Properties to simplify expressions.

Combine like terms.

Online Edition
Tutorial Videos

Countdown Week 2

Power Presentations with PowerPoint®

Warm Up

Add.

1. 427 + 35 462

2. 1.06 + 0.74 1.80

3. $6\frac{1}{6} + 3\frac{5}{6}$ 10

Multiply.

4. 25(8) 200

5. 1.3(22) 28.6

6. $4\frac{2}{5}\left(3\frac{1}{3}\right)$ $14\frac{2}{3}$

Also available on transparency

Math Humor

Q: Why was the math teacher upset with Cupid?

A: He kept changing "like terms" to "love terms."

State Resources

go.hrw.com
State Resources Online
KEYWORD: MA7 Resources

1-7 Simplifying Expressions

Objectives
Use the Commutative, Associative, and Distributive Properties to simplify expressions.

Combine like terms.

Vocabulary
term
like terms
coefficient

Who uses this?
Triathletes can use the Commutative, Associative, and Distributive Properties to calculate overall times mentally.

A triathlon is an endurance race that includes swimming, biking, and running. The winner is determined by adding the times for each of the three events.

The Commutative and Associative Properties of Addition and Multiplication allow you to rearrange an expression to simplify it.

Properties of Addition and Multiplication

WORDS	NUMBERS	ALGEBRA
Commutative Property You can add numbers in any order and multiply numbers in any order.	$2 + 7 = 7 + 2$ $3 \cdot 9 = 9 \cdot 3$	$a + b = b + a$ $ab = ba$
Associative Property When you are only adding or only multiplying, you can group any of the numbers together.	$(6 + 8) + 2 = 6 + (8 + 2)$ $(7 \cdot 4) \cdot 5 = 7 \cdot (4 \cdot 5)$	$(a + b) + c = a + (b + c)$ $(ab)c = a(bc)$

EXAMPLE 1 Using the Commutative and Associative Properties

Simplify each expression.

A $4 \cdot 9 \cdot 25$

$9 \cdot 4 \cdot 25$ *Use the Commutative Property of Multiplication.*

$9 \cdot (4 \cdot 25)$ *Use the Associative Property of Multiplication to make groups of compatible numbers.*

$9 \cdot 100$

900

B $25 + 48 + 75$

$25 + 75 + 48$ *Use the Commutative Property of Addition.*

$(25 + 75) + 48$ *Use the Associative Property of Addition to make groups of compatible numbers.*

$100 + 48$

148

Helpful Hint
Compatible numbers help you do math mentally. Try to make multiples of 5 or 10. They are simpler to use when multiplying.

CHECK IT OUT! Simplify each expression.

1a. $15\frac{1}{3} + 4 + 1\frac{2}{3}$ **21** **1b.** $410 + 58 + 90 + 2$ **560** **1c.** $\frac{1}{2} \cdot 7 \cdot 8$ **28**

1 Introduce

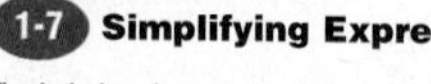

1-7 Simplifying Expressions

The desks in a classroom are arranged in two sections as shown.

1. Write a product that gives the number of desks in Section A.
2. Write a product that gives the number of desks in Section B.
3. Now add the two products to get an expression for the total number of desks.
4. There is another way to find the total number of desks. First write a sum to find the total number of rows in the classroom. Then multiply this sum by the number of desks in each row.
5. Verify that the expressions you wrote in Steps 3 and 4 give the same total number of desks.
6. The Distributive Property states that $a(b + c) = ab + ac$. Explain how the above problem is an example of this property.

Section A
Section B

THINK AND DISCUSS

7. **Describe** how you can use the Distributive Property to simplify $7(8 + 4)$ in two different ways.
8. **Discuss** whether the Distributive Property works with subtraction. That is, it is true that $a(b - c) = ab - ac$?

Motivate

Write 18 + 17 + 2 + 3 on the board. Show students how to simplify the expression using the order of operations (adding from left to right). Then show students that changing the order and grouping the numbers in a different way can make it easier to perform the operations mentally: (18 + 2) + (17 + 3) = 20 + 20 = 40. Tell students that this lesson will introduce properties that can make it easier to do mental math.

Explorations and answers are provided in *Alternate Openers: Explorations Transparencies.*

Student to Student

Commutative and Associative Properties

Lorna Anderson
Pearson High School

I used to get the Commutative and Associative Properties mixed up.

To remember the Commutative Property, I think of people commuting back and forth from work. When people commute, they move. I can move the numbers around without changing the value of the expression.

For the Associative Property, I think of associating with my friends. They're the group I hang out with. In math, it's about how numbers are grouped.

The Distributive Property is used with addition to simplify expressions.

Distributive Property

WORDS	NUMBERS	ALGEBRA
You can multiply a number by a sum or multiply each addend by the number and then add. The result is the same.	$3(4 + 8) = 3(4) + 3(8)$	$a(b + c) = ab + ac$

The Distributive Property also works with subtraction because subtraction is the same as adding the opposite.

EXAMPLE 2 **Using the Distributive Property with Mental Math**

Helpful Hint

Break the greater factor into a sum that contains a multiple of 10.

Write each product using the Distributive Property. Then simplify.

A $15(103)$

$15(100 + 3)$ — *Rewrite 103 as 100 + 3.*
$15(100) + 15(3)$ — *Use the Distributive Property.*
$1500 + 45$ — *Multiply.*
1545 — *Add.*

B $6(19)$

$6(20 - 1)$ — *Rewrite 19 as 20 − 1.*
$6(20) - 6(1)$ — *Use the Distributive Property.*
$120 - 6$ — *Multiply.*
114 — *Subtract.*

Write each product using the Distributive Property. Then simplify.

2a. $9(52)$ $9(50) + 9(2) = 468$
2b. $12(98)$ $12(100) - 12(2) = 1176$
2c. $7(34)$ $7(30) + 7(4) = 238$

The **terms** of an expression are the parts to be added or subtracted. **Like terms** are terms that contain the same variables raised to the same powers. Constants are also like terms.

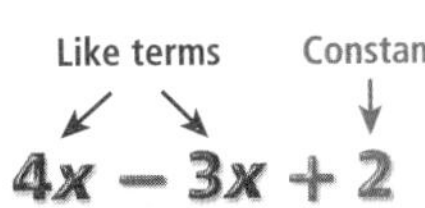

Power Presentations with PowerPoint®

Additional Examples

Example 1

Simplify each expression.

A. $\frac{1}{3}(5)(33)$ 55

B. $45 + 16 + 55 + 4$ 120

Example 2

Write each product using the Distributive Property. Then simplify.

A. $5(59)$ $5(60 - 1) = 295$

B. $8(33)$ $8(30 + 3) = 264$

INTERVENTION

Questioning Strategies

EXAMPLE 1

- How do you decide which numbers to group together?

EXAMPLE 2

- How do you decide how to "break up" a factor in order to use the Distributive Property?

Reading Math The word *distribute* means "to share among many" or "to deliver to members of a group." Point out to students how the everyday meaning is similar to the mathematical meaning.

ENGLISH LANGUAGE LEARNERS

2 Teach

Guided Instruction

Show examples of the properties with real numbers before showing their algebraic forms. Reinforce the fact that the variables and exponents do not change when combining like terms.

Reaching All Learners

Through Auditory Cues

Have students replace variables with the names of everyday objects to determine whether terms can be combined.

$5a + 3c$
Read: 5 apples + 3 chairs
(cannot be combined)

$5a + 3a$
Read: 5 apples + 3 apples = 8 apples
$5a + 3a = 8a$

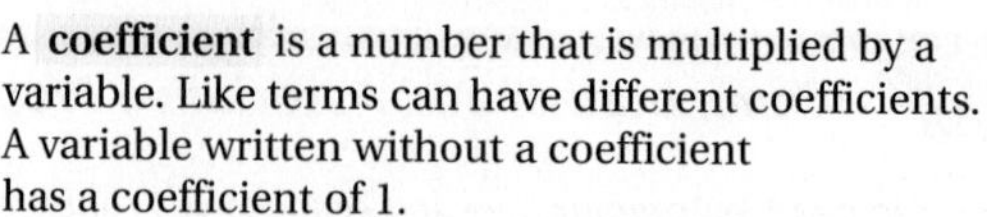

A **coefficient** is a number that is multiplied by a variable. Like terms can have different coefficients. A variable written without a coefficient has a coefficient of 1.

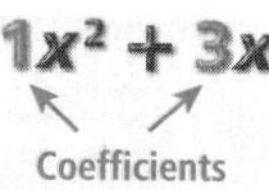

Using the Distributive Property can help you combine like terms. You can factor out the common factor to simplify the expression.

$7x^2 - 4x^2 = (7 - 4)x^2$ *Factor out x^2 from both terms.*
$= (3)x^2$ *Perform operations in parentheses.*
$= 3x^2$

Notice that you can combine like terms by adding or subtracting the coefficients and keeping the variables and exponents the same.

EXAMPLE 3 Combining Like Terms

Simplify each expression by combining like terms.

A $12x + 30x$

$12x + 30x$ *12x and 30x are like terms.*
$42x$ *Add the coefficients.*

B $6.8y^2 - y^2$

$6.8y^2 - y^2$ *A variable without a coefficient has a coefficient of 1.*
$6.8y^2 - 1y^2$ *$6.8y^2$ and $1y^2$ are like terms.*
$5.8y^2$ *Subtract the coefficients.*

C $4n + 11n^2$

$4n + 11n^2$ *4n and $11n^2$ are not like terms. Do not combine.*

Caution!
Add or subtract only the coefficients.
$6.8y^2 - y^2 \neq 6.8$

CHECK IT OUT! Simplify each expression by combining like terms.

3a. $16p + 84p$ **100p** **3b.** $-20t - 8.5t$ **−28.5t** **3c.** $3m^2 + m^3$ **$3m^2 + m^3$**

EXAMPLE 4 Simplifying Algebraic Expressions

Simplify $2(x + 6) + 3x$. Justify each step with an operation or property.

	Procedure	Justification
1.	$2(x + 6) + 3x$	
2.	$2(x) + 2(6) + 3x$	Distributive Property
3.	$2x + 12 + 3x$	Multiply.
4.	$2x + 3x + 12$	Commutative Property of Addition
5.	$(2x + 3x) + 12$	Associative Property of Addition
6.	$5x + 12$	Combine like terms.

CHECK IT OUT! Simplify each expression. Justify each step with an operation or property.

4a. $6(x - 4) + 9$ **4b.** $-12x - 5x + 3a + x$

Power Presentations with PowerPoint®

Additional Examples

Example 3

Simplify each expression by combining like terms.

A. $72p - 25p$ $47p$

B. $\frac{3}{4}x^4 + x^4$ $\frac{7}{4}x^4$

C. $0.5m + 2.5n$ $0.5m + 2.5n$

Example 4

Simplify $14x + 4(2 + x)$. Justify each step with an operation or property.

$14x + 4(2 + x)$
$14x + 4(2) + 4(x)$ Distrib. Prop.
$14x + 8 + 4x$ Multiply.
$14x + 4x + 8$ Comm. Prop. (Add.)
$(14x + 4x) + 8$ Assoc. Prop. (Add.)
$18x + 8$ Combine like terms.

Also available on transparency

INTERVENTION
Questioning Strategies

EXAMPLE 3

- What must be true about the coefficients of two like terms if adding them results in 0?

EXAMPLE 4

- How do you decide which property to use first?

Teaching Tip **Multiple Representations** In **Example 3,** show students that they should get the same value when the original expression and simplified expression are evaluated for the same value of the variable.

3 Close

Summarize

Ask students which property is illustrated in each equation.

$m + (n + p) = (m + n) + p$ Assoc. (Add.)
$m(n + p) = mn + mp$ Distributive
$m + n = n + m$ Comm. (Add.)

ONGOING ASSESSMENT and INTERVENTION

***Diagnose Before* the Lesson**
1-7 Warm Up, TE p. 46

***Monitor During* the Lesson**
Check It Out! Exercises, SE pp. 46–48
Questioning Strategies, TE pp. 47–48

***Assess After* the Lesson**
1-7 Lesson Quiz, TE p. 51
Alternative Assessment, TE p. 51

Answers to *Check It Out!*

4a. $6(x - 4) + 9$
$6(x) - 6(4) + 9$ Dist. Prop.
$6x - 24 + 9$ Multiply.
$6x - 15$ Combine like terms.

4b. $-12x - 5x + 3a + x$
$-12x - 5x + x + 3a$ Comm. Prop. of Add.
$-16x + 3a$ Combine like terms.

THINK AND DISCUSS

1. Tell which property is described by this sentence: When adding three numbers, you can add the first number to the sum of the second and third numbers, or you can add the third number to the sum of the first and second numbers.

2. **GET ORGANIZED** Copy and complete the graphic organizer below. In each box, give an example to illustrate the given property.

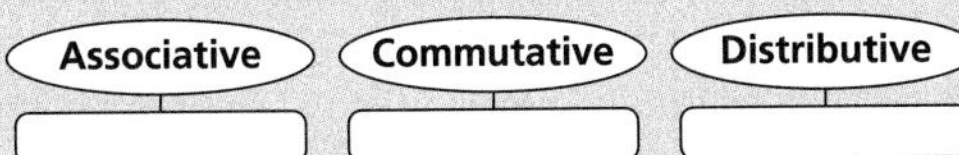

Answers to *Think and Discuss*

1. The sentence describes the Associative Property of Addition.
2. See p. A2.

1-7 Exercises

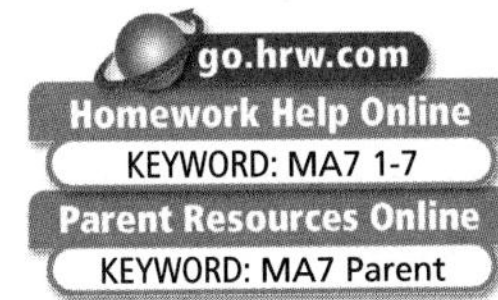

GUIDED PRACTICE

1. **Vocabulary** The ___?___ Property states the following: $(a + b) + c = a + (b + c)$. (*Associative, Commutative,* or *Distributive*) **Associative**

SEE EXAMPLE 1 p. 46

Simplify each expression.

2. $-12 + 67 + 12 + 23$ **90**
3. $16 + 2\frac{1}{2} + 4 + 1\frac{1}{2}$ **24**
4. $27 + 98 + 73$ **198**
5. $\frac{1}{3} \cdot 8 \cdot 21$ **56**
6. $2 \cdot 38 \cdot 50$ **3800**
7. $50 \cdot 118 \cdot 20$ **118,000**

SEE EXAMPLE 2 p. 47

Write each product using the Distributive Property. Then simplify.

8. $14(1002)$ **14,028**
9. $16(19)$ **304**
10. $9(38)$ **342**
11. $8(57)$ **456**
12. $12(112)$ **1344**
13. $7(109)$ **763**

SEE EXAMPLE 3 p. 48

Simplify each expression by combining like terms.

14. $6x + 10x$ **$16x$**
15. $35x - 15x$ **$20x$**
16. $-3a + 9a$ **$6a$**
17. $-8r - r$ **$-9r$**
18. $17x^2 + x$ **$17x^2 + x$**
19. $3.2x + 4.7x$ **$7.9x$**

SEE EXAMPLE 4 p. 48

Simplify each expression. Justify each step with an operation or property.

20. $5(x + 3) - 7x$
21. $9(a - 3) - 4$
22. $5x^2 - 2(x - 3x^2)$
23. $6x - x - 3x^2 + 2x$
24. $12x + 8x + t - 7x$
25. $4a - 2(a - 1)$

PRACTICE AND PROBLEM SOLVING

Simplify each expression.

26. $53 + 28 + 17 + 12$ **110**
27. $5 \cdot 14 \cdot 20$ **1400**
28. $6 \cdot 3 \cdot 5$ **90**
29. $4.5 + 7.1 + 8.5 + 3.9$ **24**

Write each product using the Distributive Property. Then simplify.

30. $9(62)$ **$9(60) + 9(2) = 558$**
31. $8(29)$ **$8(30) - 8(1) = 232$**
32. $11(25)$ **$11(20) + 11(5) = 275$**
33. $6(53)$ **$6(50) + 6(3) = 318$**

Answers

8. $14(1000) + 14(2) = 14{,}028$
9. $16(20) - 16(1) = 304$
10. $9(40) - 9(2) = 342$
11. $8(60) - 8(3) = 456$
12. $12(100) + 12(12) = 1344$
13. $7(100) + 7(9) = 763$
20. $15 - 2x$
21. $9a - 31$
22. $11x^2 - 2x$
23. $7x - 3x^2$
24. $13x + t$
25. $2a + 2$

20–25. For justifications, see p. A12.

1-7 Exercises

Assignment Guide

Assign *Guided Practice* exercises as necessary.

If you finished Examples **1–2**
Basic 26–33, 44, 46–51
Average 26–33, 45–51
Advanced 26–33, 45–51

If you finished Examples **1–4**
Basic 26–44, 46–54, 57–60, 67–75
Average 26–43, 46–50 even, 52–62, 67–75
Advanced 26–42 even, 44–75

Homework Quick Check
Quickly check key concepts.
Exercises: 26, 30, 34, 42, 46, 54

State Resources

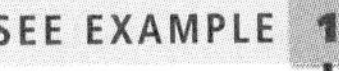

go.hrw.com
State Resources Online
KEYWORD: MA7 Resources

Exercise 57 requires students to simplify an expression that involves π. This exercise prepares students for the Multi-Step Test Prep on page 60.

Answers

38. $4y + 33$
39. $-3x - 14$
40. $x + 1$
41. $11x + 3x^2$
42. $x - 3y$
43. $13y - 10$

38–43. For justifications, see p. A12.

45a. Amy: 98:21; Julie: 81:12; Mardi: 83:39; Sabine: 63:47

55. $10 - (7 - 3) = 10 - 4 = 6$
$(10 - 7) - 3 = 3 - 3 = 0$
No; when the numbers are associated differently, the answers are different.

56. Possible answer: newspaper delivery; the newspaper is delivered to all the houses on one block. A newspaper is delivered to each house on the block.
$n(a + b + c + d) = na + nb + nc + nd$
n = newspaper
a, b, c, d = houses on the block

Independent Practice	
For Exercises	See Example
26–29	1
30–33	2
34–37	3
38–43	4

Extra Practice
Skills Practice p. S5
Application Practice p. S28

Simplify each expression by combining like terms.

34. $3x + 9x$ **12x**
35. $14x^2 - 5x^2$ **$9x^2$**
36. $-7x + 8x$ **x**
37. $3x^2 - 4$ **$3x^2 - 4$**

Simplify each expression. Justify each step with an operation or property.

38. $4(y + 6) + 9$
39. $-7(x + 2) + 4x$
40. $3x + 2 - 2x - 1$
41. $5x - 3x + 3x^2 + 9x$
42. $8x + 2x - 3y - 9x$
43. $7y - 3 + 6y - 7$

44. **Estimation** Tavon bought a binder, 3 spiral notebooks, and a pen. The binder cost \$4.89, the notebooks cost \$1.99 each, and the pen cost \$2.11. About how much did Tavon spend on school supplies? **about \$13**

45. **Sports** In a triathlon, athletes race in swimming, biking, and running events. The athlete with the shortest total time to complete the events is the winner.

Times from Triathlon

Athlete	Swim (min:s)	Bike (min:s)	Run (min:s)
Amy	18:51	45:17	34:13
Julie	17:13	40:27	23:32
Mardi	19:09	38:58	25:32
Sabine	13:09	31:37	19:01

a. Find the total time for each athlete. (*Hint:* 1 minute = 60 seconds)
b. Use the total times for the athletes to determine the order in which they finished the triathlon. **Sabine, Julie, Mardi, Amy**

Name the property that is illustrated in each equation.

46. $5 + x = x + 5$ **Comm. Prop. of Add.**
47. $x - 2 = -2 + x$ **Comm. Prop. of Add.**
48. $2 + (3 + y) = (2 + 3) + y$ **Assoc. Prop. of Add.**
49. $3(2r - 7) = 3(2r) - 3(7)$ **Distrib. Prop.**
50. $(2 + g) + 3 = 2 + (g + 3)$ **Assoc. Prop. of Add.**
51. $45x - 35 = 5(9x) - 5(7)$ **Distrib. Prop.**

Geometry Give an expression in simplified form for the perimeter of each figure.

52. 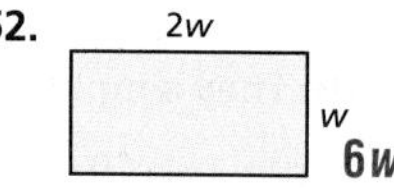

6w

53. 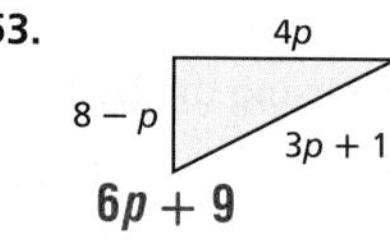

6p + 9

54. 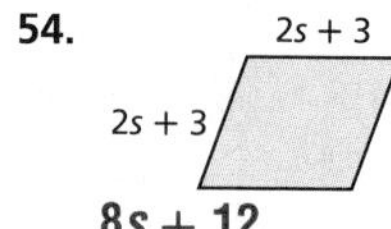

8s + 12

55. **Critical Thinking** Evaluate $a - (b - c)$ and $(a - b) - c$ for $a = 10$, $b = 7$, and $c = 3$. Based on your answers, explain whether there is an Associative Property of Subtraction.

56. **Write About It** Describe a real-world situation that can be represented by the Distributive Property. Translate your situation into an algebraic expression. Define each variable you use.

57. This problem will prepare you for the Multi-Step Test Prep on page 60.

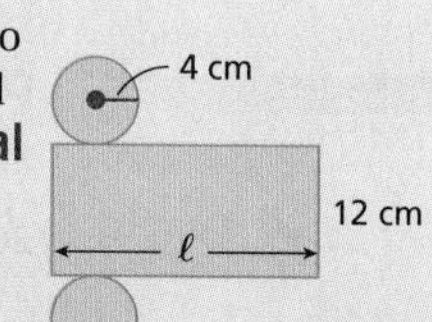

a. The diagram shows a pattern of shapes that can be folded to make a cylinder. How is the length ℓ of the rectangle related to the circumference of (distance around) each circle? **equal**
b. An expression for the circumference of each circle is $2\pi r$. Write an expression for the area of the rectangle. **96π cm^2**
c. Write an expression for the total area of the figures. Leave the symbol π in your expression. **$2(16\pi) + 96\pi = 128\pi$ cm^2**

1-7 PRACTICE A
1-7 PRACTICE C
1-7 PRACTICE B

Simplify each expression.

1. $18 + 9 + 1 + 12$ **40**
2. $7 \cdot 15 \cdot 2$ **210**
3. $3 + 4\frac{1}{2} + 11 + 5\frac{1}{2}$ **24**
4. $-5 \cdot 7 \cdot 20$ **–700**
5. $-12 + 3 + 12 + 19$ **22**
6. $-1 \cdot 5 \cdot 9 \cdot 2$ **–90**

Write each product using the Distributive Property. Then simplify.

7. $14(12)$ **$14(10) + 14(2)$; 168**
8. $5(47)$ **$5(50) - 5(3)$; 235**
9. $4(106)$ **$4(100) + 4(6)$; 424**

Simplify each expression by combining like terms.

10. $16x + 27x$ **$43x$**
11. $-4m + 12m$ **$8m$**
12. $6t^2 - 2t^2$ **$4t^2$**
13. $-5w^3 + 18w^3$ **$13w^3$**
14. $4p + 7p^2$ **$4p + 7p^2$**
15. $-2.6d - 3.4d$ **$-6d$**

Simplify each expression. Justify each step.

16. $4(x + 9) + 5x$
$4x + 36 + 5x$ Dist. Property;
$4x + 5x + 36$ Comm. Property;
$(4x + 5x) + 36$ Assoc. Property;
$9x + 36$ Combine Like Terms

17. $-12d + 3 + 14d + 18$
$-12d + 14d + 3 + 18$ Comm.
$(-12d + 14d) + (3 + 18)$ Assoc.
$2d + 21$ Combine Like Terms

Give an expression in simplified form for the perimeter of each figure.

18. 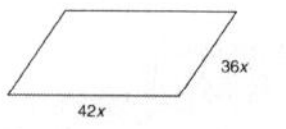 (parallelogram with sides $36x$ and $42x$) **$156x$**
19. 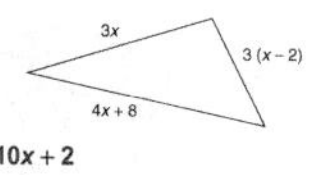 (triangle with sides $3x$, $3(x - 2)$, $4x + 8$) **$10x + 2$**

1-7 READING STRATEGIES

The Commutative, Associative, and Distributive Properties are used to simplify expressions and combine like terms. By connecting each property with a vocabulary word that has the same root, you will better understand how to use each property.

Commutative Property → think "**commute**": to travel back and forth
Ex: $7 \cdot 5 = 5 \cdot 7$ → changing the order is okay for + and ×

Associative Property → think "**associate**": to be in a group with
Ex: $(9 + 8) + 2 = 9 + (8 + 2)$ → changing the grouping is okay for + and ×

Distributive Property → think "**distribute**": to spread out to all
Ex: $2(8 + 3) = 2 \cdot 8 + 2 \cdot 3$ → the lead number is multiplied by all in ( )

Answer each problem.

1. Give an example of the Commutative Property for addition.
Possible answer: $18 + 9 + 2 = 18 + 2 + 9$
2. Write a non-mathematical sentence using the word "distribute."
Possible answer: Mr. Wiley will distribute the test to all the students.

An expression is simplified below. Justify each step of the process by naming the property that was used or by writing "combine like terms."

$27 + 3(2x + 6) + 2x$
$27 + 6x + 18 + 2x$ 3. **Distributive Property**
$27 + 18 + 6x + 2x$ 4. **Commutative Property**
$(27 + 18) + (6x + 2x)$ 5. **Associative Property**
$45 + (6x + 2x)$ 6. **combine like terms**
$45 + 8x$ 7. **combine like terms**

Use the properties above to simplify each expression.

8. $8 \cdot 3 \cdot 5$ **120**
9. $7(3 + x) + 6$ **$27 + 7x$**
10. $12x + 4(8x + 2) + 8x$ **$52x + 8$**

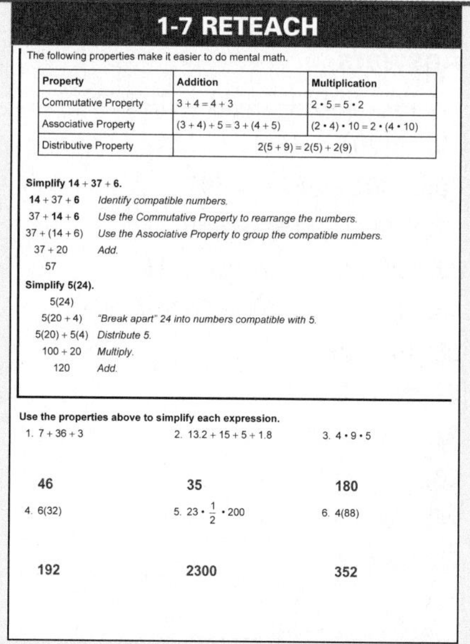

1-7 RETEACH

The following properties make it easier to do mental math.

Property	Addition	Multiplication
Commutative Property	$3 + 4 = 4 + 3$	$2 \cdot 5 = 5 \cdot 2$
Associative Property	$(3 + 4) + 5 = 3 + (4 + 5)$	$(2 \cdot 4) \cdot 10 = 2 \cdot (4 \cdot 10)$
Distributive Property	$2(5 + 9) = 2(5) + 2(9)$	

Simplify 14 + 37 + 6.

$14 + 37 + 6$ *Identify compatible numbers.*
$37 + 14 + 6$ *Use the Commutative Property to rearrange the numbers.*
$37 + (14 + 6)$ *Use the Associative Property to group the compatible numbers.*
$37 + 20$ *Add.*
57

Simplify 5(24).

$5(24)$
$5(20 + 4)$ *"Break apart" 24 into numbers compatible with 5.*
$5(20) + 5(4)$ *Distribute 5.*
$100 + 20$ *Multiply.*
120 *Add.*

Use the properties above to simplify each expression.

1. $7 + 36 + 3$ **46**
2. $13.2 + 15 + 5 + 1.8$ **35**
3. $4 \cdot 9 \cdot 5$ **180**
4. $6(32)$ **192**
5. $23 \cdot \frac{1}{2} \cdot 200$ **2300**
6. $4(88)$ **352**

TEST PREP

58. Ariel has 19 more CDs than her sister Tiffany has. Victor has 3 times as many CDs as Ariel has. Tiffany has x CDs. Which expression can be used to show how many CDs the three have in total?

   Ⓐ $19 + 3x$ Ⓑ $51 + 3x$ Ⓒ $76 + 3x$ **Ⓓ $76 + 5x$**

59. Which expression can be used to represent the perimeter of the rectangle?

   Ⓕ $16k$ Ⓗ $3k + 13$
   Ⓖ $32k$ **Ⓙ $6k + 26$**

   (rectangle: side $3 + k$, bottom $2(k + 5)$)

60. Which equation is an example of the Distributive Property?

   Ⓐ $(25 + 18) + 33 = 25 + (18 + 33)$ **Ⓒ $33 \cdot 25 + 33 \cdot 18 = 33 \cdot (25 + 18)$**
   Ⓑ $33 + (25 \cdot 18) = (25 \cdot 18) + 33$ Ⓓ $3 + 25 \cdot 33 + 18 = 18 + 33 \cdot 25 + 33$

CHALLENGE AND EXTEND

Simplify.

61. $4[3(x + 9) + 2]$ **$12x + 116$**
62. $-3[(x - 2) + 5(x - 2)]$ **$-18x + 36$**
63. $(2b + 5) - (8b + 6) + 3(b - 2)$ **$-3b - 7$**
64. $\frac{1}{2}[(10 - g) + (-6 + 3g)]$ **$2 + g$**

65. Fill in the missing justifications.

Procedure	Justification
$11e - 7 - 3e = 11e + (-7) + (-3e)$	Definition of subtraction
$= 11e + (-3e) + (-7)$	a. **Comm. Prop. of Add.**
$= [11e + (-3e)] + (-7)$	b. **Assoc. Prop. of Add.**
$= [11 + (-3)]e + (-7)$	c. **Distributive Property**
$= 8e + (-7)$	d. **Rule for subtraction**
$= 8e - 7$	Definition of subtraction

66. Fill in the missing justifications.

Procedure	Justification
$\frac{a + b}{c} = \frac{1}{c}(a + b)$	Definition of division
$= \frac{1}{c}(a) + \frac{1}{c}(b)$	a. **Distributive Property**
$= \frac{a}{c} + \frac{b}{c}$	b. **Multiplication**

SPIRAL REVIEW

Give the area of the figure described. *(Previous course)*

67. square; $s = 6$ ft **36 ft²**
68. parallelogram; $b = 7$ mm, $h = 13$ mm **91 mm²**

Simplify each expression. *(Lesson 1-4)*

69. 2^6 **64**
70. 18^2 **324**
71. $-\left(\frac{1}{2}\right)^3$ **$-\frac{1}{8}$**
72. $\left(-\frac{1}{2}\right)^2$ **$\frac{1}{4}$**

Simplify each expression. *(Lesson 1-6)*

73. $3 + 4 - 10 \div 2 + 1$ **3**
74. $\frac{8^2 - 6^2}{8^2 + 6^2}$ **$\frac{7}{25}$**
75. $2 - [6 - 8 \div (3 + 1)]$ **-2**

COMMON ERROR ALERT

Students may not see that the Commutative Property of Addition applies to **Exercise 47.** Show them that the left side can be written as $x + (-2)$.

TEST PREP DOCTOR In **Exercise 58,** students may try to use a different variable for the number of CDs each person has. Tell students to start by writing expressions for the number of CDs Ariel and Victor have, using the variable x. Then students can find the total number of CDs. Students who chose **C** may not have completely distributed when simplifying the expression.

Journal

Describe how the Commutative and Associative Properties are alike and how they are different for both addition and multiplication.

ALTERNATIVE ASSESSMENT

Have students explain how each of the properties learned in this lesson can be used to perform mental math. Then have them write and simplify an algebraic expression that uses at least two of the properties.

Power Presentations with PowerPoint®

1-7 Lesson Quiz

Simplify each expression.

1. $165 + 27 + 3 + 5$ 200
2. $\frac{1}{3}(2)(12)$ 8

Write each product using the Distributive Property. Then simplify.

3. $5(\$1.99)$
   $5(\$2) - 5(\$0.01) = \$9.95$
4. $6(13)$ $6(10) + 6(3) = 78$

Simplify each expression. Justify each step with an operation or property.

5. $\frac{2}{5}x^3 + \frac{1}{5}x^3$ $\frac{3}{5}x^3$
6. $14c^2 - 9c$ $14c^2 - 9c$
7. $301x - x$ $300x$
8. $24a + b^2 + 3a + 2b^2$
   $27a + 3b^2$

Also available on transparency

1-7 PROBLEM SOLVING

Write the correct answer.

1. An English teacher gives students 1 point for reading a magazine article, 5 points for reading a chapter of a book, and 20 points for completing an entire book. If Sue reads 4 magazine articles, 7 chapters, and completes 2 books this term, how many points will she earn?

   79

2. A recipe for chocolate chip cookies calls for $2\frac{1}{2}$ cups of flour, 1 cup of butter, $\frac{1}{2}$ cup of brown sugar, $\frac{3}{4}$ cup of sugar, and 1 cup of chocolate chips. Find the total number of cups of ingredients.

   $5\frac{3}{4}$ cups

3. A rectangular desktop has a length of $3(x + 2)$ units and a width of $x - 7$ units. Write an expression, in simplified form, for the perimeter of the desktop.

   $8x - 2$

4. Lucy is k years old. She has a sister who is three years younger than she is and another sister who is five years less than twice Lucy's age. Write an expression, in simplified form, for the sum of the three girls' ages.

   $4k - 8$

Use the table below for questions 5–8. The table which shows expected flight times to and from New York City and five other cities. The legs of each trip vary in time due to the wind. Select the best answer.

Expected Flight Times

City	Inbound (h)	Outbound (h)
Mexico City	5.5	4.5
Paris	7.25	8.0
San Diego	5.4	4.75
Atlanta	2.3	2
Rome	7.75	8.5

5. Find the sum of the expected outbound flight times

   A 23 h **C 27.75 h**
   B 26 h D 28.25 h

6. If Marty plans to travel from New York to Paris and back in February, and then from New York to Rome and back in April, what will be his total flight time for both trips?

   F 15.25 h H 31.0 h
   G 16.25 h **J 31.5 h**

7. Juan's flight time to San Diego was x hours longer than expected. His flight back was y hours less than expected. Which expression shows Juan's total flight time?

   A $10.15xy$ **C $10.15 + x - y$**
   B $5.4x - 4.75y$ D $5.4x(4.75y)$

8. Last month, Heather flew from New York to Atlanta and back twice a week for 3 weeks. What was her total flight time if there were no delays?

   F 12.9 h H 19.8 h
   G 13.8 h **J 25.8 h**

1-7 CHALLENGE

Sometimes it is helpful to use the Distributive Property more than once.

Write the product 82(63) using the Distributive Property. Then simplify.

82(63)	
(80 + 2) (60 + 3)	*Rewrite 82 as 80 + 2, and rewrite 63 as 60 + 3.*
(80 + 2) (60) + (80 + 2) (3)	*Use the Distributive Property to distribute (80 + 2).*
80(60) + 2(60) + 80(3) + 2(3)	*Distribute 60 through (80 + 2). Do the same for 3.*
4800 + 120 + 240 + 6	*Multiply.*
5166	*Add.*

Write each product using the Distributive Property. Then simplify.

1. 51(74)
   (50 + 1)(70 + 4);
   (50 + 1)(70) + (50 + 1)(4);
   50(70) + 1(70) + 50(4) + 1(4);
   3500 + 70 + 200 + 4;
   3774

2. 39(92)
   [40 + (–1)](90 + 2);
   [40 + (–1)](90) + [40 + (–1)](2);
   40(90) + (–1)(90) + 40(2) + (–1)(2);
   3600 – 90 + 80 – 2;
   3588

3. 96(98)
   [100 + (–4)][100 + (–2)];
   [100 + (–4)](100) + [100 + (–4)](–2);
   100(100) + (–4)(100) + 100(–2) + (–4)(–2);
   10,000 – 400 – 200 + 8;
   9408

You can also distribute several times to simplify algebraic expressions.

Use the Distributive Property to simplify the product $(x + 5)(x - 4)$

$(x + 5)(x - 4)$	
$(x + 5)[x + (-4)]$	*To subtract 4, add –4.*
$(x + 5)(x) + (x + 5)(-4)$	*Distribute (x + 5).*
$x(x) + 5(x) + x(-4) + 5(-4)$	*Distribute x through (x + 5). Do the same for –4.*
$x^2 + 5x - 4x - 20$	*Multiply. x(x) can be written as the power x^2.*
$x^2 + x - 20$	*Combine like terms.*

Use the Distributive Property to simplify each product.

4. $(x + 3)(x + 8)$
   $(x + 3)(x) + (x + 3)(8)$
   $x(x) + 3(x) + x(8) + 3(8)$
   $x^2 + 3x + 8x + 24$
   $x^2 + 11x + 24$

5. $(x - 2)(x + 7)$
   $[x + (-2)](x + 7)$
   $[x + (-2)](x) + [x + (-2)](7)$
   $x(x) + (-2)(x) + x(7) + (-2)(7)$
   $x^2 - 2x + 7x - 14$
   $x^2 + 5x - 14$

6. $(a + b)(c + d)$
   $(a + b)(c) + (a + b)(d)$
   $ac + bc + ad + bd$

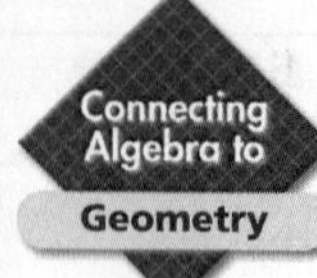

Organizer

Pacing:
Traditional $\frac{1}{2}$ day
Block $\frac{1}{4}$ day

Objective: Apply algebra skills of simplifying expressions to finding perimeters of polygons.

Online Edition

Teach

Remember

Students review and apply the concept of perimeter as the sum of the side lengths of a polygon.

Inclusion To make sure every side of the polygon is added, have students write a blank that can be filled in with an expression for the length of each side. For example, a triangle has three sides, so students should first write three blanks:

______ + ______ + ______

Close

Assess

Have students draw a rectangle and label the length and width with algebraic expressions. Have them write and simplify an expression for the perimeter. Then have them double the length of each side and write and simplify an expression for the perimeter of the new figure.

State Resources

go.hrw.com
State Resources Online
KEYWORD: MA7 Resources

Connecting Algebra to Geometry

Perimeter

The distance around a geometric figure is called the *perimeter*. You can use what you have learned about combining like terms to simplify expressions for perimeter.

A closed figure with straight sides is called a *polygon*. To find the perimeter of a polygon, add the lengths of the sides.

Example 1

A Write an expression for the perimeter of the quadrilateral.

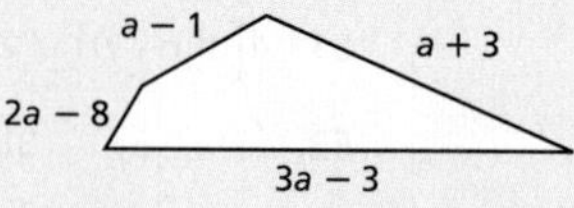

Add the lengths of the four sides.

$P = (a + 3) + (2a - 8) + (3a - 3) + (a - 1)$

Combine like terms to simplify.

$P = (a + 2a + 3a + a) + (3 - 8 - 3 - 1)$

$= 7a - 9$ *This is a general expression for the perimeter.*

B Find the perimeter of this quadrilateral for $a = 5$.

Substitute 5 for a.

$P = 7(5) - 9$ *Multiply; then subtract.*

$= 35 - 9$

$= 26$ *This is the perimeter when $a = 5$.*

Try This

Write and simplify an expression for the perimeter of each figure.

1. **$6x + 3$**

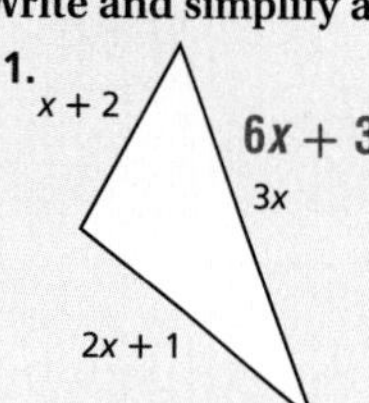

2. **$5b + 3$**

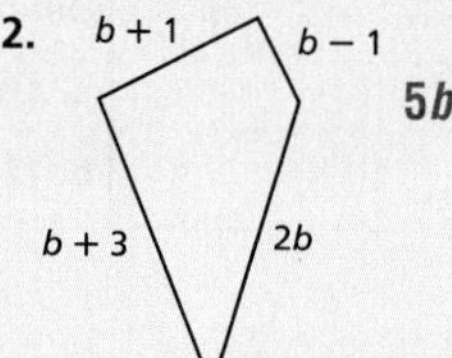

3. **$6m$**

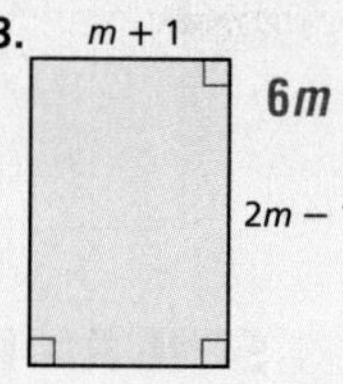

Find the perimeter of each figure for the given value of the variable.

4. $k = 3$ **10**

5. $n = 10$ **68**

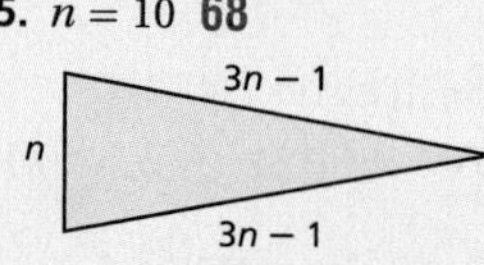

6. $y = 4$ **34**

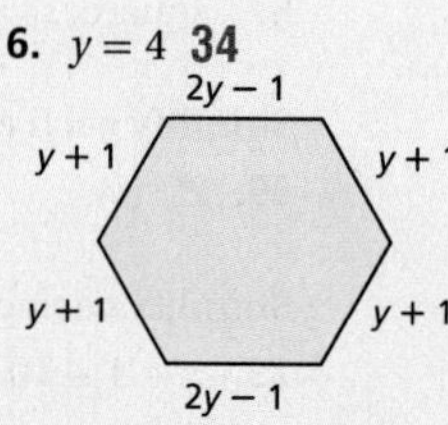

Combining like terms is one way to explore what happens to the perimeter when you double the sides of a triangle or other polygon.

Example 2

What happens to the perimeter of this triangle when you double the length of each side?

Write an expression for the perimeter of the smaller triangle. Combine like terms to simplify the expression.

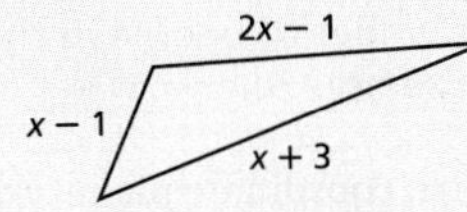

$(x - 1) + (2x - 1) + (x + 3)$

$(x + 2x + x) + (-1 - 1 + 3)$

$4x + 1$ *Perimeter of small triangle*

Double the length of each side of the triangle.

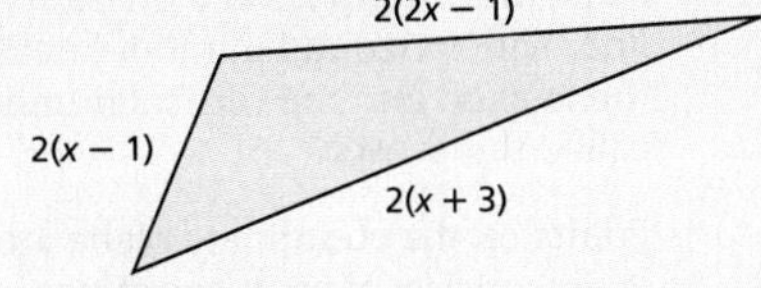

$2(x - 1) = 2x - 2$

$2(2x - 1) = 4x - 2$

$2(x + 3) = 2x + 6$

Find the perimeter of the larger triangle. Combine like terms to simplify.

$(2x - 2) + (4x - 2) + (2x + 6)$ *Add the lengths of the sides.*

$(2x + 4x + 2x) + (-2 - 2 + 6)$ *Use the Associative and Commutative Properties of Addition and combine like terms.*

$8x + 2$ *Perimeter of large triangle*

Use the Distributive Property to show that the new perimeter is twice the original perimeter.

$8x + 2 = 2(4x + 1)$

Try This

Each set of expressions represents the side lengths of a triangle. Use the Distributive Property to show that doubling the side lengths doubles the perimeter.

7. $2p + 1$	**8.** $c - 1$	**9.** $w + 5$	**10.** $h - 2$
$3p + 2$	$2c + 1$	$w + 5$	$3h$
$5p$	$3c - 1$	$3w - 1$	$2h + 3$

Solve each problem.

11. Use the triangles in Example 2. Find the side lengths and perimeters for $x = 5$.

12. The sides of a quadrilateral are $2x - 1$, $x + 3$, $3x + 1$, and $x - 1$. Double the length of each side. Then find an expression for the perimeter of the new figure.
$4x - 2$, $2x + 6$, $6x + 2$, $2x - 2$; $14x + 4$

13. What happens to the perimeter of this trapezoid when you triple the length of each side? Use the variables *a*, *b*, *b*, and *c* for the lengths of the sides. Explain your answer using the Distributive Property.

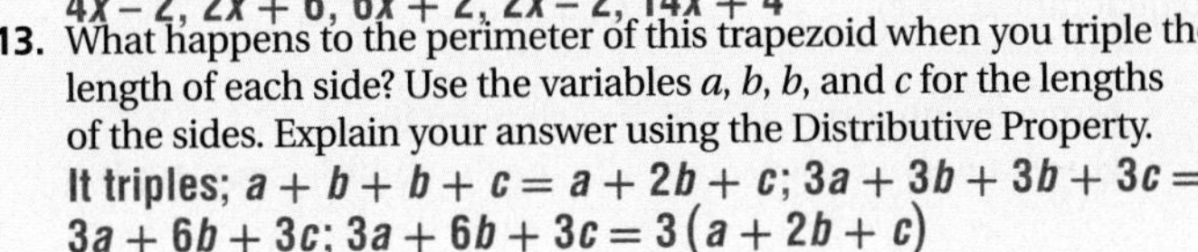
It triples; $a + b + b + c = a + 2b + c$; $3a + 3b + 3b + 3c = 3a + 6b + 3c$; $3a + 6b + 3c = 3(a + 2b + c)$

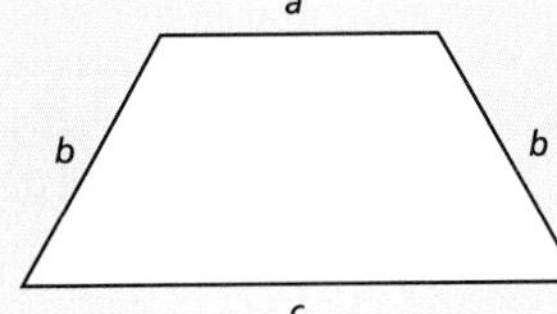

Answers

7. Perimeter: $10p + 3$; Double perimeter: $20p + 6$; Distrib. Prop: $20p + 6 = 2(10p + 3)$
8. Perimeter: $6c - 1$; Double perimeter: $12c - 2$; Distrib. Prop: $12c - 2 = 2(6c - 1)$
9. Perimeter: $5w + 9$; Double perimeter: $10w + 18$; Distrib. Prop: $10w + 18 = 2(5w + 9)$
10. Perimeter: $6h + 1$; Double perimeter: $12h + 2$; Distrib. Prop: $12h + 2 = 2(6h + 1)$
11. small triangle: 9, 4, 8; 21; large triangle: 18, 8, 16; 42

Connecting Algebra to Geometry 53

1-8 Organizer

Pacing: Traditional 1 day
Block $\frac{1}{2}$ day

Objectives: Graph ordered pairs in the coordinate plane.

Graph functions from ordered pairs.

Online Edition
Tutorial Videos, Interactivity

Countdown Week 2

Power Presentations with PowerPoint®

Warm Up

1. Draw and label a number line. Then plot the points −2, 0, and 4.

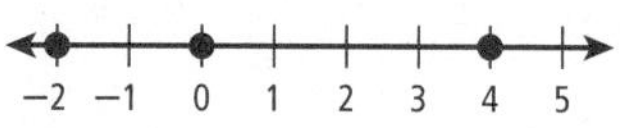

Evaluate each expression for the given value of *x*.

2. $2x + 1$ for $x = 3$ 7
3. $-\frac{1}{4}x + 3$ for $x = 8$ 1
4. $|x + 6|$ for $x = -10$ 4

Also available on transparency

Math Humor

Q: Why was the math teacher upset with one of the students?

A: He kept asking, "What's the point?"

1-8 Introduction to Functions

Objectives
Graph ordered pairs in the coordinate plane.

Graph functions from ordered pairs.

Vocabulary
coordinate plane
axes
origin
x-axis
y-axis
ordered pair
x-coordinate
y-coordinate
quadrant
input
output

Why learn this?
You can use functions to determine how the cost of a caricature is affected by the number of people in the picture. (See Example 3.)

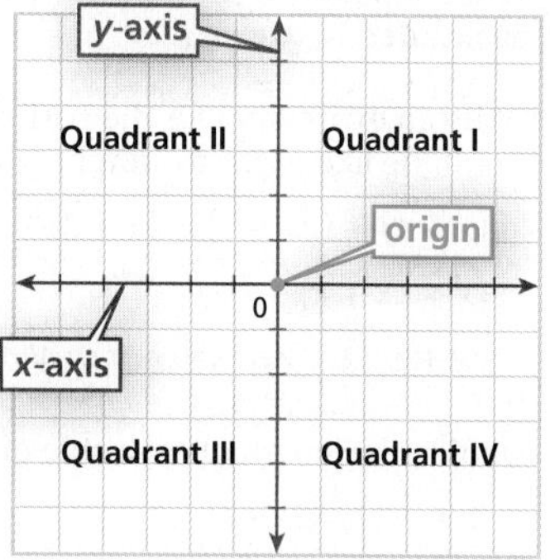

The **coordinate plane** is formed by the intersection of two perpendicular number lines called **axes**. The point of intersection, called the **origin**, is at 0 on each number line. The horizontal number line is called the ***x*-axis**, and the vertical number line is called the ***y*-axis**.

Points on the coordinate plane are described using ordered pairs. An **ordered pair** consists of an ***x*-coordinate** and a ***y*-coordinate** and is written (x, y). Points are often named by a capital letter.

EXAMPLE 1 Graphing Points in the Coordinate Plane

Reading Math
The *x*-coordinate tells how many units to move left or right from the origin. The *y*-coordinate tells how many units to move up or down.

Graph each point.

A $M(3, 4)$
Start at the origin.
Move 3 units right and 4 units up.

B $N(-2, 0)$
Start at the origin. Move 2 units left.

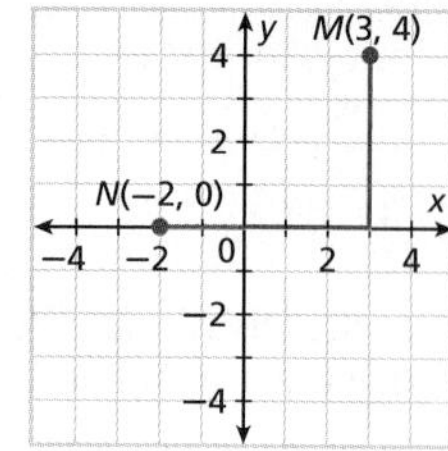

CHECK IT OUT! Graph each point.

1a. $R(2, -3)$ **1b.** $S(0, 2)$ **1c.** $T(-2, 6)$

1a, 1b, 1c.

Look at the graph at the top of this lesson. The axes divide the coordinate plane into four **quadrants**. Points that lie on an axis are not in any quadrant.

EXAMPLE 2 Locating Points in the Coordinate Plane

Name the quadrant in which each point lies.

A P
Quadrant III

B Q
Quadrant II

C R
no quadrant (*x*-axis)

D S
Quadrant IV

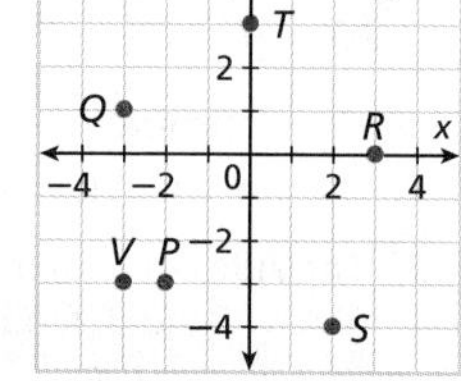

CHECK IT OUT! Name the quadrant in which each point lies.

2a. T none   **2b.** U Q I   **2c.** V Q III   **2d.** W Q II

State Resources

go.hrw.com
State Resources Online
KEYWORD: MA7 Resources

1 Introduce

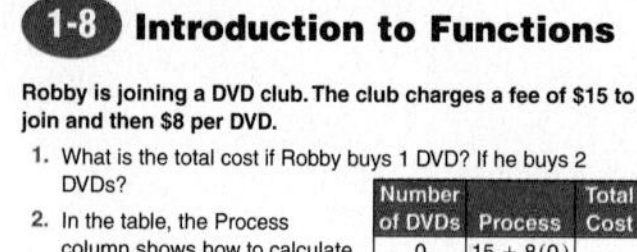

EXPLORATION

1-8 Introduction to Functions

Robby is joining a DVD club. The club charges a fee of $15 to join and then $8 per DVD.

1. What is the total cost if Robby buys 1 DVD? If he buys 2 DVDs?
2. In the table, the Process column shows how to calculate the total cost for a given number of DVDs. Complete the table.
3. Suppose Robby buys *n* DVDs. What is the total cost in terms of *n*?

Number of DVDs	Process	Total Cost
0	15 + 8(0)	
1	15 + 8(1)	
2		$31
3		$39
4	15 + 8(4)	
5		$55

4. Use the expressions you wrote to find the total cost of buying 14 DVDs.
5. In this situation, you can think of the expression as a machine. You input a number of DVDs and the machine outputs the total cost. What is the output when the input is 7?

THINK AND DISCUSS

6. **Describe** two different methods for finding the total cost of buying 10 DVDs.
7. **Explain** how you can find the number of DVDs that Robby can buy for $63.

Motivate

Pose the following problem: "Suppose the cost of a movie ticket is $8.50. How could we find the total cost for 3 people to attend the movie? 5 people? *x* people?"

cost = \$8.50(3); cost = \$8.50(5); cost = \$8.50*x*

Point out that the last equation represents a function, and can thus be used to find the cost of any number of people to attend the movie.

Explorations and answers are provided in *Alternate Openers: Explorations Transparencies.*

An equation that contains two variables can be used as a rule to generate ordered pairs. When you substitute a value for x, you generate a value for y. The value substituted for x is called the **input**, and the value generated for y is called the **output**.

Output ↓ Input ↓

$y = 10x + 5$

In a *function*, the value of y (the output) is determined by the value of x (the input). All of the equations in this lesson represent functions.

EXAMPLE 3 Art Application

A caricature artist charges his clients a \$5 setup fee plus \$10 for every person in a picture. Write a rule for the artist's fee. Write ordered pairs for the artist's fee when there are 1, 2, 3, and 4 people in the picture.

Writing Math

The artist's fee is determined by the number of people in the picture, so the number of people is the input and the artist's fee is the output.

Let y represent the artist's fee and x represent the number of people in a picture.

Artist's fee	is	\$5	plus	\$10	for each	person.
y	$=$	5	$+$	10	$\cdot$	x

$y = 5 + 10x$

Number of People in Picture	Rule	Fee	Ordered Pair
x (input)	$y = 5 + 10x$	y (output)	(x, y)
1	$y = 5 + 10(1)$	15	(1, 15)
2	$y = 5 + 10(2)$	25	(2, 25)
3	$y = 5 + 10(3)$	35	(3, 35)
4	$y = 5 + 10(4)$	45	(4, 45)

3. What if...? The artist increased his fees to a \$10 setup fee plus \$20 for every person. Write a rule for the new fee. Write ordered pairs for the fee when there are 1, 2, 3, and 4 people.

$y = 10 + 20x$; (1, 30), (2, 50), (3, 70), (4, 90)

When you graph ordered pairs generated by a function, they may create a pattern.

EXAMPLE 4 Generating and Graphing Ordered Pairs

Generate ordered pairs for each function using the given values for x. Graph the ordered pairs and describe the pattern.

A $y = 4x - 3; x = -1, 0, 1, 2$

Input	Output	Ordered Pair
x	y	(x, y)
−1	$4(-1) - 3 = -7$	(−1, −7)
0	$4(0) - 3 = -3$	(0, −3)
1	$4(1) - 3 = 1$	(1, 1)
2	$4(2) - 3 = 5$	(2, 5)

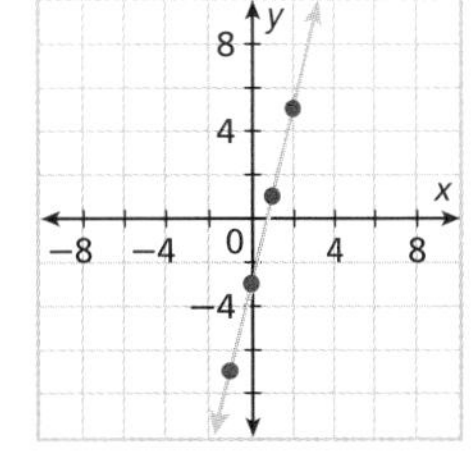

The points form a straight line.

Power Presentations with PowerPoint®

Additional Examples

Example 1

Graph each point.

A. (−4, 4) **B.** (0, −5)

C. (−2, −3)

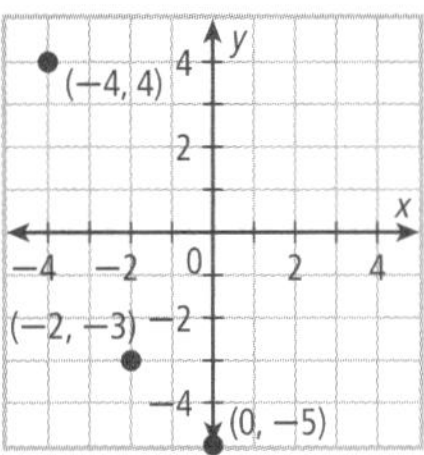

Example 2

Name the quadrant in which each point lies.

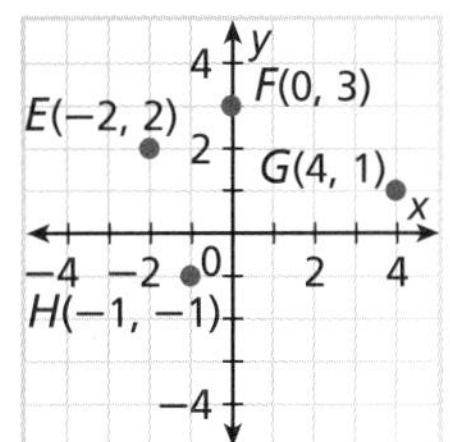

A. *E* II **B.** *F* none (y-axis)

C. *G* I **D.** *H* III

Example 3

An engraver charges a setup fee of \$10 plus \$2 for every word engraved. Write a rule for the engraver's fee. Write ordered pairs for the engraver's fee when there are 5, 10, 15, and 20 words engraved. $y = 10 + 2x$; (5, 20), (10, 30), (15, 40), (20, 50)

2 Teach

Guided Instruction

Have students practice graphing in the first quadrant alone before moving on to all four quadrants. Make sure students are comfortable with substitution, absolute value, and exponents before using equations to generate ordered pairs.

Reaching All Learners

Through Multiple Representations

Show a coordinate plane with several points plotted. Label each point with a blank set of coordinates: (,). Have students fill in the coordinates for each point, and then fill in a corresponding x-y table.

INTERVENTION

Questioning Strategies

EXAMPLE 1

- How do you know which direction to move for each coordinate in an ordered pair?

EXAMPLE 2

- How can you tell when an ordered pair will lie on the x-axis? the y-axis?

EXAMPLE 3

- What kinds of numbers are not reasonable for values of x? What does this indicate about the reasonable values of y?

Power Presentations with PowerPoint®

Additional Examples

Example 4

Generate ordered pairs for each function using the given values for *x*. Graph the ordered pairs and describe the pattern.

A. $y = 2x + 1$; $x = -2, -1, 0, 1, 2$

$(-2, -3)$
$(-1, -1)$
$(0, 1)$
$(1, 3)$
$(2, 5)$

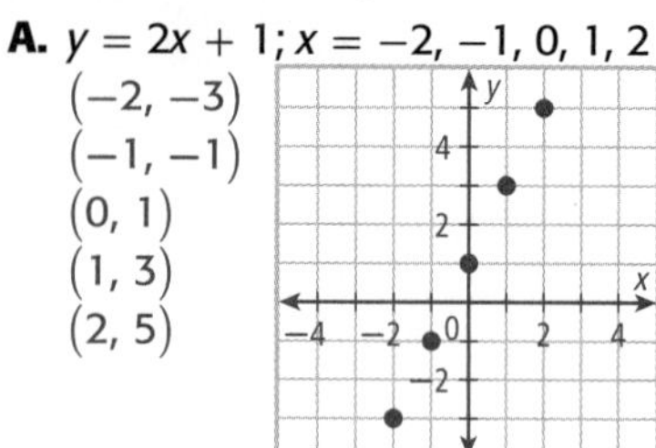

The points form a straight line.

B. $y = x^2 - 3$; $x = -2, -1, 0, 1, 2$

$(-2, 1)$
$(-1, -2)$
$(0, -3)$
$(1, -2)$
$(2, 1)$

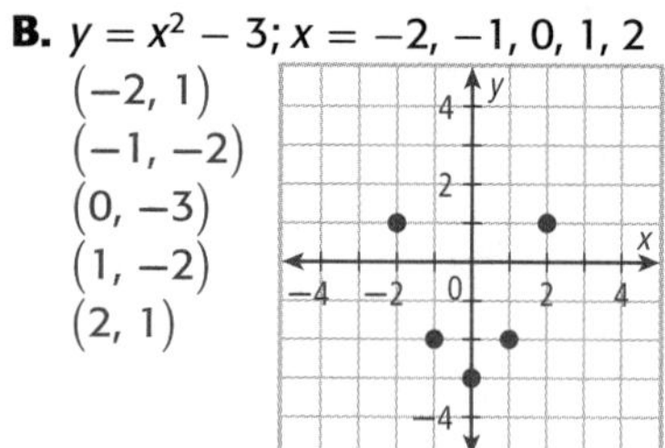

The points form a U shape.

C. $y = |x - 2|$; $x = 0, 1, 2, 3, 4$

$(0, 2)$
$(1, 1)$
$(2, 0)$
$(3, 1)$
$(4, 2)$

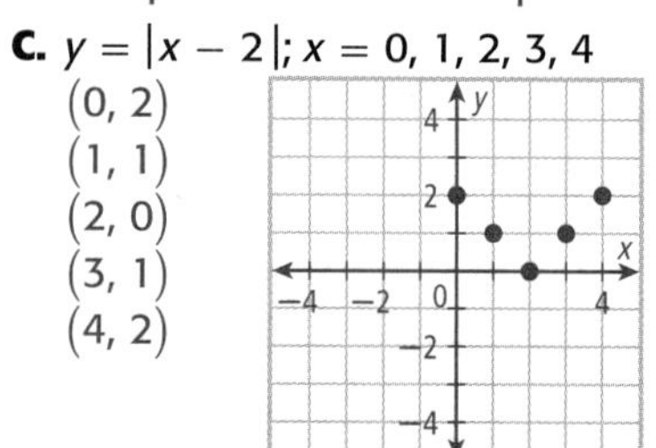

The points form a V shape.

INTERVENTION
Questioning Strategies

EXAMPLE 

- Explain why the points in the graph for **Example 4C** will never fall below the *x*-axis.

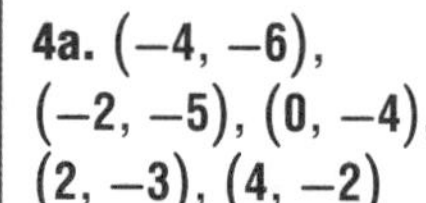

4a. $(-4, -6)$, $(-2, -5)$, $(0, -4)$, $(2, -3)$, $(4, -2)$

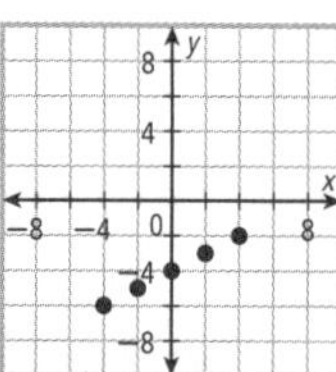

4b. $(-3, 30)$, $(-1, 6)$, $(0, 3)$, $(1, 6)$, $(3, 30)$

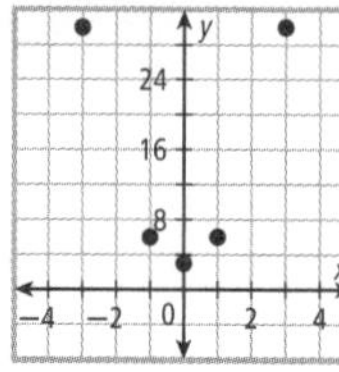

4c. $(0, 2)$, $(1, 1)$, $(2, 0)$, $(3, 1)$, $(4, 2)$

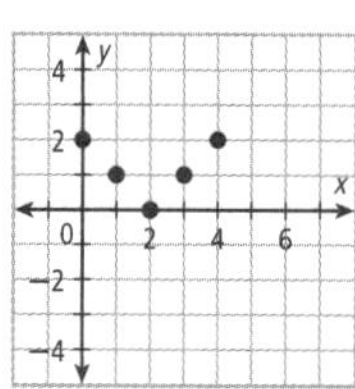

Generate ordered pairs for each function using the given values for *x*. Graph the ordered pairs and describe the pattern.

B $y = 2x^2 + 1$; $x = -2, -1, 0, 1, 2$

Input	Output	Ordered Pair
x	*y*	(*x*, *y*)
-2	$2(-2)^2 + 1 = 9$	$(-2, 9)$
-1	$2(-1)^2 + 1 = 3$	$(-1, 3)$
0	$2(0)^2 + 1 = 1$	$(0, 1)$
1	$2(1)^2 + 1 = 3$	$(1, 3)$
2	$2(2)^2 + 1 = 9$	$(2, 9)$

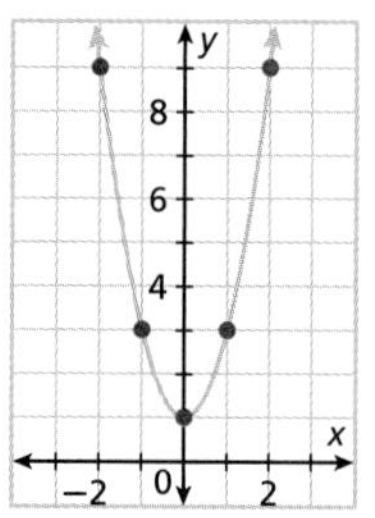

The points form a U shape.

C $y = |x + 3|$; $x = -5, -4, -3, -2, -1$

Input	Output	Ordered Pair
x	*y*	(*x*, *y*)
-5	$\lvert -5 + 3\rvert = \lvert -2\rvert = 2$	$(-5, 2)$
-4	$\lvert -4 + 3\rvert = \lvert -1\rvert = 1$	$(-4, 1)$
-3	$\lvert -3 + 3\rvert = \lvert 0\rvert = 0$	$(-3, 0)$
-2	$\lvert -2 + 3\rvert = \lvert 1\rvert = 1$	$(-2, 1)$
-1	$\lvert -1 + 3\rvert = \lvert 2\rvert = 2$	$(-1, 2)$

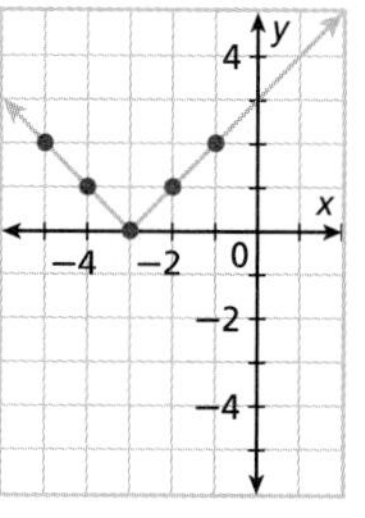

The points form a V shape.

Generate ordered pairs for each function using the given values for *x*. Graph the ordered pairs and describe the pattern.

4a. $y = \frac{1}{2}x - 4$; $x = -4, -2, 0, 2, 4$ **line**

4b. $y = 3x^2 + 3$; $x = -3, -1, 0, 1, 3$ **U shape**

4c. $y = |x - 2|$; $x = 0, 1, 2, 3, 4$ **V shape**

In Chapter 4, you will learn more about functions. You will study the relationship between the shape of a graph and the rule that generates the ordered pairs.

THINK AND DISCUSS

1. Describe how to graph the ordered pair $(-3, 6)$.
2. Give an example of a point that lies on the *y*-axis.

3. **GET ORGANIZED** Copy and complete the graphic organizer. In each blank, write "positive" or "negative."

Quadrant II		Quadrant I
x is ?. *y* is ?.	The Coordinate Plane	*x* is ?. *y* is ?.
x is ?. *y* is ?.		*x* is ?. *y* is ?.
Quadrant III		Quadrant IV

3 Close

Summarize

Remind students that the *x*-coordinate indicates left or right movement, while the *y*-coordinate indicates up or down movement. Have students make a chart to help them recognize which quadrant a point lies in, based on the signs of the coordinates.

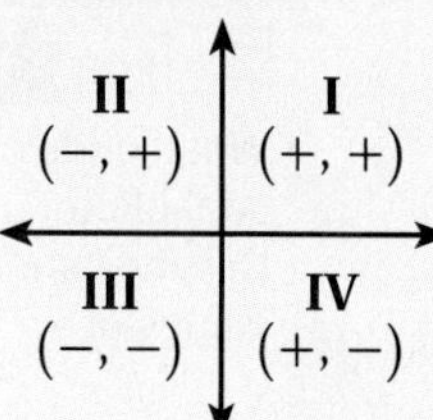

ONGOING ASSESSMENT and INTERVENTION 

***Diagnose Before* the Lesson**
1-8 Warm Up, TE p. 54

***Monitor During* the Lesson**
Check It Out! Exercises, SE pp. 54–56
Questioning Strategies, TE pp. 55–56

***Assess After* the Lesson**
1-8 Lesson Quiz, TE p. 59
Alternative Assessment, TE p. 59

Answers to *Think and Discuss*

1. Start at the origin, and move 3 units left. Then move up 6 units.
2. Check students' work. The *x*-coordinate must be 0; possible answer: (0, 4).
3. See p. A2.

go.hrw.com
Homework Help Online
KEYWORD: MA7 1-8
Parent Resources Online
KEYWORD: MA7 Parent

1-8 Exercises

GUIDED PRACTICE

1. **Vocabulary** Explain why the order in an *ordered pair* is important.

SEE EXAMPLE 1 p. 54

Graph each point.

2. $J(4, 5)$ 3. $K(-3, 2)$ 4. $L(6, 0)$ 5. $M(1, -7)$

SEE EXAMPLE 2 p. 54

Name the quadrant in which each point lies.

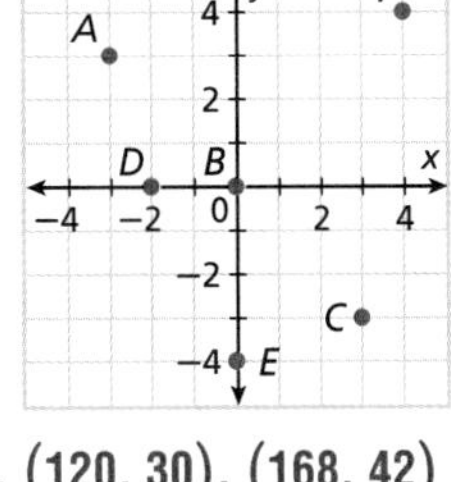

6. A **Q II** 7. B **none** 8. C **Q IV**
9. D **none** 10. E **none** 11. F **Q I**

SEE EXAMPLE 3 p. 55

12. **Multi-Step** The number of counselors at a summer camp must be equal to $\frac{1}{4}$ the number of campers. Write a rule for the number of counselors that must be at the camp. Write ordered pairs for the number of counselors when there are 76, 100, 120, and 168 campers. $y = \frac{1}{4}x$; **(76, 19), (100, 25), (120, 30), (168, 42)**

SEE EXAMPLE 4 p. 55

Generate ordered pairs for each function for $x = -2, -1, 0, 1$, and 2. Graph the ordered pairs and describe the pattern.

13. $y = x + 2$ **line** 14. $y = -x$ **line** 15. $y = -2|x|$ **V shape** 16. $y = \frac{1}{2}x^2$ **U shape**

PRACTICE AND PROBLEM SOLVING

Independent Practice	
For Exercises	See Example
17–20	1
21–26	2
27	3
28–31	4

Extra Practice
Skills Practice p. S5
Application Practice p. S28

Graph each point.

17. $D(2, 8)$ 18. $E(-2, -7)$ 19. $F(0, -5)$ 20. $G(4, -4)$

Name the quadrant in which each point lies.

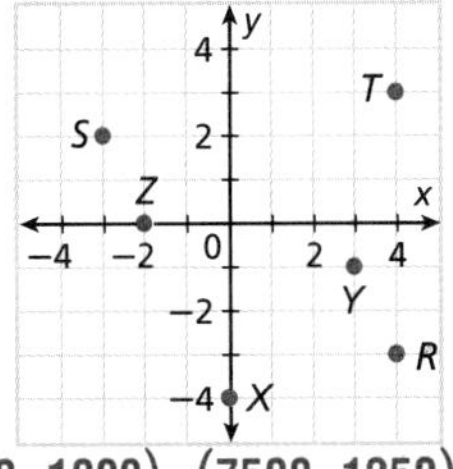

21. X **none** 22. Y **Q IV** 23. Z **none**
24. R **Q IV** 25. S **Q II** 26. T **Q I**

27. **Multi-Step** Jeremy's wages include a \$500 base salary plus $\frac{1}{10}$ of his sales. Write a rule for the total amount of Jeremy's paycheck. Write ordered pairs for the amount of Jeremy's paycheck when his sales are \$500, \$3000, \$5000, and \$7500. $y = 500 + 0.10x$; **(500, 550), (3000, 800), (5000, 1000), (7500, 1250)**

Generate ordered pairs for each function for $x = -2, -1, 0, 1$, and 2. Graph the ordered pairs and describe the pattern.

28. $y = 6 - 2x$ **line** 29. $y = -(x^2)$ **U shape** 30. $y = 3|x|$ **V shape** 31. $y = x^2 + 3$ **U shape**

Geometry Graph each point and connect them in the order they are listed. Connect the last point to the first. Describe the figure drawn.

32. $(-1, 1), (4, 1), (4, -4), (-1, -4)$ 33. $(-6, 3), (2, -2), (-7, -3)$
34. $(4, 4), (6, 2), (5, -1), (3, -1), (2, 2)$ 35. $(-6, 5), (4, 5), (4, 7), (-6, 7)$

36. **Multi-Step** The salary at Beth's company is \$32,000 for someone with no experience and increases by \$2700 per year of experience. Write a rule for the salary at Beth's company. Write ordered pairs for the salaries for employees with 0, 2, 5, and 7 years of experience.
$y = 32{,}000 + 2700x$; **(0, 32,000), (2, 37,400), (5, 45,500), (7, 50,900)**

Assignment Guide

Assign *Guided Practice* exercises as necessary.

If you finished Examples **1–2**
Basic 17–26, 32–35
Average 17–26, 32–35
Advanced 17–26, 32–35

If you finished Examples **1–4**
Basic 17–40, 42–45, 48, 50–53, 62–72
Average 17–35, 37, 41–55, 62–72
Advanced 17–27, 28–34 even, 37, 38, 41–47, 49–72

Homework Quick Check
Quickly check key concepts.
Exercises: 20, 24, 27, 28, 34, 42

Teaching Tip
Kinesthetic For exercises like **Exercises 13–16,** students may have difficulty determining if a pattern is V-shaped or U-shaped by observation only. Have them place a straight edge along the pattern to see if the points are lined up (a V shape) or curved (a U shape).

Answers

1. The first coordinate tells which way to move left or right. The second coordinate tells which way to move up or down. If you switch the direction of each coordinate, you will not get the same point.

State Resources

Answers

2–5.

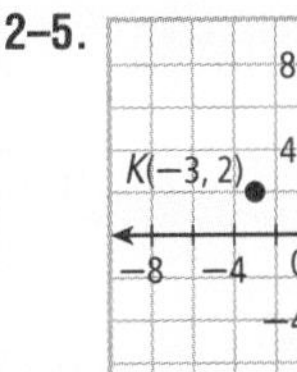
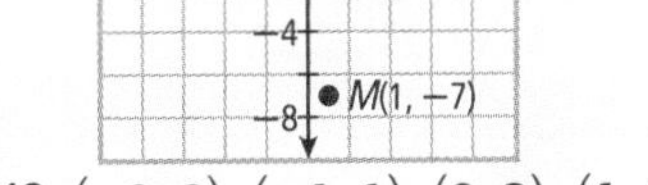

13. (−2, 0), (−1, 1), (0, 2), (1, 3), (2, 4)
14. (−2, 2), (−1, 1), (0, 0), (1, −1), (2, −2)
15. (−2, −4), (−1, −2), (0, 0), (1, −2), (2, −4)
16. $(-2, 2), \left(-1, \frac{1}{2}\right), (0, 0), \left(1, \frac{1}{2}\right), (2, 2)$
13–16. For graphs, see p. A12.

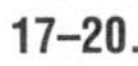
17–20.

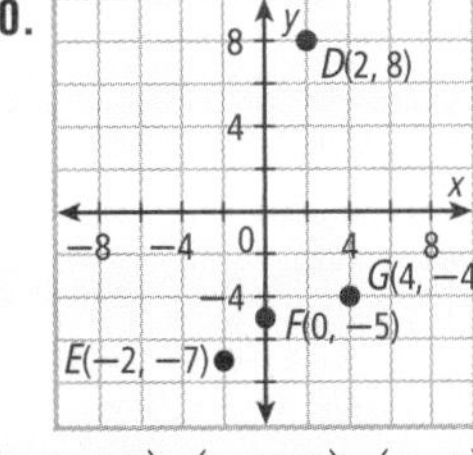

28. (−2, 10), (−1, 8), (0, 6), (1, 4), (2, 2)
29. (−2, −4), (−1, −1), (0, 0), (1, −1), (2, −4)
30. (−2, 6), (−1, 3), (0, 0), (1, 3), (2, 6)
31. (−2, 7), (−1, 4), (0, 3), (1, 4), (2, 7)
28–31. For graphs, see p. A12.
32–35. See pp. A12–A13.

Exercise 37 involves writing a rule and generating ordered pairs that represent the cost of fabric. This exercise prepares students for the Multi-Step Test Prep on page 60.

Answers

37c.

f	c
1	2.90
2	5.80
3	8.70
4	11.60
5	14.50

38. $(-2, 5)$, $(-1, 4)$, $(0, 3)$, $(1, 4)$, $(2, 5)$; V shape

39. $(-4, -5)$, $(-2, -4)$, $(0, -3)$, $(2, -2)$, $(4, -1)$; line

40. $(-5, 26)$, $(-3, 10)$, $(-1, 2)$, $(1, 2)$, $(3, 10)$, $(5, 26)$; U shape

38–40, 42–45. For graphs, see p. A13.

47a. Both ordered pairs have positive coordinates, but to graph $(4, 2)$, you move right 4 units and then up 2 units. To graph $(2, 4)$, you move right 2 units and then up 4 units.

b. The coordinates of the second point are the opposite of the coordinates of the first point. To graph $(4, 2)$, move right and then up. To graph $(-4, -2)$, move left and then down.

49. For graph, see p. A13.

MULTI-STEP TEST PREP

37. This problem will prepare you for the Multi-Step Test Prep on page 60.

a. A room decorator wants to purchase fabric. Each yard of fabric costs \$2.90. Write a rule for the cost of the fabric. Let c equal the total cost and f equal the number of yards of fabric. **$c = 2.90f$**

b. Which variable is the input and which variable is the output? **f is input; c is output.**

c. Make a table showing the cost of 1, 2, 3, 4, and 5 yards of fabric.

d. How many whole yards can the decorator purchase if she has \$21.00? **7 yards**

Write an equation for each rule. Use the given values for x to generate ordered pairs. Graph the ordered pairs and describe the pattern.

38. y is equal to 3 more than the absolute value of x; $x = -2, -1, 0, 1,$ and 2. **$y = 3 + |x|$**

39. y is equal to the sum of one half of x and -3; $x = -4, -2, 0, 2,$ and 4. **$y = \frac{1}{2}x + (-3)$**

40. y is equal to the sum of x squared and 1; $x = -5, -3, -1, 1, 3,$ and 5. **$y = x^2 + 1$**

41. Business An events planner is preparing for a 5K race. She will buy enough water bottles for 50 volunteers, plus $1\frac{1}{2}$ times the number of runners who preregister for the race. **$y = 50 + 1.5x$**

a. Write an equation for the number of water bottles the planner should buy.

b. Generate ordered pairs for the number of water bottles the event planner will buy for the following numbers of preregistered runners: 100, 150, 200, 250, and 300. **(100, 200); (150, 275); (200, 350); (250, 425); (300, 500)**

LINK — Math History

RENÉ DESCARTES.

The coordinate plane is also called the Cartesian plane. This name comes from the mathematician Rene Descartes (1596–1650), who is credited with developing the coordinate system.

Give the coordinates of three points that fit the given description. Graph the points and describe the pattern. **42–45. Possible coordinates given.**

42. The x-coordinate is 1 less than the y-coordinate. **(1, 2), (2, 3), (3, 4); line**

43. The sum of the x-coordinate and y-coordinate is 5. **(1, 4), (2, 3), (3, 2); line**

44. The x-coordinate is 2 times the y-coordinate. **(2, 1), (4, 2), (6, 3); line**

45. The quotient of the x-coordinate and y-coordinate is 3. **(3, 1), (6, 2), (9, 3); line**

46. Critical Thinking Lance wrote five ordered pairs for which the y-coordinate was the opposite of the x-coordinate. Then he graphed the ordered pairs. What pattern did the points make? **The points make a line that passes from Quadrant II through the origin and into Quadrant IV.**

47. Write About It Graph the point $(4, 2)$.

a. How is graphing the point $(4, 2)$ different from graphing the point $(2, 4)$?

b. How is graphing the point $(4, 2)$ different from graphing the point $(-4, -2)$?

48. ///ERROR ANALYSIS/// Two students graphed the point $(4, 6)$. Which is incorrect? Explain the error. **A; the first number was used as the y-coordinate and the second number was used as the x-coordinate.**

A

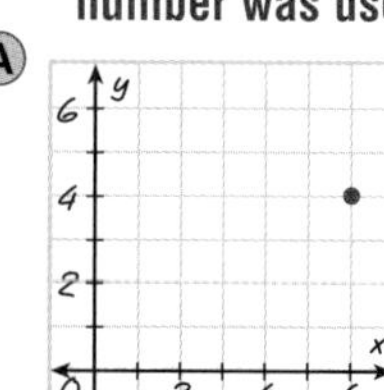

B

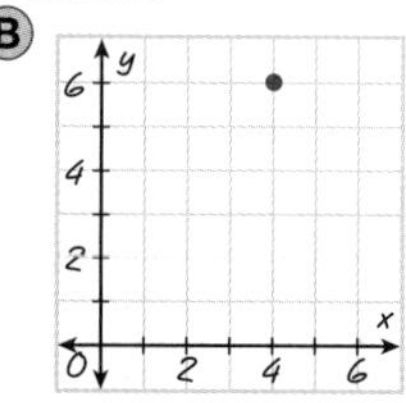

49. Generate ordered pairs for $y = x$, graph the points, and connect them to make a line. Do the same for $y = x + 2$ using the same values for x. How is the line for $y = x + 2$ different from the line for $y = x$?

49. The line for $y = x + 2$ is 2 units higher than the line for $y = x$ at every value of x.

1-8 PRACTICE A
1-8 PRACTICE C
1-8 PRACTICE B

Graph each point.

1. $G(2, 2)$
2. $M(3, 8)$
3. $X(4, -7)$
4. $L(-6, -1)$
5. $K(8, 0)$
6. $T(-2, 5)$

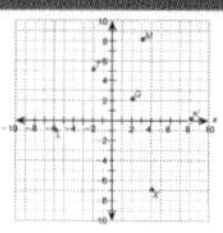

Name the quadrant in which each point lies.

7. A **Q I**
8. B **Q II**
9. C **Q III**
10. D **Q I**
11. E **Q IV**
12. F **none**

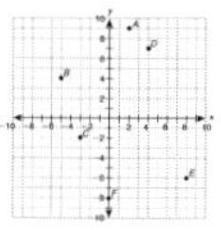

13. Generate ordered pairs for $y = |x - 4|$ using $x = 2, 3, 4, 5$ and 6. Graph the ordered pairs and describe the pattern.

Input	Output	Ordered Pair
x	y	(x, y)
2	$y = \|2 - 4\| = 2$	(2, 2)
3	$y = \|3 - 4\| = 1$	(3, 1)
4	$y = \|4 - 4\| = 0$	(4, 0)
5	$y = \|5 - 4\| = 1$	(5, 1)
6	$y = \|6 - 4\| = 2$	(6, 2)

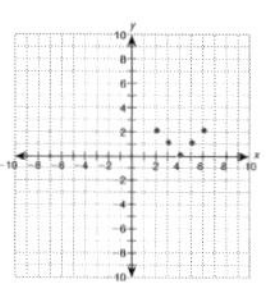

The points form a V-shape.

14. The number of chaperones at a school field trip must be $\frac{1}{5}$ the number of students attending, plus the 2 teacher sponsors. Write a rule for the number of chaperones that must be on the trip. Write ordered pairs to represent the number of chaperones that must attend the trip when there are 120, 150, 200, and 210 students.

$y = \frac{1}{5}x + 2$; (120, 26), (150, 32), (200, 42), (210, 44)

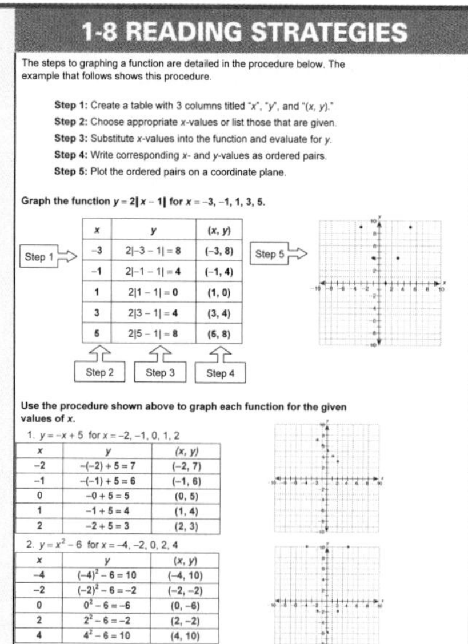

1-8 READING STRATEGIES

The steps to graphing a function are detailed in the procedure below. The example that follows shows this procedure.

Step 1: Create a table with 3 columns titled "x", "y", and "(x, y)."
Step 2: Choose appropriate x-values or list those that are given.
Step 3: Substitute x-values into the function and evaluate for y.
Step 4: Write corresponding x- and y-values as ordered pairs.
Step 5: Plot the ordered pairs on a coordinate plane.

Graph the function $y = 2|x - 1|$ for $x = -3, -1, 1, 3, 5$.

x	y	(x, y)
−3	$2\|-3 - 1\| = 8$	(−3, 8)
−1	$2\|-1 - 1\| = 4$	(−1, 4)
1	$2\|1 - 1\| = 0$	(1, 0)
3	$2\|3 - 1\| = 4$	(3, 4)
5	$2\|5 - 1\| = 8$	(5, 8)

Step 1, Step 2, Step 3, Step 4, Step 5

Use the procedure shown above to graph each function for the given values of x.

1. $y = -x + 5$ for $x = -2, -1, 0, 1, 2$

x	y	(x, y)
−2	$-(-2) + 5 = 7$	(−2, 7)
−1	$-(-1) + 5 = 6$	(−1, 6)
0	$-0 + 5 = 5$	(0, 5)
1	$-1 + 5 = 4$	(1, 4)
2	$-2 + 5 = 3$	(2, 3)

2. $y = x^2 - 6$ for $x = -4, -2, 0, 2, 4$

x	y	(x, y)
−4	$(-4)^2 - 6 = 10$	(−4, 10)
−2	$(-2)^2 - 6 = -2$	(−2, −2)
0	$0^2 - 6 = -6$	(0, −6)
2	$2^2 - 6 = -2$	(2, −2)
4	$4^2 - 6 = 10$	(4, 10)

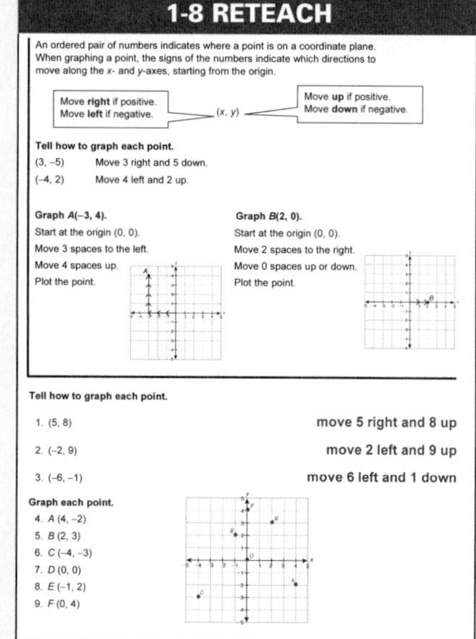

1-8 RETEACH

An ordered pair of numbers indicates where a point is on a coordinate plane. When graphing a point, the signs of the numbers indicate which directions to move along the x- and y-axes, starting from the origin.

(x, y) — Move **right** if positive. Move **left** if negative. / Move **up** if positive. Move **down** if negative.

Tell how to graph each point.

(3, −5) Move 3 right and 5 down.
(−4, 2) Move 4 left and 2 up.

Graph $A(-3, 4)$.
Start at the origin (0, 0).
Move 3 spaces to the left.
Move 4 spaces up.
Plot the point.

Graph $B(2, 0)$.
Start at the origin (0, 0).
Move 2 spaces to the right.
Move 0 spaces up or down.
Plot the point.

Tell how to graph each point.

1. (5, 8) **move 5 right and 8 up**
2. (−2, 9) **move 2 left and 9 up**
3. (−6, −1) **move 6 left and 1 down**

Graph each point.

4. $A(4, -2)$
5. $B(2, 3)$
6. $C(-4, -3)$
7. $D(0, 0)$
8. $E(-1, 2)$
9. $F(0, 4)$

TEST PREP

50. Which equation could be used to generate the ordered pairs (2, 7) and (6, 9)?

Ⓐ $y = 9 - x$ Ⓑ $y = \frac{3}{2}x^2 + 1$ **Ⓒ** $y = \frac{1}{2}x + 6$ Ⓓ $y = x + 5$

51. Which table of ordered pairs is generated when the values 1, 2, 3, and 4 are substituted for x in the equation $y = 2x - 4$?

Ⓕ

x	y
1	−3
2	−2
3	−1
4	0

Ⓖ

x	y
1	−2
2	0
3	2
4	4

Ⓗ

x	y
1	−2
2	0
3	1
4	2

Ⓙ

x	y
1	−3
2	−1
3	2
4	4

52. For which point on the graph is $x > \frac{7}{2}$ and $y < \frac{8}{3}$?

Ⓐ A Ⓒ C
Ⓑ B **Ⓓ** D

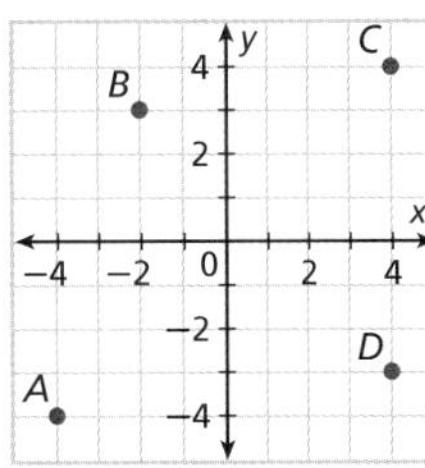

53. Which ordered pair describes the point (2, 5) shifted 3 units right and 2 units down?

Ⓕ (0, 8) **Ⓗ** (5, 3)
Ⓖ (2, 3) Ⓙ (5, 5)

CHALLENGE AND EXTEND

Graph each point.

54. $W(x + 4,\ y - 8)$ for $x = 5$ and $y = 2$ **(9, −6)**

55. $X(5 - x,\ y^2)$ for $x = -1$ and $y = 3$ **(6, 9)**

56. $Y(x + y,\ y - x)$ for $x = 6$ and $y = 3$ **(9, −3)**

57. $Z(xy,\ x^2y)$ for $x = -1$ and $y = 4$ **(−4, 4)**

58. Graph several ordered pairs that have an x-coordinate of 3. Describe the pattern.

59. Graph several ordered pairs that have a y-coordinate of 6. Describe the pattern.

58. The points make a vertical line at $x = 3$.

59. The points make a horizontal line at $y = 6$.

60. Find the perimeter of a rectangle whose vertices have the coordinates $A(3, 6)$, $B(3, -2)$, $C(-1, -2)$, and $D(-1, 6)$. **24 units**

61. **Multi-Step** The coordinates of three vertices of a rectangle are $J(-4, -2)$, $K(2, -2)$, and $L(2, 5)$. Find the coordinates of the fourth vertex. What is the area of the rectangle?
The coordinates of the fourth vertex are (−4, 5). The area of the rectangle is 42 square units.

SPIRAL REVIEW

Give the name of each figure. *(Previous course)*

62. **quadrilateral**

63. **cylinder**

64. 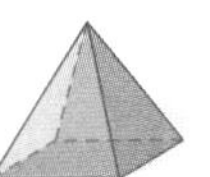
pyramid

65. 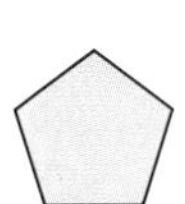
pentagon

Write all classifications that apply to each real number. *(Lesson 1-5)*

66. $\sqrt{36}$ 67. $\sqrt{6}$ 68. $\frac{1}{9}$ 69. -32

66. ℚ, terminating decimal, ℤ, 𝕎, ℕ

67. irrational

68. ℚ, repeating decimal

69. ℚ, terminating decimal, ℤ

Simplify each expression. *(Lesson 1-7)*

70. $\frac{1}{5} \cdot 18 \cdot 25$ **90**

71. $x^2 + 3x$ **$x^2 + 3x$**

72. $2a - b + a + 4b$ **$3a + 3b$**

COMMON ERROR ALERT

In **Exercise 39,** students may see the phrase "one-half of x and -3" and translate it as $\frac{1}{2}(x + (-3))$. Remind students to read the entire phrase so they can correctly place grouping symbols.

TEST PREP DOCTOR + In **Exercise 49,** students may test only the first ordered pair in the first equation and then choose **A.** Remind students to test both ordered pairs instead.

Answers

54–57. For graph, see p. A13.

Journal

Have students write instructions for graphing any ordered pair. Make sure they address graphing ordered pairs that contain 0.

ALTERNATIVE ASSESSMENT

Have students write a function, generate and graph five ordered pairs, and describe the pattern.

Power Presentations with PowerPoint®

1-8 Lesson Quiz

Graph each point. Name the quadrant in which each point lies.

1. (2, 0) None
2. (−3, −4) III
3. (1, −1) IV
4. (−5, 4) II

5. A cable company charges \$50 to set up a movie channel and \$3.00 per movie watched. Write a rule for the company's fee. Write ordered pairs for the fee when a person watches 1, 2, 3, or 4 movies.
$y = 50 + 3x$; (1, 53), (2, 56), (3, 59), (4, 62)

6. Generate ordered pairs for $y = x^2 - 5$ using $x = -2, -1, 0, 1$, and 2. Graph the ordered pairs and describe the pattern.
(−2, −1)
(−1, −4)
(0, −5)
(1, −4)
(2, −1)
The pattern is U-shaped.

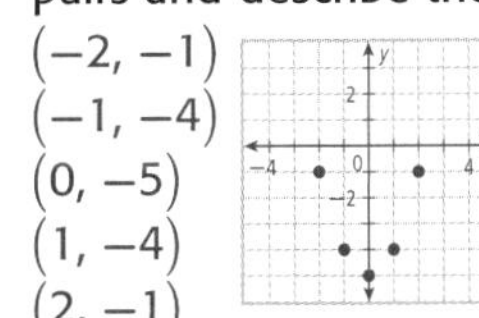

Also available on transparency

1-8 PROBLEM SOLVING

Write the correct answer.

1. The number of teachers at a university is $\frac{1}{15}$ the number of students. Write a rule for the number of teachers at the university.
$y = \frac{1}{15}x$

2. Use the rule in problem 1 to write ordered pairs for the number of teachers when there are 1230, 1500, 3045, and 4515 students.
(1230, 82), (1500, 100); (3045, 203), (4515, 301)

3. The starting salary for a new teacher in a certain school district is \$29,000 plus \$2100 for each year of previous teaching experience. Write a rule for the starting salary of a teacher in this school district.
$y = 29{,}000 + 2100x$

4. Use the rule in problem 3 to write ordered pairs for the starting salaries of teachers with 0, 3, 5, and 10 years of teaching experience.
(0, 29,000), (3, 35,300); (5, 39,500), (10, 50,000)

A class officer will buy picture frames as favors for the prom. To ensure she has enough frames, she plans to buy frames for the 18 teacher chaperones plus 1.2 times the number of students who buy tickets to the prom. Select the best answer.

5. Which rule represents the number of frames the class officer will buy?
A $y = 19.2 + x$
B $y = 19.2x$
C $y = 18x + 1.2$
D $y = 18 + 1.2x$

6. How many picture frames will the class officer buy if 225 students buy tickets to the prom?
F 244 H 270
G 252 **J** 288

7. Since both the number of students who buy tickets and the number of frames the class officer will buy cannot be negative, which quadrant will the ordered pairs that satisfy the rule in problem 5 lie in?
A Quadrant I C Quadrant III
B Quadrant II D Quadrant IV

8. If the class officer generates and graphs ordered pairs for the rule in problem 5, which statement would be true?
F The points would form a line.
G The points would form a U-shape.
H The points would form a V-shape.
J There will be no pattern.

1-8 CHALLENGE

Brandi decides to make and sell rag dolls. Her set up costs are \$150 for a new sewing machine and patterns. The fabric costs \$5 for each doll.

1. Write a rule for Brandi's cost of making dolls. Let y represent cost and x represent the number of dolls.
$y = 150 + 5x$

2. Find and graph ordered pairs for Brandi's cost of making 0, 10, 20, and 50 dolls. Describe the pattern, and then draw a line or curve that shows the pattern. Label it *Cost*.
(0, 150), (10, 200), (20, 250), (50, 400); the points form a straight line.

Brandi makes an income of \$10 for each doll she sells.

3. Write a rule for Brandi's income. Let y represent income and x represent the number of dolls.
$y = 10x$

4. Find and graph ordered pairs for Brandi's income from selling dolls. Describe the pattern, and then draw a line or curve that shows the pattern. Label it *Income*.
sample ordered pairs: (0, 0), (10, 100), (20, 200), (50, 500); the points form a straight line.

Use your graph to answer Exercises 6–10.

5. A business has a *profit* when its income is greater than its costs. From the graph, how do you know when Brandi has a profit? **when the line for income is above the line for cost**

6. A business has a *loss* when its costs are greater than its income. From the graph, how do you know when Brandi has a loss? **when the line for income is below the line for cost**

7. If Brandi only makes and sells 10 dolls, does she have a profit or a loss? How much profit or loss? **a loss of \$100**

8. If Brandi makes and sells 40 dolls, does she have a profit or a loss? How much profit or loss? **a profit of \$50**

9. A business *breaks even* when its costs equals its income. How many dolls would Brandi need to make and sell to break even? **30 dolls**

Organizer

Objective: Assess students' ability to apply concepts and skills in Lesson 1-6 through Lesson 1-8 in a real-world format.

 **Online Edition**

Resources

 ***Algebra I Assessments***
www.mathtekstoolkit.org

Problem	Text Reference
1	Lesson 1-7
2	Lesson 1-7
3	Lesson 1-6
4	Lesson 1-7
5	Lesson 1-8

Answers

1. 108 ft², 108 ft², 126 ft², 126 ft²; 636 ft²
5. See p. A13.

State Resources

MULTI-STEP TEST PREP

The Tools of Algebra

Design Time Lori's family and Marie's family are redecorating a room in each other's home. They have three days for the decorating project, which will be filmed for a local TV show.

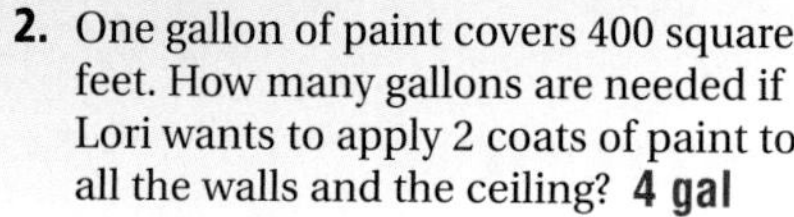

1. Lori decides to paint Marie's room a shade of blue. She measures the height and width of each wall in the rectangular room. She finds that two walls have a width of 12 feet and the other two have a width of 14 feet. The ceiling is 9 feet high. Find the area of each wall. Find the total area of all four walls plus the ceiling.

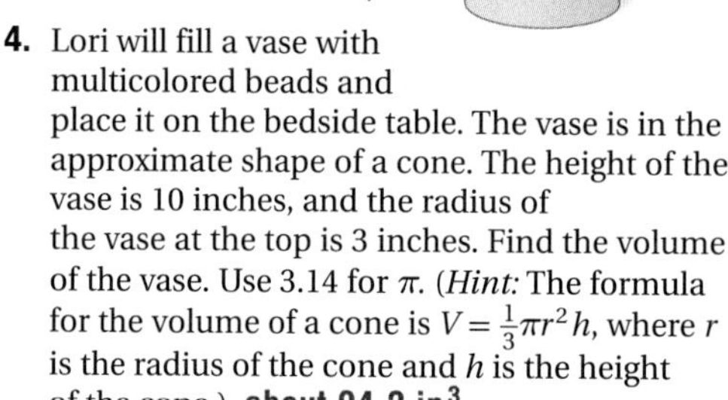

2. One gallon of paint covers 400 square feet. How many gallons are needed if Lori wants to apply 2 coats of paint to all the walls and the ceiling? **4 gal**
3. Lori decided to build a bedside table in the shape of a cylinder and cover all of its surfaces except the bottom with yellow fabric. The fabric costs $2.50 per square yard. The table has a radius of 1 foot and a height of 2 feet. What is the cost to cover the table? Use 3.14 for π. **$4.35**

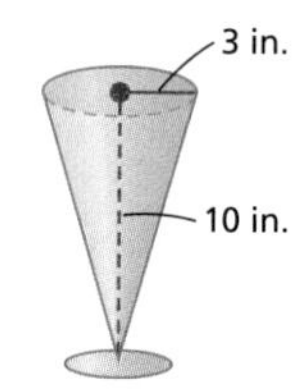

4. Lori will fill a vase with multicolored beads and place it on the bedside table. The vase is in the approximate shape of a cone. The height of the vase is 10 inches, and the radius of the vase at the top is 3 inches. Find the volume of the vase. Use 3.14 for π. (*Hint:* The formula for the volume of a cone is $V = \frac{1}{3}\pi r^2 h$, where r is the radius of the cone and h is the height of the cone.) **about 94.2 in³**

3 in.
10 in.

5. Lori wants to create a border around the room using stickers. She can purchase a package of 5 stickers for $6.00. Make a table to show the cost of 1, 2, 3, 4, and 5 packages of stickers. Make another table to show the cost based on the number of stickers (not the number of packages). How many stickers can Lori purchase if she has $32 left in her budget?

INTERVENTION

Scaffolding Questions

1. How can you find the area of one wall? width times height How can you find the area of the ceiling? width of one wall times width of adjacent wall
2. Why is the number of gallons rounded up to the next whole number? Paint is sold in full gallons.
3. How can you find the area of the top of the table? πr^2 How can you find the area of the curved surface? $2\pi rh$ How do you convert ft² into yd²? divide by 3^2
4. How do you find the volume of a cone? $\frac{1}{3}\pi r^2 h$
5. What are the input values in the second table? multiples of 5

Extension

Refer to Problem 2. Paint is sometimes sold in quarts. How many gallons and quarts of paint would Lori need to buy in order to have the least amount of paint left over? 3 gallons and 1 quart

CHAPTER 1

SECTION 1B

Quiz for Lessons 1-6 Through 1-8

1-6 Order of Operations

Simplify each expression.

1. $-6 + 12 \div (-3)$ **−10**
2. $30 - 9 + 4$ **25**
3. $(6 - 8) \cdot (7 - 5)$ **−4**
4. $8 \cdot [8 - (4 - 2)]$ **48**
5. $\frac{23 - 3 \cdot 5}{4}$ **2**
6. $|3 - 9| \div 2 + 5$ **8**

Translate each word phrase into a numerical expression.

7. the quotient of 16 and the difference of 9 and −7 $\frac{16}{9 - (-7)}$
8. the product of 5 and the sum of 6 and 4 $5(6 + 4)$
9. The area of a trapezoid can be found using the expression $\frac{1}{2}(b_1 + b_2)h$. Find the area of the trapezoid shown. 16 cm^2

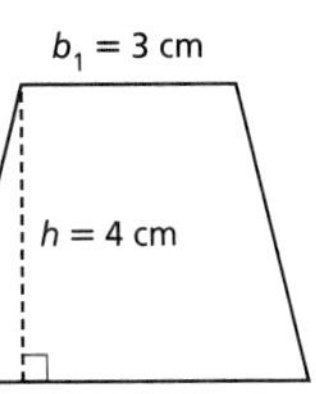

1-7 Simplifying Expressions

Simplify each expression.

10. $75 + 32 + 25$ **132**
11. $5 \cdot 18 \cdot 20$ **1800**
12. $\frac{1}{4} \cdot 19 \cdot 8$ **38**

Write each product using the Distributive Property. Then simplify.

13. $7(67)$ $7(70) - 7(3) = 469$
14. $9(29)$ $9(30) - 9(1) = 261$
15. $17(18)$ $17(20) - 17(2) = 306$
16. $8(106)$ $8(100) + 8(6) = 848$

Simplify each expression by combining like terms.

17. $4k + 15k$ $19k$
18. $x^2 + 22x^2$ $23x^2$
19. $-2g + 5g$ $3g$

Simplify each expression. Justify each step with an operation or property.

20. $3(x + 2) - 3x$ **6**
21. $x - 6x^2 + 3x + 4x^2$ $4x - 2x^2$
22. $-2(3x + 2y + 4x - 5y)$ $-14x + 6y$

1-8 Introduction to Functions

Graph each point.

23. $A(0, -3)$
24. $B(-2, -3)$
25. $C(1, 4)$

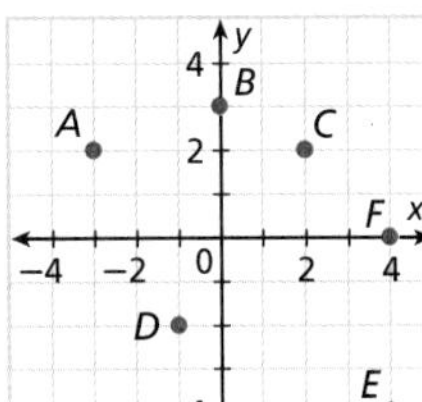

Name the quadrant in which each point lies.

26. A **Q II**
27. B **None**
28. C **Q I**
29. D **Q III**
30. E **Q IV**
31. F **None**

Generate ordered pairs for each function for $x = -2, -1, 0, 1,$ and 2. Graph the ordered pairs and describe the pattern.

32. $y = x^2 + 1$ **U shape**
33. $y = x - 1$ **line**
34. $y = -|x|$ **V shape**
35. $y = 3x + 3$ **line**

36. A swimming pool contains 30,000 gallons of water. The pool is drained at a rate of 100 gallons per minute. Write a rule for the amount of water in the pool when x minutes have gone by. Write ordered pairs for the amount of water in the pool when 30, 60, 90, and 120 minutes have gone by. $y = 30{,}000 - 100x$; (30, 27,000), (60, 24,000), (90, 21,000), (120, 18,000)

READY TO GO ON?

SECTION 1B

Organizer

Objective: Assess students' mastery of concepts and skills in Lessons 1-6 through 1-8.

Resources

Assessment Resources
Section 1B Quiz

Teacher One Stop™
Test & Practice Generator

INTERVENTION

Resources

Ready to Go On? Intervention and Enrichment **Worksheets**

Ready to Go On? **CD-ROM**

Ready to Go On? **Online**

my.hrw.com

Answers

20–22. For justifications, see p. A13.
23–25. See p. A13.
32–35. For graphs, see p. A13.

READY TO GO ON? Diagnose and Prescribe

Ready to Go On? Intervention	*Ready to Go On? Intervention,* Section 1B: Worksheets	CD-ROM	Online
Lesson 1-6	1-6 Intervention	Activity 1-6	Diagnose and Prescribe Online
Lesson 1-7	1-7 Intervention	Activity 1-7	
Lesson 1-8	1-8 Intervention	Activity 1-8	

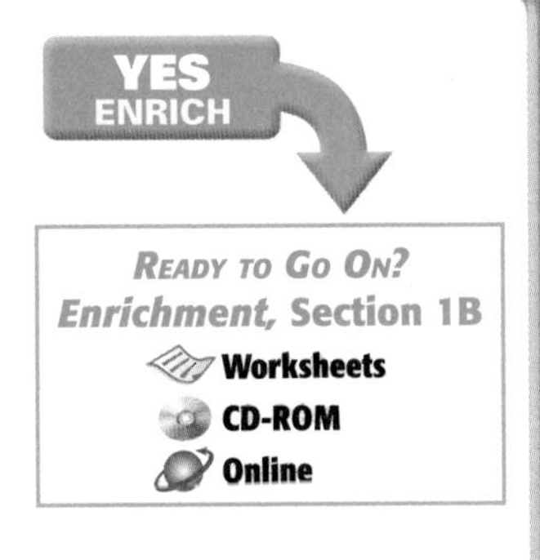

Ready to Go On? Enrichment, Section 1B
Worksheets
CD-ROM
Online

CHAPTER 1 Study Guide: Review

Organizer

Objective: Help students organize and review key concepts and skills presented in Chapter 1.

Online Edition
Multilingual Glossary

Countdown Week 2

Resources

Teacher One Stop™
PuzzleView
Test & Practice Generator

***Multilingual Glossary* Online**
go.hrw.com
KEYWORD: MA7 Glossary

Lesson *Tutorial Videos* CD-ROM

Answers

1. constant
2. whole numbers
3. coefficient
4. origin
5. 1.99g
6. $t + 3$
7. 5
8. 5
9. 6
10. $150 \div m$; 30; 25; 15

CHAPTER 1

Study Guide: Review

Vocabulary

Complete the sentences below with vocabulary words from the list above.

1. A(n) __?__ is a value that does not change.
2. The __?__ include the natural numbers and zero.
3. A(n) __?__ is the numerical factor of a term that contains a variable.
4. The __?__ is the point where the axes of a coordinate plane intersect.

1-1 Variables and Expressions *(pp. 6–11)*

EXAMPLES

■ **Barbara has saved d dollars for a $65 sweater. Write an expression for the amount of money she still needs to buy the sweater.**

$65 - d$ *Think: d dollars less than the price of the sweater.*

■ **Evaluate $b - a$ for $a = 7$ and $b = 15$.**

$b - a = 15 - 7$ *Substitute the values for the variables.*
$= 8$

EXERCISES

5. Grapes cost $1.99 per pound. Write an expression for the cost of g pounds of grapes.
6. Today's temperature is 3 degrees warmer than yesterday's temperature t. Write an expression for today's temperature.

Evaluate each expression for $p = 5$ and $q = 1$.

7. qp
8. $p \div q$
9. $q + p$
10. Each member of the art club will make the same number of posters to advertise their club. They will make 150 posters total. Write an expression for how many posters each member will make if there are m members. Find how many posters each member will make if there are 5, 6, and 10 members.

1-2 Adding and Subtracting Real Numbers *(pp. 14–19)*

EXAMPLES

Add or subtract.

- $-4 + (-9)$

  $-4 + (-9)$ *The signs are the same.*

  $(4 + 9 = 13)$ *Add the absolute values and use the sign of the numbers.*

  -13

- $-8 - (-3)$

  $-8 + 3$ *To subtract −3, add 3.*

  -5

EXERCISES

Add or subtract.

11. $-2 + (-12)$ **12.** $-6 + 1.4$ **13.** $9\frac{1}{4} + \left(-4\frac{3}{4}\right)$

14. $\frac{1}{2} - \frac{3}{2}$ **15.** $-8 - 16$ **16.** $6.7 - (-7.6)$

17. A trail starts at an elevation of 2278 feet. It descends 47 feet to a campsite. What is the elevation of the campsite?

1-3 Multiplying and Dividing Real Numbers *(pp. 20–25)*

EXAMPLES

Multiply or divide.

- $-12(9)$

  $-12(9) = -108$

- $-\frac{5}{6} \div \left(-\frac{3}{4}\right)$

  $$-\frac{5}{6} \div \left(-\frac{3}{4}\right) = -\frac{5}{6}\left(-\frac{4}{3}\right) = \frac{(-5)(-4)}{6(3)} = \frac{20}{18} = \frac{10}{9}$$

EXERCISES

Multiply or divide if possible.

18. $-5(-18)$ **19.** $0 \cdot 10$ **20.** $-4(3.8)$

21. $-56 \div 7$ **22.** $0 \div 0.75$ **23.** $9 \div 0$

Divide.

24. $4 \div \frac{4}{9}$ **25.** $-\frac{1}{2} \div \frac{3}{4}$ **26.** $\frac{6}{7} \div \frac{2}{5}$

27. An exercise program recommends that a person walk at least 10,000 steps every day. At this rate, how many steps would the person walk in 1 year?

1-4 Powers and Exponents *(pp. 26–31)*

EXAMPLES

- **Simplify -3^4.**

  $-3^4 = -1 \cdot 3 \cdot 3 \cdot 3 \cdot 3$ *Find the product of −1 and four 3's.*

  $= -81$

- **Write −216 as a power of −6.**

  $-216 = (-6)(-6)(-6)$ *The product of three −6's is −216.*

  $= (-6)^3$

EXERCISES

Write each expression as repeated multiplication. Then simplify the expression.

28. 4^3 **29.** $(-3)^3$ **30.** $(-3)^4$

31. -5^2 **32.** $\left(\frac{2}{3}\right)^3$ **33.** $\left(-\frac{4}{5}\right)^2$

Write each number as a power of the given base.

34. 16; base 2 **35.** −1000; base −10

36. 64; base −8 **37.** 12; base 12

38. The interior of a safe is shaped like a cube with edges 9 inches long. What is the volume of the interior of the safe?

Answers

11. -14
12. -4.6
13. $4\frac{1}{2}$
14. -1
15. -24
16. 14.3
17. 2231 ft
18. 90
19. 0
20. -15.2
21. -8
22. 0
23. undefined
24. 9
25. $-\frac{2}{3}$
26. $\frac{15}{7}$
27. 3,650,000 steps
28. $4 \cdot 4 \cdot 4 = 64$
29. $(-3)(-3)(-3) = -27$
30. $(-3)(-3)(-3)(-3) = 81$
31. $-1 \cdot 5 \cdot 5 = -25$
32. $\left(\frac{2}{3}\right)\left(\frac{2}{3}\right)\left(\frac{2}{3}\right) = \frac{8}{27}$
33. $\left(-\frac{4}{5}\right)\left(-\frac{4}{5}\right) = \frac{16}{25}$
34. 2^4
35. $(-10)^3$
36. $(-8)^2$
37. 12^1
38. 729 in^3

Answers

39. 6
40. 4
41. −7
42. −12
43. $\frac{5}{6}$
44. $\frac{1}{3}$
45. rational number, terminating decimal, integer, whole number, natural number
46. rational number, terminating decimal, integer, whole number
47. rational number, terminating decimal, integer
48. rational number, terminating decimal
49. irrational number
50. rational number, repeating decimal
51. 3.6 ft
52. 23
53. 8
54. 6
55. $\frac{1}{2}$
56. −18
57. 0
58. 62
59. 10
60. 8
61. 10
62. $8 + 7(-2)$
63. $\frac{12}{8+3}$
64. $4\sqrt{20 - x}$
65. 168 ft

1-5 Roots and Real Numbers (pp. 32–37)

EXAMPLES

Find each root.

■ $-\sqrt{64}$

$8^2 = 64$

$-\sqrt{64} = -8$

■ $\sqrt{\frac{16}{81}}$

$\left(\frac{4}{9}\right)^2 = \frac{4}{9} \cdot \frac{4}{9} = \frac{16}{81}$

$\sqrt{\frac{16}{81}} = \frac{4}{9}$

■ **Write all classifications that apply to −7.**

$-7 = \frac{-7}{1} = -7.0$

rational number, terminating decimal, integer

EXERCISES

Find each root.

39. $\sqrt{36}$ **40.** $\sqrt[3]{64}$ **41.** $-\sqrt{49}$

42. $-\sqrt{144}$ **43.** $\sqrt{\frac{25}{36}}$ **44.** $\sqrt[3]{\frac{1}{27}}$

Write all the classifications that apply to each real number.

45. 21 **46.** 0 **47.** −13

48. 0.8 **49.** $\sqrt{3}$ **50.** $\frac{5}{6}$

51. A tabletop is shaped like a square with an area of 13 square feet. Find the length of one side of the table to the nearest tenth of a foot.

1-6 Order of Operations (pp. 40–45)

EXAMPLES

■ **Simplify $18 - 3\left(\frac{15-7}{4}\right)^2$.**

$18 - 3\left(\frac{15-7}{4}\right)^2$

$18 - 3\left(\frac{8}{4}\right)^2$ *Simplify the numerator.*

$18 - 3(2)^2$ *Simplify inside parentheses.*

$18 - 3 \cdot 4$ *Simplify powers.*

$18 - 12$ *Multiply.*

6 *Subtract.*

■ **Evaluate $-5\sqrt{40 - x} + 12$ for $x = 4$.**

$-5\sqrt{40 - 4} + 12$ *Substitute the value for x.*

$-5\sqrt{36} + 12$ *Simplify inside the square root symbol.*

$-5(6) + 12$ *Find the square root.*

$-30 + 12$ *Multiply.*

-18 *Add.*

EXERCISES

Simplify each expression.

52. $5 \cdot 4 + 3$ **53.** $17 + 3(-3)$

54. $[8 + (2 - 6)^2] \div 4$ **55.** $\frac{4^2 - 11}{10}$

56. $|12 - 3 \cdot 7| \cdot (-2)$ **57.** $\sqrt{4 \cdot 5 + 5} - 5$

Evaluate each expression for the given value of x.

58. $48 - x + 29$ for $x = 15$

59. $x + 4 \cdot 6 - 10$ for $x = -4$

60. $8(x - 8)^3$ for $x = 9$

61. $[(3 - x)^2 + 4] \div 2$ for $x = 7$

Translate each word phrase into a numerical or algebraic expression.

62. the sum of 8 and the product of 7 and −2

63. the quotient of 12 and the sum of 8 and 3

64. 4 times the square root of x less than 20

65. The expression $16t^2 + vt$ can be used to find the distance in feet traveled by a falling object. The initial speed is v (ft/s), and time is t (s). Find the distance traveled in 3 s by a falling object with an initial speed of 8 ft/s.

1-7 Simplifying Expressions (pp. 46–51)

EXAMPLES

Simplify each expression.

- $-6f^2 - 8f + 3f^2$
  $-6f^2 + 3f^2 - 8f$ *Commutative Property*
  $-3f^2 - 8f$ *Combine like terms.*

- $3x - 4y$
  $3x - 4y$ *There are no like terms. It cannot be simplified.*

- $5x^2 - 3(x - 2) - x$
  $5x^2 - 3x - 3(-2) - x$ *Distributive Property*
  $5x^2 - 3x + 6 - x$ *Multiply.*
  $5x^2 - 3x - x + 6$ *Commutative Property*
  $5x^2 - 4x + 6$ *Combine like terms.*

EXERCISES

Simplify each expression.

66. $18 + 26 - 8 + 4$ **67.** $60 \cdot 27 \cdot \frac{1}{6}$

Write each product using the Distributive Property. Then simplify.

68. $13(103)$ **69.** $18(99)$

Simplify each expression.

70. $20x - 16x$ **71.** $2y^2 + 5y^2$

72. $6(x + 4) - 2x$ **73.** $-2(x^2 - 1) + 4x^2$

74. $-2y + 3y^2 - 3y + y$ **75.** $7y + 3y - a - 2y$

76. Rita bought a sandwich, 2 bottles of water, and an apple for lunch. The sandwich cost \$4.99, the bottles of water cost \$1.48 each, and the apple cost \$0.89. About how much did Rita spend on lunch?

1-8 Introduction to Functions (pp. 54–59)

EXAMPLES

- **Generate ordered pairs for the function using the given values for x. Graph the ordered pairs and describe the pattern.**
  $y = x + 2$; $x = -4, -3, -2, -1, 0$

Input	Output	Ordered Pair
x	y	(x, y)
−4	−4 + 2 = −2	(−4, −2)
−3	−3 + 2 = −1	(−3, −1)
−2	−2 + 2 = 0	(−2, 0)
−1	−1 + 2 = 1	(−1, 1)
0	0 + 2 = 2	(0, 2)

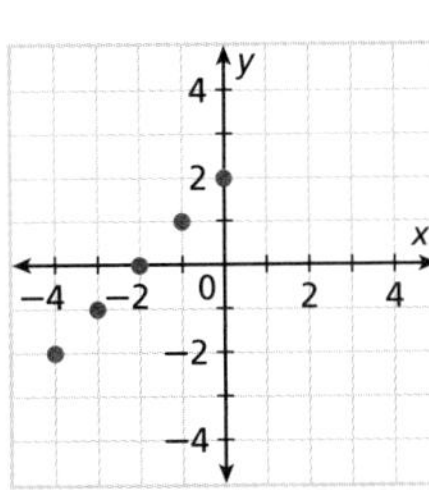

The points form a straight line.

EXERCISES

Graph each point.

77. $A(2, 3)$ **78.** $B(-1, 4)$

79. $C(0, 8)$ **80.** $D(5, -3)$

Name the quadrant in which each point lies.

81. R
82. S
83. T
84. U
85. V
86. W

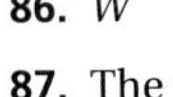

87. The price of an item with tax is equal to the price of the item plus $\frac{1}{20}$ of the price. Write a rule for the price with tax. Write ordered pairs for the price with tax of items that cost \$2, \$15, \$30, and \$40.

88. Generate ordered pairs for the function $y = \frac{1}{4}x^2$ for $x = -4, -1, 0, 1$, and 4. Graph the ordered pairs and describe the pattern.

Answers

66. 40
67. 270
68. $13(100) + 13(3) = 1339$
69. $18(100) - 18(1) = 1782$
70. $4x$
71. $7y^2$
72. $4x + 24$
73. $2x^2 + 2$
74. $-4y + 3y^2$
75. $8y - a$
76. \$9
77–80.

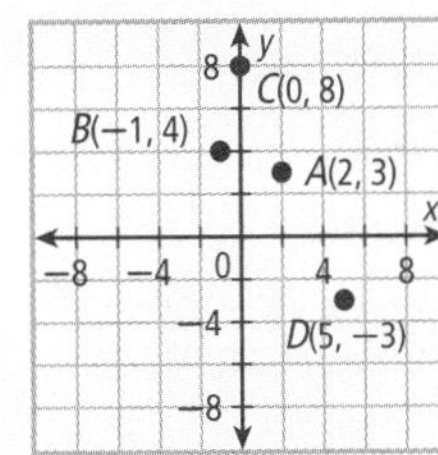

81. I
82. IV
83. I
84. II
85. III
86. IV
87. $y = p + \frac{1}{20}p$; (\$2, \$2.10), (\$15, \$15.75), (\$30, \$31.50), (\$40, \$42)
88. $(-4, 4)$, $\left(-1, \frac{1}{4}\right)$, $(0, 0)$, $\left(1, \frac{1}{4}\right)$, $(4, 4)$; U shape

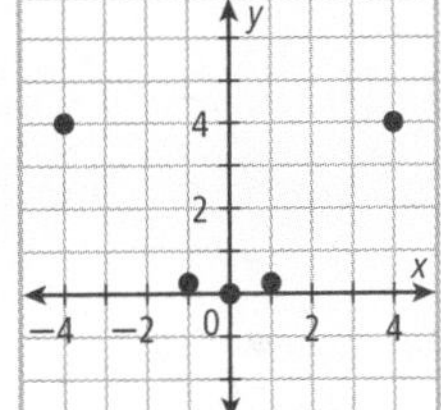

Organizer

Objective: Assess students' mastery of concepts and skills in Chapter 1.

 Online Edition

Resources

 ***Assessment Resources***

Chapter 1 Tests

- Free Response (Levels A, B, C)
- Multiple Choice (Levels A, B, C)
- Performance Assessment

Teacher One Stop™

Test & Practice Generator

Answers

22. rational, terminating decimal, integer, whole number, natural number
23. irrational
24. rational, terminating decimal, integer
25. rational, terminating decimal

33–36.

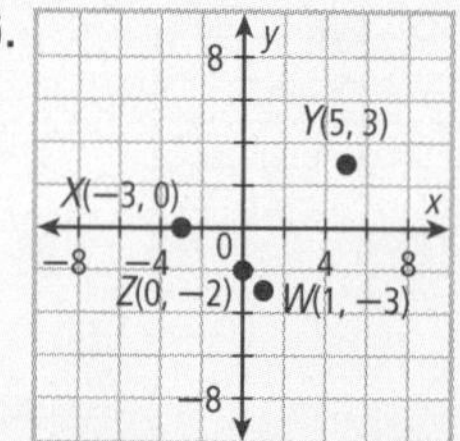

37. (−2, −5)
(−1, −3)
(0, −1)
(1, 1)
(2, 3)
line

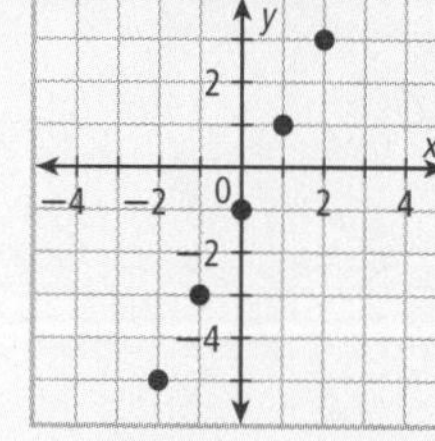

Evaluate each expression for $a = 2$, $b = 3$, and $c = 6$.

1. $c - a$ **4**
2. ab **6**
3. $c \div a$ **3**
4. $\frac{c}{b}$ **2**
5. $b - a$ **1**
6. Give two ways to write $n - 5$ in words. **five less than *n*; the difference of *n* and 5**
7. Nate runs 8 miles each week. Write an expression for the number of miles he runs in n weeks. Find the number of miles Nate runs in 5 weeks. **8*n*; 40 mi**

Add or subtract.

8. $-5 + 8$ **3**
9. $-3 - 4$ **−7**
10. $4 + (-7)$ **−3**
11. $7 - (-2)$ **9**

The table shows the lowest temperatures recorded in four states.

12. How much greater is the lowest temperature in Hawaii than the lowest temperature in Alaska? **92°F**
13. How much greater is the lowest temperature in Texas than the lowest temperature in Nebraska? **24°F**

Lowest Temperatures in Four States

Location	Temperature (°F)
Prospect Creek, Alaska	−80
Camp Clarke, Nebraska	−47
Mauna Kea, Hawaii	12
Seminole, Texas	−23

Multiply or divide if possible.

14. $(-3)(-6)$ **18**
15. $-\frac{1}{2} \div \frac{1}{4}$ **−2**
16. $12 \div (-3)$ **−4**
17. $0 \div (-4)$ **0**

Simplify each expression.

18. 5^4 **625**
19. $\left(-\frac{4}{5}\right)^3$ $\mathbf{-\frac{64}{125}}$
20. 2^5 **32**
21. -6^2 **−36**

Write all classifications that apply to each real number.

22. 30
23. $\sqrt{6}$
24. −12
25. $\frac{1}{2}$

Evaluate each expression for the given value of x.

26. $\frac{-2-6}{x^2}$ for $x = 2$ **−2**
27. $8(x - 1)^2$ for $x = 11$ **800**
28. $22 + [-2(19 - x)]$ for $x = 7$ **−2**
29. Does the phrase "2 times the sum of a number and 5" represent the same expression as the phrase "the sum of 2 times a number and 5"? Explain why or why not. **No; the first phrase represents the expression $2(n + 5)$, and the second phrase represents the expression $2n + 5$.**

Simplify each expression.

30. $5\frac{1}{4} + 7 + 2\frac{3}{4}$ **15**
31. $-2(x + 5) + 4x$ $\mathbf{2x - 10}$
32. $3x + 2x^2 - x$ $\mathbf{2x + 2x^2}$

Graph each point.

33. $W(1, -3)$
34. $X(-3, 0)$
35. $Y(5, 3)$
36. $Z(0, -2)$
37. Generate ordered pairs for $y = 2x - 1$ for $x = -2, -1, 0, 1, 2$. Graph the ordered pairs and describe the pattern.

COLLEGE ENTRANCE EXAM PRACTICE

CHAPTER 1

FOCUS ON SAT*

The SAT is often used to predict academic success at the college level. SAT scores are used to compare the math and verbal reasoning skills of students from all over the world.

In each section of SAT questions, the easier questions are at the beginning of the section and harder questions come later. Answer as many of the easy questions as you can first, and then move on to the more challenging questions.

You may want to time yourself as you take this practice test. It should take you about 8 minutes to complete.

1. The number 0 is NOT an example of which of the following?
   - (A) Real numbers
   - (B) Rational numbers
   - (C) Whole numbers
   - (D) Integers
   - (E) Natural numbers

2. A clothing store opens with 75 pairs of jeans on a sale table. By noon, 10 pairs have been sold. As of 2:00, another 8 pairs have been sold. A clerk then restocks with 12 pairs. Receipts show that 18 pairs of jeans were sold after 2:00. How many pairs of jeans are left at the end of the day?
   - (A) 23
   - (B) 27
   - (C) 36
   - (D) 51
   - (E) 123

3. If Jack is three times as old as his sister Judy, which of the following expressions represents Jack's age if Judy is j years old?
   - (A) $3 \div j$
   - (B) $3j$
   - (C) $j + 3$
   - (D) $3 - j$
   - (E) $\frac{1}{3}j$

4. Which of the following is equal to -3^4?
   - (A) 81
   - (B) 12
   - (C) -12
   - (D) -64
   - (E) -81

5. What is the result after applying the following sequence of operations to a number n in the given order?

   1. Subtract 2.
   2. Divide by 3.
   3. Add 7.
   4. Multiply by -1.

   - (A) $\frac{n-2}{3} + 7(-1)$
   - (B) $\frac{(-n-2)+7}{3}$
   - (C) $-\left(-\frac{2}{3} + 7\right)n$
   - (D) $-\left(\frac{n-2}{3} + 7\right)$
   - (E) $n - \frac{2}{3} + 7(-1)$

6. Which expression is equivalent to $8(6 + x)$?
   - (A) $48x$
   - (B) $8x + 14$
   - (C) $8x + 48$
   - (D) $x + 14$
   - (E) $x + 48$

*SAT is a registered trademark of the College Board, which was not involved in the production of, and does not endorse, this product.

COLLEGE ENTRANCE EXAM PRACTICE CHAPTER 1

Objective: Provide practice for college entrance exams such as the SAT.

 PREMIER **Online Edition**

Resources

College Entrance Exam Practice

Questions on the SAT represent the following content areas:

Number and Operation, 20–25%

Algebra and Functions, 35–40%

Geometry and Measurement, 25–30%

Data Analysis, Statistics, and Probability, 10–15%

Items on this page focus on:

- Number and Operation

Text References:

Item	1	2	3	4	5	6
Lesson	1-5	1-2	1-1	1-4	1-6	1-7

TEST PREP DOCTOR

1. Students may choose **C** because they do not remember the difference between whole numbers and natural numbers. Remind students that whole numbers are all of the natural numbers and 0.
2. Students who chose **B** may have subtracted the 12 pairs restocked instead of adding them. Students who chose **C** may have found the total number of pairs of jeans sold for the day.
3. Students may choose **C** if they did not read the question carefully; Jack is three times as old as Judy, not three years older than Judy. Students who choose answer **E** may think that Judy is three times as old as Jack.
4. Students may choose **A** because they used -3 as the base of the power. Remind students that the exponent applies only to the number right before it, and that -3^4 can be thought of as $(-1)(3^4)$.
5. Students may choose **E** if they did not perform each step on the entire expression obtained from the previous step. Remind students of the need to use grouping symbols when translating words into algebraic expressions.
6. Students may choose **E** because they do not understand the Distributive Property. Ask students about the meaning of the word *distribute* and discuss how it can be applied to an algebraic expression.

Organizer

Objective: Provide students with opportunities to learn and practice common test-taking strategies.

Online Edition

This Test Tackler focuses on how to correctly fill in a grid when answering a gridded-response item. Students often solve the test item correctly, but fill in the answer grid incorrectly. This strategy involves students reviewing the rules for how to fill in a grid, and then looking at filled-in grids and identifying why the response was marked as incorrect.

Standardized Test Strategies

Gridded Response: Fill in Answer Grids Correctly

When responding to a test item that requires you to place your answer in a grid, you must fill out the grid on your answer sheet correctly, or the item will be marked as incorrect.

EXAMPLE 1

Gridded Response: Simplify the expression $12^2 - 3(10 + 4)$.

$$12^2 - 3(10 + 4)$$
$$12^2 - 3(14)$$
$$144 - 3(14)$$
$$144 - 42$$
$$102$$

The expression simplifies to 102.

- Write your answer in the answer boxes at the top of the grid.
- Put only one digit in each box. Do not leave a blank box in the middle of an answer.
- Shade the bubble for each digit in the same column as the digit in the answer box.

EXAMPLE 2

Gridded Response: Evaluate the expression $ba \div c$ for $a = -7$, $b = 2$, and $c = -6$.

$$ba \div c$$
$$(2)(-7) \div (-6)$$
$$-14 \div (-6)$$
$$\frac{7}{3} = 2\frac{1}{3} = 2.\overline{3}$$

The expression simplifies to $\frac{7}{3}$, $2\frac{1}{3}$, or $2.\overline{3}$.

- Mixed numbers and repeating decimals cannot be gridded, so you must grid the answer as $\frac{7}{3}$.
- Write your answer in the answer boxes at the top of the grid.
- Put only one digit or symbol in each box. On some grids, the fraction bar and the decimal point have a designated box. Do not leave a blank box in the middle of an answer.
- Shade the bubble for each digit or symbol in the same column as the digit in the answer box.

On many grids you cannot grid a negative number because the grid does not include the negative sign. If you get a negative answer to a test item, you may need to recalculate the problem.

Read each sample and then answer the questions that follow.

Sample A

A student correctly evaluated an expression and got $\frac{8}{15}$ as a result. Then the student filled in the grid as shown.

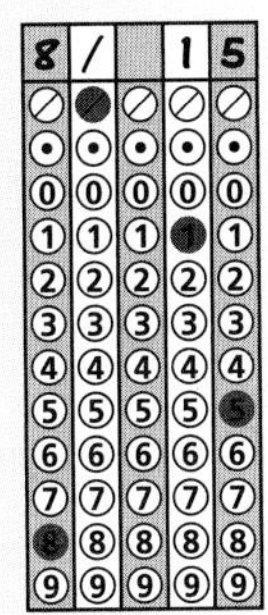

1. What error did the student make when filling in the grid?
2. Explain how to fill in the answer correctly.

Sample B

The square root of 6.25 is 2.5. This answer is displayed in the grid.

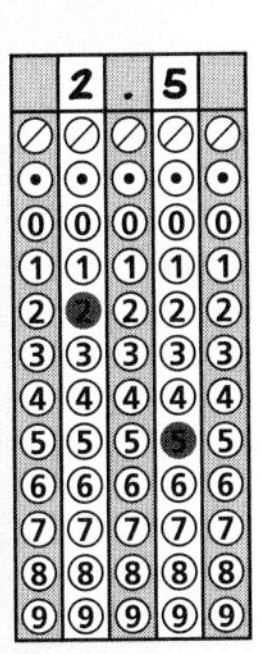

3. What error did the student make when filling in the grid?
4. Explain how to fill in the answer correctly.

Sample C

A student correctly simplified the expression $2\frac{1}{8} + 3\frac{5}{8} + \frac{7}{8}$. Then the student filled in the grid as shown.

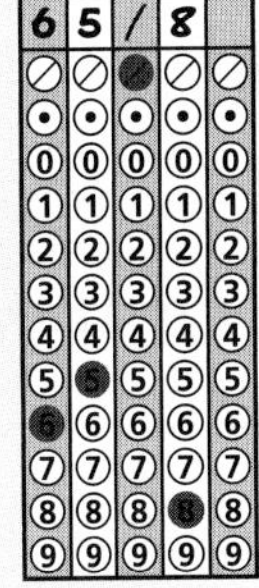

5. What answer does the grid show?
6. Explain why you cannot fill in a mixed number.
7. Write the answer $6\frac{5}{8}$ in two forms that could be entered in the grid correctly.

Sample D

A student added −10 and 25 and got an answer of 15. Then the student filled in the grid as shown.

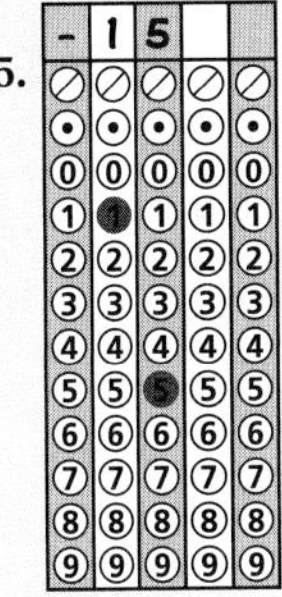

8. What error does the grid show?
9. Another student got an answer of −15. Explain why the student knew this answer was wrong.

Answers

Possible answers:

1. There should not be a space between the fraction bar and the next number.
2. Do not leave spaces in the middle of the answer.
3. The decimal point must be shaded in.
4. Shade 2, the decimal point, and 5.
5. 65 eighths
6. Because the whole number and numerator of a mixed number would be written next to each other, together they would look like the numerator of an improper fraction.
7. 6.625 or $\frac{53}{8}$
8. Negative numbers cannot be entered into the grid.
9. The student knew that there was no bubble to fill in for a negative sign. You should be able to fill in a correct answer, so the student knew that the negative answer was not correct.

Answers to Test Items

A. See answers to Problems 1 and 2.

B. See answers to Problems 3 and 4.

C. See answer to Problem 7.

D. See answer to Problem 9.

State Resources

go.hrw.com
State Resources Online
KEYWORD: MA7 Resources

Organizer

Objective: Provide review and practice for Chapter 1 and standardized tests.

Resources

 ***Assessment Resources***

Chapter 1 Cumulative Test

State Resources

CUMULATIVE ASSESSMENT, CHAPTERS 1

Multiple Choice

1. Eric is collecting gifts for a charity event. He needs 150 gifts. So far he has collected x gifts. Which expression represents how many gifts Eric still needs to collect?

Ⓐ $150 + x$
Ⓑ $150 - x$
Ⓒ $x - 150$
Ⓓ $150 \div x$

2. An online store sells birdhouses for $34.95 each. For each order, there is a one-time shipping and handling fee of $7.50. Which expression can be used to represent the cost of ordering x birdhouses?

Ⓕ $x + 34.95 + 7.50$
Ⓖ $(34.95 + 7.50)x$
Ⓗ $7.50x + 34.95$
Ⓙ $34.95x + 7.50$

3. Which equation could have generated the table?

x	y
−2	5
−1	2
0	1
1	2
2	5

Ⓐ $y = -2x + 1$
Ⓑ $y = x + 1$
Ⓒ $y = |2x| + 1$
Ⓓ $y = x^2 + 1$

4. The equation $C = \frac{5}{9}(F - 32)$ relates the Celsius temperature C to the Fahrenheit temperature F. What is the Celsius temperature if the Fahrenheit temperature is −13 degrees?

Ⓕ −45 °C
Ⓖ −39.2 °C
Ⓗ −25 °C
Ⓙ −10.6 °C

5. Which equation is NOT true?

Ⓐ $55 + 27 + 45 = 100 + 27$
Ⓑ $5 \cdot 7 \cdot \frac{2}{5} = 2 \cdot 7$
Ⓒ $14(126) = 14(100) + 14(26)$
Ⓓ $31(152) = 30(150) + 1(2)$

6. The volume of a sphere with radius r is $\frac{4\pi r^3}{3}$. The radius of a ball is 4 inches. What is the volume of the ball in cubic inches?

Ⓕ 16π in^3
Ⓖ $\frac{64\pi}{3}$ in^3
Ⓗ $\frac{256\pi}{3}$ in^3
Ⓙ $\frac{4096\pi}{3}$ in^3

7. Which of the following real numbers is a terminating decimal?

Ⓐ π
Ⓑ $\frac{3}{2}$
Ⓒ $\frac{4}{9}$
Ⓓ $\frac{1}{3}$

8. At one time, a U.S. dollar had the same value as 11.32 Mexican pesos. To the nearest hundredth, how many Mexican pesos were equal to 16 U.S. dollars at that time?

Ⓕ 1.41 pesos
Ⓖ 4.68 pesos
Ⓗ 27.32 pesos
Ⓙ 181.12 pesos

Answers

1. B
2. J
3. D
4. H
5. D
6. H
7. B
8. J
9. D
10. J
11. 283.6
12. 35.5
13. 1.8

Read each question carefully. Be sure you understand what the question is asking before looking at the answer choices or beginning your calculations.

9. Tickets to a festival cost $5.00 each, and lunch costs $8.50 per person. Renting a bus to and from the festival costs $47.00. Which expression gives the cost of x people going to the festival?

   (A) $5.00 + 8.50 + 47.00$
   (B) $5.00x + 8.50 + 47.00$
   (C) $5.00 + 8.50x + 47.00$
   (D) $5.00x + 8.50x + 47.00$

10. Tariq cut a rectangular piece of paper in half to make two triangles, as shown.

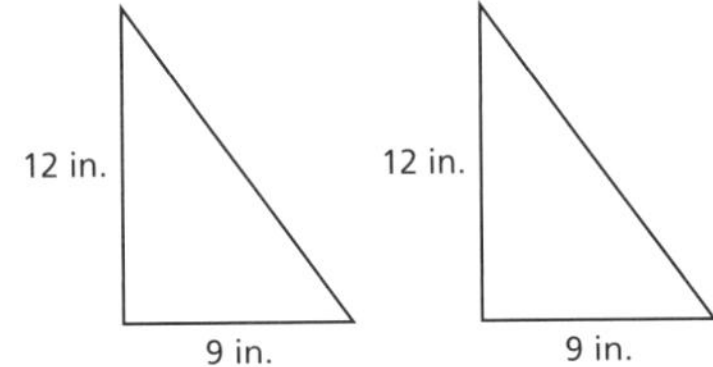

   What was the area of the rectangle?

   (F) 42 inches
   (G) 54 square inches
   (H) 72 inches
   (J) 108 square inches

Gridded Response

11. A scientist prepares 4 beakers of an acid solution. Each beaker contains 70.9 milliliters of the solution. How many milliliters of acid solution did the scientist prepare in all?

12. At an accident scene, an insurance inspector finds a skid mark 60 feet long. The inspector can determine how fast the car was going in miles per hour when the driver applied the breaks by using the expression $\sqrt{21d}$, where d is the length of the skid mark in feet. To the nearest tenth, what was the speed of the car that left the skid mark?

13. The area of a circle with radius r is πr^2. What is the area in square meters of the robot sumo-wrestling ring shown below? Use 3.14 for π. Round to the nearest tenth.

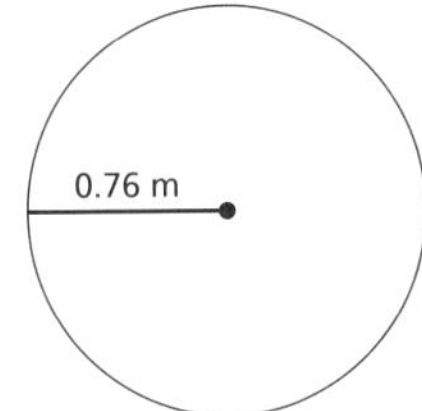

Short Response

14. Dee is using a coordinate plane to make a map of her town. Each square on the grid represents 1 square mile. She plots her house at the origin. Her school is 3 miles east and 2 miles north of her house.

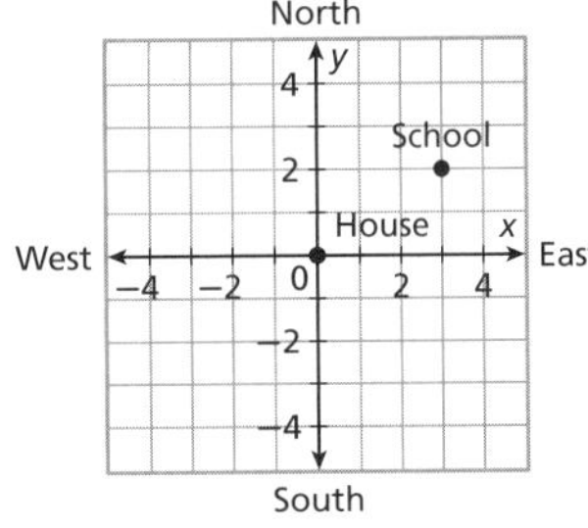

   a. Write an ordered pair to show where Dee plotted the point for her school.
   b. The post office is 4 miles east of Dee's house. Write an ordered pair to show where Dee should plot a point for the post office.
   c. The bank is 3 miles north and 3 miles west of the school. Which is closer to Dee's house, the post office or the bank? Explain your answer.

15. As part of a challenge problem, a math teacher writes the following expression on the board:

$$-(-x).$$

   a. If x is 12, what is the value of the expression?
   b. If x is a negative number, is the value of the expression positive or negative? Explain how you found your answer.
   c. Simplify the expression.

Extended Response

16. Fatima enrolled in a traveler rewards program. She begins with 10,000 bonus points. For every trip she takes, she collects 3000 bonus points.

   a. Write a rule for the number of bonus points Fatima has after x trips.
   b. Make a table showing the number of bonus points Fatima has after 0, 1, 2, 3, 4, and 5 trips.
   c. Graph the ordered pairs from the table. Describe the pattern formed by the points.
   d. When Fatima has collected 20,000 bonus points, she gets a free vacation. How many trips does Fatima need to take to get a free vacation?

Short-Response Rubric

Items 14–15

2 Points = The student's answer is an accurate and complete execution of the task or tasks.

1 Point = The student's answer contains attributes of an appropriate response but is flawed.

0 Points = The student's answer contains no attributes of an appropriate response.

Extended-Response Rubric

Item 16

4 Points = The student correctly writes an expression in part **a** and a complete table in part **b,** makes a graph and describes the pattern in part **c,** and answers part **d,** showing all work.

3 Points = The student correctly writes an expression in part **a** and a complete table in part **b** but does not describe the pattern in part **c,** or the student correctly answers parts **a** and **b** but does not provide a complete graph in part **c.**

2 Points = The student answers all parts correctly but does not show any work or explanation, or the student correctly answers parts **a** and **b** but does not correctly answer parts **c** and **d.**

1 Point = The student does not give a correct expression in part **a** but performs the correct operations in the other parts of the problem, or the student attempts to answer all parts of the problem, but does not correctly answer any part.

0 Points = The student does not answer correctly and does not attempt all parts of the problem.

Answers

14a. (3, 2)

b. (4, 0)

c. Post office; possible answer: I plotted a point for the bank at (0, 5). There are 4 squares from the post office to Dee's house, and 5 squares from the bank to Dee's house, so the post office is closer.

15a. 12

b. Negative; possible answer: The innermost negative sign makes the negative number positive. The negative sign on the outside then makes the number negative again.

c. x

16a. $10{,}000 + 3000x$

b.

Trips	Bonus Points
0	10,000
1	13,000
2	16,000
3	19,000
4	22,000
5	25,000

c.

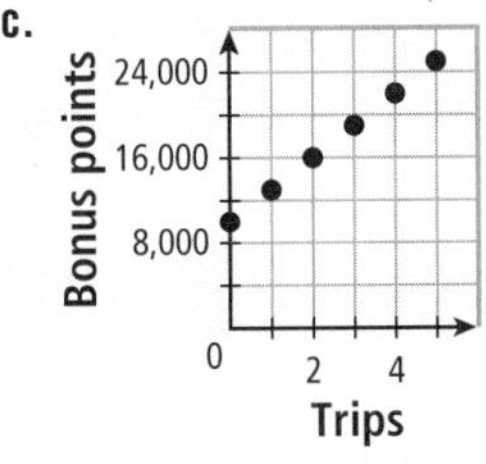

The points form a line.

d. 4 trips

CHAPTER 2

Equations

Section 2A

Equations and Formulas

2-1 Algebra Lab Model One-Step Equations
2-1 Solving Equations by Adding or Subtracting
Connecting Algebra to Geometry Area of Composite Figures
2-2 Solving Equations by Multiplying or Dividing
2-3 Technology Lab Solve Equations by Graphing
2-3 Solving Two-Step and Multi-Step Equations
2-4 Algebra Lab Model Equations with Variables on Both Sides
2-4 Solving Equations with Variables on Both Sides
2-5 Solving for a Variable
2-6 Solving Absolute-Value Equations

Section 2B

Proportion and Percent

2-7 Rates, Ratios, and Proportions
2-8 Applications of Proportions
2-9 Percents
2-10 Applications of Percents
2-11 Percent Increase and Decrease
2-11 Algebra Lab Explore Changes in Population

Pacing Guide for 45-Minute Classes

Teacher One Stop™
Calendar Planner®

Chapter 2

Countdown Weeks 3, 4, 5

DAY 1	DAY 2	DAY 3	DAY 4	DAY 5
2-1 Algebra Lab 2-1 Lesson	2-1 Lesson Connecting Algebra to Geometry	2-2 Lesson	2-3 Technology Lab 2-3 Lesson	2-3 Lesson
DAY 6	**DAY 7**	**DAY 8**	**DAY 9**	**DAY 10**
2-4 Algebra Lab 2-4 Lesson	2-4 Lesson	2-5 Lesson	2-6 Lesson	Multi-Step Test Prep Ready to Go On?
DAY 11	**DAY 12**	**DAY 13**	**DAY 14**	**DAY 15**
2-7 Lesson	2-8 Lesson	2-9 Lesson	2-10 Lesson	2-11 Lesson
DAY 16	**DAY 17**	**DAY 18**	**DAY 19**	
2-11 Algebra Lab	Multi-Step Test Prep Ready to Go On?	Chapter 2 Review	Chapter 2 Test	

Pacing Guide for 90-Minute Classes

Teacher One Stop™
Calendar Planner®

Chapter 2

DAY 1	DAY 2	DAY 3	DAY 4	DAY 5
2-1 Algebra Lab 2-1 Lesson Connecting Algebra to Geometry	2-2 Lesson 2-3 Technology Lab 2-3 Lesson	2-3 Lesson 2-4 Algebra Lab 2-4 Lesson	2-4 Lesson 2-5 Lesson	2-6 Lesson Multi-Step Test Prep Ready to Go On?
DAY 6	**DAY 7**	**DAY 8**	**DAY 9**	**DAY 10**
2-7 Lesson 2-8 Lesson	2-9 Lesson 2-10 Lesson	2-11 Lesson 2-11 Algebra Lab	Multi-Step Test Prep Ready to Go On? Chapter 2 Review	Chapter 2 Test 3-1 Lesson

ONGOING ASSESSMENT and INTERVENTION

	DIAGNOSE	PRESCRIBE
Assess Prior Knowledge	**Before Chapter 2**	
	Diagnose readiness for the chapter.	Prescribe intervention.
	Are You Ready? SE p. 73	***Are You Ready? Intervention***
Formative Assessment	**Before Every Lesson**	
	Diagnose readiness for the lesson.	Prescribe intervention.
	Warm Up TE	**Reteach** CRB
	During Every Lesson	
	Diagnose understanding of lesson concepts.	Prescribe intervention.
	Check It Out! SE **Questioning Strategies** TE **Think and Discuss** SE **Write About It** SE **Journal** TE	**Reading Strategies** CRB ***Success for Every Learner*** ***Lesson Tutorial Videos***
	After Every Lesson	
	Diagnose mastery of lesson concepts.	Prescribe intervention.
	Lesson Quiz TE **Test Prep** SE ***Test and Practice Generator***	**Reteach** CRB **Test Prep Doctor** TE ***Homework Help Online***
	Before Chapter 2 Testing	
	Diagnose mastery of concepts in chapter.	Prescribe intervention.
	Ready to Go On? SE pp. 119, 153 **Multi-Step Test Prep** SE pp. 118, 152 **Section Quizzes** AR ***Test and Practice Generator***	***Ready to Go On? Intervention*** **Scaffolding Questions** TE pp. 118, 152 **Reteach** CRB ***Lesson Tutorial Videos***
	Before High Stakes Testing	
	Diagnose mastery of benchmark concepts.	Prescribe intervention.
	College Entrance Exam Practice SE p. 159 **Standardized Test Prep** SE pp. 162–163	***College Entrance Exam Practice***
Summative Assessment	**After Chapter 2**	
	Check mastery of chapter concepts.	Prescribe intervention.
	Multiple-Choice Tests (Forms A, B, C) **Free-Response Tests (Forms A, B, C)** **Performance Assessment** AR **Cumulative Test** AR ***Test and Practice Generator***	**Reteach** CRB ***Lesson Tutorial Videos***

KEY: **SE** = *Student Edition* **TE** = *Teacher's Edition* **CRB** = *Chapter Resource Book* **AR** = *Assessment Resources*  Available online Available on CD- or DVD-ROM

Lesson Resources

Before the Lesson

Prepare ***Teacher One Stop*** SPANISH 
- Editable lesson plans
- Calendar Planner
- Easy access to all chapter resources

Lesson Transparencies
- Teacher Tools

Teach the Lesson

Introduce ***Alternate Openers: Explorations***

Lesson Transparencies
- Warm Up
- Problem of the Day

Teach ***Lesson Transparencies***
- Teaching Transparencies

Know-It Notebook™
- Vocabulary
- Key Concepts

Power Presentations 

Lesson Tutorial Videos SPANISH 

Interactive Online Edition 
- Lesson Activities
- Lesson Tutorial Videos

Lab Activities

Lab Resources Online 

Online Interactivities 

TechKeys

Practice the Lesson

Practice ***Chapter Resources***
- Practice A, B, C

Practice and Problem Solving Workbook SPANISH

IDEA Works!® Modified Worksheets and Tests

ExamView Test and Practice Generator SPANISH

Homework Help Online

Online Interactivities SPANISH

Interactive Online Edition
- Homework Help

Apply ***Chapter Resources***
- Problem Solving SPANISH

Practice and Problem Solving Workbook SPANISH

Interactive Online Edition
- Chapter Project

Project Teacher Support

After the Lesson

Reteach ***Chapter Resources***
- Reteach
- Reading Strategies ELL

Success for Every Learner

Review ***Interactive Answers and Solutions***

Solutions Key

Know-It Notebook™
- Big Ideas
- Chapter Review

Extend ***Chapter Resources***
- Challenge

Technology Highlights for the Teacher

Power Presentations

Dynamic presentations to engage students. Complete PowerPoint® presentations for every lesson in Chapter 2.

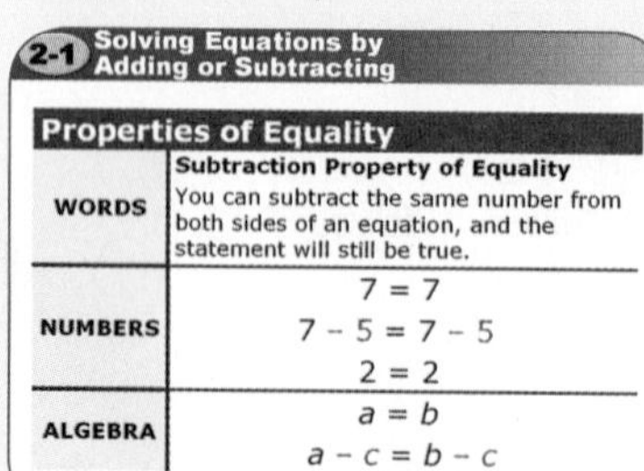

Teacher One Stop SPANISH

Easy access to Chapter 2 resources and assessments. Includes lesson planning, test generation, and puzzle creation software.

Premier Online Edition SPANISH

Chapter 2 includes Tutorial Videos, Lesson Activities, Lesson Quizzes, Homework Help, and Chapter Project.

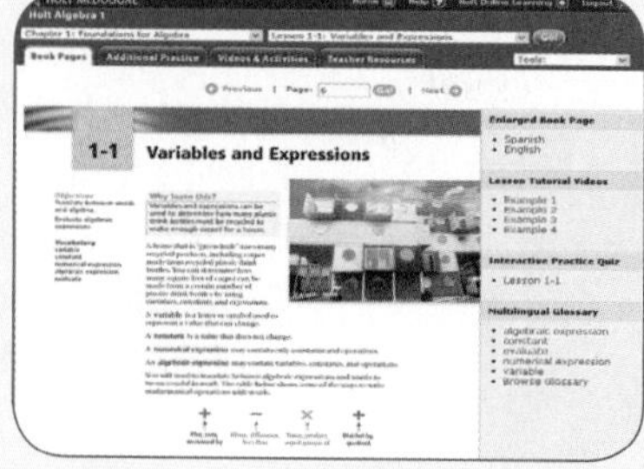

KEY: **SE** = *Student Edition* **TE** = *Teacher's Edition* ELL English Language Learners SPANISH Spanish version available — Available online — Available on CD- or DVD-ROM

Reaching All Learners

Teaching tips to help all learners appear throughout the chapter. A few that target specific students are included in the lists below.

All Learners

Lab Activities
Practice and Problem Solving Workbook SPANISH
Know-It Notebook

Special Needs Students

Practice A .... CRB
Reteach .... CRB
Reading Strategies .... CRB
Are You Ready? .... SE p. 73
Inclusion .... TE pp. 78, 79, 86, 134, 140, 146
IDEA Works!® Modified Worksheets and Tests
Ready to Go On? Intervention SPANISH
Know-It Notebook
Online Interactivities SPANISH
Lesson Tutorial Videos SPANISH

Developing Learners

Practice A .... CRB
Reteach .... CRB
Reading Strategies .... CRB
Are You Ready? .... SE p. 73
Vocabulary Connections .... SE p. 74
Questioning Strategies .... TE
Ready to Go On? Intervention SPANISH
Know-It Notebook
Homework Help Online
Online Interactivities SPANISH
Lesson Tutorial Videos 

On-Level Learners

Practice B .... CRB
Problem Solving .... CRB
Vocabulary Connections .... SE p. 74
Questioning Strategies .... TE
Ready to Go On? Intervention SPANISH
Know-It Notebook
Homework Help Online
Online Interactivities SPANISH

Advanced Learners

Practice C .... CRB
Challenge .... CRB
Challenge Exercises .... SE
Reading and Writing Math *Extend* .... TE p. 75
Critical Thinking .... TE pp. 93, 135, 145
Are You Ready? Enrichment SPANISH
Ready To Go On? Enrichment SPANISH

English Language Learners

ENGLISH LANGUAGE LEARNERS

Reading Strategies .... CRB
Are You Ready? Vocabulary .... SE p. 73
Vocabulary Connections .... SE p. 74
Vocabulary Review .... SE p. 154
English Language Learners .... TE pp. 75, 85, 134, 165
Success for Every Learner
Know-It Notebook
Multilingual Glossary
Lesson Tutorial Videos 

Technology Highlights for Reaching All Learners

Lesson Tutorial Videos SPANISH

Starring Holt authors Ed Burger and Freddie Renfro! Live tutorials to support every lesson in Chapter 2.

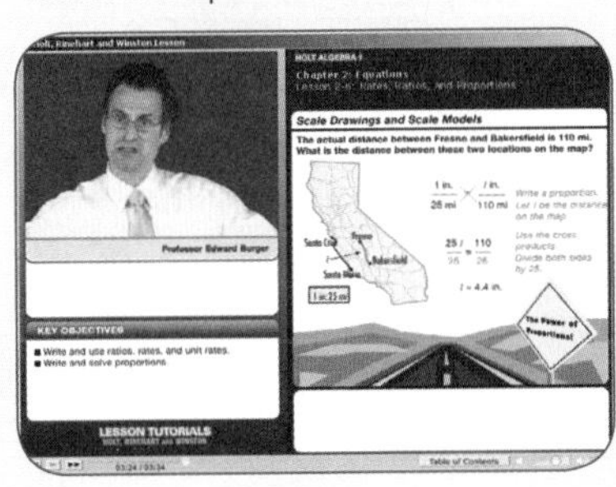

Multilingual Glossary

Searchable glossary includes definitions in English, Spanish, Vietnamese, Chinese, Hmong, Korean, and 4 other languages.

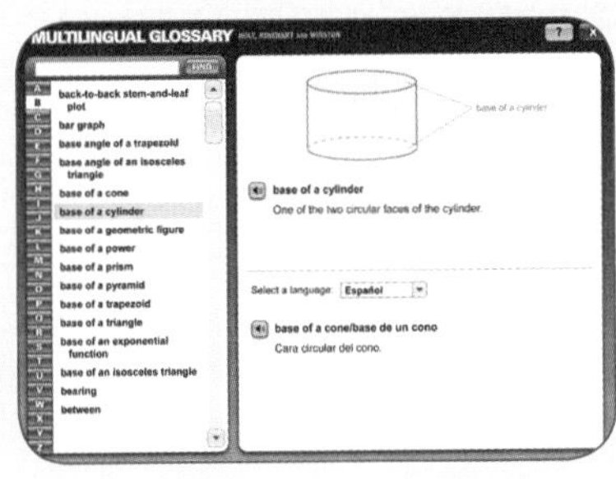

Online Interactivities

Interactive tutorials provide visually engaging alternative opportunities to learn concepts and master skills.

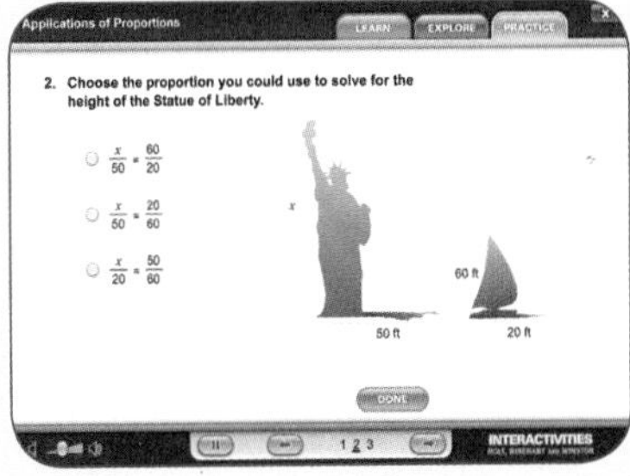

KEY: **SE** = *Student Edition* **TE** = *Teacher's Edition* **CRB** = *Chapter Resource Book* SPANISH Spanish version available · Available online · Available on CD- or DVD-ROM

Ongoing Assessment

Assessing Prior Knowledge

Determine whether students have the prerequisite concepts and skills for success in Chapter 2.

Are You Ready? SPANISH .... SE p. 73
Warm Up .... TE

Test Preparation

Provide review and practice for Chapter 2 and standardized tests.

Multi-Step Test Prep .... SE pp. 118, 152
Study Guide: Review .... SE pp. 154–157
Test Tackler .... SE pp. 160–161
Standardized Test Prep .... SE pp. 162–163
College Entrance Exam Practice .... SE p. 159
Countdown to Testing .... SE pp. C4–C27
IDEA Works!® Modified Worksheets and Tests

Alternative Assessment

Assess students' understanding of Chapter 2 concepts and combined problem-solving skills.

Chapter 2 Project .... SE p. 72
Alternative Assessment .... TE
Performance Assessment SPANISH .... AR
Portfolio Assessment SPANISH .... AR

Lesson Assessment

Provide formative assessment for each lesson of Chapter 2.

Questioning Strategies .... TE
Think and Discuss .... SE
Check It Out! Exercises .... SE
Write About It .... SE
Journal .... TE
Lesson Quiz .... TE
Alternative Assessment .... TE
IDEA Works!® Modified Worksheets and Tests

Weekly Assessment

Provide formative assessment for each section of Chapter 2.

Multi-Step Test Prep .... SE pp. 118, 152
Ready to Go On? SPANISH .... SE pp. 119, 153
Section Quizzes SPANISH .... AR
Test and Practice Generator SPANISH .... *Teacher One Stop*

Chapter Assessment

Provide summative assessment of Chapter 2 mastery.

Chapter 2 Test .... SE p. 158
Chapter Test (Levels A, B, C) SPANISH .... AR
- Multiple Choice
- Free Response

Cumulative Test SPANISH .... AR
Test and Practice Generator SPANISH .... *Teacher One Stop*
IDEA Works!® Modified Worksheets and Tests

Technology Highlights for Assessment

Are You Ready? SPANISH

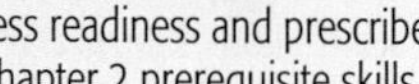

Automatically assess readiness and prescribe intervention for Chapter 2 prerequisite skills.

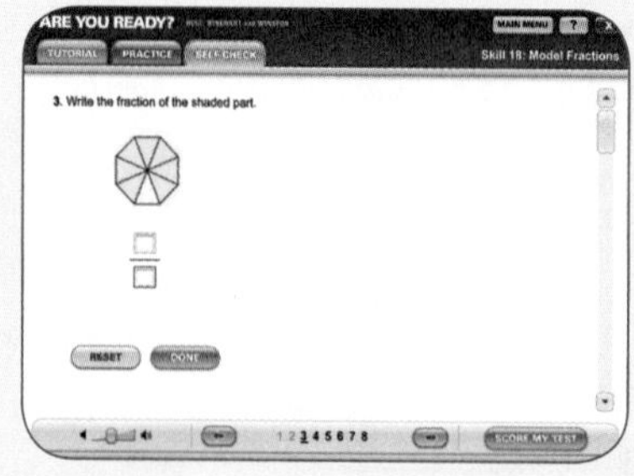

Ready to Go On?

Automatically assess understanding of and prescribe intervention for Sections 2A and 2B.

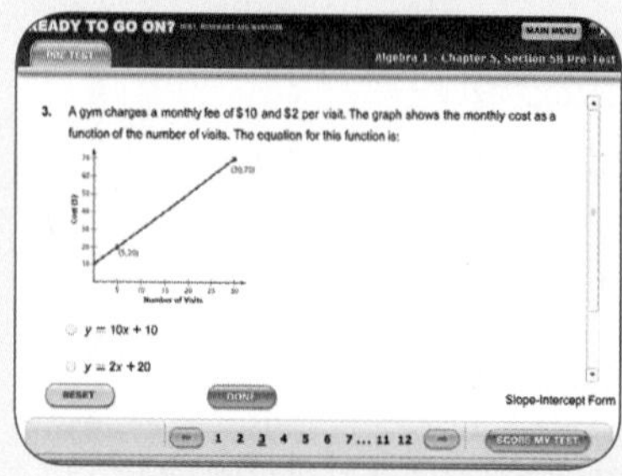

Test and Practice Generator SPANISH

Use Chapter 2 problem banks to create assessments and worksheets to print out or deliver online. Includes dynamic problems.

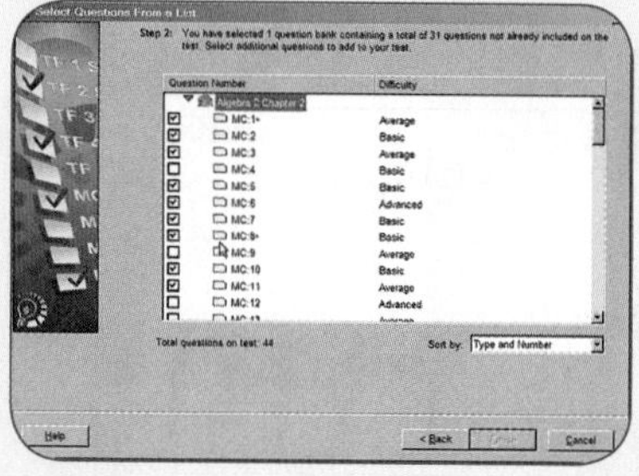

KEY: **SE** = *Student Edition* **TE** = *Teacher's Edition* **AR** = *Assessment Resources* SPANISH Spanish version available  Available online Available on CD- or DVD-ROM

Three levels (A, B, C) of multiple-choice and free-response chapter tests, along with a performance assessment, are available in the *Assessment Resources*.

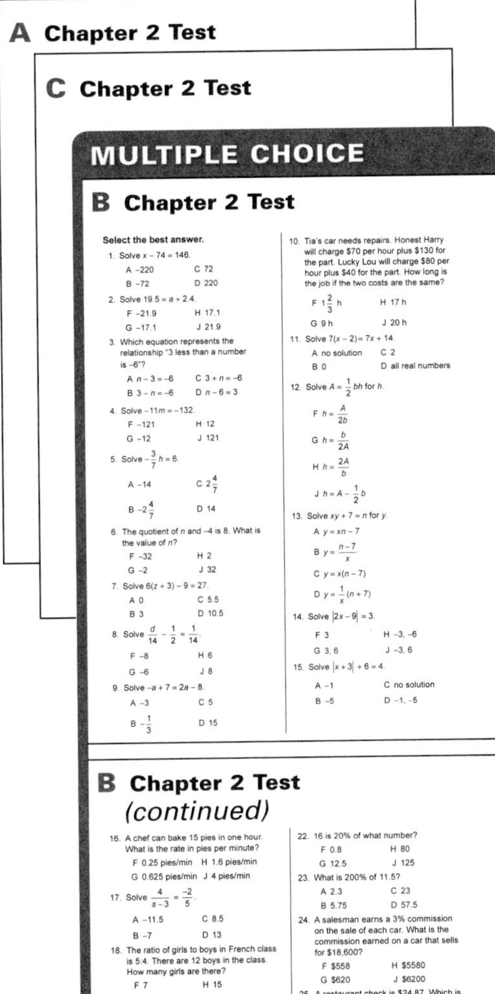

A Chapter 2 Test

C Chapter 2 Test

MULTIPLE CHOICE

B Chapter 2 Test

Select the best answer.

1. Solve $x - 74 = 146$.
   A −220 C 72
   B −72 D 220
2. Solve $19.5 = a + 2.4$.
   F −21.9 H 17.1
   G −17.1 J 21.9
3. Which equation represents the relationship "3 less than a number is −6"?
   A $n - 3 = -6$ C $3 + n = -6$
   B $3 - n = -6$ D $n - 6 = 3$
4. Solve $-11m = -132$.
   F −121 H 12
   G −12 J 121
5. Solve $-\frac{3}{7}h = 6$.
   A −14 C $2\frac{4}{7}$
   B $-2\frac{4}{7}$ D 14
6. The quotient of n and −4 is 8. What is the value of n?
   F −32 H 2
   G −2 J 32
7. Solve $6(z + 3) - 9 = 27$.
   A 0 C 5.5
   B 3 D 10.5
8. Solve $\frac{d}{14} - \frac{1}{2} = \frac{1}{14}$.
   F −8 H 6
   G −6 J 8
9. Solve $-a + 7 = 2a - 8$.
   A −3 C 5
   B $-\frac{1}{3}$ D 15
10. Tia's car needs repairs. Honest Harry will charge $70 per hour plus $130 for the part. Lucky Lou will charge $80 per hour plus $40 for the part. How long is the job if the two costs are the same?
    F $1\frac{2}{3}$ h H 17 h
    G 9 h J 20 h
11. Solve $7(x - 2) = 7x + 14$.
    A no solution C 2
    B 0 D all real numbers
12. Solve $A = \frac{1}{2}bh$ for h.
    F $h = \frac{A}{2b}$
    G $h = \frac{b}{2A}$
    H $h = \frac{2A}{b}$
    J $h = A - \frac{1}{2}b$
13. Solve $xy + 7 = n$ for y.
    A $y = xn - 7$
    B $y = \frac{n-7}{x}$
    C $y = x(n - 7)$
    D $y = \frac{1}{x}(n + 7)$
14. Solve $|2x - 9| = 3$.
    F 3 H −3, −6
    G 3, 6 J −3, 6
15. Solve $|x + 3| + 6 = 4$.
    A −1 C no solution
    B −5 D −1, −5

B Chapter 2 Test (continued)

16. A chef can bake 15 pies in one hour. What is the rate in pies per minute?
    F 0.25 pies/min H 1.6 pies/min
    G 0.625 pies/min J 4 pies/min
17. Solve $\frac{4}{s-3} = \frac{-2}{5}$.
    A −11.5 C 8.5
    B −7 D 13
18. The ratio of girls to boys in French class is 5:4. There are 12 boys in the class. How many girls are there?
    F 7 H 15
    G 10 J 17
19. A rectangle has a length of 5 cm and a width of 3 cm. Every dimension is doubled to form a second rectangle. What is the ratio of the perimeters of the two rectangles?
    A 1:2 C 1:4
    B 1:3 D 1:8
20. Kris is 1.5 meters tall and casts a shadow 4 meters long. At the same time, a statue casts a shadow 12 meters long. What is the height of the statue?
    F 4.5 m H 24 m
    G 10.6 m J 32 m
21. $ABCDEF \sim RSTUVQ$. Find x.
    A 2.25 in. C 10 in.
    B 6.75 in. D 12 in.
22. 16 is 20% of what number?
    F 0.8 H 80
    G 12.5 J 125
23. What is 200% of 11.5?
    A 2.3 C 23
    B 5.75 D 57.5
24. A salesman earns a 3% commission on the sale of each car. What is the commission earned on a car that sells for $18,600?
    F $558 H $5580
    G $620 J $6200
25. A restaurant check is $24.87. Which is the best estimate of a 15% tip?
    A $1.25 C $3.75
    B $2.50 D $5.00
26. Find the percent decrease from 40 to 25.
    F 37.5% H 62.5%
    G 60% J 160%
27. What is the result when 70 is increased by 80%?
    A 14 C 126
    B 56 D 150
28. Juanita sold a scarf for $24. Her wholesale cost was $10. What was the percent markup? Round to the nearest tenth, if needed.
    F 41.7% H 140%
    G 58.3% J 336%
29. Before using his coupon, Ben owed $87 for a tuxedo rental. After he used the coupon, he owed $69.60. What percent discount did Ben receive?
    A 20% C 75%
    B 25% D 80%

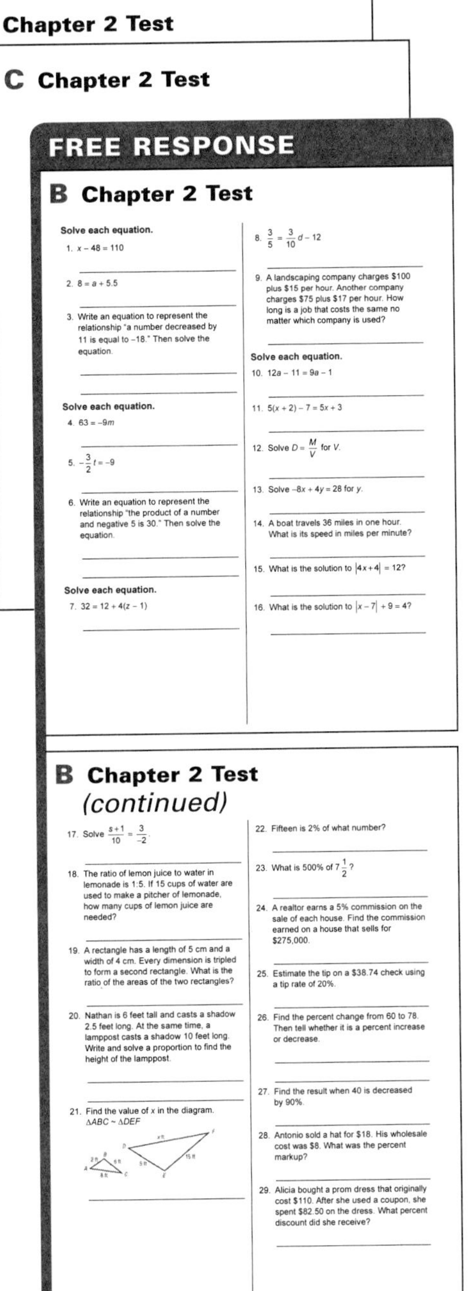

A Chapter 2 Test

C Chapter 2 Test

FREE RESPONSE

B Chapter 2 Test

Solve each equation.

1. $x - 48 = 110$ ________
2. $8 = a + 5.5$ ________
3. Write an equation to represent the relationship "a number decreased by 11 is equal to −18." Then solve the equation. ________

Solve each equation.

4. $63 = -9m$ ________
5. $-\frac{3}{2}t = -9$ ________
6. Write an equation to represent the relationship "the product of a number and negative 5 is 30." Then solve the equation. ________

Solve each equation.

7. $32 = 12 + 4(z - 1)$ ________
8. $\frac{3}{5} = \frac{3}{10}d - 12$ ________
9. A landscaping company charges $100 plus $15 per hour. Another company charges $75 plus $17 per hour. How long is a job that costs the same no matter which company is used? ________

Solve each equation.

10. $12a - 11 = 9a - 1$ ________
11. $5(x + 2) - 7 = 5x + 3$ ________
12. Solve $D = \frac{M}{V}$ for V. ________
13. Solve $-8x + 4y = 28$ for y. ________
14. A boat travels 36 miles in one hour. What is its speed in miles per minute? ________
15. What is the solution to $|4x + 4| = 12$? ________
16. What is the solution to $|x - 7| + 9 = 4$? ________

B Chapter 2 Test (continued)

17. Solve $\frac{s+1}{10} = \frac{3}{-2}$. ________
18. The ratio of lemon juice to water in lemonade is 1:5. If 15 cups of water are used to make a pitcher of lemonade, how many cups of lemon juice are needed? ________
19. A rectangle has a length of 5 cm and a width of 4 cm. Every dimension is tripled to form a second rectangle. What is the ratio of the areas of the two rectangles? ________
20. Nathan is 6 feet tall and casts a shadow 2.5 feet long. At the same time, a lamppost casts a shadow 10 feet long. Write and solve a proportion to find the height of the lamppost. ________
21. Find the value of x in the diagram. $\triangle ABC \sim \triangle DEF$ ________
22. Fifteen is 2% of what number? ________
23. What is 500% of $7\frac{1}{2}$? ________
24. A realtor earns a 5% commission on the sale of each house. Find the commission earned on a house that sells for $275,000. ________
25. Estimate the tip on a $38.74 check using a tip rate of 20%. ________
26. Find the percent change from 60 to 78. Then tell whether it is a percent increase or decrease. ________
27. Find the result when 40 is decreased by 90%. ________
28. Antonio sold a hat for $18. His wholesale cost was $8. What was the percent markup? ________
29. Alicia bought a prom dress that originally cost $110. After she used a coupon, she spent $82.50 on the dress. What percent discount did she receive? ________

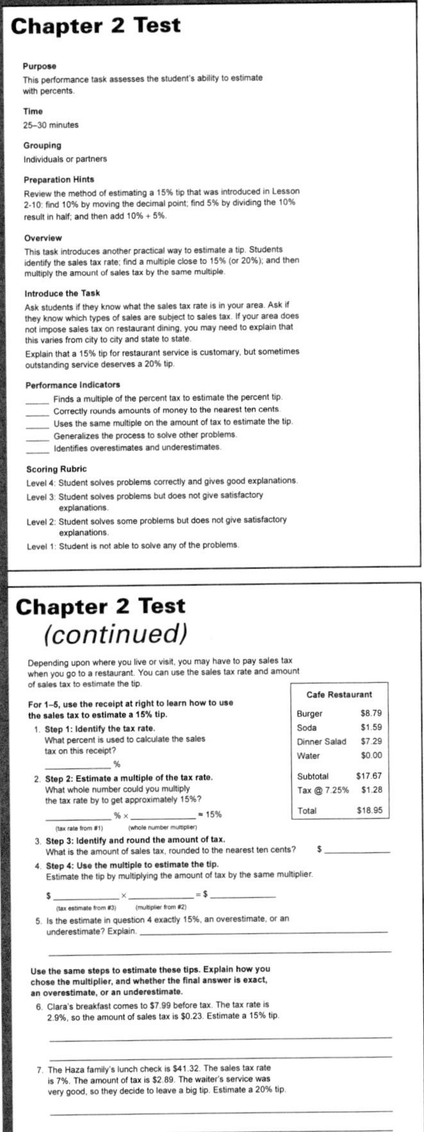

PERFORMANCE ASSESSMENT

Chapter 2 Test

Purpose
This performance task assesses the student's ability to estimate with percents.

Time
25–30 minutes

Grouping
Individuals or partners

Preparation Hints
Review the method of estimating a 15% tip that was introduced in Lesson 2-10: find 10% by moving the decimal point; find 5% by dividing the 10% result in half; and then add 10% + 5%.

Overview
This task introduces another practical way to estimate a tip. Students identify the sales tax rate; find a multiple close to 15% (or 20%); and then multiply the amount of sales tax by the same multiple.

Introduce the Task
Ask students if they know what the sales tax rate is in your area. Ask if they know which types of sales are subject to sales tax. If your area does not impose sales tax on restaurant dining, you may need to explain that this varies from city to city and state to state.

Explain that a 15% tip for restaurant service is customary, but sometimes outstanding service deserves a 20% tip.

Performance Indicators
_____ Finds a multiple of the percent tax to estimate the percent tip.
_____ Correctly rounds amounts of money to the nearest ten cents.
_____ Uses the same multiple on the amount of tax to estimate the tip.
_____ Generalizes the process to solve other problems.
_____ Identifies overestimates and underestimates.

Scoring Rubric
Level 4: Student solves problems correctly and gives good explanations.
Level 3: Student solves problems but does not give satisfactory explanations.
Level 2: Student solves some problems but does not give satisfactory explanations.
Level 1: Student is not able to solve any of the problems.

Chapter 2 Test (continued)

Depending upon where you live or visit, you may have to pay sales tax when you go to a restaurant. You can use the sales tax rate and amount of sales tax to estimate the tip.

Cafe Restaurant	
Burger	$8.79
Soda	$1.59
Dinner Salad	$7.29
Water	$0.00
Subtotal	$17.67
Tax @ 7.25%	$1.28
Total	$18.95

For 1–5, use the receipt at right to learn how to use the sales tax to estimate a 15% tip.

1. **Step 1: Identify the tax rate.** What percent is used to calculate the sales tax on this receipt? ________ %
2. **Step 2: Estimate a multiple of the tax rate.** What whole number could you multiply the tax rate by to get approximately 15%?
   ________ % × ________ ≈ 15%
   (tax rate from #1) (whole number multiplier)
3. **Step 3: Identify and round the amount of tax.** What is the amount of sales tax, rounded to the nearest ten cents? $ ________
4. **Step 4: Use the multiple to estimate the tip.** Estimate the tip by multiplying the amount of tax by the same multiplier.
   $ ________ × ________ = $ ________
   (tax estimate from #3) (multiplier from #2)
5. Is the estimate in question 4 exactly 15%, an overestimate, or an underestimate? Explain. ________

Use the same steps to estimate these tips. Explain how you chose the multiplier, and whether the final answer is exact, an overestimate, or an underestimate.

6. Clara's breakfast comes to $7.99 before tax. The tax rate is 2.9%, so the amount of sales tax is $0.23. Estimate a 15% tip. ________
7. The Haza family's lunch check is $41.32. The sales tax rate is 7%. The amount of tax is $2.89. The waiter's service was very good, so they decide to leave a big tip. Estimate a 20% tip. ________

Teacher One Stop™ 

Test & Practice Generator

Create and customize Chapter 2 Tests. Instantly generate multiple test versions, answer keys, and Spanish versions of test items.

Modified chapter tests that address special learning needs are available in *IDEA Works!® Modified Worksheets and Tests.*

CHAPTER 2

SECTION 2A
Equations and Formulas

On page 118, students write, solve, and graph equations to model real-world firefighting situations.

Exercises designed to prepare students for success on the Multi-Step Test Prep can be found in each lesson.

SECTION 2B
Proportion and Percent

On page 152, students apply ratios and proportions to model a real-world shopping situation.

Exercises designed to prepare students for success on the Multi-Step Test Prep can be found in each lesson.

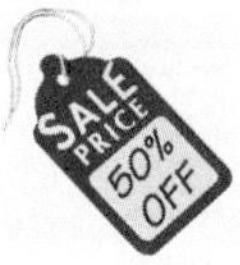

SALE PRICE 50% OFF

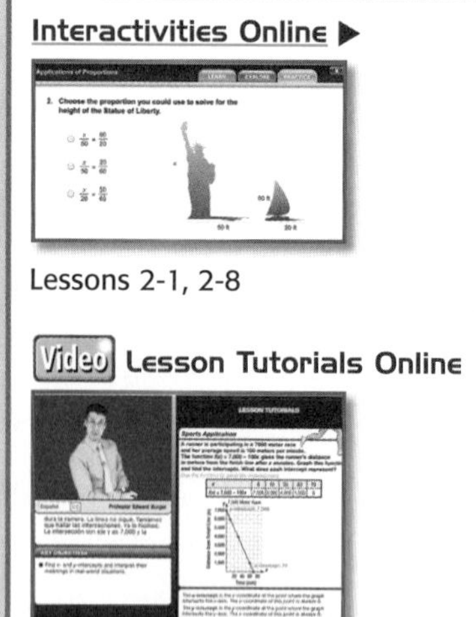

Lessons 2-1, 2-8

Lesson Tutorial Videos are available for EVERY example.

CHAPTER 2

Equations

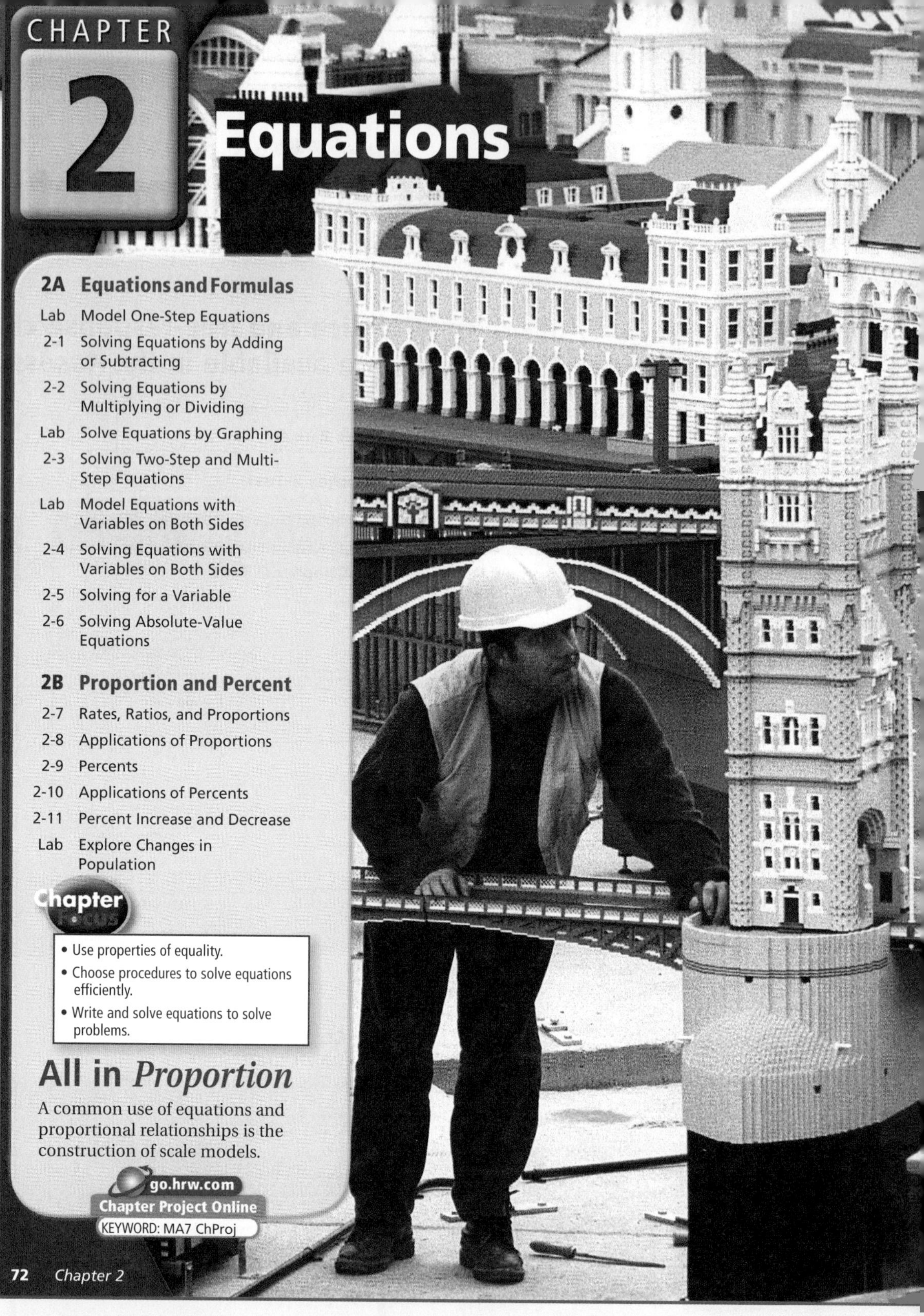

Chapter FOCUS

- Use properties of equality.
- Choose procedures to solve equations efficiently.
- Write and solve equations to solve problems.

All in *Proportion*

A common use of equations and proportional relationships is the construction of scale models.

go.hrw.com
Chapter Project Online
KEYWORD: MA7 ChProj

All in Proportion

About the Project

In the Chapter Project, students make careful measurements and use scale and proportion to design their own miniature quilts.

Project Resources

All project resources for teachers and students are provided online.

Materials:

- All in Proportion worksheet
- colored paper, ruler, scissors, glue

CHAPTER 2

ARE YOU READY?

Vocabulary

Match each term on the left with a definition on the right.

1. constant **E**
2. expression **A**
3. order of operations **C**
4. variable **D**

A. a mathematical phrase that contains operations, numbers, and/or variables
B. a mathematical statement that two expressions are equivalent
C. a process for evaluating expressions
D. a symbol used to represent a quantity that can change
E. a value that does not change

Order of Operations

Simplify each expression.

5. $(7 - 3) \div 2$ **2**
6. $4 \cdot 6 \div 3$ **8**
7. $12 - 3 + 1$ **10**
8. $2 \cdot 10 \div 5$ **4**
9. $125 \div 5^2$ **5**
10. $7 \cdot 6 + 5 \cdot 4$ **62**

Add and Subtract Integers

Add or subtract.

11. $-15 + 19$ **4**
12. $-6 - (-18)$ **12**
13. $6 + (-8)$ **−2**
14. $-12 + (-3)$ **−15**

Add and Subtract Fractions

Perform each indicated operation. Give your answer in the simplest form.

15. $\frac{1}{4} + \frac{2}{3}$ $\mathbf{\frac{11}{12}}$
16. $1\frac{1}{2} - \frac{3}{4}$ $\mathbf{\frac{3}{4}}$
17. $\frac{3}{8} + \frac{2}{3}$ $\mathbf{\frac{25}{24}}$
18. $\frac{3}{2} - \frac{2}{3}$ $\mathbf{\frac{5}{6}}$

Evaluate Expressions

Evaluate each expression for the given value of the variable.

19. $2x + 3$ for $x = 7$ **17**
20. $3n - 5$ for $n = 7$ **16**
21. $13 - 4a$ for $a = 2$ **5**
22. $3y + 5$ for $y = 5$ **20**

Connect Words and Algebra

23. Janie bought 4 apples and 6 bananas. Each apple cost $0.75, and each banana cost $0.60. Write an expression representing the total cost. **4(0.75) + 6(0.60)**
24. A rectangle has a width of 13 inches and a length of ℓ inches. Write an expression representing the area of the rectangle. **13ℓ**
25. Write a phrase that could be modeled by the expression $n + 2n$. **Possible answer: a number plus 2 times itself**

ARE YOU READY?

Organizer

Objective: Assess students' understanding of prerequisite skills.

Assessing Prior Knowledge

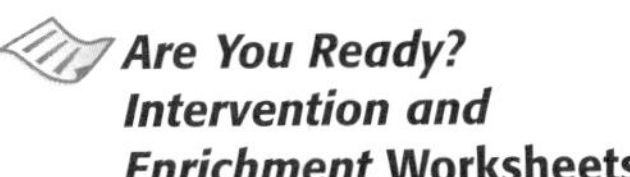

Diagnose and Prescribe

Use this page to determine whether intervention is necessary or whether enrichment is appropriate.

Resources

Are You Ready? Intervention and Enrichment **Worksheets**

my.hrw.com

ARE YOU READY?

Diagnose and Prescribe

NO INTERVENE

Prerequisite Skill	*Are You Ready? Intervention,* Chapter 2: Worksheets	CD-ROM	Online
Order of Operations	Skill 55	Activity 55	Diagnose and Prescribe Online
Add and Subtract Integers	Skill 51	Activity 51	
Add and Subtract Fractions	Skill 48	Activity 48	
Evaluate Expressions	Skill 60	Activity 60	
Connect Words and Algebra	Skill 58	Activity 58	

YES ENRICH

***Are You Ready? Enrichment,* Chapter 2**

Worksheets
CD-ROM
Online

CHAPTER 2 Study Guide: Preview

Organizer

Objective: Help students organize the new concepts they will learn in Chapter 2.

Online Edition
Multilingual Glossary

Resources

Teacher One Stop™
PuzzleView

***Multilingual Glossary* Online**
go.hrw.com
KEYWORD: MA7 Glossary

Possible answers to *Vocabulary Connections*

1. *Equal, equality, equalize* and *equator*; they all have something to do with being the same.
2. A literal equation might have letters in it.
3. They are the same.
4. You can put the two meanings together to get "for each hundred."

CHAPTER 2

Study Guide: Preview

Where You've Been

Previously, you

- practiced using operations in algebra.
- used variables to represent quantities.
- wrote expressions to represent situations.
- simplified and evaluated expressions.

In This Chapter

You will study

- how to use inverse operations to solve equations containing variables.
- writing equations to represent situations.
- simplifying equations before solving.

Where You're Going

You can use the skills in this chapter

- to compare unit prices for consumer products.
- to calculate percentages in taxes, tips, interest, and commissions.
- to create or interpret scale models and drawings.
- to solve problems in science courses and all future math courses.

Key Vocabulary/Vocabulario

equation	ecuación
formula	fórmula
identity	identidad
indirect measurement	medición indirecta
literal equation	ecuación literal
percent	porcentaje
percent change	porcentaje de cambio
proportion	proporción
ratio	razón
unit rate	tasa unitaria

Vocabulary Connections

To become familiar with some of the vocabulary terms in the chapter, consider the following. You may refer to the chapter, the glossary, or a dictionary if you like.

1. The word **equation** begins with the root *equa-*. List some other words that begin with *equa-*. What do all these words have in common?
2. The word *literal* means "of letters." How might a **literal equation** be different from an equation like $3 + 5 = 8$?
3. One definition of **identity** is "exact sameness." An equation consists of two expressions. If an equation is an *identity,* what do you think is true about the expressions?
4. The word *per* means "for each," and the word *cent* means "hundred." How can you use these meanings to understand the term **percent**?

Study Strategy: Use Your Own Words

Explaining a concept using your own words will help you better understand it. For example, learning to solve equations might seem difficult if the textbook doesn't use the same words that you would use.

As you work through each lesson:

- Identify the important ideas from the explanation in the book.
- Use your own words to explain the important ideas you identified.

What Arturo Reads	What Arturo Writes
To evaluate an expression is to find its value.	*Evaluate an expression*—find the value.
To evaluate an algebraic expression, substitute numbers for the variables in the expression and then simplify the expression.	Substitute a number for each variable (letter), and find the answer.
A replacement set is a set of numbers that can be substituted for a variable.	*Replacement set*—numbers that can be substituted for a letter.

Try This

Rewrite each paragraph in your own words.

1. Two numbers are opposites if their sum is 0. A number and its opposite are on opposite sides of zero on a number line, but are the same distance from zero.
2. The Commutative and Associative Properties of Addition and Multiplication allow you to rearrange an expression to simplify it.
3. The terms of an expression are the parts to be added or subtracted. Like terms are terms that contain the same variables raised to the same powers. Constants are also like terms.

Organizer

Objective: Help students apply strategies to understand and retain key concepts.

ENGLISH LANGUAGE LEARNERS

Study Strategy: Use Your Own Words

Discuss Students benefit from listening to each other explain their methods for solving equations.

Encourage students to find many ways to say the same thing.

Extend As students work through Chapter 2, have them discuss how they would rephrase word problems in the exercises. Ask them to first divide the problem into parts, and then identify the information given and what the problem asks.

Answers to *Try This*

1–3. Check students' work.

Reading Connection

The Golden Ratio
by Mario Livio

Livio claims that phi, the Golden Ratio, is "the world's most astonishing number," and he may be right. He explains the ratio's relationships to phenomena from plant growth to galaxy structure. Helpfully, he gently debunks the belief that phi has innately aesthetic qualities.

Activity In the Fibonacci sequence, each term is the sum of the two previous terms (1, 1, 2, 3, 5, 8, 13, 21, ...). Phi is approximately 1.618034. Have students use calculators to make a list of the quotients of succeeding terms in the Fibonacci sequence ($1 \div 1$, $2 \div 1$, $3 \div 2$, $5 \div 3$, etc.). They'll find that the longer their lists, the closer to phi the quotients will be.

SECTION 2A

Equations and Formulas

One-Minute Section Planner

Lesson	Lab Resources	Materials
2-1 Algebra Lab Model One-Step Equations • Use algebra tiles to model and solve one-step equations. ☐ SAT-10 ☐ NAEP ☐ ACT ☐ SAT ☐ SAT Subject Tests	***Algebra Lab Activities*** 2-1 Lab Recording Sheet	**Required** algebra tiles (MK)
Lesson 2-1 Solving Equations by Adding or Subtracting • Solve one-step equations in one variable by using addition or subtraction. ☑ SAT-10 ☑ NAEP ☑ ACT ☑ SAT ☑ SAT Subject Tests		**Optional** balance scale with weights, pencil holder
Lesson 2-2 Solving Equations by Multiplying or Dividing • Solve one-step equations in one variable by using multiplication or division. ☑ SAT-10 ☑ NAEP ☑ ACT ☑ SAT ☑ SAT Subject Tests		
Lesson 2-3 Technology Lab Solve Equations by Graphing • Use a graphing calculator to solve two-step equations by graphing. ☐ SAT-10 ☑ NAEP ☐ ACT ☐ SAT ☐ SAT Subject Tests		**Required** graphing calculator
Lesson 2-3 Solving Two-Step and Multi-Step Equations • Solve equations in one variable that contain more than one operation. ☑ SAT-10 ☑ NAEP ☑ ACT ☑ SAT ☑ SAT Subject Tests		
2-4 Algebra Lab Model Equations with Variables on Both Sides • Use algebra tiles to model and solve equations with variables terms on both sides. ☐ SAT-10 ☐ NAEP ☐ ACT ☐ SAT ☐ SAT Subject Tests	***Algebra Lab Activities*** 2-4 Lab Recording Sheet	**Required** algebra tiles (MK)
Lesson 2-4 Solving Equations with Variables on Both Sides • Solve equations in one variable that contain variables on both sides. ☑ SAT-10 ☑ NAEP ☑ ACT ☑ SAT ☑ SAT Subject Tests		**Optional** colored pencils (MK), index cards, graphing calculator
Lesson 2-5 Solving for a Variable • Solve a formula for a given variable. • Solve an equation in two or more variables for one of the variables. ☐ SAT-10 ☑ NAEP ☐ ACT ☐ SAT ☐ SAT Subject Tests		
Lesson 2-6 Solving Absolute-Value Equations • Solve equations in one variable that contain absolute-value expressions. ☐ SAT-10 ☐ NAEP ☑ ACT ☑ SAT ☐ SAT Subject Tests		

Note: If NAEP is checked, the content is tested on either the Grade 8 or the Grade 12 NAEP assessment.

MK = *Manipulatives Kit*

Math Background

Professional Learning

SOLUTIONS OF EQUATIONS

Lessons 2-1 to 2-4

Before they solve equations, students need to understand what is meant by a solution. A *solution* of an equation in one variable is a value of the variable that makes the equation true. The equation $5(x + 2) - 3x = 18$, for example, is neither true nor false until a specific value replaces x. It is worthwhile to have students test various values of x in the left-hand side of the equation.

x	$5(x + 2) - 3x$
1	12
2	14
3	16
4	18

The table shows that $x = 1$, $x = 2$, and $x = 3$ are not solutions of the equation and that $x = 4$ is a solution. The one-step equations that students solve in this chapter have exactly one real-number solution, but this is not true of all equations. Lesson 2-4 introduces equations with infinitely many solutions and equations with no solutions.

It may be useful to highlight a common mistake at this point. When asked to prove that two quantities are equal, students sometimes set the quantities equal and work to show an identity. The identity is then taken as proof that the original equation is true. This is a logical error. For example, suppose you are asked to show that $3 = 4$. Using the method described above, set $3 = 4$. Then it is true that $4 = 3$. Adding the two red equations gives $7 = 7$, which is certainly true, but that does not mean the original statement, $3 = 4$, is true. (The problem with this argument lies in the fact that not every step is reversible.)

SOLVING EQUATIONS

Lessons 2-1 to 2-4

Solving equations is one of the most important skills in K-12 mathematics. As previously shown, it is sometimes possible to find a solution by testing values of the variable, but this is generally not the most efficient solution method. In this chapter, students learn to solve an equation by transforming it into equivalent equations. *Equivalent equations* are equations that have the same solution set.

During the solution process, each transformation of an equation should be backed up by a general mathematical principle. As such, a proper justification for a step in the solution of an equation is not simply a description of what was done to the equation ("I added 3 to both sides."), but rather a general principle, such as the Addition Property of Equality ("equals added to equals are equal"), which students are introduced to in this chapter. The figure shows how this general principle may be understood in terms of a balanced scale: identical weights added to both sides of a balanced scale will preserve the balance.

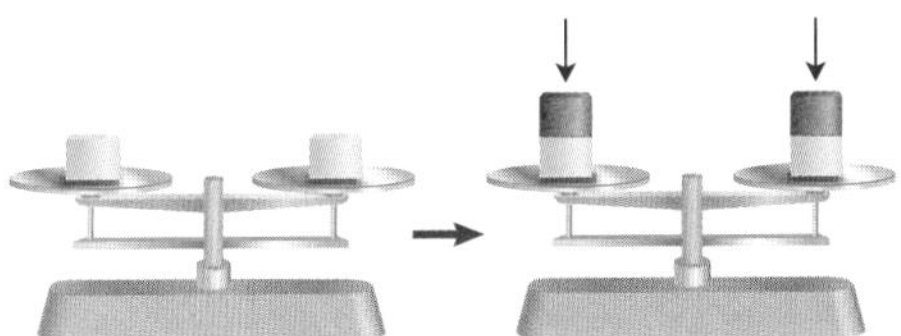

In the same way, identical quantities added to both sides of an equation will preserve the equality. A similar analogy can be made for the Subtraction Property of Equality.

ABSOLUTE-VALUE EQUATIONS

Lesson 2-6

The absolute value of a number is the number's distance from 0 on a number line. More generally, $|x - a|$ represents the distance between x and a. Thus, the equation $|x - 1| = 3$ asks, "Which values of x are 3 units away from 1?"

As the figure shows, there are two values of x that are 3 units away from 1, -2 and 4. So, this absolute-value equation has two solutions.

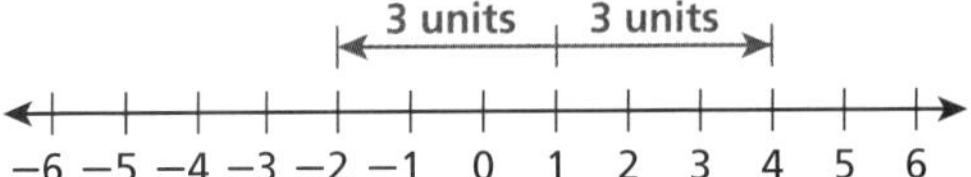

It is also possible for an absolute-value equation to have one solution, no solutions, or infinitely many solutions.

Organizer

Use with Lesson 2-1

Pacing:
Traditional $\frac{1}{2}$ day
Block $\frac{1}{4}$ day

Objective: Use algebra tiles to model and solve one-step equations.

Materials: algebra tiles

Online Edition
Algebra Tiles

Countdown Week 3

Resources

Algebra Lab Activities
2-1 Lab Recording Sheet

Teach

Discuss

Encourage students to first state which tile they are going to isolate. Algebra tiles can be found in the Manipulatives Kit (MK).

Alternative Approach

Use the transparency mat and transparency algebra tiles (MK).

Close

Key Concept

You can solve one-step equations by first adding the same number of tiles to both sides to create zero pairs.

Assessment

Journal Have students explain how to model and solve one-step equations with algebra tiles.

State Resources

Model One-Step Equations

You can use algebra tiles and an equation mat to model and solve equations. To find the value of the variable, place or remove tiles to get the x-tile by itself on one side of the mat. You must place or remove the same number of yellow tiles or the same number of red tiles on both sides.

Use with Lesson 2-1

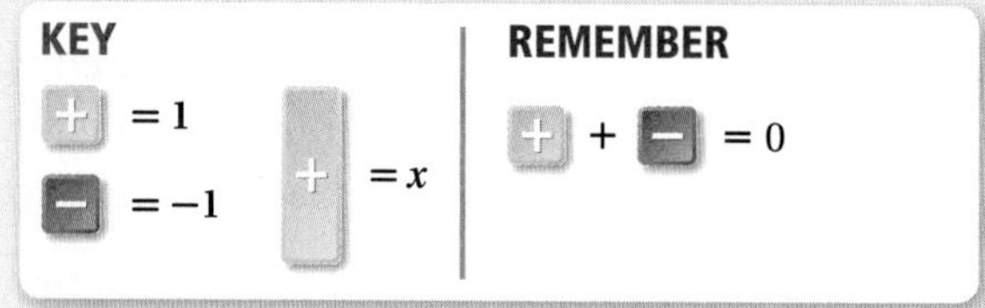

Activity

Use algebra tiles to model and solve $x + 6 = 2$.

MODEL		ALGEBRA
	Model $x + 6$ on the left side of the mat and 2 on the right side of the mat.	$x + 6 = 2$
	Place 6 red tiles on both sides of the mat. This represents adding −6 to both sides of the equation.	$x + 6 + (-6) = 2 + (-6)$
	Remove zero pairs from both sides of the mat.	$x + 0 = 0 + (-4)$
	One x-tile is equivalent to 4 red tiles.	$x = -4$

Try This

Use algebra tiles to model and solve each equation.

1. $x + 2 = 5$ **3**
2. $x - 7 = 8$ **15**
3. $x - 5 = 9$ **14**
4. $x + 4 = 7$ **3**

2-1 Solving Equations by Adding or Subtracting

Objective
Solve one-step equations in one variable by using addition or subtraction.

Vocabulary
equation
solution of an equation

Who uses this?
Athletes can use an equation to estimate their maximum heart rates. (See Example 4.)

An **equation** is a mathematical statement that two expressions are equal. A **solution of an equation** is a value of the variable that makes the equation true.

To find solutions, *isolate the variable.* A variable is isolated when it appears by itself on one side of an equation, and not at all on the other side. Isolate a variable by using inverse operations, which "undo" operations on the variable.

An equation is like a balanced scale. To keep the balance, perform the same operation on both sides.

Inverse Operations

Add x. ⟷ Subtract x.

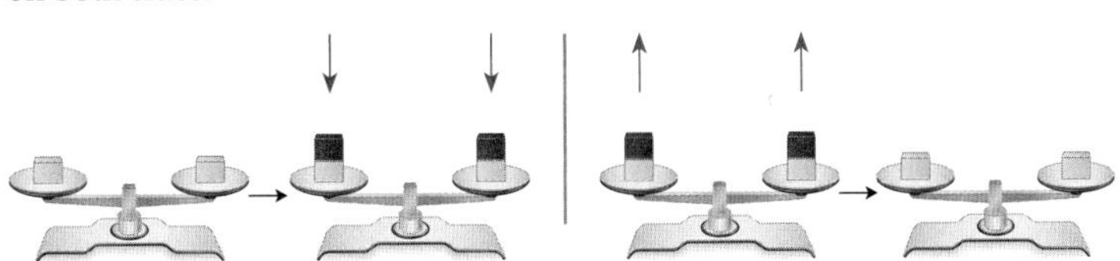

EXAMPLE 1 Solving Equations by Using Addition

Solve each equation.

A $x - 10 = 4$

$$\begin{aligned} x - 10 &= \quad 4 \\ \underline{+10} & \quad \underline{+10} \\ x \quad &= \quad 14 \end{aligned}$$

Since 10 is subtracted from x, add 10 to both sides to undo the subtraction.

Check $\begin{array}{c|c} x - 10 = 4 \\ \hline 14 - 10 & 4 \\ 4 & 4 \checkmark \end{array}$

To check your solution, substitute 14 for x in the original equation.

B $\frac{2}{5} = m - \frac{1}{5}$

$$\begin{aligned} \frac{2}{5} &= m - \frac{1}{5} \\ \underline{+\frac{1}{5}} & \quad \underline{+\frac{1}{5}} \\ \frac{3}{5} &= m \end{aligned}$$

Since $\frac{1}{5}$ is subtracted from m, add $\frac{1}{5}$ to both sides to undo the subtraction.

Writing Math

Solutions are sometimes written in a *solution set.* For Example 1A, the solution set is {14}. For Example 1B, the solution set is $\left\{\frac{3}{5}\right\}$.

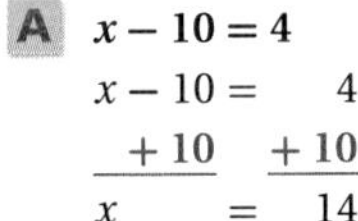

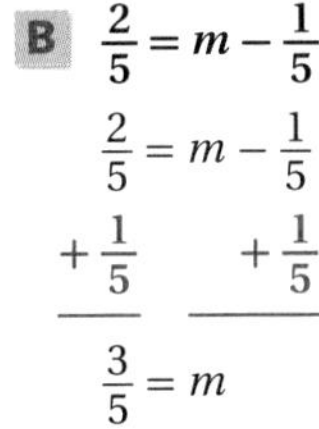

CHECK IT OUT! Solve each equation. Check your answer.

1a. $n - 3.2 = 5.6$ **8.8** **1b.** $-6 = k - 6$ **0** **1c.** $16 = m - 9$ **25**

2-1 Organizer

Pacing: Traditional 1 day
Block $\frac{1}{2}$ day

Objective: Solve one-step equations in one variable by using addition or subtraction.

Online Edition
Tutorial Videos, Interactivity

Countdown Week 3

Power Presentations with PowerPoint®

Warm Up

Simplify.

1. $-\frac{2}{3} + 4\frac{1}{3}$ $3\frac{2}{3}$

2. $-0.51 + (-0.29)$ -0.8

Give the opposite of each number.

3. 8 -8 **4.** $-\frac{2}{3}$ $\frac{2}{3}$

Evaluate each expression for $a = 3$ and $b = -2$.

5. $a + 5$ 8 **6.** $12 - b$ 14

Also available on transparency

Math Humor

Parent: Why do you have that sheet of paper in a bowl of water?

Student: It's my homework. I'm trying to *dissolve* an equation.

State Resources

1 Introduce

EXPLORATION

2-1 Solving Equations by Adding or Subtracting

Each of the following problems shows a scale that is balanced.

1. How many ■ are equal to one ▲?

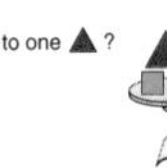

2. How many ● are equal to one ◣?

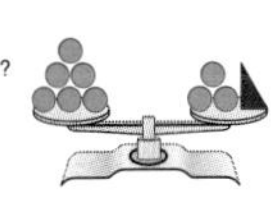

3. How many ● are equal to one ★?

THINK AND DISCUSS

4. Describe how you solved each problem.

Motivate

Place a balance scale with equal weights on each side where all students can see it. Ask them what will happen if you add or subtract an equal amount of weight on both sides. Demonstrate each. Tell the students that equations are like balance scales; both sides must always be kept equal, which means that you must perform the same operation on both sides.

Explorations and answers are provided in *Alternate Openers: Explorations Transparencies.*

go.hrw.com
State Resources Online
KEYWORD: MA7 Resources

Power Presentations with PowerPoint®

Additional Examples

Example 1

Solve each equation.

A. $y - 8 = 24$ 32

B. $\frac{5}{16} = z - \frac{7}{16}$ $\frac{3}{4}$

Example 2

Solve each equation.

A. $m + 17 = 33$ 16

B. $4.2 = t + 1.8$ 2.4

Example 3

Solve $-\frac{5}{11} + p = -\frac{2}{11}$. $\frac{3}{11}$

INTERVENTION

Questioning Strategies

EXAMPLES 1–2

- What is the goal when solving equations?
- What happens when you add or subtract the same amount on both sides of the equation?
- How do you know when to add and when to subtract?

EXAMPLE 3

- How is this problem like those in **Example 1**? How is it different?

Multiple Representations When discussing the Addition and Subtraction Properties of Equality, give students examples of how subtraction can be written as "adding the opposite." For example, $x - 4 = 6$ is equivalent to $x + (-4) = 6$.

Teaching Tip

Inclusion Students may have difficulty assigning a variable to represent a quantity in a real-world problem. Reinforce often that a variable represents the unknown. Students can copy a problem and circle the unknown quantity. This is the quantity that should be represented by the variable.

EXAMPLE 2 Solving Equations by Using Subtraction

Solve each equation. Check your answer.

A $x + 7 = 9$

$$\begin{aligned} x + 7 &= 9 \\ \underline{-7} \quad & \underline{-7} \\ x &= 2 \end{aligned}$$

Since 7 is added to x, subtract 7 from both sides to undo the addition.

Check $x + 7 = 9$

$2 + 7$	9
9	9 ✓

To check your solution, substitute 2 for x in the original equation.

B $0.7 = r + 0.4$

$$\begin{aligned} 0.7 &= r + 0.4 \\ \underline{-0.4} \quad & \underline{-0.4} \\ 0.3 &= r \end{aligned}$$

Since 0.4 is added to r, subtract 0.4 from both sides to undo the addition.

Check $0.7 = r + 0.4$

0.7	$0.3 + 0.4$
0.7	0.7 ✓

To check your solution, substitute 0.3 for r in the original equation.

Solve each equation. Check your answer.

2a. $d + \frac{1}{2} = 1$ $\frac{1}{2}$ **2b.** $-5 = k + 5$ **−10** **2c.** $6 + t = 14$ **8**

Remember that subtracting is the same as adding the opposite. When solving equations, you will sometimes find it easier to add an opposite to both sides instead of subtracting. For example, this method may be useful when the equation contains negative numbers.

EXAMPLE 3 Solving Equations by Adding the Opposite

Solve $-8 + b = 2$.

$$\begin{aligned} -8 + b &= 2 \\ \underline{+8} \quad & \underline{+8} \\ b &= 10 \end{aligned}$$

Since −8 is added to b, add 8 to both sides.

Solve each equation. Check your answer.

3a. $-2.3 + m = 7$ **9.3** **3b.** $-\frac{3}{4} + z = \frac{5}{4}$ **2** **3c.** $-11 + x = 33$ **44**

Student to Student

Zero As a Solution

Ama Walker
Carson High School

I used to get confused when I got a solution of 0. But my teacher reminded me that 0 is a number just like any other number, so it can be a solution of an equation. Just check your answer and see if it works.

$$\begin{aligned} x + 6 &= 6 \\ \underline{-6} \quad & \underline{-6} \\ x &= 0 \end{aligned}$$

Check $x + 6 = 6$

$0 + 6$	6
6	6 ✓

2 Teach

Guided Instruction

Before solving equations, review how to determine whether a given value is a solution of an equation. Emphasize that when solving equations, you want to find the value of the variable that makes the equation true. So the final answer will be in the form *variable = number*. This is why you want to isolate the variable. Discuss how to find a solution by using the inverse operation to "undo" the operation in the equation. Finally, demonstrate how to check the answer by substituting into the original equation.

Reaching All Learners

Through Concrete Manipulatives

Have one student hold a closed container of pencils in one hand and 5 pencils in the other hand. Have another student hold 12 pencils. Tell the class that both students have the same number of pencils. Ask the class how they can figure out the number of pencils in the container without opening it. Give or take pencils away from each student as suggestions are made. When the class has arrived at an answer, check by counting the number of pencils in the container.

EXAMPLE 4 ***Fitness Application***

A person's maximum heart rate is the highest rate, in beats per minute, that the person's heart should reach. One method to estimate maximum heart rate states that your age added to your maximum heart rate is 220. Using this method, write and solve an equation to find the maximum heart rate of a 15-year-old.

Age	added to	maximum heart rate	is	220.
a	$+$	r	$=$	220

$a + r = 220$ — *Write an equation to represent the relationship.*

$15 + r = 220$ — *Substitute 15 for a. Since 15 is added to r, subtract 15 from both sides to undo the addition.*

$\underline{-15 \quad\; -15}$

$r = 205$

The maximum heart rate for a 15-year-old is 205 beats per minute. Since age added to maximum heart rate is 220, the answer should be less than 220. So 205 is a reasonable answer.

4. What if...? Use the method above to find a person's age if the person's maximum heart rate is 185 beats per minute.
35 years old

The properties of equality allow you to perform inverse operations, as in the previous examples. These properties say that you can perform the same operation on both sides of an equation.

Properties of Equality

WORDS	NUMBERS	ALGEBRA
Addition Property of Equality You can add the same number to both sides of an equation, and the statement will still be true.	$3 = 3$ $3 + 2 = 3 + 2$ $5 = 5$	$a = b$ $a + c = b + c$
Subtraction Property of Equality You can subtract the same number from both sides of an equation, and the statement will still be true.	$7 = 7$ $7 - 5 = 7 - 5$ $2 = 2$	$a = b$ $a - c = b - c$

THINK AND DISCUSS

1. Describe how the Addition and Subtraction Properties of Equality are like a balanced scale.

2. GET ORGANIZED Copy and complete the graphic organizer. In each box, write an example of an equation that can be solved by using the given property, and solve it.

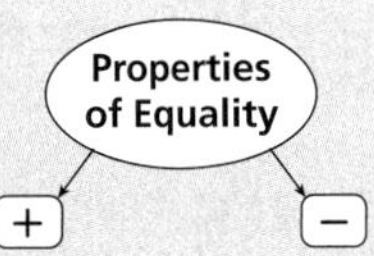

COMMON ERROR ALERT

Students sometimes use the operation that appears in an equation rather than using the inverse operation. For example, a student may try to solve $x - 3 = 9$ and get $x = 6$, which is incorrect. Have students first practice naming the operation in the equation and then identifying the inverse operation.

Inclusion Continue to use the balance scale analogy throughout the lesson. Draw a simple scale (a line with a triangle under the equal sign) under equations as a reminder to always add or subtract the same amount to both sides to keep the equation in balance.

$x - 7 = 10$

Power Presentations with PowerPoint®

Additional Examples

Example 4

Over 20 years, the population of a town decreased by 275 people to a population of 850. Write and solve an equation to find the original population.

$p - 275 = 850$; 1125

INTERVENTION 

Questioning Strategies

EXAMPLE 4

- What are the variables in this situation?
- What is the unknown variable?
- How can you check that your answer is reasonable?

3 Close

Summarize

Ask students what they would do to each side to solve each of the following equations.

$5 = c - 7$	Add 7.
$-3 + x = 14$	Add 3.
$-14 = h + 6$	Subtract 6.

ONGOING ASSESSMENT and INTERVENTION 

***Diagnose Before* the Lesson**
2-1 Warm Up, TE p. 77

***Monitor During* the Lesson**
Check It Out! Exercises, SE pp. 77–79
Questioning Strategies, TE p. 78–79

***Assess After* the Lesson**
2-1 Lesson Quiz, TE p. 82
Alternative Assessment, TE p. 82

Answers to *Think and Discuss*

1. Possible answer: If a scale is balanced, then you can add or remove the same weight on both sides without affecting the balance. Similarly, in an equation, the Addition and Subtraction Properties of Equality say that you can add or subtract the same value on both sides without affecting the equality.
2. See p. A2.

2-1 Exercises

Assignment Guide

Assign *Guided Practice* exercises as necessary.

If you finished Examples **1–2**
Basic 21–40, 51–53
Average 21–40, 51, 72, 73
Advanced 21–40, 71–78

If you finished Examples **1–4**
Basic 21–50, 51–66, 64–70, 79–87
Average 21–57, 59–74, 79–87
Advanced 21–49, 58–64, 63–87

Homework Quick Check
Quickly check key concepts.
Exercises: 24, 34, 42, 49, 59, 63

Answers

20. Possible answer: the weight of the diamond was reduced by about 50 carats, resulting in a diamond that weighed about 70 carats. So the original weight will be close to 50 + 70 = 120 carats. So 112 carats is a reasonable answer.

49. Possible answer: Luis deposited \$500 and now has about \$4700. So the original amount will be close to 4700 − 500 = \$4200. So \$4232 is a reasonable answer.

State Resources

2-1 Exercises

go.hrw.com
Homework Help Online
KEYWORD: MA7 2-1
Parent Resources Online
KEYWORD: MA7 Parent

GUIDED PRACTICE

1. **Vocabulary** Will the *solution of an equation* such as $x - 3 = 9$ be a variable or a number? Explain. **Possible answer: The solution of an equation is a number. It is a value for the variable that works in the equation.**

Solve each equation. Check your answer.

SEE EXAMPLE 1 p. 77

2. $s - 5 = 3$ **8**
3. $17 = w - 4$ **21**
4. $k - 8 = -7$ **1**
5. $x - 3.9 = 12.4$ **16.3**
6. $8.4 = y - 4.6$ **13**
7. $\frac{3}{8} = t - \frac{1}{8}$ $\mathbf{\frac{1}{2}}$

SEE EXAMPLE 2 p. 78

8. $t + 5 = -25$ **−30**
9. $9 = s + 9$ **0**
10. $42 = m + 36$ **6**
11. $2.8 = z + 0.5$ **2.3**
12. $b + \frac{2}{3} = 2$ $\mathbf{\frac{4}{3}}$
13. $n + 1.8 = 3$ **1.2**

SEE EXAMPLE 3 p. 78

14. $-10 + d = 7$ **17**
15. $20 = -12 + v$ **32**
16. $-46 + q = 5$ **51**
17. $2.8 = -0.9 + y$ **3.7**
18. $-\frac{2}{3} + c = \frac{2}{3}$ $\mathbf{\frac{4}{3}}$
19. $-\frac{5}{6} + p = 2$ $\mathbf{\frac{17}{6}}$

SEE EXAMPLE 4 p. 79

20. **Geology** In 1673, the Hope diamond was reduced from its original weight by about 45 carats, resulting in a diamond weighing about 67 carats. Write and solve an equation to find how many carats the original diamond weighed. Show that your answer is reasonable. **$w - 45 = 67$; 112 carats**

PRACTICE AND PROBLEM SOLVING

Independent Practice

For Exercises	See Example
21–30	1
31–40	2
41–48	3
49	4

Extra Practice
Skills Practice p. S6
Application Practice p. S29

Solve each equation. Check your answer.

21. $1 = k - 8$ **9**
22. $u - 15 = -8$ **7**
23. $x - 7 = 10$ **17**
24. $-9 = p - 2$ **−7**
25. $\frac{3}{7} = p - \frac{1}{7}$ $\mathbf{\frac{4}{7}}$
26. $q - 0.5 = 1.5$ **2**
27. $6 = t - 4.5$ **10.5**
28. $4\frac{2}{3} = r - \frac{1}{3}$ **5**
29. $6 = x - 3$ **9**
30. $1.75 = k - 0.75$
31. $19 + a = 19$ **0**
32. $4 = 3.1 + y$ **0.9**
33. $m + 20 = 3$ **−17**
34. $-12 = c + 3$ **−15**
35. $v + 2300 = -800$
36. $b + 42 = 300$ **258**
37. $3.5 = n + 4$ **−0.5**
38. $b + \frac{1}{2} = \frac{1}{2}$ **0**
39. $x + 5.34 = 5.39$
40. $2 = d + \frac{1}{4}$ $\mathbf{\frac{7}{4}}$
41. $-12 + f = 3$ **15**
42. $-9 = -4 + g$ **−5**
43. $-1200 + j = 345$
44. $90 = -22 + a$ **112**
45. $26 = -4 + y$ **30**
46. $1\frac{3}{4} = -\frac{1}{4} + w$ **2**
47. $-\frac{1}{6} + h = \frac{1}{6}$ $\mathbf{\frac{1}{3}}$
48. $-5.2 + a = -8$

30. 2.5
35. −3100
39. 0.05
43. 1545
48. −2.8

49. **Finance** Luis deposited \$500 into his bank account. He now has \$4732. Write and solve an equation to find how much was in his account before the deposit. Show that your answer is reasonable. **$a + 500 = 4732$; \$4232**

50. **/// ERROR ANALYSIS ///** Below are two possible solutions to $x + 12.5 = 21.6$. Which is incorrect? Explain the error.

50. Solution B is incorrect. The Addition Property of Equality was used and $x + 25$ is what truly appears on the left side of the equation.

A
x + 12.5 = 21.6
− 12.5 − 12.5
x = 9.1

B
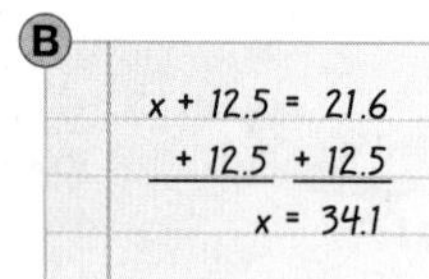

2-1 READING STRATEGIES

To solve equations, you must know many mathematical words and phrases. Look at the diagram below to help you better understand this vocabulary.

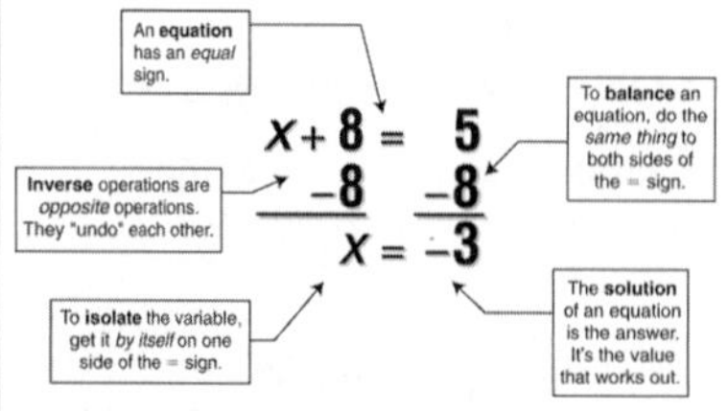

An **equation** has an *equal* sign.
To **balance** an equation, do the *same thing* to both sides of the = sign.
Inverse operations are *opposite* operations. They "undo" each other.
$x + 8 = 5$
$-8 \quad -8$
$x = -3$
To **isolate** the variable, get it *by itself* on one side of the = sign.
The **solution** of an equation is the answer. It's the value that works out.

Answer each of the following.
1. What is the **inverse** operation of subtraction? addition
2. If you add 5 to the right side of an equation, how do you keep the equation **balanced**? Add 5 to the left side.
3. How do you **isolate** the variable in the equation $p - 4 = 12$? Add 4 to both sides.

Solve each equation.
4. $m - 9 = 4$ $m = 13$
5. $13 = g + 8$ $g = 5$
6. $k + 5.8 = 2.8$ $k = -3$
7. $-3 = t + 12$ $t = -15$
8. $-30 = y - 32$ $y = 2$
9. $-2 + h = 9$ $h = 11$

2-1 RETEACH

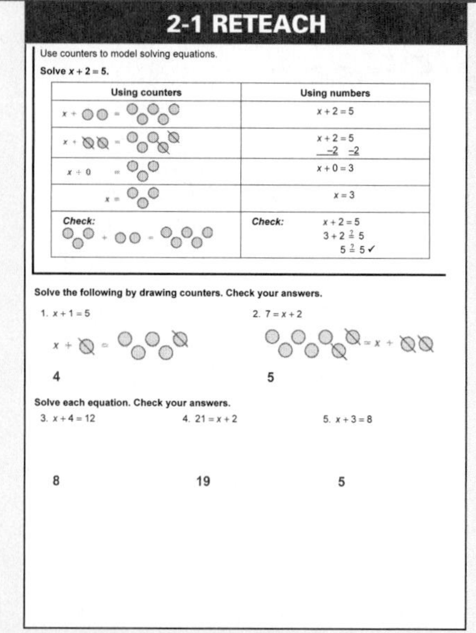
Use counters to model solving equations.
Solve $x + 2 = 5$.

Using counters	Using numbers
	$x + 2 = 5$
	$x + 2 = 5$, $-2 \quad -2$
$x + 0 =$	$x + 0 = 3$
$x =$	$x = 3$
Check:	Check: $x + 2 = 5$, $3 + 2 \stackrel{?}{=} 5$, $5 \stackrel{?}{=} 5$ ✓

Solve the following by drawing counters. Check your answers.
1. $x + 1 = 5$ 4
2. $7 = x + 2$ 5

Solve each equation. Check your answers.
3. $x + 4 = 12$ 8
4. $21 = x + 2$ 19
5. $x + 3 = 8$ 5

Write an equation to represent each relationship. Then solve the equation.

51. Ten less than a number is equal to 12. **$x - 10 = 12$; $x = 22$**
52. A number decreased by 13 is equal to 7. **$x - 13 = 7$; $x = 20$**
53. Eight more than a number is 16. **$x + 8 = 16$; $x = 8$**
54. A number minus 3 is –8. **$x - 3 = -8$; $x = -5$**
55. The sum of 5 and a number is 6. **$5 + x = 6$; $x = 1$**
56. Two less than a number is –5. **$x - 2 = -5$; $x = -3$**
57. The difference of a number and 4 is 9. **$x - 4 = 9$; $x = 13$**

LINK

Geology

The ocean depths are home to many odd-looking creatures. The anglerfish pictured above, known as the common black devil, may appear menacing but reaches a maximum length of only about 5 inches.

58. **Geology** The sum of the Atlantic Ocean's average depth (in feet) and its greatest depth is 43,126. Use the information in the graph to write and solve an equation to find the average depth of the Atlantic Ocean. Show that your answer is reasonable.

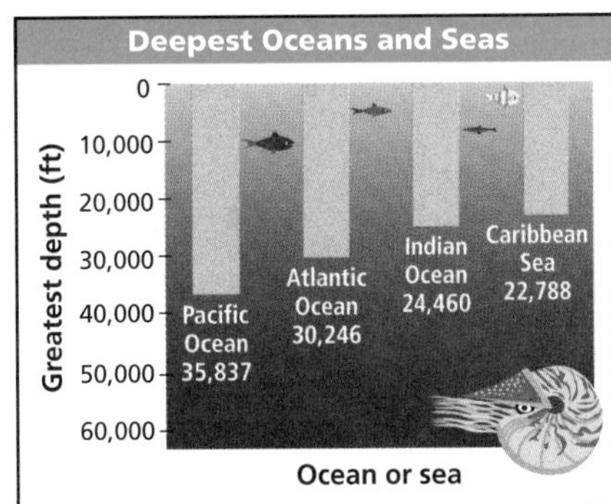

59. **School** Helene's marching band needs money to travel to a competition. Band members have raised \$560. They need to raise a total of \$1680. Write and solve an equation to find how much more they need. Show that your answer is reasonable. **$m + 560 = 1680$; \$1120**

60. **Economics** When you receive a loan to make a purchase, you often must make a down payment in cash. The amount of the loan is the purchase cost minus the down payment. Riva made a down payment of \$1500 on a used car. She received a loan of \$2600. Write and solve an equation to find the cost of the car. Show that your answer is reasonable. **$c - 1500 = 2600$; \$4100**

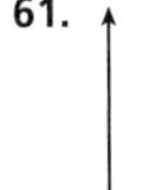

Geometry The angles in each pair are complementary. Write and solve an equation to find each value of x. (*Hint:* The measures of complementary angles add to 90°.)

61. 

$63 + x = 90$; $x = 27$

62. 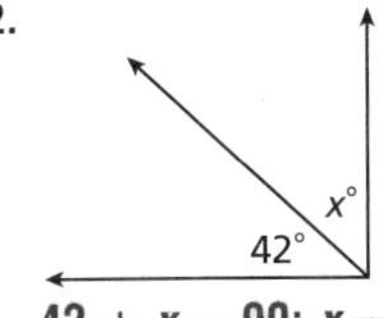

$42 + x = 90$; $x = 48$

63. 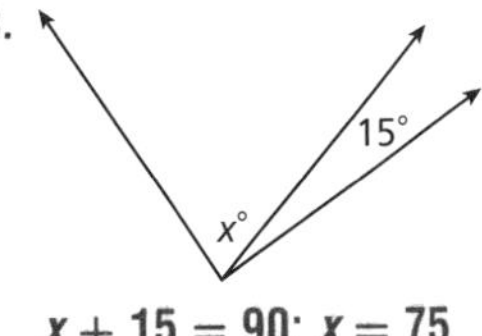

$x + 15 = 90$; $x = 75$

MULTI-STEP TEST PREP

64. This problem will prepare you for the Multi-Step Test Prep on page 118.

Rates are often used to describe how quickly something is moving or changing.

a. A wildfire spreads at a rate of 1000 acres per day. How many acres will the fire cover in 2 days? Show that your answer is reasonable. **2000 acres**

b. How many acres will the fire cover in 5 days? Explain how you found your answer. **5000 acres; multiply 5 days by 1000 acres per day.**

c. Another wildfire spread for 7 days and covered a total of 780 square miles. How can you estimate the number of square miles the fire covered per day? **Divide 780 by 7.**

Teaching Tip

Geometry In **Exercises 61–63,** students are asked to write equations for complementary angles. Two angles are complementary if their sum is 90°. Remind students that complementary angles need not be adjacent. The angles below are complementary.

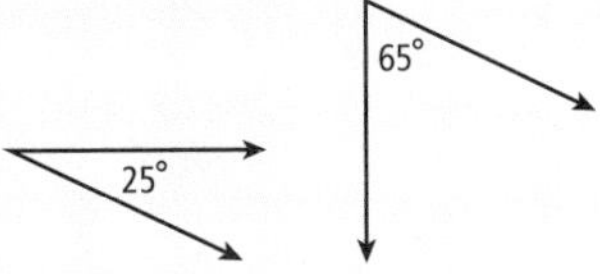

MULTI-STEP TEST PREP **Exercise 64** involves using rates to predict how quickly a fire will spread and how much land it will cover. This exercise prepares students for the Multi-Step Test Prep on page 118.

Answers

58. $a + 30{,}246 = 43{,}126$; 12,880; Possible answer: the greatest depth is about 30,000 feet. The sum of this number and the average is about 43,000 feet. So the average will be close to $43{,}000 - 30{,}000 = 13{,}000$. So 12,880 ft is a reasonable answer.

59. Possible answer: The band needs about \$1700 and they have raised about \$600. So the amount they need will be close to $1700 - 600 = 1100$. So \$1120 is a reasonable answer.

60. Possible answer: the total cost should be more than the down payment and more than the loan amount, so \$4100 is a reasonable answer.

64a. For explanation, see p. A13.

2-1 PROBLEM SOLVING

Write the correct answer.

1. Michelle withdrew \$120 from her bank account. She now has \$3345 in her account. Write and solve an equation to find how much money m was in her account before she made the withdrawal.
   $m - 120 = 3345$;
   \$3465

2. Max lost 23 pounds while on a diet. He now weighs 184 pounds. Write and solve an equation to find his initial weight w.
   $w - 23 = 184$;
   207 lbs

3. Earth takes 365 days to orbit the Sun. Mars takes 687 days. Write and solve an equation to find how many more days d Mars takes than Earth to orbit the Sun.
   $365 + d = 687$;
   322 days

4. In 1990, 53.4% of commuters took public transportation in New York City, which was 19.9% greater than the percentage in San Francisco. Write and solve an equation to find what percentage of commuters p took public transportation in San Francisco.
   $p + 19.9 = 53.4$;
   33.5%

Use the circle graph below to answer questions 5–7. Select the best answer. The circle graph shows the colors for SUVs as percents of the total number of SUVs manufactured in 2000 in North America.

5. The percent of silver SUVs increased by 7.9% between 1998 and 2000. If x% of SUVs were silver in 1998, which equation represents this relationship?
   A $x + 7.9 = 14.1$ C $7.9x = 14.1$
   B $x - 7.9 = 14.1$ D $7.9 - x = 14.1$

6. Solve the equation from problem 5. What is the value of x?
   F 1.8 H 7.1
   G 6.2 J 22

7. The sum of the percents of dark red SUVs and white SUVs was 26.3%. What was the percent of dark red SUVs?
   A 2.3% C 12.2%
   B 3.2% D 18%

Percent of SUVs by Color

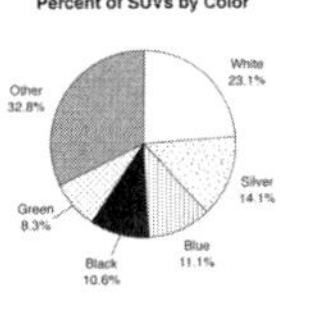

2-1 CHALLENGE

The function of an odometer is to measure the distance that a vehicle has traveled, either in miles or in kilometers. When you use an odometer for this purpose, you can answer the question, "How far have I traveled?" The reasoning that you used to answer the question can be applied to stating and solving new related problems.

Answer the following questions.

1. You are on a trip traveling from town A to town B. When you start the trip, your odometer reading is 37,538 miles. When you get to town B, your odometer reading is 37,781.
   a. Write an equation relating your initial reading, distance traveled, and final reading. **Let x represent the distance traveled. $37{,}538 + x = 37{,}781$**
   b. Find the distance traveled from town A to town B. **243 miles**

2. Let s represent the initial reading, d represent the distance traveled, and e represent the final reading. Write an addition equation relating s, d, and e.
   $s + d = e$

3. Using your equation from Exercise 2, solve for the specified variable.
   a. $s =$ **$e - d$** b. $d =$ **$e - s$** c. $e =$ **$s + d$**

4. Use one of the equations that you wrote in Exercise 3 and the given values to find the value of the third variable.
   a. $s = 27{,}281$ and $e = 28{,}978$ **$d = 1697$**
   b. $e = 17{,}349$ and $d = 197$ **$s = 17{,}152$**
   c. $s = 62{,}979$ and $d = 798$ **$e = 63{,}777$**
   d. $s = 69{,}876$ and $e = 70{,}987$ **$d = 1111$**

The water level in a storage tank is currently $10\frac{1}{2}$ feet.

5. Water is drained from the tank, and the level drops $2\frac{5}{6}$ feet. Find the new water level.
   $7\frac{2}{3}$ feet

6. Let o represent the original water level, d represent the change in water level, and f represent the final water level. Write three equations relating o, d, and f.
   $f = o + d$, $o = f - d$, and $d = f - o$

7. The water level rises $1\frac{3}{4}$ feet from $7\frac{2}{3}$ feet. Choose an equation from Exercise 6 and find the new water level.
   $9\frac{5}{12}$ feet

2-1 PRACTICE A

2-1 PRACTICE C

2-1 PRACTICE B

Solve each equation. Check your answers.

1. $g - 7 = 15$ **$g = 22$**
2. $t + 4 = 6$ **$t = 2$**
3. $13 = m - 7$ **$m = 20$**
4. $x + 3.4 = 9.1$ **$x = 5.7$**
5. $n - \frac{3}{8} = \frac{1}{8}$ **$n = \frac{1}{2}$**
6. $p - \frac{1}{3} = \frac{2}{3}$ **$p = 1$**
7. $-6 + k = 32$ **$k = 38$**
8. $7 = w + 9.3$ **$w = -2.3$**
9. $8 = r + 12$ **$r = -4$**
10. $y - 57 = -40$ **$y = 17$**
11. $-5.1 + b = -7.1$ **$b = -2$**
12. $a + 15 = 15$ **$a = 0$**

13. Marietta was given a raise of \$0.75 an hour, which brought her hourly wage to \$12.25. Write and solve an equation to determine Marietta's hourly wage before her raise. Show that your answer is reasonable.
   $x + 0.75 = 12.25$; \$11.50; Marietta received a raise, so her previous wage should be less than \$12.25.

14. Brad grew $4\frac{1}{4}$ inches this year and is now $56\frac{7}{8}$ inches tall. Write and solve an equation to find Brad's height at the start of the year. Show that your answer is reasonable.
   $x + 4\frac{1}{4} = 56\frac{7}{8}$; $52\frac{5}{8}$ in.; Brad's height increased, so his previous height should be less than $56\frac{7}{8}$ inches.

15. Heather finished a race in 58.4 seconds, which was 2.6 seconds less than her practice time. Write and solve an equation to find Heather's practice time. Show that your answer is reasonable.
   $x - 2.6 = 58.4$; 61 s; Heather's race time was less than her practice time, so her practice time should be greater than 58.4 s.

16. The radius of Earth is 6378.1 km, which is 2981.1 km longer than the radius of Mars. Write and solve an equation to determine the radius of Mars. Show that your answer is reasonable.
   $x + 2981.1 = 6378.1$; 3397 km; Earth is larger than Mars, so the radius of Mars should be less than 6378.1 km.

TEST PREP DOCTOR In **Exercise 68,** 32 is being subtracted from *x*, so students should look for a situation that shows a decrease of 32. Choice **A** has a withdrawal of 32.

If a student selects **H** in **Exercise 69,** he or she may have subtracted 18 from both sides of the equation.

Journal

Have students explain the Addition and Subtraction Properties of Equality, and how they are used to solve equations.

ALTERNATIVE ASSESSMENT

Have students write and solve four equations: two that can be solved using the Addition Property of Equality, and two that can be solved using the Subtraction Property of Equality.

Power Presentations with PowerPoint®

2-1 Lesson Quiz

Solve each equation.

1. $r - 4 = -8$ $\quad -4$

2. $\frac{5}{12} = s - \frac{11}{12}$ $\quad \frac{16}{12}$, or $\frac{4}{3}$

3. $m + 13 = 58$ $\quad 45$

4. $0.75 = n + 0.6$ $\quad 0.15$

5. $-5 + c = 22$ $\quad 27$

6. This year a high school had 578 sophomores enrolled. This is 89 less than the number enrolled last year. Write and solve an equation to find the number of sophomores enrolled last year.
$s - 89 = 578$; $s = 667$

Also available on transparency

65. Statistics The range of a set of scores is 28, and the lowest score is 47. Write and solve an equation to find the highest score. (*Hint:* In a data set, the range is the difference between the highest and the lowest values.) Show that your answer is reasonable. **$h - 47 = 28$; 75**

66. Write About It Describe a real-world situation that can be modeled by $x + 5 = 25$. Tell what the variable represents in your situation. Then solve the equation and tell what the solution means in the context of your problem.

67. Critical Thinking Without solving, tell whether the solution of $-3 + z = 10$ will be greater than 10 or less than 10. Explain. **Possible answer: greater than 10 because you will add a positive number to both sides**

TEST PREP

68. Which situation is best represented by $x - 32 = 8$?

Ⓐ Logan withdrew $32 from her bank account. After her withdrawal, her balance was $8. How much was originally in her account?

Ⓑ Daniel has 32 baseball cards. Joseph has 8 fewer baseball cards than Daniel. How many baseball cards does Joseph have?

Ⓒ Room A contains 32 desks. Room B has 8 fewer desks. How many desks are in Room B?

Ⓓ Janelle bought a bag of 32 craft sticks for a project. She used 8 craft sticks. How many craft sticks does she have left?

69. For which equation is $a = 8$ a solution?

Ⓕ $15 - a = 10$ Ⓖ $10 + a = 23$ Ⓗ $a - 18 = 26$ Ⓙ $a + 8 = 16$

70a. $g - 18 = 22$
b. $40

70. Short Response Julianna used a gift card to pay for an $18 haircut. The remaining balance on the card was $22.

a. Write an equation that can be used to determine the original value of the card.

b. Solve your equation to find the original value of the card.

CHALLENGE AND EXTEND

Solve each equation. Check your answer.

71. $3\frac{1}{5} + b = \frac{4}{5}$ $\quad -\frac{12}{5}$

72. $x - \frac{7}{4} = \frac{2}{3}$ $\quad \frac{29}{12}$

73. $x + \frac{7}{4} = \frac{2}{3}$ $\quad -\frac{13}{12}$

74. $x - \frac{4}{9} = \frac{4}{9}$ $\quad \frac{8}{9}$

75. If $p - 4 = 2$, find the value of $5p - 20$. **10**

76. If $t + 6 = 21$, find the value of $-2t$. **−30**

77. If $x + 3 = 15$, find the value of $18 + 6x$. **90**

78. If $2 + n = -11$, find the value of $6n$. **−78**

SPIRAL REVIEW

Multiply or divide. *(Lesson 1-3)*

79. $-63 \div (-7)$ **9**

80. $\frac{3}{7} \div \left(-\frac{4}{7}\right)$ $\quad -\frac{3}{4}$

81. $(-12)(-6)$ **72**

Give the side length of a square with the given area. *(Lesson 1-5)*

82. $225\ m^2$ **15 m**

83. $36\ ft^2$ **6 ft**

84. $100\ cm^2$ **10 cm**

Simplify each expression. *(Lesson 1-6)*

85. $8[-5 - (3 + 2)]$ **−80**

86. $1 - [4^2 - (12 - 15)^2]$ **−6**

87. $\frac{-12 + (-6)}{6}$ **−3**

Answers

65. Possible answer: the range is about 30 and the lowest score is about 50. So the highest score will be close to 30 + 50 = 80. So 75 is a reasonable answer.

66. Possible answer: If you add 5 yr to Sue's age, you get her cousin's age. Her cousin is 25. How old is Sue? *x* represents Sue's age. *x* = 20; this means Sue is 20 years old.

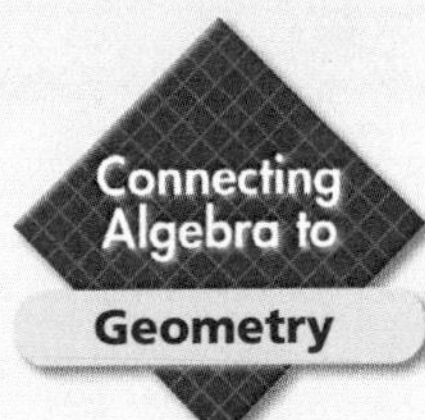

Area of Composite Figures

Review the area formulas for squares, rectangles, and triangles in the table below.

Squares	Rectangles	Triangles
s	ℓ, w	h, b
$A = s^2$	$A = \ell w$	$A = \frac{1}{2}bh$

A *composite figure* is a figure that is composed of basic shapes. You can divide composite figures into combinations of squares, rectangles, and triangles to find their areas.

Example

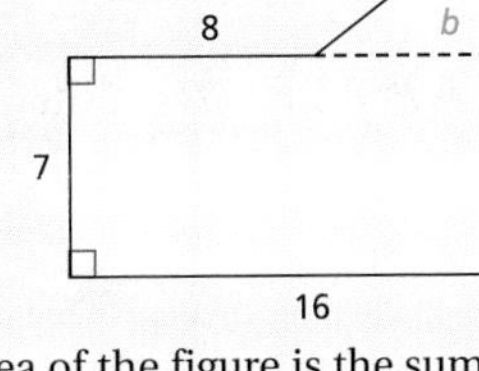

Find the area of the figure shown.

Divide the figure into a rectangle and a right triangle. Notice that you do not know the base or the height of the triangle. Use b and h to represent these lengths.

The bottom of the rectangle is 16 units long; the top of the rectangle is 8 units long plus the base of the triangle. Use this information to write and solve an equation.

$$\begin{aligned} b + 8 &= 16 \\ -8 &\quad -8 \\ b &= 8 \end{aligned}$$

The right side of the figure is 13 units long: 7 units from the rectangle plus the height of the triangle. Use this information to write and solve an equation.

$$\begin{aligned} h + 7 &= 13 \\ -7 &\quad -7 \\ h &= 6 \end{aligned}$$

The area of the figure is the sum of the areas of the rectangle and the triangle.

Area of rectangle ↓ Area of triangle ↓

$A = \ell w + \frac{1}{2}bh$

$A = 16(7) + \frac{1}{2}(8)(6)$

$A = 112 + 24$

$A = 136$ square units

Try This

Find the area of each composite figure.

1. **314 units^2**

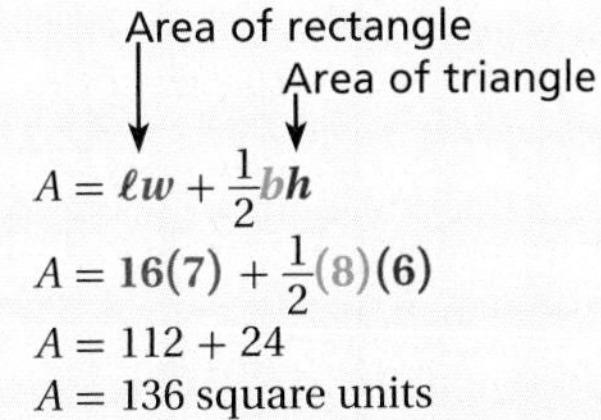

2. **672 units^2**

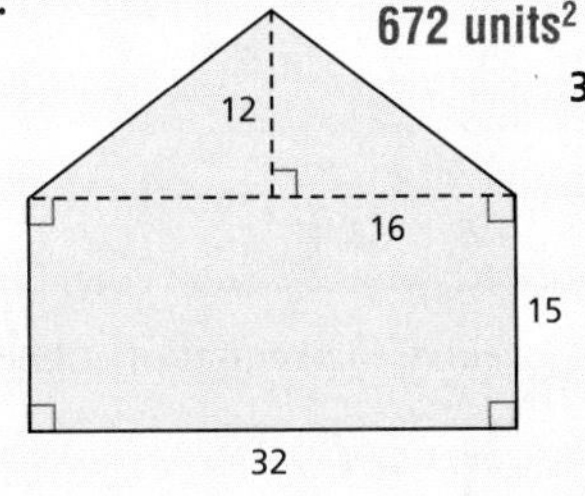

3. **330 units^2**

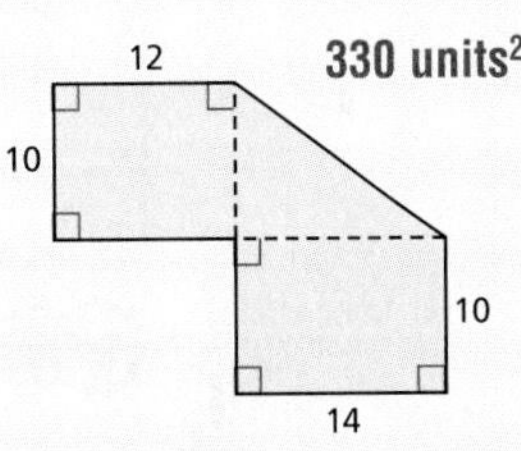

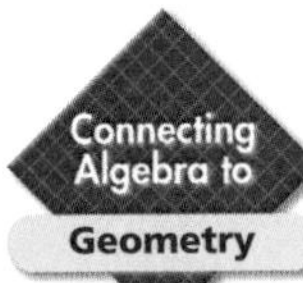

Organizer

Pacing:
Traditional $\frac{1}{2}$ day
Block $\frac{1}{4}$ day

Objective: Apply algebra skills to finding areas of geometric figures.

Teach

Remember

Students review and apply area formulas for geometric figures.

Visual Have students decide how to divide the composite figure and then draw and label each part separately.

Close

Assess

Have students divide the figure in **Exercise 1** differently than the first time they found the area. Have them show algebraically that the area is still the same.

State Resources

2-2 Organizer

Pacing: Traditional 1 day
Block $\frac{1}{2}$ day

Objective: Solve one-step equations in one variable by using multiplication or division.

Online Edition
Tutorial Videos

Countdown Week 3

Power Presentations with PowerPoint®

Warm Up

Evaluate each expression.

1. $(-7)(2.8)$ -19.6

2. $0.96 \div 6$ 0.16

3. $(-9)(-9)$ 81

4. $\left(\frac{5}{6}\right)\left(\frac{6}{5}\right)$ 1

5. $\left(\frac{8}{15}\right)\left(\frac{5}{4}\right)$ $\frac{2}{3}$

6. $\left(\frac{3}{4}\right)(2.4)$ 1.8

Also available on transparency

Math Humor

Teacher: Why don't you have your homework today?

Student: I divided by zero and the paper vanished into thin air!

2-2 Solving Equations by Multiplying or Dividing

Objective
Solve one-step equations in one variable by using multiplication or division.

Who uses this?
Pilots can make quick calculations by solving one-step equations. (See Example 4.)

Solving an equation that contains multiplication or division is similar to solving an equation that contains addition or subtraction. Use inverse operations to undo the operations on the variable.

Remember that an equation is like a balanced scale. To keep the balance, whatever you do on one side of the equation, you must also do on the other side.

Inverse Operations
Multiply by *x*. ⟷ Divide by *x*.

EXAMPLE 1 Solving Equations by Using Multiplication

Solve each equation. Check your answer.

A $-4 = \frac{k}{-5}$

$(-5)(-4) = (-5)\left(\frac{k}{-5}\right)$ *Since k is divided by −5, multiply both sides by −5 to undo the division.*

$20 = k$

Check $-4 = \frac{k}{-5}$ *To check your solution, substitute 20 for k in the original equation.*

-4	$\frac{20}{-5}$
-4	-4 ✓

B $\frac{m}{3} = 1.5$

$(3)\left(\frac{m}{3}\right) = (3)(1.5)$ *Since m is divided by 3, multiply both sides by 3 to undo the division.*

$m = 4.5$

Check $\frac{m}{3} = 1.5$ *To check your solution, substitute 1.5 for m in the original equation.*

$\frac{4.5}{3}$	1.5
1.5	1.5 ✓

Solve each equation. Check your answer.

1a. $\frac{p}{5} = 10$ **50** **1b.** $-13 = \frac{y}{3}$ **−39** **1c.** $\frac{c}{8} = 7$ **56**

State Resources

1 Introduce

EXPLORATION

2-2 Solving Equations by Multiplying or Dividing

Complete the tables by evaluating the expressions for the given values of *x*.

1.

x	$4x$
1	
4	
7	
9	

2.

x	$\frac{x}{3}$
3	
12	
18	
30	

Complete the tables by finding the values of *x*.

3.

x	$4x$
	8
	20
	24
	48

4.

x	$\frac{x}{3}$
	2
	3
	5
	15

THINK AND DISCUSS

5. **Explain** how you evaluated the expressions in Problems 1 and 2.

6. **Explain** how you found the values of *x* in Problems 3 and 4.

Motivate

Ask students what operation is being performed on each variable, and by what number.

$5x = 10$ multiplication by 5

$12 = \frac{p}{6}$ division by 6

Tell students that in this lesson, they will "undo" these operations to solve the equations, just as they had to "undo" addition and subtraction in the previous lesson.

Explorations and answers are provided in *Alternate Openers: Explorations Transparencies.*

EXAMPLE 2 Solving Equations by Using Division

Solve each equation. Check your answers.

A $7x = 56$

$\frac{7x}{7} = \frac{56}{7}$ *Since x is multiplied by 7, divide both sides by 7 to undo the multiplication.*

$x = 8$

Check $7x = 56$ *To check your solution, substitute 8 for x in the original equation.*

$7(8)$	56
56	56 ✓

B $13 = -2w$

$\frac{13}{-2} = \frac{-2w}{-2}$ *Since w is multiplied by −2, divide both sides by −2 to undo the multiplication.*

$-6.5 = w$

Check $13 = -2w$ *To check your solution, substitute −6.5 for w in the original equation.*

13	$-2(-6.5)$
13	13 ✓

Solve each equation. Check your answer.

2a. $16 = 4c$ **4** **2b.** $0.5y = -10$ **−20** **2c.** $15k = 75$ **5**

Remember that dividing is the same as multiplying by the reciprocal. When solving equations, you will sometimes find it easier to multiply by a reciprocal instead of dividing. This is often true when an equation contains fractions.

EXAMPLE 3 Solving Equations That Contain Fractions

Solve each equation.

A $\frac{5}{9}v = 35$

$\left(\frac{9}{5}\right)\frac{5}{9}v = \left(\frac{9}{5}\right)35$ *The reciprocal of $\frac{5}{9}$ is $\frac{9}{5}$. Since v is multiplied by $\frac{5}{9}$, multiply both sides by $\frac{9}{5}$.*

$v = 63$

B $\frac{5}{2} = \frac{4y}{3}$

$\frac{5}{2} = \frac{4y}{3}$

$\frac{5}{2} = \frac{4}{3}y$ *$\frac{4y}{3}$ is the same as $\frac{4}{3}y$.*

$\left(\frac{3}{4}\right)\frac{5}{2} = \left(\frac{3}{4}\right)\frac{4}{3}y$ *The reciprocal of $\frac{4}{3}$ is $\frac{3}{4}$. Since y is multiplied by $\frac{4}{3}$, multiply both sides by $\frac{3}{4}$.*

$\frac{15}{8} = y$

CHECK IT OUT! Solve each equation. Check your answer.

3a. $-\frac{1}{4} = \frac{1}{5}b$ $-\frac{5}{4}$ **3b.** $\frac{4j}{6} = \frac{2}{3}$ **1** **3c.** $\frac{1}{6}w = 102$ **612**

COMMON ERROR ALERT

When solving problems using division, some students may automatically divide the larger number by the smaller number every time. For example, a student may try to solve $6x = 3$ by dividing both sides by 3. Remind students that they must isolate the variable, and that the variable is being multiplied by 6, not by 3.

Power Presentations with PowerPoint®

Additional Examples

Example 1

Solve each equation.

A. $-8 = \frac{j}{3}$ -24

B. $\frac{n}{6} = 2.8$ 16.8

Example 2

Solve each equation.

A. $9y = 108$ 12

B. $-4.8 = -6v$ 0.8

Example 3

Solve each equation.

A. $\frac{5}{6}w = -20$ -24

B. $\frac{3}{16} = \frac{1}{8}z$ $\frac{3}{2}$, or $1\frac{1}{2}$

2 Teach

Guided Instruction

Review multiplication and division of signed numbers, as well as how to find the reciprocal of a number. Show how to solve equations by using multiplication and division to undo the operation shown. Remind students that the coefficient of a single variable is 1, so the coefficient of $-x$ is -1.

Reading Math Remind students that $-x = 3$ can be read as "the opposite of x equals 3."

ENGLISH LANGUAGE LEARNERS

Reaching All Learners

Through Visual Cues

Have students create a chart they can use as a reference on class work or homework.

When Solving Equations	
I see...	**I use...**
Addition	Subtraction
Subtraction	Addition
Multiplication	Division
Division	Multiplication

INTERVENTION

Questioning Strategies

EXAMPLE 1

- What operation is used to isolate the variable? Why?

EXAMPLE 2

- What operation is used to isolate the variable? Why?
- How do you know which number to divide both sides by?

EXAMPLE 3

- What is the product of any number and its reciprocal? How does that help you solve equations?

Power Presentations with PowerPoint®

Additional Examples

Example 4

Ciro puts $\frac{1}{4}$ of the money he earns from mowing lawns into a college education fund. This year Ciro added $285 to his college education fund. Write and solve an equation to find how much money Ciro earned mowing lawns this year. $\frac{1}{4}m = 285$; $1140

INTERVENTION

Questioning Strategies

EXAMPLE 4

- What are the variables in the situation?
- What operation is needed to solve the equation?

Inclusion The expression 7*x* means 7 of whatever quantity *x* represents. To help students understand this, give a real-world example. If 7 CDs cost $56, but you only want to buy 1 CD, how would you find the cost?

EXAMPLE 4 Aviation Application

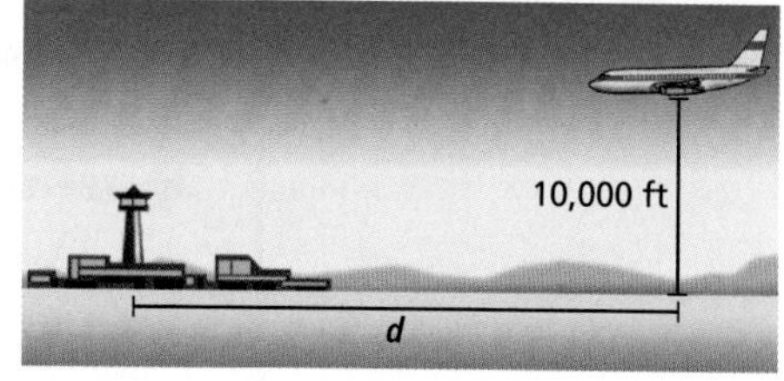

The distance in miles from the airport that a plane should begin descending, divided by 3, equals the plane's height above the ground in thousands of feet. If a plane is 10,000 feet above the ground, write and solve an equation to find the distance at which the pilot should begin descending.

The equation uses the plane's height above the ground in *thousands* of feet. So substitute 10 for *h*, not 10,000.

Distance **divided by 3** **equals** **height in thousands of feet.**

$$\frac{d}{3} = h$$ *Write an equation to represent the relationship.*

$$\frac{d}{3} = 10$$ *Substitute 10 for h. Since d is divided by 3, multiply both sides by 3 to undo the division.*

$$(3)\frac{d}{3} = (3)10$$

$$d = 30$$

The pilot should begin descending 30 miles from the airport.

CHECK IT OUT! **4. What if...?** A plane began descending 45 miles from the airport. Use the equation above to find how high the plane was flying when the descent began. **15,000 ft**

You have now used four properties of equality to solve equations. These properties are summarized in the box below.

Know it! Note

Properties of Equality

WORDS	NUMBERS	ALGEBRA
Addition Property of Equality You can add the same number to both sides of an equation, and the statement will still be true.	$3 = 3$ $3 + 2 = 3 + 2$ $5 = 5$	$a = b$ $a + c = b + c$
Subtraction Property of Equality You can subtract the same number from both sides of an equation, and the statement will still be true.	$7 = 7$ $7 - 5 = 7 - 5$ $2 = 2$	$a = b$ $a - c = b - c$
Multiplication Property of Equality You can multiply both sides of an equation by the same number, and the statement will still be true.	$6 = 6$ $6(3) = 6(3)$ $18 = 18$	$a = b$ $ac = bc$
Division Property of Equality You can divide both sides of an equation by the same nonzero number, and the statement will still be true.	$8 = 8$ $\frac{8}{4} = \frac{8}{4}$ $2 = 2$	$a = b$ $(c \neq 0)$ $\frac{a}{c} = \frac{b}{c}$

3 Close

Summarize

Ask students to explain which property of equality should be used to solve each equation.

$-4y = 20$	Div. Prop. of Eq.
$-7 + f = -\frac{1}{2}$	Add. Prop. of Eq.
$15 = p + 4$	Subt. Prop. of Eq.
$\frac{x}{33} = -9$	Mult. Prop. of Eq.

ONGOING ASSESSMENT and INTERVENTION

***Diagnose Before* the Lesson**
2-2 Warm Up, TE p. 84

***Monitor During* the Lesson**
Check It Out! Exercises, SE pp. 84–86
Questioning Strategies, TE pp. 85–86

***Assess After* the Lesson**
2-2 Lesson Quiz, TE p. 90
Alternative Assessment, TE p. 90

THINK AND DISCUSS

1. Tell how the Multiplication and Division Properties of Equality are similar to the Addition and Subtraction Properties of Equality.

2. **GET ORGANIZED** Copy and complete the graphic organizer. In each box, write an example of an equation that can be solved by using the given property, and solve it.

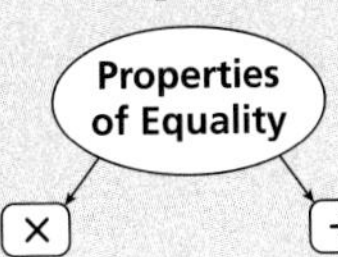

Answers to *Think and Discuss*

1. Possible answer: All 4 properties tell you that if you perform the same operation on both sides of an equation, the equality will still hold.
2. See p. A2.

2-2 Exercises

GUIDED PRACTICE

Solve each equation. Check your answer.

SEE EXAMPLE 1 p. 84

1. $\frac{k}{4} = 8$ **32**
2. $\frac{z}{3} = -9$ **−27**
3. $-2 = \frac{w}{-7}$ **14**
4. $6 = \frac{t}{-5}$ **−30**
5. $\frac{g}{1.9} = 10$ **19**
6. $2.4 = \frac{b}{5}$ **12**

SEE EXAMPLE 2 p. 85

7. $4x = 28$ **7**
8. $-64 = 8c$ **−8**
9. $-9j = -45$ **5**
10. $84 = -12a$ **−7**
11. $4m = 10$ **2.5**
12. $2.8 = -2h$ **−1.4**

SEE EXAMPLE 3 p. 85

13. $\frac{1}{2}d = 7$ **14**
14. $15 = \frac{5}{6}f$ **18**
15. $\frac{2}{3}s = -6$ **−9**
16. $9 = -\frac{3}{8}r$ **−24**
17. $\frac{1}{10} = \frac{4}{5}y$ $\mathbf{\frac{1}{8}}$
18. $\frac{1}{4}v = -\frac{3}{4}$ **−3**

SEE EXAMPLE 4 p. 86

19. **Recreation** The Baseball Birthday Batter Package at a minor league ballpark costs $192. The package includes tickets, drinks, and cake for a group of 16 children. Write and solve an equation to find the cost per child. **16*c* = 192; $12**
20. **Nutrition** An orange contains about 80 milligrams of vitamin C, which is 10 times as much as an apple contains. Write and solve an equation to find the amount of vitamin C in an apple. **80 = 10*a*; 8 mg**

PRACTICE AND PROBLEM SOLVING

Solve each equation. Check your answer.

21. $\frac{x}{2} = 12$ **24**
22. $-40 = \frac{b}{5}$ **−200**
23. $-\frac{j}{6} = 6$ **−36**
24. $-\frac{n}{3} = -4$ **12**
25. $-\frac{q}{5} = 30$ **−150**
26. $1.6 = \frac{d}{3}$ **4.8**
27. $\frac{v}{10} = 5.5$ **55**
28. $\frac{h}{8.1} = -4$ **−32.4**
29. $5t = -15$ **−3**
30. $49 = 7c$ **7**
31. $-12 = -12u$ **1**
32. $-7m = 63$ **−9**
33. $-52 = -4c$ **13**
34. $11 = -2z$ **−5.5**
35. $5f = 1.5$ **0.3**
36. $-8.4 = -4n$ **2.1**

2-2 Exercises

Assignment Guide

Assign *Guided Practice* exercises as necessary.

If you finished Examples **1–2**
Basic 21–36, 52–55
Average 21–36, 52, 54, 61–64
Advanced 22–36 even, 52–56, 61–64, 88–91

If you finished Examples **1–4**
Basic 21–57, 59–75, 77–81, 95–104
Average 21–47, 48–54 even, 56–76, 77–88, 95–104
Advanced 22–42, 48–54 even, 58–104 even

Homework Quick Check
Quickly check key concepts.
Exercises: 22, 32, 38, 46, 50, 74

State Resources

go.hrw.com
State Resources Online
KEYWORD: MA7 Resources

Teaching Tip **Earth Science Link** In **Exercise 46,** a relationship is given between people's weight on Earth and their weight on the Moon. Students may also be interested to know that people's weight on Pluto is about $\frac{7}{100}$ their weight on Earth, and their weight on Jupiter is about twice their weight on Earth.

Teaching Tip **Geometry** In **Exercises 48–51,** students must write an equation for the perimeter of a square. All four sides of a square have equal length, so the formula can be written in the form $4s = P$.

Answers

46. Possible answer: the person's weight on the moon is about 15 lb. Estimate that the answer will be close to $15 \cdot 6 = 90$. So 96 lb is reasonable.

59. Possible answer: Dion's calls cost $0.05/min. If he talked for 300 min, the cost would be $300(0.05) = \$15$. This is close to the cost given in the problem, $13.80. So 276 min is reasonable.

60. Possible answer: the amount of caffeine in the soft drink should be about $\frac{200}{5} = 40$ mg. So 37 mg is reasonable.

Independent Practice	
For Exercises	See Example
21–28	1
29–36	2
37–44	3
45	4

Extra Practice
Skills Practice p. S6
Application Practice p. S29

46. $\frac{1}{6}w = 16$; 96 lb

Solve each equation. Check your answer.

37. $\frac{5}{2}k = 5$ **2**
38. $-9 = \frac{3}{4}d$ **−12**
39. $-\frac{5}{8}b = 10$ **−16**
40. $-\frac{4}{5}g = -12$ **15**
41. $\frac{4}{7}t = -2$ **−3.5**
42. $-\frac{4}{5}p = \frac{2}{3}$ $-\frac{5}{6}$
43. $\frac{2}{3} = -\frac{1}{3}q$ **−2**
44. $-\frac{5}{8} = -\frac{3}{4}a$ $\frac{5}{6}$

45. **Finance** After taxes, Alexandra's take-home pay is $\frac{7}{10}$ of her salary before taxes. Write and solve an equation to find Alexandra's salary before taxes for the pay period that resulted in $392 of take-home pay. $\frac{7}{10}s = 392$; **$560**

46. **Earth Science** Your weight on the Moon is about $\frac{1}{6}$ of your weight on Earth. Write and solve an equation to show how much a person weighs on Earth if he weighs 16 pounds on the Moon. How could you check that your answer is reasonable?

47. **ERROR ANALYSIS** For the equation $\frac{x}{3} = 15$, a student found the value of x to be 5. Explain the error. What is the correct answer? **The student divided both sides by 3 instead of multiplying both sides by 3; 45.**

Geometry The perimeter of a square is given. Write and solve an equation to find the length of each side of the square.

48. $P = 36$ in. $4s = 36$; 9 in.
49. $P = 84$ in. $4s = 84$; 21 in.
50. $P = 100$ yd $4s = 100$; 25 yd
51. $P = 16.4$ cm $4s = 16.4$; 4.1 cm

Write an equation to represent each relationship. Then solve the equation.

52. Five times a number is 45. $5x = 45$; $x = 9$
53. A number multiplied by negative 3 is 12. $-3x = 12$; $x = -4$
54. A number divided by 4 is equal to 10. $\frac{x}{4} = 10$; $x = 40$
55. The quotient of a number and 3 is negative 8. $\frac{x}{3} = -8$; $x = -24$

LINK **Statistics**

American Robert P. Wadlow (1918–1940) holds the record for world's tallest man—8 ft 11.1 in. He also holds world records for the largest feet and hands.

Source: Guinness World Records 2005

56. **Statistics** The mean height of the students in Marta's class is 60 in. There are 18 students in her class. Write and solve an equation to find the total measure of all students' heights. (*Hint:* The mean is found by dividing the sum of all data values by the number of data values.) $\frac{x}{18} = 60$; 1080

57. **Finance** Lisa earned $6.25 per hour at her after-school job. Each week she earned $50. Write and solve an equation to show how many hours she worked each week. $6.25h = 50$; 8 h

58. **Critical Thinking** Will the solution of $\frac{x}{2.1} = 4$ be greater than 4 or less than 4? Explain. **Greater than 4; you are multiplying 4 by a positive number greater than 1.**

59. **Consumer Economics** Dion's long-distance phone bill was $13.80. His long-distance calls cost $0.05 per minute. Write and solve an equation to find the number of minutes he was charged for. Show that your answer is reasonable. $0.05m = 13.80$; 276 min

60. **Nutrition** An 8 oz cup of coffee has about 184 mg of caffeine. This is 5 times as much caffeine as in a 12 oz soft drink. Write and solve an equation to find about how much caffeine is in a 12 oz caffeinated soft drink. Round your answer to the nearest whole number. Show that your answer is reasonable. $5c = 184$; 37 mg

Use the equation $8y = 4x$ to find y for each value of x.

	x	$4x$	$8y = 4x$	y
61.	−4	$4(-4) = -16$	$8y = -16$	−2
62.	−2	−8	$8y = -8$	−1
63.	0	0	$8y = 0$	0
64.	2	8	$8y = 8$	1

2-2 PRACTICE A
2-2 PRACTICE C
2-2 PRACTICE B

Solve each equation. Check your answers.

1. $\frac{d}{8} = 6$ $d = 48$
2. $-5 = \frac{n}{2}$ $n = -10$
3. $2p = 54$ $p = 27$
4. $\frac{-t}{2} = 12$ $t = -24$
5. $-40 = -4x$ $x = 10$
6. $\frac{2r}{3} = 16$ $r = 24$
7. $-49 = 7y$ $y = -7$
8. $-15 = -\frac{3n}{5}$ $n = 25$
9. $9m = 6$ $m = \frac{2}{3}$
10. $\frac{v}{-3} = -6$ $v = 18$
11. $2.8 = \frac{b}{4}$ $b = 11.2$
12. $\frac{3r}{4} = \frac{1}{8}$ $r = \frac{1}{6}$

Answer each of the following.

13. The perimeter of a regular pentagon is 41.5 cm. Write and solve an equation to determine the length of each side of the pentagon. $5x = 41.5$; 8.3 cm
14. In June 2005, Peter mailed a package from his local post office in Fayetteville, North Carolina to a friend in Radford, Virginia for $2.07. The first-class rate at the time was $0.23 per ounce. Write and solve an equation to determine the weight of the package. $0.23x = 2.07$; 9 oz
15. Lola spends one-third of her allowance on movies. She spends $8 per week at the movies. Write and solve an equation to determine Lola's weekly allowance. $\frac{1}{3}x = 8$; $24

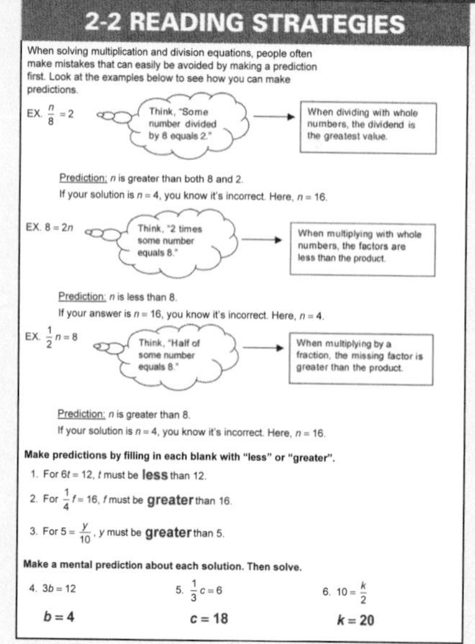
2-2 READING STRATEGIES

When solving multiplication and division equations, people often make mistakes that can easily be avoided by making a prediction first. Look at the examples below to see how you can make predictions.

EX. $\frac{n}{8} = 2$ Think, "Some number divided by 8 equals 2." → When dividing with whole numbers, the dividend is the greatest value.

Prediction: n is greater than both 8 and 2.
If your solution is $n = 4$, you know it's incorrect. Here, $n = 16$.

EX. $8 = 2n$ Think, "2 times some number equals 8." → When multiplying with whole numbers, the factors are less than the product.

Prediction: n is less than 8.
If your answer is $n = 16$, you know it's incorrect. Here, $n = 4$.

EX. $\frac{1}{2}n = 8$ Think, "Half of some number equals 8." → When multiplying by a fraction, the missing factor is greater than the product.

Prediction: n is greater than 8.
If your solution is $n = 4$, you know it's incorrect. Here, $n = 16$.

Make predictions by filling in each blank with "less" or "greater".

1. For $6t = 12$, t must be **less** than 12.
2. For $\frac{1}{4}f = 16$, f must be **greater** than 16.
3. For $5 = \frac{y}{10}$, y must be **greater** than 5.

Make a mental prediction about each solution. Then solve.

4. $3b = 12$ $b = 4$
5. $\frac{1}{3}c = 6$ $c = 18$
6. $10 = \frac{k}{2}$ $k = 20$

2-2 RETEACH

Solve equations involving multiplication and division by performing the inverse operation.

Solve $\frac{x}{5} = 4$.

$\frac{x}{5} = 4$ — *x is divided by 5.*
$5 \cdot \frac{x}{5} = 4 \cdot 5$ — *Multiply both sides by 5.*
$\frac{5x}{5} = 20$ — *Simplify.*
$x = 20$

Check: $\frac{x}{5} = 4$
$\frac{20}{5} \stackrel{?}{=} 4$
$4 \stackrel{?}{=} 4$ ✓

Solve $-3x = 27$.

$-3x = 27$ — *x is multiplied by −3.*
$\frac{-3x}{-3} = \frac{27}{-3}$ — *Divide both sides by −3.*
$x = -9$ — *Simplify.*

Check: $-3x = 27$
$-3(-9) \stackrel{?}{=} 27$
$27 \stackrel{?}{=} 27$ ✓

Circle the correct word in each sentence. Then solve the equation.

1. $\frac{x}{-2} = 7$
x is multiplied/divided by −2.
To solve, multiply/divide both sides by −2.
$x = -14$

2. $5m = -40$
m is multiplied/divided by 5.
To solve, multiply/divide both sides by 5.
$m = -8$

Solve each equation. Check your answers.

3. $-2x = -20$ 10
4. $\frac{w}{5} = -7$ −35
5. $6z = -42$ −7

65. This problem will prepare you for the Multi-Step Test Prep on page 118.

a. The formula for the mean of a data set is mean $= \frac{\text{sum of data values}}{\text{number of data values}}$. One summer, there were 1926 wildfires in Arizona. Which value does this number represent in the formula? **number of data values**

b. The mean number of acres burned by each wildfire was 96.21. Which value does this number represent in the formula? **mean**

c. Use the formula and information given to find how many acres were burned by wildfires in Arizona that summer. Round your answer to the nearest acre. Show that your answer is reasonable. **185,300 acres**

Solve each equation. Check your answer.

66. $\frac{m}{6} = 1$ **6**

67. $4x = 28$ **7**

68. $1.2h = 14.4$ **12**

69. $\frac{1}{5}x = 121$ **605**

70. $2w = 26$ **13**

71. $4b = \frac{3}{4}$ $\mathbf{\frac{3}{16}}$

72. $5y = 11$ $\mathbf{\frac{11}{5}}$**, or 2.2**

73. $\frac{n}{1.9} = 3$ **5.7**

Biology Use the table for Exercises 74 and 75.

Average Weight			
Animal	**At Birth (g)**	**Adult Female (g)**	**Adult Male (g)**
Hamster	2	130	110
Guinea pig	85	800	1050
Rat	5	275	480

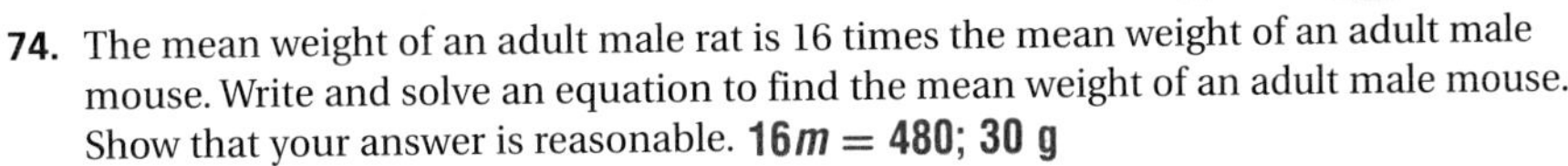

74. The mean weight of an adult male rat is 16 times the mean weight of an adult male mouse. Write and solve an equation to find the mean weight of an adult male mouse. Show that your answer is reasonable. **16*m* = 480; 30 g**

75. $\mathbf{\frac{2}{3}g = 2}$**; 3 g**

75. On average, a hamster at birth weighs $\frac{2}{3}$ the weight of a gerbil at birth. Write and solve an equation to find the average weight of a gerbil at birth. Show that your answer is reasonable.

76. Write About It Describe a real-world situation that can be modeled by $3x = 42$. Solve the equation and tell what the solution means in the context of your problem.

76. Possible answer: Ryan has 3 times as many baseball cards as David. Ryan has 42 cards. How many cards does David have? *x* = 14; this represents the number of cards that David has.

77. Which situation does NOT represent the equation $\frac{d}{2} = 10$?

Ⓐ Leo bought a box of pencils. He gave half of them to his brother. They each got 10 pencils. How many pencils were in the box Leo bought?

Ⓑ Kasey evenly divided her money from baby-sitting into two bank accounts. She put $10 in each account. How much did Kasey earn?

Ⓒ Gilbert cut a piece of ribbon into 2-inch strips. When he was done, he had ten 2-inch strips. How long was the ribbon to start?

Ⓓ Mattie had 2 more CDs than her sister Leona. If Leona had 10 CDs, how many CDs did Mattie have?

78. Which equation below shows a correct first step for solving $3x = -12$?

Ⓕ $3x + 3 = -12 + 3$

Ⓖ $3x - 3 = -12 - 3$

Ⓗ $3(3x) = 3(-12)$

Ⓙ $\frac{3x}{3} = \frac{-12}{3}$

Exercise 65 involves using the formula for the mean of a data set to find the total acreage burned by wildfires. This exercise prepares students for the Multi-Step Test Prep on page 118.

Answers

65c. Possible answer: there were about 1900 fires and the mean acreage burned was about 100. So the total acres burned will be close to 1900(100) = 190,000. So 185,300 is reasonable.

74. Possible answer: an adult male rat weighs about 500 g, and this is about 20 times the weight of an adult mouse. So the mouse will weigh close to $\frac{500}{20} = 25$ g. So 30 g is reasonable.

75. Possible answer: a hamster weighs 2 g, so the gerbil's weight will be greater than 2 g. So 3 g is reasonable.

2-2 PROBLEM SOLVING

Write the correct answer.

1. John threw a surprise birthday party for his friend. Food, drinks, and a DJ cost $480 for a group of 32 people. Write and solve an equation to find the cost *c* per person.

   $32c = 480$;
   $15

2. One serving of soybeans contains 10 grams of protein, which is 4 times the amount in one serving of kale. Write and solve an equation to find the amount of protein *x* in one serving of kale.

   $4x = 10$;
   2.5 grams

3. Maria earned $10.50 per hour working at an ice cream shop. She earned $147 each week before taxes. Write and solve an equation to find the number of hours *h* she worked each week.

   $10.50h = 147$;
   14 hours

4. Ben is saving $\frac{1}{5}$ of his weekly pay to buy a car. Write and solve an equation to find what weekly pay *w* results in savings of $61.50.

   $\frac{1}{5}w = 61.50$;
   $307.50

Use the table below to answer questions 5–7. Select the best answer. The table shows the maximum speed in miles per hour for various animals.

Animal	mi/h
Falcon	200
Zebra	40
Cat (domestic)	30
Black Mamba Snake	20
Snail	0.03

5. The speed of a snail is how many times that of a cat?

   A $\frac{1}{1000}$ C 100
   B $\frac{1}{100}$ D 1000

6. A cheetah's maximum speed of 70 mi/h is *x* times faster than a black mamba snake's maximum speed. Which equation shows this relationship?

   F $20 + x = 70$ H $70 = \frac{20}{x}$
   G $20 = 70x$ **J** $70 = 20x$

7. Use your equation in problem 6 to find how many times faster a cheetah is than a black mamba snake if they are both traveling at their maximum speed.

   A 0.3 times C 10 times
   B 3.5 times D 50 times

2-2 CHALLENGE

The Multiplication Property of Equality states that if *a*, *b*, and *c* are numbers and $a = b$, then $ac = bc$. That is, when you multiply each side of an equation by a fixed number, the resulting products are equal.

By itself, you can use the Multiplication Property of Equality to solve equations of the form $ax = b$ as well as equations of the form $\frac{x}{a} = b$.

You can see this fact at work in the solution below.

$$3x = 6$$
$$\frac{1}{3}(3x) = \frac{1}{3}(6)$$
$$\left[\frac{1}{3}(3)\right]x = \frac{1}{3}(6)$$
$$1x = \frac{1}{3}(6)$$
$$x = 2$$

Notice that you multiply by a fraction whose numerator is 1, that is, by the reciprocal of *a*.

Solve each equation by using only the Multiplication Property of Equality. Show your work.

1. $4x = 12$ **$x = 3$**
2. $-3x = 15$ **$x = -5$**
3. $-7x = -21$ **$x = 3$**
4. $10t = 12$ **$t = \frac{6}{5}$**
5. $18w = 9$ **$w = \frac{1}{2}$**
6. $-3d = -90$ **$d = 30$**
7. Suppose that $a \neq 0$. Using the process that you followed in Exercises 1–6, solve $ax = b$ for *x*.

   $ax = b$; $\frac{1}{a} \cdot ax = \frac{1}{a} \cdot b$; $1 \cdot x = \frac{1}{a} \cdot b$; $x = \frac{b}{a}$
8. Use the Division Property of Equality to solve $ax = b$ for *x*.

   $\frac{ax}{a} = \frac{b}{a}$; $1x = \frac{b}{a}$; $x = \frac{b}{a}$
9. Compare the method of solving an equation of the form $ax = b$ by using the Multiplication Property of Equality with that of solving the same type of equation by using the Division Property of Equality.

   Using the Multiplication Property of Equality, multiply each side of the equation by the reciprocal of the coefficient of the *x*-term. Using the Division Property of Equality, divide each side of the equation by the coefficient of the *x*-term. By either method, the solution is the same.

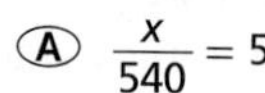

TEST PREP DOCTOR + In Exercise 79, students who chose **D** probably understand that the sum is being divided by 5, but may not understand that the unknown is each angle measure. Point out that the sum is 540, so if written as a division, the equation would be $\frac{540}{5} = x$. Remind students that a sum is that same as repeated multiplication, so the sum of 5 equal angles can be expressed as $5x$, which leads to choosing **B.**

Journal

The equation $\frac{3}{4}x = 7.2$ could be solved using either all fractions or all decimals. Have students explain which way they would solve it and why, and then have them solve it.

ALTERNATIVE ASSESSMENT

Have students make a two-column chart. On the left side, tell them to write and solve three equations by using the Multiplication Property of Equality. On the right side, tell them to write and solve three equations by using the Division Property of Equality. Then have them write a real-world scenario for one equation from each side.

Power Presentations with PowerPoint®

2-2 Lesson Quiz

Solve each equation.

1. $-3 = \frac{m}{-7}$ 21
2. $\frac{x}{100} = 0.028$ 2.8
3. $8y = 4$ $\frac{1}{2}$
4. $126 = -9q$ −14
5. $\frac{2}{5}m = 16$ 40
6. $\frac{15}{16}c = \frac{25}{48}$ $\frac{5}{9}$
7. A person's weight on Venus is about $\frac{9}{10}$ his or her weight on Earth. Write and solve an equation to find how much a person weighs on Earth if he or she weighs 108 pounds on Venus. $108 = \frac{9}{10}w$; 120 lb

Also available on transparency

79. In a regular pentagon, all of the angles are equal in measure. The sum of the angle measures is 540°. Which of the following equations could be used to find the measure of each angle?

(A) $\frac{x}{540} = 5$ (C) $540x = 5$

(B) $5x = 540$ (D) $\frac{x}{5} = 540$

80. For which equation is $m = 10$ a solution?

(F) $5 = 2m$ (G) $5m = 2$ (H) $\frac{m}{2} = 5$ (J) $\frac{m}{10} = 2$

81. Short Response Luisa bought 6 cans of cat food that each cost the same amount. She spent a total of $4.80.

a. Write an equation to determine the cost of one can of cat food. Tell what each part of your equation represents.

b. Solve your equation to find the cost of one can of cat food. Show each step.

81a. $6c = 4.80$; 6 is the number of cans of cat food; c is the cost per can; 4.80 is the total cost.

b. $c = \$0.80$

CHALLENGE AND EXTEND

Solve each equation. Check your answer.

82. $\left(3\frac{1}{5}\right)b = \frac{4}{5}$ $\frac{1}{4}$ **83.** $\left(1\frac{1}{3}\right)x = 2\frac{2}{3}$ 2 **84.** $\left(5\frac{4}{5}\right)x = -52\frac{1}{5}$ −9

85. $\left(-2\frac{9}{10}\right)k = -26\frac{1}{10}$ 9 **86.** $\left(1\frac{2}{3}\right)w = 15\frac{1}{3}$ $\frac{46}{5}$ **87.** $\left(2\frac{1}{4}\right)d = 4\frac{1}{2}$ 2

Find each indicated value.

88. If $2p = 4$, find the value of $6p + 10$. **22** **89.** If $6t = 24$, find the value of $-5t$. **−20**

90. If $3x = 15$, find the value of $12 - 4x$. **−8** **91.** If $\frac{n}{2} = -11$, find the value of $6n$. **−132**

92. To isolate x in $ax = b$, what should you divide both sides by? ***a***

93. To isolate x in $\frac{x}{a} = b$, what operation should you perform on both sides of the equation? **Multiply both sides by *a*.**

94. Travel The formula $d = rt$ gives the distance d that is traveled at a rate r in time t.

a. If $d = 400$ and $r = 25$, what is the value of t? **16**

b. If $d = 400$ and $r = 50$, what is the value of t? **8**

c. **What if...?** How did t change when r increased from 25 to 50? ***t* is divided in half (from 16 to 8).**

d. **What if...?** If r is doubled while d remains the same, what is the effect on t? ***t* is divided in half.**

SPIRAL REVIEW

Find each square root. *(Lesson 1-5)*

95. $\sqrt{144}$ **12** **96.** $\sqrt{196}$ **14** **97.** $\sqrt{625}$ **25** **98.** $-\sqrt{9}$ **−3**

Write and solve an equation that could be used to answer each question. *(Lesson 2-1)*

99. Lisa's age plus Sean's age is 17. Sean is 11 years old. How old is Lisa? **6 years old**

100. The length of a rectangle is 6 feet more than the width of the rectangle. The length is 32 feet. What is the width of the rectangle? **26 ft**

Solve each equation. Check your answer. *(Lesson 2-1)*

101. $2 = a - 4$ **6** **102.** $x - 12 = -3$ **9** **103.** $z - 5 = 11$ **16** **104.** $-4 = x + 5$ **−9**

Solve Equations by Graphing

You can use graphs to solve equations. As you complete this activity, you will learn some of the connections between graphs and equations.

Use with Lesson 2-3

go.hrw.com
Lab Resources Online
KEYWORD: MA11 LAB2

Solve $3x - 4 = 5$.

1 Press [Y=]. In Y_1, enter the left side of the equation, $3x - 4$.

In Y_2, enter the right side of the equation, 5.

[Y=] 5 [ENTER]

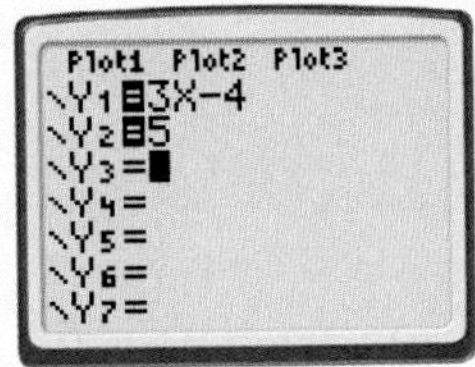

2 Press [GRAPH]. Press [TRACE]. The display will show the x- and y-values of a point on the first line. Press the right arrow key several times. Notice that the x- and y-values change.

Y1=3X-4
X=2.9787234 Y=4.9361702

3 Continue to trace as close as possible to the intersection of the two lines. The x-value of this point 2.9787..., is an approximation of the solution. The solution is about 3.

4 While still in trace mode, to check, press 3 [ENTER]. The display will show the y-value when $x = 3$. When $x = 3$, $y = 5$. So 3 is the solution. You can also check this solution by substituting 3 for x in the equation:

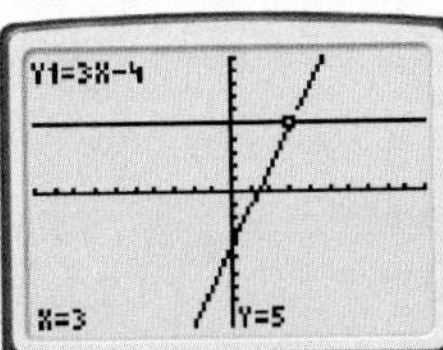

Check

$3x - 4$	$= 5$
$3(3) - 4$	5
$9 - 4$	5
5	5 ✓

Try This

1. Solve $3x - 4 = 2$, $3x - 4 = 17$, and $3x - 4 = -7$ by graphing. **2; 7; −1**
2. What does each line represent? **Each line represents one side of the equation.**
3. Describe a procedure for finding the solution of $3x - 4 = y$ for any value of y.
4. Solve $\frac{1}{2}x - 7 = -4$, $\frac{1}{2}x - 7 = 0$, and $\frac{1}{2}x - 7 = 2$ by graphing. **6; 14; 18**

Organizer

Use with Lesson 2-3

Pacing:
Traditional $\frac{1}{2}$ day
Block $\frac{1}{4}$ day

Objective: Use a graphing calculator to solve two-step equations by graphing.

Materials: graphing calculator

Online Edition
Graphing Calculator, TechKeys

Countdown Week 3

Teach

Discuss

Have students use the Table feature to make a table of values for $y = 3x - 4$. Find x when $y = 5$. Discuss how this solution method relates to solving by graphing.

Close

Key Concept

For an equation in the form *expression = constant*, graph *y = expression* and *y = constant*. The solution is the x-coordinate of the point where the two graphs intersect.

Assessment

Journal Have students explain how to solve an equation by graphing. They should include an example in their explanation.

Answers

3. Graph $y = 3x - 4$ and $y =$ *given value*. Find the intersection point of the two lines. The intersection point's x-coordinate is the solution.

Teaching Tip

Technology Students should set the window to the standard view before the activity. Press [ZOOM] and select **6:ZStandard**.

State Resources

2-3 Organizer

Pacing: Traditional $1\frac{1}{2}$ days
Block $\frac{3}{4}$ day

Objective: Solve equations in one variable that contain more than one operation.

Online Edition
Tutorial Videos

Countdown Week 3

Power Presentations with PowerPoint®

Warm Up

Evaluate each expression.

1. $9 - 3(-2)$ 15
2. $3(-5 + 7)$ 6
3. $12\left(\frac{3 + (-7)}{12}\right)$ -4
4. $26 - 4(7 - 5)$ 18

Simplify each expression.

5. $10c + c$ $11c$
6. $8.2b + 3.8b - 12b$ 0
7. $5m + 2(2m - 7)$ $9m - 14$
8. $6x - (2x + 5)$ $4x - 5$

Also available on transparency

Math Humor

Q: How do equations get into shape?

A: They do multi-step aerobics.

2-3 Solving Two-Step and Multi-Step Equations

Objective
Solve equations in one variable that contain more than one operation.

Why learn this?
Equations containing more than one operation can model real-world situations, such as the cost of a music club membership.

Alex belongs to a music club. In this club, students can buy a student discount card for \$19.95. This card allows them to buy CDs for \$3.95 each. After one year, Alex has spent \$63.40.

To find the number of CDs c that Alex bought, you can solve an equation.

Cost of discount card ↓
Cost per CD → $3.95c + 19.95 = 63.40$ ← Total cost

Notice that this equation contains multiplication and addition. Equations that contain more than one operation require more than one step to solve. Identify the operations in the equation and the order in which they are applied to the variable. Then use inverse operations and work backward to undo them one at a time.

$$3.95c + 19.95 = 63.40$$

Operations in the Equation		To Solve
❶ First c is **multiplied** by 3.95.		❶ **Subtract** 19.95 from both sides of the equation.
❷ Then 19.95 is **added**.		❷ Then **divide** both sides by 3.95.

EXAMPLE 1 Solving Two-Step Equations

Solve $10 = 6 - 2x$. Check your answer.

$10 = 6 - 2x$ *First x is multiplied by −2. Then 6 is added.*
$\underline{-6 \quad -6}$ *Work backward: Subtract 6 from both sides.*
$4 = -2x$ *Since x is multiplied by −2, divide both sides by −2 to undo the multiplication.*
$\frac{4}{-2} = \frac{-2x}{-2}$
$-2 = 1x$
$-2 = x$

Check

$10 = 6 - 2x$	
10	$6 - 2(-2)$
10	$6 - (-4)$
10	10 ✓

CHECK IT OUT! Solve each equation. Check your answer.

1a. $-4 + 7x = 3$ **1** **1b.** $1.5 = 1.2y - 5.7$ **6** **1c.** $\frac{n}{7} + 2 = 2$ **0**

State Resources

go.hrw.com
State Resources Online
KEYWORD: MA7 Resources

1 Introduce

EXPLORATION

2-3 Solving Two-Step and Multi-Step Equations

Juan wants to rent a bike while on vacation. The sign posted on the rental stand says "\$10 fee plus \$3 per hour."

1. Juan writes the expression $10 + 3h$ to find the cost of renting a bike for h hours. Complete the table.

Hours h	Cost $10 + 3h$
1	
2	
3	
4	
5	

2. Find the hours that correspond to the costs in the table.

Hours h	Cost $10 + 3h$
	28
	34
	40
	43
	46

THINK AND DISCUSS

3. **Explain** how you evaluated $10 + 3h$ for a given value of h.

4. **Describe** how you completed the table in Problem 2. What process did you use?

Motivate

Tell students that in the morning, you get in your car, start it, drive to school, turn off the car, and get out. To undo this chain of events, you get in the car, start it, drive home, turn off the car, and get out. Stress that your "undoing" must be exactly in reverse order; otherwise you might get out of the car while it is still running.

Solving equations with more than one operation is similar. The variable is isolated by reversing the order of operations that were used on it.

Explorations and answers are provided in *Alternate Openers: Explorations Transparencies.*

EXAMPLE 2 Solving Two-Step Equations That Contain Fractions

Solve $\frac{q}{15} - \frac{1}{5} = \frac{3}{5}$.

Method 1 Use fraction operations.

$\frac{q}{15} - \frac{1}{5} = \frac{3}{5}$ — *Since $\frac{1}{5}$ is subtracted from $\frac{q}{15}$, add $\frac{1}{5}$ to both sides to undo the subtraction.*

$+\frac{1}{5} \quad +\frac{1}{5}$

$\frac{q}{15} = \frac{4}{5}$ — *Since q is divided by 15, multiply both sides by 15 to undo the division.*

$15\left(\frac{q}{15}\right) = 15\left(\frac{4}{5}\right)$

$q = \frac{15 \cdot 4}{5}$ — *Simplify.*

$q = \frac{60}{5}$

$q = 12$

Method 2 Multiply by the least common denominator (LCD) to clear the fractions.

$\frac{q}{15} - \frac{1}{5} = \frac{3}{5}$

$15\left(\frac{q}{15} - \frac{1}{5}\right) = 15\left(\frac{3}{5}\right)$ — *Multiply both sides by 15, the LCD of the fractions.*

$15\left(\frac{q}{15}\right) - 15\left(\frac{1}{5}\right) = 15\left(\frac{3}{5}\right)$ — *Distribute 15 on the left side.*

$q - 3 = 9$ — *Simplify.*

$+3 \quad +3$ — *Since 3 is subtracted from q, add 3 to both sides to undo the subtraction.*

$q = 12$

Solve each equation. Check your answer.

2a. $\frac{2x}{5} - \frac{1}{2} = 5$ **$\frac{55}{4}$** **2b.** $\frac{3}{4}u + \frac{1}{2} = \frac{7}{8}$ **$\frac{1}{2}$** **2c.** $\frac{1}{5}n - \frac{1}{3} = \frac{8}{3}$ **15**

Equations that are more complicated may have to be simplified before they can be solved. You may have to use the Distributive Property or combine like terms before you begin using inverse operations.

EXAMPLE 3 Simplifying Before Solving Equations

Solve each equation.

A $6x + 3 - 8x = 13$

$6x + 3 - 8x = 13$

$6x - 8x + 3 = 13$ — *Use the Commutative Property of Addition.*

$-2x + 3 = 13$ — *Combine like terms.*

$-3 \quad -3$ — *Since 3 is added to −2x, subtract 3 from both sides to undo the addition.*

$-2x = 10$

$\frac{-2x}{-2} = \frac{10}{-2}$ — *Since x is multiplied by −2, divide both sides by −2 to undo the multiplication.*

$x = -5$

COMMON ERROR ALERT

When clearing fractions in an equation, students may forget to multiply every term by the LCD, especially when one of the terms is not a fraction. For instance, in **Example 2,** they may write $15 \cdot \frac{q}{15} - \frac{1}{5} = 15 \cdot \frac{3}{5}$, and then fail to multiply 15 by $-\frac{1}{5}$ on the left side. Remind them to use parentheses to show multiplication by the LCD and to distribute the LCD to each term.

Power Presentations with PowerPoint®

Additional Examples

Example 1

Solve each equation.

A. $18 = 4a + 10$ 2

B. $5t - 2 = -32$ −6

Example 2

Solve each equation.

A. $\frac{y}{8} - \frac{3}{4} = \frac{5}{4}$ 16

B. $\frac{2}{3}r + \frac{3}{4} = \frac{7}{12}$ $-\frac{1}{4}$

Example 3

Solve each equation.

A. $8x - 21 - 5x = -15$ 2

B. $10y - (4y + 8) = -20$ −2

2 Teach

Guided Instruction

Remind students that the goal in solving equations is to isolate the variable. Emphasize using the Distributive Property as needed before combining like terms, and make special note of distributing a negative number. Encourage students to work carefully and do all their work on paper. Trying to solve multi-step equations mentally often results in careless errors.

Reaching All Learners

Through Critical Thinking

Have students create their own multi-step equation by writing a simple equation and performing operations, one at a time, on both sides. For example:

$x = 3$

$x + 2 = 5$ Add 2.

$4(x + 2) = 20$ Multiply by 4.

Then have students solve their own multi-step equation. They should get back to their original equation.

INTERVENTION

Questioning Strategies

EXAMPLE 1

- What steps need to be taken to isolate the variable? Why?

EXAMPLE 2

- What happens to the fractions in an equation when both sides are multiplied by the LCD?

EXAMPLE 3

- How do you know what signs go with each term in the equation?

Power Presentations with PowerPoint®

Additional Examples

Example 4

Jan joined the dining club at the local café for a fee of \$29.95. Being a member entitles her to save \$2.50 every time she buys lunch. So far, Jan calculates that she has saved a total of \$12.55 by joining the club. Write and solve an equation to find how many times Jan has eaten lunch at the café. $12.55 = 2.50c - 29.95$; $c = 17$

INTERVENTION

Questioning Strategies

EXAMPLE 4

- How do you decide what the variable will represent?
- What operations are needed to solve the equation?

Helpful Hint

You can think of an opposite sign as a coefficient of -1.
$-(x + 2) = -1(x + 2)$ and $-x = -1x$.

Solve each equation.

B $9 = 6 - (x + 2)$

$9 = 6 + (-1)(x + 2)$	*Write subtraction as addition of the opposite.*
$9 = 6 + (-1)(x) + (-1)(2)$	*Distribute −1 on the right side.*
$9 = 6 - x - 2$	*Simplify.*
$9 = 6 - 2 - x$	*Use the Commutative Property of Addition.*
$9 = 4 - x$	*Combine like terms.*
$\underline{-4 \quad -4}$	*Since 4 is added to −x, subtract 4 from both sides to undo the addition.*
$5 = -x$	
$\frac{5}{-1} = \frac{-x}{-1}$	*Since x is multiplied by −1, divide both sides by −1 to undo the multiplication.*
$-5 = x$	

Solve each equation. Check your answer.

3a. $2a + 3 - 8a = 8$ $-\frac{5}{6}$

3b. $-2(3 - d) = 4$ **5**

3c. $4(x - 2) + 2x = 40$ **8**

EXAMPLE 4 Problem-Solving Application

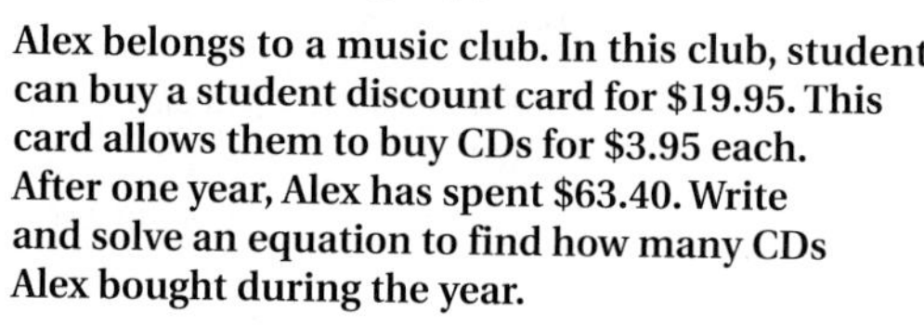

Alex belongs to a music club. In this club, students can buy a student discount card for \$19.95. This card allows them to buy CDs for \$3.95 each. After one year, Alex has spent \$63.40. Write and solve an equation to find how many CDs Alex bought during the year.

1 Understand the Problem

The **answer** will be the number of CDs that Alex bought during the year.

List the important information:

- Alex paid \$19.95 for a student discount card.
- Alex pays \$3.95 for each CD purchased.
- After one year, Alex has spent \$63.40.

2 Make a Plan

Let c represent the number of CDs that Alex purchased. That means Alex has spent \$3.95c. However, Alex must also add the amount spent on the card. Write an equation to represent this situation.

total cost	=	cost of compact discs	+	cost of discount card
63.40	=	3.95c	+	19.95

Solve

$$63.40 = 3.95c + 19.95$$
$$\underline{-19.95 \qquad -19.95}$$
$$43.45 = 3.95c$$
$$\frac{43.45}{3.95} = \frac{3.95c}{3.95}$$
$$11 = c$$

Since 19.95 is added to 3.95c, subtract 19.95 from both sides to undo the addition.

Since c is multiplied by 3.95, divide both sides by 3.95 to undo the multiplication.

Alex bought 11 CDs during the year.

Look Back

Check that the answer is reasonable. The cost per CD is about \$4, so if Alex bought 11 CDs, this amount is about $11(4) = \$44$.

Add the cost of the discount card, which is about \$20: $44 + 20 = 64$. So the total cost was about \$64, which is close to the amount given in the problem, \$63.40.

4. Sara paid \$15.95 to become a member at a gym. She then paid a monthly membership fee. Her total cost for 12 months was \$735.95. How much was the monthly fee? **\$60**

EXAMPLE 5 Solving Equations to Find an Indicated Value

If $3a + 12 = 30$, find the value of $a + 4$.

Step 1 Find the value of a.

$$3a + 12 = 30$$
$$\underline{-12 \quad -12}$$
$$3a = 18$$
$$\frac{3a}{3} = \frac{18}{3}$$
$$a = 6$$

Since 12 is added to 3a, subtract 12 from both sides to undo the addition.

Since a is multiplied by 3, divide both sides by 3 to undo the multiplication.

Step 2 Find the value of $a + 4$.

$a + 4$

$6 + 4$ — *To find the value of a + 4, substitute 6 for a.*

10 — *Simplify.*

5. If $2x + 4 = -24$, find the value of $3x$. **-42**

THINK AND DISCUSS

1. Explain the steps you would follow to solve $2x + 1 = 7$. How is this procedure different from the one you would follow to solve $2x - 1 = 7$?

2. GET ORGANIZED Copy and complete the graphic organizer. In each box, write and solve a multi-step equation. Use addition, subtraction, multiplication, and division at least one time each.

Solving Multi-Step Equations	

COMMON ERROR ALERT

When solving equations, students sometimes write only numbers, not numbers with their operation, on each side. This can lead to careless errors. For example:

$$3x + 12 = 45$$
$$\underline{\quad 12 \quad 12}$$
$$3x \quad = 57$$

Emphasize to students the importance of writing every part of each step.

Power Presentations with PowerPoint®

Additional Examples

Example 5

A. If $4a + 0.2 = 5$, find the value of $a - 1$. 0.2

B. If $3d - (9 - 2d) = 51$, find the value of $3d$. 36

INTERVENTION

Questioning Strategies

EXAMPLE 5

- What are the two main steps in solving these types of problems?

3 Close

Summarize

Ask students what they would do as a first step in solving each of the following:

- $7x - 3 = 29$ Add 3 to both sides.
- $5y - 2(y - 6) = 43$ Distribute -2.
- $-\frac{1}{3}x + \frac{3}{4} = \frac{7}{12}$ Multiply both sides by 12, or subtract $\frac{3}{4}$ from both sides.
- $25 = -m - 9 + 3m$ Combine like terms.

ONGOING ASSESSMENT and INTERVENTION

***Diagnose Before* the Lesson**
2-3 Warm Up, TE p. 92

***Monitor During* the Lesson**
Check It Out! Exercises, SE pp. 92–95
Questioning Strategies, TE pp. 93–94

***Assess After* the Lesson**
2-3 Lesson Quiz, TE p. 98
Alternative Assessment, TE p. 98

Answers to *Think and Discuss*

1. Possible answer: To solve $2x + 1 = 7$, first subtract 1 from both sides, and then divide both sides by 2. To solve $2x - 1 = 7$, first add 1 to both sides, then divide by 2.
2. See p. A2.

2-3 Exercises

Assignment Guide

Assign *Guided Practice* exercises as necessary.

If you finished Examples **1–3**
- **Basic** 24–41, 47–51, 54–61
- **Average** 24–41, 47–51, 54–61, 74, 75
- **Advanced** 24–41, 48, 54–61, 74–77

If you finished Examples **1–5**
- **Basic** 24–63, 67, 69–73, 81–92
- **Average** 24–51, 53–61 even, 62, 63, 65, 67–92,
- **Advanced** 24–46, 48, 50, 55–61 even, 62–92

Homework Quick Check
Quickly check key concepts.
Exercises: 24, 32, 40, 42, 44, 48, 50

Answers

47. $2x + 100 = 180$
48. $2x + 115 = 180$
49. $4x + 40 = 180$

State Resources

2-3 Exercises

go.hrw.com
Homework Help Online
KEYWORD: MA7 2-3
Parent Resources Online
KEYWORD: MA7 Parent

GUIDED PRACTICE

Solve each equation. Check your answer.

SEE EXAMPLE 1 p. 92

1. $4a + 3 = 11$ **2**
2. $8 = 3r - 1$ **3**
3. $42 = -2d + 6$ **−18**
4. $x + 0.3 = 3.3$ **3**
5. $15y + 31 = 61$ **2**
6. $9 - c = -13$ **22**

SEE EXAMPLE 2 p. 93

7. $\frac{x}{6} + 4 = 15$ **66**
8. $\frac{1}{3}y + \frac{1}{4} = \frac{5}{12}$ $\mathbf{\frac{1}{2}}$
9. $\frac{2}{7}j - \frac{1}{7} = \frac{3}{14}$ $\mathbf{\frac{5}{4}}$
10. $15 = \frac{a}{3} - 2$ **51**
11. $4 - \frac{m}{2} = 10$ **−12**
12. $\frac{x}{8} - \frac{1}{2} = 6$ **52**

SEE EXAMPLE 3 p. 93

13. $28 = 8x + 12 - 7x$ **16**
14. $2y - 7 + 5y = 0$ **1**
15. $2.4 = 3(m + 4)$ **−3.2**
16. $3(x - 4) = 48$ **20**
17. $4t + 7 - t = 19$ **4**
18. $5(1 - 2w) + 8w = 15$ **−5**

SEE EXAMPLE 4 p. 94

19. **Transportation** Paul bought a student discount card for the bus. The card cost \$7 and allows him to buy daily bus passes for \$1.50. After one month, Paul spent \$29.50. How many daily bus passes did Paul buy? **15 passes**

SEE EXAMPLE 5 p. 95

20. If $3x - 13 = 8$, find the value of $x - 4$. **3**
21. If $3(x + 1) = 7$, find the value of $3x$. **4**
22. If $-3(y - 1) = 9$, find the value of $\frac{1}{2}y$. **−1**
23. If $4 - 7x = 39$, find the value of $x + 1$. **−4**

PRACTICE AND PROBLEM SOLVING

Independent Practice	
For Exercises	See Example
24–29	1
30–35	2
36–41	3
42	4
43–46	5

Extra Practice
Skills Practice p. S6
Application Practice p. S29

Solve each equation. Check your answer.

24. $5 = 2g + 1$ **2**
25. $6h - 7 = 17$ **4**
26. $0.6v + 2.1 = 4.5$ **4**
27. $3x + 3 = 18$ **5**
28. $0.6g + 11 = 5$ **−10**
29. $32 = 5 - 3t$ **−9**
30. $2d + \frac{1}{5} = \frac{3}{5}$ $\mathbf{\frac{1}{5}}$
31. $1 = 2x + \frac{1}{2}$ $\mathbf{\frac{1}{4}}$
32. $\frac{z}{2} + 1 = \frac{3}{2}$ **1**
33. $\frac{2}{3} = \frac{4j}{6}$ **1**
34. $\frac{3}{4} = \frac{3}{8}x - \frac{3}{2}$ **6**
35. $\frac{1}{5} - \frac{x}{5} = -\frac{2}{5}$ **3**
36. $6 = -2(7 - c)$ **10**
37. $5(h - 4) = 8$ $\mathbf{\frac{28}{5}}$
38. $-3x - 8 + 4x = 17$ **25**
39. $4x + 6x = 30$ **3**
40. $2(x + 3) = 10$ **2**
41. $17 = 3(p - 5) + 8$ **8**
42. **Consumer Economics** Jennifer is saving money to buy a bike. The bike costs \$245. She has \$125 saved, and each week she adds \$15 to her savings. How long will it take her to save enough money to buy the bike? **8 weeks**
43. If $2x + 13 = 17$, find the value of $3x + 1$.
44. If $-(x - 1) = 5$, find the value of $-4x$.
45. If $5(y + 10) = 40$, find the value of $\frac{1}{4}y$.
46. If $9 - 6x = 45$, find the value of $x - 4$.

43. 7
44. 16
45. $-\frac{1}{2}$
46. −10

Geometry Write and solve an equation to find the value of x for each triangle. (*Hint:* The sum of the angle measures in any triangle is 180°.)

47. **40** 30°, $(2x + 7)°$, 63°

48. **32.5** 115°, $x°$, $x°$

49. **35**

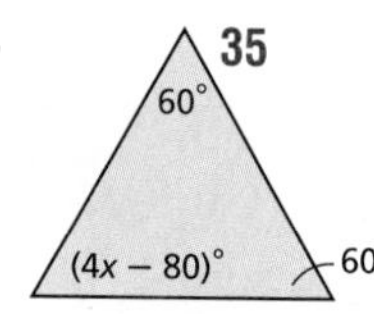

2-3 READING STRATEGIES

Use the example below to understand the procedure for solving multi-step equations. Not all problems will require all the steps.

Solve $-2(x - 5) + 4x = 17$.

$-2(x - 5) + 4x = 17$
$-2x + 10 + 4x = 17$ → 1. Use the Distributive Property.

$-2x + 10 + 4x = 17$
$2x + 10 = 17$ → 2. Identify and combine like terms.

$2x + 10 = 17$
$-10 \quad -10$ → 3. "Undo" addition (and subtraction).
$\frac{2x}{2} = \frac{7}{2}$ → 4. "Undo" division (and multiplication).
$x = 3.5$

Answer each question.

1. If an equation does not need the Distributive Property, what should you look for next?
like terms
2. To solve the equation $5x - 3 = 22$, would you "undo" subtraction or multiplication first?
subtraction
3. Describe how you would solve $\frac{1}{5}x + 3 = 28$.
Subtract 3 from both sides, then multiply by 5.

Solve each equation using the procedure shown. Show all your steps.

4. $3n - 1 = 14$ **$n = 5$**
5. $3(d - 4) = 9$ **$d = 7$**
6. $-4(j + 2) - 3j = 6$ **$j = -2$**

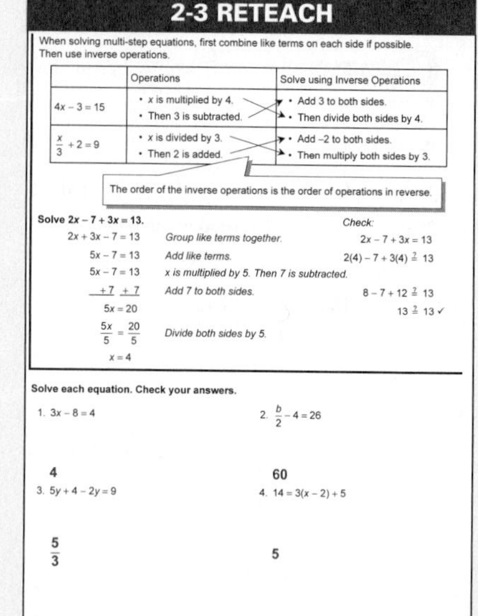

2-3 RETEACH

When solving multi-step equations, first combine like terms on each side if possible. Then use inverse operations.

	Operations	Solve using Inverse Operations
$4x - 3 = 15$	• x is multiplied by 4. • Then 3 is subtracted.	• Add 3 to both sides. • Then divide both sides by 4.
$\frac{x}{3} + 2 = 9$	• x is divided by 3. • Then 2 is added.	• Add −2 to both sides. • Then multiply both sides by 3.

The order of the inverse operations is the order of operations in reverse.

Solve $2x - 7 + 3x = 13$.

$2x + 3x - 7 = 13$ *Group like terms together.*
$5x - 7 = 13$ *Add like terms.*
$5x - 7 = 13$ *x is multiplied by 5. Then 7 is subtracted.*
$+7 \quad +7$ *Add 7 to both sides.*
$5x = 20$
$\frac{5x}{5} = \frac{20}{5}$ *Divide both sides by 5.*
$x = 4$

Check:
$2x - 7 + 3x = 13$
$2(4) - 7 + 3(4) \stackrel{?}{=} 13$
$8 - 7 + 12 \stackrel{?}{=} 13$
$13 \stackrel{?}{=} 13$ ✓

Solve each equation. Check your answers.

1. $3x - 8 = 4$ **4**
2. $\frac{b}{2} - 4 = 26$ **60**
3. $5y + 4 - 2y = 9$ $\mathbf{\frac{5}{3}}$
4. $14 = 3(x - 2) + 5$ **5**

Write an equation to represent each relationship. Solve each equation.

50. Seven less than twice a number equals 19. $2n - 7 = 19$; $n = 13$

51. Eight decreased by 3 times a number equals 2. $8 - 3n = 2$; $n = 2$

52. The sum of two times a number and 5 is 11. $2n + 5 = 11$; $n = 3$

LINK **History**

Martin Luther King Jr. entered college at age 15. During his life he earned 3 degrees and was awarded 20 honorary degrees.

Source: lib.lsu.edu

53. **History** In 1963, Dr. Martin Luther King Jr. began his famous "I have a dream" speech with the words "Five score years ago, a great American, in whose symbolic shadow we stand, signed the Emancipation Proclamation." The proclamation was signed by President Abraham Lincoln in 1863.
    a. Using the dates given, write and solve an equation that can be used to find the number of years in a score. $1963 - 5s = 1863$; $s = 20$
    b. How many score would represent 60? 3

Solve each equation. Check your answer.

54. $3t + 44 = 50$ 2
55. $3(x - 2) = 18$ 8
56. $15 = \frac{c}{3} - 2$ 51
57. $2x + 6.5 = 15.5$ 4.5
58. $3.9w - 17.9 = -2.3$ 4
59. $17 = x - 3(x + 1)$
60. $5x + 9 = 39$ 6
61. $15 + 5.5m = 70$ 10

59. −10

Biology Use the graph for Exercises 62 and 63.

62. The height of an ostrich is 20 inches more than 4 times the height of a kiwi. Write and solve an equation to find the height of a kiwi. Show that your answer is reasonable.

62. $4k + 20 = 108$; 22 in.

63. Five times the height of a kakapo minus 70 equals the height of an emu. Write and solve an equation to find the height of a kakapo. Show that your answer is reasonable.

63. $5k - 70 = 60$; 26 in.

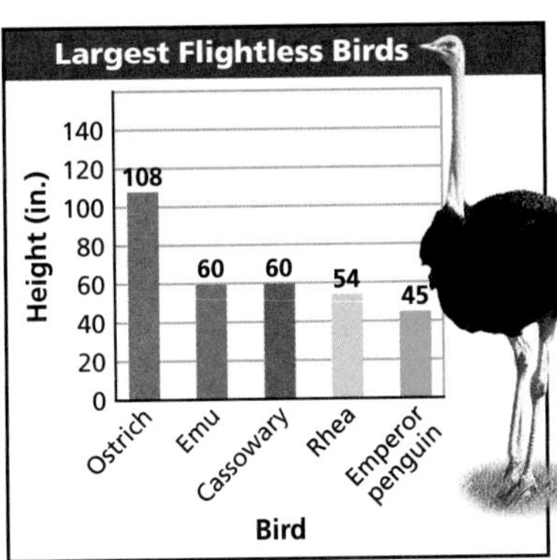

Source: The Top Ten of Everything

64. The sum of two consecutive whole numbers is 57. What are the two numbers? (*Hint:* Let n represent the first number. Then $n + 1$ is the next consecutive whole number.) 28 and 29

65. Stan's, Mark's, and Wayne's ages are consecutive whole numbers. Stan is the youngest, and Wayne is the oldest. The sum of their ages is 111. Find their ages. Stan: 36; Mark: 37; Wayne: 38

66. The sum of two consecutive even whole numbers is 206. What are the two numbers? (*Hint:* Let n represent the first number. What expression can you use to represent the second number?) 102 and 104

MULTI-STEP TEST PREP

67. This problem will prepare you for the Multi-Step Test Prep on page 118.
    a. The cost of fighting a certain forest fire is \$225 per acre. Complete the table.
    b. Write an equation for the relationship between the cost c of fighting the fire and the number of acres n. $c = 225n$

Cost of Fighting Fire

Acres	Cost (\$)
100	22,500
200	45,000
500	112,500
1000	225,000
1500	337,500
n	$225n$

MULTI-STEP TEST PREP Exercise 67 involves developing a pattern to write an expression that describes cost. This exercise prepares students for the Multi-Step Test Prep on page 118.

Answers

62. Possible answer: the height of an ostrich will be more than 4 times the height of a kiwi. 108 is more than $4(22) = 88$, so 22 in. is reasonable.

63. Possible answer: the height of a kakapo will be more than $\frac{1}{5}$ the height of the emu. 26 is more than $\frac{1}{5}(60) = 12$, so it is a reasonable answer.

2-3 PROBLEM SOLVING

Write the correct answer.

1. Stephen belongs to a movie club in which he pays an annual fee of \$39.95 and then rents DVDs for \$0.99 each. In one year, Stephen spent \$55.79. Write and solve an equation to find how many DVDs d he rented.
   $39.95 + 0.99d = 55.79$; 16 DVDs
2. In 2003, the population of Zimbabwe was about 12.6 million, which was 1 million more than 4 times the population in 1950. Write and solve an equation to find the population p of Zimbabwe in 1950.
   $12.6 = 4p + 1$
   2.9 million
3. Maggie's brother is three years younger than twice her age. The sum of their ages is 24. How old is Maggie?
   9 years old
4. Kate is saving to take an SAT prep course that costs \$350. So far, she has saved \$180, and she adds \$17 to her savings each week. How many more weeks must she save to be able to afford the course?
   10 weeks

Use the graph below to answer questions 5–7. Select the best answer. The graph shows the population density (number of people per square mile) of various states given in the 2000 census.

5. One seventeenth of Rhode Island's population density minus 17 equals the population density of Colorado. What is Rhode Island's population density?
   A 425 C 714
   B 697 **D** 1003
6. One more than sixteen times the population density of New Mexico equals the population density of Texas. To the nearest whole number, what is New Mexico's population density?
   F 5 H 13
   G 8 J 63
7. Three times the population density of Missouri minus 26 equals the population density of California. What is Missouri's population density?
   A 64 C 98
   B 81 D 729

Population Density

California 217, Colorado 42, Massachusetts 810, New Jersey 1135, Texas 80

2-3 CHALLENGE

Many concepts of algebra can be applied to a wide range of geometry problems.

Suppose that you want to design a box. The base of the box will be a square that is 10 inches on each side, and the box will be h inches tall. The surface area of the box (that is, the area of cardboard needed to make the box, assuming no overlap) is given by $4 \cdot 10 \cdot h + 2 \cdot 10 \cdot 10$, or $40h + 200$. For a surface area of 360 square inches, you would solve $40h + 200 = 360$ in order to find the height of the box.

h in. 10 in. 10 in.

The base of a rectangular box is to be a square that is 10 inches on each side. For each given surface area, find the corresponding height of the box.

1. 360 square inches 4 inches
2. 520 square inches 8 inches
3. 240 square inches 1 inch
4. 560 square inches 9 inches
5. 800 square inches 15 inches
6. 480 square inches 7 inches

Now suppose that you want to design a cylindrical box whose base is a circle with a radius of 5 inches. The surface area of the cylindrical box is given by $50\pi + 10\pi h$.

The base of a cylindrical box will be a circle with a radius of 5 inches. For each given surface area, find the corresponding height of the box.

7. 80π square inches 3 inches
8. 120π square inches 7 inches
9. 110π square inches 6 inches
10. 160π square inches 11 inches
11. 200π square inches 15 inches
12. 90π square inches 4 inches

Another geometric application of two-step equations relates to the interior angles of a polygon. If the polygon has n sides, the sum of the measures of its angles is $180n - 360$ degrees.

120° 110° 60° 70°

For example, in a triangle, $n = 3$, so the measures of the angles add up to 180°. For a trapezoid, $n = 4$, so the measures of the angles add up to 360°.

In the following exercises, the sum of the measures of the interior angles of a polygon is given. Find the number of sides of the polygon.

13. 540° 5 sides
14. 1800° 12 sides
15. 900° 7 sides
16. 2880° 18 sides

2-3 PRACTICE A

2-3 PRACTICE C

2-3 PRACTICE B

Solve each equation. Check your answers.

1. $-4x + 7 = 11$ $x = -1$
2. $17 = 5y - 3$ $y = 4$
3. $-4 = 2p + 10$ $p = -7$
4. $3m + 4 = 1$ $m = -1$
5. $12.5 = 2g - 3.5$ $g = 8$
6. $-13 = -h - 7$ $h = 6$
7. $-6 = \frac{y}{5} + 4$ $y = -50$
8. $\frac{7}{9} = 2n + \frac{1}{9}$ $n = \frac{1}{3}$
9. $-\frac{4}{5}t + \frac{2}{5} = \frac{2}{3}$ $t = -\frac{1}{3}$
10. $-(x - 10) = 7$ $x = 3$
11. $-2(b + 5) = -6$ $b = -2$
12. $8 = 4(q - 2) + 4$ $q = 3$
13. If $3x - 8 = -2$, find the value of $x - 6$. −4
14. If $-2(3y + 5) = -4$, find the value of $5y$. −5

Answer each of the following.

15. The two angles shown form a right angle. Write and solve an equation to find the value of x. $(3x - 5)°$ $(2x)°$ $3x - 5 + 2x = 90$; 19
16. For her cellular phone service, Vera pays \$32 a month, plus \$0.75 for each minute over the allowed minutes in her plan. Vera received a bill for \$47 last month. For how many minutes did she use her phone beyond the allowed minutes? 20 minutes

TEST PREP DOCTOR In **Exercise 70,** have students write expressions for each person. Greg: g; Lin: $g + 4$; Fran: $3(g + 4)$ Asking for the number of shirts Greg sold is the same as asking to solve for g. Students who chose **C** may not have distributed 3 through the quantity $(g + 4)$.

Students who chose **F** in **Exercise 71** probably found the correct value of m, but may not have substituted it into $7m - 5$.

Journal

Have students explain to a friend who missed the lesson how to solve a two-step equation. Students should write and solve a word problem as part of their explanation.

ALTERNATIVE ASSESSMENT

Have students create a multi-step equation. Ask students to describe the solution steps and explain why each step is performed. Check that students understand reversing the order of operations applied to the variable.

Power Presentations with PowerPoint®

2-3 Lesson Quiz

Solve each equation.

1. $4y + 8 = 2$ $\quad -\frac{3}{2}$
2. $\frac{3}{4}a + 14 = 8$ $\quad -8$
3. $2y + 29 - 8y = 5$ $\quad 4$
4. $3(x - 9) = 30$ $\quad 19$
5. $x - (12 - x) = 38$ $\quad 25$
6. $\frac{z}{6} - \frac{5}{8} = \frac{7}{8}$ $\quad 9$
7. If $3b - (6 - b) = -22$, find the value of $7b$. $\quad -28$
8. Josie bought 4 cases of sports drinks for an upcoming meet. After talking to her coach, she bought 3 more cases and spent an additional $6.95 on other items. Her receipts totaled $74.15. Write and solve an equation to find how much each case of sports drinks cost.
   $4c + 3c + 6.95 = 74.15$; $9.60

Also available on transparency

68. Possible answer: Distribute 2 or subtract 3 from both sides.

68. **Critical Thinking** The equation $2(m - 8) + 3 = 17$ has more than one solution method. Give at least two different "first steps" to solve this equation.

69. **Write About It** Write a series of steps that you can use to solve any multi-step equation. **Possible answer: Simplify both sides if necessary. Find the term containing the variable. Undo any addition or subtraction on this term by using inverse operations. Then undo any multiplication or division on this term by using inverse operations.**

TEST PREP

70. Lin sold 4 more shirts than Greg. Fran sold 3 times as many shirts as Lin. In total, the three sold 51 shirts. Which represents the number of shirts Greg sold?
    (A) $3g = 51$ (B) $3 + g = 51$ (C) $8 + 5g = 51$ **(D)** $16 + 5g = 51$

71. If $\frac{4m - 3}{7} = 3$, what is the value of $7m - 5$?
    (F) 6 (G) 10.5 **(H)** 37 (J) 68.5

72. The equation $c = 48 + 0.06m$ represents the cost c of renting a car and driving m miles. Which statement best describes this cost?
    (A) The cost is a flat rate of $0.06 per mile.
    (B) The cost is $0.48 for the first mile and $0.06 for each additional mile.
    (C) The cost is a $48 fee plus $0.06 per mile.
    (D) The cost is a $6 fee plus $0.48 per mile.

73. **Gridded Response** A telemarketer earns $150 a week plus $2 for each call that results in a sale. Last week she earned a total of $204. How many of her calls resulted in sales? **27**

CHALLENGE AND EXTEND

Solve each equation. Check your answer.

74. $\frac{9}{2}x + 18 + 3x = \frac{11}{2}$ $\quad -\frac{5}{3}$
75. $\frac{15}{4}x - 15 = \frac{33}{4}$ $\quad 6\frac{1}{5}$
76. $(x + 6) - (2x + 7) - 3x = -9$ $\quad 2$
77. $(4x + 2) - (12x + 8) + 2(5x - 3) = 6 + 11$ $\quad 14.5$
78. Find a value for b so that the solution of $4x + 3b = -1$ is $x = 2$. $\quad -3$
79. Find a value for b so that the solution of $2x - 3b = 0$ is $x = -9$. $\quad -6$
80. **Business** The formula $p = nc - e$ gives the profit p when a number of items n are each sold at a cost c and expenses e are subtracted.
    a. If $p = 2500$, $n = 2000$, and $e = 800$, what is the value of c? **1.65**
    b. If $p = 2500$, $n = 1000$, and $e = 800$, what is the value of c? **3.3**
    c. **What if...?** If n is divided in half while p and e remain the same, what is the effect on c? **c doubles.**

SPIRAL REVIEW

Write all classifications that apply to each real number. *(Lesson 1-5)*

81. $\sqrt{3}$ irrational
82. -58 integer, rational, terminating decimal
83. $2\frac{1}{3}$ repeating decimal, rational
84. 0.17 terminating decimal, rational

Write each product using the Distributive Property. Then simplify. *(Lesson 1-7)*

85. $8(61)$ $\quad 8(60) + 8(1) = 488$
86. $9(28)$ $\quad 9(20) + 9(8) = 252$
87. $11(28)$ $\quad 11(20) + 11(8) = 308$
88. $13(21)$ $\quad 13(20) + 13(1) = 273$

Solve each equation. Check your answer. *(Lesson 2-1)*

89. $17 = k + 4$ $\quad 13$
90. $x - 18 = 3$ $\quad 21$
91. $a + 6 = -12$ $\quad -18$
92. $-7 = q - 7$ $\quad 0$

Model Equations with Variables on Both Sides

Algebra tile models can help you understand how to solve equations with variables on both sides.

Use with Lesson 2-4

KEY

 $= 1$

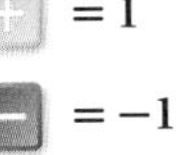 $= -1$

 $= x$

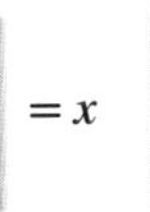 $= -x$

REMEMBER

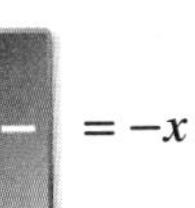 + 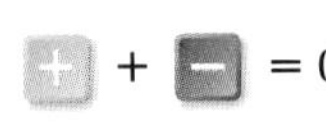 $= 0$

Activity

Use algebra tiles to model and solve $5x - 2 = 2x + 10$.

MODEL		ALGEBRA
	Model $5x - 2$ on the left side of the mat and $2x + 10$ on the right side. *Remember that $5x - 2$ is the same as $5x + (-2)$.*	$5x - 2 = 2x + 10$
	Remove 2 x-tiles from both sides. This represents subtracting 2x from both sides of the equation.	$5x - 2 - 2x = 2x - 2x + 10$ $3x - 2 = 10$
	Place 2 yellow tiles on both sides. This represents adding 2 to both sides of the equation. *Remove zero pairs.*	$3x - 2 + 2 = 10 + 2$ $3x = 12$
	Separate each side into 3 equal groups. *Each group is $\frac{1}{3}$ of the side.* *One x-tile is equivalent to 4 yellow tiles.*	$\frac{1}{3}(3x) = \frac{1}{3}(12)$ $x = 4$

Try This

Use algebra tiles to model and solve each equation.

1. $3x + 2 = 2x + 5$ **3** **2.** $5x + 12 = 2x + 3$ **−3** **3.** $9x - 5 = 6x + 13$ **6** **4.** $x = -2x + 9$ **3**

Organizer

Use with Lesson 2-4

Pacing:

Traditional $\frac{1}{2}$ day

Block $\frac{1}{4}$ day

Objective: Use algebra tiles to model and solve equations with variables on both sides.

Materials: algebra tiles

Online Edition

Algebra Tiles

Countdown Week 4

Resources

Algebra Lab Activities

2-4 Lab Recording Sheet

Teach

Discuss

Explain that the first objective is to get *x*-tiles on only one side. Then solve using methods previously learned.

Close

Key Concept

You may add or remove the same number of *x*-tiles on both sides.

Assessment

Journal Have students explain each step in solving one of the equations in *Try This*.

State Resources

Teacher to Teacher

Sometimes students wonder how to subtract tiles from both sides if there are not enough tiles to take away.

"How can I take away 12 when I have only 3?" a student might ask about **Problem 2** in *Try This.*

Show students how to subtract from both sides by adding negative tiles and then removing zero pairs. I find that using this method really helps students remember that subtraction is defined as adding an opposite.

Sue Pippen

Darien, IL

2-4 Organizer

Pacing: Traditional $1\frac{1}{2}$ days
Block $\frac{3}{4}$ day

Objective: Solve equations in one variable that contain variable terms on both sides.

Online Edition
Tutorial Videos

Countdown Week 4

Power Presentations with PowerPoint®

Warm Up

Simplify.

1. $4x - 10x$ $-6x$
2. $-7(x - 3)$ $-7x + 21$
3. $\frac{1}{3}(6x + 9)$ $2x + 3$
4. $15 - (x - 2)$ $17 - x$

Solve.

5. $3x + 2 = 8$ 2
6. $\frac{1}{3}x - \frac{1}{3} = 9$ 28

Also available on transparency

Math Humor

Q: Why did the variable add its opposite?

A: To get to the other side.

2-4 Solving Equations with Variables on Both Sides

Objective
Solve equations in one variable that contain variable terms on both sides.

Vocabulary
identity

Why learn this?
You can compare prices and find the best value.

Many phone companies offer low rates for long-distance calls without requiring customers to sign up for their services. To compare rates, solve an equation with variables on both sides.

To solve an equation like this, use inverse operations to "collect" variable terms on one side of the equation.

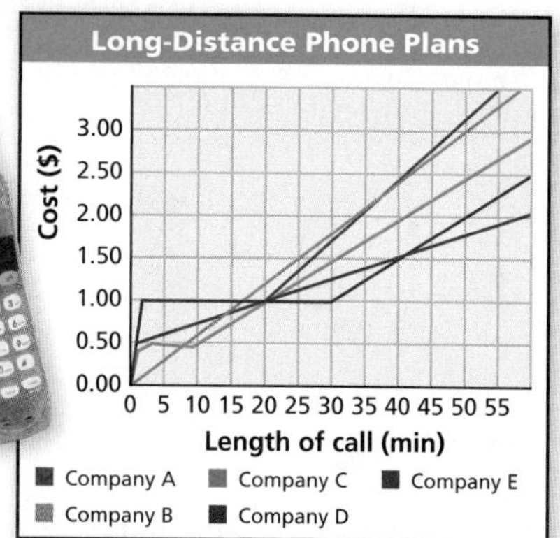

EXAMPLE 1 Solving Equations with Variables on Both Sides

Solve each equation.

A $7k = 4k + 15$

$$7k = 4k + 15$$
$$\underline{-4k \quad -4k}$$
$$3k = 15$$
To collect the variable terms on one side, subtract 4k from both sides.

$$\frac{3k}{3} = \frac{15}{3}$$
$$k = 5$$
Since k is multiplied by 3, divide both sides by 3 to undo the multiplication.

B $5x - 2 = 3x + 4$

$$5x - 2 = 3x + 4$$
$$\underline{-3x \qquad -3x}$$
$$2x - 2 = 4$$
To collect the variable terms on one side, subtract 3x from both sides.

$$\underline{+2 \qquad +2}$$
$$2x = 6$$
Since 2 is subtracted from 2x, add 2 to both sides to undo the subtraction.

$$\frac{2x}{2} = \frac{6}{2}$$
$$x = 3$$
Since x is multiplied by 2, divide both sides by 2 to undo the multiplication.

Check $5x - 2 = 3x + 4$
To check your solution, substitute 3 for x in the original equation.

$5(3) - 2$	$3(3) + 4$
$15 - 2$	$9 + 4$
13	13 ✓

Helpful Hint
Equations are often easier to solve when the variable has a positive coefficient. Keep this in mind when deciding on which side to "collect" variable terms.

Solve each equation. Check your answer.

1a. $4b + 2 = 3b$ **−2**
1b. $0.5 + 0.3y = 0.7y - 0.3$ **2**

To solve more complicated equations, you may need to first simplify by using the Distributive Property or combining like terms.

State Resources

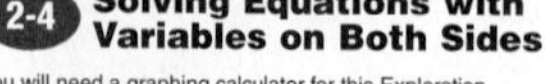
go.hrw.com
State Resources Online
KEYWORD: MA7 Resources

1 Introduce

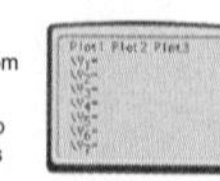

EXPLORATION

2-4 Solving Equations with Variables on Both Sides

You will need a graphing calculator for this Exploration.

A receptionist is buying plants to decorate the lobby of an office building. The receptionist wants to have the plants delivered. Flower City charges $50 plus $6 per plant. Plants for Less charges $8 per plant.

1. Write an expression that gives the cost of buying plants from Flower City.
2. Write an expression that gives the cost of buying plants from Plants for Less.
3. On your graphing calculator, press Y=. Then enter the expressions from Problems 1 and 2 in Y_1 and Y_2.
4. Use your calculator's table feature to find out what number of plants costs the same from both companies.

THINK AND DISCUSS

5. **Explain** which company the receptionist should use if 20 plants are needed for the lobby.
6. **Describe** another method you could use to find the number of plants that costs the same from both companies.

Motivate

Draw a balance scale on the board. On one side, draw a 6-ounce weight and an unknown weight. On the other side, draw a 4-ounce weight and two unknown weights. Ask students what the unknown weight must be in order to balance the scale.   2 oz

Remind students that adding or removing an equal amount on both sides of a balanced scale will maintain the balance. This is true even when the weight being added or removed is unknown.

Explorations and answers are provided in *Alternate Openers: Explorations Transparencies.*

EXAMPLE 2 Simplifying Each Side Before Solving Equations

Solve each equation.

A $2(y+6)=3y$

$$\begin{aligned} 2(y+6) &= 3y \\ 2(y)+2(6) &= 3y \\ 2y+12 &= 3y \\ -2y \quad & \quad -2y \\ 12 &= y \end{aligned}$$

Distribute 2 to the expression in parentheses.

To collect the variable terms on one side, subtract 2y from both sides.

Check $2(y+6)=3y$

$2(12+6)$	$3(12)$
$2(18)$	36
36	36 ✓

To check your solution, substitute 12 for y in the original equation.

B $2k-5=3(1-2k)$

$$\begin{aligned} 2k-5 &= 3(1-2k) \\ 2k-5 &= 3(1)-3(2k) \\ 2k-5 &= 3-6k \\ +6k \quad & \quad +6k \\ 8k-5 &= 3 \\ +5 \quad & \quad +5 \\ 8k &= 8 \\ \frac{8k}{8} &= \frac{8}{8} \\ k &= 1 \end{aligned}$$

Distribute 3 to the expression in parentheses.

To collect the variable terms on one side, add 6k to both sides.

Since 5 is subtracted from 8k, add 5 to both sides.

Since k is multiplied by 8, divide both sides by 8.

C $3-5b+2b=-2-2(1-b)$

$$\begin{aligned} 3-5b+2b &= -2-2(1-b) \\ 3-5b+2b &= -2-2(1)-2(-b) \\ 3-5b+2b &= -2-2+2b \\ 3-3b &= -4+2b \\ +3b \quad & \quad +3b \\ 3 &= -4+5b \\ +4 \quad & \quad +4 \\ 7 &= 5b \\ \frac{7}{5} &= \frac{5b}{5} \\ 1.4 &= b \end{aligned}$$

Distribute −2 to the expression in parentheses.

Combine like terms.

Add 3b to both sides.

Since −4 is added to 5b, add 4 to both sides.

Since b is multiplied by 5, divide both sides by 5.

Solve each equation. Check your answer.

2a. $\frac{1}{2}(b+6)=\frac{3}{2}b-1$ **4**

2b. $3x+15-9=2(x+2)$ **−2**

An **identity** is an equation that is always true, no matter what value is substituted for the variable. The solutions of an identity are all real numbers. Some equations are always false. These equations have no solutions.

COMMON ERROR ALERT

Students may try to combine the like terms that they see in an equation. For example, $5x-2=3x+4$ becomes $8x-2=4$. Remind students that they must instead "undo" the addition of $3x$ on the right side.

Power Presentations with PowerPoint®

Additional Examples

Example 1

Solve $7n-2=5n+6$. 4

Example 2

Solve $4-6a+4a=-1-5(7-2a)$. $\frac{10}{3}$

INTERVENTION

Questioning Strategies

EXAMPLE 1

- How do you decide which variable term to add to or subtract from one side of the equation?

EXAMPLE 2

- How are the equations in the second example different from those in the first example?
- How do you know when one side of an equation is not simplified?
- How do you simplify each side of an equation?
- Why is it important to simplify each side of an equation before you add or subtract terms on each side?

Visual To remind students to include negative values in their multiplication when distributing, as in **Example 2B,** circle the negative number that is to be distributed, perhaps with a colored pencil (MK).

2 Teach

Guided Instruction

Before solving equations with variables on both sides, review the steps used to solve equations with a variable on one side. Then review how to combine like terms and how to simplify using the Distributive Property. Show students that adding or subtracting the variable terms on each side, before adding and subtracting constant terms, results in a one-step equation like those from earlier lessons.

Reaching All Learners

Through Cooperative Learning

Give each student a card with an expression such as $2x+4$ or $3x-7$ written on it. Have students pair up and solve the equation that is formed by setting their expressions equal to each other. Students should pair up with as many students as time allows. For advanced learners, expressions should require simplifying.

Power Presentations with PowerPoint®

Additional Examples

Example 3

Solve each equation.

A. $10 - 5x + 1 = 7x + 11 - 12x$
all real numbers

B. $12x - 3 + x = 5x - 4 + 8x$
no solution

Example 4

Jon and Sara are planting tulip bulbs. Jon has planted 60 bulbs and is planting at a rate of 44 bulbs per hour. Sara has planted 96 bulbs and is planting at a rate of 32 bulbs per hour. In how many hours will Jon and Sara have planted the same number of bulbs? How many bulbs will that be? 3 h; 192 bulbs

Number Sense Encourage students to add and subtract variable terms so that the result is a positive coefficient. Often this means to subtract the variable term with the lesser coefficient on both sides.

INTERVENTION
Questioning Strategies

EXAMPLE 3

- What is the solution of an equation if the last line is a true statement? a false statement?

EXAMPLE 4

- Which phrase in the question indicates what the variable will represent?

Writing Math

The solution set for Example 3B is an empty set—it contains no elements. The empty set can be written as ∅ or {}.

EXAMPLE 3 Infinitely Many Solutions or No Solutions

Solve each equation.

A $x + 4 - 6x = 6 - 5x - 2$

$x + 4 - 6x = 6 - 5x - 2$	*Identify like terms.*
$4 - 5x = 4 - 5x$	*Combine like terms on the left and the right.*
$\underline{+5x} \quad \underline{+5x}$	*Add 5x to both sides.*
$4 = 4$ ✓	*True statement*

The equation $x + 4 - 6x = 6 - 5x - 2$ is an identity. All values of x will make the equation true. All real numbers are solutions.

B $-8x + 6 + 9x = -17 + x$

$-8x + 6 + 9x = -17 + x$	*Identify like terms.*
$x + 6 = -17 + x$	*Combine like terms.*
$\underline{-x} \quad \underline{-x}$	*Subtract x from both sides.*
$6 = -17$ ✗	*False statement*

The equation $-8x + 6 + 9x = -17 + x$ is always false. There is no value of x that will make the equation true. There are no solutions.

Solve each equation.

3a. $4y + 7 - y = 10 + 3y$ **no solution**

3b. $2c + 7 + c = -14 + 3c + 21$ **all real numbers**

EXAMPLE 4 *Consumer Application*

The long-distance rates of two phone companies are shown in the table. How long is a call that costs the same amount no matter which company is used? What is the cost of that call?

Phone Company	Charges
Company A	36¢ plus 3¢ per minute
Company B	6¢ per minute

Let m represent minutes, and write expressions for each company's cost.

When is 36¢	plus	3¢ per minute	times number of minutes	the same as	6¢ per minute	times number of minutes ?
36	+	3	(m)	=	6	(m)

$36 + 3m = 6m$	
$\underline{-3m} \quad \underline{-3m}$	*To collect the variable terms on one side, subtract 3m from both sides.*
$36 = 3m$	
$\frac{36}{3} = \frac{3m}{3}$	*Since m is multiplied by 3, divide both sides by 3 to undo the multiplication.*
$12 = m$	

The charges will be the same for a 12-minute call using either phone service. To find the cost of this call, evaluate either expression for $m = 12$:

$$36 + 3m = 36 + 3(12) = 36 + 36 = 72 \qquad 6m = 6(12) = 72$$

The cost of a 12-minute call through either company is 72¢.

4. Four times Greg's age, decreased by 3 is equal to 3 times Greg's age, increased by 7. How old is Greg? **10 years old**

Close

Summarize

Draw the triangle below on the board:

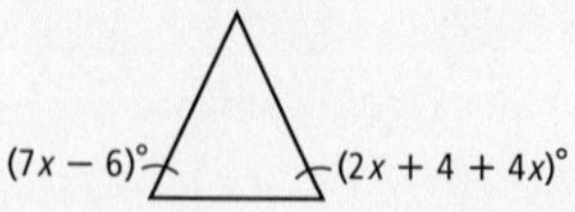

(triangle with labeled angles $(7x - 6)°$ and $(2x + 4 + 4x)°$)

Tell students that the triangle is isosceles and that the labeled angles have the same measure. Have them write and solve an equation for x, explaining each step. Then have them find the measure of each angle.
$x = 10$; each angle measures 64°.

ONGOING ASSESSMENT and INTERVENTION

***Diagnose Before* the Lesson**
2-4 Warm Up, TE p. 100

***Monitor During* the Lesson**
Check It Out! Exercises, SE pp. 100–102
Questioning Strategies, TE pp. 101–102

***Assess After* the Lesson**
2-4 Lesson Quiz, TE p. 106
Alternative Assessment, TE p. 106

THINK AND DISCUSS

1. Tell which of the following is an identity. Explain your answer.

   a. $4(a+3)-6=3(a+3)-6$ b. $8.3x-9+0.7x=2+9x-11$

2. **GET ORGANIZED** Copy and complete the graphic organizer. In each box, write an example of an equation that has the indicated number of solutions.

An equation with variables on both sides can have...

one solution: | many solutions: | no solution:

Answers to *Think and Discuss*

1. Equation b, $8.3x - 9 + 0.7x = 2 + 9x - 11$, is an identity. The equation simplifies to $9x - 9 = 9x - 9$, which is true for all values of x.
2. See p. A3.

2-4 Exercises

go.hrw.com
Homework Help Online
KEYWORD: MA7 2-4
Parent Resources Online
KEYWORD: MA7 Parent

GUIDED PRACTICE

1. **Vocabulary** How can you recognize an identity?

Solve each equation. Check your answer.

SEE EXAMPLE 1 p. 100

2. $2c-5=c+4$ **9**
3. $8r+4=10+2r$ **1**
4. $2x-1=x+11$ **12**
5. $28-0.3y=0.7y-12$ **40**

SEE EXAMPLE 2 p. 101

6. $-2(x+3)=4x-3$ $-\frac{1}{2}$
7. $3c-4c+1=5c+2+3$ $-\frac{2}{3}$
8. $5+3(q-4)=2(q+1)$ **9**
9. $5-(t+3)=-1+2(t-3)$ **3**

SEE EXAMPLE 3 p. 102

10. $7x-4=-2x+1+9x-5$
11. $8x+6-9x=2-x-15$ **no solution**
12. $6y=8-9+6y$ **no solution**
13. $6-2x-1=4x+8-6x-3$ **all real numbers**

SEE EXAMPLE 4 p. 102

14. **Consumer Economics** A house-painting company charges $376 plus $12 per hour. Another painting company charges $280 plus $15 per hour.
    a. How long is a job for which both companies will charge the same amount? **32 h**
    b. What will that cost be? **$760**

PRACTICE AND PROBLEM SOLVING

Solve each equation. Check your answer.

15. $7a-17=4a+1$ **6**
16. $2b-5=8b+1$ **−1**
17. $4x-2=3x+4$ **6**
18. $2x-5=4x-1$ **−2**
19. $8x-2=3x+12.25$ **2.85**
20. $5x+2=3x$ **−1**
21. $3c-5=2c+5$ **10**
22. $-17-2x=6-x$ **−23**
23. $3(t-1)=9+t$ **6**
24. $5-x-2=3+4x+5$ **−1**
25. $2(x+4)=3(x-2)$ **14**
26. $3m-10=2(4m-5)$ **0**
27. $5-(n-4)=3(n+2)$ $\frac{3}{4}$
28. $6(x+7)-20=6x$
29. $8(x+1)=4x-8$ **−4**
30. $x-4-3x=-2x-3-1$
31. $-2(x+2)=-2x+1$
32. $2(x+4)-5=2x+3$

28. no solution
30. all real numbers
31. no solution
32. all real numbers

Assignment Guide

Assign *Guided Practice* exercises as necessary.

If you finished Examples **1–2**
Basic 15–30, 35–37, 38–52 even
Average 15–30, 38–52 even, 54, 60, 63
Advanced 15–30, 42–52 even, 54, 64, 65, 68, 69

If you finished Examples **1–4**
Basic 15–52, 54, 55, 57, 59–63, 73–86
Average 15–37, 38–52 even, 53–63, 66–69, 73–86
Advanced 15–34, 36, 42–52 even, 54–86

Homework Quick Check
Quickly check key concepts.
Exercises: 20, 26, 32, 34, 36, 54

State Resources

go.hrw.com
State Resources Online
KEYWORD: MA7 Resources

Answers

1. Possible answer: After simplifying, the expressions on either side of the equal sign are the same.
10. all real numbers

Geometry For **Exercise 53,** remind students that perimeter is the distance around a figure. Students may benefit from writing $P_1 = P_2$, and then substituting P_1 and P_2 with expressions for each perimeter.

Exercise 54 involves writing an equation to represent a real-world relationship. This exercise prepares students for the Multi-Step Test Prep on page 118.

Answers

52a. Possible answer: For 100 mi, Rapid Rental charges \$40 + \$15 + \$25 = \$80. Capital Cars charges \$45 + \$35 = \$80.

54a. Possible answer: the total acreage in the next 2 days will be about 100 more than 420, so 540 is reasonable.

Independent Practice

For Exercises	See Example
15–22	1
23–29	2
30–32	3
33	4

Extra Practice

Skills Practice p. S6

Application Practice p. S29

33. **Sports** Justin and Tyson are beginning an exercise program to train for football season. Justin weighs 150 lb and hopes to gain 2 lb per week. Tyson weighs 195 lb and hopes to lose 1 lb per week.
    a. If the plan works, in how many weeks will the boys weigh the same amount? **15**
    b. What will that weight be? **180 lb**

Write an equation to represent each relationship. Then solve the equation.

34. Three times the sum of a number and 4 is the same as 18 more than the number.
35. A number decreased by 30 is the same as 14 minus 3 times the number.
36. Two less than 2 times a number is the same as the number plus 64.

34. $3(x + 4) = 18 + x$; $x = 3$

35. $x - 30 = 14 - 3x$; $x = 11$

36. $2x - 2 = x + 64$; $x = 66$

Solve each equation. Check your answer.

37. $2x - 2 = 4x + 6$ **−4**
38. $3x + 5 = 2x + 2$ **−3**
39. $4x + 3 = 5x - 4$ **7**
40. $-\frac{2}{5}p + 2 = \frac{1}{5}p + 11$ **−15**
41. $5x + 24 = 2x + 15$ **−3**
42. $5x - 10 = 14 - 3x$ **3**
43. $12 - 6x = 10 - 5x$ **2**
44. $5x - 7 = -6x - 29$ **−2**
45. $1.8x + 2.8 = 2.5x + 2.1$ **1**
46. $2.6x + 18 = 2.4x + 22$ **20**
47. $1 - 3x = 2x + 8$ $-\frac{7}{5}$
48. $\frac{1}{2}(8 - 6h) = h$ **1**
49. $3(x + 1) = 2x + 7$ **4**
50. $9x - 8 + 4x = 7x + 16$ **4**
51. $3(2x - 1) + 5 = 6(x + 1)$

51. no solution

52. **Travel** Rapid Rental Car company charges a \$40 rental fee, \$15 for gas, and \$0.25 per mile driven. For the same car, Capital Cars charges \$45 for rental and gas and \$0.35 per mile.
    a. Find the number of miles for which the companies' charges will be the same. Then find that charge. Show that your answers are reasonable. **100 mi; \$80**
    b. The Barre family estimates that they will drive about 95 miles during their vacation to Hershey, Pennsylvania. Which company should they rent their car from? Explain. **Capital Cars; the cost would be less.**
    c. **What if...?** The Barres have extended their vacation and now estimate that they will drive about 120 miles. Should they still rent from the same company as in part **b**? Why or why not? **No; now Rapid Rental would be cheaper.**
    d. Give a general rule for deciding which company to rent from. **Less than 100 mi—use Capital; more than 100 mi—use Rapid.**

53. **Geometry** The triangles shown have the same perimeter. What is the value of x? **9**

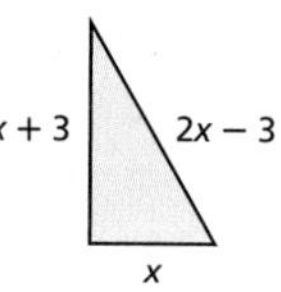

54c. $80d$

d. $420 + 60d = 80d$; $d = 21$ days; the number of days it will take the firefighters to put out the fire

54. This problem will prepare you for the Multi-Step Test Prep on page 118.
    a. A fire currently covers 420 acres and continues to spread at a rate of 60 acres per day. How many total acres will be covered in the next 2 days? Show that your answer is reasonable. **540 acres**
    b. Write an expression for the total area covered by the fire in d days. **$420 + 60d$**
    c. The firefighters estimate that they can put out the fire at a rate of 80 acres per day. Write an expression for the total area that the firefighters can put out in d days.
    d. Set the expressions in parts **b** and **c** equal. Solve for d. What does d represent?

2-4 PRACTICE A

2-4 PRACTICE C

2-4 PRACTICE B

Solve each equation. Check your answers.

1. $3d + 8 = 2d - 17$ $d = -25$
2. $2n - 7 = 5n - 10$ $n = 1$
3. $p - 15 = 13 - 6p$ $p = 4$
4. $-t + 5 = t - 19$ $t = 12$
5. $15x - 10 = -9x + 2$ $x = \frac{1}{2}$
6. $1.8r + 9 = -5.7r - 6$ $r = -2$
7. $2y + 3 = 3(y + 7)$ $y = -18$
8. $4n + 6 - 2n = 2(n + 3)$ all real numbers
9. $6m - 8 = 2 + 9m - 1$ $m = -3$
10. $-v + 5 + 6v = 1 + 5v + 3$ no solution
11. $2(3b - 4) = 8b - 11$ $b = \frac{3}{2}$
12. $5(r - 1) = 2(r - 4) - 6$ $r = -3$

Answer each of the following.

13. Janine has job offers at two companies. One company offers a starting salary of \$28,000 with a raise of \$3000 each year. The other company offers a starting salary of \$36,000 with a raise of \$2000 each year.
    a. After how many years would Janine's salary be the same with both companies? **8 years**
    b. What would that salary be? **\$52,000**
14. Xian and his cousin both collect stamps. Xian has 56 stamps, and his cousin has 80 stamps. Both have recently joined different stamp-collecting clubs. Xian's club will send him 12 new stamps per month, and his cousin's club will send him 8 new stamps per month.
    a. After how many months will Xian and his cousin have the same number of stamps? **6 months**
    b. How many stamps will that be? **128 stamps**

2-4 READING STRATEGIES

Use the sequence chain below to guide you in solving equations.

Sequence Chain: *Solving Equations*

Can you use the Distributive Property? If yes, do it. If no, →

Can you combine any like terms? If yes, do it. If no, →

Are there variable terms on both sides of the = sign? If yes, collect them on one side. If no, →

Is a number being added to or subtracted from the variable? If yes, do the opposite to both sides. If no, →

Is the variable multiplied or divided by a number? If yes, do the opposite to both sides. If no, →

Does your answer check using substitution? If yes, you're done! If no, try again.

Answer each question.

1. What is the first thing to look for when solving an equation?
   Look for an opportunity to use the Distributive Property.
2. What should you do before collecting the variables on one side of the equal sign?
   Combine any like terms.
3. Describe the first step in solving the equation $3x - 4 = 2x + 19$.
   Collect the variable terms on one side of the equal sign.

Solve each equation using the sequence chain.

4. $7p - 2 = 9p + 10$ $p = -6$
5. $8 + 4x = 3(x - 1) + 12$ $x = 1$
6. $-2(t + 2) + 5t = 6t + 2$ $t = -2$

2-4 RETEACH

Variables must be collected on the same side of the equation before the equation can be solved.

Solve $10x = 2x - 16$.

		Check:
$10x = 2x - 16$		$10x = 2x - 16$
$-2x \quad -2x$	*Add −2x to both sides.*	$10(-2) \stackrel{?}{=} 2(-2) - 16$
$8x = -16$		$-20 \stackrel{?}{=} -4 - 16$
$\frac{8x}{8} = \frac{-16}{8}$	*Divide both sides by 8.*	$-20 \stackrel{?}{=} -20$ ✓
$x = -2$		

Solve $3x = 5(x + 2)$.

		Check:
$3x = 5x + 10$	*Distribute.*	$3x = 5(x + 2)$
$-5x \quad -5x$	*Add −5x to both sides.*	$3(-5) \stackrel{?}{=} 5(-5 + 2)$
$-2x = 10$		$-15 \stackrel{?}{=} 5(-3)$
$\frac{-2x}{-2} = \frac{10}{-2}$	*Divide both sides by −2.*	$-15 \stackrel{?}{=} -15$ ✓
$x = -5$		

Write the first step you would take to solve each equation.

1. $3x + 2 = 7x$ **Possible answers: add $-3x$ to each side, add $-7x$ to each side**
2. $-4x - 6 = -10x$ **Possible answers: add $4x$ to each side, add $10x$ to each side**
3. $15x + 7 = -3x$ **Possible answers: add $3x$ to each side, add $-15x$ to each side**

Solve each equation. Check your answer.

4. $4x + 2 = 5(x + 10)$ −48
5. $-10 + y + 3 = 4y - 13$ 2
6. $3(t + 7) + 2 = 6t - 2 + 2t$ 5

A cheetah's body is well designed for fast running. Its tail acts like a boat's rudder to help it make sharp turns. Its spine acts like a spring to propel it forward.

Source: www.cheetahspot.com

55. Critical Thinking Write an equation with variables on both sides that has no solution. **Possible answer: $2x + 6 = x + 5 + x$**

56. Biology The graph shows the maximum recorded speeds of the four fastest mammals.

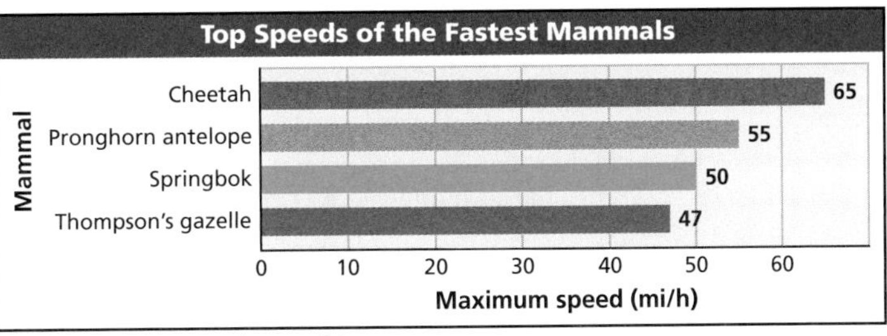

Source: The Top 10 of Everything

a. Write an expression for the distance in miles that a Thompson's gazelle can run at top speed in x hours. **$47x$**

b. Write an expression for the distance in miles that a cheetah can run at top speed in x hours. **$65x$**

c. A cheetah and a Thompson's gazelle are running at their top speeds. The cheetah is one mile behind the gazelle. Write an expression for the distance the cheetah must run to catch up with the gazelle. **$47x + 1$**

d. Write and solve an equation that represents how long the cheetah will have to run at top speed to catch up with the gazelle. **$47x + 1 = 65x$**

e. A cheetah can maintain its top speed for only 300 yards. Will the cheetah be able to catch the gazelle? Explain.

56d. $\frac{1}{18}$ h, or about $3\frac{1}{3}$ min

56e. No; the cheetah can only maintain its top speed for about 0.003 h, or about 11 s.

57. Write About It Write a series of steps that you can use to solve any equation with variables on both sides.
Possible answer: Simplify both sides if necessary. Collect the variable terms on one side by using inverse operations. Then isolate the variable using inverse operations.

58. Lindsey's monthly magazine subscription costs \$1.25 per issue. Kenzie's monthly subscription costs \$1.50 per issue, but she received her first 2 issues free. Which equation can be used to find the number of months after which the girls will have paid the same amount?

Ⓐ $1.25m = 1.50m - 2$ Ⓑ $1.25m = 1.50m - 2m$ **Ⓒ** $1.25m = 1.50(m - 2)$ Ⓓ $1.25m = 3m - 1.50$

59. What is the numerical solution of the equation *7 times a number equals 3 less than 5 times that number*?

Ⓕ -1.5 Ⓖ 0.25 Ⓗ $\frac{2}{3}$ Ⓙ 4

60. Three packs of markers cost \$9.00 less than 5 packs of markers. Which equation best represents this situation?

Ⓐ $5x + 9 = 3x$ **Ⓑ** $3x + 9 = 5x$ Ⓒ $3x - 9 = 5x$ Ⓓ $9 - 3x = 5x$

61. Nicole has \$120. If she saves \$20 per week, in how many days will she have \$500?

Ⓕ 19 Ⓖ 25 **Ⓗ** 133 Ⓙ 175

62. Gridded Response Solve $-2(x - 1) + 5x = 2(2x - 1)$. **4**

COMMON ERROR ALERT

In **Exercise 51,** students may write 0 instead of *no solution*, thinking that they are writing "zero solutions." Remind students that no solution means that there is no number, including zero, that will make the statement true.

In **Exercise 58,** only Kenzie's cost (the right side) needs to be analyzed. Have students simplify the right side of **C** so that every choice is in simplified form. Tell students that the cost of two issues at \$1.50 each is \$3.00. This amount is subtracted from the total cost of m issues at \$1.50 per issue.

If students chose **C** in **Exercise 60,** they are probably subtracting \$9 from the lesser cost. Tell students to replace the word *cost* with *is the same as*, to see where the equal sign should go. The correct choice, **B,** is the result of then adding 9 to both sides.

2-4 PROBLEM SOLVING

Write the correct answer.

1. Claire purchased just enough fencing to border either a rectangular or triangular garden, as shown, whose perimeters are the same. 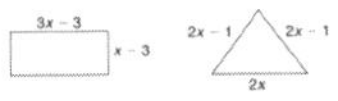
   (Rectangle: $3x - 3$, $x - 3$; Triangle: $2x - 1$, $2x - 1$, $2x$)
   How many feet of fencing did she buy?
   28 feet
2. Celia and Ryan are starting a nutrition program. Celia currently consumes 1200 calories a day and will increase that number by 100 calories each day. Ryan currently consumes 3230 calories a day and will decrease that number by 190 each day. They will continue this pattern until they are both consuming the same number of calories per day. In how many days will that be?
   7 days
3. A moving company charges \$800 plus \$16 per hour. Another moving company charges \$720 plus \$21 per hour. How long is a job that costs the same no matter which company is used?
   16 hours
4. Aaron needs to take out a loan to purchase a motorcycle. At one bank, he would pay \$2500 initially and \$150 each month for the loan. At another bank, he would pay \$3000 initially and \$125 each month. After how many months will the two loan payments be the same?
   20 months

Use the table below to answer questions 5–7. Select the best answer. The table shows the membership fees of three different gyms.

Gym	Fees
Workout Now	\$200 plus \$45 per month
Community Gym	\$50 plus \$55 per month
Ultra Sports Club	\$20 plus \$60 per month

5. After how many months will the fees for Workout Now and Community Gym be the same?
   A 2.5 **B** 15 C 25 D 30
6. Sal joined Workout Now for the number of months found in problem 5. How much did he pay?
   F \$695 **G** \$875 H \$1325 J \$1550
7. After how many months will the fees for Workout Now and Ultra Sports Club be the same?
   A 7 B 10 **C** 12 D 15

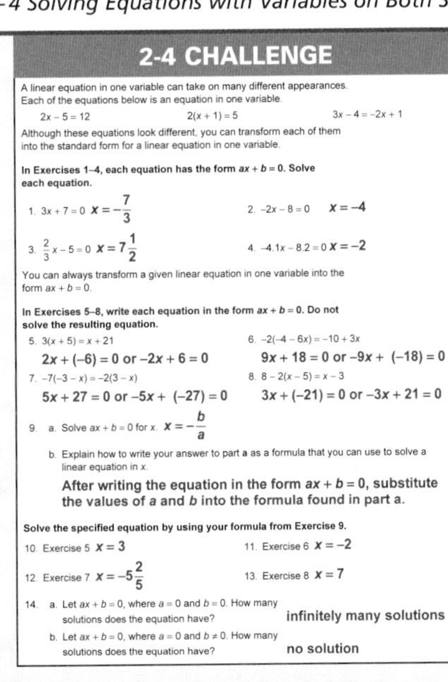

2-4 CHALLENGE

A linear equation in one variable can take on many different appearances. Each of the equations below is an equation in one variable.

$2x - 5 = 12$ $2(x + 1) = 5$ $3x - 4 = -2x + 1$

Although these equations look different, you can transform each of them into the standard form for a linear equation in one variable.

In Exercises 1–4, each equation has the form $ax + b = 0$. Solve each equation.

1. $3x + 7 = 0$ **$x = -\frac{7}{3}$**
2. $-2x - 8 = 0$ **$x = -4$**
3. $\frac{2}{3}x - 5 = 0$ **$x = 7\frac{1}{2}$**
4. $-4.1x - 8.2 = 0$ **$x = -2$**

You can always transform a given linear equation in one variable into the form $ax + b = 0$.

In Exercises 5–8, write each equation in the form $ax + b = 0$. Do not solve the resulting equation.

5. $3(x + 5) = x + 21$
   $2x + (-6) = 0$ or $-2x + 6 = 0$
6. $-2(-4 - 6x) = -10 + 3x$
   $9x + 18 = 0$ or $-9x + (-18) = 0$
7. $-7(-3 - x) = -2(3 - x)$
   $5x + 27 = 0$ or $-5x + (-27) = 0$
8. $8 - 2(x - 5) = x - 3$
   $3x + (-21) = 0$ or $-3x + 21 = 0$
9. a. Solve $ax + b = 0$ for x. **$x = -\frac{b}{a}$**
   b. Explain how to write your answer to part **a** as a formula that you can use to solve a linear equation in x.
   After writing the equation in the form $ax + b = 0$, substitute the values of a and b into the formula found in part a.

Solve the specified equation by using your formula from Exercise 9.

10. Exercise 5 **$x = 3$**
11. Exercise 6 **$x = -2$**
12. Exercise 7 **$x = -5\frac{2}{5}$**
13. Exercise 8 **$x = 7$**
14. a. Let $ax + b = 0$, where $a = 0$ and $b = 0$. How many solutions does the equation have? **infinitely many solutions**
    b. Let $ax + b = 0$, where $a = 0$ and $b \neq 0$. How many solutions does the equation have? **no solution**

CHALLENGE AND EXTEND

Solve each equation.

63. $4x + 2[4 - 2(x + 2)] = 2x - 4$ **2**

64. $\frac{x+5}{2} + \frac{x-1}{2} = \frac{x-1}{3}$ $-\frac{7}{2}$

65. $\frac{2}{3}w - \frac{1}{4} = \frac{2}{3}\left(w - \frac{1}{4}\right)$ **no solution**

66. $-5 - 7 - 3f = -f - 2(f + 6)$ **all real numbers**

67. $\frac{2}{3}x + \frac{1}{2} = \frac{3}{5}x - \frac{5}{6}$ **−20**

68. $x - \frac{1}{4} = \frac{x}{3} + 7\frac{3}{4}$ **12**

69. Find three consecutive integers such that twice the greatest integer is 2 less than 3 times the least integer. **6, 7, 8**

70. Find three consecutive integers such that twice the least integer is 12 more than the greatest integer. **14, 15, 16**

71. Rob had twice as much money as Sam. Then Sam gave Rob 1 quarter, 2 nickels, and 3 pennies. Rob then gave Sam 8 dimes. If they now have the same amount of money, how much money did Rob originally have? Check your answer. **$1.68**

SPIRAL REVIEW

Write an expression for the perimeter of each figure. *(Lesson 1-1)*

72. square with side x cm **$4x$ cm**

73. equilateral triangle with side y cm **$3y$ cm**

Multiply or divide. *(Lesson 1-3)*

74. $6.1 \div 0$ **undefined**

75. $3(-21)$ **−63**

76. $0 \div \frac{7}{8}$ **0**

77. $\frac{2}{5} \div \frac{1}{10}$ **4**

78. $5 \div (-5)$ **−1**

79. $\frac{-16}{-8}$ **2**

80. $-1000 \div (-0.001)$ **1,000,000**

81. $500(-0.25)$ **−125**

Solve each equation. Check your answer. *(Lesson 2-3)*

82. $4x - 44 = 8$ **13**

83. $2(x - 3) = 24$ **15**

84. $-1 = \frac{x}{4} - 3$ **8**

85. $2x + 6 = 12$ **3**

Career Path

KEYWORD: MA7 Career

Beth Simmons
Biology major

Q: What math classes did you take in high school?
A: Algebra 1 and 2, Geometry, and Precalculus

Q: What math classes have you taken in college?
A: Two calculus classes and a calculus-based physics class

Q: How do you use math?
A: I use math a lot in physics. Sometimes I would think a calculus topic was totally useless, and then we would use it in physics class! In biology, I use math to understand populations.

Q: What career options are you considering?
A: When I graduate, I could teach, or I could go to graduate school and do more research. I have a lot of options.

Journal

Have students explain the difference between solving an equation that has all real numbers as solutions and solving an equation that has no solutions.

ALTERNATIVE ASSESSMENT

Have students write and solve

- an equation with variables on both sides,
- an equation with variables on both sides that needs to be simplified on both sides before solving,
- an equation with infinitely many solutions, and
- an equation with no solutions.

Power Presentations with PowerPoint®

2-4 Lesson Quiz

Solve each equation.

1. $7x + 2 = 5x + 8$ 3
2. $4(2x - 5) = 5x + 4$ 8
3. $6 - 7(a + 1) = -3(2 - a)$ $\frac{1}{2}$
4. $4(3x + 1) - 7x = 6 + 5x - 2$ all real numbers
5. $\frac{2}{3}(3x + 9) = 8x$ 1
6. A painting company charges $250 base plus $16 per hour. Another painting company charges $210 base plus $18 per hour. How long is a job for which the two companies costs are the same? 20 h

Also available on transparency

2-5 Solving for a Variable

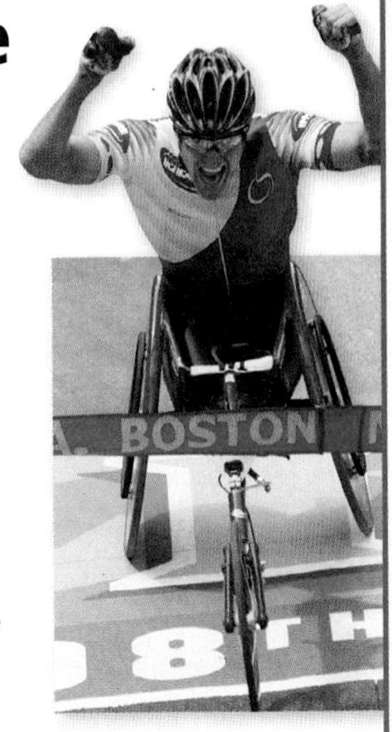

Objectives
Solve a formula for a given variable.

Solve an equation in two or more variables for one of the variables.

Vocabulary
formula
literal equation

Who uses this?

Athletes can "rearrange" the distance formula to calculate their average speed.

Many wheelchair athletes compete in marathons, which cover about 26.2 miles. Using the time t it took to complete the race, the distance d, and the *formula* $d = rt$, racers can find their average speed r.

A **formula** is an equation that states a rule for a relationship among quantities.

In the formula $d = rt$, d is isolated. You can "rearrange" a formula to isolate any variable by using inverse operations. This is called *solving for a variable.*

Know it! Note

Solving for a Variable	
Step 1	Locate the variable you are asked to solve for in the equation.
Step 2	Identify the operations on this variable and the order in which they are applied.
Step 3	Use inverse operations to undo operations and isolate the variable.

EXAMPLE 1 ***Sports Application***

In 2004, Ernst Van Dyk won the wheelchair race of the Boston Marathon with a time of about 1.3 hours. The race was about 26.2 miles. What was his average speed? Use the formula $d = rt$ and round your answer to the nearest tenth.

The question asks for speed, so first solve the formula $d = rt$ for r.

$d = rt$ — *Locate r in the equation.*

$\frac{d}{t} = \frac{rt}{t}$ — *Since r is multiplied by t, divide both sides by t to undo the multiplication.*

$\frac{d}{t} = r$, or $r = \frac{d}{t}$

Now use this formula and the information given in the problem.

$$r = \frac{d}{t} \approx \frac{26.2}{1.3}$$
$$\approx 20.2$$

Van Dyk's average speed was about 20.2 miles per hour.

Helpful Hint

A number divided by itself equals 1. For $t \neq 0$, $\frac{t}{t} = 1$.

1. Solve the formula $d = rt$ for t. Find the time in hours that it would take Van Dyk to travel 26.2 miles if his average speed was 18 miles per hour. Round to the nearest hundredth. **about 1.46 h**

2-5 Organizer

Pacing: Traditional 1 day
Block $\frac{1}{2}$ day

Objectives: Solve a formula for a given variable.

Solve an equation in two or more variables for one of the variables.

Online Edition
Tutorial Videos

Countdown Week 4

Power Presentations with PowerPoint®

Warm Up

Solve each equation.

1. $5 + x = -2$ -7

2. $8m = 43$ $\frac{43}{8}$

3. $\frac{c + 5}{4} = 6$ 19

4. $0.3s + 0.6 = 1.5$ 3

5. $10k - 6 = 9k + 2$ 8

Also available on transparency

Math Humor

Q: If you give 15 cents to one friend and 10 cents to another friend, what time is it?

A: A quarter to two.

1 Introduce

EXPLORATION

2-5 Solving for a Variable

Mei is planning a rectangular plot for her vegetable garden. She wants the plot to have an area of 24 ft².

ℓ | $\ell w = 24$ ft² | w

1. Mei considers various lengths for the plot. Complete the table to show the corresponding width for each length.
2. Explain how you found each width.
3. Write an equation that gives the width w of the plot for any length ℓ.

Length ℓ (ft)	Width w (ft)	Area A (ft²)
1		24
2		24
3		24
4		24
6		24
8		24

THINK AND DISCUSS

4. **Explain** how you can use your equation to find the width of the plot when the length is 15 feet.
5. **Describe** how the equation you wrote in Problem 3 is related to the original area equation $\ell w = 24$.

Motivate

Show students these two equivalent equations that relate the area of a rectangle to its length and width: $A = \ell w$ and $\ell = \frac{A}{w}$. Explain that the first equation is more convenient if you know the length and the width and want to find the area. The second equation is more convenient if you know the area and the width and want to find the length.

Explorations and answers are provided in *Alternate Openers: Explorations Transparencies.*

State Resources

Power Presentations with PowerPoint®

Additional Examples

Example 1

The formula $C = \pi d$ gives the circumference of a circle C in terms of its diameter d. The circumference of a bowl is 18 inches. What is the bowl's diameter? Leave the symbol π in your answer.

$\frac{18}{\pi}$ in.

Example 2

A. The formula for the area of a triangle is $A = \frac{1}{2}bh$, where b is the length of the base and h is the height. Solve for h.

$h = \frac{2A}{b}$

B. Solve the formula for a person's typing speed for e.

$e = \frac{ms - w}{-10}$

Example 3

A. Solve $x + y = 15$ for x.

$x = 15 - y$

B. Solve $pq = x$ for q. $q = \frac{x}{p}$

INTERVENTION

Questioning Strategies

EXAMPLES 1–3

- How is solving for a variable similar to solving an equation? How is it different?

EXAMPLE 2 **Solving Formulas for a Variable**

A **The formula for a Fahrenheit temperature in terms of degrees Celsius is $F = \frac{9}{5}C + 32$. Solve for C.**

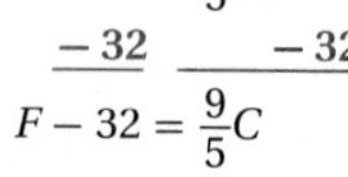

$$F = \frac{9}{5}C + 32$$ *Locate C in the equation.*

$$\underline{-32 \quad\quad -32}$$ *Since 32 is added to $\frac{9}{5}C$, subtract 32 from both sides to undo the addition.*

$$F - 32 = \frac{9}{5}C$$

$$\left(\frac{5}{9}\right)(F - 32) = \left(\frac{5}{9}\right)\frac{9}{5}C$$ *Since C is multiplied by $\frac{9}{5}$, divide both sides by $\frac{9}{5}$ $\left(\text{multiply by } \frac{5}{9}\right)$ to undo the multiplication.*

$$\frac{5}{9}(F - 32) = C$$

Remember!

Dividing by a fraction is the same as multiplying by the reciprocal.

B **The formula for a person's typing speed is $s = \frac{w - 10e}{m}$, where s is speed in words per minute, w is number of words typed, e is number of errors, and m is number of minutes typing. Solve for w.**

$$s = \frac{w - 10e}{m}$$ *Locate w in the equation.*

$$m(s) = m\left(\frac{w - 10e}{m}\right)$$ *Since w − 10e is divided by m, multiply both sides by m to undo the division.*

$$ms = w - 10e$$

$$\underline{+10e \quad\quad +10e}$$ *Since 10e is subtracted from w, add 10e to both sides to undo the subtraction.*

$$ms + 10e = w$$

CHECK IT OUT! 2. The formula for an object's final velocity f is $f = i - gt$, where i is the object's initial velocity, g is acceleration due to gravity, and t is time. Solve for i. $i = f + gt$

A formula is a type of *literal equation.* A **literal equation** is an equation with two or more variables. To solve for one of the variables, use inverse operations.

EXAMPLE 3 **Solving Literal Equations for a Variable**

A **Solve $m - n = 5$ for m.**

$$m - n = 5$$ *Locate m in the equation.*

$$\underline{+n \quad +n}$$ *Since n is subtracted from m, add n to both sides to undo the subtraction.*

$$m = 5 + n$$

B **Solve $\frac{m}{k} = x$ for k.**

$$\frac{m}{k} = x$$ *Locate k in the equation.*

$$k\left(\frac{m}{k}\right) = kx$$ *Since k appears in the denominator, multiply both sides by k.*

$$m = kx$$

$$\frac{m}{x} = \frac{kx}{x}$$ *Since k is multiplied by x, divide both sides by x to undo the multiplication.*

$$\frac{m}{x} = k$$

CHECK IT OUT! **3a.** Solve $5 - b = 2t$ for t. $t = \frac{5 - b}{2}$ **3b.** Solve $D = \frac{m}{V}$ for V. $V = \frac{m}{D}$

2 Teach

Guided Instruction

Solve $x + 7 = 9$ and $\frac{x}{7} = 9$. Then replace the 7 with y and solve for x again. Show that the procedures are the same, but the answers are in a different form.

Teaching Tip **Visual** Have students circle the variable for which they are solving. On the board, circle this variable as well, or write the variable in a different color.

3 Close

Summarize

Ask students to identify the first step in solving each of the following literal equations for x.

$abx = c$	Divide both sides by ab.
$ax + b = c$	Subtract b from both sides.
$\frac{x - a}{b} = c$	Multiply both sides by b.

ONGOING ASSESSMENT and INTERVENTION

***Diagnose Before* the Lesson**
2-5 Warm Up, TE p. 107

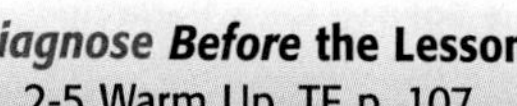

***Monitor During* the Lesson**
Check It Out! Exercises, SE pp. 107–108
Questioning Strategies, TE p. 108

***Assess After* the Lesson**
2-5 Lesson Quiz, TE p. 111
Alternative Assessment, TE p. 111

THINK AND DISCUSS

1. Describe a situation in which a formula could be used more easily if it were "rearranged." Include the formula in your description.
2. Explain how to solve $P = 2\ell + 2w$ for w.
3. **GET ORGANIZED** Copy and complete the graphic organizer. Write a formula that is used in each subject. Then solve the formula for each of its variables.

Common Formulas	
Subject	**Formula**
Geometry	
Physical science	
Earth science	

Answers to *Think and Discuss*

1. Possible answer: The formula $d = rt$ is more useful in the form $\frac{d}{r} = t$ when you need to determine the time it takes to travel a certain distance at a certain speed.
2. Isolate w on the right side of the equation by subtracting 2ℓ from both sides and then dividing both sides by 2.
3. See p. A3.

2-5 Exercises

GUIDED PRACTICE

1. **Vocabulary** Explain why a *formula* is a type of *literal equation*.

SEE EXAMPLE 1 p. 107

2. **Construction** The formula $a = 46c$ gives the floor area a in square meters that can be wired using c circuits.
   a. Solve $a = 46c$ for c. $c = \frac{a}{46}$
   b. If a room is 322 square meters, how many circuits are required to wire this room? **7 circuits**

SEE EXAMPLE 2 p. 108

3. The formula for the volume of a rectangular prism with length ℓ, width w, and height h is $V = \ell wh$. Solve this formula for w.

SEE EXAMPLE 3 p. 108

4. Solve $st + 3t = 6$ for s. $s = \frac{6 - 3t}{t}$
5. Solve $m - 4n = 8$ for m. $m = 4n + 8$
6. Solve $\frac{f + 4}{g} = 6$ for f. $f = 6g - 4$
7. Solve $b + c = \frac{10}{a}$ for a. $a = \frac{10}{b + c}$

PRACTICE AND PROBLEM SOLVING

Independent Practice	
For Exercises	**See Example**
8	1
9	2
10–13	3

Extra Practice
Skills Practice p. S6
Application Practice p. S29

8. **Geometry** The formula $C = 2\pi r$ relates the circumference C of a circle to its radius r. (Recall that π is the constant ratio of circumference to diameter.)
   a. Solve $C = 2\pi r$ for r. $r = \frac{C}{2\pi}$
   b. If a circle's circumference is 15 inches, what is its radius? Leave the symbol π in your answer. $\frac{7.5}{\pi}$ **in.**

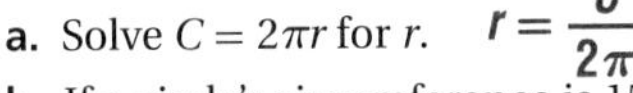

C is the distance around the circle.
r is the distance from the center of the circle to any point on the circle.

9. **Finance** The formula $A = P + I$ shows that the total amount of money A received from an investment equals the principal P (the original amount of money invested) plus the interest I. Solve this formula for I. $I = A - P$
10. Solve $-2 = 4r + s$ for s. $s = -2 - 4r$
11. Solve $xy - 5 = k$ for x. $x = \frac{k + 5}{y}$
12. Solve $\frac{m}{n} = p - 6$ for n. $\frac{m}{p - 6} = n$
13. Solve $\frac{x - 2}{y} = z$ for y. $\frac{x - 2}{z} = y$

Assignment Guide

Assign *Guided Practice* exercises as necessary.

If you finished Examples **1–3**
Basic 8–31, 34–37, 46–54
Average 8–13, 20–41, 46–54
Advanced 8–13, 20–28 even, 29–54

Homework Quick Check
Quickly check key concepts.
Exercises: 8, 9, 10, 12, 24, 28, 30

Answers

1. A literal equation contains more than one variable. A formula shows how to determine the value of one variable when you know the value(s) of one or more other variables. So a formula always contains more than one variable, making it a literal equation.

3. $w = \frac{V}{\ell h}$

State Resources

Diversity Exercise 30 is about baseball and may use terms unfamiliar to some students. Have students familiar with baseball discuss the meanings of *run, earned run, inning,* etc.

Exercise 34 involves using a known rate to find data values and then displaying that data visually. This exercise prepares students for the Multi-Step Test Prep on page 118.

Answers

14. $n = \frac{S + 360}{180}$
15. $x = 5(a + g)$
16. $b = \frac{2A}{h}$
17. $x = \frac{y - b}{m}$
18. $n = \frac{a - 1}{3}$
19. $T = \frac{PV}{nR}$
20. $T = R - M$
21. $T = M + R$
22. $R = \frac{PV}{nT}$
23. $b = \frac{c - 2a}{2}$
24. $c = \frac{-4p}{9}$
25. $r = 7 - ax$
26. $y = \frac{2 - 3x}{7}$
27. $x = \frac{5 - 4y}{3}$
28. $b = \frac{y - 3x}{3}$
32. Possible answer: Use inverse operations to isolate the indicated variable on one side of the equation. Be sure the variable is the only expression on one side of the equation and doesn't appear on the other side.

34c. For graph, see p. A14.

2-5 PRACTICE A
2-5 PRACTICE C
2-5 PRACTICE B

Answer each of the following.

1. The formula $C = 2\pi r$ relates the radius r of a circle to its circumference C. Solve the formula for r.
   $r = \frac{C}{2\pi}$
2. The formula $y = mx + b$ is called the slope-intercept form of a line. Solve this formula for m.
   $m = \frac{y - b}{x}$

Solve for the indicated variable.

3. $4c = d$ for c — $c = \frac{d}{4}$
4. $n - 6m = 8$ for n — $n = 8 + 6m$
5. $2p + 5r = q$ for p — $p = \frac{q - 5r}{2}$
6. $-10 = xy + z$ for x — $x = \frac{-10 - z}{y}$
7. $\frac{a}{b} = c$ for b — $b = \frac{a}{c}$
8. $\frac{h - 4}{j} = k$ for j — $j = \frac{h - 4}{k}$

Answer each of the following.

9. The formula $c = 5p + 215$ relates c, the total cost in dollars of hosting a birthday party at a skating rink, to p, the number of people attending.
   a. Solve the formula $c = 5p + 215$ for p. $p = \frac{c - 215}{5}$
   b. If Allie's parents are willing to spend \$300 for a party, how many people can attend? 17
10. The formula for the area of a triangle is $A = \frac{1}{2}bh$, where b represents the length of the base and h represents the height.
    a. Solve the formula $A = \frac{1}{2}bh$ for b. $b = \frac{2A}{h}$
    b. If a triangle has an area of 192 mm², and the height measures 12 mm, what is the measure of the base? 32 mm

Solve for the indicated variable.

14. $S = 180n - 360$ for n	15. $\frac{x}{5} - g = a$ for x	16. $A = \frac{1}{2}bh$ for b
17. $y = mx + b$ for x	18. $a = 3n + 1$ for n	19. $PV = nRT$ for T
20. $T + M = R$ for T	21. $M = T - R$ for T	22. $PV = nRT$ for R
23. $2a + 2b = c$ for b	24. $5p + 9c = p$ for c	25. $ax + r = 7$ for r
26. $3x + 7y = 2$ for y	27. $4y + 3x = 5$ for x	28. $y = 3x + 3b$ for b

29. **Estimation** The table shows the flying time and distance traveled for five flights on a certain airplane.
    a. Use the data in the table to write a rule that *estimates* the relationship between flying time t and distance traveled d.
    b. Use your rule from part **a** to estimate the time that it takes the airplane to fly 1300 miles.
    c. Solve your rule for d.
    d. Use your rule from part **c** to estimate the distance the airplane can fly in 8 hours.

29a. Possible answer: $t \approx \frac{d}{500}$
b. Possible answer: about 2.6 h
c. Possible answer: $d \approx 500t$
d. Possible answer: about 4000 mi

Flying Times

Flight	Time (h)	Distance (mi)
A	2	1018
B	3	1485
C	4	2103
D	5	2516
E	6	2886

30. **Sports** To find a baseball pitcher's earned run average (ERA), you can use the formula $Ei = 9r$, where E represents ERA, i represents number of innings pitched, and r represents number of earned runs allowed. Solve the equation for E. What is a pitcher's ERA if he allows 5 earned runs in 18 innings pitched? $E = \frac{9r}{i}$; **2.5**

31. **Meteorology** For altitudes up to 36,000 feet, the relationship between temperature and altitude can be described by the formula $t = -0.0035a + g$, where t is the temperature in degrees Fahrenheit, a is the altitude in feet, and g is the ground temperature in degrees Fahrenheit. Solve this formula for a.

31. $a = \frac{t - g}{-0.0035}$

32. **Write About It** In your own words, explain how to solve a literal equation for one of the variables.
33. **Critical Thinking** How is solving $a - ab = c$ for a different from the problems in this lesson? How might you solve this equation for a?

33. Possible answer: The variable a appears in 2 terms. Use the Distributive Property to write $a - ab$ as $a(1 - b)$, and then divide both sides by $1 - b$.

34. This problem will prepare you for the Multi-Step Test Prep on page 118.
    a. Suppose firefighters can extinguish a wildfire at a rate of 60 acres per day. Use this information to complete the table.
    b. Use the last row in the table to write an equation for acres A extinguished in terms of the number of days d.
    c. Graph the points in the table with *Days* on the horizontal axis and *Acres* on the vertical axis. Describe the graph. **The graph is a line.**

b. $A = 60d$

Days	Acres
1	60
2	**120**
3	180
4	**240**
5	**300**
d	**$60d$**

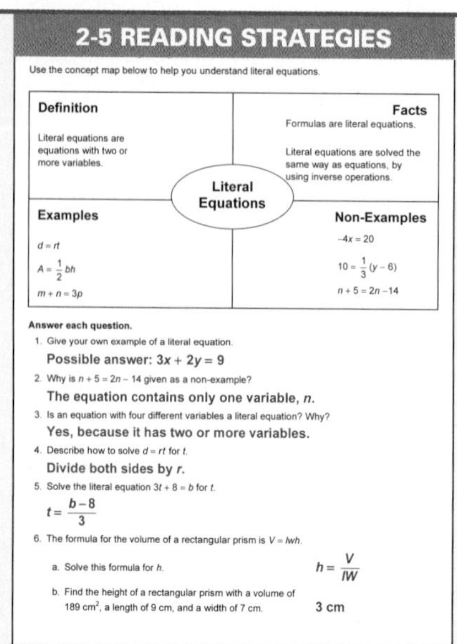

2-5 READING STRATEGIES

Use the concept map below to help you understand literal equations.

Literal Equations

Definition
Literal equations are equations with two or more variables.

Facts
Formulas are literal equations.
Literal equations are solved the same way as equations, by using inverse operations.

Examples
$d = rt$
$A = \frac{1}{2}bh$
$m + n = 3p$

Non-Examples
$-4x = 20$
$10 = \frac{1}{3}(y - 6)$
$n + 5 = 2n - 14$

Answer each question.

1. Give your own example of a literal equation.
   Possible answer: $3x + 2y = 9$
2. Why is $n + 5 = 2n - 14$ given as a non-example?
   The equation contains only one variable, n.
3. Is an equation with four different variables a literal equation? Why?
   Yes, because it has two or more variables.
4. Describe how to solve $d = rt$ for t.
   Divide both sides by r.
5. Solve the literal equation $3t + 8 = b$ for t.
   $t = \frac{b - 8}{3}$
6. The formula for the volume of a rectangular prism is $V = lwh$.
   a. Solve this formula for h. $h = \frac{V}{lw}$
   b. Find the height of a rectangular prism with a volume of 189 cm², a length of 9 cm, and a width of 7 cm. **3 cm**

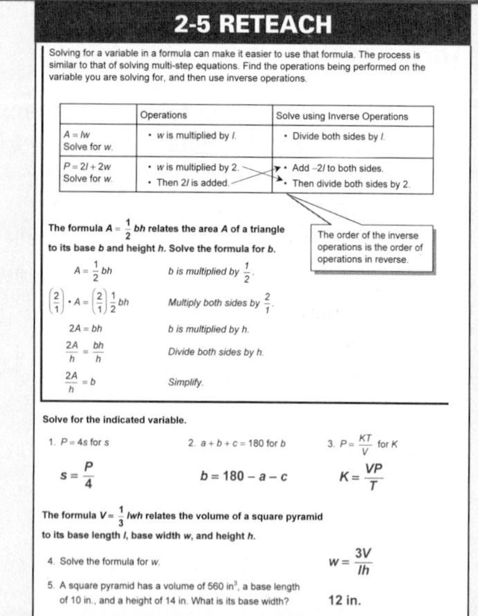

2-5 RETEACH

Solving for a variable in a formula can make it easier to use that formula. The process is similar to that of solving multi-step equations. Find the operations being performed on the variable you are solving for, and then use inverse operations.

	Operations	Solve using Inverse Operations
$A = lw$ Solve for w.	• w is multiplied by l.	• Divide both sides by l.
$P = 2l + 2w$ Solve for w.	• w is multiplied by 2. • Then $2l$ is added.	• Add $-2l$ to both sides. • Then divide both sides by 2.

The order of the inverse operations is the order of operations in reverse.

The formula $A = \frac{1}{2}bh$ relates the area A of a triangle to its base b and height h. Solve the formula for b.

$A = \frac{1}{2}bh$	*b is multiplied by $\frac{1}{2}$.*
$\left(\frac{2}{1}\right) \cdot A = \left(\frac{2}{1}\right)\frac{1}{2}bh$	*Multiply both sides by $\frac{2}{1}$.*
$2A = bh$	*b is multiplied by h.*
$\frac{2A}{h} = \frac{bh}{h}$	*Divide both sides by h.*
$\frac{2A}{h} = b$	*Simplify.*

Solve for the indicated variable.

1. $P = 4s$ for s — $s = \frac{P}{4}$
2. $a + b + c = 180$ for b — $b = 180 - a - c$
3. $P = \frac{KT}{V}$ for K — $K = \frac{VP}{T}$

The formula $V = \frac{1}{3}lwh$ relates the volume of a square pyramid to its base length l, base width w, and height h.

4. Solve the formula for w. $w = \frac{3V}{lh}$
5. A square pyramid has a volume of 560 in³, a base length of 10 in., and a height of 14 in. What is its base width? **12 in.**

TEST PREP

35. Which equation is the result of solving $9 + 3x = 2y$ for x?

Ⓐ $\frac{9 + 3y}{2} = x$ Ⓑ $\frac{2}{3}y - 9 = x$ **Ⓒ** $x = \frac{2}{3}y - 3$ Ⓓ $x = 2y - 3$

36. Which of the following is a correct method for solving $2a - 5b = 10$ for b?

Ⓕ Add $5b$ to both sides, then divide both sides by 2.
Ⓖ Subtract $5b$ from both sides, then divide both sides by 2.
Ⓗ Divide both sides by 5, then add $2a$ to both sides.
Ⓙ Subtract $2a$ from both sides, then divide both sides by -5.

37. The formula for the volume of a rectangular prism is $V = \ell wh$. Anna wants to make a cardboard box with a length of 7 inches, a width of 5 inches, and a volume of 210 cubic inches. Which variable does Anna need to solve for in order to build her box?

Ⓐ V Ⓑ ℓ Ⓒ w **Ⓓ** h

CHALLENGE AND EXTEND

Solve for the indicated variable.

38. $3.3x + r = 23.1$ for x 39. $\frac{2}{5}a - \frac{3}{4}b = c$ for a 40. $\frac{3}{5}x + 1.4y = \frac{2}{5}$ for y

41. $t = \frac{d}{500} + \frac{1}{2}$ for d 42. $s = \frac{1}{2}gt^2$ for g 43. $v^2 = u^2 + 2as$ for s

44. Solve $y = mx + 6$ for m. What can you say about y if $m = 0$?

45. **Entertainment** The formula $S = \frac{h \cdot w \cdot f \cdot t}{35{,}000}$ gives the approximate size in kilobytes (Kb) of a compressed video. The variables h and w represent the height and width of the frame measured in pixels, f is the number of frames per second (fps) the video plays, and t is the time the video plays in seconds. Estimate the time a movie trailer will play if it has a frame height of 320 pixels, has a frame width of 144 pixels, plays at 15 fps, and has a size of 2370 Kb. **120 s**

38. $x = \frac{23.1 - r}{3.3}$
39. $a = \frac{5}{2}\left(c + \frac{3}{4}b\right)$
40. $y = \frac{\frac{2}{5} - \frac{3}{5}x}{1.4}$
41. $d = 500\left(t - \frac{1}{2}\right)$
42. $g = \frac{2s}{t^2}$
43. $s = \frac{v^2 - u^2}{2a}$
44. $m = \frac{y - 6}{x}$; if $m = 0$, $y = 6$

SPIRAL REVIEW

46. Jill spent $\frac{1}{4}$ of the money she made baby-sitting. She made \$40 baby-sitting. How much did she spend? *(Previous course)* **\$10**

47. In one class, $\frac{3}{5}$ of the students are boys. There are 30 students in the class. How many are girls? *(Previous course)* **12**

Evaluate each expression for the given value of x. *(Lesson 1-6)*

48. $3 + 2 \cdot x + 4$ for $x = 3$ **13** 49. $24 \div 4 - x$ for $x = 12$ **−6** 50. $43 - 62 + x$ for $x = 15$ **−4**

Solve each equation. Check your answer. *(Lesson 2-1)*

51. $18 = -2 + w$ **20** 52. $2 = -3 + c$ **5** 53. $-8 + k = 4$ **12** 54. $-15 + a = -27$ **−12**

COMMON ERROR ALERT

Students may subtract when they should divide. In **Exercise 30,** for example, they may write $r = 9E - i$. Ask students which operation is being performed on r and what will "undo" it.

TEST PREP DOCTOR In **Exercise 35,** students who chose **B** or **D** most likely did not divide every term by 3.

Students who chose **F** in **Exercise 36** probably solved the equation for a. Encourage students to read the question carefully.

Journal

Have students discuss the differences in solving the following literal equations for x: $\frac{x}{7} - y = t$ and $\frac{x - y}{7} = t$.

ALTERNATIVE ASSESSMENT

Have students explain how to solve for each of the three variables in the following literal equation: $q + r = \frac{p}{5}$.

Power Presentations with PowerPoint®

2-5 Lesson Quiz

Solve for the indicated variable.

1. $V = \frac{1}{3}Ah$ for h $h = \frac{3V}{A}$
2. $P = R - C$ for C $C = R - P$
3. $2x + 7y = 14$ for y $y = \frac{14 - 2x}{7}$
4. $\frac{m}{x} = k - 6$ for m $m = x(k - 6)$
5. $R = \frac{C - S}{t}$ for C $C = Rt + S$

Euler's formula, $V - E + F = 2$, relates the number of vertices V, the number of edges E, and the number of faces F of a polyhedron.

6. Solve Euler's formula for F. $F = 2 - V + E$
7. How many faces does a polyhedron with 8 vertices and 12 edges have? 6

Also available on transparency

2-5 PROBLEM SOLVING

Use the table below, which shows some track and field gold medal winners, to answer questions 1–4. Round all answers to the nearest tenth.

2000 Summer Olympics		
Gold Medal Winner	Race	Time (s)
M. Greene, USA	100 m	9.87
K. Kenteris, Greece	200 m	20.09
M. Johnson, USA	400 m	43.84
A. Garcia, Cuba	110 m hurdles	13.00

1. Solve the formula $d = rt$ for r. $r = \frac{d}{t}$
2. Find Johnson's average speed in meters per second. **9.1 m/s**
3. Find Garcia's average speed in meters per second. **8.5 m/s**
4. The world record of 19.32 seconds in the 200-meter race was set by Michael Johnson in 1996. Find the difference between Johnson's average speed and Kenteris' average speed. **0.4 m/s**

Select the best answer.

5. The cost to mail a letter in the United States in 2008 was \$0.41 for the first ounce and \$0.26 for each additional ounce. Solve $C = 0.41 + 0.26(z - 1)$ for z.
   A $z = \frac{C - 0.41}{0.26}$
   B $z = \frac{C - 0.41}{0.26} + 1$
   C $z = \frac{C + 0.15}{0.26}$
   D $z = C - 0.67$
6. The formula $V = \frac{Bh}{3}$ shows how to find the volume of a pyramid. Solve for B.
   F $B = \frac{3V}{h}$ H $B = 3Vh$
   G $B = 3V - h$ J $B = 3V + h$
7. Degrees Celsius and degrees Fahrenheit are related by the equation $C = \frac{5}{9}(F - 32)$. Solve for F.
   A $F = 9C + 27$ C $F = \frac{5}{9}C + 32$
   B $F = \frac{9}{5}C$ **D** $F = \frac{9}{5}C + 32$
8. The cost of operating an electrical device is given by the formula $C = \frac{Wtc}{1000}$ where W is the power in watts, t is the time in hours, and c is the cost in cents per kilowatt-hour. Solve for W.
   F $W = 1000C - tc$
   G $W = \frac{Ctc}{1000}$
   H $W = 1000C + tc$
   J $W = \frac{1000C}{tc}$

2-5 CHALLENGE

When you put your money in a savings account, the bank may pay you *simple interest*. Let P represent the dollar amount of your deposit (the principal), let r represent the interest rate, and let t represent the number of years. The amount of interest you earn, I, is given by the *simple interest formula:* $I = Prt$.

Note that banks typically use percents to describe their interest rates. Percent means "per hundred," so an interest rate of 5% means that you should use $r = \frac{5}{100}$, or 0.05.

Use the simple interest formula to solve the following problems:

1. If $P = 2500$, $r = 0.03$, and $t = 5$, what is I? **$I = 375$**
2. If $r = 0.025$, $t = 3$, and $I = 150$, what is P? **$P = 2000$**
3. If $P = 500$, $r = 0.06$, and $I = 150$, what is t? **$t = 5$ years**
4. If $P = 3000$, $t = 4$, and $I = 384$, what is r? **$r = 0.032$ or 3.2%**
5. Kevin is making a deposit of \$1800 at his local bank. The bank pays 6.5% simple interest ($r = 0.065$). If Kevin leaves his deposit at the bank for 3 years, how much interest will he earn? **\$351**
6. Cecelia made a deposit of \$600 at a bank paying 4% simple interest ($r = 0.04$). How long should she leave her deposit at the bank in order to earn \$72 in interest? **3 years**
7. Darryl opened an account at a bank which paid 5.5% simple interest ($r = 0.055$). After 6 years, he had earned \$726 in interest. What was the amount of his original deposit? **\$2200**
8. Sophia deposited \$150 at a savings and loan association paying simple interest. If she earned \$27 in interest after 6 years, what was the interest rate? **0.03 or 3%**
9. Nathan made a deposit of \$650 at a bank paying 3.8% simple interest ($r = 0.038$). If he leaves his deposit at the bank for 10 years, how much interest will he earn? **\$247**
10. Susie made a deposit of \$980 at a credit union paying 7% simple interest ($r = 0.07$). How long should she leave her deposit at the credit union in order to earn \$343 in interest? **5 years**
11. Guillermo deposited \$1350 at a bank paying simple interest. If he earned \$109.35 in 3 years, what was the interest rate? **0.027 or 2.7%**

2-6 Organizer

Pacing: Traditional 1 day
Block $\frac{1}{2}$ day

Objectives: Solve equations in one variable that contain absolute-value expressions.

Online Edition
Tutorial Videos

Countdown Week 4

Power Presentations with PowerPoint®

Warm Up

Solve.

1. $x - 10 = 4$ 14
2. $s + 5 = -2$ −7
3. $32 = -8y$ −4
4. $\frac{m+4}{2} = 7$ 10
5. $-14 = x - 5$ −9
6. $2t + 5 = 45$ 20

Also available on transparency

Math Humor

Question: How is the equation $|x| = 8$ similar to a chemist's laboratory?

Answer: Both have multiple solutions.

State Resources

2-6 Solving Absolute-Value Equations

Objective
Solve equations in one variable that contain absolute-value expressions.

Why learn this?
Engineers can solve absolute-value equations to calculate the length of the deck of a bridge. (See Example 3.)

Recall that the absolute value of a number is that number's distance from zero on a number line. For example, $|-5| = 5$ and $|5| = 5$.

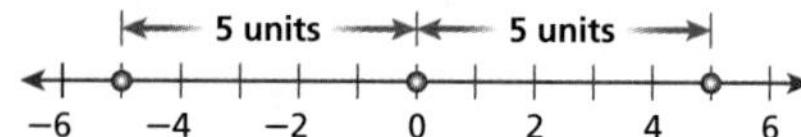

For any nonzero absolute value, there are exactly two numbers with that absolute value. For example, both 5 and −5 have an absolute value of 5.

To write this statement using algebra, you would write $|x| = 5$. This equation asks, "What values of x have an absolute value of 5?" The solutions are 5 and −5. Notice that this equation has two solutions.

Know it! Note

Absolute-Value Equations

WORDS	NUMBERS
The equation $\|x\| = a$ asks, "What values of x have an absolute value of a?" The solutions are a and the opposite of a.	$\|x\| = 5$ $x = 5$ or $x = -5$
GRAPH	**ALGEBRA**
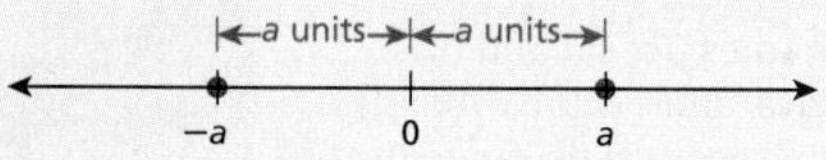 (number line: a units, a units; points $-a$, 0, a)	$\|x\| = a$ $x = a$ or $x = -a$ $(a \geq 0)$

To solve absolute-value equations, perform inverse operations to isolate the absolute-value expression on one side of the equation. Then you must consider two cases.

EXAMPLE 1 Solving Absolute-Value Equations

Solve each equation.

A $|x| = 4$

$|x| = 4$ *Think: What numbers are 4 units from 0?*

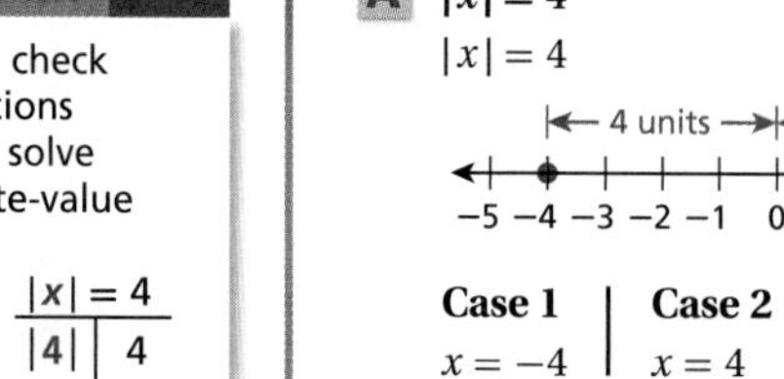
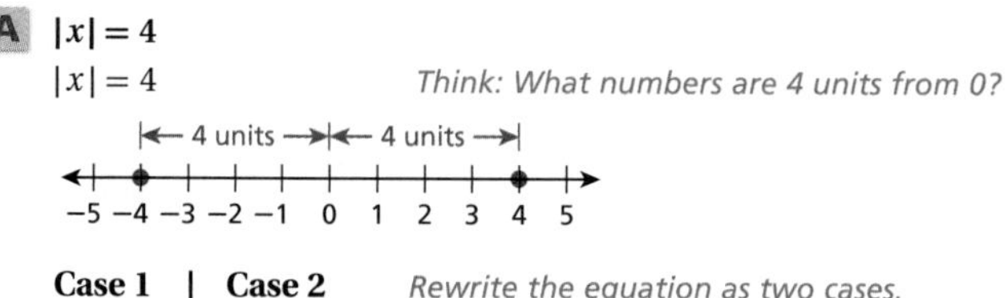

Case 1	**Case 2**
$x = -4$	$x = 4$

Rewrite the equation as two cases.

The solutions are −4 and 4.

Helpful Hint

Be sure to check both solutions when you solve an absolute-value equation.

$\|x\| = 4$		$\|x\| = 4$	
$\|-4\|$	4	$\|4\|$	4
4	4 ✓	4	4 ✓

1 Introduce

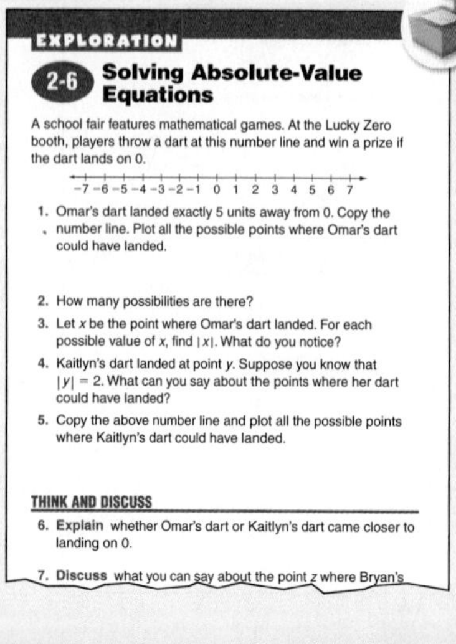

EXPLORATION

2-6 Solving Absolute-Value Equations

A school fair features mathematical games. At the Lucky Zero booth, players throw a dart at this number line and win a prize if the dart lands on 0.

−7 −6 −5 −4 −3 −2 −1 0 1 2 3 4 5 6 7

1. Omar's dart landed exactly 5 units away from 0. Copy the number line. Plot all the possible points where Omar's dart could have landed.
2. How many possibilities are there?
3. Let x be the point where Omar's dart landed. For each possible value of x, find $|x|$. What do you notice?
4. Kaitlyn's dart landed at point y. Suppose you know that $|y| = 2$. What can you say about the points where her dart could have landed?
5. Copy the above number line and plot all the possible points where Kaitlyn's dart could have landed.

THINK AND DISCUSS

6. **Explain** whether Omar's dart or Kaitlyn's dart came closer to landing on 0.
7. **Discuss** what you can say about the point z where Bryan's

Motivate

Present the following situation to the class. In a game show, two contestants guess the price of a DVD player. The contestants each make different guesses, and both differ from the actual price by \$15. The actual price of the DVD player is \$169. What guesses do the contestants make? 154, 184

Tell students they will learn how to use absolute-value equations to solve problems like this.

Explorations and answers are provided in *Alternate Openers: Explorations Transparencies.*

Solve each equation.

B $4|x+2| = 24$

$$\frac{4|x+2|}{4} = \frac{24}{4}$$ *Since $|x+2|$ is multiplied by 4, divide both sides by 4 to undo the multiplication.*

$$|x+2| = 6$$ *Think: What numbers are 6 units from 0?*

Case 1	Case 2
$x+2=-6$	$x+2=6$
$-2 \quad -2$	$-2 \quad -2$
$x = -8$	$x = 4$

Rewrite the equation as two cases. Since 2 is added to x, subtract 2 from both sides of the equation.

The solutions are –8 and 4.

CHECK IT OUT! Solve each equation. Check your answer.

1a. $|x| - 3 = 4$ **−7, 7** **1b.** $8 = |x - 2.5|$ **−5.5, 10.5**

The table summarizes the steps for solving absolute-value equations.

Solving an Absolute-Value Equation
1. Use inverse operations to isolate the absolute-value expression.
2. Rewrite the resulting equation as two cases that do not involve absolute values.
3. Solve the equation in each of the two cases.

Not all absolute-value equations have two solutions. If the absolute-value expression equals 0, there is one solution. If an equation states that an absolute value is negative, there are no solutions.

EXAMPLE 2 Special Cases of Absolute-Value Equations

Solve each equation.

A $|x+3| + 4 = 4$

$$|x+3| + 4 = 4$$
$$-4 \quad -4$$
$$|x+3| = 0$$
Since 4 is added to $|x+3|$, subtract 4 from both sides to undo the addition.

$$x+3 = 0$$
$$-3 \quad -3$$
$$x = -3$$
There is only one case. Since 3 is added to x, subtract 3 from both sides to undo the addition.

B $5 = |x+2| + 8$

$$5 = |x+2| + 8$$
$$-8 \quad -8$$
Since 8 is added to $|x+2|$, subtract 8 from both sides to undo the addition.

$$-3 = |x+2| \ \text{✗}$$ *Absolute value cannot be negative.*

This equation has no solution.

Remember!
Absolute value must be nonnegative because it represents a distance.

CHECK IT OUT! Solve each equation.

2a. $2 - |2x - 5| = 7$ **no solution** **2b.** $-6 + |x - 4| = -6$ **4**

COMMON ERROR ALERT

In **Example 1B,** students may try to distribute 4 over the absolute value bars. Remind students that their first step should be to isolate the absolute-value expression by dividing both sides by the number in front of the absolute-value bars.

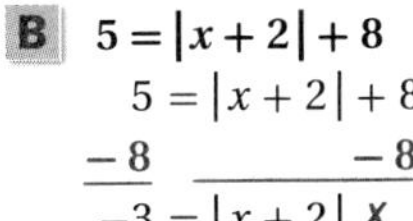

Power Presentations with PowerPoint®

Additional Examples

Example 1

Solve each equation.

A. $|x| = 12$ $-12, 12$

B. $3|x+7| = 24$ $-15, 1$

Example 2

Solve each equation.

A. $-8 = |x+2| - 8$ -2

B. $3 + |x+4| = 0$ no solution

INTERVENTION
Questioning Strategies

EXAMPLE 1

- What does *absolute value* mean?
- How is the absolute-value sign similar to parentheses? How is it different?
- Why must you consider two cases when solving absolute-value equations?

EXAMPLE 2

- How can you tell when an absolute-value equation has one solution?
- How can you tell when an absolute-value equation has no solution?

2 Teach

Guided Instruction

Review with students the concept of absolute value. Remind them that the absolute value of a number represents its distance from 0. Because distance can be in the positive or negative direction, there can be as many as two possible solutions for an absolute-value equation. Because distance is always nonnegative, there is no solution when an absolute-value expression is equal to a negative number.

Reaching All Learners

Through Concrete Manipulatives

To help students focus on first isolating the absolute-value expression, have them place a small object or piece of paper over the absolute-value expression in an equation. Then have them "isolate" the object or piece of paper by using inverse operations. Lastly, have students remove the small object or piece of paper and rewrite the equation with two cases.

Teaching Tip **Auditory** When reading absolute-value expressions aloud, students often confuse expressions of the type $|x+4|$ and $|x| + 4$. Be sure they read the first equation as "the absolute value of the quantity x plus four" and the second equation as "the absolute value of x plus four."

Power Presentations with PowerPoint®

Additional Examples

Example 3

A support beam for a building must be 3.5 meters long. It is acceptable for the beam to differ from the ideal length by 3 millimeters. Write and solve an absolute-value equation to find the minimum and maximum acceptable lengths for the beam.
$|x - 3.5| = 0.003$; 3.497 m; 3.503 m

INTERVENTION

Questioning Strategies

EXAMPLE 3

- What is the relationship between millimeters and meters?
- What must be true about the minimum and maximum lengths when you plot these values on a number line?

Answers to *Think and Discuss*

1. Divide both sides by $\frac{1}{5}$ (or multiply both sides by 5). Then write two cases: $x - 3 = -10$ and $x - 3 = 10$. Solve these equations to get $x = -7$ or $x = 13$.
2. See p. A3.

EXAMPLE 3 *Engineering Application*

Sydney Harbour Bridge in Australia is 1149 meters long. Because of changes in temperature, the bridge can expand or contract by as much as 420 millimeters. Write and solve an absolute-value equation to find the minimum and maximum lengths of the bridge.

First convert millimeters to meters.

420 mm = 0.4 2 0 m *Move the decimal point three places to the left.*

The length of the bridge can vary by 0.42 m, so find two numbers that are 0.42 units away from 1149 on a number line.

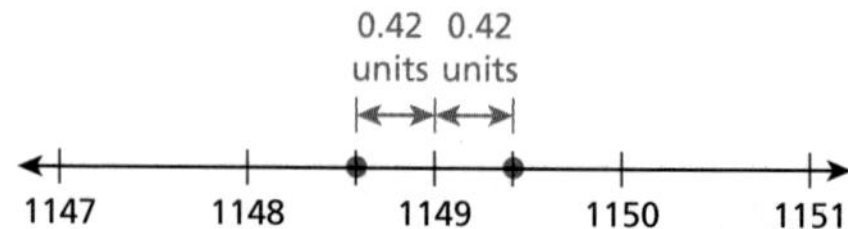

You can find these numbers by using the absolute-value equation $|x - 1149| = 0.42$. Solve the equation by rewriting it as two cases.

Case 1	Case 2	
$x - 1149 = -0.42$	$x - 1149 = 0.42$	*Since 1149 is subtracted from x, add 1149 to both sides of each equation.*
$\underline{+1149 \quad +1149}$	$\underline{+1149 \quad +1149}$	
$x = 1148.58$	$x = 1149.42$	

The minimum length of the bridge is 1148.58 m, and the maximum length is 1149.42 m.

3. $|x - 134| = 0.18$; min. height: 133.82 m; max. height: 134.18 m

3. Sydney Harbour Bridge is 134 meters tall. The height of the bridge can rise or fall by 180 millimeters because of changes in temperature. Write and solve an absolute-value equation to find the minimum and maximum heights of the bridge.

THINK AND DISCUSS

1. Explain the steps you would use to solve the equation $\frac{1}{5}|x - 3| = 2$.

2. **GET ORGANIZED** Copy and complete the graphic organizer. In each box, write an example of an absolute-value equation that has the indicated number of solutions, and then solve.

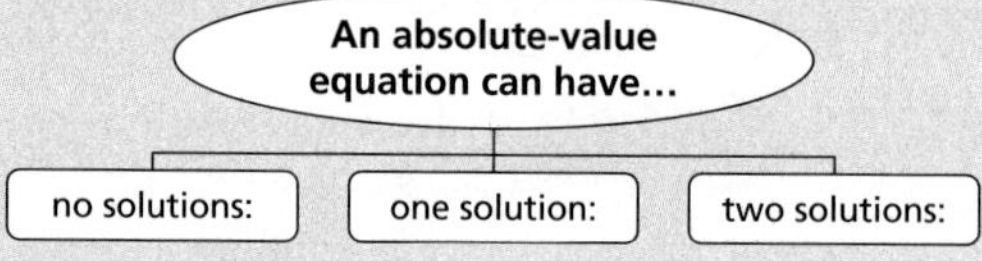

3 Close

Summarize

Ask students to summarize the steps in solving an absolute-value equation.

1. Isolate the absolute-value expression.
2. Rewrite the equation as two cases.
3. Solve for the variable in both cases.
4. Check.

Then ask, "When will there be two solutions? one solution? no solution?" When the expression equals a positive number, equals zero, and equals a negative number, respectively.

ONGOING ASSESSMENT

and INTERVENTION

***Diagnose Before* the Lesson**
2-6 Warm Up, TE p. 112

***Monitor During* the Lesson**
Check It Out! Exercises, SE pp. 113–114
Questioning Strategies, TE pp. 113–114

***Assess After* the Lesson**
2-6 Lesson Quiz, TE p. 117
Alternative Assessment, TE p. 117

2-6 Exercises

go.hrw.com
Homework Help Online
KEYWORD: MA11 2-6
Parent Resources Online
KEYWORD: MA7 Parent

GUIDED PRACTICE

Solve each equation.

SEE EXAMPLE 1 p. 112

1. $|x| = 6$ **−6, 6**
2. $9 = |x + 5|$ **−14, 4**
3. $|3x| + 2 = 8$ **−2, 2**
4. $2|x| = 18$ **−9, 9**
5. $\left|x + \frac{1}{2}\right| = 1$ **$-\frac{3}{2}, \frac{1}{2}$**
6. $|x - 3| - 6 = 2$ **−5, 11**

SEE EXAMPLE 2 p. 113

7. $-8 = |x|$ **no solution**
8. $|x| = 0$ **0**
9. $|x + 4| = -7$ **no solution**
10. $7 = |3x + 9| + 7$ **−3**
11. $|2.8 - x| + 1.5 = 1.5$ **2.8**
12. $5|x + 7| + 14 = 8$ **no solution**

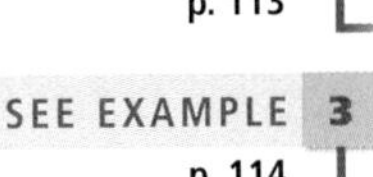
SEE EXAMPLE 3 p. 114

13. **Communication** Barry's walkie-talkie has a range of 2 mi. Barry is traveling on a straight highway and is at mile marker 207. Write and solve an absolute-value equation to find the minimum and maximum mile marker from 207 that Barry's walkie-talkie will reach. **$|x - 207| = 2$; mile markers 205 and 209**

PRACTICE AND PROBLEM SOLVING

Independent Practice	
For Exercises	See Example
14–22	1
23–28	2
29	3

Extra Practice
Skills Practice p. S6
Application Practice p. S29

Solve each equation.

14. $|x| = \frac{1}{5}$ **$-\frac{1}{5}, \frac{1}{5}$**
15. $|2x - 4| = 22$ **−9, 13**
16. $18 = 3|x - 1|$ **−5, 7**
17. $-2|x| = -4$ **−2, 2**
18. $3|x| - 12 = 18$ **−10, 10**
19. $|x - 42.04| = 23.24$ **18.8, 65.28**
20. $\left|\frac{2}{3}x - \frac{2}{3}\right| = \frac{2}{3}$ **0, 2**
21. $|3x + 1| = 13$ **$-\frac{14}{3}$, 4**
22. $|-2x + 3| = 5.8$ **−1.4, 4.4**
23. $|4x| + 9 = 9$ **0**
24. $8 = 7 - |x|$ **no solution**
25. $|x| + 6 = 12 - 6$ **0**
26. $|x - 3| + 14 = 5$ **no solution**
27. $0 = \left|\frac{2}{3} - x\right|$ **$\frac{2}{3}$**
28. $3 + |x - 1| = 3$ **1**

29. **Space Shuttle** The diameter of a valve for the space shuttle must be within 0.001 mm of 5 mm. Write and solve an absolute-value equation to find the boundary values for the acceptable diameters of the valve.

29. $|x - 5| = 0.001$; 4.999 mm; 5.001 mm

30. The two numbers that are 5 units from 3 on the number line are represented by the equation $|n - 3| = 5$. What are these two numbers? Graph the solutions. **8, −2**

31. Write and solve an absolute-value equation that represents two numbers x that are 2 units from 7 on a number line. Graph the solutions.

31. $|x - 7| = 2$; 5, 9

32. **Manufacturing** A quality control inspector at a bolt factory examines random bolts that come off the assembly line. Any bolt whose diameter differs by more than 0.04 mm from 6.5 mm is sent back. Write and solve an absolute-value equation to find the maximum and minimum diameters of an acceptable bolt.

32. $|x - 6.5| = 0.04$; 6.54 mm; 6.46 mm

33. **Construction** A brick company guarantees to fill a contractor's order to within 5% accuracy. A contractor orders 1500 bricks. Write and solve an absolute-value equation to find the maximum and minimum number of bricks guaranteed.

33. $|x - 1500| = 75$; 1575 bricks; 1425 bricks

34. **Multi-Step** A machine prints posters and then trims them to the correct size. The equation $|\ell - 65.1| = 0.2$ gives the maximum and minimum acceptable lengths for the posters in inches. Does a poster with a length of 64.8 inches fall within the acceptable range? Why or why not? **No; the acceptable range is from 64.9 to 65.3.**

2-6 Exercises

Assignment Guide

Assign *Guided Practice* exercises as necessary.

If you finished Examples **1–3**

Basic 14–29, 32, 33, 35–38, 45–49, 53–63
Average 14–29, 32–50, 53–63
Advanced 14–28 even, 29, 32–63

Homework Quick Check
Quickly check key concepts.
Exercises: 16, 24, 28, 29, 32

Answers

30.

31.
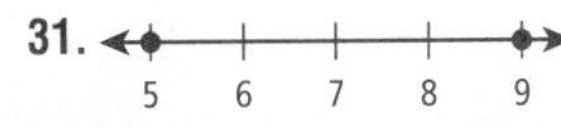

State Resources

go.hrw.com
State Resources Online
KEYWORD: MA7 Resources

MULTI-STEP TEST PREP Exercise 44 involves using absolute-value equations to describe water pressures. This exercise prepares students for the Multi-Step Test Prep on page 118.

Answers

39. When the abs.-value expression is equal to a pos. number, there are 2 solutions. If the abs.-value expression is equal to 0, there is 1 solution, and if the abs.-value expression is equal to a neg. number, there are no solutions.
40. When x is nonneg., the expressions are equal, but when x is neg., the expressions are not equal.
41. Abs. value represents a distance, so it can never be neg.

Write an absolute-value equation whose solutions are graphed on the number line.

35. 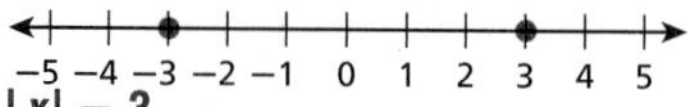 (number line from −5 to 5) $|x| = 3$

36. 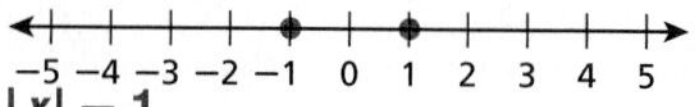 (number line from −5 to 5) $|x| = 1$

37. 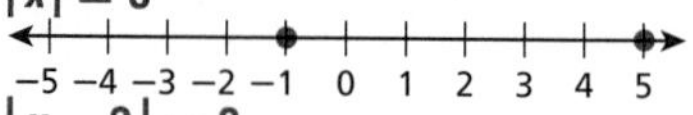 (number line from −5 to 5) $|x - 2| = 3$

38. 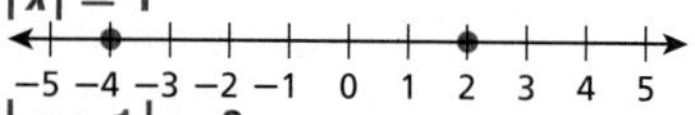 (number line from −5 to 5) $|x + 1| = 3$

Tell whether each statement is sometimes, always, or never true. Explain.

39. An absolute-value equation has two solutions. **sometimes**
40. The value of $|x + 4|$ is equal to the value of $|x| + 4$. **sometimes**
41. The absolute value of a number is nonnegative. **always**
42. **Temperature** A thermostat is set so that the temperature in a laboratory freezer stays within 2.5 °F of 2 °F. Write and solve an absolute-value equation to find the maximum and minimum temperatures in the freezer. $|x - 2| = 2.5$; **−0.5 °F; 4.5 °F**
43. **Recreation** To ensure safety, boaters must be aware of wind conditions while they are on the water. A particular anemometer gives a measurement of wind speed within a certain amount of the true wind speed, as shown in the table.

Measured Wind Speed (mi/h)	True Wind Speed (mi/h)
20	15–25
22	17–27
24	19–29
26	21–31
28	23–33
30	25–35

a. Use the table to write an absolute-value equation for the minimum and maximum possible true wind speeds t for the measured wind speed shown on the anemometer.
b. Solve your equation from part **a.** Check that the solution is correct by comparing it to the values given in the table when the measured wind speed is 24 mi/h.
c. Will your equation work for all of the values in the table? Explain.
d. Explain what your equation says about the instrument's measurements.

43a. $|t - 24| = 5$
b. 19; 29
c. yes, if you change the left side so that the measured wind speed is being subtracted from t
d. The measurements are correct to within 5 mi/h.

MULTI-STEP TEST PREP

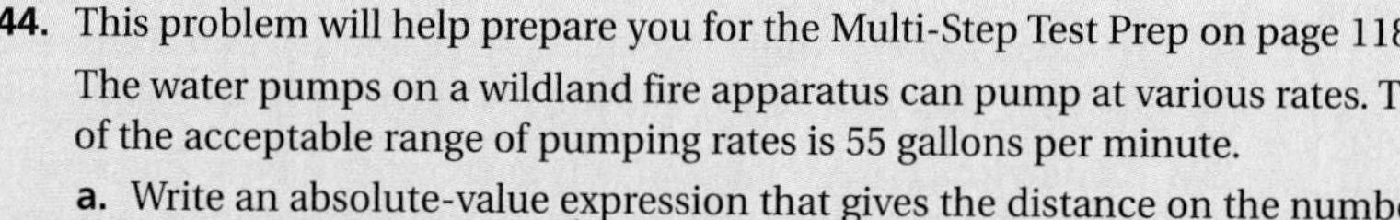

44. This problem will help prepare you for the Multi-Step Test Prep on page 118.
The water pumps on a wildland fire apparatus can pump at various rates. The center of the acceptable range of pumping rates is 55 gallons per minute.
a. Write an absolute-value expression that gives the distance on the number line of a pump's rate r from 55. $|r - 55|$
b. The smallest and largest pumps have rates that differ by 45 gallons per minute from the rate at the center of the range. Write an absolute-value equation for the rates of these pumps. $|r - 55| = 45$
c. Find the least and greatest rates that are acceptable for a wildland fire apparatus. **10 gal/min, 100 gal/min**

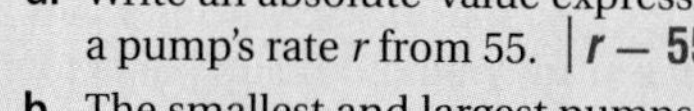

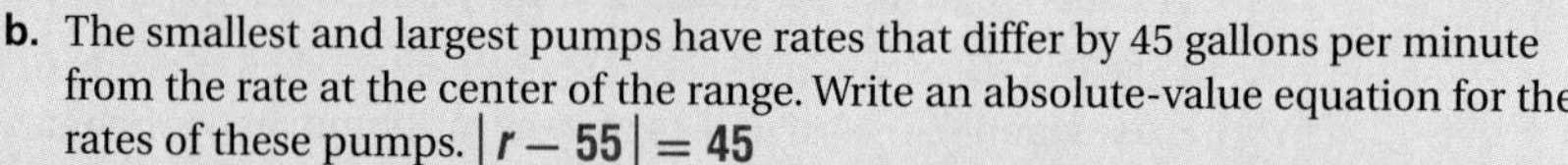

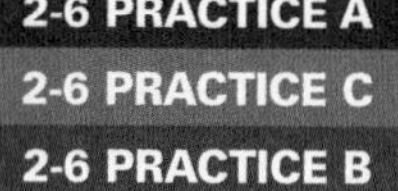

2-6 PRACTICE A
2-6 PRACTICE C
2-6 PRACTICE B

Solve each equation.

1. $|x| = 12$ {−12, 12}
2. $|x| = \frac{1}{2}$ $\left\{-\frac{1}{2}, \frac{1}{2}\right\}$
3. $|x| - 6 = 4$ {−10, 10}
4. $5 + |x| = 14$ {−9, 9}
5. $3|x| = 24$ {−8, 8}
6. $|x + 3| = 10$ {−13, 7}
7. $|x - 1| = 2$ {−1, 3}
8. $4|x - 5| = 12$ {−2, 8}
9. $|x + 2| - 3 = 9$ {−14, 10}
10. $|6x| = 18$ {−3, 3}
11. $|x - 1| = 0$ {1}
12. $|x - 3| + 2 = 2$ {3}
13. How many solutions does the equation $|x + 7| = 1$ have? **two**
14. How many solutions does the equation $|x + 7| = 0$ have? **one**
15. How many solutions does the equation $|x + 7| = -1$ have? **none**

Leticia sets the thermostat in her apartment to 68 degrees. The actual temperature in her apartment can vary from this by as much as 3.5 degrees.

16. Write an absolute-value equation that you can use to find the minimum and maximum temperature. $|x - 68| = 3.5$
17. Solve the equation to find the minimum and maximum temperature. **64.5°; 71.5°**

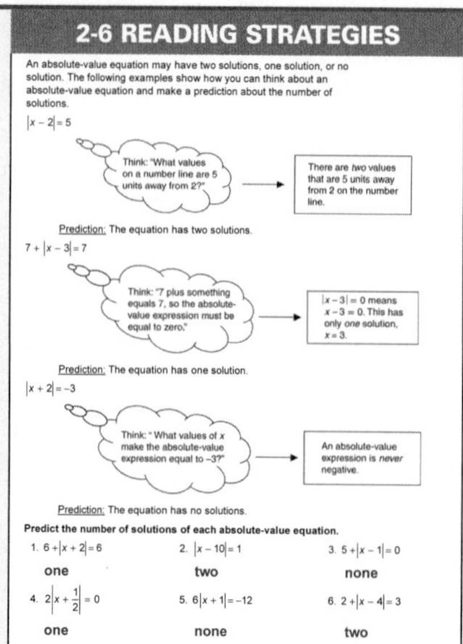

2-6 READING STRATEGIES

An absolute-value equation may have two solutions, one solution, or no solution. The following examples show how you can think about an absolute-value equation and make a prediction about the number of solutions.

$|x - 2| = 5$

Think: "What values on a number line are 5 units away from 2?" → There are *two* values that are 5 units away from 2 on the number line.

Prediction: The equation has two solutions.

$7 + |x - 3| = 7$

Think: "7 plus something equals 7, so the absolute-value expression must be equal to zero." → $|x - 3| = 0$ means $x - 3 = 0$. This has only *one* solution, $x = 3$.

Prediction: The equation has one solution.

$|x + 2| = -3$

Think: "What values of x make the absolute-value expression equal to −3?" → An absolute-value expression is *never* negative.

Prediction: The equation has no solutions.

Predict the number of solutions of each absolute-value equation.

1. $6 + |x + 2| = 6$ **one**
2. $|x - 10| = 1$ **two**
3. $5 + |x - 1| = 0$ **none**
4. $2\left|x + \frac{1}{2}\right| = 0$ **one**
5. $6|x + 1| = -12$ **none**
6. $2 + |x - 4| = 3$ **two**

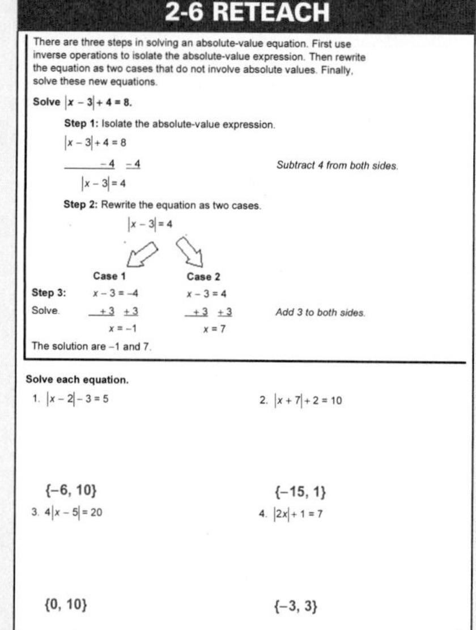

2-6 RETEACH

There are three steps in solving an absolute-value equation. First use inverse operations to isolate the absolute-value expression. Then rewrite the equation as two cases that do not involve absolute values. Finally, solve these new equations.

Solve $|x - 3| + 4 = 8$.

Step 1: Isolate the absolute-value expression.

$|x - 3| + 4 = 8$
$\quad -4 \quad -4$ *Subtract 4 from both sides.*
$|x - 3| = 4$

Step 2: Rewrite the equation as two cases.

$|x - 3| = 4$

Step 3: Solve.

	Case 1	Case 2	
	$x - 3 = -4$	$x - 3 = 4$	
	$+3 \quad +3$	$+3 \quad +3$	*Add 3 to both sides.*
	$x = -1$	$x = 7$	

The solution are −1 and 7.

Solve each equation.

1. $|x - 2| - 3 = 5$ {−6, 10}
2. $|x + 7| + 2 = 10$ {−15, 1}
3. $4|x - 5| = 20$ {0, 10}
4. $|2x| + 1 = 7$ {−3, 3}

45. Possible answer: no; when an absolute-value expression equals 0, there is only one equation to solve. When an absolute-value expression equals a negative number, there is no equation to solve.

46. No; no matter what value of a is chosen, there will always be two solutions: $a + 1$ and $a - 1$.

45. Write About It Do you agree with the following statement: "To solve an absolute-value equation, you need to solve two equations." Why or why not?

46. Critical Thinking Is there a value of a for which the equation $|x - a| = 1$ has exactly one solution? Explain.

TEST PREP

47. Which situation could be modeled by the equation $|x - 65| = 3$?

Ⓐ Two numbers on the number line are 65 units away from 3.

Ⓑ The length of a carpet is 3 inches less than 65 inches.

Ⓒ The maximum and minimum weights of wrestlers on the team are within 3 kg of 65 kg.

Ⓓ The members of an exercise club for seniors are all between 63 and 67 years old.

48. For which of the following is $n = -3$ a solution?

Ⓕ $|n - 1| = 2$ Ⓖ $|n + 2| = -1$ Ⓗ $|n - 2| = 1$ **Ⓙ** $|n + 1| = 2$

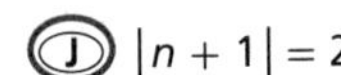

49. The minimum and maximum sound levels at a rock concert are 90 decibels and 95 decibels. Which equation models this situation?

Ⓐ $|x - 90| = 5$ **Ⓑ** $|x - 92.5| = 2.5$ Ⓒ $|x - 92.5| = 5$ Ⓓ $|x - 95| = 2.5$

CHALLENGE AND EXTEND

50. 18 in.; the solutions to the equation are 18 and −46, but since x represents a length, the negative solution is not reasonable.

50. The perimeter of a rectangle is 100 inches. The length of the rectangle is $|2x - 4|$ inches, and the width is x inches. What are the possible values of x? Explain.

51. Fill in the missing reasons to justify each step in solving the equation $3|2x + 1| = 21$.

Statements	Reasons
1. $3\|2x + 1\| = 21$	1. Given
2. $\|2x + 1\| = 7$	2. Div. Prop. of Eq.
3. $2x + 1 = -7$ or $2x + 1 = 7$	3. Definition of absolute value
4. $2x = -8$ or $2x = 6$	4. Subtr. Prop. of Eq.
5. $x = -4$ or $x = 3$	5. Div. Prop. of Eq.

52. Solve $|x| = |x + 1|$. (*Hint:* Consider two cases: $x \geq 0$ and $x < 0$.) $-\frac{1}{2}$

SPIRAL REVIEW

53. Sabrina is building a bookcase for her room. She has a piece of wood that is $4\frac{3}{8}$ ft long and estimates that she wants to use about $\frac{2}{5}$ of it. How much wood does she want to use? *(Lesson 1-3)* $1\frac{3}{4}$ ft

Solve each equation. Check your answer. *(Lesson 2-1)*

54. $5 = p - 4.5$ **9.5** 55. $-2 = y + 6\frac{1}{2}$ $-8\frac{1}{2}$ 56. $-12 + q = 3$ **15** 57. $y - 4.3 = -5.7$ **−1.4**

Solve for the indicated variable. *(Lesson 2-5)*

58. $m + 5n = 7$ for m $m = 7 - 5n$

59. $S = T + R$ for T $T = S - R$

60. $2y + 3x = 1$ for y $y = \frac{1 - 3x}{2}$

61. $\frac{3 + w}{z} = x$ for w $w = xz - 3$

62. $c + d = \frac{5}{e}$ for e $e = \frac{5}{c + d}$

63. $6M - N = S$ for N $N = 6M - S$

COMMON ERROR ALERT

When writing an absolute-value equation of the form $|x - k| = a$, students sometimes confuse the values that should be used for k and a. In **Exercise 42,** students may write $|x - 2.5| = 2$. Explain that the value that represents the variation (in this case, 2.5) should appear alone on one side of the equation, so the correct equation is $|x - 2| = 2.5$.

TEST PREP DOCTOR In **Exercise 48,** choice **G** can be immediately eliminated because an absolute value is never negative. Therefore, the equation in **G** has no solution.

Journal

Have students write a step-by-step guide to solving absolute-value equations. Ask students to solve a sample equation to illustrate the steps.

ALTERNATIVE ASSESSMENT

Have students write and solve absolute-value equations that have two solutions, one solution, and no solution.

Power Presentations with PowerPoint®

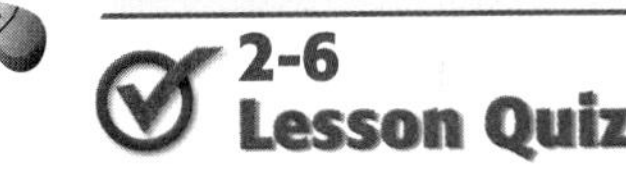

2-6 Lesson Quiz

Solve each equation.

1. $15 = |x|$ −15, 15
2. $2|x - 7| = 14$ 0, 14
3. $|x + 1| - 9 = -9$ −1
4. $|5 + x| - 3 = -2$ −6, −4
5. $7 + |x - 8| = 6$ no solution
6. Inline skates typically have wheels with a diameter of 74 mm. The wheels are manufactured so that the diameters vary from this value by at most 0.1 mm. Write and solve an absolute-value equation to find the minimum and maximum diameters of the wheels. $|x - 74| = 0.1$; 73.9 mm; 74.1 mm

Also available on transparency

2-6 PROBLEM SOLVING

Write the correct answer.

1. A machine manufactures wheels with a diameter of 70 cm. It is acceptable for the diameter of a wheel to be within 0.02 cm of this value. Write and solve an absolute-value equation to find the minimum and maximum acceptable diameters.
   $|x - 70| = 0.02$; 69.98 cm; 70.02 cm

2. A pedestrian bridge is 53 meters long. Due to changes in temperature, the bridge may expand or contract by as much as 21 millimeters. Write and solve an absolute-value equation to find the minimum and maximum lengths of the bridge.
   $|x - 53| = 0.021$; 52.979 m; 53.021 m

3. Two numbers on a number line are represented by the absolute-value equation $|n - 5| = 6$. What are the two numbers?
   −1 and 11

4. A jewelry maker cuts pieces of wire to shape into earrings. The equation $|x - 12.2| = 0.3$ gives the minimum and maximum acceptable lengths of the wires in centimeters. What is the minimum acceptable length of a wire?
   11.9 cm

The table shows the recommended daily intake of several minerals for adult women. Use the table for questions 5–7. Select the best answer.

5. Which absolute-value equation gives the minimum and maximum recommended intakes for zinc?
   A $|x - 8| = 32$ C $|x - 16| = 24$
   B $|x - 24| = 16$ D $|x - 40| = 32$

6. For which mineral are the minimum and maximum recommended intakes given by the absolute-value equation $|x - 31.5| = 13.5$?
   F Fluoride H Zinc
   G Iron J None of these

7. Jason writes an equation for the minimum and maximum intakes of fluoride. He writes it in the form $|x - b| = c$. What is the value of b?
   A 3 **C** 6.5
   B 3.5 D 7

Mineral	Daily Minimum (mg)	Daily Maximum (mg)
Fluoride	3	10
Iron	18	45
Zinc	8	40

Source: http://www.supplementquality.com/news/multi_mineral_chart.html

2-6 CHALLENGE

It is sometimes useful to construct an equation from given solutions. For example, consider the solutions −3 and 7. To write an absolute-value equation with these solutions, first plot the points on a number line.

Find the value that is midway between −3 and 7. One way to do this is to find the mean:

$\frac{-3 + 7}{2} = \frac{4}{2} = 2$

Now find the distance of −3 and 7 from this midpoint. The distance is 5 units.

The required absolute-value equation will be in the form $|x - m| = d$, where m is the midpoint and d is the distance of each solution from the midpoint. Therefore, the absolute-value equation with the solutions −3 and 7 is $|x - 2| = 5$.

1. Show how to check that −3 and 7 are solutions of $|x - 2| = 5$.
   $|(-3) - 2| = |-5| = 5; |7 - 2| = |5| = 5$

2. Are there other absolute-value equations with the same solutions? If so, give an example of such an equation. (*Hint:* Consider performing the same operation on each side of the equation $|x - 2| = 5$.)
   yes; possible answer: $|x - 2| + 1 = 6$

Write an absolute-value equation with the given solutions.

3. 1, 9 $|x - 5| = 4$
4. −4, 8 $|x - 2| = 6$
5. −5, 11 $|x - 3| = 8$
6. −9, −1 $|x + 5| = 4$
7. $-\frac{1}{3}, \frac{1}{3}$ $|x| = \frac{1}{3}$
8. 5, 6 $|x - 5.5| = 0.5$
9. −4.5, 9.5 $|x - 2.5| = 7$
10. $-\frac{1}{2}, \frac{5}{2}$ $|x - 1| = \frac{3}{2}$

Organizer

Objective: Assess students' ability to apply concepts and skills in Lessons 2-1 through 2-6 in a real-world format.

Online Edition

Resources

Algebra I Assessments

www.mathtekstoolkit.org

Problem	Text Reference
1	Previous course
2	Lessons 2-1, 2-2
3	Lessons 2-1, 2-2, 2-3
4	Technology Lab 2-3
5	Previous course

State Resources

Equations and Formulas

All Fired Up A large forest fire in the western United States burns for 14 days, spreading to cover approximately 3850 acres. Firefighters do their best to contain the fire, but hot temperatures and high winds may prompt them to request additional support.

1. The fire spreads at an average rate of how many acres per day? **275 acres**
2. Officials estimate that the fire will spread to cover 9075 acres before it is contained. At this rate, how many more days will it take for the fire to cover an area of 9075 acres? Answer this question using at least two different methods. **19 days**
3. Additional help arrives, and the firefighters contain the fire in 7 more days. In total, how many acres does the fire cover before it is contained? **5775 acres**
4. If the fire had spread to cover an area of 7000 acres, it would have reached Bowman Valley. Explain how the graph shows that firefighters stopped the spread of the fire before it reached Bowman Valley. **The red line does not reach the green horizontal line, which represents 7000.**

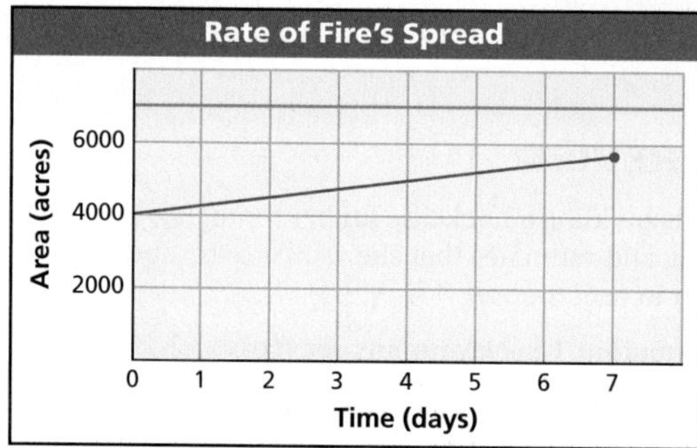

5. The total cost of fighting the fire for 21 days was approximately \$1,440,000. What was the approximate cost per acre of fighting the fire? **about \$250**

INTERVENTION

Scaffolding Questions

1. What words indicate a *rate* of spread? acres per day
2. How many acres have already been burned by the fire? 3850 What is the rate of spread of the fire that you found in **Problem 1**? 275 acres per day
3. How many acres were covered during the first 14 days? 3850 How can you find the total number of acres covered during the 21 days? Add 275(7) to the number of acres already burned, 3850.
4. What does the horizontal axis represent? number of days What does the vertical axis represent? number of acres
5. What information do you need to find the cost per acre? total cost and total number of acres burned

Extension

How many acres of land were saved by bringing in additional firefighters? How much time was saved by bringing in additional firefighters? 3300 acres; 12 days

CHAPTER 2

SECTION 2A

Quiz for Lessons 2-1 Through 2-6

2-1 Solving Equations by Adding or Subtracting

Solve each equation.

1. $x - 32 = -18$ **14**
2. $1.1 = m - 0.9$ **2**
3. $j + 4 = -17$ **−21**
4. $\frac{9}{8} = g + \frac{1}{2}$ $\frac{5}{8}$
5. When she first purchased it, Soledad's computer had 400 GB of hard drive space. After six months, there were only 313 GB available. Write and solve an equation to find the amount of hard drive space that Soledad used in the first six months. **$313 + s = 400$; 87 GB**

2-2 Solving Equations by Multiplying or Dividing

Solve each equation.

6. $\frac{h}{3} = -12$ **−36**
7. $-2.8 = \frac{w}{-3}$ **8.4**
8. $42 = 3c$ **14**
9. $-0.1b = 3.7$ **−37**
10. A fund-raiser raised \$2400, which was $\frac{3}{5}$ of the goal. Write and solve an equation to find the amount of the goal. **$\frac{3}{5}g = 2400$; \$4000**

2-3 Solving Two-Step and Multi-Step Equations

Solve each equation.

11. $2r + 20 = 200$ **90**
12. $\frac{3}{5}k + 5 = 7$ $\frac{10}{3}$
13. $5n + 6 - 3n = -12$ **−9**
14. $4(x - 7) = 2$ **7.5**
15. A taxicab company charges \$2.10 plus \$0.80 per mile. Carmen paid a fare of \$11.70. Write and solve an equation to find the number of miles she traveled. **$2.10 + 0.80m = 11.70$; 12 mi**

2-4 Solving Equations with Variables on Both Sides

Solve each equation.

16. $4x - 3 = 2x + 5$ **4**
17. $3(2x - 5) = 2(3x - 2)$ **no solution**
18. $2(2t - 3) = 6(t + 2)$ **−9**
19. $7(x + 5) = -7(x + 5)$ **−5**
20. On the first day of the year, Diego had \$700 in his savings account and started spending \$35 a week. His brother Juan had \$450 and started saving \$15 a week. After how many weeks will the brothers have the same amount? What will that amount be? **5 weeks; \$525**

2-5 Solving for a Variable

21. $x = \frac{12 - 3y}{2}$, or $6 - \frac{3}{2}y$

21. Solve $2x + 3y = 12$ for x.
22. Solve $\frac{x}{r} = v$ for x. **$x = rv$**
23. Solve $5j + s = t - 2$ for t. **$t = 5j + s + 2$**
24. Solve $h + p = 3(k - 8)$ for k. **$k = \frac{h + p}{3} + 8$**

2-6 Solving Absolute-Value Equations

Solve each equation.

25. $|r| = 7$ **7, −7**
26. $|h + 4| = 11$ **7, −15**
27. $|2x + 4| = 0$ **−2**
28. $16 = 7|p + 3| + 30$ **no solution**

SECTION 2A

Organizer

Objective: Assess students' mastery of concepts and skills in Lessons 2-1 through 2-6.

Resources

 ***Assessment Resources***
Section 2A Quiz

 **Teacher One Stop™**
Test & Practice Generator

INTERVENTION

Resources

 ***Ready to Go On? Intervention and Enrichment*** **Worksheets**

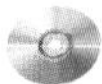 ***Ready to Go On?*** **CD-ROM**

my.hrw.com

READY TO GO ON? Diagnose and Prescribe

NO INTERVENE

Ready to Go On? Intervention	*Ready to Go On? Intervention, Section 2A* Worksheets	CD-ROM	Online
Lesson 2-1	2-1 Intervention	Activity 2-1	Diagnose and Prescribe Online
Lesson 2-2	2-2 Intervention	Activity 2-2	
Lesson 2-3	2-3 Intervention	Activity 2-3	
Lesson 2-4	2-4 Intervention	Activity 2-4	
Lesson 2-5	2-5 Intervention	Activity 2-5	
Lesson 2-6	2-6 Intervention	Activity 2-6	

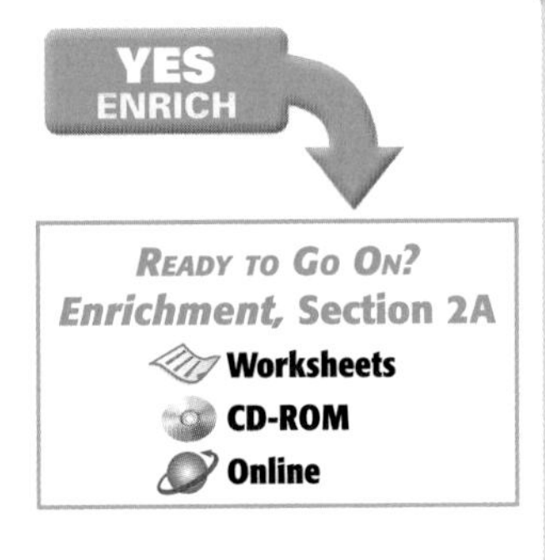

SECTION

2B Proportion and Percent

One-Minute Section Planner

Lesson	Lab Resources	Materials
Lesson 2-7 Rates, Ratios, and Proportions • Write and use ratios, rates, and unit rates. • Write and solve proportions. ☑ SAT-10 ☑ NAEP ☑ ACT ☑ SAT ☑ SAT Subject Tests	***Algebra Lab Activities*** 2-7 Algebra Lab	**Optional** rulers (MK), USA or state map
Lesson 2-8 Applications of Proportions • Use proportions to solve problems involving geometric figures. • Use proportions and similar figures to measure objects indirectly. ☑ SAT-10 ☑ NAEP ☑ ACT ☑ SAT ☑ SAT Subject Tests	***Algebra Lab Activities*** 2-8 Algebra Lab	**Optional** colored pencils (MK), graph paper
Lesson 2-9 Percents • Solve problems involving percents. ☑ SAT-10 ☑ NAEP ☑ ACT ☑ SAT ☑ SAT Subject Tests		**Optional** newspapers, graph paper
Lesson 2-10 Applications of Percents • Use common applications of percents. • Estimate with percents. ☑ SAT-10 ☑ NAEP ☑ ACT ☑ SAT ☑ SAT Subject Tests	***Technology Lab Activities*** 2-10 Technology Lab	**Optional** restaurant menus, graphing calculator
Lesson 2-11 Percent Increase and Decrease • Find percent increase and decrease. ☑ SAT-10 ☑ NAEP ☑ ACT ☑ SAT ☑ SAT Subject Tests		
2-11 Algebra Lab Explore Changes in Population • Use tables and graphs to describe changes in populations. ☐ SAT-10 ☑ NAEP ☐ ACT ☑ SAT ☑ SAT Subject Tests	***Algebra Lab Activities*** 2-11 Lab Recording Sheet	**Required** graph paper

Note: If NAEP is checked, the content is tested on either the Grade 8 or the Grade 12 NAEP assessment.

MK = *Manipulatives Kit*

PROPORTIONS

Lessons 2-7 to 2-8

A *proportion* is an equation that states that two ratios are equivalent. The method for solving a proportion, such as $\frac{x}{3} = \frac{5}{8}$, is the same as the method for solving any equation; it requires that the equation be transformed into simpler equivalent equations via a series of mathematically justifiable steps. For example, a possible first step in solving $\frac{x}{3} = \frac{5}{8}$ is to multiply both sides by $3 \cdot 8$, or 24. This step is justified by the Multiplication Property of Equality. The resulting equation, $8x = 15$, can be solved by dividing both sides by 8 (Division Property of Equality).

Performing the above multiplication step on a general proportion leads to the Cross Products Property: If $\frac{a}{b} = \frac{c}{d}$, where $b \neq 0$ and $d \neq 0$, then $ad = bc$. To see why this is true, multiply both sides of the proportion by bd.

$\frac{a}{b} = \frac{c}{d}$	
$(bd)\frac{a}{b} = (bd)\frac{c}{d}$	*Multiplication Prop. of Eq.*
$\frac{bda}{b} = \frac{bdc}{d}$	*Multiply.*
$da = bc$	*Simplify.*
$ad = bc$	*Commutative Prop. of Mult.*

Students often use the Cross Products Property without understanding its underlying mathematics; it is simply a "trick." Understanding the mathematical reasons *why* they may use this property is important for students. More generally, students should realize that there are no tricks in mathematics; every step or operation can be justified with a property, definition, etc.

PROPORTIONAL RELATIONSHIPS, UNIT RATES, AND SLOPE

Lesson 2-7

The concept of slope, which will be introduced in Chapter 5, is one of the central ideas in an Algebra 1 course. For students to become fluent in working with slope, they should be able to approach the concept from multiple points of view. Proportions and proportional relationships offer one illuminating entry point.

One way to define a *proportional relationship* is as a relationship that can be expressed as $y = mx$ for a nonzero constant m. A set of ordered pairs (x, y) forms a proportional relationship if $\frac{y}{x}$ is constant for every ordered pair. Students have seen such relationships in a variety of real-world settings. For example, if raisins cost \$1.50 per pound, then $y = 1.5x$ gives the total cost y of x pounds of raisins. The table shows some ordered pairs that satisfy this relationship.

Pounds, *x*	1	2	3	4
Cost (\$), *y*	1.5	3	4.5	6

Notice that $\frac{1.5}{1} = \frac{3}{2} = \frac{4.5}{3} = \frac{6}{4}$. For every ordered pair in the table, $\frac{y}{x} = 1.5$. This is because the *unit rate* for this situation is \$1.50/lb.

The graph of a proportional relationship is a straight line through the origin.

Cost of Raisins

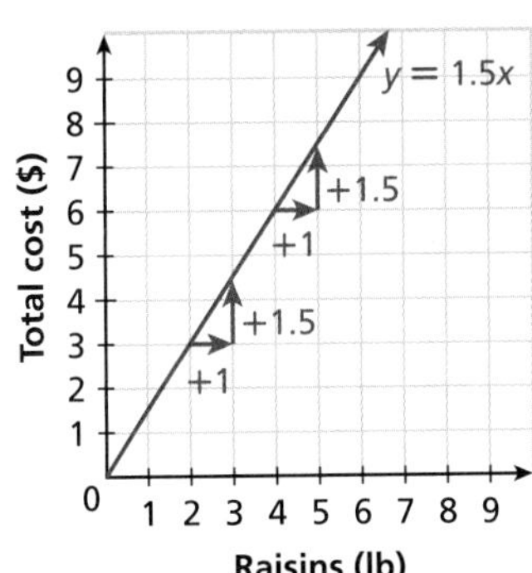

Notice that the slope of the line is 1.5. This means that an increase of one pound causes the total cost to increase by \$1.50.

In Chapter 5, students will see several different but equivalent ways of looking at slope: rise over run, change in y divided by change in x, and rate of change. For proportional relationships, slope can also be viewed as a unit rate. In the example, the unit rate is \$1.50/lb, and the slope of the related linear function, $y = 1.5x$, is 1.5. In Chapter 5, students will learn that these types of functions are called *direct variations.*

2-7 Organizer

Pacing: Traditional 1 day
Block $\frac{1}{2}$ day

Objectives: Write and use ratios, rates, and unit rates.

Write and solve proportions.

Algebra Lab
In *Algebra Lab Activities*

Online Edition
Tutorial Videos

Countdown Week 4

Power Presentations with PowerPoint®

Warm Up

Solve each equation. Check your answer.

1. $6x = 36$ 6
2. $\frac{x}{4} = 12$ 48
3. $5m = 18$ 3.6
4. $\frac{r}{21} = -3$ −63
5. $8y = 18.4$ 2.3

Multiply.

6. $8\left(\frac{7}{8}\right)$ 7
7. $12\left(\frac{5}{6}\right)$ 10

Also available on transparency

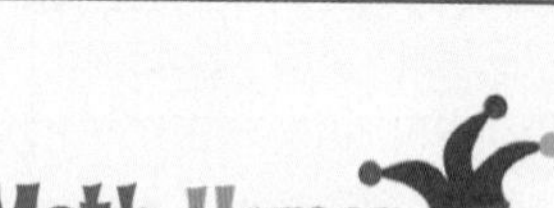

Math Humor

Q: What did the circle see when sailing on the ocean?

A: Pi rates.

2-7 Rates, Ratios, and Proportions

Objectives
Write and use ratios, rates, and unit rates.

Write and solve proportions.

Vocabulary

ratio	proportion
rate	cross products
scale	scale drawing
unit rate	scale model
conversion factor	dimensional analysis

Why learn this?
Ratios and proportions are used to draw accurate maps. (See Example 5.)

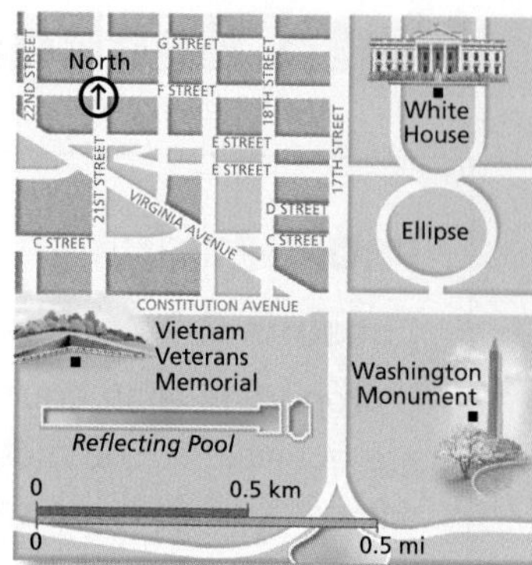

A **ratio** is a comparison of two quantities by division. The ratio of a to b can be written $a{:}b$ or $\frac{a}{b}$, where $b \neq 0$. Ratios that name the same comparison are said to be *equivalent.*

A statement that two ratios are equivalent, such as $\frac{1}{12} = \frac{2}{24}$, is called a **proportion**.

EXAMPLE 1 Using Ratios

The ratio of faculty members to students at a college is 1:15. There are 675 students. How many faculty members are there?

$\frac{\text{faculty}}{\text{students}} \to \frac{1}{15}$ *Write a ratio comparing faculty to students.*

$\frac{1}{15} = \frac{x}{675}$ *Write a proportion. Let x be the number of faculty members.*

$675\left(\frac{x}{675}\right) = 675\left(\frac{1}{15}\right)$ *Since x is divided by 675, multiply both sides of the equation by 675.*

$x = 45$

There are 45 faculty members.

Reading Math

Read the proportion $\frac{1}{15} = \frac{x}{675}$ as "1 is to 15 as x is to 675."

CHECK IT OUT! 1. The ratio of games won to games lost for a baseball team is 3:2. The team won 18 games. How many games did the team lose? **12**

A **rate** is a ratio of two quantities with different units, such as $\frac{34 \text{ mi}}{2 \text{ gal}}$. Rates are usually written as *unit rates.* A **unit rate** is a rate with a second quantity of 1 unit, such as $\frac{17 \text{ mi}}{1 \text{ gal}}$, or 17 mi/gal. You can convert any rate to a unit rate.

EXAMPLE 2 Finding Unit Rates

Takeru Kobayashi of Japan ate 53.5 hot dogs in 12 minutes to win a contest. Find the unit rate in hot dogs per minute. Round to the nearest hundredth.

$\frac{53.5}{12} = \frac{x}{1}$ *Write a proportion to find an equivalent ratio with a second quantity of 1.*

$4.46 \approx x$ *Divide on the left side to find x.*

The unit rate is approximately 4.46 hot dogs per minute.

CHECK IT OUT! 2. Cory earns \$52.50 in 7 hours. Find the unit rate in dollars per hour. **\$7.50/h**

State Resources

1 Introduce

EXPLORATION

2-7 Rates, Ratios, and Proportions

You can use fractions to compare quantities. For example, the number of stars compared to the number of squares is $\frac{4}{8}$, or $\frac{1}{2}$.

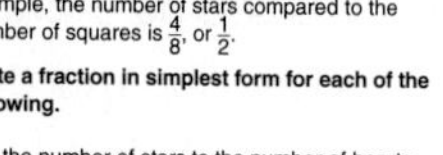

Write a fraction in simplest form for each of the following.

1. the number of stars to the number of hearts

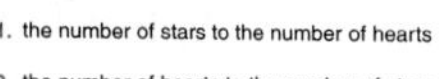

2. the number of hearts to the number of stars

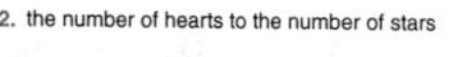

3. the number of squares to the number of hearts
4. the number of hearts to the number of squares

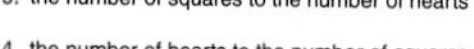

5. the number of hearts to the total number of figures
6. the total number of figures to the number of hearts

THINK AND DISCUSS

7. **Describe** how the fractions in Problems 1 and 2 are related to each other.
8. **Explain** what it means when a fraction comparing the number of boys in a class to the number of girls in the class is greater than 1.

Motivate

Show students the following table of cell phone costs for two different plans.

Plan	Minutes	Cost \$
A	800	50
B	600	40

See if students can find the cost per minute for each plan. A: 6.25 cents; B: 6.67 cents Explain that these are *unit rates*, because they are the cost for *one unit* (one minute). Unit rates allow you to compare items of different sizes.

Explorations and answers are provided in *Alternate Openers: Explorations Transparencies.*

Dimensional analysis is a process that uses rates to convert measurements from one unit to another. A rate such as $\frac{12 \text{ in.}}{1 \text{ ft}}$, in which the two quantities are equal but use different units, is called a **conversion factor**. To convert from one set of units to another, multiply by a conversion factor.

EXAMPLE 3 Using Dimensional Analysis

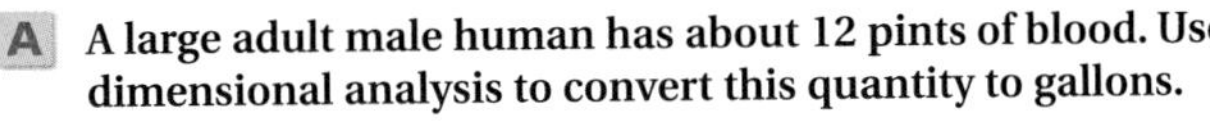

A **A large adult male human has about 12 pints of blood. Use dimensional analysis to convert this quantity to gallons.**

Helpful Hint

In Example 3A Step 1, "pt" appears to divide out, leaving "qt," as the unit. Use this strategy of "dividing out" units when using dimensional analysis.

Step 1 Convert pints to quarts.

$12 \text{ pt} \cdot \frac{1 \text{ qt}}{2 \text{ pt}}$ *Multiply by a conversion factor whose first quantity is quarts and whose second quantity is pints.*

6 qt

12 pints is 6 quarts.

Step 2 Convert quarts to gallons.

$6 \text{ qt} \cdot \frac{1 \text{ gal}}{4 \text{ qt}}$ *Multiply by a conversion factor whose first quantity is gallons and whose second quantity is quarts.*

$\frac{6}{4} \text{ gal} = 1\frac{1}{2} \text{ gal}$

A large adult male human has about $1\frac{1}{2}$ gallons of blood.

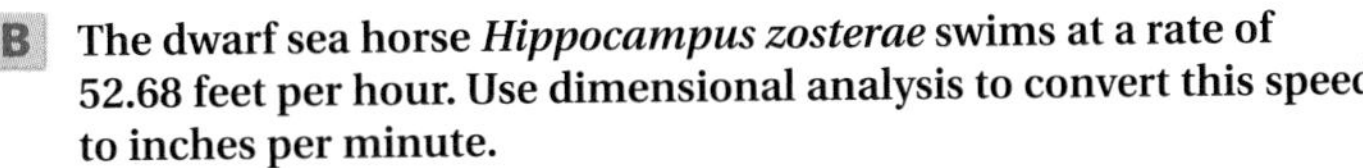

B **The dwarf sea horse *Hippocampus zosterae* swims at a rate of 52.68 feet per hour. Use dimensional analysis to convert this speed to inches per minute.**

Use the conversion factor $\frac{12 \text{ in.}}{1 \text{ ft}}$ to convert feet to inches, and use the conversion factor $\frac{1 \text{ h}}{60 \text{ min}}$ to convert hours to minutes.

$$\frac{52.68 \text{ ft}}{1 \text{ h}} \cdot \frac{12 \text{ in.}}{1 \text{ ft}} \cdot \frac{1 \text{ h}}{60 \text{ min}} = \frac{10.536 \text{ in.}}{1 \text{ min}}$$

The speed is 10.536 inches per minute.

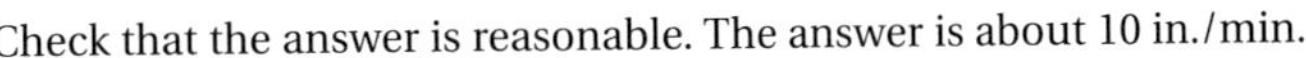

Check that the answer is reasonable. The answer is about 10 in./min.

- There are 60 min in 1 h, so 10 in./min is $60(10) = 600$ in./h.
- There are 12 in. in 1 ft, so 600 in./h is $\frac{600}{12} = 50$ ft/h. This is close to the rate given in the problem, 52.68 ft/h.

Hippocampus zosterae

CHECK IT OUT! 3. A cyclist travels 56 miles in 4 hours. Use dimensional analysis to convert the cyclist's speed to feet per second. Round your answer to the nearest tenth, and show that your answer is reasonable. **20.5 ft/s**

In the proportion $\frac{a}{b} = \frac{c}{d}$, the products $a \cdot d$ and $b \cdot c$ are called **cross products**. You can solve a proportion for a missing value by using the Cross Products Property.

Know it! Note

Cross Products Property

WORDS	NUMBERS	ALGEBRA
In a proportion, cross products are equal.	$\frac{2}{3} \times \frac{4}{6}$ $2 \cdot 6 = 3 \cdot 4$	If $\frac{a}{b} \times \frac{c}{d}$ and $b \neq 0$ and $d \neq 0$, then $ad = bc$.

2 Teach

Guided Instruction

Before teaching ratios and rates, review how to solve one-step equations with multiplication and division. When solving proportions, remind students to use the Distributive Property when a numerator or denominator has more than one term.

Reaching All Learners

Through Modeling

Have students work in groups of two or three. Assign each group a ruler (MK) and a task of finding certain measurements (include dimensions for the room, desks, tables, shelves, doors, and so on). Collect and present all measurements. Have students determine a scale that would let them draw a diagram of their classroom on a sheet of paper. Then have them use that scale to draw the diagram.

COMMON ERROR ALERT

When converting rates, students may write the conversion factor upside down. Stress to students that the unwanted units must "divide out."

Power Presentations with PowerPoint®

Additional Examples

Example 1

The ratio of the number of bones in the human skull to the number of bones in the ears is 11:3. There are 22 bones in the skull. How many bones are in the ears? 6

Example 2

Ralf Laue of Germany flipped a pancake 416 times in 120 seconds to set the world record. Find the unit rate in flips per second. Round to the nearest hundredth. about 3.47 flips/s

Example 3

A. A fast sprinter can run 100 yards in approximately 10 seconds. Use dimensional analysis to convert 100 yards to miles. Round to the nearest hundredth. (*Hint:* There are 1760 yards in a mile.) 0.06 mi

B. A cheetah can run at a rate of 60 miles per hour in short bursts. What is this speed in feet per minute? 5280 ft/min

INTERVENTION

Questioning Strategies

EXAMPLE 1

- How do you know if the number of students should be written as the first or second quantity in the ratio?
- What does the ratio 1:15 mean?

EXAMPLE 2

- In the ratio $\frac{53.5}{12}$, what does 53.5 represent? What does 12 represent?
- When you solve this proportion, what are you solving for?

EXAMPLE 3

- What is a conversion factor?
- How do you find a conversion factor?

Answer to *Check It Out!*

3. For explanation, see p. A14.

Power Presentations with PowerPoint®

Additional Examples

Example 4

Solve each proportion.

A. $\frac{3}{9} = \frac{5}{m}$ 15

B. $\frac{6}{y-3} = \frac{2}{7}$ 24

Example 5

A contractor has a blueprint for a house drawn to the scale 1 in:3 ft.

A. A wall on the blueprint is 6.5 inches long. How long is the actual wall? 19.5 ft

B. One wall of the house will be 12 feet long when it is built. How long is the wall on the blueprint? 4 in.

INTERVENTION

Questioning Strategies

EXAMPLE 4

- How could you solve these equations by multiplying both sides by the same number?

EXAMPLE 5

- If the scale is represented by a ratio less than 1, what do we know about the actual object?
- If the scale is represented by a ratio greater than 1, what do we know about the actual object?

Teaching Tip **Math Background** Students may be curious why the cross-products property works. If you rewrite the ratios with bd as the denominator, then ad and bc will be the equal numerators. For example, $\frac{2}{3} = \frac{4}{6} = \frac{12}{18}$. Here, $\frac{a}{b} = \frac{2}{3}$, $\frac{c}{d} = \frac{4}{6}$, $bd = 18$, and $ad = bc = 12$.

EXAMPLE 4 Solving Proportions

Solve each proportion.

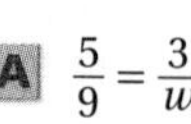

A $\frac{5}{9} = \frac{3}{w}$

$\frac{5}{9} \times \frac{3}{w}$

$5(w) = 9(3)$ *Use cross products.*

$5w = 27$

$\frac{5w}{5} = \frac{27}{5}$ *Divide both sides by 5.*

$w = \frac{27}{5}$

B $\frac{8}{x+10} = \frac{1}{12}$

$\frac{8}{x+10} \times \frac{1}{12}$

$8(12) = 1(x+10)$ *Use cross products.*

$96 = x + 10$

$-10 \quad -10$ *Subtract 10 from both sides.*

$86 = x$

CHECK IT OUT! Solve each proportion.

4a. $\frac{-5}{2} = \frac{y}{8}$ **−20**

4b. $\frac{g+3}{5} = \frac{7}{4}$ **5.75**

A **scale** is a ratio between two sets of measurements, such as 1 in:5 mi. A **scale drawing** or **scale model** uses a scale to represent an object as smaller or larger than the actual object. A map is an example of a scale drawing.

EXAMPLE 5 Scale Drawings and Scale Models

A **On the map, the distance from Chicago to Evanston is 0.625 in. What is the actual distance?**

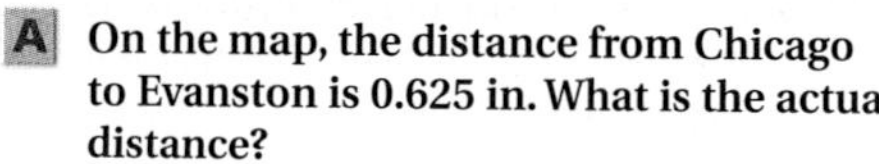

$\frac{\text{map}}{\text{actual}} \rightarrow \frac{1 \text{ in.}}{18 \text{ mi}}$ *Write the scale as a fraction.*

$\frac{1}{18} \times \frac{0.625}{x}$ *Let x be the actual distance.*

$x \cdot 1 = 18(0.625)$ *Use cross products to solve.*

$x = 11.25$

The actual distance is 11.25 mi.

Waukegan

North Chicago

Highland Park

Evanston

1 in:18 mi

Chicago

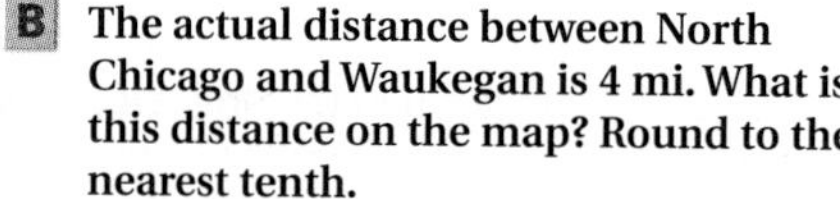

B **The actual distance between North Chicago and Waukegan is 4 mi. What is this distance on the map? Round to the nearest tenth.**

$\frac{\text{map}}{\text{actual}} \rightarrow \frac{1 \text{ in.}}{18 \text{ mi}}$ *Write the scale as a fraction.*

$\frac{1}{18} \times \frac{x}{4}$ *Let x be the distance on the map.*

$4 = 18x$ *Use cross products to solve the proportion.*

$\frac{4}{18} = \frac{18x}{18}$ *Since x is multiplied by 18, divide both sides by 18 to undo the multiplication.*

$0.2 \approx x$ *Round to the nearest tenth.*

The distance on the map is about 0.2 in.

Reading Math

A scale written without units, such as 32:1, means that 32 units of any measure correspond to 1 unit of that same measure.

CHECK IT OUT! **5.** A scale model of a human heart is 16 ft long. The scale is 32:1. How many inches long is the actual heart it represents? **6 in.**

3 Close

Summarize

Review with students how to find unit rates and solve proportions. Caution students to be careful when writing proportions to represent applications. The variable that is the first quantity of one ratio must also be the first quantity of the other. The variable that is the second quantity of one ratio must also be the second quantity of the other.

ONGOING ASSESSMENT and INTERVENTION

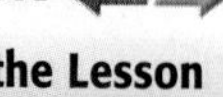

***Diagnose Before* the Lesson**
2-7 Warm Up, TE p. 120

***Monitor During* the Lesson**
Check It Out! Exercises, SE pp. 120–122
Questioning Strategies, TE pp. 121–122

***Assess After* the Lesson**
2-7 Lesson Quiz, TE p. 126
Alternative Assessment, TE p. 126

THINK AND DISCUSS

1. Explain two ways to solve the proportion $\frac{t}{4} = \frac{3}{5}$.
2. How could you show that the answer to Example 5A is reasonable?

3. **GET ORGANIZED** Copy and complete the graphic organizer. In each box, write an example of each use of ratios.

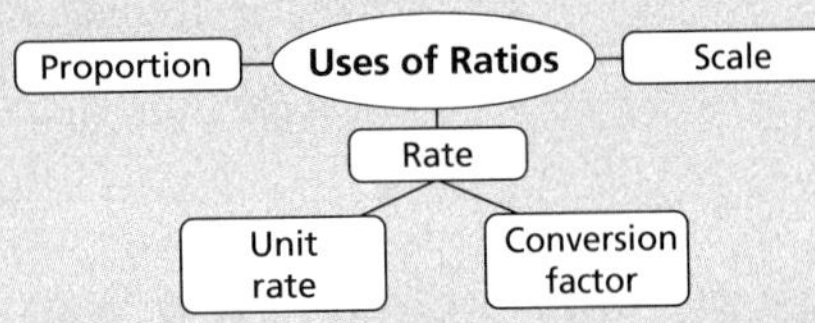

Answers to *Think and Discuss*

1. Possible answer: by using cross-products; by multiplying both sides by 4 to isolate t
2. Possible answer: One in. on the map represents 18 mi. So 0.625 in. will represent a little more than half of 18 mi. So 11.25 mi is reasonable.
3. See p. A3.

2-7 Exercises

go.hrw.com
Homework Help Online
KEYWORD: MA11 2-7
Parent Resources Online
KEYWORD: MA7 Parent

GUIDED PRACTICE

1. **Vocabulary** What does it mean when two ratios form a *proportion*? **The ratios are equivalent.**

SEE EXAMPLE 1 p. 120

2. The ratio of the sale price of a jacket to the original price is 3:4. The original price is \$64. What is the sale price? **\$48**
3. **Chemistry** The ratio of hydrogen atoms to oxygen atoms in water is 2:1. If an amount of water contains 341 trillion atoms of oxygen, how many hydrogen atoms are there? **682 trillion**

SEE EXAMPLE 2 p. 120

4. A computer's fan rotates 2000 times in 40 seconds. Find the unit rate in rotations per second. **50 rotations/s**
5. Twelve cows produce 224,988 pounds of milk. Find the unit rate in pounds per cow. **18,749 lb/cow**
6. A yellow jacket can fly 4.5 meters in 9 seconds. Find the unit rate in meters per second. **0.5 m/s**

SEE EXAMPLE 3 p. 121

7. Lydia wrote $4\frac{1}{2}$ pages of her science report in one hour. What was her writing rate in pages per minute? **0.075 page/min**
8. A model airplane flies 18 feet in 2 seconds. What is the airplane's speed in miles per hour? Round your answer to the nearest hundredth. **6.14 mi/h**
9. A vehicle uses 1 tablespoon of gasoline to drive 125 yards. How many miles can the vehicle travel per gallon? Round your answer to the nearest mile. (*Hint:* There are 256 tablespoons in a gallon.) **18 mi/gal**

SEE EXAMPLE 4 p. 122

Solve each proportion.

10. $\frac{3}{z} = \frac{1}{8}$ **24**
11. $\frac{x}{3} = \frac{1}{5}$ $\mathbf{\frac{3}{5}}$
12. $\frac{b}{4} = \frac{3}{2}$ **6**
13. $\frac{f+3}{12} = \frac{7}{2}$ **39**
14. $\frac{-1}{5} = \frac{3}{2d}$ **−7.5**
15. $\frac{3}{14} = \frac{s-2}{21}$ **6.5**
16. $\frac{-4}{9} = \frac{7}{x}$ **−15.75**
17. $\frac{3}{s-2} = \frac{1}{7}$ **23**
18. $\frac{10}{h} = \frac{52}{13}$ **2.5**

2-7 Exercises

Assignment Guide

Assign *Guided Practice* exercises as necessary.

If you finished Examples **1–3**
Basic 20–25
Average 20–25, 63
Advanced 20–25, 63

If you finished Examples **1–5**
Basic 20–41, 44–62, 66–78
Average 20–38, 40–50, 57–63, 66–78
Advanced 20–38, 46–78

Homework Quick Check
Quickly check key concepts.
Exercises: 20, 22, 24, 32, 38, 40

State Resources

go.hrw.com
State Resources Online
KEYWORD: MA7 Resources

Answers

24. Possible answer: 11.9 ft in 3 days is roughly equivalent to 12 ft in 72 h, or $\frac{12}{72} = \frac{1}{6}$ ft/h. There are 12 in. in 1 ft, so this speed is equivalent to $\frac{12}{6} = 2$ in./h. So 1.98 is reasonable.

39. Possible answer: 70 euro will be worth more than \$60, so \$84 is reasonable.

SEE EXAMPLE 5
p. 122

19. **Archaeology** Stonehenge II in Hunt, Texas, is a scale model of the ancient construction in Wiltshire, England. The scale of the model to the original is 3:5. The Altar Stone of the original construction is 4.9 meters tall. Write and solve a proportion to find the height of the model of the Altar Stone. $\frac{3}{5} = \frac{h}{4.9}$; **2.94 m**

Alfred Sheppard, one of the builders of Stonehenge II.

PRACTICE AND PROBLEM SOLVING

Independent Practice

For Exercises	See Example
20–21	1
22–23	2
24–25	3
26–37	4
38	5

Extra Practice
Skills Practice p. S7
Application Practice p. S29

20. **Gardening** The ratio of the height of a bonsai ficus tree to the height of a full-size ficus tree is 1:9. The bonsai ficus is 6 inches tall. What is the height of a full-size ficus? **54 in.**

21. **Manufacturing** At one factory, the ratio of defective light bulbs produced to total light bulbs produced is about 3:500. How many light bulbs are expected to be defective when 12,000 are produced? **72**

22. Four gallons of gasoline weigh 25 pounds. Find the unit rate in pounds per gallon. **6.25 lb/gal**

23. Fifteen ounces of gold cost \$6058.50. Find the unit rate in dollars per ounce. **\$403.90/oz**

24. **Biology** The tropical giant bamboo can grow 11.9 feet in 3 days. What is this rate of growth in inches per hour? Round your answer to the nearest hundredth, and show that your answer is reasonable. **1.98 in./h**

25. **Transportation** The maximum speed of the Tupolev Tu-144 airliner is 694 m/s. What is this speed in kilometers per hour? **2498.4 km/h**

Solve each proportion.

26. $\frac{v}{6} = \frac{1}{2}$ **3**
27. $\frac{2}{5} = \frac{4}{y}$ **10**
28. $\frac{2}{h} = \frac{-5}{6}$ **−2.4**
29. $\frac{3}{10} = \frac{b+7}{20}$ **−1**
30. $\frac{5t}{9} = \frac{1}{2}$ **0.9**
31. $\frac{2}{3} = \frac{6}{q-4}$ **13**
32. $\frac{x}{8} = \frac{7.5}{20}$ **3**
33. $\frac{3}{k} = \frac{45}{18}$ **1.2**
34. $\frac{6}{a} = \frac{15}{17}$ **6.8**
35. $\frac{9}{2} = \frac{5}{x+1}$ $\mathbf{\frac{1}{9}}$
36. $\frac{3}{5} = \frac{x}{100}$ **60**
37. $\frac{38}{19} = \frac{n-5}{20}$ **45**

38. **Science** The image shows a dust mite as seen under a microscope. The scale of the drawing to the dust mite is 100:1. Use a ruler to measure the length of the dust mite in the image in millimeters. What is the actual length of the dust mite? **0.3 mm**

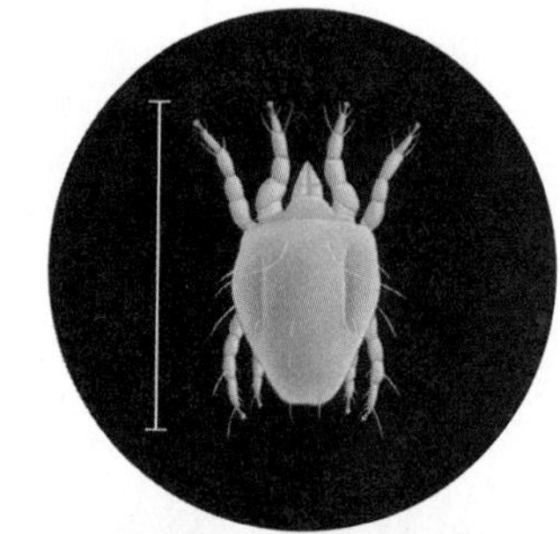

39. **Finance** On a certain day, the exchange rate was 60 U.S. dollars for 50 euro. How many U.S. dollars were 70 euro worth that day? Show that your answer is reasonable. **\$84**

40. **Environmental Science** An environmental scientist wants to estimate the number of carp in a pond. He captures 100 carp, tags all of them, and releases them. A week later, he captures 85 carp and records how many have tags. His results are shown in the table. Write and solve a proportion to estimate the number of carp in the pond.

Status	Number Captured
Tagged	20
Not tagged	65

40. $\frac{20}{85} = \frac{100}{c}$; 425 carp

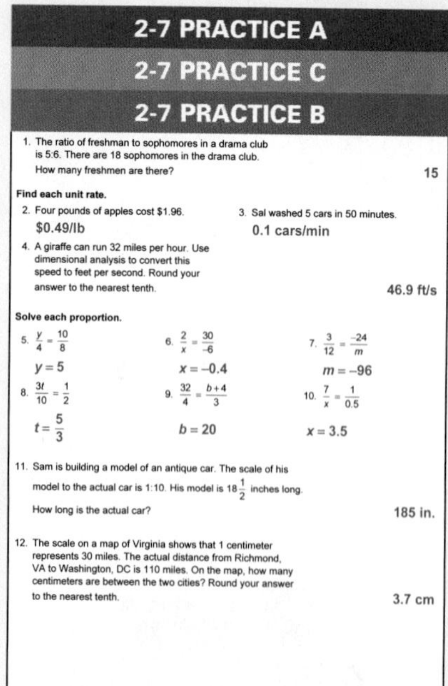

2-7 PRACTICE A
2-7 PRACTICE C
2-7 PRACTICE B

1. The ratio of freshman to sophomores in a drama club is 5:6. There are 18 sophomores in the drama club. How many freshmen are there? **15**

Find each unit rate.

2. Four pounds of apples cost \$1.96. **\$0.49/lb**
3. Sal washed 5 cars in 50 minutes. **0.1 cars/min**
4. A giraffe can run 32 miles per hour. Use dimensional analysis to convert this speed to feet per second. Round your answer to the nearest tenth. **46.9 ft/s**

Solve each proportion.

5. $\frac{y}{4} = \frac{10}{8}$ $y = 5$
6. $\frac{2}{x} = \frac{30}{-6}$ $x = -0.4$
7. $\frac{3}{12} = \frac{-24}{m}$ $m = -96$
8. $\frac{3t}{10} = \frac{1}{2}$ $t = \frac{5}{3}$
9. $\frac{32}{4} = \frac{b+4}{3}$ $b = 20$
10. $\frac{7}{x} = \frac{1}{0.5}$ $x = 3.5$

11. Sam is building a model of an antique car. The scale of his model to the actual car is 1:10. His model is $18\frac{1}{2}$ inches long. How long is the actual car? **185 in.**

12. The scale on a map of Virginia shows that 1 centimeter represents 30 miles. The actual distance from Richmond, VA to Washington, DC is 110 miles. On the map, how many centimeters are between the two cities? Round your answer to the nearest tenth. **3.7 cm**

2-7 READING STRATEGIES

The diagram below shows the connections between several related vocabulary terms and gives an example of each.

Ratio: comparison of two quantities. Ex. $\frac{3}{5}$
Scale: ratio between two measurements. Ex. 3 in:5 mi
Rate: ratio of two quantities with different units. Ex. $\frac{3\text{ ft}}{5\text{ sec}}$
Conversion Factor: rate in which two quantities are equal. Ex. $\frac{1\text{ yd}}{3\text{ ft}}$
Unit Rate: rate with a second quantity of one unit. Ex. $\frac{0.6\text{ ft}}{1\text{ sec}}$

Answer each question.

1. There are 16 ounces in a pound. Write this as a conversion factor. $\frac{16\text{ oz}}{1\text{ lb}}$ or $\frac{1\text{ lb}}{16\text{ oz}}$
2. Is $\frac{1\text{ ft}}{2\text{ sec}}$ a unit rate? Explain. **no; the second quality is not 1.**
3. Why is $\frac{12\text{ inches}}{1\text{ foot}}$ a conversion factor? **The two quantities are equal.**
4. Fill in the blanks with the most appropriate vocabulary terms:
   A rate is a type of **ratio.**
   A unit rate is a type of **rate.**
   So, a unit rate is also a type of **ratio.**
5. Write $\frac{84\text{ pages}}{3\text{ hours}}$ as a unit rate. **28 pg/hr**
6. A *proportion* is an equation showing two equal ratios. Give an example.
   Possible answer: $\frac{1}{2} = \frac{12}{24}$

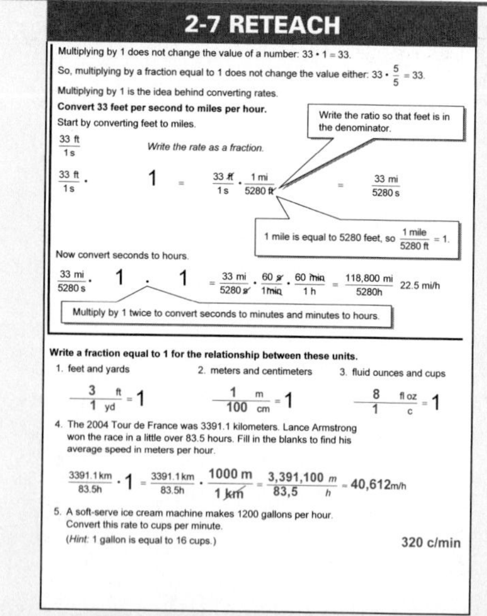

2-7 RETEACH

Multiplying by 1 does not change the value of a number: $33 \cdot 1 = 33$.

So, multiplying by a fraction equal to 1 does not change the value either: $33 \cdot \frac{5}{5} = 33$.

Multiplying by 1 is the idea behind converting rates.

Convert 33 feet per second to miles per hour.

Start by converting feet to miles.

$\frac{33\text{ ft}}{1\text{ s}}$ *Write the rate as a fraction.*

$\frac{33\text{ ft}}{1\text{ s}} \cdot 1 = \frac{33\text{ ft}}{1\text{ s}} \cdot \frac{1\text{ mi}}{5280\text{ ft}} = \frac{33\text{ mi}}{5280\text{ s}}$

Write the ratio so that feet is in the denominator.

1 mile is equal to 5280 feet, so $\frac{1\text{ mile}}{5280\text{ ft}} = 1$.

Now convert seconds to hours.

$\frac{33\text{ mi}}{5280\text{ s}} \cdot 1 \cdot 1 = \frac{33\text{ mi}}{5280\text{ s}} \cdot \frac{60\text{ s}}{1\text{ min}} \cdot \frac{60\text{ min}}{1\text{ h}} = \frac{118{,}800\text{ mi}}{5280\text{h}}$ 22.5 mi/h

Multiply by 1 twice to convert seconds to minutes and minutes to hours.

Write a fraction equal to 1 for the relationship between these units.

1. feet and yards $\frac{3\text{ ft}}{1\text{ yd}} = 1$
2. meters and centimeters $\frac{1\text{ m}}{100\text{ cm}} = 1$
3. fluid ounces and cups $\frac{8\text{ fl oz}}{1\text{ c}} = 1$
4. The 2004 Tour de France was 3391.1 kilometers. Lance Armstrong won the race in a little over 83.5 hours. Fill in the blanks to find his average speed in meters per hour.
   $\frac{3391.1\text{ km}}{83.5\text{h}} \cdot 1 = \frac{3391.1\text{ km}}{83.5\text{h}} \cdot \frac{1000\text{ m}}{1\text{ km}} = \frac{3{,}391{,}100\ m}{83{,}5\ h} = 40{,}612\text{m/h}$
5. A soft-serve ice cream machine makes 1200 gallons per hour. Convert this rate to cups per minute. (*Hint*: 1 gallon is equal to 16 cups.) **320 c/min**

41. Possible answer: The denominator in the first ratio is the number of varsity members, but in the second ratio it is the total number of people on the team.

41. **ERROR ANALYSIS** Below is a bonus question that appeared on an algebra test and a student's response.

> The ratio of junior varsity members to varsity members on the track team is 3:5. There are 24 members on the team. Write a proportion to find the number of junior varsity members. $\frac{3}{5} = \frac{x}{24}$

The student did not receive the bonus points. Why is this proportion incorrect?

LINK Sports

The records for the women's 100-meter dash and the women's 200-meter dash were set by Florence Griffith-Joyner, known as "Flo Jo." She is still referred to as the world's fastest woman.

42. **Sports** The table shows world record times for women's races of different distances.

World Records (Women)	
Distance (m)	Time (s)
100	10.5
200	21.3
800	113.3
5000	864.7

a. Find the speed in meters per second for each race. Round your answers to the nearest hundredth.

b. Which race has the fastest speed? the slowest?

c. **Critical Thinking** Give a possible reason why the speeds are different.

43. **Entertainment** Lynn, Faith, and Jeremy are film animators. In one 8-hour day, Lynn rendered 203 frames, Faith rendered 216 frames, and Jeremy rendered 227 frames. How many more frames per hour did Faith render than Lynn did? **1.625**

Solve each proportion.

44. $\frac{x-1}{3} = \frac{x+1}{5}$ **4**
45. $\frac{m}{3} = \frac{m+4}{7}$ **3**
46. $\frac{1}{x-3} = \frac{3}{x-5}$ **2**
47. $\frac{a}{2} = \frac{a-4}{30}$ $-\frac{2}{7}$

48. $\frac{3}{2y} = \frac{16}{y+2}$ $\frac{6}{29}$
49. $\frac{n+3}{5} = \frac{n-1}{2}$ $\frac{11}{3}$
50. $\frac{1}{y} = \frac{1}{6y-1}$ $\frac{1}{5}$
51. $\frac{2}{n} = \frac{4}{n+3}$ **3**

52. $\frac{5t-3}{-2} = \frac{t+3}{2}$ **0**
53. $\frac{3}{d+3} = \frac{4}{d+12}$ **24**
54. $\frac{3x+5}{14} = \frac{x}{3}$ **3**
55. $\frac{5}{2n} = \frac{8}{3n-24}$ **−120**

56. **Decorating** A particular shade of paint is made by mixing 5 parts red paint with 7 parts blue paint. To make this shade, Shannon mixed 12 quarts of blue paint with 8 quarts of red paint. Did Shannon mix the correct shade? Explain.

57. **Write About It** Give three examples of proportions. How do you know they are proportions? Then give three nonexamples of proportions. How do you know they are not proportions?

58. This problem will prepare you for the Multi-Step Test Prep on page 152.

a. Marcus is shopping for a new jacket. He finds one with a price tag of $120. Above the rack is a sign that says that he can take off $\frac{1}{5}$. Find out how much Marcus can deduct from the price of the jacket. **$24**

b. What price will Marcus pay for the jacket? **$96**

c. Copy the model below. Complete it by placing numerical values on top and the corresponding fractional parts below.

$0	? **$24**	$48	? **$72**	? **$96**	$120
0	$\frac{1}{5}$	? $\frac{2}{5}$	? $\frac{3}{5}$	$\frac{4}{5}$	1

d. Explain how this model shows proportional relationships.

MULTI-STEP TEST PREP Exercise 58 involves using proportions to find sale prices. This exercise prepares students for the Multi-Step Test Prep on page 152.

Answers

42a. 9.52 m/s; 9.39 m/s; 7.06 m/s; 5.78 m/s

b. 100 m; 5000 m

c. Possible answer: Runners can maintain a very high speed for a short distance, but over a longer distance their speed drops.

56. No; $\frac{5}{7}$ is not proportional to $\frac{8}{12}$.

57. Possible answer: $\frac{1}{2} = \frac{3}{6}$; $\frac{1}{4} = \frac{5}{20}$; $\frac{3}{7} = \frac{6}{14}$; they are proportions because the cross products are equal; $\frac{1}{2} \neq \frac{5}{6}$; $\frac{1}{2} \neq \frac{6}{7}$; $\frac{3}{4} \neq \frac{2}{3}$; they are not proportions because their cross products are not equal.

58d. Possible answer: It shows that $\frac{1}{5}$ out of 1 is the same as 24 out of 120, $\frac{2}{5}$ out of 1 is the same as 48 out of 120, etc.

2-7 PROBLEM SOLVING

Write the correct answer.

1. A donut shop bakes 4 dozen donuts every 18 minutes. Find the unit rate to the nearest hundredth.
2.67 donuts/minute

2. At one time, the ratio of in-state to out-of-state tuition at Texas A & M University in College Station, Texas was about 3:11. About how much was the out-of-state tuition if the in-state tuition at that time was about $2400?
$8800

3. The birth rate in Namibia is 35 babies to every 1000 people. In 2001, the country had a population of about 1,800,000 people. How many babies were there?
63,000 babies

4. A boat travels 160 miles in 5 hours. What is its speed in miles per minute?
0.53 mi/min

Use the table below to answer questions 5–8. Select the best answer. The table shows the ratio of female to male students at various institutions in 2002.

Institution	female:male
Massachusetts Institute of Technology	41:59
Tulane University	53:47
US Naval Academy	1:19
Georgia Institute of Technology	29:71
University of Massachusetts at Amherst	51:49
Baylor University	29:21

5. If there are 209 women at the US Naval Academy, how many men are there?
A 11 **C 3971**
B 190 D 4180

6. If there are 7282 male students at the Georgia Institute of Technology, how many females are there?
F 2427 H 8282
G 2974 J 17,828

7. If there are 4959 male students at Baylor University, which proportion can be used to find the number of female students?
A $\frac{21}{4959} = \frac{x}{21}$ C $\frac{21}{29} = \frac{x}{4959}$
B $\frac{21}{4959} = \frac{x}{29}$ **D** $\frac{29}{21} = \frac{x}{4959}$

8. For which institution is the ratio of female to male students the greatest?
F Baylor University
G Tulane University
H University of Massachusetts at Amherst
J US Naval Academy

2-7 CHALLENGE

In Lesson 2-7, you learned that in a true proportion, the cross products are equal.

If $\frac{a}{b} = \frac{c}{d}$, then $ad = bc$.

The proof to the statement above is shown at right.

$\frac{a}{b} = \frac{c}{d}$
$bd\left(\frac{a}{b}\right) = bd\left(\frac{c}{d}\right)$ Multiplication Property of Equality
$da = bc$ Inverse Property of Multiplication
$ad = bc$ Commutative Property of Multiplication

Using $\frac{a}{b} = \frac{c}{d}$, you can write and prove that other proportions involving a, b, c, and d are true.

In each proportion, assume that the denominator is not equal to 0.

1. Let $\frac{a}{b} = \frac{c}{d}$, where $a = 5$, $b = 7$, $c = 15$, and $d = 21$. Verify that the cross products are equal.
bc: 7 • 15 = 105; ad: 5 • 21 = 105

2. a. Let $\frac{a}{b} = \frac{c}{d}$. What can be done to each side of $\frac{a}{b} = \frac{c}{d}$, in order to get $\frac{d}{c} = \frac{b}{a}$?
Multiply each side by $\frac{bd}{ac}$

b. Justify each step in the reasoning below in order to show that $\frac{d}{c} = \frac{b}{a}$.

$\frac{a}{b} = \frac{c}{d}$
$ad = bc$ **Cross-Product Property;**
$\left(\frac{1}{ac}\right)ad = \left(\frac{1}{ac}\right)bc$ **Multiplication Property of Equality;**
$\frac{d}{c} = \frac{b}{a}$ **Identity Property of Multiplication**

3. Let $\frac{a}{b} = \frac{c}{d}$. Show that $\frac{d}{b} = \frac{c}{a}$. Write your reasons to the right of your steps.

$\frac{a}{b} = \frac{c}{d}$
$ad = bc$ **Cross-Product Property;**
$\left(\frac{1}{ab}\right)ad = \left(\frac{1}{ab}\right)bc$ **Multiplication Property of Equality;**
$\frac{d}{b} = \frac{c}{a}$ **Identity Property of Multiplication**

TEST PREP DOCTOR In **Exercise 60,** students who chose **H** or **J** may have merely multiplied or divided 4 and 20. Have students think of Brett's speed as 4 mi per 60 min, or 1 mi per 15 min. Therefore after 20 min (just over 15 min), Brett will be at 1.3 mi, which is just over a mile.

Teaching Tip **Geometry** For **Exercise 63,** point out that if the ratios of the angle measures are 4:5, then one is 4 times a number and the other is 5 times the same number. This leads to the equation $4x + 5x = 90$, which students can solve.

Journal

Have students write about how to find and use unit rates to get the best deal.

ALTERNATIVE ASSESSMENT

Have students use a map to determine the actual distances between three towns. Then have them plan a trip to visit all three towns and return to their starting point. They should also explain how much more gas a vehicle that gets 12 mi/gal will need than a vehicle that gets 25 mi/gal.

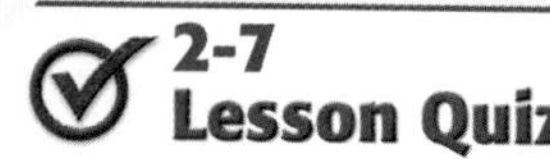

Power Presentations with PowerPoint®

2-7 Lesson Quiz

1. In a school, the ratio of boys to girls is 4:3. There are 216 boys. How many girls are there? 162
2. Nuts cost $10.75 for 3 pounds. Find the unit rate in dollars per pound. $3.58/lb
3. Sue washes 25 cars in 5 hours. Find the unit rate in cars per hour. 5 cars/h
4. A car travels 180 miles in 4 hours. Use dimensional analysis to convert the car's speed to feet per minute. 3960 ft/min

Solve each proportion.

5. $\frac{8}{12} = \frac{g}{9}$ 6
6. $\frac{3}{z-4} = \frac{2}{8}$ 16
7. A scale model of a car is 9 inches long. The scale is 1:18. How many inches long is the car it represents? 162 in.

Also available on transparency

TEST PREP

59. One day the U.S. dollar was worth approximately 100 yen. An exchange of 2500 yen was made that day. What was the value of the exchange in dollars?
 (A) $25 (B) $400 (C) $2500 (D) $40,000

60. Brett walks at a speed of 4 miles per hour. He walks for 20 minutes in a straight line at this rate. Approximately what distance does Brett walk?
 (F) 0.06 miles (G) 1.3 miles (H) 5 miles (J) 80 miles

61. A shampoo company conducted a survey and found that 3 out of 8 people use their brand of shampoo. Which proportion could be used to find the expected number of users n in a city of 75,000 people?
 (A) $\frac{3}{8} = \frac{75{,}000}{n}$ (B) $\frac{3}{75{,}000} = \frac{n}{8}$ (C) $\frac{8}{3} = \frac{n}{75{,}000}$ (D) $\frac{3}{8} = \frac{n}{75{,}000}$

62. A statue is 3 feet tall. The display case for a model of the statue can fit a model that is no more than 9 inches tall. Which of the scales below allows for the tallest model of the statue that will fit in the display case?
 (F) 2:1 (G) 1:1 (H) 1:3 (J) 1:4

CHALLENGE AND EXTEND

63. **Geometry** Complementary angles are two angles whose measures add up to 90°. The ratio of the measures of two complementary angles is 4:5. What are the measures of the angles? **40°; 50°**

64. A customer wanted 24 feet of rope. The clerk at the hardware store used what she thought was a yardstick to measure the rope, but the yardstick was actually 2 inches too short. How many inches were missing from the customer's piece of rope? **16 in.**

65. **Population** The population density of Jackson, Mississippi, is 672.2 people per square kilometer. What is the population density in people per square meter? Show that your answer is reasonable. (*Hint:* There are 1000 meters in 1 kilometer. How many square meters are in 1 square kilometer?) **0.0006722 people/m²**

SPIRAL REVIEW

Evaluate each expression. *(Lesson 1-4)*

66. 8^2 **64**
67. $(-3)^3$ **−27**
68. $(-3)^2$ **9**
69. $-\left(\frac{1}{2}\right)^5$ $-\frac{1}{32}$

Write the power represented by each geometric model. *(Lesson 1-4)*

70. **6³**

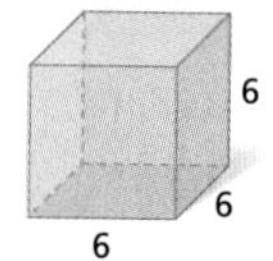

71. **10²**

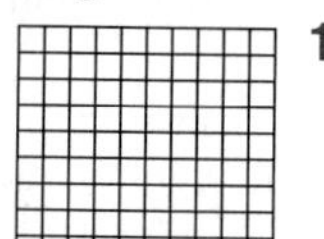

72. **y³**

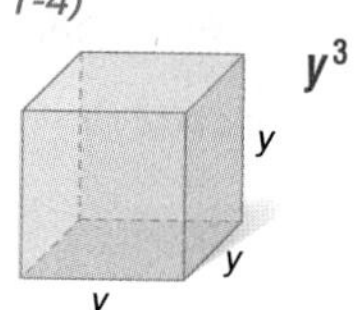

Solve each equation. Check your answer. *(Lesson 2-4)*

73. $2x - 12 = 5x + 3$ **−5**
74. $3a - 4 = 6 - 7a$ **1**
75. $3x - 4 = 2x + 4$ **8**

Solve for the indicated variable. *(Lesson 2-5)*

76. $y = mx + b$ for b — $b = y - mx$
77. $PV = nRT$ for V — $V = \frac{nRT}{P}$
78. $A = \frac{1}{2}bh$ for h — $h = \frac{2A}{b}$

2-8 Applications of Proportions

Objectives
Use proportions to solve problems involving geometric figures.

Use proportions and similar figures to measure objects indirectly.

Vocabulary
similar
corresponding sides
corresponding angles
indirect measurement
scale factor

Why learn this?
Proportions can be used to find the heights of tall objects, such as totem poles, that would otherwise be difficult to measure. (See Example 2.)

Similar figures have exactly the same shape but not necessarily the same size.

Corresponding sides of two figures are in the same relative position, and **corresponding angles** are in the same relative position. Two figures are similar if and only if the lengths of corresponding sides are proportional and all pairs of corresponding angles have equal measures.

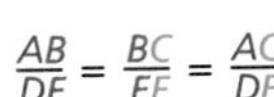

Reading Math
- $\overline{AB}$ means segment AB. AB means the length of $\overline{AB}$.
- $\angle A$ means angle A. $m\angle A$ means the measure of angle A.

$\frac{AB}{DE} = \frac{BC}{EF} = \frac{AC}{DF}$

$m\angle A = m\angle D$
$m\angle B = m\angle E$
$m\angle C = m\angle F$

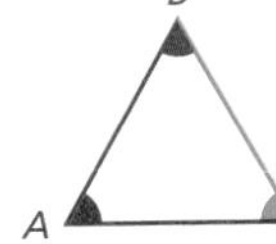

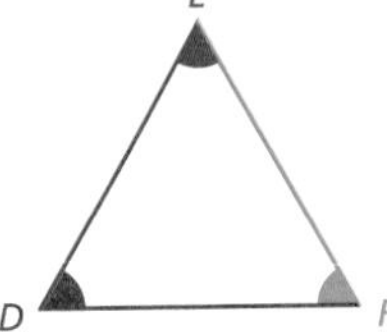

When stating that two figures are similar, use the symbol ~. For the triangles above, you can write $\triangle ABC \sim \triangle DEF$. Make sure corresponding vertices are in the same order. It would be incorrect to write $\triangle ABC \sim \triangle EFD$.

You can use proportions to find missing lengths in similar figures.

EXAMPLE 1 Finding Missing Measures in Similar Figures

Find the value of x in each diagram.

A $\triangle RST \sim \triangle BCD$

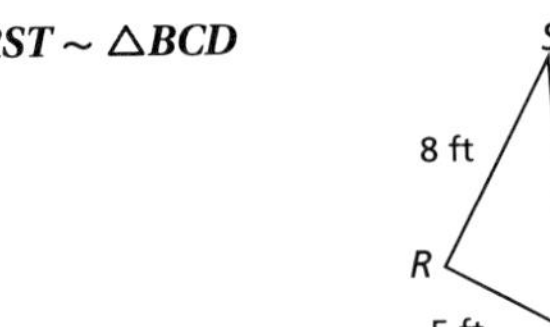

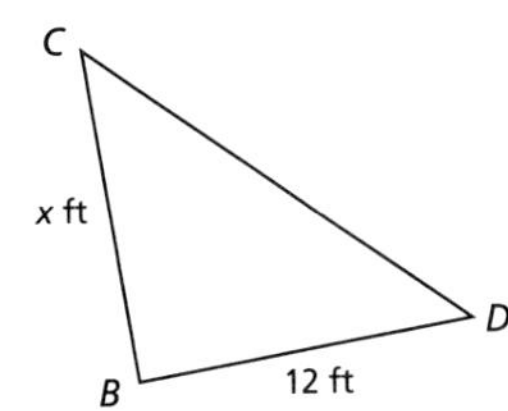

R corresponds to B, S corresponds to C, and T corresponds to D.

$\frac{5}{12} = \frac{8}{x}$ — $\frac{RT}{BD} = \frac{RS}{BC}$

$5x = 96$ — *Use cross products.*

$\frac{5x}{5} = \frac{96}{5}$ — *Since x is multiplied by 5, divide both sides by 5 to undo the multiplication.*

$x = 19.2$

The length of $\overline{BC}$ is 19.2 ft.

2-8 Organizer

Pacing: Traditional 1 day
Block $\frac{1}{2}$ day

Objectives: Use proportions to solve problems involving geometric figures.

Use proportions and similar figures to measure objects indirectly.

Algebra Lab
In *Algebra Lab Activities*

Online Edition
Tutorial Videos, Interactivity

Countdown Week 5

Power Presentations with PowerPoint®

Warm Up

Evaluate each expression for $a = 3$, $b = -2$, and $c = 5$.

1. $4a - b$ 14 **2.** $3b^2 - 5$ 7

3. $ab - 2c$ −16

Solve each proportion.

4. $\frac{6}{m} = \frac{2}{3}$ 9 **5.** $\frac{x}{8} = \frac{4}{5}$ 6.4

Also available on transparency

Math Humor

Q: Why did the variable break up with the constant?

A: The constant was incapable of change.

1 Introduce

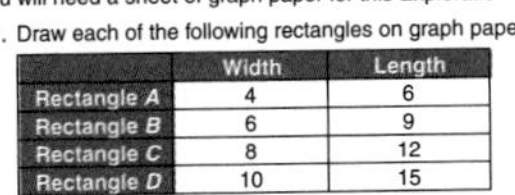

EXPLORATION

2-8 Applications of Proportions

You will need a sheet of graph paper for this Exploration.

1. Draw each of the following rectangles on graph paper.

	Width	Length
Rectangle A	4	6
Rectangle B	6	9
Rectangle C	8	12
Rectangle D	10	15

2. What do you notice about the shapes of the rectangles?
3. What is the ratio of the width of rectangle *A* to the width of rectangle *D*?
4. What is the ratio of the length of rectangle *A* to the length of rectangle *D*?
5. What do you notice about the two ratios you calculated?

THINK AND DISCUSS

6. Compare the ratio of the widths of any two of the rectangles to the ratio of their lengths. What can you say about the ratios?

Motivate

Draw and label a 4 by 6 rectangle. Ask for the perimeter and area. 20 units; 24 square units Ask students what they think each dimension should be multiplied by if they want the perimeter and area to be twice as big. Change the dimensions as suggested and find the new perimeter and area to see if the students guessed correctly. Tell students that in this lesson, they will learn how changing the dimensions of shapes affects the perimeter, area, and volume.

Explorations and answers are provided in *Alternate Openers: Explorations Transparencies.*

State Resources

Power Presentations with PowerPoint®

Additional Examples

Example 1

Find the value of *x* in each diagram.

A. $\triangle MNP \sim \triangle STU$ $9\frac{1}{3}$

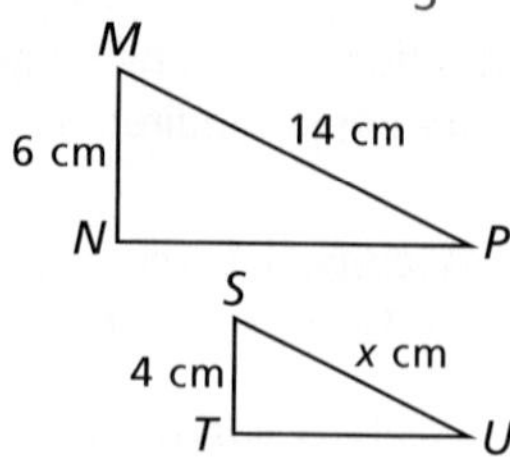

B. $ABCDE \sim FGHJK$ 2.5

D E
14 in.
A
C B 10 in.
F x in.
K G
J H
3.5 in.

Example 2

A flagpole casts a shadow that is 75 ft long at the same time a 6-foot-tall man casts a shadow that is 9 ft long. Write and solve a proportion to find the height of the flag pole. $\frac{75}{9} = \frac{h}{6}$; 50 ft

INTERVENTION

Questioning Strategies

EXAMPLE 1

- If you know the lengths of the sides of two figures, how can you show that the figures are similar?
- What are some ways you can check to see if your answers are reasonable?

EXAMPLE 2

- How do you set up a proportion involving similar triangles?

Multiple Representations There is more than one correct way to set up a proportion. In **Example 2,** students could write $\frac{\text{man's height}}{\text{man's shadow}} = \frac{\text{flagpole's height}}{\text{flagpole's shadow}}$.

Find the value of x in each diagram.

B $FGHJKL \sim MNPQRS$

F G
4 cm
L H
K J
2 cm

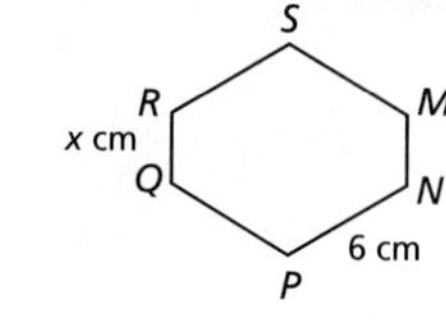

$\frac{6}{4} = \frac{x}{2}$ $\frac{NP}{GH} = \frac{RQ}{KJ}$

$4x = 12$ *Use cross products.*

$\frac{4x}{4} = \frac{12}{4}$ *Since x is multiplied by 4, divide both sides by 4 to undo the multiplication.*

$x = 3$

The length of $\overline{QR}$ is 3 cm.

1. Find the value of x in the diagram if $ABCD \sim WXYZ$. **2.8 in.**

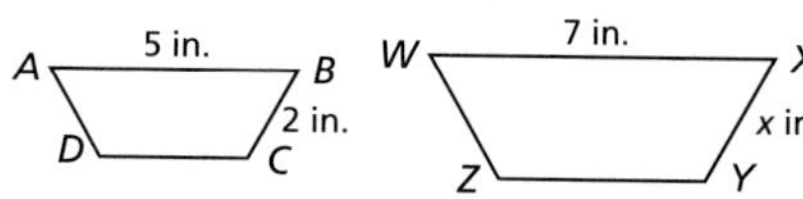

You can solve a proportion involving similar triangles to find a length that is not easily measured. This method of measurement is called **indirect measurement**. If two objects form right angles with the ground, you can apply indirect measurement using their shadows.

EXAMPLE 2 ***Measurement Application***

A totem pole casts a shadow 45 feet long at the same time that a 6-foot-tall man casts a shadow that is 3 feet long. Write and solve a proportion to find the height of the totem pole.

Helpful Hint

A height of 90 ft seems reasonable for a totem pole. If you got 900 or 9000 ft, that would not be reasonable, and you should check your work.

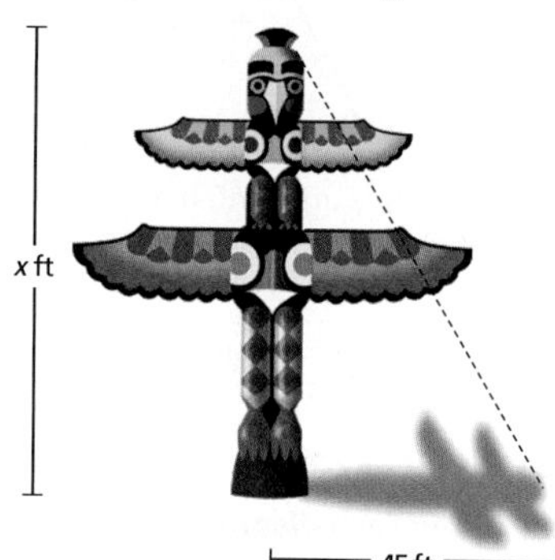

Both the man and the totem pole form right angles with the ground, and their shadows are cast at the same angle. You can form two similar right triangles.

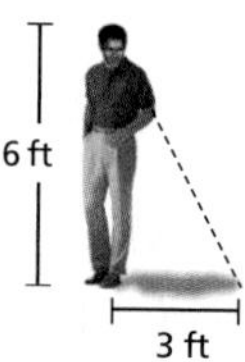

$\frac{6}{x} = \frac{3}{45}$ $\frac{\text{man's height}}{\text{pole's height}} = \frac{\text{man's shadow}}{\text{pole's shadow}}$

$3x = 270$ *Use cross products. Since x is multiplied by 3, divide both sides by 3 to undo the multiplication.*

$\frac{3x}{3} = \frac{270}{3}$

$x = 90$

The totem pole is 90 feet tall.

2a. A forest ranger who is 150 cm tall casts a shadow 45 cm long. At the same time, a nearby tree casts a shadow 195 cm long. Write and solve a proportion to find the height of the tree.

2b. A woman who is 5.5 feet tall casts a shadow 3.5 feet long. At the same time, a building casts a shadow 28 feet long. Write and solve a proportion to find the height of the building.

2a. $\frac{150}{x} = \frac{45}{195}$; 650 cm

2b. $\frac{5.5}{x} = \frac{3.5}{28}$; 44 ft

2 Teach

Guided Instruction

Review how to solve proportions before showing how they are applied. In **Example 1,** encourage students to read the statement of similarity before setting up the proportion, because sometimes one of the figures is rotated.

Visual In similarity statements, use colored pencils (MK) to color or circle two corresponding letters to show that they are the endpoints of corresponding sides. In $\triangle ABC \sim \triangle MNO$, $\overline{AC}$ corresponds to $\overline{MO}$.

Reaching All Learners

Through World Math

Have students research the heights of various landmarks around the world. (You may wish to assign a different landmark to each student.) Then have each student write an indirect measurement problem about his or her landmark. Display or distribute these problems and have students solve some of the problems written by other students.

If every dimension of a figure is multiplied by the same number, the result is a similar figure. The multiplier is called a **scale factor**.

EXAMPLE 3 Changing Dimensions

A **Every dimension of a 2-by-4-inch rectangle is multiplied by 1.5 to form a similar rectangle. How is the ratio of the perimeters related to the ratio of corresponding sides? How is the ratio of the areas related to the ratio of corresponding sides?**

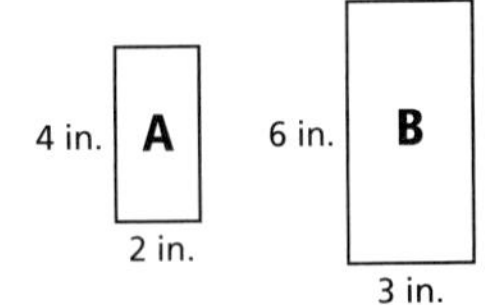

	Rectangle A	Rectangle B
$P = 2\ell + 2w$	$2(2) + 2(4) = 12$	$2(6) + 2(3) = 18$
$A = \ell w$	$4(2) = 8$	$6(3) = 18$

Sides: $\frac{4}{6} = \frac{2}{3}$ Perimeters: $\frac{12}{18} = \frac{2}{3}$ Areas: $\frac{8}{18} = \frac{4}{9} = \left(\frac{2}{3}\right)^2$

The ratio of the perimeters is equal to the ratio of corresponding sides. The ratio of the areas is the square of the ratio of corresponding sides.

Helpful Hint

A scale factor between 0 and 1 reduces a figure. A scale factor greater than 1 enlarges it.

B **Every dimension of a cylinder with radius 4 cm and height 6 cm is multiplied by $\frac{1}{2}$ to form a similar cylinder. How is the ratio of the volumes related to the ratio of corresponding dimensions?**

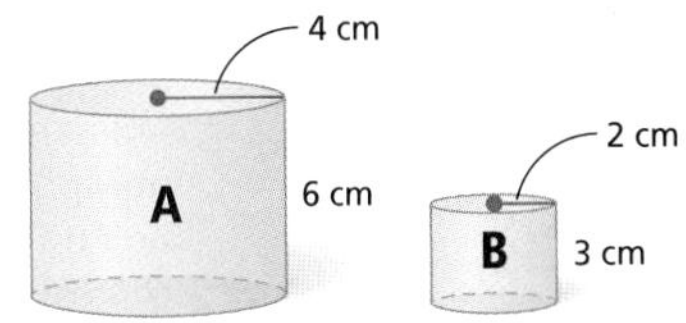

	Cylinder A	Cylinder B
$V = \pi r^2 h$	$\pi(4)^2(6) = 96\pi$	$\pi(2)^2(3) = 12\pi$

Radii: $\frac{4}{2} = \frac{2}{1} = 2$ Heights: $\frac{6}{3} = \frac{2}{1} = 2$ Volumes: $\frac{96\pi}{12\pi} = \frac{8}{1} = 8 = 2^3$

The ratio of the volumes is the cube of the ratio of corresponding dimensions.

3. A rectangle has width 12 inches and length 3 inches. Every dimension of the rectangle is multiplied by $\frac{1}{3}$ to form a similar rectangle. How is the ratio of the perimeters related to the ratio of the corresponding sides? **The ratio of the perimeters is equal to the ratio of the corresponding sides.**

THINK AND DISCUSS

1. Name some pairs of real-world items that appear to be similar figures.

2. **GET ORGANIZED** Copy and complete the graphic organizer. In the top box, sketch and label two similar triangles. Then list the corresponding sides and angles in the bottom boxes.

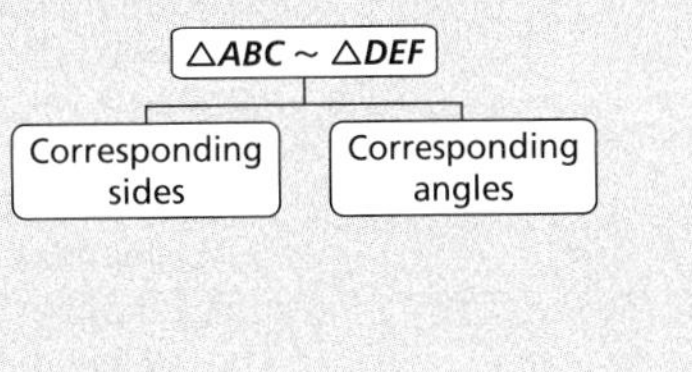

COMMON ERROR ALERT

Students often divide in the wrong order to get the scale factor, and may say that a scale factor is $\frac{1}{4}$ when it is 4. Remind students that a scale factor of greater than 1 enlarges the figure.

Power Presentations with PowerPoint®

Additional Examples

Example 3

A. The radius of a circle with radius 8 in. is multiplied by 1.75 to get a circle with radius 14 in. How is the ratio of the circumferences related to the ratio of the radii? How is the ratio of the areas related to the ratio of the radii? The ratio of the circumferences is equal to the ratio of the radii. The ratio of the areas is the square of the ratio of the radii.

B. Every dimension of a rectangular prism with length 12 cm, width 3 cm, and height 9 cm is multiplied by $\frac{1}{3}$ to get a similar rectangular prism. How is the ratio of the volumes related to the ratio of the corresponding dimensions? The ratio of the volumes is the cube of the ratio of the corresponding dimensions.

INTERVENTION
Questioning Strategies

EXAMPLE 3

- What is meant by the dimensions of a rectangular prism?
- If you know the scale factor and perimeter of the original figure, how can you find the perimeter of the new figure? the area of the new figure?

3 Close

Summarize

Have students describe what happens to a scale drawing when the scale of 1 in:50 ft is changed to 1 in:20 ft. The drawing becomes 2.5 times as large.

ONGOING ASSESSMENT and INTERVENTION

***Diagnose Before* the Lesson**
2-8 Warm Up, TE p. 127

***Monitor During* the Lesson**
Check It Out! Exercises, SE pp. 128–129
Questioning Strategies, TE p. 128–129

***Assess After* the Lesson**
2-8 Lesson Quiz, TE p. 132
Alternative Assessment, TE p. 132

Answers to *Think and Discuss*

1. Possible answers: a model airplane and the real airplane it represents; a baseball and a softball; a photograph and its enlargement
2. See p. A3.

2-8 Exercises

Assignment Guide

Assign *Guided Practice* exercises as necessary.

If you finished Examples **1–3**
Basic 6–17, 20, 22, 24–26, 30–41
Average 6–13, 14–18 even, 20–27, 30–41
Advanced 6–12, 14–41

Homework Quick Check
Quickly check key concepts.
Exercises: 6, 8, 9, 10, 12, 14, 21

Answers

10. Possible answer: the width is less than the length for the baby blanket, so the width on the mother's blanket will also be less than the length. Since 5 ft is less than $6\frac{1}{4}$ ft, 5 ft is a reasonable answer.

State Resources

go.hrw.com
State Resources Online
KEYWORD: MA7 Resources

2-8 Exercises

go.hrw.com
Homework Help Online
KEYWORD: MA11 2-8
Parent Resources Online
KEYWORD: MA7 Parent

GUIDED PRACTICE

1. **Vocabulary** What does it mean for two figures to be *similar*?
They are the same shape but not necessarily the same size.

SEE EXAMPLE 1 p. 127

Find the value of x in each diagram.

2. $\triangle ABC \sim \triangle DEF$ **5.6 m**

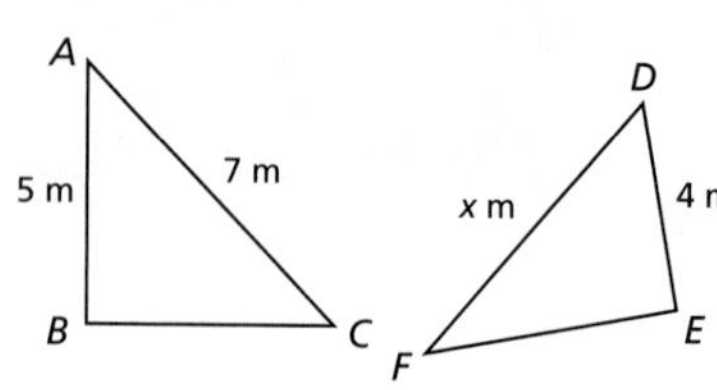

3. $RSTV \sim WXYZ$ **10 ft**

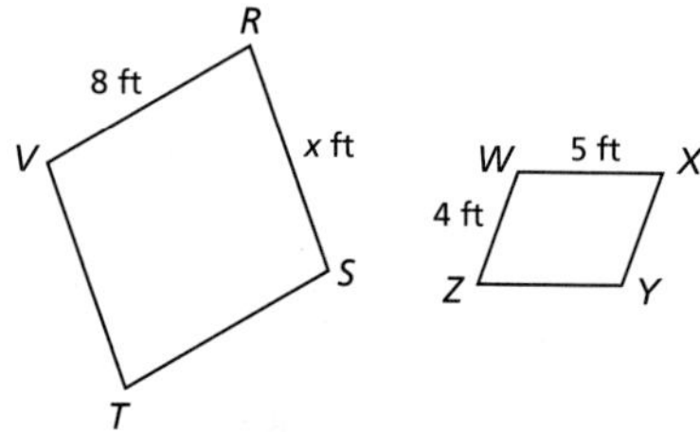

SEE EXAMPLE 2 p. 128

4. Roger is 5 feet tall and casts a shadow 3.5 feet long. At the same time, the flagpole outside his school casts a shadow 14 feet long. Write and solve a proportion to find the height of the flagpole. $\frac{5}{h} = \frac{3.5}{14}$**; 20 ft**

SEE EXAMPLE 3 p. 129

5. A rectangle has length 12 feet and width 8 feet. Every dimension of the rectangle is multiplied by $\frac{3}{4}$ to form a similar rectangle. How is the ratio of the areas related to the ratio of corresponding sides?
The ratio of the areas is the square of the ratio of the corresponding side lengths.

PRACTICE AND PROBLEM SOLVING

Independent Practice

For Exercises	See Example
6–7	1
8	2
9	3

Extra Practice
Skills Practice p. S7
Application Practice p. S29

Find the value of x in each diagram.

6. $\triangle LMN \sim \triangle RST$ **8 m**

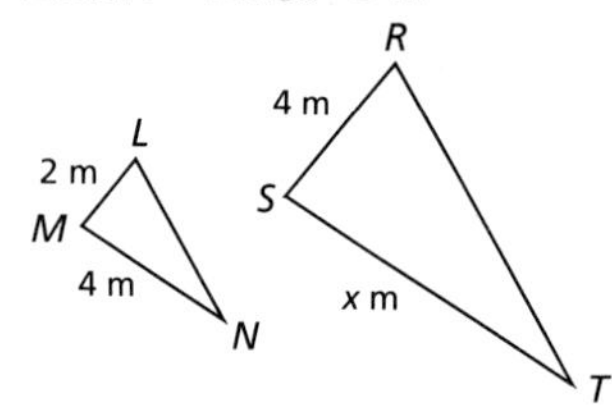

7. prism A ~ prism B **7 in.**

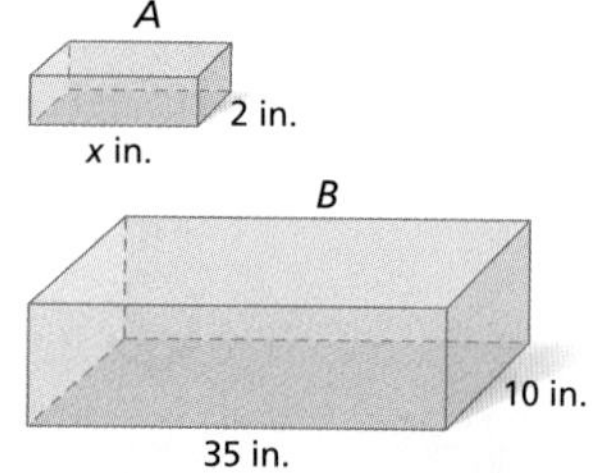

8. Write and solve a proportion to find the height of the taller tree in the diagram at right. $\frac{18}{h} = \frac{20}{42}$**; 37.8 ft**

9. A triangle has side lengths of 5 inches, 12 inches, and 15 inches. Every dimension is multiplied by $\frac{1}{5}$ to form a new triangle. How is the ratio of the perimeters related to the ratio of corresponding sides?
The ratio of the perimeters is equal to the ratio of the corresponding side lengths.

10. **Hobbies** For a baby shower gift, Heather crocheted a baby blanket whose length was $2\frac{1}{2}$ feet and whose width was 2 feet. She plans to crochet a proportionally larger similar blanket for the baby's mother. If she wants the length of the mother's blanket to be $6\frac{1}{4}$ feet, what should the width be? Show that your answer is reasonable. **5 ft**

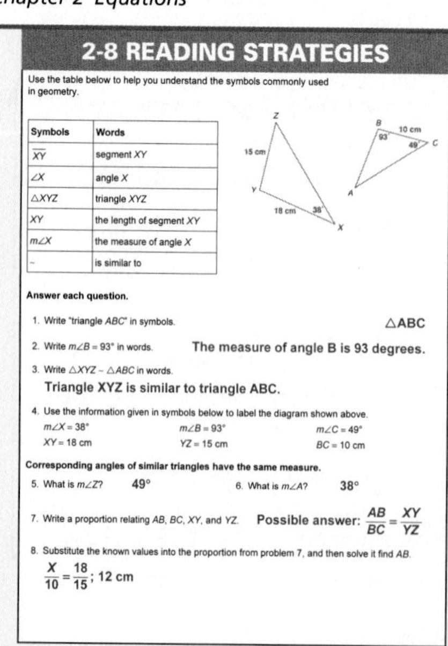

2-8 READING STRATEGIES

Use the table below to help you understand the symbols commonly used in geometry.

Symbols	Words
$\overline{XY}$	segment XY
$\angle X$	angle X
$\triangle XYZ$	triangle XYZ
XY	the length of segment XY
$m\angle X$	the measure of angle X
~	is similar to

Answer each question.

1. Write "triangle ABC" in symbols. **△ABC**
2. Write $m\angle B = 93°$ in words. **The measure of angle B is 93 degrees.**
3. Write $\triangle XYZ \sim \triangle ABC$ in words.
Triangle XYZ is similar to triangle ABC.
4. Use the information given in symbols below to label the diagram shown above.
$m\angle X = 38°$ $m\angle B = 93°$ $m\angle C = 49°$
$XY = 18$ cm $YZ = 15$ cm $BC = 10$ cm

Corresponding angles of similar triangles have the same measure.

5. What is $m\angle Z$? **49°**
6. What is $m\angle A$? **38°**
7. Write a proportion relating AB, BC, XY, and YZ. **Possible answer:** $\frac{AB}{BC} = \frac{XY}{YZ}$
8. Substitute the known values into the proportion from problem 7, and then solve it find AB.
$\frac{X}{10} = \frac{18}{15}$**; 12 cm**

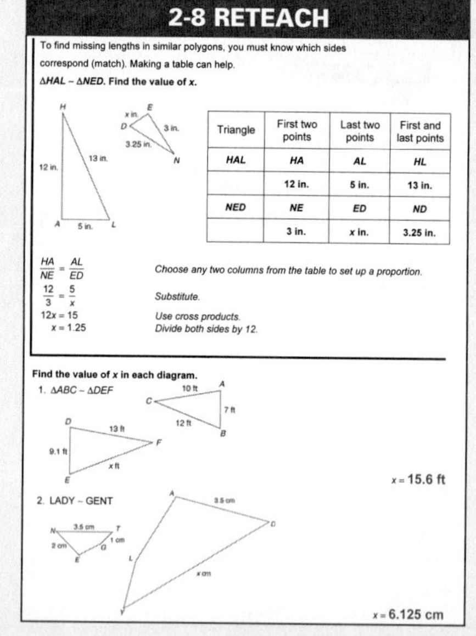

2-8 RETEACH

To find missing lengths in similar polygons, you must know which sides correspond (match). Making a table can help.

$\triangle HAL \sim \triangle NED$. Find the value of x.

Triangle	First two points	Last two points	First and last points
HAL	***HA***	***AL***	***HL***
	12 in.	**5 in.**	**13 in.**
NED	***NE***	***ED***	***ND***
	3 in.	***x* in.**	**3.25 in.**

$\frac{HA}{NE} = \frac{AL}{ED}$ *Choose any two columns from the table to set up a proportion.*
$\frac{12}{3} = \frac{5}{x}$ *Substitute.*
$12x = 15$ *Use cross products.*
$x = 1.25$ *Divide both sides by 12.*

Find the value of x in each diagram.

1. $\triangle ABC \sim \triangle DEF$

$x = 15.6$ ft

2. LADY ~ GENT

$x = 6.125$ cm

Our Homes Are Made for Families!

Our Easton model includes a 120-square-foot family room. In the new Weston model, we've doubled the dimensions of the family room!

120 ft²
Family room

11. **Real Estate** Refer to the home builder's advertisement. The family rooms in both models are rectangular. How much carpeting is needed to carpet the family room in the Weston model? **480 ft²**

12. A rectangle has an area of 16 ft². Every dimension is multiplied by a scale factor, and the new rectangle has an area of 64 ft². What was the scale factor? **2**

13. A cone has a volume of 98π cm³. Every dimension is multiplied by a scale factor, and the new cone has a volume of 6272π cm³. What was the scale factor? **4**

Find the value of x in each diagram.

14. $FGHJK \sim MNPQR$ **9 m**

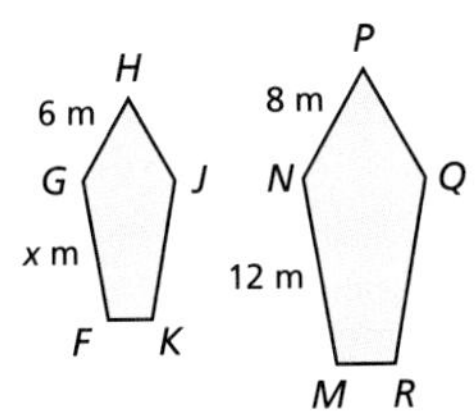

15. cylinder $A \sim$ cylinder B **2.8 ft**

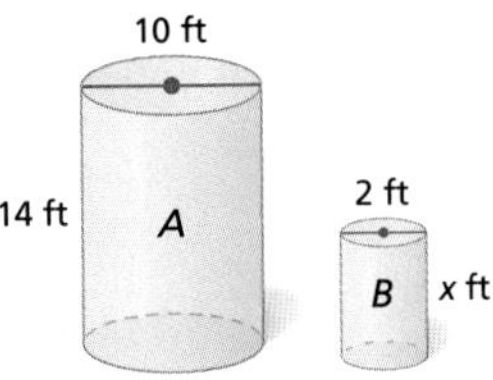

16. $\triangle BCD \sim \triangle FGD$ **8.75 ft**

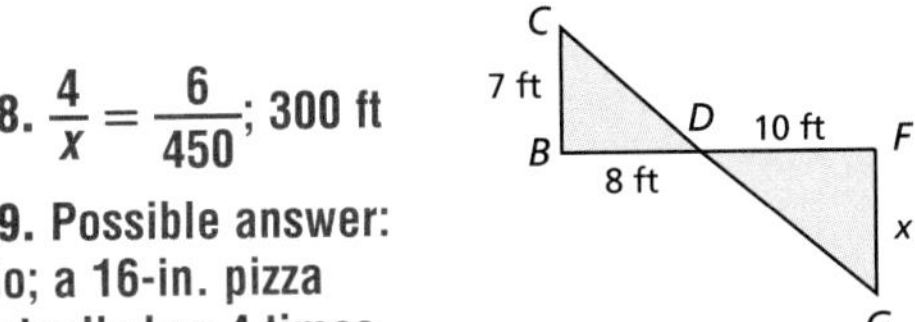

17. $\triangle RST \sim \triangle QSV$ **4 cm**

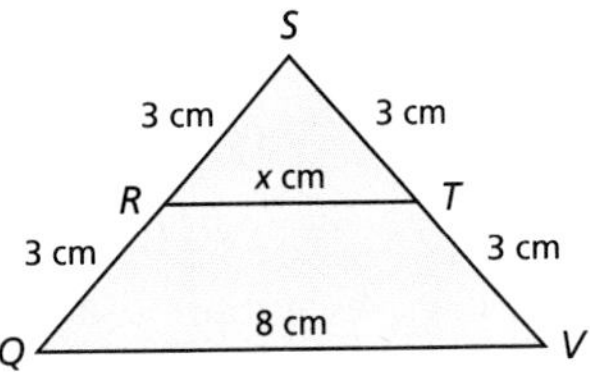

18. $\frac{4}{x} = \frac{6}{450}$**; 300 ft**

19. Possible answer: No; a 16-in. pizza actually has 4 times the area, so the cost should be 4 times as much.

18. A tower casts a 450 ft shadow at the same time that a 4 ft child casts a 6 ft shadow. Write and solve a proportion to find the height of the tower.

19. **Write About It** At Pizza Palace, a pizza with a diameter of 8 inches costs $6.00. The restaurant manager says that a 16-inch pizza should be priced at $12.00 because it is twice as large. Do you agree? Explain why or why not.

MULTI-STEP TEST PREP

20. This problem will prepare you for the Multi-Step Test Prep on page 152.

Another common application of proportion is *percents*. A percent is a ratio of a number to 100. For example, $80\% = \frac{80}{100}$.

a. Write 12%, 18%, 25%, 67%, and 98% as ratios. $\frac{12}{100}; \frac{18}{100}; \frac{25}{100}; \frac{67}{100}; \frac{98}{100}$

b. Percents can also be written as decimals. Write each of your ratios from part **a** as a decimal. **0.12; 0.18; 0.25; 0.67; 0.98**

c. What do you notice about a percent and its decimal equivalent?

You will learn more about percents and their connections to proportions in upcoming lessons.

MULTI-STEP TEST PREP Exercise 20 involves using ratios to find percents. This exercise prepares students for the Multi-Step Test Prep on page 152.

Answers

20c. The decimal is the percent with its decimal point moved 2 places to the left and the % symbol removed.

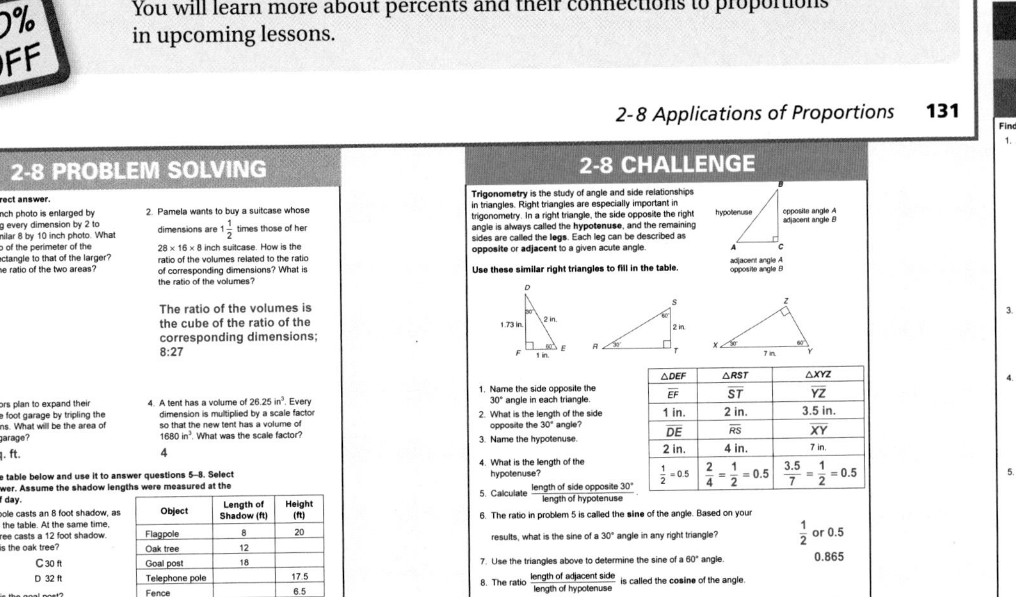

2-8 PROBLEM SOLVING

Write the correct answer.

1. A 4 by 5 inch photo is enlarged by multiplying every dimension by 2 to form a similar 8 by 10 inch photo. What is the ratio of the perimeter of the smaller rectangle to that of the larger? What is the ratio of the two areas?

1:2
1:4

2. Pamela wants to buy a suitcase whose dimensions are $1\frac{1}{2}$ times those of her 28 × 16 × 8 inch suitcase. How is the ratio of the volumes related to the ratio of corresponding dimensions? What is the ratio of the volumes?

The ratio of the volumes is the cube of the ratio of the corresponding dimensions; 8:27

3. The Taylors plan to expand their 80 square foot garage by tripling the dimensions. What will be the area of the new garage?

720 sq. ft.

4. A tent has a volume of 26.25 in³. Every dimension is multiplied by a scale factor so that the new tent has a volume of 1680 in³. What was the scale factor?

4

Complete the table below and use it to answer questions 5–8. Select the best answer. Assume the shadow lengths were measured at the same time of day.

Object	Length of Shadow (ft)	Height (ft)
Flagpole	8	20
Oak tree	12	
Goal post	18	
Telephone pole		17.5
Fence		6.5

5. The flagpole casts an 8 foot shadow, as shown in the table. At the same time, the oak tree casts a 12 foot shadow. How tall is the oak tree?

A 4.8 ft **C** 30 ft
B 24 ft D 32 ft

6. How tall is the goal post?

F 7.2 ft H 38 ft
G 30 ft **J** 45 ft

7. What is the length of the telephone pole's shadow?

A 5.5 ft C 25.5 ft
B 7 ft D 43.8 ft

8. What is the length of the fence's shadow?

F 1.5 ft H 16.25 ft
G 2.6 ft J 21.5 ft

2-8 CHALLENGE

Trigonometry is the study of angle and side relationships in triangles. Right triangles are especially important in trigonometry. In a right triangle, the side opposite the right angle is always called the **hypotenuse**, and the remaining sides are called the **legs**. Each leg can be described as **opposite** or **adjacent** to a given acute angle.

hypotenuse; opposite angle A, adjacent angle B; adjacent angle A, opposite angle B

Use these similar right triangles to fill in the table.

1. Name the side opposite the 30° angle in each triangle.
2. What is the length of the side opposite the 30° angle?
3. Name the hypotenuse.
4. What is the length of the hypotenuse?
5. Calculate $\frac{\text{length of side opposite } 30°}{\text{length of hypotenuse}}$.

$\triangle DEF$	$\triangle RST$	$\triangle XYZ$
$\overline{EF}$	$\overline{ST}$	$\overline{YZ}$
1 in.	2 in.	3.5 in.
$\overline{DE}$	$\overline{RS}$	$\overline{XY}$
2 in.	4 in.	7 in.
$\frac{1}{2} = 0.5$	$\frac{2}{4} = \frac{1}{2} = 0.5$	$\frac{3.5}{7} = \frac{1}{2} = 0.5$

6. The ratio in problem 5 is called the **sine** of the angle. Based on your results, what is the sine of a 30° angle in any right triangle? **$\frac{1}{2}$ or 0.5**

7. Use the triangles above to determine the sine of a 60° angle. **0.865**

8. The ratio $\frac{\text{length of adjacent side}}{\text{length of hypotenuse}}$ is called the **cosine** of the angle.

a. Use the triangles above to determine the cosine of a 30° angle. **0.865**

b. Use the triangles above to determine the cosine of a 60° angle. **$\frac{1}{2}$ or 0.5**

9. Explain how the sines of 30° and 60° are related to the cosines of 30° and 60°.

The sine of a 30° angle equals the cosine of a 60° angle. The sine of a 60° angle equals the cosine of 30° angle.

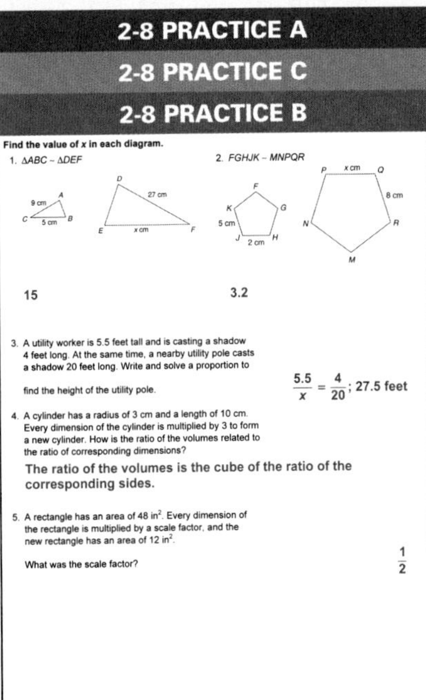

2-8 PRACTICE A
2-8 PRACTICE C
2-8 PRACTICE B

Find the value of x in each diagram.

1. $\triangle ABC \sim \triangle DEF$

15

2. $FGHJK \sim MNPQR$

3.2

3. A utility worker is 5.5 feet tall and is casting a shadow 4 feet long. At the same time, a nearby utility pole casts a shadow 20 feet long. Write and solve a proportion to find the height of the utility pole. $\frac{5.5}{x} = \frac{4}{20}$**; 27.5 feet**

4. A cylinder has a radius of 3 cm and a length of 10 cm. Every dimension of the cylinder is multiplied by 3 to form a new cylinder. How is the ratio of the volumes related to the ratio of corresponding dimensions?

The ratio of the volumes is the cube of the ratio of the corresponding sides.

5. A rectangle has an area of 48 in². Every dimension of the rectangle is multiplied by a scale factor, and the new rectangle has an area of 12 in². What was the scale factor? **$\frac{1}{2}$**

TEST PREP DOCTOR In **Exercise 24,** the radius of the first ball is twice the radius of the second. Since $2^3 = 8$, to find the volume of the smaller sphere, divide 800 by 8.

In **Exercise 25,** students can look at the first ratio in each similarity statement and check that the letters *S* and *G* are in the same positions as *M* and *W*. Only choice **G** has them placed incorrectly.

Journal

Give students the following problem: You and a friend are discussing the height of a tree. Explain how to use proportions to find this height.

ALTERNATIVE ASSESSMENT

Charlene is making a quilt out of rectangular blocks. The pattern for each block is 6 in. by 9 in. If she reduces the blocks to $\frac{2}{3}$ this size and uses 21 blocks for the width and 24 blocks for the length, what will be the dimensions and area of the quilt? Show all of your work and explain how you got your answer.

Power Presentations with PowerPoint®

2-8 Lesson Quiz

Find the value of *x* in each diagram.

1. $\triangle ABC \sim \triangle MLK$ 34

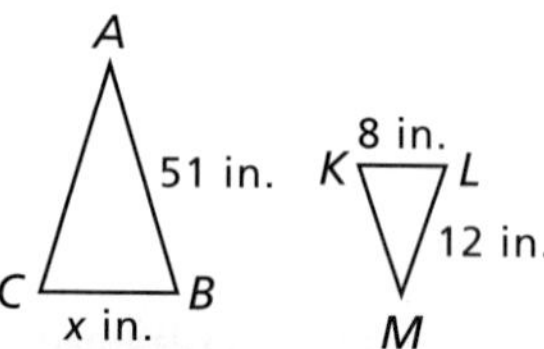

2. $RSTU \sim WXYZ$ 7

28 cm, R, S, U, T, 20 cm; x cm, W, X, Z, Y, 5 cm

3. A girl that is 5 ft tall casts a shadow 4 ft long. At the same time, a tree casts a shadow 24 ft long. How tall is the tree? 30 ft

4. The lengths of the sides of a square are multiplied by 2.5. How is the ratio of the areas related to the ratio of the sides? The ratio of the areas is the square of the ratio of the sides.

Also available on transparency

21. $\frac{1.5}{x} = \frac{4.5}{36}$; 12 m

21. A lighthouse casts a shadow that is 36 meters long. At the same time, a person who is 1.5 meters tall casts a shadow that is 4.5 meters long. Write and solve a proportion to find the height of the lighthouse.

22. In the diagram, $\triangle ABC \sim \triangle DEC$. What is the distance across the river from *A* to *B*? **96 m**

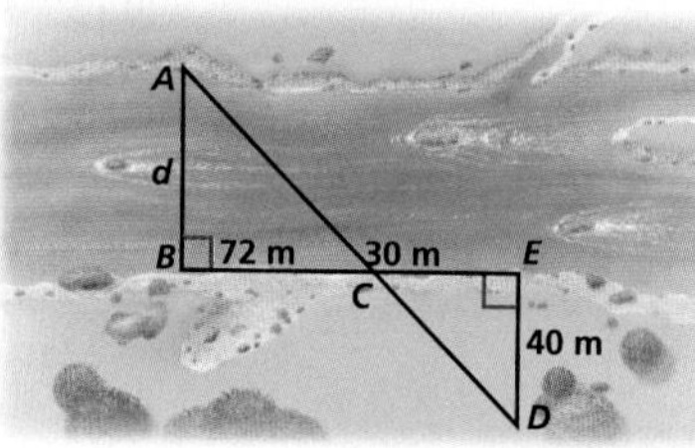

23. Critical Thinking If every dimension of a two-dimensional figure is multiplied by *k*, by what quantity is the area multiplied? k^2

24. A beach ball holds 800 cubic inches of air. Another beach ball has a radius that is half that of the larger ball. How much air does the smaller ball hold?

Ⓐ 400 cubic inches
Ⓑ 200 cubic inches
Ⓒ 100 cubic inches
Ⓓ 80 cubic inches

25. For two similar triangles, $\frac{SG}{MW} = \frac{GT}{WR} = \frac{TS}{RM}$. Which statement below is NOT correct?

Ⓕ $\triangle SGT \sim \triangle MWR$
Ⓖ $\triangle GST \sim \triangle MRW$
Ⓗ $\triangle TGS \sim \triangle RWM$
Ⓙ $\triangle GTS \sim \triangle WRM$

26. Gridded Response A rectangle has length 5 centimeters and width 3 centimeters. A similar rectangle has length 7.25 centimeters. What is the width in centimeters of this rectangle? **4.35**

CHALLENGE AND EXTEND

27. $w = 4$; $x = 7.5$; $y = 8$

27. Find the values of *w*, *x*, and *y* given that $\triangle ABC \sim \triangle DEF \sim \triangle GHJ$.

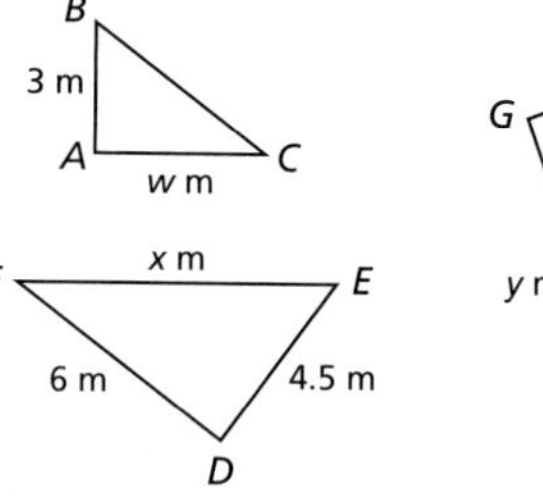

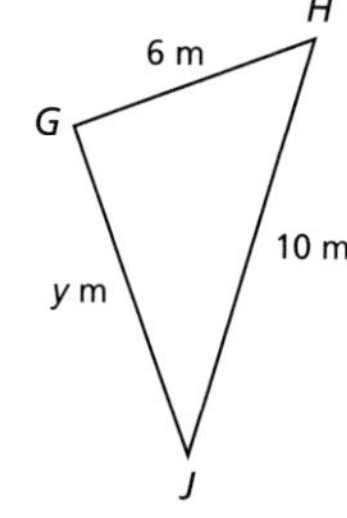

28. $\triangle RST \sim \triangle VWX$ and $\frac{RT}{VX} = b$.

What is $\frac{\text{area of } \triangle RST}{\text{area of } \triangle VWX}$? b^2

29. Multi-Step Rectangles *A* and *B* are similar. The area of *A* is 30.195 cm². The length of *B* is 6.1 cm. Each dimension of *B* is $\frac{2}{3}$ the corresponding dimension of *A*. What is the perimeter of *B*? **16.6 cm**

SPIRAL REVIEW

Add or subtract. *(Lesson 1-2)*

30. $-9 - 2$ **−11** **31.** $-7 + (-5)$ **−12** **32.** $12 - (-18)$ **30** **33.** $19 - 65$ **−46**

Generate ordered pairs for each function for $x = -2, -1, 0, 1, 2$. *(Lesson 1-8)*

34. $y = 2x$ **35.** $y = x^2$ **36.** $y = 6 - x$ **37.** $y = 3x - 1$

Solve each proportion. *(Lesson 2-7)*

38. $\frac{x}{8} = \frac{1}{4}$ **2** **39.** $\frac{6}{x} = \frac{3}{16}$ **32** **40.** $\frac{5}{12} = \frac{-4}{f}$ **−9.6** **41.** $\frac{3}{10} = \frac{x+1}{15}$ **3.5**

Answers

34. (−2, −4); (−1, −2); (0, 0); (1, 2); (2, 4)
35. (−2, 4); (−1, 1); (0, 0); (1, 1); (2, 4)
36. (−2, 8); (−1, 7); (0, 6); (1, 5); (2, 4)
37. (−2, −7); (−1, −4); (0, −1); (1, 2); (2, 5)

2-9 Percents

Objective
Solve problems involving percents.

Vocabulary
percent

Who uses this?
Jewelers use percents to determine the purity of precious metals. (See Example 4.)

A **percent** is a ratio that compares a number to 100. For example, $25\% = \frac{25}{100}$.

To find the fraction equivalent of a percent, write the percent as a ratio with a denominator of 100. Then simplify.

$$25\% = \frac{25}{100} = \frac{1}{4}$$

To find the decimal equivalent of a percent, divide by 100.

$$25\% = \frac{25}{100} = 0.25$$

Some Common Equivalents

Percent	10%	20%	25%	$33\frac{1}{3}\%$	40%	50%	60%	$66\frac{2}{3}\%$	75%	80%	100%
Fraction	$\frac{1}{10}$	$\frac{1}{5}$	$\frac{1}{4}$	$\frac{1}{3}$	$\frac{2}{5}$	$\frac{1}{2}$	$\frac{3}{5}$	$\frac{2}{3}$	$\frac{3}{4}$	$\frac{4}{5}$	1
Decimal	0.1	0.2	0.25	$0.\overline{3}$	0.4	0.5	0.6	$0.\overline{6}$	0.75	0.8	1.0

The greatest percent shown in the table is 100%, or 1. But percents can be greater than 100%. For example, $120\% = \frac{120}{100} = 1.2$. You can also find percents that are less than 1%. For example, $0.5\% = \frac{0.5}{100} = 0.005$.

You can use the proportion $\frac{\text{part}}{\text{whole}} = \frac{\text{percent}}{100}$ to find unknown values.

EXAMPLE 1 Finding the Part

A Find 50% of 20.

Method 1 Use a proportion.

$\frac{\text{part}}{\text{whole}} = \frac{\text{percent}}{100}$ *Use the percent proportion.*

$\frac{x}{20} = \frac{50}{100}$ *Let x represent the part.*

$100x = 1000$ *Find the cross products.*

$x = 10$ *Since x is multiplied by 100, divide both sides by 100 to undo the multiplication.*

50% of 20 is 10.

Check 50% is the same as $\frac{1}{2}$, and $\frac{1}{2}$ of 20 is 10. ✓

2-9 Organizer

Pacing: Traditional 1 day
Block $\frac{1}{2}$ day

Objective: Solve problems involving percents.

Online Edition
Tutorial Videos

Countdown Week 5

Power Presentations with PowerPoint®

Warm Up

Change each percent to a decimal.

1. 73% 0.73 **2.** 112% 1.12

3. 0.6% 0.006 **4.** 1% 0.01

Change each fraction or mixed number to a decimal.

5. $\frac{1}{2}$ 0.5 **6.** $\frac{1}{3}$ $0.\overline{3}$

7. $\frac{4}{5}$ 0.8 **8.** $1\frac{1}{5}$ 1.2

Solve each proportion.

9. $\frac{3}{x} = \frac{2}{8}$ 12 **10.** $\frac{x}{7} = \frac{6}{10}$ 4.2

Also available on transparency

Math Humor

Son: Dad, what does it mean when someone tells me to give 110%?

Dad: It means they didn't take Algebra 1.

1 Introduce

EXPLORATION

2-9 Percents

You will need a sheet of graph paper for this Exploration.

In the grid, 5 out of the 100 squares are shaded. One way to say "out of 100" is "percent." You can say that 5% of the squares are shaded.

Draw a 10-by-10 grid on graph paper. Then answer the following questions.

1. Shade one column of the grid, as shown. This represents $\frac{1}{10}$ of the grid. What percent of the grid is shaded? Record the percent in the table.

Fraction	$\frac{1}{10}$	$\frac{2}{10} = \frac{1}{5}$	$\frac{3}{10}$	$\frac{4}{10} = \frac{2}{5}$	$\frac{5}{10} = \frac{1}{2}$	$\frac{6}{10} = \frac{3}{5}$	$\frac{7}{10}$	$\frac{8}{10} = \frac{4}{5}$	$\frac{9}{10}$	$\frac{10}{10} = 1$
Percent										

2. Shade another column of the grid to find the percent that is equal to $\frac{2}{10}$ (or $\frac{1}{5}$). Record the result in the table. Continue in this way until the table is complete.

THINK AND DISCUSS

3. Explain how to shade $\frac{1}{...}$ of the grid. How many squares

Motivate

Ask students for three different ways to describe how much of the square is shaded. $\frac{4}{5}$; 0.8; 80%

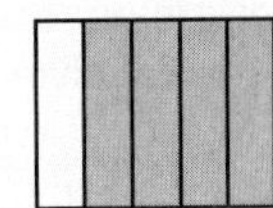

Explain to students that in order to work successfully with percents, it is important to know the different ways that percents can be represented.

Explorations and answers are provided in *Alternate Openers: Explorations Transparencies.*

State Resources

Teaching Tip **Reading Math** Encourage students to translate percent problems into mathematics by using the following: *of* means multiply, *is* means equal, and *what* means the variable. ENGLISH LANGUAGE LEARNERS

Power Presentations with PowerPoint®

Additional Examples

Example 1

A. Find 30% of 80. 24

B. Find 120% of 15. 18

Example 2

A. What percent of 45 is 35? Round your answer to the nearest tenth. 77.8%

B. 230 is what percent of 200? 115%

Example 3

A. 38% of what number is 85? Round your answer to the nearest tenth. 223.7

B. 20 is 0.4% of what number? 5000

INTERVENTION

Questioning Strategies

EXAMPLES 1–3

- Identify any similarities you see between using an equation and using a proportion.
- How can you determine the reasonableness of your answer?

Inclusion Emphasize the need for organized work when changing fractional percents to decimals. First change the fractional percent to a decimal percent, then change the percent to decimal form. Skipping a step often results in an error.

Multiple Representations Students may find it beneficial to draw a model when making estimations until they are able to represent the situation numerically.

B **Find 105% of 72.**

Method 2 Use an equation.

$x = 105\%$ of 72	*Write an equation. Let x represent the part.*
$x = 1.05(72)$	*Write the percent as a decimal and multiply.*
$x = 75.6$	

105% of 72 is 75.6.

1a. Find 20% of 60. **12** **1b.** Find 210% of 8. **16.8** **1c.** Find 4% of 36. **1.44**

EXAMPLE 2 Finding the Percent

Helpful Hint

Before solving, decide what is a reasonable answer. For Example 2A, 50% of 60 is 30, so the answer will be less than 50% of 60.

A **What percent of 60 is 15?**

Method 1 Use a proportion.

$\frac{\text{part}}{\text{whole}} = \frac{\text{percent}}{100}$	*Use the percent proportion.*
$\frac{15}{60} = \frac{x}{100}$	*Let x represent the percent.*
$60x = 1500$	*Find the cross products.*
$\frac{60x}{60} = \frac{1500}{60}$	*Since x is multiplied by 60, divide both sides by 60 to undo the multiplication.*
$x = 25$	

15 is 25% of 60.

B **440 is what percent of 400?**

Method 2 Use an equation.

$440 = x \cdot 400$	*Write an equation. Let x represent the percent.*
$440 = 400x$	*Since x is multiplied by 400, divide both sides by 400 to undo the multiplication.*
$\frac{440}{400} = \frac{400x}{400}$	
$1.1 = x$	*The answer is a decimal.*
$110\% = x$	*Write the decimal as a percent. This answer is reasonable; 440 is more than 100% of 400.*

440 is 110% of 400.

2a. What percent of 35 is 7? **20%** **2b.** 27 is what percent of 9? **300%**

EXAMPLE 3 Finding the Whole

A **40% of what number is 14?**

Method 1 Use a proportion.

$\frac{\text{part}}{\text{whole}} = \frac{\text{percent}}{100}$	*Use the percent proportion.*
$\frac{14}{x} = \frac{40}{100}$	*Let x represent the whole.*
$40x = 1400$	*Find the cross products.*
$\frac{40x}{40} = \frac{1400}{40}$	*Since x is multiplied by 40, divide both sides by 40 to undo the multiplication.*
$x = 35$	

40% of 35 is 14.

Teach

Guided Instruction

Be sure that students can convert between fractions, decimals, and percents, including those less than 1% or greater than 100%, before solving problems involving percents. Have students practice stating whether a problem is about finding the part, the whole, or the percent before they solve it. Encourage estimating before solving as well as asking if the answer makes sense. This will be beneficial when solving common applications of percents.

Reaching All Learners

Through Number Sense

Encourage students to quickly find 50% and 25% of any number by dividing in half, then in half again. For example:

	50%	25%
80	40	20
48	24	12

Students can check the reasonableness of an answer. If asked to find 35% of 48, the student knows the answer is between 12 and 24.

B **40 is 0.8% of what number?**

Method 2 Use an equation.

$40 = 0.8\% \text{ of } x$ — *Write an equation. Let x represent the whole.*

$40 = 0.008 \cdot x$ — *Write the percent as a decimal.*

$\frac{40}{0.008} = \frac{0.008x}{0.008}$ — *Since x is multiplied by 0.008, divide both sides by 0.008 to undo the multiplication.*

$5000 = x$

40 is 0.8% of 5000.

3a. 120% of what number is 90? **75**

3b. 48 is 15% of what number? **320**

EXAMPLE  **4** ***Career Application***

Jewelers use the karat system to determine the amount of pure gold in jewelry. Pure gold is 24 karat, meaning the item is 100% gold. A 14-karat gold ring contains 14 parts gold and 10 parts other metal. What percent of the ring is gold? Round your answer to the nearest percent.

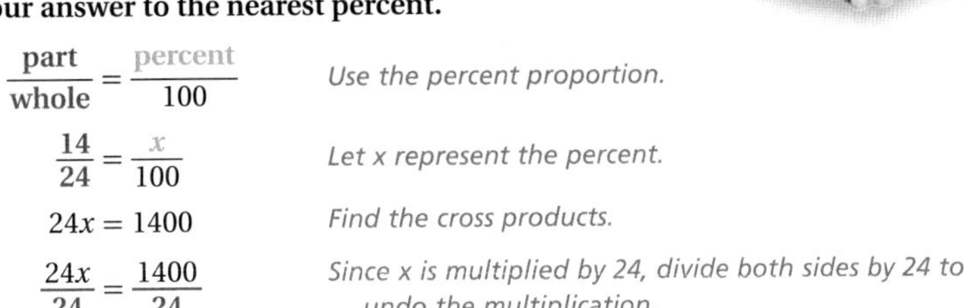

$\frac{\text{part}}{\text{whole}} = \frac{\text{percent}}{100}$ — *Use the percent proportion.*

$\frac{14}{24} = \frac{x}{100}$ — *Let x represent the percent.*

$24x = 1400$ — *Find the cross products.*

$\frac{24x}{24} = \frac{1400}{24}$ — *Since x is multiplied by 24, divide both sides by 24 to undo the multiplication.*

$x = 58.\overline{3}$

A 14-karat gold ring is approximately 58% gold.

4. Use the information above to find the number of karats in a bracelet that is 42% gold. Round your answer to the nearest whole number. **10 karats**

THINK AND DISCUSS

1. Describe the numerical value of the percent when the part is greater than the whole. Give an example.

2. 64% of a number is 32. Is the number greater than or less than 32? Explain.

Know it! Note

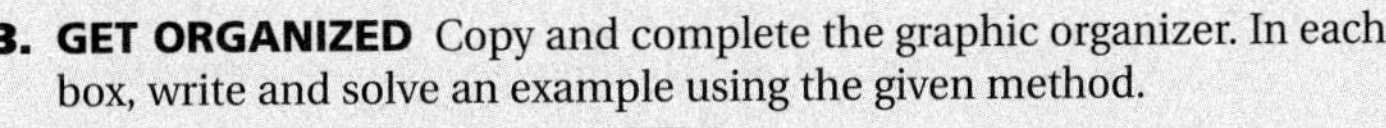

3. GET ORGANIZED Copy and complete the graphic organizer. In each box, write and solve an example using the given method.

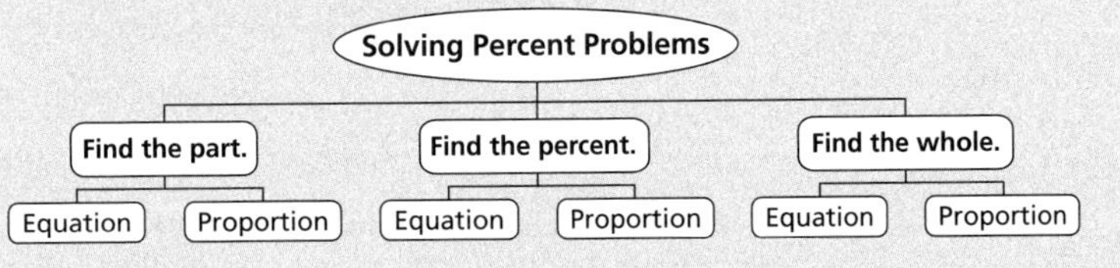

COMMON ERROR ALERT

Students may be confused as to when to change a percent to a decimal. When using the proportion method shown in **Example 3A,** the percent is not changed to decimal form because the percent number is divided by 100 as part of the proportion. When using the equation method shown in **Example 3B,** point out that dividing the percent number by 100 is equivalent to changing it to decimal form.

Power Presentations with PowerPoint®

Additional Examples

Example 4

The serving size of a popular orange drink is 12 oz. The drink is advertised as containing 5% orange juice. How many ounces of orange juice are in one serving size? 0.6 oz

INTERVENTION

Questioning Strategies

EXAMPLE 4

- What is your strategy for determining which number is the percent? the part? the whole?

Teaching Tip **Critical Thinking** Encourage students to estimate answers before solving problems. Advise students always to ask themselves, "Does my answer make sense?"

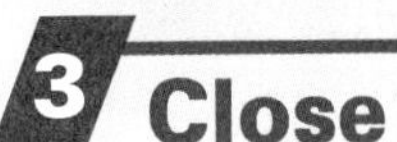

3 Close

Summarize

For each problem below, have students state whether they are finding the part, the whole, or the percent. Then have them find each value and round to the nearest tenth if necessary.

1. What percent of 120 is 24?
percent; 20%

2. Find 130% of 12.
part; 15.6

3. 40% of what number is 32?
whole; 80

ONGOING ASSESSMENT and INTERVENTION 

***Diagnose Before* the Lesson**
2-9 Warm Up, TE p. 133

***Monitor During* the Lesson**
Check It Out! Exercises, SE pp. 134–135
Questioning Strategies, TE pp. 134–135

***Assess After* the Lesson**
2-9 Lesson Quiz, TE p. 138
Alternative Assessment, TE p. 138

Answers to *Think and Discuss*

1. If the part is greater than the whole, then the percent is greater than 100%. Possible answer: If the whole is 20 and the part is 25, then the percent is 125%.
2. Greater than 32; 64% is less than 100%, so 32 is less than the whole. So the whole is greater than 32.
3. See p. A3.

2-9 Exercises

Assignment Guide

Assign *Guided Practice* exercises as necessary.

If you finished Examples **1–2**
- **Basic** 15–22, 28–47, 50–53
- **Average** 15–22, 28–47, 65, 67–69
- **Advanced** 15–22, 28–46 even, 65, 67–69

If you finished Examples **1–4**
- **Basic** 15–48, 50, 52, 54, 56, 59–64, 71–77
- **Average** 15–27, 28–46 even, 48–69, 71–77
- **Advanced** 15–27, 28–46 even, 48–77

Homework Quick Check
Quickly check key concepts.
Exercises: 18, 20, 24, 27, 48, 55

State Resources

2-9 Exercises

go.hrw.com
Homework Help Online
KEYWORD: MA11 2-9
Parent Resources Online
KEYWORD: MA7 Parent

GUIDED PRACTICE

1. Possible answer: a number compared to 100

SEE EXAMPLE 1 p. 133

1. **Vocabulary** In your own words, write a definition of *percent*.
2. Find 75% of 40. **30**
3. Find $12\frac{1}{2}$% of 168. **21**
4. Find 115% of 57. **65.55**
5. Find 70% of 8. **5.6**

SEE EXAMPLE 2 p. 134

6. What percent of 40 is 25? **62.5%**
7. What percent of 225 is 180? **80%**
8. 57 is what percent of 30? **190%**
9. 1 is what percent of 8? **12.5%**

SEE EXAMPLE 3 p. 134

10. 28 is 32% of what number? **87.5**
11. 4% of what number is 7? **175**
12. 16 is 10% of what number? **160**
13. 105% of what number is 37.8? **36**

SEE EXAMPLE 4 p. 135

14. **Nutrition** A certain granola bar has 2 grams of fiber. This is 8% of the recommended daily value. How many grams of fiber are recommended daily? **25 g**

PRACTICE AND PROBLEM SOLVING

Independent Practice

For Exercises	See Example
15–18	1
19–22	2
23–26	3
27	4

Extra Practice
Skills Practice p. S7
Application Practice p. S29

Find each value. Round to the nearest tenth if necessary.

15. 60% of 80 **48**
16. 35% of 90 **31.5**
17. $\frac{1}{2}$% of 500 **2.5**
18. 210% of 30 **63**
19. What percent of 52 is 13? **25%**
20. What percent of 9 is 27? **300%**
21. 11 is what percent of 22? **50%**
22. 5 is what percent of 67? **7.5%**
23. 36 is 90% of what number? **40**
24. 8.2 is 2% of what number? **410**
25. $4\frac{1}{2}$% of what number is 23? **511.1**
26. 16% of what number is 94? **587.5**
27. **Nutrition** A certain can of iced tea contains 4% of the recommended daily allowance of sodium. The recommended daily allowance is 2500 milligrams. How many milligrams of sodium are in the can of iced tea? **100 mg**

Write each decimal or fraction as a percent.

28. $\frac{5}{4}$ **125%**
29. 0.02 **2%**
30. 0.27 **27%**
31. $\frac{2}{25}$ **8%**
32. $\frac{7}{7}$ **100%**
33. 0.64 **64%**
34. $\frac{31}{100}$ **31%**
35. 0.85 **85%**
36. 0.003 **0.3%**
37. $\frac{17}{20}$ **85%**

Write each percent as a decimal and as a fraction.

38. 23%
39. 52%
40. 12.5%
41. 90%
42. 87.2%
43. 112%
44. 29%
45. 6%
46. 1.5%
47. $\frac{3}{5}$%

38. $0.23; \frac{23}{100}$
39. $0.52; \frac{13}{25}$
40. $0.125; \frac{1}{8}$
41. $0.90; \frac{90}{100}$
42. $0.872; \frac{109}{125}$
43. $1.12; \frac{28}{25}$
44. $0.29; \frac{29}{100}$
45. $0.06; \frac{3}{50}$
46. $0.015; \frac{3}{200}$
47. $0.006; \frac{3}{500}$

48. **Estimation** To estimate 26% of 400, think:

$$26\% \text{ is close to } 25\% \text{ and } 25\% = \frac{1}{4}$$

$$\frac{1}{4} \text{ of } 400 = 100.$$

Therefore, 26% of 400 is about 100.

Use a similar method to estimate 48% of 610 and 73% of 820. Then check your estimates by finding each percent. **Estimates: 305; 600; Actual: 292.8; 598.6**

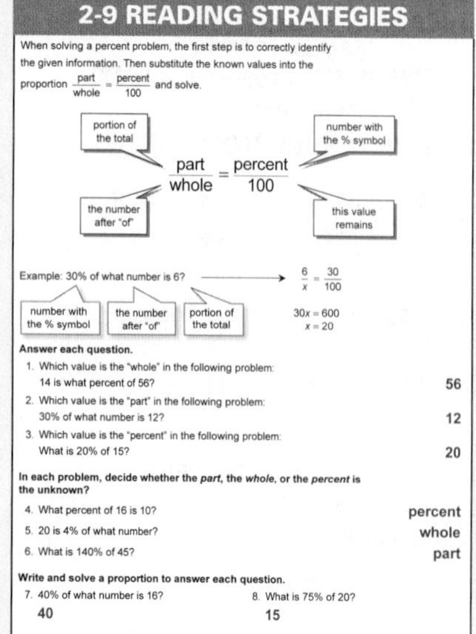
2-9 READING STRATEGIES

When solving a percent problem, the first step is to correctly identify the given information. Then substitute the known values into the proportion $\frac{\text{part}}{\text{whole}} = \frac{\text{percent}}{100}$ and solve.

$$\frac{\text{part}}{\text{whole}} = \frac{\text{percent}}{100}$$

Example: 30% of what number is 6? → $\frac{6}{x} = \frac{30}{100}$

$30x = 600$
$x = 20$

Answer each question.

1. Which value is the "whole" in the following problem: 14 is what percent of 56? **56**
2. Which value is the "part" in the following problem: 30% of what number is 12? **12**
3. Which value is the "percent" in the following problem: What is 20% of 15? **20**

In each problem, decide whether the *part*, the *whole*, or the *percent* is the unknown?

4. What percent of 16 is 10? **percent**
5. 20 is 4% of what number? **whole**
6. What is 140% of 45? **part**

Write and solve a proportion to answer each question.

7. 40% of what number is 16? **40**
8. What is 75% of 20? **15**

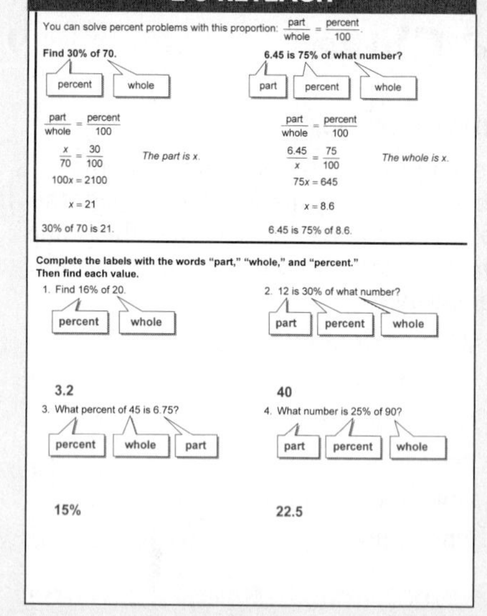
2-9 RETEACH

You can solve percent problems with this proportion: $\frac{\text{part}}{\text{whole}} = \frac{\text{percent}}{100}$.

Find 30% of 70.

$\frac{\text{part}}{\text{whole}} = \frac{\text{percent}}{100}$

$\frac{x}{70} = \frac{30}{100}$ *The part is x.*

$100x = 2100$

$x = 21$

30% of 70 is 21.

6.45 is 75% of what number?

$\frac{\text{part}}{\text{whole}} = \frac{\text{percent}}{100}$

$\frac{6.45}{x} = \frac{75}{100}$ *The whole is x.*

$75x = 645$

$x = 8.6$

6.45 is 75% of 8.6.

Complete the labels with the words "part," "whole," and "percent." Then find each value.

1. Find 16% of 20.

3.2

2. 12 is 30% of what number?

40

3. What percent of 45 is 6.75?

15%

4. What number is 25% of 90?

22.5

49. 0.5 is greater than $\frac{1}{2}$% because $\frac{1}{2}$% = 0.005.

49. **Critical Thinking** Which is greater, 0.5 or $\frac{1}{2}$%? Explain.

Write each list in order from least to greatest.

50. $\frac{1}{20}$, 5.3%, 5.1, 0.005, $\frac{1}{2}$

51. 1.1, 11%, $\frac{1}{10}$, 0.001, 1%

52. $\frac{3}{8}$, 29%, $\frac{2}{5}$, 0.25, 38%

53. 0.49, 82%, 0.94, $\frac{4}{5}$, $\frac{5}{9}$

54. **Biology** On average, sloths spend 16.5 hours per day sleeping. What percent of the day do sloths spend sleeping? Round your answer to the nearest percent. **69%**

55. **Entertainment** The numbers of various types of movies rented over a period of time are indicated in the graph.
   a. What percent of the movies rented were comedies? **40%**
   b. What type of movie made up 25% of the rentals?
   c. What percent of the movies rented were in the "other" category? **3%**
   d. **What if...?** If 25 of the comedy rentals had instead been action rentals, what percent of the movies rented would have been comedies? Round your answer to the nearest tenth. **36.9%**

55b. action

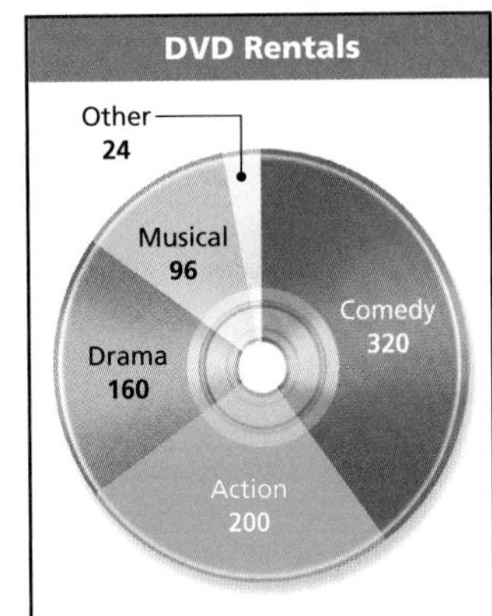

56. **Multi-Step** According to the 2000 U.S. Census, 138,053,563 Americans are male, and 143,368,343 Americans are female. About what percent of the population is male? female? Round your answers to the nearest percent. **49%; 51%**

57. Complete each statement in the table below. Describe any patterns you see in the completed table.

1% of 400 is 4.	100% of **12** is 12.	**25**% of 80 is 20.
2% of **200** is 4.	50% of **24** is 12.	**50**% of 40 is 20.
4% of **100** is 4.	25% of **48** is 12.	**100**% of 20 is 20.
8% of **50** is 4.	12.5% of **96** is 12.	**200**% of 10 is 20.

58. **Write About It** Explain the advantages of using the proportion method to solve percent problems. Then, explain the advantages of using the equation method to solve percent problems.

MULTI-STEP TEST PREP

59. This problem will prepare you for the Multi-Step Test Prep on page 152.

Kathryn found a new dress at the mall. The price tag reads \$90. The sign above the rack of dresses says that all items on the rack are 40% off.
   a. Set up a proportion to find 40% of \$90. This is the amount of the discount.
   b. How much will Kathryn pay for the dress? Show that your answer is reasonable.
   c. Copy and complete the model below. Explain how this model can help you answer the above questions in another way.

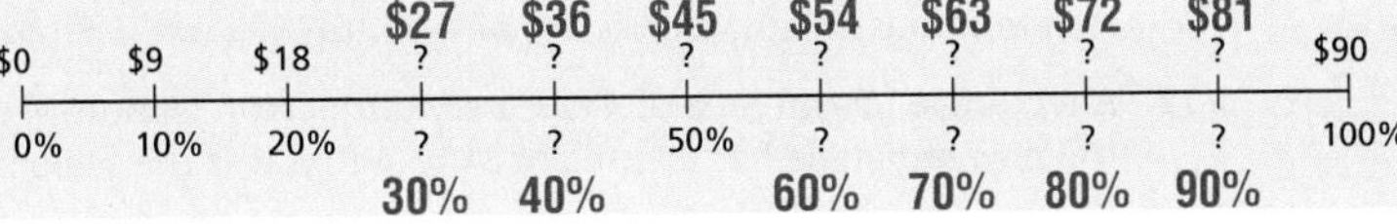

Exercise 59 involves using proportions to find discounts and sale prices. This exercise prepares students for the Multi-Step Test Prep on page 152.

Answers

50. 0.005, $\frac{1}{20}$, 5.3%, $\frac{1}{2}$, 5.1
51. 0.001, 1%, $\frac{1}{10}$, 11%, 1.1
52. 0.25, 29%, $\frac{3}{8}$, 38%, $\frac{2}{5}$
53. 0.49, $\frac{5}{9}$, $\frac{4}{5}$, 82%, 0.94
57. Possible answer: As the percent doubles, the missing value is divided by two, and vice versa.
58. Possible answer: the equation method may require fewer steps. The proportion method is good if you can't remember how to set up the equation, because the proportion method will work for any type of percent problem.

59a. $\frac{x}{90} = \frac{40}{100}$; \$36

b. \$54

Possible answer: the discount is 40%, so the sale price will be more than half of \$90, or \$45. So \$54 is reasonable.

c. Possible answer: \$90 is divided into 10 groups, and each group represents 10%. So 4 of the groups represent 40%.

2-9 PROBLEM SOLVING

Use the table below, which shows the recommended daily allowance of food components for a 2000-calorie diet, to answer questions 1–8. Round your answers to the nearest tenth.

Component	Recommended Daily Allowance
Total fat	65 g
Saturated fat	20 g
Cholesterol	300 mg
Sodium	2400 mg
Total Carbohydrates	300 g
Fiber	25 g

1. One serving of oatmeal contains 16% of the recommended daily allowance of fiber. How many grams of fiber are in one serving?
   4 grams
2. A certain can of soup contains 30% of the recommended daily allowance of sodium. How many milligrams of sodium are in one can?
   720 mg
3. One serving of pure Vermont maple syrup contains 53 grams of total carbohydrates. What percent of the recommended daily allowance is this?
   17.7%
4. One serving of pumpkin pie contains 12 total grams of fat. What percent of the recommended daily allowance is this?
   18.5%

Select the best answer.

5. A certain nutrition bar contains 15% of the recommended daily allowance of saturated fat. How many grams of saturated fat are in the bar?
   A 2.5 g C 4 g
   B 3 g D 5 g
6. One serving of plain yogurt contains 6 mg of cholesterol. What percent of the recommended daily allowance is this?
   F 2% H 20%
   G 5% J 50%
7. A cereal contains 90 mg of potassium, and this is 3% of the recommended daily allowance. What is the recommended daily allowance of potassium?
   A 27 mg C 300 mg
   B 270 mg **D** 3000 mg
8. A slice of whole grain bread contains 7 grams of fiber. What percent of the recommended daily allowance is this?
   F 18% **H** 28%
   G 25% J 30%

2-9 CHALLENGE

During a sale, the markdown of an item often becomes the focal point of the advertisement, such as "25% off". When you save 25%, or $\frac{1}{4}$, of the cost of the item, you pay $1 - \frac{1}{4}$, or $\frac{3}{4}$, of the cost. Frequently, a markup on an item is made before a sale starts. If an item is marked up by 25%, or $\frac{1}{4}$, the new cost becomes $1 + \frac{1}{4}$, or $\frac{5}{4}$, of the old cost.

In the exercises below, a coat originally costs \$130.

1. The merchant marks the coat up by 25%. Find the new price of the coat. **\$162.50**
2. After the markup is made, the merchant marks the coat down by 40%. Find the sale price of the coat after it is marked up and then marked down. **\$97.50**
3. Chris thought that the sale price of the coat after the markup and then the markdown should result in a 15% reduction in the original cost of the coat. Use reasoning to show that this is not correct.
   85% of \$130 is \$110.50, not \$97.50
4. In the box at right, a three-step process has taken place. Given your work in Exercises 1 and 2, describe the process.
   a 30% markup followed by a 15% markdown

   Step 1: 240
   Step 2: $\left(1+\frac{3}{10}\right)240$
   Step 3: $\left(1-\frac{15}{100}\right)\left[\left(1+\frac{3}{10}\right)240\right]$
5. An item is marked up by a given percent and is then marked down by a given percent. Explain how to find the sale price.
   Multiply the original amount by one plus the decimal or fractional form of the markup and then multiply that amount by one minus the decimal or fractional form of the markdown.

In some sale situations, a merchant will mark an item down and then mark the item down again.

6. Find the sale price of the coat after a 25% markdown. **\$97.50**
7. After the markdown in Exercise 6, the merchant marked the item down 40%. Find the sale price after the second markdown. **\$58.50**
8. In the box at right, a three-step process has taken place. Given your work in Exercises 6 and 7, describe the process.
   a 30% markdown followed by a 15% markdown

   Step 1: 130
   Step 2: $\left(1-\frac{3}{10}\right)130$
   Step 3: $\left(1-\frac{15}{100}\right)\left[\left(1-\frac{3}{10}\right)130\right]$
9. Explain how to find the sale price of an item after it is marked down by a given percent and then marked down by another percent.
   Multiply the original amount by one minus the decimal or fractional form of the markdown and then multiply that amount by one minus the decimal or fractional form of the next markdown.

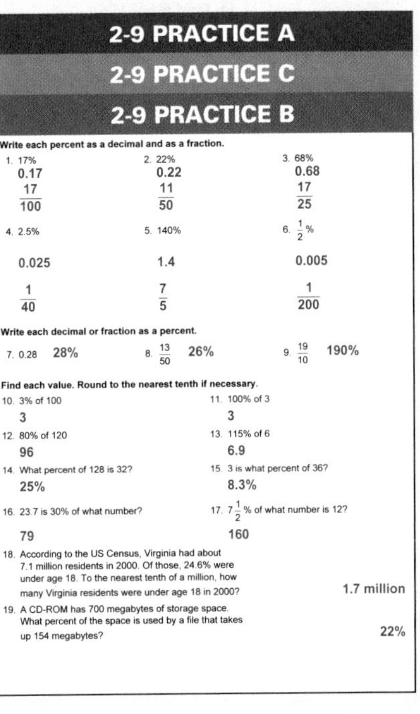

2-9 PRACTICE A
2-9 PRACTICE C
2-9 PRACTICE B

Write each percent as a decimal and as a fraction.

1. 17% **0.17** $\frac{17}{100}$
2. 22% **0.22** $\frac{11}{50}$
3. 68% **0.68** $\frac{17}{25}$
4. 2.5% **0.025** $\frac{1}{40}$
5. 140% **1.4** $\frac{7}{5}$
6. $\frac{1}{2}$% **0.005** $\frac{1}{200}$

Write each decimal or fraction as a percent.

7. 0.28 **28%**
8. $\frac{13}{50}$ **26%**
9. $\frac{19}{10}$ **190%**

Find each value. Round to the nearest tenth if necessary.

10. 3% of 100 **3**
11. 100% of 3 **3**
12. 80% of 120 **96**
13. 115% of 6 **6.9**
14. What percent of 128 is 32? **25%**
15. 3 is what percent of 36? **8.3%**
16. 23.7 is 30% of what number? **79**
17. $7\frac{1}{2}$% of what number is 12? **160**
18. According to the US Census, Virginia had about 7.1 million residents in 2000. Of those, 24.6% were under age 18. To the nearest tenth of a million, how many Virginia residents were under age 18 in 2000? **1.7 million**
19. A CD-ROM has 700 megabytes of storage space. What percent of the space is used by a file that takes up 154 megabytes? **22%**

TEST PREP DOCTOR In **Exercise 61,** students who chose **G** may not have used the correct number as the *part* in their proportion, or they may not have taken $\frac{1}{2}$ of the resulting percent. If students used the proportion $\frac{x}{100} = \frac{14}{35}$, then $x = 40$. Dividing this in half would yield the correct answer of 20%. Or, if students take $\frac{1}{2}$ of 14 students, the proportion will be $\frac{x}{100} = \frac{7}{35}$.

In **Exercise 63,** first change percents to decimals to eliminate incorrect answers. Next, change fractions to decimals to quickly determine the correct order.

Journal

Ask students to explain how they would estimate the following: 52% of what number is 28? Then have them solve the problem to see how close they were to their estimate.

ALTERNATIVE ASSESSMENT

Have students find three different advertisements in newspapers that specify a certain percent reduction in price. Instruct students to set up a proportion for each advertisement and solve the problem. Then have them create a word problem for each advertisement, first asking to find the part, then the whole, and then the percent.

Power Presentations with PowerPoint®

2-9 Lesson Quiz

Find each value. Round to the nearest tenth if necessary.

1. Find 20% of 80. 16
2. What percent of 160 is 20? 12.5%
3. 35% of what number is 40? 114.3
4. 120 is what percent of 80? 150%
5. Find 320% of 8. 25.6
6. 65 is 0.5% of what number? 13,000
7. A survey at a local school showed that 38% of students chose chocolate ice cream as their favorite ice cream. Eight hundred students took the survey. How many chose chocolate ice cream? 304

Also available on transparency

TEST PREP

60. Which proportion can be used to find 14% of 60?

Ⓐ $\frac{x}{100} = \frac{60}{14}$ Ⓑ $\frac{14}{100} = \frac{60}{x}$ Ⓒ $\frac{x}{100} = \frac{14}{60}$ Ⓓ $\frac{14}{100} = \frac{x}{60}$

61. Raul surveyed 35 students about their preferred lunch. Fourteen preferred chicken. Half of those students preferred chicken with barbecue sauce. What percent should Raul report as preferring chicken with barbecue sauce?

Ⓕ 20% Ⓖ 40% Ⓗ 50% Ⓙ 80%

62. After an election in a small town, the newspaper reported that 42% of the registered voters actually voted. If 12,000 people voted, which equation can be used to find the number of registered voters?

Ⓐ $v = 42 \cdot 12{,}000$ Ⓑ $v = 0.42 \cdot 12{,}000$ Ⓒ $42v = 12{,}000$ Ⓓ $0.42v = 12{,}000$

63. Which list is in order from least to greatest?

Ⓕ $\frac{1}{2}$, 20%, 33%, 0.625, $\frac{1}{8}$, 1 Ⓗ $\frac{1}{8}$, $\frac{1}{2}$, 0.625, 1, 20%, 30%

Ⓖ $\frac{1}{8}$, 20%, 33%, $\frac{1}{2}$, 0.625, 1 Ⓙ 0.625, $\frac{1}{8}$, $\frac{1}{2}$, 1, 20%, 30%

64. Moises saves 8% of his weekly paycheck in his savings account. He deposited $18.80 from his last paycheck into his savings account. Which is the best estimate of the total amount of Moises's last paycheck?

Ⓐ $26 Ⓑ $100 Ⓒ $160 Ⓓ $200

CHALLENGE AND EXTEND

Find each value. Round to the nearest tenth if necessary.

65. What percent of 16 is 2.75? **17.2%**

66. 22 is 73.5% of what number? **29.9**

67. 121.3% of 73 is what number? **88.5**

68. What percent of 8000 is 6525? **81.6%**

69. Find 10% of 8 and 8% of 10. What do you notice? Try this with several other pairs of numbers. Do you think this relationship will be true for all pairs of numbers? Why or why not?

69. They're equal; yes; x% of y is $\frac{x}{100} \cdot y$ and y% of x is $\frac{y}{100} \cdot x$. Both expressions are equivalent to $\frac{xy}{100}$.

70. Chemistry A chemist has 20 milliliters of a solution that is 40% acid. She wants to increase the acid content of the solution to make it a 50%-acid solution. How many milliliters of pure acid should she add to the solution? (*Hint:* Begin by finding the number of milliliters of acid in the original solution.) **4 mL**

SPIRAL REVIEW

Simplify each expression. *(Lesson 1-7)*

71. $32 + 47 + 28 + 13$ **120**

72. $4 \cdot 23 \cdot 25$ **2300**

73. $8 \cdot 4 \cdot 5$ **160**

74. $44 + 27 + 56$ **127**

75. A picture has a width of 4 in. and a length of 6 in. It is enlarged on a copier, and the new length is 9 in. What is the new width? *(Lesson 2-8)* **6 in.**

76. A picture has a width of 4 in. and a length of 6 in. It is reduced on a copier, and the new length is 4.8 in. What is the new width? *(Lesson 2-8)* **3.2 in.**

77. A rectangle has an area of 9 ft^2. Every dimension is multiplied by a scale factor, and the new rectangle has an area of 81 ft^2. What was the scale factor? *(Lesson 2-8)* **3**

2-10 Applications of Percents

Objectives
Use common applications of percents.
Estimate with percents.

Vocabulary
commission
interest
sales tax
principal
tip

Who uses this?
Sales representatives use percents to calculate their total pay.

A **commission** is money paid to a person or a company for making a sale. Usually the commission is a percent of the sale amount.

EXAMPLE 1 ***Business Application***

Ms. Barns earns a base salary of \$42,000 plus a 1.5% commission on sales. Her total sales one year were \$700,000. Find her total pay for the year.

Caution!
You must convert a percent to a decimal or a fraction before doing any calculations with it.

total pay = base salary + commission	*Write the formula for total pay.*
= base salary + % of total sales	*Write the formula for commission.*
= 42,000 + 1.5% of 700,000	*Substitute values given in the problem.*
= 42,000 + (0.015)(700,000)	*Write the percent as a decimal.*
= 42,000 + 10,500	*Multiply.*
= 52,500	*Add.*

Ms. Barns's total pay was \$52,500.

CHECK IT OUT! **1.** A telemarketer earns \$350 per week plus a 12% commission on sales. Find her total pay for a week in which her sales are \$940. **\$462.80**

Interest is the amount of money charged for borrowing money, or the amount of money earned when saving or investing money. **Principal** is the amount borrowed or invested. Simple interest is interest paid only on the principal.

Simple Interest Paid Annually

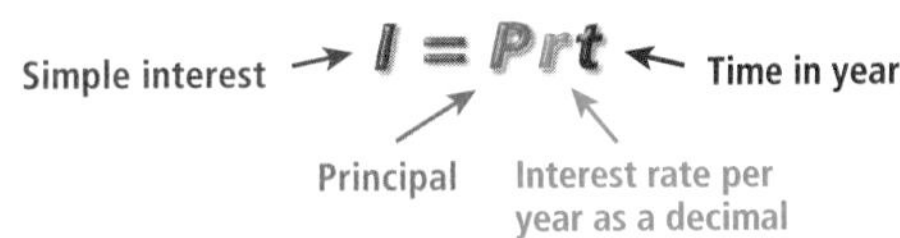

EXAMPLE 2 ***Finance Application***

A **Find the simple interest paid annually for 2 years on a \$900 loan at 16% per year.**

$I = Prt$	*Write the formula for simple interest.*
$I = (900)(0.16)(2)$	*Substitute known values. Write the interest rate as a decimal.*
$I = 288$	

The amount of interest is \$288.

2-10 Organizer

Pacing: Traditional 1 day
Block $\frac{1}{2}$ day

Objectives: Use common applications of percents.
Estimate with percents.

Technology Lab
In *Technology Lab Activities*

Online Edition
Tutorial Videos

Countdown Week 5

Power Presentations with PowerPoint®

Warm Up

1. Write 0.03 as a percent. 3%
2. Write $4\frac{1}{2}$% as a decimal. 0.045

Find each value. Round to the nearest tenth if necessary.

3. Find 10% of 53. 5.3
4. Find $2\frac{1}{2}$% of 50. 1.25

Solve for *x*.

5. $40 = (x)\left(\frac{1}{2}\right)(20)$ 4
6. $114 = (36)\left(\frac{1}{12}\right)(x)$ 38

Also available on transparency

Math Humor

Banker: Do you have any interest in taking out a loan?
Customer: If there's no interest, I'm interested!

1 Introduce

EXPLORATION

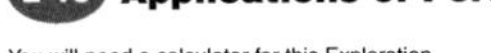

2-10 Applications of Percents

You will need a calculator for this Exploration.

1. The table shows the masses of several rocks in a geology museum. For each rock, use your calculator to find 10% of the mass and 1% of the mass. Record the results in the table.

Mass (kg)	10% of Mass (kg)	1% of Mass (kg)
4.1		
10.5		
143.9		
2010.6		

2. Describe any patterns you see in the table.
3. Another rock in the museum is composed of 10% copper and 1% zinc. The mass of the rock is 67.1 kg. Explain how you can use mental math to find the mass of the copper and the mass of the zinc. Then find each mass.

THINK AND DISCUSS

4. **Explain** how to use mental math to find 10% of a number.
5. **Explain** how to use mental math to find 5% of a number.

Motivate

Copy the table below onto the board and ask students to continue the pattern. Explain to students that the table represents an annual interest rate of 3%. Ask students how much interest is earned from a million dollars.

Principal (\$)	100	1000	10,000
Interest (\$)	3	30	300

Explorations and answers are provided in *Alternate Openers: Explorations Transparencies.*

State Resources

go.hrw.com
State Resources Online
KEYWORD: MA7 Resources

Power Presentations with PowerPoint®

Additional Examples

Example 1

Mr. Cortez earns a base salary of \$26,000 plus a sales commission of 5%. His total sales for one year were \$300,000. Find his total pay for the year. \$41,000

Example 2

A. Find the simple interest paid for 3 years on a \$2500 loan at 11.5% per year. \$862.50

B. After 6 months, the simple interest earned on an investment of \$5000 was \$45. Find the interest rate. 1.8%

Example 3

A. Lunch at a restaurant is \$27.88. Estimate a 15% tip. about \$4.50

B. The sales tax rate is 7.25%. Estimate the sales tax on a book that costs \$19.97. about \$1.40

INTERVENTION
Questioning Strategies

EXAMPLE 1

- Explain why someone who makes a base salary plus commission can never make less than the base salary.

EXAMPLE 2

- What unit is used for time in the formula?
- How can you "rearrange" the formula to make solving for the rate more convenient?

EXAMPLE 3

- How can you use the estimation techniques presented in **Example 3** to determine the reasonableness of your answer in **Example 1**?

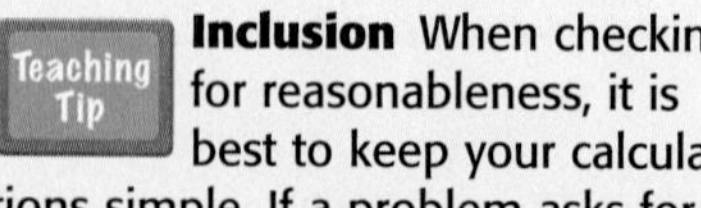

Inclusion When checking for reasonableness, it is best to keep your calculations simple. If a problem asks for 20% or 30%, simply check that your answer is less than half. If the problem requires 70% or 80%, check that your answer is more than half.

Helpful Hint

When you are using the formula $I = Prt$ to find simple interest paid annually, t represents time in years. One month is $\frac{1}{12}$ year. In Example 2B, $t = \frac{3}{12}$.

B **After 3 months the simple interest earned annually on an investment of \$7000 was \$63. Find the interest rate.**

$I = Prt$ — *Write the formula for simple interest.*

$63 = (7000)(r)\left(\frac{3}{12}\right)$ — *Substitute the given values.*

$63 = 1750r$ — *Multiply $7000\left(\frac{3}{12}\right)$. Since r is multiplied by 1750, divide both sides by 1750 to undo the multiplication.*

$\frac{63}{1750} = \frac{1750r}{1750}$

$0.036 = r$

The interest rate is 3.6%.

CHECK IT OUT!

2a. Find the simple interest earned after 2 years on an investment of \$3000 at 4.5% interest earned annually. **\$270**

2b. The simple interest paid on a loan after 6 months was \$306. The annual interest rate was 8%. Find the principal. **\$7650**

A **tip** is an amount of money added to a bill for service. It is usually a percent of the bill before *sales tax* is added. **Sales tax** is a percent of an item's cost.

Sales tax and tips are sometimes estimated instead of calculated exactly. When estimating percents, use percents that you can calculate mentally.

- Find 10% of a number by moving the decimal point one place to the left.
- Find 1% of a number by moving the decimal point two places to the left.
- Find 5% of a number by finding $\frac{1}{2}$ of 10% of the number.

EXAMPLE 3 Estimating with Percents

A **The dinner check for Maria's family is \$67.95. Estimate a 15% tip.**

Step 1 First round \$67.95 to \$70.

Step 2 Think: $15\% = 10\% + 5\%$

$10\% \text{ of } \$70 = \$7.00$ — *Move the decimal point one place left.*

Step 3 Think: $5\% = 10\% \div 2$

$= \$7.00 \div 2 = \$3.50$

Step 4 $15\% = 10\% + 5\%$

$= \$7.00 + \$3.50 = \$10.50$

The tip should be about \$10.50.

Helpful Hint

A 6.25% sales tax rate means that for every \$100 you spend, you would pay \$6.25 in sales tax.

B **The sales tax rate is 6.25%. Estimate the sales tax on a shirt that costs \$29.50.**

Step 1 First round 6.25% to 6% and \$29.50 to \$30.

Step 2 Think: $6\% = 6(1\%)$

$1\% \text{ of } \$30 = \$0.30$ — *Move the decimal point 2 places left.*

Step 3 $6\% = 6(1\%)$

$= 6(\$0.30) = \$1.80$

The sales tax is about \$1.80.

CHECK IT OUT!

3a. Estimate a 15% tip on a check for \$21.98. **about \$3.30**

3b. Estimate the tax on shoes that cost \$68.50 when the sales tax rate is 8.25% **about \$5.60**

2 Teach

Guided Instruction

Be sure students are able to identify the part, percent, and whole in percent problems before beginning the applications in this lesson.

Make sure students understand the importance of estimating tips and sales tax for use in everyday life. Also point out that any percent problem can be estimated and encourage students to do so in order to check the reasonableness of their answers.

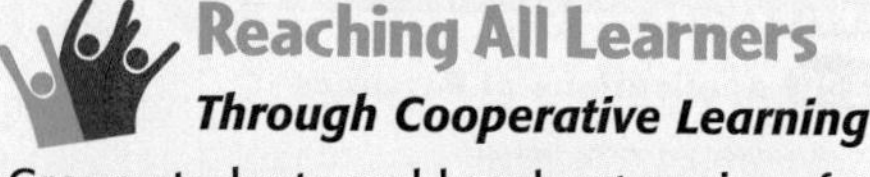

Reaching All Learners
Through Cooperative Learning

Group students and hand out copies of menus from local restaurants so that each group is "eating at the same restaurant." Have groups list what each person would choose for dinner. This should include drinks, salads, soups, entrees, desserts, etc. Have groups total their order and estimate the tip for excellent service (20%), average service (15%), and service that needs improvement (10%).

THINK AND DISCUSS

1. Explain how commission, interest, sales tax, and tips are alike.
2. When the sales tax rate is 8.25%, the tax on a $10 purchase is $0.83. Is the tax on $20 twice as much? Explain.

3. **GET ORGANIZED** Copy and complete the graphic organizer. In each box, write an example of each type of application and find the answer.

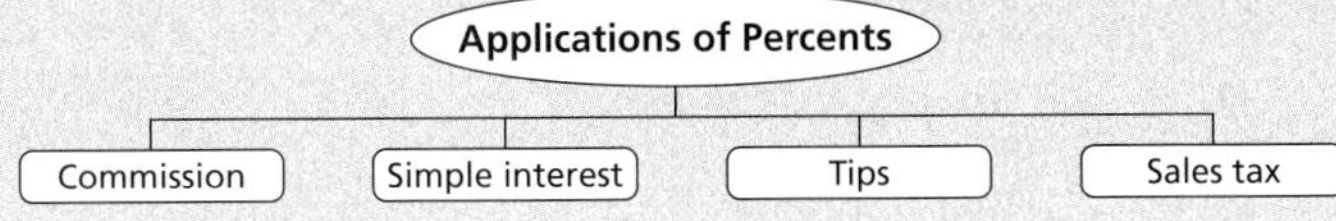

Answers to *Think and Discuss*

1. Possible answer: Each is a percent of an amount of money.
2. Possible answer: No; sales tax is rounded up to the next cent. 8.25% of $10 is $0.825, which gets rounded to $0.83. 8.25% of $20 is $1.65, which is not 2 times $0.83.
3. See p. A3

2-10 Exercises

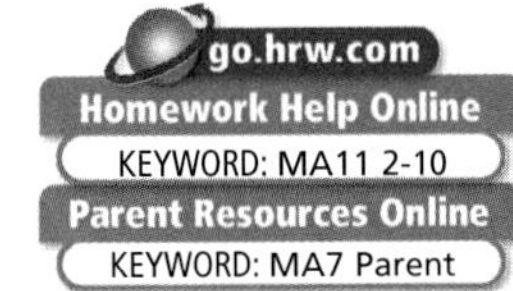

GUIDED PRACTICE

1. **Vocabulary** How are *commission* and *tips* alike? How are they different?

SEE EXAMPLE 1 p. 139

2. A sales representative earns a 2.5% commission on sales. Find the commission earned when the total sales are $80,700. **$2017.50**
3. Karen earns a salary of $28,600 per year plus a 4.25% commission on sales. Find her total earnings for a year when the sales are $310,000. **$41,775**

SEE EXAMPLE 2 p. 139

4. Find the amount of simple interest earned after 2 years on $480 invested at a 7% annual interest rate. **$67.20**
5. Find the number of years it would take for $1200 to earn simple interest of $324 at an annual interest rate of 6% per year. **$4\frac{1}{2}$ yr**
6. Find the total amount owed after 6 months on a loan of $900 at an annual simple interest rate of 8.5%. **$938.25**

SEE EXAMPLE 3 p. 140

7. Estimate a 15% tip on a $42.65 check. **about $6.45**
8. Estimate the tax on a $198 stereo when the sales tax is 5.25%. **about $10**

PRACTICE AND PROBLEM SOLVING

Independent Practice

For Exercises	See Example
9–10	1
11–13	2
14–15	3

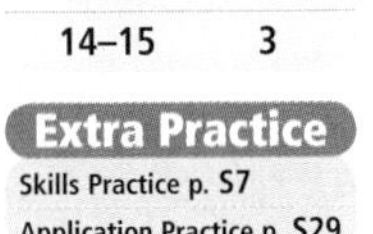

Extra Practice
Skills Practice p. S7
Application Practice p. S29

9. A boat salesperson earns a 2.5% commission on the sale of each boat. Find the commission earned on a boat that sells for $18,500. **$462.50**
10. A cell phone distributor earns a yearly salary of $28,000 plus a 17.5% commission on sales. Find the total earnings for a year when the sales are $38,000. **$34,650**
11. Find the simple interest paid after 3 months on a loan of $9700 borrowed at an annual interest rate of 11%. **$266.75**
12. After 8 months, $750 simple interest was owed on a loan of $9000. Find the annual interest rate. **12.5%**

2-10 Exercises

Assignment Guide

Assign *Guided Practice* exercises as necessary.

If you finished Examples **1–3**
Basic 9–23, 25–29, 35–43
Average 9–14, 16–31, 35–43
Advanced 9–14 even, 16–24, 26–43

Homework Quick Check
Quickly check key concepts.

Exercises: 10, 12, 14, 18, 20, 22

Answers

1. They are alike because they are both ways to earn money, and they are both usually a percent of some amount. They are different because a commission is usually a fixed percent of an amount, and tips will likely vary from one customer to another.

State Resources

3 Close

Summarize

Have students estimate each answer. Then have them find the actual answer.

- A real estate agent earns 4% commission. Her sales are $850,000. How much is her commission? about $36,000; $34,000
- The sales tax rate is 6%. How much is the sales tax on a $119 bike? about $7.20; $7.14

ONGOING ASSESSMENT and INTERVENTION

***Diagnose Before* the Lesson**
2-10 Warm Up, TE p. 139

***Monitor During* the Lesson**
Check It Out! Exercises, SE pp. 139–140
Questioning Strategies, TE p. 140

***Assess After* the Lesson**
2-10 Lesson Quiz, TE p. 143
Alternative Assessment, TE p. 143

Exercise 26 involves using percents to find sales tax. This exercise prepares students for the Multi-Step Test Prep on page 152.

Answers

20a. Possible answer: The book costs about \$6, and the CD costs about \$15. So the total price before tax would be about \$6 + \$15 = \$21. The tax is about 6%, or 6 • 1%. 1% of 21 is \$0.21, and 6(0.21) ≈ \$1.20. So the total cost would be about \$21 + \$1.20, or about \$22.20.

21. Possible answer: the commission is about 5% of \$55. 10% of \$55 is \$5.50, so 5% will be half of that, or \$2.75. So \$2.89 is reasonable.

22a. Alvarez: \$200,000; Brown: \$125,000

23. They earn the same amount because 0.04 × 3 and 0.03 × 4 both equal 0.12. So they both earn 0.12 × \$1000, or \$120.

13. How long will it take \$680 to earn \$102 in simple interest at an annual interest rate of 3%? **5 yr**
14. Estimate the tip on a \$19.65 check using a tip rate of 15%. **about \$3**
15. Estimate the tax on tires that cost \$498 with a 6.25% sales tax. **about \$30**

Use $I = Prt$ to complete the table. All interest rates are annual.

	I	=	P	×	r	×	t
16.	**\$3227.25**		\$8275		13%		3 years
17.	\$3969		**\$50,400**		10.5%		9 months
18.	\$23.75		\$950		**5%**		6 months
19.	\$380		\$4750		4%		**2 yr**

LINK Technology

Koopa is a Gulf Coast box turtle from Hartford, Connecticut. His paintings have sold for hundreds of dollars at online auctions.

20. Chris has \$21.50. He wants a book for \$5.85 and a CD for \$14.99. The sales tax is 6.25%.
    a. How could Chris estimate whether he has enough to buy the book and the CD?
    b. Does he have enough money to buy the book and the CD? **no**
21. **Technology** An online auction company charges sellers a commission fee of 5.25% of an item's final selling price. If you sell an item for \$55, what fee will you pay to the auction company? Show that your answer is reasonable. **\$2.89**
22. **Business** Sometimes business partners do not share the ownership of a business equally. Instead, they each own a percent of the business, and each receives that percent of the profits. Alvarez, Brown, and Chow are partners in a business that earned \$500,000. Alvarez owns 40% of the business. Chow received \$175,000.
    a. How much money did Alvarez and Brown each receive?
    b. What percent of the business is owned by Brown? by Chow? **25%; 35%**
23. **Write About It** Lewis invested \$1000 at 3% annual simple interest for 4 years. Lisa invested \$1000 at 4% annual simple interest for 3 years. Explain why Lewis and Lisa earned the same amount of interest.
24. **Critical Thinking** To estimate a tip of 15%, Amy tips \$1.00 for every \$6.00 in the total bill. Is this method reasonable? Why or why not? **Possible answer: yes; $\frac{1}{6} \approx 17\%$**
25. **///ERROR ANALYSIS///** Which solution is incorrect? Explain the error.

A
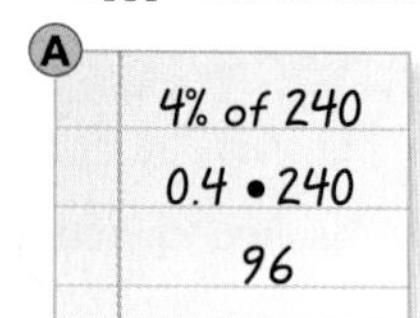

B
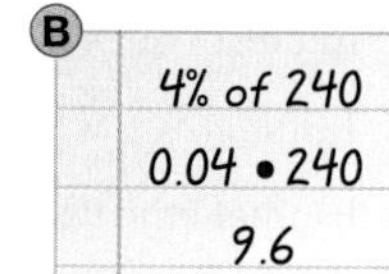

A is incorrect because 4% = 0.04, not 0.4.

26. This problem will prepare you for the Multi-Step Test Prep on page 152.
    a. Juan is shopping for a new CD player. He finds one he likes for \$225. The sales tax is 7.5%. What will be the total cost of the CD player? **\$241.88**
    b. The salesperson tells Juan that a sale starts tomorrow, and the CD player will be reduced to \$157.50. What is the total cost, including tax, that Juan will pay if he buys the CD player tomorrow? **\$169.31**
    c. How much will Juan save if he buys the CD player tomorrow? **\$72.57**

2-10 PRACTICE A

2-10 PRACTICE C

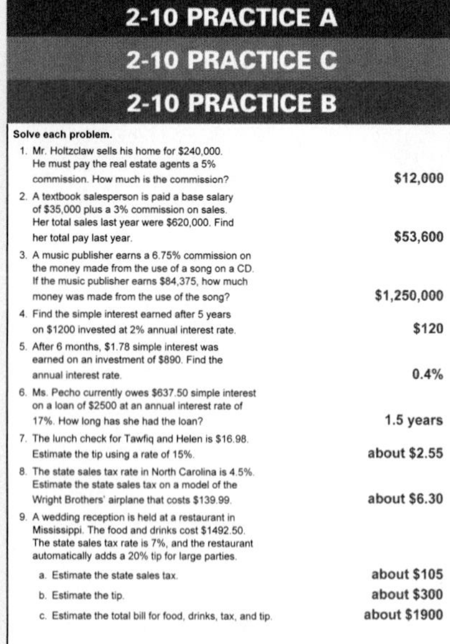

2-10 PRACTICE B

Solve each problem.

1. Mr. Holtzclaw sells his home for \$240,000. He must pay the real estate agents a 5% commission. How much is the commission? **\$12,000**
2. A textbook salesperson is paid a base salary of \$35,000 plus a 3% commission on sales. Her total sales last year were \$620,000. Find her total pay last year. **\$53,600**
3. A music publisher earns a 6.75% commission on the money made from the use of a song on a CD. If the music publisher earns \$84,375, how much money was made from the use of the song? **\$1,250,000**
4. Find the simple interest earned after 5 years on \$1200 invested at 2% annual interest rate. **\$120**
5. After 6 months, \$1.78 simple interest was earned on an investment of \$890. Find the annual interest rate. **0.4%**
6. Ms. Pecho currently owes \$637.50 simple interest on a loan of \$2500 at an annual interest rate of 17%. How long has she had the loan? **1.5 years**
7. The lunch check for Tawfiq and Helen is \$16.98. Estimate the tip using a rate of 15%. **about \$2.55**
8. The state sales tax rate in North Carolina is 4.5%. Estimate the state sales tax on a model of the Wright Brothers' airplane that costs \$139.99. **about \$6.30**
9. A wedding reception is held at a restaurant in Mississippi. The food and drinks cost \$1492.50. The state sales tax rate is 7%, and the restaurant automatically adds a 20% tip for large parties.
   a. Estimate the state sales tax. **about \$105**
   b. Estimate the tip. **about \$300**
   c. Estimate the total bill for food, drinks, tax, and tip. **about \$1900**

2-10 READING STRATEGIES

Study the models and examples that follow.

Total Pay = Base Salary + Rate of Commission × Total Sales

Ex. A person's total pay based on a \$32,000 salary and 2.5% commission on \$400,000 in sales is represented by:
Total Pay = 32,000 + 0.025 × 400,000

Simple Interest = Principal × Interest Rate × Years

Ex. The interest earned after 8 years on a \$6500 investment at an interest rate of 3% is represented by:
Simple Interest = 6500 × 0.03 × 8

Tip = Tip Rate × Charges

Ex. The tip for a bill of \$32.75 with a tip rate of 16% is represented by:
Tip = 0.16 × 32.75

Tax = Tax Rate × Charges

Ex. The taxes on a purchase of \$12 with a tax rate of 4% is represented by:
Tax = 0.04 × 12

Use the written models above as a guide to write a numerical model for each situation. Then solve.

1. Madison makes a base salary of \$52,600 plus 2% commission on her sales. If she had \$842,000 in sales last year, what was her total pay? **total pay = 52,600 + 0.02 × 842,000; \$69,440**
2. Jaylin is taking out a loan of \$6300. How much simple interest will he pay on the loan over a period of 5 years at a rate of 5%? **simple interest = 6300 × 0.05 × 5; \$1575**
3. Gregory has a restaurant bill of \$74.50 and would like to leave of tip of 18%. How much should he leave for the tip? **tip = 0.18 × 74.50; \$13.41**
4. What are the taxes due on the purchase of a car costing \$24,500 in the state of North Carolina, where the sales tax rate is 4.5%? **tax = 0.045 × 24,500; \$1102.50**

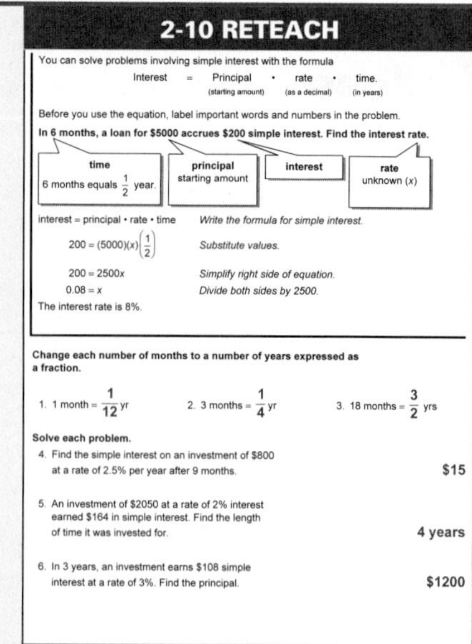

2-10 RETEACH

You can solve problems involving simple interest with the formula

Interest = Principal (starting amount) • rate (as a decimal) • time (in years).

Before you use the equation, label important words and numbers in the problem.

In 6 months, a loan for \$5000 accrues \$200 simple interest. Find the interest rate.

interest = principal • rate • time — *Write the formula for simple interest.*

$200 = (5000)(x)\left(\frac{1}{2}\right)$ — *Substitute values.*

$200 = 2500x$ — *Simplify right side of equation.*

$0.08 = x$ — *Divide both sides by 2500.*

The interest rate is 8%.

Change each number of months to a number of years expressed as a fraction.

1. 1 month = $\frac{1}{12}$ yr
2. 3 months = $\frac{1}{4}$ yr
3. 18 months = $\frac{3}{2}$ yrs

Solve each problem.

4. Find the simple interest on an investment of \$800 at a rate of 2.5% per year after 9 months. **\$15**
5. An investment of \$2050 at a rate of 2% interest earned \$164 in simple interest. Find the length of time it was invested for. **4 years**
6. In 3 years, an investment earns \$108 simple interest at a rate of 3%. Find the principal. **\$1200**

TEST PREP

27. Which account earns the most simple interest after 1 year? Assume that interest is paid annually.
    - Ⓐ $5000 at 8% per year
    - Ⓑ $10,000 at 4% per year
    - Ⓒ $8000 at 4.8% per year
    - **Ⓓ** $4000 at 10.2% per year

28. Craig earns $200 per week plus 8% commission on sales. Joan earns $150 per week plus 12% commission on sales. Last week, both had sales of $1500. Who earned more money?
    - Ⓕ Craig earned more than Joan.
    - **Ⓖ** Joan earned more than Craig.
    - Ⓗ Both earned the same amount.
    - Ⓙ Cannot be determined

29. **Short Response** If 2% of a number is 300, what is 6% of the number? Explain how you got your answer. **900; possible answer: 6% is 3 times 2%, so I multiplied 300 by 3.**

CHALLENGE AND EXTEND

30. **Multi-Step** A lunch check for Mark and a friend was $19.50 before the 6% sales tax was added. Mark wants to leave a tip of at least 20%. He has no coins, and he does not want to wait for change. What is the least amount he should leave to pay the check, tax, and tip? **$25**

31. The final cost of an item was $50. This included 6% sales tax. What was the price of the item before tax? **$47.17**

Finance A stockbroker earns a commission based on the amount of a transaction according to the table below.

Stockbroker's Commissions				
Transaction	$0–$10,000	For each additional dollar up to $20,000	For each additional dollar up to $40,000	For each additional dollar over $40,000
Commission	0.5%	0.4%	0.3%	0.2%

For example, the commission on a transaction of $11,000 is 0.5% of $10,000 plus 0.4% of $1000. Use the table for Exercises 32–34.

32. Find the amount of commission earned on a transaction of $15,000. **$70**
33. Find the amount of commission earned on a transaction of $21,000. **$93**
34. Find the amount of commission earned on a transaction of $100,000. **$270**

SPIRAL REVIEW

Compare. Write <, >, or =. *(Lesson 1-5)*

35. $\sqrt{65}$ **>** 8
36. 7 **<** $\sqrt{51}$
37. 9 **>** $\sqrt{80}$
38. $\sqrt{196}$ **=** 14

Solve each equation. Check your answer. *(Lesson 2-6)*

39. $|x - 7| = 5$ **12, 2**
40. $|3x| + 5 = 14$ **−3, 3**
41. $8|3x - 10| - 12 = 20$ **$2, \frac{14}{3}$**

Find each value. Round to the nearest tenth if necessary. *(Lesson 2-9)*

42. 40% of 60 is what number? **24**
43. What percent of 26 is 13? **50%**
44. 22 is what percent of 99? **22.2%**
45. 80% of what number is 64? **80**

2-10 PROBLEM SOLVING

Write the correct answer.

1. Use the formula $I = PRT$ to find the simple interest paid annually for 3 years on a $1260 loan at 13% per year.
   $491.40
2. A snack food distributor earns $400 a week plus a 4% commission on sales. What is her total pay for a week in which her sales are $1080?
   $443.20
3. After 8 months, the simple interest earned annually on an investment of $4500 is $165. What is the interest rate?
   5.5%
4. Estimate the tax on a digital camera that costs $399 with a 6.25% sales tax.
   $24

Vira recorded her weekend expenses to start budgeting her money. Use Vira's weekend spending list to answer questions 5–9. Select the best answer.

5. What is the tip on Saturday's dinner?
   A $3.62 **C** $10.86
   B $7.24 D $14.48
6. Estimate the tax on Vira's new shoes.
   F $4.50 H $6.30
   G $5.40 J $7.20
7. What is the tip on Sunday's breakfast?
   A $0.26 C $1.28
   B $0.64 **D** $2.55
8. What is the tip on Vira's manicure?
   F $0.13 **H** $1.30
   G $0.26 J $2.60
9. At what percent rate did Vira tip the taxi driver?
   A about 5% C about 15%
   B about 10% D about 20%

Weekend Spending

Saturday:
Dinner
$72.40 + 15% tip
Taxi
$22 + $2 tip

Sunday:
Breakfast
$12.75 + 20% tip
Manicure
$13 + 10% tip
New shoes
$89 + 6.25% sales tax

2-10 CHALLENGE

Nathan goes to a Thai restaurant for dinner. He sits down, looks at his menu, and then realizes that he left his wallet at home!

Luckily, Nathan finds $16 in the pocket of his jacket. He needs to know how much he can spend on his meal given that he must pay 5% for sales tax and leave 15% for a tip.

Answer the questions below to help Nathan first estimate, and then exactly calculate, how much he can spend on the meal alone.

Use mental math to complete the table.

	Cost of Meal	5% Sales Tax (10% ÷ 2)	15% Tip (10% + 5%)	Total Cost
1.	$15	$1.50 ÷ 2 = $0.75	$1.50 + $0.75 = $2.25	**$18.00**
2.	$14	**$0.70**	**$2.10**	**$16.80**
3.	$13	**$0.65**	**$1.95**	**$15.60**
4.	$12	**$0.60**	**$1.80**	**$14.40**
5.	$11	**$0.55**	**$1.65**	**$13.20**

6. To the nearest dollar, what is the cost of the most expensive meal Nathan can order? **$13**

Now use algebra to find an exact cost.

7. Let x represent the amount that Nathan spends on his meal. He needs to add 5% for tax and another 15% for tip, and the total needs to equal $16.
   Write an equation that models this situation. $16 = x + 0.05x + 0.15x$
8. Solve your equation in problem 7. To the nearest cent, what is the cost of the most expensive meal Nathan can order? **$13.33**

Now generalize the problem for a new situation.

Nathan finds more money in his pants, so that he now has $20. However, he wants to streamline his estimation and calculation.

9. Using your prior work, find the value of the ratio $\frac{\text{cost of meal}}{\text{total cost}}$. $\frac{5}{6}$
10. Use your ratio as a scale factor to find the most he can spend on his meal now. $\$20 \cdot \frac{5}{6} \approx \$16.67$

TEST PREP DOCTOR In **Exercise 27,** show students that choice **B** has twice the principal as **A** but half the interest rate; thus the amounts are equal. Choice **C** has twice the principal as **D** but less than half the interest rate. Therefore, **D** must be the correct choice.

Journal

For a job that pays a commission, have students explain whether they would prefer to have a $10,000 increase in their base salary or a 1% increase in their percent commission. Remind students to use examples to explain their reasoning.

ALTERNATIVE ASSESSMENT

Have students write four different percent problems using commission, simple interest, tips, and sales tax. For commission and simple interest, students should show how they check the reasonableness of their answers. For tips and sales tax, students should estimate their answer and then check it against the solution.

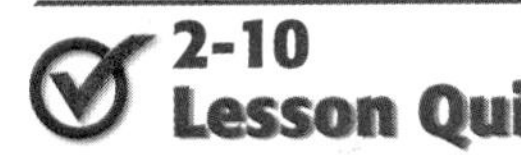

Power Presentations with PowerPoint®

2-10 Lesson Quiz

1. A computer salesperson earns a base salary of $32,000 per year plus a commission of 6% on total sales. Total sales for one year were $350,000. Find the salesperson's total pay for the year. $53,000
2. Find the simple interest paid for 9 months on a $500 loan at 8% per year. $30
3. After 2 years the simple interest earned on an investment of $4000 was $216. Find the interest rate. 2.7%
4. A family's dinner check was $38.82. Estimate a 15% tip. about $6.00
5. The sales tax rate is 7.1%. Estimate the sales tax on a television set that costs $399. about $28

Also available on transparency

2-11 Organizer

Pacing: Traditional 1 day
Block $\frac{1}{2}$ day

Objective: Find percent increase and decrease.

Online Edition
Tutorial Videos

Countdown Week 5

Power Presentations with PowerPoint®

Warm Up

1. Find 30% of 40. 12
2. Find 28% of 60. 16.8

Solve for *x*.

3. $22 = x(50)$ 0.44
4. $17.2 = x(86)$ 0.2
5. 20 is what percent of 80? 25%
6. 36 is what percent of 30? 120%

Also available on transparency

Math Humor

Q: Why did the shopper think the store was selling everything wholesale?

A: Because the store had two "half-off" sales.

State Resources

go.hrw.com
State Resources Online
KEYWORD: MA7 Resources

2-11 Percent Increase and Decrease

Objective
Find percent increase and decrease.

Vocabulary
percent change
percent increase
percent decrease
discount
markup

Who uses this?
Consumers can use percent change to determine how much money they can save. (See Example 3.)

"May I suggest you read the sign again, Sir."

A **percent change** is an increase or decrease given as a percent of the original amount. **Percent increase** describes an amount that has grown and **percent decrease** describes an amount that has been reduced.

Know it! Note — **Percent Change**

$$\text{percent change} = \frac{\text{amount of increase or decrease}}{\text{original amount}}, \text{ expressed as a percent}$$

EXAMPLE 1 Finding Percent Increase or Decrease

Find each percent change. Tell whether it is a percent increase or decrease.

A from 25 to 49

$$\begin{aligned}\text{percent change} &= \frac{\text{amount of increase}}{\text{original amount}}\\ &= \frac{49-25}{25}\\ &= \frac{24}{25} && \textit{Simplify the numerator.}\\ &= 0.96\\ &= 96\% && \textit{Write the answer as a percent.}\end{aligned}$$

25 to 49 is an increase, so a change from 25 to 49 is a 96% increase.

B from 50 to 45

$$\begin{aligned}\text{percent change} &= \frac{\text{amount of decrease}}{\text{original amount}}\\ &= \frac{50-45}{50}\\ &= \frac{5}{50} && \textit{Simplify the numerator.}\\ &= \frac{1}{10} && \textit{Simplify the fraction.}\\ &= 10\% && \textit{Write the answer as a percent.}\end{aligned}$$

50 to 45 is a decrease, so a change from 50 to 45 is a 10% decrease.

Helpful Hint

Before solving, decide what is a reasonable answer. For Example 1A, 25 to 50 would be a 100% increase. So 25 to 49 should be slightly less than 100%.

Find each percent change. Tell whether it is a percent increase or decrease.

1a. from 200 to 110 **45% decrease**
1b. from 25 to 30 **20% increase**
1c. from 80 to 115 **43.75% increase**

1 Introduce

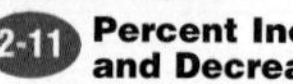
EXPLORATION

2-11 Percent Increase and Decrease

The manager of an electronics store is thinking about raising the price of a CD player. The CD player currently sells for $80.

1. Complete the table to find out how the price would change under several different plans.

	Percent Increase in Price	Dollar Amount of Increase	New Price
Plan A	5%		
Plan B	10%		
Plan C	12%		
Plan D	15%		

2. Which of the plans in the table should the manager choose for the price to be as high as possible but no greater than $90?
3. The owner of the store suggests a 9% increase in the price. What is the new price of the CD player in this case?

THINK AND DISCUSS

4. **Describe** how to use mental math to find the new price of an item when its original price is increased by 1%.
5. **Explain** how the price of an item would change if it were increased by 100%.

Motivate

Tell students that a discount coupon offers $10 off the purchase price or a 20% discount on the purchase price. Immediately ask students for a show of hands to determine which discount they would choose. Remind them that they cannot know the amount of the 20% discount unless they know the purchase price. The 20% could be greater than, less than, or equal to $10.

Explorations and answers are provided in *Alternate Openers: Explorations Transparencies.*

EXAMPLE 2 Finding the Result of a Percent Increase or Decrease

A **Find the result when 30 is increased by 20%.**

$0.20(30) = 6$ *Find 20% of 30. This is the amount of the increase.*

$30 + 6 = 36$ *It is a percent increase, so add 6 to the original amount.*

30 increased by 20% is 36.

B **Find the result when 65 is decreased by 80%.**

$0.80(65) = 52$ *Find 80% of 65. This is the amount of the decrease.*

$65 - 52 = 13$ *It is a percent decrease, so subtract 52 from 65.*

65 decreased by 80% is 13.

2a. Find the result when 72 is increased by 25%. **90**

2b. Find the result when 10 is decreased by 40%. **6**

Common applications of percent change are *discounts* and *markups*.

A **discount** is an amount by which an original price is reduced.

discount = % of **original price**

final price = **original price** − **discount**

A **markup** is an amount by which a wholesale cost is increased.

markup = % of **wholesale cost**

final price = **wholesale cost** + **markup**

EXAMPLE 3 Discounts

A **Admission to the museum is $8. Students receive a 15% discount. How much is the discount? How much do students pay?**

Method 1 A discount is a percent decrease. So find $8 decreased by 15%.

$0.15(8) = 1.20$ *Find 15% of 8. This is the amount of the discount.*

$8 - 1.20 = 6.80$ *Subtract 1.20 from 8. This is the student price.*

Method 2 Subtract percent discount from 100%.

$100\% - 15\% = \mathbf{85\%}$ *Students pay 85% of the regular price, $8.*

$\mathbf{0.85(8) = 6.80}$ *Find 85% of 8. This is the student price.*

$8 - \mathbf{6.80} = 1.20$ *Subtract 6.80 from 8. This is the amount of the discount.*

By either method, the discount is $1.20. Students pay $6.80.

B **Christo used a coupon and paid $7.35 for a pizza that normally costs $10.50. Find the percent discount.**

$\$10.50 - \$7.35 = \$3.15$ *Think: 3.15 is what percent of 10.50? Let x represent the percent.*

$3.15 = x(10.50)$

$\frac{3.15}{10.50} = \frac{x \cdot 10.50}{10.50}$ *Since x is multiplied by 10.50, divide both sides by 10.50 to undo the multiplication.*

$0.3 = x$

$30\% = x$ *Write the answer as a percent.*

The discount is 30%.

Helpful Hint

Before solving, decide what is a reasonable answer. For Example 3A, a 25% discount is $2 off. So a 15% discount will be less than $2 off.

3a. A $220 bicycle was on sale for 60% off. Find the sale price. **$88**

3b. Ray paid $12 for a $15 T-shirt. What was the percent discount? **20%**

2 Teach

Guided Instruction

Check that students can easily change percents to decimals and calculate any percent of a number. Point out that markups and discounts are applications of percent increase and decrease problems. They are finding the amount of change and dividing by the original amount. Have students use estimation to check for reasonableness of their answers. Remind students that markups should be greater than the original amount, and discounts should be less.

Reaching All Learners

Through Critical Thinking

Tell students that a $300 item is on sale at 20% off. Show that to find the amount of discount, you can calculate $0.20(300) = 60$. Then the final price is $300 - 60 = 240$. By substitution, this can be written as $300 - 0.20(300)$. If 300 is replaced by x, the expression becomes $x - 0.20x$, or $0.80x$. This shows that 20% off any price is equal to 80% of that price. Have students use similar reasoning to show that a 75% markup is 175% of the wholesale price.

COMMON ERROR ALERT

In finding percent discount and percent markup, students may use the wrong number in the denominator. Stress that it should be the original amount, so for discounts, it is the regular price, and for markups, it is the wholesale cost.

Power Presentations with PowerPoint®

Additional Examples

Example 1

Find each percent change. Tell whether it is a percent increase or decrease.

A. from 8 to 10 25% increase

B. from 75 to 30 60% decrease

Example 2

A. Find the result when 12 is increased by 50%. 18

B. Find the result when 55 is decreased by 60%. 22

Example 3

A. The entrance fee at an amusement park is $35. People over the age of 65 receive a 20% discount. What is the amount of the discount? How much do people over 65 pay? $7; $28

B. A student paid $31.20 for art supplies that normally cost $52.00. Find the percent discount. 40%

INTERVENTION

Questioning Strategies

EXAMPLE 1

- How do you determine which value is the original amount?
- Can the original amount ever be equal to zero? Explain.

EXAMPLE 2

- How is finding the result of a percent increase similar to finding the result of a percent decrease? How is it different?

EXAMPLE 3

- What does 100% minus the percent of discount give you?

Power Presentations with PowerPoint®

Additional Examples

Example 4

The wholesale cost of a DVD is \$7. The markup is 85%. What is the amount of the markup? What is the selling price? \$5.95; \$12.95

INTERVENTION

Questioning Strategies

EXAMPLE 4

- When finding percent markup, which cost is the amount of the markup always divided by?
- How is a markup similar to sales tax?

Inclusion Students may be confused by percent increases that are 100% or greater. Lead them to the conclusion that a 100% increase means that a quantity has doubled. Have them write several word phrases that all describe a 100% increase. If necessary, do the same for a 150% increase, 200% increase, etc.

EXAMPLE 4 Markups

A **Kaleb buys necklaces at a wholesale cost of \$48 each. He then marks up the price by 75% and sells the necklaces. What is the amount of the markup? What is the selling price?**

Method 1

A markup is a percent increase. So find \$48 increased by 75%.

$0.75(48) = 36$	*Find 75% of 48. This is the amount of the markup.*
$48 + 36 = 84$	*Add to 48. This is the selling price.*

Method 2

Add percent markup to 100%.

$100\% + 75\% = 175\%$	*The selling price is 175% of the wholesale price, \$48.*
$1.75(48) = 84$	*Find 175% of 48. This is the selling price.*
$84 - 48 = 36$	*Subtract from 84. This is the amount of the markup.*

By either method, the amount of the markup is \$36. The selling price is \$84.

B **Lars purchased a daily planner for \$32. The wholesale cost was \$25. What was the percent markup?**

$32 - 25 = 7$	*Find the amount of the markup.*
$7 = x(25)$	*Think: 7 is what percent of 25? Let x represent the percent.*
$\frac{7}{25} = \frac{25x}{25}$	*Since x is multiplied by 25, divide both sides by 25 to undo the multiplication.*
$0.28 = x$	
$28\% = x$	*Write the answer as a percent.*

The markup was 28%.

4a. A video game has a 70% markup. The wholesale cost is \$9. What is the selling price? **\$15.30**

4b. What is the percent markup on a car selling for \$21,850 that had a wholesale cost of \$9500? **130%**

THINK AND DISCUSS

1. 80% of a number is the same as a ?% decrease from that number. A 30% increase from a number is the same as ?% of that number.
2. A markup of 200% will result in a final cost that is how many times the wholesale cost?
3. What information would you need to find the percent change in your school's population over the last ten years?

4. **GET ORGANIZED** Copy and complete the graphic organizer. In each box, write and solve an example of the given type of problem.

Percent Increase	Percent Decrease	Discount	Markup

3 Close

Summarize

Ask students the following questions:

A \$60 item has a 20% discount. Describe a way to find

- the final price. 60(0.80)
- the amount of discount. 60(0.20)

A \$60 item is marked up 20%. Describe a way to find

- the selling price. 60(1.20)
- the amount of markup. 60(0.20)

ONGOING ASSESSMENT and INTERVENTION

***Diagnose Before* the Lesson**
2-11 Warm Up, TE p. 144

***Monitor During* the Lesson**
Check It Out! Exercises, SE pp. 144–146
Questioning Strategies, TE pp. 145–146

***Assess After* the Lesson**
2-11 Lesson Quiz, TE p. 149
Alternative Assessment, TE p. 149

Answers to *Think and Discuss*

1. 20%; 130%
2. 3
3. The population 10 yr ago and the population today
4. See p. A3.

2-11 Exercises

go.hrw.com
Homework Help Online
KEYWORD: MA11 2-11
Parent Resources Online
KEYWORD: MA7 Parent

GUIDED PRACTICE

1. **Vocabulary** Compare *percent increase* and *percent decrease.*

SEE EXAMPLE 1 p. 144

Find each percent change. Tell whether it is a percent increase or decrease

2. 25 to 45 **80% increase**
3. 10 to 8 **20% decrease**
4. 400 to 300 **25% decrease**
5. 16 to 18 **12.5% increase**
6. 40 to 50 **25% increase**
7. 50 to 40 **20% decrease**

SEE EXAMPLE 2 p. 144

8. Find the result when 40 is increased by 85%. **74**
9. Find the result when 60 is increased by 3%. **61.8**
10. Find the result when 350 is decreased by 10%. **315**
11. Find the result when 16 is decreased by 50%. **8**

SEE EXAMPLE 3 p. 145

12. What is the final price on a $185 leather jacket that is on sale for 40% off? **$111**
13. Neal bought a book on sale for $3.60. It was originally priced at $12. What was Neal's discount as a percent? **70%**

SEE EXAMPLE 4 p. 146

14. Yolanda bought a video that was priced at a 65% markup over the manufacturer's cost of $12. What was Yolanda's cost? **$19.80**
15. Randy sells hats for $12.35. The wholesale cost of each hat is $6.50. What is Randy's markup as a percent? **90%**

PRACTICE AND PROBLEM SOLVING

Independent Practice

For Exercises	See Example
16–27	1
28–31	2
32–33	3
34–35	4

Extra Practice
Skills Practice p. S7
Application Practice p. S29

Find each percent change. Tell whether it is a percent increase or decrease.

16. 50 to 60
17. 4 to 3
18. 96 to 84
19. 9 to 45
20. 32 to 30
21. 15 to 19.5
22. 150 to 180
23. 17 to 14.45
24. 20 to 15
25. 265 to 318
26. 35 to 105
27. 300 to 275
28. Find the result when 24 is increased by 75%. **42**
29. Find the result when 240 is increased by 5%. **252**
30. Find the result when 30 is decreased by 85%. **4.5**
31. Find the result when 8 is decreased by 5%. **7.6**
32. The cost of Hisako's school supplies was $49.80. She had a coupon for 30% off the entire purchase. What was the final price? **$34.86**
33. With the purchase of 10 greeting cards, Addie received a discount. She paid $26.35 for the cards that would normally have cost $31. What percent discount did Addie receive? **15%**
34. Irma sells boxing gloves in her sporting goods store for a 9% markup over the manufacturer's cost of $40. What is the selling price of the gloves? **$43.60**
35. Bottled water in a certain vending machine costs $1.50. This price is a markup from the wholesale cost of $0.20. What is the markup as a percent? **650%**
36. **Critical Thinking** Is the percent increase from 50 to 80 the same as the percent decrease from 80 to 50? Why or why not?

16. 20% increase
17. 25% decrease
18. 12.5% decrease
19. 400% increase
20. 6.25% decrease
21. 30% increase
22. 20% increase
23. 15% decrease
24. 25% decrease
25. 20% increase
26. 200% increase
27. $8\frac{1}{3}$% decrease

2-11 Exercises

Assignment Guide

Assign *Guided Practice* exercises as necessary.

If you finished Examples **1–2**
Basic 16–31, 41–48
Average 16–31, 40, 45–48, 58–60
Advanced 16–31, 45–48, 57–60

If you finished Examples **1–4**
Basic 16–35, 37–44, 49–56, 64–77
Average 16–40, 50–61, 64–77
Advanced 16–26 even, 28–40, 45–48, 50–77

Homework Quick Check
Quickly check key concepts.
Exercises: 22, 30, 32, 34, 38, 40

Answers

1. Percent increase and percent decrease are both percent changes that can be found using the formula percent change $= \frac{\text{amount of change}}{\text{original amount}}$. If the new amount is greater than the original amount, there is a percent increase. If the new amount is less than the original amount, there is a percent decrease.
36. No; the increase is 60%, and the decrease is 37.5%. The amount of change is 30 in both cases, but 30 is a greater percent of 50 than it is of 80.

State Resources

Exercise 51 involves finding the original price of an item when given the percent discount and discounted price. This exercise prepares students for the Multi-Step Test Prep on page 152.

Answers

39. Possible answer: the graph shows that a child grows about 3 in. from age 2 to age 3. The height at age 2 is about 33 inches. So the percent increase is $\frac{3}{33} \approx 9\%$.

40. Possible answer: Duncan's percent increase is $\frac{3}{20} = \frac{15}{100}$, which is equivalent to 15%.

51c. Possible answer: This model shows a number divided up into 10 equal parts. We know that 60% of the number is 18. This means 30% of the number is 9. You can use these 2 numbers to determine the pattern—each part has a value of 3. So you can fill in the diagram to find that the number (100%) is 30.

61. Possible answer: if the original bottle had 64 fl oz, then 25% of that is $\frac{64}{4} = 16$. Add 16 to the original amount and you get $64 + 16 = 80$, which is the amount given in the problem.

62. Possible answer: if the original price was \$30, then 30% is about $\frac{1}{3}$ of that, or \$10. A discount of \$10 would give a sale price of \$20, which is close to the sale price given in the problem, \$21. So \$30 is reasonable.

Multi-Step The graph shows the average height of a child from birth to age 4. Use the graph for Exercises 37–39.

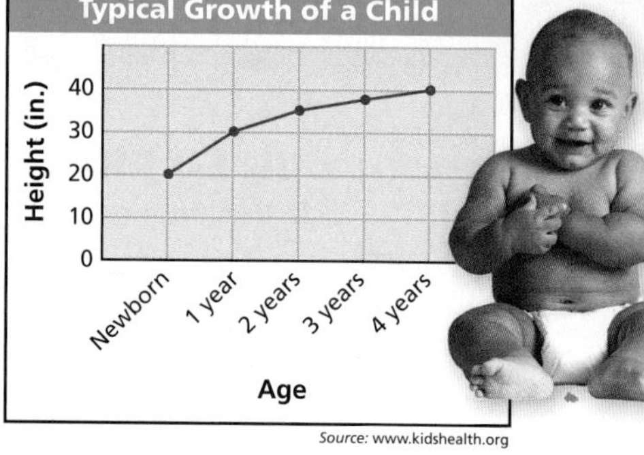

37. By what percent does a child's height increase from birth to age 1 year? **50%**

38. By what percent does a child's height increase from birth to age 4 years? **100%**

39. **Estimation** Estimate the amount and percent of increase in a child's height from age 2 to age 3. Show that your estimate is reasonable. **Possible answer: about 3 in.; about 9%**

40. **Employment** Last summer, Duncan charged \$20 to mow a lawn in his neighborhood. This summer, he'll charge \$23. What is the percent increase in Duncan's price? Show that your answer is reasonable. **15%**

Copy and complete the table.

	Original Amount	New Amount	Percent Change
41.	12	**18**	50% increase
42.	\$48	\$42.24	**12% decrease**
43.	$4\frac{1}{2}$	$13\frac{1}{2}$	**200% increase**
44.	8525	**6820**	20% decrease

Find each missing number.

45. 20 increased by **20**% is 24.
46. 80 decreased by **5**% is 76.
47. 120 decreased by 50% is **60**.
48. 200 increased by **5**% is 210.

49. **Nutrition** A can of soup had 480 mg of sodium per serving. The sodium was reduced to 360 mg per serving so that the soup could be advertised as "low sodium." What was the percent change in sodium content? **25% decrease**

50. **Write About It** Dana is shopping for shoes at a store advertising "everything 45% off." Describe a method she could use to estimate the discount and final price on a pair of shoes.

50. Possible answer: 45% is about 50%, so Dana could estimate both the discount and the final price by finding half the regular price.

51. This problem will prepare you for the Multi-Step Test Prep on page 152.
   a. Robert finds a shirt on a sale rack. All items on the rack are 40% off. The price on his shirt is missing. When the clerk scans the bar code, he tells Robert that the sale price of the shirt is \$18. What percent of the original price is \$18? **60%**
   b. Set up a proportion to find the original price of the shirt. $\frac{60}{100} = \frac{18}{x}$; $x = \$30$
   c. Copy and complete the model below and explain how it helps you to solve this problem in another way.

\$0	**\$3**	**\$6**	\$9	**\$12**	**\$15**	\$18	**\$21**	**\$24**	**\$27**	**\$30**
0%	10%	20%	30%	**40%**	**50%**	60%	**70%**	**80%**	**90%**	100%

2-11 PRACTICE A
2-11 PRACTICE C
2-11 PRACTICE B

Find each percent change. Tell whether it is a percent increase or decrease.

1. 8 to 10 — 25% increase
2. 50 to 20 — 60% decrease
3. 120 to 54 — 55% decrease
4. 12 to 96 — 700% increase
5. 72 to 108 — 50% increase
6. 2 to 1.3 — 35% decrease

Solve each problem.

7. Find the result when 20 is increased by 35%. 27
8. Find the result when 40 is increased by 64%. 65.6
9. Find the result when 68 is decreased by 25%. 51
10. Find the result when 120 is decreased by 15%. 102
11. A pharmacy discount card gives the user 40% off prescriptions. Mr. Allen's cholesterol medication normally costs \$96.50. What is the final price with the discount card? \$57.90
12. A gas station purchases fuel at a wholesale price of \$1.75 per gallon. The price is marked up 8%. What is the selling price per gallon? \$1.89
13. San Francisco's Bay Area Rapid Transit (BART) sells \$48 tickets at a discount price of \$45. What is the percent discount? 6.25%
14. A recording company sells a music CD for the wholesale price of \$12.75. A record store marks up the price to \$19.89. What is the markup as a percent? 56%

Find each missing number.

15. 50 increased by 20% is **60**.
16. 10 increased by **200** % is 30.
17. 200 decreased by 55% is **90**.
18. 60 decreased by **25** % is 45.

2-11 READING STRATEGIES

Study the chart below. It summarizes the similarities and differences between markups and discounts.

MARKUPS	Contrast	DISCOUNTS
It's a percent increase.	Type of change	It's a percent decrease.
Addition	Operation on original price/cost	Subtraction

Compare
- Both are a percent change.
- Both are found using a percent of a number.
- Both are applications involving money.

Answer each question.

1. Does a discount increase or decrease an original price? decrease
2. Is a sale considered a markup or a discount? discount
3. A clothing manager is computing markups. Are the new prices greater than or less than the original prices? greater than
4. Is \$950 + 0.15 × \$950 a model of a markup or a discount? markup

Calculate the final price/cost for each of the following.

5. 40% markup on \$87.50 — \$122.50
6. 25% discount on \$18 — \$13.50

2-11 RETEACH

Use this formula to calculate percent increase and percent decrease:

$$\text{percent change} = \frac{\text{to} - \text{from}}{\text{from}}$$

If the change was an increase, then the percent change will be positive.
If the change was a decrease, then the percent change will be negative.

Find the percent change from 70 to 28.

from = 70, to = 28

$\text{percent change} = \frac{\text{to} - \text{from}}{\text{from}}$ — Write the formula.

$= \frac{28 - 70}{70} = \frac{-42}{70}$ — Substitute values for "to" and "from."

$= -0.60$ — The decimal 0.60 means 60%. A negative percent change means a decrease.

The change is a 60% decrease.

Find the percent change from 12 to 15.

$\text{percent change} = \frac{\text{to} - \text{from}}{\text{from}}$

$= \frac{15 - 12}{12} = \frac{3}{12}$

$= \frac{1}{4}$ — The fraction $\frac{1}{4}$ means 25%. A positive percent change means an increase.

The change is a 25% increase.

Find each percent change. Tell whether it is a percent increase or decrease.

1. from 75 to 90 — 20% increase
2. from 140 to 84 — 40% decrease
3. from 98 to 147 — 50% increase
4. from 8 to 2 — 75% decrease
5. from 200 to 91 — 54.5% decrease
6. from 12 to 30 — 150% increase

TEST PREP

52. Lucia gets film developed at Photo King, where 24 prints cost \$7.80. This week, Photo King is having a sale, and 24 prints cost \$6.63. What percent of the regular cost will Lucia save?

 (A) 15%   (B) 17%   (C) 25%   (D) 85%

53. Which of these does NOT represent "200 decreased by 45%"?

 (F) 200(0.55)   (G) 110   (H) 200 − 0.45   (J) 200(1 − 0.45)

54. Which of these represents a 15% increase?

 (A) A price is marked up from \$12.50 to \$15.
 (B) Joanna's bank account balance grew from \$127.50 to \$150.
 (C) A baseball card's value rose from \$6 to \$6.15.
 (D) Luis's hourly wage was raised from \$8 to \$9.20.

55. The original price of an item was \$199. During a sale, the price was reduced by 45%. Then, during a clearance sale, the price was reduced an additional 20%. What was the final price?

 (F) \$71.91   (G) \$87.56   (H) \$98.97   (J) \$101.89

56. **Gridded Response** A skateboard that sells for \$65 is on sale for 15% off. What is the sale price in dollars? **55.25**

CHALLENGE AND EXTEND

Find each missing number.

57. **200** increased by 15% is 230.
58. **32** increased by 50% is 48.
59. **625** decreased by 20% is 500.
60. **14.5** decreased by 70% is 4.35.

61. 64 fl oz 61. The label on a bottle of orange juice says "now 25% more." The bottle has 80 fluid ounces of juice. What was the original volume? Show that your answer is reasonable.

62. Angelina paid \$21 for a backpack that was 30% off. What was the original price? Show that your answer is reasonable. **\$30**

63. **Multi-Step** Mr. Hansen owns a bookstore. He buys used books at 25% of the cover price and sells them at a 45% markup of what he paid. Jerry sold Mr. Hansen three books with cover prices of \$7.95, \$5.95, and \$12.10. If Jerry bought back his books, how much would he pay? **\$9.43**

SPIRAL REVIEW

Find the complement and the supplement of each angle. *(Previous course)*

64. 65° **25°; 115°**
65. 10° **80°; 170°**
66. 45° **45°; 135°**
67. 30° **60°; 150°**

Solve each equation. Check your answer. *(Lessons 2-1 and 2-2)*

68. $-15 + x = -3$ **12**
69. $x + 16 = -4$ **−20**
70. $r - 3 = 6$ **9**
71. $n - (-10) = 67$ **57**
72. $98 = 7z$ **14**
73. $\frac{x}{3} = 12$ **36**
74. $-x = 4$ **−4**
75. $\frac{x}{5} = -20$ **−100**

Estimate each amount. *(Lesson 2-10)*

76. the tip on a \$60.65 check using a tip rate of 15% **about \$9**
77. the tax on a \$70 DVD player when the sales tax is 6% **about \$4.20**

2-11 PROBLEM SOLVING

Write the correct answer.

1. The entrance fee at an art museum is \$22. Senior citizens receive a 15% discount. How much do seniors pay?

 \$18.70

2. Kylie paid \$38.62 to fill the gas tank of her Jeep. Two weeks ago, she paid \$34.18 to fill the tank. Find the percent increase.

 13%

3. In 2001, the population of Barbados was approximately 275,000. In 2002, the population increased by 0.5%. What was the approximate population of Barbados in 2002?

 276,375

4. A shoe salesman marked up a pair of sandals in the spring by 75% and advertised them for \$42.00. In the fall, he put them on sale at a 30% discount. What was the original price of the sandals, before the markup? How much were they selling for after the fall discount?

 \$24; \$29.40

Use the table below to answer questions 5–7. The table shows the U.S. population by region as given in the 1990 and 2000 Census. Select the best answer.

Region	Population (1990)	Population (2000)
Northeast	50,809,229	53,594,378
Midwest	59,668,632	64,392,776
South	85,445,930	100,236,820
West	52,786,082	63,197,932

5. By what percent did the population of the South increase from 1990 to 2000?

 A 14.8% C 18.6%
 B 17.3% D 19.8%

6. By what percent did the population of the West increase from 1990 to 2000?

 F 16.5% **H** 19.7%
 G 18.1% J 21.1%

7. Which statement is NOT true?

 A The percent increase in the West was twice that of the Northeast.
 B The Northeast had the smallest percent change.
 C The South had the greatest increase in population.
 D All regions had a percent increase.

2-11 CHALLENGE

This game is for 2, 3, or 4 players. It gives you a chance to practice calculating percent increase and decrease. As the game progresses, your calculations are likely to become more challenging.

Preparation:

- Cut out the 24 game pieces below. You can make the pieces sturdier by mounting them on cardboard with glue or tape.
- Place all the game pieces face down on a table and mix them up.
- Each player needs a sheet of paper and a pencil. A calculator is optional.

Game Play:

- Each player writes 100 (the starting score) on his or her paper.
- In Round 1, each player takes one game piece at random from the pile. The player then calculates a new score by increasing or decreasing the original 100 points by the percent stated on the game piece.
- In Round 2, each player takes another game piece and calculates a new score by increasing or decreasing his or her score from Round 1. Continue playing for six rounds or until all pieces have been taken.
- The winner is the player with the highest score after Round 6.

increase 5%	increase 10%	increase 25%	increase 30%	increase 50%	increase 60%
increase 75%	increase 80%	increase 90%	increase 100%	increase 125%	increase 150%
decrease 5%	decrease 10%	decrease 20%	decrease 25%	decrease 30%	decrease 40%
decrease 50%	decrease 55%	decrease 60%	decrease 65%	decrease 70%	decrease 75%

COMMON ERROR ALERT

In **Exercise 36,** students may believe that because the difference is 30 in both cases, the percent increase and decrease are the same. Remind them that percent increase or decrease also depends on the original number (the denominator).

TEST PREP DOCTOR Encourage students to estimate to eliminate answers that are clearly incorrect. In **Exercise 52,** the amount of decrease is about \$1, and the original price is about \$8, so **D** can be excluded immediately.

Journal

Have students give the result of decreasing \$100 by 10% and then increasing that amount by 10%. Is the result \$100? Have students explain.

ALTERNATIVE ASSESSMENT

Have students create a discount problem and a markup problem and solve both. The discount solution should give the amount of the discount and the final price. The markup solution should give the amount of the markup and the selling price.

Power Presentations with PowerPoint®

2-11 Lesson Quiz

Find each percent change. Tell whether it is a percent increase or decrease.

1. from 20 to 28 40% increase
2. from 80 to 62 22.5% decrease
3. from 500 to 100 80% decrease
4. Find the result when 120 is increased by 40%. 168
5. Find the result when 70 is decreased by 20%. 56
6. A movie ticket costs \$9. On Mondays, tickets are 20% off. What is the amount of the discount? How much would a ticket cost on a Monday? \$1.80; \$7.20
7. A bike helmet costs \$24. The wholesale cost was \$15. What was the percent markup? 60%

Also available on transparency

Organizer

Use with Lesson 2-11

Pacing:
Traditional 1 day
Block $\frac{1}{2}$ day

Objective: Use tables and graphs to describe changes in populations.

Materials: graph paper

Online Edition

Countdown Week 5

Resources

Algebra Lab Activities
2-11 Lab Recording Sheet

Teach

Discuss

Be sure students understand that the actual *amount* of a percent increase/decrease over a period of time does not remain constant, even though the percent itself may.

Answers to *Activity 1*

4.

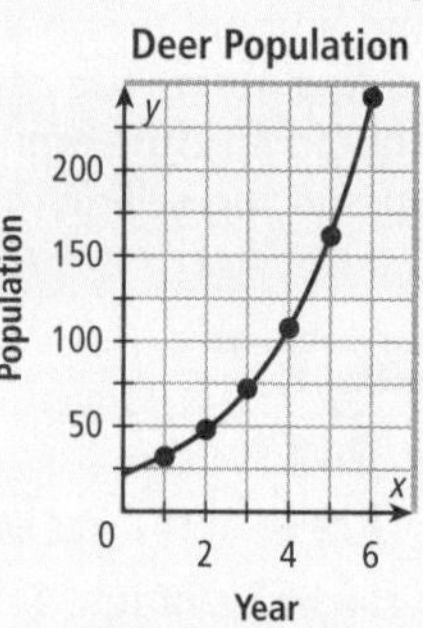

State Resources

Explore Changes in Population

Use with Lesson 2-11

You can use percents to describe changes in populations. A population may grow by a certain percent or decrease by a certain percent. Explore changing populations in these activities.

Activity 1

A team of biologists is studying a population of deer. There are 32 deer in the first year of the study. Due to a lack of predators, the biologists find that the herd grows by 50% every year.

1. Copy and complete the table. The first two rows have been completed for you.

Year	Percent Increase	Amount of Increase	Population
1			32
2	50%	$0.50 \cdot 32 = 16$	$32 + 16 = 48$
3	50%	**24**	**72**
4	50%	**36**	**108**
5	50%	**54**	**162**
6	50%	**81**	**243**

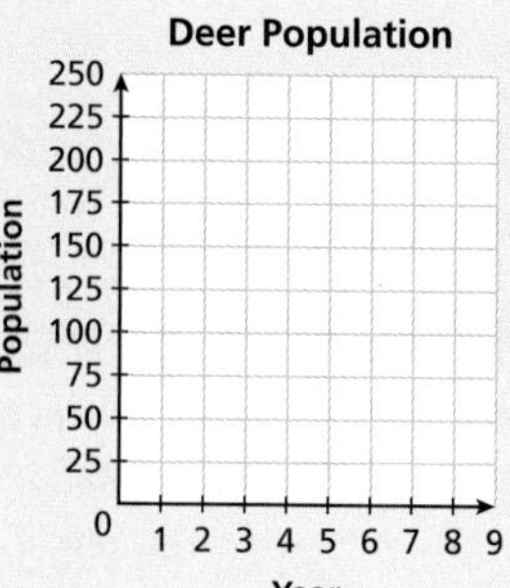

2. Describe the percent increase from year to year.
The percent increase remains the same from year to year.
3. Describe the amount of increase from year to year.
The amount of increase increases from year to year.
4. Copy the grid above onto graph paper. Plot the year and the population of deer on the graph as six ordered pairs (year, population). Connect the points with a smooth curve.
5. Describe the shape of your graph. **It is a curve that rises slowly at first, then more steeply.**

Try This

A researcher places 10 bacteria on a dish. This species increases by 100% every hour.

1. Copy and complete the table below.

Hour	0	1	2	3	4	5
Amount of Increase		**10**	**20**	**40**	**80**	**160**
Bacteria	10	**20**	**40**	**80**	**160**	**320**

2. Graph points from the table as (hour, bacteria). Connect the points with a smooth curve.
3. Compare this graph with the graph of the deer population.
4. Why does the amount of increase change when the percent of increase stays the same?

Answers to *Try This*

2.

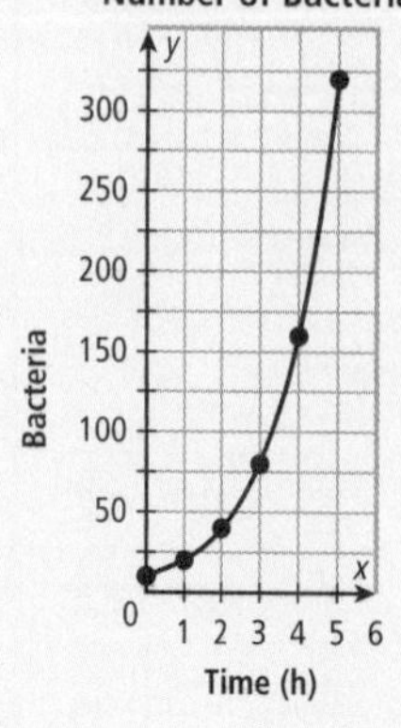

3. It is the same general shape, but it is steeper.
4. Finding the same percent of 2 different amounts gives 2 different results. A certain percent of the greater amount is greater than the same percent of the lesser amount.

Activity 2

A second team of biologists is studying a population of wolves. There are 3125 wolves in the first year. The biologists find that this population decreases by 40% every year.

1. **Make a Prediction** Based on your results in Activity 1, what do you think will happen to the amount of decrease each year?
Possible answer: The amount of decrease will grow smaller from year to year.
2. Copy and complete the table below. The first two rows have been completed for you.

Year	Percent Decrease	Amount of Decrease	Population
1			3125
2	40%	0.40 · 3125 = 1250	3125 − 1250 = 1875
3	40%	**750**	**1125**
4	40%	**450**	**675**
5	40%	**270**	**405**
6	40%	**162**	**243**

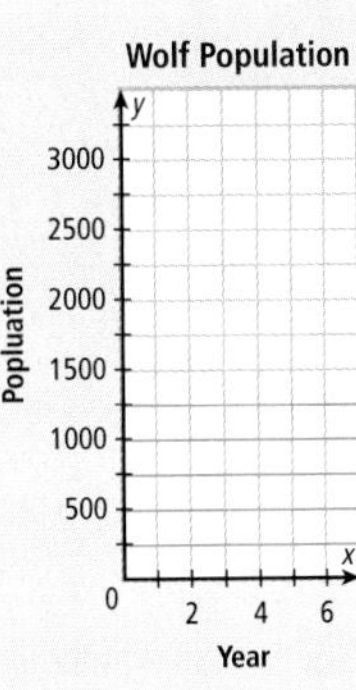

3. What happens to the amount of decrease in the wolf population from year to year? Was your prediction from Problem 1 correct?
The amount of decrease grows smaller from year to year.
4. **Make a Prediction** Copy the grid above onto graph paper. Based on your results in Activity 1, what do you think the graph of ordered pairs (year, population) will look like? **Possible answer: a curve**
5. Plot the year and the population of wolves on the graph as six ordered pairs (year, population). Connect the points with a smooth curve.
6. Describe the shape of your graph. Was your prediction from Problem 4 correct?
It is a curve that drops steeply at first, then less steeply.

Try This

A half-life is the amount of time it takes half of an amount of radioactive substance to decay into another substance. Tritium is a radioactive form of hydrogen with a half-life of 12.3 years. In other words, after one half-life of 12.3 years, an amount of tritium will have decreased by 50%.

5. Suppose you start with 128 grams of tritium. Copy and complete the table below.
6. Make a graph that shows how much tritium is left after 0, 1, 2, 3, 4, and 5 half-lives.
7. Compare this graph with the graph of the wolf population.
8. Describe the graph of a population that increases by a fixed percent. Why does the graph have this shape?
9. Describe the graph of a population that decreases by a fixed percent. Why does the graph have this shape?

Half-lives	0	1	2	3	4	5
Percent Decrease	0	50%	50%	50%	50%	50%
Amount of Decrease (g)		**64**	**32**	**16**	**8**	**4**
Tritium Remaining (g)	128	**64**	**32**	**16**	**8**	**4**

Close

Key Concept

A decreasing population will decrease by a smaller amount each year, while an increasing population will increase by a larger amount each year. As a result, the graphed points will form a curve that behaves in the same way.

Journal Have students calculate the changes in the first five years for a population of 500 that decreases by 20% each year. What do they think will happen to the population in 10 years? 20 years? Ask students to explain their reasoning.

Answers to *Activity 2*

5.

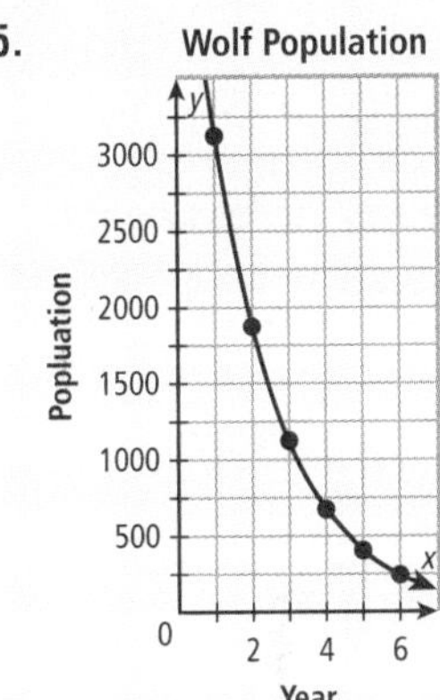

Answers to *Try This*

6.

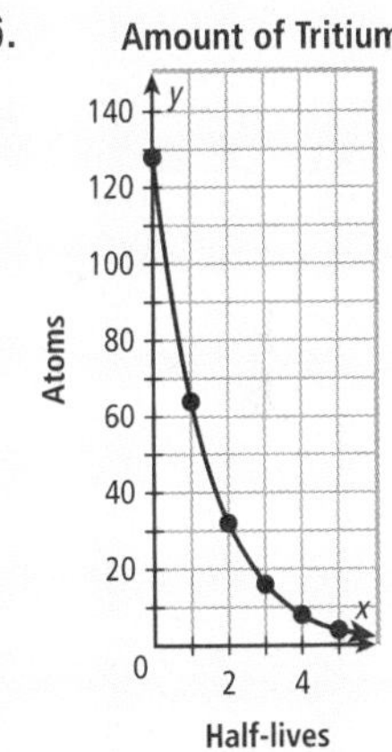

7. Possible answer: They both decrease sharply at the beginning and then less sharply later.
8. Possible answer: The graph rises from left to right, and any section of the graph is steeper than any section to the left of it; each time the population increases, the amount of increase grows larger.
9. Possible answer: The graph falls from left to right, and any section of the graph is less steep than any section to the left of it; each time the population decreases, the amount of decrease grows smaller.

Organizer

Objective: Assess students' ability to apply concepts and skills in Lessons 2-7 through 2-11 in a real-world format.

 Online Edition

Resources

 ***Algebra I Assessments***
www.mathtekstoolkit.org

Problem	Text Reference
1	Lessons 2-9, 2-10, 2-11
2	Lessons 2-9, 2-10, 2-11
3	Lesson 2-11
4	Lessons 2-9, 2-10, 2-11
5	Lesson 2-10

Answers

3. Maria; Paula took the additional $\frac{1}{4}$ off the original price, but it is actually off the reduced price. Since the reduced price is less than the original price, the additional discount will be less.

State Resources

CHAPTER 2

MULTI-STEP TEST PREP

SECTION 2B

Percentages

Bargain Hunters Maria is on her high school's lacrosse team, and her friend Paula is on the softball team. The girls notice an advertisement in the newspaper for a clearance sale at their favorite sporting goods store. The ad shows an additional $\frac{1}{4}$ off the already reduced prices of 60% off. Maria and Paula head to the store to shop for bargains.

1. Maria finds a lacrosse stick with a regular price of \$65. Find the sale price of the lacrosse stick prior to the additional $\frac{1}{4}$ off. **\$26**
2. Find the sale price of Maria's lacrosse stick with the additional $\frac{1}{4}$ off. **\$19.50**
3. Paula says that with the extra $\frac{1}{4}$ off, the total discount is 85% off. Maria thinks the discount is less than that. Who is correct? Explain your reasoning.
4. Paula finds a softball glove with a price tag that is not readable. The sales clerk scans the bar code and says the sale price, including the extra $\frac{1}{4}$ off, is \$16.50. What was the original price of the softball glove? Show your reasoning. **\$55**
5. Sales tax is 7.8%. Find the total amount that the girls will pay for the lacrosse stick and the softball glove together, including tax. **\$38.81**

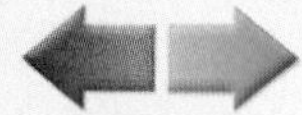

INTERVENTION

Scaffolding Questions

1. What does $\frac{1}{4}$ off mean? The price has been reduced by $\frac{1}{4}$, or 25%.
2. How can this problem be solved using proportions? $\frac{3}{4} = \frac{x}{26}$
3. One of the girls is incorrect. What common error did she make? Paula added successive discounts instead of multiplying.
4. If the final sale price, including the extra 25% off, is \$16.50, then \$16.50 is what percent of the first sale price? 75
5. Explain at least two ways to calculate the price with tax included. Possible answer: Find the tax and add to the price, or multiply the price by 1.078.

Extension

What is the total discount at the sporting goods store, as a single percent? Explain how you found your answer. 70%; possible answer: If p represents the original price, then $0.4p$ is the price after the first discount of 60%. $0.75(0.4p) = 0.3p$ is the price after the additional 25% off. This is 70% less than the original price.

Quiz for Lessons 2-7 Through 2-11

2-7 Rates, Ratios, and Proportions

1. Last week, the ratio of laptops to desktops sold at a computer store was 2:3. Eighteen desktop models were sold. How many laptop models were sold? **12**
2. Anita read 150 pages in 5 hours. What is her reading rate in pages per minute? **$\frac{1}{2}$ page/min**
3. Twenty-six crackers contain 156 Calories. Find the unit rate in Calories per cracker. **6 Calories/cracker**
4. A store developed 1024 photographs in 8 hours. Find the unit rate in photographs per hour. **128 photographs/h**

Solve each proportion.

5. $\frac{-18}{n} = \frac{9}{2}$ **−4**
6. $\frac{d}{5} = \frac{2}{4}$ **2.5**
7. $\frac{4}{12} = \frac{r+2}{16}$ **$\frac{10}{3}$**
8. $\frac{-3}{7} = \frac{6}{x+6}$ **−20**

2-8 Applications of Proportions

Find the value of n in each diagram.

9. $\triangle RST \sim \triangle XYZ$ **6 cm**

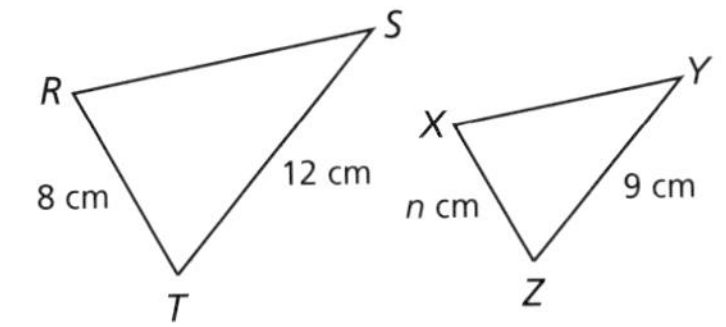

10. $ABCD \sim FGHJ$ **0.25 yd**

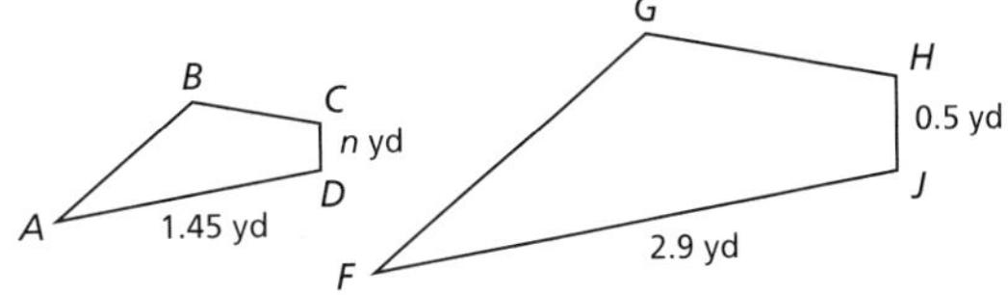

2-9 Percents

11. Find 40% of 25. **10**
12. Find 130% of 9. **11.7**
13. 35 is what percent of 70? **50%**
14. What percent of 400 is 640? **160%**
15. 16 is 80% of what number? **20**
16. 200% of what number is 28? **14**
17. A volunteer at the zoo is responsible for feeding the animals in 15 exhibits in the reptile house. This represents 20% of the total exhibits in the reptile house. How many exhibits are in the reptile house? **75**

2-10 Applications of Percents

18. Peter earns $32,000 per year plus a 2.5% commission on his jewelry sales. Find Peter's total salary for the year when his sales are valued at $420,000. **$42,500**
19. Estimate the tax on a $21,899 car when the tax rate is 5%. **about $1100**

2-11 Percent Increase and Decrease

Find each percent change. Tell whether it is a percent increase or decrease.

20. from 60 to 66
21. from 48 to 12
22. from 200 to 80
23. from 9.8 to 14.7
24. Andrea purchased a picture frame for $14.56. This price was a 30% markup from the wholesale cost. What was the wholesale cost? **$11.20**

20. 10% increase **21. 75% decrease** **22. 60% decrease** **23. 50% increase**

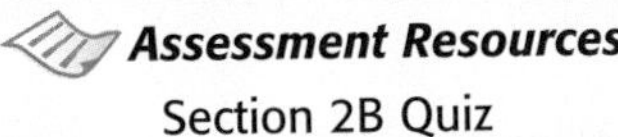

SECTION 2B

Organizer

Objective: Assess students' mastery of concepts and skills in Lessons 2-7 through 2-11.

Resources

Assessment Resources
Section 2B Quiz

Teacher One Stop™
Test & Practice Generator

INTERVENTION

Resources

***Ready to Go On? Intervention and Enrichment* Worksheets**

***Ready to Go On?* CD-ROM**

***Ready to Go On?* Online**

my.hrw.com

READY TO GO ON? Diagnose and Prescribe

Ready to Go On? Intervention	*Ready to Go On? Intervention,* Section 2B		
	Worksheets	CD-ROM	Online
Lesson 2-7	2-7 Intervention	Activity 2-7	Diagnose and Prescribe Online
Lesson 2-8	2-8 Intervention	Activity 2-8	
Lesson 2-9	2-9 Intervention	Activity 2-9	
Lesson 2-10	2-10 Intervention	Activity 2-10	
Lesson 2-11	2-11 Intervention	Activity 2-11	

Ready to Go On? Enrichment, Section 2B
Worksheets
CD-ROM
Online

Organizer

Objective: Help students organize and review key concepts and skills in Chapter 2.

Online Edition
Multilingual Glossary

Resources

Teacher One Stop™
Test & Practice Generator

Multilingual Glossary Online
go.hrw.com
KEYWORD: MA7 Glossary

Lesson Tutorial Videos CD-ROM

Answers

1. literal equation
2. ratio
3. $b = 36$
4. $x = -2$
5. $a = -21$
6. $y = 18$
7. $z = \frac{9}{8}$
8. $w = \frac{7}{3}$
9. $27 + s = 108$; 81
10. $x = 7$
11. $n = -\frac{10}{3}$
12. $n = -90$
13. $x = 13$
14. $y = 0$
15. $r = -2$

CHAPTER 2 Study Guide: Review

Vocabulary

Complete the sentences below with vocabulary words from the list above.

1. A formula is a type of a(n) ___?___.
2. A(n) ___?___ is used to compare two quantities by division.

2-1 Solving Equations by Adding or Subtracting *(pp. 77–82)*

EXAMPLES

Solve each equation. Check your answer.

■ $x - 12 = -8.3$
$ +12 \quad +12$
$x = 3.7$

Check $x - 12 = -8.3$

$3.7 - 12$	-8.3
-8.3	-8.3 ✓

■ $-7.8 = 5 + t$
$ -5 \quad -5$
$-12.8 = t$

Check $-7.8 = 5 + t$

-7.8	$5 + (-12.8)$
-7.8	-7.8 ✓

EXERCISES

Solve each equation. Check your answer.

3. $b - 16 = 20$
4. $4 + x = 2$
5. $9 + a = -12$
6. $-7 + y = 11$
7. $z - \frac{1}{4} = \frac{7}{8}$
8. $w + \frac{2}{3} = 3$
9. Robin needs 108 signatures for her petition. So far, she has 27. Write and solve an equation to determine how many more signatures she needs.

2-2 Solving Equations by Multiplying or Dividing *(pp. 84–90)*

EXAMPLES

Solve each equation.

■ $\frac{z}{2.4} = 12$
$(2.4)\frac{z}{2.4} = (2.4)12$
$z = 28.8$

■ $-8x = 148$
$\frac{-8x}{-8} = \frac{148}{-8}$
$x = -18.5$

EXERCISES

Solve each equation. Check your answer.

10. $35 = 5x$
11. $-3n = 10$
12. $-30 = \frac{n}{3}$
13. $\frac{x}{-5} = -2.6$
14. $5y = 0$
15. $-4.6r = 9.2$

2-3 Solving Two-Step and Multi-Step Equations *(pp. 92–98)*

EXAMPLE

■ Solve $\frac{3x}{5} - \frac{x}{4} + \frac{1}{2} = \frac{6}{5}$.

$$\frac{3x}{5} - \frac{x}{4} + \frac{1}{2} = \frac{6}{5}$$

$$20\left(\frac{3x}{5} - \frac{x}{4} + \frac{1}{2}\right) = 20\left(\frac{6}{5}\right)$$ *Multiply by the LCD.*

$$12x - 5x + 10 = 24$$

$$7x + 10 = 24$$ *Combine like terms.*

$$\underline{-10} \quad \underline{-10}$$

$$7x = 14$$

$$\frac{7x}{7} = \frac{14}{7}$$

$$x = 2$$

EXERCISES

Solve each equation. Check your answer.

16. $4t - 13 = 57$

17. $5 - 2y = 15$

18. $\frac{k}{5} - 6 = 2$

19. $\frac{5}{6}f - \frac{3}{4}f + \frac{3}{4} = \frac{1}{2}$

20. $7x - 19x = 6$

21. $4 + 3a - 6 = 43$

22. If $8n + 22 = 70$, find the value of $3n$.

23. If $0 = 6n - 36$, find the value of $n - 5$.

24. The sum of the measures of two angles is 180°. One angle measures $3a$ and the other angle measures $2a - 25$ Find a. Then find the measure of each angle.

2-4 Solving Equations with Variables on Both Sides *(pp. 100–106)*

EXAMPLE

■ Solve $x + 7 = 12 + 3x - 7x$.

$$x + 7 = 12 + 3x - 7x$$

$$x + 7 = 12 - 4x$$ *Combine like terms.*

$$\underline{+4x} \quad \underline{+4x}$$

$$5x + 7 = 12$$

$$\underline{-7} \quad \underline{-7}$$

$$5x = 5$$

$$\frac{5x}{5} = \frac{5}{5}$$

$$x = 1$$

EXERCISES

Solve each equation. Check your answer.

25. $4x + 2 = 3x$

26. $-3r - 8 = -5r - 12$

27. $-a - 3 + 7 = 3a$

28. $-(x - 4) = 2x + 6$

29. $\frac{2}{3}n = 4n - \frac{10}{3}n - \frac{1}{2}$

30. $0.2(7 + 2t) = 0.4t + 1.4$

31. One photo shop charges \$0.36 per print. Another photo shop charges \$2.52 plus \$0.08 per print. Juan finds that the cost of printing his photos is the same at either shop. How many photos does Juan have to print?

2-5 Solving for a Variable *(pp. 107–111)*

EXAMPLE

■ Solve $A = P + Prt$ for r.

$$A = P + Prt$$

$$\underline{-P} \quad \underline{-P}$$

$$A - P = Prt$$

$$\frac{A - P}{Pt} = \frac{Prt}{Pt}$$

$$\frac{A - P}{Pt} = r$$

EXERCISES

Solve for the indicated variable.

32. $C = \frac{360}{n}$ for n

33. $S = \frac{n}{2}(a + \ell)$ for a

34. The formula $a = \frac{d}{g}$ gives the average gas mileage a of a vehicle that uses g gallons of gas to travel d miles. Use the formula to find how many gallons of gas a vehicle with an average gas mileage of 20.2 miles per gallon will use to travel 75 miles. Round your answer to the nearest tenth.

Answers

16. $t = 17.5$
17. $y = -5$
18. $k = 40$
19. $f = -3$
20. $x = -\frac{1}{2}$
21. $a = 15$
22. 18
23. 1
24. $a = 41$; 123°; 57°
25. $x = -2$
26. $r = -2$
27. $a = 1$
28. $x = -\frac{2}{3}$
29. no solution
30. all real numbers
31. 9
32. $n = \frac{360}{C}$
33. $a = \frac{2S}{n} - \ell$
34. 3.7 gal

Answers

35. $x = 15, -27$
36. $y = 7, 3$
37. $y = 9, -9$
38. $x = 17.4, -6.6$
39. $g = -4, -8$
40. $x = \frac{5}{7}, -\frac{5}{7}$
41. $|x - 55| = 5$; min. speed: 50 mi/h; max. speed: 60 mi/h
42. $3\frac{1}{3}$c
43. 1080 m/h
44. 0.85 mi/min
45. $n = 1.6$
46. $x = 54$
47. $k = 5$
48. $x = -3$
49. 2.5
50. 16 ft
51. The ratio of the areas is the square of the ratio of the radii.

2-6 Solving Absolute-Value Equations *(pp. 112–117)*

EXAMPLES

■ **Solve $3|y + 4| = 30$.**

$$\frac{3|y+4|}{3} = \frac{|30|}{3} \quad \textit{Divide both sides by 3.}$$

$$|y + 4| = 10$$

Case 1

$$y + 4 = 10$$
$$\underline{-4 \quad -4}$$
$$y = 6$$

Case 2

$$y + 4 = -10$$
$$\underline{-4 \quad -4}$$
$$y = -14$$

EXERCISES

Solve each equation. Check your answer.

35. $|x + 6| = 21$
36. $7|y - 5| = 14$
37. $3|y| + 4 = 31$
38. $12 = |x - 5.4|$
39. $|g + 6| + 12 = 14$
40. $|x| = \frac{5}{7}$
41. Jason is driving his car at 55 mi/h. He needs to keep his car within 5 mi/h of his current speed. Write and solve an absolute-value equation to find Jason's maximum and minimum speeds.

2-7 Rates, Ratios, and Proportions *(pp. 120–126)*

■ **The ratio of skateboarders to bikers in an extreme sports contest is 7:2. There are 91 skateboarders. How many bikers are there?**

$$\frac{\text{skateboarders} \rightarrow 7}{\text{bikers} \rightarrow 2} \quad \textit{Write a proportion.}$$

$$\frac{7}{2} \times \frac{91}{x} \quad \textit{Let x be the number of bikers.}$$

$$7 \cdot x = 2 \cdot 91 \quad \textit{Use cross products.}$$

$$7x = 182$$

$$\frac{7x}{7} = \frac{182}{7} \quad \textit{Solve for x.}$$

$$x = 26$$

There are 26 bikers.

42. A recipe for a casserole calls for 2 cups of rice. The recipe makes 6 servings of casserole. How many cups of rice will you need to make 10 servings of casserole?

Use dimensional analysis to convert each rate. Round your answer to the nearest hundredth if necessary.

43. 30 cm/s to m/h
44. 75 ft/s to mi/min

Solve each proportion. Check your answer.

45. $\frac{n}{8} = \frac{2}{10}$
46. $\frac{2}{9} = \frac{12}{x}$
47. $\frac{3}{k} = \frac{9}{15}$
48. $\frac{1}{3} = \frac{x}{x - 6}$

2-8 Applications of Proportions *(pp. 127–132)*

■ **When Janelle stood next to the Washington Monument, she cast a 1.2-foot-long shadow, and the monument cast a 111-foot-long shadow. Janelle is 6 feet tall. How tall is the monument?**

$$\frac{x}{111} = \frac{6}{1.2} \quad \textit{Write a proportion.}$$

$$1.2x = 666 \quad \textit{Use cross products.}$$

$$\frac{1.2x}{1.2} = \frac{666}{1.2} \quad \textit{Solve for x.}$$

The monument is 555 feet tall.

49. Find the value of x in the diagram.

$\triangle ABC \sim \triangle DEF$

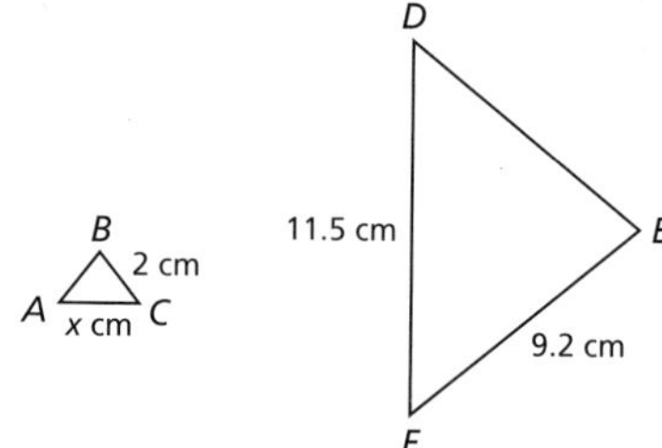

50. A tree casts a shadow that is 14 ft long at the same time that a nearby 2-foot-tall pole casts a shadow that is 1.75 ft long. How tall is the tree?
51. A circle has a radius of 9 inches. The radius is multiplied by $\frac{2}{3}$ to form a second circle. How is the ratio of the areas related to the ratio of the radii?

2-9 Percents *(pp. 133–138)*

EXAMPLES

■ **Earth's surface area is about 197 million square miles. About 58 million square miles is land. What percent is water?**

197 million − 58 million = 139 million

$\frac{\text{part}}{\text{whole}} = \frac{\text{percent}}{100}$

$\frac{139}{197} = \frac{n}{100}$

$197n = 13{,}900$ *Use cross products.*

$n = 70.56$ *Solve for n.*

About 71% of Earth's surface area is water.

EXERCISES

52. Find 2.3% of 230.
53. Find 115% of 2700.
54. What percent of 18 is 12? Round your answer to the nearest tenth of a percent.
55. What percent of 14 is 56?
56. 90% of what number is 120? Round the number to the nearest tenth.
57. 90 is 37.5% of what number?
58. A student answered 32 questions correctly and 8 incorrectly. What percent of the questions were answered correctly?

2-10 Applications of Percents *(pp. 139–143)*

■ **After 10 months, the simple interest earned on $3000 was $52.50. Find the interest rate.**

197 million − 58 million = 139 million

$I = Prt$

$52.5 = 3000(r)\left(\frac{10}{12}\right)$ *Substitute.*

$52.5 = 2500r$ *Multiply.*

$\frac{52.5}{2500} = \frac{2500r}{2500}$ *Solve for r.*

$0.021 = r$

The interest rate is 2.1%. *Write as a percent.*

59. A salesperson earns a base salary of $36,000 plus $2\frac{1}{2}$% commission on sales. His total sales for one year was $500,000. Find the salesperson's total pay for that year.
60. Find the simple interest paid for 10 years on a $10,000 loan at 9% per year.
61. The sales tax rate is 8%. Estimate the tax on a jacket that costs $69.95.
62. Estimate the tip on a $10.75 check using a tip rate of 20%.

2-11 Percent Increase and Decrease *(pp. 144–149)*

Find each percent change. Tell whether it is a percent increase or decrease.

■ from 50 to 56

$\text{percent change} = \frac{\text{amount of increase}}{\text{original amount}}$

$= \frac{56-50}{50} = \frac{6}{50} = 0.12 = 12\%$

The change is a 12% increase.

■ from 120 to 72

$\text{percent change} = \frac{\text{amount of decrease}}{\text{original amount}}$

$= \frac{120-72}{120} = \frac{48}{120} = 0.40 = 40\%$

The change is a 40% decrease.

Find each percent change. Tell whether it is a percent increase or decrease. Round your answer to the nearest percent.

63. from 19 to 26
64. from 42 to 28
65. Find the result when 65 is increased by 40%.
66. Find the result when 150 is decreased by 15%.
67. Tom sells sunglasses that he buys wholesale for $2.50 each. He then marks up the price 150%. What is the amount of the markup? What is the selling price?
68. The original price of a shirt was $79.99. It is on sale for $49.99. What is the percent discount? Round to the nearest tenth.

Answers

52. 5.29
53. 3105
54. 66.7%
55. 400%
56. 133.3
57. 240
58. 80%
59. $48,500
60. $9000
61. about $5.60
62. about $2.20
63. 37% increase
64. 33% decrease
65. 91
66. 127.5
67. $3.75; $6.25
68. 37.5%

Organizer

Objective: Assess students' mastery of concepts and skills in Chapter 2.

 **Online Edition**

Resources

 ***Assessment Resources***

Chapter 2 Tests

- Free Response (Levels A, B, C)
- Multiple Choice (Levels A, B, C)
- Performance Assessment

Teacher One Stop™
Test & Practice Generator

State Resources

Solve each equation.

1. $y - 7 = 2$ **9**
2. $x + 12 = 19$ **7**
3. $-5 + z = 8$ **13**
4. $9x = 72$ **8**
5. $\frac{m}{-8} = -2.5$ **20**
6. $\frac{7}{8}a = 42$ **48**
7. $15 = 3 - 4x$ **−3**
8. $\frac{2a}{3} + \frac{1}{5} = \frac{7}{6}$ **1.45**
9. $8 - (b - 2) = 11$ **−1**
10. $-2x + 4 = 5 - 3x$ **1**
11. $3(q - 2) + 2 = 5q - 7 - 2q$ **no solution**
12. $5z = -3(z + 7)$ **−2.625**

Solve for the indicated variable.

13. $r - 2s = 14$ for s $\boldsymbol{s = \frac{r - 14}{2}}$
14. $V = \frac{1}{3}bh$ for b $\boldsymbol{b = \frac{3V}{h}}$
15. $P = 2(\ell + w)$ for ℓ $\boldsymbol{\ell = \frac{P}{2} - w}$

Solve each equation.

16. $|x - 14| = 21$ **35, −7**
17. $13 = |y + 2| - 3$ **14, −18**
18. $4|z| = 20$ **5, −5**
19. $3|x| + 5 = 8$ **1, −1**
20. $3|g + 1| + 5 = 7$ $\boldsymbol{-\frac{5}{3}, -\frac{1}{3}}$
21. $|2v| = 6$ **3, −3**
22. A store sells 3 videotapes for $4.99. Find the unit rate in dollars per videotape. Round to the nearest cent. **$1.66/videotape**
23. Twenty-five students use 120 sheets of paper. Find the unit rate in sheets per student. **4.8 sheets/student**
24. Nutritionists recommend that teenagers consume 1300 milligrams of calcium per day. Use dimensional analysis to convert this rate to grams per year. **474.5 g/yr**

Solve each proportion.

25. $\frac{5}{4} = \frac{x}{12}$ **15**
26. $\frac{8}{2z} = \frac{15}{60}$ **16**
27. $\frac{x + 10}{10} = \frac{18}{12}$ **5**
28. The scale on a map is 1 inch:500 miles. If two cities are 875 miles apart, how far apart are they on the map? **1.75 in.**

Find the value of x in each diagram. Round your answer to the nearest tenth.

29. $\triangle EFG \sim \triangle RTS$ **24 in.**
30. $HJKL \sim WXYZ$ **1.7 m**

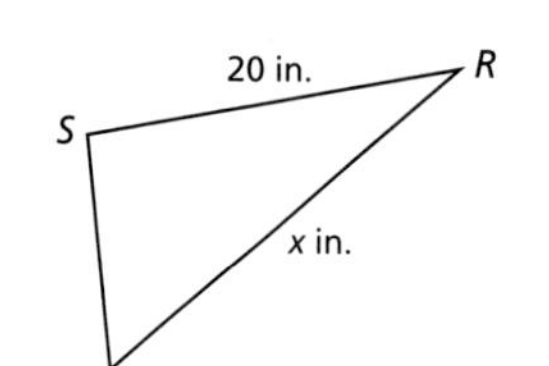

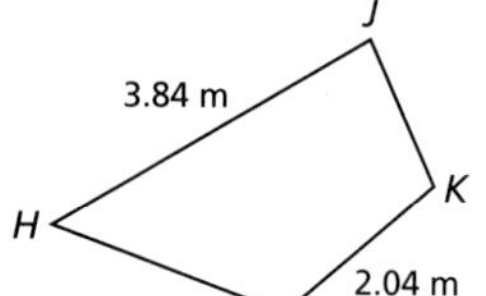

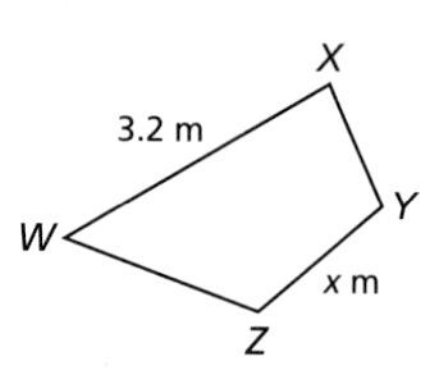

31. What is 23% of 46? **10.58**
32. 37.5 is 60% of what number? **62.5**
33. What percent of 175 is 35? **20%**
34. Find the simple interest earned after 5 years on an investment of $2000 at 3.2% per year. **$320**
35. A lunch check is $27.95. Estimate a 15% tip. **about $4.50**

Find each percent change. Tell whether it is a percent increase or decrease.

36. from 180 to 234 **30% increase**
37. from 12 to 48 **300% increase**
38. from 56 to 21 **62.5% decrease**

COLLEGE ENTRANCE EXAM PRACTICE

CHAPTER 2

FOCUS ON ACT

The ACT Mathematics Test is one of four tests in the ACT. You have 60 minutes to answer 60 multiple-choice questions. The questions cover material typically taught through the end of eleventh grade. You will need to know some basic formulas.

You may want to time yourself as you take this practice test. It should take you about 6 minutes to complete.

HOT TIP! There is no penalty for incorrect answers on the ACT. If you are unsure of the correct answer, eliminate as many answer choices as possible. Then make your best guess. Be sure you have marked an answer for every question before time runs out.

1. At a certain high school, the ratio of left-handed to right-handed basketball players is 1:4. If there are a total of 20 players on the team, how many players are right-handed?

(A) 1
(B) 4
(C) 5
(D) 12
(E) 16

2. If $y - 3 = \frac{2}{5}(x + 1)$, then $x = ?$

(F) $\frac{5(y-3)-2}{2}$
(G) $y - \frac{22}{5}$
(H) $\frac{2(y-3)}{5} - 1$
(J) $\frac{2(y+1)+15}{5}$
(K) $\frac{5}{2}y - 4$

3. What is $\frac{1}{5}$% of 20?

(A) 0.004
(B) 0.04
(C) 0.4
(D) 4
(E) 100

4. If $x - 3 = 4 - 2(x + 5)$, then $x = ?$

(F) -3
(G) -1
(H) 1
(J) $\frac{3}{2}$
(K) $\frac{11}{3}$

5. If $\triangle ABC \sim \triangle DEF$, what is the length of $\overline{AC}$?

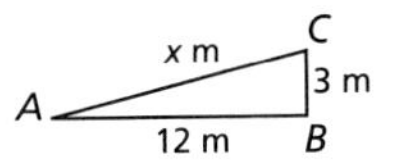

(A) 2.6 meters
(B) 3.5 meters
(C) 7 meters
(D) 14 meters
(E) 15 meters

6. A movie theater makes 30% of its revenue from concession sales. If concession sales were $174,000, what was the total revenue?

(F) $52,200
(G) $121,800
(H) $248,570
(J) $580,000
(K) $746,000

COLLEGE ENTRANCE EXAM PRACTICE CHAPTER 2

Organizer

Objective: Provide practice for college entrance exams such as the ACT.

Resources

College Entrance Exam Practice

Questions on the ACT represent the following content areas:

Pre-Algebra, 23%
Elementary Algebra, 17%
Intermediate Algebra, 15%
Coordinate Geometry, 15%
Plane Geometry, 23%
Trigonometry, 7%

Items on this page focus on:
- Pre-Algebra
- Elementary Algebra
- Plane Geometry

Text References:

Item	1	2	3	4	5	6
Lesson	2-7	2-5	2-9	2-4	2-8	2-9

TEST PREP DOCTOR

1. Students who chose **B** most likely found the number of *left*-handed players. Remind students to read each question carefully.

2. Students who chose **H** probably multiplied the left side of the equation by $\frac{2}{5}$ and eliminated $\frac{2}{5}$ from the right side. Remind students that the inverse operation for multiplication is division, so they should *divide* both sides of the equation by $\frac{2}{5}$.

3. Students who chose **D** probably found $\frac{1}{5}$ of 20 instead of $\frac{1}{5}$% of 20.
Remind students that percent means "part of 100," so they should divide $\frac{1}{5}$ by 100 before multiplying by 20.

4. Students who chose **F** may have subtracted 3 from both sides instead of adding 3. Remind students that they should always check their answers to avoid errors caused by simple mistakes.

5. Students who chose **B** probably did not set up the proportion correctly. Remind students that in similar triangles, corresponding sides are proportional, and the similarity statement indicates which sides correspond.

6. Students who chose **F** most likely found 30% of the concession sales. Remind students how to set up an equation to find the whole when the percent and the part are known.

Organizer

Objective: Provide opportunities to learn and practice common test-taking strategies.

TEST PREP DOCTOR + This Test Tackler focuses on using logic and estimation to eliminate answer choices. While this strategy may not always yield a single answer, it may save students time by eliminating some of the choices. In addition, it helps students analyze items before they begin to work.

State Resources

TEST TACKLER

Standardized Test Strategies

Multiple Choice: Eliminate Answer Choices

You can answer some problems without doing many calculations. Use logic to eliminate answer choices and save time.

EXAMPLE 1

Which number is the square of 123,765?

(A) 15,317,775,225 (C) 15,317,775,230

(B) 15,317,775,233 (D) 15,317,775,227

Your calculator will not help you on this question. Due to rounding, any of the answer choices are possible.

But you can use this fact to eliminate three of the answer choices:

The square of any number ending in 5 is also a number ending in 5.

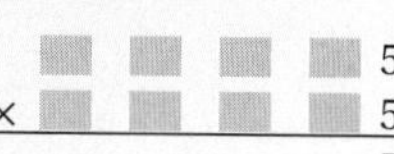

The only answer choice that ends in 5 is A, 15,317,775,225.

EXAMPLE 2

What is a possible area of the wooden triangle shown?

(F) 11 square feet (H) 14 square feet

(G) 20 square feet (J) 24 square feet

4 ft

7 ft

The triangle is inside a rectangle with an area of $7 \times 4 = 28$ square feet.

If the triangle had the same base and height as the rectangle, its area would be half the area of the rectangle, 14 square feet.

However, the triangle fits inside the rectangle, so its area must be less than 14 square feet.

The only answer choice that is less than 14 square feet is F, 11 square feet.

Try to eliminate unreasonable answer choices. Some choices may be too great or too small, have incorrect units, or not be divisible by a necessary number.

Read each test item and answer the questions that follow.

Item A
The top speed of a three-toed sloth is 0.12 miles per hour. About how many feet can a sloth travel in an hour?

Ⓐ 0.12 feet
Ⓑ 600 feet
Ⓒ 2.27 feet
Ⓓ 7500 inches

1. Are there any answer choices you can eliminate immediately? If so, which choices and why?
2. Describe how you can use estimation to find the correct answer.

Item B
A city park is shaped like a triangle. The Liberty Street side of the park is 120 feet long, and the First Avenue side is 50 feet long.

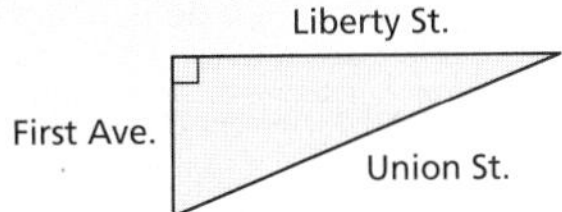

What is the approximate length of the side of the park that faces Union Street?

Ⓕ 25 feet
Ⓖ 110 inches
Ⓗ 65 feet
Ⓙ 130 feet

3. Can any of the answer choices be eliminated immediately? If so, which choices and why?
4. Are there any properties you can use to solve this problem? If so, what are they?
5. Describe how to find the correct answer without doing any calculations.

Item C
Approximately how long will the average 18-year-old have slept in his lifetime?

Ⓐ 6 weeks
Ⓑ 6 months
Ⓒ 6 years
Ⓓ 6 decades

6. Which answer choice can be eliminated immediately? Why?
7. Explain how to use mental math to solve this problem.

Item D
Sheila's paychecks for February and March were equal. If she worked every day during both months, for which month was her daily pay lower?

Ⓕ February
Ⓖ March
Ⓗ Her daily pay did not change.
Ⓙ Cannot be determined

8. What do you need to know to solve this problem?
9. Describe how you can find the correct answer.

Item E
Greg tripled the number of baseball cards he had last week. Which of these could be the number of cards Greg has now?

Ⓐ 100
Ⓑ 200
Ⓒ 150
Ⓓ 250

10. The number of cards that Greg has now must be divisible by what number? How can you tell if a number is divisible by this number?
11. Describe how to find the answer to this problem.

Answers

Possible answers:

1. **D;** the units are incorrect
2. 0.12 mi is about $\frac{1}{10}$ mile, and 1 mile is about 5000 ft, so the answer should be close to $\frac{1}{10}(5000)$, or 500 ft. **B** is the only choice close to 500 ft.
3. **G;** the units are incorrect
4. Pythagorean Theorem, Triangle Inequality Theorem
5. Union Street is the hypotenuse of a right triangle, which means it is the longest side. So Union Street must be longer than 120 ft and 50 ft. **J** is the only choice greater than both of these distances.
6. **D;** 6 decades = 60 years, which is longer than 18 years.
7. People sleep 6–8 hours each day, or 6 to 8 out of each 24. This is about $\frac{1}{4}$ to $\frac{1}{3}$ of each day An 18-year-old will spend about $\frac{1}{4}$ to $\frac{1}{3}$ of 18 years asleep, which is about 4.5 to 6 years. **C** is the correct response.
8. the number of days in February and in March
9. February always has fewer days than March. If Sheila made the same amount of money each month, her daily pay must have been lower in March. **G** is the correct response.
10. 3; the sum of the digits will be divisible by 3.
11. Add the digits of each response and check if the sum is divisible by 3. **C** is the only choice divisible by 3.

Answers to Test Items

A. B
B. J
C. C
D. G
E. C

Organizer

Objective: Provide review and practice for Chapters 1–2 and standardized tests.

PREMIER Online Edition

Resources

Assessment Resources

Chapter 2 Cumulative Test

go.hrw.com
KEYWORD: MA7 TestPrep

State Resources

go.hrw.com
State Resources Online
KEYWORD: MA7 Resources

CHAPTER 2

STANDARDIZED TEST PREP

CUMULATIVE ASSESSMENT, CHAPTERS 1–2

Multiple Choice

1. What operation does ◊ represent if $x \lozenge 2.2 = 4.5$ when $x = 9.9$?

Ⓐ Addition

Ⓑ Subtraction

Ⓒ Multiplication

Ⓓ Division

2. A couple earns $4819.25 a month. They pay 9.5% of their monthly income as the monthly payment on their car. To the nearest dollar, how much does the couple pay for their monthly car payment?

Ⓕ $458 Ⓗ $4578

Ⓖ $507 Ⓙ $4810

3. Every dimension of cylinder *A* is multiplied by 4 to make cylinder *B*. What is the ratio of the volume of cylinder *A* to the volume of cylinder *B*?

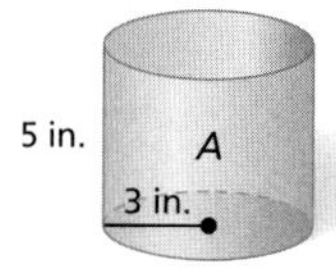

Ⓐ $\frac{1}{64}$ Ⓒ $\frac{1}{4}$

Ⓑ $\frac{1}{16}$ Ⓓ $\frac{1}{3}$

4. A clock loses 5 minutes every day. How much time will it lose in 2 hours?

Ⓕ 0.417 second Ⓗ 240 seconds

Ⓖ 25 seconds Ⓙ 600 seconds

5. A statue is 8 feet tall. The display case for a model of the statue is 18 inches tall. Which scale allows for the tallest model of the statue that will fit in the display case?

Ⓐ 1 inch:2 inches Ⓒ 1 inch:5 inches

Ⓑ 1 inch:7 inches Ⓓ 1 inch:10 inches

6. What is the value of $-|6^2|$?

Ⓕ −36 Ⓗ −8

Ⓖ −12 Ⓙ −3

7. Mr. Phillips wants to install hardwood flooring in his den. The flooring costs $25.86 per square yard. The blueprint below shows his house. What other information do you need in order to find the total cost of the flooring?

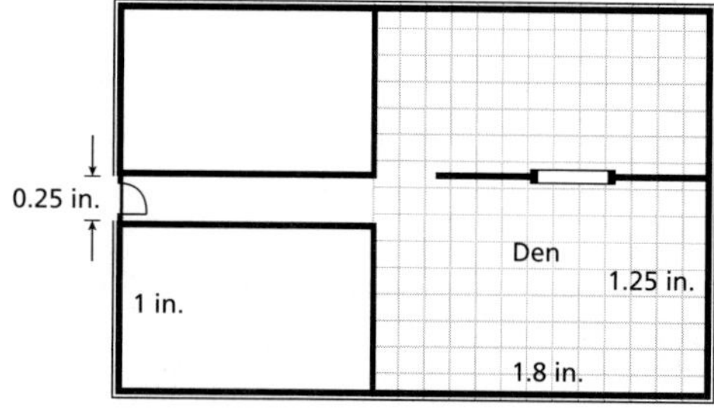

Ⓐ The lengths and widths of the adjoining rooms in the blueprint

Ⓑ The total area of the blueprint

Ⓒ The scale of inches in the blueprint to yards in the house

Ⓓ The width of the den

8. What value of *n* makes the equation below have no solution?

$$2x + 2 = nx - 3$$

Ⓕ −2

Ⓖ 0

Ⓗ 2

Ⓙ 3

9. Which of the equations below represents the second step of the solution process?

Step 1: $3(5x - 2) + 27 = -24$
Step 2: ☐
Step 3: $15x + 21 = -24$
Step 4: $15x = -45$
Step 5: $x = -3$

Ⓐ $3(5x + 27) - 2 = -24$

Ⓑ $3(5x + 25) = -24$

Ⓒ $15x - 2 + 27 = -24$

Ⓓ $15x - 6 + 27 = -24$

Answers

1. D
2. F
3. A
4. G
5. B
6. F
7. C
8. H
9. D
10. G
11. C
12. 6
13. 0.032
14. 64
15. 16.5
16. 3

If you are stuck on a problem, skip it and come back later. Another problem might remind you of something that will help. If you feel yourself become tense, take a few deep breaths to relax.

10. Cass drove 3 miles to school, and then she drove m miles to a friend's house. The total mileage for these two trips was 8 miles. Which equation CANNOT be used to determine the number of miles Cass drove?

Ⓕ $3 + m = 8$

Ⓖ $3 - m = 8$

Ⓗ $8 - 3 = m$

Ⓙ $8 - m = 3$

11. If $\frac{20}{x} = \frac{4}{x-5}$, which of the following is a true statement?

Ⓐ $x(x - 5) = 80$

Ⓑ $20x = 4(x - 5)$

Ⓒ $20(x - 5) = 4x$

Ⓓ $24 = 2x - 5$

Gridded Response

12. Four times a number is two less than six times the same number minus ten. What is the number?

13. Melissa invested her savings in a retirement account that pays simple interest. A portion of her account record is shown below. What is the interest rate on Melissa's account? Write your answer as a decimal.

Date	Transaction	Amount	Balance
8/1	Beginning deposit	\$6000.00	\$6000.00
8/31	Interest payment	\$192.00	\$6192.00
9/1	Withdrawal	\$1000.00	\$5192.00
9/30	Interest payment	\$166.14	\$5358.14

14. At 2:45 P.M. you are 112 miles from Dallas. You want to be in Dallas at 4:30 P.M. What is the average number of miles per hour you must travel to be on time?

15. A cyclist travels 45 miles in 4 hours. How many feet does she travel in one second?

16. A bike rental shop charges a one-time charge of \$8 plus an hourly fee to rent a bike. Dan paid \$24.50 to rent a bike for $5\frac{1}{2}$ hours. Find the bike shop's hourly fee in dollars.

Short Response

17. Alex buys 5 calendars to give as gifts. Each calendar has the same price. When the cashier rings up Alex's calendars, the total cost before tax is \$58.75.

a. Write and solve an equation to find the cost of each calendar.

b. The total cost of Alex's calendars after tax is \$63.45. Find the percent sales tax. Show your work and explain in words how you found your answer.

c. Alex's friend Keisha buys some calendars for the same price. She uses her 15% discount card. The total cost before tax is \$39.95. How many calendars did Keisha buy? Show your work and explain in words how you found your answer.

18. Is the percent increase from 50 to 100 the same as the percent decrease from 100 to 50? Explain your reasoning in words.

Extended Response

19. Korena is putting a decorative border around her rectangular flower garden. The total perimeter of the garden is 200 feet.

a. Draw three different rectangles that could represent Korena's flower garden. Label the dimensions of your rectangles.

b. Use the table to show the lengths and widths of five different rectangles that could represent Korena's flower garden. Do not use any of your rectangles from part **a.**

Possible Dimensions of Korena's Garden		
Length (ℓ)	Width (w)	Perimeter (P)

c. The length of Korena's garden is 4 times its width. Explain how to use the perimeter formula $P = 2\ell + 2w$ to find the dimensions of Korena's garden.

d. Find the dimensions of Korena's garden.

Short-Response Rubric

Items 17–18

2 Points = The student's answer is an accurate and complete execution of the task or tasks.

1 Point = The student's answer contains attributes of an appropriate response but is flawed.

0 Points = The student's answer contains no attributes of an appropriate response.

Extended-Response Rubric

Item 19

4 Points = The student correctly draws three different rectangles in part **a**, lists five more different rectangles in part **b**, answers and explains part **c**, and answers part **d**, showing all work.

3 Points = The student correctly draws some rectangles in part **a** and lists some rectangles in part **b** but does not identify eight different possibilities, or the student correctly answers parts **a**, **b**, and **c** but does not correctly answer part **d**.

2 Points = The student answers all parts correctly but does not show any work or explanation, or the student correctly answers parts **a** and **b** but does not correctly answer parts **c** and **d**.

1 Point = The student finds four or fewer rectangles to fit the situation but does not correctly answer other parts of the problem, or the student attempts to answer all parts of the problem but does not correctly answer any part.

0 Points = The student does not answer correctly and does not attempt all parts of the problem.

Answers

17a. $5c = 58.75$; \$11.75

b. 8%

c. 4

18. No; the percent of increase from 50 to 100 is 100%, while the percent of decrease from 100 to 50 is 50%.

19a. Possible answer:

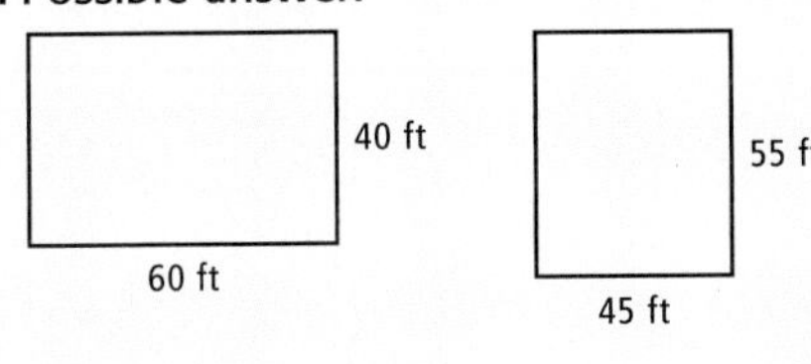

b. Possible answers:

Possible Dimensions of Korena's Garden		
Length (ℓ)	Width (w)	Perimeter (P)
30	70	200
25	75	200
50	50	200
15	85	200
10	90	200

c. Substitute $4w$ for ℓ in $P = 2\ell + 2w$ and solve for w. Substitute this value for w in $P = 2\ell + 2w$ and solve for ℓ.

d. 20 ft by 80 ft

Organizer

Objective: Choose appropriate problem-solving strategies and use them with skills from Chapters 1 and 2 to solve real-world problems.

Bullfrogs

Reading Strategies

Remind students that information needed for a problem may not be in the question itself. **Problem 3** asks how far the largest bullfrog in Illinois could jump. Ask students where on the page it states the length of the largest bullfrog. in the introductory paragraph

Using Data Have students find how much farther a 5-inch bullfrog can jump than a 4-inch bullfrog. 15 in.

State Resources

Bullfrogs

The bullfrog is the largest frog in Illinois. Adult bullfrogs are usually between $3\frac{1}{2}$ and 6 inches in length, but some have been known to grow even larger. The largest recorded bullfrog found in Illinois was 8 inches long and weighed more than a pound!

Choose one or more strategies to solve each problem.

1. A bullfrog jumping up a hill is 8 feet from the top. Each time it jumps, it moves forward 18 inches. However, mud on the hill causes it to slide backward 2 inches after each jump. How many jumps will it take the frog to reach the top of the hill? **6**
2. A certain pond is home to 120 bullfrog tadpoles. This is 90 more than 3 times the number of adult bullfrogs that live in a second pond. How many adult bullfrogs live in the second pond? **10**

For 3–5, use the table.

3. How far could the largest recorded bullfrog in Illinois jump? **120 in.**
4. If a bullfrog is $4\frac{1}{2}$ inches long, what is its maximum jumping distance? **67.5 in.**
5. A certain adult bullfrog can jump $8\frac{3}{4}$ feet. This bullfrog must be at least how long? **7 in.**

Jumping Distances of Bullfrogs

Length of Bullfrog (in.)	Maximum Jumping Distance (in.)
4	60
5	75
6	90

Problem-Solving Focus

For **Problem 1,** focus on the strategy "Use Logical Reasoning." Ask students how far the bullfrog actually advances after each jump. 16 in. Ask how many total inches he needs to travel. 96 in. Ask what operation will find the number of 16-inch jumps in 96 in. division

For **Problem 3,** students may apply the strategy "Find a Pattern" to the data in the table. They can use their pattern to answer the question. The numbers in the left column increase by 1. The numbers in the right column increase by 15.

The Great Snake Migration

When temperatures drop, large numbers of snakes leave the swamps of southern Illinois. Some travel just a few hundred feet, while others travel several miles, to Snake Road, a 3-mile-long road on the western edge of the Shawnee Forest. In this area, you can see as many as 40 to 50 snakes in a day, including cottonmouth water moccasins, rattlesnakes, and copperheads.

Choose one or more strategies to solve each problem.

1. In one hour, a researcher saw six snakes crossing Snake Road—three moccasins, a rattlesnake, a garter snake, and a diamondback water snake, though not in that order. The second snake to cross was a moccasin, and the other two moccasins crossed one after the other. The diamondback crossed before the garter snake. The first snake to cross was not the garter snake or the diamondback. A moccasin crossed last. In what order did the snakes cross Snake Road? **rattlesnake, moccasin, diamondback, garter, moccasin, moccasin**

For 2, use the table.

In 2001–2002, several Illinois hospitals were asked how many vials of antivenom they had available to treat snake bites. The results are shown in the table. For example, 37 hospitals reported that they had between 1 and 4 vials of antivenom available.

Antivenom Survey Results						
Vials	0	1–4	5–9	10–14	15–19	20+
Hospitals	■	37	14	6	0	10

2. The number of hospitals with no antivenom available to treat snake bites was 6 less than 3 times the number of hospitals that had 1–4 vials. How many hospitals had no antivenom with which to treat snake bites? What percent of the total number of hospitals surveyed does this represent? Round your answer to the nearest percent. **105; 61%**

The Great Snake Migration

Reading Strategies

ENGLISH LANGUAGE LEARNERS

Students may be unfamiliar with the word *antivenom.* Tell students that anti- means against. Ask students to use this information and context clues in the sentence to define both *venom* and *antivenom.* Venom is something in a snakebite that makes people sick; antivenom treats snakebites.

Using Data Discuss with students how to interpret the intervals in the table. Ask them what 20+ means. 20 or more

Problem-Solving Focus

Encourage students to use the four-step problem-solving process for **Problem 1.** Focus on the last step: **(4) Look Back.** After students think they have the correct order, have them read the problem again, placing a check mark next to each snake in their list as each sentence they read correctly describes its position.

Inequalities

Section 3A

Simple Inequalities

3-1 Graphing and Writing Inequalities
3-2 Solving Inequalities by Adding or Subtracting
3-3 Solving Inequalities by Multiplying or Dividing

Section 3B

Multi-Step and Compound Inequalities

3-4 Solving Two-Step and Multi-Step Inequalities
3-5 Solving Inequalities with Variables on Both Sides
3-6 **Algebra Lab** Truth Tables and Compound Statements
3-6 Solving Compound Inequalities
Connecting Algebra to Geometry Triangle Inequality
3-7 Solving Absolute-Value Inequalities

Pacing Guide for 45-Minute Classes

Teacher One Stop™
Calendar Planner®

Chapter 1

Countdown Weeks 6, 7

DAY 1	DAY 2	DAY 3	DAY 4	DAY 5
3-1 Lesson	3-2 Lesson	3-3 Lesson	Multi-Step Test Prep Ready to Go On?	3-4 Lesson
DAY 6	**DAY 7**	**DAY 8**	**DAY 9**	**DAY 10**
3-5 Lesson	3-6 Algebra Lab 3-6 Lesson	3-6 Lesson Connecting Algebra to Geometry	3-7 Lesson	Multi-Step Test Prep Ready to Go On?
DAY 11	**DAY 12**			
Chapter 3 Review	Chapter 3 Test			

Pacing Guide for 90-Minute Classes

Teacher One Stop™
Calendar Planner®

Chapter 1

DAY 1	DAY 2	DAY 3	DAY 4	DAY 5
Chapter 2 Test 3-1 Lesson	3-2 Lesson 3-3 Lesson	Multi-Step Test Prep Ready to Go On? 3-4 Lesson	3-5 Lesson 3-6 Algebra Lab 3-6 Lesson	3-6 Lesson Connecting Algebra to Geometry 3-7 Lesson
DAY 6	**DAY 7**			
Multi-Step Test Prep Ready to Go On? Chapter 3 Review	Chapter 3 Test 4-1 Lesson			

ONGOING ASSESSMENT and INTERVENTION

	DIAGNOSE	PRESCRIBE
Assess Prior Knowledge	**Before Chapter 3**	
	Diagnose readiness for the chapter.	Prescribe intervention. 
	Are You Ready? SE p. 167	***Are You Ready? Intervention***
Formative Assessment	**Before Every Lesson**	
	Diagnose readiness for the lesson.	Prescribe intervention.
	Warm Up TE	**Reteach** CRB
	During Every Lesson	
	Diagnose understanding of lesson concepts.	Prescribe intervention.
	Check It Out! SE	**Reading Strategies** CRB
	Questioning Strategies TE	***Success for Every Learner***
	Think and Discuss SE	***Lesson Tutorial Videos***
	Write About It SE	
	Journal TE	
	After Every Lesson	
	Diagnose mastery of lesson concepts.	Prescribe intervention.
	Lesson Quiz TE	**Reteach** CRB
	Test Prep SE	**Test Prep Doctor** TE
	Test and Practice Generator	***Homework Help* Online**
	 **Before Chapter 3 Testing**	
	Diagnose mastery of concepts in chapter.	Prescribe intervention.
	Ready to Go On? SE pp. 189, 219	***Ready to Go On? Intervention***
	Multi-Step Test Prep SE pp. 188, 218	**Scaffolding Questions** TE pp. 188, 218
	Section Quizzes AR	**Reteach** CRB
	Test and Practice Generator	***Lesson Tutorial Videos***
	Before High Stakes Testing	
	Diagnose mastery of benchmark concepts.	Prescribe intervention.
	College Entrance Exam Practice SE p. 225	***College Entrance Exam Practice***
	Standardized Test Prep SE pp. 228–229	
Summative Assessment	**After Chapter 3**	
	Check mastery of chapter concepts.	Prescribe intervention.
	Multiple-Choice Tests (Forms A, B, C)	**Reteach** CRB
	Free-Response Tests (Forms A, B, C)	***Lesson Tutorial Videos***
	Performance Assessment AR	
	Cumulative Test AR	
	Test and Practice Generator	

KEY: **SE** = *Student Edition* **TE** = *Teacher's Edition* **CRB** = *Chapter Resource Book* **AR** = *Assessment Resources*  Available online Available on CD- or DVD-ROM

Lesson Resources

Before the Lesson

Prepare ***Teacher One Stop*** SPANISH
- Editable lesson plans
- Calendar Planner
- Easy access to all chapter resources

Lesson Transparencies
- Teacher Tools

Teach the Lesson

Introduce ***Alternate Openers: Explorations***

Lesson Transparencies
- Warm Up
- Problem of the Day

Teach ***Lesson Transparencies***
- Teaching Transparencies

Know-It Notebook™
- Vocabulary
- Key Concepts

Power Presentations

Lesson Tutorial Videos SPANISH

Interactive Online Edition
- Lesson Activities
- Lesson Tutorial Videos

Lab Activities

Lab Resources Online

Online Interactivities SPANISH

TechKeys

Practice the Lesson

Practice ***Chapter Resources***
- Practice A, B, C

Practice and Problem Solving Workbook SPANISH

IDEA Works!® Modified Worksheets and Tests

ExamView Test and Practice Generator SPANISH

Homework Help Online

Online Interactivities SPANISH

Interactive Online Edition
- Homework Help

Apply ***Chapter Resources***
- Problem Solving SPANISH

Practice and Problem Solving Workbook SPANISH

Interactive Online Edition
- Chapter Project

Project Teacher Support

After the Lesson

Reteach ***Chapter Resources***
- Reteach
- Reading Strategies ELL

Success for Every Learner

Review ***Interactive Answers and Solutions***

Solutions Key

Know-It Notebook™
- Big Ideas
- Chapter Review

Extend ***Chapter Resources***
- Challenge

Technology Highlights for the Teacher

Power Presentations

Dynamic presentations to engage students. Complete PowerPoint® presentations for every lesson in Chapter 3.

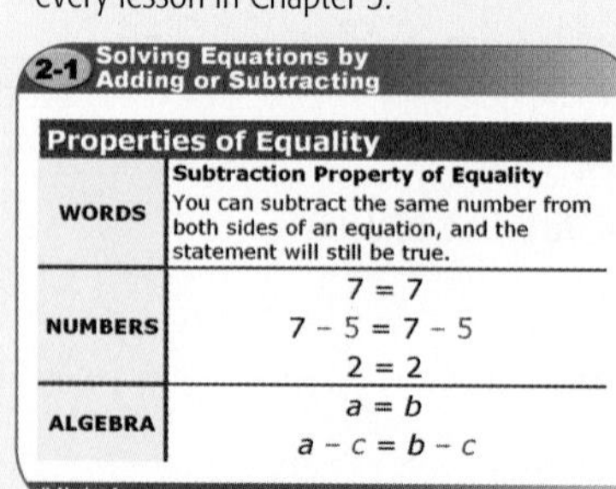

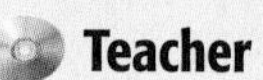

Teacher One Stop SPANISH

Easy access to Chapter 3 resources and assessments. Includes lesson planning, test generation, and puzzle creation software.

Premier Online Edition SPANISH

Chapter 3 includes Tutorial Videos, Lesson Activities, Lesson Quizzes, Homework Help, and Chapter Project.

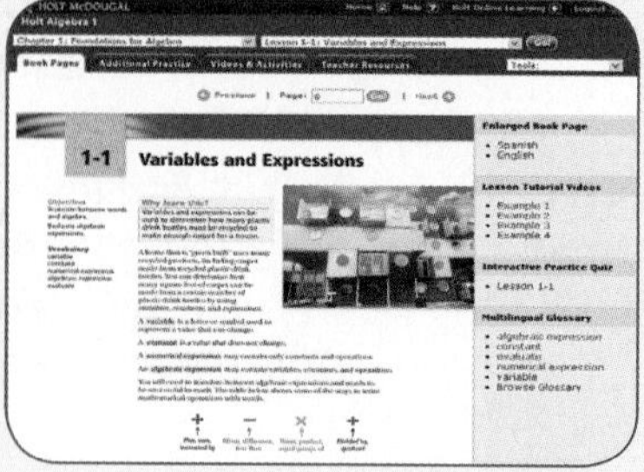

KEY: **SE** = *Student Edition* **TE** = *Teacher's Edition* ELL English Language Learners SPANISH Spanish version available Available online Available on CD- or DVD-ROM

CHAPTER 3

Reaching All Learners

Teaching tips to help all learners appear throughout the chapter. A few that target specific students are included in the lists below.

All Learners

Lab Activities
Practice and Problem Solving Workbook SPANISH
Know-It Notebook

Special Needs Students

Practice A .... CRB
Reteach .... CRB
Reading Strategies .... CRB
Are You Ready? .... SE p. 167
Inclusion .... TE pp. 173, 186, 194
IDEA Works!® Modified Worksheets and Tests
Ready to Go On? Intervention SPANISH
Know-It Notebook
Online Interactivities  SPANISH
Lesson Tutorial Videos SPANISH

Developing Learners

Practice A .... CRB
Reteach .... CRB
Reading Strategies .... CRB
Are You Ready? .... SE p. 167
Vocabulary Connections .... SE p. 168
Questioning Strategies .... TE
Ready to Go On? Intervention SPANISH
Know-It Notebook
Homework Help Online
Online Interactivities SPANISH
 *Lesson Tutorial Videos*  SPANISH

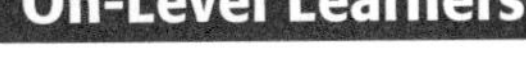

On-Level Learners

Practice B .... CRB
Problem Solving .... CRB
Vocabulary Connections .... SE p. 168
Questioning Strategies .... TE
Ready to Go On? Intervention SPANISH
Know-It Notebook
Homework Help Online
Online Interactivities SPANISH

Advanced Learners

Practice C .... CRB
Challenge .... CRB
Challenge Exercises .... SE
Reading and Writing Math *Extend* .... TE p. 169
Critical Thinking .... TE pp. 172, 177
Are You Ready? Enrichment SPANISH
Ready To Go On? Enrichment SPANISH

ENGLISH LANGUAGE LEARNERS

English Language Learners

Reading Strategies .... CRB
Are You Ready? Vocabulary .... SE p. 167
Vocabulary Connections .... SE p. 168
Vocabulary Review .... SE p. 220
English Language Learners .... TE pp. 171, 179, 206
Success for Every Learner
Know-It Notebook
Multilingual Glossary
Lesson Tutorial Videos  SPANISH

Technology Highlights for Reaching All Learners

Lesson Tutorial Videos SPANISH

Starring Holt authors Ed Burger and Freddie Renfro! Live tutorials to support every lesson in Chapter 3.

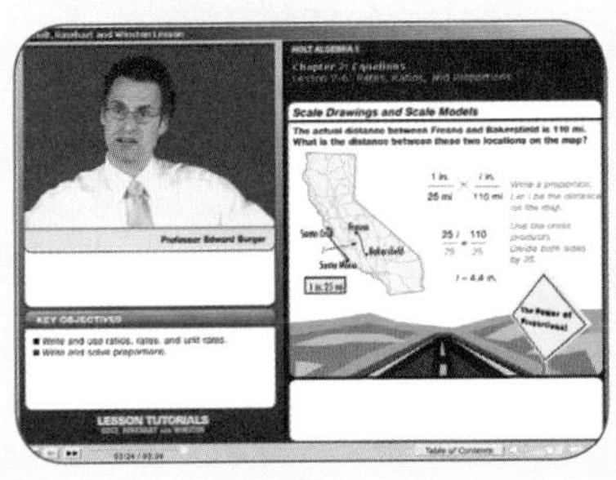

Multilingual Glossary

Searchable glossary includes definitions in English, Spanish, Vietnamese, Chinese, Hmong, Korean, and 4 other languages.

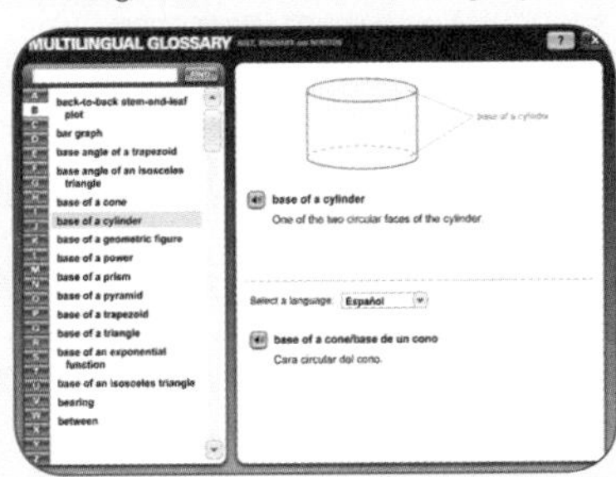

Online Interactivities

Interactive tutorials provide visually engaging alternative opportunities to learn concepts and master skills.

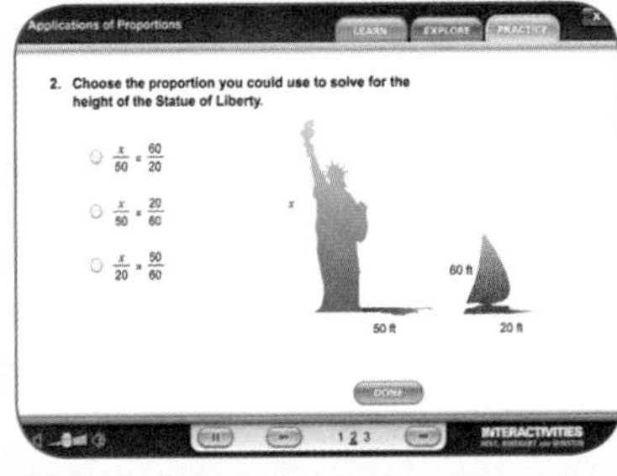

KEY: **SE** = *Student Edition* **TE** = *Teacher's Edition* **CRB** = *Chapter Resource Book* SPANISH Spanish version available; Available online; Available on CD- or DVD-ROM

CHAPTER 3

Ongoing Assessment

Assessing Prior Knowledge

Determine whether students have the prerequisite concepts and skills for success in Chapter 3.

Are You Ready? SPANISH .... SE p. 167
Warm Up .... TE

Test Preparation

Provide review and practice for Chapter 3 and standardized tests.

Multi-Step Test Prep .... SE pp. 188, 218
Study Guide: Review .... SE pp. 220–223
Test Tackler .... SE pp. 226–227
Standardized Test Prep .... SE pp. 228–229
College Entrance Exam Practice .... SE p. 225
Countdown to Testing .... SE pp. C4–C27
IDEA Works!® Modified Worksheets and Tests

Alternative Assessment

Assess students' understanding of Chapter 3 concepts and combined problem-solving skills.

Chapter 3 Project .... SE p. 166
Alternative Assessment .... TE
Performance Assessment SPANISH .... AR
Portfolio Assessment SPANISH .... AR

Lesson Assessment

Provide formative assessment for each lesson of Chapter 3.

Questioning Strategies .... TE
Think and Discuss .... SE
Check It Out! Exercises .... SE
Write About It .... SE
Journal .... TE
Lesson Quiz .... TE
Alternative Assessment .... TE
IDEA Works!® Modified Worksheets and Tests

Weekly Assessment

Provide formative assessment for each section of Chapter 3.

Multi-Step Test Prep .... SE pp. 188, 218
Ready to Go On? SPANISH .... SE pp. 189, 219
Section Quizzes SPANISH .... AR
Test and Practice Generator SPANISH .... *Teacher One Stop*

Chapter Assessment

Provide summative assessment of Chapter 3 mastery.

Chapter 3 Test .... SE p. 224
Chapter Test (Levels A, B, C) SPANISH .... AR
• Multiple Choice • Free Response
Cumulative Test SPANISH .... AR
Test and Practice Generator SPANISH .... *Teacher One Stop*
IDEA Works!® Modified Worksheets and Tests

Technology Highlights for Assessment

Are You Ready? SPANISH

Automatically assess readiness and prescribe intervention for Chapter 3 prerequisite skills.

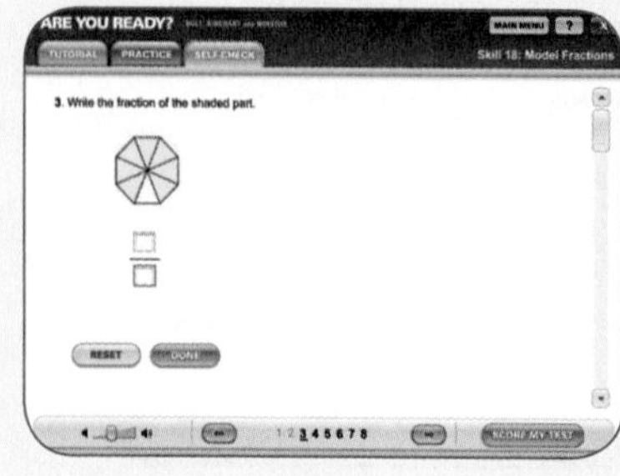

Ready to Go On?

Automatically assess understanding of and prescribe intervention for Sections 3A and 3B.

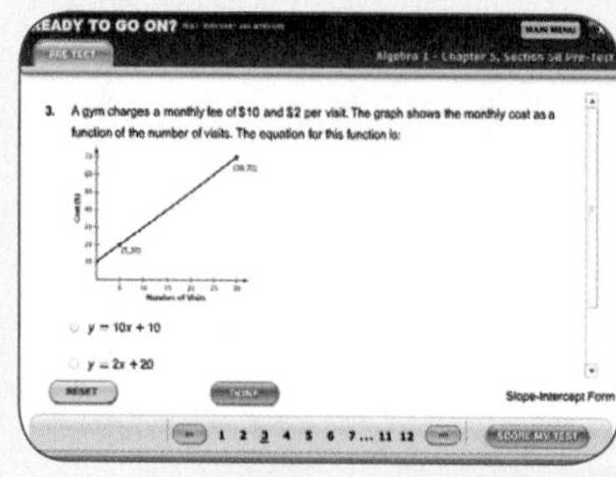

Test and Practice Generator SPANISH

Use Chapter 3 problem banks to create assessments and worksheets to print out or deliver online. Includes dynamic problems.

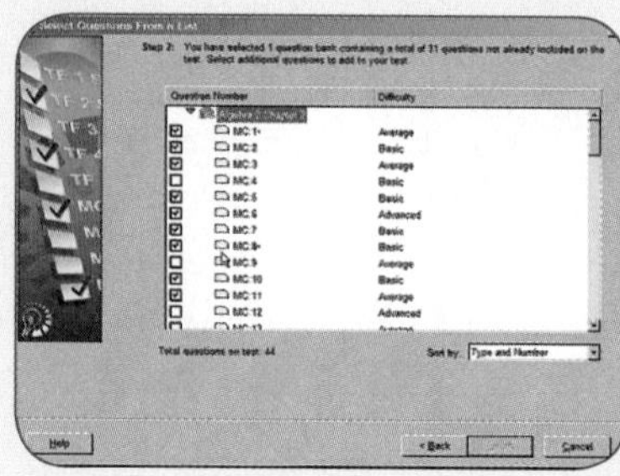

KEY: **SE** = *Student Edition* **TE** = *Teacher's Edition* **AR** = *Assessment Resources* SPANISH Spanish version available  Available online Available on CD- or DVD-ROM

Three levels (A, B, C) of multiple-choice and free-response chapter tests, along with a performance assessment, are available in the *Assessment Resources*.

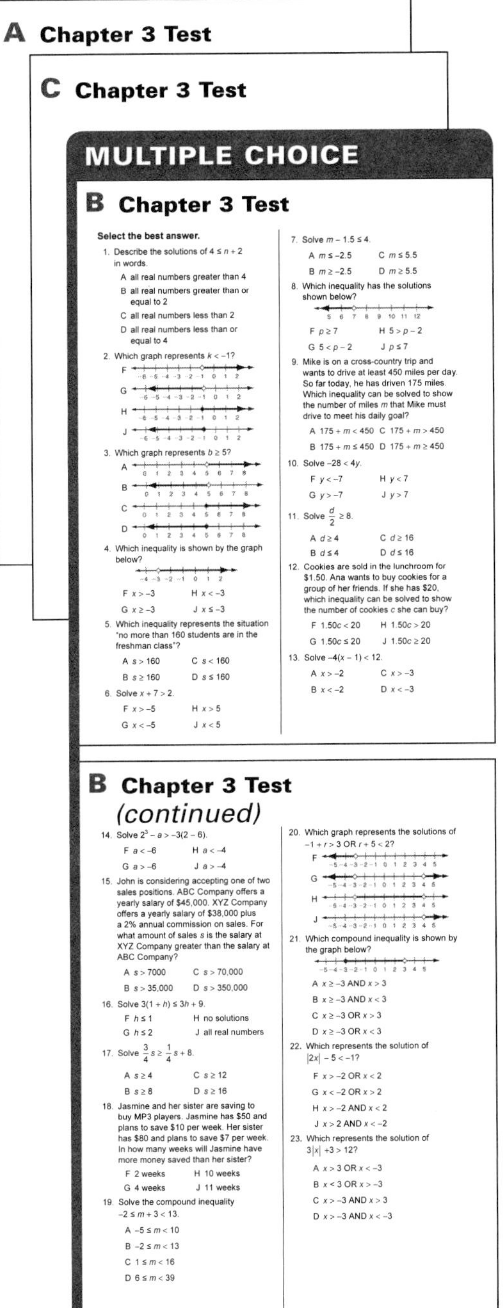

A Chapter 3 Test

C Chapter 3 Test

MULTIPLE CHOICE

B Chapter 3 Test

Select the best answer.

1. Describe the solutions of $4 \le n + 2$ in words.
   A all real numbers greater than 4
   B all real numbers greater than or equal to 2
   C all real numbers less than 2
   D all real numbers less than or equal to 4
2. Which graph represents $k < -1$?
   F G H J
3. Which graph represents $b \ge 5$?
   A B C D
4. Which inequality is shown by the graph below?
   F $x > -3$ H $x < -3$
   G $x \ge -3$ J $x \le -3$
5. Which inequality represents the situation "no more than 160 students are in the freshman class"?
   A $s > 160$ C $s < 160$
   B $s \ge 160$ D $s \le 160$
6. Solve $x + 7 > 2$.
   F $x > -5$ H $x > 5$
   G $x < -5$ J $x < 5$
7. Solve $m - 1.5 \le 4$.
   A $m \le -2.5$ C $m \le 5.5$
   B $m \ge -2.5$ D $m \ge 5.5$
8. Which inequality has the solutions shown below?
   F $p \ge 7$ H $5 > p - 2$
   G $5 < p - 2$ J $p \le 7$
9. Mike is on a cross-country trip and wants to drive at least 450 miles per day. So far today, he has driven 175 miles. Which inequality can be solved to show the number of miles m that Mike must drive to meet his daily goal?
   A $175 + m < 450$ C $175 + m > 450$
   B $175 + m \le 450$ D $175 + m \ge 450$
10. Solve $-28 < 4y$.
   F $y < -7$ H $y < 7$
   G $y > -7$ J $y > 7$
11. Solve $\frac{d}{2} \ge 8$.
   A $d \ge 4$ C $d \ge 16$
   B $d \le 4$ D $d \le 16$
12. Cookies are sold in the lunchroom for $1.50. Ana wants to buy cookies for a group of her friends. If she has $20, which inequality can be solved to show the number of cookies c she can buy?
   F $1.50c < 20$ H $1.50c > 20$
   G $1.50c \le 20$ J $1.50c \ge 20$
13. Solve $-4(x - 1) < 12$.
   A $x > -2$ C $x > -3$
   B $x < -2$ D $x < -3$

B Chapter 3 Test *(continued)*

14. Solve $2^3 - a > -3(2 - 6)$.
   F $a < -6$ H $a < -4$
   G $a > -6$ J $a > -4$
15. John is considering accepting one of two sales positions. ABC Company offers a yearly salary of $45,000. XYZ Company offers a yearly salary of $38,000 plus a 2% annual commission on sales. For what amount of sales s is the salary at XYZ Company greater than the salary at ABC Company?
   A $s > 7000$ C $s > 70,000$
   B $s > 35,000$ D $s > 350,000$
16. Solve $3(1 + h) \le 3h + 9$.
   F $h \le 1$ H no solutions
   G $h \le 2$ J all real numbers
17. Solve $\frac{3}{4}s \ge \frac{1}{4}s + 8$.
   A $s \ge 4$ C $s \ge 12$
   B $s \ge 8$ D $s \ge 16$
18. Jasmine and her sister are saving to buy MP3 players. Jasmine has $50 and plans to save $10 per week. Her sister has $80 and plans to save $7 per week. In how many weeks will Jasmine have more money saved than her sister?
   F 2 weeks H 10 weeks
   G 4 weeks J 11 weeks
19. Solve the compound inequality $-2 \le m + 3 < 13$.
   A $-5 \le m < 10$
   B $-2 \le m < 13$
   C $1 \le m < 16$
   D $6 \le m < 39$
20. Which graph represents the solutions of $-1 + r > 3$ OR $r + 5 < 2$?
   F G H J
21. Which compound inequality is shown by the graph below?
   A $x \ge -3$ AND $x > 3$
   B $x \ge -3$ AND $x < 3$
   C $x \ge -3$ OR $x > 3$
   D $x \ge -3$ OR $x < 3$
22. Which represents the solution of $|2x| - 5 < -1$?
   F $x > -2$ OR $x < 2$
   G $x < -2$ OR $x > 2$
   H $x > -2$ AND $x < 2$
   J $x > 2$ AND $x < -2$
23. Which represents the solution of $3|x| + 3 > 12$?
   A $x > 3$ OR $x < -3$
   B $x < 3$ OR $x > -3$
   C $x > -3$ AND $x > 3$
   D $x > -3$ AND $x < -3$

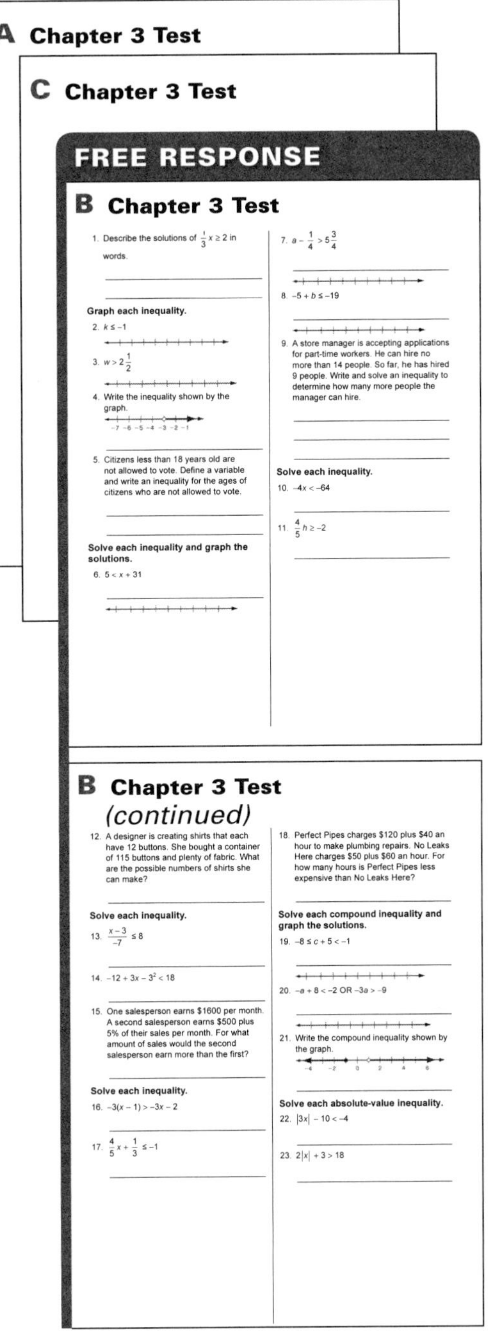

A Chapter 3 Test

C Chapter 3 Test

FREE RESPONSE

B Chapter 3 Test

1. Describe the solutions of $\frac{1}{3}x \ge 2$ in words.

Graph each inequality.

2. $k \le -1$
3. $w > 2\frac{1}{2}$
4. Write the inequality shown by the graph.
5. Citizens less than 18 years old are not allowed to vote. Define a variable and write an inequality for the ages of citizens who are not allowed to vote.

Solve each inequality and graph the solutions.

6. $5 < x + 31$
7. $a - \frac{1}{4} > 5\frac{3}{4}$
8. $-5 + b \le -19$
9. A store manager is accepting applications for part-time workers. He can hire no more than 14 people. So far, he has hired 9 people. Write and solve an inequality to determine how many more people the manager can hire.

Solve each inequality.

10. $-4x < -64$
11. $\frac{4}{5}h \ge -2$

B Chapter 3 Test *(continued)*

12. A designer is creating shirts that each have 12 buttons. She bought a container of 115 buttons and plenty of fabric. What are the possible numbers of shirts she can make?

Solve each inequality.

13. $\frac{x-3}{-7} \le 8$
14. $-12 + 3x - 3^2 < 18$
15. One salesperson earns $1600 per month. A second salesperson earns $500 plus 5% of their sales per month. For what amount of sales would the second salesperson earn more than the first?

Solve each inequality.

16. $-3(x - 1) > -3x - 2$
17. $\frac{4}{5}x + \frac{1}{3} \le -1$
18. Perfect Pipes charges $120 plus $40 an hour to make plumbing repairs. No Leaks Here charges $50 plus $60 an hour. For how many hours is Perfect Pipes less expensive than No Leaks Here?

Solve each compound inequality and graph the solutions.

19. $-8 \le c + 5 < -1$
20. $-a + 8 < -2$ OR $-3a > -9$
21. Write the compound inequality shown by the graph.

Solve each absolute-value inequality.

22. $|3x| - 10 < -4$
23. $2|x| + 3 > 18$

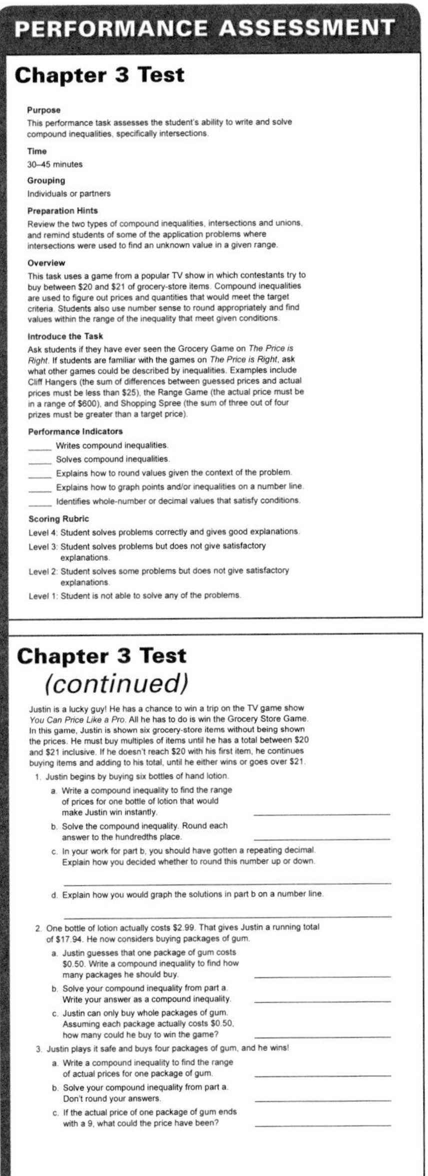

PERFORMANCE ASSESSMENT

Chapter 3 Test

Purpose
This performance task assesses the student's ability to write and solve compound inequalities, specifically intersections.

Time
30–45 minutes

Grouping
Individuals or partners

Preparation Hints
Review the two types of compound inequalities, intersections and unions, and remind students of some of the application problems where intersections were used to find an unknown value in a given range.

Overview
This task uses a game from a popular TV show in which contestants try to buy between $20 and $21 of grocery-store items. Compound inequalities are used to figure out prices and quantities that would meet the target criteria. Students also use number sense to round appropriately and find values within the range of the inequality that meet given conditions.

Introduce the Task
Ask students if they have ever seen the Grocery Game on *The Price is Right*. If students are familiar with the games on *The Price is Right*, ask what other games could be described by inequalities. Examples include Cliff Hangers (the sum of differences between guessed prices and actual prices must be less than $25), the Range Game (the actual price must be in a range of $600), and Shopping Spree (the sum of three out of four prizes must be greater than a target price).

Performance Indicators
____ Writes compound inequalities.
____ Solves compound inequalities.
____ Explains how to round values given the context of the problem.
____ Explains how to graph points and/or inequalities on a number line.
____ Identifies whole-number or decimal values that satisfy conditions.

Scoring Rubric
Level 4: Student solves problems correctly and gives good explanations.
Level 3: Student solves problems but does not give satisfactory explanations.
Level 2: Student solves some problems but does not give satisfactory explanations.
Level 1: Student is not able to solve any of the problems.

Chapter 3 Test *(continued)*

Justin is a lucky guy! He has a chance to win a trip on the TV game show *You Can Price Like a Pro*. All he has to do is win the Grocery Store Game. In this game, Justin is shown six grocery-store items without being shown the prices. He must buy multiples of items until he has a total between $20 and $21 inclusive. If he doesn't reach $20 with his first item, he continues buying items and adding to his total, until he either wins or goes over $21.

1. Justin begins by buying six bottles of hand lotion.
   a. Write a compound inequality to find the range of prices for one bottle of lotion that would make Justin win instantly.
   b. Solve the compound inequality. Round each answer to the hundredths place.
   c. In your work for part b, you should have gotten a repeating decimal. Explain how you decided whether to round this number up or down.
   d. Explain how you would graph the solutions in part b on a number line.
2. One bottle of lotion actually costs $2.99. That gives Justin a running total of $17.94. He now considers buying packages of gum.
   a. Justin guesses that one package of gum costs $0.50. Write a compound inequality to find how many packages he should buy.
   b. Solve your compound inequality from part a. Write your answer as a compound inequality.
   c. Justin can only buy whole packages of gum. Assuming each package actually costs $0.50, how many could he buy to win the game?
3. Justin plays it safe and buys four packages of gum, and he wins!
   a. Write a compound inequality to find the range of actual prices for one package of gum.
   b. Solve your compound inequality from part a. Don't round your answers.
   c. If the actual price of one package of gum ends with a 9, what could the price have been?

Teacher One Stop™ SPANISH

Test & Practice Generator

Create and customize Chapter 3 Tests. Instantly generate multiple test versions, answer keys, and Spanish versions of test items.

Modified chapter tests that address special learning needs are available in *IDEA Works!®* *Modified Worksheets and Tests.*

CHAPTER 3

Inequalities

Chapter Focus

- Solve multi-step inequalities.
- Write and solve inequalities to solve problems.

For a *Good* Cause

You can use the concepts in this chapter to plan for a fund-raising event. Inequalities help you determine how to reach your fund-raising goals.

go.hrw.com
Chapter Project Online
KEYWORD: MA7 ChProj

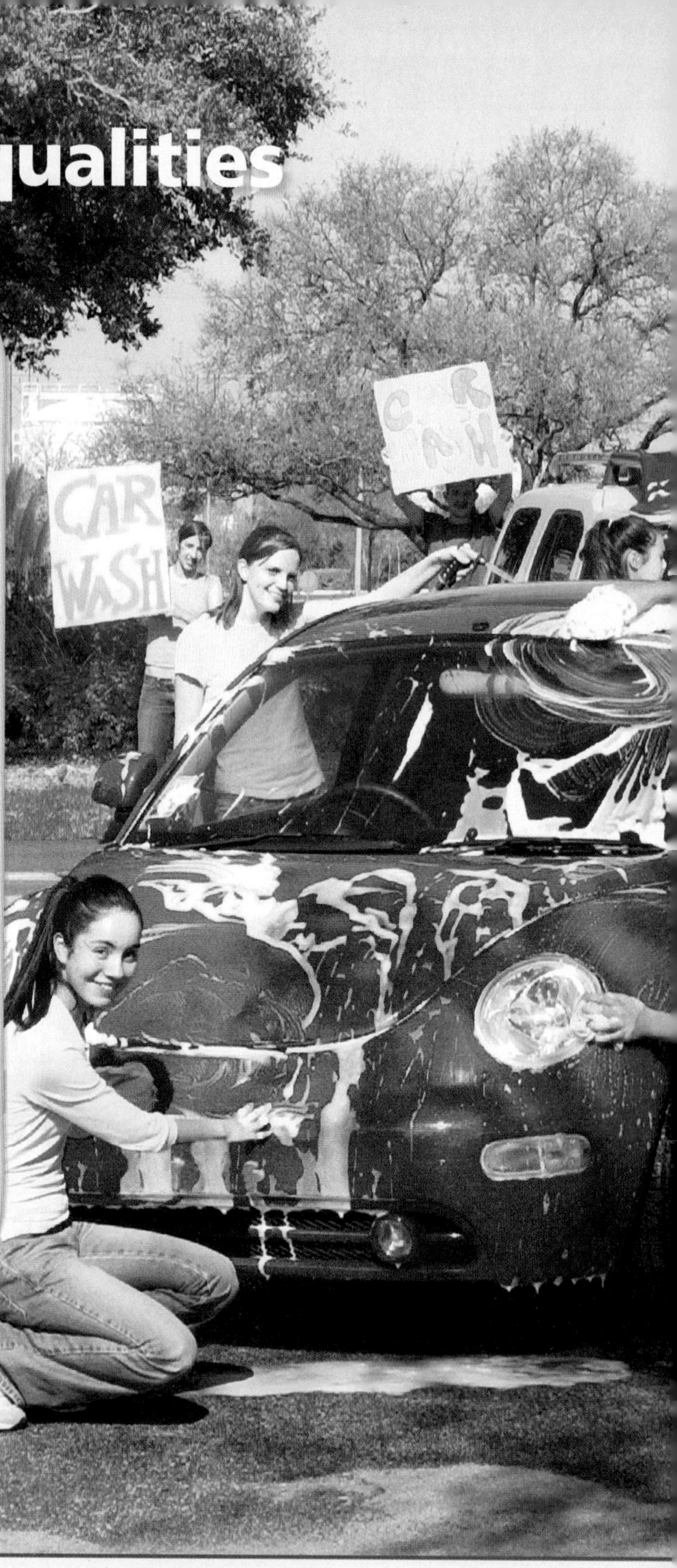

SECTION 3A

Simple Inequalities

On page 188, students write, solve, and graph inequalities to model the cost of travel, lodging, and entertainment while on a vacation.

Exercises designed to prepare students for success on the Multi-Step Test Prep can be found in each lesson.

SECTION 3B

Multi-Step and Compound Inequalities

On page 218, students write, solve, and graph inequalities to determine the costs associated with recording a CD at a studio.

Exercises designed to prepare students for success on the Multi-Step Test Prep can be found in each lesson.

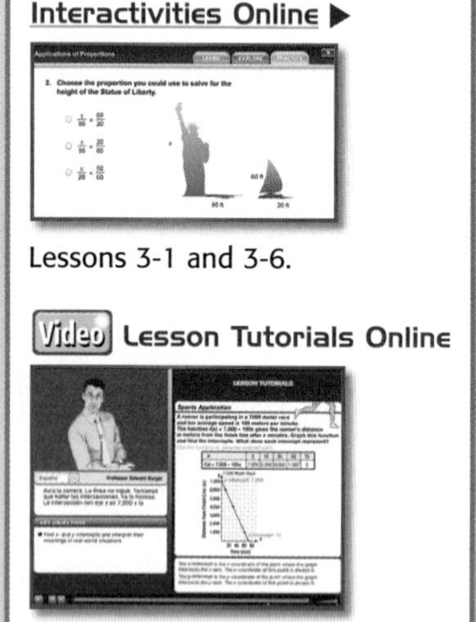

Interactivities Online ▶

Lessons 3-1 and 3-6.

Video Lesson Tutorials Online

Lesson Tutorial Videos are available for EVERY example.

For a Good Cause

About the Project

A car wash is a great way to raise money for an organization. In the chapter project students plan a car wash and decide how much to charge. Then students decide how many custom T-shirts to buy in order to promote the event. Students must write and solve inequalities to help them make these decisions.

Project Resources

All project resources for teachers and students are provided online.

Materials:

- none

ARE YOU READY?

Vocabulary

Match each term on the left with a definition on the right.

1. equation **B**
2. evaluate **E**
3. inverse operations **F**
4. like terms **D**
5. solution of an equation **C**

A. mathematical phrase that contains operations, numbers, and/ or variables
B. mathematical statement that two expressions are equivalent
C. value of a variable that makes a statement true
D. terms that contain the same variables raised to the same powers
E. to find the value of an expression
F. operations that undo each other

Evaluate Expressions

Evaluate each expression for $a = 2$ and $b = 6$.

6. $b - a$ **4**
7. ab **12**
8. $b \div a$ **3**
9. $a + b$ **8**

Compare and Order Real Numbers

Compare. Write <, >, or =.

10. 10 < 21
11. 5.27 > 5.23
12. 20% = 0.2
13. $\frac{1}{3} < \frac{2}{5}$

Combine Like Terms

Simplify each expression by combining like terms.

14. $6x + x$ **$7x$**
15. $-8a + 3a$ **$-5a$**
16. $9x^2 - 15x^2$ **$-6x^2$**
17. $2.1x + 4.3x$ **$6.4x$**

Distributive Property

Simplify each expression.

18. $2(x + 3)$ **$2x + 6$**
19. $(3 - d)5$ **$15 - 5d$**
20. $4(r - 1)$ **$4r - 4$**
21. $3(4 + m)$ **$12 + 3m$**

Solve One-Step Equations

Solve.

22. $s - 3 = 8$ **11**
23. $-7x = 21$ **-3**
24. $y + 11 = 2$ **-9**
25. $\frac{h}{2} = 6$ **12**
26. $t + 2 = -2$ **-4**
27. $6x = 42$ **7**
28. $r - 8 = -13$ **-5**
29. $\frac{y}{3} = -12$ **-36**

CHAPTER 3

ARE YOU READY?

Organizer

Objective: Assess students' understanding of prerequisite skills.

Assessing Prior Knowledge

INTERVENTION

Diagnose and Prescribe

Use this page to determine whether intervention is necessary or whether enrichment is appropriate.

Resources

 ***Are You Ready? Intervention and Enrichment*** **Worksheets**

 ***Are You Ready?*** **CD-ROM**

 ***Are You Ready?*** **Online**

my.hrw.com

ARE YOU READY?
Diagnose and Prescribe

Prerequisite Skill	*Are You Ready? Intervention,* Chapter 3: Worksheets	CD-ROM	Online
Evaluate Expressions	Skill 60	Activity 60	Diagnose and Prescribe Online
Compare and Order Real Numbers	Skill 16	Activity 16	
Combine Like Terms	Skill 57	Activity 57	
Distributive Property	Skill 56	Activity 56	
Solve One-Step Equations	Skill 68	Activity 68	

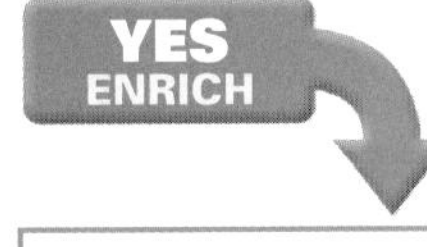

Are You Ready? Enrichment, Chapter 3
- Worksheets
- CD-ROM
- Online

Organizer

Objective: Help students organize the new concepts they will learn in Chapter 3.

Online Edition
Multilingual Glossary

Resources

Teacher One Stop™
PuzzleView

***Multilingual Glossary* Online**
go.hrw.com
KEYWORD: MA7 Glossary

Possible answers to *Vocabulary Connections*

1. An inequality states that two things are not equal.
2. A compound inequality is made of two or more simple inequalities.
3. The intersection of two graphs is the place where the two graphs overlap.
4. *Unite, unify, unit, unicycle, uniform, universal;* each word has the word *one* in its definition.

CHAPTER 3 Study Guide: Preview

Where You've Been

Previously, you

- learned the properties of equality.
- solved equations by using inverse operations.
- solved equations with variables on both sides.

In This Chapter

You will study

- the properties of inequality.
- how to solve inequalities by using inverse operations.
- how to solve inequalities with variables on both sides.
- how to solve compound inequalities.

Where You're Going

You can use the skills in this chapter

- in all your future math classes, including Geometry.
- in other classes, such as Health, Chemistry, Physics, and Economics.
- in the real world to plan a budget, to find cost-efficient services, and to set financial goals.

Key Vocabulary/Vocabulario

compound inequality	desigualdad compuesta
inequality	desigualdad
intersection	intersección
solution of an inequality	solución de una desigualdad
union	unión

Vocabulary Connections

To become familiar with some of the vocabulary terms in the chapter, consider the following. You may refer to the chapter, the glossary, or a dictionary if you like.

1. The prefix *in-* means "not." An *equality* states that two things are equal. Use these meanings to write your own definition for the word **inequality**.
2. The word *compound* means "consisting of two or more parts." What do you think a **compound inequality** might be?
3. The **intersection** of two roads is the place where the two roads overlap. What do you think the *intersection* of two graphs would be?
4. The word **union** begins with the root *uni-*. List some other words that begin with *uni-*. What do all of these words have in common?

Study Strategy: Use Your Notes Effectively

Taking notes helps you arrange, organize, and process information from your textbook and class lectures. In addition to taking notes, you need to use your notes before and after class effectively.

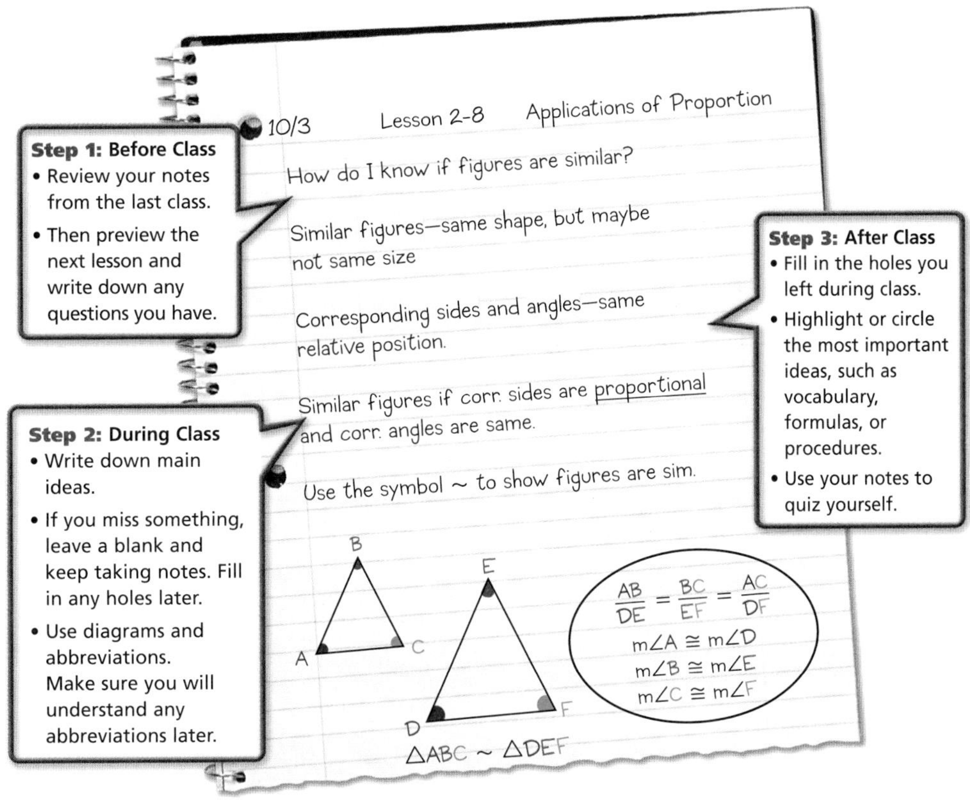

Try This

1. Look at the next lesson in your textbook. Write down some questions you have about the material in that lesson. Leave space between each question so that you can write the answers during the next class.
2. Look at the notes you took during the last class. List three ways you can improve your note-taking skills.

Reading and Writing Math CHAPTER 3

Organizer

Objective: Help students apply strategies to understand and retain key concepts.

Study Strategy: Use Your Notes Effectively

Discuss Notes are most helpful when they are well organized. Students may wish to divide their notebooks into sections for class notes, definitions, formulas, homework, scrap work, review, etc.

Extend Abbreviations can be used when taking notes to save space and time. Some students use *b/c* for *because* or *s/t* for *sometimes*. Ask students to share other abbreviations they use.

Answers to *Try This*

1–2. Check students' work.

Mathematical Mysteries
by Calvin C. Clawson

Human began counting at least 35,000 years ago, according to this fascinating inquiry into the wonder of numbers. Counting and ordering numbers allowed early humans to establish that one set of objects was larger than another, and the concept of inequality was born. The author's account of the first million years or so of numbers, plus chapters on sequences and series, prime numbers, and a host of other algebra-related topics make for entertaining and enlightening reading.

Activity Ask students to read Chapter 1, "Discovery of the Number Sequence," and then to report on the significance of a baboon thigh bone with 29 notches found in Africa's Lebembo Mountains.

SECTION

3A Simple Inequalities

One-Minute Section Planner

Lesson	Lab Resources	Materials
Lesson 3-1 Graphing and Writing Inequalities • Identify solutions of inequalities with one variable. • Write and graph inequalities with one variable. ☑ SAT-10 ☑ NAEP ☑ ACT ☑ SAT ☑ SAT Subject Tests		
Lesson 3-2 Solving Inequalities by Adding or Subtracting • Solve one-step inequalities by using addition. • Solve one-step inequalities by using subtraction. ☑ SAT-10 ☑ NAEP ☑ ACT ☑ SAT ☑ SAT Subject Tests	***Algebra Lab Activities*** 3-2 Algebra Lab	Optional index cards
Lesson 3-3 Solving Inequalities by Multiplying or Dividing • Solve one-step inequalities by using multiplication. • Solve one-step inequalities by using division. ☑ SAT-10 ☑ NAEP ☑ ACT ☑ SAT ☑ SAT Subject Tests	***Technology Lab Activities*** 3-3 Technology Lab	

Note: If NAEP is checked, the content is tested on either the Grade 8 or Grade 12 NAEP assessment.

MK *Manipulatives Kit*

Math Background

Professional Learning

INEQUALITIES

Lessons 3-1 to 3-3

One of the basic building blocks of mathematics is the Law of Trichotomy. This axiom says that given any two real numbers, a and b, exactly one of the following is true:

$$a = b,\ a < b, \text{ or } a > b.$$

In the first case, a and b are related by an equality. In the second and third cases, a and b are related by an *inequality.*

To understand inequalities, it is necessary to understand their connection to the real number line. For example, the inequality $-2 < 3$, which states that -2 is less than 3, means that -2 is to the left of 3 on the number line.

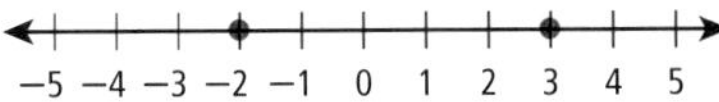

A *solution* of an algebraic inequality is any value of the variable that makes the inequality true. Thus, the solution set of $x < 3$ contains every value on the number line to the left of 3, since any of these values, when substituted in the inequality, result in a true statement. This solution set, consisting of infinitely many elements, can be shown as a ray on the number line. (The empty circle at 3 indicates that $x = 3$ is not a solution.)

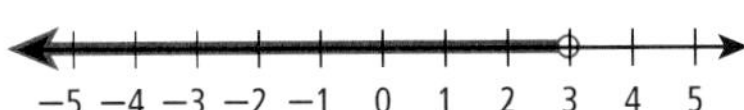

SOLVING INEQUALITIES

Lessons 3-1 to 3-3

Solving an inequality in one variable is similar to solving an equation in one variable. The goal is to isolate the variable on one side of the inequality by writing a series of equivalent inequalities—that is, a series of inequalities with the same solution set.

The Addition and Subtraction Properties of Inequality are analogous to their counterparts for equations: the same quantity may be added to or subtracted from both sides of an inequality. For multiplication and division there is an important caveat.

Consider the inequality $a > b$. By the Subtraction Property of Inequality, $a - a > b - a$ or, equivalently, $0 > b - a$. Applying the Subtraction Property of Inequality again shows that $0 - b > b - a - b$ or $-b > -a$, which is the same as $-a < -b$. In other words, when both sides of the inequality are multiplied by -1, the direction of the inequality is reversed. More generally, the direction of the inequality is reversed when both sides of an inequality are multiplied or divided by any negative number.

TRANSFORMATIONS

Lessons 3-1 to 3-3

We can use transformations to examine solutions of inequalities. For example, compare the graph of $x < 3$ with the graph of $x - 2 < 3$.

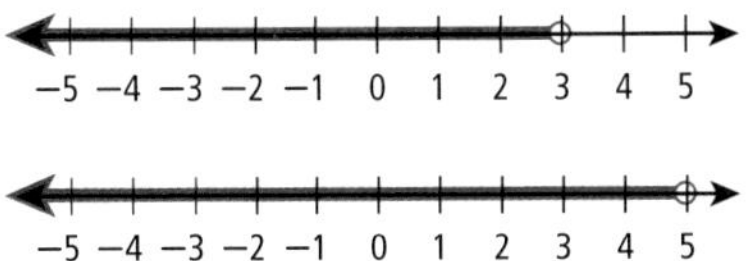

Notice that the graphs are identical except that the graph of $x - 2 < 3$ has been shifted 2 units to the right. In general, the graph of $x - a < k$ is the same as that of $x < k$, but shifted a units to the right (if $a > 0$) or $|a|$ units to the left (if $a < 0$).

The coefficient of x represents the stretching or shrinking of the graph. For example, the graph of $6x < 3$ is shown below.

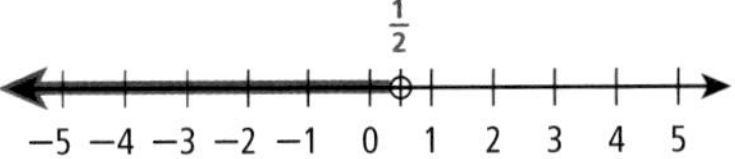

As compared to the graph of $x < 3$, the ray is contracted toward the origin by a factor of 6.

Finally, the graph of $-x < 3$ is shown below.

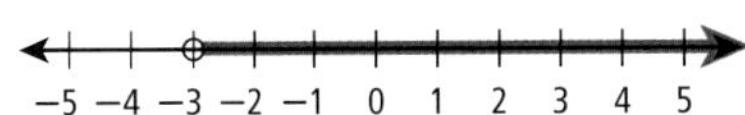

Comparing this to the graph of $x < 3$ shows that the negative sign in front of x reflects the ray about the origin.

3-1 Organizer

Pacing: Traditional 1 day
Block $\frac{1}{2}$ day

Objectives: Identify solutions of inequalities in one variable.

Write and graph inequalities in one variable.

Online Edition
Tutorial Videos, Interactivity

Countdown Week 6

Power Presentations with PowerPoint®

Warm Up

Compare. Write <, >, or =.

1. $-3 < 2$ **2.** $6.5 > 6.3$

3. $\frac{1}{2} > -\frac{3}{4}$ **4.** $0.25 = \frac{1}{4}$

Tell whether the inequality $x < 5$ is true or false for the following values of x.

5. $x = -10$ T **6.** $x = 5$ F

7. $x = 4.99$ T **8.** $x = -\frac{1}{5}$ T

Also available on transparency

Q: Why did the Moore family name their son Lester?

A: So he could be called either "Moore" or "Les."

3-1 Graphing and Writing Inequalities

Objectives
Identify solutions of inequalities in one variable.

Write and graph inequalities in one variable.

Vocabulary
inequality
solution of an inequality

Who uses this?
Members of a crew team can use inequalities to be sure they fall within a range of weights. (See Example 4.)

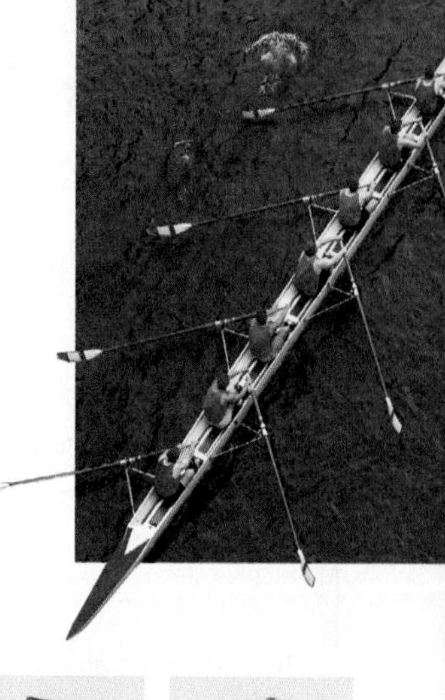

The athletes on a lightweight crew team must weigh 165 pounds or less. The acceptable weights for these athletes can be described using an *inequality.*

An **inequality** is a statement that two quantities are not equal. The quantities are compared by using one of the following signs:

$A < B$
A is less than *B*.

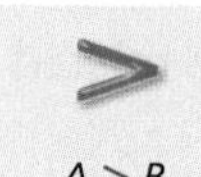
$A > B$
A is greater than *B*.

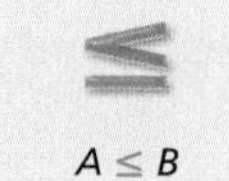
$A \le B$
A is less than or equal to *B*.

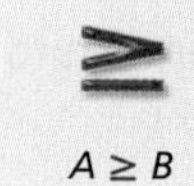
$A \ge B$
A is greater than or equal to *B*.

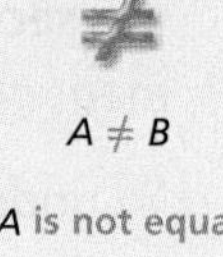
$A \ne B$
A is not equal to *B*.

A **solution of an inequality** is any value of the variable that makes the inequality true.

EXAMPLE 1 Identifying Solutions of Inequalities

Describe the solutions of $3 + x < 9$ in words.

Test values of *x* that are positive, negative, and 0.

x	-2.75	0	5.99	6	6.01	6.1
$3 + x$	0.25	3	8.99	9	9.01	9.1
$3 + x \overset{?}{<} 9$	$0.25 \overset{?}{<} 9$	$3 \overset{?}{<} 9$	$8.99 \overset{?}{<} 9$	$9 \overset{?}{<} 9$	$9.01 \overset{?}{<} 9$	$9.1 \overset{?}{<} 9$
Solution?	Yes	Yes	Yes	No	No	No

When the value of x is a number less than 6, the value of 3 + x is less than 9.
When the value of x is 6, the value of 3 + x is equal to 9.
When the value of x is a number greater than 6, the value of 3 + x is greater than 9.

The solutions of $3 + x < 9$ are numbers less than 6.

Writing Math
The solutions of the inequality in Example 1 can be written in *set-builder notation* as $\{x \mid x < 6\}$, which is read as "the set of all real numbers *x* such that *x* is less than 6."

1. Describe the solutions of $2p > 8$ in words.
all real numbers greater than 4

State Resources

State Resources Online
KEYWORD: MA7 Resources

1 Introduce

EXPLORATION

3-1 Graphing and Writing Inequalities

You can use a number line to help you see relationships among numbers.

1. Plot the following numbers on the number line: $-5, 6, -3.5, 0, 1.5, -2, -7$.
   $-10\ -8\ -6\ -4\ -2\ 0\ 2\ 4\ 6\ 8\ 10$
2. Which of the numbers that you plotted are greater than or equal to -5?
3. Name and plot three additional numbers that are greater than or equal to -5.
   $-10\ -8\ -6\ -4\ -2\ 0\ 2\ 4\ 6\ 8\ 10$
4. Draw a ray connecting all the numbers that are greater than or equal to -5.
   $-10\ -8\ -6\ -4\ -2\ 0\ 2\ 4\ 6\ 8\ 10$

THINK AND DISCUSS

5. **Describe** how the ray would be different if you plot and connect numbers that are less than or equal to -5.
6. **Explain** how you could draw a ray to show all numbers that are greater than or equal to $4\frac{1}{2}$.

Motivate

Make some statements like "There are fewer than 30 students in this class" and "The temperature will be at least 70 degrees tomorrow." Ask students what the phrases "fewer than" and "at least" mean. Ask students for other phrases that indicate a comparison.

Explorations and answers are provided in *Alternate Openers: Explorations Transparencies.*

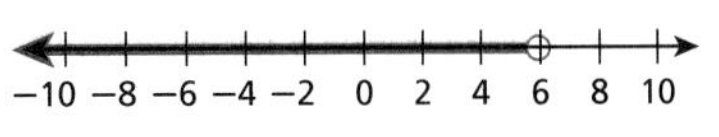

An inequality like $3 + x < 9$ has too many solutions to list. You can use a graph on a number line to show all the solutions.

The solutions are shaded and an arrow shows that the solutions continue past those shown on the graph. To show that an endpoint is a solution, draw a solid circle at the number. To show that an endpoint is not a solution, draw an empty circle.

Graphing Inequalities

WORDS	ALGEBRA	GRAPH
All real numbers less than 5	$x < 5$	−4 −3 −2 −1 0 1 2 3 4 5 6
All real numbers greater than −1	$x > -1$	−4 −3 −2 −1 0 1 2 3 4 5 6
All real numbers less than or equal to $\frac{1}{2}$	$x \le \frac{1}{2}$	-2 $-1\frac{1}{2}$ -1 $-\frac{1}{2}$ 0 $\frac{1}{2}$ 1
All real numbers greater than or equal to 0	$x \ge 0$	−4 −3 −2 −1 0 1 2 3 4 5 6

EXAMPLE 2 Graphing Inequalities

Graph each inequality.

A $b < -1.5$

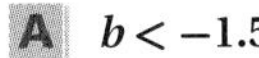

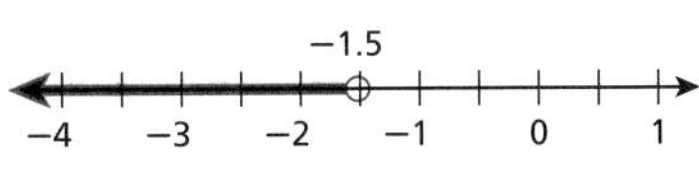

Draw an empty circle at −1.5.

Shade all the numbers less than −1.5 and draw an arrow pointing to the left.

B $r \ge 2$

Draw a solid circle at 2.

Shade all the numbers greater than 2 and draw an arrow pointing to the right.

CHECK IT OUT! Graph each inequality.

2a. $c > 2.5$ **2b.** $2^2 - 4 \ge w$ **2c.** $m \le -3$

2a. 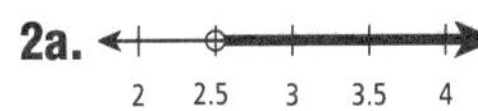 **2b.** 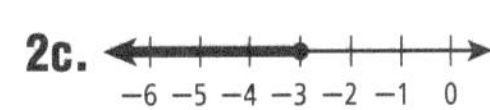 **2c.**

Student to Student

Graphing Inequalities

Victor Solomos
Palmer High School

To know which direction to shade a graph, I write inequalities with the variable on the left side of the inequality symbol. I know that the symbol has to point to the same number after I rewrite the inequality.

For example, I write $4 < y$ as $y > 4$.

Now the inequality symbol points in the direction that I should draw the shaded arrow on my graph.

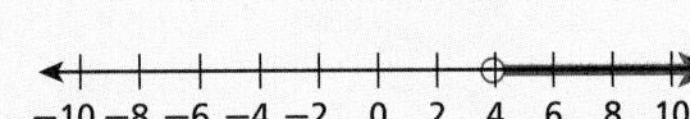

2 Teach

Guided Instruction

Review the inequality symbols before identifying solutions of inequalities. Focus on building an understanding of inequalities, rather than solving inequalities. Procedures for solving will be addressed in subsequent lessons.

Reading Math Before **Example 4,** have students use the phrases "no more than," "no less than," "at most," and "at least" in everyday sentences. ENGLISH LANGUAGE LEARNERS

Reaching All Learners

Through Cognitive Strategies

Use the DISC method to graph inequalities:

Draw—Draw a number line and a circle at the endpoint.

Include?—Look at the inequality sign to determine whether the circle should be solid or empty.

Shade—Shade in the correct direction.

Check—Substitute a value on the solution side into the inequality to check that the inequality is true.

COMMON ERROR ALERT

When students find that $x = 6$ does not make the inequality in **Example 1** true, some students believe the solution should be numbers less than 5. Remind them of the numbers between 5 and 6.

Power Presentations with PowerPoint®

Additional Examples

Example 1

Describe the solutions of $x - 6 \ge 4$ in words. all real numbers greater than or equal to 10

Example 2

Graph each inequality.

A. $m \ge \frac{3}{4}$

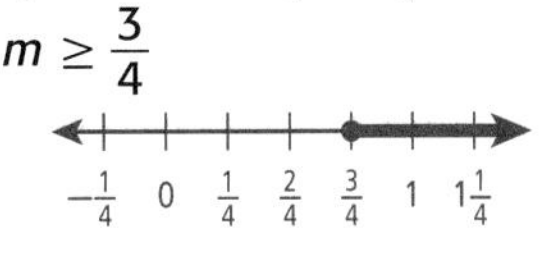

B. $t < 5(-1 + 3)$

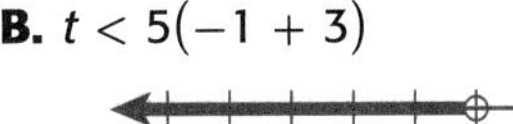

INTERVENTION

Questioning Strategies

EXAMPLE 1

- Why is it important to test values for the variable that are positive, negative, and zero?

EXAMPLE 2

- How do you decide which way to shade the graph?

Teaching Tip **Communicating Math** Some people refer to a solid circle as "closed" and an empty circle as "open."

Teaching Tip **Geometry** A *ray* is a part of a line that extends indefinitely in one direction from an endpoint. Many of the graphs in these exercises are rays.

Power Presentations with PowerPoint®

Additional Examples

Example 3

Write the inequality shown by each graph.

A. 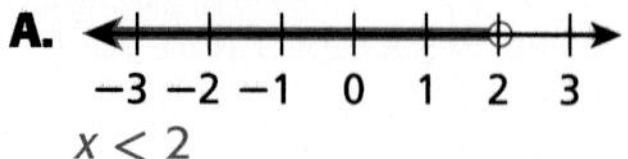

$x < 2$

B. 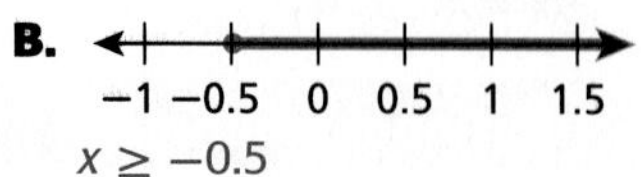

$x \geq -0.5$

Example 4

Ray's dad told him not to turn on the air conditioner unless the temperature is at least 85 °F. Define a variable and write an inequality for the temperatures at which Ray can turn on the air conditioner. Graph the solutions.

t = temperature in °F; $t \geq 85$

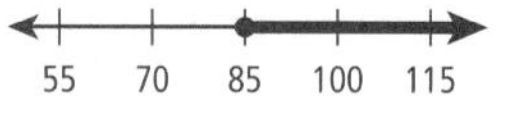

INTERVENTION

Questioning Strategies

EXAMPLE 3

- What does an empty or solid circle tell you? What does the direction of the arrow tell you?

EXAMPLE 4

- Do you think all the values that were shaded are reasonable answers in this situation?

Critical Thinking Discuss with students what types of problems might have answers that can only be whole numbers, positive numbers, etc.

EXAMPLE 3 Writing an Inequality from a Graph

Write the inequality shown by each graph.

A 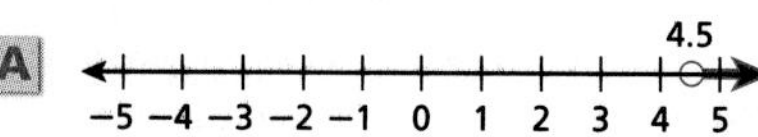

Use any variable. The arrow points to the right, so use either > or ≥.
The empty circle at 4.5 means that 4.5 is not a solution, so use >.

$h > 4.5$

B 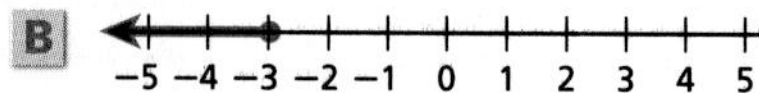

Use any variable. The arrow points to the left, so use either < or ≤.
The solid circle at −3 means that −3 is a solution, so use ≤.

$m \leq -3$

CHECK IT OUT! 3. Write the inequality shown by the graph.

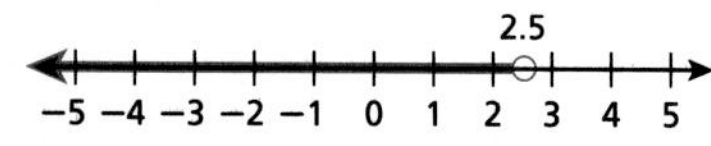

$x < 2.5$

EXAMPLE 4 *Sports Application*

The members of a lightweight crew team can weigh no more than 165 pounds each. Define a variable and write an inequality for the acceptable weights of the team members. Graph the solutions.

Let w represent the weights that are allowed.

Athletes may weigh	no more than	165 pounds.
w	$\leq$	165

$w \leq 165$

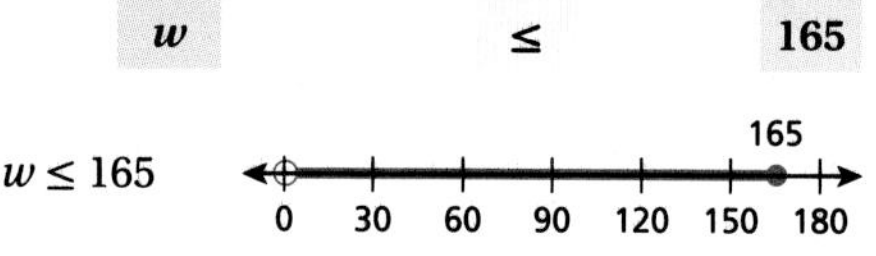

Stop the graph at 0 because a person's weight must be a positive number.

Reading Math

"No more than" means "less than or equal to."

"At least" means "greater than or equal to."

CHECK IT OUT! 4. A store's employees earn at least $8.25 per hour. Define a variable and write an inequality for the amount the employees may earn per hour. Graph the solutions.

d = amount employee can earn per hour; $d \geq 8.25$

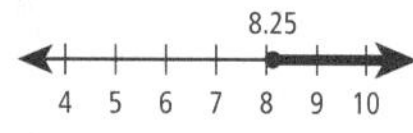

THINK AND DISCUSS

1. Compare the solutions of $x > 2$ and $x \geq 2$.

2. **GET ORGANIZED** Copy and complete the graphic organizer. Draw a graph in the first row and write the correct inequality in the second row.

Inequality	Graph
$x > 1$	
	−5 −4 −3 −2 −1 0 1

3 Close

Summarize

Make sure students can describe the solutions of inequalities in words. Stress the need to test positive and negative values as well as zero. Remind students that there are many numbers between consecutive integers.

When graphing inequalities that represent real-world situations, students should consider which values are reasonable in the context.

ONGOING ASSESSMENT and INTERVENTION

Diagnose ***Before*** **the Lesson**
3-1 Warm Up, TE p. 170

Monitor ***During*** **the Lesson**
Check It Out! Exercises, SE pp. 170–172
Questioning Strategies, TE pp. 170–172

Assess ***After*** **the Lesson**
3-1 Lesson Quiz, TE p. 175
Alternative Assessment, TE p. 175

Answers to *Think and Discuss*

1. Both graphs include the real numbers greater than 2. The graph of $x \geq 2$ also includes 2.
2. See p. A3.

3-1 Exercises

go.hrw.com
Homework Help Online
KEYWORD: MA7 3-1
Parent Resources Online
KEYWORD: MA7 Parent

GUIDED PRACTICE

1. **Vocabulary** How is a *solution of an inequality* like a solution of an equation?
A solution of an inequality makes the inequality true when substituted for the variable.

SEE EXAMPLE 1 p. 170

Describe the solutions of each inequality in words.

2. $g - 5 \geq 6$ 3. $-2 < h + 1$ 4. $20 > 5t$ 5. $5 - x \leq 2$

SEE EXAMPLE 2 p. 171

Graph each inequality.

6. $x < -5$ 7. $c \geq 3\frac{1}{2}$ 8. $(4 - 2)^3 > m$ 9. $p \geq \sqrt{17 + 8}$

SEE EXAMPLE 3 p. 172

Write the inequality shown by each graph.

10. −6 −5 −4 −3 −2 −1 0 1 2 3 4 $a \leq -2$

11. $-8\frac{1}{2}$ −9 −8 −7 −6 −5 −4 −3 −2 −1 0 1 $b > -8\frac{1}{2}$

12. 5.5 −4 −3 −2 −1 0 1 2 3 4 5 6 $c < 5.5$

13. −7 −12 −10 −8 −6 −4 −2 0 $d < -7$

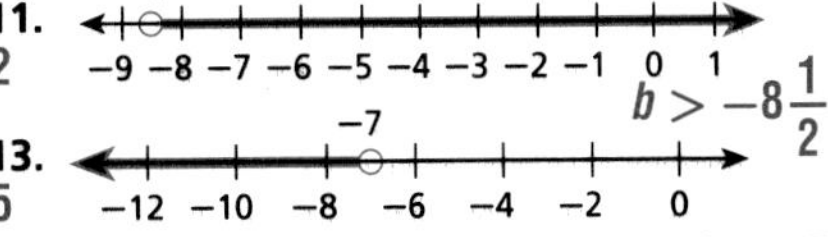

14. −4 −3 −2 −1 0 1 2 3 4 5 6 $e \geq 3$

15. −2 0 2 4 6 8 10 12 14 16 18 $f \leq 14$

SEE EXAMPLE 4 p. 172

Define a variable and write an inequality for each situation. Graph the solutions.

16. There must be at least 20 club members present in order to hold a meeting.
m = members present; $m \geq 20$ where m is a whole number

17. A trainer advises an athlete to keep his heart rate under 140 beats per minute.
r = heart rate; $r < 140$ where r is positive

PRACTICE AND PROBLEM SOLVING

Independent Practice	
For Exercises	See Example
18–21	1
22–25	2
26–31	3
32–33	4

Extra Practice
Skills Practice p. S8
Application Practice p. S30

Describe the solutions of each inequality in words.

18. $-2t > -8$ 19. $0 > w - 2$ 20. $3k > 9$ 21. $\frac{1}{2}b \leq 6$

Graph each inequality.

22. $7 < x$ 23. $t \leq -\frac{1}{2}$ 24. $d > 4(5 - 8)$ 25. $t \leq 3^2 - 2^2$

Write the inequality shown by each graph.

26. −4 −3 −2 −1 0 1 2 3 4 5 6 $u \geq 5$

27. −11 −16 −14 −12 −10 −8 −6 −4 $v < -11$

28. −3.5 −6 −5 −4 −3 −2 −1 0 1 2 3 4 $w > -3.5$

29. −3.3 −5 −4 −3 −2 −1 0 1 2 3 4 5 $x > -3.3$

30. −5 −4 −3 −2 −1 0 1 2 3 4 5 $y < 4$

31. 9 −2 0 2 4 6 8 10 12 14 16 18 $z \geq 9$

Define a variable and write an inequality for each situation. Graph the solutions.

32. The maximum speed allowed on Main Street is 25 miles per hour. s = speed; $s \leq 25$ where s is nonnegative

33. Applicants must have at least 5 years of experience.
y = years of experience; $y \geq 5$

3-1 Exercises

Assignment Guide

Assign *Guided Practice* exercises as necessary.

If you finished Examples **1–2**
Basic 18–25, 34–41, 50–53
Average 18–25, 34–41, 62–64, 67
Advanced 18–25, 34–41, 62–66

If you finished Examples **1–4**
Basic 18–45, 50–53, 56–61, 70–81
Average 18–33, 34–48 even, 54–68, 70–81
Advanced 18–33, 38–45, 54–56, 58–81

Homework Quick Check
Quickly check key concepts.
Exercises: 18, 22, 28, 32, 40, 42

Teaching Tip
Inclusion For exercises like **Exercises 32–33,** have students ask themselves a question to decide whether the endpoint is a solution. For example, for **Exercise 32,** ask "Is 25 miles per hour allowed?" Yes, so the graph should have a solid circle.

Answers

2. all real numbers greater than or equal to 11
3. all real numbers greater than −3
4. all real numbers less than 4
5. all real numbers greater than or equal to 3
6. −6 −5 −4 −3 −2 −1 0

State Resources

7. 3 $3\frac{1}{2}$ 4 $4\frac{1}{2}$ 5
8. 0 2 4 6 8 10 12
9. 0 1 2 3 4 5 6
16.
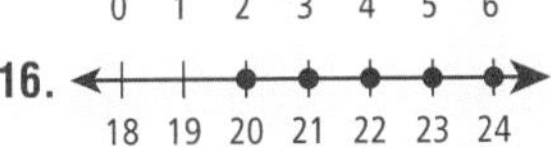
17.
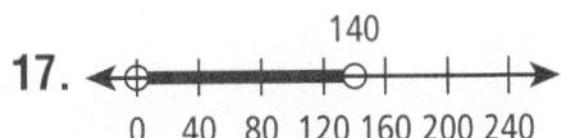
18. all real numbers less than 4
19. all real numbers less than 2
20. all real numbers greater than 3
21. all real numbers less than or equal to 12
22.
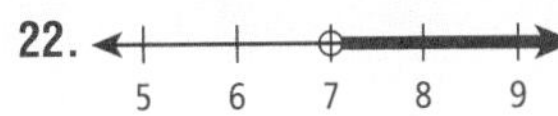
23.

24. −12 −9 −6 −3 0
25. 0 1 2 3 4 5 6
32.
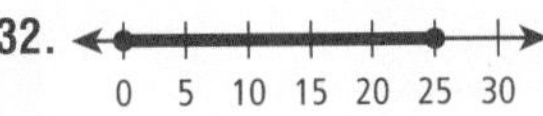
33.
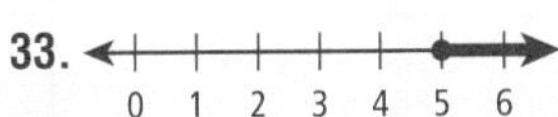

Exercise 55 involves using inequalities to describe how much money can be spent shopping. This exercise prepares students for the Multi-Step Test Prep on page 188.

Answers

34. x is greater than 7.
35. h is less than –5.
36. d is less than or equal to 23.
37. r is greater than or equal to –2.

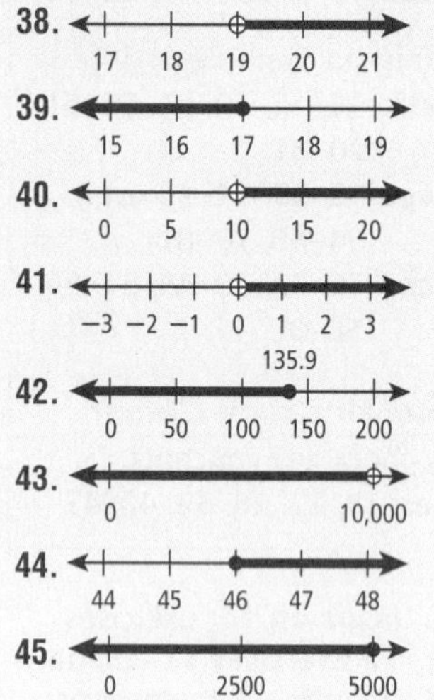

46. x represents the distance in miles between two locations.
47. x represents the age in years of a child at a childcare center when x is positive.
48. x represents the hour on an analog clock when x is a natural number.
49. x represents the number of millions of albums sold by a popular band.

Write each inequality in words.

34. $x > 7$ **35.** $h < -5$ **36.** $d \le 23$ **37.** $r \ge -2$

Write each inequality with the variable on the left. Graph the solutions.

38. $19 < g$ **$g > 19$** **39.** $17 \ge p$ **$p \le 17$** **40.** $10 < e$ **$e > 10$** **41.** $0 < f$ **$f > 0$**

Define a variable and write an inequality for each situation. Graph the solutions.

42. t = temperature; $t \le 135.9$

42. The highest temperature ever recorded on Earth was 135.9 °F at Al Aziziyah, Libya, on September 13, 1922.

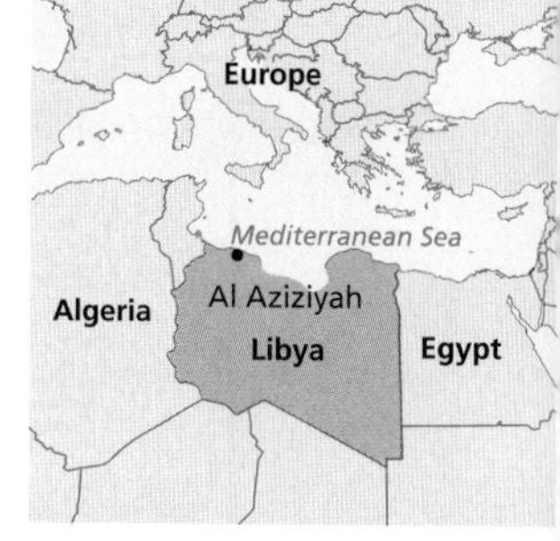

43. Businesses with profits less than $10,000 per year will be shut down. **p = profits; $p < 10{,}000$**

44. You must be at least 46 inches tall to ride a roller coaster at an amusement park. **h = height; $h \ge 46$**

45. Due to a medical condition, a hiker can hike only in areas with an elevation no more than 5000 feet above sea level. **e = elevation; $e \le 5000$**

Write a real-world situation that could be described by each inequality.

46. $x \ge 0$ **47.** $x < 10$ **48.** $x \le 12$ **49.** $x > 8.5$

Match each inequality with its graph.

50. $x \ge 5$ **A**

51. $x < 5$ **D**

52. $x > 5$ **B**

53. $x \le 5$ **C**

A. –2 –1 0 1 2 3 4 5 6 7 8

B. –2 –1 0 1 2 3 4 5 6 7 8

C. –2 –1 0 1 2 3 4 5 6 7 8

D. –2 –1 0 1 2 3 4 5 6 7 8

54. ERROR ANALYSIS Two students graphed the inequality $4 > b$. Which graph is incorrect? Explain the error. **A is incorrect; it should be drawn with an empty circle.**

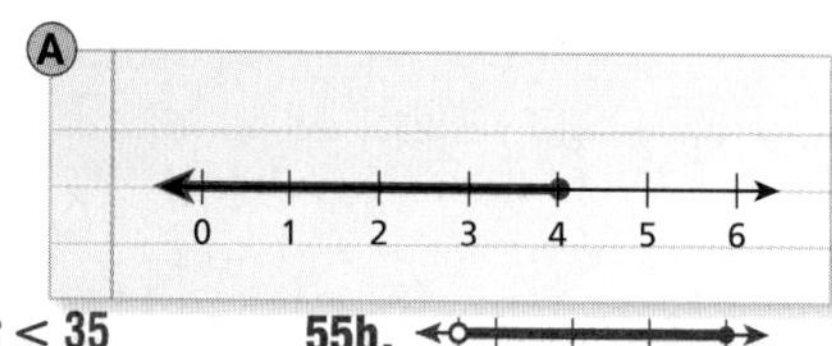

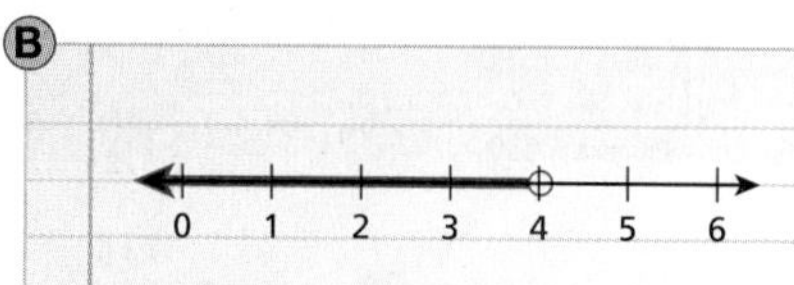

55a. $125 - s \ge 90$; $s \le 35$ where s is nonnegative

55b. 0 5 15 25 35

55c. $s + 15 \le 35$; $s \le 20$ where s is nonnegative

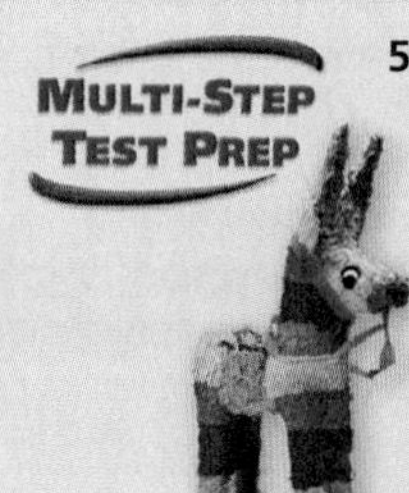

MULTI-STEP TEST PREP

55. This problem will prepare you for the Multi-Step Test Prep on page 188.

a. Mirna earned $125 baby-sitting during the spring break. She needs to save $90 for the German Club trip. She wants to spend the remainder of the money shopping. Write an inequality to show how much she can spend.

b. Graph the inequality you wrote in part **a.**

c. Mirna spends $15 on a bracelet. Write an inequality to show how much money she has left to spend.

3-1 PRACTICE A

3-1 PRACTICE C

3-1 PRACTICE B

Describe the solutions of each inequality in words.

1. $2m \ge 6$ all real numbers greater than or equal to 3
2. $t + 3 < 8$ all real numbers less than 5
3. $1 < x - 5$ all real numbers greater than 6
4. $-10 \ge \frac{1}{2}c$ all real numbers less than or equal to –20

Graph each inequality.

5. $x > -7$ (–9 –8 –7 –6 –5 –4)
6. $p \ge 2^3$ (6 7 8 9 10 11)
7. $4.5 \ge r$ (3 3.5 4.0 4.5 5.0 5.5)
8. $y < -\sqrt{14 - 5}$ (–6 –5 –4 –3 –2 –1)

Write the inequality shown by each graph.

9. (6 7 8 9) $a > 6$
10. (–5 –4 –3 –2 –1 0) $b \le -2$
11. (7 7.5 8.0 8.5 9.0 9.5) $c < 8.5$
12. (35 40 45 50 55 60) $d \ge 45$

Define a variable and write an inequality for each situation. Graph the solutions.

13. Josephine sleeps more than 7 hours each night.
s = hours of sleep; $s > 7$; (5 6 7 8 9 10)

14. In 1955, the minimum wage in the U.S. was $0.75 per hour.
w = wage; $w \ge 0.75$; (0.65 0.70 0.75 0.80 0.85 0.90)

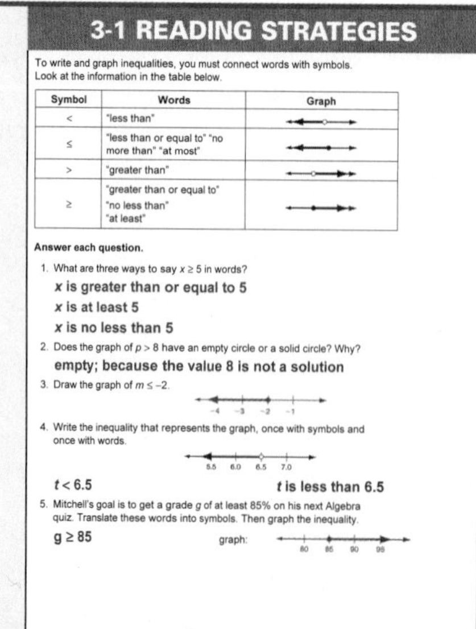

3-1 READING STRATEGIES

To write and graph inequalities, you must connect words with symbols. Look at the information in the table below.

Symbol	Words	Graph
$<$	"less than"	
$\le$	"less than or equal to" "no more than" "at most"	
$>$	"greater than"	
$\ge$	"greater than or equal to" "no less than" "at least"	

Answer each question.

1. What are three ways to say $x \ge 5$ in words?
x is greater than or equal to 5
x is at least 5
x is no less than 5
2. Does the graph of $p > 8$ have an empty circle or a solid circle? Why?
empty; because the value 8 is not a solution
3. Draw the graph of $m \le -2$.
–4 –3 –2 –1
4. Write the inequality that represents the graph, once with symbols and once with words.
5.5 6.0 6.5 7.0
$t < 6.5$ **t is less than 6.5**
5. Mitchell's goal is to get a grade g of at least 85% on his next Algebra quiz. Translate these words into symbols. Then graph the inequality.
$g \ge 85$ graph: 80 85 90 95

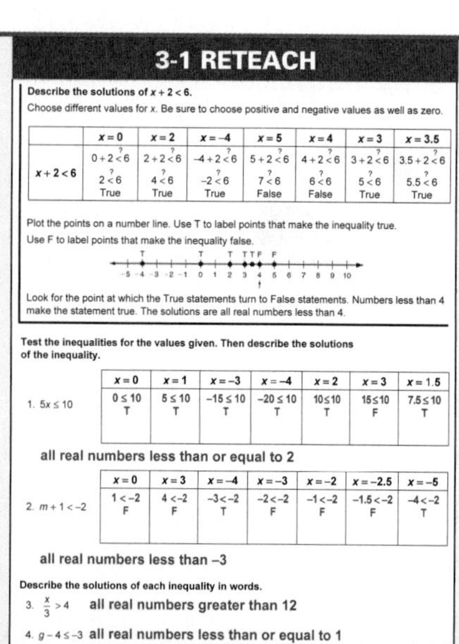

3-1 RETEACH

Describe the solutions of $x + 2 < 6$.

Choose different values for x. Be sure to choose positive and negative values as well as zero.

	$x = 0$	$x = 2$	$x = -4$	$x = 5$	$x = 4$	$x = 3$	$x = 3.5$
$x + 2 < 6$	$0 + 2 \overset{?}{<} 6$ $2 \overset{?}{<} 6$ True	$2 + 2 \overset{?}{<} 6$ $4 \overset{?}{<} 6$ True	$-4 + 2 \overset{?}{<} 6$ $-2 \overset{?}{<} 6$ True	$5 + 2 \overset{?}{<} 6$ $7 \overset{?}{<} 6$ False	$4 + 2 \overset{?}{<} 6$ $6 \overset{?}{<} 6$ False	$3 + 2 \overset{?}{<} 6$ $5 \overset{?}{<} 6$ True	$3.5 + 2 \overset{?}{<} 6$ $5.5 \overset{?}{<} 6$ True

Plot the points on a number line. Use T to label points that make the inequality true.
Use F to label points that make the inequality false.

T T T T T F F
–5 –4 –3 –2 –1 0 1 2 3 4 5 6 7 8 9 10

Look for the point at which the True statements turn to False statements. Numbers less than 4 make the statement true. The solutions are all real numbers less than 4.

Test the inequalities for the values given. Then describe the solutions of the inequality.

1. $5x \le 10$

$x = 0$	$x = 1$	$x = -3$	$x = -4$	$x = 2$	$x = 3$	$x = 1.5$
$0 \le 10$ T	$5 \le 10$ T	$-15 \le 10$ T	$-20 \le 10$ T	$10 \le 10$ T	$15 \le 10$ F	$7.5 \le 10$ T

all real numbers less than or equal to 2

2. $m + 1 < -2$

$x = 0$	$x = 3$	$x = -4$	$x = -3$	$x = -2$	$x = -2.5$	$x = -5$
$1 < -2$ F	$4 < -2$ F	$-3 < -2$ T	$-2 < -2$ F	$-1 < -2$ F	$-1.5 < -2$ F	$-4 < -2$ T

all real numbers less than –3

Describe the solutions of each inequality in words.

3. $\frac{x}{3} > 4$ **all real numbers greater than 12**
4. $g - 4 \le -3$ **all real numbers less than or equal to 1**

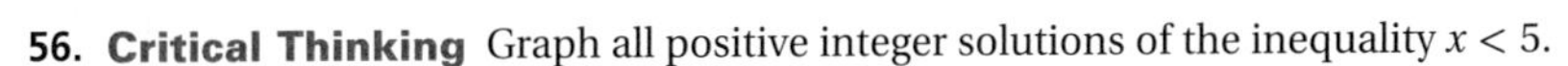

56. **Critical Thinking** Graph all positive integer solutions of the inequality $x < 5$.

57. **Write About It** Explain how to write an inequality that is modeled by a graph. What characteristics do you look for in the graph?

58. **Write About It** You were told in the lesson that the phrase "no more than" means "less than or equal to" and the phrase "at least" means "greater than or equal to."
    a. What does the phrase "at most" mean? **less than or equal to**
    b. What does the phrase "no less than" mean? **greater than or equal to**

TEST PREP

59. Which is NOT a solution of the inequality $5 - 2x \geq -3$?
    Ⓐ 0 Ⓑ 2 Ⓒ 4 **Ⓓ 5**

60. Which is NOT a solution of the inequality $3 - x < 2$?
    Ⓕ 1 Ⓖ 2 Ⓗ 3 Ⓙ 4

61. Which graph represents the solutions of $-2 \leq 1 - t$?

Ⓐ 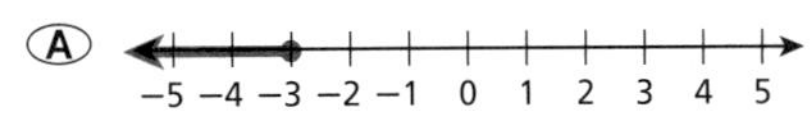

Ⓒ 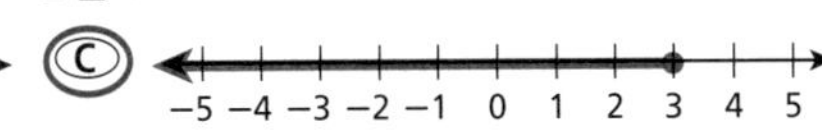

Ⓑ 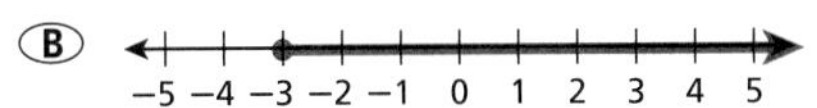

Ⓓ 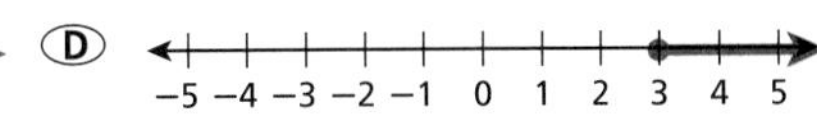

CHALLENGE AND EXTEND

Describe the values for x and y that make each inequality true.

62. $x + y \leq |x + y|$ **62. all real numbers**

63. $x^2 < xy$ **63. any nonzero numbers such that x and y have the same sign and $|x| < |y|$**

64. $x - y \geq y - x$ **any numbers such that y is less than or equal to x**

Complete each statement. Write < or >.

65. If $a > b$, then b **<** a.

66. If $x > y$ and $y > z$, then x **>** z.

67. Name a value of x that makes the statement $0.35 < x < 1.27$ true. **any number between 0.35 and 1.27**

68. Is $\frac{5}{6}$ a solution of $x < 1$? How many solutions of $x < 1$ are between 0 and 1? **68. yes; infinitely many**

69. **Write About It** Explain how to graph all the solutions of $x \neq 5$.
    Draw an empty circle at 5. Then draw arrows going left and right from 5.

SPIRAL REVIEW

Add or subtract. *(Lesson 1-2)*

70. $-7 + 5$ **−2**
71. $6 - (-4)$ **10**
72. $8 - 13$ **−5**
73. $12 + (-5)$ **7**

Simplify each expression. *(Lesson 1-7)*

74. $x + 3x$ **4x**
75. $x + (x + 1) + (x + 2)$ **3x + 3**
76. $5 + (x + 3) + 5 + 2(x + 3)$ **3x + 19**

77. There are twice as many girls in Sally's class as boys. Write a rule for the number of girls in Sally's class. Find the number of girls if there are 8 boys. *(Lesson 1-8)* **77. $g = 2b$; 16**

78. A video club charges a \$12 membership fee plus \$2.00 for each movie rental. Write a rule for the cost of renting x videos. Find the cost of renting 3, 7, and 15 videos. *(Lesson 1-8)* **$c = 12 + 2x$; 18; 26; 42**

Solve each equation. Check your answer. *(Lesson 2-4)*

79. $2b - 6 = b + 3$ **$b = 9$**
80. $-3(2 - x) = 5x + 2$ **$x = -4$**
81. $2(y + 1) = 2y + 1$ **no solution**

3-1 PROBLEM SOLVING

Write the correct answer.

1. A citizen must be at least 35 years old in order to run for the Presidency of the United States. Define a variable and write an inequality for this situation.
   a = age of person;
   $a \geq 35$

2. A certain elevator can hold no more than 2500 pounds. Define a variable and write an inequality for this situation.
   w = weight; $w \leq 2500$

3. Approximately 30% of the land on Earth is forested, but this percent is decreasing due to construction. Write and graph an inequality for this situation.
   f = percent forested;
   $f \leq 30$
   0 10 20 30 40 50 60

4. Khalil weighed 125 pounds before he started to gain weight to play football. Write and graph an inequality for this situation.
   w = weight; $w \geq 125$
   100 120 140 160

The Sanchez family is visiting an amusement park. When they enter the park, they receive a brochure which lists several requirements and restrictions. Select the best answer.

5. You must be at least 50 inches tall to ride The Wild Tornado roller coaster. Which of the following inequalities fits this situation?
   A $h \leq 50$ **C $h \geq 50$**
   B $h < 50$ D $h > 50$

6. Children less than 12 years old must be accompanied by an adult inside The Haunted House. Which of the following inequalities shows the ages of children who require an adult inside the house?
   F $y \leq 12$ H $y \geq 12$
   G $y < 12$ J $y > 12$

7. Totland is an area of the amusement park set aside for children who are 6 years old or younger. Which of the following inequalities represents the ages of children who are allowed in Totland?
   A $a \leq 6$ C $a \geq 6$
   B $a < 6$ D $a > 6$

8. The Bumpy Cars will not be turned on if there are 5 or more empty cars. Which of the following inequalities shows the possible numbers of empty cars if the ride is going to start?
   F $c \leq 5$ H $c \geq 5$
   G $c < 5$ J $c > 5$

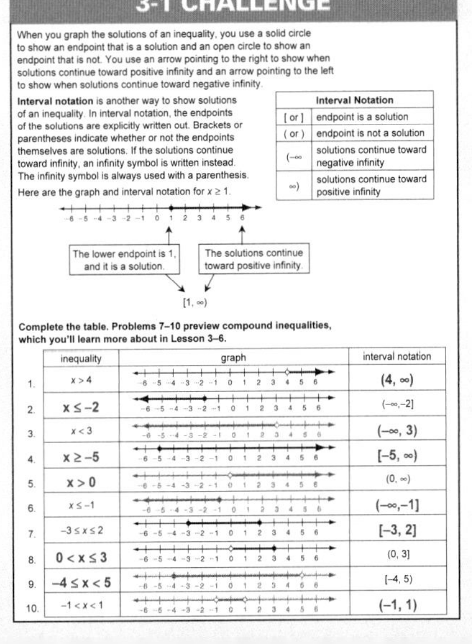

3-1 CHALLENGE

When you graph the solutions of an inequality, you use a solid circle to show an endpoint that is a solution and an open circle to show an endpoint that is not. You use an arrow pointing to the right to show when solutions continue toward positive infinity and an arrow pointing to the left to show when solutions continue toward negative infinity.

Interval notation is another way to show solutions of an inequality. In interval notation, the endpoints of the solutions are explicitly written out. Brackets or parentheses indicate whether or not the endpoints themselves are solutions. If the solutions continue toward infinity, an infinity symbol is written instead. The infinity symbol is always used with a parenthesis.

Interval Notation	
[or]	endpoint is a solution
(or)	endpoint is not a solution
(−∞	solutions continue toward negative infinity
∞)	solutions continue toward positive infinity

Here are the graph and interval notation for $x \geq 1$.

The lower endpoint is 1, and it is a solution.
The solutions continue toward positive infinity.
[1, ∞)

Complete the table. Problems 7–10 preview compound inequalities, which you'll learn more about in Lesson 3–6.

	inequality	graph	interval notation
1.	$x > 4$		**(4, ∞)**
2.	**$x \leq -2$**		(−∞, −2]
3.	$x < 3$		**(−∞, 3)**
4.	**$x \geq -5$**		**[−5, ∞)**
5.	**$x > 0$**		(0, ∞)
6.	$x \leq -1$		**(−∞, −1]**
7.	$-3 \leq x \leq 2$		**[−3, 2]**
8.	**$0 < x \leq 3$**		(0, 3]
9.	**$-4 \leq x < 5$**		[−4, 5)
10.	$-1 < x < 1$		**(−1, 1)**

TEST PREP DOCTOR Choices **B** and **C** in **Exercise 61** include zero as a solution. Substitute 0 for t to determine whether the inequality is true or false.

Answers

56. 0 1 2 3 4 5 6

57. Look for a solid or empty circle. A solid circle tells you to use ≤ or ≥, and an empty circle tells you to use < or >. Then look at the direction of the arrow. An arrow pointing left tells you to use < or ≤, and an arrow pointing right tells you to use > or ≥.

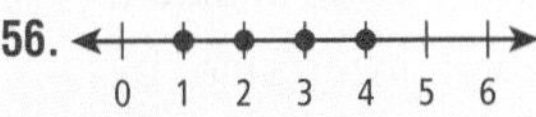

Journal

The phrase "x is not less than 7" means that x is greater than or equal to 7. The algebraic inequality is $x \geq 7$. Explain the meaning of the following statements and write an algebraic inequality for each:

1) x is not greater than 7.
2) x is not less than or equal to 7.
3) x is not greater than or equal to 7.

ALTERNATIVE ASSESSMENT

Write four inequalities using each of the following inequality symbols: <, ≤, >, ≥. Then graph each inequality.

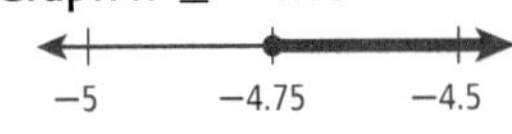

Power Presentations with PowerPoint®

3-1 Lesson Quiz

1. Describe the solutions of $7 < x + 4$. all real numbers greater than 3
2. Graph $h \geq -4.75$
   −5 −4.75 −4.5

Write the inequality shown by each graph.

3. 0 1 2 3 4 5 6
   $x \geq 3$
4. −6 −5.5 −5
   $x < -5.5$
5. A cell phone plan offers free minutes for no more than 250 minutes per month. Define a variable and write an inequality for the possible numbers of free minutes. Graph the solutions. $m \leq 250$ where m is nonneg.
   0 250

Also available on transparency

3-2 Organizer

Pacing: Traditional 1 day
Block $\frac{1}{2}$ day

Objectives: Solve one-step inequalities by using addition.

Solve one-step inequalities by using subtraction.

Algebra Lab
In *Algebra Lab Activities*

Online Edition
Tutorial Videos

Countdown Week 6

Power Presentations with PowerPoint®

Warm Up

Write an inequality for each situation.

1. The temperature must be at least -10°F. $x \geq -10$
2. The temperature must be no more than 90°F. $x \leq 90$

Solve each equation.

3. $x - 4 = 10$ 14
4. $15 = x + 1.1$ 13.9

Also available on transparency

Q: Why did the parents think their little variable was sick?

A: The nurse said he had to be isolated.

3-2 Solving Inequalities by Adding or Subtracting

Objectives
Solve one-step inequalities by using addition.

Solve one-step inequalities by using subtraction.

Who uses this?
You can use inequalities to determine how many more photos you can take. (See Example 2.)

Tenea has a cell phone that also takes pictures. After taking some photos, Tenea can use a one-step inequality to determine how many more photos she can take.

Solving one-step inequalities is much like solving one-step equations. To solve an inequality, you need to isolate the variable using the properties of inequality and inverse operations.

Know it! Note

Properties of Inequality

Addition and Subtraction

WORDS	NUMBERS	ALGEBRA
Addition You can add the same number to both sides of an inequality, and the statement will still be true.	$3 < 8$ $3 + 2 < 8 + 2$ $5 < 10$	$a < b$ $a + c < b + c$
Subtraction You can subtract the same number from both sides of an inequality, and the statement will still be true.	$9 < 12$ $9 - 5 < 12 - 5$ $4 < 7$	$a < b$ $a - c < b - c$

These properties are also true for inequalities that use the symbols >, ≥, and ≤.

EXAMPLE 1 Using Addition and Subtraction to Solve Inequalities

Solve each inequality and graph the solutions.

Helpful Hint
Use an inverse operation to "undo" the operation in an inequality. If the inequality contains addition, use subtraction to undo the addition.

A $x + 9 < 15$

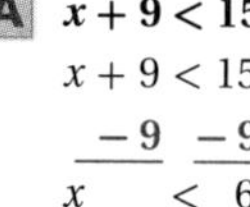

$$\begin{aligned} x + 9 &< 15 \\ -9 & \quad -9 \\ x &< 6 \end{aligned}$$

Since 9 is added to x, subtract 9 from both sides to undo the addition.

−10 −8 −6 −4 −2 0 2 4 6 8 10

B $d - 3 > -6$

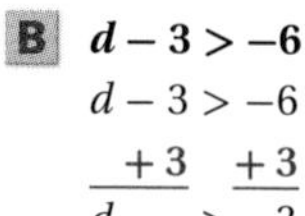

$$\begin{aligned} d - 3 &> -6 \\ +3 & \quad +3 \\ d &> -3 \end{aligned}$$

Since 3 is subtracted from d, add 3 to both sides to undo the subtraction.

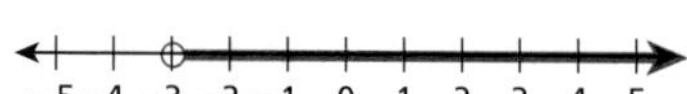

1 Introduce

EXPLORATION

3-2 Solving Inequalities by Adding or Subtracting

Use number lines to graph inequalities and to find patterns.

1. Graph the solutions of $x \leq 5$ on the number line.
   −10 −8 −6 −4 −2 0 2 4 6 8 10
2. Test each value in the table to determine if it is a solution of the inequality $x + 2 \leq 7$. Record your results.

x	−7	−5.5	−3	−1.5	0	2	5	6.5	8
Solution of $x + 2 \leq 7$? (Yes/No)									

3. Plot the values that are solutions of $x + 2 \leq 7$ on the number line. Then connect the points to form a ray.
   −10 −8 −6 −4 −2 0 2 4 6 8 10
4. What do you notice about the solutions you graphed in Step 1 and in Step 3?
5. How is the inequality $x + 2 \leq 7$ related to the inequality $x \leq 5$?

THINK AND DISCUSS

6. **Explain** how the solutions of $x \geq 3$ are related to the solutions of $x + 7 \geq 10$.

Motivate

Pose the following situation: Maria's mother told her that she should practice piano for at least 45 minutes. She has already practiced for 20 minutes. Ask students how they would determine the number of minutes that Maria still needs to practice. Tell students that they could use a one-step inequality to solve the problem.

Explorations and answers are provided in *Alternate Openers: Explorations Transparencies.*

State Resources

go.hrw.com
State Resources Online
KEYWORD: MA7 Resources

Solve each inequality and graph the solutions.

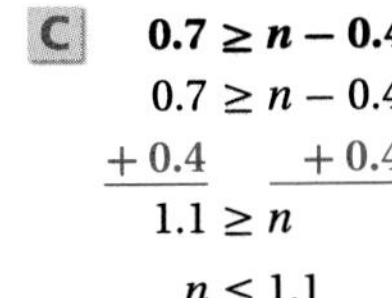

C $0.7 \geq n - 0.4$

$$\begin{aligned} 0.7 &\geq n - 0.4 \\ +0.4 &\quad\; +0.4 \\ 1.1 &\geq n \\ n &\leq 1.1 \end{aligned}$$

Since 0.4 is subtracted from n, add 0.4 to both sides to undo the subtraction.

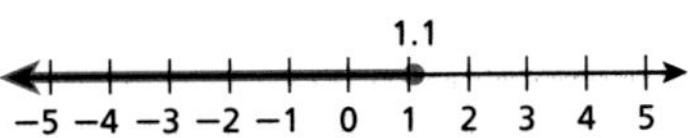

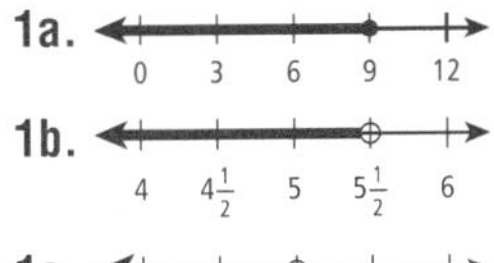

Solve each inequality and graph the solutions.

1a. $s + 1 \leq 10$ $s \leq 9$ **1b.** $2\frac{1}{2} > -3 + t$ $t < 5\frac{1}{2}$ **1c.** $q - 3.5 < 7.5$ $q < 11$

Since there can be an infinite number of solutions to an inequality, it is not possible to check all the solutions. You can check the endpoint and the direction of the inequality symbol.

The solutions of $x + 9 < 15$ are given by $x < 6$.

Step 1 Check the endpoint.

Substitute 6 for x in the related equation $x + 9 = 15$. The endpoint should be a solution of the equation.

$x + 9 = 15$	
$6 + 9$	15
15	15 ✓

Step 2 Check the inequality symbol.

Substitute a number less than 6 for x in the original inequality. The number you choose should be a solution of the inequality.

$x + 9 < 15$		
$4 + 9$	<	15
13	<	15 ✓

EXAMPLE **2** ***Problem Solving Application***

The memory in Tenea's camera phone allows her to take up to 20 pictures. Tenea has already taken 16 pictures. Write, solve, and graph an inequality to show how many more pictures Tenea could take.

1 Understand the Problem

The **answer** will be an inequality and a graph that show all the possible numbers of pictures that Tenea can take.

List the important information:

- Tenea can take up to, or *at most*, 20 pictures.
- Tenea has taken 16 pictures already.

2 Make a Plan

Write an inequality.

Let p represent the remaining number of pictures Tenea can take.

Number taken	plus	number remaining	is at most	20 pictures.
16	+	p	≤	20

COMMON ERROR ALERT

Students may assume that the symbol in the original inequality statement indicates the direction of the arrow in the graph. Remind students that this is only true when the variable is on the left side.

Power Presentations with PowerPoint®

Additional Examples

Example 1

Solve each inequality and graph the solutions.

A. $x + 12 < 20$ $x < 8$

0 2 4 6 8

B. $d - 5 > -7$ $d > -2$

−3 −2 −1 0 1 2 3

C. $0.9 \geq n - 0.3$ $n \leq 1.2$

1.2
0 1 2

Example 2

Sami has a gift card. She has already used \$14 of the total value, which was \$30. Write, solve, and graph an inequality to show how much more she can spend. $14 + g \leq 30$; $g \leq 16$ where g is nonneg.

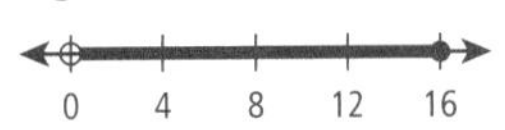

INTERVENTION

Questioning Strategies

EXAMPLE 1

- How is solving inequalities similar to solving equations?
- How are the solutions of an inequality different from the solution of an equation?

EXAMPLE 2

- What will the solutions represent?
- What two things need to be checked when checking the solutions to an inequality?

2 Teach

Guided Instruction

Discuss which operations are used to undo addition and subtraction when solving equations. Tell students to solve an inequality as they would an equation. Encourage students to always check the endpoint and the inequality symbol.

Visual Some students may find it easier to rewrite the original inequality with the variable on the left, so that when the inequality is solved, the inequality symbol points in the direction of the shading.

Reaching All Learners

Through Critical Thinking

Have students work in pairs. Each pair should make two sets of index cards: one set with one-step inequalities and another with the corresponding solutions and graphs. Have each pair trade cards with another pair. The students can then work together to match each inequality to its graph.

Power Presentations with PowerPoint®

Additional Examples

Example 3

Mrs. Lawrence wants to buy an antique bracelet at an auction. She is willing to bid no more than \$550. So far, the highest bid is \$475. Write and solve an inequality to determine the amount Mrs. Lawrence can add to the bid. Check your answer.

$475 + x \leq 550; x \leq 75$

INTERVENTION 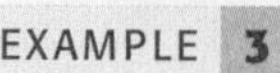

Questioning Strategies

EXAMPLE 3

- What words in the problem tell you which inequality symbol to use?

 **Solve**

$$\begin{aligned} 16 + p &\leq 20 \\ -16 \quad & \quad -16 \\ p &\leq 4 \end{aligned}$$

Since 16 is added to p, subtract 16 from both sides to undo the addition.

It is not reasonable for Tenea to take a negative or fractional number of pictures, so graph the nonnegative integers less than or equal to 4.

Tenea could take 0, 1, 2, 3, or 4 more pictures.

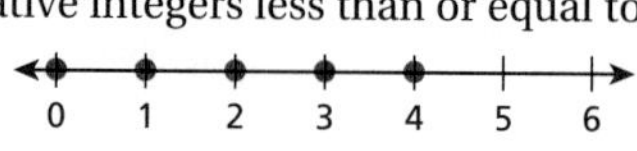

 **Look Back**

Check Check the endpoint, 4.

$$\begin{array}{c|c} 16 + p = 20 & \\ \hline 16 + 4 & 20 \\ 20 & 20 \checkmark \end{array}$$

Check a number less than 4.

$$\begin{array}{c|c|c} 16 + p & \leq & 20 \\ \hline 16 + 2 & \leq & 20 \\ 18 & \leq & 20 \checkmark \end{array}$$

Adding 0, 1, 2, 3, or 4 more pictures will not exceed 20.

2. The Recommended Dietary Allowance (RDA) of iron for a female in Sarah's age group (14–18 years) is 15 mg per day. Sarah has consumed 11 mg of iron today. Write and solve an inequality to show how many more milligrams of iron Sarah can consume without exceeding the RDA.

$11 + m \leq 15$; $m \leq 4$ where m is nonnegative; Sarah can consume 4 mg or less without exceeding the RDA.

EXAMPLE 3 *Sports Application*

Josh can bench press 220 pounds. He wants to bench press at least 250 pounds. Write and solve an inequality to determine how many more pounds Josh must lift to reach his goal. Check your answer.

Let p represent the number of additional pounds Josh must lift.

220 pounds	plus	additional pounds	is at least	250 pounds.
220	+	p	≥	250

$$\begin{aligned} 220 + p &\geq 250 \\ -220 \quad & \quad -220 \\ p &\geq 30 \end{aligned}$$

Since 220 is added to p, subtract 220 from both sides to undo the addition.

Check Check the endpoint, 30.

$$\begin{array}{c|c} 220 + p = 250 & \\ \hline 220 + 30 & 250 \\ 250 & 250 \checkmark \end{array}$$

Check a number greater than 30.

$$\begin{array}{c|c|c} 220 + p & \geq & 250 \\ \hline 220 + 40 & \geq & 250 \\ 260 & \geq & 250 \checkmark \end{array}$$

Josh must lift at least 30 additional pounds to reach his goal.

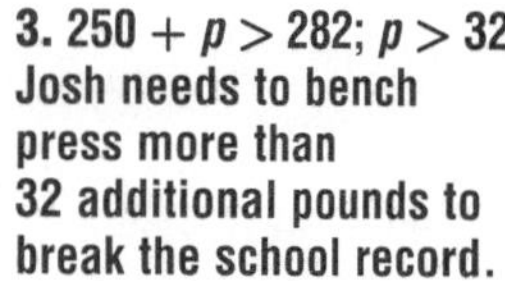

3. **What if...?** Josh has reached his goal of 250 pounds and now wants to try to break the school record of 282 pounds. Write and solve an inequality to determine how many more pounds Josh needs to break the school record. Check your answer.

3. $250 + p > 282$; $p > 32$; Josh needs to bench press more than 32 additional pounds to break the school record.

3 Close

Summarize

Remind students to solve one-step inequalities by using inverse operations. For the following solutions, ask students what two values of the variable they would check.

Possible answers:

$12 < c$ 12, 15

$d \geq -3$ −3, 0

$-7 > b$ −10, −7

ONGOING ASSESSMENT

and INTERVENTION 

***Diagnose Before* the Lesson**
3-2 Warm Up, TE p. 176

***Monitor During* the Lesson**
Check It Out! Exercises, SE pp. 177–178
Questioning Strategies, TE pp. 177–178

***Assess After* the Lesson**
3-2 Lesson Quiz, TE p. 181
Alternative Assessment, TE p. 181

THINK AND DISCUSS

1. Show how to check your solution to Example 1B.
2. Explain how the Addition and Subtraction Properties of Inequality are like the Addition and Subtraction Properties of Equality.
3. **GET ORGANIZED** Copy and complete the graphic organizer. In each box, write an inequality that you must use the specified property to solve. Then solve and graph the inequality.

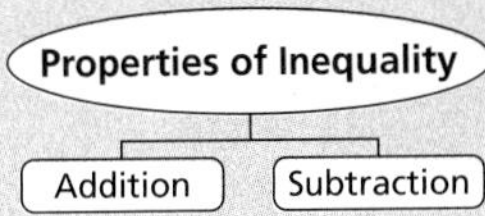

Answers to *Think and Discuss*

1.

$d - 3 = -6$		$d - 3 > -6$		
$-3 - 3$	-6	$0 - 3$	$>$	-6
-6	-6 ✓	-3	$>$	-6 ✓

2. You can add or subtract the same number on both sides of an equation or an inequality, and the statement will still be true.
3. See p. A3.

3-2 Exercises

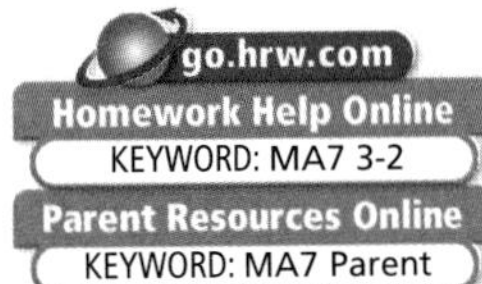

Assignment Guide

Assign *Guided Practice* exercises as necessary.

If you finished Examples **1–3**
Basic 7–23, 25–31, 34–39, 47–56
Average 7–25, 30–42, 47–56
Advanced 8–12 even, 13–25, 30–56

Homework Quick Check
Quickly check key concepts.
Exercises: 8, 10, 11, 12, 14, 24

GUIDED PRACTICE

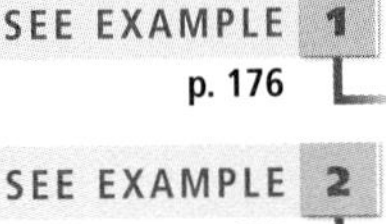

SEE EXAMPLE 1 p. 176

Solve each inequality and graph the solutions.

1. $12 < p + 6$ **$p > 6$**
2. $w + 3 \geq 4$ **$w \geq 1$**
3. $-5 + x \leq -20$ **$x \leq -15$**
4. $z - 2 > -11$ **$z > -9$**

SEE EXAMPLE 2 p. 177

5. **Health** For adults, the maximum safe water temperature in a spa is 104 °F. The water temperature in Bill's spa is 102 °F. The temperature is increased by t °F. Write, solve, and graph an inequality to show the values of t for which the water temperature is still safe. **$102 + t \leq 104$; $t \leq 2$ where t is nonnegative**

SEE EXAMPLE 3 p. 178

6. **Consumer Economics** A local restaurant will deliver food to your house if the purchase amount of your order is at least \$25.00. The total for part of your order is \$17.95. Write and solve an inequality to determine how much more you must spend for the restaurant to deliver your order. **$17.95 + d \geq 25.00$; $d \geq 7.05$**

PRACTICE AND PROBLEM SOLVING

Independent Practice	
For Exercises	See Example
7–10	1
11	2
12	3

Extra Practice
Skills Practice p. S8
Application Practice p. S30

Solve each inequality and graph the solutions.

7. $a - 3 \geq 2$ **$a \geq 5$**
8. $2.5 > q - 0.8$ **$q < 3.3$**
9. $-45 + x < -30$ **$x < 15$**
10. $r + \frac{1}{4} \leq \frac{3}{4}$ **$r \leq \frac{1}{2}$**
11. **Engineering** The maximum load for a certain elevator is 2000 pounds. The total weight of the passengers on the elevator is 1400 pounds. A delivery man who weighs 243 pounds enters the elevator with a crate of weight w. Write, solve, and graph an inequality to show the values of w that will not exceed the weight limit of the elevator. **$1400 + 243 + w \leq 2000$; $w \leq 357$ where w is nonnegative**
12. **Transportation** The gas tank in Mindy's car holds at most 15 gallons. She has already filled the tank with 7 gallons of gas. She will continue to fill the tank with g gallons more. Write and solve an inequality that shows all values of g that Mindy can add to the car's tank. **$7 + g \leq 15$; $g \leq 8$ where g is nonnegative**

Write an inequality to represent each statement. Solve the inequality and graph the solutions.

13. Ten less than a number x is greater than 32. **$x - 10 > 32$; $x > 42$**
14. A number n increased by 6 is less than or equal to 4. **$n + 6 \leq 4$; $n \leq -2$**
15. A number r decreased by 13 is at most 15. **$r - 13 \leq 15$; $r \leq 28$**

Reading Math Exercise 11 requires that students understand the phrases "maximum load," "not exceed," and "weight limit." Have students discuss which phrase indicates the inequality symbol for this problem. ENGLISH LANGUAGE LEARNERS

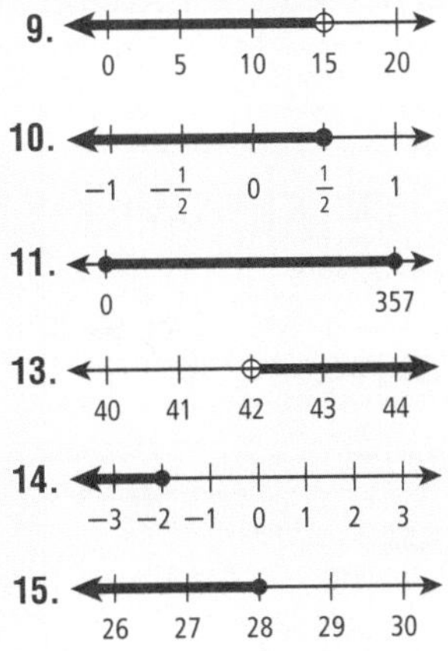

State Resources

Answers

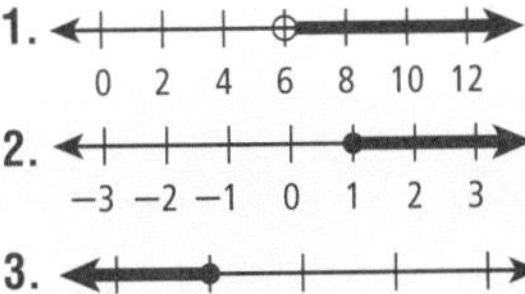

3. (number line: −20 −15 −10 −5 0)

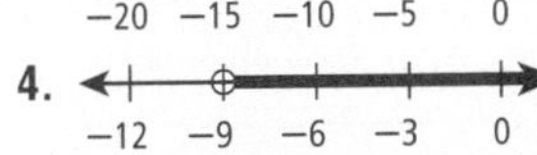

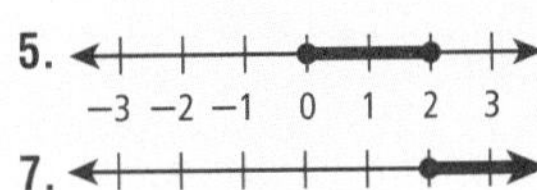

7. (number line: 0 1 2 3 4 5 6)

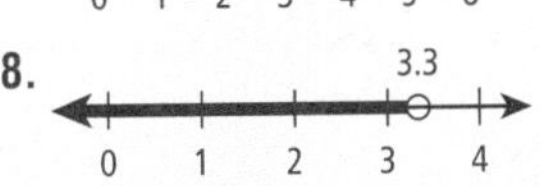

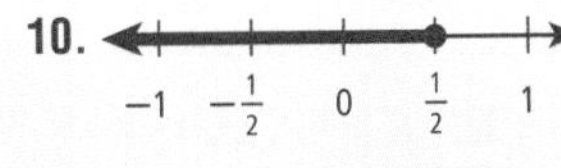

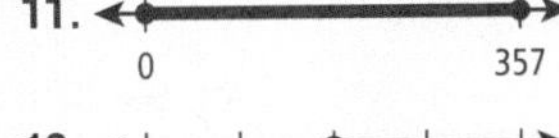

11. (number line: 0, 357)

13. (number line: 40 41 42 43 44)

14. (number line: −3 −2 −1 0 1 2 3)

15. (number line: 26 27 28 29 30)

Math Background In **Exercise 27,** students may need to be reminded that subtraction is addition of the opposite.

Exercise 35 involves using inequalities to describe the number of miles that can be driven on a trip. This exercise prepares students for the Multi-Step Test Prep on page 188.

Answers

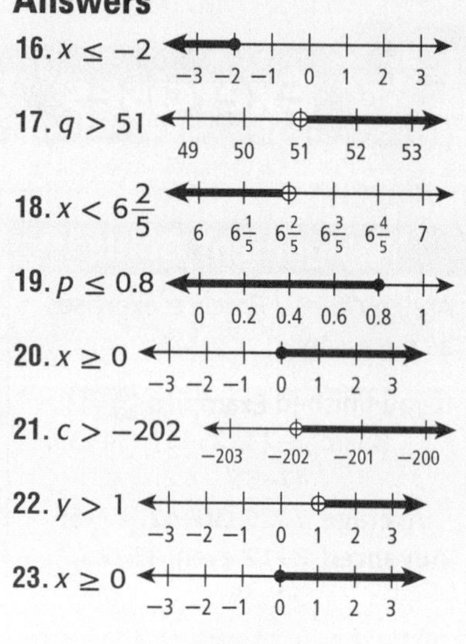
16. $x \le -2$
17. $q > 51$
18. $x < 6\frac{2}{5}$
19. $p \le 0.8$
20. $x \ge 0$
21. $c > -202$
22. $y > 1$
23. $x \ge 0$
25.

30. It is a reasonable answer. If you round each number to the nearest integer and then solve the inequality $12 + x < 22$, the solution is $x < 10$.

31. $936 + 4254 + p \le 45{,}611$; $5190 + p \le 45{,}611$; $p \le 40{,}421$ where p is nonnegative

33. When you isolate the variable in each inequality, you get $x \ge 2$ and $x \ge 2$.

34–35. See p. A14.

3-2 PRACTICE A

3-2 PRACTICE C

3-2 PRACTICE B

Solve each inequality and graph the solutions.

1. $b + 8 > 15$ — $b > 7$
2. $t - 5 \ge -2$ — $t \ge 3$
3. $-4 + x \ge 1$ — $x \ge 5$
4. $g + 8 < 2$ — $g < -6$
5. $-9 \ge m - 9$ — $m \le 0$
6. $15 > d + 19$ — $d < -4$

Answer each question.

7. Jessica makes overtime pay when she works more than 40 hours in a week. So far this week she has worked 29 hours. She will continue to work h hours this week. Write, solve, and graph an inequality to show the values of h that will allow Jessica to earn overtime pay. $29 + h > 40$; $h > 11$
8. Henry's MP3 player has 512MB of memory. He has already downloaded 287MB and will continue to download m more megabytes. Write and solve an inequality that shows how many more megabytes he can download. $287 + m \le 512$; $m \le 225$
9. Eleanor needs to read at least 97 pages of a book for homework. She has read 34 pages already. Write and solve an inequality that shows how many more pages p she must read. $34 + p \ge 97$; $p \ge 63$

Solve each inequality and graph the solutions.

16. $x + 4 \le 2$ **17.** $-12 + q > 39$ **18.** $x + \frac{3}{5} < 7$ **19.** $4.8 \ge p + 4$

20. $-12 \le x - 12$ **21.** $4 < 206 + c$ **22.** $y - \frac{1}{3} > \frac{2}{3}$ **23.** $x + 1.4 \ge 1.4$

LINK Health

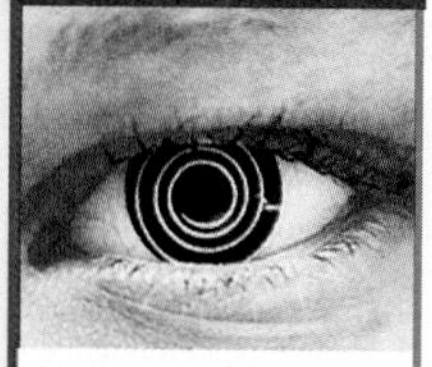

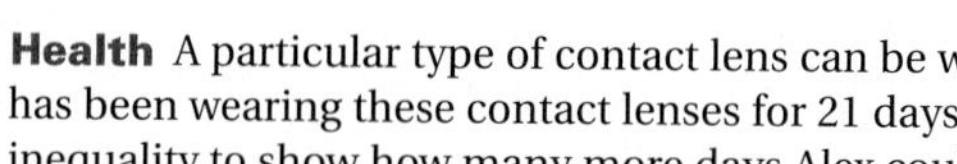

Special-effects contact lenses are sometimes part of costumes for movies. All contact lenses should be worn under an eye doctor's supervision.

24. Use the inequality $s + 12 \ge 20$ to fill in the missing numbers.
a. $s \ge$ **8** b. $s +$ **22** ≥ 30 c. $s - 8 \ge$ **0**

25. Health A particular type of contact lens can be worn up to 30 days in a row. Alex has been wearing these contact lenses for 21 days. Write, solve, and graph an inequality to show how many more days Alex could wear his contact lenses.
$21 + d \le 30$; $d \le 9$ where d is nonnegative

Solve each inequality and match the solutions to the correct graph.

26. $1 \le x - 2$ — **$x \ge 3$; C**
27. $8 > x - (-5)$ — **$x < 3$; B**
28. $x + 6 > 9$ — **$x > 3$; A**
29. $-4 \ge x - 7$ — **$x \le 3$; D**

A. (open circle at 3, shaded right; −5 −4 −3 −2 −1 0 1 2 3 4 5)
B. (open circle at 3, shaded left; −5 −4 −3 −2 −1 0 1 2 3 4 5)
C. (closed circle at 3, shaded right; −5 −4 −3 −2 −1 0 1 2 3 4 5)
D. (closed circle at 3, shaded left; −5 −4 −3 −2 −1 0 1 2 3 4 5)

30. Estimation Is $x < 10$ a reasonable estimate for the solutions to the inequality $11.879 + x < 21.709$? Explain your answer.

31. Sports At the Seattle Mariners baseball team's home games, there are 45,611 seats in the four areas listed in the table. Suppose all the suite level and club level seats during a game are filled. Write and solve an inequality to determine how many people p could be sitting in the other types of seats.

Mariners Home Game Seating

Type of Seat	Number of Seats
Main bowl	24,399
Upper bowl	16,022
Club level	4,254
Suite level	936

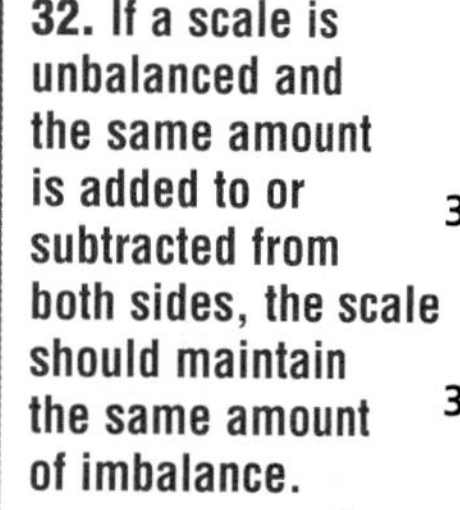
32. If a scale is unbalanced and the same amount is added to or subtracted from both sides, the scale should maintain the same amount of imbalance.

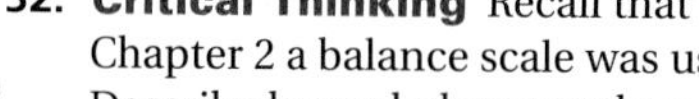
32. Critical Thinking Recall that in Chapter 2 a balance scale was used to model solving equations. Describe how a balance scale could model solving inequalities.

33. Critical Thinking Explain why $x + 4 \ge 6$ and $x - 4 \ge -2$ have the same solutions.

34. Write About It How do the solutions of $x + 2 \ge 3$ differ from the solutions of $x + 2 > 3$? How do the graphs of the solutions differ?

MULTI-STEP TEST PREP

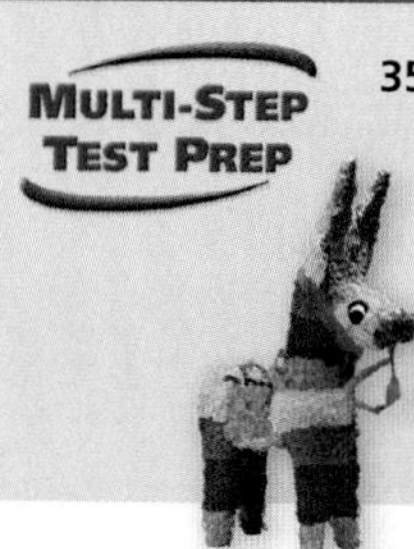

35. This problem will prepare you for the Multi-Step Test Prep on page 188.
a. Daryl finds that the distance from Columbus, Ohio, to Washington, D.C., is 411 miles. What is the round-trip distance?
b. Daryl can afford to drive a total of 1000 miles. Write an inequality to show the number of miles m he can drive while in Washington, D.C.
c. Solve the inequality and graph the solutions on a number line. Show that your answer is reasonable.

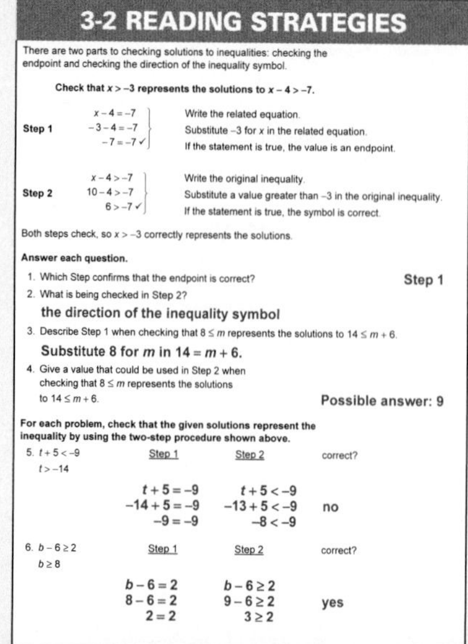
3-2 READING STRATEGIES

There are two parts to checking solutions to inequalities: checking the endpoint and checking the direction of the inequality symbol.

Check that $x > -3$ represents the solutions to $x - 4 > -7$.

Step 1: $x - 4 = -7$; $-3 - 4 = -7$; $-7 = -7$ ✓ — Write the related equation. Substitute −3 for x in the related equation. If the statement is true, the value is an endpoint.

Step 2: $x - 4 > -7$; $10 - 4 > -7$; $6 > -7$ ✓ — Write the original inequality. Substitute a value greater than −3 in the original inequality. If the statement is true, the symbol is correct.

Both steps check, so $x > -3$ correctly represents the solutions.

Answer each question.

1. Which Step confirms that the endpoint is correct? Step 1
2. What is being checked in Step 2? the direction of the inequality symbol
3. Describe Step 1 when checking that $8 \le m$ represents the solutions to $14 \le m + 6$. Substitute 8 for m in $14 = m + 6$.
4. Give a value that could be used in Step 2 when checking that $8 \le m$ represents the solutions to $14 \le m + 6$. Possible answer: 9

For each problem, check that the given solutions represent the inequality by using the two-step procedure shown above.

5. $t + 5 < -9$; $t > -14$ — Step 1: $t + 5 = -9$; $-14 + 5 = -9$; $-9 = -9$. Step 2: $t + 5 < -9$; $-13 + 5 < -9$; $-8 < -9$. correct? no
6. $b - 6 \ge 2$; $b \ge 8$ — Step 1: $b - 6 = 2$; $8 - 6 = 2$; $2 = 2$. Step 2: $b - 6 \ge 2$; $9 - 6 \ge 2$; $3 \ge 2$. correct? yes

3-2 RETEACH

The method for solving one-step inequalities by adding is just like the method for solving one-step equations by adding.

Solve $x - 2 = 1$ and graph the solution. $x - 2 = 1$; $+2\ \ +2$ Add 2 to each side. $x = 3$

Solve $x - 2 \ge 1$ and graph the solutions. $x - 2 \ge 1$; $+2\ \ +2$ Add 2 to each side. $x \ge 3$

Solve $-4 = a - 3$ and graph the solution. $-4 = a - 3$; $+3\ \ +3$ Add 3 to each side. $-1 = a$

Solve $-4 > a - 3$ and graph the solutions. $-4 > a - 3$; $+3\ \ +3$ Add 3 to each side. $-1 > a$; $a < -1$

Solve each inequality and graph the solutions.

1. $b - 4 < 3$ — $b > 7$
2. $x - 5 < -2$ — $x < 3$
3. $-10 > -6 + x$ — $x < -4$
4. $1 \le f - 3$ — $f \ge 4$

TEST PREP

36. Which is a reasonable solution of $4.7367 + p < 20.1784$?
   (A) 15 (B) 16 (C) 24 (D) 25

37. Which statement can be modeled by $x + 3 \le 12$?
   (F) Sam has 3 bottles of water. Together, Sam and Dave have at most 12 bottles of water.
   (G) Jennie sold 3 cookbooks. To earn a prize, Jennie must sell at least 12 cookbooks.
   (H) Peter has 3 baseball hats. Peter and his brothers have fewer than 12 baseball hats.
   (J) Kathy swam 3 laps in the pool this week. She must swim more than 12 laps.

38. Which graph represents the solutions of $p + 3 < 1$?

(A) 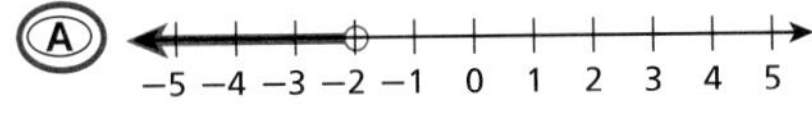

(C) 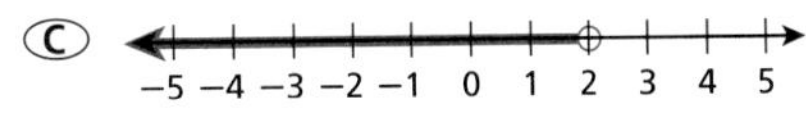

(B) −5 −4 −3 −2 −1 0 1 2 3 4 5

(D) −5 −4 −3 −2 −1 0 1 2 3 4 5

39. Which inequality does NOT have the same solutions as $n + 12 \le 26$?
   (F) $n \le 14$ (G) $n + 6 \le 20$ (H) $10 \ge n - 4$ (J) $n - 12 \le 14$

CHALLENGE AND EXTEND

Solve each inequality and graph the solutions.

40. $6\frac{9}{10} \ge 4\frac{4}{5} + x$ **$x \le 2\frac{1}{10}$** 41. $r - 1\frac{2}{5} \le 3\frac{7}{10}$ **$r \le 5\frac{1}{10}$** 42. $6\frac{2}{3} + m > 7\frac{1}{6}$ **$m > \frac{1}{2}$**

Determine whether each statement is sometimes, always, or never true. Explain.

43. $a + b > a - b$
   Sometimes; when b is positive, the inequality is true.
44. If $a > c$, then $a + b > c + b$.
   Always; adding the same number to both sides keeps the statement true.
45. If $a > b$ and $c > d$, then $a + c > b + d$.
   45. Always; a and c are the two greater numbers, so their sum will be greater than that of the two lesser numbers.
46. If $x + b > c$ and $x > 0$ have the same solutions, what is the relationship between b and c? **b and c are equal.**

SPIRAL REVIEW

Solve each equation for the indicated variable. (Lesson 2-5)

47. $2x + 3y = 9$ for y **$y = 3 - \frac{2}{3}x$** 48. $P = 4s$ for s **$s = \frac{P}{4}$** 49. $2 + ab = c$ for a **$a = \frac{c-2}{b}$**

50. $p + e = f$ for e **$e = f - p$** 51. $2s - k = 11$ for k **$k = 2s - 11$** 52. $5m + n = 0$ for m **$m = -\frac{n}{5}$**

Find the value of x in each diagram of similar figures. (Lesson 2-8)

53. **$x = 10$**

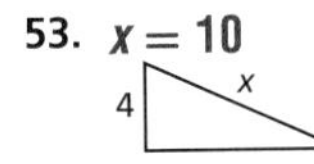

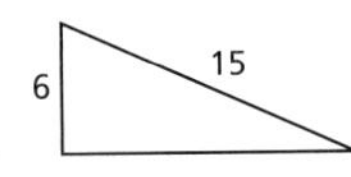

54. **$x = 15$**

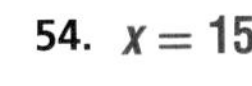

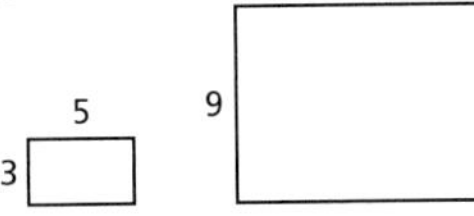

Write the inequality shown by each graph. (Lesson 3-1)

55. **$x \ge -1$** 56. **$x < 4$**

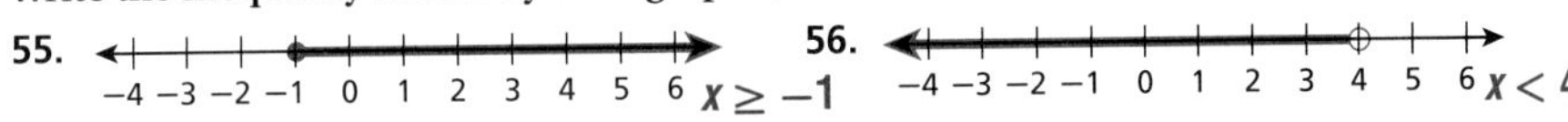

TEST PREP DOCTOR + If students have difficulty selecting the correct statement in **Exercise 37,** remind them that the inequality indicates 12 is the greatest value the expression can equal.

In **Exercise 38,** students who chose **D** may not have remembered that the less-than symbol means the graph will be shaded to the left of the endpoint.

Answers

40. 2 $2\frac{1}{10}$ $2\frac{2}{10}$ $2\frac{3}{10}$ $2\frac{4}{10}$

41. 5 $5\frac{1}{10}$ $5\frac{2}{10}$ $5\frac{3}{10}$ $5\frac{4}{10}$

42. −1 $-\frac{1}{2}$ 0 $\frac{1}{2}$ 1

Journal

Explain why the solutions to the inequality $x + 3 \ge 12$ are not only those numbers greater than or equal to 12.

ALTERNATIVE ASSESSMENT

Have students write a real-world situation that can be modeled by a one-step inequality. Ask students to write, solve, and graph the inequality and explain the meaning of the solution in the context of the situation.

Power Presentations with PowerPoint®

3-2 Lesson Quiz

Solve each inequality and graph the solutions.

1. $13 < x + 7$ $x > 6$
   0 2 4 6 8
2. $-6 + h \ge 15$ $h \ge 21$
   15 18 21 24 27
3. $6.7 + y \le -2.1$ $y \le -8.8$
   −8.8
   −10 −8 −6 −4 −2 0
4. A restaurant has room for 120 customers. There are 72 customers dining. Write and solve an inequality to show how many more people can eat at the restaurant.
   $x + 72 \le 120$; $x \le 48$ where x is a whole number

Also available on transparency

3-2 PROBLEM SOLVING

Write the correct answer.

1. Sumiko is allowed to watch no more than 10 hours of television each week. She has watched 4 hours of television already. Write and solve an inequality to show how many more hours of television Sumiko can watch.
   $4 + h \le 10$; $h \le 6$
2. A satellite will be released into an orbit of more than 400 miles above the Earth. The rocket carrying it is currently 255 miles above Earth. Write and solve an inequality to show how much higher the rocket must climb before it releases the satellite.
   $m + 255 > 400$; $m > 145$
3. Wayne's homework is to solve at least 20 questions from his textbook. So far, he has completed 9 of them. Write, solve, and graph an inequality to show how many more problems Wayne must complete.
   $q + 9 \ge 20$; $q \ge 11$
   9 10 11 12 13 14 15 16
4. Felix wants to get at least one hour of exercise each day. Today, he has run for 40 minutes. Write, solve, and graph an inequality that shows how much longer Felix needs to exercise to reach his goal.
   $40 + e \ge 60$; $e \ge 20$
   0 10 20 30 40 50 60 70

The high school has been raising money for charity and the class that raises the most will be awarded a party at the end of the year. The table below shows how much money each class has raised so far. Use this information to answer questions 5–7.

Class	Amount Raised ($)
Seniors	870
Juniors	650
Sophomores	675
First-Years	590

5. The school has a goal of raising at least $3000. Which inequality shows how much more money m they need to raise to reach their goal?
   A $m \ge 215$ C $m \le 215$
   B $m < 215$ D $m > 2785$
6. The juniors would like to raise more money than the seniors. The seniors have completed their fundraising for the year. Which expression shows how much more money j the juniors must raise to overtake the seniors?
   F $j \le 220$ H $j \ge 220$
   G $j < 220$ **J** $j > 220$
7. A local business has agreed to donate no more than half as much as the senior class raises. Which inequality shows how much money b the business will contribute?
   A $\frac{1}{2}(870) \le b$ **C** $\frac{1}{2}(870) \ge b$
   B $870 \le \frac{1}{2}b$ D $870 \ge \frac{1}{2}b$

3-2 CHALLENGE

Susan has 200 feet of fencing and wants to use it to enclose a rectangular garden. She knows that the formula for the perimeter of a rectangle is $P = 2(L + W)$. Susan also knows that the area A of a rectangle is found by using $A = LW$.

W L

Answer the following questions in order to help Susan plan how to use the fencing.

1. Susan can either use some or all of the fencing. Write an inequality that describes how much fencing she could use. **$0 < P \le 200$**
2. Would a length of 70 feet and a width of 40 feet satisfy the inequality in Exercise 1? Explain.
   No; because $2(70 + 40) = 220$ feet is greater than 200 feet
3. a. If Susan decides to use all of the fencing and chooses a length of 20 feet, find the width. **80 feet**
   b. What would the length be if she chooses a width of 20 feet? **80 feet**
   c. Given these dimensions, find the area of the garden. **1600 square feet**
4. a. If Susan decides to use all of the fencing and chooses a length of 40 feet, find the width. **60 feet**
   b. What would the length be if she chooses a width of 40 feet? **60 feet**
   c. Given these dimensions, find the area of the garden. **2400 square feet**
5. What conclusion can you draw from Exercises 3 and 4?
   If the dimensions are reversed, the area remains the same.
6. a. If Susan would like the length and the width to be as close to one another as possible and to be whole numbers, what might the dimensions be? **50 feet by 50 feet**
   b. Given her intention in part **a**, what shape is she trying to achieve? **a square**
   c. Given your answer to part **a**, find the area of the garden. **2500 square feet**
7. Susan's friend, Jack, has 160 feet of fencing. He wants to use all his fencing to make a garden with the greatest possible area. Without using inequalities, what dimensions should he choose? **40 feet by 40 feet**

3-3 Organizer

Pacing: Traditional 1 day
Block $\frac{1}{2}$ day

Objectives: Solve one-step inequalities by using multiplication.

Solve one-step inequalities by using division.

Technology Lab
In *Technology Lab Activities*

Online Edition
Tutorial Videos

Countdown Week 6

Power Presentations with PowerPoint®

Warm Up

Solve each equation.

1. $-5a = 30$ $\quad -6$
2. $-\frac{2}{5}x = 4$ $\quad -10$
3. $\frac{y}{-5} = \frac{-3}{8}$ $\quad 1\frac{7}{8}$
4. $-\frac{3}{4}x = \frac{6}{11}$ $\quad -\frac{8}{11}$

Graph each inequality.

5. $x \geq -10$ (number line: −15 −10 −5 0)
6. $x < -3$ (number line: −5 −4 −3 −2 −1)

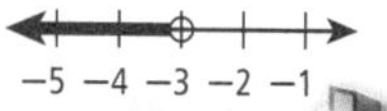

Also available on transparency

Math Humor

Q: What did the teacher do to prepare for class?

A: She made a "less-than" plan. (Lesson plan)

State Resources

go.hrw.com
State Resources Online
KEYWORD: MA7 Resources

3-3 Solving Inequalities by Multiplying or Dividing

Objectives
Solve one-step inequalities by using multiplication.

Solve one-step inequalities by using division.

Who uses this?
You can solve an inequality to determine how much you can buy with a certain amount of money. (See Example 3.)

"This is all I have, so I'll take 3 pencils, 3 notebooks, a binder, and 0.9 calculators."

Jonny Hawkins/CartoonResource.com

Remember, solving inequalities is similar to solving equations. To solve an inequality that contains multiplication or division, undo the operation by dividing or multiplying both sides of the inequality by the same number.

The rules below show the properties of inequality for multiplying or dividing by a positive number. The rules for multiplying or dividing by a negative number appear later in this lesson.

Know it! Note

Properties of Inequality

Multiplication and Division by Positive Numbers

WORDS	NUMBERS	ALGEBRA
Multiplication You can multiply both sides of an inequality by the same *positive* number, and the statement will still be true.	$7 < 12$ $7(3) < 12(3)$ $21 < 36$	If $a < b$ and $c > 0$, then $ac < bc$.
Division You can divide both sides of an inequality by the same *positive* number, and the statement will still be true.	$15 < 35$ $\frac{15}{5} < \frac{35}{5}$ $3 < 7$	If $a < b$ and $c > 0$, then $\frac{a}{c} < \frac{b}{c}$.

These properties are also true for inequalities that use the symbols $>$, $\geq$, and $\leq$.

EXAMPLE 1 **Multiplying or Dividing by a Positive Number**

Solve each inequality and graph the solutions.

A $3x > -27$

$$3x > -27$$ *Since x is multiplied by 3, divide both sides by 3 to undo the multiplication.*

$$\frac{3x}{3} > \frac{-27}{3}$$

$$x > -9$$

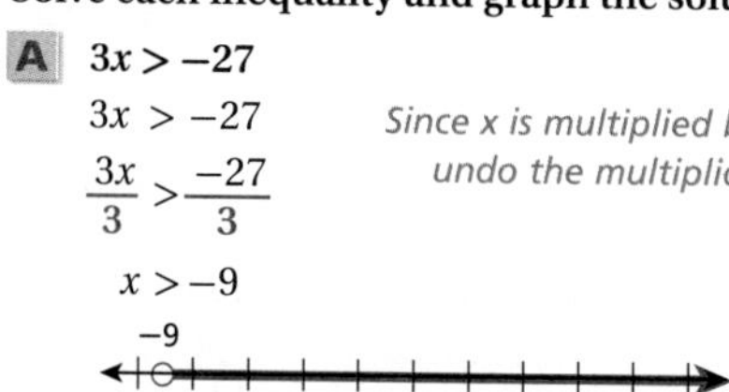

1 Introduce

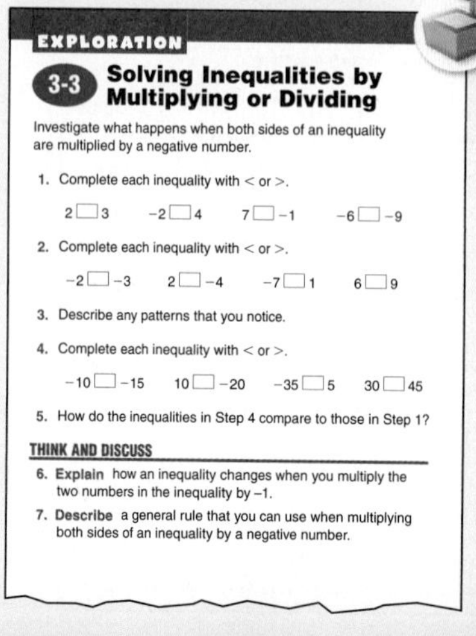

EXPLORATION

3-3 Solving Inequalities by Multiplying or Dividing

Investigate what happens when both sides of an inequality are multiplied by a negative number.

1. Complete each inequality with < or >.
   2 ☐ 3   −2 ☐ 4   7 ☐ −1   −6 ☐ −9
2. Complete each inequality with < or >.
   −2 ☐ −3   2 ☐ −4   −7 ☐ 1   6 ☐ 9
3. Describe any patterns that you notice.
4. Complete each inequality with < or >.
   −10 ☐ −15   10 ☐ −20   −35 ☐ 5   30 ☐ 45
5. How do the inequalities in Step 4 compare to those in Step 1?

THINK AND DISCUSS

6. **Explain** how an inequality changes when you multiply the two numbers in the inequality by −1.
7. **Describe** a general rule that you can use when multiplying both sides of an inequality by a negative number.

Motivate

Pose the following situation: "Bradley has $50 of birthday money to spend at a resale store. He wants to buy some used video games that cost $11 each." Ask students how they could determine the number of video games Bradley can buy. Tell students that they could use a one-step inequality. Tell students that there are special rules when multiplying or dividing both sides of an inequality by a negative number.

Explorations and answers are provided in *Alternate Openers: Explorations Transparencies.*

1a. 

1b. −18 −16 −14 −12 −10

1c. 34 35 36 37 38

Solve each inequality and graph the solutions.

B $\frac{2}{3}r < 6$

$\frac{2}{3}r < 6$ — *Since r is multiplied by $\frac{2}{3}$, multiply both sides by the reciprocal of $\frac{2}{3}$.*

$\frac{3}{2}\left(\frac{2}{3}r\right) < \frac{3}{2}(6)$

$r < 9$

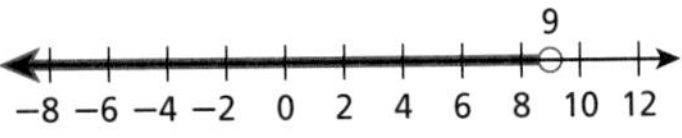

Solve each inequality and graph the solutions.

1a. $4k > 24$ $k > 6$ **1b.** $-50 \geq 5q$ $q \leq -10$ **1c.** $\frac{3}{4}g > 27$ $g > 36$

What happens when you multiply or divide both sides of an inequality by a negative number?

Look at the number line below.

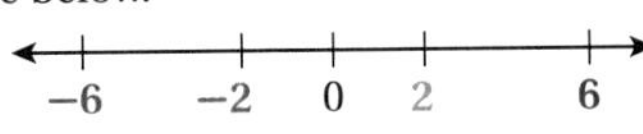

$2 < 6$		$6 > -2$	
$-2 \;\blacksquare\; -6$	*Multiply both sides by −1.*	$-6 \;\blacksquare\; 2$	*Multiply both sides by −1.*
$-2 > -6$	*Use the number line to determine the direction of the inequality.*	$-6 < 2$	*Use the number line to determine the direction of the inequality.*

Notice that when you multiply (or divide) both sides of an inequality by a negative number, you must reverse the inequality symbol. This means there is another set of properties of inequality for multiplying or dividing by a negative number.

Properties of Inequality

Multiplication and Division by Negative Numbers

WORDS	NUMBERS	ALGEBRA
Multiplication If you multiply both sides of an inequality by the same *negative* number, you must reverse the inequality symbol for the statement to still be true.	$8 > 4$ $8(-2) < 4(-2)$ $-16 < -8$	If $a > b$ and $c < 0$, then $ac < bc$.
Division If you divide both sides of an inequality by the same *negative* number, you must reverse the inequality symbol for the statement to still be true.	$12 > 4$ $\frac{12}{-4} < \frac{4}{-4}$ $-3 < -1$	If $a > b$ and $c < 0$, then $\frac{a}{c} < \frac{b}{c}$.

These properties are also true for inequalities that use the symbols <, ≥, and ≤.

COMMON ERROR ALERT

Students may change the inequality symbol when any number in the inequality is negative. Remind them that the inequality symbol is changed only when multiplying or dividing both sides by a negative number.

Power Presentations with PowerPoint®

Additional Examples

Example 1

Solve each inequality and graph the solutions.

A. $7x > -42$ $x > -6$

−8 −6 −4 −2 0

B. $2.4 \leq \frac{m}{3}$ $m \geq 7.2$

7.2
0 2 4 6 8

C. $\frac{3}{4}r < 12$ $r < 16$

0 4 8 12 16

INTERVENTION

Questioning Strategies

EXAMPLE 1

- How do you know whether to multiply or divide?

2 Teach

Guided Instruction

Review solving one-step equations using multiplication and division. Multiply both sides of a true inequality, like 2 < 6, by both a positive and negative number, to show that the statement is still true after it is multiplied by the positive number, but false after it is multiplied by the negative number. The false statement becomes true when the inequality sign is changed. Remind students how to check their solutions.

Reaching All Learners

Through Modeling

Draw a number line with 1 and 3 plotted.

Ask if it is correct to write 1 < 3. yes

Multiply both numbers by −1 and plot the products.

Ask if it is correct to write −1 < −3. no Why? −1 is further to the right. Ask if it is correct to write −1 > −3. yes What changed? the direction of the sign Use similar steps to show dividing both sides of a numerical inequality by −1.

Power Presentations with PowerPoint®

Additional Examples

Example 2

Solve each inequality and graph the solutions.

A. $-12x > 84$ $\quad x < -7$

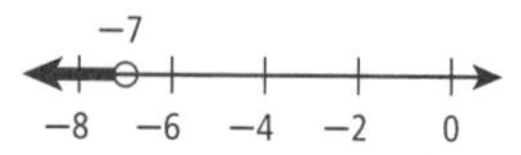

B. $-8 \le \dfrac{x}{-3}$ $\quad x \le 24$

0 6 12 18 24

Example 3

Jill has a $20 gift card to an art supply store where 4 oz tubes of paint are $4.30 each after tax. What are the possible numbers of tubes that Jill can buy?

0, 1, 2, 3, or 4 tubes

INTERVENTION

Questioning Strategies

EXAMPLE 2

- What must be done to both sides of an inequality to make the inequality symbol change?

EXAMPLE 3

- Why would the solutions of the inequality be graphed as individual points?

Caution!

Do not change the direction of the inequality symbol just because you see a negative sign. For example, you do not change the symbol when solving $4x < -24$.

EXAMPLE 2 Multiplying or Dividing by a Negative Number

Solve each inequality and graph the solutions.

A $-8x > 72$

$\dfrac{-8x}{-8} < \dfrac{72}{-8}$ — *Since x is multiplied by −8, divide both sides by −8. Change > to <.*

$x < -9$

−15 −12 −9 −6 −3 0 3

B $-3 \le \dfrac{x}{-5}$

$-5(-3) \ge -5\left(\dfrac{x}{-5}\right)$ — *Since x is divided by −5, multiply both sides by −5. Change ≤ to ≥.*

$15 \ge x$ (or $x \le 15$)

15
−2 0 2 4 6 8 10 12 14 16 18

CHECK IT OUT! Solve each inequality and graph the solutions.

2a. $10 \ge -x$ $\quad x \ge -10$

−10 −8 −6 −4 −2

2b. $4.25 > -0.25h$ $\quad h > -17$

−19 −18 −17 −16 −15

EXAMPLE 3 *Consumer Application*

Ryan has a $16 gift card for a health store where a smoothie costs $2.50 with tax. What are the possible numbers of smoothies that Ryan can buy?

Let s represent the number of smoothies Ryan can buy.

$2.50	times	number of smoothies	is at most	$16.00.
2.50	•	s	≤	16.00

$2.50s \le 16.00$

$\dfrac{2.50s}{2.50} \le \dfrac{16.00}{2.50}$ — *Since s is multiplied by 2.50, divide both sides by 2.50. The symbol does not change.*

$s \le 6.4$ — *Ryan can buy only a whole number of smoothies.*

Ryan can buy 0, 1, 2, 3, 4, 5, or 6 smoothies.

CHECK IT OUT! **3.** A pitcher holds 128 ounces of juice. What are the possible numbers of 10-ounce servings that one pitcher can fill?

$10g \le 128$; $g \le 12.8$; 0, 1, 2, 3, 4, 5, 6, 7, 8, 9, 10, 11, or 12 servings

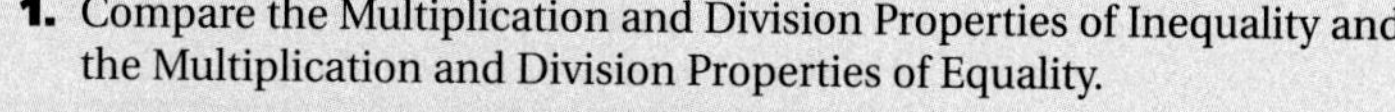

THINK AND DISCUSS

1. Compare the Multiplication and Division Properties of Inequality and the Multiplication and Division Properties of Equality.

2. **GET ORGANIZED** Copy and complete the graphic organizer. In each cell, write and solve an inequality.

Solving Inequalities by Using Multiplication and Division		
	By a Positive Number	By a Negative Number
Divide		
Multiply		

3 Close

Summarize

Remind students that solving one-step inequalities is like solving one-step equations, except they must remember to change the sign of the inequality when multiplying or dividing by a negative number. Write the following on the board, and ask if the inequality sign would change when solving.

$2x > -10$	no
$-3b \le 12$	yes
$5 > -10n$	yes
$-16 < 4t$	no

ONGOING ASSESSMENT and INTERVENTION

Diagnose Before **the Lesson**
3-3 Warm Up, TE p. 182

Monitor During **the Lesson**
Check It Out! Exercises, SE pp. 183–184
Questioning Strategies, TE pp. 183–184

Assess After **the Lesson**
3-3 Lesson Quiz, TE p. 187
Alternative Assessment, TE p. 187

Answers to *Think and Discuss*

1. They are alike because you can multiply or divide both sides by a positive number and the inequality or equation will still be true. They are different because you have to reverse the inequality symbol if you multiply or divide both sides by a negative number.
2. See p. A4.

3-3 Exercises

GUIDED PRACTICE

Solve each inequality and graph the solutions.

SEE EXAMPLE 1 p. 182

1. $3b > 27$
2. $-40 \geq 8b$
3. $\frac{d}{3} > 6$
4. $24d \leq 6$
5. $1.1m \leq 1.21$
6. $\frac{2}{3}k > 6$
7. $9s > -18$
8. $\frac{4}{5} \geq \frac{r}{2}$

SEE EXAMPLE 2 p. 184

9. $-2x < -10$
10. $\frac{b}{-2} \geq 8$
11. $-3.5n < 1.4$
12. $4 > -8g$
13. $\frac{d}{-6} < \frac{1}{2}$
14. $-10h \geq -6$
15. $12 > \frac{t}{-6}$
16. $-\frac{1}{2}m \geq -7$

SEE EXAMPLE 3 p. 184

17. **Travel** Tom saved \$550 to go on a school trip. The cost for a hotel room, including tax, is \$80 per night. What are the possible numbers of nights Tom can stay at the hotel? **0, 1, 2, 3, 4, 5, or 6 nights**

PRACTICE AND PROBLEM SOLVING

Independent Practice

For Exercises	See Example
18–29	1
30–41	2
42	3

Extra Practice
Skills Practice p. S8
Application Practice p. S30

Solve each inequality and graph the solutions.

18. $10 < 2t$
19. $\frac{1}{3}j \leq 4$
20. $-80 < 8c$
21. $21 > 3d$
22. $\frac{w}{4} \geq -2$
23. $\frac{h}{4} \leq \frac{2}{7}$
24. $6y < 4.2$
25. $12c \leq -144$
26. $\frac{4}{5}x \geq \frac{2}{5}$
27. $6b \geq \frac{3}{5}$
28. $-25 > 10p$
29. $\frac{b}{8} \leq -2$
30. $-9a > 81$
31. $\frac{1}{2} < \frac{r}{-3}$
32. $-6p > 0.6$
33. $\frac{y}{-4} > -\frac{1}{2}$
34. $-\frac{1}{6}f < 5$
35. $-2.25t < -9$
36. $24 \leq -10w$
37. $-11z > 121$
38. $\frac{3}{5} < \frac{f}{-5}$
39. $-k \geq 7$
40. $-2.2b < -7.7$
41. $16 \geq -\frac{4}{3}p$

42. **Camping** The rope Roz brought with her camping gear is 54 inches long. Roz needs to cut shorter pieces of rope that are each 18 inches long. What are the possible number of pieces Roz can cut? **0, 1, 2, or 3**

Solve each inequality and graph the solutions.

43. $-8x < 24$
44. $3t \leq 24$
45. $\frac{1}{4}x < 5$
46. $\frac{4}{5}p \geq -24$
47. $54 \leq -9p$
48. $3t > -\frac{1}{2}$
49. $-\frac{3}{4}b > -\frac{3}{2}$
50. $216 > 3.6r$

Write an inequality for each statement. Solve the inequality and graph the solutions.

51. The product of a number and 7 is not less than 21. **$7x \geq 21$; $x \geq 3$**
52. The quotient of h and -6 is at least 5. **$\frac{h}{-6} \geq 5$; $h \leq -30$**
53. The product of $-\frac{4}{5}$ and b is at most -16. **$-\frac{4}{5}b \leq -16$; $b \geq 20$**
54. Ten is no more than the quotient of t and 4. **$10 \leq \frac{t}{4}$; $t \geq 40$**
55. **Write About It** Explain how you know whether to reverse the inequality symbol when solving an inequality.
56. **Geometry** The area of a rectangle is at most 21 square inches. The width of the rectangle is 3.5 inches. What are the possible measurements for the length of the rectangle? **$\ell \leq 6$ in. where ℓ is positive**

55. You reverse the symbol only when you multiply or divide both sides of the inequality by the same negative number.

Assignment Guide

Assign *Guided Practice* exercises as necessary.

If you finished Examples **1–3**
Basic 18–60, 64–70, 78–87
Average 18–56, 61–70, 72, 78–87
Advanced 18–42, 44–50 even, 51–56, 61, 63, 66–87

Homework Quick Check
Quickly check key concepts.
Exercises: 20, 34, 42, 50, 54, 62

Answers

1. $b > 9$
2. $b \leq -5$
3. $d > 18$

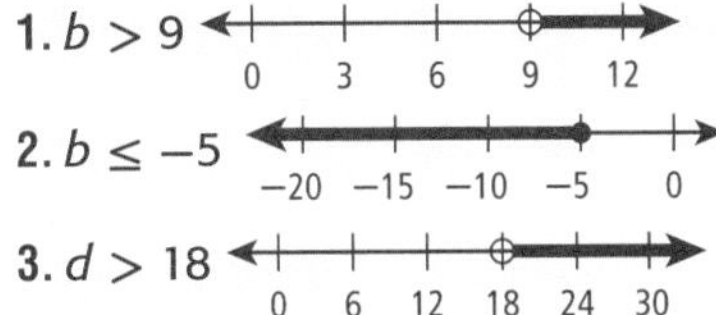

4. $d \leq \frac{1}{4}$

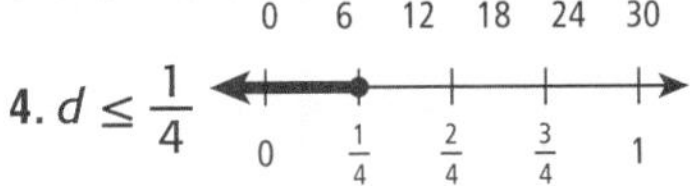

5. $m \leq 1.1$
6. $k > 9$
7. $s > -2$
8. $r \leq \frac{8}{5}$
9. $x > 5$
10. $b \leq -16$
11. $n > -0.4$

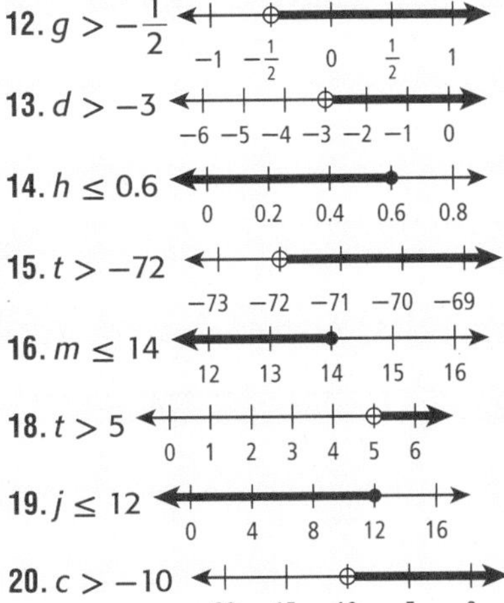

12. $g > -\frac{1}{2}$
13. $d > -3$
14. $h \leq 0.6$
15. $t > -72$
16. $m \leq 14$
18. $t > 5$
19. $j \leq 12$
20. $c > -10$
21. $d < 7$
22. $w \geq -8$
23. $h \leq \frac{8}{7}$
24. $y < 0.7$
25. $c \leq -12$
26. $x \geq \frac{1}{2}$

27–41, 43–50. See p. A14.
51–54. For graphs, see p. A14.

State Resources

Inclusion Some students may get confused in **Exercise 59** because the inequality changes direction twice: once when dividing both sides by a negative number, and again when rewriting the expression with the variable on the left. Encourage students to write down every step, and not to attempt to do two steps at once.

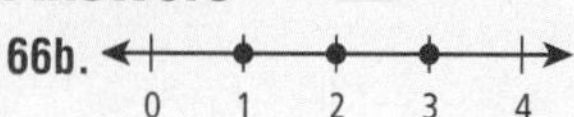

Exercise 66 involves writing and solving an inequality in which the reasonable answers are restricted to natural numbers. This exercise prepares students for the Multi-Step Test Prep on page 188.

Answers

66b. (number line from 0 to 4 with points at 1, 2, 3)

Solve each inequality and match the solution to the correct graph.

57. $-0.5t \geq 1.5$ **$t \leq -3$; C**

58. $\frac{1}{9}t \leq -3$ **$t \leq -27$; D**

59. $-13.5 \leq -4.5t$ **$t \leq 3$; A**

60. $\frac{t}{-6} \leq -\frac{1}{2}$ **$t \geq 3$; B**

A.  (number line −5 to 5)

B. 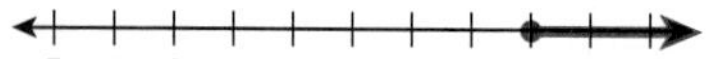 (number line −5 to 5)

C.  (number line −5 to 5)

D. 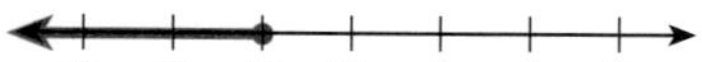 (number line −45, −36, −27, −18, −9, 0, 9)

LINK Animals

Orangutans weigh about 3.5 pounds at birth. As adults, female orangutans can weigh as much as 110 pounds, and male orangutans can weigh up to 300 pounds.

61. **Animals** A wildlife shelter is home to birds, mammals, and reptiles. If cat chow is sold in 20 lb bags, what is the least number of bags of cat chow needed for one year at this shelter? **26 bags**

Food Consumed at a Wildlife Shelter per Week

Type of Food	Amount of Food (lb)
Grapes	4
Mixed seed	10
Peanuts	5
Cat chow	10
Kitten chow	5

62. **Education** In order to earn an A in a college math class, a student must score no less than 90% of all possible points. One semester, students with at least 567 points earned an A in the class. Write an inequality to show the numbers of points possible. **$p \leq 630$ where p is a whole number**

63. **Critical Thinking** Explain why you cannot solve an inequality by multiplying both sides by zero. **Multiplying both sides of an inequality by zero makes both sides equal zero, so there is no longer an inequality to solve.**

64. **///ERROR ANALYSIS///** Two students have different answers for a homework problem. Which answer is incorrect? Explain the error.

A is incorrect. Both sides are divided by a positive number, so the inequality symbol should not be reversed.

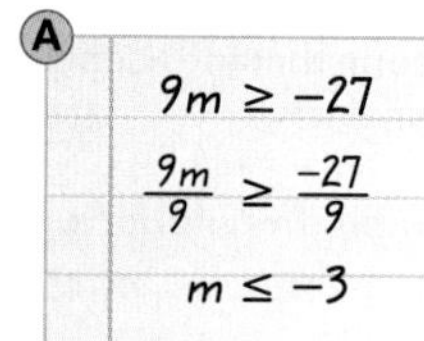

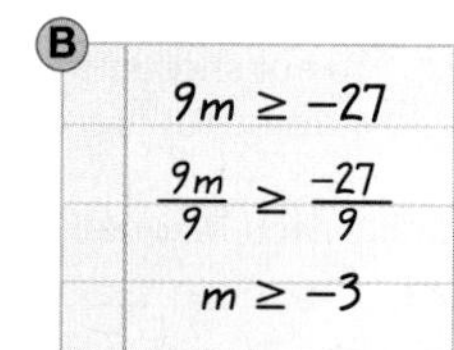

65. Jan has a budget of $800 for catering. The catering company charges $12.50 per guest. Write and solve an inequality to show the numbers of guests Jan can invite. **$12.5g \leq 800$; $g \leq 64$ where g is a whole number**

MULTI-STEP TEST PREP

66. This problem will prepare you for the Multi-Step Test Prep on page 188.
    a. The Swimming Club can spend a total of $250 for hotel rooms for its spring trip. One hotel costs $75 per night. Write an inequality to find the number of rooms the club can reserve at this hotel. Let n be the number of rooms. **$75n \leq 250$**
    b. Solve the inequality you wrote in part **a.** Graph the solutions on a number line. Make sure your answer is reasonable. **$n \leq 3.33$; n must be a natural number.**
    c. Another hotel offers a rate of $65 per night. Does this allow the club to reserve more rooms? Explain your reasoning. **$65n \leq 250$; $n \leq 3.85$; no, they still can reserve only 3 or fewer rooms.**

3-3 PRACTICE A
3-3 PRACTICE C
3-3 PRACTICE B

Solve each inequality and graph the solutions.

1. $4a > 32$ — **$a > 8$**
2. $-7y < 21$ — **$y > -3$**
3. $1.5n \leq -18$ — **$n \leq -12$**
4. $-\frac{3}{8}c \geq 9$ — **$c \leq -24$**
5. $\frac{y}{5} > 4$ — **$y > 20$**
6. $2s \leq -3$ — **$s \leq -1.5$**
7. $-\frac{1}{3}b < -6$ — **$b > 18$**
8. $\frac{z}{-8} \geq -0.25$ — **$z \leq 2$**

Write and solve an inequality for each problem.

9. Phil has a strip of wood trim that is 16 feet long. He needs 5-foot pieces to trim some windows. What are the possible numbers of pieces he can cut?
   $5p \leq 16$; $p \leq 3.2$; 0, 1, 2, or 3 pieces
10. A teacher buys a 128-ounce bottle of juice and serves it in 5-ounce cups. What are the possible numbers of cups she can fill?
    $5s \leq 128$; $s \leq 25.6$; 0 to 25 cups
11. At an online bookstore, Kendra bought 4 copies of the same book for the members of her book club. She got free shipping because her total was at least $50. What was the minimum price of each book?
    $4b \geq 50$; $b \geq 12.50$; $12.50 each

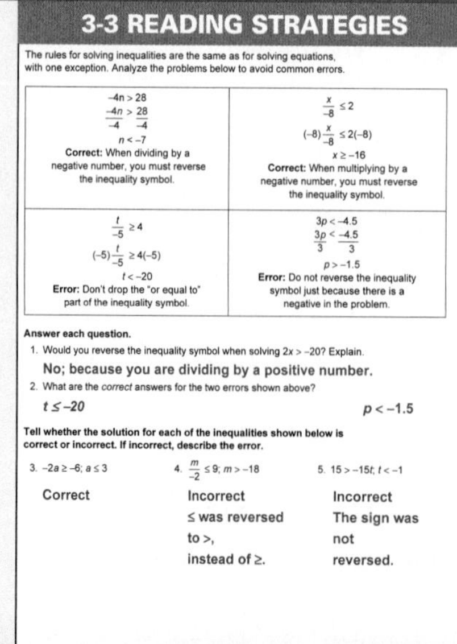

3-3 READING STRATEGIES

The rules for solving inequalities are the same as for solving equations, with one exception. Analyze the problems below to avoid common errors.

$-4n > 28$; $\frac{-4n}{-4} > \frac{28}{-4}$; $n < -7$. **Correct:** When dividing by a negative number, you must reverse the inequality symbol.	$\frac{x}{-8} \leq 2$; $(-8)\frac{x}{-8} \leq 2(-8)$; $x \geq -16$. **Correct:** When multiplying by a negative number, you must reverse the inequality symbol.
$\frac{t}{-5} \geq 4$; $(-5)\frac{t}{-5} \geq 4(-5)$; $t < -20$. **Error:** Don't drop the "or equal to" part of the inequality symbol.	$3p < -4.5$; $\frac{3p}{3} < \frac{-4.5}{3}$; $p > -1.5$. **Error:** Do not reverse the inequality symbol just because there is a negative in the problem.

Answer each question.

1. Would you reverse the inequality symbol when solving $2x > -20$? Explain.
   No; because you are dividing by a positive number.
2. What are the *correct* answers for the two errors shown above?
   $t \leq -20$ **$p < -1.5$**

Tell whether the solution for each of the inequalities shown below is correct or incorrect. If incorrect, describe the error.

3. $-2a \geq -6$; $a \leq 3$ — **Correct**
4. $\frac{m}{-2} \leq 9$; $m > -18$ — **Incorrect ≤ was reversed to >, instead of ≥.**
5. $15 > -15t$; $t < -1$ — **Incorrect The sign was not reversed.**

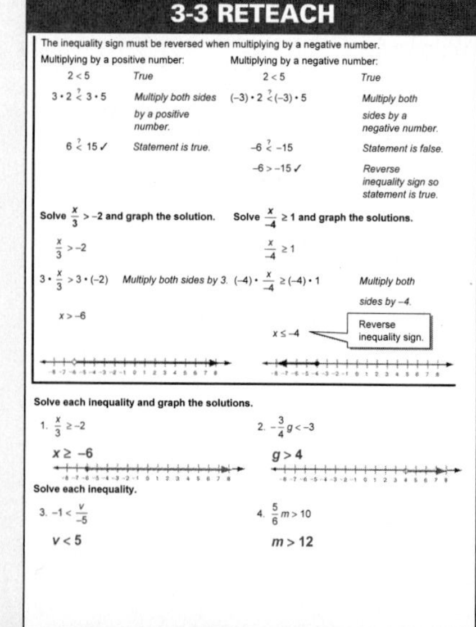

3-3 RETEACH

The inequality sign must be reversed when multiplying by a negative number.

Multiplying by a positive number:		Multiplying by a negative number:	
$2 < 5$	*True*	$2 < 5$	*True*
$3 \cdot 2 \overset{?}{<} 3 \cdot 5$	*Multiply both sides by a positive number.*	$(-3) \cdot 2 \overset{?}{<} (-3) \cdot 5$	*Multiply both sides by a negative number.*
$6 \overset{?}{<} 15$ ✓	*Statement is true.*	$-6 \overset{?}{<} -15$	*Statement is false.*
		$-6 > -15$ ✓	*Reverse inequality sign so statement is true.*

Solve $\frac{x}{3} > -2$ and graph the solution.

$\frac{x}{3} > -2$

$3 \cdot \frac{x}{3} > 3 \cdot (-2)$ *Multiply both sides by 3.*

$x > -6$

Solve $\frac{x}{-4} \geq 1$ and graph the solutions.

$\frac{x}{-4} \geq 1$

$(-4) \cdot \frac{x}{-4} \geq (-4) \cdot 1$ *Multiply both sides by −4.*

$x \leq -4$ Reverse inequality sign.

Solve each inequality and graph the solutions.

1. $\frac{x}{3} \geq -2$ — **$x \geq -6$**
2. $-\frac{3}{4}g < -3$ — **$g > 4$**

Solve each inequality.

3. $-1 < \frac{v}{-5}$ — **$v < 5$**
4. $\frac{5}{6}m > 10$ — **$m > 12$**

TEST PREP

67. Which inequality does NOT have the same solutions as $-\frac{2}{3}y > 4$?

    (A) $12 < -2y$ (C) $-\frac{3}{4}y > \frac{9}{2}$

    (B) $\frac{y}{2} < -12$ (D) $-3y > 18$

68. The solutions of which inequality are NOT represented by the following graph?

    −5 −4 −3 −2 −1 0 1 2 3 4 5

    (F) $\frac{x}{2} \geq -2$ (H) $3x \geq -12$

    (G) $-5x \geq 20$ (J) $-7x \leq 28$

69. Which inequality can be used to find the number of 39-cent stamps you can purchase for $4.00?

    (A) $0.39s \geq 4.00$ (C) $\frac{s}{0.39} \leq 4.00$

    (B) $0.39s \leq 4.00$ (D) $\frac{4.00}{0.39} \leq s$

70. **Short Response** Write three different inequalities that have the same solutions as $x > 4$. Show your work and explain each step.
    Possible answer: $2x > 8$, $\frac{1}{4}x > 1$, $3x > 12$

CHALLENGE AND EXTEND

71. $g \leq -\frac{14}{5}$
72. $x < 12.375$
73. $m > \frac{4}{15}$
74. $f \geq 4$

Solve each inequality.

71. $2\frac{1}{3} \leq -\frac{5}{6}g$ 72. $\frac{2x}{3} < 8.25$ 73. $2\frac{5}{8}m > \frac{7}{10}$ 74. $3\frac{3}{5}f \geq 14\frac{2}{5}$

75. **Estimation** What is the greatest possible integer solution of the inequality $3.806x < 19.902$? **$x = 5$**

76. **Critical Thinking** The Transitive Property of Equality states that if $a = b$ and $b = c$, then $a = c$. Is there a Transitive Property of Inequality using the symbol <? Give an example to support your answer. **yes; $2 < 3$ and $3 < 4 \rightarrow 2 < 4$**

77. **Critical Thinking** The Symmetric Property of Equality states that if $a = b$, then $b = a$. Is there a Symmetric Property of Inequality? Give an example to support your answer. **no; $0 < 1$ but $1 \not< 0$**

SPIRAL REVIEW

Write the power represented by each geometric model. *(Lesson 1-4)*

78. **3^2** 79. **2^3** 80. 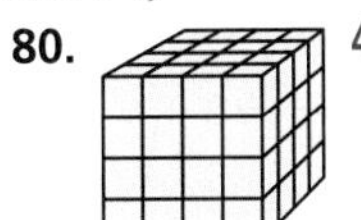 **4^3**

Find each unit rate. *(Lesson 2-7)*

81. Twelve gallons of gas cost $22.68. Find the unit rate in dollars per gallon. **$1.89/gal**
82. A tree grows four feet in six years. Find the unit rate in feet per year. **$\frac{2}{3}$ ft/yr**
83. A student types 105 words in 3 minutes. Find the unit rate in words per minute. **35 words/min**

87. 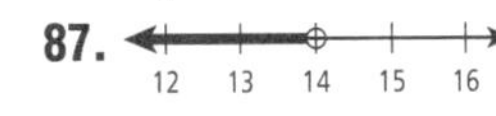
12 13 14 15 16

Solve each inequality and graph the solutions. *(Lesson 3-2)*

84. $x + 5 \geq 3$ **$x \geq -2$** 85. $t - \frac{1}{4} < \frac{3}{4}$ **$t < 1$** 86. $4 > x - 1$ **$x < 5$** 87. $6 > b - 8$ **$b < 14$**

TEST PREP DOCTOR In **Exercise 69,** students who chose **A** or **D** may understand that the cost per stamp is multiplied by the number of stamps, but not that the cost must be less than or equal to $4. Students who chose **C** may not understand the relationship between the cost of the stamps and the number of stamps that can be purchased.

Journal

Have students explain why someone might change the direction of the inequality symbol twice when solving a one-step inequality with multiplication or division.

ALTERNATIVE ASSESSMENT

Have students work in groups to explain solving one-step inequalities. The report should include using each property of inequality, at least one real-world problem, and an explanation of why and when the inequality symbol is changed.

Power Presentations with PowerPoint®

3-3 Lesson Quiz

Solve each inequality and graph the solutions.

1. $8x < -24$ $x < -3$
   −6 −5 −4 −3 −2 −1 0
2. $-5x \geq 30$ $x \leq -6$
   −8 −6 −4 −2 0
3. $\frac{x}{5} > 4$ $x > 20$
   0 10 20 30 40
4. $\frac{x}{-8} \leq \frac{-3}{4}$ $x \geq 6$
   0 2 4 6 8
5. A soccer coach plans to order more shirts for her team. Each shirt costs $9.85. She has $77 left in her uniform budget. What are the possible numbers of shirts she can buy?
   0, 1, 2, 3, 4, 5, 6, or 7 shirts

Also available on transparency

3-3 PROBLEM SOLVING

Write and solve an inequality for each situation.

1. Karin has $3 to spend in the arcade. The game she likes costs 50¢ per play. What are the possible numbers of times that she can play?
   $0.50g \leq 3$; $g \leq 6$
   0, 1, 2, 3, 4, 5, or 6
2. Tyrone has $21 and wants to buy juice drinks for his soccer team. There are 15 players on his team. How much can each drink cost so that Tyrone can buy one drink for each person?
   $15d \leq 21$; $d \leq 1.40$;
   up to $1.40
3. A swimming pool is 7 feet deep and is being filled at the rate of 2.5 feet per hour. How long can the pool be left unattended without the water overflowing?
   $2.5h \leq 7$; $h \leq 2.8$;
   up to 2.8 hours
4. Megan is making quilts that require 11 feet of cloth each. She has 50 feet of cloth. What are the possible numbers of quilts that she can make?
   $11q \leq 50$; $q \leq 4.54$;
   0, 1, 2, 3, or 4

Alyssa, Reggie, and Cassie are meeting some friends at the movies and have stopped at the refreshment stand. The table below shows some of the items for sale and their prices. Use this information to answer questions 5–7.

Menu Item	Price($)
Popcorn	3.50
Drink	3.00
Hot Dog	2.50
Nachos	2.50
Fruit Snack	2.00

5. Alyssa has $7 and would like to buy fruit snacks for as many of her friends as possible. Which inequality below can be solved to find the number of fruit snacks f she can buy?
   A $2f \leq 7$ C $7f \leq 2$
   B $2f < 7$ D $7f < 2$
6. Reggie brought $13 and is going to buy popcorn for the group. Which answer below shows the possible numbers of popcorns p Reggie can buy for his friends?
   F 0, 1, or 2 H 0, 1, 2, 3, or 4
   G 0, 1, 2, or 3 J 0, 1, 2, 3, 4, or 5
7. The movie theater donates 12% of its sales to charity. From Cassie's purchases, the theater will donate at least $2.15. Which inequality below shows the amount of money m that Cassie spent at the refreshment stand?
   A $m \geq 17.92$ C $m \geq 25.80$
   B $m \leq 17.92$ D $m \leq 25.80$

3-3 CHALLENGE

You will need a centimeter ruler for this activity.

1. Consider the inequality $-1 < 3$. Write the inequality you get when you multiply both sides by −2. **$2 > -6$**
2. On the top number line, plot a point at −1. On the bottom number line, plot the value you get when you multiply by −2. Use your ruler to connect the two points with a straight segment.
3. Similarly, on the top, plot a point at 3. On the bottom, plot the value you get when you multiply by −2. Connect the two points with a segment.
4. Explain how the graph illustrates that you *reverse* an inequality when you multiply both sides by a negative number.
   The segments cross each other showing that the value that was lesser (−1) now corresponds to the value that is greater (2), and vice versa.
5. The two segments should intersect along the dashed segment connecting the zeroes. Measure the two pieces of the dashed segment. How is the ratio of the two lengths related to the factor −2?
   The ratio of these lengths is the absolute value of −2: $\frac{\text{bottom}}{\text{top}} = \frac{2.4 \text{ cm}}{1.2 \text{ cm}} = 2$.
6. Try it again. Multiply both sides of the inequality $9 < 15$ by $-\frac{1}{3}$.
   Plot points and connect them. Do you see the same patterns?
   yes; the segments cross each other and the ratio of the lengths of the pieces of the dashed segment is still the absolute value of the factor: $\frac{\text{bottom}}{\text{top}} = \frac{0.9 \text{ cm}}{2.7 \text{ cm}} = \frac{1}{3}$.
7. Where along the dashed line would the segments intersect if you multiplied both sides of any inequality by −1?
   The segments would intersect at the midpoint of the dashed line.

Organizer

Objective: Assess students' ability to apply concepts and skills in Lessons 3-1 through 3-3 in a real-world format.

 **Online Edition**

Resources

 ***Algebra I Assessments***
www.mathtekstoolkit.org

Problem	Text Reference
1	Lessons 3-1
2	Lessons 3-2
3	Lessons 3-3
4	Lesson 1-3
5	Lessons 1-2 and 1-3

Answers

1. 615 mi
2. $532 + m \leq 615$; $m \leq 83$ where m is nonnegative

3. $58n \leq 200$; $n \leq 3.45$; they can reserve a maximum of 3 rooms.

State Resources

CHAPTER 3

MULTI-STEP TEST PREP

SECTION 3A

Simple Inequalities

Remember the Alamo! The Spanish Club is planning a trip for next summer. They plan to travel from Fort Worth, Texas, to San Antonio, Texas. They can spend only $550 for the entire trip.

1. The treasurer of the club budgets $60 for gasoline. The current gas price is $1.95/gallon. The school van gets an average of 20 miles per gallon of gasoline. Determine how many miles they can drive on this budget. Round your answer to the nearest mile.
2. The distance from Fort Worth to San Antonio is 266 miles. Write an inequality that can be used to solve for the number of miles m that they can drive while in San Antonio. Solve your inequality and graph the solutions.
3. The treasurer budgeted $200 for hotel rooms for one night. The club chose a hotel that charges $58 per night. Write an inequality that can be used to solve for the number of rooms they can reserve n. What is the maximum number of rooms that they can reserve in the hotel?
4. Use the maximum number of rooms you found in part **3.** How much will the club spend on hotel rooms? **58(3) = $174**
5. The club members plan to spend $80 on food. They also want to see attractions in San Antonio, such as SeaWorld and the Alamo.

   Write an inequality that can be solved to find the amount of money available for seeing attractions. What is the maximum amount the club can spend seeing attractions?
   $314 + a \leq 550$; $a \leq 236$
6. Write a summary of the budget for the Spanish Club trip. Include the amount they plan to spend on gasoline, hotel rooms, food, and attractions.

6.

Gasoline	**$60**
Hotel rooms	**$174**
Food	**$80**
Attractions	**+ $236**
	$550

INTERVENTION 

Scaffolding Questions

1. What equation relates the number of gallons, price per gallon, and total price? total price = (price per gallon)(gallons)
2. How can you find the total distance for the round trip? Double the distance between the cities.
3. Should you round your answer up or down? Round down, because they don't have enough money for 4 rooms.
4. What operation should you use to find the cost of the hotel rooms? multiplication

5–6. What values do you need to find the amount left for seeing attractions? total budgeted amount, cost of gas, cost of hotel rooms, and cost of food

Extension

Describe any adjustments you would make to the budget. Possible answer: Transfer money from the hotel room budget to food or attractions. Students may want to make other changes.

CHAPTER **3**

SECTION 3A

Quiz for Lessons 3-1 Through 3-3

3-1 Graphing and Writing Inequalities

Describe the solutions of each inequality in words.

1. $-2 < r$ 2. $t - 1 \le 7$ 3. $2s \ge 6$ 4. $4 > 5 - x$

Graph each inequality.

5. $x > -2$ 6. $m \le 1\frac{1}{2}$ 7. $g < \sqrt{8 + 1}$ 8. $h \ge 2^3$

5. −3 −2 −1 0 1 2 3

6. 0 $\frac{1}{2}$ 1 $1\frac{1}{2}$ 2

7. 0 1 2 3 4 5 6

8. 0 4 8 12 16

Write the inequality shown by each graph.

9. 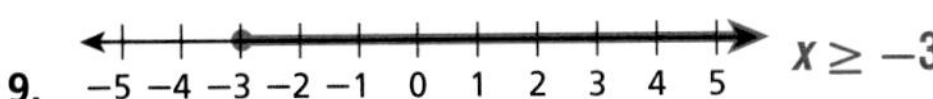 $x \ge -3$

10. 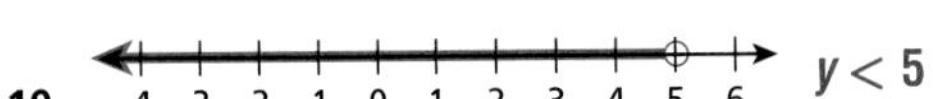 $y < 5$

11. 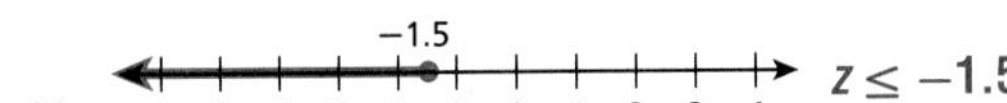 $z \le -1.5$

Write an inequality for each situation and graph the solutions.

12. You must purchase at least 5 tickets to receive a discount.
13. Children under 13 are not admitted to certain movies without an adult.
14. A cell phone plan allows up to 250 free minutes per month.

3-2 Solving One-Step Inequalities by Adding or Subtracting

Solve each inequality and graph the solutions.

15. $k + 5 \le 7$ 16. $4 > p - 3$ 17. $r - 8 \ge -12$ 18. $-3 + p < -6$

19. Allie must sell at least 50 gift baskets for the band fund-raiser. She already sold 36 baskets. Write and solve an inequality to determine how many more baskets Allie must sell for the fund-raiser. **$36 + b \ge 50$; $b \ge 14$; Allie must sell at least 14 more baskets.**

20. Dante has at most \$12 to spend on entertainment each week. So far this week, he spent \$7.50. Write and solve an inequality to determine how much money Dante can spend on entertainment the rest of the week. **$7.50 + m \le 12$; $m \le 4.50$; Dante can spend \$4.50 at most.**

3-3 Solving One-Step Inequalities by Multiplying or Dividing

Solve each inequality and graph the solutions.

21. $-4x < 8$ **$x > -2$** 22. $\frac{d}{3} \ge -3$ **$d \ge -9$** 23. $\frac{3}{4}t \le 12$ **$t \le 16$** 24. $8 > -16c$ **$c > -\frac{1}{2}$**

25. A spool of ribbon is 80 inches long. Riley needs to cut strips of ribbon that are 14 inches long. What are the possible numbers of strips that Riley can cut? **0, 1, 2, 3, 4, or 5**

READY TO GO ON?

Organizer

Objective: Assess students' mastery of concepts and skills in Lessons 3-1 through 3-3.

Resources

 ***Assessment Resources***
Section 3A Quiz

Teacher One Stop™
Test & Practice Generator

INTERVENTION 

Resources

 ***Ready to Go On? Intervention and Enrichment* Worksheets**

 ***Ready to Go On?* CD-ROM**

 ***Ready to Go On?* Online**

my.hrw.com

Answers

1–4, 12–18. See p. A14.
21–24. For graphs, see p. A14.

READY TO GO ON?
Diagnose and Prescribe

NO INTERVENE

Ready to Go On? Intervention	*Ready to Go On? Intervention,* Section 3A: Worksheets	CD-ROM	Online
Lesson 3-1	3-1 Intervention	Activity 3-1	Diagnose and Prescribe Online
Lesson 3-2	3-2 Intervention	Activity 3-2	
Lesson 3-3	3-3 Intervention	Activity 3-3	

YES ENRICH

SECTION **3B**

Multi-Step and Compound Inequalities

One-Minute Section Planner

Lesson	Lab Resources	Materials
Lesson 3-4 Solving Two-Step and Multi-Step Inequalities • Solve inequalities that contain more than one operation. ☑ SAT-10 ☑ NAEP ☑ ACT ☑ SAT ☑ SAT Subject Tests		
Lesson 3-5 Solving Inequalities with Variables on Both Sides • Solve inequalities that contain variable terms on both sides. ☑ SAT-10 ☑ NAEP ☑ ACT ☑ SAT ☑ SAT Subject Tests	***Algebra Lab Activities*** 3-5 Algebra Lab ***Technology Lab Activities*** 3-5 Technology Lab	**Optional** graphing calculator
3-6 Algebra Lab Truth Tables and Compound Statements • Determine whether compound statements are true or false. ☐ SAT-10 ☐ NAEP ☐ ACT ☐ SAT ☐ SAT Subject Tests	***Algebra Lab Activities*** 3-6 Lab Recording Sheet	
Lesson 3-6 Solving Compound Inequalities • Solve compound inequalities with one variable. • Graph solution sets of compound inequalities with one variable. ☑ SAT-10 ☑ NAEP ☑ ACT ☑ SAT ☑ SAT Subject Tests		**Optional** blank transparency, yellow and blue transparency markers, graphing calculator
Lesson 3-7 Solving Absolute-Value Inequalities • Solve inequalities with one variable involving absolute-value expressions. ☑ SAT-10 ☐ NAEP ☑ ACT ☑ SAT ☑ SAT Subject Tests		

Note: If NAEP is checked, the content is tested on either the Grade 8 or Grade 12 NAEP assessment.

MK = *Manipulatives Kit*

COMPOUND INEQUALITIES

Lesson 3-6

A *compound inequality* is a pair of inequalities linked by the word AND or by the word OR. To understand compound inequalities, it is important to understand the logic behind the words AND and OR and to recognize the uses of these words in basic set theory.

Consider the compound inequality $x \geq -2$ AND $x < 4$. If a value of x is a solution of the compound inequality, the word AND means that both inequalities must be true. The first two number lines below show solutions of the two inequalities; the third number line shows the points that both graphs have in common.

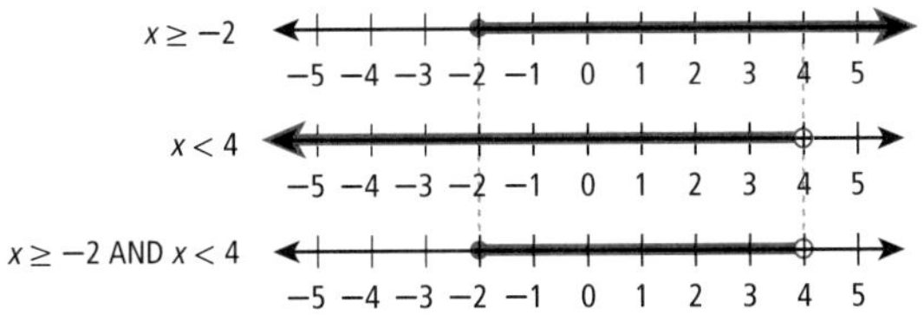

Thus, the solution set of the compound inequality $x \geq -2$ AND $x < 4$ is the *intersection* of the solution sets of $x \geq -2$ and $x < 4$. Graphically, this intersection is a line segment without one of its endpoints. Note that compound inequalities involving AND can often be written in a shorthand form: $-2 \leq x < 4$.

Now consider the compound inequality $x < -2$ OR $x \geq 4$. If a value of x is a solution of this compound inequality, the word OR means that x must be a solution of at least one of the two inequalities. Here the solution set is the *union* of the solution sets of $x < -2$ and $x \geq 4$. This is shown in the third number line below.

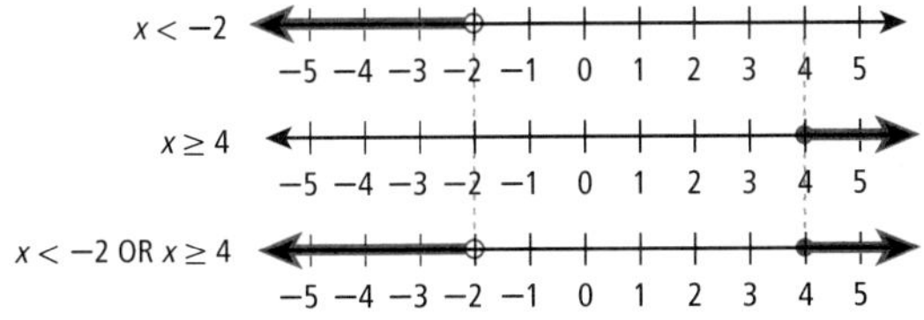

When working with compound inequalities that involve OR, students may be tempted to combine the two inequalities in a single statement, such as $-2 > x \geq 4$. This is a logical error. (For instance, the statement asserts that $-2 > 4$, which is false.) Many compound inequalities involving AND can be written in this shorthand form, but inequalities involving OR cannot.

ABSOLUTE-VALUE INEQUALITIES

Lesson 3-7

Absolute-value inequalities may be written using compound inequalities. Since the absolute value of x gives the distance of x from 0 on a number line, an inequality such as $|x| < 3$ represents all points less than 3 units from 0; that is, $x > -3$ AND $x < 3$, or $-3 < x < 3$. Similarly, $|x| > 3$ is the set of all points more than 3 units from 0, which is the compound inequality $x < -3$ OR $x > 3$.

One of the key ideas of Lesson 3-7 is that absolute-value inequalities may be used to express a range of values. The absolute value of $x - a$ gives the distance between x and a on a number line. Therefore, the absolute-value inequality $|x - a| < k$ states that the distance between x and a is less than k. In other words, the inequality represents the set of all values of x that are less than k units from a.

This idea is useful in a variety of real-world applications. For example, suppose that a machine is set to cut pieces of fabric that are 2 meters long. For quality-assurance purposes, the pieces of fabric may differ from this length by at most 3 millimeters or 0.003 meter. The range of acceptable lengths is expressed by the inequality $|x - 2| \leq 0.003$. That is, the distance on a number line from x to 2 is at most 0.003. Equivalently, the relationship can be expressed with the compound inequality $-0.003 \leq x - 2 \leq 0.003$. By the Addition Property of Inequality, it is permissible to add 2 to each part of the inequality, which gives the range of acceptable lengths as $1.997 \leq x \leq 2.003$.

3-4 Organizer

Pacing: Traditional 1 day
Block $\frac{1}{2}$ day

Objective: Solve inequalities that contain more than one operation.

Online Edition
Tutorial Videos

Countdown Week 6

Power Presentations with PowerPoint®

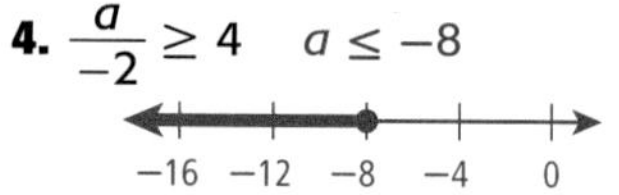

Warm Up

Solve each equation.

1. $2x - 5 = -17$ $\quad -6$
2. $\frac{2x - 4}{3} = 8$ $\quad 14$

Solve each inequality and graph the solutions.

3. $5 < t + 9$ $\quad t > -4$

−6 −5 −4 −3 −2 −1 0

4. $\frac{a}{-2} \geq 4$ $\quad a \leq -8$

−16 −12 −8 −4 0

Also available on transparency

Math Humor

Q: What did the doctor say to the multi-step inequality?

A: I can solve your problem with a few operations.

3-4 Solving Two-Step and Multi-Step Inequalities

Objective
Solve inequalities that contain more than one operation.

Who uses this?
Contestants at a county fair can solve an inequality to find how many pounds a prize-winning pumpkin must weigh. (See Example 3.)

At the county fair, contestants can enter contests that judge animals, recipes, crops, art projects, and more. Sometimes an average score or average weight is used to determine the winner of the blue ribbon. A contestant can use a multi-step inequality to determine what score or weight is needed in order to win.

Inequalities that contain more than one operation require more than one step to solve. Use inverse operations to undo the operations in the inequality one at a time.

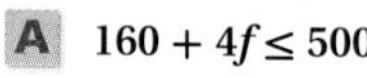

EXAMPLE 1 Solving Multi-Step Inequalities

Solve each inequality and graph the solutions.

A $160 + 4f \leq 500$

$$160 + 4f \leq 500$$
$$\underline{-160 \qquad -160}$$

Since 160 is added to 4f, subtract 160 from both sides to undo the addition.

$$4f \leq 340$$
$$\frac{4f}{4} \leq \frac{340}{4}$$

Since f is multiplied by 4, divide both sides by 4 to undo the multiplication.

$$f \leq 85$$

85
0 10 20 30 40 50 60 70 80 90 100

B $7 - 2t \leq 21$

$$7 - 2t \leq 21$$
$$\underline{-7 \qquad -7}$$

Since 7 is added to −2t, subtract 7 from both sides to undo the addition.

$$-2t \leq 14$$
$$\frac{-2t}{-2} \geq \frac{14}{-2}$$

Since t is multiplied by −2, divide both sides by −2 to undo the multiplication. Change ≤ to ≥.

$$t \geq -7$$

−7
−12 −10 −8 −6 −4 −2 0

CHECK IT OUT! Solve each inequality and graph the solutions.

1a. $-12 \geq 3x + 6$ $\quad x \leq -6$ **1b.** $\frac{x + 5}{-2} > 3$ $\quad x < -11$ **1c.** $\frac{1 - 2n}{3} \geq 7$ $\quad n \leq -10$

1a. −8 −6 −4 −2 0

1b. −13 −12 −11 −10 −9

1c. −12 −11 −10 −9 −8

State Resources

go.hrw.com
State Resources Online
KEYWORD: MA7 Resources

1 Introduce

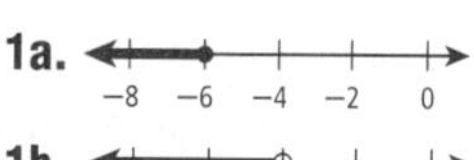

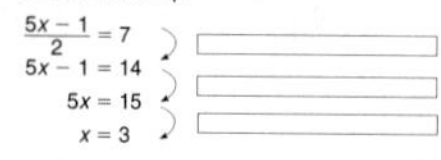

EXPLORATION

3-4 Solving Two-Step and Multi-Step Inequalities

Explore the similarities and differences between solving equations and inequalities.

1. Consider the following steps in solving the equation $\frac{5x-1}{2} = 7$. Fill in the rectangles to explain what was done at each step.

$\frac{5x-1}{2} = 7$
$5x - 1 = 14$
$5x = 15$
$x = 3$

2. Use the same steps to solve the inequality $\frac{5x-1}{2} > 7$.
3. How is the solution of the inequality $\frac{5x-1}{2} > 7$ different from the solution of the equation $\frac{5x-1}{2} = 7$?
4. What would you need to do differently if the inequality was $\frac{5x-1}{-2} > 7$?

THINK AND DISCUSS

5. **Explain** how solving an inequality is similar to solving an equation.
6. **Explain** how solving an inequality is different from solving an equation.

Motivate

An online movie-rental company has two movie-rental plans. Plan A costs \$10 per month plus \$3 for each movie rental. Plan B costs \$20 per month for unlimited movie rentals. Discuss with students how to determine the number of movie rentals in one month for which plan A is less than plan B.

Tell students that they could use a two-step inequality, which they will learn to solve in this lesson.

Explorations and answers are provided in *Alternate Openers: Explorations Transparencies.*

To solve more complicated inequalities, you may first need to simplify the expressions on one or both sides by using the order of operations, combining like terms, or using the Distributive Property.

EXAMPLE 2 Simplifying Before Solving Inequalities

Solve each inequality and graph the solutions.

A $-4 + (-8) < -5c - 2$

$-12 < -5c - 2$ — *Combine like terms. Since 2 is subtracted from −5c, add 2 to both sides to undo the subtraction.*

$\underline{+2 \quad\quad +2}$

$-10 < -5c$

$\frac{-10}{-5} > \frac{-5c}{-5}$ — *Since c is multiplied by −5, divide both sides by −5 to undo the multiplication. Change < to >.*

$2 > c \text{ (or } c < 2)$

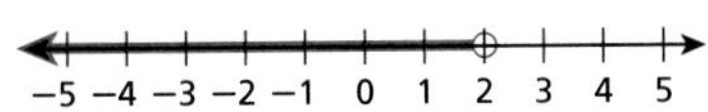

B $-3(3 - x) < 4^2$

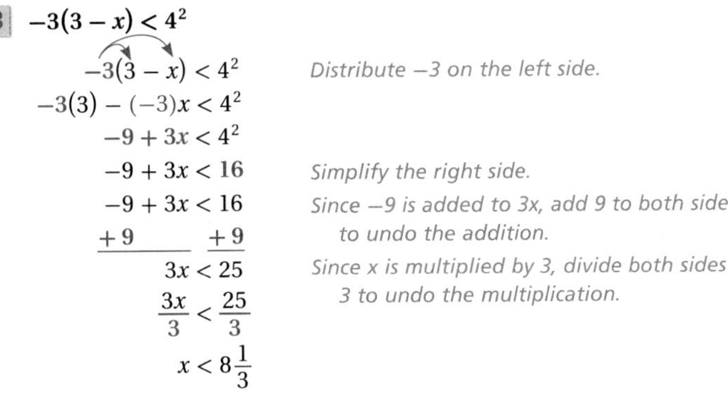

$-3(3 - x) < 4^2$ — *Distribute −3 on the left side.*

$-3(3) - (-3)x < 4^2$

$-9 + 3x < 4^2$

$-9 + 3x < 16$ — *Simplify the right side.*

$-9 + 3x < 16$ — *Since −9 is added to 3x, add 9 to both sides to undo the addition.*

$\underline{+9 \quad\quad +9}$

$3x < 25$ — *Since x is multiplied by 3, divide both sides by 3 to undo the multiplication.*

$\frac{3x}{3} < \frac{25}{3}$

$x < 8\frac{1}{3}$

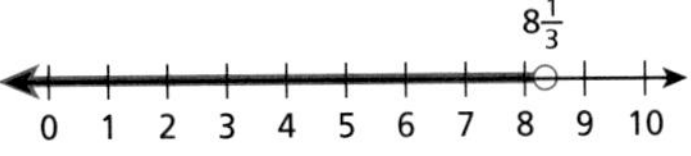

C $\frac{4}{5}x + \frac{1}{2} > \frac{3}{5}$

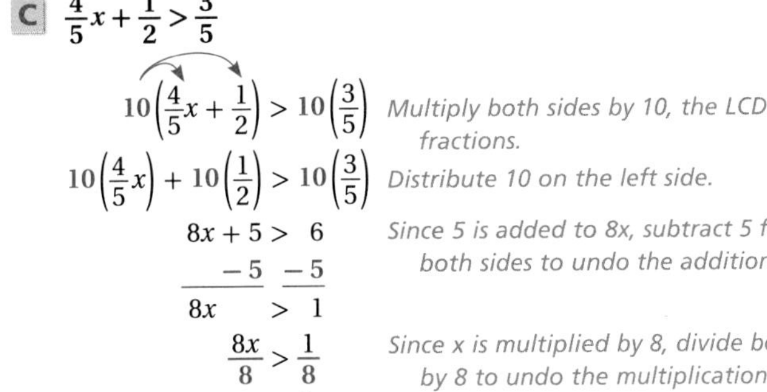

$10\left(\frac{4}{5}x + \frac{1}{2}\right) > 10\left(\frac{3}{5}\right)$ — *Multiply both sides by 10, the LCD of the fractions.*

$10\left(\frac{4}{5}x\right) + 10\left(\frac{1}{2}\right) > 10\left(\frac{3}{5}\right)$ — *Distribute 10 on the left side.*

$8x + 5 > 6$ — *Since 5 is added to 8x, subtract 5 from both sides to undo the addition.*

$\underline{-5 \quad -5}$

$8x > 1$

$\frac{8x}{8} > \frac{1}{8}$ — *Since x is multiplied by 8, divide both sides by 8 to undo the multiplication.*

$x > \frac{1}{8}$

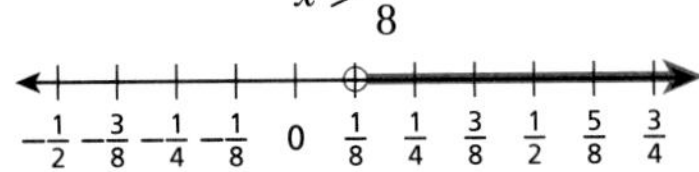

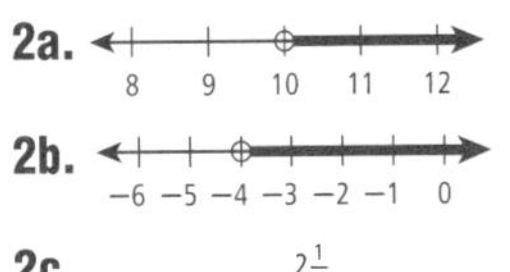

2c. $2\frac{1}{3}$ 0 1 2 3 4

CHECK IT OUT! Solve each inequality and graph the solutions.

2a. $2m + 5 > 5^2$ $m > 10$ **2b.** $3 + 2(x + 4) > 3$ $x > -4$ **2c.** $\frac{5}{8} < \frac{3}{8}x - \frac{1}{4}$ $x > 2\frac{1}{3}$

COMMON ERROR ALERT

When the variable is on the right side of the inequality, some students may have difficulty rewriting it with the variable on the left. For example, a student might rewrite $2 > c$ as $c > 2$. Suggest that they choose a number for c that makes the inequality true. If $2 > 1$, then $1 < 2$, so if $2 > c$, then $c < 2$.

Power Presentations with PowerPoint®

Additional Examples

Example 1

Solve each inequality and graph the solutions.

A. $45 + 2b > 61$ $b > 8$

0 4 8 12 16

B. $8 - 3y \geq 29$ $y \leq -7$

−8 −7 −6 −5 −4

Example 2

Solve each inequality and graph the solutions.

A. $2 - (-10) > -4t$ $t > -3$

−6 −5 −4 −3 −2 −1 0

B. $-4(2 - x) \leq 8$ $x \leq 4$

−2 0 2 4 6

C. $\frac{2}{3}f + \frac{1}{2} > \frac{1}{3}$ $f > -\frac{1}{4}$

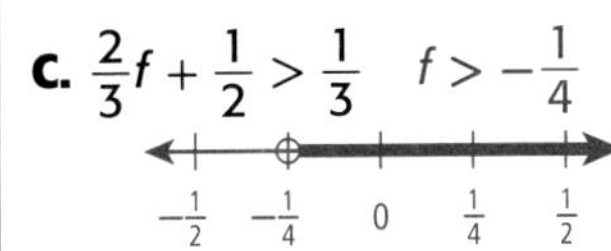

2 Teach

Guided Instruction

Review the properties of inequality and remind students that the inequality symbol must be reversed when multiplying or dividing both sides of an inequality by a negative number. Also remind students to check their solution by checking the endpoint and the inequality symbol.

Reaching All Learners

Through Visual Cues

Give students several multi-step inequalities. Ask students to identify the operations performed on the variable (in order). Ask students to identify the steps to solve the inequality (in order). They can make a chart, as shown below.

Inequality	Operations on Variable	Operations to Solve
$5 > \frac{3p + 2}{4}$	1. Multiply by 3.	3. Divide by 3.
	2. Add 2.	2. Subtract 2.
	3. Divide by 4.	1. Multiply by 4.

INTERVENTION

Questioning Strategies

EXAMPLE 1

- What operations would you use to solve the inequality? Why?

EXAMPLE 2

- What is the difference between simplifying and solving?

Power Presentations with PowerPoint®

Additional Examples

Example 3

To rent a certain vehicle, Rent-A-Ride charges $55.00 per day with unlimited miles. The cost of renting a similar vehicle at We Got Wheels is $38.00 per day plus $0.20 per mile. For what number of miles is the cost at Rent-A-Ride less than the cost at We Got Wheels? more than 85 miles

INTERVENTION

Questioning Strategies

EXAMPLE 3

- How do you know which inequality symbol to use?

EXAMPLE 3 Gardening Application

To win the blue ribbon for the Heaviest Pumpkin Crop at the county fair, the average weight of John's two pumpkins must be greater than 819 lb. One of his pumpkins weighs 887 lb. What is the least number of pounds the second pumpkin could weigh in order for John to win the blue ribbon?

Let p represent the weight of the second pumpkin. The average weight of the pumpkins is the sum of each weight divided by 2.

(887	plus	p)	divided by	2	must be greater than	819.
(887	+	p)	÷	2	>	819

$$\frac{887+p}{2} > 819$$ *Since 887 + p is divided by 2, multiply both sides by 2 to undo the division.*

$$2\left(\frac{887+p}{2}\right) > 2(819)$$

$$887 + p > 1638$$ *Since 887 is added to p, subtract 887 from both sides to undo the addition.*

$$\underline{-887 \qquad -887}$$

$$p > 751$$

The second pumpkin must weigh more than 751 pounds.

Check Check the endpoint, 751.

$$\frac{887+p}{2} = 819$$

$\frac{887+751}{2}$	819
$\frac{1638}{2}$	819
819	819 ✓

Check a number greater than 751.

$$\frac{887+p}{2} > 819$$

$\frac{887+755}{2}$	>	819
$\frac{1642}{2}$	>	819
821	>	819 ✓

3. The average of Jim's two test scores must be at least 90 to make an A in the class. Jim got a 95 on his first test. What scores can Jim get on his second test to make an A in the class?
Jim's score must be at least 85.

THINK AND DISCUSS

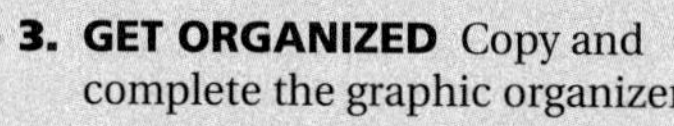

1. The inequality $v \geq 25$ states that 25 is the ___?___. (*value of v, minimum value of v,* or *maximum value of v*)
2. Describe two sets of steps for solving the inequality $\frac{x+5}{3} > 7$.
3. **GET ORGANIZED** Copy and complete the graphic organizer.

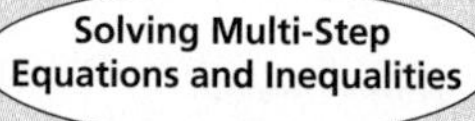

3 Close

Summarize

Have students solve and graph the following inequalities.

$8 - 3x < 20$ $x > -4$ (number line: −6 −5 −4 −3 −2)

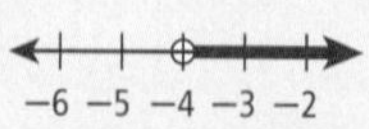

$5 - 13 \geq 16t$ $t \leq -\frac{1}{2}$ (number line: −2 $-1\frac{1}{2}$ −1 $-\frac{1}{2}$ 0)

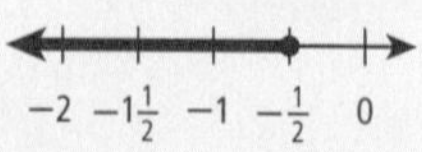

$-2(1 - y) < 4^2$ $y < 9$ (number line: 0 3 6 9 12)

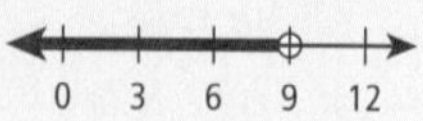

$\frac{1}{5}p - \frac{1}{3} > \frac{2}{3}$ $p > 5$ (number line: 2 3 4 5 6)

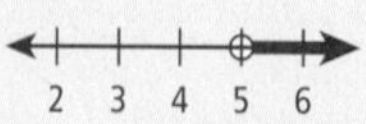

ONGOING ASSESSMENT and INTERVENTION

***Diagnose Before* the Lesson**
3-4 Warm Up, TE p. 190

***Monitor During* the Lesson**
Check It Out! Exercises, SE pp. 190–192
Questioning Strategies, TE pp. 190–192

***Assess After* the Lesson**
3-4 Lesson Quiz, TE p. 195
Alternative Assessment, TE p. 195

Answers to *Think and Discuss*

1. minimum value of v
2. 1. Multiply both sides by 3, and then subtract 5 from both sides.
   2. Rewrite the left side as $\frac{x}{3} + \frac{5}{3}$, subtract $\frac{5}{3}$ from both sides, and then multiply both sides by 3.
3. See p. A4.

3-4 Exercises

go.hrw.com
Homework Help Online
KEYWORD: MA7 3-4
Parent Resources Online
KEYWORD: MA7 Parent

GUIDED PRACTICE

Solve each inequality and graph the solutions.

SEE EXAMPLE 1 p. 190

1. $2m + 1 > 13$ 2. $2d + 21 \leq 11$ 3. $6 \leq -2x + 2$ 4. $4c - 7 > 5$

5. $\frac{4 + x}{3} > -4$ 6. $1 < 0.2x - 0.7$ 7. $\frac{3 - 2x}{3} \leq 7$ 8. $2x + 5 \geq 2$

SEE EXAMPLE 2 p. 191

9. $4(x + 2) > 6$ 10. $\frac{1}{4}x + \frac{2}{3} < \frac{3}{4}$ 11. $4 - x + 6^2 \geq 21$

12. $4 - x > 3(4 - 2)$ 13. $0.2(x - 10) > -1.8$ 14. $3(j + 41) \leq 35$

SEE EXAMPLE 3 p. 192

15. **Business** A sales representative is given a choice of two paycheck plans. One choice includes a monthly base pay of $300 plus 10% commission on his sales. The second choice is a monthly salary of $1200. For what amount of sales would the representative make more money with the first plan? **sales of more than $9000**

PRACTICE AND PROBLEM SOLVING

Independent Practice	
For Exercises	See Example
16–27	1
28–36	2
37	3

Extra Practice
Skills Practice p. S9
Application Practice p. S30

Solve each inequality and graph the solutions.

16. $4r - 9 > 7$ 17. $3 \leq 5 - 2x$ 18. $\frac{w + 3}{2} > 6$ 19. $11w + 99 < 77$

20. $9 \geq \frac{1}{2}v + 3$ 21. $-4x - 8 > 16$ 22. $8 - \frac{2}{3}z \leq 2$ 23. $f + 2\frac{1}{2} < -2$

24. $\frac{3n - 8}{5} \geq 2$ 25. $-5 > -5 - 3w$ 26. $10 > \frac{5 - 3p}{2}$ 27. $2v + 1 > 2\frac{1}{3}$

28. $4(x + 3) > -24$ 29. $4 > x - 3(x + 2)$ 30. $-18 \geq 33 - 3h$

31. $-2 > 7x - 2(x - 4)$ 32. $9 - (9)^2 > 10x - x$ 33. $2a - (-3)^2 \geq 13$

34. $6 - \frac{x}{3} + 1 > \frac{2}{3}$ 35. $12(x - 3) + 2x > 6$ 36. $15 \geq 19 + 2(q - 18)$

37. **Communications** One cell phone company offers a plan that costs $29.99 and includes unlimited night and weekend minutes. Another company offers a plan that costs $19.99 and charges $0.35 per minute during nights and weekends. For what numbers of night and weekend minutes does the second company's plan cost more than the first company's plan? **starting at 29 min**

Solve each inequality and graph the solutions.

38. $-12 > -4x - 8$ 39. $5x + 4 \leq 14$ 40. $\frac{2}{3}x - 5 > 7$

41. $x - 3x > 2 - 10$ 42. $5 - x - 2 > 3$ 43. $3 < 2x - 5(x + 3)$

44. $\frac{1}{6} - \frac{2}{3}m \geq \frac{1}{4}$ 45. $4 - (r - 2) > 3 - 5$ 46. $0.3 - 0.5n + 1 \geq 0.4$

47. $6^2 > 4(x + 2)$ 48. $-4 - 2n + 4n > 7 - 2^2$ 49. $\frac{1}{4}(p - 10) \geq 6 - 4$

50. Use the inequality $-4t - 8 \leq 12$ to fill in the missing numbers.
   a. $t \geq$ **−5** b. $t + 4 \geq$ **−1** c. $t -$ **5** ≥ 0
   d. $t + 10 \geq$ **5** e. $3t \geq$ **−15** f. $\frac{t}{\mathbf{1}} \geq -5$

Answers

4. $c > 3$
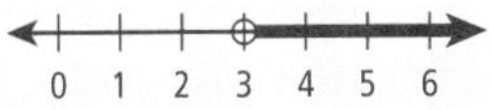

5. $x > -16$
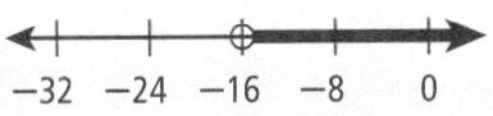

6. $x > 8.5$
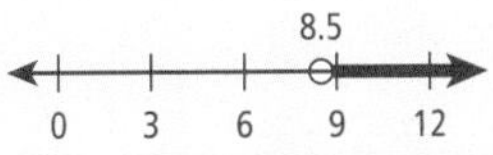

7. $x \geq -9$
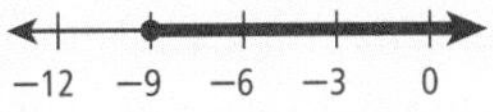

8. $x \geq -\frac{3}{2}$
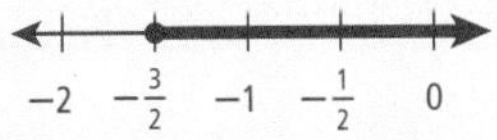

9. $x > -\frac{1}{2}$
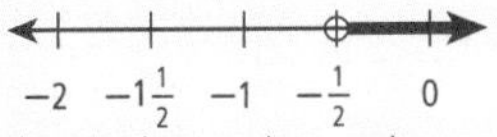

10. $x < \frac{1}{3}$
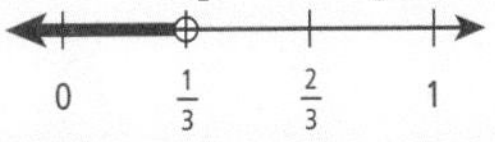

11. $x \leq 19$
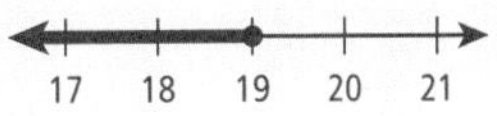

12. $x < -2$
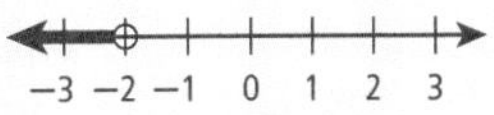

13. $x > 1$
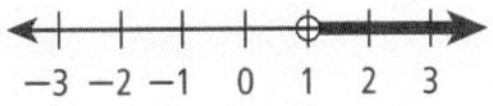

14. $j \leq -29\frac{1}{3}$
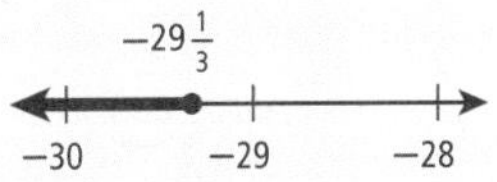

16–36, 38–49. See pp. A14–A15.

3-4 Exercises

Assignment Guide

Assign *Guided Practice* exercises as necessary.

If you finished Examples **1–2**
Basic 16–36, 38–49, 51–58
Average 16–36, 38–49, 50–54, 68–70
Advanced 16–36, 38–48 even, 50–54, 68–76

If you finished Examples **1–3**
Basic 16–49, 51–62, 64–67, 77–86
Average 16–37, 38–48 even, 50–70, 77–86
Advanced 16–26 even, 28–37, 38–48 even, 50–86

Homework Quick Check
Quickly check key concepts.
Exercises: 18, 32, 37, 46, 54, 60

Teaching Tip **Math Background** There is more than one way to solve problems with fractions. **Exercise 44** could be solved by subtracting $\frac{1}{6}$ from both sides and then multiplying both sides by $-\frac{3}{2}$, by subtracting $\frac{1}{6}$ from both sides and then dividing both sides by $-\frac{2}{3}$, or by multiplying both sides by the LCD and then solving.

Answers

1. $m > 6$
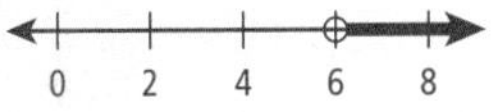

2. $d \leq -5$
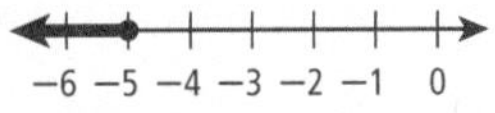

3. $x \leq -2$
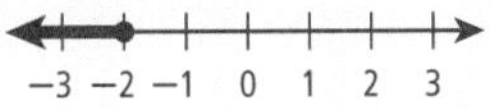

State Resources

go.hrw.com
State Resources Online
KEYWORD: MA7 Resources

Teaching Tip **Reading Math** In **Exercise 53,** students may incorrectly interpret the inequality as $4n + 12 \leq 16$. Remind students that the product of a sum requires parentheses.

Teaching Tip **Inclusion** In **Exercise 60,** students must write an inequality using the formula for the area of a triangle where the height is a sum, $\frac{1}{2}(5)(2x + 3) < 55$. Students may distribute 5 and $\frac{1}{2}$ before using inverse operations, or they may multiply both sides by $\frac{2}{5}$ before using inverse operations.

MULTI-STEP TEST PREP **Exercise 61** involves using an inequality to find the number of CDs a band can have made. This exercise prepares students for the Multi-Step Test Prep on page 218.

Answers

51. $\frac{1}{2}x + 9 < 33$; $x < 48$

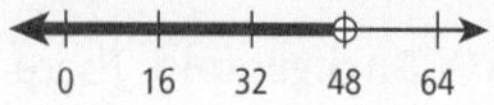

52. $6 \leq 4 - 2x$; $x \leq -1$

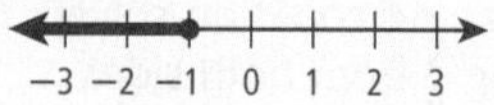

53. $4(x + 12) \leq 16$; $x \leq -8$

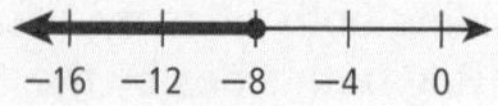

54. $\frac{1}{2}x + \frac{2}{3}x < 14$; $x < 12$

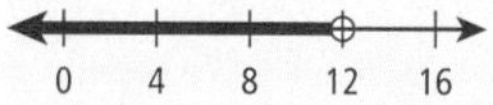

Write an inequality for each statement. Solve the inequality and graph the solutions.

51. One-half of a number, increased by 9, is less than 33.
52. Six is less than or equal to the sum of 4 and $-2x$.
53. The product of 4 and the sum of a number and 12 is at most 16.
54. The sum of half a number and two-thirds of the number is less than 14.

Solve each inequality and match the solution to the correct graph.

55. $4x - 9 \geq 7$ **$x \geq 4$; B**

A. 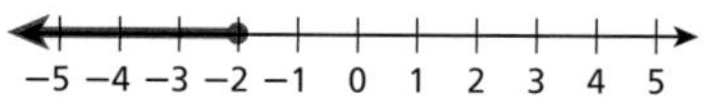

56. $-6 \geq 3(x - 2)$ **$x \leq 0$; D**

B. 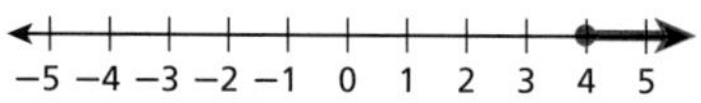

57. $-2x - 6 \geq -4 + 2$ **$x \leq -2$; A**

C. 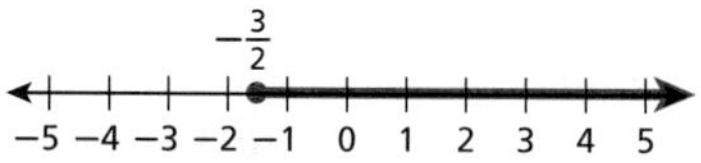

58. $\frac{1}{2} - \frac{1}{3}x \leq \left(\frac{2}{3} + \frac{1}{3}\right)^2$ **$x \geq -\frac{3}{2}$; C**

D. 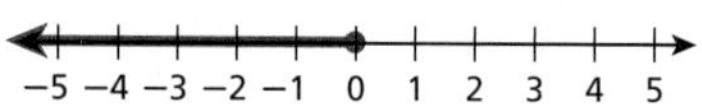

59. **Entertainment** A digital video recorder (DVR) records television shows on an internal hard drive. To use a DVR, you need a subscription with a DVR service company. Two companies advertise their charges for a DVR machine and subscription service.

For what numbers of months will a consumer pay less for the machine and subscription at Easy Electronics than at Cable Solutions? **24 months or more**

60. **Geometry** The area of the triangle shown is less than 55 square inches.
   a. Write an inequality that can be used to find x.
   b. Solve the inequality you wrote in part **a.** **$x < 9.5$**
   c. What is the maximum height of the triangle? **22 in.**

60a. $\frac{1}{2}(5)(2x + 3) < 55$

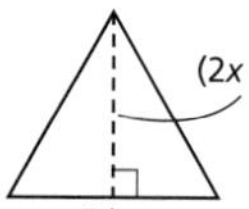

MULTI-STEP TEST PREP

61. This problem will prepare you for the Multi-Step Test Prep on page 218.
   a. A band wants to create a CD of their last concert. They received a donation of $500 to cover the cost. The total cost is $350 plus $3 per CD. Complete the table to find a relationship between the number of CDs and the total cost.

Number	Process	Cost
1	350 + 3	353
2	**350 + 3(2)**	**356**
3	**350 + 3(3)**	**359**
10	**350 + 3(10)**	**380**
n	**350 + 3(*n*)**	**350 + 3(*n*)**

   b. Write an equation for the cost c of the CDs based on the number of CDs n. **$c = 350 + 3n$**
   c. Write an inequality that can be used to determine how many CDs can be made with the $500 donation. Solve the inequality and determine how many CDs the band can have made from the $500 donation.
   $350 + 3n \leq 500$; $n \leq 50$; 50 CDs or fewer

3-4 PRACTICE A
3-4 PRACTICE C
3-4 PRACTICE B

Solve each inequality and graph the solutions.

1. $-3a + 10 < -11$
   $a > 7$
2. $4x - 12 \geq 20$
   $x \geq 8$
3. $\frac{2k - 3}{-5} > 7$
   $k < -16$
4. $-\frac{1}{5}z + \frac{2}{3} \leq 2$
   $z \geq -6\frac{2}{3}$
5. $6(n - 8) \geq -18$
   $n \geq 5$
6. $10 - 2(3x + 4) < 11$
   $x > -1\frac{1}{2}$
7. $7 + 2c - 4^2 \leq -9$
   $c \leq 0$
8. $15p + 3(p - 1) > 3(2^3)$
   $p > 1\frac{1}{2}$

Write and solve an inequality for each problem.

9. A full-year membership to a gym costs $325 upfront with no monthly charge. A monthly membership costs $100 upfront and $30 per month. For what numbers of months is it less expensive to have a monthly membership?
   $30m + 100 < 325$; $m < 7.5$; 1, 2, 3, 4, 5, 6, or 7 months
10. The sum of the lengths of any two sides of a triangle must be greater than the length of the third side. What are the possible values of x for this triangle? (3x) cm, (x + 5) cm, 40 cm
   $x + 5 + 3x > 40$; $x > 8.75$

3-4 READING STRATEGIES

The chart below summarizes the similarities and differences between multi-step equations and multi-step inequalities when there is a variable on one side.

MULTI-STEP EQUATION Ex: $3x + 4 = 19$	Contrast	MULTI-STEP INEQUALITY Ex: $3x + 4 > 19$
1	Number of solutions	infinitely many
$x = 5$	Way solution is shown	$x > 5$
always remains =	Symbol	reverses when × or ÷ by a negative

Compare

First step in solving both is using the Distributive Property, when possible.

For both, use inverse operations to isolate the variable.

Answer each question.

1. Why are solutions to inequalities graphed on number lines?
   to show the infinitely many solutions
2. Show what the solution $x = 5$ looks like when graphed on a number line.
3. What one value is the solution to the equation $3(x + 4) = 9$? −1
4. List five values that are solutions to the inequality $3(x + 4) < 9$. Possible Answer: −2, −3, −4, −5, −6
5. Do $-2x + 3 = 7$ and $-2x + 3 \geq 7$ have any solutions in common? yes
   If so, what? −2

3-4 RETEACH

When solving inequalities with more than one step, use inverse operations to isolate the variable. The order of the inverse operations is the order of the operations in reverse. You can check your solution by substituting the endpoint and another point in the solution back into the original inequality.

Solve $-5x + 3 < 23$ and graph the solutions.

$-5x + 3 < 23$
$-3 \quad -3$
$-5x < 20$ *Add −3 to each side.*
$\frac{-5x}{-5} < \frac{20}{-5}$ *Divide both sides by −5.*
$x > -4$ *Reverse the inequality sign.*

Check:

Try −4.	Try 6.
$-5x + 3 < 23$	$-5x + 3 < 23$
$-5(-4) + 3 \overset{?}{<} 23$	$-5(6) + 3 \overset{?}{<} 23$
$20 + 3 \overset{?}{<} 23$	$-30 + 3 \overset{?}{<} 23$
$23 \overset{?}{<} 23$ ✗	$-27 \overset{?}{<} 23$ ✓

The endpoint −4 is not a solution. The open circle on the graph is correct. The value 6 is a solution. The direction of the inequality symbol is correct.

Solve each inequality and graph the solutions.

1. $-3e - 10 \leq -4$
   $e \geq -2$
2. $\frac{c}{2} + 8 > 11$
   $c > 6$
3. $15 \leq 3 - 4s$
   $s \leq -3$
4. $\frac{3}{4}j + 1 > 4$
   $j > 4$

62. **Critical Thinking** What is the least whole number that is a solution of $4r - 4.9 > 14.95$? **$r = 5$**

63. **Write About It** Describe two sets of steps to solve $2(x + 3) > 10$.
1. Divide both sides by 2, and then subtract 3 from both sides.
2. Distribute 2 on the left side, subtract 6 from both sides, and then divide both sides by 2.

TEST PREP

64. What are the solutions of $3y > 2x + 4$ when $y = 6$?
   (A) $7 > x$ (B) $x > 7$ (C) $x > 11$ (D) $11 > x$

65. Cecilia has $30 to spend at a carnival. Admission costs $5.00, lunch will cost $6.00, and each ride ticket costs $1.25. Which inequality represents the number of ride tickets x that Cecilia can buy?
   (F) $30 - (5 - 6) + 1.25x \le 30$
   (G) $5 + 6 + 1.25x \le 30$
   (H) $30 - (5 + 6) \le 1.25x$
   (J) $30 + 1.25x \le 5 + 6$

66. Which statement is modeled by $2p + 5 < 11$?
   (A) The sum of 5 and 2 times p is at least 11.
   (B) Five added to the product of 2 and p is less than 11.
   (C) Two times p plus 5 is at most 11.
   (D) The product of 2 and p added to 5 is 11.

67. **Gridded Response** A basketball team scored 8 points more in its second game than in its first. In its third game, the team scored 42 points. The total number of points scored in the three games was more than 150. What is the least number of points the team might have scored in its *second* game? **59**

CHALLENGE AND EXTEND

Solve each inequality and graph the solutions.

68. $3(x + 2) - 6x + 6 \le 0$ **$x \ge 4$**
69. $-18 > -(2x + 9) - 4 + x$ **$x > 5$**
70. $\frac{2 + x}{2} - (x - 1) > 1$ **$x < 2$**

Write an inequality for each statement. Graph the solutions.

71. x is a positive number. **$x > 0$**
72. x is a negative number. **$x < 0$**
73. x is a nonnegative number. **$x \ge 0$**
74. x is not a positive number. **$x \le 0$**
75. x times negative 3 is positive. **$-3x > 0$**
76. The opposite of x is greater than 2. **$-x > 2$**

SPIRAL REVIEW

Find each root. *(Lesson 1-5)*

77. $\sqrt{49}$ **7**
78. $-\sqrt{144}$ **−12**
79. $\sqrt{\frac{4}{9}}$ **$\frac{2}{3}$**
80. $\sqrt{196}$ **14**
81. $\sqrt[3]{-729}$ **−9**
82. $\sqrt{10{,}000}$ **100**

83. Video rental store A charges a membership fee of $25 and $2 for each movie rental. Video rental store B charges a membership fee of $10 and $2.50 for each movie. Find the number of movie rentals for which both stores' charges are the same. *(Lesson 2-4)* **30 movies**

Solve each inequality and graph the solutions. *(Lesson 3-3)*

84. $2x < -8$ **$x < -4$**
85. $\frac{a}{-2} \le -3$ **$a \ge 6$**
86. $\frac{1}{4} < \frac{t}{12}$ **$t > 3$**

TEST PREP DOCTOR + For **Exercise 66,** the verbal translation for the left side of the inequality is correct for all four choices. Choice **D** can be eliminated because *is* means "equal." "At least" and "at most" both indicate or-equal-to symbols.

Answers

68–76, 84–86. For graphs, see p. A15.

Journal

Write about the differences and similarities in solving a multi-step inequality and a multi-step equation. Include a comparison of the solutions and the methods of checking the solutions.

ALTERNATIVE ASSESSMENT

Instruct students to write a real-world problem that can be modeled by an inequality that requires at least two steps to solve. Ask students to solve the inequality explaining each step. Students should explain the meaning of the solution in the context of the problem.

Power Presentations with PowerPoint®

3-4 Lesson Quiz

Solve each inequality and graph the solutions.

1. $13 - 2x \ge 21$ $x \le -4$
   −6 −5 −4 −3 −2 −1 0
2. $-11 + 2 < 3p$ $p > -3$
   −6 −5 −4 −3 −2 −1 0
3. $2^3 < -2(3 - t)$ $t > 7$
   4 5 6 7 8
4. $\frac{1}{3}n + \frac{1}{2} < \frac{2}{3}$ $n < \frac{1}{2}$
   −1 $-\frac{1}{2}$ 0 $\frac{1}{2}$ 1
5. A video store has two movie-rental plans. Plan A includes a $25 membership fee plus $1.25 for each movie rental. Plan B costs $40 for unlimited movie rentals. For what number of movie rentals is plan B less than plan A?
   more than 12 movies

Also available on transparency

3-4 PROBLEM SOLVING

Write and solve an inequality for each situation.

1. Jillene is playing in a basketball tournament and scored 24 points in her first game. If she averages over 20 points for both games, she will receive a trophy. How many points can Jillene score in the second game and receive a trophy?
   $\frac{p + 24}{2} > 20$; $p > 16$
2. Marcus has accepted a job selling cell phones. He will be paid $1500 plus 15% of his sales each month. He needs to earn at least $2430 to pay his bills. For what amount of sales will Marcus be able to pay his bills?
   $1500 + 0.15s \ge 2430$; $s \ge 6200$
3. A 15-foot-tall cedar tree is growing at a rate of 2 feet per year beneath power lines that are 58 feet above the ground. The power company will have to prune or remove the tree before it reaches the lines. How many years can the power company wait before taking action?
   $15 + 2y < 58$; $y < 21.5$
4. Binh brought $23 with her to the county fair. She purchased a $5 T-shirt and now wants to buy some locally grown plants for $2.50 each. What are the numbers of plants that she can purchase with her remaining money?
   $5 + 2.5p \le 23$; $p \le 7.2$; 0, 1, 2, 3, 4, 5, 6, or 7 plants

Benedict, Ricardo, and Charlie are considering opportunities for summer work. The table below shows the jobs open to them and the pay for each. Use this information to answer questions 5–7.

Job	Pay
Mowing Lawns	$15 per lawn
Baby-Sitting	$5.50 per hour
Tutoring	$9 per session

5. Benedict has saved $91 from last year and would like to baby-sit to earn enough to buy a mountain bike. A good quality bike costs at least $300. What numbers of hours h can Benedict baby-sit to reach his goal?
   A $h \ge 14$ **C** $h \ge 38$
   B $h \ge 23$ D $h \ge 71$
6. Ricardo has agreed to tutor for the school. He owes his older brother $59 and would like to end the summer with at least $400 in savings. How many sessions s can Ricardo tutor to meet his goal?
   F $s \ge 31$ **H** $s \ge 51$
   G $s \ge 38$ J $s \ge 83$
7. Charlie has agreed to mow his neighbor's lawn each week and will also baby-sit some hours. If he makes $100 or more each week, his parents will charge him rent. How many hours h should Charlie agree to baby-sit each week to avoid paying rent?
   A $h \le 15$ C $h \le 21$
   B $h \ge 15$ D $h \ge 21$

3-4 CHALLENGE

As you have already seen, when you solve a linear equation, you find a definite value. If the variable is equal to 3, then the number line is divided into three parts: the number 3, those numbers greater than 3, and those numbers less than 3. When you deal with multiple inequalities, you divide the number line into even more parts.

In Exercises 1–3, use the number line below.

−4 −3 −2 −1 0 1 2 3 4 5 6 7 8 9 10 x

1. Draw a graph showing the solutions to $x \ge 3$ and $x < 7$.
   −4 −3 −2 −1 0 1 2 3 4 5 6 7 8 9 10 x
2. What integers satisfy both of these inequalities? **3, 4, 5, 6**
3. What inequalities describe your response in Exercise 2?
   $x \ge 3$ and $x \le 6$ where x is an integer.

On a certain freeway, the minimum allowable speed is 40 miles per hour, and the maximum allowable speed is 55 miles per hour.

Use the information above to answer Exercises 4–6.

4. Write an inequality for each driving situation.
   a. A motorist is driving too fast. **$x > 55$**
   b. A motorist is driving too slow. **$x > 0$ and $x < 40$**
5. Is it technically correct to say that the speed limit is exactly 55 miles per hour?
   No, since there is a lower limit as well as an upper limit
6. Write multiple inequalities for each situation.
   a. The driver's speed is within the speed limits. **$x \ge 40$ and $x \le 55$**
   b. The driver's speed is outside of the speed limits. **$x > 0$ and $x < 40$ or $x > 55$**

People use multiple inequalities when they deal with real-estate situations.

7. John and Marsha would like to buy a house priced at $185,000, plus or minus $5,000.
   a. What are the maximum and minimum house price that they are willing to pay? **maximum: $190,000; minimum: $180,000**
   b. Write a pair of inequalities describing their price range.
   $x \ge \$180{,}000$ and $x \le \$190{,}000$
8. Use inequalities to describe the following sentence: "We sell houses priced at $80,000, plus or minus $5,000, to houses priced at $250,000, plus or minus $5,000."
   $x \ge \$75{,}000$ and $x \le \$255{,}000$

3-5 Organizer

Pacing: Traditional 1 day
Block $\frac{1}{2}$ day

Objective: Solve inequalities that contain variable terms on both sides.

Algebra Lab
In *Algebra Lab Activities*

Technology Lab
In *Technology Lab Activities*

Online Edition
Tutorial Videos

Countdown Week 6

Power Presentations with PowerPoint®

Warm Up

Solve each equation.

1. $2x = 7x + 15$ $\quad x = -3$
2. $3y - 21 = 4 - 2y$ $\quad y = 5$
3. $2(3z + 1) = -2(z + 3)$
   $z = -1$
4. $3(p - 1) = 3p + 2$
   no solution
5. Solve and graph $5(2 - b) > 5^2$. $\quad b < -3$

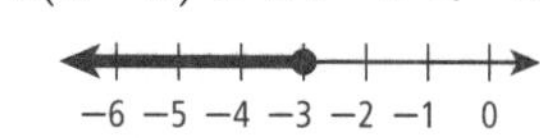

Also available on transparency

Math Humor

Q: What did Miss Manners say to the inequality symbol?
A: It's not polite to point.

State Resources

3-5 Solving Inequalities with Variables on Both Sides

Objective
Solve inequalities that contain variable terms on both sides.

Who uses this?
Business owners can use inequalities to find the most cost-efficient services. (See Example 2.)

Some inequalities have variable terms on both sides of the inequality symbol. You can solve these inequalities like you solved equations with variables on both sides.

Use the properties of inequality to "collect" all the variable terms on one side and all the constant terms on the other side.

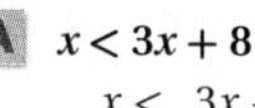

Helpful Hint

Your first step can also be to subtract $3x$ from both sides to get $-2x < 8$. When you divide by a negative number, remember to reverse the inequality symbol.

EXAMPLE 1 Solving Inequalities with Variables on Both Sides

Solve each inequality and graph the solutions.

A $x < 3x + 8$

$$\begin{aligned} x &< 3x + 8 \\ -x &\quad\; -x \\ \hline 0 &< 2x + 8 \\ -8 &\quad\;\; -8 \\ \hline -8 &< 2x \\ \frac{-8}{2} &< \frac{2x}{2} \\ -4 &< x \text{ (or } x > -4) \end{aligned}$$

To collect the variable terms on one side, subtract x from both sides.

Since 8 is added to 2x, subtract 8 from both sides to undo the addition.

Since x is multiplied by 2, divide both sides by 2 to undo the multiplication.

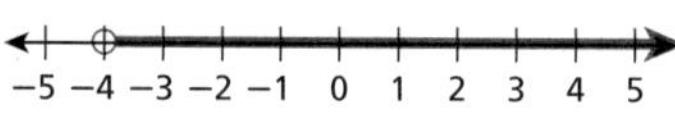

B $6x - 1 \le 3.5x + 4$

$$\begin{aligned} 6x - 1 &\le 3.5x + 4 \\ -6x \quad &\quad -6x \\ \hline -1 &\le -2.5x + 4 \\ -4 &\quad\quad\;\; -4 \\ \hline -5 &\le -2.5x \\ \frac{-5}{-2.5} &\ge \frac{-2.5x}{-2.5} \\ 2 &\ge x \end{aligned}$$

Subtract 6x from both sides.

Since 4 is added to −2.5x, subtract 4 from both sides to undo the addition.

Since x is multiplied by −2.5, divide both sides by−2.5 to undo the multiplication. Reverse the inequality symbol.

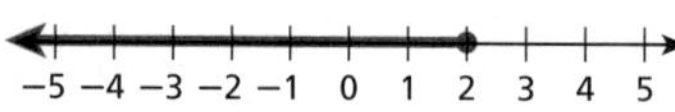

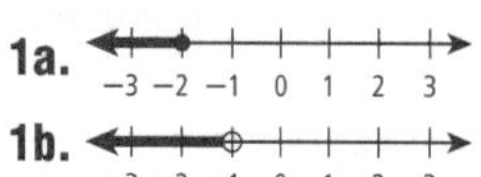

Solve each inequality and graph the solutions.

1a. $4x \ge 7x + 6$ $\quad x \le -2$ **1b.** $5t + 1 < -2t - 6$ $\quad t < -1$

1 Introduce

EXPLORATION

3-5 Solving Inequalities with Variables on Both Sides

Using a graphing calculator, follow the steps below to explore the inequality $5x < 2x + 9$.

1. Press [Y=]. Enter **5X** for **Y1** and **2X + 9** for **Y2**.
2. Press [2nd] [GRAPH]. Use the arrow keys to scroll up and down the table. For which values of x is **Y1** less than **Y2**?
3. Substitute several of the x-values from step 2 in the inequality $5x < 2x + 9$. Are they solutions of the inequality?
4. What are the solutions of $5x < 2x + 9$? Graph the solutions on a number line.

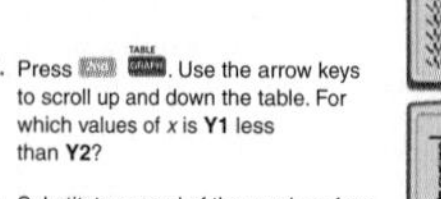

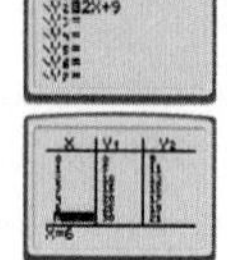

THINK AND DISCUSS

5. **Discuss** whether the table shows *all* solutions of $5x < 2x + 9$.
6. **Explain** how you could use a calculator to find solutions of the inequality $7x - 1 \ge 2x + 9$.

Motivate

Present two ski-ticket plans to students. Plan A costs $45 per day and includes equipment and the lift ticket; plan B costs $350 for the season and includes equipment but not the $20 lift ticket. Discuss with students how to determine the number of days for which plan A costs less than plan B. $45x < 350 + 20x$ Tell students that they could use an inequality with variables on both sides, which they will learn to solve in this lesson.

Explorations and answers are provided in *Alternate Openers: Explorations Transparencies*.

EXAMPLE 2 Business Application

The *Daily Info* charges a fee of \$650 plus \$80 per week to run an ad. The *People's Paper* charges \$145 per week. For how many weeks will the total cost at *Daily Info* be less expensive than the cost at *People's Paper*?

Let w be the number of weeks the ad runs in the paper.

Daily Info fee	plus	\$80 per week	times	number of weeks	is less expensive than	*People's Paper* charge per week	times	number of weeks.
\$650	+	\$80	•	w	<	\$145	•	w

$650 + 80w < 145w$

$-80w \quad -80w$ — *Subtract 80w from both sides.*

$650 < 65w$ — *Since w is multiplied by 65, divide both sides by 65 to undo the multiplication.*

$\frac{650}{65} < \frac{65w}{65}$

$10 < w$

The total cost at *Daily Info* is less than the cost at *People's Paper* if the ad runs for more than 10 weeks.

2. A-Plus Advertising charges a fee of \$24 plus \$0.10 per flyer to print and deliver flyers. Print and More charges \$0.25 per flyer. For how many flyers is the cost at A-Plus Advertising less than the cost at Print and More? **more than 160 flyers**

You may need to simplify one or both sides of an inequality before solving it. Look for like terms to combine and places to use Distributive Property.

EXAMPLE 3 Simplifying Each Side Before Solving

Solve each inequality and graph the solutions.

A $6(1 - x) < 3x$

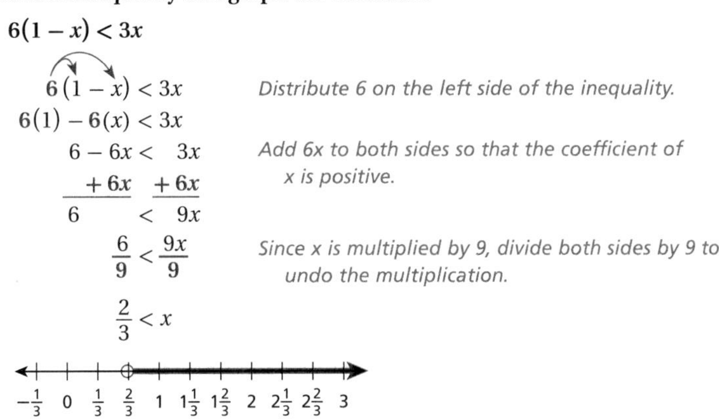

$6(1 - x) < 3x$ — *Distribute 6 on the left side of the inequality.*

$6(1) - 6(x) < 3x$

$6 - 6x < 3x$ — *Add 6x to both sides so that the coefficient of x is positive.*

$+6x \quad +6x$

$6 < 9x$

$\frac{6}{9} < \frac{9x}{9}$ — *Since x is multiplied by 9, divide both sides by 9 to undo the multiplication.*

$\frac{2}{3} < x$

Power Presentations with PowerPoint®

Additional Examples

Example 1

Solve each inequality and graph the solutions.

A. $y \le 4y + 18$ $y \ge -6$

−8 −6 −4 −2 0

B. $4m - 3 < 2m + 6$ $m < \frac{9}{2}$

$\frac{8}{2}$ $\frac{9}{2}$ $\frac{10}{2}$ $\frac{11}{2}$ $\frac{12}{2}$

Example 2

The Home Cleaning Company charges \$312 to power-wash the siding of a house plus \$12 for each window. Power Clean charges \$36 per window, and the price includes power-washing the siding. How many windows must a house have to make the total cost from The Home Cleaning Company less expensive than Power Clean?

more than 13 windows

Example 3

Solve each inequality and graph the solutions.

A. $2(k - 3) > 6 + 3k - 3$

$k < -9$

−12 −9 −6 −3 0

B. $0.9y \ge 0.4y - 0.5$ $y \ge -1$

−3 −2 −1 0 1 2 3

2 Teach

Guided Instruction

Before solving inequalities with variables on both sides, review the steps used to solve equations with variables on both sides.

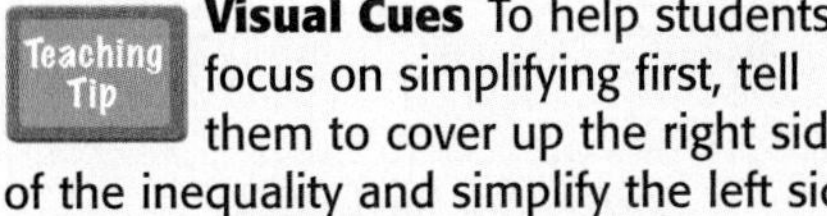

Teaching Tip **Visual Cues** To help students focus on simplifying first, tell them to cover up the right side of the inequality and simplify the left side. Then cover the left side and simplify the right side.

Reaching All Learners

Through Communication

Give students one inequality at a time. For each, ask the following questions.

- On which side of the inequality would you gather the variable terms? Why?
- Would the inequality symbol need to be reversed?

Example: $3x + 1 < 4x$

Possible answers: right, to keep the variable positive; not unless you rewrite the solutions of the inequality with the variable on the left

INTERVENTION

Questioning Strategies

EXAMPLE 1

- How do you decide on which side of the inequality to gather the variable terms?

EXAMPLE 2

- How do you know which inequality symbol to use?

EXAMPLE 3

- How can you tell when an expression is simplified?

Power Presentations with PowerPoint®

Additional Examples

Example 4

Solve each inequality.

A. $2x - 7 \le 5 + 2x$
all real numbers

B. $2(3y - 2) - 4 \ge 3(2y + 7)$
no solutions

INTERVENTION

Questioning Strategies

EXAMPLE 4

- How can you tell whether the solution of an inequality is *all real numbers* or whether the inequality has *no solutions*?

In Example 3B, you can also multiply each term in the inequality by the same power of 10 to clear the decimals.
$10(1.6x) \le 10(-0.2x) + 10(0.9)$
$16x \le -2x + 9$

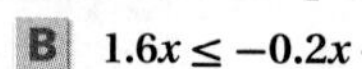

Solve each inequality and graph the solutions.

B $1.6x \le -0.2x + 0.9$

$1.6x \le -0.2x + 0.9$
$\underline{+0.2x \quad +0.2x}$ *Since −0.2x is added to 0.9, subtract −0.2x from both sides. Subtracting −0.2x is the same as adding 0.2x.*
$1.8x \le 0.9$
$\frac{1.8x}{1.8} \le \frac{0.9}{1.8}$ *Since x is multiplied by 1.8, divide both sides by 1.8 to undo the multiplication.*
$x \le \frac{1}{2}$

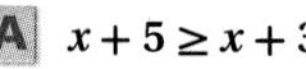

CHECK IT OUT! **Solve each inequality and graph the solutions. Check your answer.**

3a. $5(2 - r) \ge 3(r - 2)$ $r \le 2$ **3b.** $0.5x - 0.3 + 1.9x < 0.3x + 6$ $x < 3$

Some inequalities are true no matter what value is substituted for the variable. For these inequalities, all real numbers are solutions.

Some inequalities are false no matter what value is substituted for the variable. These inequalities have no solutions.

If both sides of an inequality are fully simplified and the same variable term appears on both sides, then the inequality has all real numbers as solutions or it has no solutions. Look at the other terms in the inequality to decide which is the case.

EXAMPLE 4 All Real Numbers as Solutions or No Solutions

Solve each inequality.

A $x + 5 \ge x + 3$

$x + 5 \ge x + 3$

The same variable term (x) appears on both sides. Look at the other terms.

For any number x, adding 5 will always result in a greater number than adding 3.

All values of x make the inequality true.
All real numbers are solutions.

B $2(x + 3) < 5 + 2x$

$2x + 6 < 5 + 2x$ *Distribute 2 on the left side.*

The same variable term ($2x$) appears on both sides. Look at the other terms.

For any number $2x$, adding 6 will never result in a lesser number than adding 5.

No values of x make the inequality true.
There are no solutions.

CHECK IT OUT! **Solve each inequality.**

4a. $4(y - 1) \ge 4y + 2$ no solutions **4b.** $x - 2 < x + 1$ all real numbers

3 Close

Summarize

Have students solve the following and explain each step.

$a + 8 > 3a$ $a < 4$

$2(x - 3) > x - 5^2$ $x > -19$

$4(1 - t) < -2(2t + 3)$ no solutions

ONGOING ASSESSMENT

and INTERVENTION

***Diagnose Before* the Lesson**
3-5 Warm Up, TE p. 196

***Monitor During* the Lesson**
Check It Out! Exercises, SE pp. 196–198
Questioning Strategies, TE pp. 197–198

***Assess After* the Lesson**
3-5 Lesson Quiz, TE p. 202
Alternative Assessment, TE p. 202

THINK AND DISCUSS

1. Explain how you would collect the variable terms to solve the inequality $5c - 4 > 8c + 2$.
2. **GET ORGANIZED** Copy and complete the graphic organizer. In each box, give an example of an inequality of the indicated type.

Answers to *Think and Discuss*

1. Possible answer: Subtract 5*c* from both sides of the inequality so that all variable terms are on the right side. Then subtract 2 from both sides so that all constant terms are on the left side.
2. See p. A4.

3-5 Exercises

go.hrw.com
Homework Help Online KEYWORD: MA7 3-5
Parent Resources Online KEYWORD: MA7 Parent

GUIDED PRACTICE

SEE EXAMPLE 1 p. 196

Solve each inequality and graph the solutions.

1. $2x > 4x - 6$ **$x < 3$**
2. $7y + 1 \leq y - 5$ **$y \leq -1$**
3. $27x + 33 > 58x - 29$ **$x < 2$**
4. $-3r < 10 - r$ **$r > -5$**
5. $5c - 4 > 8c + 2$ **$c < -2$**
6. $4.5x - 3.8 \geq 1.5x - 2.3$ **$x \geq \frac{1}{2}$**

SEE EXAMPLE 2 p. 197

7. **School** The school band will sell pizzas to raise money for new uniforms. The supplier charges \$100 plus \$4 per pizza. If the band members sell the pizzas for \$7 each, how many pizzas will they have to sell to make a profit? **at least 34 pizzas**

SEE EXAMPLE 3 p. 197

Solve each inequality and graph the solutions.

8. $5(4 + x) \leq 3(2 + x)$ **$x \leq -7$**
9. $-4(3 - p) > 5(p + 1)$ **$p < -17$**
10. $2(6 - x) < 4x$ **$x > 2$**
11. $4x > 3(7 - x)$ **$x > 3$**
12. $\frac{1}{2}f + \frac{3}{4} \geq \frac{1}{4}f$ **$f \geq -3$**
13. $-36.72 + 5.65t < 0.25t$ **$t < 6.8$**

SEE EXAMPLE 4 p. 198

Solve each inequality.

14. $2(x - 2) \leq -2(1 - x)$ **all real numbers**
15. $4(y + 1) < 4y + 2$ **no solutions**
16. $4v + 1 < 4v - 7$ **no solutions**
17. $b - 4 \geq b - 6$ **all real numbers**
18. $3(x - 5) > 3x$ **no solutions**
19. $2k + 7 \geq 2(k + 14)$ **no solutions**

PRACTICE AND PROBLEM SOLVING

Solve each inequality and graph the solutions.

20. $3x \leq 5x + 8$ **$x \geq -4$**
21. $9y + 3 > 4y - 7$ **$y > -2$**
22. $1.5x - 1.2 < 3.1x - 2.8$ **$x > 1$**
23. $7 + 4b \geq 3b$ **$b \geq -7$**
24. $7 - 5t < 4t - 2$ **$t > 1$**
25. $2.8m - 5.2 > 0.8m + 4.8$ **$m > 5$**
26. **Geometry** For what values of x is the area of the rectangle greater than the area of the triangle? **$x > 8$**

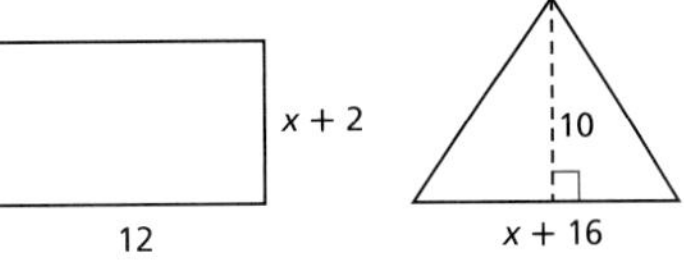

Assignment Guide

Assign *Guided Practice* exercises as necessary.

If you finished Examples **1–2**
Basic 20–26, 39–42, 44, 49, 52–56, 60
Average 20–26, 42, 44, 49, 52–56, 66
Advanced 20–26, 42, 44, 49, 52–56, 66

If you finished Examples **1–4**
Basic 20–49, 51–58, 60–65, 73–76
Average 20–38, 40–48 even, 49–51, 56–66, 73–76
Advanced 24, 26, 27–38, 40–48 even, 49–51, 56–59, 61–76

Homework Quick Check
Quickly check key concepts.
Exercises: 24, 26, 28, 38, 40, 44

Answers

1. 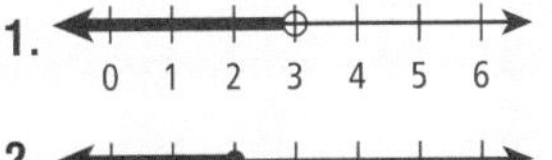

2. −3 −2 −1 0 1 2 3

3. 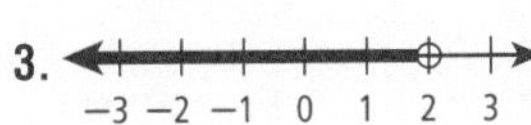

4. 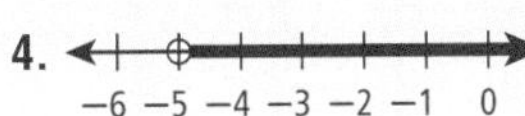

5. −3 −2 −1 0 1 2 3

6. 0 $\frac{1}{2}$ 1 $1\frac{1}{2}$ 2

8. 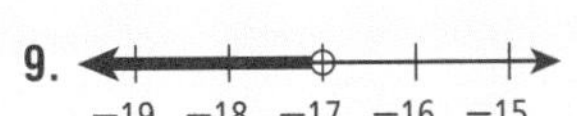

9. −19 −18 −17 −16 −15

10. −3 −2 −1 0 1 2 3

11. 0 1 2 3 4 5 6

12. −6 −5 −4 −3 −2 −1 0

13. 6 6.2 6.4 6.6 6.8

20. −6 −5 −4 −3 −2 −1 0

21. −3 −2 −1 0 1 2 3

22. −3 −2 −1 0 1 2 3

23. −9 −8 −7 −6 −5

24. −3 −2 −1 0 1 2 3

25. 0 1 2 3 4 5 6

MULTI-STEP TEST PREP Exercise 51 requires writing and solving multi-step inequalities in order to solve problems relating cost and profit. This exercise prepares students for the Multi-Step Test Prep on page 218.

Answers

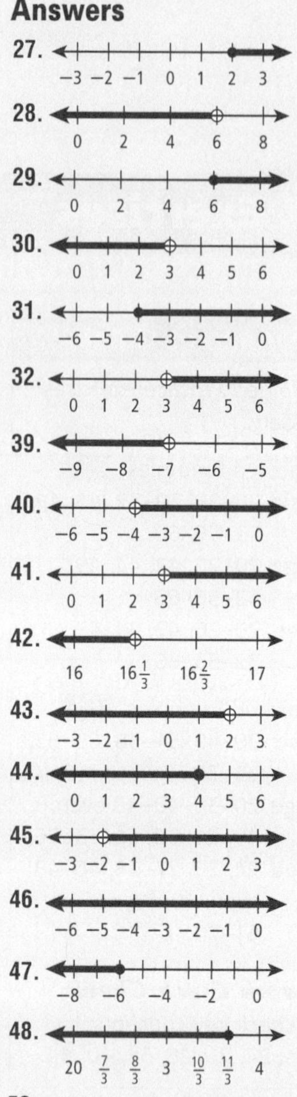

Independent Practice	
For Exercises	See Example
20–25	1
26	2
27–32	3
33–38	4

Extra Practice
Skills Practice p. S9
Application Practice p. S30

Solve each inequality and graph the solutions.

27. $4(2 - x) \le 5(x - 2)$ **$x \ge 2$**
28. $-3(n + 4) < 6(1 - n)$ **$n < 6$**
29. $9(w + 2) \le 12w$ **$w \ge 6$**
30. $4.5 + 1.3t > 3.8t - 3$ **$t < 3$**
31. $\frac{1}{2}r + \frac{2}{3} \ge \frac{1}{3}r$ **$r \ge -4$**
32. $2(4 - n) < 3n - 7$ **$n > 3$**

33. no solutions

Solve each inequality.

33. $3(2 - x) < -3(x - 1)$
34. $7 - y > 5 - y$ **all real numbers**
35. $3(10 + z) \le 3z + 36$ **all real numbers**
36. $-5(k - 1) \ge 5(2 - k)$ **no solutions**
37. $4(x - 1) \le 4x$ **all real numbers**
38. $3(v - 9) \ge 15 + 3v$ **no solutions**

Solve each inequality and graph the solutions.

39. $3t - 12 > 5t + 2$ **$t < -7$**
40. $-5(y + 3) - 6 < y + 3$ **$y > -4$**
41. $3x + 9 - 5x < x$ **$x > 3$**
42. $18 + 9p > 12p - 31$ **$p < 16\frac{1}{3}$**
43. $2(x - 5) < -3x$ **$x < 2$**
44. $-\frac{2}{5}x \le \frac{4}{5} - \frac{3}{5}x$ **$x \le 4$**
45. $-2(x - 7) - 4 - x < 8x + 32$ **$x > -2$**
46. $-3(2r - 4) \ge 2(5 - 3r)$ **all real numbers**
47. $-7x - 10 + 5x \ge 3(x + 4) + 8$ **$x \le -6$**
48. $-\frac{1}{3}(n + 8) + \frac{1}{3}n \le 1 - n$ **$n \le \frac{11}{3}$**

LINK

Recreation

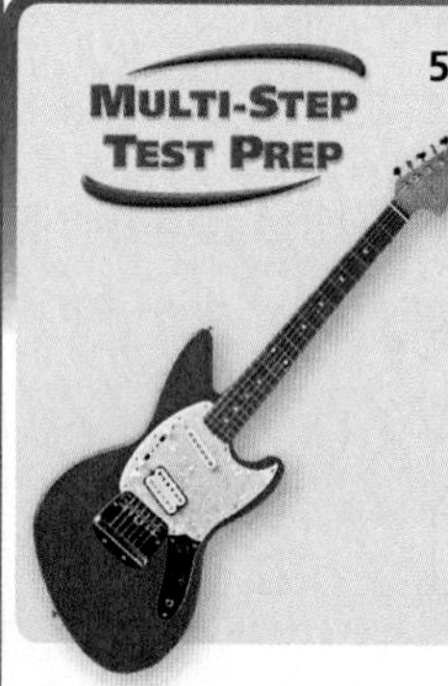

The American Kitefliers Association has over 4000 members in 35 countries. Kitefliers participate in festivals, competitions, and kite-making workshops.

49. **Recreation** A red kite is 100 feet off the ground and is rising at 8 feet per second. A blue kite is 180 feet off the ground and is rising at 5 feet per second. How long will it take for the red kite to be higher than the blue kite? Round your answer to the nearest second. **27 s**

50. **Education** The table shows the enrollment in Howard High School and Phillips High School for three school years.

School Enrollment			
	Year 1	Year 2	Year 3
Howard High School	1192	1188	1184
Phillips High School	921	941	961

a. How much did the enrollment change each year at Howard? **decreased by 4**

b. Use the enrollment in year 1 and your answer from part **a** to write an expression for the enrollment at Howard in any year x. **$1192 - 4(x - 1)$**

c. How much did the enrollment change each year at Phillips? **increased by 20**

d. Use the enrollment in year 1 and your answer from part **c** to write an expression for the enrollment at Phillips in any year x. **$921 + 20(x - 1)$**

e. Assume that the pattern in the table continues. Use your expressions from parts **b** and **d** to write an inequality that can be solved to find the year in which the enrollment at Phillips High School will be greater than the enrollment at Howard High School. Solve your inequality and graph the solutions.
$1192 - 4(x - 1) < 921 + 20(x - 1)$; $x \ge 13$ where x is a whole number

MULTI-STEP TEST PREP

51. This problem will prepare you for the Multi-Step Test Prep on page 218.

a. The school orchestra is creating a CD of their last concert. The total cost is \$400 + 4.50 per CD. Write an expression for the cost of creating the CDs based on the number of CDs n. **$400 + 4.50n$**

b. The orchestra plans to sell the CDs for \$12. Write an expression for the amount the orchestra earns from the sale of n CDs. **$12n$**

c. In order for the orchestra to make a profit, the amount they make selling the CDs must be greater than the cost of creating the CDs. Write an inequality that can be solved to find the number of CDs the orchestra must sell in order to make a profit. Solve your inequality. **$400 + 4.50n < 12n$; $n > 53\frac{1}{3}$; 54 CDs or more**

3-5 PRACTICE A
3-5 PRACTICE C
3-5 PRACTICE B

Solve each inequality and graph the solutions.

1. $2x + 30 \ge 7x$ **$x \le 6$**
2. $2k + 6 < 5k - 3$ **$k > 3$**
3. $3b - 2 \le 2b + 1$ **$b \le 3$**
4. $2(3n + 7) > 5n$ **$n > -14$**
5. $5s - 9 < 2(s - 6)$ **$s < -1$**
6. $-3(3x + 5) \ge -5(2x - 2)$ **$x \ge 25$**
7. $1.4z + 2.2 > 2.6z - 0.2$ **$z < 2$**
8. $\frac{7}{8}p - \frac{1}{4} \le \frac{1}{2}p$ **$p \le \frac{2}{3}$**

Solve each inequality.

9. $v + 1 > v - 6$ **all real numbers**
10. $3(x + 4) \le 3x$ **no solutions**
11. $-2(8 - 3x) \ge 6x + 2$ **no solution**

Write and solve an inequality for each problem.

12. Ian wants to promote his band on the Internet. Site A offers website hosting for \$4.95 per month with a \$49.95 startup fee. Site B offers website hosting for \$9.95 per month with no startup fee. For how many months would Ian need to keep the website for Site B to be less expensive than Site A?
$9.95m < 4.95m + 49.95$; $m < 9.99$; for 0 to 9 months

13. For what values of x is the area of the rectangle greater than the perimeter? (rectangle: 7 by $x + 2$)
$7(x + 2) > 7 + (x + 2) + 7 + (x + 2)$; $x > 0.8$

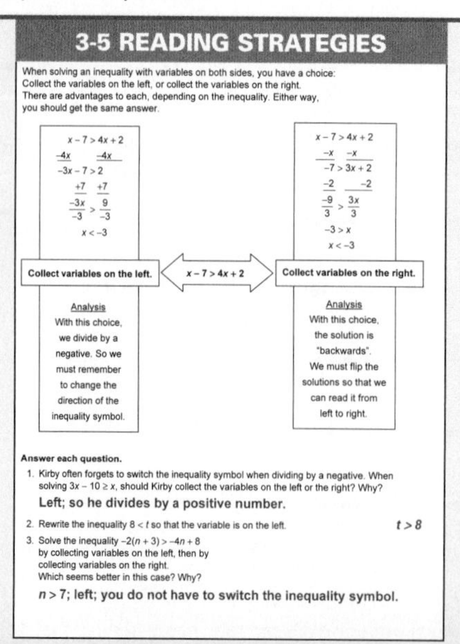

3-5 READING STRATEGIES

When solving an inequality with variables on both sides, you have a choice: Collect the variables on the left, or collect the variables on the right. There are advantages to each, depending on the inequality. Either way, you should get the same answer.

$x - 7 > 4x + 2$

Collect variables on the left.

$x - 7 > 4x + 2$
$-4x \quad -4x$
$-3x - 7 > 2$
$+7 \quad +7$
$\frac{-3x}{-3} > \frac{9}{-3}$
$x < -3$

Analysis: With this choice, we divide by a negative. So we must remember to change the direction of the inequality symbol.

Collect variables on the right.

$x - 7 > 4x + 2$
$-x \quad -x$
$-7 > 3x + 2$
$-2 \quad -2$
$\frac{-9}{3} > \frac{3x}{3}$
$-3 > x$
$x < -3$

Analysis: With this choice, the solution is "backwards". We must flip the solutions so that we can read it from left to right.

Answer each question.

1. Kirby often forgets to switch the inequality symbol when dividing by a negative. When solving $3x - 10 \ge x$, should Kirby collect the variables on the left or the right? Why?
Left; so he divides by a positive number.
2. Rewrite the inequality $8 < t$ so that the variable is on the left. **$t > 8$**
3. Solve the inequality $-2(n + 3) > -4n + 8$ by collecting variables on the left, then by collecting variables on the right. Which seems better in this case? Why?
$n > 7$; left; you do not have to switch the inequality symbol.

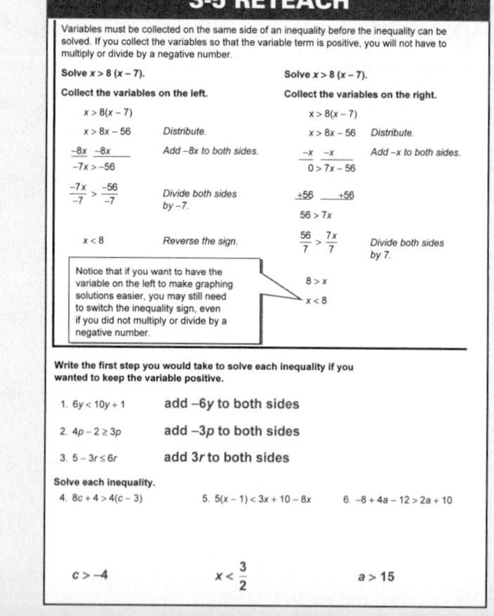

3-5 RETEACH

Variables must be collected on the same side of an inequality before the inequality can be solved. If you collect the variables so that the variable term is positive, you will not have to multiply or divide by a negative number.

Solve $x > 8(x - 7)$.

Collect the variables on the left.

$x > 8(x - 7)$
$x > 8x - 56$ *Distribute.*
$-8x \quad -8x$ *Add −8x to both sides.*
$-7x > -56$
$\frac{-7x}{-7} > \frac{-56}{-7}$ *Divide both sides by −7.*
$x < 8$ *Reverse the sign.*

Solve $x > 8(x - 7)$.

Collect the variables on the right.

$x > 8(x - 7)$
$x > 8x - 56$ *Distribute.*
$-x \quad -x$ *Add −x to both sides.*
$0 > 7x - 56$
$+56 \quad +56$
$56 > 7x$
$\frac{56}{7} > \frac{7x}{7}$ *Divide both sides by 7.*
$8 > x$
$x < 8$

Notice that if you want to have the variable on the left to make graphing solutions easier, you may still need to switch the inequality sign, even if you did not multiply or divide by a negative number.

Write the first step you would take to solve each inequality if you wanted to keep the variable positive.

1. $6y < 10y + 1$ **add $-6y$ to both sides**
2. $4p - 2 \ge 3p$ **add $-3p$ to both sides**
3. $5 - 3r \le 6r$ **add $3r$ to both sides**

Solve each inequality.

4. $8c + 4 > 4(c - 3)$ **$c > -4$**
5. $5(x - 1) < 3x + 10 - 8x$ **$x < \frac{3}{2}$**
6. $-8 + 4a - 12 > 2a + 10$ **$a > 15$**

Write an inequality to represent each relationship. Solve your inequality.

52. $2x + 4 > \frac{2}{3}x$; $x > -3$

52. Four more than twice a number is greater than two-thirds of the number.

53. Ten less than five times a number is less than six times the number decreased by eight. **$5x - 10 < 6x - 8$; $x > -2$**

54. The sum of a number and twenty is less than four times the number decreased by one. **$x + 20 < 4x - 1$; $x > 7$**

55. $\frac{3}{4}x \geq x - 5$; $x \leq 20$

55. Three-fourths of a number is greater than or equal to five less than the number.

56. **Entertainment** Use the table to determine how many movies you would have to rent for Video View to be less expensive than Movie Place. **20 movies or more**

	Membership Fee ($)	Cost per Rental ($)
Movie Place	None	2.99
Video View	19.99	1.99

57. **Geometry** In an acute triangle, all angles measure less than 90°. Also, the sum of the measures of any two angles is greater than the measure of the third angle. Can the measures of an acute triangle be x, $x - 1$, and $2x$? Explain.

58. **Write About It** Compare the steps you would follow to solve an inequality to the steps you would follow to solve an equation.

59. **Critical Thinking** How can you tell just by looking at the inequality $x > x + 1$ that it has no solutions? **x can never be greater than itself plus 1.**

60. **///ERROR ANALYSIS///** Two students solved the inequality $5x < 3 - 4x$. Which is incorrect? Explain the error.

B is incorrect; the student should have added $4x$ to both sides to undo the subtraction.

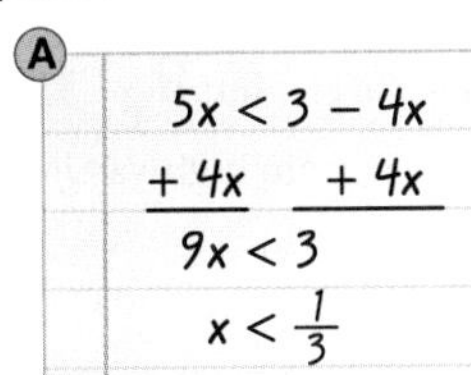

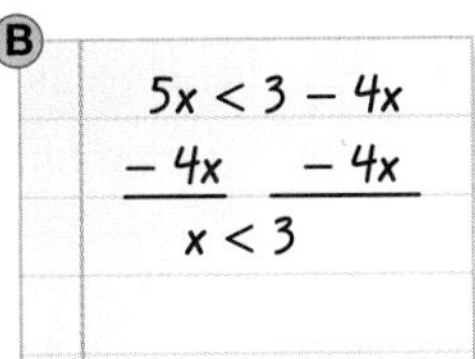

TEST PREP

61. If $a - b > a + b$, which statement is true?
    - (A) The value of a is positive.
    - (B) The value of b is positive.
    - (C) The value of a is negative.
    - **(D)** The value of b is negative.

62. If $-a < b$, which statement is always true?
    - (F) $a < b$
    - (G) $a > b$
    - (H) $a < -b$
    - **(J)** $a > -b$

63. Which is a solution of the inequality $7(2 - x) > 4(x - 2)$?
    - **(A)** -2
    - (B) 2
    - (C) 4
    - (D) 7

64. Which is the graph of $-5x < -2x - 6$?

(F) 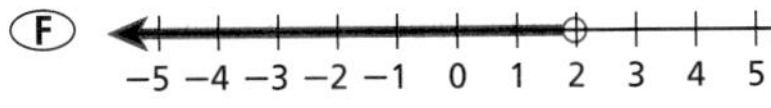

(H) 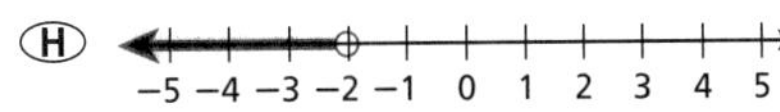

(G) 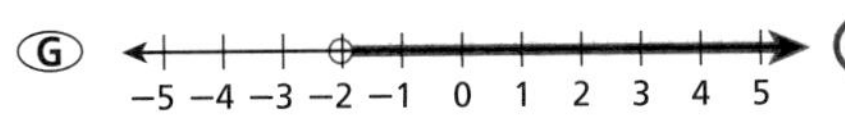

(J) 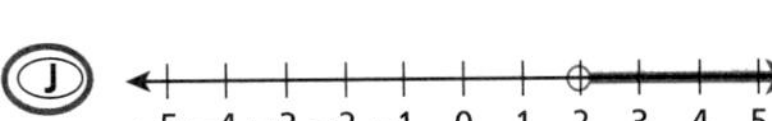

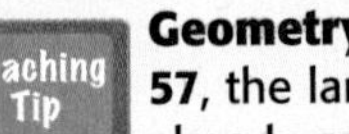

Geometry For **Exercise 57**, the largest angle is already greater than either of the other two, so students only need to check if the sum of the measures of the two smaller angles (x and $x - 1$) is greater than the measure of the largest angle ($2x$). The problem could also be solved by writing and solving an equation. Set the sum of the angle measures equal to 180, solve for x, and then substitute x back into each expression. One angle is greater than 90°, so it is not acute.

In **Exercise 61,** tell students to solve for either variable. Both will result in the inequality $b < 0$.

In **Exercise 63,** students who chose **C** or **D** may not have changed the inequality sign when dividing both sides by a negative number. Students who chose **B** chose the endpoint, which is not included in the solutions.

Answers

57. No; the sum of the angle measures x and $x - 1$ would need to be greater than $2x$. $x + (x - 1) > 2x$: $2x - 1 > 2x$ has no solutions.

58. The steps are identical except when you multiply or divide both sides of an inequality by a negative number, when you must reverse the inequality symbol.

3-5 PROBLEM SOLVING

Write and solve an inequality for each situation.

1. Rosa has decided to sell pet rocks at an art fair for $5 each. She has paid $50 to rent a table at the fair and it costs her $2 to package each rock with a set of instructions. For what numbers of sales will Rosa make a profit?
   $5r > 50 + 2r$; $r > 16$

2. Jamie has a job paying $25,000 and expects to receive a $1000 raise each year. Wei has a job paying $19,000 a year and expects a $1500 raise each year. For what span of time is Jamie making more money than Wei?
   $25{,}000 + 1000y > 19{,}000 + 1500y$; $y < 12$

3. Sophia types 75 words per minute and is just starting to write a term paper. Patton already has 510 words written and types at a speed of 60 words per minute. For what numbers of minutes will Sophia have more words typed than Patton?
   $75m > 510 + 60m$; $m > 34$

4. Keith is racing his little sister Pattie and has given her a 15 foot head start. She runs 5 ft/sec and he is chasing at 8 ft/sec. For how long can Pattie stay ahead of Keith?
   $15 + 5s > 8s$; $s < 5$

The table below shows the population of four cities in 2004 and the amount of population change from 2003. Use this table to answer questions 5–6.

City	Population (2004)	Population Change (from 2003)
Lakewood, CO	141,301	–830
Vallejo, CA	118,349	–1155
Carrollton, TX	117,823	+1170
Manchester, NH	109,310	+261

5. If the trends in this table continue, after how many years y will the population of Manchester, NH, be more than the population of Vallejo, CA? Round your answer to the nearest tenth of a year.
   - A $y > 0.2$
   - **B** $y > 6.4$
   - C $y > 34.6$
   - D $y > 78.6$

6. If the trends in this table continue, for how long x will the population of Carrollton, TX be less than the population of Lakewood, CO? Round your answer to the nearest tenth of a year.
   - **F** $x < 11.7$
   - G $x < 14.6$
   - H $x < 20.1$
   - J $x < 28.3$

3-5 CHALLENGE

The grid at right shows the graphs of two functions, $y_1 = x + 3$ and $y_2 = 2x - 1$. These functions can be graphed by creating a table of ordered pairs for each function and then plotting the ordered pairs. The ordered pairs of each function form straight lines as shown.

1. For what value of x is $y_1 = y_2$? What happens to the graphs at this x-value?
   $x = 4$; the lines intersect

2. For what values of x is $y_1 > y_2$? What happens to the graphs for these x-values?
   $x < 4$; the line for y_1 is above (greater than) the line for y_2

3. The equation $y_1 = x + 3$ tells you that y_1 is the same as the expression $x + 3$. Likewise, $y_2 = 2x - 1$ tells you that y_2 is the same as $2x - 1$. Use this information to rewrite $y_1 > y_2$ using the variable x.
   $y_1 > y_2$
   $x + 3 > 2x - 1$

4. Solve the inequality in problem 3. How do the solutions relate to your answer for problem 2?
   $x < 4$; same solutions as problem 2

5. Explain how you could use the graph to solve this inequality: $2x - 1 \geq x + 3$.
   Possible answer: Find the x-values for which the line for y_2 is either above (greater than) or intersects (equal to) the line for y_1. The solutions are $x \geq 4$.

6. Generate ordered pairs for the functions below. For each, plot the points, connect them with straight lines, and label as in the example above.

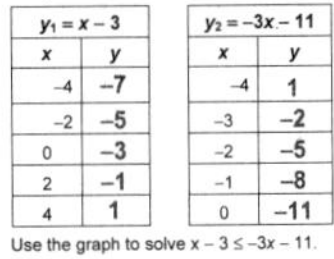

$y_1 = x - 3$	
x	y
–4	**–7**
–2	**–5**
0	**–3**
2	**–1**
4	**1**

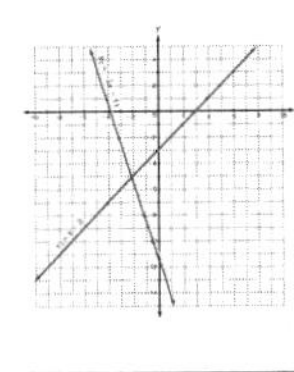

$y_2 = -3x - 11$	
x	y
–4	**1**
–3	**–2**
–2	**–5**
–1	**–8**
0	**–11**

Use the graph to solve $x - 3 \leq -3x - 11$.
$x \leq -2$

65. Short Response Write a real-world situation that could be modeled by the inequality $7x + 4 > 4x + 13$. Explain how the inequality relates to your situation.

Possible answer: parking lot A starts with 4 cars and 7 more cars park each hour. Parking lot B starts with 13 cars and 4 more cars park each hour. The inequality helps you find that parking lot A has more cars than parking lot B after 3 hours.

CHALLENGE AND EXTEND

Solve each inequality.

66. $2\frac{1}{2} + 2x \geq 5\frac{1}{2} + 2\frac{1}{2}x$ **$x \leq -6$**

67. $1.6x - 20.7 > 6.3x - (-2.2x)$ **$x < -3$**

68. $1.3x - 7.5x < 8.5x - 29.4$ **$x > 2$**

69. $-4w + \frac{-8 - 37}{9} \leq \frac{75 - 3}{9} + 3w$ **$w \geq -1\frac{6}{7}$**

70. Replace the square and circle with numbers so that the inequality has all real numbers as solutions. □ $- 2x <$ ○ $- 2x$ **Check students' work: the number in the square should be less than the number in the circle.**

71. Replace the square and circle with numbers so that the inequality has no solutions. □ $- 2x <$ ○ $- 2x$ **Check students' work: the number in the square should be greater than the number in the circle.**

72. Critical Thinking Explain whether there are any numbers that can replace the square and circle so that the inequality has all real numbers as solutions. □ $+ 2x <$ ○ $+ x$ **Check students' work: if the same number is added to both sides and x is negative, the inequality is an identity.**

SPIRAL REVIEW

73. The ratio of the width of a rectangle to the length is 2 : 5. The length is 65 inches. Find the width. *(Lesson 2-7)* **26 in.**

74. Find the simple interest paid after 6 months on a loan of $5000 borrowed at a rate of 9%. *(Lesson 2-10)* **$225**

Define a variable and write an inequality for each situation. Graph the solutions. *(Lesson 3-1)*

75. Participants must be at least 14 years old. **y = years; $y \geq 14$**

76. The maximum speed on a certain highway is 60 miles per hour. **s = speed; $s \leq 60$ where s is nonnegati**

Career Path

go.hrw.com
Career Resources Online
KEYWORD: MA7 Career

Katie Flannigan
Culinary Arts program

Q: What math classes did you take in high school?
A: Algebra 1, Geometry, and Algebra 2

Q: What math classes have you taken since high school?
A: I have taken a basic accounting class and a business math class.

Q: How do you use math?
A: I use math to estimate how much food I need to buy. I also use math when adjusting recipe amounts to feed large groups of people.

Q: What are your future plans?
A: I plan to start my own catering business. The math classes I took will help me manage the financial aspects of my business.

Journal

Given $n \geq 4n + 9$, have students explain how they decide on which side of the inequality to gather the variable terms and why. Then have students solve the inequality, explaining each step.

ALTERNATIVE ASSESSMENT

Have students write, solve, and graph an inequality that has variables on both sides and that needs to be simplified before applying inverse operations.

Power Presentations with PowerPoint®

3-5 Lesson Quiz

Solve each inequality and graph the solutions.

1. $t < 5t + 24$ $t > -6$

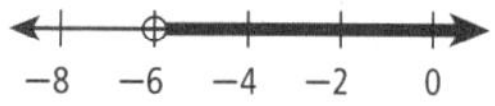

2. $5x - 9 \leq 4.1x - 81$
$x \leq -80$

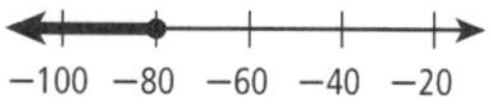

3. $4b + 4(1 - b) > b - 9$
$b < 13$

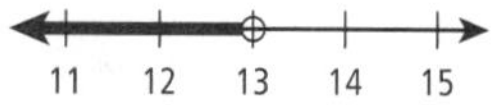

4. Rick bought a photo printer and supplies for $186.90, which will allow him to print photos for $0.29 each. A photo store charges $0.55 to print each photo. How many photos must Rick print before his total cost is less than getting prints made at the photo store? more than 718 photos

Solve each inequality.

5. $2y - 2 \geq 2(y + 7)$
no solutions

6. $2(-6r - 5) < -3(4r + 2)$
all real numbers

Also available on transparency

Answers

75.
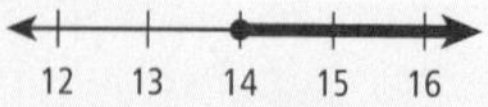

76.
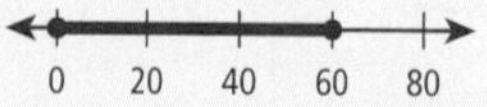

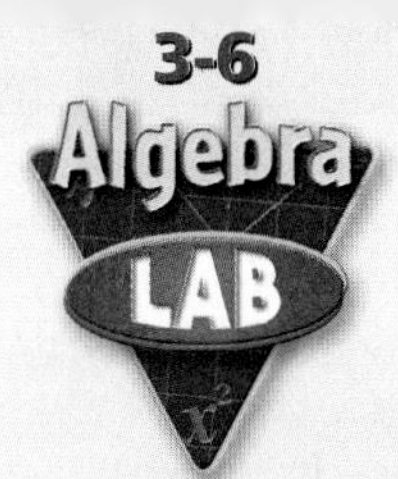

Truth Tables and Compound Statements

A compound statement is formed by combining two or more simple statements. A compound statement is either true or false depending on whether its simple statements are true or false.

Use with Lesson 3-6

• Let *P* be "Cindy is at least 17 years old." • Let *Q* be "Cindy has a driver's license."

If...	then *P* is	and *Q* is	so *P* AND *Q* is
Cindy is 18 years old. Cindy has a driver's license.	True	True	True
Cindy is 17 years old. Cindy does not have a driver's license.	True	False	False
Cindy is 16 years old. Cindy has a driver's license.	False	True	False
Cindy is 15 years old. Cindy does not have a driver's license.	False	False	False

P **AND** *Q* is true when ______?______. **both *P* AND *Q* are true**

Try This

For each pair of simple statements, tell whether *P* AND *Q* is true or false.

1. *P:* Many birds can fly; *Q:* A zebra is an animal. ***P* AND *Q* is true.**

• Let *P* be "Paul plays tennis." • Let *Q* be "Paul has brown eyes."

If...	then *P* is	and *Q* is	so *P* OR *Q* is
Paul plays tennis. Paul has brown eyes.	True	True	True
Paul plays tennis. Paul has green eyes.	True	False	True
Paul does not play tennis. Paul has brown eyes.	False	True	True
Paul does not play tennis. Paul has green eyes.	False	False	False

P **OR** *Q* is true when ______?______. **either *P* OR *Q* is true**

Try This

For each pair of simple statements, tell whether *P* OR *Q* is true or false.

2. *P:* The number 12 is even; *Q:* The number 12 is a composite number. ***P* OR *Q* is true.**

Teacher to Teacher

I usually introduce the topic of truth tables with AND or OR sentences when working with inequalities and absolute values. Students learn that "the absolute value of an expression is less than a number" is an AND statement, and "the absolute value of an expression is greater than a number" is an OR statement.

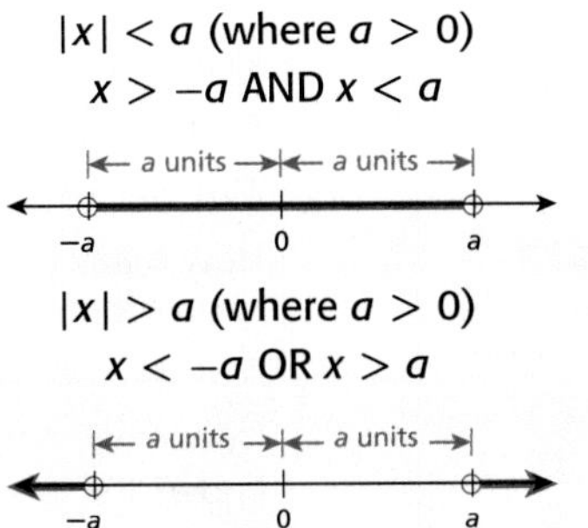

John Remensky
Library, PA

Organizer

Use with Lesson 3-6

Pacing:
Traditional $\frac{1}{2}$ day
Block $\frac{1}{4}$ day

Objective: Determine whether compound statements are true or false.

Online Edition

Countdown Week 7

Resources

Algebra Lab Activities
3-6 Lab Recording Sheet

Teach

Discuss

P and *Q* are variables that are replaced by phrases, rather than by numbers.

Teaching Tip **Math Background** *P* AND *Q* can be written as $P \wedge Q$. *P* OR *Q* can be written as $P \vee Q$.

Close

Key Concept

An AND statement is true if *both* statements are true. An OR statement is true if *at least one* of the statements is true.

Assessment

Journal Have students explain how to determine if a compound statement with AND is true, and how to determine if a compound statement with OR is true. Explanations should include examples.

State Resources

3-6 Organizer

Pacing: Traditional 1 day
Block $\frac{1}{2}$ day

Objectives: Solve compound inequalities in one variable.

Graph solution sets of compound inequalities in one variable.

Online Edition
Tutorial Videos, Interactivity

Countdown Week 7

Warm Up

Solve each inequality.

1. $x + 3 \le 10$ $\quad x \le 7$
2. $23 < -2x + 3$ $\quad -10 > x$

Solve each inequality and graph the solutions.

3. $4x + 1 \le 25$ $\quad x \le 6$

0 2 4 6 8

4. $0 \ge 3x + 3$ $\quad -1 \ge x$

−3 −2 −1 0 1 2 3

Also available on transparency

Math Humor

Q: How does a math teacher get a compound fracture?

A: She breaks her hAND.

3-6 Solving Compound Inequalities

Objectives
Solve compound inequalities in one variable.

Graph solution sets of compound inequalities in one variable.

Vocabulary
compound inequality
intersection
union

Who uses this?
A lifeguard can use compound inequalities to describe the safe pH levels in a swimming pool. (See Example 1.)

The inequalities you have seen so far are simple inequalities. When two simple inequalities are combined into one statement by the words AND or OR, the result is called a **compound inequality**.

Know it! Note

Compound Inequalities

WORDS	ALGEBRA	GRAPH
All real numbers greater than 2 AND less than 6	$x > 2$ AND $x < 6$ $2 < x < 6$	0 2 4 6 8
All real numbers greater than or equal to 2 AND less than or equal to 6	$x \ge 2$ AND $x \le 6$ $2 \le x \le 6$	0 2 4 6 8
All real numbers less than 2 OR greater than 6	$x < 2$ OR $x > 6$	0 2 4 6 8
All real numbers less than or equal to 2 OR greater than or equal to 6	$x \le 2$ OR $x \ge 6$	0 2 4 6 8

EXAMPLE 1 ***Chemistry Application***

A water analyst recommends that the pH level of swimming pool water be between 7.2 and 7.6 inclusive. Write a compound inequality to show the pH levels that are within the recommended range. Graph the solutions.

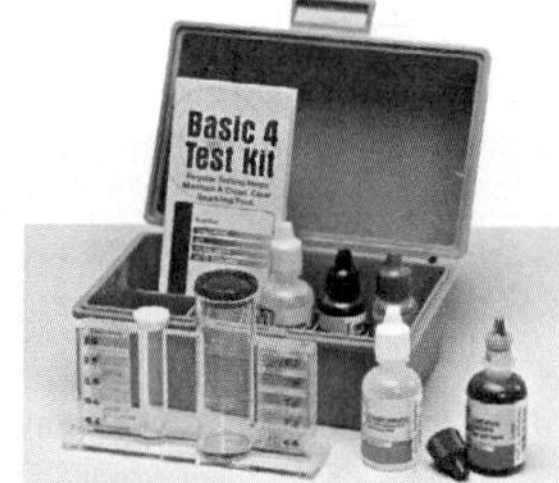

Helpful Hint

The phrase "between 7.2 and 7.6 *inclusive*" means that the numbers 7.2 and 7.6 are included in the solutions. Use a solid circle for endpoints that are solutions.

Let p be the pH level of swimming pool water.

7.2	is less than or equal to	pH level	is less than or equal to	7.6
7.2	$\le$	p	$\le$	7.6

$7.2 \le p \le 7.6$

7.1 7.2 7.3 7.4 7.5 7.6 7.7

State Resources

1 Introduce

EXPLORATION

3-6 Solving Compound Inequalities

Using a graphing calculator, follow the steps below to find the values of x when $2x + 1$ is between −3 and 7.

1. Press [Y=]. Enter **2X + 1** for **Y1**, **−3** for **Y2**, and **7** for **Y3**.
2. Press [GRAPH] to graph the functions.
3. Press [TRACE] and use the arrow keys to move the cursor. Find the x-values where the graph of $y = 2x + 1$ crosses the horizontal lines.
4. For which values of x is $2x + 1$ between −3 and 7?
5. Press [2nd] [TABLE] to examine these functions in a table. For which values of x is $2x + 1$ between −3 and 7? Graph these values on a number line.

−10 −8 −6 −4 −2 0 2 4 6 8 10

THINK AND DISCUSS

6. **Explain** how the solution to this problem is different from the solutions to problems you studied earlier in the chapter.
7. **Explain** how the graph of this solution looks different from the graphs you studied earlier in the chapter.

Motivate

Read the sentences and follow-up questions below.

Max will take his brother or sister to the concert.

How many people will Max take? 1 How do you know? the word *or*

Max will take his brother and sister to the concert.

How many people will Max take? 2 How do you know? the word *and*

The words *or* and *and* can be used to represent the solutions of a compound inequality.

Explorations and answers are provided in *Alternate Openers: Explorations Transparencies.*

1. The free chlorine level in a pool should be between 1.0 and 3.0 parts per million inclusive. Write a compound inequality to show the levels that are within this range. Graph the solutions.
$1.0 \le c \le 3.0$

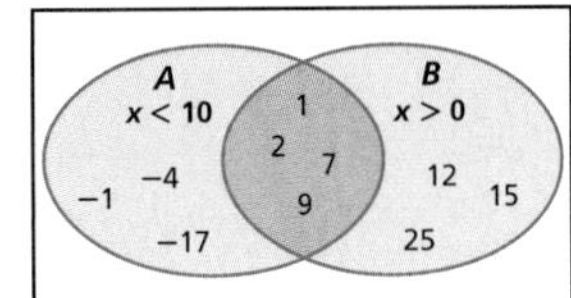

In this diagram, oval A represents some integer solutions of $x < 10$, and oval B represents some integer solutions of $x > 0$. The overlapping region represents numbers that belong in both ovals. Those numbers are solutions of *both* $x < 10$ *and* $x > 0$.

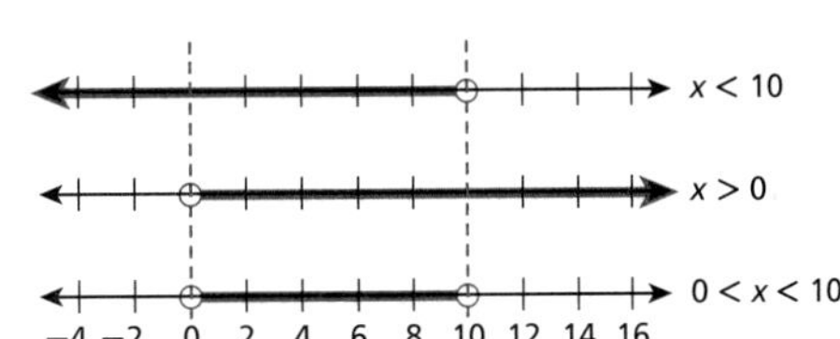

You can graph the solutions of a compound inequality involving AND by using the idea of an overlapping region. The overlapping region is called the **intersection** and shows the numbers that are solutions of both inequalities.

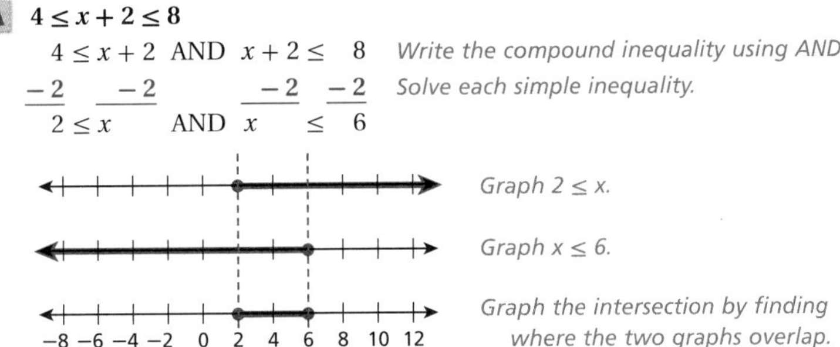

EXAMPLE 2 Solving Compound Inequalities Involving AND

Solve each compound inequality and graph the solutions.

A $4 \le x + 2 \le 8$

$4 \le x + 2$ AND $x + 2 \le 8$ *Write the compound inequality using AND.*

$\underline{-2 \quad\; -2} \qquad \underline{-2 \quad -2}$ *Solve each simple inequality.*

$2 \le x$ AND $x \le 6$

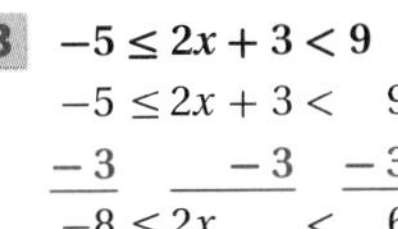

Graph $2 \le x$.

Graph $x \le 6$.

Graph the intersection by finding where the two graphs overlap.

−8 −6 −4 −2 0 2 4 6 8 10 12

B $-5 \le 2x + 3 < 9$

$-5 \le 2x + 3 < 9$ *Since 3 is added to 2x, subtract 3 from each part of the inequality.*

$\underline{-3 \qquad -3 \quad -3}$

$-8 \le 2x < 6$

$\frac{-8}{2} \le \frac{2x}{2} < \frac{6}{2}$ *Since x is multiplied by 2, divide each part of the inequality by 2.*

$-4 \le x < 3$

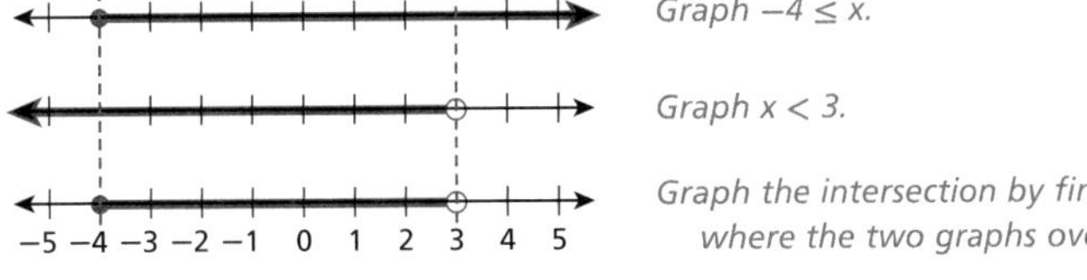

Graph $-4 \le x$.

Graph $x < 3$.

Graph the intersection by finding where the two graphs overlap.

−5 −4 −3 −2 −1 0 1 2 3 4 5

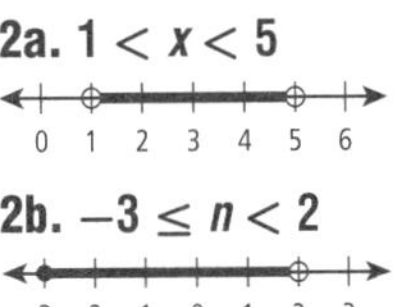

Remember!

The statement $-5 \le 2x + 3 \le 9$ consists of two inequalities connected by AND. Example 2B shows a "shorthand" method for solving this type of inequality.

2a. $1 < x < 5$

0 1 2 3 4 5 6

2b. $-3 \le n < 2$

−3 −2 −1 0 1 2 3

Solve each compound inequality and graph the solutions.

2a. $-9 < x - 10 < -5$ **2b.** $-4 \le 3n + 5 < 11$

COMMON ERROR ALERT

Students may be confused when using the shorthand method for AND in **Example 2B.** When reading the expression $a < x < b$, students can say, "x is greater than a AND x is less than b." Students can also say, "a is less than x AND x is less than b." This shorthand method for writing a compound inequality exists only for the AND statement.

Power Presentations with PowerPoint®

Additional Examples

Example 1

The pH level of a popular shampoo is between 6.0 and 6.5 inclusive. Write a compound inequality to show the pH levels of this shampoo. Graph the solutions. $6.0 \le p \le 6.5$

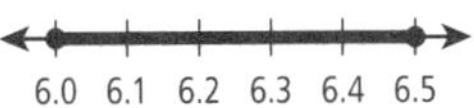

6.0 6.1 6.2 6.3 6.4 6.5

Example 2

Solve each compound inequality and graph the solutions.

A. $-5 < x + 1 < 2$ $-6 < x < 1$

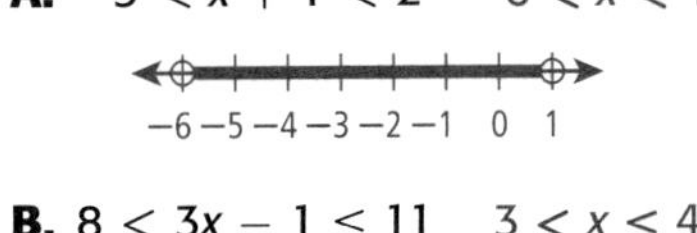

−6 −5 −4 −3 −2 −1 0 1

B. $8 < 3x - 1 \le 11$ $3 < x \le 4$

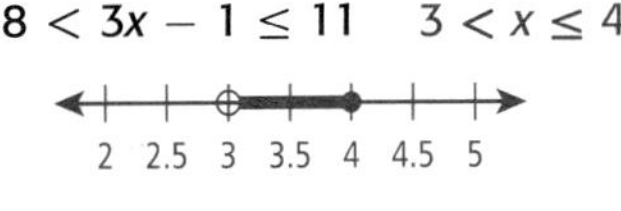

2 2.5 3 3.5 4 4.5 5

INTERVENTION
Questioning Strategies

EXAMPLE 1

- How would the solution change if the range of given values were not inclusive?

EXAMPLE 2

- How do you write a compound inequality as two simple inequalities?

2 Teach

Guided Instruction

Review solving multi-step inequalities. Solve compound inequalities with AND and then OR, and then discuss the differences between the two. Help students make the connection between AND and intersection and between OR and union.

Reaching All Learners
Through Kinesthetic Experience

Assign each student a number. (Assign 1–20 to twenty students.) Then have students stand when you read statements that describe their number. For instance:

- greater than 15 OR less than 2;
- less than 12 AND greater than or equal to 8;
- greater than or equal to 3 AND less than or equal to 3;
- greater than 2 OR less than 3

Power Presentations with PowerPoint®

Additional Examples

Example 3

Solve each compound inequality and graph the solutions.

A. $8 + t \geq 7$ OR $8 + t < 2$

$t \geq -1$ OR $t < -6$

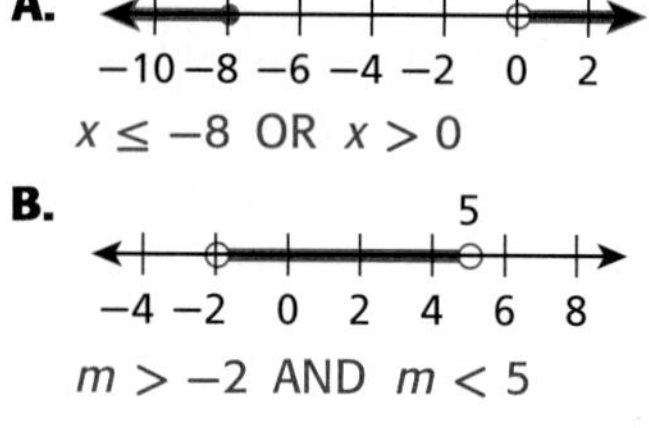

B. $4x \leq 20$ OR $3x > 21$

$x \leq 5$ OR $x > 7$

Example 4

Write the compound inequality shown by each graph.

A. $x \leq -8$ OR $x > 0$

B. $m > -2$ AND $m < 5$

INTERVENTION

Questioning Strategies

EXAMPLE 3

- Describe a characteristic of the graph of the solutions of a compound inequality involving OR.

EXAMPLE 4

- How do you know whether a graph represents a compound inequality that involves AND or OR?

Teaching Tip **Reading Math** Discuss the everyday meanings of *intersection* and *union*. The intersection of two streets is where they cross each other. A labor union is an organization of workers who join together. English Language Learners

In this diagram, circle A represents some integer solutions of $x < 0$, and circle B represents some integer solutions of $x > 10$. The combined shaded regions represent numbers that are solutions of *either* $x < 0$ *or* $x > 10$.

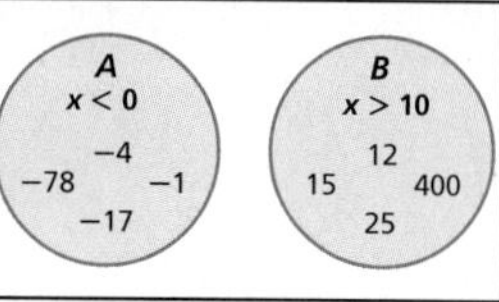

You can graph the solutions of a compound inequality involving OR by using the idea of combining regions. The combined regions are called the **union** and show the numbers that are solutions of either inequality.

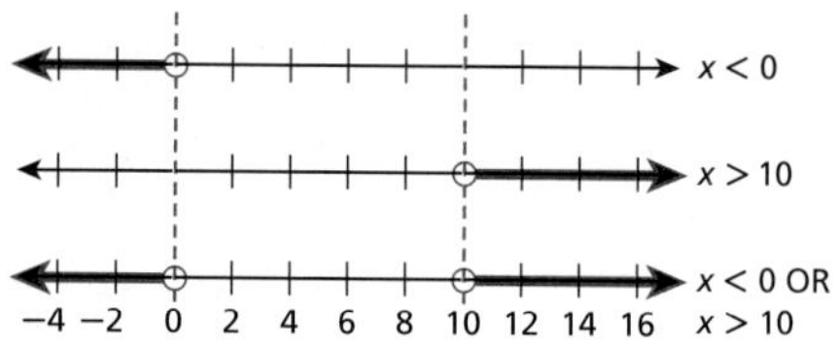

EXAMPLE 3 **Solving Compound Inequalities Involving OR**

Solve each compound inequality and graph the solutions.

A $-4 + a > 1$ **OR** $-4 + a < -3$

$-4 + a > 1$ OR $-4 + a < -3$

$\underline{+4} \quad \underline{+4} \quad \underline{+4} \quad \underline{+4}$ *Solve each simple inequality.*

$a > 5$ OR $a < 1$

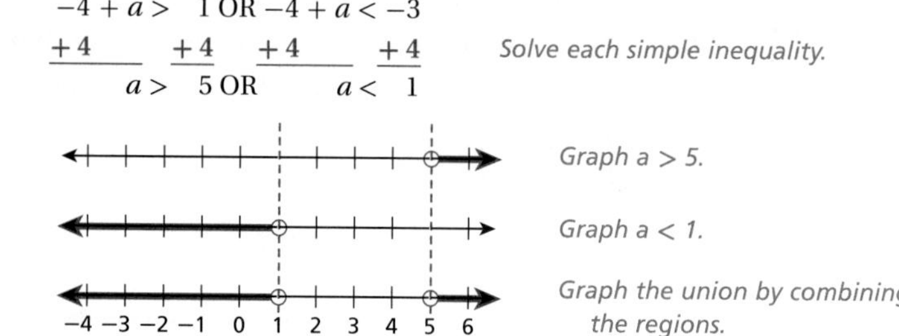

B $2x \leq 6$ **OR** $3x > 12$

$2x \leq 6$ OR $3x > 12$

$\frac{2x}{2} \leq \frac{6}{2}$ $\frac{3x}{3} > \frac{12}{3}$ *Solve each simple inequality.*

$x \leq 3$ OR $x > 4$

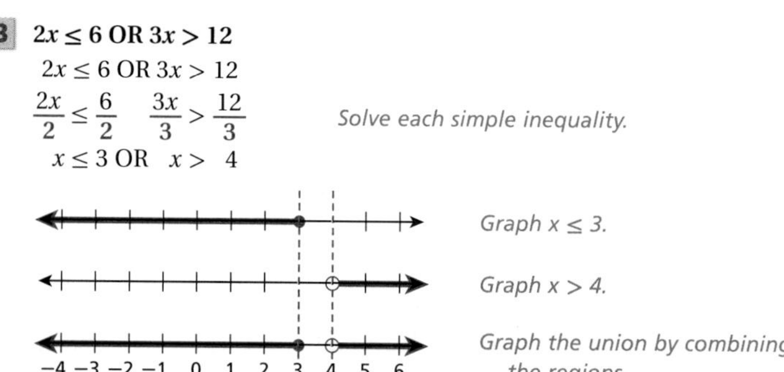

CHECK IT OUT! **Solve each compound inequality and graph the solutions.**

3a. $2 + r < 12$ OR $r + 5 > 19$ **$r < 10$ OR $r > 14$**

3b. $7x \geq 21$ OR $2x < -2$ **$x \geq 3$ OR $x < -1$**

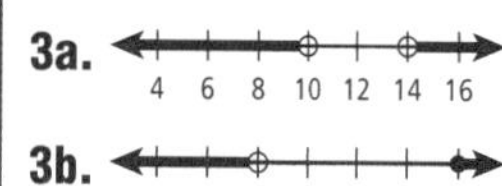

Every solution of a compound inequality involving AND must be a solution of both parts of the compound inequality. If no numbers are solutions of *both* simple inequalities, then the compound inequality has no solutions.

The solutions of a compound inequality involving OR are not always two separate sets of numbers. There may be numbers that are solutions of both parts of the compound inequality.

EXAMPLE 4 Writing a Compound Inequality from a Graph

Write the compound inequality shown by each graph.

A 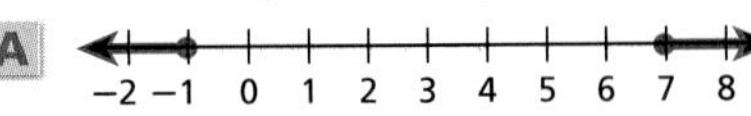

The shaded portion of the graph is not between two values, so the compound inequality involves OR.

On the left, the graph shows an arrow pointing left, so use either $<$ or $\leq$. The solid circle at -1 means -1 is a solution, so use $\leq$.

$x \leq -1$

On the right, the graph shows an arrow pointing right, so use either $>$ or $\geq$. The solid circle at 7 means 7 is a solution, so use $\geq$.

$x \geq 7$

The compound inequality is $x \leq -1$ OR $x \geq 7$.

B 

The shaded portion of the graph is between the values 0 and 6, so the compound inequality involves AND.

The shaded values are to the right of 0, so use $>$ or $\geq$. The solid circle at 0 means 0 is a solution, so use $\geq$.

$x \geq 0$

The shaded values are to the left of 6, so use $<$ or $\leq$. The empty circle at 6 means 6 is not a solution, so use $<$.

$x < 6$

The compound inequality is $x \geq 0$ AND $x < 6$.

Writing Math

The compound inequality in Example 4B can also be written with the variable between the two endpoints. $0 \leq x < 6$

CHECK IT OUT! Write the compound inequality shown by the graph.

4a.  $-9 < y < -2$

4b. $x \leq -3$ OR $x \geq 2$

THINK AND DISCUSS

1. Describe how to write the compound inequality $y > 4$ AND $y \leq 12$ without using the joining word AND.
2. **GET ORGANIZED** Copy and complete the graphic organizers. Write three solutions in each of the three sections of the diagram. Then write each of your nine solutions in the appropriate column or columns of the table.

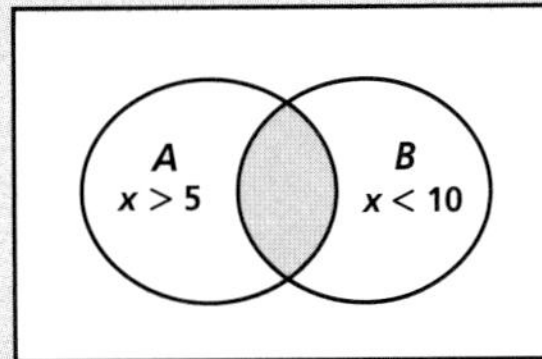

$x > 5$ AND $x < 10$	$x > 5$ OR $x < 10$

Teaching Tip **Visual** Use color to help students compare AND and OR statements. On a transparency, graph the solutions of $x < 3$ with a yellow marker and the solutions of $x < 7$ with a blue marker. Show that the solution set for $x < 3$ AND $x < 7$ is the green area described by $x < 3$. Then discuss the solution set for $x < 3$ OR $x < 7$. The solution is anywhere the graph is shaded, as described by $x < 7$.

Teaching Tip **Multiple Representations** Sometimes a parenthesis is used for an empty circle and a square bracket is used for a solid circle. The values described by $a < x \leq b$ can also be written as $(a, b]$, a notation used more often in higher-level math. The symbols may also be used on a graph.

3 Close

Summarize

Remind students that solving compound inequalities requires solving two separate inequalities.

Emphasize that an AND statement represents an intersection, and the solutions will be those values that make both inequalities true.

An OR statement represents a union, and the solutions combine two sets of numbers, which may or may not overlap. The solutions make either inequality true.

ONGOING ASSESSMENT and INTERVENTION

Diagnose ***Before*** **the Lesson**
3-6 Warm Up, TE p. 204

Monitor ***During*** **the Lesson**
Check It Out! Exercises, SE pp. 205–207
Questioning Strategies, TE pp. 205–206

Assess ***After*** **the Lesson**
3-6 Lesson Quiz, TE p. 210
Alternative Assessment, TE p. 210

Answers to *Think and Discuss*

1. $y > 4$ can be written as $4 < y$. Combine the inequalities $4 < y$ and $y \leq 12$ to write $4 < y \leq 12$.
2. See p. A4.

3-6 Exercises

Assignment Guide

Assign *Guided Practice* exercises as necessary.

If you finished Examples **1–2**
Basic 15–19, 30–35, 42
Average 15–19, 30–35, 45
Advanced 15–19, 30–35, 42, 43, 45, 51

If you finished Examples **1–4**
Basic 15–40, 42, 45, 47–50, 57–65
Average 15–29, 30–40 even, 42–54, 57–65
Advanced 15–29, 34, 36–40 even, 42–65

Homework Quick Check
Quickly check key concepts.
Exercises: 15, 18, 20, 26, 34, 42

Answers

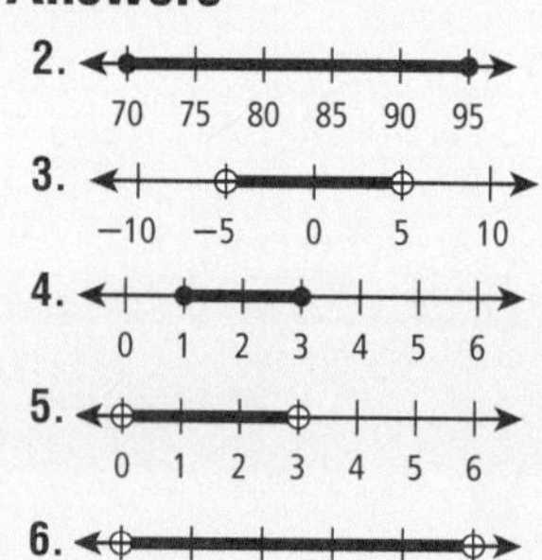

7–10, 15–23. For graphs, see p. A15.

28. $82.4 \le f \le 659.2$

State Resources

3-6 Exercises

go.hrw.com
Homework Help Online
KEYWORD: MA7 3-6
Parent Resources Online
KEYWORD: MA7 Parent

GUIDED PRACTICE

1. **Vocabulary** The graph of a(n) __?__ shows all values that are solutions to both simple inequalities that make a compound inequality. (*union* or *intersection*) **intersection**

SEE EXAMPLE 1 p. 204

2. **Biology** An iguana needs to live in a warm environment. The temperature in a pet iguana's cage should be between 70 °F and 95 °F inclusive. Write a compound inequality to show the temperatures that are within the recommended range. Graph the solutions. $70 \le t \le 95$

Solve each compound inequality and graph the solutions.

SEE EXAMPLE 2 p. 205

3. $-3 < x + 2 < 7$ $-5 < x < 5$
4. $5 \le 4x + 1 \le 13$ $1 \le x \le 3$
5. $2 < x + 2 < 5$ $0 < x < 3$
6. $11 < 2x + 3 < 21$ $4 < x < 9$

SEE EXAMPLE 3 p. 206

7. $x + 2 < -6$ OR $x + 2 > 6$ $x < -8$ OR $x > 4$
8. $r - 1 < 0$ OR $r - 1 > 4$ $r < 1$ OR $r > 5$
9. $n + 2 < 3$ OR $n + 3 > 7$ $n < 1$ OR $n > 4$
10. $x - 1 < -1$ OR $x - 5 > -1$ $x < 0$ OR $x > 4$

SEE EXAMPLE 4 p. 207

Write the compound inequality shown by each graph.

11. 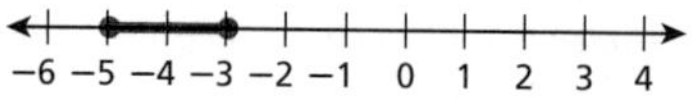 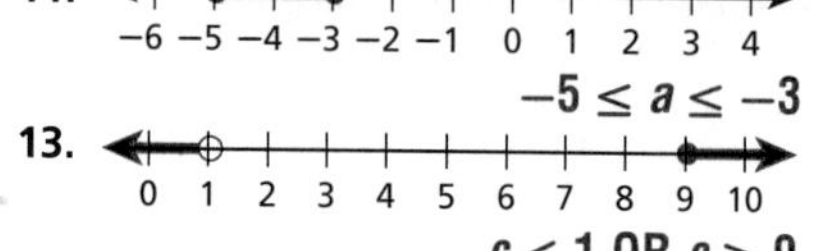 $-5 \le a \le -3$
12. 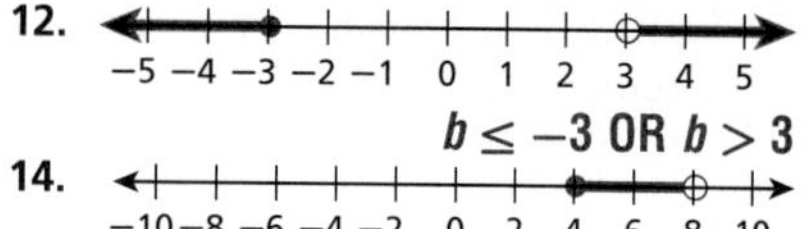 $b \le -3$ OR $b > 3$
13. (number line 0 to 10) $c < 1$ OR $c \ge 9$
14. 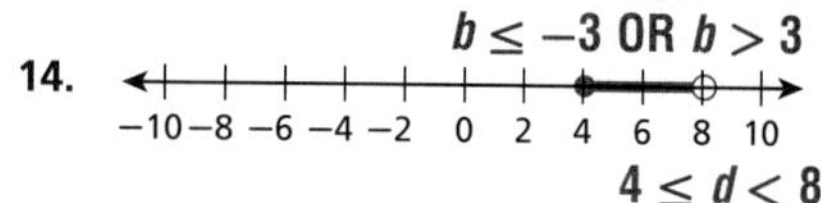 $4 \le d < 8$

PRACTICE AND PROBLEM SOLVING

For Exercises	See Example
15	1
16–19	2
20–23	3
24–27	4

Extra Practice
Skills Practice p. S9
Application Practice p. S30

15. **Meteorology** One layer of Earth's atmosphere is called the stratosphere. At one point above Earth's surface the stratosphere extends from an altitude of 16 km to an altitude of 50 km. Write a compound inequality to show the altitudes that are within the range of the stratosphere. Graph the solutions. $16 \le k \le 50$

Solve each compound inequality and graph the solutions.

16. $-1 < x + 1 < 1$ $-2 < x < 0$
17. $1 \le 2n - 5 \le 7$ $3 \le n \le 6$
18. $-2 < x - 2 < 2$ $0 < x < 4$
19. $5 < 3x - 1 < 17$ $2 < x < 6$
20. $x - 4 < -7$ OR $x + 3 > 4$ $x < -3$ OR $x > 1$
21. $2x + 1 < 1$ OR $x + 5 > 8$ $x < 0$ OR $x > 3$
22. $x + 1 < 2$ OR $x + 5 > 8$ $x < 1$ OR $x > 3$
23. $x + 3 < 0$ OR $x - 2 > 0$ $x < -3$ OR $x > 2$

Write the compound inequality shown by each graph.

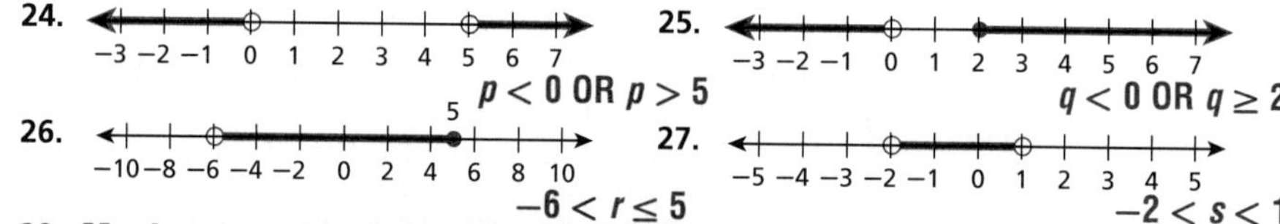

24. $p < 0$ OR $p > 5$
25. $q < 0$ OR $q \ge 2$
26. $-6 < r \le 5$
27. $-2 < s < 1$

28. **Music** A typical acoustic guitar has a range of three octaves. When the guitar is tuned to "concert pitch," the range of frequencies for those three octaves is between 82.4 Hz and 659.2 Hz inclusive. Write a compound inequality to show the frequencies that are within the range of a typical acoustic guitar. Graph the solutions.

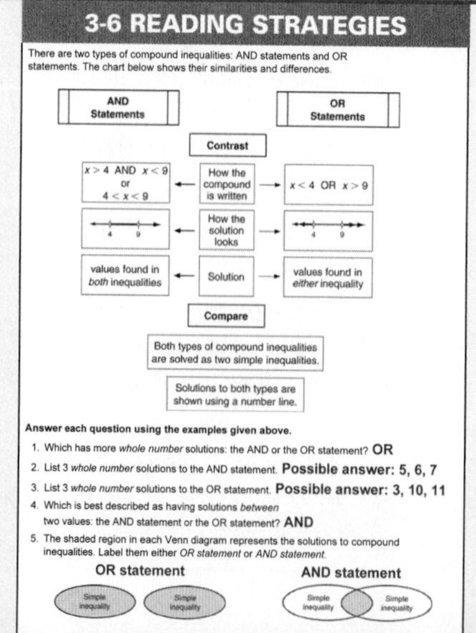

3-6 READING STRATEGIES

There are two types of compound inequalities: AND statements and OR statements. The chart below shows their similarities and differences.

Answer each question using the examples given above.
1. Which has more whole number solutions: the AND or the OR statement? OR
2. List 3 whole number solutions to the AND statement. Possible answer: 5, 6, 7
3. List 3 whole number solutions to the OR statement. Possible answer: 3, 10, 11
4. Which is best described as having solutions between two values: the AND statement or the OR statement? AND
5. The shaded region in each Venn diagram represents the solutions to compound inequalities. Label them either OR statement or AND statement.

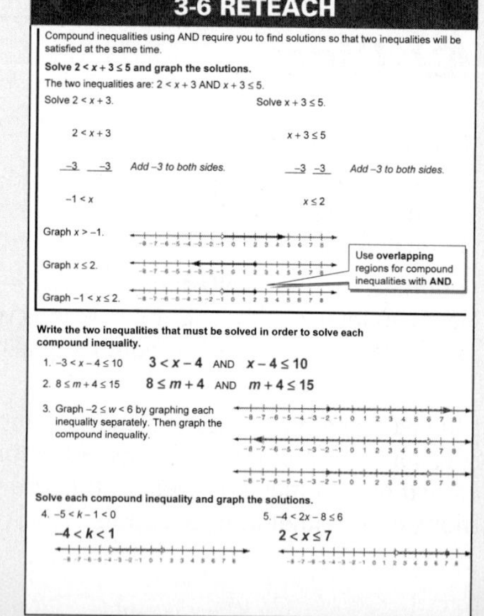

3-6 RETEACH

Compound inequalities using AND require you to find solutions so that two inequalities will be satisfied at the same time.

Write the two inequalities that must be solved in order to solve each compound inequality.
1. $-3 \le x - 4 \le 10$ $3 < x - 4$ AND $x - 4 \le 10$
2. $8 \le m + 4 \le 15$ $8 \le m + 4$ AND $m + 4 \le 15$

Solve each compound inequality and graph the solutions.
4. $-5 < k - 1 < 0$ $-4 < k < 1$
5. $-4 < 2x - 8 \le 6$ $2 < x \le 7$

MULTI-STEP TEST PREP

29. This problem will prepare you for the Multi-Step Test Prep on page 218.

Jenna's band is going to record a CD at a recording studio. They will pay \$225 to use the studio for one day and \$80 per hour for sound technicians. Jenna has \$200 and can reasonably expect to raise up to an additional \$350 by taking pre-orders for the CDs.

a. Explain how the inequality $200 \le 225 + 80n \le 550$ can be used to find the number of hours Jenna and her band can afford to use the studio and sound technicians.

b. Solve the inequality. Are there any numbers in the solution set that are not reasonable in this situation? **$-0.3125 \le n \le 4.0625$; n cannot be negative**

c. Suppose Jenna raises \$350 in pre-orders. How much more money would she need to raise if she wanted to use the studio and sound technicians for 6 hours? **\$155**

Write and graph a compound inequality for the numbers described.

30. all real numbers between −6 and 6 **$-6 < x < 6$**

31. all real numbers less than or equal to 2 and greater than or equal to 1 **$1 \le x \le 2$**

32. all real numbers greater than 0 and less than 15 **$0 < x < 15$**

33. all real numbers between −10 and 10 inclusive **$-10 \le x \le 10$**

34. Transportation The cruise-control function on Georgina's car should keep the speed of the car within 3 mi/h of the set speed. Write a compound inequality to show the acceptable speeds s if the set speed is 55 mi/h. Graph the solutions. **$52 \le x \le 58$**

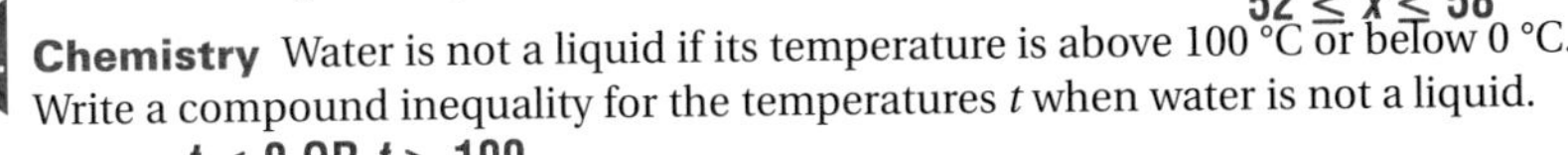

LINK

Chemistry

The element gallium is in a solid state at room temperature but becomes a liquid at about 30 °C. Gallium stays in a liquid state until it reaches a temperature of about 2204 °C.

35. Chemistry Water is not a liquid if its temperature is above 100 °C or below 0 °C. Write a compound inequality for the temperatures t when water is not a liquid. **$t < 0$ OR $t > 100$**

Solve each compound inequality and graph the solutions.

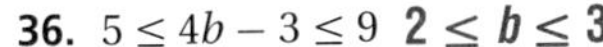

36. $5 \le 4b - 3 \le 9$ **$2 \le b \le 3$**

37. $-3 < x - 1 < 4$ **$-2 < x < 5$**

38. $r + 2 < -2$ OR $r - 2 > 2$ **$r < -4$ OR $r > 4$**

39. $2a - 5 < -5$ OR $3a - 2 > 1$ **$a < 0$ OR $a > 1$**

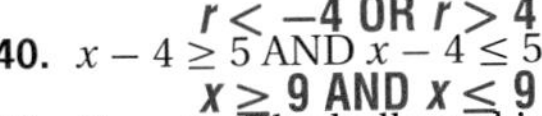

40. $x - 4 \ge 5$ AND $x - 4 \le 5$ **$x \ge 9$ AND $x \le 9$**

41. $n - 4 < -2$ OR $n + 1 > 6$ **$n < 2$ OR $n > 5$**

42. Sports The ball used in a soccer game may not weigh more than 16 ounces or less than 14 ounces at the start of the match. After $1\frac{1}{2}$ ounces of air was added to a ball, the ball was approved for use in a game. Write and solve a compound inequality to show how much the ball might have weighed before the air was added. **$12.5 \le w \le 14.5$**

43. Meteorology Tornado damage is rated using the Fujita scale shown in the table. A tornado has a wind speed of 200 miles per hour. Write and solve a compound inequality to show how many miles per hour the wind speed would need to increase for the tornado to be rated "devastating" but not "incredible." **$7 \le m \le 60$**

Fujita Tornado Scale

Category	Type	Wind Speed (mi/h)
F0	Weak	40 to 72
F1	Moderate	73 to 112
F2	Significant	113 to 157
F3	Severe	158 to 206
F4	Devastating	207 to 260
F5	Incredible	261 to 318

44. Possible answer: Margaret is expecting between 25 and 35 guests; $25 \le g \le 35$ where g is a natural number

44. Give a real-world situation that can be described by a compound inequality. Write the inequality that describes your situation.

45. Write About It How are the graphs of the compound inequality $x < 3$ AND $x < 7$ and the compound inequality $x < 3$ OR $x < 7$ different? How are the graphs alike? Explain.

MULTI-STEP TEST PREP **Exercise 29** involves using inequalities to find the number of hours a band can afford to rent a recording studio. This exercise prepares students for the Multi-Step Test Prep on page 218.

Answers

29a. 225 + 80n gives the cost of the studio and technicians. The band will spend between \$200 and \$550.

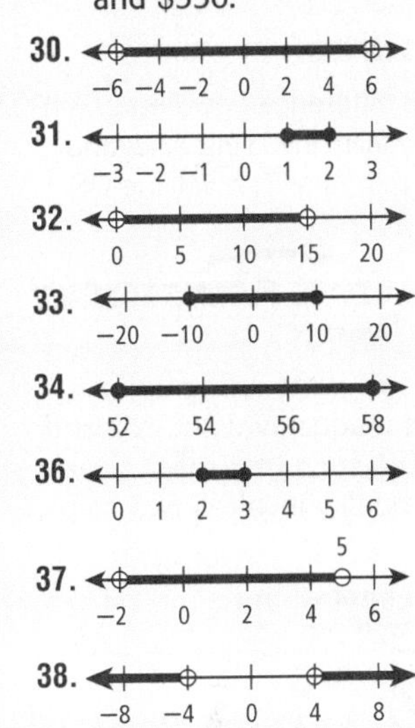

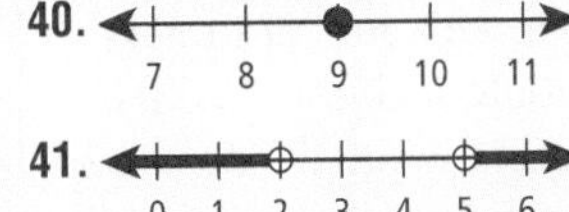

45. Both graphs include numbers less than 3. The graph of $x < 3$ AND $x < 7$ does not include numbers greater than or equal to 3. The graph of $x < 3$ OR $x < 7$ also includes all numbers less than 7.

3-6 PROBLEM SOLVING

Write and solve an inequality for each situation.

1. The Mexican Tetra is a tropical fish that requires a water temperature between 68 and 77 degrees Fahrenheit, inclusive. An aquarium is heated 8 degrees so that a Tetra can live in it. What temperatures could the water have been before the heating?
   $68 \le t + 8 \le 77$; $60 \le t \le 69$
2. Nerissa's car can travel between 380 and 410 miles on a full tank of gas. She filled her gas tank and drove 45 miles. How many more miles can she drive without running out of gas?
   $380 \le m + 45 \le 410$; $335 \le m \le 365$
3. A local company is hiring trainees with less than 1 year of experience and managers with 5 or more years of experience. Graph the solutions.
   $y < 1$ OR $y \ge 5$
4. Marty's allowance is doubled and is now between \$10 and \$15, inclusive. What amounts could his allowance have been before the increase? Graph the solutions.
   $10 \le 2a \le 15$; $5 \le a \le 7.5$

The elliptical orbits of planets bring them closer to and farther from the Sun at different times. The closest (perihelion) and furthest (aphelion) points are given for three planets below. Use this data to answer questions 5–7.

Planet	Perihelion (in 10^6 km)	Aphelion (in 10^6 km)
Uranus	2741.3	3003.6
Neptune	4444.5	4545.7
Pluto	4435.0	7304.3

5. Which inequality represents the distances d from the sun to Neptune?
   A $d \le 4444.5$
   B $d \le 4545.7$
   C $4444.5 \le d \le 4545.7$
   D $d = 4444.5$ OR $d \ge 4545.7$
6. A NASA probe is traveling between Uranus and Neptune. It is currently between their orbits. Which inequality shows the possible distance p from the probe to the Sun?
   F $1542.1 < p < 1703.2$
   G $2741.3 < p < 4545.7$
   H $3003.6 < p < 4444.5$
   J $7185.8 < p < 7549.3$
7. At what distances o do the orbits of Neptune and Pluto overlap?
   A $4435.0 \le o \le 4444.5$
   B $4435.0 \le o \le 4545.7$
   C $4444.5 \le o \le 7304.3$
   D $4545.7 \le o \le 7304.3$

3-6 CHALLENGE

The inequality $a \le x \le b$, where $a < b$, is the set of all real numbers between a and b, including a and b. The corresponding set of points on the number line is called a *closed inverval.*

In Exercises 1–7, n is an integer and $n - \frac{1}{4} \le x \le n + \frac{1}{4}$. Graph the solutions for the given values of n on the number line below.

1. $n = 0$
2. $n = 0$ or $n = 1$
3. $n = 0$ or $n = -1$
4. $n = -2, -1, 0, 1,$ or 2
5. $n = -3, -2, -1, 0, 1, 2,$ or 3
6. $n = -4, -3, -2, -1, 0, 1, 2, 3,$ or 4
7. Suppose that the graphs for all values of n are shown on the number line. Describe the graph.
   Answers may vary. Sample answer: closed intervals centered at each integer with each interval being $\frac{1}{2}$ unit long

Let n be an integer. For each set of intervals on the given number line, write a compound inequality involving n, x, and a conjunction to describe the entire graph.

8. **$n \le x \le n + \frac{1}{2}$**
9. **$2n \le x \le 2n + 1$**
10. **$4n - 1 \le x \le 4n + 1$**
11. a. Let n be a nonzero integer. Describe the interval $1 - \frac{1}{n} \le x \le 1 + \frac{1}{n}$.
    Answers may vary. Sample answers: The center of the interval is 1, and its length is $\frac{2}{n}$.
    b. What can you say about the interval as n gets larger?

3-6 PRACTICE A

3-6 PRACTICE C

3-6 PRACTICE B

Write the compound inequality shown by each graph.

1. **$-2 < x < 4$**
2. **$x < -3$ OR $x \ge 3$**
3. **$x \le -15$ OR $x \ge -8$**
4. **$0 \le x < 20$**

Solve each compound inequality and graph the solutions.

5. $-15 < x - 8 < -4$ **$-7 < x < 4$**
6. $12 \le 4n < 28$ **$3 \le n < 7$**
7. $-2 \le 3b + 7 \le 13$ **$-3 \le b \le 2$**
8. $x - 3 < -3$ OR $x - 3 \ge 3$ **$x < 0$ OR $x \ge 6$**
9. $5k \le -20$ OR $2k \ge 8$ **$k \le -4$ OR $k \ge 4$**
10. $2s + 3 \le 7$ OR $3s + 5 > 26$ **$s \le 2$ OR $s > 7$**

Write a compound inequality for each problem. Graph the solutions.

11. The human ear can distinguish sounds between 20 Hz and 20,000 Hz, inclusive. **$20 \le h \le 20{,}000$**
12. For a man to box as a welterweight, he must weigh more than 140 lbs, but at most 147 lbs. **$140 < w \le 147$**

TEST PREP DOCTOR In **Exercise 48,** students who chose **F** solved only the second inequality. Students who chose **J** graphed the solutions as an OR statement.

In **Exercise 49,** students can start by looking at the open circle at 2 and determining that the correct symbol is <. This immediately eliminates all choices but **B.**

Journal

Explain the difference between graphing an inequality involving AND and graphing an inequality involving OR.

ALTERNATIVE ASSESSMENT

Have students write and graph a compound inequality with AND and one with OR, such that solving each simple inequality involves two steps.

Power Presentations with PowerPoint®

3-6 Lesson Quiz

1. The target heart rate during exercise for a 15-year-old is between 154 and 174 beats per minute inclusive. Write a compound inequality to show the heart rates that are within the target range. Graph the solutions. $154 \le h \le 174$

144 154 164 174 184

Solve each compound inequality and graph the solutions.

2. $2 \le 2w + 4 \le 12$
   $-1 \le w \le 4$

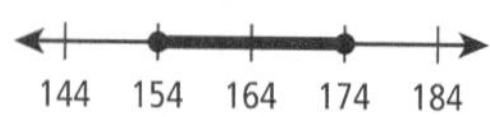

3. $3 + r > -2$ OR $3 + r < -7$
   $r > -5$ OR $r < -10$

−10 −9 −8 −7 −6 −5 −4

Write the compound inequality shown by each graph.

4. −7; −10 −8 −6 −4 −2 0 2
   $x < -7$ OR $x \ge 0$
5. −2 −1 0 1 2 3 4
   $-2 \le a < 4$

Also available on transparency

46. **Critical Thinking** If there is no solution to a compound inequality, does the compound inequality involve OR or AND? Explain. **An inequality with OR always has solutions because the two simple inequalities do not have to be true at the same time. A compound inequality with no solutions must involve AND.**

TEST PREP

47. Which of the following describes the solutions of $-x + 1 > 2$ OR $x - 1 > 2$?
    (A) all real numbers greater than 1 or less than 3
    (B) all real numbers greater than 3 or less than 1
    (C) all real numbers greater than −1 or less than 3
    (D) all real numbers greater than 3 or less than −1

48. Which of the following is a graph of the solutions of $x - 3 < 2$ AND $x + 3 > 2$?

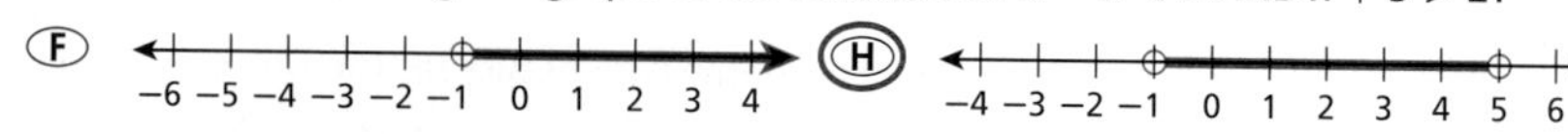

(F) −6 −5 −4 −3 −2 −1 0 1 2 3 4 **(H)** −4 −3 −2 −1 0 1 2 3 4 5 6

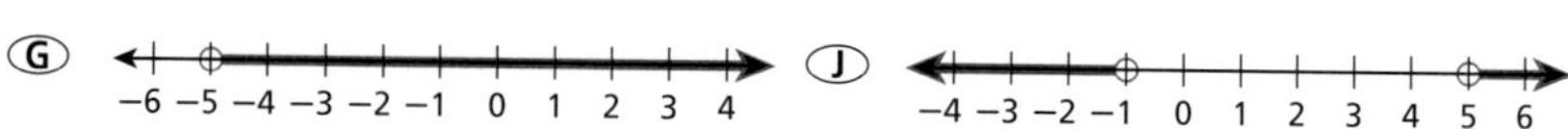

(G) −6 −5 −4 −3 −2 −1 0 1 2 3 4 (J) −4 −3 −2 −1 0 1 2 3 4 5 6

49. Which compound inequality is shown by the graph?

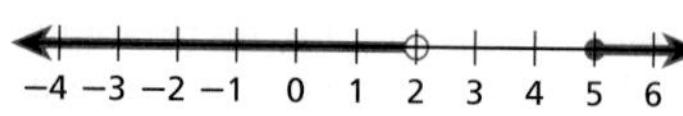

−4 −3 −2 −1 0 1 2 3 4 5 6

(A) $x \le 2$ OR $x > 5$ (C) $x \le 2$ OR $x \ge 5$
(B) $x < 2$ OR $x \ge 5$ (D) $x \ge 2$ OR $x > 5$

50. Which of the following is a solution of $x + 1 \ge 3$ AND $x + 1 \le 3$?
    (F) 0 (G) 1 **(H)** 2 (J) 3

CHALLENGE AND EXTEND

Solve and graph each compound inequality.

51. $2c - 10 < 5 - 3c < 7c$ $0.5 < c < 3$
52. $5p - 10 < p + 6 < 3p$ $3 < p < 4$
53. $2s \le 18 - s$ OR $5s \ge s + 36$
54. $9 - x \ge 5x$ OR $20 - 3x \le 17$
55. Write a compound inequality that represents all values of x that are NOT solutions to $x < -1$ OR $x > 3$. $-1 \le x \le 3$
56. For the compound inequality $x + 2 \ge a$ AND $x - 7 \le b$, find values of a and b for which the only solution is $x = 1$. $a = 3$; $b = -6$

53. $s \le 6$ OR $s \ge 9$

54. $x \le 1\frac{1}{2}$ OR $x \ge 1$

SPIRAL REVIEW

Simplify each expression. Justify each step. *(Lesson 1-7)*

57. $4(x - 3) + 7$ $4x - 5$
58. $5x - 4y - x + 3y$ $4x - y$
59. $6a - 3(a - 1)$ $3a + 3$

Generate ordered pairs for each function for $x = -2, -1, 0, 1,$ and 2. Graph the ordered pairs and describe the pattern. *(Lesson 1-8)*

60. $y = -2x + 2$ line
61. $y = x^2 - 1$ U-shaped
62. $y = x^2 + (-2)$ U-shaped

Solve each inequality and graph the solutions. *(Lesson 3-4)*

63. $3m - 5 < 1$ $m < 2$
64. $2(x + 4) > 6$ $x > -1$
65. $11 \le 7 - 2x$ $x \le -2$

Answers

51. 0.5 1 1.5 2 2.5 3
52. 0 1 2 3 4 5 6
53. 0 3 6 9 12

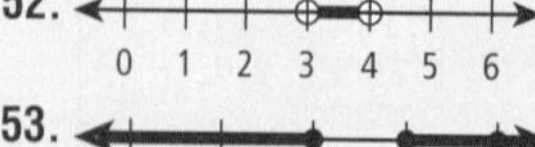

54. 0 $\frac{1}{2}$ 1 $1\frac{1}{2}$ 2

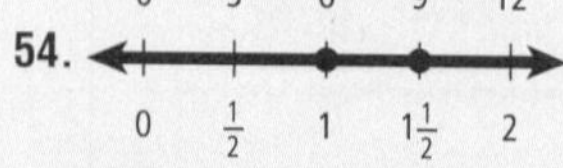

57. $4(x - 3) + 7$
    $4x - 12 + 7$ Dist. Prop.
    $4x - 5$ Combine like terms.
58. $5x - 4y - x + 3y$
    $5x - x - 4y + 3y$ Comm. Prop. of Add.
    $4x - y$ Combine like terms.
59. $6a - 3(a - 1)$
    $6a - 3a + 3$ Dist. Prop.
    $3a + 3$ Combine like terms.

60–65. For graphs, see p. A15.

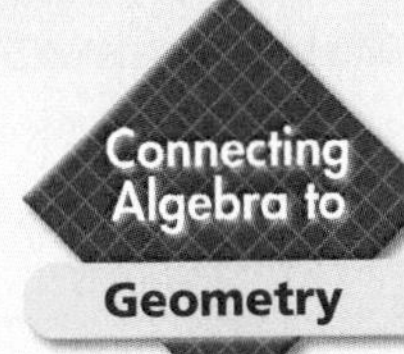

Triangle Inequality

For any triangle, the sum of the lengths of any two sides is greater than the length of the third side.

The sides of this triangle are labeled a, b, and c. You can use the Triangle Inequality to write three statements about the triangle.

$a + b > c$ $\quad a + c > b$ $\quad b + c > a$

Unless all three of the inequalities are true, the lengths a, b, and c cannot form a triangle.

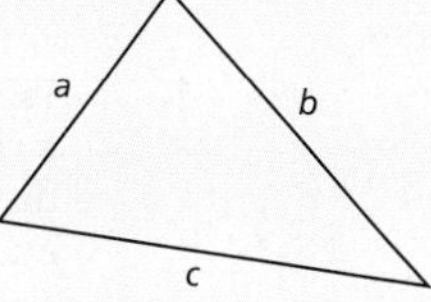

Example 1

Can three side lengths of 25 cm, 15 cm, and 5 cm form a triangle?

a. $25 + 15 > 5$
$40 > 5$ *True*

b. $25 + 5 > 15$
$30 > 15$ *True*

c. $15 + 5 > 25$
$20 > 25$ *False*

One of the inequalities is false, so the three lengths will not make a triangle. The situation is shown in the figure to the right.

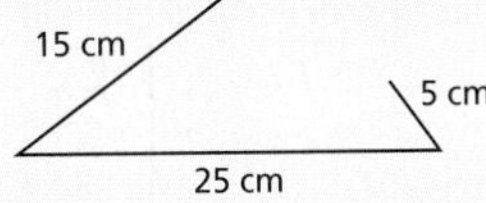

Example 2

Two sides of a triangle measure 8 ft and 10 ft. What is the range of lengths of the third side?

Start by writing three statements about the triangle. Use x for the unknown side length.

a. $8 + 10 > x$
$18 > x$
The third side must be shorter than 18 ft.

b. $8 + x > 10$
$8 + x - 8 > 10 - 8$
$x > 2$
The third side must be longer than 2 ft.

c. $x + 10 > 8$
$x + 10 - 10 > 8 - 10$
$x > -2$
This provides no new useful information.

From part **a,** the third side must be shorter than 18 ft. And from part **b,** it must be longer than 2 ft. An inequality showing this is $2 < x < 18$.

Try This

Decide whether the three lengths given can form a triangle. If not, explain.

1. 14 ft, 30 ft, 10 ft **no; 14 ft + 10 ft < 30 ft**
2. 11 cm, 8 cm, 17 cm **yes**
3. $6\frac{1}{2}$ yd, 3 yd, $2\frac{3}{4}$ yd **3. no; 3 yd + $2\frac{3}{4}$ yd < $6\frac{1}{2}$ yd**

Write a compound inequality for the range of lengths of the third side of each triangle.

4. 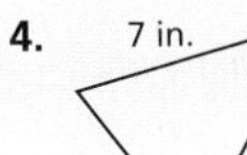 

5. 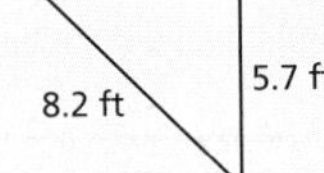

6. 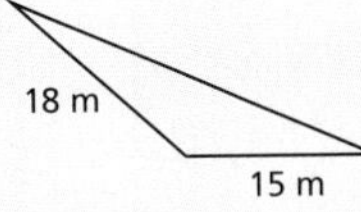

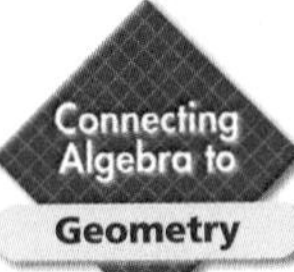

Organizer

Pacing:
Traditional $\frac{1}{2}$ day
Block $\frac{1}{4}$ day

Objective: Apply the algebra skills of solving inequalities to finding possible side lengths of triangles.

 **Online Edition**

 **Countdown Week 7**

Teach

Remember

Students review and apply the geometric properties of triangles.

 **Kinesthetic** Students may better understand the Triangle Inequality if they attempt to make triangles from various lengths of straw or spaghetti.

Close

Assess

Have students give three possible side lengths for the third side of the triangles in **Problems 4–6.**

Answers

4. 0 in. < x < 14 in.
5. 2.5 ft < x < 13.9 ft
6. 3 m < x < 33 m

State Resources

go.hrw.com
State Resources Online
KEYWORD: MA7 Resources

3-7 Organizer

Pacing: Traditional 1 day
Block $\frac{1}{2}$ day

Objective: Solve inequalities in one variable involving absolute-value expressions.

Online Edition
Tutorial Videos

Countdown Week 7

Power Presentations with PowerPoint®

Warm Up

Solve each inequality and graph the solutions.

1. $x + 7 < 4$ $\quad x < -3$

−5 −4 −3 −2 −1 0 1

2. $14x \geq 28$ $\quad x \geq 2$

−1 0 1 2 3 4 5 6

3. $5 + 2x > 1$ $\quad x > -2$

−5 −4 −3 −2 −1 0 1

Also available on transparency

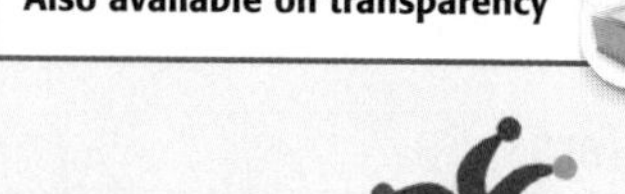

Q: What does an absolute-value expression work on when it goes to the gym?

A: Its "abs"!

3-7 Solving Absolute-Value Inequalities

Objective
Solve inequalities in one variable involving absolute-value expressions.

Why learn this?
You can solve an absolute-value inequality to determine the safe range for the pressure of a fire extinguisher. (See Example 3.)

When an inequality contains an absolute-value expression, it can be rewritten as a compound inequality. The inequality $|x| < 5$ describes all real numbers whose distance from 0 is less than 5 units. The solutions are all numbers between -5 and 5, so $|x| < 5$ can be rewritten as $-5 < x < 5$ or as $x > -5$ AND $x < 5$.

Absolute-Value Inequalities Involving <

WORDS	NUMBERS
The inequality $\|x\| < a$ (when $a > 0$) asks, "What values of x have an absolute value less than a?" The solutions are numbers between $-a$ and a.	$\|x\| < 5$ $-5 < x < 5$ $x > -5$ AND $x < 5$
GRAPH	**ALGEBRA**
← a units →← a units → $-a$ 0 a	$\|x\| < a$ (when $a > 0$) $-a < x < a$ $x > -a$ AND $x < a$

The same properties are true for inequalities that use the symbol $\leq$.

EXAMPLE 1 Solving Absolute-Value Inequalities Involving <

Solve each inequality and graph the solutions.

Helpful Hint
Just as you do when solving absolute-value equations, you first isolate the absolute-value expression when solving absolute-value inequalities.

A $|x| + 3 < 12$

$$\begin{aligned} |x| + 3 &< 12 \\ -3 \quad & \;\; -3 \\ |x| &< 9 \end{aligned}$$

Since 3 is added to $|x|$, subtract 3 from both sides to undo the addition.

$x > -9$ AND $x < 9$ *Write as a compound inequality.*

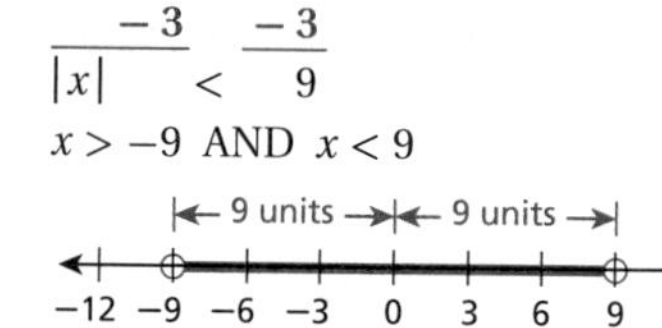

B $|x + 4| \leq 2$

$x + 4 \geq -2$ AND $x + 4 \leq 2$ *Write as a compound inequality.*

$\quad -4 \;\; -4 \qquad\quad -4 \;\; -4$ *Solve each inequality.*

$x \geq -6$ AND $x \leq -2$ *Write as a compound inequality.*

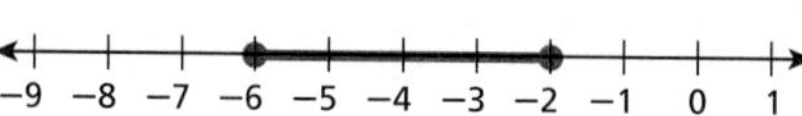

State Resources

go.hrw.com
State Resources Online
KEYWORD: MA7 Resources

1 Introduce

EXPLORATION

3-7 Solving Absolute-Value Inequalities

In this activity, you will investigate the inequality $|x| < 2$.

1. Copy and complete the table.

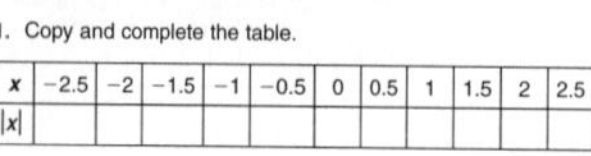

x	−2.5	−2	−1.5	−1	−0.5	0	0.5	1	1.5	2	2.5
$\|x\|$											

2. Circle all the values of x for which $|x| < 2$.
3. Copy the number line. Shade all the values of x on the number line for which $|x| < 2$.

−7 −6 −5 −4 −3 −2 −1 0 1 2 3 4 5 6 7

4. Is the value −1.9 included in the shaded region? Why or why not?
5. Are the values 2 and −2 included in the shaded region? Why or why not?
6. What can you say about the distance of x from 0 on the number line if you know that $|x| < 2$?

THINK AND DISCUSS

7. **Describe** the region you shaded using a compound inequality.
8. **Explain** how the shaded region would be different for the

Motivate

Present the following situation to the class: To get a B on an exam, a student's score must be no more than 5 points away from 85. Ask students what scores result in a B. Plot these values on a number line. Then explain that an absolute-value inequality can be used to describe the set of scores.

Explorations and answers are provided in *Alternate Openers: Explorations Transparencies.*

Solve each inequality and graph the solutions.

1a. $2|x| \le 6$ $-3 \le x \le 3$

1b. $|x + 3| - 4.5 \le 7.5$ $-15 \le x \le 9$

The inequality $|x| > 5$ describes all real numbers whose distance from 0 is greater than 5 units. The solutions are all numbers less than -5 or greater than 5. The inequality $|x| > 5$ can be rewritten as the compound inequality $x < -5$ OR $x > 5$.

Absolute-Value Inequalities Involving >

WORDS	NUMBERS
The inequality $\|x\| > a$ (when $a > 0$) asks, "What values of x have an absolute value greater than a?" The solutions are numbers less than $-a$ or greater than a.	$\|x\| > 5$ $x < -5$ OR $x > 5$
GRAPH	**ALGEBRA**
← a units →← a units → $-a$ 0 a	$\|x\| > a$ (when $a > 0$) $x < -a$ OR $x > a$

The same properties are true for inequalities that use the symbol $\ge$.

EXAMPLE 2 Solving Absolute-Value Inequalities Involving >

Solve each inequality and graph the solutions.

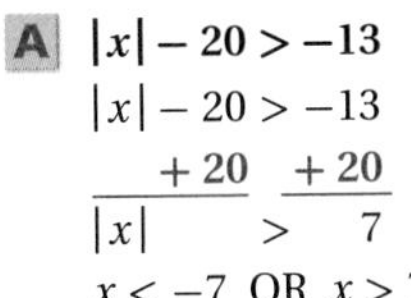

A $|x| - 20 > -13$

$$|x| - 20 > -13$$
$$\underline{+20 \quad +20}$$
$$|x| > 7$$

Since 20 is subtracted from $|x|$, add 20 to both sides to undo the subtraction.

$x < -7$ OR $x > 7$ *Write as a compound inequality.*

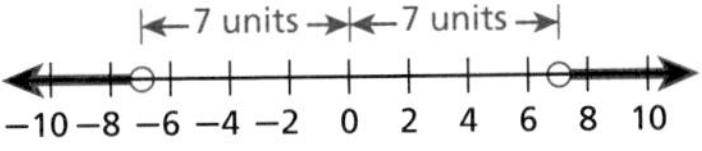

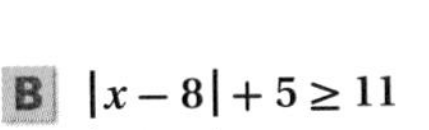

B $|x - 8| + 5 \ge 11$

$$|x - 8| + 5 \ge 11$$
$$\underline{-5 \quad -5}$$
$$|x - 8| \ge 6$$

Since 5 is added to $|x - 8|$, subtract 5 from both sides to undo the addition.

$x - 8 \le -6$ OR $x - 8 \ge 6$ *Write as a compound inequality.*

$\underline{+8 \quad +8} \qquad \underline{+8 \quad +8}$ *Solve each inequality.*

$x \le 2$ OR $x \ge 14$ *Write as a compound inequality.*

Solve each inequality and graph the solutions.

2a. $|x| + 10 \ge 12$

2b. $\left|x + 2\frac{1}{2}\right| + \frac{1}{2} \ge 4$

2a. $x \le -2$ OR $x \ge 2$

2b. $x \le -6$ OR $x \ge 1$

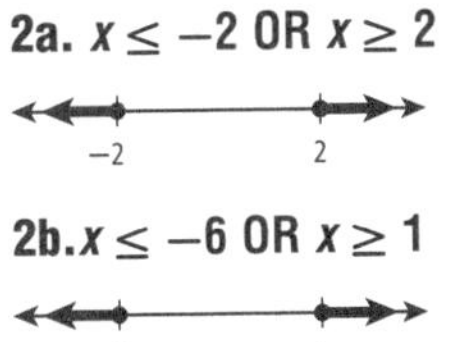

COMMON ERROR ALERT

In **Example 1B,** students may try to subtract 4 from both sides of the inequality as a first step. Remind students that they must first remove the absolute-value symbol by writing a compound inequality.

Power Presentations with PowerPoint®

Additional Examples

Example 1

Solve each inequality and graph the solutions.

A. $|x| - 3 < -1$ $-2 < x < 2$

B. $|x - 1| \le 2$ $-1 \le x \le 3$

Example 2

Solve each inequality and graph the solutions.

A. $|x| + 14 \ge 19$ $x \le -5$ OR $x \ge 5$

B. $3 + |x + 2| > 5$ $x < -4$ OR $x > 0$

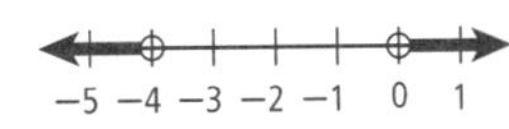

INTERVENTION

Questioning Strategies

EXAMPLE 1

- Why does an absolute-value inequality with a less-than symbol indicate an AND statement?

EXAMPLE 2

- Why does an absolute-value inequality with a greater-than symbol indicate an OR statement?

Reading Math Have students read $|x|$ as "the distance from zero" to help them visualize what the graph of an absolute-value inequality will look like. For example, $|x| < 3$ can be read as "the distance from zero is less than 3."

2 Teach

Guided Instruction

Remind students that the absolute value of a number is its distance from 0 on a number line. Then briefly review how to solve compound inequalities.

Use number lines and simple absolute-value inequalities like $|x| < 5$ and $|x| > 5$ to show why less-than symbols indicate an AND statement and greater-than symbols indicate an OR statement.

Reaching All Learners

Through Auditory Cues

Stress the word *than* when saying "less than" and stress the suffix *-er* when saying "greater." Then the appropriate compound word almost rhymes with the inequality in the following phrase: "Less than is AND, greater is OR."

Power Presentations with PowerPoint®

Additional Examples

Example 3

A pediatrician recommends that a baby's bath water be 95 °F, but it is acceptable for the temperature to vary from this amount by as much as 3 °F. Write and solve an absolute-value inequality to find the range of acceptable temperatures. Graph the solutions.

$|t - 95| \leq 3$; $92 \leq t \leq 98$

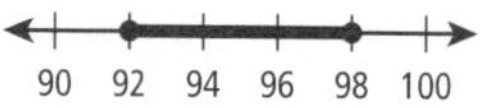

90 92 94 96 98 100

Example 4

Solve each inequality.

A. $|x + 4| - 5 > -8$ all real numbers

B. $|x - 2| + 9 < 7$ no solutions

INTERVENTION
Questioning Strategies

EXAMPLE 3

- How can you use an inequality to represent the phrase "at most"?

EXAMPLE 4

- How can you tell when an absolute-value inequality will have all real numbers as its solutions?
- How can you tell when an absolute-value inequality will have no solutions?

EXAMPLE 3 Safety Application

Some fire extinguishers contain pressurized water. The water pressure should be 162.5 psi (pounds per square inch), but it is acceptable for the pressure to differ from this value by at most 12.5 psi. Write and solve an absolute-value inequality to find the range of acceptable pressures. Graph the solutions.

Let p represent the actual water pressure of a fire extinguisher.

The difference between p and the ideal pressure	is at most	12.5 psi.
$\|p - 162.5\|$	$\leq$	12.5

$|p - 162.5| \leq 12.5$

$p - 162.5 \geq -12.5$ AND $p - 162.5 \leq 12.5$ *Solve the two inequalities.*

$\underline{+162.5 \quad +162.5} \qquad \underline{+162.5 \quad +162.5}$

$p \geq 150$ AND $p \leq 175$

140 145 150 155 160 165 170 175 180 185 190

The range of acceptable pressures is $150 \leq p \leq 175$.

CHECK IT OUT! **3.** A dry-chemical fire extinguisher should be pressurized to 125 psi, but it is acceptable for the pressure to differ from this value by at most 75 psi. Write and solve an absolute-value inequality to find the range of acceptable pressures. Graph the solutions.

3. $|p - 125| \leq 75$; $50 \leq p \leq 200$

25 50 75 100 125 150 175 200 225

When solving an absolute-value inequality, you may get a statement that is true for all values of the variable. In this case, all real numbers are solutions of the original inequality. If you get a false statement when solving an absolute-value inequality, the original inequality has no solutions.

EXAMPLE 4 Special Cases of Absolute-Value Inequalities

Solve each inequality.

A $|x - 6| + 7 > 2$

$|x - 6| + 7 > 2$

$\underline{\quad -7 \quad -7}$ *Subtract 7 from both sides.*

$|x - 6| > -5$ *Absolute-value expressions are always nonnegative. Therefore, the statement is true for all values of x.*

All real numbers are solutions.

B $|x + 12| - 5 \leq -6$

$|x + 12| - 5 \leq -6$

$\underline{\quad +5 \quad +5}$ *Add 5 to both sides.*

$|x + 12| \leq -1$ *Absolute-value expressions are always nonnegative. Therefore, the statement is false for all values of x.*

The inequality has no solutions.

Remember!

An absolute value represents a distance, and distance cannot be less than 0.

CHECK IT OUT! **Solve each inequality.**

4a. $|x| - 9 \geq -11$ all real numbers

4b. $4|x - 3.5| \leq -8$ no solutions

3 Close

Summarize

Solve each absolute-value inequality.

1. $4 + |x| < 16$ $\quad -12 < x < 12$
2. $|x - 3| + 5 \leq -8$ $\quad$ no solutions
3. $|x + 1| - 4 \geq 3$ $\quad x \leq -8$ OR $x \geq 6$
4. $2|x + 6| > -10$ $\quad$ all real numbers

ONGOING ASSESSMENT and INTERVENTION

***Diagnose Before* the Lesson**
3-7 Warm Up, TE p. 212

***Monitor During* the Lesson**
Check It Out! Exercises, SE pp. 213–214
Questioning Strategies, TE pp. 212–214

***Assess After* the Lesson**
3-7 Lesson Quiz, TE p. 217
Alternative Assessment, TE p. 217

THINK AND DISCUSS

1. Describe how the solutions of $7|x| \le 21$ are different from the solutions of $7|x| < 21$.
2. **GET ORGANIZED** Copy and complete the graphic organizer. In each box, write an example of the indicated type of absolute-value inequality and then solve.

Absolute-Value Inequalities → AND, OR

Answers to *Think and Discuss*

1. Possible answer: The solutions of $7|x| \le 21$ are all values of x between -3 and 3, inclusive. The solutions of $7|x| < 21$ are all values of x between -3 and 3, not including these values.
2. See p. A4.

3-7 Exercises

go.hrw.com
Homework Help Online
KEYWORD: MA11 3-7
Parent Resources Online
KEYWORD: MA7 Parent

GUIDED PRACTICE

Solve each inequality and graph the solutions.

SEE EXAMPLE 1 p. 212

1. $|x| - 5 \le -2$
2. $|x+1| - 7.8 < 6.2$
3. $|3x| + 2 < 8$
4. $4|x| \le 20$
5. $|x-5| + 1 < 2$
6. $\left|x + \frac{1}{2}\right| - \frac{1}{2} \le 3\frac{1}{2}$

SEE EXAMPLE 2 p. 213

7. $|x| - 6 > 16$
8. $|x| + 2.9 > 8.6$
9. $2|x| \ge 8$
10. $|x+2| > 7$
11. $|x-3| + 2 \ge 4$
12. $|x+5| - 4\frac{1}{2} \ge 7\frac{1}{2}$

SEE EXAMPLE 3 p. 214

13. **Nutrition** A nutritionist recommends that an adult male consume 55 grams of fat per day. It is acceptable for the fat intake to differ from this amount by at most 25 grams. Write and solve an absolute-value inequality to find the range of fat intake that is acceptable. Graph the solutions.

SEE EXAMPLE 4 p. 214

Solve each inequality.

14. $|x| + 8 \le 2$ **no solutions**
15. $|x+3| < -5$ **no solutions**
16. $|x+4| \ge -8$ **all real numbers**
17. $|x-5| + \frac{1}{3} > -1$ **all real numbers**
18. $|3x| + 7 > 2$ **all real numbers**
19. $|x-7| + 3.5 \le 2$ **no solutions**

PRACTICE AND PROBLEM SOLVING

Independent Practice	
For Exercises	See Example
20–25	1
26–31	2
32	3
33–38	4

Extra Practice
Skills Practice p. S9
Application Practice p. S30

Solve each inequality and graph the solutions.

20. $|x| + 6 \le 10$
21. $|x-3| < 1$
22. $|x-2| - 8 \le -3$
23. $|5x| < 15$
24. $|x-2.4| + 4 \le 6.4$
25. $4 + |x+3| < 7$
26. $|x-1| > 2$
27. $6|x| \ge 60$
28. $|x-4| + 3 > 8$
29. $2|x+2| \ge 16$
30. $3 + |x-4| > 4$
31. $\left|x - \frac{1}{2}\right| + 9 > 10\frac{1}{2}$
32. The thermostat for a sauna is set to 175 °F, but the actual temperature of the sauna may vary by as much as 12 °F. Write and solve an absolute-value inequality to find the range of possible temperatures. Graph the solutions.

Solve each inequality.

33. $12 + |x| \le 10$ **no solutions**
34. $\left|x + \frac{3}{5}\right| - 2 > -4$ **all real numbers**
35. $|x+1| + 5 \ge 4$ **all real numbers**
36. $|4x| - 3 < -6$ **no solutions**
37. $3|x-4| \le -9$ **no solutions**
38. $|2x| + 9 \ge 9$ **all real numbers**

Assignment Guide

Assign *Guided Practice* exercises as necessary.

If you finished Examples **1–2**
- **Basic** 20–31, 45–48
- **Average** 20–31, 39, 40, 45–48
- **Advanced** 20–31, 39, 40, 45–48, 58, 59

If you finished Examples **1–4**
- **Basic** 20–38, 42–52, 55–57, 61–70
- **Average** 20–44, 46–52 even, 53–58, 61–72
- **Advanced** 20–44 even, 45–72

Homework Quick Check
Quickly check key concepts.
Exercises: 8, 10, 11, 12, 14, 24

Answers

1. $-3 \le x \le 3$
2. $-15 < x < 13$

State Resources

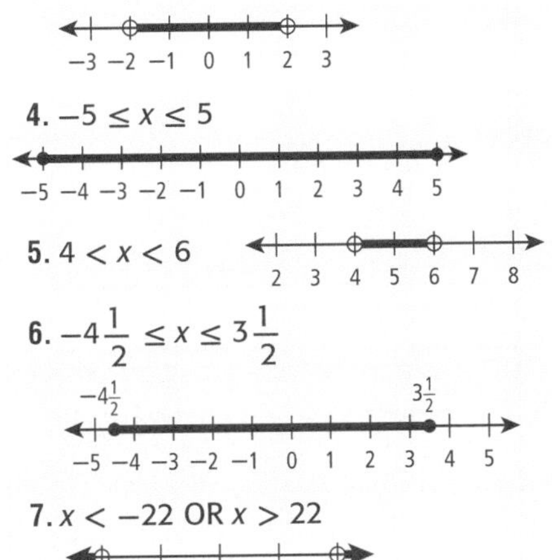

8. $x < -5.7$ OR $x > 5.7$
9. $x \le -4$ OR $x \ge 4$
10. $x < -9$ OR $x > 5$
11. $x \le 1$ OR $x \ge 5$
12. $x \le -17$ OR $x \ge 7$
13. $|x - 55| \le 25$; $30 \le x \le 80$

20–32. See pp. A15–A16.

Exercise 52 involves using absolute-value inequalities to determine the range of possible prices for a CD. This exercise prepares students for the Multi-Step Test Prep on page 218.

Answers

39. Absolute-value expressions are always nonneg.
40. Absolute-value expressions are always nonneg.
41. Possible answer: $|x + 1| > -5$ has all real numbers as solutions, but $|x - 7| < 0$ has no solutions.
42. $|x| \le 15$; $-15 \le x \le 15$

    −30 −15 0 15 30
43. $|x - 2| \le 3$; $-1 \le x \le 5$

    −1 5
44. $|x - 8| \ge 2$; $x \le 6$ OR $x \ge 10$

    5 6 7 8 9 10 11
45. $|a| \le 2$
46. $|b| > 3$
47. $|c| \ge 6\frac{1}{2}$
48. $|d| < 7$
49. a. 10,010 Hz

    b. $|x - 10{,}010| \le 9990$
50. European eel: $|x - 23| \le 11$;
    Rainbow trout: $|x - 15| \le 11$;
    Sea bass: $|x - 21| \le 9$

Tell whether each statement is sometimes, always, or never true. Explain.

39. The value of $|x + 1|$ is greater than -5. **always**
40. The value of $|x - 7|$ is less than 0. **never**
41. An absolute-value inequality has all real numbers as solutions. **sometimes**

Write and solve an absolute-value inequality for each expression. Graph the solutions on a number line.

42. All numbers whose absolute value is less than or equal to 15
43. All numbers less than or equal to 3 units from 2 on the number line
44. All numbers at least 2 units from 8 on the number line

Write an absolute-value inequality for each graph.

45. −5 −4 −3 −2 −1 0 1 2 3 4 5
46. −5 −4 −3 −2 −1 0 1 2 3 4 5
47. $-6\frac{1}{2}$ $6\frac{1}{2}$ −10 −8 −6 −4 −2 0 2 4 6 8 10
48. −7 7 −10 −8 −6 −4 −2 0 2 4 6 8 10

49. **Multi-Step** The frequency of a sound wave determines its pitch. The human ear can detect a wide range of frequencies, from 20 Hz (very low notes) to 20,000 Hz (very high notes).
    a. What frequency is at the middle of the range?
    b. Write an absolute-value inequality for the range of frequencies the human ear can detect.

50. **Biology** The diagram shows the temperature range at which several fish species can survive. For each species, write an absolute-value inequality that gives the range of temperatures at which it can survive.

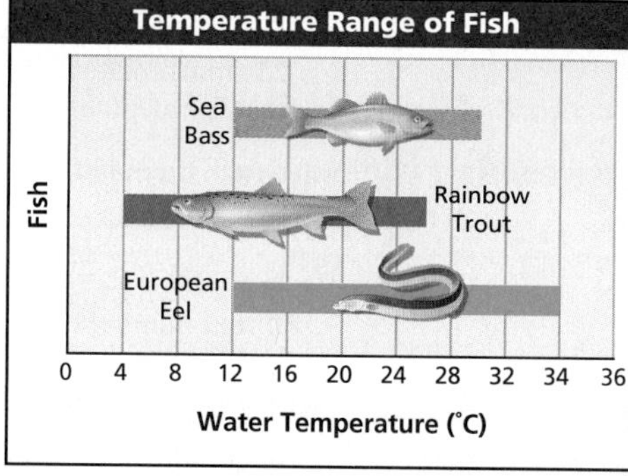

51. **Entertainment** On a game show, a contestant must guess a secret two-digit number. The secret number is 23. Write an absolute-value inequality that shows that the contestant's guess is more than 12 numbers away from the secret number. $|n - 23| > 12$

MULTI-STEP TEST PREP

52. This problem will help prepare you for the Multi-Step Test Prep on page 218.

    The manager of a band recommends that the band sell its CDs for $8.75. The band decides to sell the CDs for p dollars.
    a. Write an absolute-value expression that tells how far the band's price is from the recommended price. $|p - 8.75|$
    b. The band wants the price of its CD to be no more than $1.25 from the recommended price. Write an absolute-value inequality that gives the range of possible prices for the CD. $|p - 8.75| \le 1.25$
    c. Solve the inequality. Write the solution as a compound inequality. $\$7.50 \le p \le \$10.00$

3-7 PRACTICE A
3-7 PRACTICE C
3-7 PRACTICE B

Solve each inequality and graph the solutions.

1. $|x| - 2 \le 3$ — $x \ge -5$ AND $x \le 5$
2. $|x + 1| + 5 < 7$ — $x > -3$ AND $x < 1$
3. $3|x - 6| \le 9$ — $x \ge 3$ AND $x \le 9$
4. $|x + 3| - 1.5 < -2.5$ — $x > -7$ AND $x < 1$
5. $|x| + 17 > 20$ — $x < -3$ OR $x > 3$
6. $|x - 6| - 7 > -3$ — $x < 2$ OR $x > 10$
7. $\frac{1}{2}|x + 5| \ge 2$ — $x \le -9$ OR $x \ge -1$
8. $2|x - 2| \ge 3$ — $x \le 0.5$ OR $x \ge 3.5$
9. The organizers of a drama club wanted to sell 350 tickets to their show. The actual sales were no more than 35 tickets from this goal. Write and solve an absolute-value inequality to find the range of the number of tickets that may have been sold.

   $|x - 350| \le 35$; $315 \le x \le 385$
10. The temperature at noon in Los Angeles on a summer day was 88 °F. During the day, the temperature varied from this by as much as 7.5 °F. Write and solve an absolute-value inequality to find the range of possible temperatures for that day.

    $|x - 88| \le 7.5$; $80.5 \le x \le 95.5$

3-7 READING STRATEGIES

You can use a number line to help you solve absolute-value inequalities that have the form $|x - b| \le c$ or $|x - b| < c$. The following steps show how to use this method to solve $|x - 1| \le 3$.

Step 1: Plot the value of b on the number line.
In $|x - 1| \le 3$, $b = 1$

Step 2: Plot the two points that are c units away from b.
In this case, $c = 3$.
3 units 3 units

Step 3: Shade the points in between.
The solution is $-2 \le x \le 4$

Answer each question.

1. When you use a number line to solve the inequality $|x - 5| < 4$, which point should you plot first? **5**
2. Which points should you plot next? **1 and 9**
3. Graph the solutions of $|x - 5| < 4$ on the number line.
4. When you use a number line to solve the inequality $|x + 1| \le 2$, which point should you plot first? (*Hint: The* inequality can be written as $|x - (-1)| \le 2$) **−1**
5. Which points should you plot next? **−3 and 1**
6. Graph the solutions of $|x + 1| \le 2$ on the number line.
7. Use this method to graph the solutions of $|x + 2| < 1$.

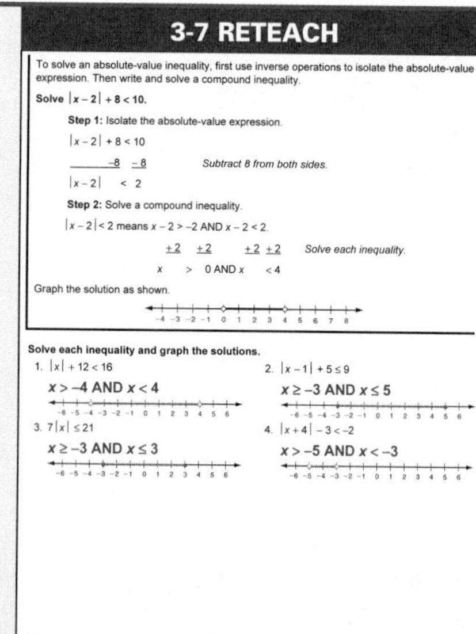
3-7 RETEACH

To solve an absolute-value inequality, first use inverse operations to isolate the absolute-value expression. Then write and solve a compound inequality.

Solve $|x - 2| + 8 < 10$.

Step 1: Isolate the absolute-value expression.

$|x - 2| + 8 < 10$

$-8 \quad -8$ *Subtract 8 from both sides.*

$|x - 2| < 2$

Step 2: Solve a compound inequality.

$|x - 2| < 2$ means $x - 2 > -2$ AND $x - 2 < 2$.

$+2 \quad +2 \qquad +2 \quad +2$ *Solve each inequality.*

$x > 0$ AND $x < 4$

Graph the solution as shown.

Solve each inequality and graph the solutions.

1. $|x| + 12 < 16$ — $x > -4$ AND $x < 4$
2. $|x - 1| + 5 \le 9$ — $x \ge -3$ AND $x \le 5$
3. $7|x| \le 21$ — $x \ge -3$ AND $x \le 3$
4. $|x + 4| - 3 < -2$ — $x > -5$ AND $x < -3$

53. Critical Thinking For which values of k does the inequality $|x| + 1 < k$ have no solutions? Explain.

54. Write About It Describe how to use an absolute-value inequality to find all the values on a number line that are within 5 units of -6.

TEST PREP

55. What is the solution of the inequality $3 + |x + 4| < 6$?
    - Ⓐ $-13 < x < 5$
    - Ⓑ $-7 < x < -1$ (circled)
    - Ⓒ $-6 < x < -2$
    - Ⓓ $1 < x < 7$

56. A thermometer gives temperature readings that may be inaccurate by at most 2 °F. The actual temperature is 75 °F. Which absolute-value inequality describes the range of temperatures that may be shown on the thermometer?
    - Ⓕ $|x - 75| \leq 2$ (circled)
    - Ⓖ $|x + 75| \leq 2$
    - Ⓗ $|x - 75| \geq 2$
    - Ⓙ $|x + 75| \geq 2$

57. The inequality $|w - 156| \leq 3$ describes the weights of members of a wrestling team. Which statement is NOT true?
    - Ⓐ All of the team members weigh no more than 159 pounds.
    - Ⓑ A team member may weigh 152 pounds. (circled)
    - Ⓒ Every member of the team is at most 3 pounds away from 156 pounds.
    - Ⓓ There are no team members who weigh 160 pounds.

CHALLENGE AND EXTEND

Write an absolute-value inequality for each graph.

58.

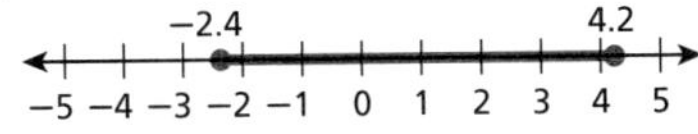

59. (number line with open circles at $-1\frac{1}{2}$ and $3\frac{1}{2}$; −5 −4 −3 −2 −1 0 1 2 3 4 5)

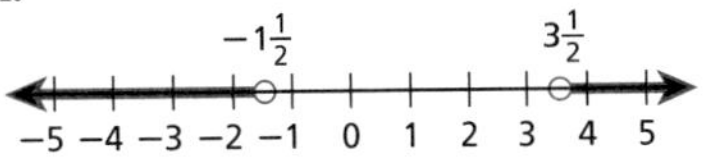

58. Possible answer: $|x - 0.9| \leq 3.3$

59. Possible answer: $|x - 1| > 2\frac{1}{2}$

60. Critical Thinking Fill in the missing reasons to justify each step in solving $|2x - 6| + 5 \leq 7$.

Statements	Reasons
1. $\lvert 2x - 6\rvert + 5 \leq 7$	Given
2. $\lvert 2x - 6\rvert \leq 2$	Subtr. Prop. of Ineq.
3. $2x - 6 \geq -2$ AND $2x - 6 \leq 2$	Definition of absolute value
4. $2x \geq 4$ AND $2x \leq 8$	Add. Prop. of Ineq.
5. $x \geq 2$ AND $x \leq 4$	Div. Prop. of Ineq.

SPIRAL REVIEW

Solve each proportion. Check your answer. *(Lesson 2-7)*

61. $\frac{x+1}{4} = \frac{5}{8}$ $1\frac{1}{2}$
62. $\frac{2}{15} = \frac{6}{y-5}$ 50
63. $\frac{12}{m+2} = \frac{8}{3}$ $2\frac{1}{2}$
64. $\frac{7+g}{10} = \frac{6}{8}$ $\frac{1}{2}$

Describe the solutions of each inequality in words. *(Lesson 3-1)*

65. $16 > 8m$
66. $c + 4 < 11$
67. $-4 \leq x + 2$
68. $0 \geq x + 7$

Solve each compound inequality and graph the solutions. *(Lesson 3-6)*

69. $-3 < x - 3 < 1$
70. $-3 \leq 2x + 1 \leq 9$
71. $x - 2 < -1$ OR $x - 2 > 2$
72. $x + 4 \leq 3$ OR $x + 4 \geq 6$

COMMON ERROR ALERT

When writing an absolute-value inequality of the form $|x - k| \leq a$, students sometimes confuse the values that should be used for k and a. In **Exercise 43**, students may write $|x - 3| \leq 2$. Explain that the value that is at the center of the range (in this case, 2) should appear inside the absolute-value expression, so the correct inequality is $|x - 2| \leq 3$.

TEST PREP DOCTOR

If students answered **H** or **J** for **Exercise 56**, remind them that the range of values is represented by AND, which corresponds to a less-than symbol. Therefore, choices **H** and **J** can be eliminated at once.

Answers

53, 54, 65–72. See p. A16.

Journal

Have students compare the steps they would use to solve $|x + 1| - 5 < 4$ with the steps they would use to solve $|x + 1| - 5 > 4$.

ALTERNATIVE ASSESSMENT

Have students write and solve an absolute-value inequality that involves AND and an absolute-value inequality that involves OR.

Power Presentations with PowerPoint®

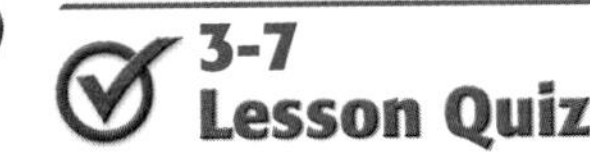

3-7 Lesson Quiz

Solve each inequality and graph the solutions.

1. $3|x| > 15$ $x < -5$ OR $x > 5$

(number line: −10 −5 0 5 10)

2. $|x + 3| + 1 < 3$ $-5 < x < -1$

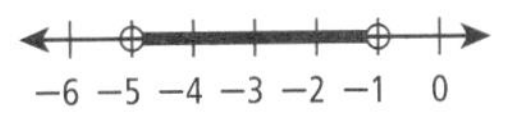

3. A number n is no more than 7 units away from 5. Write and solve an absolute-value inequality to show the range of possible values for n.
$|n - 5| \leq 7$; $-2 \leq n \leq 12$

Solve each inequality.

4. $|3x| + 1 < 1$ no solutions

5. $|x + 2| - 3 \geq -6$ all real numbers

Also available on transparency

3-7 PROBLEM SOLVING

Write the correct answer.

1. A carpenter cuts boards that are 2 meters long. It is acceptable for the length to differ from this value by at most 0.05 meters. Write and solve an absolute-value inequality to find the range of acceptable lengths.
   $|x - 2| \leq 0.05$;
   $1.95 \leq x \leq 2.05$

2. During a workout, Vince tries to keep his heart rate at 134 beats per minute. His actual heart rate varies from this value by as much as 8 beats per minute. Write and solve an absolute-value inequality to find Vince's range of heart rates.
   $|x - 134| \leq 8$;
   $126 \leq x \leq 142$

3. Mai thinks of a secret number. She says that her secret number is more than 11 units away from 50. Write an absolute-value inequality that gives the possible values of Mai's number.
   $|x - 50| > 11$

4. Boxes of cereal are supposed to weigh 15.3 ounces each. A quality-control manager finds that the boxes are no more than 0.4 ounces away from this weight. Write an absolute-value inequality that gives the range of possible weights of the boxes.
   $|x - 15.3| \leq 0.4$

The table gives the typical lifespan for several mammals. Use the table for questions 5-7. Select the best answer.

5. Which absolute-value inequality gives the number of years a goat may live?
   A $|x - 6| \leq 11$ C $|x - 24| \leq 6$
   B $|x - 15| \leq 9$ D $|x - 30| \leq 9$

6. Which mammal has a lifespan that can be represented by the absolute-value inequality $|x - 12.5| \leq 2.5$?
   F Antelope H Otter
   G Koala J Wolf

7. The inequality $|x - 17| \leq c$ gives the number of years a panda may live. What is the value of c?
   A 3 C 14
   B 6 D 20

Mammal	Lifespan (years)	Mammal	Lifespan (years)
Antelope	10 to 25	Otter	15 to 20
Goat	6 to 24	Panda	14 to 20
Koala	10 to 15	Wolf	13 to 15

Source: http://www.sandiegozoo.org/animalbytes/a-mammal.html

3-7 CHALLENGE

When you solve a multi-step inequality, you may need to simplify expressions, combine like terms, or use the Distributive Property. This also applies when you solve inequalities that involve absolute values.

For example, to solve $3(|x| + 4) < 18$, you can first use the Distributive Property on the left side of the equation to write $3|x| + 12 < 18$.

1. Show how to finish solving the above inequality. Graph the solutions.
   $3|x| < 6$; $|x| < 2$; $x > -2$ AND $x < 2$

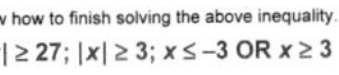

In some cases, you may need to combine like terms. For example, to solve $6|x| - 5 + 3|x| \geq 22$, first combine the absolute-value terms to write $9|x| - 5 \geq 22$.

2. Show how to finish solving the above inequality. Graph the solutions.
   $9|x| \geq 27$; $|x| \geq 3$; $x \leq -3$ OR $x \geq 3$

Solve each inequality and graph the solutions.

3. $5|x| + 1 - 3|x| \leq 3$
   $x \geq -1$ AND $x \leq 1$

4. $2(5 + |x|) < 13$
   $x > -\frac{3}{2}$ AND $x < \frac{3}{2}$

5. $7|x + 1| - 5|x + 1| > 4$
   $x < -3$ OR $x > 1$

6. $3(|x - 2| + 1) \geq -1$
   all real numbers

Organizer

Objective: Assess students' ability to apply concepts and skills in Lessons 3-4 through 3-7 in a real-world format.

Online Edition

Resources

Algebra I Assessments
www.mathtekstoolkit.org

Problem	Text Reference
1	Lesson 3-4
2	Lesson 3-4
3	Lesson 3-4
4	Lesson 3-5
5	Lesson 3-5
6	Lesson 3-6

State Resources

MULTI-STEP TEST PREP

Multi-Step and Compound Inequalities

Guitar Picks Cullen and his band are interested in recording a CD of their music. The recording studio charges \$450 to record the music and then charges \$5 for each CD. The band is required to spend at least \$1000 for the total of the recording and CD charges.

1. Write an equation for the cost c of the CDs based on the number of CDs n. $c = 450 + 5n$
2. Write an inequality that can be used to determine the minimum number of CDs that must be burned at this studio to meet the \$1000 total. $450 + 5n \geq 1000$
3. Solve your inequality from Problem 2. $n \geq 110$ where n is a natural number
4. The band orders the minimum number of CDs found in Problem 3. They want to sell the CDs and make at least as much money as they spent for the recording studio and making the CDs. Write an inequality that can be solved to determine the minimum amount the band should charge for their CDs. $110x \geq 1000$
5. Solve your inequality from Problem 4. $x \geq 9.\overline{09}$
6. If the band has 30 more CDs made than the minimum number found in Problem 3 and charges the minimum price found in Problem 5, will they make a profit? If so, how much profit will the band make? **yes; \$122.60**

INTERVENTION

Scaffolding Questions

1. What is the cost if Cullen's band purchases only 1 CD? \$455 What is the cost if the band purchases 10 CDs? \$500

2–3. What inequality symbol is indicated by the word *minimum*? greater than or equal to Would a graph of the inequality be shaded or have individual points? Explain. individual points, because they must buy whole numbers of CDs

4–5. What expression can be used to represent the amount made from selling the CDs? $110x$ Would the endpoint on a graph of the inequality have an empty or a solid circle? solid

6. How is the profit from the sale of CDs determined? sales minus cost

Extension

Write and solve an inequality to find the number of CDs they would need to purchase and sell for \$9 each in order to make at least \$200 profit. $200 \leq 9x - (450 + 5x)$; $x \geq 162.5$; at least 163 CDs

CHAPTER 3

SECTION 3B

Quiz for Lessons 3-4 Through 3-7

3-4 Solving Two-Step and Multi-Step Inequalities

Solve each inequality and graph the solutions.

1. $2x + 3 < 9$ $x < 3$
2. $3t - 2 > 10$ $t > 4$
3. $7 \geq 1 - 6r$ $r \geq -1$

Solve each inequality.

4. $2(x - 3) > -1$ $x > 2.5$
5. $\frac{1}{3}a + \frac{1}{2} > \frac{2}{3}$ $a > \frac{1}{2}$
6. $15 < 5(m - 7)$ $m > 10$
7. $2 + (-6) > 0.8p$ $p < -5$
8. The average of Mindy's two test scores must be at least 92 to make an A in the class. Mindy got an 88 on her first test. What scores can she get on her second test to make an A in the class? **Mindy must make a score of 96 or higher.**

3-5 Solving Inequalities with Variables on Both Sides

Solve each inequality and graph the solutions.

9. $5x < 3x + 8$ $x < 4$
10. $6p - 3 > 9p$ $p < -1$
11. $r - 8 \geq 3r - 12$ $r \leq 2$

Solve each inequality.

12. $3(y + 6) > 2(y + 4)$ $y > -10$
13. $4(5 - g) \geq g$ $g \leq 4$
14. $4x < 4(x - 1)$ no solutions
15. $3(1 - x) \geq -3(x + 2)$ all real numbers
16. Phillip has \$100 in the bank and deposits \$18 per month. Gil has \$145 in the bank and deposits \$15 per month. For how many months will Gil have a larger bank balance than Phillip? **15 mo**

3-6 Solving Compound Inequalities

Solve each compound inequality and graph the solutions.

17. $-2 \leq x + 3 < 9$ $-5 \leq x < 6$
18. $m + 2 < -1$ OR $m - 2 > 6$ $m < -3$ OR $m > 8$
19. $-3 \geq x - 1 > 2$ no solutions
20. $-2 > r + 2$ OR $r + 4 < 5$ $r < 1$
21. It is recommended that a certain medicine be stored in temperatures above 32 °F and below 70 °F. Write a compound inequality to show the acceptable storage temperatures for this medicine. $32 < t < 70$

3-7 Solving Absolute-Value Inequalities

Solve each inequality and graph the solutions.

22. $|x| + 9 \leq 12$ $-3 \leq x \leq 3$
23. $|x + 7| - 15 < 6$ $-28 < x < 14$
24. $4.5|x| \geq 31.5$ $x \leq -7$ OR $x \geq 7$

Solve each inequality.

25. $|x - 2| \leq 14$ $-12 \leq x \leq 16$
26. $|x| - 9.2 < -5.7$ $-3.5 < x < 3.5$
27. $\frac{1}{2} + 2|x| > -4$ all real numbers
28. $7 + |3x| > 13$ $x < -2$ OR $x > 2$
29. Eli attended a concert. The decibel level of the music averaged 110 decibels but varied by 22 decibels from the average. Write and solve an absolute-value inequality to find the decibel range. Graph the solutions. $|d - 110| \leq 22$; $88 \leq d \leq 132$

READY TO GO ON? SECTION 3B

Organizer

Objective: Assess students' mastery of concepts and skills in Lessons 3-4 through 3-7.

Resources

 ***Assessment Resources***
Section 3B Quiz

Teacher One Stop™
Test & Practice Generator

INTERVENTION

Resources

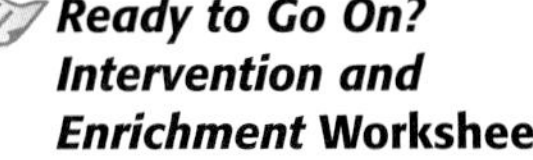

Ready to Go On? Intervention and Enrichment Worksheets

 ***Ready to Go On?* CD-ROM**

 ***Ready to Go On?* Online**

my.hrw.com

Answers

1–3, 9–11, 17–20, 22–24, 29. For graphs, see p. A16.

READY TO GO ON? Diagnose and Prescribe

NO INTERVENE

Ready to Go On? Intervention	READY TO GO ON? *Intervention*, Section 3B Worksheets	CD-ROM	Online
Lesson 3-4	3-4 Intervention	Activity 3-4	Diagnose and Prescribe Online
Lesson 3-5	3-5 Intervention	Activity 3-5	
Lesson 3-6	3-6 Intervention	Activity 3-6	
Lesson 3-7	3-7 Intervention	Activity 3-7	

YES ENRICH

READY TO GO ON? Enrichment, Section 3B

Worksheets

 CD-ROM

 Online

Organizer

Objective: Help students organize and review key concepts and skills presented in Chapter 3.

Online Edition
Multilingual Glossary

Countdown Week 7

Resources

Teacher One Stop™
PuzzleView
Test & Practice Generator

***Multilingual Glossary* Online**
go.hrw.com
KEYWORD: MA7 Glossary

Lesson Tutorial Videos
CD-ROM

Answers

1. inequality
2. union
3. compound inequality
4. intersection
5. solution of an inequality

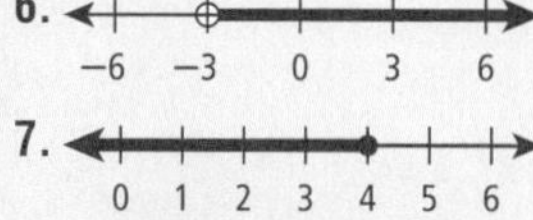

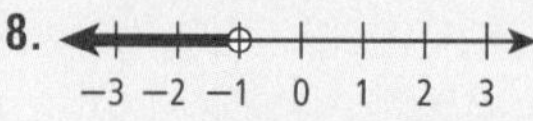

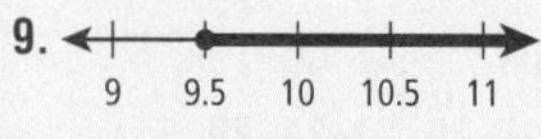

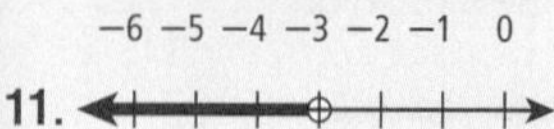

11\. 0 1 2 3 4 5 6

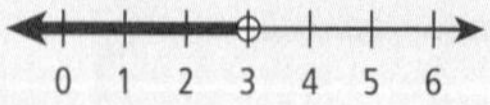

12. $a < 2$
13. $k \geq -3.5$
14. $q < -10$
15. t = temperature; $t \geq 72$

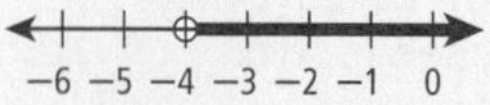

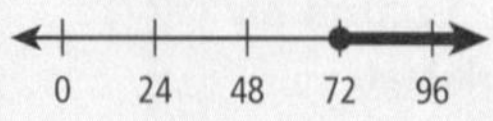

16. s = students; $s \leq 12$ where s is a natural number

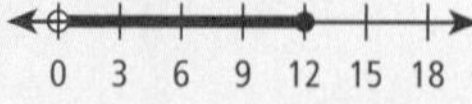

17. m = minutes; $m < 30$ where m is non-negative

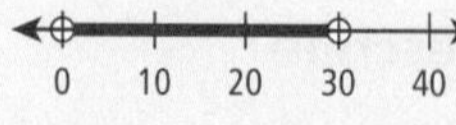

CHAPTER 3 Study Guide: Review

Vocabulary

compound inequality . . . . 204 **intersection** . . . . 205 **union** 206
inequality . . . . 170 **solution of an inequality** 170

Complete the sentences below with vocabulary words from the list above.

1. A(n) ___?___ is a mathematical statement that two quantities are not equal.
2. The numbers that are solutions to either inequality of a compound inequality is the ___?___.
3. A statement formed by combining two simple inequalities with the words AND or OR is a(n) ___?___.
4. The numbers that are solutions to both inequalities of a compound inequality is the ___?___.
5. Any value that makes the inequality true is a(n) ___?___.

3-1 Graphing and Writing Inequalities *(pp. 170–175)*

EXAMPLES

■ **Graph the inequality $y > -1$.**

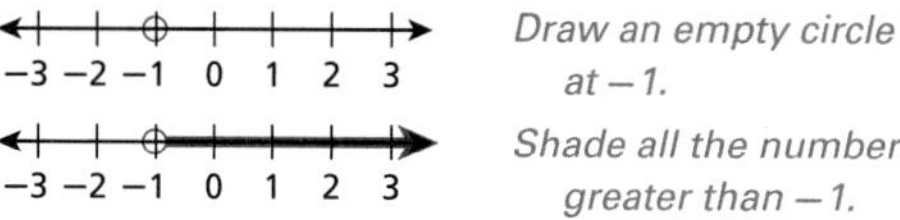

■ **Write the inequality shown by the graph.**

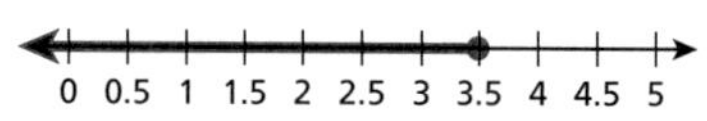

$n \leq 3.5$ *Use the variable n.*
The arrow points left, so use either < or ≤. The solid circle means 3.5 is a solution, so use ≤.

■ **Write an inequality for the situation and graph the solutions.**

Applicants for a driver's permit must be at least 16 years old.

age	must be at least	16 years
a	$\geq$	16

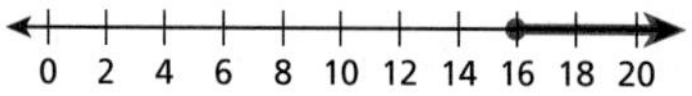

0 2 4 6 8 10 12 14 16 18 20

EXERCISES

Graph each inequality.

6. $x > -3$
7. $p \leq 4$
8. $-1 > t$
9. $r \geq 9.5$
10. $2(3 - 5) < k$
11. $w < 3$

Write the inequality shown by each graph.

12.

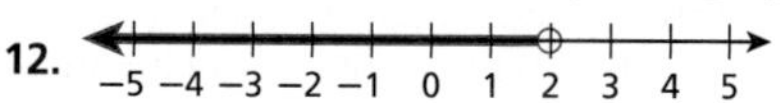

13\. 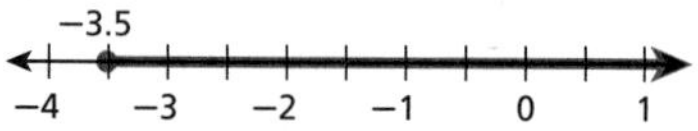 −3.5
−4 −3 −2 −1 0 1

14\. −12 −10 −8 −6 −4 −2 0

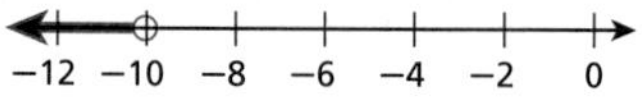

Define a variable and write an inequality for each situation. Graph the solutions.

15. The temperature must be at least 72 °F.
16. No more than 12 students were present.
17. It takes less than 30 minutes to complete the lab activity.

3-2 Solving Inequalities by Adding or Subtracting (pp. 176–181)

EXAMPLES

Solve each inequality and graph the solutions.

- $x + 6 > 2$

$$\begin{array}{rl} x + 6 > & 2 \\ -6 & -6 \\ \hline x \quad > & -4 \end{array}$$

Since 6 is added to x, subtract 6 from both sides.

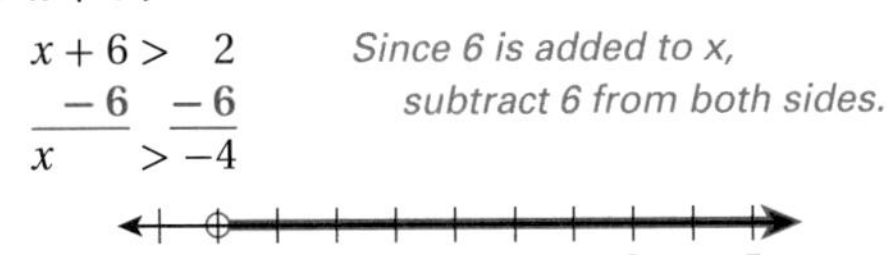

- $n - 1.3 < 3.2$

$$\begin{array}{rl} n - 1.3 < & 3.2 \\ +1.3 & +1.3 \\ \hline n \quad < & 4.5 \end{array}$$

Since 1.3 is subtracted from x, add 1.3 to both sides.

EXERCISES

Solve each inequality and graph the solutions.

18. $t + 3 < 10$

19. $k - 7 \leq -5$

20. $-1 < m + 4$

21. $x + 2.3 \geq 6.8$

22. $w - 3 < 6.5$

23. $4 > a - 1$

24. $h - \frac{1}{4} < \frac{3}{4}$

25. $5 > 7 + v$

26. Tammy wants to run at least 10 miles per week. So far this week, she ran 4.5 miles. Write and solve an inequality to determine how many more miles Tammy must run this week to reach her goal.

27. Rob has a gift card for \$50. So far, he has selected a shirt that costs \$32. Write and solve an inequality to determine the additional amount Rob could spend without exceeding the gift card limit.

3-3 Solving Inequalities by Multiplying or Dividing (pp. 182–187)

EXAMPLES

- **Solve $\frac{p}{-3} \leq 6$ and graph the solutions.**

$$\frac{p}{-3} \leq 6$$

Since p is divided by −3, multiply both sides by −3.

$$-3 \cdot \frac{p}{-3} \geq -3 \cdot 6$$

$$p \geq -18$$

Change ≤ to ≥.

- **Pizzas cost \$5.50 each. What are the possible numbers of pizzas that can be purchased with \$30?**

Let n represent the number of pizzas that can be purchased.

\$5.50	times	number of pizzas	is at most	\$30.
5.50	•	n	≤	30

$$5.50n \leq 30$$

$$\frac{5.50n}{5.50} \leq \frac{30}{5.50}$$

Since n is multiplied by 5.50, divide both sides by 5.50.

$$n \leq 5\frac{5}{11}$$

Only a whole number of pizzas can be purchased, so 0, 1, 2, 3, 4, or 5 pizzas can be purchased.

EXERCISES

Solve each inequality and graph the solutions.

28. $3a \leq 15$

29. $-18 < 6t$

30. $\frac{p}{4} > 2$

31. $\frac{2}{5}x \leq -10$

32. $-3n < -18$

33. $\frac{g}{-2} > 6$

34. $-2k < 14$

35. $-3 > \frac{1}{3}r$

36. $27 < -9h$

37. $-0.4g > -1$

38. Notebooks cost \$1.39 each. What are the possible numbers of notebooks that can be purchased with \$10?

39. A senior class is selling lanyards as a fundraiser. The profit for each lanyard is \$0.75. Write and solve an inequality to determine the number of lanyards the class must sell to make a profit of at least \$250.

Answers

18. $t < 7$

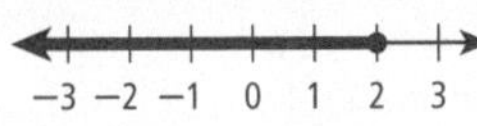

19. $k \leq 2$

20. $m > -5$

21. $x \geq 4.5$

22. $w < 9.5$

23. $a < 5$

24. $h < 1$

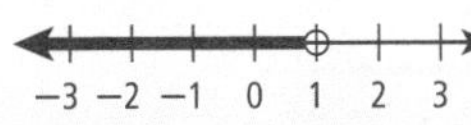

25. $v < -2$

26. $4.5 + m \geq 10$; $m \geq 5.5$; Tammy must run 5.5 mi or more.

27. $32 + d \leq 50$; $d \leq 18$; Rob can spend \$18 or less.

28. $a \leq 5$

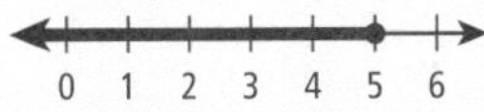

29. $t > -3$

30. $p > 8$

31. $x \leq -25$

32. $n > 6$

33. $g < -12$

34. $k > -7$

35. $r < -9$

36. $h < -3$

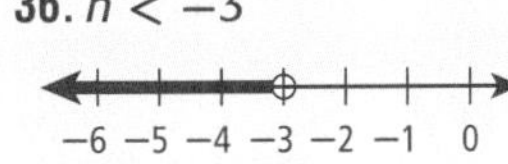

37. $g < 2.5$

38. 0, 1, 2, 3, 4, 5, 6, 7

39. $0.75n \geq 250$; $n \geq 333\frac{1}{3}$; they must sell at least 334 lanyards.

Answers

40. $x < 5$

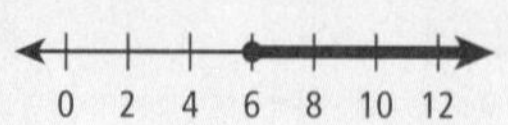

41. $t \geq 6$

0 2 4 6 8 10 12

42. $m > -11$

−12 −11 −10 −9 −8

43. $x < -1$

−3 −2 −1 0 1 2 3

44. $h > -3$

−6 −5 −4 −3 −2 −1 0

45. $x > 1\frac{1}{2}$

0 $\frac{1}{2}$ 1 $1\frac{1}{2}$ 2

46. $b \leq 10$

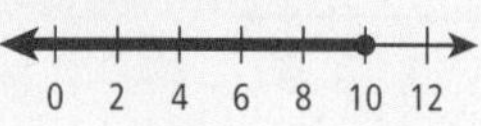

47. $y > 3\frac{1}{2}$

3 $3\frac{1}{2}$ 4 $4\frac{1}{2}$ 5

48. $n > -15$

−20 −15 −10 −5 0

49. 0, 1, 2, 3, 4, 5, 6, 7, 8, 9, 10, 11, 12, or 13

50. $m < -1$

−3 −2 −1 0 1 2 3

51. $y \geq -2$

−3 −2 −1 0 1 2 3

52. $c < -3$

−6 −5 −4 −3 −2 −1 0

53. $q \leq -4$

−6 −5 −4 −3 −2 −1 0

54. $x > 2$

−3 −2 −1 0 1 2 3

55. $t < 3$

0 1 2 3 4 5 6

56. no solutions

57. all real numbers

58. $p > -\frac{1}{2}$

−1 $-\frac{1}{2}$ 0 $\frac{1}{2}$ 1

3-4 Solving Two-Step and Multi-Step Inequalities *(pp. 190–195)*

EXAMPLES

Solve each inequality and graph the solutions.

■ $18 + 3t > -12$

$$18 + 3t > -12$$
$$-18 \quad -18$$
$$3t > -30$$

Since 18 is added to 3t, subtract 18 from both sides.

$$\frac{3t}{3} > \frac{-30}{3}$$
$$t > -10$$

Since t is multiplied by 3, divide both sides by 3.

−12 −10 −8 −6 −4 −2 0

■ $3^2 - 5 \leq 2(1 + x)$

$$3^2 - 5 \leq 2(1 + x)$$
$$9 - 5 \leq 2(1 + x)$$

Simplify the left side using order of operations.

$$4 \leq 2(1 + x)$$
$$4 \leq 2(1) + 2(x)$$

Distribute 2 on the right side.

$$4 \leq 2 + 2x$$
$$-2 \quad -2$$
$$2 \leq 2x$$

Since 2 is added to 2x, subtract 2 from both sides

$$\frac{2}{2} \leq \frac{2x}{2}$$
$$1 \leq x$$

Since x is multiplied by 2, divide both sides by 2.

−5 −4 −3 −2 −1 0 1 2 3 4 5

EXERCISES

Solve each inequality and graph the solutions.

40. $3x + 4 < 19$
41. $7 \leq 2t - 5$
42. $\frac{m + 3}{2} > -4$
43. $2(x + 5) < 8$
44. $-4(2 - 5) > (-3)^2 - h$
45. $\frac{1}{5}x + \frac{1}{2} > \frac{4}{5}$
46. $0.5(b - 2) \leq 4$
47. $\frac{1}{3}y - \frac{1}{2} > \frac{2}{3}$
48. $6 - 0.2n < 9$
49. Carl's Cable Company charges \$55 for monthly service plus \$4 for each pay-per-view movie. Teleview Cable Company charges \$110 per month with no fee for movies. For what number of movies is the cost of Carl's Cable Company less than the cost of Teleview?

3-5 Solving Inequalities with Variables on Both Sides *(pp. 196–202)*

EXAMPLES

■ **Solve $b + 16 < 3b$ and graph the solutions.**

$$b + 16 > 3b$$
$$-b \quad -b$$
$$16 > 2b$$

Subtract b from both sides so that the coefficient of b is positive.

$$\frac{16}{2} > \frac{2b}{2}$$
$$8 > b$$

Since b is multiplied by 2, divide both sides by 2.

−8 −6 −4 −2 0 2 4 6 8 10 12

■ **Solve the inequality $3(1 + k) > 4 + 3k$.**

$3 + 3k > 4 + 3k$ *Distribute 3 on the left side.*

The same variable term ($3k$) appears on both sides.

For any number $3k$, adding 3 will never result in a greater number than adding 4.

There are no solutions.

EXERCISES

Solve each inequality and graph the solutions.

50. $5 + 2m < -3m$
51. $y \leq 6 + 4y$
52. $4c - 7 > 9c + 8$
53. $-3(2 - q) \geq 6(q + 1)$
54. $2(5 - x) < 3x$
55. $3.5t - 1.8 < 1.6t + 3.9$

Solve each inequality.

56. $d - 2 < d - 4$
57. $2(1 - x) > -2(1 + x)$
58. $4(1 - p) < 4(2 + p)$
59. $3w + 1 > 3(w - 1)$
60. $5(4 - k) < 5k$
61. $3(c + 1) > 3c + 5$
62. Hanna has a savings account with a balance of \$210 and deposits \$16 per month. Faith has a savings account with a balance of \$175 and deposits \$20 per month. Write and solve an inequality to determine the number of months Hanna's account balance will be greater than Faith's account balance.

59. all real numbers

60. $k > 2$

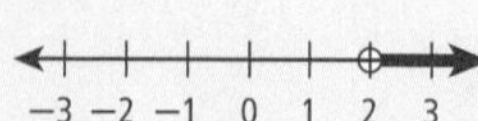

61. no solutions

62. $210 + 16m > 175 + 20m$; $8.75 > m$

3-6 Solving Compound Inequalities *(pp. 204–210)*

EXAMPLES

Solve each compound inequality and graph the solutions.

■ $-3 < c + 5 \leq 11$

$\quad -5 \quad\; -5 \;\; -5$

$-8 < c \quad\; \leq 6$

Since 5 is added to c, subtract 5 from each part of the inequality.

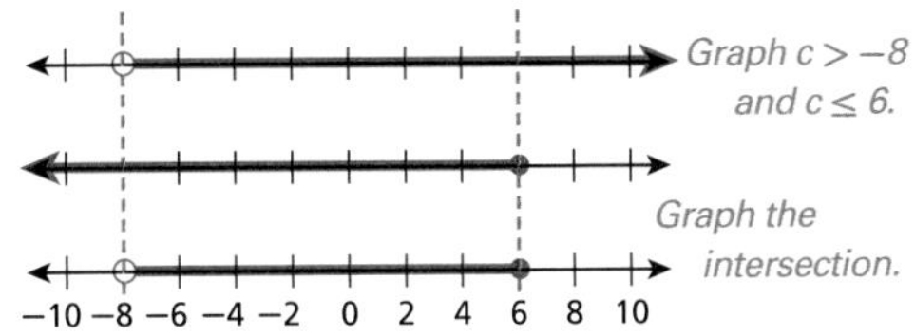

■ $-2 + t \geq 2$ OR $t + 3 < 1$

$\quad +2 \quad\; +2 \qquad -3 \quad -3$

$\quad\; t \geq 4$ OR $\quad t < -2$

Solve the simple inequalities.

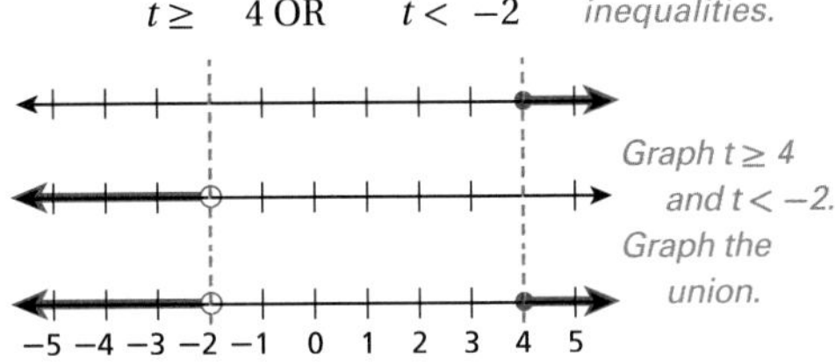

EXERCISES

Solve each compound inequality and graph the solutions.

63. $-4 < t + 6 < 10$

64. $-8 < k - 2 \leq 5$

65. $-3 + r > 4$ OR $r + 1 < -1$

66. $2 > n + 3 > 5$

67. $12 \geq p + 7 > 5$

68. $3 < s + 9$ OR $1 > s - 4$

69. One day, the high temperature was 84 °F and the low temperature was 68 °F. Write a compound inequality to represent the day's temperatures.

70. The table shows formulas for the recommended heart rates during exercise for a person who is *a* years old. Write and solve a compound inequality to determine the heart rate range for a 16-year-old person.

Recommended Heart Rate Range	
Lower Limit	$0.5 \times (220 - a)$
Upper Limit	$0.9 \times (220 - a)$

3-7 Solving Absolute-Value Inequalities *(pp. 212–217)*

EXAMPLES

Solve each inequality and graph the solutions.

■ $|x| + 4 < 9$

$|x| + 4 < 9$

$\quad\; -4 \;\; -4$ *Subtract 4 from both sides.*

$|x| \quad < 5$

$x > -5$ AND $x < 5$ *Write as a compound inequality.*

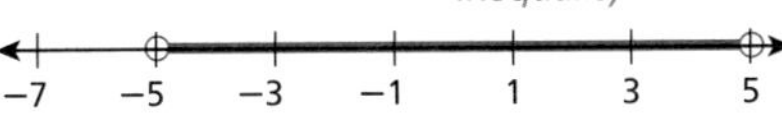

■ $|x - 3| + 7 \geq 13$

$\qquad\quad -7 \;\; -7$ *Subtract 7 from both sides.*

$|x - 3| \quad \geq 6$

$x - 3 \leq -6$ OR $x - 3 \geq 6$ *Solve the two inequalities.*

$\quad +3 \;\; +3 \qquad\quad +3 \;\; +3$

$x \quad \leq -3$ OR $x \quad \geq 9$

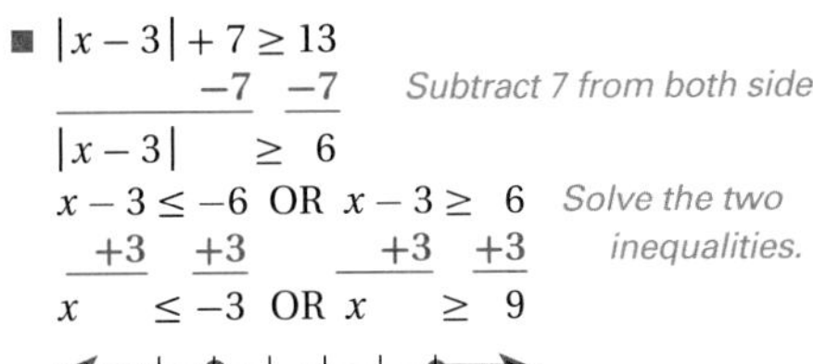

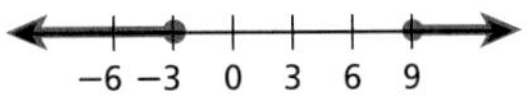

EXERCISES

Solve each inequality and graph the solutions.

71. $|x| - 7 \leq 15$

72. $|x + 4| > 8$

73. $6|x| \leq 24$

74. $|x + 9| + 11 < 20$

75. $3|x| \geq 9$

76. $4|2x| < 24$

Solve the inequality.

77. $|x| - 5.4 > 8.5$

78. $|5.2 + x| < 7.3$

79. $|x - 7| + 10 \geq 12$

80. $14|x| - 15 \geq 41$

81. $\left|x - \frac{1}{2}\right| + 4 \leq \frac{5}{2}$

82. $|x + 5.5| - 6.4 \leq 4.9$

83. The water depth for a pool is set to 6 ft, but the actual depth of the pool may vary by as much as 4 in. Write and solve an absolute-value inequality to find the range of possible water depths in inches. Graph the solutions.

Answers

63. $-10 < t < 4$

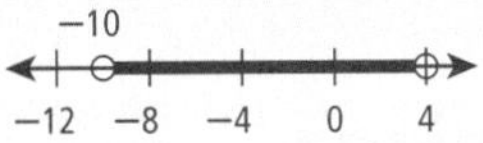

64. $-6 < k \leq 7$

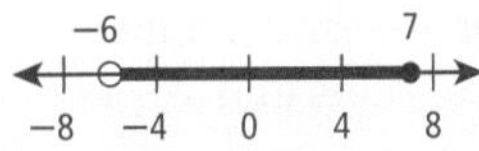

65. $r > 7$ OR $r < -2$

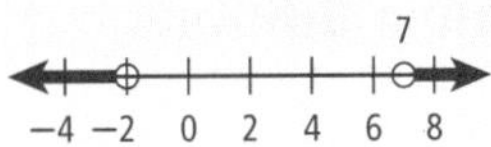

66. no solutions

67. $-2 < p \leq 5$

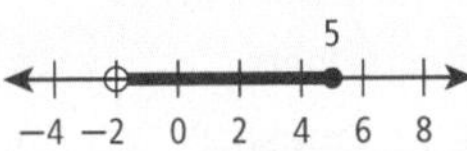

68. all real numbers

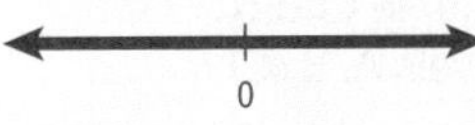

69. $68 \leq t \leq 84$

70. $102 \leq n \leq 183.6$

71. $-22 \leq x \leq 22$

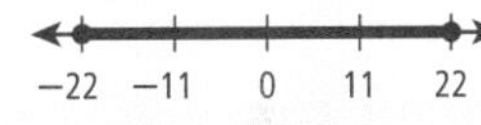

72. $x < -12$ OR $x > 4$

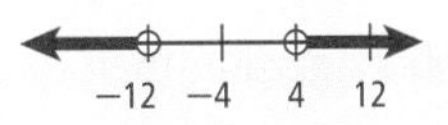

73. $-4 \leq x \leq 4$

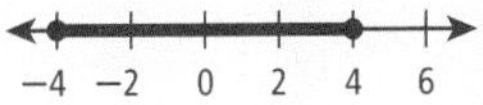

74. $-18 < x < 0$

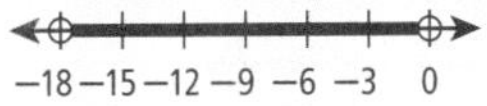

75. $x \leq -3$ OR $x \geq 3$

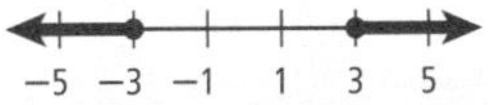

76. $-3 < x < 3$

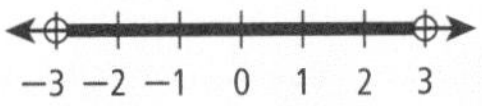

77. $x < -13.9$ OR $x > 13.9$

78. $-12.5 < x < 2.1$

79. $x \leq 5$ OR $x \geq 9$

80. $x \leq -4$ OR $x \geq 4$

81. no solutions

82. $-16.8 \leq x \leq 5.8$

83. $|d - 72| \leq 4$; $68 \leq d \leq 76$

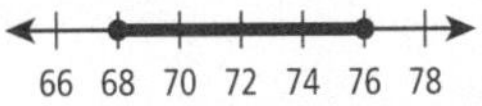

Organizer

Objective: Assess students' mastery of concepts and skills in Chapter 3.

Online Edition

Resources

Assessment Resources

Chapter 3 Tests
- Free Response (Levels A, B, C)
- Multiple Choice (Levels A, B, C)
- Performance Assessment

Teacher One Stop™

Test & Practice Generator

Answers

1. all real numbers greater than or equal to −6
2. all real numbers greater than 4
3. all real numbers less than or equal to −2
4. all real numbers less than or equal to 8
5. −6 −5 −4 −3 −2 −1 0
6. 2 2.5 3 3.5 4
7. −6 −5 −4 −3 −2 −1 0
8. −16 −12 −8 −4 0

State Resources

Describe the solutions of each inequality in words.

1. $-6 \le m$ 2. $3t > 12$ 3. $-x \ge 2$ 4. $2 + b \le 10$

Graph each inequality.

5. $b > -3$ 6. $2.5 < c$ 7. $y \le -\sqrt{25}$ 8. $3 - (4 + 7) \ge h$

Write the inequality shown by each graph.

9. −5 −4 −3 −2 −1 0 1 2 3 4 5 **$d < 1$**

10. −4.5; −5 −4 −3 −2 −1 0 **$p \ge -4.5$**

Write an inequality for the situation and graph the solutions.

11. Madison must run a mile in no more than 9 minutes to qualify for the race.
$m \le 9$ where m is nonnegative

Solve each inequality and graph the solutions.

12. $d - 5 > -7$ **$d > -2$** 13. $f + 4 < -3$ **$f < -7$** 14. $4.5 \ge s + 3.2$ **$s \le 1.3$** 15. $g + (-2) \le 9$ **$g \le 11$**

16. Students need at least 75 hours of volunteer service to meet their graduation requirement. Samir has already completed 48 hours. Write and solve an inequality to determine how many more hours he needs to complete.
$48 + h \ge 75$; $h \ge 27$; Samir needs at least 27 more hours.

Solve each inequality and graph the solutions.

17. $-2c \le 2$ **$c \ge -1$** 18. $3 > \frac{k}{2}$ **$k < 6$** 19. $\frac{4}{5}x \le -8$ **$x \le -10$** 20. $\frac{b}{3} > -7$ **$b > -21$**

21. Marco needs to buy premium gasoline for his car. He has \$20 in his wallet. Write and solve an inequality to determine how many gallons of gas Marco can buy.
$2.25g \le 20$; $g \le 8.89$; Marco can buy 8.89 gallons or less.

Gasoline Prices (\$)		
Regular	Plus	Premium
2.05	2.12	2.25

Solve each inequality and graph the solutions.

22. $3x - 8 < 4$ **$x < 4$** 23. $-2(c - 3) > 4$ **$c < 1$** 24. $5 \le \frac{3}{4}n - 2^4$ **$n \ge 28$** 25. $3 - 2a \le -15 + (-9)$ **$a \ge 13\frac{1}{2}$**

Solve each inequality.

26. $2k - 6 > 3k + 2$ **$k < -8$** 27. $2(5 - f) \le f + 12$ **$f \ge -\frac{2}{3}$** 28. $\frac{3}{2}d \le -\frac{1}{2}d + 6$ **$d \le 3$**

Solve each compound inequality and graph the solutions.

29. $-1 \le x - 3 < 3$ **$2 \le x < 6$** 30. $t + 7 < 3$ OR $t - 1 > 4$ **$t < -4$ OR $t > 5$** 31. $4 \le d - 2 < 5$ **$6 \le d < 7$**

32. The driving school instructor has asked Lina to stay within 2 miles of the posted speed limits. The current road has a speed limit of 45 mi/h. Write a compound inequality to show Lina's acceptable speeds s. **$43 \le s \le 47$**

Solve each inequality.

33. $|x - 3| + 7 < 17$ **$-7 < x < 13$** 34. $6|x| + 4 \ge 16$ **$x \le -2$ OR $x \ge 2$** 35. $|x + 12| \le 23$ **$-35 \le x \le 11$**

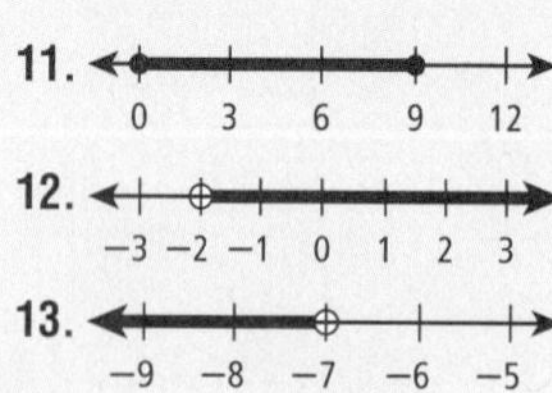
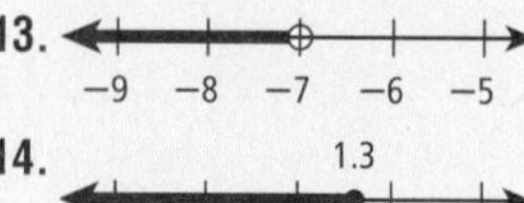
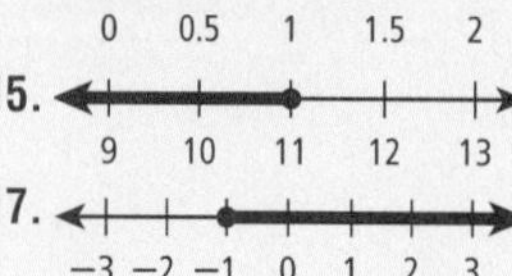
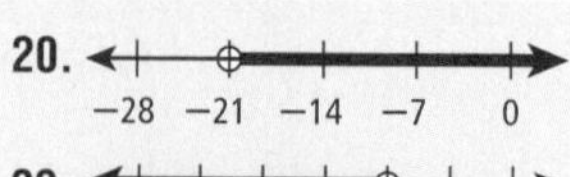
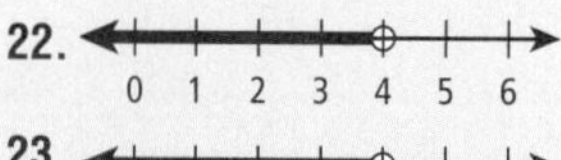
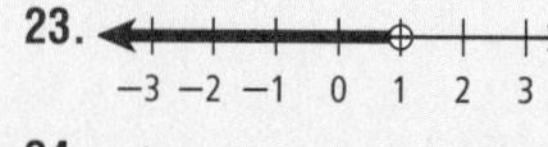
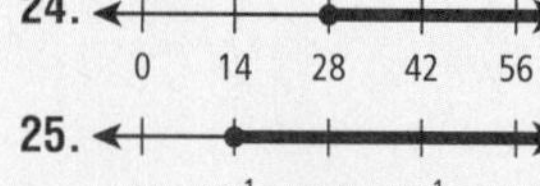
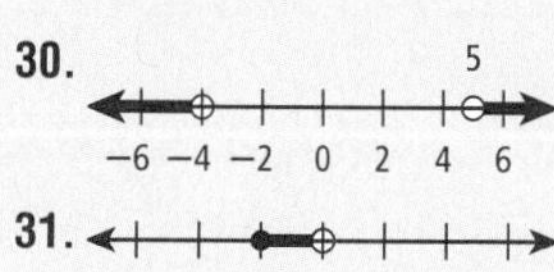

College Entrance Exam Practice

CHAPTER 3

FOCUS ON SAT STUDENT-PRODUCED RESPONSES

Ten questions on the SAT require you to enter your answer in a special grid like the one shown. You do not have to write your answer in the boxes at the top of the grid, but doing this may help you avoid errors when filling in the grid. The circles must be filled in correctly for you to receive credit.

You cannot enter a zero in the first column of the grid. This is to encourage you to give a more accurate answer when you need to round. For example, $\frac{1}{16}$ written as a decimal is 0.0625. This should be entered in the grid as .063 instead of 0.06.

You may want to time yourself as you take this practice test. It should take you about 9 minutes to complete.

1. Mailing a standard-sized letter in 2005 by first-class mail cost \$0.37 for a letter weighing 1 ounce or less and \$0.23 for each additional ounce. How much did it cost, in dollars, to send a standard-sized letter that weighed 3 ounces? **0.83**

2. If $p = q - 2$ and $\frac{q}{3} = 9$, what is the value of p? **25**

3. Give the maximum value of x if $12 - 3(x + 1) \geq \frac{1}{2}(3 - 5)$. $\mathbf{\frac{10}{3}}$

4. Give the minimum value of x if $2x + y \leq 7x - 9$ and $y = -3$. $\mathbf{\frac{6}{5}}$

5. For what integer value of x is $2x - 9 < 5$ and $x - 1 > 4$? **6**

6. What is the minimum value of z that satisfies the inequality $z - 7.3 \geq 4.1$? **11.4**

7. To be eligible for financial aid, Alisa must work at least 15 hours per week in a work-study program. She wants to spend at least 5 more hours studying than working each week. What is the minimum number of hours per day (Monday through Friday) that she must study to meet this goal and be eligible for financial aid? **4**

8. For all real numbers a and b, define the operation # as follows:

$$a \# b = 2a - b$$

Given $a = 3$ and $a \# b = 1$, what is the value of b? **5**

College Entrance Exam Practice

CHAPTER 3

Organizer

Objective: Provide practice for college entrance exams such as the SAT.

Premier Online Edition

Resources

College Entrance Exam Practice

Questions on the SAT represent the following math content areas:

Number and Operations, 20–25%

Algebra and Functions, 35–40%

Geometry and Measurement, 25–30%

Data Analysis, Statistics, and Probability, 10–15%

Items on this page focus on:

- Number and Operations
- Algebra and Functions

Text References:

Item	1	2	3	4	5	6	7
Lesson	1-8	2-2	3-4	3-5	3-4	3-2	3-4

TEST PREP DOCTOR

1. Students who answered 1.06 may have found the cost of 3 additional ounces instead of 2 additional ounces.
2. Students who answered 1 may have incorrectly solved for q and then substituted $q = 3$ into the first equation.
3. Students who gave an answer greater than $\frac{10}{3}$ may have forgotten to reverse the inequality symbol when multiplying or dividing by a negative number.
4. Students who gave an answer less than −24 may have substituted −3 for x instead of y. Urge students to read each test item carefully.
5. Students who gave an answer other than 6 that is between 5 and 7 may have solved correctly, but did not remember to give an integer answer.
6. Students who gave an answer of 3.2 may have subtracted instead of adding.
7. Students may have difficulty working with two inequalities. Suggest that students first write the inequality and then test several values to determine whether their answer is reasonable.
8. Students may have difficulty approaching the problem. Suggest that students write the given equation and then substitute 1 for the expression on the left side and 3 for a on the right side.

Organizer

Objective: Provide opportunities to learn and practice common test-taking strategies.

TEST PREP DOCTOR This Test Tackler focuses on writing full-credit answers to short-response test items. Students benefit from knowing how their answers will be scored. By seeing examples of answers that do not earn full credit, students are reminded that they must pay attention to all parts of the question to receive full credit for an answer.

State Resources

State Resources Online
KEYWORD: MA7 Resources

Standardized Test Strategies

Short Response: Understand Short Response Scores

To answer a short-response question completely, you must show how you solved the problem and explain your answer. Short response questions are scored using a 2-point scoring rubric. A sample scoring rubric is provided below.

EXAMPLE 1

Short Response An online company offers free shipping if the cost of the order is at least \$35. Your order currently totals \$26.50. Write an inequality to show how much more you need to spend to qualify for free shipping. Solve the inequality and explain what your answer means.

2-point response:

Let c be the amount I must add to my order.
c plus the amount I already ordered must be at least \$35.
c + 26.50 ≥ 35

$c + 26.50 \geq 35$
$c + 26.50 - 26.50 \geq 35 - 26.50$
$c \geq 8.50$

Check:
$8.50 + 26.50 \geq 35$ ✓

To get free shipping on the order, I must spend at least \$8.50 more since \$8.50 + \$26.50 is at least \$35.

The student wrote and solved an inequality correctly. The student showed all work and explained the meaning of the solution to the inequality.

1-point response:

$c + 26.50 > 35$
$c > 8.50$
\$8.50

The student gave a correct answer, but the inequality symbol shown in the student's work is incorrect. No explanation was given.

0-point response:

\$9.25

The student gave an answer that satisfies the problem but did not show any work or give an explanation.

Scoring Rubric:

2 points: The student writes and correctly solves an inequality, showing all work. Student defines the variable, answers the question in a complete sentence, and provides an explanation.

1 point: The student writes and correctly solves an inequality but does not show all work, does not define the variable, or does not provide an explanation.

1 point: The student writes and solves an inequality but gives an incorrect answer. The student shows all work and provides an explanation for the answer.

0 points: The student gives no response or provides a solution without showing any work or explanation.

Read short-response test items carefully. If you are allowed to write in the test booklet, underline or circle the parts of the question that tell you what your answer must include. Be sure to explain how you get your answer in complete sentences.

Read each sample and answer the questions that follow by using the scoring rubric below.

Scoring Rubric:

2 points: The student demonstrates a thorough understanding of the concept, correctly answers the question, and provides a complete explanation.

1 point: The student correctly answers the question but does not show all work or does not provide an explanation.

1 point: The student makes minor errors resulting in an incorrect solution but shows and explains understanding of the concept.

0 points: The student gives a response but shows no work or explanation, or the student gives no response.

Sample A

Short Response Write a real-world situation that can be modeled by the inequality $25s - 75 \geq 250$. Solve for s and explain how the value of s relates to your situation.

Student's Answer

A painter rents a booth at the county fair for \$75. The artist sells his paintings for \$25 each. If he makes at least \$250 in profit, he can buy a new easel.

The artist has to sell at least 13 paintings.

1. What score should the student's answer receive? Explain your reasoning.
2. What additional information, if any, should the student's answer include in order to receive full credit?

Sample B

Short Response How do the solutions of $3s - 10 < 15 - 2s$ and $-34 + 9s \leq 4s - 9$ differ? How are the solutions alike? Include a graph in your explanation.

Student's Answer

Solve both inequalities.

$3s - 10 < 15 - 2s$	$-34 + 9s \leq 4s - 9$
$+2s \quad\quad +2s$	$\quad -4s \quad -4s$
$5s - 10 < 15$	$-34 + 5s \leq -9$
$+10 \quad +10$	$+34 \quad\quad +34$
$5s < 25$	$5s \leq 25$
$\frac{5s}{5} < \frac{25}{5}$	$\frac{5s}{5} \leq \frac{25}{5}$
$s < 5$	$s \leq 5$

Blue graph: $s<5$ Red graph: $s \leq 5$

0 5

3. What score should the student's answer receive? Explain your reasoning.
4. What additional information, if any, should the student's answer include in order to receive full credit?

Sample C

Short Response Explain the difference between the solution of the equation $x - 6 = 2x + 9$ and the solutions of the inequality $x - 6 < 2x + 9$.

Student's Answer

The equation has a solution of $x = -15$, and the inequality has a solution of $x > -15$. The equation is true only when x equals -15. The inequality is true for all values greater than -15.

5. What score should the student's answer receive? Explain your reasoning.
6. What additional information, if any, should the student's answer include in order to receive full credit?

Answers

1. 1; the student did not show how he or she got the answer 13.
2. The student should explain how he or she got the answer by showing each step he or she followed to solve the inequality.
3. 1; the student did not explain how the graphs and solutions differ or how they are alike.
4. The student should explain that the solutions of the two inequalities are the same except that one includes 5 and the other does not.
5. 1; the student did not show the steps he or she followed to solve the equation or the inequality.
6. The student should show each step he or she followed to solve the equation and the inequality.

Answers to Test Items

A. See answer to Problem 2.
B. See answer to Problem 4.
C. See answer to Problem 6.

CHAPTER 3 STANDARDIZED TEST PREP

Organizer

Objective: Provide review and practice for Chapters 1–3 and standardized tests.

PREMIER Online Edition

Resources

Assessment Resources
Chapter 3 Cumulative Test

go.hrw.com
KEYWORD: MA7 TestPrep

State Resources

go.hrw.com
State Resources Online
KEYWORD: MA7 Resources

CHAPTER 3 STANDARDIZED TEST PREP

go.hrw.com
State Test Practice Online
KEYWORD: MA7 TestPrep

CUMULATIVE ASSESSMENT, CHAPTERS 1–3

Multiple Choice

1. Which algebraic expression means "5 less than y"?

Ⓐ $5 - y$
Ⓑ $y - 5$
Ⓒ $5 < y$
Ⓓ $5 \div y$

2. Which expression is equivalent to $5 + 2(x - 5)$?

Ⓕ $2x$
Ⓖ $2x + 5$
Ⓗ $2x - 5$
Ⓙ $7x - 35$

3. If $t + 8 = 2$, find the value of $2t$.

Ⓐ -12
Ⓑ -6
Ⓒ 12
Ⓓ 20

4. The length of the rectangle is $2(x + 1)$ meters and the perimeter is 60 meters. What is the length of the rectangle?

2(x + 1)
4

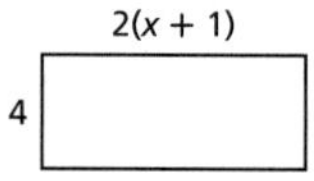

Ⓕ 12 meters
Ⓖ 26 meters
Ⓗ 28 meters
Ⓙ 56 meters

5. Samantha opened a bank account in June and deposited some money. She deposited twice that amount in August. At the end of August, Samantha had less than $600 in her account. If she made no other withdrawals or deposits, which inequality could be used to determine the maximum amount Samantha could have deposited in June?

Ⓐ $2x < 600$
Ⓑ $2x > 600$
Ⓒ $3x < 600$
Ⓓ $3x > 600$

6. Which proportion could be used to determine the ratio of the areas of these similar rectangles?

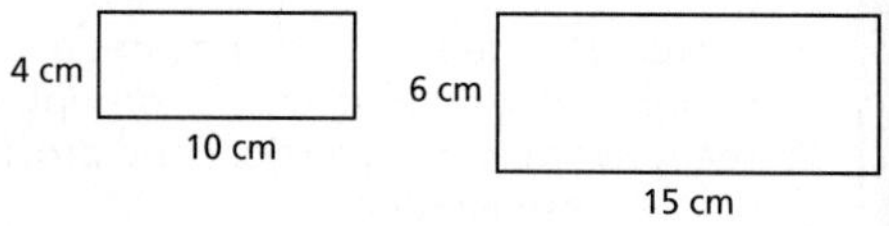

4 cm
10 cm
6 cm
15 cm

Ⓕ $\frac{2}{3}$
Ⓖ $\frac{2}{5}$
Ⓗ $\frac{4}{9}$
Ⓙ $\frac{4}{25}$

7. For which inequality is -2 a solution?

Ⓐ $2x < -4$
Ⓑ $-2x < 4$
Ⓒ $-2x > -4$
Ⓓ $-2x < -4$

8. Which graph shows the solutions of $-2(1 - x) < 3(x - 2)$?

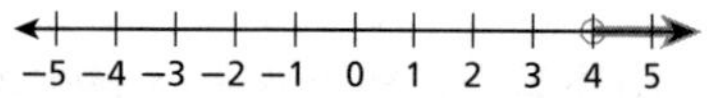

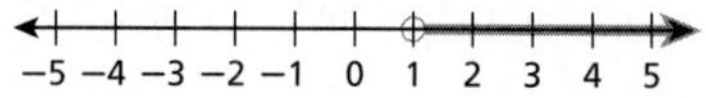

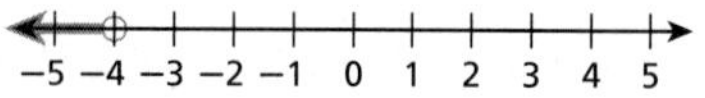

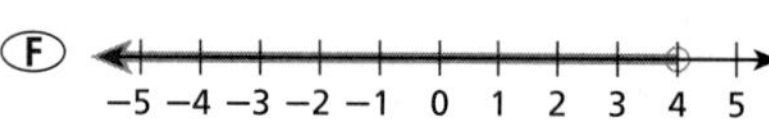

Ⓕ
−5 −4 −3 −2 −1 0 1 2 3 4 5

Ⓖ
−5 −4 −3 −2 −1 0 1 2 3 4 5

Ⓗ
−5 −4 −3 −2 −1 0 1 2 3 4 5

Ⓙ
−5 −4 −3 −2 −1 0 1 2 3 4 5

9. Which compound inequality has no solution?

Ⓐ $x > 1$ OR $x < -2$
Ⓑ $x < 1$ AND $x > -2$
Ⓒ $x < 1$ OR $x < -2$
Ⓓ $x > 1$ AND $x < -2$

Answers

1. B
2. H
3. A
4. G
5. C
6. H
7. C
8. G
9. D
10. G
11. D

To check your answer, use a different method to solve the problem from the one you originally used. If you made a mistake the first time, you are unlikely to make the same mistake when you solve the problem a different way.

0. Which inequality has the same solutions as $p < -2$?

Ⓕ $p + 1 < -2$

Ⓖ $p + 4 < 2$

Ⓗ $2p + 1 < -4$

Ⓙ $3p < -12$

1. What is the greatest integer solution of $5 - 3m > 11$?

Ⓐ 0

Ⓑ −1

Ⓒ −2

Ⓓ −3

ridded Response

2. The sum of the measures of any two sides of a triangle must be greater than the measure of the third side. What is the greatest possible integer value for x?

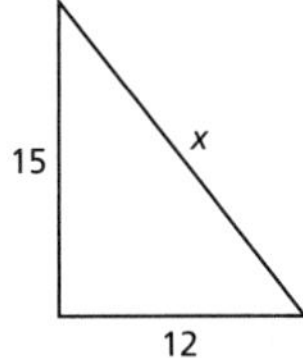

3. After 2 years, the simple interest paid on an investment of $2500 was $175. What percent was the interest rate?

4. Amy's bowling score in her third game was 10 points less than her score in the first game and 5 points more than her score in the second game. The total points for all three games was no more than 275. What is the greatest number of points Amy could have scored in her first game?

5. Trevor needs a 93 on his second quiz to have a quiz average of 90. What score did Trevor receive on his first quiz?

6. The radius of a circle can be determined by the formula $r = \sqrt{\frac{A}{\pi}}$. What is the length in meters of the radius of a circle that has an area of 314 square meters? (Use 3.14 for π.)

Short Response

17. Write 2 different inequalities that have the same solution as $n > 3$ such that

a. the first inequality uses the symbol > and requires addition or subtraction to solve.

b. the second inequality uses the symbol < and requires multiplication or division to solve.

18. Alison has twice as many video games as Kyle. Maurice has 5 more video games than Alison. The total number of video games is less than 40.

a. Write an inequality to represent this situation.

b. Solve the inequality to determine the greatest number of video games Maurice could have. Justify each step in your solution.

19. Donna's Deli delivers lunches for $7 per person plus a $35 delivery fee. Larry's Lunches delivers lunches for $11 per person.

a. Write an expression to represent the cost of x lunches from Donna's Deli. Write an expression to represent the cost of ordering x lunches from Larry's Lunches.

b. Write an inequality to determine the number of lunches for which the cost of Larry's Lunches is less than the cost of Donna's Deli.

c. Solve the inequality and explain what the answer means. Which restaurant charges less for an order of 10 lunches?

Extended Response

20. Aleya has two employment opportunities. Company A offered her a yearly salary of $31,000. Company B offered her a similar position with a yearly salary of $27,000 plus 2.5% commission on her total sales for the year.

a. Let x represent Aleya's total sales for the year at company B. Write an expression to represent the total income after one year at company B.

b. Use your expression from part **a** to write an inequality that could be solved to determine the amount of sales for which the yearly income at company A would be greater than that at company B.

c. Solve the inequality from part **b** and explain the meaning of the solution in relation to Aleya's decision to work for company A or company B.

d. How much more than the salary at company A would Aleya make after one year at company B if her total sales for the year were $200,000?

Short-Response Rubric

Items 17–19

2 Points = The student's answer is an accurate and complete execution of the task or tasks.

1 Point = The student's answer contains attributes of an appropriate response but is flawed.

0 Points = The student's answer contains no attributes of an appropriate response.

Extended-Response Rubric

Item 20

4 Points = The student correctly writes an expression in part **a,** and an inequality in part **b.** The solution in part **c** is correct, and the student correctly explains what the answer means in the context of the problem. The student gives a correct answer to part **d.**

3 Points = The student correctly writes an expression in part **a** and an inequality in part **b.** The solution in part **c** is correct, but the student does not explain the meaning of the answer in the context of the problem. The student gives a correct answer to part **d.**

2 Points = The student answers all parts correctly but does not show any work or explanation; or the student correctly answers parts **a** and **b** but does not correctly answer parts **c** and **d.**

1 Point = The student correctly writes an expression in part **a** but does not correctly answer the other parts of the problem; or the student attempts to answer all parts of the problem but does not correctly answer any part.

0 Points = The student does not answer correctly and does not attempt all parts of the problem.

Answers

12. 28

13. 3.6

14. 100

15. 87

16. 10

17a. Possible answer: $n + 5 > 8$

b. Possible answer: $-2n < -6$

18a. $k + 2k + (2k + 5) < 40$

b. Maurice can have up to 17 videos.

19a. $35 + 7x$; $11x$

b. $35 + 7x > 11x$

c. $x < 8.75$; Larry's costs less when 8 lunches or fewer are ordered. Donna's costs less for 10 lunches.

20a. $27{,}000 + 0.025x$

b. $31{,}000 > 27{,}000 + 0.025x$

c. $x < 160{,}000$; Aleya should work for company A if her sales will be less than $160,000.

d. $1000

Functions

Section 4A

Function Concepts

4-1 Graphing Relationships
4-2 Relations and Functions
4-2 Algebra Lab The Vertical-Line Test
4-3 Algebra Lab Model Variable Relationships
4-3 Writing Functions
4-4 Graphing Functions
4-4 Technology Lab Connect Function Rules, Tables, and Graphs

Section 4B

Applying Functions

4-5 Scatter Plots and Trend Lines
4-5 Technology Lab Interpret Scatter Plots and Trend Lines
Connecting Algebra to Data Analysis Median-Fit Line
4-6 Arithmetic Sequences

Pacing Guide for 45-Minute Classes

Teacher One Stop™
Calendar Planner®

Chapter 4

Countdown Weeks 8, 9

DAY 1	DAY 2	DAY 3	DAY 4	DAY 5
4-1 Lesson	4-2 Lesson	4-2 Algebra Lab 4-3 Algebra Lab	4-3 Lesson	4-4 Lesson
DAY 6	**DAY 7**	**DAY 8**	**DAY 9**	**DAY 10**
4-4 Technology Lab Multi-Step Test Prep	Ready to Go On? 4-5 Lesson	4-5 Lesson 4-5 Technology Lab	Connecting Algebra to Data Analysis	4-6 Lesson
DAY 11	**DAY 12**	**DAY 13**		
Multi-Step Test Prep Ready to Go On?	Chapter 4 Review	Chapter 4 Test		

Pacing Guide for 90-Minute Classes

Teacher One Stop™
Calendar Planner®

Chapter 4

DAY 1	DAY 2	DAY 3	DAY 4	DAY 5
Chapter 3 Test 4-1 Lesson	4-2 Lesson 4-2 Algebra Lab 4-3 Algebra Lab	4-3 Lesson 4-4 Lesson	4-4 Technology Lab Multi-Step Test Prep Ready to Go On? 4-5 Lesson	4-5 Lesson 4-5 Technology Lab Connecting Algebra to Data Analysis
DAY 6	**DAY 7**			
4-6 Lesson Multi-Step Test Prep Ready to Go On?	Chapter 4 Review Chapter 4 Test			

ONGOING ASSESSMENT and INTERVENTION

	DIAGNOSE	PRESCRIBE
Assess Prior Knowledge	**Before Chapter 4**	
	Diagnose readiness for the chapter.	Prescribe intervention.
	Are You Ready? SE p. 231	***Are You Ready? Intervention***
Formative Assessment	**Before Every Lesson**	
	Diagnose readiness for the lesson.	Prescribe intervention.
	Warm Up TE	**Reteach** CRB
	During Every Lesson	
	Diagnose understanding of lesson concepts.	Prescribe intervention.
	Check It Out! SE	**Reading Strategies** CRB
	Questioning Strategies TE	***Success for Every Learner***
	Think and Discuss SE	***Lesson Tutorial Videos***
	Write About It SE	
	Journal TE	
	After Every Lesson	
	Diagnose mastery of lesson concepts.	Prescribe intervention.
	Lesson Quiz TE	**Reteach** CRB
	Test Prep SE	**Test Prep Doctor** TE
	Test and Practice Generator	***Homework Help Online***
	Before Chapter 4 Testing	
	Diagnose mastery of concepts in chapter.	Prescribe intervention.
	Ready to Go On? SE pp. 265, 283	***Ready to Go On? Intervention***
	Multi-Step Test Prep SE pp. 264, 282	**Scaffolding Questions** TE pp. 264, 282
	Section Quizzes AR	**Reteach** CRB
	Test and Practice Generator	***Lesson Tutorial Videos***
	Before High Stakes Testing	
	Diagnose mastery of benchmark concepts.	Prescribe intervention.
	College Entrance Exam Practice SE p. 289	***College Entrance Exam Practice***
	Standardized Test Prep SE pp. 292–293	
Summative Assessment	**After Chapter 4**	
	Check mastery of chapter concepts.	Prescribe intervention.
	Multiple-Choice Tests (Forms A, B, C)	**Reteach** CRB
	Free-Response Tests (Forms A, B, C)	***Lesson Tutorial Videos***
	Performance Assessment AR	
	Cumulative Test AR	
	Test and Practice Generator	

KEY: **SE** = *Student Edition* **TE** = *Teacher's Edition* **CRB** = *Chapter Resource Book* **AR** = *Assessment Resources*  Available online 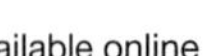 Available on CD- or DVD-ROM

CHAPTER 4

Lesson Resources

Before the Lesson

Prepare *Teacher One Stop* 
- Editable lesson plans
- Calendar Planner
- Easy access to all chapter resources

Lesson Transparencies
- Teacher Tools

Teach the Lesson

Introduce *Alternate Openers: Explorations*

Lesson Transparencies 
- Warm Up
- Problem of the Day

Teach *Lesson Transparencies*
- Teaching Transparencies

Know-It Notebook™
- Vocabulary
- Key Concepts

Power Presentations 

Lesson Tutorial Videos 

Interactive Online Edition 
- Lesson Activities
- Lesson Tutorial Videos

Lab Activities

Lab Resources Online 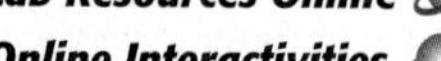

Online Interactivities 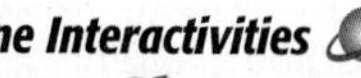

TechKeys 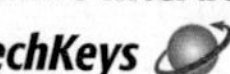

Practice the Lesson

Practice *Chapter Resources*
- Practice A, B, C

Practice and Problem Solving Workbook SPANISH

IDEA Works!® Modified Worksheets and Tests

ExamView Test and Practice Generator 

Homework Help Online

Online Interactivities 

Interactive Online Edition 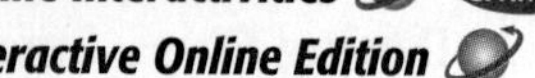
- Homework Help

Apply *Chapter Resources*
- Problem Solving SPANISH

Practice and Problem Solving Workbook SPANISH

Interactive Online Edition
- Chapter Project

Project Teacher Support 

After the Lesson

Reteach *Chapter Resources*
- Reteach
- Reading Strategies ELL

Success for Every Learner

Review *Interactive Answers and Solutions*

Solutions Key

Know-It Notebook™ 
- Big Ideas
- Chapter Review

Extend *Chapter Resources*
- Challenge

Technology Highlights for the Teacher

Power Presentations

Dynamic presentations to engage students. Complete PowerPoint® presentations for every lesson in Chapter 4.

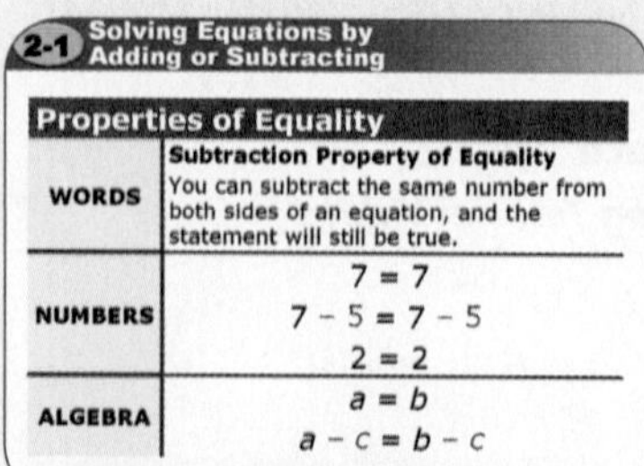

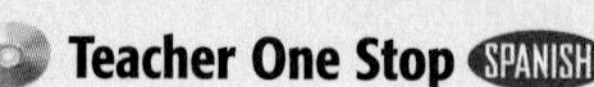

Teacher One Stop SPANISH

Easy access to Chapter 4 resources and assessments. Includes lesson planning, test generation, and puzzle creation software.

Premier Online Edition SPANISH

Chapter 4 includes Tutorial Videos, Lesson Activities, Lesson Quizzes, Homework Help, and Chapter Project.

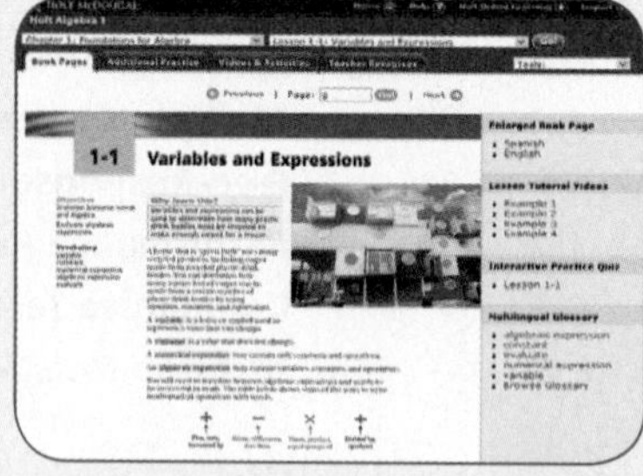

KEY: **SE** = *Student Edition* **TE** = *Teacher's Edition* 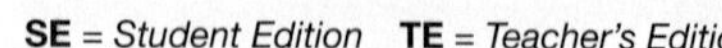  ELL English Language Learners 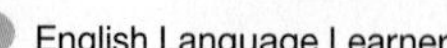  SPANISH Spanish version available 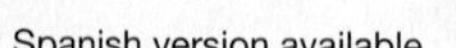 Available online 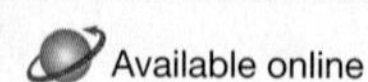 Available on CD- or DVD-R

Reaching All Learners

Teaching tips to help all learners appear throughout the chapter. A few that target specific students are included in the lists below.

All Learners

- ***Lab Activities***
- ***Practice and Problem Solving Workbook*** SPANISH
- ***Know-It Notebook***

Special Needs Students

- **Practice A** .... CRB
- **Reteach** .... CRB
- **Reading Strategies** .... CRB
- **Are You Ready?** .... SE p. 231
- **Inclusion** .... TE pp. 236, 252, 259
- ***IDEA Works!® Modified Worksheets and Tests***
- ***Ready to Go On? Intervention*** SPANISH
- ***Know-It Notebook***
- ***Online Interactivities*** SPANISH
- ***Lesson Tutorial Videos*** SPANISH

Developing Learners

- **Practice A** .... CRB
- **Reteach** .... CRB
- **Reading Strategies** .... CRB
- **Are You Ready?** .... SE p. 231
- **Vocabulary Connections** .... SE p. 232
- **Questioning Strategies** .... TE
- ***Ready to Go On? Intervention*** SPANISH
- ***Know-It Notebook***
- ***Homework Help Online***
- ***Online Interactivities*** SPANISH
- ***Lesson Tutorial Videos*** 

On-Level Learners

- **Practice B** .... CRB
- **Problem Solving** .... CRB
- **Vocabulary Connections** .... SE p. 232
- **Questioning Strategies** .... TE
- ***Ready to Go On? Intervention*** SPANISH
- ***Know-It Notebook***
- ***Homework Help Online***
- ***Online Interactivities*** SPANISH

Advanced Learners

- **Practice C** .... CRB
- **Challenge** .... CRB
- **Challenge Exercises** .... SE
- **Reading and Writing Math** *Extend* .... TE p. 233
- **Critical Thinking** .... TE p. 259
- ***Are You Ready? Enrichment*** SPANISH
- ***Ready To Go On? Enrichment*** SPANISH

English Language Learners

ENGLISH LANGUAGE LEARNERS

- **Reading Strategies** .... CRB
- **Are You Ready? Vocabulary** .... SE p. 231
- **Vocabulary Connections** .... SE p. 232
- **Vocabulary Review** .... SE p. 284
- **English Language Learners** .... TE pp. 233, 249, 251 277, 278, 295
- ***Success for Every Learner***
- ***Know-It Notebook***
- ***Multilingual Glossary***
- ***Lesson Tutorial Videos*** 

Technology Highlights for Reaching All Learners

Lesson Tutorial Videos SPANISH

Starring Holt authors Ed Burger and Freddie Renfro! Live tutorials to support every lesson in Chapter 4.

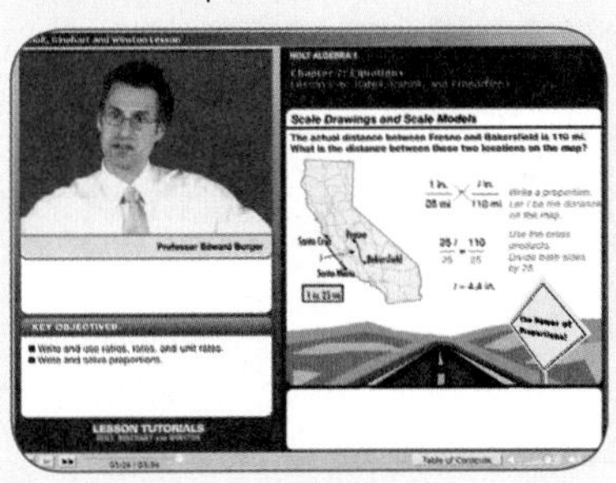

Multilingual Glossary

Searchable glossary includes definitions in English, Spanish, Vietnamese, Chinese, Hmong, Korean, and 4 other languages.

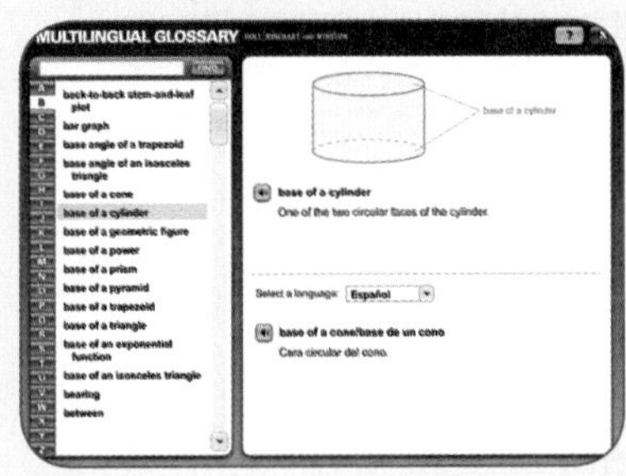

Online Interactivities

Interactive tutorials provide visually engaging alternative opportunities to learn concepts and master skills.

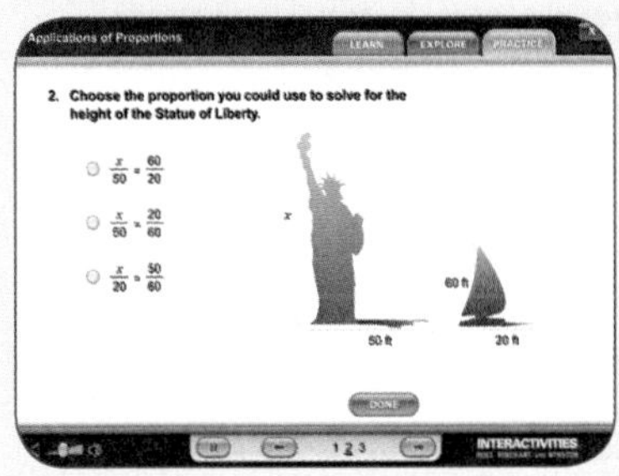

KEY: **SE** = *Student Edition* **TE** = *Teacher's Edition* **CRB** = *Chapter Resource Book* SPANISH Spanish version available; Available online; Available on CD- or DVD-ROM

CHAPTER 4

Ongoing Assessment

Assessing Prior Knowledge

Determine whether students have the prerequisite concepts and skills for success in Chapter 4.

Are You Ready? SPANISH .... SE p. 231
Warm Up .... TE

Test Preparation

Provide review and practice for Chapter 4 and standardized tests.

Multi-Step Test Prep .... SE pp. 264, 282
Study Guide: Review .... SE pp. 284–287
Test Tackler .... SE pp. 290–291
Standardized Test Prep .... SE pp. 292–293
College Entrance Exam Practice .... SE p. 289
Countdown to Testing .... SE pp. C4–C27
IDEA Works!® Modified Worksheets and Tests

Alternative Assessment

Assess students' understanding of Chapter 4 concepts and combined problem-solving skills.

Chapter 4 Project .... SE p. 230
Alternative Assessment .... TE
Performance Assessment SPANISH .... AR
Portfolio Assessment SPANISH .... AR

Lesson Assessment

Provide formative assessment for each lesson of Chapter 4.

Questioning Strategies .... TE
Think and Discuss .... SE
Check It Out! Exercises .... SE
Write About It .... SE
Journal .... TE
Lesson Quiz .... TE
Alternative Assessment .... TE
IDEA Works!® Modified Worksheets and Tests

Weekly Assessment

Provide formative assessment for each section of Chapter 4.

Multi-Step Test Prep .... SE pp. 264, 282
Ready to Go On? SPANISH .... SE pp. 265, 283
Section Quizzes SPANISH .... AR
Test and Practice Generator SPANISH .... *Teacher One Stop*

Chapter Assessment

Provide summative assessment of Chapter 4 mastery.

Chapter 4 Test .... SE p. 288
Chapter Test (Levels A, B, C) SPANISH .... AR
• Multiple Choice • Free Response
Cumulative Test SPANISH .... AR
Test and Practice Generator SPANISH .... *Teacher One Stop*
IDEA Works!® Modified Worksheets and Tests

Technology Highlights for Assessment

Are You Ready? SPANISH

Automatically assess readiness and prescribe intervention for Chapter 4 prerequisite skills.

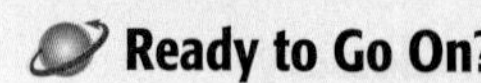

Ready to Go On?

Automatically assess understanding of and prescribe intervention for Sections 4A and 4B.

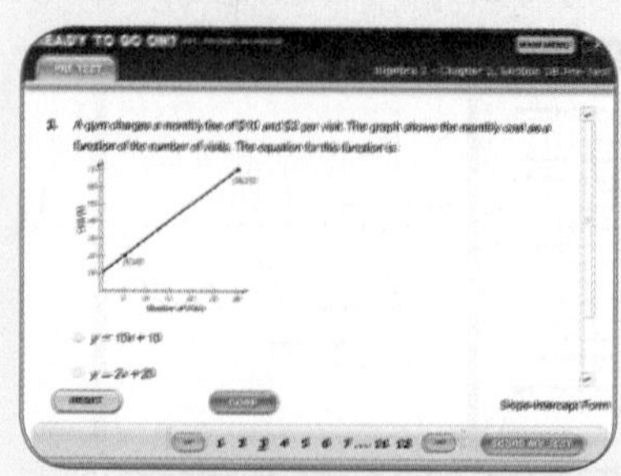

Test and Practice Generator SPANISH

Use Chapter 4 problem banks to create assessments and worksheets to print out or deliver online. Includes dynamic problems.

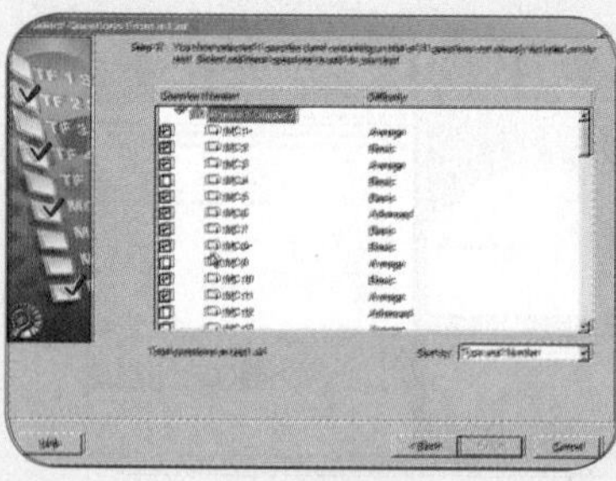

KEY: **SE** = *Student Edition* **TE** = *Teacher's Edition* **AR** = *Assessment Resources* SPANISH Spanish version available Available online  Available on CD- or DVD-ROM

Three levels (A, B, C) of multiple-choice and free-response chapter tests, along with a performance assessment, are available in the *Assessment Resources.*

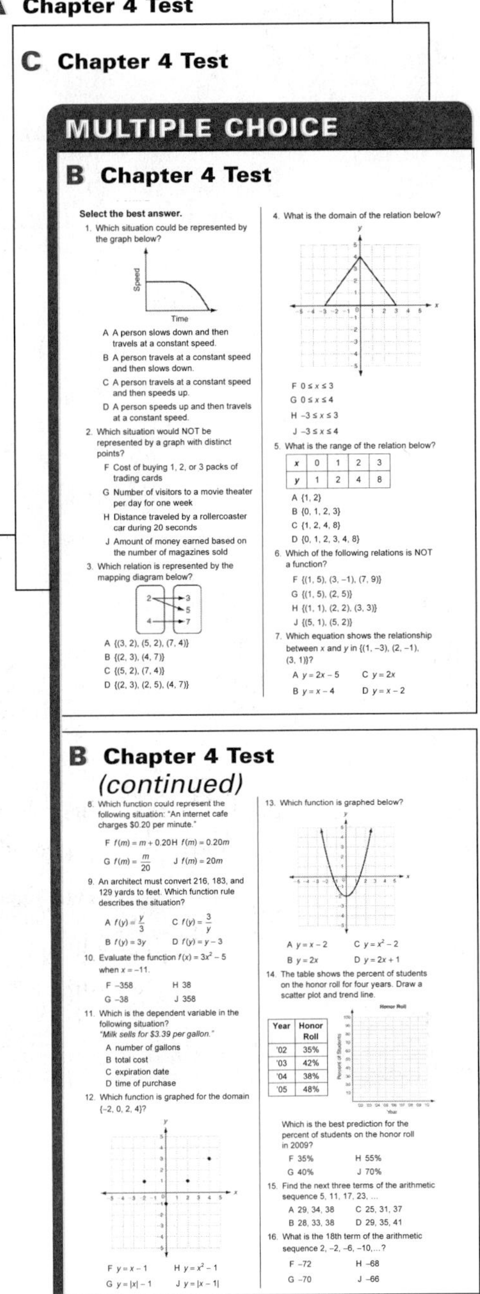

A Chapter 4 Test

C Chapter 4 Test

MULTIPLE CHOICE

B Chapter 4 Test

Select the best answer.

1. Which situation could be represented by the graph below?

A A person slows down and then travels at a constant speed.
B A person travels at a constant speed and then slows down.
C A person travels at a constant speed and then speeds up.
D A person speeds up and then travels at a constant speed.

2. Which situation would NOT be represented by a graph with distinct points?

F Cost of buying 1, 2, or 3 packs of trading cards
G Number of visitors to a movie theater per day for one week
H Distance traveled by a rollercoaster car during 20 seconds
J Amount of money earned based on the number of magazines sold

3. Which relation is represented by the mapping diagram below?

A {(3, 2), (5, 2), (7, 4)}
B {(2, 3), (4, 7)}
C {(5, 2), (7, 4)}
D {(2, 3), (2, 5), (4, 7)}

4. What is the domain of the relation below?

F $0 \le x \le 3$
G $0 \le x \le 4$
H $-3 \le x \le 3$
J $-3 \le x \le 4$

5. What is the range of the relation below?

x	0	1	2	3
y	1	2	4	8

A {1, 2}
B {0, 1, 2, 3}
C {1, 2, 4, 8}
D {0, 1, 2, 3, 4, 8}

6. Which of the following relations is NOT a function?

F {(1, 5), (3, −1), (7, 9)}
G {(1, 5), (2, 5)}
H {(1, 1), (2, 2), (3, 3)}
J {(5, 1), (5, 2)}

7. Which equation shows the relationship between x and y in {(1, −3), (2, −1), (3, 1)}?

A $y = 2x - 5$ C $y = 2x$
B $y = x - 4$ D $y = x - 2$

B Chapter 4 Test (continued)

8. Which function could represent the following situation: "An internet cafe charges $0.20 per minute."

F $f(m) = m + 0.20$ H $f(m) = 0.20m$
G $f(m) = \frac{m}{20}$ J $f(m) = 20m$

9. An architect must convert 216, 183, and 129 yards to feet. Which function rule describes the situation?

A $f(y) = \frac{y}{3}$ C $f(y) = \frac{3}{y}$
B $f(y) = 3y$ D $f(y) = y - 3$

10. Evaluate the function $f(x) = 3x^2 - 5$ when $x = -11$.

F −358 H 38
G −38 J 358

11. Which is the dependent variable in the following situation? "Milk sells for $3.39 per gallon."

A number of gallons
B total cost
C expiration date
D time of purchase

12. Which function is graphed for the domain {−2, 0, 2, 4}?

F $y = x - 1$ H $y = x^2 - 1$
G $y = |x| - 1$ J $y = |x - 1|$

13. Which function is graphed below?

A $y = x - 2$ C $y = x^2 - 2$
B $y = 2x$ D $y = 2x + 1$

14. The table shows the percent of students on the honor roll for four years. Draw a scatter plot and trend line.

Year	Honor Roll
'02	35%
'03	42%
'04	38%
'05	48%

Which is the best prediction for the percent of students on the honor roll in 2009?

F 35% H 55%
G 40% J 70%

15. Find the next three terms of the arithmetic sequence 5, 11, 17, 23, ...

A 29, 34, 38 C 25, 31, 37
B 28, 33, 38 D 29, 35, 41

16. What is the 18th term of the arithmetic sequence 2, −2, −6, −10, ...?

F −72 H −68
G −70 J −66

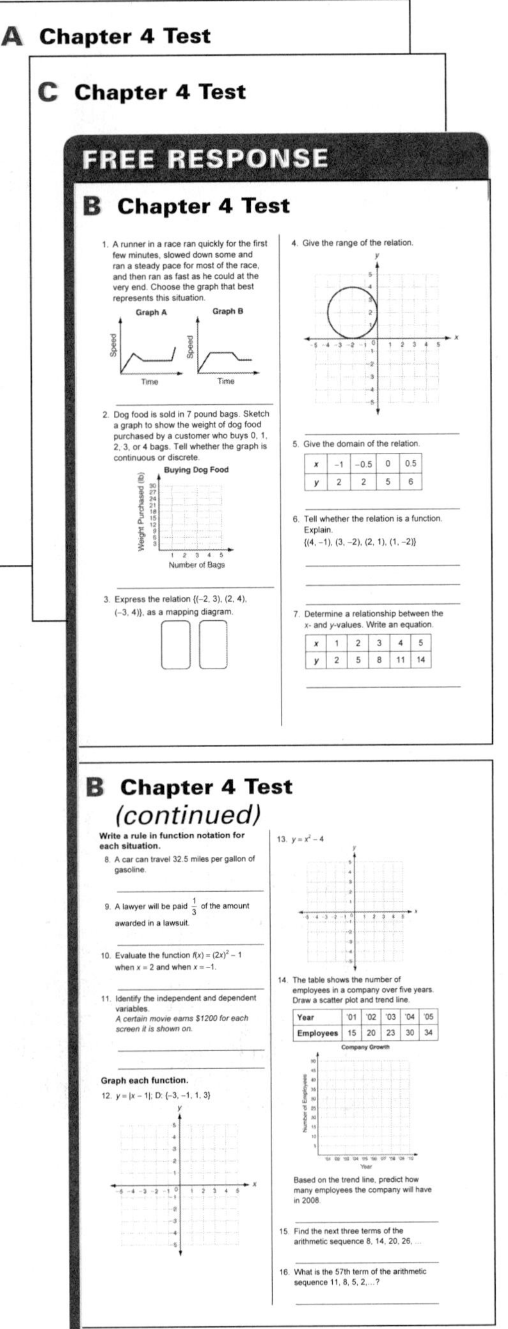

A Chapter 4 Test

C Chapter 4 Test

FREE RESPONSE

B Chapter 4 Test

1. A runner in a race ran quickly for the first few minutes, slowed down some and ran a steady pace for most of the race, and then ran as fast as he could at the very end. Choose the graph that best represents this situation.

Graph A Graph B

2. Dog food is sold in 7 pound bags. Sketch a graph to show the weight of dog food purchased by a customer who buys 0, 1, 2, 3, or 4 bags. Tell whether the graph is continuous or discrete.

Buying Dog Food

3. Express the relation {(−2, 3), (2, 4), (−3, 4)}, as a mapping diagram.

4. Give the range of the relation.

5. Give the domain of the relation.

x	−1	−0.5	0	0.5
y	2	2	5	6

6. Tell whether the relation is a function. Explain.
{(4, −1), (3, −2), (2, 1), (1, −2)}

7. Determine a relationship between the x- and y-values. Write an equation.

x	1	2	3	4	5
y	2	5	8	11	14

B Chapter 4 Test (continued)

Write a rule in function notation for each situation.

8. A car can travel 32.5 miles per gallon of gasoline.

9. A lawyer will be paid $\frac{1}{3}$ of the amount awarded in a lawsuit.

10. Evaluate the function $f(x) = (2x)^2 - 1$ when $x = 2$ and when $x = -1$.

11. Identify the independent and dependent variables.
A certain movie earns $1200 for each screen it is shown on.

Graph each function.

12. $y = |x - 1|$; D: {−3, −1, 1, 3}

13. $y = x^2 - 4$

14. The table shows the number of employees in a company over five years. Draw a scatter plot and trend line.

Year	'01	'02	'03	'04	'05
Employees	15	20	23	30	34

Company Growth

Based on the trend line, predict how many employees the company will have in 2008.

15. Find the next three terms of the arithmetic sequence 8, 14, 20, 26, ...

16. What is the 57th term of the arithmetic sequence 11, 8, 5, 2, ...?

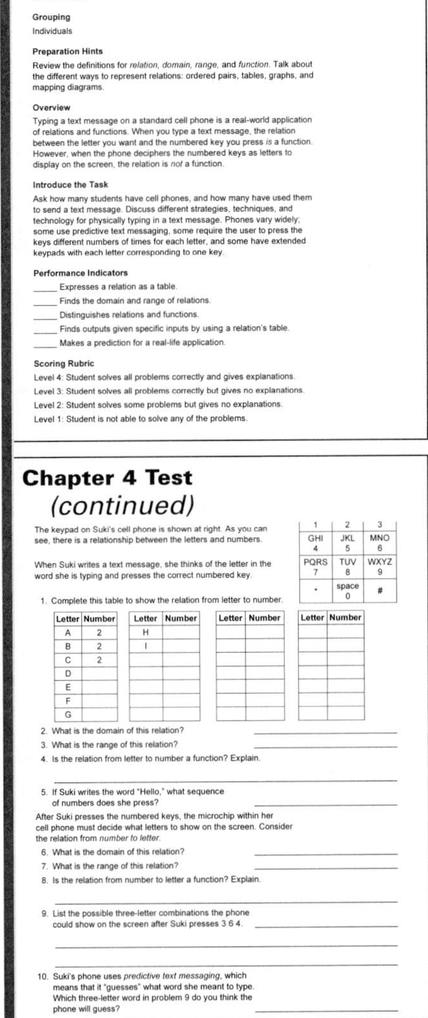

PERFORMANCE ASSESSMENT

Chapter 4 Test

Purpose
This performance task assesses the student's ability to find the domain and range of relations, and to identify functions.

Time
25–40 minutes

Grouping
Individuals

Preparation Hints
Review the definitions for *relation, domain, range,* and *function.* Talk about the different ways to represent relations: ordered pairs, tables, graphs, and mapping diagrams.

Overview
Typing a text message on a standard cell phone is a real-world application of relations and functions. When you type a text message, the relation between the letter you want and the numbered key you press *is* a function. However, when the phone deciphers the numbered keys as letters to display on the screen, the relation is *not* a function.

Introduce the Task
Ask how many students have cell phones, and how many have used them to send a text message. Discuss different strategies, techniques, and technology for physically typing in a text message. Phones vary widely; some use predictive text messaging, some require the user to press the keys different numbers of times for each letter, and some have extended keypads with each letter corresponding to one key.

Performance Indicators
____ Expresses a relation as a table.
____ Finds the domain and range of relations.
____ Distinguishes relations and functions.
____ Finds outputs given specific inputs by using a relation's table.
____ Makes a prediction for a real-life application.

Scoring Rubric
Level 4: Student solves all problems correctly and gives explanations.
Level 3: Student solves all problems correctly but gives no explanations.
Level 2: Student solves some problems but gives no explanations.
Level 1: Student is not able to solve any of the problems.

Chapter 4 Test (continued)

The keypad on Suki's cell phone is shown at right. As you can see, there is a relationship between the letters and numbers.

1	2 ABC	3 DEF
GHI 4	JKL 5	MNO 6
PQRS 7	TUV 8	WXYZ 9
*	space 0	#

When Suki writes a text message, she thinks of the letter in the word she is typing and presses the correct numbered key.

1. Complete this table to show the relation from letter to number.

Letter	Number
A	2
B	2
C	2
D	
E	
F	
G	
H	
I	

2. What is the domain of this relation?
3. What is the range of this relation?
4. Is the relation from letter to number a function? Explain.
5. If Suki writes the word "Hello," what sequence of numbers does she press?

After Suki presses the numbered keys, the microchip within her cell phone must decide what letters to show on the screen. Consider the relation from *number to letter.*

6. What is the domain of this relation?
7. What is the range of this relation?
8. Is the relation from number to letter a function? Explain.
9. List the possible three-letter combinations the phone could show on the screen after Suki presses 3 6 4.
10. Suki's phone uses *predictive text messaging,* which means that it "guesses" what word she meant to type. Which three-letter word in problem 9 do you think the phone will guess?

Teacher One Stop™ 
Test & Practice Generator

Create and customize Chapter 4 Tests. Instantly generate multiple test versions, answer keys, and Spanish versions of test items.

Modified chapter tests that address special learning needs are available in *IDEA Works!*® *Modified Worksheets and Tests.*

CHAPTER 4

SECTION 4A
Function Concepts

On page 264, students use a graph to write an equation of a function that models the volume of water in a pool.

Exercises designed to prepare students for success on the Multi-Step Test Prep can be found in each lesson.

SECTION 4B
Applying Functions

On page 282, students create a scatter plot and trend line to model a real-world travel situation.

Exercises designed to prepare students for success on the Multi-Step Test Prep can be found in each lesson.

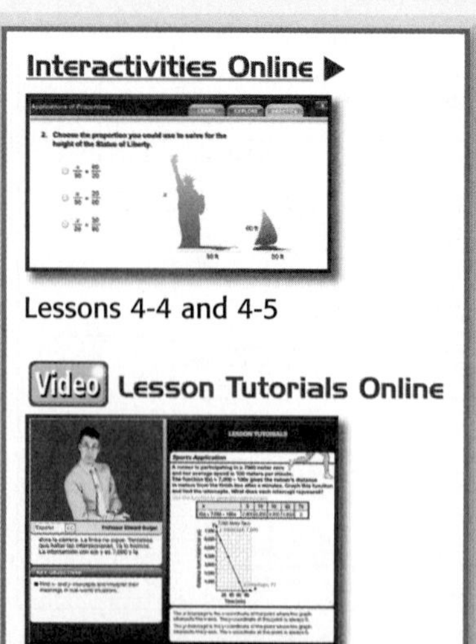

Interactivities Online ▶

Lessons 4-4 and 4-5

Video Lesson Tutorials Online

Lesson Tutorial Videos are available for EVERY example.

CHAPTER 4

Functions

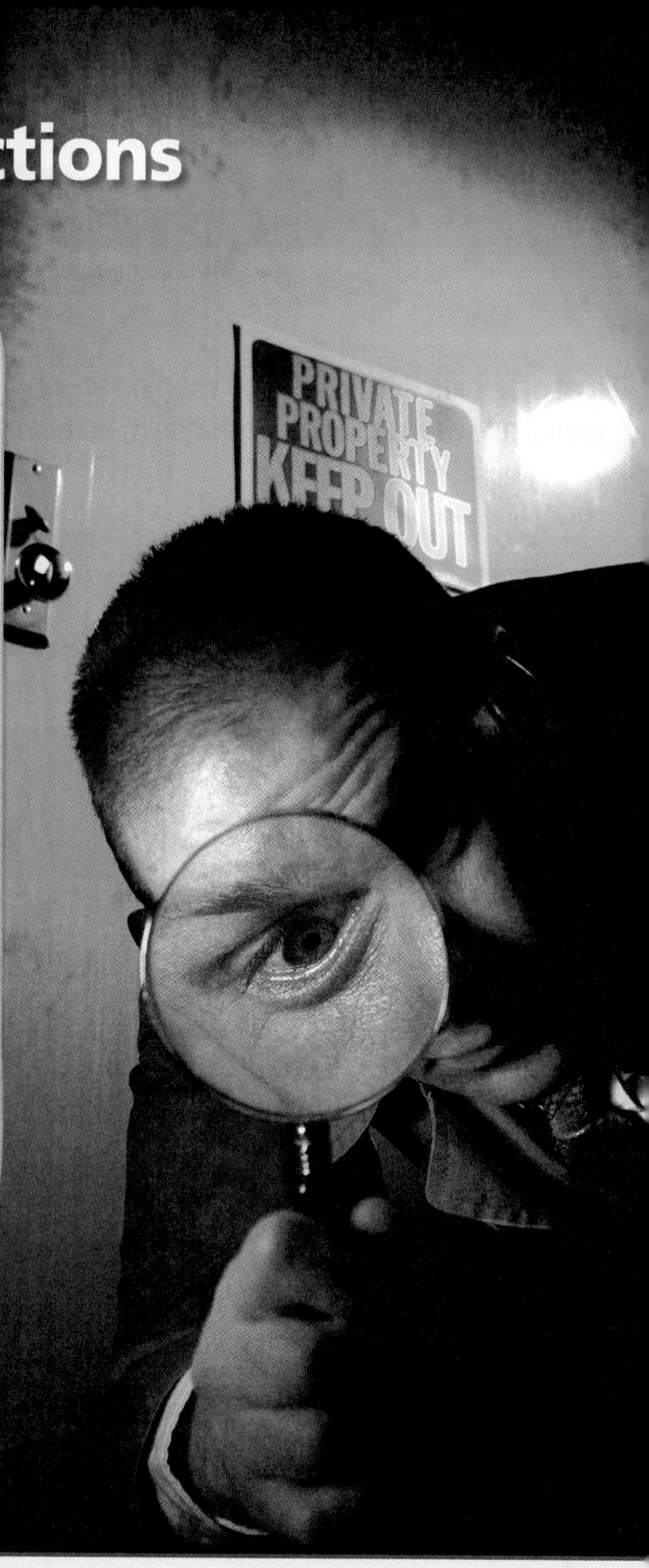

Chapter Focus

- Use tables, diagrams, graphs, and equations to describe functions.
- Translate among representations of functions.
- Use functions to represent, analyze, and solve problems.

Is That *Your* Foot?

Criminologists use measurements, such as the size of footprints, and functions to help them identify criminals.

go.hrw.com
Chapter Project Online
KEYWORD: MA7 ChProj

PRIVATE PROPERTY KEEP OUT

Is That Your Foot?

About the Project

In the first activity of the Chapter Project, students determine their walking rate and then graph a function to predict how far they can walk in 8 hours. In the second activity, students determine whether there is a correlation between foot length and height by creating and interpreting a scatter plot and its trend line.

Project Resources

All project resources for teachers and students are provided online.

Materials:

- Activity 1: stopwatch, tape measure (ft) (MK)
- Activity 2: tape measure (cm)

ARE YOU READY?

Vocabulary

Match each term on the left with a definition on the right.

1. absolute value **D**
2. algebraic expression **C**
3. input **F**
4. output **B**
5. x-axis **E**

A. a letter used to represent a value that can change
B. the value generated for y
C. a group of numbers, symbols, and variables with one or more operations
D. the distance of a number from zero on the number line
E. the horizontal number line in the coordinate plane
F. a value substituted for x

Ordered Pairs

Graph each point on the same coordinate plane.

6. $(-2, 4)$ 7. $(0, -5)$ 8. $(1, -3)$ 9. $(4, 2)$
10. $(3, -2)$ 11. $(-1, -2)$ 12. $(-1, 3)$ 13. $(-4, 0)$

Function Tables

Generate ordered pairs for each function for $x = -2, -1, 0, 1, 2$.

14. $y = -2x - 1$ 15. $y = x + 1$ 16. $y = -x^2$
17. $y = \frac{1}{2}x + 2$ 18. $y = (x + 1)^2$ 19. $y = (x - 1)^2$

Solve Multi-Step Equations

Solve each equation. Check your answer.

20. $17x - 15 = 12$ **$\frac{27}{17}$** 21. $-7 + 2t = 7$ **7** 22. $-6 = \frac{p}{3} + 9$ **−45**
23. $5n - 10 = 35$ **9** 24. $3r - 14 = 7$ **7** 25. $9 = \frac{x}{2} + 1$ **16**
26. $-2.4 + 1.6g = 5.6$ **5** 27. $34 - 2x = 12$ **11** 28. $2(x + 5) = -8$ **−9**

Solve for a Variable

Solve each equation for the indicated variable.

29. $A = \ell w$ for w **$w = \frac{A}{\ell}$** 30. $V = \ell wh$ for w **$w = \frac{V}{\ell h}$** 31. $A = bh$ for h **$h = \frac{A}{b}$**
32. $C = 2\pi r$ for r **$r = \frac{C}{2\pi}$** 33. $I = Prt$ for P **$P = \frac{I}{rt}$** 34. $V = \frac{1}{3}\ell wh$ for h **$h = \frac{3V}{\ell w}$**

CHAPTER 4

ARE YOU READY?

Organizer

Objective: Assess students' understanding of prerequisite skills.

Assessing Prior Knowledge

INTERVENTION

Diagnose and Prescribe

Use this page to determine whether intervention is necessary or whether enrichment is appropriate.

Resources

***Are You Ready? Intervention and Enrichment* Worksheets**

***Are You Ready?* CD-ROM**

***Are You Ready?* Online**

my.hrw.com

Answers

6–19. See p. A16.

NO INTERVENE

ARE YOU READY? Diagnose and Prescribe

YES ENRICH

Prerequisite Skill	*Are You Ready? Intervention,* Chapter 4 Worksheets	CD-ROM	Online
Ordered Pairs	Skill 79	Activity 79	Diagnose and Prescribe Online
Function Tables	Skill 78	Activity 78	
Solve Multi-Step Equations	Skill 69	Activity 69	
Solve for a Variable	Skill 72	Activity 72	

***Are You Ready? Enrichment,* Chapter 4**

Worksheets

CD-ROM

Online

CHAPTER 4 Study Guide: Preview

Organizer

Objective: Help students organize the new concepts they will learn in Chapter 4.

Online Edition
Multilingual Glossary

Resources

Teacher One Stop™
PuzzleView

***Multilingual Glossary* Online**
go.hrw.com
KEYWORD: MA7 Glossary

Possible answers to *Vocabulary Connections*

1. Relying on someone or something else; the value of a dependent variable relies on the value of another variable.
2. Function notation is a method of writing special types of relations.
3. The two data sets have no relationship.
4. Something about them is the same. When you subtract two consecutive numbers in the list, the answer is the same as when you subtract two other consecutive numbers.

CHAPTER 4 Study Guide: Preview

Where You've Been

Previously, you

- were introduced to functions when you generated and graphed ordered pairs.
- stated rules for relationships among values.
- represented and interpreted data using bar graphs and circle graphs.

In This Chapter

You will study

- relationships between variables and determine whether a relation is a function.
- relationships in function notation.
- how trend lines on scatter plots can help you make predictions.

Where You're Going

You can use the skills in this chapter

- to find values of a function from a graph.
- to analyze data and make predictions in other courses, such as Chemistry.
- to calculate total earnings for a certain hourly rate.

Key Vocabulary/Vocabulario

arithmetic sequence	sucesión aritmética
common difference	diferencia común
correlation	correlación
dependent variable	variable dependiente
domain	dominio
function	función
function notation	notación de función
independent variable	variable independiente
no correlation	sin correlación
range	rango
relation	relación
scatter plot	diagrama de dispersión
sequence	sucesión

Vocabulary Connections

To become familiar with some of the vocabulary terms in the chapter, consider the following. You may refer to the chapter, the glossary, or a dictionary if you like.

1. What does the word *dependent* mean? What do you think is true about the value of a **dependent variable**?
2. A *function* is a special type of relation and *notation* is a method of writing. What do you suppose is meant by **function notation**?
3. The word *correlation* means "relationship." What might it mean if two sets of data have **no correlation**?
4. What does it mean when someone says that two people have something in *common*? If *difference* is the answer to a subtraction problem, what might it mean for a list of numbers to have a **common difference**?

Reading Strategy: Read and Interpret Math Symbols

It is essential that as you read through each lesson of the textbook, you can interpret mathematical symbols.

Common Math Symbols

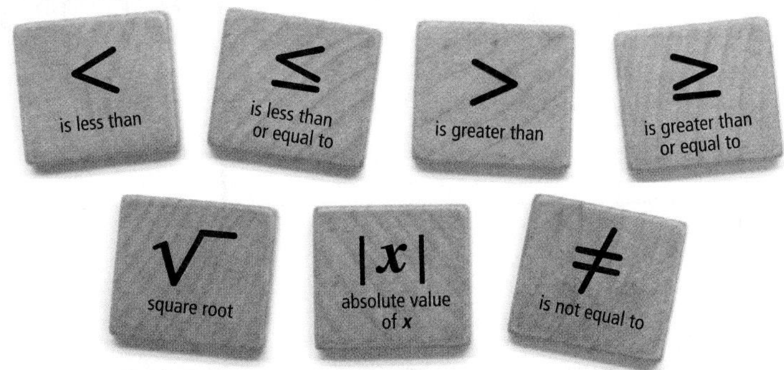

You must be able to translate symbols into words . . .

Using Symbols	Using Words
$3\left(\frac{x}{12}\right) - 1 = 21$	Three times the quotient of *x* and 12, minus 1 **equals** 21.
$25x + 6 \geq 17$	Twenty-five times *x* plus 6 **is greater than or equal** to 17.
$\|x\| > 14$	The **absolute value** of *x* **is greater than** 14.
$\sqrt{60 + x} \leq 40$	The **square root** of the sum of 60 and *x* **is less than or equal** to 40.

. . . and words into symbols.

Using Words	Using Symbols
The height of the shed **is at least** 9 feet.	$h \geq 9$ ft
The distance **is at most** one tenth of a mile.	$d \leq 0.1$ mi
The silo contains **more than** 600 cubic feet of corn.	$c > 600$ ft^3

Try This

Translate the symbols into words.

1. $x \leq \sqrt{10}$
2. $|x| + 2 > 45$
3. $-5 \leq x < 8$
4. $-6 - \frac{1}{5}x = -32$

Translate the words into symbols.

5. There are less than 15 seconds remaining.
6. The tax rate is 8.25 percent of the cost.
7. Ann counted over 100 pennies.
8. Joe can spend at least $22 but no more than $30.

Organizer

Objective: Help students apply strategies to understand and retain key concepts.

ENGLISH LANGUAGE LEARNERS

Reading Strategy: Read and Interpret Math Symbols

Discuss Mathematics is considered an "international language" because the same symbols are used all around the world.

Extend As students work through Chapter 4, point out how symbols make writing some answers (such as domain and range) easier than if they had used only words.

Answers to *Try This*

Possible answers:

1. *x* is less than or equal to the square root of 10.
2. The sum of the absolute value of *x* and 2 is greater than 45.
3. *x* is greater than or equal to negative 5 and is less than 8.
4. Negative 6 minus $\frac{1}{5}$ times *x* is equal to negative 32.
5. $t < 15$
6. $r = 0.0825$
7. $a > 100$
8. $22 \leq s \leq 30$

Reading Connection

***The Man Who Counted* by Malba Tahan**

This is a book of classic puzzles written in an exotic style reminiscent of *1001 Arabian Nights*. A Persian mathematician travels the countryside. At each stop, a situation arises that requires an elegant solution to a math problem.

Activity After students study arithmetic sequences, have them read Chapter 16, *The Game Plan*. Ask them to explain the method used to allot grains of com to the chess-board squares and to compare that method with an arithmetic sequence.

SECTION 4A Function Concepts

One-Minute Section Planner

Lesson	Lab Resources	Materials
Lesson 4-1 Graphing Relationships • Match simple graphs with situations. • Graph a relationship. ☐ SAT-10 ☑ NAEP ☐ ACT ☑ SAT ☐ SAT Subject Tests	***Technology Lab Activities*** 4-1 Technology Lab	
Lesson 4-2 Relations and Functions • Identify functions. • Find the domain and range of relations and functions. ☑ SAT-10 ☑ NAEP ☑ ACT ☑ SAT ☑ SAT Subject Tests		
4-2 Algebra Lab The Vertical-Line Test • Determine if a relation is a function. ☑ SAT-10 ☑ NAEP ☑ ACT ☑ SAT ☐ SAT Subject Tests	***Algebra Lab Activities*** 4-2 Lab Recording Sheet	**Optional** graphing calculator
4-3 Algebra Lab Model Variable Relationships • Use models to represent algebraic relationships. ☐ SAT-10 ☐ NAEP ☐ ACT ☐ SAT ☐ SAT Subject Tests	***Algebra Lab Activities*** 4-3 Lab Recording Sheet	**Optional** square tiles
Lesson 4-3 Writing Functions • Identify independent and dependent variables. • Write an equation in function notation and evaluate a function for given input values. ☑ SAT-10 ☑ NAEP ☑ ACT ☑ SAT ☑ SAT Subject Tests	***Algebra Lab Activities*** 4-3 Algebra Lab	
Lesson 4-4 Graphing Functions • Graph functions given a limited domain. • Graph functions given a domain of all real numbers. ☐ SAT-10 ☑ NAEP ☑ ACT ☑ SAT ☑ SAT Subject Tests		**Optional** graphing calculator, scale, pennies
4-4 Technology Lab Connect Function Rules, Tables, and Graphs • Use a graphing calculator to make the connections among function rules, tables, and graphs. ☑ SAT-10 ☑ NAEP ☑ ACT ☑ SAT ☐ SAT Subject Tests	***Technology Lab Activities*** 4-4 Lab Recording Sheet	**Required** graphing calculator

Note: If NAEP is checked, the content is tested on either the Grade 8 or Grade 12 NAEP assessment.

MK = *Manipulatives Kit*

RELATIONS AND FUNCTIONS

Lesson 4-2

Many students have the mistaken belief that relations and functions must be described by equations. Presenting relations and functions as sets of ordered pairs right from the start helps avoid this misconception.

A *relation* is simply a set of ordered pairs. For a given relation, the set of all first values (or x-values) is the *domain.* The set of all second values (or y-values) is the *range.*

The ordered pairs in a relation may be given as a set. For example, the relation described by the set $\{(-1, 2), (4, 0), (4, 3), (7, -5)\}$ consists of four ordered pairs. The ordered pairs may also be presented in a table, graph, or a mapping diagram. This mapping diagram below describes the same relation as the set of ordered pairs.

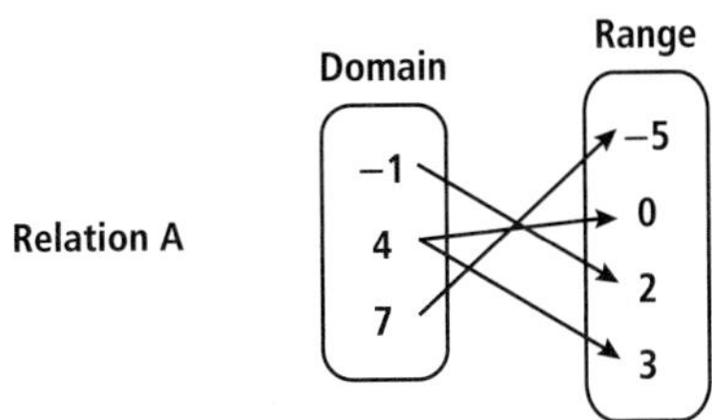

A relation can be described by the way it matches domain and range values. Relation A is *one-to-many.* This means there is at least one domain value (in this case, 4) that is paired with more than one range value (0 and 3).

A relation is *many-to-one* if more than one domain value is paired with a single range value. Relation B, shown below, is many-to-one because the domain values 0 and 9 are both paired with the range value 8.

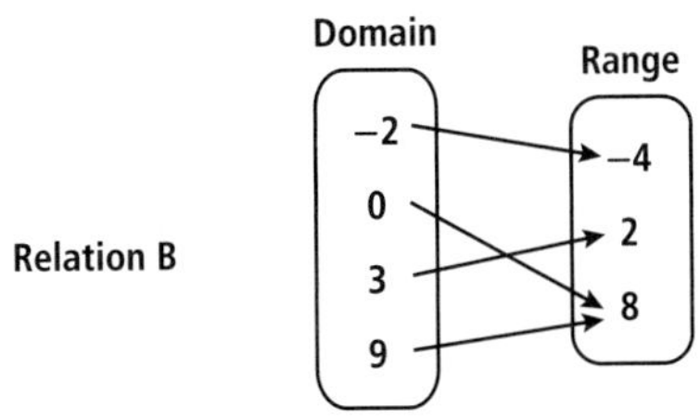

A relation is *one-to-one* if each domain value is paired with a unique range value and each range value is paired with a unique domain value. Relation C is one-to-one.

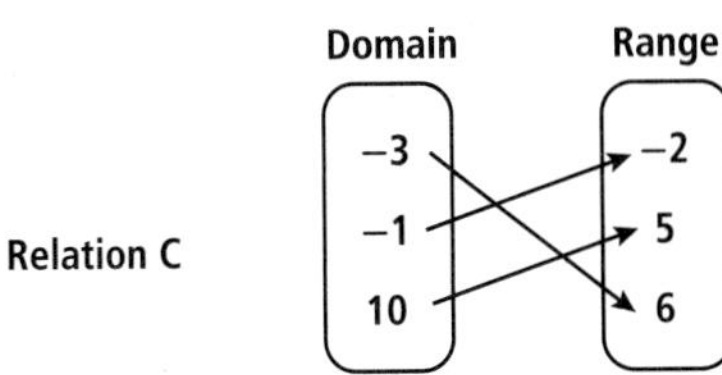

FUNCTIONS

Lessons 4-2, 4-3

A *function* is a relation in which each domain value is paired with exactly one range value. Thus, every function is a relation, but not every relation is a function. In the above examples, relations B and C are functions. Relation A is not a function because the domain value 4 is paired with more than one range value.

The definition of *function* may seem somewhat arbitrary to students. It is helpful to explicitly point out the important role that functions play in real-world situations. For example, a meteorologist might study the relation in which each day of the year is paired with the daily high temperature in Los Angeles. It would not make sense if one domain value (a day of the year) were paired with more than one range value (a high temperature). This relation is a function, as are most relations that describe real-world situations. This example illustrates that a function does not have to be defined with an equation or formula; the function above is not described by any formula that we understand.

The real-world example also illustrates why the first value of a function is the *independent variable* and the second value is the *dependent variable.* The second value (e.g., temperature) *depends* on the first value (e.g., day of the year).

Functions may be one-to-one or many-to-one. The function that gives the daily high temperature in Los Angeles is likely to be many-to-one, as there may be several days that are paired with the same temperature. However, by definition a function cannot be one-to-many.

4-1 Organizer

Pacing: Traditional 1 day
Block $\frac{1}{2}$ day

Objectives: Match simple graphs with situations.

Graph a relationship.

Technology Lab
In Technology Lab Activities

Online Edition
Tutorial Videos

Countdown Week 8

Power Presentations with PowerPoint®

Warm Up

State whether each word or phrase represents an amount that is increasing, decreasing, or constant.

1. stays the same constant
2. rises increasing
3. drops decreasing
4. slows down decreasing

Also available on transparency

Math Humor

Q: What do a math teacher and an English teacher have in common?

A: They can both make a "pair-a-graph."

4-1 Graphing Relationships

Objectives
Match simple graphs with situations.

Graph a relationship.

Vocabulary
continuous graph
discrete graph

Who uses this?
Cardiologists can use graphs to analyze their patients' heartbeats. (See Example 2.)

Graphs can be used to illustrate many different situations. For example, trends shown on a cardiograph can help a doctor see how the patient's heart is functioning.

To relate a graph to a given situation, use key words in the description.

EXAMPLE 1 Relating Graphs to Situations

The air temperature was constant for several hours at the beginning of the day and then rose steadily for several hours. It stayed the same temperature for most of the day before dropping sharply at sundown. Choose the graph that best represents this situation.

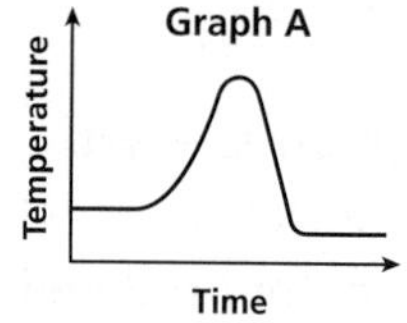

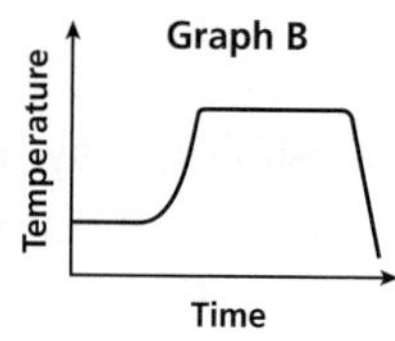

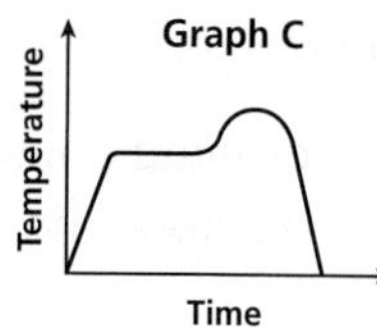

Step 1 Read the graphs from left to right to show time passing.

Step 2 List key words in order and decide which graph shows them.

Key Words	Segment Description	Graphs
Was constant	Horizontal	Graphs A and B
Rose steadily	Slanting upward	Graphs A and B
Stayed the same	Horizontal	Graph B
Dropped sharply	Slanting downward	Graph B

Step 3 Pick the graph that shows all the key phrases in order.

horizontal, slanting upward, horizontal, slanting downward

The correct graph is B.

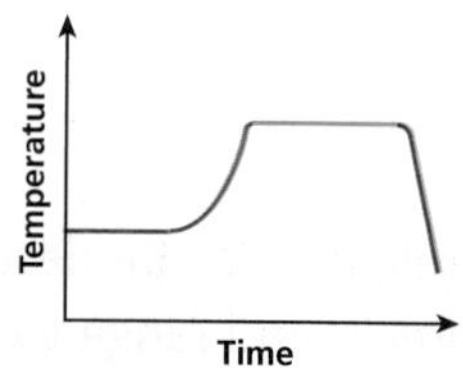

1. The air temperature increased steadily for several hours and then remained constant. At the end of the day, the temperature increased slightly again before dropping sharply. Choose the graph above that best represents this situation. **C**

State Resources

go.hrw.com
State Resources Online
KEYWORD: MA7 Resources

1 Introduce

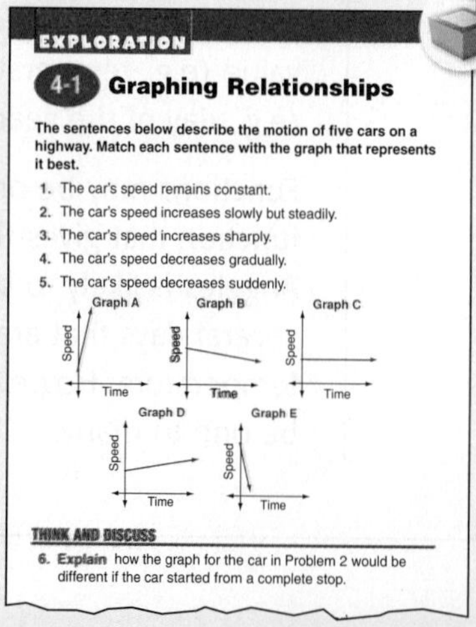

EXPLORATION

4-1 Graphing Relationships

The sentences below describe the motion of five cars on a highway. Match each sentence with the graph that represents it best.

1. The car's speed remains constant.
2. The car's speed increases slowly but steadily.
3. The car's speed increases sharply.
4. The car's speed decreases gradually.
5. The car's speed decreases suddenly.

Graph A, Graph B, Graph C, Graph D, Graph E (Speed vs. Time)

THINK AND DISCUSS

6. **Explain** how the graph for the car in Problem 2 would be different if the car started from a complete stop.

Motivate

Have students state what would happen to the height of an ice cube in the following situations.

It is placed in a refrigerator. decrease slowly

It is placed in a hot oven. decrease quickly

It is placed in a freezer. stay the same

Explorations and answers are provided in *Alternate Openers: Explorations Transparencies.*

As seen in Example 1, some graphs are connected lines or curves called **continuous graphs**. Some graphs are only distinct points. These are called **discrete graphs**.

The graph on theme-park attendance is an example of a discrete graph. It consists of distinct points because each year is distinct and people are counted in whole numbers only. The values between the whole numbers are not included, since they have no meaning for the situation.

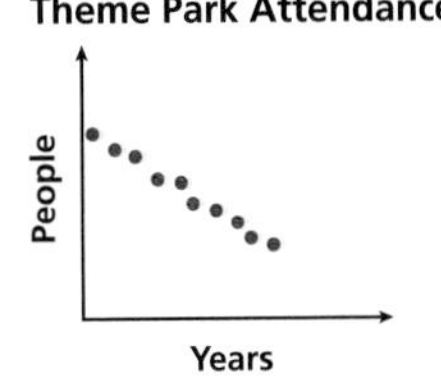

EXAMPLE 2 Sketching Graphs for Situations

Sketch a graph for each situation. Tell whether the graph is continuous or discrete.

A **Simon is selling candles to raise money for the school dance. For each candle he sells, the school will get $2.50. He has 10 candles that he can sell.**

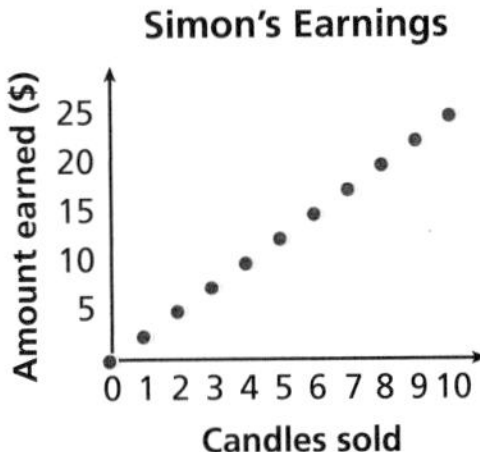

The amount earned (y-axis) increases by $2.50 for each candle Simon sells (x-axis).

Since Simon can only sell whole numbers of candles, the graph is 11 distinct points.

The graph is discrete.

B **Angelique's heart rate is being monitored while she exercises on a treadmill. While walking, her heart rate remains the same. As she increases her pace, her heart rate rises at a steady rate. When she begins to run, her heart rate increases more rapidly and then remains high while she runs. As she decreases her pace, her heart rate slows down and returns to her normal rate.**

As time passes during her workout (moving left to right along the x-axis), her heart rate (y-axis) does the following:

- remains the same,
- rises at a steady rate,
- increases more rapidly (steeper than previous segment),
- remains high,
- slows down,
- and then returns to her normal rate.

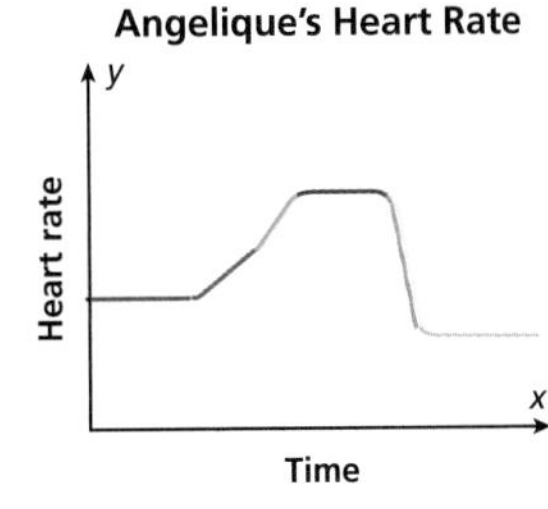

The graph is continuous.

Sketch a graph for each situation. Tell whether the graph is continuous or discrete.

2a. Jamie is taking an 8-week keyboarding class. At the end of each week, she takes a test to find the number of words she can type per minute. She improves each week.

2b. Henry begins to drain a water tank by opening a valve. Then he opens another valve. Then he closes the first valve. He leaves the second valve open until the tank is empty.

2a. discrete;

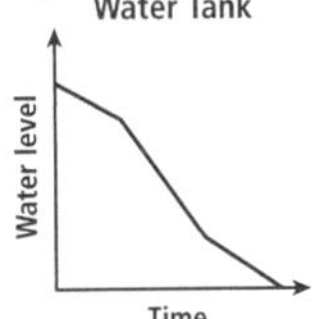

b. continuous

Water Tank

Water level

Time

Power Presentations with PowerPoint®

Additional Examples

Example 1

Each day several leaves fall from a tree. One day a gust of wind blows off many leaves. Eventually, there are no more leaves on the tree. Choose the graph that best represents this situation. B

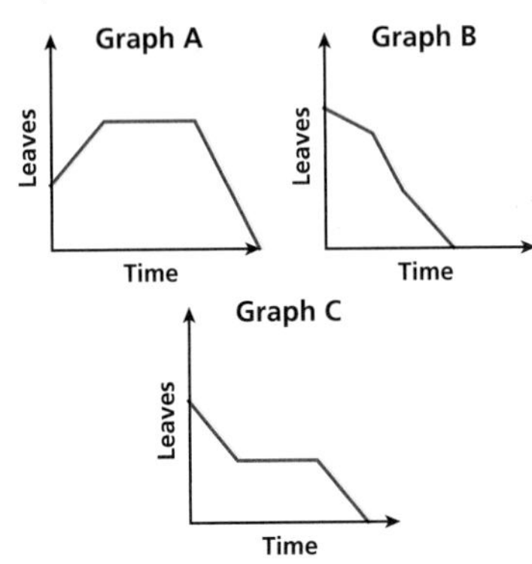

Example 2

Sketch a graph for each situation. Tell whether the graph is continuous or discrete.

A. A truck driver enters a street, drives at a constant speed, stops at a light, and then continues. continuous

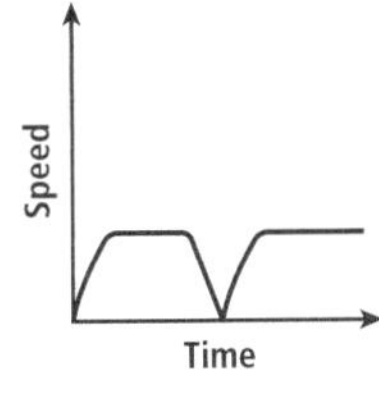

B. A small bookstore sold between 5 and 8 books each day for 7 days. discrete; possible answer:

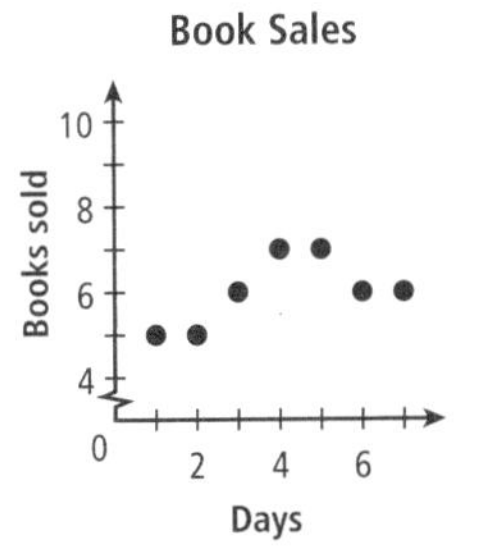

2 Teach

Guided Instruction

Explain that all graphs should be read from left to right. Encourage students to write down key phrases from a situation in the order they appear to help with matching situations to graphs. Help students identify which label to put on which axis by having them ask themselves which variable depends on the other variable. For instance, "Does time depend on distance, or does distance depend on time?" The dependent variable (distance) goes on the y-axis.

Reaching All Learners

Through Cooperative Learning

Put students in groups of three or four. Instruct each group to write a situation on one piece of paper and draw a corresponding graph on a separate piece of paper. Collect all graphs and shuffle them; then collect all situations and shuffle. Randomly label graphs A, B, C, . . . , and situations 1, 2, 3, ... Display all graphs and situations on the wall. Have groups match each graph with the correct description.

INTERVENTION

Questioning Strategies

EXAMPLES 1–2

- What are some phrases used to describe a graph that slants upward? downward? remains constant?
- How do you know when to use discrete points instead of connected segments or curves?

Inclusion Some students may interpret a horizontal line to mean that the x-value is constant. Label some points on the line to show that it is the y-value that is constant.

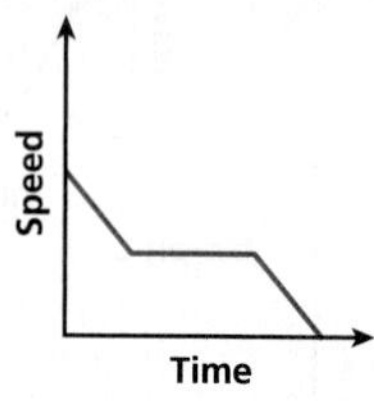

Power Presentations with PowerPoint®

Additional Examples

Example 3

Write a possible situation for the given graph.

Possible answer: A car approaching traffic slows down, drives at a constant speed, and then slows down until coming to a complete stop.

INTERVENTION

Questioning Strategies

EXAMPLE 3

- What part of the graph shows "increased steadily"? "remained unchanged"? "decreased steadily"?

When sketching or interpreting a graph, pay close attention to the labels on each axis. Both graphs below show a relationship about a child going down a slide. **Graph A** represents the child's *distance from the ground* over time. **Graph B** represents the child's *speed* over time.

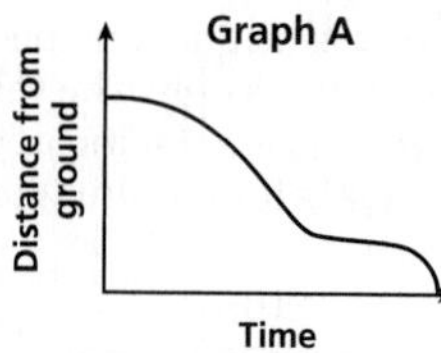

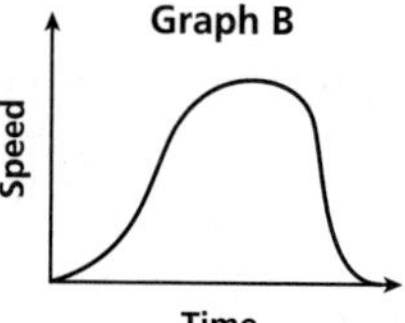

EXAMPLE 3 Writing Situations for Graphs

Write a possible situation for the given graph.

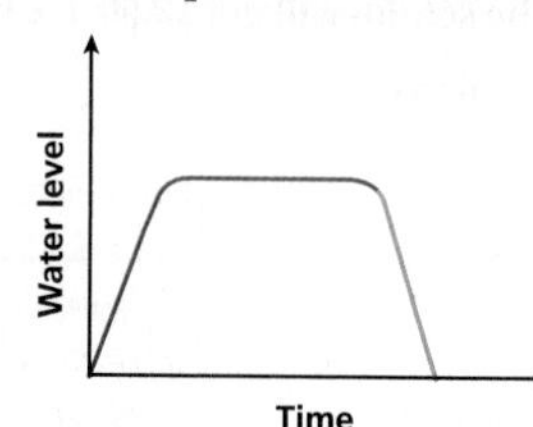

Step 1 Identify labels.
x-axis: time y-axis: water level

Step 2 Analyze sections.
Over time, the water level
- **increases steadily,**
- **remains unchanged,**
- and then **decreases steadily.**

Possible Situation: A watering can is **filled with water.** It **sits for a while** until some flowers are planted. The water is then **emptied** on top of the planted flowers.

3. Write a possible situation for the given graph.

Possible answer: When the number of students reaches a certain point, the number of pizzas bought increases.

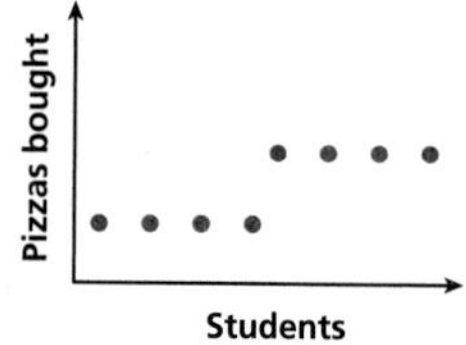

THINK AND DISCUSS

1. Should a graph of age related to height be a continuous graph or a discrete graph? Explain.
2. Give an example of a situation that, when graphed, would include a horizontal segment.
3. **GET ORGANIZED** Copy and complete the graphic organizer. Write an example of key words that suggest the given segments on a graph. One example for each segment is given for you.

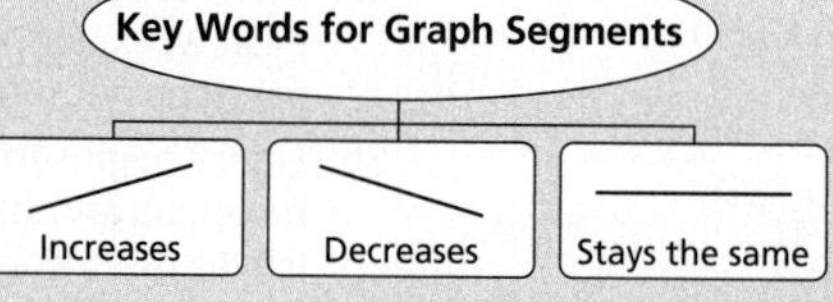

3 Close

Summarize

Be sure students understand what the axes are representing. For example, if a person runs uphill at a *constant* speed, then a speed vs. time graph will be horizontal, but a distance or height vs. time graph will slant upward. Review what a graph of speed vs. time would look like for the following.

Someone is running downhill with an increasing speed. slant upward

Someone is running on a flat path at a decreasing speed. slant downward

ONGOING ASSESSMENT and INTERVENTION

***Diagnose Before* the Lesson**
4-1 Warm Up, TE p. 234

***Monitor During* the Lesson**
Check It Out! Exercises, SE pp. 234–236
Questioning Strategies, TE pp. 235–236

***Assess After* the Lesson**
4-1 Lesson Quiz, TE p. 239
Alternative Assessment, TE p. 239

Answers to *Think and Discuss*

1. Continuous; if you plot distinct points, you could always plot more points between any pair of points.
2. Possible answer: Speed related to time—a runner runs a race and keeps a steady pace for part of it.
3. See p. A4.

go.hrw.com
Homework Help Online
KEYWORD: MA7 4-1
Parent Resources Online
KEYWORD: MA7 Parent

GUIDED PRACTICE

Vocabulary Apply the vocabulary from this lesson to answer each question.

continuous **1.** A __?__ graph is made of connected lines or curves. (*continuous* or *discrete*)

discrete **2.** A __?__ graph is made of only distinct points. (*continuous* or *discrete*)

SEE EXAMPLE 1 p. 234

Choose the graph that best represents each situation.

3. A person alternates between running and walking. B

4. A person gradually speeds up to a constant running pace. A

5. A person walks, gradually speeds up to a run, and then slows back down to a walk. C

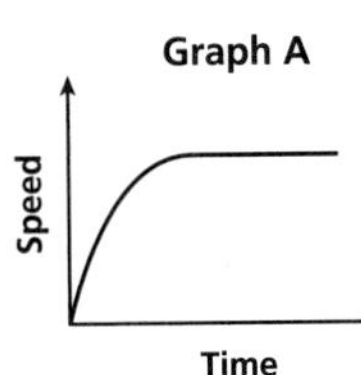

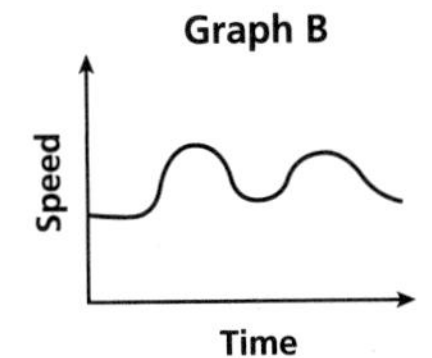

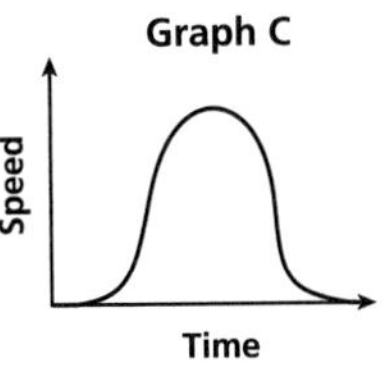

SEE EXAMPLE 2 p. 235

6. Maxine is buying extra pages for her photo album. Each page holds exactly 8 photos. Sketch a graph to show the maximum number of photos she can add to her album if she buys 1, 2, 3, or 4 extra pages. Tell whether the graph is continuous or discrete.

SEE EXAMPLE 3 p. 236

Write a possible situation for each graph.

7.

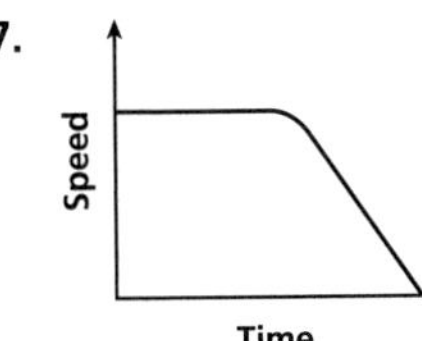

8.

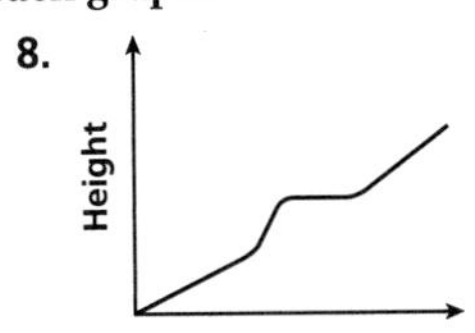

9.

PRACTICE AND PROBLEM SOLVING

Independent Practice

For Exercises	See Example
10–12	1
13	2
14–16	3

Extra Practice
Skills Practice p. S10
Application Practice p. S31

Choose the graph that best represents each situation.

10. A flag is raised up a flagpole quickly at the beginning and then more slowly near the top. C

11. A flag is raised up a flagpole in a jerky motion, using a hand-over-hand method. A

12. A flag is raised up a flagpole at a constant rate of speed. B

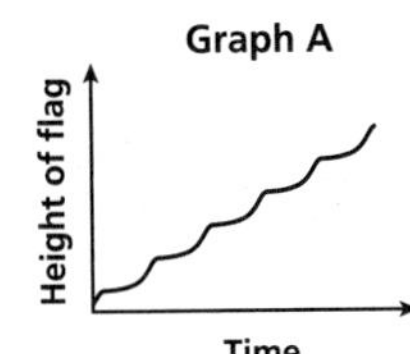

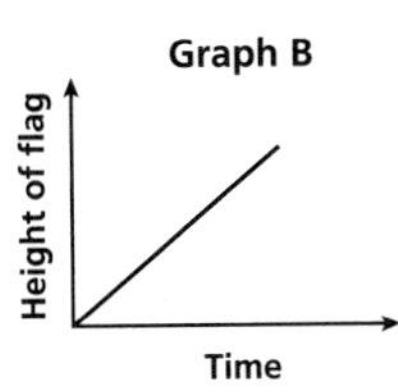

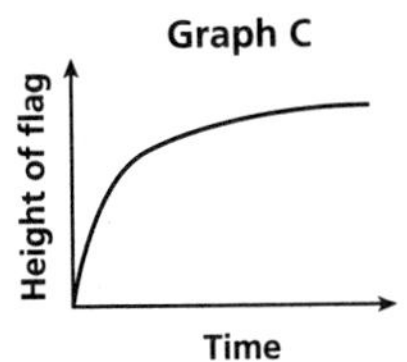

Assignment Guide

Assign *Guided Practice* exercises as necessary.

If you finished Examples **1–3**
Basic 10–18, 22–25, 29–37
Average 10–25, 28–37
Advanced 10–37

Homework Quick Check
Quickly check key concepts.
Exercises: 10, 12, 13, 14, 18

Teaching Tip **Kinesthetic** For **Exercises 3–5,** you may want to have students act out the events happening in the situation to more easily match them to each graph.

Teaching Tip **Communicating Math** Point out to students that some graphs start at (0, 0), like the one in **Exercise 8,** which begins with a height of 0, while some start higher on the vertical axis, like the one in **Exercise 7,** which begins with a positive speed.

State Resources

Answers

6. discrete

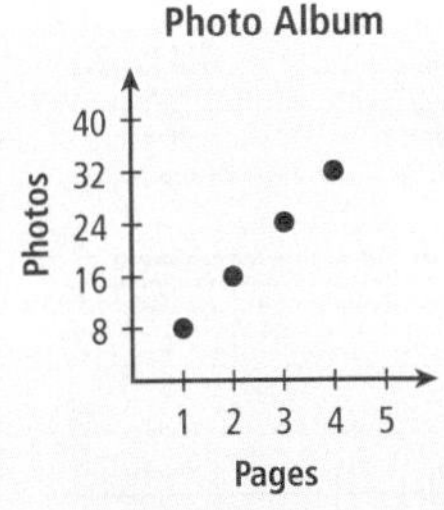

7–9. Possible answers given.

7. A car is moving at a constant speed for several minutes. When it approaches a red light, it slows down and comes to a stop.

8. A plant grows steadily and then has a growth spurt during the rainy season. It remains the same height for a while and then grows steadily again.

9. The more servings you eat, the more Calories you consume.

go.hrw.com
State Resources Online
KEYWORD: MA7 Resources

Data Collection To help students complete **Exercise 17,** see *Technology Lab Activities.*

Exercise 22 involves sketching a graph to describe a situation. This exercise prepares students for the Multi-Step Test Prep on page 264.

Answers

14–16, 18. Possible answers given.

14. A student is driven to school. The distance from home remains constant while the student is at school. Then the distance decreases during the ride back home.

15. The cost of a long-distance phone call increases for the first few minutes and then increases at a slower rate for the remainder of the call.

16. Park attendance steadily declines over the course of a week due to bad weather.

18. The horse starts at the gate, increases speed very quickly, then keeps a fairly steady pace, and then increases speed again at the end of the race. After crossing the finish line the horse slows to a stop.

19–22. See p. A16.

13. For six months, a puppy gained weight at a steady rate. Sketch a graph to illustrate the weight of the puppy during that time period. Tell whether the graph is continuous or discrete. **continuous**

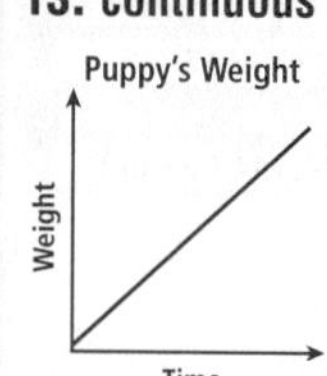

Write a possible situation for each graph.

14. **15.**

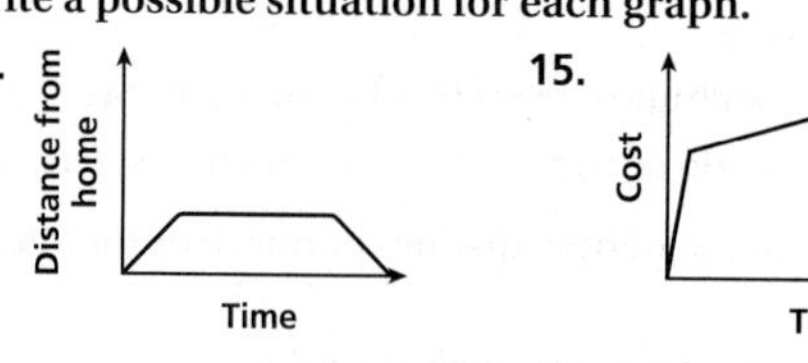

16.

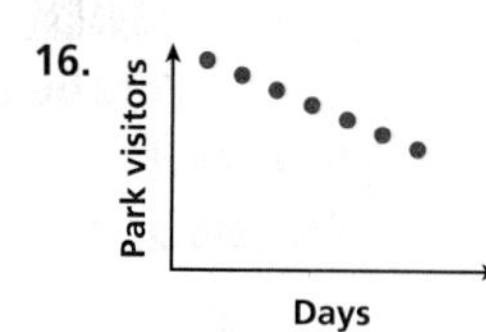

17. Data Collection Use a graphing calculator and motion detector for the following. **17a–c. Check students' work.**

a. On a coordinate plane, draw a graph relating distance from a starting point walking at various speeds and time.

b. Using the motion detector as the starting point, walk away from the motion detector to make a graph on the graphing calculator that matches the one you drew.

c. Compare your walking speeds to each change in steepness on the graph.

Sports

On November 1, 1938, the underdog Seabiscuit beat the heavily favored Triple-Crown winner War Admiral in a historic horse race at Pimlico Race Course in Baltimore, Maryland.

18. Sports The graph shows the speed of a horse during and after a race. Use it to describe the changing pace of the horse during the race.

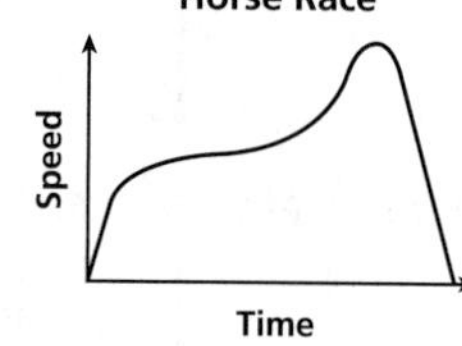

19. Recreation You hike up a mountain path starting at 10 A.M. You camp overnight and then walk back down the same path at the same pace at 10 A.M. the next morning. On the same set of axes, graph the relationship between distance from the top of the mountain and the time of day for both the hike up and the hike down. What does the point of intersection of the graphs represent?

20. Critical Thinking Suppose that you sketched a graph of speed related to time for a brick that fell from the top of a building. Then you sketched a graph for speed related to time for a ball that was rolled down a hill and then came to rest. How would the graphs be the same? How would they be different?

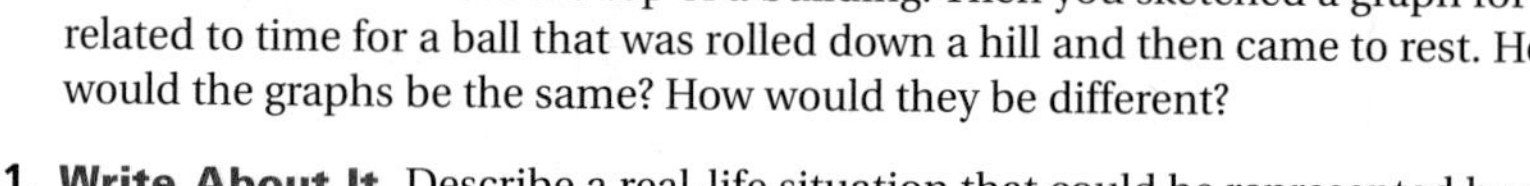

21. Write About It Describe a real-life situation that could be represented by a distinct graph. Then describe a real-life situation that could be represented by a continuous graph.

MULTI-STEP TEST PREP

22. This problem will prepare you for the Multi-Step Test Prep on page 264.

A rectangular pool that is 4 feet deep at all places is being filled at a constant rate.

a. Sketch a graph to show the depth of the water as it increases over time.

b. The side view of another swimming pool is shown. If the pool is being filled at a constant rate, sketch a graph to show the depth of the water as it increases over time.

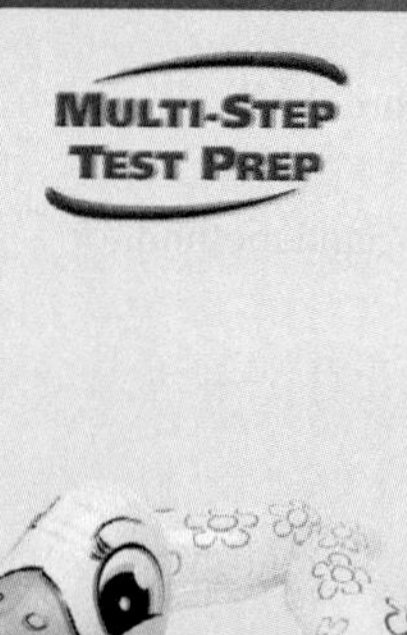

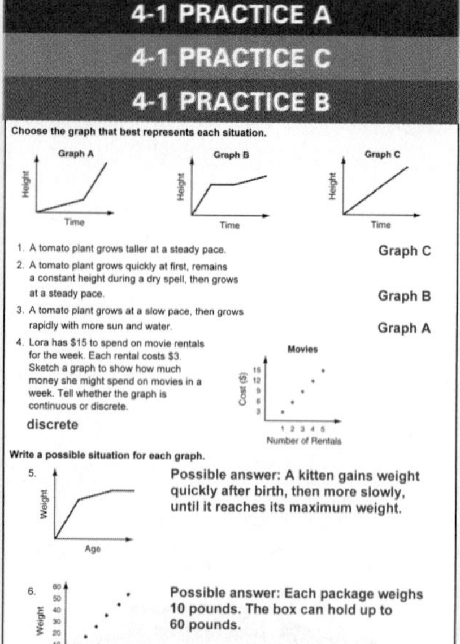

4-1 PRACTICE A
4-1 PRACTICE C
4-1 PRACTICE B

Choose the graph that best represents each situation.

Graph A, Graph B, Graph C

1. A tomato plant grows taller at a steady pace. **Graph C**
2. A tomato plant grows quickly at first, remains a constant height during a dry spell, then grows at a steady pace. **Graph B**
3. A tomato plant grows at a slow pace, then grows rapidly with more sun and water. **Graph A**
4. Lora has $15 to spend on movie rentals for the week. Each rental costs $3. Sketch a graph to show how much money she might spend on movies in a week. Tell whether the graph is continuous or discrete. **discrete**

Write a possible situation for each graph.

5. **Possible answer: A kitten gains weight quickly after birth, then more slowly, until it reaches its maximum weight.**

6. **Possible answer: Each package weighs 10 pounds. The box can hold up to 60 pounds.**

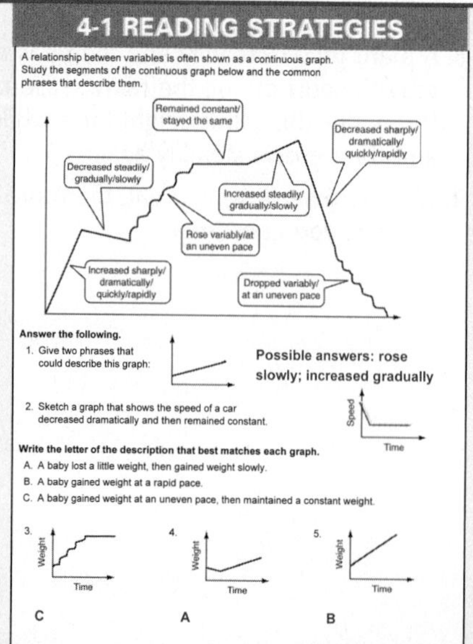

4-1 READING STRATEGIES

A relationship between variables is often shown as a continuous graph. Study the segments of the continuous graph below and the common phrases that describe them.

Remained constant/stayed the same; Decreased sharply/dramatically/quickly/rapidly; Decreased steadily/gradually/slowly; Increased steadily/gradually/slowly; Rose variably/at an uneven pace; Increased sharply/dramatically/quickly/rapidly; Dropped variably/at an uneven pace

Answer the following.

1. Give two phrases that could describe this graph: **Possible answers: rose slowly; increased gradually**
2. Sketch a graph that shows the speed of a car decreased dramatically and then remained constant.

Write the letter of the description that best matches each graph.

A. A baby lost a little weight, then gained weight slowly.
B. A baby gained weight at a rapid pace.
C. A baby gained weight at an uneven pace, then maintained a constant weight.

3. **C** 4. **A** 5. **B**

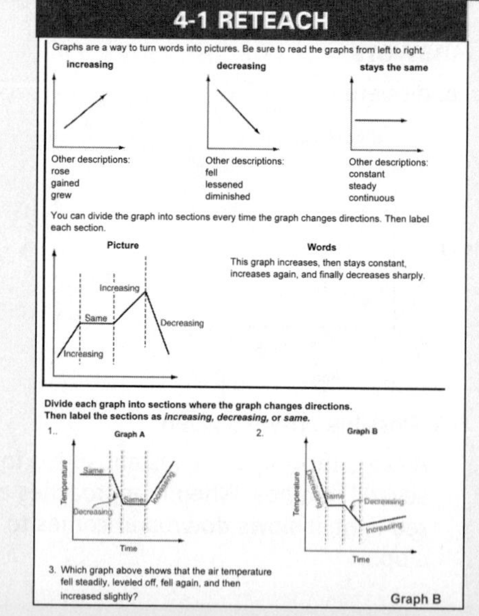

4-1 RETEACH

Graphs are a way to turn words into pictures. Be sure to read the graphs from left to right.

increasing	decreasing	stays the same
Other descriptions: rose, gained, grew	Other descriptions: fell, lessened, diminished	Other descriptions: constant, steady, continuous

You can divide the graph into sections every time the graph changes directions. Then label each section.

Picture — Words: This graph increases, then stays constant, increases again, and finally decreases sharply.

Divide each graph into sections where the graph changes directions. Then label the sections as *increasing, decreasing,* or *same.*

1. Graph A 2. Graph B

3. Which graph above shows that the air temperature fell steadily, leveled off, fell again, and then increased slightly? **Graph B**

23. Which situation would NOT be represented by a distinct graph?

Ⓐ Amount of money earned based on the number of cereal bars sold
Ⓑ Number of visitors to a grocery store per day for one week
Ⓒ The amount of iced tea in a pitcher at a restaurant during the lunch hour
Ⓓ The total cost of buying 1, 2, or 3 CDs at the music store

24. Which situation is best represented by the graph?

Ⓕ A snowboarder starts at the bottom of the hill and takes a ski lift to the top.
Ⓖ A cruise boat travels at a steady pace from the port to its destination.
Ⓗ An object falls from the top of a building and gains speed at a rapid pace before hitting the ground.
Ⓙ A marathon runner starts at a steady pace and then runs faster at the end of the race before stopping at the finish line.

Speed / Time

25. **Short Response** Marla participates in a triathlon consisting of swimming, biking, and running. Would a graph of Marla's speed during the triathlon be a continuous graph or a distinct graph? Explain. **Possible answer: The graph would be continuous because Marla is constantly moving at all times.**

CHALLENGE AND EXTEND

Pictured are three vases and graphs representing the height of water as it is poured into each of the vases at a constant rate. Match each vase with the correct graph.

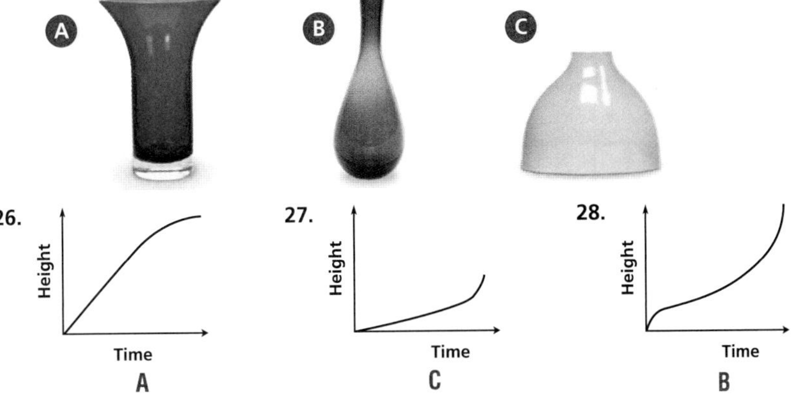

SPIRAL REVIEW

Evaluate each expression. *(Lesson 1-4)*

29. -2^3 **−8**   30. 4^4 **256**   31. $\left(\frac{1}{3}\right)^2$ $\frac{1}{9}$

Generate ordered pairs for each function for $x = -2, -1, 0, 1,$ and 2. Graph the ordered pairs and describe the pattern. *(Lesson 1-8)*

32. $y = x - 2$ 33. $2x + y = 1$ 34. $y = |x - 1|$ 35. $y = x^2 + 2$

Write and solve an equation to represent each relationship. *(Lesson 2-1)*

36. A number increased by 11 is equal to 3.   37. Five less than a number is equal to −2.

36. $n + 11 = 3$; −8
37. $n - 5 = -2$; 3

For **Exercise 23,** students should look for a situation where both units can be broken into fractions. Time and the liquid measurement in choice **C** can both be fractional.

Answers

32–35. See pp. A16–A17.

Journal

Write a situation in which the graph would contain either one vertical or one horizontal segment. Draw the graph.

ALTERNATIVE ASSESSMENT

Have students write and graph a situation described by a distinct graph and a situation described by a continuous graph.

Power Presentations with PowerPoint®

4-1 Lesson Quiz

1. Write a possible situation for the given graph.

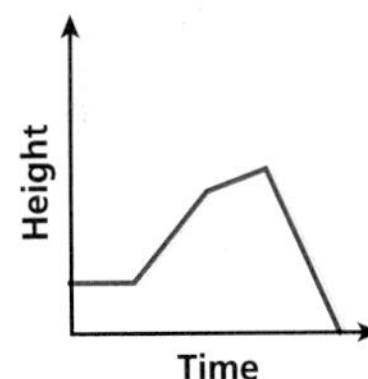

Possible answer: The level of water in a bucket stays constant. A steady rain raises the level. The rain slows down. Someone dumps the bucket.

2. A pet store is selling puppies for $50 each. It has 8 puppies to sell. Sketch a graph for this situation.

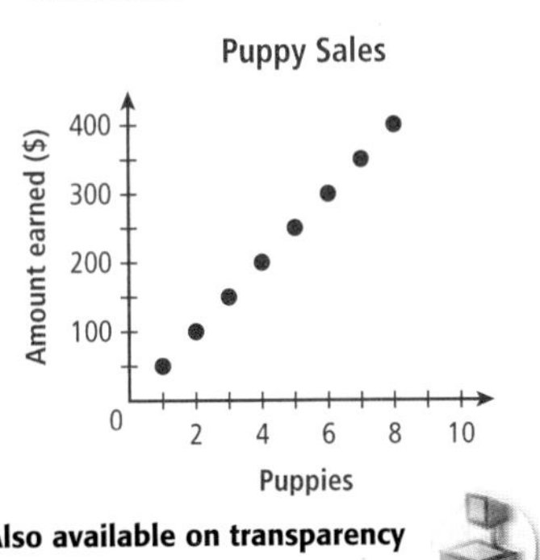

Also available on transparency

4-1 PROBLEM SOLVING

Sketch a graph for the given situation. Tell whether the graph is discrete or continuous.

1. A giraffe is born 6 feet tall and continues to grow at a steady rate until it is fully grown.

Height / Time

continuous

2. The price of a used car is discounted $200 each week.

Price / Weeks

discrete

3. A city planner buys more buses as the population of her city grows.

Number of Buses / Population

discrete

4. Joseph is sky-diving. At first, he is free-falling rapidly and then he releases his parachute to slow his descent until he reaches the ground.

Height Above Ground / Time

continuous

Choose the graph that best represents the situation.

5. Rebekah turns on the oven and sets it to 300 °F. She bakes a tray of cookies and then turns the oven off.
A Graph 1 **C** Graph 3
B Graph 2 D Graph 4

6. Leon puts ice cubes in his soup to cool it down before eating it.
F Graph 1 H Graph 3
G Graph 2 **J** Graph 4

7. Barlee has the flu and her temperature rises slowly until it reaches 101 °F.
A Graph 1 C Graph 3
B Graph 2 D Graph 4

8. On a hot day, Karin walks into and out of an air-conditioned building.
F Graph 1 H Graph 3
G Graph 2 J Graph 4

Graph 1, Graph 2, Graph 3, Graph 4: Temperature / Time

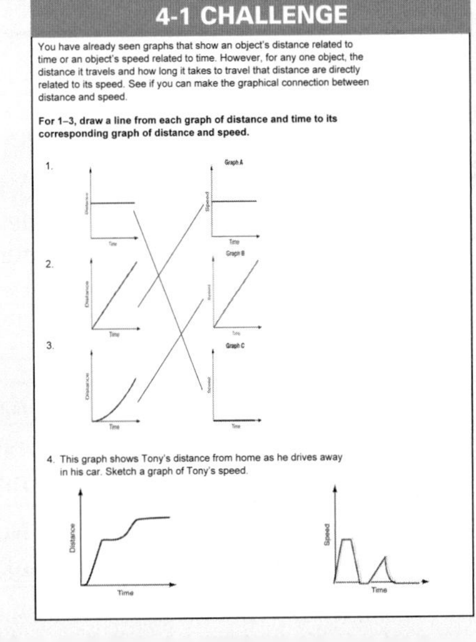
4-1 CHALLENGE

You have already seen graphs that show an object's distance related to time or an object's speed related to time. However, for any one object, the distance it travels and how long it takes to travel that distance are directly related to its speed. See if you can make the graphical connection between distance and speed.

For 1–3, draw a line from each graph of distance and time to its corresponding graph of distance and speed.

1.
2.
3.

Graph A
Graph B
Graph C

4. This graph shows Tony's distance from home as he drives away in his car. Sketch a graph of Tony's speed.

Distance / Time   Speed / Time

4-2 Organizer

Pacing: Traditional 1 day
Block $\frac{1}{2}$ day

Objectives: Identify functions.
Find the domain and range of relations and functions.

Online Edition
Tutorial Videos

Countdown Week 8

Power Presentations with PowerPoint®

Warm Up

1. Generate ordered pairs for the function $y = x + 3$ for $x = -2, -1, 0, 1,$ and 2. Graph the ordered pairs.
$(-2, 1), (-1, 2), (0, 3), (1, 4), (2, 5)$

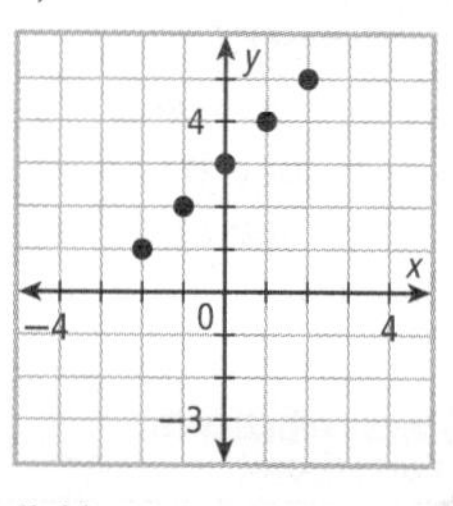

Also available on transparency

Math Humor

Q: Why did the *y*-variable leave the city?

A: He was more at home on the range.

State Resources

4-2 Relations and Functions

Objectives
Identify functions.

Find the domain and range of relations and functions.

Vocabulary
relation
domain
range
function

Why learn this?
You can use a relation to show finishing positions and scores in a track meet.

In Lesson 4-1, you saw relationships represented by graphs. Relationships can also be represented by a set of ordered pairs, called a **relation**.

In the scoring system of some track meets, **first place** is worth 5 points, **second place** is worth 3 points, third place is worth 2 points, and **fourth place** is worth 1 point. This scoring system is a relation, so it can be shown as ordered pairs, $\{(1, 5), (2, 3), (3, 2), (4, 1)\}$. You can also show relations in other ways, such as tables, graphs, or *mapping diagrams*.

EXAMPLE 1 Showing Multiple Representations of Relations

Express the relation for the track meet scoring system, $\{(1, 5), (2, 3), (3, 2), (4, 1)\}$, as a table, as a graph, and as a mapping diagram.

Table

Track Scoring	
Place	**Points**
1	5
2	3
3	2
4	1

Write all x-values under "Place" and all y-values under "Points."

Graph

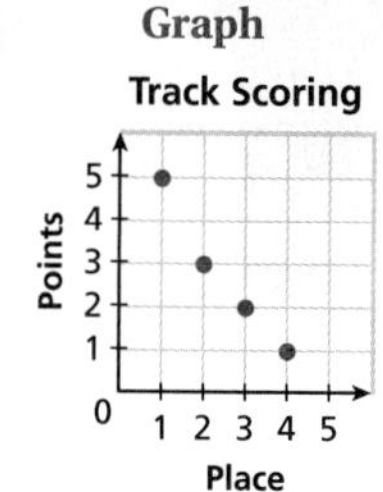

Use the x- and y-values to plot the ordered pairs.

Mapping Diagram

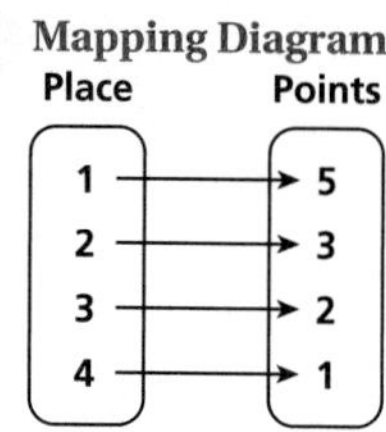

Write all x-values under "Place" and all y-values under "Points." Draw an arrow from each x-value to its corresponding y-value.

1. Express the relation $\{(1, 3)\ (2, 4), (3, 5)\}$ as a table, as a graph, and as a mapping diagram.

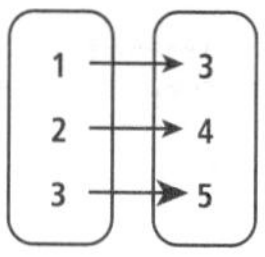

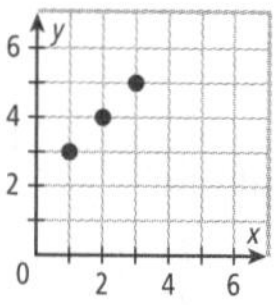

1.

x	y
1	3
2	4
3	5

1 → 3
2 → 4
3 → 5

(Graph: y-axis 2, 4, 6; x-axis 0, 2, 4, 6)

The **domain** of a relation is the set of first coordinates (or *x*-values) of the ordered pairs. The **range** of a relation is the set of second coordinates (or *y*-values) of the ordered pairs. The domain of the track meet scoring system is $\{1, 2, 3, 4\}$. The range is $\{5, 3, 2, 1\}$.

1 Introduce

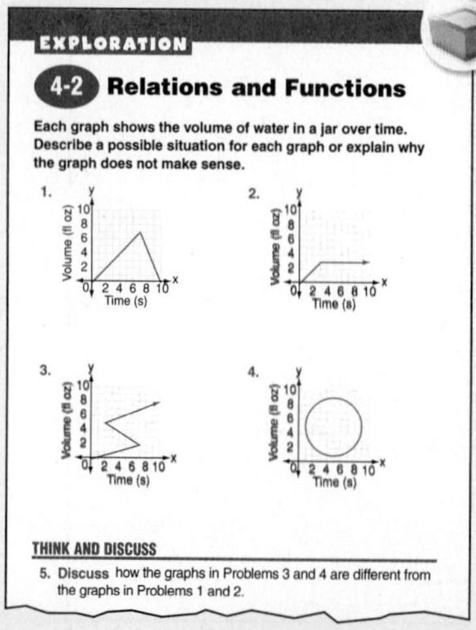

EXPLORATION

4-2 Relations and Functions

Each graph shows the volume of water in a jar over time. Describe a possible situation for each graph or explain why the graph does not make sense.

1. (Graph: Volume (fl oz) vs. Time (s))
2. (Graph: Volume (fl oz) vs. Time (s))
3. (Graph: Volume (fl oz) vs. Time (s))
4. (Graph: Volume (fl oz) vs. Time (s))

THINK AND DISCUSS

5. Discuss how the graphs in Problems 3 and 4 are different from the graphs in Problems 1 and 2.

Motivate

Display the following chart and have students determine if the examples could contain negative numbers or fractions and decimals.

	Negative Numbers?	Fractions and Decimals?
Ages of Students	No	Yes
Temperatures in Antarctica	Yes	Yes
Number of Desks in Classrooms	No	No

EXAMPLE 2 Finding the Domain and Range of a Relation

Give the domain and range of the relation.

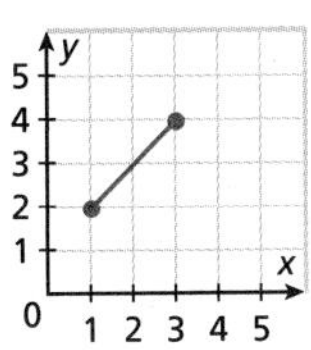

The domain is all x-values from 1 through 3, inclusive.

The range is all y-values from 2 through 4, inclusive.

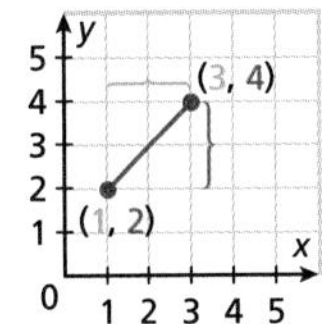

D: $1 \le x \le 3$ R: $2 \le y \le 4$

Give the domain and range of each relation.

2a.

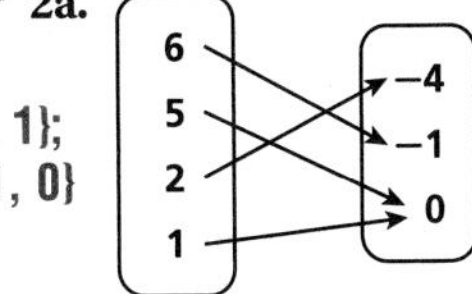

D: {6, 5, 2, 1}; R: {−4, −1, 0}

2b.

x	y
1	1
4	4
8	1

D: {1, 4, 8}; R: {1, 4}

A **function** is a special type of relation that pairs each domain value with exactly one range value.

EXAMPLE 3 Identifying Functions

Give the domain and range of each relation. Tell whether the relation is a function. Explain.

Field Trip	
Students x	**Buses y**
75	2
68	2
125	3

D: {75, 68, 125}
R: {2, 3}

Even though 2 appears twice in the table, it is written only once when writing the range.

This relation is a function. Each domain value is paired with exactly one range value.

Writing Math

When there is a finite number of values in a domain or range, list the values inside braces.

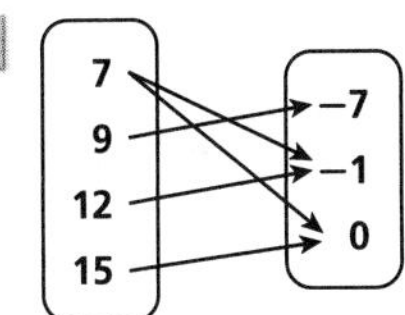

Use the arrows to determine which domain values correspond to each range value.

D: {7, 9, 12, 15}
R: {−7, −1, 0}

This relation is not a function. Each domain value does not have exactly one range value. The domain value 7 is paired with the range values −1 and 0.

COMMON ERROR ALERT

Students may have difficulty remembering how to determine whether a relation is a function. Tell students to think of x as a person and y as a place. A person cannot be in more than one place at a time, but more than one person can be at the same place.

Power Presentations with PowerPoint®

Additional Examples

Example 1

Express the relation {(2, 3), (4, 7), (6, 8)} as a table, as a graph, and as a mapping diagram.

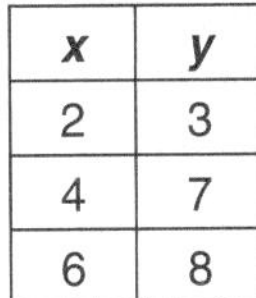

x	y
2	3
4	7
6	8

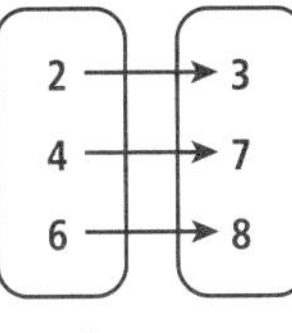

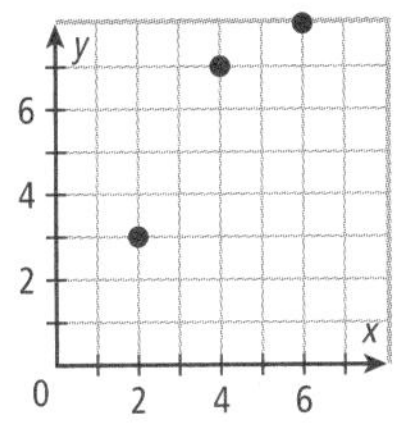

Example 2

Give the domain and range of the relation.

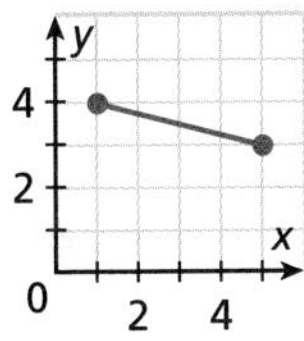

D: $1 \le x \le 5$
R: $3 \le y \le 4$

2 Teach

Guided Instruction

Remind students that an ordered pair consists of (x, y). In **Examples 2** and **3,** encourage students to list the ordered pairs when given a mapping diagram, following one arrow at a time.

Communicating Math Another way to write a domain or range is by using set-builder notation. For example, the domain $\{x \mid 1 \le x \le 3\}$ is read, "all x such that x is greater than or equal to 1 and x is less than or equal to 3."

Reaching All Learners

Through Cognitive Strategies

Show students the following to help them remember which values are in the domain and which are in the range.

- ***x*** **and** ***y*** are in alphabetical order.
- **D**omain and **r**ange are in alphabetical order.

So the x-values make up the domain, and the y-values make up the range.

INTERVENTION

Questioning Strategies

EXAMPLE 1

- Which representation do you prefer? Why?

EXAMPLE 2

- When are the domain and range of a relation a continuous interval of values? When are they distinct numbers?

Power Presentations with PowerPoint®

Additional Examples

Example 3

Give the domain and range of each relation. Tell whether the relation is a function. Explain.

A. {(3, −2), (5, −1), (4, 0), (3, 1)} D: {3, 5, 4}; R: {−2, −1, 0, 1}; no; 3 is paired with −2 and 1.

B.

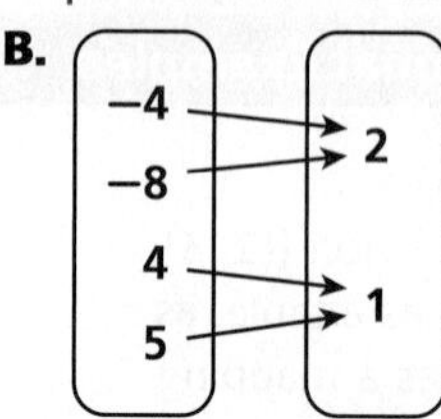

D: {−8, −4, 4, 5}; R: {2, 1}; yes; each domain element is paired with exactly one range element.

C.

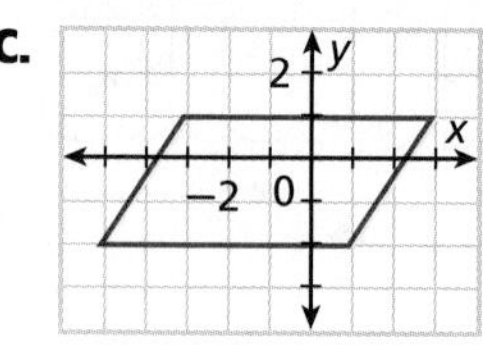

D: $-5 \le x \le 3$; R: $-2 \le y \le 1$; no; nearly all domain values have more than one range value.

INTERVENTION
Questioning Strategies

EXAMPLE 3

- Which of the displays (mapping diagram, table, or graph) is easiest for determining if a relation is a function? Why?

Helpful Hint

To find the domain and range of a graph, it may help to draw lines to see the *x*- and *y*-values.

3a. D: {−6, −4, 1, 8}; R: {1, 2, 9}; yes; each domain value is paired with exactly one range value.

b. D: {2, 3, 4}; R: {−5, −4, −3}; no; the domain value 2 is paired with both −5 and −4.

Give the domain and range of each relation. Tell whether the relation is a function. Explain.

C

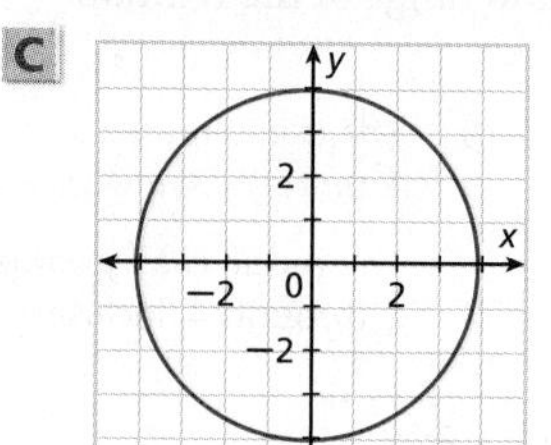

Draw lines to see the domain and range values.

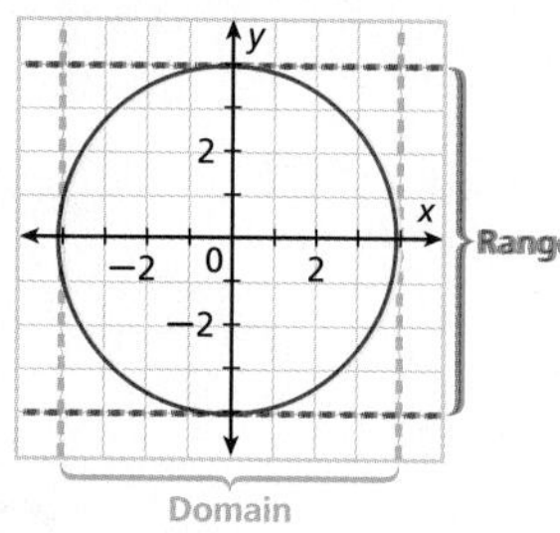

D: $-4 \le x \le 4$ R: $-4 \le y \le 4$

x	4	0	0	−4
y	0	4	−4	0

To compare domain and range values, make a table using points from the graph.

This relation is not a function because there are several domain values that have more than one range value. For example, the domain value 0 is paired with both 4 and −4.

Give the domain and range of each relation. Tell whether the relation is a function. Explain.

3a. $\{(8, 2), (-4, 1), (-6, 2), (1, 9)\}$ **3b.**

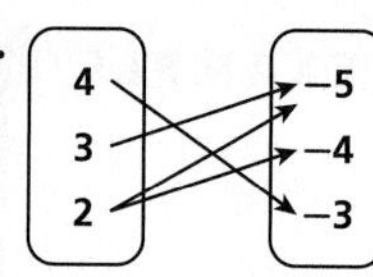

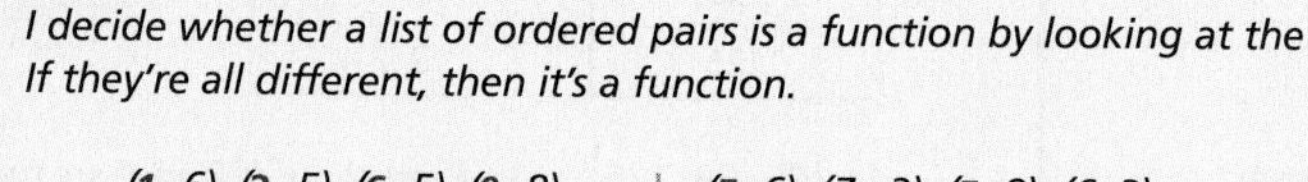

Student to Student

Functions

I decide whether a list of ordered pairs is a function by looking at the x-values. If they're all different, then it's a function.

(1, 6), (2, 5), (6, 5), (0, 8)	*(5, 6), (7, 2), (5, 8), (6, 3)*
All different x-values	*Same x-value* (with different *y*-values)
Function	*Not a function*

Eric Dawson
Boone High School

THINK AND DISCUSS

1. Describe how to tell whether a set of ordered pairs is a function.
2. Can the graph of a vertical line segment represent a function? Explain.

3. **GET ORGANIZED** Copy and complete the graphic organizer by explaining when a relation is a function and when it is not a function.

A relation is...	
A function if...	Not a function if...

3 Close

Summarize

Ask students to name the four different ways relations are represented in this lesson. list of ordered pairs, table, graph, mapping diagram Write each of the following on the board. Have students find the domain and range and tell whether the relation is a function.

{(1, 4), (2, 4), (3, 5)}
D: {1, 2, 3}; R: {4, 5}; yes

{(1, 4), (2, 5), (2, 6)}
D: {1, 2}; R: {4, 5, 6}; no

ONGOING ASSESSMENT and INTERVENTION

***Diagnose Before* the Lesson**
4-2 Warm Up, TE p. 240

***Monitor During* the Lesson**
Check It Out! Exercises, SE pp. 240–242
Questioning Strategies, TE pp. 241–242

***Assess After* the Lesson**
4-2 Lesson Quiz, TE p. 246
Alternative Assessment, TE p. 246

Answers to *Think and Discuss*

1. A set of ordered pairs is a function if each *x*-value is assigned exactly one *y*-value.
2. No; the graph of a vertical line segment cannot represent a function because there is only one element in the domain and it is assigned many different elements in the range.
3. See p. A4.

4-2 Exercises

GUIDED PRACTICE

Vocabulary Apply the vocabulary from this lesson to answer each question.

1. Use a mapping diagram to show a relation that is not a *function*.
2. The set of x-values for a relation is also called the __?__. (*domain* or *range*) **domain**

SEE EXAMPLE 1 p. 240

Express each relation as a table, as a graph, and as a mapping diagram.

3. $\{(1, 1), (1, 2)\}$
4. $\left\{(-1, 1), \left(-2, \frac{1}{2}\right), \left(-3, \frac{1}{3}\right), \left(-4, \frac{1}{4}\right)\right\}$
5. $\{(-1, 1), (-3, 3), (5, -5), (-7, 7)\}$
6. $\{(0, 0), (2, -4), (2, -2)\}$

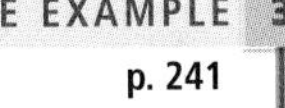

SEE EXAMPLE 2 p. 241

Give the domain and range of each relation.

7. $\{(-5, 7), (0, 0), (2, -8), (5, -20)\}$
8. $\{(1, 2), (2, 4), (3, 6), (4, 8), (5, 10)\}$
9.

x	3	5	2	8	6
y	9	25	4	81	36

10. 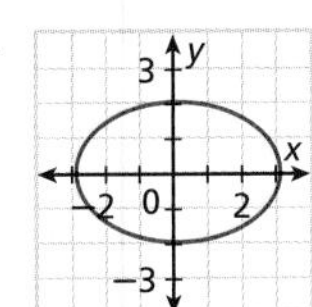

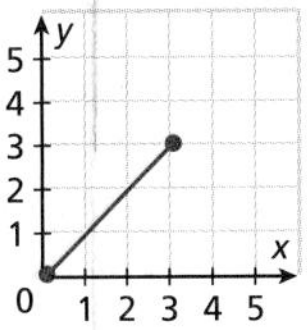

7. D: {−5, 0, 2, 5}; R: {−20, −8, 0, 7}
8. D: {1, 2, 3, 4, 5}; R: {2, 4, 6, 8, 10}
9. D: {2, 3, 5, 6, 8}; R: { 4, 9, 25, 36, 81}
10. D: $0 \le x \le 3$; R: $0 \le y \le 3$

SEE EXAMPLE 3 p. 241

Multi-Step Give the domain and range of each relation. Tell whether the relation is a function. Explain.

11. $\{(1, 3), (1, 0), (1, -2), (1, 8)\}$
12. $\{(-2, 1), (-1, 2), (0, 3), (1, 4)\}$
13.

x	−2	−1	0	1	2
y	1	1	1	1	1

14. 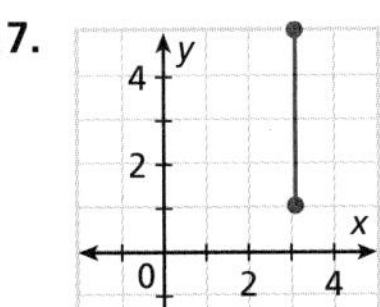

PRACTICE AND PROBLEM SOLVING

Independent Practice

For Exercises	See Example
15–16	1
17–18	2
19–20	3

Extra Practice
Skills Practice p. S10
Application Practice p. S31

Express each relation as a table, as a graph, and as a mapping diagram.

15. $\{(-2, -4), (-1, -1), (0, 0), (1, -1), (2, -4)\}$
16. $\left\{(2, 1), \left(2, \frac{1}{2}\right), (2, 2), \left(2, 2\frac{1}{2}\right)\right\}$

Give the domain and range of each relation.

17. (graph) **D: {3}; R: $1 \le y \le 5$**

18.

x	y
4	4
5	5
6	6
7	7
8	8

D: {4, 5, 6, 7, 8}; R: {4, 5, 6, 7, 8}

4-2 Exercises

Assignment Guide

Assign *Guided Practice* exercises as necessary.

If you finished Examples **1–3**
Basic 15–26, 29, 30, 32–35, 39–42
Average 15–20, 22–24, 27–37, 39–42
Advanced 15–20, 22, 24, 26–29, 31–42

Homework Quick Check
Quickly check key concepts.
Exercises: 16, 18, 20, 22, 24

Visual Encourage students to write out some of the ordered pairs in **Exercise 17** to help them determine the domain and range.

Answers

1. Possible answer:

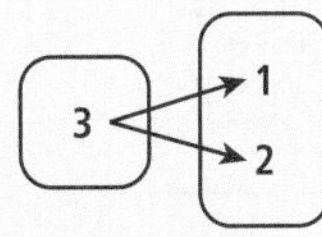

3–6. See p. A17.

11. D: {1}; R: {−2, 0, 3, 8}; no; the domain value 1 is paired with several different range values.
12. D: {−2, −1, 0, 1}; R: {1, 2, 3, 4}; yes; each domain value is paired with exactly one range value.
13. D: {−2, −1, 0, 1, 2}; R: {1}; yes; each element in the domain is paired with exactly one element in the range.

State Resources

14. D: $-3 \le x \le 3$; R: $-2 \le y \le 2$; no; almost every domain value is paired with 2 range values.

15.

x	y
−2	−4
−1	−1
0	0
1	−1
2	−4

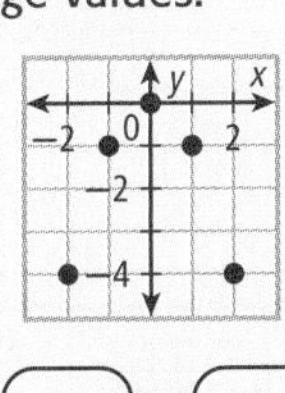

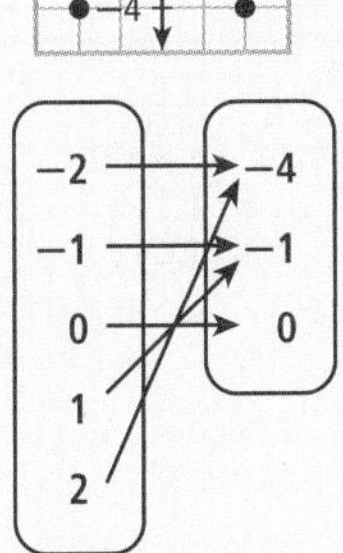

16.

x	y
2	1
2	$\frac{1}{2}$
2	2
2	$2\frac{1}{2}$

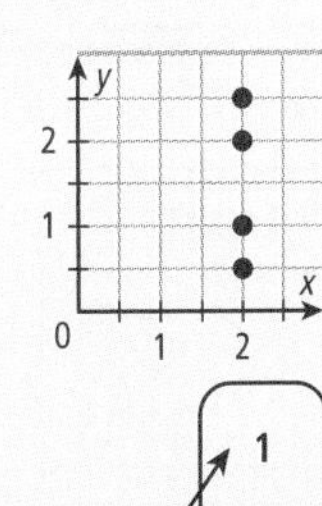

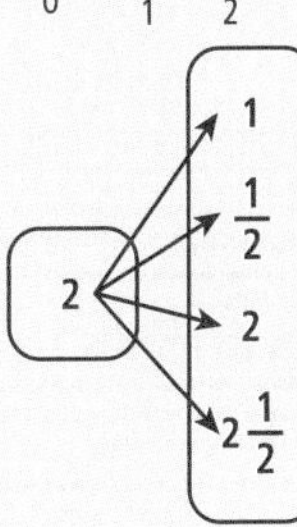

go.hrw.com
State Resources Online
KEYWORD: MA7 Resources

Geometry In **Exercise 22,** remind students that the area of a square with side length s is s^2.

Answers

21. Yes; each domain value is paired with exactly one range value.

x	y
1	125
2	175
3	225
4	275

24a.

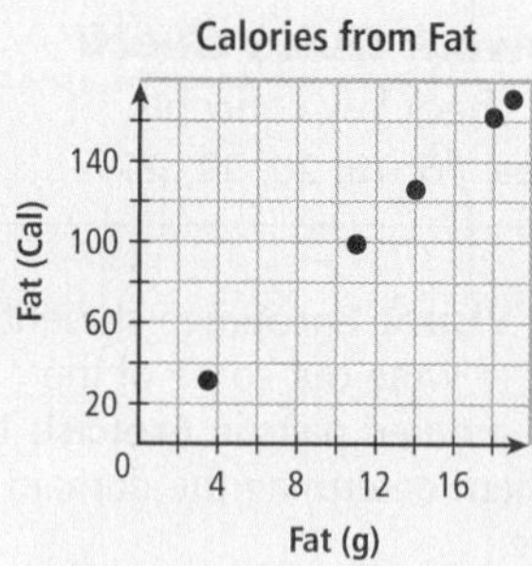

b. Yes; each domain value is paired with exactly one range value.

25.

Hours x	Cost y
1	9
2	11
3	13
4	15
5	15

Yes; each domain value is paired with exactly one range value.

26. See p. A17.

Multi-Step Give the domain and range of each relation. Tell whether the relation is a function. Explain.

19. D: $-2 \le x \le 2$; R: $0 \le y \le 2$

Yes; each domain value is paired with exactly one range value.

20. 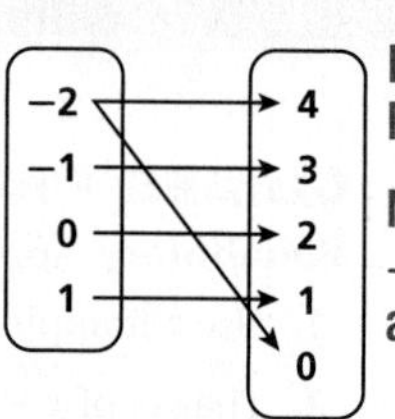

D: {−2, −1, 0, 1}; R: {0, 1, 2, 3, 4};

No; the domain valu[e] −2 is paired with 4 and 0.

21. **Consumer Application** An electrician charges a base fee of $75 plus $50 for each hour of work. Create a table that shows the amount the electrician charges for 1, 2, 3, and 4 hours of work. Let x represent the number of hours and y represent the amount charged for x hours. Is this relation a function? Explain.

22. **Geometry** Write a relation as a set of ordered pairs in which the x-value represents the side length of a square and the y-value represents the area of that square. Use a domain of 2, 4, 6, 9, and 11. **{(2, 4), (4, 16), (6, 36), (9, 81), (11, 121)}**

23. **Multi-Step** Create a mapping diagram to display the numbers of days in 1, 2, 3, and 4 weeks. Is this relation a function? Explain.

23. Yes; each domain value is paired with exactly one range value.

Weeks	Days
1	7
2	14
3	21
4	28

24. **Nutrition** The illustrations list the number of grams of fat and the number of Calories from fat for selected foods.

a. Create a graph for the relation between grams of fat and Calories from fat.

b. Is this relation a function? Explain.

Hamburger
Fat (g): 14
Fat (Cal): 126

Cheeseburger
Fat (g): 18
Fat (Cal): 162

Grilled chicken filet
Fat (g): 3.5
Fat (Cal): 31.5

Breaded chicken filet
Fat (g): 11
Fat (Cal): 99

Taco salad
Fat (g): 19
Fat (Cal): 171

25. **Recreation** A shop rents canoes for a $7 equipment fee plus $2 per hour, with a maximum cost of $15 per day. Express the number of hours x and the cost y as a relation in table form, and find the cost to rent a canoe for 1, 2, 3, 4, and 5 hours. Is this relation a function? Explain.

26. **Health** You can burn about 6 Calories per minute bicycling. Let x represent the number of minutes bicycled, and let y represent the number of Calories burned.

a. Write ordered pairs to show the number of Calories burned by bicycling for 60, 120, 180, 240, or 300 minutes. Graph the ordered pairs.

b. Find the domain and range of the relation.

c. Does this graph represent a function? Explain.

27. **Critical Thinking** For a function, can the number of elements in the range be greater than the number of elements in the domain? Explain.

27. No; if the number of range values is greater than the number of domain values, then there must be a domain value that is paired with more than one range value.

28. **Critical Thinking** Tell whether each statement is true or false. If false, explain why.

a. All relations are functions.

b. All functions are relations. **true**

28a. False; a relation that has several of the same domain values paired with different range values is not a function.

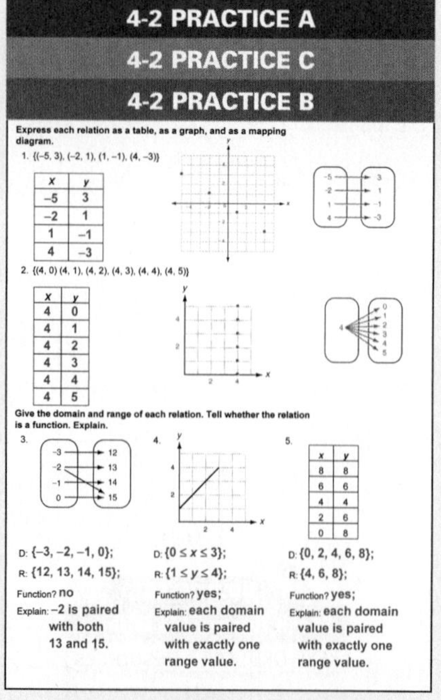

4-2 PRACTICE A

4-2 PRACTICE C

4-2 PRACTICE B

Express each relation as a table, as a graph, and as a mapping diagram.

1. {(−5, 3), (−2, 1), (1, −1), (4, −3)}

x	y
−5	3
−2	1
1	−1
4	−3

2. {(4, 0) (4, 1), (4, 2), (4, 3), (4, 4), (4, 5)}

x	y
4	0
4	1
4	2
4	3
4	4
4	5

Give the domain and range of each relation. Tell whether the relation is a function. Explain.

3.

4.

5.

x	y
8	8
6	6
4	4
2	6
0	8

3. D: {−3, −2, −1, 0}; R: {12, 13, 14, 15}; Function? no; Explain: −2 is paired with both 13 and 15.

4. D: $\{0 \le x \le 3\}$; R: $\{1 \le y \le 4\}$; Function? yes; Explain: each domain value is paired with exactly one range value.

5. D: {0, 2, 4, 6, 8}; R: {4, 6, 8}; Function? yes; Explain: each domain value is paired with exactly one range value.

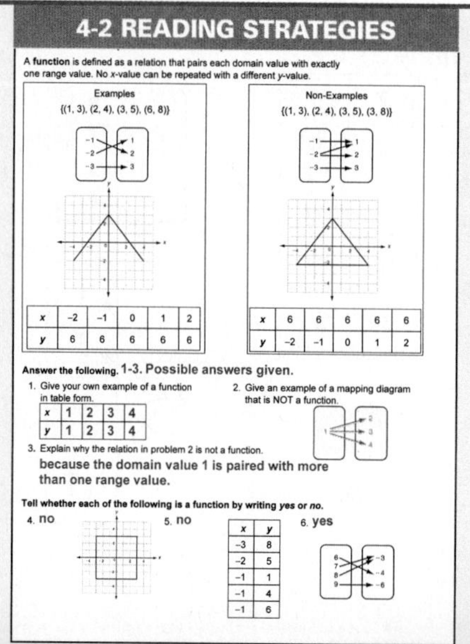

4-2 READING STRATEGIES

A **function** is defined as a relation that pairs each domain value with exactly one range value. No x-value can be repeated with a different y-value.

Examples: {(1, 3), (2, 4), (3, 5), (6, 8)}

Non-Examples: {(1, 3), (2, 4), (3, 5), (3, 8)}

x	−2	−1	0	1	2
y	6	6	6	6	6

x	6	6	6	6	6
y	−2	−1	0	1	2

Answer the following. 1–3. Possible answers given.

1. Give your own example of a function in table form.

x	1	2	3	4
y	1	2	3	4

2. Give an example of a mapping diagram that is NOT a function.

3. Explain why the relation in problem 2 is not a function. because the domain value 1 is paired with more than one range value.

Tell whether each of the following is a function by writing *yes* or *no*.

4. no

5. no

x	y
−3	8
−2	5
−1	1
−1	4
−1	6

6. yes

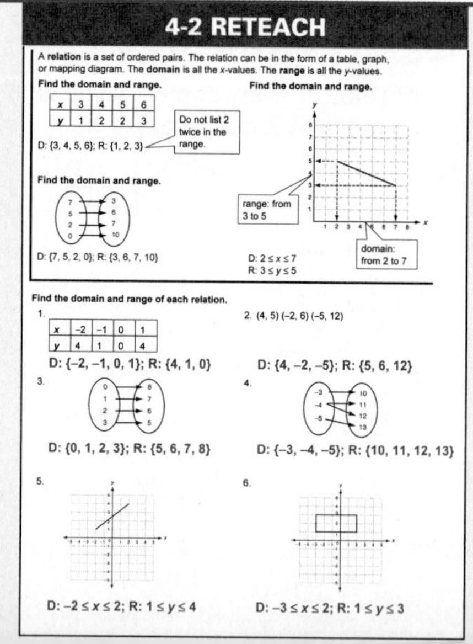

4-2 RETEACH

A **relation** is a set of ordered pairs. The relation can be in the form of a table, graph, or mapping diagram. The **domain** is all the x-values. The **range** is all the y-values.

Find the domain and range.

x	3	4	5	6
y	1	2	2	3

D: {3, 4, 5, 6}; R: {1, 2, 3} — Do not list 2 twice in the range.

Find the domain and range.

D: {7, 5, 2, 0}; R: {3, 6, 7, 10}

Find the domain and range.

range: from 3 to 5; domain: from 2 to 7

D: $2 \le x \le 7$; R: $3 \le y \le 5$

Find the domain and range of each relation.

1.

x	−2	−1	0	1
y	4	1	0	4

D: {−2, −1, 0, 1}; R: {4, 1, 0}

2. (4, 5) (−2, 6) (−5, 12)

D: {4, −2, −5}; R: {5, 6, 12}

3. D: {0, 1, 2, 3}; R: {5, 6, 7, 8}

4. D: {−3, −4, −5}; R: {10, 11, 12, 13}

5. D: $-2 \le x \le 2$; R: $1 \le y \le 4$

6. D: $-3 \le x \le 2$; R: $1 \le y \le 3$

MULTI-STEP TEST PREP

29. This problem will prepare you for the Multi-Step Test Prep on page 264.

a. The graph shows the amount of water being pumped into a pool over a 5-hour time period. Find the domain and range.

b. Does the graph represent a function? Explain.

c. Give the time and volume as ordered pairs at 2 hours and at 3 hours 30 minutes.

29a. D: $0 \le t \le 5$; R: $0 \le v \le 750$

b. Yes; each x-value is paired with exactly one y-value.

c. (2, 300); (3.5, 525)

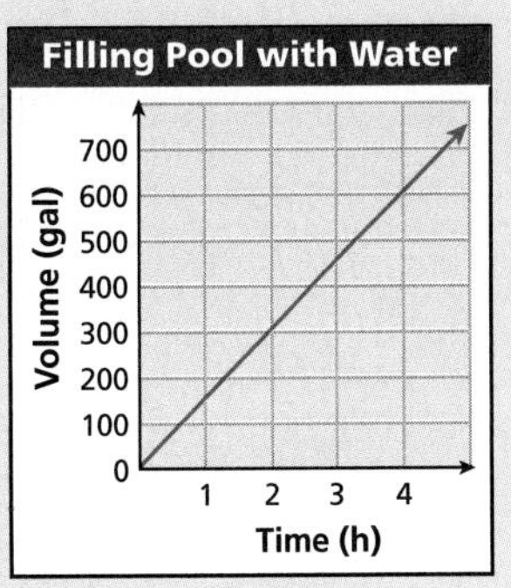

30. **ERROR ANALYSIS** When asked whether the relation $\{(-4, 16), (-2, 4), (0, 0), (2, 4)\}$ is a function, a student stated that the relation is not a function because 4 appears twice. What error did the student make? How would you explain to the student why this relation is a function?

31. **Write About It** Describe a real-world situation for a relation that is NOT a function. Create a mapping diagram to show why the relation is not a function.

TEST PREP

32. Which of the following relations is NOT a function?

Ⓐ $\{(6, 2), (-1, 2), (-3, 2), (-5, 2)\}$

Ⓑ

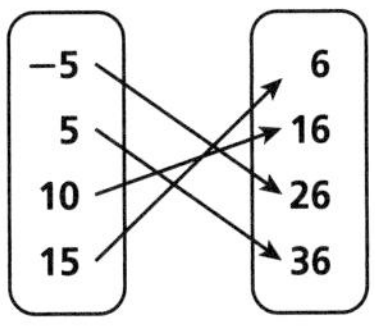

Ⓒ

x	3	5	7
y	1	15	30

Ⓓ

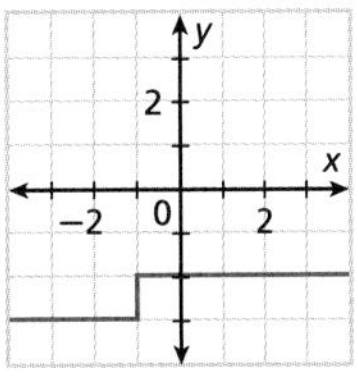

33. Which is NOT a correct way to describe the function $\{(-3, 2), (1, 8), (-1, 5), (3, 11)\}$?

Ⓕ

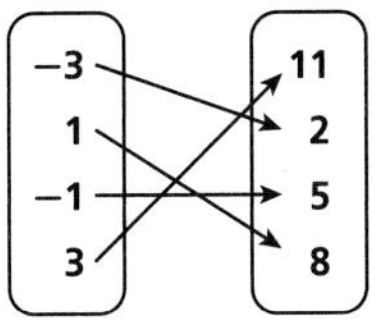

Ⓗ Domain: $\{-3, 1, -1, 3\}$

Range: $\{2, 8, 5, 11\}$

Ⓖ

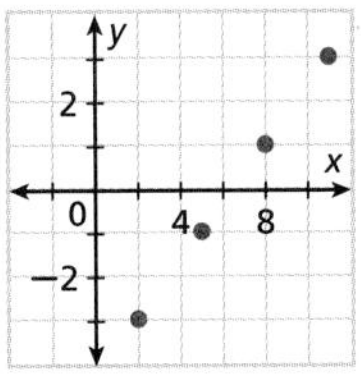

Ⓙ

x	y
−3	2
−1	5
1	8
3	11

MULTI-STEP TEST PREP **Exercise 29** involves finding the domain and range of a graph. This exercise prepares students for the Multi-Step Test Prep on page 264.

TEST PREP DOCTOR For **Exercise 32,** choices **A, B,** and **C** can be eliminated because no x-values are repeated.

Students who chose **F** in **Exercise 33** may not understand that in a mapping diagram, the domain and range values can be listed in an order other than that given. Students who chose **H** may not understand that in the domain and range, the x- and y-values can be listed out of order. Remind students that order does not matter.

Answers

30. The student thought that since there are two 4's, one element in the domain is paired with more than one element in the range. The relation is a function because each x-value is paired with exactly one y-value. A relation is a function even if a y-value has more than one x-value paired with it.

31. Possible answer: Packages being sent from a warehouse contain different numbers of items. One package contains 1 item, another package contains 3 items, and yet another package contains 5 items.

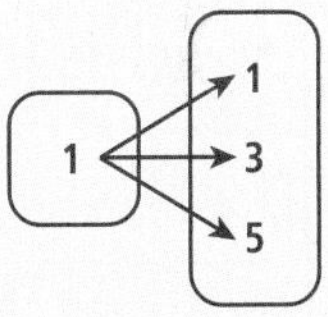

4-2 PROBLEM SOLVING

Give the domain and range of each relation and tell whether it is a function.

1. The mapping diagram shows the ages x and grade level y of four children.

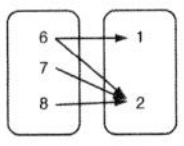

D: {6, 7, 8};
R: {1, 2};
no

2.

Age x	Shoe Size y
6	8
9	10
12	10
15	10.5
18	11

D: {6, 9, 12, 15, 18};
R: {8, 10, 10.5, 11};
yes

3. The list represents the number of cars sold and the bonus received by the salespeople of a car dealership.
{(1, 50), (2, 50), (3, 100), (4, 150)}
D: {1, 2, 3, 4};
R: {50, 100, 150};
yes

4. A 2-inch-tall plant grows at a rate of 2.5 inches every week for 5 weeks. Let x represent the number of weeks and y represent the height of the plant.
D: {0, 1, 2, 3, 4, 5};
R: {2, 4.5, 7, 9.5, 12, 14.5};
yes

Use the graph below to answer questions 5–6. A conservation group has been working to increase the population of a herd of Asian elephants. The graph shows the results of their efforts. Select the correct answer.

5. Which relation represents the information in the graph?
A {(1, 4.5), (2, 6), (3, 10), (4, 14.5)}
B {(1, 5), (2, 6), (3, 10), (4, 15)}
C {(4.5, 1), (6, 2), (10, 3), (14.5, 4)}
D {(5, 1), (6, 2), (10, 3), (15, 4)}

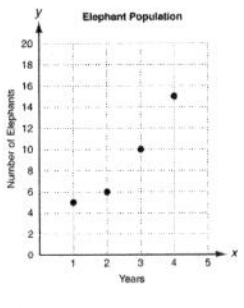

6. What is the range of the relation shown in the graph?
F {0, 1, 2, 3, 4, 5}
G {1, 2, 3, 4}
H {4.5, 6, 10, 14.5}
J {5, 6, 10, 15}

4-2 CHALLENGE

A function is a correspondence, f, between two sets, A and B, such that each member of A is assigned exactly one member of B. The diagram shows a function as a dynamic process.

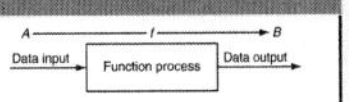

In Exercises 1–3, suppose that the input set, A, is the set of integers. Describe the range of each function.

1. f: Multiply each integer, n, by 5. multiples of 5: . . . , −15, −10, −5, 0, 5, 10, 15, . . .
2. g: Multiply each integer, n, by a fixed integer, k. multiples of k: kn
3. h: Divide the input integer, n, by 10 and write the remainder, r. 0, 1, 2, 3, 4, 5, 6, 7, 8, 9

In Exercises 4–6, write a function rule that represents the function described.

4. j: the coordinate of the point halfway between each distinct pair of points on a number line
If P has coordinate a, Q has coordinate b, assign $\frac{a+b}{2}$.
5. k: the distance of each point from 0
If P has coordinate a, assign $|a|$.
6. m: the length of the line segment determined by each distinct pair of points on the number line
If P has coordinate a and Q has coordinate b, assign $|a - b|$.

In Exercises 7 and 8, the domain of each function is the set of all squares.

7. a. Write a function, P, that gives the perimeter of any square. If the length of a side of square X is s, then P(square X) = $4s$.
b. Write a function, A, that gives the area of any square. If the length of a side of square X is s, then A(square X) = s^2.

8. a. Using the diagram below, describe the function that moves the square from A to B. The function rotates square A 120° counterclockwise about point O.
b. What is the range of the function in part **a**?
The set of all squares.

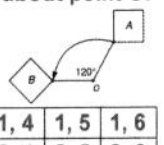

9. Suppose that you roll two number cubes. The sum of the numbers that are showing can be represented by a function.
a. In the space at the right, make a table showing the members of the domain.
b. What is the range of the function?
{2, 3, 4, 5, 6, 7, 8, 9, 10, 12}

1, 1	1, 2	1, 3	1, 4	1, 5	1, 6
2, 1	2, 2	2, 3	2, 4	2, 5	2, 6
3, 1	3, 2	3, 3	3, 4	3, 5	3, 6
4, 1	4, 2	4, 3	4, 4	4, 5	4, 6
5, 1	5, 2	5, 3	5, 4	5, 5	5, 6
6, 1	6, 2	6, 3	6, 4	6, 5	6, 6

Journal

Have students explain how to determine whether a graphed relation is a function.

ALTERNATIVE ASSESSMENT

Have students write a list of four ordered pairs. Instruct them to write this relation as a table, a graph, and a mapping diagram. Have them find the domain and range and explain whether their relation is a function.

Power Presentations with PowerPoint®

4-2 Lesson Quiz

1. Express the relation {(−2, 5), (−1, 4), (1, 3), (2, 4)} as a table, as a graph, and as a mapping diagram.

x	y
−2	5
−1	4
1	3
2	4

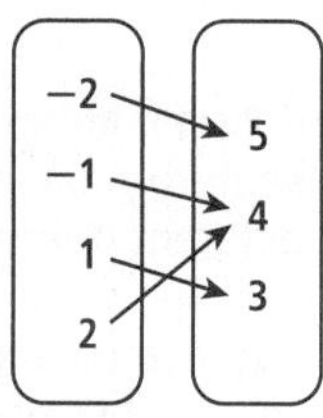

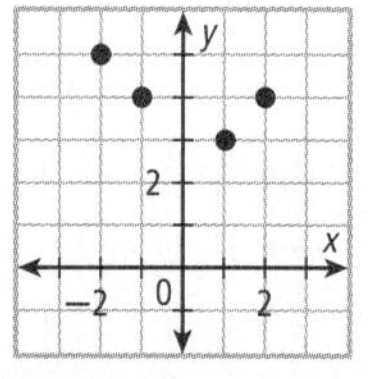

2. Give the domain and range of the relation.

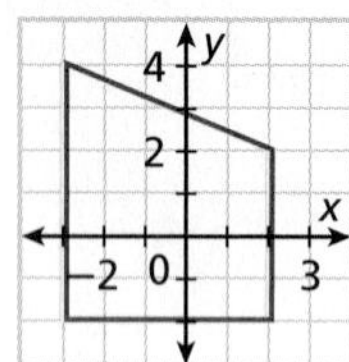

D: $-3 \le x \le 2$; R: $-2 \le y \le 4$

3. Give the domain and range of the relation. Tell whether the relation is a function. Explain.

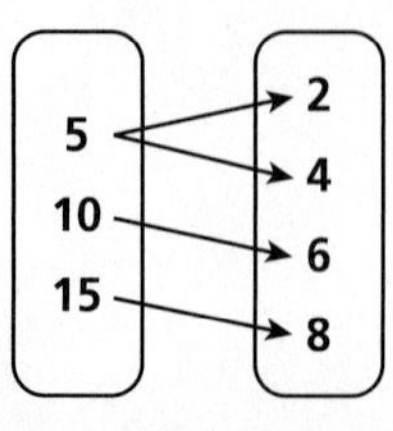

D: {5, 10, 15}; R: {2, 4, 6, 8}; no; 5 is paired with 2 and 4.

Also available on transparency

34. Which graph represents a function?

Ⓐ 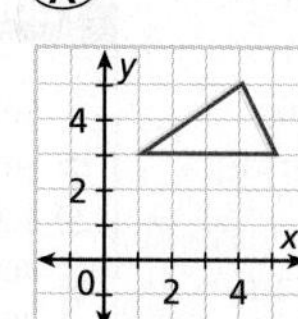

Ⓑ 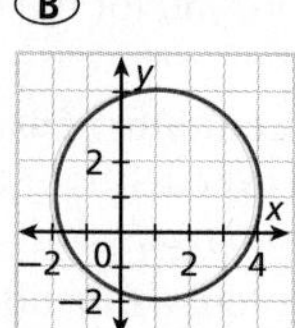

Ⓒ 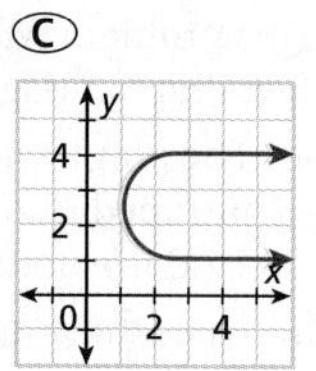

Ⓓ 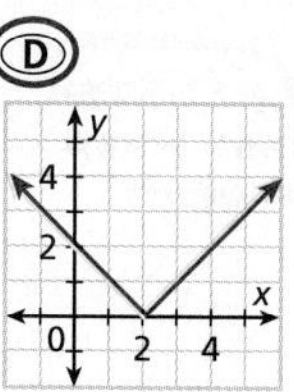

35. Extended Response Use the table for the following.

x	−3	−1	0	1	3
y	5	7	9	11	13

a. Express the relation as ordered pairs.

b. Give the domain and range of the relation.

c. Does the relation represent a function? Explain your answer.
Yes; each domain value is paired with exactly one range value.

35a. {(−3, 5), (−1, 7), (0, 9), (1, 11), (3, 13)}

b. D: {−3, −1, 0, 1, 3}; R: {5, 7, 9, 11, 13}

CHALLENGE AND EXTEND

36. What values of a make the relation $\{(a, 1), (2, 3), (4, 5)\}$ a function? Explain.

37. What values of b make the relation $\{(5, 6), (7, 8), (9, b)\}$ a function? Explain.

38. The *inverse* of a relation is created by interchanging the x- and y- coordinates of each ordered pair in the relation.

a. Find the inverse of the following relation: $\{(-2, 5), (0, 4), (3, -8), (7, 5)\}$.

b. Is the original relation a function? Why or why not? Is the inverse of the relation a function? Why or why not?

c. The statement "If a relation is a function, then the inverse of the relation is also a function" is sometimes true. Give an example of a relation and its inverse that are both functions. Then give an example of a relation and its inverse that are both not functions.

SPIRAL REVIEW

39. The ratio of a rectangle's width to its length is 3 : 4. The length of the rectangle is 36 cm. Write and solve a proportion to find the rectangle's width. *(Lesson 2-7)* $\mathbf{\frac{3}{4} = \frac{x}{36}}$**; 27 cm**

40. A scale drawing of a house is drawn with a scale of 1 in. : 16 ft. Find the actual length of a hallway that is $\frac{5}{8}$ in. on the scale drawing. *(Lesson 2-7)* **10 ft**

41. Penny wants to drink at least 64 ounces of water today. She has consumed 45 ounces of water so far. Write, solve, and graph an inequality to determine how many more ounces of water Penny must drink to reach her goal. *(Lesson 3-2)*

42. The local pizza parlor sold the following number of pizzas over 10 days. Sketch a graph for the situation. Tell whether the graph is continuous or discrete. *(Lesson 4-1)*

Time (days)	1	2	3	4	5	6	7	8	9	10
Pizzas Sold	5	11	2	4	8	10	3	6	12	1

41. $\mathbf{x + 45 \ge 64}$**;** $\mathbf{x \ge 19}$

17 18 19 20 21 22 23

42. discrete;

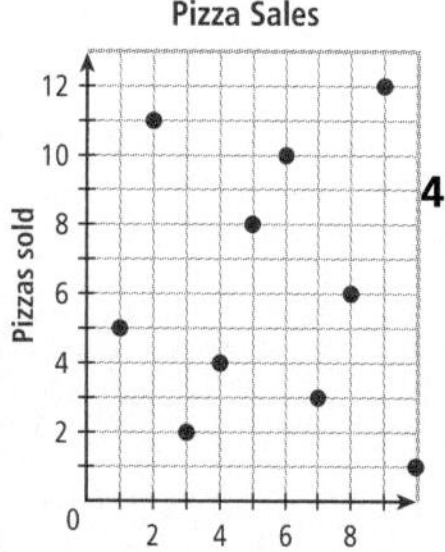

Answers

36. All real numbers except 2 and 4; values in the domain cannot repeat.

37. All real numbers; values in the range can repeat.

38a. {(5, −2), (4, 0), (−8, 3), (5, 7)}

b. The original relation is a function because each domain value is paired with exactly one range value. The inverse is not a function because a domain value has more than one range value paired with it.

38c. Possible answer: Relation: {(1, 2), (2, 3), (3, 4)}; Inverse: {(2, 1), (3, 2), (4, 3)}; Relation: {(1, 1), (1, 2), (2, 2), (2, 4)}; Inverse: {(1, 1), (2, 1), (2, 2), (4, 2)}

The Vertical-Line Test

The *vertical-line test* can be used to visually determine whether a graphed relation is a function.

Use with Lesson 4-2

Activity

Table 1	
x	y
−2	−5
−1	−3
0	−1
1	1
2	3
3	5

1. Look at the values in Table 1. Is every x-value paired with exactly one y-value? If not, what x-value(s) are paired with more than one y-value? **yes**
2. Is the relation a function? Explain. **Yes; each x-value has exactly one y-value.**
3. Graph the points from the Table 1. Draw a vertical line through each point of the graph. Does any vertical line touch more than one point?

Table 2	
x	y
−2	−3
1	4
0	5
1	2
2	3
3	5

4. Look at the values in Table 2. Is every x-value paired with exactly one y-value? If not, what x-value(s) are paired with more than one y-value? **No; the x-value 1 has two y-values: 2 and 4.**
5. Is the relation a function? Explain. **No; an x-value has more than one y-value.**
6. Graph the points from the Table 2. Draw a vertical line through each point of the graph. Does any vertical line touch more than one point?
7. What is the x-value of the two points that are on the same vertical line? Is that x-value paired with more than one y-value? **1; yes**
8. Write a statement describing how to use a vertical line to tell if a relation is a function. This is called the vertical-line test. **Possible answer: A relation is a function if there are no vertical lines that intersect the graph at more than one point.**
9. Why does the vertical-line test work? **The vertical-line test works because it shows if there is more than 1 y-value for an x-value.**

Try This

Use the vertical-line test to determine whether each relation is a function. If a relation is not a function, list two ordered pairs that show the same x-value with two different y-values.

1.
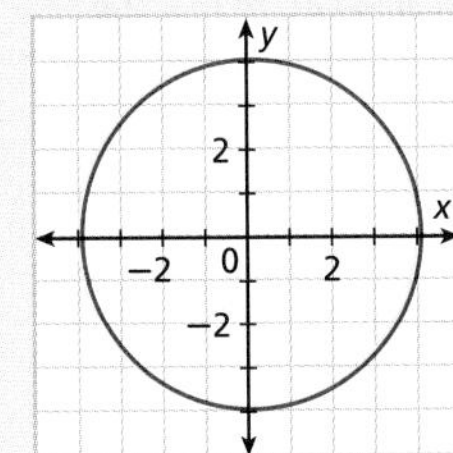

1. no; possible answer: (0, −4), (0, 4)

2. **2. yes**
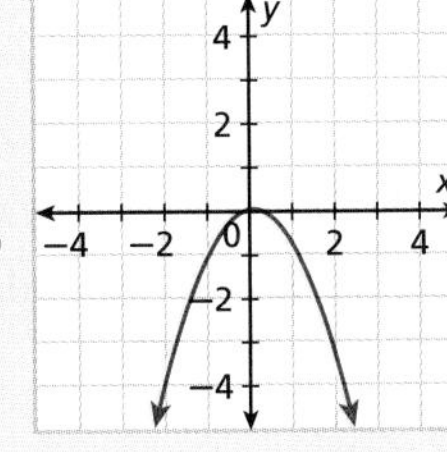

3.
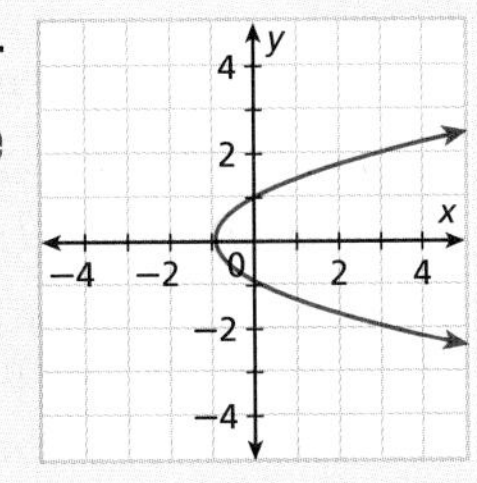

3. no; possible answer: (3, 2), (3, −2)

Answers to Activity

3. no

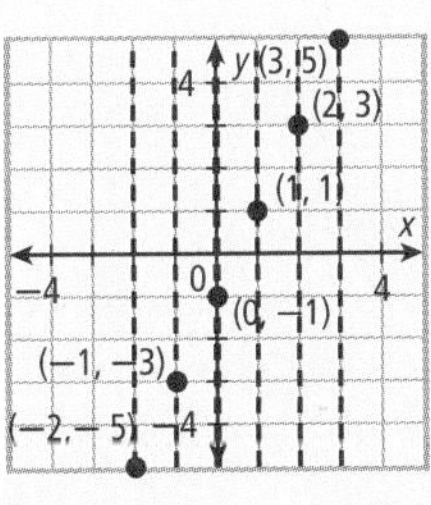

6. yes

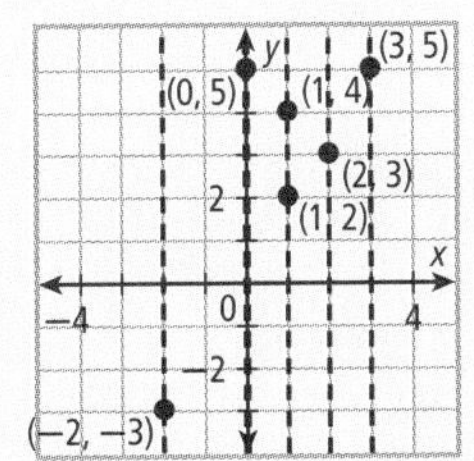

Organizer

Use with Lesson 4-2

Pacing:
Traditional $\frac{1}{2}$ day
Block $\frac{1}{4}$ day

Objective: Determine if a relation is a function.

Online Edition
Graphing Calculator

Countdown Week 8

Lab Resources

Algebra Lab Activities
4-2 Lab Recording Sheet

Teach

Discuss

A vertical line has the same x-value for each y-value.

Alternative Approach

To perform the vertical-line test with a graphing calculator, press GRAPH 2nd PRGM (DRAW), choose **4:Vertical**, and use arrow keys to move the vertical line across the graph.

Close

Key Concept

If any vertical line touches the graph no more than once, then the graphed relation is a function.

Assessment

Journal Have students graph a relation that is not a function and explain why it is not a function.

State Resources

Organizer

Use with Lesson 4-3

Pacing:

Traditional $\frac{1}{2}$ day

Block $\frac{1}{4}$ day

Objective: Use models to represent algebraic relationships.

Online Edition

Countdown Week 8

Resources

Algebra Lab Activities

4-3 Lab Recording Sheet

Teach

Discuss

The expression for the number of blocks is *length of tabletop plus product of 2 and height of base.* Only the height of the base changes.

Alternative Approach

Use square tiles to model the pattern.

Close

Key Concept

You can use models to find a pattern, and algebra to describe it.

Assessment

Journal Sketch a model of a table with a length of 6 and a base of 4 columns. Extend the pattern by three terms by adding rows of blocks to the table's base. Have students write expressions for each term of the pattern.

Model Variable Relationships

Use with Lesson 4-3

You can use models to represent an algebraic relationship. Using these models, you can write an algebraic expression to help describe and extend patterns.

The diagrams below represent the side views of tables. Each has a tabletop and a base. Copy and complete the chart using the pattern shown in the diagrams.

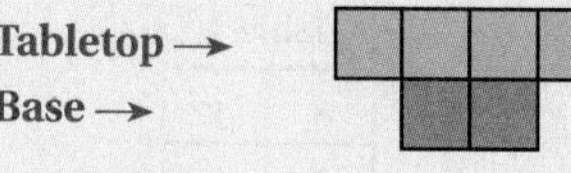

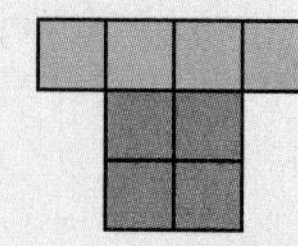

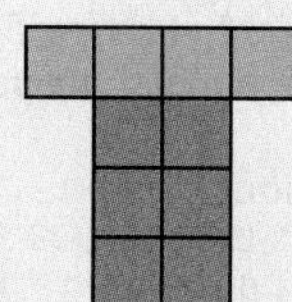

TERM NUMBER	FIGURE	DESCRIPTION OF FIGURE	EXPRESSION FOR NUMBER OF BLOCKS	VALUE OF TERM (NUMBER OF BLOCKS)	ORDERED PAIR
1		length of tabletop = 4 height of base = 1	$4 + (2)1$	6	(1, 6)
2		length of tabletop = 4 height of base = 2	$4 + (2)2$	8	(2, 8)
3		length of tabletop = 4 height of base = 3	$4 + (2)3$	10	(3, 10)
4		length of tabletop = 4 height of base = 4	$4 + (2)4$	12	(4, 12)
5		length of tabletop = 4 height of base = 5	$4 + (2)5$	14	(5, 14)
n		length of tabletop = 4 height of base = n	$4 + 2n$		$(n, 4 + 2n)$

Try This

1. Explain why you must multiply the height of the base by 2. **There are 2 base columns.**
2. What does the ordered pair (1, 6) mean? **The height of the base is 1 block, and a total of 6 blocks are in the table.**
3. Does the ordered pair (10, 24) belong in this pattern? Why or why not? **Yes; if the height of the table is 10 blocks, a total of 24 blocks will be in the table: $4 + 2(10) = 24$.**
4. Which expression from the table describes how you would find the total number of blocks for any term number n? **$4 + 2n$**
5. Use your rule to find the 25th term in this pattern. **54**

Answers to Activity

4.

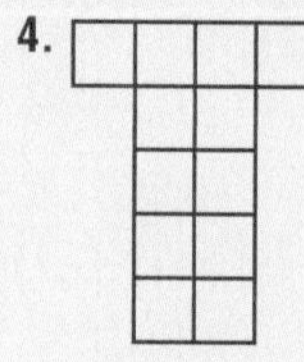

5.

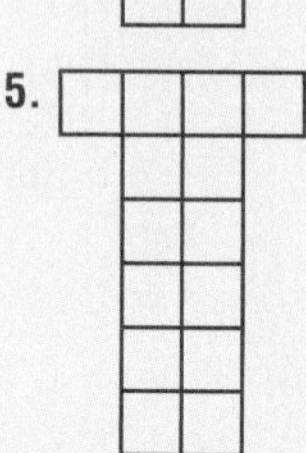

4-3 Writing Functions

Objectives
Identify independent and dependent variables.

Write an equation in function notation and evaluate a function for given input values.

Vocabulary
independent variable
dependent variable
function rule
function notation

Why learn this?
You can use a function rule to calculate how much money you will earn for working specific amounts of time.

Suppose Tasha baby-sits and charges $5 per hour.

Time Worked (h) x	1	2	3	4
Amount Earned ($) y	5	10	15	20

The amount of money Tasha earns is $5 times the number of hours she works. Write an equation using two different variables to show this relationship.

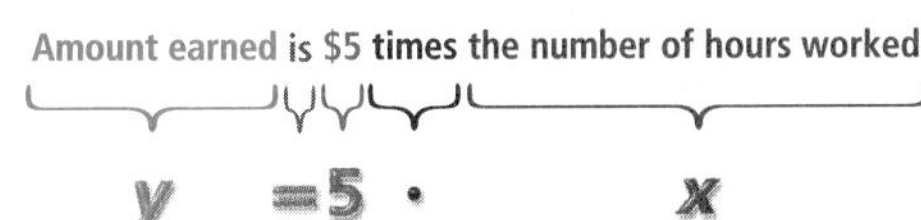

Tasha can use this equation to find how much money she will earn for any number of hours she works.

EXAMPLE 1 **Using a Table to Write an Equation**

Determine a relationship between the x- and y-values. Write an equation.

x	1	2	3	4
y	-2	-1	0	1

Step 1 List possible relationships between the first x- and y-values.

$1 - 3 = -2$ or $1(-2) = -2$

Step 2 Determine if one relationship works for the remaining values.

$2 - 3 = -1$ ✓ $\quad 2(-2) \neq -1$ ✗

$3 - 3 = 0$ ✓ $\quad 3(-2) \neq 0$ ✗

$4 - 3 = 1$ ✓ $\quad 4(-2) \neq 1$ ✗

The first relationship works. The value of y is 3 less than x.

Step 3 Write an equation.

$y = x - 3$ *The value of y is 3 less than x.*

1. Determine a relationship between the x- and y-values in the relation $\{(1, 3), (2, 6), (3, 9), (4, 12)\}$. Write an equation. $y = 3x$

The equation in Example 1 describes a function because for each x-value (input), there is only one y-value (output).

4-3 Organizer

Pacing: Traditional 1 day
Block $\frac{1}{2}$ day

Objectives: Identify independent and dependent variables.

Write an equation in function notation and evaluate a function for given input values.

Algebra Lab
In *Algebra Lab Activities*

Online Edition
Tutorial Videos

Countdown Week 8

Power Presentations with PowerPoint®

Warm Up

Evaluate each expression for $a = 2$, $b = -3$, and $c = 8$.

1. $a + 3c$ 26
2. $ab - c$ -14
3. $\frac{1}{2}c + b$ 1
4. $4c - b$ 35
5. $b^a + c$ 17

Also available on transparency

Math Humor

Q: Why did the x-variable move back home?

A: She was more comfortable in her own domain.

Introduce

EXPLORATION

4-3 Writing Functions

Dan has $100 in his savings account. His grandmother promises to deposit $25 into the account for each day Dan helps her during his summer vacation.

1. Complete the table to show how much money will be in Dan's account for each given number of days Dan works for his grandmother.
2. How much money will be in Dan's account if he works x days?

Days x	Process	Total in Account ($) y
0		
1	100 + 25(1)	
2	100 + 25(2)	
3		
5		225
10		

3. Write an equation that shows the relationship between x (the number of days Dan works) and y (the total in his account).

THINK AND DISCUSS

4. **Discuss** whether the above relationship is a function.
5. **Explain** how you can use your equation to find the total in Dan's account if he works 20 days.

Motivate

ENGLISH LANGUAGE LEARNERS

Have students describe the meaning of the following phrases: Possible answers:

- independently wealthy doesn't need a job
- Independence Day day of freedom
- working independently doesn't need help
- dependent child needs a parent
- insulin dependent needs insulin
- dependent on friends needs friends

Explorations and answers are provided in *Alternate Openers: Explorations Transparencies.*

State Resources

go.hrw.com
State Resources Online
KEYWORD: MA7 Resources

Power Presentations with PowerPoint®

Additional Examples

Example 1

Determine a relationship between the x- and y-values. Write an equation. $y = \frac{x}{5}$

x	5	10	15	20
y	1	2	3	4

Example 2

Identify the independent and dependent variables in each situation.

A. A painter must measure a room before deciding how much paint to buy. ind.: measurement of room; dep.: amount of paint

B. The height of a candle decreases for every hour it burns. ind.: time; dep.: height of candle

C. A veterinarian must weigh an animal before determining the amount of medication. ind.: weight of animal; dep.: amount of medication

INTERVENTION

Questioning Strategies

EXAMPLE 1

- As the x-value is increasing, what is happening to the y-value?
- What situation could this table of numbers represent?

EXAMPLE 2

- What is another situation where you would have independent and dependent variables?

The input of a function is the **independent variable**. The output of a function is the **dependent variable**. The value of the dependent variable *depends* on, or is a function of, the value of the independent variable. For Tasha, the amount she earns depends on, or is a function of, the amount of time she works.

Helpful Hint

There are several different ways to describe the variables of a function.

Independent Variable	Dependent Variable
x-values	y-values
Domain	Range
Input	Output
x	$f(x)$

EXAMPLE 2 Identifying Independent and Dependent Variables

Identify the independent and dependent variables in each situation.

A **In the winter, more electricity is used when the temperature goes down, and less is used when the temperature rises.**

The amount of electricity used *depends on* the temperature.

Dependent: amount of electricity Independent: temperature

B **The cost of shipping a package is based on its weight.**

The cost of shipping a package *depends on* its weight.

Dependent: cost Independent: weight

C **The faster Ron walks, the quicker he gets home.**

The time it takes Ron to get home *depends on* the speed he walks.

Dependent: time Independent: speed

Identify the independent and dependent variables in each situation.

2a. A company charges $10 per hour to rent a jackhammer. **2a. ind.: time; dep.: cost**

2b. Apples cost $0.99 per pound. **ind.: pounds; dep.: cost**

An algebraic expression that defines a function is a **function rule**. $5 \cdot x$ in the equation about Tasha's earnings is a function rule.

If x is the independent variable and y is the dependent variable, then **function notation** for y is $f(x)$, read "f of x," where f names the function. When an equation in two variables describes a function, you can use function notation to write it.

The dependent variable	is	a function of	the independent variable.
y	is	a function of	x.
y	$=$	f	(x)

Since $y = f(x)$, Tasha's earnings, $y = 5x$, can be rewritten in function notation by substituting $f(x)$ for y: $f(x) = 5x$. Sometimes functions are written using y, and sometimes functions are written using $f(x)$.

EXAMPLE 3 Writing Functions

Identify the independent and dependent variables. Write an equation in function notation for each situation.

A **A lawyer's fee is $200 per hour for her services.**

The fee for the lawyer depends on how many hours she works.

Dependent: fee Independent: hours

Let h represent the number of hours the lawyer works.

The function for the lawyer's fee is $f(h) = 200h$.

2 Teach

Guided Instruction

If students have a hard time finding a relationship in **Example 1,** have them first test the four basic operations. (Is the same value added to each x, subtracted from each x, etc.?) If those don't work, then it may be a square, square root, or combination of operations. In **Examples 2** and **3,** encourage students to rewrite each statement using the words *depends on* before choosing which variables are independent and dependent.

Reaching All Learners

Through Communication

Designate a group of four students as the "function machine." This group must create a secret function rule. Other students give input values to the group, and the group must state the output value. The other students must guess the secret function rule. Students can explain how they deduced the secret function rule.

Through Graphic Organizers

Divide students into groups and have them write examples of dependent relationships in various formats.

For example:

- I get cranky when I don't eat.
- If I don't work, then I don't get paid.

Independent	Dependent
• when I don't eat • if I don't work	• I get cranky • then I don't get paid

Identify the independent and dependent variables. Write an equation in function notation for each situation.

B **The admission fee to a local carnival is $8. Each ride costs $1.50.**

The total cost depends on the number of rides ridden, plus $8.

Dependent: total cost Independent: number of rides

Let r represent the number of rides ridden.

The function for the total cost of the carnival is $f(r) = 1.50r + 8$.

Identify the independent and dependent variables. Write an equation in function notation for each situation.

3a. ind.: pounds; dep.: cost; $f(x) = 1.69x$

3a. Steven buys lettuce that costs $1.69/lb.

3b. An amusement park charges a $6.00 parking fee plus $29.99 per person. ind.: people; dep.: cost; $f(x) = 6 + 29.99x$

You can think of a function as an input-output machine. For Tasha's earnings, $f(x) = 5x$, if you input a value x, the output is $5x$.

If Tasha wanted to know how much money she would earn by working 6 hours, she could input 6 for x and find the output. This is called *evaluating the function.*

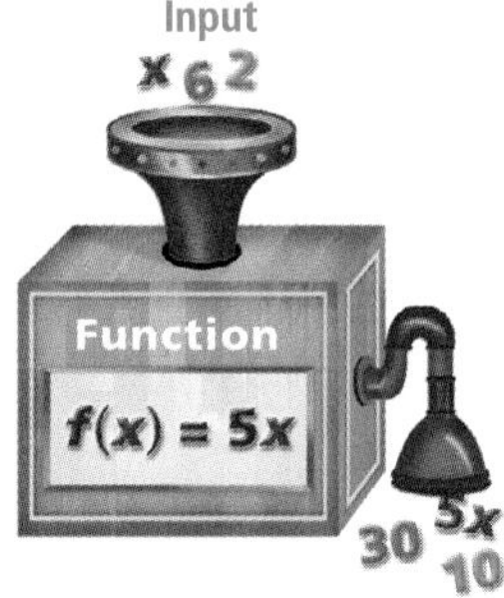

EXAMPLE 4 **Evaluating Functions**

Evaluate each function for the given input values.

A **For $f(x) = 5x$, find $f(x)$ when $x = 6$ and when $x = 7.5$.**

$f(x) = 5x$

$f(6) = 5(6)$ *Substitute 6 for x.*

$= 30$ *Simplify.*

$f(x) = 5x$

$f(7.5) = 5(7.5)$ *Substitute 7.5 for x.*

$= 37.5$ *Simplify.*

Reading Math

Functions can be named with any letter; *f*, *g*, and *h* are the most common. You read $f(6)$ as "*f* of 6," and $g(2)$ as "*g* of 2."

B **For $g(t) = 2.30t + 10$, find $g(t)$ when $t = 2$ and when $t = -5$.**

$g(t) = 2.30t + 10$

$g(2) = 2.30(2) + 10$

$= 4.6 + 10$

$= 14.6$

$g(t) = 2.30t + 10$

$g(-5) = 2.30(-5) + 10$

$= -11.5 + 10$

$= -1.5$

C **For $h(x) = \frac{1}{2}x - 3$, find $h(x)$ when $x = 12$ and when $x = -8$.**

$h(x) = \frac{1}{2}x - 3$

$h(12) = \frac{1}{2}(12) - 3$

$= 6 - 3$

$= 3$

$h(x) = \frac{1}{2}x - 3$

$h(-8) = \frac{1}{2}(-8) - 3$

$= -4 - 3$

$= -7$

Evaluate each function for the given input values.

4a. $h(1) = 1$; $h(-3) = -7$

4a. For $h(c) = 2c - 1$, find $h(c)$ when $c = 1$ and $c = -3$.

4b. For $g(t) = \frac{1}{4}t + 1$, find $g(t)$ when $t = -24$ and $t = 400$.

$g(-24) = -5$; $g(400) = 101$

COMMON ERROR ALERT

Students might mistake the notation $f(x)$ as meaning f times x. Remind them that $f(x)$ is the notation of a function and, in a function, is interchangeable with y.

Power Presentations with PowerPoint®

Additional Examples

Example 3

Identify the independent and dependent variables. Write an equation in function notation for each situation.

A. A math tutor charges $35 per hour. ind.: time; dep.: cost; $f(h) = 35h$

B. A fitness center charges a $100 initiation fee plus $40 per month. ind.: number of months; dep.: total cost; $f(m) = 100 + 40m$

Example 4

Evaluate each function for the given input values.

A. For $f(x) = 3x + 2$, find $f(x)$ when $x = 7$ and when $x = -4$. $f(7) = 23$; $f(-4) = -10$

B. For $g(t) = 1.5t - 5$, find $g(t)$ when $t = 6$ and when $t = -2$. $g(6) = 4$; $g(-2) = -8$

C. For $h(r) = \frac{1}{3}r + 2$, find $h(r)$ when $r = 600$ and when $r = -12$. $h(600) = 202$; $h(-12) = -2$

INTERVENTION

Questioning Strategies

EXAMPLE 3

- How could you write the equation without using function notation?
- Does $f(x)$ represent domain or range?

EXAMPLE 4

- How is evaluating a function like solving an equation? How is it different?

Teaching Tip **Auditory** Tell students that the ***in***put is the ***in***dependent variable. ENGLISH LANGUAGE LEARNERS

Teaching Tip

Inclusion Encourage students to identify the dependent and independent variables in **Example 5** before attempting to write the function.

Power Presentations with PowerPoint®

Additional Examples

Example 5

Joe has enough money to purchase 1, 2, or 3 DVDs at $15.00 each.

Write a function to describe the situation. Find the reasonable domain and range for the function. $f(x) = 15x$; D: {1, 2, 3}; R: {15, 30, 45}

INTERVENTION

Questioning Strategies

EXAMPLE 5

- What do you look for when finding the reasonable domain?
- How do you find the reasonable range once you have determined the reasonable domain?

When a function describes a real-world situation, every real number is not always reasonable for the domain and range. For example, a number representing the length of an object cannot be negative, and only whole numbers can represent a number of people.

EXAMPLE 5 Finding the Reasonable Domain and Range of a Function

Manuel has already sold $20 worth of tickets to the school play. He has 4 tickets left to sell at $2.50 per ticket. Write a function to describe how much money Manuel can collect from selling tickets. Find the reasonable domain and range for the function.

Money collected from ticket sales	is	$2.50	per	ticket	plus	the $20 already sold.
$f(x)$	=	$2.50	•	x	+	20

If he sells x more tickets, he will have collected $f(x) = 2.50x + 20$ dollars.

Manuel has only 4 tickets left to sell, so he could sell 0, 1, 2, 3, or 4 tickets. A reasonable domain is {0, 1, 2, 3, 4}.

Substitute these values into the function rule to find the range values.

x	0	1	2	3	4
f(x)	2.50(0) + 20 = 20	2.50(1) + 20 = 22.50	2.50(2) + 20 = 25	2.50(3) + 20 = 27.50	2.50(4) + 20 = 30

The reasonable range for this situation is {$20, $22.50, $25, $27.50, $30}.

5. The settings on a space heater are the whole numbers from 0 to 3. The total number of watts used for each setting is 500 times the setting number. Write a function to describe the number of watts used for each setting. Find the reasonable domain and range for the function.
$f(x) = 500x$; D: {0, 1, 2, 3}; R: {0, 500, 1000, 1500}

THINK AND DISCUSS

1. When you input water into an ice machine, the output is ice cubes. Name another real-world object that has an input and an output.
2. How do you identify the independent and dependent variables in a situation?
3. Explain how to find reasonable domain values for a function.

4. **GET ORGANIZED** Copy and complete the graphic organizer. Use the function $y = x + 3$ and the domain {−2, −1, 0, 1, 2}.

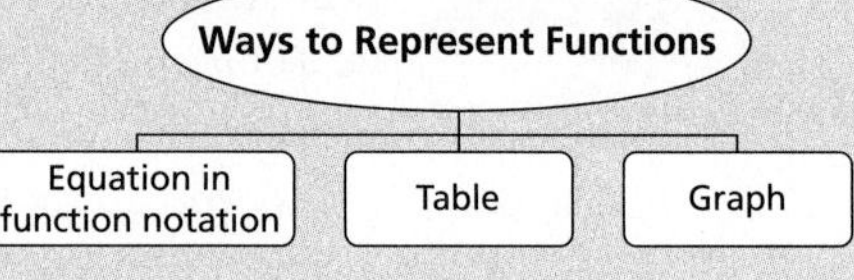

3 Close

Summarize

Remind students that you need to know the value of the independent variable to be able to determine the value of the dependent variable. Then have students write an equation for the following situations using function notation.

A cable TV service charges $50 for hookup and $30 per month. $f(m) = 50 + 30m$

A library charges $0.25 for every day that a book is late. $f(d) = 0.25d$

ONGOING ASSESSMENT and INTERVENTION

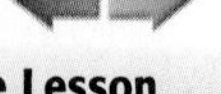

***Diagnose Before* the Lesson**
4-3 Warm Up, TE p. 249

***Monitor During* the Lesson**
Check It Out! Exercises, SE pp. 249–252
Questioning Strategies, TE pp. 250–252

***Assess After* the Lesson**
4-3 Lesson Quiz, TE p. 255
Alternative Assessment, TE p. 255

Answers to *Think and Discuss*

Possible answers:

1. a toaster
2. If one data set depends on the other, the first data set represents the dependent variable, and the other data set represents the independent variable.
3. Find what makes sense for the real-world situation. Time, for example, would not be negative.
4. See p. A4.

4-3 Exercises

go.hrw.com
Homework Help Online
KEYWORD: MA7 4-3
Parent Resources Online
KEYWORD: MA7 Parent

GUIDED PRACTICE

Vocabulary Apply the vocabulary from this lesson to answer each question.

1. The output of a function is the __?__ variable. (*independent* or *dependent*) **dependent**
2. An algebraic expression that defines a function is a __?__. (*function rule* or *function notation*) **function rule**

SEE EXAMPLE 1 p. 249

Determine a relationship between the x- and y-values. Write an equation.

3.

x	1	2	3	4
y	−1	0	1	2

$y = x - 2$

4. $\{(1, 4), (2, 7), (3, 10), (4, 13)\}$ $y = 3x + 1$

SEE EXAMPLE 2 p. 250

Identify the independent and dependent variables in each situation.

5. A small-size bottle of water costs \$1.99 and a large-size bottle of water costs \$3.49. **ind.: size of bottle; dep.: cost of water**
6. An employee receives 2 vacation days for every month worked. **ind.: months worked; dep.: vacation days available**

SEE EXAMPLE 3 p. 250

Identify the independent and dependent variables. Write an equation in function notation for each situation. ind.: hours; dep.: cost; $f(h) = 75h$

7. An air-conditioning technician charges customers \$75 per hour.
8. An ice rink charges \$3.50 for skates and \$1.25 per hour. **ind.: hours; dep.: cost;** $f(x) = 3.50 + 1.25x$

SEE EXAMPLE 4 p. 251

Evaluate each function for the given input values.

9. For $f(x) = 7x + 2$, find $f(x)$ when $x = 0$ and when $x = 1$. $f(0) = 2$; $f(1) = 9$
10. For $g(x) = 4x - 9$, find $g(x)$ when $x = 3$ and when $x = 5$. $g(3) = 3$; $g(5) = 11$
11. For $h(t) = \frac{1}{3}t - 10$, find $h(t)$ when $t = 27$ and when $t = -15$. $h(27) = -1$; $h(-15) = -15$

SEE EXAMPLE 5 p. 252

12. A construction company uses beams that are 2, 3, or 4 meters long. The measure of each beam must be converted to centimeters. Write a function to describe the situation. Find the reasonable domain and range for the function. (*Hint*: 1 m = 100 cm) $f(\ell) = 100\ell$; D: {2, 3, 4}; R: {200, 300, 400}

PRACTICE AND PROBLEM SOLVING

Independent Practice

For Exercises	See Example
13–14	1
15–16	2
17–19	3
20–22	4
23	5

Extra Practice
Skills Practice p. S10
Application Practice p. S31

Determine a relationship between the x- and y-values. Write an equation.

13.

x	1	2	3	4
y	−2	−4	−6	−8

$y = -2x$

14. $\{(1, -1), (2, -2), (3, -3), (4, -4)\}$ $y = -x$

Identify the independent and dependent variables in each situation.

15. Gardeners buy fertilizer according to the size of a lawn. **ind.: size of lawn; dep.: cost**
16. The cost to gift wrap an order is \$3 plus \$1 per item wrapped. **ind.: items wrapped; dep.: cost**

Identify the independent and dependent variables. Write an equation in function notation for each situation.

17. To rent a DVD, a customer must pay \$3.99 plus \$0.99 for every day that it is late. **ind.: days late; dep.: total cost;** $f(x) = 3.99 + 0.99x$
18. Stephen charges \$25 for each lawn he mows. **ind.: lawns mowed; dep.: amount earned;** $f(x) = 25x$
19. A car can travel 28 miles per gallon of gas. **ind.: gallons of gas; dep.: miles;** $f(x) = 28x$

4-3 Exercises

Assignment Guide

Assign *Guided Practice* exercises as necessary.

If you finished Examples **1–3**
Basic 13–19, 29
Average 13–19, 29
Advanced 13–19, 29

If you finished Examples **1–5**
Basic 13–35, 38–44
Average 13–36, 38–44
Advanced 13–24, 29, 31–44

Homework Quick Check
Quickly check key concepts.
Exercises: 14, 16, 18, 20, 23, 24

State Resources

Exercise 32 involves determining relationships between two variables. This exercise prepares students for the Multi-Step Test Prep on page 264.

Answers

31. Possible answer: The cost of a hotel room is a function of how many nights you stay. The cost is the dependent variable because it depends on the number of nights; therefore, the number of nights is the independent variable.

Evaluate each function for the given input values.

20. For $f(x) = x^2 - 5$, find $f(x)$ when $x = 0$ and when $x = 3$. **$f(0) = -5$; $f(3) = 4$**
21. For $g(x) = x^2 + 6$, find $g(x)$ when $x = 1$ and when $x = 2$. **$g(1) = 7$; $g(2) = 10$**
22. For $f(x) = \frac{2}{3}x + 3$, find $f(x)$ when $x = 9$ and when $x = -3$. **$f(9) = 9$; $f(-3) = 1$**
23. A mail-order company charges \$5 per order plus \$2 per item in the order, up to a maximum of 4 items. Write a function to describe the situation. Find the reasonable domain and range for the function. **$f(n) = 2n + 5$; D: {1, 2, 3, 4}; R: {\$7, \$9, \$11, \$13}**

LINK Transportation

Air Force One refers to two specially configured Boeing 747-200B airplanes. The radio call sign when the president is aboard either aircraft or any Air Force aircraft is "Air Force One."

24. **Transportation** Air Force One can travel 630 miles per hour. Let h be the number of hours traveled. The function $d = 630h$ gives the distance d in miles that Air Force One travels in h hours.
    a. Identify the independent and dependent variables. Write $d = 630h$ using function notation. **ind.: hours; dep.: distance; $f(h) = 630h$**
    b. What are reasonable values for the domain and range in the situation described? **D: $x \geq 0$; R: $y \geq 0$**
    c. How far can Air Force One travel in 12 hours? **7560 mi**
25. Complete the table for $g(z) = 2z - 5$.

z	1	2	3	4
$g(z)$	**−3**	**−1**	**1**	**3**

26. Complete the table for $h(x) = x^2 + x$.

x	0	1	2	3
$h(x)$	**0**	**2**	**6**	**12**

27. **Estimation** For $f(x) = 3x + 5$, estimate the output when $x = -6.89$, $x = 1.01$, and $x = 4.67$. **$f(-6.89) \approx -16$; $f(1.01) \approx 8$; $f(4.67) \approx 20$**
28. **Transportation** A car can travel 30 miles on a gallon of gas and has a 20-gallon gas tank. Let g be the number of gallons of gas the car has in its tank. The function $d = 30g$ gives the distance d in miles that the car travels on g gallons.
    a. What are reasonable values for the domain and range in the situation described?
    b. How far can the car travel on 12 gallons of gas? **360 mi**
29. **Critical Thinking** Give an example of a real-life situation for which the reasonable domain consists of 1, 2, 3, and 4 and the reasonable range consists of 2, 4, 6, and 8.
30. **ERROR ANALYSIS** Rashid saves \$150 each month. He wants to know how much he will have saved in 2 years. He writes the rule $s = m + 150$ to help him figure out how much he will save, where s is the amount saved and m is the number of months he saves. Explain why his rule is incorrect.

31. **Write About It** Give a real-life situation that can be described by a function. Identify the independent variable and the dependent variable.

28a. D: $\{0 \leq g \leq 20\}$ R: $\{0 \leq d \leq 600\}$

29. Possible answer: There can be a maximum of 4 bowlers on one bowling lane, and each bowler needs to rent 2 shoes.

30. Rashid must multiply \$150 by the number of months he saves for, not add the number of months to 150.

MULTI-STEP TEST PREP

32. This problem will prepare you for the Multi-Step Test Prep on page 264.

    The table shows the volume v of water pumped into a pool after t hours.
    a. Determine a relationship between the time and the volume of water and write an equation. **$v = 1250t$**
    b. Identify the independent and dependent variables. **ind.: time; dep.: volume**
    c. If the pool holds 10,000 gallons, how long will it take to fill? **8h**

Amount of Water in Pool	
Time (h)	Volume (gal)
0	0
1	1250
2	2500
3	3750
4	5000

4-3 PRACTICE A
4-3 PRACTICE C
4-3 PRACTICE B

Determine a relationship between the x- and y-values. Write an equation.

1.

x	−4	−3	−2	−1
y	−1	0	1	2

$y = x + 3$

2. {(2, 3), (3, 5), (4, 7), (5, 9)} **$y = 2x - 1$**

Identify the independent and dependent variables in each situation.

3. Ice cream sales increase when the temperature rises.
   I: **temperature;** D: **ice cream sales**
4. Food for the catered party costs \$12.75 per person.
   I: **number of people;** D: **cost of food**

Identify the independent and dependent variables. Write a rule in function notation for each situation.

5. Carson charges \$7 per hour for yard work.
   I: number of hours; D: total charge; $f(h) = 7h$
6. Kay donates twice what Ed donates.
   I: Ed's donation; D: Kay's donation; $f(d) = 2d$

Evaluate each function for the given input values.

7. For $f(x) = 5x + 1$, find $f(x)$ when $x = 2$ and when $x = 3$. **11; 16**
8. For $g(x) = -4x$, find $g(x)$ when $x = -6$ and when $x = 2$. **24; −8**
9. For $h(x) = x - 3$, find $h(x)$ when $x = 3$ and when $x = 1$. **0; −2**

Complete the following.

10. An aerobics class is being offered once a week for 6 weeks. The registration fee is \$15 and the cost for each class attended is \$10. Write a function rule to describe the total cost of the class. Find a reasonable domain and range for the function. **$f(x) = 15 + 10x$; D: {0, 1, 2, 3, 4, 5, 6}; R: {15, 25, 35, 45, 55, 65, 75}**

4-3 READING STRATEGIES

To read and write functions, you must understand what is meant by an *independent variable* and a *dependent variable*.

domain — x-value — Independent Variable — x — input

range — y-value — Dependent Variable — f(x) — output

Carmen attends a school with a dress code. She went shopping and found acceptable shirts for \$15 each. Her mother has allowed her to buy up to 5 new shirts for the school year.

Independent variable: number of shirts
Dependent variable: total cost
The function that represents this relation is $f(x) = 15x$.
Reasonable domain (x-values): {1, 2, 3, 4, 5}
Reasonable range (y-values): {15, 30, 45, 60, 75}
When $x = 5$, $f(x) = 75$.
So, 5 shirts will cost \$75.

Answer the following based on the situation below.

Molly is making greeting cards for 5 of her friends. Each card is to have 4 ribbons.

1. Identify each as either the independent or the dependent variable.
   "number of ribbons used" **dependent**
   "number of cards made" **independent**
2. Write a function for the relation. **$f(x) = 4x$**
3. What is the reasonable domain for this function? **D: {1, 2, 3, 4, 5}**
4. What is the reasonable range for this function? **R: {4, 8, 12, 16, 20}**
5. How many ribbons will Molly use if she makes 3 cards? **12 ribbons**
6. How many ribbons will Molly use if she makes 5 cards? **20 ribbons**

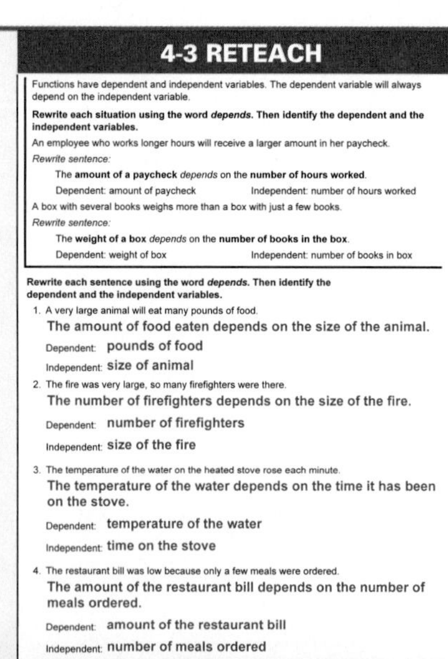

4-3 RETEACH

Functions have dependent and independent variables. The dependent variable will always depend on the independent variable.

Rewrite each situation using the word *depends*. Then identify the dependent and the independent variables.

An employee who works longer hours will receive a larger amount in her paycheck.

Rewrite sentence:

The **amount of a paycheck** *depends* on the **number of hours worked**.

Dependent: amount of paycheck Independent: number of hours worked

A box with several books weighs more than a box with just a few books.

Rewrite sentence:

The **weight of a box** *depends* on the **number of books in the box**.

Dependent: weight of box Independent: number of books in box

Rewrite each sentence using the word *depends*. Then identify the dependent and the independent variables.

1. A very large animal will eat many pounds of food.
   The amount of food eaten depends on the size of the animal.
   Dependent: **pounds of food**
   Independent: **size of animal**
2. The fire was very large, so many firefighters were there.
   The number of firefighters depends on the size of the fire.
   Dependent: **number of firefighters**
   Independent: **size of the fire**
3. The temperature of the water on the heated stove rose each minute.
   The temperature of the water depends on the time it has been on the stove.
   Dependent: **temperature of the water**
   Independent: **time on the stove**
4. The restaurant bill was low because only a few meals were ordered.
   The amount of the restaurant bill depends on the number of meals ordered.
   Dependent: **amount of the restaurant bill**
   Independent: **number of meals ordered**

TEST PREP

33. Marsha buys x pens at \$0.70 per pen and one pencil for \$0.10. Which function gives the total amount Marsha spends?

   (A) $c(x) = 0.70x + 0.10x$ (C) $c(x) = (0.70 + 0.10)x$

   (B) $c(x) = 0.70x + 1$ **(D)** $c(x) = 0.70x + 0.10$

34. Belle is buying pizzas for her daughter's birthday party, using the prices in the table. Which equation best describes the relationship between the total cost c and the number of pizzas p?

Pizzas	Total Cost (\$)
5	26.25
10	52.50
15	78.75

   (F) $c = 26.25p$ (H) $c = p + 26.25$

   (G) $c = 5.25p$ (J) $c = 6p - 3.75$

35. **Gridded Response** What is the value of $f(x) = 5 - \frac{1}{2}x$ when $x = 3$? **3.5**

CHALLENGE AND EXTEND

D: $0 \le x \le 100$; R: $32 \le x \le 212$

36. The formula to convert a temperature that is in degrees Celsius x to degrees Fahrenheit $f(x)$ is $f(x) = \frac{9}{5}x + 32$. What are reasonable values for the domain and range when you convert to Fahrenheit the temperature of water as it rises from 0° to 100° Celsius?

37. **Math History** In his studies of the motion of free-falling objects, Galileo Galilei found that regardless of its mass, an object will fall a distance d that is related to the square of its travel time t in seconds. The modern formula that describes free-fall motion is $d = \frac{1}{2}gt^2$, where g is the acceleration due to gravity and t is the length of time in seconds the object falls. Find the distance an object falls in 3 seconds. (*Hint*: Research to find acceleration due to gravity in meters per second squared.) **44.1 m**

SPIRAL REVIEW

Solve each equation. Check your answer. *(Lesson 2-3)*

38. $5x + 2 - 7x = -10$ **6** 39. $3(2 - y) = 15$ **−3** 40. $\frac{2}{3}p - \frac{1}{2} = \frac{1}{6}$ **1**

Find the value of x in each diagram. *(Lesson 2-8)*

41. $\triangle ABC \sim \triangle DEF$ **2** 42. $QRST \sim LMNP$ **6**

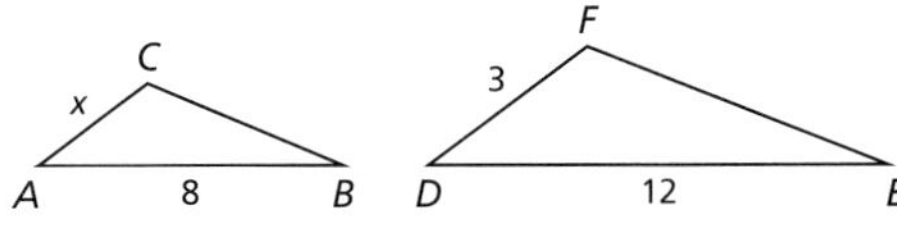

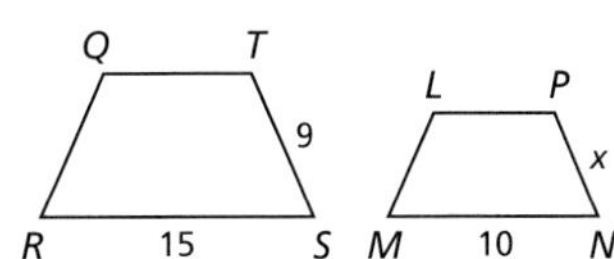

Give the domain and range of each relation. Tell whether the relation is a function. Explain. *(Lesson 4-2)*

43. 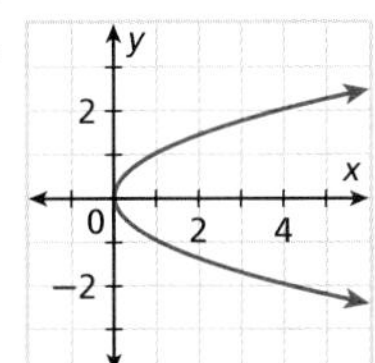

D: $x \ge 0$; R: all real numbers; no; some domain values are paired with more than one range value.

44.

x	y
−3	4
−1	2
0	0
1	2
3	−4

D: {−3, −1, 0, 1, 3}; R: {4, 2, 0, −4}; yes; each domain value is paired with exactly one range value.

4-3 PROBLEM SOLVING

Identify the independent and dependent variables. Write a rule in function notation for each situation.

1. Each state receives electoral votes based on the number of representatives it has in the House of Representatives.

Representatives	2	4	6	8
Electoral Votes	4	6	8	10

I: number of representatives; D: number of electoral votes; $f(r) = r + 2$

2. Terry has 30 pieces of gum and gives 2 pieces to each of his friends.

I: number of friends; D: pieces of gum Terry has left $f(x) = 30 - 2x$

3. Ronaldo is buying bacon that costs \$4.29 per pound.

I: pounds of bacon; D: total price; $f(b) = 4.29b$

4. A personal trainer charges \$50 for the first session and \$40 for every session thereafter.

I: number of sessions; D: total cost; $f(s) = 50 + 40(s - 1)$

International travel and business require the conversion of American dollars into foreign currency. During part of 2005, one American dollar was worth 6 Croatian Kuna. Select the best answer.

5. An American bank wishes to convert d dollars into kuna. Which function rule describes the situation?

   A $f(d) = \frac{d}{6}$ C $f(d) = \frac{6}{d}$

   B $f(d) = 6d$ D $f(d) = d + 6$

6. A Croatian company already has \$100,000 and is going to convert k kuna into dollars. Which function rule can be used to determine the total amount of American dollars this company will have?

   F $f(x) = 100{,}000 + 6k$

   G $f(x) = 100{,}000 + \frac{k}{6}$

   H $f(x) = 100{,}000k + 6$

   J $f(x) = 100{,}000 + \frac{6}{k}$

7. Macon has \$100 and is thinking about converting some of it into kuna. What is a reasonable range for this situation?

   A $0 \le y \le 6$ C $0 \le y \le 100$

   B $0 \le y \le 16.7$ D $0 \le y \le 600$

8. Robin converts x dollars into y kuna. Which expression is the independent variable in this situation?

   F x H $6x$

   G y J $6y$

9. Jakov converts n kuna into c dollars. Which expression is the dependent variable in this situation?

   A n C $\frac{n}{6}$

   B c D $\frac{c}{6}$

4-3 CHALLENGE

A Celsius thermometer shows a reading of 40 °C. While you are looking at this thermometer, the local weather report on the radio gives a temperature of 104 °F. When you change to another local station, you hear a report of 112 °F.

40°

1. Use the formula $F = \frac{9}{5}C + 32$ to find the Fahrenheit temperature corresponding to 40 °C. **104°F**
2. Why do you suppose that you heard a different Fahrenheit temperature on one of the radio stations?

   Answers may vary. Sample answer: the 112°F may have been a "heat index" reading.
3. Explain why $F = \frac{9}{5}C + 32$ represents a function.

   For each value of C there is exactly 1 value for F.
4. Complete the following ordered pairs for (C, F) by using the formula $F = \frac{9}{5}C + 32$:

   a. (25, **77**) b. (−10, **14**) c. (18, **64.4**) d. (**30**, 86)
5. In part **d** of Exercise 4, you solved for C given F. Use the appropriate properties of equality to solve $F = \frac{9}{5}C + 32$ for C in terms of F. **$C = \frac{5}{9}(F - 32)$**
6. Use the formula found in Exercise 5 to complete the following ordered pairs (C, F).

   a. **15**, 59) b. (**25**, 77) c. (**−20**, −4) d. (**$26\frac{2}{3}$**, 80)
7. Is this formula for C in terms of F also a function? Why or why not?

   Yes; for each value of F, there is exactly one value of C.
8. Functions that "undo" each other are called *inverse* functions. Start with 35 °C and use the first formula to find a value of F. Then use this value of F in the second formula to find a value of C. What happens?

   The result is the original 35.
9. Find the temperature at which the Celsius and the Fahrenheit temperatures are equivalent.

   There is no temperature equivalent in both systems.

TEST PREP DOCTOR + Exercise 33 states that one pencil is purchased for \$0.10. Therefore, the function must contain 0.10 as a constant (not multiplied by the variable). This is true only in choice **D.**

Journal

Have students give the meaning of $f(3) = 12$, and then create a function such that $f(3) = 12$.

ALTERNATIVE ASSESSMENT

Have students choose a math formula and write the formula in function notation, stating which is the dependent variable and which is the independent variable. Then have them evaluate their function for three appropriate domain values.

Power Presentations with PowerPoint®

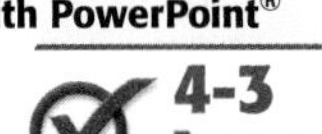

4-3 Lesson Quiz

Identify the independent and dependent variables. Write an equation in function notation for each situation.

1. A buffet charges \$8.95 per person. ind.: number of people; dep.: cost; $f(p) = 8.95p$
2. A moving company charges \$130 for weekly truck rental plus \$1.50 per mile. ind.: miles; dep.: cost; $f(m) = 130 + 1.50m$

Evaluate each function for the given input values.

3. For $g(t) = \frac{1}{4}t - 3$, find $g(t)$ when $t = 20$ and when $t = -12$. $g(20) = 2$; $g(-12) = -6$
4. For $f(x) = 6x - 1$, find $f(x)$ when $x = 3.5$ and when $x = -5$. $f(3.5) = 20$; $f(-5) = -31$

Write a function to describe the situation. Find the reasonable domain and range for the function.

5. A theater can be rented for exactly 2, 3, or 4 hours. The cost is a \$100 deposit plus \$200 per hour. $f(h) = 100 + 200h$; D: {2, 3, 4}; R: {500, 700, 900}

Also available on transparency

4-4 Organizer

Pacing: Traditional 1 day
Block $\frac{1}{2}$ day

Objectives: Graph functions given a limited domain.

Graph functions given a domain of all real numbers.

Online Edition
Tutorial Videos, Interactivity, TechKeys

Countdown Week 9

Power Presentations with PowerPoint®

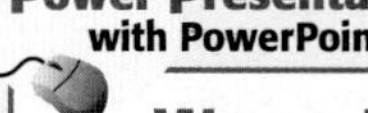

Warm Up

Solve each equation for *y*.

1. $2x + y = 3 \quad y = -2x + 3$
2. $-x + 3y = -6 \quad y = \frac{1}{3}x - 2$
3. $4x - 2y = 8 \quad y = 2x - 4$
4. Generate ordered pairs for $y = \frac{1}{2}x + 1$ using $x = -4, -2, 0, 2,$ and 4. $(-4, -1), (-2, 0), (0, 1), (2, 2), (4, 3)$

Also available on transparency

Math Humor

Psychology Teacher: Can anyone use "dysfunction" in a sentence?
Math Student: I can! "Dysfunction" is really hard to graph.

4-4 Graphing Functions

Objectives
Graph functions given a limited domain.
Graph functions given a domain of all real numbers.

Who uses this?
Scientists can use a function to make conclusions about rising sea level.

Sea level is rising at an approximate rate of 2.5 millimeters per year. If this rate continues, the function $y = 2.5x$ can describe how many millimeters y sea level will rise in the next x years.

One way to understand functions such as the one above is to graph them. You can graph a function by finding ordered pairs that satisfy the function.

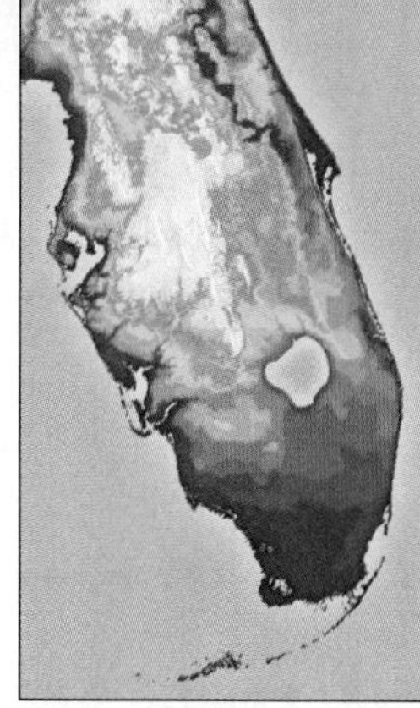
Current Florida coastline.

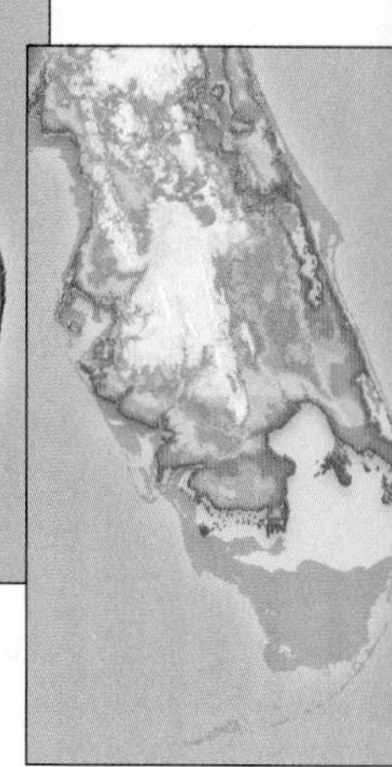
Possible Florida coastline in 2400 years.

EXAMPLE 1 Graphing Solutions Given a Domain

Graph each function for the given domain.

A $-x + 2y = 6$; D: $\{-4, -2, 0, 2\}$

Step 1 Solve for y since you are given values of the domain, or x.

$$-x + 2y = 6$$
$$\underline{+x \qquad\quad +x}$$ *Add x to both sides.*
$$2y = x + 6$$
$$\frac{2y}{2} = \frac{x+6}{2}$$ *Since y is multiplied by 2, divide both sides by 2.*
$$y = \frac{x}{2} + \frac{6}{2}$$ *Rewrite $\frac{x+6}{2}$ as two separate fractions.*
$$y = \frac{1}{2}x + 3$$ *Simplify.*

Helpful Hint
Sometimes solving for y first makes it easier to substitute values of x and find an ordered pair.
To review solving for a variable, see Lesson 2-5.

Step 2 Substitute the given values of the domain for x and find values of y.

x	$y = \frac{1}{2}x + 3$	(x, y)
−4	$y = \frac{1}{2}(-4) + 3 = 1$	$(-4, 1)$
−2	$y = \frac{1}{2}(-2) + 3 = 2$	$(-2, 2)$
0	$y = \frac{1}{2}(0) + 3 = 3$	$(0, 3)$
2	$y = \frac{1}{2}(2) + 3 = 4$	$(2, 4)$

Step 3 Graph the ordered pairs.

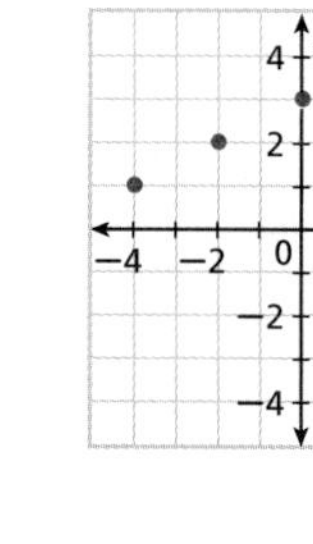

1 Introduce

EXPLORATION

4-4 Graphing Functions

You can use a calculator to graph ordered pairs that satisfy a function.

1. Complete the table for the function $y = 3x - 2$.

x	−1	0	1	2	3
y					

2. Enter the ordered pairs into your calculator as follows. Press STAT and select **1:Edit.** Then enter the x-values under **L1** and enter the corresponding y-values under **L2.**
3. To graph the ordered pairs, press 2nd Y= and select **1:Plot1.** Then select **On** and press ENTER. To display the graph, press GRAPH.

THINK AND DISCUSS

4. **Describe** the graph.
5. **Explain** how you could graph another ordered pair that satisfies the function.

Motivate

Display the following graph:

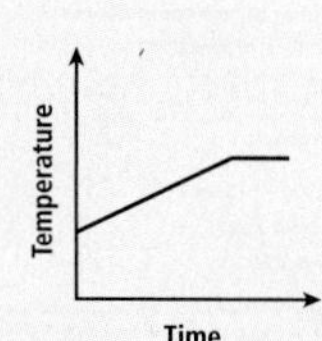

1. Describe the graph.
Possible answer: The temperature increases and then remains constant.
2. Can you determine what the temperature will be after 3 hours? If so, what is it? cannot be determined

Explorations and answers are provided in *Alternate Openers: Explorations Transparencies.*

State Resources

go.hrw.com
State Resources Online
KEYWORD: MA7 Resources

Graph each function for the given domain.

B $f(x) = |x|$; D: $\{-2, -1, 0, 1, 2\}$

Step 1 Use the given values of the domain to find values of $f(x)$.

x	$f(x) = \|x\|$	$(x, f(x))$
−2	$f(x) = \|-2\| = 2$	(−2, 2)
−1	$f(x) = \|-1\| = 1$	(−1, 1)
0	$f(x) = \|0\| = 0$	(0, 0)
1	$f(x) = \|1\| = 1$	(1, 1)
2	$f(x) = \|2\| = 2$	(2, 2)

Step 2 Graph the ordered pairs.

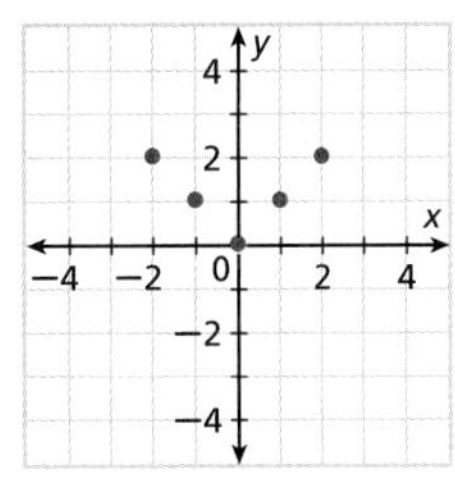

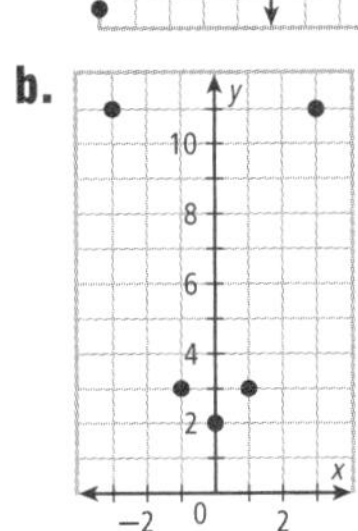

1a.

b.

Graph each function for the given domain.

1a. $-2x + y = 3$; D: $\{-5, -3, 1, 4\}$

1b. $f(x) = x^2 + 2$; D: $\{-3, -1, 0, 1, 3\}$

If the domain of a function is all real numbers, any number can be used as an input value. This process will produce an infinite number of ordered pairs that satisfy the function. Therefore, arrowheads are drawn at both "ends" of a smooth line or curve to represent the infinite number of ordered pairs. If a domain is not given, assume that the domain is all real numbers.

Graphing Functions Using a Domain of All Real Numbers	
Step 1	Use the function to generate ordered pairs by choosing several values for x.
Step 2	Plot enough points to see a pattern for the graph.
Step 3	Connect the points with a line or smooth curve.

EXAMPLE 2 Graphing Functions

Graph each function.

A $2x + 1 = y$

Step 1 Choose several values of x and generate ordered pairs.

x	$2x + 1 = y$	(x, y)
−3	$2(-3) + 1 = -5$	(−3, −5)
−2	$2(-2) + 1 = -3$	(−2, −3)
−1	$2(-1) + 1 = -1$	(−1, −1)
0	$2(0) + 1 = 1$	(0, 1)
1	$2(1) + 1 = 3$	(1, 3)
2	$2(2) + 1 = 5$	(2, 5)
3	$2(3) + 1 = 7$	(3, 7)

Step 2 Plot enough points to see a pattern.

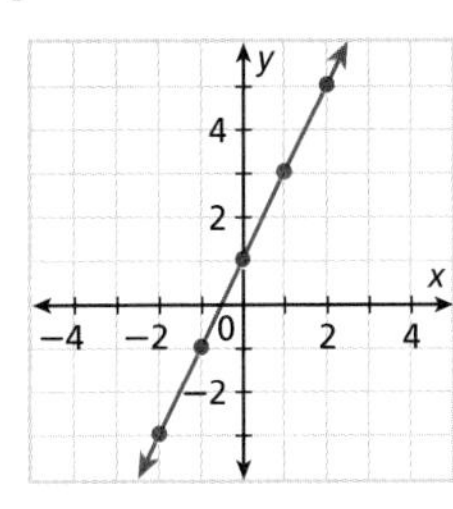

Helpful Hint

When choosing values of x, be sure to choose both positive and negative values. You may not need to graph all the points to see the pattern.

Step 3 The ordered pairs appear to form a line. Draw a line through all the points to show all the ordered pairs that satisfy the function. Draw arrowheads on both "ends" of the line.

2 Teach

Guided Instruction

Be sure students can solve for y and graph ordered pairs before beginning this lesson. Point out that graphing a function with given values for the domain will yield distinct points, while graphing a function using all real numbers yields a continuous graph. This is shown by arrows on the graphs of continuous functions. Stress the importance of choosing several points (positive, negative, and zero values) when graphing to determine the pattern.

Reaching All Learners

Through Modeling

The function $y = 2.5x$ describes the mass in grams of a stack of x pennies minted after 1982. Have students create a table of values and graph the function.

Obtain a scale (in grams) and several pennies (post-1982). Ask students to use their graph to predict the mass of a given number of pennies.

Measure the mass of the pennies to check the answers given. Repeat with a different number of pennies.

Power Presentations with PowerPoint®

Additional Examples

Example 1

Graph each function for the given domain.

A. $x - 3y = -6$; D: $\{-3, 0, 3, 6\}$

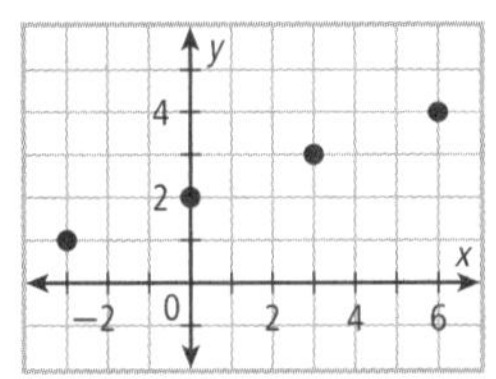

B. $f(x) = x^2 - 3$; D: $\{-2, -1, 0, 1, 2\}$

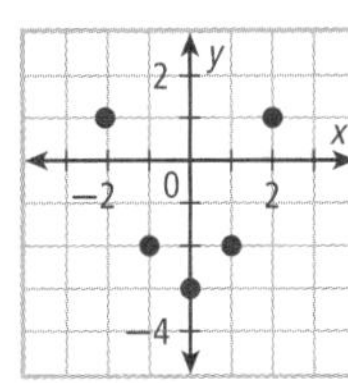

Example 2

Graph each function.

A. $-3x + 2 = y$

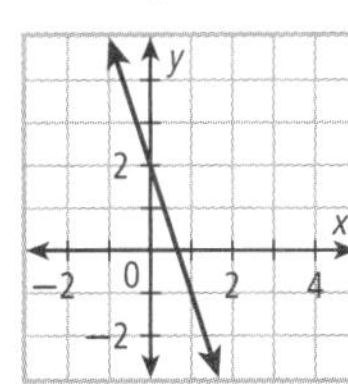

B. $g(x) = |x| + 2$

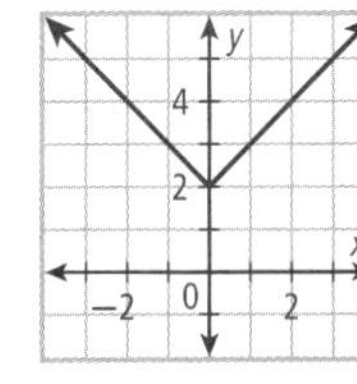

INTERVENTION

Questioning Strategies

EXAMPLE 1

- What is a benefit to solving for y when graphing a function?
- When creating the table, what did you notice about the y-values relative to the x-values?

EXAMPLE 2

- What is the difference between this example and **Example 1**?

Power Presentations with PowerPoint®

Additional Examples

Example 3

Use a graph of the function $f(x) = -\frac{1}{2}x + 4$ to find the value of $f(x)$ when $x = -4$. Check your answer. $f(-4) = 6$

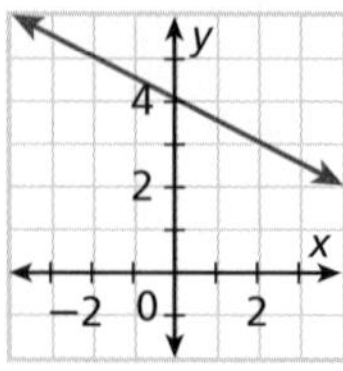

Example 4

A mouse can run 3.5 meters per second. The function $y = 3.5x$ describes the distance in meters the mouse can run in x seconds. Graph the function. Use the graph to estimate how many meters a mouse can run in 2.5 seconds. about 8.75 meters

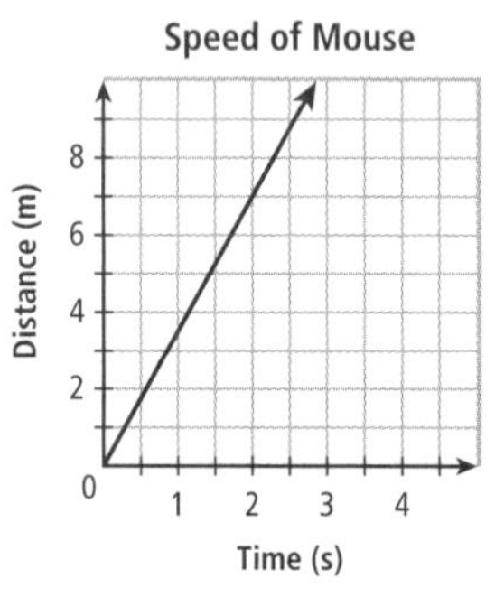

INTERVENTION
Questioning Strategies

EXAMPLE 3

- Can the graph be used to find the value of y if x is a fractional number? Explain.

EXAMPLE 4

- If you wanted an exact answer, what could you do?

Graph each function.

B $y = x^2$

Step 1 Choose several values of x and generate ordered pairs.

x	$y = x^2$	(x, y)
-3	$y = (-3)^2 = 9$	$(-3, 9)$
-2	$y = (-2)^2 = 4$	$(-2, 4)$
-1	$y = (-1)^2 = 1$	$(-1, 1)$
0	$y = (0)^2 = 0$	$(0, 0)$
1	$y = (1)^2 = 1$	$(1, 1)$
2	$y = (2)^2 = 4$	$(2, 4)$

Step 2 **Plot enough points** to see a pattern.

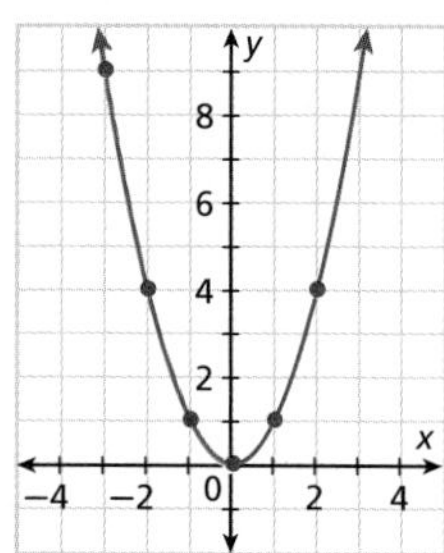

Step 3 The ordered pairs appear to form an almost U-shaped graph. **Draw a smooth curve** through the points to show all the ordered pairs that satisfy the function. Draw arrowheads on the "ends" of the curve.

Check If the graph is correct, any point on it will satisfy the function. Choose an ordered pair on the graph that was not in your table, such as $(3, 9)$. Check whether it satisfies $y = x^2$.

y	$= x^2$	
9	3^2	*Substitute the values for x and y into the function. Simplify.*
9	9 ✓	*The ordered pair (3, 9) satisfies the function.*

2a. [graph]

2b. [graph]

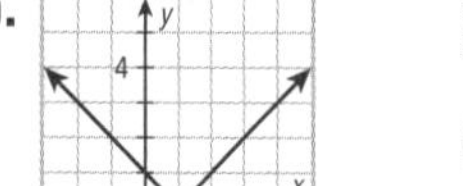

CHECK IT OUT! Graph each function.

2a. $f(x) = 3x - 2$ **2b.** $y = |x - 1|$

EXAMPLE 3 Finding Values Using Graphs

Use a graph of the function $f(x) = \frac{1}{3}x + 2$ to find the value of $f(x)$ when $x = 6$. Check your answer.

Locate 6 on the x-axis. Move up to the graph of the function. Then move **left** to the y-axis to find the corresponding value of y.

$f(x) = 4$

Writing Math

"The value of y is 4 when $x = 6$" can also be written as $f(6) = 4$.

Check Use substitution.

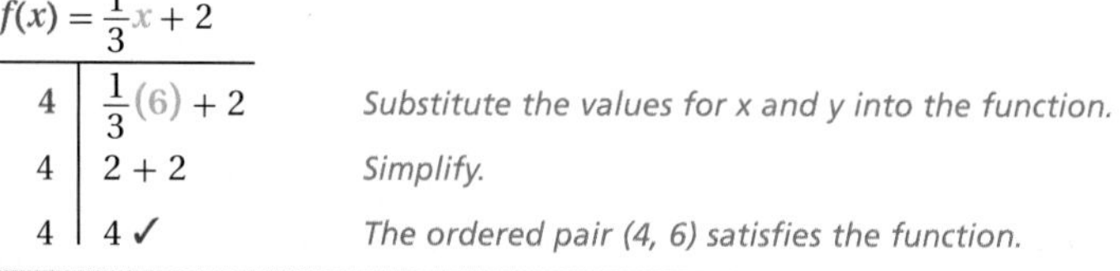

$f(x)$	$= \frac{1}{3}x + 2$	
4	$\frac{1}{3}(6) + 2$	*Substitute the values for x and y into the function.*
4	$2 + 2$	*Simplify.*
4	4 ✓	*The ordered pair (4, 6) satisfies the function.*

CHECK IT OUT! **3.** Use the graph above to find the value of x when $f(x) = 3$. Check your answer. **3**

Reaching All Learners
Through Multiple Representations

The period of revolution for Mars (compared to Earth) is approximately 1.88 Earth years. Have students find their age in Mars years by using the function $y = \frac{1}{1.88}x$ or $y = 0.5319x$, where y = age in Mars years and x = age in Earth years.

Have students create a table of values and graph the function. Use the graph to estimate various ages in Mars years.

Recall that in real-world situations you may have to limit the domain to make answers reasonable. For example, quantities such as time, distance, and number of people can be represented using only nonnegative values. When both the domain and the range are limited to nonnegative values, the function is graphed only in Quadrant I.

EXAMPLE  4 Problem-Solving Application

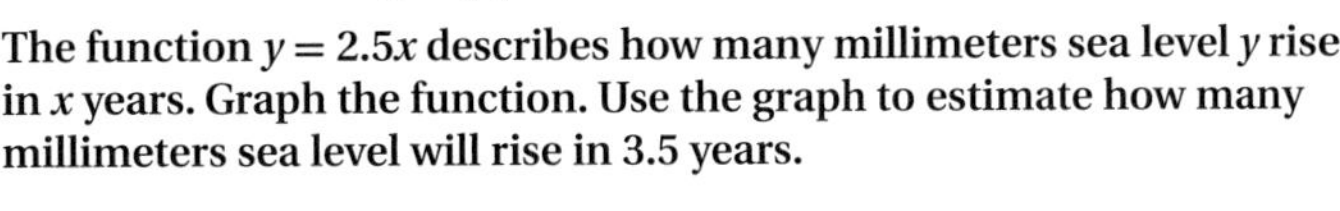

The function $y = 2.5x$ describes how many millimeters sea level y rises in x years. Graph the function. Use the graph to estimate how many millimeters sea level will rise in 3.5 years.

1 Understand the Problem

The **answer** is a graph that can be used to find the value of y when x is 3.5.

List the important information:

- The function $y = 2.5x$ describes how many millimeters sea level rises.

2 Make a Plan

Think: What values should I use to graph this function? Both, the number of years sea level has risen and the distance sea level rises, cannot be negative. Use only nonnegative values for both the domain and the range. The function will be graphed in Quadrant I.

 3 Solve

Choose several nonnegative values of x to find values of y. Then graph the ordered pairs.

x	$y = 2.5x$	(x, y)
0	$y = 2.5(0) = 0$	$(0, 0)$
1	$y = 2.5(1) = 2.5$	$(1, 2.5)$
2	$y = 2.5(2) = 5$	$(2, 5)$
3	$y = 2.5(3) = 7.5$	$(3, 7.5)$
4	$y = 2.5(4) = 10$	$(4, 10)$

Draw a line through the points to show all the ordered pairs that satisfy this function.

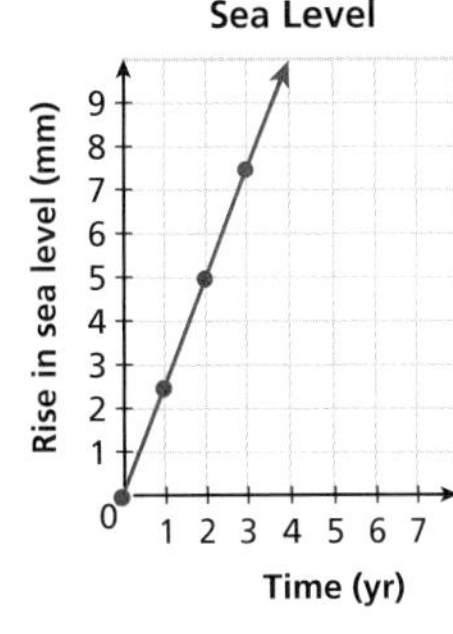

Use the graph to estimate the y-value when x is 3.5.
Sea level will rise about 8.75 millimeters in 3.5 years.

 4 Look Back

As the number of years increases, sea level also increases, so the graph is reasonable. When x is between 3 and 4, y is between 7.5 and 10. Since 3.5 is between 3 and 4, it is reasonable to estimate y to be 8.75 when x is 3.5.

4. The fastest recorded Hawaiian lava flow moved at an average speed of 6 miles per hour. The function $y = 6x$ describes the distance y the lava moved on average in x hours. Graph the function. Use the graph to estimate how many miles the lava moved after 5.5 hours.

4. Possible answer: about 32.5 mi

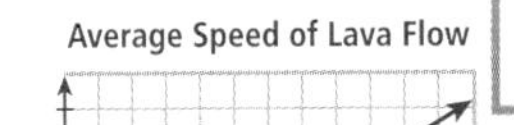

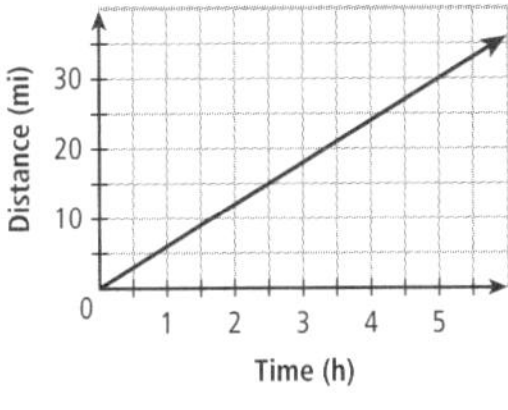

COMMON ERROR ALERT

In **Example 4,** students may simply evaluate the function for $x = 3.5$ rather than using the graph. Tell students that equations will become more complicated later, and they must learn to read values from a graph.

Teaching Tip **Inclusion** When graphing a function, suggest that students choose simple values for x, such as 0, 1, and 2. They should also be sure to choose negative values when the domain is all real numbers.

Teaching Tip **Critical Thinking** Discuss with students what negative values of x could represent. For example, if x represents time in years, lead them to see that an x-value of -2 could represent 2 years ago.

3 Close

Summarize

Have students name the steps for graphing a function. solve for y, choose points for x, generate ordered pairs, graph Remind students that the points are not connected when the domain is a finite set of values. The points are connected when the domain is the set of all real numbers. When not otherwise stated, the domain will be the set of real numbers.

ONGOING ASSESSMENT and INTERVENTION 

***Diagnose Before* the Lesson**
4-4 Warm Up, TE p. 256

***Monitor During* the Lesson**
Check It Out! Exercises, SE pp. 257–259
Questioning Strategies, TE pp. 257–259

***Assess After* the Lesson**
4-4 Lesson Quiz, TE p. 262
Alternative Assessment, TE p. 262

Answers to *Think and Discuss*

1. Possible answer: Graph the function by plotting points and connecting them with a line or smooth curve. Then use the graph to determine all possible values of *y* (the range).
2. Locate the given value on the *x*-axis. Move up or down to the graph, and then left or right to the *y*-axis to find the *y*-value.
3. See p. A4.

4-4 Exercises

Assignment Guide

Assign *Guided Practice* exercises as necessary.

If you finished Examples **1–2**
- **Basic** 13–24, 40–43
- **Average** 13–24, 45–47, 62
- **Advanced** 13–24, 45–47, 62

If you finished Examples **1–4**
- **Basic** 13–55, 58–61, 64–71
- **Average** 13–62, 64–71
- **Advanced** 13–43, 45–71

Homework Quick Check
Quickly check key concepts.
Exercises: 14, 22, 26, 27, 34, 50

Math Background
For **Exercise 10,** remind students that $-x^2$ is the same as $-(x^2)$.

Answers

1–10, 12–24. See pp. A17–A18.

State Resources

THINK AND DISCUSS

1. How do you find the range of a function if the domain is all real numbers?

2. Explain how to use a graph to find the value of a function for a given value of *x*.

3. GET ORGANIZED Copy and complete the graphic organizer. Explain how to graph a function for each situation.

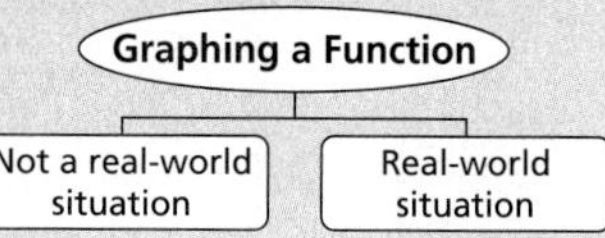

4-4 Exercises

GUIDED PRACTICE

SEE EXAMPLE 1 p. 256

Graph each function for the given domain.

1. $3x - y = 1$; D: $\{-3, -1, 0, 4\}$
2. $f(x) = -|x|$; D: $\{-5, -3, 0, 3, 5\}$
3. $f(x) = x + 4$; D: $\{-5, -3, 0, 4\}$
4. $y = x^2 - 1$; D: $\{-3, -1, 0, 1, 3\}$

SEE EXAMPLE 2 p. 257

Graph each function.

5. $f(x) = 6x + 4$
6. $y = \frac{1}{2}x + 4$
7. $x + y = 0$
8. $y = |x| - 4$
9. $f(x) = 2x^2 - 7$
10. $y = -x^2 + 5$

SEE EXAMPLE 3 p. 258

11. Use a graph of the function $f(x) = \frac{1}{2}x - 2$ to find the value of *y* when $x = 2$. Check your answer. $y = -1$

SEE EXAMPLE 4 p. 259

12. **Oceanography** The floor of the Atlantic Ocean is spreading at an average rate of 1 inch per year. The function $y = x$ describes the number of inches *y* the ocean floor spreads in *x* years. Graph the function. Use the graph to estimate the number of inches the ocean floor will spread in $10\frac{1}{2}$ years.

PRACTICE AND PROBLEM SOLVING

Independent Practice

For Exercises	See Example
13–16	1
17–24	2
25–26	3
27	4

Extra Practice
Skills Practice p. S12
Application Practice p. S31

Graph each function for the given domain.

13. $2x + y = 4$; D: $\{-3, -1, 4, 7\}$
14. $y = |x| - 1$; D: $\{-4, -2, 0, 2, 4\}$
15. $f(x) = -7x$; D: $\{-2, -1, 0, 1\}$
16. $y = (x + 1)^2$; D: $\{-2, -1, 0, 1, 2\}$

Graph each function.

17. $y = -3x + 5$
18. $f(x) = 3x$
19. $x + y = 8$
20. $f(x) = 2x + 2$
21. $y = -|x| + 10$
22. $f(x) = -5 + x^2$
23. $y = |x + 1| + 1$
24. $y = (x - 2)^2 - 1$
25. Use a graph of the function $f(x) = -2x - 3$ to find the value of *y* when $x = -4$. Check your answer. $y = 5$
26. Use a graph of the function $f(x) = \frac{1}{3}x + 1$ to find the value of *y* when $x = 6$. Check your answer. $y = 3$

4-4 READING STRATEGIES

Whether graphing a function with a limited domain, or a domain of all real numbers, the procedure is almost the same. The steps of the procedure are listed below and shown in the following example.

Step 1: Create a three-column table headed "x", "$f(x)$", and "$(x, f(x))$".
Step 2: Write the given or chosen domain values in the "x" column.
Step 3: Substitute the domain values into the function and evaluate for $f(x)$.
Step 4: Write corresponding x- and $f(x)$-values as ordered pairs.
Step 5: Plot the ordered pairs on a coordinate grid.
Step 6: If the domain is all real numbers, connect the points with a smooth line/curve and put arrows on both ends.

Graph the function $f(x) = |x - 2|$.

x	$f(x)$	$(x, f(x))$
6	$\lvert 6-2\rvert = \lvert 4\rvert = 4$	(6, 4)
4	$\lvert 4-2\rvert = \lvert 2\rvert = 2$	(4, 2)
2	$\lvert 2-2\rvert = \lvert 0\rvert = 0$	(2, 0)
0	$\lvert 0-2\rvert = \lvert -2\rvert = 2$	(0, 2)
−2	$\lvert -2-2\rvert = \lvert -4\rvert = 4$	(−2, 4)

Step1 Step2 Step3 Step4 Step5 Step6

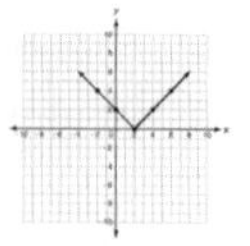

Graph each function using the procedure shown above.

1. $f(x) = x^2 - 8$; D: $\{-4, -2, 0, 2, 4\}$

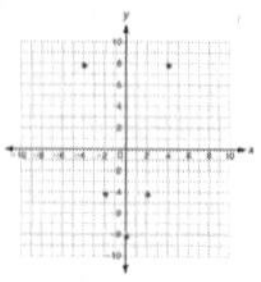

2. $f(x) = -2x + 3$

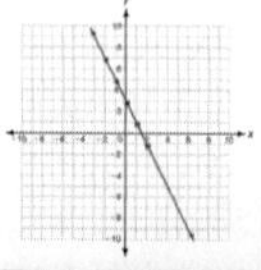

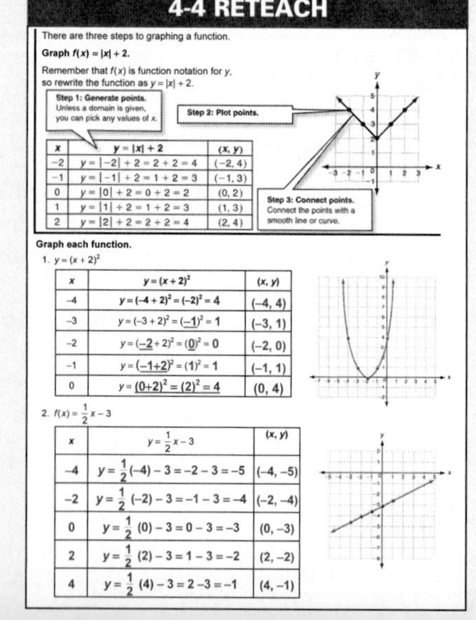

4-4 RETEACH

There are three steps to graphing a function.

Graph $f(x) = |x| + 2$.

Remember that $f(x)$ is function notation for y, so rewrite the function as $y = |x| + 2$.

Step 1: Generate points. Unless a domain is given, you can pick any values of x.

Step 2: Plot points.

x	$y = \lvert x\rvert + 2$	(x, y)
−2	$y = \lvert -2\rvert + 2 = 2 + 2 = 4$	(−2, 4)
−1	$y = \lvert -1\rvert + 2 = 1 + 2 = 3$	(−1, 3)
0	$y = \lvert 0\rvert + 2 = 0 + 2 = 2$	(0, 2)
1	$y = \lvert 1\rvert + 2 = 1 + 2 = 3$	(1, 3)
2	$y = \lvert 2\rvert + 2 = 2 + 2 = 4$	(2, 4)

Step 3: Connect points. Connect the points with a smooth line or curve.

Graph each function.

1. $y = (x + 2)^2$

x	$y = (x + 2)^2$	(x, y)
−4	$y = (-4 + 2)^2 = (-2)^2 = 4$	(−4, 4)
−3	$y = (-3 + 2)^2 = (-1)^2 = 1$	(−3, 1)
−2	$y = (-2 + 2)^2 = (0)^2 = 0$	(−2, 0)
−1	$y = (-1 + 2)^2 = (1)^2 = 1$	(−1, 1)
0	$y = (0 + 2)^2 = (2)^2 = 4$	(0, 4)

2. $f(x) = \frac{1}{2}x - 3$

x	$y = \frac{1}{2}x - 3$	(x, y)
−4	$y = \frac{1}{2}(-4) - 3 = -2 - 3 = -5$	(−4, −5)
−2	$y = \frac{1}{2}(-2) - 3 = -1 - 3 = -4$	(−2, −4)
0	$y = \frac{1}{2}(0) - 3 = 0 - 3 = -3$	(0, −3)
2	$y = \frac{1}{2}(2) - 3 = 1 - 3 = -2$	(2, −2)
4	$y = \frac{1}{2}(4) - 3 = 2 - 3 = -1$	(4, −1)

27. Transportation An electric motor scooter can travel at 0.25 miles per minute. The function $y = 0.25x$ describes the number of miles y the scooter can travel in x minutes. Graph the function. Use the graph to estimate the number of miles an electric motor scooter travels in 15 minutes.

Graph each function.

28. $f(x) = x - 1$ **29.** $12 - x - 2y = 0$ **30.** $3x - y = 13$

31. $y = x^2 - 2$ **32.** $x^2 - y = -4$ **33.** $2x^2 = f(x)$

34. $f(x) = |2x| - 2$ **35.** $y = |-x|$ **36.** $-|2x + 1| = y$

37. Find the value of x so that $(x, 12)$ satisfies $y = 4x + 8$. **1**

38. Find the value of x so that $(x, 6)$ satisfies $y = -x - 4$. **−10**

39. Find the value of y so that $(-2, y)$ satisfies $y = -2x^2$. **−8**

For each function, determine whether the given points are on the graph.

40. $y = 7x - 2$; $(1, 5)$ and $(2, 10)$ **yes; no** **41.** $y = |x| + 2$; $(3, 5)$ and $(-1, 3)$ **yes; yes**

42. $y = x^2$; $(1, 1)$ and $(-3, -9)$ **yes; no** **43.** $y = \frac{1}{4}x - 2$; $\left(1, -\frac{3}{4}\right)$ and $(4, -1)$ **no; yes**

44. ERROR ANALYSIS Student A says that $(3, 2)$ is on the graph of $y = 4x - 5$, but student B says that it is not. Who is incorrect? Explain the error.

Student A; student A substituted the coordinates of the ordered pair incorrectly, and student B substituted them correctly.

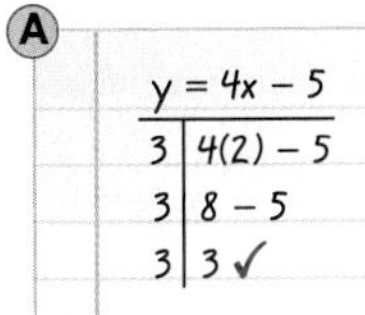
A

	$y = 4x - 5$
3	$4(2) - 5$
3	$8 - 5$
3	3 ✓

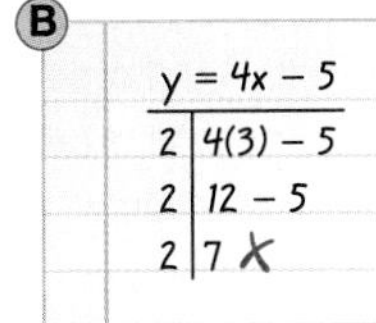
B

	$y = 4x - 5$
2	$4(3) - 5$
2	$12 - 5$
2	7 ✗

Determine whether $(0, -7)$, $\left(-6, -\frac{5}{3}\right)$, and $(-2, -3)$ lie on the graph of each function.

45. $x + 3y = -11$ **no; yes; yes** **46.** $y + |x| = -1$ **no; no; yes** **47.** $x^2 - y = 7$ **yes; no; yes**

For each function, find three ordered pairs that lie on the graph of the function.

48. $-6 = 3x + 2y$ **49.** $y = 1.1x + 2$

50. $y = \frac{4}{5}x$ **51.** $y = 3x - 1$

52. $y = |x| + 6$ **53.** $y = x^2 - 5$

54. Critical Thinking Graph the functions $y = |x|$ and $y = -|x|$. Describe how they are alike. How are they different?

54. Possible answer: The graphs are alike because they are both V shaped. They are different because the graph of $y = |x|$ opens upward and the graph of $y = -|x|$ opens downward.

MULTI-STEP TEST PREP

55. This problem will prepare you for the Multi-Step Test Prep on page 264.

A pool containing 10,000 gallons of water is being drained. Every hour, the volume of the water in the pool decreases by 1500 gallons.

a. Write an equation to describe the volume v of water in the pool after h hours.

b. How much water is in the pool after 1 hour?

c. Create a table of values showing the volume of the water in gallons in the pool as a function of the time in hours and graph the function.

Exercise 55 involves writing an equation and creating a table of values. This exercise prepares students for the Multi-Step Test Prep on page 264.

Answers

27. about 3.75 mi

Electric Scooter Mileage

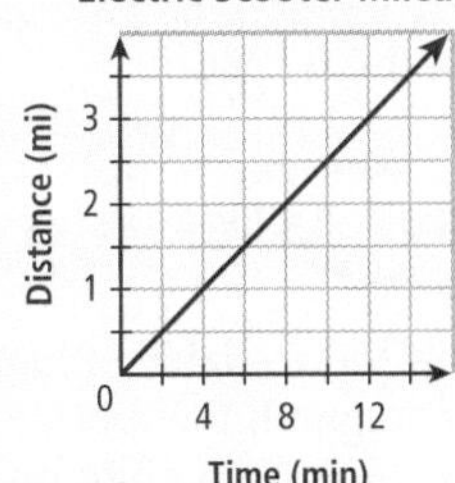

28–36. See p. A18.

48–53. Possible answers given.

48. $(0, -3)$, $(-2, 0)$, $(2, -6)$

49. $(0, 2)$, $(1, 3.1)$, $(-1, 0.9)$

50. $(0, 0)$, $\left(1, \frac{4}{5}\right)$, $\left(-1, -\frac{4}{5}\right)$

51. $(0, -1)$, $(1, 2)$, $(-2, -7)$

52. $(0, 6)$, $(1, 7)$, $(2, 8)$

53. $(0, -5)$, $(1, -4)$, $(-1, -4)$

55. See p. A18.

4-4 PROBLEM SOLVING

In 1998, Hurricane Bonnie approached the United States at a speed of 8 miles per hour. The function $y = 8x$ describes how many miles y Hurricane Bonnie traveled in x hours.

1. Complete the table by generating ordered pairs.

x	$y = 8x$	(x, y)
0	0	(0, 0)
1	8	(1, 8)
2	16	(2, 16)
3	24	(3, 24)
4	32	(4, 32)

2. Graph the function $y = 8x$.

Hurricane Bonnie

3. Use the graph to estimate how far Hurricane Bonnie traveled in 3.5 hours.

28 miles

Select the correct answer.

4. The graph below shows the relation between the cost of an item and the sales tax due. Which function is graphed below?

Sales Tax

A $y = \frac{6}{x}$ C $y = \frac{x}{6}$

B $y = 0.06x$ D $y = 6x$

5. The graph below shows the relation between Jeremy's age and the number of times per year he refused to eat his brussel sprouts. Which function is graphed for the domain {1, 2, 3, 4, 5}?

Brussel Sprouts

F $y = 30 - x$ **H** $y = 30 - x^2$

G $y = x + 28$ J $y = 29x$

4-4 CHALLENGE

When the output of one function is used as the input of another, you have a **composition of functions.** The notation $f(g(x))$ means you input x into function g, and then use that output as the input for function f.

For 1–5, use the functions $f(x) = x^2 - 4$ and $g(x) = -2x$.

1. Use this table to find $f(g(x))$ for each x-value.

x	$g(x) = -2x$	$g(x)$	$f(x) = x^2 - 4$	$f(g(x))$
−2	$g(-2) = -2(-2) = 4$	4	$f(4) = 4^2 - 4 = 16 - 4 = 12$	12
	$g(-1) = -2(-1) = 2$	2	$f(2) = 2^2 - 4 = 4 - 4 = 0$	0
	$g(0) = -2(0) = 0$	0	$f(0) = 0^2 - 4 = 0 - 4 = -4$	−4
	$g(1) = -2(1) = -2$	−2	$f(-2) = (-2)^2 - 4 = 4 - 4 = 0$	0
	$g(2) = -2(2) = -4$	−4	$f(-4) = (-4)^2 - 4 = 16 - 4 = 12$	12

2. Use the first and last columns of the table to graph the function $y = f(g(x))$. Connect the points with a smooth curve.

Here is the algebra to find a "one-step" rule for $y = f(g(x))$.

$y = f(g(x))$ *Write the composite function.*

$y = f(-2x)$ *Because $g(x) = -2x$, substitute $-2x$ for $g(x)$.*

$y = (-2x)^2 - 4$ *Substitute $-2x$ for x in $f(x) = x^2 - 4$.*

$y = 4x^2 - 4$ *Simplify the power: $(-2x)^2 = (-2x)(-2x) = (-2)(-2)(x)(x) = 4x^2$.*

3. Use a similar process to find a one-step rule for $y = g(f(x))$.

$y = -2x^2 + 8$

4. Complete the table below for $y = g(f(x))$. Then graph the function. Use the same coordinate plane at right.

x	$y = g(f(x)) = -2x^2 + 8$	$(x, g(f(x)))$
−2	$g(f(-2)) = -2(-2)^2 + 8 = -8 + 8 = 0$	(−2, 0)
−1	$g(f(-1)) = -2(-1)^2 + 8 = -2 + 8 = 6$	(−1, 6)
0	$g(f(0)) = -2(0)^2 + 8 = 0 + 8 = 8$	(0, 8)
1	$g(f(1)) = -2(1)^2 + 8 = -2 + 8 = 6$	(1, 6)
2	$g(f(2)) = -2(2)^2 + 8 = -8 + 8 = 0$	(2, 0)

5. Is $f(g(x))$ the same as $g(f(x))$? No

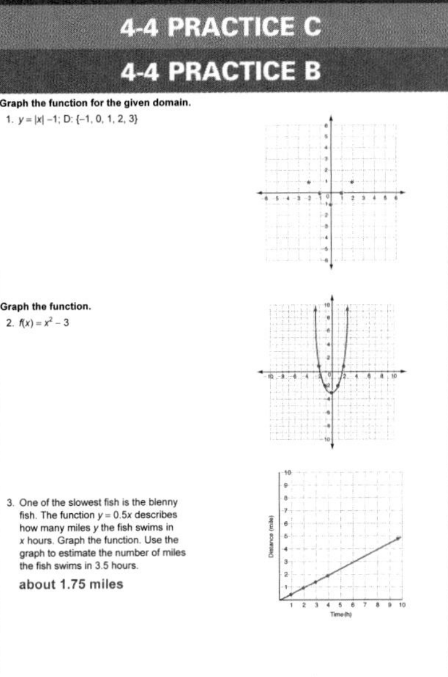

4-4 PRACTICE A

4-4 PRACTICE C

4-4 PRACTICE B

Graph the function for the given domain.

1. $y = |x| - 1$; D: {−1, 0, 1, 2, 3}

Graph the function.

2. $f(x) = x^2 - 3$

3. One of the slowest fish is the blenny fish. The function $y = 0.5x$ describes how many miles y the fish swims in x hours. Graph the function. Use the graph to estimate the number of miles the fish swims in 3.5 hours.

about 1.75 miles

TEST PREP DOCTOR In **Exercise 61,** if statement **I** is true, then statement **III** must also be true. Students who chose **H** may have confused the x- and y-axes.

Journal

Use $y = x^2 + 1$ to explain how you choose points when graphing a function. Graph the function.

ALTERNATIVE ASSESSMENT

Create a function, write a table of four ordered pairs, and graph the function. Write an ordered pair for a point on the graph that is not included in the table.

Power Presentations with PowerPoint®

4-4 Lesson Quiz

1. Graph the function for the given domain.
$3x + y = 4$; D: $\{-1, 0, 1, 2\}$

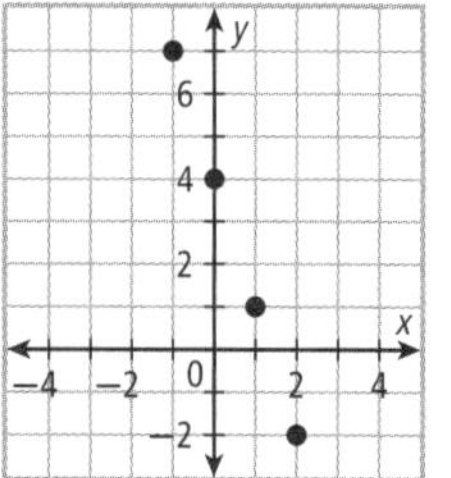

2. Graph the function
$y = |x + 3|$.

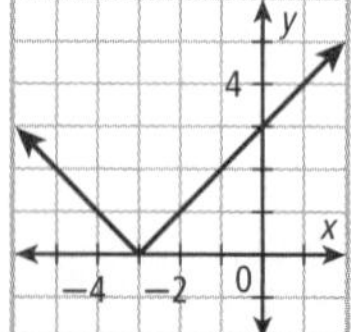

3. The function $y = 3x$ describes the distance (in inches) a giant tortoise walks in x seconds. Graph the function. Use the graph to estimate how many inches the tortoise will walk in 5.5 seconds.
about 16.5 in.

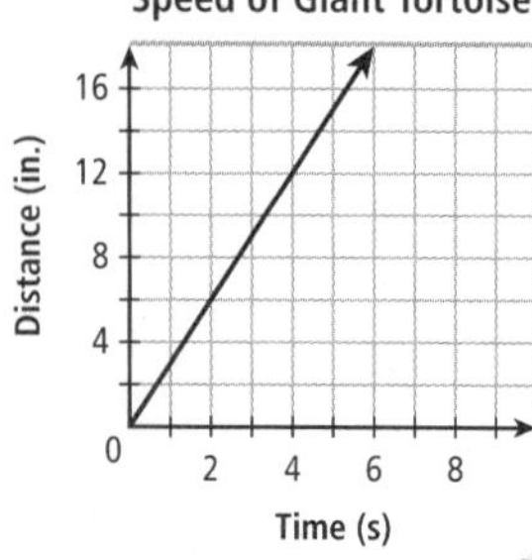

Also available on transparency

56. **Estimation** Use the graph to estimate the value of y when $x = 2.117$. $y \approx -2$

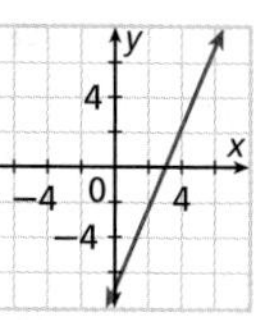

57. **Write About It** Why is a graph a convenient way to show the ordered pairs that satisfy a function?
A graph can represent all ordered pairs that satisfy a function, even when there are infinitely many.

TEST PREP

58. Which function is graphed?
Ⓐ $2y - 3x = 2$ (circled)　Ⓒ $y = 2x - 1$
Ⓑ $5x + y = 1$　Ⓓ $y = 5x + 8$

59. Which ordered pair is NOT on the graph of $y = 4 - |x|$?
Ⓕ $(0, 4)$　Ⓗ $(-1, 3)$
Ⓖ $(4, 0)$　Ⓙ $(3, -1)$ (circled)

60. Which function has $(3, 2)$ on its graph?
Ⓐ $2x - 3y = 12$　Ⓒ $y = -\frac{2}{3}x + 4$ (circled)
Ⓑ $-2x - 3y = 12$　Ⓓ $y = -\frac{3}{2}x + 4$

61. Which statement(s) is true about the function $y = x^2 + 1$?
I. All points on the graph are above the origin.
II. All ordered pairs have positive x-values.
III. All ordered pairs have positive y-values.
Ⓕ I Only　Ⓖ II Only　Ⓗ I and II　Ⓙ I and III (circled)

CHALLENGE AND EXTEND

62. Graph the function $y = x^3$. Make sure you have enough ordered pairs to see the shape of the graph.

63. The temperature of a liquid that started at 64 °F is increasing by 4 °F per hour. Write a function that describes the temperature of the liquid over time. Graph the function to show the temperatures over the first 10 hours.

SPIRAL REVIEW

Write the power represented by each geometric model. *(Lesson 1-4)*

64. 3^2

65. 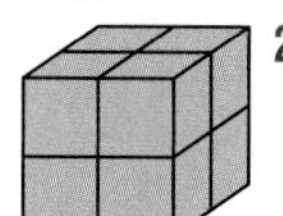 2^3

66. 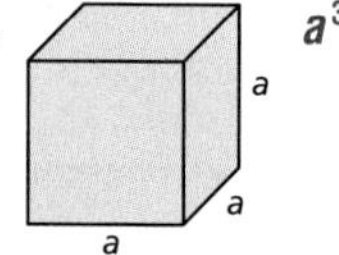 a^3

Solve each inequality and graph the solutions. *(Lesson 3-3)*

67. $5p < -20$ $p < -4$
68. $18 > -9k$ $k > -2$
69. $\frac{3}{4}b \geq 15$ $b \geq 20$

Evaluate each function for the given input values. *(Lesson 4-3)*

70. For $f(x) = -2x - 3$, find $f(x)$ when $x = -4$ and when $x = 2$. **5; −7**

71. For $h(t) = \frac{2}{3}t + 1$, find $h(t)$ when $t = -6$ and when $t = 9$. **−3; 7**

Answers

62.

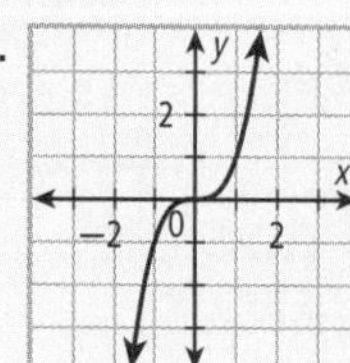

63. $y = 4x + 64$

Liquid Temperature
(Temperature (°F) vs. Time (h))

4-4 Technology LAB

Connect Function Rules, Tables, and Graphs

You can use a graphing calculator to understand the connections among function rules, tables, and graphs.

Use with Lesson 4-4

go.hrw.com
Lab Resources Online
KEYWORD: MA7 Lab4

Activity

Make a table of values for the function $f(x) = 4x + 3$. Then graph the function.

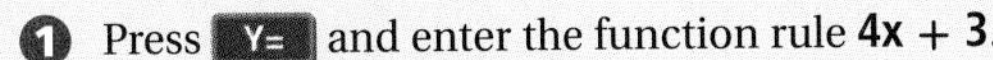

1. Press Y= and enter the function rule **4x + 3**.

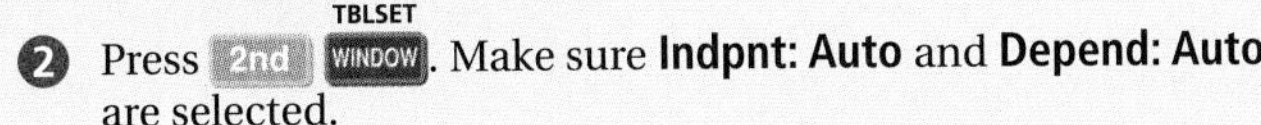

2. Press 2nd WINDOW (TBLSET). Make sure **Indpnt: Auto** and **Depend: Auto** are selected.

TABLE SETUP
TblStart=1
ΔTbl=1
Indpnt: Auto Ask
Depend: Auto Ask

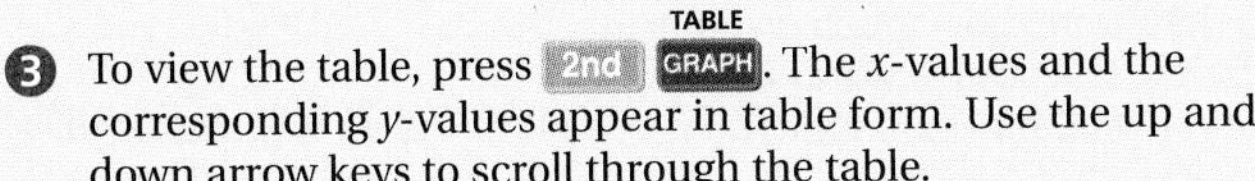

3. To view the table, press 2nd GRAPH (TABLE). The x-values and the corresponding y-values appear in table form. Use the up and down arrow keys to scroll through the table.

X	Y1
1	7
2	11
3	15
4	19
5	23
6	27
7	31

X=3

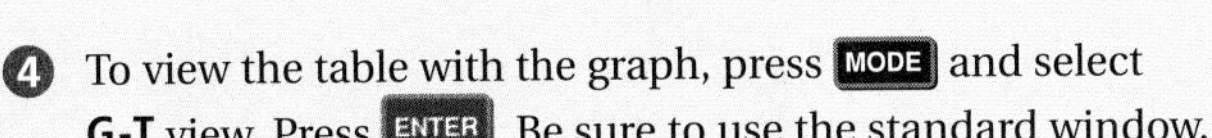

4. To view the table with the graph, press MODE and select **G-T** view. Press ENTER. Be sure to use the standard window.

5. Press TRACE to see both the graph and a table of values.
6. Press the left arrow key several times to move the cursor. Notice that the point on the graph and the values in the table correspond.

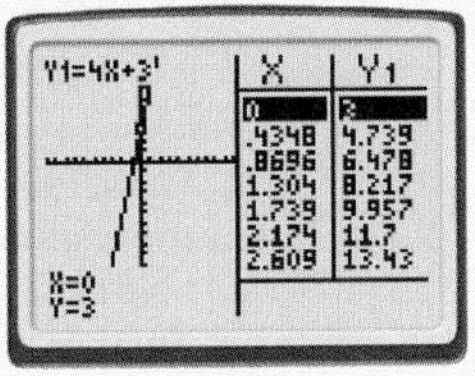

X	Y1
0	3
.4348	4.739
.8696	6.478
1.304	8.217
1.739	9.957
2.174	11.7
2.609	13.43

Try This

Make a table of values for each function. Then graph the function.

1. $f(x) = 2x - 1$
2. $f(x) = 1.5x$
3. $f(x) = \frac{1}{2}x + 2$
4. Explain the relationship between a function, its table of values, and the graph of the function.

The table of values and graph of the function show ordered pairs that satisfy the function.

Technology LAB Organizer

Use with Lesson 4-4

Pacing:
Traditional $\frac{1}{2}$ day
Block $\frac{1}{4}$ day

Objective: Use a graphing calculator to make the connections among equations, tables, and graphs.

Materials: Graphing calculator

PREMIER **Online Edition**
Graphing Calculator

Countdown Week 9

Resources

Technology Lab Activities
4-4 Lab Recording Sheet

Teach

Discuss

Point out to students that all pairs of decimal values in the table are also ordered pairs.

Close

Key Concept

Equations, tables, and graphs can represent the same ordered pairs in different formats.

Assessment

Journal Create a function rule. Make a table of function values and list three ordered pairs. Then graph the ordered pairs and sketch the line or curve.

State Resources

Answers to *Try This*

1.

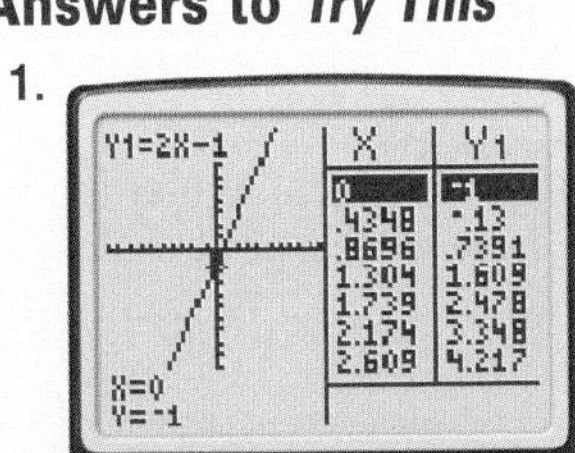

X	Y1
0	-1
.4348	-.13
.8696	.7391
1.304	1.609
1.739	2.478
2.174	3.348
2.609	4.217

2.

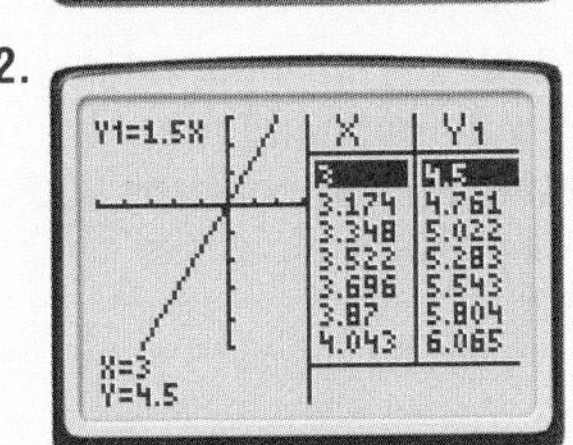

X	Y1
3	4.5
3.174	4.761
3.348	5.022
3.522	5.283
3.696	5.543
3.87	5.804
4.043	6.065

3.

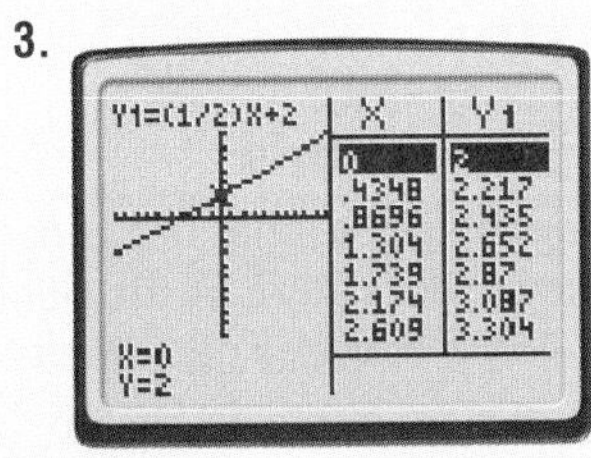

X	Y1
0	2
.4348	2.217
.8696	2.435
1.304	2.652
1.739	2.87
2.174	3.087
2.609	3.304

Teaching Tip

Technology Point out to students that **TblStart** defines the x-value at which the table values start and that **ΔTbl** defines the increment at which the x-values increase. Have students change these values if they are not already set to 1.

Organizer

Objective: Assess students' ability to apply concepts and skills in Lessons 4-1 through 4-4 in a real-world format.

Resources

Algebra I Assessments
www.mathtekstoolkit.org

Problem	Text Reference
1	Lesson 4-1
2	Lesson 4-2
3	Lesson 4-4
4	Lesson 4-4
5	Lesson 4-3

State Resources

CHAPTER 4

MULTI-STEP TEST PREP

SECTION 4A

Function Concepts

Down the Drain The graph shows the relationship between the number of hours that have passed since a pool began to drain and the amount of water in the pool.

Pool Draining
(Graph: Volume (gal) 200–1400 vs. Time (h) 1–8)

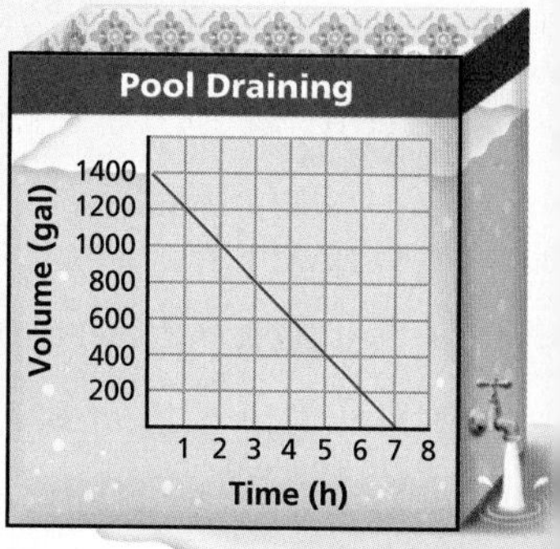

1. Describe in words the relationship between the amount of water in the pool and the number of hours that have passed since the pool began to drain.
2. What are the domain and range for the graph?
3. Use the graph to determine how much water is in the pool after 3 hours. How much water is in the pool after $4\frac{1}{2}$ hours? **800 gal; 500 gal**
4. Copy and complete the table.

2. $0 \le t \le 7$; $0 \le v \le 1400$

Draining Pool	
Time (h)	Volume (gal)
0	1400
1	1200
2	1000
3	800
4	600
5	400
6	200
7	0

5. Write an equation to describe the relationship between the volume v and the time t. Use the equation to find how much water is in the pool after 5.2 hours.
$v = 1400 - 200t$; 360 gal

1. Possible answer: The pool begins with 1400 gallons. As time goes on, the volume of water decreases by 200 gallons per hour.

INTERVENTION

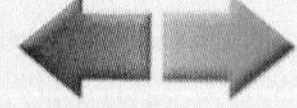

Scaffolding Questions

1. When draining the pool, what happens to the volume of the water? As the pool drains, the volume of water decreases.
2. Does the volume depend on time, or does time depend on the volume? Volume depends on time.
3. Which axis is labeled with hours? horizontal Which axis is labeled with the amount of water? vertical
4. What volume does the graph show at 1 hour? 1200 at 2 hours? 1000
5. What is the rate at which the water is decreasing per hour as the pool drains? The water is decreasing at 200 gallons per hour.

Extension

Write a function that describes the relationship between the volume V and the time t for a pool that initially contains 800 gallons and drains at 100 gallons per hour. $V(t) = 800 - 100t$

Quiz for Lessons 4-1 Through 4-4

4-1 Graphing Relationships

Choose the graph that best represents each situation.

1. A person bungee jumps from a high platform. B
2. A person jumps on a trampoline in a steady motion. A

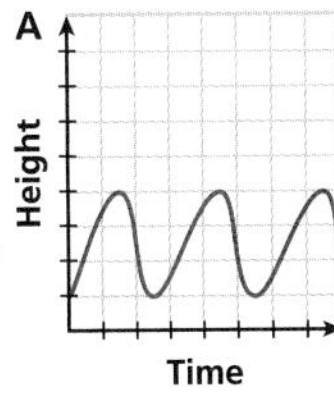

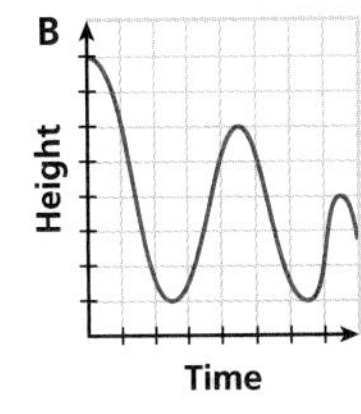

3. Xander takes a quiz worth 100 points. Each question is worth 20 points. Sketch a graph to show his score if he misses 1, 2, 3, 4, or 5 questions.

4-2 Relations and Functions

Give the domain and range of each relation. Tell whether the relation is a function. Explain.

4. 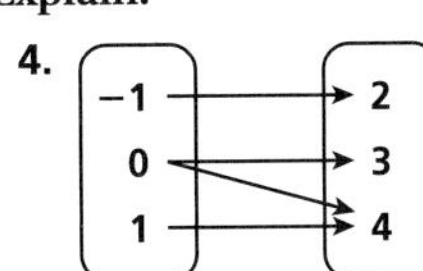

5.

x	−2	−2	0	2	2
y	3	3	3	3	3

6. 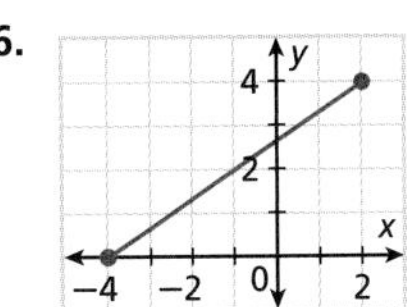

4-3 Writing Functions

Determine a relationship between the x- and y-values. Write an equation.

7.

x	1	2	3	4
y	−6	−5	−4	−3

y is 7 less than x; $y = x - 7$.

8.

x	1	2	3	4
y	−3	−6	−9	−12

y is −3 times the value of x; $y = -3x$.

9. A printer can print 8 pages per minute. Identify the dependent and independent variables for the situation. Write an equation in function notation.
ind.: minutes; dep.: pages; $f(m) = 8m$

Evaluate each function for the given input values.

10. For $f(x) = 3x - 1$, find $f(x)$ when $x = 2$. 5
11. For $g(x) = x^2 - x$, find $g(x)$ when $x = -2$. 6
12. A photographer charges a sitting fee of \$15 plus \$3 for each pose. Write a function to describe the situation. Find a reasonable domain and range for up to 5 poses.
$f(x) = 15 + 3x$, D: $\{1, 2, 3, 4, 5\}$; R: $\{18, 21, 24, 27, 30\}$

4-4 Graphing Functions

Graph each function for the given domain.

13. $2x - y = 3$; D: $\{-2, 0, 1, 3\}$
14. $y = 4 - x^2$; D: $\{-1, 0, 1, 2\}$
15. $y = 3 - 2x$; D: $\{-1, 0, 1, 3\}$

Graph each function.

16. $x + y = 6$
17. $y = |x| - 3$
18. $y = x^2 + 1$
19. The function $y = 8x$ represents how many miles y a certain storm travels in x hours. Graph the function and estimate the number of miles the storm travels in 10.5 h.

Organizer

Objective: Assess students' mastery of concepts and skills in Lessons 4-1 through 4-4.

Resources

Assessment Resources
Section 4A Quiz

Teacher One Stop™
Test & Practice Generator

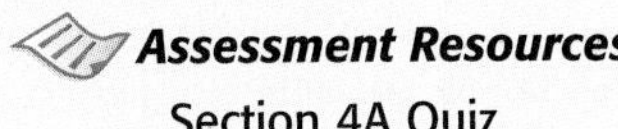

Resources

Ready to Go On? Intervention and Enrichment Worksheets

***Ready to Go On?* CD-ROM**

***Ready to Go On?* Online**

my.hrw.com

Answers

3. See p. A18.
4. D: {−1, 0, 1}; R: {2, 3, 4}; no; the x-value 0 is assigned to the y-value 3 and the y-value 4.
5, 6, 13–19. See p. A18.

READY TO GO ON? Diagnose and Prescribe

NO INTERVENE

Ready to Go On? Intervention	Worksheets	CD-ROM	Online
	Ready to Go On? Intervention, Section 4A		
Lesson 4-1	4-1 Intervention	Activity 4-1	Diagnose and Prescribe Online
Lesson 4-2	4-2 Intervention	Activity 4-2	
Lesson 4-3	4-3 Intervention	Activity 4-3	
Lesson 4-4	4-4 Intervention	Activity 4-4	

YES ENRICH

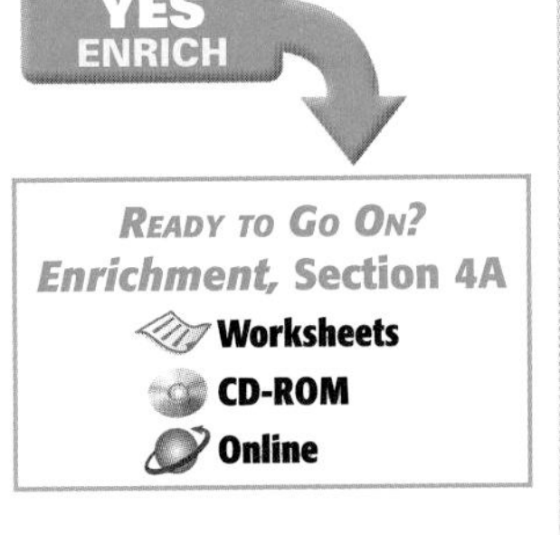

SECTION **4B**

Applying Functions

One-Minute Section Planner

Lesson	Lab Resources	Materials
Lesson 4-5 Scatter Plots and Trend Lines • Create and interpret scatter plots. • Use trend lines to make predictions. ☑ SAT-10 ☑ NAEP ☐ ACT ☑ SAT ☑ SAT Subject Tests	***Algebra Lab Activities*** 4-5 Algebra Lab (A) 4-5 Algebra Lab (B) 4-5 Algebra Lab (C)	**Optional** uncooked spaghetti, centimeter cubes (MK)
4-5 Technology Lab Interpret Scatter Plots and Trend Lines • Use a graphing calculator to graph a trend line on a scatter plot. ☑ SAT-10 ☑ NAEP ☐ ACT ☑ SAT ☑ SAT Subject Tests	***Technology Lab Activities*** 4-5 Lab Recording Sheet	**Required** graphing calculator
Lesson 4-6 Arithmetic Sequences • Recognize and extend an arithmetic sequence. • Find a given term of an arithmetic sequence. ☑ SAT-10 ☑ NAEP ☑ ACT ☑ SAT ☑ SAT Subject Tests		

Note: If NAEP is checked, the content is tested on either the Grade 8 or the Grade 12 NAEP assessment.

MK = *Manipulatives Kit*

USING RELATIONS AND FUNCTIONS

Lesson 4-5

Scatter plots provide an efficient way to present, analyze, and describe large quantities of data. As such, they are one of the most important applications of relations.

A scatter plot is a graph that shows *bivariate data*; that is, data for which there are two variables for each observation. Each point on the scatter plot represents one data pair. The scatter plot below shows the area and the number of counties for the seven smallest U.S. states. Each point represents the data pair for a single state. Rhode Island has an area of approximately 1500 square miles and 5 counties. This is represented by the ordered pair (1.5, 5).

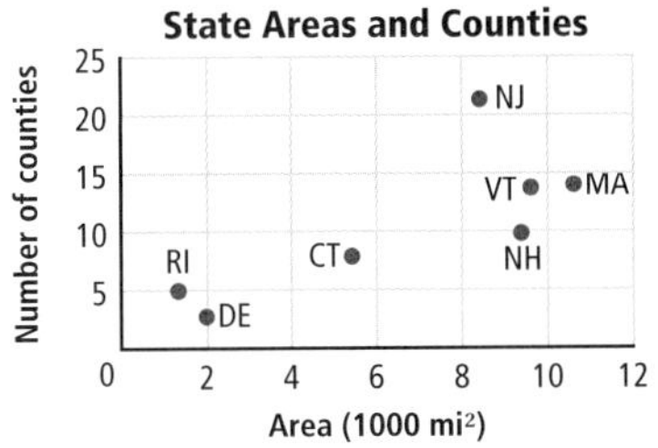

Students are often tempted to connect points on a scatter plot. It is essential that students understand that a scatter plot shows all of the collected data and that a path that is drawn by connecting the points is meaningless.

A *correlation* describes the relationship between the two data sets in a scatter plot. A *positive correlation* means that both sets of data values tend to increase together. The scatter plot of state areas and counties shows a positive correlation. A *negative correlation* means that one set of data values tends to increase as the other decreases. A scatter plot that shows the number of hours a group of people spend reading and the number of hours they spend watching television would likely show a negative correlation.

More specifically, the *correlation coefficient* measures the degree of similarity between two data sets. The correlation coefficient is a value between -1 and 1, where -1 indicates a perfect negative correlation (the data points all fall on a downward slanting line) and 1 indicates a perfect positive correlation (the data points all fall on an upward-slanting line). The closer the coefficient is to -1 or 1, the stronger the correlation, and the more closely the data points resemble a straight line. A coefficient of 0 means the data show *no correlation*, and in this case the scatter plot's points may appear to be randomly distributed.

ARITHMETIC SEQUENCES

Lesson 4-6

A *sequence* is a type of function whose domain is the natural numbers, {1, 2, 3, ...}. Each natural number is paired with a term of the sequence; hence the range is the terms of the sequence. The figure shows how the natural numbers are paired with the terms of the sequence formed by positive multiples of 3.

1	2	3	4	...	n
3	6	9	12	...	
a_1	a_2	a_3	a_4	...	a_n

In an *arithmetic sequence,* all pairs of successive terms differ by the same nonzero constant, called the *common difference.* Equivalently, each term is equal to the previous term plus the common difference. The above sequence is arithmetic with common difference 3.

The nth term of an arithmetic sequence with common difference d is given by $a_n = a_1 + (n - 1)d$. Students are sometimes puzzled by the use of $n - 1$. Exploring simple cases can help students see why $n - 1$ makes sense. For example, to find the 2nd term of the sequence, start with the first term and add the common difference once. To find the 3rd term, start with the first term and add the common difference twice. Generally, to find the nth term, start with the first term and add the common difference $n - 1$ times, as stated in the formula.

4-5 Organizer

Pacing: Traditional 1 day
Block $\frac{1}{2}$ day

Objectives: Create and interpret scatter plots.

Use trend lines to make predictions.

Algebra Labs
In Algebra Lab Activities

Online Edition
Tutorial Videos, Interactivity, TechKeys

Countdown Week 9

Power Presentations with PowerPoint®

Warm Up

Graph each point.

1. $A(3, 2)$ **2.** $B(-3, 3)$

3. $C(-2, -1)$ **4.** $D(0, -3)$

5. $E(1, 0)$ **6.** $F(3, -2)$

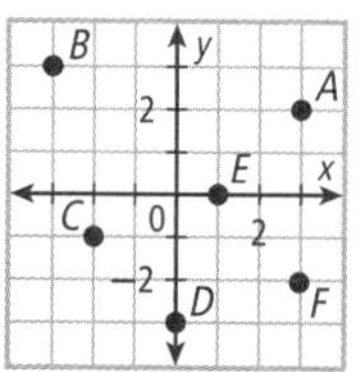

Also available on transparency

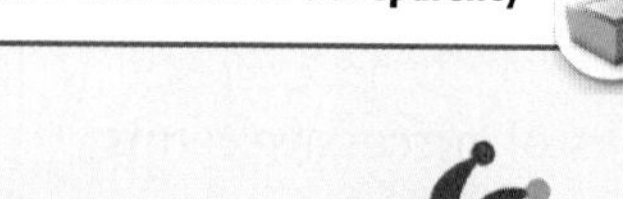

Q: What should you title a graph showing the relative diameters and weights of a batch of pancakes?

A: The Batter Plot!

State Resources

State Resources Online
KEYWORD: MA7 Resources

4-5 Scatter Plots and Trend Lines

Objectives
Create and interpret scatter plots.

Use trend lines to make predictions.

Vocabulary
scatter plot
correlation
positive correlation
negative correlation
no correlation
trend line

Who uses this?
Ecologists can use scatter plots to help them analyze data about endangered species, such as ocelots. (See Example 1.)

In this chapter, you have examined relationships between sets of ordered pairs, or data. Displaying data visually can help you see relationships.

A **scatter plot** is a graph with points plotted to show a possible relationship between two sets of data. A scatter plot is an effective way to display some types of data.

EXAMPLE 1 **Graphing a Scatter Plot from Given Data**

The table shows the number of species added to the list of endangered and threatened species in the United States during the given years. Graph a scatter plot using the given data.

Increase in List							
Calendar Year	1996	1997	1998	1999	2000	2001	2002
Species	91	79	62	11	39	10	9

Source: U.S. Fish and Wildlife Service

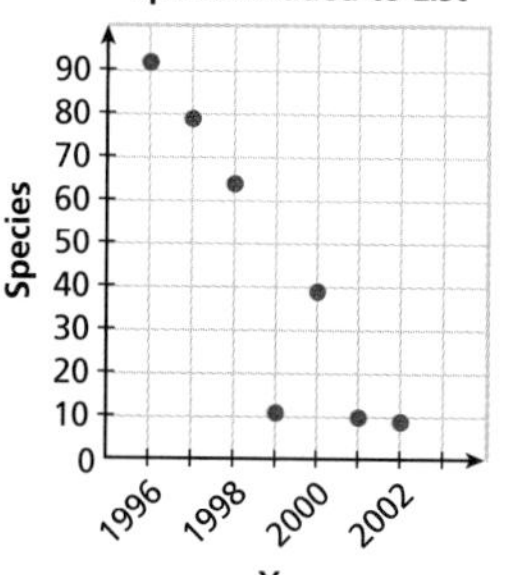

Use the table to make ordered pairs for the scatter plot.

The x-value represents the calendar year and the y-value represents the number of species added.

Plot the ordered pairs.

Helpful Hint
The point (2000, 39) tells you that in the year 2000, the list increased by 39 species.

CHECK IT OUT!

1. The table shows the number of points scored by a high school football team in the first four games of a season. Graph a scatter plot using the given data.

Game	1	2	3	4
Score	6	21	46	34

1.

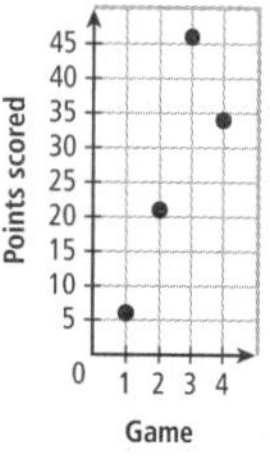

A **correlation** describes a relationship between two data sets. A graph may show the correlation between data. The correlation can help you analyze trends and make predictions. There are three types of correlations between data.

1 Introduce

EXPLORATION

4-5 Scatter Plots and Trend Lines

The table and graph show the high temperatures for certain days and the number of lemonades sold at a deli on those days.

High Temperature (°F)	Lemonades Sold
25	43
40	55
58	60
70	72
81	70
92	80

1. What does the point (40, 55) represent?

2. Describe the relationship between the high temperature and the number of lemonades sold.

THINK AND DISCUSS

3. **Explain** how you could use the graph to predict the number of lemonades that would be sold on a day when the high temperature is 100°.

4. **Describe** the likely appearance of a graph showing the high temperature and the number of hot cocoas sold.

Motivate

Tell students that when 100 fish were placed in a pond, a fisherman caught 5. The next year, 150 fish were placed in the pond, and the fisherman caught 8. Ask students how many fish they think the fisherman would catch in a year when only 50 fish were placed in the pond. Have students explain their reasoning. Possible answer: 2; the fisherman caught more when there were more fish in the pond, so he is likely to catch fewer when fewer fish are in the pond.

Explorations and answers are provided in *Alternate Openers: Explorations Transparencies.*

Correlations

Positive Correlation	Negative Correlation	No Correlation
Both sets of data values increase.	One set of data values increases as the other set decreases.	There is no relationship between the data sets.

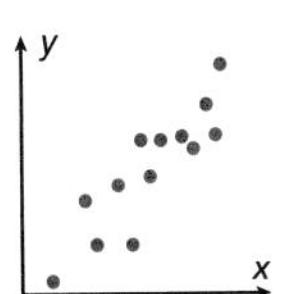

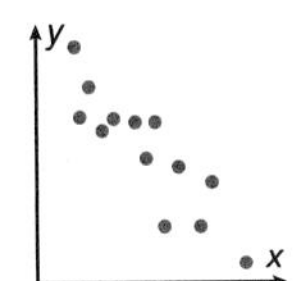

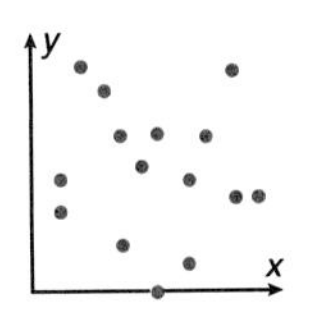

In the endangered species graph, as time increases, the number of new species added decreases. So the correlation between the data is negative.

EXAMPLE 2 Describing Correlations from Scatter Plots

Describe the correlation illustrated by the scatter plot.

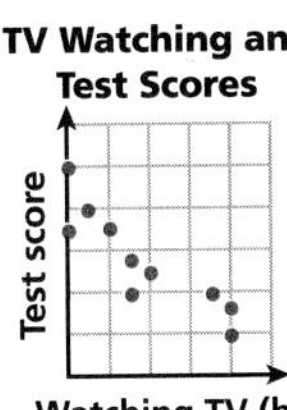

As the number of hours spent watching TV increased, test scores decreased.

There is a negative correlation between the two data sets.

2. Describe the correlation illustrated by the scatter plot.

positive

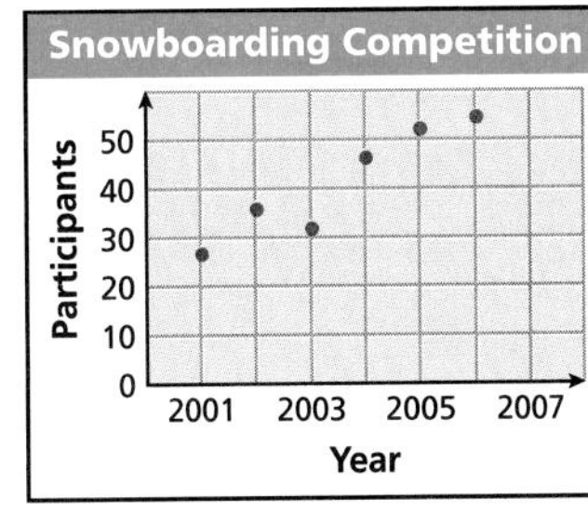

EXAMPLE 3 Identifying Correlations

Identify the correlation you would expect to see between each pair of data sets. Explain.

A **the number of empty seats in a classroom and the number of students seated in the class**

You would expect to see a negative correlation. As the number of students increases, the number of empty seats decreases.

B **the number of pets a person owns and the number of books that person read last year**

You would expect to see no correlation. The number of pets a person owns has nothing to do with how many books the person has read.

2 Teach

Guided Instruction

When working through **Example 2,** show students a graph of a perfect positive correlation (points form a straight line), strong positive correlation (points almost form a straight line), and weak positive correlation (generally going up, but points spread out). Then do the same for negative correlation.

Visual For smaller graphs, a piece of uncooked spaghetti works well when trying to place a trend line.

Reaching All Learners

Through Kinesthetic Experience

Build a tower of centimeter cubes by adding one cube at random time intervals. Centimeter cubes can be found in the Manipulatives Kit (MK). Have a volunteer record how many cubes are in place every second. Have another student graph a scatter plot of the data. Point out the connection between the growing tower of cubes, the passage of time, and the positive correlation in the scatter plot.

Power Presentations with PowerPoint®

Additional Examples

Example 1

The table shows the number of cookies in a jar from the time since they were baked. Graph a scatter plot using the given data.

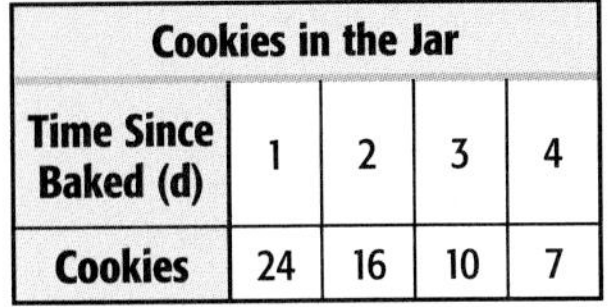

Cookies in the Jar				
Time Since Baked (d)	1	2	3	4
Cookies	24	16	10	7

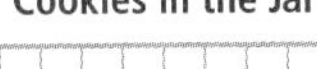

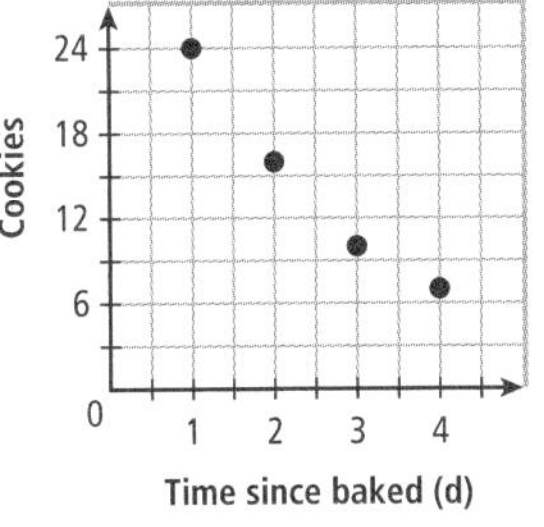

Example 2

Describe the correlation illustrated by the scatter plot.

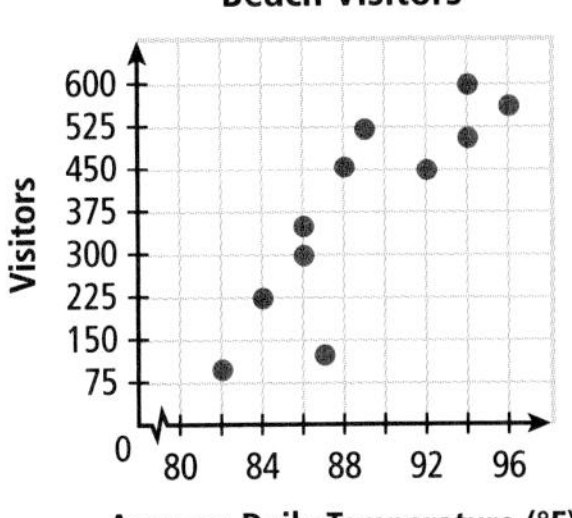

positive

Example 3

Identify the correlation you would expect to see between each pair of data sets. Explain.

A. The average temperature in a city and the number of speeding tickets given in the city
No correlation; the number of speeding tickets has nothing to do with the temperature.

B. The number of people in an audience and ticket sales
Positive; as ticket sales increase, the number of people in the audience increases.

C. The time since the start of a race and a runner's distance to the finish line Negative; as the time increases, the distance to the finish line decreases.

Power Presentations with PowerPoint®

Additional Examples

Example 4

Choose the scatter plot that best represents the relationship between the age of a car and the amount of money spent each year on repairs. Explain.

Graph A

Yearly Repair Costs

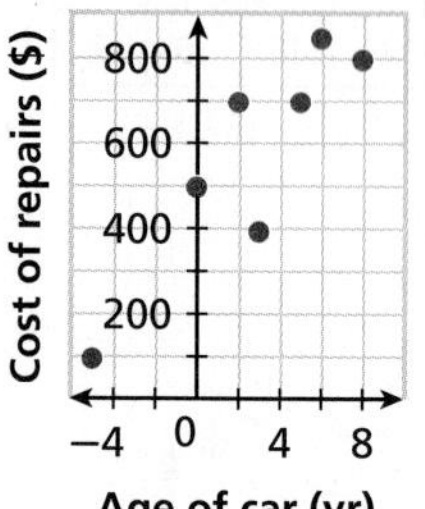

Graph B

Yearly Repair Costs

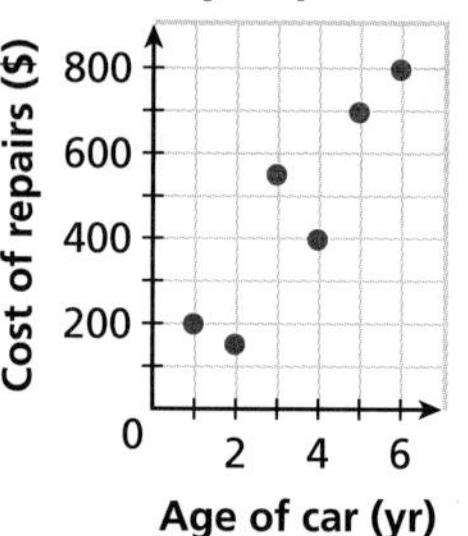

Graph C

Yearly Repair Costs

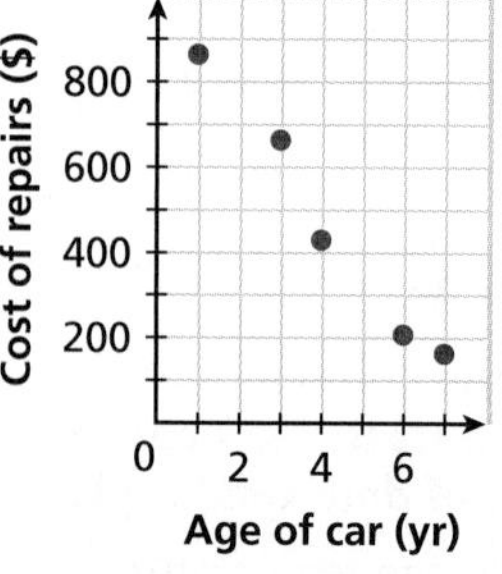

B; graph A shows negative age; graph C shows costs decreasing, a negative correlation.

INTERVENTION

Questioning Strategies

EXAMPLE 1

- What do the points being graphed represent?

EXAMPLES 2–4

- What does a scatter plot look like if there is no correlation between the data sets? positive correlation? negative correlation?

Identify the correlation you would expect to see between each pair of data sets. Explain.

C **the monthly rainfall and the depth of water in a reservoir**

You would expect to see a positive correlation. As more rain falls, there is more water in the reservoir.

Identify the correlation you would expect to see between each pair of data sets. Explain.

3a. the temperature in Houston and the number of cars sold in Boston

3b. the number of members in a family and the size of the family's grocery bill

3c. the number of times you sharpen your pencil and the length of your pencil **Negative; as the number of times you sharpen your pencil increases, the length of the pencil decreases.**

3a. No correlation; the temperature in Houston has nothing to do with the number of cars sold in Boston.

b. Positive; as the number of family members increases, more food is needed, so the grocery bill increases too.

EXAMPLE 4 Matching Scatter Plots to Situations

Choose the scatter plot that best represents the relationship between the number of days since a sunflower seed was planted and the height of the plant. Explain.

Graph A

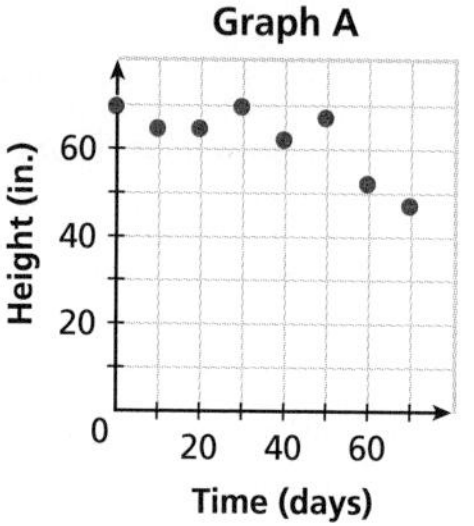

Graph B

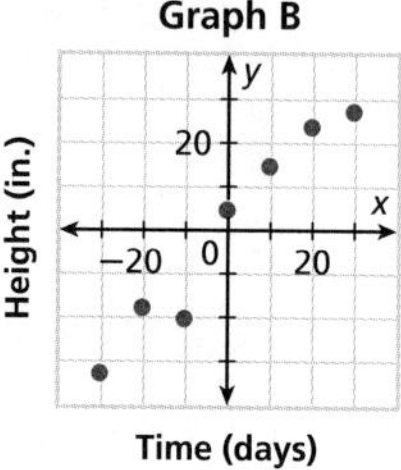

Graph C

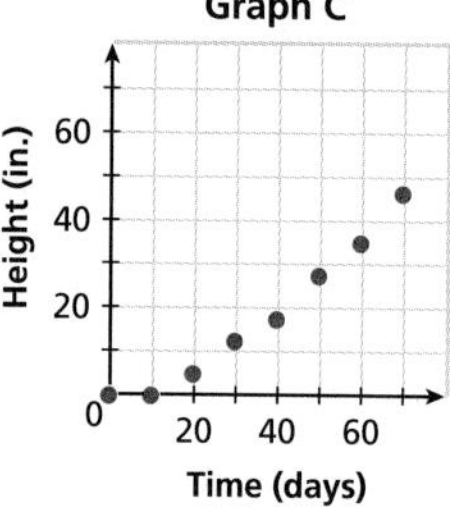

There will be a positive correlation between the number of days and the height because the plant will grow each day.

Graph A has a negative correlation, so it is incorrect.

Neither the number of days nor the plant heights can be negative.

Graph B shows negative values, so it is incorrect.

This graph shows all positive coordinates and a positive correlation, so it could represent the data sets.

Graph C is the correct scatter plot.

4. Choose the scatter plot that best represents the relationship between the number of minutes since a pie has been taken out of the oven and the temperature of the oven. Explain.

Graph A

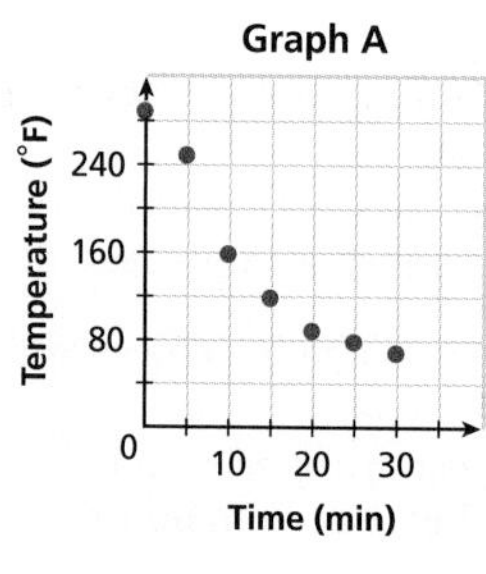

Graph B

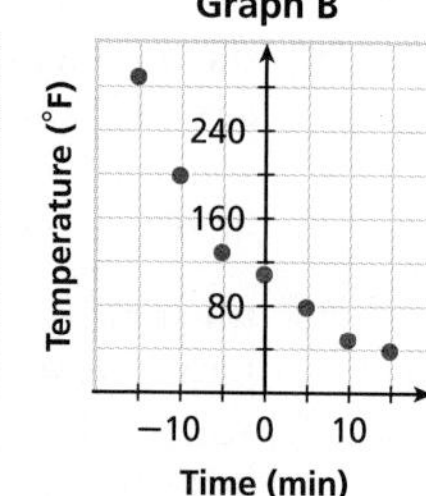

Graph C

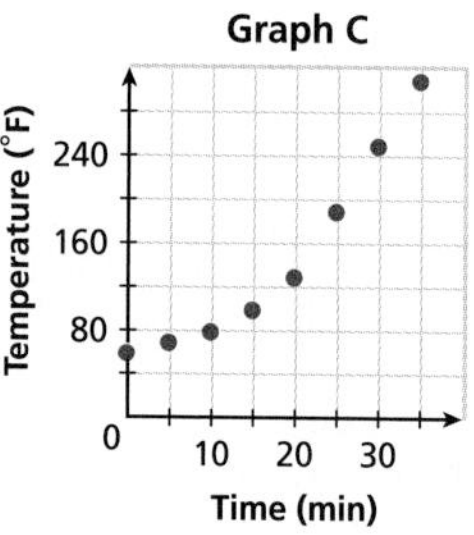

4. Graph A; it cannot be graph B because graph B shows negative minutes; it cannot be graph C because graph C shows the temperature of the oven increasing, a positive correlation.

You can graph a line on a scatter plot to help show a relationship in the data. This line, called a **trend line,** helps show the correlation between data sets more clearly. It can also be helpful when making predictions based on the data.

EXAMPLE 5 ***Fund-raising Application***

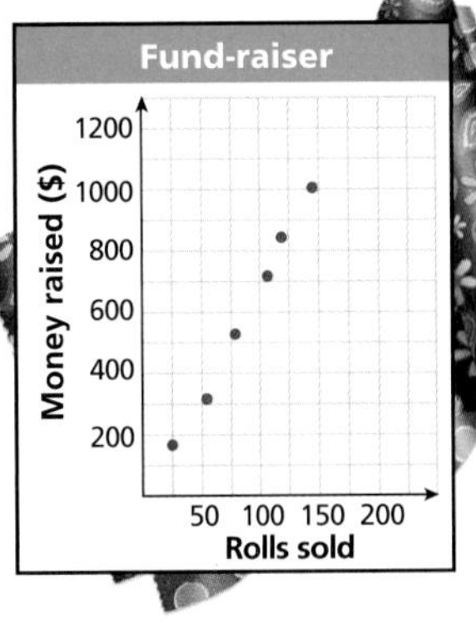

The scatter plot shows a relationship between the total amount of money collected and the total number of rolls of wrapping paper sold as a school fund-raiser. Based on this relationship, predict how much money will be collected when 175 rolls have been sold.

Draw a trend line and use it to make a prediction.

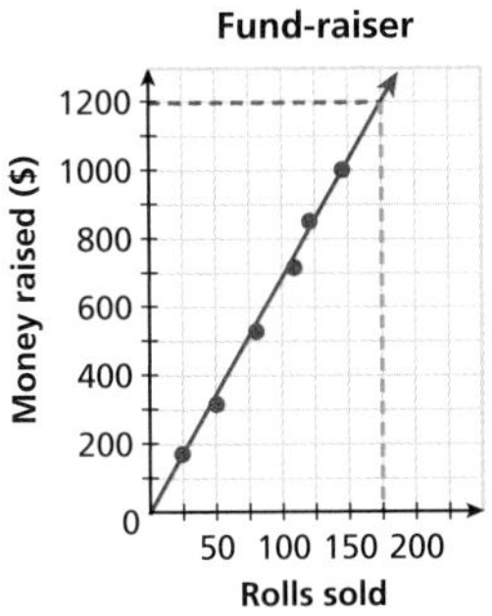

Fund-raiser

Draw a line that has about the same number of points above and below it. Your line may or may not go through data points.

Find the point on the line whose x-value is 175. The corresponding y-value is 1200.

Based on the data, $1200 is a reasonable prediction of how much money will be collected when 175 rolls have been sold.

5. Based on the trend line above, predict how many wrapping paper rolls need to be sold to raise $500. **about 75 rolls**

THINK AND DISCUSS

1. Is it possible to make a prediction based on a scatter plot with no correlation? Explain your answer.

Know it! Note

2. GET ORGANIZED Copy and complete the graphic organizer with either a scatter plot, a real-world example, or both.

	Graph	Example
Positive Correlation	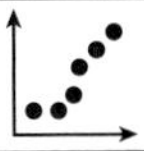	
Negative Correlation		The amount of water in a watering can and the number of flowers watered
No Correlation		

Power Presentations with PowerPoint®

Additional Examples

Example 5

The scatter plot shows a relationship between the total amount of money collected at the concession stand and the total number of tickets sold at a movie theater. Based on this relationship, predict how much money will be collected at the concession stand when 150 tickets have been sold.
about $720

Concession Stand Sales

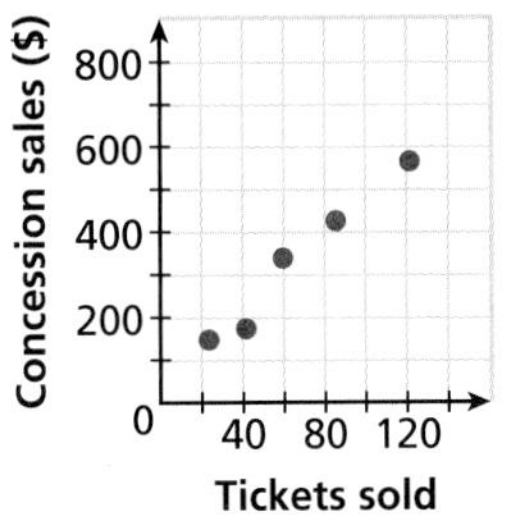

INTERVENTION
Questioning Strategies

EXAMPLE 5

- How do you decide where to draw the trend line?

Reading Math Explain to students that in math, *trend* means "tendency," not "fashion." A *trend* line shows where the data *tend* to lie.

3 Close

Summarize

Tell students that in a positive correlation, the values of the variables tend to go in the same direction; that is, as the values of the first variable increase, so do the values of the second variable. In a negative correlation, the opposite is true. As the values of the first variable increase, the values of the second variable tend to decrease. Have students give real-world examples of each type.

ONGOING ASSESSMENT and INTERVENTION

***Diagnose Before* the Lesson**
4-5 Warm Up, TE p. 266

***Monitor During* the Lesson**
Check It Out! Exercises, SE pp. 266–267
Questioning Strategies, TE pp. 266–267

***Assess After* the Lesson**
4-5 Lesson Quiz, TE p. 273
Alternative Assessment, TE p. 273

Answers to *Think and Discuss*

1. No; no correlation means that there is no relationship and the points on the graph show no pattern.
2. See p. A4.

4-5 Exercises

Assignment Guide

Assign *Guided Practice* exercises as necessary.

If you finished Examples **1–3**
Basic 14–18
Average 14–18
Advanced 14–18

If you finished Examples **1–5**
Basic 14–23, 25–27, 29–31, 34–41
Average 14–32, 34–41
Advanced 14–24, 26–41

Homework Quick Check
Quickly check key concepts.
Exercises: 14, 16, 18, 20, 21, 22

Answers

2. Possible answer: A graph with a negative correlation shows one set of values decreasing as the other set increases, while a graph with no correlation shows no relationship between the sets of values.

4.

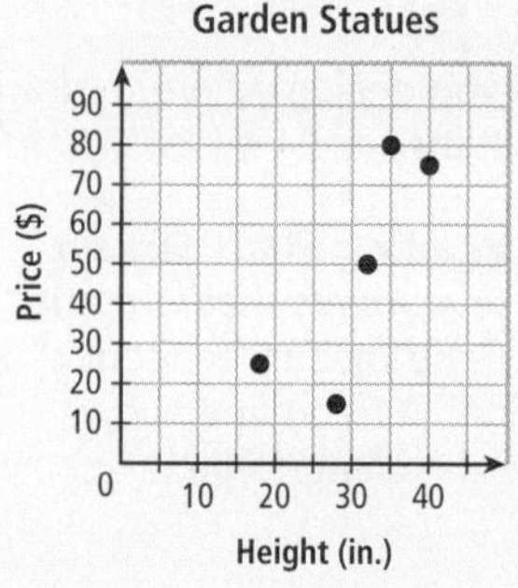

State Resources

4-5 Exercises

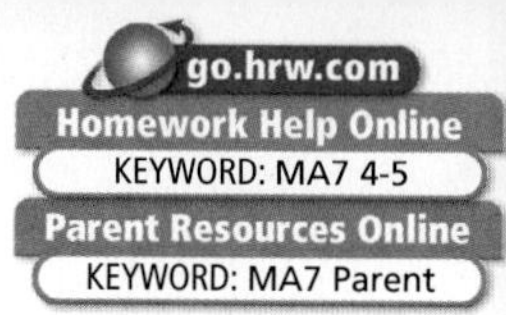

GUIDED PRACTICE

Vocabulary Apply the vocabulary from this lesson to answer each question.

1. Give an example of a graph that is not a *scatter plot*. **Possible answer: a circle graph**
2. How is a scatter plot that shows *no correlation* different from a scatter plot that shows a *negative correlation*?
3. Does a *trend line* always pass through every point on a scatter plot? Explain.

3. No; a trend line just fits the pattern of data points, so it usually does not pass through every point.

SEE EXAMPLE 1 p. 266

4. Graph a scatter plot using the given data.

Garden Statue	Cupid	Gnome	Lion	Flamingo	Wishing well
Height (in.)	32	18	35	28	40
Price ($)	50	25	80	15	75

SEE EXAMPLE 2 p. 267

Describe the correlation illustrated by each scatter plot.

5. **positive**

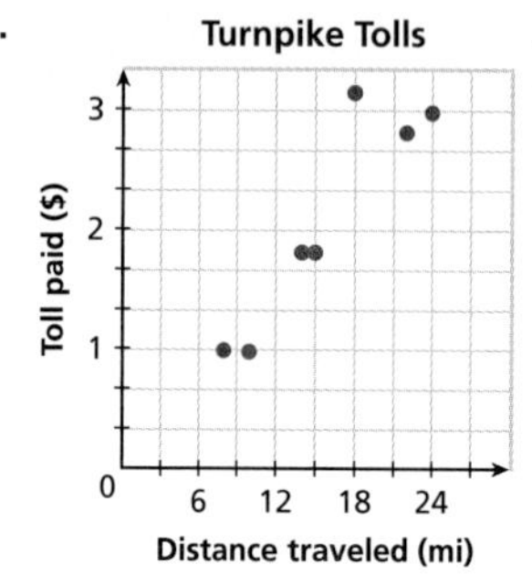

6. **negative**

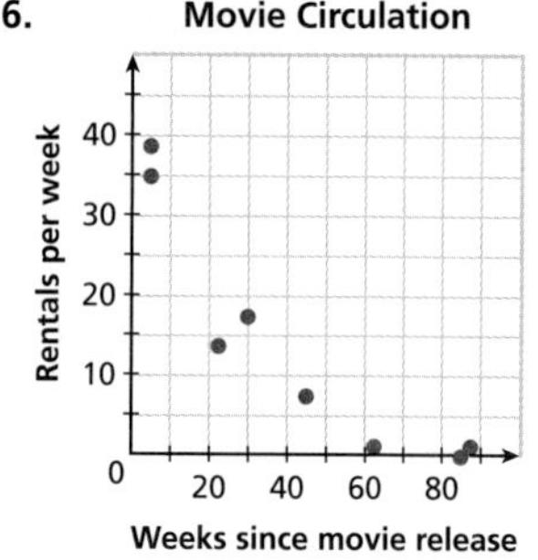

SEE EXAMPLE 3 p. 267

Identify the correlation you would expect to see between each pair of data sets. Explain.

7. the volume of water poured into a container and the amount of empty space left in the container **Neg.; as more water is poured, less space remains.**
8. a person's shoe size and the length of the person's hair **No correlation; there is no relationship.**
9. the outside temperature and the number of people at the beach **Pos.; as temperature increases, the number of people at the beach increases.**

SEE EXAMPLE 4 p. 268

Choose the scatter plot that best represents the described relationship. Explain.

10. age of car and number of miles traveled **B; there should be a pos. correlation.**
11. age of car and sales price of car **A; there should be a neg. correlation.**
12. age of car and number of states traveled to **C; there should be no correlation.**

Graph A

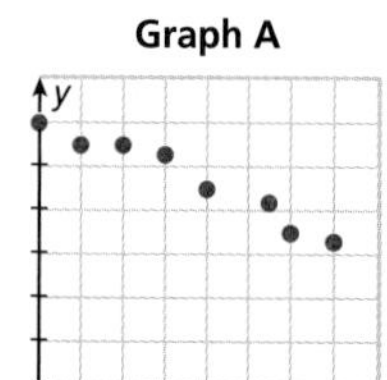

Graph B

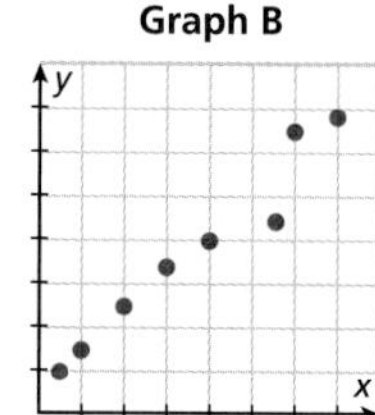

Graph C

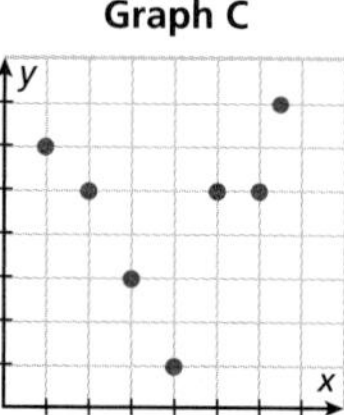

Teacher to Teacher

To reinforce the concepts of scatter plots and trend lines, I use an exercise where the students guess the ages of various celebrities. Then students make a scatter plot showing the relationship between their guesses and the actual ages of the celebrities. This helps them to discover the trend line. Because of the topic, students are very involved.

Lendy Jones
Killeen, TX

SEE EXAMPLE 5
p. 270

13. **Transportation** The scatter plot shows the total number of miles passengers flew on U.S. domestic flights in the month of April for the years 1997–2004. Based on this relationship, predict how many miles passengers flew in April 2008.
Possible answer: 53 million

U.S. Domestic Air Travel in April

Miles (billions): 0, 36, 38, 40, 42, 44, 46, 48, 50, 52
Year: 1998, 2002, 2006

Answers

14. **Train Arrival**

Passengers: 25, 50, 75, 100, 125, 150, 175
Arrival Time (A.M.): 6:00, 7:30, 9:00, 10:30

PRACTICE AND PROBLEM SOLVING

Independent Practice

For Exercises	See Example
14	1
15–16	2
17–18	3
19–20	4
21	5

Extra Practice
Skills Practice p. S12
Application Practice p. S31

14. Graph a scatter plot using the given data.

Train Arrival Time	6:45 A.M.	7:30 A.M.	8:15 A.M.	9:45 A.M.	10:30 A.M.
Passengers	160	148	194	152	64

Describe the correlation illustrated by each scatter plot.

15. **Nascar** **positive**

Best finish: 1, 2, 3, 4, 5, 6, 7
Rank: 0, 1, 2, 3, 4, 5, 6, 7

16. **Concert Ticket Costs** **negative**

Ticket cost ($): 10, 20, 30, 40, 50, 60, 70
Row: 0, 10, 20, 30

Identify the correlation you would expect to see between each pair of data sets. Explain.

17. the speed of a runner and the distance she can cover in 10 minutes

17. Pos.; greater speed results in more distance covered in a given time.

18. the year a car was made and the total mileage **Neg.; cars made in higher-numbered years are newer and should have lower mileage.**

Choose the scatter plot that best represents the described relationship. Explain.

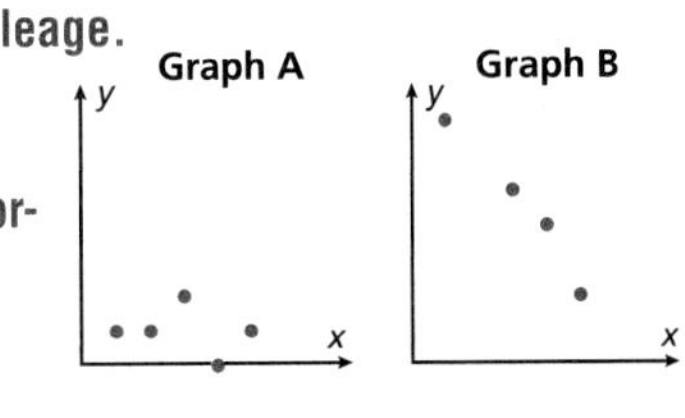

19. the number of college classes taken and the number of roommates **A; there should be no correlation.**

20. the number of college classes taken and the hours of free time. **B; there should be a neg. correlation.**

LINK
Ecology

The ocelot population in Texas is dwindling due in part to their habitat being destroyed. The ocelot population at Laguna Atascosa National Wildlife Refuge is monitored by following 5–10 ocelots yearly by radio telemetry.

21. **Ecology** The scatter plot shows a projection of the average ocelot population living in Laguna Atascosa National Wildlife Refuge near Brownsville, Texas. Based on this relationship, predict the number of ocelots living at the wildlife refuge in 2014 if nothing is done to help manage the ocelot population.

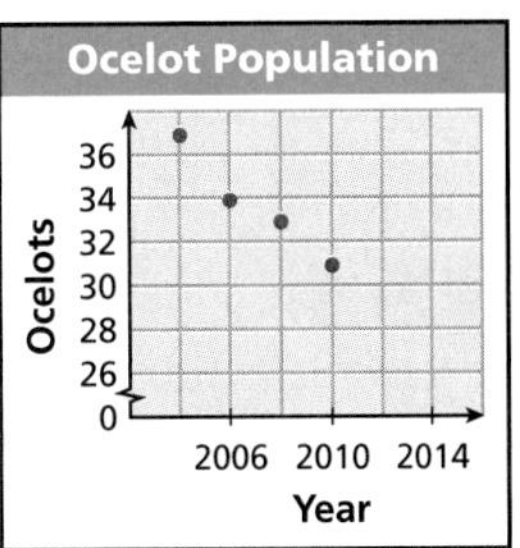

Possible answer: 25

4-5 READING STRATEGIES

The relationship between two variables can be described as having a *positive correlation*, a *negative correlation*, or *no correlation*. The sentence below can be used as a model to help you determine what type of relationship best fits each situation.

"As the (independent *x*-variable) increases, the (dependent *y*-variable) (increase/decrease/shows no pattern)."

If the dependent *y*-variable...

- increases ⇒ positive correlation
- decreases ⇒ negative correlation
- shows no pattern ⇒ no correlation

Determine the correlation between the amount of time a block of ice sits at room temperature and the amount of ice that remains.

MODEL: As the amount of time a block of ice sits in room temperature increases, the amount of ice that remains decreases.

CORRELATION: There is a negative correlation.

For each relationship, fill in the blanks using the model. Then identify the type of correlation found between the two sets of data.

1. the number of children in a family and the monthly cost of food

As the number of children in a family increases, the monthly cost of food increases.

CORRELATION: positive

2. the population of cities in the U.S. and the average February temperature

As the population of cities in the U.S. increases, the average February temperature shows no pattern.

CORRELATION: none

3. **Maggie's 10K Training**

Finishing Time (minutes): 40, 45, 50, 55, 60, 65, 70
Number of Practice Runs: 1, 2, 3, 4, 5, 6, 7, 8, 9, 10

As the number of practice runs increases, the finish time decreases.

CORRELATION: negative

4-5 RETEACH

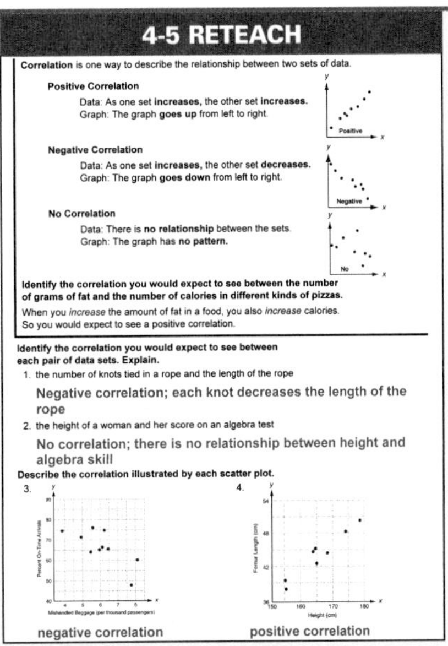

Correlation is one way to describe the relationship between two sets of data.

Positive Correlation
Data: As one set **increases,** the other set **increases.**
Graph: The graph **goes up** from left to right.

Negative Correlation
Data: As one set **increases,** the other set **decreases.**
Graph: The graph **goes down** from left to right.

No Correlation
Data: There is **no relationship** between the sets.
Graph: The graph has **no pattern.**

Identify the correlation you would expect to see between the number of grams of fat and the number of calories in different kinds of pizzas.

When you *increase* the amount of fat in a food, you also *increase* calories. So you would expect to see a positive correlation.

Identify the correlation you would expect to see between each pair of data sets. Explain.

1. the number of knots tied in a rope and the length of the rope

Negative correlation; each knot decreases the length of the rope

2. the height of a woman and her score on an algebra test

No correlation; there is no relationship between height and algebra skill

Describe the correlation illustrated by each scatter plot.

3. Percent On-Time Arrivals: 40, 50, 60, 70, 80, 90; Mishandled Baggage (per thousand passengers): 4, 5, 6, 7, 8

negative correlation

4. Femur Length (cm): 36, 42, 48, 54; Height (cm): 150, 160, 170, 180

positive correlation

4-5 PRACTICE A
4-5 PRACTICE C
4-5 PRACTICE B

Graph a scatter plot using the given data.

1. The table shows the percent of people ages 18–24 who reported they voted in the presidential elections. Graph a scatter plot using the given data.

Year	1988	1992	1996	2000	2004
% of 18-24 year olds	36	43	32	32	42

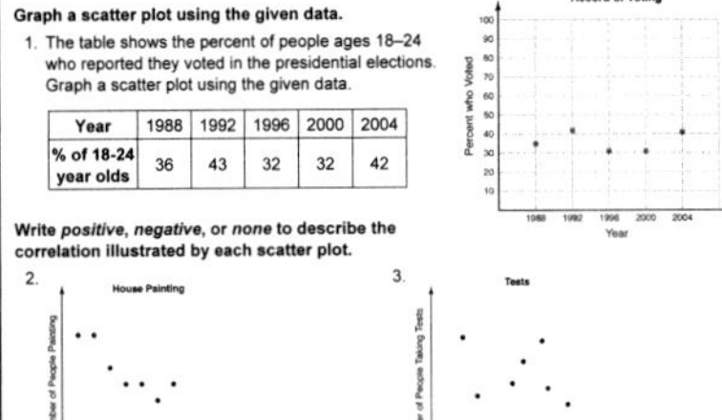

Write *positive*, *negative*, or *none* to describe the correlation illustrated by each scatter plot.

2. House Painting — Number of People Painting; Time (h)

negative

3. Tests — Number of People Taking Tests; Temperature

none

4. Identify the correlation you would expect to see between the number of pets a person has and the number of times they go to a pet store. Explain.

positive correlation; having more pets means needing more food, toys, etc.

Neal kept track of the number of minutes it took him to assemble sandwiches at his restaurant. The information is in the table below.

Number of sandwiches	1	2	4	6	7
Minutes	3	4	5	6	7

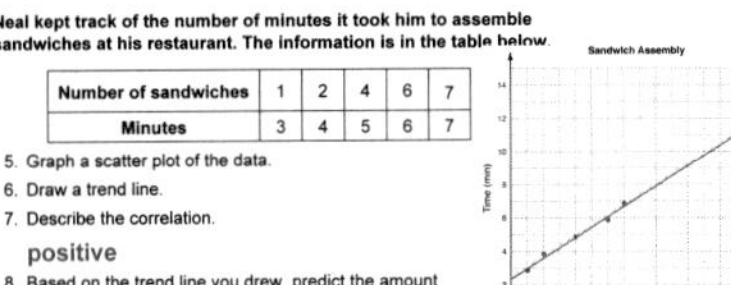

5. Graph a scatter plot of the data.
6. Draw a trend line.
7. Describe the correlation.

positive

8. Based on the trend line you drew, predict the amount of time it will take Neal to assemble 12 sandwiches.

about 10 minutes

Exercise 27 involves using a trend line to make a prediction. This exercise prepares students for the Multi-Step Test Prep on page 282.

Answers

26. Fewer people will buy an item if the price goes up. So there is a negative correlation between the price of an item and the number of people buying the item.

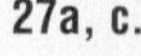

27a, c.

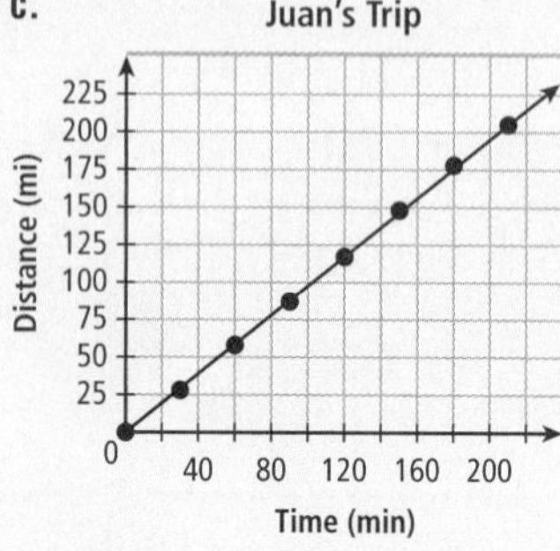

b. Positive; as time increases, the number of miles also increases.

c. Possible answer: about 235 mi

23. Pos.; as the number of left shoes sold increases, the number of right shoes sold also increases, because people need shoes for both feet.

24a, c.

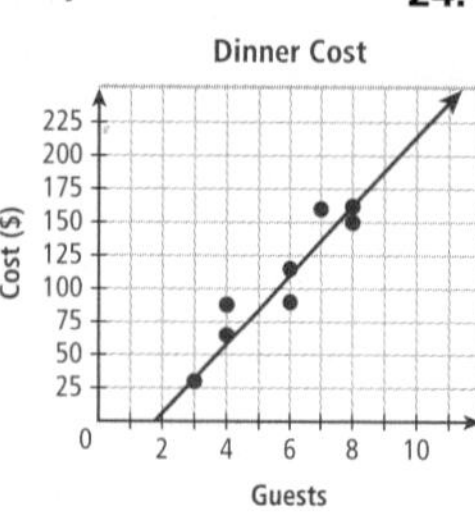

b. Pos.; as the number of guests increases, the cost increases.

d. Possible answer: about $230

e. The cost will increase.

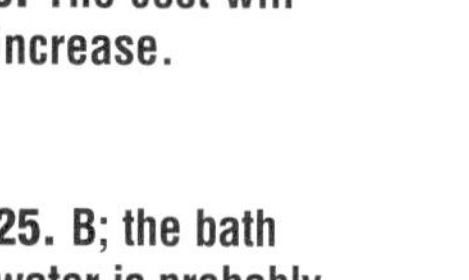

25. B; the bath water is probably hot at first, but as time passes, the temperature decreases.

22. **Estimation** Angie enjoys putting jigsaw puzzles together. The scatter plot shows the number of puzzle pieces and the time in minutes it took her to complete each of her last six puzzles. Use the trend line to estimate the time in minutes it will take Angie to complete a 1200-piece puzzle. **Possible answer: 600 min**

Puzzle Completion

23. **Critical Thinking** Describe the correlation between the number of left shoes sold and the number of right shoes sold.

24. Roma had guests for dinner at her house eight times and has recorded the number of guests and the total cost for each meal in the table.

Guests	3	4	4	6	6	7	8	8
Cost ($)	30	65	88	90	115	160	150	162

a. Graph a scatter plot of the data.

b. Describe the correlation.

c. Draw a trend line.

d. Based on the trend line you drew, predict the cost of dinner for 11 guests.

e. **What if...?** Suppose that each cost in the table increased by $5. How will this affect the cost of dinner for 11 guests?

25. **/// ERROR ANALYSIS ///** Students graphed a scatter plot for the temperature of hot bath water and time if no new water is added. Which graph is incorrect? Explain the error.

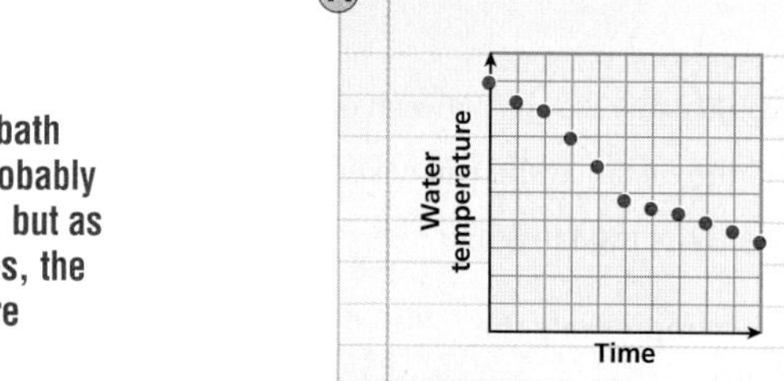

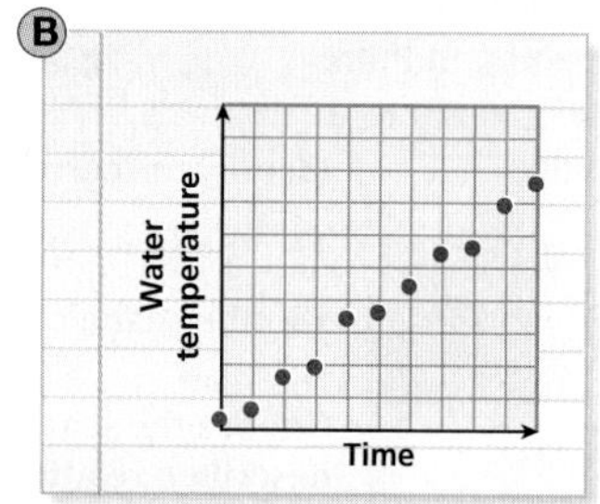

26. **Critical Thinking** Will more people or fewer people buy an item if the price goes up? Explain the relationship and describe the correlation.

MULTI-STEP TEST PREP

27. This problem will prepare you for the Multi-Step Test Prep on page 282.

Juan and his parents are visiting a university 205 miles from their home. As they travel, Juan uses the car odometer and his watch to keep track of the distance.

a. Make a scatter plot for this data set.

b. Describe the correlation. Explain.

c. Draw a trend line for the data and predict the distance Juan would have traveled going to a university 4 hours away.

Time (min)	Distance (mi)
0	0
30	28
60	58
90	87
120	117
150	148
180	178
210	205

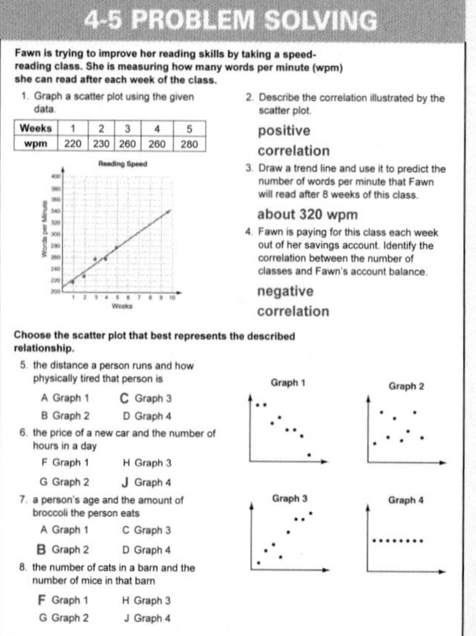

4-5 PROBLEM SOLVING

Fawn is trying to improve her reading skills by taking a speed-reading class. She is measuring how many words per minute (wpm) she can read after each week of the class.

1. Graph a scatter plot using the given data.

Weeks	1	2	3	4	5
wpm	220	230	260	260	280

Reading Speed

2. Describe the correlation illustrated by the scatter plot.

positive correlation

3. Draw a trend line and use it to predict the number of words per minute that Fawn will read after 8 weeks of this class.

about 320 wpm

4. Fawn is paying for this class each week out of her savings account. Identify the correlation between the number of classes and Fawn's account balance.

negative correlation

Choose the scatter plot that best represents the described relationship.

5. the distance a person runs and how physically tired that person is

A Graph 1 C Graph 3
B Graph 2 D Graph 4

6. the price of a new car and the number of hours in a day

F Graph 1 H Graph 3
G Graph 2 J Graph 4

7. a person's age and the amount of broccoli the person eats

A Graph 1 C Graph 3
B Graph 2 D Graph 4

8. the number of cats in a barn and the number of mice in that barn

F Graph 1 H Graph 3
G Graph 2 J Graph 4

Graph 1 Graph 2 Graph 3 Graph 4

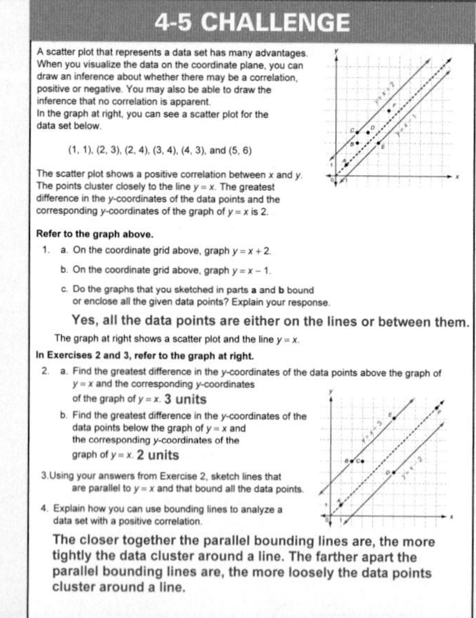

4-5 CHALLENGE

A scatter plot that represents a data set has many advantages. When you visualize the data on the coordinate plane, you can draw an inference about whether there may be a correlation, positive or negative. You may also be able to draw the inference that no correlation is apparent.
In the graph at right, you can see a scatter plot for the data set below.

(1, 1), (2, 3), (2, 4), (3, 4), (4, 3), and (5, 6)

The scatter plot shows a positive correlation between x and y. The points cluster closely to the line $y = x$. The greatest difference in the y-coordinates of the data points and the corresponding y-coordinates of the graph of $y = x$ is 2.

Refer to the graph above.

1. a. On the coordinate grid above, graph $y = x + 2$.

b. On the coordinate grid above, graph $y = x - 1$.

c. Do the graphs that you sketched in parts **a** and **b** bound or enclose all the given data points? Explain your response.

Yes, all the data points are either on the lines or between them.

The graph at right shows a scatter plot and the line $y = x$.

In Exercises 2 and 3, refer to the graph at right.

2. a. Find the greatest difference in the y-coordinates of the data points above the graph of $y = x$ and the corresponding y-coordinates of the graph of $y = x$. 3 units

b. Find the greatest difference in the y-coordinates of the data points below the graph of $y = x$ and the corresponding y-coordinates of the graph of $y = x$. 2 units

3. Using your answers from Exercise 2, sketch lines that are parallel to $y = x$ and that bound all the data points.

4. Explain how you can use bounding lines to analyze a data set with a positive correlation.

The closer together the parallel bounding lines are, the more tightly the data cluster around a line. The farther apart the parallel bounding lines are, the more loosely the data points cluster around a line.

28. **Write About It** Conduct a survey of your classmates to find the number of siblings they have and the number of pets they have. Predict whether there will be a positive, negative, or no correlation. Then graph the data in a scatter plot. What is the relationship between the two data sets? Was your prediction correct?
Check students' work.

TEST PREP

29. Which graph is the best example of a negative correlation?

Ⓐ 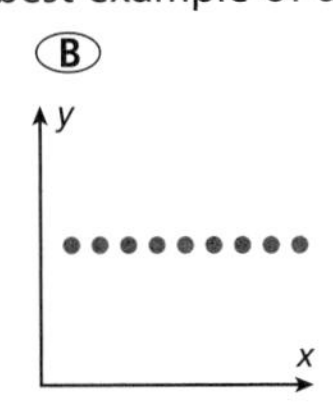

Ⓑ 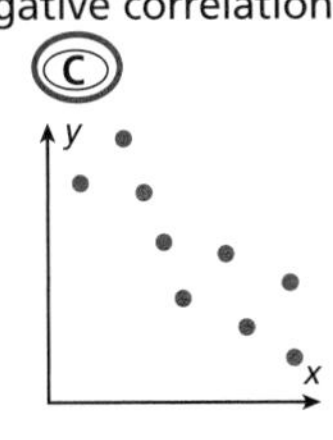

Ⓒ 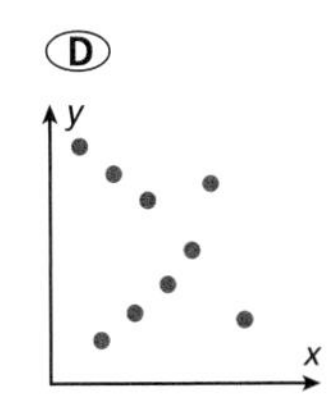

Ⓓ

30. Which situation best describes a positive correlation?
    - Ⓕ The amount of rainfall on Fridays
    - Ⓖ The height of a candle and the amount of time it stays lit
    - **Ⓗ** The price of a pizza and the number of toppings added
    - Ⓙ The temperature of a cup of hot chocolate and the length of time it sits

31. **Short Response** Write a real-world situation for the graph. Explain your answer.

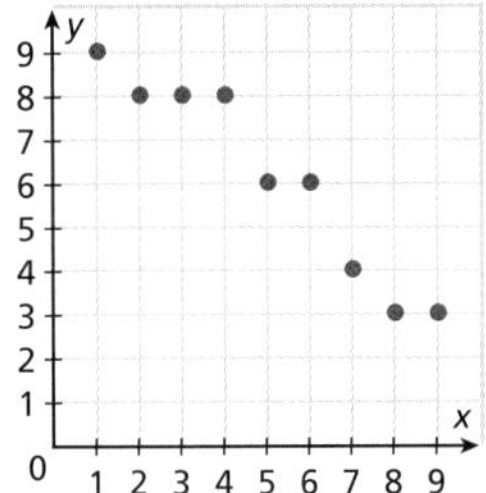

31. Possible answer: The number of milk cartons at the grocery store varies with the number of people who pass by the milk. Each person who passes by either takes milk or does not. If the person does not, the same number of cartons remain.

CHALLENGE AND EXTEND

32. Describe a situation that involves a positive correlation. Gather data on the situation. Make a scatter plot showing the correlation. Use the scatter plot to make a prediction. Repeat for a negative correlation and for no correlation.
Check students' work.
33. Research an endangered or threatened species in your state. Gather information on its population for several years. Make a scatter plot using the data you gather. Is there a positive or negative correlation? Explain. Draw a trend line and make a prediction about the species population over the next 5 years. **Check students' work.**

SPIRAL REVIEW

Write an equation to represent each relationship. Then solve the equation. *(Lesson 2-4)*

34. Five times a number increased by 2 is equal to twice the number decreased by 4.
$5n + 2 = 2n - 4; -2$
35. Five times the sum of a number and 2 is equal to 8 less than twice the number.
$5(n + 2) = 2n - 8; -6$

Solve each inequality. *(Lesson 3-5)*

36. $4(6 + x) \geq -2x$ **$x \geq -4$**
37. $3(x - 1) > 3x$ **no solutions**
38. $2(3 - x) < 2(1 + x)$ **$x > 1$**

Graph each function. *(Lesson 4-4)*

39. $y = 2x - 3$
40. $y = -|x| + 3$
41. $y = x^2 - 4$

Answers

39. 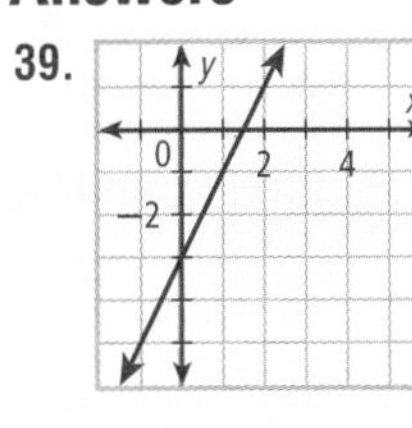

40. 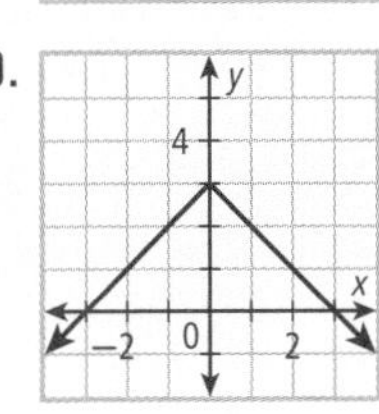

41.  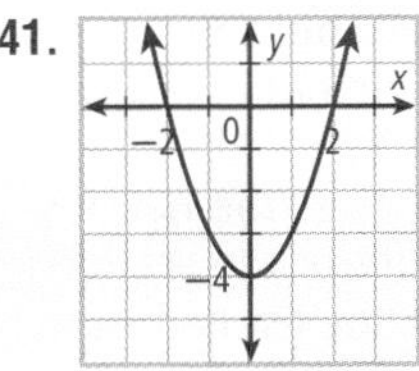

TEST PREP DOCTOR Students who choose **B** or **D** for **Exercise 29** may be confusing no correlation with negative correlation. Students who chose **G** or **J** in **Exercise 30** chose situations that describe negative correlations.

Journal

Have students describe how to identify positive and negative correlations from a scatter plot.

ALTERNATIVE ASSESSMENT

Have students create a scatter plot showing population over time for an endangered species and predict its population in 2020.

Power Presentations with PowerPoint®

4-5 Lesson Quiz

For Items 1 and 2, identify the correlation you would expect to see between each pair of data sets. Explain.

1. The outside temperature in the summer and the cost of the electric bill Positive; as the outside temperature increases, the electric bill increases because of the use of the air conditioner.
2. The price of a car and the number of passengers it seats No correlation; a very expensive car could seat only 2 passengers.
3. The scatter plot shows the number of orders placed for flowers before Valentine's Day at one shop. Based on this relationship, predict the number of flower orders placed on February 12. about 45

Valentine's Day Orders

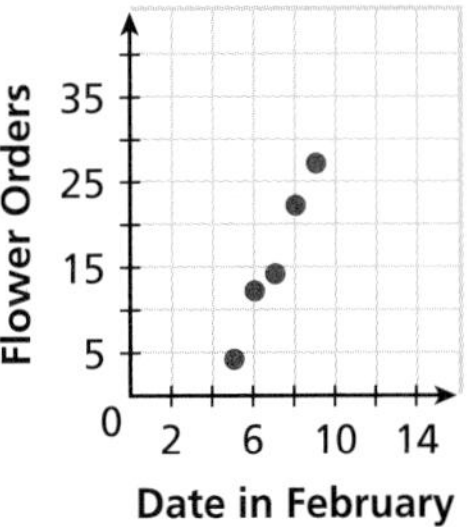

Also available on transparency

Organizer

Use with Lesson 4-5

Pacing:
Traditional $\frac{1}{2}$ day
Block $\frac{1}{4}$ day

Objective: Use a graphing calculator to graph a trend line on a scatter plot.

Materials: graphing calculator

Online Edition
Graphing Calculator

Countdown Week 9

Resources

Technology Lab Activities
4-5 Lab Recording Sheet

Teach

Discuss

When viewing the values of a and b in the equation of the trend line $y = ax + b$, point out that $0.5079441502x - 26.78767453 = 0.5079441502x + (-26.78767453)$.

Close

Key Concept

A trend line can help you interpret a scatter plot.

Assessment

Journal Have students outline the steps for using a calculator to find the equation of a trend line.

Answer to *Try This*

1. For graph, see p. A19.

State Resources

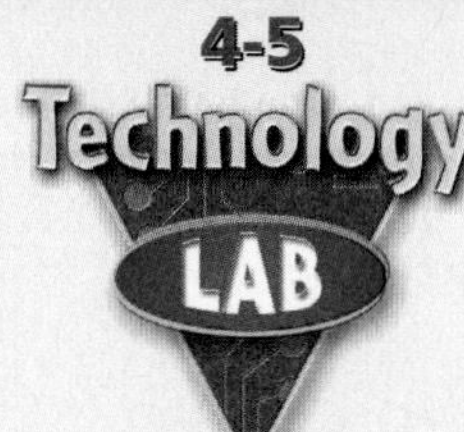

Interpret Scatter Plots and Trend Lines

You can use a graphing calculator to graph a trend line on a scatter plot.

Use with Lesson 4-5

Activity

The table shows the recommended dosage of a particular medicine as related to a person's weight. Graph a scatter plot of the given data. Draw the trend line. Then predict the dosage for a person weighing 240 pounds.

Weight (lb)	90	100	110	125	140	155	170	180	200
Dosage (mg)	20	25	30	35	40	53	60	66	75

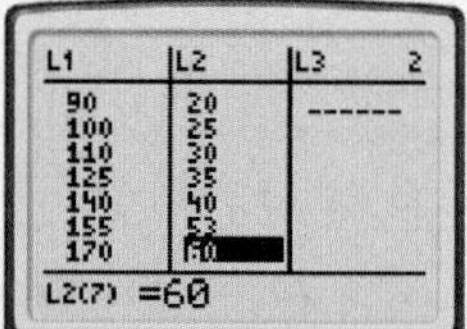

1. First enter the data. Press STAT and select **1: Edit**. In **L1**, enter the first weight. Press ENTER. Continue entering all weights. Use ▶ to move to **L2**. Enter the first dosage. Press ENTER. Continue entering all dosages.

2. To view the scatter plot, press 2nd Y=. Select **Plot 1**. Select **On**, the first plot type, and the plot mark +. Press ZOOM. Select **9: ZoomStat**. You should see a scatter plot of the data.

3. To find the trend line, press STAT and select the **CALC** menu. Select **LinReg (ax+b)**. Press ENTER. This gives you the values of a and b in the trend line.

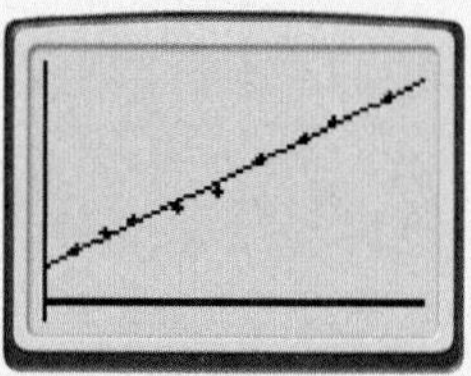

4. To enter the equation for the trend line, press Y=, and then input **.5079441502x – 26.78767453**. Press GRAPH.

5. Now predict the dosage for a weight of 240 pounds. Press VARS. Select **Y-VARS** menu and select **1:Function**. Select **1:Y1**. Enter **(240)**. Press ENTER. The dosage is about 95 milligrams.

Try This

1. The table shows the price of a stock over an 8-month period. Graph a scatter plot of the given data. Draw the trend line. Then predict what the price of one share of stock will be in the twelfth month. **about $73.54**

Month	1	2	3	4	5	6	7	8
Price ($)	32	35	37	41	46	50	54	59

Teaching Tip

Technology Point out to students that **Xlist** gives the name of the list of data used for the x-values of the scatter plot and that **Ylist** gives the name of the list used for the y-values of the scatter plot. Students can change the list names to **L1** and **L2** by pressing 2nd 1 (L1) and 2nd 2 (L2).

Teaching Tip

Technology Instead of entering the equation for the trend line manually, students can press Y= VARS, select **5:Statistics**, scroll right to **EQ**, and then select **1:RegEQ**.

Median-Fit Line

You have learned about trend lines. Now you will learn about another line of fit called the *median-fit line.*

Example

At a water raft rental shop, a group of up to four people can rent a single raft. The table shows the number of rafts rented to different groups of people one morning. Graph the median-fit line for the data.

People *x*	1	2	4	5	5	5	7	9	10	11	12	15
Rafts Rented *y*	1	1	1	3	4	5	4	7	5	3	4	6

1. Plot the points on a coordinate plane.

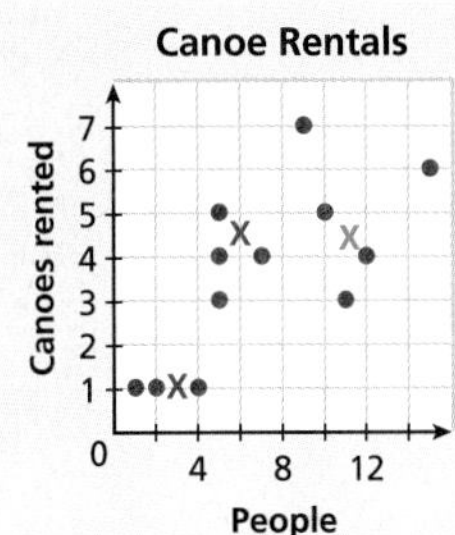

2. Divide the data into three sections of equal size. Find the medians of the *x*-values and the *y*-values for each section. Plot the three median points with an X.

1	2	4	5	5	5	7	9	10	11	12	15
1	1	1	3	4	5	4	7	5	3	4	6

Median point: (3, 1) | Median point: (6, 4.5) | Median point: (11.5, 4.5)

3. Connect the outside, or first and third, median points with a line.

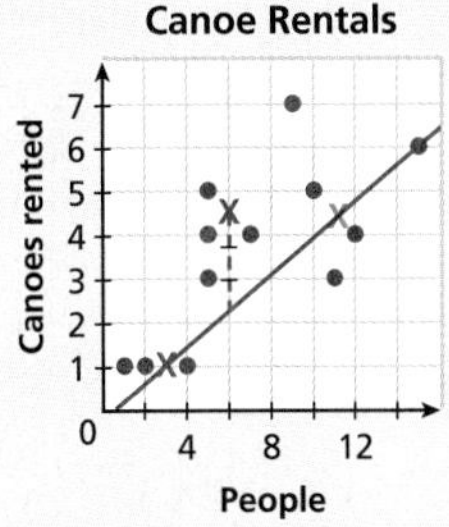

4. Lightly draw a dashed line straight down from the middle median point to the line just drawn. Mark the dashed line to create three equal segments.

5. Keeping your ruler parallel to the first line you drew, move your ruler to the mark closest to the line. Draw the line. This is the median-fit line.

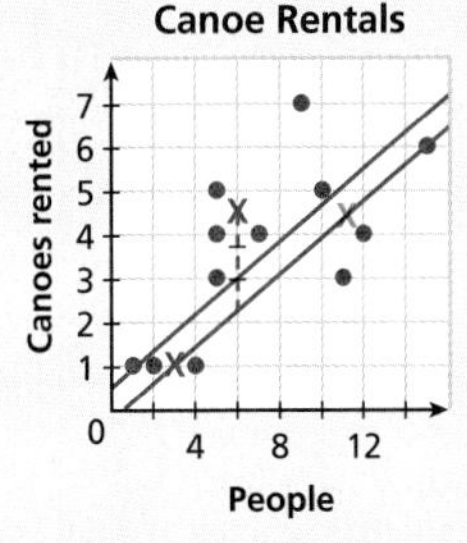

Try This

1. A manager at a restaurant kept track one afternoon of the number of people in a party and the time it took to seat them. Graph the median-fit line for the data.
2. Use your median-fit line to predict the time it would take to seat a party of 6. **4 min**

People *x*	3	7	8	8	10	12
Wait Time *y* (min)	1	5	3	9	6	6

Answers to *Try This*

Organizer

Pacing:
Traditional 1 day
Block $\frac{1}{2}$ day

Objective: Apply the algebra skills learned in Lesson 4-5 to approximate a median-fit line.

Teach

Remember

Students review and reinforce the concept of finding the median, plotting points on a coordinate plane, and drawing trend lines.

Remind students that for an ordered data set with an odd number of values, the median is the middle value. For an ordered data set with an even number of values, the median is the average of the two middle values.

Point out to students that only one set of data values can be ordered from least to greatest. In this case, *x*-values are ordered, not *y*-values.

Close

Assess

Using the data in the example, have students demonstrate finding the median points for the second and third sections.

State Resources

4-6 Organizer

Pacing: Traditional 1 day
Block $\frac{1}{2}$ day

Objectives: Recognize and extend an arithmetic sequence.

Find a given term of an arithmetic sequence.

Online Edition
Tutorial Videos

Countdown Week 9

Power Presentations with PowerPoint®

Warm Up

Simplify.

1. $5 + (-7)$ -2 **2.** $\frac{2}{3} + \frac{1}{3} + \frac{1}{3}$ $\frac{4}{3}$

3. $5.3 + 0.8$ 6.1 **4.** $6(4 - 1)$ 18

5. $-3(2 - 5)$ 9 **6.** $\frac{12}{5}\left(\frac{10}{3} + \frac{5}{4}\right)$ 11

Evaluate.

7. $\frac{3}{4} + h$ for $h = -2$ $-\frac{5}{4}$

8. $n - 2.8$ for $n = 5.1$ 2.3

9. $6(x - 1)$ for $x = 5$ 24

10. $10 + (5 - 1)s$ for $s = -4$ -6

Also available on transparency

Math Humor

Teacher: Is something wrong with your printer? Your history paper is covered in dots.

Student: Those are ellipses. After the first paragraph, imagine the rest!

4-6 Arithmetic Sequences

Objectives
Recognize and extend an arithmetic sequence.

Find a given term of an arithmetic sequence.

Vocabulary
sequence
term
arithmetic sequence
common difference

Why learn this?
The distance between you and a lightning strike can be approximated by using an arithmetic sequence.

During a thunderstorm, you can estimate your distance from a lightning strike by counting the number of seconds from the time you see the lightning until the time you hear the thunder.

Time (s)	Distance (mi)	
1	0.2	
2	0.4	+0.2
3	0.6	+0.2
4	0.8	+0.2
5	1.0	+0.2
6	1.2	+0.2
7	1.4	+0.2
8	1.6	+0.2

When you list the times and distances in order, each list forms a *sequence.* A **sequence** is a list of numbers that may form a pattern. Each number in a sequence is a **term**.

In the distance sequence, each distance is 0.2 mi greater than the previous distance. When the terms of a sequence differ by the same nonzero number d, the sequence is an **arithmetic sequence** and d is the **common difference**. The distances in the table form an arithmetic sequence with $d = 0.2$.

The variable a is often used to represent terms in a sequence. The variable a_9, read "a sub 9," is the ninth term in a sequence. To designate any term, or the nth term, in a sequence, you write a_n, where n can be any number.

To find a term in an arithmetic sequence, add d to the previous term.

Know it! Note

Finding a Term of an Arithmetic Sequence

The nth term of an arithmetic sequence with common difference d is

$$a_n = a_{n-1} + d.$$

EXAMPLE 1 **Identifying Arithmetic Sequences**

Determine whether each sequence appears to be an arithmetic sequence. If so, find the common difference and the next three terms in the sequence.

A 12, 8, 4, 0, ...

Step 1 Find the difference between successive terms.

12, 8, 4, 0, ...
−4 −4 −4

Add −4 to each term to find the next term. The common difference is −4.

Step 2 Use the common difference to find the next 3 terms.

12, 8, 4, 0, −4, −8, −12
−4 −4 −4

$a_n = a_{n-1} + d$

The sequence appears to be an arithmetic sequence with a common difference of −4. The next 3 terms are −4, −8, −12.

Reading Math
The three dots at the end of a sequence are called an ellipsis. They mean that the sequence continues and can be read as "and so on."

State Resources

go.hrw.com
State Resources Online
KEYWORD: MA7 Resources

1 Introduce

EXPLORATION

4-6 Arithmetic Sequences

Mei collects postcards. On August 1, she has 10 cards in her collection. She decides to buy three cards every day thereafter for the rest of the month.

1. The table shows the number of postcards in Mei's collection. Complete the table for the first six days of August.

Day of Month	1	2	3	4	5	6
Postcards	10	13	16			

2. How many postcards will Mei have on August 10 (day 10)?
3. How many postcards will Mei have on August 15 (day 15)?
4. Find a shortcut that you can use to find the number of postcards Mei will have at the end of the month (day 31).

THINK AND DISCUSS

5. **Explain** how you found the shortcut to determine the number of postcards Mei will have on day 31.
6. **Describe** a general rule you can use to find the number of postcards Mei will have on day n.

Motivate

Display the following list of numbers. Ask students to find the next 3 numbers.

1, 2, 4, 8, 16, _, _, _

Tell students that this list of numbers is a *sequence* because it is a list of numbers that form a pattern. Explain that in this lesson they will learn about a type of sequence called an arithmetic sequence.

Explorations and answers are provided in *Alternate Openers: Explorations Transparencies.*

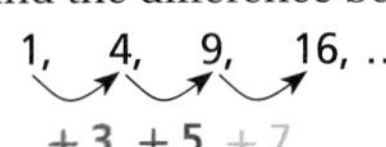

B 1, 4, 9, 16, ...

Find the difference between successive terms.

1, 4, 9, 16, ...
+3 +5 +7

The difference between successive terms is not the same.

This sequence is not an arithmetic sequence.

CHECK IT OUT! **Determine whether each sequence appears to be an arithmetic sequence. If so, find the common difference and the next three terms.**

1a. $-\frac{3}{4}, -\frac{1}{4}, \frac{1}{4}, \frac{3}{4}, \ldots$ **1a. yes;** $\frac{1}{2}; \frac{5}{4}, \frac{7}{4}, \frac{9}{4}$

1b. $-4, -2, 1, 5, \ldots$ **no**

To find the nth term of an arithmetic sequence when n is a large number, you need an equation or rule. Look for a pattern to find a rule for the sequence below.

1	2	3	4...	n	← Position
↓	↓	↓	↓		
3,	5,	7,	9...		← Term
a_1	a_2	a_3	a_4	a_n	

The sequence starts with 3. The common difference d is 2. You can use the first term and the common difference to write a rule for finding a_n.

Words	Numbers	Algebra
1st term	3	a_1
2nd term = 1st term plus common difference	3 + (1)2 = 5	$a_1 + 1d$
3nd term = 1st term plus 2 common differences	3 + (2)2 = 7	$a_1 + 2d$
4th term = 1st term plus 3 common differences	3 + (3)2 = 9	$a_1 + 3d$
⋮	⋮	⋮
nth term = 1st term plus $(n - 1)$ common differences	$3 + (n - 1)2$	$a_1 + (n - 1)d$

The pattern in the table shows that to find the nth term, add the first term to the product of $(n - 1)$ and the common difference.

Finding the nth Term of an Arithmetic Sequence

The nth term of an arithmetic sequence with common difference d and first term a_1 is

$$a_n = a_1 + (n - 1)d.$$

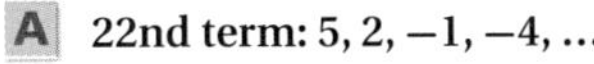

EXAMPLE 2 **Finding the nth Term of an Arithmetic Sequence**

Find the indicated term of each arithmetic sequence.

A **22nd term: 5, 2, −1, −4, ...**

Step 1 Find the common difference.

5, 2, −1, −4, ...
−3 −3 −3

The common difference is −3.

2 Teach

Guided Instruction

Remind students that they had to look for a pattern when they were writing equations earlier in this chapter. Tell them that they will also look for a pattern when identifying an arithmetic sequence. Then review the Distributive Property and the order of operations with students. When teaching the formula for the nth term in an arithmetic sequence, point out that students will need to calculate $n - 1$ first because it is in parentheses.

ENGLISH LANGUAGE LEARNERS

Reaching All Learners

Through Cognitive Strategies

Challenge students to identify the best way to memorize vocabulary terms and formulas like the one on this page. Suggest the following methods:

- Writing the information over and over again.
- Making up a song or chant.
- Creating flash cards to use with a partner.
- Writing sentences with the vocabulary and working problems with the formulas.

COMMON ERROR ALERT

Students sometimes get confused when finding the nth term. Tell students that if they are finding the 6th term, they will be multiplying the common difference d by 5, 6 − 1. The reason is that the formula uses the first term of a sequence as a constant. Ask students what number they would multiply the common difference by if they were looking for the 20th term of an arithmetic sequence. 19

Power Presentations with PowerPoint®

Additional Examples

Example 1

Determine whether each sequence appears to be an arithmetic sequence. If so, find the common difference and the next three terms.

A. 9, 13, 17, 21, . . . yes; 4; 25, 29, 33

B. 10, 8, 5, 1, . . . no

Example 2

Find the indicated term of each arithmetic sequence.

A. 16th term: 4, 8, 12, 16, . . . 64

B. 25th term: $a_1 = -5$; $d = -2$ −53

INTERVENTION

Questioning Strategies

EXAMPLE 1

- How is identifying an arithmetic sequence similar to identifying a function rule?

EXAMPLE 2

- How do you know what number to substitute for d?
- How do you know what number to substitute for n?

Math Background A sequence is said to be *recursively defined* if the nth term is defined by using the terms that precede it. The box on page 276 shows the recursive definition of an arithmetic sequence. The box on this page shows the *iterative* definition.

Power Presentations with PowerPoint®

Additional Examples

Example 3

A bag of cat food weighs 18 pounds at the beginning of day 1. Each day, the cats are fed 0.5 pound of food. How much does the bag of cat food weigh at the beginning of day 30? 3.5 lb

INTERVENTION

Questioning Strategies

EXAMPLE 3

- How can you identify d in a word problem?
- How do you solve the problem once you know the values of a_1, d, and n?

Reading Math Point out the key words in **Example 3** that will help students put the information in a formula. Tell students that *each* or *every* with a time word such as *day* or *hour* signals that the following number is d. Explain that the number to substitute for n may be indicated by an ordinal number. The first term of the sequence is a number that can be associated with the words *at the start* or *first.* ENGLISH LANGUAGE LEARNERS

Step 2 Find the 22nd term.

$a_n = a_1 + (n - 1)d$	*Write the rule to find the nth term.*
$a_{22} = 5 + (22 - 1)(-3)$	*Substitute 5 for a_1, 22 for n, and −3 for d.*
$= 5 + (21)(-3)$	*Simplify the expression in parentheses.*
$= 5 - 63$	*Multiply.*
$= -58$	*Subtract.*

B **15th term: $a_1 = 7$; $d = 3$**

$a_n = a_1 + (n - 1)d$	*Write the rule to find the nth term.*
$a_{15} = 7 + (15 - 1)3$	*Substitute 7 for a_1, 15 for n, and 3 for d.*
$= 7 + (14)3$	*Simplify the expression in parentheses.*
$= 7 + 42$	*Multiply.*
$= 49$	*Add.*

Find the indicated term of each arithmetic sequence.

2a. 60th term: 11, 5, −1, −7, ... **−343**

2b. 12th term: $a_1 = 4.2$; $d = 1.4$ **19.6**

EXAMPLE 3 *Travel Application*

The odometer on a car reads 60,473 on day 1. Every day, the car is driven 54 miles. If this pattern continues, what is the odometer reading on day 20?

Notice that the sequence for the situation is arithmetic with $d = 54$ because the odometer reading will increase by 54 miles per day.

Since the odometer reading on day 1 is 60,473 miles, $a_1 = 60{,}473$.

Since you want to find the odometer reading on day 20, you will need to find the 20th term of the sequence, so $n = 20$.

$a_n = a_1 + (n - 1)d$	*Write the rule to find the nth term.*
$a_{20} = 60{,}473 + (20 - 1)54$	*Substitute 60,473 for a_1, 54 for d, and 21 for n.*
$= 60{,}473 + (19)54$	*Simplify the expression in parentheses.*
$= 60{,}473 + 1026$	*Multiply.*
$= 61{,}499$	*Add.*

The odometer will read 61,499 miles on day 20.

3. Each time a truck stops, it drops off 250 pounds of cargo. After stop 1, its cargo weighed 2000 pounds. How much does the load weigh after stop 6? **750 lb**

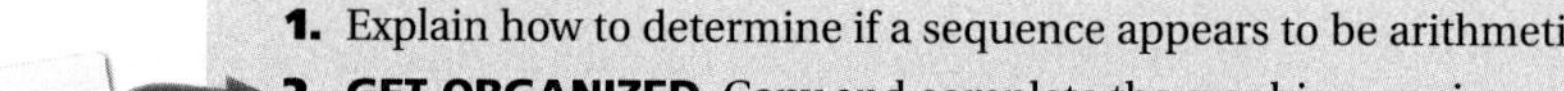

THINK AND DISCUSS

1. Explain how to determine if a sequence appears to be arithmetic.
2. **GET ORGANIZED** Copy and complete the graphic organizer with steps for finding the nth term of an arithmetic sequence.

Finding the *n*th Term of an Arithmetic Sequence → 1. → 2.

3 Close

Summarize

Display the formula $a_n = a_1 + (n - 1)d$. Have students define each variable in the formula. Then have them find the value of each variable and the 24th term of the following arithmetic sequence.

10, 4, −2, −8, . . .

In the formula, a_n is the nth term, a_1 is the first term, n is the term number, and d is the common difference. $a_1 = 10$, $n = 24$, $d = -6$, $a_{24} = -128$.

ONGOING ASSESSMENT and INTERVENTION

Diagnose **Before** the Lesson
4-6 Warm Up, TE p. 276

Monitor **During** the Lesson
Check It Out! Exercises, SE pp. 277–278
Questioning Strategies, TE pp. 277–278

Assess **After** the Lesson
4-6 Lesson Quiz, TE p. 281
Alternative Assessment, TE p. 281

Answers to *Think and Discuss*

Possible answers:

1. If the sequence has a common difference, it could be an arithmetic sequence.
2. See p. A4.

go.hrw.com
Homework Help Online
KEYWORD: MA7 4-6
Parent Resources Online
KEYWORD: MA7 Parent

GUIDED PRACTICE

1. **Vocabulary** When trying to find the nth term of an arithmetic sequence you must first know the ___?___. (*common difference* or *sequence*) **common difference**

SEE EXAMPLE 1 p. 276

Multi-Step Determine whether each sequence appears to be an arithmetic sequence. If so, find the common difference and the next three terms.

2. 2, 8, 14, 20, ... **yes; 6; 26, 32, 38**
3. 2.1, 1.4, 0.7, 0, ... **yes; −0.7; −0.7, −1.4, −2.1**
4. 1, 1, 2, 3, ... **no**
5. 0.1, 0.3, 0.9, 2.7, ... **no**

SEE EXAMPLE 2 p. 277

Find the indicated term of each arithmetic sequence.

6. 21st term: 3, 8, 13, 18, ... **103**
7. 18th term: $a_1 = -2$; $d = -3$ **−53**

SEE EXAMPLE 3 p. 278

8. **Shipping** To package and ship an item, it costs $5.75 for the first pound and $0.75 for each additional pound. What is the cost of shipping a 12-pound package? **$14**

PRACTICE AND PROBLEM SOLVING

For Exercises	See Example
9–12	1
13–14	2
15	3

Independent Practice

Extra Practice
Skills Practice p. S12
Application Practice p. S31

Multi-Step Determine whether each sequence appears to be an arithmetic sequence. If so, find the common difference and the next three terms.

9. −1, 10, −100, 1,100, ... **no**
10. 0, −2, −4, −6, ... **yes; −2; −8, −10, −12**
11. −22, −31, −40, −49, ... **yes; −9; −58, −67, −76**
12. 0.2, 0.5, 0.9, 1.1, ... **no**

Find the indicated term of each arithmetic sequence.

13. 31st term: 1.40, 1.55, 1.70, ... **5.9**
14. 50th term: $a_1 = 2.2$; $d = 1.1$ **56.1**

15. **Travel** Rachel signed up for a frequent-flier program. She receives 4300 frequent-flier miles for her first round trip and 1300 frequent-flier miles for each additional round-trip. How many frequent-flier miles will she have after 5 round-trips? **9500 mi**

Find the common difference for each arithmetic sequence.

16. 0, 6, 12, 18, ... **6**
17. $\frac{1}{2}, \frac{3}{4}, 1, \frac{5}{4}, \ldots$ $\mathbf{\frac{1}{4}}$
18. 107, 105, 103, 101, ... **−2**
19. 7.9, 5.7, 3.5, 1.3, ... **−2.2**
20. $\frac{1}{5}, \frac{2}{5}, \frac{3}{5}, \frac{4}{5}, \ldots$ $\mathbf{\frac{1}{5}}$
21. 4.25, 4.32, 4.39, 4.46, ... **0.07**

Find the next four terms in each arithmetic sequence.

22. −4, −7, −10, −13, ... **−16, −19, −22, −25**
23. $\frac{1}{8}, 0, -\frac{1}{8}, -\frac{1}{4}, \ldots$
24. 505, 512, 519, 526, ... **533, 540, 547, 554**
25. 1.8, 1.3, 0.8, 0.3, ... **−0.2, −0.7, −1.2, −1.7**
26. $\frac{2}{3}, \frac{4}{3}, 2, \frac{8}{3}, \ldots$ $\mathbf{\frac{10}{3}, 4, \frac{14}{3}, \frac{16}{3}}$
27. −1.1, −0.9, −0.7, −0.5 **−0.3, −0.1, 0.1, 0.3**

23. $\mathbf{-\frac{3}{8}, -\frac{1}{2}, -\frac{5}{8}, -\frac{3}{4}}$

Find the given term of each arithmetic sequence.

28. 5, 10, 15, 20, ...; 17th term **85**
29. 121, 110, 99, 88, ...; 10th term **22**
30. −2, −5, −8, −11, ...; 41st term **−122**
31. −30, −22, −14, −6, ...; 20th term **122**

32. **Critical Thinking** Is the sequence $5a - 1, 3a - 1, a - 1, -a - 1, \ldots$ arithmetic? If not, explain why not. If so, find the common difference and the next three terms. **Yes (when $a \neq 0$); the common difference is $-2a$; $-3a - 1, -5a - 1, -7a - 1$.**

4-6 Exercises

Assignment Guide

Assign *Guided Practice* exercises as necessary.

If you finished Examples **1–3**
Basic 9–38, 41–44, 48–53
Average 10–14 even, 15–45, 47–53
Advanced 10–14 even, 15–53

Homework Quick Check
Quickly check key concepts.
Exercises: 10, 14, 15, 20, 30, 36

State Resources

Exercise 41 involves using an arithmetic sequence to calculate distance. This exercise prepares students for the Multi-Step Test Prep on page 282.

Answers

38a. 1, 1, 2, 3, 5, 8, 13, 21, 34, 55; no; there is no common difference.

b. Yes; every 3rd term is divisible by 2; every 3rd term is the sum of 2 odd numbers.

c. Every 4th term is divisible by 3, and every 5th term is divisible by 5.

40. Possible answer: Find the difference between two successive terms. If the terms of the sequence become greater in value, then the common difference is positive. If the terms of the sequence become lesser in value, then the common difference is negative.

33a. Because you pay $2 per lap, the relationship could be represented by an arithmetic sequence in which $d = 2$.

b. $9, $11, $13, $15; $a_n = 2n + 7$

33. Recreation The rates for a go-cart course are shown.

JESSIKA'S SPEEDWAY
License: $7
Per Lap: $2

a. Explain why the relationship described on the flyer could be represented by an arithmetic sequence.

b. Find the cost for 1, 2, 3, and 4 laps. Write a rule to find the nth term of the sequence.

c. How much would 15 laps cost? **$37**

d. **What if...?** After 9 laps, you get the 10th one free. Will the sequence still be arithmetic? Explain.
No; the sequence will not increase by 2 from the 9th term to the 10th term.

LINK Number Theory

Fibonacci numbers occur frequently throughout nature. The number of petals on many flowers are numbers of the Fibonacci sequence. Two petals on a flower are rare but 3, 5, and even 34 petals are common.

Find the given term of each arithmetic sequence.

34. 2.5, 8.5, 14.5, 20.5, ...; 30th term **176.5**

35. 189.6, 172.3, 155, 137.7, ...; 18th term **−104.5**

36. $\frac{1}{4}, \frac{3}{4}, \frac{5}{4}, \frac{7}{4}, \ldots$; 15th term $\mathbf{\frac{29}{4}}$

37. $\frac{2}{3}, \frac{11}{12}, \frac{7}{6}, \frac{17}{12}, \ldots$; 25th term $\mathbf{\frac{20}{3}}$

38. Number Theory The sequence 1, 1, 2, 3, 5, 8, 13, ... is a famous sequence called the Fibonacci sequence. After the first two terms, each term is the sum of the previous two terms.

a. Write the first 10 terms of the Fibonacci sequence. Is the Fibonacci sequence arithmetic? Explain.

b. Notice that the third term is divisible by 2. Are the 6th and 9th terms also divisible by 2? What conclusion can you draw about every third term? Why is this true?

c. Can you find any other patterns? (*Hint:* Look at every 4th and 5th term.)

39. Entertainment Seats in a concert hall are arranged in the pattern shown.

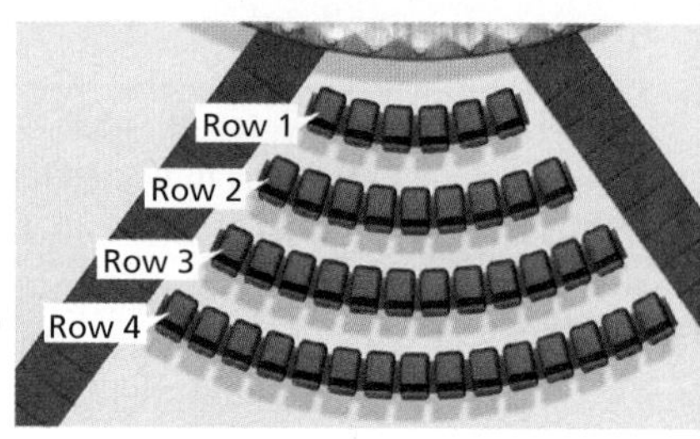

a. The numbers of seats in the rows form an arithmetic sequence. Write a rule for the arithmetic sequence.

b. How many seats are in the 15th row? **48**

c. A ticket costs $40. Suppose every seat in the first 10 rows is filled. What is the total revenue from those seats? **$7800**

d. **What if...?** An extra chair is added to each row. Write the new rule for the arithmetic sequence and find the new total revenue from the first 10 rows.
$a_n = 7 + 3(n - 1)$; **$8200**

39a. $a_n = 6 + 3(n - 1)$

40. Write About It Explain how to find the common difference of an arithmetic sequence. How can you determine whether the arithmetic sequence has a positive common difference or a negative common difference?

MULTI-STEP TEST PREP

41. This problem will prepare you for the Multi-Step Test Prep on page 282.

Juan is traveling to visit universities. He notices mile markers along the road. He records the mile marker every 10 minutes. His father is driving at a constant speed.

Time Interval	Mile Marker
1	520
2	509
3	498
4	**487**
5	**476**
6	**465**

a. Copy and complete the table.

b. Write the rule for the sequence. $a_n = 520 + (n - 1)(-11)$

c. What does the common difference represent? **c. number of miles per interval**

d. If this sequence continues, find the mile marker for time interval 10. **421**

STATE

4-6 PRACTICE A

4-6 PRACTICE C

4-6 PRACTICE B

Determine whether each sequence is an arithmetic sequence. If so, find the common difference and the next three terms.

1. −10, −7, −4, −1, ...
arithmetic; $d = 3$; 2, 5, 8

2. 0, 1.5, 3, 4.5, ...
arithmetic; $d = 1.5$; 6, 7.5, 9

3. 5, 8, 12, 17, ...
not arithmetic

4. −20, −20.5, −21, −21.5, ...
arithmetic; $d = -0.5$; −22, −22.5, 23

Find the indicated term of each arithmetic sequence.

5. 28th term: 0, −4, −8, −12, ...
−108

6. 15th term: 2, 3.5, 5, 6.5, ...
23

7. 37th term: $a_1 = -3$; $d = 2.8$
97.8

8. 14th term: $a_1 = 4.2$; $d = -5$
−60.8

9. 17th term; $a_1 = 2.3$; $d = -2.3$
−34.5

10. 92nd term; $a_1 = 1$; $d = 0.8$
73.8

11. A movie rental club charges $4.95 for the first month's rentals. The club charges $18.95 for each additional month. How much is the total cost for one year? **$213.40**

12. A carnival game awards a prize if Kasey can shoot a basket. The charge is $5.00 for the first shot, then $2.00 for each additional shot. Kasey needed 11 shots to win a prize. What is the total amount Kasey spent to win a prize? **$25.00**

4-6 READING STRATEGIES

Use the concept map below to help you understand arithmetic sequences.

Arithmetic Sequence

Definition
An arithmetic sequence is a list of numbers whose terms all differ by the same non-zero number.

Formula
The nth term of an arithmetic sequence can be found using
$a_n = a_1 + (n - 1)d$
where a_1 is the first term and d is the common difference.

Examples
−2, 1, 4, 7, 10, ...
+3 +3 +3 +3
9, 7.5, 6, 4.5, 3, ...
−1.5 −1.5 −1.5 −1.5

Non-Examples
−4, −3, −1, 2, 6, ...
+1 +2 +3 +4
1, 2, 4, 8, 16, ...
×2 ×2 ×2 ×2

Answer each question.

1. Explain why −4, −3, −1, 2, 6, ... is given as a non-example of an arithmetic sequence.
The terms do not all differ by the same number.

2. Explain why 1, 2, 4, 8, 16, ... is given as a non-example of an arithmetic sequence.
The same number is being multiplied, not added, to each term.

3. Give an example of an arithmetic sequence whose common difference is 5.
Possible answer: 1, 6, 11, 16, 21, ...

4. Find the common difference and the next 3 terms of the sequence 8, $7\frac{1}{2}$, 7, $6\frac{1}{2}$, 6, ...
$-\frac{1}{2}$; $5\frac{1}{2}$, 5, $4\frac{1}{2}$

Find the indicated term of each arithmetic sequence using the formula given above.

5. 25th term: −14, −8, −2, 4, 10, ...
130

6. 18th term: 122, 120, 118, 116, 114, ...
88

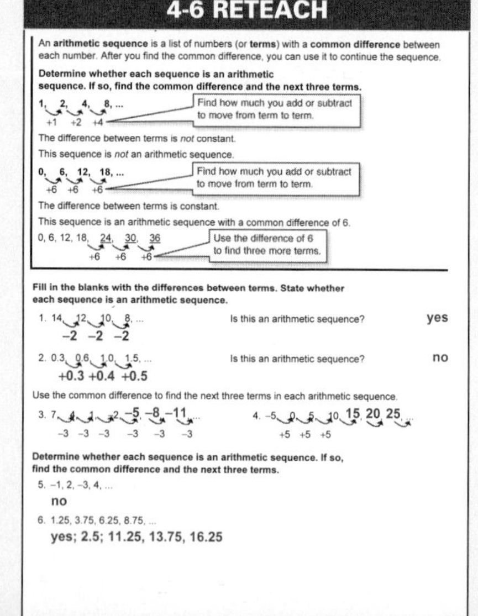

4-6 RETEACH

An **arithmetic sequence** is a list of numbers (or **terms**) with a **common difference** between each number. After you find the common difference, you can use it to continue the sequence.

Determine whether each sequence is an arithmetic sequence. If so, find the common difference and the next three terms.

1, 2, 4, 8, ...
+1 +2 +4
Find how much you add or subtract to move from term to term.

The difference between terms is *not* constant.

This sequence is *not* an arithmetic sequence.

0, 6, 12, 18, ...
+6 +6 +6
Find how much you add or subtract to move from term to term.

The difference between terms is constant.

This sequence is an arithmetic sequence with a common difference of 6.

0, 6, 12, 18, 24, 30, 36
+6 +6 +6
Use the difference of 6 to find three more terms.

Fill in the blanks with the differences between terms. State whether each sequence is an arithmetic sequence.

1. 14, 12, 10, 8, ...
−2 −2 −2
Is this an arithmetic sequence? **yes**

2. 0.3, 0.6, 1.0, 1.5, ...
+0.3 +0.4 +0.5
Is this an arithmetic sequence? **no**

Use the common difference to find the next three terms in each arithmetic sequence.

3. 7, 4, 1, −2, **−5**, **−8**, **−11**, ...
−3 −3 −3 −3 −3 −3

4. −5, 0, 5, 10, **15**, **20**, **25**, ...
+5 +5 +5

Determine whether each sequence is an arithmetic sequence. If so, find the common difference and the next three terms.

5. −1, 2, −3, 4, ...
no

6. 1.25, 3.75, 6.25, 8.75, ...
yes; 2.5; 11.25, 13.75, 16.25

TEST PREP

42. What are the next three terms in the arithmetic sequence −21, −12, −3, 6, … ?

   (A) 9, 12, 15 (B) 15, 24, 33 (C) 12, 21, 27 (D) 13, 20, 27

43. What is the common difference for the data listed in the second column?

   (F) −1.8 (H) 2.8
   (G) 1.8 (J) −3.6

Altitude (ft)	Boiling Point of Water (°F)
1000	210.2
2000	208.4
3000	206.6

44. Which of the following sequences is NOT arithmetic?

   (A) −4, 2, 8, 14, … (B) 9, 4, −1, −6, … (C) 2, 4, 8, 16, … (D) $\frac{1}{3}, 1\frac{1}{3}, 2\frac{1}{3}, 3\frac{1}{3}, \ldots$

CHALLENGE AND EXTEND

45. The first term of an arithmetic sequence is 2, and the common difference is 9. Find two consecutive terms of the sequence that have a sum of 355. What positions in the sequence are the terms? **173 and 182; 20th and 21st terms**

46. The 60th term of an arithmetic sequence is 106.5, and the common difference is 1.5. What is the first term of the sequence? **18**

47. **Athletics** Verona is training for a marathon. The first part of her training schedule is shown below.

Session	1	2	3	4	5	6
Distance Run (mi)	3.5	5	6.5	8	9.5	11

Session 16; yes; she increases the amount she runs by 1.5 miles each time.

a. If Verona continues this pattern, during which training session will she run 26 miles? Is her training schedule an arithmetic sequence? Explain.

b. If Verona's training schedule starts on a Monday and she runs every third day, on which day will she run 26 miles? **Thursday**

SPIRAL REVIEW

48. Three sides of a triangle are represented by x, $x + 3$ and $x + 5$. The perimeter of the triangle is 35 units. Solve for x. *(Lesson 2-3)* **9**

49. The length of a rectangle is 2 and the width is represented by $x + 4$. The area of the rectangle is 40 square units. Find the width of the rectangle. *(Lesson 2-3)* **20**

Solve each compound inequality and graph the solutions. *(Lesson 3-6)*

50. $4 < 2n + 6 \le 20$ **$-1 < n \le 7$**

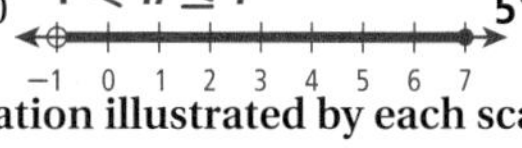

   −1 0 1 2 3 4 5 6 7

51. $t + 5 > 7$ OR $2t - 8 < -12$ **$t < -2$ OR $t > 2$**

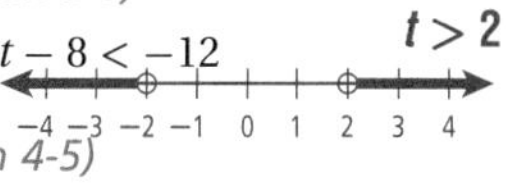

   −4 −3 −2 −1 0 1 2 3 4

Describe the correlation illustrated by each scatter plot. *(Lesson 4-5)*

52. Household Televisions

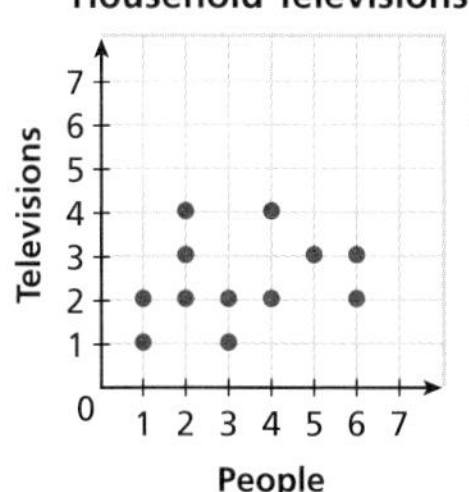

no correlation

53. Safe Heart Rate

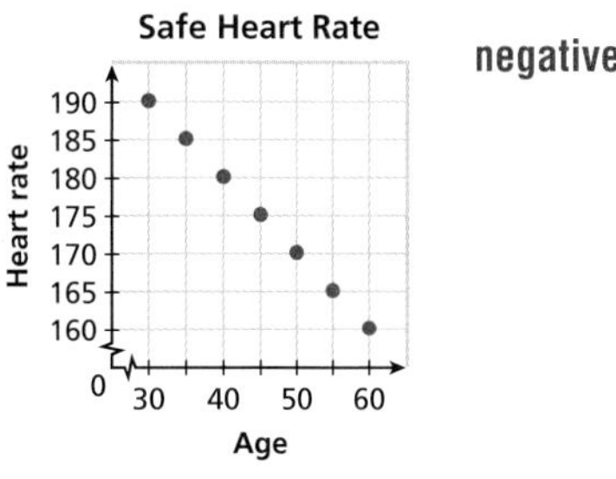

negative

TEST PREP DOCTOR In **Exercise 43,** tell students to note that the data in the second column are decreasing. This means that the common difference will be negative. They can eliminate choices **G** and **H.** Students who chose **J** may not understand what the common difference is. Remind them that d is the difference between consecutive terms.

In **Exercise 44,** point out to students that although choice **C** does have a pattern, it is not arithmetic. You cannot add the same number to each term to get the next term.

Journal

Have students compare and contrast determining whether a sequence is arithmetic to determining whether a function is linear.

ALTERNATIVE ASSESSMENT

Have students create three arithmetic sequences. Then have them find the 10th, 25th, and 100th terms for each sequence.

Power Presentations with PowerPoint®

4-6 Lesson Quiz

Determine whether each sequence appears to be an arithmetic sequence. If so, find the common difference and the next three terms.

1. 3, 9, 27, 81, . . . no
2. 5, 6.5, 8, 9.5, . . . yes; 1.5; 11, 12.5, 14

Find the indicated term of each arithmetic sequence.

3. 23rd term: −4, −7, −10, −13, . . . −70
4. 40th term: 2, 7, 12, 17, . . . 197
5. 7th term: $a_1 = -12, d = 2$ 0
6. 34th term: $a_1 = 3.2, d = 2.6$ 89
7. On day 1, Zelle has knitted 61 rows of a scarf. Each following day she adds 17 more rows. How many total rows has Zelle knitted on day 16? 316 rows

Also available on transparency

4-6 PROBLEM SOLVING

Find the indicated term of each arithmetic sequence.

1. Darnell has a job and his saving his paychecks each week.

Weeks	1	2	3	4
Savings	$130	$260	$390	$520

How much will Darnell have saved after 11 weeks?

$1430

2. A tube containing 3 ounces of toothpaste is being used at a rate of 0.15 ounces per day. How much toothpaste will be in the tube after one week?

1.95 ounces

3. A new car costs $13,000 and is depreciating by $900 each year. How much will the car be worth after 4 years?

$9400

4. Jessie is playing an arcade game that costs 50¢ for the first game and 25¢ to continue if she loses. How much will she spend on the game if she continues 9 times?

$2.75

Use the graph below to answer questions 5–9. The graph shows the size of Ivor's ant colony over the first four weeks. Assume the ant population will continue to grow at the same rate. Select the best answer.

Ivor's Ant Farm

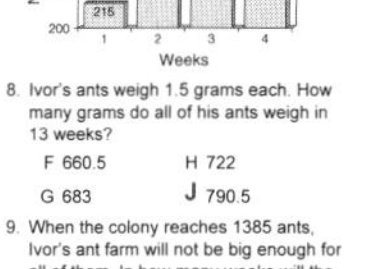

Number of Ants: 300, 275, 250, 225, 200; Weeks: 1, 2, 3, 4; bars: 215, 241, 267, 293

5. Which of the following shows how many ants Ivor will have in the next three weeks?

   A 315, 341, 367
   B 317, 343, 369
   C 318, 334, 350
   D 319, 345, 371

6. Which rule can be used to find how large the colony will be in n weeks?

   F $a_n = 215 + 26n$
   G $a_n = 215n + 26$
   H $a_n = 215(n - 1) + 26$
   J $a_n = 215 + 26(n - 1)$

7. How many ants will Ivor have in 27 weeks?

   A 891 C 5616
   B 917 D 5831

8. Ivor's ants weigh 1.5 grams each. How many grams do all of his ants weigh in 13 weeks?

   F 660.5 H 722
   G 683 **J** 790.5

9. When the colony reaches 1385 ants, Ivor's ant farm will not be big enough for all of them. In how many weeks will the ant population be too large?

   A 45 C 47
   B 46 D 48

4-6 CHALLENGE

The sequence of numbers below is known as the sequence of whole numbers. At an early age, children learn to count by using whole numbers.

0, 1, 2, 3, 4, 5, 6, 7, 8, 9, 10, 11, 12, 13, 14, ...

When you divide each whole number by a fixed number of your choice, you can create a new sequence. The diagram at the right will help you recall the meaning of the terms related to division.

3 ← quotient
divisor → 6)23 ← dividend
18

In Exercises 1–6, consider the set of whole numbers. Write the first 10 terms of the sequence defined by the specified division.

1. the remainder you get when you divide by 1 **0, 0, 0, 0, . . .**
2. the remainder you get when you divide by 2 **0, 1, 0, 1, 0, . . .**
3. the remainder you get when you divide by 3 **0, 1, 2, 0, 1, 2, . . .**
4. the remainder you get when you divide by 4 **0, 1, 2, 3, 0, 1, 2, 3, . . .**
5. the remainder you get when you divide by 5 **0, 1, 2, 3, 4, 0, 1, 2, 3, 4, . . .**
6. the remainder you get when you divide by 6 **0, 1, 2, 3, 4, 5, 0, 1, 2, 3, 4, 5, . . .**
7. a. Suppose that you divide each of the whole numbers by 12. Without writing any division or remainders, write a conjecture about the sequence of remainders that you think you will get.

   The sequence will range from 0 to 11 and then repeat the pattern from 0 to 11. 0, 1, 2, 3, 4, 5, 6, 7, 8, 9, 10, 11, 0, 1, 2, 3, 4, 5, 6, 7, 8, 9, 10, 11, . . .

   b. Write a brief justification of your conjecture from part **a.**

   The remainder will always be a whole number ranging from 0 to 1 less than the divisor. The remainders repeat because every whole number is either a multiple of the divisor or a multiple of the divisor plus a whole number between 1 and 1 less than the divisor inclusive.

8. a. The following sequence of remainders is the result of dividing each whole number by an unknown number. By what number are the whole numbers being divided?

   0, 1, 2, 3, 4, 5, 6, 7, 8, 9, 0, 1, 2, 3, 4, 5, 6, 7, 8, 9, 0, 1, 2, 3, 4, 5, 6, 7, 8, 9, ...

   10

   b. Write a brief justification of your conjecture from part **a.**

   Every whole number divided by 10 will give a remainder that is a whole number from 0 to 9 inclusive.

9. It is noon. Use division and remainders to find what time will be 99 hours from now.

   3:00 P.M.

Organizer

Objective: Assess students' ability to apply concepts and skills in Lessons 4-5 through 4-6 in a real-world format.

Online Edition

Resources

Algebra I Assessments

www.mathtekstoolkit.org

Problem	Text References
1	Lesson 4-5
2	Lesson 4-5
3	Lesson 4-5
4	Lesson 4-6
5	Lesson 4-6

State Resources

STATE

Applying Functions

College Knowledge Myra is helping her brother plan a college visit 10 hours away from their home. She creates a table listing approximate travel times and distances from their home.

Time (h)	Distance (mi)
0	0
2	123
3	190
4	207
6	355
8	472
10	657

1. Create a scatter plot for the data.
2. Draw a trend line through the data.
3. Based on the trend line, how many miles will they have traveled after 5 hours? **Possible answer: 300 miles**
4. If Myra's brother decided to visit a college 13 hours away from their home, approximately how many miles will they travel? **approximately 800 miles**
5. To find the average speed for the entire trip, find $\frac{\text{change in distance}}{\text{change in time}}$ between the initial ordered pair and the final ordered pair. Include the units. **65.7 mi/h**

1, 2.

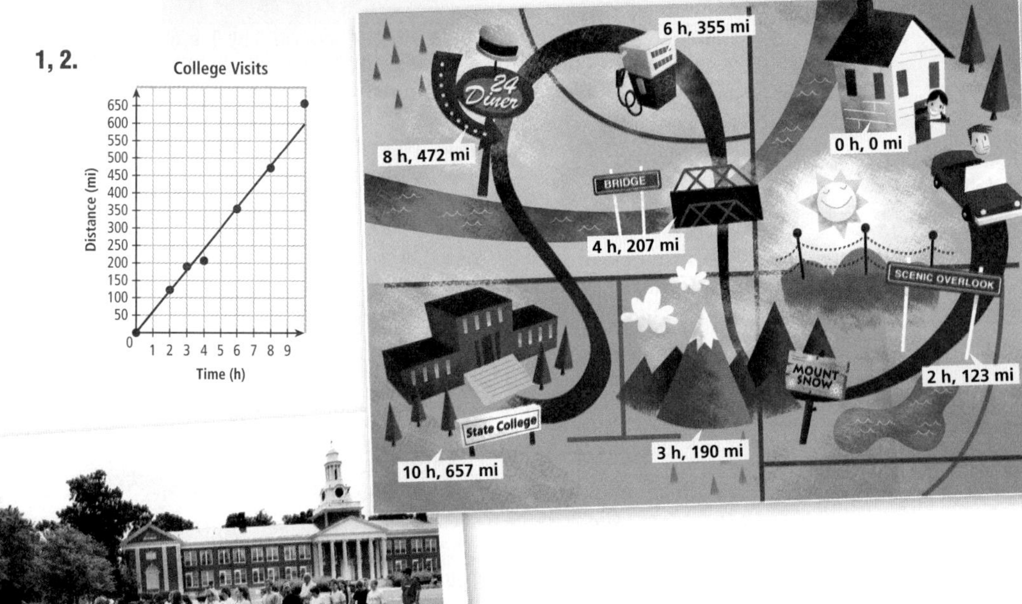

INTERVENTION

Scaffolding Questions

1. What are two points that will be graphed? Possible answer: (0, 0), (4, 207)
2. Does the trend line have to go through all the points? no

3–4. How do you use a trend line to make predictions? Find the point on the graph with the given x-value and use it to identify the corresponding y-value.

5. What is the total change in distance? 657 mi What is the total change in time? 10 h

Extension

Based on the scatter plot, how far away would you estimate the college to be if Myra and her brother traveled for 15 hours? about 985 mi

SECTION 4B

Quiz for Lessons 4-5 Through 4-6

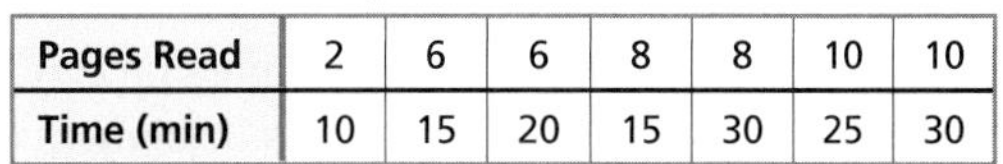

1. (scatter plot: Time (min) vs. Pages read)

4-5 Scatter Plots and Trend Lines

The table shows the time it takes different people to read a given number of pages.

Pages Read	2	6	6	8	8	10	10
Time (min)	10	15	20	15	30	25	30

1. Graph a scatter plot using the given data.
2. Describe the correlation illustrated by the scatter plot. **positive**

Choose the scatter plot that best represents the described relationship. Explain.

3. number of movie tickets sold and number of available seats **A**
4. number of movie tickets sold and amount of concession sales **B**
5. number of movie tickets sold and length of movie **C**

Graph A

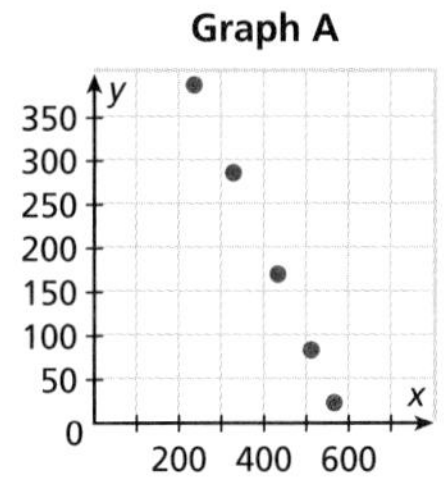

Graph B

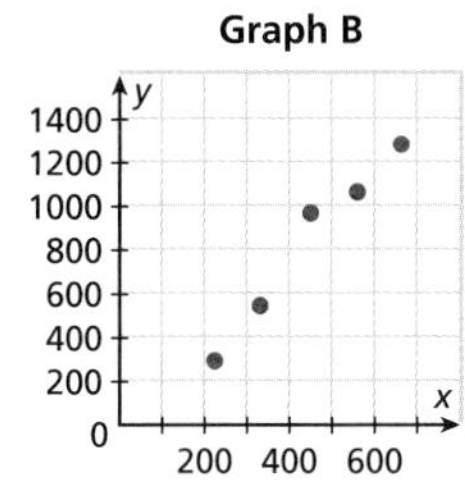

Graph C

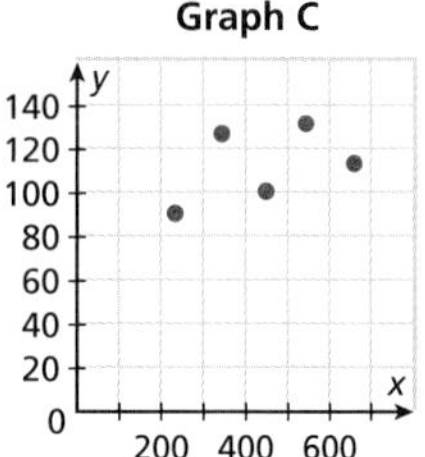

6. The scatter plot shows the estimated annual sales for an electronics and appliance chain of stores for the years 2004–2009. Based on this relationship, predict the annual sales in 2012.
Possible answer: 16.5 million

Estimated Annual Sales

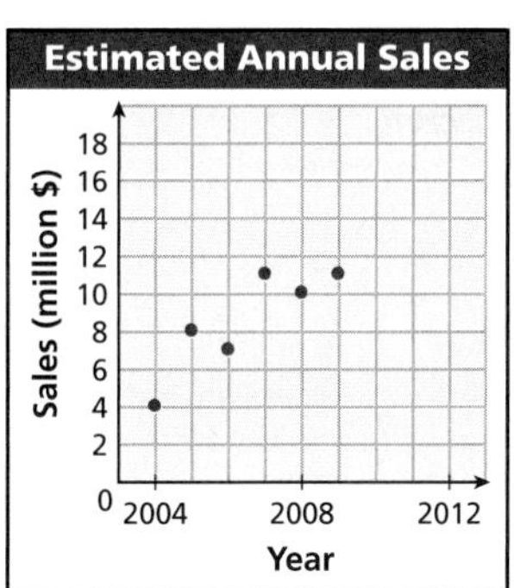

4-6 Arithmetic Sequences

Determine whether each sequence appears to be an arithmetic sequence. If so, find the common difference and the next three terms.

7. 7, 3, −1, −5, … **yes; −4; −9, −13, −17**
8. 3, 6, 12, 24, … **no**
9. −3.5, −2, −0.5, 1, … **yes; 1.5; 2.5, 4, 5.5**

Find the indicated term of the arithmetic sequence.

10. 31st term: 12, 7, 2, −3, … **−138**
11. 22nd term: $a_1 = 6$; $d = 4$ **90**
12. With no air resistance, an object would fall 16 feet during the first second, 48 feet during the second second, 80 feet during the third second, 112 feet during the fourth second, and so on. How many feet will the object fall during the ninth second? **272 ft**

READY TO GO ON?

SECTION 4B

Organizer

Objective: Assess students' mastery of concepts and skills in Lessons 4-5 through 4-6.

Resources

Assessment Resources
Section 4B Quiz

Teacher One Stop™
Test & Practice Generator

INTERVENTION

Resources

Ready to Go On? Intervention and Enrichment Worksheets

***Ready to Go On?* CD-ROM**

***Ready to Go On?* Online**

my.hrw.com

NO INTERVENE

READY TO GO ON? Diagnose and Prescribe

Ready to Go On? Intervention	*Ready to Go On? Intervention*, Section 4B: Worksheets	CD-ROM	Online
Lesson 4-5	4-5 Intervention	Activity 4-5	Diagnose and Prescribe Online
Lesson 4-6	4-6 Intervention	Activity 4-6	

YES ENRICH

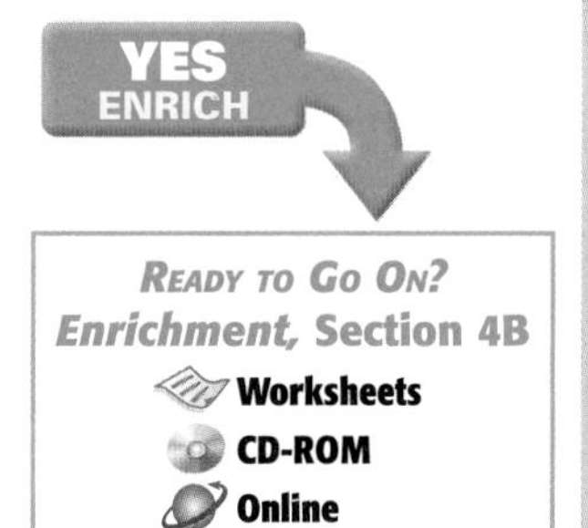

Ready to Go On? Enrichment, Section 4B
Worksheets
CD-ROM
Online

Study Guide: Review

Organizer

Objective: Help students organize and review key concepts and skills presented in Chapter 4.

PREMIER **Online Edition**
Multilingual Glossary

Resources

Teacher One Stop™
PuzzleView
Test & Practice Generator

***Multilingual Glossary* Online**
go.hrw.com
KEYWORD: MA7 Glossary

Lesson Tutorial Videos
CD-ROM

Answers

1. domain
2. negative correlation
3. term
4. continuous

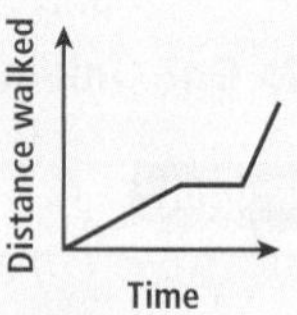

5. continuous

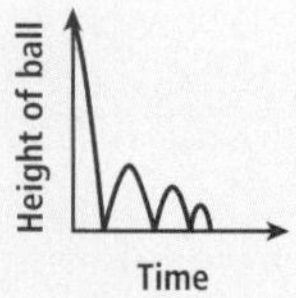

6. continuous

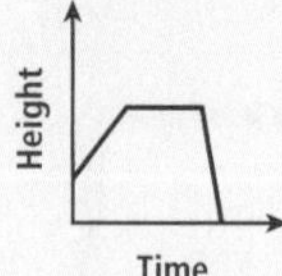

7. Possible answer: A family buys a fish tank and some fish. After two weeks, they buy some more fish. After two more weeks, they even buy more fish.
8. Possible answer: A monkey swings from a high branch to a lower branch. He climbs along the branch. Then he jumps to a higher branch and takes a nap.

CHAPTER 4

Study Guide: Review

Vocabulary

arithmetic sequence	276	**function**	241	**range**	240
common difference	276	**function notation**	250	**relation**	240
continuous graph	235	**function rule**	250	**scatter plot**	266
correlation	266	**independent variable**	250	**sequence**	276
dependent variable	250	**negative correlation**	267	**term**	276
discrete graph	235	**no correlation**	267	**trend line**	269
domain	240	**positive correlation**	267		

Complete the sentences below with vocabulary words from the list above.

1. The set of x-coordinates of the ordered pairs of a relation is called the ___?___.
2. If one set of data values increases as another set of data values decreases, the relationship can be described as having a(n) ___?___.
3. A sequence is an ordered list of numbers where each number is a(n) ___?___.

4-1 Graphing Relationships *(pp. 234–239)*

EXAMPLES

Sketch a graph for each situation. Tell whether the graph is continuous or discrete.

- A parking meter has a limit of 1 hour. The cost is \$0.25 per 15 minutes and the meter accepts quarters only.

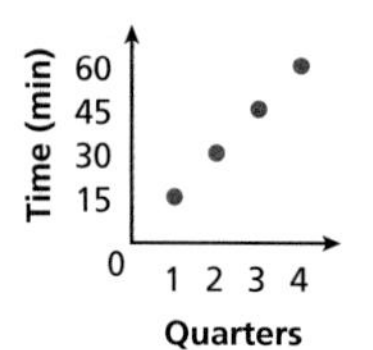

Since only quarters are accepted, the points are not connected.

The graph is discrete.

- Ian bought a cup of coffee. At first, he sipped slowly. As it cooled, he drank more quickly. The last bit was cold, and he dumped it out.

As time passes the coffee was **sipped slowly, drank more quickly,** and then **dumped out.**

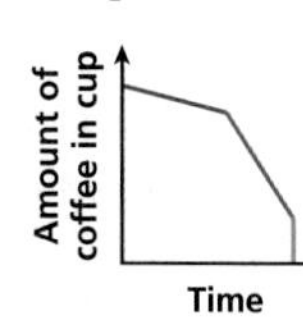

The graph is continuous.

EXERCISES

Sketch a graph for each situation. Tell whether the graph is continuous or discrete.

4. A girl was walking home at a steady pace. Then she stopped to talk to a friend. After her friend left, she jogged the rest of the way home.
5. A ball is dropped from a second story window and bounces to a stop on the patio below.
6. Jason was on the second floor when he got a call to attend a meeting on the sixth floor. He took the stairs. After the meeting, he took the elevator to the first floor.

Write a possible situation for each graph.

7. 8.

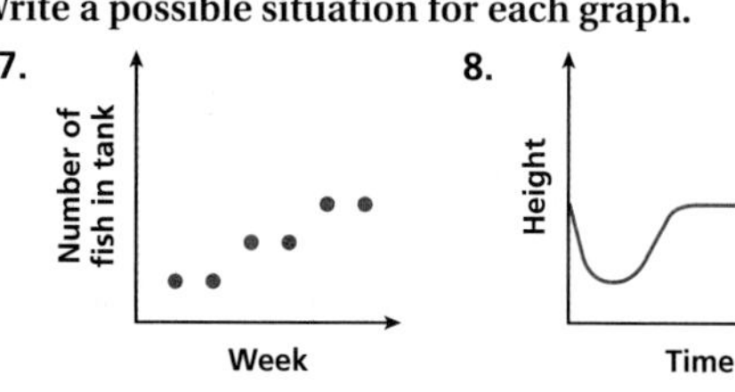

4-2 Relations and Functions *(pp. 240–246)*

EXAMPLES

■ Express the relation $\{(2, 15), (4, 12), (5, 7), (7, 2)\}$ as a table, as a graph, and as a mapping diagram.

Table

x	y
2	15
4	12
5	7
7	2

Graph

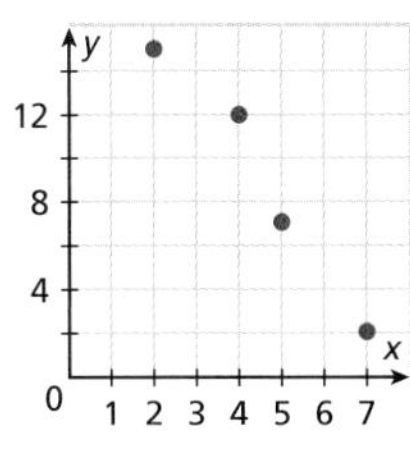

Mapping Diagram

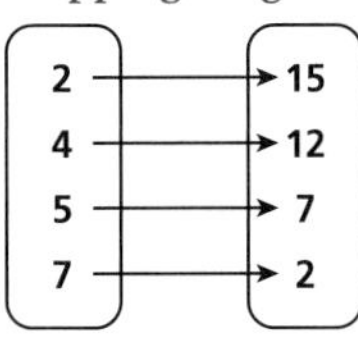

Give the domain and range of each relation. Tell whether the relation is a function. Explain.

■

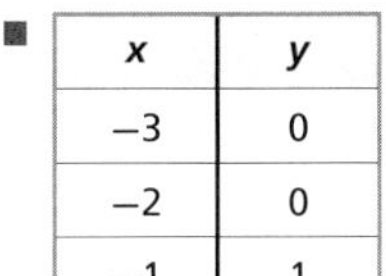

x	y
−3	0
−2	0
−1	1

D: $\{-3, -2, -1\}$

R: $\{0, 1\}$

The relation is a function because each domain value is paired with exactly one range value.

■

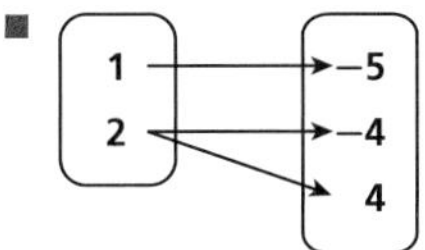

D: $\{1, 2\}$

R: $\{-5, -4, 4\}$

The relation is not a function because one domain value is paired with two range values.

■

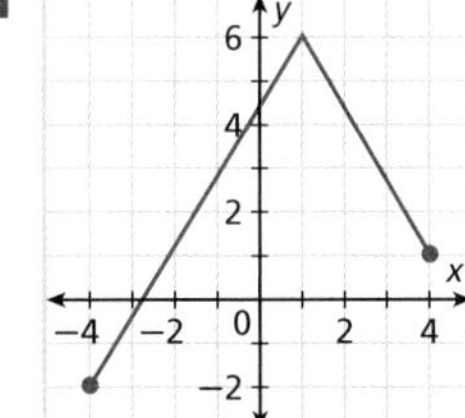

D: $-4 \le x \le 4$

R: $-2 \le y \le 6$

The relation is a function because every x-value is paired with exactly one y-value.

EXERCISES

Express each relation as a table, as a graph, and as a mapping diagram.

9. $\{(-1, 0), (0, 1), (2, 1)\}$
10. $\{(-2, -1), (-1, 1), (2, 3), (3, 4)\}$

Give the domain and range of each relation.

11. $\{(-4, 5), (-2, 3), (0, 1), (2, -1)\}$
12. $\{(-2, -1)\ (-1, 0), (0, -1), (1, 0), (2, -1)\}$

13.

x	0	1	4	1	4
y	0	−1	−2	1	2

14.

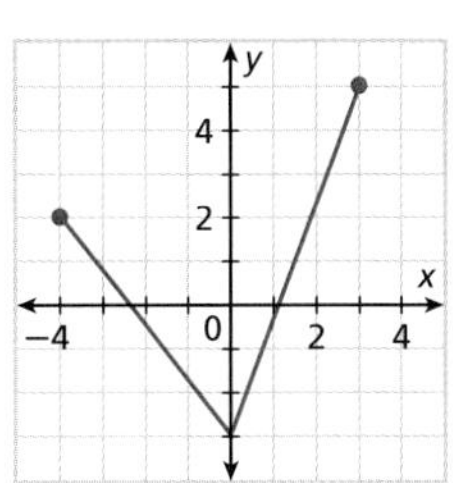

Give the domain and range of each relation. Tell whether the relation is a function. Explain.

15. $\{(-5, -3), (-3, -2), (-1, -1), (1, 0)\}$

16.

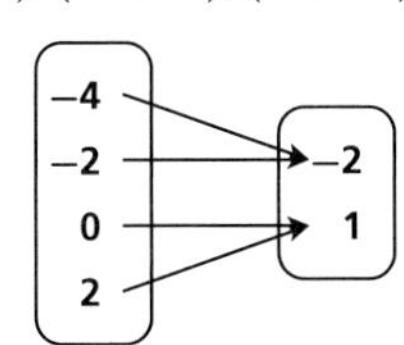

17.

x	1	2	3	4	1
y	3	2	1	0	−1

18. A local parking garage charges \$5.00 for the first hour plus \$1.50 for each additional hour or part of an hour. Write a relation as a set of ordered pairs in which the x-value represents the number of hours and the y-value represents the cost for x hours. Use a domain of 1, 2, 3, 4, 5. Is this relation a function? Explain.

19. A baseball coach is taking the team for ice cream. Four students can ride in each car. Create a mapping diagram to show the number of cars needed to transport 8, 10, 14, and 16 students. Is this relation a function? Explain.

Answers

9.

x	−1	0	2
y	0	1	1

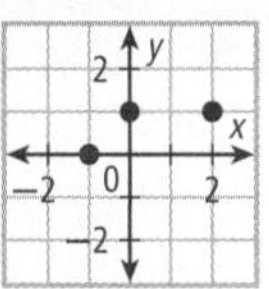

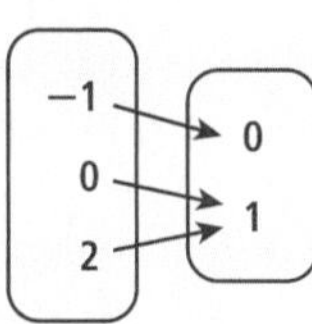

10.

x	−2	−1	2	3
y	−1	1	3	4

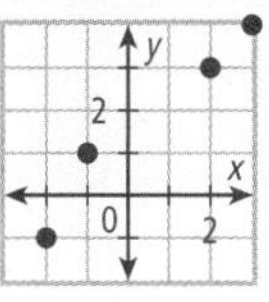

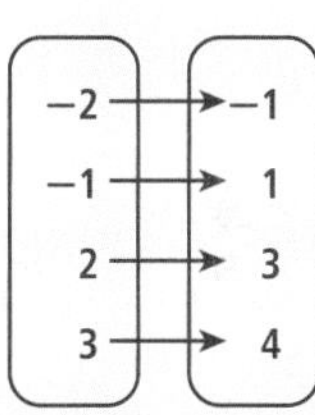

11. D: $\{-4, -2, 0, 2\}$; R: $\{-1, 1, 3, 5\}$
12. D: $\{-2, -1, 0, 1, 2\}$; R: $\{-1, 0\}$
13. D: $\{0, 1, 4\}$; R: $\{-2, -1, 0, 1, 2\}$
14. D: $-4 \le x \le 3$; R: $-3 \le y \le 5$
15. D: $\{-5, -3, -1, 1\}$; R: $\{-3, -2, -1, 0\}$; yes; every element of the domain is assigned to exactly one element in the range.
16. D: $\{-4, -2, 0, 2\}$; R: $\{-2, 1\}$; yes; each element of the domain is assigned to exactly one element in the range.
17. D: $\{1, 2, 3, 4\}$; R: $\{-1, 0, 1, 2, 3\}$; no; the x-value 1 is assigned to the y-value 3 and the y-value −1.
18. $\{(1, 5.00), (2, 6.50), (3, 8.00), (4, 9.50), (5, 11.00)\}$; yes; each x-value has exactly one y-value.
19.

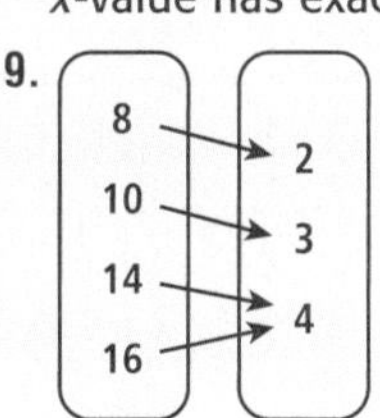

Yes; each element in the domain is assigned to exactly one element in the range.

Answers

20. y is 7 less than x; $y = x - 7$.
21. y is 9 times x; $y = 9x$.
22. ind.: number of cakes; dep.: cost; $f(c) = 6c$
23. ind.: number of CDs Raul will buy; dep.: number of CDs Tim will buy; $g(n) = 2n$
24. 14
25. −11
26. 6; −1
27.

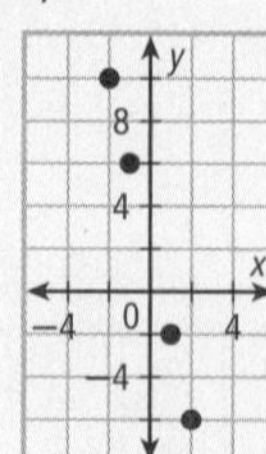

28.

29.

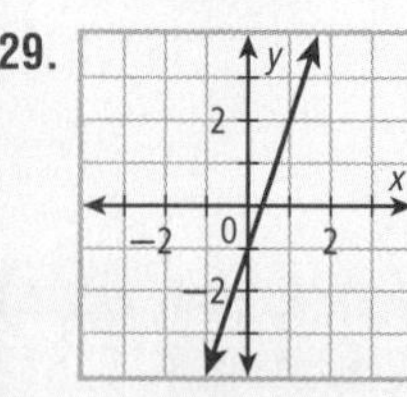

30.

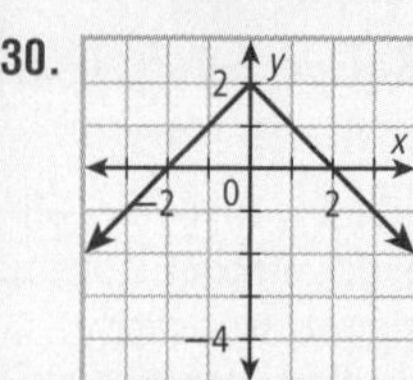

31.

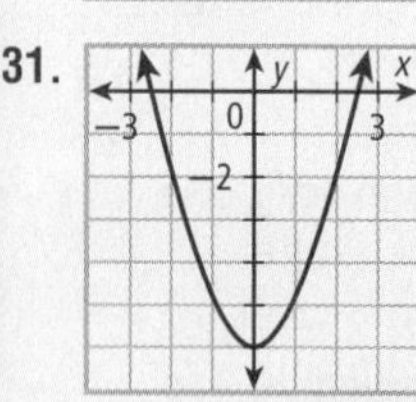

32.

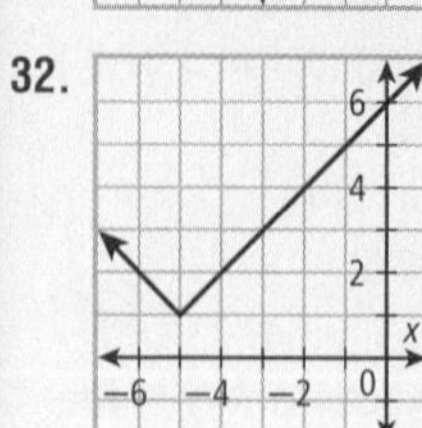

4-3 Writing Functions *(pp. 249–255)*

EXAMPLES

- **Determine a relationship between the x- and y-values in the table. Write an equation.**

x	1	2	3	4
y	−3	−6	−9	−12

What are possible relationships between the x-values and the y-values?

$1 - 4 = -3$ $\quad 1(-3) = -3$

$2 - 4 \neq -6$ ✗ $\quad 2(-3) = -6$ ✓

$3(-3) = -9$ ✓

$4(-3) = -12$ ✓

$y = -3x$ *Write an equation.*

- **Nia earns \$5.25 per hour. Identify the independent and dependent variables. Write an equation in function notation for the situation.**

  Nia's pay depends on the number of hours she works.
  Dependent: pay
  Independent: hours

  Let h represent the number of hours Nia works.
  The function for Nia's pay is $f(h) = 5.25h$.

EXERCISES

Determine the relationship between the x- and y-values. Write an equation.

20.

x	1	2	3	4
y	−6	−5	−4	−3

21. $\{(1, 9), (2, 18), (3, 27), (4, 36)\}$

Identify the independent and dependent variables. Write an equation in function notation for the situation.

22. A baker spends \$6 on ingredients for each cake he bakes.
23. Tim will buy twice as many CDs as Raul.

Evaluate each function for the given input values.

24. For $f(x) = -2x + 4$, find $f(x)$ when $x = -5$.
25. For $g(n) = -n^2 - 2$, find $g(n)$ when $n = -3$.
26. For $h(t) = 7 - |t + 3|$, find $h(t)$ when $t = -4$ and when $t = 5$.

4-4 Graphing Functions *(pp. 256–262)*

EXAMPLE

- **Graph the function $y = 3x - 1$.**

Step 1 Choose several values of x to generate ordered pairs.

x	$y = 3x - 1$	y
−1	$y = 3(-1) - 1 = -4$	−4
0	$y = 3(0) - 1 = -1$	−1
1	$y = 3(1) - 1 = 2$	2
2	$y = 3(2) - 1 = 5$	5

Step 2 Plot enough points to see a pattern.

Step 3 Draw a line through the points to show all the ordered pairs that satisfy this function.

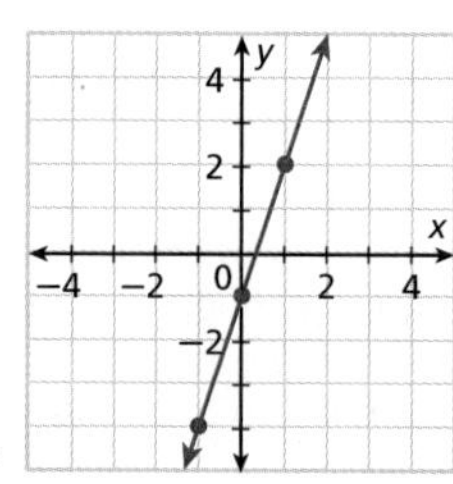

EXERCISES

Graph each function for the domain $\{-2, -1, 1, 2\}$.

27. $4x + y = 2$
28. $y = (1 - x)^2$

Graph each function.

29. $3x - y = 1$
30. $y = 2 - |x|$
31. $y = x^2 - 6$
32. $y = |x + 5| + 1$
33. The function $y = 6.25x$ describes the amount of money y Peter gets paid after x hours. Graph the function. Use the graph to estimate how much money Peter gets paid after 7 hours.

33.

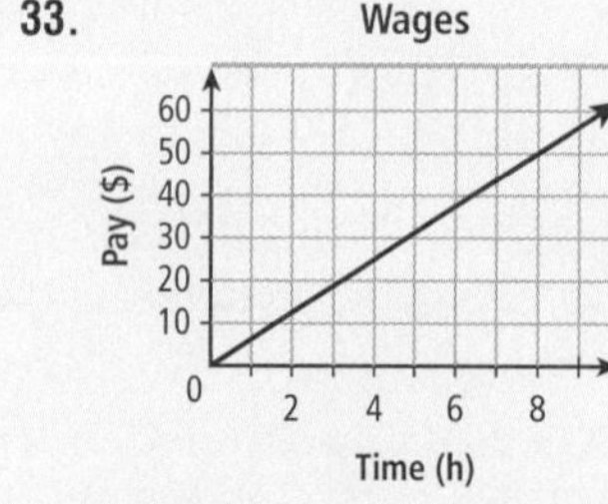

Possible answer: about \$44

4-5 Scatter Plots and Trend Lines *(pp. 266–273)*

EXAMPLE

- **The graph shows the amount of money in a savings account. Based on this relationship, predict how much money will be in the account in month 7.**

Draw a line that has about the same number of points above and below it. Your line may or may not go through data points.

Find the point on the line whose x-value is 7.

Based on the data, $90 is a reasonable prediction.

EXERCISES

34. The table shows the value of a car for the given years. Graph a scatter plot using the given data. Describe the correlation illustrated by the scatter plot.

Year	2000	2001	2002	2003
Value (thousand $)	28	25	23	20

35. The graph shows the results of a 2003–2004 survey on class size at the given grade levels. Based on this relationship, predict the class size for the 9th grade.

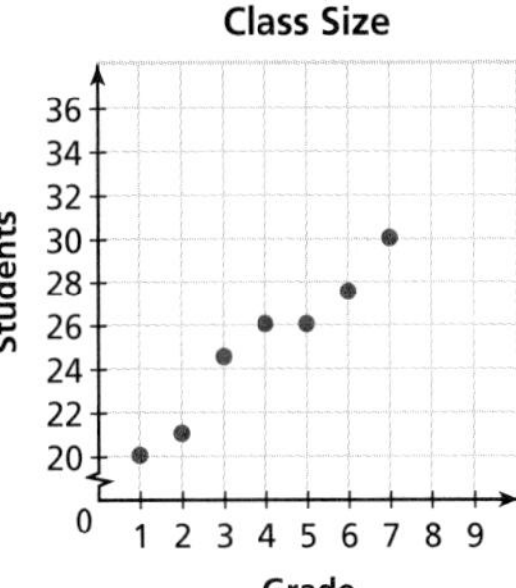

4-6 Arithmetic Sequences *(pp. 276–281)*

EXAMPLES

- **Determine whether the sequence appears to be arithmetic. If so, find the common difference and the next three terms.**

−8, −5 ,−2 , 1,...

Step 1 Find the difference between successive terms.

−8, −5, −2, 1,... *The common difference is 3.*
+3 +3 +3

Step 2 Use the common difference to find the next 3 terms.

−8, −5, −2, 1, 4, 7, 10
+3 +3 +3

- **Find the 18th term of the arithmetic sequence for which $a_1 = -4$ and $d = 6$.**

$a_n = a_1 + (n - 1)d$ *Write the rule.*
$a_{18} = -4 + (18 - 1)6$ *Substitute.*
$= -4 + (17)6$ *Simplify.*
$= -4 + 102$ *Simplify.*
$= 98$

The 18th term is 98.

EXERCISES

Determine whether each sequence appears to be arithmetic. If so, find the common difference and the next three terms.

36. 20, 14, 8, 2,...

37. −15, −12, −9, −4,...

38. 5, 4, 2, −1,...

39. −8, −5.5, −3, −0.5,...

Find the indicated term of each arithmetic sequence.

40. 31st term: −15, −11, −7, −3,...

41. 24th term: $a_1 = 7$; $d = -3$

42. 17th term: $a_1 = -20$; $d = 2.5$

43. Marie has $180 in a savings account in week 1. She plans to deposit $12 each following week. Assuming that she does not withdraw any money from her account, what will her balance be in week 20?

44. The table shows the temperature at the given heights above sea level. Use an arithmetic sequence to find the temperature at 8000 feet above sea level.

Height Above Sea Level (thousand feet)	1	2	3	4
Temperature (°C)	30	23.5	17	10.5

Answers

34.

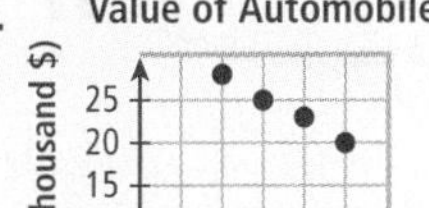

Negative; as the time increases, the value of the automobile decreases.

35. Possible answer: 33

36. yes; −6; −4, −10, −16

37. no

38. no

39. yes; 2.5; 2, 4.5, 7

40. 105

41. −62

42. 20

43. $408

44. −15.5 °C

Study Guide: Review 287

Organizer

Objective: Assess students' mastery of concepts and skills in Chapter 4.

Online Edition

Resources

Assessment Resources

Chapter 4 Tests

- Free Response (Levels A, B, C)
- Multiple Choice (Levels A, B, C)
- Performance Assessment

Teacher One Stop™

Test & Practice Generator

Answers

9. 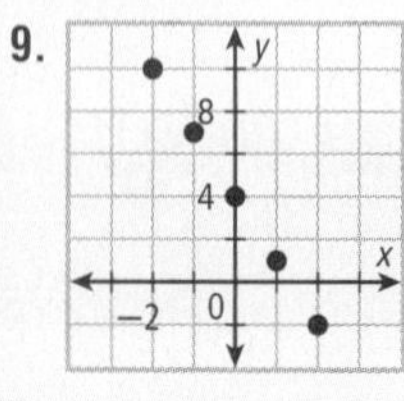

10. 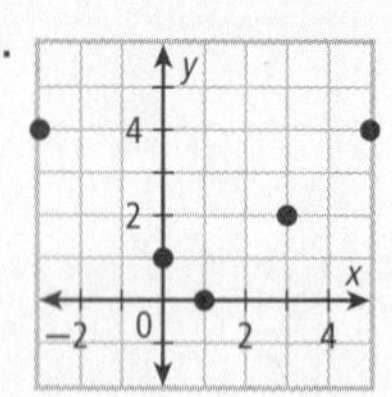

State Resources

CHAPTER 4 CHAPTER TEST

Choose the graph that best represents each situation.

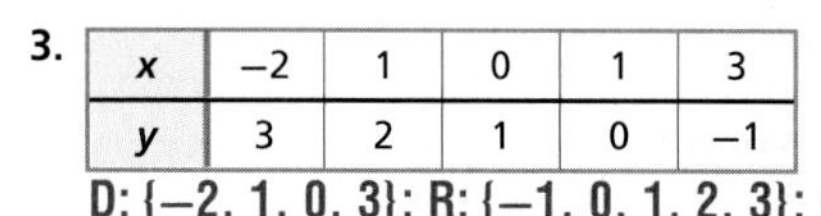

1. A person walks leisurely, stops, and then continues walking. **A**
2. A person jogs, then runs, and then jogs again. **B**

Give the domain and range for each relation.
Tell whether the relation is a function. Explain.

3.

x	−2	1	0	1	3
y	3	2	1	0	−1

D: {−2, 1, 0, 3}; R: {−1, 0, 1, 2, 3}; no; the x-value 1 is assigned to the y-value 2 and the y-value 0.

4. 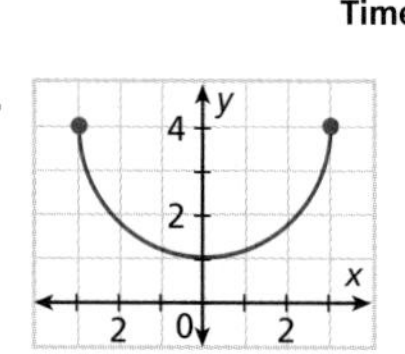

D: $-3 \le x \le 3$; R: $1 \le y \le 4$; yes; each element in the domain is assigned to exactly one element in the range.

5. Bowling costs \$3 per game plus \$2.50 for shoe rental. Identify the independent and dependent variables. Write an equation in function notation for the situation.
ind.: games played; dep.: total cost; $y = 3x + 2.50$

Evaluate each function for the given input values.

6. For $f(x) = -3x + 4$, find $f(x)$ when $x = -2$. **10**
7. For $f(x) = 2x^2$, find $f(x)$ when $x = -3$. **18**
8. An engraver charges a \$10 fee plus \$6 for each line of engraving. Write a function to describe the situation. Find a reasonable domain and range for the function for up to 8 lines.
$y = 10 + 6x$; D: {1, 2, 3, 4, 5, 6, 7, 8}; R: {16, 22, 28, 34, 40, 46, 52, 58}

Graph each function for the given domain.

9. $3x + y = 4$; D: {−2, −1, 0, 1, 2}
10. $y = |x - 1|$; D: {−3, 0, 1, 3, 5}
11. $y = x^2 - 1$; D: {−2, −1, 0, 1, 2}

Graph each function.

12. $y = x - 5$
13. $y = x^2 - 5$
14. $y = |x| + 3$
15. The function $y = 30x$ describes the amount of interest y earned in a savings account in x years. Graph the function. Use the graph to estimate the total amount of interest earned in 7 years.

The table shows possible recommendations for the amount of sleep that children should get every day.

Age (yr)	1	2	3	4	5	14
Sleep Needed (h)	14	13	12	12	11	9

16. Graph a scatter plot of the given data.
17. Describe the correlation illustrated by the scatter plot. **17. Negative; as the child's age increases, the number of hours of sleep needed decreases.**
18. Predict how many hours of sleep a 16-year-old needs. **Possible answer: 7 h**

Determine whether each sequence appears to be an arithmetic sequence. If so, find the common difference and the next three terms.

19. 11, 6, 1, −4,... **yes; −5; −9, −14, −19**
20. −4, −3, −1, 2,... **no**
21. 7, 21, 30, 45,... **no**

Find the indicated term of the arithmetic sequence.

22. 32nd term: 18, 11, 4, −3,... **−199**
23. 24th term: $a_1 = 4$; $d = 6$ **142**
24. Mandy's new job has a starting salary of \$16,000 and annual increases of \$800. How much will she earn during her fifth year? **\$19,200**

11. 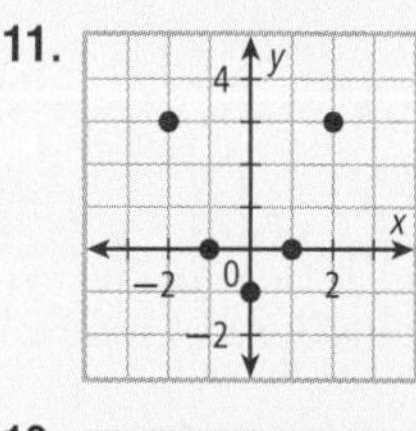

12. 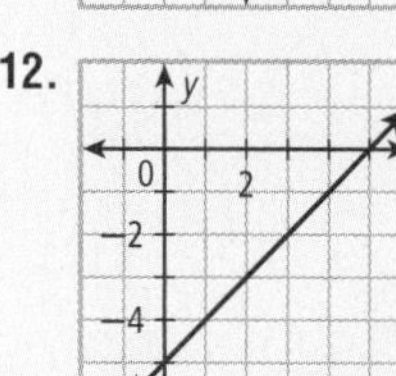

13. 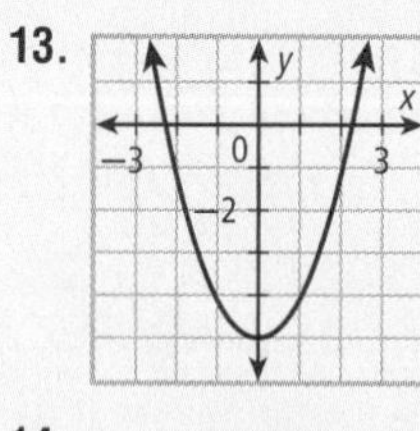

14. 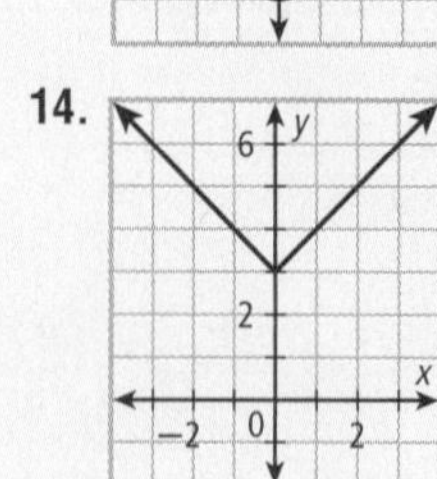

15. Possible answer: \$210

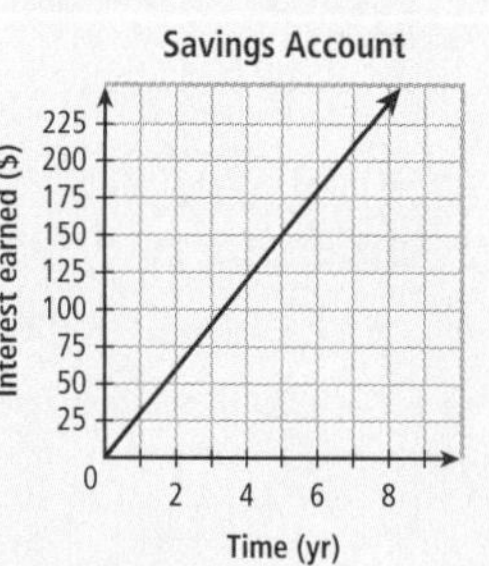

16. See p. A19.

COLLEGE ENTRANCE EXAM PRACTICE

FOCUS ON ACT

Questions on the ACT Mathematics Test do not require the use of a calculator, but you may bring one to use with the test. Make sure that it is a calculator that is on the approved list for the ACT.

You may want to time yourself as you take this practice test. It should take you about 6 minutes to complete.

When taking the test, you will be more comfortable using a calculator that you are used to. If you already have a calculator, make sure it is one of the permitted calculators. If you plan to use a new one, make sure to practice using it before the test.

1. The soccer team is ordering new uniforms. There is a one-time setup charge of \$50.00, and each uniform costs \$23.50. Which of the following best describes the total cost C for ordering uniforms for p players?

   (A) $C = 23.50p$

   (B) $C = 50p$

   (C) $C = 73.50p$

   (D) $C = 23.50p + 50$

   (E) $C = 50p + 23.50$

2. In the given relation, what domain value corresponds to the range value -2?
   $\{(-1, 2), (-2, 4), (2, 5), (0, -2), (2, 0)\}$

   (F) -2

   (G) 0

   (H) 2

   (J) 4

   (K) 5

3. Evaluate $h(x) = \frac{1}{2}(5 - 6x) + 9x$ when $x = \frac{2}{3}$.

   (A) $\frac{9}{2}$

   (B) $\frac{13}{2}$

   (C) 7

   (D) $\frac{19}{2}$

   (E) $\frac{23}{2}$

4. What is the seventh term of the arithmetic sequence $-4, -1, 2 \ldots$?

   (F) 5

   (G) 10

   (H) 11

   (J) 14

   (K) 17

5. The graph of which function is shown below?

   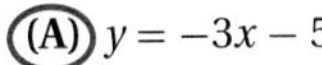
   (A) $y = -3x - 5$

   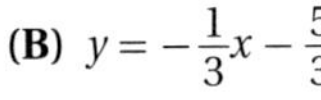
   (B) $y = -\frac{1}{3}x - \frac{5}{3}$

   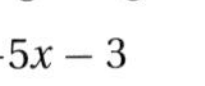
   (C) $y = -5x - 3$

   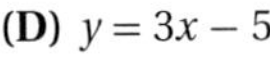
   (D) $y = 3x - 5$

   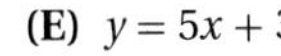
   (E) $y = 5x + 3$

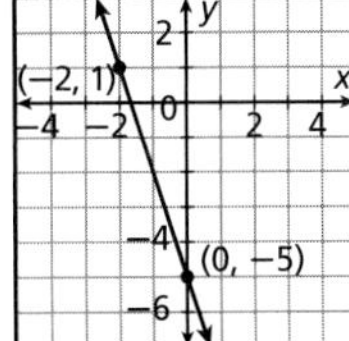

6. Which of the following relations is NOT a function?

   (F) $\{(0, 1), (1, 2), (2, 3), (3, 4)\}$

   (G) $\{(1, 2), (2, 2), (3, 3), (4, 3)\}$

   (H) $\{(0, 2), (2, 4), (4, 1), (1, 3)\}$

   (J) $\{(1, 3), (4, 2), (2, 0), (3, 4)\}$

   (K) $\{(0, 2), (1, 3), (4, 3), (1, 2)\}$

Organizer

Objective: Provide practice for college entrance exams such as the ACT.

PREMIER **Online Edition**

Resources

College Entrance Exam Practice

Questions on the ACT represent the following content areas:

Pre-Algebra, 23%

Elementary Algebra, 17%

Intermediate Algebra, 15%

Coordinate Geometry, 15%

Plane Geometry, 23%

Trigonometry, 7%

Items on this page focus on:

- Elementary Algebra
- Coordinate Geometry

Text References:

Item	1	2	3	4	5	6
Lesson	4-3	4-2	4-3	4-6	4-4	4-2

TEST PREP DOCTOR

1. Students who chose **A** did not take into account the setup charge for the order. Students who chose **C** added the one-time setup charge to the price for each uniform.
2. Students who chose **J** may not understand the meaning of the terms *domain* and *range*. Students who selected a different incorrect answer may not have read the problem carefully.
3. Students who chose **E** found $h\left(\frac{3}{2}\right)$ instead of $h\left(\frac{2}{3}\right)$. Students who chose **A** may have tried to simplify the expression before evaluating it and may not have applied the distributive property correctly.
4. Students who chose **G** may have incorrectly remembered the formula for finding the nth term of an arithmetic sequence as $a_n = a_1 + (d - 1)n$. Suggest to students that when the term to be found is a low-numbered term of the sequence, they can add the common difference repeatedly to find the result.
5. Students who chose **B** reversed the values of x and y in the definition of the function.
6. Students who chose **G** may think that a function is a relation in which each element of the range corresponds to exactly one element of the domain.

Organizer

Objective: Provide opportunities to learn and practice common test-taking strategies.

This Test Tackler explains how extended-response test items are scored and demonstrates how to create a response that is deserving of full credit. Explain to students that extended-response questions are longer and more complex than short-response questions and that the scoring rubric used is based on a 4-point scale rather than a 2-point scale. Use the analogy that these questions are like essay questions in an English class; they require complete explanations to receive full credit.

Extended Response: Understand the Scores

Extended response test items are typically multipart questions that require a high level of thinking. The responses are scored using a 4-point rubric. To receive full credit, you must correctly answer all parts of the question and provide a clear explanation. A partial answer is worth 2 or 3 points, an incorrect solution is worth 1 point, and no response is worth 0 points.

EXAMPLE 1

Extended Response A train traveling from Boston, Massachusetts, to Richmond, Virginia, averages about 55 miles per hour. Define variables, write an equation, make a table, and draw a graph to show the distance the train travels in 5 hours.

Here are examples of four different responses and their scores using the rubric shown.

4-point response:

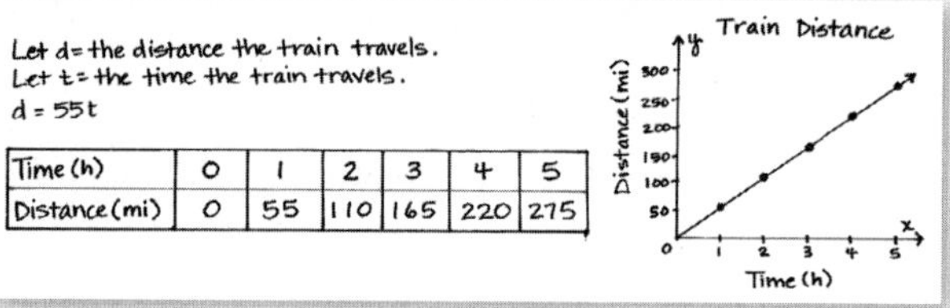

3-point response:

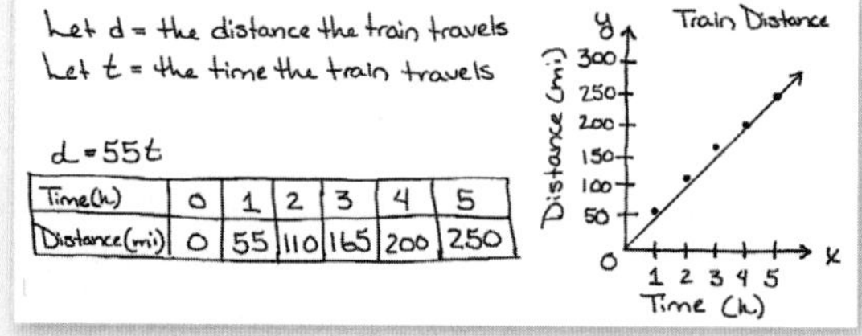

The student shows all of the work, but there are two minor computation errors when t = 4 and t = 5.

2-point response:

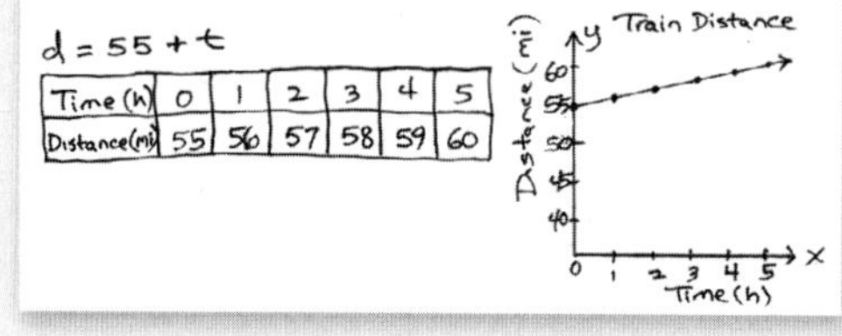

The student writes an incorrect equation and uses it to create an incorrect table and graph.

1-point response:

$d = 55t$

The student does not answer two parts of the question.

TEST PREP DOCTOR +

As you read through each test item, ask students to determine how many parts are in each question. Encourage students to underline key words in the question: *List, Explain, Solve,* etc.

Never leave an extended-response test item blank. At least try to define variables or write equations where appropriate. You will get some points just for trying.

Read each test item and answer the questions that follow using the rubric below.

Scoring Rubric:

4 points: The student shows all of the work, correctly answers all parts of the question, and provides a clear explanation.

3 points: The student shows most of the work and provides a clear explanation but has a minor computation error, or the student shows all of the work and arrives at a correct solution but does not provide a clear explanation.

2 points: The student makes major errors resulting in an incorrect solution, or the student gives a correct solution but does not show any work nor provide an explanation.

1 point: The student shows no work and gives an incorrect solution.

0 points: The student gives no response.

Item A

Extended Response Draw a graph that is a function. Explain why it is a function. Then draw a graph that is NOT a function. Explain why it is not a function.

1. What should be included in a 4-point response?
2. Explain how would you score the response below.

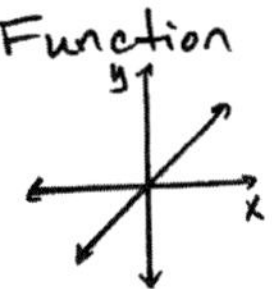

Function — Not a function

The first graph is a function because each x-value has exactly one y-value. When $x=1$, $y=1$. The second graph is not a function because there is more than one y-value for each x-value. When $x=1$, $y=1$, and $y=-1$. Therefore, the second graph is not a function.

Item B

Extended Response A car travels at a steady rate of 60 miles per hour. Identify the independent and dependent variables. Describe the domain and range. Write an equation to describe the situation.

3. Ana wrote the response below.

The equation is $y = 60x$. The independent variable is time and the dependent variable is distance. The domain and range are all real numbers.

Explain how would you score Ana's response.

4. If you did not give Ana full credit, what should be added to Ana's response, if anything, so that it receives full credit?

Item C

Extended Response Lara bought 8 notebooks and 4 binders. She spent \$14 total without tax. How much did each notebook cost if each binder cost \$2.50? Write an equation and find the solution.

5. Explain how would you score the response below.

Let s = the cost of each notebook.
Let b = the cost of each binder.
$8s + 4b = 14$
$8s + 4(2.50) = 14$
$8s + 10 = 14$
$8s = 4$
$s = 2$ The notebooks cost \$2 each

6. If you did not give the response full credit, what should be added to the response, if anything, so that it receives full credit?

Answers

1. Possible answer: a graph of a function and an explanation of why it is a function; a graph of a relation that is not a function and an explanation of why it is not a function
2. Possible answer: The response is worth 4 points because it has two graphs, one of which is a function and one of which is not a function. The explanations are complete and clearly written.
3. Possible answer: 3; Ana answered 2 of the sections correctly, but the domain and range are not all real numbers.
4. The domain and range should be all real numbers greater than or equal to zero.
5. Possible answer: The response is worth 3 points because the student showed all of the work and completed all parts of the question, but in the last step of the equation, the student divided incorrectly.
6. Change the last step to $s = 0.5$ and then state that the notebooks cost \$0.50.

State Resources

Answers to Test Items

A. See answer to Problem 2.

B. The equation is $y = 60x$. The independent variable is time and the dependent variable is distance. The domain and range are all real numbers greater than or equal to zero.

C. \$0.50; let s = the cost of each spiral notebook, let b = the cost of each binder purchased, $8s + 4b = 14$

go.hrw.com
State Resources Online
KEYWORD: MA7 Resources

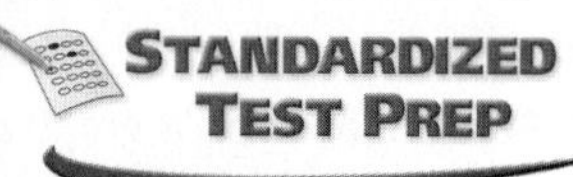

Organizer

Objective: Provide review and practice for Chapters 1–4 and standardized tests.

 Online Edition

Resources

 ***Assessment Resources***

Chapter 4 Cumulative Test

go.hrw.com
KEYWORD: MA7 TestPrep

CUMULATIVE ASSESSMENT, CHAPTERS 1–4

Multiple Choice

1. Find the value of $|a| - b^2$ when $a = -3$ and $b = -5$.
   Ⓐ -28 Ⓑ -22 Ⓒ -7 Ⓓ 4

2. Benito has x apples. He cuts each apple in half and gives each half to a different horse. Which expression represents the number of horses Benito feeds?
   Ⓕ $x \cdot \frac{1}{2}$ Ⓖ $x \div \frac{1}{2}$ Ⓗ $x \cdot 1\frac{1}{2}$ Ⓙ $x \div 1\frac{1}{2}$

3. If the value of a^5 is positive, then which is true?
   Ⓐ a is positive.
   Ⓑ a is negative.
   Ⓒ a^5 is odd.
   Ⓓ a^5 is even.

4. Find the value of $\frac{2a}{a^3}$ if $4 - a = -6$.
   Ⓕ $\frac{1}{50}$ Ⓖ $\frac{1}{2}$ Ⓗ 8 Ⓙ 10

5. There are 36 flowers in a bouquet. Two-thirds of the flowers are roses. One-fourth of the roses are red. What percent of the bouquet is made up of red roses?
   Ⓐ 9% Ⓑ $16\frac{2}{3}\%$ Ⓒ 25% Ⓓ $66\frac{2}{3}\%$

6. A large tree should be planted at least 70 feet away from a power line. Which inequality shows the acceptable number of feet x between a large tree and a power line?
   Ⓕ $x < 70$ Ⓖ $x \le 70$ Ⓗ $x > 70$ Ⓙ $x \ge 70$

7. Which statement is modeled by $3f + 2 > -16$?
   Ⓐ Two added to 3 times f is at least -16.
   Ⓑ Three times the sum of f and 2 is at most -1
   Ⓒ The sum of 2 and 3 times f is more than -1
   Ⓓ The product of $3f$ and 2 is no more than -1

8. Jo Ann needs at least 3 pounds of peaches for a recipe. At the market, she calculates that she has enough money to buy 5 pounds at most. Which graph shows all possible numbers of pounds of peaches Jo Ann can buy so that she has enough for the recipe?
   Ⓕ 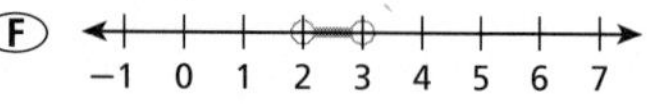
   Ⓖ 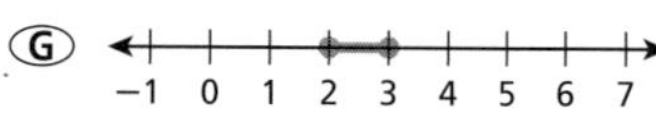
   Ⓗ 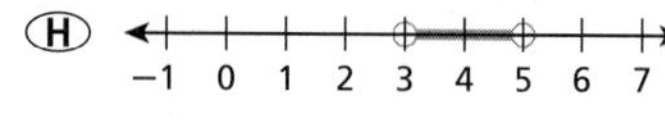
   Ⓙ 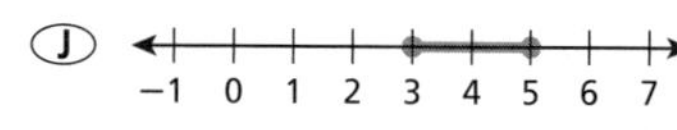

9. A bird flies from the ground to the top of a tree, sits there and sings for a while, flies down to the top of a picnic table to eat crumbs, and then flies back to the top of the tree to sing some more. Which graph best represents this situation?

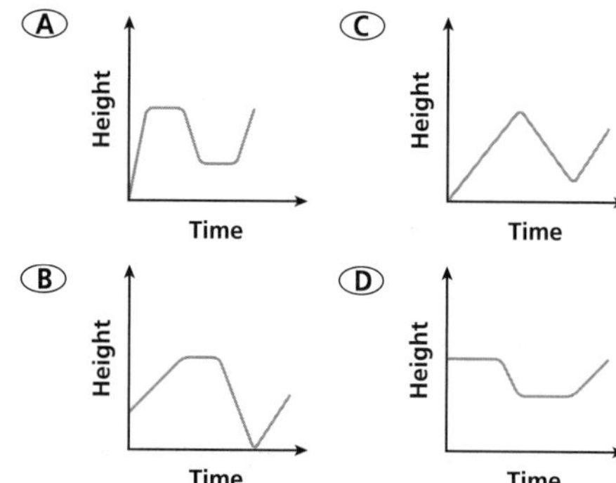

10. Which relation is NOT a function?
   Ⓕ $\{(1, -5), (3, 1), (-5, 4), (4, -2)\}$
   Ⓖ $\{(2, 7), (3, 7), (4, 7), (5, 8)\}$
   Ⓗ $\{(1, -5), (-1, 6), (1, 5), (6, -3)\}$
   Ⓙ $\{(3, -2), (5, -6), (7, 7), (8, 8)\}$

Answers

1. B
2. G
3. A
4. F
5. B
6. J
7. C
8. J
9. A
10. H
11. D
12. F
13. B
14. 9
15. 72
16. 414

State Resources

If possible, use the same calculator you usually use in math class. A timed test is not the right place to figure out where buttons are and how they work. Also, replace your batteries the night before the test. If your batteries run out, you may be given a replacement calculator you are not familiar with.

1. The graph below shows a function.

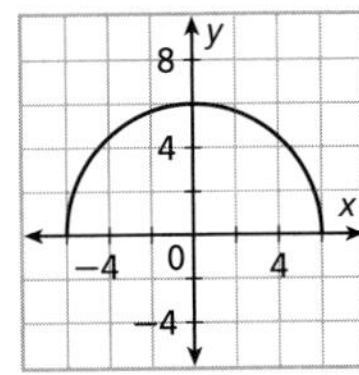

What is the domain of the function?

Ⓐ $x \geq 0$

Ⓑ $x \geq -6$

Ⓒ $0 \leq x \leq 6$

Ⓓ $-6 \leq x \leq 6$

2. Which situation best describes a negative correlation?

Ⓕ The speed of a runner and the time it takes to run a race

Ⓖ The number of apples in a bag and the weight of the bag of apples

Ⓗ The time it takes to repair a car and the amount of the bill

Ⓙ The number of people in a household and the amount of mail in their mailbox

3. Which of the following is a solution of $x + 1 \leq \frac{3}{2}$ AND $x - 1 \geq -\frac{5}{4}$?

Ⓐ $\frac{3}{2}$

Ⓑ $\frac{1}{3}$

Ⓒ $-\frac{1}{3}$

Ⓓ $-\frac{3}{2}$

Gridded Response

4. What is the value of x when $3(x + 7) - 6x = 4 - (x + 1)$?

5. For $h(x) = x^3 + 2x$, find $h(4)$.

6. WalkieTalkie phone company charges $18.00 for basic phone service per month and $0.15 per minute for long distance calls. Arena Calls charges $80.00 per month with no fee for long distance calls. What is the minimum number of minutes of long distance calls for which the cost of WalkieTalkie is more than the cost of Arena Calls?

Short Response

17. A function is graphed below.

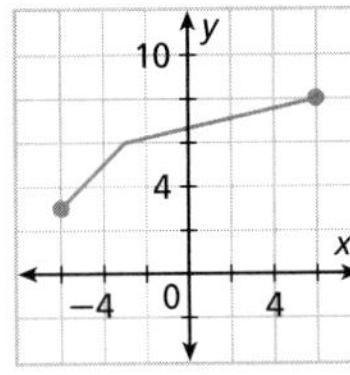

What is the domain and range of the function?

18. Rory made a pentagon by cutting two triangles from a square piece of cardboard as shown.

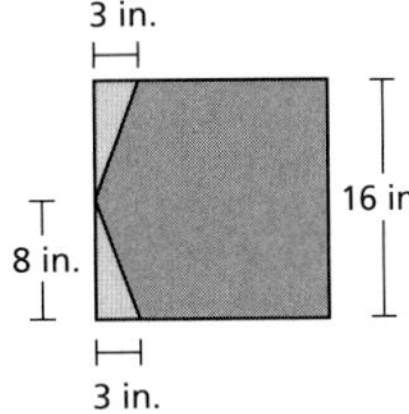

What is the area of the pentagon? Show your work or explain how you got your answer.

19. The manager of a new restaurant needs at most 12 servers. He has already hired 7 servers.

a. Write and solve an inequality to determine how many more servers the manager could hire.

b. Graph the solutions to the inequality you solved in part **a.**

20. Study the sequence below.

18, 24.5, 31, 37.5, 44,...

a. Could this sequence be arithmetic? Explain.

b. Find the 100th term of the sequence. Show your work.

Extended Response

21. A relation is shown in the table.

a. Express the relation as a mapping diagram.

b. Is the relation a function? Explain why or why not.

c. Write a possible real-life situation for the relation.

x	y
2	12
3	15
3	18
5	40
6	64

Short-Response Rubric

Items 17–20

2 Points = The student's answer is an accurate and complete execution of the task or tasks.

1 Point = The student's answer contains attributes of an appropriate response but is flawed.

0 Points = The student's answer contains no attributes of an appropriate response.

Extended-Response Rubric

Item 21

4 Points = The student draws the correct mapping diagram in part **a,** gives the correct answer and explanation in part **b,** and writes a possible real-world situation in part **c.**

3 Points = The student draws the correct mapping diagram in part **a,** gives the correct answer but not the correct explanation in part **b,** and writes a possible real-world situation in part **c.**

2 Points = The student draws the correct mapping diagram in part **a,** gives the correct answer and an incorrect explanation in part **b,** and writes an incorrect real-world situation in part **c;** or the student attempts to answer all parts and correctly answers one part.

1 Point = The student draws the mapping diagram with a minor error in part **a,** gives the correct answer but no explanation in part **b,** and attempts to write a possible real-world situation in part **c;** or the student attempts to answer all parts of the problem but does not correctly answer any part.

0 Points = The student does not answer correctly and does not attempt all parts of the problem.

Answers

17. D: $-6 \leq x \leq 6$
R: $3 \leq y \leq 8$

18. 232 in^2

19a. Let s = the number of servers that the manager will hire.
$7 + s \leq 12$
$s \leq 5$ where s is a whole number

b. 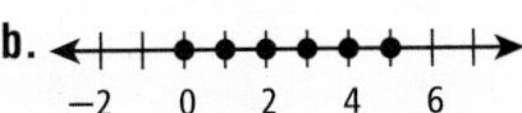

20a. Yes; there is a common difference of 6.5.

b. 661.5
$a_{100} = 18 + 99(6.5)$
$a_{100} = 661.5$

21a.

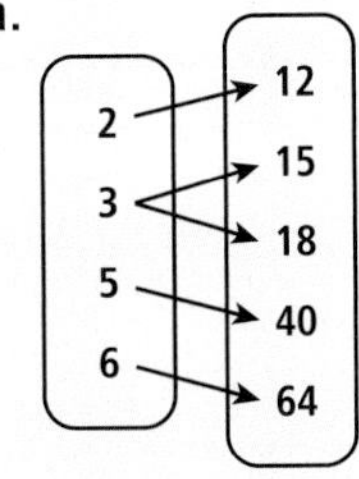

b. No; 3 is mapped to two different values.

c. Possible answer: There were 5 different field trips. The x-values are the number of chaperones, and the y-values are the number of students on each trip.

Organizer

Objective: Choose appropriate problem-solving strategies and use them with skills from Chapters 3 and 4 to solve real-world problems.

The World's Largest Weathervane

Reading Strategies

Remind students that they should read a word problem at least two times, once to learn the general idea and again to obtain specific information.

Using Data Have students use the bar graph to make comparison statements such as "The amount of snowfall in January is about four times the amount in March."

Problem-Solving Focus

Encourage students to use the four-step problem-solving process for **Problems 1–2.** Focus on the second step: **(2) Make a Plan.** Ask students what equation the second sentence in **Problem 1** translates into. $h = 2\ell - 4$ Then ask how they can use this equation to solve the problem. Substitute 26 for ℓ. **Problem 2** can be solved similarly, but with an inequality.

State Resources

The World's Largest Weather Vane

The world's largest working weather vane weighs approximately 4300 pounds and is located in Montague, Michigan. Weather vanes are used to indicate the direction of the wind. When the wind blows, the vane points in the direction from which the wind is coming.

Choose one or more strategies to solve each problem.

1. The arrow on the world's largest weather vane has a length of 26 feet. The height of the weather vane is 4 feet shorter than twice its length. What is the height of the world's largest weather vane? **48 ft**

At the base of the weather vane is a working weather station. Weather stations include instruments such as thermometers, rain gauges, and wind gauges that measure different characteristics of the weather. The data gathered from weather stations are used to make predictions about future weather.

For 2 and 3, use the graph.

2. The data in the graph represent the average snowfall for each month, measured over a 30-year time period. The average amount of snowfall received in April is less than $\frac{1}{4}$ of the average snowfall in March. What is the greatest possible average snowfall for April? Round to the nearest tenth of an inch. **1.9 in.**
3. Which month do you predict will get the most snowfall next year? Explain your reasoning.

January; the data shows that January has the greatest average snowfall for the past 30 years, so it is most likely that January will have the most snowfall next year.

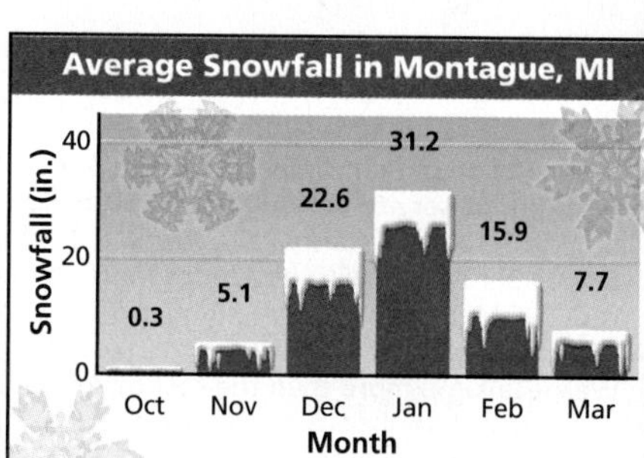
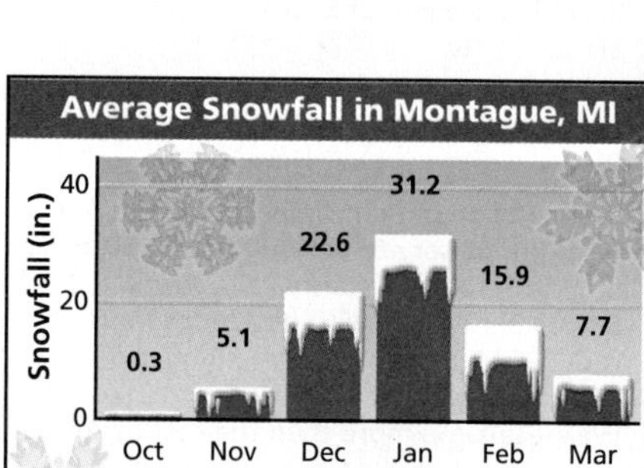

Maple Syrup

Michigan produces about 90,000 gallons of maple syrup each year. This places the state among the top ten states in U.S. production of maple syrup. Maple syrup is made from the sap of maple trees, but only about 1% of Michigan's maple trees are used in maple syrup production.

Choose one or more strategies to solve each problem.

1. The standard sugar concentration level of maple syrup is 66%. At certain levels above 66%, the product develops into maple cream, soft maple sugar, or hard maple sugar. The sugar concentration never reaches 100%, even in hard maple sugar. What is the range of sugar concentration levels in the various maple products? Show your answer on a number line. $0.66 \le c < 1$

0.66 1

For 2 and 3, use the table.

Sweetener	Calories (per tbsp)
Blackstrap molasses	43
Granulated sugar	46
Maple syrup	50
Corn syrup	57
Honey	64

2. How many Calories are in 1 cup of maple syrup? (*Hint*: 4 tbsp $= \frac{1}{4}$c) **800 Calories**
3. Approximately how many tablespoons of maple syrup would you need to have the same number of Calories that are in 7 tablespoons of honey? Round to the nearest tablespoon. **9 tbsp**
4. It takes 40 gallons of maple sap to make 1 gallon of maple syrup. Each tap hole in a maple tree will produce about 10 gallons of sap in an average year. How many gallons of maple syrup could be made with the sap from 20 tap holes? **5 gal**
5. It is recommended that maple trees be at least 10 inches in diameter before they are tapped. Only one tap should be placed in trees that are 10 to 18 inches in diameter, while 2 taps can be placed in trees greater than 18 inches in diameter. An orchard has 130 trees that are less than 10 inches in diameter, 104 trees that are 10–18 inches in diameter, and 48 trees that are greater than 18 inches in diameter. What is the maximum number of tap holes this orchard should have? **200**

Real-World Connections

Maple Syrup

Reading Strategies

ENGLISH LANGUAGE LEARNERS

Tell students to underline key words when reading a problem. In **Problem 1,** for example, *never reaches* are key words because they will be used to decide whether an open or closed circle should be used on the number line.

Using Data Ask students how the information in the table is arranged. from least to greatest Calories Have students find the range of Calories for the sweeteners listed in the table. 64 − 43 = 21

Problem-Solving Focus

The information in **Problem 5** can be organized into a table. Ask students what the three categories of trees at the orchard are. less than 10 inches, 10–18 inches, and greater than 18 inches in diameter

Then ask them how many trees are in each category. 130, 104, and 48 Then ask them how many taps are in each type of tree. 0, 1, and 2 Have students put the information into a table.

Category	<10	10–18	>18
Number of Trees	130	104	48
Number of Taps per Tree	0	1	2

Ask students how to use the table to answer the question. Multiply the numbers in the second and third rows. Then add those products.

Linear Functions

Section 5A
Characteristics of Linear Functions

Section 5B
Using Linear Functions

Pacing Guide for 45-Minute Classes

Teacher One Stop™
Calendar Planner®

Chapter 5

Countdown Weeks 10, 11, 12

DAY 1	DAY 2	DAY 3	DAY 4	DAY 5
5-1 Lesson	5-2 Lesson	Connecting Algebra to Geometry 5-3 Lesson	5-3 Lesson 5-3 Algebra Lab	5-4 Lesson
DAY 6	**DAY 7**	**DAY 8**	**DAY 9**	**DAY 10**
5-5 Lesson	5-6 Lesson	Multi-Step Test Prep Ready to Go On?	5-7 Lesson	5-8 Lesson
DAY 11	**DAY 12**	**DAY 13**	**DAY 14**	**DAY 15**
5-8 Technology Lab Connecting Algebra to Data Analysis	5-9 Lesson	5-9 Lesson 5-10 Technology Lab	5-10 Lesson	Multi-Step Test Prep Ready to Go On?
DAY 16	**DAY 17**	**DAY 18**		
EXTENSION	Chapter 5 Review	Chapter 5 Test		

Pacing Guide for 90-Minute Classes

Teacher One Stop™
Calendar Planner®

Chapter 5

DAY 1	DAY 2	DAY 3	DAY 4	DAY 5
5-1 Lesson 5-2 Lesson	Connecting Algebra to Geometry 5-3 Lesson 5-3 Algebra Lab	5-4 Lesson 5-5 Lesson	5-6 Lesson Multi-Step Test Prep Ready to Go On?	5-7 Lesson 5-8 Lesson
DAY 6	**DAY 7**	**DAY 8**	**DAY 9**	
5-8 Technology Lab Connecting Algebra to Data Analysis 5-9 Lesson	5-9 Lesson 5-10 Technology Lab 5-10 Lesson	Multi-Step Test Prep Ready to Go On? EXTENSION	Chapter 5 Review Chapter 5 Test	

ONGOING ASSESSMENT and INTERVENTION

	DIAGNOSE	PRESCRIBE
Assess Prior Knowledge	**Before Chapter 5** Diagnose readiness for the chapter. **Are You Ready?** SE p. 297	Prescribe intervention. ***Are You Ready? Intervention***
Formative Assessment	**Before Every Lesson** Diagnose readiness for the lesson. **Warm Up** TE	Prescribe intervention. **Reteach** CRB
	During Every Lesson Diagnose understanding of lesson concepts. **Check It Out!** SE **Questioning Strategies** TE **Think and Discuss** SE **Write About It** SE **Journal** TE	Prescribe intervention. **Reading Strategies** CRB ***Success for Every Learner*** ***Lesson Tutorial Videos***
	After Every Lesson Diagnose mastery of lesson concepts. **Lesson Quiz** TE **Test Prep** SE ***Test and Practice Generator***	Prescribe intervention. **Reteach** CRB **Test Prep Doctor** TE ***Homework Help Online***
	Before Chapter 5 Testing Diagnose mastery of concepts in chapter. **Ready to Go On?** SE pp. 343, 377 **Multi-Step Test Prep** SE pp. 342, 376 **Section Quizzes** AR ***Test and Practice Generator***	Prescribe intervention. ***Ready to Go On? Intervention*** **Scaffolding Questions** TE pp. 342, 376 **Reteach** CRB ***Lesson Tutorial Videos***
	Before High Stakes Testing Diagnose mastery of benchmark concepts. **College Entrance Exam Practice** SE p. 387 **Standardized Test Prep** SE pp. 390–391	Prescribe intervention. ***College Entrance Exam Practice***
Summative Assessment	**After Chapter 5** Check mastery of chapter concepts. **Multiple-Choice Tests (Forms A, B, C)** **Free-Response Tests (Forms A, B, C)** **Performance Assessment** AR **Cumulative Test** AR ***Test and Practice Generator***	Prescribe intervention. **Reteach** CRB ***Lesson Tutorial Videos***

KEY: **SE** = *Student Edition* **TE** = *Teacher's Edition* **CRB** = *Chapter Resource Book* **AR** = *Assessment Resources*  Available online Available on CD- or DVD-ROM

CHAPTER 5

Lesson Resources

Before the Lesson

Prepare

Teacher One Stop SPANISH 
- Editable lesson plans
- Calendar Planner
- Easy access to all chapter resources

Lesson Transparencies
- Teacher Tools

Teach the Lesson

Introduce

Alternate Openers: Explorations

Lesson Transparencies
- Warm Up 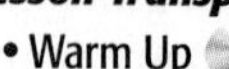
- Problem of the Day

Teach

Lesson Transparencies
- Teaching Transparencies

Know-It Notebook™
- Vocabulary
- Key Concepts

Power Presentations

Lesson Tutorial Videos SPANISH 

Interactive Online Edition
- Lesson Activities
- Lesson Tutorial Videos

Lab Activities

Lab Resources Online

Online Interactivities SPANISH 

TechKeys

Practice the Lesson

Practice

Chapter Resources
- Practice A, B, C

Practice and Problem Solving Workbook SPANISH

IDEA Works!® Modified Worksheets and Tests

ExamView Test and Practice Generator SPANISH 

Homework Help Online

Online Interactivities SPANISH 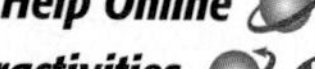

Interactive Online Edition 
- Homework Help 

Apply

Chapter Resources
- Problem Solving SPANISH

Practice and Problem Solving Workbook SPANISH

Interactive Online Edition
- Chapter Project

Project Teacher Support

After the Lesson

Reteach

Chapter Resources
- Reteach
- Reading Strategies ELL

Success for Every Learner

Review

Interactive Answers and Solutions

Solutions Key

Know-It Notebook™
- Big Ideas
- Chapter Review

Extend

Chapter Resources
- Challenge

Technology Highlights for the Teacher

Power Presentations

Dynamic presentations to engage students. Complete PowerPoint® presentations for every lesson in Chapter 5.

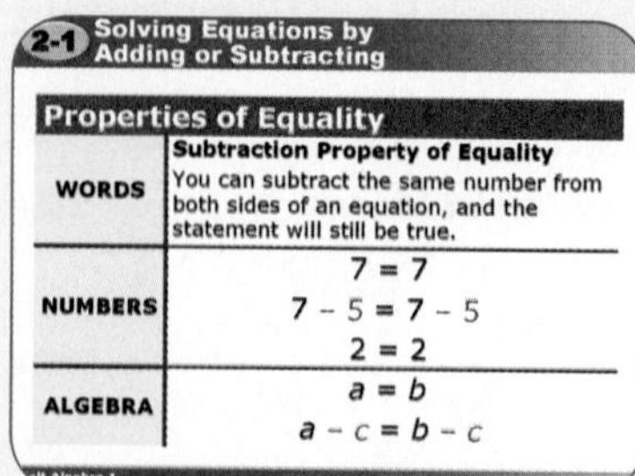

Teacher One Stop SPANISH

Easy access to Chapter 5 resources and assessments. Includes lesson planning, test generation, and puzzle creation software.

Premier Online Edition SPANISH

Chapter 5 includes Tutorial Videos, Lesson Activities, Lesson Quizzes, Homework Help, and Chapter Project.

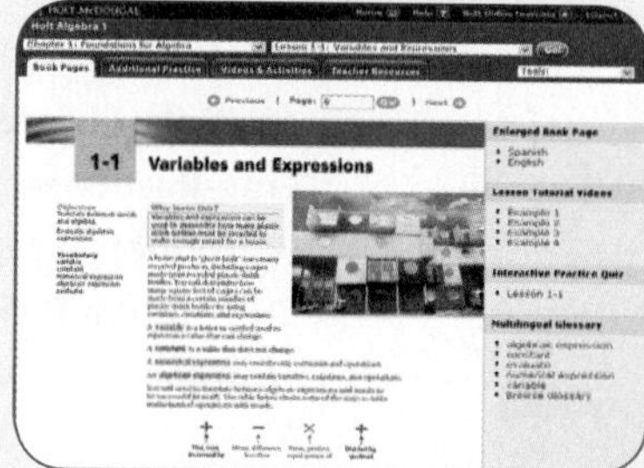

KEY: **SE** = *Student Edition* **TE** = *Teacher's Edition*  ELL English Language Learners SPANISH Spanish version available  Available online Available on CD- or DVD-RO

Reaching All Learners

Teaching tips to help all learners appear throughout the chapter. A few that target specific students are included in the lists below.

All Learners

Lab Activities
Practice and Problem Solving Workbook SPANISH 
Know-It Notebook

Special Needs Students

Practice A .... CRB
Reteach .... CRB
Reading Strategies .... CRB
Are You Ready? .... SE p. 297
Inclusion .... TE pp. 317, 318, 331, 334, 337, 346, 354
IDEA Works!® Modified Worksheets and Tests
Ready to Go On? Intervention SPANISH
Know-It Notebook
Online Interactivities SPANISH
Lesson Tutorial Videos SPANISH

Developing Learners

Practice A .... CRB
Reteach .... CRB
Reading Strategies .... CRB
Are You Ready? .... SE p. 297
Vocabulary Connections .... SE p. 298
Questioning Strategies .... TE
Ready to Go On? Intervention SPANISH
Know-It Notebook
Homework Help Online
Online Interactivities SPANISH
Lesson Tutorial Videos SPANISH 

On-Level Learners

Practice B .... CRB
Problem Solving .... CRB
Vocabulary Connections .... SE p. 298
Questioning Strategies .... TE
Ready to Go On? Intervention SPANISH
Know-It Notebook
Homework Help Online 
Online Interactivities SPANISH

Advanced Learners

Practice C .... CRB
Challenge .... CRB
Challenge Exercises .... SE
Reading and Writing Math *Extend* .... TE p. 299
Critical Thinking .... TE p. 338
Are You Ready? Enrichment SPANISH
Ready To Go On? Enrichment SPANISH

English Language Learners

ENGLISH LANGUAGE LEARNERS

Reading Strategies .... CRB
Are You Ready? Vocabulary .... SE p. 297
Vocabulary Connections .... SE p. 298
Vocabulary Review .... SE p. 382
English Language Learners .... TE pp. 301, 308, 317, 346
Success for Every Learner
Know-It Notebook
Multilingual Glossary
Lesson Tutorial Videos SPANISH 

Technology Highlights for Reaching All Learners

Lesson Tutorial Videos SPANISH

Starring Holt authors Ed Burger and Freddie Renfro! Live tutorials to support every lesson in Chapter 5.

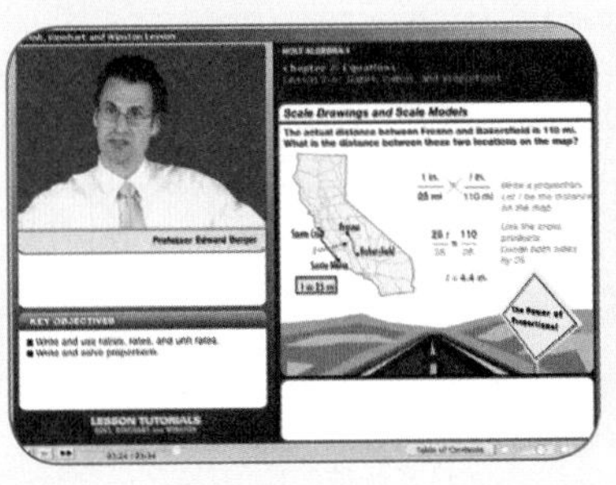

Multilingual Glossary

Searchable glossary includes definitions in English, Spanish, Vietnamese, Chinese, Hmong, Korean, and 4 other languages.

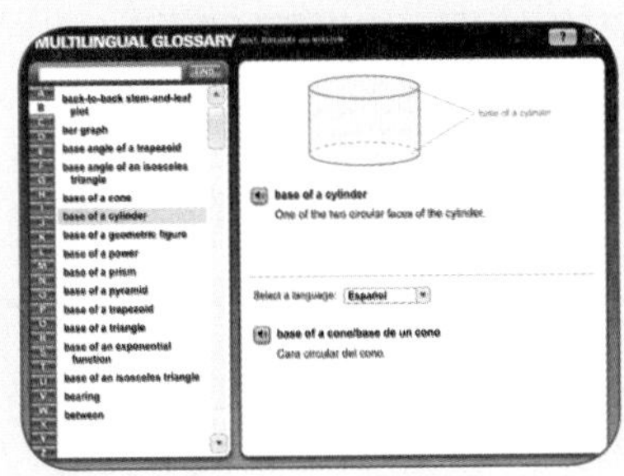

Online Interactivities

Interactive tutorials provide visually engaging alternative opportunities to learn concepts and master skills.

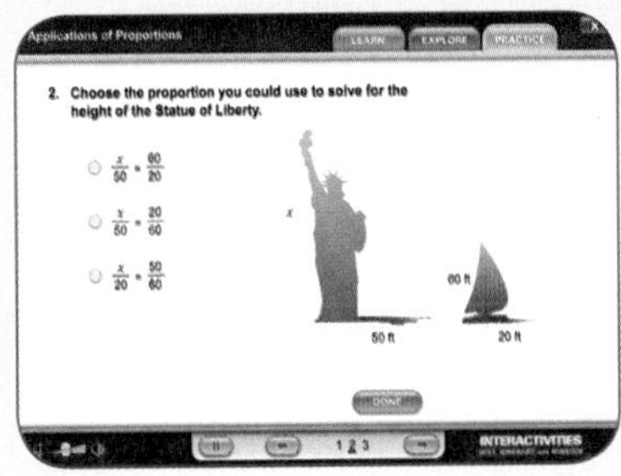

KEY: **SE** = *Student Edition* **TE** = *Teacher's Edition* **CRB** = *Chapter Resource Book* SPANISH Spanish version available · Available online · Available on CD- or DVD-ROM

Ongoing Assessment

Assessing Prior Knowledge

Determine whether students have the prerequisite concepts and skills for success in Chapter 5.

Are You Ready? SPANISH .... SE p. 297
Warm Up .... TE

Test Preparation

Provide review and practice for Chapter 5 and standardized tests.

Multi-Step Test Prep .... SE pp. 342, 376
Study Guide: Review .... SE pp. 382–385
Test Tackler .... SE pp. 388–389
Standardized Test Prep .... SE pp. 390–391
College Entrance Exam Practice .... SE p. 387
Countdown to Testing .... SE pp. C4–C27
IDEA Works!® Modified Worksheets and Tests

Alternative Assessment

Assess students' understanding of Chapter 5 concepts and combined problem-solving skills.

Chapter 5 Project .... SE p. 296
Alternative Assessment .... TE
Performance Assessment SPANISH .... AR
Portfolio Assessment SPANISH .... AR

Lesson Assessment

Provide formative assessment for each lesson of Chapter 5.

Questioning Strategies .... TE
Think and Discuss .... SE
Check It Out! Exercises .... SE
Write About It .... SE
Journal .... TE
Lesson Quiz .... TE
Alternative Assessment .... TE
IDEA Works!® Modified Worksheets and Tests

Weekly Assessment

Provide formative assessment for each section of Chapter 5.

Multi-Step Test Prep .... SE pp. 342, 376
Ready to Go On? SPANISH .... SE pp. 343, 377
Section Quizzes SPANISH .... AR
Test and Practice Generator SPANISH .... *Teacher One Stop*

Chapter Assessment

Provide summative assessment of Chapter 5 mastery.

Chapter 5 Test .... SE p. 386
Chapter Test (Levels A, B, C) SPANISH .... AR
- Multiple Choice
- Free Response

Cumulative Test SPANISH .... AR
Test and Practice Generator SPANISH .... *Teacher One Stop*
IDEA Works!® Modified Worksheets and Tests

Technology Highlights for Assessment

Are You Ready? SPANISH

Automatically assess readiness and prescribe intervention for Chapter 5 prerequisite skills.

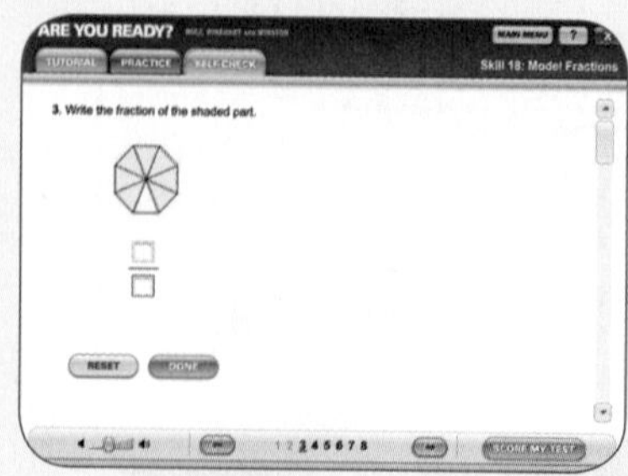

Ready to Go On?

Automatically assess understanding of and prescribe intervention for Sections 5A and 5B.

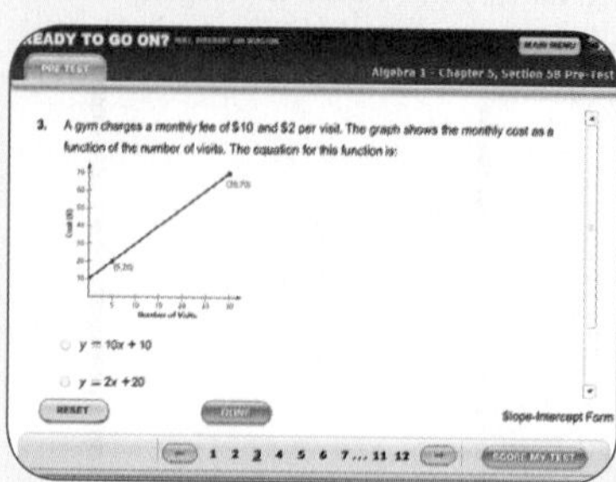

Test and Practice Generator SPANISH

Use Chapter 5 problem banks to create assessments and worksheets to print out or deliver online. Includes dynamic problems.

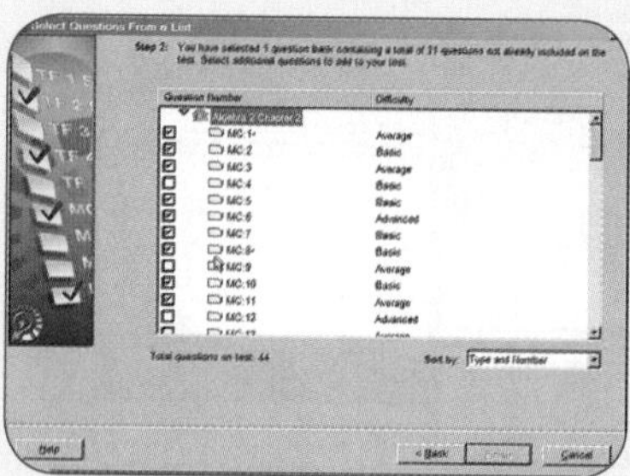

KEY: **SE** = *Student Edition* **TE** = *Teacher's Edition* **AR** = *Assessment Resources*  Spanish version available  Available online Available on CD- or DVD-ROM

Three levels (A, B, C) of multiple-choice and free-response chapter tests, along with a performance assessment, are available in the *Assessment Resources.*

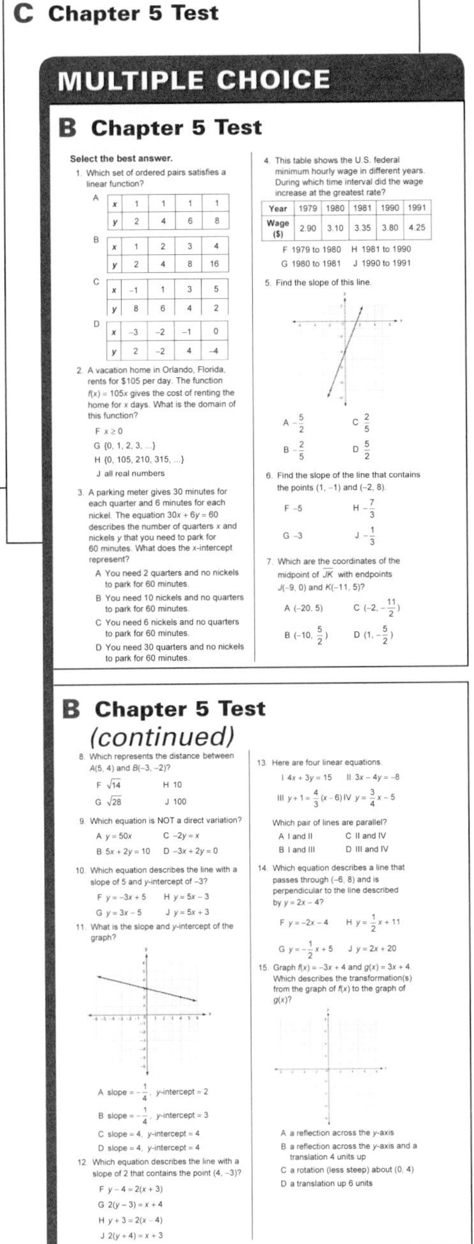

A Chapter 5 Test

C Chapter 5 Test

MULTIPLE CHOICE

B Chapter 5 Test

Select the best answer.

1. Which set of ordered pairs satisfies a linear function?

A

x	1	1	1	1
y	2	4	6	8

B

x	1	2	3	4
y	2	4	8	16

C

x	−1	1	3	5
y	8	6	4	2

D

x	−3	−2	−1	0
y	2	−2	4	−4

2. A vacation home in Orlando, Florida, rents for $105 per day. The function $f(x) = 105x$ gives the cost of renting the home for x days. What is the domain of this function?

F $x \geq 0$
G $\{0, 1, 2, 3, ...\}$
H $\{0, 105, 210, 315, ...\}$
J all real numbers

3. A parking meter gives 30 minutes for each quarter and 6 minutes for each nickel. The equation $30x + 6y = 60$ describes the number of quarters x and nickels y that you need to park for 60 minutes. What does the x-intercept represent?

A You need 2 quarters and no nickels to park for 60 minutes.
B You need 10 nickels and no quarters to park for 60 minutes.
C You need 6 nickels and no quarters to park for 60 minutes.
D You need 30 quarters and no nickels to park for 60 minutes.

4. This table shows the U.S. federal minimum hourly wage in different years. During which time interval did the wage increase at the greatest rate?

Year	1979	1980	1981	1990	1991
Wage ($)	2.90	3.10	3.35	3.80	4.25

F 1979 to 1980 H 1981 to 1990
G 1980 to 1981 J 1990 to 1991

5. Find the slope of this line.

A $-\frac{5}{2}$ C $\frac{2}{5}$
B $-\frac{2}{5}$ D $\frac{5}{2}$

6. Find the slope of the line that contains the points (1, −1) and (−2, 8).

F −5 H $-\frac{7}{3}$
G −3 J $-\frac{1}{3}$

7. Which are the coordinates of the midpoint of $\overline{JK}$ with endpoints $J(-9, 0)$ and $K(-11, 5)$?

A (−20, 5) C $(-2, -\frac{11}{2})$
B $(-10, \frac{5}{2})$ D $(1, -\frac{5}{2})$

B Chapter 5 Test (continued)

8. Which represents the distance between $A(5, 4)$ and $B(-3, -2)$?

F $\sqrt{14}$ H 10
G $\sqrt{28}$ J 100

9. Which equation is NOT a direct variation?

A $y = 50x$ C $-2y = x$
B $5x + 2y = 10$ D $-3x + 2y = 0$

10. Which equation describes the line with a slope of 5 and y-intercept of −3?

F $y = -3x + 5$ H $y = 5x - 3$
G $y = 3x - 5$ J $y = 5x + 3$

11. What is the slope and y-intercept of the graph?

A slope $= -\frac{1}{4}$, y-intercept = 2
B slope $= -\frac{1}{4}$, y-intercept = 3
C slope = 4, y-intercept = 4
D slope = 4, y-intercept = 4

12. Which equation describes the line with a slope of 2 that contains the point (4, −3)?

F $y - 4 = 2(x + 3)$
G $2(y - 3) = x + 4$
H $y + 3 = 2(x - 4)$
J $2(y + 4) = x + 3$

13. Here are four linear equations.

I $4x + 3y = 15$ II $3x - 4y = -8$
III $y + 1 = \frac{4}{3}(x - 6)$ IV $y = \frac{3}{4}x - 5$

Which pair of lines are parallel?

A I and II C II and IV
B I and III D III and IV

14. Which equation describes a line that passes through (−6, 8) and is perpendicular to the line described by $y = 2x - 4$?

F $y = -2x - 4$ H $y = \frac{1}{2}x + 11$
G $y = -\frac{1}{2}x + 5$ J $y = 2x + 20$

15. Graph $f(x) = -3x + 4$ and $g(x) = 3x + 4$. Which describes the transformation(s) from the graph of $f(x)$ to the graph of $g(x)$?

A a reflection across the y-axis
B a reflection across the y-axis and a translation 4 units up
C a rotation (less steep) about (0, 4)
D a translation up 6 units

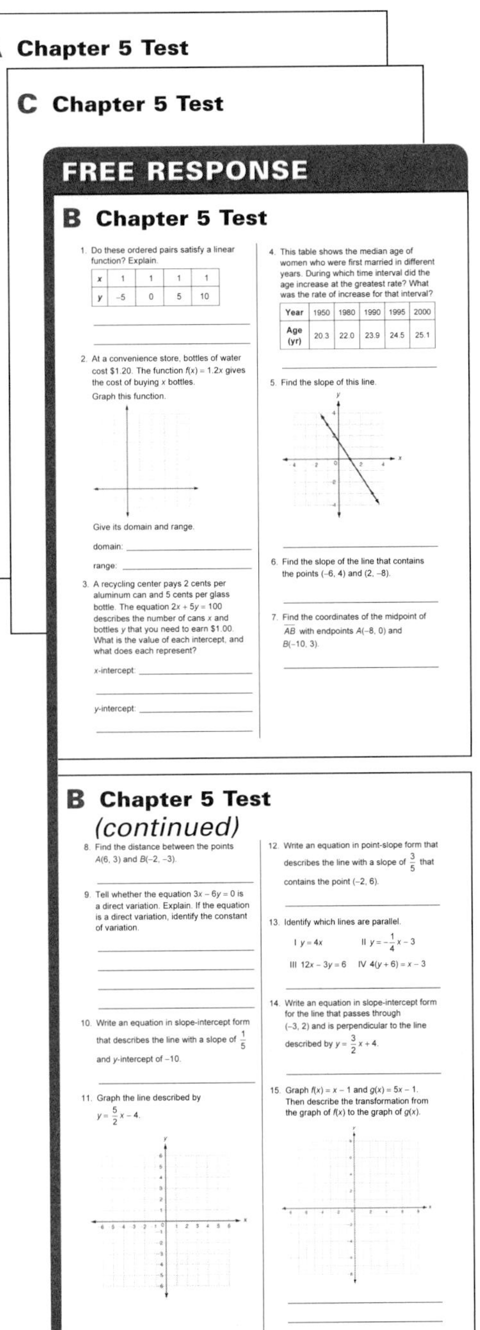

A Chapter 5 Test

C Chapter 5 Test

FREE RESPONSE

B Chapter 5 Test

1. Do these ordered pairs satisfy a linear function? Explain.

x	1	1	1	1
y	−5	0	5	10

2. At a convenience store, bottles of water cost $1.20. The function $f(x) = 1.2x$ gives the cost of buying x bottles.

Graph this function.

Give its domain and range.

domain: ____________

range: ____________

3. A recycling center pays 2 cents per aluminum can and 5 cents per glass bottle. The equation $2x + 5y = 100$ describes the number of cans x and bottles y that you need to earn $1.00. What is the value of each intercept, and what does each represent?

x-intercept: ____________

y-intercept: ____________

4. This table shows the median age of women who were first married in different years. During which time interval did the age increase at the greatest rate? What was the rate of increase for that interval?

Year	1950	1980	1990	1995	2000
Age (yr)	20.3	22.0	23.9	24.5	25.1

5. Find the slope of this line.

6. Find the slope of the line that contains the points (−6, 4) and (2, −8).

7. Find the coordinates of the midpoint of $\overline{AB}$ with endpoints $A(-8, 0)$ and $B(-10, 3)$.

B Chapter 5 Test (continued)

8. Find the distance between the points $A(6, 3)$ and $B(-2, -3)$.

9. Tell whether the equation $3x - 6y = 0$ is a direct variation. Explain. If the equation is a direct variation, identify the constant of variation.

10. Write an equation in slope-intercept form that describes the line with a slope of $\frac{1}{5}$ and y-intercept of −10.

11. Graph the line described by $y = \frac{5}{2}x - 4$.

12. Write an equation in point-slope form that describes the line with a slope of $\frac{3}{5}$ that contains the point (−2, 6).

13. Identify which lines are parallel.

I $y = 4x$ II $y = -\frac{1}{4}x - 3$
III $12x - 3y = 6$ IV $4(y + 6) = x - 3$

14. Write an equation in slope-intercept form for the line that passes through (−3, 2) and is perpendicular to the line described by $y = \frac{3}{2}x + 4$.

15. Graph $f(x) = x - 1$ and $g(x) = 5x - 1$. Then describe the transformation from the graph of $f(x)$ to the graph of $g(x)$.

PERFORMANCE ASSESSMENT

Chapter 5 Test

Purpose

This performance task assesses the student's ability to write the equation of a trend line in slope-intercept form or point-slope form.

Time

40–55 minutes

Grouping

Partners

Preparation Hints

Review the concept of a *trend line.* Remind students that in Lesson 4-5 they used the graph of a trend line to make predictions. Now that students can write the equation of a line, they can also use the equation to make predictions.

Overview

Students graph a trend line that they feel fits a scatter plot well. Depending upon whether the y-intercept is visible, they use either slope-intercept form or point-slope form to write the equation of the trend line. Lastly, they use the trend line to make predictions (both interpolation and extrapolation).

Introduce the Task

Ask what students know about automobile fuel economy. Some students may have heard the terms *MPG* or *mileage* to describe miles per gallon, or heard their parents discussing fuel economy when purchasing a new car. Ask whether students know what types of automobiles get better or poorer mileage, and what types of factors influence fuel economy. Lastly, ask whether any students know about (or even own) a hybrid automobile.

Performance Indicators

_____ Draws a line that appropriately summarizes the trend of linear data.
_____ Identifies or calculates features of the line necessary to write a linear equation (slope, y-intercept, or collinear points).
_____ Writes the equation of the trend line in slope-intercept or point-slope form.
_____ Uses the trend line's equation to make predictions.

Scoring Rubric

Level 4: Student solves all problems correctly and gives explanations.
Level 3: Student solves all problems correctly but gives no explanations.
Level 2: Student solves some problems but gives no explanations.
Level 1: Student is not able to solve any of the problems.

Chapter 5 Test *(continued)*

For 1–6, use this data about engine size in liters x and highway fuel economy in miles per gallon y for a few model-year 2005 automobiles.

Engine size (L)	1.0	1.5	2.0	2.4	3.5	3.8	4.2	4.4	5.0	5.9
Highway (mi/gal)	66	39	31	28	25	26	24	26	20	17

1. Discuss with your partner what a good trend line for this data would look like. Using a ruler, add a trend line to the scatter plot. Make the line intersect the y-axis.
2. Estimate the y-intercept of your line. ____________
3. Estimate the slope of your line. Explain how you did this. ____________
4. Write the equation of your line in slope-intercept form. ____________
5. Use your equation to estimate the highway fuel economy of an automobile with a 3.0 L engine. ____________
6. One data point represents a hybrid automobile that uses both electricity and gasoline fuel. Which point do you think is the hybrid? How is that data point different from the rest? ____________

For 7–9, use this data about the number of new hybrid automobile registrations y in each year x in the U.S.

Year	2000	2001	2002	2003
Registrations (thousands)	6.5	19.0	34.5	43.4

7. Draw a trend line that passes through two of the data points. Explain why you choose those two points.
8. Because the x-axis doesn't start at zero, you can't see the y-intercept. So, use the two points you chose in question 7 to write the equation of the line in point-slope form. ____________
9. Assuming the linear trend continues, use your equation to estimate the number of new registrations in 2007. ____________

Teacher One Stop™ 

Test & Practice Generator

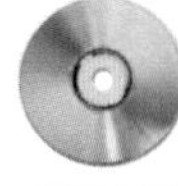

Create and customize Chapter 5 Tests. Instantly generate multiple test versions, answer keys, and Spanish versions of test items.

Modified chapter tests that address special learning needs are available in *IDEA Works!®* *Modified Worksheets and Tests.*

SECTION **5A**

Characteristics of Linear Functions

On page 342, students write, graph, and evaluate algebraic expressions to describe maximum heart rates during exercise.

Exercises designed to prepare students for success on the Multi-Step Test Prep can be found in each lesson.

SECTION **5B**

Using Linear Functions

On page 376, students use linear equations to model and solve problems involving walking at constant speeds. They describe how changing slope affects the graph of this function.

Exercises designed to prepare students for success on the Multi-Step Test Prep can be found in each lesson.

Interactivities Online ▶

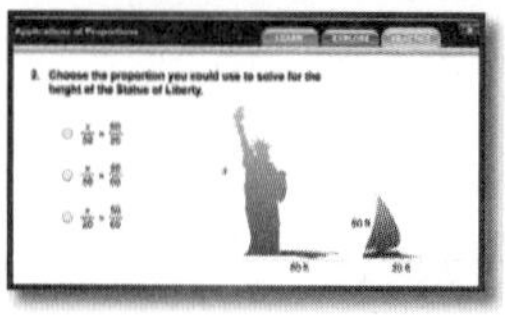

Lessons 5-3, 5-7 and 5-9

Video Lesson Tutorials Online

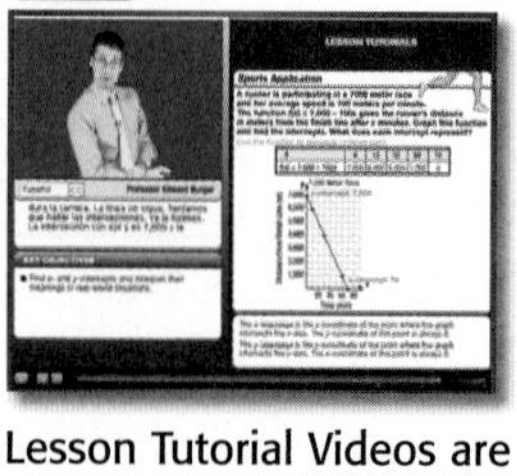

Lesson Tutorial Videos are available for EVERY example.

CHAPTER 5

Linear Functions

Chapter Focus

- Translate among different representations of linear functions.
- Find and interpret slopes and intercepts of linear equations that model real-world problems
- Solve real-world problems involving linear equations.

Take *Flight*

You can use linear functions to describe patterns and relationships in flight times.

go.hrw.com
Chapter Project Online
KEYWORD: MA7 ChProj

Take Flight

About the Project

In the Chapter Project, students research distances and flight times between several locations. Students then graph a scatter plot of the data and analyze a trend line in terms of slope, intercepts, and transformations of the graph of $y = x$.

Project Resources

All project resources for teachers and students are provided online.

Materials:

- graphing calculator or graph paper

ARE YOU READY?

Vocabulary

Match each term on the left with a definition on the right.

1. coefficient **E**
2. coordinate plane **C**
3. transformation **A**
4. perpendicular **B**

A. a change in the size or position of a figure
B. forming right angles
C. a two-dimensional system formed by the intersection of a horizontal number line and a vertical number line
D. an ordered pair of numbers that gives the location of a point
E. a number that is multiplied by a variable

Ordered Pairs

Graph each point on the same coordinate plane.

5. $A(2, 5)$
6. $B(-1, -3)$
7. $C(-5, 2)$
8. $D(4, -4)$
9. $E(-2, 0)$
10. $F(0, 3)$
11. $G(8, 7)$
12. $H(-8, -7)$

Solve for a Variable

Solve each equation for the indicated variable.

13. $2x + y = 8; y$ **$y = 8 - 2x$**
14. $5y = 5x - 10; y$ **$y = x - 2$**
15. $2y = 6x - 8; y$ **$y = 3x - 4$**
16. $10x + 25 = 5y; y$ **$y = 2x + 5$**

Evaluate Expressions

Evaluate each expression for the given value of the variable.

17. $4g - 3; g = -2$ **−11**
18. $8p - 12; p = 4$ **20**
19. $4x + 8; x = -2$ **0**
20. $-5t - 15; t = 1$ **−20**

Connect Words and Algebra

21. The value of a stock begins at $0.05 and increases by $0.01 each month. Write an equation representing the value of the stock v in any month m. **$v = 0.05 + 0.01m$**
22. Write a situation that could be modeled by the equation $b = 100 - s$. **Possible answer: The amount of money in your bank account equals $100 minus the amount spent.**

Rates and Unit Rates

Find each unit rate.

23. 322 miles on 14 gallons of gas **23 mi/gal**
24. $14.25 for 3 pounds of deli meat **$4.75/lb**
25. 32 grams of fat in 4 servings **8 g/serving**
26. 120 pictures on 5 rolls of film **24 pictures/roll**

ARE YOU READY?

Organizer

Objective: Assess students' understanding of prerequisite skills.

Assessing Prior Knowledge

INTERVENTION

Diagnose and Prescribe

Use this page to determine whether intervention is necessary or whether enrichment is appropriate.

Resources

***Are You Ready? Intervention and Enrichment* Worksheets**

***Are You Ready?* CD-ROM**

***Are You Ready?* Online**

Answers

5–12. See p. A19.

ARE YOU READY?

Diagnose and Prescribe

NO INTERVENE

Prerequisite Skill	*Are You Ready? Intervention,* Chapter 5 — Worksheets	CD-ROM	Online
Ordered Pairs	Skill 79	Activity 79	Diagnose and Prescribe Online
Solve for a Variable	Skill 72	Activity 72	
Evaluate Expressions	Skill 60	Activity 60	
Connect Words and Algebra	Skill 58	Activity 58	
Rates and Unit Rates	Skill 13	Activity 13	

YES ENRICH

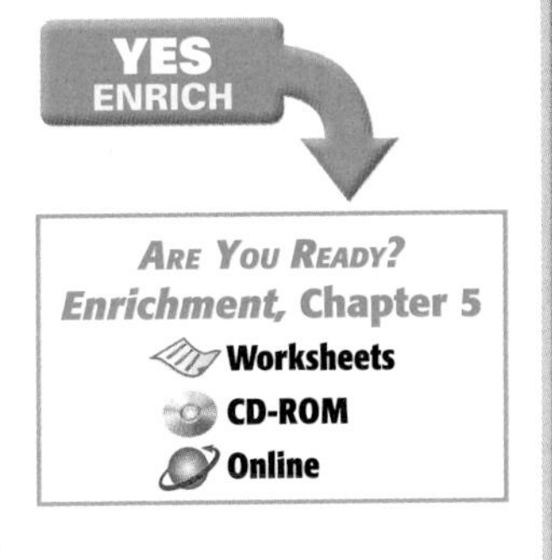

Are You Ready? Enrichment, Chapter 5
Worksheets
CD-ROM
Online

Organizer

Objective: Help students organize the new concepts they will learn in Chapter 5.

Online Edition
Multilingual Glossary

Resources

Teacher One Stop™
PuzzleView

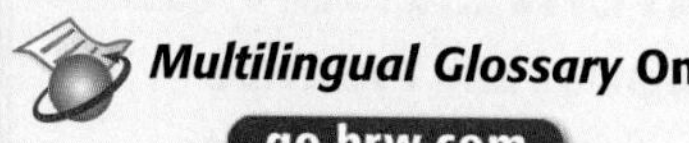
***Multilingual Glossary* Online**
go.hrw.com
KEYWORD: MA7 Glossary

Possible answers to *Vocabulary Connections*

1. a line
2. where a graph intersects the x-axis
3. a slant or an incline
4. functions that are somehow related or have similar characteristics

CHAPTER 5

Study Guide: Preview

Where You've Been

Previously, you

- wrote equations in function notation.
- graphed functions.
- identified the domain and range of functions.
- identified independent and dependent variables.

In This Chapter

You will study

- writing and graphing linear functions.
- identifying and interpreting the components of linear graphs, including the x-intercept, y-intercept, and slope.
- graphing and analyzing families of functions.

Where You're Going

You can use the skills in this chapter

- to solve systems of linear equations in Chapter 6.
- to identify rates of change in linear data in biology and economics.
- to make calculations and comparisons in your personal finances.

Key Vocabulary/Vocabulario

constant of variation	constante de variación
direct variation	variación directa
family of functions	familia de funciones
linear function	función lineal
parallel lines	líneas paralelas
perpendicular lines	líneas perpendiculares
slope	pendiente
transformation	transformación
x-intercept	intersección con el eje x
y-intercept	intersección con el eje y

Vocabulary Connections

To become familiar with some of the vocabulary terms in the chapter, consider the following. You may refer to the chapter, the glossary, or a dictionary if you like.

1. What shape do you think is formed when a **linear function** is graphed on a coordinate plane?
2. The meaning of *intercept* is similar to the meaning of *intersection*. What do you think an **x-intercept** might be?
3. **Slope** is a word used in everyday life, as well as in mathematics. What is your understanding of the word *slope*?
4. A family is a group of related people. Use this concept to define **family of functions**.

Study Strategy: Use Multiple Representations

Representing a math concept in more than one way can help you understand it more clearly. As you read the explanations and example problems in your text, note the use of tables, lists, graphs, diagrams, and symbols, as well as words to explain a concept.

From Lesson 4-4:

In this example from Chapter 4, the given function is described using an equation, a table, ordered pairs, and a graph.

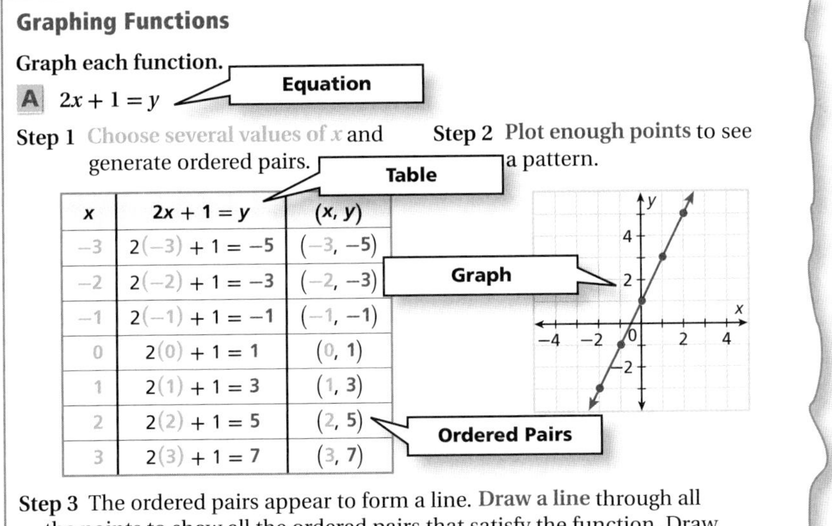

Graphing Functions

Graph each function.

A $2x + 1 = y$ — **Equation**

Step 1 Choose several values of x and generate ordered pairs. — **Table**

x	$2x + 1 = y$	(x, y)
−3	$2(-3) + 1 = -5$	$(-3, -5)$
−2	$2(-2) + 1 = -3$	$(-2, -3)$
−1	$2(-1) + 1 = -1$	$(-1, -1)$
0	$2(0) + 1 = 1$	$(0, 1)$
1	$2(1) + 1 = 3$	$(1, 3)$
2	$2(2) + 1 = 5$	$(2, 5)$
3	$2(3) + 1 = 7$	$(3, 7)$

Ordered Pairs

Step 2 Plot enough points to see a pattern. — **Graph**

Step 3 The ordered pairs appear to form a line. Draw a line through all the points to show all the ordered pairs that satisfy the function. Draw arrowheads on both "ends" of the line.

Try This

1. If an employee earns \$8.00 an hour, $y = 8x$ gives the total pay y the employee will earn for working x hours. For this equation, make a table of ordered pairs and a graph. Explain the relationships between the equation, the table, and the graph. How does each one describe the situation?
2. What situations might make one representation more useful than another?

Organizer

Objective: Help students apply strategies to understand and retain key concepts.

Study Strategy: Use Multiple Representations

Discuss Students make key mathematical connections when they see the same concept presented in various formats side by side.

For the example presented, the numbers in the domain of $2x + 1 = y$ appear in green and are also the x-coordinates of the points plotted on the graph. The numbers in the range appear in blue and are also the y-coordinates of the points plotted on the graph.

Extend As students work through the application problems in Chapter 5, have them discuss which representation they think is best for that problem and why.

Answers to *Try This*

1–2. See p. A19.

Reading Connection

Strength in Numbers
by Sherman K. Stein

This is a careful, beautifully written book covering topics from arithmetic to calculus. Stein expounds on each in a way that will enlighten algebra students and delight their teachers. He continually reinforces the important idea that the more mathematics a person knows, the more career options are available to him or her.

Activity After students study the slope of a line, direct them to Chapter 28, *How Steep is a Curve?* Ask them to explain how a curve can have a slope and how it can be measured. Then ask: How is the slope of a curve like the slope of a line? How is it different?

SECTION 5A

Linear Functions

One-Minute Section Planner

Lesson	Lab Resources	Materials
Lesson 5-1 Identifying Linear Functions • Identify linear functions and linear equations. • Graph linear functions that represent real-world situations and give their domain and range. ☑ SAT-10 ☑ NAEP ☑ ACT ☑ SAT ☑ SAT Subject Tests	***Algebra Lab Activities*** 5-1 Algebra Lab	**Optional** graphing calculator
Lesson 5-2 Using Intercepts • Find *x*- and *y*-intercepts and interpret their meanings in real-world situations. • Use *x*- and *y*-intercepts to graph lines. ☑ SAT-10 ☑ NAEP ☑ ACT ☑ SAT ☑ SAT Subject Tests		
Lesson 5-3 Rate of Change and Slope • Find rates of change and slopes. • Relate a constant rate of change to the slope of a line. ☑ SAT-10 ☑ NAEP ☑ ACT ☑ SAT ☑ SAT Subject Tests	***Technology Lab Activities*** 5-3 Technology Lab	
5-3 Algebra Lab Explore Constant Changes • Explore the relationship between constant change and the slope of a line. ☑ SAT-10 ☐ NAEP ☑ ACT ☑ SAT ☑ SAT Subject Tests	***Algebra Lab Activities*** 5-3 Lab Recording Sheet	
Lesson 5-4 The Slope Formula • Find slope by using the slope formula. ☑ SAT-10 ☑ NAEP ☑ ACT ☑ SAT ☑ SAT Subject Tests		**Optional** number cubes (MK)
Lesson 5-5 The Midpoint and Distance Formulas • Apply the formula for midpoint. • Use the Distance Formula to find the distance between two points. ☑ SAT-10 ☑ NAEP ☑ ACT ☑ SAT ☐ SAT Subject Tests		**Optional** index cards
Lesson 5-5 Direct Variation • Identify, write, and graph direct variation. ☑ SAT-10 ☑ NAEP ☑ ACT ☑ SAT ☑ SAT Subject Tests		**Optional** ruler (MK), graphing calculator

Note: If NAEP is checked, the content is tested on either the Grade 8 or the Grade 12 NAEP assessment.

MK = *Manipulatives Kit*

LINEAR FUNCTIONS

Lesson 5-1

A solution of a linear equation in two variables, x and y, is an ordered pair, (a, b), such that when a is substituted for x and b is substituted for y the resulting equation is true. Thus the ordered pair $(2, 5)$ is a solution of $y = 3x - 1$ because $5 = 3(2) - 1$ is a true statement. The ordered pair $(5, 4)$ is not a solution of the equation because $4 \neq 3(5) - 1$.

In contrast to linear equations in one variable, linear equations in two variables have infinitely many solutions. It is important for students to understand the connection between the solutions of a linear equation and the graph of the equation—the graph of an equation is precisely the set of ordered pairs that are solutions of the equation.

A specific example helps to clarify this last point. The graph of $y = 3x - 1$ consists of all ordered pairs (a, b) such that $b = 3a - 1$. In other words, the graph consists of all ordered pairs of the form $(a, 3a - 1)$. As shown above, the point $(2, 5)$ satisfies this relationship and so it must lie on the graph. Conversely, the point $(1, 2)$ lies on the graph, so it must be a solution of the equation, and indeed $2 = 3(1) - 1$. It was also shown above that $(5, 4)$ is *not* a solution of the equation; therefore this point does *not* lie on the graph.

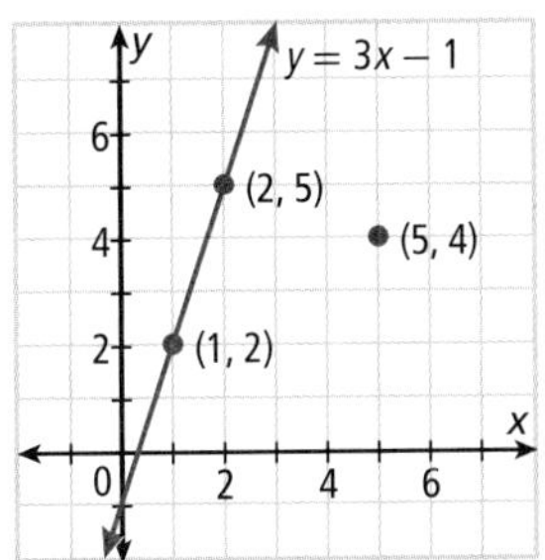

SLOPE

Lessons 5-3, 5-4

The slope of a line is defined as the ratio of rise to run for *any pair* of points on the line.

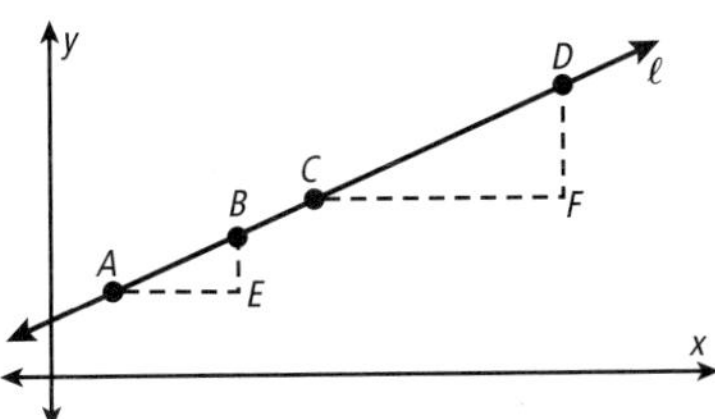

To see why the slope of line ℓ is the same whether points A and B are used or points C and D are used, draw $\overline{AE}$ and $\overline{CF}$ parallel to the x-axis, and $\overline{BE}$ and $\overline{DF}$ parallel to the y-axis. Then $\overline{AE}$ and $\overline{CF}$ are parallel (since they are both parallel to the x-axis) and $\angle A \cong \angle C$, since they are corresponding angles formed by parallel lines cut by a transversal. By a similar argument, $\angle B \cong \angle D$. Thus, $\triangle ABE$ is similar to $\triangle CDF$. Corresponding sides of similar triangles are proportional so $\frac{BE}{DF} = \frac{AE}{CF}$, which can be rewritten as $\frac{BE}{AE} = \frac{DF}{CF}$. This shows that the ratio of rise to run (slope) is the same for both pairs of points.

DIRECT VARIATION

Lesson 5-6

A *direct variation* is a linear relationship that can be written in the form $y = kx$, where k is a nonzero constant. A direct variation is a proportional relationship because the ratio $\frac{y}{x}$ is constant for every ordered pair for which $x \neq 0$.

There are two ways in which a function may fail to represent a direct variation. The first category includes linear functions with a nonzero constant ($y = mx + b$, where $b \neq 0$). These functions have constant slope, but the ratio $\frac{y}{x}$ is not constant for every ordered pair. Therefore, they are neither proportional nor direct variations.

The second category includes functions whose slope may vary between different pairs of points, in other words, nonlinear functions. The varying slope of nonlinear functions is the basis of differential calculus, which students may study in future classes.

5-1 Organizer

Pacing: Traditional 1 day
Block $\frac{1}{2}$ day

Objectives: Identify linear functions and linear equations.

Graph linear functions that represent real-world situations and give their domain and range.

Algebra Lab
In *Algebra Lab Activities*

Online Edition
Tutorial Videos, Graphing Calculator

Countdown Week 10

Power Presentations with PowerPoint®

Warm Up

1. Solve $2x - 3y = 12$ for y.
$y = \frac{2}{3}x - 4$
2. Graph $y = \frac{1}{5}x + 1$ for D: $\{-10, -5, 0, 5, 10\}$.

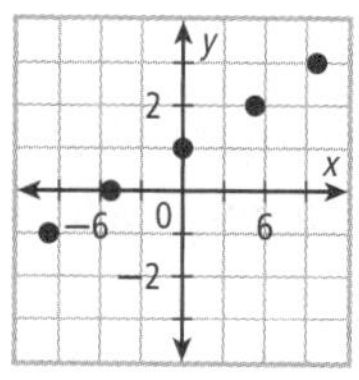

Also available on transparency

Math Humor

Q: How are linear functions similar to Cupid?

A: They have a partner for every number.

State Resources

5-1 Identifying Linear Functions

Objectives
Identify linear functions and linear equations.

Graph linear functions that represent real-world situations and give their domain and range.

Vocabulary
linear function
linear equation

Why learn this?
Linear functions can describe many real-world situations, such as distances traveled at a constant speed.

Most people believe that there is no speed limit on the German autobahn. However, many stretches have a speed limit of 120 km/h. If a car travels continuously at this speed, $y = 120x$ gives the number of kilometers y that the car would travel in x hours. Solutions are shown in the graph.

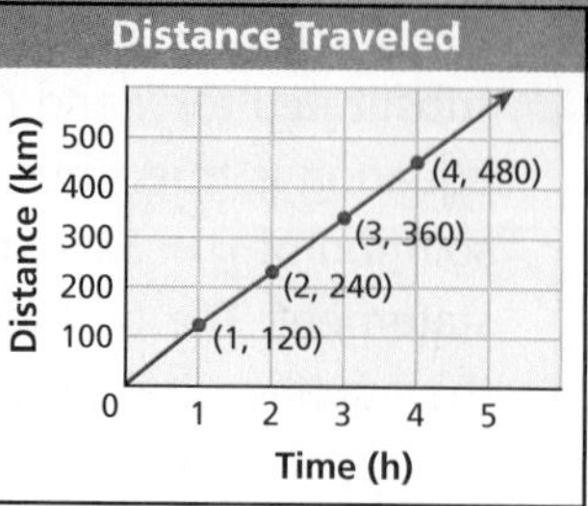

The graph represents a function because each domain value (x-value) is paired with exactly one range value (y-value). Notice that the graph is a straight line. A function whose graph forms a straight line is called a **linear function**.

EXAMPLE 1 **Identifying a Linear Function by Its Graph**

Identify whether each graph represents a function. Explain. If the graph does represent a function, is the function linear?

A

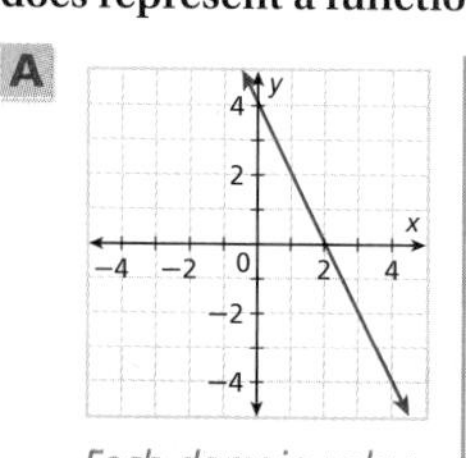

Each domain value is paired with exactly one range value. The graph forms a line.

linear function

B

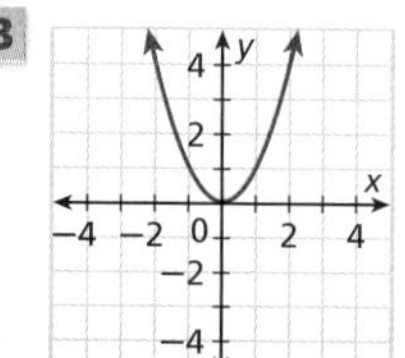

Each domain value is paired with exactly one range value. The graph is not a line.

not a linear function

C

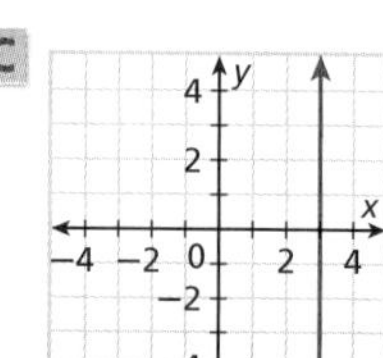

The only domain value, 3, is paired with many different range values.

not a function

CHECK IT OUT! Identify whether each graph represents a function. Explain. If the graph does represent a function, is the function linear?

1a.

1b.

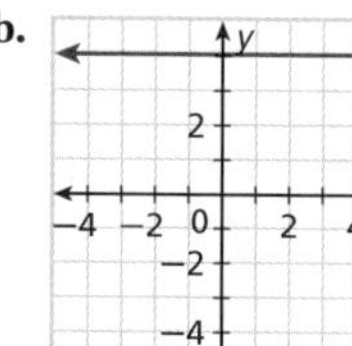

1c.

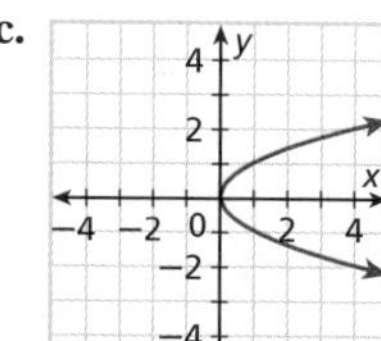

1a. Yes; each domain value is paired with exactly one range value; yes.

1b. Yes; each domain value is paired with exactly one range value; yes.

1c. No; each domain value is not paired with exactly one range value.

1 Introduce

EXPLORATION

5-1 Identifying Linear Functions

The table shows the fees that a DVD rental company charges for movie rentals.

Movies	2	4	6	8	10
Cost ($)	8	12	16	20	24

1. Which is the independent variable and which is the dependent variable?
2. For every increase of two movies, by how much does the cost increase?
3. Make a graph of the data.
4. What do you notice about the points that you plotted?

THINK AND DISCUSS

5. **Explain** how you know this relationship is a function.
6. **Describe** how to use your graph to predict the cost of renting 12 movies.

Motivate

Pose this situation: During a storm, snow fell at a rate of 0.5 in./h. The equation $y = 0.5x$ gives the number of inches of snow y that fell in x hours. Then have students graph ordered-pair solutions for this equation. Ask the following questions:

- What pattern do the points form? a line
- Is the relation a function? yes
- Why? Possible answer: Each x is paired with exactly one y.

Explorations and answers are provided in *Alternate Openers: Explorations Transparencies.*

You can sometimes identify a linear function by looking at a table or a list of ordered pairs. In a linear function, a constant change in x corresponds to a constant change in y.

	x	y	
	−2	7	
+1	−1	4	−3
+1	0	1	−3
+1	1	−2	−3
+1	2	−5	−3

In this table, a constant change of +1 in x corresponds to a constant change of −3 in y. These points satisfy a linear function.

The points from this table lie on a line.

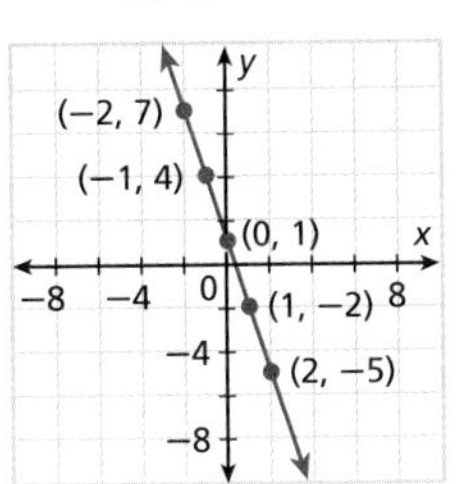

	x	y	
	−2	6	
+1	−1	3	−3
+1	0	2	−1
+1	1	3	+1
+1	2	6	+3

In this table, a constant change of +1 in x does *not* correspond to a constant change in y. These points do *not* satisfy a linear function.

The points from this table do not lie on a line.

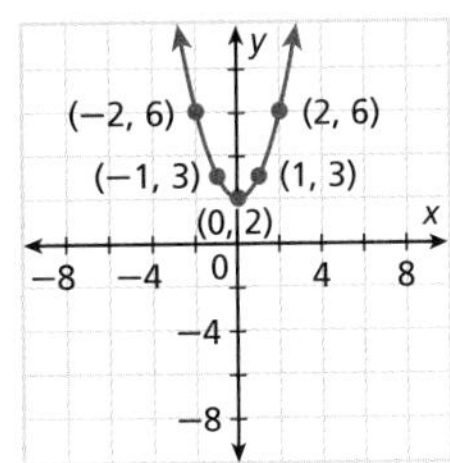

Caution!

If you find a constant change in the y-values, check for a constant change in the x-values. Both need to be constant for the function to be linear.

EXAMPLE 2 Identifying a Linear Function by Using Ordered Pairs

Tell whether each set of ordered pairs satisfies a linear function. Explain.

A $\{(2, 4), (5, 3), (8, 2), (11, 1)\}$

	x	y	
	2	4	
+3	5	3	−1
+3	8	2	−1
+3	11	1	−1

Write the ordered pairs in a table. Look for a pattern.

A constant change of +3 in x corresponds to a constant change of −1 in y.

These points satisfy a linear function.

B $\{(-10, 10), (-5, 4), (0, 2), (5, 0)\}$

	x	y	
	−10	10	
+5	−5	4	−6
+5	0	2	−2
+5	5	0	−2

Write the ordered pairs in a table. Look for a pattern.

A constant change of +5 in x corresponds to different changes in y.

These points do not satisfy a linear function.

2. Tell whether the set of ordered pairs $\{(3, 5), (5, 4), (7, 3), (9, 2), (11, 1)\}$ satisfies a linear function. Explain.

2. Yes; a constant change of +2 in x corresponds to a constant change of −1 in y.

Power Presentations with PowerPoint®

Additional Examples

Example 1

Identify whether each graph represents a function. Explain. If the graph does represent a function, is the function linear?

A.

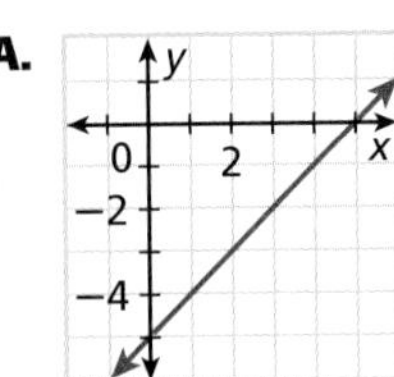

Yes; each domain value is paired with exactly one range value; yes.

B.

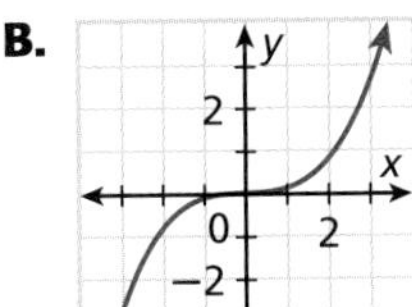

Yes; each domain value is paired with exactly one range value; no.

C.

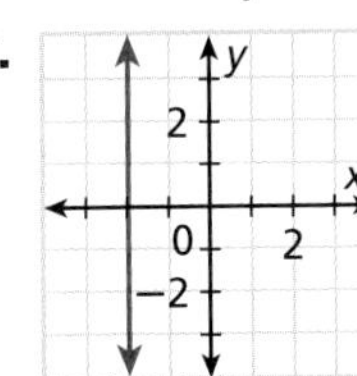

No; each domain value is not paired with exactly one range value.

Example 2

Tell whether each set of ordered pairs satisfies a linear function. Explain.

A. $\{(0, -3), (4, 0), (8, 3), (12, 6), (16, 9)\}$ Yes; a constant change of +4 in x corresponds to a constant change of +3 in y.

B. $\{(-4, 13), (-2, 1), (0, -3), (2, 1), (4, 13)\}$ No; a constant change of +2 in x corresponds to different changes in y.

2 Teach

Guided Instruction

Before working through **Examples 1** and **2,** review how to determine whether a relation is a function from ordered pairs and from a graph. In **Example 1B,** point out that the relation is a function, but not a linear function, because the graph is not a straight line. Introduce the standard form of a linear equation and practice writing several equations in standard form.

Reading Math Point out that the word *linear* includes the word *line*. ENGLISH LANGUAGE LEARNERS

Reaching All Learners

Through Visual Cues

Have students write five ordered pairs where the change between the x-values is constant. Have half the class select their y-values so that the change between each is also constant. Have the other half choose their y-values so that the change is not constant. Graph some examples of each on the board. Show that the points lie on a straight line only when the change is also constant between the y-values.

INTERVENTION

Questioning Strategies

EXAMPLE 1

- When is the graph of a line a function? When is it *not* a function?

EXAMPLE 2

- What is the relationship between change in x and change in y?

Power Presentations with PowerPoint®

Additional Examples

Example 3

Tell whether each function is linear. If so, graph the function.

A. $x = 2y + 4$ yes

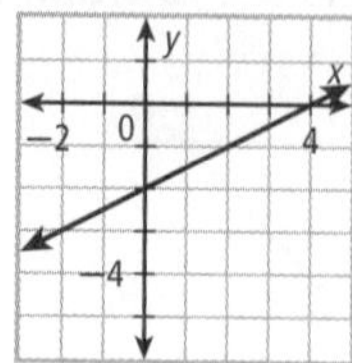

B. $xy = 4$ no

INTERVENTION

Questioning Strategies

EXAMPLE 3

- What is the standard form of a linear equation?
- If an equation is in standard form, what are the exponents of x and y?

Technology Have students use a graphing calculator to graph the functions in **Example 3** to quickly verify which are linear and which are not.

Multiple Representations Students should be aware that there is more than one way (in fact, infinitely many ways) to write a linear equation in standard form. This is because for any linear equation $Ax + By = C$, you can multiply or divide both sides of the equation by any nonzero constant and the resulting equation will be equivalent. For instance, in **Example 3A**, you can multiply both sides of $-x + y = 3$ by -1 and get the equivalent equation $x - y = -3$, which is also in standard form.

Another way to determine whether a function is linear is to look at its equation. A function is linear if it is described by a *linear equation.* A **linear equation** is any equation that can be written in the *standard form* shown below.

Standard Form of a Linear Equation

$Ax + By = C$ where A, B, and C are real numbers and A and B are not both 0

Notice that when a linear equation is written in standard form

- x and y both have exponents of 1.
- x and y are not multiplied together.
- x and y do not appear in denominators, exponents, or radical signs.

Linear		Not Linear	
$3x + 2y = 10$	*Standard form*	$3xy + x = 1$	*x and y are multiplied.*
$y - 2 = 3x$	*Can be written as* $3x - y = -2$	$x^3 + y = -1$	*x has an exponent other than 1.*
$-y = 5x$	*Can be written as* $5x + y = 0$	$x + \frac{6}{y} = 12$	*y is in a denominator.*

For any two points, there is exactly one line that contains them both. This means you need only two ordered pairs to graph a line.

EXAMPLE 3 Graphing Linear Functions

Tell whether each function is linear. If so, graph the function.

A $y = x + 3$

$$\begin{aligned} y &= x + 3 && \textit{Write the equation in standard form.} \\ -x & \quad -x && \textit{Subtraction Property of Equality} \\ y - x &= 3 \\ -x + y &= 3 && \textit{The equation is in standard form } (A = -1, B = 1, C = 3). \end{aligned}$$

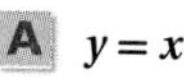

Remember!

- $y - x = y + (-x)$
- $y + (-x) = -x + y$
- $-x = -1x$
- $y = 1y$

The equation can be written in standard form, so the function is linear.

To graph, choose three values of x, and use them to generate ordered pairs. (You only need two, but graphing three points is a good check.)

x	$y = x + 3$	(x, y)
0	$y = 0 + 3 = 3$	$(0, 3)$
1	$y = 1 + 3 = 4$	$(1, 4)$
2	$y = 2 + 3 = 5$	$(2, 5)$

Plot the points and connect them with a straight line.

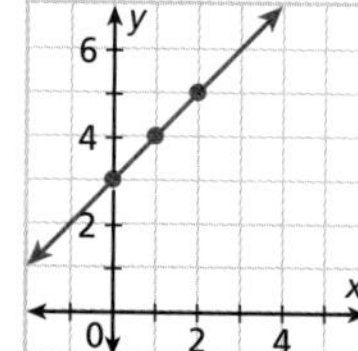

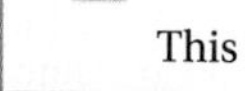

B $y = x^2$

This is not linear, because x has an exponent other than 1.

Tell whether each function is linear. If so, graph the function.

3a. $y = 5x - 9$ **3b.** $y = 12$ **3c.** $y = 2^x$ no

3a. yes

3b. yes

For linear functions whose graphs are not horizontal, the domain and range are all real numbers. However, in many real-world situations, the domain and range must be restricted. For example, some quantities cannot be negative, such as time.

Sometimes domain and range are restricted even further to a set of points. For example, a quantity such as number of people can only be whole numbers. When this happens, the graph is not actually connected because every point on the line is not a solution. However, you may see these graphs shown connected to indicate that the linear pattern, or trend, continues.

COMMON ERROR ALERT

Students might think that any equation with x and y on the left side is in standard form. Remind them of the other conditions: the exponents of x and y are 1; x and y are not multiplied together; and x and y are not in denominators, exponents, or radical signs.

EXAMPLE  Career Application

Sue rents a manicure station in a salon and pays the salon owner \$5.50 for each manicure she gives. The amount Sue pays each day is given by $f(x) = 5.50x$, where x is the number of manicures. Graph this function and give its domain and range.

Choose several values of x and make a table of ordered pairs.

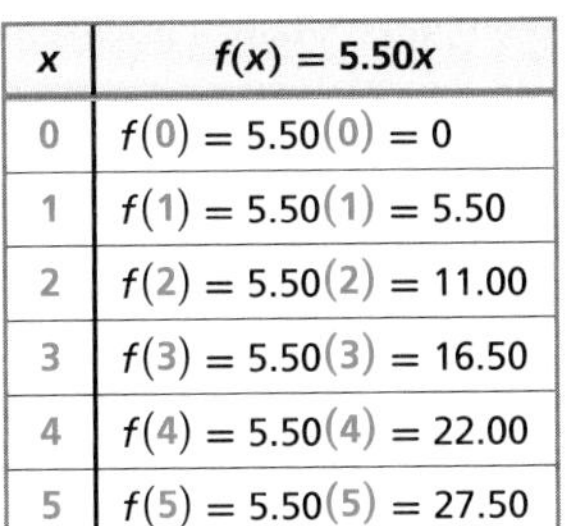

x	$f(x) = 5.50x$
0	$f(0) = 5.50(0) = 0$
1	$f(1) = 5.50(1) = 5.50$
2	$f(2) = 5.50(2) = 11.00$
3	$f(3) = 5.50(3) = 16.50$
4	$f(4) = 5.50(4) = 22.00$
5	$f(5) = 5.50(5) = 27.50$

Graph the ordered pairs.

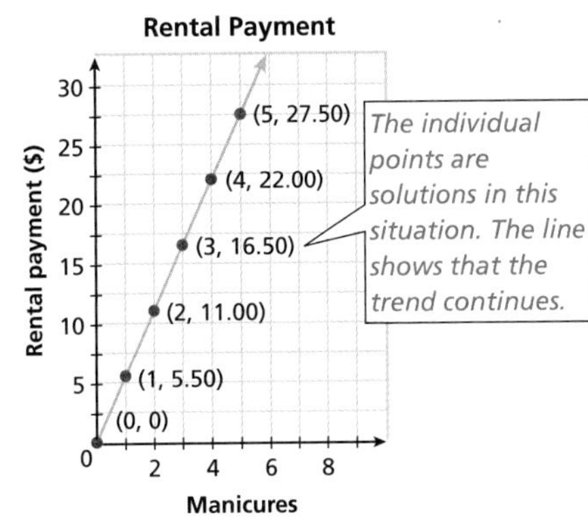

The number of manicures must be a whole number, so the domain is $\{0, 1, 2, 3, \ldots\}$. The range is $\{0, 5.50, 11.00, 16.50, \ldots\}$.

Remember!

$f(x) = y$, so in Example 4, graph the function values (dependent variable) on the y-axis.

4. Rental Payment (graph: Rental payment (\$) vs. Manicures)

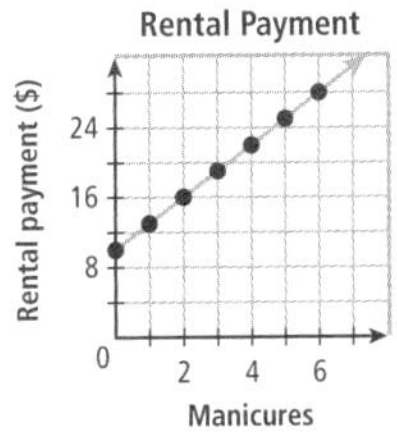

D: {0, 1, 2, 3, ...}

R: {\$10, \$13, \$16, \$19, ...}

4. What if...? At another salon, Sue can rent a station for \$10.00 per day plus \$3.00 per manicure. The amount she would pay each day is given by $f(x) = 3x + 10$, where x is the number of manicures. Graph this function and give its domain and range.

Power Presentations with PowerPoint®

Additional Examples

Example 4

The distance in centimeters that a Mars rover can travel at top speed is given by the function $f(x) = 5x$, where x is the time in seconds. Graph this function and give its domain and range.

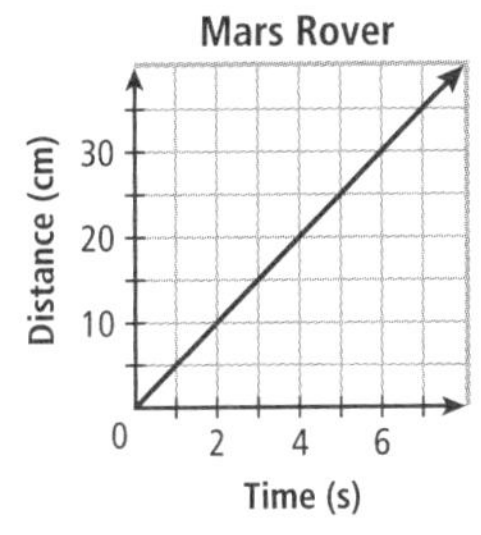

D: $x \geq 0$; R: $y \geq 0$

THINK AND DISCUSS

1. Suppose you are given five ordered pairs that satisfy a function. When you graph them, four lie on a straight line, but the fifth does not. Is the function linear? Why or why not?
2. In Example 4, why is every point on the line not a solution?
3. **GET ORGANIZED** Copy and complete the graphic organizer. In each box, describe how to use the information to identify a linear function. Include an example.

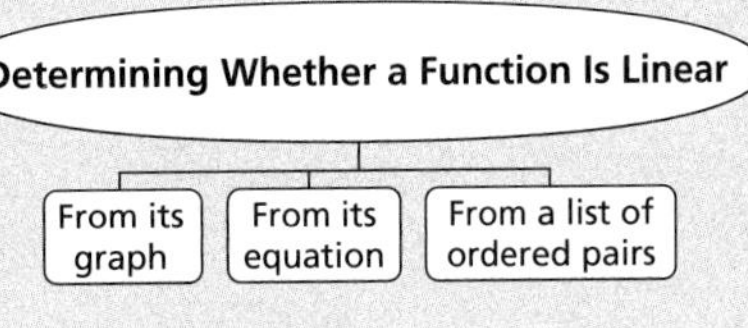

INTERVENTION

Questioning Strategies

EXAMPLE 4

- How do you decide what a reasonable domain is?

3 Close

Summarize

Remind students that a function may or may not be linear, and that a linear equation may or may not represent a function.

For example:

- $y = x + 2$ is a linear function.
- $y = x^2$ is a function but is not linear.
- $x = 4$ is a linear equation but is not a function.

ONGOING ASSESSMENT and INTERVENTION

***Diagnose Before* the Lesson**
5-1 Warm Up, TE p. 300

***Monitor During* the Lesson**
Check It Out! Exercises, SE pp. 300–303
Questioning Strategies, TE pp. 301–303

***Assess After* the Lesson**
5-1 Lesson Quiz, TE p. 306
Alternative Assessment, TE p. 306

Answers to *Think and Discuss*

1. No; all the points of the function must form a line in order for it to be a linear function.
2. It is only possible to do a whole number of manicures, so the points whose x-coordinates are not whole numbers have no meaning in this situation.
3. See p. A5.

Assignment Guide

Assign *Guided Practice* exercises as necessary.

If you finished Examples **1–2**
- **Basic** 15–20, 26–29
- **Average** 15–20, 26–29, 60
- **Advanced** 15–20, 26–29, 60

If you finished Examples **1–4**
- **Basic** 15–49, 54, 55, 57–59, 64–72
- **Average** 15–25, 30–54, 53–72
- **Advanced** 15–25, 30–54, 53–72

Homework Quick Check

Quickly check key concepts.
Exercises: 16, 18, 24, 25, 34, 36, 38

Answers

2. Each domain value is paired with exactly one range value.
3. Each domain value is paired with exactly one range value.
4. Each domain value is paired with exactly one range value.
5. A constant change of −1 in *x* corresponds to a constant change of +2 in *y*.
6. There is a constant change in *y*, but there is not a corresponding constant change in *x*.
7. A constant change of −2 in *x* corresponds to a constant change of −2 in *y*.
8. For explanation, see p. A19.

9, 10, 12. For graphs, see p. A19.
13, 14. See p. A19.
15–20. For explanations, see p. A19.

State Resources

5-1 Exercises

go.hrw.com
Homework Help Online
KEYWORD: MA7 5-1
Parent Resources Online
KEYWORD: MA7 Parent

GUIDED PRACTICE

1. **Vocabulary** Is the *linear equation* $3x - 2 = y$ in standard form? Explain. **No; it is not in the form $Ax + By = C$.**

SEE EXAMPLE 1 p. 300

Identify whether each graph represents a function. Explain. If the graph does represent a function, is the function linear?

2. 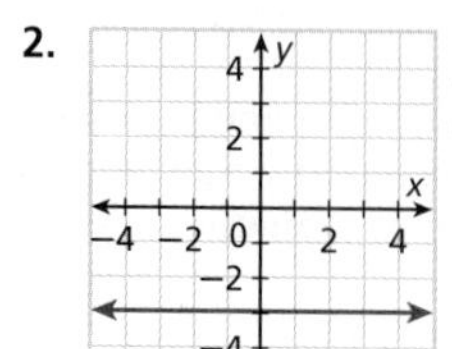 **yes; yes**

3. 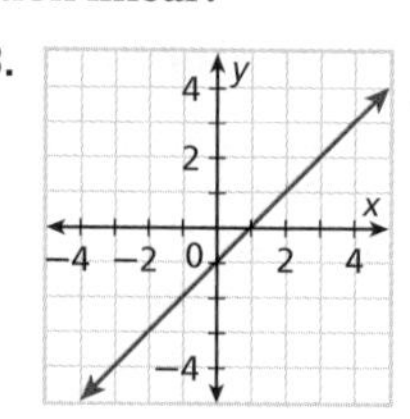 **yes; yes**

4. 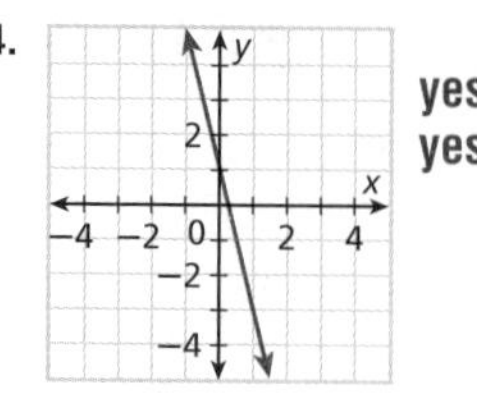 **yes; yes**

SEE EXAMPLE 2 p. 301

Tell whether the given ordered pairs satisfy a linear function. Explain.

5.

x	5	4	3	2	1
y	0	2	4	6	8

yes

6.

x	1	4	9	16	25
y	1	2	3	4	5

no

7. $\{(0, 5), (-2, 3), (-4, 1), (-6, -1), (-8, -3)\}$ **yes**
8. $\{(2, -2), (-1, 0), (-4, 1), (-7, 3), (-10, 6)\}$ **no**

SEE EXAMPLE 3 p. 302

Tell whether each function is linear. If so, graph the function.

9. $2x + 3y = 5$ **yes**
10. $2y = 8$ **yes**
11. $\frac{x^2 + 3}{5} = y$ **no**
12. $\frac{x}{5} = \frac{y}{3}$ **yes**

SEE EXAMPLE 4 p. 303

13. **Transportation** A train travels at a constant speed of 75 mi/h. The function $f(x) = 75x$ gives the distance that the train travels in x hours. Graph this function and give its domain and range.
14. **Entertainment** A movie rental store charges a \$6.00 membership fee plus \$2.50 for each movie rented. The function $f(x) = 2.50x + 6$ gives the cost of renting x movies. Graph this function and give its domain and range.

PRACTICE AND PROBLEM SOLVING

Independent Practice

For Exercises	See Example
15–17	1
18–20	2
21–24	3
25	4

Extra Practice
Skills Practice p. S12
Application Practice p. S32

Identify whether each graph represents a function. Explain. If the graph does represent a function, is the function linear?

15. 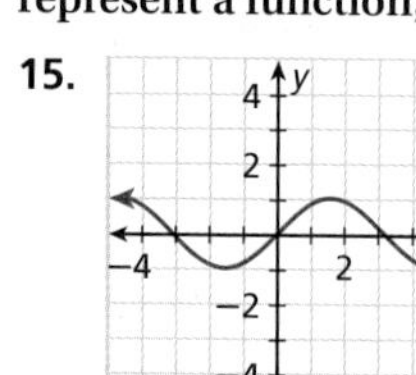 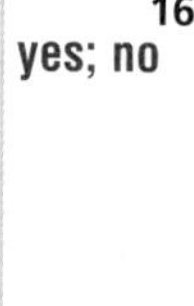 **yes; no**

16. 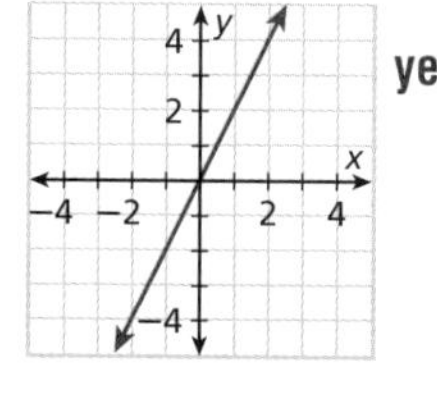 **yes; yes**

17. 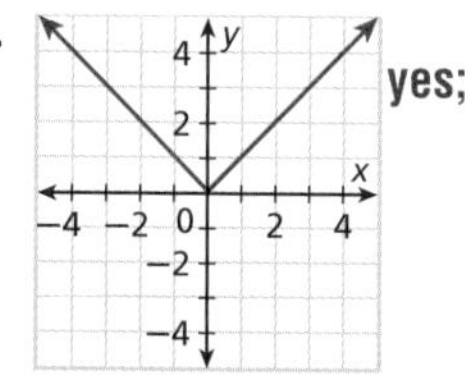 **yes; no**

Tell whether the given ordered pairs satisfy a linear function. Explain.

18.

x	−3	0	3	6	9
y	−2	−1	0	2	4

no

19.

x	−1	0	1	2	3
y	−3	−2	−1	0	1

yes

20. $\{(3, 4), (0, 2), (-3, 0), (-6, -2), (-9, -4)\}$ **yes**

5-1 READING STRATEGIES

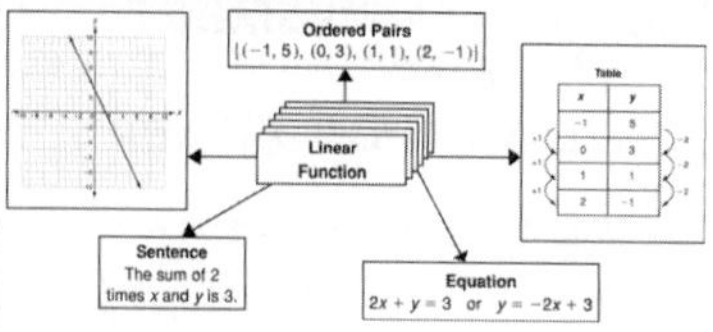

Linear functions can be represented in many forms. The same function is represented below in five different ways.

Linear Function

Ordered Pairs {(−1, 5), (0, 3), (1, 1), (2, −1)}

Table

x	y
−1	5
0	3
1	1
2	−1

Sentence The sum of 2 times *x* and *y* is 3.

Equation $2x + y = 3$ or $y = -2x + 3$

Answer each of the following.

1. Write the following linear function as an equation: "The sum of *x* and 4*y* is 9."
   $x + 4y = 9$
2. Does the graph at right represent a linear function? Tell why or why not.
   yes;
   Each domain value is paired with exactly one range value.
3. Represent the list of ordered pairs in table form: {(6, −3), (4, −1), (2, 0), (0, 2), (−2, 3)}. It this a linear function? Tell why or why not.
   no; A constant change of +2 in *x* does not correspond to a constant change in *y*.

x	6	4	2	0	−2
y	−3	−1	0	2	3

4. Write $y = -x + 4$ in standard form $(Ax + By = C)$.
   $x + y = 4$

5-1 RETEACH

You can determine if a function is linear by its graph, ordered pairs, or equation.

Identify whether the graph represents a linear function.

Step 1: Determine whether the graph is a function.

Every *x*-value is paired with exactly one *y*-value; therefore, the graph is a function. Continue to step 2.

Step 2: Determine whether the graph is a straight line.

Conclusion: Because this graph is a function and a straight line, this graph represents a linear function.

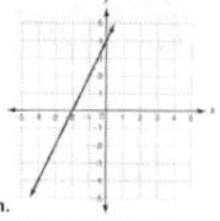

Identify whether {(4, 3), (6, 4), (8, 6)} represents a linear function.

Step 1: Write the ordered pairs in a table.

Step 2: Find the amount of change in each variable. Determine if the amounts are constant.

Conclusion: Although the *x*-values show a constant change, the *y*-values do not. Therefore, this set of ordered pairs does not represent a linear function.

x	y
4	3
6	4
8	6

Identify whether the function $y = 5x - 2$ is a linear function.

Try to write the equation in standard form $(Ax + By = C)$.

$$y = 5x - 2$$
$$-5x \quad -5x$$
$$-5x + y = -2$$

In standard form, *x* and *y*
- have exponents of 1
- are not multiplied together
- are not in denominators, exponents, or radical signs

Conclusion: Because the function can be written in standard form, (A = −5, B = 1, C = −2), the function is a linear function.

Tell whether each graph, set of ordered pairs, or equation represents a linear function. Write *yes* or *no*.

1. 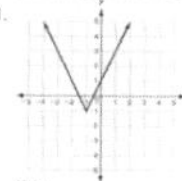 no
2. 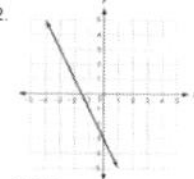 yes
3. yes

x	y
−9	5
−5	10
−1	15

4. {(−3, 5), (−2, 8), (−1, 12)} no
5. $2y = -3x^2$ no
6. $y = 4x - 7$ yes

21. yes

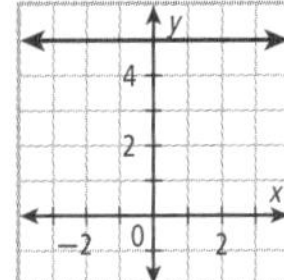

22. yes

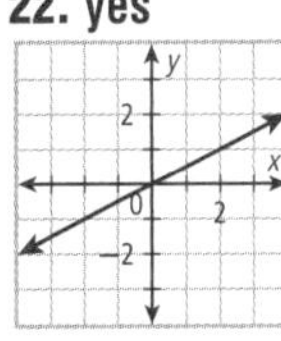

24. yes

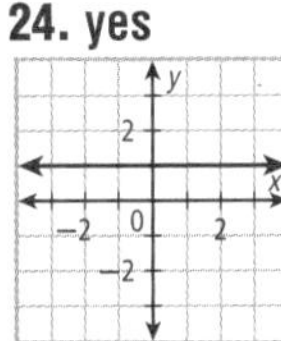

27. yes; yes

Tell whether each function is linear. If so, graph the function.

21. $y = 5$ **22.** $4y - 2x = 0$ **23.** $\frac{3}{x} + 4y = 10$ **no** **24.** $5 + 3y = 8$

25. Transportation The gas tank in Tony's car holds 15 gallons, and the car can travel 25 miles for each gallon of gas. When Tony begins with a full tank of gas, the function $f(x) = -\frac{1}{25}x + 15$ gives the amount of gas $f(x)$ that will be left in the tank after traveling x miles (if he does not buy more gas). Graph this function and give its domain and range.

Tell whether the given ordered pairs satisfy a function. If so, is it a linear function?

26. $\{(2, 5), (2, 4), (2, 3), (2, 2), (2, 1)\}$ **no; no** **27.** $\{(-8, 2), (-6, 0), (-4, -2), (-2, -4), (0, -6)\}$

28.

x	−10	−6	−2	2	4
y	0	0.25	0.50	0.75	1

yes; no

29.

x	−5	−1	3	7	11
y	1	1	1	1	1

yes; yes

Tell whether each equation is linear. If so, write the equation in standard form and give the values of *A*, *B*, and *C*.

30. $2x - 8y = 16$ **31.** $y = 4x + 2$ **32.** $2x = \frac{y}{3} - 4$ **33.** $\frac{4}{x} = y$ **no**

34. $\frac{x+4}{2} = \frac{y-4}{3}$ **35.** $x = 7$ **36.** $xy = 6$ **no** **37.** $3x - 5 + y = 2y - 4$

38. $y = -x + 2$ **39.** $5x = 2y - 3$ **40.** $2y = -6$ **41.** $y = \sqrt{x}$ **no**

Graph each linear function.

42. $y = 3x + 7$ **43.** $y = x + 25$ **44.** $y = 8 - x$ **45.** $y = 2x$

46. $-2y = -3x + 6$ **47.** $y - x = 4$ **48.** $y - 2x = -3$ **49.** $x = 5 + y$

50. Measurement One inch is equal to approximately 2.5 centimeters. Let x represent inches and y represent centimeters. Write an equation in standard form relating x and y. Give the values of A, B, and C. **$2.5x - y = 0$; $A = 2.5$, $B = -1$, $C = 0$**

51. Wages Molly earns $8.00 an hour at her job.

a. Let x represent the number of hours that Molly works. Write a function using x and $f(x)$ that describes Molly's pay for working x hours. **$f(x) = 8x$**

b. Graph this function and give its domain and range.

52. Write About It For $y = 2x - 1$, make a table of ordered pairs and a graph. Describe the relationships between the equation, the table, and the graph.

53. Critical Thinking Describe a real-world situation that can be represented by a linear function whose domain and range must be limited. Give your function and its domain and range.

54. This problem will prepare you for the Multi-Step Test Prep on page 342.

a. Juan is running on a treadmill. The table shows the number of Calories Juan burns as a function of time. Explain how you can tell that this relationship is linear by using the table.

b. Create a graph of the data.

c. How can you tell from the graph that the relationship is linear? **The graph forms a line.**

Time (min)	Calories
3	27
6	54
9	81
12	108
15	135
18	162
21	189

Exercise 54 involves creating a graph from a table and determining whether the relationship is linear. This exercise prepares students for the Multi-Step Test Prep on page 342.

Answers

25.

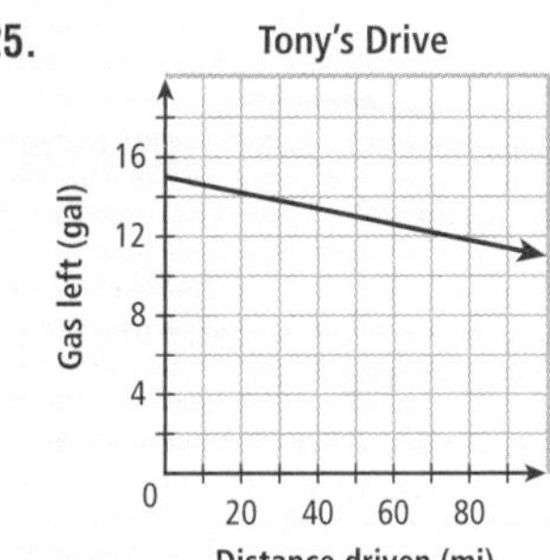

D: $0 \le x \le 375$; R: $0 \le y \le 15$

30. yes; $2x - 8y = 16$; $A = 2$; $B = -8$; $C = 16$

31. yes; $-4x + y = 2$; $A = -4$; $B = 1$; $C = 2$

32. yes; $2x - \frac{1}{3}y = -4$; $A = 2$; $B = -\frac{1}{3}$; $C = -4$

34. yes; $3x - 2y = -20$; $A = 3$; $B = -2$; $C = -20$

35. yes; $x = 7$; $A = 1$; $B = 0$; $C = 7$

37. yes; $3x - y = 1$; $A = 3$; $B = -1$; $C = 1$

38. yes; $x + y = 2$; $A = 1$, $B = 1$, $C = 2$

39. yes; $5x - 2y = -3$; $A = 5$, $B = -2$, $C = -3$

40. yes; $2y = -6$; $A = 0$, $B = 2$, $C = -6$

42–49, 51b–54b. See pp. A19–A20.

5-1 PROBLEM SOLVING

Write the correct answer.

1. A daycare center charges a $75 enrollment fee plus $100 per week. The function $f(x) = 100x + 75$ gives the cost of daycare for x weeks. Graph this function and give its domain and range.
   D: {0, 1, 2, 3, ...};
   R: {$75, $175, $275, $375, ...}

Cost of Daycare — Cost (dollars); Number of Weeks

2. A family swimming pool holds 60 m³ of water. The function $f(x) = 60 - 0.18x$ gives the cubic meters of water in the pool, taking into account water lost to evaporation over x days. Graph this function and give its domain and range.
   D: $x \ge 0$;
   R: $0 \le y \le 60$

Amount of Water in Swimming Pool — Volume of Water in Pool (m³); Day

Elijah is using a rowing machine. The table shows how many Calories he can burn for certain lengths of time. Select the best answer.

Time (min)	Calories
2	24
4	48
6	72
8	96
10	120

3. Which function could be used to describe the number of Calories burned after x minutes?
   F $y = 12 + x$ H $xy = 12$
   G $x + y = 12$ **J** $y = 12x$

4. What is the domain of the function?
   A {0, 1, 2, 3, ...} **C** $x \ge 0$
   B {2, 4, 6, ...} D $x \ge 2$

5. What is the range of the function?
   F {0, 12, 24, 36, ...} **H** $y \ge 0$
   G {24, 48, 72, ...} J $y \ge 24$

6. Elijah graphed the function in problem 4. Which best describes the graph?
   A It is a line that increases from left to right.
   B It is a line that decreases from left to right.
   C It forms a U-shape.
   D It forms a V-shape.

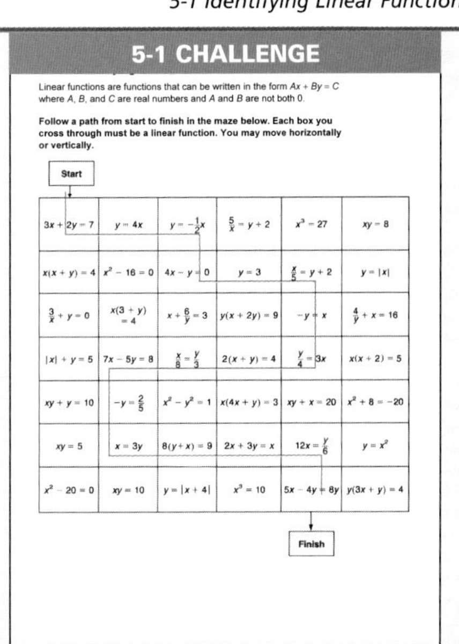

5-1 CHALLENGE

Linear functions are functions that can be written in the form $Ax + By = C$ where A, B, and C are real numbers and A and B are not both 0.

Follow a path from start to finish in the maze below. Each box you cross through must be a linear function. You may move horizontally or vertically.

Start

$3x + 2y = 7$	$y = 4x$	$y = -\frac{1}{2}x$	$\frac{5}{x} = y + 2$	$x^3 = 27$	$xy = 8$
$x(x + y) = 4$	$x^2 - 16 = 0$	$4x - y = 0$	$y = 3$	$\frac{x}{5} = y + 2$	$y = \lvert x \rvert$
$\frac{3}{x} + y = 0$	$x(3 + y) = 4$	$x + \frac{6}{y} = 3$	$y(x + 2y) = 9$	$-y = x$	$\frac{4}{y} + x = 16$
$\lvert x \rvert + y = 5$	$7x - 5y = 8$	$\frac{x}{8} = \frac{y}{3}$	$2(x + y) = 4$	$\frac{y}{4} = 3x$	$x(x + 2) = 5$
$xy + y = 10$	$-y = \frac{2}{5}$	$x^2 - y^2 = 1$	$x(4x + y) = 3$	$xy + x = 20$	$x^2 + 8 = -20$
$xy = 5$	$x = 3y$	$8(y + x) = 9$	$2x + 3y = x$	$12x = \frac{y}{6}$	$y = x^2$
$x^2 - 20 = 0$	$xy = 10$	$y = \lvert x + 4 \rvert$	$x^3 = 10$	$5x - 4y = 8y$	$y(3x + y) = 4$

Finish

5-1 PRACTICE A

5-1 PRACTICE C

5-1 PRACTICE B

Identify whether each graph represents a function. Explain. If the graph does represent a function, is the function linear?

1. function (not linear); each domain value is paired with exactly one range value.

2. not a function; several domain values are paired with two range values.

3. Which set of ordered pairs satisfies a linear function? Explain.
   Set A: {(5, 1), (4, 4), (3, 9), (2, 16), (1, 25)}
   Set B: {(1, −5), (2, −3), (3, −1), (4, 1), (5, 3)}
   Set B; A constant change of +1 in x corresponds to a constant change of +2 in y.

4. Write $y = -2x$ in standard form. Then graph the function.
   $2x + y = 0$

5. In 2005, the Shabelle River in Somalia rose an estimated 5.25 inches every hour for 15 hours. The increase in water level is represented by the function $f(x) = 5.25x$, where x is the number of hours. Graph this function and give its domain and range.
   D: $0 \le x \le 15$; R: $0 \le y \le 78.75$

TEST PREP DOCTOR Students who did not choose **C** in **Exercise 57** may not understand that in a linear function, x or y cannot be in the denominator of a fraction.

Journal

Have students explain how to identify a linear function from its graph and from its equation.

ALTERNATIVE ASSESSMENT

Have students write a real-world problem that can be represented by a linear function. Then have them write the function rule and determine a reasonable domain and range.

Power Presentations with PowerPoint®

5-1 Lesson Quiz

Tell whether each set of ordered pairs satisfies a linear function. Explain.

1. $\{(-3, 10), (-1, 9), (1, 7), (3, 4), (5, 0)\}$ No; a constant change of +2 in x corresponds to different changes in y.
2. $\{(3, 4), (5, 7), (7, 10), (9, 13), (11, 16)\}$ Yes; a constant change of +2 in x corresponds to a constant change of +3 in y.

Tell whether each function is linear. If so, graph the function.

3. $y = 3 - 2^x$ no
4. $3y = 12$ yes

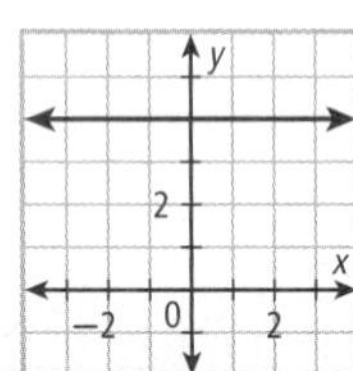

5. The cost of a can of iced-tea mix at SaveMore Grocery is \$4.75. The function $f(x) = 4.75x$ gives the cost of x cans of iced-tea mix. Graph this function and give its domain and range.

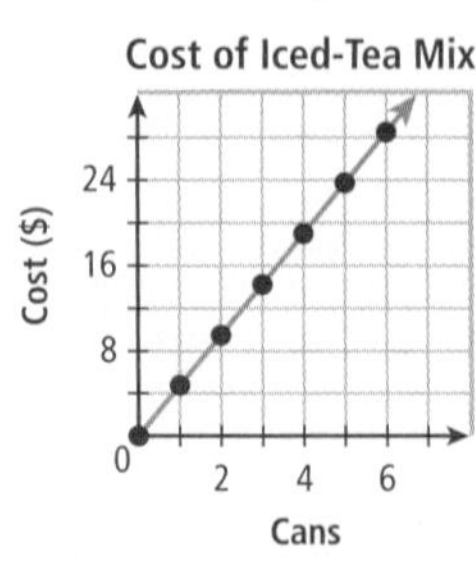

D: {0, 1, 2, 3, . . .}
R: {0, 4.75, 9.50, 14.25, . . .}

Also available on transparency

55. **Physical Science** A ball was dropped from a height of 100 meters. Its height above the ground in meters at different times after its release is given in the table. Do these ordered pairs satisfy a linear function? Explain. **No; each constant change in time (+ 1 s) is not accompanied by a constant change in height.**

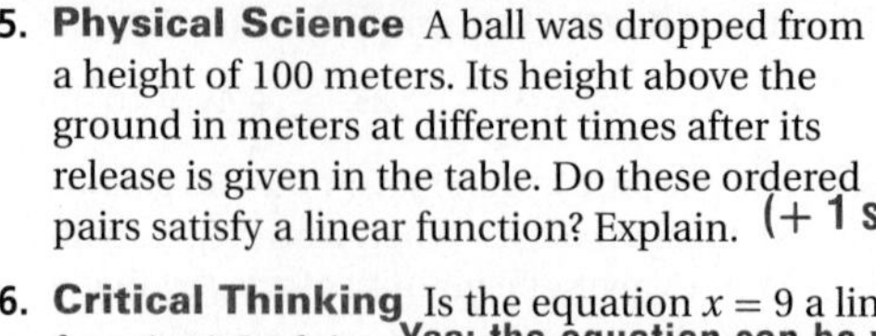

Time (s)	0	1	2	3
Height (m)	100	90.2	60.8	11.8

56. **Critical Thinking** Is the equation $x = 9$ a linear equation? Does it describe a linear function? Explain. **Yes; the equation can be written in stand. form with $A = 1$, $B = 0$, and $C = 9$. No; all solutions are ordered pairs with x-value 9. The x-value 9 corresponds to more than one y-value.**

TEST PREP

57. Which is NOT a linear function?
 (A) $y = 8x$ (B) $y = x + 8$ **(C)** $y = \frac{8}{x}$ (D) $y = 8 - x$

58. The speed of sound in 0 °C air is about 331 feet per second. Which function could be used to describe the distance in feet d that sound will travel in air in s seconds?
 (F) $d = s + 331$ **(G)** $d = 331s$ (H) $s = 331d$ (J) $s = 331 - d$

59. **Extended Response** Write your own linear function. Show that it is a linear function in at least three different ways. Explain any connections you see between your three methods.

CHALLENGE AND EXTEND

60. What equation describes the x-axis? the y-axis? Do these equations represent linear functions?
 $y = 0$; $x = 0$; the first describes a linear function, but the second does not.

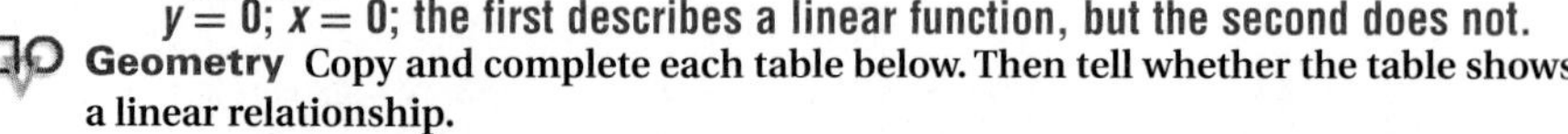

Geometry Copy and complete each table below. Then tell whether the table shows a linear relationship.

61.

Perimeter of a Square	
Side Length	Perimeter
1	4
2	8
3	12
4	16

linear

62.

Area of a Square	
Side Length	Area
1	1
2	4
3	9
4	16

not linear

63.

Volume of a Cube	
Side Length	Volume
1	1
2	8
3	27
4	64

not linear

SPIRAL REVIEW

Simplify each expression. *(Lesson 1-4)*

64. 8^2 **64**
65. $(-1)^3$ **−1**
66. $(-4)^4$ **256**
67. $\left(\frac{1}{3}\right)^2$ $\mathbf{\frac{1}{9}}$

Solve each equation. Check your answer. *(Lesson 2-4)*

68. $6m + 5 = 3m - 4$ **−3**
69. $2(t - 4) = 3 - (3t + 1)$ **2**
70. $9y + 5 - 2y = 2y + 5 - y + 3$ $\mathbf{\frac{1}{2}}$

Find the value of x in each diagram. *(Lesson 2-8)*

71. $\triangle ABC \sim \triangle DEF$ **9**

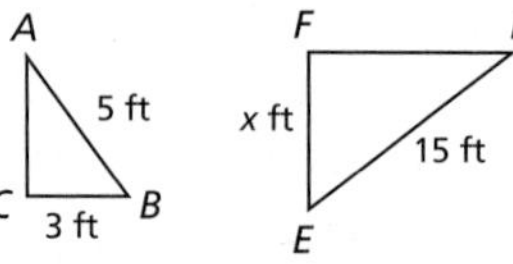

72. $ABCD \sim QRST$ **9**

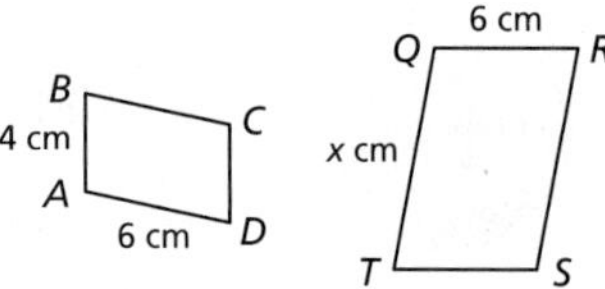

Answers

59. Possible answer: $3x + 2y = 7$; it is a linear equation because it can be written in standard form with $A = 3$, $B = 2$, and $C = 7$.
 A table of values also shows it is a linear function:

x	y
−3	8
−2	6.5
−1	5
0	3.5
1	2
2	0.5

Each constant change in x (+1) is accompanied by a constant change in y (−1.5).
The graph shows a linear function.

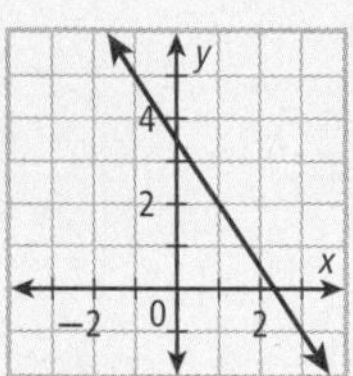

Both the graph and the table show solutions to the equation.

5-2 Using Intercepts

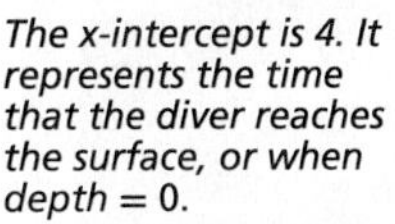

Objectives
Find x- and y-intercepts and interpret their meanings in real-world situations.

Use x- and y-intercepts to graph lines.

Vocabulary
y-intercept
x-intercept

Who uses this?
Divers can use intercepts to determine the time a safe ascent will take.

A diver explored the ocean floor 120 feet below the surface and then ascended at a rate of 30 feet per minute. The graph shows the diver's elevation below sea level during the ascent.

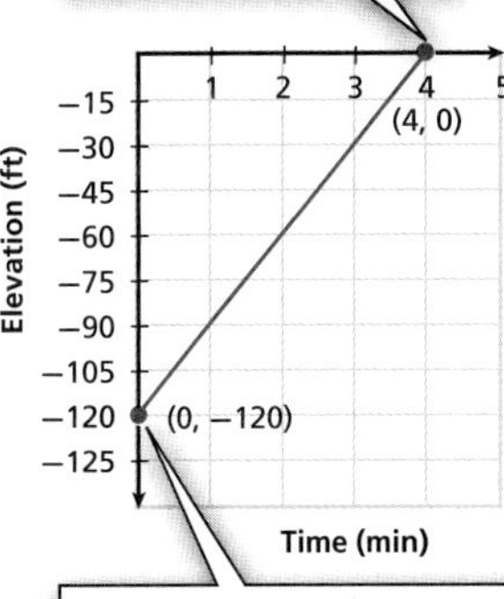

The ***y*-intercept** is the y-coordinate of the point where the graph intersects the y-axis. The x-coordinate of this point is always 0.

The ***x*-intercept** is the x-coordinate of the point where the graph intersects the x-axis. The y-coordinate of this point is always 0.

The y-intercept is −120. It represents the diver's elevation at the start of the ascent, when time = 0.

EXAMPLE  1 **Finding Intercepts**

Find the x- and y-intercepts.

A

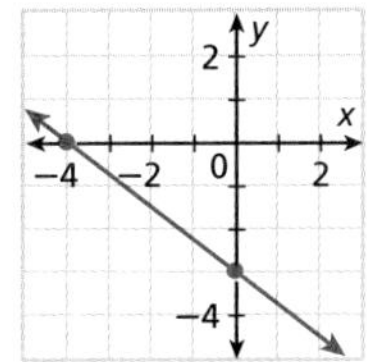

The graph intersects the x-axis at (−4, 0).
The x-intercept is −4.

The graph intersects the y-axis at (0, −3).
The y-intercept is −3.

B $3x - 2y = 12$

To find the x-intercept, replace y with 0 and solve for x.

$$3x - 2y = 12$$
$$3x - 2(0) = 12$$
$$3x - 0 = 12$$
$$3x = 12$$
$$\frac{3x}{3} = \frac{12}{3}$$
$$x = 4$$

The x-intercept is 4.

To find the y-intercept, replace x with 0 and solve for y.

$$3x - 2y = 12$$
$$3(0) - 2y = 12$$
$$0 - 2y = 12$$
$$-2y = 12$$
$$\frac{-2y}{-2} = \frac{12}{-2}$$
$$y = -6$$

The y-intercept is −6.

Find the x- and y-intercepts.

1a. *x*-int.: −2; *y*-int.: 3

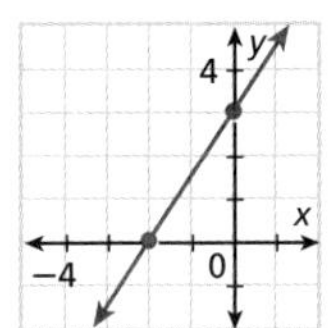

1b. $-3x + 5y = 30$ *x*-int.: −10; *y*-int.: 6

1c. $4x + 2y = 16$ *x*-int.: 4; *y*-int.: 8

5-2 Organizer

Pacing: Traditional 1 day
Block $\frac{1}{2}$ day

Objectives: Find x- and y-intercepts and interpret their meanings in real-world situations.

Use x- and y-intercepts to graph lines.

Online Edition
Tutorial Videos

Countdown Week 10

Power Presentations with PowerPoint®

Warm Up

Solve each equation.

1. $5x + 0 = -10$ −2
2. $33 = 0 + 3y$ 11
3. $\frac{4}{5}x + \frac{1}{10} = \frac{9}{10}$ 1
4. $2x + 14 = -3x + 4$ −2
5. $-5y - 1 = 7y + 5$ $-\frac{1}{2}$

Also available on transparency

Teacher: Where's the graph of your function?

Student: It was intercepted on the way to school.

1 Introduce

5-2 Using Intercepts

Katarina's family is traveling from Brownsville, Texas, to their home in Laredo, Texas. The distance from Brownsville to Laredo is 200 miles, and Katarina's mother is driving at a speed of 50 miles per hour.

1. Complete the table.

Time from Start of Trip (h)	0	1	2	3	4
Distance to Laredo (mi)	200	150			

2. Make a graph of the data.
3. What is the starting distance? What point on the graph corresponds to the starting distance? Where is this point located?
4. How long does it take to reach Laredo? What point on the graph corresponds to this time? Where is this point located?

THINK AND DISCUSS

5. **Explain** how you could use a graph to find the time it would take to reach Laredo if Katarina's mother drove at a speed of 40 miles per hour.
6. **Describe** what it means for a point to lie on the y-axis in a graph of distance versus time.

Motivate

Have students graph $3x + 4y = 12$ by generating ordered pairs for x and y using the following table.

x	y
−2	4.5
0	3
2	1.5
4	0

Then have students circle the rows of the table that include 0. Ask students where these points are located on the graph. the axes

Explorations and answers are provided in *Alternate Openers: Explorations Transparencies.*

State Resources

Power Presentations with PowerPoint®

Additional Examples

Example 1

Find the *x*- and *y*-intercepts.

A.

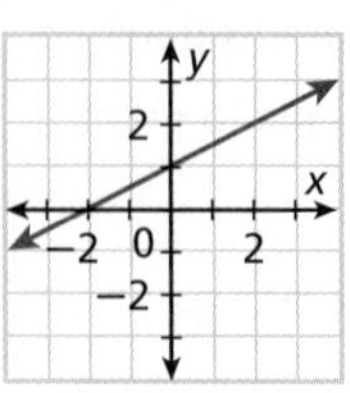

x-int.: −2; *y*-int.: 1

B. $5x - 2y = 10$
x-int.: 2; *y*-int.: −5

Example 2

Trish can run the 200 m dash in 25 s. The function $f(x) = 200 - 8x$ gives the distance remaining to run after *x* seconds. Graph this function and find the intercepts. What does each intercept represent?

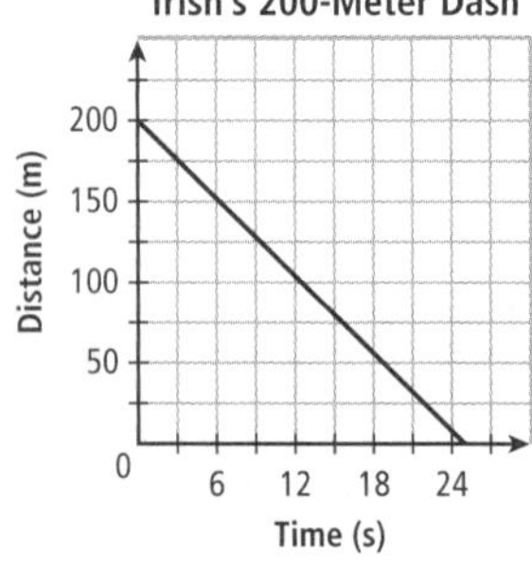

x-int.: 25; *y*-int.: 200

x-int.: the time when Trish finishes the race, when the distance remaining is 0

y-int.: the number of meters Trish has to run at the start of the race, when the time passed is 0

Student to Student — *Finding Intercepts*

Madison Stewart
Jefferson High School

I use the "cover-up" method to find intercepts. To use this method, make sure the equation is in standard form first.

If I have $4x - 3y = 12$:

First, I cover 4x with my finger and solve the equation I can still see.

$- 3y = 12$
$y = -4$

The y-intercept is −4.

Then I cover −3y with my finger and do the same thing.

$4x = 12$
$x = 3$

The x-intercept is 3.

EXAMPLE 2 ***Travel Application***

2a.

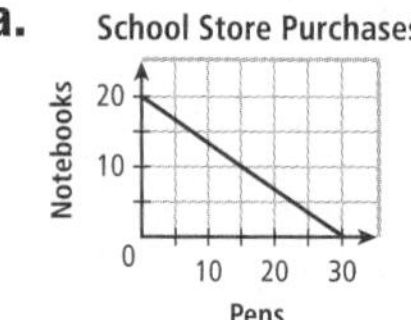

x-int.: 30; y-int.: 20

2b. x-int.: pens that can be purchased if no notebooks are purchased; y-int.: notebooks that can be purchased if no pens are purchased

The Sandia Peak Tramway in Albuquerque, New Mexico, travels a distance of about 4500 meters to the top of Sandia Peak. Its speed is 300 meters per minute. The function $f(x) = 4500 - 300x$ gives the tram's distance in meters from the top of the peak after *x* minutes. Graph this function and find the intercepts. What does each intercept represent?

Neither time nor distance can be negative, so choose several nonnegative values for x. Use the function to generate ordered pairs.

x	0	2	5	10	15
$f(x) = 4500 - 300x$	4500	3900	3000	1500	0

Graph the ordered pairs. Connect the points with a line.

Caution!

The graph is not the path of the tram. Even though the line is descending, the graph describes the distance from the peak as the tram goes *up* the mountain.

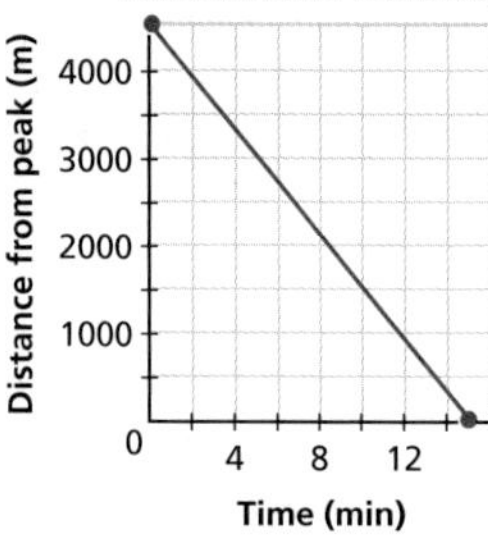

- *y*-intercept: 4500. This is the starting distance from the top (time = 0).
- *x*-intercept: 15. This the time when the tram reaches the peak (distance = 0).

CHECK IT OUT!

2. The school store sells pens for \$2.00 and notebooks for \$3.00. The equation $2x + 3y = 60$ describes the number of pens *x* and notebooks *y* that you can buy for \$60.
   a. Graph the function and find its intercepts.
   b. What does each intercept represent?

INTERVENTION

Questioning Strategies

EXAMPLE 1

- What point on a graph corresponds to the *x*-intercept? the *y*-intercept?
- What intercept do you find by substituting zero for *x*?

EXAMPLE 2

- Why is the graph of only the first quadrant shown?
- What do other points on the graph, such as (5, 160), (10, 120), and so on, represent?

2 Teach

Guided Instruction

Show how to find the intercepts from a graph and then from an equation. Show students the "cover-up" method of finding intercepts from an equation (described in Student to Student) and ask students why it works. The value covered up always becomes zero.

ENGLISH LANGUAGE LEARNERS

Reading Math Have students familiar with football explain the meaning of *interception* in that sport. Then ask the class how it relates to an intercept in math.

Reaching All Learners

Through Number Sense

Give students the following scenario: *You have \$25, and you spend \$5 per week.* Tell students that the function $y = 25 - 5x$ describes the amount of money *y* they will have after *x* weeks. Have them find ordered pairs for $x = 0, 1, 2, 3, 4,$ and 5. (0, 25), (1, 20), (2, 15), (3, 10), (4, 5), (5, 0) Graph the ordered pairs, labeling each as follows: (week 1, \$20 left).

Discuss why the value of *y* when $x = 6$ is not reasonable in this situation. You have no money left to spend after the 5th week.

Remember, to graph a linear function, you need to plot only two ordered pairs. It is often simplest to find the ordered pairs that contain the intercepts.

EXAMPLE 3 Graphing Linear Equations by Using Intercepts

Use intercepts to graph the line described by each equation.

A $2x - 4y = 8$

Step 1 Find the intercepts.

x-intercept:	*y*-intercept:
$2x - 4y = 8$	$2x - 4y = 8$
$2x - 4(0) = 8$	$2(0) - 4y = 8$
$2x = 8$	$-4y = 8$
$\frac{2x}{2} = \frac{8}{2}$	$\frac{-4y}{-4} = \frac{8}{-4}$
$x = 4$	$y = -2$

Step 2 Graph the line.

Plot (4, 0) and (0, −2).

Connect with a straight line.

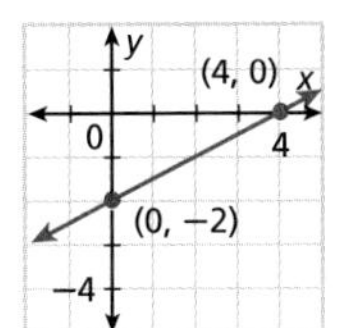

B $\frac{2}{3}y = 4 - \frac{1}{2}x$

Step 1 Write the equation in standard form.

$6\left(\frac{2}{3}y\right) = 6\left(4 - \frac{1}{2}x\right)$ *Multiply both sides by 6, the LCD of the fractions, to clear the fractions.*

$4y = 24 - 3x$

$3x + 4y = 24$ *Write the equation in standard form.*

Step 2 Find the intercepts.

x-intercept:	*y*-intercept:
$3x + 4y = 24$	$3x + 4y = 24$
$3x + 4(0) = 24$	$3(0) + 4y = 24$
$3x = 24$	$4y = 24$
$\frac{3x}{3} = \frac{24}{3}$	$\frac{4y}{4} = \frac{24}{4}$
$x = 8$	$y = 6$

Step 3 Graph the line.

Plot (8, 0) and (0, 6).

Connect with a straight line.

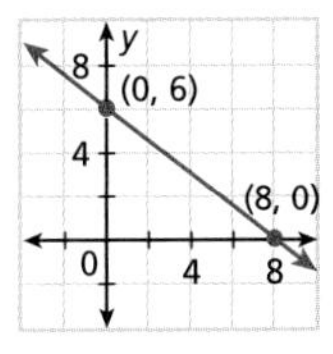

Helpful Hint

You can use a third point to check your line. Either choose a point from your graph and check it in the equation, or use the equation to generate a point and check that it is on your graph.

Use intercepts to graph the line described by each equation.

3a. $-3x + 4y = -12$ **3b.** $y = \frac{1}{3}x - 2$

3a.

3b.

THINK AND DISCUSS

1. A function has *x*-intercept 4 and *y*-intercept 2. Name two points on the graph of this function.
2. What is the *y*-intercept of $2.304x + y = 4.318$? What is the *x*-intercept of $x - 92.4920y = -21.5489$?

3. **GET ORGANIZED** Copy and complete the graphic organizer.

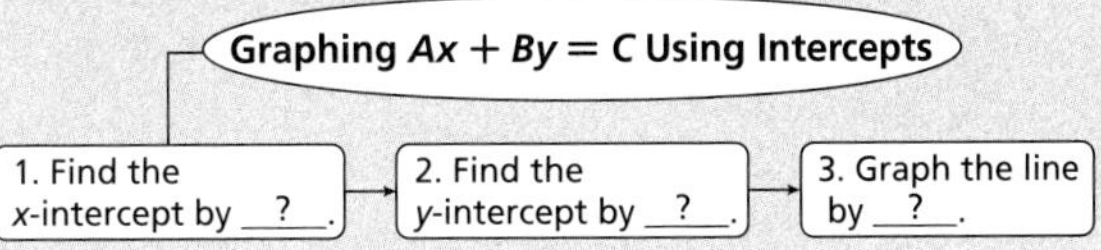

Power Presentations with PowerPoint®

Additional Examples

Example 3

Use intercepts to graph the line described by each equation.

A. $3x - 7y = 21$

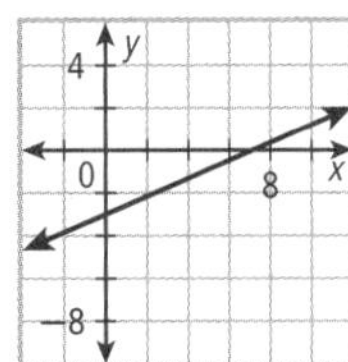

B. $y = -x + 4$

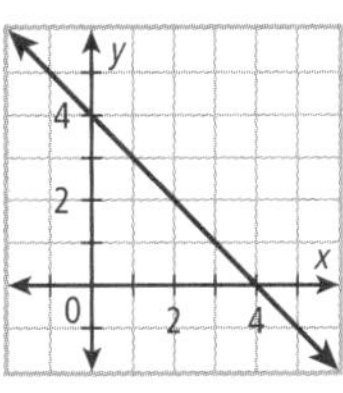

INTERVENTION

Questioning Strategies

EXAMPLE 3

- What is the difference between graphing a line using intercepts and graphing a line by generating a table of ordered pairs?

3 Close

Summarize

Review the definitions of *x*- and *y*-intercepts and how to find them from a graph and from an equation.

Tell students that finding intercepts is especially useful for graphing lines, because it is often quicker than generating ordered pairs, especially when the equation is written in standard form.

ONGOING ASSESSMENT

and INTERVENTION 

***Diagnose Before* the Lesson**
5-2 Warm Up, TE p. 307

***Monitor During* the Lesson**
Check It Out! Exercises, SE pp. 307–309
Questioning Strategies, TE pp. 308–309

***Assess After* the Lesson**
5-2 Lesson Quiz, TE p. 312
Alternative Assessment, TE p. 312

Answers to *Think and Discuss*

1. (4, 0) and (0, 2)
2. 4.318; −21.5489
3. See p. A5.

Assignment Guide

Assign *Guided Practice* exercises as necessary.

If you finished Examples **1–3**

Basic 13–29, 34–38, 40–42, 48–54

Average 13–33, 38–42, 44, 46, 48–54

Advanced 14–20 even, 22–33, 38–54

Homework Quick Check

Quickly check key concepts.
Exercises: 14, 18, 22, 24, 26, 30

Answers

8a. Refrigeration Tank Temperature

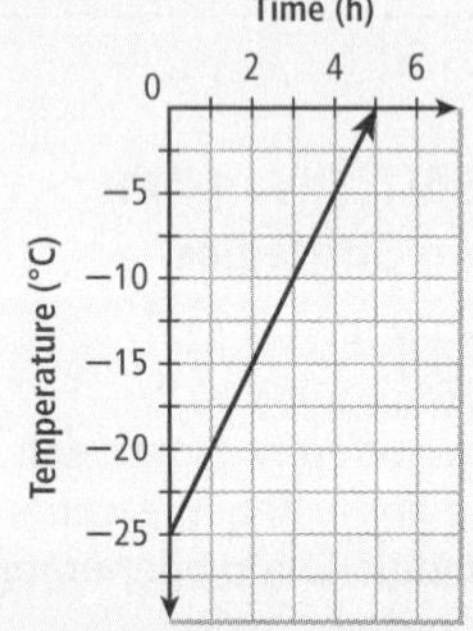

b. x-int.: time when temp. = 0 °C; y-int.: initial temp.

9–12. See p. A20.

22a. For graph, see p. A20.

b. See p. A20.

23a. For graph, see p. A20.

b. See p. A20.

State Resources

5-2 Exercises

go.hrw.com
Homework Help Online
KEYWORD: MA7 5-2
Parent Resources Online
KEYWORD: MA7 Parent

GUIDED PRACTICE

1. **Vocabulary** The ___?___ is the *y*-coordinate of the point where a graph crosses the *y*-axis. (*x-intercept* or *y-intercept*) **y-intercept**

SEE EXAMPLE 1 p. 307

2. x-int.: –5; y-int.: 1
3. x-int.: 2; y-int.: –4
4. x-int.: –3; y-int.: –2

Find the *x*- and *y*-intercepts.

2.

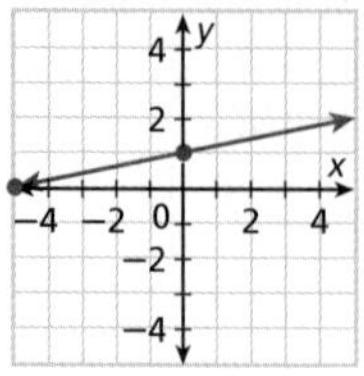

3.

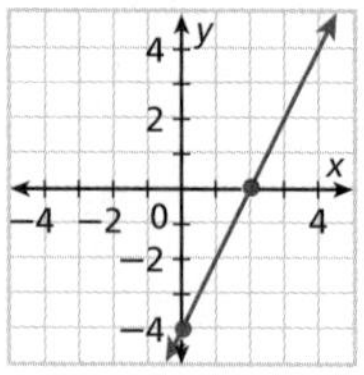

4.

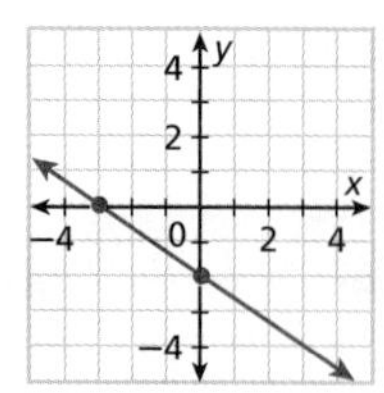

5. $2x - 4y = 4$ **x-int.: 2; y-int.: –1**

6. $-2y = 3x - 6$ **x-int.: 2; y-int.: 3**

7. $4y + 5x = 2y - 3x + 16$ **x-int.: 2; y-int.: 8**

SEE EXAMPLE 2 p. 308

8. **Biology** To thaw a specimen stored at –25 °C, the temperature of a refrigeration tank is raised 5 °C every hour. The temperature in the tank after *x* hours can be described by the function $f(x) = -25 + 5x$.
   a. Graph the function and find its intercepts. **x-int.: 5; y-int.: –25**
   b. What does each intercept represent?

SEE EXAMPLE 3 p. 309

Use intercepts to graph the line described by each equation.

9. $4x - 5y = 20$
10. $y = 2x + 4$
11. $\frac{1}{3}x - \frac{1}{4}y = 2$
12. $-5y + 2x = -10$

PRACTICE AND PROBLEM SOLVING

Independent Practice

For Exercises	See Example
13–21	1
22–23	2
24–29	3

Extra Practice
Skills Practice p. S12
Application Practice p. S32

16. x-int.: 2; y-int.: 4
17. x-int.: –4; y-int.: 2
18. x-int.: –8; y-int.: 2
19. x-int.: 2; y-int.: 8
20. x-int.: 5; y-int.: –15
21. x-int.: $\frac{1}{8}$; y-int.: –1

Find the *x*- and *y*-intercepts.

13.

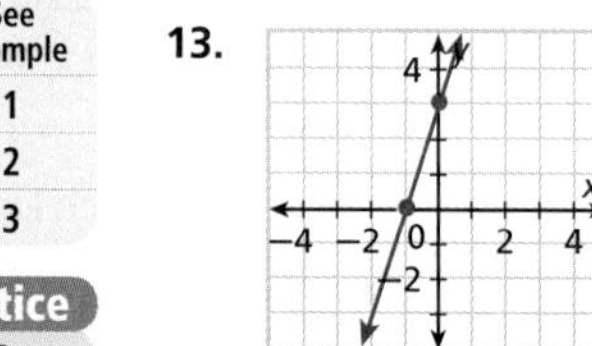

x-int.: –1; y-int.: 3

14.

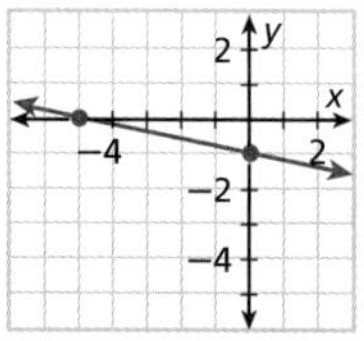

x-int.: –5; y-int.: –1

15.

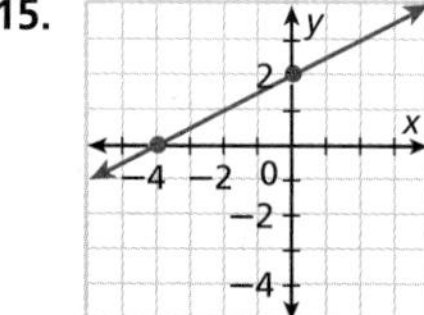

x-int.: –4; y-int.: 2

16. $6x + 3y = 12$
17. $4y - 8 = 2x$
18. $-2y + x = 2y - 8$
19. $4x + y = 8$
20. $y - 3x = -15$
21. $2x + y = 10x - 1$

22. **Environmental Science** A fishing lake was stocked with 300 bass. Each year, the population decreases by 25. The population of bass in the lake after *x* years is represented by the function $f(x) = 300 - 25x$. **x-int.: 12; y-int.: 300**
    a. Graph the function and find its intercepts.
    b. What does each intercept represent?

23. **Sports** Julie is running a 5-kilometer race. She runs 1 kilometer every 5 minutes. Julie's distance from the finish line after *x* minutes is represented by the function $f(x) = 5 - \frac{1}{5}x$.
    a. Graph the function and find its intercepts. **x-int.: 25; y-int.: 5**
    b. What does each intercept represent?

5-2 READING STRATEGIES

Study the chart below to compare and contrast *x*- and *y*-intercepts.

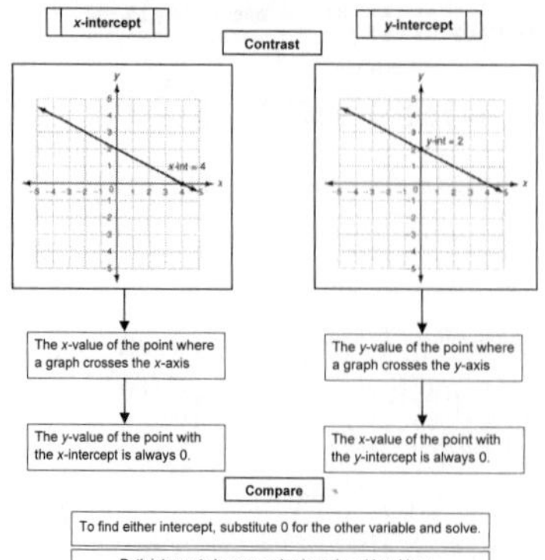

x-intercept | Contrast | y-intercept

The x-value of the point where a graph crosses the x-axis

The y-value of the point where a graph crosses the y-axis

The y-value of the point with the x-intercept is always 0.

The x-value of the point with the y-intercept is always 0.

Compare

To find either intercept, substitute 0 for the other variable and solve.

Both intercepts have meaning in real-world problems.

Find the x- and y-intercepts.
1. $3x - 2y = 6$
2.
3. The graph intersects the two axes at (–3, 0) and (0, 5).

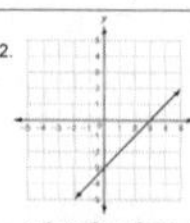

x-int: 2; y-int: –3 x-int: 3; y-int: –3 x-int: –3; y-int: 5

5-2 RETEACH

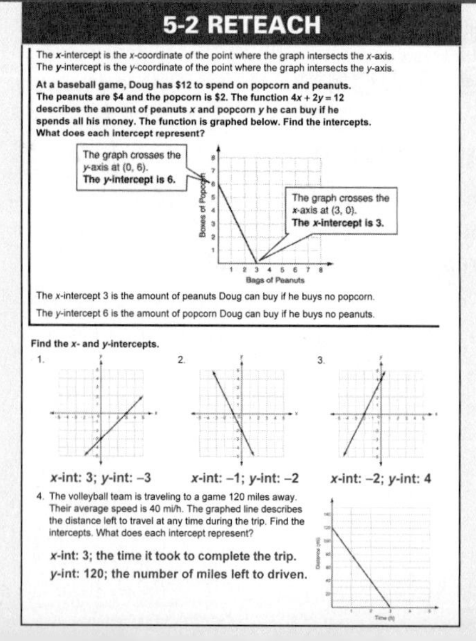

The x-intercept is the x-coordinate of the point where the graph intersects the x-axis.
The y-intercept is the y-coordinate of the point where the graph intersects the y-axis.

At a baseball game, Doug has $12 to spend on popcorn and peanuts. The peanuts are $4 and the popcorn is $2. The function $4x + 2y = 12$ describes the amount of peanuts x and popcorn y he can buy if he spends all his money. The function is graphed below. Find the intercepts. What does each intercept represent?

The graph crosses the y-axis at (0, 6). **The y-intercept is 6.**

The graph crosses the x-axis at (3, 0). **The x-intercept is 3.**

The x-intercept 3 is the amount of peanuts Doug can buy if he buys no popcorn.
The y-intercept 6 is the amount of popcorn Doug can buy if he buys no peanuts.

Find the x- and y-intercepts.

1. x-int: 3; y-int: –3
2. x-int: –1; y-int: –2
3. x-int: –2; y-int: 4

4. The volleyball team is traveling to a game 120 miles away. Their average speed is 40 mi/h. The graph below describes the distance left to travel at any time during the trip. Find the intercepts. What does each intercept represent?

x-int: 3; the time it took to complete the trip.
y-int: 120; the number of miles left to driven.

Use intercepts to graph the line described by each equation.

24. $4x - 6y = 12$
25. $2x + 3y = 18$
26. $\frac{1}{2}x - 4y = 4$
27. $y - x = -1$
28. $5x + 3y = 15$
29. $x - 3y = -1$

LINK **Biology**

Bamboo is the world's fastest-growing woody plant. Some varieties can grow more than 30 centimeters a day and up to 40 meters tall.

30. **Biology** A bamboo plant is growing 1 foot per day. When you first measure it, it is 4 feet tall.
    a. Write an equation to describe the height y, in feet, of the bamboo plant x days after you measure it. $y = x + 4$
    b. What is the y-intercept? 4
    c. What is the meaning of the y-intercept in this problem? orig. height of bamboo plant

31. **Estimation** Look at the scatter plot and trend line. x-int.: 600; y-int.: 7.5
    a. Estimate the x- and y-intercepts.
    b. What is the real-world meaning of each intercept?

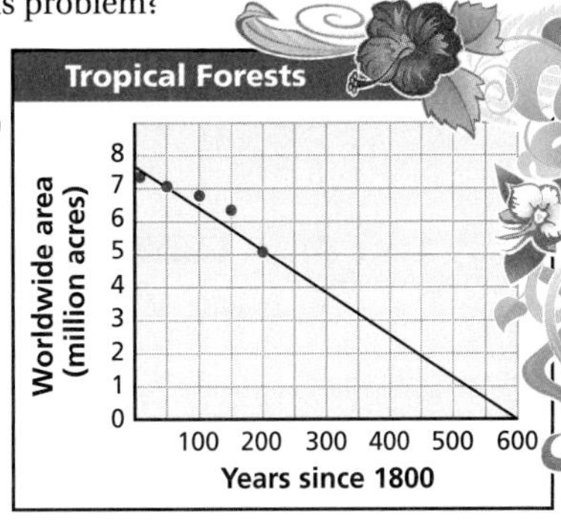

32. **Personal Finance** A bank employee notices an abandoned checking account with a balance of \$412. If the bank charges a \$4 monthly fee for the account, the function $b = 412 - 4m$ shows the balance b in the account after m months.
    a. Graph the function and give its domain and range. (*Hint:* The bank will keep charging the monthly fee even after the account is empty.)
    b. Find the intercepts. What does each intercept represent?
    c. When will the bank account balance be 0? after 103 mo (8 yr 7 mo)

32b. x-int.: 103; y-int.: 412; y-int.: balance when bank employee noticed account; x-int.: number of months from that time until account has \$0

33. **Critical Thinking** Complete the following to learn about intercepts and horizontal and vertical lines.
    a. Graph $x = -6$, $x = 1$, and $x = 5$. Find the intercepts.
    b. Graph $y = -3$, $y = 2$, and $y = 7$. Find the intercepts.
    c. Write a rule describing the intercepts of linear equations whose graphs are horizontal and vertical lines.

33c. Horiz.: For $y = c$, the y-int. is c, and there is no x-int. Vert.: For $x = k$, the x-int. is k, and there is no y-int.

Match each equation with a graph.

34. $-2x - y = 4$ **D**
35. $y = 4 - 2x$ **A**
36. $2y + 4x = 8$ **A**
37. $4x - 2y = 8$ **B**

A.

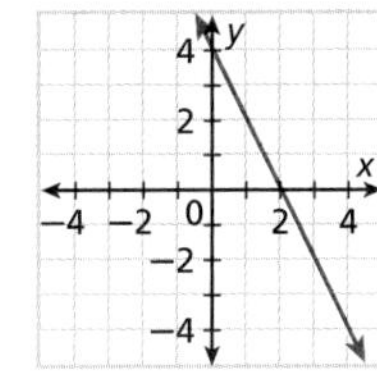

B.

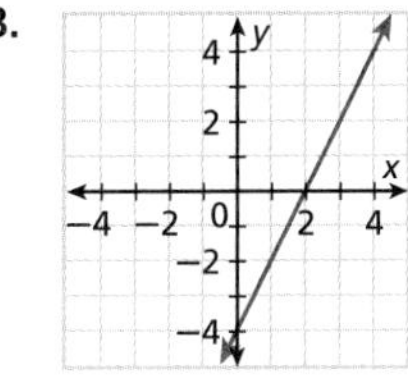

C.

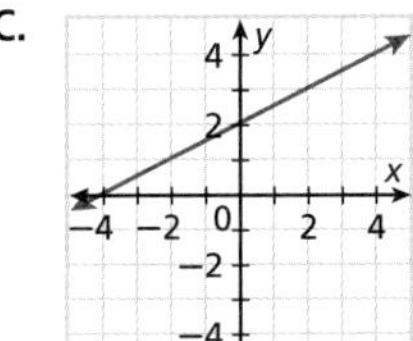

D.

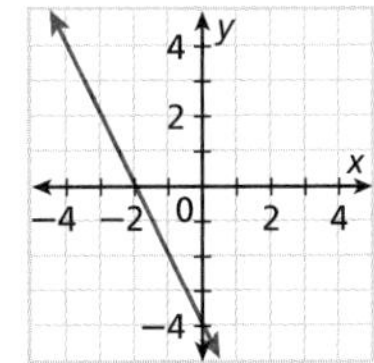

COMMON ERROR ALERT

Students may combine intercepts to form a point. In **Exercise 9,** for example, a student might take the x-intercept (5) and the y-intercept (−4) to form the point (5, −4). Remind students that the intercepts give you two separate points: (5, 0) and (0, −4).

Answers

24.

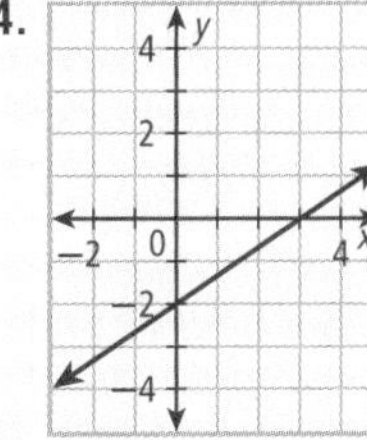

25.

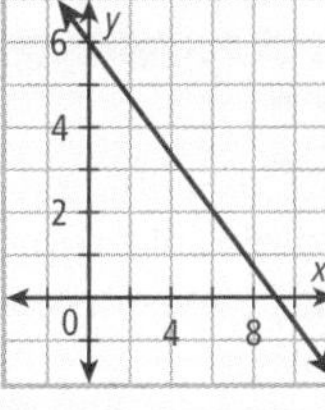

26.

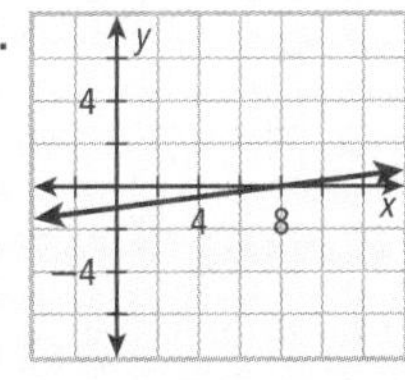

27.

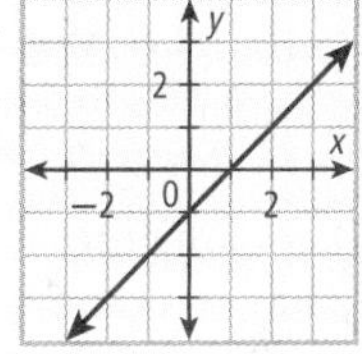

28, 29, 31b, 32a, 33a, 33b. See p. A20.

5-2 PROBLEM SOLVING

Write the correct answer.

1. Naima has \$40 to spend on refreshments for herself and her friends at the movie theater. The equation $5x + 2y = 40$ describes the number of large popcorns x and small drinks y she can buy. Graph this function and find its intercepts.
   y-int: 20; x-int: 8

2. Turner is reading a 400-page book. He reads 4 pages every 5 minutes. The number of pages Turner has left to read after x minutes is represented by the function $f(x) = 400 - \frac{4}{5}x$. Graph this function and find its intercepts.
   y-int: 400; x-int: 500

The graph shows the distance of an elevator at Chimney Rock, North Carolina, from its destination as a function of time. Use the graph to answer questions 3–6. Select the best answer.

3. What is the x-intercept of this function?
   A 0 C 258
   B 30 D 300
4. What does the x-intercept represent?
   F the total distance the elevator travels
   G the number of seconds that have passed for any given distance
   H the number of seconds it takes the elevator to reach its destination
   J the distance that the elevator has traveled at any given time
5. What is the y-intercept for this function?
   A 0 **C** 258
   B 30 D 300
6. What does the y-intercept represent?
   F the total distance the elevator travels
   G the number of seconds that have passed for any given distance
   H the number of seconds it takes the elevator to reach its destination
   J the distance that the elevator has traveled at any given time

5-2 CHALLENGE

You can use the **distance formula** to find the distance between two ordered pairs.

$$d = \sqrt{(x_2 - x_1)^2 + (y_2 - y_1)^2}$$

where (x_1), (y_1) represents the first ordered pair and (x_2), (y_2) represents the second ordered pair.

Find the distance between the ordered pairs. Round your answer to the nearest tenth.

1. (3, 0) and (0, 5) ≈5.8 units
2. (−4, 0) and (0, 2) ≈4.5 units

Find the x- and y-intercepts of each equation. Use the intercepts to graph the equations on the same grid. Then find the perimeter of the geometric figure formed by the lines. Round all distances to the nearest tenth.

3. $-x + y = 4$ x-int: −4 y-int: 4
   $-x + y = -4$ x-int: 4 y-int: −4
   $x + y = 4$ x-int: 4 y-int: 4
   $x + y = -4$ x-int: −4 y-int: −4

   Perimeter: ≈22.6 units

4. $8y + 9x = 72$ x-int: 8 y-int: 9
   $4y - 9x = 36$ x-int: −4 y-int: 9
   $16y - 9x = -72$ x-int: 8 y-int: −4.5

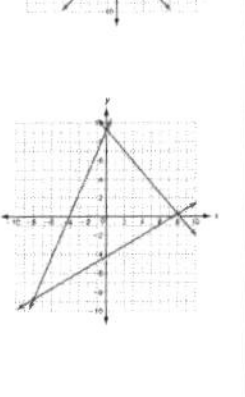

   Perimeter: ≈50.1 units

5-2 PRACTICE A
5-2 PRACTICE C
5-2 PRACTICE B

Find the x- and y-intercepts.

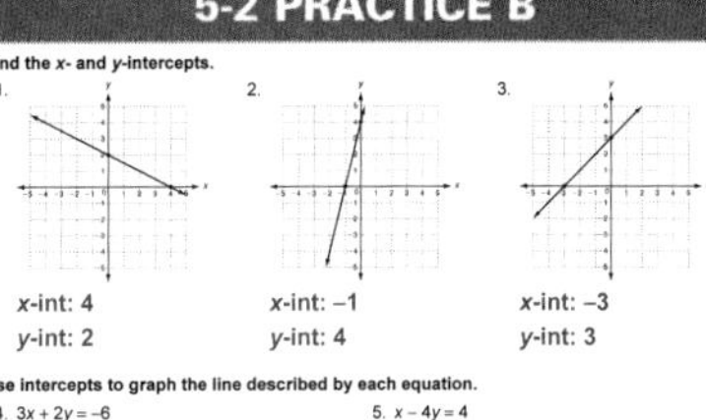

1. x-int: 4 y-int: 2
2. x-int: −1 y-int: 4
3. x-int: −3 y-int: 3

Use intercepts to graph the line described by each equation.

4. $3x + 2y = -6$
5. $x - 4y = 4$

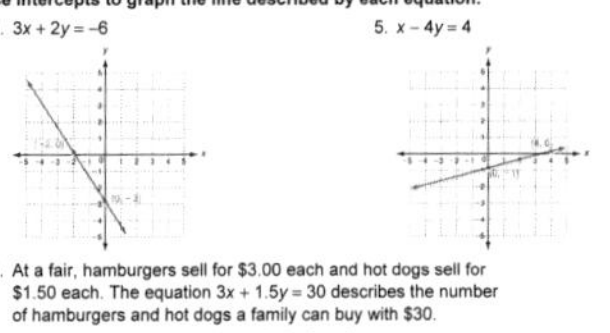

6. At a fair, hamburgers sell for \$3.00 each and hot dogs sell for \$1.50 each. The equation $3x + 1.5y = 30$ describes the number of hamburgers and hot dogs a family can buy with \$30.
   a. Find the intercepts and graph the function.
   x-int: 10; y-int: 20
   b. What does each intercept represent?
   x-int: the number of hamburgers they can buy if they buy no hot dogs. y-int: the number of hot dogs they can buy if they buy no hamburgers.

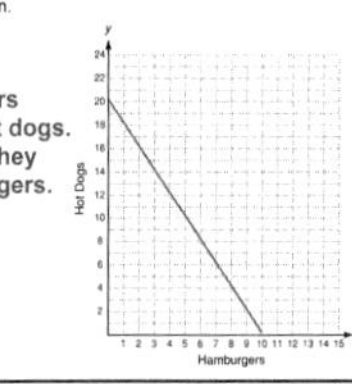

Exercise 38 involves identifying and interpreting *x*- and *y*-intercepts. This exercise prepares students for the Multi-Step Test Prep on page 342.

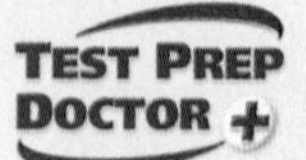

Students who chose **B** in **Exercise 40** may have chosen the coefficient of *x*. Students who chose **C** found the *y*-intercept instead of the *x*-intercept.

Journal

Have students explain how to find the intercepts of $5x - 8y = 40$.

Have students write an equation in standard form, find the intercepts, and then graph the line using the intercepts.

Power Presentations with PowerPoint®

5-2 Lesson Quiz

1. An amateur filmmaker has \$6000 to make a film that costs \$75/h to produce. The function $f(x) = 6000 - 75x$ gives the amount of money left to make the film after *x* hours of production. Graph this function and find the intercepts. What does each intercept represent?

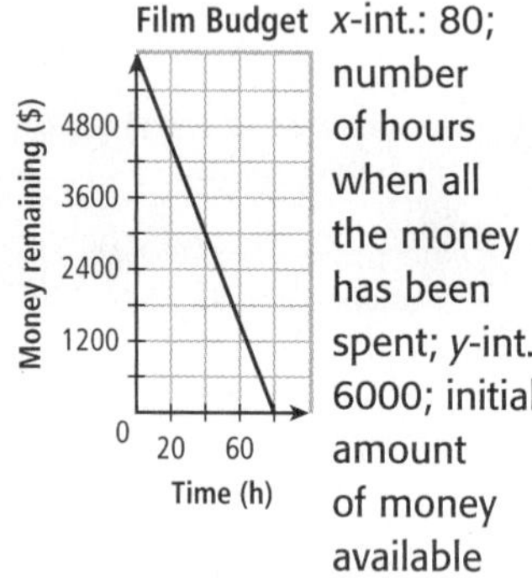

x-int.: 80; number of hours when all the money has been spent; *y*-int.: 6000; initial amount of money available

2. Use intercepts to graph the line described by $\frac{1}{4}x = 2 - \frac{1}{3}y$.

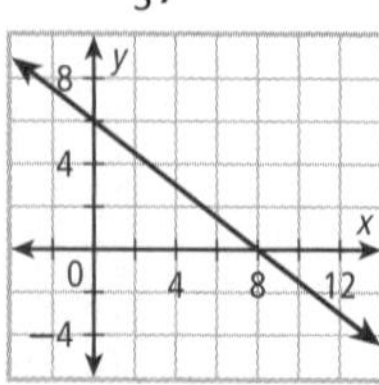

Also available on transparency

MULTI-STEP TEST PREP

38. This problem will prepare you for the Multi-Step Test Prep on page 342.

Kristyn rode a stationary bike at the gym. She programmed the timer for 20 minutes. The display counted backward to show how much time remained in her workout. It also showed her mileage.

a. What are the intercepts? **x-int.: 20; y-int.: 1.75**

b. What do the intercepts represent? **x-int.: time remaining when Kristyn started her workout; y-int.: total distance Kristyn covered**

Time Remaining (min)	Distance Covered (mi)
20	0
16	0.35
12	0.70
8	1.05
4	1.40
0	1.75

39. **Write About It** Write a real-world problem that could be modeled by a linear function whose *x*-intercept is 5 and whose *y*-intercept is 60.

40. Which is the *x*-intercept of $-2x = 9y - 18$?
 (A) −9 (B) −2 (C) 2 **(D) 9**

41. Which of the following situations could be represented by the graph?

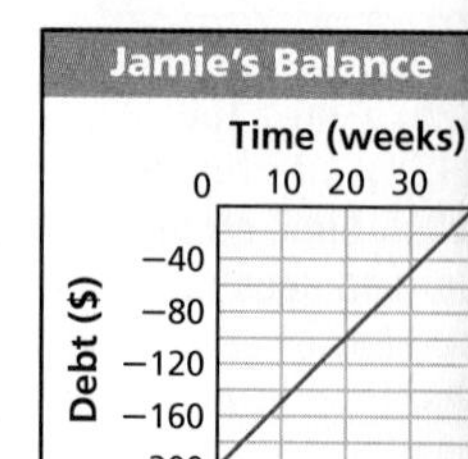

 (F) Jamie owed her uncle \$200. Each week for 40 weeks she paid him \$5.
 (G) Jamie owed her uncle \$200. Each week for 5 weeks she paid him \$40.
 (H) Jamie owed her uncle \$40. Each week for 5 weeks she paid him \$200.
 (J) Jamie owed her uncle \$40. Each week for 200 weeks she paid him \$5.

42. **Gridded Response** What is the *y*-intercept of $60x + 55y = 660$? **12**

CHALLENGE AND EXTEND

Use intercepts to graph the line described by each equation.

43. $\frac{1}{2}x + \frac{1}{5}y = 1$
44. $0.5x - 0.2y = 0.75$
45. $y = \frac{3}{8}x + 6$
46. For any linear equation $Ax + By = C$, what are the intercepts? **x-int.: $\frac{C}{A}$; y-int.: $\frac{C}{B}$**
47. Find the intercepts of $22x - 380y = 20{,}900$. Explain how to use the intercepts to determine appropriate scales for the graph.

47. x-int.: 950; y-int.: −55; possible answer: scale on x-axis should include numbers from 0 to a number a little greater than 950; scale on y-axis should include numbers from a little less than −55 to 0.

SPIRAL REVIEW

48. Marlon's fish tank is 80% filled with water. Based on the measurements shown, what volume of the tank is NOT filled with water? *(Lesson 2-9)* **600 in³**

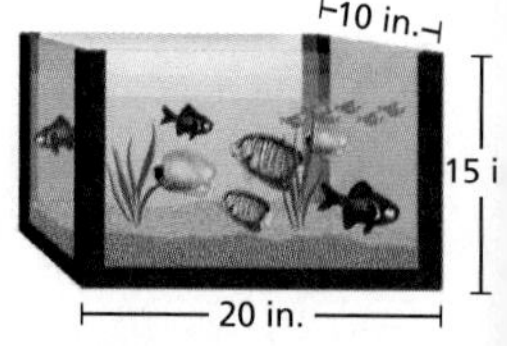

Solve each inequality and graph the solutions. *(Lesson 3-3)*

49. $3c > 12$ **$c > 4$**
50. $-4 \geq \frac{t}{2}$ **$t \leq -8$**
51. $\frac{1}{2}m \geq -3$ **$m \geq -6$**
52. $-2w > 14$ **$w < -7$**

Tell whether the given ordered pairs satisfy a linear function. Explain. *(Lesson 5-1)*

53. $\{(-2, 0), (0, 3), (2, 6), (4, 9), (6, 12)\}$ **yes**
54. $\{(0, 0), (1, 1), (4, 2), (9, 3), (16, 4)\}$ **no**

Answers

39. Possible answer: Jen wants to save \$60. Each week she will earn \$12. The function shows how much money Jen has left to save each week.

43.

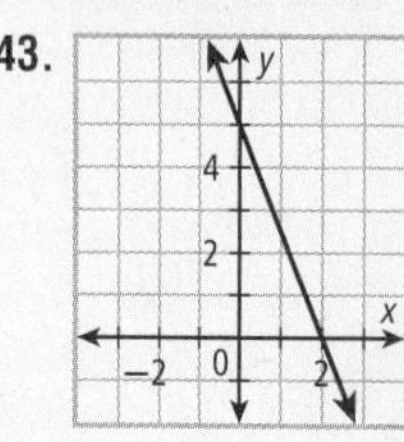

44.

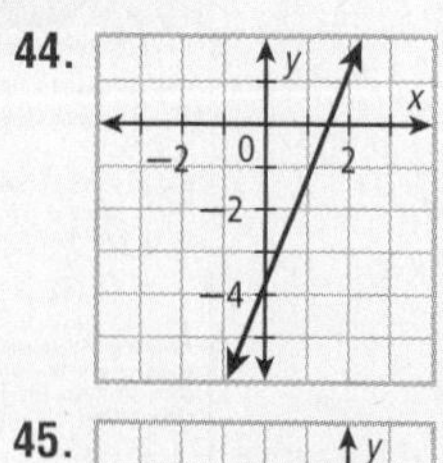

45.

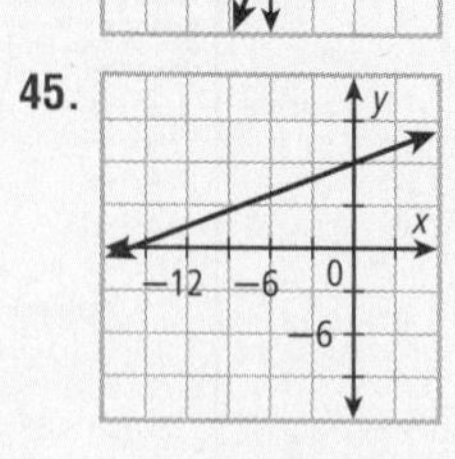

49. 1 2 3 4 5 6 7

50.

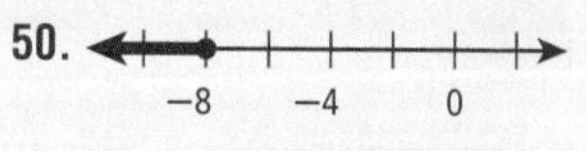

51.

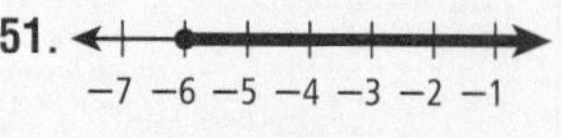

52.

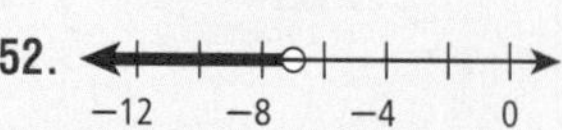

53. Possible answer: A constant change in *x* of 2 corresponds to a constant change in *y* of 3.

54. Possible answer: When graphed, the points do not lie on a line.

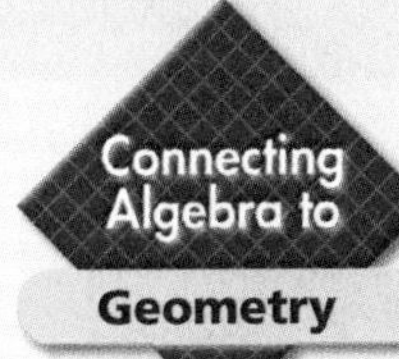

Area in the Coordinate Plane

Lines in the coordinate plane can form the sides of polygons. You can use points on these lines to help you find the areas of these polygons.

Example

Find the area of the triangle formed by the x-axis, the y-axis, and the line described by $3x + 2y = 18$.

Step 1 Find the intercepts of $3x + 2y = 18$.

x-intercept:	**y-intercept:**
$3x + 2y = 18$	$3x + 2y = 18$
$3x + 2(0) = 18$	$3(0) + 2y = 18$
$3x = 18$	$2y = 18$
$x = 6$	$y = 9$

Step 2 Use the intercepts to graph the line. The x-intercept is 6, so plot $(6, 0)$. The y-intercept is 9, so plot $(0, 9)$. Connect with a straight line. Then shade the triangle formed by the line and the axes, as described.

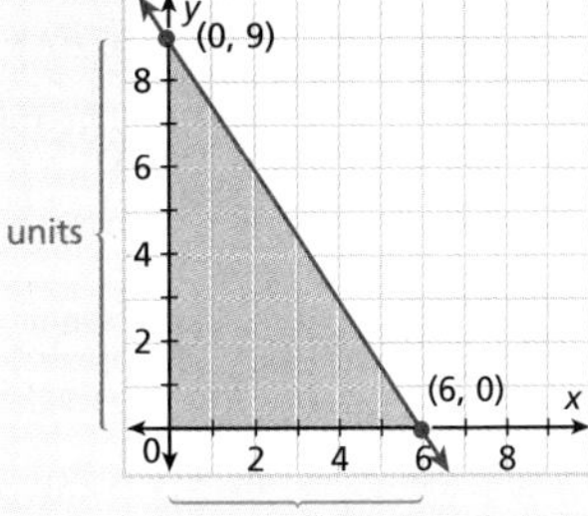

Step 3 Recall that the area of a triangle is given by $A = \frac{1}{2}bh$.

- The length of the base is 6.
- The height is 9.

Step 4 Substitute these values into the formula.

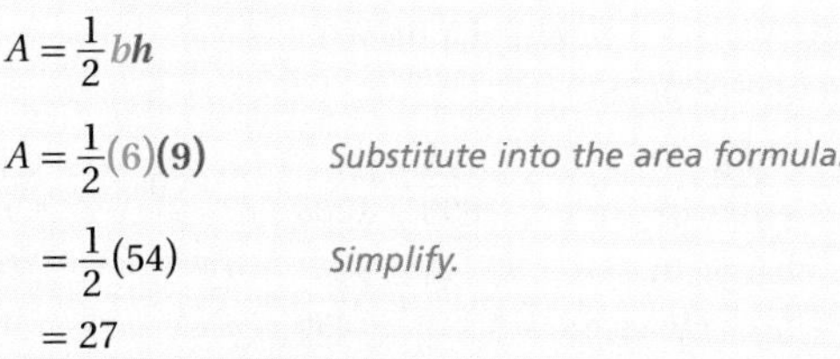

$$A = \frac{1}{2}bh$$

$$A = \frac{1}{2}(6)(9) \quad \textit{Substitute into the area formula.}$$

$$= \frac{1}{2}(54) \quad \textit{Simplify.}$$

$$= 27$$

The area of the triangle is 27 square units.

Try This

1. Find the area of the triangle formed by the x-axis, the y-axis, and the line described by $3x + 2y = 12$. **12 sq. units**
2. Find the area of the triangle formed by the x-axis, the y-axis, and the line described by $y = 6 - x$. **18 sq. units**
3. Find the area of the polygon formed by the x-axis, the y-axis, the line described by $y = 6$, and the line described by $x = 4$. **24 sq. units**

Connecting Algebra to Geometry

Organizer

Pacing:
Traditional $\frac{1}{2}$ day
Block $\frac{1}{4}$ day

Objective: Apply algebra skills to finding areas of geometric figures in the coordinate plane.

Online Edition

Countdown Week 10

Teach

Remember

Students review and apply the formulas for the areas of triangles and rectangles.

Discuss with students how identifying the intercepts of the line determines the base and height of the triangle.

Close

Assess

Use the triangle from the example. Have students change the equation of the line so that the area of the triangle increases. Then have them find the area of the new triangle.
Possible answer: $8x + 9y = 72$; 36 square units

State Resources

go.hrw.com
State Resources Online
KEYWORD: MA7 Resources

5-3 Organizer

Pacing: Traditional 1 day
Block $\frac{1}{2}$ day

Objectives: Find rates of change and slopes.

Relate a constant rate of change to the slope of a line.

Technology Lab
In Technology Lab Activities

Online Edition
Tutorial Videos, Interactivity

Countdown Week 10

Power Presentations with PowerPoint®

Warm Up

1. Find the x- and y-intercepts of $2x - 5y = 20$. x-int.: 10; y-int.: −4

Describe the correlation shown by the scatter plot.

2.

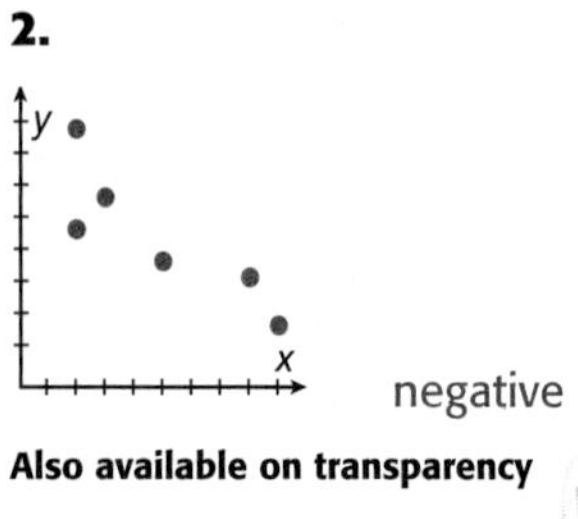

negative

Also available on transparency

Q: Why were the math students getting up and sprinting around the classroom?

A: Their teacher kept saying rise and run.

5-3 Rate of Change and Slope

Objectives
Find rates of change and slopes.

Relate a constant rate of change to the slope of a line.

Vocabulary
rate of change
rise
run
slope

Why learn this?
Rates of change can be used to find how quickly costs have increased.

In 1985, the cost of sending a 1-ounce letter was 22 cents. In 1988, the cost was 25 cents. How fast did the cost change from 1985 to 1988? In other words, at what *rate* did the cost change?

A **rate of change** is a ratio that compares the amount of change in a dependent variable to the amount of change in an independent variable.

$$\text{rate of change} = \frac{\text{change in dependent variable}}{\text{change in independent variable}}$$

EXAMPLE 1 ***Consumer Application***

The table shows the cost of mailing a 1-ounce letter in different years. Find the rate of change in cost for each time interval. During which time interval did the cost increase at the greatest rate?

Year	1988	1990	1991	2004	2008
Cost (¢)	25	25	29	37	42

Step 1 Identify the dependent and independent variables.

dependent: cost **independent: year**

Step 2 Find the rates of change.

1988 to 1990 $\frac{\text{change in cost}}{\text{change in years}} = \frac{25 - 25}{1990 - 1988} = \frac{0}{2} = 0$ $\frac{0 \text{ cents}}{\text{year}}$

1990 to 1991 $\frac{\text{change in cost}}{\text{change in years}} = \frac{29 - 25}{1991 - 1990} = \frac{4}{1} = 4$ $\frac{4 \text{ cents}}{\text{year}}$

1991 to 2004 $\frac{\text{change in cost}}{\text{change in years}} = \frac{37 - 29}{2004 - 1991} = \frac{8}{13} \approx 0.62 \approx$ $\frac{0.62 \text{ cents}}{\text{year}}$

2004 to 2008 $\frac{\text{change in cost}}{\text{change in years}} = \frac{42 - 37}{2008 - 2004} = \frac{5}{4} = 1.25$ $\frac{1.25 \text{ cents}}{\text{year}}$

The cost increased at the greatest rate from 1990 to 1991.

Caution!
A rate of change of 1.25 cents per year for a 4-year period means that the *average* change was 1.25 cents per year. The *actual* change in each year may have been different.

1. The table shows the balance of a bank account on different days of the month. Find the rate of change for each time interval. During which time interval did the balance decrease at the greatest rate?

Day	1	6	16	22	30
Balance ($)	550	285	210	210	175

1. day 1 to day 6: −53; day 6 to day 16: −7.5; day 16 to day 22: 0; day 22 to day 30: −4.375; from day 1 to day 6

State Resources

go.hrw.com
State Resources Online
KEYWORD: MA7 Resources

1 Introduce

EXPLORATION

5-3 Rate of Change and Slope

An electronics company has several factories that make stereos. Each factory produces the stereos at a steady pace throughout the day.

1. Over a period of 8 hours, factory A produces 400 stereos. Complete the table.

Time (h)	1	2	3	4	5	6	7	8
Stereos Produced								400

2. Over a period of 6 hours, factory B produces 360 stereos. Complete the table.

Time (h)	1	2	3	4	5	6	7	8
Stereos Produced						360		

3. How many stereos does each factory produce per hour?
4. Graph a linear function for each of the factories on the same coordinate plane.
5. How do the graphs compare?

THINK AND DISCUSS

6. **Explain** how you found the number of stereos that each factory produces per hour.
7. **Discuss** how a graph for factory C, which produces 75 stereos per hour, would compare to the other factories' graphs.

Motivate

Have students graph a line with x-intercept 3 and y-intercept 4. On the same grid, have them graph a line with x-intercept 5 and y-intercept 1. Ask how the lines are the same. Both are slanting in the same direction. Ask how the lines are different. One is steeper than the other.

Tell students that in this section they will learn how to indicate the steepness and direction of a line.

Explorations and answers are provided in *Alternate Openers: Explorations Transparencies.*

EXAMPLE 2 Finding Rates of Change from a Graph

Graph the data from Example 1 and show the rates of change.

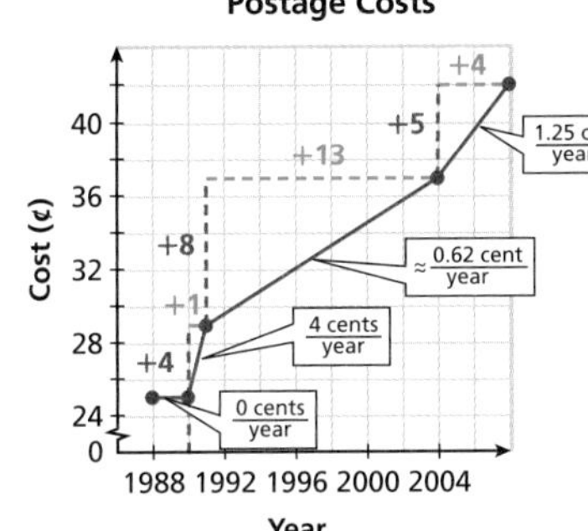

Graph the ordered pairs. The vertical blue segments show the changes in the dependent variable, and the horizontal green segments show the changes in the independent variable.

Notice that the greatest rate of change is represented by the steepest of the red line segments.

Also notice that between 1988 and 1990, when the cost did not change, the red line segment is horizontal.

2\.

Bank Balance

Balance ($); Day; −$53/day; −$7.50/day; $0/day; −$4.38/day

CHECK IT OUT! **2.** Graph the data from Check It Out Problem 1 and show the rates of change.

If all of the connected segments have the same rate of change, then they all have the same steepness and together form a straight line. The constant rate of change of a nonvertical line is called the *slope* of the line.

Slope of a Line

The **rise** is the difference in the **y-values** of two points on a line.

The **run** is the difference in the **x-values** of two points on a line.

The **slope** of a line is the ratio of rise to run for any two points on the line.

$$\text{slope} = \frac{\text{rise}}{\text{run}} = \frac{\text{change in } y}{\text{change in } x}$$

(Remember that y is the **dependent variable** and x is the independent variable.)

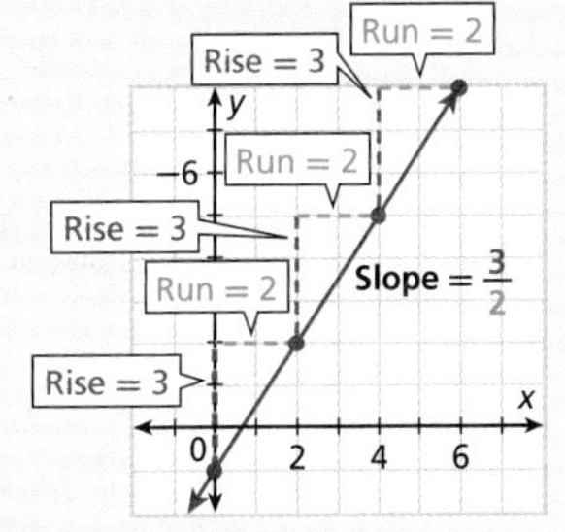

EXAMPLE  Finding Slope

Find the slope of the line.

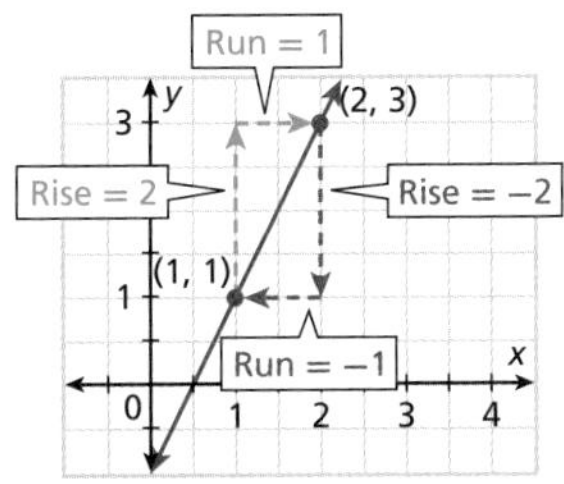

Begin at one point and count vertically to find the rise.

Then count horizontally to the second point to find the run. $\text{slope} = \frac{2}{1} = 2$

It does not matter which point you start with. The slope is the same. $\text{slope} = \frac{-2}{-1} = 2$

Caution!

Pay attention to the scales on the axes. One square on the grid may not represent 1 unit. In Example 3, each square represents $\frac{1}{2}$ unit.

3. Find the slope of the line that contains $(0, -3)$ and $(5, -5)$. $-\frac{2}{5}$

2 Teach

Guided Instruction

Connect the meaning of rate of change to the fact that the independent variable is represented on the horizontal axis, and the dependent variable on the vertical axis. Explain that a positive slope means the rate of change is positive, and a negative slope means the rate of change is negative. Point out that a horizontal line has 0 slope, no change in y-values, and 0 rate of change. By contrast, a vertical line has undefined slope and undefined rate of change.

Reaching All Learners

Through Multiple Representations

Show students how to use a "T-Chart" to find the slope.

x	y
1	1
2	4
3	7

+1, +1 (x); +3, +3 (y)

$$\text{Slope} = \frac{\text{change in } y}{\text{change in } x} = \frac{+3}{+1} = 3$$

This method works whether the ordered pairs are given in a table or a list, or selected from a graph.

Power Presentations with PowerPoint®

Additional Examples

Example 1

The table shows the average temperature (°F) for five months in a certain city. Find the rate of change in temperature for each time period. During which time period did the temperature increase at the greatest rate?

Month	2	3	5	7	8
Temp. (°F)	56	56	63	71	72

2 to 3: 0; 3 to 5: 3.5; 5 to 7: 4; 7 to 8: 1; from months 5 to 7

Example 2

Graph the data from Additional Example 1 and show the rates of change.

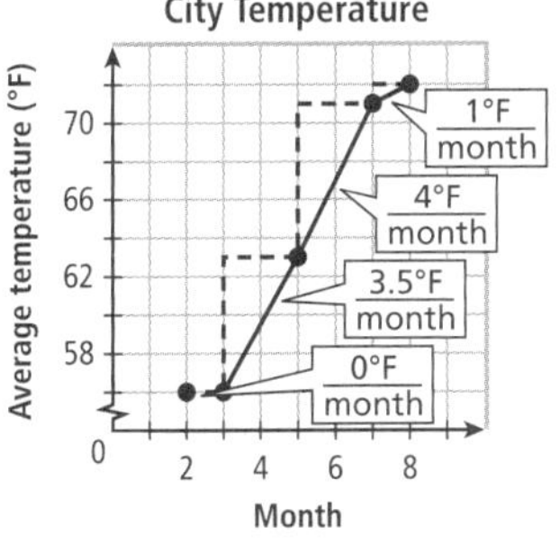

Example 3

Find the slope of the line.

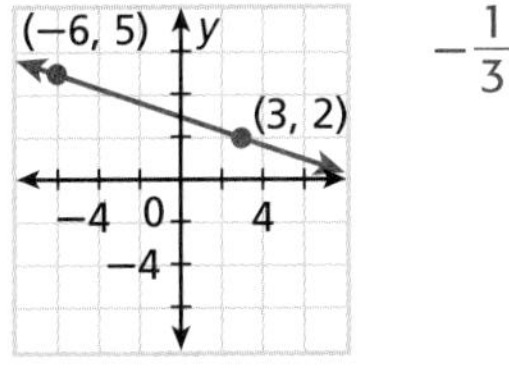

$-\frac{1}{3}$

INTERVENTION

Questioning Strategies

EXAMPLE 1

- In a rate of change, the change in which variable goes in the numerator? the denominator?

EXAMPLE 2

- Which variable is dependent? Which is independent?

EXAMPLE 3

- Does it matter which point you start at to find the slope?
- What does a positive slope look like? negative slope? zero slope?

Power Presentations with PowerPoint®

Additional Examples

Example 4

Find the slope of each line.

A.

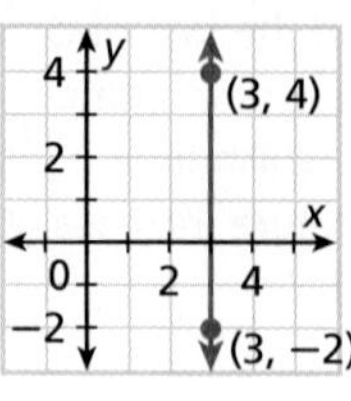

undefined

B.

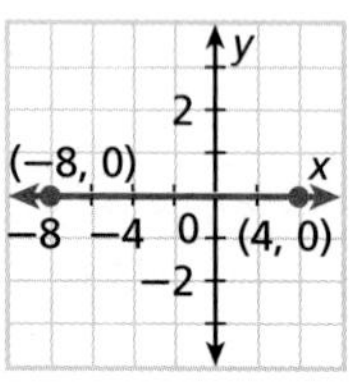

0

Example 5

Tell whether the slope of each line is positive, negative, zero, or undefined.

A.

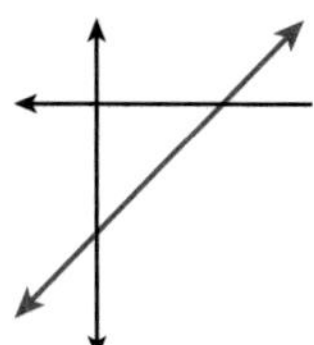

positive

B.

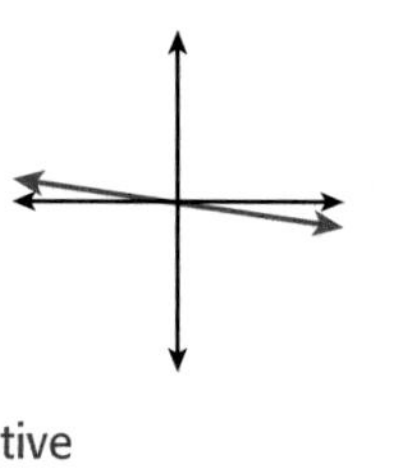

negative

INTERVENTION

Questioning Strategies

EXAMPLE 4

- Why is the slope of a vertical line undefined?

EXAMPLE 5

- Why don't you need points to determine whether the slope is positive, negative, zero, or undefined?

EXAMPLE 4 Finding Slopes of Horizontal and Vertical Lines

Find the slope of each line.

A

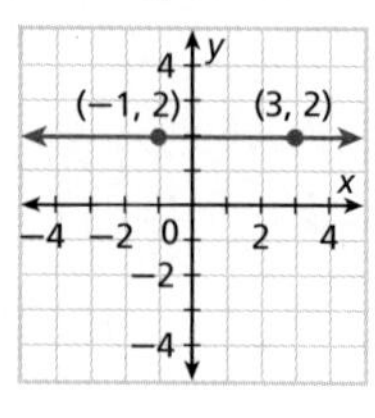

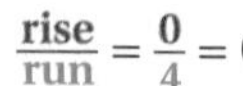

$\frac{\text{rise}}{\text{run}} = \frac{0}{4} = 0$

The slope is 0.

B

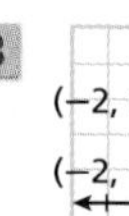

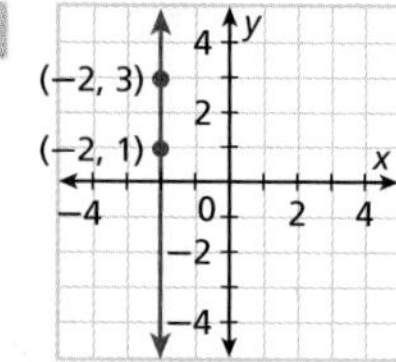

$\frac{\text{rise}}{\text{run}} = \frac{2}{0}$ *You cannot divide by 0.*

The slope is undefined.

CHECK IT OUT! Find the slope of each line.

4a. undef.

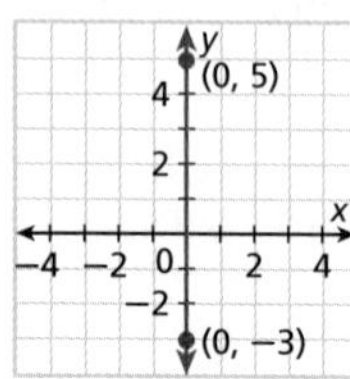

4b. 0

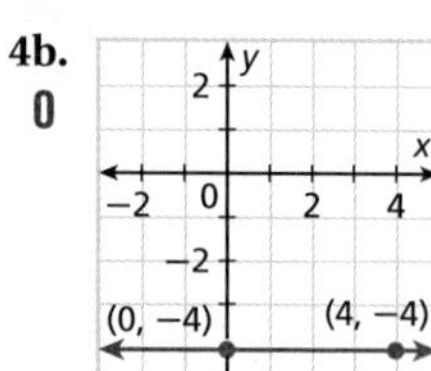

As shown in the previous examples, slope can be positive, negative, zero, or undefined. You can tell which of these is the case by looking at the graph of a line—you do not need to calculate the slope.

Know it! Note

Positive Slope	Negative Slope	Zero Slope	Undefined Slope
Line rises from left to right.	Line falls from left to right.	Horizontal line	Vertical line

EXAMPLE 5 Describing Slope

Tell whether the slope of each line is positive, negative, zero, or undefined.

A

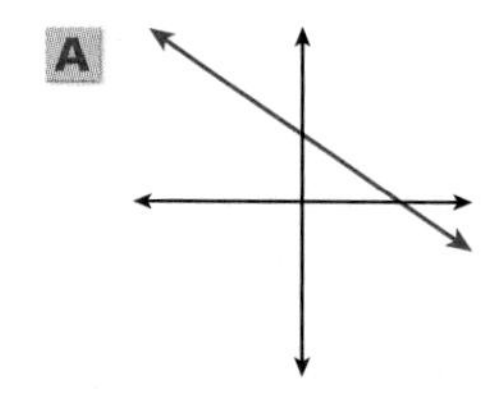

The line falls from left to right.

The slope is negative.

B

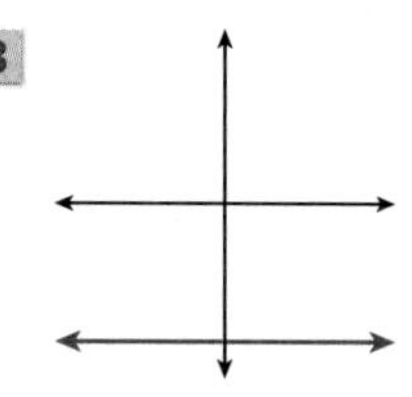

The line is horizontal.

The slope is 0.

Reaching All Learners

Through Cognitive Strategies

To help students remember the slopes of horizontal and vertical lines, remind them to think about which line has a rise of 0. Since a horizontal line does not rise at all, the rise is 0, and the slope is 0.

Through Auditory Cues

To help students interpret the meanings of different slopes, emphasize reading the graph *from left to right*.

Positive slope → *y*-values increase ***from left to right.***

Negative slope → *y*-values decrease ***from left to right.***

Zero slope → *y*-values have zero change ***from left to right.***

Undefined slope → There is ***NO left to right;*** the line is vertical.

CHECK IT OUT! Tell whether the slope of each line is positive, negative, zero, or undefined.

5a. undef.

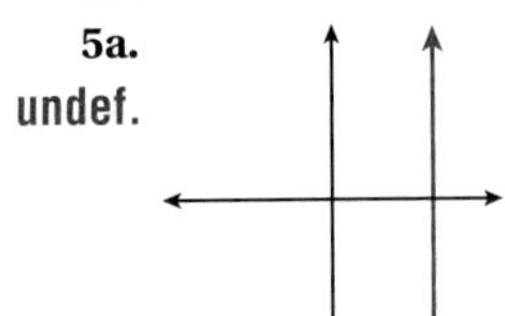

5b. pos.

A line's slope is a measure of its steepness. Some lines are steeper than others. As the absolute value of the slope increases, the line becomes steeper. As the absolute value of the slope decreases, the line becomes less steep.

Comparing Slopes

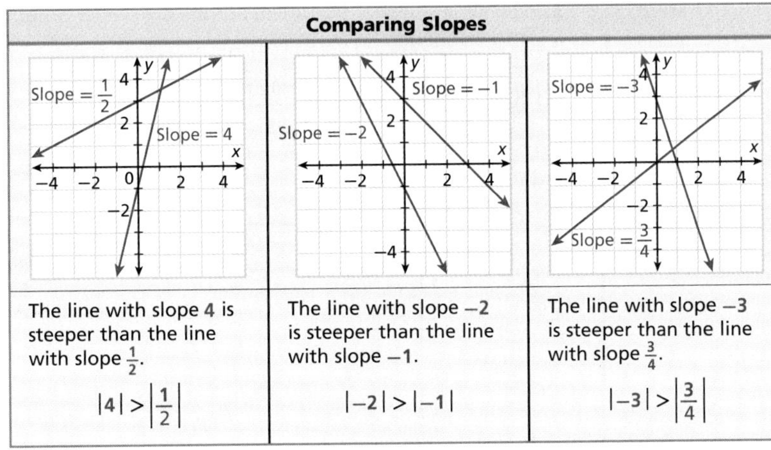

The line with slope 4 is steeper than the line with slope $\frac{1}{2}$. $\lvert 4 \rvert > \left\lvert \frac{1}{2} \right\rvert$	The line with slope −2 is steeper than the line with slope −1. $\lvert -2 \rvert > \lvert -1 \rvert$	The line with slope −3 is steeper than the line with slope $\frac{3}{4}$. $\lvert -3 \rvert > \left\lvert \frac{3}{4} \right\rvert$

THINK AND DISCUSS

1. What is the rise shown in the graph? What is the run? What is the slope?
2. The rate of change of the profits of a company over one year is negative. How have the profits of the company changed over that year?
3. Would you rather climb a hill with a slope of 4 or a hill with a slope of $\frac{5}{2}$? Explain your answer.

4. **GET ORGANIZED** Copy and complete the graphic organizer. In each box, sketch a line whose slope matches the given description.

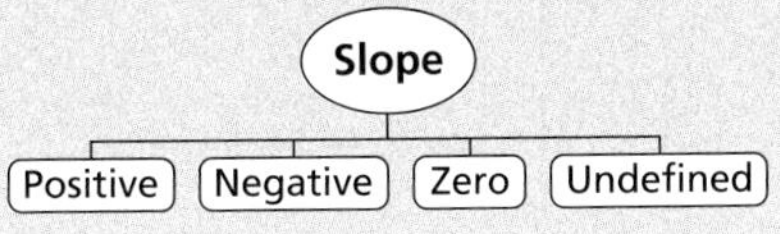

COMMON ERROR ALERT

Students may write 0 for the slope of a vertical line, thinking that "0" and "undefined" are the same. Remind students that 0 is a real number; it is not undefined.

Reading Math The words *gradient, slant,* and *incline* have meanings similar to *slope.* ENGLISH LANGUAGE LEARNERS

Inclusion Point out that in the slope ratio, the rise (change in *y*-values) is recorded before the run (change in *x*-values). This is the opposite of students' understanding from working in the coordinate plane. Everything up until now has been *x*-values (horizontal) first and then *y*-values (vertical) second. Direct students' attention to this difference.

3 Close

Summarize

Ask students to give descriptions of lines with the following slopes:

1. $m = 0$ horizontal line
2. $m = \frac{1}{50}$
   line rising from left to right, not steep
3. $m = -10$
   line falling from left to right, steep
4. $m = \frac{2}{0}$ vertical line

ONGOING ASSESSMENT and INTERVENTION

***Diagnose Before* the Lesson**
5-3 Warm Up, TE p. 314

***Monitor During* the Lesson**
Check It Out! Exercises, SE pp. 314–317
Questioning Strategies, TE pp. 315–316

***Assess After* the Lesson**
5-3 Lesson Quiz, TE p. 321
Alternative Assessment, TE p. 321

Answers to *Think and Discuss*

1. 6 units; 5 units; $\frac{6}{5}$
2. decreased
3. Possible answer: $\frac{5}{2}$, because it is less steep
4. See p. A5.

5-3 Exercises

Assignment Guide

Assign *Guided Practice* exercises as necessary.

If you finished Examples **1–3**
Basic 12–15, 24, 26, 27
Average 12–15, 23, 24, 26, 27, 32
Advanced 12–15, 23, 24, 27, 32, 33

If you finished Examples **1–5**
Basic 10–20, 22, 27, 29–31, 34–41
Average 12–32, 34–41
Advanced 12–25, 27–41

Homework Quick Check
Quickly check key concepts.
Exercises: 12, 13, 14, 16, 18, 24

Teaching Tip

Inclusion Emphasize the difference between non-constant rates of change and constant rates of change (slope). The graph of **Exercise 3** will show different slopes, indicating different rates of change. The graph of **Exercise 4** shows the same slope, so the rate of change is constant.

State Resources

5-3 Exercises

GUIDED PRACTICE

1. **Vocabulary** The *slope* of any nonvertical line is __?__. (*positive* or *constant*) **constant**

SEE EXAMPLE 1 p. 314

2. The table shows the volume of gasoline in a gas tank at different times. Find the rate of change for each time interval. During which time interval did the volume decrease at the greatest rate?

Time (h)	0	1	3	6	7
Volume (gal)	12	9	5	1	1

hour 0 to hour 1: −3; hour 1 to hour 3: −2; hour 3 to hour 6: $-\frac{4}{3}$; hour 6 to hour 7: 0; from hour 0 to hour 1

SEE EXAMPLE 2 p. 315

3. The table shows a person's heart rate over time. Graph the data and show the rates of change.

Time (min)	0	2	5	7	10
Heart Rate (beats/min)	64	92	146	84	64

Find the slope of each line.

SEE EXAMPLE 3 p. 315

4. 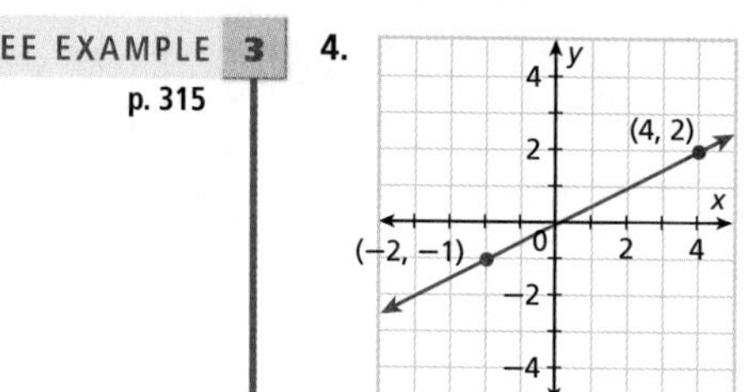

$\frac{1}{2}$

5. 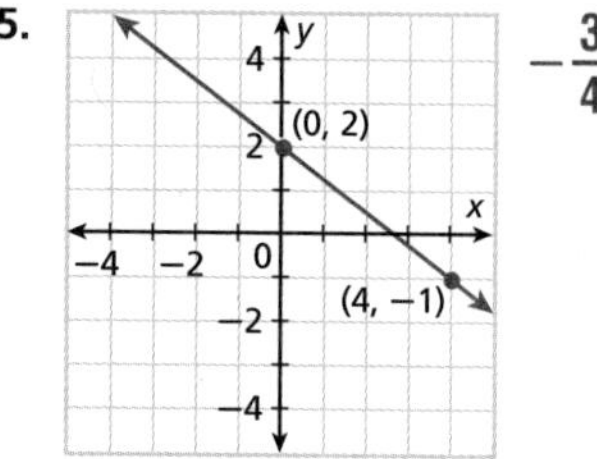

$-\frac{3}{4}$

SEE EXAMPLE 4 p. 316

6. 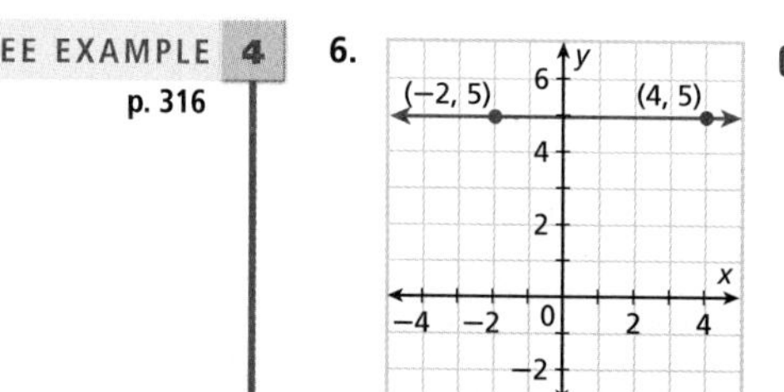

0

7. 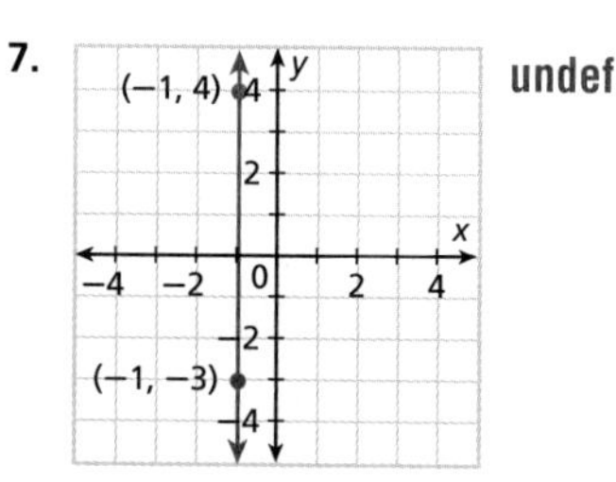

undef.

SEE EXAMPLE 5 p. 316

Tell whether the slope of each line is positive, negative, zero, or undefined.

8. **neg.**

9. **undef.**

10. **zero**

11. **pos.**

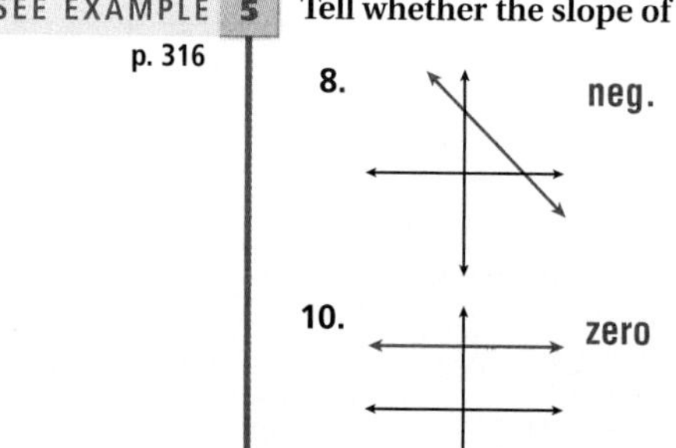

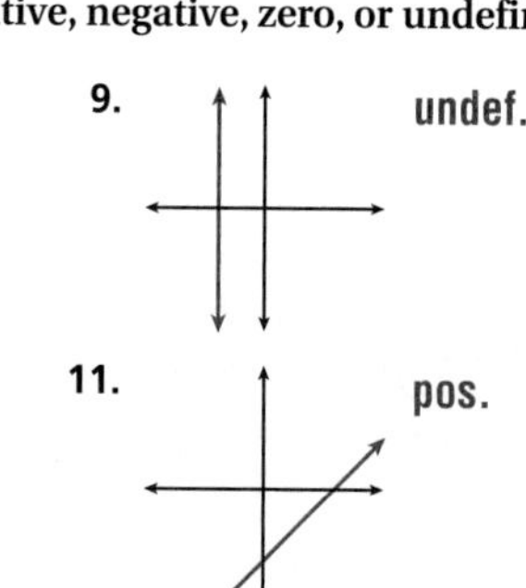

Answers

3.

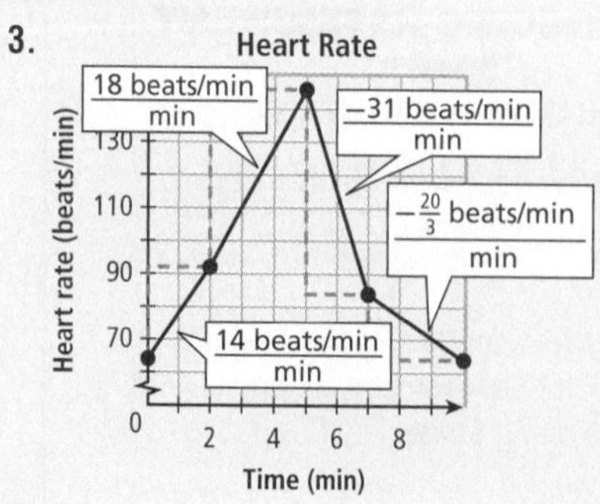

PRACTICE AND PROBLEM SOLVING

Independent Practice	
For Exercises	See Example
12	1
13	2
14–15	3
16–17	4
18–19	5

Extra Practice
Skills Practice p. S12
Application Practice p. S32

12. The table shows the length of a baby at different ages. Find the rate of change for each time interval. Round your answers to the nearest tenth. During which time interval did the baby have the greatest growth rate? **month 3 to month 9: 0.7; month 9 to month 18: 0.5; month 18 to month 26: 0.4; month 26 to month 33: 0.3; from 3 months to 9 months**

Age (mo)	3	9	18	26	33
Length (in.)	23.5	27.5	31.6	34.5	36.7

13. The table shows the distance of an elevator from the ground floor at different times. Graph the data and show the rates of change.

Time (s)	0	15	23	30	35
Distance (m)	30	70	0	45	60

Find the slope of each line.

14. 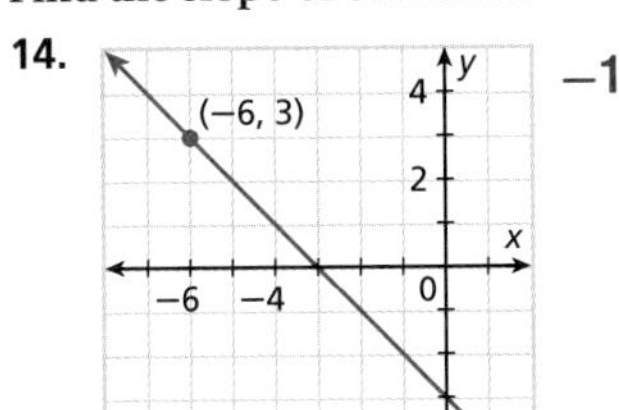

−1

15. 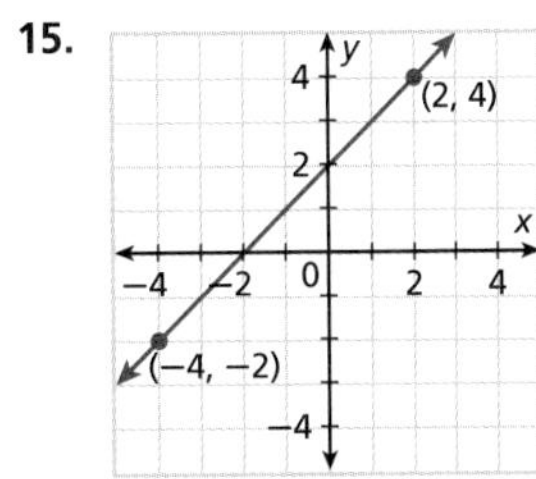

1

16. 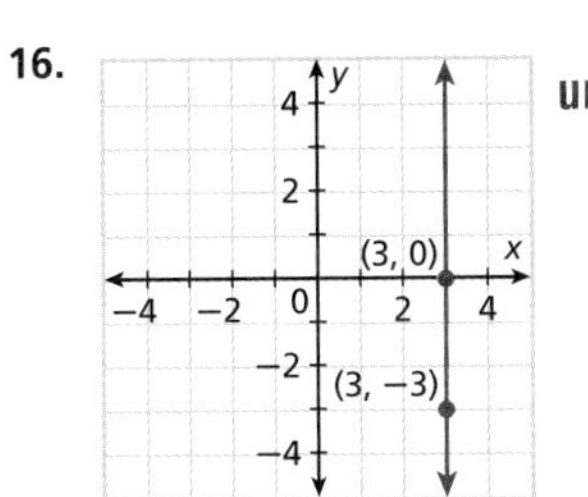

undef.

17. 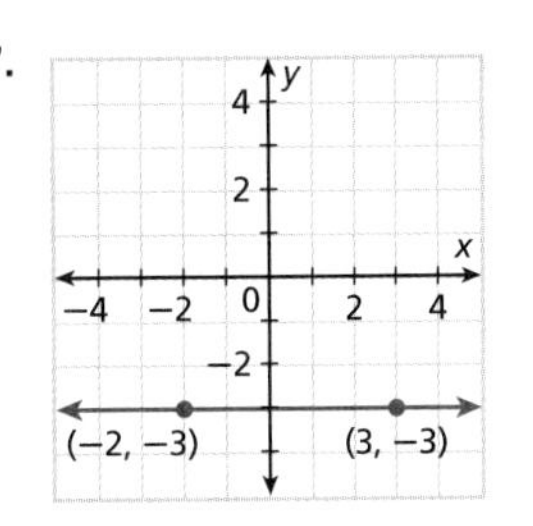

0

Tell whether the slope of each line is positive, negative, zero, or undefined.

18. **pos.**

19. 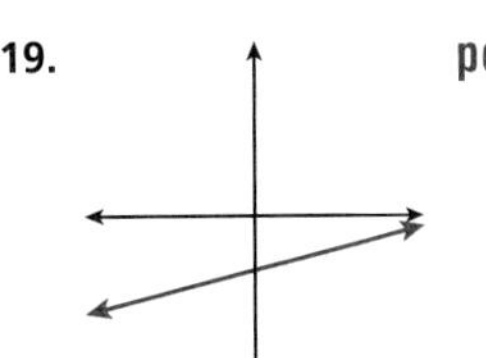 **pos.**

LINK Travel

The Incline Railway's climb up Lookout Mountain has been called "America's Most Amazing Mile." A round-trip on the railway lasts about 1.5 hours.

20. **Travel** The Lookout Mountain Incline Railway in Chattanooga, Tennessee, is the steepest passenger railway in the world. A section of the railway has a slope of about 0.73. In this section, a vertical change of 1 unit corresponds to a horizontal change of what length? Round your answer to the nearest hundredth. **1.37**

21. **Critical Thinking** In Lesson 5-1, you learned that in a linear function, a constant change in *x* corresponds to a constant change in *y*. How is this related to slope?

Answers

13. 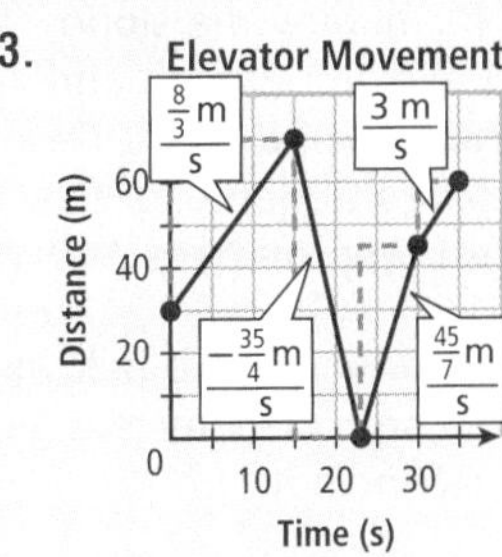

21. Possible answer: Slope is the ratio of change in *y* to change in *x*, and, for a line, it is always constant.

5-3 PRACTICE A
5-3 PRACTICE C
5-3 PRACTICE B

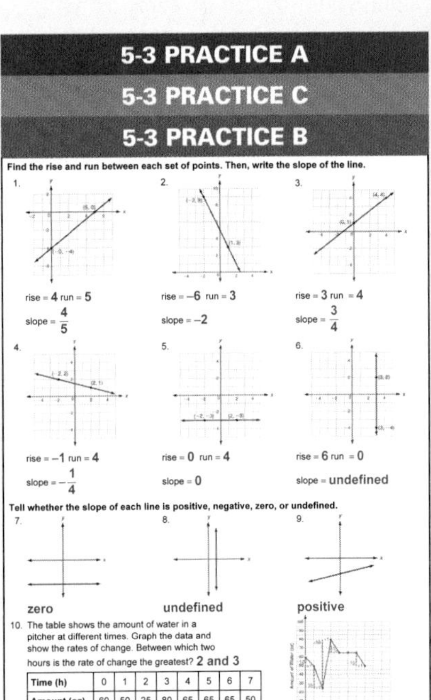

Find the rise and run between each set of points. Then, write the slope of the line.

1. rise = 4 run = 5, slope = $\frac{4}{5}$
2. rise = −6 run = 3, slope = −2
3. rise = 3 run = 4, slope = $\frac{3}{4}$
4. rise = −1 run = 4, slope = $-\frac{1}{4}$
5. rise = 0 run = 4, slope = 0
6. rise = 6 run = 0, slope = undefined

Tell whether the slope of each line is positive, negative, zero, or undefined.

7. zero
8. undefined
9. positive

10. The table shows the amount of water in a pitcher at different times. Graph the data and show the rates of change. Between which two hours is the rate of change the greatest? 2 and 3

Time (h)	0	1	2	3	4	5	6	7
Amount (oz)	60	50	25	80	65	65	65	50

Exercise 22 involves finding the slope from a graph and describing the rate of change. This exercise prepares students for the Multi-Step Test Prep on page 342.

Data Collection To help students complete **Exercise 28,** see *Technology Lab Activities.*

Answers

24a.

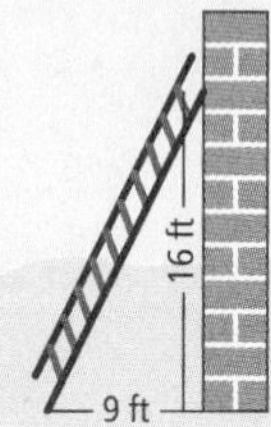

25. Possible answer: The slope of a horizontal line will always be 0 because the *y*-coordinates of any 2 points will be the same. Therefore, the numerator in the slope formula will always be 0. The slope of a vertical line will always be undefined because the *x*-coordinates of any 2 points will be the same. Therefore, the denominator in the slope formula will always be 0. Since you can't divide by 0, the slope will always be undefined.

26a.

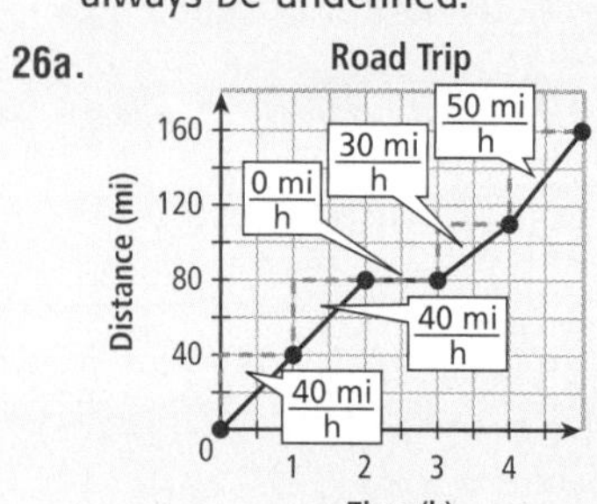

28a. Walk toward or away from the motion detector at a constant rate. A line has constant slope, and in this case slope represents $\frac{\text{distance}}{\text{time}}$, or rate. So keeping the rate constant will result in a line.

b. Positive slope: walk away from the detector; negative slope: walk toward the detector.

c. Stand still—as time passes, your distance from the detector does not change. This graph is a horizontal line.

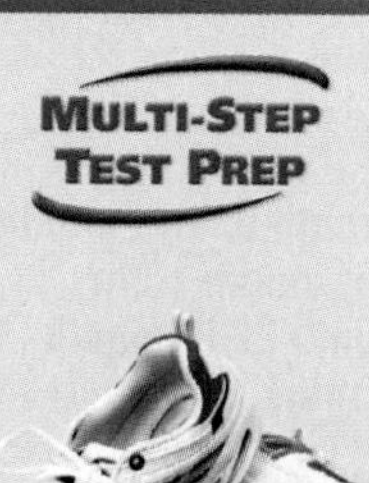

MULTI-STEP TEST PREP

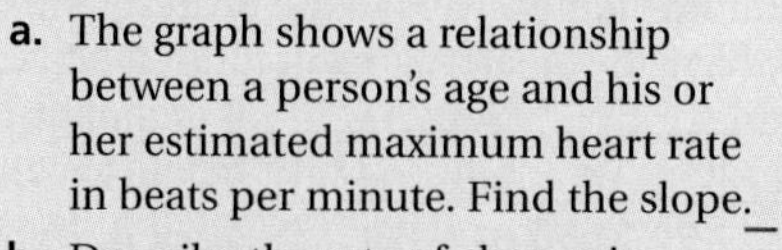

22. This problem will prepare you for the Multi-Step Test Prep on page 342.
    a. The graph shows a relationship between a person's age and his or her estimated maximum heart rate in beats per minute. Find the slope. **−1**
    b. Describe the rate of change in this situation. **For each yr that a person ages, their max. heart rate decreases by 1 beat/min.**

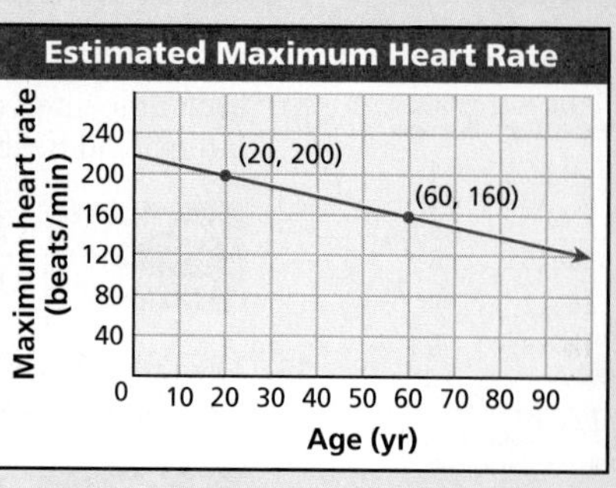

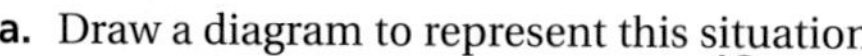

23. $\frac{8.5}{9} \approx 0.9444$

23. **Construction** Most staircases in use today have 9-inch treads and $8\frac{1}{2}$-inch risers. What is the slope of a staircase with these measurements?

24. A ladder is leaned against a building. The bottom of the ladder is 9 feet from the building. The top of the ladder is 16 feet above the ground.
    a. Draw a diagram to represent this situation.
    b. What is the slope of the ladder? $\frac{16}{9}$

25. **Write About It** Why will the slope of any horizontal line be 0? Why will the slope of any vertical line be undefined?

26. The table shows the distance traveled by a car during a five-hour road trip.

Time (h)	0	1	2	3	4	5
Distance (mi)	0	40	80	80	110	160

    a. Graph the data and show the rates of change.
    b. The rate of change represents the average speed. During which hour was the car's average speed the greatest? **the fifth**

27a. Possible answer: (16, 420)
b. Possible answer: (26, 650)
c. Possible answer: 23

27. **Estimation** The graph shows the number of files scanned by a computer virus detection program over time.
    a. Estimate the coordinates of point *A*.
    b. Estimate the coordinates of point *B*.
    c. Use your answers from parts **a** and **b** to estimate the rate of change (in files per second) between points *A* and *B*.

28. **Data Collection** Use a graphing calculator and a motion detector for the following. Set the equipment so that the graph shows distance on the *y*-axis and time on the *x*-axis.
    a. Experiment with walking in front of the motion detector. How must you walk to graph a straight line? Explain.
    b. Describe what you must do differently to graph a line with a positive slope vs. a line with a negative slope.
    c. How can you graph a line with slope 0? Explain.

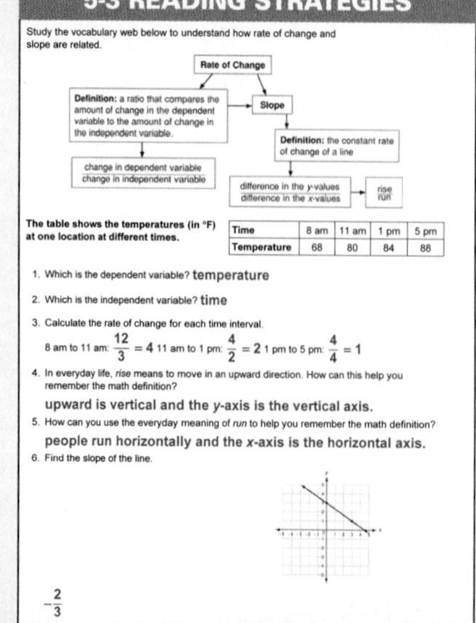

5-3 READING STRATEGIES

Study the vocabulary web below to understand how rate of change and slope are related.

Rate of Change → Definition: a ratio that compares the amount of change in the dependent variable to the amount of change in the independent variable. → $\frac{\text{change in dependent variable}}{\text{change in independent variable}}$

Rate of Change → Slope → Definition: the constant rate of change of a line → $\frac{\text{difference in the } y\text{-values}}{\text{difference in the } x\text{-values}}$ → $\frac{\text{rise}}{\text{run}}$

The table shows the temperatures (in °F) at one location at different times.

Time	8 am	11 am	1 pm	5 pm
Temperature	68	80	84	88

1. Which is the dependent variable? **temperature**
2. Which is the independent variable? **time**
3. Calculate the rate of change for each time interval.
   8 am to 11 am: $\frac{12}{3} = 4$ 11 am to 1 pm: $\frac{4}{2} = 2$ 1 pm to 5 pm: $\frac{4}{4} = 1$
4. In everyday life, *rise* means to move in an upward direction. How can this help you remember the math definition?
   upward is vertical and the *y*-axis is the vertical axis.
5. How can you use the everyday meaning of *run* to help you remember the math definition?
   people run horizontally and the *x*-axis is the horizontal axis.
6. Find the slope of the line.
   $-\frac{2}{3}$

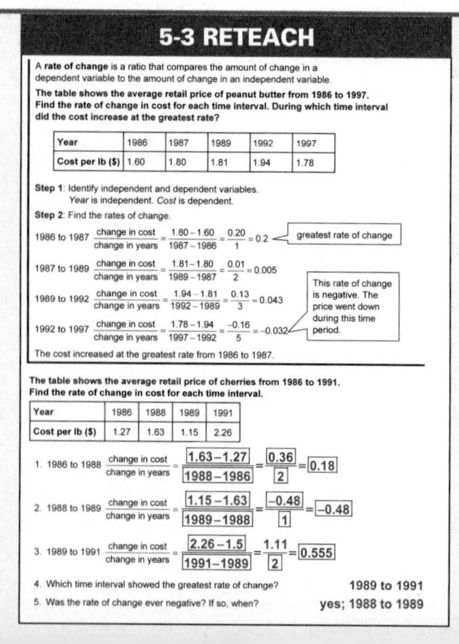

5-3 RETEACH

A **rate of change** is a ratio that compares the amount of change in a dependent variable to the amount of change in an independent variable.

The table shows the average retail price of peanut butter from 1986 to 1997. Find the rate of change in cost for each time interval. During which time interval did the cost increase at the greatest rate?

Year	1986	1987	1989	1992	1997
Cost per lb ($)	1.60	1.80	1.81	1.94	1.78

Step 1: Identify independent and dependent variables.
Year is independent. *Cost* is dependent.

Step 2: Find the rates of change.

1986 to 1987 $\frac{\text{change in cost}}{\text{change in years}} = \frac{1.80-1.60}{1987-1986} = \frac{0.20}{1} = 0.2$ (greatest rate of change)

1987 to 1989 $\frac{\text{change in cost}}{\text{change in years}} = \frac{1.81-1.80}{1989-1987} = \frac{0.01}{2} = 0.005$

1989 to 1992 $\frac{\text{change in cost}}{\text{change in years}} = \frac{1.94-1.81}{1992-1989} = \frac{0.13}{3} = 0.043$

1992 to 1997 $\frac{\text{change in cost}}{\text{change in years}} = \frac{1.78-1.94}{1997-1992} = \frac{-0.16}{5} = -0.032$ (This rate of change is negative. The price went down during this time period.)

The cost increased at the greatest rate from 1986 to 1987.

The table shows the average retail price of cherries from 1986 to 1991. Find the rate of change in cost for each time interval.

Year	1986	1988	1989	1991
Cost per lb ($)	1.27	1.63	1.15	2.26

1. 1986 to 1988 $\frac{\text{change in cost}}{\text{change in years}} = \frac{1.63-1.27}{1988-1986} = \frac{0.36}{2} = 0.18$
2. 1988 to 1989 $\frac{\text{change in cost}}{\text{change in years}} = \frac{1.15-1.63}{1989-1988} = \frac{-0.48}{1} = -0.48$
3. 1989 to 1991 $\frac{\text{change in cost}}{\text{change in years}} = \frac{2.26-1.5}{1991-1989} = \frac{1.11}{2} = 0.555$
4. Which time interval showed the greatest rate of change? **1989 to 1991**
5. Was the rate of change ever negative? If so, when? **yes; 1988 to 1989**

29. The slope of which line has the greatest absolute value?

Ⓐ line *A*   **(C)** line *C*
Ⓑ line *B*   Ⓓ line *D*

30. For which line is the run equal to 0?

Ⓐ line *A*   Ⓒ line *C*
Ⓑ line *B*   **(D)** line *D*

31. Which line has a slope of 4?

Ⓕ
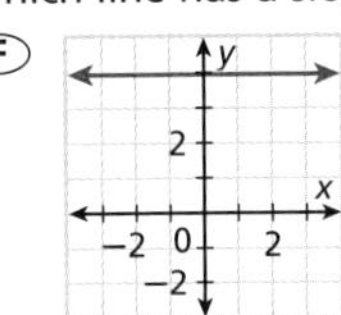

Ⓗ
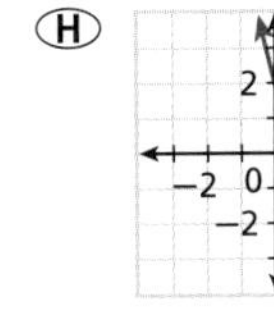

(G)
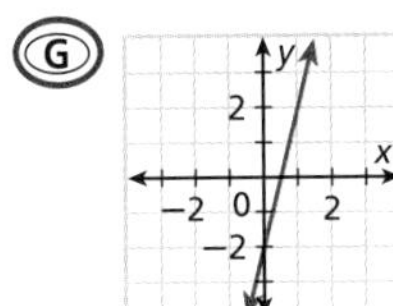

Ⓙ
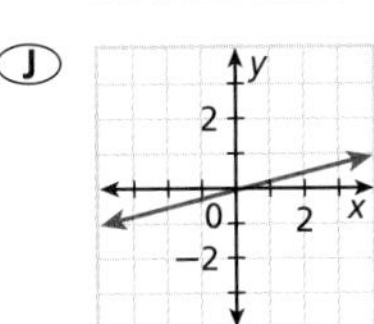

CHALLENGE AND EXTEND

32. **Recreation** Tara and Jade are hiking up a hill. Each has a different stride. The run for Tara's stride is 32 inches, and the rise is 8 inches. The run for Jade's stride is 36 inches. What is the rise of Jade's stride? **9 in.**

33. **Economics** The table shows cost in dollars charged by an electric company for various amounts of energy in kilowatt-hours.

Energy (kWh)	0	200	400	600	1000	2000
Cost ($)	3	3	31	59	115	150

a. Graph the data and show the rates of change.
b. Compare the rates of change for each interval. Are they all the same? Explain.
c. What do the rates of change represent?
d. Describe in words the electric company's billing plan.

SPIRAL REVIEW

37. D: {3}; R: {4, 2, 0, −2}; no
38. D: {−4, −2, 0, 2, 4}; R: {0, 2, 4}; yes
39. *x*-int.: 3; *y*-int.: 6
40. *x*-int.: −3; *y*-int.: −9
41. *x*-int.: $\frac{1}{4}$; *y*-int.: $\frac{1}{2}$

Add or subtract. *(Lesson 1-2)*

34. $-5 + 15$ **10**   35. $9 - 11$ **−2**   36. $-5 - (-25)$ **20**

Find the domain and range of each relation, and tell whether the relation is a function. *(Lesson 4-2)*

37. $\{(3, 4), (3, 2), (3, 0), (3, -2)\}$

38.

x	0	2	4	−2	−4
y	0	2	4	2	4

Find the *x*- and *y*-intercepts. *(Lesson 5-2)*

39. $2x + y = 6$ 40. $y = -3x - 9$ 41. $2y = -4x + 1$

Answers

33a.

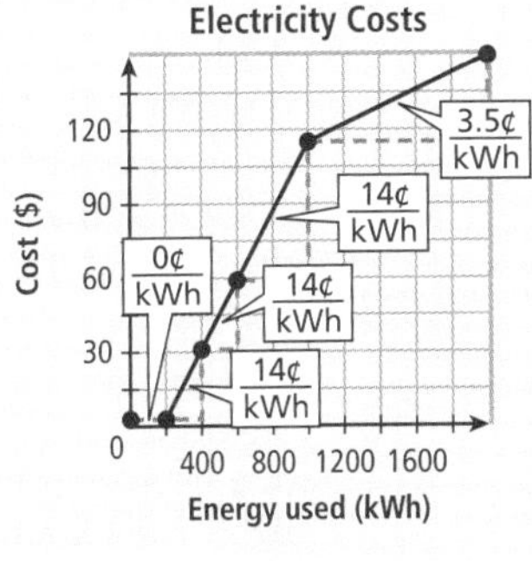

b. 0 kWh to 200 kWh: 0; 200 kWh to 400 kWh: 0.14; 400 kWh to 600 kWh: 0.14; 600 kWh to 1000 kWh: 0.14; 1000 kWh to 2000 kWh: 0.035; the rates of change for 200 kWh to 400 kWh, 400 kWh to 600 kWh, and 600 kWh to 1000 kWh are equivalent.

c. the cost per kilowatt-hour

d. Up to 200 kWh costs $3.00. Between 200 and 1000 kWh costs $0.14 per kWh. Between 1000 and 2000 kWh costs $0.035 per kWh.

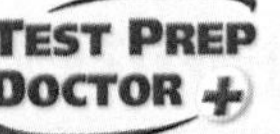

In **Exercise 31,** choices **F** and **H** can be eliminated immediately—the line in choice **F** has zero slope, and the line in choice **H** has a negative slope.

Journal

Have students compare a line with a slope of 3 and a line with a slope of $\frac{1}{3}$. Ask them to explain how they are alike, how they are different, and which line is steeper.

ALTERNATIVE ASSESSMENT

Have students explain how to tell whether the slope of a line is positive, negative, zero, or undefined simply by looking at the graph. They should include sketches in their answer.

Power Presentations with PowerPoint®

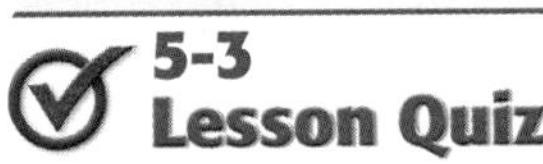

5-3 Lesson Quiz

1. The table shows the number of bikes made by a company for certain days. Find the rate of change for each time period. During which time period did the number of bikes increase at the fastest rate?

Day	1	2	5	7	11
Bikes	32	35	47	47	61

1 to 2: 3; 2 to 5: 4; 5 to 7: 0; 7 to 11: 3.5; from days 2 to 5

Find the slope of each line.

2. $-\frac{1}{3}$

3.
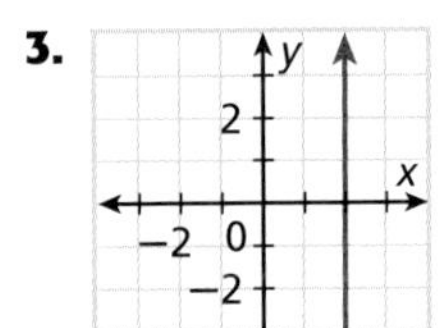
undefined

Also available on transparency

Organizer

Use with Lesson 5-3

Pacing:
Traditional $\frac{1}{2}$ day
Block $\frac{1}{4}$ day

Objective: Explore the relationship between constant change and the slope of a line.

Online Edition

Countdown Week 10

Lab Resources

Algebra Lab Activities
5-3 Lab Recording Sheet

Teach

Discuss

Encourage students to identify the independent and dependent variables for each situation.

Alternative Approach

Have students write the function rule for each scenario and compare the number multiplied by the independent variable with the amount of constant change.

Answers to *Activity 1*

2. The number of books Janice reads per week; the number of books read increases by 2 each week.

State Resources

Use with Lesson 5-3

Explore Constant Changes

There are many real-life situations in which the amount of change is constant. In these activities, you will explore what happens when

- a quantity increases by a constant amount.
- a quantity decreases by a constant amount.

Activity 1

Janice has read 7 books for her summer reading club. She plans to read 2 books each week for the rest of the summer. The table shows the total number of books that Janice will have read after different numbers of weeks have passed.

1. What number is added to the number of books in each row to get the number of books in the next row? **2**
2. What does your answer to Problem 1 represent in Janice's situation? Describe the meaning of the constant change.
3. Graph the ordered pairs from the table. Describe how the points are related.
4. Look again at your answer to Problem 1. Explain how this number affects your graph.

Janice's Summer Reading	
Week	**Total Books Read**
0	7
1	9
2	11
3	13
4	15
5	17

Try This

At a particular college, a full-time student must take at least 12 credit hours per semester and may take up to 18 credit hours per semester. Tuition costs $200 per credit hour.

1. Copy and complete the table by using the information above.
2. What number is added to the cost in each row to get the cost in the next row? **200**
3. What does your answer to Problem 2 above represent in the situation? Describe the meaning of the constant change.
4. Graph the ordered pairs from the table. Describe how the points are related.
5. Look again at your answer to Problem 2. Explain how this number affects your graph.
6. Compare your graphs from Activity 1 and Problem 4. How are they alike? How are they different?
7. **Make a Conjecture** Describe the graph of any situation that involves repeated addition of a positive number. Why do you think your description is correct?

Possible answer: It will be a line that ascends from left to right because the *y*-values will keep increasing by the same amount.

Tuition Costs	
Credit Hours	**Cost ($)**
12	**2400**
13	**2600**
14	**2800**
15	**3000**
16	**3200**
17	**3400**
18	**3600**

3. Janice's Summer Reading

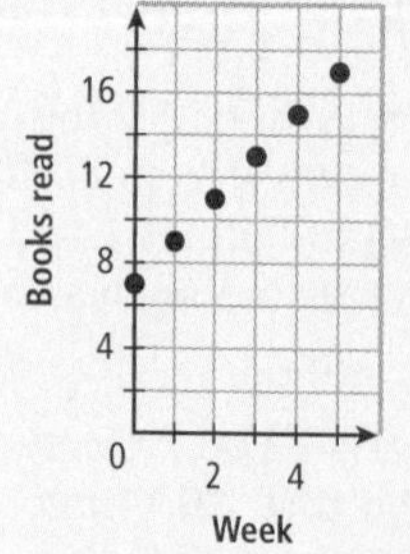

The points lie on a line that ascends from left to right.

4. Possible answer: The *y*-coordinate of each point is 2 greater than that of the previous point.

Answers to *Try This*

3. The cost of one credit hour; each additional credit hour increases the cost of tuition by $200.
4. Tuition Costs

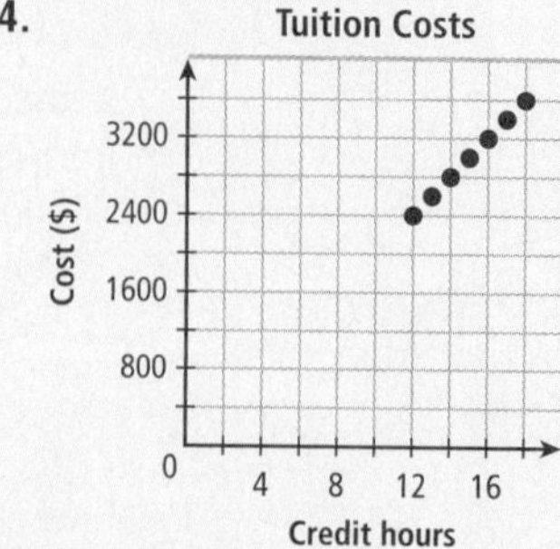

The points lie on a line that ascends from left to right.

5. Possible answer: The *y*-coordinate of each point is 200 greater than that of the previous point.
6. Possible answer: They are both points on lines that ascend from left to right. The tuition graph forms a steeper line.

Activity 2

An airplane is 3000 miles from its destination. The plane is traveling at a rate of 540 miles per hour. The table shows how far the plane is from its destination after various amounts of time have passed.

Airplane's Distance	
Time (h)	Distance to Destination (mi)
0	3000
1	2460
2	1920
3	1380
4	840

1. What number is subtracted from the distance in each row to get the distance in the next row? **540**
2. What does your answer to Problem 1 represent in the situation? Describe the meaning of the constant change.
3. Graph the ordered pairs from the table. Describe how the points are related.
4. Look again at your answer to Problem 1. Explain how this number affects your graph.

Try This

A television game show begins with 20 contestants. Each week, the players vote 2 contestants off the show.

Game Show	
Week	Contestants Remaining
0	20
1	**18**
2	**16**
3	**14**
4	**12**
5	**10**
6	**8**

8. Copy and complete the table by using the information above.
9. What number is subtracted from the number of contestants in each row to get the number of contestants in the next row? **2**
10. What does your answer to Problem 9 represent in the situation? Describe the meaning of the constant change.
11. Graph the ordered pairs from the table. Describe how the points are related.
12. Look again at your answer to Problem 9. Explain how this number affects your graph.
13. Compare your graphs from Activity 2 and Problem 11. How are they alike? How are they different?
14. **Make a Conjecture** Describe the graph of any situation that involves repeated subtraction of a positive number. Why do you think your description is correct?
15. Compare your two graphs from Activity 1 with your two graphs from Activity 2. How are they alike? How are they different?
16. **Make a Conjecture** How are graphs of situations involving repeated subtraction different from graphs of situations involving repeated addition? Explain your answer.

14. Possible answer: It will be a line that descends from left to right because you will keep decreasing the *y*-values by the same amount.

15. Possible answer: They both form lines. In Act. 1, the lines were ascending from left to right. In Act. 2, the lines were descending from left to right.

16. Possible answer: When situations involve repeated subt., the line is descending. When situations involve repeated add., the line is ascending.

Teacher to Teacher

Jennifer J. Southers
Piedmont, SC

When I introduce slope, I use a motion detector to motivate the lesson. I have a student walk at a normal pace toward the detector while the class watches the graph appear on the overhead panel. We discuss how the axes are labeled (distance-time). Students make and test conjectures about how to make the line more or less steep (walk faster or slower) and about how to change the direction of the graph (walk toward or away from the detector).

We discuss the units of the slope (m/s) and determine that this is speed, a rate of change. This also helps students remember that the slope of a horizontal line is zero (standing still, having zero speed), and that a vertical line has undefined slope, since it cannot be created by the detector. By starting in this fashion, I can always refer back to the motion detector activity as students continue to learn about slope.

Close

Key Concept

If a situation involves a quantity that increases or decreases by a constant amount, the data points will form a straight line. The steepness of the line is determined by the amount of increase or decrease.

Assessment

Journal Create a word problem involving a situation that uses repeated addition or subtraction. Write at least five ordered pairs and graph the line. Explain how the graph is related to the situation.

Answers to *Activity 2*

2. The plane's speed; the distance to the destination is decreasing by 540 mi each hour.
3.

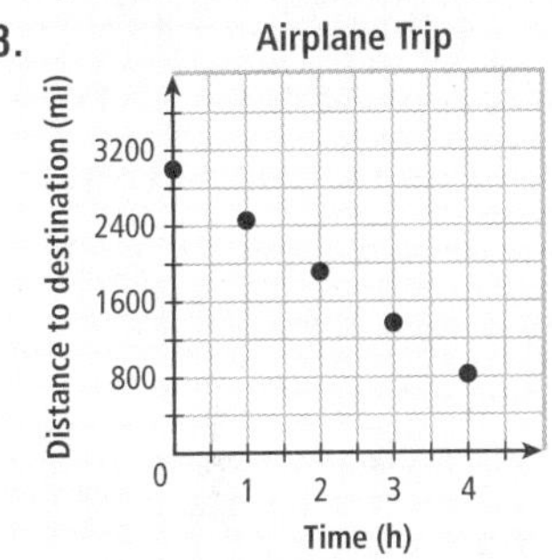

The points lie on a line that descends from left to right.

4. Possible answer: The *y*-coordinate of each point is 540 less than that of the previous point.

Answers to *Try This*

10. The number of contestants voted off each week; the total number of contestants is decreasing by 2 each week.
11.

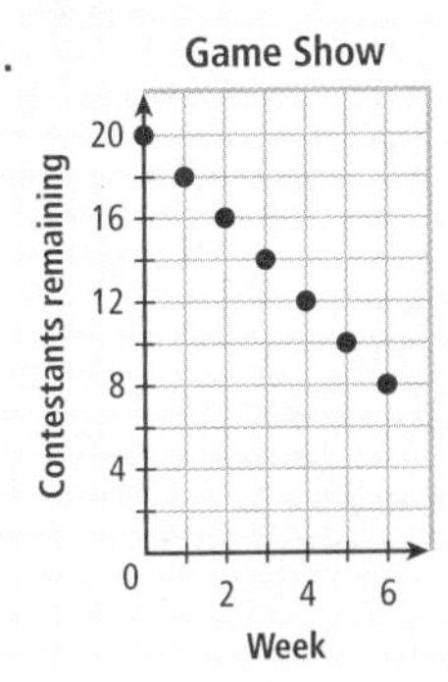

The points lie on a line that descends from left to right.

12. Possible answer: The *y*-coordinate of each point is 2 less than that of the previous point.
13. Possible answer: Both are points on lines that descend from left to right. The airplane graph is steeper.

5-4 Organizer

Pacing: Traditional 1 day
Block $\frac{1}{2}$ day

Objective: Find slope by using the slope formula.

Online Edition
Tutorial Videos

Countdown Week 11

Power Presentations with PowerPoint®

Warm Up

Add or subtract.

1. $4 + (-6)$ -2 **2.** $-3 + 5$ 2

3. $-7 - 7$ -14 **4.** $2 - (-1)$ 3

Find the *x*- and *y*-intercepts.

5. $x + 2y = 8$ *x*-int.: 8; *y*-int.: 4

6. $3x + 5y = -15$ *x*-int.: -5; *y*-int.: -3

Also available on transparency

Math Humor

A baker told his assistant to halve the filling recipe for a cake. When the baker asked for the filling, the assistant replied, "But I ate it!"

"Why did you do that?" demanded the baker.

"You told me to have it!"

5-4 The Slope Formula

Objective
Find slope by using the slope formula.

Why learn this?
You can use the slope formula to find how quickly a quantity, such as the amount of water in a reservoir, is changing. (See Example 3.)

In Lesson 5-3, slope was described as the constant rate of change of a line. You saw how to find the slope of a line by using its graph.

There is also a formula you can use to find the slope of a line, which is usually represented by the letter m. To use this formula, you need the coordinates of two different points on the line.

Know it! Note

Slope Formula

WORDS	FORMULA	EXAMPLE
The slope of a line is the ratio of the difference in *y*-values to the difference in *x*-values between any two different points on the line.	If (x_1, y_1) and (x_2, y_2) are any two different points on a line, the slope of the line is $m = \frac{y_2 - y_1}{x_2 - x_1}$.	If $(2, -3)$ and $(1, 4)$ are two points on a line, the slope of the line is $m = \frac{4-(-3)}{1-2} = \frac{7}{-1} = -7$.

EXAMPLE 1 **Finding Slope by Using the Slope Formula**

Reading Math
The small numbers to the bottom right of the variables are called subscripts. Read x_1 as "*x* sub one" and y_2 as "*y* sub two."

Find the slope of the line that contains $(4, -2)$ and $(-1, 2)$.

$m = \frac{y_2 - y_1}{x_2 - x_1}$ *Use the slope formula.*

$= \frac{2-(-2)}{-1-4}$ *Substitute $(4, -2)$ for (x_1, y_1) and $(-1, 2)$ for (x_2, y_2).*

$= \frac{4}{-5}$ *Simplify.*

$= -\frac{4}{5}$

The slope of the line that contains $(4, -2)$ and $(-1, 2)$ is $-\frac{4}{5}$.

CHECK IT OUT!

1a. Find the slope of the line that contains $(-2, -2)$ and $(7, -2)$. **0**

1b. Find the slope of the line that contains $(5, -7)$ and $(6, -4)$. **3**

1c. Find the slope of the line that contains $\left(\frac{3}{4}, \frac{7}{5}\right)$ and $\left(\frac{1}{4}, \frac{2}{5}\right)$. **2**

State Resources

go.hrw.com
State Resources Online
KEYWORD: MA7 Resources

1 Introduce

EXPLORATION

5-4 The Slope Formula

In this Exploration, you will investigate a shortcut for finding the slope of a line.

1. What is the rise from point *A* to point *B*?
2. What is the run from point *A* to point *B*?
3. What is the slope of the line?
4. Explain how you could have found the rise by using only the *y*-coordinates of the two points, without seeing the graph.
5. Explain how you could have found the run by using only the *x*-coordinates of the two points, without seeing the graph.

THINK AND DISCUSS

6. **Describe** a general method you can use to find the slope of a line if you are given the coordinates of two points on the line.
7. **Explain** how you could use your method to find the slope of the line that contains the points (5, 8) and (10, 18).

Motivate

Display the graph of a line (not horizontal or vertical) and plot and label two points whose coordinates are fractions or decimals. Ask students how they would find the slope. Possible answer: Count the rise and run and then find $\frac{\text{rise}}{\text{run}}$. Because the coordinates are not integers, counting rise and run is more difficult, and an error is likely. Tell students that in this lesson, they will learn a formula to find the slope without counting.

Explorations and answers are provided in *Alternate Openers: Explorations Transparencies.*

Sometimes you are not given two points to use in the formula. You might have to choose two points from a graph or a table.

EXAMPLE 2 Finding Slope from Graphs and Tables

Each graph or table shows a linear relationship. Find the slope.

A

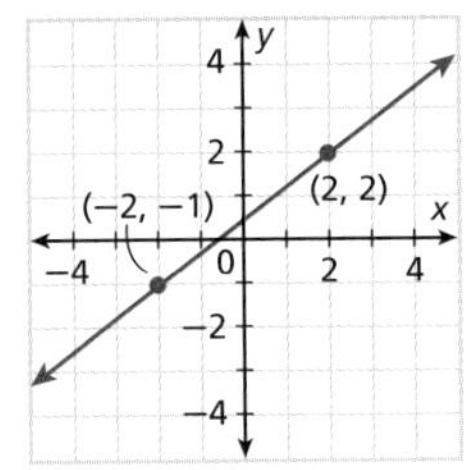

Let (2, 2) be (x_1, y_1) and (−2, −1) be (x_2, y_2).

$m = \frac{y_2 - y_1}{x_2 - x_1}$ *Use the slope formula.*

$= \frac{-1 - 2}{-2 - 2}$ *Substitute (2, 2) for (x_1, y_1) and (−2, −1) for (x_2, y_2).*

$= \frac{-3}{-4}$ *Simplify.*

$= \frac{3}{4}$

B

x	2	2	2	2
y	0	1	3	5

Step 1 Choose any two points from the table. Let (2, 0) be (x_1, y_1) and (2, 3) be (x_2, y_2).

Step 2 Use the slope formula.

$m = \frac{y_2 - y_1}{x_2 - x_1}$ *Use the slope formula.*

$= \frac{3 - 0}{2 - 2}$ *Substitute (2, 0) for (x_1, y_1) and (2, 3) for (x_2, y_2).*

$= \frac{3}{0}$ *Simplify.*

The slope is undefined.

Each graph or table shows a linear relationship. Find the slope.

2a. $\frac{1}{2}$

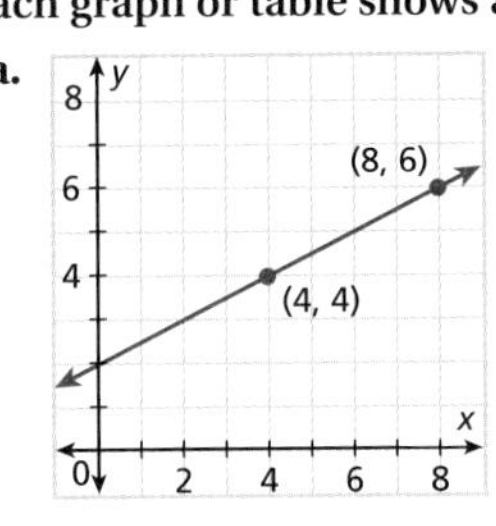

2b. −3

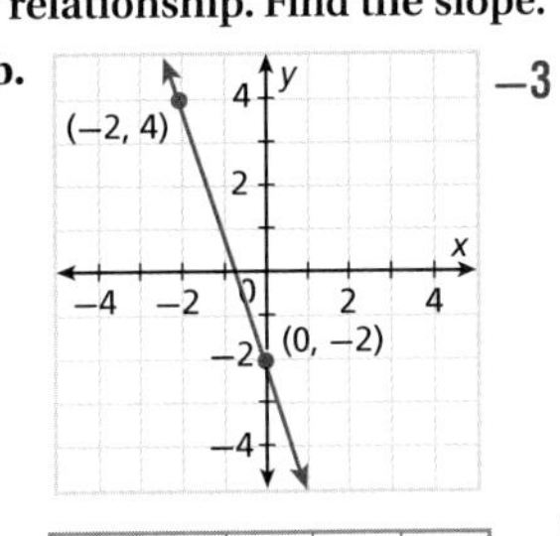

2c. 2

x	0	2	5	6
y	1	5	11	13

2d. $-\frac{3}{2}$

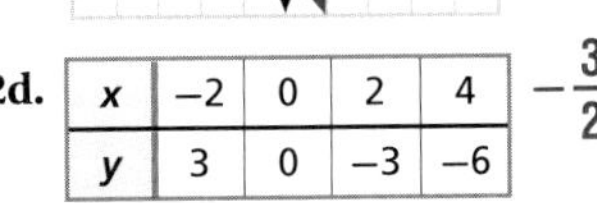

x	−2	0	2	4
y	3	0	−3	−6

Remember that slope is a rate of change. In real-world problems, finding the slope can give you information about how a quantity is changing.

COMMON ERROR ALERT

When using the slope formula, students may subtract the *x*- and *y*-values in different orders. Encourage students to label their ordered pairs *first* and *second* so that the *x*- and *y*-values are always subtracted in the same order.

Power Presentations with PowerPoint®

Additional Examples

Example 1

Find the slope of the line that contains (2, 5) and (8, 1). $-\frac{2}{3}$

Example 2

Each graph or table shows a linear relationship. Find the slope.

A. 2

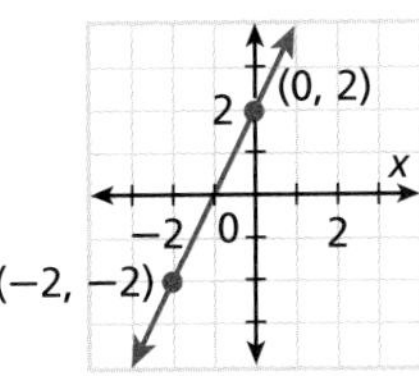

B.

x	−2	−1	0	1
y	5	3	1	−1

−2

INTERVENTION

Questioning Strategies

EXAMPLE 1

- If a line has slope 0, what will be true about the *y*-coordinates of any two points on that line?
- If a line has undefined slope, what will be true about the *x*-coordinates of any two points on that line?

EXAMPLE 2

- When you are given more than one point, how do you know which points to use in the slope formula?
- How could you check your answers?

Visual For problems like those in **Example 1,** students can check that their answer is reasonable by plotting the two points and connecting them with a line. They can then check that the direction of the line matches the sign of the slope.

2 Teach

Guided Instruction

Be sure students understand slope as the ratio of rise to run. Be sure that students can see that both methods—using the slope formula and using a graph to count rise and run—yield the same result.

Multiple Representations It is important for students to realize that the slope of a line is always the same, no matter which two points on the line are used to determine the slope. Use examples to demonstrate this.

Reaching All Learners

Through Cooperative Learning

Divide the class into groups of 3–5 students. Each group will need four number cubes. These can be found in the Manipulatives Kit (MK). One member of the group rolls the number cubes. Each member then uses the rolled numbers to create two ordered pairs and calculates the slope of the line between these two points. The student who finds the steepest slope wins the round and receives one point. (Note that a negative slope may be steeper than a positive one.) Play until one student reaches five points.

EXAMPLE 3 Environmental Science Application

The graph shows how much water is in a reservoir at different times. Find the slope of the line. Then tell what the slope represents.

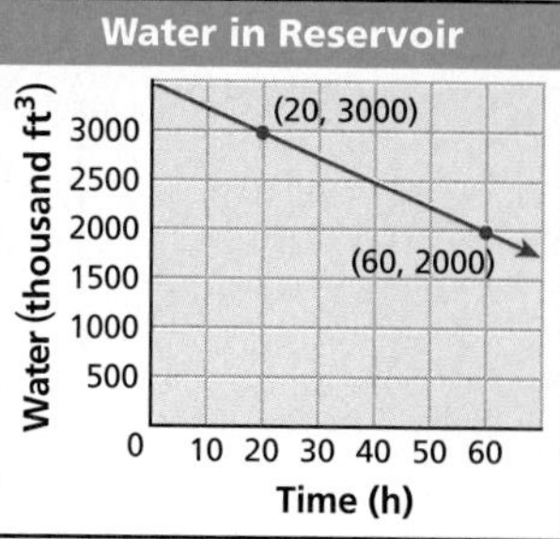

Step 1 Use the slope formula.

$$m = \frac{y_2 - y_1}{x_2 - x_1}$$

$$= \frac{2000 - 3000}{60 - 20}$$

$$= \frac{-1000}{40} = -25$$

Step 2 Tell what the slope represents.

In this situation, y represents **volume of water** and x represents time.

So slope represents $\frac{\text{change in volume}}{\text{change in time}}$ in units of $\frac{\text{thousands of cubic feet}}{\text{hours}}$.

A slope of -25 means the amount of water in the reservoir is decreasing (negative change) at a rate of 25 thousand cubic feet each hour.

3. The graph shows the height of a plant over a period of days. Find the slope of the line. Then tell what the slope represents.

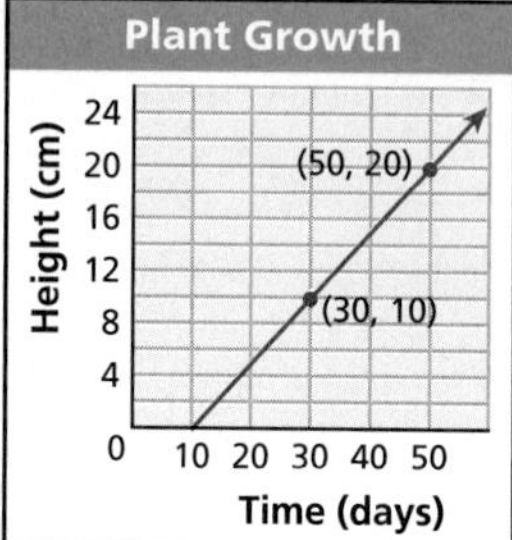

$\frac{1}{2}$; the height of the plant is increasing at a rate of 1 cm every 2 days.

If you know the equation that describes a line, you can find its slope by using any two ordered-pair solutions. It is often easiest to use the ordered pairs that contain the intercepts.

EXAMPLE 4 Finding Slope from an Equation

Find the slope of the line described by $6x - 5y = 30$.

Step 1 Find the x-intercept.

$$6x - 5y = 30$$

$$6x - 5(0) = 30 \quad \textit{Let } y = 0.$$

$$6x = 30$$

$$\frac{6x}{6} = \frac{30}{6}$$

$$x = 5$$

Step 2 Find the y-intercept.

$$6x - 5y = 30$$

$$6(0) - 5y = 30 \quad \textit{Let } x = 0.$$

$$-5y = 30$$

$$\frac{-5y}{-5} = \frac{30}{-5}$$

$$y = -6$$

Step 3 The line contains $(5, 0)$ and $(0, -6)$. Use the slope formula.

$$m = \frac{y_2 - y_1}{x_2 - x_1} = \frac{-6 - 0}{0 - 5} = \frac{-6}{-5} = \frac{6}{5}$$

4. Find the slope of the line described by $2x + 3y = 12$. $-\frac{2}{3}$

Power Presentations with PowerPoint®

Additional Examples

Example 3

The graph shows the average electricity costs (in dollars) for operating a refrigerator for several months. Find the slope of the line. Then tell what the slope represents.

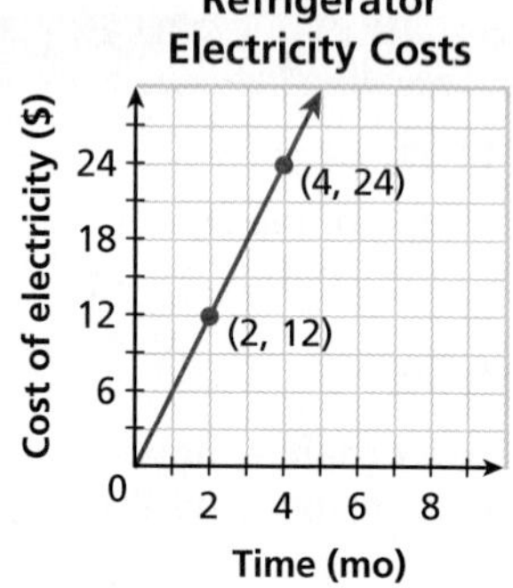

slope = 6; cost to run refrigerator is $6/mo

Example 4

Find the slope of the line described by $4x - 2y = 16$. 2

INTERVENTION

Questioning Strategies

EXAMPLE 3

- What kind of slope represents a negative rate of change? a positive rate of change?
- What does time 0 represent?

EXAMPLE 4

- Do you have to find the x- and y-intercepts to find the slope? Explain why or why not.
- How could you solve this problem by graphing?

Math Background Point out to students that the slope formula is the change in y divided by the corresponding change in x, which can also be represented with the Greek letter Δ (delta): $\frac{\Delta y}{\Delta x}$, which is read "delta y over delta x."

3 Close

Summarize

Write the coordinates $A(9, 2)$ and $B(5, -1)$ on the board. Have half of the class use the slope formula with A as (x_1, y_1), and have the other half use B as (x_1, y_1). Compare answers. Each method will give a slope of $\frac{3}{4}$. Remind students that it does not matter which point you choose to be (x_1, y_1), but once the choice is made, you must subtract the y-coordinates and x-coordinates in the same order.

ONGOING ASSESSMENT and INTERVENTION

***Diagnose Before* the Lesson**
5-4 Warm Up, TE p. 324

***Monitor During* the Lesson**
Check It Out! Exercises, SE pp. 324–326
Questioning Strategies, TE pp. 325–326

***Assess After* the Lesson**
5-4 Lesson Quiz, TE p. 329
Alternative Assessment, TE p. 329

THINK AND DISCUSS

1. The slope of a line is the difference of the ___?___ divided by the difference of the ___?___ for any two points on the line.
2. Two points lie on a line. When you substitute their coordinates into the slope formula, the value of the denominator is 0. Describe this line.

3. **GET ORGANIZED** Copy and complete the graphic organizer. In each box, describe how to find slope using the given method.

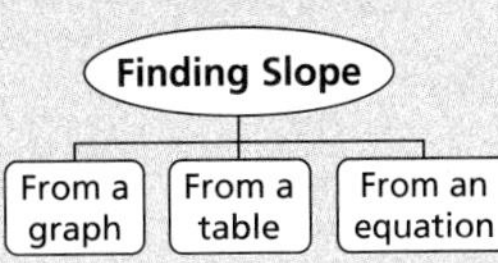
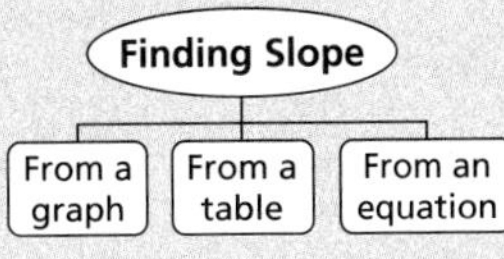

Answers to *Think and Discuss*

1. *y*-values; *x*-values
2. vertical line
3. See p. A5.

5-4 Exercises

go.hrw.com
Homework Help Online
KEYWORD: MA7 5-4
Parent Resources Online
KEYWORD: MA7 Parent

GUIDED PRACTICE

SEE EXAMPLE 1 p. 324

Find the slope of the line that contains each pair of points.

1. $(3, 6)$ and $(6, 9)$ **1**
2. $(2, 7)$ and $(4, 4)$ $-\frac{3}{2}$
3. $(-1, -5)$ and $(-9, -1)$ $-\frac{1}{2}$

SEE EXAMPLE 2 p. 325

Each graph or table shows a linear relationship. Find the slope.

4. $\frac{1}{2}$

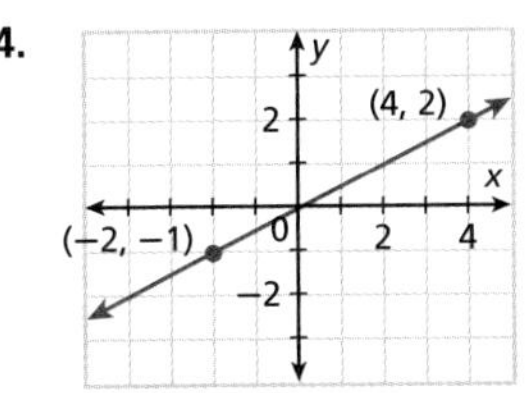

5. **10**

x	*y*
0	25
2	45
4	65
6	85

SEE EXAMPLE 3 p. 326

Find the slope of each line. Then tell what the slope represents.

6.

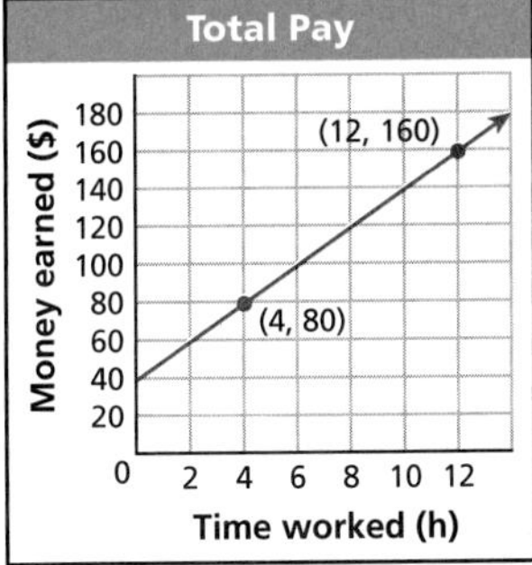

6. 10; the money earned is increasing at a rate of $10/h.

7.

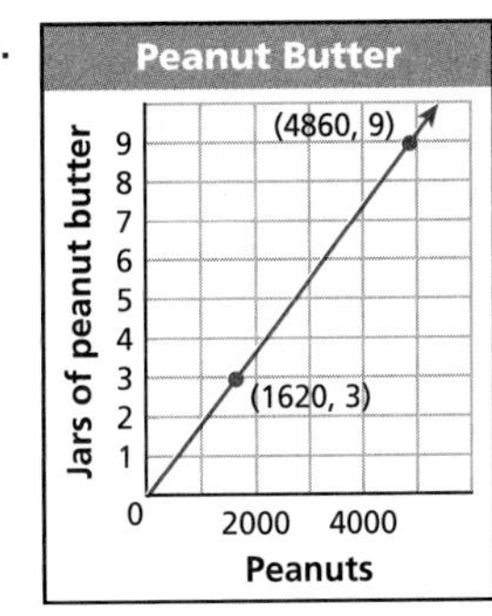

7. $\frac{1}{540}$; for each jar of peanut butter, 540 peanuts are needed.

SEE EXAMPLE 4 p. 326

Find the slope of the line described by each equation.

8. $8x + 2y = 96$ **−4**
9. $5x = 90 - 9y$ $-\frac{5}{9}$
10. $5y = 160 + 9x$ $\frac{9}{5}$

5-4 Exercises

Assignment Guide

Assign *Guided Practice* exercises as necessary.

If you finished Examples **1–2**
Basic 11–15, 22
Average 11–15, 22, 29, 30
Advanced 11–15, 29–36

If you finished Examples **1–4**
Basic 11–22, 25–28, 38–48
Average 11–28, 32–48
Advanced 11–20, 22–48

Homework Quick Check
Quickly check key concepts.
Exercises: 12, 14, 16, 18, 22

State Resources

go.hrw.com
State Resources Online
KEYWORD: MA7 Resources

Exercise 25 involves writing a function to describe a relationship, calculating the slope, and interpreting the slope in a real-world context. This exercise prepares students for the Multi-Step Test Prep on page 342.

Answers

23b. The speed and the slope are both equal to the dist. divided by time.

PRACTICE AND PROBLEM SOLVING

Independent Practice

For Exercises	See Example
11–13	1
14–15	2
16–17	3
18–20	4

Extra Practice

Skills Practice p. S12
Application Practice p. S32

Find the slope of the line that contains each pair of points.

11. (2, 5) and (3, 1) **−4**
12. (−9, −5) and (6, −5) **0**
13. (3, 4) and (3, −1) **undef.**

Each graph or table shows a linear relationship. Find the slope.

14.

x	y
1	18.5
2	22
3	25.5
4	29

$\frac{7}{2}$

15. 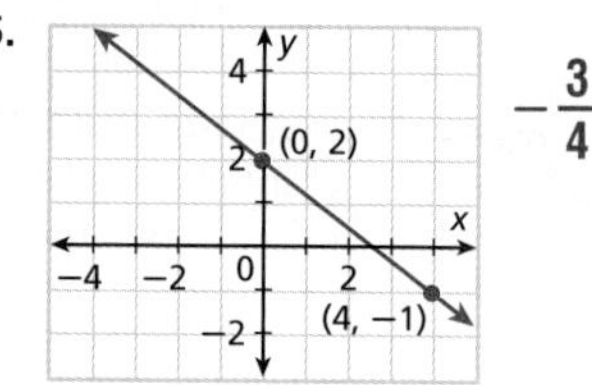

$-\frac{3}{4}$

Find the slope of each line. Then tell what the slope represents.

16. 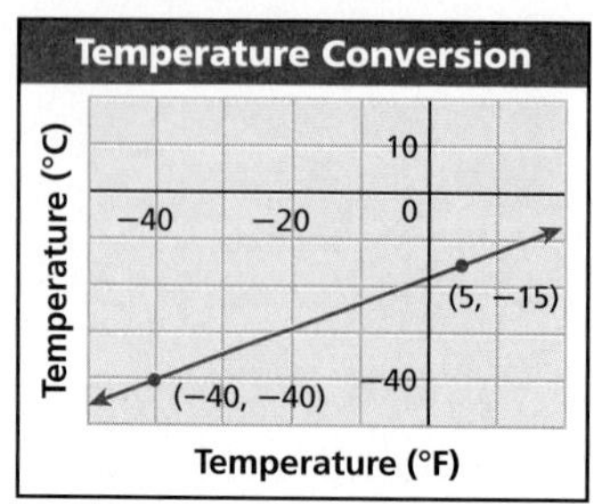

17. 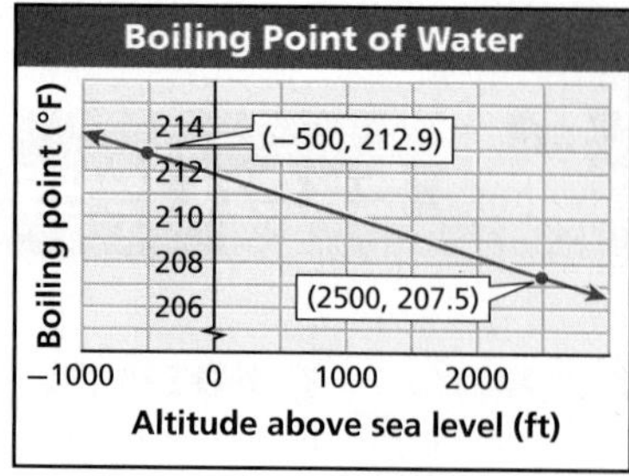

16. $\frac{5}{9}$; temp. in Celsius is increasing at a rate of 5 °C for each 9 °F.

17. $-\frac{9}{5000}$; the boiling point is decreasing at a rate of 9 °F for each 5000 ft above sea level.

Find the slope of the line described by each equation.

18. $7x + 13y = 91$ **$-\frac{7}{13}$**
19. $5y = 130 - 13x$ **$-\frac{13}{5}$**
20. $7 - 3y = 9x$ **−3**

21. **///ERROR ANALYSIS///** Two students found the slope of the line that contains (−6, 3) and (2, −1). Who is incorrect? Explain the error. **Student B. The student did not use the same coordinate pair order in the denom. as in the num.**

A: $m = \frac{-1-3}{2-(-6)} = \frac{-4}{8} = -\frac{1}{2}$

B: 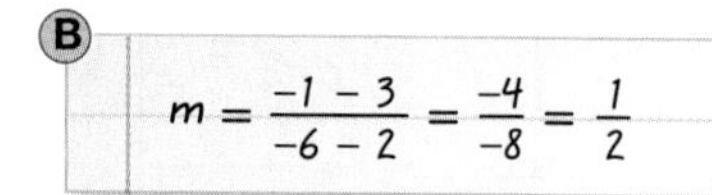
$m = \frac{-1-3}{-6-2} = \frac{-4}{-8} = \frac{1}{2}$

22. **Environmental Science** The table shows how the number of cricket chirps per minute changes with the air temperature.

Temperature (°F)	40	50	60	70	80	90
Chirps per minute	0	40	80	120	160	200

a. Find the rates of change. **The rate of change for each interval is $\frac{4 \text{ chirps/min}}{1\ °\text{F}}$.**
b. Is the graph of the data a line? If so, what is the slope? If not, explain why not. **yes; 4**

23. **Critical Thinking** The graph shows the distance traveled by two cars.

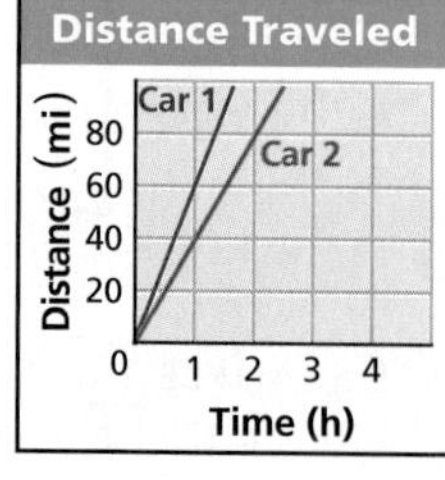

a. Which car is going faster? How much faster? **car 1; 20 mi/h**
b. How are the speeds related to slope?
c. At what rate is the distance between the cars changing? **20 mi/h**

24. **Write About It** You are given the coordinates of two points on a line. Describe two different ways to find the slope of that line.

24. Possible answer: Given the 2 pts. (x_1, y_1) and (x_2, y_2), you could substitute into the slope formula or graph the 2 points, connect with a line, and count the rise and run.

5-4 PRACTICE A
5-4 PRACTICE C
5-4 PRACTICE B

Find the slope of the line that contains each pair of points.

1. (2, 8) and (1, −3)
2. (−4, 0) and (−6, −2)
3. (0, −2) and (4, −7)

Each graph or table shows a linear relationship. Find the slope.

4. $\frac{3}{5}$
5. 1.25

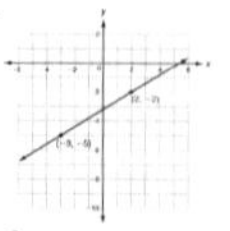

x	y
1	3.75
2	5
3	6.25
4	7.50
5	8.75

6. $-\frac{3}{4}$

Find the slope of each line. Then tell what the slope represents.

7. $\frac{3}{2}$; the salary increases $3 every 2 years.
8. $-\frac{400}{3}$; the number of people remaining decreases by 400 every 3 hours.

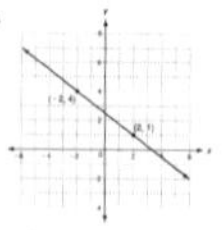

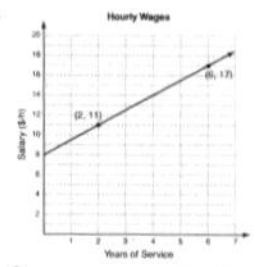

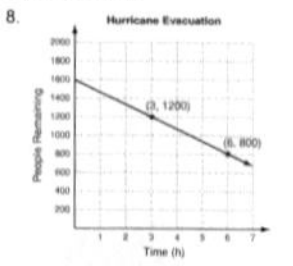

Find the slope of the line described by each equation.

9. $3x + 4y = 24$ $-\frac{3}{4}$
10. $8x + 48 = 3y$ $\frac{8}{3}$

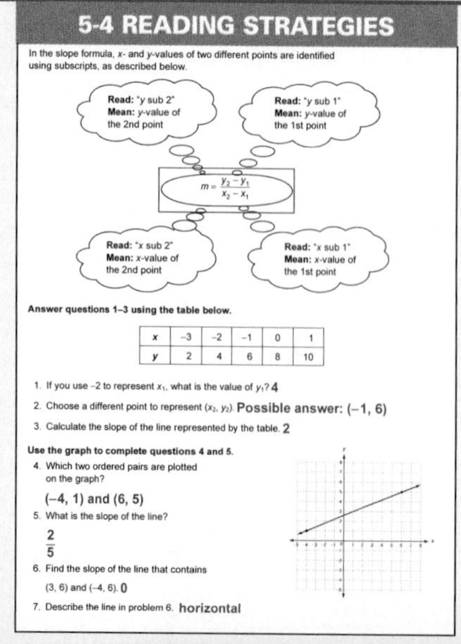
5-4 READING STRATEGIES

In the slope formula, x- and y-values of two different points are identified using subscripts, as described below.

Read: "y sub 2" Mean: y-value of the 2nd point
Read: "y sub 1" Mean: y-value of the 1st point
$m = \frac{y_2 - y_1}{x_2 - x_1}$
Read: "x sub 2" Mean: x-value of the 2nd point
Read: "x sub 1" Mean: x-value of the 1st point

Answer questions 1–3 using the table below.

x	−3	−2	−1	0	1
y	2	4	6	8	10

1. If you use −2 to represent x_1, what is the value of y_1? 4
2. Choose a different point to represent (x_2, y_2). Possible answer: (−1, 6)
3. Calculate the slope of the line represented by the table. 2

Use the graph to complete questions 4 and 5.

4. Which two ordered pairs are plotted on the graph? (−4, 1) and (6, 5)
5. What is the slope of the line? $\frac{2}{5}$
6. Find the slope of the line that contains (3, 6) and (−4, 6). 0
7. Describe the line in problem 6. horizontal

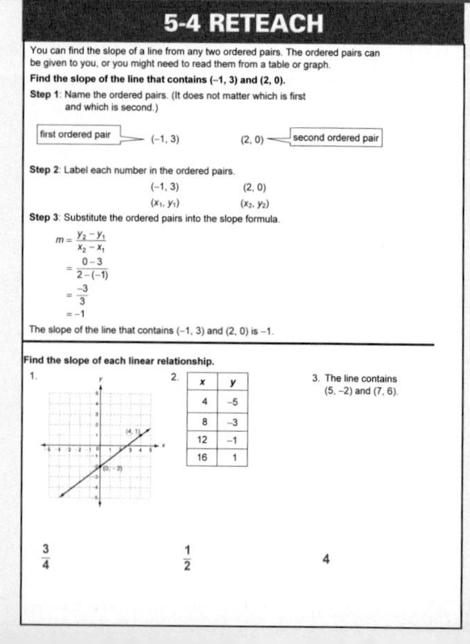
5-4 RETEACH

You can find the slope of a line from any two ordered pairs. The ordered pairs can be given to you, or you might need to read them from a table or graph.

Find the slope of the line that contains (−1, 3) and (2, 0).

Step 1: Name the ordered pairs. (It does not matter which is first and which is second.)

first ordered pair (−1, 3) (2, 0) second ordered pair

Step 2: Label each number in the ordered pairs.

(−1, 3) (x_1, y_1) (2, 0) (x_2, y_2)

Step 3: Substitute the ordered pairs into the slope formula.

$m = \frac{y_2 - y_1}{x_2 - x_1} = \frac{0-3}{2-(-1)} = \frac{-3}{3} = -1$

The slope of the line that contains (−1, 3) and (2, 0) is −1.

Find the slope of each linear relationship.

1. $\frac{3}{4}$
2. $\frac{1}{2}$

x	y
4	−5
8	−3
12	−1
16	1

3. The line contains (5, −2) and (7, 6). 4

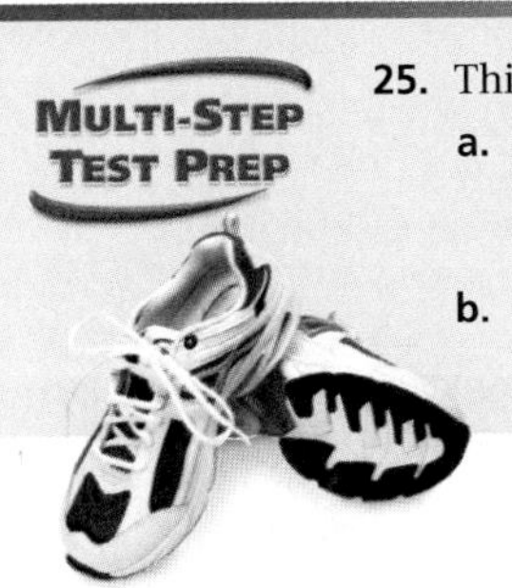

MULTI-STEP TEST PREP

25. This problem will prepare you for the Multi-Step Test Prep on page 342.

a. One way to estimate your maximum heart rate is to subtract your age from 220. Write a function to describe the relationship between maximum heart rate y and age x. **$y = 220 - x$**

b. The graph of this function is a line. Find its slope. Then tell what the slope represents.

TEST PREP

26. The equation $2y + 3x = -6$ describes a line with what slope?

Ⓐ $\frac{3}{2}$ Ⓑ 0 Ⓒ $\frac{1}{2}$ **Ⓓ** $-\frac{3}{2}$

27. A line with slope $-\frac{1}{3}$ could pass through which of the following pairs of points?

Ⓕ $\left(0, -\frac{1}{3}\right)$ and $(1, 1)$ Ⓗ $(0, 0)$ and $\left(-\frac{1}{3}, -\frac{1}{3}\right)$

Ⓖ $(-6, 5)$ and $(-3, 4)$ Ⓙ $(5, -6)$ and $(4, 3)$

28. Gridded Response Find the slope of the line that contains $(-1, 2)$ and $(5, 5)$. **$\frac{1}{2}$, or 0.5**

CHALLENGE AND EXTEND

Find the slope of the line that contains each pair of points.

29. $(a, 0)$ and $(0, b)$ **$-\frac{b}{a}$** **30.** $(2x, y)$ and $(x, 3y)$ **$-\frac{2y}{x}$** **31.** (x, y) and $(x + 2, 3 - y)$ **$\frac{3}{2} - y$**

Find the value of x so that the points lie on a line with the given slope.

32. $(x, 2)$ and $(-5, 8)$, $m = -1$ **1** **33.** $(4, x)$ and $(6, 3x)$, $m = \frac{1}{2}$ **$\frac{1}{2}$**

34. $(1, -3)$ and $(3, x)$, $m = -1$ **−5** **35.** $(-10, -4)$ and (x, x), $m = \frac{1}{7}$ **−3**

36. A line contains the point $(1, 2)$ and has a slope of $\frac{1}{2}$. Use the slope formula to find another point on this line. **Possible answer: (3, 3)**

37. The points $(-2, 4)$, $(0, 2)$, and $(3, x - 1)$ all lie on the same line. What is the value of x? (*Hint:* Remember that the slope of a line is constant for any two points on the line.) **0**

SPIRAL REVIEW

Solve each inequality and graph the solutions. *(Lesson 3-7)*

38. $|x| + 5 < 16$ **39.** $|x + 8| < 3$ **40.** $3|x| \le 12$

41. $|x| - 11 \ge -4$ **42.** $|x - 6| > 10$ **43.** $|x + 1| \ge 7$

Tell whether the given ordered pairs satisfy a linear function. *(Lesson 5-1)*

44. $\{(1, 1), (2, 4), (3, 9), (4, 16)\}$ **no** **45.** $\{(9, 0), (8, -5), (5, -20), (3, -30)\}$ **yes**

Use the intercepts to graph the line described by each equation. *(Lesson 5-2)*

46. $x - y = 5$ **47.** $3x + y = 9$ **48.** $y = 5x + 10$

TEST PREP DOCTOR In **Exercise 26,** students who chose **A** may have subtracted the coordinates in different orders or made an error in integer subtraction.

Answers

25b.

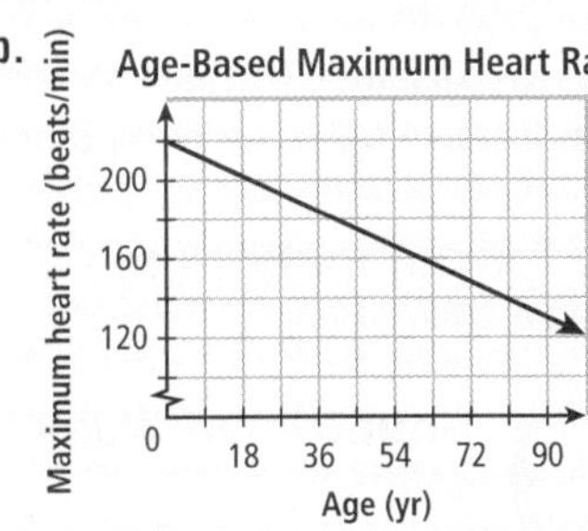

The slope is −1; for every year increase, the max. heart rate decreases 1 beat/min.

38–43, 46–48. See p. A20.

Journal

Have students describe similarities and differences between each method of finding slope—counting the rise and run and using the formula.

ALTERNATIVE ASSESSMENT

Have students graph four lines with different slopes—one positive, one negative, one zero, and one undefined. They should then label two points on each and find each slope by using the slope formula.

Power Presentations with PowerPoint®

5-4 Lesson Quiz

1. Find the slope of the line that contains $(5, 3)$ and $(-1, 4)$. $-\frac{1}{6}$

2. Find the slope of the line. Then tell what the slope represents.

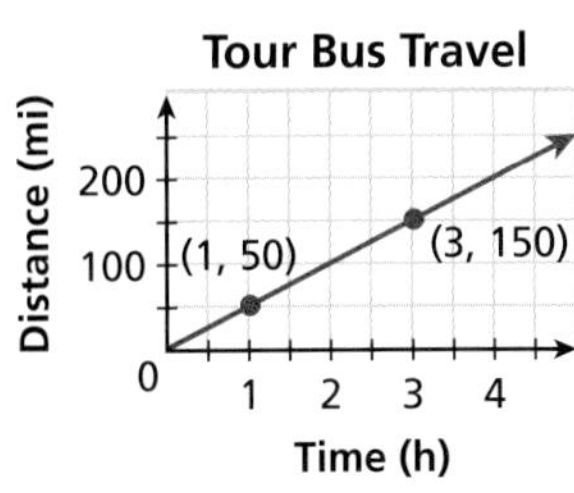

50; speed of bus is 50 mi/h

3. Find the slope of the line described by $x + 2y = 8$. $-\frac{1}{2}$

Also available on transparency

5-4 PROBLEM SOLVING

Write the correct answer.

1. The graph shows the number of emergency kits assembled by volunteers over a period of days. Find the slope of the line. Then tell what the slope represents.

Emergency Kits Prepared by Volunteers — (2, 24), (6, 72); Number of Kits Assembled; Number of Days

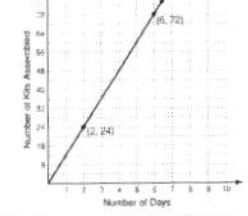

12; the number of kits assembled per day.

2. The graph shows how much flour is in a bag at different times. Find the slope of the line. Then tell what the slope represents.

Amount of Flour in Bag — (2, 4.6), (5, 4); Weight of Flour (lb); Days Since Purchase

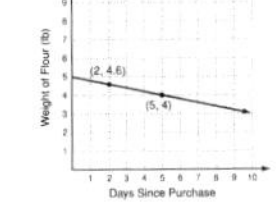

0.2; the number of pounds of flour used per day.

3. The function $20x - y = 250$ describes the profit y Bridget can make from selling x pairs of earrings. The graph of this function is a line. Find its slope. **20**

The graph below shows the cost of membership at Fabulously Fit. Use the graph to answer questions 4–7. Select the best answer.

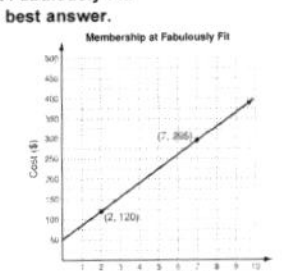

Membership at Fabulously Fit — (2, 120), (7, 295); Cost ($); Number of Months

4. What is the slope of the line?
A 24 C 50
B 35 D 70

5. What does the slope represent?
F the enrollment fee
G the late payment fee
H the total cost of membership
J the monthly membership fee

6. A second line is graphed that shows the cost of membership at The Fitness Studio. The line contains (0, 35) and (5, 85). What is the slope of this line?
A 10 C 45
B 20 D 50

7. How much greater is the monthly fee at Fabulously Fit than The Fitness Studio?
F \$15 H \$35
G \$25 J \$40

5-4 CHALLENGE

When two variables x and y are related and (x_1, y_1) and (x_2, y_2) satisfy the relationship, you can write the quotient as shown at right. The quotient is called a *difference quotient*. $\frac{y_2 - y_1}{x_2 - x_1}$

The difference quotient can have different meanings in different situations.

In Exercises 1–5, use the grid at the right.

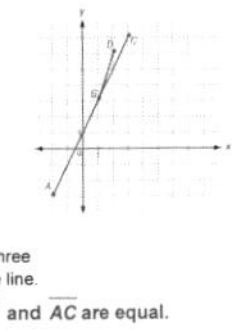

1. Graph and connect $A(-2, -3)$, $B(1, 3)$, and $C(3, 7)$.
2. Calculate the slope of $\overline{AB}$ and of $\overline{BC}$. **Slope of $\overline{AB}$ = Slope of $\overline{BC}$ = 2**
3. On the same grid, graph $D(2, 6)$. Connect A, B and D.
4. Calculate the slope of $\overline{AB}$ and of $\overline{BD}$. **Slope of $\overline{AB}$ = 2; Slope of $\overline{BD}$ = 3**
5. Explain how to use a difference quotient to determine whether three points are collinear, that is, whether three points lie on the same line.
Points A, B, and C lie on a line if the slopes of $\overline{AB}$, $\overline{BC}$ and $\overline{AC}$ are equal.

Another application of the difference quotient is the measurement of the *grade*, or steepness, of a road. A grade of 3% means that the road surface rises 3 feet for every horizontal run of 100 feet. A roadway that slopes down has a negative grade.

6. If the vertical rise of a highway is 150 feet when the horizontal run is 5000 feet, what is the grade of the road? **3%**
7. If the grade of a road is 5%, what is the vertical rise of the road when the horizontal run is 6000 feet? **300 feet**
8. On a certain stretch of road, the point 420 feet east of point A is 24 feet lower than point A. Point B, 600 feet east of A, is 36 feet lower than point A.
a. Find the grade of the road surface between points A and B. **6%**
b. Would a motorist driving along a stretch of road from point B to point A report the same grade for the road as a motorist driving from A to B would report? Explain your response.
No; the uphill grade is positive and the downhill grade is negative.

In economics, the additional cost to produce one more unit of an item is called the *marginal cost* of the item. Marginal cost is found by computing the difference quotient, or $\frac{\text{difference in manufacturing cost}}{\text{difference in units made}}$.

9. The cost that a manufacturer pays for producing 5 pairs of shoes is \$113. The cost to produce 12 pairs of shoes is \$127. Use a difference quotient to find the marginal cost. **\$2**

5-5 Organizer

Pacing: Traditional 1 day
Block $\frac{1}{2}$ day

Objectives: Apply the formula for midpoint.

Use the Distance Formula to find the distance between two points.

Online Edition
Tutorial Videos

Countdown Week 11

Power Presentations with PowerPoint®

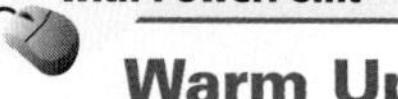

Warm Up

Simplify.

1. $\frac{-4+9}{2}$ $\frac{5}{2}$
2. $\frac{7+(-3)}{2}$ 2
3. $(6 - 10)^2$ 16
4. $(-1 - 5)^2$ 36

Find each square root to the nearest tenth.

5. $\sqrt{18}$ 4.2
6. $\sqrt{60}$ 7.7
7. $\sqrt{84}$ 9.2
8. $\sqrt{37}$ 6.1

Also available on transparency

Math Humor

Q: What's the midpoint of an algebra test?

A: The point where fear of not having enough time to finish overcomes the fear of not having studied enough.

State Resources

5-5 The Midpoint and Distance Formulas

Objectives
Apply the formula for midpoint.
Use the Distance Formula to find the distance between two points.

Vocabulary
midpoint

Why learn this?
You can use the coordinate plane to model and solve problems involving distances, such as the distance across a lake. (See Example 4.)

In Lesson 5-4, you used the coordinates of points to determine the slope of lines. You can also use coordinates to determine the *midpoint* of a line segment on the coordinate plane.

The **midpoint** of a line segment is the point that divides the segment into two congruent segments. *Congruent segments* are segments that have the same length.

You can find the midpoint of a segment by using the coordinates of its endpoints. Calculate the average of the *x*-coordinates and the average of the *y*-coordinates of the endpoints.

Know it! Note

Midpoint Formula

The midpoint M of $\overline{AB}$ with endpoints $A(x_1, y_1)$ and $B(x_2, y_2)$ is

$$M\left(\frac{x_1 + x_2}{2}, \frac{y_1 + y_2}{2}\right).$$

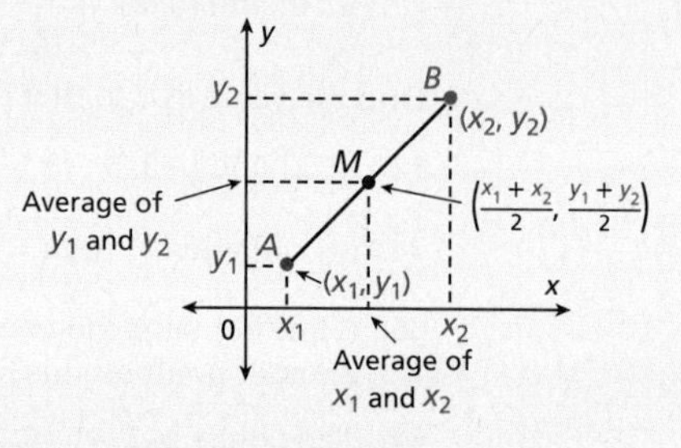

EXAMPLE 1 **Finding the Coordinates of a Midpoint**

Remember!
A segment is named by its endpoints. The notation $\overline{CD}$ is read "segment CD."

Find the coordinates of the midpoint of $\overline{CD}$ with endpoints $C(-2, -1)$ and $D(4, 2)$.

$M\left(\frac{x_1 + x_2}{2}, \frac{y_1 + y_2}{2}\right)$ *Write the formula.*

$M\left(\frac{-2 + 4}{2}, \frac{-1 + 2}{2}\right)$ *Substitute.*

$M\left(\frac{2}{2}, \frac{1}{2}\right) = M\left(1, \frac{1}{2}\right)$ *Simplify.*

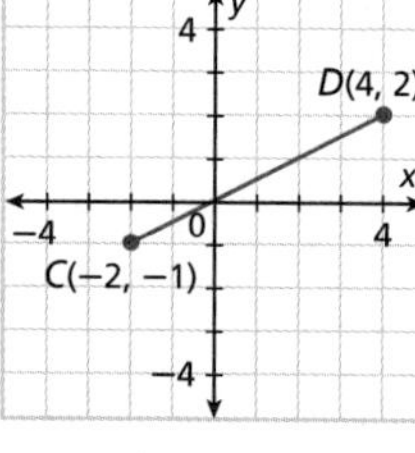

1. Find the coordinates of the midpoint of $\overline{EF}$ with endpoints $E(-2, 3)$ and $F(5, -3)$. $\left(\frac{3}{2}, 0\right)$

1 Introduce

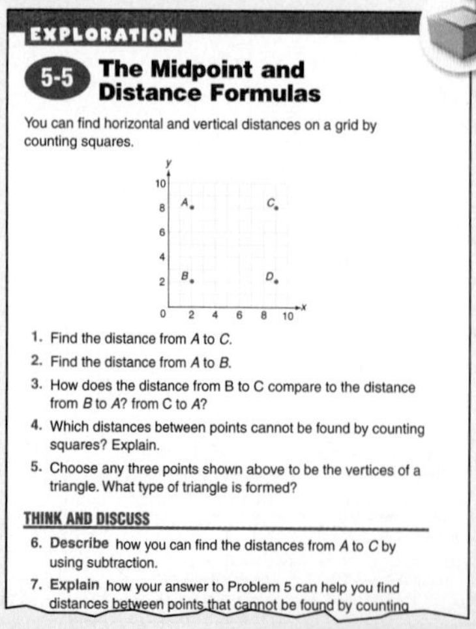

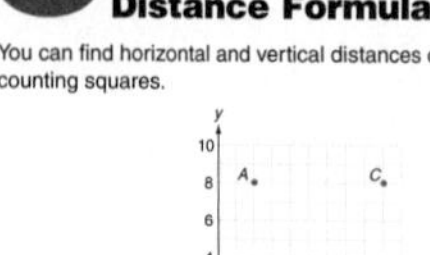

EXPLORATION

5-5 The Midpoint and Distance Formulas

You can find horizontal and vertical distances on a grid by counting squares.

1. Find the distance from A to C.
2. Find the distance from A to B.
3. How does the distance from B to C compare to the distance from B to A? from C to A?
4. Which distances between points cannot be found by counting squares? Explain.
5. Choose any three points shown above to be the vertices of a triangle. What type of triangle is formed?

THINK AND DISCUSS

6. **Describe** how you can find the distances from A to C by using subtraction.
7. **Explain** how your answer to Problem 5 can help you find distances between points that cannot be found by counting

Motivate

Ask students how they could find the length of horizontal or vertical line segments on the coordinate plane. Count the number of units between the endpoints. Ask whether this method could be used to find the length of segments that are not horizontal or vertical. No, the number of units could only be estimated. Explain that in this lesson students will learn a formula they can use to determine the length of any segment on the coordinate plane.

Explorations and answers are provided in *Alternate Openers: Explorations Transparencies.*

EXAMPLE 2 Finding the Coordinates of an Endpoint

M is the midpoint of $\overline{AB}$. A has coordinates $(2, 2)$, and M has coordinates $(4, -3)$. Find the coordinates of B.

Step 1 Let the coordinates of B equal (x, y).

Step 2 Use the Midpoint Formula.

$$(4, -3) = \left(\frac{2+x}{2}, \frac{2+y}{2}\right)$$

Step 3 Find the x-coordinate. Find the y-coordinate.

x-coordinate		y-coordinate
$4 = \frac{2+x}{2}$	*Set the coordinates equal.*	$-3 = \frac{2+y}{2}$
$2(4) = 2\left(\frac{2+x}{2}\right)$	*Multiply both sides by 2.*	$2(-3) = 2\left(\frac{2+y}{2}\right)$
$8 = 2 + x$	*Simplify.*	$-6 = 2 + y$
$-2 \quad -2$	*Subtract 2 from both sides.*	$-2 \quad -2$
$6 = x$	*Simplify.*	$-8 = y$

The coordinates of B are $(6, -8)$.

Check Graph points A and B and midpoint M.

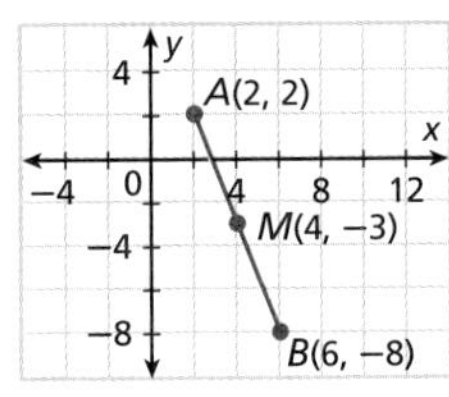

Point M appears to be the midpoint of $\overline{AB}$.

2. S is the midpoint of $\overline{RT}$. R has coordinates $(-6, -1)$, and S has coordinates $(-1, 1)$. Find the coordinates of T. **(4, 3)**

You can also use coordinates to find the distance between two points or the length of a line segment. To find the length of segment PQ, draw a horizontal segment from P and a vertical segment from Q to form a right triangle.

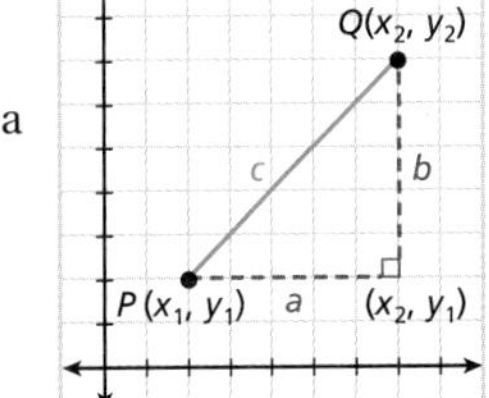

Remember!

The *Pythagorean Theorem* states that if a right triangle has legs of lengths a and b and a hypotenuse of length c, then $a^2 + b^2 = c^2$.

$c^2 = a^2 + b^2$ *Pythagorean Theorem*

$c = \sqrt{a^2 + b^2}$ *Solve for c. Use the positive square root to represent distance.*

$$PQ = \sqrt{\underbrace{(x_2 - x_1)^2}_{\text{Length of horizontal segment}} + \underbrace{(y_2 - y_1)^2}_{\text{Length of vertical segment}}}$$

This equation represents the Distance Formula.

Distance Formula

In a coordinate plane, the distance d between two points (x_1, y_1) and (x_2, y_2) is

$$d = \sqrt{(x_2 - x_1)^2 + (y_2 - y_1)^2}.$$

Power Presentations with PowerPoint®

Additional Examples

Example 1

Find the coordinates of the midpoint of $\overline{GH}$ with endpoints $G(-4, 3)$ and $H(6, -2)$. $\left(1, \frac{1}{2}\right)$

Example 2

P is the midpoint of $\overline{NQ}$. N has coordinates $(-5, 4)$, and P has coordinates $(-1, 3)$. Find the coordinates of Q. $(3, 2)$

INTERVENTION

Questioning Strategies

EXAMPLE 1

- In the Midpoint Formula, why is each sum divided by 2?
- When will a coordinate of the midpoint be a fraction?
- If both x-coordinates of the endpoints are positive, why must the x-coordinate of the midpoint also be positive?

EXAMPLE 2

- How do you use the Midpoint Formula to write equations for the coordinates of the endpoint?
- How can you check your answer by substituting values into the Midpoint Formula?

Inclusion Students may find only one coordinate of a midpoint, forgetting that an ordered pair has two coordinates. To avoid this, have students write (,) on their paper when solving midpoint problems, and then fill in each coordinate as they find it.

Visual Point out to students that when using the Distance Formula, they can find the value of the expression $(x_2 - x_1)$ by counting the number of units between x_2 and x_1 on the x-axis. Likewise, they can find the value of the expression $(y_2 - y_1)$ by counting the number of units between y_2 and y_1 on the y-axis.

2 Teach

Guided Instruction

Before teaching the Midpoint Formula, remind students how to find the average of two numbers. Connect the idea of average to the idea of midpoint. Also emphasize the relationship between the Distance Formula and the Pythagorean Theorem. Use a given segment to form the hypotenuse of a right triangle with horizontal and vertical legs. Then use the Pythagorean Theorem and the lengths of the legs to find the length of the given segment.

Reaching All Learners

Through Cognitive Strategies

Have students use mental math to estimate the midpoint of a segment or the distance between two points on the coordinate plane. Then have them use the formulas to calculate exact answers. If their estimates are not close to their calculated answers, students should check their work to make sure they have not made a careless mistake.

Power Presentations with PowerPoint®

Additional Examples

Example 3

Use the Distance Formula to find the distance, to the nearest hundredth, from $A(-2, -2)$ to $B(4, 3)$. 7

Example 4

Each unit on the map represents 100 meters. To the nearest tenth of a meter, how far is it from the roller coaster to the Ferris wheel? 721.1 m

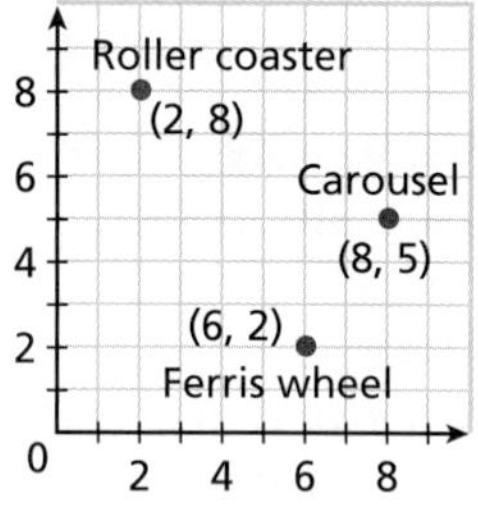

INTERVENTION

Questioning Strategies

EXAMPLE 3

- Why can you subtract each pair of coordinates in either order?

EXAMPLE 4

- If you did not have a calculator, how could you estimate the square root?

Answers to *Think and Discuss*

1. Yes; $\frac{x_2 + x_1}{2} = \frac{x_1 + x_2}{2}$ and $\frac{y_2 + y_1}{2} = \frac{y_1 + y_2}{2}$.
2. See p. A5.

EXAMPLE 3 Finding Distance in the Coordinate Plane

Use the Distance Formula to find the distance, to the nearest hundredth, from $A(-2, 3)$ to $B(2, -2)$.

$d = \sqrt{(x_2 - x_1)^2 + (y_2 - y_1)^2}$ *Distance Formula*

$d = \sqrt{[2 - (-2)]^2 + (-2 - 3)^2}$ *Substitute (−2, 3) for (x_1, y_1) and (2, −2) for (x_2, y_2).*

$d = \sqrt{4^2 + (-5)^2}$ *Subtract.*

$d = \sqrt{16 + 25}$ *Simplify powers.*

$d = \sqrt{41}$ *Add.*

$d \approx 6.40$ *Find the square root to the nearest hundredth.*

3. Use the Distance Formula to find the distance, to the nearest hundredth, from $R(3, 2)$ to $S(-3, -1)$. **6.71**

EXAMPLE 4 *Geography Application*

Each unit on the map of Lake Okeechobee represents 1 mile. Delia and her father plan to travel from point A near the town of Okeechobee to point B at Pahokee. To the nearest tenth of a mile, how far do Delia and her father plan to travel?

$d = \sqrt{(x_2 - x_1)^2 + (y_2 - y_1)^2}$

$d = \sqrt{(33 - 22)^2 + (13 - 39)^2}$ *Substitute.*

$d = \sqrt{11^2 + (-26)^2}$ *Subtract.*

$d = \sqrt{121 + 676}$ *Simplify powers.*

$d = \sqrt{797}$ *Add.*

$d \approx 28.2$ *Find the square root to the nearest tenth.*

Delia and her father plan to travel about 28.2 miles.

4. Jacob takes a boat from Pahokee to Clewiston. To the nearest tenth of a mile, how far does he travel? **17.7 mi**

THINK AND DISCUSS

1. If you use the formula $M\left(\frac{x_2 + x_1}{2}, \frac{y_2 + y_1}{2}\right)$ to find the midpoint of a segment, will you get the correct coordinates for the midpoint? Explain.

2. **GET ORGANIZED** Copy and complete the graphic organizer. In each box, write a formula. Then make a sketch that will illustrate the formula.

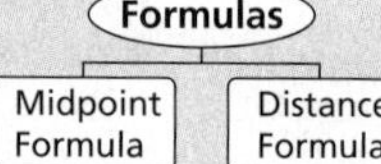

3 Close

Summarize

Have students consider the points $A(8, 5)$ and $B(12, 15)$. What is the horizontal distance between the points? 4 units What is the vertical distance between the points? 10 units How can you use the horizontal and vertical distances to find the length of $\overline{AB}$? Substitute 4 for $(x_2 - x_1)$ and substitute 10 for $(y_2 - y_1)$ in the Distance Formula. Then simplify.

and INTERVENTION

***Diagnose Before* the Lesson**
5-5 Warm Up, TE p. 330

***Monitor During* the Lesson**
Check It Out! Exercises, SE pp. 330–332
Questioning Strategies, TE pp. 331–332

***Assess After* the Lesson**
5-5 Lesson Quiz, TE p. 335
Alternative Assessment, TE p. 335

5-5 Exercises

GUIDED PRACTICE

1. **Vocabulary** In your own words, describe the *midpoint* of a line segment.

SEE EXAMPLE 1 p. 330

Find the coordinates of the midpoint of each segment.

2. $\overline{AB}$ with endpoints $A(4, -6)$ and $B(-4, 2)$ **(0, −2)**
3. $\overline{CD}$ with endpoints $C(0, -8)$ and $D(3, 0)$ $\left(1\frac{1}{2}, -4\right)$
4. $\overline{EF}$ with endpoints $E(-8, 17)$ and $F(-12, -16)$ $\left(-10, \frac{1}{2}\right)$

SEE EXAMPLE 2 p. 331

5. M is the midpoint of $\overline{LN}$. L has coordinates $(-3, -1)$, and M has coordinates $(0, 1)$. Find the coordinates of N. **(3, 3)**
6. B is the midpoint of $\overline{AC}$. A has coordinates $(-3, 4)$, and B has coordinates $\left(-1\frac{1}{2}, 1\right)$. Find the coordinates of C. **(0, −2)**

SEE EXAMPLE 3 p. 332

Use the Distance Formula to find the distance, to the nearest hundredth, between each pair of points.

7. $A(1, -2)$ and $B(-4, -4)$ **5.39**
8. $X(-2, 7)$ and $Y(-2, -8)$ **15.00**
9. $V(2, -1)$ and $W(-4, 8)$ **10.82**

SEE EXAMPLE 4 p. 332

10. **Recreation** Each unit on the map of a public park represents 1 kilometer. To the nearest tenth of a kilometer, what is the distance from the campground to the waterfall? **3.9 km**

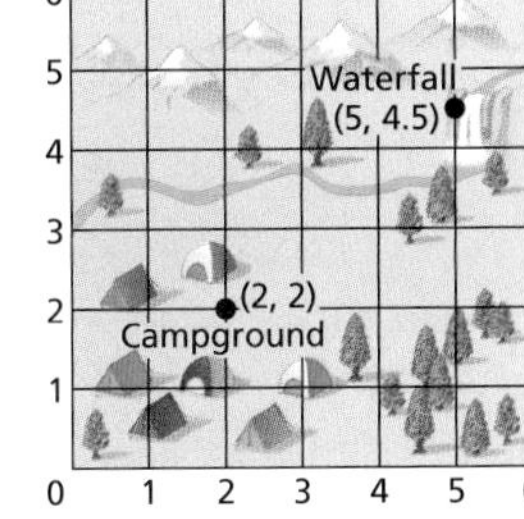

PRACTICE AND PROBLEM SOLVING

Independent Practice	
For Exercises	See Example
11–12	1
13–15	2
16–19	3
20	4

Extra Practice
Skills Practice p. S12
Application Practice p. S32

Find the coordinates of the midpoint of each segment.

11. $\overline{XY}$ with endpoints $X(-3, -7)$ and $Y(-1, 1)$ **(−2, −3)**
12. $\overline{MN}$ with endpoints $M(12, -7)$ and $N(-5, -2)$ $\left(3\frac{1}{2}, -4\frac{1}{2}\right)$
13. M is the midpoint of $\overline{QR}$. Q has coordinates $(-3, 5)$, and M has coordinates $(7, -9)$. Find the coordinates of R. **(17, −23)**
14. D is the midpoint of $\overline{CE}$. E has coordinates $(-3, -2)$, and D has coordinates $\left(2\frac{1}{2}, 1\right)$. Find the coordinates of C. **(8, 4)**
15. Y is the midpoint of $\overline{XZ}$. X has coordinates $(0, -1)$, and Y has coordinates $\left(1, -4\frac{1}{2}\right)$. Find the coordinates of Z. **(2, −8)**

Use the Distance Formula to find the distance, to the nearest hundredth, between each pair of points.

16. $U(0, 1)$ and $V(-3, -9)$ **10.44**
17. $M(10, -1)$ and $N(2, -5)$ **8.94**
18. $P(-10, 1)$ and $Q(5, 5)$ **15.52**
19. $F(6, 15)$ and $G(4, 24)$ **9.22**
20. **Astronomy** Each unit on the map of a section of a moon represents 1 kilometer. To the nearest tenth of a kilometer, what is the distance between the two craters? **78.3 km**

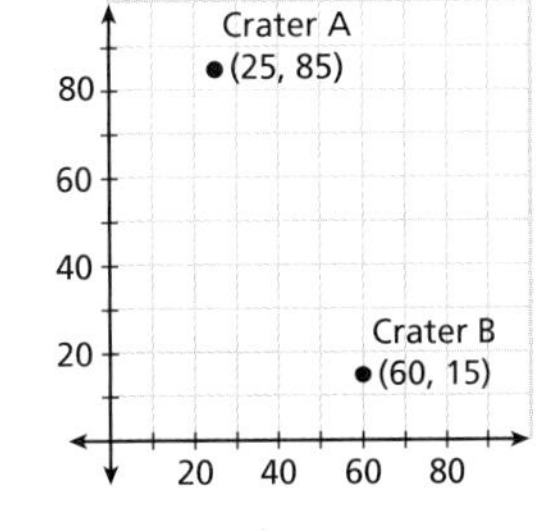

5-5 READING STRATEGIES

For any line segment, you can find the location of the midpoint and the distance between the endpoints.

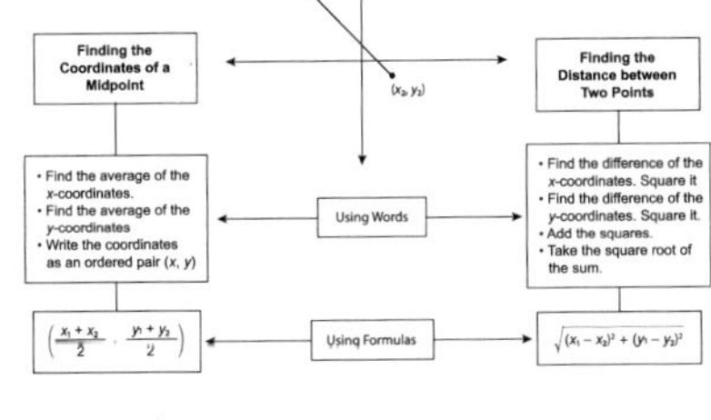

Answer each question.

1. In the formula for finding a midpoint, why is each sum divided by 2?
   Divide by 2 when averaging two numbers.
2. What is the last step in finding the distance between two points?
   Taking a square root.
3. When finding a distance, can the first two steps be switched? Explain.
   Yes, the sums of the squares can be added in any order.
4. Find the coordinates of the midpoint of the segment whose endpoints are at (2, 9) and (8, −1). Then find the distance between the endpoints.
   (5, 4); ≈ 11.7

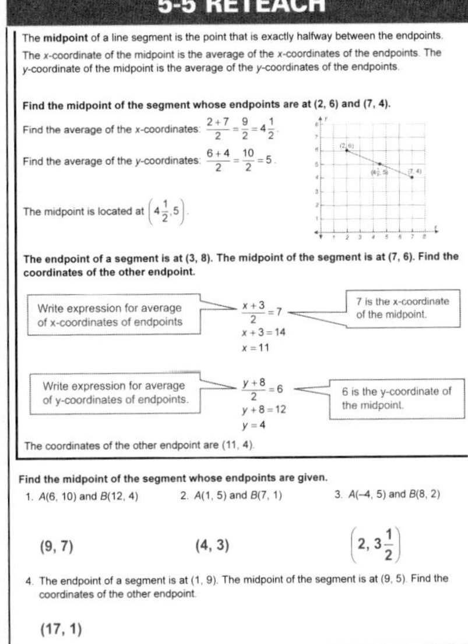

5-5 RETEACH

The **midpoint** of a line segment is the point that is exactly halfway between the endpoints. The *x*-coordinate of the midpoint is the average of the *x*-coordinates of the endpoints. The *y*-coordinate of the midpoint is the average of the *y*-coordinates of the endpoints.

Find the midpoint of the segment whose endpoints are at (2, 6) and (7, 4).

Find the average of the *x*-coordinates: $\frac{2+7}{2} = \frac{9}{2} = 4\frac{1}{2}$.

Find the average of the *y*-coordinates: $\frac{6+4}{2} = \frac{10}{2} = 5$.

The midpoint is located at $\left(4\frac{1}{2}, 5\right)$.

The endpoint of a segment is at (3, 8). The midpoint of the segment is at (7, 6). Find the coordinates of the other endpoint.

Write expression for average of x-coordinates of endpoints: $\frac{x+3}{2} = 7$ (7 is the x-coordinate of the midpoint.)
$x + 3 = 14$
$x = 11$

Write expression for average of y-coordinates of endpoints: $\frac{y+8}{2} = 6$ (6 is the y-coordinate of the midpoint.)
$y + 8 = 12$
$y = 4$

The coordinates of the other endpoint are (11, 4).

Find the midpoint of the segment whose endpoints are given.

1. $A(6, 10)$ and $B(12, 4)$ **(9, 7)**
2. $A(1, 5)$ and $B(7, 1)$ **(4, 3)**
3. $A(-4, 5)$ and $B(8, 2)$ $\left(2, 3\frac{1}{2}\right)$
4. The endpoint of a segment is at (1, 9). The midpoint of the segment is at (9, 5). Find the coordinates of the other endpoint. **(17, 1)**

5-5 Exercises

Assignment Guide

Assign *Guided Practice* exercises as necessary.

If you finished Examples **1–2**
- **Basic** 11–15, 22
- **Average** 11–15, 22, 30
- **Advanced** 11–15, 29, 30, 32

If you finished Examples **1–4**
- **Basic** 11–27, 29, 31, 34–38, 44–49
- **Average** 11–31, 33–39, 44–49
- **Advanced** 11–24, 28–49

Homework Quick Check
Quickly check key concepts.
Exercises: 12, 14, 18, 20, 24

Visual In **Exercises 2–9**, encourage students to graph the points on a coordinate plane so that they can determine whether their answers are reasonable.

Answers

1. Possible answer: The midpoint of a segment is the point that divides the segment into two congruent parts.

State Resources

Exercise 34 involves finding the distance between two points on the coordinate plane. This exercise prepares students for the Multi-Step Test Prep on page 342.

Inclusion For **Exercise 28,** students may need to be reminded of the formula $d = rt$, which can be solved for t to yield $t = \frac{d}{r}$.

Geometry In **Exercise 29,** students can use either πd or $2\pi r$ to find the circumference.

Answers

23. Possible answer: 30; approximate the coordinates using the compatible numbers (−5, 2) and (15, −23). Substituting these values into the Distance Formula yields $\sqrt{20^2 + (-25)^2} \approx \sqrt{1025}$. Use a perfect square to estimate the square root: $\sqrt{1025} \approx \sqrt{900} = 30$.
25. 13.42
26. 8.54
27. 14.32
32. See p. A20.
33. When 2 points lie on a horizontal or vertical line, they share a common x-coordinate or a common y-coordinate. To find the distance between the points, find the absolute value of the difference of the other coordinates.

For Exercises 21 and 22, use the map, and round your answers to the nearest tenth of a mile. Each unit on the map represents 1 mile.

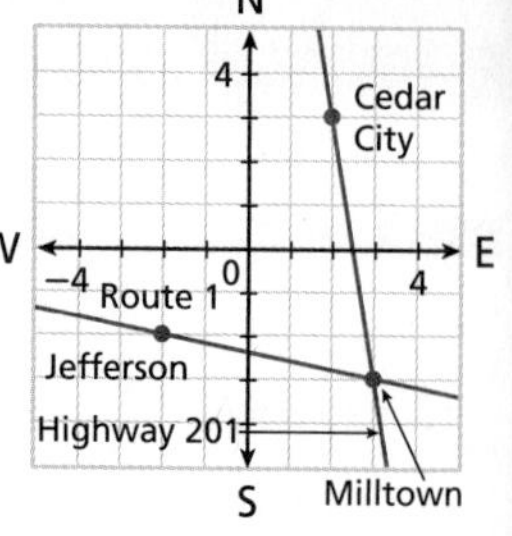

21. How far is it from Cedar City to Milltown along Highway 201? **6.1 mi**

22. A car breaks down on Route 1 halfway between Jefferson and Milltown. A tow truck is sent out from Jefferson. How far does the truck travel to reach the car? **2.5 mi**

23. **Estimation** Estimate the distance between the points (−5.21, 1.84) and (16.62, −23.19). Explain how you determined your answer.

24. **Geometry** The coordinates of the vertices of ΔABC are $A(1, 4)$, $B(-2, -1)$, and $C(3, -2)$. Find the perimeter of ΔABC to the nearest whole number. **17**

Find the distance, to the nearest hundredth, between each pair of points.

25. $J(0, 3)$ and $K(-6, -9)$
26. $L(-5, 2)$ and $M(-8, 10)$
27. $N(4, -6)$ and $P(-2, 7)$

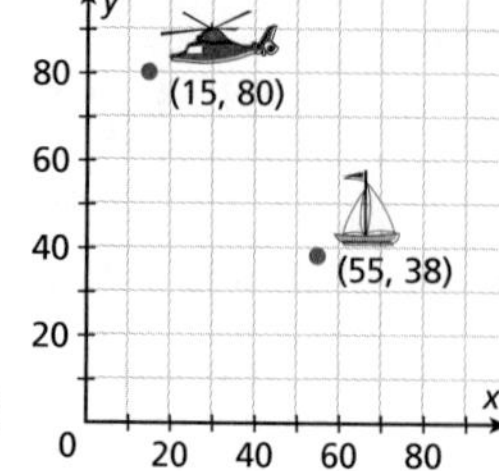

28. **Aviation** A Coast Guard helicopter receives a distress signal from a boat. The units on the map represent miles. To the nearest minute, how long will it take the helicopter to reach the boat if the helicopter travels at an average speed of 75 miles per hour? **46 min**

29. **Geometry** A diameter of a circle has endpoints (−2, −5) and (2, 1).
    a. Find the length of the diameter to the nearest tenth. **7.2**
    b. Find the coordinates of the center of the circle. **(0, −2)**
    c. Find the circumference of the circle to the nearest whole number. **23**

30. **Travel** A group of tourists is traveling by camel in the desert. They are following a straight path from point (2, 4) to point (8, 12) on a map. Each unit on the map represents 1 mile. An oasis lies at the midpoint of the path. The group has already traveled 3.2 miles. How much farther do they need to go to reach the oasis? **1.8 mi**

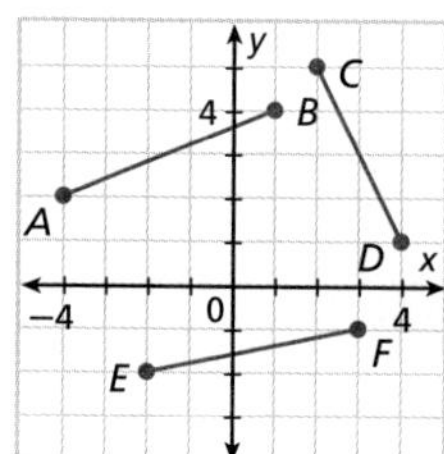

31. **Multi-Step** Use the Distance Formula to order $\overline{AB}$, $\overline{CD}$, and $\overline{EF}$ from shortest to longest. $\overline{CD}$**,** $\overline{EF}$**,** $\overline{AB}$

32. **Critical Thinking** Rebecca found the x-coordinate of the midpoint of $\overline{AB}$ with endpoints $A(x_1, y_1)$ and $B(x_2, y_2)$ by dividing the difference between x_2 and x_1 by 2 and then adding the quotient to x_1. Did this method give the correct x-coordinate for the midpoint? Explain.

33. **Write About It** Explain why the Distance Formula is not needed to find the distance between two points that lie on a horizontal or vertical line.

34. This problem will help you prepare for the Multi-Step Test Prep on page 342.

    On a map of a city park, the ordered pairs (3, 5) and (8, 17) mark the starting and ending points of a straight jogging trail. Each unit on the map represents 0.1 mile.
    a. What is the length of the trail in miles? **1.3 mi**
    b. How many back-and-forth trips would Marisol need to make on the trail in order to run at least 7 miles? **3**

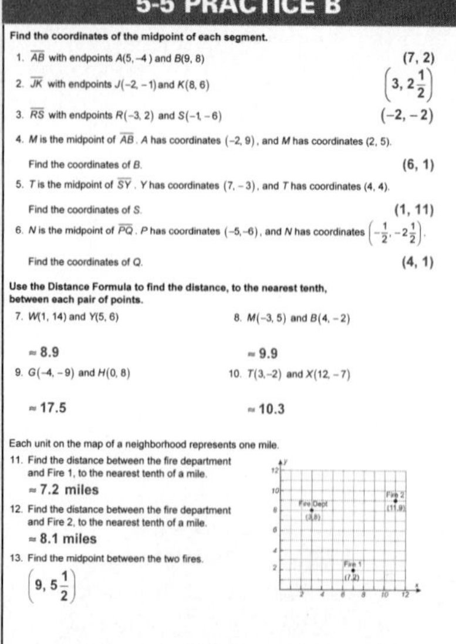

5-5 PRACTICE A
5-5 PRACTICE C
5-5 PRACTICE B

Find the coordinates of the midpoint of each segment.

1. $\overline{AB}$ with endpoints $A(5, -4)$ and $B(9, 8)$ **(7, 2)**
2. $\overline{JK}$ with endpoints $J(-2, -1)$ and $K(8, 6)$ $\left(3, 2\frac{1}{2}\right)$
3. $\overline{RS}$ with endpoints $R(-3, 2)$ and $S(-1, -6)$ **(−2, −2)**
4. M is the midpoint of $\overline{AB}$. A has coordinates (−2, 9), and M has coordinates (2, 5). Find the coordinates of B. **(6, 1)**
5. T is the midpoint of $\overline{SY}$. Y has coordinates (7, −3), and T has coordinates (4, 4). Find the coordinates of S. **(1, 11)**
6. N is the midpoint of $\overline{PQ}$. P has coordinates (−5, −6), and N has coordinates $\left(-\frac{1}{2}, -2\frac{1}{2}\right)$. Find the coordinates of Q. **(4, 1)**

Use the Distance Formula to find the distance, to the nearest tenth, between each pair of points.

7. $W(1, 14)$ and $Y(5, 6)$ **≈ 8.9**
8. $M(-3, 5)$ and $B(4, -2)$ **≈ 9.9**
9. $G(-4, -9)$ and $H(0, 8)$ **≈ 17.5**
10. $T(3, -2)$ and $X(12, -7)$ **≈ 10.3**

Each unit on the map of a neighborhood represents one mile.

11. Find the distance between the fire department and Fire 1, to the nearest tenth of a mile. **≈ 7.2 miles**
12. Find the distance between the fire department and Fire 2, to the nearest tenth of a mile. **≈ 8.1 miles**
13. Find the midpoint between the two fires. $\left(9, 5\frac{1}{2}\right)$

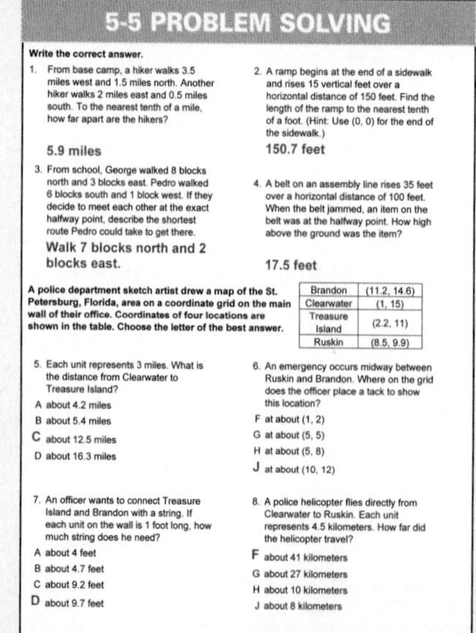

5-5 PROBLEM SOLVING

Write the correct answer.

1. From base camp, a hiker walks 3.5 miles west and 1.5 miles north. Another hiker walks 2 miles east and 0.5 miles south. To the nearest tenth of a mile, how far apart are the hikers? **5.9 miles**
2. A ramp begins at the end of a sidewalk and rises 15 vertical feet over a horizontal distance of 150 feet. Find the length of the ramp to the nearest tenth of a foot. (Hint: Use (0, 0) for the end of the sidewalk.) **150.7 feet**
3. From school, George walked 8 blocks north and 3 blocks east. Pedro walked 6 blocks south and 1 block west. If they decide to meet each other at the exact halfway point, describe the shortest route Pedro could take to get there. **Walk 7 blocks north and 2 blocks east.**
4. A belt on an assembly line rises 35 feet over a horizontal distance of 100 feet. When the belt jammed, an item on the belt was at the halfway point. How high above the ground was the item? **17.5 feet**

A police department sketch artist drew a map of the St. Petersburg, Florida, area on a coordinate grid on the main wall of their office. Coordinates of four locations are shown in the table. Choose the letter of the best answer.

Brandon	(11.2, 14.6)
Clearwater	(1, 15)
Treasure Island	(2.2, 11)
Ruskin	(8.5, 9.9)

5. Each unit represents 3 miles. What is the distance from Clearwater to Treasure Island?
   A about 4.2 miles
   B about 5.4 miles
   C about 12.5 miles
   D about 16.3 miles
6. An emergency occurs midway between Ruskin and Brandon. Where on the grid does the officer place a tack to show this location?
   F at about (1, 2)
   G at about (5, 5)
   H at about (5, 8)
   J at about (10, 12)
7. An officer wants to connect Treasure Island and Brandon with a string. If each unit on the wall is 1 foot long, how much string does he need?
   A about 4 feet
   B about 4.7 feet
   C about 9.2 feet
   D about 9.7 feet
8. A police helicopter flies directly from Clearwater to Ruskin. Each unit represents 4.5 kilometers. How far did the helicopter travel?
   F about 41 kilometers
   G about 27 kilometers
   H about 10 kilometers
   J about 8 kilometers

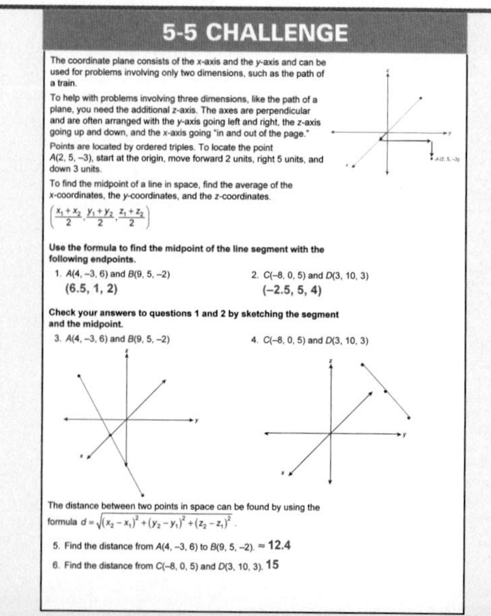

5-5 CHALLENGE

The coordinate plane consists of the x-axis and the y-axis and can be used for problems involving only two dimensions, such as the path of a train.

To help with problems involving three dimensions, like the path of a plane, you need the additional z-axis. The axes are perpendicular and are often arranged with the y-axis going left and right, the z-axis going up and down, and the x-axis going "in and out of the page."

Points are located by ordered triples. To locate the point $A(2, 5, -3)$, start at the origin, move forward 2 units, right 5 units, and down 3 units.

To find the midpoint of a line in space, find the average of the x-coordinates, the y-coordinates, and the z-coordinates.

$$\left(\frac{x_1 + x_2}{2}, \frac{y_1 + y_2}{2}, \frac{z_1 + z_2}{2}\right)$$

Use the formula to find the midpoint of the line segment with the following endpoints.

1. $A(4, -3, 6)$ and $B(9, 5, -2)$ **(6.5, 1, 2)**
2. $C(-8, 0, 5)$ and $D(3, 10, 3)$ **(−2.5, 5, 4)**

Check your answers to questions 1 and 2 by sketching the segment and the midpoint.

3. $A(4, -3, 6)$ and $B(9, 5, -2)$
4. $C(-8, 0, 5)$ and $D(3, 10, 3)$

The distance between two points in space can be found by using the formula $d = \sqrt{(x_2 - x_1)^2 + (y_2 - y_1)^2 + (z_2 - z_1)^2}$.

5. Find the distance from $A(4, -3, 6)$ to $B(9, 5, -2)$. **≈ 12.4**
6. Find the distance from $C(-8, 0, 5)$ and $D(3, 10, 3)$. **15**

35. Which segment has a length closest to 4 units?

Ⓐ $\overline{EF}$ Ⓒ $\overline{JK}$

Ⓑ $\overline{GH}$ Ⓓ $\overline{LM}$

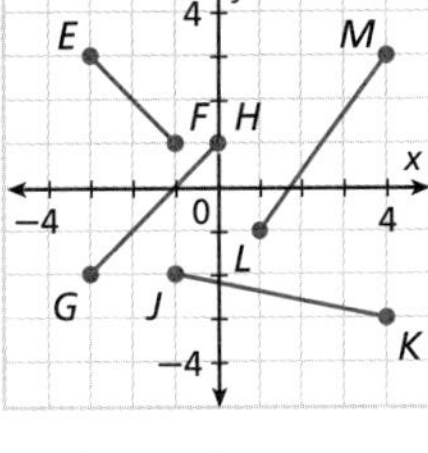

36. What is the distance between the points (7, −3) and (−5, 6)?

Ⓕ 4 Ⓗ 15

Ⓖ 9 Ⓙ 21

37. A coordinate plane is placed over the map of a town. A library is located at (−5, 1), and a museum is located at (3, 5). What is the distance, to the nearest tenth, from the library to the museum?

Ⓐ 4.5 units Ⓑ 5.7 units Ⓒ 6.3 units Ⓓ 8.9 units

38. **Short Response** Brian is driving along a straight highway. His truck can travel 22 miles per gallon of gasoline, and it has 2 gallons of gas remaining. On a map, the truck's current location is (7, 12), and the nearest gas station on the highway is located at (16, 52). Each unit on the map represents 1 mile. Will the truck reach the gas station before running out of gas? Support your answer.

CHALLENGE AND EXTEND

40. $\left(-2a, \frac{3}{2}a\right)$

39. **Geometry** Find the area of a trapezoid with vertices $A(-4, 2)$, $B(0, 4)$, $C(3, 3)$, and $D(-3, 0)$. (*Hint:* The formula for the area of a trapezoid is $A = \frac{1}{2}h(b_1 + b_2)$.) **12.5 square units**

40. X has coordinates $(a, 3a)$, and Y has coordinates $(-5a, 0)$. Find the coordinates of the midpoint of $\overline{XY}$.

41. The coordinates of P are $(a - 5, 0)$. The coordinates of Q are $(a + 1, a)$. The distance between P and Q is 10 units. Find the value of a. **±8**

42. Find two points on the y-axis that are a distance of 5 units from (4, 2). **(0, 5); (0, −1)**

43. The coordinates of S are (4, 5). The coordinates of the midpoint of $\overline{ST}$ are (−1, −7). Find the length of $\overline{ST}$. **26**

SPIRAL REVIEW

44. In the 2007–2008 season, the Orlando Magic won 52 games and lost 30 games. What percent of its games did the team win? Round your answer to the nearest percent. *(Lesson 2-9)* **63%**

Solve each inequality and graph the solutions. *(Lesson 3-5)*

45. $4x < 7x + 6$ **$x > -2$** 46. $4y + 3 \geq 5y - 8$ **$y \leq 11$** 47. $6(z + 2) > 3z$ **$z > -4$**

Find the slope of each line. *(Lesson 5-3)*

48. 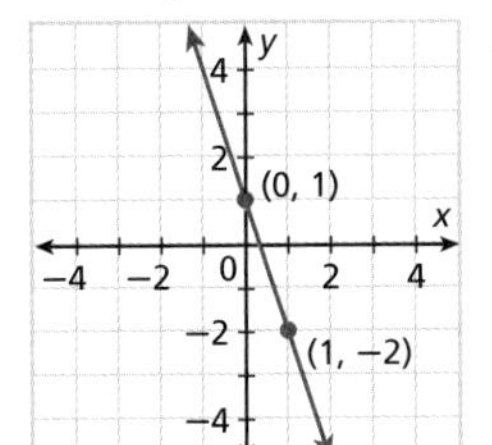

−3

49. 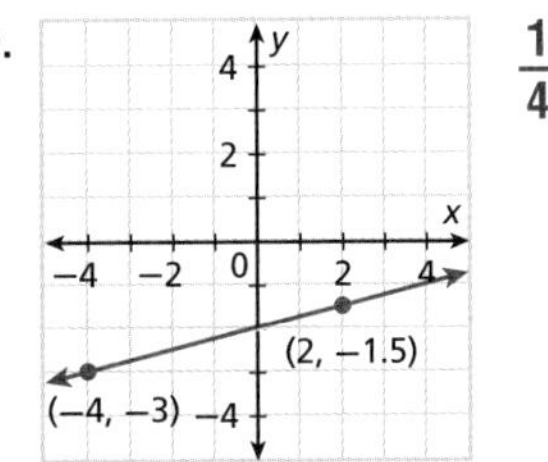

$\frac{1}{4}$

Answers

38. Yes; the distance to the gas station is 41 miles, and Brian can drive up to 44 miles on the gas currently in the tank.

45. 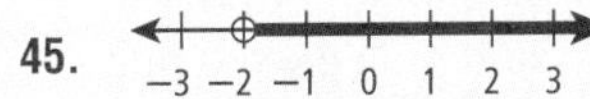

46.
6 7 8 9 10 11 12

47.
−5 −4 −3 −2 −1 0 1

TEST PREP DOCTOR If students have difficulty getting started with **Exercise 38**, point out that the problem has three steps. First, determine the distance Brian can drive on 2 gallons of gas. Next, determine the distance between the truck and the gas station. Lastly, compare the distances from steps 1 and 2.

Journal

Have students explain how the Distance Formula can be used to determine the distance between two locations on a map.

ALTERNATIVE ASSESSMENT

Give students two index cards. Have them write the coordinates of a point on each card. Coordinates should be whole numbers ranging from 0 to 10. Shuffle the cards, and have students pick two at random. For the points they picked, students must find the distance between them and the coordinates of the midpoint of the segment that joins them.

Power Presentations with PowerPoint®

5-5 Lesson Quiz

1. Find the coordinates of the midpoint of $\overline{AB}$ with endpoints $A(-1, 4)$ and $B(4, -3)$. $\left(\frac{3}{2}, \frac{1}{2}\right)$

2. M is the midpoint of $\overline{AB}$. A has coordinates (−5, 7), and M has coordinates (−1, 8). Find the coordinates of B. (3, 9)

3. Use the Distance Formula to find the distance, to the nearest hundredth, from $A(-1, -3)$ to $B(7, -1)$. 8.25

4. Each unit on the map represents 1 meter. To the nearest tenth of a meter, what is the distance from the fountain to the statue? 18.0 m

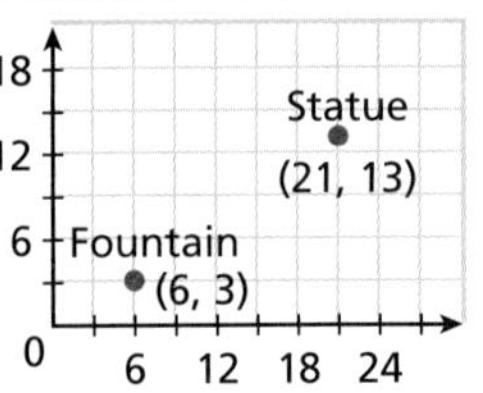

Also available on transparency

5-6 Organizer

Pacing: Traditional 1 day
Block $\frac{1}{2}$ day

Objective: Identify, write, and graph direct variation.

Online Edition
Tutorial Videos

Countdown Week 11

Power Presentations with PowerPoint®

Warm Up

Solve for *y*.

1. $3 + y = 2x$ $\quad y = 2x - 3$
2. $6x = 3y$ $\quad y = 2x$

Write an equation that describes the relationship.

3.

x	1	2	3	4
y	3	6	9	12

$y = 3x$

Solve for *x*.

4. $\frac{3}{5} = \frac{x}{15}$ $\quad 9$
5. $\frac{6}{2} = \frac{1.5}{x}$ $\quad 0.5$

Also available on transparency

Math Humor

Parent: How is your math homework going?

Child: Well, *m* is negative, so at least I'm on the down slope!

5-6 Direct Variation

Objective
Identify, write, and graph direct variation.

Vocabulary
direct variation
constant of variation

Who uses this?
Chefs can use direct variation to determine ingredients needed for a certain number of servings.

Paella is a rice dish that originated in Valencia, Spain.

A recipe for paella calls for 1 cup of rice to make 5 servings. In other words, a chef needs 1 cup of rice for every 5 servings.

Rice (c) *x*	1	2	3	4
Servings *y*	5	10	15	20

The equation $y = 5x$ describes this relationship. In this relationship, the number of servings *varies directly* with the number of cups of rice.

A **direct variation** is a special type of linear relationship that can be written in the form $y = kx$, where k is a nonzero constant called the **constant of variation**.

EXAMPLE 1 Identifying Direct Variations from Equations

Tell whether each equation represents a direct variation. If so, identify the constant of variation.

A $y = 4x$

This equation represents a direct variation because it is in the form $y = kx$. The constant of variation is 4.

B $-3x + 5y = 0$

$$-3x + 5y = 0 \qquad \textit{Solve the equation for y.}$$
$$\underline{+3x \qquad\quad +3x} \qquad \textit{Since } -3x \textit{ is added to } 5y, \textit{ add } 3x \textit{ to both sides.}$$
$$5y = 3x$$
$$\frac{5y}{5} = \frac{3x}{5} \qquad \textit{Since y is multiplied by 5, divide both sides by 5.}$$
$$y = \frac{3}{5}x$$

This equation represents a direct variation because it can be written in the form $y = kx$. The constant of variation is $\frac{3}{5}$.

C $2x + y = 10$

$$2x + y = 10 \qquad \textit{Solve the equation for y.}$$
$$\underline{-2x \qquad\quad -2x} \qquad \textit{Since } 2x \textit{ is added to y, subtract } 2x \textit{ from both sides.}$$
$$y = -2x + 10$$

This equation does not represent a direct variation because it cannot be written in the form $y = kx$.

Tell whether each equation represents a direct variation. If so, identify the constant of variation.

1a. $3y = 4x + 1$ **1b.** $3x = -4y$ **1c.** $y + 3x = 0$

1a. no
1b. yes; $-\frac{3}{4}$
1c. yes; -3

1 Introduce

EXPLORATION

5-6 Direct Variation

You will need a graphing calculator for this Exploration.

1. Use your calculator to graph the following functions in the same viewing window.
$y = 3x$
$y = \frac{1}{2}x$
$y = 5x$

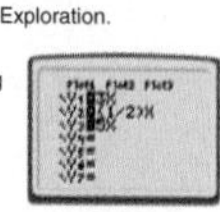

2. What do you notice about the graphs? What do they all have in common?
3. Make a table for the function $y = 3x$ as follows. Press [Y=] and delete the functions that have been entered for **Y2** and **Y3**. Then press [2nd] [TABLE] to view the table for **Y1**.
4. Choose any row of the table except the row for $x = 0$. Divide the *y*-value by the *x*-value. What is the result? Is this true for every row of the table?
5. Follow the same procedure to examine the tables for $y = \frac{1}{2}x$ and $y = 5x$. For each row (except $x = 0$), divide the *y*-value by the *x*-value. Describe the results for each function.

THINK AND DISCUSS

6. **Predict** what would happen if you made a table of values for $y = 7x$ and divided any *y*-value by its corresponding *x*-value (except $x = 0$).
7. **Describe** the graph of an equation that has the form $y = kx$.

Motivate

Have a volunteer count the number of people present in the classroom and multiply the number by 2. Ask what the product could represent in relation to the number of people in the room. Possible answer: number of shoes What could the product represent if you multiplied by 10? Possible answer: number of fingers

Tell students that these are examples of direct variations.

Explorations and answers are provided in Alternate Openers: Explorations Transparencies.

State Resources

What happens if you solve $y = kx$ for k?

$$y = kx$$

$$\frac{y}{x} = \frac{kx}{x} \quad \textit{Divide both sides by } x \ (x \neq 0).$$

$$\frac{y}{x} = k$$

So, in a direct variation, the ratio $\frac{y}{x}$ is equal to the constant of variation. Another way to identify a direct variation is to check whether $\frac{y}{x}$ is the same for each ordered pair (except where $x = 0$).

EXAMPLE 2 Identifying Direct Variations from Ordered Pairs

Tell whether each relationship is a direct variation. Explain.

A

x	1	3	5
y	6	18	30

Method 1 Write an equation.

$y = 6x$ *Each y-value is 6 times the corresponding x-value.*

This is a direct variation because it can be written as $y = kx$, where $k = 6$.

Method 2 Find $\frac{y}{x}$ for each ordered pair.

$\frac{6}{1} = 6$ $\qquad \frac{18}{3} = 6$ $\qquad \frac{30}{5} = 6$

This is a direct variation because $\frac{y}{x}$ is the same for each ordered pair.

B

x	2	4	8
y	−2	0	4

Method 1 Write an equation.

$y = x - 4$ *Each y-value is 4 less than the corresponding x-value.*

This is not a direct variation because it cannot be written as $y = kx$.

Method 2 Find $\frac{y}{x}$ for each ordered pair.

$\frac{-2}{2} = -1$ $\qquad \frac{0}{4} = 0$ $\qquad \frac{4}{8} = \frac{1}{2}$

This is not a direct variation because $\frac{y}{x}$ is not the same for all ordered pairs.

CHECK IT OUT! **Tell whether each relationship is a direct variation. Explain.**

2a.

x	y
−3	0
1	3
3	6

2b.

x	y
2.5	−10
5	−20
7.5	−30

2c.

x	y
−2	5
1	3
4	1

2a. No; possible answer: the value of $\frac{y}{x}$ is not the same for each ordered pair.

2b. Yes; possible answer: the value of $\frac{y}{x}$ is the same for each ordered pair.

2c. No; possible answer: the value of $\frac{y}{x}$ is not the same for each ordered pair.

If you know one ordered pair that satisfies a direct variation, you can write the equation. You can also find other ordered pairs that satisfy the direct variation.

2 Teach

Guided Instruction

Review writing an equation from a table. Remind students that they are looking for a consistent relationship between x and y in which y is always a constant multiple of x. Before **Example 3,** review solving a proportion by using cross products.

Visual Some students may find a table of values easier to read if the values are written in columns rather than rows.

Reaching All Learners

Through Multiple Representations

Have students work in small groups. Using a ruler (MK), each group should measure and record the thickness of one algebra book. Then have them measure and record the height of 2 algebra books, 3 algebra books, and so on, until all group members' books are on the stack. Using these data, ask each group to explain how the relationship between the number of books and the height of the stack models a direct variation.

COMMON ERROR ALERT

Students may have trouble differentiating between a direct variation and a simple linear relationship like $y = x + 2$. Explain that although both $y = 2x$ and $y = x + 2$ are linear functions, the relationship between x and y in a direct variation always has a y-intercept of 0.

Power Presentations with PowerPoint®

Additional Examples

Example 1

Tell whether each equation represents a direct variation. If so, identify the constant of variation.

A. $y = 3x$ yes; 3

B. $3x + y = 8$ no

C. $-4x + 3y = 0$ yes; $\frac{4}{3}$

Example 2

Tell whether each relationship is a direct variation. Explain.

A.

x	2	4	6
y	6	12	18

Yes; possible answer: the value of $\frac{y}{x}$ is the same for each ordered pair.

B.

x	1	3	7
y	−2	0	4

No; possible answer: the value of $\frac{y}{x}$ is not the same for each ordered pair.

INTERVENTION

Questioning Strategies

EXAMPLE 1

- Is the constant of variation always the coefficient of x? Explain.

EXAMPLE 2

- Why does finding $\frac{y}{x}$ for each ordered pair tell you whether the relationship is a direct variation?
- If the coefficient of x is 1, can the relationship be a direct variation? Explain.

Inclusion Point out that a linear equation cannot be a direct variation if the value of C is nonzero when the equation is written in standard form ($Ax + By = C$).

Power Presentations with PowerPoint®

Additional Examples

Example 3

The value of y varies directly with x, and $y = 3$ when $x = 9$. Find y when $x = 21$. 7

Example 4

A group of people are tubing down a river at an average speed of 2 mi/h. Write a direct variation equation that gives the number of miles y that the people will float in x hours. Then graph.

$y = 2x$

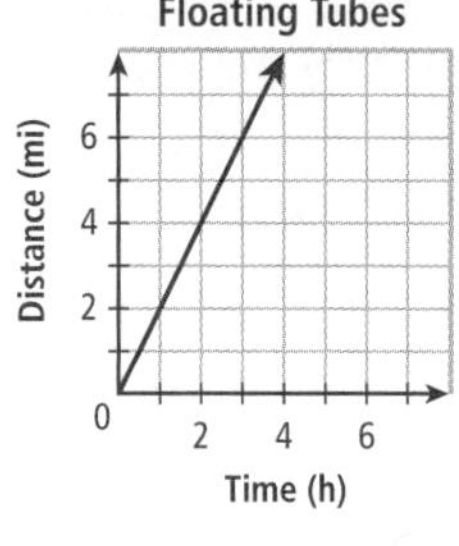

INTERVENTION
Questioning Strategies

EXAMPLE 3

- If you use a proportion to find y, how can you then find k?

EXAMPLE 4

- How can you "see" the constant of variation in the ordered pairs? in the graph?

Critical Thinking Ask students whether the graph in **Example 4** appears to suggest that the three-toed sloth is *not* "an extremely slow animal." Point out that the steep slope represents a rate of 6 ft/min, which is equivalent to about 0.07 mi/h.

EXAMPLE 3 Writing and Solving Direct Variation Equations

The value of y varies directly with x, and $y = 6$ when $x = 12$. Find y when $x = 27$.

Method 1 Find the value of k and then write the equation.

$y = kx$	*Write the equation for a direct variation.*
$6 = k(12)$	*Substitute 6 for y and 12 for x. Solve for k.*
$\frac{1}{2} = k$	*Since k is multiplied by 12, divide both sides by 12.*

The equation is $y = \frac{1}{2}x$. When $x = 27$, $y = \frac{1}{2}(27) = 13.5$.

Method 2 Use a proportion.

$\frac{6}{12} = \frac{y}{27}$	*In a direct variation, $\frac{y}{x}$ is the same for all values of x and y.*
$12y = 162$	*Use cross products.*
$y = 13.5$	*Since y is multiplied by 12, divide both sides by 12.*

3. The value of y varies directly with x, and $y = 4.5$ when $x = 0.5$. Find y when $x = 10$. **90**

EXAMPLE 4 Graphing Direct Variations

The three-toed sloth is an extremely slow animal. On the ground, it travels at a speed of about 6 feet per minute. Write a direct variation equation for the distance y a sloth will travel in x minutes. Then graph.

Step 1 Write a direct variation equation.

distance	=	6 feet per minute	times	number of minutes
y	=	6	•	x

Step 2 Choose values of x and generate ordered pairs.

x	$y = 6x$	(x, y)
0	$y = 6(0) = 0$	(0, 0)
1	$y = 6(1) = 6$	(1, 6)
2	$y = 6(2) = 12$	(2, 12)

Step 3 Graph the points and connect.

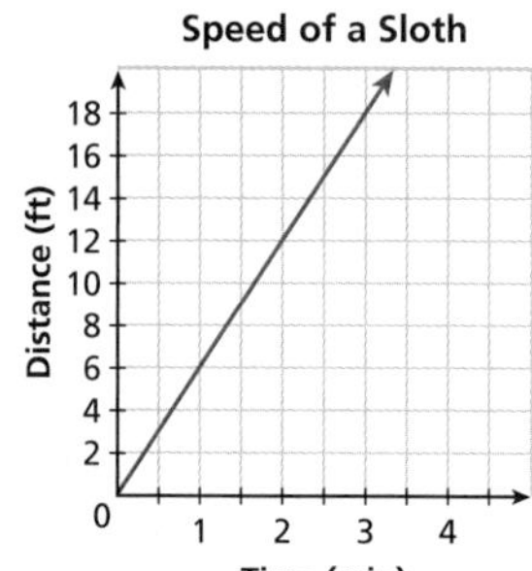

4. $y = 4x$

Perimeter of a Square

Perimeter

Side length

4. The perimeter y of a square varies directly with its side length x. Write a direct variation equation for this relationship. Then graph.

Look at the graph in Example 4. It passes through (0, 0) and has a slope of 6. The graph of any direct variation $y = kx$

- is a line through (0, 0).
- has a slope of k.

3 Close

Summarize

Ask students if each relationship or equation below is a direct variation. If so, have them identify the constant of variation.

x	0	3	6
y	2	8	14

no; $\frac{2}{0} \neq \frac{8}{3} \neq \frac{14}{6}$

$x - 4y = 0$ yes; $\frac{1}{4}$

$5x + 10 = y$ no; cannot be written in the form $y = kx$.

ONGOING ASSESSMENT

and INTERVENTION

***Diagnose Before* the Lesson**
5-6 Warm Up, TE p. 336

***Monitor During* the Lesson**
Check It Out! Exercises, SE pp. 336–338
Questioning Strategies, TE pp. 337–338

***Assess After* the Lesson**
5-6 Lesson Quiz, TE p. 341
Alternative Assessment, TE p. 341

THINK AND DISCUSS

1. How do you know that a direct variation is linear?
2. How does the graph of a direct variation differ from the graphs of other types of linear relationships?

3. **GET ORGANIZED** Copy and complete the graphic organizer. In each box, describe how you can use the given information to identify a direct variation.

Recognizing a Direct Variation		
From an Equation	From Ordered Pairs	From a Graph

Answers to *Think and Discuss*

Possible answers:

1. It can be written in standard form $kx - y = 0$ with $A = k$, $B = -1$, and $C = 0$.
2. The graph of a direct variation always passes through the origin and is neither horizontal nor vertical.
3. See p. A5.

5-6 Exercises

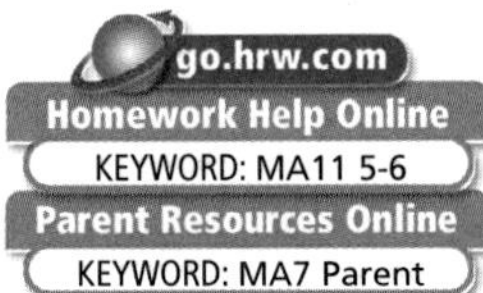

GUIDED PRACTICE

1. **Vocabulary** If x varies directly with y, then the relationship between the two variables is said to be a __?__. (*direct variation* or *constant of variation*) **direct variation**

SEE EXAMPLE 1 p. 336

Tell whether each equation represents a direct variation. If so, identify the constant of variation.

2. $y = 4x + 9$ **no**
3. $2y = -8x$ **yes; −4**
4. $x + y = 0$ **yes; −1**

SEE EXAMPLE 2 p. 337

Tell whether each relationship is a direct variation. Explain.

5. **no**

x	10	5	2
y	12	7	4

6. **yes**

x	3	−1	−4
y	−6	2	8

SEE EXAMPLE 3 p. 338

7. The value of y varies directly with x, and $y = -3$ when $x = 1$. Find y when $x = -6$. **18**
8. The value of y varies directly with x, and $y = 6$ when $x = 18$. Find y when $x = 12$. **4**

SEE EXAMPLE 4 p. 338

9. **Wages** Cameron earns $7 per hour at her after-school job. The total amount of her paycheck varies directly with the amount of time she works. Write a direct variation equation for the amount of money y that she earns for working x hours. Then graph. $y = 7x$

PRACTICE AND PROBLEM SOLVING

Tell whether each equation represents a direct variation. If so, identify the constant of variation.

10. $y = \frac{1}{6}x$ **yes;** $\frac{1}{6}$
11. $4y = x$ **yes;** $\frac{1}{4}$
12. $x = 2y - 12$ **no**

Tell whether each relationship is a direct variation. Explain.

13. **yes**

x	6	9	17
y	13.2	19.8	37.4

14. **yes**

x	−6	3	12
y	4	−2	−8

Answers

5. Possible answer: The value of $\frac{y}{x}$ is not the same for each ordered pair.
6. Possible answer: The value of $\frac{y}{x}$ is the same for each ordered pair.
9.

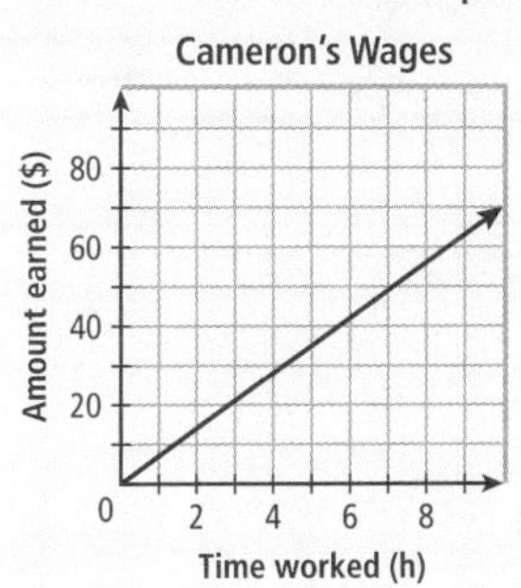

13. Possible answer: The value of $\frac{y}{x}$ is the same for each ordered pair.
14. Possible answer: The value of $\frac{y}{x}$ is the same for each ordered pair.

5-6 Exercises

Assignment Guide

Assign *Guided Practice* exercises as necessary.

If you finished Examples **1–2**
Basic 10–14, 18, 19
Average 10–14, 18, 19
Advanced 10–14, 18, 19, 46

If you finished Examples **1–4**
Basic 10–37, 40–44, 47–55
Average 10–17, 20–44, 46–55
Advanced 10–17, 20–55

Homework Quick Check
Quickly check key concepts.
Exercises: 10, 14, 16, 17, 22, 36

State Resources

go.hrw.com
State Resources Online
KEYWORD: MA7 Resources

Exercise 40 involves writing an equation of direct variation and determining the constant of variation. This exercise prepares students for the Multi-Step Test Prep on page 342.

Answers

17. Cost of Gasoline

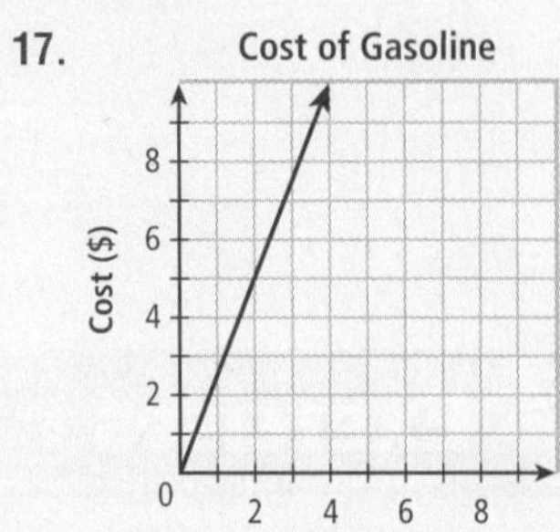

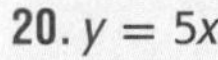

20. $y = 5x$

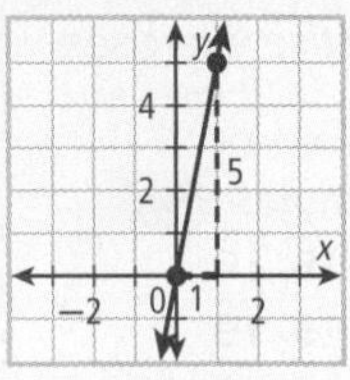

$k = 5$; graph shows slope $= 5$

21. $y = -3x$

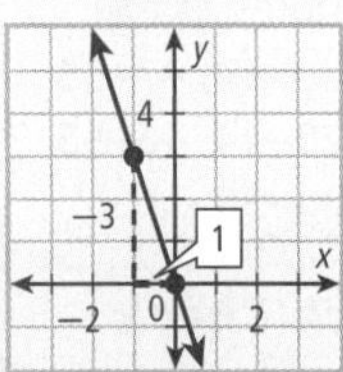

$k = -3$; graph shows slope $= -3$

22–35, 37b, 38. See pp. A20–A21.

39. Possible answer: The ratio $\frac{y}{x}$ is the same for all ordered pairs in a direct var., so you can write a proportion using any two ordered pairs.

Independent Practice	
For Exercises	See Example
10–12	1
13–14	2
15–16	3
17	4

Extra Practice
Skills Practice p. S13
Application Practice p. S32

15. The value of y varies directly with x, and $y = 8$ when $x = -32$. Find y when $x = 64$. **−16**
16. The value of y varies directly with x, and $y = \frac{1}{2}$ when $x = 3$. Find y when $x = 1$. $\frac{1}{6}$
17. While on his way to school, Norman saw that the cost of gasoline was $2.50 per gallon. Write a direct variation equation to describe the cost y of x gallons of gas. Then graph. **$y = 2.50x$**

Tell whether each relationship is a direct variation. Explain your answer.

18. The equation $-15x + 4y = 0$ relates the length of a videotape in inches x to its approximate playing time in seconds y. **Yes; it can be written as $y = \frac{15}{4}x$.**
19. The equation $y - 2.00x = 2.50$ relates the cost y of a taxicab ride to distance x of the cab ride in miles. **No; it cannot be written in the form $y = kx$.**

Each ordered pair is a solution of a direct variation. Write the equation of direct variation. Then graph your equation and show that the slope of the line is equal to the constant of variation.

20. $(2, 10)$	21. $(-3, 9)$	22. $(8, 2)$	23. $(1.5, 6)$
24. $(7, 21)$	25. $(1, 2)$	26. $(2, -16)$	27. $\left(\frac{1}{7}, 1\right)$
28. $(-2, 9)$	29. $(9, -2)$	30. $(4, 6)$	31. $(3, 4)$
32. $(5, 1)$	33. $(1, -6)$	34. $\left(-1, \frac{1}{2}\right)$	35. $(7, 2)$

LINK
Astronomy

The Mars rover *Spirit* landed on Mars in January 2004 and immediately began sending photos of the planet's surface back to Earth.

36. **Astronomy** Weight varies directly with gravity. A Mars lander weighed 767 pounds on Earth but only 291 pounds on Mars. Its accompanying Mars rover weighed 155 pounds on Mars. How much did it weigh on Earth? Round your answer to the nearest pound. **409 lb**
37. **Environment** Mischa bought an energy-efficient washing machine. She will save about 15 gallons of water per wash load.
    a. Write an equation of direct variation to describe how many gallons of water y Mischa saves for x loads of laundry she washes. **$y = 15x$**
    b. Graph your direct variation from part **a.** Is every point on the graph a solution in this situation? Why or why not?
    c. If Mischa does 2 loads of laundry per week, how many gallons of water will she have saved at the end of a year? **1560 gal**
38. **Critical Thinking** If you double an x-value in a direct variation, will the corresponding y-value double? Explain.

39. **Write About It** In a direct variation $y = kx$, k is sometimes called the "constant of proportionality." How are proportions related to direct variations?

MULTI-STEP TEST PREP

40. This problem will prepare you for the Multi-Step Test Prep on page 342.
    Rhea exercised on a treadmill at the gym. When she was finished, the display showed that she had walked at an average speed of 3 miles per hour.
    a. Write an equation that gives the number of miles y that Rhea would cover in x hours if she walked at this speed. **$y = 3x$**
    b. Explain why this is a direct variation and find the value of k. What does this value represent in Rhea's situation? **It is written in the form $y = kx$, where $k = 3$. This value represents the speed at which Rhea is walking.**

5-6 PRACTICE A
5-6 PRACTICE C
5-6 PRACTICE B

Tell whether each equation is a direct variation. If so, identify the constant of variation.

1. $y = 3x$ **yes; 3**
2. $y = 2x - 9$ **no**
3. $2x + 3y = 0$ **yes; $-\frac{2}{3}$**
4. $3y = 9x$ **yes; 3**

Find the value of $\frac{y}{x}$ for each ordered pair. Then, tell whether each relationship is a direct variation.

5.

x	6	15	21
y	2	5	7
$\frac{y}{x}$	$\frac{1}{3}$	$\frac{1}{3}$	$\frac{1}{3}$

yes

6.

x	6	10	25
y	24	40	100
$\frac{y}{x}$	4	4	4

yes

7.

x	10	15	20
y	3	5	9
$\frac{y}{x}$	$\frac{3}{10}$	$\frac{1}{3}$	$\frac{9}{20}$

no

8. The value of y varies directly with x, and $y = -18$ when $x = 6$. Find y when $x = -8$.
   Find k: $-3 = k$
   Use k to find y: $y = kx$; $y = (-3)(-8)$; $y = 24$
9. The value of y varies directly with x, and $y = \frac{1}{2}$ when $x = 5$. Find y when $x = 30$.
   Find k: $\frac{1}{10} = k$
   Use k to find y: $y = kx$; $y = \left(\frac{1}{10}\right)(30)$; $y = 3$
10. The amount of interest earned in a savings account varies directly with the amount of money in the account. A certain bank offers a 2% savings rate. Write a direct variation equation for the amount of interest y earned on a balance of x. Then graph.
    $y = 0.02x$
11. Another bank offers a different savings rate. If an account with $400 earns interest of $6, how much interest is earned by an account with $1800?
    $27

Interest
Interest Earned ($)
Amount in Account ($)

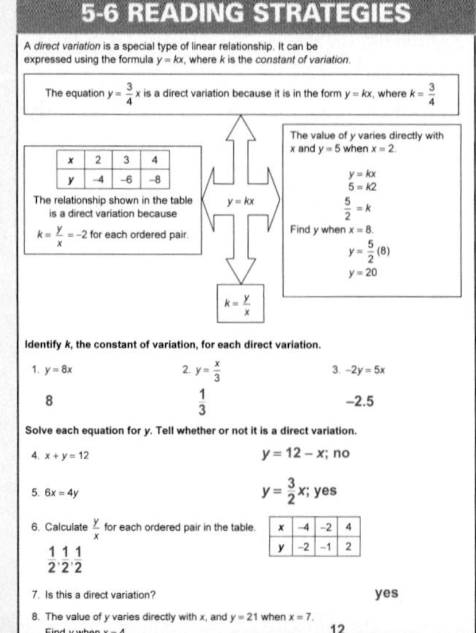

5-6 READING STRATEGIES

A *direct variation* is a special type of linear relationship. It can be expressed using the formula $y = kx$, where k is the *constant of variation*.

The equation $y = \frac{3}{4}x$ is a direct variation because it is in the form $y = kx$, where $k = \frac{3}{4}$

x	2	3	4
y	−4	−6	−8

The relationship shown in the table is a direct variation because $k = \frac{y}{x} = -2$ for each ordered pair.

$y = kx$

The value of y varies directly with x and $y = 5$ when $x = 2$.
$y = kx$
$5 = k2$
$\frac{5}{2} = k$
Find y when $x = 8$.
$y = \frac{5}{2}(8)$
$y = 20$

$k = \frac{y}{x}$

Identify k, the constant of variation, for each direct variation.

1. $y = 8x$ **8**
2. $y = \frac{x}{3}$ **$\frac{1}{3}$**
3. $-2y = 5x$ **−2.5**

Solve each equation for y. Tell whether or not it is a direct variation.

4. $x + y = 12$ **$y = 12 - x$; no**
5. $6x = 4y$ **$y = \frac{3}{2}x$; yes**
6. Calculate $\frac{y}{x}$ for each ordered pair in the table.

x	−4	−2	4
y	−2	−1	2

$\frac{1}{2}, \frac{1}{2}, \frac{1}{2}$

7. Is this a direct variation? **yes**
8. The value of y varies directly with x, and $y = 21$ when $x = 7$. Find y when $x = 4$. **12**

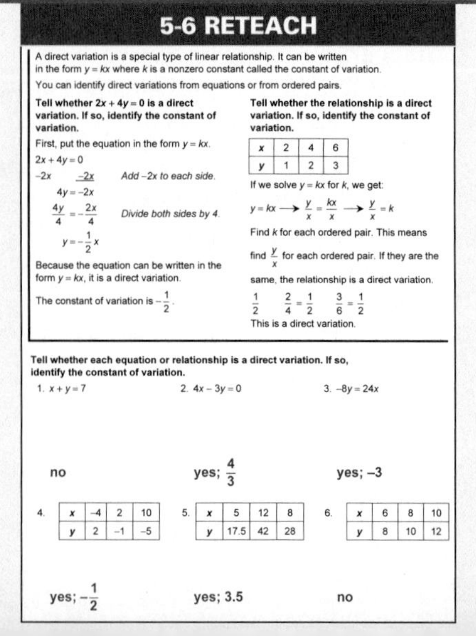

5-6 RETEACH

A direct variation is a special type of linear relationship. It can be written in the form $y = kx$ where k is a nonzero constant called the constant of variation.

You can identify direct variations from equations or from ordered pairs.

Tell whether $2x + 4y = 0$ is a direct variation. If so, identify the constant of variation.

First, put the equation in the form $y = kx$.
$2x + 4y = 0$
$-2x \quad -2x$ *Add −2x to each side.*
$4y = -2x$
$\frac{4y}{4} = -\frac{2x}{4}$ *Divide both sides by 4.*
$y = -\frac{1}{2}x$

Because the equation can be written in the form $y = kx$, it is a direct variation.

The constant of variation is $-\frac{1}{2}$.

Tell whether the relationship is a direct variation. If so, identify the constant of variation.

x	2	4	6
y	1	2	3

If we solve $y = kx$ for k, we get:

$y = kx \longrightarrow \frac{y}{x} = \frac{kx}{x} \longrightarrow \frac{y}{x} = k$

Find k for each ordered pair. This means find $\frac{y}{x}$ for each ordered pair. If they are the same, the relationship is a direct variation.

$\frac{1}{2} \quad \frac{2}{4} = \frac{1}{2} \quad \frac{3}{6} = \frac{1}{2}$
This is a direct variation.

Tell whether each equation or relationship is a direct variation. If so, identify the constant of variation.

1. $x + y = 7$ **no**
2. $4x - 3y = 0$ **yes; $\frac{4}{3}$**
3. $-8y = 24x$ **yes; −3**

4.

x	−4	2	10
y	2	−1	−5

yes; $-\frac{1}{2}$

5.

x	5	12	8
y	17.5	42	28

yes; 3.5

6.

x	6	8	10
y	8	10	12

no

TEST PREP

41. Which equation does NOT represent a direct variation?

   Ⓐ $y = \frac{1}{3}x$ Ⓑ $y = -2x$ **Ⓒ** $y = 4x + 1$ Ⓓ $6x - y = 0$

42. Identify which set of data represents a direct variation.

   Ⓕ

x	1	2	3
y	1	2	3

   Ⓗ

x	1	2	3
y	3	5	7

   Ⓖ

x	1	2	3
y	0	1	2

   Ⓙ

x	1	2	3
y	3	4	5

43. Two yards of fabric cost $13, and 5 yards of fabric cost $32.50. Which equation relates the cost of the fabric c to its length ℓ?

   Ⓐ $c = 2.6\ell$ **Ⓑ** $c = 6.5\ell$ Ⓒ $c = 13\ell$ Ⓓ $c = 32.5\ell$

44. **Gridded Response** A car is traveling at a constant speed. After 3 hours, the car has traveled 180 miles. If the car continues to travel at the same constant speed, how many hours will it take to travel a total of 270 miles? **4.5**

CHALLENGE AND EXTEND

45b.

Gas Mileage

Hybrid, SUV; Distance (mi): 20, 40, 60, 80; Gas used (gal): 0, 2, 4, 6

45. **Transportation** The function $y = 20x$ gives the number of miles y that a sport-utility vehicle (SUV) can travel on x gallons of gas. The function $y = 60x$ gives the number of miles y that a hybrid car can travel on x gallons of gas.
   a. If you drive 120 miles, how much gas will you save by driving the hybrid instead of the SUV? **4 gal**
   b. Graph both functions on the same coordinate plane. Will the lines ever meet other than at the origin? Explain. **No; the lines begin at (0, 0) and then move apart.**
   c. **What if...?** Shannon drives 15,000 miles in one year. How many gallons of gas will she use if she drives the SUV? the hybrid? **750 gal; 250 gal**

46. Suppose the equation $ax + by = c$, where a, b, and c are real numbers, describes a direct variation. What do you know about the value of c? $\mathbf{c = 0}$

SPIRAL REVIEW

Solve for the indicated variable. *(Lesson 2-5)*

47. $p + 4q = 7; p$ $\mathbf{p = 7 - 4q}$

48. $\frac{s-5}{t} = 2; s$ $\mathbf{s = 2t + 5}$

49. $xy + 2y = 4; x$ $\mathbf{x = \frac{4 - 2y}{y}}$

Determine a relationship between the x- and y-values and write an equation. *(Lesson 4-3)*

50. $\mathbf{y = x - 6}$

x	y
1	−5
2	−4
3	−3
4	−2

51. $\mathbf{y = -2x}$

x	y
1	−2
2	−4
3	−6
4	−8

52. $\mathbf{y = -3x}$

x	y
−3	9
−2	6
−1	3
0	0

Find the slope of the line described by each equation. *(Lesson 5-4)*

53. $4x + y = -9$ $\mathbf{-4}$

54. $6x - 3y = -9$ $\mathbf{2}$

55. $5x = 10y - 5$ $\mathbf{\frac{1}{2}}$

5-6 PROBLEM SOLVING

Write the correct answer.

1. Wesley earns $6.50 per hour at the bookstore. The total amount of his paycheck varies directly with the number of hours he works. Write a direct variation equation for the amount of money y Wesley earns for working x hours.
   $y = 6.5x$

2. The equation $-4x + y = 0$ relates the number of pages in a photo album y to the number of pictures in the album x. Tell whether the relationship is a direct variation. Explain your answer.
   yes; it can be written as $y = 4x$.

3. The formula $9x - 5y = -160$ relates the temperature in degrees Fahrenheit y to the temperature in degrees Celsius x. Tell whether the relationship is a direct variation. Explain your answer.
   no; it cannot be written in the form $y = kx$

4. The number of miles driven varies directly with the number of gallons of gas used. Erin drove 297 miles on 9 gallons of gas. How far would she be able to drive on 14 gallons of gas?
   462 miles

Select the best answer.

5. The table shows the relationship between the number of lemons purchased and their cost.

Lemons x	1	2	3	4
Cost y	0.1	0.2	0.3	0.4

   Is the relationship a direct variation?
   A Yes; it can be written as $y = 0.1x$.
   B Yes; it can be written as $y = 10x$.
   C No; it cannot be written as $y = kx$.
   D No; the relationship is not a function.

6. The table shows the relationship between the hours since sunrise and the temperature in degrees Celsius.

Hour x	1	2	3	4
Temp. y	25	26	28	32

   Is the relationship a direct variation?
   F Yes; it can be written as $y = 25x$.
   G Yes; it can be written as $y = 8x$.
   H No; it cannot be written as $y = kx$.
   J No; the relationship is not a function.

7. The Diaz family is driving at a constant speed on the highway so their distance varies directly with their speed. They traveled 17.5 miles in 15 minutes. How far did they travel in 2 hours?
   A 50 miles **C** 140 miles
   B 70 miles D 262.5 miles (17.5 times 15)

8. On July 26, 2005, it rained a record 37 inches in Mumbai, India, in a 24-hour period. Which equation of direct variation relates the number of inches of rain y to the number of hours x?
   F $y = \frac{24}{37}x$ H $y = 24x$
   G $y = \frac{37}{24}x$ J $y = 37x$

5-6 CHALLENGE

In Lesson 5.3, you learned that when y varies directly as x, there is a nonzero number, k, such that $y = kx$. There are many situations in which one variable varies directly with another variable.

A 700-gallon tank contains 500 gallons of a certain liquid. Three pumps feed three different ingredients into the tank at its top. A discharge pump at the base of the tank removes the mixed ingredients. The rates at which the pipes feed and remove liquid are shown at right.

Pump 1:	5 gallons per minute
Pump 2:	10 gallons per minute
Pump 3:	15 gallons per minute
Discharge pump:	35 gallons per minute

Pump 1, Pump 2, Pump 3, Discharge

Let t represent the amount of time for which each pipe is operating.

1. Write a direct-variation relationship for the gallons supplied by each pump. Then find the amount of time that it takes for each pump to fill the tank to capacity if each works alone.
   a. pump 1 **$y = 5t$, 40 minutes**
   b. pump 2 **$y = 10t$, 20 minutes**
   c. pump 3 **$y = 15t$, $13\frac{1}{3}$ minutes**

2. On certain occasions, some pumps are turned on at the same time. Write a direct-variation relationship for each combination of pumps operating simultaneously.
   a. pump 1 and pump 2 $y = 15t$
   b. pump 2 and pump 3 $y = 25t$
   c. pump 1, pump 2, and pump 3 $y = 30t$

3. At noon, the tank contains 500 gallons of solution. At noon, all pumps, and the discharge pump, are turned on simultaneously.
   a. Write an equation for the quantity, Q, of solution t minutes after noon. $Q = 500 + 30t - 35t$
   b. Is the tank filling or emptying? At what rate is this happening? **emptying at 5 gallons per minute**
   c. After how many minutes will the tank be full or empty? **after 100 minutes, the tank will be empty**

4. At noon, the tank contains 500 gallons of solution and all feeder pumps are turned on. At 12:06 p.m., the discharge pump is turned on.
   a. Write an equation or equations for the quantity, Q, of solution t minutes after noon. $Q = 500 + 30(t + 6) - 35t$, or $Q = 680 - 5t$
   b. How many minutes after noon will the tank either be full or be empty? **after 136 minutes, the tank will be empty**

TEST PREP DOCTOR Students might eliminate the correct choice **F** in **Exercise 42** because they do not understand that the constant of variation can be 1.

Journal

Have students explain how a rate of change, a slope, and a constant of variation are related.

ALTERNATIVE ASSESSMENT

Have students write two equations of direct variation involving common conversion factors, such as 12 inches:1 foot. Then have them graph the equations and identify the constants of variation.

Power Presentations with PowerPoint®

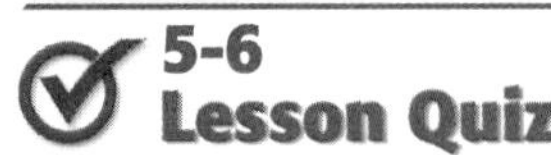

5-6 Lesson Quiz

Tell whether each equation represents a direct variation. If so, identify the constant of variation.

1. $2y = 6x$ yes; 3

2. $3x = 4y - 7$ no

Tell whether each relationship is a direct variation. Explain.

3.

x	−4	0	8
y	2	3	5

   no; $\frac{2}{-4} \neq \frac{3}{0} \neq \frac{5}{8}$

4. 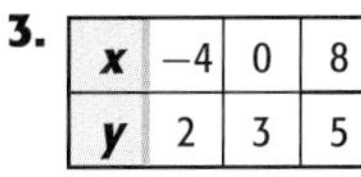

x	1	3	7
y	4.3	12.9	30.1

   yes; $\frac{4.3}{1} = \frac{12.9}{3} = \frac{30.1}{7}$

5. The value of y varies directly with x, and $y = -8$ when $x = 20$. Find y when $x = -4$. 1.6

6. Apples cost $0.80 per pound. Write a direct variation equation to describe the cost y of x pounds of apples. Then graph. $y = 0.8x$

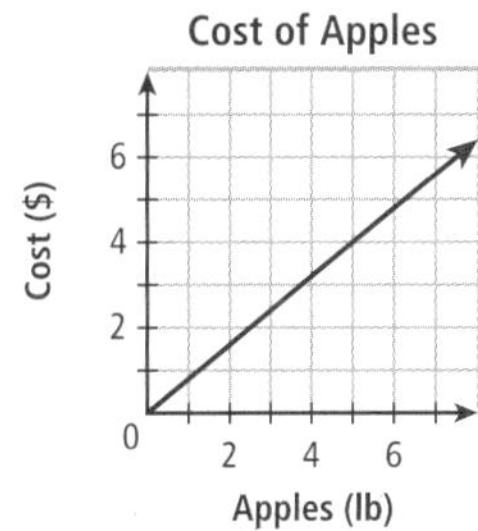

Also available on transparency

Organizer

Objective: Assess students' ability to apply concepts and skills in Lessons 5-1 through 5-6 in a real-world format.

Online Edition

Resources

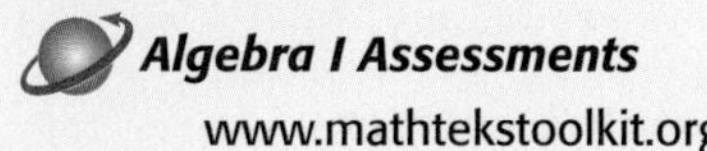

www.mathtekstoolkit.org

Problem	Text Reference
1	Lessons 4-3, 5-1
2	Lessons 5-1, 5-2, 5-3, 5-4
3	Lesson 5-2
4	Lessons 5-3, 5-4
5	Lessons 5-2, 5-3, 5-4
6	Lesson 1-1
7	Lesson 2-9

Answers

1. For table, see p. A21.

2–5, 7. See p. A21.

State Resources

CHAPTER 5

SECTION 5A

Characteristics of Linear Functions

Heart Health People who exercise need to be aware of their maximum heart rate.

1. One way to estimate your maximum heart rate m is to subtract 85% of your age in years from 217. Create a table of values that shows the maximum heart rates for people ages 13 to 18. Then write an equation to describe the data in the table. $m = 217 - 0.85a$
2. Use your table from Problem 1 to graph the relationship between age and maximum heart rate. What are the intercepts? What is the slope?
3. What do the intercepts represent in this situation?
4. What does the slope represent? Explain why the slope is negative.
5. Another formula for estimating maximum heart rate is $m = 206.3 - 0.711a$, where a represents age in years. Describe how this equation is different from your equation in Problem 1. Include slope and intercepts in your description.
6. Which equation gives a higher maximum heart rate for people ages 75 and younger? **the first equation**
7. To be exercising in your *aerobic training zone* means that your heart rate is 70% to 80% of your maximum heart rate. Write two equations that someone could use to estimate the range of heart rates that are within his or her aerobic training zone. Use your equation for maximum heart rate from Problem 1.

Scaffolding Questions

1. What are the independent and dependent variables? independent: age; dependent: maximum heart rate
2. How can you find the slope? Possible answer: Once you know the intercepts, use (255.29, 0) and (0, 217) in the slope formula.
3. What does $a = 0$ represent? age of 0 yr What does $m = 0$ represent? max. heart rate of 0 beats/min Are these values reasonable in this situation? no
4. Does the maximum heart rate increase or decrease with age? How do you know? Decrease; the graph falls from left to right.

5–7. Discuss the variables, intercepts, and slopes in the formulas described.

Extension

Find your maximum heart rate using the method given in **Problem 5.** Then find the range of heart rates that are within your aerobic training zone using this method and the information given in **Problem 7.** Possible answer: For age 14, the maximum rate is about 196 beats/min, and the range is about 137–157 beats/min.

CHAPTER 5

SECTION 5A

Quiz for Lessons 5-1 Through 5-6

5-1 Identifying Linear Functions

Tell whether the given ordered pairs satisfy a linear function. Explain.

1.

x	−2	−1	0	1	2
y	1	0	1	4	9

1. No; a constant change of +1 in x corresponds to diff. changes in y.

2. $\{(-3, 8), (-2, 6), (-1, 4), (0, 2), (1, 0)\}$
Yes; a constant change of +1 in x corresponds to a constant change of −2 in y.

5-2 Using Intercepts

Use intercepts to graph the line described by each equation.

3. $2x - 4y = 16$ 4. $-3y + 6x = -18$ 5. $y = -3x + 3$

5-3 Rate of Change and Slope

6. The chart gives the amount of water in a rain gauge in inches at various times. Graph the data and show the rates of change.

Time (h)	1	2	3	4	5
Rain (in.)	0.2	0.4	0.7	0.8	1.0

5-4 The Slope Formula

Find the slope of each line. Then tell what the slope represents.

7. 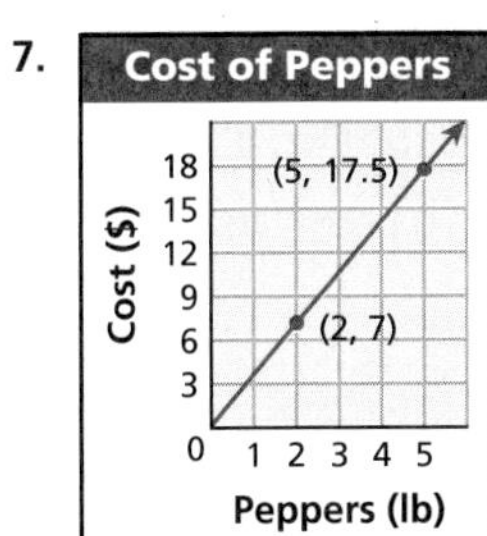

3.5; peppers cost \$3.50/lb.

8. 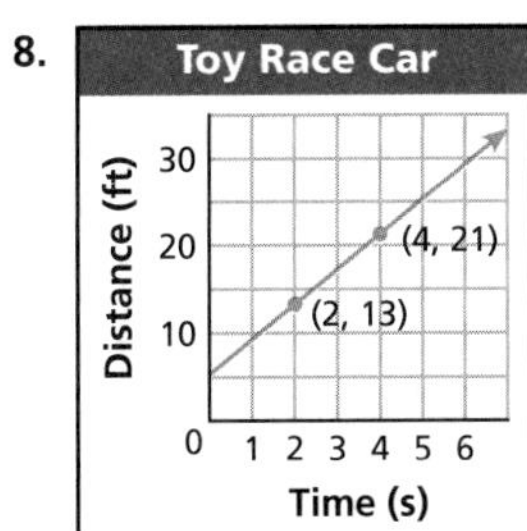

4; speed is 4 ft/s.

9. 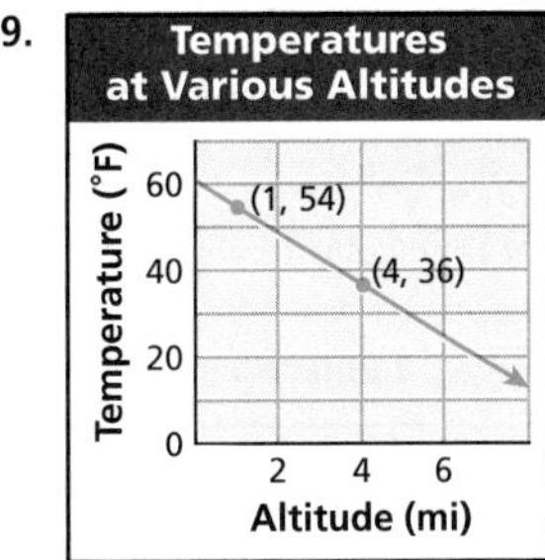

−6; temp. decreases 6 °F/mi.

5-5 The Midpoint and Distance Formulas

10. Find the coordinates of the midpoint of $\overline{XY}$ with endpoints $X(-4, 6)$ and $Y(3, 8)$. $\left(-\frac{1}{2}, 7\right)$

11. On a treasure map, the coordinates of a crooked palm tree are (3, 6), and the coordinates of a buried treasure chest are (12, 18). Each unit on the map represents 10 feet. What is the distance in feet between the palm tree and the treasure chest? 150 ft

5-6 Direct Variation

Tell whether each relationship is a direct variation. If so, identify the constant of variation.

12.

x	1	4	8	12
y	3	6	10	14

no

13.

x	−6	−2	0	3
y	−3	−1	0	1.5

yes; $\frac{1}{2}$

READY TO GO ON? SECTION 5A

Organizer

Objective: Assess students' mastery of concepts and skills in Lessons 5-1 through 5-6.

Resources

Assessment Resources
Section 5A Quiz

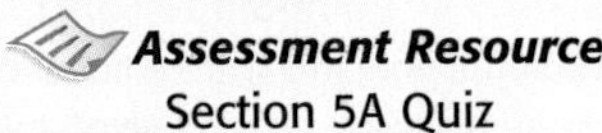

Test & Practice Generator

Answers

3. 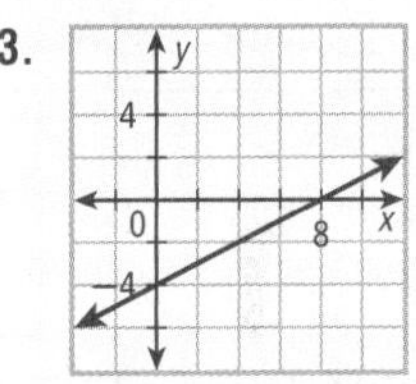

4. 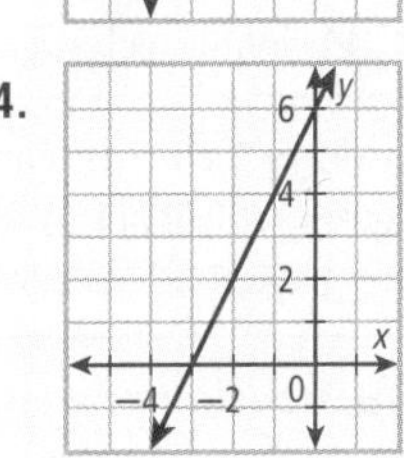

5, 6. See p. A21.

INTERVENTION

Resources

Ready to Go On? Intervention and Enrichment Worksheets

Ready to Go On? CD-ROM

READY TO GO ON? Diagnose and Prescribe

NO INTERVENE

Ready to Go On? Intervention	Ready to Go On? Intervention, Section 5A: Worksheets	CD-ROM	Online
Lesson 5-1	5-1 Intervention	Activity 5-1	Diagnose and Prescribe Online
Lesson 5-2	5-2 Intervention	Activity 5-2	
Lesson 5-3	5-3 Intervention	Activity 5-3	
Lesson 5-4	5-4 Intervention	Activity 5-4	
Lesson 5-5	5-5 Intervention	Activity 5-5	
Lesson 5-6	5-6 Intervention	Activity 5-6	

YES ENRICH

Ready to Go On? Enrichment, Section 5A

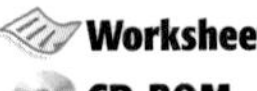

Worksheets
CD-ROM
Online

SECTION
5B Using Linear Functions

One-Minute Section Planner

Lesson	Lab Resources	Materials
Lesson 5-7 Slope-Intercept Form • Write a linear equation in slope-intercept form. • Graph a line using slope-intercept form. ☑ SAT-10 ☑ NAEP ☑ ACT ☑ SAT ☑ SAT Subject Tests	***Algebra Lab Activities*** 5-7 Algebra Lab (A) 5-7 Algebra Lab (B)	**Optional** graphing calculator, masking tape, rope or string, graph paper
Lesson 5-8 Point-Slope Form • Graph a line and write a linear equation using point-slope form. • Write a linear equation given two points. ☑ SAT-10 ☑ NAEP ☑ ACT ☑ SAT ☑ SAT Subject Tests		
5-8 Technology Lab Graph Linear Functions • Use a graphing calculator to graph lines. ☐ SAT-10 ☐ NAEP ☑ ACT ☑ SAT ☑ SAT Subject Tests	***Technology Lab Activities*** 5-8 Lab Recording Sheet	**Required** graphing calculator
Lesson 5-9 Slopes of Parallel and Perpendicular Lines • Identify and graph parallel and perpendicular lines. • Write equations to describe lines parallel or perpendicular to a given line. ☑ SAT-10 ☑ NAEP ☑ ACT ☑ SAT ☑ SAT Subject Tests	***Algebra Lab Activities*** 5-9 Algebra Lab	**Required** graphing calculator
5-10 Technology Lab The Family of Linear Functions • Use a graphing calculator to explore families of functions. ☐ SAT-10 ☐ NAEP ☐ ACT ☑ SAT ☑ SAT Subject Tests	***Technology Lab Activities*** 5-10 Lab Recording Sheet	**Required** graphing calculator
Lesson 5-10 Transforming Linear Functions • Describe how changing slope and *y*-intercept affect the graph of a linear function. ☐ SAT-10 ☑ NAEP ☐ ACT ☑ SAT ☑ SAT Subject Tests		**Optional** graphing calculator, index cards, graph paper
Extension Absolute-Value Functions • Graph absolute-value functions • Identify characteristics of absolute-value functions and their graphs. ☑ SAT-10 ☐ NAEP ☑ ACT ☐ SAT ☐ SAT Subject Tests		**Optional** tracing paper

Note: If NAEP is checked, the content is tested on either the Grade 8 or the Grade 12 NAEP assessment.

MK = *Manipulatives Kit*

MORE ON LINEAR FUNCTIONS

Lessons 5-7, 5-8, 5-10

Any linear function may be written in slope-intercept form, $y = mx + b$, where m is the slope of the line and b is the y-intercept. It is useful to understand how m and b affect the appearance of the line.

For nonnegative values of m, the graph of $y = mx$ is a *rotation* of the graph of $y = x$. The greater the value of m, the steeper the resulting line. The figure shows how $y = 2x$ represents a rotation of $y = x$. When m is negative, the line is reflected across the x-axis, as seen in the graph of $y = -2x$.

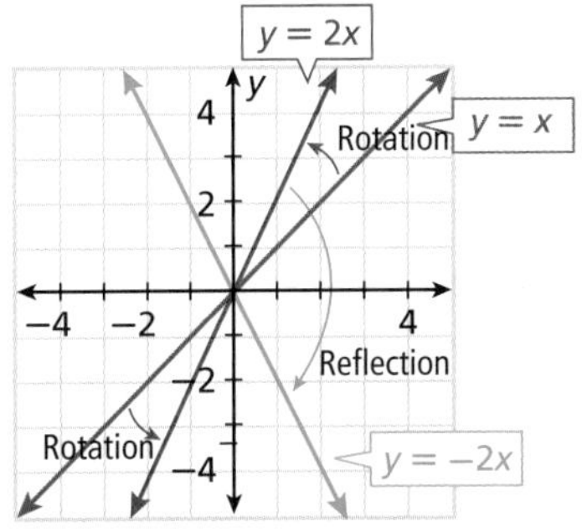

In general, the graph of $y = mx + b$ is a *vertical translation* of the graph of $y = mx$. If b is positive, the translation is upward by b units. If b is negative, the translation is downward by $|b|$ units. Comparing the graphs of $y = x$, $y = x + 3$, $y = x - 2$, and $y = x - 4$ illustrates this.

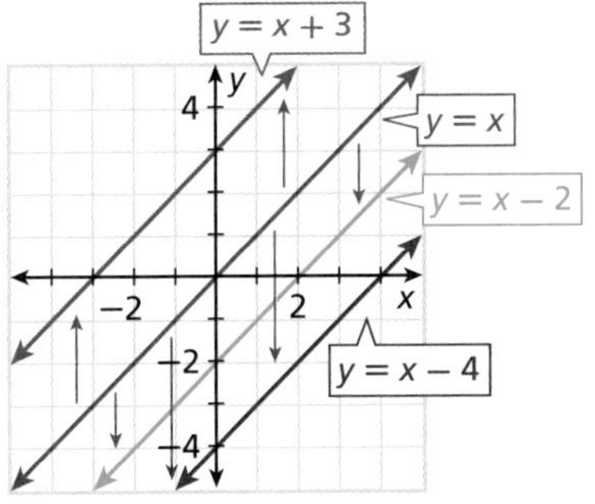

Putting all of these ideas together shows that the graph of every linear function is the result of one or more transformations of the graph of the *parent function* $y = x$. For example, to get the graph of $y = -5x + 3$, the graph of $y = x$ is first rotated, then reflected across the x-axis, and then translated upward by 3 units.

PERPENDICULAR LINES

Lesson 5-9

Two nonvertical lines are perpendicular if and only if the product of their slopes is -1 (or, equivalently, if and only if their slopes are opposite reciprocals). Students should understand the logic of the phrase *if and only if.* It means that the statement is true "in both directions": if nonvertical lines are perpendicular, then the product of their slopes is -1; if the product of the slopes is -1, then the lines are perpendicular.

Students should also be aware that they will have to accept this result as true until they are able to prove it in a geometry course. The main steps in the proof that nonvertical perpendicular lines have slopes whose product is -1 are outlined below.

Assume perpendicular lines k and ℓ intersect at P and that line ℓ has positive slope m. Then it is possible to construct a right triangle PQR that has its hypotenuse along line ℓ and has legs of length m and 1 as shown. Extend $\overline{PR}$ through P and mark off a length of m along the line (at point S). Construct a perpendicular at S to form right triangle TPS. Basic facts from geometry and the ASA triangle congruence theorem show that $\triangle PQR \cong \triangle TPS$. Thus, $\overline{TS} \cong \overline{PR}$ and so $TS = 1$. The slope of $\overline{TP}$ must be $-\frac{1}{m}$, and $-\frac{1}{m} \cdot m = -1$.

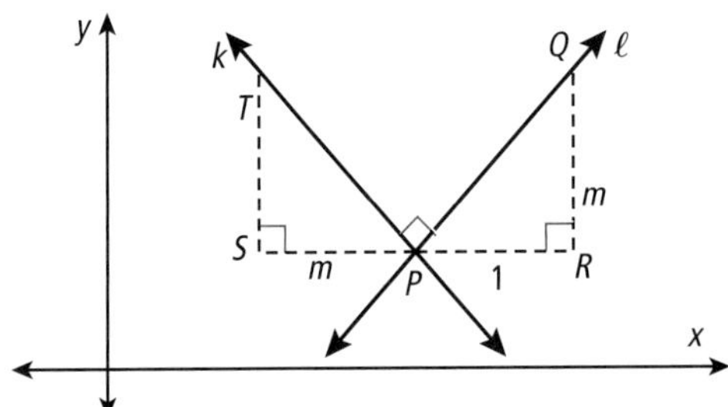

5-7 Organizer

Pacing: Traditional 1 day
Block $\frac{1}{2}$ day

Objectives: Write a linear equation in slope-intercept form.

Graph a line using slope-intercept form.

Online Edition
Tutorial Videos, Interactivity

Countdown Week 11

Power Presentations with PowerPoint®

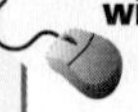

Warm Up

Find each *y*-intercept.

1. $y = 3x + 2$ 2
2. $5x - 3y = 12$ −4

Find each slope.

3. $y = \frac{2}{3}x$ $\frac{2}{3}$
4. $6x + 2y = 6$ −3

Solve each equation for *y*.

5. $4x + 2y = 10$ $y = -2x + 5$
6. $3x + 2 = 6y$ $y = \frac{1}{2}x + \frac{1}{3}$

Also available on transparency

Math Humor

Q: Why was the scientist smiling as he worked?

A: His graph had a great plot!

5-7 Slope-Intercept Form

Objectives
Write a linear equation in slope-intercept form.

Graph a line using slope-intercept form.

Who uses this?
Consumers can use slope-intercept form to model and calculate costs, such as the cost of renting a moving van. (See Example 4.)

You have seen that you can graph a line if you know two points on the line. Another way is to use the slope of the line and the point that contains the *y*-intercept.

EXAMPLE 1 Graphing by Using Slope and *y*-intercept

Graph the line with slope −2 and *y*-intercept 4.

Step 1 The *y*-intercept is 4, so the line contains (0, 4). Plot (0, 4).

Step 2 Slope $= \frac{\text{change in } y}{\text{change in } x} = \frac{-2}{1}$

Count 2 units down and 1 unit right from (0, 4) and plot another point.

Step 3 Draw the line through the two points.

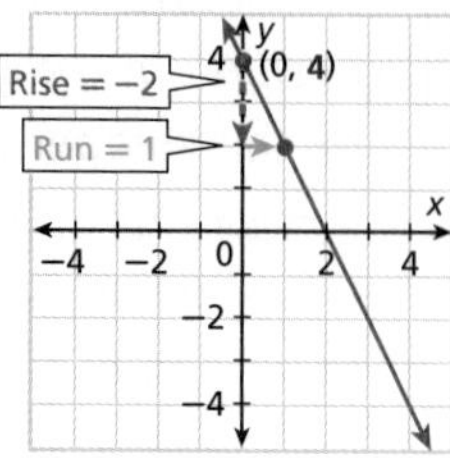

Writing Math
Any integer can be written as a fraction with 1 in the denominator.
$-2 = \frac{-2}{1}$

CHECK IT OUT! **Graph each line given the slope and *y*-intercept.**
1a. slope = 2, *y*-intercept = −3 **1b.** slope = $-\frac{2}{3}$, *y*-intercept = 1

1a.

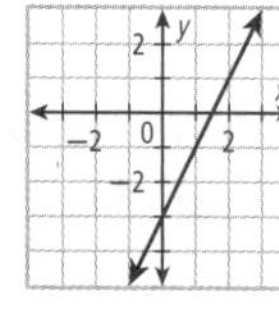

1b.

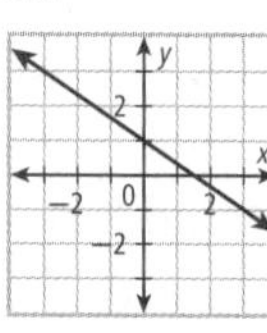

If you know the slope of a line and the *y*-intercept, you can write an equation that describes the line.

Step 1 If a line has slope 2 and the *y*-intercept is 3, then $m = 2$ and (0, 3) is on the line. Substitute these values into the slope formula.

Slope formula → $m = \frac{y_2 - y_1}{x_2 - x_1}$ $2 = \frac{y - 3}{x - 0}$ ← *Since you don't know* (x_2, y_2), *use* (x, y).

Step 2 Solve for *y*: $2 = \frac{y - 3}{x - 0}$

$2 = \frac{y - 3}{x}$ *Simplify the denominator.*

$2 \cdot x = \left(\frac{y - 3}{x}\right) \cdot x$ *Multiply both sides by x.*

$2x = y - 3$

$\underline{+3} \quad \underline{+3}$ *Add 3 to both sides.*

$2x + 3 = y$, or $y = 2x + 3$

State Resources

State Resources Online
KEYWORD: MA7 Resources

1 Introduce

EXPLORATION

5-7 Slope-Intercept Form

You will need graph paper or a graphing calculator for this activity.

1. Graph each function in the table. Once you have made each graph, find the slope of the line and the *y*-intercept. Record your results in the table.

Function	Slope	*y*-intercept
$y = 3x + 2$		
$y = -2x + 4$		
$y = \frac{1}{2}x - 3$		
$y = x + 1$		

2. Describe any patterns you notice in the table.
3. Use your results to predict the slope of the line described by $y = -5x + 7$.
4. Use your results to predict the *y*-intercept of the function $y = -3x - 2$.

THINK AND DISCUSS

5. **Predict** what the graph of $y = \frac{2}{3}x + 4$ will look like.
6. **Explain** how you could write a linear function whose *y*-intercept is 21 and whose graph has a slope of 3.

Motivate

Ask students how they would graph the function $y = 2x + 3$. Possible answers: generate ordered pairs; use intercepts

Then tell students that in this lesson, they will learn a quick way to graph linear functions. It does not involve generating ordered pairs and uses only one intercept.

Explorations and answers are found in *Alternate Openers: Explorations Transparencies.*

Slope-Intercept Form of a Linear Equation

If a line has slope m and the y-intercept is b, then the line is described by the equation $y = mx + b$.

Any linear equation can be written in slope-intercept form by solving for y and simplifying. In this form, you can immediately see the slope and y-intercept. Also, you can quickly graph a line when the equation is written in slope-intercept form.

EXAMPLE 2 Writing Linear Equations in Slope-Intercept Form

Write the equation that describes each line in slope-intercept form.

A slope $= \frac{1}{3}$, y-intercept $= 6$

$y = mx + b$ — *Substitute the given values for m and b.*

$y = \frac{1}{3}x + 6$ — *Simplify if necessary.*

B slope $= 0$, y-intercept $= -5$

$y = mx + b$

$y = 0x + (-5)$

$y = -5$

C

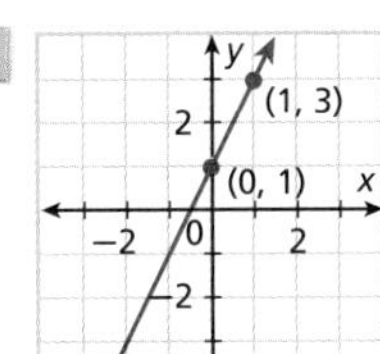

Step 1 Find the y-intercept. The graph crosses the y-axis at $(0, 1)$, so $b = 1$.

Step 2 Find the slope. The line contains the points $(0, 1)$ and $(1, 3)$.

$m = \frac{y_2 - y_1}{x_2 - x_1}$ — *Use the slope formula.*

$m = \frac{3 - 1}{1 - 0} = \frac{2}{1} = 2$ — *Substitute (0, 1) for (x_1, y_1) and (1, 3) for (x_2, y_2).*

Step 3 Write the equation.

$y = mx + b$ — *Write the slope-intercept form.*

$y = 2x + 1$ — *Substitute 2 for m and 1 for b.*

D slope $= 4$, $(2, 5)$ is on the line

Step 1 Find the y-intercept.

$y = mx + b$ — *Write the slope-intercept form.*

$5 = 4(2) + b$ — *Substitute 4 for m, 2 for x, and 5 for y.*

$5 = 8 + b$ — *Solve for b. Since 8 is added to b, subract 8 from both sides to undo the addition.*

$\underline{-8 \quad -8}$

$-3 = b$

Step 2 Write the equation.

$y = mx + b$ — *Write the slope-intercept form.*

$y = 4x + (-3)$ — *Substitute 4 for m and −3 for b.*

$y = 4x - 3$

Write the equation that describes each line in slope-intercept form.

2a. slope $= -12$, y-intercept $= -\frac{1}{2}$

2b. slope $= 1$, y-intercept $= 0$

2c. slope $= 8$, $(-3, 1)$ is on the line.

2a. $y = -12x - \frac{1}{2}$

2b. $y = x$

2c. $y = 8x + 25$

Power Presentations with PowerPoint®

Additional Examples

Example 1

Graph the line with slope $-\frac{2}{5}$ and y-intercept 4.

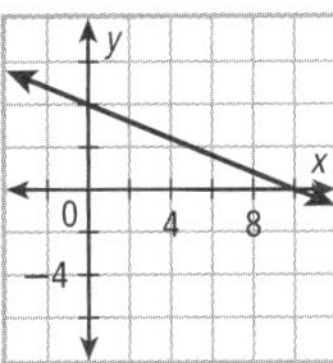

Example 2

Write the equation that describes each line in slope-intercept form.

A. slope $= \frac{1}{4}$; y-intercept $= 4$

$y = \frac{1}{4}x + 4$

B. slope $= -9$; y-intercept $= -\frac{5}{4}$

$y = -9x - \frac{5}{4}$

C.

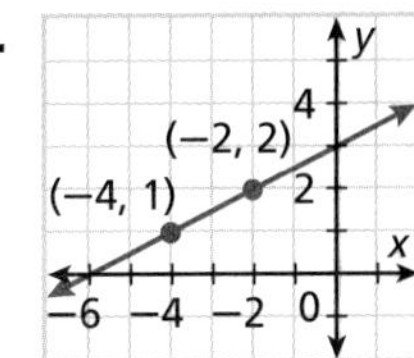

$y = 3x + \frac{1}{2}$

D. slope $= 2$; $(3, 4)$ is on the line. $y = 2x - 2$

INTERVENTION
Questioning Strategies

EXAMPLE 1

- What is the first step when graphing a line given the slope and y-intercept?

EXAMPLE 2

- What does b represent?
- What do the equation and graph look like if $b = 0$?

2 Teach

Guided Instruction

Remind students that slope is the ratio of rise over run. Graph a line such as $y = -\frac{1}{2}x + 2$ in two ways, once using a slope of $\frac{-1}{2}$ and once using a slope of $\frac{1}{-2}$, to show that they result in the same line. In **Example 3,** remind students that they can quickly check that their graph is reasonable by looking at the slope. Lines with positive slopes rise from left to right, and lines with negative slopes fall from left to right.

Reaching All Learners
Through Kinesthetic Experience

Use masking tape to outline a coordinate plane on a floor of square tiles. Then give a pair of students a length of rope. Announce an equation in slope-intercept form, and have the two students move around on the plane so that when they hold the rope taut, it represents the line described by the given equation, with each of them as two points on the line. A third student can check that these two points satisfy the equation.

Power Presentations with PowerPoint®

Additional Examples

Example 3

Write each equation in slope-intercept form. Then graph the line described by the equation.

A. $y = 3x - 1$ $\quad y = 3x - 1$

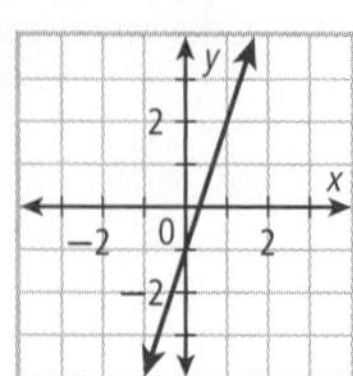

B. $2y + 3x = 6$ $\quad y = -\frac{3}{2}x + 3$

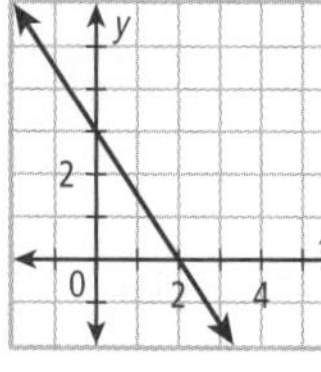

INTERVENTION

Questioning Strategies

EXAMPLE 3

- Does the coefficient of x in a linear equation always equal the slope? Explain.

Multiple Representations Remind students that they could use the intercepts to graph the equation in **Example 3B.**

3a. $y = \frac{2}{3}x$

3b. $y = -3x + 5$

Helpful Hint

To divide $(8 - 3x)$ by 2, you can multiply by $\frac{1}{2}$ and use the Distributive Property.

$\frac{8 - 3x}{2} = \frac{1}{2}(8 - 3x)$

$= \frac{1}{2}(8) + \frac{1}{2}(-3x)$

$= 4 - \frac{3}{2}x$

3c. $y = -4$

EXAMPLE 3 Using Slope-Intercept Form to Graph

Write each equation in slope-intercept form. Then graph the line described by the equation.

A $y = 4x - 3$

$y = 4x - 3$ is in the form $y = mx + b$.

slope: $m = 4 = \frac{4}{1}$

y-intercept: $b = -3$

Step 1 Plot $(0, -3)$.

Step 2 Count **4 units up** and **1 unit right** and plot another point.

Step 3 Draw the line connecting the two points.

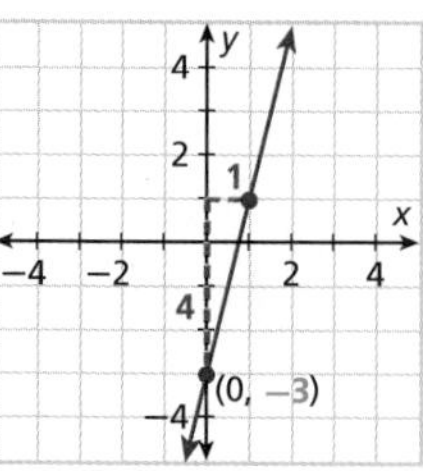

B $y = -\frac{2}{3}x + 2$

$y = -\frac{2}{3}x + 2$ is in the form $y = mx + b$.

slope: $m = -\frac{2}{3} = \frac{-2}{3}$

y-intercept: $b = 2$

Step 1 Plot $(0, 2)$

Step 2 Count **2 units down** and **3 units right** and plot another point.

Step 3 Draw the line connecting the two points.

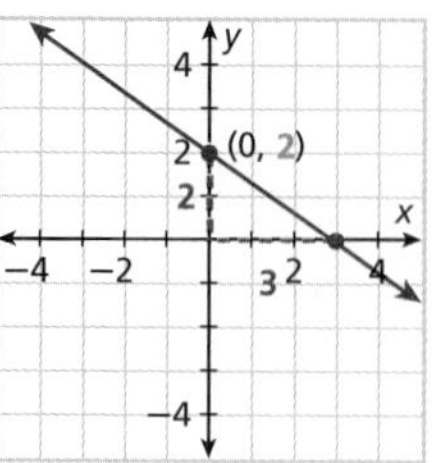

C $3x + 2y = 8$

Step 1 Write the equation in slope-intercept form by solving for y.

$$\begin{aligned} 3x + 2y &= 8 \\ -3x \quad & \quad -3x \end{aligned}$$ *Subtract 3x from both sides.*

$$2y = 8 - 3x$$

$$\frac{2y}{2} = \frac{8 - 3x}{2}$$ *Since y is multiplied by 2, divide both sides by 2.*

$$y = 4 - \frac{3}{2}x$$ $\quad \frac{3x}{2} = \frac{3}{2}x$

$$y = -\frac{3}{2}x + 4$$ *Write the equation in the form $y = mx + b$.*

Step 2 Graph the line.

$y = -\frac{3}{2}x + 4$ is in the form $y = mx + b$.

slope: $m = -\frac{3}{2} = \frac{-3}{2}$

y-intercept: $b = 4$

- Plot $(0, 4)$.
- Then count **3 units down** and **2 units right** and plot another point.
- Draw the line connecting the two points.

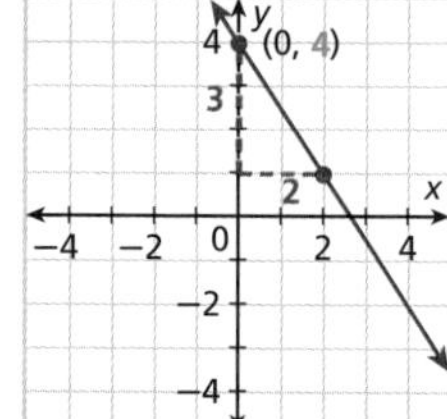

Write each equation in slope-intercept form. Then graph the line described by the equation.

3a. $y = \frac{2}{3}x$ **3b.** $6x + 2y = 10$ **3c.** $y = -4$

Teaching Tip **Inclusion** Students may confuse rise and run when counting slope on a graph. Draw $\frac{\updownarrow}{\leftrightarrow}$ on the board to help them remember which number goes up or down and which goes left or right.

Teaching Tip **Diversity** In **Check it Out 4,** the term *caterer* may be unfamiliar to some students. Explain that a caterer prepares food that is served at a special event, such as a wedding.

ENGLISH LANGUAGE LEARNERS

EXAMPLE 4 Consumer Application

To rent a van, a moving company charges \$30.00 plus \$0.50 per mile. The cost as a function of the number of miles driven is shown in the graph.

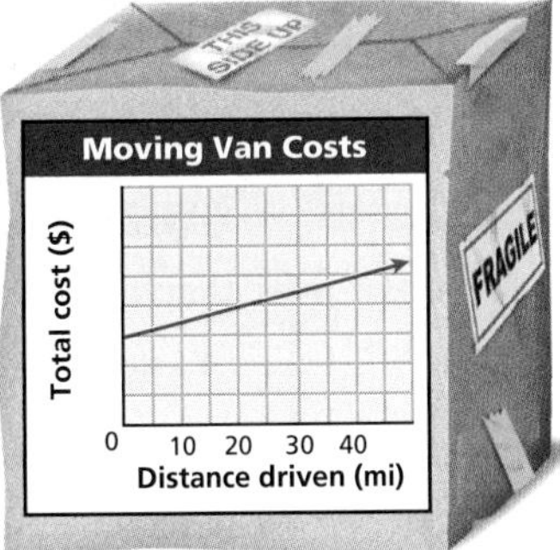

a. Write an equation that represents the cost as a function of the number of miles.

Cost	is	\$0.50 per mile	times	miles	plus	\$30.00
y	=	0.5	•	x	+	30

An equation is $y = 0.5x + 30$.

b. Identify the slope and y-intercept and describe their meanings.

The y-intercept is 30. This is the cost for 0 miles, or the initial fee of \$30.00.

The slope is 0.5. This is the rate of change of the cost: \$0.50 per mile.

c. Find the cost of the van for 150 miles.

$y = 0.5x + 30$

$= 0.5(150) + 30 = 105$ *Substitute 150 for x in the equation.*

The cost of the van for 150 miles is \$105.

4. A caterer charges a \$200 fee plus \$18 per person served. The cost as a function of the number of guests is shown in the graph.
   a. Write an equation that represents the cost as a function of the number of guests. **$y = 18x + 200$**
   b. Identify the slope and y-intercept and describe their meanings.
   c. Find the cost of catering an event for 200 guests. **\$3800**

4b. slope: 18; cost per person; y-int: 200; fee

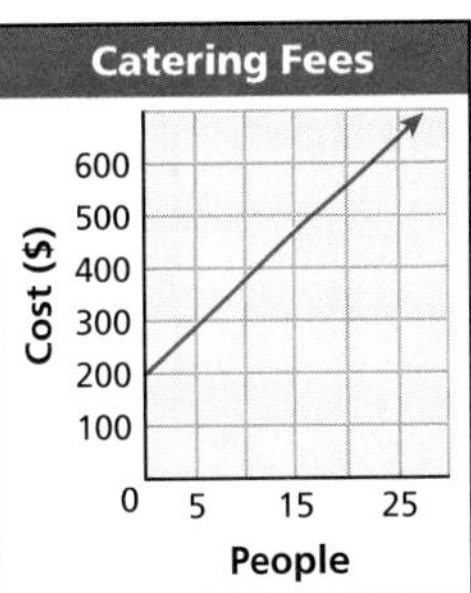

THINK AND DISCUSS

1. If a linear function has a y-intercept of b, at what point does its graph cross the y-axis?
2. Where does the line described by $y = 4.395x - 23.75$ cross the y-axis?
3. **GET ORGANIZED** Copy and complete the graphic organizer.

Know it! Note

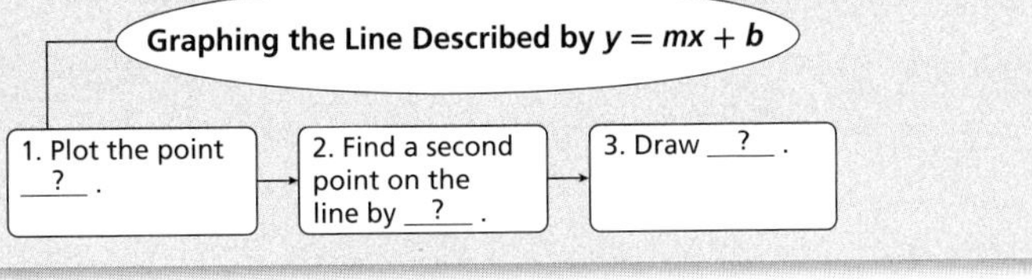

Power Presentations with PowerPoint®

Additional Examples

Example 4

A closet organizer charges a \$100 initial consultation fee plus \$30 per hour. The cost as a function of the number of hours worked is graphed below.

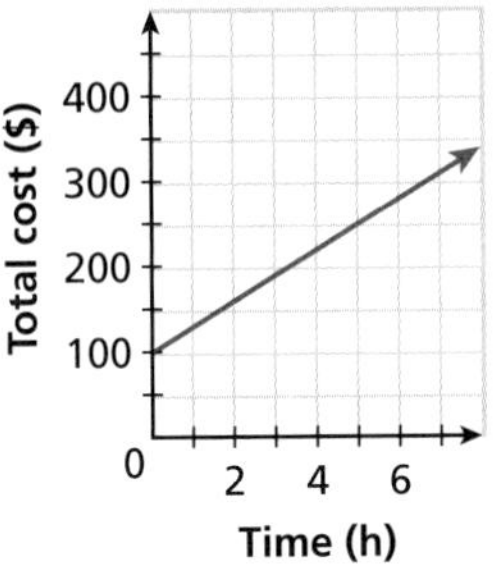

a. Write an equation that represents the cost as a function of the number of hours.
$y = 30x + 100$

b. Identify the slope and y-intercept and describe their meanings. y-int.: 100; the cost for 0 h, or the initial fee of \$100. Slope: 30; the rate of change of the cost: \$30/h.

c. Find the cost if the organizer works 12 hours. \$460

INTERVENTION 
Questioning Strategies

EXAMPLE 4

- Why doesn't the graph start at the origin?

3 Close

Summarize

Review slope-intercept form, reminding students that an integer slope can be written with a denominator of 1. Review how to write an equation of a line in slope-intercept form when given the slope and y-intercept or when given the slope and a point on the line.

ONGOING ASSESSMENT and INTERVENTION 

***Diagnose Before* the Lesson**
5-7 Warm Up, TE p. 344

***Monitor During* the Lesson**
Check It Out! Exercises, SE pp. 344–347
Questioning Strategies, TE pp. 345–347

***Assess After* the Lesson**
5-7 Lesson Quiz, TE p. 350
Alternative Assessment, TE p. 350

Answers to *Think and Discuss*

1. $(0, b)$
2. $(0, -23.75)$
3. See p. A5.

Assignment Guide

Assign *Guided Practice* exercises as necessary.

If you finished Examples **1–2**
Basic 14–22
Average 14–22, 42
Advanced 14–22, 42

If you finished Examples **1–4**
Basic 14–27, 32–41, 45–50
Average 14–31, 35–42, 45–50
Advanced 14–31, 35–50

Homework Quick Check
Quickly check key concepts.
Exercises: 14, 18, 20, 24, 26, 36

Answers

1. 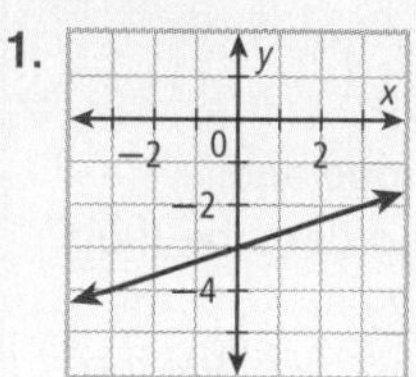
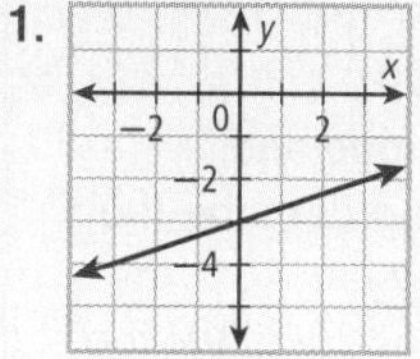

2–4. See p. A21.
10–12. For graphs, see p. A22.
14–17. See p. A22.

State Resources

5-7 Exercises

GUIDED PRACTICE

SEE EXAMPLE 1 p. 344

Graph each line given the slope and y-intercept.

1. slope $= \frac{1}{3}$, y-intercept $= -3$
2. slope $= 0.5$, y-intercept $= 3.5$
3. slope $= 5$, y-intercept $= -1$
4. slope $= -2$, y-intercept $= 2$

SEE EXAMPLE 2 p. 345

Write the equation that describes each line in slope-intercept form.

5. 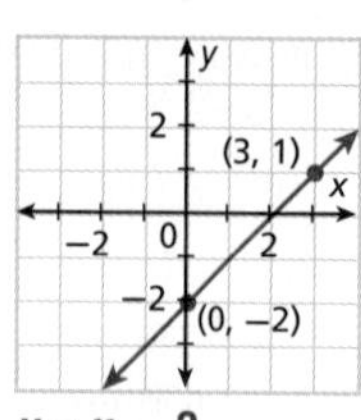

$y = x - 2$

6. slope $= 8$, y-intercept $= 2$ $\quad y = 8x + 2$
7. slope $= 0$, y-intercept $= -3$ $\quad y = -3$
8. slope $= 5$, $(2, 7)$ is on the line. $\quad y = 5x - 3$
9. slope $= -2$, $(1, -3)$ is on the line. $\quad y = -2x - 1$

SEE EXAMPLE 3 p. 346

Write each equation in slope-intercept form. Then graph the line described by the equation.

10. $y = \frac{2}{5}x - 6$ $\quad y = \frac{2}{5}x - 6$
11. $3x - y = 1$ $\quad y = 3x - 1$
12. $2x + y = 4$ $\quad y = -2x + 4$

SEE EXAMPLE 4 p. 347

13. Helen is in a bicycle race. She has already biked 10 miles and is now biking at a rate of 18 miles per hour. Her distance as a function of time is shown in the graph.
    a. Write an equation that represents the distance Helen has biked as a function of time. $\quad y = 18x + 10$
    b. Identify the slope and y-intercept and describe their meanings.
    c. How far will Helen have biked after 2 hours? $\quad$ 46 mi

13b. slope: 18; Helen's speed; y-int.: 10; dist. she has already biked

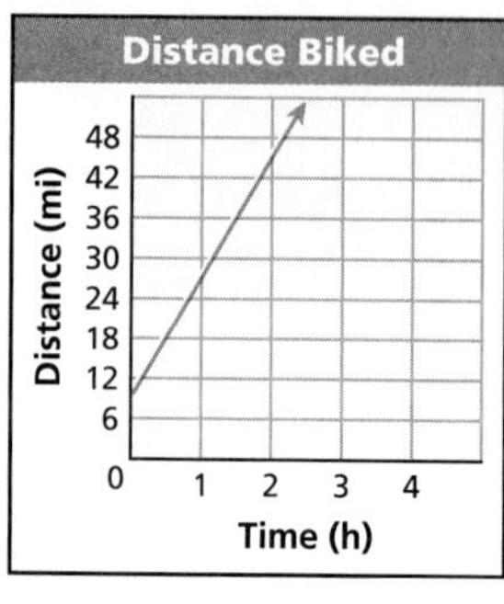

PRACTICE AND PROBLEM SOLVING

For Exercises	See Example
14–17	1
19–22	2
23–25	3
26	4

Independent Practice

Extra Practice
Skills Practice p. S13
Application Practice p. S32

Graph each line given the slope and y-intercept.

14. slope $= \frac{1}{4}$, y-intercept $= 7$
15. slope $= -6$, y-intercept $= -3$
16. slope $= 1$, y-intercept $= -4$
17. slope $= -\frac{4}{5}$, y-intercept $= 6$

Write the equation that describes each line in slope-intercept form.

18. 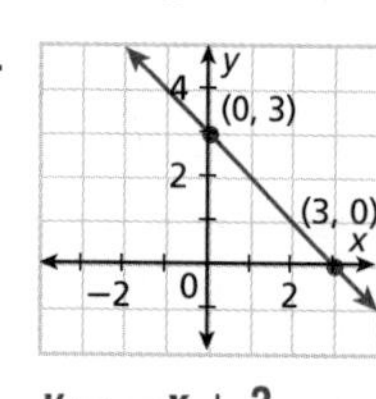

$y = -x + 3$

19. slope $= 5$, y-intercept $= -9$ $\quad y = 5x - 9$
20. slope $= -\frac{2}{3}$, y-intercept $= 2$ $\quad y = -\frac{2}{3}x + 2$
21. slope $= -\frac{1}{2}$, $(6, 4)$ is on the line. $\quad y = -\frac{1}{2}x + 7$
22. slope $= 0$, $(6, -8)$ is on the line. $\quad y = -8$

5-7 READING STRATEGIES

The procedure outlined below shows how to graph a line using slope-intercept form.

Graph the line described by $2x + y = 4$.

Step 1: Rewrite in slope-intercept form.
$2x + y = 4$
$-2x \quad -2x$
$y = -2x + 4$

Step 2: Identify the slope and y-intercept.
$y = mx + b$
$m = -2 = \frac{-2}{1}$
$b = 4$

Step 3: Plot the point $(0, b)$

Step 4: Plot a second point using the slope.

Step 5: Draw a line through the points.

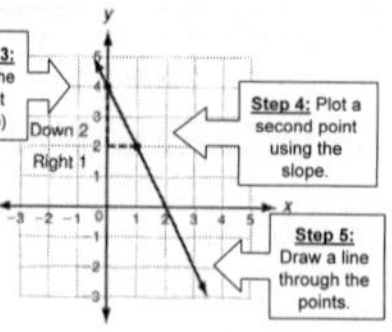

Down 2
Right 1

Answer the following.

1. What is the benefit of always writing slope as a fraction?
   With a fraction, you have a "rise" and "run" for graphing.
2. What point would you plot first if $b = -8$? $\quad (0, -8)$

Identify the slope and y-intercept for each equation.

3. $y = 5x + 12$ $\quad m$: 5 $\quad b$: 12
4. $y = -3x$ $\quad m$: −3 $\quad b$: 0
5. $y = x - 4$ $\quad m$: 1 $\quad b$: −4
6. $3y = x + 9$ $\quad m$: $\frac{1}{3}$ $\quad b$: 12

Graph the line described by each equation.

7. $3x + y = 2$ 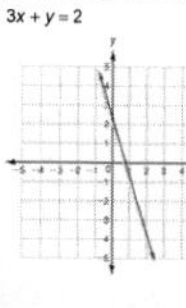
8. $x - 2y = 6$

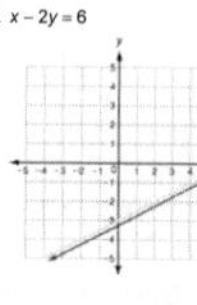

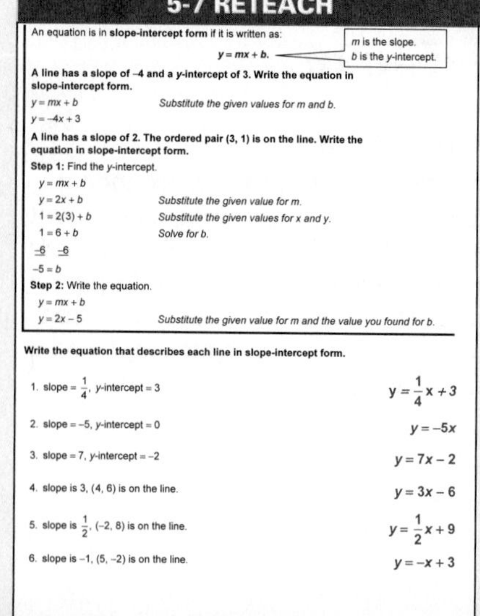

5-7 RETEACH

An equation is in **slope-intercept form** if it is written as:

$y = mx + b$. — m is the slope. b is the y-intercept.

A line has a slope of −4 and a y-intercept of 3. Write the equation in slope-intercept form.

$y = mx + b$ — *Substitute the given values for m and b.*
$y = -4x + 3$

A line has a slope of 2. The ordered pair (3, 1) is on the line. Write the equation in slope-intercept form.

Step 1: Find the y-intercept.
$y = mx + b$
$y = 2x + b$ — *Substitute the given value for m.*
$1 = 2(3) + b$ — *Substitute the given values for x and y.*
$1 = 6 + b$ — *Solve for b.*
$-6 \quad -6$
$-5 = b$

Step 2: Write the equation.
$y = mx + b$
$y = 2x - 5$ — *Substitute the given value for m and the value you found for b.*

Write the equation that describes each line in slope-intercept form.

1. slope $= \frac{1}{4}$, y-intercept $= 3$ $\quad y = \frac{1}{4}x + 3$
2. slope $= -5$, y-intercept $= 0$ $\quad y = -5x$
3. slope $= 7$, y-intercept $= -2$ $\quad y = 7x - 2$
4. slope is 3, $(4, 6)$ is on the line. $\quad y = 3x - 6$
5. slope is $\frac{1}{2}$, $(-2, 8)$ is on the line. $\quad y = \frac{1}{2}x + 9$
6. slope is −1, $(5, -2)$ is on the line. $\quad y = -x + 3$

Write each equation in slope-intercept form. Then graph the line described by the equation.

23. $-\frac{1}{2}x + y = 4$ **24.** $\frac{2}{3}x + y = 2$ **25.** $2x + y = 8$

26. Fitness Pauline's health club has an enrollment fee of \$175 and costs \$35 per month. Total cost as a function of number of membership months is shown in the graph.

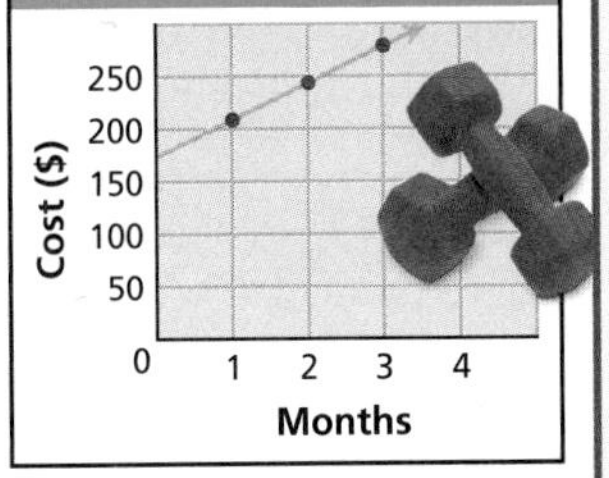

a. Write an equation that represents the total cost as a function of months. **$y = 35x + 175$**

b. Identify the slope and y-intercept and describe their meanings.

c. Find the cost of one year of membership. **\$595**

Health Club Membership Costs

Cost (\$): 0, 50, 100, 150, 200, 250; Months: 0, 1, 2, 3, 4

26b. slope: 35; monthly cost; y-int.: 175; enrollment fee

27. A company rents video games. The table shows the linear relationship between the number of games a customer can rent at one time and the monthly cost of the service.

a. Graph the relationship.

b. Write an equation that represents the monthly cost as a function of games rented at one time. **$y = 4x + 10$**

Games Rented at One Time	1	2	3
Monthly Cost (\$)	14	18	22

Critical Thinking Tell whether each situation is possible or impossible. If possible, draw a sketch of the graphs. If impossible, explain.

28. Two different lines have the same slope. **possible**

29. Two different linear functions have the same y-intercept. **possible**

30. Two intersecting lines have the same slope. **impossible**

31. A linear function does not have a y-intercept. **impossible**

Match each equation with its corresponding graph.

32. 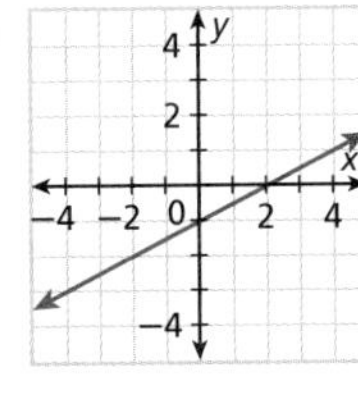 **B** **33.** 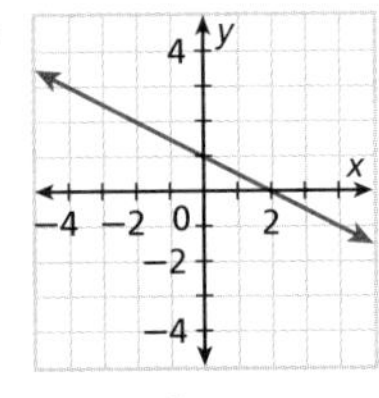  **C** **34.** 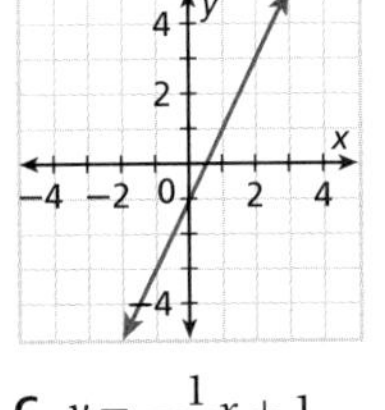 **A**

A. $y = 2x - 1$ B. $y = \frac{1}{2}x - 1$ C. $y = -\frac{1}{2}x + 1$

35. Possible answer: $x = -4$; no; because it has an undef. slope and no y-int.

35. Write About It Write an equation that describes a vertical line. Can you write this equation in slope-intercept form? Why or why not?

36. This problem will prepare you for the Multi-Step Test Prep on page 376.

a. Ricardo and Sam walk from Sam's house to school. Sam lives 3 blocks from Ricardo's house. The graph shows their distance from Ricardo's house as they walk to school. Create a table of these values.

b. Find an equation for the distance as a function of time.

c. What are the slope and y-intercept? What do they represent in this situation?

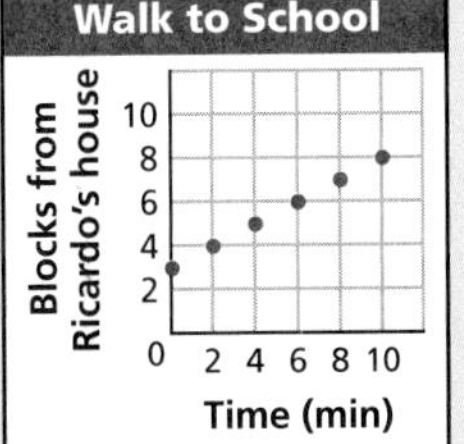

Exercise 36 involves graphing and interpreting a linear equation in slope-intercept form. This exercise prepares students for the Multi-Step Test Prep on page 376.

Answers

23–25, 27a. See p. A22.

28. 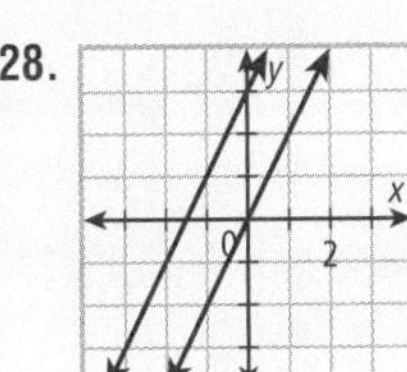

29. 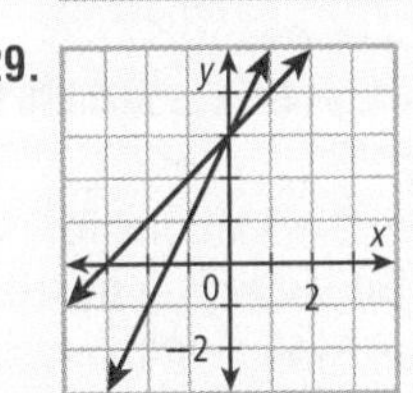

30. Lines with the same slope are par. and therefore cannot intersect.

31. If a lin. func. does not have a y-int., then its graph does not intersect the y-axis. The y-axis is vert. so the only lines that do not intersect the y-axis are also vert. But vert. lines cannot be graphs of functions. All nonvert. lines will intersect the y-axis, so every lin. func. will have a y-int.

36a.

x	y
0	3
2	4
4	5
6	6
8	7
10	8

b. $y = \frac{1}{2}x + 3$

c. slope: $\frac{1}{2}$; boys' walking speed; y-int.: 3; dist. from Sam's house to Ricardo's house

5-7 PROBLEM SOLVING

The cost of food for an honor roll dinner is \$300 plus \$10 per student. The cost of the food as a function of the number of students is shown in the graph. Write the correct answer.

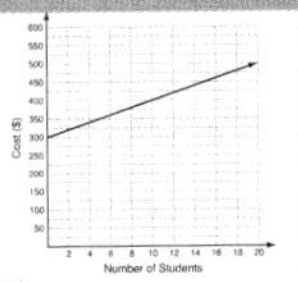

1. Write an equation that represents the cost as a function of the number of students.

   $y = 10x + 300$

2. Identify the slope and y-intercept and describe their meanings.

   slope: 10, rate of the change of the cost: \$10 per student; y-int: 300, the initial fee (the cost for 0 students)

3. Find the cost of the food for 50 students. **\$800**

Laura is on a two-day hike in the Smoky Mountains. She hiked 8 miles on the first day and is hiking at a rate of 3 mi/h on the second day. Her total distance as a function of time is shown in the graph. Select the best answer.

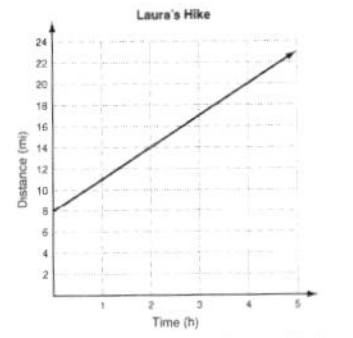

Laura's Hike

4. Which equation represents Laura's total distance as a function of time?

   A $y = 3x$ **C** $y = 3x + 8$
   B $y = 8x$ D $y = 8x + 3$

5. What does the slope represent?

   F Laura's total distance after one day
   G Laura's total distance after two days
   H the number of miles Laura hiked per hour on the first day
   J the number of miles Laura hikes per hour on the second day

6. What does the y-intercept represent?

   A Laura's total distance after one day
   B Laura's total distance after two days
   C the number of miles Laura hiked per hour on the first day
   D the number of miles Laura hikes per hour on the second day

7. What will be Laura's total distance if she hikes for 6 hours on the second day?

   F 14 miles **H** 26 miles
   G 18 miles J 28 miles

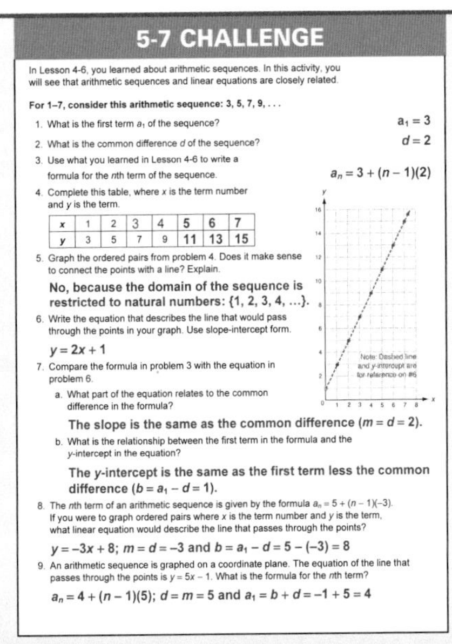

5-7 CHALLENGE

In Lesson 4-6, you learned about arithmetic sequences. In this activity, you will see that arithmetic sequences and linear equations are closely related.

For 1–7, consider this arithmetic sequence: 3, 5, 7, 9, . . .

1. What is the first term a_1 of the sequence? $a_1 = 3$
2. What is the common difference d of the sequence? $d = 2$
3. Use what you learned in Lesson 4-6 to write a formula for the nth term of the sequence. $a_n = 3 + (n - 1)(2)$
4. Complete this table, where x is the term number and y is the term.

x	1	2	3	4	5	6	7
y	3	5	7	9	11	13	15

5. Graph the ordered pairs from problem 4. Does it make sense to connect the points with a line? Explain.

   No, because the domain of the sequence is restricted to natural numbers: {1, 2, 3, 4, ...}.

6. Write the equation that describes the line that would pass through the points in your graph. Use slope-intercept form.

   $y = 2x + 1$

7. Compare the formula in problem 3 with the equation in problem 6.

   a. What part of the equation relates to the common difference in the formula?

   The slope is the same as the common difference ($m = d = 2$).

   b. What is the relationship between the first term in the formula and the y-intercept in the equation?

   The y-intercept is the same as the first term less the common difference ($b = a_1 - d = 1$).

8. The nth term of an arithmetic sequence is given by the formula $a_n = 5 + (n - 1)(-3)$. If you were to graph ordered pairs where x is the term number and y is the term, what linear equation would describe the line that passes through the points?

   $y = -3x + 8$; $m = d = -3$ and $b = a_1 - d = 5 - (-3) = 8$

9. An arithmetic sequence is graphed on a coordinate plane. The equation of the line that passes through the points is $y = 5x - 1$. What is the formula for the nth term?

   $a_n = 4 + (n - 1)(5)$; $d = m = 5$ and $a_1 = b + d = -1 + 5 = 4$

Note: Dashed line and y-intercept are for reference on #6

5-7 PRACTICE A

5-7 PRACTICE C

5-7 PRACTICE B

Write the equation that describes each line in slope-intercept form.

1. slope = 4; y-intercept = −3

   y = $y = 4x - 3$

2. slope = −2; y-intercept = 0

   y = $y = -2x$

3. slope = $-\frac{1}{3}$; y-intercept = 6

   y = $y = -\frac{1}{3}x + 6$

4. slope = $\frac{2}{5}$, (10, 3) is on the line.

   Find the y-intercept $y = mx + b$

   $3 = \left(\frac{2}{5}\right)10 + b$

   $3 = 4 + b$

   $-1 = b$

   Write the equation: $y = \frac{2}{5}x - 1$

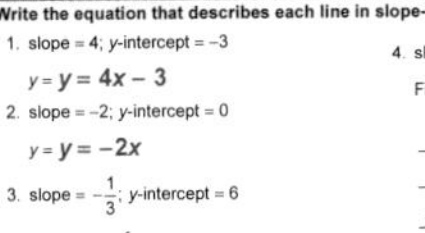
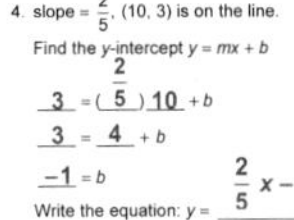

Write each equation in slope-intercept form. Then graph the line described by the equation.

5. $y + x = 3$ 6. $y + 4 = \frac{4}{3}x$ 7. $5x - 2y = 10$

   $y = -x + 3$ $y = \frac{4}{3}x - 4$ $y = \frac{5}{2}x - 5$

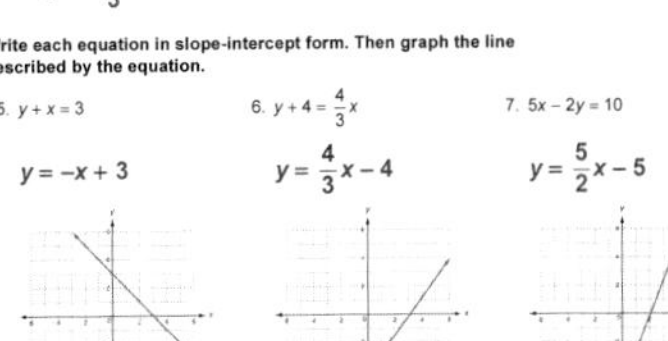

8. Daniel works as a volunteer in a homeless shelter. So far, he has worked 22 hours, and he plans to continue working 3 hours per week. His hours worked as a function of time is shown in the graph.

   a. Write an equation that represents the hours Daniel will work as a function of time. $y = 3x + 22$

   b. Identify the slope and y-intercept and describe their meanings. slope: 3; number of hours per week; y-int: 22; hours already worked

   c. Find the number of hours worked after 16 weeks. 70 hours

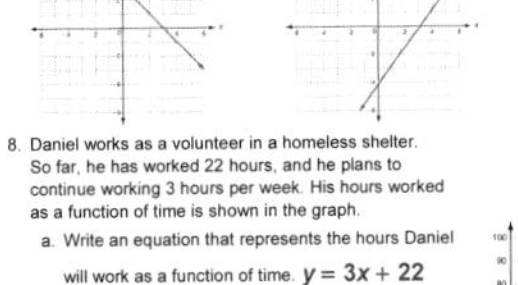

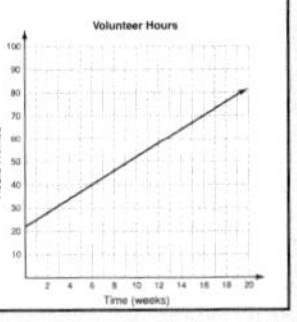

In **Exercise 37,** students who chose **C** chose a function whose graph has the same slope, but not the same y-intercept. Students who chose **D** may have forgotten to divide by -2.

Journal

Have students describe three different ways to graph a line.

Have students write equations for 4 lines: one whose slope is a positive integer, one whose slope is a negative integer, and two whose slopes are fractions. Three should be in slope-intercept form, and one in standard form. Then have them trade equations with a partner, who will ensure that the above conditions are met and then graph the lines.

Power Presentations with PowerPoint®

5-7 Lesson Quiz

Write the equation that describes each line in slope-intercept form.

1. slope $= 3$, y-intercept $= -2$ $y = 3x - 2$
2. slope $= 0$, y-intercept $= \frac{1}{2}$ $y = \frac{1}{2}$
3. slope $= \frac{3}{2}$, $(2, 7)$ is on the line. $y = \frac{3}{2}x + 4$

Write each equation in slope-intercept form. Then graph the line described by the equation.

4. $6x + 2y = 10$ $y = -3x + 5$

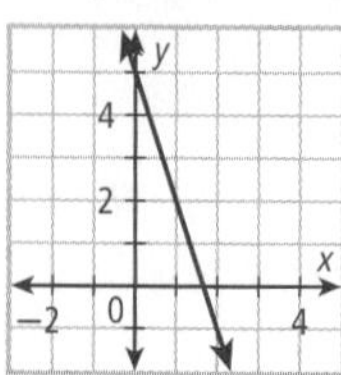

5. $x - y = 6$ $y = x - 6$

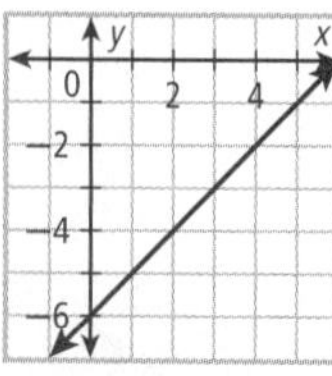

37. Which function has the same y-intercept as $y = \frac{1}{2}x - 2$?

  Ⓐ $2x + 3y = 6$ **Ⓑ $x + 4y = -8$** Ⓒ $-\frac{1}{2}x + y = 4$ Ⓓ $\frac{1}{2}x - 2y = -2$

38. What is the slope-intercept form of $x - y = -8$?

  Ⓕ $y = -x - 8$ Ⓖ $y = x - 8$ Ⓗ $y = -x + 8$ **Ⓙ $y = x + 8$**

39. Which function has a y-intercept of 3?

  Ⓐ $2x - y = 3$ **Ⓑ $2x + y = 3$** Ⓒ $2x + y = 6$ Ⓓ $y = 3x$

40. **Gridded Response** What is the slope of the line described by $-6x = -2y + 5$? **3**

41. **Short Response** Write a function whose graph has the same slope as the line described by $3x - 9y = 9$ and the same y-intercept as $8x - 2y = 6$. Show your work. $y = \frac{1}{3}x - 3$

CHALLENGE AND EXTEND

42. $y = -\frac{A}{B}x + \frac{C}{B}$; slope $= -\frac{A}{B}$; y-int.: $\frac{C}{B}$

42. The standard form of a linear equation is $Ax + By = C$. Rewrite this equation in slope-intercept form. What is the slope? What is the y-intercept?

43. What value of n in the equation $nx + 5 = 3y$ would give a line with slope -2? **−6**

44. If b is the y-intercept of a linear function whose graph has slope m, then $y = mx + b$ describes the line. Below is an incomplete justification of this statement. Fill in the missing information.

Statements	Reasons
1. $m = \frac{y_2 - y_1}{x_2 - x_1}$	1. Slope formula
2. $m = \frac{y - b}{x - 0}$	2. By definition, if b is the y-intercept, then $(\mathbf{0}, b)$ is a point on the line. (x, y) is any other point on the line.
3. $m = \frac{y - b}{x}$	3. **Any number minus 0 is the number itself.**
4. $m\,\mathbf{x} = y - b$	4. Multiplication Property of Equality (Multiply both sides of the equation by x.)
5. $mx + b = y$, or $y = mx + b$	5. **Addition Property of Equality (Add b to both sides.)**

SPIRAL REVIEW

Define a variable and write an inequality for each situation. Graph the solutions. *(Lesson 3-1)*

45. Molly has, at most, 2 hours to work out at the gym today. **h = hours; $h \le 2$ where h is nonnegative**

46. Mishenko is hoping to save at least \$300 this month. **s = savings; $s \ge 300$**

Solve each inequality. *(Lesson 3-5)*

47. $3n \le 2n + 8$ **$n \le 8$**
48. $4x - 4 > 2(x + 5)$ **$x > 7$**
49. $2(2t + 1) > 6t + 8$ **$t < -3$**

50. The amount of water conditioner needed for an aquarium varies directly with the capacity of the aquarium. For every 10 gallons of water, you need 1 teaspoon of conditioner. Write a direct variation equation for the amount of water conditioner y needed for an aquarium that holds x gallons of water. Then graph. *(Lesson 5-6)* $y = \frac{1}{10}x$

Answers

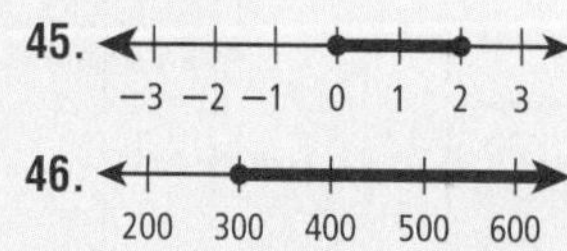

50.

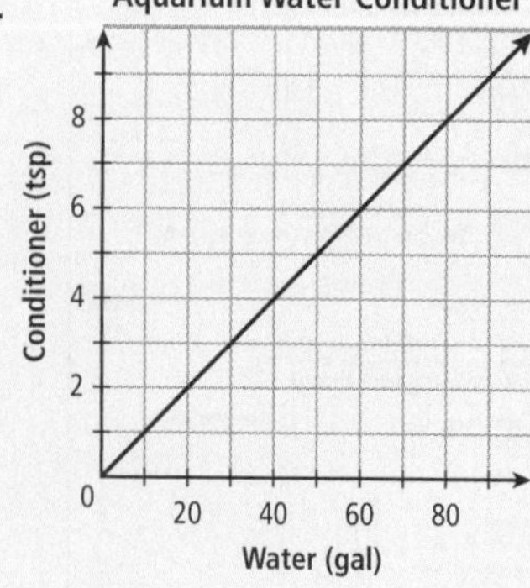

5-8 Point-Slope Form

Objectives
Graph a line and write a linear equation using point-slope form.
Write a linear equation given two points.

Why learn this?
You can use point-slope form to represent a cost function, such as the cost of placing a newspaper ad. (See Example 5.)

If you know the slope and any point on the line, you can write an equation of the line by using the slope formula. For example, suppose a line has a slope of 3 and contains (2, 1). Let (x, y) be any other point on the line.

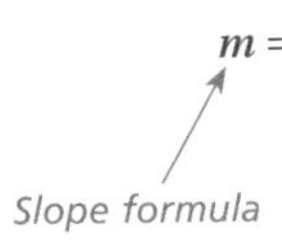

$$m = \frac{y_2 - y_1}{x_2 - x_1} \longrightarrow 3 = \frac{y-1}{x-2}$$ *Substitute into the slope formula.*

Slope formula

$$3(x-2) = \left(\frac{y-1}{x-2}\right)(x-2)$$ *Multiplication Property of Equality*

$$3(x-2) = y - 1$$ *Simplify.*

$$y - 1 = 3(x-2)$$

Point-Slope Form of a Linear Equation

The line with slope m that contains the point (x_1, y_1) can be described by the equation $y - y_1 = m(x - x_1)$.

EXAMPLE 1 Writing Linear Equations in Point-Slope Form

Write an equation in point-slope form for the line with the given slope that contains the given point.

A slope $= \frac{5}{2}$; $(-3, 0)$

$y - y_1 = m(x - x_1)$ *Write the point-slope form.*

$y - 0 = \frac{5}{2}[x - (-3)]$ *Substitute $\frac{5}{2}$ for m, −3 for x_1, and 0 for y_1.*

$y - 0 = \frac{5}{2}(x + 3)$ *Rewrite subtraction of negative numbers as addition.*

B slope $= -7$; $(4, 2)$

$y - y_1 = m(x - x_1)$

$y - 2 = -7(x - 4)$

C slope $= 0$; $(-2, -3)$

$y - y_1 = m(x - x_1)$

$y - (-3) = 0[x - (-2)]$

$y + 3 = 0(x + 2)$

CHECK IT OUT! Write an equation in point-slope form for the line with the given slope that contains the given point.

1a. slope $= 2$; $\left(\frac{1}{2}, 1\right)$ $y - 1 = 2\left(x - \frac{1}{2}\right)$

1b. slope $= 0$; $(3, -4)$ $y + 4 = 0(x - 3)$

5-8 Organizer

Pacing: Traditional 1 day
Block $\frac{1}{2}$ day

Objectives: Graph a line and write a linear equation using point-slope form.

Write a linear equation given two points.

Online Edition
Tutorial Videos

Countdown Week 11

Power Presentations with PowerPoint®

Warm Up

Find the slope of the line containing each pair of points.

1. (0, 2) and (3, 4) $\frac{2}{3}$
2. (−2, 8) and (4, 2) −1
3. (3, 3) and (12, −15) −2

Write the following equations in slope-intercept form.

4. $y - 5 = 3(x + 2)$ $y = 3x + 11$
5. $3x + 4y + 20 = 0$
   $y = -\frac{3}{4}x - 5$

Also available on transparency

Math Humor

Q: What did the horizontal line say to the vertical line?

A: It was nice running into you.

1 Introduce

EXPLORATION

5-8 Point-Slope Form

In this activity, you will investigate another way to write linear equations.

1a. Does the line described by $y - 4 = 5(x - 3)$ contain the point (3, 4)? How do you know?
b. What is the slope of the line described by $y - 4 = 5(x - 3)$?
2a. Does the line described by $y - 2 = \frac{1}{2}(x - 1)$ contain the point (1, 2)? How do you know?
b. What is the slope of the line described by $y - 2 = \frac{1}{2}(x - 1)$?
3a. Does the line described by $y - 6 = -3(x - 12)$ contain the point (12, 6)? How do you know?
b. What is the slope of the line described by $y - 6 = -3(x - 12)$?
4. Describe any patterns you notice in Problems 1–3.

THINK AND DISCUSS

5. **Explain** how you can use the patterns you discovered to make some predictions about the line described by $y + 2 = -2(x + 3)$.
6. **Discuss** what equation you think describes a line with slope 4 that contains the point (5, 8). Explain your reasoning.

Motivate

Plot the points (−3, 2) and (1, −6) on a coordinate grid. Ask students to find the slope of the line that contains these two points. −2 Then ask what additional information they would need to write the equation of the line using slope-intercept form. the *y*-intercept

Tell students that in this lesson, they will learn a new formula to write an equation of a line, using any two points on the line.

Explorations and answers are found in *Alternate Openers: Explorations Transparencies.*

State Resources

Power Presentations with PowerPoint®

Additional Examples

Example 1

Write an equation in point-slope form for the line with the given slope that contains the given point.

A. slope $= \frac{1}{6}$; $(5, 1)$

$y - 1 = \frac{1}{6}(x - 5)$

B. slope $= -4$; $(0, 3)$

$y - 3 = -4(x - 0)$

C. slope $= 1$; $(-1, -4)$

$y + 4 = 1(x + 1)$

Example 2

Graph the line described by each equation.

A. $y - 1 = 2(x - 3)$

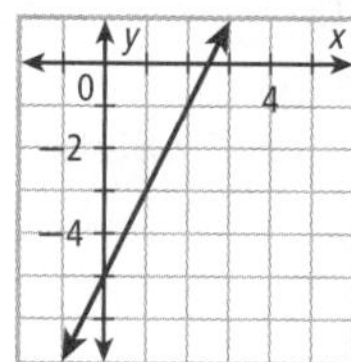

B. $y - 4 = \frac{3}{4}(x + 2)$

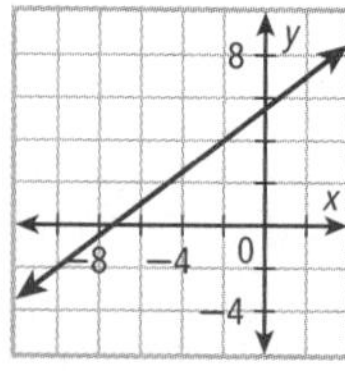

C. $y + 3 = 0(x - 4)$

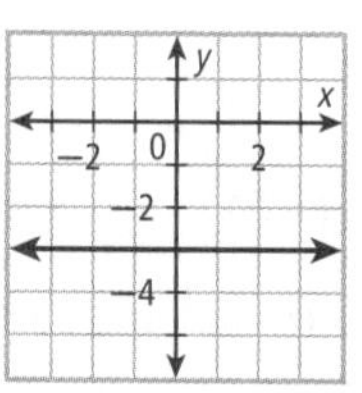

In Lesson 5-7, you graphed a line given its equation in slope-intercept form. You can also graph a line when given its equation in point-slope form. Start by using the equation to identify a point on the line. Then use the slope of the line to identify a second point.

EXAMPLE 2 Using Point-Slope Form to Graph

Graph the line described by each equation.

A $y - 1 = 3(x - 1)$

$y - 1 = 3(x - 1)$ is in the form $y - y_1 = m(x - x_1)$.

The line contains the point $(1, 1)$.

slope: $m = 3 = \frac{3}{1}$

Step 1 Plot $(1, 1)$.

Step 2 Count 3 units up and 1 unit right and plot another point.

Step 3 Draw the line connecting the two points.

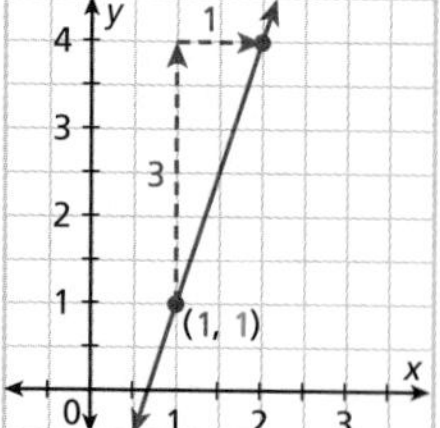

B $y + 2 = -\frac{1}{2}(x - 3)$

Step 1 Write the equation in point-slope form: $y - y_1 = m(x - x_1)$.

$y - (-2) = -\frac{1}{2}(x - 3)$ *Rewrite addition of 2 as subtraction of −2.*

Step 2 Graph the line.

The line contains the point $(3, -2)$.

slope: $m = -\frac{1}{2} = \frac{1}{-2}$

- Plot $(3, -2)$.
- Count 1 unit up and 2 units left and plot another point.
- Draw the line connecting the two points.

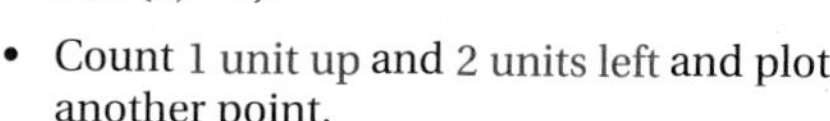

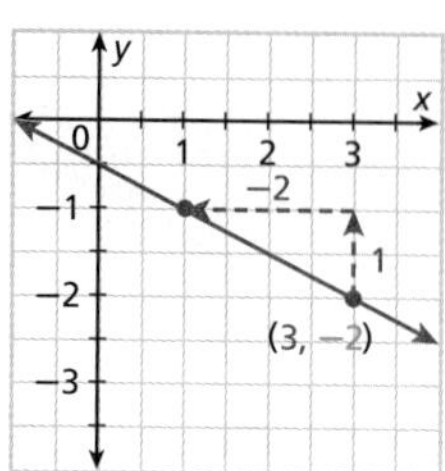

Helpful Hint

For a negative fraction, you can write the negative sign in one of three places.

$-\frac{1}{2} = \frac{-1}{2} = \frac{1}{-2}$

CHECK IT OUT! **Graph the line described by each equation.**

2a. $y + 2 = -(x - 2)$ **2b.** $y + 3 = -2(x - 1)$

2a.

2b.

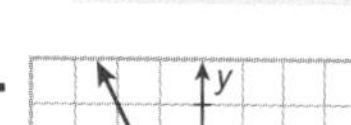

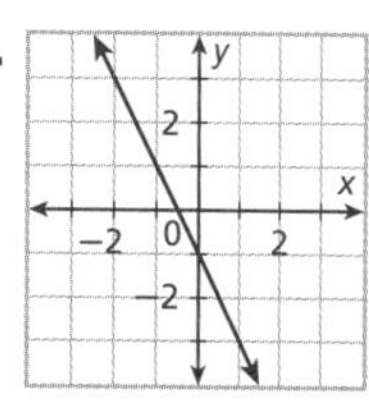

EXAMPLE 3 Writing Linear Equations in Slope-Intercept Form

Write the equation that describes each line in slope-intercept form.

A **slope $= -4$, $(-1, -2)$ is on the line.**

Step 1 Write the equation in point-slope form: $y - y_1 = m(x - x_1)$.

$y - (-2) = -4[x - (-1)]$

Step 2 Write the equation in slope-intercept form by solving for y.

$y - (-2) = -4[x - (-1)]$

$y + 2 = -4(x + 1)$ *Rewrite subtraction of negative numbers as addition. Distribute −4 on the right side.*

$y + 2 = -4x - 4$

$\underline{-2} \quad \underline{-2}$ *Subtract 2 from both sides.*

$y = -4x - 6$

INTERVENTION

Questioning Strategies

EXAMPLE 1

- How do you use the point to write the equation?

EXAMPLE 2

- How could you check that the graph is reasonable?

2 Teach

Guided Instruction

Show students that they can graph a line starting at *any* point on the line if they know the slope, by counting vertically and horizontally from that point. Show how point-slope form comes from the slope formula, and show how it also simplifies to slope-intercept form. Ask students why you might want to rewrite an equation that is in point-slope form in slope-intercept form. Possible answer: because you can quickly graph when an equation is written in slope-intercept form

Reaching All Learners

Through Auditory Cues

Have students work in pairs to quiz each other out loud about the various forms of a linear equation. Have one student state a linear equation, such as $3x + y = 8$ or $y = 2x + 2$, and have the other tell which form the equation is in (standard, slope-intercept, or point-slope). Then have students reverse roles. If time permits, reverse the exercise, so that the first student states a form and the second student gives an equation in that form.

B **(1, −4) and (3, 2) are on the line.**

Step 1 Find the slope.

$$m = \frac{y_2 - y_1}{x_2 - x_1} = \frac{2 - (-4)}{3 - 1} = \frac{6}{2} = 3$$

Step 2 Substitute the slope and one of the points into the point-slope form. Then write the equation in slope-intercept form.

$y - y_1 = m(x - x_1)$

$y - 2 = 3(x - 3)$ *Use (3, 2).*

$y - 2 = 3x - 9$ *Distribute 3 on the right side.*

$y = 3x - 7$ *Add 2 to both sides.*

C **x-intercept = −2, y-intercept = 4**

Step 1 Use the intercepts to find two points: (−2, 0) and (0, 4).

Step 2 Find the slope.

$$m = \frac{y_2 - y_1}{x_2 - x_1} = \frac{4 - 0}{0 - (-2)} = \frac{4}{2} = 2$$

Step 3 Write the equation in slope-intercept form.

$y = mx + b$ *Write the slope-intercept form.*

$y = 2x + 4$ *Substitute 2 for m and 4 for b.*

Write the equation that describes each line in slope-intercept form.

3a. slope $= \frac{1}{3}$, (−3, 1) is on the line. $y = \frac{1}{3}x + 2$

3b. (1, −2) and (3, 10) are on the line. $y = 6x - 8$

EXAMPLE 4 Using Two Points to Find Intercepts

The points (4, 8) and (−1, −12) are on a line. Find the intercepts.

Step 1 Find the slope.

$$m = \frac{y_2 - y_1}{x_2 - x_1} = \frac{-12 - 8}{-1 - 4} = \frac{-20}{-5} = 4$$

Step 2 Write the equation in slope-intercept form.

$y - y_1 = m(x - x_1)$ *Write the point-slope form.*

$y - 8 = 4(x - 4)$ *Substitute (4, 8) for (x_1, y_1) and 4 for m.*

$y - 8 = 4x - 16$ *Distribute 4 on the right side.*

$y = 4x - 8$ *Add 8 to both sides.*

Step 3 Find the intercepts.

x-intercept:

$y = 4x - 8$ *Replace y with 0 and solve for x.*

$0 = 4x - 8$

$8 = 4x$

$2 = x$

y-intercept:

$y = 4x - 8$ *Use the slope-intercept form to identify the y-intercept.*

$b = -8$

The x-intercept is 2, and the y-intercept is −8.

4. The points (2, 15) and (−4, −3) are on a line. Find the intercepts. **x-intercept: −3, y-intercept: 9**

COMMON ERROR ALERT

When calculating slope, students may put negative numbers in the y_1 and x_1 positions but forget to change subtraction of a negative number to addition. Remind them that subtracting a negative number is the same as adding a positive number.

Power Presentations with PowerPoint®

Additional Examples

Example 3

Write the equation that describes each line in slope-intercept form.

A. slope = 3, (−1, 4) is on the line. $y = 3x + 7$

B. (2, −3) and (4, 1) are on the line. $y = 2x - 7$

C. x-intercept $= \frac{1}{4}$, y-intercept = 1 $y = -4x + 1$

Example 4

The points (10, −3) and (5, −2) are on a line. Find the intercepts. x-int.: −5; y-int.: −1

INTERVENTION

Questioning Strategies

EXAMPLE 3

- How do you switch from point-slope form to slope-intercept form?
- Given two points, what are the steps in writing an equation of the line through those points?

EXAMPLE 4

- How do you determine the intercepts once you have written the linear equation in slope-intercept form?

Teaching Tip **Communicating Math** Once students have been introduced to multiple methods for graphing a line, discuss with them which method is easiest for different situations.

Power Presentations with PowerPoint®

Additional Examples

Example 5

The cost to stain a deck is a linear function of the deck's area. The costs to stain 100, 250, and 400 square feet are shown in the table. Write an equation in slope-intercept form that represents the function. Then find the cost to stain a deck whose area is 75 square feet.

Area (ft^2)	Cost ($)
100	150
250	337.50
400	525

$y = 1.25x + 25$; $118.75

INTERVENTION

Questioning Strategies

EXAMPLE 5

- How can you find a point on the line?
- How can you find the slope of the line?

Inclusion Encourage students to look for ways to make problems easier to solve. In **Example 5,** any two points can be used to find the slope, but some pairs may be easier to work with than others.

EXAMPLE 5 Problem-Solving Application

The cost to place an ad in a newspaper for one week is a linear function of the number of lines in the ad. The costs for 3, 5, and 10 lines are shown. Write an equation in slope-intercept form that represents the function. Then find the cost of an ad that is 18 lines long.

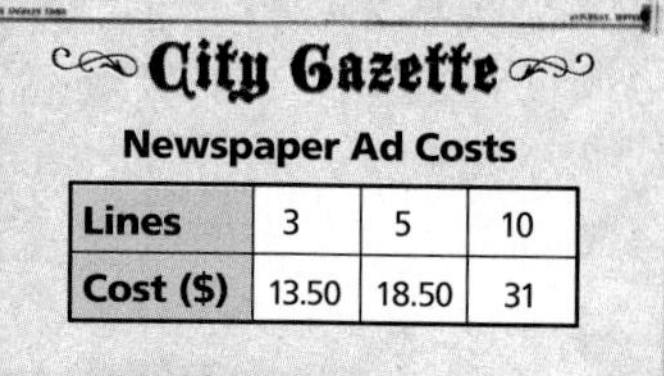

City Gazette

Newspaper Ad Costs

Lines	3	5	10
Cost ($)	13.50	18.50	31

1 Understand the Problem

- The **answer** will have two parts—an equation in slope-intercept form and the cost of an ad that is 18 lines long.
- The ordered pairs given in the table satisfy the equation.

2 Make a Plan

First, find the slope. Then use point-slope form to write the equation. Finally, write the equation in slope-intercept form.

3 Solve

Step 1 Choose any two ordered pairs from the table to find the slope.

$$m = \frac{y_2 - y_1}{x_2 - x_1} = \frac{18.50 - 13.50}{5 - 3} = \frac{5}{2} = 2.5$$ *Use (3, 13.50) and (5, 18.50).*

Step 2 Substitute the slope and any ordered pair from the table into the point-slope form.

$y - y_1 = m(x - x_1)$

$y - 31 = 2.5(x - 10)$ *Use (10, 31).*

Step 3 Write the equation in slope-intercept form by solving for y.

$y - 31 = 2.5(x - 10)$

$y - 31 = 2.5x - 25$ *Distribute 2.5.*

$y = 2.5x + 6$ *Add 31 to both sides.*

Step 4 Find the cost of an ad containing 18 lines by substituting 18 for x.

$y = 2.5x + 6$

$y = 2.5(18) + 6 = 51$

The cost of an ad containing 18 lines is $51.

4 Look Back

Check the equation by substituting the ordered pairs (3, 13.50) and (5, 18.50).

$y = 2.5x + 6$	
13.50	2.5(3) + 6
13.5	7.5 + 6
13.5	13.5 ✓

$y = 2.5x + 6$	
18.50	2.5(5) + 6
18.5	12.5 + 6
18.5	18.5 ✓

CHECK IT OUT!

5. What if...? At a different newspaper, the costs to place an ad for one week are shown. Write an equation in slope-intercept form that represents this linear function. Then find the cost of an ad that is 21 lines long.

Lines	Cost ($)
3	12.75
5	17.25
10	28.50

$y = 2.25x + 6$; $53.25

3 Close

Summarize

Ask students what they would need to do *first*, given the following information, before writing an equation in slope-intercept form.

slope and (0, 3)	Use the point (0, 3) to identify the y-intercept.
slope and (2, 2)	Write the equation in point-slope form.
2 points on the line	Find the slope.
point-slope form	Simplify.

ONGOING ASSESSMENT and INTERVENTION

Diagnose Before the Lesson
5-8 Warm Up, TE p. 351

Monitor During the Lesson
Check It Out! Exercises, SE pp. 351–354
Questioning Strategies, TE pp. 352–354

Assess After the Lesson
5-8 Lesson Quiz, TE p. 358
Alternative Assessment, TE p. 358

THINK AND DISCUSS

1. How are point-slope form and slope-intercept form alike? different?
2. When is point-slope form useful? When is slope-intercept form useful?

3. **GET ORGANIZED** Copy and complete the graphic organizer. In each box, describe how to find the equation of a line by using the given method.

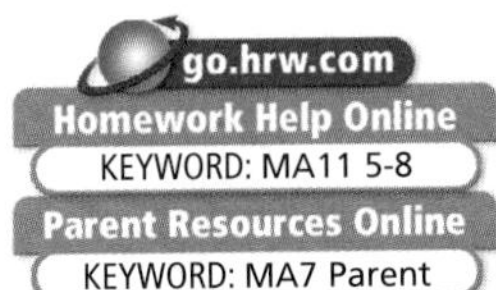

Answers to *Think and Discuss*

1. Both are based on the slope and a point. Slope-int.: uses the point that contains the y-int.; point-slope: can use any point.
2. Point slope: when you know the slope and a point or 2 points; slope-int.: when you know the slope and the y-int.
3. See p. A5.

5-8 Exercises

go.hrw.com
Homework Help Online
KEYWORD: MA11 5-8
Parent Resources Online
KEYWORD: MA7 Parent

GUIDED PRACTICE

SEE EXAMPLE 1 p. 351

Write an equation in point-slope form for the line with the given slope that contains the given point.

1. slope $= \frac{1}{5}$; $(2, -6)$ $y + 6 = \frac{1}{5}(x - 2)$
2. slope $= -4$; $(1, 5)$ $y - 5 = -4(x - 1)$
3. slope $= 0$; $(3, -7)$ $y + 7 = 0(x - 3)$

SEE EXAMPLE 2 p. 352

Graph the line described by each equation.

4. $y - 1 = -(x - 3)$
5. $y + 2 = -2(x + 4)$
6. $y + 1 = -\frac{1}{2}(x + 4)$

SEE EXAMPLE 3 p. 352

Write the equation that describes each line in slope-intercept form.

7. slope $= -\frac{1}{3}$, $(-3, 8)$ is on the line.
8. slope $= 2$; $(1, 1)$ is on the line.
9. $(-2, 2)$ and $(2, -2)$ are on the line.
10. $(1, 1)$ and $(-5, 3)$ are on the line.
11. x-intercept $= 8$, y-intercept $= 4$
12. x-intercept $= -2$, y-intercept $= 3$

SEE EXAMPLE 4 p. 353

Each pair of points is on a line. Find the intercepts.

13. $(5, 2)$ and $(7, 4)$ **x-int.: 3; y-int.: −3**
14. $(-1, 5)$ and $(-3, -5)$ **x-int.: −2; y-int.: 10**
15. $(2, 9)$ and $(-4, -9)$ **x-int.: −1; y-int.: 3**

SEE EXAMPLE 5 p. 354

16. **Measurement** An oil tank is being filled at a constant rate. The depth of the oil is a function of the number of minutes the tank has been filling, as shown in the table. Write an equation in slope-intercept form that represents this linear function. Then find the depth of the oil after one-half hour. $y = \frac{1}{5}x + 3$; 9 ft

Time (min)	Depth (ft)
0	3
10	5
15	6

PRACTICE AND PROBLEM SOLVING

Write an equation in point-slope form for the line with the given slope that contains the given point.

17. slope $= \frac{2}{9}$; $(-1, 5)$
18. slope $= 0$; $(4, -2)$ $y + 2 = 0(x - 4)$
19. slope $= 8$; $(1, 8)$ $y - 8 = 8(x - 1)$

17. $y - 5 = \frac{2}{9}(x + 1)$

Assignment Guide

Assign *Guided Practice* exercises as necessary.

If you finished Examples **1–3**
- **Basic** 17–30, 37–39, 44–49
- **Average** 17–30, 37–39, 44–48
- **Advanced** 17–30, 37–39, 44–48, 56–58

If you finished Examples **1–5**
- **Basic** 17–39, 43–49, 52–55, 59–63
- **Average** 17–39, 43–48, 50–56, 59–63
- **Advanced** 17–48, 50–63

Homework Quick Check
Quickly check key concepts.
Exercises: 18, 20, 24, 32, 34, 36

State Resources

go.hrw.com
State Resources Online
KEYWORD: MA7 Resources

Answers

4. 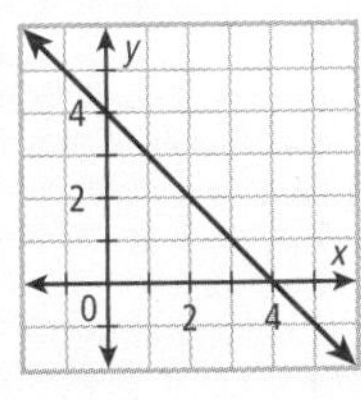

5. 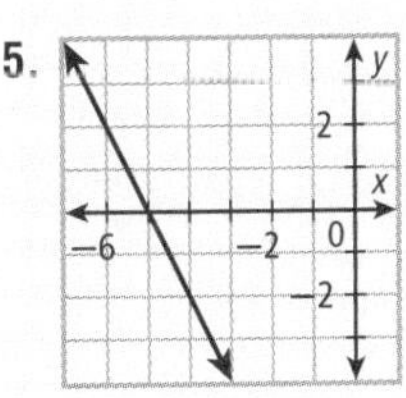

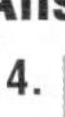

6. (graph)

7. $y = -\frac{1}{3}x + 7$
8. $y = 2x - 1$
9. $y = -x$
10. $y = -\frac{1}{3}x + \frac{4}{3}$
11. $y = -\frac{1}{2}x + 4$
12. $y = \frac{3}{2}x + 3$

Science Link Exercise 35 involves finding the boiling point of water in degrees Fahrenheit. Students can check their equation by substituting the altitude at sea level (0) into the equation and checking that the boiling temperature is 212 °F.

Answers

20.

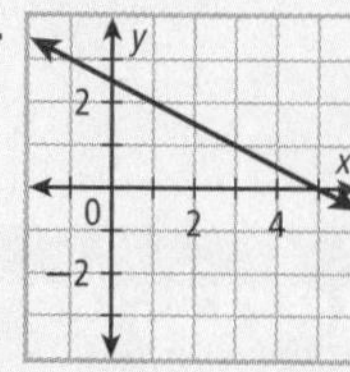

21.

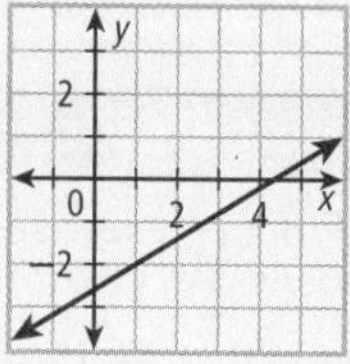

22.

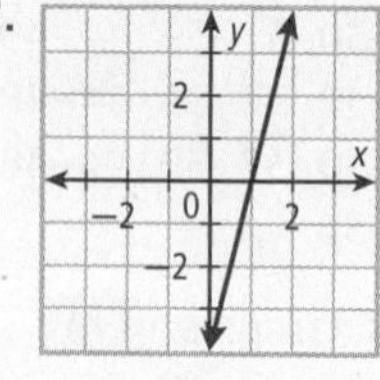

23. $y = -\frac{2}{7}x + 1$

24. $y = \frac{4}{5}x + 13$

25. $y = -6x + 57$

26. $y = \frac{1}{7}x + 7$

27. $y = -\frac{11}{2}x + 18$

28. $y = -5x - 3$

29. $y = 2x - 6$

30. $y = \frac{1}{4}x - 1$

31. x-int.: 1; y-int.: −2

32. x-int.: 6; y-int.: 8

33. x-int.: −6; y-int.: 9

35. $y = -\frac{1}{500}x + 212$; 200 °F

36b. −0.95; the change in the amount in dollars remaining on the card after each download

c. 20; the initial amount in dollars on the card

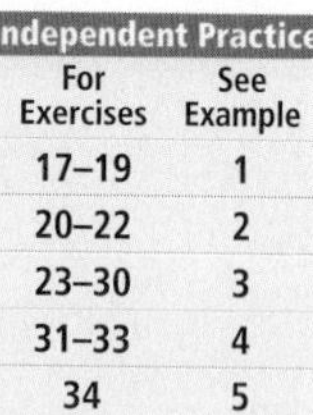

Independent Practice	
For Exercises	See Example
17–19	1
20–22	2
23–30	3
31–33	4
34	5

Extra Practice

Skills Practice p. S13

Application Practice p. S32

Graph the line described by each equation.

20. $y - 4 = -\frac{1}{2}(x + 3)$

21. $y + 2 = \frac{3}{5}(x - 1)$

22. $y - 0 = 4(x - 1)$

Write the equation that describes each line in slope-intercept form.

23. slope $= -\frac{2}{7}$, (14, −3) is on the line.

24. slope $= \frac{4}{5}$, (−15, 1) is on the line.

25. slope = −6, (9, 3) is on the line.

26. (7, 8) and (−7, 6) are on the line.

27. (2, 7) and (4, −4) are on the line.

28. (−1, 2) and (4, −23) are on the line.

29. x-intercept = 3, y-intercept = −6

30. x-intercept = 4, y-intercept = −1

Each pair of points is on a line. Find the intercepts.

31. (−1, −4) and (6, 10)

32. (3, 4) and (−6, 16)

33. (4, 15) and (−2, 6)

34. **History** The amount of fresh water left in the tanks of a 19th-century clipper ship is a linear function of the time since the ship left port, as shown in the table. Write an equation in slope-intercept form that represents the function. Then find the amount of water that will be left in the ship's tanks 50 days after leaving port. **$y = -45x + 3600$; 1350 gal**

Fresh Water Aboard Ship	
Time (days)	Amount (gal)
1	3555
8	3240
15	2925

Science

As altitude increases, the amount of breathable oxygen decreases. At elevations above 8000 feet, this can cause altitude sickness. To prevent this, mountain climbers often use tanks containing a mixture of air and pure oxygen.

35. **Science** At higher altitudes, water boils at lower temperatures. This relationship between altitude and boiling point is linear. At an altitude of 1000 feet, water boils at 210 °F. At an altitude of 3000 feet, water boils at 206 °F. Write an equation in slope-intercept form that represents this linear function. Then find the boiling point at 6000 feet.

36. **Consumer Economics** Lora has a gift card from an online music store where all downloads cost the same amount. After downloading 2 songs, the balance on her card was \$18.10. After downloading a total of 5 songs, the balance was \$15.25.
    a. Write an equation in slope-intercept form that represents the amount in dollars remaining on the card as a function of songs downloaded. **$y = -0.95x + 20$**
    b. Identify the slope of the line and tell what the slope represents.
    c. Identify the y-intercept of the line and tell what it represents.
    d. How many additional songs can Lora download when there is \$15.25 left on the card? **16 songs**

Graph the line with the given slope that contains the given point.

37. slope = −3; (2, 4)

38. slope $= -\frac{1}{4}$; (0, 0)

39. slope $= \frac{1}{2}$; (−2, −1)

Tell whether each statement is sometimes, always, or never true.

40. A line described by the equation $y = mx + b$ contains the point (0, b). **always**

41. The slope of the line that contains the points (0, 0) and (c, d) is negative if both c and d are negative. **never**

42. The y-intercept of the graph of $y - y_1 = m(x - x_1)$ is negative if y_1 is negative. **sometimes**

43. **Meteorology** Snowfall accumulates at an average rate of 2.5 inches per hour during a snowstorm. Two hours after the snowstorm begins, the average depth of snow on the ground is 11 inches.
    a. Write an equation in point-slope form that represents the depth of the snow in inches as a function of hours since the snowstorm began. **$y - 11 = 2.5(x - 2)$**
    b. How much snow is on the ground when the snowstorm starts? **6 in.**
    c. The snowstorm begins at 2:15 P.M. and continues until 6:30 P.M. How much snow is on the ground at the end of the storm? **$16\frac{5}{8}$ in.**

Answers

37.

38.

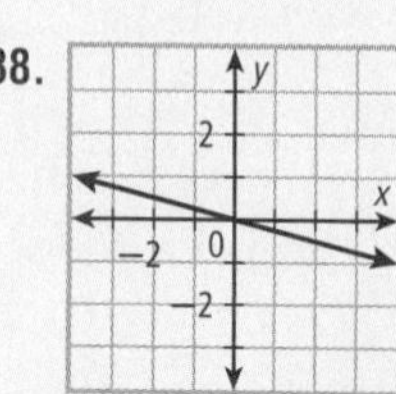

39.

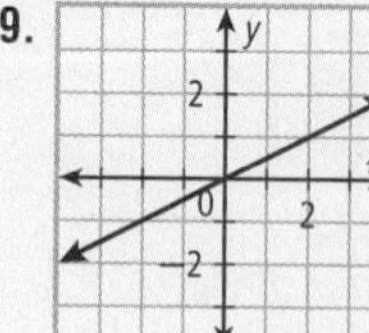

Write an equation in point-slope form that describes each graph.

44. Possible answer: $y + 3 = -(x - 2)$

45. Possible answer: $y - 3 = \frac{3}{2}(x - 3)$

46. Possible answer: $y - 1 = \frac{2}{5}(x - 3)$

44.

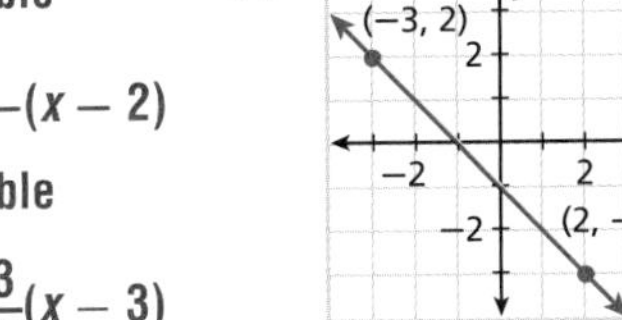

45.

46.

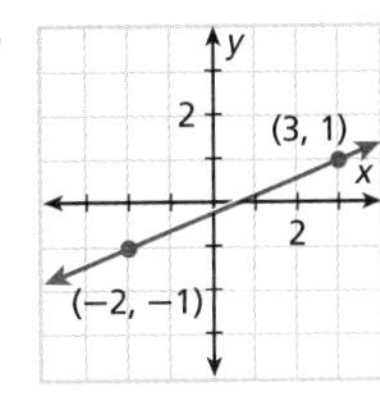

The tables show linear relationships between *x* and *y*. Copy and complete the tables.

47.

x	−2	0	**4**	7
y	−18	**−8**	12	27

48.

x	−4	1	0	**6**
y	14	4	**6**	−6

49. ///**ERROR ANALYSIS**/// Two students used point-slope form to find an equation that describes the line with slope −3 through (−5, 2). Who is incorrect? Explain the error.

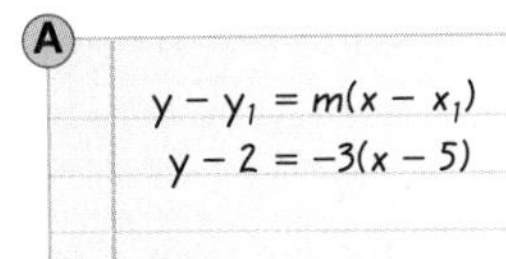

Ⓐ
$y - y_1 = m(x - x_1)$
$y - 2 = -3(x - 5)$

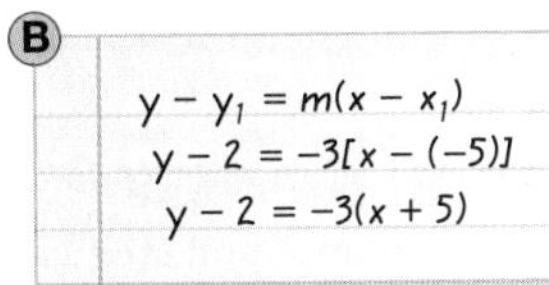

Ⓑ
$y - y_1 = m(x - x_1)$
$y - 2 = -3[x - (-5)]$
$y - 2 = -3(x + 5)$

Student A is incorrect. Student A incorrectly wrote $x - (-5)$ as $x - 5$ instead of $x + 5$.

50. Possible answer: When you know a point and the slope, you can immediately use point-slope form. When you know 2 points, first use them to find the slope. Then use point-slope form, just like in the first case.

50. Critical Thinking Compare the methods for finding the equation that describes a line when you know

- a point on the line and the slope of the line.
- two points on the line.

How are the methods alike? How are they different?

51. Write About It Explain why the first statement is false but the second is true.

- All linear equations can be written in point-slope form.
- All linear equations that describe functions can be written in point-slope form.

51. Possible answer: Linear equations that describe vert. lines cannot be written in point-slope form because they have undef. slope. All non-vert. lines represent functions, and they can all be written in point-slope form.

52. Multi-Step The table shows the mean scores on a standardized test for several different years.

Years Since 1985	0	5	10	17	21
Mean Combined Score	994	1009	1001	1016	1020

a. Make a scatter plot of the data and add a trend line to your graph.

b. Use your trend line to estimate the slope and *y*-intercept, and write an equation in slope-intercept form. **Possible answer: slope: 1.5; *y*-int.: 994; $y = 1.5x + 994$**

c. What do the slope and *y*-intercept represent in this situation? **slope: number of points by which mean score is increasing each year; *y*-int.: mean score in 1985**

53. This problem will prepare you for the Multi-Step Test Prep on page 376.

a. Stephen is walking from his house to his friend Sharon's house. When he is 12 blocks away, he looks at his watch. He looks again when he is 8 blocks away and finds that 6 minutes have passed. Write two ordered pairs for these data in the form (time, blocks). **(0, 12) and (6, 8)**

b. Write a linear equation for these two points. $y = -\frac{2}{3}x + 12$

c. What is the total amount of time it takes Stephen to reach Sharon's house? Explain how you found your answer. **18 min**

Teaching Tip **Statistics** In **Exercise 52,** remind students that a trend line should have about the same number of points below it as above it.

Exercise 53 involves using two points to write an equation for a line. This exercise prepares students for the Multi-Step Test Prep on page 376.

Answers

52a.

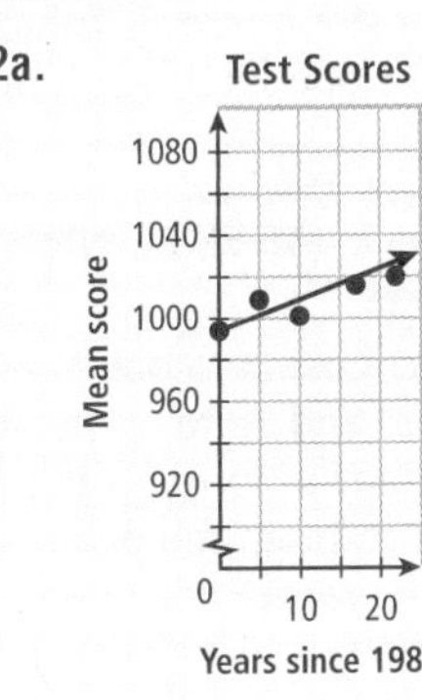

5-8 READING STRATEGIES

The point-slope form of a line can be used when writing linear equations.

Equation	Writing Equations in Point-Slope Form
$y - y_1 = m(x - x_1)$	A line with slope 3 which contains the point (−6, 2) can be written in point-slope form as $y - 2 = 3[x - (-6)]$, or $y - 2 = 3(x + 6)$.
Changing Point-Slope Form to Slope-Intercept Form	**Uses**
$y - 2 = 3(x + 6)$ $y - 2 = 3x + 18$ $y = 3x + 20$	The point-slope form can be used to write a linear equation when given either... • a point and the slope • two points ...and then simplified to slope-intercept form to graph.

Point-Slope Form

Complete the following.

1. What two pieces of information do you need to write an equation in point-slope form? **the slope of the line and one point on the line**
2. In the concept map above, it states that you can write an equation in point-slope form if given two points on the line. What piece of information do you still need and how can you get it? **the slope; you can substitute the coordinates of the two given points into the slope formula.**
3. Write an equation in point-slope form for the line with slope 4 that contains (3, −10). **$y + 10 = 4(x - 3)$**
4. Write an equation in slope-intercept form for the line that contains points (2, −5) and (−4, 7). **$y = -2x - 1$**

5-8 RETEACH

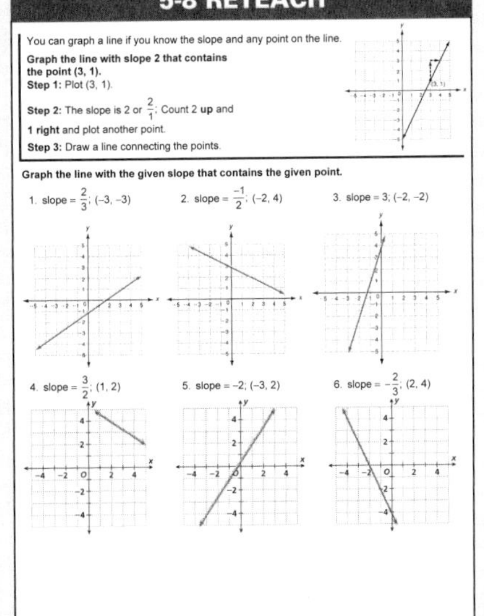

You can graph a line if you know the slope and any point on the line.

Graph the line with slope 2 that contains the point (3, 1).

Step 1: Plot (3, 1).

Step 2: The slope is 2 or $\frac{2}{1}$. Count 2 up and 1 right and plot another point.

Step 3: Draw a line connecting the points.

Graph the line with the given slope that contains the given point.

1. slope $= \frac{2}{3}$; (−3, −3)
2. slope $= \frac{-1}{2}$; (−2, 4)
3. slope = 3; (−2, −2)
4. slope $= \frac{3}{2}$; (1, 2)
5. slope = −2; (−3, 2)
6. slope $= -\frac{2}{3}$; (2, 4)

5-8 PRACTICE A

5-8 PRACTICE C

5-8 PRACTICE B

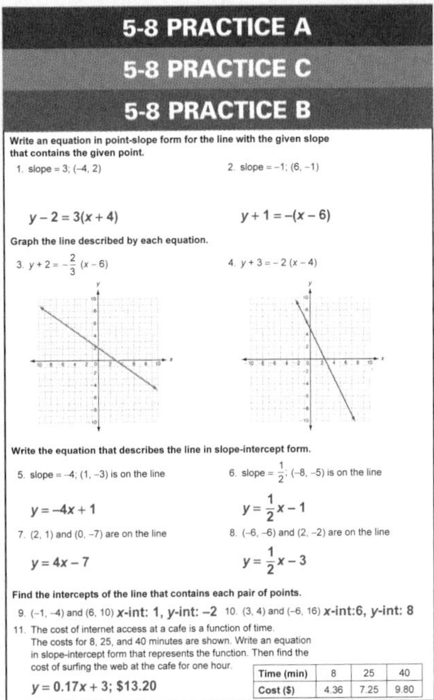

Write an equation in point-slope form for the line with the given slope that contains the given point.

1. slope = 3; (−4, 2) **$y - 2 = 3(x + 4)$**
2. slope = −1; (6, −1) **$y + 1 = -(x - 6)$**

Graph the line described by each equation.

3. $y + 2 = -\frac{2}{3}(x - 6)$
4. $y + 3 = -2(x - 4)$

Write the equation that describes the line in slope-intercept form.

5. slope = −4; (1, −3) is on the line **$y = -4x + 1$**
6. slope $= \frac{1}{2}$; (−8, −5) is on the line **$y = \frac{1}{2}x - 1$**
7. (2, 1) and (0, −7) are on the line **$y = 4x - 7$**
8. (−6, −6) and (2, −2) are on the line **$y = \frac{1}{2}x - 3$**

Find the intercepts of the line that contains each pair of points.

9. (−1, −4) and (6, 10) **x-int: 1, y-int: −2**
10. (3, 4) and (−6, 16) **x-int: 6, y-int: 8**

11. The cost of internet access at a cafe is a function of time. The costs for 8, 25, and 40 minutes are shown. Write an equation in slope-intercept form that represents the function. Then find the cost of surfing the web at the cafe for one hour. **$y = 0.17x + 3$; $13.20**

Time (min)	8	25	40
Cost ($)	4.36	7.25	9.80

TEST PREP DOCTOR In Exercise 54, students who chose **B** most likely reversed x_1 and y_1 in the point-slope form. Students who chose **A** probably added x_1 and y_1.

Answers

59, 60. For graphs, see p. A22.

61. See p. A22.

Journal

Have students describe a situation in which the point-slope form is more useful than the slope-intercept form.

ALTERNATIVE ASSESSMENT

Have students choose two points on a coordinate grid and write an equation in slope-intercept form for the line that passes through the points. Then have them graph the line and check their work by making sure their two original points are on the line.

Power Presentations with PowerPoint®

5-8 Lesson Quiz

Write an equation in point-slope form for the line with the given slope that contains the given point.

1. slope = −1; (0, 9)
   $y - 9 = -(x - 0)$
2. slope = $-\frac{1}{3}$; (3, −6)
   $y + 6 = -\frac{1}{3}(x - 3)$

Write the equation that describe each line in slope-intercept form.

3. slope = −2, (2, 1) is on the line.
   $y = -2x + 5$
4. (0, 4) and (−7, 2) are on the line.
   $y = \frac{2}{7}x + 4$
5. The cost to take a taxi from the airport is a linear function of the distance driven. The costs for 5, 10, and 20 miles are shown in the table. Write an equation in slope-intercept form that represents the function.

Distance (mi)	Cost ($)
5	14
10	22
20	38

$y = 1.6x + 6$

Also available on transparency

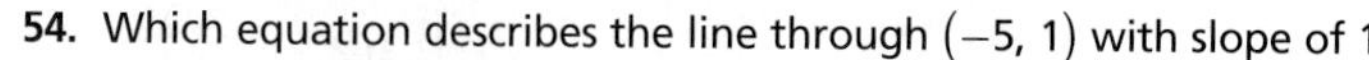

TEST PREP

54. Which equation describes the line through (−5, 1) with slope of 1?
    Ⓐ $y + 1 = x - 5$ Ⓒ $y - 1 = -5(x - 1)$
    Ⓑ $y + 5 = x - 1$ Ⓓ $y - 1 = x + 5$
55. A line contains (4, 4) and (5, 2). What are the slope and y-intercept?
    Ⓕ slope = −2; y-intercept = 2 Ⓗ slope = −2; y-intercept = 12
    Ⓖ slope = 1.2; y-intercept = −2 Ⓙ slope = 12; y-intercept = 1.2

CHALLENGE AND EXTEND

56. A linear function has the same y-intercept as $x + 4y = 8$ and its graph contains the point (2, 7). Find the slope and y-intercept. **slope: $\frac{5}{2}$; y-int.: 2**
57. Write the equation of a line in slope-intercept form that contains $\left(\frac{3}{4}, \frac{1}{2}\right)$ and has the same slope as the line described by $y + 3x = 6$. $y = -3x + \frac{11}{4}$
58. Write the equation of a line in slope-intercept form that contains $\left(-\frac{1}{2}, -\frac{1}{3}\right)$ and $\left(1\frac{1}{2}, 1\right)$. y

SPIRAL REVIEW

Solve each compound inequality and graph the solutions. *(Lesson 3-6)*

59. $-4 \le x + 2 \le 1$ $-6 \le x \le -1$
60. $m - 5 > -7$ AND $m + 1 < 2$ $m > -2$ AN

61. A group of hikers is walking the Appalachian Trail. The function $y = 12x$ describes how many miles y the group has traveled in x days. Graph the function. Then use the graph to estimate how many miles the group will hike in 18 days. *(Lesson 4-4)*

Write the equation that describes each line in slope-intercept form. *(Lesson 5-7)*

62. slope = 3, y-intercept = −5
    $y = 3x - 5$
63. slope = −2, (2, 4) is on the line
    $y = -2x + 8$

Career Path

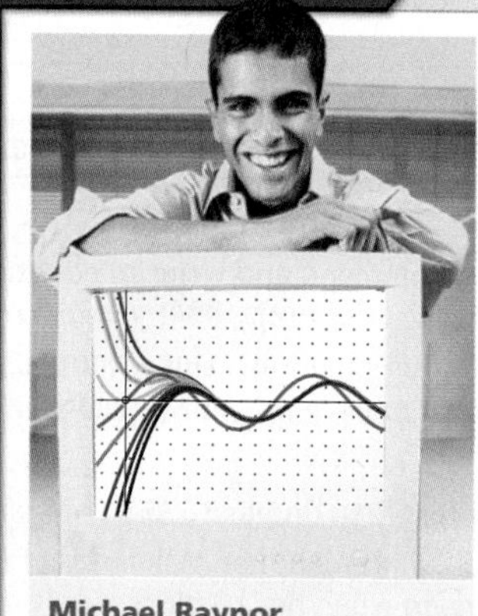

Michael Raynor
Data mining major

Q: What math classes did you take in high school?
A: Algebra 1 and 2, Geometry, and Statistics

Q: What math classes have you taken in college?
A: Applied Statistics, Data Mining Methods, Web Mining, and Artificial Intelligence

Q: How do you use math?
A: Once for a class, I used software to analyze basketball statistics. What I learned helped me develop strategies for our school team.

Q: What are your future plans?
A: There are many options for people with data mining skills. I could work in banking, pharmaceuticals, or even the military. But my dream job is to develop game strategies for an NBA team.

5-8 PROBLEM SOLVING

Write the correct answer.

1. The number of students in a school has been increasing at a constant rate. The table shows the number of students in the school for certain numbers of years since 1995.

Years Since 1995	Number of Students
0	118
5	124
10	130

Write an equation in point-slope form that represents this linear function.

Possible answer:
$y - 130 = 1.2(x - 10)$

Write the equation in slope-intercept form.

$y = 1.2x + 118$

Assuming the rate of change remains constant, how many students will be in the school in 2010?

136

2. Toni is finishing a scarf at a constant rate. The table shows the number of hours Toni has spent knitting this week and the corresponding number of rows in the scarf.

Toni's Knitting	
Hours	Rows of Knitting
2	38
4	44
6	50

Write an equation in slope-intercept form that represents this linear function.

$y = 3x + 32$

3. A photo lab manager graphed the cost of having photos developed as a function of the number of photos in the order. The graph is a line with a slope of $\frac{1}{10}$ that passes through (10, 6). Write an equation in slope-intercept form that describes the cost to have photos developed. How much does it cost to have 25 photos developed?

$y = \frac{1}{10}x + 5$; $7.50

The cost of a cell phone for one month is a linear function of the number of minutes used. The total cost for 20, 35, and 40 additional minutes are shown. Select the best answer.

Cell-Phone Costs			
Number of Additional Minutes	20	35	40
Total Cost	$48	$54	$56

4. What is the slope of the line represented in the table?
   A 0.1 C 2
   B 0.4 D 2.5
5. What would be the monthly cost if 60 additional minutes were used?
   F $64 H $84
   G $72 J $150
6. What does the y-intercept of the function represent?
   A total cost of the bill
   B cost per additional minute
   C number of additional minutes used
   D cost with no additional minutes used

5-8 CHALLENGE

The objective of this game is to write and graph linear equations such that each line passes through as many points as possible. Each equation must be written in slope-intercept form, but you may use point-slope form as part of your work.

Two-player version:

- Each player takes a turn writing and graphing one linear equation that passes through points on the graph. Allow time for the player to make calculations. Check each other's work for accuracy—sometimes a line may come close to a point but not actually intersect it.
- The player scores 5 points for each point on the graph that the line passes through. If the line passes through a point that was previously intersected by a line, the player does not get credit for it.
- After all points have been used, tally your scores to see who wins.

Single-player version:

- Try to write equations for the fewest number of lines that intersect all of the points.
- If other students in your class are playing as single players, compare results to see who was able to use the fewest lines. Challenge yourselves to find ways to further reduce the number of lines that you used.

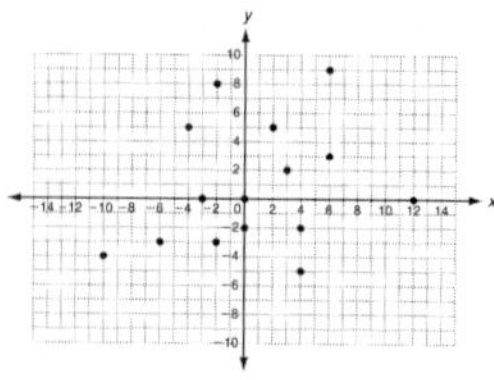

Tell how to make a game board that would result in a tie.

Plot an even number of pairs of points such that the two points in each pair are collinear but neither point is collinear with any other plotted point.

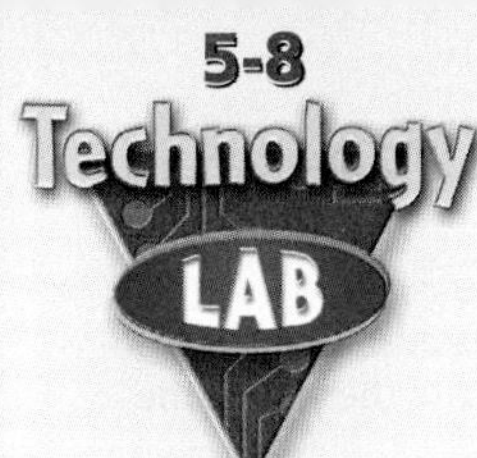

Graph Linear Functions

You can use a graphing calculator to quickly graph lines whose equations are in point-slope form. To enter an equation into your calculator, it must be solved for y, but it does not necessarily have to be in slope-intercept form.

Use with Lesson 5-8

go.hrw.com
Lab Resources Online
KEYWORD: MA11 LAB5

Activity

Graph the line with slope 2 that contains the point (2, 6.09).

1. Use point-slope form.

$$y - y_1 = m(x - x_1)$$
$$y - 6.09 = 2(x - 2)$$

2. Solve for y by adding 6.09 to both sides of the equation.

$$y - 6.09 = 2(x - 2)$$
$$\underline{+6.09} \quad \underline{+6.09}$$
$$y = 2(x - 2) + 6.09$$

3. Enter this equation into your calculator.

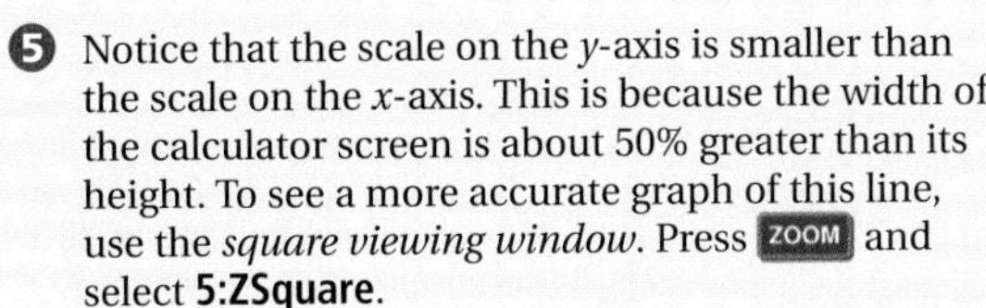

Y= 2 (X,T,θ,n − 2) + 6.09 ENTER

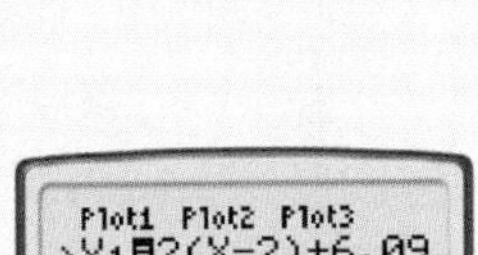

4. Graph in the *standard viewing window* by pressing ZOOM and selecting **6:ZStandard**. In this window, both the x- and y-axes go from −10 to 10.

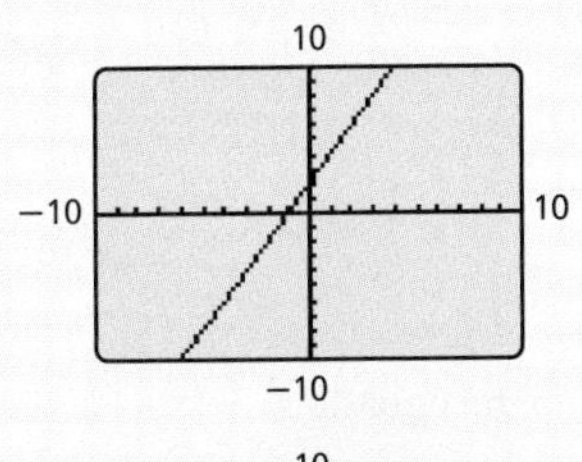

5. Notice that the scale on the y-axis is smaller than the scale on the x-axis. This is because the width of the calculator screen is about 50% greater than its height. To see a more accurate graph of this line, use the *square viewing window*. Press ZOOM and select **5:ZSquare**.

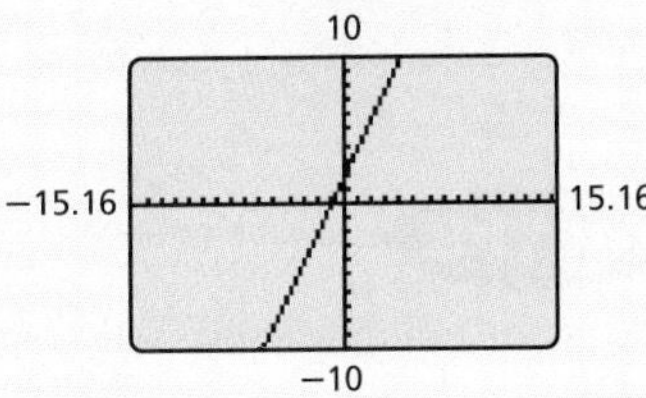

Try This

1. Graph the function represented by the line with slope −1.5 that contains the point (2.25, −3). View the graph in the standard viewing window.
2. Now view the graph in the square viewing window. Press WINDOW and write down the minimum and maximum values on the x- and y-axes.
3. In which graph does the line appear steeper? Why?
4. Explain why it might sometimes be useful to look at a graph in a square window.

Organizer

Use with Lesson 5-8

Pacing:
Traditional $\frac{1}{2}$ day
Block $\frac{1}{4}$ day

Objective: Use a graphing calculator to graph lines.

Materials: graphing calculator

Online Edition
Graphing Calculator, TechKeys

Countdown Week 12

Resources

Technology Lab Activities
5-8 Lab Recording Sheet

Teach

Discuss

Have students compare the graph in the two viewing windows. Discuss how the scale of the viewing window can distort a graph.

Close

Key Concept

Before graphing a function on a calculator, you must first solve for y. The scale of the axes in the viewing window affects the appearance of the slope of a line.

Assessment

Journal Have students explain the difference between the standard viewing window and the square viewing window.

Teaching Tip

Technology Caution students not to confuse the negative key (−) with the subtraction key −.

State Resources

go.hrw.com
State Resources Online
KEYWORD: MA7 Resources

Answers

1.

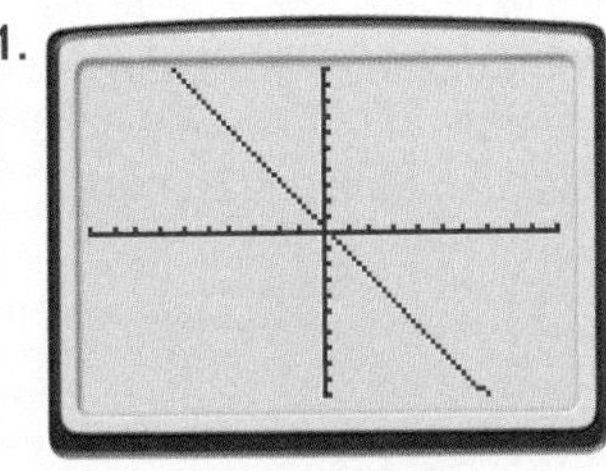

2.

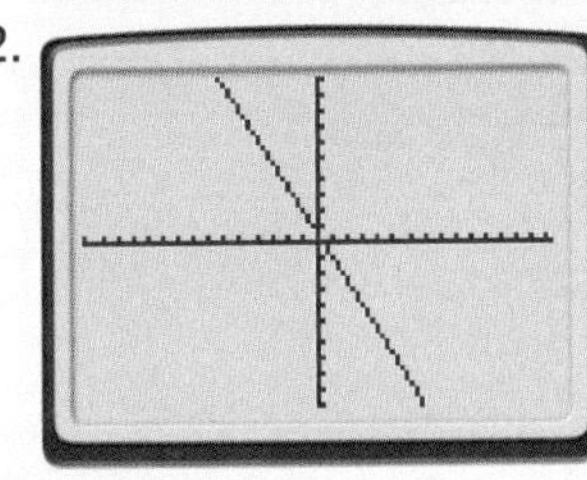

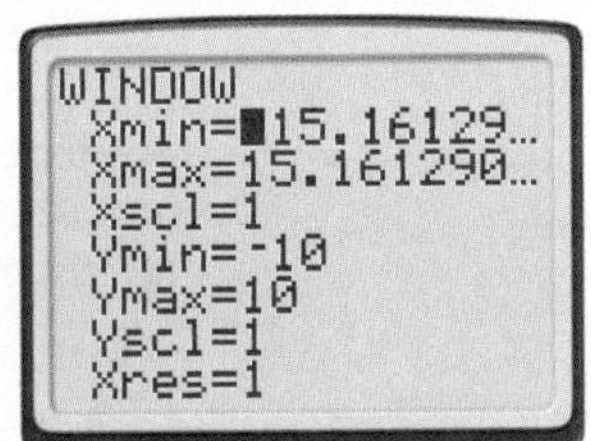

3. The second graph; the stand. window has the same number of units on each axis. Since the calc. screen is more horiz. than vert., the units on the x-axis are larger than the units on the y-axis. This makes the line appear less steep than it really is. In the square window, the units on each axis are the same size, so the slope of the line is represented more accurately.
4. Possible answer: When you want an accurate representation of the slope of a line, a square window would help avoid skewing the line.

Organizer

Pacing:
Traditional $\frac{1}{2}$ day
Block $\frac{1}{4}$ day

Objective: Write and interpret a linear equation for a trend line on a scatter plot.

Online Edition

Teach

Remember

Students review the slope formula, the definition of y-intercept, and the slope-intercept form of a linear equation.

Discuss

Be sure students understand that the equation of a trend line cannot be used to make predictions with absolute certainty. Instead, it is used to make a "best guess" based on the available data.

Close

Assess

Use the graph from the example. Have students describe another method, different from the one shown, to find the equation of the trend line. Possible answer: After finding the slope, substitute that value and one of the ordered pairs on the trend line into the point-slope form.

Interpreting Trend Lines

In Chapter 4 you learned how to draw trend lines on scatter plots. Now you will learn how to find the equations of trend lines and write them in slope-intercept form.

Example

Write an equation for the trend line on the scatter plot.

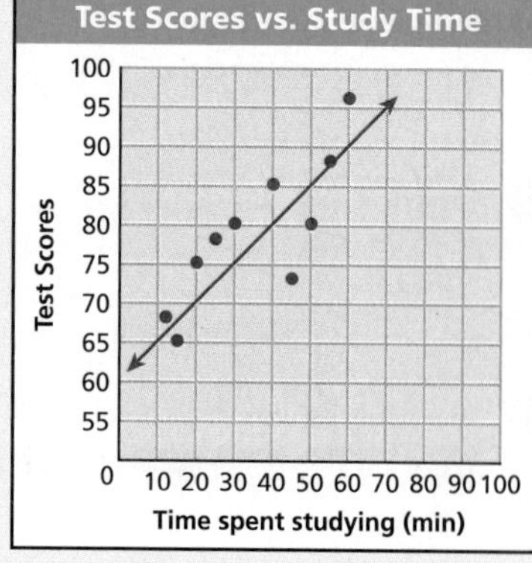

Two points on the trend line are (30, 75) and (60, 90).

To find the slope of the line that contains (30, 75) and (60, 90), use the slope formula.

$m = \frac{y_2 - y_1}{x_2 - x_1}$ *Use the slope formula.*

$m = \frac{90 - 75}{60 - 30}$ *Substitute (30, 75) for (x_1, y_1) and (60, 90) for (x_2, y_2).*

$m = \frac{15}{30}$ *Simplify.*

$m = \frac{1}{2}$

Use the slope and the point (30, 75) to find the y-intercept of the line.

$y = mx + b$ *Slope-intercept form*

$75 = \frac{1}{2}(30) + b$ *Substitute $\frac{1}{2}$ for m, 30 for x, and 75 for y.*

$75 = 15 + b$ *Solve for b.*

$60 = b$

Write the equation.

$y = \frac{1}{2}x + 60$ *Substitute $\frac{1}{2}$ for m and 60 for b.*

Try This

1. In the example above, what is the meaning of the slope? **1. Every two minutes spent studying results in a one-point increase in the test score.**
2. What does the y-intercept represent? **The score of a student who spent no time studying**
3. Use the equation to predict the test score of a student who spent 25 minutes studying. **72.5**
4. Use the table to create a scatter plot. Draw a trend line and find the equation of your trend line. Tell the meaning of the slope and y-intercept. Then use your equation to predict the race time of a runner who ran 40 miles in training.

Distance Run in Training (mi)	12	15	16	18	21	23	24	25	33
Race Time (min)	65	64	55	58	55	50	50	47	36

Answers to *Try This*

4. Possible answers:

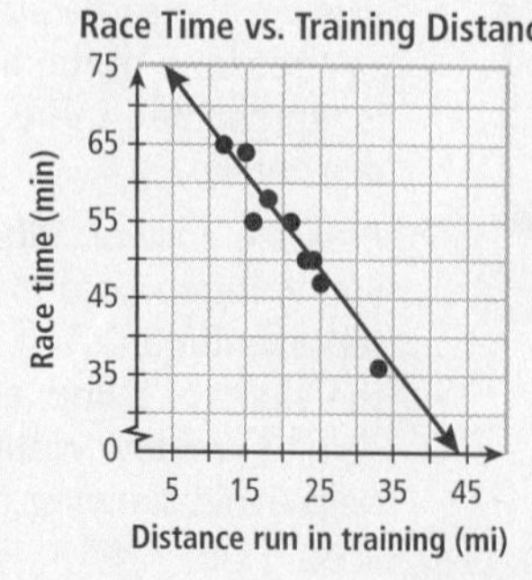

$y = -\frac{5}{4}x + 80$; the slope, $-\frac{5}{4}$, indicates that every 4 miles run in training decreases the race time by 5 minutes; the y-intercept, 80, indicates the race time of someone who did not run any distance in training; 30 min

5-9 Slopes of Parallel and Perpendicular Lines

Objectives
Identify and graph parallel and perpendicular lines.

Write equations to describe lines parallel or perpendicular to a given line.

Vocabulary
parallel lines
perpendicular lines

Why learn this?
Parallel lines and their equations can be used to model costs, such as the cost of a booth at a farmers' market.

To sell at a particular farmers' market for a year, there is a \$100 membership fee. Then you pay \$3 for each hour that you sell at the market. However, if you were a member the previous year, the membership fee is reduced to \$50.

- The red line shows the total cost if you are a new member.
- The blue line shows the total cost if you are a returning member.

These two lines are *parallel.* **Parallel lines** are lines in the same plane that have no points in common. In other words, they do not intersect.

Farmers' Market Fees

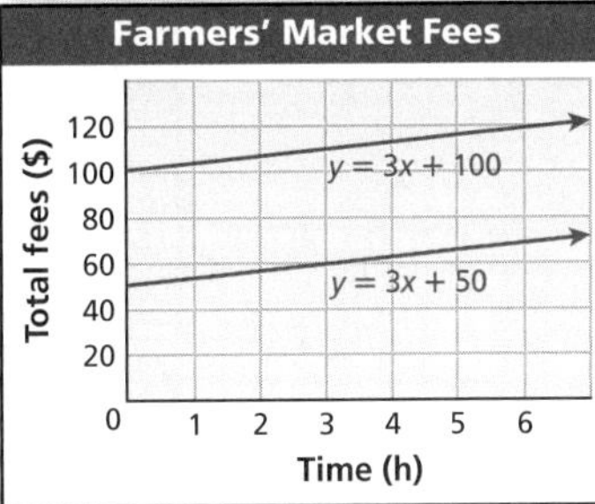

Know it! Note — **Parallel Lines**

WORDS	Two different nonvertical lines are parallel if and only if they have the same slope.	All different vertical lines are parallel.
GRAPH	$y = \frac{1}{2}x + 5$; $y = \frac{1}{2}x + 1$	$x = 2$; $x = 4$

EXAMPLE 1 Identifying Parallel Lines

Identify which lines are parallel.

A $y = \frac{4}{3}x + 3$; $y = 2$; $y = \frac{4}{3}x - 5$; $y = -3$

The lines described by $y = \frac{4}{3}x + 3$ and $y = \frac{4}{3}x - 5$ both have slope $\frac{4}{3}$. These lines are parallel. The lines described by $y = 2$ and $y = -3$ both have slope 0. These lines are parallel.

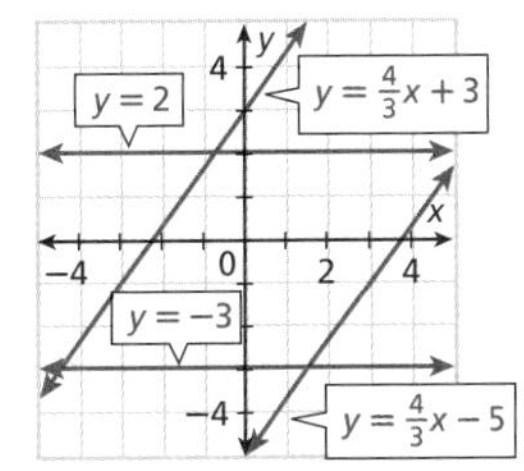

5-9 Organizer

Pacing: Traditional $1\frac{1}{2}$ days
Block $\frac{3}{4}$ day

Objectives: Identify and graph parallel and perpendicular lines.

Write equations to describe lines parallel or perpendicular to a given line.

Algebra Lab
In *Algebra Lab Activities*

Online Edition
Tutorial Videos, Interactivity

Countdown Week 12

Power Presentations with PowerPoint®

Warm Up

Find the reciprocal.

1. 2 $\frac{1}{2}$ **2.** $\frac{1}{3}$ 3

3. $-\frac{3}{4}$ $-\frac{4}{3}$

Find the slope of the line that passes through each pair of points.

4. (2, 2) and (−1, 3) $-\frac{1}{3}$

5. (3, 4) and (4, 6) 2

6. (5, 1) and (0, 0) $\frac{1}{5}$

Also available on transparency

Math Humor

Q: What did the lines do at the gym to avoid each other?

A: They used the parallel bars.

1 Introduce

EXPLORATION

5-9 Slopes of Parallel and Perpendicular Lines

You will need graph paper or a graphing calculator for this Exploration.

1. Graph $y = 2x + 3$ and $y = 2x - 2$ so that you can see both graphs at the same time. What do you notice about the lines?
2. Compare the slopes of the lines.
3. Repeat this process with $y = \frac{1}{3}x + 2$ and $y = \frac{1}{3}x$. What do you notice about the lines? What are the slopes of the lines?

THINK AND DISCUSS

4. **Discuss** any conjectures that you can make based on your findings.
5. **Describe** what you would expect to be true, based on your conjectures, about the graphs of $y = \frac{2}{3}x - 2$ and $y = \frac{2}{3}x - 5$.

Motivate

Have students use a graphing calculator to graph $y = 4x + 3$ and $y = 4x - 1$. Ask students where the lines intersect. They do not intersect.

Have students graph $y = 4x + 3$ and $y = -\frac{1}{4}x + 3$.

Tell students to estimate the measures of the angles at the intersection of the two lines. 90°

Explorations and answers are provided in *Alternate Openers: Explorations Transparencies.*

State Resources

Power Presentations with PowerPoint®

Additional Examples

Example 1

Identify which lines are parallel.

A. $y = \frac{5}{3}x - 2$; $y = x$;

$y = \frac{5}{3}x + 4$; $y = x + 1$

$y = \frac{5}{3}x - 2$ and $y = \frac{5}{3} + 4$;

$y = x$ and $y = x + 1$

B. $y = 2x - 3$; $y = -\frac{2}{3}x + 3$;

$2x + 3y = 8$; $y + 1 = 3(x - 3)$

$y = -\frac{2}{3}x + 3$

and $2x + 3y = 8$

Example 2

Show that *JKLM* is a parallelogram.

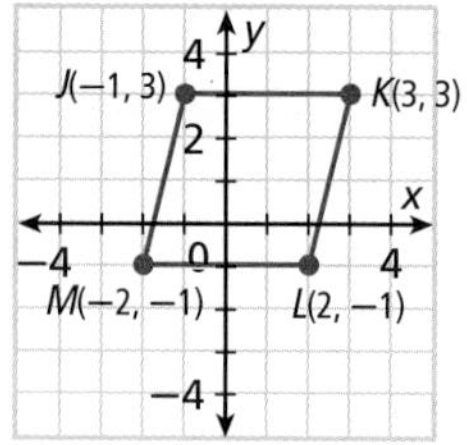

Slope of $\overline{JK} = 0$; slope of $\overline{KL} = 4$; slope of $\overline{ML} = 0$; slope of $\overline{JM} = 4$; $\overline{JK}$ is par. to $\overline{ML}$ because they are both horiz. $\overline{KL}$ is par. to $\overline{JM}$ because they have the same slope. Since opposite sides are par., *JKLM* is a parallelogram.

INTERVENTION

Questioning Strategies

EXAMPLE 1

- What is always true about the slopes of parallel lines?
- Can functions whose graphs are parallel lines have the same *y*-intercept? Explain.

EXAMPLE 2

- Why is it not necessary to calculate the slopes of horizontal and vertical lines?

Identify which lines are parallel.

B $y = 3x + 2$; $y = -\frac{1}{2}x + 4$; $x + 2y = -4$; $y - 5 = 3(x - 1)$

Write all equations in slope-intercept form to determine the slopes.

$y = 3x + 2$ slope-intercept form ✓	$y = -\frac{1}{2}x + 4$ slope-intercept form ✓
$x + 2y = -4$ $\underline{-x \qquad -x}$ $2y = -x - 4$ $\frac{2y}{2} = \frac{-x-4}{2}$ $y = -\frac{1}{2}x - 2$	$y - 5 = 3(x - 1)$ $y - 5 = 3x - 3$ $\underline{+5 \qquad +5}$ $y = 3x + 2$

The lines described by $y = 3x + 2$ and $y - 5 = 3(x - 1)$ have the same slope, but they are not parallel lines. They are the same line.

The lines described by $y = -\frac{1}{2}x + 4$ and $x + 2y = -4$ represent parallel lines. They each have slope $-\frac{1}{2}$.

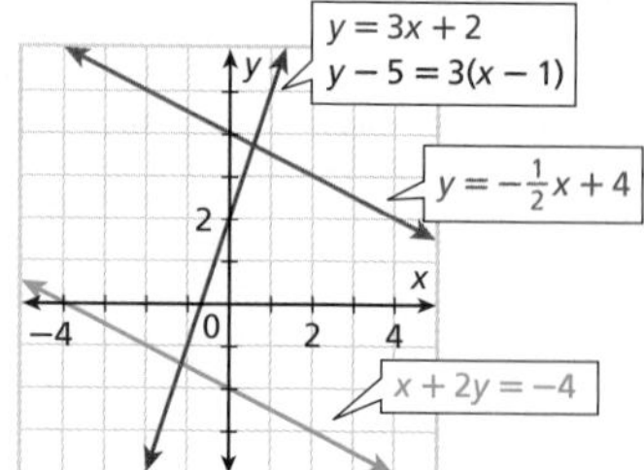

CHECK IT OUT! Identify which lines are parallel.

1a. $y = 2x + 2$; $y = 2x + 1$; $y = -4$; $x = 1$

1b. $y = \frac{3}{4}x + 8$; $-3x + 4y = 32$; $y = 3x$; $y - 1 = 3(x + 2)$

1a. $y = 2x + 2$ **and** $y = 2x + 1$ **1b.** $y = 3x$ **and** $y - 1 = 3(x + 2)$

EXAMPLE 2 Geometry

Geometry Application

Show that *ABCD* is a parallelogram.

Use the ordered pairs and the slope formula to find the slopes of $\overline{AB}$ and $\overline{CD}$.

slope of $\overline{AB} = \frac{7 - 5}{4 - (-1)} = \frac{2}{5}$

slope of $\overline{CD} = \frac{3 - 1}{4 - (-1)} = \frac{2}{5}$

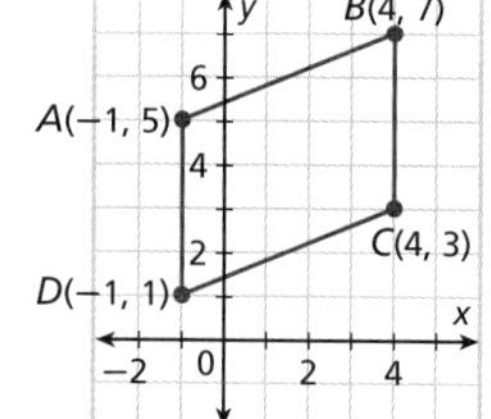

$\overline{AB}$ is parallel to $\overline{CD}$ because they have the same slope.

$\overline{AD}$ is parallel to $\overline{BC}$ because they are both vertical.

Therefore, *ABCD* is a parallelogram because both pairs of opposite sides are parallel.

Remember!

In a parallelogram, opposite sides are parallel.

2. slope of $\overline{AB} = 0$; slope of $\overline{BC} = \frac{5}{3}$; slope of $\overline{CD} = 0$; slope of $\overline{AD} = \frac{5}{3}$; $\overline{AB}$ is par. to $\overline{CD}$ because they have the same slope. $\overline{AD}$ is par. to $\overline{BC}$ because they have the same slope. Since opp. sides are par., *ABCD* is a parallelogram.

CHECK IT OUT! **2.** Show that the points $A(0, 2)$, $B(4, 2)$, $C(1, -3)$, and $D(-3, -3)$ are the vertices of a parallelogram.

2 Teach

Guided Instruction

Start the lesson by reviewing how to rewrite equations that are in standard and point-slope form in slope-intercept form. Then work through **Examples 1** and **2.** Prior to **Example 3,** remind students that reciprocals, like $\frac{3}{7}$ and $\frac{7}{3}$, have a product of 1. Opposite reciprocals, like $\frac{2}{3}$ and $-\frac{3}{2}$, have a product of -1. Then work through the remaining examples.

Reaching All Learners

Through Communication

Divide the class into small groups. Have the groups develop and present one of the following:

- a 60-second TV commercial about parallel or perpendicular lines
- a two-minute news segment about how to use parallel and perpendicular lines in geometry
- a brief infomercial about the equations of parallel and perpendicular lines

Perpendicular lines are lines that intersect to form right angles (90°).

Perpendicular Lines

WORDS	Two nonvertical lines are perpendicular if and only if the product of their slopes is −1.	Vertical lines are perpendicular to horizontal lines.
GRAPH	$y = -\frac{2}{3}x + 3$; $y = \frac{3}{2}x - 2$	$y = 3$; $x = 2$

EXAMPLE 3 Identifying Perpendicular Lines

Identify which lines are perpendicular: $x = -2$; $y = 1$; $y = -4x$; $y + 2 = \frac{1}{4}(x + 1)$.

The graph described by $x = -2$ is a vertical line, and the graph described by $y = 1$ is a horizontal line. These lines are perpendicular.

The slope of the line described by $y = -4x$ is -4. The slope of the line described by $y + 2 = \frac{1}{4}(x - 1)$ is $\frac{1}{4}$.

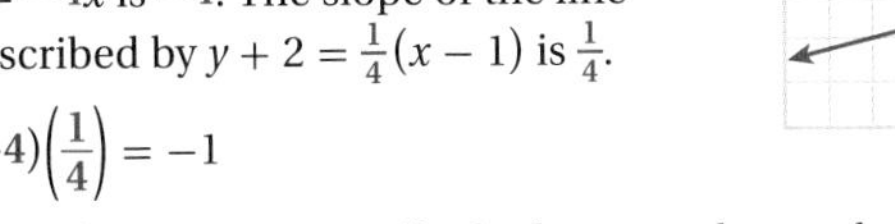

$$(-4)\left(\frac{1}{4}\right) = -1$$

These lines are perpendicular because the product of their slopes is −1.

4. slope of $\overline{PQ} = 2$; slope of $\overline{QR} = -1$; slope of $\overline{PR} = -\frac{1}{2}$; $\overline{PQ}$ is perp. to $\overline{PR}$ because the product of their slopes is −1. Since PQR contains a rt. angle, PQR is a rt. triangle.

3. Identify which lines are perpendicular: $y = -4$; $y - 6 = 5(x + 4)$; $x = 3$; $y = -\frac{1}{5}x + 2$.

$y = -4$ and $x = 3$; $y - 6 = 5(x + 4)$ and $y = -\frac{1}{5}x + 2$

EXAMPLE 4 Geometry Application

Geometry

Show that PQR is a right triangle.

If PQR is a right triangle, $\overline{PQ}$ will be perpendicular to $\overline{QR}$.

$$\text{slope of } \overline{PQ} = \frac{3 - 1}{3 - 0} = \frac{2}{3}$$

$$\text{slope of } \overline{QR} = \frac{3 - 0}{3 - 5} = \frac{3}{-2} = -\frac{3}{2}$$

$\overline{PQ}$ is perpendicular to $\overline{QR}$ because $\frac{2}{3}\left(-\frac{3}{2}\right) = -1$.

Therefore, PQR is a right triangle because it contains a right angle.

Helpful Hint

A right triangle contains one right angle. In Example 4, $\angle P$ and $\angle R$ are clearly not right angles, so the only possibility is $\angle Q$.

4. Show that $P(1, 4)$, $Q(2, 6)$, and $R(7, 1)$ are the vertices of a right triangle.

COMMON ERROR ALERT

Students might always use the coefficient of x for slope, regardless of the form of the equation. Tell students to always check the form of the equation first, because the coefficient of x may change when the equation is written in slope-intercept form.

Power Presentations with PowerPoint®

Additional Examples

Example 3

Identify which lines are perpendicular: $y = 3$; $x = -2$; $y = 3x$; $y = -\frac{1}{3}(x - 4)$. $y = 3$ and $x = -2$; $y = 3x$ and $y = -\frac{1}{3}(x - 4)$

Example 4

Show that ABC is a right triangle.

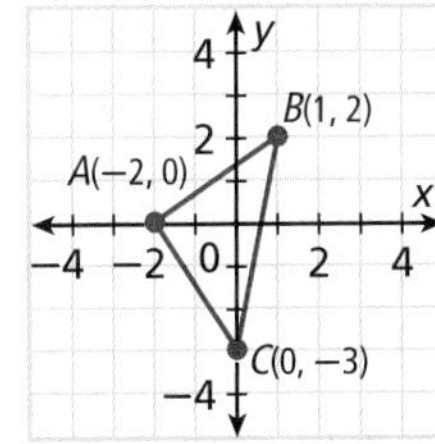

Slope of $\overline{AB} = \frac{2}{3}$; slope of $\overline{AC} = -\frac{3}{2}$; $\overline{AB}$ is perp. to $\overline{AC}$ because the product of their slopes is −1. Since ABC contains a rt. angle, ABC is a rt. triangle.

Teaching Tip

Geometry Have students think of geometric shapes that have parallel or perpendicular sides. Their list could include squares, rhombuses, rectangles, and trapezoids, as well as parallelograms and right triangles.

INTERVENTION

Questioning Strategies

EXAMPLE 3

- What is true about the slopes of perpendicular lines?
- Can perpendicular lines have the same y-intercept? Explain.

EXAMPLE 4

- What is true about the intersection of two perpendicular lines?
- What is the maximum number of right angles a triangle could contain?

Power Presentations with PowerPoint®

Additional Examples

Example 5

A. Write an equation in slope-intercept form for the line that passes through (4, 10) and is parallel to the line described by $y = 3x + 8$. $y = 3x - 2$

B. Write an equation in slope-intercept form for the line that passes through (2, −1) and is perpendicular to the line described by $y = 2x - 5$. $y = -\frac{1}{2}x$

INTERVENTION

Questioning Strategies

EXAMPLE 5

- How do you know what to substitute for *m* if you are writing an equation for a line parallel to a given line? for a line perpendicular to a given line?

Visual Encourage students to check their work in **Example 5** by graphing.

Technology When using a graphing calculator, lines may not appear perpendicular in the standard window. This is because units on the *x*-axis are larger than units on the *y*-axis. To view a more accurate graph, have students use the square window by pressing ZOOM and selecting **5:ZSquare**.

EXAMPLE 5 Writing Equations of Parallel and Perpendicular Lines

A **Write an equation in slope-intercept form for the line that passes through (4, 5) and is parallel to the line described by $y = 5x + 10$.**

Step 1 Find the slope of the line.

$y = 5x + 10$ *The slope is 5.*

The parallel line also has a slope of 5.

Step 2 Write the equation in point-slope form.

$y - y_1 = m(x - x_1)$ *Use point-slope form.*

$y - 5 = 5(x - 4)$ *Substitute 5 for m, 4 for x_1, and 5 for y_1.*

Step 3 Write the equation in slope-intercept form.

$y - 5 = 5(x - 4)$

$y - 5 = 5x - 20$ *Distributive Property*

$y = 5x - 15$ *Addition Property of Equality*

B **Write an equation in slope-intercept form for the line that passes through (3, 2) and is perpendicular to the line described by $y = 3x - 1$.**

Step 1 Find the slope of the line.

$y = 3x - 1$ *The slope is 3.*

The perpendicular line has a slope of $-\frac{1}{3}$, because $3\left(-\frac{1}{3}\right) = -1$.

Step 2 Write the equation in point-slope form.

$y - y_1 = m(x - x_1)$ *Use point-slope form.*

$y - 2 = -\frac{1}{3}(x - 3)$ *Substitute $-\frac{1}{3}$ for m, 3 for x_1, and 2 for y_1.*

Step 3 Write the equation in slope-intercept form.

$y - 2 = -\frac{1}{3}(x - 3)$

$y - 2 = -\frac{1}{3}x + 1$ *Distributive Property*

$y = -\frac{1}{3}x + 3$ *Addition Property of Equality*

Helpful Hint

If you know the slope of a line, the slope of a perpendicular line will be the "opposite reciprocal."

$\frac{2}{3} \rightarrow -\frac{3}{2}$

$\frac{1}{5} \rightarrow -5$

$-7 \rightarrow \frac{1}{7}$

5a. Write an equation in slope-intercept form for the line that passes through (5, 7) and is parallel to the line described by $y = \frac{4}{5}x - 6$.

5b. Write an equation in slope-intercept form for the line that passes through (−5, 3) and is perpendicular to the line described by $y = 5x$.

5a. $y = \frac{4}{5}x + 3$ **5b.** $y = -\frac{1}{5}x + 2$

THINK AND DISCUSS

1. Are the lines described by $y = \frac{1}{2}x$ and $y = 2x$ perpendicular? Explain.
2. Describe the slopes and *y*-intercepts when two nonvertical lines are parallel.
3. **GET ORGANIZED** Copy and complete the graphic organizer. In each box, sketch an example and describe the slopes.

Parallel lines	Perpendicular lines

3 Close

Summarize

Remind students that they will need to know the slopes of lines to determine whether the lines are parallel, perpendicular, or neither. Tell students that equations can be presented in many ways, and that they may need to rewrite equations in slope-intercept form before deciding on the value of the slope.

ONGOING ASSESSMENT and INTERVENTION

***Diagnose Before* the Lesson**
5-9 Warm Up, TE p. 361

***Monitor During* the Lesson**
Check It Out! Exercises, SE pp. 362–364
Questioning Strategies, TE pp. 362–364

***Assess After* the Lesson**
5-9 Lesson Quiz, TE p. 367
Alternative Assessment, TE p. 367

Answers to *Think and Discuss*

1. No; the product of their slopes is 1, not −1.
2. The slopes are the same, and the *y*-intercepts are different.
3. See p. A5.

go.hrw.com
Homework Help Online
KEYWORD: MA11 5-9
Parent Resources Online
KEYWORD: MA7 Parent

GUIDED PRACTICE

1. **Vocabulary** ____?____ lines have the same slope. (*Parallel* or *Perpendicular*) **Parallel**

SEE EXAMPLE 1 p. 361

Identify which lines are parallel.

2. $y = 6$; $y = 6x + 5$; $y = 6x - 7$; $y = -8$ **$y = 6x + 5$ and $y = 6x - 7$; $y = 6$ and $y = -8$**

3. $y = \frac{3}{4}x - 1$; $y = -2x$; $y - 3 = \frac{3}{4}(x - 5)$; $y - 4 = -2(x + 2)$

SEE EXAMPLE 2 p. 362

4. **Geometry** Show that $ABCD$ is a trapezoid. (*Hint:* In a trapezoid, exactly one pair of opposite sides is parallel.)

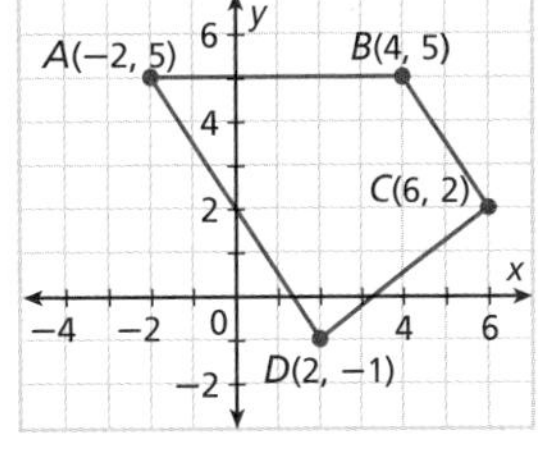

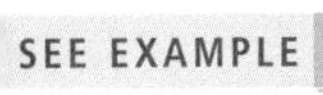

SEE EXAMPLE 3 p. 363

Identify which lines are perpendicular.

5. $y = \frac{2}{3}x - 4$; $y = -\frac{3}{2}x + 2$; $y = -1$; $x = 3$

6. $y = -\frac{3}{7}x - 4$; $y - 4 = -7(x + 2)$;
$y - 1 = \frac{1}{7}(x - 4)$; $y - 7 = \frac{7}{3}(x - 3)$

SEE EXAMPLE 4 p. 363

7. **Geometry** Show that $PQRS$ is a rectangle. (*Hint:* In a rectangle, all four angles are right angles.)

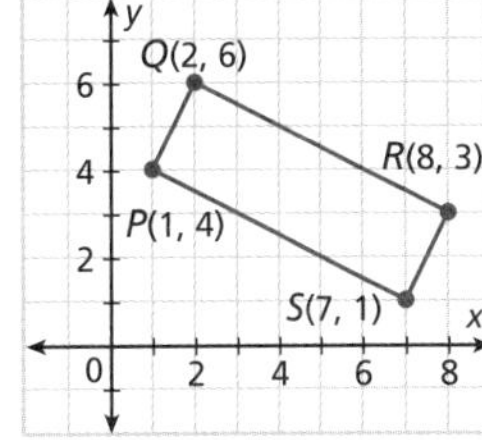

SEE EXAMPLE 5 p. 364

8. Write an equation in slope-intercept form for the line that passes through (5, 0) and is perpendicular to the line described by $y = -\frac{5}{2}x + 6$. **$y = \frac{2}{5}x - 2$**

PRACTICE AND PROBLEM SOLVING

Independent Practice

For Exercises	See Example
9–11	1
12	2
13–15	3
16	4
17	5

Extra Practice
Skills Practice p. S13
Application Practice p. S32

Identify which lines are parallel.

9. $x = 7$; $y = -\frac{5}{6}x + 8$; $y = -\frac{5}{6}x - 4$; $x = -9$

10. $y = -x$; $y - 3 = -1(x + 9)$; $y - 6 = \frac{1}{2}(x - 14)$; $y + 1 = \frac{1}{2}x$

11. $y = -3x + 2$; $y = \frac{1}{2}x - 1$; $-x + 2y = 17$; $3x + y = 27$

12. **Geometry** Show that $LMNP$ is a parallelogram.

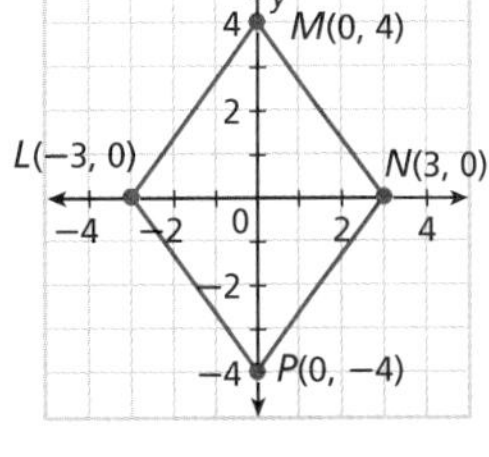

Identify which lines are perpendicular.

13. $y = 6x$; $y = \frac{1}{6}x$; $y = -\frac{1}{6}x$; $y = -6x$

14. $y - 9 = 3(x + 1)$; $y = -\frac{1}{3}x + 5$; $y = 0$; $x = 6$

15. $x - 6y = 15$; $y = 3x - 2$; $y = -3x - 3$; $y = -6x - 8$; $3y = -x - 11$

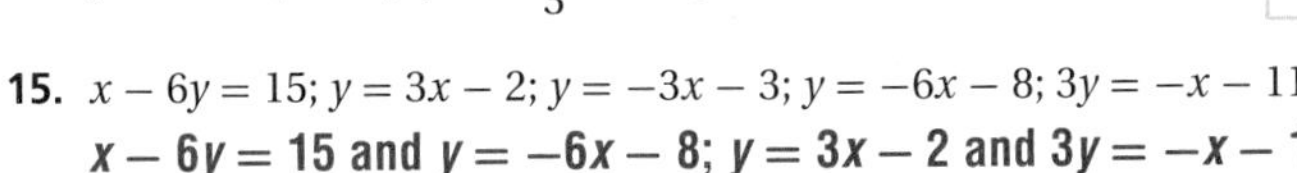
$x - 6y = 15$ and $y = -6x - 8$; $y = 3x - 2$ and $3y = -x - 11$

Assignment Guide

Assign *Guided Practice* exercises as necessary.

If you finished Examples **1–3**
Basic 9–15, 18–21
Average 9–15, 18–21, 49
Advanced 9–15, 18–21, 49, 56, 57

If you finished Examples **1–5**
Basic 9–45, 51–54, 59–68
Average 9–17, 18–44 even, 46–54, 56–68
Advanced 9–17, 18–44 even, 46–68

Homework Quick Check
Quickly check key concepts.
Exercises: 10, 12, 14, 16, 26, 42

Answers

3. $y = \frac{3}{4}x - 1$ and $y - 3 = \frac{3}{4}(x - 5)$

4. slope of $\overline{AD} = -\frac{3}{2}$; slope of $\overline{BC} = -\frac{3}{2}$; $\overline{AD}$ and $\overline{BC}$ are par. because they have the same slope. Therefore, $ABCD$ is a trapezoid.

5. $y = \frac{2}{3}x - 4$ and $y = -\frac{3}{2}x + 2$; $y = -1$ and $x = 3$

6. $y = -\frac{3}{7}x - 4$ and $y - 7 = \frac{7}{3}(x - 3)$; $y - 4 = -7(x + 2)$ and $y - 1 = \frac{1}{7}(x - 4)$

State Resources

Answers

7. slope of $\overline{PQ} = 2$; slope of $\overline{QR} = -\frac{1}{2}$; slope of $\overline{RS} = 2$; slope of $\overline{PS} = -\frac{1}{2}$
$\overline{PQ}$ is perp. to $\overline{QR}$ because the product of their slopes is -1. $\overline{QR}$ is perp. to $\overline{RS}$ because the product of their slopes is -1. $\overline{RS}$ is perp. to $\overline{PS}$ because the product of their slopes is -1. $\overline{PS}$ is perp. to $\overline{PQ}$ because the product of their slopes is -1. Therefore all the angles are rt. angles, and $PQRS$ is a rectangle.

9. $x = 7$ and $x = -9$; $y = -\frac{5}{6}x + 8$ and $y = -\frac{5}{6}x - 4$

10. $y = -x$ and $y - 3 = -1(x + 9)$

11. $y = -3x + 2$ and $3x + y = 27$; $y = \frac{1}{2}x - 1$ and $-x + 2y = 17$

12. slope of $\overline{LM} = \frac{4}{3}$; slope of $\overline{MN} = -\frac{4}{3}$; slope of $\overline{PN} = \frac{4}{3}$; slope of $\overline{LP} = -\frac{4}{3}$
$\overline{LM}$ is par. to $\overline{PN}$ because they have the same slope. $\overline{MN}$ is par. to $\overline{LP}$ because they have the same slope. Since opp. sides are par., $LMNP$ is a parallelogram.

13. $y = 6x$ and $y = -\frac{1}{6}x$; $y = \frac{1}{6}x$ and $y = -6x$

14. $y - 9 = 3(x + 1)$ and $y = -\frac{1}{3}x + 5$; $y = 0$ and $x = 6$

Exercise 51 involves writing and graphing functions. This exercise prepares students for the Multi-Step Test Prep on page 376.

Answers

16. slope of $\overline{AB} = -\frac{1}{4}$; slope of $\overline{BC} = 4$; $\overline{AB}$ is perp. to $\overline{BC}$ because the product of their slopes is -1. Since ABC contains a rt. angle, ABC is a rt. triangle.

48. Possible answer: No; par. lines have no points in common. If they had the same *y*-int., they would both intersect the *y*-axis at the same place, and they could not be par.

50. Possible answer: First find the slope of $y - 3 = -6(x - 3)$. Since it is written in point-slope form, you can immediately tell that the slope is -6. Then find the *y*-int. of $y - 3 = -6(x - 3)$ by solving for *y*: $y = -6x + 21$. So the *y*-int. is 21. Choose any other *y*-int. *b* and write the equation $y = -6x + b$. This line will be par. to $y - 3 = -6(x - 3)$.

51c. No; the lines are par. and never intersect, so Flora and Dan will never be at the same place at the same time during their walk. Because Dan is walking at the same pace as Flora, Flora will not be able to catch up.

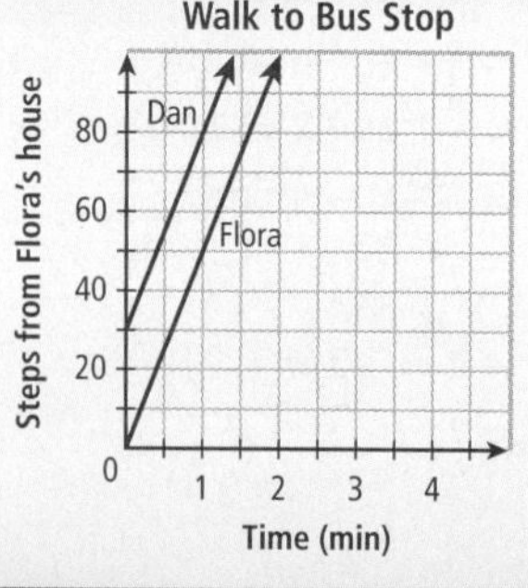

22. $y = 3x + 4$
23. $y = \frac{1}{2}x - 5$
24. $y = \frac{1}{4}x - 1$
25. $y = 2x + 5$
26. $y = \frac{5}{2}x - \frac{25}{2}$
27. $y = 3x + 13$
28. $y = 4$
29. $y = -x + 5$
30. $y = -\frac{2}{3}x + \frac{23}{3}$
31. $y = 4x - 23$
32. $y = \frac{1}{2}x - 4$
33. $y = -\frac{3}{4}x$
34. $y = \frac{1}{3}x - 4$
35. $y = -x + 1$
36. $y = -\frac{4}{3}x - 3$
37. $y = \frac{2}{5}x - \frac{31}{5}$
38. $y = \frac{1}{3}x - \frac{14}{3}$
39. $y = -\frac{1}{5}x - \frac{11}{5}$
40. $y = \frac{3}{2}x - 1$
41. $y = -\frac{1}{2}x - \frac{1}{2}$
42. $y = 4x - 11$
43. $y = \frac{1}{2}x + 6$
44. $y = -x + 5$
45. $y = x - 3$

16. **Geometry** Show that *ABC* is a right triangle.

17. Write an equation in slope-intercept form for the line that passes through $(0, 0)$ and is parallel to the line described by $y = -\frac{6}{7}x + 1$. $y = -\frac{6}{7}x$

Without graphing, tell whether each pair of lines is parallel, perpendicular, or neither.

18. $x = 2$ and $y = -5$ **perp.**
19. $y = 7x$ and $y - 28 = 7(x - 4)$ **neither**
20. $y = 2x - 1$ and $y = \frac{1}{2}x + 2$ **neither**
21. $y - 3 = \frac{1}{4}(x - 3)$ and $y + 13 = \frac{1}{4}(x + 1)$ **par.**

Write an equation in slope-intercept form for the line that is parallel to the given line and that passes through the given point.

22. $y = 3x - 7$; $(0, 4)$
23. $y = \frac{1}{2}x + 5$; $(4, -3)$
24. $4y = x$; $(4, 0)$
25. $y = 2x + 3$; $(1, 7)$
26. $5x - 2y = 10$; $(3, -5)$
27. $y = 3x - 4$; $(-2, 7)$
28. $y = 7$; $(2, 4)$
29. $x + y = 1$; $(2, 3)$
30. $2x + 3y = 7$; $(4, 5)$
31. $y = 4x + 2$; $(5, -3)$
32. $y = \frac{1}{2}x - 1$; $(0, -4)$
33. $3x + 4y = 8$; $(4, -3)$

Write an equation in slope-intercept form for the line that is perpendicular to the given line and that passes through the given point.

34. $y = -3x + 4$; $(6, -2)$
35. $y = x - 6$; $(-1, 2)$
36. $3x - 4y = 8$; $(-6, 5)$
37. $5x + 2y = 10$; $(3, -5)$
38. $y = 5 - 3x$; $(2, -4)$
39. $-10x + 2y = 8$; $(4, -3)$
40. $2x + 3y = 7$; $(4, 5)$
41. $4x - 2y = -6$; $(3, -2)$
42. $-2x - 8y = 16$; $(4, 5)$
43. $y = -2x + 4$; $(-2, 5)$
44. $y = x - 5$; $(0, 5)$
45. $x + y = 2$; $(8, 5)$

46. Write an equation describing the line that is parallel to the *y*-axis and that is 6 units to the right of the *y*-axis. $x = 6$

47. Write an equation describing the line that is perpendicular to the *y*-axis and that is 4 units below the *x*-axis. $y = -4$

48. **Critical Thinking** Is it possible for two linear functions whose graphs are parallel lines to have the same *y*-intercept? Explain.

49. **Estimation** Estimate the slope of a line that is perpendicular to the line through $(2.07, 8.95)$ and $(-1.9, 25.07)$. **Possible answer: about** $\frac{1}{4}$

50. **Write About It** Explain in words how to write an equation in slope-intercept form that describes a line parallel to $y - 3 = -6(x - 3)$.

51. This problem will prepare you for the Multi-Step Test Prep on page 376.
    a. Flora walks from her home to the bus stop at a rate of 50 steps per minute. Write a rule that gives her distance from home (in steps) as a function of time. $y = 50x$
    b. Flora's neighbor Dan lives 30 steps closer to the bus stop. He begins walking at the same time and at the same pace as Flora. Write a rule that gives Dan's distance from *Flora's* house as a function of time. $y = 50x + 30$
    c. Will Flora meet Dan along the walk? Use a graph to help explain your answer.

5-9 PRACTICE A

5-9 PRACTICE C

5-9 PRACTICE B

Identify which lines are parallel.

1. $y = 3x + 4$; $y = 4$; $y = 3x$; $y = 3$
   $y = 3x + 4$ and $y = 3x$; $y = 4$ and $y = 3$
2. $y = \frac{1}{2}x + 4$; $x = \frac{1}{2}$; $2x + y = 1$; $y = \frac{1}{2}x + 1$
   $y = \frac{1}{2}x + 4$ and $y = \frac{1}{2}x + 1$
3. Find the slope of each segment.
   slope of $\overline{AB}$: $-\frac{2}{3}$
   slope of $\overline{AD}$: undefined
   slope of $\overline{DC}$: $-\frac{2}{3}$
   slope of $\overline{BC}$: undefined
   Explain why *ABCD* is a parallelogram.
   The opposite sides have the same slope which means they are parallel. A quadrilateral is a parallelogram if the opposite sides are parallel.

Identify which lines are perpendicular.

4. $y = 5$; $y = \frac{1}{8}x$; $x = 2$; $y = 8x - 5$
   $y = 5$ and $x = 2$
5. $y = -2$; $y = -\frac{1}{2}x - 4$; $y - 4 = 2(x + 3)$; $y = -2x$
   $y = -\frac{1}{2}x - 4$ and $y - 4 = 2(x + 3)$
6. Show that *ABC* is a right triangle.
   slope of $\overline{AB} = \frac{1}{4}$; slope of $\overline{BC} = -4$; $\overline{AB}$ is perpendicular to $\overline{BC}$ because $\frac{1}{4}(-4) = -1$. *ABC* is a right triangle because it contains a right angle.

5-9 READING STRATEGIES

Parallel lines		Perpendicular lines
Parallel lines never intersect.	Contrast	Perpendicular lines intersect to form right angles.
The slopes of parallel lines are the same.	Compare	The slopes of perpendicular lines have a product of -1.

Both parallel and perpendicular lines can be identified by their equations.

Both parallel and perpendicular lines have applications in geometry.

Possible answers are given for 1 and 2.

1. Write an equation of a line parallel to $y = 3x + 4$.
   $y = 3x + 3$
2. Write an equation of a line perpendicular to $y = 3x + 4$.
   $y = -\frac{1}{3}x + 3$

$A(9, -4)$, $B(-3, 0)$ and $C(1, 4)$ are the vertices of a triangle.

3. Find the slope of $\overline{AB}$. $-\frac{1}{3}$
4. Find the slope of $\overline{BC}$. 1
5. Find the slope of $\overline{AC}$. -1
6. Is *ABC* a right triangle? Why? yes, $\overline{BC}$ and $\overline{AC}$ are perpendicular because $1(-1) = -1$.

5-9 RETEACH

Two lines are **parallel** if they lie in the same plane and have no points in common. The lines will never intersect.

Identify which lines are parallel.

$y = -2x + 4$; $y = 3x + 4$; $y = -2x - 1$

If lines have the same slope, but different *y*-intercepts, they are parallel lines.

$y = -2x + 4$	$y = 3x + 4$	$y = -2x - 1$
$m = -2$,	$m = 3$	$m = -2$
$b = 4$	$b = 4$	$b = -1$

$y = -2x + 4$ and $y = -2x - 1$ are parallel.

Two lines are **perpendicular** if they intersect to form right angles.

Identify which lines are perpendicular.

If the product of the slopes of two lines is -1, the two lines are perpendicular.

$y = -3x + 1$	$y = 3x + 2$	$y = -\frac{1}{3}x + 3$
$m = -3$	$m = 3$	$m = -\frac{1}{3}$

Because $3\left(-\frac{1}{3}\right) = -1$, $y = 3x + 2$ and $y = -\frac{1}{3}x + 3$ are perpendicular.

Identify which two lines are parallel. Then graph the parallel lines.

1. $y = 4x + 2$; $y = 2x + 1$; $y = 2x - 3$
   $y = 2x + 1$; $y = 2x - 3$

Identify which two lines are perpendicular. Then graph the perpendicular lines.

2. $y = -\frac{2}{3}x + 2$; $y = \frac{3}{2}x + 1$; $y = \frac{2}{3}x - 3$
   $y = -\frac{2}{3}x + 2$; $y = \frac{3}{2}x + 1$

52. Which describes a line parallel to the line described by $y = -3x + 2$?

(A) $y = -3x$ (B) $y = \frac{1}{3}x$ (C) $y = 2 - 3x$ (D) $y = \frac{1}{3}x + 2$

53. Which describes a line passing through $(3, 3)$ that is perpendicular to the line described by $y = \frac{3}{5}x + 2$?

(F)
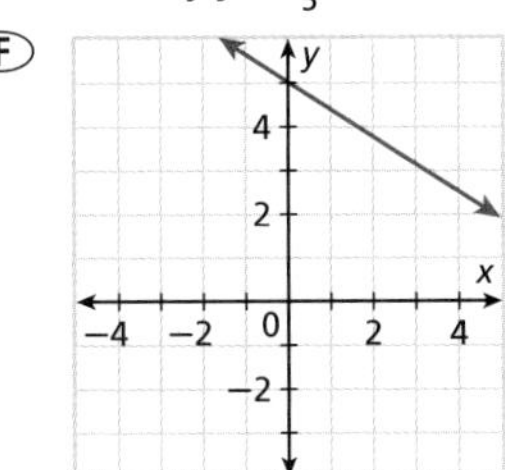

(H)
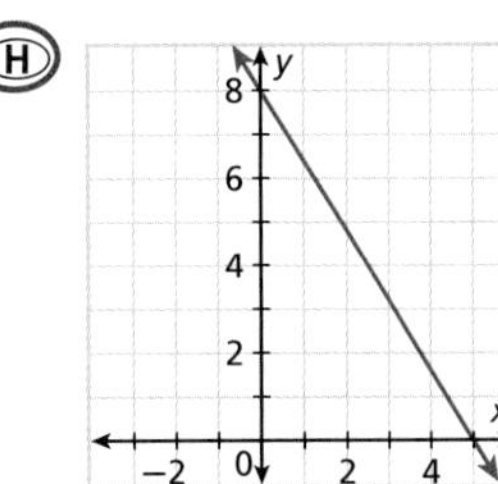

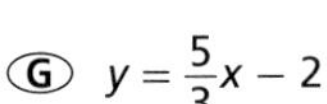

(G) $y = \frac{5}{3}x - 2$ (J) $y = \frac{3}{5}x + \frac{6}{5}$

54. **Gridded Response** The graph of a linear function $f(x)$ is parallel to the line described by $2x + y = 5$ and contains the point $(6, -2)$. What is the y-intercept of $f(x)$? **10**

CHALLENGE AND EXTEND

55. Three or more points that lie on the same line are called *collinear points*. Explain why the points A, B, and C must be collinear if the line containing A and B has the same slope as the line containing B and C.

56. The lines described by $y = (a + 12)x + 3$ and $y = 4ax$ are parallel. What is the value of a? **4**

57. The lines described by $y = (5a + 3)x$ and $y = -\frac{1}{2}x$ are perpendicular. What is the value of a? $-\frac{1}{5}$

58. **Geometry** The diagram shows a square in the coordinate plane. Use the diagram to show that the diagonals of a square are perpendicular. **The slope of one diagonal is $\frac{a-0}{a-0} = \frac{a}{a} = 1$. The slope of the other diagonal is $\frac{0-a}{a-0} = \frac{-a}{a} = -1$. The product of the slopes is $1(-1) = -1$, so the diagonals are perp.**

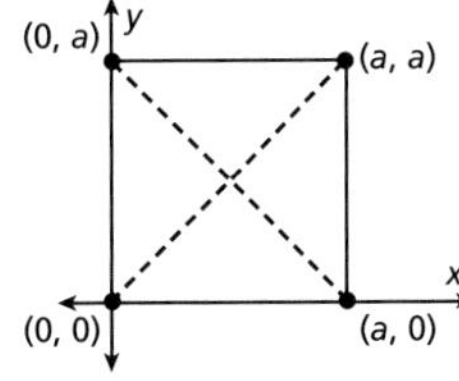

SPIRAL REVIEW

59. The record high temperature for a given city is 112 °F. The morning temperature today was 94 °F and the temperature will increase t degrees. Write and solve an inequality to find all values of t that would break the record for the high temperature. *(Lesson 3-2)* **$94 + t > 112$; $t > 18$**

Graph each function. *(Lesson 4-4)*

60. $y = -3x + 5$ 61. $y = x - 1$ 62. $y = x^2 - 3$

Write an equation in slope-intercept form for the line with the given slope that contains the given point. *(Lesson 5-8)*

63. slope $= \frac{2}{3}$; $(6, -1)$ 64. slope $= -5$; $(2, 4)$ 65. slope $= -\frac{1}{2}$; $(-1, 0)$

66. slope $= -\frac{1}{3}$; $(2, 7)$ 67. slope $= 0$; $(-3, 3)$ 68. slope $= \frac{1}{5}$; $(-4, -2)$

63. $y = \frac{2}{3}x - 5$
64. $y = -5x + 14$
65. $y = -\frac{1}{2}x - \frac{1}{2}$
66. $y = -\frac{1}{3}x + \frac{23}{3}$
67. $y = 3$
68. $y = \frac{1}{5}x - \frac{6}{5}$

Students who chose **C** for **Exercise 52** chose the same line, not a parallel line.

Students who chose **J** in **Exercise 53** found a line parallel to the given line, not perpendicular to it.

Answers

55, 60–62. See p. A22.

Journal

Have students explain how to write the equation of a line that is perpendicular to a given line, such as $y - 2 = 3(x + 1)$.

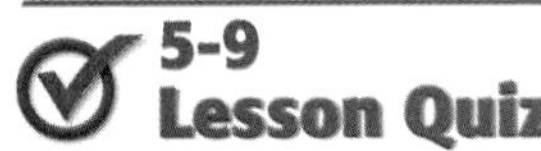

Have students write three equations: one in standard form, one in slope-intercept form, and one in point-slope form. Have them write equations of lines parallel to each line. Then have them write equations of lines perpendicular to each line.

Power Presentations with PowerPoint®

5-9 Lesson Quiz

Write an equation in slope-intercept form for the line described.

1. contains the point $(8, -12)$ and is parallel to $y = -\frac{3}{4}x - 9$ $y = -\frac{3}{4}x - 6$
2. contains the point $(4, -3)$ and is perpendicular to $y = 4x + 5$ $y = -\frac{1}{4}x - 2$
3. Show that $WXYZ$ is a rectangle.

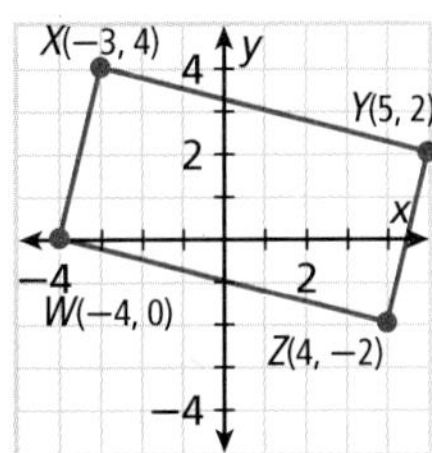

Slope of $\overline{XY} = -\frac{1}{4}$; slope of $\overline{YZ} = 4$; slope of $\overline{WZ} = -\frac{1}{4}$; slope of $\overline{XW} = 4$; the product of the slopes of adjacent sides is -1. Therefore, all angles are rt. angles, and $WXYZ$ is a rectangle.

Also available on transparency

5-9 PROBLEM SOLVING

Write the correct answer.

1. Hamid is making a stained-glass window. He needs a piece of glass that is a perfect parallelogram. Hamid lays a piece of glass that he has cut on a coordinate grid. Show that the glass is in the shape of a parallelogram.
The top and bottom are parallel because they are both horizontal. The sides are parallel because they both have a slope of $-\frac{5}{3}$. It is a parallelogram because both pairs of opposite sides are parallel.

2. Norelle's garden is shown at right. Is her garden in the shape of a right triangle? Justify your answer.
The slope of AB is $\frac{1}{4}$, the slope of AC is $-\frac{7}{4}$, and the slope of BC is $-\frac{1}{4}$. None of the slopes have a product of –1 so no sides are perpendicular.

The graph shows a street map. Use it to answer questions 3–5.

3. The district plans to add Industrial Road next year. It will run perpendicular to Smith Ave. and pass through (–14, 2). What equation will describe the location of Industrial Road?
A $y = 14 - x$ C $y = -14$
B $y = x - 14$ D $x = -14$

4. In two years, the business district plans to add Stock Street. It will run parallel to Market Blvd. and pass through (–1, 5). What equation will describe the location of Stock Street?
F $y = -7x + 12$ H $y = \frac{1}{7}x + \frac{34}{7}$
G $y = -7x - 2$ J $y = \frac{1}{7}x + \frac{36}{7}$

5. What is the slope of a street parallel to Bear Street?
A –7 C $\frac{1}{7}$
B $-\frac{1}{7}$ D 7

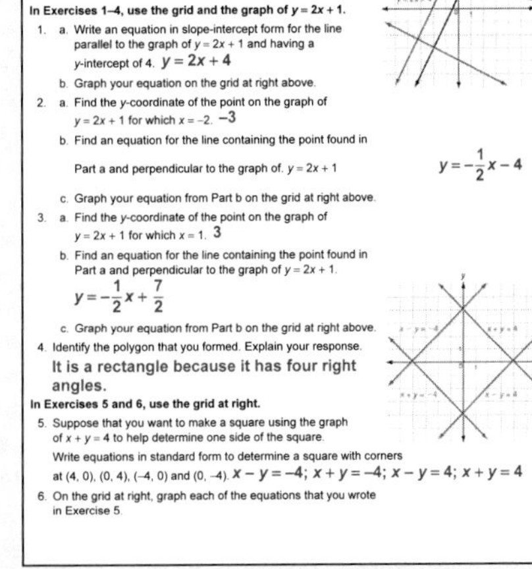

5-9 CHALLENGE

Two facts about parallel and perpendicular lines are summarized below.

If two nonvertical lines are parallel, then their slopes are equal.

If two nonvertical lines are perpendicular, then their slopes are negative reciprocals of one another.

You can use these facts if you want to construct special polygons on the coordinate plane.

In Exercises 1–4, use the grid and the graph of $y = 2x + 1$.

1. a. Write an equation in slope-intercept form for the line parallel to the graph of $y = 2x + 1$ and having a y-intercept of 4. $y = 2x + 4$
b. Graph your equation on the grid at right above.
2. a. Find the y-coordinate of the point on the graph of $y = 2x + 1$ for which $x = -2$. -3
b. Find an equation for the line containing the point found in Part a and perpendicular to the graph of $y = 2x + 1$. $y = -\frac{1}{2}x - 4$
c. Graph your equation from Part b on the grid at right above.
3. a. Find the y-coordinate of the point on the graph of $y = 2x + 1$ for which $x = 1$. 3
b. Find an equation for the line containing the point found in Part a and perpendicular to the graph of $y = 2x + 1$. $y = -\frac{1}{2}x + \frac{7}{2}$
c. Graph your equation from Part b on the grid at right above.
4. Identify the polygon that you formed. Explain your response. It is a rectangle because it has four right angles.

In Exercises 5 and 6, use the grid at right.

5. Suppose that you want to make a square using the graph of $x + y = 4$ to help determine one side of the square. Write equations in standard form to determine a square with corners at (4, 0), (0, 4), (–4, 0) and (0, –4). $x - y = -4$; $x + y = -4$; $x - y = 4$; $x + y = 4$
6. On the grid at right, graph each of the equations that you wrote in Exercise 5.

Organizer

Use with Lesson 5-10

Pacing:

Traditional $\frac{1}{2}$ day
Block $\frac{1}{4}$ day

Objective: Use a graphing calculator to explore the family of linear functions.

Materials: graphing calculator

PREMIER **Online Edition**
Graphing Calculator, TechKeys

Resources

Technology Lab Activities
5-10 Lab Recording Sheet

Teach

Discuss

The order in which the equations are entered into the **Y1** editor will be the same order in which the lines are graphed. Before pressing GRAPH, note if the values of b in the equations are starting out negative or positive, and if they are in ascending or descending order.

Close

Key Concept

Changing b shifts a graph up or down. Changing m turns a graph so it is steeper or less steep.

Assessment

Journal Have students compare and contrast the graphs of $y = x$, $y = x + 10$, and $y = 10x$.

State Resources

go.hrw.com
State Resources Online
KEYWORD: MA7 Resources

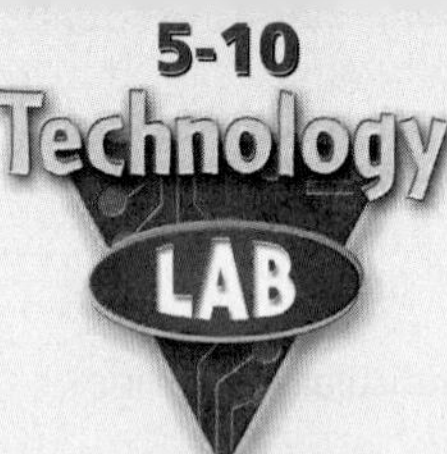

5-10 Technology LAB

The Family of Linear Functions

Use with Lesson 5-10

A *family of functions* is a set of functions whose graphs have basic characteristics in common. For example, all linear functions form a family. You can use a graphing calculator to explore families of functions.

go.hrw.com
Lab Resources Online
KEYWORD: MA11 LAB5

Activity

Graph the lines described by $y = x - 2$, $y = x - 1$, $y = x$, $y = x + 1$, $y = x + 2$, $y = x + 3$, and $y = x + 4$. How does the value of b affect the graph described by $y = x + b$?

1. All of the functions are in the form $y = x + b$. Enter them into the **Y=** editor.

   Y= X,T,θ,n − 2 ENTER
   X,T,θ,n − 1 ENTER

   and so on.

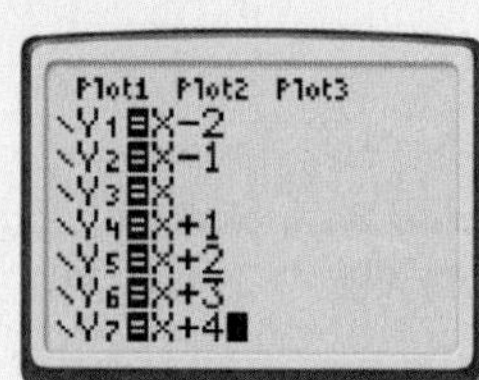

2. Press ZOOM and select **6:Zstandard.** Think about the different values of b as you watch the graphs being drawn. Notice that the lines are all parallel.

3. It appears that the value of b in $y = x + b$ shifts the graph up or down—up if b is positive and down if b is negative.

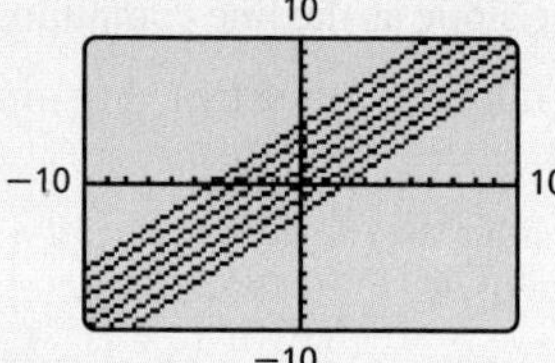

Try This

1. Make a prediction about the lines described by $y = 2x - 3$, $y = 2x - 2$, $y = 2x - 1$, $y = 2x$, $y = 2x + 1$, $y = 2x + 2$, and $y = 2x + 3$. Then graph. Was your prediction correct?
2. Now use your calculator to explore what happens to the graph of $y = mx$ when you change the value of m.
   a. **Make a Prediction** How do you think the lines described by $y = -2x$, $y = -x$, $y = x$, and $y = 2x$ will be related? How will they be alike? How will they be different?
   b. Graph the functions given in part **a.** Was your prediction correct?
   c. How is the effect of m different when m is positive from when m is negative?

2c. When m is pos., the graph slopes upward from left to right and greater values of m mean steeper lines. When m is neg., the graph slopes downward from left to right and greater values of m mean less steep lines.

Answers

1. They will all be par. lines.

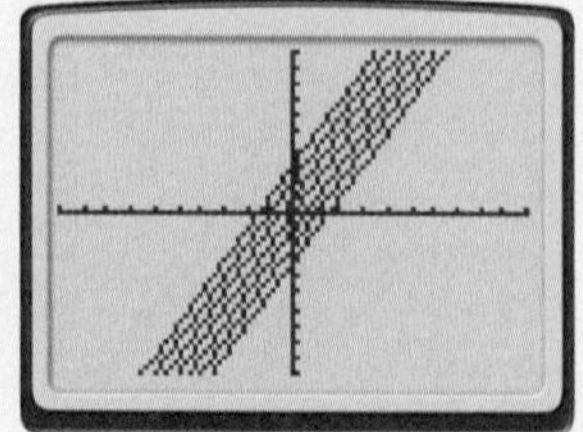

2a. They will all pass through (0, 0) but have different slopes.

2b.

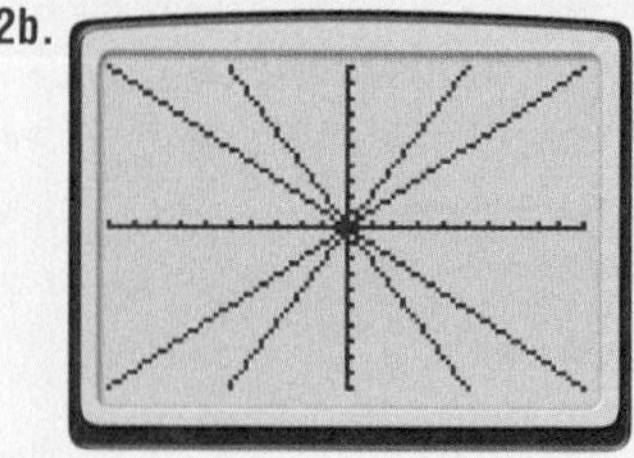

5-10 Transforming Linear Functions

Objective
Describe how changing slope and y-intercept affect the graph of a linear function.

Vocabulary
family of functions
parent function
transformation
translation
rotation
reflection

Who uses this?
Business owners can use transformations to show the effects of price changes, such as the price of trophy engraving. (See Example 5.)

A **family of functions** is a set of functions whose graphs have basic characteristics in common. For example, all linear functions form a family because all of their graphs are the same basic shape.

A **parent function** is the most basic function in a family. For linear functions, the parent function is $f(x) = x$.

The graphs of all other linear functions are *transformations* of the graph of the parent function, $f(x) = x$. A **transformation** is a change in position or size of a figure.

There are three types of transformations—*translations, rotations,* and *reflections.*

Look at the four functions and their graphs below.

Remember!
Function notation—$f(x)$, $g(x)$, and so on—can be used in place of y.
$y = f(x)$

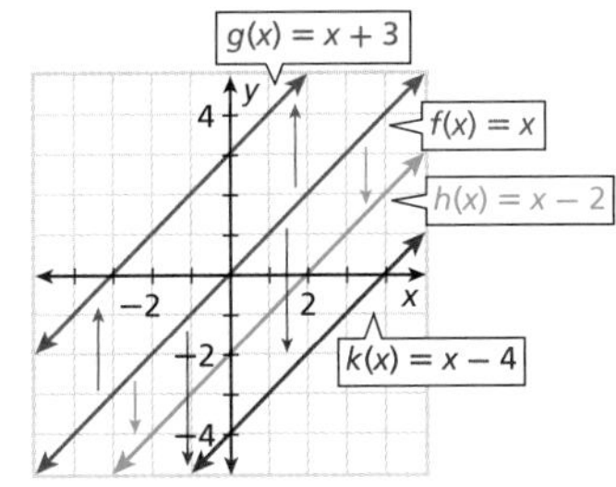

Notice that all of the lines above are parallel. The slopes are the same but the y-intercepts are different.

The graphs of $g(x) = x + 3$, $h(x) = x - 2$, and $k(x) = x - 4$ are vertical *translations* of the graph of the parent function, $f(x) = x$. A **translation** is a type of transformation that moves every point the same distance in the same direction. You can think of a translation as a "slide."

Vertical Translation of a Linear Function

When the y-intercept b is changed in the function $f(x) = mx + b$, the graph is translated vertically.

- If b increases, the graph is translated up.
- If b decreases, the graph is translated down.

5-10 Organizer

Pacing: Traditional 1 day
Block $\frac{1}{2}$ day

Objective: Describe how changing slope and y-intercept affect the graph of a linear function.

Online Edition
Tutorial Videos

Countdown Week 12

Power Presentations with PowerPoint®

Warm Up

Identify the slope and y-intercept.

1. $y = x + 4$ $m = 1; b = 4$

2. $y = -3x$ $m = -3; b = 0$

Compare and contrast the graphs of each pair of equations.

3. $y = 2x + 4$ and $y = 2x - 4$
same slope, par.; diff. intercepts

4. $y = 2x + 4$ and $y = -2x + 4$
same y-intercepts; diff. slopes but same steepness

Also available on transparency

Q: Why did the student need directions during math class?

A: He was lost in translation.

State Resources

1 Introduce

EXPLORATION

5-10 Transforming Linear Functions

You will need graph paper or a graphing calculator for this Exploration.

1. Graph $y = 2x + 3$.
2. Write a new linear function of the form $y = 2x + b$, where b is any number of your choice. Graph this function on the same coordinate plane as $y = 2x + 3$. How does the graph of the new function compare to that of $y = 2x + 3$?
3. Repeat the process several times, choosing different values for b and graphing the new functions on the same coordinate plane. Be sure to try some values greater than 3 and some less than 3.
4. What happened to the graph of $y = 2x + 3$ when you replaced 3 with a number greater than 3?
5. What happened to the graph of $y = 2x + 3$ when you replaced 3 with a number less than 3?

THINK AND DISCUSS

6. **Describe** how you would change $y = -7x + 1$ if you wanted to slide its graph down.
7. **Describe** how you would change $y = -7x + 1$ if you wanted to slide its graph up by 5 units.

Motivate

Students most likely studied translations and reflections of geometric figures in previous grades, but they may recognize only informal names such as *slide*, *turn*, and *flip*. Review these concepts with them. Tell students that graphs of functions are geometric figures too, and that they can also be translated and reflected. Tell students that they will learn how such changes to a graph can be related directly to the equation that describes the function.

Explorations and answers are provided in *Alternate Openers: Explorations Transparencies.*

Power Presentations with PowerPoint®

Additional Examples

Example 1

Graph $f(x) = 2x$ and $g(x) = 2x - 6$. Then describe the transformation from the graph of $f(x)$ to the graph of $g(x)$.

trans. 6 units down

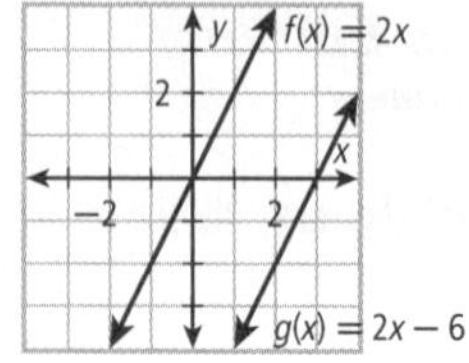

Example 2

Graph $f(x) = x$ and $g(x) = 5x$. Then describe the transformation from the graph of $f(x)$ to the graph of $g(x)$.

rot. about (0, 0) (steeper)

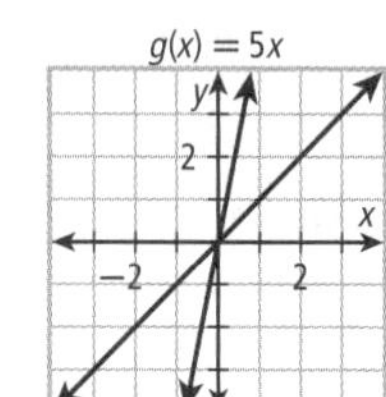

INTERVENTION

Questioning Strategies

EXAMPLE 1

- What part of a linear function indicates which way the line will shift vertically?

EXAMPLE 2

- How can you tell if a transformed function will be steeper or less steep than the original function?

Technology Notice that the slopes appear different on the calculator screen than on the paper graph. By using a square window, you can see the true slope represented on the calculator screen.

EXAMPLE 1 Translating Linear Functions

1\.

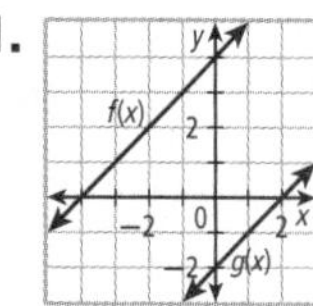

trans. 6 units down

Graph $f(x) = x$ and $g(x) = x - 5$. Then describe the transformation from the graph of $f(x)$ to the graph of $g(x)$.

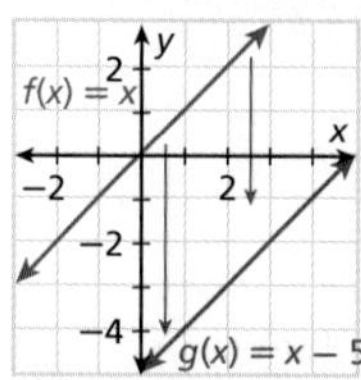

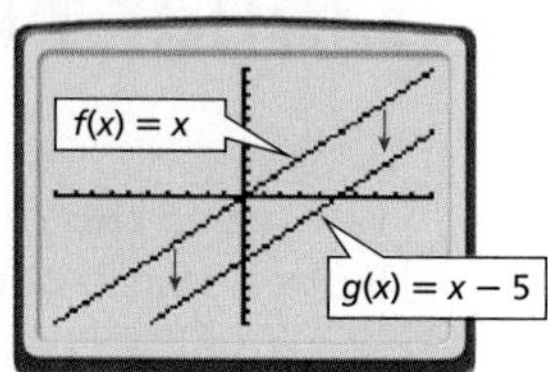

The graph of $g(x) = x - 5$ is the result of translating the graph of $f(x) = x$ 5 units down.

1\. Graph $f(x) = x + 4$ and $g(x) = x - 2$. Then describe the transformation from the graph of $f(x)$ to the graph of $g(x)$.

The graphs of $g(x) = 3x$, $h(x) = 5x$, and $k(x) = \frac{1}{2}x$ are *rotations* of the graph of $f(x) = x$. A **rotation** is a transformation about a point. You can think of a rotation as a "turn." The *y*-intercepts are the same, but the slopes are different.

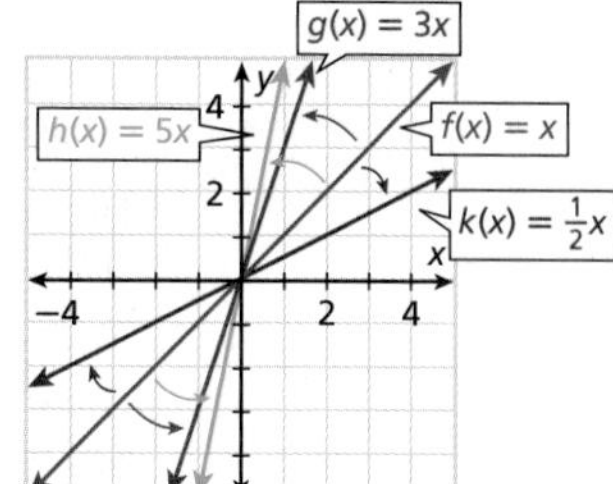

Know it! Note

Rotation of a Linear Function

When the slope *m* is changed in the function $f(x) = mx + b$ it causes a rotation of the graph about the point (0, *b*), which changes the line's steepness.

EXAMPLE 2 Rotating Linear Functions

Graph $f(x) = x + 2$ and $g(x) = 2x + 2$. Then describe the transformation from the graph of $f(x)$ to the graph of $g(x)$.

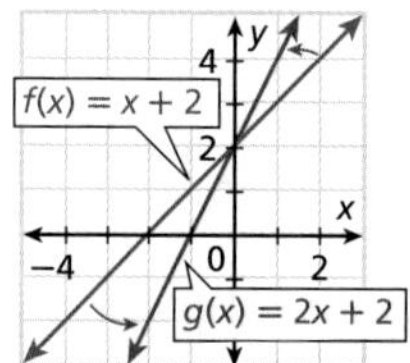

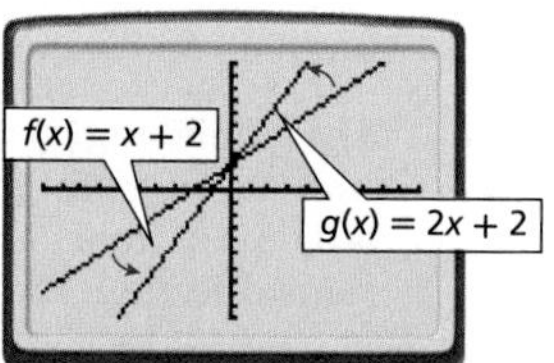

2\.

rot. about (0, −1) (less steep)

The graph of $g(x) = 2x + 2$ is the result of rotating the graph of $f(x) = x + 2$ about (0, 2). The graph of $g(x)$ is steeper than the graph of $f(x)$.

2\. Graph $f(x) = 3x - 1$ and $g(x) = \frac{1}{2}x - 1$. Then describe the transformation from the graph of $f(x)$ to the graph of $g(x)$.

2 Teach

Guided Instruction

Review graphing linear equations with an emphasis on slope and *y*-intercept before beginning this lesson. For each transformation of a linear function, encourage students to ask themselves if the *y*-intercept and/or the slope will change, and in which direction. This lesson will help prepare students for transformations of nonlinear functions, which are an important concept later in this course as well as in future mathematics courses.

Reaching All Learners

Through Kinesthetic Experience

Give each student three index cards and have them write *translation* on the first, *rotation* on the second, and *reflection* on the third. Write the functions listed below on the board one at a time. Instruct students to hold up the correct card(s) to describe the transformation from $f(x)$ to $g(x)$.

$f(x) = x$, $g(x) = 4x$ rotation

$f(x) = x$, $g(x) = x - 6$ translation

$f(x) = x$, $g(x) = -5x$ rotation

$f(x) = 2x$, $g(x) = -2x$ rotation, reflection

The diagram shows the *reflection* of the graph of $f(x) = 2x$ across the y-axis, producing the graph of $g(x) = -2x$. A **reflection** is a transformation across a line that produces a mirror image. You can think of a reflection as a "flip" over a line.

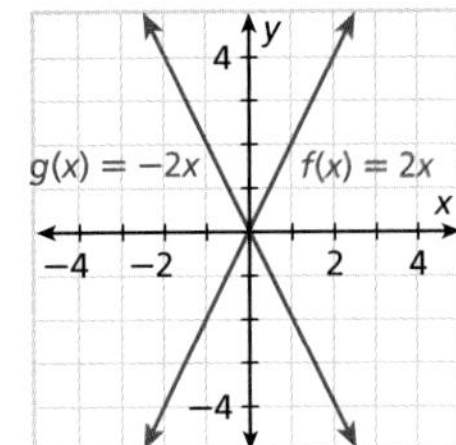

Reflection of a Linear Function

When the slope m is multiplied by -1 in $f(x) = mx + b$, the graph is reflected across the y-axis.

EXAMPLE 3 Reflecting Linear Functions

Graph $f(x)$. Then reflect the graph of $f(x)$ across the y-axis. Write a function $g(x)$ to describe the new graph.

A $f(x) = x$

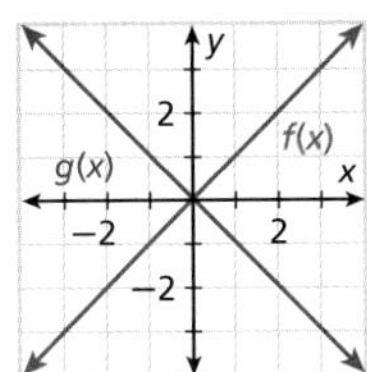

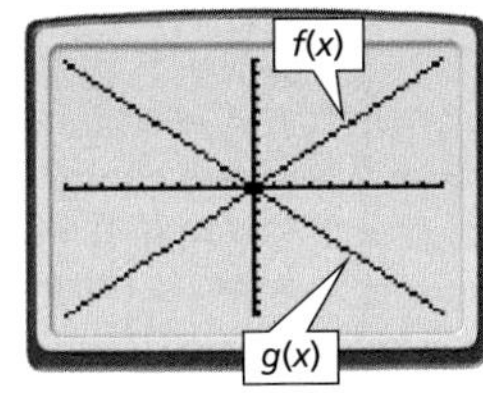

To find $g(x)$, multiply the value of m by -1.

In $f(x) = x$, $m = 1$.

$1(-1) = -1$ *This is the value of m for g(x).*

$g(x) = -x$

B $f(x) = -4x - 1$

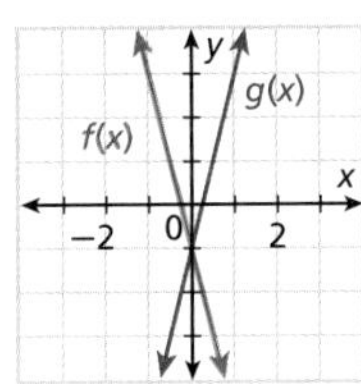

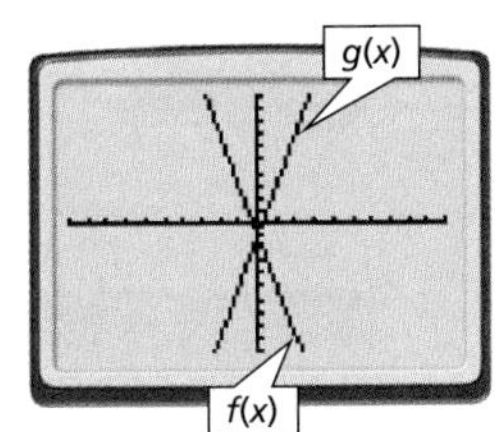

To find $g(x)$, multiply the value of m by -1.

In $f(x) = -4x - 1$, $m = -4$.

$-4(-1) = 4$ *This is the value of m for g(x).*

$g(x) = 4x - 1$

3. Graph $f(x) = \frac{2}{3}x + 2$. Then reflect the graph of $f(x)$ across the y-axis. Write a function $g(x)$ to describe the new graph.

3.

$g(x) = -\frac{2}{3}x + 2$

COMMON ERROR ALERT

Students might think that a positive slope will always be steeper than a negative slope because the positive value is greater. To show this is not true, have students graph $f(x) = -6x$ and $g(x) = 2x$. Explain that it is necessary to take the absolute value of each slope before comparing them.

Power Presentations with PowerPoint®

Additional Examples

Example 3

Graph $f(x) = 2x + 2$. Then reflect the graph of $f(x)$ across the y-axis. Write a function $g(x)$ to describe the new graph.

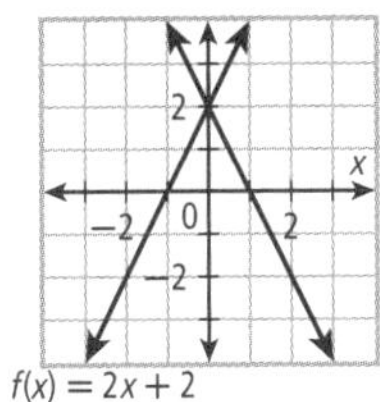

$g(x) = -2x + 2$

INTERVENTION

Questioning Strategies

EXAMPLE 3

- How does the slope change in a reflection? How does the y-intercept change?

Teaching Tip

Math Background Some students may notice that a reflection of a linear function can also be described as a rotation. This is true for linear functions, because both are the result of changing the slope. However, this is not the case for other functions that students will study later in this course and in future courses. Be sure students connect the concepts "multiply by −1" and "reflection."

Power Presentations with PowerPoint®

Additional Examples

Example 4

Graph $f(x) = x$ and $g(x) = 2x - 3$. Then describe the transformations from the graph of $f(x)$ to the graph of $g(x)$.

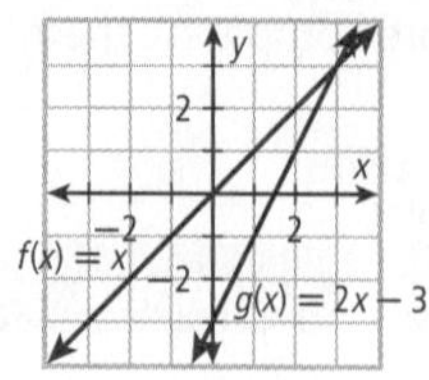

rot. about (0, 0) (steeper) and trans. 3 units down

Example 5

A florist charges $25 for a vase plus $4.50 for each flower. The total charge for the vase and flowers is given by the function $f(x) = 4.50x + 25$. How will the graph change if the vase's cost is raised to $35? if the charge per flower is lowered to $3.00?

translated 10 units up; rotated about (0, 25) (less steep)

INTERVENTION

Questioning Strategies

EXAMPLE 4

- Does the order of multiple transformations make a difference on the resulting graph? Explain.

EXAMPLE 5

- Do you think a translation or a rotation will have more effect on the overall cost? Explain your reasoning.

4.

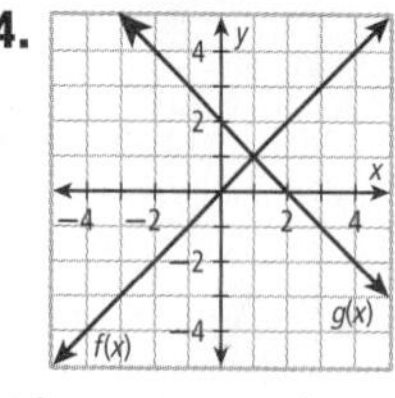

ref. across *y*-axis, trans. 2 units up

EXAMPLE 4 Multiple Transformations of Linear Functions

Graph $f(x) = x$ and $g(x) = 3x + 1$. Then describe the transformations from the graph of $f(x)$ to the graph of $g(x)$.

Find transformations of $f(x) = x$ that will result in $g(x) = 3x + 1$:

- Multiply $f(x)$ by 3 to get $h(x) = 3x$. This rotates the graph about (0, 0) and makes it steeper.
- Then add 1 to $h(x)$ to get $g(x) = 3x + 1$. This translates the graph 1 unit up.

The transformations are a rotation and a translation.

4. Graph $f(x) = x$ and $g(x) = -x + 2$. Then describe the transformations from the graph of $f(x)$ to the graph of $g(x)$.

EXAMPLE 5 Business Application

A trophy company charges $175 for a trophy plus $0.20 per letter for the engraving. The total charge for a trophy with x letters is given by the function $f(x) = 0.20x + 175$. How will the graph change if the trophy's cost is lowered to $172? if the charge per letter is raised to $0.50?

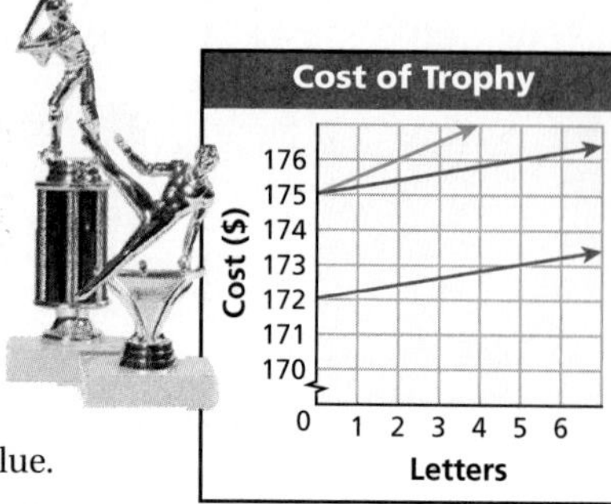

$f(x) = 0.20x + 175$ is graphed in blue.

If the trophy's cost is lowered to $172, the new function is $g(x) = 0.20x + 172$. The original graph will be translated 3 units down.

If the charge per letter is raised to $0.50, the new function is $h(x) = 0.50x + 175$. The original graph will be rotated about (0, 175) and become steeper.

5. **What if...?** How will the graph change if the charge per letter is lowered to $0.15? if the trophy's cost is raised to $180?

rotated about (0, 175) (less steep); translated 5 units up

THINK AND DISCUSS

1. Describe the graph of $f(x) = x + 3.45$
2. Look at the graphs in Example 5. For each line, is every point on the line a solution in this situation? Explain.
3. **GET ORGANIZED** Copy and complete the graphic organizer. In each box, sketch a graph of the given transformation of $f(x) = x$, and label it with a possible equation.

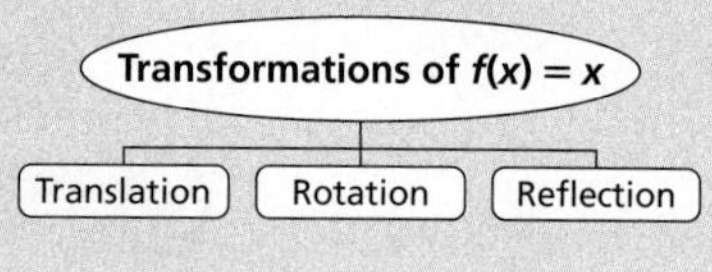

3 Close

Summarize

Ask students to state how each transformation affects the slope and *y*-intercept.

translation
same slope, diff. *y*-int.

rotation
diff. slope, same *y*-int.

reflection
opp. slope, same *y*-int.

ONGOING ASSESSMENT and INTERVENTION

***Diagnose Before* the Lesson**
5-10 Warm Up, TE p. 369

***Monitor During* the Lesson**
Check It Out! Exercises, SE pp. 370–372
Questioning Strategies, TE pp. 370–372

***Assess After* the Lesson**
5-10 Lesson Quiz, TE p. 375
Alternative Assessment, TE p. 375

Answers to *Think and Discuss*

1. translation of $f(x) = x$ up 3.45 units
2. No; there can only be a whole number of letters, so points whose *x*-coordinates are not whole numbers have no meaning in this situation.
3. See p. A6.

go.hrw.com
Homework Help Online
KEYWORD: MA11 5-10
Parent Resources Online
KEYWORD: MA7 Parent

GUIDED PRACTICE

Vocabulary Apply the vocabulary from this lesson to answer each question.

1. Changing the value of b in $f(x) = mx + b$ results in a __?__ of the graph. (*translation* or *reflection*) **translation**
2. Changing the value of m in $f(x) = mx + b$ results in a __?__ of the graph. (*translation* or *rotation*) **rotation**

Graph $f(x)$ and $g(x)$. Then describe the transformation from the graph of $f(x)$ to the graph of $g(x)$.

SEE EXAMPLE 1 p. 370

3. $f(x) = x$, $g(x) = x - 4$
4. $f(x) = x$, $g(x) = x + 1$
5. $f(x) = x$, $g(x) = x + 2$
6. $f(x) = x$, $g(x) = x - 6.5$

SEE EXAMPLE 2 p. 370

7. $f(x) = x$, $g(x) = \frac{1}{4}x$
8. $f(x) = \frac{1}{5}x + 3$, $g(x) = x + 3$
9. $f(x) = 2x - 2$, $g(x) = 4x - 2$
10. $f(x) = x + 1$, $g(x) = \frac{1}{2}x + 1$

Graph $f(x)$. Then reflect the graph of $f(x)$ across the y-axis. Write a function $g(x)$ to describe the new graph.

SEE EXAMPLE 3 p. 371

11. $f(x) = -\frac{1}{5}x$ $\mathbf{g(x) = \frac{1}{5}x}$
12. $f(x) = 2x + 4$ $\mathbf{g(x) = -2x + 4}$
13. $f(x) = \frac{1}{3}x - 6$ $\mathbf{g(x) = -\frac{1}{3}x - 6}$
14. $f(x) = 5x - 1$ $\mathbf{g(x) = -5x - 1}$

Graph $f(x)$ and $g(x)$. Then describe the transformations from the graph of $f(x)$ to the graph of $g(x)$.

SEE EXAMPLE 4 p. 372

15. $f(x) = x$, $g(x) = 2x - 2$
16. $f(x) = x$, $g(x) = \frac{1}{3}x + 1$
17. $f(x) = -x - 1$, $g(x) = -4x$
18. $f(x) = -x$, $g(x) = -\frac{1}{2}x - 3$

SEE EXAMPLE 5 p. 372

19. **Entertainment** For large parties, a restaurant charges a reservation fee of $25, plus $15 per person. The total charge for a party of x people is $f(x) = 15x + 25$. How will the graph of this function change if the reservation fee is raised to $50? if the per-person charge is lowered to $12?

PRACTICE AND PROBLEM SOLVING

Independent Practice

For Exercises	See Example
20–21	1
22–23	2
24–25	3
26–27	4
28	5

Extra Practice
Skills Practice p. S13
Application Practice p. S32

Graph $f(x)$ and $g(x)$. Then describe the transformation(s) from the graph of $f(x)$ to the graph of $g(x)$.

20. $f(x) = x$, $g(x) = x + \frac{1}{2}$
21. $f(x) = x$, $g(x) = x - 4$
22. $f(x) = \frac{1}{5}x - 1$, $g(x) = \frac{1}{10}x - 1$
23. $f(x) = x + 2$, $g(x) = \frac{2}{3}x + 2$

Graph $f(x)$. Then reflect the graph of $f(x)$ across the y-axis. Write a function $g(x)$ to describe the new graph.

24. $f(x) = 6x$ $\mathbf{g(x) = -6x}$
25. $f(x) = -3x - 2$ $\mathbf{g(x) = 3x - 2}$

Graph $f(x)$ and $g(x)$. Then describe the transformations from the graph of $f(x)$ to the graph of $g(x)$.

26. $f(x) = 2x$, $g(x) = 4x - 1$
27. $f(x) = -7x + 5$, $g(x) = -14x$

Assignment Guide

Assign *Guided Practice* exercises as necessary.

If you finished Examples **1–3**
Basic 20–25, 30, 40, 44
Average 20–25, 30, 40, 51
Advanced 20–25, 30, 51, 52

If you finished Examples **1–5**
Basic 20–35, 39–44, 47, 49, 50, 53–61
Average 20–28, 35–51, 53–61
Advanced 20–28, 36–61

Homework Quick Check
Quickly check key concepts.
Exercises: 20, 22, 24, 26, 28, 42

Answers

3.

trans. 4 units down

4.

trans. 1 unit up

State Resources

Answers

5.

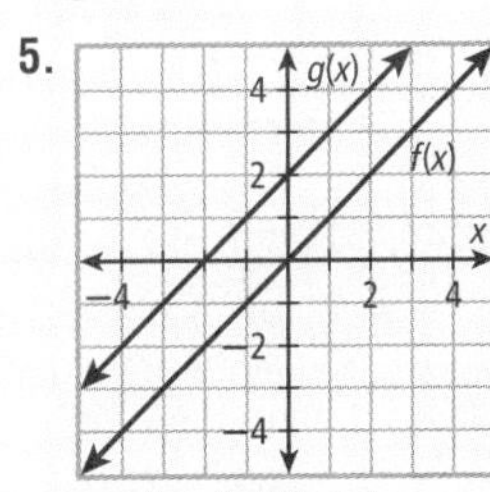

trans. 2 units up

6.

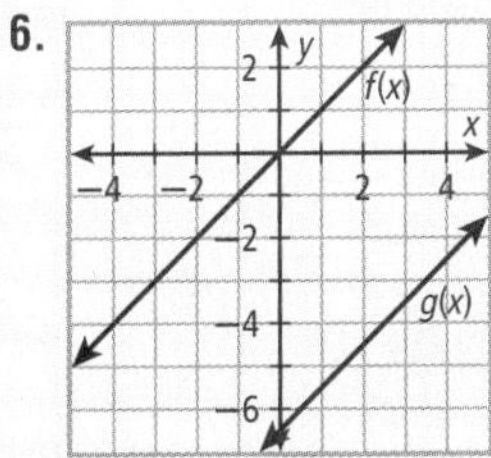

trans. 6.5 units down

7.

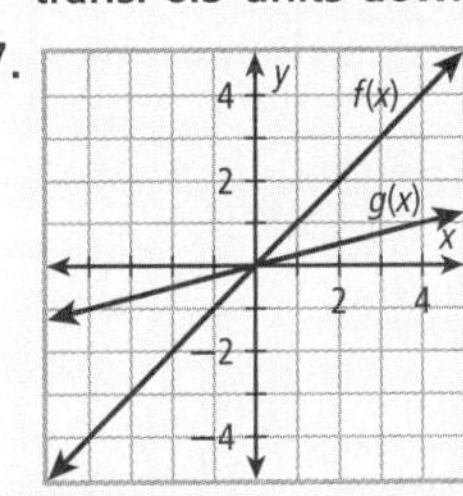

rot. about (0, 0) (less steep)

8.

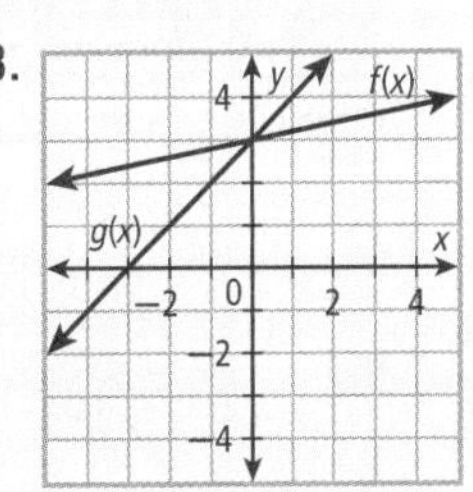

rot. about (0, 3) (steeper)

9, 10. See p. A22.
11–14. For graphs, see p. A22.
15–23. See pp. A22–A23.
24, 25. For graphs, see p. A23.
26, 27. See p. A23.

Exercise 48 involves a translation of a line. This exercise prepares students for the Multi-Step Test Prep on page 376.

Answers

28. trans. 2 units down; rot. about (0, 2) (steeper)
29. ref. across y-axis

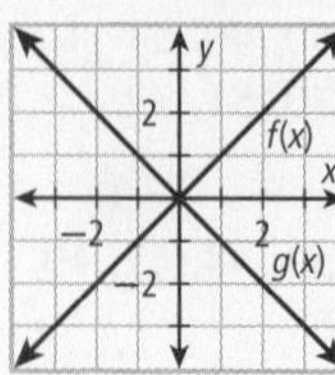

opp. slopes—same steepness but in opp. directions; same y-int.

30. trans. 8 units up

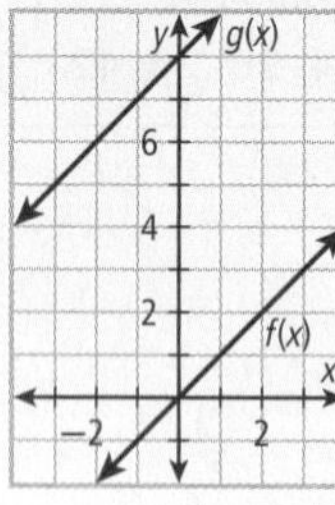

same slope but diff. y-intercepts

31. rot. about (0, 0) (steeper)

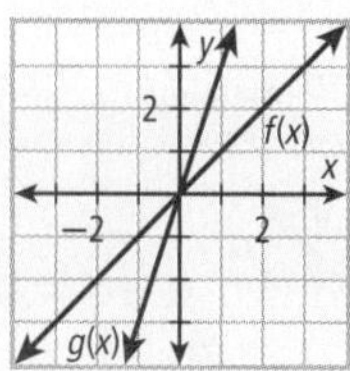

diff. slopes and same y-int.

32–34. See p. A23.
35–38b. For graphs, see p. A23.
38c–44, 47, 48. See p. A23.

28. **School** The number of chaperones on a field trip must include 1 teacher for every 4 students, plus 2 parents total. The function describing the number of chaperones for a trip of x students is $f(x) = \frac{1}{4}x + 2$. How will the graph change if the number of parents is reduced to 0? if the number of teachers is raised to 1 for every 3 students?

Describe the transformation(s) on the graph of $f(x) = x$ that result in the graph of $g(x)$. Graph $f(x)$ and $g(x)$, and compare the slopes and intercepts.

29. $g(x) = -x$
30. $g(x) = x + 8$
31. $g(x) = 3x$
32. $g(x) = -\frac{2}{7}x$
33. $g(x) = 6x - 3$
34. $g(x) = -2x + 1$

Sketch the transformed graph. Then write a function to describe your graph.

35. Rotate the graph of $f(x) = -x + 2$ until it has the same steepness in the opposite direction. **$g(x) = x + 2$**
36. Reflect the graph of $f(x) = x - 1$ across the y-axis, and then translate it 4 units down. **$g(x) = -x - 5$**
37. Translate the graph of $f(x) = \frac{1}{6}x - 10$ six units up. **$g(x) = \frac{1}{6}x - 4$**
38. **Hobbies** A book club charges a membership fee of \$20 and then \$12 for each book purchased.
    a. Write and graph a function to represent the cost y of membership in the club based on the number of books purchased x. **$y = 12x + 20$**
    b. **What if...?** Write and graph a second function to represent the cost of membership if the club raises its membership fee to \$30. **$y = 12x + 30$**
    c. Describe the relationship between your graphs from parts **a** and **b**.

LINK

Hobbies

Seattle librarian Nancy Pearl started the first citywide reading program, "If All Seattle Reads the Same Book," in 1998. Many cities have since emulated this program, attempting to unite communities by having everyone read the same book at the same time.

45c. Commission changes to 25%; base pay changes to \$400.

Describe the transformation(s) on the graph of $f(x) = x$ that result in the graph of $g(x)$.

39. $g(x) = x - 9$
40. $g(x) = -x$
41. $g(x) = 5x$
42. $g(x) = -\frac{2}{3}x + 1$
43. $g(x) = -2x$
44. $g(x) = \frac{1}{5}x$
45. **Careers** Kelly works as a salesperson. She earns a weekly base salary plus a commission that is a percent of her total sales. Her total weekly pay is described by $f(x) = 0.20x + 300$, where x is total sales in dollars.
    a. What is Kelly's weekly base salary? **\$300**
    b. What percent of total sales does Kelly receive as commission? **20%**
    c. **What if...?** What is the change in Kelly's salary plan if the weekly pay function changes to $g(x) = 0.25x + 300$? to $h(x) = 0.2x + 400$?
46. **Critical Thinking** To transform the graph of $f(x) = x$ into the graph of $g(x) = -x$, you can reflect the graph of $f(x)$ across the y-axis. Find another transformation that will have the same result. **Possible answer: ref. across x-axis**

47. **Write About It** Describe how a reflection across the y-axis affects each point on a graph. Give an example to illustrate your answer.

48. This problem will prepare you for the Multi-Step Test Prep on page 376.
    a. Maria is walking from school to the softball field at a rate of 3 feet per second. Write a rule that gives her distance from school (in feet) as a function of time (in seconds). Then graph.
    b. Give a real-world situation that could be described by a line parallel to the one in part **a**.
    c. What does the y-intercept represent in each of these situations?

5-10 PRACTICE A
5-10 PRACTICE C
5-10 PRACTICE B

Graph $f(x)$ and $g(x)$. Then describe the transformation from the graph of $f(x)$ to the graph of $g(x)$.

1. $f(x) = x$; $g(x) = x + 3$
   translation 3 units up
2. $f(x) = \frac{1}{3}x - 4$; $g(x) = \frac{1}{4}x - 4$
   rotation (less steep) about (0, −4)
3. $f(x) = x$; $g(x) = 2x - 5$
   rotation (steeper) about (0, 0) and translation 5 units down
4. Graph $f(x) = -3x + 1$. Then reflect the graph of $f(x)$ across the y-axis. Write a function $g(x)$ to describe the new graph.
   $g(x) = 3x + 1$
5. The cost of hosting a party at a horse farm is a flat fee of \$250, plus \$5 per person. The total charge for a party of x people is $f(x) = 5x + 250$. How will the graph of this function change if the flat fee is lowered to \$200? if the per-person rate is raised to \$8?
   The graph will be translated 50 units down. The graph will be rotated about (0, 250) and become steeper.

5-10 READING STRATEGIES

The table shows three types of transformations.

Transformation	Translation	Rotation	Reflection
Description	When b in $y = mx + b$ increases (decreases), the line is translated up (down).	When $\lvert m \rvert$ in $y = mx + b$ increases (decreases), the line becomes more steep (less steep).	When m in $y = mx + b$ is multiplied by −1, the line is reflected across the y-axis.
Graph			
Equations	$f(x) = -3x + 2$ $g(x) = -3x - 3$	$f(x) = -3x + 2$ $g(x) = -1x + 2$	$f(x) = -3x + 2$ $g(x) = 3x + 2$

Answer the following.

1. Look at the graph of the translation. How many vertical units is $f(x)$ shifted down to $g(x)$? **5**
   Look at the related functions. Subtract the y-intercept of $g(x)$ from the y-intercept of $f(x)$. **2 − (−3) = 5**
2. Look at the graph of the rotation. Which graph is steeper? **$f(x)$**
   Look at the slopes of the related functions. For which function is the absolute value of the slope greater? **$f(x)$**
3. Look at the graph of the reflection. Which axis is a line of symmetry? **y-axis**
   Look at the slopes of the related functions. Are they the same or opposite? **opposite**

Describe the transformation from the graph of $f(x)$ to the graph of $g(x)$.

4. $f(x) = 4x - 3$, $g(x) = 2x - 3$ **rotation (less steep) about (0, −3)**
5. $f(x) = -2x + 2$, $g(x) = 2x + 2$ **reflection about y-axis**
6. $f(x) = x + 2$, $g(x) = x + 8$ **translation 6 units up**

5-10 RETEACH

The function $f(x) = x$ is called the parent function for the family of linear functions.

Changing the y-intercept will shift the line up or down. This is called a **translation**.

Graph $f(x) = x$, $g(x) = x + 2$, and $h(x) = x - 4$. Describe the transformations.

shift 2 up
parent function
shift 4 down

The y-intercept of $g(x)$ is 2 so the graph shifts up 2 units from $f(x)$. The y-intercept of $h(x)$ is −4 so the graph shifts down 4 units from $f(x)$.

Changing the slope of a line will change the steepness of the line. This is called a **rotation.**

Graph $f(x) = x$, $g(x) = 4x$, and $h(x) = \frac{1}{2}x$.

Describe the transformations.

line is steeper
line is less steep

The slope of $g(x)$ is 4 so the line is steeper than $f(x)$ which has a slope of 1. The slope of $h(x)$ is $\frac{1}{2}$ and it is less steep.

1. Graph $f(x) = x$ and $g(x) = x + 3$. Then describe the transformation from the graph of $f(x)$ to the graph of $g(x)$.
   translation 3 units up

Describe the transformations from the graph of $f(x)$ to the graph of $g(x)$.

2. $f(x) = x$; $g(x) = \frac{1}{3}x$ **rotation (less steep)**
3. $f(x) = x$; $g(x) = x - 5$ **translation 5 units down**
4. $f(x) = x$; $g(x) = 6x$ **rotation (steeper)**

TEST PREP

49. Which best describes the effect on $f(x) = 2x - 5$ if the slope changes to 10?

(A) Its graph becomes less steep.
(B) Its graph moves 15 units up.
(C) Its graph makes 10 complete rotations.
(D) The x-intercept becomes $\frac{1}{2}$.

50. Given $f(x) = 22x - 182$, which does NOT describe the effect of increasing the y-intercept by 182?

(F) The new line passes through the origin.
(G) The new x-intercept is 0.
(H) The new line is parallel to the original.
(J) The new line is steeper than the original.

CHALLENGE AND EXTEND

51. You have seen that the graph of $g(x) = x + 3$ is the result of translating the graph of $f(x) = x$ three units up. However, you can also think of this as a *horizontal* translation—that is, a translation left or right. Graph $g(x) = x + 3$. Describe the horizontal translation of the graph of $f(x) = x$ to get the graph of $g(x) = x + 3$. **trans. 3 units to the left**

52. If $c > 0$, how can you describe the translation that transforms the graph of $f(x) = x$ into the graph of $g(x) = x + c$ as a horizontal translation? $g(x) = x - c$ as a horizontal translation? **trans. c units to the left; trans. c units to the right**

SPIRAL REVIEW

Give an expression in simplest form for the perimeter of each figure. *(Lesson 1-7)*

53. **15x**

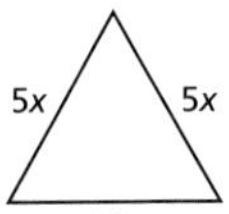

54. **8y + 4**

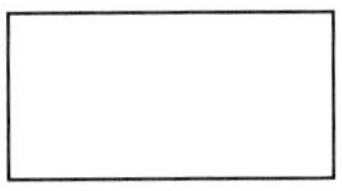

Identify the correlation you would expect to see between each pair of data sets. Explain. *(Lesson 4-5)*

55. the temperature and the number of people at the local ice cream parlor **pos.; as it gets hotter, more people buy ice cream.**
56. the amount of electricity used and the total electric bill **pos.; as you use more electricity, your electric bill increases.**
57. the number of miles driven after a fill-up and the amount of gasoline in the tank **neg.; as you drive farther, the amount of gasoline in the tank decreases.**

Identify which lines are parallel. *(Lesson 5-9)*

58. $y = -2x + 3$; $y = 2x$; $y = -2$; $y = -2x - 4$; $y = \frac{1}{2}x$; $y - 1 = -\frac{1}{2}(x + 6)$

59. $y = \frac{3}{5}x + 8$; $y = -\frac{3}{5}x$; $y + 1 = -\frac{3}{5}(x - 2)$; $y = \frac{5}{3}x + 9$; $y = 3x + 5$

Identify which lines are perpendicular. *(Lesson 5-9)*

60. $3x - 5y = 5$; $5y = -2x - 15$; $y = 3x + 5$; $5x + 3y = -21$; $y = \frac{5}{2}x - 2$

61. $x = 4$; $2y + x = 6$; $3x - y = 12$; $y = 2x + 3$; $y = -3$

TEST PREP DOCTOR In **Exercise 49,** the answer must be **A** or **D** because changing slope affects steepness and possibly the x-intercept. Choice **A** can be eliminated because the increase in the absolute value of the slope indicates that the line will be steeper.

Answers

51. For graph, see p. A23.
58–61. See p. A23.

Journal

Have students explain the changes in the slope and y-intercept for a rotation, a translation, and a reflection.

ALTERNATIVE ASSESSMENT

Have students write possible functions representing transformations according to the following directions:

1. Rotate the graph of $f(x) = x$.
2. Translate the graph of $f(x) = x - 4$ up.
3. Reflect the graph of $f(x) = -3x$.

Power Presentations with PowerPoint®

5-10 Lesson Quiz

Describe the transformation from the graph of $f(x)$ to the graph of $g(x)$.

1. $f(x) = 4x$, $g(x) = x$
rot. about (0, 0) (less steep)
2. $f(x) = x - 1$, $g(x) = x + 6$
trans. 7 units up
3. $f(x) = \frac{1}{5}x$, $g(x) = 2x$
rot. about (0, 0) (steeper)
4. $f(x) = 5x$, $g(x) = -5x$
ref. over y-axis, rot. about (0, 0)
5. $f(x) = x$, $g(x) = x - 4$
trans. 4 units down
6. $f(x) = -3x$, $g(x) = -x + 1$
rot. about (0, 0) (less steep), trans. 1 unit up
7. A cashier gets a \$50 bonus for working on a holiday plus \$9/h. The total holiday salary is given by the function $f(x) = 9x + 50$. How will the graph change if the bonus is raised to \$75? if the hourly rate is raised to \$12/h?
translated 25 units up; rotated about (0, 50) (steeper)

Also available on transparency

5-10 PROBLEM SOLVING

Write the correct answer.

1. The number of camp counselors at a day camp must include 1 counselor for every 8 campers, plus 3 camp directors. The function describing the number of counselors is $f(x) = \frac{1}{8}x + 3$ where x is the number of campers. How will the graph change if the number of camp directors is reduced to 2?
translation 1 unit down

2. A city water service has a base cost of \$12 per month plus \$1.50 per hundred cubic feet (HCF) of water. Write a function $f(x)$ to represent the cost of water as a function of x, amount used. Then write a second function $g(x)$ to represent the cost if the rate rises to \$1.60 per HCF.
$f(x) = 1.50x + 12$; $g(x) = 1.60x + 12$;
How would the graph of $g(x)$ compare to the graph of $f(x)$?
it would be rotated about (0, 12), steeper.

3. Owen earns a base salary plus a commission that is a percent of his total sales. His total weekly pay is described by $f(x) = 0.15x + 325$, where x is his total sales in dollars. What is the change in Owen's salary plan if his total weekly pay function changes to $g(x) = 0.20x + 325$?
His commission is raised to 20%.

An attorney charges \$250 per hour. The graph represents the cost of the attorney as a function of time. Select the best answer.

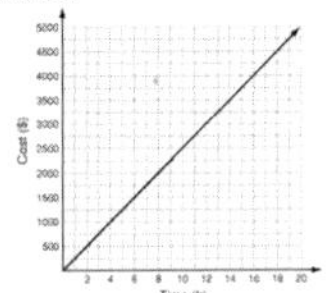

4. When a traveling fee is added to the attorney's rate for cases outside the city limits, the graph is translated up 50 units. What function $h(x)$ would describe the attorney's rate with the traveling fee?
A $h(x) = 250x - 50$
B $h(x) = 250x + 50$
C $h(x) = 200x$
D $h(x) = 300x$

5. The attorney's paralegal has an hourly rate of \$150. How would you transform the graph of $f(x)$ into a graph for the paralegal's rate?
F Reflect it over the y-axis.
G Translate it down 100 units.
H Translate it to the left 100 units.
J Rotate it clockwise about (0, 0).

6. Which hourly rate would NOT make the attorney's graph steeper?
A \$225
B \$275
C \$300
D \$325

5-10 CHALLENGE

For 1–5, use the two points and line graphed at right.

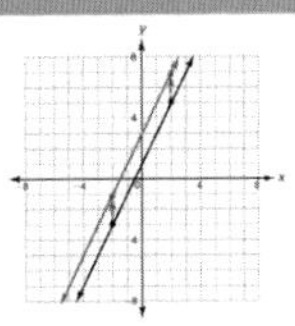

1. Write an equation in point-slope form for the line. Circle the point that you used as (x_1, y_1).
$y + 3 = 2(x + 2)$ OR $y - 5 = 2(x - 2)$
2. Translate the line up 2 units by doing the following:
a. Translate each of the two points up 2 units and plot a new point. Each translated point is an **image** of the original point. Circle the image of the point that you used in problem 1.
b. Connect the two new points with a line.
3. Use the coordinates of the image that you circled to write an equation in point-slope form for the new line. **$y + 1 = 2(x + 2)$ OR $y - 7 = 2(x - 2)$**
4. Compare your equations for problems 1 and 3. What indicates that there was a vertical translation up 2 units?
In the form $y - y_1 = m(x - x_1)$, the value of y_1, increased by 2 units.
5. Suppose that the *original* line is translated down 6 units. Without graphing the transformation, write an equation in point-slope form for the new line. **$y + 9 = 2(x + 2)$ OR $y + 1 = 2(x - 2)$**

For 6–10, use the graph at right.

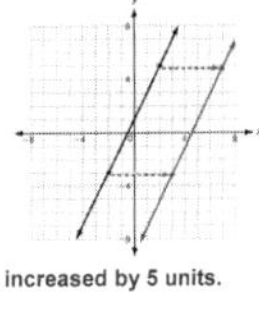

6. Translate the line right 5 units. (Use a process similar to problem 2.) Again, circle the image of the point that you used in problem 1.
7. Use the coordinates of the image that you circled to write an equation in point-slope form for the new line.
$y + 3 = 2(x - 3)$ OR $y - 5 = 2(x - 7)$
8. Compare your equations for problems 1 and 7. What indicates a horizontal translation right 5 units?
In the form $y - y_1 = m(x - x_1)$, the value of x_1, increased by 5 units.
9. Suppose that the *original* line was translated left 3 units. Without graphing the transformation, write an equation in point-slope form for the new line. **$y + 3 = 2(x + 5)$ OR $y - 5 = 2(x + 1)$**
10. The equation $y - 3 = -4(x + 2)$ is transformed into $y + 1 = -4(x - 7)$. Describe the transformations from the graph of the first line to the graph of the second.
Translated down 4 units and right 9 units.

Organizer

Objective: Assess students' ability to apply concepts and skills in Lessons 5-7 through 5-10 in a real-world format.

Online Edition

Resources

Algebra I Assessments

www.mathtekstoolkit.org

Problem	Text Reference
1	Lesson 1-8
2	Lessons 5-3, 5-4
3	Lesson 5-1
4	Lesson 5-8
5	Lesson 5-10

Answers

3.

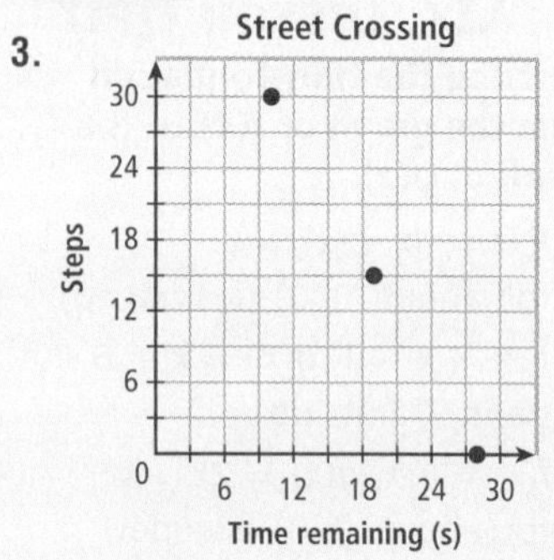

State Resources

CHAPTER 5

MULTI-STEP TEST PREP

SECTION 5B

Using Linear Functions

Take a Walk! All intersections in Durango, Colorado, have crossing signals with timers. Once the signal changes to walk, the timer begins at 28 seconds and counts down to show how much time pedestrians have to cross the street.

1. Pauline counted her steps as she crossed the street. She counted 15 steps with 19 seconds remaining. When she reached the opposite side of the street, she had counted a total of 30 steps and had 10 seconds remaining. Copy and complete the table below using these values.

Time Remaining (s)	28	**19**	**10**
Steps	0	**15**	**30**

2. Find the average rate of change for Pauline's walk. **$-\frac{5}{3}$, or $-1\frac{2}{3}$, steps/s**

3. Sketch a graph of the points in the table, or plot them on your graphing calculator.

4. Find an equation that describes the line through the points. **$y = -\frac{5}{3}x + \frac{140}{3}$**

5. How would the graph change if Pauline increased her speed? What if she decreased her speed? **The line would become steeper; the line would become less steep.**

INTERVENTION

Scaffolding Questions

1–2. What are the independent and dependent variables? ind.: time remaining; dep.: steps

3–4. Will the points go upward or downward from left to right? Explain. Downward; as time remaining increases, number of steps taken decreases. What does the slope represent? steps per time remaining

5a. How can you find the equation for the relationship? Possible answer: Use point-slope form.

5b. In terms of the number of steps, what does it mean to increase or decrease speed? If speed increases, the number of steps increases; if speed decreases, the number of steps decreases.

Extension

Change the given situation in such a way that the graph is a vertical translation of your graph in **Problem 3.** Possible answer: Pauline walks at the same speed, but the dist. across the street is longer.

READY TO GO ON?

CHAPTER 5

SECTION 5B

Quiz for Lessons 5-7 Through 5-10

5-7 Slope-Intercept Form

Graph each line given the slope and y-intercept.

1. slope $= \frac{1}{4}$; y-intercept $= 2$
2. slope $= -3$; y-intercept $= 5$
3. slope $= -1$; y-intercept $= -6$

Write each equation in slope-intercept form. Then graph the line described by the equation.

4. $2x + y = 5$ **$y = -2x + 5$**
5. $2x - 6y = 6$ **$y = \frac{1}{3}x - 1$**
6. $3x + y = 3x - 4$ **$y = -4$**
7. **Entertainment** At a chili cook-off, people pay a \$3.00 entrance fee and \$0.50 for each bowl of chili they taste. The graph shows the total cost per person as a function of the number of bowls of chili tasted. **a. $y = 0.5x + 3$**

   a. Write an equation that represents the total cost per person as a function of the number of bowls of chili tasted.

   b. Identify the slope and y-intercept and describe their meanings.
   slope: 0.5; cost per bowl of chili; y-int.: 3; entrance fee

5-8 Point-Slope Form

Graph the line with the given slope that contains the given point.

8. slope $= -3$; $(0, 3)$
9. slope $= -\frac{2}{3}$; $(-3, 5)$
10. slope $= 2$; $(-3, -1)$

Write an equation in slope-intercept form for the line through the two points.

11. $(3, 1)$ and $(4, 3)$ **$y = 2x - 5$**
12. $(-1, -1)$ and $(1, 7)$ **$y = 4x + 3$**
13. $(1, -4)$ and $(-2, 5)$ **$y = -3x - 1$**

5-9 Slopes of Parallel and Perpendicular Lines

Identify which lines are parallel.

14. $y = -2x$; $y = 2x + 1$; $y = 2x$; $y = 2(x + 5)$ **$y = 2x + 1$, $y = 2x$, and $y = 2(x + 5)$**
15. $-3y = x$; $y = -\frac{1}{3}x + 1$; $y = -3x$; $y + 2 = x + 4$ **$-3y = x$ and $y = -\frac{1}{3}x + 1$**

Identify which lines are perpendicular.

16. $y = -4x - 1$; $y = \frac{1}{4}x$; $y = 4x - 6$; $x = -4$
17. $y = -\frac{3}{4}x$; $y = \frac{3}{4}x - 3$; $y = \frac{4}{3}x$; $y = 4$; $x = 3$
18. Write an equation in slope-intercept form for the line that passes through $(5, 2)$ and is parallel to the line described by $3x - 5y = 15$. **$y = \frac{3}{5}x - 1$**
19. Write an equation in slope-intercept form for the line that passes through $(3, 5)$ and is perpendicular to the line described by $y = -\frac{3}{2}x - 2$. **$y = \frac{2}{3}x + 3$**

5-10 Transforming Linear Functions

Graph $f(x)$ and $g(x)$. Then describe the transformation(s) from the graph of $f(x)$ to the graph of $g(x)$.

20. $f(x) = 5x$, $g(x) = -5x$ **ref. across y-axis; rot. about (0, 0)**
21. $f(x) = \frac{1}{2}x - 1$, $g(x) = \frac{1}{2}x + 4$ **trans. 5 units up**
22. An attorney charges an initial fee of \$250 and then \$150 per hour. The total bill after x hours is $f(x) = 150x + 250$. How will the graph of this function change if the initial fee is reduced to \$200? if the hourly rate is increased to \$175?
translated 50 units down; rotated about (0, 250) and steeper

READY TO GO ON?

SECTION 5B

Organizer

Objective: Assess students' mastery of concepts and skills in Lessons 5-7 through 5-10.

Resources

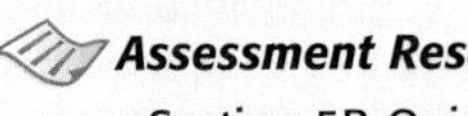

Assessment Resources
Section 5B Quiz

Teacher One Stop™
Test & Practice Generator

INTERVENTION

Resources

Ready to Go On? Intervention and Enrichment Worksheets

***Ready to Go On?* CD-ROM**

***Ready to Go On?* Online**

my.hrw.com

Answers

1–3. See p. A23.
4–6. For graphs, see p. A24.
8–10, 16, 17. See p. A24.
20–21. For graphs, see p. A24.

READY TO GO ON?

Diagnose and Prescribe

Ready to Go On? Intervention	*Ready to Go On? Intervention,* Section 5B: Worksheets	CD-ROM	Online
Lesson 5-7	5-7 Intervention	Activity 5-7	Diagnose and Prescribe Online
Lesson 5-8	5-8 Intervention	Activity 5-8	
Lesson 5-9	5-9 Intervention	Activity 5-9	
Lesson 5-10	5-10 Intervention	Activity 5-10	

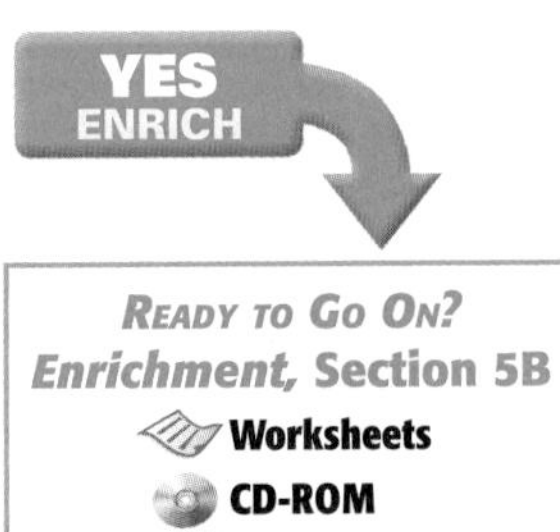

CHAPTER 5 **Organizer**

Pacing: Traditional 1 day
Block $\frac{1}{2}$ day

Objectives: Graph absolute-value functions.

Identify characteristics of absolute-value functions and their graphs.

Using the Extension

In Chapter 5, students learn to graph a linear function and identify characteristics of the graph, such as its slope and *x*- and *y*-intercepts. In this extension, students learn to graph an absolute-value function and identify characteristics of the graph, such as its vertex and axis of symmetry.

Teaching Tip **Kinesthetic** Have students graph $f(x) = x$ on a piece of tracing paper. Tell them to fold up the bottom of the graph along the *x*-axis so the bottom of the graph meets the top. Say that this is the graph of $f(x) = |x|$; all the *y*-values that were negative are now positive.

State Resources

EXTENSION Absolute-Value Functions

Objectives
Graph absolute-value functions.

Identify characteristics of absolute-value functions and their graphs.

Vocabulary
absolute-value function
axis of symmetry
vertex

An **absolute-value function** is a function whose rule contains an absolute-value expression. To graph an absolute-value function, choose several values of *x* and generate some ordered pairs.

x	$f(x) = \lvert x \rvert$
−2	2
−1	1
0	0
1	1
2	2

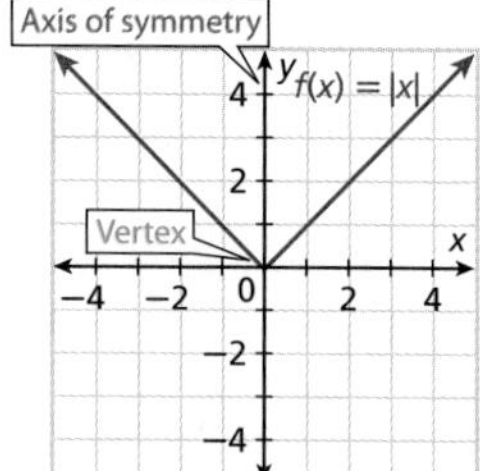

Absolute-value graphs are composed of two linear pieces. The **axis of symmetry** is the line that divides the graph into two congruent halves. The **vertex** is the "corner" point on the graph.

From the table and the graph of $f(x) = |x|$, you can tell that

- the axis of symmetry is the *y*-axis ($x = 0$).
- the vertex is $(0, 0)$.
- the domain (x-values) is the set of all real numbers.
- the range (y-values) is described by $y \geq 0$.
- the *x*-intercept and the *y*-intercept are both 0.
- the slope of the left linear piece is −1 and the slope of the right linear piece is 1.

EXAMPLE 1 Absolute-Value Functions

Graph $f(x) = |2x| - 1$ and label the axis of symmetry and the vertex. Identify the intercepts, give the domain and range, and find the slope of each piece.

Choose positive, negative, and zero values for x, and find ordered pairs.

x	−2	−1	0	1	2
$f(x) = \lvert 2x \rvert - 1$	3	1	−1	1	3

Plot the ordered pairs and connect them.

From the table and the graph, you can tell that

- the axis of symmetry is the *y*-axis ($x = 0$).
- the vertex is $(0, -1)$.
- the *x*-intercepts are $\frac{1}{2}$ and $-\frac{1}{2}$.
- the *y*-intercept is −1.
- the domain is all real numbers.
- the range is described by $y \geq -1$.
- the slope of the left piece is −2 and the slope of the right piece is 2.

1 Introduce

Motivate

Ask students to do the following:

Find the range for $f(x) = x$ if D: {−2, −1, 0, 1, 2}. R: {−2, −1, 0, 1, 2}

Find the range for $f(x) = |x|$ if D: {−2, −1, 0, 1, 2}. R: {2, 1, 0, 1, 2}

How are the ranges similar? Both contain 0, 1, 2.

How are the ranges different? The first contains −2 and −1; the second does not.

2 Teach

Guided Instruction

When graphing absolute-value functions by generating ordered pairs, encourage students to substitute zero, positive, and negative values for *x*. Point out that the absolute-value functions in this extension are translations of the parent function $f(x) = |x|$.

Visual Graphs of absolute-value functions will have a V-shape.

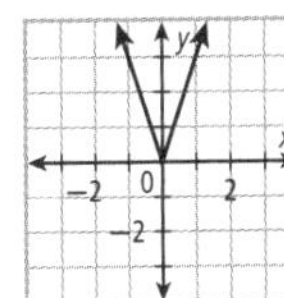

1. Graph $f(x) = 3|x|$ and label the axis of symmetry and the vertex. Identify the intercepts, give the domain and range, and find the slope of each piece.

axis of symm.: $x = 0$; vertex: $(0, 0)$; x-int.: 0; y-int.: 0; D: all real numbers; R: $y \geq 0$; left slope: -3; right slope: 3

The parent function for absolute-value functions is $f(x) = |x|$. The graphs of all other absolute-value functions are transformations of the graph of $f(x) = |x|$.

For $f(x) = a|x - b| + c$

WORDS	EXAMPLES	WORDS	EXAMPLES
Opening Direction • If $a > 0$, the graph opens upward. • If $a < 0$, the graph opens downward.	$f(x) = \|x\|$ $g(x) = -\|x\|$	Horizontal Translation • If $b > 0$, the graph is translated b units right from $f(x) = \|x\|$. • If $b < 0$, the graph is translated b units left from $f(x) = \|x\|$.	$h(x) = \|x + 2\|$ $f(x) = \|x\|$ $g(x) = \|x - 2\|$
Width • If $\|a\| > 1$, the graph is narrower than the graph of $f(x) = \|x\|$. • If $\|a\| < 1$, the graph is wider than the graph of $f(x) = \|x\|$. The slopes of the two linear pieces are a and $-a$.	$g(x) = 3\|x\|$ $f(x) = \|x\|$ $h(x) = \frac{1}{2}\|x\|$	Vertical Translation • If $c > 0$, the graph is translated c units up from $f(x) = \|x\|$. • If $c < 0$, the graph is translated c units down from $f(x) = \|x\|$.	$g(x) = \|x\| + 2$ $f(x) = \|x\|$ $h(x) = \|x\| - 2$

EXAMPLE  Transforming Absolute-Value Functions

Describe the transformations from the graph of $f(x) = |x|$ to the graph of $g(x)$. Then graph both functions.

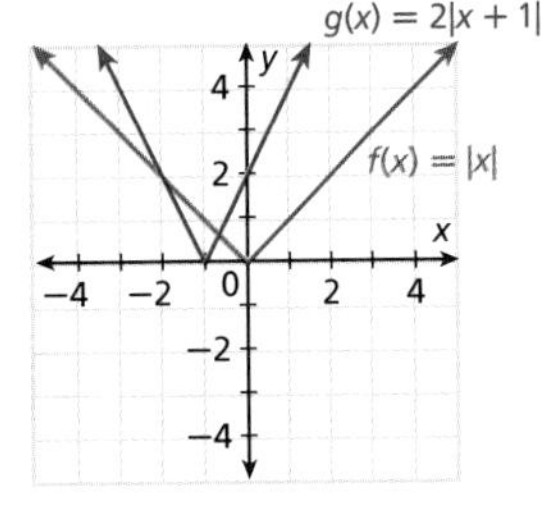

A $g(x) = 2|x + 1|$

Identify a, b, and c.

$g(x) = 2|x + 1| = 2|x - (-1)| + 0$

- $a = 2$: graph is narrower
- $b = -1$: translated 1 unit left
- $c = 0$: no vertical translation

COMMON ERROR ALERT

Students may assume that the range in **Example 1** should contain only positive values. Show students that the substitution of any point between $-\frac{1}{2}$ and $+\frac{1}{2}$ will yield a negative number for this function. Point out how this differs from **Check it Out 1,** where there is no constant term.

Power Presentations with PowerPoint®

Additional Examples

Example 1

Graph each absolute-value function and label the axis of symmetry and the vertex. Identify the intercepts, give the domain and range, and find the slope of each piece.

A. $f(x) = |x| + 1$

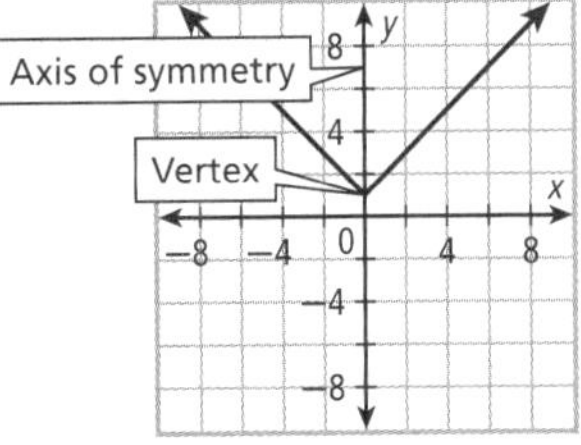

axis of symmetry: $x = 0$; vertex: $(0, 1)$; x-int.: none; y-int.: 1; D: all real numbers; R: $y \geq 1$; left slope: -1; right slope: 1

B. $f(x) = |x - 4|$

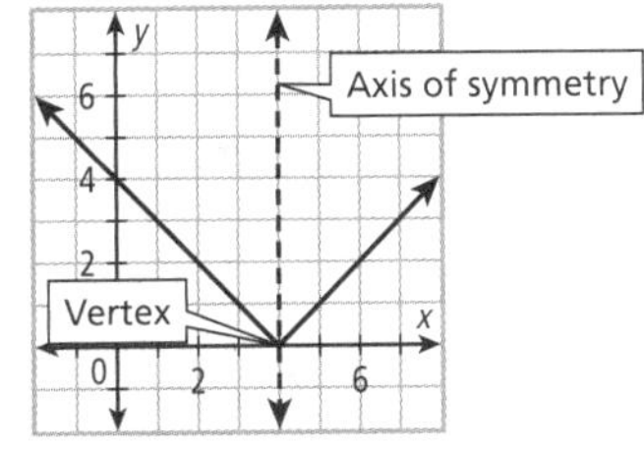

axis of symmetry: $x = 4$; vertex: $(4, 0)$; x-int.: 4; y-int.: 4; D: all real numbers; R: $y \geq 0$; left slope: -1; right slope: 1

INTERVENTION
Questioning Strategies

EXAMPLE 

- How many x- and y-intercepts are possible for an absolute-value function? Explain.
- How can you determine the axis of symmetry simply by looking at the function rule?

Power Presentations with PowerPoint®

Additional Examples

Example 2

Describe the transformations from the graph of $f(x) = |x|$ to the graph of $g(x)$. Then graph both functions.

A. $g(x) = 2|x - 3|$

narrowed and trans. 3 units right

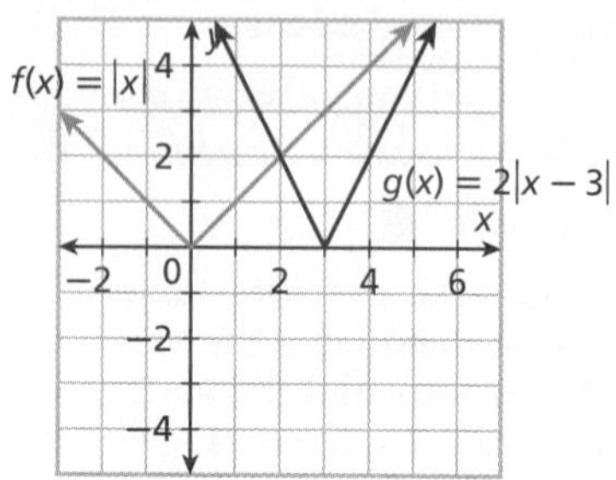

B. $g(x) = -|x + 2| + 1$

refl. across x-axis, trans. 2 units left and 1 unit up

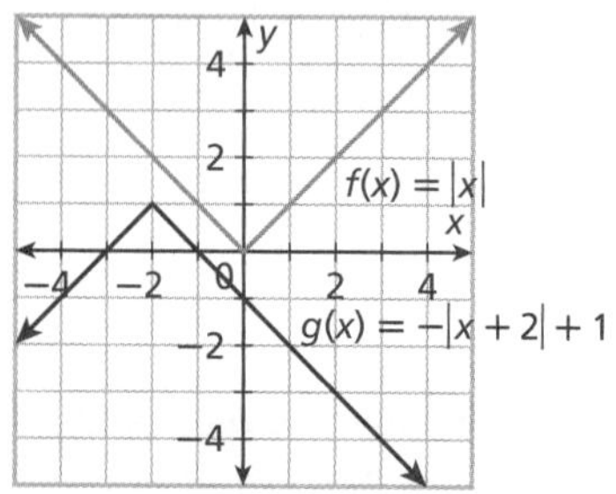

Example 3

Graph $f(x) = |3x| + 3$. Identify the vertex and give the minimum or maximum value of the function.

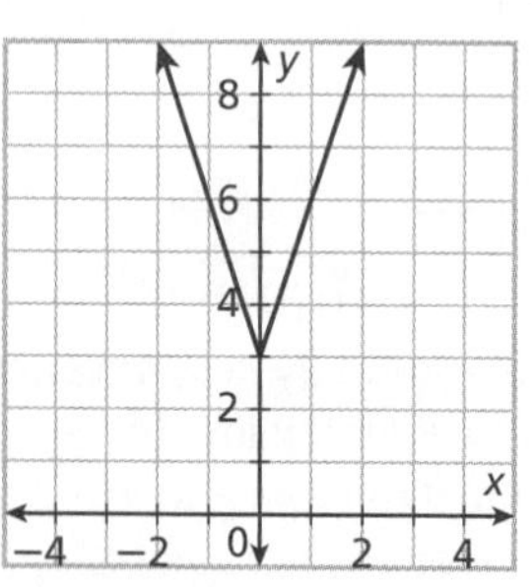

vertex: (0, 3); minimum: 3

INTERVENTION
Questioning Strategies

EXAMPLE 2

- How will the graphs of an absolute-value function and its transformation look on the same coordinate plane?

EXAMPLE 3

- Is the vertex of an absolute-value function always a minimum or maximum point? Explain.

2a.

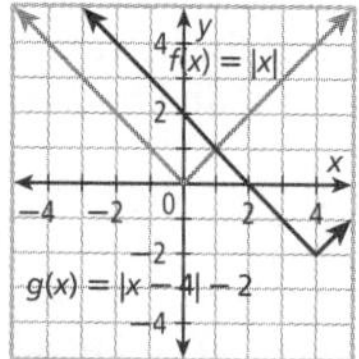
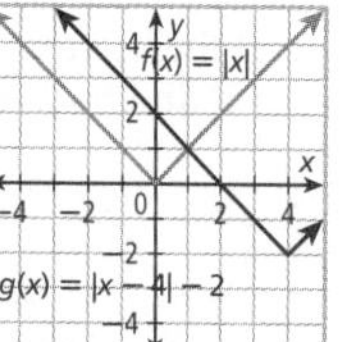

translated 4 units right and 2 units down

2b.

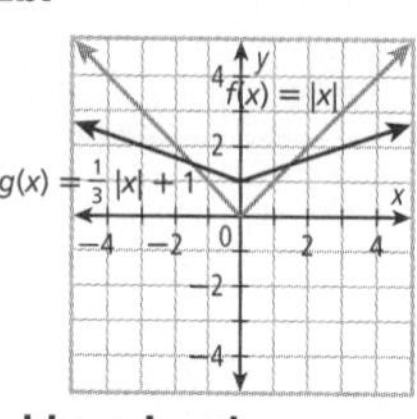

widened and translated 1 unit up

3a.

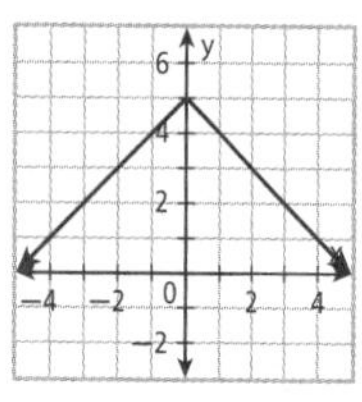

vertex: (0, 5); maximum: 5

3b.

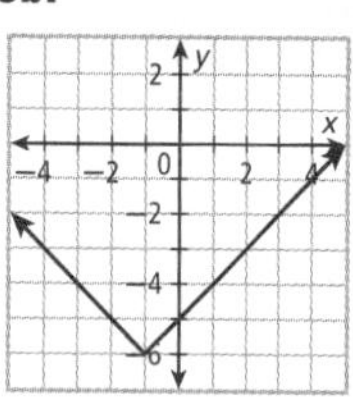

vertex: (−1, −6); minimum: −6

Describe the transformations from the graph of $f(x) = |x|$ to the graph of $g(x)$. Then graph both functions.

B $g(x) = -|x - 3| + 2$

Identify a, b, and c.

$g(x) = -|x - 3| + 2 = -1|x - 3| + 2$

- $a = -1$: graph opens downward and width is unchanged
- $b = 3$: translated 3 units right
- $c = 2$: translated 2 units up

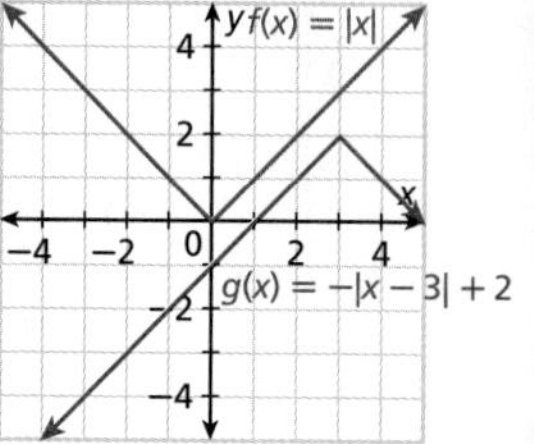

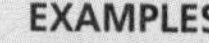

CHECK IT OUT! Describe the transformations from the graph of $f(x) = |x|$ to the graph of $g(x)$. Then graph both functions.

2a. $g(x) = |x - 4| - 2$ **2b.** $g(x) = \frac{1}{3}|x| + 1$

Minimum and Maximum Values of Absolute-Value Functions

WORDS	If the graph of an absolute-value function opens upward, the y-value of the vertex is the **minimum** value of the function.	If the graph of an absolute-value function opens downward, the y-value of the vertex is the **maximum** value of the function.
EXAMPLES	$f(x) = 2|x| - 2$ 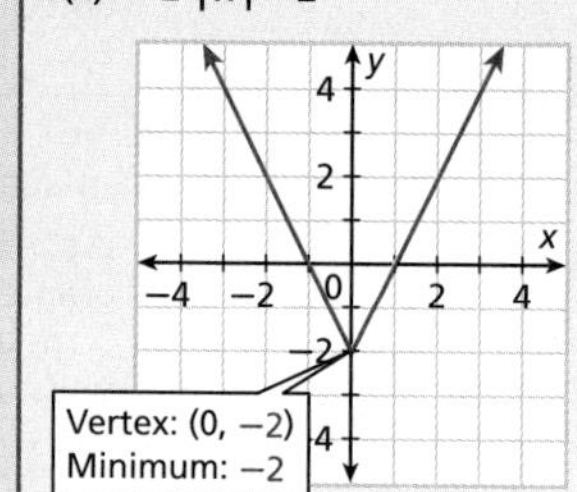	$f(x) = -|x - 1|$ 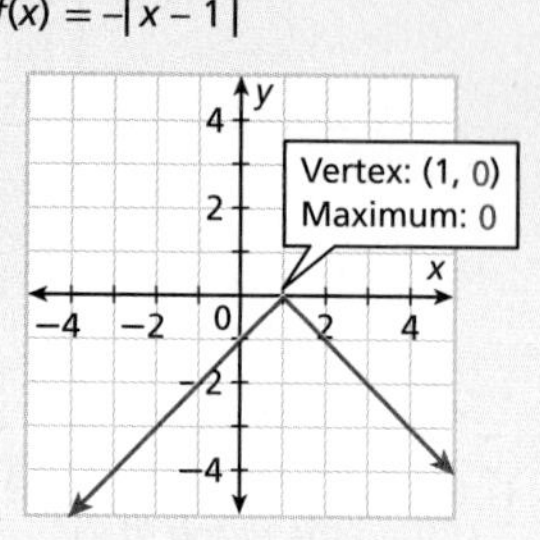

EXAMPLE 3 **Identifying the Minimum or Maximum**

Graph $f(x) = |x + 3| - 5$. Identify the vertex and give the minimum or maximum value of the function.

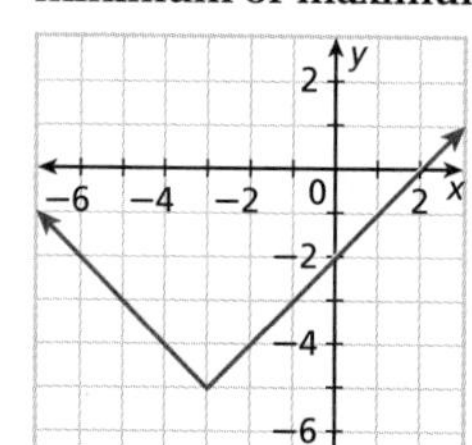

The vertex is (−3, −5).

The graph opens upward, so the function has a minimum.

The minimum is −5.

CHECK IT OUT! Graph each absolute-value function. Identify the vertex and give the minimum or maximum value of the function.

3a. $f(x) = -|x| + 5$ **3b.** $f(x) = |x + 1| - 6$

EXAMPLE 4 ***Sports Application***

In a charity race, a water stand for the runners is halfway between the start and finish lines. The function $y = \left|\frac{x}{8} - 3\right|$ models Riley's distance y in miles from the water stand x minutes into the race.

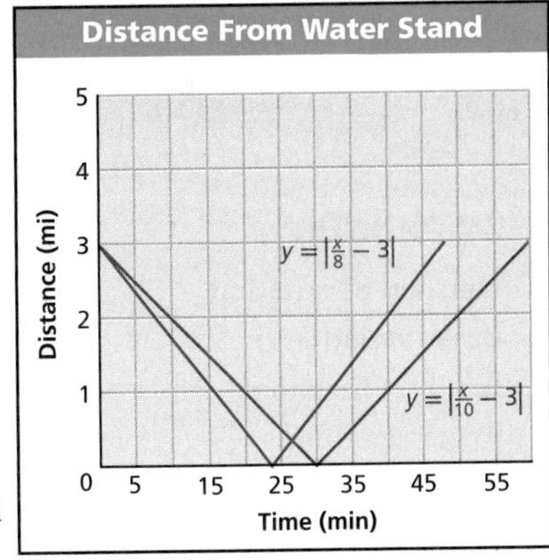

A How long is the race?

$y = \left|\frac{x}{8} - 3\right|$ is graphed in blue.

At the start of the race ($x = 0$), Riley is 3 mi from the water stand. The water stand is halfway between the start and finish lines, so the race is 6 mi.

B How much time does it take Riley to reach the water stand?

When Riley reaches the water stand, $y = 0$. This happens when $x = 24$. It takes Riley 24 min to reach the water stand.

C The function $y = \left|\frac{x}{10} - 3\right|$ models Dean's distance from the water stand during the same race. Compare Dean's graph to Riley's graph. What can you conclude about Dean's speed?

$y = \left|\frac{x}{10} - 3\right|$ is graphed in red. Both graphs start at the same point, but Dean's graph is translated to the right. It takes him more time to reach the water stand and to finish the race. Therefore, he is running more slowly than Riley.

4. How would the graph be different for someone who runs faster than Riley? **shifted left and linear pieces would be steeper**

EXTENSION Exercises

Graph each absolute-value function and label the axis of symmetry and the vertex. Identify the intercepts, give the domain and range, and find the slope of each piece. Identify the maximum or minimum.

1. $f(x) = |x| + 3$
2. $f(x) = |x + 3|$
3. $f(x) = \frac{1}{2}|x|$
4. $f(x) = |x - 3|$

Tell whether each statement is sometimes, always, or never true.

5. The absolute value of a number is negative. **never**
6. An absolute-value function has an x-intercept. **sometimes**
7. An absolute-value function has two y-intercepts. **never**

Write a function to describe each of the following.

8. The graph of $f(x) = |x|$ is translated 2 units right. **$g(x) = |x - 2|$**
9. The graph of $f(x) = |x|$ is narrowed and reflected across the x-axis. **Possible answer: $g(x) = -|4x|$**
10. **Critical Thinking** Suppose that an absolute-value function has no x-intercepts. What can you say about the function rule? **Possible answer: It is in the form $|x| + c$, where $c > 0$.**

Power Presentations with PowerPoint®

Additional Examples

Example 4

Rosa and Tony are hiking a mountain trail. Two-thirds of the way up the trail is a scenic overlook. The function $y = |2x - 6|$, graphed below, models Rosa's and Tony's distance y in miles from the overlook after hiking for x hours.

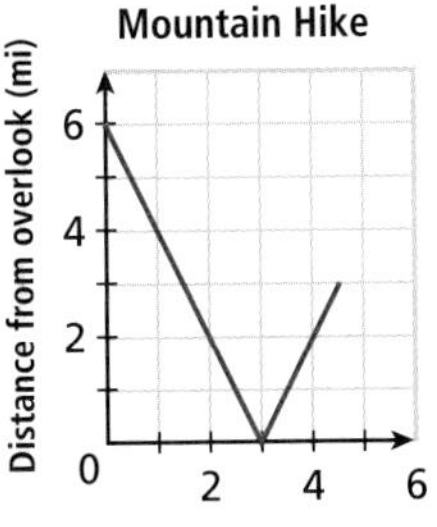

A. How long is the trail? 9 mi

B. How long does it take Rosa and Tony to reach the overlook? 3 h

INTERVENTION

Questioning Strategies

EXAMPLE 4

- What are the domain and range of the functions?

3 Close

Summarize

Ask students to give the axis of symmetry and vertex for the following functions.

1. $f(x) = |x - 5|$
   axis of symmetry: $x = 5$; vertex: $(5, 0)$
2. $f(x) = |x| - 5$
   axis of symmetry: $x = 0$; vertex: $(0, -5)$
3. $f(x) = |x| + 4$
   axis of symmetry: $x = 0$; vertex: $(0, 4)$
4. $f(x) = |x + 4|$
   axis of symmetry: $x = -4$; vertex: $(-4, 0)$

Answers

1. axis of symmetry: $x = 0$; vertex: $(0, 3)$; x-int.: none; y-int.: 3; D: all real numbers; R: $y \geq 3$; left slope: -1; right slope: 1; minimum: 3

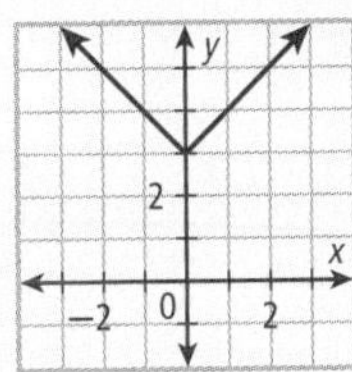

2–4. See p. A24.

Organizer

Objective: Help students organize and review key concepts and skills presented in Chapter 5.

Online Edition
Multilingual Glossary

Countdown Week 12

Resources

Teacher One Stop™
PuzzleView
Test & Practice Generator

***Multilingual Glossary* Online**
go.hrw.com
KEYWORD: MA7 Glossary

Lesson Tutorial Videos
CD-ROM

Answers

1. translation; rotation; reflection
2. *y*-intercept
3. slope; *y*-intercept
4. No; a constant change of +2 in *x* corresponds to different changes in *y*.
5. Yes; a constant change of +1 in *x* corresponds to a constant change of +2 in *y*.
6. Yes; a constant change of +1 in *x* corresponds to a constant change of −2 in *y*.
7. No; a constant change of −1 in *y* corresponds to different changes in *x*.
8. $5x + y = 1$; $A = 5$; $B = 1$; $C = 1$
9. $x + 6y = -2$; $A = 1$; $B = 6$; $C = -2$
10. $7x - 4y = 0$; $A = 7$, $B = -4$, $C = 0$
11. $y = 9$; $A = 0$; $B = 1$; $C = 9$
12. Cupcake Sales (graph: Amount earned ($) vs. Cupcakes sold)

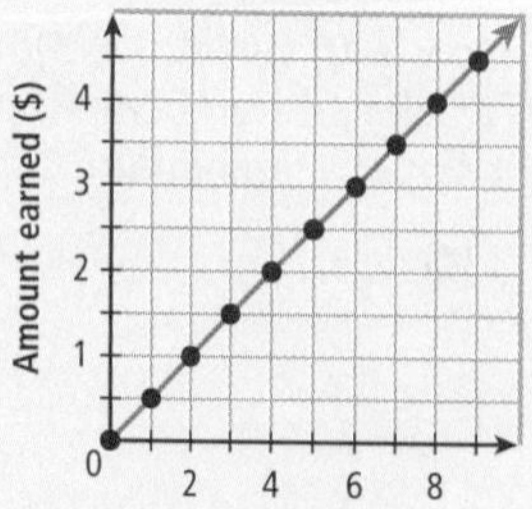

D: whole numbers;
R: nonneg. multiples of 0.5

CHAPTER 5

Study Guide: Review

Vocabulary

Complete the sentences below with vocabulary words from the list above. Words may be used more than once.

1. A(n) ___?___ is a "slide," a(n) ___?___ is a "turn," and a(n) ___?___ is a "flip."
2. The *x*-coordinate of the point that contains the ___?___ is always 0.
3. In the equation $y = mx + b$, the value of *m* is the ___?___ , and the value of *b* is the ___?___ .

5-1 Identifying Linear Functions *(pp. 300–306)*

EXAMPLES

Tell whether each function is linear. If so, graph the function.

■ $y = -3x + 2$

$$y = -3x + 2$$
$$\underline{+3x \quad +3x}$$
$$3x + y = \quad 2$$

Write the equation in standard form.

This is a linear function.

Generate ordered pairs.

x	$y = -3x + 2$	(*x*, *y*)
−2	$y = -3(-2) + 2 = 8$	(−2, 8)
0	$y = -3(0) + 2 = 2$	(0, 2)
2	$y = -3(2) + 2 = -4$	(2, −4)

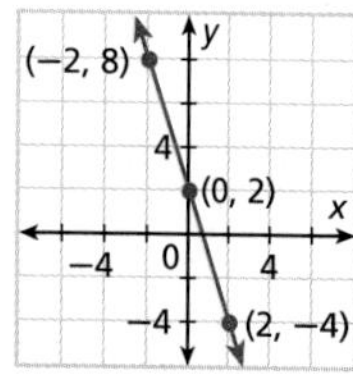

Plot the points and connect them with a straight line.

■ $y = 2x^3$

This is not a linear function because *x* has an exponent other than 1.

EXERCISES

Tell whether the given ordered pairs satisfy a linear function. Explain.

4.

x	*y*
−3	3
−1	1
1	1
3	3

5.

x	*y*
0	−3
1	−1
2	1
3	3

6. $\{(-2, 5), (-1, 3), (0, 1), (1, -1), (2, -3)\}$
7. $\{(1, 7), (3, 6), (6, 5), (9, 4), (13, 3)\}$

Each equation below is linear. Write each equation in standard form and give the values of *A*, *B*, and *C*.

8. $y = -5x + 1$
9. $\frac{x + 2}{2} = -3y$
10. $4y = 7x$
11. $9 = y$
12. Helene is selling cupcakes for $0.50 each. The function $f(x) = 0.5x$ gives the total amount of money Helene makes after selling *x* cupcakes. Graph this function and give its domain and range.

5-2 Using Intercepts *(pp. 307–312)*

EXAMPLE

- **Find the x- and y-intercepts of $2x + 5y = 10$.**

Let $y = 0$.	Let $x = 0$.
$2x + 5(0) = 10$	$2(0) + 5y = 10$
$2x + 0 = 10$	$0 + 5y = 10$
$2x = 10$	$5y = 10$
$\frac{2x}{2} = \frac{10}{2}$	$\frac{5y}{5} = \frac{10}{5}$
$x = 5$	$y = 2$
The x-intercept is 5.	The y-intercept is 2.

EXERCISES

Find the x- and y-intercepts.

13.

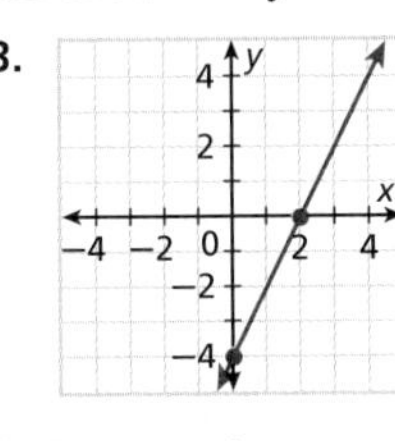

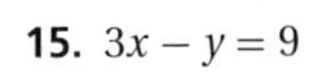

14.

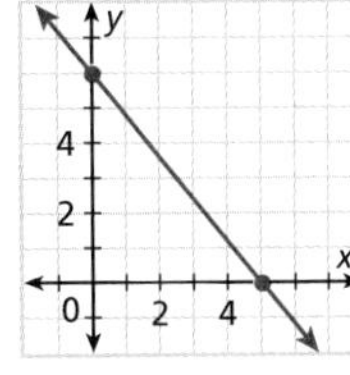

15. $3x - y = 9$
16. $-2x + y = 1$
17. $-x + 6y = 18$
18. $3x - 4y = 1$

5-3 Rate of Change and Slope *(pp. 314–321)*

EXAMPLE

- **Find the slope of the line.**

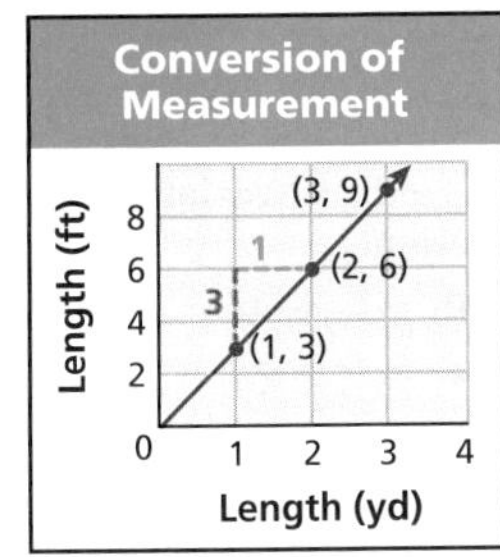

$$\text{slope} = \frac{\text{change in } y}{\text{change in } x} = \frac{3}{1} = 3$$

EXERCISES

19. Graph the data and show the rates of change.

Time (s)	Distance (ft)
0	0
1	16
2	64
3	144
4	256

20. Find the slope of the line graphed below.

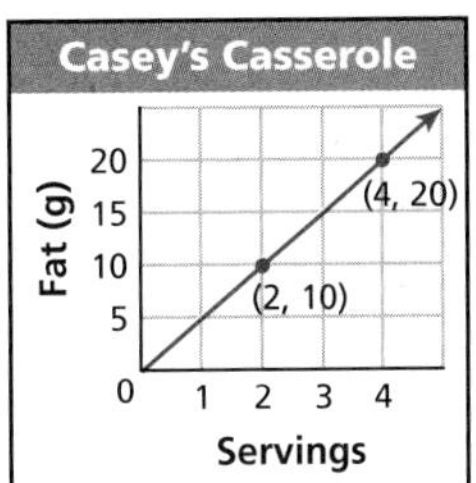

5-4 The Slope Formula *(pp. 324–329)*

EXAMPLE

- **Find the slope of the line described by $2x - 3y = 6$.**

Step 1 Find the x- and y-intercepts.

Let $y = 0$.	Let $x = 0$.
$2x - 3(0) = 6$	$2(0) - 3y = 6$
$2x = 6$	$-3y = 6$
$x = 3$	$y = -2$

The line contains $(3, 0)$ and $(0, -2)$.

Step 2 Use the slope formula.

$$m = \frac{y_2 - y_1}{x_2 - x_1} = \frac{-2 - 0}{0 - 3} = \frac{-2}{-3} = \frac{2}{3}$$

EXERCISES

Find the slope of the line described by each equation.

21. $4x + 3y = 24$
22. $y = -3x + 6$
23. $x + 2y = 10$
24. $3x = y + 3$
25. $y + 2 = 7x$
26. $16x = 4y + 1$

Find the slope of the line that contains each pair of points.

27. $(1, 2)$ and $(2, -3)$
28. $(4, -2)$ and $(-5, 7)$
29. $(-3, -6)$ and $(4, 1)$
30. $\left(\frac{1}{2}, 2\right)$ and $\left(\frac{3}{4}, \frac{5}{2}\right)$
31. $(2, 2)$ and $(2, 7)$
32. $(1, -3)$ and $(5, -3)$

Answers

13. x-int.: 2; y-int.: −4
14. x-int.: 5; y-int.: 6
15. x-int.: 3; y-int.: −9
16. x-int.: $-\frac{1}{2}$; y-int.: 1
17. x-int.: −18; y-int.: 3
18. x-int.: $\frac{1}{3}$; y-int.: $-\frac{1}{4}$
19.

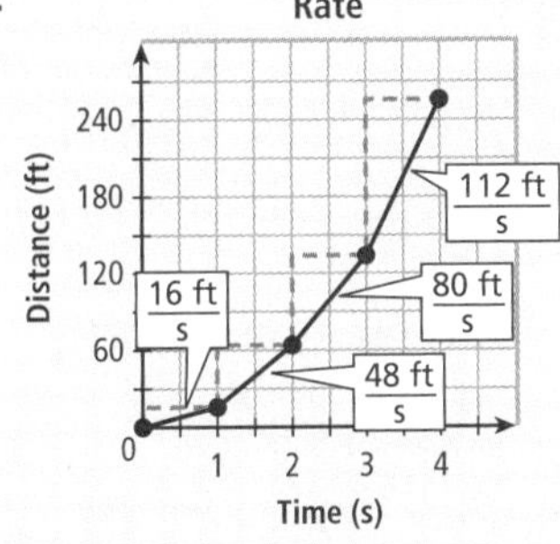

20. 5
21. $-\frac{4}{3}$
22. −3
23. $-\frac{1}{2}$
24. 3
25. 7
26. 4
27. −5
28. −1
29. 1
30. 2
31. undefined
32. 0

Answers

33. (15, 15)
34. $\left(-\frac{1}{2}, -9\right)$
35. 7.81 units
36. 15.65 units
37. 2.2 mi
38. yes; -6
39. yes; 1
40. no
41. yes; $-\frac{1}{2}$
42. -12
43. $y = 8x$

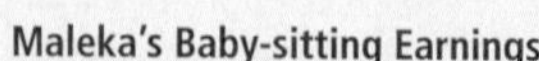

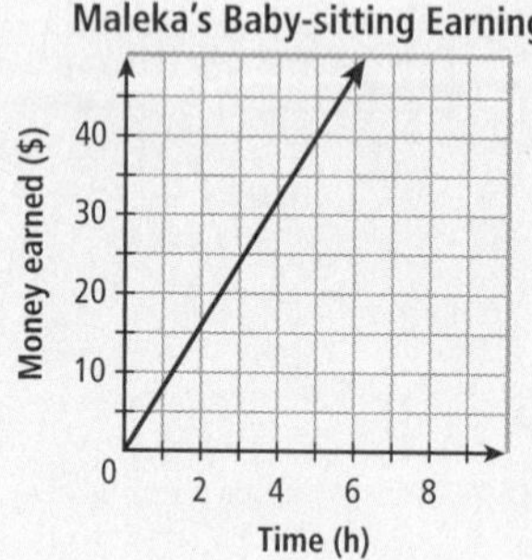

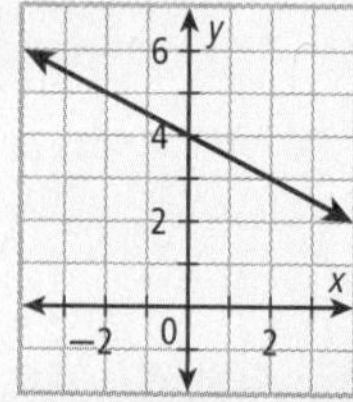

45.

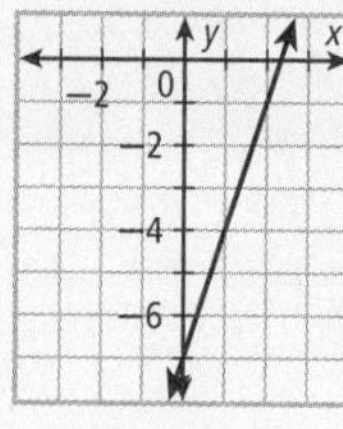

46. $y = \frac{1}{3}x + 5$
47. $y = 4x - 9$

5-5 The Midpoint and Distance Formulas *(pp. 330–335)*

EXAMPLE

- **Find the coordinates of the midpoint of $\overline{AB}$ with endpoints $A(-4, 3)$ and $B(5, -6)$**

$M\left(\frac{x_1 + x_2}{2}, \frac{y_1 + y_2}{2}\right)$ *Write the formula.*

$M\left(\frac{-4 + 5}{2}, \frac{3 + (-6)}{2}\right) = M\left(\frac{1}{2}, -\frac{3}{2}\right)$

- **Use the Distance Formula to find the distance, to the nearest hundredth, from $C(-4, 1)$ to $D(5, -3)$.**

$d = \sqrt{(x_2 - x_1)^2 + (y_2 - y_1)^2}$

$d = \sqrt{[5 - (-4)]^2 + (-3 - 1)^2}$

$d = \sqrt{9^2 + (-4)^2}$ *Subtract within grouping symbols.*

$d = \sqrt{97} \approx 9.85$ *Simplify and estimate.*

EXERCISES

Find the coordinates of the midpoint of each segment.

33. $\overline{EF}$ with endpoints $E(9, 12)$ and $F(21, 18)$
34. $\overline{GH}$ with endpoints $G(-5, -7)$ and $H(4, -11)$

Use the Distance Formula to find the distance, to the nearest hundredth, between each pair of points.

35. $J(3, 10)$ and $K(-2, 4)$
36. $L(-6, 0)$ and $M(8, -7)$
37. Each unit on a map of a forest represents 1 mile. To the nearest tenth of a mile, what is the distance from a ranger station at (1, 2) on the map to a river crossing at (2, 4)?

5-6 Direct Variation *(pp. 336–341)*

EXAMPLE

- **Tell whether $6x = -4y$ represents a direct variation. If so, identify the constant of variation.**

$6x = -4y$

$\frac{6x}{-4} = \frac{-4y}{-4}$ *Solve the equation for y.*

$-\frac{6}{4}x = y$

$y = -\frac{3}{2}x$ *Simplify.*

This equation represents a direct variation because it can be written in the form $y = kx$, where $k = -\frac{3}{2}$.

EXERCISES

Tell whether each equation is a direct variation. If so, identify the constant of variation.

38. $y = -6x$
39. $x - y = 0$
40. $y + 4x = 3$
41. $2x = -4y$
42. The value of y varies directly with x, and $y = -8$ when $x = 2$. Find y when $x = 3$.
43. Maleka charges $8 per hour for baby-sitting. The amount of money she makes varies directly with the number of hours she baby-sits. Write a direct variation equation for the amount y Maleka earns for baby-sitting x hours. Then graph.

5-7 Slope-Intercept Form *(pp. 344–350)*

EXAMPLE

- **Graph the line with slope $= -\frac{4}{5}$ and y-intercept $= 8$.**

Step 1 Plot $(0, 8)$.

Step 2 For a slope of $\frac{-4}{5}$, count 4 down and 5 right from $(0, 8)$. Plot another point.

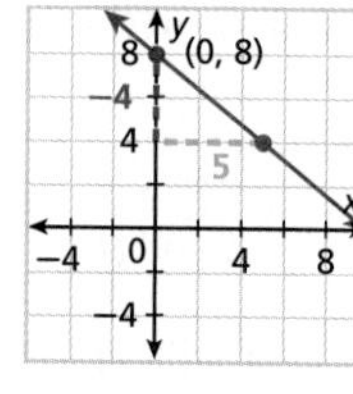

Step 3 Connect the two points with a line.

EXERCISES

Graph each line given the slope and y-intercept.

44. slope $= -\frac{1}{2}$; y-intercept $= 4$
45. slope $= 3$; y-intercept $= -7$

Write the equation that describes each line in slope-intercept form.

46. slope $= \frac{1}{3}$, y-intercept $= 5$
47. slope $= 4$, $(1, -5)$ is on the line.

5-8 Point-Slope Form *(pp. 351–358)*

EXAMPLE

- **Write an equation in slope-intercept form for the line through $(4, -1)$ and $(-2, 8)$.**

Step 1 Find the slope.

$$m = \frac{y_2 - y_1}{x_2 - x_1} = \frac{8-(-1)}{-2-4} = \frac{9}{-6} = -\frac{3}{2}$$

Step 2 Write the point-slope form.

$y - 8 = -\frac{3}{2}[x - (-2)]$ *Substitute into the point-slope form.*

$y - 8 = -\frac{3}{2}(x + 2)$

Step 3 Write the slope-intercept form.

$y = -\frac{3}{2}x + 5$ *Solve for y.*

EXERCISES

Graph the line described by each equation.

48. $y + 3 = \frac{1}{2}(x - 4)$ **49.** $y - 1 = -(x + 3)$

Write the equation that describes each line in slope-intercept form.

50. slope = 2, (1, 3) is on the line.

51. slope = −5, (−6, 4) is on the line.

52. (1, 4) and (3, 8) are on the line.

53. (−2, 4) and (−1, 6) are on the line.

5-9 Slopes of Parallel and Perpendicular Lines *(pp. 361–367)*

EXAMPLE

- **Write an equation in slope-intercept form for the line that passes through $(4, -2)$ and is perpendicular to the line described by $y = -4x + 3$.**

The slope of $y = -4x + 3$ is -4.

The perpendicular line has a slope of $\frac{1}{4}$ and contains $(4, -2)$.

$y + 2 = \frac{1}{4}(x - 4)$ *Substitute into the point-slope form.*

$y = \frac{1}{4}x - 3$ *Solve for y.*

EXERCISES

Identify which lines are parallel.

54. $y = -\frac{1}{3}x$; $y = 3x + 2$; $y = -\frac{1}{3}x - 6$; $y = 3$

55. $y - 2 = -4(x - 1)$; $y = 4x - 4$; $y = \frac{1}{4}x$; $y = -4x - 2$

Identify which lines are perpendicular.

56. $y - 1 = -5(x - 6)$; $y = \frac{1}{5}x + 2$; $y = 5$; $y = 5x + 8$

57. $y = 2x$; $y - 2 = 3(x + 1)$; $y = \frac{2}{3}x - 4$; $y = -\frac{1}{3}x$

58. Write an equation in slope-intercept form for the line that passes through $(1, -1)$ and is parallel to the line described by $y = 2x - 4$.

5-10 Transforming Linear Functions *(pp. 369–375)*

EXAMPLE

- **Graph $f(x) = \frac{1}{2}x$ and $g(x) = 4x + 2$. Then describe the transformation(s) from the graph of $f(x)$ to the graph of $g(x)$.**

  - Multiply $f(x) = \frac{1}{2}x$ by 8 to get $h(x) = 4x$. This rotates the graph about (0, 0), making it steeper.
  - Then add 2 to $h(x) = 4x$ to get $g(x) = 4x + 2$. This translates the graph 2 units up.

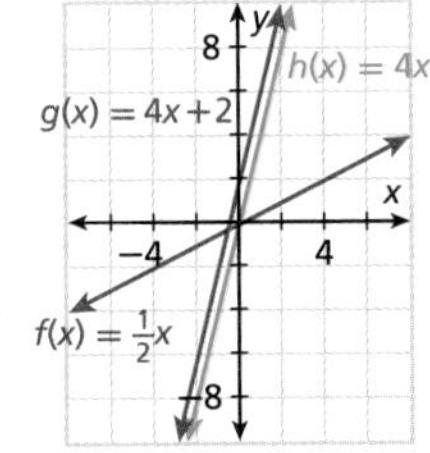

EXERCISES

Graph $f(x)$ and $g(x)$. Then describe the transformation(s) from the graph of $f(x)$ to the graph of $g(x)$.

59. $f(x) = x$, $g(x) = x + 4$

60. $f(x) = 4x$, $g(x) = -4x$

61. $f(x) = \frac{1}{3}x - 2$, $g(x) = -\frac{1}{3}x - 2$

62. The entrance fee at a carnival is \$3 and each ride costs \$1. The total cost for x rides is $f(x) = x + 3$. How will the graph of this function change if the entrance fee is increased to \$5? if the cost per ride is increased to \$2?

Answers

48.
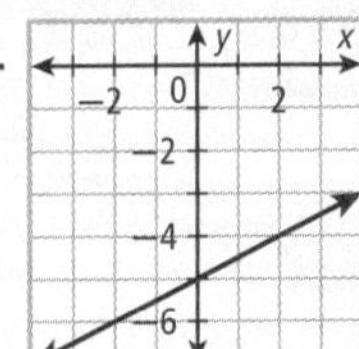

49.
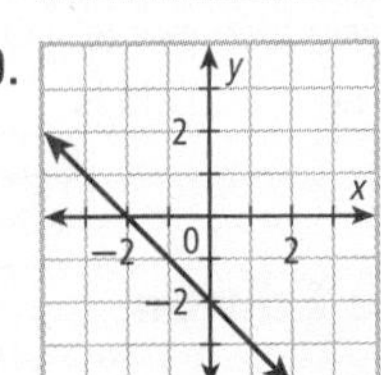

50. $y = 2x + 1$

51. $y = -5x - 26$

52. $y = 2x + 2$

53. $y = 2x + 8$

54. $y = -\frac{1}{3}x$ and $y = -\frac{1}{3}x - 6$

55. $y - 2 = -4(x - 1)$ and $y = -4x - 2$

56. $y - 1 = -5(x - 6)$ and $y = \frac{1}{5}x + 2$

57. $y - 2 = 3(x + 1)$ and $y = -\frac{1}{3}x$

58. $y = 2x - 3$

59.
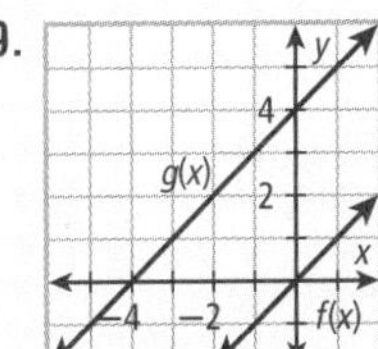

trans. 4 units up

60.
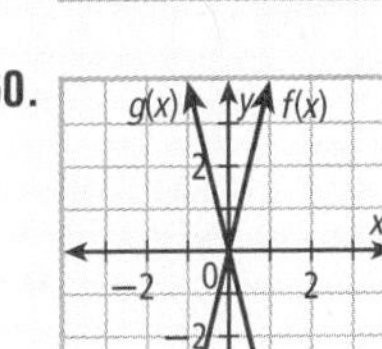

ref. across *y*-axis

61.
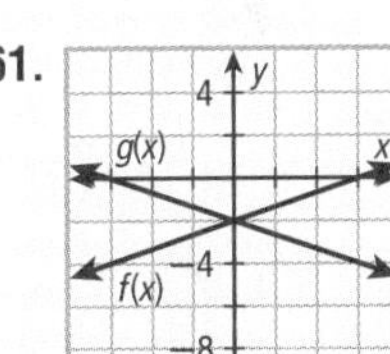

ref. across *y*-axis

62. trans. 2 units up; rot. about (0, 3) (steeper)

Study Guide: Review 385

Organizer

Objective: Assess students' mastery of concepts and skills in Chapter 5.

 Online Edition

Resources

 ***Assessment Resources***

Chapter 5 Tests

- Free Response (Levels A, B, C)
- Multiple Choice (Levels A, B, C)
- Performance Assessment

Teacher One Stop™
Test & Practice Generator

Answers

1. 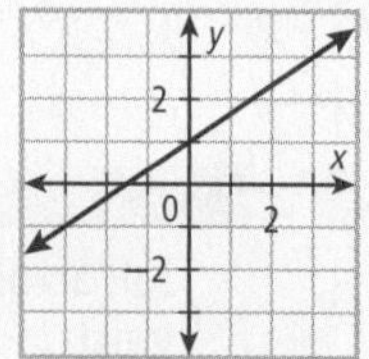

State Resources

CHAPTER 5 CHAPTER TEST

Tell whether each function is linear. If so, graph the function.

1. $3y = 2x + 3$ **yes**
2. $y = x(4 + x)$ **no**
3. Lily plans to volunteer at the tutoring center for 45 hours. She can tutor 3 hours per week. The function $f(x) = 45 - 3x$ gives the number of hours she will have left to tutor after x weeks. Graph the function and find its intercepts. What does each intercept represent?
4. The table shows the number of guppies in an aquarium over time. Graph the data and show the rates of change.

Time (mo)	0	1	2	5	8
Guppies	4	4	10	25	31

Find the slope of each line. Then tell what the slope represents.

5. 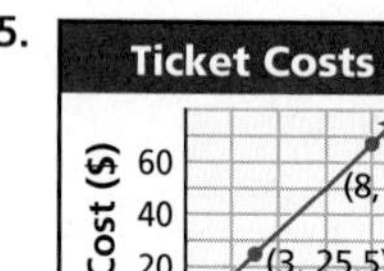

6. 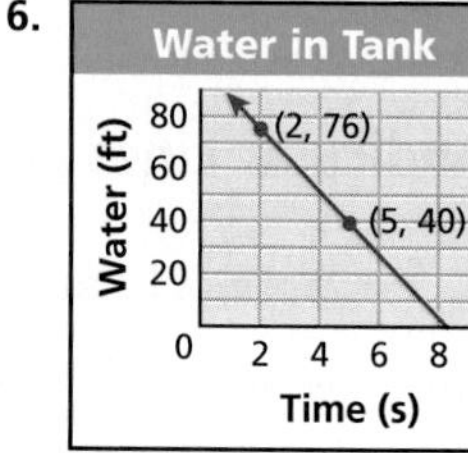

7. 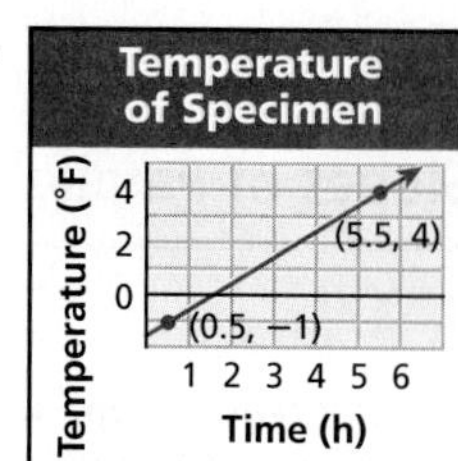

8. Each unit on a map of a bay represents 1 kilometer. Two buoys are located at (1, 5) and (3, 6) on the map. To the nearest tenth of a kilometer, what is the distance between the two buoys? **2.2 km**
9. In orbit around Earth, a space shuttle travels at a speed of about 5 miles per second. Write a direct variation equation for the distance y the space shuttle will travel in x seconds. Then graph. $\mathbf{y = 5x}$
10. Write the equation $2x - 2y = 4$ in slope-intercept form. Then graph the line described by the equation. $\mathbf{y = x - 2}$

Write the equation that describes each line in slope-intercept form.

11. slope $= -2$, y-intercept $= 7$ $\mathbf{y = -2x + 7}$
12. slope $= 4$, $(-3, 3)$ is on the line. $\mathbf{y = 4x + 15}$
13. $(1, 5)$ and $(-2, 8)$ are on the line. $\mathbf{y = -x + 6}$
14. x-intercept $= 3$, y-intercept $= -3$ $\mathbf{y = x - 3}$

Write an equation in point-slope form for the line with the given slope that contains the given point.

15. slope $= -1$; $(1, 3)$ $\mathbf{y - 3 = -(x - 1)}$
16. slope $= 5$; $(-3, 2)$ $\mathbf{y - 2 = 5(x + 3)}$
17. Write an equation in slope-intercept form for the line that passes through $(0, 6)$ and is parallel to the line described by $y = 2x + 3$. $\mathbf{y = 2x + 6}$

Graph $f(x)$ and $g(x)$. Then describe the transformation(s) from the graph of $f(x)$ to the graph of $g(x)$.

18. $f(x) = 8x$, $g(x) = 4x$
19. $f(x) = -x + 2$, $g(x) = -x - 1$
20. $f(x) = 3x$, $g(x) = 6x - 1$

3. 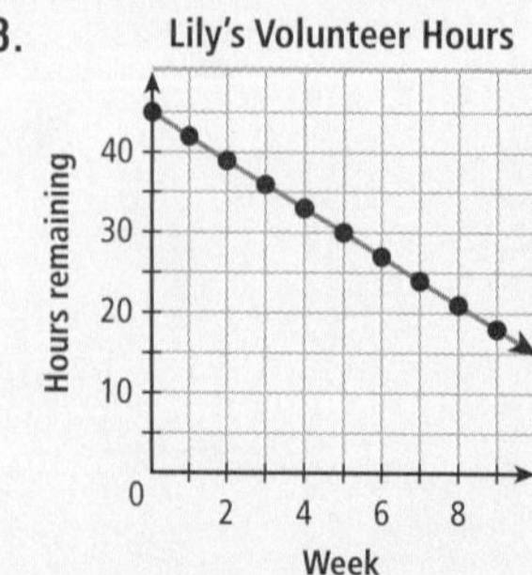

x-int.: 15; y-int.: 45; x-int.: number of weeks that will have passed when Lily has no vol. hours remaining; y-int.: orig. number of vol. hours

4. 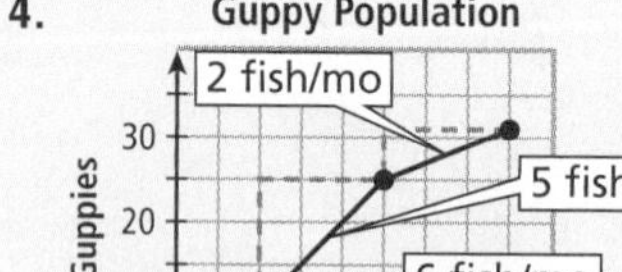

5. slope $= 8.5$; \$8.50/ticket
6. slope $= -12$; height decreases by 12 ft/s
7. slope $= 1$; temperature increases by 1 °F/h

9. trans. 3 units down

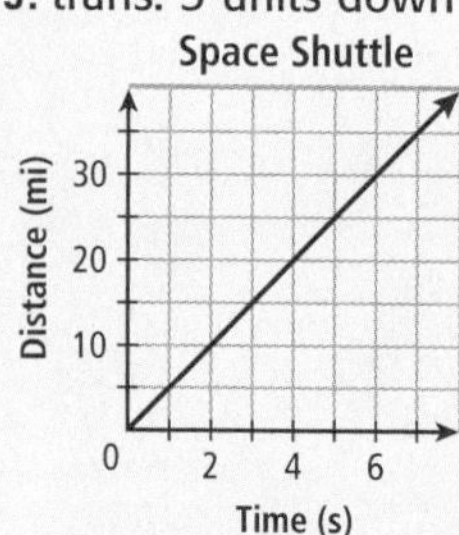

10. 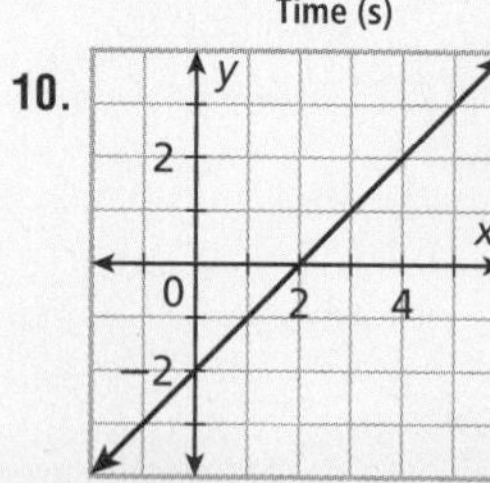

18–20. See p. A24.

College Entrance Exam Practice

FOCUS ON SAT

SAT scores are based on the total number of items answered correctly minus a fraction of the number of multiple-choice questions answered incorrectly. No points are subtracted for questions unanswered.

On the SAT, there is a penalty for incorrect answers on multiple-choice items. Guess only when you can eliminate at least one of the answer choices.

You may want to time yourself as you take this practice test. It should take you about 7 minutes to complete.

1. The line through $A(1, -3)$ and $B(-2, d)$ has slope -2. What is the value of d?

   (A) $-\frac{3}{2}$

   (B) -1

   (C) $\frac{1}{2}$

   (D) 3

   (E) 5

2. The ordered pairs $\{(0, -3), (4, -1), (6, 0), (10, 2)\}$ satisfy a pattern. Which is NOT true?

   (A) The pattern is linear.

   (B) The pattern can be described by $2x - 4y = 12$.

   (C) The ordered pairs lie on a line.

   (D) $(-4, 1)$ satisfies the same pattern.

   (E) The set of ordered pairs is a function.

3. If y varies directly as x, what is the value of x when $y = 72$?

x	7	12	
y	28	48	72

   (A) 17

   (B) 18

   (C) 24

   (D) 28

   (E) 36

4. The line segment between the points $(4, 0)$ and $(2, -2)$ forms one side of a rectangle. Which of the following coordinates could determine another vertex of that rectangle?

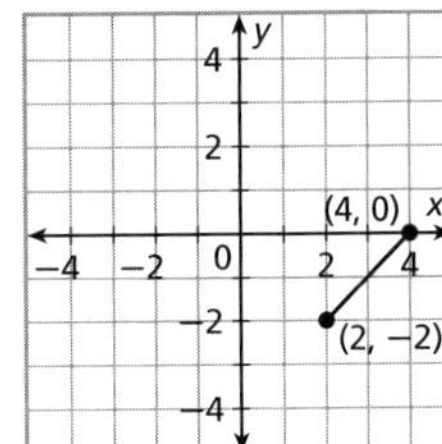

   (A) $(-2, 6)$

   (B) $(-2, -2)$

   (C) $(0, 6)$

   (D) $(1, 2)$

   (E) $(4, 6)$

5. Which of the following has the same slope as the line described by $2x - 3y = 3$?

   (A) $3x - 2y = 2$

   (B) $\frac{2}{3}x - y = -2$

   (C) $2x - 2y = 3$

   (D) $\frac{1}{3}x - 2y = -2$

   (E) $-2x - 3y = 2$

Organizer

Objective: Provide practice for college entrance exams such as the SAT.

Resources

College Entrance Exam Practice

Questions on the SAT represent the following math content areas:

Number and Operations, 20–25%

Algebra and Functions, 35–40%

Geometry and Measurement, 25–30%

Data Analysis, Statistics, and Probability, 10–15%

Items on this page focus on:

- Algebra and Functions
- Geometry and Measurement

Text References:

Item	1	2	3	4	5
Lesson	5-3	5-1	5-6	5-9	5-7

1. Students who chose **A** may have inverted the slope formula. Students who chose **E** most likely used addition in the slope formula instead of subtraction.
2. Students who did not choose **D** should review terminology and properties of linear functions.
3. Students who chose **A** most likely assumed that the difference between x-values was constant. Remind students to look for a value of k so that the given values satisfy $y = kx$.
4. Students who did not choose **A** may not have verified that the line segments forming adjacent sides were perpendicular. Remind students that a rectangle has four right angles.
5. Students who chose **C** selected a function with the same x-coefficient as the given function, but not the same slope. Students who chose **A** selected an answer with the same y-intercept as the given function.

Organizer

Objective: Provide opportunities to learn and practice common test-taking strategies.

TEST PREP DOCTOR This Test Tackler focuses on how to recognize the distracters given in multiple-choice test items. Tell students that the "wrong" answer choices given in multiple-choice items are not randomly written, but are created based on common student errors.

Standardized Test Strategies

Multiple Choice: Recognize Distracters

In multiple-choice items, the options that are incorrect are called *distracters*. This is an appropriate name, because these incorrect options can distract you from the correct answer.

Test writers create distracters by using common student errors. Beware! Even if the answer you get when you work the problem is one of the options, it may not be the correct answer.

EXAMPLE 1

What is the y-intercept of $4x + 10 = -2y$?

Ⓐ 10 Ⓒ −2.5

Ⓑ 5 Ⓓ −5

Look at each option carefully.

Ⓐ This is a distracter. The y-intercept would be 10 if the function was $4x + 10 = y$. A common error is to ignore the coefficient of y.

Ⓑ This is a distracter. Another common error is to divide by 2 instead of −2 when solving for y.

Ⓒ This is a distracter. One of the most common errors students make is confusing the x-intercept and the y-intercept. This distracter is actually the *x-intercept* of the given line.

Ⓓ This is the correct answer.

EXAMPLE 2

What is the equation of a line with a slope of −4 that contains (2, −3)?

Ⓕ $y - 3 = -4(x - 2)$ Ⓗ $y + 3 = -4(x - 2)$

Ⓖ $y - 2 = -4(x + 3)$ Ⓙ $y + 4 = -3(x - 2)$

Look at each option carefully.

Ⓕ This is a distracter. Students often make errors with positive and negative signs. You would get this answer if you simplified $y - (-3)$ as $y - 3$.

Ⓖ This is a distracter. You would get this answer if you switched the x-coordinate and the y-coordinate.

Ⓗ This is the correct answer.

Ⓙ This is a distracter. You would get this answer if you substituted the given values incorrectly in the point-slope equation.

When you calculate an answer to a multiple-choice test item, try to solve the problem again with a different method to make sure your answer is correct.

Read each test item and answer the questions that follow.

Item A
A line contains $(1, 2)$ and $(-2, 14)$. What are the slope and y-intercept?

Ⓐ Slope $= -4$; y-intercept $= -2$

Ⓑ Slope $= 4$; y-intercept $= 6$

Ⓒ Slope $= -\frac{1}{4}$; y-intercept $= 1$

Ⓓ Slope $= -4$; y-intercept $= 6$

1. What common error does the slope in choice B represent?
2. The slope given in choice A is correct, but the y-intercept is not. What error was made when finding the y-intercept?
3. What formula can you use to find the slope of a line? How was this formula used incorrectly to get the slope in choice C?

Item B
Which of these functions has a graph that is NOT parallel to the line described by $y = \frac{1}{2}x + 4$?

Ⓕ $y = 6 - \frac{1}{2}x$

Ⓖ $y = \frac{1}{2}x + 6$

Ⓗ $-2y = -x + 1$

Ⓙ $2y = x$

4. When given two linear functions, describe how to determine whether their graphs are parallel.
5. Which is the correct answer? Describe the errors a student might make to get each of the distracters.

Item C
Which of these lines has a slope of -3?

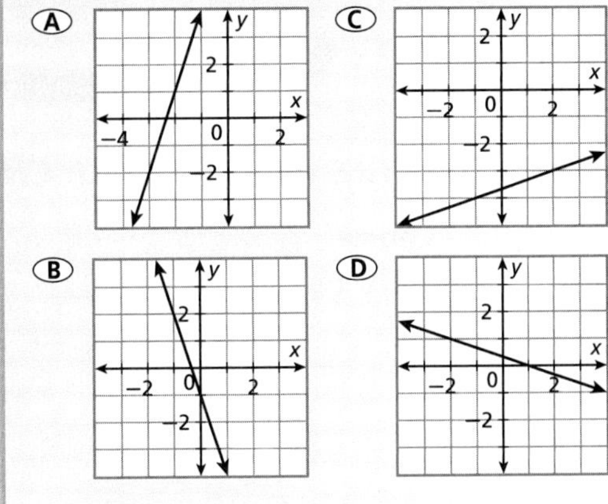

6. Which two answer choices can be eliminated immediately? Why?
7. Decribe how to find the slope of a line from its graph.
8. What common error does choice A represent?
9. What common error does choice D represent?
10. Which is the correct answer?

Item D
Which is NOT a linear function?

Ⓕ $f(x) = 4 + x$

Ⓖ $f(x) = -x - 4$

Ⓗ $f(x) = 4x^2$

Ⓙ $f(x) = \frac{1}{4}x$

11. When given a function rule, how can you tell if the function is linear?
12. What part of the function given in choice G might make someone think it is not linear?
13. What part of the function given in choice J might make someone think it is not linear?
14. What part of the function given in choice H makes it NOT linear?

TEST PREP DOCTOR + Show students how common errors, such as dropping negative signs or switching the x- and y-coordinates, will lead to an incorrect answer. Point out instances in which that incorrect answer is given as one of the answer choices. Any error analysis that students can do on a regular basis will help them to recognize distracters. Use **Problems 1, 9,** and **10** to discuss common errors with linear functions.

Answers

1. The slope should be -4 instead of 4. An error was made with the neg. sign.
2. Possible answer: When $y = mx + b$ was solved for b using the point $(1, 2)$, 4 was subtracted from both sides instead of -4.
3. $m = \frac{y_2 - y_1}{x_2 - x_1}$; the formula was incorrectly inverted.
4. They have the same slope.
5. **F** is the correct answer because it is the only option whose slope is not equal to $\frac{1}{2}$.
   Possible answers: You might get **G** or **J** if you do not read the question correctly and think you were looking for a line par. to $y = \frac{1}{2}x + 4$. You might get **H** if you divide by 2 instead of -2 when solving for y.
6. **A** and **C**; a line with a negative slope falls from left to right, so the correct answer cannot be **A** or **C**.
7. Possible answer: Locate 2 points on the graph. Begin at one of the points and count the rise and the run to the second point. Divide the rise by the run.
8. The slope of the line in **A** is 3. The line increases from left to right. The question asked for a slope of -3.
9. The slope of the line in **D** is $-\frac{1}{3}$, not -3. The rise is -1 and the run is 3.
10. B
11. When a linear equation is written in standard form, x and y both have exponents of 1, x and y are not multiplied together, and x and y do not appear in denominators or in exponents.
12. the negative sign
13. the fraction
14. x has an exponent of 2.

Answers to Test Items

A. D

B. F

C. B

D. H

State Resources

go.hrw.com
State Resources Online
KEYWORD: MA7 Resources

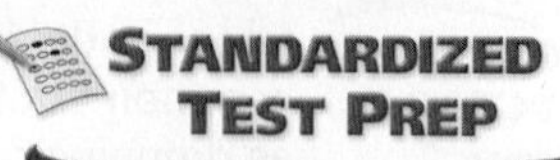

Organizer

Objective: Provide review and practice for Chapters 1–5 and standardized tests.

Online Edition

Resources

Assessment Resources

Chapter 5 Cumulative Test

go.hrw.com
KEYWORD: MA7 TestPrep

State Resources

go.hrw.com
State Resources Online
KEYWORD: MA7 Resources

go.hrw.com
State Test Practice Online
KEYWORD: MA7 TestPrep

CUMULATIVE ASSESSMENT, CHAPTERS 1–5

Multiple Choice

1. What is the value of $2 - [1 - (2 - 1)]$?
   - (A) −2
   - (B) 0
   - (C) 2
   - (D) 4

2. Frank borrowed $5000 with an annual simple interest rate. The amount of interest he owed after 6 months was $300. What is the interest rate of the loan?
   - (F) 1%
   - (G) 6%
   - (H) 10%
   - (J) 12%

3. Patty's Pizza charges $5.50 for a large pizza plus $0.30 for each topping. Pizza Town charges $5.00 for a large pizza plus $0.40 for each topping. Which inequality can you use to find the number of toppings x so that the cost of a pizza at Pizza Town is greater than the cost of a pizza at Patty's Pizza?
   - (A) $(5 + 0.4)x > (5.5 + 0.3)x$
   - (B) $5.5x + 0.3 > 5x + 0.4$
   - (C) $5.5 + 0.3x > 5 + 0.4x$
   - (D) $5 + 0.4x > 5.5 + 0.3x$

4. The side length of a square s can be determined by the formula $s = \sqrt{A}$ where A represents the area of the square. What is the side length of a square with area 0.09 square meter?
   - (F) 0.0081 meters
   - (G) 0.81 meters
   - (H) 0.03 meters
   - (J) 0.3 meters

5. What is the value of $f(x) = -3 - x$ when $x = -7$?
   - (A) −10
   - (B) −4
   - (C) 4
   - (D) 10

6. Which relationship is a direct variation?

   (F)

x	1	2	3	4
y	−1	0	1	2

   (G)

x	1	2	3	4
y	0	−1	−2	−3

   (H)

   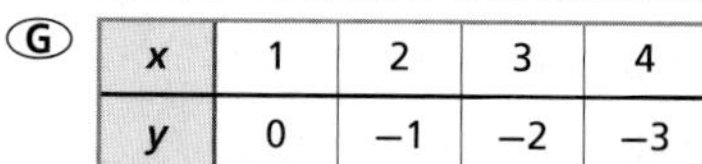

x	1	2	3	4
y	3	5	7	9

   (J)

   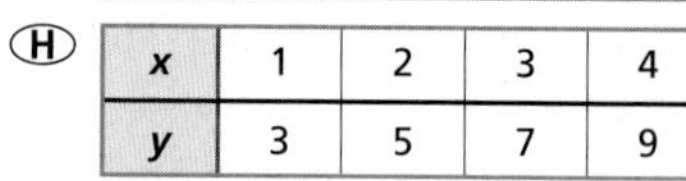

x	1	2	3	4
y	3	6	9	12

7. Which function has x-intercept −2 and y-intercept 4
   - (A) $2x - y = 4$
   - (B) $2y - x = 4$
   - (C) $y - 2x = 4$
   - (D) $x - 2y = 4$

8. Which equation describes the relationship between x and y in the table below?

x	−8	−4	0	4	8
y	2	1	0	−1	−2

   - (F) $y = -4x$
   - (G) $y = -\frac{1}{4}x$
   - (H) $y = 4x$
   - (J) $y = \frac{1}{4}x$

9. Which graph is described by $x - 3y = -3$?

   (A)
   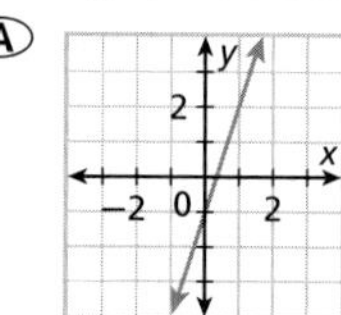

   (C)
   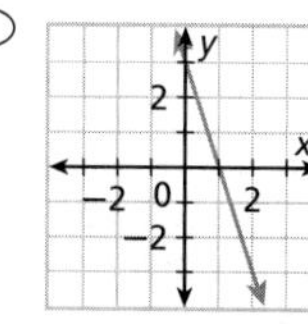

   (B)
   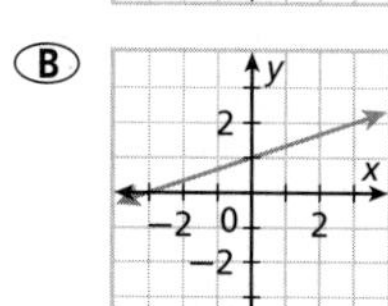

   (D)
   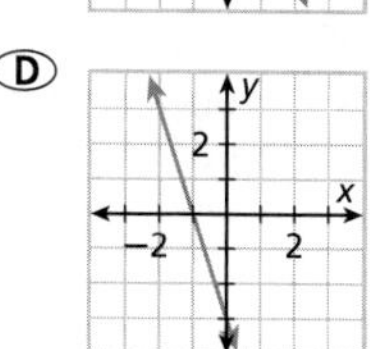

Answers

1. C
2. J
3. D
4. J
5. C
6. J
7. C
8. G
9. B
10. G
11. C
12. H
13. C
14. 10.5
15. 7.5
16. 14

When answering multiple-choice test items, check that the test item number matches the number on your answer sheet, especially if you skip test items that you plan to come back to.

10. Which steps could you use to graph the line that has slope 2 and contains the point $(-1, 3)$?

Ⓕ Plot $(-1, 3)$. Move 1 unit up and 2 units right and plot another point.

Ⓖ Plot $(-1, 3)$. Move 2 units up and 1 unit right and plot another point.

Ⓗ Plot $(-1, 3)$. Move 1 unit up and 2 units left and plot another point.

Ⓙ Plot $(-1, 3)$. Move 2 units up and 1 unit left and plot another point.

11. Which line is parallel to the line described by $2x + 3y = 6$?

Ⓐ $3x + 2y = 6$ Ⓒ $2x + 3y = -6$

Ⓑ $3x - 2y = -6$ Ⓓ $2x - 3y = 6$

12. Which function's graph is NOT perpendicular to the line described by $4x - y = -2$?

Ⓕ $y + \frac{1}{4}x = 0$ Ⓗ $3y = \frac{3}{4}x + 3$

Ⓖ $\frac{1}{2}x = 10 - 2y$ Ⓙ $y = -\frac{1}{4}x + \frac{3}{2}$

13. Company A charges \$30 plus \$0.40 per mile for a car rental. The total charge for m miles is given by $f(m) = 30 + 0.4m$. For a similar car, company B charges \$30 plus \$0.30 per mile. The total charge for m miles is given by $g(m) = 30 + 0.3m$. Which best describes the transformation from the graph of $f(m)$ to the graph of $g(m)$?

Ⓐ Translation up

Ⓑ Translation down

Ⓒ Rotation

Ⓓ Reflection

Gridded Response

14. What is the value of x in the diagram below?

$\triangle ABC \sim \triangle DEF$

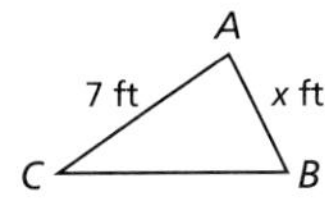

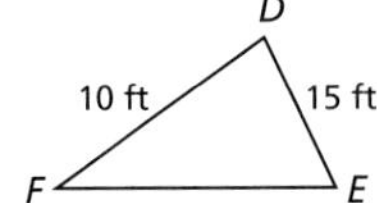

15. What is the 46th term in the arithmetic sequence $-1.5, -1.3, -1.1, -0.9, \ldots$?

16. What is the y-intercept of $y - 2 = 3(x + 4)$?

Short Response

17. A video store charges a \$10 membership fee plus \$2 for each movie rental. The total cost for x movie rentals is given by $f(x) = 2x + 10$.

a. Graph this function.

b. Give a reasonable domain and range.

18. The table below shows the federal minimum wage in different years.

Year	1960	1970	1980	1990	2000
Minimum Wage (\$)	1.00	1.60	3.10	3.80	5.15

a. Find the rate of change for each ten-year time period. Show your work.

b. During which time period did the minimum wage increase the fastest? Explain what the rate of change for this time period means.

19. a. Find the slope of the line below.

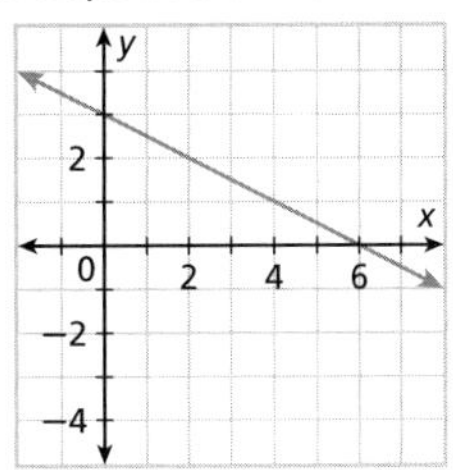

b. Write an equation in slope-intercept form for a line that is perpendicular to the line in part **a** and has the same y-intercept as the function in part **a.** Show your work and explain how you found your answer.

Extended Response

20. The relationship between the wind speed at a given temperature and the apparent temperature is approximately linear. The table shows the apparent temperature at various wind speeds when the actual temperature is t °F.

Wind Speed (mi/h)	5	10	15
Apparent Temperature (°F)	36	34	32

a. Write an equation in slope-intercept form that describes the data in the table. Explain how you found your answer.

b. What does the slope mean in this situation?

c. What is the actual temperature t? Explain.

d. Determine the apparent temperature when the wind speed is 12 miles per hour. Show your work.

Short-Response Rubric

Items 17–19

2 Points = The student's answer is an accurate and complete execution of the task or tasks.

1 Point = The student's answer contains attributes of an appropriate response but is flawed.

0 Points = The student's answer contains no attributes of an appropriate response.

Extended-Response Rubric

Item 20

4 Points = The student writes the correct equation and explanation and shows all work in part **a,** gives the correct explanation for the slope in part **b,** gives the correct answer and explanation in part **c,** and determines the correct answer and shows all work in part **d.**

3 Points = The student writes the correct equation and explanation but does not show all work in part **a,** gives the correct explanation for the slope in part **b,** gives the correct answer and some explanation in part **c,** and determines the correct answer and shows some work in part **d.**

2 Points = The student writes the correct equation and explanation but shows no work in part **a,** gives the correct explanation for the slope in part **b,** gives the correct answer but no explanation in part **c,** and determines the correct answer and shows some work in part **d;** or the student attempts to answer all parts and correctly answers only two parts.

1 Point = The student writes the correct equation but gives no explanation and shows no work in part **a,** gives the correct explanation for the slope in part **b,** gives the correct answer but no explanation in part **c,** and determines the correct answer but shows no work in part **d;** or the student attempts to answer all parts of the problem but does not correctly answer any part.

0 Points = The student does not answer correctly and does not attempt all parts of the problem.

Answers

17a.

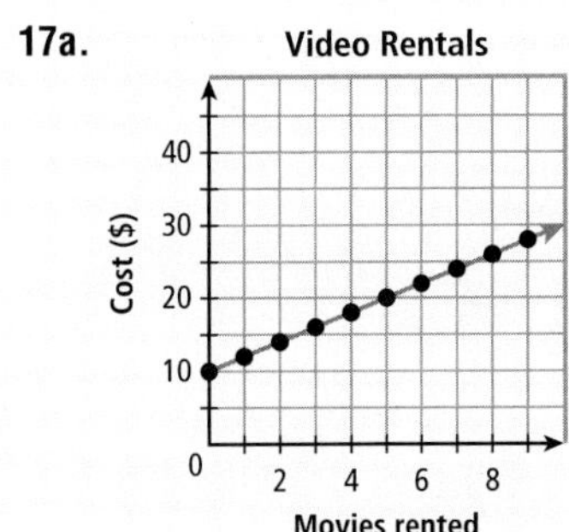

b. D: whole numbers; R: even whole numbers greater than or equal to 10

18a. 1960 to 1970: 0.06; 1970 to 1980: 0.15; 1980 to 1990: 0.07; 1990 to 2000: 0.135

b. 1970 to 1980; on average, min. wage increased by \$0.15 per year during this time period.

19a. $-\frac{1}{2}$

b. $y = 2x + 3$

20a. $y = -\frac{2}{5}x + 38$

b. the amount by which the apparent temp. decreases each time the wind speed increases by 1 mi/h

c. 38°F

d. 33.2°F

Systems of Equations and Inequalities

Section 6A

Systems of Linear Equations

6-1 Technology Lab Solve Linear Equations by Using a Spreadsheet
6-1 Solving Systems by Graphing
6-2 Algebra Lab Model Systems of Linear Equations
6-2 Solving Systems by Substitution
6-3 Solving Systems by Elimination
Connecting Algebra to Number Theory Solving Classic Problems
6-4 Solving Special Systems

Section 6B

Linear Inequalities

6-5 Solving Linear Inequalities
6-6 Solving Systems of Linear Inequalities
6-6 Technology Lab Solve Systems of Linear Inequalities

Pacing Guide for 45-Minute Classes

Teacher One Stop™
Calendar Planner®

Chapter 6

Countdown Weeks 13, 14

DAY 1	DAY 2	DAY 3	DAY 4	DAY 5
6-1 Technology Lab 6-1 Lesson	6-1 Lesson 6-2 Algebra Lab	6-2 Lesson	6-3 Lesson	Connecting Algebra to Number Theory
DAY 6	**DAY 7**	**DAY 8**	**DAY 9**	**DAY 10**
6-4 Lesson	Multi-Step Test Prep Ready to Go On?	6-5 Lesson	6-6 Lesson	6-6 Lesson 6-6 Technology Lab
DAY 11	**DAY 12**	**DAY 13**		
Multi-Step Test Prep Ready to Go On?	Chapter 6 Review	Chapter 6 Test		

Pacing Guide for 90-Minute Classes

Teacher One Stop™
Calendar Planner®

Chapter 6

DAY 1	DAY 2	DAY 3	DAY 4	DAY 5
6-1 Technology Lab 6-1 Lesson 6-2 Algebra Lab	6-2 Lesson 6-3 Lesson	Connecting Algebra to Number Theory 6-4 Lesson	Multi-Step Test Prep Ready to Go On? 6-5 Lesson	6-6 Lesson 6-6 Technology Lab
DAY 6	**DAY 7**			
Multi-Step Test Prep Ready to Go On? Chapter 6 Review	Chapter 6 Test 7-1 Lesson			

ONGOING ASSESSMENT and INTERVENTION

	DIAGNOSE	PRESCRIBE
Assess Prior Knowledge	**Before Chapter 6**	
	Diagnose readiness for the chapter.	Prescribe intervention.
	Are You Ready? SE p. 393	***Are You Ready? Intervention***
Formative Assessment	**Before Every Lesson**	
	Diagnose readiness for the lesson.	Prescribe intervention.
	Warm Up TE	**Reteach** CRB
	During Every Lesson	
	Diagnose understanding of lesson concepts.	Prescribe intervention.
	Check It Out! SE	**Reading Strategies** CRB
	Questioning Strategies TE	***Success for Every Learner***
	Think and Discuss SE	***Lesson Tutorial Videos***
	Write About It SE	
	Journal TE	
	After Every Lesson	
	Diagnose mastery of lesson concepts.	Prescribe intervention.
	Lesson Quiz TE	**Reteach** CRB
	Test Prep SE	**Test Prep Doctor** TE
	Test and Practice Generator	***Homework Help Online***
	Before Chapter 6 Testing	
	Diagnose mastery of concepts in chapter.	Prescribe intervention.
	Ready to Go On? SE pp. 427, 443	***Ready to Go On? Intervention***
	Multi-Step Test Prep SE pp. 426, 442	**Scaffolding Questions** TE pp. 426, 442
	Section Quizzes AR	**Reteach** CRB
	Test and Practice Generator	***Lesson Tutorial Videos***
	Before High Stakes Testing	
	Diagnose mastery of benchmark concepts.	Prescribe intervention.
	College Entrance Exam Practice SE p. 449	***College Entrance Exam Practice***
	Standardized Test Prep SE pp. 452–453	
Summative Assessment	**After Chapter 6**	
	Check mastery of chapter concepts.	Prescribe intervention.
	Multiple-Choice Tests (Forms A, B, C)	**Reteach** CRB
	Free-Response Tests (Forms A, B, C)	***Lesson Tutorial Videos***
	Performance Assessment AR	
	Cumulative Test AR	
	Test and Practice Generator	

KEY: **SE** = *Student Edition* **TE** = *Teacher's Edition* **CRB** = *Chapter Resource Book* **AR** = *Assessment Resources*  Available online Available on CD- or DVD-ROM

CHAPTER 6

Lesson Resources

Before the Lesson

Prepare

Teacher One Stop  
- Editable lesson plans
- Calendar Planner
- Easy access to all chapter resources

Lesson Transparencies
- Teacher Tools

Teach the Lesson

Introduce

Alternate Openers: Explorations

Lesson Transparencies
- Warm Up
- Problem of the Day

Teach

Lesson Transparencies
- Teaching Transparencies

Know-It Notebook™
- Vocabulary
- Key Concepts

Power Presentations 

Lesson Tutorial Videos 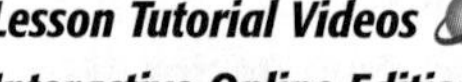

Interactive Online Edition
- Lesson Activities
- Lesson Tutorial Videos

Lab Activities

Lab Resources Online

Online Interactivities   

TechKeys

Practice the Lesson

Practice

Chapter Resources
- Practice A, B, C

Practice and Problem Solving Workbook SPANISH

IDEA Works!® Modified Worksheets and Tests

ExamView Test and Practice Generator 

Homework Help Online

Online Interactivities 

Interactive Online Edition
- Homework Help

Apply

Chapter Resources
- Problem Solving SPANISH

Practice and Problem Solving Workbook SPANISH

Interactive Online Edition
- Chapter Project

Project Teacher Support

After the Lesson

Reteach

Chapter Resources
- Reteach
- Reading Strategies ELL

Success for Every Learner

Review

Interactive Answers and Solutions

Solutions Key

Know-It Notebook™
- Big Ideas
- Chapter Review

Extend

Chapter Resources
- Challenge

Technology Highlights for the Teacher

 **Power Presentations**

Dynamic presentations to engage students. Complete PowerPoint® presentations for every lesson in Chapter 6.

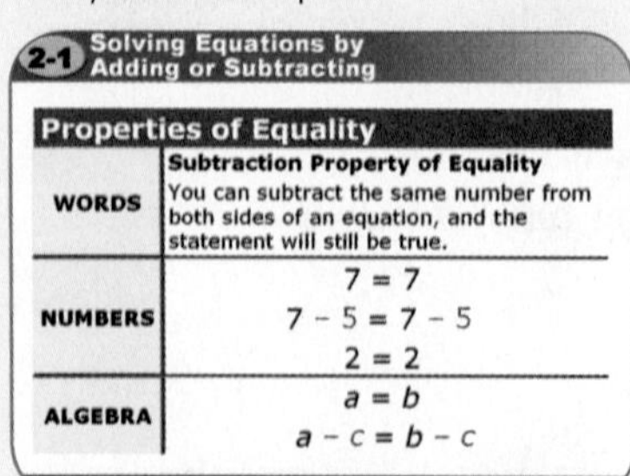

 **Teacher One Stop** SPANISH

Easy access to Chapter 6 resources and assessments. Includes lesson planning, test generation, and puzzle creation software.

 **Premier Online Edition** SPANISH

Chapter 6 includes Tutorial Videos, Lesson Activities, Lesson Quizzes, Homework Help, and Chapter Project.

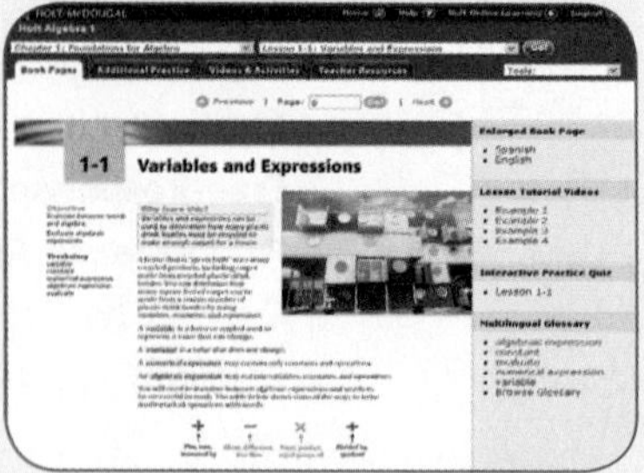

KEY: **SE** = *Student Edition* **TE** = *Teacher's Edition*  English Language Learners 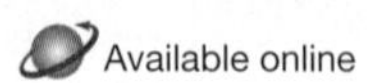 Spanish version available Available online 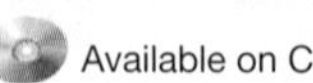 Available on CD- or DVD-R

Reaching All Learners

Teaching tips to help all learners appear throughout the chapter. A few that target specific students are included in the lists below.

All Learners

Lab Activities
Practice and Problem Solving Workbook SPANISH
Know-It Notebook

Special Needs Students

Practice A .... CRB
Reteach .... CRB
Reading Strategies .... CRB
Are You Ready? .... SE p. 393
Inclusion .... TE pp. 401, 405, 419
IDEA Works!® Modified Worksheets and Tests
Ready to Go On? Intervention SPANISH
Know-It Notebook
Online Interactivities  SPANISH
Lesson Tutorial Videos  SPANISH

Developing Learners

Practice A .... CRB
Reteach .... CRB
Reading Strategies .... CRB
Are You Ready? .... SE p. 393
Vocabulary Connections .... SE p. 394
Questioning Strategies .... TE
Ready to Go On? Intervention SPANISH
Know-It Notebook
Homework Help Online
Online Interactivities  SPANISH
Lesson Tutorial Videos   SPANISH

On-Level Learners

Practice B .... CRB
Problem Solving .... CRB
Vocabulary Connections .... SE p. 394
Questioning Strategies .... TE
Ready to Go On? Intervention SPANISH
Know-It Notebook
Homework Help Online 
Online Interactivities SPANISH

Advanced Learners

Practice C .... CRB
Challenge .... CRB
Challenge Exercises .... SE
Reading and Writing Math *Extend* .... TE p. 395
Critical Thinking .... TE pp. 412, 424
Are You Ready? Enrichment SPANISH
Ready To Go On? Enrichment SPANISH

English Language Learners

ENGLISH LANGUAGE LEARNERS

Reading Strategies .... CRB
Are You Ready? Vocabulary .... SE p. 393
Vocabulary Connections .... SE p. 394
Vocabulary Review .... SE p. 444
English Language Learners .... TE pp. 409, 412
Success for Every Learner
Know-It Notebook
Multilingual Glossary
Lesson Tutorial Videos  SPANISH 

Technology Highlights for Reaching All Learners

Lesson Tutorial Videos SPANISH

Starring Holt authors Ed Burger and Freddie Renfro! Live tutorials to support every lesson in Chapter 6.

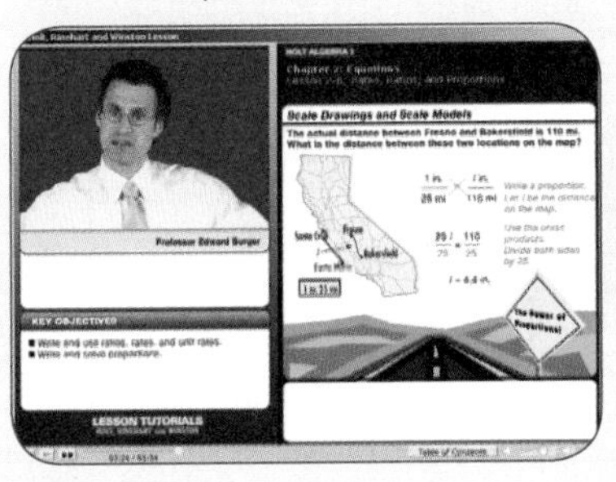

Multilingual Glossary

Searchable glossary includes definitions in English, Spanish, Vietnamese, Chinese, Hmong, Korean, and 4 other languages.

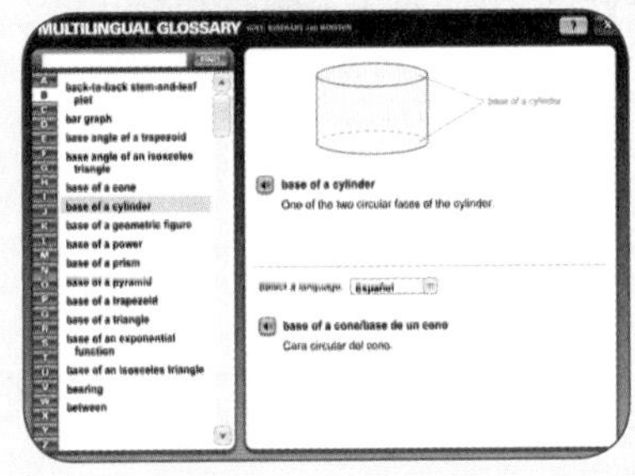

Online Interactivities

Interactive tutorials provide visually engaging alternative opportunities to learn concepts and master skills.

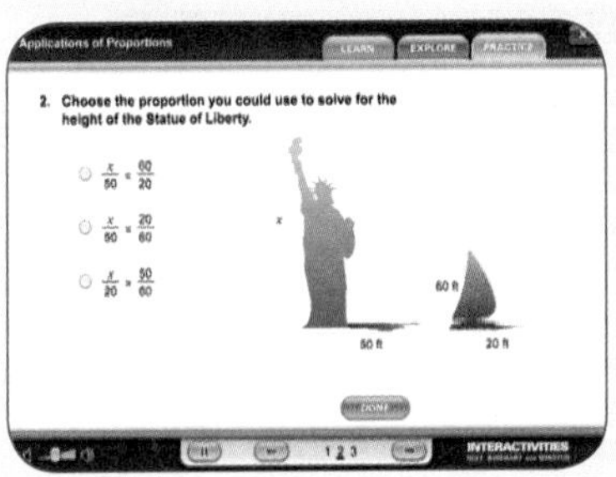

KEY: **SE** = *Student Edition* **TE** = *Teacher's Edition* **CRB** = *Chapter Resource Book* SPANISH Spanish version available — Available online — Available on CD- or DVD-ROM

Assessing Prior Knowledge

Determine whether students have the prerequisite concepts and skills for success in Chapter 6.

Are You Ready? SPANISH .... SE p. 393
Warm Up .... TE

Test Preparation

Provide review and practice for Chapter 6 and standardized tests.

Multi-Step Test Prep .... SE pp. 426, 442
Study Guide: Review .... SE pp. 444–447
Test Tackler .... SE pp. 450–451
Standardized Test Prep .... SE pp. 452–453
College Entrance Exam Practice .... SE p. 449
Countdown to Testing .... SE pp. C4–C27
IDEA Works!® Modified Worksheets and Tests

Alternative Assessment

Assess students' understanding of Chapter 6 concepts and combined problem-solving skills.

Chapter 6 Project .... SE p. 392
Alternative Assessment .... TE
Performance Assessment SPANISH .... AR
Portfolio Assessment SPANISH .... AR

Lesson Assessment

Provide formative assessment for each lesson of Chapter 6.

Questioning Strategies .... TE
Think and Discuss .... SE
Check It Out! Exercises .... SE
Write About It .... SE
Journal .... TE
Lesson Quiz .... TE
Alternative Assessment .... TE
IDEA Works!® Modified Worksheets and Tests

Weekly Assessment

Provide formative assessment for each section of Chapter 6.

Multi-Step Test Prep .... SE pp. 426, 442
Ready to Go On? SPANISH .... SE pp. 427, 443
Section Quizzes SPANISH .... AR
Test and Practice Generator SPANISH .... *Teacher One Stop*

Chapter Assessment

Provide summative assessment of Chapter 6 mastery.

Chapter 6 Test .... SE p. 448
Chapter Test (Levels A, B, C) SPANISH .... AR
- Multiple Choice
- Free Response

Cumulative Test SPANISH .... AR
Test and Practice Generator SPANISH .... *Teacher One Stop*
IDEA Works!® Modified Worksheets and Tests

Technology Highlights for Assessment

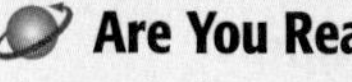

Are You Ready? SPANISH

Automatically assess readiness and prescribe intervention for Chapter 6 prerequisite skills.

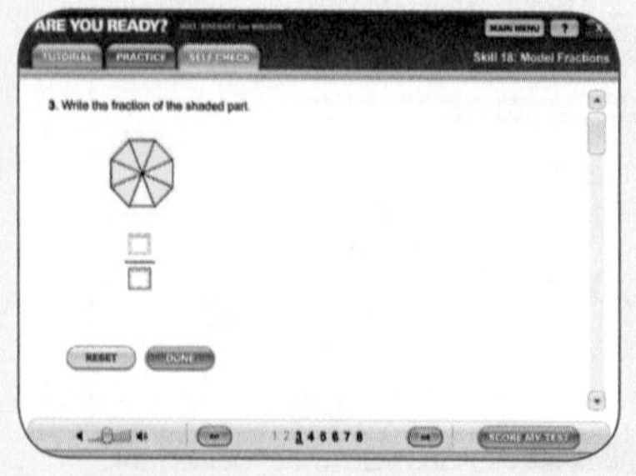

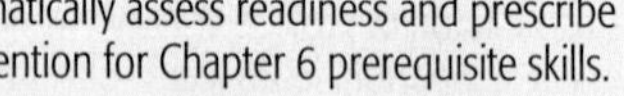

Ready to Go On?

Automatically assess understanding of and prescribe intervention for Sections 6A and 6B.

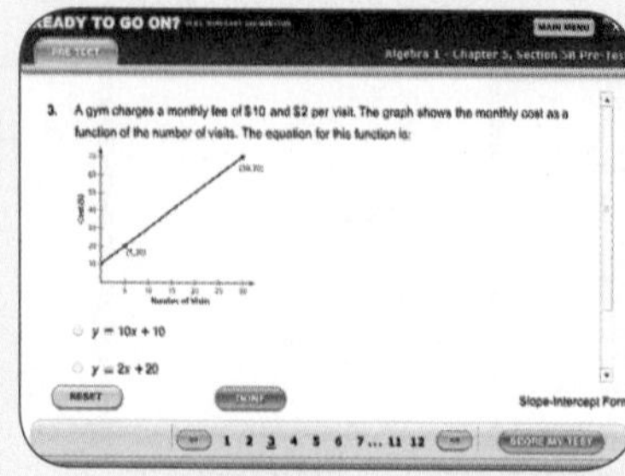

Test and Practice Generator SPANISH

Use Chapter 6 problem banks to create assessments and worksheets to print out or deliver online. Includes dynamic problems.

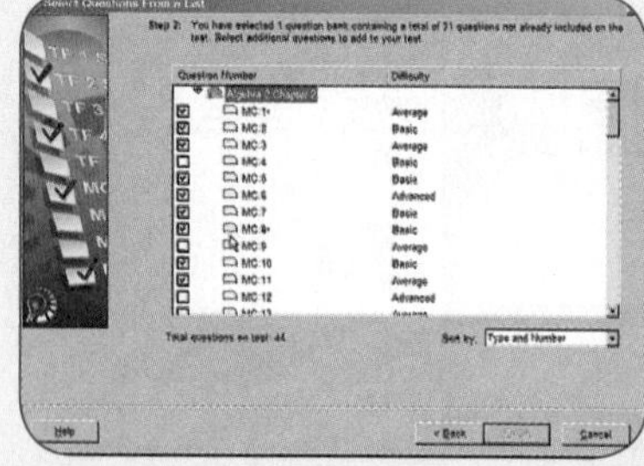

KEY: **SE** = *Student Edition* **TE** = *Teacher's Edition* **AR** = *Assessment Resources*  Spanish version available 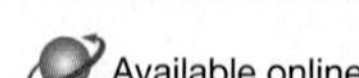  Available on CD- or DVD-ROM

CHAPTER 6

Formal Assessment

Three levels (A, B, C) of multiple-choice and free-response chapter tests, along with a performance assessment, are available in the *Assessment Resources.*

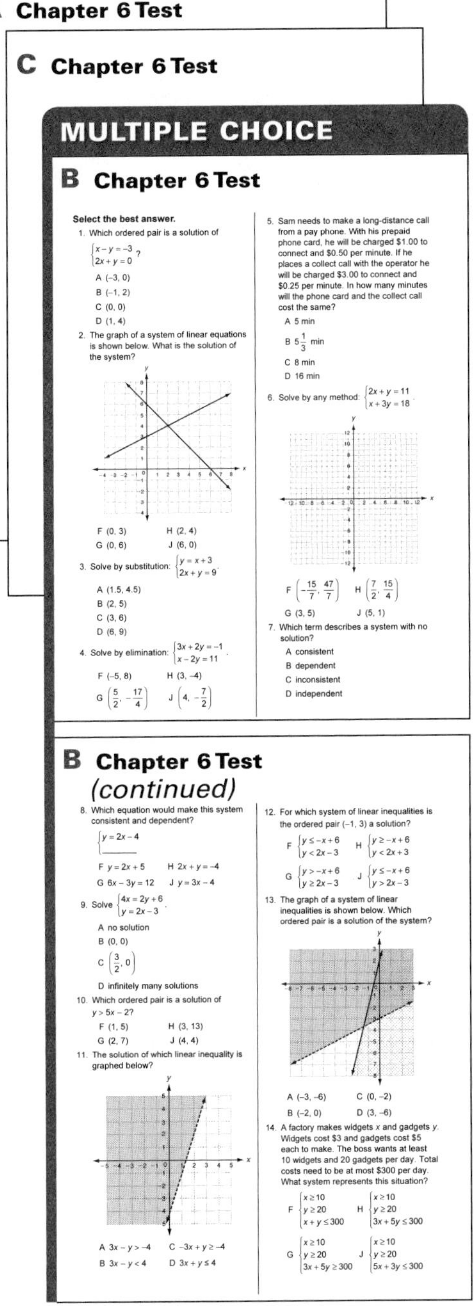

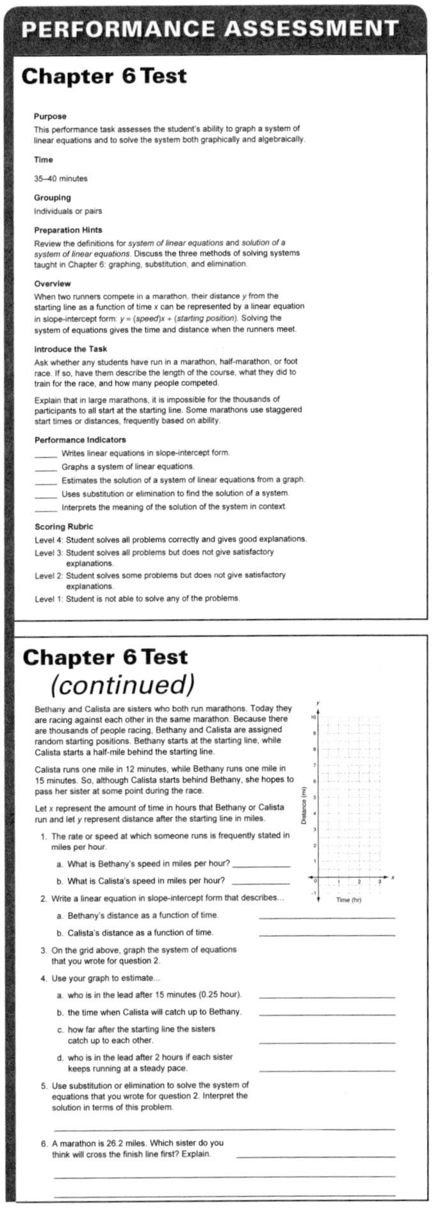

A Chapter 6 Test

C Chapter 6 Test

MULTIPLE CHOICE

B Chapter 6 Test

Select the best answer.

1. Which ordered pair is a solution of $\begin{cases} x - y = -3 \\ 2x + y = 0 \end{cases}$?
A (−3, 0)
B (−1, 2)
C (0, 0)
D (1, 4)

2. The graph of a system of linear equations is shown below. What is the solution of the system?
F (0, 3) H (2, 4)
G (0, 6) J (6, 0)

3. Solve by substitution: $\begin{cases} y = x + 3 \\ 2x + y = 9 \end{cases}$
A (1.5, 4.5)
B (2, 5)
C (3, 6)
D (6, 9)

4. Solve by elimination: $\begin{cases} 3x + 2y = -1 \\ x - 2y = 11 \end{cases}$
F (−5, 8) H (3, −4)
G $\left(\frac{5}{2}, -\frac{17}{4}\right)$ J $\left(4, -\frac{7}{2}\right)$

5. Sam needs to make a long-distance call from a pay phone. With his prepaid phone card, he will be charged $1.00 to connect and $0.50 per minute. If he places a collect call with the operator he will be charged $3.00 to connect and $0.25 per minute. In how many minutes will the phone card and the collect call cost the same?
A 5 min
B $5\frac{1}{3}$ min
C 8 min
D 16 min

6. Solve by any method: $\begin{cases} 2x + y = 11 \\ x + 3y = 18 \end{cases}$
F $\left(-\frac{15}{7}, \frac{47}{7}\right)$ H $\left(\frac{7}{2}, \frac{15}{4}\right)$
G (3, 5) J (5, 1)

7. Which term describes a system with no solution?
A consistent
B dependent
C inconsistent
D independent

B Chapter 6 Test (continued)

8. Which equation would make this system consistent and dependent? $\begin{cases} y = 2x - 4 \\ \_\_\_\_ \end{cases}$
F $y = 2x + 5$ H $2x + y = -4$
G $6x - 3y = 12$ J $y = 3x - 4$

9. Solve $\begin{cases} 4x = 2y + 6 \\ y = 2x - 3 \end{cases}$.
A no solution
B (0, 0)
C $\left(\frac{3}{2}, 0\right)$
D infinitely many solutions

10. Which ordered pair is a solution of $y > 5x - 2$?
F (1, 5) H (3, 13)
G (2, 7) J (4, 4)

11. The solution of which linear inequality is graphed below?
A $3x - y > -4$ C $-3x + y \ge -4$
B $3x - y < 4$ D $3x + y \le 4$

12. For which system of linear inequalities is the ordered pair (−1, 3) a solution?
F $\begin{cases} y \le -x + 6 \\ y < 2x - 3 \end{cases}$ H $\begin{cases} y \ge -x + 6 \\ y < 2x + 3 \end{cases}$
G $\begin{cases} y > -x + 6 \\ y \ge 2x - 3 \end{cases}$ J $\begin{cases} y \le -x + 6 \\ y > 2x - 3 \end{cases}$

13. The graph of a system of linear inequalities is shown below. Which ordered pair is a solution of the system?
A (−3, −6) C (0, −2)
B (−2, 0) D (3, −6)

14. A factory makes widgets *x* and gadgets *y*. Widgets cost $3 and gadgets cost $5 each to make. The boss wants at least 10 widgets and 20 gadgets per day. Total costs need to be at most $300 per day. What system represents this situation?
F $\begin{cases} x \ge 10 \\ y \ge 20 \\ x + y \le 300 \end{cases}$ H $\begin{cases} x \ge 10 \\ y \ge 20 \\ 3x + 5y \le 300 \end{cases}$
G $\begin{cases} x \ge 10 \\ y \ge 20 \\ 3x + 5y \ge 300 \end{cases}$ J $\begin{cases} x \ge 10 \\ y \ge 20 \\ 5x + 3y \le 300 \end{cases}$

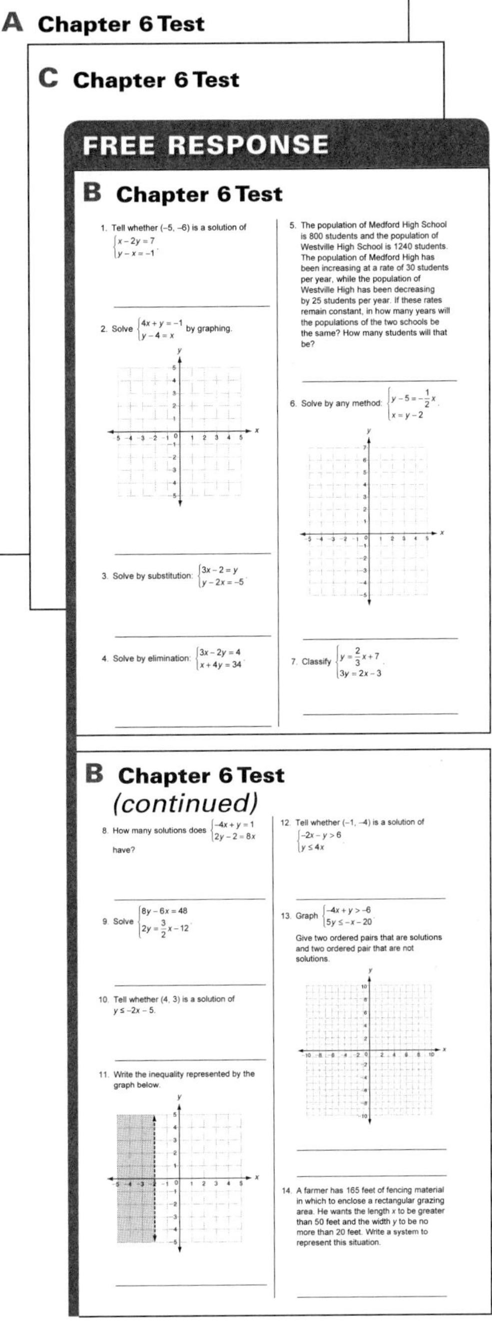

A Chapter 6 Test

C Chapter 6 Test

FREE RESPONSE

B Chapter 6 Test

1. Tell whether (−5, −6) is a solution of $\begin{cases} x - 2y = 7 \\ y - x = -1 \end{cases}$.

2. Solve $\begin{cases} 4x + y = -1 \\ y - 4 = x \end{cases}$ by graphing.

3. Solve by substitution: $\begin{cases} 3x - 2 = y \\ y - 2x = -5 \end{cases}$

4. Solve by elimination: $\begin{cases} 3x - 2y = 4 \\ x + 4y = 34 \end{cases}$

5. The population of Medford High School is 800 students and the population of Westville High School is 1240 students. The population of Medford High has been increasing at a rate of 30 students per year, while the population of Westville High has been decreasing by 25 students per year. If these rates remain constant, in how many years will the populations of the two schools be the same? How many students will that be?

6. Solve by any method: $\begin{cases} y - 5 = -\frac{1}{2}x \\ x = y - 2 \end{cases}$

7. Classify $\begin{cases} y = \frac{2}{3}x + 7 \\ 3y = 2x - 3 \end{cases}$

B Chapter 6 Test (continued)

8. How many solutions does $\begin{cases} -4x + y = 1 \\ 2y - 2 = 8x \end{cases}$ have?

9. Solve $\begin{cases} 8y - 6x = 48 \\ 2y = \frac{3}{2}x - 12 \end{cases}$

10. Tell whether (4, 3) is a solution of $y \le -2x - 5$.

11. Write the inequality represented by the graph below.

12. Tell whether (−1, −4) is a solution of $\begin{cases} -2x - y > 6 \\ y \le 4x \end{cases}$

13. Graph $\begin{cases} -4x + y > -6 \\ 5y \le -x - 20 \end{cases}$
Give two ordered pairs that are solutions and two ordered pair that are not solutions.

14. A farmer has 165 feet of fencing material in which to enclose a rectangular grazing area. He wants the length *x* to be greater than 50 feet and the width *y* to be no more than 20 feet. Write a system to represent this situation.

PERFORMANCE ASSESSMENT

Chapter 6 Test

Purpose

This performance task assesses the student's ability to graph a system of linear equations and to solve the system both graphically and algebraically.

Time

35–40 minutes

Grouping

Individuals or pairs

Preparation Hints

Review the definitions for *system of linear equations* and *solution of a system of linear equations.* Discuss the three methods of solving systems taught in Chapter 6: graphing, substitution, and elimination.

Overview

When two runners compete in a marathon, their distance *y* from the starting line as a function of time *x* can be represented by a linear equation in slope-intercept form: *y* = (*speed*)*x* + (*starting position*). Solving the system of equations gives the time and distance when the runners meet.

Introduce the Task

Ask whether any students have run in a marathon, half-marathon, or foot race. If so, have them describe the length of the course, what they did to train for the race, and how many people competed.

Explain that in large marathons, it is impossible for the thousands of participants to all start at the starting line. Some marathons use staggered start times or distances, frequently based on ability.

Performance Indicators

____ Writes linear equations in slope-intercept form.
____ Graphs a system of linear equations.
____ Estimates the solution of a system of linear equations from a graph.
____ Uses substitution or elimination to find the solution of a system.
____ Interprets the meaning of the solution of the system in context.

Scoring Rubric

Level 4: Student solves all problems correctly and gives good explanations.
Level 3: Student solves all problems but does not give satisfactory explanations.
Level 2: Student solves some problems but does not give satisfactory explanations.
Level 1: Student is not able to solve any of the problems.

Chapter 6 Test (continued)

Bethany and Calista are sisters who both run marathons. Today they are racing against each other in the same marathon. Because there are thousands of people racing, Bethany and Calista are assigned random starting positions. Bethany starts at the starting line, while Calista starts a half-mile behind the starting line.

Calista runs one mile in 12 minutes, while Bethany runs one mile in 15 minutes. So, although Calista starts behind Bethany, she hopes to pass her sister at some point during the race.

Let *x* represent the amount of time in hours that Bethany or Calista run and let *y* represent distance after the starting line in miles.

1. The rate or speed at which someone runs is frequently stated in miles per hour.
a. What is Bethany's speed in miles per hour? ____
b. What is Calista's speed in miles per hour? ____
2. Write a linear equation in slope-intercept form that describes...
a. Bethany's distance as a function of time. ____
b. Calista's distance as a function of time. ____
3. On the grid above, graph the system of equations that you wrote for question 2.
4. Use your graph to estimate...
a. who is in the lead after 15 minutes (0.25 hour). ____
b. the time when Calista will catch up to Bethany. ____
c. how far after the starting line the sisters catch up to each other. ____
d. who is in the lead after 2 hours if each sister keeps running at a steady pace. ____
5. Use substitution or elimination to solve the system of equations that you wrote for question 2. Interpret the solution in terms of this problem.
6. A marathon is 26.2 miles. Which sister do you think will cross the finish line first? Explain.

Teacher One Stop™ 

Test & Practice Generator

Create and customize Chapter 6 Tests. Instantly generate multiple test versions, answer keys, and Spanish versions of test items.

Modified chapter tests that address special learning needs are available in *IDEA Works!*® *Modified Worksheets and Tests.*

CHAPTER 6

SECTION **6A**

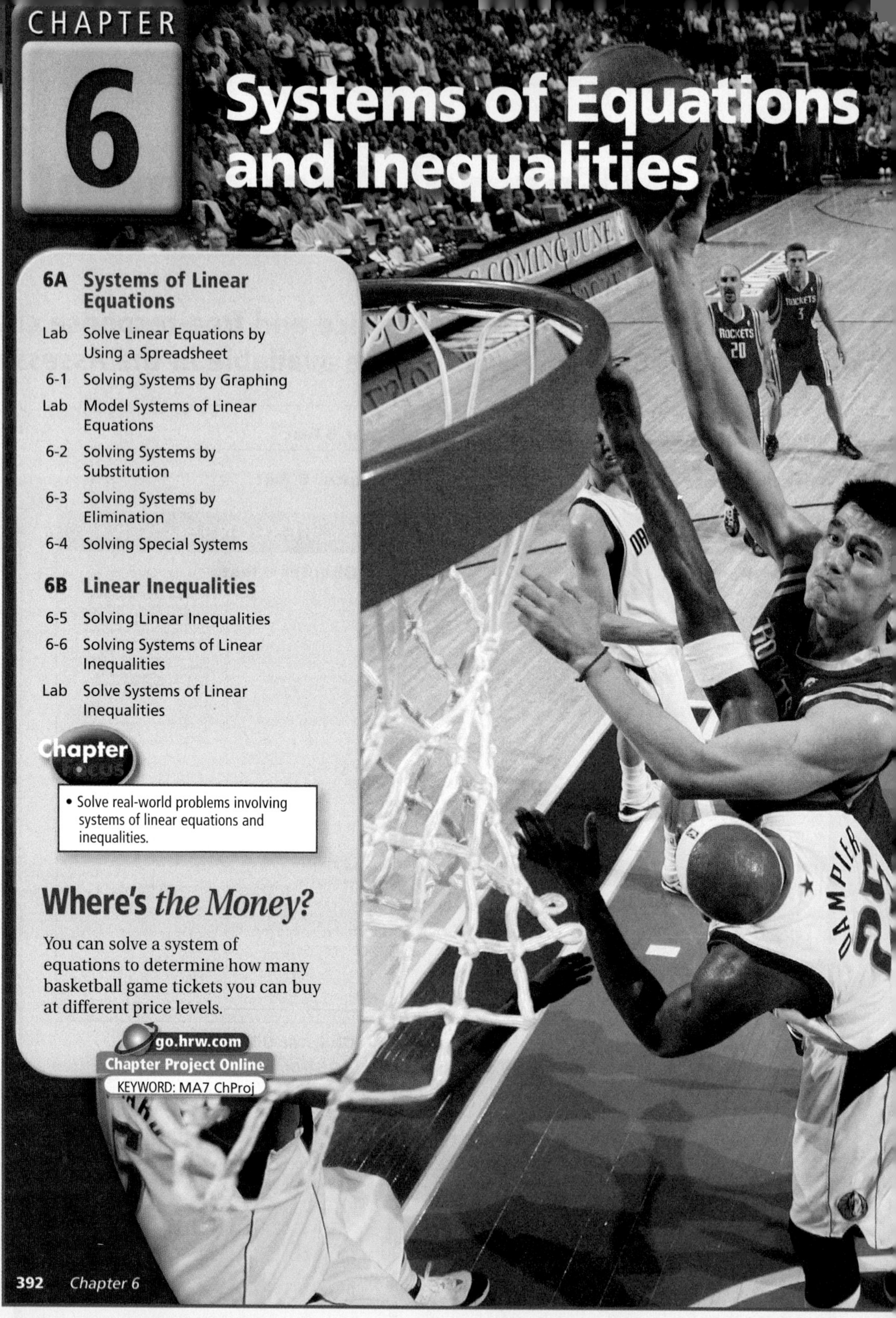

Systems of Linear Equations

On page 426, students write and solve systems of equations to help them make good business decisions.

Exercises designed to prepare students for success on the Multi-Step Test Prep can be found in each lesson.

SECTION **6B**

Linear Inequalities

On page 442, students write and graph systems of inequalities to model a real-world sales situation.

Exercises designed to prepare students for success on the Multi-Step Test Prep can be found in each lesson.

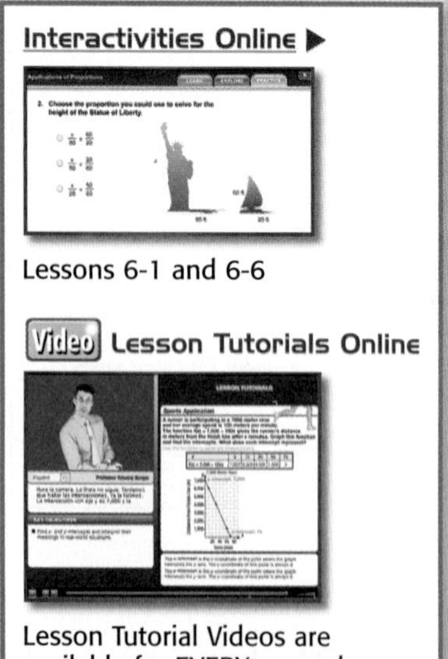

CHAPTER 6

Systems of Equations and Inequalities

Chapter Focus

- Solve real-world problems involving systems of linear equations and inequalities.

Where's *the Money?*

You can solve a system of equations to determine how many basketball game tickets you can buy at different price levels.

go.hrw.com
Chapter Project Online
KEYWORD: MA7 ChProj

392 Chapter 6

Where's the Money?

About the Project

In the Chapter Project, students research current salaries for professional athletes. Students then use the data to write a system of equations to determine whether the salaries overlap and where. Students also write a system of equations to determine how many game tickets they can buy at each price level.

Project Resources

All project resources for teachers and students are provided online.

ARE YOU READY?

Vocabulary

Match each term on the left with a definition on the right.

1. inequality **B**
2. linear equation **F**
3. ordered pair **A**
4. slope **E**
5. solution of an equation **D**

A. a pair of numbers (x, y) that represent the coordinates of a point

B. a statement that two quantities are not equal

C. the y-value of the point at which the graph of an equation crosses the y-axis

D. a value of the variable that makes the equation true

E. the ratio of the vertical change to the horizontal change for a nonvertical line

F. an equation whose graph is a straight line

Graph Linear Functions

Graph each function.

6. $y = \frac{3}{4}x + 1$ 7. $y = -3x + 5$ 8. $y = x - 6$
9. $x + y = 4$ 10. $y = -\frac{2}{3}x + 4$ 11. $y = -5$

Solve Multi-Step Equations

Solve each equation.

12. $-7x - 18 = 3$ **$x = -3$** 13. $12 = -3n + 6$ **$n = -2$** 14. $\frac{1}{2}d + 30 = 32$ **$d = 4$**
15. $-2p + 9 = -3$ **$p = 6$** 16. $33 = 5y + 8$ **$y = 5$** 17. $-3 + 3x = 27$ **$x = 10$**

Solve for a Variable

Solve each equation for y.

18. $7x + y = 4$ **$y = -7x + 4$** 19. $y + 2 = -4x$ **$y = -4x - 2$** 20. $8 = x - y$ **$y = x - 8$**
21. $x + 2 = y - 5$ **$y = x + 7$** 22. $2y - 3 = 12x$ **$y = 6x + \frac{3}{2}$** 23. $y + \frac{3}{4}x = 4$ **$y = -\frac{3}{4}x + 4$**

Evaluate Expressions

Evaluate each expression for the given value of the variable.

24. $t - 5$ for $t = 7$ **2** 25. $9 - 2a$ for $a = 4$ **1** 26. $\frac{1}{2}x - 2$ for $x = 14$ **5**
27. $n + 15$ for $n = 37$ **52** 28. $9c + 4$ for $c = \frac{1}{3}$ **7** 29. $16 + 3d$ for $d = 5$ **31**

Solve and Graph Inequalities

Solve and graph each inequality.

30. $b - 9 \geq 1$ **$b \geq 10$** 31. $-2x < 10$ **$x > -5$** 32. $3y \leq -3$ **$y \leq -1$** 33. $\frac{1}{3}y \leq 5$ **$y \leq 15$**

Organizer

Objective: Assess students' understanding of prerequisite skills.

Assessing Prior Knowledge

INTERVENTION

Diagnose and Prescribe

Use this page to determine whether intervention is necessary or whether enrichment is appropriate.

Resources

***Are You Ready? Intervention and Enrichment* Worksheets**

***Are You Ready?* CD-ROM**

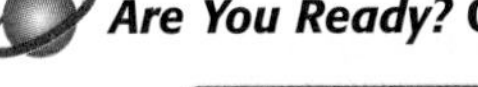

***Are You Ready?* Online**

my.hrw.com

Answers

6–11. See p. A24.

30–33. For graphs, see p. A24.

ARE YOU READY?

Diagnose and Prescribe

NO INTERVENE

Prerequisite Skill	*Are You Ready?* Intervention, Chapter 6		
	Worksheets	CD-ROM	Online
Graph Linear Functions	Skill 75	Activity 75	
Solve Multi-Step Equations	Skill 69	Activity 69	
Solve for a Variable	Skill 72	Activity 72	Diagnose and Prescribe Online
Evaluate Expressions	Skill 60	Activity 60	
Solve and Graph Inequalities	Skill 74	Activity 74	

YES ENRICH

Are You Ready? Enrichment, Chapter 6

Worksheets

CD-ROM

Online

Study Guide: Preview

Organizer

Objective: Help students organize the new concepts they will learn in Chapter 6.

Online Edition
Multilingual Glossary

Resources

Teacher One Stop™
PuzzleView

***Multilingual Glossary* Online**
go.hrw.com
KEYWORD: MA7 Glossary

Answers to *Vocabulary Connections*

1. Possible answer: A system of linear equations is a group of linear equations, rather than just one linear equation.
2. none
3. independent system
4. any ordered pair that makes the inequality true

CHAPTER 6

Study Guide: Preview

Where You've Been

Previously, you
- solved one-step and multi-step equations.
- solved one-step and multi-step inequalities.
- graphed linear equations on a coordinate plane.

In This Chapter

You will study
- how to find a solution that satisfies two linear equations.
- how to find solutions that satisfy two linear inequalities.
- how to graph one or more linear inequalities on a coordinate plane.

Where You're Going

You can use the skills in this chapter
- to determine which purchases are better deals.
- in other classes, such as Economics and Chemistry.
- to solve linear equations that involve three or more variables in future math classes.

Key Vocabulary/Vocabulario

consistent system	sistema consistente
dependent system	sistema dependiente
inconsistent system	sistema inconsistente
independent system	sistema independiente
linear inequality	desigualdad lineal
solution of a linear inequality	solución de una desigualdad lineal
system of linear equations	sistema de ecuaciones lineales

Vocabulary Connections

To become familiar with some of the vocabulary terms in the chapter, consider the following. You may refer to the chapter, the glossary, or a dictionary if you like.

1. The word *system* means "a group." How do you think a **system of linear equations** is different from a linear equation?
2. A **consistent system** has *at least one* solution. How many solutions do you think an **inconsistent system** has?
3. A **dependent system** has infinitely many solutions. Which vocabulary term above means a system with *exactly one* solution?
4. In Chapter 5, you saw that a solution of a linear equation was an ordered pair that made the equation true. Modify this to define **solution of a linear inequality**.

394 Chapter 6

Writing Strategy: Write a Convincing Argument/Explanation

The Write About It icon appears throughout the book. These icons identify questions that require you to write a complete argument or explanation. Writing a convincing argument or explanation shows that you have a solid understanding of a concept.

To be effective, an argument or explanation should include

- evidence, work, or facts.
- a complete response that will answer or explain.

From Lesson 2-10

23. Write About It Lewis invested $1000 at 3% simple interest for 4 years. Lisa invested $1000 at 4% simple interest for 3 years. Explain why Lewis and Lisa earned the same amount of interest.

Step 1 **Identify what you need to answer or explain.**
Explain why Lewis and Lisa earned the same amount of interest.

Step 2 **Give evidence, work, or facts that are needed to answer the question.**
Use the formula for simple interest to find the amount of interest earned: $I = Prt$.

Lewis: $P = 1000, r = 0.03, t = 4$

$I = Prt = 1000(0.03)(4) = 120$

$I = 1000(0.12) = \$120$

Lisa: $P = 1000, r = 0.04, t = 3$

$I = Prt = 1000(0.04)(3) = 120$

$I = 1000(0.12) = \$120$

Step 3 **Write a complete response that answers or explains.**
Lewis and Lisa both invested the same amount of money, $1000. They earned the same amount of interest because 0.04×3 and 0.03×4 both equal 0.12. They both earned $0.12 \times \$1000$, or $120.

Try This

Write a convincing argument or explanation.

1. What is the least whole number that is a solution of $12x + 15.4 > 118.92$? Explain.
2. Which equation has an error? Explain the error.

   A. $4(6 \cdot 5) = (4)6 \cdot (4)5$ **B.** $4(6 \cdot 5) = (4 \cdot 6)5$

CHAPTER 6

Organizer

Objective: Help students apply strategies to understand and retain key concepts.

Writing Strategy: Write a Convincing Argument/Explanation

Discuss A convincing argument or explanation leaves no doubt in the mind of the reader. There is no point at which the reader can say "Why?" or "How did you get that?"

Extend As students work through the *Write About It* problems in Chapter 6, encourage them to write as thoroughly as possible. Have students check each other's work, checking for adequate evidence and completed work shown.

Answers to *Try This*

Possible answers:

1. The actual answer is $x > 8.62\overline{6}$. The nearest whole number that is greater than $8.62\overline{6}$ is 9.
2. Equation A is the equation with the error. The Distributive Property does not work over multiplication, only over addition or subtraction.

Reading Connection

Mathematicians Are People, Too: Stories from the Lives of Great Mathematicians, Volume 2 **by Luetta & Wilbert Reimer**

Here are intriguing tales of 15 ground-breaking mathematicians. The authors stress the human side of these men and women, almost (but not completely!) convincing us that they're just like us.

Activity After students have solved systems by graphing, have them read Chapter 5, *René Descartes.* Ask them to report on Descartes's development of the Cartesian coordinate system, and to judge whether the story that the idea occurred to Descartes while watching a fly on the ceiling is myth or reality.

SECTION
6A Systems of Linear Equations

One-Minute Section Planner

Lesson	Lab Resources	Materials
6-1 Technology Lab Solve Linear Equations by Using a Spreadsheet • Use a spreadsheet to model real-world linear relationships. ☐ SAT-10 ☐ NAEP ☐ ACT ☐ SAT ☐ SAT Subject Tests	***Technology Lab Activities*** 6-1 Lab Recording Sheet	**Required** spreadsheet software **Optional** graphing calculator
Lesson 6-1 Solving Systems by Graphing • Identify solutions of systems of linear equations in two variables. • Solve systems of linear equations in two variables by graphing. ☐ SAT-10 ☐ NAEP ☑ ACT ☑ SAT ☑ SAT Subject Tests		**Required** graph paper **Optional** graphing calculator
6-2 Algebra Lab Model Systems of Linear Equations • Use algebra tiles to model and solve systems of linear equations. ☐ SAT-10 ☐ NAEP ☑ ACT ☑ SAT ☑ SAT Subject Tests	***Algebra Lab Activities*** 6-2 Lab Recording Sheet	**Required** algebra tiles (MK)
Lesson 6-2 Solving Systems by Substitution • Solve systems of linear equations in two variables by substitution. ☐ SAT-10 ☐ NAEP ☑ ACT ☑ SAT ☐ SAT Subject Tests		**Optional** graphing calculator
Lesson 6-3 Solving Systems by Elimination • Solve systems of linear equations in two variables by elimination. • Compare and choose an appropriate method for solving systems of linear equations. ☐ SAT-10 ☐ NAEP ☑ ACT ☑ SAT ☐ SAT Subject Tests	***Algebra Lab Activities*** 6-3 Algebra Lab	**Optional** graphing calculator, transparent algebra tiles (MK), algebra tiles (MK)
Lesson 6-4 Solving Special Systems • Solve special systems of linear equations in two variables. • Classify systems of linear equations and determine the number of solutions. ☐ SAT-10 ☐ NAEP ☑ ACT ☐ SAT ☐ SAT Subject Tests	***Algebra Lab Activities*** 6-4 Algebra Lab	**Optional** graphing calculator

Note: If NAEP is checked, the content is tested on either the Grade 8 or the Grade 12 NAEP assessment.

MK = *Manipulatives Kit*

SYSTEMS OF LINEAR EQUATIONS

Lessons 6-1 to 6-4

A *system of linear equations* is a set of two or more linear equations that each contain two or more variables. In this course, the systems consist of two equations that each contain two variables. A *solution* of such a system is an ordered pair that satisfies both equations. Consider the system $\begin{cases} x + y = 5 \\ y - x = -1 \end{cases}$. The ordered pair (3, 2) is a solution of the system because it satisfies both equations: $3 + 2 = 5$ and $2 - 3 = -1$.

The graph of an equation is the set of all of its solutions. Therefore, if an ordered pair is a solution of two linear equations, it must lie on both graphs. In other words, the solution is the *intersection* of the graphs. The intersection of the graphs of $x + y = 5$ and $y - x = -1$ is (3, 2).

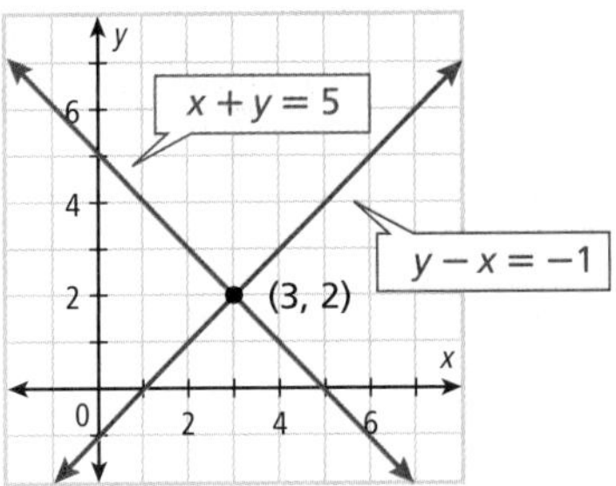

This graphic representation leads naturally to the conclusions that some systems may have no solutions (lines may be parallel) and that some systems may have infinitely many solutions (lines may be coincident).

Graphing is an intuitive way to solve systems, and it visually reinforces the meaning of a solution. Graphing also highlights the connection between algebra and geometry; in particular, it shows that you can solve a problem presented in purely algebraic terms by using geometric methods.

ALGEBRAIC METHODS

Lessons 6-2 to 6-4

The intersection point of two lines may not have integer coordinates, thereby motivating the need for algebraic methods of solving systems. In general, the goal of algebraic methods is to eliminate a variable so that the techniques for solving single-variable equations may be used.

As an example of an algebraic method, one can solve both equations in a system for y to get two equations that can be set equal to each other. Solving both equations for y in the system discussed earlier gives $y = 5 - x$ and $y = x - 1$. The two expressions for y must be equal, so $5 - x = x - 1$. Solving shows that $x = 3$, and substituting this value of x into either of the original equations gives $y = 2$.

This method is called the *substitution method*. In general, solve either equation for either variable and then substitute into the other equation. This yields an equation that can be solved using previously learned skills. In future math courses, students will see that the substitution method is useful for solving systems when one or more of the equations are not linear.

Although the substitution method works with any system, it may be awkward to use when no variable term has a coefficient of 1. In this case, the *elimination method* may be a better choice.

Students should understand that the elimination method is based on the properties of equality.

For example, to solve $\begin{cases} 2x + 3y = 11 \\ -6x + 5y = -19 \end{cases}$, you can multiply both sides of the first equation by 3 using the Multiplication Property of Equality. To solve the resulting system, $\begin{cases} 6x + 9y = 33 \\ -6x + 5y = -19 \end{cases}$, you can add the two equations together to eliminate the x-terms. This is justified by the Addition Property of Equality since you are adding equal quantities, $-6x + 5y$ and -19, to both sides of the first equation. The result is one equation in one variable, $14y = 14$, that is easy to solve for y. Then substitute to find x.

In general, elimination works well for systems of all linear equations containing any number of variables, and it is a fundamental process in the study of linear algebra.

Organizer

Use with Lesson 6-1

Pacing:
Traditional $\frac{1}{2}$ day
Block $\frac{1}{4}$ day

Objective: Use a spreadsheet to model real-world linear relationships.

Materials: spreadsheet software

Countdown Week 13

Lab Resources

Technology Lab Activities
6-1 Lab Recording Sheet

Teach

Discuss

Ask students what the breakeven point represents. Lead them to see that it is when the cost and sales are equal and profit is thus 0.

Close

Key Concept

You can use a spreadsheet to view the expressions evaluated for many values at a time and observe the pattern.

Assessment

Journal Have students explain what a breakeven point is and how, given the cost and sales equations, they can use a spreadsheet to find this point.

State Resources

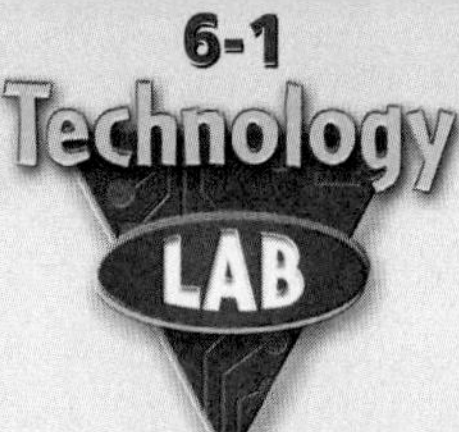

6-1 Technology LAB: Solve Linear Equations by Using a Spreadsheet

Use with Lesson 6-1

You can use a spreadsheet to answer "What if...?" questions. By changing one or more values, you can quickly model different scenarios.

go.hrw.com
Lab Resources Online
KEYWORD: MA7 Lab6

Activity

Company Z makes DVD players. The company's costs are $400 per week plus $20 per DVD player. Each DVD player sells for $45. How many DVD players must company Z sell in one week to make a profit?

Let n represent the number of DVD players company Z sells in one week.

$c = 400 + 20n$ *The total cost is $400 plus $20 times the number of DVD players made.*

$s = 45n$ *The total sales income is $45 times the number of DVD players sold.*

$p = s - c$ *The total profit is the sales income minus the total cost.*

1. Set up your spreadsheet with columns for number of DVD players, total cost, total income, and profit.

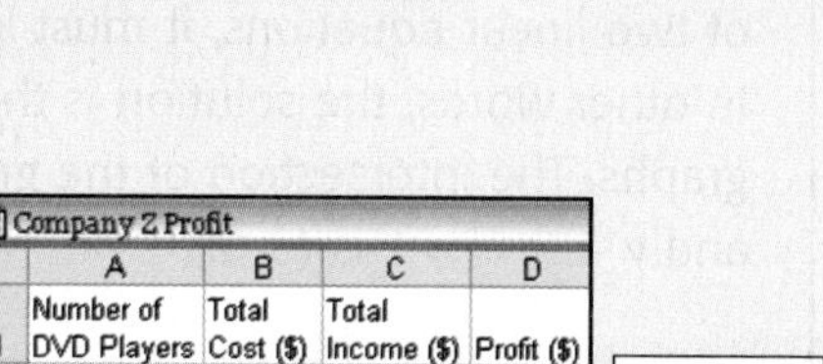

Company Z Profit

	A	B	C	D
1	Number of DVD Players	Total Cost ($)	Total Income ($)	Profit ($)
2	1	420	45	-375

2. Under Number of DVD Players, enter 1 in cell A2.
3. Use the equations above to enter the formulas for total cost, total sales, and total profit in row 2.
   - In cell B2, enter the formula for total cost.
   - In cell C2, enter the formula for total sales income.
   - In cell D2, enter the formula for total profit.
4. Fill columns A, B, C, and D by selecting cells A1 through D1, clicking the small box at the bottom right corner of cell D2, and dragging the box down through several rows.
5. Find the point where the profit is $0. This is known as the breakeven point, where total cost and total income are the same.

Company Z Profit

	A	B	C	D
1	Number of DVD Players	Total Cost ($)	Total Income ($)	Profit ($)
16	15	700	675	-25
17	16	720	720	0
18	17	740	765	25

Breakeven point

Profit begins.

Company Z must sell 17 DVD players to make a profit. The profit is $25.

Try This

For Exercises 1 and 2, use the spreadsheet from the activity.

1. If company Z sells 10 DVD players, will they make a profit? Explain. What if they sell 16?
2. Company Z makes a profit of $225 dollars. How many DVD players did they sell? **25**

For Exercise 3, make a spreadsheet.

3. Company Y's costs are $400 per week plus $20 per DVD player. They want the breakeven point to occur with sales of 8 DVD players. What should the sales price be? **$70**

Answers to *Try This*

1. Company Z will not make a profit; it will lose $150. If it sells 16 DVD players it still will not make a profit; it will only break even.

6-1 Solving Systems by Graphing

Objectives
Identify solutions of systems of linear equations in two variables.

Solve systems of linear equations in two variables by graphing.

Vocabulary
system of linear equations
solution of a system of linear equations

Why learn this?
You can compare costs by graphing a system of linear equations. (See Example 3.)

Sometimes there are different charges for the same service or product at different places. For example, Bowl-o-Rama charges \$2.50 per game plus \$2 for shoe rental while Bowling Pinz charges \$2 per game plus \$4 for shoe rental. A *system of linear equations* can be used to compare these charges.

A **system of linear equations** is a set of two or more linear equations containing two or more variables. A **solution of a system of linear equations** with two variables is an ordered pair that satisfies each equation in the system. So, if an ordered pair is a solution, it will make both equations true.

EXAMPLE 1 Identifying Solutions of Systems

Tell whether the ordered pair is a solution of the given system.

A $(4, 1); \begin{cases} x + 2y = 6 \\ x - y = 3 \end{cases}$

$x + 2y = 6$	
$4 + 2(1)$	6
$4 + 2$	6
6	6 ✓

$x - y = 3$	
$4 - 1$	3
3	3 ✓

Substitute 4 for x and 1 for y in each equation in the system.

The ordered pair $(4, 1)$ makes both equations true.
$(4, 1)$ is a solution of the system.

B $(-1, 2); \begin{cases} 2x + 5y = 8 \\ 3x - 2y = 5 \end{cases}$

$2x + 5y = 8$	
$2(-1) + 5(2)$	8
$-2 + 10$	8
8	8 ✓

$3x - 2y = 5$	
$3(-1) - 2(2)$	5
$-3 - 4$	5
-7	5 ✗

Substitute −1 for x and 2 for y in each equation in the system.

The ordered pair $(-1, 2)$ makes one equation true, but not the other.
$(-1, 2)$ is not a solution of the system.

Helpful Hint
If an ordered pair does not satisfy the first equation in the system, there is no need to check the other equations.

CHECK IT OUT! Tell whether the ordered pair is a solution of the given system.

1a. $(1, 3); \begin{cases} 2x + y = 5 \\ -2x + y = 1 \end{cases}$ yes **1b.** $(2, -1); \begin{cases} x - 2y = 4 \\ 3x + y = 6 \end{cases}$ no

6-1 Organizer

Pacing: Traditional 1 day
Block $\frac{1}{2}$ day

Objectives: Identify solutions of systems of linear equations in two variables.

Solve systems of linear equations in two variables by graphing.

Online Edition
Tutorial Videos, Interactivity, Graphing Calculator

Countdown Week 13

Power Presentations with PowerPoint®

Warm Up

Evaluate each expression for $x = 1$ and $y = -3$.

1. $x - 4y$ 13

2. $-2x + y$ −5

Write each equation in slope-intercept form.

3. $y - x = 1$ $y = x + 1$

4. $2x + 3y = 6$ $y = -\frac{2}{3}x + 2$

5. $0 = 5y + 5x$ $y = -x$

Also available on transparency

Math Humor

Teacher: What is the name of the formula that describes the phases of the moon?
Student: The lunear (linear) equation

1 Introduce

EXPLORATION

6-1 Solving Systems by Graphing

You will need a graphing calculator for this Exploration.

1. Press [Y=] and enter the equations $y = 2x - 5$ and $y = -x + 4$ as **Y1** and **Y2**.
2. Press [2nd] [GRAPH] to view a table of values for the two equations.
3. Use the table to find an x-value that produces the same y-value for both equations. Write this x-value and the corresponding y-value as an ordered pair.
4. Use the arrow keys to scroll up and down the table. Does there appear to be any other x-value that produces the same y-value for both equations?
5. Press [GRAPH] to view a graph of the equations.

THINK AND DISCUSS

6. **Describe** the graph of the functions.
7. **Explain** what happens on the graph at the point that you found in Step 3.

Motivate

Have students choose an ordered pair that is a solution of $y = x + 1$. Point out that there are infinitely many ordered-pair solutions. Then ask which of the ordered pairs is also a solution of $y = 5 - x$. Let them try several pairs. Tell students that there is only one ordered pair that is a solution of both equations. $(2, 3)$ Then explain that this lesson will show a method for finding that pair.

Explorations and answers are provided in *Alternate Openers: Explorations Transparencies.*

State Resources

go.hrw.com
State Resources Online
KEYWORD: MA7 Resources

Power Presentations with PowerPoint®

Additional Examples

Example 1

Tell whether the ordered pair is a solution of the given system.

A. $(5, 2)$; $\begin{cases} \frac{2}{5}x - y = 0 \\ 3x - y = 13 \end{cases}$ yes

B. $(-2, 2)$; $\begin{cases} x + 3y = 4 \\ -x + y = 2 \end{cases}$ no

Example 2

Solve each system by graphing. Check your answer.

A. $\begin{cases} y = x \\ y = -2x - 3 \end{cases}$ $(-1, -1)$

B. $\begin{cases} y = x - 6 \\ y + \frac{1}{3}x = -1 \end{cases}$ $\left(\frac{15}{4}, -\frac{9}{4}\right)$

INTERVENTION

Questioning Strategies

EXAMPLE 1

- How do you know when an ordered pair is a solution of a system of linear equations?

EXAMPLE 2

- What does the intersection of the two lines represent?

Technology In **Example 2B,** make sure that students know how to find the point of intersection on a graphing calculator.

After both lines are graphed, press

CALC TRACE and then choose 5.

All solutions of a linear equation are on its graph. To find a solution of a system of linear equations, you need a point that each line has in common. In other words, you need their point of intersection.

$\begin{cases} y = 2x - 1 \\ y = -x + 5 \end{cases}$

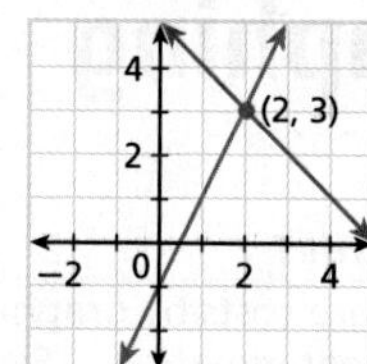

The point $(2, 3)$ is where the two lines intersect and is a solution of both equations, so $(2, 3)$ is the solution of the system.

EXAMPLE 2 Solving a System of Linear Equations by Graphing

Helpful Hint

Sometimes it is difficult to tell exactly where the lines cross when you solve by graphing. It is good to confirm your answer by substituting it into both equations.

Solve each system by graphing. Check your answer.

A $\begin{cases} y = x - 3 \\ y = -x - 1 \end{cases}$

Graph the system.

The solution appears to be at $(1, -2)$.

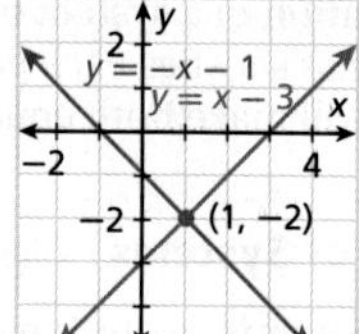

Check Substitute $(1, -2)$ into the system.

$y = x - 3$	
-2	$1 - 3$
-2	-2 ✓

$y = -x - 1$	
-2	$-1 - 1$
-2	-2 ✓

The solution is $(1, -2)$.

B $\begin{cases} x + y = 0 \\ y = -\frac{1}{2}x + 1 \end{cases}$

$$\begin{aligned} x + y &= 0 \\ \underline{-x } & \underline{-x} \\ y &= -x \end{aligned}$$ *Rewrite the first equation in slope-intercept form.*

Graph using a calculator and then use the intersection command.

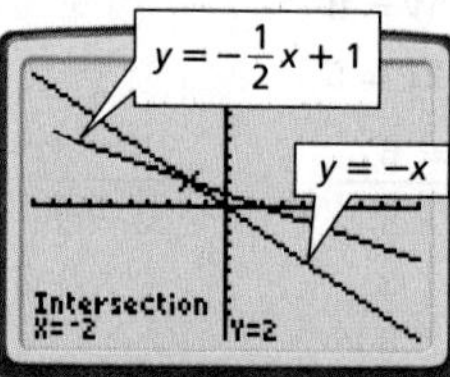

Check Substitute $(-2, 2)$ into the system.

$x + y = 0$	
$-2 + 2$	0
0	0 ✓

$y = -\frac{1}{2}x + 1$	
2	$-\frac{1}{2}(-2) + 1$
2	$1 + 1$
2	2 ✓

The solution is $(-2, 2)$.

Solve each system by graphing. Check your answer.

2a. $\begin{cases} y = -2x - 1 \\ y = x + 5 \end{cases}$ $(-2, 3)$ **2b.** $\begin{cases} y = \frac{1}{3}x - 3 \\ 2x + y = 4 \end{cases}$ $(3, -2)$

2 Teach

Guided Instruction

Before teaching students to solve a system by graphing, review slope-intercept form and how to write an equation in that form.

Communicating Math Warn students that the brace, {, is not always used to indicate a system of equations. A standardized test might omit the symbol and simply say that the equations are a system.

Reaching All Learners

Through Multiple Representations

Have students copy and complete the table for the system of equations.

$\begin{cases} y = -2x + 9 \\ y = x + 3 \end{cases}$

x	$y_1 = -2x + 9$	$y_2 = x + 3$
0	9	3
1	7	4
2	5	5
3	3	6

Graph the system, and discuss similarities between the table and the graph. For example, from the table, you can see that when $x = 0$, the y-value of one equation is 9, and the y-value of the other equation is 3. On the graph you can see that the point $(0, 9)$ is on one line and the point $(0, 3)$ is on the other line.

EXAMPLE 3 Problem-Solving Application

Bowl-o-Rama charges $2.50 per game plus $2 for shoe rental, and Bowling Pinz charges $2 per game plus $4 for shoe rental. For how many games will the cost to bowl be the same at both places? What is that cost?

1 Understand the Problem

The **answer** will be the number of games played for which the total cost is the same at both bowling alleys. **List the important information:**

- Game price: Bowl-o-Rama $2.50 Bowling Pinz: $2
- Shoe-rental fee: Bowl-o-Rama $2 Bowling Pinz: $4

2 Make a Plan

Write a system of equations, one equation to represent the price at each company. Let x be the number of games played and y be the total cost.

	Total cost	is	price per game	times	games	plus	shoe rental.
Bowl-o-Rama	y	=	2.5	•	x	+	2
Bowling Pinz	y	=	2	•	x	+	4

3 Solve

Graph $y = 2.5x + 2$ and $y = 2x + 4$. The lines appear to intersect at $(4, 12)$. So, the cost at both places will be the same for 4 games bowled and that cost will be $12.

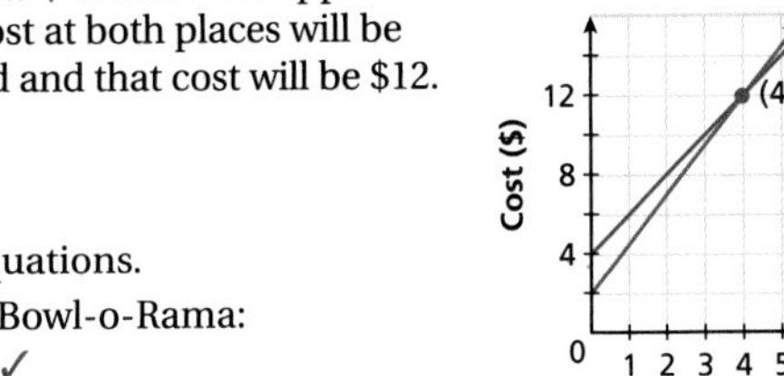

4 Look Back

Check $(4, 12)$ using both equations.
Cost of bowling 4 games at Bowl-o-Rama:
$\$2.5(4) + \$2 = 10 + 2 = 12$ ✓
Cost of bowling 4 games at Bowling Pinz:
$\$2(4) + \$4 = 8 + 4 = 12$ ✓

CHECK IT OUT! 3. Video club A charges $10 for membership and $3 per movie rental. Video club B charges $15 for membership and $2 per movie rental. For how many movie rentals will the cost be the same at both video clubs? What is that cost? **5 movies; $25**

THINK AND DISCUSS

1. Explain how to use a graph to solve a system of linear equations.
2. Explain how to check a solution of a system of linear equations.
3. **GET ORGANIZED** Copy and complete the graphic organizer. In each box, write a step for solving a linear system by graphing. More boxes may be added.

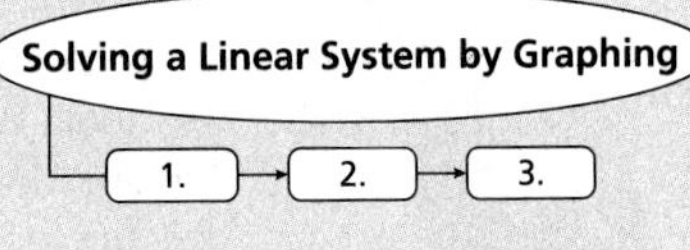

COMMON ERROR ALERT

Students sometimes have difficulty correctly assigning x and y variables in word problems, such as in **Example 3.** Remind them that the value of y cannot be determined unless the value of x is known. In other words, y is dependent on x.

Power Presentations with PowerPoint®

Additional Examples

Example 3

Wren and Jenni are reading the same book. Wren is on page 14 and reads 2 pages every night. Jenni is on page 6 and reads 3 pages every night. After how many nights will they have read the same number of pages? 8 nights How many pages will that be? 30 pages

INTERVENTION

Questioning Strategies

EXAMPLE 3

- What does the graph show on the left side of the point of intersection?
- What does the graph show on the right side of the point of intersection?

Visual Cues In **Example 3** students may benefit from using a table to organize the information.

	Shoe Rental	Game Price
Bowl-o-Rama	$2.00	$2.50
Bowling Pinz	$4.00	$2.00

3 Close

Summarize

Have students graph the equations below to determine whether each ordered pair is the solution of the given system. Have them check their work by substituting the ordered pair into the system of equations.

1. $(0, -2)$; $\begin{cases} y = x - 2 \\ 4y + \frac{1}{2}x = -8 \end{cases}$ yes
2. $(3, 6)$; $\begin{cases} y + 3x = 9 \\ y = 2x \end{cases}$ no

ONGOING ASSESSMENT and INTERVENTION

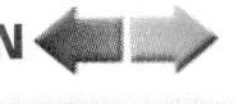

Diagnose ***Before*** **the Lesson**
6-1 Warm Up, TE p. 397

Monitor ***During*** **the Lesson**
Check It Out! Exercises, SE pp. 397–399
Questioning Strategies, TE pp. 398–399

Assess ***After*** **the Lesson**
6-1 Lesson Quiz, TE p. 402
Alternative Assessment, TE p. 402

Answers to *Think and Discuss*

1. Locate the point of intersection. The ordered pair is a solution of the system.
2. Substitute the x- and y-values of the ordered pair into all of the equations. If all equations are true, the solution is correct.
3. See p. A6.

Assignment Guide

Assign *Guided Practice* exercises as necessary.

If you finished Examples **1–3**

Basic 9–22, 28–30, 33–42

Average 9–16, 18–22, 26–42

Advanced 9–16, 18–42

Homework Quick Check

Quickly check key concepts.
Exercises: 10, 14, 16, 18, 22

Answers

17a. $\begin{cases} y = 2x \\ y = 16 + 0.50x \end{cases}$

b.

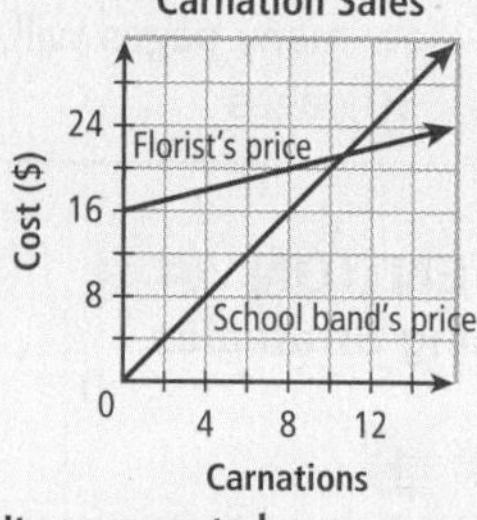

It represents how many carnations need to be sold to break even.

c. No; because the solution is not a whole number of carnations; 11 carnations.

18a. Hats Off: $c = 5h + 50$; Top Stuff: $c = 6h + 25$

b. 25 hats; $175; for graph, see p. A24.

State Resources

6-1 Exercises

go.hrw.com
Homework Help Online
KEYWORD: MA7 6-1
Parent Resources Online
KEYWORD: MA7 Parent

GUIDED PRACTICE

1. **Vocabulary** Describe a *solution of a system of linear equations.* **an ordered pair that satisfies both equations**

SEE EXAMPLE 1 p. 397

Tell whether the ordered pair is a solution of the given system.

2. $(2, -2)$; $\begin{cases} 3x + y = 4 \\ x - 3y = -4 \end{cases}$ **no**
3. $(3, -1)$; $\begin{cases} x - 2y = 5 \\ 2x - y = 7 \end{cases}$ **yes**
4. $(-1, 5)$; $\begin{cases} -x + y = 6 \\ 2x + 3y = 13 \end{cases}$ **yes**

SEE EXAMPLE 2 p. 398

Solve each system by graphing. Check your answer.

5. $\begin{cases} y = \frac{1}{2}x \\ y = -x + 3 \end{cases}$ **(2, 1)**
6. $\begin{cases} y = x - 2 \\ 2x + y = 1 \end{cases}$ **(1, –1)**
7. $\begin{cases} -2x - 1 = y \\ x + y = 3 \end{cases}$ **(–4, 7)**

SEE EXAMPLE 3 p. 399

8. To deliver mulch, Lawn and Garden charges $30 per cubic yard of mulch plus a $30 delivery fee. Yard Depot charges $25 per cubic yard of mulch plus a $55 delivery fee. For how many cubic yards will the cost be the same? What will that cost be? **5 yd^3; $180**

PRACTICE AND PROBLEM SOLVING

Independent Practice

For Exercises	See Example
9–11	1
12–15	2
16	3

Extra Practice
Skills Practice p. S14
Application Practice p. S33

Tell whether the ordered pair is a solution of the given system.

9. $(1, -4)$; $\begin{cases} x - 2y = 8 \\ 4x - y = 8 \end{cases}$ **no**
10. $(-2, 1)$; $\begin{cases} 2x - 3y = -7 \\ 3x + y = -5 \end{cases}$ **yes**
11. $(5, 2)$; $\begin{cases} 2x + y = 12 \\ -3y - x = -11 \end{cases}$ **yes**

Solve each system by graphing. Check your answer.

12. $\begin{cases} y = \frac{1}{2}x + 2 \\ y = -x - 1 \end{cases}$ **(–2, 1)**
13. $\begin{cases} y = x \\ y = -x + 6 \end{cases}$ **(3, 3)**
14. $\begin{cases} -2x - 1 = y \\ x = -y + 3 \end{cases}$ **(–4, 7)**
15. $\begin{cases} x + y = 2 \\ y = x - 4 \end{cases}$ **(3, –1)**

16. **Multi-Step** Angelo runs 7 miles per week and increases his distance by 1 mile each week. Marc runs 4 miles per week and increases his distance by 2 miles each week. In how many weeks will Angelo and Marc be running the same distance? What will that distance be? **3 weeks; 10 mi**

17. **School** The school band sells carnations on Valentine's Day for $2 each. They buy the carnations from a florist for $0.50 each, plus a $16 delivery charge.
    a. Write a system of equations to describe the situation.
    b. Graph the system. What does the solution represent?
    c. Explain whether the solution shown on the graph makes sense in this situation. If not, give a reasonable solution.

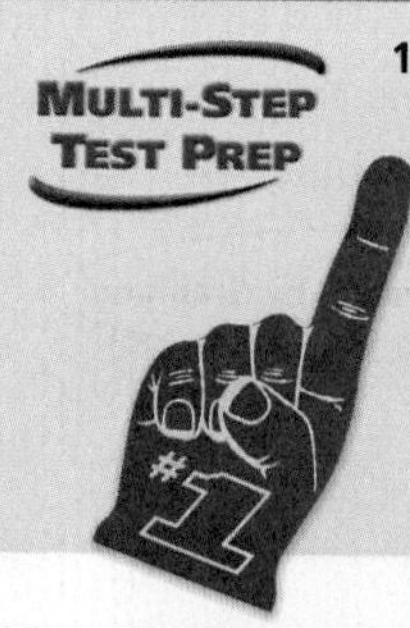

18. This problem will prepare you for the Multi-Step Test Prep on page 426.
    a. The Warrior baseball team is selling hats as a fund-raiser. They contacted two companies. Hats Off charges a $50 design fee and $5 per hat. Top Stuff charges a $25 design fee and $6 per hat. Write an equation for each company's pricing.
    b. Graph the system of equations from part **a**. For how many hats will the cost be the same? What is that cost?
    c. Explain when it is cheaper for the baseball team to use Top Stuff and when it is cheaper to use Hats Off. **fewer than 25 hats: Top Stuff; more than 25 hats: Hats Off**

6-1 READING STRATEGIES

In the example below, the steps show how to set up and solve a system of linear equations.

A teacher needs to rent video equipment. Rent All charges $60 plus $12 for each hour. Rent It Here charges $80 plus $10 per hour. After how many hours is the cost of renting video equipment the same from both companies?

1. Define variables for the unknowns.
   - Let x = number of rental hours
   - Let y = total cost
2. Write a system of linear equations.
   $\begin{cases} y = 12x + 60 \text{ (Rent All)} \\ y = 10x + 80 \text{ (Rent It Here)} \end{cases}$
3. Graph the equations on the same grid.
4. Identify the point of intersection.
5. Write your answer as a sentence.

Video Equipment Rental (Total Cost ($) vs. Rental Hours; point (10, 180))

After 10 hours, the cost of renting video equipment is $180 from both companies.

Derek is going to have a party catered. Good Eats charges $120 plus $10 per person. Food Fare charges $150 plus $8 per person. Complete the following to find the number of people for which the total cost is the same for both catering companies.

1. Define the variables. Let x = **number of people**. Let y = **total cost**
2. Write a system of linear equations. $\begin{cases} y = 10x + 120 \\ y = 8x + 150 \end{cases}$
3. Graph the equations.
4. What is the point of intersection? **(15, 270)**
5. Write your answer. **For 15 people, the total cost will be $270 with both catering companies.**

Catering Costs (Total Cost ($) vs. Number of People)

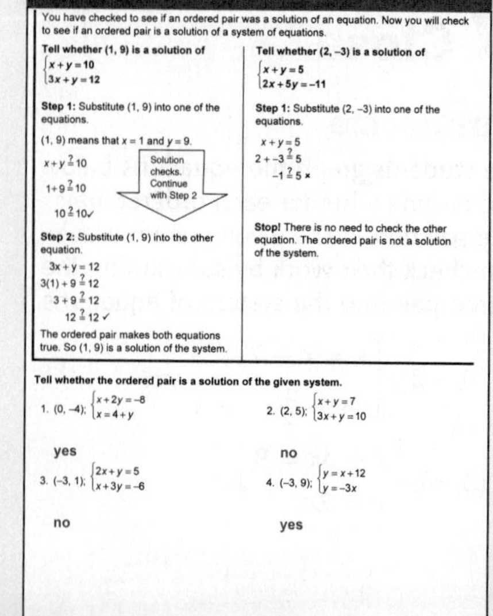

6-1 RETEACH

You have checked to see if an ordered pair was a solution of an equation. Now you will check to see if an ordered pair is a solution of a system of equations.

Tell whether (1, 9) is a solution of $\begin{cases} x + y = 10 \\ 3x + y = 12 \end{cases}$

Step 1: Substitute (1, 9) into one of the equations.

(1, 9) means that $x = 1$ and $y = 9$.

$x + y \stackrel{?}{=} 10$
$1 + 9 \stackrel{?}{=} 10$
$10 \stackrel{?}{=} 10$ ✓

Solution checks. Continue with Step 2

Step 2: Substitute (1, 9) into the other equation.

$3x + y = 12$
$3(1) + 9 \stackrel{?}{=} 12$
$3 + 9 \stackrel{?}{=} 12$
$12 \stackrel{?}{=} 12$ ✓

The ordered pair makes both equations true. So (1, 9) is a solution of the system.

Tell whether (2, –3) is a solution of $\begin{cases} x + y = 5 \\ 2x + 5y = -11 \end{cases}$

Step 1: Substitute (2, –3) into one of the equations.

$x + y = 5$
$2 + -3 \stackrel{?}{=} 5$
$-1 \stackrel{?}{=} 5$ ×

Stop! There is no need to check the other equation. The ordered pair is not a solution of the system.

Tell whether the ordered pair is a solution of the given system.

1. $(0, -4)$; $\begin{cases} x + 2y = -8 \\ x = 4 + y \end{cases}$ **yes**
2. $(2, 5)$; $\begin{cases} x + y = 7 \\ 3x + y = 10 \end{cases}$ **no**
3. $(-3, 1)$; $\begin{cases} 2x + y = 5 \\ x + 3y = -6 \end{cases}$ **no**
4. $(-3, 9)$; $\begin{cases} y = x + 12 \\ y = -3x \end{cases}$ **yes**

Graphing Calculator Use a graphing calculator to graph and solve the systems of equations in Exercises 19–22. Round your answer to the nearest tenth.

19. $\begin{cases} y = 4.7x + 2.1 \\ y = 1.6x - 5.4 \end{cases}$ **(−2.4, −9.3)**

20. $\begin{cases} 4.8x + 0.6y = 4 \\ y = -3.2x + 2.7 \end{cases}$ **(0.8, 0.1)**

21. $\begin{cases} y = \frac{5}{4}x - \frac{2}{3} \\ \frac{8}{3}x + y = \frac{5}{9} \end{cases}$ **(0.3, −0.3)**

22. $\begin{cases} y = 6.9x + 12.4 \\ y = -4.1x - 5.3 \end{cases}$ **(−1.6, 1.3)**

LINK

Landscaping

Middleton Place Gardens, South Carolina, are the United States' oldest landscaped gardens. The gardens were established in 1741 and opened to the public in the 1920s.

23. Landscaping The gardeners at Middleton Place Gardens want to plant a total of 45 white and pink hydrangeas in one flower bed. In another flower bed, they want to plant 120 hydrangeas. In this bed, they want 2 times the number of white hydrangeas and 3 times the number of pink hydrangeas as in the first bed. Use a system of equations to find how many white and how many pink hydrangeas the gardeners should buy altogether. **45 white; 120 pink**

24. Fitness Rusty burns 5 Calories per minute swimming and 11 Calories per minute jogging. In the morning, Rusty burns 200 Calories walking and swims for x minutes. In the afternoon, Rusty will jog for x minutes. How many minutes must he jog to burn at least as many Calories y in the afternoon as he did in the morning? Round your answer up to the next whole number of minutes. **34 min**

25. A tree that is 2 feet tall is growing at a rate of 1 foot per year. A 6-foot tall tree is growing at a rate of 0.5 foot per year. In how many years will the trees be the same height? **8 yr**

26. Critical Thinking Write a real-world situation that could be represented by the system $\begin{cases} y = 3x + 10 \\ y = 5x + 20 \end{cases}$.

27. Write About It When you graph a system of linear equations, why does the intersection of the two lines represent the solution of the system?
Every point on a line satisfies the related linear equation. A point that is on both lines (the intersection point) satisfies both equations.

TEST PREP

28. Taxi company A charges $4 plus $0.50 per mile. Taxi company B charges $5 plus $0.25 per mile. Which system best represents this problem?

Ⓐ $\begin{cases} y = 4x + 0.5 \\ y = 5x + 0.25 \end{cases}$

Ⓒ $\begin{cases} y = -4x + 0.5 \\ y = -5x + 0.25 \end{cases}$

Ⓑ $\begin{cases} y = 0.5x + 4 \\ y = 0.25x + 5 \end{cases}$

Ⓓ $\begin{cases} y = -0.5x + 4 \\ y = -0.25x + 5 \end{cases}$

29. Which system of equations represents the given graph?

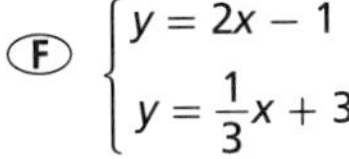

Ⓕ $\begin{cases} y = 2x - 1 \\ y = \frac{1}{3}x + 3 \end{cases}$

Ⓗ $\begin{cases} y = 2x + 1 \\ y = \frac{1}{3}x - 3 \end{cases}$

Ⓖ $\begin{cases} y = -2x + 1 \\ y = 2x - 3 \end{cases}$

Ⓙ $\begin{cases} y = -2x - 1 \\ y = 3x - 3 \end{cases}$

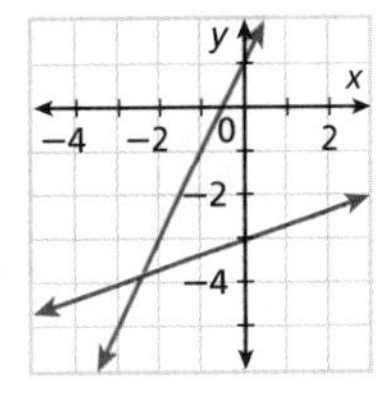

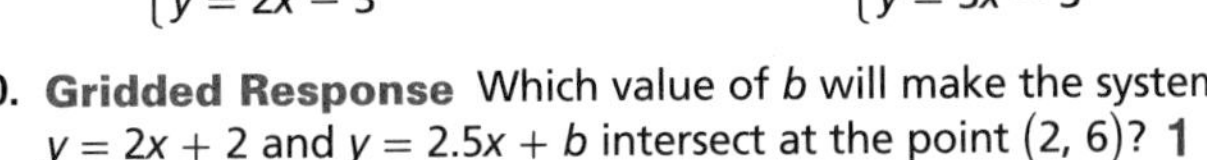

30. Gridded Response Which value of b will make the system $y = 2x + 2$ and $y = 2.5x + b$ intersect at the point $(2, 6)$? **1**

COMMON ERROR ALERT

In **Exercises 5–7** and **12–15,** students may get the wrong answer because of inaccurate graphs. Caution students to use a straightedge when drawing lines.

MULTI-STEP TEST PREP **Exercise 18** involves writing a system of equations to compare pricing options. This exercise prepares students for the Multi-Step Test Prep on page 426.

Teaching Tip **Inclusion** In **Exercise 23,** encourage students to check that they answered the question asked in the problem.

TEST PREP DOCTOR In **Exercise 28,** choices **C** and **D** can be eliminated because the situation in the problem requires lines with positive slopes.

Choices **G** and **J** can be eliminated in **Exercise 29** because the graph shows two lines with positive slopes.

Answers

26. Possible answer: Store A rents carpet cleaners for a fee of $10, plus $3 per day. Store B rents carpet cleaners for a fee of $20, plus $5 per day. For how many days rental will the costs be the same?

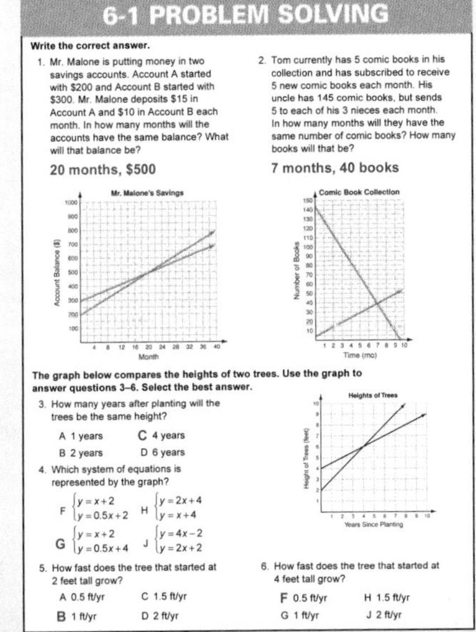

6-1 PROBLEM SOLVING

Write the correct answer.

1. Mr. Malone is putting money in two savings accounts. Account A started with $200 and Account B started with $300. Mr. Malone deposits $15 in Account A and $10 in Account B each month. In how many months will the accounts have the same balance? What will that balance be?

20 months, $500

Mr. Malone's Savings (Account Balance ($) vs. Month)

2. Tom currently has 5 comic books in his collection and has subscribed to receive 5 new comic books each month. His uncle has 145 comic books, but sends 5 to each of his 3 nieces each month. In how many months will they have the same number of comic books? How many books will that be?

7 months, 40 books

Comic Book Collection (Number of Books vs. Time (mo))

The graph below compares the heights of two trees. Use the graph to answer questions 3–6. Select the best answer.

Heights of Trees (Height of Trees (feet) vs. Years Since Planting)

3. How many years after planting will the trees be the same height?

A 1 years **C** 4 years
B 2 years D 6 years

4. Which system of equations is represented by the graph?

F $\begin{cases} y = x + 2 \\ y = 0.5x + 2 \end{cases}$ H $\begin{cases} y = 2x + 4 \\ y = x + 4 \end{cases}$

G $\begin{cases} y = x + 2 \\ y = 0.5x + 4 \end{cases}$ J $\begin{cases} y = 4x - 2 \\ y = 2x + 2 \end{cases}$

5. How fast does the tree that started at 2 feet tall grow?

A 0.5 ft/yr C 1.5 ft/yr
B 1 ft/yr D 2 ft/yr

6. How fast does the tree that started at 4 feet tall grow?

F 0.5 ft/yr H 1.5 ft/yr
G 1 ft/yr J 2 ft/yr

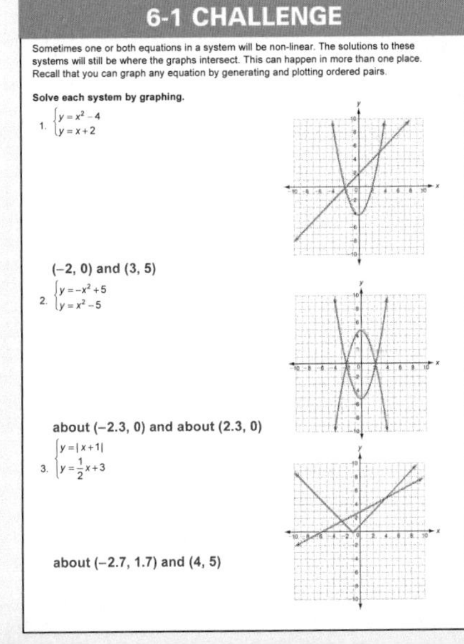

6-1 CHALLENGE

Sometimes one or both equations in a system will be non-linear. The solutions to these systems will still be where the graphs intersect. This can happen in more than one place. Recall that you can graph any equation by generating and plotting ordered pairs.

Solve each system by graphing.

1. $\begin{cases} y = x^2 - 4 \\ y = x + 2 \end{cases}$

(−2, 0) and (3, 5)

2. $\begin{cases} y = -x^2 + 5 \\ y = x^2 - 5 \end{cases}$

about (−2.3, 0) and about (2.3, 0)

3. $\begin{cases} y = |x + 1| \\ y = \frac{1}{2}x + 3 \end{cases}$

about (−2.7, 1.7) and (4, 5)

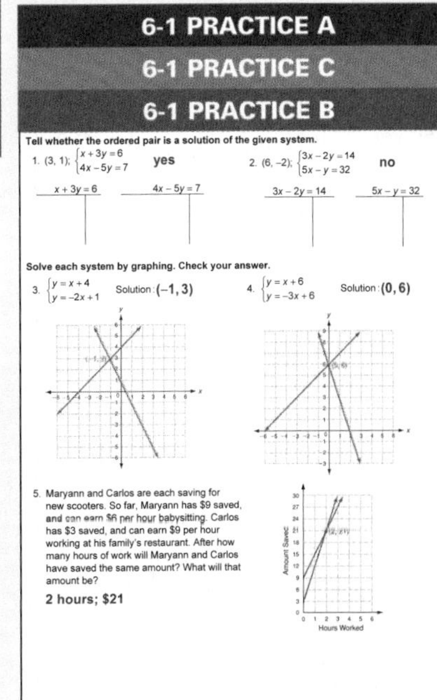

6-1 PRACTICE A
6-1 PRACTICE C
6-1 PRACTICE B

Tell whether the ordered pair is a solution of the given system.

1. (3, 1); $\begin{cases} x + 3y = 6 \\ 4x - 5y = 7 \end{cases}$ **yes**

$x + 3y = 6$ | $4x - 5y = 7$

2. (6, −2); $\begin{cases} 3x - 2y = 14 \\ 5x - y = 32 \end{cases}$ **no**

$3x - 2y = 14$ | $5x - y = 32$

Solve each system by graphing. Check your answer.

3. $\begin{cases} y = x + 4 \\ y = -2x + 1 \end{cases}$ Solution: **(−1, 3)**

4. $\begin{cases} y = x + 6 \\ y = -3x + 6 \end{cases}$ Solution: **(0, 6)**

5. Maryann and Carlos are each saving for new scooters. So far, Maryann has $9 saved, and can earn $6 per hour babysitting. Carlos has $3 saved, and can earn $9 per hour working at his family's restaurant. After how many hours of work will Maryann and Carlos have saved the same amount? What will that amount be?

2 hours; $21

(Amount Saved vs. Hours Worked)

CHALLENGE AND EXTEND

31. **Entertainment** If the pattern in the table continues, in what month will the number of sales of VCRs and DVD players be the same? What will that number be? **month 11; 400**

Total Number Sold				
Month	1	2	3	4
VCRs	500	490	480	470
DVD Players	250	265	280	295

32. Long Distance Inc. charges a \$1.45 connection charge and \$0.03 per minute. Far Away Calls charges a \$1.52 connection charge and \$0.02 per minute.

a. For how many minutes will a call cost the same from both companies? What is that cost? **7 min; \$1.66**

b. When is it better to call using Long Distance Inc.? Far Away Calls? Explain.

c. **What if...?** Long Distance Inc. raised its connection charge to \$1.50 and Far Away Calls decreased its connection charge by 2 cents. How will this affect the graphs? Now which company is better to use for calling long distance? Why?

32b. It is better to use Long Distance Inc. if the call is under 7 minutes. If the call is over 7 minutes, it is better to use Far Away Calls.

c. The graphs will intersect the *y*-axis at 1.5. Far Away Calls is cheaper because it costs less per minute.

SPIRAL REVIEW

Solve each equation. *(Lesson 2-2)*

33. $18 = \frac{3}{7}x$ **42** 34. $-\frac{x}{5} = 12$ **−60** 35. $-6y = -13.2$ **2.2** 36. $\frac{2}{5} = \frac{y}{12}$ $4\frac{4}{5}$

Describe the solutions of each inequality in words. *(Lesson 3-1)*

37. $3c < 15$ 38. $\frac{1}{3}x \geq 9$ 39. $5 + a > 11$

37. numbers less than 5

38. numbers greater than or equal to 27

39. numbers greater than 6

Solve each inequality and graph the solutions. *(Lesson 3-4)*

40. $4(2x + 1) > 28$ 41. $3^3 + 9 \leq -4c$ 42. $\frac{1}{8}x + \frac{3}{5} \leq \frac{3}{8}$

Career Path

go.hrw.com
Career Resources Online
KEYWORD: MA7 Career

Ethan Reynolds
Applied Sciences major

Q: What math classes did you take in high school?

A: Career Math, Algebra, and Geometry

Q: What are you studying and what math classes have you taken?

A: I am really interested in aviation. I am taking Statistics and Trigonometry. Next year I will take Calculus.

Q: How is math used in aviation?

A: I use math to interpret aeronautical charts. I also perform calculations involving wind movements, aircraft weight and balance, and fuel consumption. These skills are necessary for planning and executing safe air flights.

Q: What are your future plans?

A: I could work as a commercial or corporate pilot or even as a flight instructor. I could also work toward a bachelor's degree in aviation management, air traffic control, aviation electronics, aviation maintenance, or aviation computer science.

Journal

Have students explain how to determine whether an ordered pair is the solution of a system of equations.

ALTERNATIVE ASSESSMENT

Have students choose a point on the coordinate grid, draw two lines through the point, and write the equations for those lines. Then have students show algebraically that the coordinates of the point of intersection are a solution of both equations.

Power Presentations with PowerPoint®

6-1 Lesson Quiz

Tell whether the ordered pair is a solution of the given system.

1. $(-3, 1)$; $\begin{cases} y = -\frac{1}{3}x \\ 4y + 12 = 3x \end{cases}$ no

2. $(2, -4)$; $\begin{cases} y - 2x = -8 \\ 4y + 13x = 10 \end{cases}$ yes

Solve the system by graphing.

3. $\begin{cases} y + 2x = 9 \\ y = 4x - 3 \end{cases}$ (2, 5)

4. Joy has 5 collectible stamps and will buy 2 more each month. Ronald has 25 collectible stamps and will sell 3 each month. After how many months will they have the same number of stamps? 4 months How many will that be? 13 stamps

Also available on transparency

Answers

40. $x > 3$

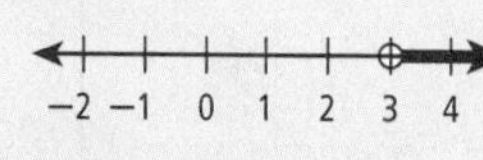

41. $c \leq -9$

−10 −8 −6 −4 −2 0 2

42. $x \leq -1\frac{4}{5}$

$-1\frac{4}{5}$

−2 $-1\frac{1}{2}$ −1 $-\frac{1}{2}$ 0

Model Systems of Linear Equations

You can use algebra tiles to model and solve some systems of linear equations.

Use with Lesson 6-2

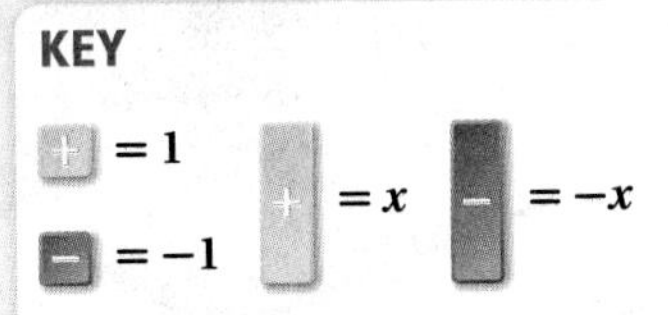

KEY

= 1   = −1   = x = $-x$

REMEMBER

When two expressions are equal, you can substitute one for the other in any expression or equation.

Activity

Use algebra tiles to model and solve $\begin{cases} y = 2x - 3 \\ x + y = 9 \end{cases}$.

MODEL		ALGEBRA
x y 9	*The first equation is solved for y. Model the second equation, $x + y = 9$, by substituting $2x - 3$ for y.*	$x + y = 9$ $x + (2x - 3) = 9$ $3x - 3 = 9$
	Add 3 yellow tiles on both sides of the mat. This represents adding 3 to both sides of the equation. *Remove zero pairs.*	$3x - 3 = 9$ $+3 \quad +3$ $3x = 12$
	Divide each side into 3 equal groups. Align one x-tile with each group on the right side. One x-tile is equivalent to 4 yellow tiles. $x = 4$	$\frac{3x}{3} = \frac{12}{3}$ $x = 4$

To solve for y, substitute 4 for x in one of the equations:

$$y = 2x - 3$$
$$= 2(4) - 3$$
$$= 5$$

The solution is (4, 5).

Try This

Model and solve each system of equations.

1. $\begin{cases} y = x + 3 \\ 2x + y = 6 \end{cases}$ **(1, 4)**
2. $\begin{cases} 2x + 3 = y \\ x + y = 6 \end{cases}$ **(1, 5)**
3. $\begin{cases} 2x + 3y = 1 \\ x = -1 - y \end{cases}$ **(−4, 3)**
4. $\begin{cases} y = x + 1 \\ 2x - y = -5 \end{cases}$ **(−4, −3)**

Organizer

Use with Lesson 6-2

Pacing:
Traditional $\frac{1}{2}$ day
Block $\frac{1}{4}$ day

Objective: Use algebra tiles to model and solve systems of linear equations.

Materials: algebra tiles

Online Edition
Algebra Tiles

Countdown Week 13

Lab Resources

Algebra Activities
6-2 Lab Recording Sheet

Teach

Discuss

You can represent either x or y with the variable tile. Make sure the variable tile represents the same variable throughout the same system. Algebra tiles can be found in the Manipulatives Kit (MK).

Close

Key Concept

You can solve a system of linear equations by modeling one variable in terms of the other, substituting that value into the other equation, and solving.

Assessment

Journal Have students explain how to use algebra tiles to solve one of the systems in the *Try This* problems.

State Resources

6-2 Organizer

Pacing: Traditional 1 day
Block $\frac{1}{2}$ day

Objective: Solve systems of linear equations in two variables by substitution.

Online Edition
Tutorial Videos

Countdown Week 13

Power Presentations with PowerPoint®

Warm Up

Solve each equation for x.

1. $y = x + 3$ $\quad x = y - 3$
2. $y = 3x - 4$ $\quad x = \dfrac{y + 4}{3}$

Simplify each expression.

3. $2(x - 5)$ $\quad 2x - 10$
4. $12 - 3(x + 1)$ $\quad 9 - 3x$

Evaluate each expression for the given value of x.

5. $\frac{2}{3}x + 8$ for $x = 6$ $\quad 12$
6. $3(x - 7)$ for $x = 10$ $\quad 9$

Also available on transparency

Math Humor

Q: Why did the chef throw the unsolved system of equations out of the restaurant?

A: The menu said, "No substitution."

6-2 Solving Systems by Substitution

Off the Mark by Mark Parisi. Cartoon copyrighted by Mark Parisi,

Objective
Solve systems of linear equations in two variables by substitution.

Why learn this?
You can solve systems of equations to help select the best value among high-speed Internet providers. (See Example 3.)

Sometimes it is difficult to identify the exact solution to a system by graphing. In this case, you can use a method called *substitution*.

The goal when using substitution is to reduce the system to one equation that has only one variable. Then you can solve this equation by the methods taught in Chapter 2.

Know it! Note

Solving Systems of Equations by Substitution	
Step 1	Solve for one variable in at least one equation, if necessary.
Step 2	Substitute the resulting expression into the other equation.
Step 3	Solve that equation to get the value of the first variable.
Step 4	Substitute that value into one of the original equations and solve.
Step 5	Write the values from Steps 3 and 4 as an ordered pair, (x, y), and check.

EXAMPLE 1 **Solving a System of Linear Equations by Substitution**

Solve each system by substitution.

A $\begin{cases} y = 2x \\ y = x + 5 \end{cases}$

Step 1 $y = 2x$, $y = x + 5$ — *Both equations are solved for y.*

Step 2 $y = x + 5$; $2x = x + 5$ — *Substitute 2x for y in the second equation.*

Step 3 $\begin{aligned} 2x &= x + 5 \\ -x &\quad -x \\ x &= 5 \end{aligned}$ — *Solve for x.*

Step 4 $y = 2x$ — *Write one of the original equations.*
$y = 2(5)$ — *Substitute 5 for x.*
$y = 10$

Step 5 $(5, 10)$ — *Write the solution as an ordered pair.*

Check Substitute $(5, 10)$ into both equations in the system.

$y = 2x$	
10	2(5)
10	10 ✓

$y = x + 5$	
10	5 + 5
10	10 ✓

Helpful Hint
You can substitute the value of one variable into *either* of the original equations to find the value of the other variable.

State Resources

go.hrw.com
State Resources Online
KEYWORD: MA7 Resources

1 Introduce

EXPLORATION

6-2 Solving Systems by Substitution

You can sometimes use the equations in a system of equations to write a new equation.

1. Consider the two equations shown here. What new equation can you write? Explain. $\quad a = b$, $a = c$
2. Use the idea from Step 1 to write a new equation based on each of the following systems.
   a. $\begin{cases} y = 2x + 1 \\ y = 3x - 4 \end{cases}$
   b. $\begin{cases} x = 3y + 2 \\ x = 5y + 4 \end{cases}$
   c. $\begin{cases} m = -4t + 2 \\ m = t - 8 \end{cases}$
   d. $\begin{cases} 3y = 2x + 7 \\ 3y = -x + 4 \end{cases}$

THINK AND DISCUSS

3. **Describe** what you notice about all of the equations you wrote in Step 2. (*Hint:* How many variables are in each equation?)
4. **Discuss** whether it would be possible to use the above method to write a new equation based on this system: $\begin{cases} y = 2x + 6 \\ y + 1 = 4x \end{cases}$

Motivate

In sports, coaches often substitute one player for another who plays the same position. Ask students to suggest other situations in which substitutions are made. Tell them that in a system of equations, you also can make substitutions. You can replace a variable in an equation with an equivalent expression.

Explorations and answers are provided in *Alternate Openers: Explorations Transparencies.*

Solve each system by substitution.

B $\begin{cases} 2x + y = 5 \\ y = x - 4 \end{cases}$

Step 1 $y = x - 4$	*The second equation is solved for y.*
Step 2 $2x + y = 5$	
$2x + (x - 4) = 5$	*Substitute x − 4 for y in the first equation.*
Step 3 $3x - 4 = 5$	*Simplify. Then solve for x.*
$\underline{\quad +4 \quad +4}$	*Add 4 to both sides.*
$3x = 9$	
$\frac{3x}{3} = \frac{9}{3}$	*Divide both sides by 3.*
$x = 3$	
Step 4 $y = x - 4$	*Write one of the original equations.*
$y = 3 - 4$	*Substitute 3 for x.*
$y = -1$	
Step 5 $(3, -1)$	*Write the solution as an ordered pair.*

C $\begin{cases} x + 4y = 6 \\ x + y = 3 \end{cases}$

Step 1 $x + 4y = 6$	*Solve the first equation for x by subtracting 4y from both sides.*
$\underline{\quad -4y \quad -4y}$	
$x = 6 - 4y$	
Step 2 $x + y = 3$	
$(6 - 4y) + y = 3$	*Substitute 6 − 4y for x in the second equation.*
Step 3 $6 - 3y = 3$	*Simplify. Then solve for y.*
$\underline{-6 \qquad -6}$	*Subtract 6 from both sides.*
$-3y = -3$	
$\frac{-3y}{-3} = \frac{-3}{-3}$	*Divide both sides by −3.*
$y = 1$	
Step 4 $x + y = 3$	*Write one of the original equations.*
$x + 1 = 3$	*Substitute 1 for y.*
$\underline{\quad -1 \quad -1}$	*Subtract 1 from both sides.*
$x = 2$	
Step 5 $(2, 1)$	*Write the solution as an ordered pair.*

Helpful Hint

Sometimes neither equation is solved for a variable. You can begin by solving either equation for either x or y.

CHECK IT OUT! Solve each system by substitution.

1a. $\begin{cases} y = x + 3 \\ y = 2x + 5 \end{cases}$ $(-2, 1)$ **1b.** $\begin{cases} x = 2y - 4 \\ x + 8y = 16 \end{cases}$ $(0, 2)$ **1c.** $\begin{cases} 2x + y = -4 \\ x + y = -7 \end{cases}$ $(3, -10)$

Sometimes you substitute an expression for a variable that has a coefficient. When solving for the second variable in this situation, you can use the Distributive Property.

COMMON ERROR ALERT

Students often think they have solved a system after finding the value of only one variable. Remind them that the solution is an ordered pair.

Power Presentations with PowerPoint®

Additional Examples

Example 1

Solve each system by substitution.

A. $\begin{cases} y = 3x \\ y = x - 2 \end{cases}$ $(-1, -3)$

B. $\begin{cases} y = x + 1 \\ 4x + y = 6 \end{cases}$ $(1, 2)$

C. $\begin{cases} x + 2y = -1 \\ x - y = 5 \end{cases}$ $(3, -2)$

INTERVENTION

Questioning Strategies

EXAMPLE 1

- How is substituting an expression for a variable similar to substituting a number for a variable? How is it different?
- In **Example 1C**, how do you know which variable to isolate?

Teaching Tip **Inclusion** Point out that in **Example 1A** both equations are written in slope-intercept form, so isolating a variable is unnecessary. In **Example 1B**, one equation is in slope-intercept form. The expression containing x from that equation can be substituted into the other equation. In **Example 1C**, neither equation is written in slope-intercept form. First, a variable must be isolated in one or both equations.

2 Teach

Guided Instruction

Review how to apply the Distributive Property and combine like terms to simplify an expression before **Example 2.** Have students practice solving by substitution when at least one equation is in slope-intercept form before having them solve systems where they first need to rewrite an equation. Remind students to check their solutions by substituting the values back into both equations or by graphing both lines and locating their intersection.

Reaching All Learners

Through Cooperative Learning

Have students work in pairs, and give them the system $\begin{cases} 2x - 4y = 10 \\ y + 5x = 3 \end{cases}$. Have one student solve the first equation for y and the other solve the second equation for y. Then have both continue independently to solve by using substitution. Each should arrive at the solution $(1, -2)$. Have them compare their work and discuss which substitution is more efficient.

Power Presentations with PowerPoint®

Additional Examples

Example 2

Solve $\begin{cases} y + 6x = 11 \\ 3x + 2y = -5 \end{cases}$ by substitution. (3, −7)

INTERVENTION

Questioning Strategies

EXAMPLE 2

- When do you need to use the Distributive Property?
- Why is it important to put the expression you are substituting for a variable in parentheses?

Multiple Representations Allowing students to check their solutions by graphing on a calculator and finding points of intersection will provide a quick check as well as emphasize that there are multiple representations of a system of linear equations.

EXAMPLE 2 Using the Distributive Property

Solve $\begin{cases} 4y - 5x = 9 \\ x - 4y = 11 \end{cases}$ by substitution.

Caution! When you solve one equation for a variable, you must substitute the value or expression into the *other* original equation, not the one that has just been solved.

Step 1 $x - 4y = 11$; $+4y \quad +4y$; $x = 4y + 11$ — *Solve the second equation for x by adding 4y to each side.*

Step 2 $4y - 5x = 9$; $4y - 5(4y + 11) = 9$ — *Substitute 4y + 11 for x in the first equation.*

Step 3 $4y - 5(4y) - 5(11) = 9$ — *Distribute −5 to the expression in parentheses. Simplify. Solve for y.*

$4y - 20y - 55 = 9$

$-16y - 55 = 9$

$+55 \quad +55$ — *Add 55 to both sides.*

$-16y = 64$

$\frac{-16y}{-16} = \frac{64}{-16}$ — *Divide both sides by −16.*

$y = -4$

Step 4 $x - 4y = 11$ — *Write one of the original equations.*

$x - 4(-4) = 11$ — *Substitute −4 for y.*

$x + 16 = 11$ — *Simplify.*

$-16 \quad -16$ — *Subtract 16 from both sides.*

$x = -5$

Step 5 $(-5, -4)$ — *Write the solution as an ordered pair.*

2. Solve $\begin{cases} -2x + y = 8 \\ 3x + 2y = 9 \end{cases}$ by substitution. **(−1, 6)**

Student to Student

Solving Systems by Substitution

Erika Chu
Terrell High School

I always look for a variable with a coefficient of 1 or −1 when deciding which equation to solve for x or y.

For the system

$\begin{cases} 2x + y = 14 \\ -3x + 4y = -10 \end{cases}$

I would solve the first equation for y because it has a coefficient of 1.

$2x + y = 14$

$y = -2x + 14$

Then I use substitution to find the values of x and y.

$-3x + 4y = -10$

$-3x + 4(-2x + 14) = -10$

$-3x + (-8x) + 56 = -10$

$-11x + 56 = -10$

$-11x = -66$

$x = 6$

$y = -2x + 14$

$y = -2(6) + 14 = 2$

The solution is (6, 2).

EXAMPLE 3 Consumer Economics Application

One high-speed Internet provider has a $50 setup fee and costs $30 per month. Another provider has no setup fee and costs $40 per month.

a. In how many months will both providers cost the same? What will that cost be?

Write an equation for each option. Let t represent the total amount paid and m represent the number of months.

	Total paid	is	setup fee	plus	cost per month	times	months.
Option 1	t	=	50	+	30	•	m
Option 2	t	=	0	+	40	•	m

Step 1 $t = 50 + 30m$ — *Both equations are solved for t.*

$t = 40m$

Step 2 $50 + 30m = 40m$ — *Substitute 50 + 30m for t in the second equation.*

Step 3 $\underline{-30m \quad -30m}$ — *Solve for m. Subtract 30m from both sides.*

$50 = 10m$

$\frac{50}{10} = \frac{10m}{10}$ — *Divide both sides by 10.*

$5 = m$

Step 4 $t = 40m$ — *Write one of the original equations.*

$= 40(5)$ — *Substitute 5 for m.*

$= 200$

Step 5 $(5, 200)$ — *Write the solution as an ordered pair.*

In 5 months, the total cost for each option will be the same—$200.

b. If you plan to cancel in 1 year, which is the cheaper provider? Explain.

Option 1: $t = 50 + 30(12) = 410$ Option 2: $t = 40(12) = 480$

Option 1 is cheaper.

3. One cable television provider has a $60 setup fee and charges $80 per month, and another provider has a $160 equipment fee and charges $70 per month.

a. In how many months will the cost be the same? What will that cost be?

b. If you plan to move in 6 months, which is the cheaper option? Explain.

3a. 10 months; $860

3b. The first option; the first option is cheaper for the first 9 months; the second option is cheaper after 10 months.

THINK AND DISCUSS

1. If you graphed the equations in Example 1A, where would the lines intersect?

2. **GET ORGANIZED** Copy and complete the graphic organizer. In each box, solve the system by substitution using the first step given. Show that each method gives the same solution.

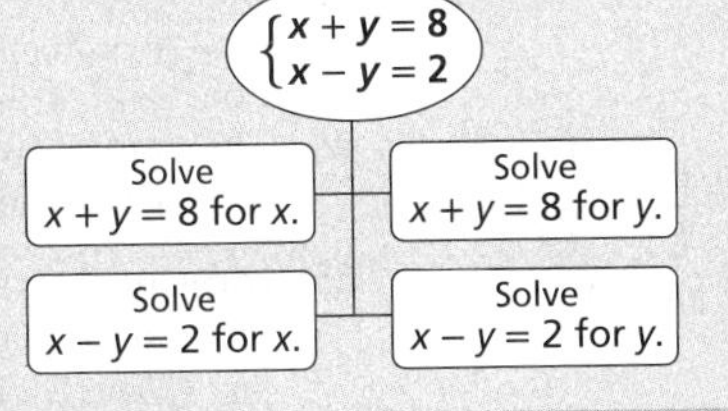

COMMON ERROR ALERT

Students may "lose" a negative sign when they substitute an expression for a variable. Encourage students to write clearly, even when solving problems on scratch paper. A poorly written minus sign can easily be mistaken for a stray pencil mark.

Power Presentations with PowerPoint®

Additional Examples

Example 3

Jenna is deciding between two cell-phone plans. The first plan has a $50 sign-up fee and costs $20 per month. The second plan has a $30 sign-up fee and costs $25 per month. After how many months will the total costs be the same? What will the cost be? If Jenna has to sign a one-year contract, which plan will be cheaper? Explain. 4 months; $130; Jenna should choose the first plan because it costs $290 for 1 year, and the second plan costs $330.

INTERVENTION
Questioning Strategies

EXAMPLE 3

- Why can you set the expressions for each option/plan equal to each other?

Visual In **Example 3,** students may benefit from using a table to organize the information.

	Setup Fee	Monthly Rate
Provider 1	$50	$30
Provider 2	$0	$40

3 Close

Summarize

Have students supply the steps they would need to take to solve the system $\begin{cases} 4x - y = 8 \\ 2x + 3y = 4 \end{cases}$ by substitution. Then have them solve it. Possible answer: Solve the first equation for y, then substitute that expression for y in the second equation. Solve for x. Substitute the value for x into the first equation and solve for y. The solution is $(2, 0)$.

ONGOING ASSESSMENT and INTERVENTION

***Diagnose Before* the Lesson**
6-2 Warm Up, TE p. 404

***Monitor During* the Lesson**
Check It Out! Exercises, SE pp. 405–407
Questioning Strategies, TE pp. 405–407

***Assess After* the Lesson**
6-2 Lesson Quiz, TE p. 410
Alternative Assessment, TE p. 410

Answers to *Think and Discuss*

1. at the point $(5, 10)$
2. See p. A6.

6-2 Exercises

Assignment Guide

Assign *Guided Practice* exercises as necessary.

If you finished Examples **1–3**

Basic 8–30, 34, 36–37, 42–50

Average 8–17, 18–30 even, 32–38, 42–50

Advanced 8–30 even, 31–50

Homework Quick Check

Quickly check key concepts.

Exercises: 10, 12, 16, 20, 26, 30

State Resources

6-2 Exercises

go.hrw.com
Homework Help Online
KEYWORD: MA7 6-2
Parent Resources Online
KEYWORD: MA7 Parent

GUIDED PRACTICE

Solve each system by substitution.

SEE EXAMPLE 1 p. 404

1. $\begin{cases} y = 5x - 10 \\ y = 3x + 8 \end{cases}$ **(9, 35)**
2. $\begin{cases} 3x + y = 2 \\ 4x + y = 20 \end{cases}$ **(18, −52)**
3. $\begin{cases} y = x + 5 \\ 4x + y = 20 \end{cases}$ **(3, 8)**

SEE EXAMPLE 2 p. 406

4. $\begin{cases} x - 2y = 10 \\ \frac{1}{2}x - 2y = 4 \end{cases}$ **(12, 1)**
5. $\begin{cases} y - 4x = 3 \\ 2x - 3y = 21 \end{cases}$ **(−3, −9)**
6. $\begin{cases} x = y - 8 \\ -x - y = 0 \end{cases}$ **(−4, 4)**

SEE EXAMPLE 3 p. 407

7. **Consumer Economics** The Strauss family is deciding between two lawn-care services. Green Lawn charges a \$49 startup fee, plus \$29 per month. Grass Team charges a \$25 startup fee, plus \$37 per month.
   a. In how many months will both lawn-care services cost the same? What will that cost be? **3 months; \$136**
   b. If the family will use the service for only 6 months, which is the better option? Explain. **Green Lawn; for 6 months, Green Lawn's service costs only \$223, while Grass Team's costs \$247.**

PRACTICE AND PROBLEM SOLVING

Independent Practice

For Exercises	See Example
8–10	1
11–16	2
17	3

Extra Practice

Skills Practice p. S14
Application Practice p. S33

Solve each system by substitution.

8. $\begin{cases} y = x + 3 \\ y = 2x + 4 \end{cases}$ **(−1, 2)**
9. $\begin{cases} y = 2x + 10 \\ y = -2x - 6 \end{cases}$ **(−4, 2)**
10. $\begin{cases} x + 2y = 8 \\ x + 3y = 12 \end{cases}$ **(0, 4)**
11. $\begin{cases} 2x + 2y = 2 \\ -4x + 4y = 12 \end{cases}$ **(−1, 2)**
12. $\begin{cases} y = 0.5x + 2 \\ -y = -2x + 4 \end{cases}$ **(4, 4)**
13. $\begin{cases} -x + y = 4 \\ 3x - 2y = -7 \end{cases}$ **(1, 5)**
14. $\begin{cases} 3x + y = -8 \\ -2x - y = 6 \end{cases}$ **(−2 −2)**
15. $\begin{cases} x + 2y = -1 \\ 4x - 4y = 20 \end{cases}$ **(3, −2)**
16. $\begin{cases} 4x = y - 1 \\ 6x - 2y = -3 \end{cases}$ $\mathbf{\left(\frac{1}{2}, 3\right)}$
17. **Recreation** Casey wants to buy a gym membership. One gym has a \$150 joining fee and costs \$35 per month. Another gym has no joining fee and costs \$60 per month.
    a. In how many months will both gym memberships cost the same? What will that cost be? **6 months; \$360**
    b. If Casey plans to cancel in 5 months, which is the better option for him? Explain.

the second option; for 5 months, it costs only \$300, while the other option costs \$325.

Solve each system by substitution. Check your answer.

18. $\begin{cases} x = 5 \\ x + y = 8 \end{cases}$ **(5, 3)**
19. $\begin{cases} y = -3x + 4 \\ x = 2y + 6 \end{cases}$ **(2, −2)**
20. $\begin{cases} 3x - y = 11 \\ 5y - 7x = 1 \end{cases}$ **(7, 10)**
21. $\begin{cases} \frac{1}{2}x + \frac{1}{3}y = 6 \\ x - y = 2 \end{cases}$ **(8, 6)**
22. $\begin{cases} x = 7 - 2y \\ 2x + y = 5 \end{cases}$ **(1, 3)**
23. $\begin{cases} y = 1.2x - 4 \\ 2.2x + 5 = y \end{cases}$ **(−9, −14.8)**
24. The sum of two numbers is 50. The first number is 43 less than twice the second number. Write and solve a system of equations to find the two numbers.
25. **Money** A jar contains n nickels and d dimes. There are 20 coins in the jar, and the total value of the coins is \$1.40. How many nickels and how many dimes are in the jar? (*Hint:* Nickels are worth \$0.05 and dimes are worth \$0.10.) **12 nickels; 8 dimes**

24. $\begin{cases} x + y = 50 \\ x = 2y - 43 \end{cases}$; **19 and 31**

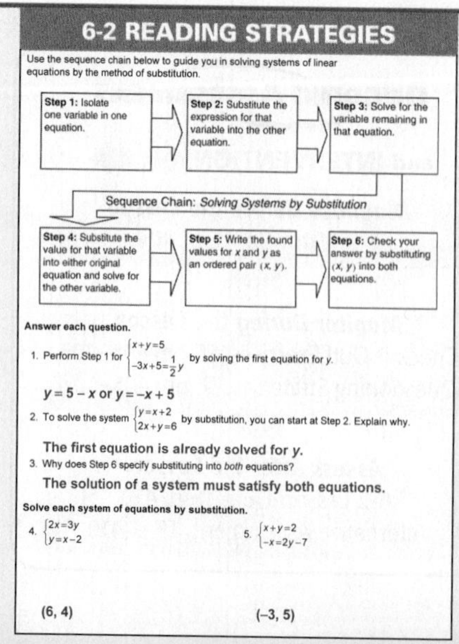

6-2 READING STRATEGIES

Use the sequence chain below to guide you in solving systems of linear equations by the method of substitution.

Sequence Chain: *Solving Systems by Substitution*

Step 1: Isolate one variable in one equation.

Step 2: Substitute the expression for that variable into the other equation.

Step 3: Solve for the variable remaining in that equation.

Step 4: Substitute the value for that variable into either original equation and solve for the other variable.

Step 5: Write the found values for x and y as an ordered pair (x, y).

Step 6: Check your answer by substituting (x, y) into both equations.

Answer each question.

1. Perform Step 1 for $\begin{cases} x+y=5 \\ -3x+5=\frac{1}{2}y \end{cases}$ by solving the first equation for y.

   $y = 5 - x$ or $y = -x + 5$

2. To solve the system $\begin{cases} y=x+2 \\ 2x+y=6 \end{cases}$ by substitution, you can start at Step 2. Explain why.

   The first equation is already solved for y.

3. Why does Step 6 specify substituting into *both* equations?

   The solution of a system must satisfy both equations.

Solve each system of equations by substitution.

4. $\begin{cases} 2x=3y \\ y=x-2 \end{cases}$ **(6, 4)**
5. $\begin{cases} x+y=2 \\ -x=2y-7 \end{cases}$ **(−3, 5)**

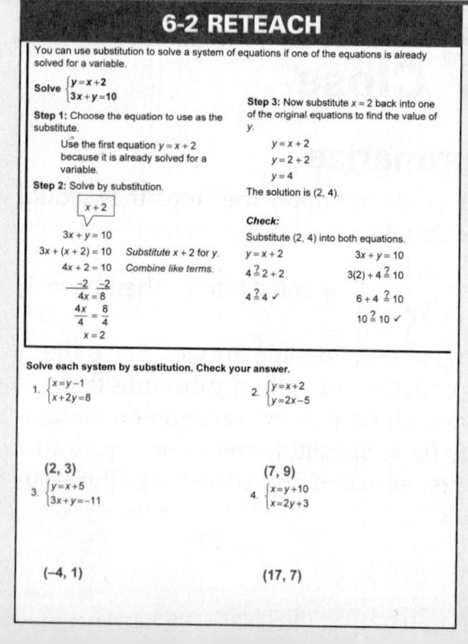

6-2 RETEACH

You can use substitution to solve a system of equations if one of the equations is already solved for a variable.

Solve $\begin{cases} y=x+2 \\ 3x+y=10 \end{cases}$

Step 1: Choose the equation to use as the substitute.

Use the first equation $y = x + 2$ because it is already solved for a variable.

Step 2: Solve by substitution.

$x + 2$

$3x + y = 10$

$3x + (x + 2) = 10$ *Substitute $x + 2$ for y.*

$4x + 2 = 10$ *Combine like terms.*

$\underline{-2 \quad -2}$

$4x = 8$

$\frac{4x}{4} = \frac{8}{4}$

$x = 2$

Step 3: Now substitute $x = 2$ back into one of the original equations to find the value of y.

$y = x + 2$

$y = 2 + 2$

$y = 4$

The solution is (2, 4).

Check:

Substitute (2, 4) into both equations.

$y = x + 2$	$3x + y = 10$
$4 \stackrel{?}{=} 2 + 2$	$3(2) + 4 \stackrel{?}{=} 10$
$4 \stackrel{?}{=} 4$ ✓	$6 + 4 \stackrel{?}{=} 10$
	$10 \stackrel{?}{=} 10$ ✓

Solve each system by substitution. Check your answer.

1. $\begin{cases} x=y-1 \\ x+2y=8 \end{cases}$ **(2, 3)**
2. $\begin{cases} y=x+2 \\ y=2x-5 \end{cases}$ **(7, 9)**
3. $\begin{cases} y=x+5 \\ 3x+y=-11 \end{cases}$ **(−4, 1)**
4. $\begin{cases} x=y+10 \\ x=2y+3 \end{cases}$ **(17, 7)**

26. **Multi-Step** Use the receipts below to write and solve a system of equations to find the cost of a large popcorn and the cost of a small drink. $\begin{cases} 3p + 2d = 21 \\ 2p + 4d = 22 \end{cases}$; popcorn: \$5; drink: \$3

27. $\begin{cases} x + y = 1000 \\ 0.05x + 0.06y = 58 \end{cases}$; \$200 at 5%; \$800 at 6%

27. **Finance** Helene invested a total of \$1000 in two simple-interest bank accounts. One account paid 5% annual interest; the other paid 6% annual interest. The total amount of interest she earned after one year was \$58. Write and solve a system of equations to find the amount invested in each account. (*Hint:* Change the interest rates into decimals first.)

Geometry Two angles whose measures have a sum of 90° are called complementary angles. For Exercises 28–30, x and y represent the measures of complementary angles. Use this information and the equation given in each exercise to find the measure of each angle.

28. $y = 4x - 10$ $x = 20°$; $y = 70°$

29. $x = 2y$ $x = 60°$; $y = 30°$

30. $y = 2(x - 15)$ $x = 40°$; $y = 50°$

31. **Aviation** With a headwind, a small plane can fly 240 miles in 3 hours. With a tailwind, the plane can fly the same distance in 2 hours. Follow the steps below to find the rates of the plane and wind.

a. Copy and complete the table. Let p be the rate of the plane and w be the rate of the wind.

	Rate	•	Time	=	Distance
With Headwind	$p - w$	•	3	=	240
With Tailwind	$p + w$	•	2	=	240

31b. $\begin{cases} 3p - 3w = 240 \\ 2p + 2w = 240 \end{cases}$

31c. plane: 100 mi/h; wind: 20 mi/h

b. Use the information in each row to write a system of equations.

c. Solve the system of equations to find the rates of the plane and wind.

32. **Write About It** Explain how to solve a system of equations by substitution.

33. **Critical Thinking** Explain the connection between the solution of a system solved by graphing and the solution of the same system solved by substitution.

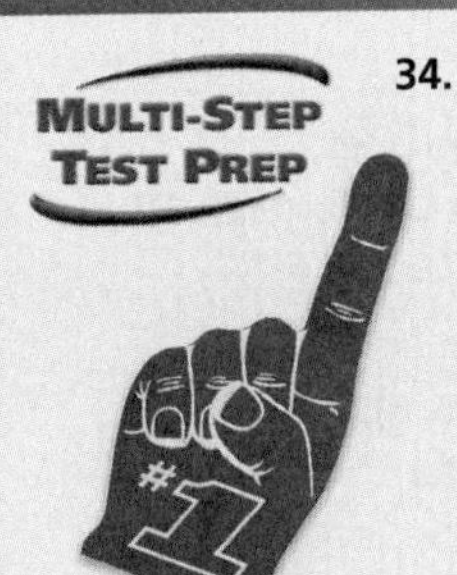

MULTI-STEP TEST PREP

34. This problem will prepare you for the Multi-Step Test Prep on page 426.

At the school store, Juanita bought 2 books and a backpack for a total of \$26 before tax. Each book cost \$8 less than the backpack.

a. Write a system of equations that can be used to find the price of each book and the price of the backpack.

b. Solve this system by substitution.

c. Solve this system by graphing. Discuss advantages and disadvantages of solving by substitution and solving by graphing.

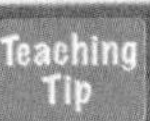

Reading Math For **Exercise 31,** help students understand the terms *headwind* and *tailwind*. A headwind blows in the direction opposite the course of the plane. A tailwind blows in the same direction as the course of the plane. ENGLISH LANGUAGE LEARNERS

Exercise 34 involves solving a system of equations by at least two different methods to find prices. This exercise prepares students for the Multi-Step Test Prep on page 426.

Answers

32. Possible answer: Solve one of the equations for either x or y. Then substitute the expression equal to x or y into the other equation. This creates a one-variable equation that can be solved. When you get the value of one variable, substitute it into one of the original equations and solve to find the value of the other variable.

33. The solution of a system solved by graphing is the same as the solution of a system solved by substitution.

34a. $\begin{cases} 2x + y = 26 \\ x = y - 8 \end{cases}$

b. book: \$6; backpack: \$14

c. Possible answer: Substitution works well since x is already isolated. Graphing requires solving both equations for y.

6-2 PROBLEM SOLVING

Write the correct answer.

1. Maribel has \$1.25 in her pocket. The money is in quarters and dimes. There are a total of 8 coins. How many quarters and dimes does Maribel have in her pocket?

3 quarters, 5 dimes

2. Fabulously Fit offers memberships for \$35 per month plus a \$50 enrollment fee. The Fitness Studio offers memberships for \$40 per month plus a \$35 enrollment fee. In how many months will the fitness clubs cost the same? What will the cost be?

3 months; \$155

3. Vong grilled 21 burgers at a block party. He grilled the same number of pounds of turkey burgers as hamburgers. Each turkey burger weighed $\frac{1}{4}$ pound and each hamburger weighed $\frac{1}{3}$ pound. How many of each did Vong grill?

12 turkey burgers, 9 beef hamburgers

4. Kate bought 3 used CDs and 1 used DVD at the bookstore. Her friend Joel bought 2 used CDs and 2 used DVDs at the same store. If Kate spent \$20 and Joel spent \$22, determine the cost of a used CD and a used DVD.

used CD \$4.50, used DVD \$6.50

Use the chart below to answer questions 5–8. Select the best answer. The chart compares the quotes that the Masons received from four different flooring contractors to tear out and replace a floor.

Contractor	Cost to tear out old floor	Cost of new floor per square foot
Smith & Son	\$250	\$8.00
V.I.P. Inc.	\$350	\$7.75
Dad's Floors	\$150	\$8.00
Floorshop	\$300	\$8.25

5. Which expression shows the total cost if the work is done by Dad's Floors?

A $8 + 150x$ C $150(8x)$
B $150 + 8x$ D $158x$

6. How many square feet would the Masons need to have installed to make the total cost of V.I.P. Inc. the same as the total cost of Floorshop?

F 10 sq ft **H** 100 sq ft
G 200 sq ft J 350 sq ft

7. When the total costs of V.I.P. Inc. and Floorshop are the same, what is the total cost?

A \$1125.00 C \$1950.00
B \$1900.00 D \$3187.50

8. How many square feet would the Masons need to have installed to make the total cost of Smith & Son the same as the total cost of V.I.P. Inc.?

F 80 sq ft **H** 400 sq ft
G 100 sq ft J 1000 sq ft

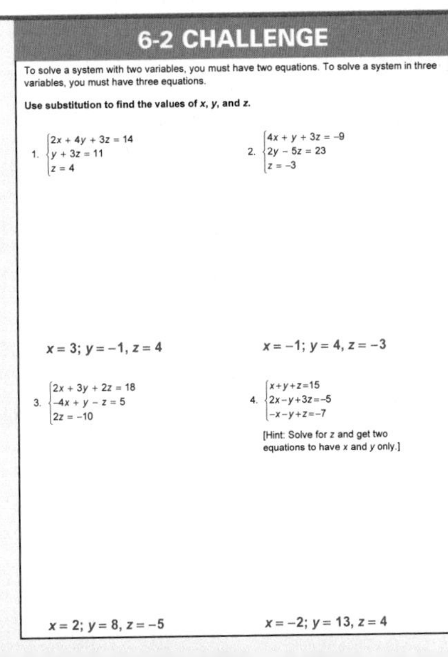

6-2 CHALLENGE

To solve a system with two variables, you must have two equations. To solve a system in three variables, you must have three equations.

Use substitution to find the values of x, y, and z.

1. $\begin{cases} 2x + 4y + 3z = 14 \\ y + 3z = 11 \\ z = 4 \end{cases}$

$x = 3$; $y = -1$, $z = 4$

2. $\begin{cases} 4x + y + 3z = -9 \\ 2y - 5z = 23 \\ z = -3 \end{cases}$

$x = -1$; $y = 4$, $z = -3$

3. $\begin{cases} 2x + 3y + 2z = 18 \\ -4x + y - z = 5 \\ 2z = -10 \end{cases}$

$x = 2$; $y = 8$, $z = -5$

4. $\begin{cases} x+y+z=15 \\ 2x-y+3z=-5 \\ -x-y+z=-7 \end{cases}$

[Hint: Solve for z and get two equations to have x and y only.]

$x = -2$; $y = 13$, $z = 4$

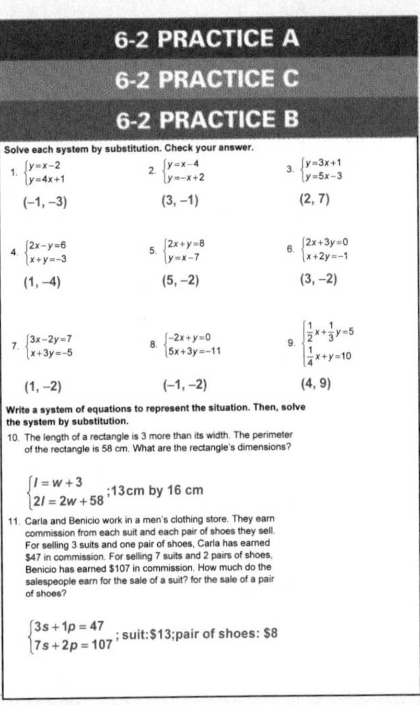

6-2 PRACTICE A

6-2 PRACTICE C

6-2 PRACTICE B

Solve each system by substitution. Check your answer.

1. $\begin{cases} y=x-2 \\ y=4x+1 \end{cases}$ $(-1, -3)$

2. $\begin{cases} y=x-4 \\ y=-x+2 \end{cases}$ $(3, -1)$

3. $\begin{cases} y=3x+1 \\ y=5x-3 \end{cases}$ $(2, 7)$

4. $\begin{cases} 2x-y=6 \\ x+y=-3 \end{cases}$ $(1, -4)$

5. $\begin{cases} 2x+y=8 \\ y=x-7 \end{cases}$ $(5, -2)$

6. $\begin{cases} 2x+3y=0 \\ x+2y=-1 \end{cases}$ $(3, -2)$

7. $\begin{cases} 3x-2y=7 \\ x+3y=-5 \end{cases}$ $(1, -2)$

8. $\begin{cases} -2x+y=0 \\ 5x+3y=-11 \end{cases}$ $(-1, -2)$

9. $\begin{cases} \frac{1}{2}x+\frac{1}{3}y=5 \\ \frac{1}{4}x+y=10 \end{cases}$ $(4, 9)$

Write a system of equations to represent the situation. Then, solve the system by substitution.

10. The length of a rectangle is 3 more than its width. The perimeter of the rectangle is 58 cm. What are the rectangle's dimensions?

$\begin{cases} l = w + 3 \\ 2l = 2w + 58 \end{cases}$;13cm by 16 cm

11. Carla and Benicio work in a men's clothing store. They earn commission from each suit and each pair of shoes they sell. For selling 3 suits and one pair of shoes, Carla has earned \$47 in commission. For selling 7 suits and 2 pairs of shoes, Benicio has earned \$107 in commission. How much do the salespeople earn for the sale of a suit? for the sale of a pair of shoes?

$\begin{cases} 3s + 1p = 47 \\ 7s + 2p = 107 \end{cases}$; suit:\$13;pair of shoes: \$8

TEST PREP DOCTOR In **Exercise 36,** students who chose **A** may have confused the variables in the second equation. Remind students that the verb *is* or *was* often represents the equal sign in an equation. The second sentence in the exercise indicates that *m* will equal some expression that contains *f*, not vice versa.

Journal

Have students write about a price comparison they could make in their own lives and how they could compare the prices with a system of equations.

ALTERNATIVE ASSESSMENT

Have students write and solve a system of linear equations that requires using the Distributive Property in the solution. Then have students write a real-world application problem that can be represented by a system of linear equations in two variables.

Power Presentations with PowerPoint®

6-2 Lesson Quiz

Solve each system by substitution.

1. $\begin{cases} y = 2x \\ y = \frac{1}{2}x - 3 \end{cases}$ $(-2, -4)$

2. $\begin{cases} x = 6y - 11 \\ 3x - 2y = -1 \end{cases}$ $(1, 2)$

3. $\begin{cases} -3x + y = -1 \\ x - y = 4 \end{cases}$ $\left(-\frac{3}{2}, -\frac{11}{2}\right)$

4. Plumber A charges $60 an hour. Plumber B charges $40 to visit your home plus $55 for each hour. For how many hours will the total cost for each plumber be the same? How much will that cost be? If a customer thinks they will need a plumber for 5 hours, which plumber should the customer hire? Explain.
8 hours; $480; plumber A; plumber A is cheaper for less than 8 hours.

Also available on transparency

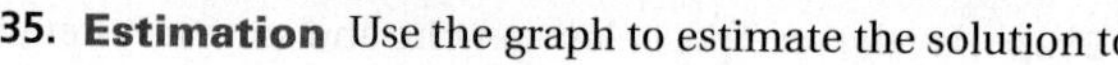

35. **Estimation** Use the graph to estimate the solution to $\begin{cases} 2x - y = 6 \\ x + y = -0.6 \end{cases}$. Round your answer to the nearest tenth. Then solve the system by substitution.
Possible estimate: (1.75, –2.5); (1.8, –2.4)

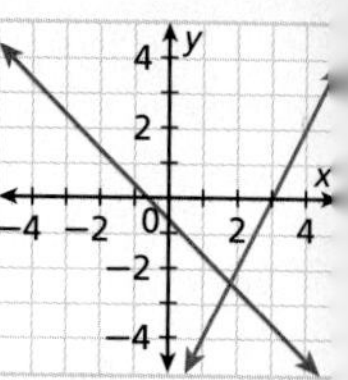

TEST PREP

36. Elizabeth met 24 of her cousins at a family reunion. The number of male cousins *m* was 6 less than twice the number of female cousins *f*. Which system can be used to find the number of male cousins and female cousins?

Ⓐ $\begin{cases} m + f = 24 \\ f = 2m - 6 \end{cases}$ Ⓑ $\begin{cases} m + f = 24 \\ f = 2m \end{cases}$ Ⓒ $\begin{cases} m = 24 + f \\ m = f - 6 \end{cases}$ **Ⓓ** $\begin{cases} f = 24 - m \\ m = 2f - 6 \end{cases}$

37. Which problem is best represented by the system $\begin{cases} d = n + 5 \\ d + n = 12 \end{cases}$?

Ⓕ Roger has 12 coins in dimes and nickels. There are 5 more dimes than nickels.
Ⓖ Roger has 5 coins in dimes and nickels. There are 12 more dimes than nickels.
Ⓗ Roger has 12 coins in dimes and nickels. There are 5 more nickels than dimes.
Ⓙ Roger has 5 coins in dimes and nickels. There are 12 more nickels than dimes.

CHALLENGE AND EXTEND

38. A car dealership has 378 cars on its lot. The ratio of new cars to used cars is 5:4. Write and solve a system of equations to find the number of new and used cars on the lot.
$\begin{cases} n + u = 378 \\ 4n = 5u \end{cases}$; **210 new cars; 168 used cars**

Solve each system by substitution.

39. $\begin{cases} 2r - 3s - t = 12 \\ s + 3t = 10 \\ t = 4 \end{cases}$ **$r = 5$; $s = -2$; $t = 4$**

40. $\begin{cases} x + y + z = 7 \\ y + z = 5 \\ 2y - 4z = -14 \end{cases}$ **$x = 2$; $y = 1$; $z = 4$**

41. $\begin{cases} a + 2b + c = 19 \\ -b + c = -5 \\ 3b + 2c = 15 \end{cases}$ **$a = 9$; $b = 5$; $c = 0$**

SPIRAL REVIEW

Write a possible situation for the given graph. *(Lesson 4-1)*

42. Height of hedge vs. Time

43.

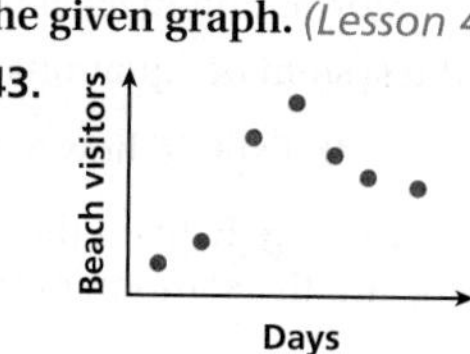

44.

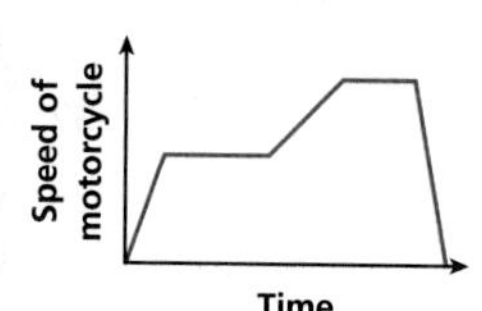

Find the *x*- and *y*-intercepts. *(Lesson 5-2)*

45. $6x - 2y = 12$ **x-int: 2; y-int: –6**

46. $-3y + x = 15$ **x-int: 15; y-int: –5**

47. $4y - 40 = -5x$ **x-int: 8; y-int: 10**

Tell whether each ordered pair is a solution of the given system. *(Lesson 6-1)*

48. $(3, 0)$; $\begin{cases} 2x - y = -6 \\ x + y = 3 \end{cases}$ **no**

49. $(-1, 4)$; $\begin{cases} y - 2x = 6 \\ x + 4y = 15 \end{cases}$ **yes**

50. $(5, 6)$; $\begin{cases} \frac{1}{3}y + x = 7 \\ 2x = 12 \end{cases}$ **no**

Answers

42. Possible answer: The hedge grows for a while, then someone trims it, and then it starts to grow again.

43. Possible answer: The weather is bad for the first 2 days, so few people are at the beach. Then the temperature warms up for the next 2 days, and the number of visitors increases. For the last 3 days, the weather is warm, but cloudy, so the number of visitors drops.

44. Possible answer: A motorcycle begins accelerating and maintains a constant speed. Then it accelerates to a faster speed, which is maintained for a while until it brakes and slows to a complete stop.

6-3 Solving Systems by Elimination

Objectives
Solve systems of linear equations in two variables by elimination.

Compare and choose an appropriate method for solving systems of linear equations.

Why learn this?
You can solve a system of linear equations to determine how many flowers of each type you can buy to make a bouquet. (See Example 4.)

Another method for solving systems of equations is *elimination*. Like substitution, the goal of elimination is to get one equation that has only one variable.

Remember that an equation stays balanced if you add equal amounts to both sides. Consider the system $\begin{cases} x - 2y = 19 \\ 5x + 2y = 1 \end{cases}$. Since $5x + 2y = 1$, you can add $5x + 2y$ to one side of the first equation and 1 to the other side and the balance is maintained.

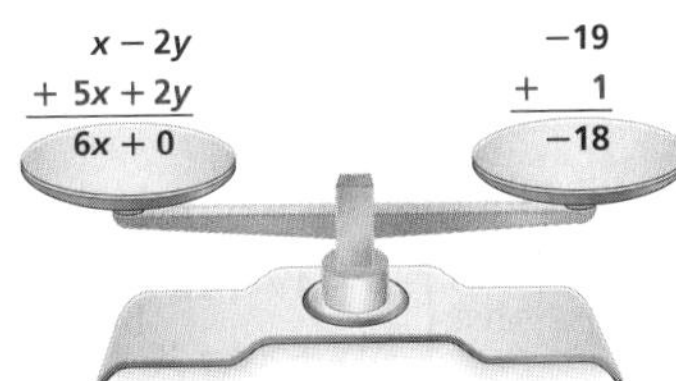

Since $-2y$ and $2y$ have **opposite coefficients**, you can eliminate the y by adding the two equations. The result is one equation that has only one variable: $6x = -18$.

When you use the elimination method to solve a system of linear equations, align all like terms in the equations. Then determine whether any like terms can be eliminated because they have opposite coefficients.

Solving Systems of Equations by Elimination	
Step 1	Write the system so that like terms are aligned.
Step 2	Eliminate one of the variables and solve for the other variable.
Step 3	Substitute the value of the variable into one of the original equations and solve for the other variable.
Step 4	Write the answers from Steps 2 and 3 as an ordered pair, (x, y), and check.

Later in this lesson you will learn how to multiply one or more equations by a number in order to produce opposites that can be eliminated.

6-3 Organizer

Pacing: Traditional 1 day
Block $\frac{1}{2}$ day

Objectives: Solve systems of linear equations in two variables by elimination.

Compare and choose an appropriate method for solving systems of linear equations.

Algebra Lab
In Algebra Lab Activities

Online Edition
Tutorial Videos

Countdown Week 13

Power Presentations with PowerPoint®

Warm Up

Simplify each expression.

1. $3x + 2y - 5x - 2y$ $\quad -2x$

2. $5(x - y) + 2x + 5y$ $\quad 7x$

3. $4y + 6x - 3(y + 2x)$ $\quad y$

4. $2y - 4x - 2(4y - 2x)$ $\quad -6y$

Write the least common multiple.

5. 3 and 6 $\quad$ 6 $\quad$ **6.** 4 and 10 $\quad$ 20

7. 6 and 8 $\quad$ 24 $\quad$ **8.** 2 and 5 $\quad$ 10

Also available on transparency

Math Humor

Teacher: What's your solution of the system of equations?

Student: Nothing – I used elimination and got rid of the whole thing!

1 Introduce

Solving Systems by Elimination

In this Exploration, you will investigate another method for solving systems of equations.

1. Consider the following system of equations: $\begin{cases} 2x - y = 5 \\ x + y = 1 \end{cases}$.
   What can you say about the expressions on either side of the equal sign in the equation $x + y = 1$?
2. In general, what happens if you add equal quantities to both sides of an equation?
3. Explain why you can add $x + y$ to the left side of $2x - y = 5$ and add 1 to the right side of $2x - y = 5$.
4. Add $x + y$ to the left side of $2x - y = 5$ and add 1 to the right side of $2x - y = 5$. What is the resulting equation?
5. Solve for x.
6. Use this value of x to find y.

THINK AND DISCUSS

7. **Explain** how you found the value of y once you knew the value of x.
8. **Describe** how you can check your solution to the system of equations.

Motivate

To introduce the word *elimination*, ask students what happens when the expressions below are simplified.

$5x + 2y + x - 2y$ *6x; y is eliminated.*

$2(x - y) - 2x + 7y$ *5y; x is eliminated.*

Tell students that in this lesson, they will eliminate variables to solve a system of equations.

Explorations and answers are provided in *Alternate Openers: Explorations Transparencies.*

State Resources

Communicating Math (Teaching Tip)

Some students may recognize the process of combining opposite terms as *cancellation* or *making zero pairs*. Use the word *eliminate* when describing the elimination method, but ask students to think of various names they have used to label this concept. This provides the students with a connection to previous learning. ENGLISH LANGUAGE LEARNERS

Power Presentations with PowerPoint®

Additional Examples

Example 1

Solve $\begin{cases} 3x - 4y = 10 \\ x + 4y = -2 \end{cases}$ by elimination. Check your answer.

(2, −1)

Example 2

Solve $\begin{cases} 2x + y = -5 \\ 2x - 5y = 13 \end{cases}$ by elimination. Check your answer.

(−1, −3)

INTERVENTION

Questioning Strategies

EXAMPLE 1

- Why is it helpful to write the system so that like terms are aligned?

EXAMPLE 2

- How do you decide what operation to use after you have aligned like terms?

Critical Thinking (Teaching Tip)

Challenge students to find two different ways to solve **Example 2** by substitution. One way is to solve each equation for 4y and then set the expressions equal to each other. Another is to divide the second equation by −2 and then isolate *x*.

EXAMPLE 1 Elimination Using Addition

Solve $\begin{cases} x - 2y = -19 \\ 5x + 2y = 1 \end{cases}$ by elimination.

Step 1	$x - 2y = -19$ $\underline{+\ 5x + 2y = \quad 1}$	*Write the system so that like terms are aligned.* *Notice that −2y and 2y are opposites.*
Step 2	$6x + 0 = -18$	*Add the equations to eliminate y.*
	$6x = -18$	*Simplify and solve for x.*
	$\frac{6x}{6} = \frac{-18}{6}$	*Divide both sides by 6.*
	$x = -3$	
Step 3	$x - 2y = -19$	*Write one of the original equations.*
	$-3 - 2y = -19$	*Substitute −3 for x.*
	$\underline{+3 \qquad +3}$	*Add 3 to both sides.*
	$-2y = -16$	
	$\frac{-2y}{-2} = \frac{-16}{-2}$	*Divide both sides by −2.*
	$y = 8$	
Step 4	$(-3, 8)$	*Write the solution as an ordered pair.*

Helpful Hint

Check your answer.

$x - 2y = -19$	
$-3 - 2(8)$	-19
$-3 - 16$	-19
-19	-19 ✓

$5x + 2y = 1$	
$5(-3) + 2(8)$	1
$-15 + 16$	1
1	1 ✓

CHECK IT OUT! **1.** Solve $\begin{cases} y + 3x = -2 \\ 2y - 3x = 14 \end{cases}$ by elimination. Check your answer. (−2, 4)

When two equations each contain the same term, you can subtract one equation from the other to solve the system. To subtract an equation, add the opposite of *each* term.

EXAMPLE 2 Elimination Using Subtraction

Solve $\begin{cases} 3x + 4y = 18 \\ -2x + 4y = 8 \end{cases}$ by elimination.

Step 1	$3x + 4y = 18$ $\underline{-(-2x + 4y = 8)}$	*Notice that both equations contain 4y.*
	$3x + 4y = 18$ $\underline{+\ 2x - 4y = -8}$	*Add the opposite of each term in the second equation.*
Step 2	$5x + 0 = 10$	*Eliminate y.*
	$5x = 10$	*Simplify and solve for x.*
	$x = 2$	
Step 3	$-2x + 4y = 8$	*Write one of the original equations.*
	$-2(2) + 4y = 8$	*Substitute 2 for x.*
	$-4 + 4y = 8$	
	$\underline{+4 \qquad +4}$	*Add 4 to both sides.*
	$4y = 12$	*Simplify and solve for y.*
	$y = 3$	
Step 4	$(2, 3)$	*Write the solution as an ordered pair.*

Remember!

Remember to check by substituting your answer into both original equations.

---

2 Teach

Guided Instruction

Review combining like terms before **Examples 1** and **2.** Review finding the least common multiple before **Example 3.** Be sure that students are comfortable with solving systems by addition or subtraction before showing them how to solve by multiplication. Discuss when each of the three methods of solving systems of linear equations is most convenient to use. Remind students that a solution is an ordered pair and that they should check their solutions.

Reaching All Learners

Through Concrete Manipulatives

Use transparency algebra tiles (MK) to model $2x + 3y = 6$ and $-2x + y = 10$. Label the *x*- and *y*-tiles.

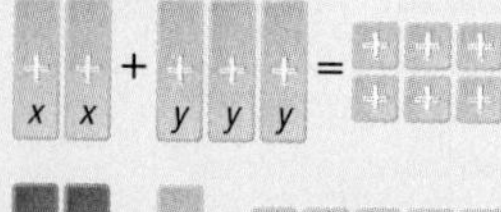

Add the tiles vertically. Remove the zero pairs. This leaves $4y = 16$. Solve for *y*. Then find *x* through substitution. (−3, 4)

CHECK IT OUT! **2.** Solve $\begin{cases} 3x + 3y = 15 \\ -2x + 3y = -5 \end{cases}$ by elimination. Check your answer. (4, 1)

In some cases, you will first need to multiply one or both of the equations by a number so that one variable has opposite coefficients.

Helpful Hint

In Example 3A, you could have also multiplied the first equation by −3 to eliminate *y*.

EXAMPLE 3 Elimination Using Multiplication First

Solve each system by elimination.

A $\begin{cases} 2x + y = 3 \\ -x + 3y = -12 \end{cases}$

Step 1 $2x + y = 3$

$+2(-x + 3y = -12)$ — *Multiply each term in the second equation by 2 to get opposite x-coefficients.*

$2x + y = 3$

$+(-2x + 6y = -24)$ — *Add the new equation to the first equation to eliminate x.*

Step 2 $7y = -21$

$y = -3$ — *Solve for y.*

Step 3 $2x + y = 3$ — *Write one of the original equations.*

$2x + (-3) = 3$ — *Substitute −3 for y.*

$+3 \quad +3$ — *Add 3 to both sides.*

$2x = 6$ — *Solve for x.*

$x = 3$

Step 4 $(3, -3)$ — *Write the solution as an ordered pair.*

B $\begin{cases} 7x - 12y = -22 \\ 5x - 8y = -14 \end{cases}$

Step 1 $2(7x - 12y = -22)$

$+(-3)(5x - 8y = -14)$ — *Multiply the first equation by 2 and the second equation by −3 to get opposite y-coefficients.*

$14x - 24y = -44$

$+(-15x + 24y = 42)$ — *Add the new equations to eliminate y.*

Step 2 $-x = -2$

$x = 2$ — *Solve for x.*

Step 3 $7x - 12y = -22$ — *Write one of the original equations.*

$7(2) - 12y = -22$ — *Substitute 2 for x.*

$14 - 12y = -22$

$-14 \quad -14$ — *Subtract 14 from both sides.*

$-12y = -36$ — *Solve for y.*

$y = 3$

Step 4 $(2, 3)$ — *Write the solution as an ordered pair.*

CHECK IT OUT! **Solve each system by elimination. Check your answer.**

3a. $\begin{cases} 3x + 2y = 6 \\ -x + y = -2 \end{cases}$ (2, 0) **3b.** $\begin{cases} 2x + 5y = 26 \\ -3x - 4y = -25 \end{cases}$ (3, 4)

COMMON ERROR ALERT

In problems like **Example 3,** students may forget to multiply both sides of the equation by a number when they create an opposite coefficient through multiplication. Remind them that the Multiplication Property of Equality requires both sides of the equation to be multiplied by the same number.

Power Presentations with PowerPoint®

Additional Examples

Example 3

Solve each system by elimination. Check your answer.

A. $\begin{cases} x + 2y = 11 \\ -3x + y = -5 \end{cases}$ (3, 4)

B. $\begin{cases} -5x + 2y = 32 \\ 2x + 3y = 10 \end{cases}$ (−4, 6)

INTERVENTION

Questioning Strategies

EXAMPLE 3

- How do you choose the number to multiply each equation by?

Science Link Systems of linear equations are commonly used in the sciences. A major field of study that uses systems of linear equations is digital signal processing (DSP). DSP has several applications, including weather forecasting, seismic (earth tremor) data processing, and image manipulation.

Teaching Tip **Number Sense** In **Example 4,** students can multiply both equations by 100 before solving. The new system will be equivalent to the original system, but it may be easier to solve because it will not contain decimals.

Teaching Tip **Visual** In **Example 4,** students may benefit from using a table to organize the information.

	Roses	Daises	Total
Number of Flowers	r	d	12
Cost of Flowers	2.50r$	1.75d$	$24.75

Power Presentations with PowerPoint®

Additional Examples

Example 4

Paige has $7.75 to buy 12 sheets of felt and card stock for her scrapbook. The felt costs $0.50 per sheet, and the card stock costs $0.75 per sheet. How many sheets of each can Paige buy?
5 sheets of felt and 7 sheets of card stock

INTERVENTION 

Questioning Strategies

EXAMPLE 4

- How do you know which numbers in the problem should be coefficients for the variables?

EXAMPLE 4 Consumer Economics Application

Sam spent $24.75 to buy 12 flowers for his mother. The bouquet contained roses and daisies. How many of each type of flower did Sam buy?

Write a system. Use r for the number of roses and d for the number of daisies.

$2.50r + 1.75d = 24.75$ *The cost of roses and daisies totals $24.75.*

$r + d = 12$ *The total number of roses and daisies is 12.*

Step 1 $2.50r + 1.75d = 24.75$

$+ (-2.50)(r + d = 12)$ *Multiply the second equation by −2.50 to get opposite r-coefficients.*

$2.50r + 1.75d = 24.75$

$+ (-2.50r - 2.50d = -30.00)$ *Add this equation to the first equation to eliminate r.*

Step 2 $-0.75d = -5.25$

$d = 7$ *Solve for d.*

Step 3 $r + d = 12$ *Write one of the original equations.*

$r + 7 = 12$ *Substitute 7 for d.*

$-7 \quad -7$ *Subtract 7 from both sides.*

$r = 5$

Step 4 $(5, 7)$ *Write the solution as an ordered pair.*

Sam can buy 5 roses and 7 daisies.

4. What if...? Sally spent $14.85 to buy 13 flowers. She bought lilies, which cost $1.25 each, and tulips, which cost $0.90 each. How many of each flower did Sally buy? **9 lilies, 4 tulips**

All systems can be solved in more than one way. For some systems, some methods may be better than others.

Systems of Linear Equations

METHOD	USE WHEN...	EXAMPLE
Graphing	• Both equations are solved for y. • You want to estimate a solution.	$\begin{cases} y = 3x + 2 \\ y = -2x + 6 \end{cases}$
Substitution	• A variable in either equation has a coefficient of 1 or −1. • Both equations are solved for the same variable. • Either equation is solved for a variable.	$\begin{cases} x + 2y = 7 \\ x = 10 - 5y \end{cases}$ or $\begin{cases} x = 2y + 10 \\ x = 3y + 5 \end{cases}$
Elimination	• Both equations have the same variable with the same or opposite coefficients. • A variable term in one equation is a multiple of the corresponding variable term in the other equation.	$\begin{cases} 3x + 2y = 8 \\ 5x + 2y = 12 \end{cases}$ or $\begin{cases} 6x + 5y = 10 \\ 3x + 2y = 15 \end{cases}$

3 Close

Summarize

Ask students which method they would use to solve each system of equations and why. Possible answers:

$\begin{cases} x + 5y = 28 \\ -x + 2y = 7 \end{cases}$ Elimination using add.; the x-terms are opposites.

$\begin{cases} y = 6 \\ y = 4x - 2 \end{cases}$ Graphing: both in slope-int. form; substitution: both are solved for y.

$\begin{cases} -2x + 5y = -17 \\ 3x - 10y = 28 \end{cases}$ Elimination using mult.; the y-terms are multiples of 5.

ONGOING ASSESSMENT and INTERVENTION

***Diagnose Before* the Lesson**
6-3 Warm Up, TE p. 411

***Monitor During* the Lesson**
Check It Out! Exercises, SE pp. 412–414
Questioning Strategies, TE pp. 412–414

***Assess After* the Lesson**
6-3 Lesson Quiz, TE p. 417
Alternative Assessment, TE p. 417

THINK AND DISCUSS

1. Explain how multiplying the second equation in a system by −1 and eliminating by adding is the same as elimination by subtraction. Give an example of a system for which this applies.
2. Explain why it does not matter which variable you solve for first when solving a system by elimination.

3. **GET ORGANIZED** Copy and complete the graphic organizer. In each box, write an example of a system of equations that you could solve using the given method.

Answers to *Think and Discuss*

1. Multiplying the second equation by −1 and adding is like adding the opposite, which is the same as subtracting; possible answer: $3x + y = 5$; $3x + 2y = 6$.
2. No matter which variable you solve for first, the answer will still be the same.
3. See p. A6.

6-3 Exercises

go.hrw.com
Homework Help Online
KEYWORD: MA7 6-3
Parent Resources Online
KEYWORD: MA7 Parent

GUIDED PRACTICE

Solve each system by elimination. Check your answer.

SEE EXAMPLE 1 p. 412

1. $\begin{cases} -x + y = 5 \\ x - 5y = -9 \end{cases}$ **(−4, 1)**
2. $\begin{cases} x + y = 12 \\ x - y = 2 \end{cases}$ **(7, 5)**
3. $\begin{cases} 2x + 5y = -24 \\ 3x - 5y = 14 \end{cases}$ **(−2, −4)**

SEE EXAMPLE 2 p. 412

4. $\begin{cases} x - 10y = 60 \\ x + 14y = 12 \end{cases}$ **(40, −2)**
5. $\begin{cases} 5x + y = 0 \\ 5x + 2y = 30 \end{cases}$ **(−6, 30)**
6. $\begin{cases} -5x + 7y = 11 \\ -5x + 3y = 19 \end{cases}$ **(−5, −2)**

SEE EXAMPLE 3 p. 413

7. $\begin{cases} 2x + 3y = 12 \\ 5x - y = 13 \end{cases}$ **(3, 2)**
8. $\begin{cases} -3x + 4y = 12 \\ 2x + y = -8 \end{cases}$ **(−4, 0)**
9. $\begin{cases} 2x + 4y = -4 \\ 3x + 5y = -3 \end{cases}$ **(4, −3)**

SEE EXAMPLE 4 p. 414

10. **Consumer Economics** Each family in a neighborhood is contributing $20 worth of food to the neighborhood picnic. The Harlin family is bringing 12 packages of buns. The hamburger buns cost $2.00 per package. The hot-dog buns cost $1.50 per package. How many packages of each type of bun did they buy?
4 packages of hamburger buns, 8 packages of hot dog buns

PRACTICE AND PROBLEM SOLVING

18. $\left(-\frac{1}{3}, -2\right)$

Solve each system by elimination. Check your answer.

Independent Practice	
For Exercises	See Example
11–13	1
14–16	2
17–19	3
20	4

Extra Practice
Skills Practice p. S14
Application Practice p. S33

11. $\begin{cases} -x + y = -1 \\ 2x - y = 0 \end{cases}$ **(−1, −2)**
12. $\begin{cases} -2x + y = -20 \\ 2x + y = 48 \end{cases}$ **(17, 14)**
13. $\begin{cases} 3x - y = -2 \\ -2x + y = 3 \end{cases}$ **(1, 5)**
14. $\begin{cases} x - y = 4 \\ x - 2y = 10 \end{cases}$ **(−2, −6)**
15. $\begin{cases} x + 2y = 5 \\ 3x + 2y = 17 \end{cases}$ $\left(6, -\frac{1}{2}\right)$
16. $\begin{cases} 3x - 2y = -1 \\ 3x - 4y = 9 \end{cases}$ $\left(-\frac{11}{3}, -5\right)$
17. $\begin{cases} x - y = -3 \\ 5x + 3y = 1 \end{cases}$ **(−1, 2)**
18. $\begin{cases} 9x - 3y = 3 \\ 3x + 8y = -17 \end{cases}$
19. $\begin{cases} 5x + 2y = -1 \\ 3x + 7y = 11 \end{cases}$ **(−1, 2)**
20. **Multi-Step** Mrs. Gonzalez bought centerpieces to put on each table at a graduation party. She spent $31.50. There are 8 tables each requiring either a candle or vase. Candles cost $3 and vases cost $4.25. How many of each type did she buy?

20. 2 candles, 6 vases

6-3 Exercises

Assignment Guide

Assign *Guided Practice* exercises as necessary.

If you finished Examples **1–2**
Basic 11–16, 21, 23
Average 11–16, 21, 23
Advanced 11–16, 21, 23

If you finished Examples **1–4**
Basic 11–23, 31, 33–35, 40–48
Average 11–21, 24–30 even, 31–48
Advanced 12–20 even, 21, 24–28 even, 31–48

Homework Quick Check

Quickly check key concepts.
Exercises: 12, 14, 18, 20

State Resources

Visual Have students use a table like the one in **Exercise 23** to help them write systems of equations that represent real-world problems. To make a generic chart, they should label the left-hand rows *Situation 1* and *Situation 2*. The column headings should be *Item 1*, *Item 2*, and *Total*. The plus sign in the third column should be changed to +/−.

Exercise 31 involves writing and solving a system of equations to help calculate savings. This exercise prepares students for the Multi-Step Test Prep on page 426.

Answers

21. $\begin{cases} \ell - w = 2 \\ 2\ell + 2w = 40 \end{cases}$; length: 11 units; width: 9 units

24. (40, −2); possible answer: elimination using subtraction; coefficients of *x*-values are the same.

25. (3, 3); possible answer: elimination using multiplication; no variables have the same coefficient, so they cannot be eliminated by addition or subtraction.

26. (3, −1); possible answer: elimination using subtraction; the *y*-terms have the same coefficients.

27. $\left(\frac{46}{7}, \frac{8}{7}\right)$; possible answer: I would use substitution because the second equation is already solved for a variable.

28–29. See p. A24.

21. **Geometry** The difference between the length and width of a rectangle is 2 units. The perimeter is 40 units. Write and solve a system of equations to determine the length and width of the rectangle. (*Hint:* The perimeter of a rectangle is $2\ell + 2w$.)

22. **ERROR ANALYSIS** Which is incorrect? Explain the error.

22. A; the student did not distribute the neg. sign to all values in the parentheses and so mistakenly added 3 to −3.

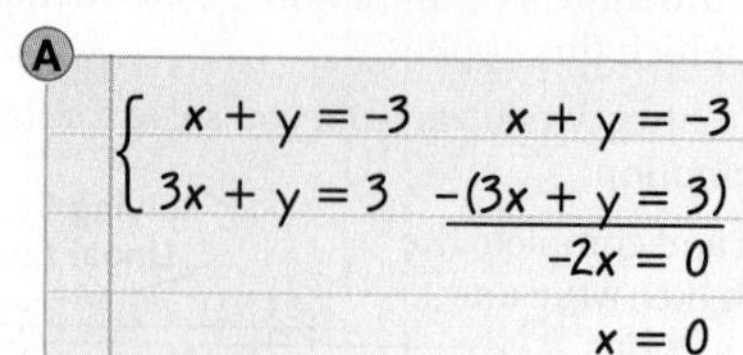

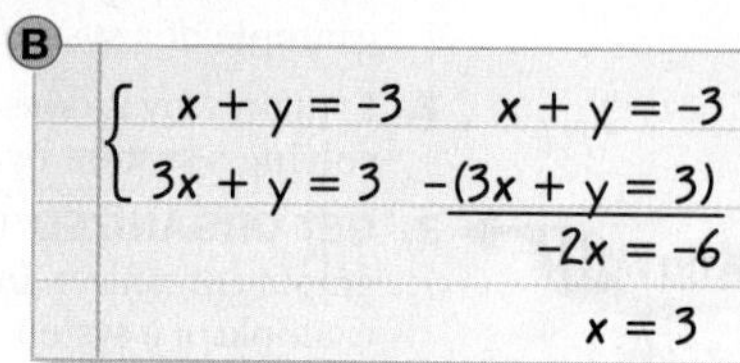

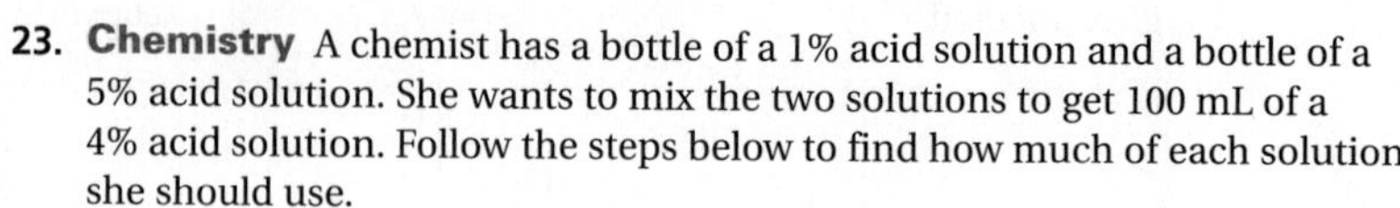

23. **Chemistry** A chemist has a bottle of a 1% acid solution and a bottle of a 5% acid solution. She wants to mix the two solutions to get 100 mL of a 4% acid solution. Follow the steps below to find how much of each solution she should use.

	1% Solution	+	5% Solution	=	4% Solution
Amount of Solution (mL)	x	+	y	=	**100**
Amount of Acid (mL)	$0.01x$	+	**0.05y**	=	$0.04(100)$

a. Copy and complete the table.

b. Use the information in the table to write a system of equations. $\begin{cases} x + y = 100 \\ 0.01x + 0.05y = 4 \end{cases}$

c. Solve the system of equations to find how much she will use from each bottle to get 100 mL of a 4% acid solution. **25 mL of the 1% solution, 75 mL of the 5% solution**

LINK Math History

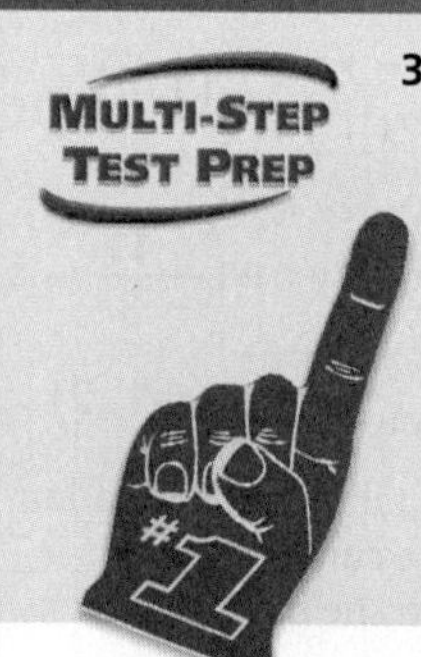

In 1247, Qin Jiushao wrote *Mathematical Treatise in Nine Sections*. Its contents included solving systems of equations and the Chinese Remainder Theorem.

Critical Thinking Which method would you use to solve each system? Explain.

24. $\begin{cases} \frac{1}{2}x - 5y = 30 \\ \frac{1}{2}x + 7y = 6 \end{cases}$

25. $\begin{cases} -x + 2y = 3 \\ 4x - 5y = -3 \end{cases}$

26. $\begin{cases} 3x - y = 10 \\ 2x - y = 7 \end{cases}$

27. $\begin{cases} 3y + x = 10 \\ x = 4y + 2 \end{cases}$

28. $\begin{cases} y = -4x \\ y = 2x + 3 \end{cases}$

29. $\begin{cases} 2x + 6y = 12 \\ 4x + 5y = 15 \end{cases}$

30. **Business** A local boys club sold 176 bags of mulch and made a total of $520. They did not sell any of the expensive cocoa mulch. Use the table to determine how many bags of each type of mulch they sold. **48 bags hardwood mulch; 128 bags pine bark mulch**

Mulch Prices ($)	
Cocoa	4.75
Hardwood	3.50
Pine Bark	2.75

31a. $\begin{cases} 3A + 2B = 16 \\ 2A + 3B = 14 \end{cases}$

MULTI-STEP TEST PREP

31. This problem will prepare you for the Multi-Step Test Prep on page 426.

a. The school store is running a promotion on school supplies. Different supplies are placed on two shelves. You can purchase 3 items from shelf A and 2 from shelf B for $16. Or you can purchase 2 items from shelf A and 3 from shelf B for $14. Write a system of equations that can be used to find the individual prices for the supplies on shelf A and on shelf B.

b. Solve the system of equations by elimination. **$A = 4$; $B = 2$**

c. If the supplies on shelf A are normally $6 each and the supplies on shelf B are normally $3 each, how much will you save on each package plan from part a? **Buying the first package will save $8; buying the second package will save $7.**

6-3 PRACTICE A

6-3 PRACTICE C

6-3 PRACTICE B

Follow the steps to solve each system by elimination.

1. $\begin{cases} 2x - 3y = 14 \\ 2x + y = -10 \end{cases}$
Subtract the second equation:
$2x - 3y = 14$
$-(2x + y = -10)$
$-4y = 24$
Solve the resulting equation:
$y = -6$
Use your answer to find the value of *x*:
$x = -2$
Solution: (−2, −6)

2. $\begin{cases} 3x + y = 17 \\ 4x + 2y = 20 \end{cases}$
Multiply the first equation by −2. Then, add the equations:
$-6x - 2y = -34$
$+ 4x + 2y = 20$
$-2x = -14$
Solve the resulting equation:
$x = 7$
Use your answer to find the value of *y*:
$y = -4$
Solution: (7, −4)

Solve each system by elimination. Check your answer.

3. $\begin{cases} x + 3y = -7 \\ -x + 2y = -8 \end{cases}$ (2, −3)

4. $\begin{cases} 3x + y = -26 \\ 2x - y = -19 \end{cases}$ (−9, 1)

5. $\begin{cases} x + 3y = -14 \\ 2x - 4y = 32 \end{cases}$ (4, −6)

6. $\begin{cases} 4x - y = -5 \\ -2x + 3y = 10 \end{cases}$ $\left(-\frac{1}{2}, 3\right)$

7. $\begin{cases} y - 3x = 11 \\ 2y - x = 2 \end{cases}$ (−4, −1)

8. $\begin{cases} -10x + y = 0 \\ 5x + 3y = -7 \end{cases}$ $\left(-\frac{1}{5}, -2\right)$

Solve.

9. Brianna's family spent $134 on 2 adult tickets and 3 youth tickets at an amusement park. Max's family spent $146 on 3 adult tickets and 2 youth tickets. What is the price of a youth ticket? $22

10. Carl bought 19 apples of 2 different varieties to make a pie. The total cost of the apples was $5.10. Granny Smith apples cost $0.25 each and Gala apples cost $0.30 each. How many of each type of apple did Carl buy? 7 Gala apples; 12 Granny Smith apples

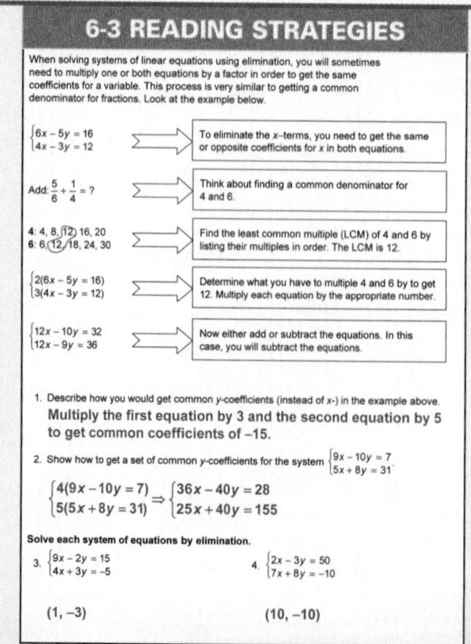

6-3 READING STRATEGIES

When solving systems of linear equations using elimination, you will sometimes need to multiply one or both equations by a factor in order to get the same coefficients for a variable. This process is very similar to getting a common denominator for fractions. Look at the example below.

$\begin{cases} 6x - 5y = 16 \\ 4x - 3y = 12 \end{cases}$	To eliminate the *x*-terms, you need to get the same or opposite coefficients for *x* in both equations.
Add: $\frac{5}{6} + \frac{1}{4} = ?$	Think about finding a common denominator for 4 and 6.
4: 4, 8, (12), 16, 20 6: 6, (12), 18, 24, 30	Find the least common multiple (LCM) of 4 and 6 by listing their multiples in order. The LCM is 12.
$\begin{cases} 2(6x - 5y = 16) \\ 3(4x - 3y = 12) \end{cases}$	Determine what you have to multiple 4 and 6 by to get 12. Multiply each equation by the appropriate number.
$\begin{cases} 12x - 10y = 32 \\ 12x - 9y = 36 \end{cases}$	Now either add or subtract the equations. In this case, you will subtract the equations.

1. Describe how you would get common *y*-coefficients (instead of *x*-) in the example above. Multiply the first equation by 3 and the second equation by 5 to get common coefficients of −15.

2. Show how to get a set of common *y*-coefficients for the system $\begin{cases} 9x - 10y = 7 \\ 5x + 8y = 31 \end{cases}$.
$\begin{cases} 4(9x - 10y = 7) \\ 5(5x + 8y = 31) \end{cases} \Rightarrow \begin{cases} 36x - 40y = 28 \\ 25x + 40y = 155 \end{cases}$

Solve each system of equations by elimination.

3. $\begin{cases} 9x - 2y = 15 \\ 4x + 3y = -5 \end{cases}$ (1, −3)

4. $\begin{cases} 2x - 3y = 50 \\ 7x + 8y = -10 \end{cases}$ (10, −10)

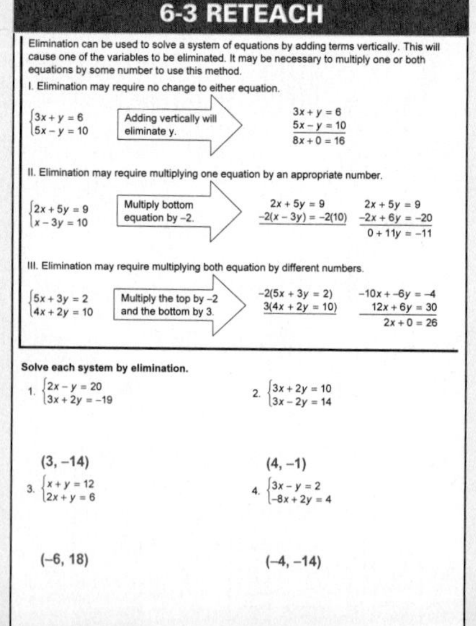

6-3 RETEACH

Elimination can be used to solve a system of equations by adding terms vertically. This will cause one of the variables to be eliminated. It may be necessary to multiply one or both equations by some number to use this method.

I. Elimination may require no change to either equation.

$\begin{cases} 3x + y = 6 \\ 5x - y = 10 \end{cases}$ → Adding vertically will eliminate *y*. → $3x + y = 6$; $5x - y = 10$; $8x + 0 = 16$

II. Elimination may require multiplying one equation by an appropriate number.

$\begin{cases} 2x + 5y = 9 \\ x - 3y = 10 \end{cases}$ → Multiply bottom equation by −2. → $2x + 5y = 9$; $-2(x - 3y) = -2(10)$ → $2x + 5y = 9$; $-2x + 6y = -20$; $0 + 11y = -11$

III. Elimination may require multiplying both equation by different numbers.

$\begin{cases} 5x + 3y = 2 \\ 4x + 2y = 10 \end{cases}$ → Multiply the top by −2 and the bottom by 3. → $-2(5x + 3y = 2)$; $3(4x + 2y = 10)$ → $-10x - 6y = -4$; $12x + 6y = 30$; $2x + 0 = 26$

Solve each system by elimination.

1. $\begin{cases} 2x - y = 20 \\ 3x + 2y = -19 \end{cases}$ (3, −14)

2. $\begin{cases} 3x + 2y = 10 \\ 3x - 2y = 14 \end{cases}$ (4, −1)

3. $\begin{cases} x + y = 12 \\ 2x + y = 6 \end{cases}$ (−6, 18)

4. $\begin{cases} 3x - y = 2 \\ -8x + 2y = 4 \end{cases}$ (−4, −14)

32. **Write About It** Solve the system $\begin{cases} 3x + y = 1 \\ 2x + 4y = -6 \end{cases}$. Explain how you can check your solution algebraically and graphically.

TEST PREP

33. A math test has 25 problems. Some are worth 2 points, and some are worth 3 points. The test is worth 60 points total. Which system can be used to determine the number of 2-point problems and the number of 3-point problems on the test?

    (A) $\begin{cases} x + y = 25 \\ 2x + 3y = 60 \end{cases}$ (B) $\begin{cases} x + y = 60 \\ 2x + 3y = 25 \end{cases}$ (C) $\begin{cases} x - y = 25 \\ 2x + 3y = 60 \end{cases}$ (D) $\begin{cases} x - y = 60 \\ 2x - 3y = 25 \end{cases}$

34. An electrician charges $15 plus $11 per hour. Another electrician charges $10 plus $15 per hour. For what amount of time will the cost be the same? What is that cost?

    (F) 1 hour; $25 (H) $1\frac{1}{2}$ hours; $30

    (G) $1\frac{1}{4}$ hours; $28.75 (J) $1\frac{3}{4}$ hours; $32.50

35. **Short Response** Three hundred fifty-eight tickets to the school basketball game on Friday were sold. Student tickets were $1.50, and nonstudent tickets were $3.25. The school made $752.25.

    a. Write a system of linear equations that could be used to determine how many student and how many nonstudent tickets were sold. Define the variables you use.

    35a. Let s = the number of student tickets sold. Let n = the number of nonstudent tickets sold; $\begin{cases} s + n = 358 \\ 1.50s + 3.25n = 752.25 \end{cases}$

    b. Solve the system you wrote in part **a.** How many student and how many nonstudent tickets were sold? **$s = 235$; $n = 123$; 235 student tickets, 123 nonstudent tickets**

CHALLENGE AND EXTEND

Solve each system by any method.

36. $\begin{cases} x + 16\frac{1}{2} = -\frac{3}{4}y \\ y = \frac{1}{2}x \end{cases}$ **$x = -12$; $y = -6$**

37. $\begin{cases} 2x + y + z = 17 \\ \frac{1}{2}z = 5 \\ x - y = 5 \end{cases}$ **$x = 4$; $y = -1$; $z = 10$**

38. $\begin{cases} x - 2y - z = -1 \\ -x + 2y + 4z = -11 \\ 2x + y + z = 1 \end{cases}$ **$x = 1$; $y = 3$; $z = -4$**

39. The sum of the digits of a two-digit number is 5. If the number is multiplied by 3, the result is 42. Write and solve a system of equations to find the number. (*Hint:* One equation involves the digits in the number. The other equation involves the values of the digits.) **$\begin{cases} x + y = 5 \\ 3(10x + y) = 42 \end{cases}$; $x = 1$; $y = 4$; the number is 14.**

SPIRAL REVIEW

Determine a relationship between the *x*- and *y*-values. Write an equation. *(Lesson 4-3)*

40.

x	1	2	3	4
y	6	7	8	9

$y = x + 5$

41.

x	1	2	3	4
y	3	6	9	12

$y = 3x$

42.

x	1	2	3	4
y	−9	−8	−7	−6

$y = x - 10$

Tell whether each equation is a direct variation. If so, identify the constant of variation. *(Lesson 5-6)*

43. $x = 2y$ **yes; $\frac{1}{2}$**

44. $y = -6x$ **yes; −6**

45. $y - 1 = x$ **no**

Solve each system by substitution. *(Lesson 6-2)*

46. $\begin{cases} y = x - 1 \\ x + y = 10 \end{cases}$ **(5.5, 4.5)**

47. $\begin{cases} x = y - 5 \\ 2x + 1 = y \end{cases}$ **(4, 9)**

48. $\begin{cases} y = 2x - 1 \\ x - y = 3 \end{cases}$ **(−2, −5)**

TEST PREP DOCTOR Students who chose **B** or **D** for **Exercise 33** may not have understood how to organize the information. Suggest that students use a table to organize the information into number of problems and number of points.

Answers

32. (1, −2); possible answer: to check the solution algebraically, substitute 1 for *x* and −2 for *y* in both equations. If both equations are true statements, the solution is correct. To check the solution graphically, graph both equations on the same coordinate plane and locate their intersection. If the intersection is (1, −2) then the solution is correct.

Journal

Have students write about which method for solving a system of equations they find the easiest.

ALTERNATIVE ASSESSMENT

Have students write a real-world situation that can be modeled by $\begin{cases} 4x + 8y = 100 \\ x + y = 15 \end{cases}$. Then have them solve the system and tell what the solution means in the context of their problem.

Power Presentations with PowerPoint®

6-3 Lesson Quiz

Solve each system by elimination.

1. $\begin{cases} 2x + y = 25 \\ 3y = 2x - 13 \end{cases}$ (11, 3)
2. $\begin{cases} -3x + 4y = -18 \\ x = -2y - 4 \end{cases}$ (2, −3)
3. $\begin{cases} -2x + 3y = -15 \\ 3x + 2y = -23 \end{cases}$ (−3, −7)
4. Harlan has $44 to buy 7 pairs of socks. Athletic socks cost $5 per pair. Dress socks cost $8 per pair. How many pairs of each can Harlan buy? 4 pairs of athletic socks and 3 pairs of dress socks

Also available on transparency

6-3 PROBLEM SOLVING

Write the correct answer.

1. Mr. Nguyen bought a package of 3 chicken legs and a package of 7 chicken wings. Ms. Dawes bought a package of 3 chicken legs and a package of 6 chicken wings. Mr. Nguyen bought 45 ounces of chicken. Ms. Dawes bought 42 ounces of chicken. How much did each chicken leg and each chicken wing weigh?
   chicken leg 8 oz., chicken wing 3 oz.
2. Jayce bought 2 bath towels and returned 3 hand towels. His sister Jayna bought 3 bath towels and 3 hand towels. Jayce's bill was $5. Jayna's bill was $45. What are the prices of a bath towel and a hand towel?
   bath towel $10, hand towel $5
3. The Lees spent $31 on movie tickets for 2 adults and 3 children. The Macias spent $26 on movie tickets for 2 adults and 2 children. What are the prices for adult and child movie tickets?
   adult ticket $8, child ticket $5
4. Last month Stephanie spent $57 on 4 allergy shots and 1 office visit. This month she spent $9 after 1 office visit and a refund for 2 allergy shots from her insurance company. How much does an office visit cost? an allergy shot?
   office visit $25, allergy shot $8

Use the chart below to answer questions 5–6. Select the best answer. The chart shows the price per pound for dried fruit.

Dried Fruit Price List			
Pineapple	Apple	Mango	Papaya
$7.50/lb	$7.00/lb	$8.00/lb	$7.25/lb

5. A customer bought 5 pounds of mango and papaya for $37.75. How many pounds of each fruit did the customer buy?
   A 2 lbs mango and 3 lbs papaya
   B 3 lbs mango and 2 lbs papaya
   C 1 lb mango and 4 lbs papaya
   D 4 lbs mango and 1 lb papaya
6. A store employee made two gift baskets of dried fruit, each costing $100. The first basket had 12 pounds of fruit x and 2 pounds of fruit y. The second basket had 4 pounds of fruit x and 9 pounds of fruit y. Which two fruits did the employee use in the baskets?
   F pineapple and apple
   G apple and mango
   H mango and papaya
   J papaya and pineapple

6-3 CHALLENGE

The elimination method can also be used for a system of three equations in three unknowns.

Three camp leaders purchased equipment for a camping trip.
Max bought 10 sleeping bags, 2 tents, and 1 can of bug repellant for $885.
Carlos bought 5 sleeping bags, 4 tents, and 1 can of bug repellant for $865.
Amy bought 9 sleeping bags, 6 tents, and 6 cans of bug repellant for $1410.
If they made their purchases at the same store, how much did each item cost?

1. Write the 3 equations: $\begin{cases} 10x + 2y + z = 885 \\ 5x + 4y + z = 865 \\ 9x + 6y + 6z = 1410 \end{cases}$
2. Subtract the second equation from the first. $5x - 2y = 20$
3. Multiply the second equation by −6 and add the second and third equations. $-21x - 18y = -3780$
4. The equations in steps 2 and 3 form a linear system in two variables. Solve this system for *x*. $x = 60$
5. Substitute the value of *x* into the first two equations. Write the resulting system. $\begin{cases} 2y + z = 285 \\ 4y + z = 565 \end{cases}$
6. Solve the system in problem 5 for *y* and *z*. $y = 140, z = 5$
7. Write the cost of each item. **sleeping bags: $60; tents: $140; bug repellant: $5**

Organizer

Pacing:
Traditional 1 day
Block $\frac{1}{2}$ day

Objective: Apply solving systems of equations to number theory puzzles.

Online Edition

Countdown Week 14

Teach

Remember

Students review and apply number theory concepts to solve classic puzzle problems.

Reading Math
Recommend to students that they start their solution by creating a "dictionary" to identify the variables they are using for the system. If they get confused, they have a reference.

Solving Classic Problems

You can use systems of linear equations to solve some "classic" math problems that are common in textbooks and puzzle books.

Example 1

Yuri is twice as old as Zack. Four years from now, the sum of their ages will be 23. How old is Yuri?

Step 1 Write a system. Let y represent Yuri's age. Let z represent Zack's age.

Yuri is twice as old as Zack.

$$y = 2z$$

In 4 years, the sum of their ages will be 23.

$$(y + 4) + (z + 4) = 23$$
$$y + z + 8 = 23$$
$$y + z = 15$$

Step 2 Solve the equations for y.

$$\begin{cases} y = 2z \\ y + z = 15 \end{cases} \rightarrow \begin{cases} y = 2z \\ y = -z + 15 \end{cases}$$

Step 3 Graph $y = 2z$ and $y = -z + 15$.

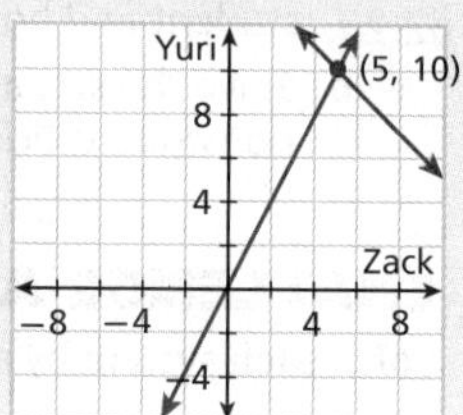

The lines appear to intersect at (5, 10).

The solution (5, 10) means that Yuri is 10 years old.

Example 2

Mandy has 11 coins in dimes and quarters. The value of her coins is $2.15. How many dimes does she have?

Step 1 Write a system. Let d be the number of dimes. Let q be the number of quarters.

The total number of coins is 11.

$$q + d = 11$$

The value of the coins is $2.15.

$$0.25q + 0.10d = 2.15$$
$$100(0.25q + 0.10d = 2.15)$$
$$25q + 10d = 215$$
$$5q + 2d = 43$$

Step 2 Solve the first equation for d.

$$d = 11 - q$$

Step 3 Substitute $11 - q$ for d in the second equation.

$$5q + 2(11 - q) = 43$$
$$3q + 22 = 43 \quad \textit{Distribute 2 and then combine like terms.}$$
$$3q = 21$$
$$q = 7 \quad \textit{Solve for q.}$$

State Resources

go.hrw.com
State Resources Online
KEYWORD: MA7 Resources

Step 4 Substitute 7 for q in one of the original equations.

$q + d = 11$

$7 + d = 11$

$d = 4$

The solution (4, 7) means that there are 4 dimes and 7 quarters. Mandy has 4 dimes.

Example 3

When the digits of a two-digit number are reversed, the new number is 45 less than the original number. The sum of the digits is 7. What is the original number?

Step 1 Write expressions for the original number and the new number. Let a represent the tens digit. Let b represent the ones digit.

The original number: $10a + b$

The new number: $10b + a$

Step 2 Write a system.

The new number is 45 less than the original number.

$10b + a = (10a + b) - 45$

$9b - 9a = -45$

$b - a = -5 \rightarrow a - b = 5$

The sum of the digits is 7.

$a + b = 7$

Step 3 Add the equations to eliminate b. Solve for a.

$$\begin{aligned} a - b &= 5 \\ +(a + b &= 7) \\ \hline 2a &= 12 \\ a &= 6 \end{aligned}$$

Step 4 Substitute 6 for a in one of the original equations.

$a + b = 7$

$6 + b = 7$

$b = 1$

The solution is (6, 1). This means that 6 is the tens digit and 1 is the ones digit. The original number is 61.

Check Check your solution using the original problem.
The sum of the digits is 7: $6 + 1 = 7$ ✓
When the digits are reversed, the new number is 45 less than the original number: $16 = 61 - 45$ ✓

Try This

1. The sum of the digits of a two-digit number is 17. When the digits are reversed, the new number is 9 more than the original number. What is the original number? **89**
2. Vic has 14 coins in nickels and quarters. The value of his coins is \$1.70. How many quarters does he have? **5 quarters**
3. Grace is 8 years older than her brother Sam. The sum of their ages is 24. How old is Grace? **16 yr old**

Some students may forget to answer the question in the problem after solving the system of equations. Tell students that the solution to the system may not be the final answer, and remind them to make sure they answer the question in the problem.

Inclusion It may be beneficial to have students practice writing systems of linear equations to model the scenarios in the *Try This* problems.

Close

Assess

Have students figure out the original number in **Example 3** if the new number is 27 more than the original. 25

6-4 Organizer

Pacing: Traditional 1 day
Block $\frac{1}{2}$ day

Objectives: Solve special systems of linear equations in two variables.

Classify systems of linear equations and determine the number of solutions.

Algebra Lab
In *Algebra Lab Activities*

Online Edition
Tutorial Videos

Countdown Week 14

Power Presentations with PowerPoint®

Warm Up

Solve each equation.

1. $2x + 3 = 2x + 4$ no solution
2. $2(x + 1) = 2x + 2$ infinitely many solutions
3. Solve $2y - 6x = 10$ for y. $y = 3x + 5$

Solve by using any method.

4. $\begin{cases} y = 3x + 2 \\ 2x + y = 7 \end{cases}$ $(1, 5)$
5. $\begin{cases} x - y = 8 \\ x + y = 4 \end{cases}$ $(6, -2)$

Also available on transparency

Math Fact !!

The solution set of an inconsistent system is the empty, or null, set, and can be symbolized with ∅ or { }.

6-4 Solving Special Systems

Objectives
Solve special systems of linear equations in two variables.

Classify systems of linear equations and determine the number of solutions.

Vocabulary
consistent system
inconsistent system
independent system
dependent system

Why learn this?
Linear systems can be used to analyze business growth, such as comic book sales. (See Example 4.)

In Lesson 6-1, you saw that when two lines intersect at a point, there is exactly one solution to the system. A system with at least one solution is a **consistent system**.

When the two lines in a system do not intersect, they are parallel lines. There are no ordered pairs that satisfy both equations, so there is no solution. A system that has no solution is an **inconsistent system**.

EXAMPLE 1 Systems with No Solution

Show that $\begin{cases} y = x - 1 \\ -x + y = 2 \end{cases}$ has no solution.

Method 1 Compare slopes and y-intercepts.

$y = x - 1 \rightarrow y = 1x - 1$ *Write both equations in slope-intercept form.*
$-x + y = 2 \rightarrow y = 1x + 2$ *The lines are parallel because they have the same slope and different y-intercepts.*

This system has no solution.

Method 2 Graph the system.
The lines are parallel.

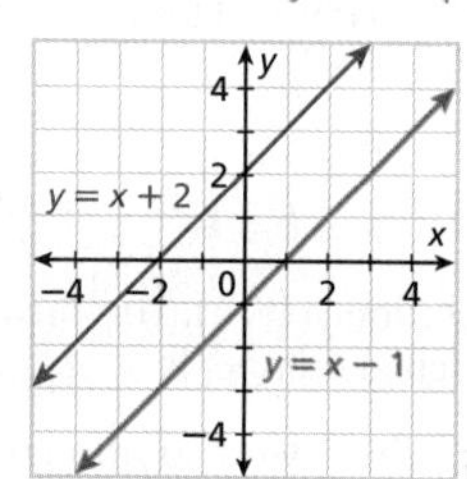

This system has no solution.

Method 3 Solve the system algebraically. Use the substitution method.

$-x + (x - 1) = 2$ *Substitute x − 1 for y in the second equation, and solve.*
$-1 = 2$ ✗ *False*

This system has no solution.

1. Possible answer: substitute $-2x + 5$ for y in the second equation.
$2x + (-2x + 5) = 1$
$5 = 1$ ✗

CHECK IT OUT! 1. Show that $\begin{cases} y = -2x + 5 \\ 2x + y = 1 \end{cases}$ has no solution.

State Resources

1 Introduce

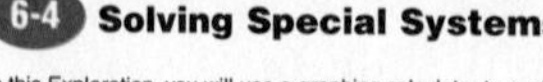

6-4 Solving Special Systems

In this Exploration, you will use a graphing calculator to explore this system of equations: $\begin{cases} y = -\frac{1}{2}x + 3 \\ x + 2y = -4 \end{cases}$.

1. Enter the equations in your calculator as **Y1** and **Y2**. Remember that you must first write each equation in the form $y = \ldots$.
2. Press [2nd] [GRAPH] to view a table of values for the equations.
3. Use the arrow keys to scroll up and down the table. Look for a solution of the system of equations by looking for a value of x for which the two y-values are equal. What do you notice?
4. Press [GRAPH] to view a graph of the functions. What do you notice about the graphs?

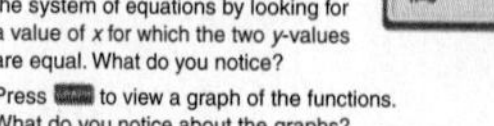

THINK AND DISCUSS

5. **Describe** what happens when you try to solve this system of equations algebraically (by substitution or by elimination).
6. **Explain** why some systems of equations do not have a solution.

Motivate

Review with students equations that have no solution, such as $x + 1 = x + 2$, and equations for which all real numbers are solutions, such as $2(x + 1) = 2x + 2$. Tell students that in this lesson, they will learn about systems of equations that either have no solution or infinitely many solutions.

Explorations and answers are provided in *Alternate Openers: Explorations Transparencies.*

If two linear equations in a system have the same graph, the graphs are coincident lines, or the same line. There are infinitely many solutions of the system because every point on the line represents a solution of both equations.

EXAMPLE 2 Systems with Infinitely Many Solutions

Show that $\begin{cases} y = 2x + 1 \\ 2x - y + 1 = 0 \end{cases}$ has infinitely many solutions.

Method 1 Compare slopes and y-intercepts.

$$y = 2x + 1 \rightarrow y = 2x + 1$$
$$2x - y + 1 = 0 \rightarrow y = 2x + 1$$

Write both equations in slope-intercept form. The lines have the same slope and the same y-intercept.

If this system were graphed, the graphs would be the same line. There are infinitely many solutions.

Method 2 Solve the system algebraically. Use the elimination method.

$$y = 2x + 1 \rightarrow -2x + y = 1$$ *Write equations to line up like terms.*

$$2x - y + 1 = 0 \rightarrow \underline{+2x - y = -1}$$ *Add the equations.*

$$0 = 0 \checkmark$$ *True. The equation is an identity.*

There are infinitely many solutions.

Caution!

$0 = 0$ is a true statement. It does not mean the system has zero solutions or no solution.

2. Show that $\begin{cases} y = x - 3 \\ x - y - 3 = 0 \end{cases}$ has infinitely many solutions.

2. Possible answer: substitute $x - 3$ for y in the second equation.

$$x - (x - 3) - 3 = 0$$
$$3 - 3 = 0$$
$$0 = 0 \checkmark$$

Consistent systems can either be independent or dependent.

- An **independent system** has exactly one solution. The graph of an independent system consists of two intersecting lines.
- A **dependent system** has infinitely many solutions. The graph of a dependent system consists of two coincident lines.

Classification of Systems of Linear Equations

CLASSIFICATION	CONSISTENT AND INDEPENDENT	CONSISTENT AND DEPENDENT	INCONSISTENT
Number of Solutions	Exactly one	Infinitely many	None
Description	Different slopes	Same slope, same y-intercept	Same slope, different y-intercepts
Graph	Intersecting lines	Coincident lines	Parallel lines

COMMON ERROR ALERT

Students might think that *infinitely many solutions* means that all ordered pairs are solutions. Remind them that the solutions are the infinite number of ordered pairs that make up the line.

Power Presentations with PowerPoint®

Additional Examples

Example 1

Show that $\begin{cases} y = x - 4 \\ -x + y = 3 \end{cases}$ has no solution.

Possible answer: Compare slopes and intercepts.

$y = x - 4$
$y = x + 3$

The lines have the same slope and diff. y-intercepts, so they are parallel.

Example 2

Show that $\begin{cases} y = 3x + 2 \\ 3x - y + 2 = 0 \end{cases}$ has infinitely many solutions.

Possible answer: Substitute $3x + 2$ for y in the second equation.

$3x - (3x + 2) + 2 = 0$
$0 = 0 \checkmark$

INTERVENTION

Questioning Strategies

EXAMPLE 1

- What is true about the graph of a system that is a false statement when it is solved algebraically?

EXAMPLE 2

- What is true about the graph of a system that is an identity when it is solved algebraically?

2 Teach

Guided Instruction

After introducing students to inconsistent systems in **Example 1** and consistent systems in **Example 2,** have students practice classifying systems. Be sure to make connections between the multiple representations of each type of system, as shown in the table on page 421.

Reaching All Learners

Through Auditory Cues

Have students work in pairs. One student describes either the graph, solution, or classification for a type of system. The other student gives the other two descriptions.

Graph	Solutions	Classification
Intersecting lines	Exactly one	Consistent, independent
Same line	Infinitely many	Consistent, dependent
Parallel lines	None	Inconsistent

Power Presentations with PowerPoint®

Additional Examples

Example 3

Classify each system. Give the number of solutions.

A. $\begin{cases} 3y = x + 3 \\ -\frac{1}{3}x + y = 1 \end{cases}$ consistent and dependent; infinitely many solutions

B. $\begin{cases} x + y = 5 \\ 4 + y = -x \end{cases}$ inconsistent; no solution

C. $\begin{cases} y = 4(x + 1) \\ y - 3 = x \end{cases}$ consistent and independent; one solution

Example 4

Jared and David both started a savings account in January. If the pattern of savings in the table continues, when will the amount in Jared's account equal the amount in David's account?

	Jan	Feb	Mar	Apr	May
Jared	25	30	35	40	45
David	40	45	50	55	60

The amount in Jared's account will never equal the amount in David's account.

INTERVENTION

Questioning Strategies

EXAMPLE 3

- How are independent and dependent systems different?
- How are consistent and inconsistent systems different?
- Is it possible for a dependent system to be inconsistent?

EXAMPLE 4

- Why are the values in the first column of the table equal to the constants in the equations?
- How do you determine the rate from the table?
- What would the graph of the system look like?

Multiple Representations Encourage students to check their solutions in **Example 3** by graphing.

EXAMPLE 3 Classifying Systems of Linear Equations

Classify each system. Give the number of solutions.

A $\begin{cases} 2y = x + 2 \\ -\frac{1}{2}x + y = 1 \end{cases}$

$2y = x + 2 \rightarrow y = \frac{1}{2}x + 1$ *Write both equations in slope-intercept form.*

$-\frac{1}{2}x + y = 1 \rightarrow y = \frac{1}{2}x + 1$ *The lines have the same slope and the same y-intercepts. They are the same.*

The system is consistent and dependent. It has infinitely many solutions.

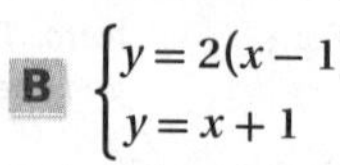

B $\begin{cases} y = 2(x - 1) \\ y = x + 1 \end{cases}$

$y = 2(x - 1) \rightarrow y = 2x - 2$ *Write both equations in slope-intercept form.*

$y = x + 1 \rightarrow y = 1x + 1$ *The lines have different slopes. They intersect.*

The system is consistent and independent. It has one solution.

3a. consistent, dependent; infinitely many solutions

3b. consistent, independent; one solution

3c. inconsistent; no solution

CHECK IT OUT! Classify each system. Give the number of solutions.

3a. $\begin{cases} x + 2y = -4 \\ -2(y + 2) = x \end{cases}$ **3b.** $\begin{cases} y = -2(x - 1) \\ y = -x + 3 \end{cases}$ **3c.** $\begin{cases} 2x - 3y = 6 \\ y = \frac{2}{3}x \end{cases}$

EXAMPLE 4 *Business Application*

The sales manager at Comics Now is comparing its sales with the sales of its competitor, Dynamo Comics. If the sales patterns continue, will the sales for Comics Now ever equal the sales for Dynamo Comics? Explain.

Comic Books Sold per Year (thousands) POW!

	2005	2006	2007	2008
Comics Now	130	170	210	250
Dynamo Comics	180	220	260	300

Use the table to write a system of linear equations. Let y represent the sales total and x represent the number of years since 2005.

	Sales total	equals	increase in sales per year	times	years	plus	beginning sales.
Comics Now	y	=	40	•	x	+	130
Dynamo Comics	y	=	40	•	x	+	180

Helpful Hint

The increase in sales is the difference between sales each year.

$\begin{cases} y = 40x + 130 \\ y = 40x + 180 \end{cases}$

$y = 40x + 130$ *Both equations are in slope-intercept form.*

$y = 40x + 180$ *The lines have the same slope, but different y-intercepts.*

The graphs of the two equations are parallel lines, so there is no solution. If the patterns continue, sales for the two companies will never be equal.

4. Yes; the graphs of the two equations have different slopes so they intersect.

CHECK IT OUT! **4.** Matt has \$100 in a checking account and deposits \$20 per month. Ben has \$80 in a checking account and deposits \$30 per month. Will the accounts ever have the same balance? Explain.

3 Close

Summarize

Give students the system $\begin{cases} y = 3x + 8 \\ \square y = \square x + \square \end{cases}$.

Have them replace the boxes with numbers so that the system has

Possible answers given:

- one solution. 1, 2, 1
- infinitely many solutions. 2, 6, 16
- no solutions. 1, 3, 5

ONGOING ASSESSMENT and INTERVENTION

***Diagnose Before* the Lesson**
6-4 Warm Up, TE p. 420

***Monitor During* the Lesson**
Check It Out! Exercises, SE pp. 420–422
Questioning Strategies, TE pp. 421–422

***Assess After* the Lesson**
6-4 Lesson Quiz, TE p. 425
Alternative Assessment, TE p. 425

THINK AND DISCUSS

1. What methods can be used to determine the number of solutions of a system of linear equations?

2. **GET ORGANIZED** Copy and complete the graphic organizer. In each box, write the word or words that describes a system with that number of solutions and sketch a graph.

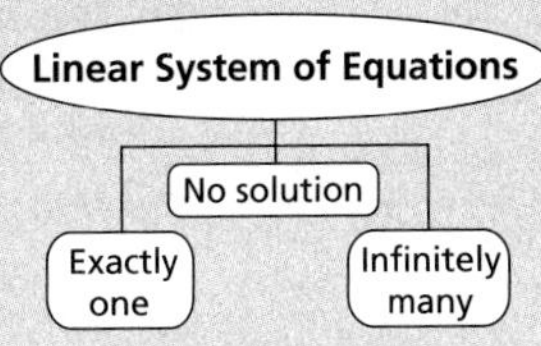

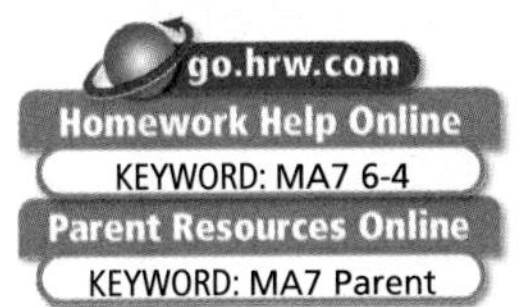

Answers to *Think and Discuss*

1. solving algebraically by substitution or elimination, comparing slopes and y-intercepts, or graphing
2. See p. A6.

6-4 Exercises

go.hrw.com
Homework Help Online
KEYWORD: MA7 6-4
Parent Resources Online
KEYWORD: MA7 Parent

GUIDED PRACTICE

1. **Vocabulary** A ___?___ system can be independent or dependent. (*consistent* or *inconsistent*) **consistent**

SEE EXAMPLE 1 p. 420

Show that each system has no solution.

2. $\begin{cases} y = x + 1 \\ -x + y = 3 \end{cases}$
3. $\begin{cases} 3x + y = 6 \\ y = -3x + 2 \end{cases}$
4. $\begin{cases} -y = 4x + 1 \\ 4x + y = 2 \end{cases}$

SEE EXAMPLE 2 p. 421

Show that each system has infinitely many solutions.

5. $\begin{cases} y = -x + 3 \\ x + y - 3 = 0 \end{cases}$
6. $\begin{cases} y = 2x - 4 \\ 2x - y - 4 = 0 \end{cases}$
7. $\begin{cases} -7x + y = -2 \\ 7x - y = 2 \end{cases}$

SEE EXAMPLE 3 p. 422

Classify each system. Give the number of solutions.

8. $\begin{cases} y = 2x + 3 \\ -2y = 2x + 6 \end{cases}$
9. $\begin{cases} y = -3x - 1 \\ 3x + y = 1 \end{cases}$
10. $\begin{cases} 9y = 3x + 18 \\ \frac{1}{3}x - y = -2 \end{cases}$

SEE EXAMPLE 4 p. 422

11. **Athletics** Micah walks on a treadmill at 4 miles per hour. He has walked 2 miles when Luke starts running at 6 miles per hour on the treadmill next to him. If their rates continue, will Luke's distance ever equal Micah's distance? Explain.
Yes; 1 hour after Luke begins, both boys will have covered 6 mi.

PRACTICE AND PROBLEM SOLVING

Show that each system has no solution.

12. $\begin{cases} y = 2x - 2 \\ -2x + y = 1 \end{cases}$
13. $\begin{cases} x + y = 3 \\ y = -x - 1 \end{cases}$
14. $\begin{cases} x + 2y = -4 \\ y = -\frac{1}{2}x - 4 \end{cases}$
15. $\begin{cases} -6 + y = 2x \\ y = 2x - 36 \end{cases}$

Show that each system has infinitely many solutions.

16. $\begin{cases} y = -2x + 3 \\ 2x + y - 3 = 0 \end{cases}$
17. $\begin{cases} y = x - 2 \\ x - y - 2 = 0 \end{cases}$
18. $\begin{cases} x + y = -4 \\ y = -x - 4 \end{cases}$
19. $\begin{cases} -9x - 3y = -18 \\ 3x + y = 6 \end{cases}$

6-4 Exercises

Assignment Guide

Assign *Guided Practice* exercises as necessary.

If you finished Examples **1–2**
Basic 12–19, 26, 31
Average 12–19, 24–32 even
Advanced 12–19, 25–29 odd

If you finished Examples **1–4**
Basic 12–23, 26, 30–31, 33–34, 37–44
Average 12–23, 24–32 even, 33–34, 37–44
Advanced 12–23, 29–44

Homework Quick Check
Quickly check key concepts.
Exercises: 16, 18, 22, 23, 28

Answers

2. Possible answer: Substitute $x + 1$ for y in the second equation.
$-x + (x + 1) = 3$
$1 = 3$ ✗

State Resources

Answers

3. Possible answer: Substitute $-3x + 2$ for y in the first equation.
$3x + (-3x + 2) = 6$
$2 = 6$ ✗

4. Possible answer: Compare slopes and intercepts.
$-y = 4x + 1 \rightarrow y = -4x - 1$
$4x + y = 2 \rightarrow y = -4x + 2$
The lines have the same slope and different y-intercepts. Therefore the lines are parallel.

5. Possible answer: Substitute $-x + 3$ for y in the second equation.
$x + (-x + 3) - 3 = 0$
$0 = 0$ ✓

6. Possible answer: Substitute $2x - 4$ for y in the second equation.
$2x - (2x - 4) - 4 = 0$
$4 - 4 = 0$
$0 = 0$ ✓

7. Possible answer: Add the two equations.
$-7x + y = -2$
$+\ 7x - y = 2$
$0 + 0 = 0$
$0 = 0$ ✓

8. cons., indep.; one sol.
9. inconsis.; no sol.
10. cons., dep.; inf. many solutions

12–19. See pp. A24–A25.

go.hrw.com
State Resources Online
KEYWORD: MA7 Resources

Teaching Tip **Critical Thinking** There are infinitely many answers to **Exercise 25.** Many students might choose \$4 for a DVD and \$1 for a video because that solution is easy to see. Encourage students to find decimal solutions, such as \$3.50 and \$2.

Teaching Tip **Visual** In dependent systems, such as in **Exercise 27,** have students substitute solutions of one equation into the other equation to show that the solutions of one equation are also solutions of the other.

MULTI-STEP TEST PREP **Exercise 30** involves writing and solving a system of equations to compare cost. This exercise prepares students for the Multi-Step Test Prep on page 426.

Answers

24. No; the graphs of the two equations are parallel lines, so there is no solution.
25. There are inf. many answers for the cost of each video game and DVD. The system is consis. and dep.

28b.

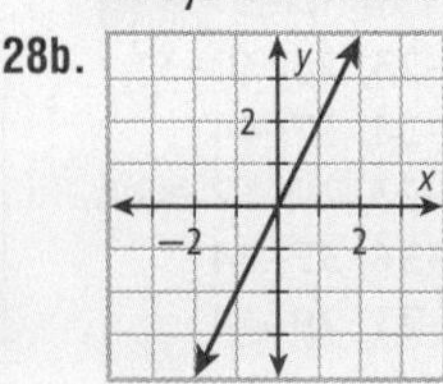

coincident lines

c. The equations are the same.
d. The graphs will now be 2 parallel lines. The equations have the same slope but different y-intercepts.

30. See p. A25.

Independent Practice

For Exercises	See Example
12–15	1
16–19	2
20–22	3
23	4

Extra Practice

Skills Practice p. S15
Application Practice p. S33

LINK Geology

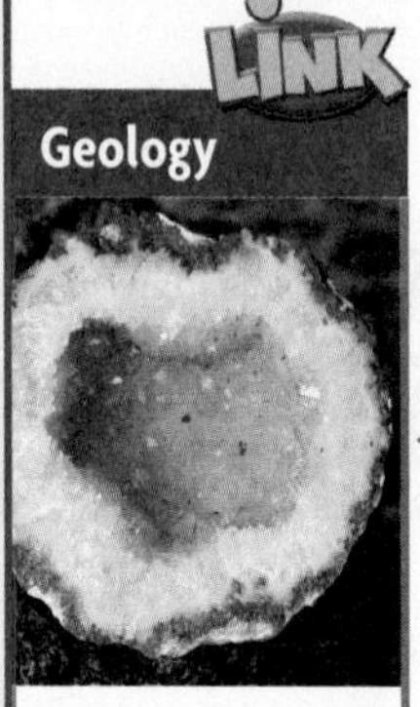

Geodes are rounded, hollow rock formations. Most are partially or completely filled with layers of colored quartz crystals. The world's largest geode was discovered in Spain in 2000. It is 26 feet long and 5.6 feet high.

Classify each system. Give the number of solutions.

20. $\begin{cases} y = -x + 5 \\ x + y = 5 \end{cases}$ **cons., dep.; inf. many solutions**

21. $\begin{cases} y = -3x + 2 \\ y = 3x \end{cases}$ **cons., indep.; one sol.**

22. $\begin{cases} y - 1 = 2x \\ y = 2x - 1 \end{cases}$ **inconsis.; no sol.**

23. **Sports** Mandy is skating at 5 miles per hour. Nikki is skating at 6 miles per hour and started 1 mile behind Mandy. If their rates stay the same, will Mandy catch up with Nikki? Explain. **Yes; the graphs of the two equations have different slopes, so they intersect.**

24. **Multi-Step** Photocopier A can print 35 copies per minute. Photocopier B can print 35 copies per minute. Copier B is started and makes 10 copies. Copier A is then started. If the copiers continue, will the number of copies from machine A ever equal the number of copies from machine B? Explain.

25. **Entertainment** One week Trey rented 4 DVDs and 2 video games for \$18. The next week he rented 2 DVDs and 1 video game for \$9. Find the rental costs for each video game and DVD. Explain your answer.

26. Rosa bought 1 pound of cashews and 2 pounds of peanuts for \$10. At the same store, Sabrina bought 2 pounds of cashews and 1 pound of peanuts for \$11. Find the cost per pound for cashews and peanuts. **cashews: \$4/lb; peanuts: \$3/lb**

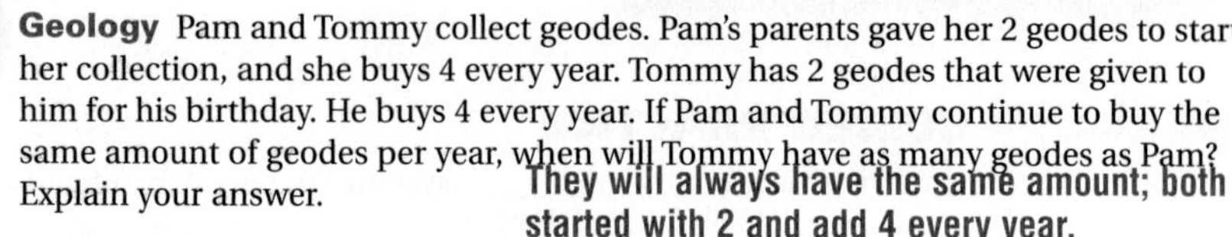

27. **Geology** Pam and Tommy collect geodes. Pam's parents gave her 2 geodes to start her collection, and she buys 4 every year. Tommy has 2 geodes that were given to him for his birthday. He buys 4 every year. If Pam and Tommy continue to buy the same amount of geodes per year, when will Tommy have as many geodes as Pam? Explain your answer. **They will always have the same amount; both started with 2 and add 4 every year.**

28. Use the data given in the tables.

x	3	4	5	6
y	6	8	10	12

x	12	13	14	15
y	24	26	28	30

a. Write an equation to describe the data in each table. **$y = 2x$; $y = 2x$**
b. Graph the system of equations from part **a.** Describe the graph.
c. How could you have predicted the graph by looking at the equations?
d. **What if...?** Each y-value in the second table increases by 1. How does this affect the graphs of the two equations? How can you tell how the graphs would be affected without actually graphing?

29. **Critical Thinking** Describe the graphs of two equations if the result of solving the system by substitution or elimination is the statement $1 = 3$. **The graph will be 2 parallel lines.**

MULTI-STEP TEST PREP

30. This problem will prepare you for the Multi-Step Test Prep on page 426.

The Crusader pep club is selling team buttons that support the sports teams. They contacted Buttons, Etc. which charges \$50 plus \$1.10 per button, and Logos, which charges \$40 plus \$1.10 per button.

a. Write an equation for each company's cost.
b. Use the system from part **a** to find when the price for both companies is the same. Explain.
c. What part of the equation should the pep club negotiate to change so that the cost of Buttons, Etc. is the same as Logos? What part of the equation should change in order to get a better price?

6-4 PRACTICE A
6-4 PRACTICE C
6-4 PRACTICE B

Solve each system of linear equations.

1. $\begin{cases} y = 2x - 3 \\ y - 2x = -3 \end{cases}$ **infinitely many solutions**

2. $\begin{cases} 3x + y = 4 \\ -3x = y - 7 \end{cases}$ **no solution**

3. $\begin{cases} y = -4x + 1 \\ 4x = -y - 6 \end{cases}$ **no solution**

4. $\begin{cases} y - x + 3 = 0 \\ x = y + 3 \end{cases}$ **infinitely many solutions**

Classify each system. Give the number of solutions.

5. $\begin{cases} y = 3(x - 1) \\ -y + 3x = 3 \end{cases}$ **consistent, dependent; infinitely many solutions**

6. $\begin{cases} y - 2x = 5 \\ x = y - 3 \end{cases}$ **consistent, independent; one solution**

7. Sabina and Lou are reading the same book. Sabina reads 12 pages a day. She had read 36 pages when Lou started the book, and Lou reads at a pace of 15 pages per day. If their reading rates continue, will Sabina and Lou ever be reading the same page on the same day? Explain. **Yes. The graphs of the two equations have different slopes. They will intersect.**

8. Brandon started jogging at 4 miles per hour. After he jogged 1 mile, his friend Anton started jogging along the same path at a pace of 4 miles per hour. If they continue to jog at the same rate, will Anton ever catch up with Brandon? Explain. **No. The graphs of the two equations are parallel lines. They will never intersect.**

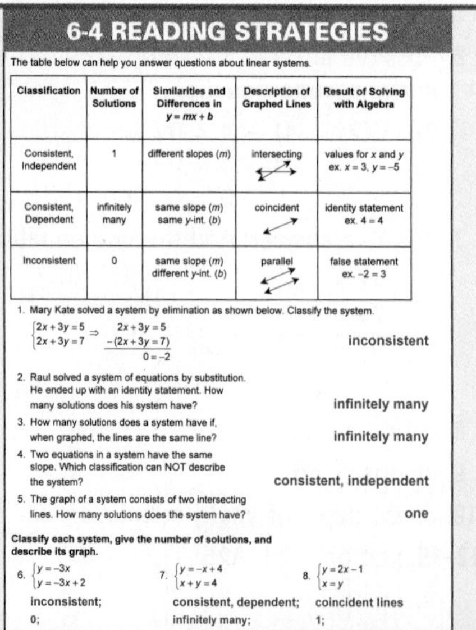

6-4 READING STRATEGIES

The table below can help you answer questions about linear systems.

Classification	Number of Solutions	Similarities and Differences in $y = mx + b$	Description of Graphed Lines	Result of Solving with Algebra
Consistent, Independent	1	different slopes (m)	intersecting	values for x and y ex. $x = 3$, $y = -5$
Consistent, Dependent	infinitely many	same slope (m) same y-int. (b)	coincident	identity statement ex. $4 = 4$
Inconsistent	0	same slope (m) different y-int. (b)	parallel	false statement ex. $-2 = 3$

1. Mary Kate solved a system by elimination as shown below. Classify the system.
$\begin{cases} 2x + 3y = 5 \\ 2x + 3y = 7 \end{cases} \Rightarrow \begin{array}{r} 2x + 3y = 5 \\ -(2x + 3y = 7) \\ \hline 0 = -2 \end{array}$ **inconsistent**
2. Raul solved a system of equations by substitution. He ended up with an identity statement. How many solutions does his system have? **infinitely many**
3. How many solutions does a system have if, when graphed, the lines are the same line? **infinitely many**
4. Two equations in a system have the same slope. Which classification can NOT describe the system? **consistent, independent**
5. The graph of a system consists of two intersecting lines. How many solutions does the system have? **one**

Classify each system, give the number of solutions, and describe its graph.

6. $\begin{cases} y = -3x \\ y = -3x + 2 \end{cases}$ **inconsistent; 0; parallel lines**

7. $\begin{cases} y = -x + 4 \\ x + y = 4 \end{cases}$ **consistent, dependent; infinitely many; coincident lines**

8. $\begin{cases} y = 2x - 1 \\ x = y \end{cases}$ **coincident lines 1; intersecting lines**

6-4 RETEACH

When solving equations in one variable, it is possible to have one solution, no solutions, or infinitely many solutions. The same results can occur when graphing systems of equations.

Solve $\begin{cases} 4x + 2y = 2 \\ 2x + y = 4 \end{cases}$.

Multiplying the second equation by -2 will eliminate the x-terms.

$4x + 2y = 2 \qquad 4x + 2y = 2$
$-2(2x + y = 4) \rightarrow \underline{-4x - 2y = -8}$
$0 + 0 = -6$
$0 = -6$ ×

The equation is a contradiction. **There is no solution.**

Solve $\begin{cases} y = 4 - 3x \\ 3x + y = 4 \end{cases}$.

Because the first equation is solved for a variable, use substitution.

$3x + y = 4$
$3x + (4 - 3x) = 4$ *Substitute* $4 - 3x$ *for* y
$0 + 4 = 4$
$4 = 4$ ✓

The equation is true for all values of x and y. **There are infinitely many solutions.**

Solve each system of linear equations algebraically.

1. $\begin{cases} y = 3x \\ 2y = 6x \end{cases}$ **infinitely many solutions**

2. $\begin{cases} y = 2x + 5 \\ y - 2x = 1 \end{cases}$ **no solution**

3. $\begin{cases} 3x - 2y = 9 \\ -6x + 4y = 1 \end{cases}$ **no solution**

31. **ERROR ANALYSIS** Student A says there is no solution to the graphed system of equations. Student B says there is one solution. Which student is incorrect? Explain the error.
Student A; the lines are not parallel, so they will intersect.

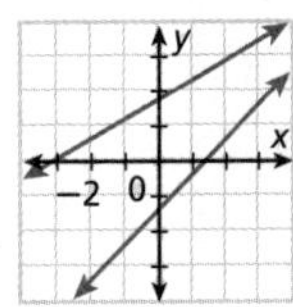

32. **Write About It** Compare the graph of a system that is consistent and independent with the graph of a system that is consistent and dependent.
The graph of a system that is consistent and independent shows 2 lines that intersect at 1 point. The graph of a system that is consistent and dependent shows only 1 line.

TEST PREP

33. Which of the following classifications fit the following system?

$$\begin{cases} 2x - y = 3 \\ 6x - 3y = 9 \end{cases}$$

Ⓐ Inconsistent and independent
Ⓑ Consistent and independent
Ⓒ Inconsistent and dependent
Ⓓ Consistent and dependent (circled)

34. Which of the following would be enough information to classify a system of two linear equations?

Ⓕ The graphs have the same slope.
Ⓖ The y-intercepts are the same.
Ⓗ The graphs have different slopes. (circled)
Ⓙ The y-intercepts are different.

CHALLENGE AND EXTEND

35. What conditions are necessary for the system $\begin{cases} y = 2x + p \\ y = 2x + q \end{cases}$ to have infinitely many solutions? no solution? **$p = q$; $p \neq q$**

36. Solve the systems in parts **a** and **b**. Use this information to make a conjecture about all solutions that exist for the system in part **c**.

a. $\begin{cases} 3x + 4y = 0 \\ 4x + 3y = 0 \end{cases}$ **(0, 0)**
b. $\begin{cases} 2x + 5y = 0 \\ 5x + 2y = 0 \end{cases}$ **(0, 0)**
c. $\begin{cases} ax + by = 0 \\ bx + ay = 0 \end{cases}$, for $a > 0$, $b > 0$, $a \neq b$ **(0, 0)**

SPIRAL REVIEW

Use the map to find the actual distances between each pair of cities. *(Lesson 2-7)*

37. from Hon to Averly **11 km**
38. from Averly to Lewers **6.25 km**

Scale
2 cm:5 km
Averly
4.4 cm
2.5 cm
Hon
Lewers
5 cm

Determine if each sequence appears to be an arithmetic sequence. If so, find the common difference and the next three terms. *(Lesson 4-6)*

39. 1, 3, 5, 9, … **no**
40. 1, 5, 9, 13, … **$d = 4$; 17, 21, 25**
41. $0, -1\frac{1}{2}, -3, -4\frac{1}{2}, \ldots$ **$d = -1\frac{1}{2}$; $-6, -7\frac{1}{2}, -9$**

Solve each system by graphing. *(Lesson 6-1)*

42. $\begin{cases} y = x - 2 \\ y = -x + 4 \end{cases}$ **(3, 1)**
43. $\begin{cases} y = 2x \\ x + y = -6 \end{cases}$ **(−2, −4)**
44. $\begin{cases} y = -\frac{1}{2}x \\ y - x = 9 \end{cases}$ **(−6, 3)**

TEST PREP DOCTOR In **Exercise 33,** students can eliminate choices **A** and **C** because inconsistent systems are not classified as independent or dependent.

For **Exercise 33,** suggest that students think of the graphs of each answer.

Journal

Have students explain how they can determine the number of solutions of a system of equations by comparing them by writing the equations in slope-intercept form and comparing m and b.

ALTERNATIVE ASSESSMENT

Have students work in pairs to make a poster that describes and classifies all three types of systems of equations. Have them include the result of solving each type algebraically.

Power Presentations with PowerPoint®

6-4 Lesson Quiz

Solve and classify each system.

1. $\begin{cases} y = 5x - 1 \\ 5x - y - 1 = 0 \end{cases}$ infinitely many solutions; consistent, dependent

2. $\begin{cases} y = 4 + x \\ -x + y = 1 \end{cases}$ no solution; inconsistent

3. $\begin{cases} y = 3(x + 1) \\ y = x - 2 \end{cases}$ $\left(-\frac{5}{2}, -\frac{9}{2}\right)$; consistent, independent

4. If the pattern in the table continues, when will sales for Hats Off equal sales for Tops? never

Hat Sales (thousands)

Year	2004	2005	2006	2007
Hats Off	6.2	8	9.8	11.6
Tops	3.5	5.3	7.1	8.9

Also available on transparency

6-4 PROBLEM SOLVING

Write the correct answer.

1. Tyra and Charmian are training for a bike race. Tyra has logged 256 miles so far and rides 48 miles per week. Charmian has logged 125 miles so far and rides 48 miles per week. If these rates continue, will Tyra's distance ever equal Charmian's distance? Explain.
No; the graphs are parallel lines so there is no solution.

2. Metroplexpress and Local Express are courier companies. Metroplexpress charges \$15 to pick up a package and \$0.50 per mile. Local Express charges \$10 to pick up a package and \$0.55 per mile. Classify this system and find its solution, if any.
consistent and independent; 100 mi and \$65

3. The Singhs start savings accounts for their twin boys. The accounts earn 5% annual interest. The initial deposit in each account is \$200. Classify this system and find its solution, if any.
consistent and dependent; infinitely many solutions

4. Frank earns \$8 per hour. Madison earns \$7.50 per hour. Frank started working after Madison had already earned \$300. If these rates continue, will Frank's earnings ever equal Madison's earnings? If so, when?
Yes; at 600 hours.

Select the best answer.

5. A studio apartment at The Oaks costs \$400 per month plus a \$350 deposit. A studio apartment at Crossroads costs \$400 per month plus a \$300 deposit. How many solutions does this system have?
A no solutions
B 1 solution
C 2 solutions
D an infinite number of solutions

6. Jane and Gary are both landscape designers. Jane charges \$75 for a consultation plus \$25 per hour. Gary charges \$50 for a consultation plus \$30 per hour. For how many hours will Jane's charges equal Gary's charges?
F never
G after 2 hours
H after 5 hours
J always

7. A tank filled with 75 liters of water loses 0.5 liter of water per hour. A tank filled with 50 liters of water loses 0.1 liter of water per hour. How would this system be classified?
A inconsistent
B dependent
C consistent and independent
D consistent and dependent

8. Simon is 3 years older than Renata. Five years ago, Renata was half as old as Simon is now. How old are Simon and Renata now?
F Simon is 13 and Renata is 10.
G Simon is 15 and Renata is 10.
H Simon is 16 and Renata is 8.
J Simon is 16 and Renata is 13.

6-4 CHALLENGE

The puzzle below contains 23 linear equations. You goal is to find paths through the puzzle such that each pair of equations along your path forms a special type of system.

You must begin in the **Start** square, and end in the **Finish** square. Moves can be horizontal, vertical, or diagonal between adjacent squares. Each individual path cannot cross itself, but your answers to 1 and 2 might cross.

	1	2	3	4
Start → ↓ ↘	$y = x + 2$	$3x = 3y - 6$	$3x + y = -1$	$8y = 8x + 16$
5	6	7	8	9
$y = 2x + 3$	$y = 3x - 1$	$y - x = 2$	$\frac{1}{3}x + \frac{1}{3}y = 1$	$3x = y + 1$
10	11	12	13	14
$2y = 6x + 6$	$2x - y = -3$	$2x + 2y = 4$	$2y - 4 = 2x$	$x - y = -2$
15	16	17	18	19
$\frac{1}{2}y = \frac{3}{2}x + \frac{1}{2}$	$3y = 2x + 1$	$3x - y = 4$	$\frac{1}{6}y = \frac{1}{3}x + \frac{1}{2}$	$\frac{1}{2}y = \frac{1}{2}x + 1$
20	21	22	23	
$10x + 15y = 5$	$-12x + 4y 5 8$	$\frac{1}{2}y = \frac{1}{3}x + \frac{1}{6}$	$x = \frac{1}{3}y + 1$	↘ ↓ → **Finish**

Find a path through the puzzle such that each pair of equations forms...

1. ...a consistent and dependent system.
Start –1 –2 –7 –13 –14 –19 – Finish

2. ...an inconsistent system.
Start –6 –10 –15 –21 –17 –23 – Finish

Organizer

Objective: Assess students' ability to apply concepts and skills in Lessons 6-1 through 6-4 in a real-world format.

Resources

Algebra I Assessments
www.mathtekstoolkit.org

Problem	Text Reference
1	Lesson 6-2
2	Lessons 6-1, 6-2, 6-3, 6-4
3	Lessons 6-1, 6-2, 6-3
4	Lessons 6-1, 6-2, 6-3
5	Lessons 6-1, 6-2, 6-3

State Resources

CHAPTER 6

MULTI-STEP TEST PREP

SECTION 6A

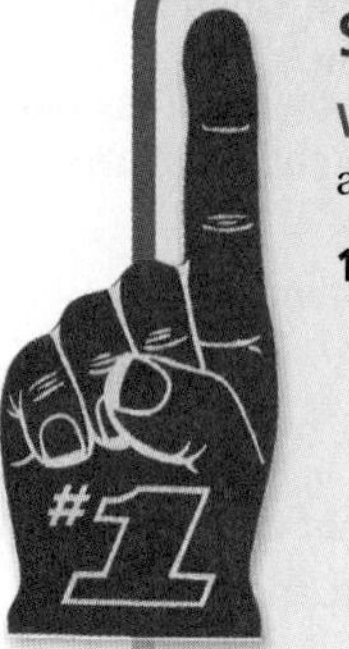

Systems of Equations

1. Spirit for You; for 100 fingers Spirit charges $285 and Go Team charges $320.

We've Got Spirit Some cheerleaders are going to sell spirit bracelets and foam fingers to raise money for traveling to away games.

Company	Design fee	Cost per item
Spirit for You	$35	$2.50
Go Team	$20	$3.00

1. Two companies, Spirit for You and Go Team, are interested in providing the foam fingers. The cheerleaders plan to sell 100 foam fingers. Based on this information, which company should they choose? Explain your reasoning.
2. The cheerleaders sold foam fingers for $5 and spirit bracelets for $4. They sold 40 more foam fingers than bracelets, and they earned $965. Write a system of equations to describe this situation.
3. Solve this system using at least two different methods. Explain each method. **$f = 125$, $b = 85$; check students' work.**
4. Using the company you chose in Problem 1, how much profit did the cheerleaders make from the foam fingers alone? (*Hint:* profit = amount earned − expenses) **$277.50**
5. What is the maximum price the cheerleaders could pay for each spirit bracelet in order to make a total profit of $500? **$1.38**

2. $\begin{cases} f = b + 40 \\ 965 = 5f + 4b \end{cases}$

INTERVENTION

Scaffolding Questions

1. **What are the variables in this problem situation?** The independent variable is the number of foam fingers. The dependent variable is the total cost.
2. **How do you calculate total sales?** For each item, multiply the number of items by the unit price, and then add the products.
3. **What are the possible ways that you can solve a system of equations?** Substitution, elimination, graphing, using a table
4. **What are expenses?** money spent to create products
5. **Which method is best for this situation? Explain.** Some students may prefer algebraic methods, while others will prefer using a graphing calculator.

Extension

If the cheerleaders needed to make a total profit of $600, would the maximum price they pay for the spirit bracelets be more or less than the answer in Problem 5? Explain. less; because they could not spend as much up front

CHAPTER 6

SECTION 6A

Quiz for Lessons 6-1 Through 6-4

6-1 Solving Systems by Graphing

Tell whether the ordered pair is a solution of the given system.

1. $(-2, 1); \begin{cases} y = -2x - 3 \\ y = x + 3 \end{cases}$ **yes**
2. $(9, 2); \begin{cases} x - 4y = 1 \\ 2x - 3y = 3 \end{cases}$ **no**
3. $(3, -1); \begin{cases} y = -\frac{1}{3}x \\ y + 2x = 5 \end{cases}$ **yes**

Solve each system by graphing.

4. $\begin{cases} y = x + 5 \\ y = \frac{1}{2}x + 4 \end{cases}$ **(−2, 3)**
5. $\begin{cases} y = -x - 2 \\ 2x - y = 2 \end{cases}$ **(0, −2)**
6. $\begin{cases} \frac{2}{3}x + y = -3 \\ 4x + y = 7 \end{cases}$ **(3, −5)**

7. **Banking** Christiana and Marlena opened their first savings accounts on the same day. Christiana opened her account with \$50 and plans to deposit \$10 every month. Marlena opened her account with \$30 and plans to deposit \$15 every month. After how many months will their two accounts have the same amount of money? What will that amount be? **4 mo; \$90**

6-2 Solving Systems by Substitution

Solve each system by substitution.

8. $\begin{cases} y = -x + 5 \\ 2x + y = 11 \end{cases}$ **(6, −1)**
9. $\begin{cases} 4x - 3y = -1 \\ 3x - y = -2 \end{cases}$ **(−1, −1)**
10. $\begin{cases} y = -x \\ y = -2x - 5 \end{cases}$ **(−5, 5)**

6-3 Solving Systems by Elimination

Solve each system by elimination.

11. $\begin{cases} x + 3y = 15 \\ 2x - 3y = -6 \end{cases}$ **(3, 4)**
12. $\begin{cases} x + y = 2 \\ 2x + y = -1 \end{cases}$ **(−3, 5)**
13. $\begin{cases} -2x + 5y = -1 \\ 3x + 2y = 11 \end{cases}$ **(3, 1)**

14. It takes Akira 10 minutes to make a black and white drawing and 25 minutes for a color drawing. On Saturday he made a total of 9 drawings in 2 hours. Write and solve a system of equations to determine how many drawings of each type Akira made. **$10x + 25y = 120$; $x + y = 9$; 7 black and white, 2 color**

6-4 Solving Special Systems

Solve each system of linear equations.

15. $\begin{cases} y = -2x - 6 \\ 2x + y = 5 \end{cases}$ **no sol.**
16. $\begin{cases} x + y = 2 \\ 2x + 2y = -6 \end{cases}$ **no sol.**
17. $\begin{cases} y = -2x + 4 \\ 2x + y = 4 \end{cases}$ **inf. many solutions**

Classify each system. Give the number of solutions.

18. $\begin{cases} 3x = -6y + 3 \\ 2y = -x + 1 \end{cases}$ **cons., dep.; inf. many solutions**
19. $\begin{cases} y = -4x + 2 \\ 4x + y = -2 \end{cases}$ **incons.; no sol.**
20. $\begin{cases} 4x - 3y = 8 \\ y = 4(x + 2) \end{cases}$ **cons., indep.; one sol.**

READY TO GO ON? SECTION 6A

Organizer

Objective: Assess students' mastery of concepts and skills in Lessons 6-1 through 6-4.

Resources

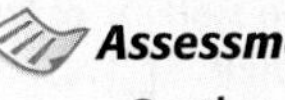
Assessment Resources
Section 6A Quiz

Teacher One Stop™
Test & Practice Generator

INTERVENTION

Resources

Ready to Go On? Intervention and Enrichment Worksheets

***Ready to Go On?* CD-ROM**

***Ready to Go On?* Online**

my.hrw.com

READY TO GO ON? Diagnose and Prescribe

NO INTERVENE

Ready to Go On? Intervention	*Ready to Go On? Intervention*, Section 6A: Worksheets	CD-ROM	Online
Lesson 6-1	6-1 Intervention	Activity 6-1	Diagnose and Prescribe Online
Lesson 6-2	6-2 Intervention	Activity 6-2	
Lesson 6-3	6-3 Intervention	Activity 6-3	
Lesson 6-4	6-4 Intervention	Activity 6-4	

YES ENRICH

Ready to Go On? Enrichment, Section 6A
Worksheets

CD-ROM

Online

SECTION

6B Linear Inequalities

One-Minute Section Planner

Lesson	Lab Resources	Materials
Lesson 6-5 Solving Linear Inequalities • Graph and solve linear inequalities in two variables. ☑ SAT-10 ☐ NAEP ☑ ACT ☑ SAT ☑ SAT Subject Tests	***Algebra Lab Activities*** 6-5 Algebra Lab	**Optional** graphing calculator, graph paper
Lesson 6-6 Solving Systems of Linear Inequalities • Graph and solve systems of linear inequalities in two variables. ☐ SAT-10 ☐ NAEP ☐ ACT ☑ SAT ☐ SAT Subject Tests		**Optional** colored pencils (MK), graphing calculator, transparency grids
6-6 Technology Lab Solve Systems of Linear Inequalities • Use a graphing calculator to view solutions of a system of linear inequalities. ☐ SAT-10 ☐ NAEP ☐ ACT ☑ SAT ☐ SAT Subject Tests	***Technology Lab Activities*** 6-6 Lab Recording Sheet	**Required** graphing calculator

Note: If NAEP is checked, the content is tested on either the Grade 8 or the Grade 12 NAEP assessment.

MK = *Manipulatives Kit*

LINEAR INEQUALITIES

Lesson 6-5

A *linear inequality in two variables* is an inequality that may be written in the form $ax + by < c$, where a and b are not both 0, and where the symbols $\leq$, $>$, or $\geq$ may be used instead of $<$. A *solution* of a linear inequality in two variables is an ordered pair that makes the inequality true. For example, (4, 5) is a solution of the linear inequality $y > \frac{1}{2}x + 1$ because $5 > \frac{1}{2}(4) + 1$ is a true statement.

Students can begin to explore solutions of inequalities in two variables by fixing the value of one variable and then testing values of the other. For $y > \frac{1}{2}x + 1$, when $x = 4$ it is easy to see that any value of y greater than 3 is a solution. That is, the ordered pairs (4, 3.1), (4, 5), and (4, 17) are all solutions of $y > \frac{1}{2}x + 1$. More generally, the solution set when $x = 4$ can be represented by the ray described by $y > 3$. This can be shown on a coordinate plane as the part of the vertical line $x = 4$ where the y-values are greater than 3.

Similarly, the solution set when $x = 6$ can be represented by the ray described by $y > 4$. Doing this for other values of x results in a collection of rays.

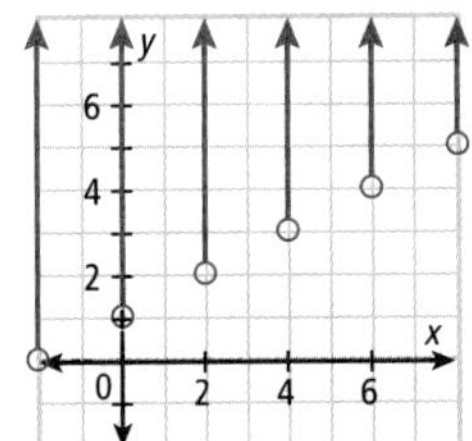

If we imagine doing this for all values of x, we see that the solution set of $y > \frac{1}{2}x + 1$ can be represented by an infinite set of rays similar to those graphed above. These rays fill the part of the coordinate plane that lies above the line $y = \frac{1}{2}x + 1$. That is, the solution set can be represented by a half plane.

The shaded region shows the half plane that represents the solution set of $y > \frac{1}{2}x + 1$. All ordered pairs in this region are solutions of the inequality.

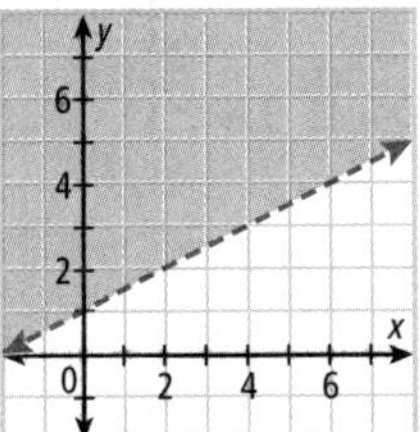

Note that the line $y = \frac{1}{2}x + 1$ is the boundary of the half plane. This boundary is shown with a dashed line because the points on the line are not solutions of the inequality. (For the inequality $y \geq \frac{1}{2}x + 1$, the points on the line *are* solutions and the boundary would be drawn as a solid line.)

Students should know how to check solutions to inequalities by selecting specific points from a graph. In the above graph, the point (4, 6) lies in the shaded region. Therefore, (4, 6) should be a solution of the inequality $y > \frac{1}{2}x + 1$. This is easily verified: $6 > \frac{1}{2}(4) + 1$ is a true statement. The point (5, 2) is *not* in the shaded region and so should *not* be a solution of the inequality. Again, this is easily verified by substituting 5 for x and 2 for y and noting that the resulting inequality is false.

SYSTEMS OF INEQUALITIES

Lesson 6-6

As discussed above, the solution set of a single inequality in two variables can be represented by a half plane. The solution set of a system of two inequalities in two variables can therefore be represented by the intersection of two half planes. Students should understand that this intersection may be an infinite region, a straight line, or the empty set. As before, specific points inside and outside the solution region should be checked in *both* inequalities to verify that the correct solution region has been identified.

6-5 Organizer

Pacing: Traditional 1 day
Block $\frac{1}{2}$ day

Objective: Graph and solve linear inequalities in two variables.

Algebra Lab
In *Algebra Lab Activities*

Online Edition
Tutorial Videos

Countdown Week 14

Power Presentations with PowerPoint®

Warm Up

Graph each inequality.

1. $x > -5$
2. $y \leq 0$
3. Write $-6x + 2y = -4$ in slope-intercept form, and graph. $y = 3x - 2$

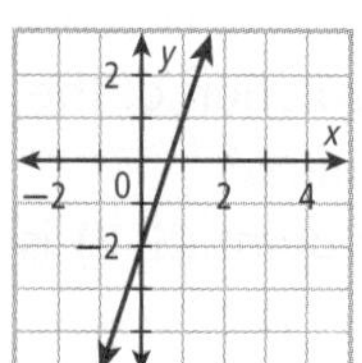

Also available on transparency

Math Humor

Q: Why did the math student name her boundary line Hope?

A: Because it was dashed.

State Resources

go.hrw.com
State Resources Online
KEYWORD: MA7 Resources

6-5 Solving Linear Inequalities

Objective
Graph and solve linear inequalities in two variables.

Vocabulary
linear inequality
solution of a linear inequality

Who uses this?
Consumers can use linear inequalities to determine how much food they can buy for an event. (See Example 3.)

A **linear inequality** is similar to a linear equation, but the equal sign is replaced with an inequality symbol. A **solution of a linear inequality** is any ordered pair that makes the inequality true.

EXAMPLE 1 Identifying Solutions of Inequalities

Tell whether the ordered pair is a solution of the inequality.

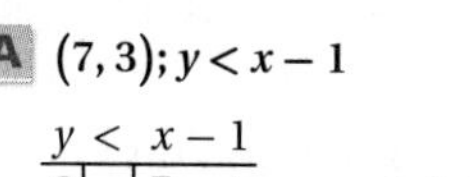

A $(7, 3); y < x - 1$

$y < x - 1$	
3	$7 - 1$
$3 <$	6 ✓

Substitute (7, 3) for (x, y).

$(7, 3)$ is a solution.

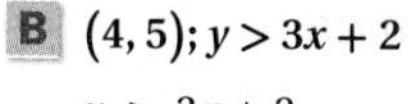

B $(4, 5); y > 3x + 2$

$y > 3x + 2$	
5	$3(4) + 2$
5	$12 + 2$
$5 >$	14 ✗

Substitute (4, 5) for (x, y).

$(4, 5)$ is not a solution.

CHECK IT OUT! **Tell whether the ordered pair is a solution of the inequality.**

1a. $(4, 5); y < x + 1$ **no** **1b.** $(1, 1); y > x - 7$ **yes**

A linear inequality describes a region of a coordinate plane called a *half-plane.* All points in the region are solutions of the linear inequality. The boundary line of the region is the graph of the related equation.

When the inequality is written as $y \leq$ or $y \geq$, the points on the boundary line are solutions of the inequality, and the line is solid.

When the inequality is written as $y <$ or $y >$, the points on the boundary line are not solutions of the inequality, and the line is dashed.

When the inequality is written as $y >$ or $y \geq$, the points above the boundary line are solutions of the inequality.

When the inequality is written as $y <$ or $y \leq$, the points below the boundary line are solutions of the inequality.

1 Introduce

EXPLORATION

6-5 Solving Linear Inequalities

You will need graph paper for this Exploration.
You will investigate how to solve linear inequalities.

1. Graph $y = 2x + 1$.
2. Choose three points above the line. Give the coordinates of each point and tell whether y is greater than, less than, or equal to $2x + 1$ at each point.
3. Now choose three points below the line. Give the coordinates of each point and tell whether y is greater than, less than, or equal to $2x + 1$ at each point.
4. Now choose three points on the line. Give the coordinates of each point and tell whether y is greater than, less than, or equal to $2x + 1$ at each point.

THINK AND DISCUSS

5. **Describe** the set of all points on the coordinate plane for which $y > 2x + 1$.
6. **Describe** the set of all points on the coordinate plane for which $y \leq 2x + 1$.

Motivate

Pose some real-world situations that can be represented by linear inequalities in two variables. For example: The cost of 5 pencils and 2 pens must be at most \$4. $5x + 2y \leq 4$ Challenge students to find many possible solutions. Possible answers: $(0.10, 1.50)$ = pencils \$0.10, pens \$1.50; $(0.25, 1.00)$ = pencils \$0.25, pens \$1.00 Ask students if negative numbers are reasonable solutions for this problem. no

Explorations and answers are provided in *Alternate Openers: Explorations Transparencies.*

Graphing Linear Inequalities	
Step 1	Solve the inequality for y.
Step 2	Graph the boundary line. Use a solid line for $\le$ or $\ge$. Use a dashed line for $<$ or $>$.
Step 3	Shade the half-plane above the line for $y >$ or $y \ge$. Shade the half-plane below the line for $y <$ or $y \le$. Check your answer.

EXAMPLE 2 Graphing Linear Inequalities in Two Variables

Graph the solutions of each linear inequality.

A $y < 3x + 4$

Step 1 The inequality is already solved for y.

Step 2 Graph the boundary line $y = 3x + 4$. Use a dashed line for $<$.

Step 3 The inequality is $<$, so shade below the line.

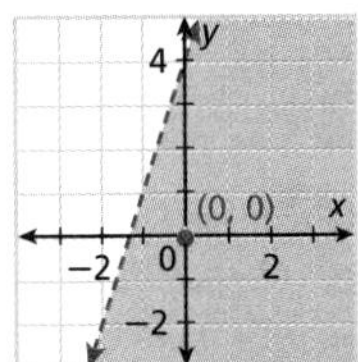

Check

y	$<$	$3x + 4$
0		$3(0) + 4$
0		$0 + 4$
0	$<$	4 ✓

Substitute (0, 0) for (x, y) because it is not on the boundary line.

The point (0, 0) satisfies the inequality, so the graph is shaded correctly.

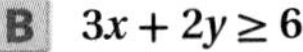

B $3x + 2y \ge 6$

Step 1 Solve the inequality for y.

$$3x + 2y \ge 6$$
$$\underline{-3x \qquad\quad -3x}$$
$$2y \ge -3x + 6$$
$$y \ge -\frac{3}{2}x + 3$$

Step 2 Graph the boundary line $y = -\frac{3}{2}x + 3$. Use a solid line for $\ge$.

Step 3 The inequality is $\ge$, so shade above the line.

Check

y	$\ge$	$\frac{3}{2}x + 3$
0		$\frac{3}{2}(0) + 3$
0		$0 + 3$
0	$\ge$	3 ✗

A false statement means that the half-plane containing (0, 0) should NOT be shaded. (0, 0) is not one of the solutions, so the graph is shaded correctly.

Helpful Hint

The point (0, 0) is a good test point to use if it does not lie on the boundary line.

2a.

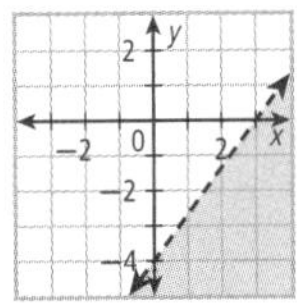

2b.

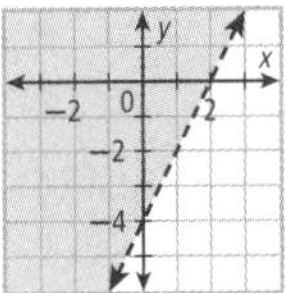

2c.

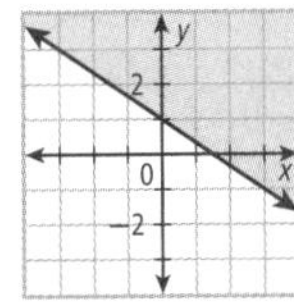

Graph the solutions of each linear inequality.

2a. $4x - 3y > 12$ **2b.** $2x - y - 4 > 0$ **2c.** $y \ge -\frac{2}{3}x + 1$

Power Presentations with PowerPoint®

Additional Examples

Example 1

Tell whether the ordered pair is a solution of the inequality.

A. $(-2, 4); y < 2x + 1$ no

B. $(3, 1); y > x - 4$ yes

Example 2

Graph the solutions of each linear inequality.

A. $y \le 2x - 3$

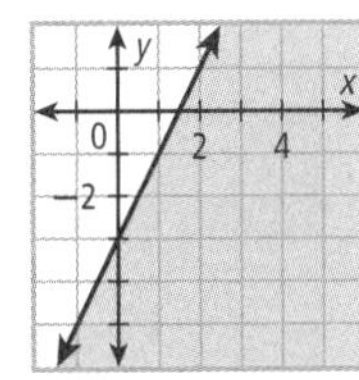

B. $5x + 2y > -8$

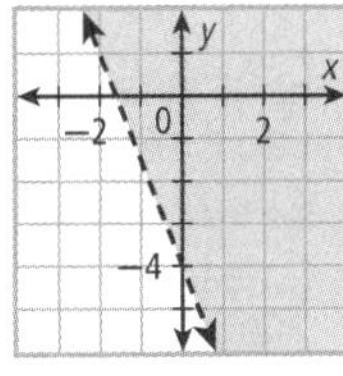

C. $4x - y + 2 \le 0$

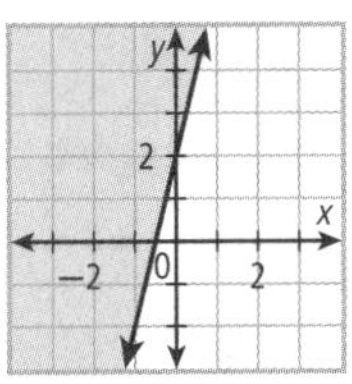

INTERVENTION

Questioning Strategies

EXAMPLE 1

- How do you know if an ordered pair is not a solution of a linear inequality?

EXAMPLE 2

- How can you check that you shaded the correct half-plane?
- Explain why the point (0, 0) should not be used as a test point if it lies on the boundary line.

2 Teach

Guided Instruction

Explain to students that graphing an inequality begins with graphing an equation. The inequality symbol determines whether the points on the boundary line are solutions (solid line) or not solutions (dashed line). Ask students to think about what the shaded part will mean before they shade. Have students test several points in the area to be shaded to determine whether they make the inequality true.

Reaching All Learners

Through Home Connection

Have students search through local advertisements and find two different items (under \$20) they would like to purchase. Tell students they have a maximum of \$125 to purchase different combinations of these two items. Have students write a linear inequality to describe the situation. Possible answer: $13.99x + 17.95y \le 125$ Then have them graph the solutions of their inequality and give at least two combinations of items they can purchase.

Power Presentations with PowerPoint®

Additional Examples

Example 3

Ada has at most 285 beads to make jewelry. A necklace requires 40 beads, and a bracelet requires 15 beads. Write a linear inequality to describe the situation. Graph the solutions, describe reasonable solutions, and then give two combinations of necklaces and bracelets Ada could make.

$40x + 15y \leq 285$

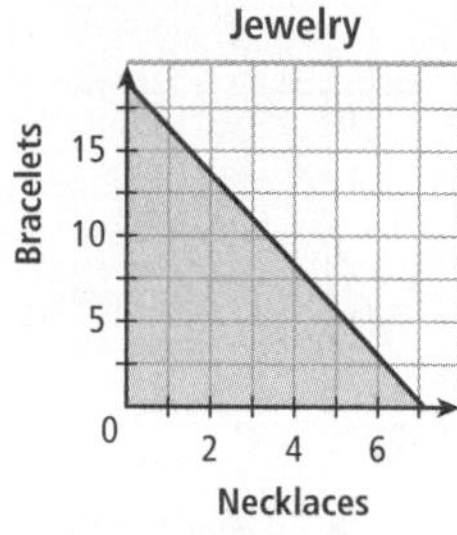

Only whole-number solutions are reasonable. Possible answer: (2 necklaces, 8 bracelets), (5 necklaces, 3 bracelets)

INTERVENTION
Questioning Strategies

EXAMPLE 3

- Can the reasonable solutions of a linear inequality include fractions or decimals? Why or why not?

Number Sense In **Example 3,** discuss with students what numbers are reasonable solutions. In many real-world situations, reasonable solutions are often nonnegative, and sometimes only whole numbers are reasonable.

3a. $2.5b + 2g \leq 6$

3b.

Olive Combinations (Green olives vs. Black olives)

3c. possible answer: (1 lb black, 1 lb green), (0.5 lb black, 2 lb green)

EXAMPLE 3 *Consumer Economics Application*

Sarah can spend at most \$7.50 on vegetables for a party. Broccoli costs \$1.25 per bunch and carrots cost \$0.75 per package.

a. Write a linear inequality to describe the situation.

Let x represent the number of bunches of broccoli and let y represent the number of packages of carrots.

Write an inequality. Use $\leq$ for "at most."

Cost of broccoli	plus	cost of carrots	is at most	\$7.50.
$1.25x$	$+$	$0.75y$	$\leq$	7.50

Solve the inequality for y.

$$1.25x + 0.75y \leq 7.50$$

$$100(1.25x + 0.75y) \leq 100(7.50)$$ *You can multiply both sides of the inequality by 100 to eliminate the decimals.*

$$125x + 75y \leq 750$$
$$-125x \qquad -125x$$ *Subtraction Property of Inequality*

$$75y \leq 750 - 125x$$

$$\frac{75y}{75} \leq \frac{750 - 125x}{75}$$ *Division Property of Inequality*

$$y \leq 10 - \frac{5}{3}x$$

b. Graph the solutions.

Step 1 Since Sarah cannot buy a negative amount of vegetables, the system is graphed only in Quadrant I. Graph the boundary line $y = -\frac{5}{3}x + 10$. Use a solid line for $\leq$.

Step 2 Shade below the line. Sarah must buy whole numbers of bunches or packages. All points on or below the line with whole-number coordinates represent combinations of broccoli and carrots that Sarah can buy.

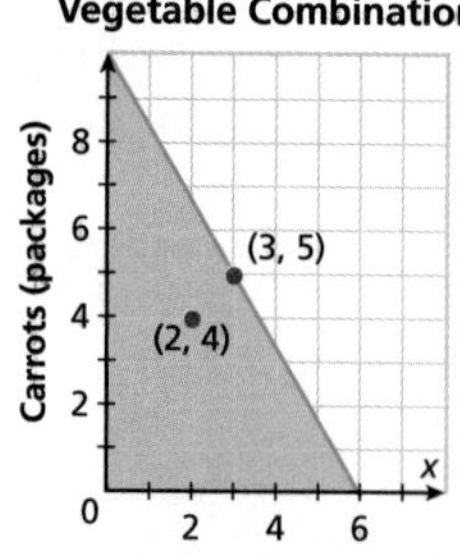

c. Give two combinations of vegetables that Sarah can buy.

Two different combinations that Sarah could buy for \$7.50 or less are 2 bunches of broccoli and 4 packages of carrots, or 3 bunches of broccoli and 5 packages of carrots.

CHECK IT OUT!

3. Dirk is going to bring two types of olives to the Honor Society induction and can spend no more than \$6. Green olives cost \$2 per pound and black olives cost \$2.50 per pound.

a. Write a linear inequality to describe the situation.

b. Graph the solutions.

c. Give two combinations of olives that Dirk could buy.

Technology Show students how to graph an inequality on a graphing calculator. Press Y= and enter the equation. Press ◄ to move the cursor to the left of Y_1. Press ENTER until the icon that looks like a region above or below a line appears. Press GRAPH. Tell students that the graphing calculator does not distinguish between solid and dashed boundary lines. They will need to decide for themselves if the line should be dashed or solid.

EXAMPLE 4 Writing an Inequality from a Graph

Write an inequality to represent each graph.

A

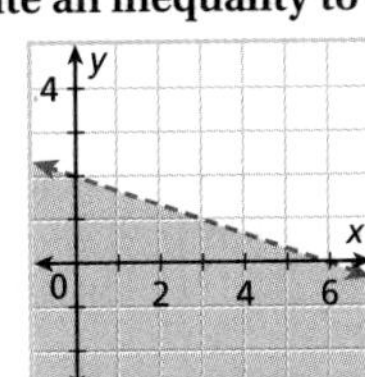

y-intercept: 2; slope: $-\frac{1}{3}$

Write an equation in slope-intercept form.

$$y = mx + b \longrightarrow y = -\frac{1}{3}x + 2$$

The graph is shaded *below* a *dashed* boundary line.

Replace = with < to write the inequality $y < -\frac{1}{3}x + 2$.

B

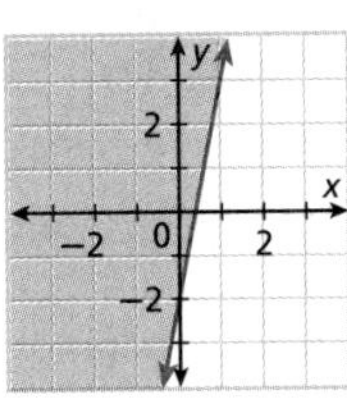

y-intercept: −2; slope: 5

Write an equation in slope-intercept form.

$$y = mx + b \longrightarrow y = 5x + (-2)$$

The graph is shaded *above* a *solid* boundary line.

Replace = with ≥ to write the inequality $y \geq 5x - 2$.

C

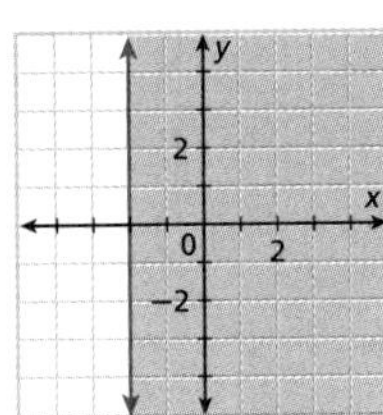

y-intercept: none; slope: undefined

The graph is a vertical line at $x = -2$.

The graph is shaded on the *right* side of a *solid* boundary line.

Replace = with ≥ to write the inequality $x \geq -2$.

CHECK IT OUT! Write an inequality to represent each graph.

4a.

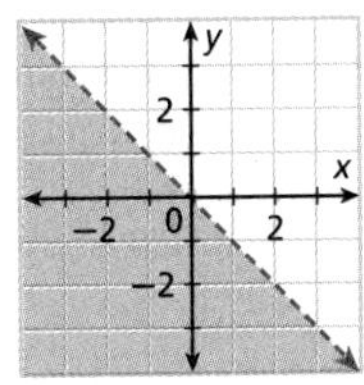

$y < -x$

4b.

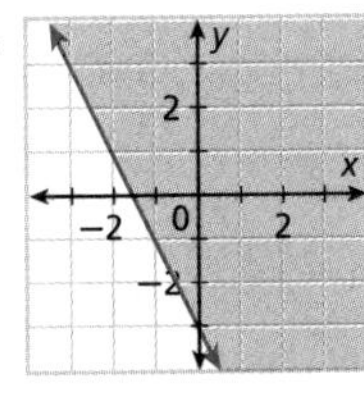

$y \geq -2x - 3$

THINK AND DISCUSS

1. Tell how graphing a linear inequality is the same as graphing a linear equation. Tell how it is different.
2. Explain how you would write a linear inequality from a graph.
3. **GET ORGANIZED** Copy and complete the graphic organizer.

Inequality	$y < 5x + 2$	$y > 7x - 3$	$y \leq 9x + 1$	$y \geq -3x - 2$
Symbol	<			
Boundary Line	Dashed			
Shading	Below			

Power Presentations with PowerPoint®

Additional Examples

Example 4

Write an inequality to represent each graph.

A.

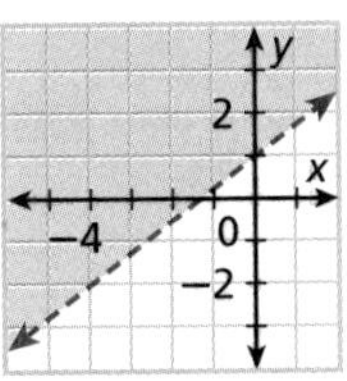

$y > \frac{3}{4}x + 1$

B.

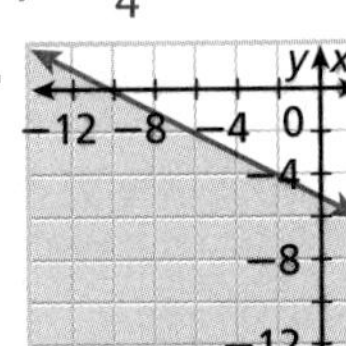

$y \leq -\frac{1}{2}x - 5$

INTERVENTION

Questioning Strategies

EXAMPLE 4

- How do you determine which inequality symbol to use?

3 Close

Summarize

For each inequality below, have students describe the boundary line and state which direction should be shaded.

1) $y < 2x + 1$ dashed; below

2) $y \geq -\frac{3}{5}x - 2$ solid; above

3) $2x - 3y \leq 6$ solid; above

4) $y > -3$ dashed; above

5) $x \leq 7$ solid; to the left

ONGOING ASSESSMENT and INTERVENTION

***Diagnose Before* the Lesson**
6-5 Warm Up, TE p. 428

***Monitor During* the Lesson**
Check It Out! Exercises, SE pp. 428–431
Questioning Strategies, TE pp. 429–431

***Assess After* the Lesson**
6-5 Lesson Quiz, TE p. 434
Alternative Assessment, TE p. 434

Answers to *Think and Discuss*

1. Possible answer: In both cases you will always graph a line. They are different because the graph of a linear inequality can be a dashed or solid line, and the graph must be shaded on one side of the line.
2. To write a linear inequality from a graph, find the equation of the boundary line. Use ≥ or ≤ for a solid boundary line. Use > or < for a dashed boundary line. If the half-plane is shaded above the line, use > or ≥, and if it is shaded below, use < or ≤.
3. See p. A6.

6-5 Exercises

Assignment Guide

Assign *Guided Practice* exercises as necessary.

If you finished Examples **1–2**
Basic 12–18, 23–27
Average 12–18, 23–27, 30–36 even
Advanced 12–18, 23–27, 30–36 even

If you finished Examples **1–4**
Basic 12–21, 22–36 even, 40–41, 43–45, 51–65,
Average 12–21, 30–42 even, 43–48, 51–65
Advanced 12–21, 30–38 even, 39–40, 43–65

Homework Quick Check
Quickly check key concepts.
Exercises: 14, 18, 19, 20, 30, 40

Answers

5–8. See p. A25.

9a. $x + y \leq 16$

b.

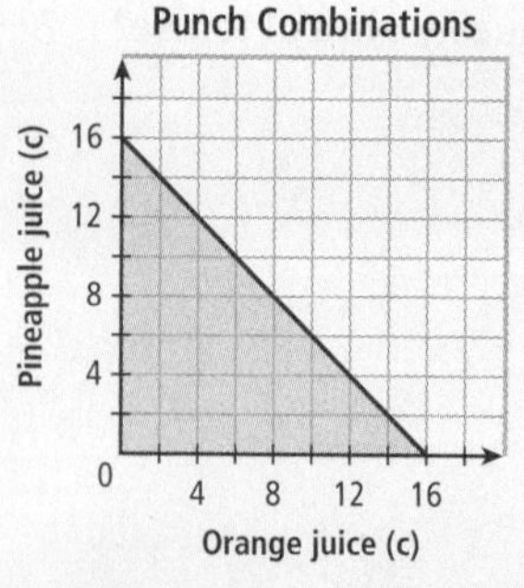

c. Possible answer: (2 c orange, 2 c pineapple), (4 c orange, 10 c pineapple)

15–19. See p. A25.

State Resources

go.hrw.com
State Resources Online
KEYWORD: MA7 Resources

6-5 Exercises

go.hrw.com
Homework Help Online
KEYWORD: MA7 6-5
Parent Resources Online
KEYWORD: MA7 Parent

GUIDED PRACTICE

1. **Vocabulary** Can a *solution of a linear inequality* lie on a dashed boundary line? Explain. **No; a dashed line means that the ordered pairs are not solutions to the linear inequality.**

SEE EXAMPLE 1 p. 428

Tell whether the ordered pair is a solution of the given inequality.

2. $(0, 3)$; $y \leq -x + 3$ **yes**
3. $(2, 0)$; $y > -2x - 2$ **yes**
4. $(-2, 1)$; $y < 2x + 4$ **no**

SEE EXAMPLE 2 p. 429

Graph the solutions of each linear inequality.

5. $y \leq -x$
6. $y > 3x + 1$
7. $-y < -x + 4$
8. $-y \geq x + 1$

SEE EXAMPLE 3 p. 430

9. **Multi-Step** Jack is making punch with orange juice and pineapple juice. He can make at most 16 cups of punch.
   a. Write an inequality to describe the situation.
   b. Graph the solutions.
   c. Give two combinations of cups of orange juice and pineapple juice that Jack can use in his punch.

SEE EXAMPLE 4 p. 431

Write an inequality to represent each graph.

10.

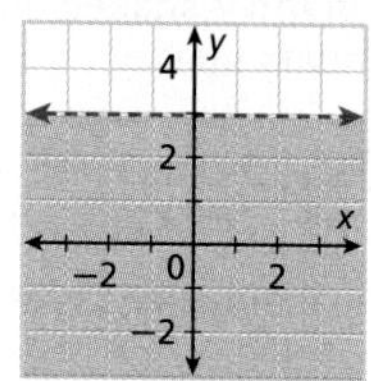

$y < 3$

11.

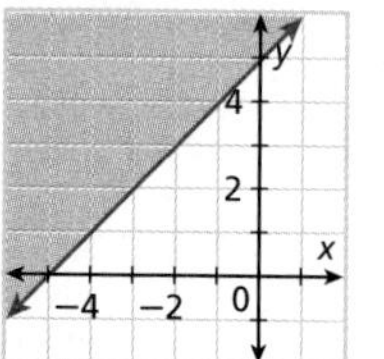

$y \geq x + 5$

PRACTICE AND PROBLEM SOLVING

Independent Practice

For Exercises	See Example
12–14	1
15–18	2
19	3
20–21	4

Extra Practice
Skills Practice p. S15
Application Practice p. S33

Tell whether the ordered pair is a solution of the given inequality.

12. $(2, 3)$; $y \geq 2x + 3$ **no**
13. $(1, -1)$; $y < 3x - 3$ **yes**
14. $(0, 7)$; $y > 4x + 7$ **no**

Graph the solutions of each linear inequality.

15. $y > -2x + 6$
16. $-y \geq 2x$
17. $x + y \leq 2$
18. $x - y \geq 0$

19. **Multi-Step** Beverly is serving hamburgers and hot dogs at her cookout. Hamburger meat costs \$3 per pound, and hot dogs cost \$2 per pound. She wants to spend no more than \$30.
   a. Write an inequality to describe the situation.
   b. Graph the solutions.
   c. Give two combinations of pounds of hamburger and hot dogs that Beverly can buy.

Write an inequality to represent each graph.

20.

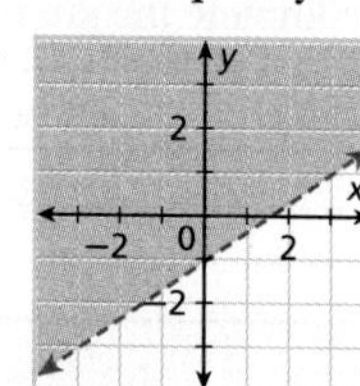

$y > \frac{2}{3}x - 1$

21.

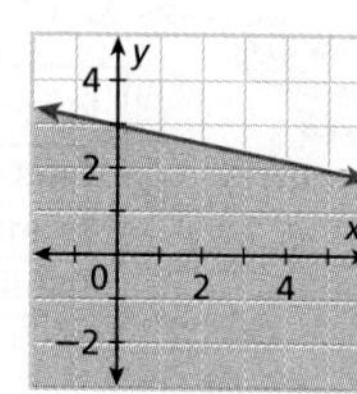

$y \leq -\frac{1}{5}x + 3$

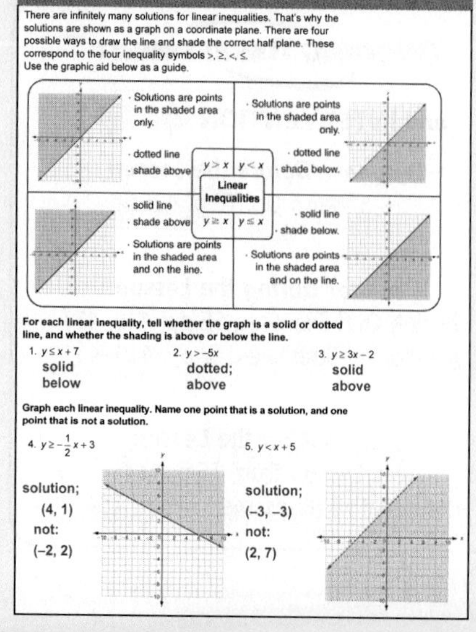

6-5 READING STRATEGIES

There are infinitely many solutions for linear inequalities. That's why the solutions are shown as a graph on a coordinate plane. There are four possible ways to draw the line and shade the correct half plane. These correspond to the four inequality symbols >, ≥, <, ≤.
Use the graphic aid below as a guide.

For each linear inequality, tell whether the graph is a solid or dotted line, and whether the shading is above or below the line.

1. $y \leq x + 7$ solid below
2. $y > -5x$ dotted; above
3. $y \geq 3x - 2$ solid above

Graph each linear inequality. Name one point that is a solution, and one point that is not a solution.

4. $y \geq -\frac{1}{2}x + 3$ solution; (4, 1) not: (−2, 2)
5. $y < x + 5$ solution; (−3, −3) not: (2, 7)

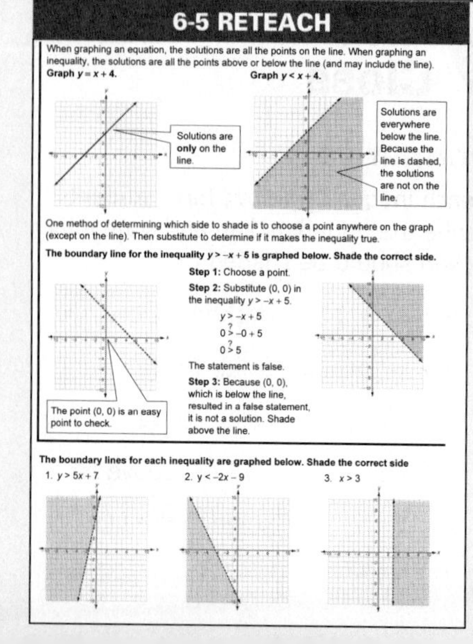

6-5 RETEACH

When graphing an equation, the solutions are all the points on the line. When graphing an inequality, the solutions are all the points above or below the line (and may include the line).

Graph $y = x + 4$. **Graph $y < x + 4$.**

One method of determining which side to shade is to choose a point anywhere on the graph (except on the line). Then substitute to determine if it makes the inequality true.

The boundary line for the inequality $y > -x + 5$ is graphed below. Shade the correct side.

Step 1: Choose a point.

Step 2: Substitute (0, 0) in the inequality $y > -x + 5$.

$y > -x + 5$
$0 \overset{?}{>} -0 + 5$
$0 \overset{?}{>} 5$

The statement is false.

Step 3: Because (0, 0), which is below the line, resulted in a false statement, it is not a solution. Shade above the line.

The boundary lines for each inequality are graphed below. Shade the correct side

1. $y > 5x + 7$
2. $y < -2x - 9$
3. $x > 3$

22b.

Electronics Sales

CD players

DVD players

0 2 4 6 8

22. **Business** An electronics store makes \$125 profit on every DVD player it sells and \$100 on every CD player it sells. The store owner wants to make a profit of at least \$500 a day selling DVD players and CD players. **a. $125x + 100y \geq 500$**
   a. Write a linear inequality to determine the number of DVD players x and the number of CD players y that the owner needs to sell to meet his goal.
   b. Graph the linear inequality.
   c. Describe the possible values of x. Describe the possible values of y. **x and y must be whole numbers.**
   d. List three combinations of DVD players and CD players that the owner could sell to meet his goal. **Possible answer: (5 DVD, 1 CD), (7 DVD, 6 CD), (9 DVD, 2 CD)**

Graph the solutions of each linear inequality.

23. $y \leq 2 - 3x$ 24. $-y < 7 + x$ 25. $2x - y \leq 4$ 26. $3x - 2y > 6$

27. **Geometry** Marvin has 18 yards of fencing that he can use to put around a rectangular garden. **$2x + 2y \leq 18$**
   a. Write an inequality to describe the possible lengths and widths of the garden.
   b. Graph the inequality and list three possible solutions to the problem.
   c. What are the dimensions of the largest *square* garden that can be fenced in with whole-number dimensions? **4 yd × 4 yd**

28. **Hobbies** Stephen wants to buy yellow tangs and clown fish for his saltwater aquarium. He wants to spend no more than \$77 on fish. At the store, yellow tangs cost \$15 each and clown fish cost \$11 each. Write and graph a linear inequality to find the number of yellow tangs x and the number of clown fish y that Stephen could purchase. Name a solution of your inequality that is not reasonable for the situation. Explain.

Graph each inequality on a coordinate plane.

29. $y > 1$ 30. $-2 < x$ 31. $x \geq -3$ 32. $y \leq 0$

33. $0 \geq x$ 34. $-12 + y > 0$ 35. $x + 7 < 7$ 36. $-4 \geq x - y$

37. **School** At a high school football game, tickets at the gate cost \$7 per adult and \$4 per student. Write a linear inequality to determine the number of adult and student tickets that need to be sold so that the amount of money taken in at the gate is at least \$280. Graph the inequality and list three possible solutions.

38. **Critical Thinking** Why must a region of a coordinate plane be shaded to show all solutions of a linear inequality? **Possible answer: It is not possible to list an infinite number of solutions, so shading is used to show all the solutions in the coordinate plane.**

39. **Write About It** Give a real-world situation that can be described by a linear inequality. Then graph the inequality and give two solutions.

Possible answer: Sammy volunteers at the hospital and the library. The total number of hours he volunteers is more than 5; $h + \ell > 5$; Check students' graphs and solutions.

MULTI-STEP TEST PREP

40. This problem will prepare you for the Multi-Step Test Prep on page 442.
   Gloria is making teddy bears. She is making boy and girl bears. She has enough stuffing to create 50 bears. Let x represent the number of girl bears and y represent the number of boy bears.
   a. Write an inequality that shows the possible number of boy and girl bears Gloria can make. **$x + y \leq 50$**
   b. Graph the inequality.
   c. Give three possible solutions for the numbers of boy and girl bears that can be made. **Possible answer: (10, 20), (30, 10), (15, 15)**

Teaching Tip

Geometry For **Exercise 27,** remind students that the formula for the perimeter of a rectangle is $P = 2\ell + 2w$ and the formula for the perimeter of a square is $P = 4s$.

MULTI-STEP TEST PREP

Exercise 40 involves writing and graphing an inequality in two variables to determine possible solutions due to constraints on materials. This exercise prepares students for the Multi-Step Test Prep on page 442.

Answers

23.

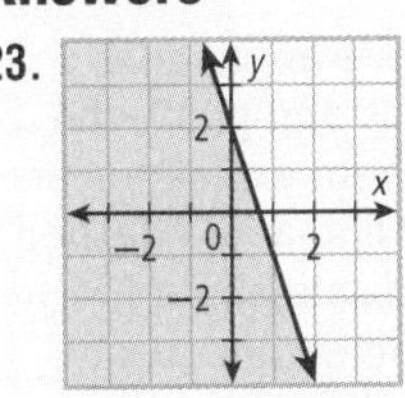

24.

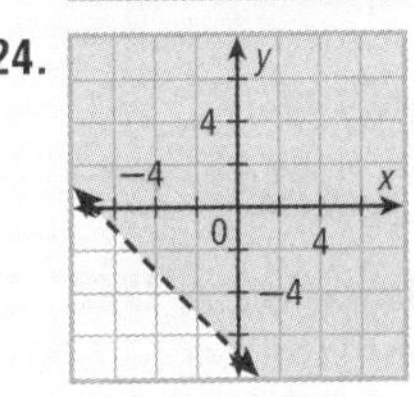

25.

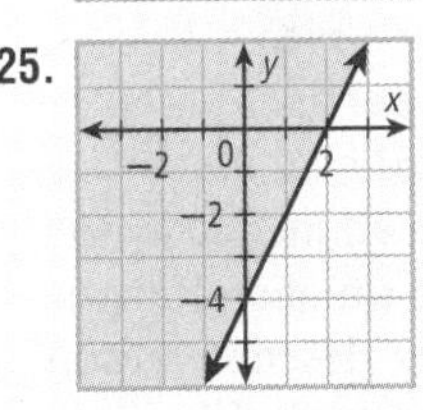

26.

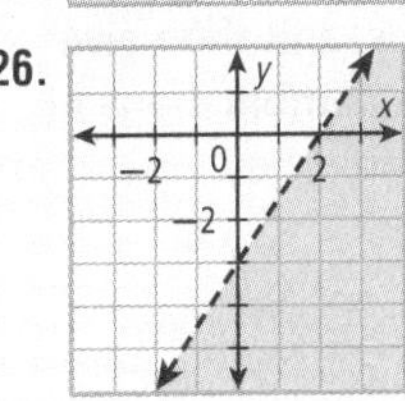

27b, 28–37, 40b. See p. A25.

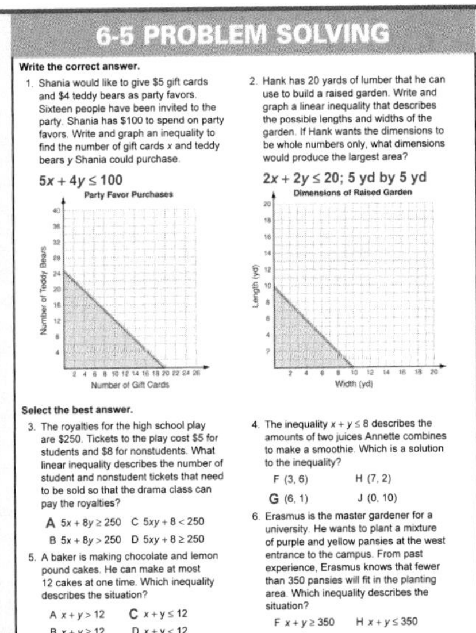

6-5 PROBLEM SOLVING

Write the correct answer.

1. Shania would like to give \$5 gift cards and \$4 teddy bears as party favors. Sixteen people have been invited to the party. Shania has \$100 to spend on party favors. Write and graph an inequality to find the number of gift cards x and teddy bears y Shania could purchase.

$5x + 4y \leq 100$

2. Hank has 20 yards of lumber that he can use to build a raised garden. Write and graph a linear inequality that describes the possible lengths and widths of the garden. If Hank wants the dimensions to be whole numbers only, what dimensions would produce the largest area?

$2x + 2y \leq 20$; 5 yd by 5 yd

Select the best answer.

3. The royalties for the high school play are \$250. Tickets to the play cost \$5 for students and \$8 for nonstudents. What linear inequality describes the number of student and nonstudent tickets that need to be sold so that the drama class can pay the royalties?
   A $5x + 8y \geq 250$ C $5xy + 8 < 250$
   B $5x + 8y > 250$ D $5xy + 8 \geq 250$

4. The inequality $x + y \leq 8$ describes the amounts of two juices Annette combines to make a smoothie. Which is a solution to the inequality?
   F (3, 6) H (7, 2)
   G (6, 1) J (0, 10)

5. A baker is making chocolate and lemon pound cakes. He can make at most 12 cakes at one time. Which inequality describes the situation?
   A $x + y > 12$ **C** $x + y \leq 12$
   B $x + y \geq 12$ D $x + y < 12$

6. Erasmus is the master gardener for a university. He wants to plant a mixture of purple and yellow pansies at the west entrance to the campus. From past experience, Erasmus knows that fewer than 350 pansies will fit in the planting area. Which inequality describes the situation?
   F $x + y \geq 350$ H $x + y \leq 350$
   G $x + y > 350$ **J** $x + y < 350$

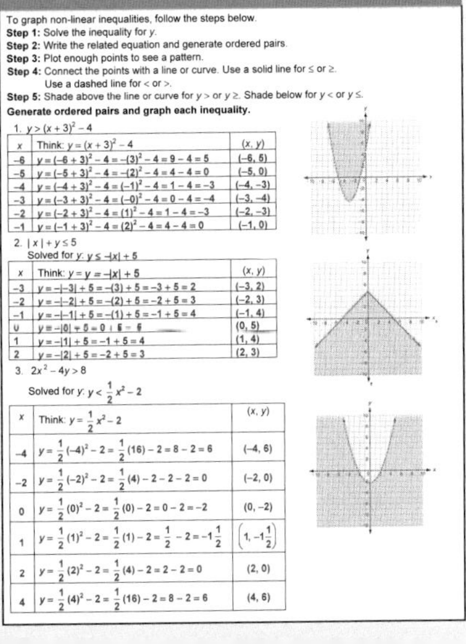

6-5 CHALLENGE

To graph non-linear inequalities, follow the steps below.
Step 1: Solve the inequality for y.
Step 2: Write the related equation and generate ordered pairs.
Step 3: Plot enough points to see a pattern.
Step 4: Connect the points with a line or curve. Use a solid line for ≤ or ≥. Use a dashed line for < or >.
Step 5: Shade above the line or curve for $y >$ or $y \geq$. Shade below for $y <$ or $y \leq$.

Generate ordered pairs and graph each inequality.

1. $y > (x + 3)^2 - 4$

x	Think: $y = (x + 3)^2 - 4$	(x, y)
−6	$y = (-6 + 3)^2 - 4 = -(3)^2 - 4 = 9 - 4 = 5$	(−6, 5)
−5	$y = (-5 + 3)^2 - 4 = -(2)^2 - 4 = 4 - 4 = 0$	(−5, 0)
−4	$y = (-4 + 3)^2 - 4 = (-1)^2 - 4 = 1 - 4 = -3$	(−4, −3)
−3	$y = (-3 + 3)^2 - 4 = (-0)^2 - 4 = 0 - 4 = -4$	(−3, −4)
−2	$y = (-2 + 3)^2 - 4 = (1)^2 - 4 = 1 - 4 = -3$	(−2, −3)
−1	$y = (-1 + 3)^2 - 4 = (2)^2 - 4 = 4 - 4 = 0$	(−1, 0)

2. $|x| + y \leq 5$
   Solved for y: $y \leq -|x| + 5$

x	Think: $y = y = -\lvert x\rvert + 5$	(x, y)
−3	$y = -\lvert -3\rvert + 5 = -(3) + 5 = -3 + 5 = 2$	(−3, 2)
−2	$y = -\lvert -2\rvert + 5 = -(2) + 5 = -2 + 5 = 3$	(−2, 3)
−1	$y = -\lvert -1\rvert + 5 = -(1) + 5 = -1 + 5 = 4$	(−1, 4)
0	$y = -\lvert 0\rvert + 5 = 0 + 5 = 5$	(0, 5)
1	$y = -\lvert 1\rvert + 5 = -1 + 5 = 4$	(1, 4)
2	$y = -\lvert 2\rvert + 5 = -2 + 5 = 3$	(2, 3)

3. $2x^2 - 4y > 8$
   Solved for y: $y < \frac{1}{2}x^2 - 2$

x	Think: $y = \frac{1}{2}x^2 - 2$	(x, y)
−4	$y = \frac{1}{2}(-4)^2 - 2 = \frac{1}{2}(16) - 2 = 8 - 2 = 6$	(−4, 6)
−2	$y = \frac{1}{2}(-2)^2 - 2 = \frac{1}{2}(4) - 2 - 2 - 2 = 0$	(−2, 0)
0	$y = \frac{1}{2}(0)^2 - 2 = \frac{1}{2}(0) - 2 = 0 - 2 = -2$	(0, −2)
1	$y = \frac{1}{2}(1)^2 - 2 = \frac{1}{2}(1) - 2 = \frac{1}{2} - 2 = -1\frac{1}{2}$	$(1, -1\frac{1}{2})$
2	$y = \frac{1}{2}(2)^2 - 2 = \frac{1}{2}(4) - 2 = 2 - 2 = 0$	(2, 0)
4	$y = \frac{1}{2}(4)^2 - 2 = \frac{1}{2}(16) - 2 = 8 - 2 = 6$	(4, 6)

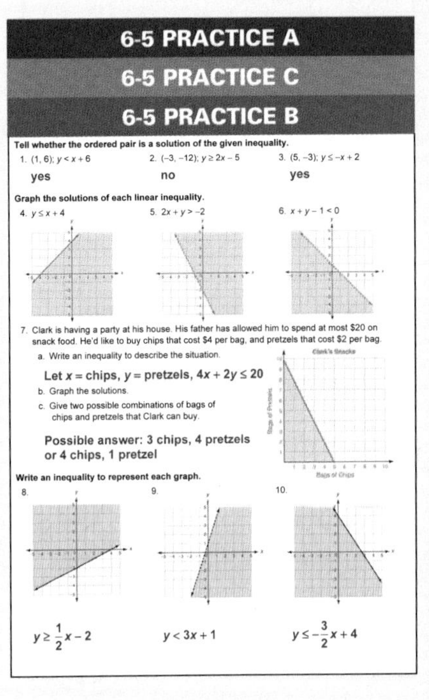

6-5 PRACTICE A
6-5 PRACTICE C
6-5 PRACTICE B

Tell whether the ordered pair is a solution of the given inequality.

1. (1, 6); $y < x + 6$ **yes**
2. (−3, −12); $y \geq 2x - 5$ **no**
3. (5, −3); $y \leq -x + 2$ **yes**

Graph the solutions of each linear inequality.

4. $y \leq x + 4$ 5. $2x + y > -2$ 6. $x + y - 1 < 0$

7. Clark is having a party at his house. His father has allowed him to spend at most \$20 on snack food. He'd like to buy chips that cost \$4 per bag, and pretzels that cost \$2 per bag.
   a. Write an inequality to describe the situation.
   Let x = chips, y = pretzels, $4x + 2y \leq 20$
   b. Graph the solutions.
   c. Give two possible combinations of bags of chips and pretzels that Clark can buy.
   Possible answer: 3 chips, 4 pretzels or 4 chips, 1 pretzel

Write an inequality to represent each graph.

8. **$y \geq \frac{1}{2}x - 2$** 9. **$y < 3x + 1$** 10. **$y \leq -\frac{3}{2}x + 4$**

In Exercise 44, choices G and J can be eliminated because the boundary line is solid.

Journal

Have students describe the steps for graphing $y \le x + 2$. Have them include how they would decide whether the boundary line is dashed or solid and how they would decide which half-plane to shade.

ALTERNATIVE ASSESSMENT

Have students write an inequality in two variables and graph the solutions. Have them explain what a solid boundary line and a dashed boundary line indicate about the solution set of a linear inequality.

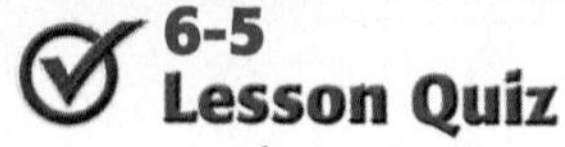

6-5 Lesson Quiz

1. You can spend at most $12.00 for drinks for a picnic. Iced tea costs $1.50 per gallon, and lemonade costs $2.00 per gallon. Write an inequality to describe the situation. Graph the solutions, describe reasonable solutions, and then give two possible combinations of drinks you could buy.
$1.50x + 2.00y \le 12.00$

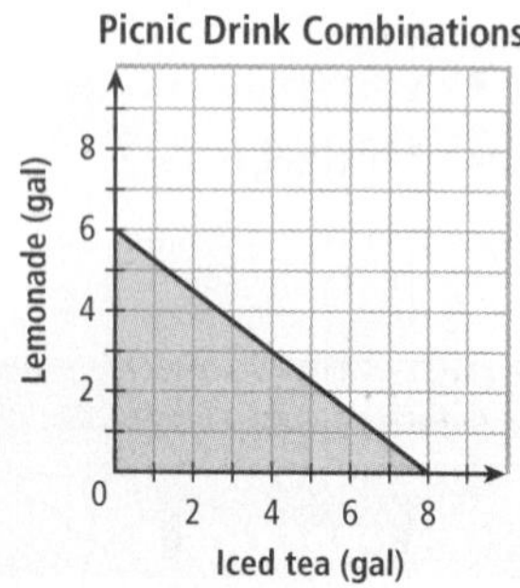

Only whole number solutions are reasonable. Possible answer: (2 gal iced tea, 3 gal lemonade), (4 gal iced tea, 1 gal lemonade)

2. Write an inequality to represent the graph.

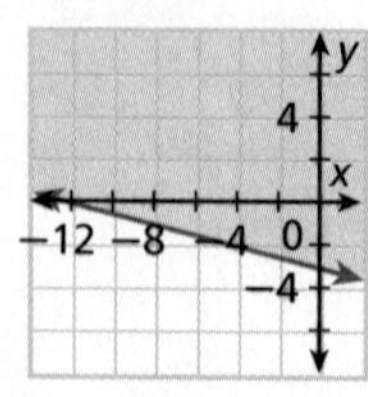

$y \ge -\frac{1}{4}x - 3$

Also available on transparency

41. **ERROR ANALYSIS** Student A wrote $y < 2x - 1$ as the inequality represented by the graph. Student B wrote $y \le 2x - 1$ as the inequality represented by the graph. Which student is incorrect? Explain the error.
Student A; the graph is a solid line.

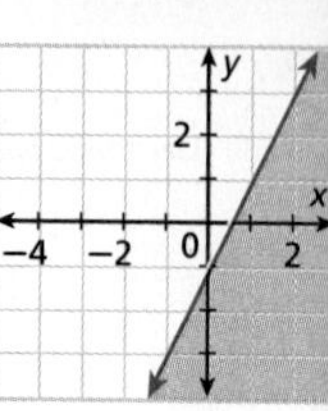

42. **Write About It** How do you decide to shade above or below a boundary line? What does this shading represent?

TEST PREP

43. Which point is a solution of the inequality $y > -x + 3$?
Ⓐ (0, 3) Ⓑ (1, 4) Ⓒ (−1, 4) Ⓓ (0, −3)

44. Which inequality is represented by the graph at right?
Ⓕ $2x + y \ge 3$ Ⓗ $2x + y \le 3$
Ⓖ $2x + y > 3$ Ⓙ $2x + y < 3$

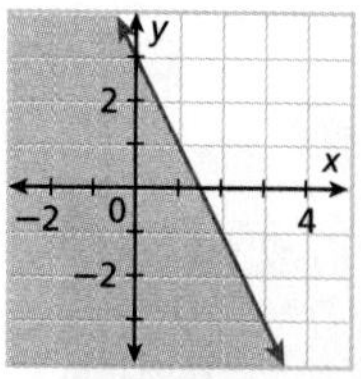

45. Which of the following describes the graph of $3 \le x$?
Ⓐ The boundary line is dashed, and the shading is to the right.
Ⓑ The boundary line is dashed, and the shading is to the left.
Ⓒ The boundary line is solid, and the shading is to the right.
Ⓓ The boundary line is solid, and the shading is to the left.

CHALLENGE AND EXTEND

Graph each inequality.

46. $0 \ge -6 - 2x - 5y$ 47. $y > |x|$ 48. $y \ge |x - 3|$

49. A linear inequality has the points (0, 3) and (−3, 1.5) as solutions on the boundary line. Also, the point (1, 1) is not a solution. Write the linear inequality. $y \ge \frac{1}{2}x + 3$

50. Two linear inequalities are graphed on the same coordinate plane. The point (0, 0) is a solution of both inequalities. The entire coordinate plane is shaded except for Quadrant I. What are the two inequalities? $x \le 0$; $y \le 0$

SPIRAL REVIEW

Tell whether each function is linear. If so, graph the function. *(Lesson 5-1)*

51. $y = 2x - 4$ **yes** 52. $y = x^2 + 2$ **no** 53. $y = 3$ **yes**

Write an equation in slope-intercept form for the line through the two points. *(Lesson 5-8)*

54. (0, 9) and (5, 2) 55. (−5, −2) and (7, 7) 56. (0, 0) and (−8, −10)
57. (−1, −2) and (1, 4) 58. (2, 2) and (6, 5) 59. (−3, 2) and (3, −1)

54. $y = -\frac{7}{5}x + 9$
55. $y = \frac{3}{4}x + \frac{7}{4}$
56. $y = \frac{5}{4}x$
57. $y = 3x + 1$
58. $y = \frac{3}{4}x + \frac{1}{2}$
59. $y = -\frac{1}{2}x + \frac{1}{2}$

Solve each system by elimination. *(Lesson 6-3)*

60. $\begin{cases} x + 6y = 14 \\ x - 6y = -10 \end{cases}$ (2, 2)
61. $\begin{cases} x + y = 13 \\ 3x + y = 9 \end{cases}$ (−2, 15)
62. $\begin{cases} 2x - 4y = 18 \\ 5x - y = 36 \end{cases}$ (7, −1)
63. $\begin{cases} 2y + x = 12 \\ y - 2x = 1 \end{cases}$ (2, 5)
64. $\begin{cases} 2y - 6x = -8 \\ y = -5x + 12 \end{cases}$ (2, 2)
65. $\begin{cases} 2x + 3y = 33 \\ y = \frac{1}{4}x \end{cases}$ (12, 3)

Answers

42. Possible answer: If the inequality is in slope-intercept form, then > or ≥ means you shade above the boundary line, and < or ≤ means you shade below the boundary line. The shading represents all the solutions of the inequality.

46.
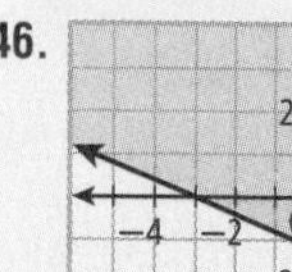

47.
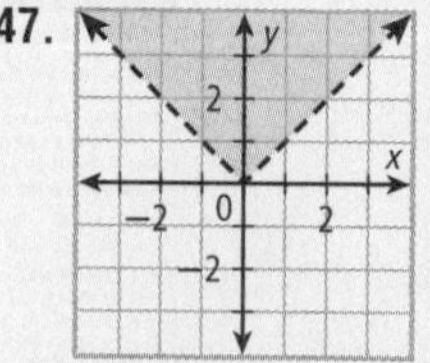

48.
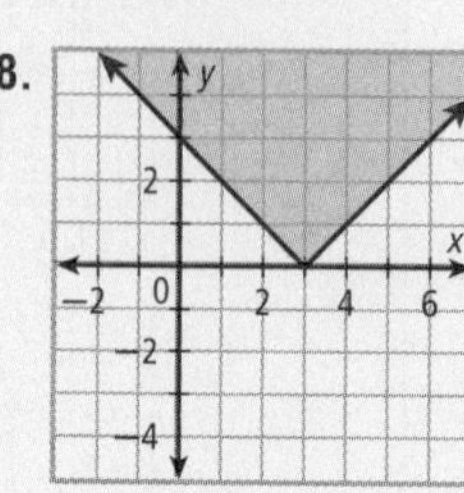

51.
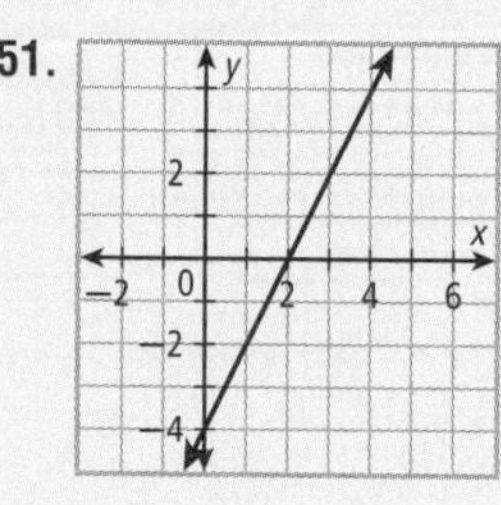

53.
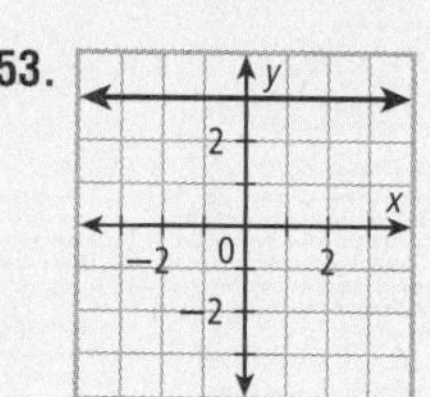

6-6 Solving Systems of Linear Inequalities

Objective
Graph and solve systems of linear inequalities in two variables.

Vocabulary
system of linear inequalities
solutions of a system of linear inequalities

Who uses this?
The owner of a surf shop can use systems of linear inequalities to determine how many surfboards and wakeboards need to be sold to make a certain profit. (See Example 4.)

A **system of linear inequalities** is a set of two or more linear inequalities containing two or more variables. The **solutions of a system of linear inequalities** are all of the ordered pairs that satisfy all the linear inequalities in the system.

Remember!
An ordered pair must be a solution of all inequalities to be a solution of the system.

EXAMPLE 1 Identifying Solutions of Systems of Linear Inequalities

Tell whether the ordered pair is a solution of the given system.

A $(2, 1); \begin{cases} y < -x + 4 \\ y \le x + 1 \end{cases}$

(2, 1)		(2, 1)	
$y < -x + 4$		$y \le x + 1$	
1	$-2 + 4$	1	$2 + 1$
$1 < 2$ ✓		$1 \le 3$ ✓	

(2, 1) is a solution to the system because it satisfies both inequalities.

B $(2, 0); \begin{cases} y \ge 2x \\ y < x + 1 \end{cases}$

(2, 0)		(2, 0)	
$y \ge 2x$		$y < x + 1$	
0	$2(2)$	0	$2 + 1$
$0 \ge 4$ ✗		$0 < 3$ ✓	

(2, 0) is not a solution to the system because it does not satisfy both inequalities.

CHECK IT OUT! Tell whether the ordered pair is a solution of the given system.

1a. $(0, 1); \begin{cases} y < -3x + 2 \\ y \ge x - 1 \end{cases}$ yes **1b.** $(0, 0); \begin{cases} y > -x + 1 \\ y > x - 1 \end{cases}$ no

To show all the solutions of a system of linear inequalities, graph the solutions of each inequality. The solutions of the system are represented by the overlapping shaded regions. Below are graphs of Examples 1A and 1B.

Example 1A

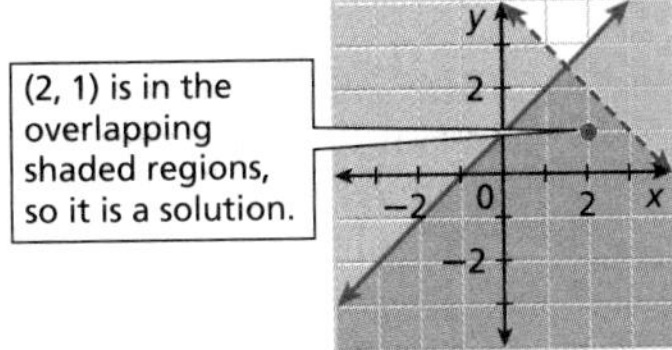

(2, 1) is in the overlapping shaded regions, so it is a solution.

Example 1B

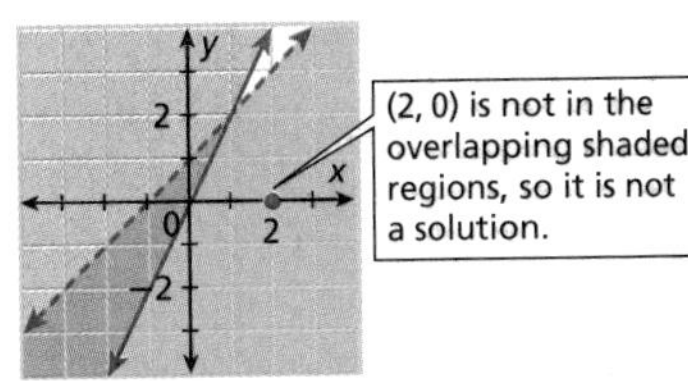

(2, 0) is not in the overlapping shaded regions, so it is not a solution.

6-6 Organizer

Pacing: Traditional $1\frac{1}{2}$ days
Block $\frac{3}{4}$ day

Objective: Graph and solve systems of linear inequalities in two variables.

Online Edition
Tutorial Videos, Interactivity

Countdown Week 14

Power Presentations with PowerPoint®

Warm Up

Solve each inequality for *y*.

1. $8x + y < 6$ $y < -8x + 6$
2. $3x - 2y > 10$ $y < \frac{3}{2}x - 5$
3. Graph the solutions of $4x + 3y > 9$.

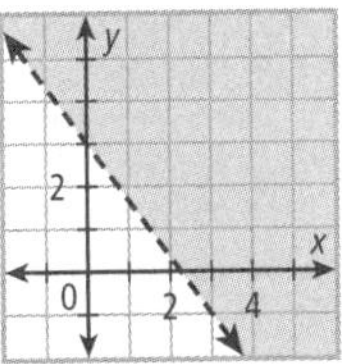

Also available on transparency

Math Humor

Q: Why did the math student wear two pairs of sunglasses?

A: He wanted to have overlapping shades.

1 Introduce

6-6 Solving Systems of Linear Inequalities

You will need a graphing calculator for this Exploration.

1. To graph the inequality $y > 2x$, first press [Y=] and enter the equation $y = 2x$ as **Y1**.
2. Use the arrow keys to move the cursor to the left of **Y1**. Then press [ENTER] two times until the icon changes from a diagonal line to a solid triangle above the line.
3. Press [GRAPH].
4. Enter the equation $y = -x + 3$ as **Y2**. Now graph the inequality $y < -x + 3$ in the same viewing window as $y > 2x$.
5. Use the arrow keys to move the cursor to the left of **Y2**. Then press [ENTER] three times until the icon changes from a diagonal line to a solid triangle below the line.
6. Press [GRAPH].

THINK AND DISCUSS

7. **Describe** what you see when you graph the two inequalities in the same window.

Motivate

Have students graph the solutions of the following compound inequality.

$x > 2$ AND $x < 5$

Tell students that, like compound inequalities, systems of inequalites have solutions that are represented by overlapping areas.

Explorations and answers are provided in *Alternate Openers: Explorations Transparencies.*

State Resources

Power Presentations with PowerPoint®

Additional Examples

Example 1

Tell whether the ordered pair is a solution of the given system.

A. $(-1, -3)$; $\begin{cases} y \le -3x + 1 \\ y < 2x + 2 \end{cases}$ yes

B. $(-1, 5)$; $\begin{cases} y < -2x - 1 \\ y \ge x + 3 \end{cases}$ no

Example 2

Graph each system of linear inequalities. Give two ordered pairs that are solutions and two that are not solutions.

A. $\begin{cases} y \le 3 \\ y > -x + 5 \end{cases}$

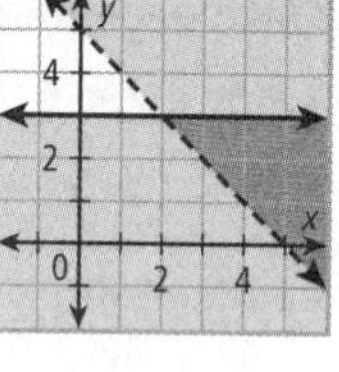

Possible answer: solutions: $(8, 1)$, $(6, 3)$; not solutions: $(-4, 4)$, $(2, 6)$

B. $\begin{cases} -3x + 2y \ge 2 \\ y < 4x + 3 \end{cases}$

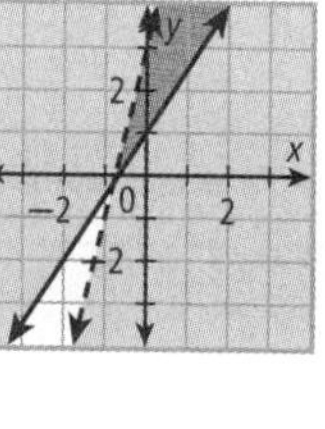

Possible answer: solutions: $(2, 6)$, $(1, 3)$; not solutions: $(0, 0)$, $(-4, 5)$

Example 3

Graph each system of linear inequalities. Describe the solutions.

A. $\begin{cases} y \le -2x - 4 \\ y > -2x + 5 \end{cases}$

no solutions

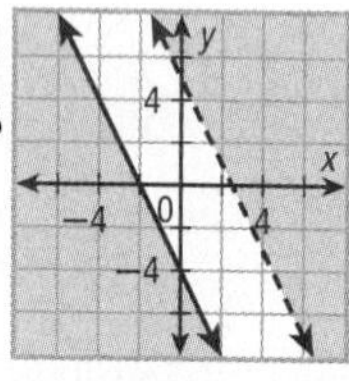

B. $\begin{cases} y > 3x - 2 \\ y < 3x + 6 \end{cases}$

all pts. between the par. lines

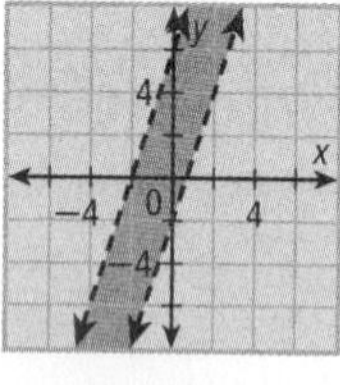

C. $\begin{cases} y \ge 4x + 6 \\ y \ge 4x - 5 \end{cases}$

same as solutions of $y \ge 4x + 6$

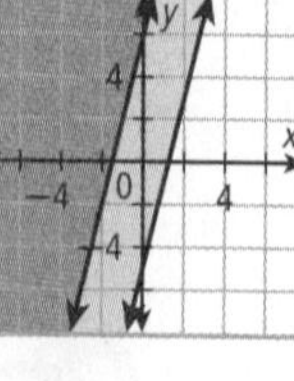

2a.

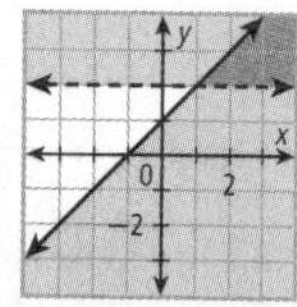

Possible answer: solutions: $(3, 3)$, $(4, 4)$; not solutions: $(-3, 1)$, $(-1, -4)$

2b.

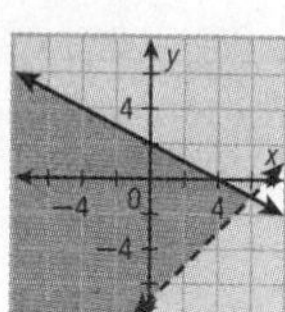

Possible answer: solutions: $(0, 0)$, $(3, -2)$; not solutions: $(4, 4)$, $(1, -6)$

3a. no solutions

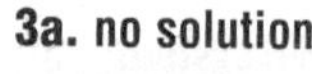

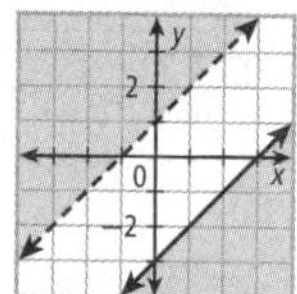

3b. all pts. between and on the parallel lines

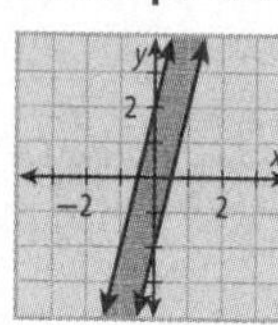

EXAMPLE 2 Solving a System of Linear Inequalities by Graphing

Graph the system of linear inequalities. Give two ordered pairs that are solutions and two that are not solutions.

$$\begin{cases} 8x + 4y \le 12 \\ y > \frac{1}{2}x - 2 \end{cases}$$

$8x + 4y \le 12$ *Solve the first inequality for y.*

$4y \le -8x + 12$

$y \le -2x + 3$

Graph the system.

$$\begin{cases} y \le -2x + 3 \\ y > \frac{1}{2}x - 2 \end{cases}$$

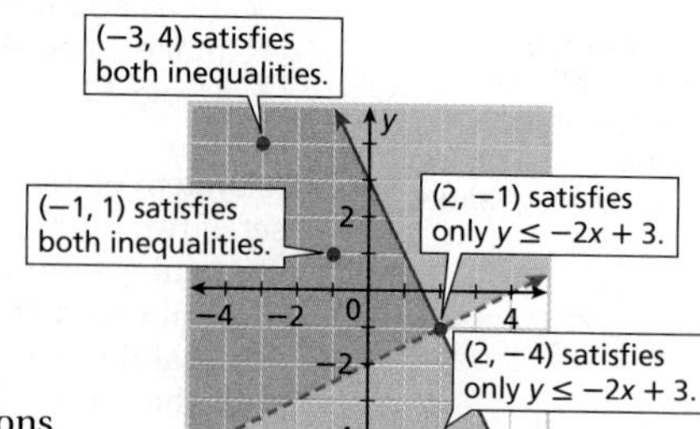

$(-1, 1)$ and $(-3, 4)$ are solutions.
$(2, -1)$ and $(2, -4)$ are not solutions.

CHECK IT OUT! **Graph each system of linear inequalities. Give two ordered pairs that are solutions and two that are not solutions.**

2a. $\begin{cases} y \le x + 1 \\ y > 2 \end{cases}$ **2b.** $\begin{cases} y > x - 7 \\ 3x + 6y \le 12 \end{cases}$

In Lesson 6-4, you saw that in systems of linear equations, if the lines are parallel, there are no solutions. With systems of linear inequalities, that is not always true.

EXAMPLE 3 Graphing Systems with Parallel Boundary Lines

Graph each system of linear inequalities. Describe the solutions.

A $\begin{cases} y < 2x - 3 \\ y > 2x + 2 \end{cases}$

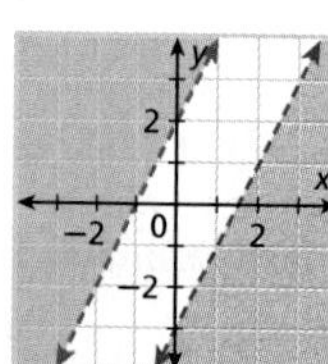

This system has no solution.

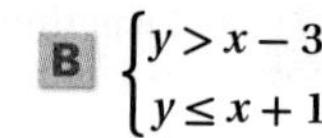

B $\begin{cases} y > x - 3 \\ y \le x + 1 \end{cases}$

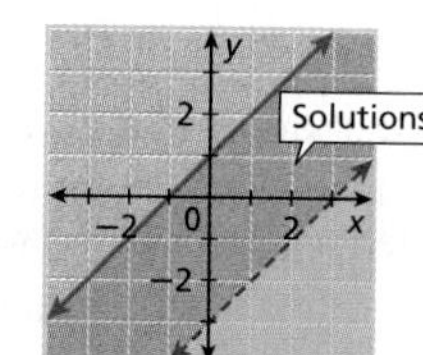

The solutions are all points between the parallel lines and on the solid line.

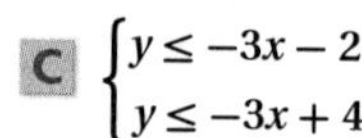

C $\begin{cases} y \le -3x - 2 \\ y \le -3x + 4 \end{cases}$

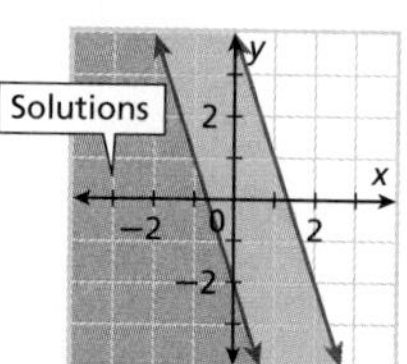

The solutions are the same as the solutions of $y \le -3x - 2$.

2 Teach

Guided Instruction

Tell students that graphing a system of inequalities is just graphing two or more inequalities on the same coordinate plane. The solution is the overlapping region. Encourage students to always use a test point to check that they shaded the correct regions.

Visual Have students shade graphs of inequalities using two different colored pencils (MK). This will make the solution area easier to see.

Have two students each graph a linear inequality in two variables on different transparencies. Then combine the two graphs by overlapping them, and have students write two ordered pairs that are solutions and two that are not. Repeat with another pair of students until all have taken a turn.

Graph each system of linear inequalities. Describe the solutions.

3a. $\begin{cases} y > x + 1 \\ y \le x - 3 \end{cases}$ **3b.** $\begin{cases} y \ge 4x - 2 \\ y \le 4x + 2 \end{cases}$ **3c.** $\begin{cases} y > -2x + 3 \\ y > -2x \end{cases}$

3c. same as solutions of $y > -2x + 3$

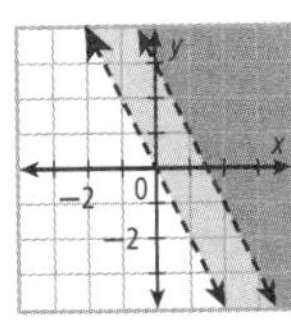

EXAMPLE 4 *Business Application*

A surf shop makes the profits given in the table. The shop owner sells at least 10 surfboards and at least 20 wakeboards per month. He wants to earn at least \$2000 a month. Show and describe all possible combinations of surfboards and wakeboards that the store owner needs to sell to meet his goals. List two possible combinations.

Profit per Board Sold (\$)	
Surfboard	150
Wakeboard	100

Step 1 Write a system of inequalities.
Let x represent the number of surfboards and y represent the number of wakeboards.

$x \ge 10$ *He sells at least 10 surfboards.*

$y \ge 20$ *He sells at least 20 wakeboards.*

$150x + 100y \ge 2000$ *He wants to earn a total of at least \$2000.*

Step 2 Graph the system.
The graph should be in only the first quadrant because sales are not negative.

Step 3 Describe all possible combinations.
To meet the sales goals, the shop could sell any combination represented by an ordered pair of whole numbers in the solution region. Answers must be whole numbers because the shop cannot sell part of a surfboard or wakeboard.

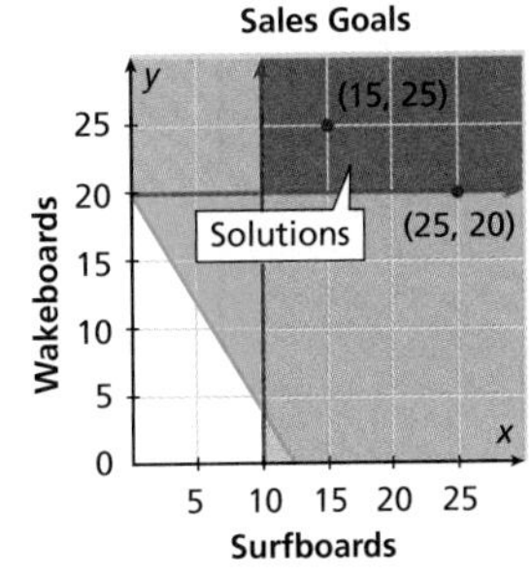

Step 4 List two possible combinations.
Two possible combinations are:
15 surfboards and 25 wakeboards
25 surfboards and 20 wakeboards

Caution!

An ordered pair solution of the system need not have whole numbers, but answers to many application problems may be restricted to whole numbers.

CHECK IT OUT!

4. At her party, Alice is serving pepper jack cheese and cheddar cheese. She wants to have at least 2 pounds of each. Alice wants to spend at most \$20 on cheese. Show and describe all possible combinations of the two cheeses Alice could buy. List two possible combinations.

Price per Pound (\$)	
Pepper Jack	4
Cheddar	2

4. Cheese Combinations

Cheddar cheese (lb); Pepper jack cheese (lb)

Possible answer:
(3 lb pepper jack, 2 lb cheddar),
(2.5 lb pepper jack, 4 lb cheddar)

THINK AND DISCUSS

1. How would you write a system of linear inequalities from a graph?

2. GET ORGANIZED Copy and complete each part of the graphic organizer. In each box, draw a graph and list one solution.

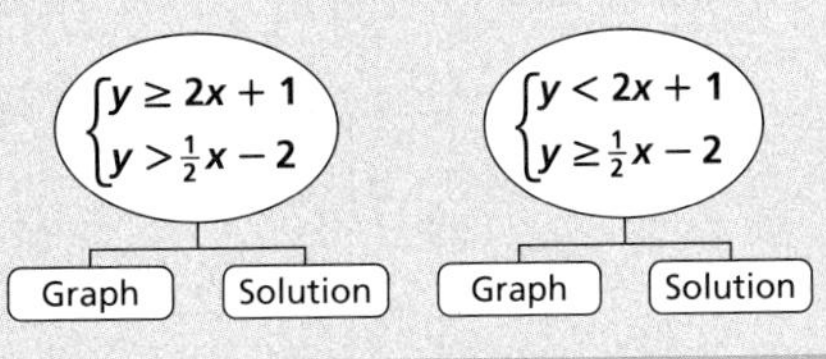

Power Presentations with PowerPoint®

Additional Examples

Example 4

In one week, Ed can mow at most 9 times and rake at most 7 times. He charges \$20 for mowing and \$10 for raking. He needs to earn more than \$125 in one week. Show and describe all the possible combinations of mowing and raking that Ed can do to meet his goal. List two possible combinations.

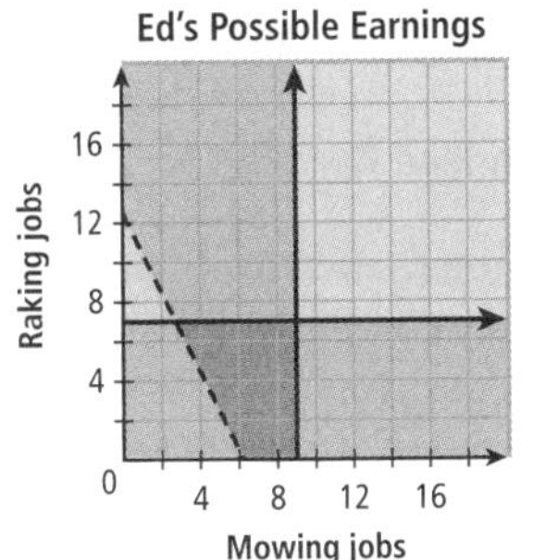

Reasonable answers must be whole numbers. Possible answer: (7 mowing, 4 raking), (8 mowing, 1 raking)

INTERVENTION
Questioning Strategies

EXAMPLE 1

- When do you need to check only one inequality? Why?

EXAMPLES 2–3

- How can you check that you shaded the correct areas?

EXAMPLE 4

- How do you choose which region to select the combinations from?

3 Close

Summarize

Emphasize that an ordered pair is a solution of a system of inequalities only if it makes every inequality in that system true. Graphically, the solutions will be in the overlapping shaded regions. Remind students that points on a boundary line are solutions if the line is solid, and are not solutions if the line is dashed. The intersection of boundary lines is a solution only if both lines are solid.

ONGOING ASSESSMENT and INTERVENTION

***Diagnose Before* the Lesson**
6-6 Warm Up, TE p. 435

***Monitor During* the Lesson**
Check It Out! Exercises, SE pp. 435–437
Questioning Strategies, TE pp. 437

***Assess After* the Lesson**
6-6 Lesson Quiz, TE p. 440
Alternative Assessment, TE p. 440

Answers to *Think and Discuss*

Possible answers:

1. To write a system of linear inequalities from a graph, write the linear inequality for each of the graphs that make up the system.
2. See p. A6.

6-6 Exercises

Assignment Guide

Assign *Guided Practice* exercises as necessary.

If you finished Examples **1–2**
Basic 16–22, 34, 35
Average 16–22, 34, 35
Advanced 16–22, 34, 35

If you finished Examples **1–4**
Basic 16–29, 30–38 even, 39, 42, 44–46, 51–60
Average 16–29, 30–42 even, 44–47, 51–60
Advanced 16–29, 30, 41–60

Homework Quick Check
Quickly check key concepts.
Exercises: 16, 22, 26, 29, 42

Answers

5–14. See pp. A25–A26.

15.

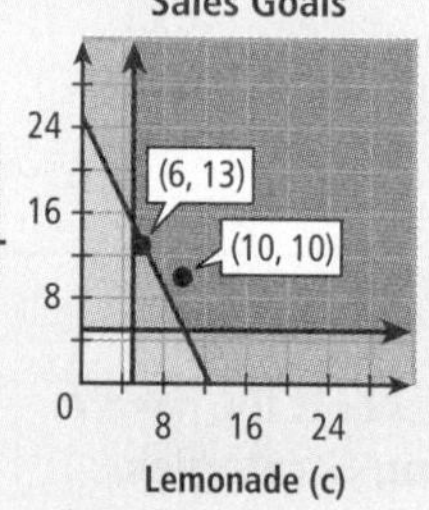

Possible answer:
(6 c lemonade, 13 cupcakes),
(10 c lemonade, 10 cupcakes)

19–28. See p. A26.

State Resources

6-6 Exercises

go.hrw.com
Homework Help Online
KEYWORD: MA7 6-6
Parent Resources Online
KEYWORD: MA7 Parent

GUIDED PRACTICE

1. **Vocabulary** A solution of a system of inequalities is a solution of ___?___ of the inequalities in the system. (*at least one* or *all*) **all**

SEE EXAMPLE 1 p. 435

Tell whether the ordered pair is a solution of the given system.

2. $(0, 0); \begin{cases} y < -x + 3 \\ y < x + 2 \end{cases}$ **yes**
3. $(0, 0); \begin{cases} y < 3 \\ y > x - 2 \end{cases}$ **yes**
4. $(1, 0); \begin{cases} y > 3x \\ y \le x + 1 \end{cases}$ **no**

SEE EXAMPLE 2 p. 436

Graph each system of linear inequalities. Give two ordered pairs that are solutions and two that are not solutions.

5. $\begin{cases} y < 2x - 1 \\ y > 2 \end{cases}$
6. $\begin{cases} x < 3 \\ y > x - 2 \end{cases}$
7. $\begin{cases} y \ge 3x \\ 3x + y \ge 3 \end{cases}$
8. $\begin{cases} 2x - 4y \le 8 \\ y > x - 2 \end{cases}$

SEE EXAMPLE 3 p. 436

Graph each system of linear inequalities. Describe the solutions.

9. $\begin{cases} y > 2x + 3 \\ y < 2x \end{cases}$
10. $\begin{cases} y \le -3x - 1 \\ y \ge -3x + 1 \end{cases}$
11. $\begin{cases} y > 4x - 1 \\ y \le 4x + 1 \end{cases}$
12. $\begin{cases} y < -x + 3 \\ y > -x + 2 \end{cases}$
13. $\begin{cases} y > 2x - 1 \\ y > 2x - 4 \end{cases}$
14. $\begin{cases} y \le -3x + 4 \\ y \le -3x - 3 \end{cases}$

SEE EXAMPLE 4 p. 437

15. **Business** Sandy makes \$2 profit on every cup of lemonade that she sells and \$1 on every cupcake that she sells. Sandy wants to sell at least 5 cups of lemonade and at least 5 cupcakes per day. She wants to earn at least \$25 per day. Show and describe all the possible combinations of lemonade and cupcakes that Sandy needs to sell to meet her goals. List two possible combinations.

PRACTICE AND PROBLEM SOLVING

Independent Practice

For Exercises	See Example
16–18	1
19–22	2
23–28	3
29	4

Extra Practice
Skills Practice p. S15
Application Practice p. S33

Tell whether the ordered pair is a solution of the given system.

16. $(0, 0); \begin{cases} y > -x - 1 \\ y < 2x + 4 \end{cases}$ **yes**
17. $(0, 0); \begin{cases} x + y < 3 \\ y > 3x - 4 \end{cases}$ **yes**
18. $(1, 0); \begin{cases} y > 3x \\ y > 3x + 1 \end{cases}$ **no**

Graph each system of linear inequalities. Give two ordered pairs that are solutions and two that are not solutions.

19. $\begin{cases} y < -3x - 3 \\ y \ge 0 \end{cases}$
20. $\begin{cases} y < -1 \\ y > 2x - 1 \end{cases}$
21. $\begin{cases} y > 2x + 4 \\ 6x + 2y \ge -2 \end{cases}$
22. $\begin{cases} 9x + 3y \le 6 \\ y > x \end{cases}$

Graph each system of linear inequalities. Describe the solutions.

23. $\begin{cases} y < 3 \\ y > 5 \end{cases}$
24. $\begin{cases} y < x - 1 \\ y > x - 2 \end{cases}$
25. $\begin{cases} x \ge 2 \\ x \le 2 \end{cases}$
26. $\begin{cases} y > -4x - 3 \\ y < -4x + 2 \end{cases}$
27. $\begin{cases} y > -1 \\ y > 2 \end{cases}$
28. $\begin{cases} y \le 2x + 1 \\ y \le 2x - 4 \end{cases}$

6-6 READING STRATEGIES

To solve a real-world problem involving inequalities, there is a lot of information that must be analyzed. Study the example below.

The perimeter of a garden must be less than 20 meters.
The width must be at least 6 meters.
Show all possible combinations of the garden's length and width.
Identify two possible solutions.

- Let x = length of garden
- Let y = width of garden

Define variables for the unknowns: "the garden's length and width."

The perimeter must be less than 20 meters: $P = 2l + 2w$; and "less than" means <.

Garden's Dimension $\begin{cases} 2x + 2y < 20 \\ y \ge 6 \end{cases}$

The width must be at least 6 meters: y = width and "at least" means ≥.

Solutions are all points in the double-shaded region, but not on the dotted line.

$y \ge 6$ solid line shaded above

Use a first-quadrant grid because length and width can only be positive values.

Rewrite $2x + 2y < 20$ in slope-intercept form: $y < -x + 10$ dotted line, shaded below

Width (m)
Length (m)

Possible solutions: $l = 2$ m, $w = 7$ m and $l = 1$ m, $w = 8$ m

Manuel is going to build a rabbit cage with a rectangular base.
The perimeter can be no greater than 30 feet.
The length must be greater than 8 feet.
Let x = length and y = width.

1. Write a system of linear inequalities to describe the possible cage sizes.

$\begin{cases} 2x + 2y \le 30 \\ x > 8 \end{cases}$

2. Graph the system to show possible dimensions.
3. Give two possible dimensions for the cage.

$l = 10$ ft, $w = 5$ ft and
$l = 11$ ft, $w = 4$ ft

Rabbit Cage
Width (ft)
Length (ft)

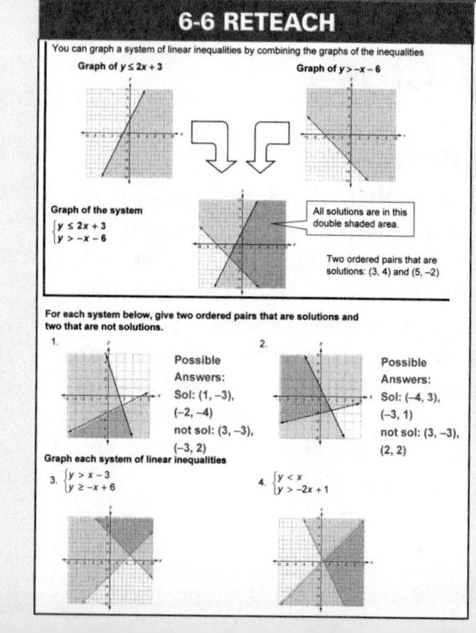

6-6 RETEACH

You can graph a system of linear inequalities by combining the graphs of the inequalities

Graph of $y \le 2x + 3$

Graph of $y > -x - 6$

Graph of the system $\begin{cases} y \le 2x + 3 \\ y > -x - 6 \end{cases}$

All solutions are in this double shaded area.

Two ordered pairs that are solutions: (3, 4) and (5, –2)

For each system below, give two ordered pairs that are solutions and two that are not solutions.

1. Possible Answers: Sol: (1, –3), (–2, –4) not sol: (3, –3), (–3, 2)

2. Possible Answers: Sol: (–4, 3), (–3, 1) not sol: (3, –3), (2, 2)

Graph each system of linear inequalities

3. $\begin{cases} y > x - 3 \\ y \ge -x + 6 \end{cases}$

4. $\begin{cases} y < x \\ y > -2x + 1 \end{cases}$

29. **Multi-Step** Linda works at a pharmacy for $15 an hour. She also baby-sits for $10 an hour. Linda needs to earn at least $90 per week, but she does not want to work more than 20 hours per week. Show and describe the number of hours Linda could work at each job to meet her goals. List two possible solutions.

30. **Farming** Tony wants to plant at least 40 acres of corn and at least 50 acres of soybeans. He wants no more than 200 acres of corn and soybeans. Show and describe all the possible combinations of the number of acres of corn and of soybeans Tony could plant. List two possible combinations.

Graph each system of linear inequalities.

31. $\begin{cases} y \geq -3 \\ y \geq 2 \end{cases}$ 32. $\begin{cases} y > -2x - 1 \\ y > -2x - 3 \end{cases}$ 33. $\begin{cases} x \leq -3 \\ x \geq 1 \end{cases}$ 34. $\begin{cases} y < 4 \\ y > 0 \end{cases}$

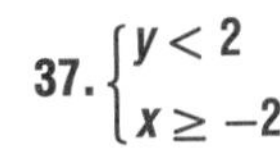
37. $\begin{cases} y < 2 \\ x \geq -2 \end{cases}$

Write a system of linear inequalities to represent each graph.

35.
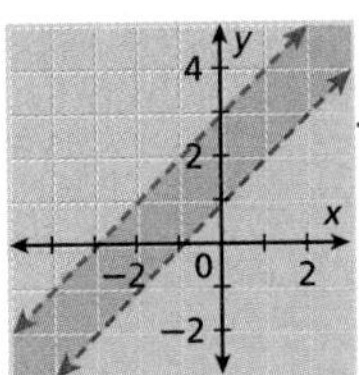
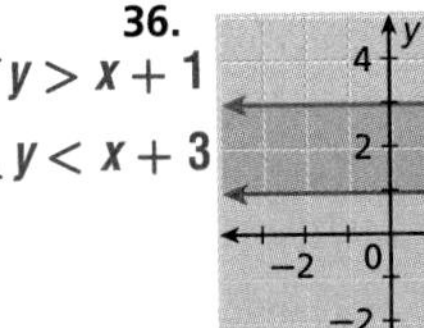
$\begin{cases} y > x + 1 \\ y < x + 3 \end{cases}$

36.
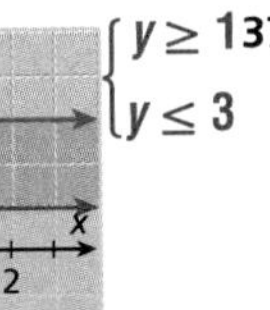
$\begin{cases} y \geq 1 \\ y \leq 3 \end{cases}$

37.
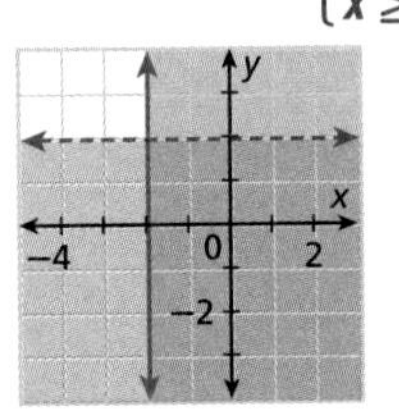

38. **Military** For males to enter the United States Air Force Academy, located in Colorado Springs, CO, they must be at least 17 but less than 23 years of age. Their standing height must be not less than 60 inches and not greater than 80 inches. Graph all possible heights and ages for eligible male candidates. Give three possible combinations.

39. **/// ERROR ANALYSIS ///** Two students wrote a system of linear inequalities to describe the graph. Which student is incorrect? Explain the error. **Student B; the inequality symbols are incorrect.**

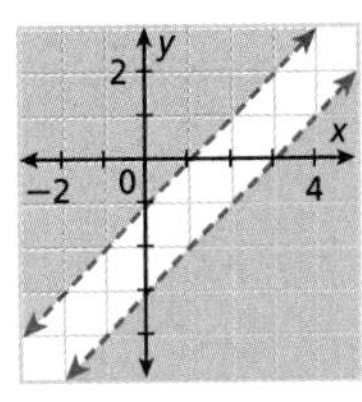

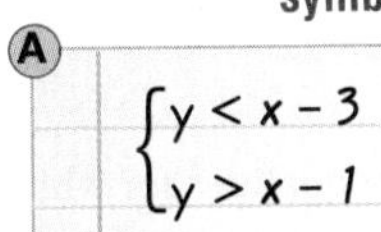
A $\begin{cases} y < x - 3 \\ y > x - 1 \end{cases}$

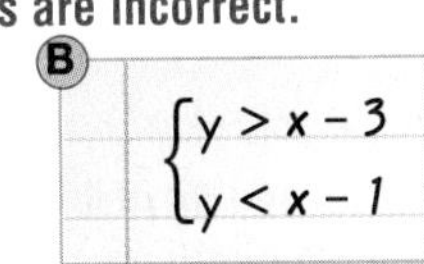
B $\begin{cases} y > x - 3 \\ y < x - 1 \end{cases}$

40. **Recreation** Vance wants to fence in a rectangular area for his dog. He wants the length of the rectangle to be at least 30 feet and the perimeter to be no more than 150 feet. Graph all possible dimensions of the rectangle.

41. **Critical Thinking** Can the solutions of a system of linear inequalities be the points on a line? Explain.

LINK Military

In 1959, the first class graduated from the Air Force Academy. The first class that included women graduated in 1980.

MULTI-STEP TEST PREP

42. This problem will prepare you for the Multi-Step Test Prep on page 442.

Gloria is starting her own company making teddy bears. She has enough bear bodies to create 40 bears. She will make girl bears and boy bears.

a. Write an inequality to show this situation.

b. Gloria will charge $15 for girl bears and $12 for boy bears. She wants to earn at least $540 a week. Write an inequality to describe this situation.

c. Graph this situation and locate the solution region.

COMMON ERROR ALERT

Students may have trouble graphing systems containing horizontal or vertical boundary lines, such as in **Exercises 5 and 6.** Remind them that the line intersects the x-axis when x is the only variable in the inequality and that the line intersects the y-axis when y is the only variable.

MULTI-STEP TEST PREP **Exercise 42** involves graphing solutions of linear inequalities to determine the number of items that need to be sold to meet earning goals. This exercise prepares students for the Multi-Step Test Prep on page 442.

Answers

29.

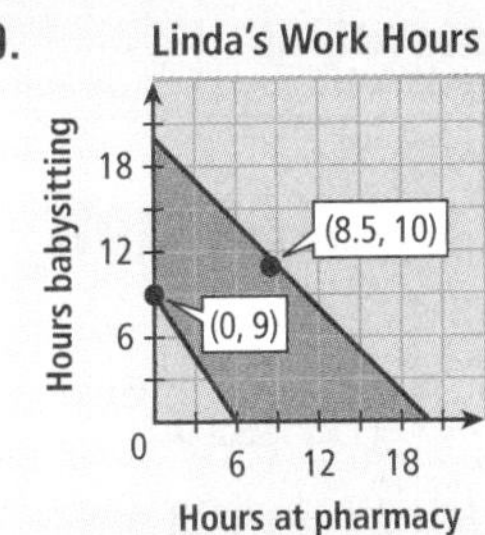

Possible answer: (0 h at pharmacy, 9 h babysitting), (8.5 h at pharmacy, 10 h babysitting)

30–34, 38, 40–42. See pp. A26–A27.

6-6 PROBLEM SOLVING

Write the correct answer.

1. Paul earns $7 per hour at the bagel shop and $12 per hour mowing lawns. Paul needs to earn at least $120 per week, but he must work less than 30 hours per week. Write and graph the system of linear inequalities that describes this situation.

$\begin{cases} 7x + 12y \geq 120 \\ x + y < 30 \end{cases}$

Hours Paul Works per Week (Mowing Lawns (hours); Bagel Shop (hours))

2. Zoe plans to knit a scarf. She wants the scarf to be more than 1 but less than 1.5 feet wide, and more than 6 but less than 8 feet long. Graph all possible dimensions of Zoe's scarf. List two possible combinations.

width of 1.25 ft, length of 7 ft; width of 1.4 ft, length of 7.5 ft

Zoe's Scarf Dimensions (Length (ft); Width (ft))

The graph shows the numbers of two types of custom wood tables that can be made to fit a client's needs. Select the best answer.

3. Which system of linear inequalities represents the graph?

A $\begin{cases} x + y \leq 15 \\ y \geq 12 - \frac{4}{3}x \end{cases}$ C $\begin{cases} x + y \geq 15 \\ y \geq \frac{4}{3}x - 12 \end{cases}$

B $\begin{cases} y \leq x + 15 \\ y \geq 12 - \frac{4}{3}x \end{cases}$ D $\begin{cases} y \leq 15 - x \\ y \leq \frac{4}{3}x - 12 \end{cases}$

4. If 6 buffet tables are built, which can NOT be the number of dining tables built?

F 4 H 8
G 6 J 10

Custom Tables (Number of Dining Tables; Number of Buffet Tables)

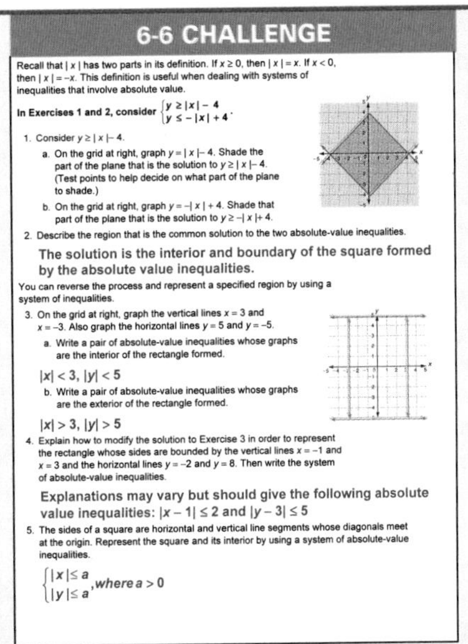
6-6 CHALLENGE

Recall that $|x|$ has two parts in its definition. If $x \geq 0$, then $|x| = x$. If $x < 0$, then $|x| = -x$. This definition is useful when dealing with systems of inequalities that involve absolute value.

In Exercises 1 and 2, consider $\begin{cases} y \geq |x| - 4 \\ y \leq -|x| + 4 \end{cases}$.

1. Consider $y \geq |x| - 4$.
   a. On the grid at right, graph $y = |x| - 4$. Shade the part of the plane that is the solution to $y \geq |x| - 4$. (Test points to help decide on what part of the plane to shade.)
   b. On the grid at right, graph $y = -|x| + 4$. Shade that part of the plane that is the solution to $y \geq -|x| + 4$.
2. Describe the region that is the common solution to the two absolute-value inequalities.

The solution is the interior and boundary of the square formed by the absolute value inequalities.

You can reverse the process and represent a specified region by using a system of inequalities.

3. On the grid at right, graph the vertical lines $x = 3$ and $x = -3$. Also graph the horizontal lines $y = 5$ and $y = -5$.
   a. Write a pair of absolute-value inequalities whose graphs are the interior of the rectangle formed.

   $|x| < 3$, $|y| < 5$

   b. Write a pair of absolute-value inequalities whose graphs are the exterior of the rectangle formed.

   $|x| > 3$, $|y| > 5$

4. Explain how to modify the solution to Exercise 3 in order to represent the rectangle whose sides are bounded by the vertical lines $x = -1$ and $x = 3$ and the horizontal lines $y = -2$ and $y = 8$. Then write the system of absolute-value inequalities.

Explanations may vary but should give the following absolute value inequalities: $|x - 1| \leq 2$ and $|y - 3| \leq 5$

5. The sides of a square are horizontal and vertical line segments whose diagonals meet at the origin. Represent the square and its interior by using a system of absolute-value inequalities.

$\begin{cases} |x| \leq a \\ |y| \leq a \end{cases}$, where $a > 0$

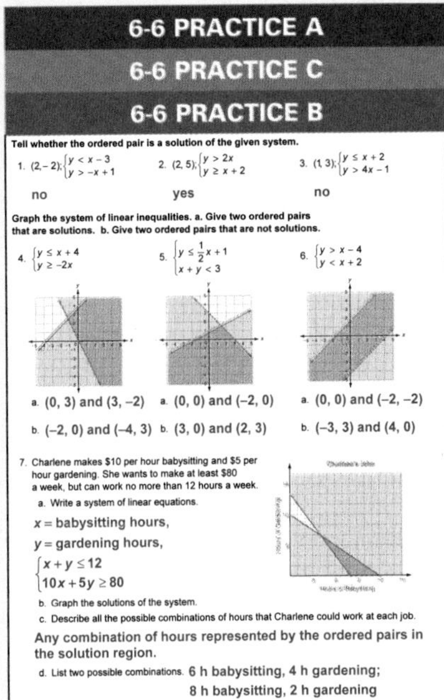
6-6 PRACTICE A
6-6 PRACTICE C
6-6 PRACTICE B

Tell whether the ordered pair is a solution of the given system.

1. $(2, -2)$; $\begin{cases} y < x - 3 \\ y > -x + 1 \end{cases}$ no

2. $(2, 5)$; $\begin{cases} y > 2x \\ y \geq x + 2 \end{cases}$ yes

3. $(1, 3)$; $\begin{cases} y \leq x + 2 \\ y > 4x - 1 \end{cases}$ no

Graph the system of linear inequalities. a. Give two ordered pairs that are solutions. b. Give two ordered pairs that are not solutions.

4. $\begin{cases} y \leq x + 4 \\ y \geq -2x \end{cases}$
   a. (0, 3) and (3, –2)
   b. (–2, 0) and (–4, 3)

5. $\begin{cases} y \leq \frac{1}{2}x + 1 \\ x + y < 3 \end{cases}$
   a. (0, 0) and (–2, 0)
   b. (3, 0) and (2, 3)

6. $\begin{cases} y > x - 4 \\ y < x + 2 \end{cases}$
   a. (0, 0) and (–2, –2)
   b. (–3, 3) and (4, 0)

7. Charlene makes $10 per hour babysitting and $5 per hour gardening. She wants to make at least $80 a week, but can work no more than 12 hours a week.
   a. Write a system of linear equations.

   x = babysitting hours,
   y = gardening hours,
   $\begin{cases} x + y \leq 12 \\ 10x + 5y \geq 80 \end{cases}$

   b. Graph the solutions of the system.
   c. Describe all the possible combinations of hours that Charlene could work at each job.

   Any combination of hours represented by the ordered pairs in the solution region.

   d. List two possible combinations. 6 h babysitting, 4 h gardening; 8 h babysitting, 2 h gardening

TEST PREP DOCTOR The graph in **Exercise 45** shows solutions between parallel lines. This is not possible when the inequality symbols are both < or both >. Choices **H** and **J** can be eliminated.

Journal

Have students describe a real-world situation that can be modeled by a system of linear inequalities in two variables and in which reasonable solutions must be whole numbers.

ALTERNATIVE ASSESSMENT

Tell students to write and graph a system of inequalities that has solutions, and identify two solutions. Then have students write and graph a system that has no solutions.

Power Presentations with PowerPoint®

6-6 Lesson Quiz

1. Graph $\begin{cases} y < x + 2 \\ 5x + 2y \geq 10 \end{cases}$. Give two ordered pairs that are solutions and two that are not solutions.

Possible answer: solutions: (4, 4), (8, 6); not solutions: (0, 0), (−2, 3)

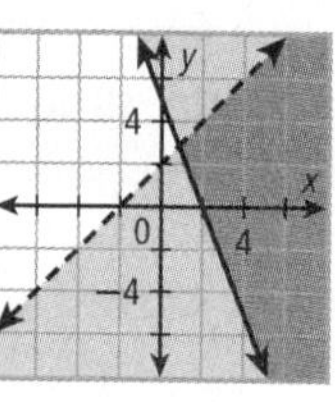

2. Dee has at most $150 to spend on restocking dolls and trains at her toy store. Dolls cost $7.50, and trains cost $5.00. Dee needs no more than 10 trains, and at least 8 dolls. Show and describe all possible combinations of dolls and trains that Dee can buy. List two possible combinations.

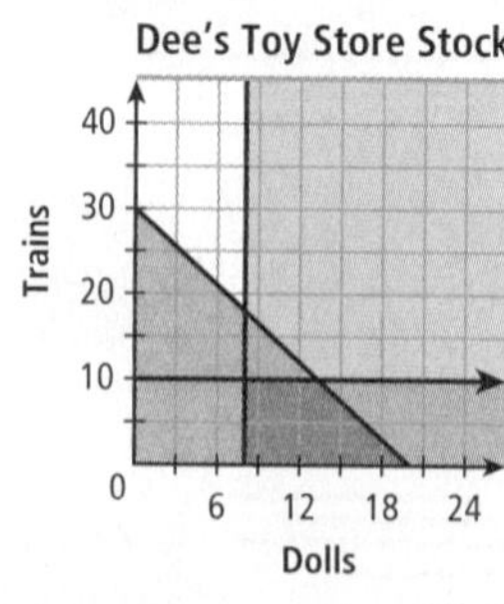

Reasonable answers must be whole numbers. Possible answer: (12 dolls, 6 trains), (16 dolls, 4 trains)

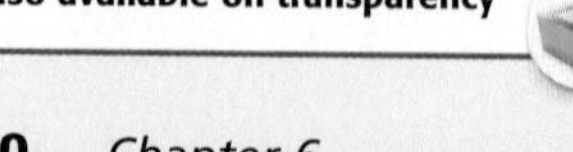
Also available on transparency

43. **Write About It** What must be true of the boundary lines in a system of two linear inequalities if there is no solution of the system? Explain.
The boundary lines must be parallel. If the boundary lines are not parallel, there will be overlap.

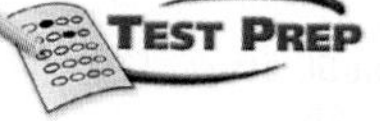

TEST PREP

44. Which point is a solution of $\begin{cases} 2x + y \geq 3 \\ y \geq -2x + 1 \end{cases}$?

Ⓐ (0, 0) Ⓑ (0, 1) Ⓒ (1, 0) **Ⓓ (1, 1)**

45. Which system of inequalities best describes the graph?

Ⓕ $\begin{cases} y < 2x - 3 \\ y > 2x + 1 \end{cases}$ Ⓗ $\begin{cases} y < 2x - 3 \\ y < 2x + 1 \end{cases}$

Ⓖ $\begin{cases} y > 2x - 3 \\ y < 2x + 1 \end{cases}$ Ⓙ $\begin{cases} y > 2x - 3 \\ y > 2x + 1 \end{cases}$

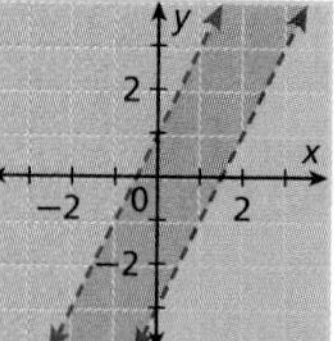

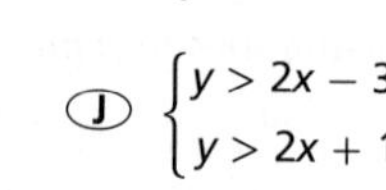

46. **Short Response** Graph and describe $\begin{cases} y + x > 2 \\ y \leq -3x + 4 \end{cases}$. Give two possible solutions of the system.

CHALLENGE AND EXTEND

47. 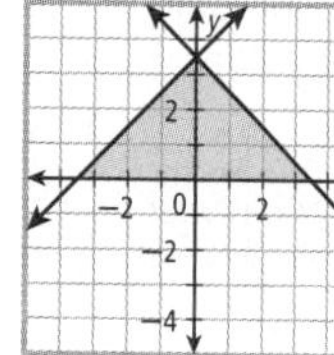

47. **Estimation** Graph the given system of inequalities. Estimate the area of the overlapping solution regions. **about 12 sq. units**
$\begin{cases} y \geq 0 \\ y \leq x + 3.5 \\ y \leq -x + 3.5 \end{cases}$

48. Write a system of linear inequalities for which $(-1, 1)$ and $(1, 4)$ are solutions and $(0, 0)$ and $(2, -1)$ are not solutions.

49. Graph $|y| < 1$.

50. Write a system of linear inequalities for which the solutions are all the points in the third quadrant. $\begin{cases} x < 0 \\ y < 0 \end{cases}$

SPIRAL REVIEW

Use the diagram to find each of the following. *(Lesson 1-6)*

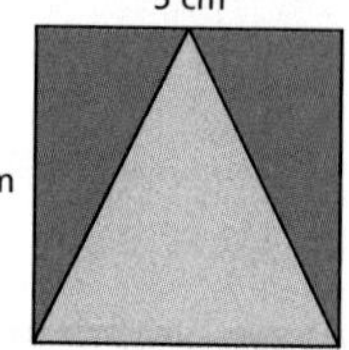

51. area of the square **25 cm²**
52. area of the yellow triangle **12.5 cm²**
53. combined area of the blue triangles **12.5 cm²**

Tell whether the given ordered pairs satisfy a linear function. *(Lesson 5-1)*

54. $\{(3, 8), (4, 6), (5, 4), (6, 2), (7, 0)\}$ **yes**
55. $\{(6, 1), (7, 2), (8, 4), (9, 7), (10, 11)\}$ **no**
56. $\{(2, 10), (7, 9), (12, 8), (17, 7), (22, 6)\}$ **yes**
57. $\{(1, -9), (3, -7), (5, -5), (7, -3), (9, -1)\}$ **yes**

Graph the solutions of each linear inequality. *(Lesson 6-5)*

58. $y \leq 2x - 1$
59. $-\frac{1}{4}x + y > 6$
60. $5 - x \geq 0$

Answers

46. 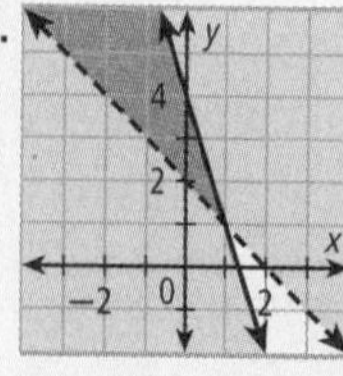

Possible answer: (0, 3), (−2, 6)

48. 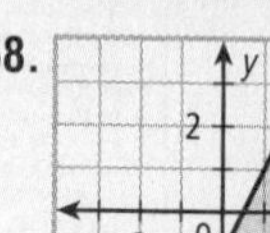
$\begin{cases} y \geq \frac{3}{2}x + \frac{5}{2} \\ y > -\frac{1}{2}x \end{cases}$

49. 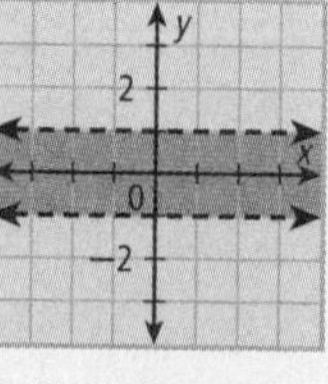

58.

59. 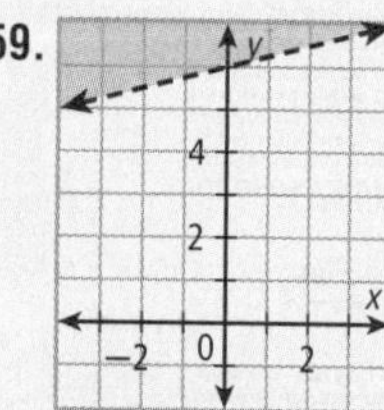

60. 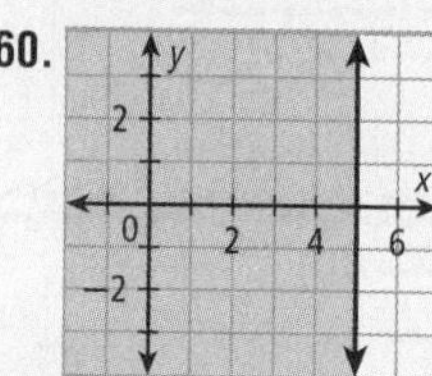

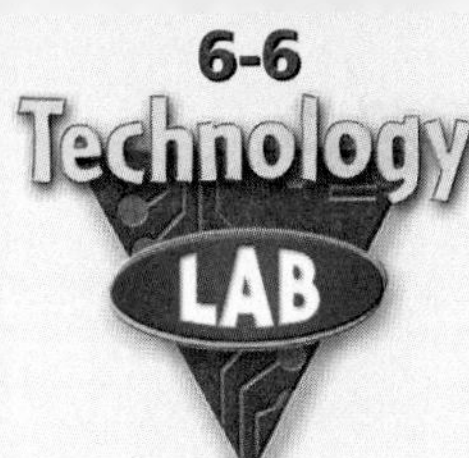

6-6 Technology LAB

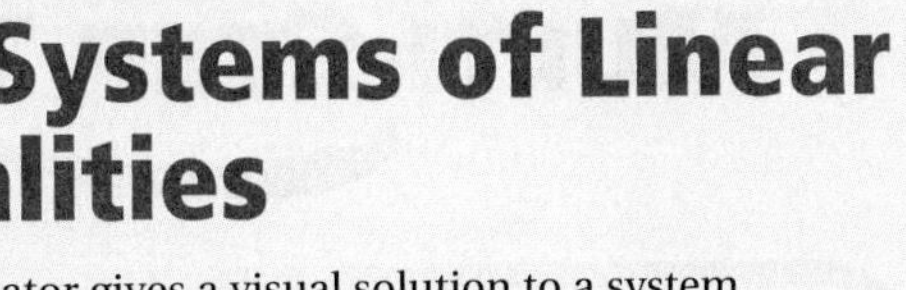

Solve Systems of Linear Inequalities

A graphing calculator gives a visual solution to a system of linear inequalities.

Use with Lesson 6-6

Activity

Graph the system $\begin{cases} y > 2x - 4 \\ 2.75y - x < 6 \end{cases}$**. Give two ordered pairs that are solutions.**

1. The first inequality is solved for y.

2. Graph the first inequality. First graph the boundary line $y = 2x - 4$. Press **Y=** and enter $2x - 4$ for **Y1**.

   The inequality contains the symbol >. The solution region is above the boundary line. Press ◀ to move the cursor to the left of **Y1**. Press **ENTER** until the icon that looks like a region above a line appears. Press **GRAPH**.

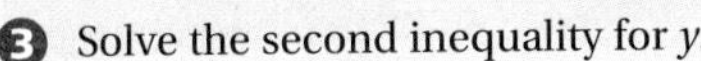

3. Solve the second inequality for y.

$$2.75y - x < 6$$
$$2.75y < x + 6$$
$$y < \frac{x + 6}{2.75}$$

4. Graph the second inequality. First graph the boundary line $y = \frac{x + 6}{2.75}$. Press **Y=** and enter $(x + 6)/2.75$ for **Y2**. The inequality contains the symbol <. The solution region is below the boundary line. Press ◀ to move the cursor to the left of **Y2**. Press **ENTER** until the icon that looks like a region below a line appears. Press **GRAPH**.

5. The solutions of the system are represented by the overlapping shaded regions. The points $(0, 0)$ and $(-1, 0)$ are in the shaded region.

Check Test $(0, 0)$ in both inequalities.

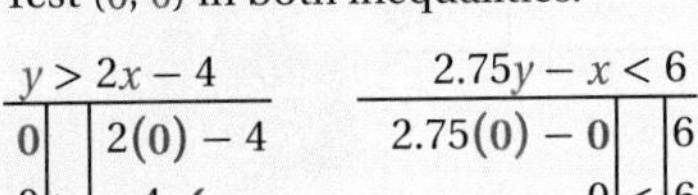

$y > 2x - 4$	
0	$2(0) - 4$
$0 >$	-4 ✓

$2.75y - x < 6$	
$2.75(0) - 0$	6
$0 <$	6 ✓

Test $(-1, 0)$ in both inequalities.

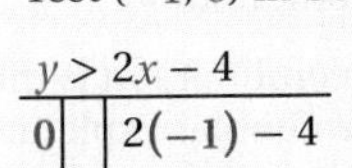

$y > 2x - 4$	
0	$2(-1) - 4$
$0 >$	-6 ✓

$2.75y - x < 6$	
$2.75(0) - (-1)$	6
$1 <$	6 ✓

Try This

Graph each system. Give two ordered pairs that are solutions.

1. $\begin{cases} x + 5y > -10 \\ x - y < 4 \end{cases}$

2. $\begin{cases} y > x - 2 \\ y \le x + 2 \end{cases}$

3. $\begin{cases} y > x - 2 \\ y \le 3 \end{cases}$

4. $\begin{cases} y < x - 3 \\ y - 3 > x \end{cases}$

Technology LAB Organizer

Use with Lesson 6-6

Pacing:
Traditional $\frac{1}{2}$ day
Block $\frac{1}{4}$ day

Objective: Use a graphing calculator to view solutions of a system of linear inequalities.

Materials: graphing calculator

Online Edition
Graphing Calculator, TechKeys

Countdown Week 14

Lab Resources

Technology Lab Activities
6-6 Lab Recording Sheet

Teach

Discuss

After the equation for the boundary line is entered, discuss how to determine whether to shade above or below the line.

Close

Key Concept

You can graph a system of inequalities on a graphing calculator by entering equations for each boundary line and graphing the solutions of each inequality.

Assessment

Journal Have students explain how to use a graphing calculator to solve a system of linear inequalities.

Answers

1–4. See p. A27.

State Resources

go.hrw.com
State Resources Online
KEYWORD: MA7 Resources

Teacher to Teacher

It is important to point out to students that when you graph a linear inequality using a graphing calculator, the boundary line will always appear solid.

Remind students that they will need to consider the points on the boundary line and decide whether or not they are included in the solution set based on the inequality symbol rather than the appearance of the graph.

Larry Ward
Corinth, TX

Organizer

Objective: Assess students' ability to apply concepts and skills in Lessons 6-5 through 6-6 in a real-world format.

Online Edition

Resources

Algebra I Assessments

www.mathtekstoolkit.org

Problem	Text Reference
1	Lessons 6-5, 6-6
2	Lesson 6-6
3	Lesson 6-6
4	Lesson 4-4
5	Lesson 6-6

Answers

2. See p. A27.

State Resources

go.hrw.com
State Resources Online
KEYWORD: MA7 Resources

CHAPTER 6

MULTI-STEP TEST PREP

SECTION 6B

Equations and Formulas

Bearable Sales Gloria makes teddy bears. She dresses some as girl bears with dresses and bows and some as boy bears with bow ties. She is running low on supplies. She has only 100 eyes, 30 dresses, and 60 ties that can be used as bows on the girls and bow ties on the boys.

1. $2x + 2y \leq 100$; $y \leq 30$; $x + y \leq 60$

1. Write the inequalities that describe this situation. Let x represent the number of boy bears and y represent the number of girl bears.
2. Graph the inequalities and locate the region showing the number of boy and girl bears Gloria can make.

3. Possible answer: (5 boys, 20 girls), (10 boys, 15 girls), (30 boys, 5 girls)

3. List at least three combinations of girl and boy bears that Gloria can make.

For 4 and 5, use the table.

4. Using the boundary line in your graph from Problem 2, copy and complete the table with the corresponding number of girl bears.

5. $240; $290; $340; $310; $280; $250

5. Gloria sells the bears for profit. She makes a profit of $8 for the girl bears and $5 for the boy bears. Use the table from Problem 4 to find the profit she makes for each given combination.

6. 20 boy bears and 30 girl bears makes a profit of $340, which is the most; it lies at the intersection of the boundary lines $y \leq 30$ and $2x + 2y \leq 100$.

6. Which combination is the most profitable? Explain. Where does it lie on the graph?

Bear Combinations	
Boy	**Girl**
0	30
10	30
20	30
30	20
40	10
50	0

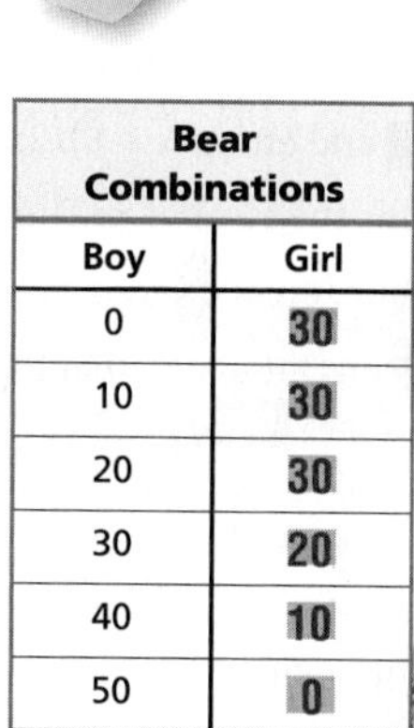

INTERVENTION

Scaffolding Questions

1. How many eyes are there per bear? 2 Which type of bear will use the dresses? girl bears Which type of bear will use the bow? both girl and boy bears
2. Can reasonable solutions be negative? no Explain. Gloria cannot sell a negative number of bears.
3. Can reasonable solutions include fractions or decimals? no Explain. Gloria cannot sell a fraction of a bear.
4. Which lines are included in the solution boundary? $y = 30$, $2x + 2y = 100$
5. What is the formula for Gloria's profit? $P = 5x + 8y$
6. How can you tell which combination is more profitable? the combination that results in the greatest value of P

Extension

What is the most profitable combination if Gloria makes a profit of $5 for girl bears and $8 for boy bears? 30 boy bears and 20 girl bears.

Quiz for Lessons 6-5 Through 6-6

6-5 Solving Linear Inequalities

Tell whether the ordered pair is a solution of the inequality.

1. $(3, -2)$; $y < -2x + 1$ **no**
2. $(2, 1)$; $y \geq 3x - 5$ **yes**
3. $(1, -6)$; $y \leq 4x - 10$ **yes**

Graph the solutions of each linear inequality.

4. $y \geq 4x - 3$
5. $3x - y < 5$
6. $2x + 3y < 9$
7. $y \leq -\frac{1}{2}x$
8. Theo's mother has given him at most $150 to buy clothes for school. The pants cost $30 each and the shirts cost $15 each. Write a linear inequality to describe the situation. Graph the solutions and give three combinations of pants and shirts that Theo could buy.

Write an inequality to represent each graph.

9. 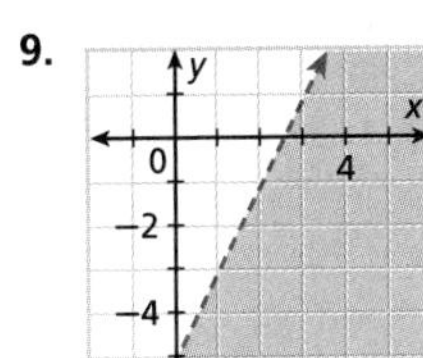
$y < 2x - 5$

10. 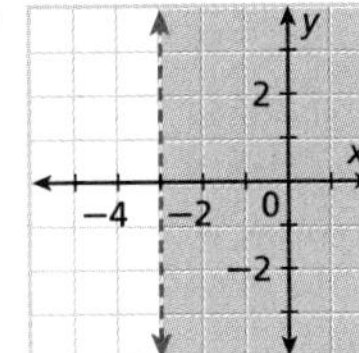
$x > -3$

11. 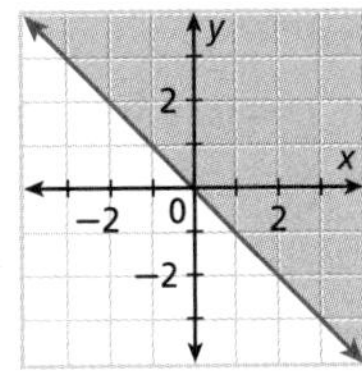
$y \geq -x$

6-6 Solving Systems of Linear Inequalities

Tell whether the ordered pair is a solution of the given system.

12. $(-3, -1)$; $\begin{cases} y > -2 \\ y < x + 4 \end{cases}$ **yes**
13. $(-3, 0)$; $\begin{cases} y \leq x + 4 \\ y \geq -2x - 6 \end{cases}$ **yes**
14. $(0, 0)$; $\begin{cases} y \geq 3x \\ 2x + y < -1 \end{cases}$ **no**

Graph each system of linear inequalities. Give two ordered pairs that are solutions and two that are not solutions.

15. $\begin{cases} y > -2 \\ y < x + 3 \end{cases}$
16. $\begin{cases} x + y \leq 2 \\ 2x + y \geq -1 \end{cases}$
17. $\begin{cases} 2x - 5y \leq -5 \\ 3x + 2y < 10 \end{cases}$

Graph each system of linear inequalities. Describe the solutions.

18. $\begin{cases} y \geq x + 1 \\ y \geq x - 4 \end{cases}$
19. $\begin{cases} y \geq 2x - 1 \\ y < 2x - 3 \end{cases}$
20. $\begin{cases} y < -3x + 5 \\ y > -3x - 2 \end{cases}$
21. A grocer sells mangos for $4/lb and apples for $3/lb. The grocer starts with 45 lb of mangos and 50 lb of apples each day. The grocer's goal is to make at least $300 by selling mangos and apples each day. Show and describe all possible combinations of mangos and apples that could be sold to meet the goal. List two possible combinations.

18. The solutions of the system are the solutions of $y \geq x + 1$.
19. The system has no solutions.
20. The solutions are between the graphs of $y = -3x + 5$ and $y = -3x - 2$.

READY TO GO ON? SECTION **6B**

Organizer

Objective: Assess students' mastery of concepts and skills in Lessons 6-5 through 6-6.

Resources

 ***Assessment Resources***
Section 6B Quiz

Teacher One Stop™
Test & Practice Generator

INTERVENTION 

Resources

 ***Ready to Go On? Intervention and Enrichment* Worksheets**

 ***Ready to Go On?* CD-ROM**

 ***Ready to Go On?* Online**

my.hrw.com

Answers

4–8, 15–17, 21. See p. A27.

READY TO GO ON?
Diagnose and Prescribe

	***Ready to Go On? Intervention,* Section 6B**		
Ready to Go On? Intervention	**Worksheets**	**CD-ROM**	**Online**
Lesson 6-5	6-5 Intervention	Activity 6-5	Diagnose and Prescribe Online
Lesson 6-6	6-6 Intervention	Activity 6-6	

***Ready to Go On? Enrichment,* Section 6B**
 **Worksheets**
CD-ROM
Online

Organizer

Objective: Help students organize and review key concepts and skills presented in Chapter 6.

Resources

Teacher One Stop™
PuzzleView
Test & Practice Generator

***Multilingual Glossary* Online**

go.hrw.com
KEYWORD: MA7 Glossary

Lesson Tutorial Videos
CD-ROM

Answers

1. independent system
2. system of linear equations
3. solution of a system of linear inequalities
4. inconsistent system
5. independent system
6. no
7. yes
8. yes
9. no
10. $(-1, -1)$
11. $(3, 4)$
12. 8 h; $10

Vocabulary

consistent system 420
dependent system 421
inconsistent system 420
independent system 421
linear inequality 428
solution of a linear inequality 428
solution of a system of linear equations 397
solutions of a system of linear inequalities 435
system of linear equations 397
system of linear inequalities 435

Complete the sentences below with vocabulary words from the list above.

1. A(n) ___?___ is a system that has exactly one solution.
2. A set of two or more linear equations that contain the same variable(s) is a(n) ___?___.
3. The ___?___ consists of all the ordered pairs that satisfy all the inequalities in the system.
4. A system consisting of equations of parallel lines with different y-intercepts is a(n) ___?___.
5. A(n) ___?___ consists of two intersecting lines.

6-1 Solving Systems by Graphing *(pp. 397–402)*

EXAMPLE

■ Solve $\begin{cases} y = 2x - 2 \\ x + 2y = 16 \end{cases}$ by graphing.

Check your answer.

$\begin{cases} y = 2x - 2 \\ y = -\frac{1}{2}x + 8 \end{cases}$ *Write the second equation in slope-intercept form.*

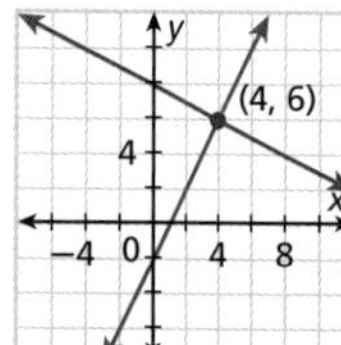

The solution appears to be at $(4, 6)$.

$y = 2x - 2$	
6	$2(4) - 2$
6	6 ✓

$x + 2y = 16$	
$4 + 2(6)$	16
16	16 ✓

The ordered pair $(4, 6)$ makes both equations true, so it is a solution of the system.

EXERCISES

Tell whether the ordered pair is a solution of the given system.

6. $(0, -5)$; $\begin{cases} y = -6x + 5 \\ x - y = 5 \end{cases}$
7. $(4, 3)$; $\begin{cases} x - 2y = -2 \\ y = \frac{1}{2}x + 1 \end{cases}$
8. $\left(1\frac{3}{4}, 7\frac{1}{4}\right)$; $\begin{cases} x + y = 9 \\ 2y = 6x + 4 \end{cases}$
9. $(-1, -1)$; $\begin{cases} y = -2x + 5 \\ 3y = 6x + 3 \end{cases}$

Solve each system by graphing. Check your answer.

10. $\begin{cases} y = 3x + 2 \\ y = -2x - 3 \end{cases}$
11. $\begin{cases} y = -\frac{1}{3}x + 5 \\ 2x - 2y = -2 \end{cases}$
12. Raheel is comparing the cost of two parking garages. Garage A charges a flat fee of $6 per car plus $0.50 per hour. Garage B charges a flat fee of $2 per car plus $1 per hour. After how many hours will the cost at garage A be the same as the cost at garage B? What will that cost be?

6-2 Solving Systems by Substitution *(pp. 404–410)*

EXAMPLE

■ Solve $\begin{cases} 2x - 3y = -2 \\ y - 3x = 10 \end{cases}$ by substitution.

Step 1 $y - 3x = 10$ *Solve the second equation for y.*

$y = 3x + 10$

Step 2 $2x - 3y = -2$ *Substitute 3x + 10 for y in the first equation.*

$2x - 3(3x + 10) = -2$

Step 3 *Solve for x.*

$2x - 9x - 30 = -2$

$-7x - 30 = -2$

$-7x = 28$

$x = -4$

Step 4 $y - 3x = 10$ *Substitute −4 for x.*

$y - 3(-4) = 10$

$y + 12 = 10$ *Find the value of y.*

$y = -2$

Step 5 $(-4, -2)$ *Write the solution as an ordered pair.*

To check the solution, substitute $(-4, -2)$ into both equations in the system.

EXERCISES

Solve each system by substitution.

13. $\begin{cases} y = x + 3 \\ y = 2x + 12 \end{cases}$

14. $\begin{cases} y = -4x \\ y = 2x - 3 \end{cases}$

15. $\begin{cases} 2x + y = 4 \\ 3x + y = 3 \end{cases}$

16. $\begin{cases} x + y = -1 \\ y = -2x + 3 \end{cases}$

17. $\begin{cases} x = y - 7 \\ -y - 2x = 8 \end{cases}$

18. $\begin{cases} \frac{1}{2}x + y = 9 \\ 3x - 4y = -6 \end{cases}$

19. The Nash family's car needs repairs. Estimates for parts and labor from two garages are shown below.

Garage	Parts ($)	Labor ($ per hour)
Motor Works	650	70
Jim's Car Care	800	55

For how many hours of labor will the total cost of fixing the car be the same at both garages? What will that cost be? Which garage will be cheaper if the repairs require 8 hours of labor? Explain.

6-3 Solving Systems by Elimination *(pp. 411–417)*

EXAMPLE

■ Solve $\begin{cases} 2x - 3y = -8 \\ x + 4y = 7 \end{cases}$ by elimination.

Step 1 *Multiply the second equation by −2.*

$2x - 3y = -8$

$+(-2)(x + 4y = 7)$

Eliminate x.

$2x - 3y = -8$

$+(-2x - 8y = -14)$

Step 2 $-11y = -22$ *Solve for y.*

$y = 2$

Step 3 *Substitute 2 for y. Simplify and solve for x.*

$2x - 3y = -8$

$2x - 3(2) = -8$

$2x - 6 = -8$

$2x = -2$

$x = -1$

Step 4 $(-1, 2)$ *Write the solution as an ordered pair.*

To check the solution, substitute $(-1, 2)$ into both equations in the system.

EXERCISES

Solve each system by elimination.

20. $\begin{cases} 4x + y = -1 \\ 2x - y = -5 \end{cases}$

21. $\begin{cases} x + 2y = -1 \\ x + y = 2 \end{cases}$

22. $\begin{cases} x + y = 12 \\ 2x + 5y = 27 \end{cases}$

23. $\begin{cases} 3x - 2y = -6 \\ \frac{1}{3}x + 3y = 9 \end{cases}$

Solve each system by any method. Explain why you chose each method. Check your answer.

24. $\begin{cases} 3x + y = 2 \\ y = -4x \end{cases}$

25. $\begin{cases} y = \frac{1}{3}x - 6 \\ y = -2x + 1 \end{cases}$

26. $\begin{cases} 2y = -3x \\ y = -2x + 2 \end{cases}$

27. $\begin{cases} x - y = 0 \\ 3x + y = 8 \end{cases}$

Answers

13. $(-9, -6)$
14. $\left(\frac{1}{2}, -2\right)$
15. $(-1, 6)$
16. $(4, -5)$
17. $(-5, 2)$
18. $(6, 6)$
19. 10 h; $1350; Motor Works; 8 hours will cost $30 less at Motor Works.
20. $(-1, 3)$
21. $(5, -3)$
22. $(11, 1)$
23. $(0, 3)$
24. $(-2, 8)$; possible answer: substitution; the second equation is already solved for *y*, and *y* has a coefficient of 1 in the first equation.
25. $(3, -5)$; possible answer: graphing; both equations are already in slope-intercept form.
26. $(4, -6)$; possible answer: substitution; the second equation is already solved for *y*.
27. $(2, 2)$; possible answer: elimination; the coefficients of the *y*-terms are opposites.

Study Guide: Review 445

Answers

28. no solution
29. infinitely many solutions
30. $(-2, -4)$
31. infinitely many solutions
32. infinitely many solutions
33. $(-1, -3)$
34. Yes; at 7 months, Tristan and Marco will have the same number of DVDs.
35. consistent, independent; one solution
36. inconsistent; no solution
37. consistent, dependent; infinitely many solutions
38. inconsistent; no solution
39. consistent, independent; one solution
40. consistent, dependent; infinitely many solutions
41. inconsistent; no solution
42. no
43. yes
44. yes
45. no

46. 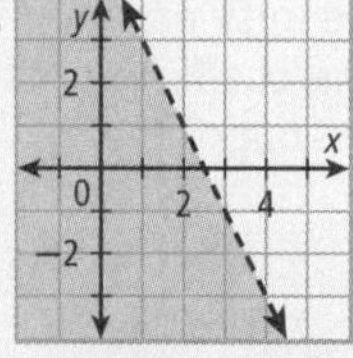

47. 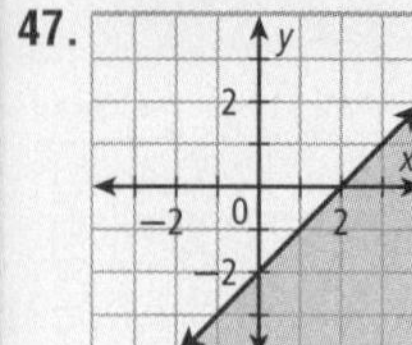

6-4 Solving Special Systems *(pp. 420–425)*

EXAMPLES

Classify each system. Give the number of solutions.

■ $\begin{cases} y = 3x + 4 \\ 6x - 2y = -8 \end{cases}$

Use the substitution method because the first equation is solved for y.

$6x - 2(3x + 4) = -8$ *Substitute $3x + 4$ for y in the second equation.*

$6x - 6x - 8 = -8$

$-8 = -8$ ✓ *True*

The equation is an identity. There are infinitely many solutions.

This system is **consistent** and **dependent.** When graphed, the two lines are coincident (the same line)—they have identical slopes and y-intercepts.

■ $\begin{cases} y = 2x - 1 \\ 2x - y = -2 \end{cases}$

Compare slopes and y-intercepts. Write both equations in slope-intercept form.

$\begin{cases} y = 2x - 1 & \Rightarrow y = 2x - 1 \\ 2x - y = -2 & \Rightarrow y = 2x + 2 \end{cases}$

The lines have the same slope and different y-intercepts. The lines are parallel.

The lines never intersect, so this system is **inconsistent**. It has **no solution.**

■ $\begin{cases} 2x - y = 6 \\ y = x - 1 \end{cases}$

Write both equations in slope-intercept form.

$\begin{cases} 2x - y = 6 & \Rightarrow y = 2x - 6 \\ y = x - 1 & \Rightarrow y = 1x - 1 \end{cases}$

The lines intersect because they have different slopes.

The system is **consistent** and **independent.** There is **one solution:** $(5, 4)$.

EXERCISES

Solve each system of linear equations.

28. $\begin{cases} y = \frac{1}{4}x - 3 \\ y = \frac{1}{4}x + 5 \end{cases}$

29. $\begin{cases} y = -x + 4 \\ x + y = 4 \end{cases}$

30. $\begin{cases} y = 3x + 2 \\ y = 2x \end{cases}$

31. $\begin{cases} -4x - y = 6 \\ \frac{1}{2}y = -2x - 3 \end{cases}$

32. $\begin{cases} x + 2y = 8 \\ y = -\frac{1}{2}x + 4 \end{cases}$

33. $\begin{cases} y - 2x = -1 \\ y + 2x = -5 \end{cases}$

34. Tristan and his friend Marco just started DVD collections. They continue to get DVDs at the rate shown in the table below. Will Tristan ever have the same number of DVDs as Marco? Explain.

DVD Collections			
	Month 1	Month 2	Month 3
Tristan	2	7	12
Marco	8	12	16

Classify each system. Give the number of solutions.

35. $\begin{cases} y = \frac{1}{2}x + 2 \\ y = \frac{1}{4}x - 8 \end{cases}$

36. $\begin{cases} y = 3x - 7 \\ y = 3x + 2 \end{cases}$

37. $\begin{cases} 2x + y = 2 \\ y - 2 = -2x \end{cases}$

38. $\begin{cases} -3x - y = -5 \\ y = -3x - 5 \end{cases}$

39. $\begin{cases} 2x + 3y = 1 \\ 3x + 2y = 1 \end{cases}$

40. $\begin{cases} x + \frac{1}{2}y = 3 \\ 2x = 6 - y \end{cases}$

41. The two parallel lines graphed below represent a system of equations. Classify the system and give the number of solutions.

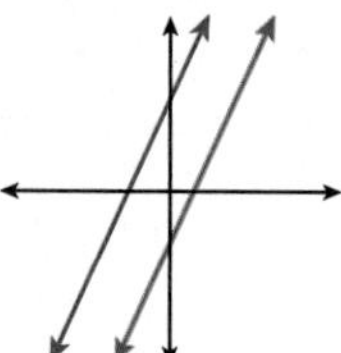

6-5 Solving Linear Inequalities *(pp. 428–434)*

EXAMPLE

- **Graph the solutions of $x - 2y < 6$.**

Step 1 Solve the inequality for y.

$$x - 2y < 6$$
$$-2y < -x + 6$$
$$y > \frac{1}{2}x - 3$$

Step 2 Graph $y = \frac{1}{2}x - 3$. Use a dashed line for $>$.

Step 3 The inequality is $>$, so shade above the boundary line.

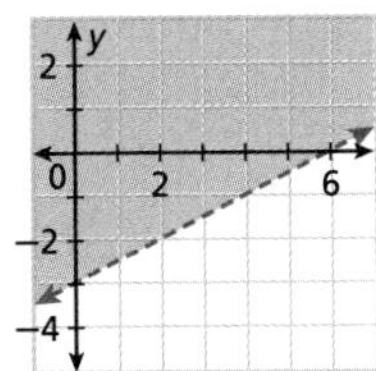

Check Substitute $(0, 0)$ for (x, y).

$$x - 2y < 6$$
$$0 - 2(0) \; | \; 6$$
$$0 < 6 \checkmark$$

(0, 0) satisfies the inequality, so the graph is shaded correctly.

EXERCISES

Tell whether the ordered pair is a solution of the inequality.

42. $(0, -3)$; $y < 2x - 3$
43. $(2, -1)$; $y \geq x - 3$
44. $(6, 0)$; $y > -3x + 4$
45. $(10, 10)$; $y \leq x - 3$

Graph the solutions of each linear inequality.

46. $y < -2x + 5$
47. $x - y \geq 2$
48. $-x + 2y \geq 6$
49. $y > -4x$
50. $x + y + 4 > 0$
51. $5 - y \geq 2x$
52. The Mathematics Club is selling pizza and lemonade to raise money for a trip. They estimate that the trip will cost at least \$450. They earn \$2 on each slice of pizza and \$1 on each bottle of lemonade. Write an inequality to describe the situation. Graph the solutions and then give two combinations of the number of pizza slices and number of lemonade bottles they could sell to meet their goal.

6-6 Solving Systems of Linear Inequalities *(pp. 435–440)*

EXAMPLES

- **Graph $\begin{cases} y < -x + 5 \\ y \geq 2x - 3 \end{cases}$. Give two ordered pairs that are solutions and two that are not solutions.**

Graph both inequalities.

The solutions of the system are represented by the overlapping shaded regions.

The points $(0, 0)$ and $(-2, 2)$ are solutions of the system.

The points $(3, -2)$ and $(4, 4)$ are not solutions.

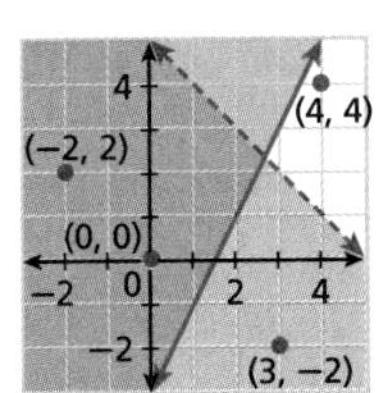

EXERCISES

Tell whether the ordered pair is a solution of the given system.

53. $(3, 3)$; $\begin{cases} y > -2x + 9 \\ y \geq x \end{cases}$
54. $(-1, 0)$; $\begin{cases} 2x - y > -5 \\ y \leq -3x - 3 \end{cases}$

Graph each system of linear inequalities. Give two ordered pairs that are solutions and two that are not solutions.

55. $\begin{cases} y \geq x + 4 \\ y > 6x - 3 \end{cases}$
56. $\begin{cases} y \leq -2x + 8 \\ y > 3x - 5 \end{cases}$
57. $\begin{cases} -x + 2y > 6 \\ x + y < 4 \end{cases}$
58. $\begin{cases} x - y > 7 \\ x + 3y \leq 15 \end{cases}$

Graph each system of linear inequalities.

59. $\begin{cases} y > -x - 6 \\ y < -x + 5 \end{cases}$
60. $\begin{cases} 4x + 2y \geq 10 \\ 6x + 3y < -9 \end{cases}$

Answers

48.
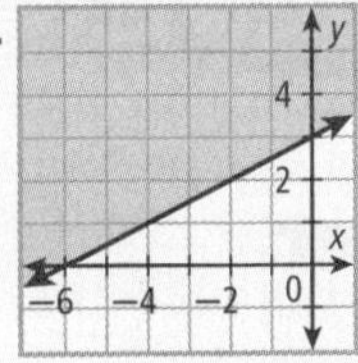

49.
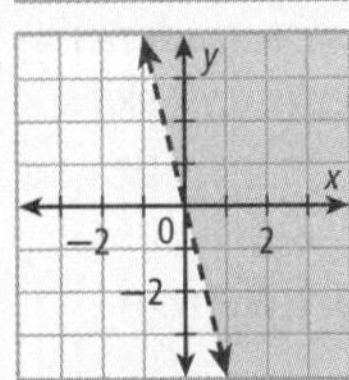

50.
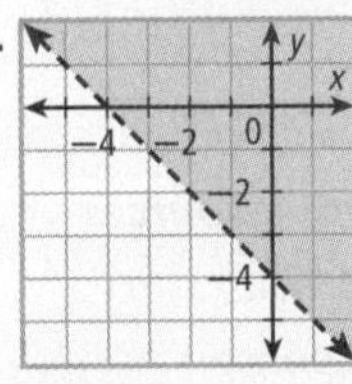

51.
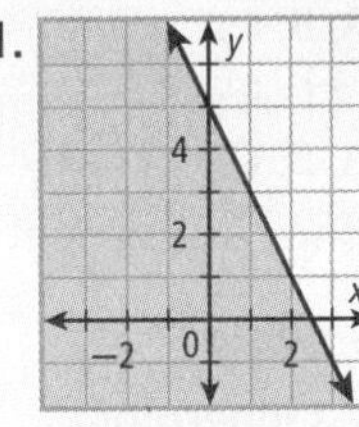

52. Let x = slices of pizza, and y = bottles of soda; $2x + y \geq 450$; possible answer: (200 slices, 50 bottles), (150 slices, 150 bottles).

Fundraising Needs

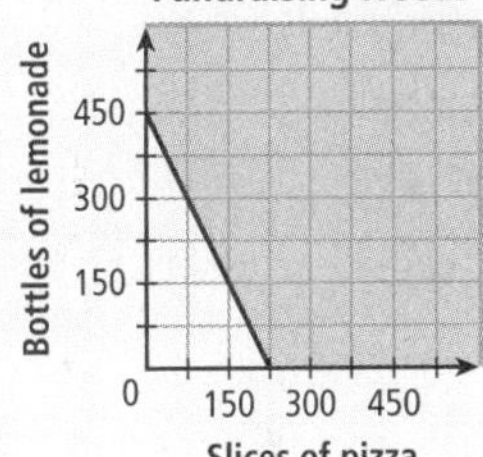

53. no
54. yes
55. Possible answer: solutions: $(-6, 6)$, $(-10, 0)$; not solutions: $(0, 0)$, $(4, -4)$

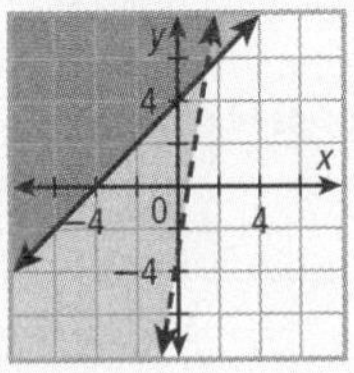

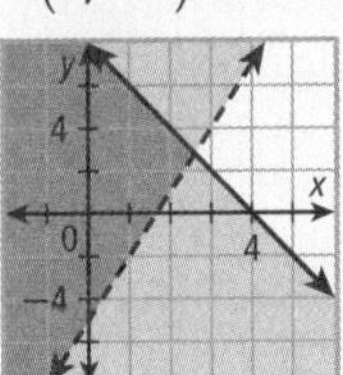

56. Possible answer: solutions: $(0, 0)$, $(-5, 0)$; not solutions: $(8, 0)$, $(3, -3)$

57. Possible answer: solutions: $(-6, 2)$, $(-8, 1)$; not solutions: $(0, 0)$, $(4, 1)$

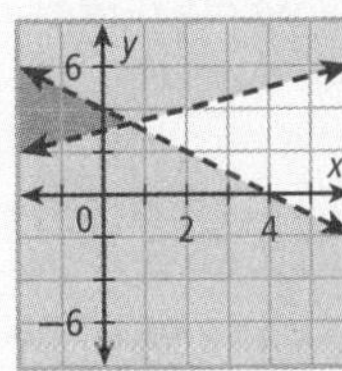

58. Possible answer: solutions: $(8, -8)$, $(9, 0)$; not solutions: $(0, 0)$, $(0, -4)$

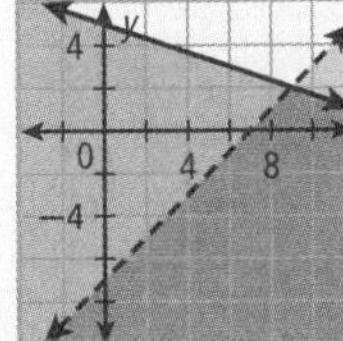

59.
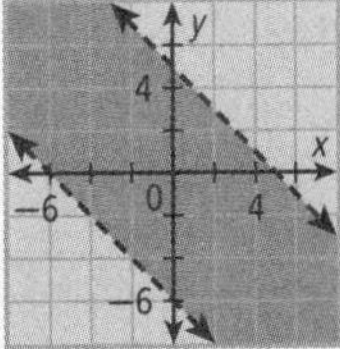

60.
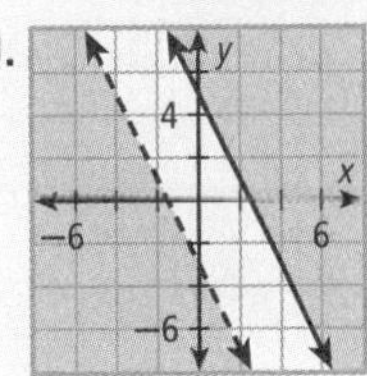

Organizer

Objective: Assess students' mastery of concepts and skills in Chapter 6.

Online Edition

Resources

Assessment Resources

Chapter 6 Tests

- Free Response (Levels A, B, C)
- Multiple Choice (Levels A, B, C)
- Performance Assessment

Teacher One Stop™

Test & Practice Generator

Answers

17.

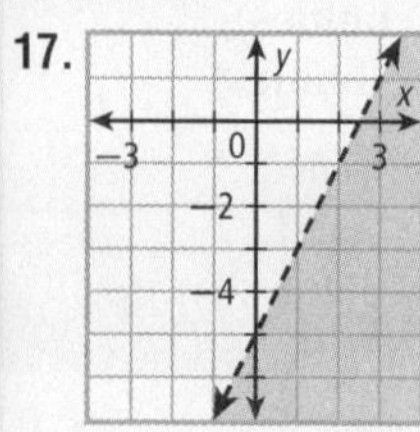

18.

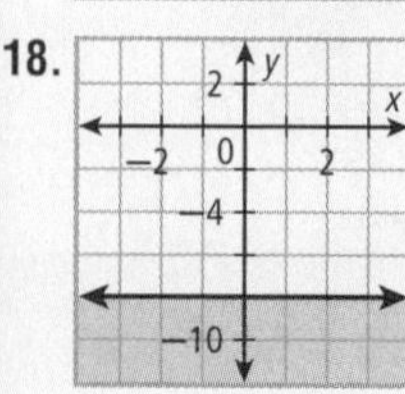

State Resources

Tell whether the ordered pair is a solution of the given system.

1. $(1, -4); \begin{cases} y = -4x \\ y = 2x - 2 \end{cases}$ **no**
2. $(0, -1); \begin{cases} 3x - y = 1 \\ x + 5y = -5 \end{cases}$ **yes**
3. $(3, 2); \begin{cases} x - 2y = -1 \\ -3x + 2y = 5 \end{cases}$ **no**

Solve each system by graphing.

4. $\begin{cases} y = x - 3 \\ y = -2x - 3 \end{cases}$ **(0, −3)**
5. $\begin{cases} 2x + y = -8 \\ y = \frac{1}{3}x - 1 \end{cases}$ **(−3, −2)**
6. $\begin{cases} y = -x + 4 \\ x = y + 2 \end{cases}$ **(3, 1)**

Solve each system by substitution.

7. $\begin{cases} y = -6 \\ y = -2x - 2 \end{cases}$ **(2, −6)**
8. $\begin{cases} -x + y = -4 \\ y = 2x - 11 \end{cases}$ **(7, 3)**
9. $\begin{cases} x - 3y = 3 \\ 2x = 3y \end{cases}$ **(−3, −2)**

10. The costs for services at two kennels are shown in the table. Joslyn plans to board her dog and have him bathed once during his stay. For what number of days will the cost for boarding and bathing her dog at each kennel be the same? What will that cost be? If Joslyn plans a week-long vacation, which is the cheaper service? Explain. **6; $195; Fido's; it will cost less per day after 6 days.**

Kennel Costs		
	Boarding ($ per day)	Bathing ($)
Pet Care	30	15
Fido's	28	27

Solve each system by elimination.

11. $\begin{cases} 3x - y = 7 \\ 2x + y = 3 \end{cases}$ **(2, −1)**
12. $\begin{cases} 4x + y = 0 \\ x + y = -3 \end{cases}$ **(1, −4)**
13. $\begin{cases} 2x + y = 3 \\ x - 2y = -1 \end{cases}$ **(1, 1)**

Classify each system. Give the number of solutions.

14. $\begin{cases} y = 6x - 1 \\ 6x - y = 1 \end{cases}$ **cons. and dep.; inf. many solutions**
15. $\begin{cases} y = -3x - 3 \\ 3x + y = 3 \end{cases}$ **incons.; no sol.**
16. $\begin{cases} 2x - y = 1 \\ -4x + y = 1 \end{cases}$ **cons. and indep.; one sol.**

Graph the solutions of each linear inequality.

17. $y < 2x - 5$
18. $-y \geq 8$
19. $y > \frac{1}{3}x$

Graph each system of linear inequalities. Give two ordered pairs that are solutions and two that are not solutions.

20. $\begin{cases} y > \frac{1}{2}x - 5 \\ y \leq 4x - 1 \end{cases}$
21. $\begin{cases} y > -x + 4 \\ 3x - y > 3 \end{cases}$
22. $\begin{cases} y \geq 2x \\ y - 2x < 6 \end{cases}$

23. Ezra and Tava sold at least 150 coupon books. Ezra sold at most 30 books more than twice the number Tava sold. Show and describe all possible combinations of the numbers of coupon books Ezra and Tava sold. List two possible combinations.

Answers

19.

20.

Possible answers: solutions: (2, 0), (4, 0); not solutions: (−2, 0), (−4, 0)

21.

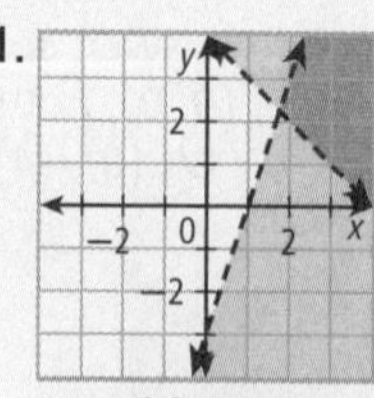

Possible answers: solutions: (6, 4), (9, 0); not solutions: (2, −4), (0, 0)

22.

Possible answers: solutions: (0, 1), (0, 2); not solutions: (−6, 0), (4, 1)

23. Ezra and Tava could have sold any combination represented by an ordered pair of whole numbers in the solutions region.

Possible answers: (Tava: 50, Ezra: 125), (Tava: 65, Ezra: 95)

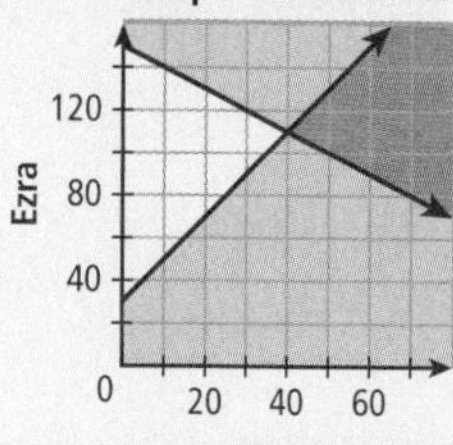

COLLEGE ENTRANCE EXAM PRACTICE

CHAPTER 6

FOCUS ON ACT

Four scores are reported for the ACT Mathematics Test: one score based on all 60 problems and one for each content area. The three content areas are: Pre-Algebra/ Elementary Algebra, Intermediate Algebra/Coordinate Geometry, and Plane Geometry/Trigonometry.

Taking classes that cover the content areas on the ACT is a good idea. This way you will have skills from each area of the test. Preparation over a long term is better than cramming at the last minute.

You may want to time yourself as you take this practice test. It should take you about 5 minutes to complete.

1. Which system of inequalities is represented by the graph?

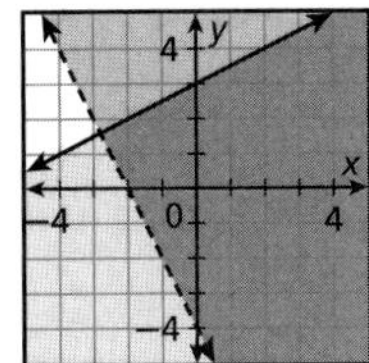

(A) $\begin{cases} -x + 2y < 6 \\ 2x + y > -4 \end{cases}$

(B) $\begin{cases} x - 2y \leq 6 \\ 2x - y \geq 4 \end{cases}$

(C) $\begin{cases} -x + 2y \leq 6 \\ 2x + y \geq 4 \end{cases}$

(D) $\begin{cases} -x + 2y \leq 6 \\ 2x + y > -4 \end{cases}$

(E) $\begin{cases} x - 2y \leq 6 \\ 2x - y > 4 \end{cases}$

2. What is the y-value of the solution of the given system?

$\begin{cases} 4x + 3y = 1 \\ -4x + 3y = -7 \end{cases}$

(F) -1

(G) 0

(H) 1

(J) 2

(K) 6

3. Wireless phone company A charges \$20 per month plus \$0.12 per minute. Wireless phone company B charges \$50 per month plus \$0.06 per minute. For how many minutes of calls will the monthly bills be the same?

(A) 80 minutes

(B) 100 minutes

(C) 160 minutes

(D) 250 minutes

(E) 500 minutes

4. Which of the following systems of equations does NOT have a solution?

(F) $\begin{cases} x + 5y = 30 \\ -4x + 5y = 10 \end{cases}$

(G) $\begin{cases} x + 5y = -30 \\ -4x + 5y = 10 \end{cases}$

(H) $\begin{cases} x + 5y = -30 \\ -4x + 5y = -10 \end{cases}$

(J) $\begin{cases} -4x + 5y = -10 \\ -8x + 10y = -20 \end{cases}$

(K) $\begin{cases} -4x + 5y = -10 \\ -4x + 5y = -30 \end{cases}$

TEST PREP DOCTOR

1. Students who chose **A** may not have assigned the appropriate inequality symbols to the dashed and solid lines. Remind students of the difference between dashed and solid lines and how they correspond to the solutions of an inequality.
2. Students who chose **H** may have found the solution for x instead of y.
3. Students who chose **A** found the value of the bill for the month, in dollars, instead of the number of minutes.
4. Students who chose **J** may not understand that coinciding lines indicate infinitely many solutions of the system. Remind students that the type of system that has no solution is represented by parallel lines.

COLLEGE ENTRANCE EXAM PRACTICE

CHAPTER 6

Organizer

Objective: Provide practice for college entrance exams such as the ACT.

Resources

College Entrance Exam Practice

Questions on the ACT represent the following content areas:

Pre-Algebra, 23%

Elementary Algebra, 17%

Intermediate Algebra, 15%

Coordinate Geometry, 15%

Plane Geometry, 23%

Trigonometry, 7%

Items on this page focus on:

- Elementary Algebra
- Coordinate Geometry

Text References:

Item	1	2	3	4
Lesson	6-6	6-3	6-1 6-2 6-3	6-4

Organizer

Objective: Provide opportunities to learn and practice common test-taking strategies.

This Test Tackler reinforces the importance of reading a test item slowly and carefully, identifying the important information, and being aware of all parts of the question. Explain to students that if they read a question too quickly, they might make assumptions that are not true, answer the wrong question, or not answer all parts of the question. Show students how to read a question for understanding by using the process shown in the example.

Standardized Test Strategies

Any Question Type: Read the Problem for Understanding

Standardized test questions may vary in format including multiple choice, gridded response, and short or extended response. No matter what format the test uses, read each question carefully and critically. Do not rush. Be sure you completely understand what you are asked to do and what your response should include.

EXAMPLE

Extended Response

An interior decorator charges a consultation fee of $50 plus $12 per hour. Another interior decorator charges a consultation fee of $5 plus $22 per hour. Write a system of equations to find the amount of time for which the cost of both decorators will be the same. Graph the system. After how many hours will the cost be the same for both decorators? What will the cost be?

Read the problem again.

What information are you given?

the consultation fees and hourly rates of two decorators

What are you asked to do?

1. Write a system of equations.
2. Graph the system.
3. Interpret the solution to the system.

What should your response include?

1. a system of equations with variables defined
2. a graph of the system
3. the time when the cost is the same for both decorators
4. the cost at that time

Read each test item and answer the questions that follow.

Item A
Short Response Which value of b will make the lines intersect at the point $(-2, 14)$?

$$\begin{cases} y = -6x + 2 \\ y = 4x + b \end{cases}$$

1. What information are you given?
2. What are you asked to do?
3. Ming's answer to this test problem was $y = 4x + 22$. Did Ming answer correctly? Explain.

Item B
Extended Response Solve the system by using elimination. Explain how you can check your solution algebraically and graphically.

$$\begin{cases} 4x + 10y = -48 \\ 6x - 10y = 28 \end{cases}$$

4. What method does the problem ask you to use to solve the system of equations?
5. What methods does the problem ask you to use to check your solution?
6. How many parts are there to this problem? List what needs to be included in your response.

Item C
Gridded Response What is the x-coordinate of the solution to this system? $\begin{cases} y = 6x + 9 \\ y = 12x - 15 \end{cases}$

7. What question is being asked?
8. A student correctly found the solution of the system to be $(4, 33)$. What should the student mark on the grid so that the answer is correct?

After you answer each item, read the item again to be sure your response includes everything that is asked for.

Item D
Short Response Write an inequality to represent the graph below. Give a real-world situation that this inequality could describe.

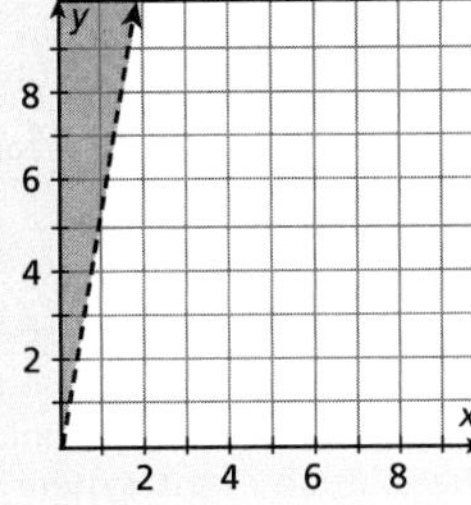

9. As part of his answer, a student wrote the following response:

The point (1, 5) is not a solution to the inequality because it lies on the line, but (2, 12) is a solution because it lies above the line.

Is his response appropriate? Explain.

10. What should the response include so that it answers all parts of the problem?

Item E
Multiple Choice Taylor bikes 50 miles per week and increases her distance by 2 miles each week. Josie bikes 30 miles per week and increases her distance by 10 miles each week. In how many weeks will Taylor and Josie be biking the same distance?

Ⓐ 2.5 weeks
Ⓑ 7.5 weeks
Ⓒ 55 weeks
Ⓓ 110 weeks

11. What question is being asked?
12. Carson incorrectly selected option C as his answer. What question did he most likely answer?

TEST PREP DOCTOR In **Item A,** students are asked for the value of b, not the equation. In **Item B,** a complete answer will show three solution methods. In **Item C,** students are asked for only the x-coordinate of the solution, not the entire ordered pair. In **Item E,** students are asked for only the solution value of the independent variable, number of weeks, not the dependent variable, number of miles.

Answers

1. a system of equations and the point of intersection
2. Find the value of b that makes the system intersect at $(-2, 14)$.
3. No; Ming found the actual equation, which is correct, but the question just asked for the value of b.
4. elimination
5. algebraically and graphically
6. three parts; solving the system using elimination, checking the solution algebraically, and checking the solution graphically
7. What is the x-coordinate of the solution of the system?
8. 4
9. No; the problem did not ask anything about solutions of the inequality.
10. The response should include an inequality that represents the graph and a real-world situation that the inequality could describe.
11. In how many weeks will the girls be biking the same distance?
12. How many miles will the girls bike during the week that they are biking the same distance?

State Resources

Answers to Test Items

A. 22
B. $(-2, -4)$
C. 4
D. $y > 5x$; Jeff opens a bank account and deposits more than $5 a week.
E. A

go.hrw.com
State Resources Online
KEYWORD: MA7 Resources

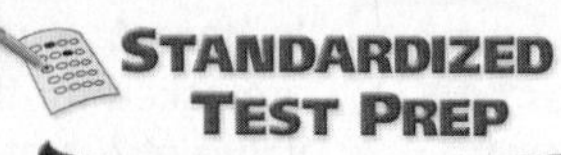

Organizer

Objective: Provide review and practice for Chapters 1–6 and standardized tests.

Resources

Assessment Resources

Chapter 6 Cumulative Test

go.hrw.com
KEYWORD: MA7 TestPrep

State Resources

State Test Practice Online
KEYWORD: MA7 TestPrep

CUMULATIVE ASSESSMENT, CHAPTERS 1–6

Multiple Choice

1. If $a > 0$ and $b < 0$, which of the following must be true?

Ⓐ $ab > 0$ Ⓒ $a + b > 0$

Ⓑ $ab < 0$ Ⓓ $a + b < 0$

2. Which of the problems below could be solved by finding the solution of this system?

$$\begin{cases} 2x + 2y = 56 \\ y = \frac{1}{3}x \end{cases}$$

Ⓕ The area of a rectangle is 56 square units. The width is one-third the length. Find the length of the rectangle.

Ⓖ The area of a rectangle is 56 square units. The length is one-third the perimeter. Find the length of the rectangle.

Ⓗ The perimeter of a rectangle is 56 units. The length is one-third more than the width. Find the length of the rectangle.

Ⓙ The perimeter of a rectangle is 56 units. The width is one-third the length. Find the length of the rectangle.

3. What is the slope of a line perpendicular to a line that passes through (3, 8) and (1, −4)?

Ⓐ $-\frac{1}{6}$ Ⓒ 2

Ⓑ $-\frac{1}{2}$ Ⓓ 6

4. Which inequality is graphed below?

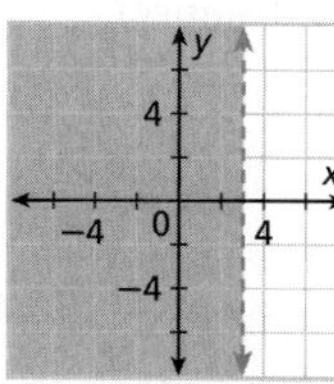

Ⓕ $-x > -3$ Ⓗ $2x < -6$

Ⓖ $-y > -3$ Ⓙ $3y < 9$

5. A chemist has a bottle of a 10% acid solution and a bottle of a 30% acid solution. He mixes the solutions together to get 500 mL of a 25% acid solution. How much of the 30% solution did he use?

Ⓐ 125 mL Ⓒ 375 mL

Ⓑ 150 mL Ⓓ 450 mL

6. Which ordered pair is NOT a solution of the system graphed below?

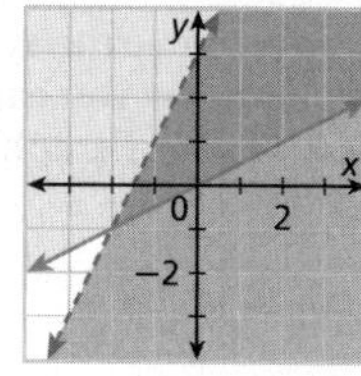

Ⓕ (0, 0) Ⓗ (1, 1)

Ⓖ (0, 3) Ⓙ (2, 1)

7. Which of the following best classifies a system of linear equations whose graph is two intersecting lines?

Ⓐ inconsistent and dependent

Ⓑ inconsistent and independent

Ⓒ consistent and dependent

Ⓓ consistent and independent

8. Which ordered pair is a solution of this system?

$$\begin{cases} 2x - y = -2 \\ \frac{1}{3}y = x \end{cases}$$

Ⓕ (0, 2) Ⓗ (2, 6)

Ⓖ (1, 3) Ⓙ (3, 8)

9. Where does the graph of $5x - 10y = 30$ cross the y-axis?

Ⓐ (0, −3) Ⓒ (6, 0)

Ⓑ $\left(0, \frac{1}{2}\right)$ Ⓓ (0, −6)

Answers

1. B
2. J
3. A
4. F
5. C
6. G
7. D
8. H
9. A
10. F
11. C
12. 26.25
13. 2
14. 5

Most standardized tests allow you to write in your test booklet. Cross out each answer choice you eliminate. This may keep you from accidentally marking an answer other than the one you think is right. However, don't draw in your math book!

10. Hillary needs markers and poster board for a project. The markers are $0.79 each and the poster board is $1.89 per sheet. She needs at least 4 sheets of poster board. Hillary has $15 to spend on project materials. Which system models this information?

Ⓕ $\begin{cases} p \geq 4 \\ 0.79m + 1.89p \leq 15 \end{cases}$

Ⓖ $\begin{cases} 0.79m \geq 1.89p \\ 4p \leq 15 \end{cases}$

Ⓗ $\begin{cases} 4p \geq 1.89 \\ m + 4p \leq 15 \end{cases}$

Ⓙ $\begin{cases} p + m \leq 15 \\ 0.79m + 1.89p \geq 4 \end{cases}$

11. Find the slope of the line described by $4x - 2y = -8$.

Ⓐ -2

Ⓑ $-\frac{1}{2}$

Ⓒ 2

Ⓓ 4

Gridded Response

12. The floor in the entranceway of Kendra's house is square and measures 6.5 feet on each side. Colored tiles have been set in the center of the floor in a square measuring 4 feet on each side. The remaining floor consists of white tiles.

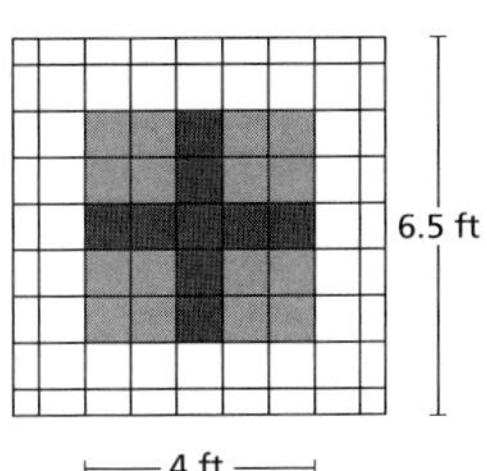

How many square feet of the entranceway floor consists of white tiles?

13. What value of y will make the line passing through $(4, -4)$ and $(-8, y)$ have a slope of $-\frac{1}{2}$?

14. What value of k will make the system $y - 5x = -1$ and $y = kx + 3$ inconsistent?

Short Response

15. The data in the table represents a linear relationship between x and y. Find the missing y-value. Explain your answer.

x	y
−3	−15
−1	−7
0	−3
2	▒
5	17

16. Graph $y > \frac{-x}{3} - 1$ on a coordinate plane. Name one point that is a solution of the inequality.

17. Marc and his brother Ty start saving money at the same time. Marc has $145 and will add $10 to his savings every week. Ty has $20 and will add $15 to his savings every week. After how many weeks will Marc and Ty have the same amount saved? What is that amount? Show your work.

18. A movie producer is looking for extras to act as office employees in his next movie. The producer needs extras that are at least 40 years old but less than 70 years old. They should be at least 60 inches tall but less than 75 inches tall. Graph all the possible combinations of ages and heights for extras that match the producer's needs. Let x represent age and y represent height. Show your work.

19. Graph the system $\begin{cases} y < -2x + 3 \\ y \geq 6x + 6 \end{cases}$.

a. Is $(0, 0)$ a solution of the system you graphed? Explain why or why not.

b. Is $(-4, 5)$ a solution of the system you graphed? Explain why or why not.

Extended Response

20. Every year, Erin knits scarves and sells them at the craft fair. This year she used $6 worth of yarn for each scarf. She also paid $50 to rent a table at the fair. She sold every scarf for $10.

a. Write a system of linear equations to represent the amount Erin spent and the amount she collected. Tell what your variables represent. Tell what each equation in the system represents.

b. Use any method to solve the system you wrote in part **a.** Show your work. How many scarves did Erin need to sell to make a profit? Explain.

c. Describe two ways you could check your solution to part **b.** Check your solution by using one of those ways. Show your work.

Short-Response Rubric

Items 15–19

2 Points = The student's answer is an accurate and complete execution of the task or tasks.

1 Point = The student's answer contains attributes of an appropriate response but is flawed.

0 Points = The student's answer contains no attributes of an appropriate response.

Extended Response Rubric

Item 20

4 Points = The student correctly writes a system of linear equations, identifying all variables and describes what each system represents, solves the system, and checks the answer in a method different from how it was solved.

3 Points = The student correctly writes a system of equations but does not identify any of the variables. The student solves the system and checks the answer.

2 Points = The student answers all parts correctly but does not show any work or explanation; or the student correctly answers parts **a** and **b** but does not check his or her work as stated in part **c.**

1 Point = The student writes a system of equations but does not correctly answer other parts of the problem; or the student attempts to answer all parts of the problem but does not correctly answer any part.

0 Points = The student does not answer correctly and does not attempt all parts of the problem.

Answers

15. 5; possible answer: find the slope of the line, then use a known point and the unknown point, substitute these coordinates into the slope ratio, and set it equal to the slope of the line. Then solve for y.

16.

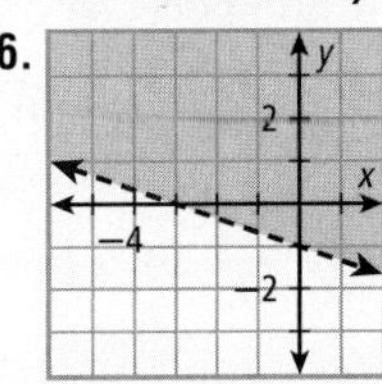

Possible answer: (3, 4)

17. 25 weeks; $395

18. Movie Extras

Height (in.) vs. Age (yr)

19.

19a. No; possible answer: it is not in the overlapping region.

b. Yes; it is in the overlapping region.

20a. Let x = the number of scarves and y = the total amount of money.

$\begin{cases} y = 6x + 50 \text{ (amount Erin spent)} \\ y = 10x \text{ (amount Erin collected)} \end{cases}$

b. Possible answer: by substitution: $10x = 6x + 50$; $12.5 = x$; 13; Erin can't sell half a scarf, and 12 scarves won't make a profit.

c. Possible answer: Graph the 2 equations and find their point of intersection. Solve for y and then substitute for x and y in both equations. (Check students' work.)

Real-World CONNECTIONS

Organizer

Objective: Choose appropriate problem-solving strategies and use them with skills from Chapters 5 and 6 to solve real-world problems.

Kayaking and Canoeing in the Pine Barrens

Reading Strategies

Have students reword **Problem 3** in their own words. Instruct them to write it so that all needed information not directly given in the problem is given and that any unnecessary information is omitted. Possible answer: A 6-hour trip must be completed by 4:30 P.M. What is the latest time the trip can begin?

Using Data Using the table for **Problems 2–3**, ask students to identify where they should start if they want to end their canoe trip at Harrisville. Oswego Lake

State Resources

Kayaking and Canoeing in the Pine Barrens

The Pine Barrens, or Pinelands, of New Jersey cover over 1 million acres in southern and central New Jersey. Kayaking on the Wading and Oswego Rivers is a popular summertime activity. There are several campgrounds and canoe and kayak rentals located along the rivers.

Choose one or more strategies to solve each problem.

1. A group of kayakers starts at Evans Bridge and kayaks to Beaver Branch. Two other groups of kayakers start at Oswego Lake. One of these groups heads toward Harrisville, and the other heads toward Bodine Field. A fourth group starts at Speedwell and kayaks to Chips Folly. Draw a mapping diagram to represent the starting and ending points of the trips. Tell whether the relation is a function. Explain.

For 2 and 3, use the table.

2. If the average speed of canoes on the river is $1\frac{1}{2}$ miles per hour, about how far is it from Oswego Lake to Beaver Branch? **6.75 mi**
3. All river trips must be completed by 4:30 P.M. What is the latest time a canoetrip can start in order to make it from Speedwell to Evans Bridge? **10:30 A.M.**

Approximate Canoe Trip Times on the Wading and Oswego Rivers

Trip	Time (h)
Evans Bridge to Beaver Branch	2
Hawkins Bridge to Evans Bridge	3
Oswego Lake to Harrisville	4
Oswego Lake to Beaver Branch	$4\frac{1}{2}$
Hawkins Bridge to Beaver Branch	5
Speedwell to Evans Bridge	6
Speedwell to Beaver Branch	8

Problem-Solving Focus

Encourage students to use the four-step problem-solving process for **Problem 2.** Focus on the first and second steps: **(1) Understand the Problem:** Ask students what they are asked to find. the distance from Oswego Lake to Beaver Branch

(2) Make a Plan: Have students find two different ways to solve the problem. Use the distance formula, $d = rt$, or make a table comparing time and distance.

Answers

1.

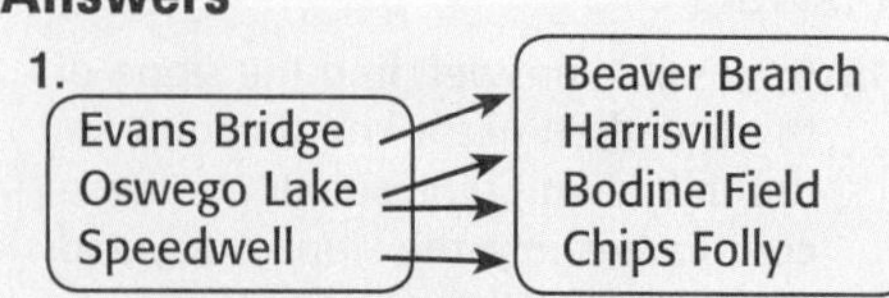

This relation is not a function because one element of the domain (Oswego Lake) is paired with more than one element of the range.

American Black Bear

American black bears are the most common bears in the United States. They can be found in 11 of the 21 counties in New Jersey. Most wild male black bears weigh between 125 and 600 pounds, while females generally weigh between 90 and 300 pounds. Their weight depends upon their age, the season of the year, and how much food is available.

Choose one or more strategies to solve each problem.

1. Black bears hibernate for about 5 months in the winter. They must store 50 to 60 pounds of fat to survive hibernation. During the month before hibernation, a black bear may consume up to 20,000 Calories per day. If a bear consumes an average of 18,500 Calories per day in the month of August, about how many total Calories will he consume that month? **about 600,000 Calories**

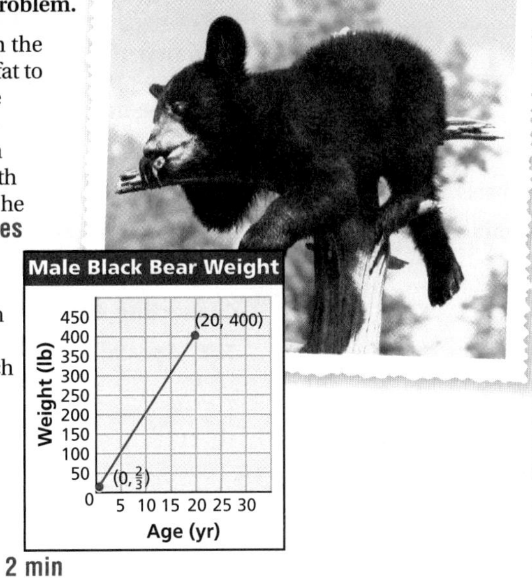

For 2, use the graph.

2. A male bear weighed $\frac{2}{3}$ pound at birth. When he died at 20 years of age, he weighed 400 pounds. Use the graph to estimate how much the bear weighed when he was 7 years old. **about 150 lb**
3. A white-tailed deer is running from a black bear at 20 miles per hour. It is $\frac{1}{3}$ mile in front of the bear. The bear is running at 30 miles per hour. How long will it take the bear to catch the deer? Assume both continue running at that same pace. **about 2 min**
4. During the hibernation months, the bear's heart rate slows to about 10 beats per minute. If the bear hibernates for 155 days, how many times will his heart beat? **2,232,000 times**

Real-World Connections

American Black Bear

Reading Strategies

ENGLISH LANGUAGE LEARNERS

In **Problem 3,** have students identify the needed information. 18,500 Calories per day for the month of August Then ask what additional information is needed to answer the question. the number of days in August

Using Data Have students explain why the graph has a segment rather than a line. Age cannot be negative, and the bear cannot live forever. Then ask why the graph does not begin at (0, 0). The bear must weigh something at birth.

Problem-Solving Focus

Encourage students to use the four-step problem-solving process for **Problem 2.** Focus on the second and third steps: **(2) Make a Plan:** What equation can you write for the speed of the deer? $y = 20x + \frac{1}{3}$ for the speed of the bear? $y = 30x$ What does x represent? number of hours **(3) Solve:** Ask students how they will solve for x. Possible answer: Solve the system by substitution.

Discuss how to convert the answer in **Problem 2** to minutes. $\frac{1}{30}$ h = $\frac{1}{30}$ of 60 min; $\frac{1}{30} \cdot 60 = 2$ min

Exponents and Polynomials

Section 7A

Exponents

Section 7B

Polynomials

Pacing Guide for 45-Minute Classes

Teacher One Stop™
Calendar Planner®

Chapter 7

Countdown Weeks 15, 16, 17

DAY 1	DAY 2	DAY 3	DAY 4	DAY 5
7-1 Lesson	7-2 Lesson	7-3 Algebra Lab	7-3 Lesson	7-4 Lesson
DAY 6	**DAY 7**	**DAY 8**	**DAY 9**	**DAY 10**
7-5 Lesson	Multi-Step Test Prep Ready to Go On?	7-6 Lesson	7-7 Algebra Lab 7-7 Lesson	7-7 Lesson 7-8 Algebra Lab
DAY 11	**DAY 12**	**DAY 13**	**DAY 14**	**DAY 15**
7-8 Lesson	Connecting Algebra to Geometry	7-9 Lesson	Multi-Step Test Prep Ready to Go On?	Chapter 7 Review
DAY 16				
Chapter 7 Test				

Pacing Guide for 90-Minute Classes

Teacher One Stop™
Calendar Planner®

Chapter 7

DAY 1	DAY 2	DAY 3	DAY 4	DAY 5
Chapter 6 Test 7-1 Lesson	7-2 Lesson 7-3 Algebra Lab	7-3 Lesson 7-4 Lesson	7-5 Lesson Multi-Step Test Prep Ready to Go On?	7-6 Lesson 7-7 Algebra Lab 7-7 Lesson
DAY 6	**DAY 7**	**DAY 8**	**DAY 9**	
7-7 Lesson 7-8 Algebra Lab 7-8 Lesson	Connecting Algebra to Geometry 7-9 Lesson	Multi-Step Test Prep Ready to Go On? Chapter 7 Review	Chapter 7 Test 8-1 Lesson	

ONGOING ASSESSMENT and INTERVENTION

	DIAGNOSE	PRESCRIBE
Assess Prior Knowledge	**Before Chapter 7**	
	Diagnose readiness for the chapter.	Prescribe intervention.
	Are You Ready? SE p. 457	***Are You Ready? Intervention***
Formative Assessment	**Before Every Lesson**	
	Diagnose readiness for the lesson.	Prescribe intervention.
	Warm Up TE	**Reteach** CRB
	During Every Lesson	
	Diagnose understanding of lesson concepts.	Prescribe intervention.
	Check It Out! SE **Questioning Strategies** TE **Think and Discuss** SE **Write About It** SE **Journal** TE	**Reading Strategies** CRB ***Success for Every Learner*** ***Lesson Tutorial Videos***
	After Every Lesson	
	Diagnose mastery of lesson concepts.	Prescribe intervention.
	Lesson Quiz TE **Test Prep** SE ***Test and Practice Generator***	**Reteach** CRB **Test Prep Doctor** TE ***Homework Help Online***
	Before Chapter 7 Testing	
	Diagnose mastery of concepts in chapter.	Prescribe intervention.
	Ready to Go On? SE pp. 495, 529 **Multi-Step Test Prep** SE pp. 494, 528 **Section Quizzes** AR ***Test and Practice Generator***	***Ready to Go On? Intervention*** **Scaffolding Questions** TE pp. 494, 528 **Reteach** CRB ***Lesson Tutorial Videos***
	Before High Stakes Testing	
	Diagnose mastery of benchmark concepts.	Prescribe intervention.
	College Entrance Exam Practice SE p. 535 **Standardized Test Prep** SE pp. 538–539	***College Entrance Exam Practice***
Summative Assessment	**After Chapter 7**	
	Check mastery of chapter concepts.	Prescribe intervention.
	Multiple-Choice Tests (Forms A, B, C) **Free-Response Tests (Forms A, B, C)** **Performance Assessment** AR **Cumulative Test** AR ***Test and Practice Generator***	**Reteach** CRB ***Lesson Tutorial Videos***

KEY: **SE** = *Student Edition* **TE** = *Teacher's Edition* **CRB** = *Chapter Resource Book* **AR** = *Assessment Resources*  Available online  Available on CD- or DVD-ROM

Lesson Resources

Before the Lesson

Prepare ***Teacher One Stop*** SPANISH 
- Editable lesson plans 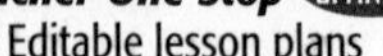
- Calendar Planner
- Easy access to all chapter resources

Lesson Transparencies
- Teacher Tools

Teach the Lesson

Introduce ***Alternate Openers: Explorations***

Lesson Transparencies
- Warm Up
- Problem of the Day

Teach ***Lesson Transparencies***
- Teaching Transparencies

Know-It Notebook™
- Vocabulary
- Key Concepts

Power Presentations

Lesson Tutorial Videos SPANISH 

Interactive Online Edition 
- Lesson Activities
- Lesson Tutorial Videos

Lab Activities

Lab Resources Online

Online Interactivities SPANISH 

TechKeys 

Practice the Lesson

Practice ***Chapter Resources***
- Practice A, B, C

Practice and Problem Solving Workbook SPANISH

IDEA Works!® Modified Worksheets and Tests

ExamView Test and Practice Generator SPANISH 

Homework Help Online

Online Interactivities SPANISH 

Interactive Online Edition 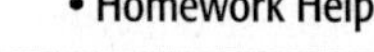
- Homework Help

Apply ***Chapter Resources***
- Problem Solving SPANISH

Practice and Problem Solving Workbook SPANISH

Interactive Online Edition 
- Chapter Project

Project Teacher Support

After the Lesson

Reteach ***Chapter Resources***
- Reteach
- Reading Strategies ELL

Success for Every Learner

Review ***Interactive Answers and Solutions***

Solutions Key

Know-It Notebook™
- Big Ideas
- Chapter Review

Extend ***Chapter Resources***
- Challenge

Technology Highlights for the Teacher

 **Power Presentations**

Dynamic presentations to engage students. Complete PowerPoint® presentations for every lesson in Chapter 7.

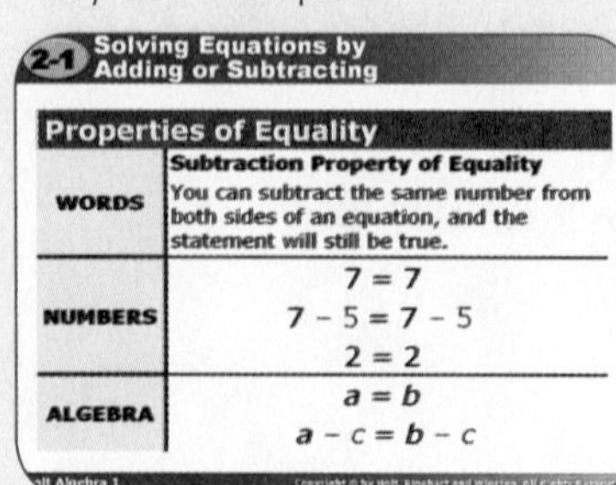

 **Teacher One Stop** SPANISH

Easy access to Chapter 7 resources and assessments. Includes lesson planning, test generation, and puzzle creation software.

 **Premier Online Edition** SPANISH

Chapter 7 includes Tutorial Videos, Lesson Activities, Lesson Quizzes, Homework Help, and Chapter Project.

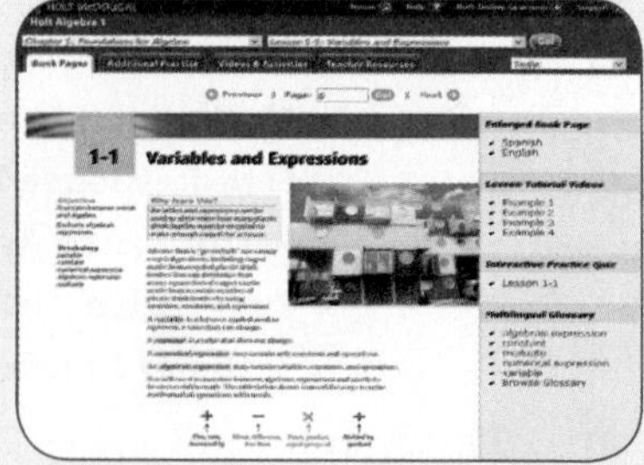

KEY: **SE** = *Student Edition* **TE** = *Teacher's Edition*  English Language Learners  Spanish version available  Available online Available on CD- or DVD-R

CHAPTER 7

Reaching All Learners

Teaching tips to help all learners appear throughout the chapter. A few that target specific students are included in the lists below.

All Learners

Lab Activities
Practice and Problem Solving Workbook SPANISH
Know-It Notebook

Special Needs Students

Practice A	CRB
Reteach	CRB
Reading Strategies	CRB
Are You Ready?	SE p. 457
Inclusion	TE pp. 461, 505, 513

IDEA Works!® Modified Worksheets and Tests
Ready to Go On? Intervention SPANISH
Know-It Notebook
Online Interactivities SPANISH
Lesson Tutorial Videos SPANISH

Developing Learners

Practice A	CRB
Reteach	CRB
Reading Strategies	CRB
Are You Ready?	SE p. 457
Vocabulary Connections	SE p. 458
Questioning Strategies	TE

Ready to Go On? Intervention SPANISH
Know-It Notebook
Homework Help Online
Online Interactivities SPANISH
Lesson Tutorial Videos SPANISH

On-Level Learners

Practice B	CRB
Problem Solving	CRB
Vocabulary Connections	SE p. 458
Questioning Strategies	TE

Ready to Go On? Intervention SPANISH
Know-It Notebook
Homework Help Online
Online Interactivities SPANISH

Advanced Learners

Practice C	CRB
Challenge	CRB
Challenge Exercises	SE
Reading and Writing Math *Extend*	TE p. 459
Critical Thinking	TE p. 515

Are You Ready? Enrichment SPANISH
Ready To Go On? Enrichment SPANISH

English Language Learners

Reading Strategies	CRB
Are You Ready? Vocabulary	SE p. 457
Vocabulary Connections	SE p. 458
Vocabulary Review	SE p. 530
English Language Learners	TE pp. 459, 476

Success for Every Learner
Know-It Notebook
Multilingual Glossary
Lesson Tutorial Videos SPANISH

Technology Highlights for Reaching All Learners

Lesson Tutorial Videos SPANISH

Starring Holt authors Ed Burger and Freddie Renfro! Live tutorials to support every lesson in Chapter 7.

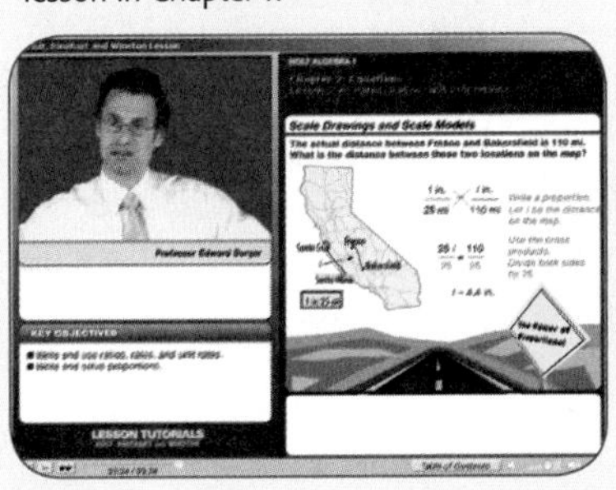

Multilingual Glossary

Searchable glossary includes definitions in English, Spanish, Vietnamese, Chinese, Hmong, Korean, and 4 other languages.

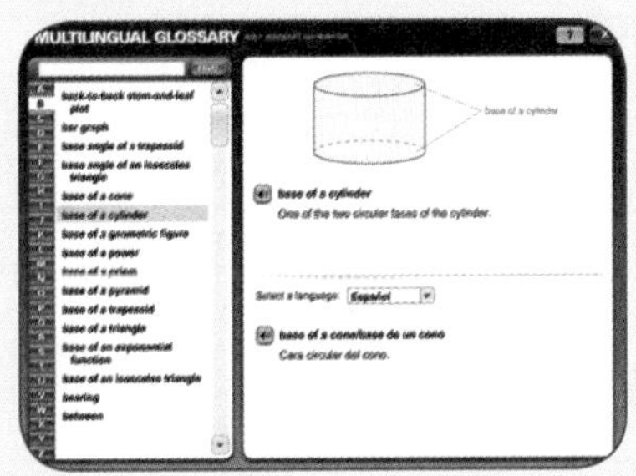

Online Interactivities

Interactive tutorials provide visually engaging alternative opportunities to learn concepts and master skills.

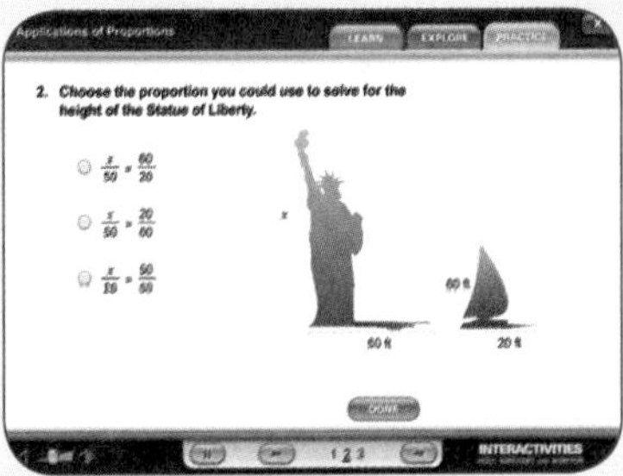

KEY: **SE** = *Student Edition* **TE** = *Teacher's Edition* **CRB** = *Chapter Resource Book* SPANISH Spanish version available · Available online · Available on CD- or DVD-ROM

Ongoing Assessment

Assessing Prior Knowledge

Determine whether students have the prerequisite concepts and skills for success in Chapter 7.

Are You Ready? SPANISH .... SE p. 457
Warm Up .... TE

Test Preparation

Provide review and practice for Chapter 7 and standardized tests.

Multi-Step Test Prep .... SE pp. 494, 528
Study Guide: Review .... SE pp. 530–533
Test Tackler .... SE pp. 536–537
Standardized Test Prep .... SE pp. 538–539
College Entrance Exam Practice .... SE p. 535
Countdown to Testing .... SE pp. C4–C27
IDEA Works!® Modified Worksheets and Tests

Alternative Assessment

Assess students' understanding of Chapter 7 concepts and combined problem-solving skills.

Chapter 7 Project .... SE p. 456
Alternative Assessment .... TE
Performance Assessment SPANISH .... AR
Portfolio Assessment SPANISH .... AR

Lesson Assessment

Provide formative assessment for each lesson of Chapter 7.

Questioning Strategies .... TE
Think and Discuss .... SE
Check It Out! Exercises .... SE
Write About It .... SE
Journal .... TE
Lesson Quiz .... TE
Alternative Assessment .... TE
IDEA Works!® Modified Worksheets and Tests

Weekly Assessment

Provide formative assessment for each section of Chapter 7.

Multi-Step Test Prep .... SE pp. 494, 528
Ready to Go On? SPANISH .... SE pp. 495, 529
Section Quizzes SPANISH .... AR
Test and Practice Generator SPANISH .... *Teacher One Stop*

Chapter Assessment

Provide summative assessment of Chapter 7 mastery.

Chapter 7 Test .... SE p. 534
Chapter Test (Levels A, B, C) SPANISH .... AR
• Multiple Choice • Free Response
Cumulative Test SPANISH .... AR
Test and Practice Generator SPANISH .... *Teacher One Stop*
IDEA Works!® Modified Worksheets and Tests

Technology Highlights for Assessment

Are You Ready? SPANISH

Automatically assess readiness and prescribe intervention for Chapter 7 prerequisite skills.

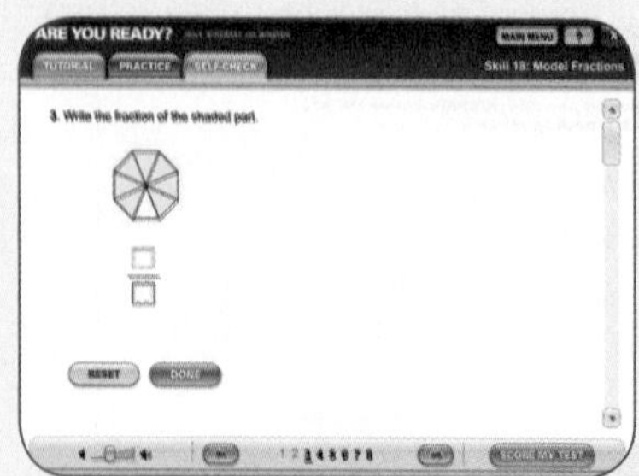

Ready to Go On?

Automatically assess understanding of and prescribe intervention for Sections 7A and 7B.

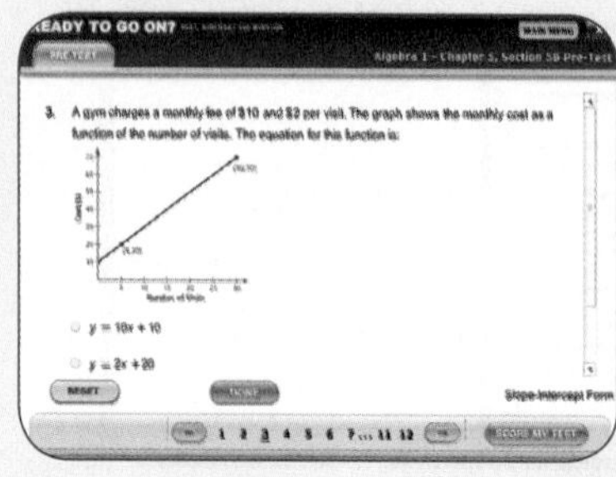

Test and Practice Generator SPANISH

Use Chapter 7 problem banks to create assessments and worksheets to print out or deliver online. Includes dynamic problems.

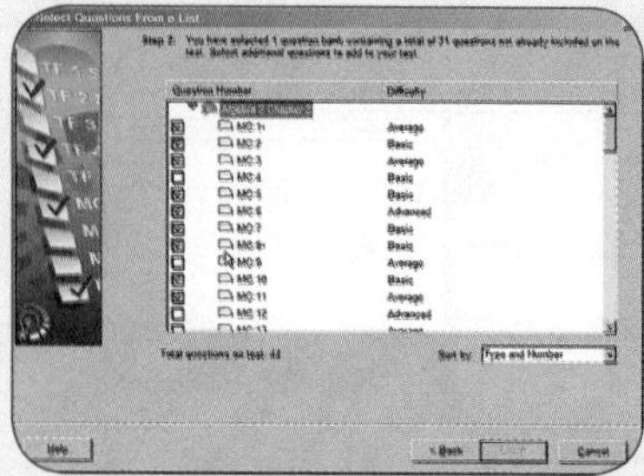

KEY: **SE** = *Student Edition* **TE** = *Teacher's Edition* **AR** = *Assessment Resources*  SPANISH Spanish version available  Available online · Available on CD- or DVD-ROM

Formal Assessment

Three levels (A, B, C) of multiple-choice and free-response chapter tests, along with a performance assessment, are available in the *Assessment Resources.*

A Chapter 7 Test

C Chapter 7 Test

MULTIPLE CHOICE

B Chapter 7 Test

Select the best answer.

1. Which of the following is equivalent to 2^{-3}?
   A $(-2)(-2)(-2)$ C $\frac{1}{(2)(2)(2)}$
   B $-\frac{1}{(2)(2)(2)}$ D $(2)(2)(2)$
2. Evaluate $(3 + x)^{-2}$ for $x = -1$.
   F -4 H $\frac{10}{9}$
   G $\frac{1}{4}$ J 10
3. Simplify $4b^{-3}$.
   A $-64b^3$ C $\frac{1}{4b^3}$
   B $\frac{1}{64b^3}$ D $\frac{4}{b^3}$
4. Which power of 10 is equivalent to 0.00001?
   F 10^{-5} H 10^4
   G 10^{-4} J 10^5
5. In 2000, the population of Texas was about 20,900,000 people. Write this population in scientific notation.
   A 2.09×10^5 C 20.9×10^6
   B 2.09×10^7 D 209×10^5
6. Which of the following is the standard form of 6.2×10^{-2}?
   F -620 H 0.062
   G $\frac{1}{620}$ J 6200
7. Simplify $y^{10} \cdot y^5$.
   A y^2 C y^{15}
   B y^5 D y^{50}
8. Simplify $(x^6)^3$.
   F x^2 H x^9
   G x^3 J x^{18}
9. Simplify $(3a^5)^2$.
   A $3a^7$ C $9a^9$
   B $3a^{10}$ D $9a^{10}$
10. In June 2005, Miami International Airport served about 8.9×10^4 airline passengers per day. Find the approximate number of airline passengers served in total during the 30 days of June.
    F 2.67×10^6 H 26.7×10^4
    G 8.01×10^7 J 80.1×10^5
11. Simplify $\frac{a^8}{a^2}$.
    A a^4 C a^{10}
    B a^6 D a^{16}
12. Simplify $\left(\frac{2y^4}{x^3}\right)^5$.
    F $\frac{2y^{20}}{x^3}$ H $\frac{32y^{20}}{x^{15}}$
    G $\frac{2y^{20}}{x^{15}}$ J $32y^9$
13. Simplify $\left(\frac{5}{b^4}\right)^{-2}$.
    A $\frac{1}{25b^4}$ C $\frac{b^8}{25}$
    B $\frac{5}{b^8}$ D $-5b^2$
14. Simplify the quotient $(7.2 \times 10^{-18}) \div (2.4 \times 10^6)$.
    F 1.728×10^{-12}
    G 3×10^{-24}
    H 3×10^{-3}
    J 4.8×10^{-24}

B Chapter 7 Test (continued)

15. Simplify $256^{\frac{1}{4}}$.
    A 4 C 6
    B 5 D 64
16. Simplify $64^{\frac{2}{3}}$.
    F 2 H 16
    G 8 J 512
17. Simplify $(x^{\frac{1}{2}})^4\sqrt[3]{x^3}$. All variables represent nonnegative numbers.
    A x^2 C $x^{2(x)}$
    B x^3 D x^9
18. When written in standard form, which polynomial has a leading coefficient of 5?
    F $-7 + 6y + 5y^2$
    G $x + 5$
    H $x^2 - 5x^3 + 2x$
    J $5y + 3y^2 - 4$
19. Classify the polynomial $3x^5 + 3$ according to its degree and number of terms.
    A cubic binomial
    B cubic trinomial
    C quintic binomial
    D quintic trinomial
20. Brett has 100 feet of fence with which to make a rectangular cage for his dog. The area of the cage in square feet is given by the polynomial $-w^2 + 50w$, where w is the width of the cage in feet. What is the area of the cage if the width is 8 feet?
    F 114 ft² H 384 ft²
    G 336 ft² J 464 ft²
21. Add $(2x^2 - 5x - 7) + (7x^2 + 3)$.
    A $2x^2 + 2x - 4$
    B $9x^2 - 5x - 4$
    C $9x^2 - 2x - 7$
    D $9x^4 - 5x - 4$
22. Subtract $(7a^2 - 3a) - (5a^2 - 5a)$.
    F $2a^2 - 8a$ H 4
    G $2a^2 + 2a$ J $12a^2 - 8a$
23. Multiply $(4rs^3)(6r^2s^5)$.
    A $10r^2s^8$ C $24r^2s^8$
    B $10r^3s^8$ D $24r^3s^8$
24. A rectangle has width w and its length is 2 units shorter than 3 times the width, or $3w - 2$. Write a polynomial for the area of the rectangle.
    F $3w^2 - 2$ H $4w - 2$
    G $3w^2 - 2w$ J $8w - 4$
25. Multiply $(x - 5)(2x + 4)$.
    A $-6x$ C $2x^2 - 20$
    B $2x^2 - 26$ D $2x^2 - 6x - 20$
26. Multiply $(b + 3)(b^2 - 5b - 7)$.
    F $b^3 - 5b^2 - 21$
    G $b^3 - 2b^2 - 22b - 21$
    H $3b^3 - 15b^2 - 21b$
    J $4b^3 - 20b^2 - 28b$
27. Multiply $(2x + 7)^2$.
    A $2x^2 + 7$ C $4x^2 + 14x + 49$
    B $4x^2 + 49$ D $4x^2 + 28x + 49$
28. Which product results in $x^2 - 100$?
    F $(x - 10)^2$
    G $(x + 10)^2$
    H $x(x - 100)$
    J $(x + 10)(x - 10)$

A Chapter 7 Test

C Chapter 7 Test

FREE RESPONSE

B Chapter 7 Test

1. Simplify 4^{-3}.
2. Evaluate $(5 - x)^{-2}$ for $x = -1$.
3. Simplify $5b^{-4}$.
4. Write 0.0000001 as a power of 10.
5. In 2000, the population of Indiana was about 6,080,000 people. Write this population in scientific notation.
6. Write 8.5×10^{-7} in standard form.

Simplify.

7. $y^7 \cdot y^3$
8. $(x^{20})^4$
9. $(2a^3)^5$
10. A computer modem can transmit 1.5×10^6 bytes per second. How many bytes can it transmit in 300 seconds? Write your answer in scientific notation.

Simplify.

11. $\frac{a^{16}}{a^4}$
12. $\left(\frac{4y^6}{x^3}\right)^2$
13. $\left(\frac{9}{b^3}\right)^{-2}$

B Chapter 7 Test (continued)

14. Simplify the quotient $(6.4 \times 10^8) \div (1.6 \times 10^{-3})$. Write the answer in scientific notation.

Simplify.

15. $32^{\frac{1}{5}}$
16. $27^{\frac{4}{3}}$
17. Simplify $(x^{\frac{1}{3}})^3\sqrt[4]{y^3}$. All variables represent nonnegative numbers.
18. When the polynomial $5x - 2x^3 + 8x^2 - 7$ is written in standard form, what is the leading coefficient?
19. Classify the polynomial $5x^2 + 9x + 1$ according to its degree and number of terms.
20. Genie has 100 feet of fence with which to make a rectangular cage for her rabbit. If she uses the wall of her house as one side, the area of the cage in square feet is given by the polynomial $-2w^2 + 100w$, where w is the width of the cage in feet. What is the area of the cage if the width is 15 feet?
21. Add $(5x^2 - 2x + 9) + (2x^2 - 4)$.
22. Subtract $(10a^2 - 6a) - (7a^2 - 8a)$.
23. Multiply $(-5rs^4)(3r^2s^3)$.
24. A rectangle has width w and its length is 4 units longer than 2 times the width, or $2w + 4$. Write a polynomial for the area of the rectangle.

Multiply.

25. $(x + 6)(3x - 8)$
26. $(b - 4)(b^2 + 3b - 2)$
27. $(3x - 4)^2$
28. $(2x + 4)(2x - 4)$

PERFORMANCE ASSESSMENT

Chapter 7 Test

Purpose
This performance task assesses the student's ability to use powers of 10 to convert between standard, period, engineering, and scientific notations.

Time
30–40 minutes

Grouping
Individuals

Preparation Hints
Review powers of 10 and scientific notation. Review the place-value names of digits in decimal numbers and define groups of digits as *periods*.

Overview
Students first rewrite numbers using periods. Then they write the periods using powers of 10, which have exponents that are always multiples of 3. Students then use engineering notation, a variation of scientific notation, to rewrite numbers.

Many scientific and graphing calculators have both a scientific notation mode (SCI) and an engineering notation mode (ENG). If you routinely use calculators in your class, you may want to allow students to use them on this activity. Calculators can be particularly beneficial for problem 16 because students can enter and compare numbers under both notations.

Introduce the Task
As a class, go over the two introductory examples. Mention that the use of the comma, space, and decimal point to separate periods is a regional, North American convention. Around the world, there are a variety of symbols used to denote separators in multi-digit numbers.

Performance Indicators
____ Rewrites numbers using words to describe periods.
____ Uses powers of 10 to represent periods.
____ Converts between standard notation and engineering notation.
____ Compares and contrasts scientific and engineering notation.

Scoring Rubric
Level 4: Student solves all problems correctly and gives a solid comparison between scientific and engineering notation.
Level 3: Student solves most problems correctly but gives a faulty comparison between scientific and engineering notation.
Level 2: Student solves a few problems and gives no comparison.
Level 1: Student is not able to solve any of the problems.

Chapter 7 Test (continued)

Commas are used to separate a large number into groups of three digits, or *periods*. Decimal numbers less than 1 can be written with spaces to distinguish periods. Periods provide a shorthand way to write the numbers.

360, 000, 000 = 360 million (millions period, thousands period, units period) 0. 000 000 045 = 45 billionths (thousandths period, millionths period, billionths period)

Write these numbers using periods (trillion, billion, million, thousand, thousandths, millionths, billionths, and trillionths).

1. 35,000,000,000,000
2. 425,000
3. 9,500,000
4. 0.000 012
5. 0.000 000 000 005
6. 0.069

Write these numbers as powers of 10.

7. 1 trillion
8. 1 billion
9. 1 million
10. 1 thousand
11. 1 thousandth
12. 1 millionth

Engineering notation is a method of writing a number with a power of 10 to emphasize the period of the number. It helps to write the period first.

0.000 000 045 = 45 **billionths** = 45×10^{-9}

Write these numbers in engineering notation.

13. 96,000,000,000
14. 108,000
15. 0.000 004
16. Based on your answers to problems 7–15, complete this table to compare and contrast scientific notation and engineering notation.

Notation	Leading factor	Power of 10
Scientific		
Engineering		

17. Convert 5.8×10^5 to engineering notation.

Teacher One Stop™ SPANISH
Test & Practice Generator

Create and customize Chapter 7 Tests. Instantly generate multiple test versions, answer keys, and Spanish versions of test items.

Modified chapter tests that address special learning needs are available in *IDEA Works!®* *Modified Worksheets and Tests.*

CHAPTER 7

SECTION 7A
Exponents

On page 494, students write, solve, and graph equations to model real-world speed-of-light situations.

Exercises designed to prepare students for success on the Multi-Step Test Prep can be found in each lesson.

SECTION 7B
Polynomials

On page 528, students multiply polynomials to model a real-world area situation.

Exercises designed to prepare students for success on the Multi-Step Test Prep can be found in each lesson.

Interactivities Online ▶

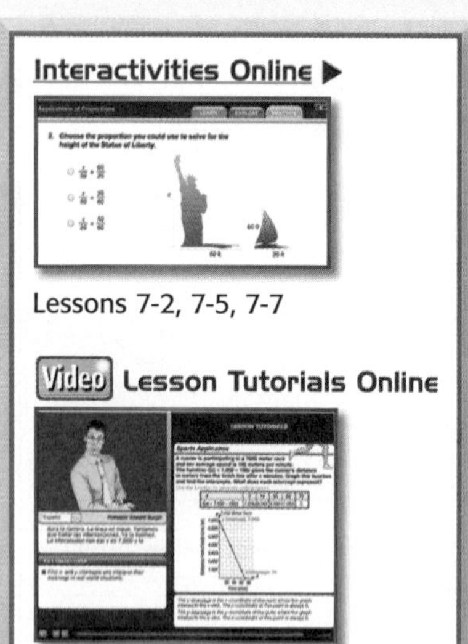

Lessons 7-2, 7-5, 7-7

Video Lesson Tutorials Online

Lesson Tutorial Videos are available for EVERY example.

CHAPTER 7

Exponents and Polynomials

Chapter Focus

- Use exponents and scientific notation to describe numbers.
- Use laws of exponents to simplify monomials.
- Perform operations with polynomials.

Every Second *Counts*

How many seconds until you graduate? The concepts in this chapter will help you find and use large numbers such as this one.

go.hrw.com
Chapter Project Online
KEYWORD: MA7 ChProj

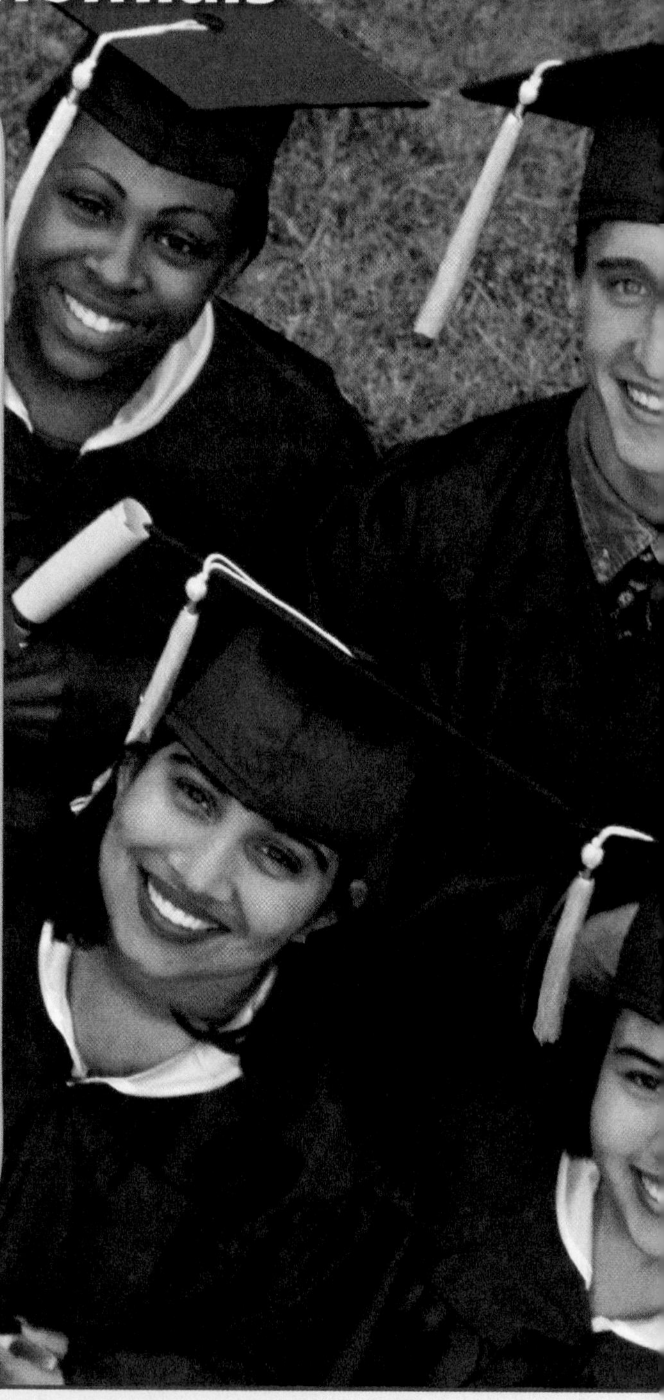

456 Chapter 7

Every Second Counts

About the Project

In the Chapter Project, students consider the passage of time in seconds. First they calculate large numbers of seconds, such as how many seconds they've been alive or how many seconds until graduation. Then they calculate fractions of seconds as they learn about a car's braking distance and driver reaction time. In each case, students use exponents and scientific notation to work with these very large and very small numbers.

Project Resources

All project resources for teachers and students are provided online.

Materials:
- calculators

ARE YOU READY?

Vocabulary

Match each term on the left with a definition on the right.

1. Associative Property **F**
2. coefficient **B**
3. Commutative Property **C**
4. exponent **D**
5. like terms **E**

A. a number that is raised to a power
B. a number that is multiplied by a variable
C. a property of addition and multiplication that states you can add or multiply numbers in any order
D. the number of times a base is used as a factor
E. terms that contain the same variables raised to the same powers
F. a property of addition and multiplication that states you can group the numbers in any order

Exponents

Write each expression using a base and an exponent.

6. $4 \cdot 4 \cdot 4 \cdot 4 \cdot 4 \cdot 4 \cdot 4$ $\mathbf{4^7}$
7. $5 \cdot 5$ $\mathbf{5^2}$
8. $(-10)(-10)(-10)(-10)$ $\mathbf{(-10)^4}$
9. $x \cdot x \cdot x$ $\mathbf{x^3}$
10. $k \cdot k \cdot k \cdot k \cdot k$ $\mathbf{k^5}$
11. 9 $\mathbf{9^1}$

Evaluate Powers

Evaluate each expression.

12. 3^4 **81**
13. -12^2 **−144**
14. 5^3 **125**
15. 2^5 **32**
16. 4^3 **64**
17. $(-1)^6$ **1**

Multiply Decimals

Multiply.

18. 0.006×10 **0.06**
19. 25.25×100 **2525**
20. 2.4×6.5 **15.6**

Combine Like Terms

Simplify each expression.

21. $6 + 3p + 14 + 9p$ $\mathbf{20 + 12p}$
22. $8y - 4x + 2y + 7x - x$ $\mathbf{10y + 2x}$
23. $(12 + 3w - 5) + 6w - 3 - 5w$ $\mathbf{4 + 4w}$
24. $6n - 14 + 5n$ $\mathbf{11n - 14}$

Squares and Square Roots

Tell whether each number is a perfect square. If so, identify its positive square root.

25. 42 **no**
26. 81 **yes; 9**
27. 36 **yes; 6**
28. 50 **no**
29. 100 **yes; 10**
30. 4 **yes; 2**
31. 1 **yes; 1**
32. 12 **no**

CHAPTER 7

ARE YOU READY?

Organizer

Objective: Assess students' understanding of prerequisite skills.

Assessing Prior Knowledge

INTERVENTION

Diagnose and Prescribe

Use this page to determine whether intervention is necessary or whether enrichment is appropriate.

Resources

 ***Are You Ready? Intervention and Enrichment* Worksheets**

 ***Are You Ready?* CD-ROM**

 ***Are You Ready?* Online**

my.hrw.com

ARE YOU READY?
Diagnose and Prescribe

Prerequisite Skill	*Are You Ready? Intervention*, Chapter 7: Worksheets	CD-ROM	Online
Exponents	Skill 7	Activity 7	Diagnose and Prescribe Online
Evaluate Powers	Skill 8	Activity 8	
Multiply Decimals	Skill 45	Activity 45	
Combine Like Terms	Skill 57	Activity 57	
Squares and Square Roots	Skill 6	Activity 6	

***Are You Ready? Enrichment*, Chapter 7**
- Worksheets
-  CD-ROM
-  Online

Organizer

Objective: Help students organize the new concepts they will learn in Chapter 7.

Online Edition
Multilingual Glossary

Resources

Teacher One Stop™
PuzzleView

***Multilingual Glossary* Online**
go.hrw.com
KEYWORD: MA7 Glossary

Answers to *Vocabulary Connections*

1. a method of writing very large and very small numbers
2. the coefficient of the first (lead) term, which is the number attached to the variable of that term
3. an expression with exactly 2 terms
4. Possible answers: tricycle, triangle, tripod; they all have three of something; an expression with exactly three terms.

CHAPTER 7

Study Guide: Preview

Where You've Been

Previously, you

- wrote and evaluated exponential expressions.
- simplified algebraic expressions by combining like terms.

In This Chapter

You will study

- properties of exponents.
- powers of 10 and scientific notation.
- how to add, subtract, and multiply polynomials by using properties of exponents and combining like terms.

Where You're Going

You can use the skills in this chapter

- to model area, perimeter, and volume in geometry.
- to express very small or very large quantities in science classes such as Chemistry, Physics, and Biology.
- in the real world to model business profits and population growth or decline.

Key Vocabulary/Vocabulario

binomial	binomio
degree of a monomial	grado de un monomio
degree of a polynomial	grado de un polinomio
leading coefficient	coeficiente principal
monomial	monomio
perfect-square trinomial	trinomio cuadrado perfecto
polynomial	polinomio
scientific notation	notación científica
standard form of a polynomial	forma estándar de un polinomio
trinomial	trinomio

Vocabulary Connections

To become familiar with some of the vocabulary terms in the chapter, consider the following. You may refer to the chapter, the glossary, or a dictionary if you like.

1. Very large and very small numbers are often encountered in the sciences. If *notation* means a method of writing something, what might **scientific notation** mean?
2. A **polynomial** written in standard form may have more than one algebraic term. What do you think the **leading coefficient** of a polynomial is?
3. A simple definition of **monomial** is "an expression with exactly one term." If the prefix *mono-* means "one" and the prefix *bi-* means "two," define the word **binomial**.
4. What words do you know that begin with the prefix *tri-*? What do they all have in common? Define the word **trinomial** based on the prefix *tri-* and the information given in Problem 3.

Reading and Writing Math

Reading Strategy: Read and Understand the Problem

Follow this strategy when solving word problems.

- Read the problem through once.
- Identify exactly what the problem asks you to do.
- Read the problem again, slowly and carefully, to break it into parts.
- Highlight or underline the key information.
- Make a plan to solve the problem.

From Lesson 6-6

29. Multi-Step Linda works at a pharmacy for $15 an hour. She also baby-sits for $10 an hour. Linda needs to earn at least $90 per week, but she does not want to work more than 20 hours per week. Show and describe the number of hours Linda could work at each job to meet her goals. List two possible solutions.

Step 1	**Identify exactly what the problem asks you to do.**	• Show and describe the number of hours Linda can work at each job and earn at least $90 per week, without working more than 20 hours per week. • List two possible solutions of the system.
Step 2	**Break the problem into parts. Highlight or underline the key information.**	• Linda has two jobs. She makes **$15 per hour** at one job and **$10 per hour** at the other job. • She wants to earn **at least $90 per week.** • She does **not** want to work **more than 20 hours per week.**
Step 3	**Make a plan to solve the problem.**	• Write a system of inequalities. • Solve the system. • Identify two possible solutions of the system.

Try This

For the problem below,

a. identify exactly what the problem asks you to do.

b. break the problem into parts. Highlight or underline the key information.

c. make a plan to solve the problem.

1. The difference between the length and the width of a rectangle is 14 units. The area is 120 square units. Write and solve a system of equations to determine the length and the width of the rectangle. (*Hint:* The formula for the area of a rectangle is $A = \ell w$.)

Reading and Writing Math

Organizer

Objective: Help students apply strategies to understand and retain key concepts.

Online Edition

ENGLISH LANGUAGE LEARNERS

Reading Strategy: Read and Understand the Problem

Discuss Key information can include more than just numbers. Words and phrases such as *not, no more than, whole number solutions, inches,* and *two different ways* can be crucial to correctly solving a problem.

Extend As you present word problems in Chapter 7 to the class, ask students what information should be highlighted and why.

Answers to *Try This*

1a. Find the length and width of the rectangle.

b. The difference between length and width is 14 units. The area is 120 square units.

c. Write and solve a system of equations.

Reading Connection

Powers of Ten
by Philip and Phylis Morrison

This is a wondrous yet practical guide to powers of 10 and exponential growth. The book begins with one billion light years. In 40 steps, each step depicting $\frac{1}{10}$ the scale of the previous step, it moves to subatomic particles.

Activity Ask students to make their own books using 1 ft (10^0 ft) as step 6, 10^1 ft as step 7, 10^2 ft as step 8, and so on, up to step 11. Then 10^{-1} ft will be step 5, 10^{-2} ft will be step 4, etc. For each step, have students name (and perhaps locate a photo of) an object near that length.

SECTION 7A

Exponents

One-Minute Section Planner

Lesson	Lab Resources	Materials
Lesson 7-1 Integer Exponents • Evaluate expressions containing zero and integer exponents. • Simplify expressions containing zero and integer exponents. ☑ SAT-10 ☐ NAEP ☑ ACT ☑ SAT ☑ SAT Subject Tests		**Optional** graphing calculator
Lesson 7-2 Powers of 10 and Scientific Notation • Evaluate and multiply by powers of 10. • Convert between standard notation and scientific notation. ☑ SAT-10 ☐ NAEP ☑ ACT ☐ SAT ☐ SAT Subject Tests		**Optional** graphing calculator
7-3 Algebra Lab Explore Properties of Exponents • Use patterns to explore multiplication properties of exponents. ☐ SAT-10 ☑ NAEP ☐ ACT ☐ SAT ☐ SAT Subject Tests	***Algebra Lab Activities*** 7-3 Lab Recording Sheet	
Lesson 7-3 Multiplication Properties of Exponents • Use multiplication properties of exponents to evaluate and simplify expressions. ☑ SAT-10 ☑ NAEP ☑ ACT ☑ SAT ☑ SAT Subject Tests		
Lesson 7-4 Division Properties of Exponents • Use division properties of exponents to evaluate and simplify expressions. ☑ SAT-10 ☑ NAEP ☑ ACT ☑ SAT ☑ SAT Subject Tests	***Technology Lab Activities*** 7-4 Technology Lab	
Lesson 7-5 Rational Exponents • Evaluate and simplify expressions containing rational exponents. ☑ SAT-10 ☑ NAEP ☑ ACT ☑ SAT ☐ SAT Subject Tests		**Optional** graphing calculator, number cubes

Note: If NAEP is checked, the content is tested on either the Grade 8 or Grade 12 NAEP assessment.

MK = *Manipulatives Kit*

Math Background

Professional Learning

EXPONENTS

Lesson 7-1

Up to this point, students have worked primarily with linear equations and linear inequalities. In Chapter 7, students move toward more complex ideas as they begin to study polynomials. Before beginning this study, students must first have an understanding of exponents.

One common difficulty students have with exponents is the use of zero. For example, students are often puzzled by the fact that any nonzero number raised to the zero power is 1. It makes sense to think of 2^4 as a product where 2 is a factor 4 times ($2^4 = 2 \cdot 2 \cdot 2 \cdot 2$), but when it comes to evaluating 2^0, how does one write a product with 2 as a factor zero times? Students should understand that 2^0 is *defined* to be 1 in order to make it consistent with the rules of exponent arithmetic. For example, in order for the Quotient of Powers Property to work in as many situations as possible, it must be true that $\frac{2^4}{2^4} = 2^{4-4} = 2^0$, but $\frac{2^4}{2^4} = 1$. Thus, $2^0 = 1$.

This idea of defining certain powers in order to create a system that is as widely consistent as possible also explains why the expression 0^0 is undefined. First, it is clear that $0^1 = 0$, $0^2 = 0$, and $0^{13} = 0$. In fact, for any value of n greater than zero, $0^n = 0$. For this reason, it might make sense to define 0^0 as zero. On the other hand, as shown above, any nonzero number raised to the zero power is 1, so it might also make sense to define 0^0 as 1. Because there is no single real number that works consistently as a definition of 0^0, this expression is considered *indeterminate* and is left undefined.

SCIENTIFIC NOTATION

LESSON 7-2

Scientific notation is an efficient way to write very large and very small numbers, such as numbers used to express distances in space. For example, the distance from the Earth to the Sun is approximately 93 million miles or 93,000,000 miles.

The key step in the translation to scientific notation is to recognize that

$$93{,}000{,}000 = 9.3 \times 10{,}000{,}000$$

and to see that 10,000,000 is a power of 10, namely 10^7. Thus, $93{,}000{,}000 = 9.3 \times 10^7$.

In general, every positive real number may be written in scientific notation, $a \times 10^n$, where $1 \le a < 10$ and n is an integer. The value of a is called the *coefficient.* A number line helps to visualize scientific notation. On the number line below, several powers of 10 are graphed.

The interval between each successive power of 10 is 10 times as large as the preceding interval. When a number is written in scientific notation, such as 6.7×10^3, the power of 10 tells which interval the number lies in and the coefficient tells where the number falls within the interval.

Numbers greater than or equal to 1 but less than 10 are written in scientific notation with an exponent of 0 since, for example,

$$\begin{aligned} 3.8 &= 3.8 \times 1 \\ &= 3.8 \times 10^0 \end{aligned}$$

Numbers greater than 0 but less than 1 are written with negative powers of 10. A specific example shows why this is the case:

$$\begin{aligned} 0.0041 &= 4.1 \times 0.001 \\ &= 4.1 \times \frac{1}{1000} \\ &= 4.1 \times 10^{-3} \end{aligned}$$

7-1 Organizer

Pacing: Traditional 1 day
Block $\frac{1}{2}$ day

Objectives: Evaluate expressions containing zero and integer exponents.

Simplify expressions containing zero and integer exponents.

Online Edition
Tutorial Videos

Countdown Week 15

Power Presentations with PowerPoint®

Warm Up

Evaluate each expression for the given values of the variables.

1. x^3y^2 for $x = -1$ and $y = 10$ $\quad -100$

2. $\frac{3x^2}{y^2}$ for $x = 4$ and $y = -7$ $\quad \frac{48}{49}$

Write each number as a power of the given base.

3. 64; base 4 $\quad 4^3$

4. -27; base -3 $\quad (-3)^3$

Also available on transparency

Math Fact !!!

The Babylonian number system had no symbol for zero. It was represented by a blank space.

7-1 Integer Exponents

Objectives
Evaluate expressions containing zero and integer exponents.

Simplify expressions containing zero and integer exponents.

Who uses this?
Manufacturers can use negative exponents to express very small measurements.

In 1930, the Model A Ford was one of the first cars to boast precise craftsmanship in mass production. The car's pistons had a diameter of $3\frac{7}{8}$ inches; this measurement could vary by at most 10^{-3} inch.

You have seen positive exponents. Recall that to simplify 3^2, use 3 as a factor 2 times: $3^2 = 3 \cdot 3 = 9$.

Remember!

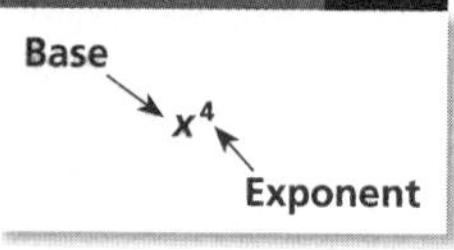

But what does it mean for an exponent to be negative or 0? You can use a table and look for a pattern to figure it out.

Power	5^5	5^4	5^3	5^2	5^1	5^0	5^{-1}	5^{-2}
Value	3125	625	125	25	5			

$\div 5 \quad \div 5 \quad \div 5 \quad \div 5$

When the exponent decreases by one, the value of the power is divided by 5. Continue the pattern of dividing by 5:

$$5^0 = \frac{5}{5} = 1 \qquad 5^{-1} = \frac{1}{5} = \frac{1}{5^1} \qquad 5^{-2} = \frac{1}{5} \div 5 = \frac{1}{25} = \frac{1}{5^2}$$

Integer Exponents

WORDS	NUMBERS	ALGEBRA
Zero exponent—Any nonzero number raised to the zero power is 1.	$3^0 = 1 \quad 123^0 = 1$ $(-16)^0 = 1 \quad \left(\frac{3}{7}\right)^0 = 1$	If $x \neq 0$, then $x^0 = 1$.
Negative exponent—A nonzero number raised to a negative exponent is equal to 1 divided by that number raised to the opposite (positive) exponent.	$3^{-2} = \frac{1}{3^2} = \frac{1}{9}$ $2^{-4} = \frac{1}{2^4} = \frac{1}{16}$	If $x \neq 0$ and n is an integer, then $x^{-n} = \frac{1}{x^n}$.

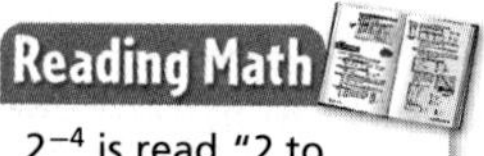

2^{-4} is read "2 to the negative fourth power."

Notice the phrase "nonzero number" in the table above. This is because 0^0 and 0 raised to a negative power are both undefined. For example, if you use the pattern given above the table with a base of 0 instead of 5, you would get $0^0 = \frac{0}{0}$. Also, 0^{-6} would be $\frac{1}{0^6} = \frac{1}{0}$. Since division by 0 is undefined, neither value exists.

State Resources

State Resources Online
KEYWORD: MA7 Resources

1 Introduce

EXPLORATION

7-1 Integer Exponents

A botanist has taken over a study of a plant whose height doubles every day. On the fourth day after the experiment began, the plant was 16 inches tall.

1. The botanist can find the height of the plant on previous days by repeatedly dividing by 2. Use this fact to complete the middle column of the table.
2. Use your knowledge of exponents to fill in the right column for days 1 and 2. Then look for patterns to complete the right column.
3. What does day 0 represent? What was the height of the plant on day 0? How can you write the height as a power?
4. What does day -1 represent? What was the height of the plant on day -1? How can you write the height as a power?

Day	Height of Plant (in.)	Height Written as a Power
4	16	2^4
3	8	2^3
2		
1		
0		
-1		
-2		
-3		

THINK AND DISCUSS

5. **Describe** the pattern in the right column of the table.
6. **Show** how you could find the height of the plant on day -4 and then write the height as a power.

Motivate

Show students the following examples and ask them to suggest a rule about the use of negative exponents.

a. $2^{-1} = \frac{1}{2}$ **b.** $2^{-3} = \frac{1}{8}$ **c.** $5^{-2} = \frac{1}{25}$

d. $3^{-2} = \frac{1}{9}$

Possible answer: The negative exponent means that you must use the reciprocal of the base and change the exponent to a positive number.

Explorations and answers are provided in *Alternate Openers: Explorations Transparencies.*

EXAMPLE 1 Manufacturing Application

The diameter for the Model A Ford piston could vary by at most 10^{-3} inch. Simplify this expression.

$$10^{-3} = \frac{1}{10^3} = \frac{1}{10 \cdot 10 \cdot 10} = \frac{1}{1000}$$

10^{-3} inch is equal to $\frac{1}{1000}$ inch, or 0.001 inch.

CHECK IT OUT! 1. A sand fly may have a wingspan up to 5^{-3} m. Simplify this expression. $\frac{1}{125}$ m

EXAMPLE 2 Zero and Negative Exponents

Simplify.

A 2^{-3}

$$2^{-3} = \frac{1}{2^3} = \frac{1}{2 \cdot 2 \cdot 2} = \frac{1}{8}$$

B 5^0

$5^0 = 1$ *Any nonzero number raised to the zero power is 1.*

Caution!

In $(-3)^{-4}$, the base is negative because the negative sign is inside the parentheses.

In -3^{-4} the base (3) is positive.

C $(-3)^{-4}$

$$(-3)^{-4} = \frac{1}{(-3)^4} = \frac{1}{(-3)(-3)(-3)(-3)} = \frac{1}{81}$$

D -3^{-4}

$$-3^{-4} = -\frac{1}{3^4} = -\frac{1}{3 \cdot 3 \cdot 3 \cdot 3} = -\frac{1}{81}$$

CHECK IT OUT! Simplify.

2a. 10^{-4} $\frac{1}{10{,}000}$ 2b. $(-2)^{-4}$ $\frac{1}{16}$ 2c. $(-2)^{-5}$ $-\frac{1}{32}$ 2d. -2^{-5} $-\frac{1}{32}$

EXAMPLE 3 Evaluating Expressions with Zero and Negative Exponents

Evaluate each expression for the given value(s) of the variable(s).

A x^{-1} for $x = 2$

2^{-1} *Substitute 2 for x.*

$2^{-1} = \frac{1}{2^1} = \frac{1}{2}$ *Use the definition $x^{-n} = \frac{1}{x^n}$.*

B a^0b^{-3} for $a = 8$ and $b = -2$

$8^0 \cdot (-2)^{-3}$ *Substitute 8 for a and −2 for b.*

$1 \cdot \frac{1}{(-2)^3}$ *Simplify expressions with exponents.*

$1 \cdot \frac{1}{(-2)(-2)(-2)}$ *Write the power in the denominator as a product.*

$1 \cdot \frac{1}{-8}$ *Simplify the power in the denominator.*

$-\frac{1}{8}$ *Simplify.*

3a. $\frac{1}{64}$
3b. 2

CHECK IT OUT! Evaluate each expression for the given value(s) of the variable(s).

3a. p^{-3} for $p = 4$ 3b. $8a^{-2}b^0$ for $a = -2$ and $b = 6$

2 Teach

Guided Instruction

Explain negative and zero exponents by demonstrating the pattern in the decreasing values of the powers. Use the definition to simplify and evaluate expressions with negative and zero exponents. Then include examples with negative exponents in the denominator. Remind students that factors with negative exponents should be simplified.

Technology Students can use the ^ or Y^x keys on their calculators to check their work in **Examples 1–3.**

Reaching All Learners

Through Graphic Organizers

Have students make a chart similar to the one below and let them refer to it during class work and homework.

0^x $(x \le 0)$	Undefined
x^0 $(x \ne 0)$	1
x^{-2} $(x \ne 0)$	$\frac{1}{x^2}$
$\frac{1}{x^{-2}}$ $(x \ne 0)$	x^2

Students will sometimes multiply the base by the negative exponent. Have these students reread the definition of a negative exponent. Point out that 10^{-3} means a number less than one, not a number less than zero.

Power Presentations with PowerPoint®

Additional Examples

Example 1

One cup is 2^{-4} gallons. Simplify this expression. $\frac{1}{16}$ gal

Example 2

Simplify.

A. 4^{-3} $\frac{1}{64}$ **B.** 7^0 1

C. $(-5)^{-4}$ $\frac{1}{625}$ **D.** -5^{-4} $-\frac{1}{625}$

Example 3

Evaluate each expression for the given value(s) of the variable(s).

A. x^{-2} for $x = 4$ $\frac{1}{16}$

B. $-2a^0b^{-4}$ for $a = 5$ and $b = -3$ $-\frac{2}{81}$

INTERVENTION

Questioning Strategies

EXAMPLES 1–2

- What is the difference between **Examples 2C** and **2D**?
- When will a term with a negative exponent have a negative value?

EXAMPLE 3

- There are no fractions in the problem. Why are there fractions in the answers?
- Why is the value of a variable irrelevant if that variable is raised to the zero power?

Inclusion In **Example 3,** some students may prefer to rewrite the expression with a positive exponent before substituting for the variable.

Power Presentations with PowerPoint®

Additional Examples

Example 4

Simplify.

A. $7w^{-4}$ $\frac{7}{w^4}$ **B.** $\frac{-5}{k^{-2}}$ $-5k^2$

C. $\frac{a^0b^{-2}}{c^{-3}d^6}$ $\frac{c^3}{b^2d^6}$

INTERVENTION

Questioning Strategies

EXAMPLE 4

- How do you decide which factors get moved to the other side of the fraction bar?
- What happens to factors with exponents of zero?

What if you have an expression with a negative exponent in a denominator, such as $\frac{1}{x^{-8}}$?

$x^{-n} = \frac{1}{x^n}$, or $\frac{1}{x^n} = x^{-n}$ — *Definition of negative exponent*

$\frac{1}{x^{-8}} = x^{-(-8)}$ — *Substitute −8 for n.*

$= x^8$ — *Simplify the exponent on the right side.*

So if a base with a negative exponent is in a denominator, it is equivalent to the same base with the opposite (positive) exponent in the numerator.

An expression that contains negative or zero exponents is not considered to be simplified. Expressions should be rewritten with only positive exponents.

EXAMPLE 4 Simplifying Expressions with Zero and Negative Exponents

Simplify.

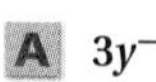

A $3y^{-2}$

$3y^{-2} = 3 \cdot y^{-2}$

$= 3 \cdot \frac{1}{y^2}$

$= \frac{3}{y^2}$

B $\frac{-4}{k^{-4}}$

$\frac{-4}{k^{-4}} = -4 \cdot \frac{1}{k^{-4}}$

$= -4 \cdot k^4$

$= -4k^4$

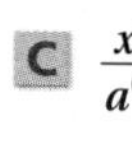

C $\frac{x^{-3}}{a^0y^5}$

$\frac{x^{-3}}{a^0y^5} = \frac{1}{x^3 \cdot 1 \cdot y^5}$ — *$a^0 = 1$ and $x^{-3} = \frac{1}{x^3}$.*

$= \frac{1}{x^3y^5}$

CHECK IT OUT! Simplify.

4a. $2r^0m^{-3}$ $\frac{2}{m^3}$ **4b.** $\frac{r^{-3}}{7}$ $\frac{1}{7r^3}$ **4c.** $\frac{g^4}{h^{-6}}$ g^4h^6

THINK AND DISCUSS

1. Complete each equation: $2b^? = \frac{2}{b^2}$, $\frac{s^{-3}}{k^?} = \frac{1}{s^3}$, $?^{-2} = \frac{1}{t^2}$

2. GET ORGANIZED Copy and complete the graphic organizer. In each box, describe how to simplify, and give an example.

Simplifying Expressions with Negative Exponents	
For a negative exponent in the numerator . . .	For a negative exponent in the denominator . . .

3 Close

Summarize

Remind students that an expression is not simplified if it has an exponent that is negative or zero.

Have students state the rules for simplifying expressions with negative exponents in their own words. Accept nontechnical answers such as the following: Make the exponent positive and move the factor to the other side of the fraction bar.

ONGOING ASSESSMENT and INTERVENTION

***Diagnose Before* the Lesson**
7-1 Warm Up, TE p. 460

***Monitor During* the Lesson**
Check It Out! Exercises, SE pp. 461–462
Questioning Strategies, TE pp. 461–462

***Assess After* the Lesson**
7-1 Lesson Quiz, TE p. 465
Alternative Assessment, TE p. 465

Answers to *Think and Discuss*

1. −2; 0; *t*
2. See p. A6.

7-1 Exercises

go.hrw.com
Homework Help Online
KEYWORD: MA7 7-1
Parent Resources Online
KEYWORD: MA7 Parent

GUIDED PRACTICE

SEE EXAMPLE 1 p. 461

1. **Medicine** A typical virus is about 10^{-7} m in size. Simplify this expression. $\frac{1}{10{,}000{,}000}$ m

SEE EXAMPLE 2 p. 461

Simplify.

2. 6^{-2} $\frac{1}{36}$
3. 3^0 1
4. -5^{-2} $-\frac{1}{25}$
5. 3^{-3} $\frac{1}{27}$
6. 1^{-8} 1
7. -8^{-3} $-\frac{1}{512}$
8. 10^{-2} $\frac{1}{100}$
9. $(4.2)^0$ 1
10. $(-3)^{-3}$ $-\frac{1}{27}$
11. 4^{-2} $\frac{1}{16}$

SEE EXAMPLE 3 p. 461

Evaluate each expression for the given value(s) of the variable(s).

12. b^{-2} for $b = -3$ $\frac{1}{9}$
13. $(2t)^{-4}$ for $t = 2$ $\frac{1}{256}$
14. $(m - 4)^{-5}$ for $m = 6$ $\frac{1}{32}$
15. $2x^0y^{-3}$ for $x = 7$ and $y = -4$ $-\frac{1}{32}$

SEE EXAMPLE 4 p. 462

Simplify.

16. $4m^0$ 4
17. $3k^{-4}$ $\frac{3}{k^4}$
18. $\frac{7}{r^{-7}}$ $7r^7$
19. $\frac{x^{10}}{d^{-3}}$ $x^{10}d^3$
20. $2x^0y^{-4}$ $\frac{2}{y^4}$
21. $\frac{f^{-4}}{g^{-6}}$ $\frac{g^6}{f^4}$
22. $\frac{c^4}{d^{-3}}$ c^4d^3
23. p^7q^{-1} $\frac{p^7}{q}$

PRACTICE AND PROBLEM SOLVING

Independent Practice	
For Exercises	See Example
24	1
25–36	2
37–42	3
43–57	4

Extra Practice
Skills Practice p. S16
Application Practice p. S34

24. **Biology** One of the smallest bats is the northern blossom bat, which is found from Southeast Asia to Australia. This bat weighs about 2^{-1} ounce. Simplify this expression. $\frac{1}{2}$ oz

Simplify.

25. 8^0 1
26. 5^{-4} $\frac{1}{625}$
27. 3^{-4} $\frac{1}{81}$
28. -9^{-2} $-\frac{1}{81}$
29. -6^{-2} $-\frac{1}{36}$
30. 7^{-2} $\frac{1}{49}$
31. $\left(\frac{2}{5}\right)^0$ 1
32. 13^{-2} $\frac{1}{169}$
33. $(-3)^{-1}$ $-\frac{1}{3}$
34. $(-4)^2$ 16
35. $\left(\frac{1}{2}\right)^{-2}$ 4
36. -7^{-1} $-\frac{1}{7}$

Evaluate each expression for the given value(s) of the variable(s).

37. x^{-4} for $x = 4$ $\frac{1}{256}$
38. $\left(\frac{2}{3}v\right)^{-3}$ for $v = 9$ $\frac{1}{216}$
39. $(10 - d)^0$ for $d = 11$ 1
40. $10m^{-1}n^{-5}$ for $m = 10$ and $n = -2$ $-\frac{1}{32}$
41. $(3ab)^{-2}$ for $a = \frac{1}{2}$ and $b = 8$ $\frac{1}{144}$
42. $4w^vx^v$ for $w = 3$, $v = 0$, and $x = -5$ 4

Simplify.

43. k^{-4} $\frac{1}{k^4}$
44. $2z^{-8}$ $\frac{2}{z^8}$
45. $\frac{1}{2b^{-3}}$ $\frac{b^3}{2}$
46. $c^{-2}d$ $\frac{d}{c^2}$
47. $-5x^{-3}$ $-\frac{5}{x^3}$
48. $4x^{-6}y^{-2}$ $\frac{4}{x^6y^2}$
49. $\frac{2f^0}{7g^{-10}}$ $\frac{2g^{10}}{7}$
50. $\frac{r^{-5}}{s^{-1}}$ $\frac{s}{r^5}$
51. $\frac{s^5}{t^{-12}}$ s^5t^{12}
52. $\frac{3w^{-5}}{x^{-6}}$ $\frac{3x^6}{w^5}$
53. b^0c^0 1
54. $\frac{2}{3}m^{-1}n^5$ $\frac{2n^5}{3m}$
55. $\frac{q^{-2}r^0}{s^0}$ $\frac{1}{q^2}$
56. $\frac{a^{-7}b^2}{c^3d^{-4}}$ $\frac{b^2d^4}{a^7c^3}$
57. $\frac{h^3k^{-1}}{6m^2}$ $\frac{h^3}{6m^2k}$

Assignment Guide

Assign *Guided Practice* exercises as necessary.

If you finished Examples **1–2**
Basic 24–36, 77, 86, 88
Average 24–36, 77, 86, 88
Advanced 24–36, 77, 100, 101

If you finished Examples **1–4**
Basic 24–77, 86–99, 102–113
Average 24–57, 58–74 even, 76–100, 102–113
Advanced 24–57, 58–74 even, 77–113

Homework Quick Check
Quickly check key concepts.
Exercises: 24, 28, 34, 42, 52, 77

State Resources

Exercise 94 involves writing an equation with a negative exponent. This exercise prepares students for the Multi-Step Test Prep on page 494.

Answers

77. red blood cell: $\frac{1}{125{,}000}$ m; white blood cell: $\frac{3}{250{,}000}$ m; platelet: $\frac{3}{1{,}000{,}000}$ m

85. Possible answer: Look at the pattern below. As the exponent goes down by 1, the value is half of what it was before.
$2^3 = 8,\ 2^2 = 4,$
$2^1 = 2,\ 2^0 = 1,$
$2^{-1} = \frac{1}{2},\ 2^{-2} = \frac{1}{4},$
$2^{-3} = \frac{1}{8} = \frac{1}{2^3}$

Evaluate each expression for $x = 3$, $y = -1$, and $z = 2$.

58. z^{-5} $\frac{1}{32}$
59. $(x + y)^{-4}$ $\frac{1}{16}$
60. $(yz)^0$ 1
61. $(xyz)^{-1}$ $-\frac{1}{6}$
62. $(xy - 3)^{-2}$ $\frac{1}{36}$
63. x^{-y} 3
64. $(yz)^{-x}$ $-\frac{1}{8}$
65. xy^{-4} 3

66. **/// ERROR ANALYSIS ///** Look at the two equations below. Which is incorrect? Explain the error.

66. Equation A is incorrect because 5 was incorrectly moved to the denom. The neg. exp. applies only to the base x.

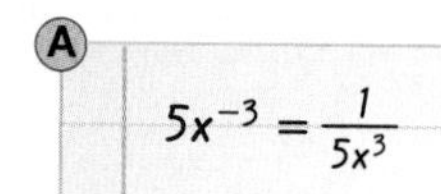
A: $5x^{-3} = \frac{1}{5x^3}$

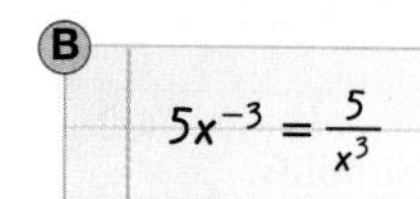
B: $5x^{-3} = \frac{5}{x^3}$

Simplify.

67. a^3b^{-2} $\frac{a^3}{b^2}$
68. $c^{-4}d^3$ $\frac{d^3}{c^4}$
69. $v^0w^2y^{-1}$ $\frac{w^2}{y}$
70. $(a^2b^{-7})^0$ 1
71. $-5y^{-6}$ $-\frac{5}{y^6}$
72. $\frac{2a^{-5}}{b^{-6}}$ $\frac{2b^6}{a^5}$
73. $\frac{2a^3}{b^{-1}}$ $2a^3b$
74. $\frac{m^2}{n^{-3}}$ m^2n^3
75. $\frac{x^{-8}}{3y^{12}}$ $\frac{1}{3x^8y^{12}}$
76. $-\frac{20p^{-1}}{5q^{-3}}$ $-\frac{4q^3}{p}$

LINK Biology

When bleeding occurs, platelets (which appear green in the image above) help to form a clot to reduce blood loss. Calcium and vitamin K are also necessary for clot formation.

77. **Biology** Human blood contains red blood cells, white blood cells, and platelets. The table shows the sizes of these components. Simplify each expression.

Blood Components	
Part	**Size (m)**
Red blood cell	$125{,}000^{-1}$
White blood cell	$3(500)^{-2}$
Platelet	$3(1000)^{-2}$

Tell whether each statement is sometimes, always, or never true.

78. If n is a positive integer, then $x^{-n} = \frac{1}{x^n}$. **always**
79. If x is positive, then x^{-n} is negative. **never**
80. If n is zero, then x^{-n} is 1. **sometimes**
81. If n is a negative integer, then $x^{-n} = 1$. **sometimes**
82. If x is zero, then x^{-n} is 1. **never**
83. If n is an integer, then $x^{-n} > 1$. **sometimes**
84. **Critical Thinking** Find the value of $2^3 \cdot 2^{-3}$. Then find the value of $3^2 \cdot 3^{-2}$. Make a conjecture about the value of $a^n \cdot a^{-n}$. **1; 1; $a^n \cdot a^{-n} = 1$**
85. **Write About It** Explain in your own words why 2^{-3} is the same as $\frac{1}{2^3}$.

Find the missing value.

86. $\frac{1}{4} = 2^{■}$ **−2**
87. $9^{-2} = \frac{1}{■}$ **81**
88. $\frac{1}{64} = ■^{-2}$ **8**
89. $\frac{■}{3} = 3^{-1}$ **1**
90. $7^{-2} = \frac{1}{■}$ **49**
91. $10^{■} = \frac{1}{1000}$ **−3**
92. $3 \cdot 4^{-2} = \frac{3}{■}$ **16**
93. $2 \cdot \frac{1}{5} = 2 \cdot 5^{■}$ **−1**

94. This problem will prepare you for the Multi-Step Test Prep on page 494.
    a. The product of the frequency f and the wavelength w of light in air is a constant v. Write an equation for this relationship. **$fw = v$**
    b. Solve this equation for wavelength. Then write this equation as an equation with f raised to a negative exponent. **b. $w = \frac{v}{f}$; $w = vf^{-1}$**
    c. The units for frequency are hertz (Hz). One hertz is one cycle per second, which is often written as $\frac{1}{s}$. Rewrite this expression using a negative exponent. **s^{-1}**

7-1 PRACTICE A
7-1 PRACTICE C
7-1 PRACTICE B

Simplify.

1. $5^{-3} = \frac{1}{5^3} = \frac{1}{125}$
2. $2^{-6} = \frac{1}{2^6} = \frac{1}{64}$
3. $(-5)^{-2}$ $\frac{1}{25}$
4. $-(4)^{-3}$ $-\frac{1}{64}$
5. -6^0 -1
6. $(7)^{-2}$ $\frac{1}{49}$

Evaluate each expression for the given value(s) of the variable(s).

7. d^{-3} for $d = -2$ $-\frac{1}{8}$
8. a^5b^{-6} for $a = 3$ and $b = 2$ $\frac{243}{64}$
9. $(b - 4)^{-2}$ for $b = 1$ $\frac{1}{9}$
10. $5z^{-x}$ for $z = -3$ and $x = 2$ $\frac{5}{9}$
11. $(5z)^{-x}$ for $z = -3$ and $x = 2$ $\frac{1}{225}$
12. $c^{-3}(16^{-2})$ for $c = 4$ $\frac{1}{16{,}384}$

Simplify.

13. t^{-4} $\frac{1}{t^4}$
14. $3r^{-5}$ $\frac{3}{r^5}$
15. $\frac{s^{-3}}{t^{-5}}$ $\frac{t^5}{s^3}$
16. $\frac{h^0}{3}$ $\frac{1}{3}$
17. $\frac{2x^{-3}y^{-2}}{z^4}$ $\frac{2}{x^3y^2z^4}$
18. $\frac{4fg^{-5}}{5h^{-3}}$ $\frac{4fh^3}{5g^5}$
19. $\frac{14a^{-4}}{20bc^{-1}}$ $\frac{7c}{10a^4b}$
20. $\frac{a^4c^2e^0}{b^{-1}d^{-3}}$ $a^4bc^2d^3$
21. $\frac{-3g^{-2}hk^{-2}}{-6h^0}$ $\frac{h}{2g^2k^2}$
22. A cooking website claims to contain 10^5 recipes. Evaluate this expression. **100,000**
23. A ball bearing has diameter 2^{-3} inches. Evaluate this expression. **$\frac{1}{8}$ inch or 0.125 inch**

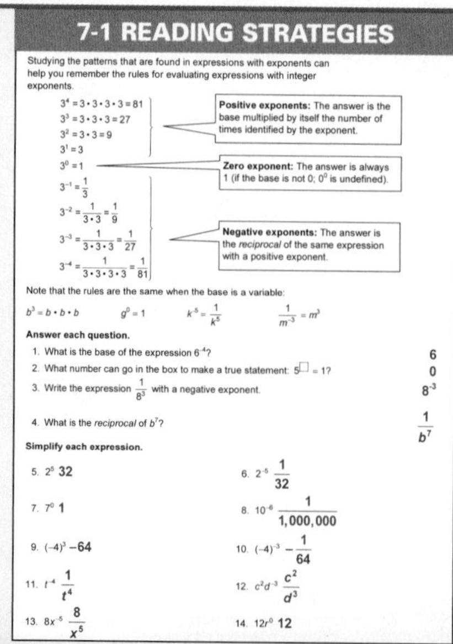

7-1 READING STRATEGIES

Studying the patterns that are found in expressions with exponents can help you remember the rules for evaluating expressions with integer exponents.

$3^4 = 3 \cdot 3 \cdot 3 \cdot 3 = 81$
$3^3 = 3 \cdot 3 \cdot 3 = 27$
$3^2 = 3 \cdot 3 = 9$
$3^1 = 3$
$3^0 = 1$
$3^{-1} = \frac{1}{3}$
$3^{-2} = \frac{1}{3 \cdot 3} = \frac{1}{9}$
$3^{-3} = \frac{1}{3 \cdot 3 \cdot 3} = \frac{1}{27}$
$3^{-4} = \frac{1}{3 \cdot 3 \cdot 3 \cdot 3} = \frac{1}{81}$

Positive exponents: The answer is the base multiplied by itself the number of times identified by the exponent.

Zero exponent: The answer is always 1 (if the base is not 0; 0^0 is undefined).

Negative exponents: The answer is the *reciprocal* of the same expression with a positive exponent.

Note that the rules are the same when the base is a variable:

$b^3 = b \cdot b \cdot b$ $\quad g^0 = 1$ $\quad k^{-5} = \frac{1}{k^5}$ $\quad \frac{1}{m^{-3}} = m^3$

Answer each question.

1. What is the base of the expression 6^{-4}? **6**
2. What number can go in the box to make a true statement: $5^{\square} = 1$? **0**
3. Write the expression $\frac{1}{8^3}$ with a negative exponent. **8^{-3}**
4. What is the *reciprocal* of b^7? **$\frac{1}{b^7}$**

Simplify each expression.

5. 2^5 **32**
6. 2^{-5} **$\frac{1}{32}$**
7. 7^0 **1**
8. 10^{-6} **$\frac{1}{1{,}000{,}000}$**
9. $(-4)^3$ **−64**
10. $(-4)^{-3}$ **$-\frac{1}{64}$**
11. t^{-4} **$\frac{1}{t^4}$**
12. c^2d^{-3} **$\frac{c^2}{d^3}$**
13. $8x^{-5}$ **$\frac{8}{x^5}$**
14. $12r^0$ **12**

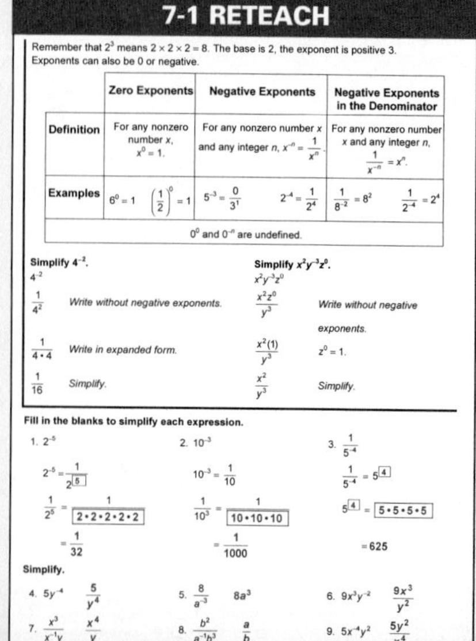

7-1 RETEACH

Remember that 2^3 means $2 \times 2 \times 2 = 8$. The base is 2, the exponent is positive 3. Exponents can also be 0 or negative.

	Zero Exponents	Negative Exponents	Negative Exponents in the Denominator
Definition	For any nonzero number x, $x^0 = 1$.	For any nonzero number x and any integer n, $x^{-n} = \frac{1}{x^n}$.	For any nonzero number x and any integer n, $\frac{1}{x^{-n}} = x^n$.
Examples	$6^0 = 1$ $\quad \left(\frac{1}{2}\right)^0 = 1$	$5^{-3} = \frac{0}{3^1}$ $\quad 2^{-4} = \frac{1}{2^4}$	$\frac{1}{8^{-2}} = 8^2$ $\quad \frac{1}{2^{-4}} = 2^4$
0^0 and 0^{-n} are undefined.			

Simplify 4^{-2}.
4^{-2}
$\frac{1}{4^2}$ *Write without negative exponents.*
$\frac{1}{4 \cdot 4}$ *Write in expanded form.*
$\frac{1}{16}$ *Simplify.*

Simplify $x^2y^{-3}z^0$.
$x^2y^{-3}z^0$
$\frac{x^2z^0}{y^3}$ *Write without negative exponents.*
$\frac{x^2(1)}{y^3}$ $z^0 = 1$.
$\frac{x^2}{y^3}$ *Simplify.*

Fill in the blanks to simplify each expression.

1. 2^{-5}
$2^{-5} = \frac{1}{2^{\boxed{5}}}$
$\frac{1}{2^5} = \frac{1}{\boxed{2 \cdot 2 \cdot 2 \cdot 2 \cdot 2}}$
$= \frac{1}{32}$

2. 10^{-3}
$10^{-3} = \frac{1}{10}$
$\frac{1}{10^3} = \frac{1}{\boxed{10 \cdot 10 \cdot 10}}$
$= \frac{1}{1000}$

3. $\frac{1}{5^{-4}}$
$\frac{1}{5^{-4}} = 5^{\boxed{4}}$
$5^{\boxed{4}} = \boxed{5 \cdot 5 \cdot 5 \cdot 5}$
$= 625$

Simplify.

4. $5y^{-4}$ **$\frac{5}{y^4}$**
5. $\frac{8}{a^{-3}}$ **$8a^3$**
6. $9x^3y^{-2}$ **$\frac{9x^3}{y^2}$**
7. $\frac{x^3}{x^{-1}y}$ **$\frac{x^4}{y}$**
8. $\frac{b^2}{a^{-1}b^3}$ **$\frac{a}{b}$**
9. $5x^{-4}y^2$ **$\frac{5y^2}{x^4}$**

TEST PREP

95. Which is NOT equivalent to the other three?

(A) $\frac{1}{25}$ (B) 5^{-2} (C) 0.04 **(D)** -25

96. Which is equal to 6^{-2}?

(F) $6(-2)$ (G) $(-6)(-6)$ (H) $-\frac{1}{6 \cdot 6}$ **(J)** $\frac{1}{6 \cdot 6}$

97. Simplify $\frac{a^3b^{-2}}{c^{-1}}$.

(A) $\frac{a^3c}{b^2}$ (B) $\frac{a^3b^2}{-c}$ (C) $\frac{a^3}{-b^2c}$ (D) $\frac{c}{a^3b^2}$

98. **Gridded Response** Simplify $\left[2^{-2} + (6 + 2)^0\right]$. **$\frac{5}{4}$, or 1.25**

99. **Short Response** If a and b are real numbers and n is a positive integer, write a simplified expression for the product $a^{-n} \cdot b^0$ that contains only positive exponents. Explain your answer. **$\frac{1}{a^n}$; $a^{-n} = \frac{1}{a^n}$ and $b^0 = 1$ for $b \neq 0$. So you have $\frac{1}{a^n} \cdot 1$, or simply $\frac{1}{a^n}$.**

CHALLENGE AND EXTEND

100.

100. **Multi-Step** Copy and complete the table of values below. Then graph the ordered pairs and describe the shape of the graph. **Possible answer: y increases more rapidly as x increases.**

x	−4	−3	−2	−1	0	1	2	3	4
$y = 2^x$	**$\frac{1}{16}$**	**$\frac{1}{8}$**	**$\frac{1}{4}$**	**$\frac{1}{2}$**	**1**	**2**	**4**	**8**	**16**

101. **Multi-Step** Copy and complete the table. Then write a rule for the values of 1^n and $(-1)^n$ when n is any negative integer. **$1^n = 1$; $(-1)^n = -1$ if n is odd, and $(-1)^n = 1$ if n is even.**

n	−1	−2	−3	−4	−5
1^n	**1**	**1**	**1**	**1**	**1**
$(-1)^n$	**−1**	**1**	**−1**	**1**	**−1**

SPIRAL REVIEW

Solve each equation. *(Lesson 2-3)*

102. $6x - 4 = 8$ **2**

103. $-9 = 3(p - 1)$ **−2**

104. $\frac{y}{5} - 8 = -12$ **−20**

105. $1.5h - 5 = 1$ **4**

106. $2w + 6 - 3w = -10$ **16**

107. $-12 = \frac{1}{2}n + 2 - n$ **28**

Identify the independent and dependent variables. Write a rule in function notation for each situation. *(Lesson 4-3)*

108. Pink roses cost $1.50 per stem. **ind.: number of roses; dep.: total cost; $f(x) = 1.50x$**

109. For dog-sitting, Beth charges a $30 flat fee plus $10 a day. **ind.: number of days; dep.: total cost; $f(x) = 10x + 30$**

Write the equation that describes each line in slope-intercept form. *(Lesson 5-7)*

110. slope = 3, y-intercept = −4

111. slope = $\frac{1}{3}$, y-intercept = 5

112. slope = 0, y-intercept = $\frac{2}{3}$

113. slope = −4, the point (1, 5) is on the line.

110. $y = 3x - 4$
111. $y = \frac{1}{3}x + 5$
112. $y = \frac{2}{3}$
113. $y = -4x + 9$

TEST PREP DOCTOR +

In **Exercise 96,** if students chose **F,** they may have used the negative exponent as a factor. If they chose **G,** they may have made the base negative because the exponent is negative.

If students chose **D** in **Exercise 97,** they probably moved every factor to the opposite side of the fraction bar, even if it had a positive exponent.

Journal

Have students use patterns to explain why any number raised to the zero power, except zero, is one.

ALTERNATIVE ASSESSMENT

Have students choose three exercises from **Exercises 37–42,** write each expression in words, and then show two different ways to evaluate each expression.

Power Presentations with PowerPoint®

7-1 Lesson Quiz

1. A square foot is 3^{-2} square yards. Simplify this expression. $\frac{1}{9}$ yd^2

Simplify.

2. 2^{-6} $\frac{1}{64}$

3. $(-7)^{-3}$ $-\frac{1}{343}$

4. 6^0 1

5. -11^2 −121

Evaluate each expression for the given value(s) of the variable(s).

6. x^{-4} for $x = 10$ $\frac{1}{10{,}000}$

7. $2a^{-1}b^{-3}$ for $a = 6$ and $b = 3$ $\frac{1}{81}$

Simplify.

8. $4y^{-5}$ $\frac{4}{y^5}$

9. $\frac{-3}{y^{-6}}$ $-3y^6$

10. $\frac{x^{-4}}{a^0y^3}$ $\frac{1}{x^4y^3}$

Also available on transparency

7-1 PROBLEM SOLVING

Write the correct answer.

1. At the 2005 World Exposition in Aichi, Japan, tiny mu-chips were embedded in the admissions tickets to prevent counterfeiting. The mu-chip was developed by Hitachi in 2003. Its area is $4^2(10)^{-2}$ square millimeters. Simplify this expression.
$\frac{4}{25}$ or 0.16 mm^2

2. Despite their name, Northern Yellow Bats are commonly found in warm, humid areas in the southeast United States. An adult has a wingspan of about 14 inches and weighs between $3(2)^{-3}$ and $3(2)^{-2}$ ounces. Simplify these expressions.
$\frac{3}{8}$ and $\frac{3}{4}$ oz

3. Saira is using the formula for the area of a circle to determine the value of π. She is using the expression Ar^{-2} where $A = 50.265$ and $r = 4$. Use a calculator to evaluate Saira's expression to find her approximation of the value of π to the nearest thousandth.
3.142

4. The volume of a freshwater tank can be expressed in terms of x, y, and z. Expressed in these terms, the volume of the tank is $x^3y^{-2}z$ liters. Determine the volume of the tank if $x = 4$, $y = 3$, and $z = 6$.
$42\frac{2}{3}$ liters

Alison has an interest in entomology, the study of insects. Her collection of insects from around the world includes the four specimens shown in the table below. Select the best answer.

Insect	Mass
Emperor Scorpion	2^{-5} kg
African Goliath Beetle	11^{-1} kg
Giant Weta	2^{-4} kg
Madagascar Hissing Cockroach	5^{-3} kg

5. Cockroaches have been found on every continent, including Antarctica. What is the mass of Alison's Madagascar Hissing Cockroach expressed as a quotient?
A $-\frac{1}{125}$ kg C $\frac{1}{15}$ kg
B $\frac{1}{125}$ kg D 125 kg

6. Many Giant Wetas are so heavy that they cannot jump. Which expression is another way to show the mass of the specimen in Alison's collection?
F $-(2)4$ kg **H** $\frac{1}{2 \cdot 2 \cdot 2 \cdot 2}$ kg
G $\left(\frac{1}{2}\right)^{-4}$ kg J $4\frac{1}{2}$ kg

7. Scorpions are closely related to spiders and horseshoe crabs. What is the mass of Alison's Emperor Scorpion expressed as a quotient?
A $-\frac{1}{32}$ kg **C** $\frac{1}{32}$ kg
B $\frac{1}{25}$ kg D 32 kg

7-1 CHALLENGE

When you write out the first several powers of x^n, where x and n are positive integers, you can discover interesting patterns in the units digits of x^n.

	x^1	x^2	x^3	x^4	x^5	x^6
$x = 2$	$2^1 = $ **2**	$2^2 = 2(2) = $ **4**	$2^3 = 2(4) = $ **8**	$2^4 = 2(8) = $ **16**	$2^5 = 2(16) = $ **32**	$2^6 = 2(32) = $ **64**

Notice that 2^1 and 2^5 have the same units digit and that 2^2 and 2^6 have the same units digit. In the exercises that follow, you can discover other number patterns involving the units digits of x^n.

In Exercises 1–10, find the first nine powers of each value of x. Using the units digit of each result, complete the table. You may find a calculator useful.

		x^1	x^2	x^3	x^4	x^5	x^6	x^7	x^8	x^9
1.	$x = 1$	1	1	1	1	1	1	1	1	1
2.	$x = 2$	2	4	8	6	2	4	8	6	2
3.	$x = 3$	3	9	7	1	3	9	7	1	3
4.	$x = 4$	4	6	4	6	4	6	4	6	4
5.	$x = 5$	5	5	5	5	5	5	5	5	5
6.	$x = 6$	6	6	6	6	6		6	6	6
7.	$x = 7$	7	9	3	1	7	9	3	1	7
0.	$x = 0$	8	4	2	6	8	4	2	6	8
9.	$x = 9$	9	1	9	1	9	1	9	1	9
10.	$x = 10$	0	0	0	0	0	0	0	0	0

Refer to the table that you completed in Exercises 1–10. Describe the pattern in the units digits of x^n.

11. 1^n **For all n, 1^n has 1 as its units digit.**

12. 2^n **The pattern is 2, 4, 8, and 6, for $n = 1, 2, 3$, and 4 and then repeats.**

13. 3^n **The pattern is 3, 9, 7, and 1, for $n = 1, 2, 3$, and 4 and then repeats.**

14. 5^n **For all $n > 0$, 5^n has 5 as its units digit.**

15. Write a rule that determines the units digit of 7^n as a function of n.
If you divide n by 4, then the units digit is 7, 9, 3, or 1, depending on whether the remainder is 1, 2, 3, or 0, respectively.

7-2 Powers of 10 and Scientific Notation

Nucleus of a silicon atom

Objectives

Evaluate and multiply by powers of 10.

Convert between standard notation and scientific notation.

Vocabulary

scientific notation

Why learn this?

Powers of 10 can be used to read and write very large and very small numbers, such as the masses of atomic particles. (See Exercise 44.)

The table shows relationships between several powers of 10.

(Arrows above the table: ÷ 10 from each power to the next; arrows below: × 10 from each power to the previous.)

Power	10^3	10^2	10^1	10^0	10^{-1}	10^{-2}	10^{-3}
Value	1000	100	10	1	$\frac{1}{10} = 0.1$	$\frac{1}{100} = 0.01$	$\frac{1}{1000} = 0.001$

- Each time you **divide by 10**, the exponent decreases by 1 and the decimal point moves one place to the left.
- Each time you **multiply by 10**, the exponent increases by 1 and the decimal point moves one place to the right.

Know it! Note

Powers of 10

WORDS	NUMBERS
Positive Integer Exponent If n is a positive integer, find the value of 10^n by starting with 1 and moving the decimal point n places to the right.	$10^4 = 1\,0,\,0\,0\,0$ 4 places
Negative Integer Exponent If n is a positive integer, find the value of 10^{-n} by starting with 1 and moving the decimal point n places to the left.	$10^{-6} = \frac{1}{10^6} = 0.0\,0\,0\,0\,0\,1$ 6 places

EXAMPLE 1 Evaluating Powers of 10

Find the value of each power of 10.

A 10^{-3}

Start with 1 and move the decimal point three places to the left.

0. 0 0 1

0.001

B 10^2

Start with 1 and move the decimal point two places to the right.

1 0 0

100

C 10^0

Start with 1 and move the decimal point zero places.

1

Writing Math

You may need to add zeros to the right or left of a number in order to move the decimal point in that direction.

7-2 Organizer

Pacing: Traditional 1 day
Block $\frac{1}{2}$ day

Objectives: Evaluate and multiply by powers of 10.

Convert between standard notation and scientific notation.

Online Edition
Tutorial Videos, Interactivity

Countdown Week 15

Power Presentations with PowerPoint®

Warm Up

Evaluate each expression.

1. 123 × 1000   123,000
2. 123 ÷ 1000   0.123
3. 0.003 × 100   0.3
4. 0.003 ÷ 100   0.00003
5. 10^4 10,000
6. 10^{-4} 0.0001
7. 23^0 1

Also available on transparency

Math Humor

Q: How did the number written in scientific notation feel after he changed into standard form?

A: Powerless.

State Resources

go.hrw.com
State Resources Online
KEYWORD: MA7 Resources

1 Introduce

EXPLORATION

7-2 Powers of 10 and Scientific Notation

You will need a calculator for this Exploration.

1. You can use the exponent key, [^], on your calculator to evaluate powers of 10. Use your calculator as needed to complete the table.

Power of 10	Value
10^5	
10^6	
10^7	
10^8	
10^9	

2. Look for patterns in the table. How is the exponent in each power of 10 related to the value of that power of 10?
3. What happens when you try to use your calculator to evaluate larger powers of 10, such as 10^{15}?

THINK AND DISCUSS

4. **Explain** how you could write the value of 10^{15}. How many zeros would you write?
5. **Describe** a general rule you can use to write the value of 10^n, where n is a positive integer.

Motivate

Have students copy the following numbers:

0.0000000000095

2,700,000,000,000,000,000,000

Ask them why the numbers are difficult to copy accurately. They have many zeros.

Say that numbers used in science and technology often contain many zeros. Scientific notation was developed to make these numbers easier to work with.

Explorations and answers are provided in *Alternate Openers: Explorations Transparencies.*

Find the value of each power of 10.

1a. 10^{-2} **0.01** 1b. 10^{5} **100,000** 1c. 10^{10} **10,000,000,000**

EXAMPLE 2 Writing Powers of 10

If you do not see a decimal point in a number, it is understood to be at the end of the number.

Write each number as a power of 10.

A 10,000,000

The decimal point is seven places to the right of 1, so the exponent is 7.

10^7

B 0.001

The decimal point is three places to the left of 1, so the exponent is −3.

10^{-3}

C 10

The decimal point is one place to the right of 1, so the exponent is 1.

10^1

CHECK IT OUT! Write each number as a power of 10.

2a. 100,000,000 $\mathbf{10^8}$ 2b. 0.0001 $\mathbf{10^{-4}}$ 2c. 0.1 $\mathbf{10^{-1}}$

You can also move the decimal point to find the product of any number and a power of 10. You start with the number instead of starting with 1.

Multiplying by Powers of 10	
If the exponent is a positive integer, move the decimal point to the right.	$125 \times 10^5 = 12{,}500{,}000$ (5 places)
If the exponent is a negative integer, move the decimal point to the left.	$36.2 \times 10^{-3} = 0.0362$ (3 places)

EXAMPLE 3 Multiplying by Powers of 10

Find the value of each expression.

A 97.86×10^6

97.8 6 0 0 0 0 *Move the decimal point 6 places to the right.*

97,860,000

B 19.5×10^{-4}

0 0 1 9.5 *Move the decimal point 4 places to the left.*

0.00195

CHECK IT OUT! Find the value of each expression.

3a. 853.4×10^5 **85,340,000** 3b. 0.163×10^{-2} **0.00163**

Scientific notation is a method of writing numbers that are very large or very small. A number written in scientific notation has two parts that are multiplied.

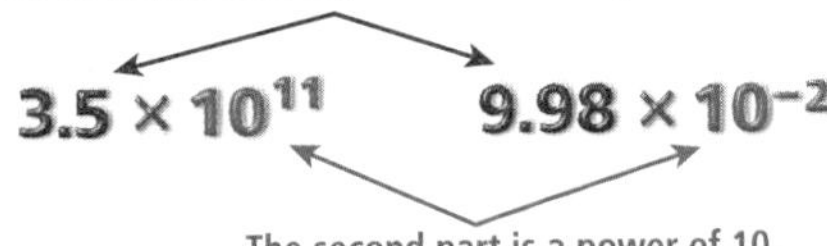

The first part is a number that is greater than or equal to 1 and less than 10.

3.5×10^{11} 9.98×10^{-2}

The second part is a power of 10.

COMMON ERROR ALERT

When writing the powers of 10 in a chart or a list, students will often start at 10, rather than 1. Remind students that $10^0 = 1$.

Power Presentations with PowerPoint®

Additional Examples

Example 1

Find the value of each power of 10.

A. 10^{-6} 0.000001

B. 10^4 10,000

C. 10^9 1,000,000,000

Example 2

Write each number as a power of 10.

A. 1,000,000 10^6

B. 0.0001 10^{-4}

C. 1000 10^3

Example 3

Find the value of each expression.

A. 23.89×10^8 2,389,000,000

B. 467×10^{-3} 0.467

INTERVENTION Questioning Strategies

EXAMPLE 1

- What does a positive exponent represent?
- What does a negative exponent represent?

EXAMPLE 2

- What pattern do you notice when you multiply repeatedly by 10?
- What pattern do you notice when you divide repeatedly by 10?

EXAMPLE 3

- Why does multiplying by a negative power of 10 result in a smaller number?

2 Teach

Guided Instruction

Show students the pattern of powers of 10. First show some with positive exponents:

$10^2 = 10 \times 10 = 100$

$10^3 = 10 \times 10 \times 10 = 1000$

Show how each is the number 1 followed by the same number of zeros as the exponent number. Then work backward for 10 to the first power, zero power, and negative powers. With negative exponents, the number of zeros is one less than the exponent number.

Reaching All Learners

Through Cooperative Learning

Separate students into groups of three. The first student writes a number in standard form. The second student writes that number in scientific notation, and the third student checks/corrects the work. Have students switch roles so that everyone has done each job at least once. Then repeat, having the first student write a number in scientific notation, the second student write that number in standard form, and the third student check/correct the work.

Power Presentations with PowerPoint®

Additional Examples

Example 4

Saturn has a diameter of about 1.2×10^5 km. Its distance from the Sun is about 1,427,000,000 km.

A. Write Saturn's diameter in standard form. 120,000 km

B. Write Saturn's distance from the Sun in scientific notation. 1.427×10^9 km

Example 5

Order the list of numbers from least to greatest.

1.3×10^{-2}, 6.3×10^3, 4.1×10^6, 2.1×10^6, 1×10^{-2}, 5.4×10^{-3}

5.4×10^{-3}, 1×10^{-2}, 1.3×10^{-2}, 6.3×10^3, 2.1×10^6, 4.1×10^6

INTERVENTION
Questioning Strategies

EXAMPLE 4

- What does it mean to write a number in standard form?

EXAMPLE 5

- When ordering numbers in scientific notation, why is the power of 10 used to determine the initial order of the numbers?

Number Sense Tell students to associate the direction the decimal point moves with the positive and negative directions on a number line: positive numbers to the right and negative numbers to the left.

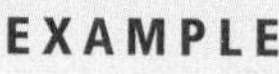

EXAMPLE 4 *Astronomy Application*

Jupiter has a diameter of about 143,000 km. Its shortest distance from Earth is about 5.91×10^8 km, and its average distance from the Sun is about 778,400,000 km. Jupiter's orbital speed is approximately 1.3×10^4 m/s.

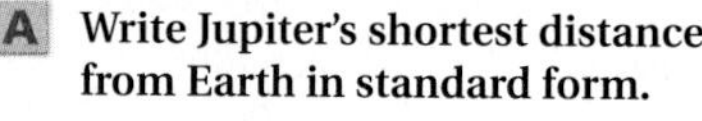

Reading Math

Standard form refers to the usual way that numbers are written.

A Write Jupiter's shortest distance from Earth in standard form.

5.91×10^8

5.9 1 0 0 0 0 0 0 — *Move the decimal point 8 places to the right.*

591,000,000 km

B Write Jupiter's average distance from the Sun in scientific notation.

778,400,000

7 7 8, 4 0 0, 0 0 0 — *Count the number of places you need to move the decimal point to get a number between 1 and 10.*

8 places

7.784×10^8 km — *Use that number as the exponent of 10.*

CHECK IT OUT!

4a. Use the information above to write Jupiter's diameter in scientific notation. 1.43×10^5 **km**

4b. Use the information above to write Jupiter's orbital speed in standard form. **13,000 m/s**

EXAMPLE 5 Comparing and Ordering Numbers in Scientific Notation

Order the list of numbers from least to greatest.

1.2×10^{-1}, 8.2×10^4, 6.2×10^5, 2.4×10^5, 1×10^{-1}, 9.9×10^{-4}

Step 1 List the numbers in order by powers of 10.

9.9×10^{-4}, 1.2×10^{-1}, 1×10^{-1}, 8.2×10^4, 6.2×10^5, 2.4×10^5

Step 2 Order the numbers that have the same power of 10.

9.9×10^{-4}, 1×10^{-1}, 1.2×10^{-1}, 8.2×10^4, 2.4×10^5, 6.2×10^5

CHECK IT OUT!

5. Order the list of numbers from least to greatest.

5.2×10^{-3}, 3×10^{14}, 4×10^{-3}, 2×10^{-12}, 4.5×10^{30}, 4.5×10^{14}

2×10^{-12}, 4×10^{-3}, 5.2×10^{-3}, 3×10^{14}, 4.5×10^{14}, 4.5×10^{30}

THINK AND DISCUSS

1. Tell why 34.56×10^4 is not correctly written in scientific notation.

Know it! Note

2. GET ORGANIZED Copy and complete the graphic organizer.

Powers of 10 and Scientific Notation
- A negative exponent corresponds to moving the decimal point ___?___.
- A positive exponent corresponds to moving the decimal point ___?___.

3 Close

Summarize

Remind students that to multiply by a positive power of 10, they should move the decimal point to the right, and to multiply by a negative power of 10, they should move the decimal point to the left.

If a number is in scientific notation, it is in the form $x \times 10^y$, with $1 \leq x < 10$ and with y being any integer.

ONGOING ASSESSMENT and INTERVENTION

***Diagnose Before* the Lesson**
7-2 Warm Up, TE p. 466

***Monitor During* the Lesson**
Check It Out! Exercises, SE pp. 467–468
Questioning Strategies, TE pp. 467–468

***Assess After* the Lesson**
7-2 Lesson Quiz, TE p. 471
Alternative Assessment, TE p. 471

Answers to *Think and Discuss*

1. 34.56 is not between 1 and 10.
2. See p. A6.

go.hrw.com
Homework Help Online
KEYWORD: MA7 7-2
Parent Resources Online
KEYWORD: MA7 Parent

GUIDED PRACTICE

1. **Vocabulary** Explain how you can tell whether a number is written in *scientific notation.* **A number written in sci. notation is a product with 2 parts: a decimal greater than or equal to 1 and less than 10 and a power of 10.**

SEE EXAMPLE 1 p. 466

Find the value of each power of 10.

2. 10^6 **1,000,000**
3. 10^{-5} **0.00001**
4. 10^{-4} **0.0001**
5. 10^8 **100,000,000**

SEE EXAMPLE 2 p. 467

Write each number as a power of 10.

6. 10,000 **10^4**
7. 0.000001 **10^{-6}**
8. 100,000,000,000,000,000 **10^{17}**

SEE EXAMPLE 3 p. 467

Find the value of each expression.

9. 650.3×10^6 **650,300,000**
10. 48.3×10^{-4} **0.00483**
11. 92×10^{-3} **0.092**

SEE EXAMPLE 4 p. 468

12. **Astronomy** A light-year is the distance that light travels in a year and is equivalent to 9.461×10^{12} km. Write this distance in standard form. **9,461,000,000,000 km**

SEE EXAMPLE 5 p. 468

13. Order the list of numbers from least to greatest.
$8.5 \times 10^{-1}, 3.6 \times 10^8, 5.85 \times 10^{-3}, 2.5 \times 10^{-1}, 8.5 \times 10^8$
$5.85 \times 10^{-3}, 2.5 \times 10^{-1}, 8.5 \times 10^{-1}, 3.6 \times 10^8, 8.5 \times 10^8$

PRACTICE AND PROBLEM SOLVING

Independent Practice

For Exercises	See Example
14–17	1
18–20	2
21–24	3
25–26	4
27	5

Extra Practice
Skills Practice p. S16
Application Practice p. S34

Find the value of each power of 10.

14. 10^3 **1000**
15. 10^{-9} **0.000000001**
16. 10^{-12} **0.000000000001**
17. 10^{14} **100,000,000,000,000**

Write each number as a power of 10.

18. 0.01 **10^{-2}**
19. 1,000,000 **10^6**
20. 0.000000000000001 **10^{-15}**

Find the value of each expression.

21. 9.2×10^4 **92,000**
22. 1.25×10^{-7} **0.000000125**
23. 42×10^{-5} **0.00042**
24. 0.05×10^7 **500,000**

25. **Biology** The human body is made of about 1×10^{13} cells. Write this number in standard form. **10,000,000,000,000**

26. **Statistics** At the beginning of the twenty-first century, the population of China was about 1,287,000,000. Write this number in scientific notation. **1.287×10^9**

27. Order the list of numbers from least to greatest.
$2.13 \times 10^{-1}, 3.12 \times 10^2, 1.23 \times 10^{-3}, 2.13 \times 10^1, 1.32 \times 10^{-3}, 3.12 \times 10^{-3}$
$1.23 \times 10^{-3}, 1.32 \times 10^{-3}, 3.12 \times 10^{-3}, 2.13 \times 10^{-1}, 2.13 \times 10^1, 3.12 \times 10^2$

28. **Health** Donnell is allergic to pollen. The diameter of a grain of pollen is between 1.2×10^{-5} m and 9×10^{-5} m. Donnell's air conditioner has a filter that removes particles larger than 3×10^{-7} m. Will the filter remove pollen? Explain.

28. Yes; the smallest grain of pollen is larger than 3×10^{-7} m.

Grain of pollen, enlarged 1300 times

29. **Entertainment** In the United States, a CD is certified platinum if it sells 1,000,000 copies. A CD that has gone 2 times platinum has sold 2,000,000 copies. How many copies has a CD sold if it has gone 27 times platinum? Write your answer in scientific notation. **2.7×10^7**

Write each number in scientific notation.

30. 40,080,000 **4.008×10^7**
31. 235,000 **2.35×10^5**
32. 170,000,000,000 **1.7×10^{11}**
33. 0.0000006 **6×10^{-7}**
34. 0.000077 **7.7×10^{-5}**
35. 0.0412 **4.12×10^{-2}**

7-2 Exercises

Assignment Guide

Assign *Guided Practice* exercises as necessary.

If you finished Examples **1–3**
Basic 14–24
Average 14–24, 53
Advanced 14–24, 53

If you finished Examples **1–5**
Basic 14–46, 48–52, 55–63
Average 14–53, 55–63
Advanced 14–45, 47–63

Homework Quick Check
Quickly check key concepts.
Exercises: 16, 18, 22, 26, 27, 36

Teaching Tip

Number Sense In **Exercises 14–17,** have students estimate whether their answer is greater than or less than 10 before finding the value. This will help them if they forget the rules for evaluating powers of 10.

Teaching Tip

Technology For **Exercises 21–24,** students can enter numbers in scientific notation into their calculators by using 2nd [EE ,] to indicate the power of 10. For example, to enter 9.2×10^4, press 9.2 2nd [EE ,] 4. To enter powers of 10, use [^] or 2nd [10^x LOG]. To enter 10^{-5}, press 10 [^] −5 or 2nd [10^x LOG](−5).

State Resources

Exercise 49 involves writing numbers in scientific notation. This exercise prepares students for the Multi-Step Test Prep on page 494.

Reading Math For **Exercise 44,** in 1.67×10^{-27}, 1.67 is called the *coefficient.*

Answers

36. no; 5×10^{-4}
37. yes
38. no; 1.2×10^{6}
39. no; 2.5×10^{2}
40. no; 1×10^{-1}
41. yes
42. no; 4.8×10^{4}
43. yes

49b. Possible answer: It would be easy to accidentally omit a 0 or add an extra 0 when writing the number in standard form. You are probably less likely to make an error when using scientific notation.

State whether each number is written in scientific notation. If not, write it in scientific notation.

36. 50×10^{-5}	37. 8.1×10^{-2}	38. 1,200,000	39. 0.25×10^{3}
40. 0.1	41. 7×10^{8}	42. 48,000	43. 3.5×10^{-6}

LINK **Chemistry**

The image above is a colored bubble-chamber photograph. It shows the tracks left by subatomic particles in a particle accelerator.

44. **Chemistry** Atoms are made of three elementary particles: protons, electrons, and neutrons. The mass of a proton is about 1.67×10^{-27} kg. The mass of an electron is about 0.000000000000000000000000000000911 kg. The mass of a neutron is about 1.68×10^{-27} kg. Which particle has the least mass? (*Hint:* Compare the numbers after they are written in scientific notation.) **electron**

45. **Communication** This bar graph shows the increase of cellular telephone subscribers worldwide.

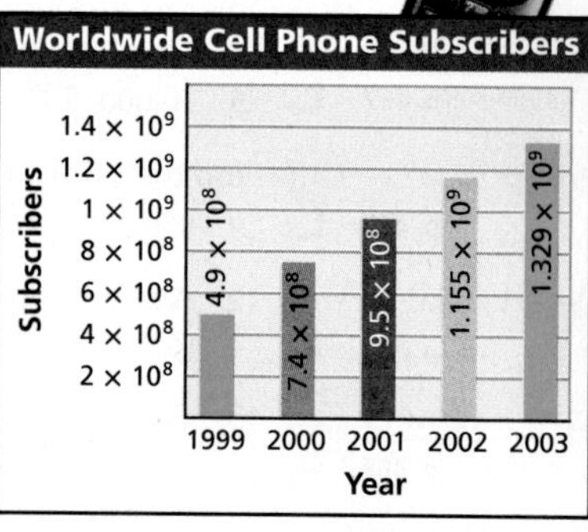

a. Write the number of subscribers for the following years in standard form: 1999, 2000, and 2003.

b. Zorah looks at the bar graph and says, "It looks like the number of cell phone subscribers nearly doubled from 2000 to 2003." Do you agree with Zorah? Use scientific notation to explain your answer.

45a. 490,000,000; 740,000,000; 1,329,000,000

b. When you double 7.4×10^{8}, you get approx. 14×10^{8}, or 1.4×10^{9} in sci. notation. 1.4 is close to 1.3, so Zorah's observation is correct.

46. **Measurement** In the metric system, the basic unit for measuring length is the meter (m). Other units for measuring length are based on the meter and powers of 10, as shown in the table.

Selected Metric Lengths	
1 millimeter (mm) = 10^{-3} m	1 dekameter (dam) = 10^{1} m
1 centimeter (cm) = 10^{-2} m	1 hectometer (hm) = 10^{2} m
1 decimeter (dm) = 10^{-1} m	1 kilometer (km) = 10^{3} m

b. $10^{-3} = 0.001$; $10^{-2} = 0.01$; $10^{-1} = 0.1$; $10^{1} = 10$; $10^{2} = 100$; $10^{3} = 1000$

a. Which lengths in the table are longer than a meter? Which are shorter than a meter? How do you know? **dam, hm, km; mm, cm, dm**

b. Evaluate each power of 10 in the table to check your answers to part **a.**

47. **Critical Thinking** Recall that $\frac{1}{10^3} = 10^{-3}$. Based on this information, complete the following statement: Dividing a number by 10^{3} is equivalent to multiplying by ▭. **10^{-3}**

48. **Write About It** When you change a number from scientific notation to standard form, explain how you know which way to move the decimal point and how many places to move it. **If the exp. is pos., move the dec. pt. that many places to the right. If the exp. is neg., move the dec. pt. that many places to the left.**

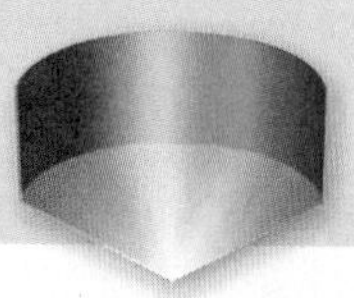

49. This problem will prepare you for the Multi-Step Test Prep on page 494.

a. The speed of light is approximately 3×10^{8} m/s. Write this number in standard form. **300,000,000**

b. Why do you think it would be better to express this number in scientific notation rather than standard form?

c. The wavelength of a shade of red light is 0.00000068 meters. Write this number in scientific notation. **6.8×10^{-7}**

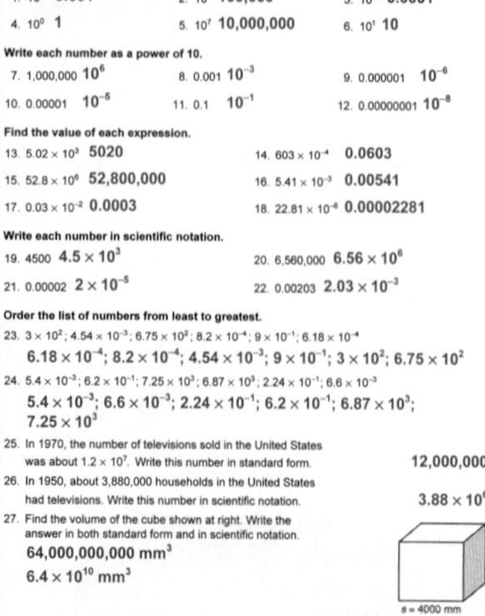

7-2 PRACTICE A
7-2 PRACTICE C
7-2 PRACTICE B

Find the value of each power of 10.

1. 10^{-3} **0.001** 2. 10^{5} **100,000** 3. 10^{-4} **0.0001**
4. 10^{0} **1** 5. 10^{7} **10,000,000** 6. 10^{1} **10**

Write each number as a power of 10.

7. 1,000,000 **10^{6}** 8. 0.001 **10^{-3}** 9. 0.000001 **10^{-6}**
10. 0.00001 **10^{-5}** 11. 0.1 **10^{-1}** 12. 0.00000001 **10^{-8}**

Find the value of each expression.

13. 5.02×10^{3} **5020** 14. 603×10^{-4} **0.0603**
15. 52.8×10^{6} **52,800,000** 16. 5.41×10^{-3} **0.00541**
17. 0.03×10^{-2} **0.0003** 18. 22.81×10^{-6} **0.00002281**

Write each number in scientific notation.

19. 4500 **4.5×10^{3}** 20. 6,560,000 **6.56×10^{6}**
21. 0.00002 **2×10^{-5}** 22. 0.00203 **2.03×10^{-3}**

Order the list of numbers from least to greatest.

23. 3×10^{2}; 4.54×10^{-3}; 6.75×10^{2}; 8.2×10^{-4}; 9×10^{-1}; 6.18×10^{-4}
6.18×10^{-4}; 8.2×10^{-4}; 4.54×10^{-3}; 9×10^{-1}; 3×10^{2}; 6.75×10^{2}

24. 5.4×10^{-3}; 6.2×10^{-1}; 7.25×10^{3}; 6.87×10^{3}; 2.24×10^{-1}; 6.6×10^{-3}
5.4×10^{-3}; 6.6×10^{-3}; 2.24×10^{-1}; 6.2×10^{-1}; 6.87×10^{3}; 7.25×10^{3}

25. In 1970, the number of televisions sold in the United States was about 1.2×10^{7}. Write this number in standard form. **12,000,000**

26. In 1950, about 3,880,000 households in the United States had televisions. Write this number in scientific notation. **3.88×10^{6}**

27. Find the volume of the cube shown at right. Write the answer in both standard form and in scientific notation. **64,000,000,000 mm^3**
6.4×10^{10} mm^3

s = 4000 mm

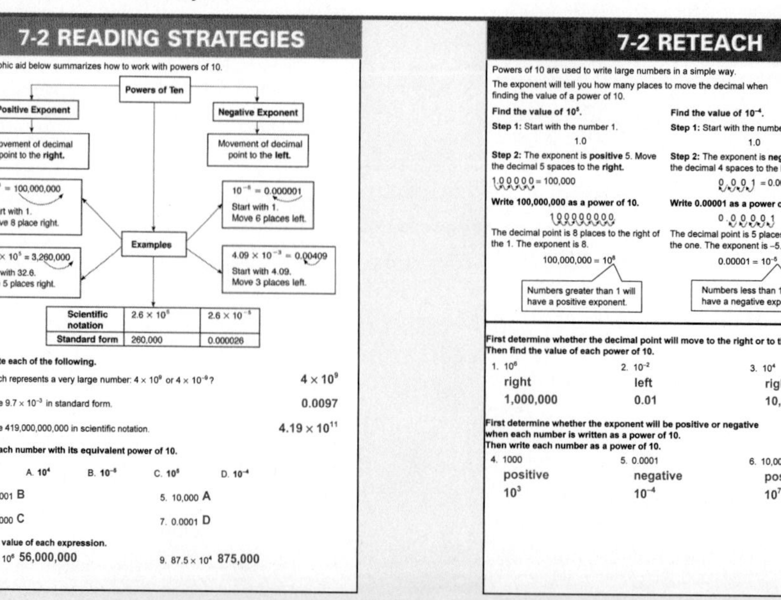

7-2 READING STRATEGIES

The graphic aid below summarizes how to work with powers of 10.

Powers of Ten

Positive Exponent — Movement of decimal point to the **right.**

Negative Exponent — Movement of decimal point to the **left.**

Examples

10^{8} = 100,000,000 Start with 1. Move 8 place right.

32.6×10^{5} = 3,260,000 Start with 32.6. Move 5 places right.

10^{-6} = 0.000001 Start with 1. Move 6 places left.

4.09×10^{-3} = 0.00409 Start with 4.09. Move 3 places left.

Scientific notation	2.6×10^{5}	2.6×10^{-5}
Standard form	260,000	0.000026

Complete each of the following.

1. Which represents a very large number: 4×10^{9} or 4×10^{-9}? **4×10^{9}**
2. Write 9.7×10^{-3} in standard form. **0.0097**
3. Write 419,000,000,000 in scientific notation. **4.19×10^{11}**

Match each number with its equivalent power of 10.

A. 10^{4} B. 10^{-5} C. 10^{5} D. 10^{-4}

4. 0.00001 **B** 5. 10,000 **A**
6. 100,000 **C** 7. 0.0001 **D**

Find the value of each expression.

8. 56×10^{6} **56,000,000** 9. 87.5×10^{4} **875,000**

7-2 RETEACH

Powers of 10 are used to write large numbers in a simple way.

The exponent will tell you how many places to move the decimal when finding the value of a power of 10.

Find the value of 10^{5}.

Step 1: Start with the number 1.

1.0

Step 2: The exponent is **positive** 5. Move the decimal 5 spaces to the **right.**

1.00000 = 100,000

Write 100,000,000 as a power of 10.

100000000

The decimal point is 8 places to the right of the 1. The exponent is 8.

100,000,000 = 10^{8}

Numbers greater than 1 will have a positive exponent.

Find the value of 10^{-4}.

Step 1: Start with the number 1.

1.0

Step 2: The exponent is **negative** 4. Move the decimal 4 spaces to the **left.**

0001 = 0.0001

Write 0.00001 as a power of 10.

0.00001

The decimal point is 5 places to the left of the one. The exponent is –5.

0.00001 = 10^{-5}

Numbers less than 1 will have a negative exponent.

First determine whether the decimal point will move to the right or to the left. Then find the value of each power of 10.

1. 10^{6} **right** **1,000,000** 2. 10^{-2} **left** **0.01** 3. 10^{4} **right** **10,000**

First determine whether the exponent will be positive or negative when each number is written as a power of 10. Then write each number as a power of 10.

4. 1000 **positive** **10^{3}** 5. 0.0001 **negative** **10^{-4}** 6. 10,000,000 **positive** **10^{7}**

TEST PREP

50. There are about 3.2×10^7 seconds in one year. What is this number in standard form?
    - (A) 0.000000032
    - (B) 0.00000032
    - (C) 32,000,000
    - (D) 320,000,000

51. Which expression is the scientific notation for 82.35?
    (F) 8.235×10^1 (G) 823.5×10^{-1} (H) 8.235×10^{-1} (J) 0.8235×10^2

52. Which statement is correct for the list of numbers below?
    2.35×10^{-8}, 0.000000029, 1.82×10^8, 1,290,000,000, 1.05×10^9
    - (A) The list is in increasing order.
    - (B) If 0.000000029 is removed, the list will be in increasing order.
    - (C) If 1,290,000,000 is removed, the list will be in increasing order.
    - (D) The list is in decreasing order.

CHALLENGE AND EXTEND

53. About 7 times; 4.7 GB, the storage of the DVD, is the same as 4700 MB, which is approx. 7 times 700 MB, the storage of the CD.

53. **Technology** The table shows estimates of computer storage. A CD-ROM holds 700 MB. A DVD-ROM holds 4.7 GB. Estimate how many times more storage a DVD has than a CD. Explain how you found your answer.

Computer Storage
1 kilobyte (KB) ≈ 1000 bytes
1 megabyte (MB) ≈ 1 million bytes
1 gigabyte (GB) ≈ 1 billion bytes

54. For parts **a–d**, use what you know about multiplying by powers of 10 and the Commutative and Associative Properties of Multiplication to find each product. Write each answer in scientific notation.
    a. $(3 \times 10^2)(2 \times 10^3)$ $\mathbf{6 \times 10^5}$
    b. $(5 \times 10^8)(1.5 \times 10^{-6})$ $\mathbf{7.5 \times 10^2}$
    c. $(2.2 \times 10^{-8})(4 \times 10^{-3})$ $\mathbf{8.8 \times 10^{-11}}$
    d. $(2.5 \times 10^{-12})(2 \times 10^6)$ $\mathbf{5 \times 10^{-6}}$
    e. Based on your answers to parts **a–d**, write a rule for multiplying numbers in scientific notation.
    f. Does your rule work when you multiply $(6 \times 10^3)(8 \times 10^5)$? Explain.
    Yes, but the answer, 48×10^8, is not in sci. notation. After multiplying, you will have to rewrite the answer in sci. notation as 4.8×10^9.

54e. First multiply the numbers, and then multiply the powers of 10 by adding the exponents.

SPIRAL REVIEW

Define a variable and write an inequality for each situation. Graph the solutions. *(Lesson 3-1)*

55. Melanie must wait at least 45 minutes for the results of her test.
56. Ulee's dog can lose no more than 8 pounds to stay within a healthy weight range.
57. Charlene must spend more than $50 to get the advertised discount.

55. Let m = number of minutes; $m \geq 45$.

56. Let p = pounds; $p \leq 8$ where p is nonneg.

57. Let m = money spent; $m > 50$.

Solve each system by elimination. *(Lesson 6-3)*

58. $\begin{cases} x + y = 8 \\ x - y = 2 \end{cases}$ **(5, 3)**
59. $\begin{cases} 2x + y = -3 \\ 2x + 3y = -1 \end{cases}$ **(−2, 1)**
60. $\begin{cases} x - 6y = -3 \\ 3x + 4y = 13 \end{cases}$ **(3, 1)**

Evaluate each expression for the given value(s) of the variable(s). *(Lesson 7-1)*

61. t^{-4} for $t = 2$ $\mathbf{\frac{1}{16}}$
62. $(-8m)^0$ for $m = -5$ **1**
63. $3a^{-3}b^0$ for $a = 5$ and $b = 6$ $\mathbf{\frac{3}{125}}$

TEST PREP DOCTOR + If students chose **A** or **D** in **Exercise 50,** they may have associated the exponent of 10 with the number of zeros in the answer.

In **Exercise 52,** encourage students to write the second and fourth numbers in the list in scientific notation as a first step.

Teaching Tip **Technology** In **Exercise 53,** you might tell students that metric prefixes are used to describe computer storage. However, bytes do not follow true metric conventions. For example, 1 kilobyte = 1024 bytes, not 1000 bytes.

Answers

55–57. For graphs, see p. A27.

Journal

Have students explain why 10^5 has 5 zeros, but 10^{-5} has only 4 zeros.

ALTERNATIVE ASSESSMENT

Have students write four numbers in scientific notation, two with positive exponents and two with negative exponents, and then arrange them from least to greatest.

Power Presentations with PowerPoint®

7-2 Lesson Quiz

Find the value of each expression.

1. 37.45×10^5 3,745,000
2. 29.3×10^{-4} 0.00293
3. The Pacific Ocean has an area of about 6.4×10^7 square miles. Its volume is about 170,000,000 cubic miles.
    a. Write the area of the Pacific Ocean in standard form. 64,000,000 mi²
    b. Write the volume of the Pacific Ocean in scientific notation. 1.7×10^8 mi³
4. Order the list of numbers from least to greatest.

3.6×10^{-3}, 1×10^{-5}, 2.7×10^2, 1.3×10^4, 3.1×10^4, 4.1×10^{-3}

1×10^{-5}, 3.6×10^{-3}, 4.1×10^{-3}, 2.7×10^2, 1.3×10^4, 3.1×10^4

Also available on transparency

7-2 PROBLEM SOLVING

Write the correct answer

1. Insects can multiply rapidly during the summer. A pair of houseflies could potentially grow to a population of 1.91×10^{20}. If all the descendants of a female cabbage aphid lived, the population could increase to 1.56×10^{24}. Which population would be larger?
   cabbage aphid
2. The graph shows the gross domestic product (GDP) for several countries around the world. Identify the country whose GDP is twice that of another country. Write the GDPs of both countries in standard form.

Gross Domestic Product in 2004 (GDP (dollars) by Country): Afghanistan 2.15×10^{10}; Cambodia 2.7×10^{10}; Ethiopia 5.4×10^{10}; Mexico 1.01×10^{12}; Poland 4.6×10^{11}

Ethiopia: $54,000,000,000; Cambodia: $27,000,000,000

3. The 2005 population estimates of five countries are listed below.

Brazil	1.86×10^8
India	1.08×10^9
Kenya	3.38×10^7
Philippines	8.79×10^7
United Kingdom	6.04×10^7

List the countries in order of population size from least to greatest.
Kenya, UK, Philippines, Brazil, India

The table shows astronomical data about several planets. Use the table to answer questions 4–7. Select the best answer.

4. An AU is an astronomical unit. One AU equals 150,000,000 km. What is that measure in scientific notation?
   A 1.50×10^8 km C 1.50×10^{10} km
   B 1.50×10^9 km D 1.50×10^{11} km
5. Suppose the mass of Mars were written in standard form. How many digits would be to the *left* of the decimal?
   F 23 H 25
   G 24 J 26
6. Which of these is the average distance from the Sun to Mercury expressed in scientific notation?
   A 0.38 AU **C** 3.8×10^{-1} AU
   B 3.8×10^1 AU D 38×10^{-2} AU
7. What is the diameter of the Earth in scientific notation?
   F 1.28×10^2 km **H** 1.28×10^4 km
   G 1.28×10^3 km J 1.28×10^5 km

Astronomical Data for the First Five Planets			
Planet	Avg. Distance from Sun (AU)	Diameter (km)	Mass (kg)
Mercury	0.38	4,880	3.20×10^{23}
Venus	0.72	12,100	4.87×10^{24}
Earth	1	12,800	5.97×10^{24}
Mars	1.52	6,790	6.42×10^{23}
Jupiter	5.20	143,000	1.90×10^{27}

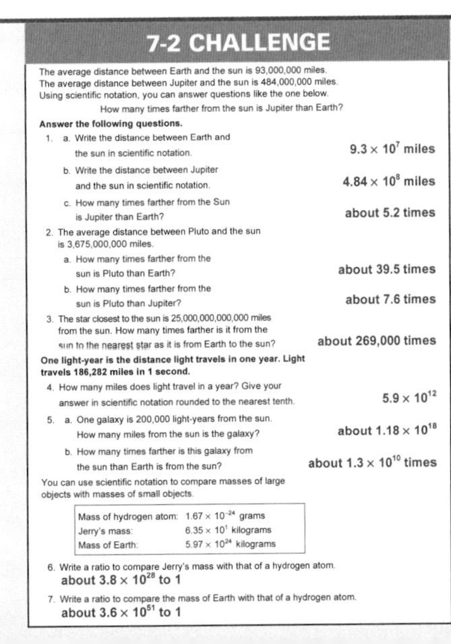

7-2 CHALLENGE

The average distance between Earth and the sun is 93,000,000 miles. The average distance between Jupiter and the sun is 484,000,000 miles. Using scientific notation, you can answer questions like the one below.

How many times farther from the sun is Jupiter than Earth?

Answer the following questions.

1. a. Write the distance between Earth and the sun in scientific notation. **9.3×10^7 miles**
   b. Write the distance between Jupiter and the sun in scientific notation. **4.84×10^8 miles**
   c. How many times farther from the Sun is Jupiter than Earth? **about 5.2 times**
2. The average distance between Pluto and the sun is 3,675,000,000 miles.
   a. How many times farther from the sun is Pluto than Earth? **about 39.5 times**
   b. How many times farther from the sun is Pluto than Jupiter? **about 7.6 times**
3. The star closest to the sun is 25,000,000,000,000 miles from the sun. How many times farther is it from the sun to the nearest star as it is from Earth to the sun? **about 269,000 times**

One light-year is the distance light travels in one year. Light travels 186,282 miles in 1 second.

4. How many miles does light travel in a year? Give your answer in scientific notation rounded to the nearest tenth. **5.9×10^{12}**
5. a. One galaxy is 200,000 light-years from the sun. How many miles from the sun is the galaxy? **about 1.18×10^{18}**
   b. How many times farther is this galaxy from the sun than Earth is from the sun? **about 1.3×10^{10} times**

You can use scientific notation to compare masses of large objects with masses of small objects.

Mass of hydrogen atom:	1.67×10^{-24} grams
Jerry's mass:	6.35×10^1 kilograms
Mass of Earth:	5.97×10^{24} kilograms

6. Write a ratio to compare Jerry's mass with that of a hydrogen atom. **about 3.8×10^{28} to 1**
7. Write a ratio to compare the mass of Earth with that of a hydrogen atom. **about 3.6×10^{51} to 1**

Organizer

Use with Lesson 7-3

Pacing:

Traditional 1 day
Block $\frac{1}{2}$ day

Objective: Use patterns to discover multiplication properties of exponents.

Online Edition

Countdown Week 15

Resources

Algebra Lab Activities
7-3 Lab Recording Sheet

Teach

Discuss

Remind students that a conjecture is an educated guess that is based on evidence but has not been proven true or false.

Discuss with students what patterns they notice in each activity. Help students represent the patterns in conjectures with words and with algebraic statements. For example, Activity 3 can be thought of as "distributing" the exponent.

go.hrw.com
State Resources Online
KEYWORD: MA7 Resources

7-3 Algebra LAB

Explore Properties of Exponents

You can use patterns to find some properties of exponents.

Use with Lesson 7-3

Activity 1

1. Copy and complete the table below.

$3^2 \cdot 3^3 = (3 \cdot 3)(3 \cdot 3 \cdot 3) = 3^{\mathbf{5}}$
$5^4 \cdot 5^2 = (\mathbf{5} \cdot \mathbf{5} \cdot \mathbf{5} \cdot \mathbf{5})(\mathbf{5} \cdot \mathbf{5}) = 5^{\mathbf{6}}$
$4^3 \cdot 4^3 = (\mathbf{4} \cdot \mathbf{4} \cdot \mathbf{4})(\mathbf{4} \cdot \mathbf{4} \cdot \mathbf{4}) = \mathbf{4}^{\mathbf{6}}$
$2^3 \cdot 2^2 = (\mathbf{2} \cdot \mathbf{2} \cdot \mathbf{2})(\mathbf{2} \cdot \mathbf{2}) = \mathbf{2}^{\mathbf{5}}$
$6^3 \cdot 6^4 = (\quad)(\quad) =$ **6 • 6 • 6; 6 • 6 • 6 • 6;** $\mathbf{6^7}$

2. Examine your completed table. Look at the two exponents in each factor and the exponent in the final answer. What pattern do you notice?
The exp. in the final answer is the sum of the exponents in the orig. problem.
3. Use your pattern to make a conjecture: $a^m \cdot a^n = a^{\blacksquare}$. $\mathbf{m + n}$

Try This

Use your conjecture to write each product below as a single power.

1. $5^3 \cdot 5^5$ $\mathbf{5^8}$
2. $7^2 \cdot 7^2$ $\mathbf{7^4}$
3. $10^8 \cdot 10^4$ $\mathbf{10^{12}}$
4. $8^7 \cdot 8^3$ $\mathbf{8^{10}}$
5. Make a table similar to the one above to explore what happens when you multiply more than two powers that have the same base. Then write a conjecture in words to summarize what you find.

Activity 2

1. Copy and complete the table below.

$(2^3)^2 = 2^3 \cdot 2^3 = (\mathbf{2} \cdot \mathbf{2} \cdot \mathbf{2})(\mathbf{2} \cdot \mathbf{2} \cdot \mathbf{2}) = 2^{\mathbf{6}}$
$(2^2)^3 = \mathbf{2^2} \cdot \mathbf{2^2} \cdot \mathbf{2^2} = (\mathbf{2} \cdot \mathbf{2})(\mathbf{2} \cdot \mathbf{2})(\mathbf{2} \cdot \mathbf{2}) = \mathbf{2}^{\mathbf{6}}$
$(4^2)^4 = \mathbf{4^2} \cdot \mathbf{4^2} \cdot \mathbf{4^2} \cdot \mathbf{4^2} = (\mathbf{4} \cdot \mathbf{4})(\mathbf{4} \cdot \mathbf{4})(\mathbf{4} \cdot \mathbf{4})(\mathbf{4} \cdot \mathbf{4}) = \mathbf{4}^{\mathbf{8}}$
$(3^4)^2 = \mathbf{3^4} \cdot \mathbf{3^4} = (\mathbf{3} \cdot \mathbf{3} \cdot \mathbf{3} \cdot \mathbf{3})(\mathbf{3} \cdot \mathbf{3} \cdot \mathbf{3} \cdot \mathbf{3}) = \mathbf{3}^{\mathbf{8}}$
$(6^3)^4 = \mathbf{6^3 \cdot 6^3 \cdot 6^3 \cdot 6^3 = (6 \cdot 6 \cdot 6)(6 \cdot 6 \cdot 6)(6 \cdot 6 \cdot 6)(6 \cdot 6 \cdot 6) = 6^{12}}$

2. Examine your completed table. Look at the two exponents in the original expression and the exponent in the final answer. What pattern do you notice?
The exp. in the final answer is the product of the exponents in the orig. problem.
3. Use your pattern to make a conjecture: $(a^m)^n = a^{\blacksquare}$. $\mathbf{mn}$

Answers to *Try This*

5. Possible answer:

$3^2 \cdot 3^3 \cdot 3^4 = (3 \cdot 3) \cdot (3 \cdot 3 \cdot 3) \cdot (3 \cdot 3 \cdot 3 \cdot 3) = 3^9$
$2^2 \cdot 2^2 \cdot 2^3 = (2 \cdot 2) \cdot (2 \cdot 2) \cdot (2 \cdot 2 \cdot 2) = 2^7$
$4^2 \cdot 4^5 \cdot 4^3 = (4 \cdot 4) \cdot (4 \cdot 4 \cdot 4 \cdot 4 \cdot 4) \cdot (4 \cdot 4 \cdot 4) = 4^{10}$
$6^2 \cdot 6^3 \cdot 6^3 \cdot 6^2 = (6 \cdot 6) \cdot (6 \cdot 6 \cdot 6) \cdot (6 \cdot 6 \cdot 6) \cdot (6 \cdot 6) = 6^{10}$

When multiplying powers with the same base, the answer is the base raised to the sum of all the exponents.

Try This

Use your conjecture to write each product below as a single power.

6. $(5^3)^2$ **5^6**
7. $(7^2)^2$ **7^4**
8. $(3^3)^4$ **3^{12}**
9. $(9^7)^3$ **9^{21}**

10. Make a table similar to the one in Activity 2 to explore what happens when you raise a power to two powers, for example, $\left[(4^2)^3\right]^3$. Then write a conjecture in words to summarize what you find.

Activity 3

1. Copy and complete the table below.

$(ab)^3 = (ab)(ab)(ab) = (a \cdot a \cdot a)(b \cdot b \cdot b) = a^{3}b^{3}$
$(mn)^4 = (mn)(mn)(mn)(mn) = (m \cdot m \cdot m \cdot m)(n \cdot n \cdot n \cdot n) = m^{4}n^{4}$
$(xy)^2 = (xy)(xy) = (x \cdot x)(y \cdot y) = x^{2}y^{2}$
$(cd)^5 = (cd)(cd)(cd)(cd)(cd) = (c \cdot c \cdot c \cdot c \cdot c)(d \cdot d \cdot d \cdot d \cdot d) = c^{5}d^{5}$
$(pq)^6 = pq \cdot pq \cdot pq \cdot pq \cdot pq \cdot pq;\ (p \cdot p \cdot p \cdot p \cdot p \cdot p) \cdot (q \cdot q \cdot q \cdot q \cdot q \cdot q);\ p^6q^6$

2. Examine your completed table. Look at the original expression and the final answer. What pattern do you notice?
To get the final answer, the exp. is "distributed" to each factor in the product.
3. Use your pattern to make a conjecture: $(ab)^n = a^{\blacksquare}b^{\blacksquare}$. **n; n**

Try This

Use your conjecture to write each power below as a product.

11. $(rs)^8$ **r^8s^8**
12. $(yz)^9$ **y^9z^9**
13. $(ab)^7$ **a^7b^7**
14. $(xz)^{12}$ **$x^{12}z^{12}$**

15. Look at the first row of your table. What property or properties allow you to write $(ab)(ab)(ab)$ as $(a \cdot a \cdot a)(b \cdot b \cdot b)$? **Assoc. and Comm. Properties of Mult.**
16. Make a table similar to the one above to explore what happens when you raise a product containing more than two factors to a power, for example, $(xyz)^7$. Then write a conjecture in words to summarize what you find. **Possible answer:**

$(abc)^3 = (abc)(abc)(abc) = (a \cdot a \cdot a)(b \cdot b \cdot b)(c \cdot c \cdot c) = a^3b^3c^3$
$(xyz)^2 = (xyz)(xyz) = (x \cdot x)(y \cdot y)(z \cdot z) = x^2y^2z^2$
$(mnpq)^4 = (mnpq)(mnpq)(mnpq)(mnpq) =$ $(m \cdot m \cdot m \cdot m)(n \cdot n \cdot n \cdot n)(p \cdot p \cdot p \cdot p)(q \cdot q \cdot q \cdot q) = m^4n^4p^4q^4$

When a product is raised to a power, the exp. is "distributed" to each factor in the product.

Close

Key Concepts

The product of two powers with the same base is the base raised to the sum of the exponents.

The power of a power is the base raised to the product of the exponents.

The power of a product is the product of each factor raised to that exponent.

Assessment

Journal Have students use numbers to show an example of each property explored.

Answers to *Try This*

10. Possible answer:

$\left[(3^2)^3\right]^4 = (3^2)^3 \cdot (3^2)^3 \cdot (3^2)^3 \cdot (3^2)^3 = 3^6 \cdot 3^6 \cdot 3^6 \cdot 3^6 = 3^{24}$
$\left[(2^2)^2\right]^3 = (2^2)^2 \cdot (2^2)^2 \cdot (2^2)^2 = 2^4 \cdot 2^4 \cdot 2^4 = 2^{12}$
$\left[(4^2)^5\right]^3 = (4^2)^5 \cdot (4^2)^5 \cdot (4^2)^5 = 4^{10} \cdot 4^{10} \cdot 4^{10} = 4^{30}$

When a power is raised to 2 powers, the final answer is the base raised to the product of all the exponents.

7-3 Organizer

Pacing: Traditional 1 day
Block $\frac{1}{2}$ day

Objective: Use multiplication properties of exponents to evaluate and simplify expressions.

Online Edition
Tutorial Videos

Countdown Week 15

Power Presentations with PowerPoint®

Warm Up

Write each expression using an exponent.

1. $2 \cdot 2 \cdot 2$ $\quad 2^3$

2. $x \cdot x \cdot x \cdot x$ $\quad x^4$

3. $\frac{1}{4 \cdot 4}$ $\quad 4^{-2}$ or $\frac{1}{4^2}$

Write each expression without using an exponent.

4. 4^3 $\quad 4 \cdot 4 \cdot 4$ **5.** y^2 $\quad y \cdot y$

6. m^{-4} $\quad \frac{1}{m \cdot m \cdot m \cdot m}$

Also available on transparency

Math Humor

Q: What do you call x^{sun}?

A: Solar power.

7-3 Multiplication Properties of Exponents

Objective
Use multiplication properties of exponents to evaluate and simplify expressions.

Who uses this?
Astronomers can multiply expressions with exponents to find the distance between objects in space. (See Example 2.)

You have seen that exponential expressions are useful when writing very small or very large numbers. To perform operations on these numbers, you can use properties of exponents. You can also use these properties to simplify your answer.

In this lesson, you will learn some properties that will help you simplify exponential expressions containing multiplication.

Know it! Note

Simplifying Exponential Expressions

An exponential expression is completely simplified if...

- There are no negative exponents.
- The same base does not appear more than once in a product or quotient.
- No powers are raised to powers.
- No products are raised to powers.
- No quotients are raised to powers.
- Numerical coefficients in a quotient do not have any common factor other than 1.

Examples	Nonexamples
$\frac{b}{a}$ $\quad x^3$ $\quad z^{12}$ $\quad a^4b^4$ $\quad \frac{s^5}{t^5}$ $\quad \frac{5a^2}{2b}$	$a^{-2}ba$ $\quad x \cdot x^2$ $\quad (z^3)^4$ $\quad (ab)^4$ $\quad \left(\frac{s}{t}\right)^5$ $\quad \frac{10a^2}{4b}$

Products of powers with the same base can be found by writing each power as repeated multiplication.

$$3^5 \cdot 3^2 = (3 \cdot 3 \cdot 3 \cdot 3 \cdot 3) \cdot (3 \cdot 3) = 3^7$$

Notice the relationship between the exponents in the factors and the exponent in the product: $5 + 2 = 7$.

Product of Powers Property

WORDS	NUMBERS	ALGEBRA
The product of two powers with the same base equals that base raised to the sum of the exponents.	$6^7 \cdot 6^4 = 6^{7+4} = 6^{11}$	If a is any nonzero real number and m and n are integers, then $a^m \cdot a^n = a^{m+n}$.

State Resources

go.hrw.com
State Resources Online
KEYWORD: MA7 Resources

1 Introduce

EXPLORATION

7-3 Multiplication Properties of Exponents

1. The expression $(x \cdot x \cdot x) \cdot (x \cdot x)$ can be evaluated two ways. As a product of two powers, it can be written as $x^3 \cdot x^2$. As a single power, it can be written as x^5. Use this information to complete the table below.

Expression	Product of Powers	Single Power
$(x \cdot x \cdot x) \cdot (x \cdot x)$	$x^3 \cdot x^2$	x^5
$(y \cdot y \cdot y \cdot y) \cdot (y \cdot y)$		
$(a \cdot a \cdot a \cdot a \cdot a) \cdot (a \cdot a \cdot a \cdot a)$		
$m \cdot (m \cdot m \cdot m \cdot m \cdot m)$		

2. Describe any patterns you see in the table above.
3. Use a similar method to complete the table below.

Expression	Product of Powers	Single Power
$(y \cdot y \cdot y) \cdot (y \cdot y) \cdot (y \cdot y)$	$y^3 \cdot y^2 \cdot y^2$	y^7
$(b \cdot b \cdot b) \cdot (b \cdot b) \cdot (b \cdot b \cdot b \cdot b)$		
$(z \cdot z) \cdot (z \cdot z \cdot z) \cdot (z \cdot z \cdot z \cdot z \cdot z)$		
$x \cdot (x \cdot x) \cdot (x \cdot x \cdot x) \cdot (x \cdot x)$		

THINK AND DISCUSS

4. **Describe** any patterns you see in the second table.
5. **Explain** how you can use your findings to write $x^{10} \cdot x^4$ as a single power.

Motivate

Draw a square on the board. Label one side x^3. Ask students for an expression for the area of the square. $x^3 \cdot x^3$

Show students that this can also be written as $(x^3)^2$, and tell them that the properties in this lesson will show them how to simplify expressions with multiple exponents, such as this one.

Explorations and answers are provided in *Alternate Openers: Explorations Transparencies.*

EXAMPLE 1 Finding Products of Powers

Simplify.

A $2^5 \cdot 2^6$

$2^5 \cdot 2^6$

2^{5+6} — *Since the powers have the same base, keep the base and add the exponents.*

2^{11}

B $4^2 \cdot 3^{-2} \cdot 4^5 \cdot 3^6$

$4^2 \cdot 3^{-2} \cdot 4^5 \cdot 3^6$ — *Group powers with the same base together.*

$(4^2 \cdot 4^5) \cdot (3^{-2} \cdot 3^6)$

$4^{2+5} \cdot 3^{-2+6}$ — *Add the exponents of powers with the same base.*

$4^7 \cdot 3^4$

C $a^4 \cdot b^5 \cdot a^2$

$a^4 \cdot b^5 \cdot a^2$

$(a^4 \cdot a^2) \cdot b^5$ — *Group powers with the same base together.*

$a^6 \cdot b^5$ — *Add the exponents of powers with the same base.*

a^6b^5

D $y^2 \cdot y \cdot y^{-4}$

$(y^2 \cdot y^1) \cdot y^{-4}$ — *Group the first two powers.*

$y^3 \cdot y^{-4}$ — *The first two powers have the same base, so add the exponents.*

y^{-1} — *The two remaining powers have the same base, so add the exponents.*

$\frac{1}{y}$ — *Write with a positive exponent.*

Remember!

A number or variable written without an exponent actually has an exponent of 1.

$10 = 10^1$

$y = y^1$

Simplify.

1a. $7^8 \cdot 7^4$ 7^{12}

1b. $3^{-3} \cdot 5^8 \cdot 3^4 \cdot 5^2$ 3×5^{10}

1c. $m \cdot n^{-4} \cdot m^4$ $\frac{m^5}{n^4}$

1d. $x \cdot x^{-1} \cdot x^{-3} \cdot x^{-4}$ $\frac{1}{x^7}$

EXAMPLE 2 *Astronomy Application*

Light from the Sun travels at about 1.86×10^5 miles per second. It takes about 500 seconds for the light to reach Earth. Find the approximate distance from the Sun to Earth. Write your answer in scientific notation.

distance = rate × time

$= (1.86 \times 10^5) \times 500$

$= (1.86 \times 10^5) \times (5 \times 10^2)$ — *Write 500 in scientific notation.*

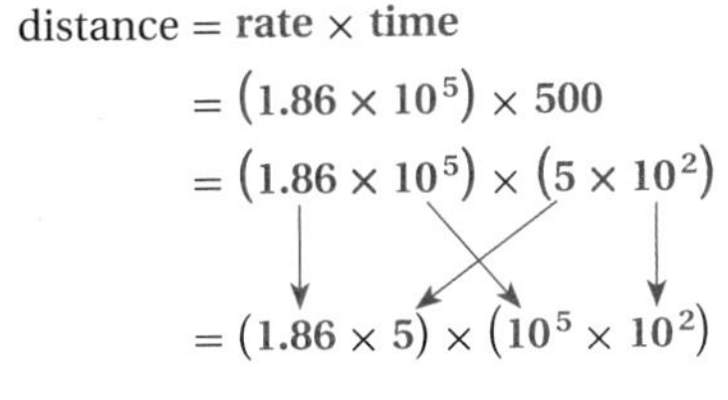

$= (1.86 \times 5) \times (10^5 \times 10^2)$ — *Use the Commutative and Associative Properties to group.*

$= 9.3 \times 10^7$ — *Multiply within each group.*

The Sun is about 9.3×10^7 miles from Earth.

2. Light travels at about 1.86×10^5 miles per second. Find the approximate distance that light travels in one hour. Write your answer in scientific notation. **6.696×10^8 mi**

Power Presentations with PowerPoint®

Additional Examples

Example 1

Simplify.

A. $3^2 \cdot 3^5$ 3^7

B. $2^4 \cdot 3^4 \cdot 2^{-2} \cdot 3^2$ $2^2 \cdot 3^6$

C. $q^3 \cdot r^2 \cdot q^6$ q^9r^2

D. $n^3 \cdot n^{-4} \cdot n$ 1

Example 2

Light from the Sun travels at about 1.86×10^5 miles per second. It takes about 15,000 seconds for the light to reach Neptune. Find the approximate distance from the Sun to Neptune. Write your answer in scientific notation.

2.79×10^9 mi

INTERVENTION

Questioning Strategies

EXAMPLE 1

- How do you know when an expression containing exponents is completely simplified?
- How do you know which powers to group together?

EXAMPLE 2

- What is the formula for distance?
- Why should you write the time in scientific notation?
- If you left the time in standard notation, how would that affect your calculations?

2 Teach

Guided Instruction

Introduce the Product of Powers Property by writing each power in the product in factored form and having students discover the relationship among the exponents. Have students discover the other properties in a similar fashion. In **Example 1,** encourage students to add the exponents of powers with the same base before rewriting negative exponents as positive exponents.

Reaching All Learners

Through Graphic Organizers

Have students create a graphic organizer to show evidence that each property works.

Product of Powers	$3^2 \cdot 3^3$ $9 \cdot 27$ 243	3^5 243
Power of a Power	$(2^3)^4$ 8^4 4096	2^{12} 4096
Power of a Product	$(2 \cdot 4)^3$ 8^3 512	$2^3 \cdot 4^3$ $8 \cdot 64$ 512

Power Presentations with PowerPoint®

Additional Examples

Example 3

Simplify.

A. $(5^2)^4$ 5^8

B. $(4^3)^0$ 1

C. $(x^3)^{-5} \cdot x^4$ $\frac{1}{x^{11}}$

INTERVENTION

Questioning Strategies

EXAMPLE 3

- What operation is performed on the exponents when a power is raised to another power?

Teaching Tip **Reading Math** Tell students that the exponent is usually read as an ordinal followed by the word *power*. For example, 7^4 is read "seven to the fourth power." Point out that 2 and 3 are exceptions to this rule. For those exponents, it is customary to say "squared" or "cubed," respectively. If students have trouble with ordinals, suggest that they make a chart with the numbers in the first column and their ordinals in the second column. ENGLISH LANGUAGE LEARNERS

To find a power of a power, you can use the meaning of exponents.

$$(4^3)^2 = 4^3 \cdot 4^3 = (4 \cdot 4 \cdot 4) \cdot (4 \cdot 4 \cdot 4) = 4^6$$

Notice the relationship between the exponents in the original power and the exponent in the final power: $3 \cdot 2 = 6$.

Power of a Power Property

WORDS	NUMBERS	ALGEBRA
A power raised to another power equals that base raised to the product of the exponents.	$(6^7)^4 = 6^{7 \cdot 4} = 6^{28}$	If a is any nonzero real number and m and n are integers, then $(a^m)^n = a^{mn}$.

EXAMPLE 3 Finding Powers of Powers

Simplify.

A $(7^4)^3$

$7^{4 \cdot 3}$	*Use the Power of a Power Property.*
7^{12}	*Simplify.*

B $(3^6)^0$

$3^{6 \cdot 0}$	*Use the Power of a Power Property.*
3^0	*Zero multiplied by any number is zero.*
1	*Any number raised to the zero power is 1.*

C $(x^2)^{-4} \cdot x^5$

$x^{2 \cdot (-4)} \cdot x^5$	*Use the Power of a Power Property.*
$x^{-8} \cdot x^5$	*Simplify the exponent of the first term.*
x^{-8+5}	*Since the powers have the same base, add the exponents.*
x^{-3}	
$\frac{1}{x^3}$	*Write with a positive exponent.*

CHECK IT OUT! Simplify.

3a. $(3^4)^5$ 3^{20} **3b.** $(6^0)^3$ 1 **3c.** $(a^3)^4 \cdot (a^{-2})^{-3}$ a^{18}

Student to Student

Multiplication Properties of Exponents

Briana Tyler
Memorial High School

Sometimes I can't remember when to add exponents and when to multiply them. When this happens, I write everything in expanded form.

For example, I would write $x^2 \cdot x^3$ as $(x \cdot x)(x \cdot x \cdot x) = x^5$. Then $x^2 \cdot x^3 = x^{2+3} = x^5$.

I would write $(x^2)^3$ as $x^2 \cdot x^2 \cdot x^2$, which is $(x \cdot x)(x \cdot x)(x \cdot x) = x^6$.

Then $(x^2)^3 = x^{2 \cdot 3} = x^6$.

This way I get the right answer even if I forget the properties.

Powers of products can be found by using the meaning of an exponent.

$$(8x)^3 = 8x \cdot 8x \cdot 8x = 8 \cdot 8 \cdot 8 \cdot x \cdot x \cdot x = 8^3x^3 = 512x^3$$

Power of a Product Property

WORDS	NUMBERS	ALGEBRA
A product raised to a power equals the product of each factor raised to that power.	$(2 \cdot 4)^3 = 2^3 \cdot 4^3$ $= 8 \cdot 64$ $= 512$	If a and b are any nonzero real numbers and n is any integer, then $(ab)^n = a^nb^n$.

EXAMPLE 4 Finding Powers of Products

Simplify.

A $(-3x)^2$

$(-3)^2 \cdot x^2$ — *Use the Power of a Product Property.*

$9x^2$ — *Simplify.*

Caution!

In Example 4B, the negative sign is not part of the base.
$-(3x)^2 = -1 \cdot (3x)^2$

B $-(3x)^2$

$-(3^2 \cdot x^2)$ — *Use the Power of a Product Property.*

$-(9 \cdot x^2)$ — *Simplify.*

$-9x^2$

C $(x^{-2} \cdot y^0)^3$

$(x^{-2})^3 \cdot (y^0)^3$ — *Use the Power of a Product Property.*

$x^{-2 \cdot 3} \cdot y^{0 \cdot 3}$ — *Use the Power of a Power Property.*

$x^{-6} \cdot y^0$ — *Simplify.*

$x^{-6} \cdot 1$ — *Write y^0 as 1.*

$\frac{1}{x^6}$ — *Write with a positive exponent.*

CHECK IT OUT! Simplify.

4a. $(4p)^3$ $\mathbf{64p^3}$ 4b. $(-5t^2)^2$ $\mathbf{25t^4}$ 4c. $(x^2y^3)^4 \cdot (x^2y^4)^{-4}$ $\mathbf{\frac{1}{y^4}}$

THINK AND DISCUSS

1. Explain why $(a^2)^3$ and $a^2 \cdot a^3$ are not equivalent expressions.

2. **GET ORGANIZED** Copy and complete the graphic organizer. In each box, supply the missing exponents. Then give an example for each property.

Multiplication Properties of Exponents		
Product of Powers Property	Power of a Power Property	Power of a Product Property
$a^m \cdot a^n = a^{\square}$	$(a^m)^n = a^{\square}$	$(ab)^n = a^{\square}b^{\square}$

COMMON ERROR ALERT

Students sometimes add exponents when a power is raised to another power. Encourage students to write out the expression in expanded form to help them remember.

Teaching Tip **Communicating Math** Have students write the Product of Powers, Power of a Power, and Power of a Product Properties in their own words. Then have volunteers read their definitions aloud.

Power Presentations with PowerPoint®

Additional Examples

Example 4

Simplify.

A. $-(2y)^2$ $-4y^2$

B. $(-2y)^3$ $-8y^3$

C. $(x^6 \cdot y^{-3})^2$ $\frac{x^{12}}{y^6}$

INTERVENTION

Questioning Strategies

EXAMPLE 4

- How does the Power of a Product Property compare with the Distributive Property?
- If a negative number is raised to an even-numbered power, is it positive or negative? Why?

3 Close

Summarize

Have students identify the property they can use to simplify each expression. Then have them simplify the expression.

$(3^2)^3$	Power of a Power; 3^6
$x^2 \cdot x^4$	Product of Powers; x^6
$(4b \cdot c^{-2})^2$	Power of a Product; $\frac{16b^2}{c^4}$

ONGOING ASSESSMENT and INTERVENTION

***Diagnose Before* the Lesson**
7-3 Warm Up, TE p. 474

***Monitor During* the Lesson**
Check It Out! Exercises, SE pp. 475–477
Questioning Strategies, TE pp. 475–477

***Assess After* the Lesson**
7-3 Lesson Quiz, TE p. 480
Alternative Assessment, TE p. 480

Answers to *Think and Discuss*

1. $(a^2)^3 = a^{2 \cdot 3} = a^6$, while $a^2 \cdot a^3 = a^{2+3} = a^5$.
2. See p. A6.

7-3 Exercises

Assignment Guide

Assign *Guided Practice* exercises as necessary.

If you finished Examples **1–2**
- **Basic** 18–22, 53, 68
- **Average** 18–22, 53, 68, 84
- **Advanced** 18–22, 53, 68, 84

If you finished Examples **1–4**
- **Basic** 18–65, 68, 75, 80–83, 98–106
- **Average** 18–43, 44–52 even, 53, 54, 56–64 even, 66–83, 84–96 even, 98–106
- **Advanced** 18–42 even, 44–54, 56–106

Homework Quick Check
Quickly check key concepts.
Exercises: 18, 22, 28, 32, 40, 42, 46

State Resources

go.hrw.com
State Resources Online
KEYWORD: MA7 Resources

7-3 Exercises

go.hrw.com
Homework Help Online
KEYWORD: MA7 7-3
Parent Resources Online
KEYWORD: MA7 Parent

GUIDED PRACTICE

SEE EXAMPLE 1 p. 475

Simplify.

1. $2^2 \cdot 2^3$ **2^5**　　2. $5^3 \cdot 5^3$ **5^6**　　3. $n^6 \cdot n^2$ **n^8**　　4. $x^2 \cdot x^{-3} \cdot x^4$ **x^3**

SEE EXAMPLE 2 p. 475

5. **Science** If you traveled in space at a speed of 1000 miles per hour, how far would you travel in 7.5×10^5 hours? Write your answer in scientific notation. **7.5×10^8 mi**

Simplify.

SEE EXAMPLE 3 p. 476

6. $(x^2)^5$ **x^{10}**　　7. $(y^4)^8$ **y^{32}**　　8. $(p^3)^3$ **p^9**
9. $(3^{-2})^2$ **$\frac{1}{3^4}$, or $\frac{1}{81}$**　　10. $(a^{-3})^4 \cdot (a^7)^2$ **a^2**　　11. $xy \cdot (x^2)^3 \cdot (y^3)^4$ **x^7y^{13}**

SEE EXAMPLE 4 p. 477

12. $(2t)^5$ **$32t^5$**　　13. $(6k)^2$ **$36k^2$**　　14. $(r^2s)^7$ **$r^{14}s^7$**
15. $(-2x^5)^3$ **$-8x^{15}$**　　16. $-(2x^5)^3$ **$-8x^{15}$**　　17. $(a^2b^2)^5 \cdot (a^{-5})^2$ **b^{10}**

PRACTICE AND PROBLEM SOLVING

Independent Practice

For Exercises	See Example
18–21	1
22	2
23–28	3
29–34	4

Extra Practice
Skills Practice p. S16
Application Practice p. S34

Simplify.

18. $3^3 \cdot 2^3 \cdot 3$ **$2^3 \cdot 3^4$**　　19. $6 \cdot 6^2 \cdot 6^3 \cdot 6^2$ **6^8**　　20. $a^5 \cdot a^0 \cdot a^{-5}$ **1**　　21. $x^7 \cdot x^{-6} \cdot y^{-3}$ **$\frac{x}{y^3}$**

22. **Geography** Rhode Island is the smallest state in the United States. Its land area is about 2.9×10^{10} square feet. Alaska, the largest state, is about 5.5×10^2 times as large as Rhode Island. What is the land area of Alaska in square feet? Write your answer in scientific notation. **1.595×10^{13} ft²**

Simplify.

23. $(2^3)^3$ **2^9, or 512**　　24. $(3^6)^0$ **1**　　25. $(x^2)^{-1}$ **$\frac{1}{x^2}$**
26. $(b^4)^6 \cdot b$ **b^{25}**　　27. $b \cdot (a^3)^4 \cdot (b^{-2})^3$ **$\frac{a^{12}}{b^5}$**　　28. $(x^4)^2 \cdot (x^{-1})^{-4}$ **x^{12}**
29. $(3x)^3$ **$27x^3$**　　30. $(5w^8)^2$ **$25w^{16}$**　　31. $(p^4q^2)^7$ **$p^{28}q^{14}$**
32. $(-4x^3)^4$ **$256x^{12}$**　　33. $-(4x^3)^4$ **$-256x^{12}$**　　34. $(x^3y^4)^3 \cdot (xy^3)^{-2}$ **x^7y^6**

Find the missing exponent in each expression.

35. $a^{■}a^4 = a^{10}$ **6**　　36. $(a^{■})^4 = a^{12}$ **3**　　37. $(a^2b^{■})^4 = a^8b^{12}$ **3**
38. $(a^3b^6)^{■} = \frac{1}{a^9b^{18}}$ **−3**　　39. $(b^2)^{-4} = \frac{1}{b^{■}}$ **8**　　40. $a^{■} \cdot a^6 = a^6$ **0**

Geometry Write an expression for the area of each figure.

41. 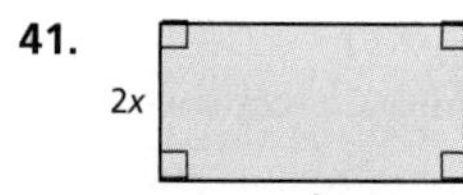

$2x^3$

42. 

a^2b^4

43. 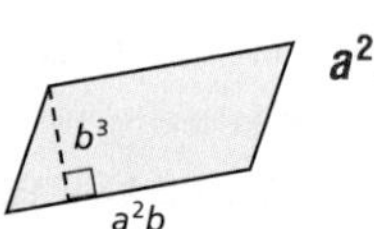

$2m^{10}n^6$

Simplify, if possible.

44. x^6y^5 **x^6y^5**　　45. $(2x^2)^2 \cdot (3x^3)^3$ **$108x^{13}$**　　46. $x^2 \cdot y^{-3} \cdot x^{-2} \cdot y^{-3}$ **$\frac{1}{y^6}$**
47. $(5x^2)(5x^2)^2$ **$125x^6$**　　48. $-(x^2)^4(-x^2)^4$ **$-x^{16}$**　　49. $a^3 \cdot a^0 \cdot 3a^3$ **$3a^6$**
50. $(ab)^3(ab)^{-2}$ **ab**　　51. $10^2 \cdot 10^{-4} \cdot 10^5$ **10^3, or 1000**　　52. $(x^2y^2)^2(x^2y)^{-2}$ **y^2**

7-3 READING STRATEGIES

The table below summarizes the multiplication properties that are needed to simplify expressions with powers.

Product of a Power	To multiply powers with the same base, keep the base and **add the exponents.**	$4^3 \cdot 4^5 = 4^{3+5} = 4^8$ $3^8 \cdot 5^6 \cdot 3^{-6} = 3^{8+(-6)} \cdot 5^6 = 3^2 \cdot 5^6$ $x^{-5} \cdot x^4 \cdot y^7 = x^{-5+4} \cdot y^7 = x^{-1}y^7 = \frac{y^7}{x}$	In general, $a^m \cdot a^n = a^{m+n}$
Power of a Power	To find the power of a power, keep the base and **multiply the exponents.**	$(4^3)^5 = 4^{3 \cdot 5} = 4^{15}$ $(8^9)^0 = 8^{9 \cdot 0} = 8^0 = 1$ $(x^2)^{-6} = x^{2 \cdot -6} = x^{-12} = \frac{1}{x^{12}}$	In general, $(a^m)^n = a^{m \cdot n}$
Power of a Product	To find the power of a product, **apply the exponent** to each factor.	$(5 \cdot 3)^2 = 5^2 \cdot 3^2 = 25 \cdot 9 = 225$ $(-4b)^3 = (-4)^3 \cdot b^3 = -64b^3$ $(x^0 \cdot y^{-1})^5 = (x^0)^5 \cdot (y^{-1})^5 = x^0 \cdot y^{-5} = \frac{1}{y^5}$	In general, $(ab)^n = a^nb^n$

Complete each of the following.

1. What do you do with the exponents to simplify $(c^4)^{-2}$? **multiply**
2. What do you do with the exponents to simplify $6^4 \cdot 6^8$? **add**
3. What is the name of the property that can be used to simplify $(6t)^{-9}$?
Power of a Product
4. $3(x + 4) = 3x + 12$ shows how the Distributive Property of Multiplication is used to simplify an expression. Which property of exponents is similar to the Distributive Property? Why?
Power of a Product; with both properties, a number is applied to all parts.

Simplify each expression.

5. $(m^3)^8$ **m^{24}**　　6. $8^4 \cdot 8^4$ **8^8**　　7. $(3v^5)^2$ **$9v^{10}$**
8. $c^{-2} \cdot d^8 \cdot c^{-3}$ **$\frac{d^8}{c^5}$**　　9. $(2 \cdot 9)^3$ **5832**　　10. $-(4y^7)^2$ **$-16y^{14}$**

7-3 RETEACH

You can multiply a power by a power by expanding each factor.

Simplify $(4^3)(4^5)$.

$(4^3)(4^5)$
$(4 \cdot 4 \cdot 4)(4 \cdot 4 \cdot 4 \cdot 4 \cdot 4)$ *Expand each factor.*
4^8 *Count the number of factors.*
The number of factors is the exponent.

Or you can use the **Product of Powers Property:**

$a^m \cdot a^n = a^{m+n}$ ($a \neq 0$, m and n are integers.)

Simplify $(4^3)(4^5)$.
$(4^3)(4^5)$
4^{3+5}
4^8

Simplify $a^4 \cdot b^5 \cdot a^{-2}$.
$a^{4+(-2)} \cdot b^5$
$a^2 \cdot b^5$
a^2b^5

You can use the **Power of a Power Property** to find a power raised to another power.

$(a^m)^n = a^{mn}$ ($a \neq 0$, m and n are integers.)

Simplify $(2^3)^2$.
$(2^3)^2$
$2^{3 \cdot 2}$
2^6

Simplify $(x^5)^4 \cdot y$.
$x^{5 \cdot 4} \cdot y$
$x^{20}y$

Simplify.

1. $2^3 \cdot 2^4$ **2^7**　　2. $8^{-2} \cdot 5^3 \cdot 8^6$ **$8^4 \cdot 5^3$**　　3. $2^4 \cdot 3^5 \cdot 2^8 \cdot 3^{-2}$ **$2^{12} \cdot 3^3$**
4. $m^8 \cdot n^4 \cdot m^7$ **$m^{15}n^4$**　　5. $(6^4)^2$ **6^8**　　6. $(4^{-3})^2$ **$\frac{1}{4^6}$**
7. $(5^{-3})^3 \cdot 4^0$ **$\frac{1}{5^9}$**　　8. $(x^2)^{-4} \cdot y^{-3}$ **$\frac{1}{x^8y^3}$**　　9. $(u^5)^{-2} \cdot (v^3)^4$ **$\frac{v^{12}}{u^{10}}$**

53. Earth: 9.3×10^7 mi; Mars: 1.4136×10^8 mi; Jupiter: 4.836×10^8 mi; Saturn: 8.928×10^8 mi

53. **Astronomy** The graph shows the approximate time it takes light from the Sun, which travels at a speed of 1.86×10^5 miles per second, to reach several planets. Find the approximate distance from the Sun to each planet in the graph. Write your answers in scientific notation. (*Hint:* Remember $d = rt$.)

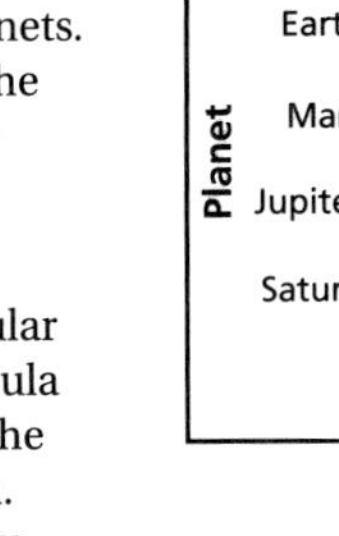

Sunlight Travel Time to Planets

Planet	Time (s)
Earth	500
Mars	760
Jupiter	2600
Saturn	4800

54. **Geometry** The volume of a rectangular prism can be found by using the formula $V = \ell wh$ where ℓ, w, and h represent the length, width, and height of the prism. Find the volume of a rectangular prism whose dimensions are $3a^2$, $4a^5$, and $4a^2b^2$. $48a^9b^2$

55. **ERROR ANALYSIS** Explain the error in each simplification below. What is the correct answer in each case?

a. $x^2 \cdot x^4 = x^8$ b. $(x^4)^5 = x^9$ c. $(x^2)^3 = x^{2^3} = x^8$

Simplify.

56. $(-3x^2)(5x^{-3})$ $-\frac{15}{x}$ 57. $(a^4b)(a^3b^{-6})$ $\frac{a^7}{b^5}$ 58. $(6w^5)(2v^2)(w^6)$ $12v^2w^{11}$

59. $15m^{12}n^9$

59. $(3m^7)(m^2n)(5m^3n^8)$ 60. $(b^2)^{-2}(b^4)^5$ b^{16} 61. $(3st)^2t^5$ $9s^2t^7$

62. $(2^2)^2(x^5y)^3$ $16x^{15}y^3$ 63. $(-t)(-t)^2(-t^4)$ t^7 64. $(2m^2)(4m^4)(8n)^2$ $512m^6n^2$

65. **Estimation** Estimate the value of each expression. Explain how you estimated.

a. $\left[(-3.031)^2\right]^3$ b. $(6.2085 \times 10^2) \times (3.819 \times 10^{-5})$

66. **Physical Science** The speed of sound at sea level is about 344 meters per second. The speed of light is about 8.7×10^5 times faster than the speed of sound. What is the speed of light in meters per second? Write your answer in scientific notation and in standard form. 2.9928×10^8 m/s; 299,280,000 m/s

67. Yes; because of the Comm. Prop. of Mult., they are both equal to x^6.

67. **Write About It** Is $(x^2)^3$ equal to $(x^3)^2$? Explain.

68. **Biology** A newborn baby has about 26,000,000,000 cells. An adult has about 1.9×10^3 times as many cells as a baby. About how many cells does an adult have? Write your answer in scientific notation. 4.94×10^{13}

Simplify.

69. $(-4k)^2 + k^2$ $17k^2$ 70. $-3z^3 + (-3z)^3$ $-30z^3$ 71. $(2x^2)^2 + 2(x^2)^2$ $6x^4$

72. $(2r)^2s^2 + 6(rs)^2 + 1$ $10r^2s^2 + 1$ 73. $(3a)^2b^3 + 3(ab)^2(2b)$ $15a^2b^3$ 74. $(x^2)(x^2)(x^2) + 3x^2$ $x^6 + 3x^2$

MULTI-STEP TEST PREP

75. This problem will prepare you for the Multi-Step Test Prep on page 494.

a. The speed of light v is the product of the frequency f and the wavelength w ($v = fw$). Wavelengths are often measured in *nanometers*. *Nano* means 10^{-9}, so 1 nanometer $= 10^{-9}$ meters. What is 600 nanometers in meters? Write your answer in scientific notation. 6×10^{-7} m

b. Use your answer from part *a* to find the speed of light in meters per second if $f = 5 \times 10^{14}$ Hz. 3×10^8 m/s

c. Explain why you can rewrite $(6 \times 10^{-7})(5 \times 10^{14})$ as $(6 \times 5)(10^{-7})(10^{14})$.

Teaching Tip

Science Link For **Exercise 53,** you can explain to students that a planet's distance from the Sun varies at different points in its orbit. This is because the planets have elliptical orbits. At a point called *perihelion*, a planet is closest to the Sun. At *aphelion*, it is farthest from the Sun. The root in both words, *helion*, comes from the Greek word for Sun.

MULTI-STEP TEST PREP **Exercise 75** involves using the formula for the speed of light. This exercise prepares students for the Multi-Step Test Prep on page 494.

Answers

55a. Exponents are multiplied but should be added; x^6.

b. Exponents are added but should be multiplied; x^{20}.

c. Exponent is written as a power but should be multiplied; x^6.

65a. 9^3, or 729; possible answer: Round -3.031 to -3.

b. 0.024; possible answer: Round 6.2085 to 6 and round 3.819 to 4.

75c. Assoc. and Comm. Properties of Mult.

7-3 PROBLEM SOLVING

Write the correct answer.

1. In the mid-nineteenth century, several landowners in Australia released domestic rabbits into the wild. Suppose 100 rabbits were released. By 1950, the population had increased about 6×10^6 times. Determine the wild rabbit population in 1950.
about 600,000,000

2. Barnard's star is the fifth closest star to the Earth, after the Sun and the stars in the Alpha Centauri system. It takes 1.86×10^8 seconds for light from Barnard's star to reach the Earth. Light travels at a speed of 1.86×10^5 miles per second. Calculate the distance from Barnard's star to the Earth.
3.46×10^{13} miles

3. Saturn's smallest moon, Tethys, has a diameter of about 6.5×10^2 miles. The diameter of Jupiter's largest moon, Ganymede, is 5 times that of Tethys. Determine the diameter of Ganymede. Write your answer in standard form and in scientific notation.
about 3250 mi or 3.25×10^3 mi

4. Delaware and Montana have roughly the same population. Delaware's area is 2.49×10^3 square miles. Montana is 59 times larger. Determine the area of Montana. Write your answer in standard form and in scientific notation.
147,000 sq mi or 1.47×10^5 sq mi

Select the best answer.

5. The formula for the volume of a cylinder is $V = 2\pi r^2h$ where r is the radius and h is the height. What is the volume of the cylinder shown below?

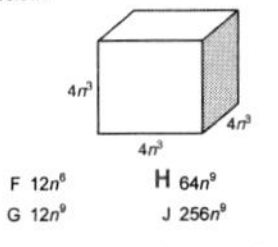

A $12\pi xy$ C $24\pi x^2y$
B $12\pi xy^2$ **D** $36\pi xy^2$

6. What is the volume of the cube shown below?

$4n^3$, $4n^3$, $4n^3$

F $12n^6$ **H** $64n^9$
G $12n^9$ J $256n^9$

7. Belize borders Mexico and Guatemala in Central America. It has an area of 2.30×10^4 square kilometers. Russia borders fourteen countries and is 7.43×10^2 times larger than Belize. What is the area of Russia?

A 1.71×10^6 sq km C 1.71×10^8 sq km
B 1.71×10^7 sq km D 1.71×10^9 sq km

8. In 1989, Voyager 2 discovered six moons that orbit Neptune. The smallest of these is Naiad, which orbits Neptune in a brief 7.2 hours, or 8.22×10^{-4} years. Neptune's orbit of the Sun takes 2×10^5 times longer than Naiad's. How long does Neptune's orbit take?

F 10.2 years H 102 years
G 16.4 years **J** 164 years

7-3 CHALLENGE

When you learned how to multiply one decimal by another, you learned to count decimal places and move the decimal point that many places to the left.

0.003×0.02 ⟶ Write 6 and move the decimal point 5 places to the left. ⟶ 0.00006

Using properties of exponents, you can understand why this rule works.

Find each product by counting decimal places and moving the decimal point.

1. 0.06×0.002 0.00012 2. 0.04×0.012 0.00048
3. 0.15×0.0006 0.00009 4. 0.09×0.00012 0.0000108

You can also find the product 0.003×0.02 by using a property of exponents that you learned. Notice that the final answer shown below agrees with the answer obtained by applying the rule for multiplication shown in the example above.

$0.003 \times 0.02 = \frac{3}{1000} \times \frac{2}{100} = \frac{3}{10^3} \times \frac{2}{10^2} = \frac{3 \times 2}{10^3 \times 10^2} = \frac{3 \times 2}{10^{3+2}} = \frac{6}{10^5} = \frac{6}{10{,}000}$ 0.00006

5. 0.06×0.002 0.00012 6. 0.04×0.012 0.00048
7. 0.15×0.0006 0.00009 8. 0.09×0.00012 0.0000108

Find each product by using a property of exponents. Show your work.

9. $0.06 \times 0.002 \times 0.003$ 0.00000036 10. $0.04 \times 0.05 \times 0.003$ 0.000006

11. Write an extension of the rule for multiplying two decimals between 0 and 1 that applies to multiplying three such decimals.
Multiply the decimals in the same way as the whole numbers. Count the number of decimal places in each of the three numbers. Find the sum of those numbers. Move the decimal point that many places to the left.

7-3 PRACTICE A
7-3 PRACTICE C
7-3 PRACTICE B

Simplify.

1. $3^4 \cdot 3^2$ 3^6 or 729 2. $2^5 \cdot 2^4$ 2^9 or 512 3. $2^3 \cdot 2^5 \cdot 2^1$ 2^9 or 512

4. $q^{-6} \cdot q^{-1}$ $\frac{1}{q^7}$ 5. $r^{-3} \cdot r^4 \cdot s^{-4}$ $\frac{r}{s^4}$ 6. $j^{-2} \cdot j^{-4} \cdot j^2$ $\frac{1}{j^4}$

7. $c^5 \cdot b^{-2} \cdot c^3$ $\frac{c^8}{b^2}$ 8. $(h^2)^5$ h^{10} 9. $(g^4)^{-2}$ $\frac{1}{g^8}$

10. $(w^8)^0$ 1 11. $(v^2)^5 \cdot v^4$ v^{14} 12. $(w^5)^{-2} \cdot w^{-3}$ $\frac{1}{w^{13}}$

13. $(f^6)^{-4} \cdot (f^{-2})^{-3}$ $\frac{1}{f^{18}}$ 14. $(a^{-2})^{-3} \cdot (a^5)^2$ a^{16} 15. $(3b)^4$ $81b^4$

16. $(-5k)^2$ $25k^2$ 17. $-(4m)^3$ $-64m^3$ 18. $(-3p)^{-2}$ $\frac{1}{9p^2}$

19. $(s^4t)^3 \cdot (s^4t^3)^2$ $s^{20}t^9$ 20. $(a^2b^4)^2 \cdot (a^{-2}b^3)^{-1} \cdot a^4$ $a^{10}b^5$ 21. $(x^3y^2)^{-4} \cdot (x^2y^{-3})^{-2}$ $\frac{1}{x^{16}y^2}$

22. The pitch of a sound is determined by the number of vibrations produced per second. The note "middle C" produces 2.62×10^2 vibrations per second. If a pianist plays middle C for 5×10^{-1} seconds, how many vibrations will occur?
1.31×10^2 or 131 vibrations

TEST PREP DOCTOR Students who chose **B** for **Exercise 80** may have recalled that any nonzero number raised to the zero power is one, but they may have forgotten to multiply by x^2.

In **Exercise 82,** 4 must be cubed because it is a factor of an expression that is being cubed. Students can eliminate choices **A** and **B** immediately because 4^3 is 64.

Journal

Have students explain how parentheses affect the expressions ab^3c^2, $(ab^3c)^2$ and $(ab)^3c^2$.

ALTERNATIVE ASSESSMENT

Have students work in small groups to create a presentation that explains the properties learned in this lesson. The presentation should include visual aids as needed.

Power Presentations with PowerPoint®

7-3 Lesson Quiz

Simplify.

1. $3^2 \cdot 3^4$ 3^6 **2.** $z^4 \cdot z^{-2} \cdot z$ z^3

3. $(x^3)^2$ x^6 **4.** $-(t^{-3})^5$ $-\frac{1}{t^{15}}$

5. $(5g)^3$ $125g^3$ **6.** $(-3f^{-4})^2$ $\frac{9}{f^8}$

7. $(x^2y)^3 \cdot (x^3y^2)^{-2}$ $\frac{1}{y}$

8. The islands of Samoa have an approximate area of 2.9×10^3 square kilometers. The area of Texas is about 2.3×10^2 times as great as that of the islands. What is the approximate area of Texas? Write your answer in scientific notation.
6.67×10^5 km^2

Also available on transparency

Critical Thinking Rewrite each expression so that it has only one exponent. (*Hint:* You may use parentheses.)

76. c^3d^3 $(cd)^3$ **77.** $36a^2b^2$ $(6ab)^2$ **78.** $\frac{8a^3}{b^3}$ $\left(\frac{2a}{b}\right)^3$ **79.** $\frac{k^{-2}}{4m^2n^2}$ $\left(\frac{1}{2kmn}\right)^2$

TEST PREP

80. Which of the following is equivalent to $x^2 \cdot x^0$?
Ⓐ 0 Ⓑ 1 Ⓒ x^2 Ⓓ x^{20}

81. Which of the following is equivalent to $(3 \times 10^5)^2$?
Ⓕ 9×10^7 Ⓖ 9×10^{10} Ⓗ 6×10^7 Ⓙ 6×10^{10}

82. What is the value of n^3 when $n = 4 \times 10^5$?
Ⓐ 1.2×10^9 Ⓑ 1.2×10^{16} Ⓒ 6.4×10^9 Ⓓ 6.4×10^{16}

83. Which represents the area of the triangle?
Ⓕ $6x^2$ Ⓗ $7x^2$
Ⓖ $12x^2$ Ⓙ $24x^2$

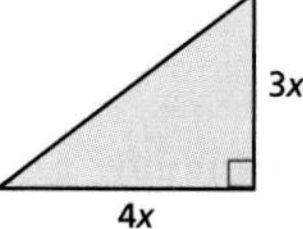

CHALLENGE AND EXTEND

Simplify.

84. $3^2 \cdot 3^x$ 3^{2+x} **85.** $(3^2)^x$ 3^{2x} **86.** $(x^yz)^2$ $x^{2y}z^2$

87. $(x+1)^{-2}(x+1)^3$ $x+1$ **88.** $(x+1)^2(x+1)^{-3}$ $\frac{1}{x+1}$ **89.** $(x^y \cdot x^z)^3$ x^{3y+3z}

90. $(4^x)^x$ 4^{x^2} **91.** $(x^x)^x$ x^{x^2} **92.** $(3x)^{2y}$ 9^yx^{2y}

Find the value of x.

93. $5^x \cdot 5^4 = 5^8$ **4** **94.** $7^3 \cdot 7^x = 7^{12}$ **9** **95.** $(4^x)^3 = 4^{12}$ **4** **96.** $(6^2)^x = 6^{16}$ **8**

97. Multi-Step The edge of a cube measures 1.2×10^{-2} m. What is the volume of the cube in cubic centimeters? **1.728 cm^3**

SPIRAL REVIEW

Find the value of x in each diagram. *(Lesson 2-8)*

98. □$ABCD \sim$ □$WXYZ$ **100** **99.** $\triangle ABC \sim \triangle RST$ **15**

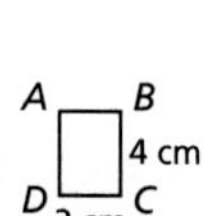

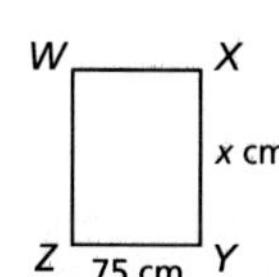

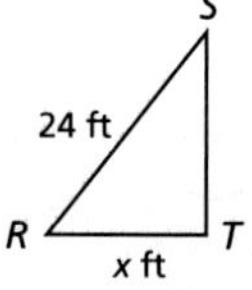

Determine whether each sequence appears to be an arithmetic sequence. If so, find the common difference and the next three terms. *(Lesson 4-6)*

100. 5, 1, −3, −7, … **yes; $d = -4$; −11, −15, −19** **101.** −3, −2, 0, 3, … **no** **102.** 0.4, 1.0, 1.6, 2.2, … **yes; $d = 0.6$; 2.8, 3.4, 4.0**

Write each number in standard form. *(Lesson 7-2)*

103. 7.8×10^6 **104.** 4.95×10^{-4} **105.** 983×10^{-1} **98.3** **106.** 0.06×10^8 **6,000,000**

103. 7,800,000
104. 0.000495

7-4 Division Properties of Exponents

Objective
Use division properties of exponents to evaluate and simplify expressions.

Who uses this?
Economists can use expressions with exponents to calculate national debt statistics. (See Example 3.)

A quotient of powers with the same base can be found by writing the powers in factored form and dividing out common factors.

$$\frac{3^5}{3^3} = \frac{\cancel{3}\cdot\cancel{3}\cdot\cancel{3}\cdot 3\cdot 3}{\cancel{3}\cdot\cancel{3}\cdot\cancel{3}} = 3\cdot 3 = 3^2$$

Notice the relationship between the exponents in the original quotient and the exponent in the final answer: $5 - 3 = 2$.

Know it! Note

Quotient of Powers Property

WORDS	NUMBERS	ALGEBRA
The quotient of two nonzero powers with the same base equals the base raised to the difference of the exponents.	$\frac{6^7}{6^4} = 6^{7-4} = 6^3$	If a is a nonzero real number and m and n are integers, then $\frac{a^m}{a^n} = a^{m-n}$.

EXAMPLE 1 Finding Quotients of Powers

Simplify.

A $\frac{3^8}{3^2}$

$\frac{3^8}{3^2} = 3^{8-2}$

$= 3^6 = 729$

B $\frac{x^5}{x^5}$

$\frac{x^5}{x^5} = x^{5-5}$

$= x^0 = 1$

C $\frac{a^5b^9}{(ab)^4}$

$\frac{a^5b^9}{(ab)^4} = \frac{a^5b^9}{a^4b^4}$

$= a^{5-4}\cdot b^{9-4}$

$= a^1 \cdot b^5$

$= ab^5$

D $\frac{2^3\cdot 3^2\cdot 5^7}{2\cdot 3^4\cdot 5^5}$

$\frac{2^3\cdot 3^2\cdot 5^7}{2\cdot 3^4\cdot 5^5} = 2^{3-1}\cdot 3^{2-4}\cdot 5^{7-5}$

$= 2^2\cdot 3^{-2}\cdot 5^2$

$= \frac{2^2\cdot 5^2}{3^2}$

$= \frac{4\cdot 25}{9} = \frac{100}{9}$

Helpful Hint
$3^6 = 729$
Both 3^6 and 729 are considered to be simplified.

Simplify.

1a. $\frac{2^9}{2^7}$ **4** **1b.** $\frac{y}{y^4}$ $\mathbf{\frac{1}{y^3}}$ **1c.** $\frac{m^5n^4}{(m^5)^2n}$ $\mathbf{\frac{n^3}{m^5}}$ **1d.** $\frac{3^5\cdot 2^4\cdot 4^3}{3^4\cdot 2^2\cdot 4^6}$ $\mathbf{\frac{3}{16}}$

7-4 Organizer

Pacing: Traditional 1 day
Block $\frac{1}{2}$ day

Objective: Use division properties of exponents to evaluate and simplify expressions.

Technology Lab
In *Technology Lab Activities*

Online Edition
Tutorial Videos

Countdown Week 15

Power Presentations with PowerPoint®

Warm Up

Simplify.

1. $(x^2)^3$ x^6 **2.** 2^{-3} $\frac{1}{2^3}$ or $\frac{1}{8}$

3. $3^2\cdot x^{-1}$ $\frac{9}{x}$ **4.** $(v^{-2}w^3)^{-3}$ $\frac{v^6}{w^9}$

5. $3^8\cdot 3^{-2}$ 3^6 **6.** $\left(\frac{y}{z}\right)^3$ $\frac{y^3}{z^3}$

Write in scientific notation.

7. 30×10^{-3} 3×10^{-2}

8. 0.16×10^7 1.6×10^6

Also available on transparency

Math Humor

Q: Why does $\frac{(xy)^2}{x^2y^2}$ refuse to be simplified?
A: One is the loneliest number.

1 Introduce

EXPLORATION

7-4 Division Properties of Exponents

1. The expression $\frac{x^5}{x^2}$ can be simplified by expanding the powers and dividing out common factors: $\frac{x^5}{x^2} = \frac{x\cdot x\cdot \cancel{x}\cdot \cancel{x}\cdot x}{\cancel{x}\cdot \cancel{x}} = x\cdot x\cdot x = x^3$. Use this information to complete the table.
2. Describe any patterns you see in the table.
3. You can use a similar method when the exponent in the denominator is greater than the exponent in the numerator. For example, $\frac{x^2}{x^5} = \frac{\cancel{x}\cdot\cancel{x}}{x\cdot\cancel{x}\cdot\cancel{x}\cdot x\cdot x} = \frac{1}{x\cdot x\cdot x} = \frac{1}{x^3} = x^{-3}$. Use this information to complete this table.

Expression	Simplified Form
$\frac{x^5}{x^2}$	x^3
$\frac{a^4}{a^2}$	
$\frac{y^7}{y^5}$	
$\frac{x^6}{x^5}$	

Expression	Simplified Form
$\frac{x^2}{x^5}$	x^{-3}
$\frac{m^3}{m^7}$	
$\frac{a^2}{a^8}$	
$\frac{x^6}{x^7}$	

THINK AND DISCUSS

4. **Explain** how the results in the second table compare to those in the first table.
5. **Describe** how you can use your findings to simplify $\frac{z^{10}}{z^{15}}$.

Motivate

Have students write out the factors in $\frac{4^9}{4^6}$.
$\frac{4\cdot 4\cdot 4\cdot 4\cdot 4\cdot 4\cdot 4\cdot 4\cdot 4}{4\cdot 4\cdot 4\cdot 4\cdot 4\cdot 4}$ Ask them how to simplify this quotient of powers. $4^3 = 64$
Explain that in this lesson they will learn properties for division of powers.

Explorations and answers are provided in *Alternate Openers: Explorations Transparencies.*

State Resources

go.hrw.com
State Resources Online
KEYWORD: MA7 Resources

Power Presentations with PowerPoint®

Additional Examples

Example 1

Simplify.

A. $\frac{2^7}{2^2}$ 2^5, or 32 **B.** $\frac{x^4}{x^3}$ x

C. $\frac{d^4e^3}{(de)^2}$ d^2e

D. $\frac{3 \cdot 4^3 \cdot 5^5}{3^2 \cdot 4^4 \cdot 5^3}$ $\frac{25}{12}$

Example 2

Simplify $(3 \times 10^{10}) \div (6 \times 10^6)$ and write the answer in scientific notation. 5×10^3

Example 3

The Colorado Department of Education spent about 4.408×10^9 dollars in fiscal year 2004–05 on public schools. There were about 7.6×10^5 students enrolled in public school. What was the average spending per student? Write your answer in standard form. $5800

INTERVENTION

Questioning Strategies

EXAMPLE 1

- Why can the Quotient of Powers Property not be used to simplify $\frac{x^4}{y^3}$?
- Is the smaller exponent always subtracted from the larger exponent? Explain.

EXAMPLE 2

- How do you know if your answer is in scientific notation?

EXAMPLE 3

- How do you know which number is the divisor?
- What mathematical operations are needed to answer the question? How do you know?

Writing Math

You can "split up" a quotient of products into a product of quotients:

$\frac{a \times c}{b \times d} = \frac{a}{b} \times \frac{c}{d}$

Example:

$\frac{3 \times 4}{5 \times 7} = \frac{3}{5} \times \frac{4}{7} = \frac{12}{35}$

EXAMPLE 2 Dividing Numbers in Scientific Notation

Simplify $(2 \times 10^8) \div (8 \times 10^5)$ and write the answer in scientific notation.

$(2 \times 10^8) \div (8 \times 10^5) = \frac{2 \times 10^8}{8 \times 10^5}$

$= \frac{2}{8} \times \frac{10^8}{10^5}$ *Write as a product of quotients.*

$= 0.25 \times 10^{8-5}$ *Simplify each quotient.*

$= 0.25 \times 10^3$ *Simplify the exponent.*

$= 2.5 \times 10^{-1} \times 10^3$ *Write 0.25 in scientific notation as 2.5×10^{-1}.*

$= 2.5 \times 10^{-1+3}$ *The second two terms have the same base, so add the exponents.*

$= 2.5 \times 10^2$ *Simplify the exponent.*

2. Simplify $(3.3 \times 10^6) \div (3 \times 10^8)$ and write the answer in scientific notation. 1.1×10^{-2}

EXAMPLE 3 *Economics Application*

In the year 2000, the United States public debt was about 5.6×10^{12} dollars. The population of the United States in that year was about 2.8×10^8 people. What was the average debt per person? Give your answer in standard form.

To find the average debt per person, divide the total debt by the number of people.

$\frac{\text{total debt}}{\text{number of people}} = \frac{5.6 \times 10^{12}}{2.8 \times 10^8}$

$= \frac{5.6}{2.8} \times \frac{10^{12}}{10^8}$ *Write as a product of quotients.*

$= 2 \times 10^{12-8}$ *Simplify each quotient.*

$= 2 \times 10^4$ *Simplify the exponent.*

$= 20{,}000$ *Write in standard form.*

The average debt per person was about $20,000.

3. In 1990, the United States public debt was about 3.2×10^{12} dollars. The population of the United States in 1990 was about 2.5×10^8 people. What was the average debt per person? Write your answer in standard form. **$12,800**

A power of a quotient can be found by first writing factors and then writing the numerator and denominator as powers.

$$\left(\frac{2}{3}\right)^3 = \frac{2}{3} \cdot \frac{2}{3} \cdot \frac{2}{3} = \frac{2 \cdot 2 \cdot 2}{3 \cdot 3 \cdot 3} = \frac{2^3}{3^3}$$

Notice that the exponents in the final answer are the same as the exponent in the original expression.

2 Teach

Guided Instruction

Review the multiplication properties of exponents because some problems in this lesson use both multiplication and division properties. Introduce the division properties in this lesson by examining the powers written in factored form first.

Reaching All Learners

Through Graphic Organizers

Have students create a graphic organizer to show evidence that each property works.

Quotient of Powers Property	$\frac{6^7}{6^4} = \frac{279{,}936}{1296}$ 216	$6^{7-4} = 6^3$ 216
Power of a Quotient Property	$\left(\frac{3}{5}\right)^4 = (0.6)^4$ 0.1296	$\frac{3^4}{5^4} = \frac{81}{625}$ 0.1296

Positive Power of a Quotient Property

WORDS	NUMBERS	ALGEBRA
A quotient raised to a positive power equals the quotient of each base raised to that power.	$\left(\frac{3}{5}\right)^4 = \frac{3}{5}\cdot\frac{3}{5}\cdot\frac{3}{5}\cdot\frac{3}{5} = \frac{3\cdot3\cdot3\cdot3}{5\cdot5\cdot5\cdot5} = \frac{3^4}{5^4}$	If a and b are nonzero real numbers and n is a positive integer, then $\left(\frac{a}{b}\right)^n = \frac{a^n}{b^n}$.

EXAMPLE 4 Finding Positive Powers of Quotients

Simplify.

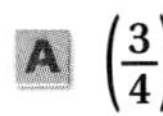

A $\left(\frac{3}{4}\right)^3$

$\left(\frac{3}{4}\right)^3 = \frac{3^3}{4^3}$ *Use the Power of a Quotient Property.*

$= \frac{27}{64}$ *Simplify.*

B $\left(\frac{2x^3}{yz}\right)^3$

$\left(\frac{2x^3}{yz}\right)^3 = \frac{(2x^3)^3}{(yz)^3}$ *Use the Power of a Quotient Property.*

$= \frac{2^3(x^3)^3}{y^3z^3}$ *Use the Power of a Product Property: $(2x^3)^3 = 2^3(x^3)^3$ and $(yz)^3 = y^3z^3$.*

$= \frac{8x^9}{y^3z^3}$ *Simplify 2^3 and use the Power of a Power Property: $(x^3)^3 = x^{3\cdot3} = x^9$.*

CHECK IT OUT! Simplify.

4a. $\left(\frac{2^3}{3^2}\right)^2$ **$\frac{2^6}{3^4}$, or $\frac{64}{81}$** 4b. $\left(\frac{ab^4}{c^2d^3}\right)^5$ **$\frac{a^5b^{20}}{c^{10}d^{15}}$** 4c. $\left(\frac{a^3b}{a^2b^2}\right)^3$ **$\frac{a^3}{b^3}$**

Remember that $x^{-n} = \frac{1}{x^n}$. What if x is a fraction?

$\left(\frac{a}{b}\right)^{-n} = \frac{1}{\left(\frac{a}{b}\right)^n} = 1 \div \left(\frac{a}{b}\right)^n$ *Write the fraction as division.*

$= 1 \div \frac{a^n}{b^n}$ *Use the Power of a Quotient Property.*

$= 1 \cdot \frac{b^n}{a^n}$ *Multiply by the reciprocal.*

$= \frac{b^n}{a^n}$ *Simplify.*

$= \left(\frac{b}{a}\right)^n$ *Use the Power of a Quotient Property.*

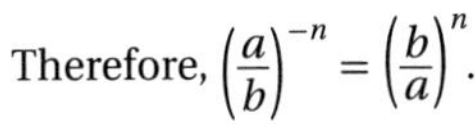

Therefore, $\left(\frac{a}{b}\right)^{-n} = \left(\frac{b}{a}\right)^n$.

COMMON ERROR ALERT

When using the Power of a Product Property in **Example 4B,** students might forget to apply the power to the coefficients of terms. Remind students to apply the power to each factor in the product, including variables and coefficients.

Power Presentations with PowerPoint®

Additional Examples

Example 4

Simplify.

A. $\left(\frac{4}{7}\right)^2$ $\frac{16}{49}$ **B.** $\left(\frac{3d^2}{ef}\right)^4$ $\frac{81d^8}{e^4f^4}$

C. $\left(\frac{2x^3}{(xy)^3}\right)^2$ $\frac{4}{y^6}$

INTERVENTION

Questioning Strategies

EXAMPLE 4

- What happened to a variable if it was in the original expression, but not in the simplified expression?

Teaching Tip

Auditory The names of the properties in this lesson sound a lot alike. Help students differentiate between the two:

Say "Quotient," and then write $\frac{\square}{\square}$.

Say "of Powers," and then write $\frac{\boxed{x^3}}{\boxed{x^2}}$.

Say "Power," and then write $(\ )^3$.

Say "of a Quotient," and then write $\left(\frac{x}{y}\right)^3$.

Power Presentations with PowerPoint®

Additional Examples

Example 5

Simplify.

A. $\left(\frac{3}{4}\right)^{-3}$ $\frac{64}{27}$

B. $\left(\frac{2x^2}{y^3}\right)^{-2}$ $\frac{y^6}{4x^4}$

C. $\left(\frac{2}{3}\right)^{-2}\left(\frac{6m}{2n}\right)^{-3}$ $\frac{n^3}{12m^3}$

INTERVENTION

Questioning Strategies

EXAMPLE 5

- How can you make a negative exponent positive?
- What is the value of $\left(\frac{1}{5}\right)^{-3}$?

Multiple Representations Discuss with students the advantages or disadvantages of different methods of simplifying. For example, in **Example 5A,** students could use the Power of a Quotient Property first: $\left(\frac{2}{5}\right)^{-3} = \frac{2^{-3}}{5^{-3}} = \frac{5^3}{2^3} = \frac{125}{8}$.

Negative Power of a Quotient Property

WORDS	NUMBERS	ALGEBRA
A quotient raised to a negative power equals the reciprocal of the quotient raised to the opposite (positive) power.	$\left(\frac{2}{3}\right)^{-4} = \left(\frac{3}{2}\right)^4 = \frac{3^4}{2^4}$	If a and b are nonzero real numbers and n is a positive integer, then $\left(\frac{a}{b}\right)^{-n} = \left(\frac{b}{a}\right)^n = \frac{b^n}{a^n}$.

EXAMPLE 5 **Finding Negative Powers of Quotients**

Simplify.

A $\left(\frac{2}{5}\right)^{-3}$

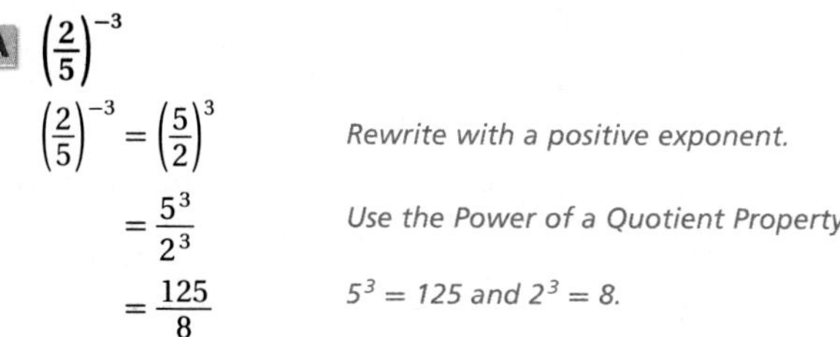

$\left(\frac{2}{5}\right)^{-3} = \left(\frac{5}{2}\right)^3$ *Rewrite with a positive exponent.*

$= \frac{5^3}{2^3}$ *Use the Power of a Quotient Property.*

$= \frac{125}{8}$ *$5^3 = 125$ and $2^3 = 8$.*

B $\left(\frac{3x}{y^2}\right)^{-3}$

$\left(\frac{3x}{y^2}\right)^{-3} = \left(\frac{y^2}{3x}\right)^3$ *Rewrite with a positive exponent.*

$= \frac{(y^2)^3}{(3x)^3}$ *Use the Power of a Quotient Property.*

$= \frac{y^6}{3^3x^3}$ *Use the Power of a Power Property: $(y^2)^3 = y^{2 \cdot 3} = y^6$. Use the Power of a Product Property: $(3x)^3 = 3^3x^3$.*

$= \frac{y^6}{27x^3}$ *Simplify the denominator.*

C $\left(\frac{3}{4}\right)^{-1}\left(\frac{2x}{3y}\right)^{-2}$

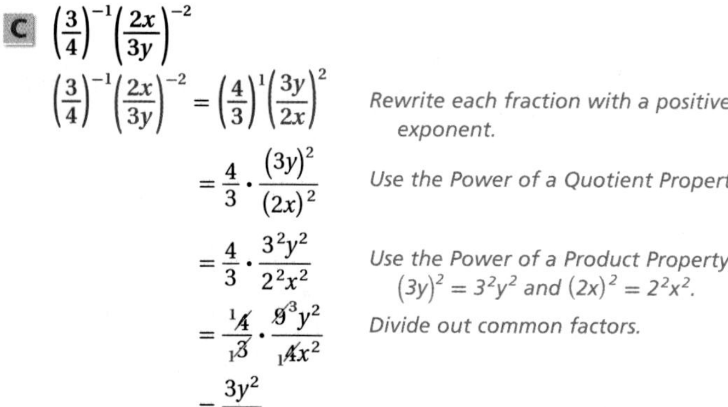

$\left(\frac{3}{4}\right)^{-1}\left(\frac{2x}{3y}\right)^{-2} = \left(\frac{4}{3}\right)^1\left(\frac{3y}{2x}\right)^2$ *Rewrite each fraction with a positive exponent.*

$= \frac{4}{3} \cdot \frac{(3y)^2}{(2x)^2}$ *Use the Power of a Quotient Property.*

$= \frac{4}{3} \cdot \frac{3^2y^2}{2^2x^2}$ *Use the Power of a Product Property: $(3y)^2 = 3^2y^2$ and $(2x)^2 = 2^2x^2$.*

$= \frac{{}^1\cancel{4}}{{}_1\cancel{3}} \cdot \frac{\cancel{9}^3y^2}{{}_1\cancel{4}x^2}$ *Divide out common factors.*

$= \frac{3y^2}{x^2}$

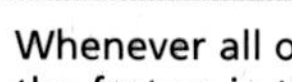

Helpful Hint

Whenever all of the factors in the numerator or the denominator divide out, replace them with 1.

Simplify.

5a. $\left(\frac{4}{3^2}\right)^{-3}$ $\frac{9^3}{4^3}$, or $\frac{729}{64}$ **5b.** $\left(\frac{2a}{b^2c^3}\right)^{-4}$ $\frac{b^8c^{12}}{16a^4}$ **5c.** $\left(\frac{s}{3}\right)^{-2}\left(\frac{9s^2}{t}\right)^{-1}$ $\frac{t}{s^4}$

3 Close

Summarize

Have students give an example of the Quotient of Powers Property and the Power of a Quotient Property.

Possible answers:

Quotient of Powers: $\frac{x^5}{x^3} = x^{5-3} = x^2$

Power of a Quotient : $\left(\frac{x}{y}\right)^3 = \frac{x^3}{y^3}$

ONGOING ASSESSMENT and INTERVENTION

***Diagnose Before* the Lesson**
7-4 Warm Up, TE p. 481

***Monitor During* the Lesson**
Check It Out! Exercises, SE pp. 481–484
Questioning Strategies, TE pp. 482–484

***Assess After* the Lesson**
7-4 Lesson Quiz, TE p. 487
Alternative Assessment, TE p. 487

THINK AND DISCUSS

1. Compare the Quotient of Powers Property and the Product of Powers Property. Then compare the Power of a Quotient Property and the Power of a Product Property.

2. **GET ORGANIZED** Copy and complete the graphic organizer. In each cell, supply the missing information. Then give an example for each property.

Answers to *Think and Discuss*

1. Possible answer: Both the Quotient of Powers Property and the Product of Powers Property require that the bases be the same. For quotients, you subtract the exponents. For products, you add the exponents. In the Power of a Quotient Property, each term is raised to the same power. In the Power of a Product Property, each factor is raised to the same power.
2. See p. A7.

7-4 Exercises

go.hrw.com
Homework Help Online
KEYWORD: MA7 7-4
Parent Resources Online
KEYWORD: MA7 Parent

GUIDED PRACTICE

SEE EXAMPLE 1 p. 481

Simplify.

1. $\frac{5^8}{5^6}$ **25**
2. $\frac{2^2 \cdot 3^4 \cdot 4^4}{2^9 \cdot 3^5}$ $\mathbf{\frac{2}{3}}$
3. $\frac{15x^6}{5x^6}$ **3**
4. $\frac{a^5b^6}{a^3b^7}$ $\mathbf{\frac{a^2}{b}}$

SEE EXAMPLE 2 p. 482

Simplify each quotient and write the answer in scientific notation.

5. $(2.8 \times 10^{11}) \div (4 \times 10^8)$ $\mathbf{7 \times 10^2}$
6. $(5.5 \times 10^3) \div (5 \times 10^8)$ $\mathbf{1.1 \times 10^{-5}}$
7. $(1.9 \times 10^4) \div (1.9 \times 10^4)$ **1**

SEE EXAMPLE 3 p. 482

8. **Sports** A star baseball player earns an annual salary of $\$8.1 \times 10^6$. There are 162 games in a baseball season. How much does this player earn per game? Write your answer in standard form. **$50,000**

Simplify.

SEE EXAMPLE 4 p. 483

9. $\left(\frac{2}{5}\right)^2$ $\mathbf{\frac{4}{25}}$
10. $\left(\frac{x^2}{xy^3}\right)^3$ $\mathbf{\frac{x^3}{y^9}}$
11. $\left(\frac{a^3}{(a^3b)^2}\right)^2$ $\mathbf{\frac{1}{a^6b^4}}$
12. $\frac{y^{10}}{y}$ $\mathbf{y^9}$

SEE EXAMPLE 5 p. 484

13. $\left(\frac{3}{4}\right)^{-2}$ $\mathbf{\frac{16}{9}}$
14. $\left(\frac{2x}{y^3}\right)^{-4}$ $\mathbf{\frac{y^{12}}{16x^4}}$
15. $\left(\frac{2}{3}\right)^{-1}\left(\frac{3a}{2b}\right)^{-2}$ $\mathbf{\frac{2b^2}{3a^2}}$
16. $\left(\frac{x^3}{y^2}\right)^{-4}$ $\mathbf{\frac{y^8}{x^{12}}}$

PRACTICE AND PROBLEM SOLVING

Simplify.

17. $\frac{3^9}{3^6}$ **27**
18. $\frac{5^4 \cdot 3^3}{5^2 \cdot 3^2}$ **75**
19. $\frac{x^8y^3}{x^3y^3}$ $\mathbf{x^5}$
20. $\frac{x^8y^4}{x^9yz}$ $\mathbf{\frac{y^3}{xz}}$

Simplify each quotient and write the answer in scientific notation.

21. $(4.7 \times 10^{-3}) \div (9.4 \times 10^3)$ $\mathbf{5 \times 10^{-7}}$
22. $(8.4 \times 10^9) \div (4 \times 10^{-5})$ $\mathbf{2.1 \times 10^{14}}$
23. $(4.2 \times 10^{-5}) \div (6 \times 10^{-3})$ $\mathbf{7 \times 10^{-3}}$
24. $(2.1 \times 10^2) \div (8.4 \times 10^5)$ $\mathbf{2.5 \times 10^{-4}}$

7-4 Exercises

Assignment Guide

Assign *Guided Practice* exercises as necessary.

If you finished Examples **1–3**
Basic 17–25, 34–37, 47
Average 17–25, 34–37, 47, 59
Advanced 17–25, 34–37, 47, 59

If you finished Examples **1–5**
Basic 17–45, 47–57, 62–71
Average 17–49, 54–60, 62–71
Advanced 17–49, 54–71

Homework Quick Check
Quickly check key concepts.
Exercises: 18, 22, 25, 28, 30, 48

State Resources

Teaching Tip

Social Studies Link For **Exercise 47,** students might be interested to know that the population density of the United States is actually rather low. Some cities are dense, but there is a lot of open land as well. In comparison, Puerto Rico has a population density of 435 people/km². Bermuda's population density is even higher, at 1211 people/km².

Answers

47. 2000: 3×10^1

 1995: 2.84×10^1

 1990: 2.65×10^1

49. Possible answer: The bases are the same, so subtract the exponent of the denominator from the exponent of the numerator: $\frac{4^5}{4^2} = 4^3 = 64$.

 When simplifying $\frac{4^2}{4^5}$, subtracting the exponents gives a negative exponent: $\frac{4^2}{4^5} = 4^{-3} = \frac{1}{4^3} = \frac{1}{64}$.

Independent Practice	
For Exercises	See Example
17–20	1
21–24	2
25	3
26–29	4
30–33	5

Extra Practice
Skills Practice p. S16
Application Practice p. S34

25. **Astronomy** The mass of Earth is about 3×10^{-3} times the mass of Jupiter. The mass of Earth is about 6×10^{24} kg. What is the mass of Jupiter? Give your answer in scientific notation. 2×10^{27} **kg**

Simplify.

26. $\left(\frac{2}{3}\right)^4$ $\frac{16}{81}$
27. $\left(\frac{a^4}{b^2}\right)^3$ $\frac{a^{12}}{b^6}$
28. $\left(\frac{a^3b^2}{ab^3}\right)^6$ $\frac{a^{12}}{b^6}$
29. $\left(\frac{xy^2}{x^3y}\right)^3$ $\frac{y^3}{x^6}$
30. $\left(\frac{1}{7}\right)^{-3}$ 343
31. $\left(\frac{x^2}{y^5}\right)^{-5}$ $\frac{y^{25}}{x^{10}}$
32. $\left(\frac{8w^7}{16}\right)^{-1}$ $\frac{2}{w^7}$
33. $\left(\frac{1}{4}\right)^{-2}\left(\frac{6x}{7}\right)^{-2}$ $\frac{196}{9x^2}$

Simplify, if possible.

34. $\frac{x^6}{x^5}$ x
35. $\frac{8d^5}{4d^3}$ $2d^2$
36. $\frac{x^2y^3}{a^2b^3}$ $\frac{x^2y^3}{a^2b^3}$
37. $\frac{(3x^3)^3}{(6x^2)^2}$ $\frac{3x^5}{4}$
38. $\frac{(5x^2)^3}{5x^2}$ $25x^4$
39. $\left(\frac{c^2a^3}{a^5}\right)^2$ $\frac{c^4}{a^4}$
40. $\left(\frac{3a}{a^3 \cdot a^0}\right)^3$ $\frac{27}{a^6}$
41. $\left(\frac{-p^4}{-5p^3}\right)^{-2}$ $\frac{25}{p^2}$
42. $\left(\frac{b^{-2}}{b^3}\right)^2$ $\frac{1}{b^{10}}$
43. $\left(\frac{10^2}{10^{-5} \cdot 10^5}\right)^{-1}$ $\frac{1}{100}$
44. $\left(\frac{x^2y^2}{x^2y}\right)^{-3}$ $\frac{1}{y^3}$
45. $\frac{(-x^2)^4}{-(x^2)^4}$ -1

46. **Critical Thinking** How can you use the Quotient of a Power Property to explain the definition of x^{-n}? (*Hint:* Think of $\frac{1}{x^n}$ as $\frac{x^0}{x^n}$.) $\frac{1}{x^n} = \frac{x^0}{x^n} = x^{0-n} = x^{-n}$

47. **Geography** *Population density* is the number of people per unit of area. The area of the United States is approximately 9.37×10^6 square kilometers. The table shows population data from the U. S. Census Bureau.

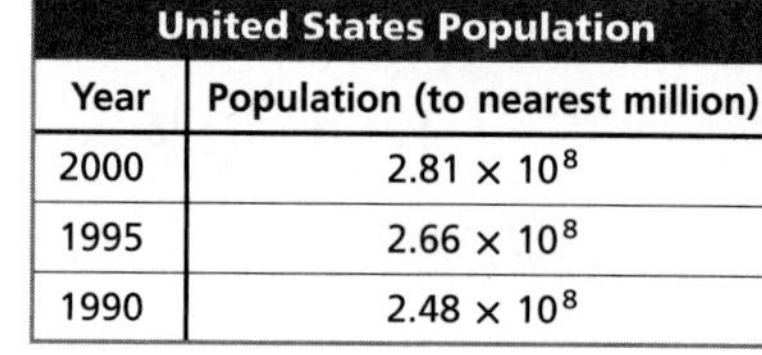

United States Population	
Year	Population (to nearest million)
2000	2.81×10^8
1995	2.66×10^8
1990	2.48×10^8

Write the approximate population density (people per square kilometer) for each of the given years in scientific notation. Round decimals to the nearest hundredth.

48. **Chemistry** The pH of a solution is a number that describes the concentration of hydrogen ions in that solution. For example, if the concentration of hydrogen ions in a solution is 10^{-4}, that solution has a pH of 4.

Lemon juice
pH 2

Apples
pH 3

Water
pH 7

Ammonia
pH 11

a. What is the concentration of hydrogen ions in lemon juice? 10^{-2}

b. What is the concentration of hydrogen ions in water? 10^{-7}

c. How many times more concentrated are the hydrogen ions in lemon juice than in water? 10^5**, or 100,000, times more concentrated**

49. **Write About It** Explain how to simplify $\frac{4^5}{4^2}$. How is it different from simplifying $\frac{4^2}{4^5}$?

Find the missing exponent(s).

50. $\frac{x^{\square}}{x^4} = x^2$ 6
51. $\frac{x^7}{x^{\square}} = x^4$ 3
52. $\left(\frac{a^2}{b^{\square}}\right)^4 = \frac{a^8}{b^{12}}$ 3
53. $\left(\frac{x^4}{y^{\square}}\right)^{-1} = \frac{y^3}{x^{\square}}$ $3; 4$

7-4 PRACTICE A

7-4 PRACTICE C

7-4 PRACTICE B

Simplify.

1. $\frac{6^7}{6^5} = 6^{7-5} = 6^{\boxed{2}} = 36$
2. $\frac{t^{12}}{t^7} = t^{\boxed{12} - \boxed{7}} = t^5$
3. $\frac{w^9}{w^2}$ w^7
4. $\frac{j^2}{j^8}$ $\frac{1}{j^6}$
5. $\frac{20m^5}{4m^2}$ $5m^3$
6. $\frac{c^3d^2}{c^2d^5}$ $\frac{c}{d^3}$
7. $\frac{(x^4)^2}{(x^3)^5}$ $\frac{1}{x^7}$
8. $\left(\frac{s^3t}{st^4}\right)^2$ $\frac{s^4}{t^6}$
9. $\left(\frac{2}{3}\right)^{-3}$ $\frac{27}{8}$
10. $\left(\frac{3a}{2b}\right)^{-4}$ $\frac{16b^4}{81a^4}$
11. $-\left(\frac{-t}{3v}\right)^{-4}$ $-\frac{81v^4}{t^4}$
12. $\left(\frac{6}{7}\right)^{-2} \cdot \left(\frac{4s}{6t}\right)^{-2}$ $\frac{49t^2}{16s^2}$
13. $\left(\frac{3c}{-2}\right)^{-1}\left(\frac{d}{4}\right)^{-2}$ $-\frac{32}{3cd^2}$
14. $\left(\left(\frac{3mn}{2}\right)^{-1}\right)^{-4}$ $\frac{81m^4n^4}{16}$

Simplify. Write the answer in scientific notation.

15. $(3.8 \times 10^5) \div (1.9 \times 10^{-6})$ 2×10^{11}
16. $(2.5 \times 10^3) \div (5 \times 10^{-4})$ 5×10^6
17. A textile factory produces 1.08×10^8 yards of fabric every year. If the factory is in operation 360 days a year, what is the average number of yards of fabric produced each day? Give your answer in standard form. **300,000 yards**
18. It takes 5 yards of fabric to manufacture a dress. If the textile factory turned their entire yearly production of 1.08×10^8 yards of fabric into dresses, how many could they make? Give your answer in scientific notation. 2.16×10^7 **dresses**

7-4 READING STRATEGIES

The table below summarizes the multiplication properties that are needed to simplify expressions with powers.

Quotient of Powers	To divide powers with the same base, keep the base and **subtract the exponents.**	$\frac{4^5}{4^3} = 4^{5-3} = 4^2 = 16$ $\frac{x^{12}y^4}{xy^6} = x^{12-1} \cdot y^{4-6} = x^{11}y^{-2} = \frac{x^{11}}{y^2}$	In general, $\frac{a^m}{a^n} = a^{m-n}$
Positive power of a Quotient	To find the positive power of a quotient, **apply the exponent** to the numerator and denominator.	$\left(\frac{2}{3}\right)^5 = \frac{2^5}{3^5} = \frac{32}{243}$ $\left(\frac{x^2y^5}{y}\right)^3 = \frac{(x^2y^5)^3}{(y)^3} = \frac{x^6y^{15}}{y^3} = x^6y^{12}$	In general, $\left(\frac{a}{b}\right)^n = \frac{a^n}{b^n}$
Negative Power of a Quotient	To find the negative power of a quotient, **apply the positive exponent** to the numerator and denominator of the **reciprocal.**	$\left(\frac{2}{3}\right)^{-5} = \left(\frac{3}{2}\right)^5 = \frac{3^5}{2^5} = \frac{243}{32}$ $\left(\frac{x^3y}{x^5}\right)^{-4} = \left(\frac{x^5}{x^3y}\right)^4 = \frac{x^{20}}{x^{12}y^4} = \frac{x^8}{y^4}$	In general, $\left(\frac{a}{b}\right)^{-n} = \left(\frac{b}{a}\right)^n = \frac{b^n}{a^n}$

Complete each of the following.

1. What do you do with the exponents to simplify $\frac{b^{13}}{b^8}$? **subtract**
2. Rewrite the expression $\left(\frac{5}{8}\right)^{-4}$ using a positive exponent. $\left(\frac{8}{5}\right)^4$
3. What is the name of the property that can be used to simplify the expression $\left(\frac{4t}{5}\right)^3$? **Positive Power of a Quotient**

Simplify each expression.

4. $\frac{12^{10}}{12^8}$ 144
5. $\left(\frac{2}{5}\right)^4$ $\frac{16}{625}$
6. $\left(\frac{9}{8}\right)^{-2}$ $\frac{64}{81}$
7. $\frac{f^3g^4}{f^7gh^5}$ $\frac{g^3}{f^4h^5}$
8. $\left(\frac{st}{t^4}\right)^{-6}$ $\frac{t^{18}}{s^6}$
9. $\left(\frac{2c^2}{c^4d}\right)^5$ $\frac{32}{c^{10}d^5}$
10. $\left(\frac{3}{2}\right)^{-3}$ $\frac{8}{27}$
11. $\left(\frac{x^3y}{xy^3}\right)^2$ $\frac{x^4}{y^4}$
12. $\left(\frac{5f^3}{g^7}\right)^{-2}$ $\frac{g^{14}}{25f^6}$

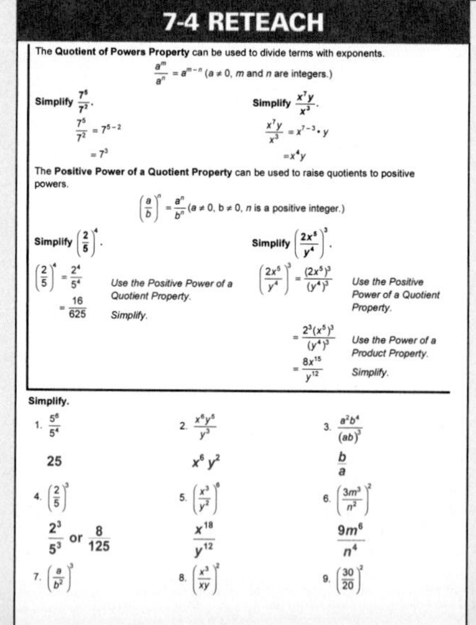

7-4 RETEACH

The **Quotient of Powers Property** can be used to divide terms with exponents.

$\frac{a^m}{a^n} = a^{m-n}$ ($a \neq 0$, m and n are integers.)

Simplify $\frac{7^5}{7^2}$.

$\frac{7^5}{7^2} = 7^{5-2}$
$= 7^3$

Simplify $\frac{x^7y}{x^3}$.

$\frac{x^7y}{x^3} = x^{7-3} \cdot y$
$= x^4y$

The **Positive Power of a Quotient Property** can be used to raise quotients to positive powers.

$\left(\frac{a}{b}\right)^n = \frac{a^n}{b^n}$ ($a \neq 0$, $b \neq 0$, n is a positive integer.)

Simplify $\left(\frac{2}{5}\right)^4$.

$\left(\frac{2}{5}\right)^4 = \frac{2^4}{5^4}$ *Use the Positive Power of a Quotient Property.*
$= \frac{16}{625}$ *Simplify.*

Simplify $\left(\frac{2x^5}{y^4}\right)^3$.

$\left(\frac{2x^5}{y^4}\right)^3 = \frac{(2x^5)^3}{(y^4)^3}$ *Use the Positive Power of a Quotient Property.*
$= \frac{2^3(x^5)^3}{(y^4)^3}$ *Use the Power of a Product Property.*
$= \frac{8x^{15}}{y^{12}}$ *Simplify.*

Simplify.

1. $\frac{5^6}{5^4}$ 25
2. $\frac{x^6y^5}{y^3}$ x^6y^2
3. $\frac{a^2b^4}{(ab)^3}$ $\frac{b}{a}$
4. $\left(\frac{2}{5}\right)^3$ $\frac{2^3}{5^3}$ or $\frac{8}{125}$
5. $\left(\frac{x^3}{y^2}\right)^6$ $\frac{x^{18}}{y^{12}}$
6. $\left(\frac{3m^3}{n^2}\right)^2$ $\frac{9m^6}{n^4}$
7. $\left(\frac{a}{b^2}\right)^3$
8. $\left(\frac{x^3}{xy}\right)^2$
9. $\left(\frac{30}{20}\right)^2$

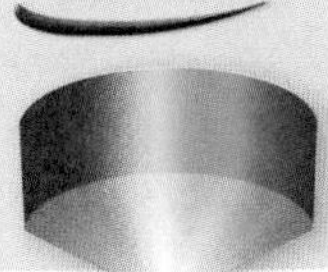

54. This problem will prepare you for the Multi-Step Test Prep on page 494.
   a. Yellow light has a wavelength of 589 nm. A nanometer (nm) is 10^{-9} m. What is 589 nm in meters? Write your answer in scientific notation. **5.89×10^{-7} m**
   b. The speed of light in air, v, is 3×10^8 m/s, and $v = fw$, where f represents the frequency in hertz (Hz) and w represents the wavelength in meters. What is the frequency of yellow light? **about 5.09×10^{14} Hz**

TEST PREP

55. Which of the following is equivalent to $(8 \times 10^6) \div (4 \times 10^2)$?

   Ⓐ 2×10^3　　**(B)** 2×10^4　　Ⓒ 4×10^3　　Ⓓ 4×10^4

56. Which of the following is equivalent to $\left(\frac{x^{12}}{3xy^4}\right)^{-2}$?

   (F) $\frac{9y^8}{x^{22}}$　　Ⓖ $\frac{3y^8}{x^{22}}$　　Ⓗ $\frac{3y^6}{x^{12}}$　　Ⓙ $\frac{6y^8}{x^{26}}$

57. Which of the following is equivalent to $\frac{(-3x)^4}{-(3x)^4}$?

   (A) -1　　Ⓑ 1　　Ⓒ $-81x^4$　　Ⓓ $\frac{1}{81x^4}$

CHALLENGE AND EXTEND

58. **Geometry** The volume of the prism at right is $V = 30x^4y^3$. Write and simplify an expression for the prism's height in terms of x and y. **$2x^2y^2$**

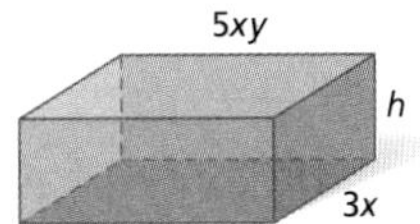

59. Simplify $\frac{3^{2x}}{3^{2x-1}}$. **3**　　60. Simplify $\frac{(x+1)^2}{(x+1)^3}$. **$\frac{1}{x+1}$**

61. Copy and complete the table below to show how the Quotient of Powers Property can be found by using the Product of Powers Property. **m; $-n$**

Statements	Reasons
1. $a^{m-n} = a^{\square + \square}$	1. Subtraction is addition of the opposite.
2. $= a^{m} \cdot a^{-n}$	2. Product of Powers Property
3. $= a^m \cdot \frac{1}{a^n}$	3. **Def. of neg. exp.**
4. $= \frac{a^m}{a^n}$	4. Multiplication can be written as division.

SPIRAL REVIEW

Find each square root. *(Lesson 1-5)*

62. $\sqrt{36}$ **6**　　63. $\sqrt{1}$ **1**　　64. $-\sqrt{49}$ **−7**　　65. $\sqrt{144}$ **12**

Solve each equation. *(Lesson 2-4)*

66. $-2(x-1) + 4x = 5x + 3$ **$-\frac{1}{3}$**　　67. $x - 1 - (4x + 3) = 5x$ **$-\frac{1}{2}$**

Simplify. *(Lesson 7-3)*

68. $3^2 \cdot 3^3$ **3^5, or 243**　69. $k^5 \cdot k^{-2} \cdot k^{-3}$ **1**　70. $(4t^5)^2$ **$16t^{10}$**　71. $-(5x^4)^3$ **$-125x^{12}$**

7-4 PROBLEM SOLVING

Write the correct answer.

1. Kudzu is a fast-growing vine that has become a nuisance in the southeastern United States. It covers 2.5×10^5 acres in Alabama. In 2004 the population of Alabama was estimated to be 4.45×10^6 people. How many acres of kudzu are there for each person in Alabama?

   0.056 acres

2. A cylindrical water tank has a volume of $6\pi x^2y^4$ cubic meters. The formula for the volume of a cylinder is πr^2h. The water tank has a radius of xy meters. What is its height?

   $6y^2$ meters

3. Voyager 2 was launched in 1979 to explore the planets of the outer solar system. The spacecraft travels an average of 4.68×10^6 kilometers in one year. Determine the speed of Voyager 2 in kilometers per hour. (*Hint*: 1 year = 8760 hours)

   5.34×10^2 km/h

4. The population of Laos is 6.22×10^6. In 2004 its gross domestic product (GDP) was $\$1.13 \times 10^{10}$. The population of Norway is 4.59×10^6. In 2004 its GDP was $\$1.83 \times 10^{11}$. What is the GDP per capita, or per person, of Laos and Norway?

   Laos: $1817;
   Norway: $39,869

Select the best answer.

5. A rectangular parking lot has an area of $10a^3b^6$ square yards. What is the width of the parking lot?

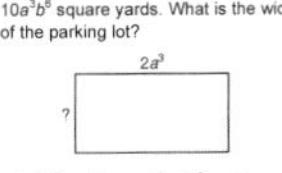

   A $5b^2$ yards　**C** $5b^6$ yards
   B $5b^3$ yards　D $25b^6$ yards

6. A storage chest is shaped like a cube. What is the volume of the storage chest?

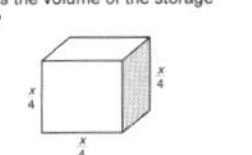

   F $\frac{x^3}{64}$ cubic units　H $\frac{32}{x^3}$ cubic units
   G $\frac{x^3}{32}$ cubic units　J $64x^3$ cubic units

7. The wavelengths of electromagnetic radiation vary greatly. Green light has a wavelength of about 5.1×10^{-7} meters. The wavelength of a U-band radio wave is 2.0×10^{-2} meters. About how much greater is the wavelength of a U-band radio wave than that of green light?

   A 2.55×10^{-9}　**C** 3.92×10^4
   B 2.55×10^{-5}　D 3.92×10^5

8. Puerto Rico has an area of 5.32×10^3 square miles and a population of 3.89×10^6. What is the population density of Puerto Rico in persons per square mile?

   F 1.37×10^{-3}　**H** 7.31×10^2
   G 1.37×10^{-2}　J 7.31×10^3

7-4 CHALLENGE

You can use the following three facts to discover a new and interesting fact about rational numbers:

- A rational number is the quotient of two integers with a nonzero denominator.
- Every integer can be written as a product of powers of prime numbers, called the *prime factorization* of the given number. For example, $120 = 2^3 3^1 5^1$.
- When dividing two powers with the same base, subtract the exponents. $\frac{10^5}{10^3} = 10^2$ and $\frac{10^3}{10^5} = \frac{1}{10^2}$

Write the prime factorization of each integer.

1. 24 **$2^3 \times 3^1$**　　2. 108 **$2^2 \times 3^3$**
3. 452 **$2^2 \times 113^1$**　　4. 1800 **$2^3 \times 3^2 \times 5^2$**

For each rational number, write the numerator and denominator by using the prime factorization of each. Then use the Quotient-of-Powers Property to simplify the result. Do not multiply out the powers of prime numbers that remain.

5. $\frac{18}{24}$ **$\frac{2 \cdot 3^2}{2^2 \cdot 3} = \frac{3}{2^2}$**
6. $\frac{48}{180}$ **$\frac{2^4 \cdot 3}{2^2 \cdot 3^2 \cdot 5} = \frac{2^2}{3 \cdot 5}$**
7. $\frac{250}{288}$ **$\frac{2 \cdot 5^3}{2^5 \cdot 3^2} = \frac{5^3}{2^4 \cdot 3^2}$**
8. $\frac{540}{1800}$ **$\frac{2^2 \cdot 3^3 \cdot 5}{2^3 \cdot 3^2 \cdot 5^2} = \frac{3}{2 \cdot 5}$**
9. Examine the final quotients that you wrote in Exercises 5–8. Explain why a prime-number base that appears in a numerator does not appear in the denominator and why a prime-number base that appears in a denominator does not appear in the numerator.

   If a prime number base b appear in the numerator (or denominator), it cannot occur in the denominator (or numerator) as well because then the rational number is not fully simplified. ex: $\frac{b^n a}{b^m c} = \frac{b^{n-m}a}{c}$

10. Let $\frac{a}{b}$ be a rational number. Write a generalization about the representation of $\frac{a}{b}$ as the quotient of prime numbers raised to powers. Illustrate your generalization by using $\frac{54}{120} = \frac{2^1 3^3}{2^3 3^1 5^1}$.

   Every rational number can be written as a quotient whose numerator is 1 or the product of prime numbers raised to positive integer exponents and whose denominator can be written as 1 or the product of prime numbers raised to positive integer exponents, and there are no prime bases common to the numerator and the denominator.

Exercise 54 involves dividing numbers written in scientific notation. This exercise prepares students for the Multi-Step Test Prep on page 494.

TEST PREP DOCTOR Students who chose **C** or **D** for **Exercise 55** may have subtracted 4 from 8 instead of dividing.

For **Exercise 56,** remind students that the exponent outside the parentheses applies to every factor inside them, including 3.

In **Exercise 57,** point out that the negative sign in the denominator will be unaffected by the exponent because it is outside the parentheses.

Journal

Have students compare and contrast multiplying and dividing two numbers that are each written in scientific notation.

ALTERNATIVE ASSESSMENT

Have students simplify $(5x^2y)^3 \cdot \left(\frac{2xy}{z^4}\right)^{-3}$ and explain at each step which property or definition they used.

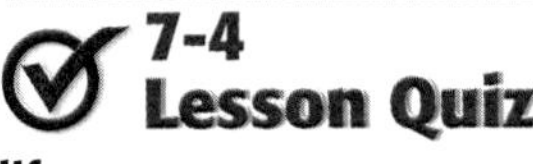

7-4 Lesson Quiz

Simplify.

1. $\frac{4^8}{4^3}$　4^5
2. $\frac{x^5y^2}{(xy)^3}$　$\frac{x^2}{y}$
3. $\left(\frac{2xy^2}{x^3y}\right)^3$　$\frac{8y^3}{x^6}$
4. $\left(\frac{4m}{n^3}\right)^{-2}$　$\frac{n^6}{16m^2}$
5. $\left(\frac{3}{c}\right)^2\left(\frac{9d^2}{2c}\right)^{-3}$　$\frac{8c}{81d^6}$
6. Simplify $(3 \times 10^{12}) \div (5 \times 10^5)$ and write the answer in scientific notation.　6×10^6
7. The Republic of Botswana has an area of 6×10^5 square kilometers. Its population is about 1.62×10^6. What is the population density of Botswana? Write your answer in standard form.

   2.7 people/km²

Also available on transparency

7-5 Organizer

Pacing: Traditional 1 day
Block $\frac{1}{2}$ day

Objective: Evaluate and simplify expressions containing rational exponents.

Online Edition
Tutorial Videos, Interactivity

Countdown Week 16

Power Presentations with PowerPoint®

Warm Up

Simplify each expression.

1. $\sqrt{36}$ 6
2. $\sqrt[5]{0}$ 0
3. $\sqrt[3]{64}$ 4
4. $\sqrt[4]{1}$ 1
5. $\sqrt[5]{100{,}000}$ 10
6. $-\sqrt[3]{27}$ −3

Also available on transparency

Math Humor

Q: What do $3\sqrt{7}$ and this textbook have in common?

A: Both have an index.

7-5 Rational Exponents

Objective
Evaluate and simplify expressions containing rational exponents.

Vocabulary
index

Why learn this?
You can use rational exponents to find the number of Calories animals need to consume each day to maintain health. (See Example 3.)

Recall that the radical symbol $\sqrt{\ }$ is used to indicate roots. The **index** is the small number to the left of the radical symbol that tells which root to take. For example, $\sqrt[3]{\ }$ represents a cube root. Since $2^3 = 2 \cdot 2 \cdot 2 = 8$, $\sqrt[3]{8} = 2$.

Another way to write nth roots is by using exponents that are fractions. For example, for $b > 1$, suppose $\sqrt{b} = b^k$.

$$\sqrt{b} = b^k$$
$$\left(\sqrt{b}\right)^2 = \left(b^k\right)^2 \quad \textit{Square both sides.}$$
$$b^1 = b^{2k} \quad \textit{Power of a Power Property}$$
$$1 = 2k \quad \textit{If } b^m = b^n \textit{, then } m = n.$$
$$\frac{1}{2} = k \quad \textit{Divide both sides by 2.}$$

So for all $b > 1$, $\sqrt{b} = b^{\frac{1}{2}}$.

Helpful Hint
When $b = 0$, $\sqrt[n]{b} = 0$.
When $b = 1$, $\sqrt[n]{b} = 1$.

Know it! Note

Definition of $b^{\frac{1}{n}}$

WORDS	NUMBERS	ALGEBRA
A number raised to the power of $\frac{1}{n}$ is equal to the nth root of that number.	$3^{\frac{1}{2}} = \sqrt{3}$ $5^{\frac{1}{4}} = \sqrt[4]{5}$ $2^{\frac{1}{7}} = \sqrt[7]{2}$	If $b > 1$ and n is an integer, where $n \geq 2$, then $b^{\frac{1}{n}} = \sqrt[n]{b}$. $b^{\frac{1}{2}} = \sqrt{b}$, $b^{\frac{1}{3}} = \sqrt[3]{b}$, $b^{\frac{1}{4}} = \sqrt[4]{b}$, and so on.

EXAMPLE 1 Simplifying $b^{\frac{1}{n}}$

Simplify each expression.

A $125^{\frac{1}{3}}$

$$125^{\frac{1}{3}} = \sqrt[3]{125} = \sqrt[3]{5^3} = 5 \quad \textit{Use the definition of } b^{\frac{1}{n}}.$$

B $64^{\frac{1}{6}} + 25^{\frac{1}{2}}$

$$64^{\frac{1}{6}} + 25^{\frac{1}{2}} = \sqrt[6]{64} + \sqrt{25} \quad \textit{Use the definition of } b^{\frac{1}{n}}.$$
$$= \sqrt[6]{2^6} + \sqrt{5^2}$$
$$= 2 + 5 = 7$$

Remember!
$\sqrt{\ }$ is equivalent to $\sqrt[2]{\ }$. See Lesson 1-5.

State Resources

go.hrw.com
State Resources Online
KEYWORD: MA7 Resources

1 Introduce

EXPLORATION

7-5 Rational Exponents

You will need a graphing calculator for this Exploration.

Recall that whole-number exponents mean repeated multiplication. For example, 3^4 3 · 3 · 3 · 3 = 81. You use a radical to show the inverse operation: $\sqrt[4]{81} = 3$.

1. You can use your calculator to evaluate radicals. To find $\sqrt[3]{4096}$, enter 3 and then press MATH. Select 5: $\sqrt[x]{\ }$, enter 4096, and press ENTER.
2. Use your calculator to help you complete the table.
3. You can also use your calculator to explore fractional exponents. To evaluate $4096^{\frac{1}{3}}$, first enter 4096. Then press ^ (1 ÷ 3) and press ENTER.
4. Use your calculator to help you complete the table.

3 ˣ√4096 16

Radical	Value
$\sqrt{4096}$	
$\sqrt[3]{4096}$	16
$\sqrt[4]{4096}$	
$\sqrt[6]{4096}$	

4096^(1/3) 16

Power	Value
$4096^{\frac{1}{2}}$	
$4096^{\frac{1}{3}}$	16
$4096^{\frac{1}{4}}$	
$4096^{\frac{1}{6}}$	

THINK AND DISCUSS

5. **Describe** what you notice about the two tables.

Motivate

Write 4^2 and 4^3 on the board and have students simplify both expressions. 16 and 64

Then write $4^{2\frac{1}{2}}$ on the board. Ask students to guess the value of this expression and explain their thinking. Possible answer: 32; the value should be between 16 and 64.

Tell students that in this lesson they will learn why $4^{2\frac{1}{2}} = 32$.

Explorations and answers are found in *Alternate Openers: Explorations Transparencies.*

Simplify each expression.

1a. $81^{\frac{1}{4}}$ **3** **1b.** $121^{\frac{1}{2}} + 256^{\frac{1}{4}}$ **15**

A fractional exponent can have a numerator other than 1, as in the expression $b^{\frac{2}{3}}$. You can write the exponent as a product in two different ways.

$$b^{\frac{2}{3}} = b^{\frac{1}{3}\cdot 2} = \left(b^{\frac{1}{3}}\right)^2 \quad \textit{Power of a Power Property} \quad = \left(\sqrt[3]{b}\right)^2 \quad \textit{Definition of } b^{\frac{1}{n}}$$

$$b^{\frac{2}{3}} = b^{2\cdot\frac{1}{3}} = \left(b^2\right)^{\frac{1}{3}} = \sqrt[3]{b^2}$$

Definition of $b^{\frac{m}{n}}$

WORDS	NUMBERS	ALGEBRA
A number raised to the power of $\frac{m}{n}$ is equal to the nth root of the number raised to the mth power.	$8^{\frac{2}{3}} = \left(\sqrt[3]{8}\right)^2 = 2^2 = 4$ $8^{\frac{2}{3}} = \sqrt[3]{8^2} = \sqrt[3]{64} = 4$	If $b > 1$ and m and n are integers, where $m \geq 1$ and $n \geq 2$, then $b^{\frac{m}{n}} = \left(\sqrt[n]{b}\right)^m = \sqrt[n]{b^m}$.

EXAMPLE 2 Simplifying Expressions with Fractional Exponents

Simplify each expression.

A $216^{\frac{2}{3}}$

$$216^{\frac{2}{3}} = \left(\sqrt[3]{216}\right)^2 \quad \textit{Definition of } b^{\frac{m}{n}}$$
$$= \left(\sqrt[3]{6^3}\right)^2$$
$$= (6)^2 = 36$$

B $32^{\frac{4}{5}}$

$$32^{\frac{4}{5}} = \left(\sqrt[5]{32}\right)^4$$
$$= \left(\sqrt[5]{2^5}\right)^4$$
$$= (2)^4 = 16$$

Simplify each expression.

2a. $16^{\frac{3}{4}}$ **8** **2b.** $1^{\frac{2}{5}}$ **1** **2c.** $27^{\frac{4}{3}}$ **81**

EXAMPLE 3 *Biology Application*

The approximate number of Calories C that an animal needs each day is given by $C = 72m^{\frac{3}{4}}$, where m is the animal's mass in kilograms. Find the number of Calories that a 16 kg dog needs each day.

$$C = 72m^{\frac{3}{4}}$$
$$= 72(16)^{\frac{3}{4}} \quad \textit{Substitute 16 for m.}$$
$$= 72 \cdot \left(\sqrt[4]{16}\right)^3 \quad \textit{Definition of } b^{\frac{m}{n}}$$
$$= 72 \cdot \left(\sqrt[4]{2^4}\right)^3$$
$$= 72 \cdot (2)^3$$
$$= 72 \cdot 8 = 576$$

The dog needs 576 Calories per day to maintain health.

3. Find the number of Calories that an 81 kg panda needs each day. **1944**

COMMON ERROR ALERT

With fractional exponents with a numerator other than 1, as in **Example 2,** students may confuse the index with the power. Write $\text{base}^{\frac{\text{power}}{\text{index}}}$ on the board for students to use as a reference.

Power Presentations with PowerPoint®

Additional Examples

Example 1

Simplify each expression.

A. $343^{\frac{1}{3}}$ 7

B. $32^{\frac{1}{5}} + 9^{\frac{1}{2}}$ 5

Example 2

Simplify each expression.

A. $81^{\frac{5}{4}}$ 243

B. $3125^{\frac{2}{5}}$ 25

Example 3

Given a cube with surface area S, the volume V of the cube can be found by using the formula $V = \left(\frac{S}{6}\right)^{\frac{3}{2}}$. Find the volume of a cube with surface area 54 m^2.

27 m^3

INTERVENTION Questioning Strategies

EXAMPLE 1

- How do you change a fractional exponent to an nth root?

EXAMPLE 2

- Will you get the same answer if you raise the number to the power before taking the root?

EXAMPLE 3

- How can you use the order of operations to solve this problem?

Multiple Representations In **Example 2,** the power can also be placed under the radical sign: $216^{\frac{2}{3}} = \sqrt[3]{216^2}$. However, it is usually more convenient to evaluate the root and then evaluate the power.

Teach

Guided Instruction

Review powers and roots by writing $5^3 = 5 \bullet 5 \bullet 5 = 125$ and $\sqrt[3]{125} = 5$. Have students practice writing several of these examples. Then present the definition of $b^{\frac{1}{n}}$ and discuss **Example 1.** Show students two special cases: $1^{\frac{1}{n}} = 1$ and $0^{\frac{1}{n}} = 0$ for all natural-number values of n. Continue with the definition of $b^{\frac{m}{n}}$ and the remaining examples. Remind students of the properties of exponents before presenting **Example 4.**

Reaching All Learners

Through Cooperative Learning

Have students work in pairs. Students take turns rolling both a red (r) and a blue (b) number cube. After each roll, the student uses the numbers shown on the cubes to complete the expression $64^{\frac{r}{b}}$. Then the student simplifies the expression or states that it cannot be simplified. The other student checks the answer and then rolls the number cubes to decide the next expression.

Remember that $\sqrt{\ }$ always indicates a nonnegative square root. When you simplify variable expressions that contain $\sqrt{\ }$, such as $\sqrt{x^2}$, the answer cannot be negative. But x may be negative. Therefore you simplify $\sqrt{x^2}$ as $|x|$ to ensure the answer is nonnegative.

When x is...	and n is...	x^n is...	and $\sqrt[n]{x^n}$ is...
Positive	Even	Positive	Positive
Negative	Even	Positive	Positive
Positive	Odd	Positive	Positive
Negative	Odd	Negative	Negative

When n is even, you must simplify $\sqrt[n]{x^n}$ to $|x|$, because you do not know whether x is positive or negative. When n is odd, simplify $\sqrt[n]{x^n}$ to x.

EXAMPLE 4 Using Properties of Exponents to Simplify Expressions

Simplify. All variables represent nonnegative numbers.

Helpful Hint

When you are told that all variables represent nonnegative numbers, you do not need to use absolute values in your answers.

A $\sqrt[3]{x^9y^3}$

$\sqrt[3]{x^9y^3} = \left(x^9y^3\right)^{\frac{1}{3}}$ — *Definition of $b^{\frac{1}{n}}$*

$= \left(x^9\right)^{\frac{1}{3}} \cdot \left(y^3\right)^{\frac{1}{3}}$ — *Power of a Product Property*

$= \left(x^{9 \cdot \frac{1}{3}}\right) \cdot \left(y^{3 \cdot \frac{1}{3}}\right)$ — *Power of a Power Property*

$= \left(x^3\right) \cdot \left(y^1\right) = x^3y$ — *Simplify exponents.*

B $\left(x^2y^{\frac{1}{2}}\right)^4 \sqrt[3]{y^3}$

$\left(x^2y^{\frac{1}{2}}\right)^4 \sqrt[3]{y^3} = \left(x^2y^{\frac{1}{2}}\right)^4 \cdot y$ — *$\sqrt[3]{y^3} = y$*

$= \left(x^{2 \cdot 4}\right) \cdot \left(y^{\frac{1}{2} \cdot 4}\right) \cdot y$ — *Power of a Product Property*

$= \left(x^8\right) \cdot \left(y^2\right) \cdot y$ — *Simplify exponents.*

$= x^8 \cdot y^{2+1} = x^8y^3$ — *Product of Powers Property*

Simplify. All variables represent nonnegative numbers.

4a. $\sqrt[4]{x^4y^{12}}$ ***xy^3***

4b. $\dfrac{\left(xy^{\frac{1}{2}}\right)^2}{\sqrt[5]{x^5}}$ ***xy***

THINK AND DISCUSS

1. Explain how to find the value of $\left(\sqrt[10]{25}\right)^5$.

2. GET ORGANIZED Copy and complete the graphic organizer. In each cell, provide the definition and a numerical example of each type of exponent.

Exponent	Definition	Numerical Example
$b^{\frac{1}{n}}$		
$b^{\frac{m}{n}}$		

Power Presentations with PowerPoint®

Additional Examples

Example 4

Simplify. All variables represent nonnegative numbers.

A. $\sqrt[4]{a^4b^{20}}$ ab^5

B. $\left(x^6y^4\right)^{\frac{1}{2}}\sqrt{y^2}$ x^3y^3

INTERVENTION

Questioning Strategies

EXAMPLE 4

- How do you use properties of exponents to simplify expressions?
- How can you check your answer after you have simplified an expression?

Answers to *Think and Discuss*

1. $\left(\sqrt[10]{25}\right)^5 = 25^{\frac{5}{10}} = 25^{\frac{1}{2}} = \sqrt{25} = 5$
2. See p. A7.

3 Close

Summarize

Have students give an equivalent expression with fractional exponents for each expression below. Then have them simplify the expression.

1. $\sqrt[4]{81}$ $81^{\frac{1}{4}}$; 3
2. $\left(\sqrt{25}\right)^3$ $25^{\frac{3}{2}}$; 125
3. $\left(\sqrt[4]{256}\right)^3$ $256^{\frac{3}{4}}$; 64

Essential Question

Be sure students can answer the lesson's essential question:

How do you simplify an expression with a rational exponent? If the exponent has the form $\frac{1}{n}$, find the nth root of the base.

If the exponent has the form $\frac{m}{n}$, find the nth root of the base raised to the mth power.

ONGOING ASSESSMENT

and INTERVENTION 

***Diagnose Before* the Lesson**
7-5 Warm Up, TE p. 488

***Monitor During* the Lesson**
Check It Out! Exercises, SE pp. 488–490
Questioning Strategies, TE pp. 489–490

***Assess After* the Lesson**
7-5 Lesson Quiz, TE p. 493
Alternative Assessment, TE p. 493

7-5 Exercises

go.hrw.com
Homework Help Online
KEYWORD: MA11 7-5
Parent Resources Online
KEYWORD: MA7 Parent

7-5 Exercises

GUIDED PRACTICE

1. **Vocabulary** In the expression $\sqrt[5]{3x}$, what is the *index*? **5**

Simplify each expression.

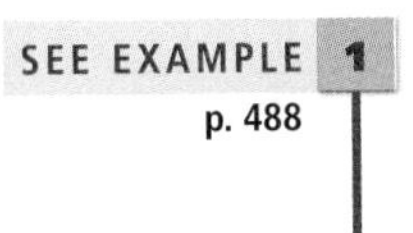

SEE EXAMPLE 1 p. 488

2. $8^{\frac{1}{3}}$ **2** 3. $16^{\frac{1}{2}}$ **4** 4. $0^{\frac{1}{6}}$ **0** 5. $27^{\frac{1}{3}}$ **3**
6. $81^{\frac{1}{2}}$ **9** 7. $216^{\frac{1}{3}}$ **6** 8. $1^{\frac{1}{9}}$ **1** 9. $625^{\frac{1}{4}}$ **5**
10. $36^{\frac{1}{2}} + 1^{\frac{1}{3}}$ **7** 11. $8^{\frac{1}{3}} + 64^{\frac{1}{2}}$ **10** 12. $81^{\frac{1}{4}} + 8^{\frac{1}{3}}$ **5** 13. $25^{\frac{1}{2}} - 1^{\frac{1}{4}}$ **4**

SEE EXAMPLE 2 p. 489

14. $81^{\frac{3}{4}}$ **27** 15. $8^{\frac{5}{3}}$ **32** 16. $125^{\frac{2}{3}}$ **25** 17. $25^{\frac{3}{2}}$ **125**
18. $36^{\frac{3}{2}}$ **216** 19. $64^{\frac{4}{3}}$ **256** 20. $1^{\frac{3}{4}}$ **1** 21. $0^{\frac{2}{3}}$ **0**

SEE EXAMPLE 3 p. 489

22. **Geometry** Given a square with area a, you can use the formula $P = 4a^{\frac{1}{2}}$ to find the perimeter P of the square. Find the perimeter of a square that has an area of 64 m^2. **32 m**

SEE EXAMPLE 4 p. 490

Simplify. All variables represent nonnegative numbers.

23. $\sqrt{x^4y^2}$ $\mathbf{x^2y}$ 24. $\sqrt[4]{z^4}$ $\mathbf{z}$ 25. $\sqrt{x^6y^6}$ $\mathbf{x^3y^3}$ 26. $\sqrt[3]{a^{12}b^6}$ $\mathbf{a^4b^2}$
27. $\left(a^{\frac{1}{2}}\right)^2\sqrt{a^2}$ $\mathbf{a^2}$ 28. $\left(x^{\frac{1}{3}}\right)^6\sqrt[4]{y^4}$ $\mathbf{x^2y}$ 29. $\dfrac{\left(z^{\frac{1}{3}}\right)^3}{\sqrt{z^2}}$ **1** 30. $\dfrac{\sqrt[3]{x^6y^9}}{x^2}$ $\mathbf{y^3}$

PRACTICE AND PROBLEM SOLVING

Independent Practice	
For Exercises	See Example
31–42	1
43–50	2
51	3
52–59	4

Extra Practice
Skills Practice p. S17
Application Practice p. S34

Simplify each expression.

31. $100^{\frac{1}{2}}$ **10** 32. $1^{\frac{1}{5}}$ **1** 33. $512^{\frac{1}{3}}$ **8** 34. $729^{\frac{1}{2}}$ **27**
35. $32^{\frac{1}{5}}$ **2** 36. $196^{\frac{1}{2}}$ **14** 37. $256^{\frac{1}{8}}$ **2** 38. $400^{\frac{1}{2}}$ **20**
39. $125^{\frac{1}{3}} + 81^{\frac{1}{2}}$ **14** 40. $25^{\frac{1}{2}} - 81^{\frac{1}{4}}$ **2** 41. $121^{\frac{1}{2}} - 243^{\frac{1}{5}}$ **8** 42. $256^{\frac{1}{4}} + 0^{\frac{1}{3}}$ **4**
43. $4^{\frac{3}{2}}$ **8** 44. $27^{\frac{2}{3}}$ **9** 45. $256^{\frac{3}{4}}$ **64** 46. $64^{\frac{5}{6}}$ **32**
47. $100^{\frac{3}{2}}$ **1000** 48. $1^{\frac{5}{3}}$ **1** 49. $9^{\frac{5}{2}}$ **243** 50. $243^{\frac{2}{5}}$ **9**

51. **Biology** Biologists use a formula to estimate the mass of a mammal's brain. For a mammal with a mass of m grams, the approximate mass B of the brain, also in grams, is given by $B = \frac{1}{8}m^{\frac{2}{3}}$. Find the approximate mass of the brain of a mouse that has a mass of 64 grams. **2g**

Simplify. All variables represent nonnegative numbers.

52. $\sqrt[3]{a^6c^9}$ $\mathbf{a^2c^3}$ 53. $\sqrt[3]{8m^3}$ $\mathbf{2m}$ 54. $\sqrt[4]{x^{16}y^4}$ $\mathbf{x^4y}$ 55. $\sqrt[3]{27x^6}$ $\mathbf{3x^2}$
56. $\left(x^{\frac{1}{2}}y^3\right)^2\sqrt{x^2}$ $\mathbf{x^2y^6}$ 57. $(a^2b^4)^{\frac{1}{2}}\sqrt[3]{b^6}$ $\mathbf{ab^4}$ 58. $\dfrac{\sqrt[3]{x^6y^6}}{yx^2}$ $\mathbf{y}$ 59. $\dfrac{\left(a^2b^{\frac{1}{2}}\right)^4}{\sqrt{b^2}}$ $\mathbf{a^8b}$

Fill in the boxes to make each statement true.

60. $256^{\frac{\square}{4}} = 4$ **1** 61. $\square^{\frac{1}{5}} = 1$ **1** 62. $225^{\frac{1}{\square}} = 15$ **2** 63. $\square^{\frac{1}{6}} = 0$ **0**
64. $64^{\frac{\square}{3}} = 16$ **2** 65. $\square^{\frac{3}{4}} = 125$ **625** 66. $27^{\frac{4}{\square}} = 81$ **3** 67. $36^{\frac{\square}{2}} = 216$ **3**

Assignment Guide

Assign *Guided Practice* exercises as necessary.

If you finished Examples **1–2**
Basic 31–50, 87, 88
Average 32–50 even, 60–78 even, 98–107
Advanced 32–50 even, 60–78 even, 86–88, 91–93, 98–107

If you finished Examples **1–4**
Basic 32–58 even, 60–80, 85, 87–90, 98–107
Average 32–58 even, 60–90, 92–96 even, 98–107
Advanced 32–80 even, 81–107

Homework Quick Check
Quickly check key concepts.
Exercises: 34, 40, 44, 51, 52, 56

State Resources

go.hrw.com
State Resources Online
KEYWORD: MA7 Resources

MULTI-STEP TEST PREP Exercise 85 involves using rational exponents to model a real-world situation related to light. This exercise prepares students for the Multi-Step Test Prep on page 494.

Answers

86. $4^{\frac{3}{2}} = 4^{3\cdot\frac{1}{2}} = (4^3)^{\frac{1}{2}} = 64^{\frac{1}{2}} = 8$; $4^{\frac{3}{2}} = 4^{\frac{1}{2}\cdot 3} = \left(4^{\frac{1}{2}}\right)^3 = 2^3 = 8$. It is often easier to take the square root first so that the remaining numbers in the calculation are smaller.

101. $n < 3$

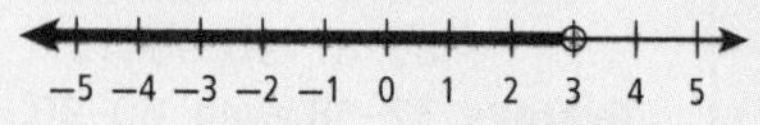

102. $x \geq 2$

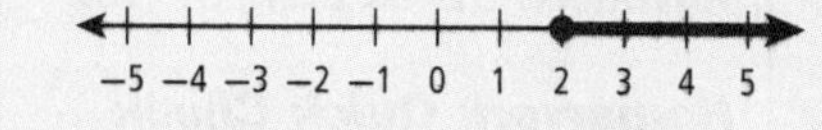

103. $y \leq -2$

−5 −4 −3 −2 −1 0 1 2 3 4 5

104. D: {2}; R: {3, 4, 5, 6}; no; the domain value 2 is paired with several different range values.

105. D: {−2, −1, −0, 1}; R: {0, 1, 2, 3}; yes; each domain value is paired with exactly one range value.

106. D: {5, 7, 9, 11}; R: {2}; yes; each domain value is paired with exactly one range value.

107. D: $1 \leq x \leq 4$; R: $2 \leq y \leq 4$; yes; each domain value is paired with exactly one range value.

Simplify each expression.

68. $\left(\frac{81}{169}\right)^{\frac{1}{2}}$ $\frac{9}{13}$

69. $\left(\frac{8}{27}\right)^{\frac{1}{3}}$ $\frac{2}{3}$

70. $\left(\frac{256}{81}\right)^{\frac{1}{4}}$ $\frac{4}{3}$

71. $\left(\frac{1}{16}\right)^{\frac{1}{2}}$ $\frac{1}{4}$

72. $\left(\frac{9}{16}\right)^{\frac{3}{2}}$ $\frac{27}{64}$

73. $\left(\frac{8}{27}\right)^{\frac{2}{3}}$ $\frac{4}{9}$

74. $\left(\frac{16}{81}\right)^{\frac{3}{4}}$ $\frac{8}{27}$

75. $\left(\frac{4}{49}\right)^{\frac{3}{2}}$ $\frac{8}{343}$

76. $\left(\frac{4}{25}\right)^{\frac{3}{2}}$ $\frac{8}{125}$

77. $\left(\frac{1}{81}\right)^{\frac{3}{4}}$ $\frac{1}{27}$

78. $\left(\frac{27}{64}\right)^{\frac{2}{3}}$ $\frac{9}{16}$

79. $\left(\frac{8}{125}\right)^{\frac{4}{3}}$ $\frac{16}{625}$

80. **Multi-Step** Scientists have found that the life span of a mammal living in captivity is related to the mammal's mass. The life span in years L can be approximated by the formula $L = 12m^{\frac{1}{5}}$, where m is the mammal's mass in kilograms. How much longer is the life span of a lion compared with that of a wolf? **12 years**

Typical Mass of Mammals	
Mammal	**Mass (kg)**
Koala	8
Wolf	32
Lion	243
Giraffe	1024

81. **Geometry** Given a sphere with volume V, the formula $r = 0.62V^{\frac{1}{3}}$ may be used to approximate the sphere's radius r. Find the approximate radius of a sphere that has a volume of 27 in³. **1.86 in.**

82. **Critical Thinking** Show that a number raised to the power $\frac{1}{3}$ is the same as the cube root of that number. (*Hint:* Use properties of exponents to find the cube of $b^{\frac{1}{3}}$. Then compare this with the cube of $\sqrt[3]{b}$. Use the fact that if two numbers have the same cube, then they are equal.)

83. **Critical Thinking** Compare $n^{\frac{2}{3}}$ and $n^{\frac{3}{2}}$ for values of n greater than 1. When simplifying each of these expressions, will the result be greater than n or less than n? Explain.

84. **/// ERROR ANALYSIS ///** Two students simplified $64^{\frac{3}{2}}$. Which solution is incorrect? Explain the error.

82. $\left(b^{\frac{1}{3}}\right)^3 = b^{\frac{1}{3}\cdot 3} = b^1 = b$. Also, by definition $\left(\sqrt[3]{b}\right)^3 = b$. Therefore, $b^{\frac{1}{3}} = \sqrt[3]{b}$.

83. $n^{\frac{2}{3}}$ will be less than n because $\frac{2}{3} < 1$. $n^{\frac{3}{2}}$ will be greater than n because $\frac{3}{2} > 1$.

84. Solution A is incorrect. The first line should be $64^{\frac{3}{2}} = \left(\sqrt{64}\right)^3$.

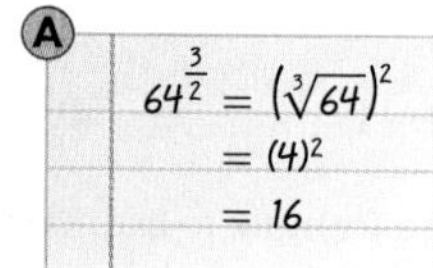

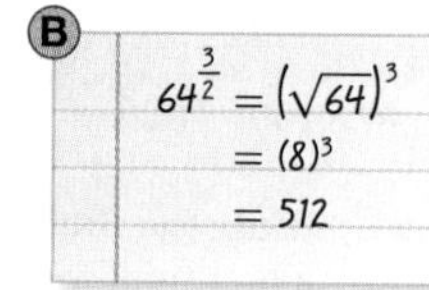

85. This problem will prepare you for the Multi-Step Test Prep on page 494. You can estimate an object's distance in inches from a light source by using the formula $d = \left(0.8\frac{L}{B}\right)^{\frac{1}{2}}$, where L is the light's luminosity in lumens and B is the light's brightness in lumens per square inch.

a. Find an object's distance to a light source with a luminosity of 4000 lumens and a brightness of 32 lumens per square inch. **10 in.**

b. Suppose the brightness of this light source decreases to 8 lumens per square inch. How does the object's distance from the source change? **The distance doubles (20 in.)**

7-5 PRACTICE A

7-5 PRACTICE C

7-5 PRACTICE B

Simplify each expression. All variables represent nonnegative numbers.

1. $27^{\frac{1}{3}}$ **3**
2. $121^{\frac{1}{2}}$ **11**
3. $0^{\frac{1}{3}}$ **0**
4. $64^{\frac{1}{2}} + 27^{\frac{1}{3}}$ **11**
5. $16^{\frac{1}{4}} + 8^{\frac{1}{3}}$ **4**
6. $100^{\frac{1}{2}} - 64^{\frac{1}{6}}$ **8**
7. $1^{\frac{1}{5}} + 49^{\frac{1}{2}}$ **8**
8. $25^{\frac{3}{2}}$ **125**
9. $32^{\frac{3}{5}}$ **8**
10. $16^{\frac{3}{4}}$ **8**
11. $1^{\frac{5}{6}}$ **1**
12. $121^{\frac{3}{2}}$ **1331**
13. $\sqrt[5]{y^5}$ **y**
14. $\sqrt{x^4y^{12}}$ **x^2y^6**
15. $\sqrt[3]{a^6b^3}$ **a^2b**
16. $(x^{\frac{1}{2}})^4\sqrt{x^6}$ **x^5**
17. $(x^{\frac{1}{3}}y)^3\sqrt{x^2y^2}$ **x^2y^4**
18. $\frac{(x^{\frac{1}{4}})^8}{\sqrt[3]{x^3}}$ **x**
19. Given a cube with volume V, you can use the formula $P = 4V^{\frac{1}{3}}$ to find the perimeter of one of the cube's square faces. Find the perimeter of a face of a cube that has volume 125 m³.
20 m

7-5 READING STRATEGIES

The table below summarizes the definitions you need when you work with fractional exponents.

Definition of $b^{\frac{1}{n}}$	A number raised to the power of $\frac{1}{n}$ is equal to the nth root of that number.	$9^{\frac{1}{2}} = \sqrt{9} = 3$ $32^{\frac{1}{5}} = \sqrt[5]{32} = 2$ $125^{\frac{1}{3}} = \sqrt[3]{125} = 5$	In general, if $b > 1$ and n is an integer where $n \geq 2$, then $b^{\frac{1}{n}} = \sqrt[n]{b}$.
Definition of $b^{\frac{m}{n}}$	A number raised to the power of $\frac{m}{n}$ is equal to the nth root of the number raised to the mth power.	$16^{\frac{3}{4}} = \left(\sqrt[4]{16}\right)^3 = 2^3 = 8$ $100^{\frac{3}{2}} = \left(\sqrt{100}\right)^3 = 10^3 = 1000$	In general, if $b > 1$ and m and n are integers where $m \geq 1$ and $n \geq 2$, then $b^{\frac{m}{n}} = \left(\sqrt[n]{b}\right)^m = \sqrt[n]{b^m}$.

Complete each of the following.

1. The expression $27^{\frac{1}{3}}$ is equal to the **3rd or cube** root of 27.
2. The expression $9^{\frac{5}{2}}$ is equal to the square root of 9 raised to the **5th** power.
3. The expression $32^{\frac{4}{5}}$ is equal to the **5th** root of 32 raised to the **4th** power.

Simplify each expression.

4. $8^{\frac{1}{3}}$ **2**
5. $81^{\frac{1}{2}}$ **9**
6. $16^{\frac{1}{4}}$ **2**
7. $400^{\frac{1}{2}}$ **20**
8. $32^{\frac{2}{5}}$ **4**
9. $81^{\frac{3}{4}}$ **27**
10. $4^{\frac{3}{2}}$ **8**
11. $16^{\frac{5}{2}}$ **1024**
12. $256^{\frac{3}{4}}$ **64**

7-5 RETEACH

To simplify a number raised to the power of $\frac{1}{n}$, write the nth root of the number.

Simplify $216^{\frac{1}{3}}$.

$216^{\frac{1}{3}} = \sqrt[3]{216} = 6$

Think: What number, when taken as a factor 3 times, is equal to 216? $6^3 = 6 \times 6 \times 6 = 216$, so $\sqrt[3]{216} = 6$.

When an expression contains two or more expressions with fractional exponents, evaluate the expressions with the exponents first, then add or subtract.

Simplify $81^{\frac{1}{2}} + 32^{\frac{1}{5}}$.

$81^{\frac{1}{2}} + 32^{\frac{1}{5}} = \sqrt{81} + \sqrt[5]{32} = 9 + 2 = 11$

Simplify each expression.

1. $64^{\frac{1}{2}}$ **8**
2. $1000^{\frac{1}{3}}$ **10**
3. $1^{\frac{1}{5}}$ **1**
4. $256^{\frac{1}{4}}$ **4**
5. $32^{\frac{1}{5}}$ **2**
6. $49^{\frac{1}{2}}$ **7**
7. $8^{\frac{1}{3}} + 16^{\frac{1}{2}}$ **6**
8. $121^{\frac{1}{2}} + 27^{\frac{1}{3}}$ **14**
9. $32^{\frac{1}{5}} + 1^{\frac{1}{2}}$ **3**
10. $81^{\frac{1}{4}} - 16^{\frac{1}{4}}$ **1**
11. $144^{\frac{1}{2}} - 125^{\frac{1}{3}}$ **7**
12. $625^{\frac{1}{4}} - 0^{\frac{1}{2}}$ **5**

86. **Write About It** You can write $4^{\frac{3}{2}}$ as $4^{3 \cdot \frac{1}{2}}$ or as $4^{\frac{1}{2} \cdot 3}$. Use the Power of a Power Property to show that both expressions are equal. Is one method easier than the other? Explain.

TEST PREP

87. What is $9^{\frac{1}{2}} + 8^{\frac{1}{3}}$?
(A) 4 **(B) 5** (C) 6 (D) 10

88. Which expression is equal to 8?
(F) $4^{\frac{3}{2}}$ (G) $16^{\frac{1}{2}}$ (H) $32^{\frac{4}{5}}$ (J) $64^{\frac{3}{2}}$

89. Which expression is equivalent to $\sqrt[3]{a^9b^3}$?
(A) a^2b (B) a^3 **(C) a^3b** (D) a^3b^3

90. Which of the following is NOT equal to $16^{\frac{3}{2}}$?
(F) $(\sqrt{16})^3$ (G) 4^3 **(H) $(\sqrt[3]{16})^2$** (J) $\sqrt{16^3}$

CHALLENGE AND EXTEND

Use properties of exponents to simplify each expression.

91. $\left(a^{\frac{1}{3}}\right)\left(a^{\frac{1}{3}}\right)\left(a^{\frac{1}{3}}\right)$ **a**
92. $\left(x^{\frac{1}{2}}\right)^5\left(x^{\frac{3}{2}}\right)$ **x^4**
93. $\left(x^{\frac{1}{3}}\right)^4\left(x^5\right)^{\frac{1}{3}}$ **x^3**

You can use properties of exponents to help you solve equations. For example, to solve $x^3 = 64$, raise both sides to the $\frac{1}{3}$ power to get $(x^3)^{\frac{1}{3}} = 64^{\frac{1}{3}}$. Simplifying both sides gives $x = 4$. Use this method to solve each equation. Check your answer.

94. $y^5 = 32$ **2**
95. $27x^3 = 729$ **3**
96. $1 = \frac{1}{8}x^3$ **2**

97. **Geometry** The formula for the surface area of a sphere S in terms of its volume V is $S = (4\pi)^{\frac{1}{3}}(3V)^{\frac{2}{3}}$. What is the surface area of a sphere that has a volume of 36π cm^3? Leave the symbol π in your answer. What do you notice? **36π cm^2; both volume and surface area are described by 36π (although the units are different).**

SPIRAL REVIEW

Solve each equation. *(Lesson 2-6)*

98. $|x + 6| = 2$ **−8, −4**
99. $|5x + 5| = 0$ **−1**
100. $|2x - 1| = 3$ **−1, 2**

Solve each inequality and graph the solutions. *(Lesson 3-4)*

101. $3n + 5 < 14$
102. $4 \le \frac{1}{2}x + 3$
103. $7 \ge 2y + 11$

Give the domain and range of each relation. Tell whether the relation is a function. Explain. *(Lesson 4-2)*

104. $\{(2, 3), (2, 4), (2, 5), (2, 6)\}$
105. $\{(-2, 0), (-1, 1), (0, 2), (1, 3)\}$

106.

x	y
5	2
7	2
9	2
11	2

107.

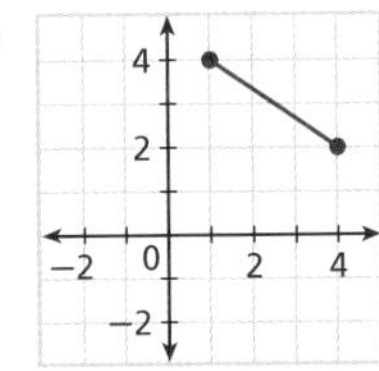

COMMON ERROR ALERT

In **Exercise 80,** students might multiply by 12 before evaluating the fifth root of m. Remind students of the order of operations: grouping symbols, exponents, multiply/divide, add/subtract. Remind them that radical signs are grouping symbols.

TEST PREP DOCTOR + If students answer **B** for **Exercise 89,** they may think that $\sqrt[3]{b^3} = 1$ or $(b^3)^{\frac{1}{3}} = 1$. Remind them that cubing a number and taking the cube root are inverse operations that "undo" each other, so $\sqrt[3]{b^3} = (b^3)^{\frac{1}{3}} = b$.

Journal

Have students write the steps they would use to simplify $729^{\frac{5}{6}}$.

ALTERNATIVE ASSESSMENT

Have students write a quiz on rational exponents. The quiz should include five problems about simplifying expressions of various types. The quiz should also include answers.

Power Presentations with PowerPoint®

7-5 Lesson Quiz

Simplify each expression.

1. $16^{\frac{1}{4}}$ 2
2. $144^{\frac{1}{2}} - 27^{\frac{1}{3}}$ 9
3. $81^{\frac{3}{2}}$ 729
4. $64^{\frac{7}{6}}$ 128
5. In an experiment, the approximate population P of a bacteria colony is given by $P = 15t^{\frac{5}{3}}$, where t is the number of days since the start of the experiment. Find the population of the colony on the 8th day. 480

Simplify. All variables represent nonnegative numbers.

6. $\sqrt[5]{x^{10}z^5}$ x^2z
7. $\left(a^4b^{\frac{1}{4}}\right)^4\sqrt[3]{b^3}$ $a^{16}b^2$

Also available on transparency

7-5 PROBLEM SOLVING

Write the correct answer.

1. For a pendulum with a length of L meters, the time in seconds that it takes the pendulum to swing back and forth is approximately $2L^{\frac{1}{2}}$. About how long does it take a pendulum that is 9 meters long to swing back and forth?
6 s

2. The Beaufort Scale is used to measure the intensity of tornados. For a tornado with Beaufort number B, the formula $v = 1.9B^{\frac{3}{2}}$ may be used to estimate the tornado's wind speed in miles per hour. Estimate the wind speed of a tornado with Beaufort number 9.
51.3 mi/h

3. Given a cube whose faces each have area A, the volume of the cube is given by the formula $V = A^{\frac{3}{2}}$. Find the volume of a cube whose faces each have an area of 64 in^2.
512 in^3

4. At a factory that makes cylindrical cans, the formula $r = \left(\frac{V}{12}\right)^{\frac{1}{2}}$ is used to find the radius of a can with volume V. What is the radius of a can whose volume is 192 cm^3?
4 cm

Given an animal's body mass m, in grams, the formula $B = 1.8m^{\frac{3}{4}}$ may be used to estimate the mass B, in grams, of the animal's brain The table shows the body mass of several birds. Use the table for questions 5–7. Select the best answer.

5. Which is the best estimate for the brain mass of a macaw?
A 9 g
B 45 g
C 125 g
D 225 g

6. How much larger is the brain mass of a barn owl compared to the brain mass of a cockatiel?
F 189 g
G 340.2 g
H 388.8 g
J 1215 g

7. An animal has a body mass given by the expression x^4. Which expression can be used to estimate the animal's brain mass?
A $B = 1.8x^3$
B $B = 1.8x^{\frac{3}{4}}$
C $B = 1.8x^{12}$
D $B = 1.8x$

Typical Body Masses of Birds

Bird	Body Mass (g)
Cockatiel	81
Guam Rail	256
Macaw	625
Barn Owl	1296

Sources:
http://www.beyondveg.com/billings-t/comp-anat/comp-anat-appx2.shtml
http://www.sandiegozoo.org/animalbytes/index.html

7-5 CHALLENGE

Find a path from start to finish in the maze below. Each box that you pass through must have a value that is *greater than or equal to* the value in the previous box. You may only move horizontally or vertically to go from one box to the next.

START

$16^{\frac{1}{4}}$	$4^{\frac{1}{2}} - 27^{\frac{1}{3}}$	$0^{\frac{1}{5}}$	$1^{\frac{2}{3}} - 8^{\frac{1}{3}}$	$216^{\frac{2}{3}}$	$8^{\frac{1}{3}} + 9^{\frac{3}{2}}$
$36^{\frac{1}{2}} - 216^{\frac{1}{3}}$	$25^{\frac{1}{2}} - 32^{\frac{2}{5}}$	$9^{\frac{1}{2}} - 8^{\frac{1}{3}}$	$1^{\frac{3}{5}}$	$64^{\frac{1}{6}}$	$100^{\frac{1}{2}} + 27^{\frac{2}{3}}$
$1^{\frac{1}{2}} - 9^{\frac{3}{2}}$	$125^{\frac{2}{3}}$	$81^{\frac{3}{4}}$	$1000^{\frac{2}{3}}$	$16^{\frac{1}{2}} - 16^{\frac{1}{4}}$	$32^{\frac{1}{5}} + 0^{\frac{3}{4}}$
$512^{\frac{2}{9}}$	$9^{\frac{1}{2}} + 3^{\frac{4}{4}}$	$32^{\frac{2}{5}}$	$27^{\frac{1}{3}}$	$121^0 + 1^{\frac{1}{2}}$	$9^{\frac{1}{2}} - 3^0$
$49^{\frac{1}{2}} + 0^{\frac{1}{2}}$	$16^{\frac{3}{4}}$	$16^{\frac{1}{4}} - 1^{\frac{3}{2}}$	$1024^{\frac{1}{10}}$	$81^{\frac{1}{4}} + 49^{\frac{1}{2}}$	$243^{\frac{4}{5}}$
$16^{\frac{3}{4}} + 32^{\frac{1}{5}}$	$100^{\frac{1}{2}}$	$625^{\frac{1}{4}}$	$128^{\frac{2}{7}}$	$144^{\frac{1}{2}} - 81^{\frac{1}{2}}$	$64^{\frac{1}{3}}$
$125^{\frac{1}{3}} - 2^0$	$81^{\frac{3}{4}} - 32^{\frac{4}{5}}$	$256^{\frac{1}{2}}$	$16^{\frac{3}{4}} + 4^{\frac{3}{2}}$	$64^{\frac{2}{3}}$	$32^{\frac{1}{5}} + 100^{\frac{1}{2}}$
$625^{\frac{1}{4}}$	$64^{\frac{5}{6}} - 125^{\frac{2}{3}}$	$243^{\frac{2}{5}}$	$125^{\frac{2}{3}}$	$128^{\frac{3}{7}}$	$243^{\frac{1}{5}}$

FINISH

SECTION 7A MULTI-STEP TEST PREP

Organizer

Objective: Assess students' ability to apply concepts and skills in Lessons 7-1 through 7-5 in a real-world format.

PREMIER Online Edition

Resources

Algebra I Assessments
www.mathtekstoolkit.org

Problem	Text Reference
1	Lesson 7-1
2	Lesson 7-2
3	Lesson 7-3
4	Lesson 7-3
5	Lesson 7-4

Answers

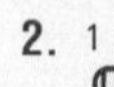

2. 1×10^{15}

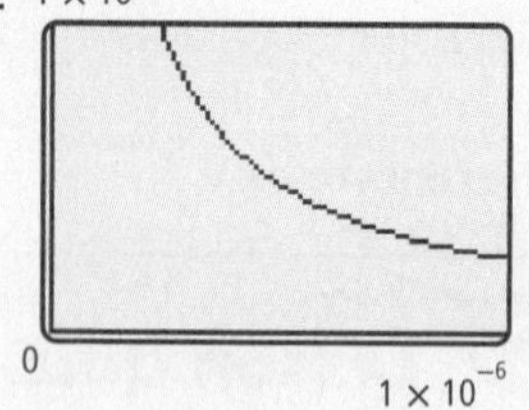

As the wavelength increases, the frequency decreases.

State Resources

CHAPTER 7

MULTI-STEP TEST PREP

SECTION 7A

Exponents

I See the Light! The speed of light is the product of its frequency f and its wavelength w. In air, the speed of light is 3×10^8 m/s.

1. $f = \frac{3 \times 10^8}{w}$; $f = (3 \times 10^8)w^{-1}$

1. Write an equation for the relationship described above, and then solve this equation for frequency. Write this equation as an equation with w raised to a negative exponent.
2. Wavelengths of visible light range from 400 to 700 nanometers (10^{-9} meters). Use a graphing calculator and the relationship you found in Problem 1 to graph frequency as a function of wavelength. Sketch the graph with the axes clearly labeled. Describe your graph.
3. The speed of light in water is $\frac{3}{4}$ of its speed in air. Find the speed of light in water. **2.25×10^8 m/s**
4. When light enters water, some colors bend more than others. How much the light bends depends on its wavelength. This is what creates a rainbow. The frequency of green light is about 5.9×10^{14} cycles per second. Find the wavelength of green light in water. **about 3.81×10^{-7} m**
5. When light enters water, colors with shorter wavelengths bend more than colors with longer wavelengths. Violet light has a frequency of 7.5×10^{14} cycles per second, and red light has a frequency of 4.6×10^{14} cycles per second. Which of these colors of light will bend more when it enters water? Justify your answer.

Violet light will bend more. Students can justify by using the inverse relationship, by using the graph, or by finding the wavelength for each color and comparing them.

INTERVENTION

Scaffolding Questions

1. What does it mean to "solve for frequency"? Isolate the variable that represents frequency.
2. What are a reasonable domain and range? Possible answer: D: 380 to 760; R: 3×10^{14} to 9×10^{14}
3. How do you enter numbers in scientific notation into a calculator? Possible answer: 3×10^{14} is entered as 3 [2nd] [,] (EE) 14 or 3 [×] [LOG] (10^x) 14.

4. What information do you need for this problem? speed of light in water Where can you find this information? answer to Problem 3
5. How does wavelength change as frequency changes? As one increases, the other decreases.

Extension

When you choose an FM radio station, you are choosing the frequency in MHz, or millions of waves per second (90 MHz = 90,000,000 waves per second). Find the wavelength for your favorite FM radio station. Possible answer: Using $w = (3 \times 10^8) f^{-1}$, FM 93.7 has an approximate wavelength of 3.2 m.

READY TO GO ON?

Quiz for Lessons 7-1 Through 7-5

7-1 Integer Exponents

Evaluate each expression for the given value(s) of the variable(s).

1. t^{-6} for $t = 2$ $\frac{1}{64}$
2. n^{-3} for $n = -5$ $-\frac{1}{125}$
3. $r^0 s^{-2}$ for $r = 8$ and $s = 10$ $\frac{1}{100}$

Simplify.

4. $5k^{-3}$ $\frac{5}{k^3}$
5. $\frac{x^4}{y^{-6}}$ x^4y^6
6. $8f^{-4}g^0$ $\frac{8}{f^4}$
7. $\frac{a^{-3}}{b^{-2}}$ $\frac{b^2}{a^3}$
8. **Measurement** Metric units can be written in terms of a base unit. The table shows some of these equivalencies. Simplify each expression.

Selected Metric Prefixes					
Milli-	Centi-	Deci-	Deka-	Hecto-	Kilo-
10^{-3}	10^{-2}	10^{-1}	10^1	10^2	10^3

7-2 Powers of 10 and Scientific Notation

9. Find the value of 10^4. **10,000**
10. Write 0.0000001 as a power of 10. 10^{-7}
11. Write 100,000,000,000 as a power of 10. 10^{11}
12. Find the value of 82.1×10^4. **821,000**
13. **Measurement** The lead in a mechanical pencil has a diameter of 0.5 mm. Write this number in scientific notation. 5×10^{-1}

7-3 Multiplication Properties of Exponents

Simplify.

14. $2^2 \cdot 2^5$ 2^7
15. $3^5 \cdot 3^{-3}$ 3^2, or 9
16. $p^4 \cdot p^5$ p^9
17. $a^3 \cdot a^{-6} \cdot a^{-2}$ $\frac{1}{a^5}$
18. **Biology** A swarm of locusts was estimated to contain 2.8×10^{10} individual insects. If each locust weighs about 2.5 grams, how much did this entire swarm weigh? Write your answer in scientific notation. 7×10^{10} g

Simplify.

19. $(3x^4)^3$ $27x^{12}$
20. $(m^3n^2)^5$ $m^{15}n^{10}$
21. $(-4d^7)^2$ $16d^{14}$
22. $(cd^6)^3 \cdot (c^5d^2)^2$ $c^{13}d^{22}$

7-4 Division Properties of Exponents

Simplify.

23. $\frac{6^9}{6^7}$ 36
24. $\frac{12a^5}{3a^2}$ $4a^3$
25. $\left(\frac{3}{5}\right)^3$ $\frac{27}{125}$
26. $\left(\frac{4p^3}{2pq^4}\right)^2$ $\frac{4p^4}{q^8}$

Simplify each quotient and write the answer in scientific notation.

27. $(8 \times 10^9) \div (2 \times 10^6)$ 4×10^3
28. $(3.5 \times 10^5) \div (7 \times 10^8)$ 5×10^{-4}
29. $(1 \times 10^4) \div (4 \times 10^4)$ 2.5×10^{-1}

7-5 Rational Exponents

Simplify each expression. All variables represent nonnegative numbers.

30. $81^{\frac{1}{2}}$ 9
31. $125^{\frac{1}{3}}$ 5
32. $4^{\frac{3}{2}}$ 8
33. $0^{\frac{2}{9}}$ 0
34. $\sqrt{x^8y^4}$ x^4y^2
35. $\sqrt[3]{r^9}$ r^3
36. $\sqrt[6]{z^{12}}$ z^2
37. $\sqrt[3]{p^3q^{12}}$ pq^4

READY TO GO ON? SECTION 7A

Organizer

Objective: Assess students' mastery of concepts and skills in Lessons 7-1 through 7-5.

Resources

Assessment Resources

Section 7A Quiz

Teacher One Stop™

Test & Practice Generator

INTERVENTION

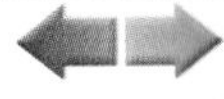

Resources

Ready to Go On? Intervention and Enrichment **Worksheets**

Ready to Go On? **CD-ROM**

Answers

8. $10^{-3} = \frac{1}{1000}$, or 0.001; $10^{-2} = \frac{1}{100}$, or 0.01; $10^{-1} = \frac{1}{10}$, or 0.1; $10^1 = 10$; $10^2 = 100$; $10^3 = 1000$

READY TO GO ON? Diagnose and Prescribe

NO INTERVENE

Ready to Go On? Intervention	READY TO GO ON? Intervention, Section 7A: Worksheets	CD-ROM	Online
Lesson 7-1	7-1 Intervention	Activity 7-1	Diagnose and Prescribe Onlinew
Lesson 7-2	7-2 Intervention	Activity 7-2	
Lesson 7-3	7-3 Intervention	Activity 7-3	
Lesson 7-4	7-4 Intervention	Activity 7-4	
Lesson 7-5	7-5 Intervention	Activity 7-5	

YES ENRICH

READY TO GO ON? Enrichment, Section 7A

Worksheets

CD-ROM

Online

SECTION

7B Polynomials

One-Minute Section Planner

Lesson	Lab Resources	Materials
Lesson 7-6 Polynomials • Classify polynomials and write polynomials in standard form. • Evaluate polynomial expressions. ☐ SAT-10 ☑ NAEP ☑ ACT ☑ SAT ☑ SAT Subject Tests		**Optional** index cards, scissors, tape, ruler (MK), 8.5-by-11 inch paper
7-7 Algebra Lab Model Polynomial Addition and Subtraction • Use algebra tiles to model polynomial addition and subtraction. ☐ SAT-10 ☑ NAEP ☐ ACT ☐ SAT ☐ SAT Subject Tests	***Algebra Lab Activities*** 7-7 Lab Recording Sheet	**Required** algebra tiles (MK)
Lesson 7-7 Adding and Subtracting Polynomials • Add and subtract polynomials. ☑ SAT-10 ☑ NAEP ☑ ACT ☐ SAT ☐ SAT Subject Tests	***Technology Lab Activities*** 7-7 Technology Lab	**Optional** books, pencils, slips of paper
7-8 Algebra Lab Model Polynomial Multiplication • Use algebra tiles to model polynomial multiplication. ☐ SAT-10 ☐ NAEP ☐ ACT ☐ SAT ☐ SAT Subject Tests	***Algebra Lab Activities*** 7-8 Lab Recording Sheet	**Required** algebra tiles (MK)
Lesson 7-8 Multiplying Polynomials • Multiply polynomials. ☐ SAT-10 ☑ NAEP ☑ ACT ☐ SAT ☐ SAT Subject Tests		
Lesson 7-9 Special Products of Binomials • Find special products of binomials ☐ SAT-10 ☑ NAEP ☑ ACT ☐ SAT ☐ SAT Subject Tests		

Note: If NAEP is checked, the content is tested on either the Grade 8 or Grade 12 NAEP assessment.

MK = *Manipulatives Kit*

Math Background

Professional Learning

TERMINOLOGY

Lesson 7-6

In order to discuss polynomials, we must agree on terminology. The basic unit is the *monomial.* A monomial is a product of a real number and one or more variables with whole-number exponents. (The real number is usually rational, particularly within the scope of Algebra 1, but this is not a requirement.) A *polynomial* is a sum of monomials. For example, the polynomial $8x^4 - 3x - 1$ may be written as $8x^4 + (-3x) + (-1)$, which is the sum of the monomials $8x^4$, $-3x$, and -1.

POLYNOMIALS

Lesson 7-6

Polynomials are in many ways analogous to counting numbers. Because our number system is base 10, all counting numbers can be written in expanded form in terms of powers of 10. For example, consider the expanded form of 653.

$$\begin{aligned} 653 &= 6 \cdot 100 + 5 \cdot 10 + 3 \cdot 1 \\ &= 6 \cdot 10^2 + 5 \cdot 10^1 + 3 \cdot 10^0 \end{aligned}$$

You can create a polynomial by replacing each of the 10s by a variable, such as x.

$$\begin{array}{ccc} 6 \cdot 10^2 + & 5 \cdot 10^1 + & 3 \cdot 10^0 \\ \downarrow & \downarrow & \downarrow \\ 6 \cdot x^2 + & 5 \cdot x^1 + & 3 \cdot x^0 \end{array}$$

This polynomial is usually written in the more familiar form $6x^2 + 5x + 3$. For counting numbers, the only permissible multipliers of the powers of 10 are the digits 0 through 9, inclusive. For polynomials, any real number can be a multiplier of the variable terms. The goal of this analogy is not to suggest that there is a correspondence between counting numbers and polynomials but to demonstrate that diverse mathematical concepts sometimes share underlying structures. As such, it makes sense to pose some of the same questions about polynomials that one might pose about counting numbers. For example, can we add, subtract, multiply, and divide polynomials? How?

POLYNOMIAL OPERATIONS

Lessons 7-7 to 7-9

Adding and subtracting polynomials is fairly straightforward because the process is nothing more than combining like terms.

$$(3x^2 + 7x + 5) + (2x + 6) = 3x^2 + 9x + 11$$

Polynomial multiplication can present greater difficulty for students, so it is essential to build gradually. Multiplication of two monomials is a natural starting point. You can use the Commutative and Associative Properties to show that $(4x)(2x) = 8x^2$.

Use the Distributive Property when multiplying a monomial and a binomial:

$$5x(2x + 3) = (5x)(2x) + (5x)(3) = 10x^2 + 15x$$

The Distributive Property is used repeatedly when multiplying a binomial by a binomial:

$$\begin{aligned} (3x + 2)(7x + 4) &= (3x)(7x + 4) + (2)(7x + 4) \\ &= 21x^2 + 12x + 14x + 8 \\ &= 21x^2 + 26x + 8 \end{aligned}$$

In fact, the Distributive Property can be used to multiply any two polynomials, regardless of the number of terms. The product will have one term for each product of a term from the first polynomial and a term from the second polynomial. So, the product of a binomial (2 terms) and a trinomial (3 terms) will have $2 \cdot 3 = 6$ terms before simplifying:

$$\begin{aligned} &(x + 2)(x^2 + 6x + 8) \\ &= (x + 2)(x^2) + (x + 2)(6x) + (x + 2)(8) \\ &= (x)(x^2) + 2(x^2) + x(6x) + 2(6x) + x(8) + 2(8) \end{aligned}$$

It is important to remember that this rule is true before the product is simplified. Clearly, some of the terms above are like terms and will be combined; the final answer will have fewer than 6 terms. In general, the product of a polynomial with m terms and a polynomial with n terms has mn terms before simplifying.

7-6 Organizer

Pacing: Traditional 1 day
Block $\frac{1}{2}$ day

Objectives: Classify polynomials and write polynomials in standard form.

Evaluate polynomial expressions.

Online Edition
Tutorial Videos

Countdown Week 16

Power Presentations with PowerPoint®

Warm Up

Evaluate each expression for the given value of *x*.

1. $2x + 3; x = 2$ 7
2. $x^2 + 4; x = -3$ 13
3. $-4x - 2; x = -1$ 2
4. $7x^2 + 2x; x = 3$ 69

Identify the coefficient in each term.

5. $4x^3$ 4
6. y^3 1
7. $2n^7$ 2
8. $-s^4$ −1

Also available on transparency

Math Humor

Q: What happened to the quadratic polynomial when he fell asleep on the beach?

A: He got second-degree burns.

7-6 Polynomials

Objectives
Classify polynomials and write polynomials in standard form.

Evaluate polynomial expressions.

Vocabulary
monomial
degree of a monomial
polynomial
degree of a polynomial
standard form of a polynomial
leading coefficient
quadratic
cubic
binomial
trinomial

Who uses this?
Pyrotechnicians can use polynomials to plan complex fireworks displays. (See Example 5.)

A **monomial** is a number, a variable, or a product of numbers and variables with whole-number exponents.

Monomials	Not Monomials
$5 \quad x \quad -7xy \quad 0.5x^4$	$-0.3x^{-2} \quad 4x - y \quad \frac{2}{x^3}$

The **degree of a monomial** is the sum of the exponents of the variables. A constant has degree 0.

EXAMPLE 1 Finding the Degree of a Monomial

Find the degree of each monomial.

A $-2a^2b^4$
The degree is 6. *Add the exponents of the variables: 2 + 4 = 6*

B 4
$4x^0$ *There is no variable, but you can write 4 as $4x^0$.*
The degree is 0.

C $8y$
$8y^1$ *A variable written without an exponent has exponent 1.*
The degree is 1.

Remember!
The *terms* of an expression are the parts being added or subtracted. See Lesson 1-7.

CHECK IT OUT! Find the degree of each monomial.
1a. $1.5k^2m$ **3** **1b.** $4x$ **1** **1c.** $2c^3$ **3**

A **polynomial** is a monomial or a sum or difference of monomials. The **degree of a polynomial** is the degree of the term with the greatest degree.

EXAMPLE 2 Finding the Degree of a Polynomial

Find the degree of each polynomial.

A $4x - 18x^5$
$4x$: degree 1 $\quad -18x^5$: degree 5 *Find the degree of each term.*
The degree of the polynomial is the greatest degree, 5.

State Resources

go.hrw.com
State Resources Online
KEYWORD: MA7 Resources

1 Introduce

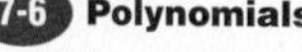

EXPLORATION

7-6 Polynomials

1. The table shows examples of expressions that are and are not *polynomials*. What are some characteristics that the polynomials have in common? Describe some ways in which the polynomials are different from the expressions that are not polynomials.

Polynomials	Not Polynomials
$4x^2 - 5x + 1$	3^x
$3y^8 - 0.5y$	$0.6x^{-1} + 7$
$\frac{1}{2}z^5 - 2z^4 + 8z^2 + \frac{3}{4}z + \frac{1}{3}$	$\frac{4}{x^2}$
$-9x^2$	$-2z^3 + 3z^2 + \frac{1}{z}$
$1.7xy$	$3xy^{-5} + 3x^2y^{-8}$
$4x^2y - x^3y^2$	$\frac{1}{xy^2} + 2$

2. What do you notice about the exponents in the polynomials?
3. Do you think $16x^2 + 2xy + 8y^{-2}$ is a polynomial? Why or why not?

THINK AND DISCUSS

4. **Show** your own examples of expressions that are and are not polynomials.
5. **Describe** how you can tell whether an expression is a polynomial.

Motivate

Write $m^3 + n^2 + p + 5$ on the board. Ask students how many terms are in the expression. 4

Then have students identify the exponent of each variable.

m: 3

n: 2

p: 1

Ask students to identify the greatest exponent. 3

Explorations and answers are provided in *Alternate Openers: Explorations Transparencies.*

Find the degree of each polynomial.

B $0.5x^2y + 0.25xy + 0.75$

$0.5x^2y$: degree 3 $\quad$ $0.25xy$: degree 2 $\quad$ 0.75: degree 0

The degree of the polynomial is the greatest degree, 3.

C $6x^4 + 9x^2 - x + 3$

$6x^4$: degree 4 $\quad$ $9x^2$: degree 2 $\quad$ $-x$: degree 1 $\quad$ 3: degree 0

The degree of the polynomial is the greatest degree, 4.

Find the degree of each polynomial.

2a. $5x - 6$ **1** $\quad$ **2b.** $x^3y^2 + x^2y^3 - x^4 + 2$ **5**

The terms of a polynomial may be written in any order. However, polynomials that contain only one variable are usually written in *standard form.*

The **standard form of a polynomial** that contains one variable is written with the terms in order from greatest degree to least degree. When written in standard form, the coefficient of the first term is called the **leading coefficient**.

EXAMPLE 3 Writing Polynomials in Standard Form

Write each polynomial in standard form. Then give the leading coefficient.

A $20x - 4x^3 + 2 - x^2$

Find the degree of each term. Then arrange them in descending order.

$$\underbrace{20x}_{1}\ \underbrace{-\,4x^3}_{3}\ \underbrace{+\,2}_{0}\ \underbrace{-\,x^2}_{2} \longrightarrow \underbrace{-\,4x^3}_{3}\ \underbrace{-\,x^2}_{2}\ \underbrace{+\,20x}_{1}\ \underbrace{+\,2}_{0}$$

Degree: 1 3 0 2 → 3 2 1 0

The standard form is $-4x^3 - x^2 + 20x + 2$. The leading coefficient is -4.

B $y^3 + y^5 + 4y$

Find the degree of each term. Then arrange them in descending order.

$$\underbrace{y^3}_{3}\ \underbrace{+\,y^5}_{5}\ \underbrace{+\,4y}_{1} \longrightarrow \underbrace{y^5}_{5}\ \underbrace{+\,y^3}_{3}\ \underbrace{+\,4y}_{1}$$

Degree: 3 5 1 → 5 3 1

The standard form is $y^5 + y^3 + 4y$. The leading coefficient is 1.

Remember!

A variable written without a coefficient has a coefficient of 1.

$y^5 = 1y^5$

Write each polynomial in standard form. Then give the leading coefficient.

3a. $16 - 4x^2 + x^5 + 9x^3$ $\quad$ **$x^5 + 9x^3 - 4x^2 + 16$; 1**

3b. $18y^5 - 3y^8 + 14y$ $\quad$ **$-3y^8 + 18y^5 + 14y$; -3**

Some polynomials have special names based on their degree and the number of terms they have.

Degree	Name
0	Constant
1	Linear
2	**Quadratic**
3	**Cubic**
4	Quartic
5	Quintic
6 or more	6th degree, 7th degree, and so on

Terms	Name
1	Monomial
2	**Binomial**
3	**Trinomial**
4 or more	Polynomial

2 Teach

Guided Instruction

Discuss with students examples and non-examples of monomials. Explain how to find the degree of a monomial and the degree of a polynomial. Be sure students get plenty of exposure to the new vocabulary in this lesson—it will be used often throughout the remainder of this chapter and Chapter 8.

Reaching All Learners

Through Kinesthetic Experience

Divide students into groups of five, and have each write a monomial on an index card in large print. They may write a constant or a monomial with a variable. Tell them the variable must be *x*, but it can be raised to any power between 1 and 4, and can have any coefficient. Then call out classifications such as *quadratic trinomial* and *quartic binomial.* Have students in each group stand and arrange themselves to form that polynomial, holding their monomial in front of them for the rest of the class to see.

COMMON ERROR ALERT

Students often confuse the degree of a polynomial with the number of terms. Students may be less likely to confuse the two if they equate the word *degree* with an exponent-related phrase such as "maximum power."

Power Presentations with PowerPoint®

Additional Examples

Example 1

Find the degree of each monomial.

A. $4p^4q^3$ $\quad$ 7

B. $7ed$ $\quad$ 2

C. 3 $\quad$ 0

Example 2

Find the degree of each polynomial.

A. $11x^7 + 3x^3$ $\quad$ 7

B. $\frac{1}{3}w^2z + \frac{1}{2}z^4 - 5$ $\quad$ 4

Example 3

Write each polynomial in standard form. Then give the leading coefficient.

A. $6x - 7x^5 + 4x^2 + 9$

$-7x^5 + 4x^2 + 6x + 9$; -7

B. $y^2 + y^6 - 3y$

$y^6 + y^2 - 3y$; 1

INTERVENTION

Questioning Strategies

EXAMPLE 1

- If a monomial has more than one variable with an exponent, how do you determine its degree?
- Why is the degree of a constant always zero?

EXAMPLE 2

- Do coefficients affect the degree of the polynomial? Explain.

EXAMPLE 3

- When is the coefficient of the first term also the leading coefficient of the polynomial?

Power Presentations with PowerPoint®

Additional Examples

Example 4

Classify each polynomial according to its degree and number of terms.

A. $5n^3 + 4n$ cubic binomial

B. $4y^6 - 5y^3 + 2y - 9$ 6th-degree polynomial

C. $-2x$ linear monomial

Example 5

A tourist accidentally drops her lip balm off the Golden Gate Bridge. The bridge is 220 feet from the water of the bay. The height of the lip balm is given by the polynomial $-16t^2 + 220$, where t is time in seconds. How far above the water will the lip balm be after 3 seconds? 76 ft

INTERVENTION 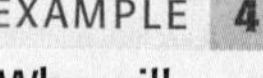

Questioning Strategies

EXAMPLE 4

- Why will a constant polynomial always be a monomial?
- How does writing a polynomial in standard form help you classify the polynomial?

EXAMPLE 5

- What step in the order of operations will never be used when evaluating a polynomial in standard form? Why?

EXAMPLE 4 Classifying Polynomials

Classify each polynomial according to its degree and number of terms.

A $5x - 6$
Degree: 1 Terms: 2 $5x - 6$ is a linear binomial.

B $y^2 + y + 4$
Degree: 2 Terms: 3 $y^2 + y + 4$ is a quadratic trinomial.

C $6x^7 + 9x^2 - x + 3$
Degree: 7 Terms: 4 $6x^7 + 9x^2 - x + 3$ is a 7th-degree polynomial.

Classify each polynomial according to its degree and number of terms.

4a. $x^3 + x^2 - x + 2$ **cubic polynomial** **4b.** 6 **constant monomial** **4c.** $-3y^8 + 18y^5 + 14y$ **8th-degree trinomial**

EXAMPLE 5 *Physics Application*

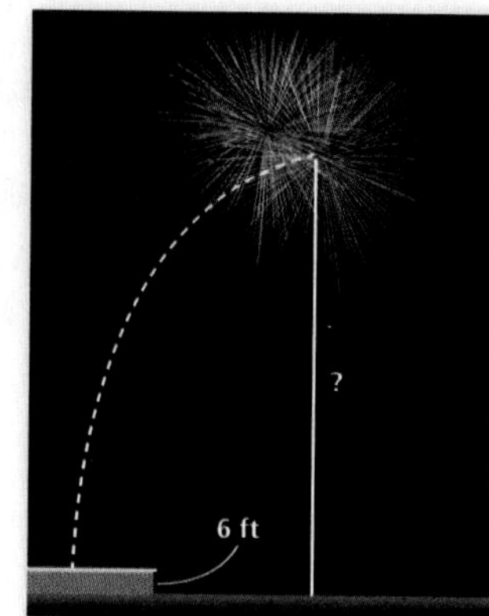

A firework is launched from a platform 6 feet above the ground at a speed of 200 feet per second. The firework has a 5-second fuse. The height of the firework in feet is given by the polynomial $-16t^2 + 200t + 6$, where t is the time in seconds. How high will the firework be when it explodes?

Substitute the time for t to find the firework's height.

$-16t^2 + 200t + 6$

$-16(5)^2 + 200(5) + 6$ *The time is 5 seconds.*

$-16(25) + 200(5) + 6$

$-400 + 1000 + 6$ *Evaluate the polynomial by using the order of operations.*

606

When the firework explodes, it will be 606 feet above the ground.

5. What if...? Another firework with a 5-second fuse is launched from the same platform at a speed of 400 feet per second. Its height is given by $-16t^2 + 400t + 6$. How high will this firework be when it explodes? **1606 ft**

THINK AND DISCUSS

1. Explain why each expression is not a polynomial: $2x^2 + 3x^{-3}$; $1 - \frac{a}{b}$.

2. GET ORGANIZED Copy and complete the graphic organizer. In each oval, write an example of the given type of polynomial.

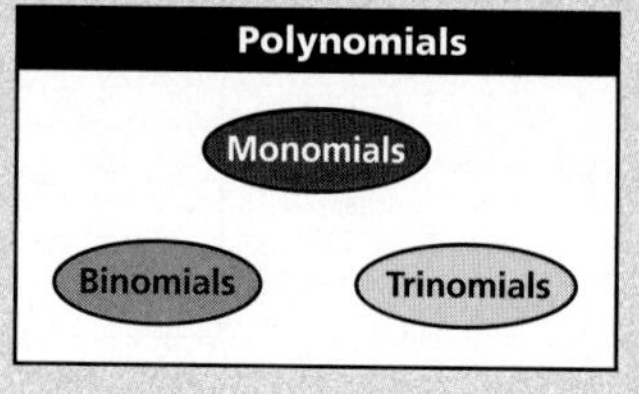

3 Close

Summarize

Have students give examples of monomials, binomials, trinomials, and polynomials of fourth and fifth degree. Write their examples on the board as they say them. For each, have students state whether the polynomial is in standard form, and if not, rewrite it in standard form.

ONGOING ASSESSMENT and INTERVENTION 

***Diagnose Before* the Lesson**
7-6 Warm Up, TE p. 496

***Monitor During* the Lesson**
Check It Out! Exercises, SE pp. 496–498
Questioning Strategies, TE pp. 497–498

***Assess After* the Lesson**
7-6 Lesson Quiz, TE p. 501
Alternative Assessment, TE p. 501

Answers to *Think and Discuss*

1. Possible answer: $2x^2 + 3x^{-3}$ contains an expression with a negative exponent. $1 - \frac{a}{b}$ contains a variable within a denominator.
2. See p. A7.

7-6 Exercises

go.hrw.com
Homework Help Online
KEYWORD: MA11 7-6
Parent Resources Online
KEYWORD: MA7 Parent

GUIDED PRACTICE

Vocabulary Match each polynomial on the left with its classification on the right.

1. $2x^3 + 6$ **d**
2. $3x^3 + 4x^2 - 7$ **c**
3. $5x^2 - 2x + 3x^4 - 6$ **a**

a. quartic polynomial
b. quadratic polynomial
c. cubic trinomial
d. cubic binomial

SEE EXAMPLE 1 p. 496

Find the degree of each monomial.

4. 10^6 **0**
5. $-7xy^2$ **3**
6. $0.4n^8$ **8**
7. 2 **0**

SEE EXAMPLE 2 p. 496

Find the degree of each polynomial.

8. $x^2 - 2x + 1$ **2**
9. $0.75a^2b - 2a^3b^5$ **8**
10. $15y - 84y^3 + 100 - 3y^2$ **3**
11. $r^3 + r^2 - 5$ **3**
12. $a^3 + a^2 - 2a$ **3**
13. $3k^4 + k^3 - 2k^2 + k$ **4**

SEE EXAMPLE 3 p. 497

Write each polynomial in standard form. Then give the leading coefficient.

14. $-2b + 5 + b^2$ **$b^2 - 2b + 5$; 1**
15. $9a^8 - 8a^9$ **$-8a^9 + 9a^8$; −8**
16. $5s^2 - 3s + 3 - s^7$ **$-s^7 + 5s^2 - 3s + 3$; −1**
17. $2x + 3x^2 - 1$ **$3x^2 + 2x - 1$; 3**
18. $5g - 7 + g^2$ **$g^2 + 5g - 7$; 1**
19. $3c^2 + 5c^4 + 5c^3 - 4$ **$5c^4 + 5c^3 + 3c^2 - 4$; 5**

SEE EXAMPLE 4 p. 498

Classify each polynomial according to its degree and number of terms.

20. $x^2 + 2x + 3$ **quadratic trinomial**
21. $x - 7$ **linear binomial**
22. $8 + k + 5k^4$ **quartic trinomial**
23. $q^2 + 6 - q^3 + 3q^4$ **quartic polynomial**
24. $5k^2 + 7k^3$ **cubic binomial**
25. $2a^3 + 4a^2 - a^4$ **quartic trinomial**

SEE EXAMPLE 5 p. 498

26. **Geometry** The surface area of a cone is approximated by the polynomial $3.14r^2 + 3.14r\ell$, where r is the radius and ℓ is the slant height. Find the approximate surface area of this cone. **301.44 cm²**

Slant height = 10 cm
6 cm

PRACTICE AND PROBLEM SOLVING

Independent Practice	
For Exercises	See Example
27–34	1
35–40	2
41–49	3
50–57	4
58	5

Extra Practice
Skills Practice p. S17
Application Practice p. S34

Find the degree of each monomial.

27. $3y^4$ **4**
28. $6k$ **1**
29. $2a^3b^2c$ **6**
30. 325 **0**
31. $2y^4z^3$ **7**
32. $9m^5$ **5**
33. p **1**
34. 5 **0**

Find the degree of each polynomial.

35. $a^2 + a^4 - 6a$ **4**
36. $3^2b - 5$ **1**
37. $3.5y^2 - 4.1y - 6$ **2**
38. $-5f^4 + 2f^6 + 10f^8$ **8**
39. $4n^3 - 2n$ **3**
40. $4r^3 + 4r^6$ **6**

Write each polynomial in standard form. Then give the leading coefficient.

41. $2.5 + 4.9t^3 - 4t^2 + t$ **$4.9t^3 - 4t^2 + t + 2.5$; 4.9**
42. $8a - 10a^2 + 2$ **$-10a^2 + 8a + 2$; −10**
43. $x^7 - x + x^3 - x^5 + x^{10}$ **$x^{10} + x^7 - x^5 + x^3 - x$; 1**
44. $-m + 7 - 3m^2$ **$-3m^2 - m + 7$; −3**
45. $3x^2 + 5x - 4 + 5x^3$ **$5x^3 + 3x^2 + 5x - 4$; 5**
46. $-2n + 1 - n^2$ **$-n^2 - 2n + 1$; −1**
47. $4d + 3d^2 - d^3 + 5$ **$-d^3 + 3d^2 + 4d + 5$; −1**
48. $3s^2 + 12s^3 + 6$ **$12s^3 + 3s^2 + 6$; 12**
49. $4x^2 - x^5 - x^3 + 1$ **$-x^5 - x^3 + 4x^2 + 1$; −1**

7-6 Exercises

Assignment Guide

Assign *Guided Practice* exercises as necessary.

If you finished Examples **1–3**
Basic 27–49
Average 27–49
Advanced 27–49

If you finished Examples **1–5**
Basic 27–78, 81–89
Average 27–79, 81–89
Advanced 27–74, 76–89

Homework Quick Check
Quickly check key concepts.
Exercises: 27, 32, 34, 42, 52, 58, 60

State Resources

Teacher to Teacher

For many students it is easier to identify the degree of each term in a polynomial when each term is written with the variables and their exponents. For example:

$5x^2y + 25xy + 75$
$= 5x^2y^1 + 25x^1y^1 + 75x^0y^0$
$5x^2y^1 \longrightarrow$ degree $2 + 1 = 3$
$25x^1y^1 \longrightarrow$ degree $1 + 1 = 2$
$75x^0y^0 \longrightarrow$ degree $0 + 0 = 0$

The highest degree is 3, so the polynomial $5x^2y + 25xy + 75$ has degree 3.

Arlane Frederick
Buffalo, NY

Exercise 74 involves expressing the area and perimeter of a rectangle as polynomials. This exercise prepares students for the Multi-Step Test Prep on page 528.

Kinesthetic Have students make (or attempt to make) the boxes for parts **a, b,** and **c** of **Exercise 63.** Give students scissors and tape and make sure they have a ruler and 8.5-by-11-inch paper (standard size of notebook or copy paper). The ruler can be found in the Manipulatives Kit (MK).

Answers

78.

Time (s)	Height (ft)
1	59
2	86
3	81
4	44

The rocket will be highest after 2 s.

Transportation

Hybrid III is the crash test dummy used by the Insurance Institute for Highway Safety. During a crash test, sensors in the dummy's head, neck, chest, legs, and feet measure and record forces. Engineers study this data to help design safer cars.

Classify each polynomial according to its degree and number of terms.

50. 12 **constant monomial**

51. $6k$ **linear monomial**

52. $3.5x^3 - 4.1x - 6$ **cubic trinomial**

53. $4g + 2g^2 - 3$ **quadratic trinomial**

54. $2x^2 - 6x$ **quadratic binomial**

55. $6 - s^3 - 3s^4$ **quartic trinomial**

56. $c^2 + 7 - 2c^3$ **cubic trinomial**

57. $-y^2$ **quadratic monomial**

58. Transportation The polynomial $3.675v + 0.096v^2$ is used by transportation officials to estimate the stopping distance in feet for a car whose speed is v miles per hour on flat, dry pavement. What is the stopping distance for a car traveling at 30 miles per hour? **196.65 ft**

Tell whether each statement is sometimes, always, or never true.

59. A monomial is a polynomial. **always**

60. A trinomial is a 3rd-degree polynomial. **sometimes**

61. A binomial is a trinomial. **never**

62. A polynomial has two or more terms. **sometimes**

63. Geometry A piece of 8.5-by-11-inch cardboard has identical squares cut from its corners. It is then folded into a box with no lid. The volume of the box in cubic inches is $4c^3 - 39c^2 + 93.5c$, where c is the side length of the missing squares in inches.

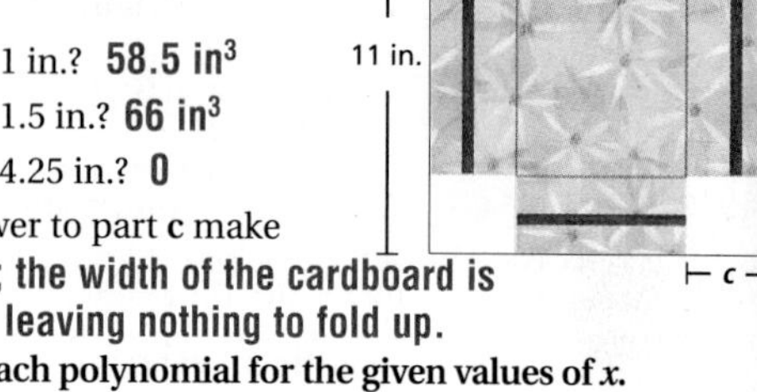

a. What is the volume of the box if $c = 1$ in.? **58.5 in³**

b. What is the volume of the box if $c = 1.5$ in.? **66 in³**

c. What is the volume of the box if $c = 4.25$ in.? **0**

d. **Critical Thinking** Does your answer to part c make sense? Explain why or why not. **Yes; the width of the cardboard is 8.5 in., so 4.25 in. cuts will meet, leaving nothing to fold up.**

Copy and complete the table by evaluating each polynomial for the given values of x.

	Polynomial	$x = -2$	$x = 0$	$x = 5$
64.	$5x - 6$	$5(-2) - 6 = -16$	$5(0) - 6 = -6$	**19**
65.	$x^5 + x^3 + 4x$	**−48**	**0**	**3270**
66.	$-10x^2$	**−40**	**0**	**−250**

Give one example of each type of polynomial. **Possible answers given.**

67. quadratic trinomial **$x^2 + 3x - 6$**

68. linear binomial **$5x - 2$**

69. constant monomial **5**

70. cubic monomial **$6x^3$**

71. quintic binomial **$x^5 - 3$**

72. 12th-degree trinomial **$2x^{12} - x + 15$**

73. Write About It Explain the steps you would follow to write the polynomial $4x^3 - 3 + 5x^2 - 2x^4 - x$ in standard form.

73. Possible answer: First identify the degree of each term. From left to right, the degrees are 3, 0, 2, 4, and 1. Arrange the terms in order of decreasing degree, and move the plus or minus sign in front of each term with it: $-2x^4 + 4x^3 + 5x^2 - x - 3$.

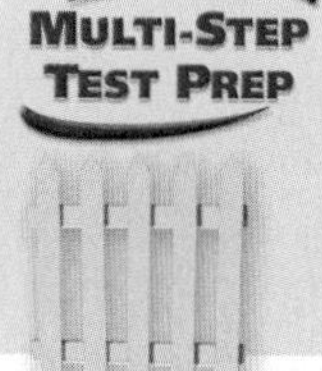

74. This problem will prepare you for the Multi-Step Test Prep on page 528.

a. The perimeter of the rectangle shown is $12x + 6$. What is the degree of this polynomial? **1**

b. The area of the rectangle is $8x^2 + 12x$. What is the degree of this polynomial? **2**

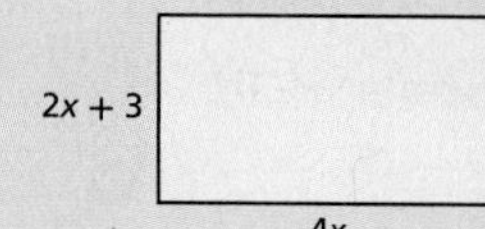

7-6 PRACTICE A
7-6 PRACTICE C
7-6 PRACTICE B

Find the degree and number of terms of each polynomial.

1. $14h^3 + 2h + 10$ **3** **3**
2. $7y - 10y^2$ **2** **2**
3. $2a^2 - 5a + 34 - 6a^4$ **4** **4**

Write each polynomial in standard form. Then, give the leading coefficient.

4. $3x^2 - 2 + 4x^8 - x$ **$4x^8 + 3x^2 - x - 2$** **4**
5. $7 - 50j + 3j^3 - 4j^2$ **$3j^3 - 4j^2 - 50j + 7$** **3**
6. $6k + 5k^4 - 4k^3 + 3k^2$ **$5k^4 - 4k^3 + 3k^2 + 6k$** **5**

Classify each polynomial by its degree and number of terms.

7. $-5t^2 + 10$ **quadratic binomial**
8. $8w - 32 + 9w^4$ **quartic trinomial**
9. $b - b^3 - 2b^2 + 5b^4$ **quartic polynomial**

Evaluate each polynomial for the given value.

10. $3m + 8 - 2m^3$ for $m = -1$ **7**
11. $4y^5 - 6y + 8y^2 - 1$ for $y = -1$ **9**
12. $2w + w^3 - \frac{1}{2}w^2$ for $w = 2$ **10**
13. An egg is thrown off the top of a building. Its height in meters above the ground can be approximated by the polynomial $300 + 2t - 4.9t^2$, where t is the time since it was thrown in seconds.
    a. How high is the egg above the ground after 5 seconds? **187.5 m**
    b. How high is the egg above the ground after 6 seconds? **135.6 m**

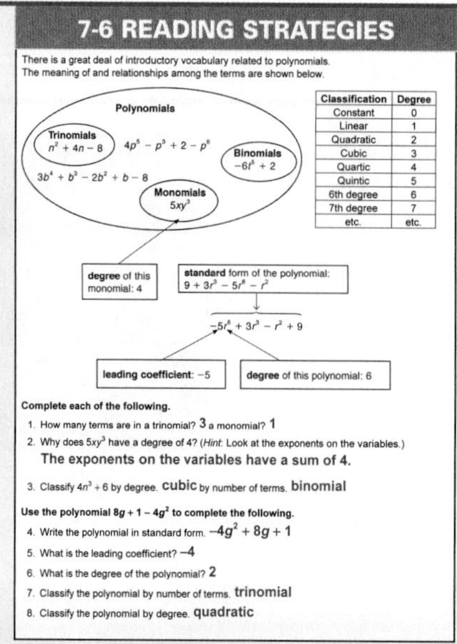

7-6 READING STRATEGIES

There is a great deal of introductory vocabulary related to polynomials. The meaning of and relationships among the terms are shown below.

Classification	Degree
Constant	0
Linear	1
Quadratic	2
Cubic	3
Quartic	4
Quintic	5
6th degree	6
7th degree	7
etc.	etc.

Complete each of the following.

1. How many terms are in a trinomial? **3** a monomial? **1**
2. Why does $5xy^3$ have a degree of 4? (*Hint:* Look at the exponents on the variables.) **The exponents on the variables have a sum of 4.**
3. Classify $4n^3 + 6$ by degree. **cubic** by number of terms. **binomial**

Use the polynomial $8g + 1 - 4g^2$ to complete the following.

4. Write the polynomial in standard form. **$-4g^2 + 8g + 1$**
5. What is the leading coefficient? **−4**
6. What is the degree of the polynomial? **2**
7. Classify the polynomial by number of terms. **trinomial**
8. Classify the polynomial by degree. **quadratic**

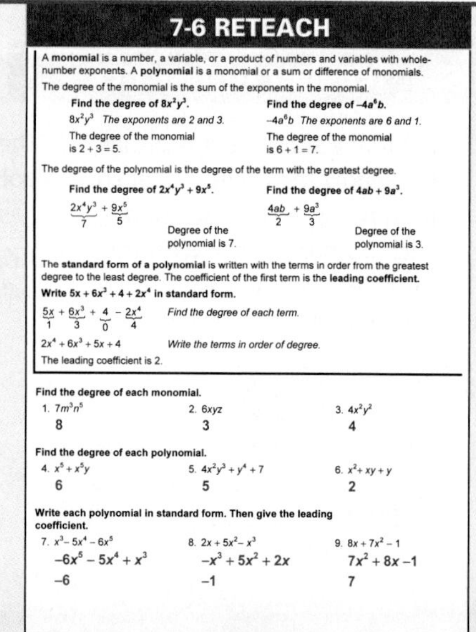

7-6 RETEACH

A **monomial** is a number, a variable, or a product of numbers and variables with whole-number exponents. A **polynomial** is a monomial or a sum or difference of monomials.

The degree of the monomial is the sum of the exponents in the monomial.

Find the degree of $8x^2y^3$.

$8x^2y^3$ *The exponents are 2 and 3.*

The degree of the monomial is $2 + 3 = 5$.

Find the degree of $-4a^6b$.

$-4a^6b$ *The exponents are 6 and 1.*

The degree of the monomial is $6 + 1 = 7$.

The degree of the polynomial is the degree of the term with the greatest degree.

Find the degree of $2x^4y^3 + 9x^5$.

$\underbrace{2x^4y^3}_{7} + \underbrace{9x^5}_{5}$ Degree of the polynomial is 7.

Find the degree of $4ab + 9a^3$.

$\underbrace{4ab}_{2} + \underbrace{9a^3}_{3}$ Degree of the polynomial is 3.

The **standard form of a polynomial** is written with the terms in order from the greatest degree to the least degree. The coefficient of the first term is the **leading coefficient.**

Write $5x + 6x^3 + 4 + 2x^4$ in standard form.

$\underbrace{5x}_{1} + \underbrace{6x^3}_{3} + \underbrace{4}_{0} - \underbrace{2x^4}_{4}$ *Find the degree of each term.*

$2x^4 + 6x^3 + 5x + 4$ *Write the terms in order of degree.*

The leading coefficient is 2.

Find the degree of each monomial.

1. $7m^3n^5$ **8**
2. $6xyz$ **3**
3. $4x^2y^2$ **4**

Find the degree of each polynomial.

4. $x^5 + x^5y$ **6**
5. $4x^2y^3 + y^4 + 7$ **5**
6. $x^2 + xy + y$ **2**

Write each polynomial in standard form. Then give the leading coefficient.

7. $x^3 - 5x^4 - 6x^5$ **$-6x^5 - 5x^4 + x^3$** **−6**
8. $2x + 5x^2 - x^3$ **$-x^3 + 5x^2 + 2x$** **−1**
9. $8x + 7x^2 - 1$ **$7x^2 + 8x - 1$** **7**

75. **ERROR ANALYSIS** Two students evaluated $4x - 3x^5$ for $x = -2$. Which is incorrect? Explain the error.

75. A is incorrect. The student incorrectly multiplied −3 by −2 before evaluating the power.

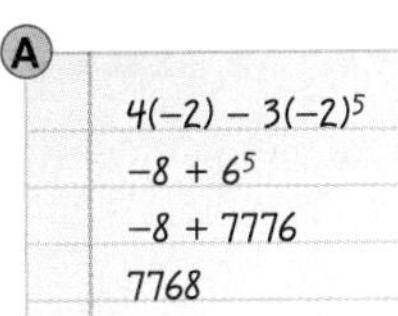

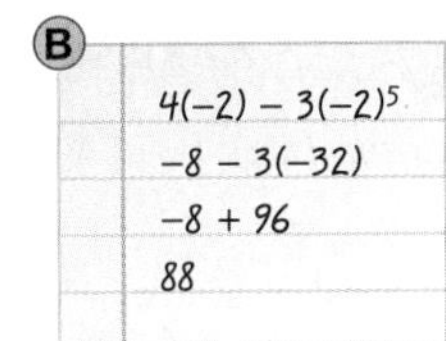

TEST PREP

76. Which polynomial has the highest degree?

Ⓐ $3x^8 - 2x^7 + x^6$ Ⓑ $5x - 100$ **Ⓒ** $25x^{10} + 3x^5 - 15$ Ⓓ $134x^2$

77. What is the value of $-3x^3 + 4x^2 - 5x + 7$ when $x = -1$?

Ⓕ 3 Ⓖ 13 Ⓗ 9 **Ⓙ** 19

78. **Short Response** A toy rocket is launched from the ground at 75 feet per second. The polynomial $-16t^2 + 75t$ gives the rocket's height in feet after t seconds. Make a table showing the rocket's height after 1 second, 2 seconds, 3 seconds, and 4 seconds. At which of these times will the rocket be the highest?

CHALLENGE AND EXTEND

79. **Medicine** Doctors and nurses use growth charts and formulas to tell whether a baby is developing normally. The polynomial $0.016m^3 - 0.390m^2 + 4.562m + 50.310$ gives the average length in centimeters of a baby boy between 0 and 10 months of age, where m is the baby's age in months.

a. What is the average length of a 2-month-old baby boy? a 5-month-old baby boy? Round your answers to the nearest centimeter. **58 cm; 65 cm**

b. What is the average length of a newborn (0-month-old) baby boy? **50.310 cm**

c. How could you find the answer to part **b** without doing any calculations?

79c. The first 3 terms of the polynomial will equal 0, so just look at the constant.

80. Consider the binomials $4x^5 + x$, $4x^4 + x$, and $4x^3 + x$.

a. Without calculating, which binomial has the greatest value for $x = 5$? **$4x^5 + x$**

b. Are there any values of x for $4x^3 + x$ which will have the greatest value? Explain.

SPIRAL REVIEW

81. Jordan is allowed 90 minutes of screen time per day. Today, he has already used m minutes. Write an expression for the remaining number of minutes Jordan has today. *(Lesson 1-1)* **$90 - m$**

82. Pens cost $0.50 each. Giselle bought p pens. Write an expression for the total cost of Giselle's pens. *(Lesson 1-1)* **$0.50p$**

Classify each system. Give the number of solutions. *(Lesson 6-4)*

83. $\begin{cases} y = -4x + 5 \\ 4x + y = 2 \end{cases}$ 84. $\begin{cases} 2x + 8y = 10 \\ 4y = -x + 5 \end{cases}$ 85. $\begin{cases} y = 3x + 2 \\ y = -5x - 6 \end{cases}$

83. incons.; no sol.

84. cons. and dep.; inf. many solutions

85. cons. and indep.; one sol.

Simplify. *(Lesson 7-4)*

86. $\frac{4^7}{4^4}$ **4^3, or 64** 87. $\frac{x^6y^4}{x^4y^9}$ **$\frac{x^2}{y^5}$** 88. $\left(\frac{2v^4}{vw^5}\right)^2$ **$\frac{4v^6}{w^{10}}$** 89. $\left(\frac{2p}{p^3}\right)^{-4}$ **$\frac{p^8}{16}$**

TEST PREP DOCTOR In **Exercise 76,** students who chose **A** may have confused degree with number of terms. Students who chose **D** may think that the coefficients are significant when determining degree.

In **Exercise 77,** students who chose **G** probably got −3 for the value of the first term.

Answers

80b. Yes; $0 < x < 1$; raising a number between 0 and 1 to a higher power results in a lesser number. So if x is between 0 and 1, the binomial with the least degree will have the greatest value.

Journal

Have students explain how to classify a polynomial according to its degree and number of terms.

ALTERNATIVE ASSESSMENT

Have students write a linear binomial and a quadratic trinomial, each with only x as a variable. Then have them evaluate each polynomial for $x = 3$.

Power Presentations with PowerPoint®

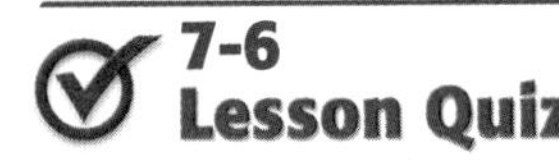

Find the degree of each polynomial.

1. $7a^3b^2 - 2a^4 + 4b - 15$ 5

2. $25x^2 - 3x^4$ 4

Write each polynomial in standard form. Then give the leading coefficient.

3. $24g^3 + 10 + 7g^5 - g^2$
$7g^5 + 24g^3 - g^2 + 10$; 7

4. $14 - x^4 + 3x^2$ $-x^4 + 3x^2 + 14$; −1

Classify each polynomial according to its degree and number of terms.

5. $18x^2 - 12x + 5$ quadratic trinomial

6. $2x^4 - 1$ quartic binomial

7. The polynomial $3.675v + 0.096v^2$ is used to estimate the stopping distance in feet for a car whose speed is v miles per hour on flat, dry pavement. What is the stopping distance for a car traveling at 70 miles per hour? 727.65 ft

Also available on transparency

7-6 PROBLEM SOLVING

Write the correct answer.

1. The surface area of a cylinder is given by the polynomial $2\pi r^2 + 2\pi rh$. A cylinder has a radius of 2 centimeters and a height of 5 centimeters. Find the surface area of the cylinder. Use 3.14 for π.
87.92 square centimeters

2. A firework is launched from the ground at a velocity of 180 feet per second. Its height after t seconds is given by the polynomial $-16t^2 + 180t$. Find the height of the firework after 2 seconds and after 5 seconds.
2 s: 296 feet
5 s: 500 feet

3. In the United Kingdom, transportation authorities use the polynomial $\frac{1}{20}v^2 + v$ for calculating the number of feet needed to stop on dry pavement. In the United States, many use the polynomial $0.096v^2$. Both formulas are based on speed v in miles per hour. Calculate the stopping distances for a car traveling 45 miles per hour in both the U.S. and the UK.
UK: 146.25 feet
US: 194.4 feet

4. A piece of cardboard that measures 2 feet by 3 feet can be folded into a box if notches are cut out of the corners. The length of the side of the notch will be the same as the height h of the resulting box. The volume of the box is given by $4h^3 - 10h^2 + 6h$. Find the volume of the box for $h = 0.25$ and $h = 0.5$.
$h = 0.25$: 0.9375 cubic feet
$h = 0.5$: 1 cubic foot

The height of a rocket in meters t seconds after it is launched is approximated by the polynomial $0.5at^2 + vt + h$ where a is always −9.8, v is the initial velocity, and h is the initial height. Use this information with the data in the chart for questions 5 – 7. Select the best answer.

Model Number	Initial Velocity (m/s)
300X	250
Q99	90
4400*i*	125

5. A 300X was launched from a height of 10 meters. What was its height after 3 seconds?
A 715.9 m C 755.5 m
B 745.3 m D 760 m

6. Marie and Bob launched their rockets at the same time from a platform 5 meters above the ground. Marie launched the 4400*i* and Bob launched the Q99. How much higher was Marie's rocket after 2 seconds?
F 35 meters H 140 meters
G 70 meters J 320 meters

7. The 4400*i* was launched from the ground at the same time the Q99 was launched from 175 meters above the ground. After how many seconds were the rockets at the same height?
A 2 s **C** 5 s
B 4 s D 6 s

7-6 CHALLENGE

Match each polynomial with the correct clue. Each polynomial can be used only once. Not every polynomial will be used.

Use these polynomials for 1 – 7.

$x^5 + x^3 + x$	$2x^4y^4 + 3x^2y^5$
$2x^4$	$x^5y - 3x^2y - xy$
$3x + 3y + 3z$	$-3xy^4$
$2xy + 5xz$	$2x^2y + 5xy^2$
$4x^2 - 3x^5 + x$	$4xyz^2 + xyz$

Use these polynomials for 8 – 14.

$4x^2 - 3x^2y$	$x^3 + x^2 + x$
$x^2 + x - 3$	$x^4 + x^3 + x^2$
$-3 + x + 4x^2$	$2x^2 - 3x^3 + 1$
$x^3y - 3xyz + z$	$x - 3$
$-x + 3$	$x^2 + y^2 + z^2 + w^2$

1. I am a monomial with degree 5. Who am I?
$-3xy^4$

2. I am a sum of monomials with degree 8. Who am I?
$2x^4y^4 + 3x^2y^5$

3. I am a trinomial with degree 5. Who am I?
$x^5 + x^3 + x$

4. I am a binomial. Both of my terms have degree 2. Who am I?
$2xy + 5xz$

5. I am a monomial with degree 4. Who am I?
$2x^4$

6. I am a binomial with degree 4. Who am I?
$4xyz^2 + xyz$

7. I am a trinomial. When you put me in standard form, my leading coefficient is −3. Who am I?
$4x^2 - 3x^5 + x$

8. I am a linear expression. My constant is −3. Who am I?
$x - 3$

9. I am a quartic trinomial. I have three different variables. Who am I?
$x^3y - 3xyz + z$

10. I am a cubic binomial. Who am I?
$4x^2 - 3x^2y$

11. I am a quadratic polynomial. I have no constants. Who am I?
$x^2 + y^2 + z^2 + w^2$

12. I am a cubic trinomial with one variable. Who am I?
$x^3 + x^2 + x$

13. I am a quadratic trinomial. When you put me in standard form, my leading coefficient is 4. Who am I?
$-3 + x + 4x^2$

14. I am a quartic trinomial. Who am I?
$x^4 + x^3 + x^2$

Organizer

Use with Lesson 7-7

Pacing:

Traditional $\frac{1}{2}$ day
Block $\frac{1}{4}$ day

Objective: Use algebra tiles to model polynomial addition and subtraction.

Materials: algebra tiles

Online Edition
Algebra Tiles

Countdown Week 16

Resources

Algebra Lab Activities
7-7 Lab Recording Sheet

Teach

Discuss

Compare like terms and like tiles. In like terms, the same variables are raised to the same powers, but the coefficients may differ. In like tiles, the size and shape are the same, but the color of the tile (whether it is positive or negative) may differ.

In **Activity 2,** remind students to add the opposite of every term in the second expression.

Encourage students to always arrange their tiles and write their answers in standard form. This will help prevent careless errors.

State Resources

Model Polynomial Addition and Subtraction

You can use algebra tiles to model polynomial addition and subtraction.

Use with Lesson 7-7

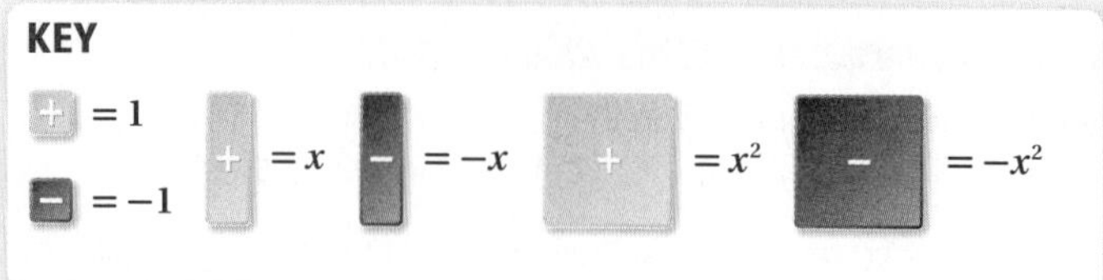

Activity 1

Use algebra tiles to find $(2x^2 - x) + (x^2 + 3x - 1)$.

MODEL	ALGEBRA
Use tiles to represent all terms from both expressions.	$(2x^2 - x) + (x^2 + 3x - 1)$
Rearrange tiles so that like tiles are together. Like tiles are the same size and shape.	$(2x^2 + x^2) + (-x + 3x) - 1$
Remove any zero pairs.	$3x^2 - x + x + 2x - 1$
The remaining tiles represent the sum.	$3x^2 + 2x - 1$

Try This

Use algebra tiles to find each sum.

1. $(-2x^2 + 1) + (-x^2)$ $\mathbf{-3x^2 + 1}$
2. $(3x^2 + 2x + 5) + (x^2 - x - 4)$ $\mathbf{4x^2 + x + 1}$
3. $(x - 3) + (2x - 2)$ $\mathbf{3x - 5}$
4. $(5x^2 - 3x - 6) + (x^2 + 3x + 6)$ $\mathbf{6x^2}$
5. $-5x^2 + (2x^2 + 5x)$ $\mathbf{-3x^2 + 5x}$
6. $(x^2 - x - 1) + (6x - 3)$ $\mathbf{x^2 + 5x - 4}$

Activity 2

Use algebra tiles to find $(2x^2 + 6) - 4x^2$.

MODEL	ALGEBRA
Use tiles to represent the terms in the first expression.	$2x^2 + 6$
To subtract $4x^2$, you would remove 4 yellow x^2-tiles, but there are not enough to do this. Remember that subtraction is the same as adding the opposite, so rewrite $(2x^2 + 6) - 4x^2$ as $(2x^2 + 6) + (-4x^2)$.	
Add 4 red x^2-tiles.	$2x^2 + 6 + (-4x^2)$
Rearrange tiles so that like tiles are together.	$2x^2 + (-4x^2) + 6$
Remove zero pairs.	$2x^2 + (-2x^2) + (-2x^2) + 6$
The remaining tiles represent the difference.	$-2x^2 + 6$

Try This

Use algebra tiles to find each difference.

7. $(6x^2 + 4x) - 3x^2$ **8.** $(2x^2 + x - 7) - 5x$ **9.** $(3x + 6) - 6$

10. $(8x + 5) - (-2x)$ **11.** $(x^2 + 2x) - (-4x^2 + x)$ **12.** $(3x^2 - 4) - (x^2 + 6x)$

13. [+] [−] represents a zero pair. Use algebra tiles to model two other zero pairs.

14. When is it not necessary to "add the opposite" for polynomial subtraction using algebra tiles? **when you have enough tiles to actually remove them to model the subtraction**

Close

Key Concept

Polynomial addition is the same as combining like terms. Polynomial subtraction can be written as polynomial addition by adding the opposite.

Assessment

Journal Have students explain how to use algebra tiles to find $(3x^2 - 4x + 1) - 5x$.

Answers to *Try This*

7. $3x^2 + 4x$

8. $2x^2 - 4x - 7$

9. $3x$

10. $10x + 5$

11. $5x^2 + x$

12. $2x^2 - 6x - 4$

13.

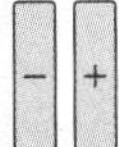

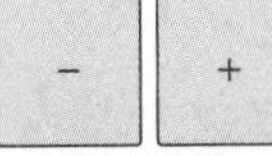

7-7 Algebra Lab **503**

7-7 Organizer

Pacing: Traditional 1 day
Block $\frac{1}{2}$ day

Objective: Add and subtract polynomials.

Technology Lab
In *Technology Lab Activities*

Online Edition
Tutorial Videos

Countdown Week 16

Power Presentations with PowerPoint®

Warm Up

Simplify each expression by combining like terms.

1. $4x + 2x$ $\quad 6x$
2. $3y + 7y$ $\quad 10y$
3. $8p - 5p$ $\quad 3p$
4. $5n + 6n^2$ $\quad$ not like terms

Simplify each expression.

5. $3(x + 4)$ $\quad 3x + 12$
6. $-2(t + 3)$ $\quad -2t - 6$
7. $-1(x^2 - 4x - 6)$
$-x^2 + 4x + 6$

Also available on transparency

Math Humor

Teacher: What is $b + b$?
Shakespeare: Is it $2b$ or not $2b$?

7-7 Adding and Subtracting Polynomials

"This one pretty much sums it up."

www.cartoonstock.com

Objective
Add and subtract polynomials.

Who uses this?
Business owners can add and subtract polynomials that model profit. (See Example 4.)

Just as you can perform operations on numbers, you can perform operations on polynomials. To add or subtract polynomials, combine like terms.

Remember!
Like terms are constants or terms with the same variable(s) raised to the same power(s). To review combining like terms, see Lesson 1-7.

EXAMPLE 1 Adding and Subtracting Monomials

Add or subtract.

A $15m^3 + 6m^2 + 2m^3$

$15m^3 + 6m^2 + 2m^3$	*Identify like terms.*
$15m^3 + 2m^3 + 6m^2$	*Rearrange terms so that like terms are together.*
$17m^3 + 6m^2$	*Combine like terms.*

B $3x^2 + 5 - 7x^2 + 12$

$3x^2 + 5 - 7x^2 + 12$	*Identify like terms.*
$3x^2 - 7x^2 + 5 + 12$	*Rearrange terms so that like terms are together.*
$-4x^2 + 17$	*Combine like terms.*

C $0.9y^5 - 0.4y^5 + 0.5x^5 + y^5$

$0.9y^5 - 0.4y^5 + 0.5x^5 + y^5$	*Identify like terms.*
$0.9y^5 - 0.4y^5 + y^5 + 0.5x^5$	*Rearrange terms so that like terms are together.*
$1.5y^5 + 0.5x^5$	*Combine like terms.*

D $2x^2y - x^2y - x^2y$

$2x^2y - x^2y - x^2y$	*All terms are like terms.*
0	*Combine.*

CHECK IT OUT! Add or subtract.

1a. $2s^2 + 3s^2 + s$ $\quad 5s^2 + s$
1b. $4z^4 - 8 + 16z^4 + 2$ $\quad 20z^4 - 6$
1c. $2x^8 + 7y^8 - x^8 - y^8$ $\quad x^8 + 6y^8$
1d. $9b^3c^2 + 5b^3c^2 - 13b^3c^2$ $\quad b^3c^2$

Polynomials can be added in either vertical or horizontal form.

In vertical form, align the like terms and add:

$$\begin{array}{r} 5x^2 + 4x + 1 \\ +\ 2x^2 + 5x + 2 \\ \hline 7x^2 + 9x + 3 \end{array}$$

In horizontal form, use the Associative and Commutative Properties to regroup and combine like terms:

$$\begin{aligned} &(5x^2 + 4x + 1) + (2x^2 + 5x + 2) \\ &= (5x^2 + 2x^2) + (4x + 5x) + (1 + 2) \\ &= 7x^2 + 9x + 3 \end{aligned}$$

State Resources

go.hrw.com
State Resources Online
KEYWORD: MA7 Resources

1 Introduce

EXPLORATION

7-7 Adding and Subtracting Polynomials

An ecologist is studying frogs and toads in a wetlands habitat. She finds that the polynomial $3x^2 + x$ models the frog population and that the polynomial $7x^2 - x$ models the toad population. In both cases, x represents the number of months.

1. Complete the table. For each month, evaluate the two polynomials to find the population of frogs and toads. Then add these values to find the total population.

Month, x	Population of Frogs, $3x^2 + x$	Population of Toads, $7x^2 - x$	Total Population
1	4	6	10
2			
3			
4			
5			
6			

2. Look for a pattern in the last column. Write a simplified polynomial that gives the total population in month x.

THINK AND DISCUSS

3. **Show** how to find the sum of the polynomials $3x^2 + x$ and $7x^2 - x$.
4. **Describe** how you could find the sum using the terms of the two polynomials that are being added.

Motivate

Display the following items: 4 books, 3 pencils, 2 books, and 5 pencils.

Ask students for a sensible way to group the items. a group of 6 books and a group of 8 pencils

Explain to students that adding and subtracting monomials is done in a similar way.

Explorations and answers are provided in *Alternate Openers: Explorations Transparencies.*

EXAMPLE 2 Adding Polynomials

Add.

A $(2x^2 - x) + (x^2 + 3x - 1)$

$(2x^2 - x) + (x^2 + 3x - 1)$	*Identify like terms.*
$(2x^2 + x^2) + (-x + 3x) + (-1)$	*Group like terms together.*
$3x^2 + 2x - 1$	*Combine like terms.*

B $(-2ab + b) + (2ab + a)$

$(-2ab + b) + (2ab + a)$	*Identify like terms.*
$(-2ab + 2ab) + b + a$	*Group like terms together.*
$0 + b + a$	*Combine like terms.*
$b + a$	*Simplify.*

C $(4b^5 + 8b) + (3b^5 + 6b - 7b^5 + b)$

$(4b^5 + 8b) + (3b^5 + 6b - 7b^5 + b)$	*Identify like terms.*
$(4b^5 + 8b) + (-4b^5 + 7b)$	*Combine like terms in the second polynomial.*
$\begin{array}{r} 4b^5 + 8b \\ + -4b^5 + 7b \\ \hline 0 \quad + 15b \end{array}$	*Use the vertical method.* *Combine like terms.*
$15b$	*Simplify.*

D $(20.2y^2 + 6y + 5) + (1.7y^2 - 8)$

$(20.2y^2 + 6y + 5) + (1.7y^2 - 8)$	*Identify like terms.*
$\begin{array}{r} 20.2y^2 + 6y + 5 \\ + 1.7y^2 + 0y - 8 \\ \hline 21.9y^2 + 6y - 3 \end{array}$	*Use the vertical method.* *Write 0y as a placeholder in the second polynomial.* *Combine like terms.*

Writing Math

When you use the Associative and Commutative Properties to rearrange the terms, the sign in front of each term must stay with that term.

2. Add $(5a^3 + 3a^2 - 6a + 12a^2) + (7a^3 - 10a)$. **$12a^3 + 15a^2 - 16a$**

To subtract polynomials, remember that subtracting is the same as adding the opposite. To find the opposite of a polynomial, you must write the opposite of *each* term in the polynomial:

$$-(2x^3 - 3x + 7) = -2x^3 + 3x - 7$$

EXAMPLE 3 Subtracting Polynomials

Subtract.

A $(2x^2 + 6) - (4x^2)$

$(2x^2 + 6) + (-4x^2)$	*Rewrite subtraction as addition of the opposite.*
$(2x^2 + 6) + (-4x^2)$	*Identify like terms.*
$(2x^2 - 4x^2) + 6$	*Group like terms together.*
$-2x^2 + 6$	*Combine like terms.*

B $(a^4 - 2a) - (3a^4 - 3a + 1)$

$(a^4 - 2a) + (-3a^4 + 3a - 1)$	*Rewrite subtraction as addition of the opposite.*
$(a^4 - 2a) + (-3a^4 + 3a - 1)$	*Identify like terms.*
$(a^4 - 3a^4) + (-2a + 3a) - 1$	*Group like terms together.*
$-2a^4 + a - 1$	*Combine like terms.*

COMMON ERROR ALERT

Students often think the terms xy^2 and x^2y are like terms. Write out all factors to show students how they are different: $xy^2 = xyy$, and $x^2y = xxy$.

Power Presentations with PowerPoint®

Additional Examples

Example 1

Add or subtract.

A. $12p^3 + 11p^2 + 8p^3$ $20p^3 + 11p^2$

B. $5x^2 - 6 - 3x + 8$ $5x^2 - 3x + 2$

C. $t^2 + 2s^2 - 4t^2 - s^2$ $-3t^2 + s^2$

D. $10m^2n + 4m^2n - 8m^2n$ $6m^2n$

Example 2

Add.

A. $(4m^2 + 5) + (m^2 - m + 6)$ $5m^2 - m + 11$

B. $(10xy + x) + (-3xy + y)$ $7xy + x + y$

C. $(6x^2 - 4y) + (3x^2 + 3y - 8x^2 - 2y)$ $x^2 - 3y$

D. $\left(\frac{1}{2}a^2 + b + 2\right) + \left(\frac{3}{2}a^2 - 4b + 5\right)$ $2a^2 - 3b + 7$

INTERVENTION

Questioning Strategies

EXAMPLE 1

- How do you identify like terms?

EXAMPLE 2

- When using a vertical format to add polynomials, what is a placeholder? How is it helpful?

Inclusion Remind students that the Commutative Property of Addition states that you can add numbers in any order. The Associative Property of Addition states that you can group any of the numbers together.

2 Teach

Guided Instruction

Review like terms before beginning this lesson. When rearranging terms, remind students to pay close attention to the sign in front of each term. Point out that in **Example 2C**, like terms in the second polynomial were simplified before the polynomials were added. Students will be less likely to make mistakes when the individual polynomials are simplified first.

Visual Cues Draw different marks around like terms so they stand out.

Reaching All Learners

Through Cooperative Learning

Prepare a bag with several small slips of paper (at least four times the number of students in class), each with one of the following: x, $2x$, $-3x$, y, $4y$, $-6y$. Have each student randomly select three or four slips of paper. Have students combine, and simplify if possible, their terms and write the resulting polynomial on a piece of paper. Then have students pair up to find the sums and differences of their polynomials. Have students pair up with as many others as time allows.

Multiple Representations Finding the opposite of a polynomial can be thought of as distributing -1.

Power Presentations with PowerPoint®

Additional Examples

Example 3

Subtract.

A. $(x^3 + 4y) - (2x^3)$ $\quad -x^3 + 4y$

B. $(7m^4 - 2m^2) - (5m^4 - 5m^2 + 8)$
$2m^4 + 3m^2 - 8$

C. $(-10x^2 - 3x + 7) - (x^2 - 9)$
$-11x^2 - 3x + 16$

D. $(9q^2 - 3q) - (q^2 - 5)$
$8q^2 - 3q + 5$

Example 4

A farmer must add the areas of two plots of land to determine the amount of seed to plant. The area of plot A can be represented by $3x^2 + 7x - 5$, and the area of plot B can be represented by $5x^2 - 4x + 11$. Write a polynomial that represents the total area of both plots of land.
$8x^2 + 3x + 6$

INTERVENTION

Questioning Strategies

EXAMPLE 3

- What is the first step in subtracting polynomials?
- Why are parentheses used when subtracting polynomials?

EXAMPLE 4

- What is the purpose of aligning terms before adding or subtracting polynomials?

Subtract.

C $(3x^2 - 2x + 8) - (x^2 - 4)$

$(3x^2 - 2x + 8) + (-x^2 + 4)$ — *Rewrite subtraction as addition of the opposite.*

$(3x^2 - 2x + 8) + (-x^2 + 4)$ — *Identify like terms.*

$\ 3x^2 - 2x + 8$ — *Use the vertical method.*

$+ -x^2 + 0x + 4$ — *Write 0x as a placeholder.*

$2x^2 - 2x + 12$ — *Combine like terms.*

D $(11z^3 - 2z) - (z^3 - 5)$

$(11z^3 - 2z) + (-z^3 + 5)$ — *Rewrite subtraction as addition of the opposite.*

$(11z^3 - 2z) + (-z^3 + 5)$ — *Identify like terms.*

$\ 11z^3 - 2z + 0$ — *Use the vertical method.*

$+ -z^3 + 0z + 5$ — *Write 0 and 0z as placeholders.*

$10z^3 - 2z + 5$ — *Combine like terms.*

3. Subtract $(2x^2 - 3x^2 + 1) - (x^2 + x + 1)$. $\mathbf{-2x^2 - x}$

EXAMPLE 4 *Business Application*

The profits of two different manufacturing plants can be modeled as shown, where x is the number of units produced at each plant.

Eastern: $-0.03x^2 + 25x - 1500$

Southern: $-0.02x^2 + 21x - 1700$

Write a polynomial that represents the difference of the profits at the eastern plant and the profits at the southern plant.

$(-0.03x^2 + 25x - 1500)$ — *Eastern plant profits*

$-(-0.02x^2 + 21x - 1700)$ — *Southern plant profits*

$\ -0.03x^2 + 25x - 1500$

$+(+0.02x^2 - 21x + 1700)$ — *Write subtraction as addition of the opposite.*

$-0.01x^2 + 4x + 200$ — *Combine like terms.*

4. Use the information above to write a polynomial that represents the total profits from both plants.
$\mathbf{-0.05x^2 + 46x - 3200}$

THINK AND DISCUSS

1. Identify the like terms in the following list: $-12x^2, -4.7y, \frac{1}{5}x^2y, y, 3xy^2, -9x^2, 5x^2y, -12x$
2. Describe how to find the opposite of $9t^2 - 5t + 8$.

3. **GET ORGANIZED** Copy and complete the graphic organizer. In each box, write an example that shows how to perform the given operation.

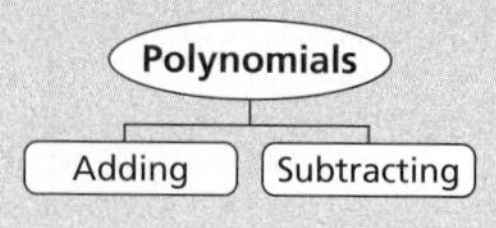

3 Close

Summarize

Have students list the steps for adding and subtracting polynomials.

1. Rewrite subtraction as addition if necessary.
2. Identify like terms.
3. Rearrange terms so that like terms are together.
4. Combine like terms.
5. Simplify if necessary.

ONGOING ASSESSMENT and INTERVENTION

***Diagnose Before* the Lesson**
7-7 Warm Up, TE p. 504

***Monitor During* the Lesson**
Check It Out! Exercises, SE pp. 504–506
Questioning Strategies, TE pp. 505–506

***Assess After* the Lesson**
7-7 Lesson Quiz, TE p. 509
Alternative Assessment, TE p. 509

Answers to *Think and Discuss*

1. $-12x^2$ and $-9x^2$; $-4.7y$ and y; $\frac{1}{5}x^2y$ and $5x^2y$
2. Take the opposite of each term: $-9t^2 + 5t - 8$.
3. See p. A7.

7-7 Exercises

go.hrw.com
Homework Help Online
KEYWORD: MA11 7-7
Parent Resources Online
KEYWORD: MA7 Parent

GUIDED PRACTICE

SEE EXAMPLE 1 p. 504

Add or subtract.

1. $7a^2 - 10a^2 + 9a$ **$-3a^2 + 9a$**
2. $13x^2 + 9y^2 - 6x^2$ **$7x^2 + 9y^2$**
3. $0.07r^4 + 0.32r^3 + 0.19r^4$ **$0.26r^4 + 0.32r^3$**
4. $\frac{1}{4}p^3 + \frac{2}{3}p^3$ **$\frac{11}{12}p^3$**
5. $5b^3c + b^3c - 3b^3c$ **$3b^3c$**
6. $-8m + 5 - 16 + 11m$ **$3m - 11$**

SEE EXAMPLE 2 p. 505

Add.

7. $(5n^3 + 3n + 6) + (18n^3 + 9)$
8. $(3.7q^2 - 8q + 3.7) + (4.3q^2 - 2.9q + 1.6)$
9. $(-3x + 12) + (9x^2 + 2x - 18)$
10. $(9x^4 + x^3) + (2x^4 + 6x^3 - 8x^4 + x^3)$

SEE EXAMPLE 3 p. 505

Subtract.

11. $(6c^4 + 8c + 6) - (2c^4)$ **$4c^4 + 8c + 6$**
12. $(16y^2 - 8y + 9) - (6y^2 - 2y + 7y)$ **$10y^2 - 13y + 9$**
13. $(2r + 5) - (5r - 6)$ **$-3r + 11$**
14. $(-7k^2 + 3) - (2k^2 + 5k - 1)$ **$-9k^2 - 5k + 4$**

SEE EXAMPLE 4 p. 506

15. **Geometry** Write a polynomial that represents the measure of angle *ABD*. **$8a^2 + 5a + 9$**

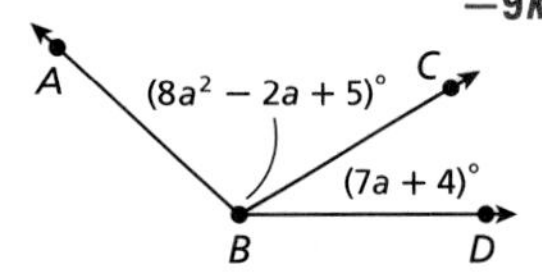

PRACTICE AND PROBLEM SOLVING

Independent Practice

For Exercises	See Example
16–24	1
25–28	2
29–32	3
33–34	4

Extra Practice
Skills Practice p. S17
Application Practice p. S34

Add or subtract.

16. $4k^3 + 6k^2 + 9k^3$
17. $5m + 12n^2 + 6n - 8m$
18. $2.5a^4 - 8.1b^4 - 3.6b^4$
19. $2d^5 + 1 - d^5$
20. $7xy - 4x^2y - 2xy$
21. $-6x^3 + 5x + 2x^3 + 4x^3$
22. $x^2 + x + 3x + 2x^2$
23. $3x^3 - 4 - x^3 - 1$
24. $3b^3 - 2b - 1 - b^3 - b$

Add.

25. $(2t^2 - 8t) + (8t^2 + 9t)$ **$10t^2 + t$**
26. $(-7x^2 - 2x + 3) + (4x^2 - 9x)$ **$-3x^2 - 11x + 3$**
27. $(x^5 - x) + (x^4 + x)$ **$x^5 + x^4$**
28. $(-2z^3 + z + 2z^3 + z) + (3z^3 - 5z^2)$ **$3z^3 - 5z^2 + 2z$**

Subtract.

29. $(t^3 + 8t^2) - (3t^3)$ **$-2t^3 + 8t^2$**
30. $(3x^2 - x) - (x^2 + 3x - x)$ **$2x^2 - 3x$**

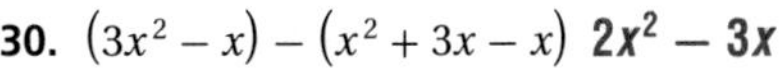

31. $(5m + 3) - (6m^3 - 2m^2)$ **$-6m^3 + 2m^2 + 5m + 3$**
32. $(3s^2 + 4s) - (-10s^2 + 6s)$ **$13s^2 - 2s$**
33. **Photography** The measurements of a photo and its frame are shown in the diagram. Write a polynomial that represents the width of the photo. **$4w^2 + 6w + 4$**

34. **Geometry** The length of a rectangle is represented by $4a + 3b$, and its width is represented by $7a - 2b$. Write a polynomial for the perimeter of the rectangle. **$22a + 2b$**

7-7 Exercises

Assignment Guide

Assign *Guided Practice* exercises as necessary.

If you finished Examples **1–2**
Basic 16–28
Average 16–28, 58
Advanced 16–28, 58

If you finished Examples **1–4**
Basic 16–43, 45–51, 53–56, 63–72
Average 16–56, 58, 63–72
Advanced 16–44, 52–72

Homework Quick Check
Quickly check key concepts.
Exercises: 24, 28, 30, 32, 33, 48

Teaching Tip

Auditory For **Exercises 1–6,** suggest to students that they say each term out loud as they do their homework to hear the difference between like and unlike terms.

State Resources

Answers

7. $23n^3 + 3n + 15$
8. $8q^2 - 10.9q + 5.3$
9. $9x^2 - x - 6$
10. $3x^4 + 8x^3$
16. $13k^3 + 6k^2$
17. $12n^2 + 6n - 3m$
18. $2.5a^4 - 11.7b^4$
19. $d^5 + 1$
20. $-4x^2y + 5xy$
21. $5x$
22. $3x^2 + 4x$
23. $2x^3 - 5$
24. $2b^3 - 3b - 1$

Exercise 53 involves writing expressions for the dimensions of a rectangle. This exercise prepares students for the Multi-Step Test Prep on page 528.

Answers

52. No; polynomial addition simply involves combining like terms. No matter what order the terms are combined in, the sum will be the same. Yes; in polynomial subtraction, the subtraction sign is distributed among all terms in the second polynomial, changing all the signs to their opposites.

53a.

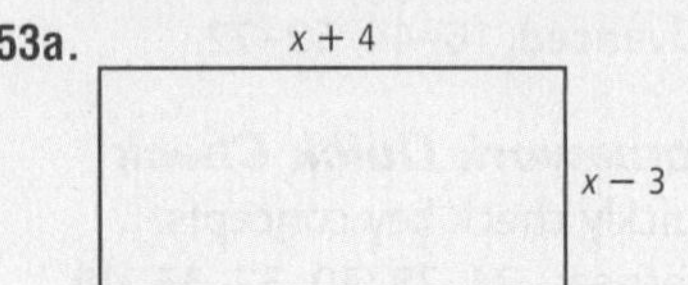

Add or subtract.

35. $(2t - 7) + (-t + 2)$ **$t - 5$**
36. $(4m^2 + 3m) + (-2m^2)$ **$2m^2 + 3m$**
37. $(4n - 2) - 2n$ **$2n - 2$**
38. $(-v - 7) - (-2v)$ **$v - 7$**
39. $(4x^2 + 3x - 6) + (2x^2 - 4x + 5)$ **$6x^2 - x - 1$**
40. $(2z^2 - 3z - 3) + (2z^2 - 7z - 1)$ **$4z^2 - 10z - 4$**
41. $(5u^2 + 3u + 7) - (u^3 + 2u^2 + 1)$
42. $(-7h^2 - 4h + 7) - (7h^2 - 4h + 11)$ **$-14h^2 - 4$**

41. $-u^3 + 3u^2 + 3u + 6$

43. **Geometry** The length of a rectangle is represented by $2x + 3$, and its width is represented by $3x + 7$. The perimeter of the rectangle is 35 units. Find the value of x.

43. $\frac{3}{2}$, or 1.5

44. **Write About It** If the parentheses are removed from $(3m^2 - 5m) + (12m^2 + 7m - 10)$, is the new expression equivalent to the original? If the parentheses are removed from $(3m^2 - 5m) - (12m^2 + 7m - 10)$, is the new expression equivalent to the original? Explain.

44. Yes; the simplified form of both expressions is $15m^2 + 2m - 10$. No; the simplified form of the orig. expression is $-9m^2 - 12m + 10$, and the simplified form of the new expression is $-9m^2 + 2m - 10$.

45. **/// ERROR ANALYSIS ///** Two students found the sum of the polynomials $(-3n^4 + 6n^3 + 4n^2)$ and $(8n^4 - 3n^2 + 9n)$. Which is incorrect? Explain the error.

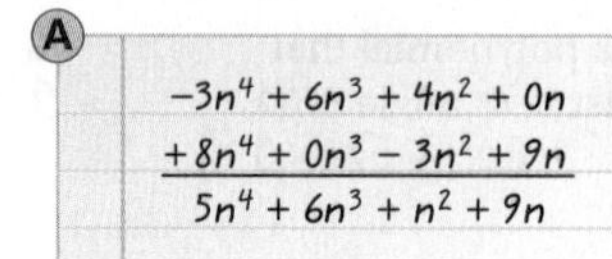

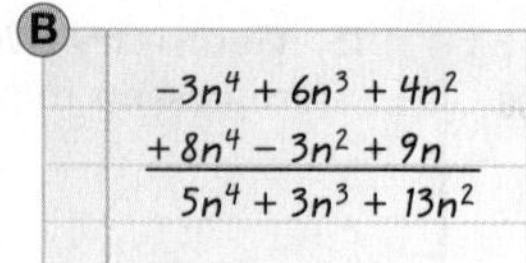

45. B is incorrect. The student incorrectly tried to combine $6n^3$ and $-3n^2$, which are not like terms, and $4n^2$ and $9n$, which are not like terms.

Copy and complete the table by finding the missing polynomials.

	Polynomial 1	Polynomial 2	Sum
46.	$x^2 - 6$	$3x^2 - 10x + 2$	**$4x^2 - 10x - 4$**
47.	$12x + 5$	**$3x + 6$**	$15x + 11$
48.	**$x^4 - 3x^2 - 9$**	$5x^4 + 8$	$6x^4 - 3x^2 - 1$
49.	$7x^3 - 6x - 3$	**$6x + 14$**	$7x^3 + 11$
50.	$2x^3 + 5x^2$	$7x^3 - 5x^2 + 1$	**$9x^3 + 1$**
51.	**$2x^2 + x - 5$**	$x + x^2 + 6$	$3x^2 + 2x + 1$

52. **Critical Thinking** Does the order in which you add polynomials affect the sum? Does the order in which you subtract polynomials affect the difference? Explain.

53. This problem will prepare you for the Multi-Step Test Prep on page 528.
    a. Ian plans to build a fenced dog pen. At first, he planned for the pen to be a square of length x feet on each side, but then he decided that a square may not be best. He added 4 feet to the length and subtracted 3 feet from the width. Draw a diagram to show the dimensions of the new pen.
    b. Write a polynomial that represents the amount of fencing that Ian will need for the new dog pen. **$4x + 2$**
    c. How much fencing will Ian need if $x = 15$? **62 ft**

7-7 PRACTICE A
7-7 PRACTICE C
7-7 PRACTICE B

Add or subtract.

1. $3m^3 + 8m^3 - 3 + m^3 - 2m^2$ **$12m^3 - 2m^2 - 3$**
2. $2pg - p^5 - 12pg + 5g - 6p^5$ **$-7p^5 - 10pg + 5g$**

Add.

3. $3k^2 - 2k + 7$ + $k - 2$ **$3k^2 - k + 5$**
4. $5x^2 - 2x + 3y$ + $6x^2 + 5x + 6y$ **$11x^2 + 3x + 9y$**
5. $11hz^3 + 3hz^2 + 8hz$ + $9hz^3 + hz^2 - 3hz$ **$20hz^3 + 4hz^2 + 5hz$**
6. $(ab^2 + 13b - 4a) + (3ab^2 + a + 7b)$ **$4ab^2 + 20b - 3a$**
7. $(4x^3 - x^2 + 4x) + (x^3 - x^2 - 4x)$ **$5x^3 - 2x^2$**

Subtract.

8. $12d^2 + 3dx + x$ $-(-4d^2 + 2dx - 8x)$ **$16d^2 + dx + 9x$**
9. $2v^5 - 3v^4 - 8$ $-(3v^5 + 2v^4 - 8)$ **$-v^5 - 5v^4$**
10. $-y^4 + 6ay^2 - y + a$ $-(-6y^4 - 2ay^2 + y)$ **$5y^4 + 8ay^2 - 2y + a$**
11. $(-r^2 + 8pr - p) - (-12r^2 - 2pr + 8p)$ **$11r^2 + 10pr - 9p$**
12. $(un - n^2 + 2un^3) - (3un^3 + n^2 + 4un)$ **$-3un - 2n^2 - un^3$**
13. Antoine is making a banner in the shape of a triangle. He wants to line the banner with a decorative border. How long will the border be? (Triangle sides: $12b - 8$, $9b + 8$, $12b - 8$)
    $33b - 8$
14. Darnell and Stephanie have competing refreshment stand businesses. Darnell's profit can be modeled with the polynomial $c^2 + 8c - 100$, where c is the number of items sold. Stephanie's profit can be modeled with the polynomial $2c^2 - 7c - 200$.
    a. Write a polynomial that represents the difference between Stephanie's profit and Darnell's profit.
    $c^2 - 15c - 100$
    b. Write a polynomial to show how much they can expect to earn if they decided to combine their businesses.
    $3c^2 + c - 300$

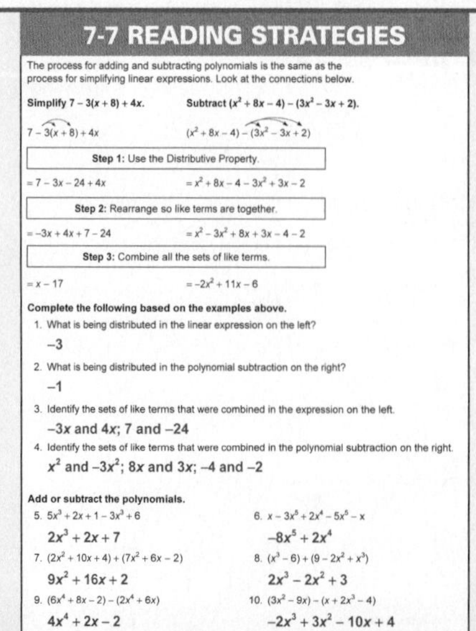

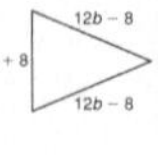

7-7 READING STRATEGIES

The process for adding and subtracting polynomials is the same as the process for simplifying linear expressions. Look at the connections below.

Simplify $7 - 3(x + 8) + 4x$. | **Subtract $(x^2 + 8x - 4) - (3x^2 - 3x + 2)$.**

$7 - 3(x + 8) + 4x$ | $(x^2 + 8x - 4) - (3x^2 - 3x + 2)$

Step 1: Use the Distributive Property.

$= 7 - 3x - 24 + 4x$ | $= x^2 + 8x - 4 - 3x^2 + 3x - 2$

Step 2: Rearrange so like terms are together.

$= -3x + 4x + 7 - 24$ | $= x^2 - 3x^2 + 8x + 3x - 4 - 2$

Step 3: Combine all the sets of like terms.

$= x - 17$ | $= -2x^2 + 11x - 6$

Complete the following based on the examples above.

1. What is being distributed in the linear expression on the left?
   -3
2. What is being distributed in the polynomial subtraction on the right?
   -1
3. Identify the sets of like terms that were combined in the expression on the left.
   $-3x$ and $4x$; 7 and -24
4. Identify the sets of like terms that were combined in the polynomial subtraction on the right.
   x^2 and $-3x^2$; $8x$ and $3x$; -4 and -2

Add or subtract the polynomials.

5. $5x^3 + 2x + 1 - 3x^3 + 6$ **$2x^3 + 2x + 7$**
6. $x - 3x^5 + 2x^4 - 5x^5 - x$ **$-8x^5 + 2x^4$**
7. $(2x^2 + 10x + 4) + (7x^2 + 6x - 2)$ **$9x^2 + 16x + 2$**
8. $(x^3 - 6) + (9 - 2x^2 + x^3)$ **$2x^3 - 2x^2 + 3$**
9. $(6x^4 + 8x - 2) - (2x^4 + 6x)$ **$4x^4 + 2x - 2$**
10. $(3x^2 - 9x) - (x + 2x^3 - 4)$ **$-2x^3 + 3x^2 - 10x + 4$**

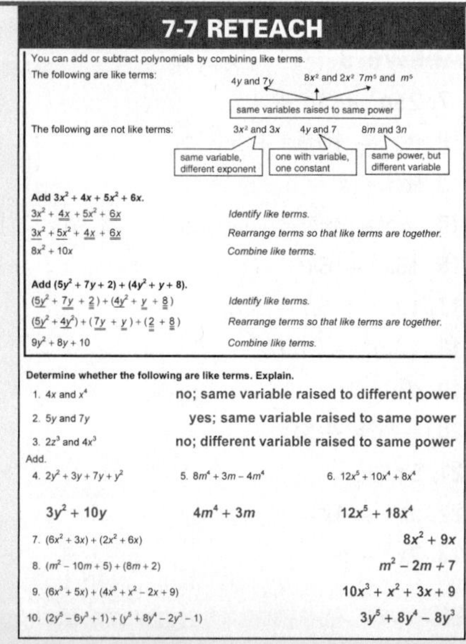

7-7 RETEACH

You can add or subtract polynomials by combining like terms.

The following are like terms: $4y$ and $7y$ | $8x^2$ and $2x^2$ | $7m^5$ and m^5 — same variables raised to same power

The following are not like terms: $3x^2$ and $3x$ (same variable, different exponent) | $4y$ and 7 (one with variable, one constant) | $8m$ and $3n$ (same power, but different variable)

Add $3x^2 + 4x + 5x^2 + 6x$.

$3x^2 + 4x + 5x^2 + 6x$ — *Identify like terms.*
$3x^2 + 5x^2 + 4x + 6x$ — *Rearrange terms so that like terms are together.*
$8x^2 + 10x$ — *Combine like terms.*

Add $(5y^2 + 7y + 2) + (4y^2 + y + 8)$.

$(5y^2 + 7y + 2) + (4y^2 + y + 8)$ — *Identify like terms.*
$(5y^2 + 4y^2) + (7y + y) + (2 + 8)$ — *Rearrange terms so that like terms are together.*
$9y^2 + 8y + 10$ — *Combine like terms.*

Determine whether the following are like terms. Explain.

1. $4x$ and x^4 **no; same variable raised to different power**
2. $5y$ and $7y$ **yes; same variable raised to same power**
3. $2z^3$ and $4x^3$ **no; different variable raised to same power**

Add.

4. $2y^2 + 3y + 7y + y^2$ **$3y^2 + 10y$**
5. $8m^4 + 3m - 4m^4$ **$4m^4 + 3m$**
6. $12x^5 + 10x^4 + 8x^4$ **$12x^5 + 18x^4$**
7. $(6x^2 + 3x) + (2x^2 + 6x)$ **$8x^2 + 9x$**
8. $(m^2 - 10m + 5) + (8m + 2)$ **$m^2 - 2m + 7$**
9. $(6x^3 + 5x) + (4x^3 + x^2 - 2x + 9)$ **$10x^3 + x^2 + 3x + 9$**
10. $(2y^5 - 6y^3 + 1) + (y^5 + 8y^4 - 2y^3 - 1)$ **$3y^5 + 8y^4 - 8y^3$**

TEST PREP

54. What is the missing term?

$(-14y^2 + 9y^2 - 12y + 3) + (2y^2 + \blacksquare - 6y - 2) = (-3y^2 - 15y + 1)$

(A) $-6y$ (B) $-3y$ **(C)** $3y$ (D) $6y$

55. Which is NOT equivalent to $-5t^3 - t$?

(F) $-(5t^3 + t)$ (H) $(t^3 + 6t) - (6t^3 + 7t)$

(G) $(2t^3 - 4t) - (-7t - 3t)$ (J) $(2t^3 - 3t^2 + t) - (7t^3 - 3t^2 + 2t)$

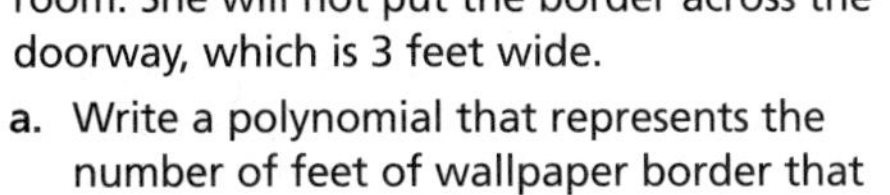

56. **Extended Response** Tammy plans to put a wallpaper border around the perimeter of her room. She will not put the border across the doorway, which is 3 feet wide.

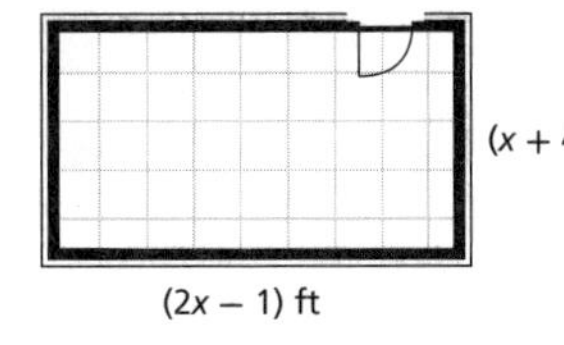

a. Write a polynomial that represents the number of feet of wallpaper border that Tammy will need. $\mathbf{6x + 3}$

b. A local store has 50 feet of the border that Tammy has chosen. What is the greatest whole-number value of x for which this amount would be enough for Tammy's room? Justify your answer.

c. Determine the dimensions of Tammy's room for the value of x that you found in part **b.** **13 ft × 11 ft**

56b. 7; If $x = 7$, Tammy will need $6(7) + 3 = 45$ feet of wallpaper border. However, if $x = 8$, Tammy will need $6(8) + 3 = 51$ feet of wallpaper border, which is more than the store has.

CHALLENGE AND EXTEND

57. **Geometry** The legs of the isosceles triangle at right measure $(x^3 + 5)$ units. The perimeter of the triangle is $(2x^3 + 3x^2 + 8)$ units. Write a polynomial that represents the measure of the base of the triangle. $\mathbf{3x^2 - 2}$

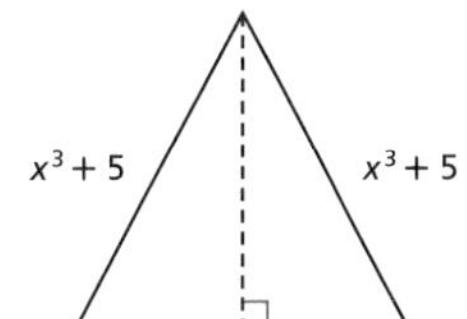

58. Write two polynomials whose sum is $4m^3 + 3m$.

59. Write two polynomials whose difference is $4m^3 + 3m$.

60. Write three polynomials whose sum is $4m^3 + 3m$.

61. Write two monomials whose sum is $4m^3 + 3m$. $\mathbf{4m^3, 3m}$

62. Write three trinomials whose sum is $4m^3 + 3m$.
$\mathbf{2m^3 + m^2 + m, m^3 + m^2 + m, m^3 - 2m^2 + m}$

58–62. Possible answers given.

58. $2m^3 + 2m$, $2m^3 + m$

59. $5m^3 + 2m$, $m^3 - m$

60. $2m^3 + m$, $m^3 + m$, $m^3 + m$

SPIRAL REVIEW

Solve each inequality and graph the solutions. *(Lesson 3-2)*

63. $d + 5 \geq -2$ $\mathbf{d \geq -7}$ 64. $15 < m - 11$ $\mathbf{m > 26}$ 65. $-6 + t < -6$ $\mathbf{t < 0}$

Write each equation in slope-intercept form. Then graph the line described by each equation. *(Lesson 5-7)*

66. $3x + y = 8$ $\mathbf{y = -3x + 8}$ 67. $2y = \frac{1}{2}x + 6$ $\mathbf{y = \frac{1}{4}x + 3}$ 68. $y = 4(-x + 1)$ $\mathbf{y = -4x + 4}$

Simplify. *(Lesson 7-3)*

69. $b^4 \cdot b^7$ $\mathbf{b^{11}}$ 70. $cd^4 \cdot (c^{-5})^3$ $\mathbf{\frac{d^4}{c^{14}}}$ 71. $(-3z^6)^2$ $\mathbf{9z^{12}}$ 72. $(j^3k^{-5})^3 \cdot (k^2)^4$ $\mathbf{\frac{j^9}{k^7}}$

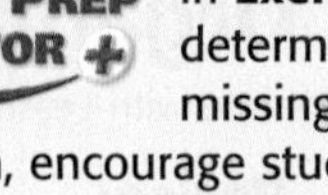

TEST PREP DOCTOR In **Exercise 54,** after determining that the missing term is a y-term, encourage students to write and solve an algebraic equation to find the coefficient:
$-12 + x - 6 = -15$.

Answers

63. Number line: −8 −7 −6 −5 −4 −3 −2 −1 0

64. Number line: 6 16 26 36 46 56 66

65. Number line: −3 −2 −1 0 1 2 3

66–68. For graphs, see p. A27.

Journal

Have students describe two different ways of adding polynomials, using examples in their descriptions.

ALTERNATIVE ASSESSMENT

Have students write four different polynomials, using any of the following as the variable part of the terms: x, y, x^2, y^2. Instruct students to pick any two of the polynomials and find the sum. Then have them find the difference of the remaining two polynomials.

Power Presentations with PowerPoint®

7-7 Lesson Quiz

Add or subtract.

1. $7m^2 + 3m + 4m^2$ $11m^2 + 3m$
2. $(r^2 + s^2) - (5r^2 + 4s^2)$
$-4r^2 - 3s^2$
3. $(10pq + 3p) + (2pq - 5p + 6pq)$ $18pq - 2p$
4. $(14d^2 - 8) + (6d^2 - 2d + 1)$
$20d^2 - 2d - 7$
5. $(2.5ab + 14b) - (-1.5ab + 4b)$ $4ab + 10b$
6. A painter must add the areas of two walls to determine the amount of paint needed. The area of the first wall is modeled by $4x^2 + 12x + 9$, and the area of the second wall is modeled by $36x^2 - 12x + 1$. Write a polynomial that represents the total area of the two walls. $40x^2 + 10$

Also available on transparency

7-7 PROBLEM SOLVING

Write the correct answer.

1. There are two boxes in a storage unit. The volume of the first box is $4x^3 + 4x^2$ cubic units. The volume of the second box is $6x^3 - 18x^2$ cubic units. Write a polynomial for the total volume of the two boxes.
$10x^3 - 14x^2$ cubic units

2. The recreation field at a middle school is shaped like a rectangle with a length of $15x$ yards and a width of $10x - 3$ yards. Write a polynomial for the perimeter of the field. Then calculate the perimeter if $x = 2$.
$50x - 6$
94 yards

3. Two cabins on opposite banks of a river are $12x^2 - 7x + 5$ feet apart. One cabin is $9x + 1$ feet from the river. The other cabin is $3x^2 + 4$ feet from the river. Write the polynomial that represents the width of the river where it passes between the two cabins. Then calculate the width if $x = 3$.

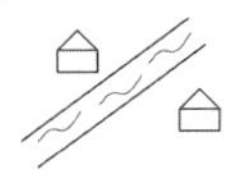

$9x^2 - 16x$; 33 feet

The circle graph represents election results for the president of the math team. Use the graph for questions 4–6. Select the best answer.

4. The angle value of Greg's sector can be modeled by $x^2 + 6x + 2$. The angle value of Dion's sector can be modeled by $7x + 20$. Which polynomial represents both sectors combined?
A $x^2 + x + 18$ C $6x^2 + 7x + 18$
B $x^2 + 13x + 22$ D $7x^2 + 6x + 22$

5. The sum of Greg and Lynn's sectors is $2x^2 + 4x - 6$. The sum of Max and Dion's sectors is $10x + 26$. Which polynomial represents how much greater Greg and Lynn's combined sectors are than Max and Dion's?
F $2x^2 + 6x + 32$ **H** $2x^2 - 6x - 32$
G $2x^2 - 6x + 20$ J $2x^2 + 14x + 20$

6. The sum of Lynn's sector and Max's sector is $2x^2 - 9x - 2$. Max's sector can be modeled by $3x + 6$. Which polynomial represents the angle value of Lynn's sector?
A $2x^2 - 6x + 4$ C $2x^2 - 12x + 8$
B $2x^2 - 6x - 4$ **D** $2x^2 - 12x - 8$

7-7 CHALLENGE

A **polynomial function** is a function whose rule is a polynomial. For example, $P(x) = 2x^3 - 4x^2 + 3x - 2$ is a polynomial function.

Like other functions, polynomial functions can be evaluated by substituting a value for the variable and simplifying.

1. For $P(x) = 2x^3 - 4x^2 + 3x - 2$, find $P(2)$. **4**

A variable, or variable expression, can be substituted for the variable in a function as well. For example, if $P(x) = 5x + 3$, then $P(a) = 5a + 3$.

2. For $P(x) = -4x^3 + x - 6$, find $P(b)$. **$-4b^3 + b - 6$**

Suppose $P(x) = 3x - 2$. Then $P(c) + P(c + 1) = 3c - 2 + 3(c + 1) - 2$
$= 3c - 2 + 3c + 3 - 2$
$= 6c - 1$

3. For $P(x) = 10 - 4x$, find $P(d) + P(2d) - P(3)$.
$22 - 12d$

4. For $P(x) = -3x^4 - 7x^3 + 2x^2 - x + 8$, find $P(g^2) + P(g)$.
$-3g^8 - 7g^6 - g^4 - 7g^3 + g^2 - g + 16$

Give an example of $Q(x)$ and $S(x)$ for each situation.

5. $Q(x)$ is a quartic binomial. $S(x)$ is a quartic trinomial. $Q(x) + S(x)$ is a quartic trinomial.
$Q(x) = x^4 + 1$; $S(x) = x^4 + x^3 + 1$

6. $Q(x)$ is a cubic trinomial. $S(x)$ is a cubic binomial. $Q(x) - S(x)$ is a quadratic monomial.
$Q(x) = x^3 + x^2 + 1$; $S(x) = x^3 + 1$

7. $Q(x)$ is a cubic trinomial. $S(x)$ is a cubic binomial. $Q(x) + S(x)$ is a quadratic binomial.
$Q(x) = x^3 + x^2 + 1$; $S(x) = -x^3 + x^2$

8. $Q(x)$ is a quintic trinomial. $S(x)$ is a quartic trinomial. $Q(x) + S(x)$ is a quintic polynomial with five terms.
$Q(x) = x^5 + x^4 + 1$; $S(x) = x^4 + x^3 + x^2$

Organizer

Use with Lesson 7-8

Pacing:
Traditional $\frac{1}{2}$ day
Block $\frac{1}{4}$ day

Objective: Use algebra tiles to model polynomial multiplication.

Materials: algebra tiles

Online Edition

Countdown Week 16

Resources

Algebra Lab Activities
7-8 Lab Recording Sheet

Teach

Discuss

In **Activity 1,** show students that they would get the same product if they placed the first factor along the top and the second factor along the left side. This is because multiplication is commutative.

In **Activity 3,** remind students that zero pairs are only those whose size and shape are the same, but whose colors are different.

Alternative Approach

Use the transparency mat and transparency algebra tiles (MK).

State Resources

go.hrw.com
State Resources Online
KEYWORD: MA7 Resources

7-8 Algebra LAB

Use with Lesson 7-8

Model Polynomial Multiplication

You can use algebra tiles to multiply polynomials. Use the length and width of a rectangle to represent the factors. The area of the rectangle represents the product.

KEY

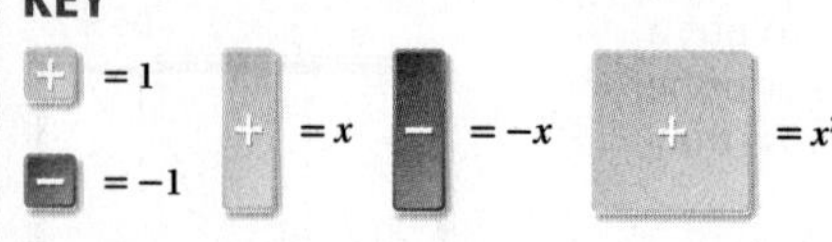

REMEMBER

- The product of two values with the same sign is positive.
- The product of two values with different signs is negative.

Activity 1

Use algebra tiles to find $2(x + 1)$.

MODEL		ALGEBRA
	Place the first factor in a column along the left side of the grid. This will be the width of the rectangle. *Place the second factor across the top of the grid. This will be the length of the rectangle.*	$2(x + 1)$
	Fill in the grid with tiles that have the same width as the tiles in the left column and the same length as the tiles in the top row.	
	The area of the rectangle inside the grid represents the product.	$x + x + 1 + 1$ $2x + 2$

The rectangle has an area of $2x + 2$, so $2(x + 1) = 2x + 2$. Notice that this is the same product you would get by using the Distributive Property to multiply $2(x + 1)$.

Try This

Use algebra tiles to find each product.

1. $3(x + 2)$ **$3x + 6$**
2. $2(2x + 1)$ **$4x + 2$**
3. $3(x + 1)$ **$3x + 3$**
4. $3(2x + 2)$ **$6x + 6$**

Activity 2

Use algebra tiles to find $2x(x - 3)$.

MODEL		ALGEBRA
	Place tiles to form the length and width of a rectangle and fill in the rectangle. The product of two values with the same sign (same color) is positive (yellow). The product of two values with different signs (different colors) is negative (red).	$2x(x - 3)$
	The area of the rectangle inside the grid represents the product. The rectangle has an area of $2x^2 - 6x$, so $2x(x - 3) = 2x^2 - 6x$.	$x^2 + x^2 - x - x - x - x - x - x$ $2x^2 - 6x$

Try This

Use algebra tiles to find each product.

5. $3x(x - 2)$ **$3x^2 - 6x$**
6. $x(2x - 1)$ **$2x^2 - x$**
7. $x(x + 1)$ **$x^2 + x$**
8. $(8x + 5)(-2x)$ **$-16x^2 - 10x$**

Activity 3

Use algebra tiles to find $(x + 1)(x - 2)$.

MODEL		ALGEBRA
	Place tiles for each factor to form the length and width of a rectangle. Fill in the grid and remove any zero pairs.	$(x + 1)(x - 2)$ $x^2 - x - x + x - 1 - 1$
	The area inside the grid represents the product. The remaining area is $x^2 - x - 2$, so $(x + 1)(x - 2) = x^2 - x - 2$.	$x^2 - x - 1 - 1$ $x^2 - x - 2$

Try This

Use algebra tiles to find each product.

9. $(x + 2)(x - 3)$ **$x^2 - x - 6$**
10. $(x - 1)(x + 3)$ **$x^2 + 2x - 3$**
11. $(x - 2)(x - 3)$ **$x^2 - 5x + 6$**
12. $(x + 1)(x + 2)$ **$x^2 + 3x + 2$**

Close

Key Concept

When multiplication is being modeled with algebra tiles, the dimensions of a rectangle represent the factors, and the area of the rectangle represents the product. The area of the rectangle can sometimes be simplified by removing zero pairs.

Assessment

Journal When using algebra tiles to model polynomial multiplication, have students explain how to determine which tiles should be placed inside the multiplication grid to form the rectangle (product). Explanations should include how to determine sizes, shapes, and colors of tiles.

7-8 Organizer

Pacing: Traditional 1 day
Block $\frac{1}{2}$ day

Objective: Multiply polynomials.

Online Edition
Tutorial Videos, Interactivity

Countdown Week 17

Power Presentations with PowerPoint®

Warm Up

Simplify.

1. 3^2 9 **2.** 2^4 16

3. 10^2 100

4. $2^3 \cdot 2^4$ 2^7 **5.** $y^5 \cdot y^4$ y^9

6. $(5^3)^2$ 5^6 **7.** $(x^2)^4$ x^8

8. $-4(x - 7)$ $-4x + 28$

Also available on transparency

Math Humor

Student A: What is *u* times *r* times *r*?

Student B: ur^2.

Student A: No, I'm not!

7-8 Multiplying Polynomials

Objective
Multiply polynomials.

Why learn this?
You can multiply polynomials to write expressions for areas, such as the area of a dulcimer. (See Example 5.)

To multiply monomials and polynomials, you will use some of the properties of exponents that you learned earlier in this chapter.

EXAMPLE 1 Multiplying Monomials

Multiply.

A $(5x^2)(4x^3)$

$(5x^2)(4x^3)$

$(5 \cdot 4)(x^2 \cdot x^3)$ *Group factors with like bases together.*

$20x^5$ *Multiply.*

B $(-3x^3y^2)(4xy^5)$

$(-3x^3y^2)(4xy^5)$

$(-3 \cdot 4)(x^3 \cdot x)(y^2 \cdot y^5)$ *Group factors with like bases together.*

$-12x^4y^7$ *Multiply.*

C $\left(\frac{1}{2}a^3b\right)(a^2c^2)(6b^2)$

$\left(\frac{1}{2}a^3b\right)(a^2c^2)(6b^2)$

$\left(\frac{1}{2} \cdot 6\right)(a^3 \cdot a^2)(b \cdot b^2)(c^2)$ *Group factors with like bases together.*

$3a^5b^3c^2$ *Multiply.*

Remember!

When multiplying powers with the same base, keep the base and add the exponents.

$x^2 \cdot x^3 = x^{2+3} = x^5$

CHECK IT OUT! Multiply.

1a. $(3x^3)(6x^2)$ $\mathbf{18x^5}$ **1b.** $(2r^2t)(5t^3)$ $\mathbf{10r^2t^4}$ **1c.** $\left(\frac{1}{3}x^2y\right)(12x^3z^2)(y^4z^5)$ $\mathbf{4x^5y^5z^7}$

To multiply a polynomial by a monomial, use the Distributive Property.

EXAMPLE 2 Multiplying a Polynomial by a Monomial

Multiply.

A $5(2x^2 + x + 4)$

$5(2x^2 + x + 4)$

$(5)2x^2 + (5)x + (5)4$ *Distribute 5.*

$10x^2 + 5x + 20$ *Multiply.*

1 Introduce

EXPLORATION

Multiplying Polynomials

You will need a graphing calculator for this Exploration. As you work through the Exploration, try to find a rule for multiplying a monomial and a polynomial.

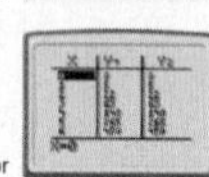

1. You can use your calculator to explore the relationship between $x(2x^2 + 3)$ and $2x^3 + 3x$. Press [Y=] and enter $x(2x^2 + 3)$ as **Y1**. Then enter $2x^3 + 3x$ as **Y2**.
2. Press [2nd] [GRAPH] to view a table of values for the two expressions. Use the arrow keys to scroll up and down the table. What do you notice about the values of **Y1** and **Y2** for each value of x? Use this information to make a conjecture about $x(2x^2 + 3)$ and $2x^3 + 3x$.

Use a calculator to predict whether each equation is true.

3. $2x(5x + 9) = 10x^2 + 18x$
4. $3x^3(2x + 9) = 6x^4 + 9$
5. $4x^2(3x - 5) = 12x^3 - 20x^2$
6. $10x^3(3x^2 - 2x) = 30x^5 - 20x^4$

THINK AND DISCUSS

7. **Describe** how to multiply a monomial and a polynomial based on your answers to Problems 3–6.

Motivate

Ask students to explain how to find the area of a rectangle with length 5 cm and width 7 cm.
$A = \ell w$, so $A = (5)(7) = 35$ cm²

Have students explain how to find the area of a rectangle with length x and width 10.
$A = \ell w$, so $A = (x)(10) = 10x$

Explain to students that in this lesson they will learn to describe area when the dimensions are polynomials.

Explorations and answers are provided in *Alternate Openers: Explorations Transparencies.*

State Resources

go.hrw.com
State Resources Online
KEYWORD: MA7 Resources

Multiply.

B $2x^2y(3x - y)$

$(2x^2y)(3x - y)$	
$(2x^2y)3x + (2x^2y)(-y)$	*Distribute $2x^2y$.*
$(2 \cdot 3)(x^2 \cdot x)y + 2(-1)(x^2)(y \cdot y)$	*Group like bases together.*
$6x^3y - 2x^2y^2$	*Multiply.*

C $4a(a^2b + 2b^2)$

$4a(a^2b + 2b^2)$	
$(4a)a^2b + (4a)2b^2$	*Distribute 4a.*
$(4)(a \cdot a^2)(b) + (4 \cdot 2)(a)(b^2)$	*Group like bases together.*
$4a^3b + 8ab^2$	*Multiply.*

Multiply.

2a. $2(4x^2 + x + 3)$ **$8x^2 + 2x + 6$**

2b. $3ab(5a^2 + b)$ **$15a^3b + 3ab^2$**

2c. $5r^2s^2(r - 3s)$ **$5r^3s^2 - 15r^2s^3$**

To multiply a binomial by a binomial, you can apply the Distributive Property more than once:

$(x + 3)(x + 2) = x(x + 2) + 3(x + 2)$	*Distribute.*
$= x(x + 2) + 3(x + 2)$	
$= x(x) + x(2) + 3(x) + 3(2)$	*Distribute again.*
$= x^2 + 2x + 3x + 6$	*Multiply.*
$= x^2 + 5x + 6$	*Combine like terms.*

Another method for multiplying binomials is called the FOIL method.

1. Multiply the **F**irst terms. F: $(x+3)(x+2) \rightarrow x \cdot x = x^2$
2. Multiply the **O**uter terms. O: $(x+3)(x+2) \rightarrow x \cdot 2 = 2x$
3. Multiply the **I**nner terms. I: $(x+3)(x+2) \rightarrow 3 \cdot x = 3x$
4. Multiply the **L**ast terms. L: $(x+3)(x+2) \rightarrow 3 \cdot 2 = 6$

$$(x+3)(x+2) = x^2 + 2x + 3x + 6 = x^2 + 5x + 6$$

F O I L

COMMON ERROR ALERT

When a binomial is raised to a power, many students make the following mistake: $(x + 4)^2 = x^2 + 4^2$. Encourage students to write the expression as the product of two binomials first and then multiply. For example, $(x + 4)^2 = (x + 4)(x + 4) = x^2 + 4x + 4x + 16 = x^2 + 8x + 16$.

Power Presentations with PowerPoint®

Additional Examples

Example 1

Multiply.

A. $(6y^3)(3y^5)$ $18y^8$

B. $(3mn^2)(9m^2n)$ $27m^3n^3$

C. $\left(\frac{1}{4}s^2t^2\right)(st)(-12st^2)$ $-3s^4t^5$

Example 2

Multiply.

A. $4(3x^2 + 4x - 8)$ $12x^2 + 16x - 32$

B. $6pq(2p - q)$ $12p^2q - 6pq^2$

C. $\frac{1}{2}x^2y(6xy + 8x^2y^2)$ $3x^3y^2 + 4x^4y^3$

INTERVENTION

Questioning Strategies

EXAMPLE 1

- How is multiplying monomials different from adding monomials?
- When multiplying monomials with exponents, why do you add the exponents?

EXAMPLE 2

- Will a monomial times a binomial always be a binomial?
- Will a monomial times a trinomial always be a trinomial? Explain.

Inclusion When using the FOIL method, encourage students to write the product after drawing each arrow rather than drawing all of the arrows at once. State: "Draw the F arrow and write the product, draw the O arrow and write the product," and so on.

2 Teach

Guided Instruction

Review the multiplication properties of exponents before beginning this lesson. Encourage students to write each step carefully to avoid making mistakes when distributing. Arrows can be drawn to help keep track of the terms that have been multiplied. Remind students that all of the methods presented in this lesson will give correct answers. Students should choose the method they are most comfortable with.

Reaching All Learners

Through Visual Cues

Show students the "FOIL face" to help them keep track of which terms to multiply.

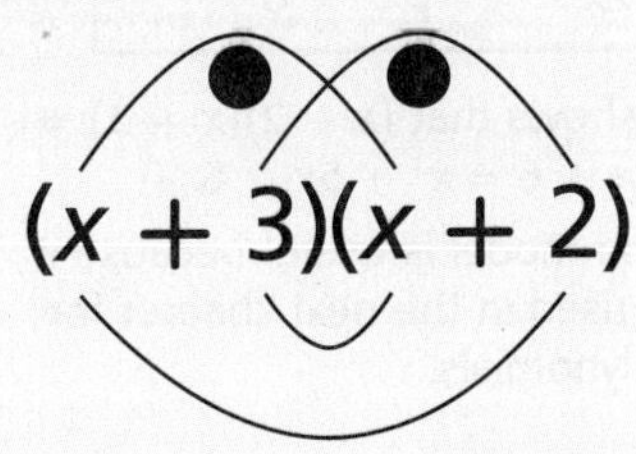

Power Presentations with PowerPoint®

Additional Examples

Example 3

Multiply.

A. $(s + 4)(s - 2)$ $s^2 + 2s - 8$

B. $(x - 4)^2$ $x^2 - 8x + 16$

C. $(8m^2 - n)(m^2 - 3n)$
$8m^4 - 25m^2n + 3n^2$

INTERVENTION

Questioning Strategies

EXAMPLE 3

- What terms from FOIL can often be combined?
- What do the signs from the last terms in each binomial tell you about the signs in the answer?

Teaching Tip **Math Background** In **Example 3C,** remind students that the terms $6a^2b$ and $-ba^2$ are like terms due to the Commutative Property of Multiplication.

EXAMPLE 3 Multiplying Binomials

Helpful Hint

In the expression $(x + 5)^2$, the base is $(x + 5)$.

$(x + 5)^2 =$
$(x + 5)(x + 5)$

Multiply.

A $(x+2)(x-5)$

$(x+2)(x-5)$	
$x(x-5)+2(x-5)$	*Distribute.*
$x(x)+x(-5)+2(x)+2(-5)$	*Distribute again.*
$x^2-5x+2x-10$	*Multiply.*
$x^2-3x-10$	*Combine like terms.*

B $(x+5)^2$

$(x+5)(x+5)$	*Write as a product of two binomials.*
$(x \cdot x)+(x \cdot 5)+(5 \cdot x)+(5 \cdot 5)$	*Use the FOIL method.*
$x^2+5x+5x+25$	*Multiply.*
$x^2+10x+25$	*Combine like terms.*

C $(3a^2-b)(a^2-2b)$

$3a^2(a^2)+3a^2(-2b)-b(a^2)-b(-2b)$	*Use the FOIL method.*
$3a^4-6a^2b-a^2b+2b^2$	*Multiply.*
$3a^4-7a^2b+2b^2$	*Combine like terms.*

3a. $(a+3)(a-4)$ **$a^2 - a - 12$**   **3b.** $(x-3)^2$ **$x^2 - 6x + 9$**   **3c.** $(2a-b^2)(a+4b^2)$ **$2a^2 + 7ab^2 - 4b^4$**

To multiply polynomials with more than two terms, you can use the Distributive Property several times. Multiply $(5x+3)$ by $(2x^2+10x-6)$:

$$(5x+3)(2x^2+10x-6) = 5x(2x^2+10x-6)+3(2x^2+10x-6)$$
$$= 5x(2x^2+10x-6)+3(2x^2+10x-6)$$
$$= 5x(2x^2)+5x(10x)+5x(-6)+3(2x^2)+3(10x)+3(-6)$$
$$= 10x^3+50x^2-30x+6x^2+30x-18$$
$$= 10x^3+56x^2-18$$

You can also use a rectangle model to multiply polynomials with more than two terms. This is similar to finding the area of a rectangle with length $(2x^2+10x-6)$ and width $(5x+3)$:

	$2x^2$	$+10x$	-6
$5x$	$10x^3$	$50x^2$	$-30x$
$+3$	$6x^2$	$30x$	-18

Write the product of the monomials in each row and column.

To find the product, add all of the terms inside the rectangle by combining like terms and simplifying if necessary.

$$10x^3+6x^2+50x^2+30x-30x-18$$
$$10x^3+56x^2-18$$

Reaching All Learners
Through Modeling

A rectangle model can also be used to display the FOIL method.

	x	$+3$
x	x^2	$3x$
$+2$	$2x$	6

This model shows that $(x + 2)(x + 3) = x^2 + 3x + 2x + 6 = x^2 + 5x + 6$.

This rectangle model is useful because it can also be used in the next chapter for factoring polynomials.

Another method that can be used to multiply polynomials with more than two terms is the vertical method. This is similar to methods used to multiply whole numbers.

$2x^2 + 10x - 6$	
$\times \quad 5x + 3$	
$6x^2 + 30x - 18$	*Multiply each term in the top polynomial by 3.*
$+ 10x^3 + 50x^2 - 30x$	*Multiply each term in the top polynomial by 5x, and align like terms.*
$10x^3 + 56x^2 + 0x - 18$	*Combine like terms by adding vertically.*
$10x^3 + 56x^2 \quad - 18$	*Simplify.*

EXAMPLE 4 Multiplying Polynomials

Helpful Hint

A polynomial with *m* terms multiplied by a polynomial with *n* terms has a product that, before simplifying, has *mn* terms. In Example 4A, there are 2 • 3, or 6, terms before simplifying.

Multiply.

A $(x + 2)(x^2 - 5x + 4)$

$(x + 2)(x^2 - 5x + 4)$	
$x(x^2 - 5x + 4) + 2(x^2 - 5x + 4)$	*Distribute.*
$x(x^2) + x(-5x) + x(4) + 2(x^2) + 2(-5x) + 2(4)$	*Distribute again.*
$x^3 + 2x^2 - 5x^2 - 10x + 4x + 8$	*Simplify.*
$x^3 - 3x^2 - 6x + 8$	*Combine like terms.*

B $(3x - 4)(-2x^3 + 5x - 6)$

$(3x - 4)(-2x^3 + 5x - 6)$	
$-2x^3 + 0x^2 + 5x - 6$	*Add $0x^2$ as a placeholder.*
$\times \quad 3x - 4$	
$8x^3 + 0x^2 - 20x + 24$	*Multiply each term in the top polynomial by −4.*
$+ -6x^4 + 0x^3 + 15x^2 - 18x$	*Multiply each term in the top polynomial by 3x, and align like terms.*
$-6x^4 + 8x^3 + 15x^2 - 38x + 24$	*Combine like terms by adding vertically.*

C $(x - 2)^3$

$[(x - 2)(x - 2)](x - 2)$	*Write as the product of three binomials.*
$[x \cdot x + x(-2) + (-2)x + (-2)(-2)](x - 2)$	*Use the FOIL method on the first two factors.*
$(x^2 - 2x - 2x + 4)(x - 2)$	*Multiply.*
$(x^2 - 4x + 4)(x - 2)$	*Combine like terms.*
$(x - 2)(x^2 - 4x + 4)$	*Use the Commutative Property of Multiplication.*
$x(x^2 - 4x + 4) + (-2)(x^2 - 4x + 4)$	*Distribute.*
$x(x^2) + x(-4x) + x(4) + (-2)(x^2) + (-2)(-4x) + (-2)(4)$	*Distribute again.*
$x^3 - 4x^2 + 4x - 2x^2 + 8x - 8$	*Simplify.*
$x^3 - 6x^2 + 12x - 8$	*Combine like terms.*

Power Presentations with PowerPoint®

Additional Examples

Example 4

Multiply.

A. $(x - 5)(x^2 + 4x - 6)$ $x^3 - x^2 - 26x + 30$

B. $(2x - 5)(-4x^2 - 10x + 3)$ $-8x^3 + 56x - 15$

C. $(x + 3)^3$ $x^3 + 9x^2 + 27x + 27$

D. $(3x + 1)(x^3 + 4x^2 - 7)$ $3x^4 + 13x^3 + 4x^2 - 21x - 7$

INTERVENTION
Questioning Strategies

EXAMPLE 4

- How is multiplying a polynomial by a binomial similar to multiplying a binomial by a binomial? How is it different?

Critical Thinking Ask students to find similarities between polynomials and real numbers. Discuss the types of operations you can use with each.

Power Presentations with PowerPoint®

Additional Examples

Example 5

The width of a rectangular prism is 3 feet less than the height, and the length of the prism is 4 feet more than the height.

a. Write a polynomial that represents the area of the base of the prism. $h^2 + h - 12$

b. Find the area of the base when the height is 5 feet. 18 ft^2

INTERVENTION

Questioning Strategies

EXAMPLE 5

- What types of polynomials did you multiply?

Multiply.

D $(2x+3)(x^2-6x+5)$

	x^2	$-6x$	$+5$
$2x$	$2x^3$	$-12x^2$	$10x$
$+3$	$3x^2$	$-18x$	15

Write the product of the monomials in each row and column.

$2x^3 + 3x^2 - 12x^2 - 18x + 10x + 15$ *Add all terms inside the rectangle.*

$2x^3 - 9x^2 - 8x + 15$ *Combine like terms.*

Multiply. $x^3 - x^2 - 6x + 18$

4a. $(x+3)(x^2-4x+6)$

4b. $(3x+2)(x^2-2x+5)$

$3x^3 - 4x^2 + 11x + 10$

EXAMPLE 5 ***Music Application***

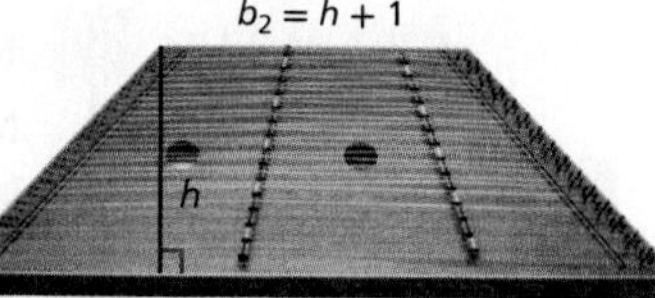

A dulcimer is a musical instrument that is sometimes shaped like a trapezoid.

A **Write a polynomial that represents the area of the dulcimer shown.**

$A = \frac{1}{2}h(b_1 + b_2)$ *Write the formula for area of a trapezoid.*

$= \frac{1}{2}h[(2h-1)+(h+1)]$ *Substitute 2h − 1 for b_1 and h + 1 for b_2.*

$= \frac{1}{2}h(3h)$ *Combine like terms.*

$= \frac{3}{2}h^2$ *Simplify.*

The area is represented by $\frac{3}{2}h^2$.

B **Find the area of the dulcimer when the height is 22 inches.**

$A = \frac{3}{2}h^2$ *Use the polynomial from part* ***a.***

$= \frac{3}{2}(22)^2$ *Substitute 22 for h.*

$= \frac{3}{2}(484) = 726$

The area is 726 square inches.

5a. $x^2 - 4x$

5b. 12 m^2

5. The length of a rectangle is 4 meters shorter than its width.

a. Write a polynomial that represents the area of the rectangle.

b. Find the area of the rectangle when the width is 6 meters.

THINK AND DISCUSS

1. Compare the vertical method for multiplying polynomials with the vertical method for multiplying whole numbers.

2. GET ORGANIZED Copy and complete the graphic organizer. In each box, multiply two polynomials using the given method.

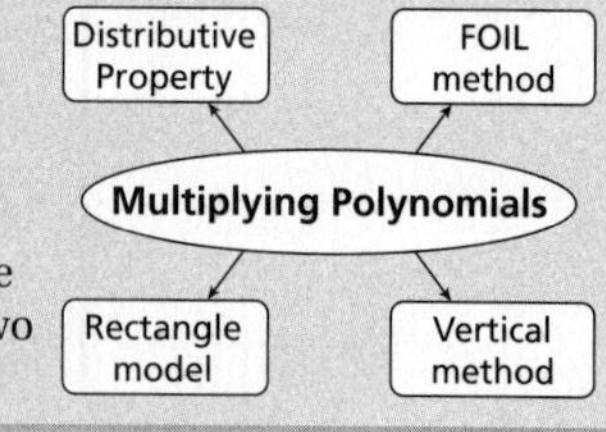

3 Close

Summarize

Ask students to multiply the following using any of the methods learned in this lesson.

$(5r^2s)(9rs)$ $45r^3s^2$

$3x^2(x^3 - 10)$ $3x^5 - 30x^2$

$(y+2)(y-5)$ $y^2 - 3y - 10$

$(x+5y)(xy+4x+7y)$

$x^2y + 4x^2 + 27xy + 5xy^2 + 35y^2$

ONGOING ASSESSMENT and INTERVENTION

Diagnose Before **the Lesson**
7-8 Warm Up, TE p. 512

Monitor During **the Lesson**
Check It Out! Exercises, SE pp. 512–516
Questioning Strategies, TE pp. 513–516

Assess After **the Lesson**
7-8 Lesson Quiz, TE p. 519
Alternative Assessment, TE p. 519

Answers to *Think and Discuss*

1. Possible answer: Both numbers and polynomials are set up in 2 rows and require you to multiply each item in the top row by an item in the bottom row. In the end, you add vertically to get the answer. When you are multiplying polynomials, the items are monomial terms. When you are multiplying numbers, the items are digits.
2. See p. A7.

go.hrw.com
Homework Help Online
KEYWORD: MA11 7-8
Parent Resources Online
KEYWORD: MA7 Parent

GUIDED PRACTICE

Multiply.

SEE EXAMPLE 1 p. 512

1. $(2x^2)(7x^4)$ 2. $(-5mn^3)(4m^2n^2)$ 3. $(6rs^2)(s^3t^2)\left(\frac{1}{2}r^4t^3\right)$
4. $\left(\frac{1}{3}a^5\right)(12a)$ 5. $(-3x^4y^2)(-7x^3y)$ 6. $(-2pq^3)(5p^2q^2)(-3q^4)$

SEE EXAMPLE 2 p. 512

7. $4(x^2 + 2x + 1)$ 8. $3ab(2a^2 + 3b^3)$ 9. $2a^3b(3a^2b + ab^2)$
10. $-3x(x^2 - 4x + 6)$ 11. $5x^2y(2xy^3 - y)$ 12. $5m^2n^3 \cdot mn^2(4m - n)$

SEE EXAMPLE 3 p. 514

13. $(x + 1)(x - 2)$ 14. $(x + 1)^2$ 15. $(x - 2)^2$
16. $(y - 3)(y - 5)$ 17. $(4a^3 - 2b)(a - 3b^2)$ 18. $(m^2 - 2mn)(3mn + n^2)$

SEE EXAMPLE 4 p. 515

19. $(x + 5)(x^2 - 2x + 3)$ 20. $(3x + 4)(x^2 - 5x + 2)$ 21. $(2x - 4)(-3x^3 + 2x - 5)$
22. $(-4x + 6)(2x^3 - x^2 + 1)$ 23. $(x - 5)(x^2 + x + 1)$ 24. $(a + b)(a - b)(b - a)$

SEE EXAMPLE 5 p. 516

25. **Photography** The length of a rectangular photograph is 3 inches less than twice the width. **$2x^2 - 3x$**
 a. Write a polynomial that represents the area of the photograph.
 b. Find the area of the photograph when the width is 4 inches. **20 in^2**

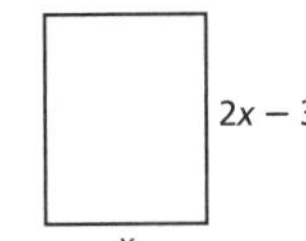
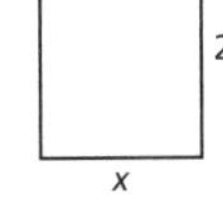

PRACTICE AND PROBLEM SOLVING

Independent Practice	
For Exercises	See Example
26–34	1
35–43	2
44–52	3
53–61	4
62	5

Extra Practice
Skills Practice p. S17
Application Practice p. S34

Multiply.

26. $(3x^2)(8x^5)$ 27. $(-2r^3s^4)(6r^2s)$ 28. $(15xy^2)\left(\frac{1}{3}x^2z^3\right)(y^3z^4)$
29. $(-2a^3)(-5a)$ 30. $(6x^3y^2)(-2x^2y)$ 31. $(-3a^2b)(-2b^3)(-a^3b^2)$
32. $(7x^2)(xy^5)(2x^3y^2)$ 33. $(-4a^3bc^2)(a^3b^2c)(3ab^4c^5)$ 34. $(12mn^2)(2m^2n)(mn)$
35. $9s(s + 6)$ 36. $9(2x^2 - 5x)$ 37. $3x(9x^2 - 4x)$
38. $3(2x^2 + 5x + 4)$ 39. $5s^2t^3(2s - 3t^2)$ 40. $x^2y^3 \cdot 5x^2y(6x + y^2)$
41. $-5x(2x^2 - 3x - 1)$ 42. $-2a^2b^3(3ab^2 - a^2b)$ 43. $-7x^3y \cdot x^2y^2(2x - y)$
44. $(x + 5)(x - 3)$ 45. $(x + 4)^2$ 46. $(m - 5)^2$
47. $(5x - 2)(x + 3)$ 48. $(3x - 4)^2$ 49. $(5x + 2)(2x - 1)$
50. $(x - 1)(x - 2)$ 51. $(x - 8)(7x + 4)$ 52. $(2x + 7)(3x + 7)$
53. $(x + 2)(x^2 - 3x + 5)$ 54. $(2x + 5)(x^2 - 4x + 3)$ 55. $(5x - 1)(-2x^3 + 4x - 3)$
56. $(x - 3)(x^2 - 5x + 6)$ 57. $(2x^2 - 3)(4x^3 - x^2 + 7)$ 58. $(x - 4)^3$
59. $(x - 2)(x^2 + 2x + 1)$ 60. $(2x + 10)(4 - x + 6x^3)$ 61. $(1 - x)^3$

62. **Geometry** The length of the rectangle at right is 3 feet longer than its width. **$x^2 + 3x$**
 a. Write a polynomial that represents the area of the rectangle.
 b. Find the area of the rectangle when the width is 5 feet. **40 ft^2**

x + 3
x

63. A square tabletop has side lengths of $(4x - 6)$ units. Write a polynomial that represents the area of the tabletop. **$16x^2 - 48x + 36$**

7-8 Exercises

Assignment Guide

Assign *Guided Practice* exercises as necessary.

If you finished Examples **1–3**
Basic 26–52, 70–78
Average 26–52, 70–78
Advanced 26–52, 70–78, 90

If you finished Examples **1–5**
Basic 26–69, 75–84, 87–89, 98–104
Average 26–65, 70–80 even, 82–93, 98–104
Advanced 26–64, 70–80 even, 82–104

Homework Quick Check
Quickly check key concepts.
Exercises: 30, 42, 46, 52, 56, 62, 69

Answers

1. $14x^6$
2. $-20m^3n^5$
3. $3r^5s^5t^5$
4. $4a^6$
5. $21x^7y^3$
6. $30p^3q^9$
7. $4x^2 + 8x + 4$
8. $6a^3b + 9ab^4$
9. $6a^5b^2 + 2a^4b^3$
10. $-3x^3 + 12x^2 - 18x$
11. $10x^3y^4 - 5x^2y^2$
12. $20m^4n^5 - 5m^3n^6$
13. $x^2 - x - 2$
14. $x^2 + 2x + 1$
15. $x^2 - 4x + 4$
16. $y^2 - 8y + 15$
17. $4a^4 - 2ab - 12a^3b^2 + 6b^3$
18. $3m^3n - 5m^2n^2 - 2mn^3$
19. $x^3 + 3x^2 - 7x + 15$
20. $3x^3 - 11x^2 - 14x + 8$
21. $-6x^4 + 12x^3 + 4x^2 - 18x + 20$
22. $-8x^4 + 16x^3 - 6x^2 - 4x + 6$
23. $x^3 - 4x^2 - 4x - 5$
24. $-a^3 + a^2b + ab^2 - b^3$
26. $24x^7$
27. $-12r^5s^5$
28. $5x^3y^5z^7$
29. $10a^4$
30. $-12x^5y^3$
31. $-6a^5b^6$
32. $14x^6y^7$
33. $-12a^7b^7c^8$
34. $24m^4n^4$
35. $9s^2 + 54s$
36. $18x^2 - 45x$
37. $27x^3 - 12x^2$
38. $6x^2 + 15x + 12$
39. $10s^3t^3 - 15s^2t^5$
40. $30x^5y^4 + 5x^4y^6$
41. $-10x^3 + 15x^2 + 5x$
42. $-6a^3b^5 + 2a^4b^4$
43. $-14x^6y^3 + 7x^5y^4$
44. $x^2 + 2x - 15$
45. $x^2 + 8x + 16$
46. $m^2 - 10m + 25$
47. $5x^2 + 13x - 6$
48. $9x^2 - 24x + 16$

49–61. See p. A27.

State Resources

go.hrw.com
State Resources Online
KEYWORD: MA7 Resources

MULTI-STEP TEST PREP Exercise 64 involves multiplying polynomials. This exercise prepares students for the Multi-Step Test Prep on page 528.

Answers

64a.

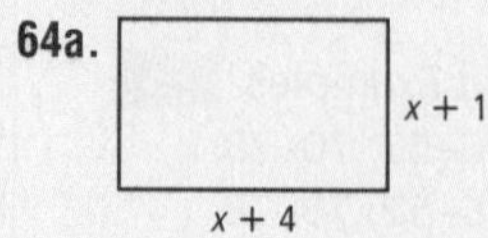

65b. $x^4 - x^3 + 2x^2 - 2x$

c. $x^4 - 5x^3 + 6x^2 + x - 3$

70. $6a^9$

71. $2x^2 - 7x - 30$

72. $3g^2 + 14g - 5$

73. $8x^2 - 16xy + 6y^2$

74. $x^2 - 9$

75. $6x^2 - 9x - 6$

76. $x^2 - 6x - 40$

77. $x^3 + 3x^2$

78. $x^3 + 3x^2 + 2x$

79. $2x^3 - 7x^2 - 10x + 24$

80. $a^3 - a^2b - ab^2 + b^3$

81. $8p^3 - 36p^2q + 54pq^2 - 27q^3$

82a.

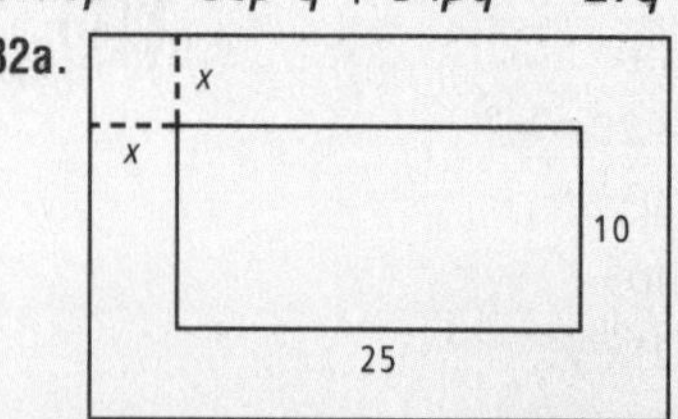

83. Possible answer: Each letter in FOIL represents a pair of terms in a certain position within the factors. The letters must account for every pairing of terms while describing first, outside, inside, and last positions. This is only possible with 2 binomials.

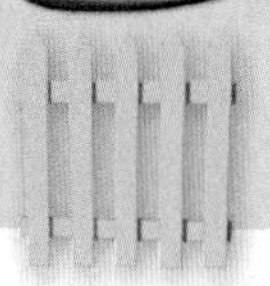

64. This problem will prepare you for the Multi-Step Test Prep on page 528.
    a. Marie is creating a garden. She designs a rectangular garden with a length of $(x + 4)$ feet and a width of $(x + 1)$ feet. Draw a diagram of Marie's garden with the length and width labeled.
    b. Write a polynomial that represents the area of Marie's garden. $x^2 + 5x + 4$
    c. What is the area when $x = 4$? **40 ft²**

65. Copy and complete the table below.

	A	Degree of A	B	Degree of B	A • B	Degree of A • B
	$2x^2$	2	$3x^5$	5	$6x^7$	7
a.	$5x^3$	3	$2x^2 + 1$	2	$10x^5 + 5x^3$	5
b.	$x^2 + 2$	2	$x^2 - x$	2		4
c.	$x - 3$	1	$x^3 - 2x^2 + 1$	3		4

d. Use the results from the table to complete the following: The product of a polynomial of degree m and a polynomial of degree n has a degree of ▒. $m + n$

Geometry Write a polynomial that represents the area of each rectangle.

66.

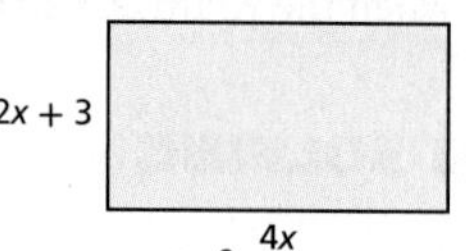

$8x^2 + 12x$

67. 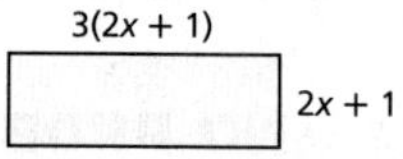 $3(2x + 1)$, $2x + 1$

$12x^2 + 12x + 3$

68.

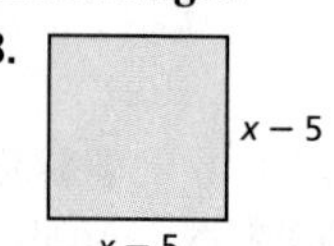

$x^2 - 10x + 25$

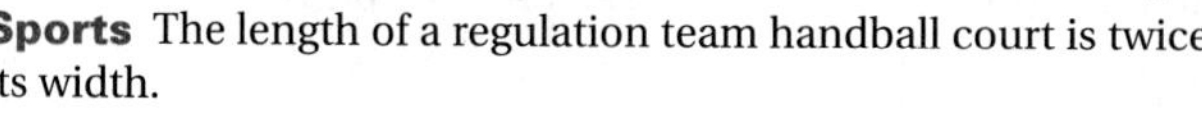

69. **Sports** The length of a regulation team handball court is twice its width.

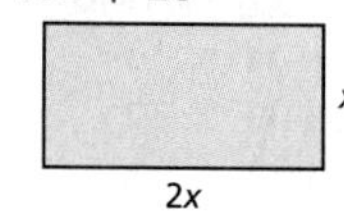

a. Write a polynomial that represents the area of the court. $2x^2$

b. The width of a team handball court is 20 meters. Find the area of the court. **800 m²**

LINK Sports

Team handball is a game with elements of soccer and basketball. It originated in Europe in the 1900s and was first played at the Olympics in 1936 with teams of 11 players. Today, a handball team consists of seven players—six court players and one goalie.

Multiply.

70. $(1.5a^3)(4a^6)$
71. $(2x + 5)(x - 6)$
72. $(3g - 1)(g + 5)$
73. $(4x - 2y)(2x - 3y)$
74. $(x + 3)(x - 3)$
75. $(1.5x - 3)(4x + 2)$
76. $(x - 10)(x + 4)$
77. $x^2(x + 3)$
78. $(x + 1)(x^2 + 2x)$
79. $(x - 4)(2x^2 + x - 6)$
80. $(a + b)(a - b)^2$
81. $(2p - 3q)^3$

82. **Multi-Step** A rectangular swimming pool is 25 feet long and 10 feet wide. It is surrounded by a fence that is x feet from each side of the pool.
    a. Draw a diagram of this situation.
    b. Write expressions for the length and width of the fenced region. (*Hint:* How much longer is one side of the fenced region than the corresponding side of the pool?) $2x + 25$; $2x + 10$
    c. Write an expression for the area of the fenced region. $4x^2 + 70x + 250$

83. **Write About It** Explain why the FOIL method can be used to multiply only two binomials at a time.

7-8 PRACTICE A

7-8 PRACTICE C

7-8 PRACTICE B

Multiply.

1. $(6m^4)(8m^2)$ — $48m^6$
2. $(5x^3)(4xy^2)$ — $20x^4y^2$
3. $(10s^5t)(7st^4)$ — $70s^6t^5$
4. $4(x^2 + 5x + 6)$ — $4x^2 + 20x + 24$
5. $2x(3x - 4)$ — $6x^2 - 8x$
6. $7xy(3x^2 + 4y + 2)$ — $21x^3y + 28xy^2 + 14xy$
7. $(x + 3)(x + 4)$ — $x^2 + 7x + 12$
8. $(x - 6)(x - 6)$ — $x^2 - 12x + 36$
9. $(x - 2)(x - 5)$ — $x^2 - 7x + 10$
10. $(2x + 5)(x + 6)$ — $2x^2 + 17x + 30$
11. $(m^3 + 3)(5m + n)$ — $5m^4 + m^3n + 15m + 3n$
12. $(a^2 + b^2)(a + b)$ — $a^3 + a^2b + ab^2 + b^3$
13. $(x + 4)(x^2 + 3x + 5)$ — $x^3 + 7x^2 + 17x + 20$
14. $(3m + 4)(m^2 - 3m + 5)$ — $3m^3 - 5m^2 + 3m + 20$
15. $(2x - 5)(4x^2 - 3x + 1)$ — $8x^3 - 26x^2 + 17x - 5$

16. **The length of a rectangle is 3 inches greater than the width.**
    a. Write a polynomial that represents the area of the rectangle. $w^2 + 3w$
    b. Find the area of the rectangle when the width is 4 inches. $28\ in^2$

17. **The length of a rectangle is 8 centimeters less than 3 times the width.**
    a. Write a polynomial that represents the area of the rectangle. $3w^2 - 8w$
    b. Find the area of the rectangle when the width is 10 centimeters. $220\ cm^2$

18. Write a polynomial to represent the volume of the rectangular prism.

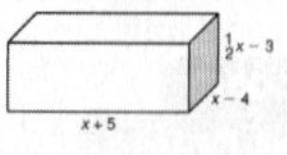

$\frac{1}{2}x - 3$, $x - 4$, $x + 5$

$\frac{1}{2}x^3 - \frac{5}{2}x^2 - 13x + 60$

7-8 READING STRATEGIES

There are several methods that can be used to multiply polynomials, depending on the number of terms. There is one procedure that can always be used, no matter how many terms there are. It is shown in the example below.

Multiply $(5x - 4)(3x^2 + x - 8)$.

$(5x - 4)(3x^2 + x - 8)$
$5x(3x^2 + x - 8) - 4(3x^2 + x - 8)$
$15x^3 + 5x^2 - 40x - 12x^2 - 4x + 32$

1 Use the Distributive Property.

$15x^3 + 5x^2 - 40x - 12x^2 - 4x + 32$
$15x^3 + (5x^2 - 12x^2) + (-40x - 4x) + 32$

2 Collect like terms.

$15x^3 + (5x^2 - 12x^2) + (-40x - 4x) + 32$
$15x^3 - 7x^2 - 44x + 32$

3 Simplify by combining like terms.

Use the procedure shown above to answer each of the following.

1. Multiplication was used six times in step 1. How many times would it be used if two binomials were being multiplied?
   4
2. In step 2, how do you know that $5x^2$ and $-12x^2$ are like terms?
   They have the same exponent on the same variable.
3. In step 3, how do you know the expression is completely simplified?
   There are no like terms.

Multiply the polynomials.

4. $-3x^3(2x^2 - 4x + 1)$ — $-6x^5 + 12x^4 - 3x^3$
5. $(2x + 5)(9x^2 + 6x)$ — $18x^3 + 57x^2 + 30x$
6. $(7x + 2)(x - 3)$ — $7x^2 - 19x - 6$
7. $(2x^3 + 6x + 8)(x^2 - 5x + 1)$ — $2x^5 - 10x^4 + 8x^3 - 22x^2 - 34x + 8$

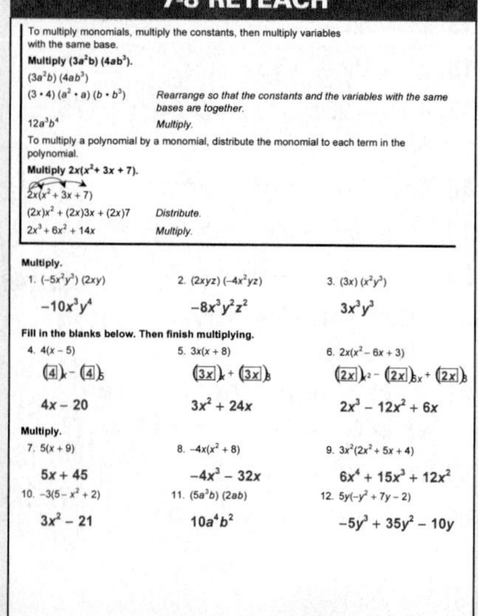

7-8 RETEACH

To multiply monomials, multiply the constants, then multiply variables with the same base.

Multiply $(3a^2b)(4ab^3)$.

$(3a^2b)(4ab^3)$
$(3 \cdot 4)(a^2 \cdot a)(b \cdot b^3)$ — *Rearrange so that the constants and the variables with the same bases are together.*
$12a^3b^4$ — *Multiply.*

To multiply a polynomial by a monomial, distribute the monomial to each term in the polynomial.

Multiply $2x(x^2 + 3x + 7)$.

$2x(x^2 + 3x + 7)$
$(2x)x^2 + (2x)3x + (2x)7$ — *Distribute.*
$2x^3 + 6x^2 + 14x$ — *Multiply.*

Multiply.

1. $(-5x^2y^3)(2xy)$ — $-10x^3y^4$
2. $(2xyz)(-4x^2yz)$ — $-8x^3y^2z^2$
3. $(3x)(x^2y^3)$ — $3x^3y^3$

Fill in the blanks below. Then finish multiplying.

4. $4(x - 5)$ — $(4)x - (4)5$ — $4x - 20$
5. $3x(x + 8)$ — $(3x)x + (3x)8$ — $3x^2 + 24x$
6. $2x(x^2 - 6x + 3)$ — $(2x)x^2 - (2x)6x + (2x)3$ — $2x^3 - 12x^2 + 6x$

Multiply.

7. $5(x + 9)$ — $5x + 45$
8. $-4x(x^2 + 8)$ — $-4x^3 - 32x$
9. $3x^2(2x^2 + 5x + 4)$ — $6x^4 + 15x^3 + 12x^2$
10. $-3(5 - x^2 + 2)$ — $3x^2 - 21$
11. $(5a^3b)(2ab)$ — $10a^4b^2$
12. $5y(-y^2 + 7y - 2)$ — $-5y^3 + 35y^2 - 10y$

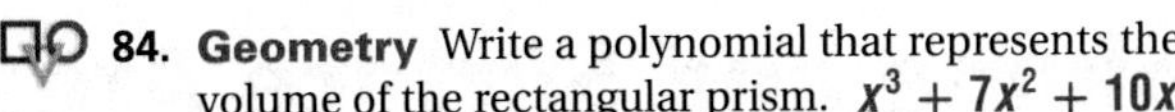

84. **Geometry** Write a polynomial that represents the volume of the rectangular prism. $x^3 + 7x^2 + 10x$

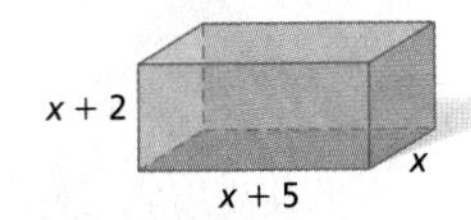

85. **Critical Thinking** Is there any value for x that would make the statement $(x + 3)^3 = x^3 + 3^3$ true? Give an example to justify your answer. **Yes; $x = 0$**

86. **Estimation** The length of a rectangle is 1 foot more than its width. Write a polynomial that represents the area of the rectangle. Estimate the width of the rectangle if its area is 25 square feet. $x^2 + x$; **4.5 ft**

TEST PREP

87. Which of the following products is equal to $a^2 - 5a - 6$?
   (A) $(a - 1)(a - 5)$ (B) $(a - 2)(a - 3)$ **(C)** $(a + 1)(a - 6)$ (D) $(a + 2)(a - 3)$

88. Which of the following is equal to $2a(a^2 - 1)$?
   (F) $2a^2 - 2a$ (G) $2a^3 - 1$ **(H)** $2a^3 - 2a$ (J) $2a^2 - 1$

89. What is the degree of the product of $3x^3y^2z$ and x^2yz?
   (A) 5 (B) 6 (C) 7 **(D)** 10

CHALLENGE AND EXTEND

Simplify.

90. $6x^2 - 2(3x^2 - 2x + 4)$ $4x - 8$
91. $x^2 - 2x(x + 3)$ $-x^2 - 6x$
92. $x(4x - 2) + 3x(x + 1)$ $7x^2 + x$

93. The diagram shows a sandbox and the frame that surrounds it.
   a. Write a polynomial that represents the area of the sandbox. $x^2 - 1$
   b. Write a polynomial that represents the area of the frame that surrounds the sandbox. $8x + 16$

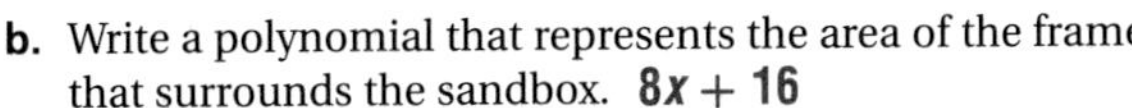

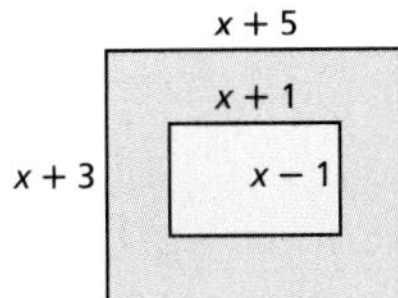

94. **Geometry** The side length of a square is $(8 + 2x)$ units. The area of this square is the same as the perimeter of another square with a side length of $(x^2 + 48)$ units. Find the value of x. $x = 4$

95. Write a polynomial that represents the product of three consecutive integers. Let x represent the first integer. $x^3 + 3x^2 + 2x$

96. Find m and n so that $x^m(x^n + x^{n-2}) = x^5 + x^3$. **Possible answer: $m = 2$; $n = 3$**

97. Find a so that $2x^a(5x^{2a-3} + 2x^{2a+2}) = 10x^3 + 4x^8$ $a = 2$

SPIRAL REVIEW

98. A stop sign is 2.5 meters tall and casts a shadow that is 3.5 meters long. At the same time, a flagpole casts a shadow that is 28 meters long. How tall is the flagpole? *(Lesson 2-8)* **20 m**

Find the distance, to the nearest hundredth, between each pair of points. *(Lesson 5-5)*

99. (2, 3) and (4, 6) **3.61**
100. (−1, 4) and (0, 8) **4.12**
101. (−3, 7) and (−6, −2) **9.49**

Graph the solutions of each linear inequality. *(Lesson 6-5)*

102. $y \le x - 2$
103. $4x - 2y < 10$
104. $-y \ge -3x + 1$

TEST PREP DOCTOR Because the last term of the polynomial in **Exercise 87** is negative, the signs of the second terms in the binomials must be different. Eliminate choices **A** and **B**.

Multiplying the first terms in **Exercise 88** gives $2a^3$, so choices **F** and **J** cannot be correct. Students who chose **G** probably did not distribute fully.

Answers

102–104. See p. A27.

Journal

Have students explain how to multiply $(2x + 3)$ by $(x + 4)$ using the method of their choice.

ALTERNATIVE ASSESSMENT

Have students count off by fours. Have the 1's write a monomial, the 2's write a binomial, the 3's write a trinomial, and the 4's write a polynomial of degree four. Rearrange the class into new groups of four, so that each new group has a monomial, a binomial, a trinomial, and a 4th-degree polynomial. (Make some groups of five students if needed.) Have students multiply pairs of their polynomials together. Each group must turn in as many pairs as possible, with work shown for each answer.

Power Presentations with PowerPoint®

7-8 Lesson Quiz

Multiply.

1. $(6s^2t^2)(3st)$ $18s^3t^3$
2. $4xy^2(x + y)$ $4x^2y^2 + 4xy^3$
3. $(x + 2)(x - 8)$ $x^2 - 6x - 16$
4. $(2x - 7)(x^2 + 3x - 4)$
   $2x^3 - x^2 - 29x + 28$
5. $6mn(m^2 + 10mn - 2)$
   $6m^3n + 60m^2n^2 - 12mn$
6. $(2x - 5y)(3x + y)$
   $6x^2 - 13xy - 5y^2$
7. A triangle has a base that is 4 cm longer than its height.
   a. Write a polynomial that represents the area of the triangle. $\frac{1}{2}h^2 + 2h$
   b. Find the area when the height is 8 cm. 48 cm²

Also available on transparency

7-8 PROBLEM SOLVING

Write the correct answer.

1. A bedroom has a length of $x + 3$ feet and a width of $x - 1$ feet. Write a polynomial to express the area of the bedroom. Then calculate the area if $x = 10$.
   $x^2 + 2x - 3$
   117 square feet

2. The length of a classroom is 4 feet longer than its width. Write a polynomial to express the area of the classroom. Then calculate the area if the width is 22 feet.
   $w^2 + 4w$
   572 square feet

3. Nicholas is determining if he can afford to buy a car. He multiplies the number of months m by $i + p + 30f$ where i represents the monthly cost of insurance, p represents the monthly car payment, and f represents the number of times he fills the gas tank each month. Write the polynomial that Nicholas can use to determine how much it will cost him to own a car both for one month and for one year.
   $i + p + 30f$; $12i + 12p + 360f$

4. A seat cushion is shaped like a trapezoid. The shorter base of the cushion is 3 inches greater than the height. The longer base is 2 inches shorter than twice the height. Write the polynomial that can be used to find the area of the cushion. (The area of a trapezoid is represented by $\frac{1}{2}h(b_1 + b_2)$.)
   $\frac{3}{2}h^2 + \frac{1}{2}h$

The volume of a pyramid can be found by using $\frac{1}{3}Bh$ where B is the area of the base and h is the height of the pyramid. The Great Pyramid of Giza has a square base, and each side is about 300 feet longer than the height of the pyramid. Select the best answer.

5. Which polynomial represents the approximate area of the base of the Great Pyramid?
   A $h + 90{,}000$
   B $2h + 90{,}000$
   C $h^2 + 600h + 90{,}000$
   D $2h^2 + 600h + 90{,}000$

6. Which polynomial represents the approximate volume of the Great Pyramid?
   F $\frac{1}{3}h^3 + 200h^2 + 30{,}000h$
   G $\frac{1}{3}h^2 + 200h + 30{,}000$
   H $h^3 + 600h^2 + 90{,}000h$
   J $3h^3 + 600h^2 + 90{,}000h$

7. The original height of the Great Pyramid was 485 feet. Due to erosion, it is now about 450 feet. Find the approximate volume of the Great Pyramid today.
   A 562,500 ft³ **C** 84,375,000 ft³
   B 616,225 ft³ D 99,623,042 ft³

7-8 CHALLENGE

Determine the missing binomial. Choose from the table below. Each binomial is used once.

$x + 4$	$x + 3$	$x - 3$
$x + 1$	$x + 6$	$x - 4$
$x + 1$	$x - 2$	$x - 6$

1. $(x + 4)(x + 2) = x^2 + 2x + 4x + 8 = x^2 + 6x + 8$
2. $(x + 1)(x + 5) = x^2 + 5x + x + 5 + = x^2 + 6x + 5$
3. $(x + 2)(x - 3) = x^2 - 3x + 2x - 6 = x^2 - x - 6$
4. $(x + 3)(x - 5) = x^2 - 2x - 15$
5. $(x + 6)(x + 1) = x^2 + 7x + 6$
6. $(x - 2)(x + 4) = x^2 + 2x - 8$
7. $(x - 3)(x + 6) = x^2 + 3x - 18$
8. $(x - 4)(x + 2) = x^2 - 2x - 8$
9. $(x - 6)(x - 5) = x^2 - 11x + 30$

The binomials missing from the following equations are not all listed in the table. Determine the missing binomials.

10. $(x + 2)(x + 7) = x^2 + 9x + 14$
11. $(x + 3)(x + 4) = x^2 + 7x + 12$
12. $(x - 6)(x - 2) = x^2 - 8x + 12$
13. $(x - 4)(x - 10) = x^2 - 14x + 40$
14. $(x + 6)(x + 3) = x^2 + 9x + 18$
15. $(x + 1)(x - 4) = x^2 - 3x - 4$
16. $(x - 2)(x - 2) = x^2 - 4x + 4$
17. $(3x - 1)(x + 2) = 3x^2 + 5x - 2$
18. $(x - 7)(2x + 3) = 2x^2 - 11x - 21$
19. $(2x - 3)(3x + 4) = 6x^2 - x - 12$

Organizer

Pacing:
Traditional 1 day
Block $\frac{1}{2}$ day

Objective: Apply polynomial operations to finding areas of geometric figures.

Online Edition

Countdown Week 17

Teach

Remember

Students review and apply volume and surface area formulas for geometric figures.

Close

Assess

The volume of any prism equals the area of the base times the height. Have students explain how to find the volume of the triangular prism in **Problem 6.** Find the area of the base. It is $2y^2 + y$. Multiply this by the height, which is $3y$. The volume is $6y^3 + 3y^2$.

State Resources

go.hrw.com
State Resources Online
KEYWORD: MA7 Resources

Volume and Surface Area

The volume V of a three-dimensional figure is the amount of space it occupies. The surface area S is the total area of the two-dimensional surfaces that make up the figure.

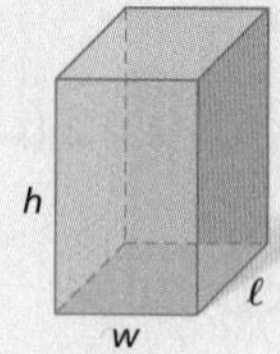

$V = \ell wh$
$S = 2(\ell w + \ell h + wh)$

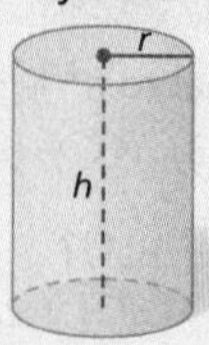

$V = \pi r^2 h$
$S = 2\pi r^2 + 2\pi rh$

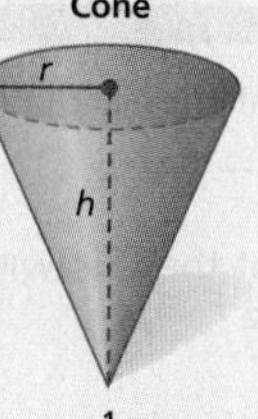

$V = \frac{1}{3}\pi r^2 h$

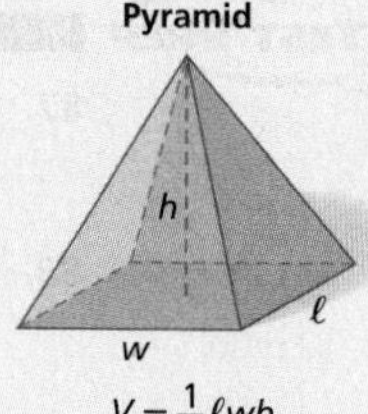

$V = \frac{1}{3}\ell wh$

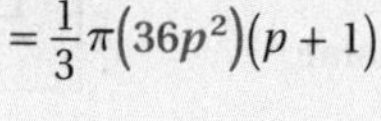

Write and simplify a polynomial expression for the volume of the cone. Leave the symbol π in your answer.

$V = \frac{1}{3}\pi r^2 h$	*Choose the correct formula.*
$= \frac{1}{3}\pi(6p)^2(p+1)$	*Substitute 6p for r and p + 1 for h.*
$= \frac{1}{3}\pi(36p^2)(p+1)$	*Use the Power of a Product Property.*
$= \frac{1}{3}(36)\pi[p^2(p+1)]$	*Use the Associative and Commutative Properties of Multiplication.*
$= 12\pi p^2(p+1)$	*Distribute $12\pi p^2$.*
$= 12\pi p^3 + 12\pi p^2$	

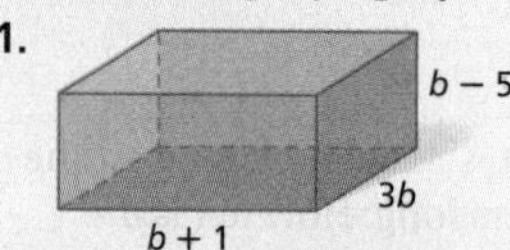

Write and simplify a polynomial expression for the volume of each figure.

1.
$3b^3 - 12b^2 - 15b$

2.
$4\pi n^3 - 16\pi n^2 + 16\pi n$

3.
$2k^3 - k^2 - 6k$

Write and simplify a polynomial expression for the surface area of each figure.

4.
$16x^2 + 30x + 6$

5.
$4\pi w^2 - 4\pi$

6.
$19y^2 + 14y$

7-9 Special Products of Binomials

Objective
Find special products of binomials.

Vocabulary
perfect-square trinomial
difference of two squares

Why learn this?
You can use special products to find areas, such as the area of a deck around a pond. (See Example 4.)

Imagine a square with sides of length $(a + b)$:

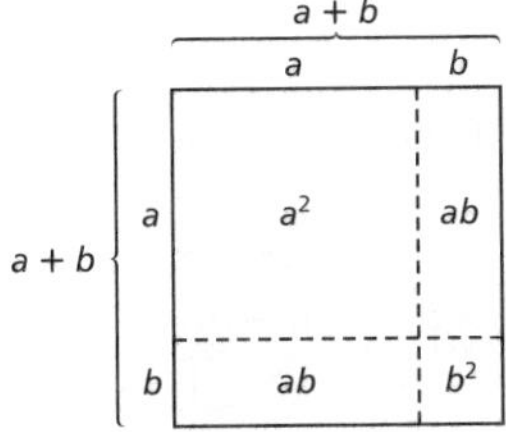

The area of this square is $(a + b)(a + b)$, or $(a + b)^2$. The area of this square can also be found by adding the areas of the smaller squares and rectangles inside. The sum of the areas inside is $a^2 + ab + ab + b^2$.

This means that $(a + b)^2 = a^2 + 2ab + b^2$.

You can use the FOIL method to verify this:

$$(a + b)^2 = (a + b)(a + b) = a^2 + ab + ab + b^2$$

F L I O

$$= a^2 + 2ab + b^2$$

A trinomial of the form $a^2 + 2ab + b^2$ is called a *perfect-square trinomial.* A **perfect-square trinomial** is a trinomial that is the result of squaring a binomial.

EXAMPLE 1 Finding Products in the Form $(a + b)^2$

Multiply.

A $(x + 4)^2$

$(a + b)^2 = a^2 + 2ab + b^2$ — *Use the rule for $(a + b)^2$.*

$(x + 4)^2 = x^2 + 2(x)(4) + 4^2$ — *Identify a and b: a = x and b = 4.*

$= x^2 + 8x + 16$ — *Simplify.*

B $(3x + 2y)^2$

$(a + b)^2 = a^2 + 2ab + b^2$ — *Use the rule for $(a + b)^2$.*

$(3x + 2y)^2 = (3x)^2 + 2(3x)(2y) + (2y)^2$ — *Identify a and b: a = 3x and b = 2y.*

$= 9x^2 + 12xy + 4y^2$ — *Simplify.*

7-9 Organizer

Pacing: Traditional 1 day
Block $\frac{1}{2}$ day

Objective: Find special products of binomials.

Online Edition
Tutorial Videos

Countdown Week 17

Power Presentations with PowerPoint®

Warm Up

Simplify.

1. 4^2 16
2. 7^2 49
3. $(-2)^2$ 4
4. $(x)^2$ x^2
5. $-(5y^2)$ $-5y^2$
6. $(m^2)^2$ m^4
7. $2(6xy)$ $12xy$
8. $2(8x^2)$ $16x^2$

Also available on transparency

Math Humor

Parent: What happened in math class today?
Student: When the teacher said to look for perfect squares, everyone looked at me.

1 Introduce

You can use the FOIL method to find the square of a binomial. For example, to find $(a + 1)^2$, first write the product as $(a + 1)(a + 1)$. Then use the FOIL method.

$$(a + 1)^2 = (a + 1)(a + 1) = a^2 + a \cdot 1 + 1 \cdot a + 1^2 = a^2 + a + a + 1 = a^2 + 2a + 1$$

1. Use the FOIL method to complete the table.

Power	Expanded Form	Product
$(a + 1)^2$	$(a + 1)(a + 1)$	$a^2 + 2a + 1$
$(a + 2)^2$		
$(a + 3)^2$		
$(a + 4)^2$		

2. Look for a pattern in the right column of the table. Use the pattern to find $(a + 5)^2$ without using the FOIL method.
3. Find $(a + 9)^2$ without using the FOIL method.

THINK AND DISCUSS

4. **Describe** a general rule you can use to find $(a + b)^2$.
5. **Show** how you can apply your rule to find $(7 + x)^2$.

Motivate

Have students find the products of the following:

$(x + 3)(x + 3)$ $x^2 + 6x + 9$

$(x + 4)(x + 4)$ $x^2 + 8x + 16$

$(x + 5)(x + 5)$ $x^2 + 10x + 25$

Discuss with students any patterns they see. Lead them to recognize that the middle term of the trinomial is two times the product of the first and last terms of the binomial.

$(a + b)(a + b) = a^2 + 2ab + b^2$

Explorations and answers are provided in *Alternate Openers: Explorations Transparencies.*

State Resources

State Resources Online
KEYWORD: MA7 Resources

Power Presentations with PowerPoint®

Additional Examples

Example 1

Multiply.

A. $(x + 3)^2$ $x^2 + 6x + 9$

B. $(4s + 3t)^2$ $16s^2 + 24st + 9t^2$

C. $(5 + m^2)^2$ $25 + 10m^2 + m^4$

Example 2

Multiply.

A. $(x - 6)^2$ $x^2 - 12x + 36$

B. $(4m - 10)^2$ $16m^2 - 80m + 100$

C. $(2x - 5y)^2$ $4x^2 - 20xy + 25y^2$

D. $(7 - r^3)^2$ $49 - 14r^3 + r^6$

INTERVENTION

Questioning Strategies

EXAMPLE 1

- How do you find the middle term?
- In which position could a perfect-square trinomial have a term with an odd exponent?

EXAMPLE 2

- How are these examples different from those in **Example 1**? What causes the differences? How are they the same?
- Why is the last term of any perfect-square trinomial always positive?

Multiply.

C $(4 + s^2)^2$

$(a + b)^2 = a^2 + 2ab + b^2$ — *Use the rule for $(a + b)^2$.*

$(4 + s^2)^2 = (4)^2 + 2(4)(s^2) + (s^2)^2$ — *Identify a and b: $a = 4$ and $b = s^2$.*

$= 16 + 8s^2 + s^4$ — *Simplify.*

D $(-m + 3)^2$

$(a + b)^2 = a^2 + 2ab + b^2$ — *Use the rule for $(a + b)^2$.*

$(-m + 3)^2 = (-m)^2 + 2(-m)(3) + 3^2$ — *Identify a and b: $a = -m$ and $b = 3$.*

$= m^2 - 6m + 9$ — *Simplify.*

CHECK IT OUT! Multiply.

1a. $(x + 6)^2$ **$x^2 + 12x + 36$**

1b. $(5a + b)^2$ **$25a^2 + 10ab + b^2$**

1c. $(1 + c^3)^2$ **$1 + 2c^3 + c^6$**

You can use the FOIL method to find products in the form $(a - b)^2$:

F L

$$(a - b)^2 = (a - b)(a - b) = a^2 - ab - ab + b^2$$

I

O

$$= a^2 - 2ab + b^2$$

A trinomial of the form $a^2 - 2ab + b^2$ is also a perfect-square trinomial because it is the result of squaring the binomial $(a - b)$.

EXAMPLE 2 Finding Products in the Form $(a - b)^2$

Multiply.

A $(x - 5)^2$

$(a - b)^2 = a^2 - 2ab + b^2$ — *Use the rule for $(a - b)^2$.*

$(x - 5)^2 = x^2 - 2(x)(5) + 5^2$ — *Identify a and b: $a = x$ and $b = 5$.*

$= x^2 - 10x + 25$ — *Simplify.*

B $(6a - 1)^2$

$(a - b)^2 = a^2 - 2ab + b^2$ — *Use the rule for $(a - b)^2$.*

$(6a - 1)^2 = (6a)^2 - 2(6a)(1) + (1)^2$ — *Identify a and b: $a = 6a$ and $b = 1$.*

$= 36a^2 - 12a + 1$ — *Simplify.*

C $(4c - 3d)^2$

$(a - b)^2 = a^2 - 2ab + b^2$ — *Use the rule for $(a - b)^2$.*

$(4c - 3d)^2 = (4c)^2 - 2(4c)(3d) + (3d)^2$ — *Identify a and b: $a = 4c$ and $b = 3d$.*

$= 16c^2 - 24cd + 9d^2$ — *Simplify.*

D $(3 - x^2)^2$

$(a - b)^2 = (a)^2 - 2ab + b^2$ — *Use the rule for $(a - b)^2$.*

$(3 - x^2)^2 = (3)^2 - 2(3)(x^2) + (x^2)^2$ — *Identify a and b: $a = 3$ and $b = x^2$.*

$= 9 - 6x^2 + x^4$ — *Simplify.*

2a. $x^2 - 14x + 49$
2b. $9b^2 - 12bc + 4c^2$
2c. $a^4 - 8a^2 + 16$

Multiply.

2a. $(x - 7)^2$ **2b.** $(3b - 2c)^2$ **2c.** $(a^2 - 4)^2$

2 Teach

Guided Instruction

Review how to multiply any two binomials before starting this section. Show the FOIL method for $(a + b)^2$ and $(a - b)^2$ next to each other, so students can better visualize the similarities and differences. Tell students that the binomials in this lesson could be multiplied using any of the methods they already know, but that certain types of binomials can be multiplied more quickly knowing these rules.

Reaching All Learners

Through Auditory Cues

Have students learn the "verbal rules" for the special products.

$(a + b)^2 = a^2 + 2ab + b^2$

$(a - b)^2 = a^2 - 2ab + b^2$

- first term squared
- plus (or minus) two times the product of both terms
- plus last term squared

Have students create a similar verbal rule for $(a + b)(a - b) = a^2 - b^2$.

You can use an area model to see that $(a + b)(a - b) = a^2 - b^2$.

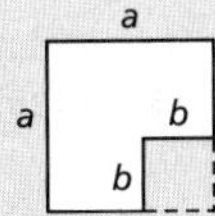

Begin with a square with area a^2. Remove a square with area b^2. The area of the new figure is $a^2 - b^2$.

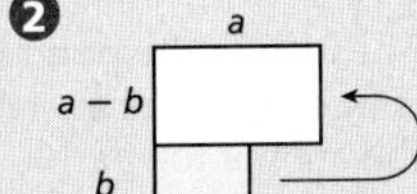

Then remove the smaller rectangle on the bottom. Turn it and slide it up next to the top rectangle.

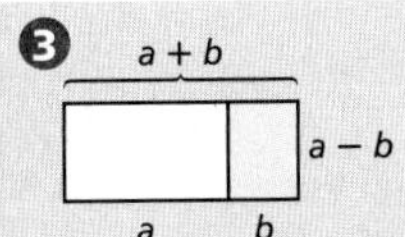

The new arrangement is a rectangle with length $a + b$ and width $a - b$. Its area is $(a + b)(a - b)$.

So $(a + b)(a - b) = a^2 - b^2$. A binomial of the form $a^2 - b^2$ is called a **difference of two squares**.

EXAMPLE 3 Finding Products in the Form $(a + b)(a - b)$

Multiply.

A $(x + 6)(x - 6)$

$(a + b)(a - b) = a^2 - b^2$ *Use the rule for $(a + b)(a - b)$.*

$(x + 6)(x - 6) = x^2 - 6^2$ *Identify a and b: $a = x$ and $b = 6$.*

$= x^2 - 36$ *Simplify.*

B $(x^2 + 2y)(x^2 - 2y)$

$(a + b)(a - b) = a^2 - b^2$ *Use the rule for $(a + b)(a - b)$.*

$(x^2 + 2y)(x^2 - 2y) = (x^2)^2 - (2y)^2$ *Identify a and b: $a = x^2$ and $b = 2y$.*

$= x^4 - 4y^2$ *Simplify.*

C $(7 + n)(7 - n)$

$(a + b)(a - b) = a^2 - b^2$ *Use the rule for $(a + b)(a - b)$.*

$(7 + n)(7 - n) = 7^2 - n^2$ *Identify a and b: $a = 7$ and $b = n$.*

$= 49 - n^2$ *Simplify.*

Multiply.

3a. $(x + 8)(x - 8)$ $x^2 - 64$ **3b.** $(3 + 2y^2)(3 - 2y^2)$ $9 - 4y^4$ **3c.** $(9 + r)(9 - r)$ $81 - r^2$

EXAMPLE 4 *Problem-Solving Application*

A square koi pond is surrounded by a gravel path. Write an expression that represents the area of the path.

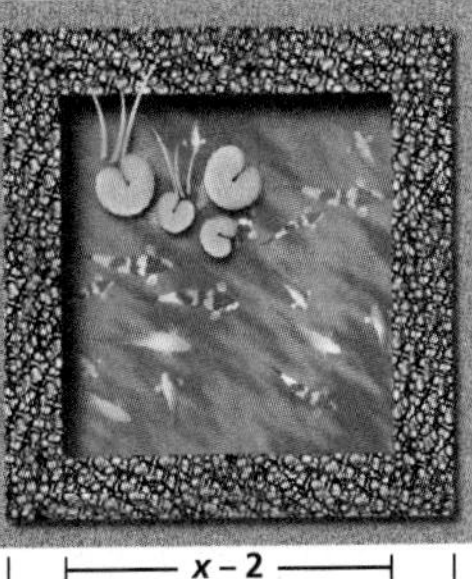

1 Understand the Problem

The **answer** will be an expression that represents the area of the path.

List the important information:

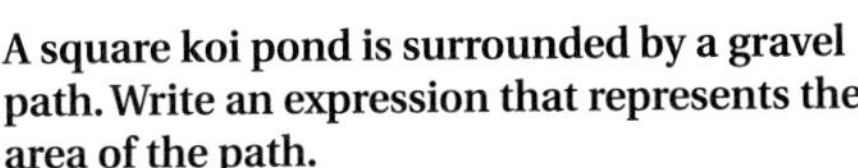

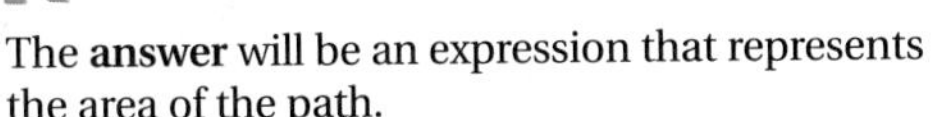

- The pond is a square with a side length of $x - 2$.
- The path has a side length of $x + 2$.

COMMON ERROR ALERT

When finding the product of $(a - b)^2$, some students might believe that the middle term and the last term will both be negative numbers. Remind them that the last term comes from a number being squared, and thus will never be a negative.

Power Presentations with PowerPoint®

Additional Examples

Example 3

Multiply.

A. $(x + 4)(x - 4)$ $x^2 - 16$

B. $(p^2 + 8q)(p^2 - 8q)$ $p^4 - 64q^2$

C. $(10 + b)(10 - b)$ $100 - b^2$

INTERVENTION

Questioning Strategies

EXAMPLE 3

- Why is there no middle term in the product $(a + b)(a - b)$?
- Why does the product $(a + b)(a - b)$ always have a minus sign between the terms?

Teaching Tip **Math Background** The binomials $(a + b)$ and $(a - b)$ are called *conjugates*. Conjugates are used in many situations because of the special property that their product is always a difference of squares.

Power Presentations with PowerPoint®

Additional Examples

Example 4

Write a polynomial that represents the area of the yard around the pool shown below. $10x + 29$

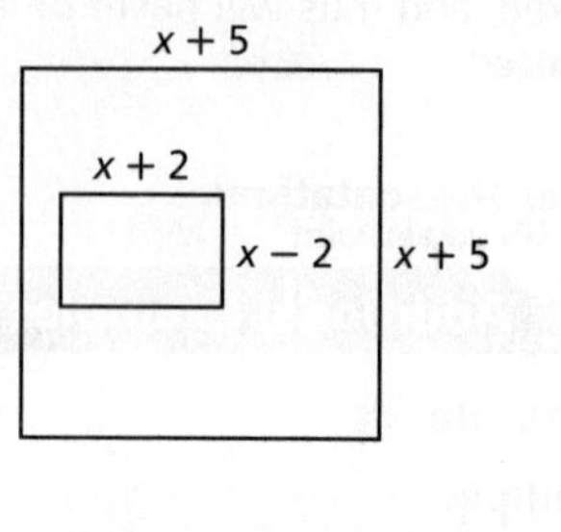

INTERVENTION

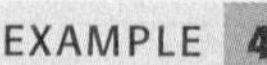

Questioning Strategies

EXAMPLE 4

- What are you finding when you are multiplying the binomials?
- What area are you asked to find?
- What operation would you need to perform to get this result?

2 Make a Plan

The area of the pond is $(x-2)^2$. The total area of the path plus the pond is $(x+2)^2$. You can subtract the area of the pond from the total area to find the area of the path.

3 Solve

Step 1 Find the total area.

$$(x+2)^2 = x^2 + 2(x)(2) + 2^2 \qquad \textit{Use the rule for } (a+b)^2\textit{: } a = x \textit{ and } b = 2.$$
$$= x^2 + 4x + 4$$

Step 2 Find the area of the pond.

$$(x-2)^2 = x^2 - 2(x)(2) + 2^2 \qquad \textit{Use the rule for } (a-b)^2\textit{: } a = x \textit{ and } b = 2.$$
$$= x^2 - 4x + 4$$

Remember!

To subtract a polynomial, add the opposite of *each* term.

Step 3 Find the area of the path.

area of path	=	total area	−	area of pond
a	=	$x^2 + 4x + 4$	−	$(x^2 - 4x + 4)$

$$= x^2 + 4x + 4 - x^2 + 4x - 4 \qquad \textit{Identify like terms.}$$
$$= (x^2 - x^2) + (4x + 4x) + (4 - 4) \qquad \textit{Group like terms together.}$$
$$= 8x$$

The area of the path is $8x$. *Combine like terms.*

4 Look Back

Suppose that $x = 10$. Then one side of the path is 12, and the total area is 12^2, or 144. Also, if $x = 10$, one side of the pond is 8, and the area of the pond is 8^2, or 64. This means the area of the path is $144 - 64 = 80$.

According to the solution above, the area of the path is $8x$. If $x = 10$, then $8x = 8(10) = 80$. ✓

4. Write an expression that represents the area of the swimming pool at right. **25**

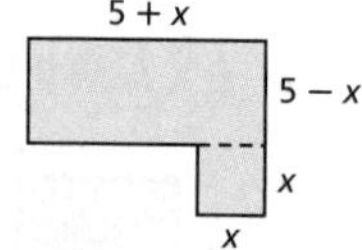

Special Products of Binomials

Perfect-Square Trinomials

$$(a+b)^2 = (a+b)(a+b) = a^2 + 2ab + b^2$$
$$(a-b)^2 = (a-b)(a-b) = a^2 - 2ab + b^2$$

Difference of Two Squares

$$(a+b)(a-b) = a^2 - b^2$$

3 Close

Summarize

Have students state whether each product is a perfect-square trinomial or a difference of two squares, and then find the product.

$(2x + 3y)^2$ perfect-square trinomial; $4x^2 + 12xy + 9y^2$

$(5m + 7)(5m - 7)$ difference of two squares; $25m^2 - 49$

$(4s - t)^2$ perfect-square trinomial; $16s^2 - 8st + t^2$

Tell students that recognizing special products will greatly help them with factoring in the next chapter.

ONGOING ASSESSMENT and INTERVENTION

***Diagnose Before* the Lesson**
7-9 Warm Up, TE p. 521

***Monitor During* the Lesson**
Check It Out! Exercises, SE pp. 522–524
Questioning Strategies, TE pp. 522–524

***Assess After* the Lesson**
7-9 Lesson Quiz, TE p. 527
Alternative Assessment, TE p. 527

THINK AND DISCUSS

1. Use the FOIL method to verify that $(a + b)(a - b) = a^2 - b^2$.
2. When a binomial is squared, the middle term of the resulting trinomial is twice the ___?___ of the first and last terms.

3. **GET ORGANIZED** Copy and complete the graphic organizer. Complete the special product rules and give an example of each.

Special Products of Binomials		
Perfect-Square Trinomials		Difference of Two Squares
$(a + b)^2 = ?$	$(a - b)^2 = ?$	$(a + b)(a - b) = ?$

Answers to *Think and Discuss*

1. $(a + b)(a - b) = a^2 - ab + ab - b^2 = a^2 - b^2$
2. product
3. See p. A7.

7-9 Exercises

GUIDED PRACTICE

1. **Vocabulary** In your own words, describe a *perfect-square trinomial*.
Possible answer: a trinomial that is the result of squaring a binomial

Multiply.

SEE EXAMPLE 1 p. 521

2. $(x + 7)^2$ 3. $(2 + x)^2$ 4. $(x + 1)^2$
5. $(2x + 6)^2$ 6. $(5x + 9)^2$ 7. $(2a + 7b)^2$

SEE EXAMPLE 2 p. 522

8. $(x - 6)^2$ 9. $(x - 2)^2$ 10. $(2x - 1)^2$
11. $(8 - x)^2$ 12. $(6p - q)^2$ 13. $(7a - 2b)^2$

SEE EXAMPLE 3 p. 523

14. $(x + 5)(x - 5)$ 15. $(x + 6)(x - 6)$ 16. $(5x + 1)(5x - 1)$
17. $(2x^2 + 3)(2x^2 - 3)$ 18. $(9 - x^3)(9 + x^3)$ 19. $(2x - 5y)(2x + 5y)$

SEE EXAMPLE 4 p. 523

20. **Geometry** Write a polynomial that represents the area of the figure. $\mathbf{2x^2 + 8x + 10}$

PRACTICE AND PROBLEM SOLVING

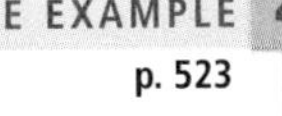

For Exercises	See Example
21–26	1
27–32	2
33–38	3
39	4

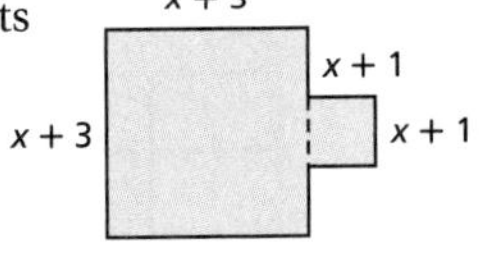

Extra Practice
Skills Practice p. S17
Application Practice p. S34

Multiply.

21. $(x + 3)^2$ 22. $(4 + z)^2$ 23. $(x^2 + y^2)^2$
24. $(p + 2q^3)^2$ 25. $(2 + 3x)^2$ 26. $(r^2 + 5t)^2$
27. $(s^2 - 7)^2$ 28. $(2c - d^3)^2$ 29. $(a - 8)^2$
30. $(5 - w)^2$ 31. $(3x - 4)^2$ 32. $(1 - x^2)^2$
33. $(a - 10)(a + 10)$ 34. $(y + 4)(y - 4)$ 35. $(7x + 3)(7x - 3)$
36. $(x^2 - 2)(x^2 + 2)$ 37. $(5a^2 + 9)(5a^2 - 9)$ 38. $(x^3 + y^2)(x^3 - y^2)$

Assignment Guide

Assign *Guided Practice* exercises as necessary.

If you finished Examples **1–2**
Basic 21–32, 53–57
Average 21–32, 53–57
Advanced 21–32, 41, 44–48 even, 54, 56

If you finished Examples **1–4**
Basic 21–63, 64, 67–70, 75–82
Average 21–40, 42–52 even, 53–73, 75–82
Advanced 21–52, 58–62, 64–82

Homework Quick Check
Quickly check key concepts.
Exercises: 22, 28, 36, 39, 42

State Resources

Answers

2. $x^2 + 14x + 49$
3. $4 + 4x + x^2$
4. $x^2 + 2x + 1$
5. $4x^2 + 24x + 36$
6. $25x^2 + 90x + 81$
7. $4a^2 + 28ab + 49b^2$
8. $x^2 - 12x + 36$
9. $x^2 - 4x + 4$
10. $4x^2 - 4x + 1$
11. $64 - 16x + x^2$
12. $36p^2 - 12pq + q^2$
13. $49a^2 - 28ab + 4b^2$
14. $x^2 - 25$
15. $x^2 - 36$
16. $25x^2 - 1$
17. $4x^4 - 9$
18. $81 - x^6$
19. $4x^2 - 25y^2$
21. $x^2 + 6x + 9$
22. $16 + 8z + z^2$
23. $x^4 + 2x^2y^2 + y^4$
24. $p^2 + 4pq^3 + 4q^6$
25. $4 + 12x + 9x^2$
26. $r^4 + 10r^2t + 25t^2$
27. $s^4 - 14s^2 + 49$
28. $4c^2 - 4cd^3 + d^6$
29. $a^2 - 16a + 64$
30. $25 - 10w + w^2$
31. $9x^2 - 24x + 16$
32. $1 - 2x^2 + x^4$
33. $a^2 - 100$
34. $y^2 - 16$
35. $49x^2 - 9$
36. $x^4 - 4$
37. $25a^4 - 81$
38. $x^6 - y^4$

Answers

64a.

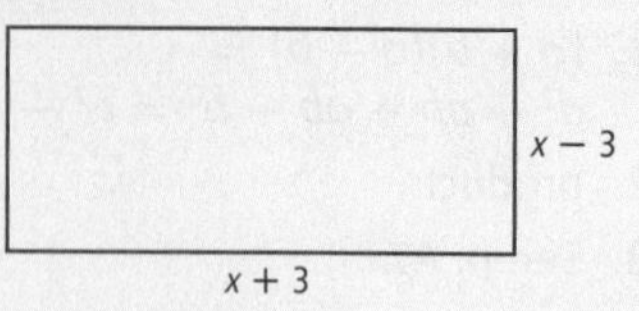

76.

77.

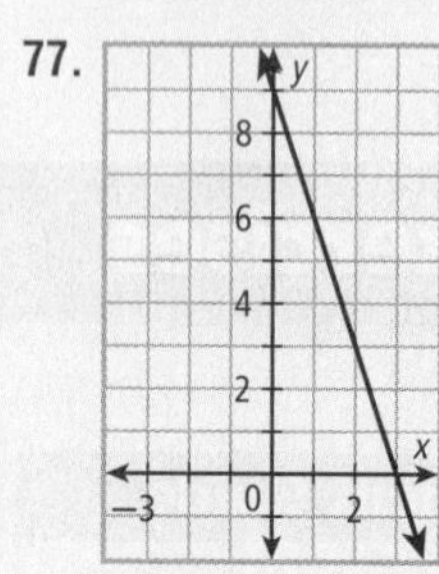

78.

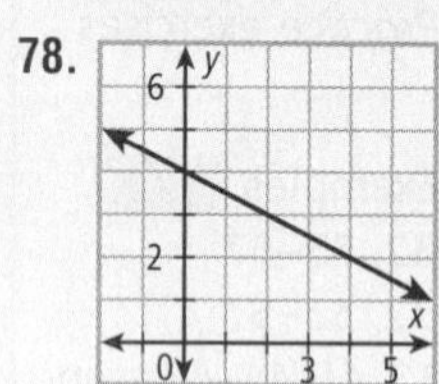

39. $\pi x^2 + 8\pi x + 16\pi$

40a. $x > 2$; values less than or equal to 2 cause the width of the rectangle to be zero or neg., which does not make sense.

49. $x^6 - 2a^3x^3 + a^6$

39. Entertainment Write a polynomial that represents the area of the circular puzzle. Remember that the formula for area of a circle is $A = \pi r^2$, where r is the radius of the circle. Leave the symbol π in your answer.

40. Multi-Step A square has sides that are $(x - 1)$ units long and a rectangle has a length of x units and a width of $(x - 2)$ units.

a. What are the possible values of x? Explain.

b. Which has the greater area, the square or the rectangle? **square**

c. What is the difference in the areas? **1 sq. unit**

Multiply.

41. $(x + y)^2$ $\mathbf{x^2 + 2xy + y^2}$
42. $(x - y)^2$ $\mathbf{x^2 - 2xy + y^2}$
43. $(x^2 + 4)(x^2 - 4)$ $\mathbf{x^4 - 16}$
44. $(x^2 + 4)^2$ $\mathbf{x^4 + 8x^2 + 16}$
45. $(x^2 - 4)^2$ $\mathbf{x^4 - 8x^2 + 16}$
46. $(1 - x)^2$ $\mathbf{1 - 2x + x^2}$
47. $(1 + x)^2$ $\mathbf{1 + 2x + x^2}$
48. $(1 - x)(1 + x)$ $\mathbf{1 - x^2}$
49. $(x^3 - a^3)(x^3 - a^3)$
50. $(5 + n)(5 + n)$ $\mathbf{25 + 10n + n^2}$
51. $(6a - 5b)(6a + 5b)$ $\mathbf{36a^2 - 25b^2}$
52. $(r - 4t^4)(r - 4t^4)$ $\mathbf{r^2 - 8rt^4 + 16t^8}$

Copy and complete the tables to verify the special products of binomials.

	a	b	$(a - b)^2$	$a^2 - 2ab + b^2$
	1	4	$(1 - 4)^2 = 9$	$1^2 - 2(1)(4) + 4^2 = 9$
53.	2	4	**4**	**4**
54.	3	2	**1**	**1**

	a	b	$(a + b)^2$	$a^2 + 2ab + b^2$
55.	1	4	**25**	**25**
56.	2	5	**49**	**49**
57.	3	0	**9**	**9**

	a	b	$(a + b)(a - b)$	$a^2 - b^2$
58.	1	4	**−15**	**−15**
59.	2	3	**−5**	**−5**
60.	3	2	**5**	**5**

LINK Math History

Beginning about 3000 B.C.E., the Babylonians lived in what is now Iraq and Turkey. Around 575 B.C.E., they built the Ishtar Gate to serve as one of eight main entrances into the city of Babylon. The image above is a relief sculpture from a restoration of the Ishtar Gate.

61. Math History The Babylonians used tables of squares and the formula $ab = \frac{(a + b)^2 - (a - b)^2}{4}$ to multiply two numbers. Use this formula to find the product $35 \cdot 24$. **840**

62. Critical Thinking Find a value of c that makes $16x^2 - 24x + c$ a perfect-square trinomial. $\mathbf{c = 9}$

63. ///ERROR ANALYSIS/// Explain the error below. What is the correct product?
$(a - b)^2 = a^2 - b^2$ **Possible answer: The square of a diff. is not the same as a diff. of squares; $a^2 - 2ab + b^2$.**

7-9 PRACTICE A

7-9 PRACTICE C

7-9 PRACTICE B

Multiply.

1. $(x + 2)^2$ $\mathbf{x^2 + 4x + 4}$
2. $(m + 4)^2$ $\mathbf{m^2 + 8m + 16}$
3. $(3 + a)^2$ $\mathbf{9 + 6a + a^2}$
4. $(2x + 5)^2$ $\mathbf{4x^2 + 20x + 25}$
5. $(3a + 2)^2$ $\mathbf{9a^2 + 12a + 4}$
6. $(6 + 5b)^2$ $\mathbf{36 + 60b + 25b^2}$
7. $(b - 3)^2$ $\mathbf{b^2 - 6b + 9}$
8. $(8 - y)^2$ $\mathbf{64 - 16y + y^2}$
9. $(a - 10)^2$ $\mathbf{a^2 - 20a + 100}$
10. $(3x - 7)^2$ $\mathbf{9x^2 - 42x + 49}$
11. $(4m - 9)^2$ $\mathbf{16m^2 - 72m + 81}$
12. $(6 - 3n)^2$ $\mathbf{36 - 36n + 9n^2}$
13. $(x + 3)(x - 3)$ $\mathbf{x^2 - 9}$
14. $(8 + y)(8 - y)$ $\mathbf{64 - y^2}$
15. $(x + 6)(x - 6)$ $\mathbf{x^2 - 36}$
16. $(5x + 2)(5x - 2)$ $\mathbf{25x^2 - 4}$
17. $(10x + 7y)(10x - 7y)$ $\mathbf{100x^2 - 49y^2}$
18. $(x^2 + 3y)(x^2 - 3y)$ $\mathbf{x^4 - 9y^2}$
19. Write a simplified expression that represents the...
    a. area of the large rectangle. $\mathbf{36 - x^2}$
    b. area of the small rectangle. $\mathbf{4 - x^2}$
    c. area of the shaded area. **32**

6 + x; 2 − x; 6 − x; 2 + x

20. The small rectangle is made larger by adding 2 units to the length and 2 units to the width.
    a. What is the new area of the smaller rectangle? $\mathbf{16 - x^2}$
    b. What is the area of the new shaded area? **20**

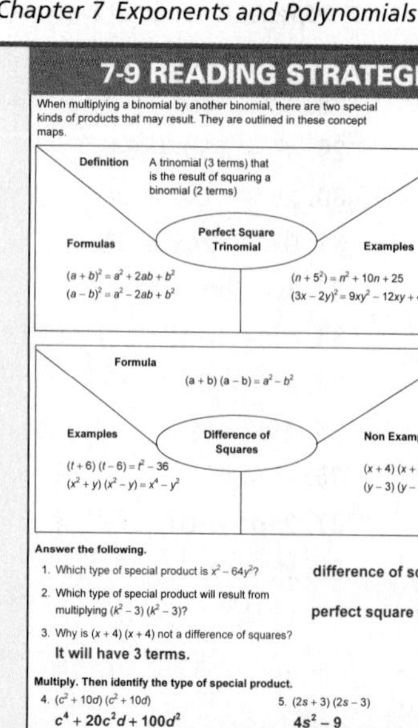

7-9 READING STRATEGIES

When multiplying a binomial by another binomial, there are two special kinds of products that may result. They are outlined in these concept maps.

Perfect Square Trinomial
Definition A trinomial (3 terms) that is the result of squaring a binomial (2 terms)
Formulas $(a + b)^2 = a^2 + 2ab + b^2$; $(a - b)^2 = a^2 - 2ab + b^2$
Examples $(n + 5^2) = n^2 + 10n + 25$; $(3x - 2y)^2 = 9xy^2 - 12xy + 4y^2$

Difference of Squares
Formula $(a + b)(a - b) = a^2 - b^2$
Examples $(t + 6)(t - 6) = t^2 - 36$; $(x^2 + y)(x^2 - y) = x^4 - y^2$
Non Examples $(x + 4)(x + 4)$; $(y - 3)(y - 3)$

Answer the following.

1. Which type of special product is $x^2 - 64y^2$? **difference of squares**
2. Which type of special product will result from multiplying $(k^2 - 3)(k^2 - 3)$? **perfect square trinomial**
3. Why is $(x + 4)(x + 4)$ not a difference of squares? **It will have 3 terms.**

Multiply. Then identify the type of special product.

4. $(c^2 + 10d)(c^2 + 10d)$ $\mathbf{c^4 + 20c^2d + 100d^2}$ **perfect square trinomial**
5. $(2s + 3)(2s - 3)$ $\mathbf{4s^2 - 9}$ **difference of squares**

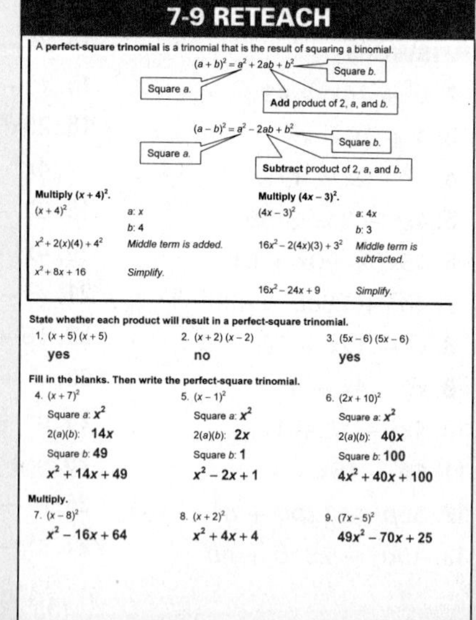

7-9 RETEACH

A **perfect-square trinomial** is a trinomial that is the result of squaring a binomial.

$(a + b)^2 = a^2 + 2ab + b^2$ — Square a. **Add** product of 2, a, and b. Square b.

$(a - b)^2 = a^2 - 2ab + b^2$ — Square a. **Subtract** product of 2, a, and b. Square b.

Multiply $(x + 4)^2$.

$(x + 4)^2$	a: x b: 4
$x^2 + 2(x)(4) + 4^2$	*Middle term is added.*
$x^2 + 8x + 16$	*Simplify.*

Multiply $(4x - 3)^2$.

$(4x - 3)^2$	a: 4x b: 3
$16x^2 - 2(4x)(3) + 3^2$	*Middle term is subtracted.*
$16x^2 - 24x + 9$	*Simplify.*

State whether each product will result in a perfect-square trinomial.

1. $(x + 5)(x + 5)$ **yes**
2. $(x + 2)(x - 2)$ **no**
3. $(5x - 6)(5x - 6)$ **yes**

Fill in the blanks. Then write the perfect-square trinomial.

4. $(x + 7)^2$ Square a: $\mathbf{x^2}$; 2(a)(b): **14x**; Square b: **49**; $\mathbf{x^2 + 14x + 49}$
5. $(x - 1)^2$ Square a: $\mathbf{x^2}$; 2(a)(b): **2x**; Square b: **1**; $\mathbf{x^2 - 2x + 1}$
6. $(2x + 10)^2$ Square a: $\mathbf{x^2}$; 2(a)(b): **40x**; Square b: **100**; $\mathbf{4x^2 + 40x + 100}$

Multiply.

7. $(x - 8)^2$ $\mathbf{x^2 - 16x + 64}$
8. $(x + 2)^2$ $\mathbf{x^2 + 4x + 4}$
9. $(7x - 5)^2$ $\mathbf{49x^2 - 70x + 25}$

64. This problem will prepare you for the Multi-Step Test Prep on page 528.
   a. Michael is fencing part of his yard. He started with a square of length x on each side. He then added 3 feet to the length and subtracted 3 feet from the width. Make a sketch to show the fenced area with the length and width labeled.
   b. Write a polynomial that represents the area of the fenced region. **$x^2 - 9$**
   c. Michael bought a total of 48 feet of fencing. What is the area of his fenced region? **135 ft^2**

65. **Critical Thinking** The polynomial $ax^2 - 49$ is a difference of two squares. Find all possible values of a between 1 and 100 inclusive. **1, 4, 9, 16, 25, 36, 49, 64, 81, 100**

66. **Write About It** When is the product of two binomials also a binomial? Explain and give an example. **When 1 binomial is in the form $a + b$ and the other is in the form $a - b$; $(x + 2)(x - 2) = x^2 - 4$**

67. What is $(5x - 6y)(5x - 6y)$?
   (A) $25x^2 - 22xy + 36y^2$
   (B) $25x^2 - 60xy + 36y^2$ (circled)
   (C) $25x^2 + 22xy + 36y^2$
   (D) $25x^2 + 60xy + 36y^2$

68. Which product is represented by the model?

$25x^2$	$10x$
$10x$	4

   (F) $(2x + 5)(2x + 5)$
   (G) $(5x - 2)(5x - 2)$
   (H) $(5x + 2)(5x - 2)$
   (J) $(5x + 2)(5x + 2)$ (circled)

69. If $a + b = 12$ and $a^2 - b^2 = 96$ what is the value of a?
   (A) 2 (B) 4 (C) 8 (D) 10 (circled)

70. If $rs = 15$ and $(r + s)^2 = 64$, what is the value of $r^2 + s^2$?
   (F) 25 (G) 30 (H) 34 (circled) (J) 49

CHALLENGE AND EXTEND

71. Multiply $(x + 4)(x + 4)(x - 4)$.
72. Multiply $(x + 4)(x - 4)(x - 4)$.
73. If $x^2 + bx + c$ is a perfect-square trinomial, what is the relationship between b and c?
74. You can multiply two numbers by rewriting the numbers as the difference of two squares. For example:

$$36 \cdot 24 = (30 + 6)(30 - 6) = 30^2 - 6^2 = 900 - 36 = 864$$

Use this method to multiply $27 \cdot 19$. Explain how you rewrote the numbers. **513; rewrite 27 as 23 + 4 and 19 as 23 − 4.**

71. $x^3 + 4x^2 - 16x - 64$
72. $x^3 - 4x^2 - 16x + 64$
73. $b = \pm 2\sqrt{c}$

SPIRAL REVIEW

75. The square paper that Yuki is using to make an origami frog has an area of 165 cm^2. Find the side length of the paper to the nearest centimeter. *(Lesson 1-5)* **13 cm**

Use intercepts to graph the line described by each equation. *(Lesson 5-2)*

76. $2x + 3y = 6$
77. $y = -3x + 9$
78. $\frac{1}{2}x + y = 4$

Add or subtract. *(Lesson 7-7)*

79. $3x^2 + 8x - 2x + 9x^2$
80. $(8m^4 + 2n - 3m^3 + 6) + (9m^3 + 5 - 4m^4)$
81. $(2p^3 + p) - (5p^3 + 9p)$
82. $(12t - 3t^2 + 10) - (-5t^2 - 7 - 4t)$

79. $12x^2 + 6x$
80. $4m^4 + 6m^3 + 2n + 11$
81. $-3p^3 - 8p$
82. $2t^2 + 16t + 17$

MULTI-STEP TEST PREP **Exercise 64** involves finding area using polynomials. This exercise prepares students for the Multi-Step Test Prep on page 528.

TEST PREP DOCTOR When multiplying binomials of the form $(a - b)(a - b)$ in **Exercise 67,** the middle term of the product is negative. Choices **C** and **D** can be eliminated.

For **Exercise 69,** $a^2 - b^2 = 96$ is the difference of two squares, so $(a + b)(a - b) = 96$, and by substitution, $12(a - b) = 96$. After dividing both sides by 12, $a - b = 8$. This equation and $a + b = 12$ form a system of linear equations, easily solved by elimination.

Journal

Have students describe three ways to find the product $(x + 2)(x + 2)$; one method must use the special products rule.

ALTERNATIVE ASSESSMENT

Have students create binomials of the form $(a + b)^2$, $(a - b)^2$, and $(a + b)(a - b)$; find each product; and describe how the special products rule is illustrated.

Power Presentations with PowerPoint®

7-9 Lesson Quiz

Multiply.

1. $(x + 7)^2$ $x^2 + 14x + 49$
2. $(x - 2)^2$ $x^2 - 4x + 4$
3. $(5x + 2y)^2$ $25x^2 + 20xy + 4y^2$
4. $(2x - 9y)^2$ $4x^2 - 36xy + 81y^2$
5. $(4x + 5y)(4x - 5y)$ $16x^2 - 25y^2$
6. $(m^2 + 2n)(m^2 - 2n)$ $m^4 - 4n^2$
7. Write a polynomial that represents the shaded area of the figure below. $14x - 85$

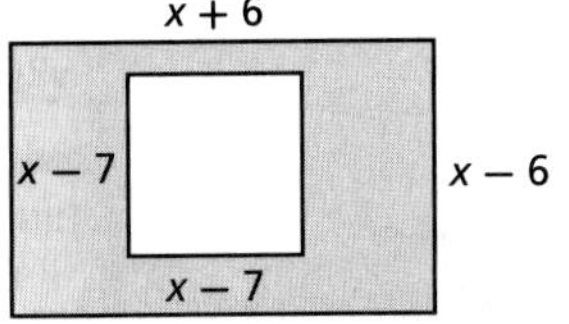

Also available on transparency

7-9 PROBLEM SOLVING

Write the correct answer.

1. This week Kyara worked $x + 4$ hours. She is paid $x - 4$ dollars per hour. Write a polynomial for the amount that Kyara earned this week. Then calculate her pay if $x = 12$.
   $x^2 - 16$
   $128

2. A museum set aside part of a large gallery for a special exhibit.

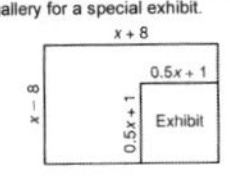

Write a polynomial for the area of the gallery that is not part of the exhibit. Then calculate the area of that section if $x = 60$.
   $0.75x^2 - x - 65$
   2575 square feet

3. Gary is building a square table for a kitchen. In his initial sketch, each side measured x inches. After rearranging some furniture, he realized he would have to add one foot to the length and remove one foot from the width and have a rectangular table instead. Write a polynomial to represent the area of the rectangular table.
   $x^2 - 144$ in^2

A fountain is in the center of a square garden. The radius of the fountain is $x - 2$ feet. The length of the garden is $2x + 4$ feet. Use this information and the diagram for questions 4 – 7. Select the best answer.

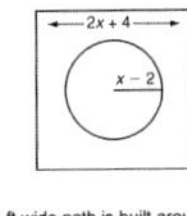

4. Which polynomial represents the area of the fountain?
   A $2\pi x - 4\pi$ C $\pi x^2 - 4\pi$
   B $\pi x^2 - 4\pi x - 4\pi$ **D** $\pi x^2 - 4\pi x + 4\pi$
5. Which polynomial represents the area of the garden, including the fountain?
   F $4x^2 + 8$ H $4x^2 + 16$
   G $4x^2 + 16x + 16$ J $4x^2 + 8x + 16$
6. Which polynomial represents the area of the garden *outside* the fountain? (Use 3.14 for π.)
   A $0.86x^2 + 28.56x + 3.44$
   B $0.86x^2 + 3.44x + 28.56$
   C $7.14x^2 + 28.56x + 3.44$
   D $7.14x^2 + 3.44x + 28.56$
7. A 3-ft wide path is built around the garden. Which expression represents the area of the path?
   F $12x + 33$ H $4x^2 + 28x + 29$
   G $24x + 84$ J $4x^2 + 40x + 100$

7-9 CHALLENGE

The expansions of $(a + b)^2$, $(a - b)^2$, and $(a + b)(a - b)$ show patterns involving a and b. You can discover other patterns involving a and b when you combine these special products.

In Exercises 1–5, use the given values of a and b to complete the table below.

	a	b	$(a+b)^2$	$(a-b)^2$	$(a+b)^2-(a-b)^2$	ab
1.	−3	5	4	64	−60	−15
2.	−2	−4	36	4	32	8
3.	3	6	81	9	72	18
4.	4	7	121	9	112	28
5.	5	−8	9	169	−160	−40

6. a. From the table, how are the values of $(a + b)^2 - (a - b)^2$ and ab related?
   The difference $(a + b)^2 - (a - b)^2$ is four times the product ab.
   b. Based on your work in Exercises 1–5 and your answer to part **a**, write a simplification of $(a + b)^2 - (a + b)^2$. $4ab$
   c. Use algebra to show that your response to part **b** is true.
   $(a^2 + 2ab + b^2) - (a^2 - 2ab + b^2) = 4ab$
7. Using a table like the one that you completed in Exercises 1–5 and the values of a and b used there, write a simplification of $(a + b)^2 + (a - b)^2$. $(a + b)^2 + (a - b)^2 = 2a^2 + 2b^2$

Write a conjecture for the simplification of each sum or difference. Try to do as much of the simplification as you can mentally.

8. $[(a^2 + b^2) + (a^2 - b^2)]^2$
   $4a^4$
9. $[(a^2 + b^2) - (a^2 - b^2)]^2$
   $4b^4$

Simplify each expression.

10. $[(a^2 + b^2) + (a^2 - b^2)]^2$
   $[(a^2 + b^2) + (a^2 - b^2)]^2$
   $= (a^2 + a^2 + b^2 - b^2)^2$
   $= (2a^2)^2 = 2^2a^4 = 4a^4$
11. $[(a^2 + b^2) - (a^2 - b^2)]^2$
   $[(a^2 + b^2) - (a^2 - b^2)]^2$
   $= (a^2 - a^2 + b^2 + b^2)^2$
   $= (2b^2)^2 = 2^2b^4 = 4b^4$

MULTI-STEP TEST PREP

SECTION 7B

Organizer

Objective: Assess students' ability to apply concepts and skills in Lessons 7-6 through 7-9 in a real-world format.

Online Edition

Resources

Algebra I Assessments

www.mathtekstoolkit.org

Problem	Text Reference
1	Lesson 7-7
2	Lesson 7-6
3	Lesson 7-8
4	Lesson 7-9
5	Lesson 7-9
6	Lesson 7-9

State Resources

go.hrw.com State Resources Online KEYWORD: MA7 Resources

Polynomials

Don't Fence Me In James has 500 feet of fencing to enclose a rectangular region on his farm for some sheep.

1. Make a sketch of three possible regions that James could enclose and give the corresponding areas.
2. If the length of the region is x, find an expression for the width. **$250 - x$**
3. Use your answer to Problem 2 to write an equation for the area of the region. **$A = x(250 - x)$**
4. Graph your equation from Problem 3 on your calculator. Sketch the graph.
5. James wants his fenced region to have the largest area possible using 500 feet of fencing. Find this area using the graph or a table of values. **15,625 ft^2**
6. What are the length and width of the region with the area from Problem 5? Describe this region. **125 ft × 125 ft; square**

1. Possible answers:

$A = 15{,}625$ ft^2

125 ft × 125 ft

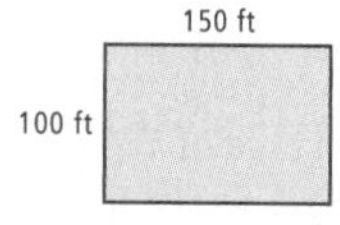

$A = 10{,}000$ ft^2

200 ft × 50 ft

$A = 15{,}000$ ft^2

150 ft × 100 ft

4.

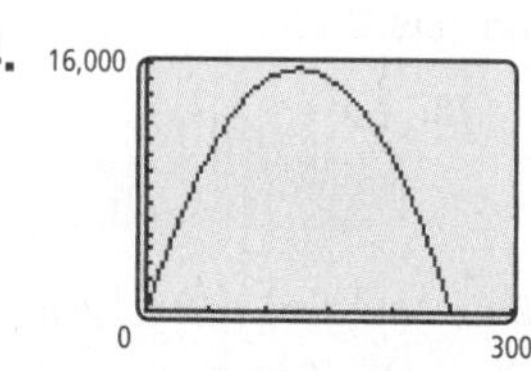

INTERVENTION

Scaffolding Questions

1. What is the perimeter of a rectangle? distance around the rectangle How is it calculated? $P = 2\ell + 2w$
2. What are some possible values for ℓ and w? Possible answers: $\ell = 40, w = 210$; $\ell = 30, w = 220$; $\ell = 45, w = 205$
3. What is the area of a rectangle? number of square units inside the rectangle How is it calculated? $A = \ell w$
4. What is an appropriate viewing window? Possible answer: $0 < x < 250$ and $0 < y < 16{,}000$
5. How can you find the greatest area from the graph or table? Graph: find the y-coordinate of the highest point; Table: find the greatest y-value.
6. How can you find the dimensions from the graph or table? Graph: find the x-coordinate of the highest point; Table: look for the greatest y-value and find its corresponding x-value.

Extension

Now James will use his fencing to create three sides of a rectangular region and build a wall for the fourth side. Now what is the greatest possible area? Describe this region. What is the minimum length of the wall? 31,250 ft^2; 125 ft × 250 ft rectangle; 250 ft

Quiz for Lessons 7-6 Through 7-9

1. $2r^6 + 4r^2 - 3r$; 2
2. $-8y^3 + y^2 + 2y + 7$; -8
3. $t^4 - 12t^3 - 4t$; 1

7-6 Polynomials

Write each polynomial in standard form and give the leading coefficient.

1. $4r^2 + 2r^6 - 3r$
2. $y^2 + 7 - 8y^3 + 2y$
3. $-12t^3 - 4t + t^4$
4. $n + 3 + 3n^2$ $3n^2 + n + 3$; 3
5. $2 + 3x^3$ $3x^3 + 2$; 3
6. $-3a^2 + 16 + a^7 + a$ $a^7 - 3a^2 + a + 16$; 1

Classify each polynomial according to its degree and number of terms.

7. $2x^3 + 5x - 4$
8. $5b^2$
9. $6p^2 + 3p - p^4 + 2p^3$
10. $x^2 + 12 - x$
11. $-2x^3 - 5 + x - 2x^7$
12. $5 - 6b^2 + b - 4b^4$
13. **Business** The function $C(x) = x^3 - 15x + 14$ gives the cost to manufacture x units of a product. What is the cost to manufacture 900 units? **\$728,986,514**

7-7 Adding and Subtracting Polynomials

Add or subtract.

14. $(10m^3 + 4m^2) + (7m^2 + 3m)$
15. $(3t^2 - 2t) + (9t^2 + 4t - 6)$
16. $(12d^6 - 3d^2) + (2d^4 + 1)$
17. $(6y^3 + 4y^2) - (2y^2 + 3y)$
18. $(7n^2 - 3n) - (5n^2 + 5n)$
19. $(b^2 - 10) - (-5b^3 + 4b)$
20. **Geometry** The measures of the sides of a triangle are shown as polynomials. Write a simplified polynomial to represent the perimeter of the triangle. $2s^3 + 4s^2 + 5s + 5$

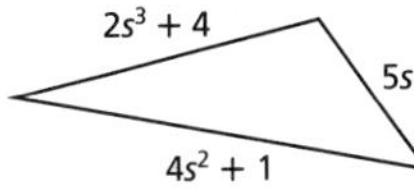

7-8 Multiplying Polynomials

Multiply.

21. $2h^3 \cdot 5h^5$
22. $(s^8t^4)(-6st^3)$
23. $2ab(5a^3 + 3a^2b)$
24. $(3k + 5)^2$
25. $(2x^3 + 3y)(4x^2 + y)$
26. $(p^2 + 3p)(9p^2 - 6p - 5)$

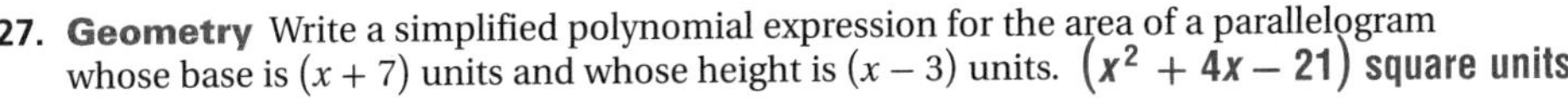

27. **Geometry** Write a simplified polynomial expression for the area of a parallelogram whose base is $(x + 7)$ units and whose height is $(x - 3)$ units. $(x^2 + 4x - 21)$ square units

7-9 Special Products of Binomials

Multiply.

28. $(d + 9)^2$
29. $(3 + 2t)^2$
30. $(2x + 5y)^2$
31. $(m - 4)^2$
32. $(a - b)^2$
33. $(3w - 1)^2$
34. $(c + 2)(c - 2)$
35. $(5r + 6)(5r - 6)$
36. **Sports** A child's basketball has a radius of $(x - 5)$ inches. Write a polynomial that represents the surface area of the basketball. (The formula for the surface area of a sphere is $S = 4\pi r^2$, where r represents the radius of the sphere.) Leave the symbol π in your answer. $(4\pi x^2 - 40\pi x + 100\pi)$ in^2

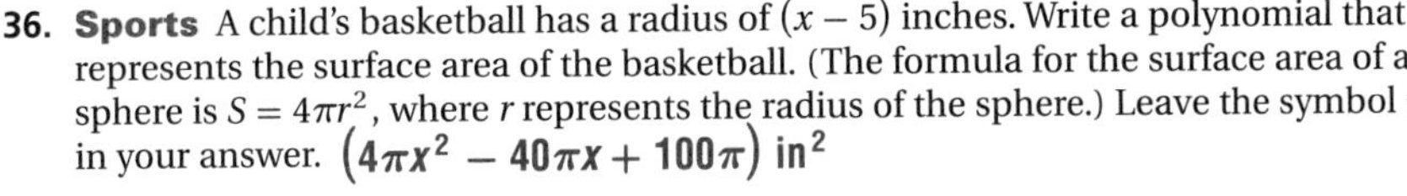

SECTION 7B

Organizer

Objective: Assess students' mastery of concepts and skills in Lessons 7-6 through 7-9.

Resources

Assessment Resources
Section 7B Quiz

Teacher One Stop™
Test & Practice Generator

INTERVENTION

Resources

Ready to Go On? Intervention and Enrichment **Worksheets**

Ready to Go On? **CD-ROM**

Ready to Go On? **Online**

my.hrw.com

Answers

7–12, 14–19. See p. A27.
21–26, 28–35. See pp. A27–A28.

READY TO GO ON? Diagnose and Prescribe

NO INTERVENE

Ready to Go On? Intervention	*Ready to Go On? Intervention,* Section 7B — Worksheets	CD-ROM	Online
Lesson 7-6	7-6 Intervention	Activity 7-6	Diagnose and Prescribe Online
Lesson 7-7	7-7 Intervention	Activity 7-7	
Lesson 7-8	7-8 Intervention	Activity 7-8	
Lesson 7-9	7-9 Intervention	Activity 7-9	

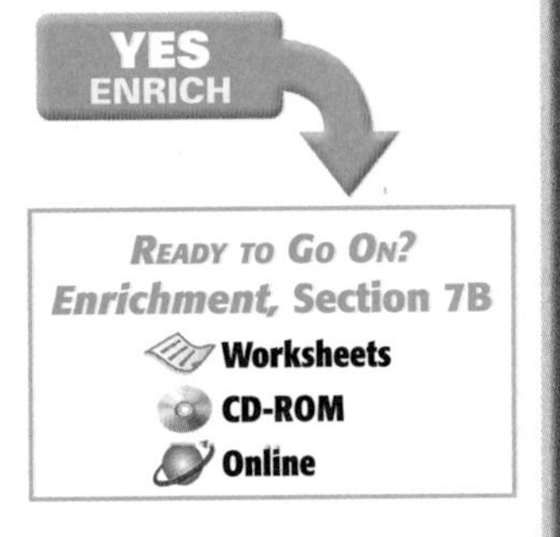

Ready to Go On? Enrichment, **Section 7B**
Worksheets
CD-ROM
Online

CHAPTER 7 **Study Guide: Review**

Organizer

Objective: Help students organize and review key concepts and skills presented in Chapter 7.

Online Edition
Multilingual Glossary

Countdown Week 17

Resources

Teacher One Stop™
PuzzleView
Test & Practice Generator

***Multilingual Glossary* Online**
go.hrw.com
KEYWORD: MA7 Glossary

Lesson Tutorial Videos
CD-ROM

Answers

1. cubic
2. standard form of a polynomial
3. monomial
4. trinomial
5. scientific notation
6. $\frac{1}{32}$ in.
7. 1
8. 1
9. $\frac{1}{125}$
10. $\frac{1}{10{,}000}$, or 0.0001
11. $\frac{1}{16}$
12. $\frac{1}{256}$
13. $\frac{27}{4}$
14. $\frac{1}{m^2}$
15. b
16. $-\frac{1}{2x^2y^4}$
17. $2b^6c^4$
18. $\frac{3a^2}{4c^2}$
19. $\frac{s^3}{qr^2}$

CHAPTER 7

Study Guide: Review

Vocabulary

binomial 497	index 488	quadratic 497
cubic 497	leading coefficient 497	scientific notation 467
degree of a monomial 496	monomial 496	standard form of a polynomial 497
degree of a polynomial 496	perfect-square trinomial 521	trinomial 497
difference of two squares 523	polynomial 496	

Complete the sentences below with vocabulary words from the list above.

1. A(n) ___?___ polynomial is a polynomial of degree 3.
2. When a polynomial is written with the terms in order from highest to lowest degree, it is in ___?___.
3. A(n) ___?___ is a number, a variable, or a product of numbers and variables with whole-number exponents.
4. A(n) ___?___ is a polynomial with three terms.
5. ___?___ is a method of writing numbers that are very large or very small.

7-1 Integer Exponents *(pp. 460–465)*

EXAMPLES

Simplify.

■ -2^{-4}

$$-2^{-4} = -\frac{1}{2^4} = -\frac{1}{2 \cdot 2 \cdot 2 \cdot 2} = -\frac{1}{16}$$

■ 3^0

$3^0 = 1$ *Any nonzero number raised to the zero power is 1.*

■ **Evaluate r^3s^{-4} for $r = -3$ and $s = 2$.**

r^3s^{-4}

$$(-3)^3(2)^{-4} = \frac{(-3)(-3)(-3)}{2 \cdot 2 \cdot 2 \cdot 2} = -\frac{27}{16}$$

■ **Simplify $\frac{a^{-3}b^4}{c^{-2}}$.**

$$\frac{a^{-3}b^4}{c^{-2}} = \frac{b^4c^2}{a^3}$$

EXERCISES

6. The diameter of a certain bearing is 2^{-5} in. Simplify this expression.

Simplify.

7. $(3.6)^0$
8. $(-1)^{-4}$
9. 5^{-3}
10. 10^{-4}

Evaluate each expression for the given value(s) of the variable(s).

11. b^{-4} for $b = 2$
12. $\left(\frac{2}{5}b\right)^{-4}$ for $b = 10$
13. $-2p^3q^{-3}$ for $p = 3$ and $q = -2$

Simplify.

14. m^{-2}
15. bc^0
16. $-\frac{1}{2}x^{-2}y^{-4}$
17. $\frac{2b^6}{c^{-4}}$
18. $\frac{3a^2c^{-2}}{4b^0}$
19. $\frac{q^{-1}r^{-2}}{s^{-3}}$

7-2 Powers of 10 and Scientific Notation *(pp. 466–471)*

EXAMPLES

- **Write 1,000,000 as a power of 10.**

1,000,000 — *The decimal point is 6 places to the right of 1.*

$1{,}000{,}000 = 10^6$

- **Find the value of 386.21×10^5.**

386.21000 — *Move the decimal point 5 places to the right.*

38,621,000

- **Write 0.000000041 in scientific notation.**

0.000000041 — *Move the decimal point 8 places to the right to get a number between 1 and 10.*

4.1×10^{-8}

EXERCISES

Find the value of each power of 10.

20. 10^7 **21.** 10^{-5}

Write each number as a power of 10.

22. 100 **23.** 0.00000000001

Find the value of each expression.

24. 3.25×10^5 **25.** 0.18×10^4

26. 17×10^{-2} **27.** 299×10^{-6}

28. Order the list of numbers from least to greatest. 6.3×10^{-3}, 1.2×10^4, 5.8×10^{-7}, 2.2×10^2

29. In 2003, the average daily value of shares traded on the New York Stock Exchange was about $\$3.85 \times 10^{10}$. Write this amount in standard form.

7-3 Multiplication Properties of Exponents *(pp. 474–480)*

EXAMPLES

Simplify.

- $5^3 \cdot 5^{-2}$

$5^3 \cdot 5^{-2}$ — *The powers have the same base.*

$5^{3+(-2)}$ — *Add the exponents.*

5^1

5

- $a^4 \cdot b^{-3} \cdot b \cdot a^{-2}$

$a^4 \cdot b^{-3} \cdot b \cdot a^{-2}$

$(a^4 \cdot a^{-2}) \cdot (b^{-3} \cdot b)$ — *Use properties to group factors.*

$a^2 \cdot b^{-2}$ — *Add the exponents of powers with the same base.*

$\frac{a^2}{b^2}$ — *Write with a positive exponent.*

- $(a^{-3}b^2)^{-2}$

$(a^{-3})^{-2} \cdot (b^2)^{-2}$ — *Power of a Product Property*

$a^6 \cdot b^{-4}$ — *Power of a Power Property*

$\frac{a^6}{b^4}$ — *Write with a positive exponent.*

EXERCISES

Simplify.

30. $5^3 \cdot 5^6$ **31.** $2^6 \cdot 3 \cdot 2^{-3} \cdot 3^3$

32. $b^2 \cdot b^8$ **33.** $r^4 \cdot r$

34. $(x^3)^4$ **35.** $(s^3)^0$

36. $(2^3)^{-1}$ **37.** $(5^2)^{-2}$

38. $(4b^3)^{-2}$ **39.** $(g^3h^2)^4$

40. $(-x^2y)^2$ **41.** $-(x^2y)^2$

42. $(x^2y^3)(xy^3)^4$ **43.** $(j^2k^3)(j^4k^6)$

44. $(5^3 \cdot 5^{-2})^{-1}$ **45.** $(mn^3)^5(mn^5)^3$

46. $(4 \times 10^8)(2 \times 10^3)$ **47.** $(3 \times 10^2)(3 \times 10^5)$

48. $(5 \times 10^3)(2 \times 10^6)$ **49.** $(7 \times 10^5)(4 \times 10^9)$

50. $(3 \times 10^{-4})(2 \times 10^5)$ **51.** $(3 \times 10^{-8})(6 \times 10^{-1})$

52. In 2003, Wyoming's population was about 5.0×10^5. California's population was about 7.1×10 times as large as Wyoming's. What was the approximate population of California? Write your answer in scientific notation.

Answers

20. 10,000,000
21. 0.00001
22. 10^2
23. 10^{-11}
24. 325,000
25. 1800
26. 0.17
27. 0.000299
28. 5.8×10^{-7}, 6.3×10^{-3}, 2.2×10^2, 1.2×10^4
29. \$38,500,000,000
30. 5^9
31. $2^3 \cdot 3^4$
32. b^{10}
33. r^5
34. x^{12}
35. 1
36. $\frac{1}{2^3}$, or $\frac{1}{8}$
37. $\frac{1}{5^4}$, or $\frac{1}{625}$
38. $\frac{1}{16b^6}$
39. $g^{12}h^8$
40. x^4y^2
41. $-x^4y^2$
42. x^6y^{15}
43. j^6k^9
44. $\frac{1}{5}$
45. m^8n^{30}
46. 8×10^{11}
47. 9×10^7
48. 1×10^{10}
49. 2.8×10^{15}
50. 6×10^1
51. 1.8×10^{-8}
52. 3.55×10^7

Answers

53. 64
54. m^5
55. $\frac{7}{32}$
56. $6b$
57. t^3v^4
58. 16
59. 5×10^1
60. 2.5×10^7
61. 9
62. 7
63. 16
64. 8
65. z^2
66. $5x^2$
67. x^4y^3
68. m^2n^4
69. 0
70. 4
71. 6
72. 1
73. $3n^2 + 2n - 4$; 3
74. $-a^6 - a^4 + 3a^3 + 2a$; -1
75. linear binomial
76. quintic monomial
77. quartic trinomial
78. constant monomial

7-4 Division Properties of Exponents *(pp. 481–487)*

EXAMPLES

■ **Simplify $\frac{x^9}{x^2}$.**

$\frac{x^9}{x^2} = x^{9-2} = x^7$ *Subtract the exponents.*

EXERCISES

Simplify.

53. $\frac{2^8}{2^2}$
54. $\frac{m^6}{m}$
55. $\frac{2^6 \cdot 4 \cdot 7^3}{2^5 \cdot 4^4 \cdot 7^2}$
56. $\frac{24b^6}{4b^5}$
57. $\frac{t^4v^5}{tv}$
58. $\left(\frac{1}{2}\right)^{-4}$

Simplify each quotient and write the answer in scientific notation.

59. $(2.5 \times 10^8) \div (0.5 \times 10^7)$
60. $(2 \times 10^{10}) \div (8 \times 10^2)$

7-5 Rational Exponents *(pp. 488–493)*

EXAMPLES

■ **Simplify $\sqrt[3]{r^6s^{12}}$.**

$\sqrt[3]{r^6s^{12}} = (r^6s^{12})^{\frac{1}{3}}$ *Definition of $b^{\frac{1}{n}}$*

$= (r^6)^{\frac{1}{3}} \cdot (s^{12})^{\frac{1}{3}}$ *Power of a Product Property*

$= \left(r^{6 \cdot \frac{1}{3}}\right) \cdot \left(s^{12 \cdot \frac{1}{3}}\right)$ *Power of a Power Property*

$= (r^2) \cdot (s^4)$ *Simplify exponents.*

$= r^2s^4$

EXERCISES

Simplify each expression.

61. $81^{\frac{1}{2}}$
62. $343^{\frac{1}{3}}$
63. $64^{\frac{2}{3}}$
64. $(2^6)^{\frac{1}{2}}$

Simplify each expression. All variables represent nonnegative numbers.

65. $\sqrt[5]{z^{10}}$
66. $\sqrt[3]{125x^6}$
67. $\sqrt{x^8y^6}$
68. $\sqrt[3]{m^6n^{12}}$

7-6 Polynomials *(pp. 496–501)*

EXAMPLES

■ **Find the degree of the polynomial $3x^2 + 8x^5$.**

$3x^2 + 8x^5$ *$8x^5$ has the highest degree.*

The degree is 5.

■ **Classify the polynomial $y^3 - 2y$ according to its degree and number of terms.**

Degree: 3
Terms: 2

The polynomial $y^3 - 2y$ is a **cubic binomial.**

EXERCISES

Find the degree of each polynomial.

69. 5
70. $8st^3$
71. $3z^6$
72. $6h$

Write each polynomial in standard form. Then give the leading coefficient.

73. $2n - 4 + 3n^2$
74. $2a - a^4 - a^6 + 3a^3$

Classify each polynomial according to its degree and number of terms.

75. $2s - 6$
76. $-8p^5$
77. $-m^4 - m^2 - 1$
78. 2

7-7 Adding and Subtracting Polynomials (pp. 504–509)

EXAMPLES

Add.

- $(h^3 - 2h) + (3h^2 + 4h) - 2h^3$
  $(h^3 - 2h) + (3h^2 + 4h) - 2h^3$
  $(h^3 - 2h^3) + (3h^2) + (4h - 2h)$
  $-h^3 + 3h^2 + 2h$

Subtract.

- $(n^3 + 5 - 6n^2) - (3n^2 - 7)$
  $(n^3 + 5 - 6n^2) + (-3n^2 + 7)$
  $(n^3 + 5 - 6n^2) + (-3n^2 + 7)$
  $n^3 + (-6n^2 - 3n^2) + (5 + 7)$
  $n^3 - 9n^2 + 12$

EXERCISES

Add or subtract.

79. $3t + 5 - 7t - 2$
80. $4x^5 - 6x^6 + 2x^5 - 7x^5$
81. $-h^3 - 2h^2 + 4h^3 - h^2 + 5$
82. $(3m - 7) + (2m^2 - 8m + 6)$
83. $(12 + 6p) - (p - p^2 + 4)$
84. $(3z - 9z^2 + 2) + (2z^2 - 4z + 8)$
85. $(10g - g^2 + 3) - (-4g^2 + 8g - 1)$
92. $(-5x^3 + 2x^2 - x + 5) - (-5x^3 + 3x^2 - 5x - 3)$

7-8 Multiplying Polynomials (pp. 512–519)

EXAMPLES

Multiply.

- $(2x - 4)(3x + 5)$
  $2x(3x) + 2x(5) - 4(3x) - 4(5)$
  $6x^2 + 10x - 12x - 20$
  $6x^2 - 2x - 20$

- $(b - 2)(b^2 + 4b - 5)$
  $b(b^2) + b(4b) - b(5) - 2(b^2) - 2(4b) - 2(-5)$
  $b^3 + 4b^2 - 5b - 2b^2 - 8b + 10$
  $b^3 + 2b^2 - 13b + 10$

EXERCISES

Multiply.

87. $(2r)(4r)$
88. $(3a^5)(2ab)$
89. $(-3xy)(-6x^2y)$
90. $(3s^3t^2)(2st^4)\left(\frac{1}{2}s^2t^8\right)$
91. $2(x^2 - 4x + 6)$
92. $-3ab(ab - 2a^2b + 5a)$
93. $(a + 3)(a - 6)$
94. $(b - 9)(b + 3)$
95. $(x - 10)(x - 2)$
96. $(t - 1)(t + 1)$
97. $(2q + 6)(4q + 5)$
98. $(5g - 8)(4g - 1)$

7-9 Special Products of Binomials (pp. 521–527)

EXAMPLES

Multiply.

- $(2h - 6)^2$
  $(2h - 6)^2 = (2h)^2 + 2(2h)(-6) + (-6)^2$
  $4h^2 - 24h + 36$

- $(4x - 3)(4x + 3)$
  $(4x - 3)(4x + 3) = (4x)^2 - 3^2$
  $16x^2 - 9$

EXERCISES

Multiply.

99. $(p - 4)^2$
100. $(x + 12)^2$
101. $(m + 6)^2$
102. $(3c + 7)^2$
103. $(2r - 1)^2$
104. $(3a - b)^2$
105. $(2n - 5)^2$
106. $(h - 13)^2$
107. $(x - 1)(x + 1)$
108. $(z + 15)(z - 15)$
109. $(c^2 - d)(c^2 + d)$
110. $(3k^2 + 7)(3k^2 - 7)$

Answers

79. $-4t + 3$
80. $-6x^6 - x^5$
81. $3h^3 - 3h^2 + 5$
82. $2m^2 - 5m - 1$
83. $p^2 + 5p + 8$
84. $-7z^2 - z + 10$
85. $3g^2 + 2g + 4$
86. $-x^2 + 4x + 8$
87. $8r^2$
88. $6a^6b$
89. $18x^3y^2$
90. $3s^6t^{14}$
91. $2x^2 - 8x + 12$
92. $-3a^2b^2 + 6a^3b^2 - 15a^2b$
93. $a^2 - 3a - 18$
94. $b^2 - 6b - 27$
95. $x^2 - 12x + 20$
96. $t^2 - 1$
97. $8q^2 + 34q + 30$
98. $20g^2 - 37g + 8$
99. $p^2 - 8p + 16$
100. $x^2 + 24x + 144$
101. $m^2 + 12m + 36$
102. $9c^2 + 42c + 49$
103. $4r^2 - 4r + 1$
104. $9a^2 - 6ab + b^2$
105. $4n^2 - 20n + 25$
106. $h^2 - 26h + 169$
107. $x^2 - 1$
108. $z^2 - 225$
109. $c^4 - d^2$
110. $9k^4 - 49$

Organizer

Objective: Assess students' mastery of concepts and skills in Chapter 7.

 Online Edition

Resources

 ***Assessment Resources***

Chapter 7 Tests
- Free Response (Levels A, B, C)
- Multiple Choice (Levels A, B, C)
- Performance Assessment

Teacher One Stop™
Test & Practice Generator

Evaluate each expression for the given value(s) of the variable(s).

1. $\left(\frac{1}{3}b\right)^{-2}$ for $b = 12$ $\frac{1}{16}$
2. $(14 - a^0b^2)^{-3}$ for $a = -2$ and $b = 4$ $-\frac{1}{8}$

Simplify.

3. $2r^{-3}$ $\frac{2}{r^3}$
4. $-3f^0g^{-1}$ $-\frac{3}{g}$
5. m^2n^{-3} $\frac{m^2}{n^3}$
6. $\frac{1}{2}s^{-5}t^3$ $\frac{t^3}{2s^5}$

Write each number as a power of 10.

7. 0.0000001 10^{-7}
8. 10,000,000,000,000 10^{13}
9. 1 10^0

Find the value of each expression.

10. 1.25×10^{-5} **0.0000125**
11. $10^8 \times 10^{-11}$ **0.001**
12. 325×10^{-2} **3.25**
13. **Technology** In 2002, there were approximately 544,000,000 Internet users worldwide. Write this number in scientific notation. 5.44×10^8

Simplify.

14. $(f^4)^3$ f^{12}
15. $(4b^2)^0$ **1**
16. $(a^3b^6)^6$ $a^{18}b^{36}$
17. $-(x^3)^5 \cdot (x^2)^6$ $-x^{27}$

Simplify each quotient and write the answer in scientific notation.

18. $(3.6 \times 10^9) \div (6 \times 10^4)$ 6×10^4
19. $(3 \times 10^{12}) \div (9.6 \times 10^{16})$ 3.125×10^{-5}

Simplify.

20. $\frac{y^4}{y}$ y^3
21. $\frac{d^2f^5}{(d^3)^2f^{-4}}$ $\frac{f^9}{d^4}$
22. $\frac{2^5 \cdot 3^3 \cdot 5^4}{2^8 \cdot 3^2 \cdot 5^4}$ $\frac{3}{8}$
23. $\left(\frac{4s}{3t}\right)^{-2} \cdot \left(\frac{2s}{6t}\right)^2$ $\frac{1}{16}$
24. **Geometry** The surface area of a cone is approximated by the polynomial $3.14r^2 + 3.14r\ell$, where r is the radius and ℓ is the slant height. Find the approximate surface area of a cone when $\ell = 5$ cm and $r = 3$ cm. **75.36 cm²**

Simplify each expression. All variables represent nonnegative numbers.

25. $\left(\frac{27}{125}\right)^{\frac{1}{3}}$ $\frac{3}{5}$
26. $\sqrt[3]{43^3}$ **43**
27. $\sqrt{25y^8}$ $5y^4$
28. $\sqrt[5]{3^5t^{10}}$ $3t^2$

Add or subtract.

29. $3a - 4b + 2a$ $5a - 4b$
30. $(2b^2 - 4b^3) - (6b^3 + 8b^2)$ $-10b^3 - 6b^2$
31. $-9g^2 + 3g - 4g^3 - 2g + 3g^2 - 4$ $-4g^3 - 6g^2 + g - 4$

Multiply.

32. $-5(r^2s - 6)$ $-5r^2s + 30$
33. $(2t - 7)(t + 4)$ $2t^2 + t - 28$
34. $(4g - 1)(4g^2 - 5g - 3)$ $16g^3 - 24g^2 - 7g + 3$
35. $(m + 6)^2$ $m^2 + 12m + 36$
36. $(3t - 7)(3t + 7)$ $9t^2 - 49$
37. $(3x^2 - 7)^2$ $9x^4 - 42x^2 + 49$
38. **Carpentry** Carpenters use a tool called a *speed square* to help them mark right angles. A speed square is a right triangle.
    a. Write a polynomial that represents the area of the speed square shown. $x^2 - x - 12$
    b. Find the area when $x = 4.5$ in. **3.75 in²**

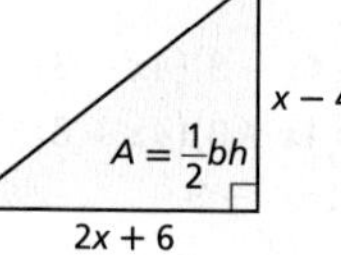

COLLEGE ENTRANCE EXAM PRACTICE

CHAPTER 7

FOCUS ON SAT

When you receive your SAT scores, you will find a percentile for each score. The percentile tells you what percent of students scored lower than you on the same test. Your percentile at the national and state levels may differ because of the different groups being compared.

You may want to time yourself as you take this practice test. It should take you about 7 minutes to complete.

HOT TIP! You may use some types of calculators on the math section of the SAT. For about 40% of the test items, a graphing calculator is recommended. Bring a calculator that you are comfortable using. You won't have time to figure out how a new calculator works.

1. If $(x + 1)(x + 4) - (x - 1)(x - 2) = 0$, what is the value of x?
   (A) -1
   (B) $-\frac{1}{4}$
   (C) 0
   (D) $\frac{1}{4}$
   (E) 1

2. Which of the following is equal to 4^5?
   I. $3^5 \times 1^5$
   II. 2^{10}
   III. $4^0 \times 4^5$
   (A) I only
   (B) II only
   (C) I and II only
   (D) II and III only
   (E) I, II, and III

3. If $x^{-4} = 81$, then $x =$
   (A) -3
   (B) $\frac{1}{4}$
   (C) $\frac{1}{3}$
   (D) 3
   (E) 9

4. What is the value of $2x^3 - 4x^2 + 3x + 1$ when $x = -2$?
   (A) -37
   (B) -25
   (C) -5
   (D) 7
   (E) 27

5. What is the area of a rectangle with a length of $x - a$ and a width of $x + b$?
   $x - a$ / $x + b$
   (A) $x^2 - a^2$
   (B) $x^2 + b^2$
   (C) $x^2 - abx + ab$
   (D) $x^2 - ax - bx - ab$
   (E) $x^2 + bx - ax - ab$

6. For integers greater than 0, define the following operations.
   $$a \square b = 2a^2 + 3b$$
   $$a \triangle b = 5a^2 - 2b$$
   What is $(a \square b) + (a \triangle b)$?
   (A) $7a^2 + b$
   (B) $-3a^2 + 5b$
   (C) $7a^2 - b$
   (D) $3a^2 - 5b$
   (E) $-3a^2 - b$

COLLEGE ENTRANCE EXAM PRACTICE CHAPTER 7

Organizer

Objective: Provide practice for college entrance exams such as the SAT.

PREMIER Online Edition

Resources

College Entrance Exam Practice

Questions on the SAT represent the following math content areas:

Number and Operations, 20–25%

Algebra and Functions, 35–40%

Geometry and Measurement, 25–30%

Data Analysis, Statistics, and Probability, 10–15%

Items on this page focus on:
- Algebra and Functions
- Geometry and Measurement

Text References:

Item	1	2	3	4	5	6
Lesson	7-8	7-1, 7-3	7-1	7-6	7-8	7-7

TEST PREP DOCTOR

1. Students who chose **A** or **E** may have made a sign error in the second term. Suggest that students use parentheses around each product of binomials until the multiplication is complete and then distribute the negative sign from the subtraction of the terms.
2. Students who chose **A, C,** or **E** may have added the bases in choice **I** and kept the exponent the same. Remind students that if the bases are the same when powers are multiplied, then they can add the exponents.
3. Students who chose **D** found the value of x if $x^4 = 81$. Suggest that students rewrite x^{-4} with a positive exponent and try again.
4. Students who chose **C** probably made a sign error in the first or second term. Remind students to be careful when using exponents with negative numbers. Be sure they understand when the negative sign is part of the base, and when it is not.
5. Students who did not choose **E** should review multiplying binomials. Remind students to be cautious of signs.
6. Students who chose **B** subtracted the two binomials instead of adding them. Remind students to read each test item carefully.

Organizer

Objective: Provide opportunities to learn and practice common test-taking strategies.

This Test Tackler explains how test item diagrams can inadvertently mislead students. If students assume that visual information from a diagram is correct, they will likely misinterpret the information. Advise students that diagrams are not always drawn to scale. Students should not rely solely on the appearance of the drawing to answer the test item. Instead they should look closely at a drawing's labels. They may even need to redraw the diagram to scale in order to better represent the problem. Explain that even though a test item may not include a diagram, it may be beneficial for students to make a quick sketch. Show students the importance of labeling their sketch with the information in the test item.

Any Question Type: Use a Diagram

When a test item includes a diagram, use it to help solve the problem. Gather as much information from the drawing as possible. However, keep in mind that diagrams are not always drawn to scale and can be misleading.

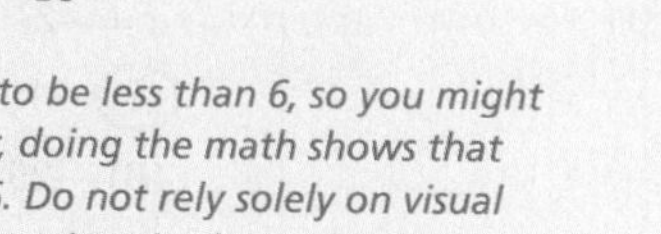

EXAMPLE 1

Multiple Choice **What is the height of the triangle when $x = 4$ and $y = 1$?**

Ⓐ 2
Ⓑ 4
Ⓒ 8
Ⓓ 16

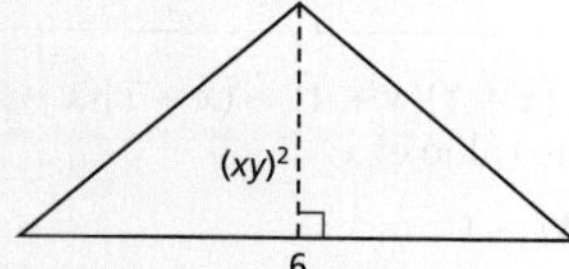

In the diagram, the height appears to be less than 6, so you might eliminate choices C and D. However, doing the math shows that the height is actually greater than 6. Do not rely solely on visual information. Always use the numbers given in the problem.

The height of the triangle is $(xy)^2$.

When $x = 4$ and $y = 1$, $(xy)^2 = (4 \cdot 1)^2 = (4)^2 = 16$.

Choice D is the correct answer.

If a test item does not have a diagram, draw a quick sketch of the problem situation. Label your diagram with the data given in the problem.

EXAMPLE 2

Short Response **A square placemat is lying in the middle of a rectangular table. The side length of the placemat is $\left(\frac{x}{2}\right)$. The length of the table is $12x$, and the width is $8x$. Write a polynomial to represent the area of the placemat. Then write a polynomial to represent the area of the table that surrounds the placemat.**

Use the information in the problem to draw and label a diagram. Then write the polynomials.

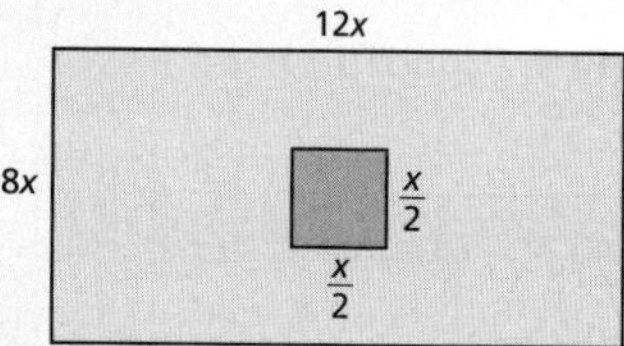

area of placemat $= s^2 = \left(\frac{x}{2}\right)^2 = \left(\frac{x}{2}\right)\left(\frac{x}{2}\right) = \frac{x^2}{4}$

area of table $= \ell w = (12x)(8x) = 96x^2$

area of table $-$ area of placemat $= 96x^2 - \frac{x^2}{4} = \frac{384x^2 - x^2}{4} = \frac{383x^2}{4}$

The area of the placemat is $\frac{x^2}{4}$.

The area of the table that surrounds the placemat is $\frac{383x^2}{4}$.

If a given diagram does not reflect the problem, draw a sketch that is more accurate. If a test item does not have a diagram, use the given information to sketch your own. Try to make your sketch as accurate as possible.

Read each test item and answer the questions that follow.

Item A
Short Response **The width of a rectangle is 1.5 feet more than 4 times its length. Write a polynomial expression for the area of the rectangle. What is the area when the length is 16.75 feet?**

1. What is the unknown measure in this problem?
2. How will drawing a diagram help you solve the problem?
3. Draw and label a sketch of the situation.

Item B
Multiple Choice **Rectangle *ABDC* is similar to rectangle *MNPO*. If the width of rectangle *ABDC* is 8, what is its length?**

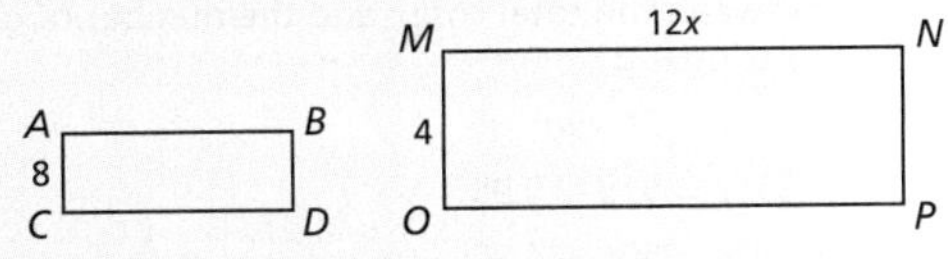

Ⓐ 2
Ⓑ $2x$
Ⓒ $24x$
Ⓓ 24

4. Look at the dimensions in the diagram. Do you think that the length of rectangle *ABDC* is greater or less than the length of rectangle *MNPO*?
5. Do you think the drawings reflect the information in the problem accurately? Why or why not?
6. Draw your own sketch to match the information in the problem.

Item C
Short Response **Write a polynomial expression for the area of triangle *QRP*. Write a polynomial expression for the area of triangle *MNP*. Then use these expressions to write a polynomial expression for the area of *QRNM*.**

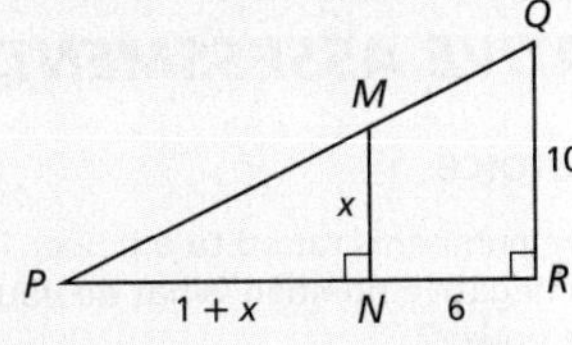

7. Describe how redrawing the figure can help you better understand the information in the problem.
8. After reading this test item, a student redrew the figure as shown below. Is this a correct interpretation of the original figure? Explain.

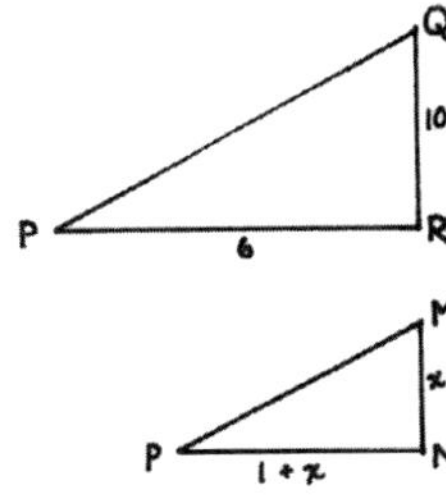

Item D
Multiple Choice **The measure of angle *XYZ* is $(x^2 + 10x + 15)°$. What is the measure of angle *XYW*?**

Ⓕ $(6x + 15)°$
Ⓖ $(2x^2 + 14x + 15)°$
Ⓗ $(14x + 15)°$
Ⓙ $(6x^2 + 15)°$

W
X
$(x^2 + 4x)°$
Y
Z

9. What information does the diagram provide that the problem does not?
10. Will the measure of angle *XYW* be less than or greater than the measure of angle *XYZ*? Explain.

Answers

1. the width
2. Possible answer: By drawing a rectangle and labeling each dimension, you will have a better understanding of what should be substituted into the area formula for length and width.
3.

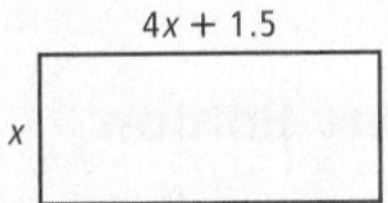

4. greater
5. No; it appears that the length of rectangle *ABDC* is less than the length of rectangle *MNPO*, and this is not consistent with the dimensions that are given.
6. Possible answer:

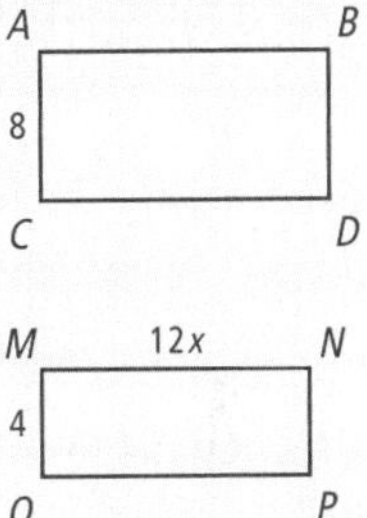

7. Possible answer: By redrawing the figures into 2 separate triangles, you can better see the base and height measures, which will help you correctly set up the area formula for each triangle.
8. No, it is not correct. The student mislabeled the base of triangle *QRP*. It should be labeled $7 + x$.
9. the measure of angle *WYZ*
10. Less than; angle *XYW* lies within angle *XYZ*, so angle *XYW* must be smaller.

Answers to Test Items

A. $4x^2 + 1.5x$; 1147.375 ft²
B. C
C. $5x + 35$; $\frac{1}{2}(x^2 + x)$; $-\frac{1}{2}x^2 + \frac{9}{2}x + 35$
D. F

State Resources

go.hrw.com
State Resources Online
KEYWORD: MA7 Resources

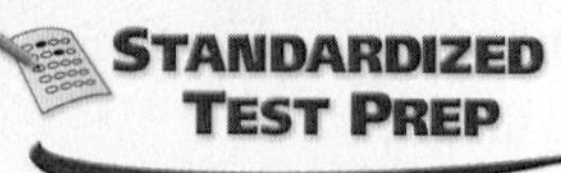

Organizer

Objective: Provide review and practice for Chapters 1–7 and standardized tests.

Online Edition

Resources

Assessment Resources

Chapter 7 Cumulative Test

State Resources

CUMULATIVE ASSESSMENT, CHAPTERS 1–7

Multiple Choice

1. A negative number is raised to a power. The result is a negative number. What do you know about the power?

Ⓐ It is an even number.

Ⓑ It is an odd number.

Ⓒ It is zero.

Ⓓ It is a whole number.

2. Which expression represents the phrase *eight less than the product of a number and two*?

Ⓕ $2 - 8x$

Ⓖ $8 - 2x$

Ⓗ $2x - 8$

Ⓙ $\frac{x}{2} - 8$

3. An Internet service provider charges a $20 set-up fee plus $12 per month. A competitor charges $15 per month. Which equation can you use to find *x*, the number of months when the total charge will be the same for both companies?

Ⓐ $15 = 20 + 12x$

Ⓑ $20 + 12x = 15x$

Ⓒ $20x + 12 = 15x$

Ⓓ $20 = 15x + 12x$

4. Which is a solution of the inequality $7 - 3(x - 3) > 2(x + 3)$?

Ⓕ 0

Ⓖ 2

Ⓗ 5

Ⓙ 12

5. One dose of Ted's medication contains 0.625 milligram, or $\frac{5}{8}$ milligram, of a drug. Which expression is equivalent to 0.625?

Ⓐ $5(4)^{-2}$

Ⓑ $5(2)^{-4}$

Ⓒ $5(-2)^{3}$

Ⓓ $5(2)^{-3}$

6. A restaurant claims to have served 352×10^6 hamburgers. What is this number in scientific notation?

Ⓕ 3.52×10^6

Ⓖ 3.52×10^8

Ⓗ 3.52×10^4

Ⓙ 352×10^6

7. Janet is ordering game cartridges from an online retailer. The retailer's prices, including shipping and handling, are given in the table below.

Game Cartridges	Total Cost ($)
1	54.95
2	104.95
3	154.95
4	204.95

Which equation best describes the relationship between the total cost *c* and the number of game cartridges *g*?

Ⓐ $c = 54.95g$

Ⓑ $c = 51g + 0.95$

Ⓒ $c = 50g + 4.95$

Ⓓ $c = 51.65g$

8. Which equation describes a line parallel to $y = 5 - 2x$?

Ⓕ $y = -2x + 8$

Ⓖ $y = 2x - 5$

Ⓗ $y = 5 + \frac{1}{2}x$

Ⓙ $y = 5 - \frac{1}{2}x$

9. A square has sides of length $x - 4$. A rectangle has a length of $x + 2$ and a width of $2x - 1$. What is the total combined area of the square and the rectangle?

Ⓐ $10x - 14$

Ⓑ $4x - 3$

Ⓒ $3x^2 - 5x + 14$

Ⓓ $3x^2 + 3x - 18$

Answers

1. B
2. H
3. B
4. F
5. D
6. G
7. C
8. F
9. C
10. J
11. C
12. H
13. $\frac{3}{4}$, or 0.75
14. 2
15. 4
16. 16

17a. $28.00

b. $19.60

Test writers develop multiple-choice test options with distracters. Distracters are incorrect options that are based on common student errors. Be cautious! Even if the answer you calculated is one of the options, it may not be the correct answer. Always check your work carefully.

10. Jennifer has a pocketful of change, all in nickels and quarters. There are 11 coins with a total value of \$1.15. Which system of equations can you use to find the number of each type of coin?

Ⓕ $\begin{cases} n + q = 11 \\ n + q = 1.15 \end{cases}$

Ⓖ $\begin{cases} n + q = 11 \\ 5n + 25q = 1.15 \end{cases}$

Ⓗ $\begin{cases} 5n + 25q = 11 \\ n + q = 1.15 \end{cases}$

Ⓙ $\begin{cases} n + q = 11 \\ 0.05n + 0.25q = 1.15 \end{cases}$

11. Which of the following is a true statement?

Ⓐ $\left[(a^m)^n\right]^p = a^{m+n+p}$

Ⓑ $\left[(a^m)^n\right]^p = a^{mn+p}$

Ⓒ $\left[(a^m)^n\right]^p = a^{mnp}$

Ⓓ $\left[(a^m)^n\right]^p = (a^{m+n})^p$

12. In 1867, the United States purchased the Alaska Territory from Russia for $\$7.2 \times 10^6$. The total area was about 6×10^5 square miles. What was the price per square mile?

Ⓕ About \$0.12 per square mile

Ⓖ About \$1.20 per square mile

Ⓗ About \$12.00 per square mile

Ⓙ About \$120.00 per square mile

Gridded Response

13. Evaluate the expression $3b^{-2}c^0$ for $b = 2$ and $c = -3$.

14. What is the slope of the line described by $-3y = -6x - 12$?

15. The quotient $(5.6 \times 10^8) \div (8 \times 10^3)$ is written in scientific notation as (7×10^n). What is the value of n?

16. The volume of a plastic cylinder is 64 cubic centimeters. A glass cylinder has the same height and a radius that is half that of the plastic cylinder. What is the volume in cubic centimeters of the glass cylinder?

Short Response

17. A sweater that normally sells for \$35 was marked down 20% and placed on the sale rack. Later, the sweater was marked down an additional 30% and placed on the clearance rack.

    a. Find the price of the sweater while on the sale rack. Show your work.

    b. Find the price of the sweater while on the clearance rack. Show your work.

18. A set of positive integers (a, b, c) is called a *Pythagorean triple* if $a^2 + b^2 = c^2$.

    a. Find a^2, b^2, and c^2 when $a = 2x$, $b = x^2 - 1$, and $c = x^2 + 1$. Show your work.

    b. Is $(2x, x^2 - 1, x^2 + 1)$ a Pythagorean triple? Explain your reasoning.

19. Ron is making an ice sculpture. The block of ice is in the shape of a rectangular prism with a length of $(x + 2)$ inches, a width of $(x - 2)$ inches, and a height of $2x$ inches.

    a. Write and simplify a polynomial expression for the volume of the block of ice. Show your work.

    b. The final volume of the ice sculpture is $(x^3 + 4x^2 - 10x + 1)$ cubic inches. Write an expression for the volume of ice that Ron carved away. Show your work.

20. Simplify the expression $(3 \cdot a^2 \cdot b^{-4} \cdot a \cdot b^{-3})^{-3}$ using two different methods. Show that the results are the same.

Extended Response

21. Look at the pentagon below.

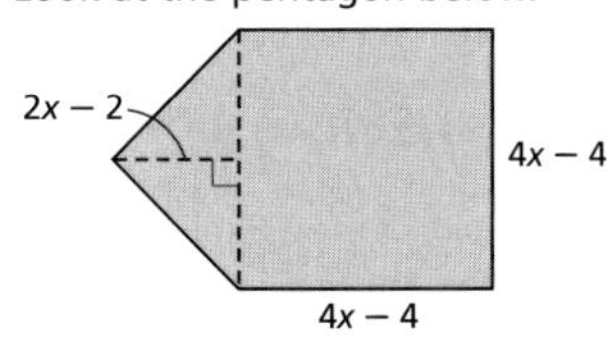

    a. Write and simplify an expression that represents the area of the pentagon. Show your work or explain your answer.

    b. Show one method of checking that your expression in part **a** is correct.

    c. The triangular part of the pentagon can be rearranged to form a square. Write the area of this square as the square of a binomial.

    d. Expand the product that you wrote in part **c.** What type of polynomial is this?

    e. Is the square of a binomial ever a binomial? Explain your reasoning.

Short-Response Rubric

Items 17–20

2 Points = The student's answer is an accurate and complete execution of the task or tasks.

1 Point = The student's answer contains attributes of an appropriate response but is flawed.

0 Points = The student's answer contains no attributes of an appropriate response.

Extended-Response Rubric

Item 21

4 Points = The student writes the correct expression with full work or explanation in part **a,** shows one method of checking the previous answer in part **b,** writes the correct area as a binomial square in part **c,** expands the product correctly and identifies the type of polynomial in part **d,** and answers correctly with explanation in part **e.**

3 Points = The student writes the correct expression with minimal work or explanation in part **a,** shows one method of checking the previous answer in part **b,** writes the area as a binomial square with minor errors in part **c,** expands the product with minor errors and identifies the type of polynomial in part **d,** and answers correctly with explanation in part **e.**

2 Points = The student answers parts **a, b,** and **e** correctly with attempted explanation; or the student answers parts **c, d,** and **e** correctly with attempted explanation.

1 Point = The student answers one part correctly but does not attempt all parts; or the student attempts to answer all parts of the problem but does not correctly answer any part.

0 Points = The student does not answer correctly and does not attempt all parts of the problem.

Answers

18a. $a^2 = (2x)^2 = 4x^2$
$b^2 = (x^2 - 1)^2 = x^4 - 2x^2 + 1$
$c^2 = (x^2 + 1)^2 = x^4 + 2x^2 + 1$

b. Yes; $(2x)^2 + (x^2 - 1)^2 = 4x^2 + x^4 - 2x^2 + 1 = x^4 + 2x^2 + 1$ and $(x^2 + 1)^2 = x^4 + 2x^2 + 1$. Because $(2x)^2 + (x^2 - 1)^2 = (x^2 + 1)^2$, the expressions form a Pythagorean triple.

19a. $(2x^3 - 8x)$ in^3

b. $(x^3 - 4x^2 + 2x - 1)$ in^3

20. $(3 \cdot a^2 \cdot b^{-4} \cdot a \cdot b^{-3})^{-3} = (3 \cdot a^3 \cdot b^{-7})^{-3} = 3^{-3} \cdot a^{-9} \cdot b^{21} = \dfrac{b^{21}}{27a^9}$;
$(3 \cdot a^2 \cdot b^{-4} \cdot a \cdot b^{-3})^{-3} = 3^{-3} \cdot a^{-6} \cdot b^{12} \cdot a^{-3} \cdot b^9 = 3^{-3} \cdot a^{-9} \cdot b^{21} = \dfrac{b^{21}}{27a^9}$

21a. $20x^2 - 40x + 20$

b. Possible answer: Substitute 5 for x in the diagram. Then the side lengths of the square are 16 units, and the height of the triangle is 8 units. The area of the square is 256 square units, and the area of the triangle is 64 square units. Add 256 to 64, which gives the area of the pentagon, 320 square units. Then substitute 5 for x in the simplified expression. It also simplifies to 320.

c. $(2x - 2)^2$

d. $4x^2 - 8x + 4$; trinomial

e. No; for any values of a and b, $(a + b)^2 = a^2 + 2ab + b^2$ and $(a - b)^2 = a^2 - 2ab + b^2$. This is always a trinomial.

Factoring Polynomials

Section 8A	Section 8B
Factoring Methods	**Applying Factoring Methods**
8-1 Factors and Greatest Common Factors	**8-5 Factoring Special Products**
8-2 Algebra Lab Model Factoring	**Connecting Algebra to Number Theory** Mental Math
8-2 Factoring by GCF	**8-6 Choosing a Factoring Method**
8-3 Algebra Lab Model Factorization of Trinomials	
8-3 Factoring $x^2 + bx + c$	
8-4 Factoring $ax^2 + bx + c$	
8-4 Technology Lab Use a Graph to Factor Polynomials	

Pacing Guide for 45-Minute Classes

Teacher One Stop™
Calendar Planner®

Countdown Weeks 17, 18

Chapter 8

DAY 1	DAY 2	DAY 3	DAY 4	DAY 5
8-1 Lesson	8-2 Algebra Lab 8-2 Lesson	8-2 Lesson 8-3 Algebra Lab	8-3 Lesson	8-4 Lesson
DAY 6	**DAY 7**	**DAY 8**	**DAY 9**	**DAY 10**
8-4 Lesson 8-4 Technology Lab	Multi-Step Test Prep Ready to Go On?	8-5 Lesson	Connecting Algebra to Geometry	8-6 Lesson
DAY 11	**DAY 12**	**DAY 18**		
Multi-Step Test Prep Ready to Go On?	Chapter 8 Review	Chapter 8 Test		

Pacing Guide for 90-Minute Classes

Teacher One Stop™
Calendar Planner®

Chapter 8

DAY 1	DAY 2	DAY 3	DAY 4	DAY 5
Chapter 7 Test 8-1 Lesson	8-2 Algebra Lab 8-2 Lesson 8-3 Algebra Lab	8-3 Lesson 8-4 Lesson	8-4 Lesson 8-4 Technology Lab Multi-Step Test Prep Ready to Go On?	8-5 Lesson Connecting Algebra to Geometry
DAY 6	**DAY 7**			
8-6 Lesson Multi-Step Test Prep Ready to Go On?	Chapter 8 Review Chapter 8 Test			

ONGOING ASSESSMENT and INTERVENTION

	DIAGNOSE	PRESCRIBE
Assess Prior Knowledge	**Before Chapter 8**	
	Diagnose readiness for the chapter. ***Are You Ready?*** SE p. 541	Prescribe intervention. ***Are You Ready? Intervention***
Formative Assessment	**Before Every Lesson**	
	Diagnose readiness for the lesson. **Warm Up** TE	Prescribe intervention. **Reteach** CRB
	During Every Lesson	
	Diagnose understanding of lesson concepts. **Check It Out!** SE **Questioning Strategies** TE **Think and Discuss** SE **Write About It** SE **Journal** TE	Prescribe intervention. **Reading Strategies** CRB ***Success for Every Learner*** ***Lesson Tutorial Videos***
	After Every Lesson	
	Diagnose mastery of lesson concepts. **Lesson Quiz** TE **Test Prep** SE ***Test and Practice Generator***	Prescribe intervention. **Reteach** CRB **Test Prep Doctor** TE ***Homework Help Online***
	Before Chapter 8 Testing	
	Diagnose mastery of concepts in chapter. ***Ready to Go On?*** SE pp. 577, 593 **Multi-Step Test Prep** SE pp. 576, 592 **Section Quizzes** AR ***Test and Practice Generator***	Prescribe intervention. ***Ready to Go On? Intervention*** **Scaffolding Questions** TE pp. 576, 592 **Reteach** CRB ***Lesson Tutorial Videos***
	Before High Stakes Testing	
	Diagnose mastery of benchmark concepts. **College Entrance Exam Practice** SE p. 599 **Standardized Test Prep** SE pp. 602–603	Prescribe intervention. ***College Entrance Exam Practice***
Summative Assessment	**After Chapter 8**	
	Check mastery of chapter concepts. **Multiple-Choice Tests (Forms A, B, C)** **Free-Response Tests (Forms A, B, C)** **Performance Assessment** AR **Cumulative Test** AR ***Test and Practice Generator***	Prescribe intervention. **Reteach** CRB ***Lesson Tutorial Videos***

KEY: **SE** = *Student Edition* **TE** = *Teacher's Edition* **CRB** = *Chapter Resource Book* **AR** = *Assessment Resources* Available online  Available on CD- or DVD-ROM

Lesson Resources

Before the Lesson

Prepare ***Teacher One Stop***  
- Editable lesson plans
- Calendar Planner
- Easy access to all chapter resources

Lesson Transparencies
- Teacher Tools

Teach the Lesson

Introduce ***Alternate Openers: Explorations***

Lesson Transparencies 
- Warm Up
- Problem of the Day

Teach ***Lesson Transparencies***
- Teaching Transparencies

Know-It Notebook™
- Vocabulary
- Key Concepts

Power Presentations 

Lesson Tutorial Videos SPANISH

Interactive Online Edition
- Lesson Activities
- Lesson Tutorial Videos

Lab Activities

Lab Resources Online 

Online Interactivities 

TechKeys

Practice the Lesson

Practice ***Chapter Resources***
- Practice A, B, C

Practice and Problem Solving Workbook SPANISH

IDEA Works!® Modified Worksheets and Tests

ExamView Test and Practice Generator 

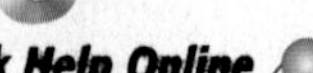
Homework Help Online

Online Interactivities 

Interactive Online Edition
- Homework Help

Apply ***Chapter Resources***
- Problem Solving SPANISH

Practice and Problem Solving Workbook SPANISH

Interactive Online Edition
- Chapter Project

Project Teacher Support 

After the Lesson

Reteach ***Chapter Resources***
- Reteach
- Reading Strategies ELL

Success for Every Learner

Review ***Interactive Answers and Solutions***

Solutions Key

Know-It Notebook™
- Big Ideas
- Chapter Review

Extend ***Chapter Resources***
- Challenge

Technology Highlights for the Teacher

 **Power Presentations**

Dynamic presentations to engage students. Complete PowerPoint® presentations for every lesson in Chapter 8.

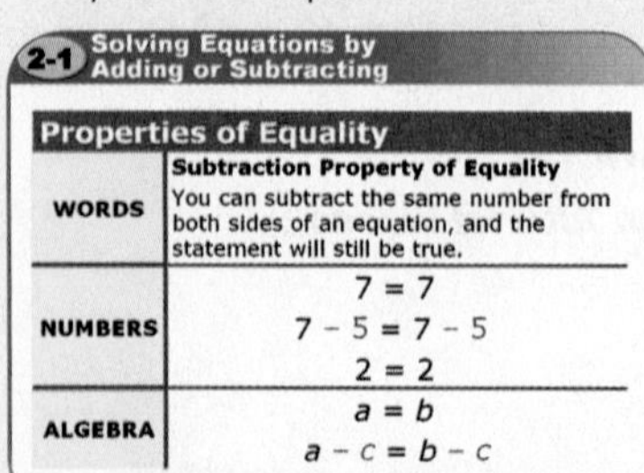

 **Teacher One Stop** SPANISH

Easy access to Chapter 8 resources and assessments. Includes lesson planning, test generation, and puzzle creation software.

 **Premier Online Edition** SPANISH

Chapter 8 includes Tutorial Videos, Lesson Activities, Lesson Quizzes, Homework Help, and Chapter Project.

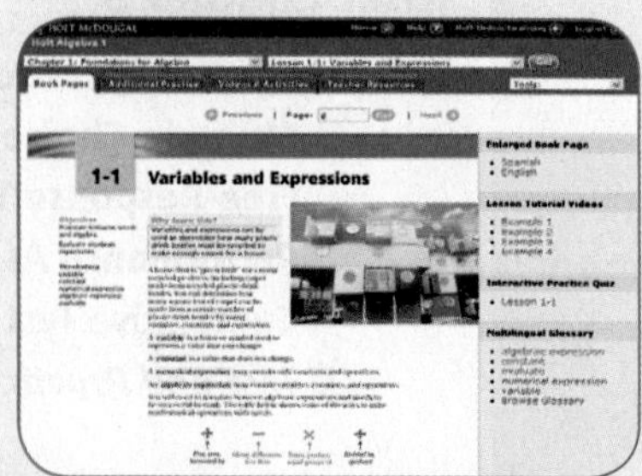

KEY: **SE** = *Student Edition* **TE** = *Teacher's Edition*  English Language Learners  Spanish version available  Available online  Available on CD- or DVD-R

Reaching All Learners

Teaching tips to help all learners appear throughout the chapter. A few that target specific students are included in the lists below.

All Learners

Lab Activities
Practice and Problem Solving Workbook SPANISH
Know-It Notebook

Special Needs Students

Practice A .... CRB
Reteach .... CRB
Reading Strategies .... CRB
Are You Ready? .... SE p. 541
Inclusion .... TE pp. 552, 562, 569, 580, 589
IDEA Works!® Modified Worksheets and Tests
Ready to Go On? Intervention SPANISH
Know-It Notebook
Online Interactivities SPANISH
Lesson Tutorial Videos SPANISH

Developing Learners

Practice A .... CRB
Reteach .... CRB
Reading Strategies .... CRB
Are You Ready? .... SE p. 541
Vocabulary Connections .... SE p. 542
Questioning Strategies .... TE
Ready to Go On? Intervention SPANISH
Know-It Notebook
Homework Help Online
Online Interactivities SPANISH
Lesson Tutorial Videos SPANISH

On-Level Learners

Practice B .... CRB
Problem Solving .... CRB
Vocabulary Connections .... SE p. 542
Questioning Strategies .... TE
Ready to Go On? Intervention SPANISH
Know-It Notebook
Homework Help Online
Online Interactivities SPANISH

Advanced Learners

Practice C .... CRB
Challenge .... CRB
Challenge Exercises .... SE
Reading and Writing Math *Extend* .... TE p. 543
Critical Thinking .... TE pp. 566, 569
Are You Ready? Enrichment SPANISH
Ready To Go On? Enrichment SPANISH

English Language Learners

ENGLISH LANGUAGE LEARNERS

Reading Strategies .... CRB
Are You Ready? Vocabulary .... SE p. 541
Vocabulary Connections .... SE p. 542
Vocabulary Review .... SE p. 594
English Language Learners .... TE pp. 543, 605
Success for Every Learner
Know-It Notebook
Multilingual Glossary
Lesson Tutorial Videos SPANISH

Technology Highlights for Reaching All Learners

Lesson Tutorial Videos SPANISH

Starring Holt authors Ed Burger and Freddie Renfro! Live tutorials to support every lesson in Chapter 8.

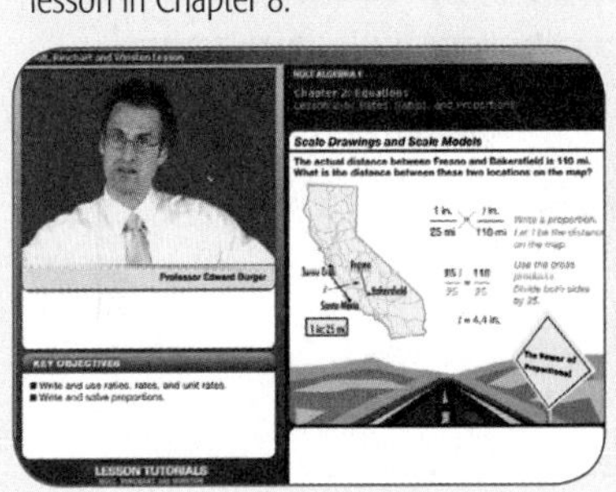

Multilingual Glossary

Searchable glossary includes definitions in English, Spanish, Vietnamese, Chinese, Hmong, Korean, and 4 other languages.

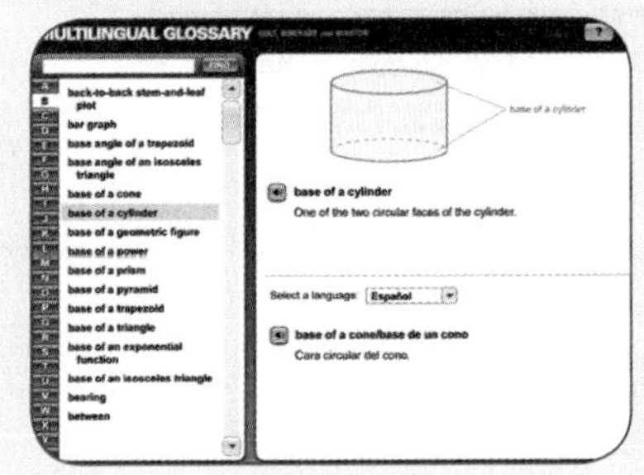

Online Interactivities

Interactive tutorials provide visually engaging alternative opportunities to learn concepts and master skills.

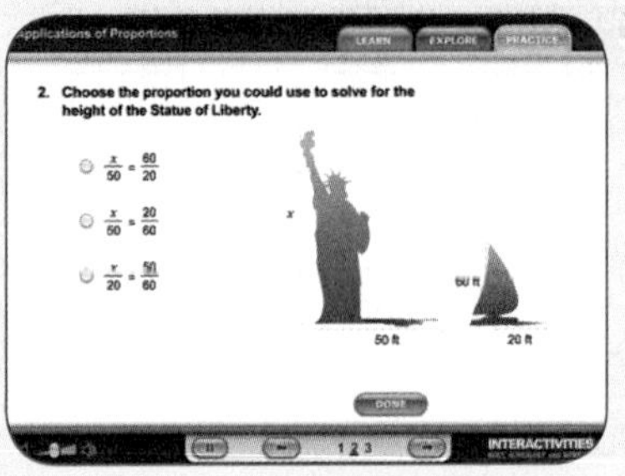

KEY: **SE** = *Student Edition* **TE** = *Teacher's Edition* **CRB** = *Chapter Resource Book* SPANISH Spanish version available; Available online; Available on CD- or DVD-ROM

Ongoing Assessment

Assessing Prior Knowledge

Determine whether students have the prerequisite concepts and skills for success in Chapter 8.

Are You Ready? SPANISH .... SE p. 541
Warm Up .... TE

Test Preparation

Provide review and practice for Chapter 8 and standardized tests.

Multi-Step Test Prep .... SE pp. 576, 592
Study Guide: Review .... SE pp. 594–597
Test Tackler .... SE pp. 600–601
Standardized Test Prep .... SE pp. 602–603
College Entrance Exam Practice .... SE p. 599
Countdown to Testing .... SE pp. C4–C27
IDEA Works!® Modified Worksheets and Tests

Alternative Assessment

Assess students' understanding of Chapter 8 concepts and combined problem-solving skills.

Chapter 8 Project .... SE p. 540
Alternative Assessment .... TE
Performance Assessment SPANISH .... AR
Portfolio Assessment SPANISH .... AR

Lesson Assessment

Provide formative assessment for each lesson of Chapter 8.

Questioning Strategies .... TE
Think and Discuss .... SE
Check It Out! Exercises .... SE
Write About It .... SE
Journal .... TE
Lesson Quiz .... TE
Alternative Assessment .... TE
IDEA Works!® Modified Worksheets and Tests

Weekly Assessment

Provide formative assessment for each section of Chapter 8.

Multi-Step Test Prep .... SE pp. 576, 592
Ready to Go On? SPANISH .... SE pp. 577, 593
Section Quizzes SPANISH .... AR
Test and Practice Generator SPANISH .... *Teacher One Stop*

Chapter Assessment

Provide summative assessment of Chapter 8 mastery.

Chapter 8 Test .... SE p. 598
Chapter Test (Levels A, B, C) SPANISH .... AR
• Multiple Choice • Free Response
Cumulative Test SPANISH .... AR
Test and Practice Generator SPANISH .... *Teacher One Stop*
IDEA Works!® Modified Worksheets and Tests

Technology Highlights for Assessment

Are You Ready? SPANISH

Automatically assess readiness and prescribe intervention for Chapter 8 prerequisite skills.

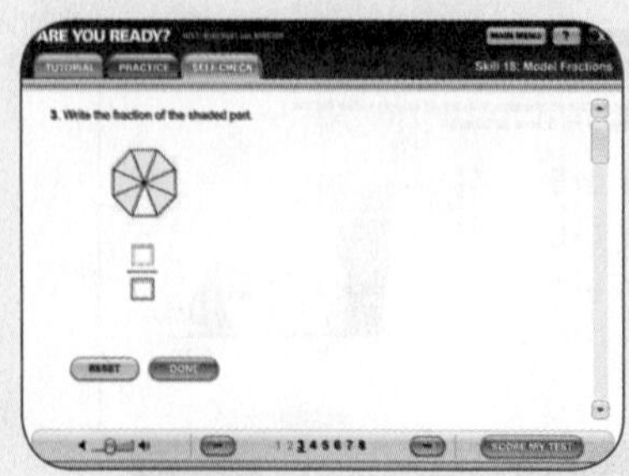

Ready to Go On?

Automatically assess understanding of and prescribe intervention for Sections 8A and 8B.

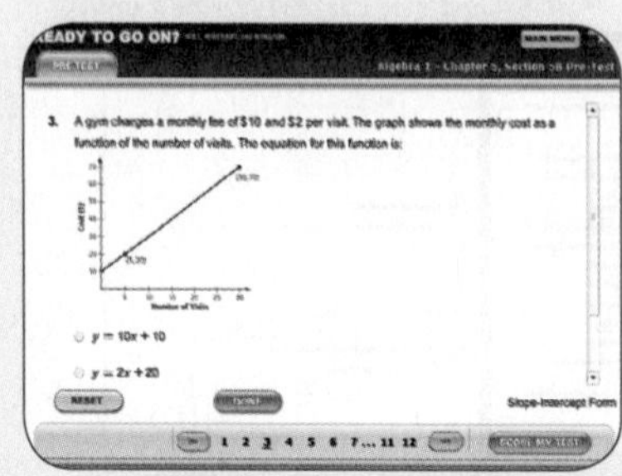

Test and Practice Generator SPANISH

Use Chapter 8 problem banks to create assessments and worksheets to print out or deliver online. Includes dynamic problems.

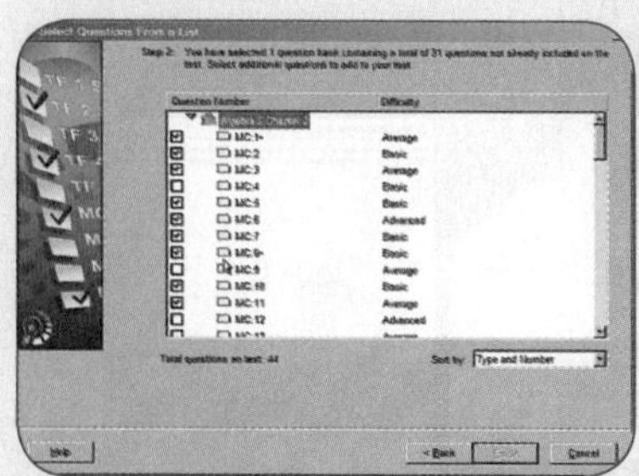

KEY: **SE** = *Student Edition* **TE** = *Teacher's Edition* **AR** = *Assessment Resources*  Spanish version available 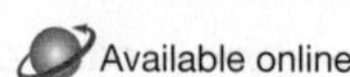 Available online  Available on CD- or DVD-ROM

Formal Assessment

Three levels (A, B, C) of multiple-choice and free-response chapter tests, along with a performance assessment, are available in the *Assessment Resources.*

A Chapter 8 Test

C Chapter 8 Test

MULTIPLE CHOICE

B Chapter 8 Test

Select the best answer.

1. Which is the prime factorization of 120?
   A $2 \cdot 2 \cdot 2 \cdot 15$ C $3 \cdot 5 \cdot 8$
   B $2 \cdot 2 \cdot 2 \cdot 3 \cdot 5$ D $10 \cdot 12$
2. Find the GCF of 42 and 70.
   F 7 H 196
   G 14 J 210
3. Find the GCF of $30x^2$ and $45x^5$.
   A $5x^2$ C $15x^2$
   B $5x^5$ D $15x^5$
4. Kyle is making flower arrangements for a wedding. He has 16 roses and 60 carnations. Each arrangement will have the same number of flowers, but roses and carnations will not appear in the same arrangement. If he puts the greatest possible number of flowers in each arrangement, how many arrangements can he make?
   F 4 H 19
   G 15 J 38
5. Factor $30y^3 - 6y^2 + 12y$ completely.
   A $y(30y^2 - 6y + 12)$
   B $3y(10y^2 - 2y + 4)$
   C $6(5y^3 - y^2 + 2y)$
   D $6y(5y^2 - y + 2)$
6. Factor $2n(n + 3) - 5(n + 3)$.
   F $(n - 3)(2n + 5)$
   G $(n + 3)(2n + 5)$
   H $(n + 3)(2n - 5)$
   J cannot be factored
7. Factor $6a^3 - 3a^2 + 8a - 4$ by grouping.
   A $(2a - 1)(3a^2 + 4)$
   B $(2a + 4)(3a^2 - 1)$
   C $(6a^3 - 3a^2)(8a - 4)$
   D cannot be factored
8. Factor $x^2 + 8x + 12$.
   F $(x + 1)(x + 12)$
   G $(x + 2)(x + 6)$
   H $(x + 3)(x + 4)$
   J cannot be factored
9. Factor $x^2 - 3x + 70$.
   A $(x - 10)(x + 7)$
   B $(x - 7)(x - 10)$
   C $(x + 5)(x + 14)$
   D cannot be factored
10. Factor $x^2 - 6x - 16$.
    F $(x - 2)(x - 8)$
    G $(x - 2)(x + 8)$
    H $(x + 2)(x - 8)$
    J cannot be factored
11. Which value of b would make $x^2 + bx - 30$ factorable?
    A −31 C 11
    B −17 D 13
12. Write the factored form of the polynomial that is modeled by this geometric diagram.

$12x^2$	$9x$
$4x$	3

    F $(x + 3)(12x + 1)$
    G $(2x + 3)(6x + 1)$
    H $(3x + 1)(4x + 3)$
    J $(12x^2 + 4x)(9x + 3)$

B Chapter 8 Test *(continued)*

13. Factor $5x^2 + 39x + 54$.
    A $(x + 2)(5x + 27)$
    B $(x + 3)(5x + 18)$
    C $(x + 6)(5x + 9)$
    D cannot be factored
14. Factor $8a^2 - 10a - 7$.
    F $(2a - 7)(4a + 1)$
    G $(2a - 1)(4a + 7)$
    H $(2a + 1)(4a - 7)$
    J cannot be factored
15. Which value of c would NOT make $3x^2 + 5x + c$ factorable?
    A −22 C 2
    B −2 D 22
16. Determine whether $n^2 - 10n - 25$ is a perfect square trinomial. If so, choose the correct factorization.
    F yes; $(n - 5)^2$
    G yes; $(n + 5)^2$
    H yes; $(n + 5)(n - 5)$
    J no
17. Determine whether $16x^2 + 24x + 9$ is a perfect square trinomial. If so, choose the correct factorization.
    A yes; $(4x - 3)^2$
    B yes; $(4x + 3)^2$
    C yes; $(4x + 3)(4x - 3)$
    D no
18. Determine whether $p^2 - 36$ is a difference of two squares. If so, choose the correct factorization.
    F yes; $(p - 6)^2$
    G yes; $(p + 6)(p - 6)$
    H yes; $(p + 18)(p - 18)$
    J no
19. Determine whether $4x^2 - 10$ is a difference of two squares. If so, choose the correct factorization.
    A yes; $(2x - 5)^2$
    B yes; $(2x + 5)(2x - 5)$
    C yes; $(2x + 10)(2x - 10)$
    D no
20. The area of a square is represented by $9z^2 - 12z + 4$. Which expression represents the perimeter of the square?
    F $3z - 2$ H $6z - 4$
    G $3z + 2$ J $12z - 8$
21. Is $x(4x^2 + 8x + 12)$ completely factored? If not, what other factoring can occur?
    A yes; the polynomial is completely factored.
    B no; 4 can be factored from each term of the trinomial.
    C no; the trinomial $4x^2 + 8x + 12$ can be factored into two binomials.
    D no; 4 can be factored from each term of the trinomial AND the resulting trinomial can be factored into two binomials.
22. Completely factor $3x^4 - 15x^3 - 18x^2$.
    F $x^2(3x + 2)(1x - 9)$
    G $3(x^2 + 1)(x^2 - 6)$
    H $3x^2(x + 1)(x - 6)$
    J cannot be factored
23. Completely factor $3m^3 + 5m^2 - 12m - 20$.
    A $(m^2 - 4)(3m + 5)$
    B $(m - 2)^2(3m + 5)$
    C $(m^2 + 4)(3m + 5)$
    D $(m + 2)(m - 2)(3m + 5)$

A Chapter 8 Test

C Chapter 8 Test

FREE RESPONSE

B Chapter 8 Test

1. Write the prime factorization of 176.

Find the GCF.

2. 54 and 144
3. $30x^2$ and $66x^5$
4. Mrs. Mendoza is organizing seating for a standardized test. 45 ninth-grade students and 120 tenth-grade students will take the test. Each row will have the same number of students, but ninth-graders and tenth-graders will not be seated in the same row. If she puts the greatest possible number of students in each row, how many rows will there be?

Factor.

5. $14y^3 + 28y^2 - 54y$
6. $n(2n + 3) + 4(2n - 3)$
7. Factor $15a^3 + 20a^2 - 6a - 8$ by grouping.

Factor each trinomial.

8. $x^2 + 9x + 18$
9. $x^2 + 7x - 30$
10. $x^2 - 5x - 50$
11. Find an integer value of b that makes $x^2 + bx + 42$ factorable, and then factor the trinomial.
    $b =$ ______
12. Write the polynomial modeled by this geometric diagram and then factor.

$18x^2$	$15x$
$6x$	5

B Chapter 8 Test *(continued)*

Factor each trinomial.

13. $3x^2 + 47x + 140$
14. $27a^2 + 42a - 5$
15. Determine whether each value of c makes $5x^2 - 22x + c$ factorable. If so, factor it.
    $c = -15$
    $c = 4$
    $c = 8$

Determine whether the trinomial is a perfect square. If so, factor it. If not, explain why.

16. $n^2 + 72n + 36$
17. $9x^2 - 30x + 25$

Determine whether the binomial is a difference of two squares. If so, factor it. If not, explain why.

18. $p^2 - 132$
19. $16x^2 - 49$
20. The area of a square in square feet is represented by $4z^2 - 36z + 81$. Find an expression for the perimeter of the square. Then find the perimeter when $z = 10$ ft.
    expression: ______
    perimeter when $z = 10$ ft: ______
21. Tell whether $x(4x^2 + 19x + 12)$ is completely factored. If not, factor it.

Factor each polynomial completely.

22. $4x^5 - 30x^4 - 16x^3$
23. $2m^3 + 3m^2 - 18m - 27$

PERFORMANCE ASSESSMENT

Chapter 8 Test

Purpose
This performance task assesses the student's ability to factor by using the GCF, to factor trinomials including perfect square trinomials, and to find the scale factor of polygons when the areas are given as algebraic expressions.

Time
30 minutes

Grouping
Individuals

Preparation Hints
Review the formulas for the areas of rectangles and circles as needed.
Review the fact that π is a number, and that it can be factored out of an expression like any other number.

Overview
Students are asked to factor expressions that represent the areas of similar rectangles and circles and identify the scale factor that was used. They are then asked to identify the relationship between the GCF of the polynomials and the scale factor.

Introduce the Task
Remind students that when every dimension of a figure is multiplied by the same number, the result is a similar figure (same shape, different size) and that the number that was the multiplier is called the scale factor. Tell students that they found scale factors in Chapter 2 as numeric values instead of algebraic expressions.

Performance Indicators
____ Factors trinomials completely.
____ Identifies the scale factor as the square of the ratio of the corresponding sides.
____ Identifies the scale factor as the square root of the GCF.
____ Evaluates polynomials.

Scoring Rubric
Level 4: Student solves all problems and gives good explanations.
Level 3: Student solves all problems, but does not give satisfactory explanations.
Level 2: Student solves only some problems, and attempts to give some explanations.
Level 1: Student is not able to solve any of the problems.

Chapter 8 Test *(continued)*

The area of rectangle A can be expressed by the polynomial $8x^2 + 2x - 3$. The area of rectangle B can be expressed by the polynomial $32x^2 + 8x - 12$.

1. Factor the expression for the area of rectangle A.
2. Factor the expression for the area of rectangle B.
3. Every dimension of rectangle A was multiplied by a scale factor to get rectangle B. What was the scale factor? Explain how you know.

The area of circle A can be expressed by the polynomial $4\pi x^2 - 20\pi x + 25\pi$. The area of circle B can be expressed by the polynomial $36\pi x^2 - 180\pi x + 225\pi$.

4. Factor the expression for the area of circle A. Then write an expression for the radius of circle A.
5. Factor the expression for the area of circle B.
6. What is the scale factor from circle A to circle B? How is it related to the GCF?
7. The area of parallelogram A is $3x^2 + 8x - 16$. The area of parallelogram B is $12x^2 + 32x - 64$. What is scale factor from parallelogram A to B?
8. The surface area of sphere A is $4\pi x^2 + 24\pi x + 36\pi$. The surface area of sphere B is $100\pi x^2 + 600\pi x + 900\pi$. What is the scale factor from sphere A to sphere B?
9. Evaluate the expressions in problem 8 for $x = 7$. (Leave your answers in terms of π.) Show how these values relate to your answer in problem 8.

Teacher One Stop™ 

Test & Practice Generator

Create and customize Chapter 8 Tests. Instantly generate multiple test versions, answer keys, and Spanish versions of test items.

Modified chapter tests that address special learning needs are available in *IDEA Works!®* *Modified Worksheets and Tests.*

CHAPTER 8

SECTION 8A

Factoring Methods

On page 576, students write and factor polynomials to model the distance traveled by an automobile.

Exercises designed to prepare students for success on the Multi-Step Test Prep can be found in each lesson.

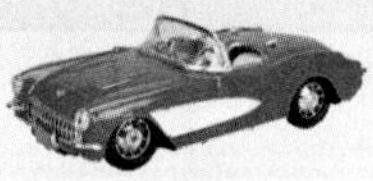

SECTION 8B

Applying Factoring Methods

On page 592, students factor polynomials to model the dimensions of a garden.

Exercises designed to prepare students for success on the Multi-Step Test Prep can be found in each lesson.

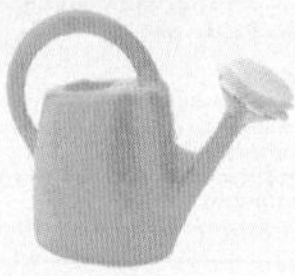

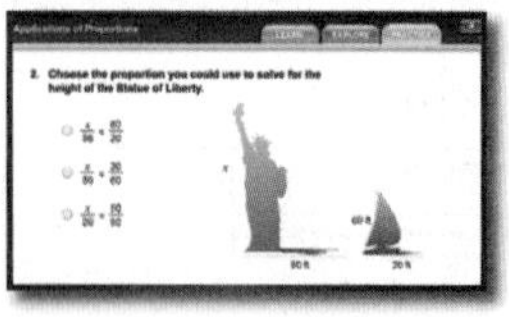

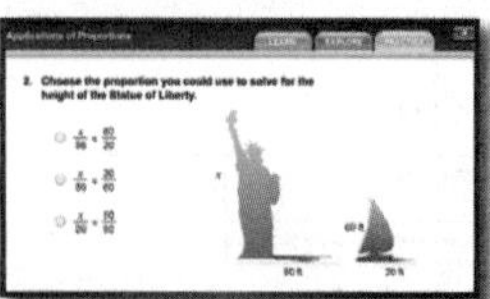

Lessons 8-3 and 8-5

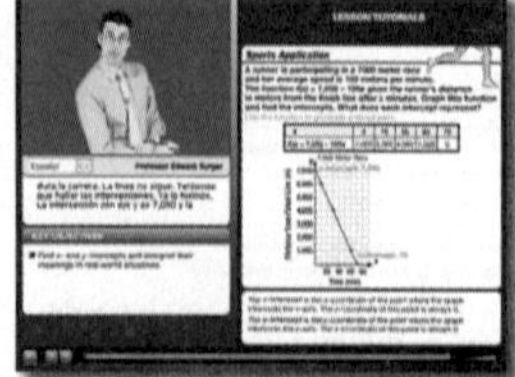

Lesson Tutorial Videos are available for EVERY example.

CHAPTER 8

Factoring Polynomials

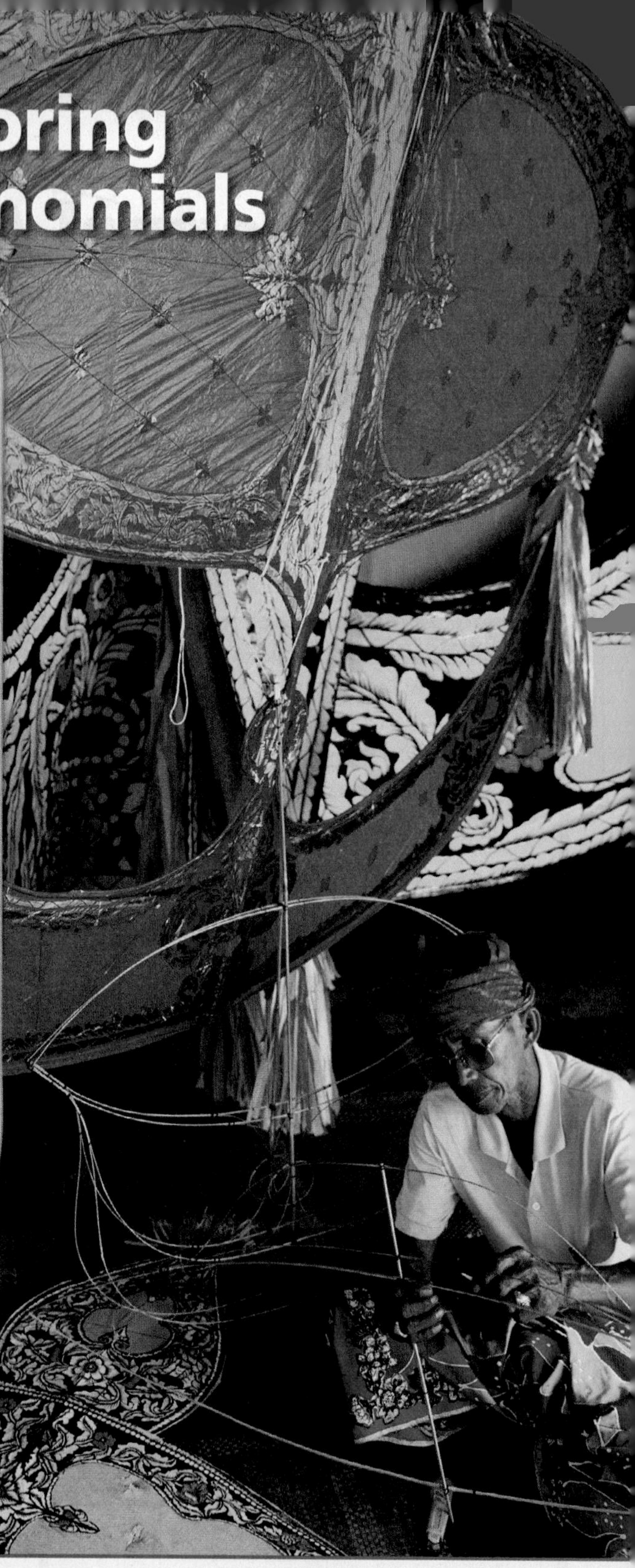

Chapter Focus

- Factor polynomials.
- Apply factoring techniques to solve problems involving area and volume.

High Fliers

You can use polynomials to model area. When given the area of a kite as a polynomial, you can factor to find the kite's dimensions.

go.hrw.com
Chapter Project Online
KEYWORD: MA7 ChProj

High Fliers

About the Project

In the Chapter Project, students use polynomials to model the area of kites and flags. When given an area expressed as a polynomial, students factor to find the dimensions of the kite or flag.

Project Resources

All project resources for teachers and students are provided online.

Match each term on the left with a definition on the right.

1. binomial B
2. composite number A
3. factor F
4. multiple C
5. prime number E

A. a whole number greater than 1 that has more than two positive factors

B. a polynomial with two terms

C. the product of any number and a whole number

D. a number that is written as the product of its prime factors

E. a whole number greater than 1 that has exactly two positive factors, itself and 1

F. a number that is multiplied by another number to get a product

Write the first four multiples of each number.

6. 3 3, 6, 9, 12 **7.** 4 4, 8, 12, 16 **8.** 8 8, 16, 24, 32 **9.** 15 15, 30, 45, 60

Tell whether the second number is a factor of the first number.

10. 20, 5 yes **11.** 50, 6 no **12.** 120, 8 yes **13.** 245, 7 yes

Tell whether each number is prime or composite. If the number is composite, write it as the product of two numbers.

14. 2 prime **15.** 7 prime **16.** 10 comp.; $10 = 2 \cdot 5$ **17.** 38 comp.; $38 = 2 \cdot 19$

18. 115 comp.; $115 = 5 \cdot 23$ **19.** 147 comp.; $147 = 21 \cdot 7$ **20.** 151 prime **21.** 93 comp.; $93 = 3 \cdot 31$

Multiply Monomials and Polynomials

Multiply.

22. $2(x + 5)$ $2x + 10$ **23.** $3h(h + 1)$ $3h^2 + 3h$ **24.** $xy(x^2 - xy^3)$ $x^3y - x^2y^4$ **25.** $6m(m^2 - 4m - 1)$ $6m^3 - 24m^2 - 6m$

Find each product.

26. $(x + 3)(x + 8)$ $x^2 + 11x + 24$ **27.** $(b - 7)(b + 1)$ $b^2 - 6b - 7$

28. $(2p - 5)(p - 1)$ $2p^2 - 7p + 5$ **29.** $(3n + 4)(2n + 3)$ $6n^2 + 17n + 12$

CHAPTER 8

Organizer

Objective: Assess students' understanding of prerequisite skills.

Assessing Prior Knowledge

INTERVENTION

Diagnose and Prescribe

Use this page to determine whether intervention is necessary or whether enrichment is appropriate.

Resources

***Are You Ready? Intervention and Enrichment* Worksheets**

***Are You Ready?* CD-ROM**

***Are You Ready?* Online**

my.hrw.com

ARE YOU READY?

Diagnose and Prescribe

Prerequisite Skill	*Are You Ready? Intervention,* Chapter 8 Worksheets	CD-ROM	Online
Multiples	Skill 1	Activity 1	Diagnose and Prescribe Online
Factors	Skill 3	Activity 3	
Prime and Composite Numbers	Skill 5	Activity 5	
Multiply Monomials and Polynomials	Skill 62	Activity 62	
Multiply Binomials	Skill 64	Activity 64	

***Are You Ready? Enrichment,* Chapter 8**
- Worksheets
- CD-ROM
- Online

CHAPTER 8 Study Guide: Preview

Organizer

Objective: Help students organize the new concepts they will learn in Chapter 8.

Online Edition
Multilingual Glossary

Resources

Teacher One Stop™
PuzzleView

***Multilingual Glossary* Online**
go.hrw.com
KEYWORD: MA7 Glossary

Answers to *Vocabulary Connections*

1. to write a number or polynomial as a multiplication of factors
2. Possible answer: Civilize/civilization, capitalize/capitalization, optimize/optimization, visualize/visualization; the suffix *-ization* indicates the result of an action that has taken place. Factorization is the result when something is factored.
3. The main part; the first coat of paint; fundamental; early stage of development; a prime factor is a basic building block of the product. It cannot be further factored.
4. A prime number has no positive factors other than 1 and itself. A prime factorization is written with factors that are all prime numbers.
5. *Common* means "alike." The greatest common factor of 2 numbers is the greatest factor that the 2 numbers share.

CHAPTER 8

Study Guide: Preview

Where You've Been

Previously, you

- used properties of exponents to evaluate and simplify expressions.
- added and subtracted polynomials by combining like terms.
- multiplied polynomials.

In This Chapter

You will study

- greatest common factors.
- how to factor polynomials.
- how to factor special products.
- how to choose a factoring method.

Where You're Going

You can use the skills in this chapter

- in Geometry to solve area problems.
- in Physics to solve quadratic equations.
- in the real world to calculate dimensions in landscaping, construction, or design work.

Key Vocabulary/Vocabulario

greatest common factor	máximo común divisor
prime factorization	factorización prima

Vocabulary Connections

To become familiar with the vocabulary terms in the chapter, consider the following. You may refer to the chapter, the glossary, or a dictionary if you like.

1. The word *factor* refers to a number or polynomial that is multiplied by another number or polynomial to form a product. What do you think the word *factor* means when it is used as a verb (action word)?
2. List some words that end with the suffixes *-ize* or *-ization*. What does the ending *-ization* seem to mean? What do you think *factorization* means?
3. The words *prime, primer, primary*, and *primitive* all come from the same root word. What are the meanings of these words? How can their meanings help you understand what a *prime factor* is?
4. What is a prime number? How might the **prime factorization** of a number differ from another factorization?
5. What does the word *common* mean? How can you use this meaning to understand the term **greatest common factor**?

542 Chapter 8

Reading Strategy: Read a Lesson for Understanding

To help you learn new concepts, you should read each lesson with a purpose. As you read a lesson, make notes. Include the main ideas of the lesson and any questions you have. In class, listen for explanations of the vocabulary, clarification of the examples, and answers to your questions.

Reading Tips

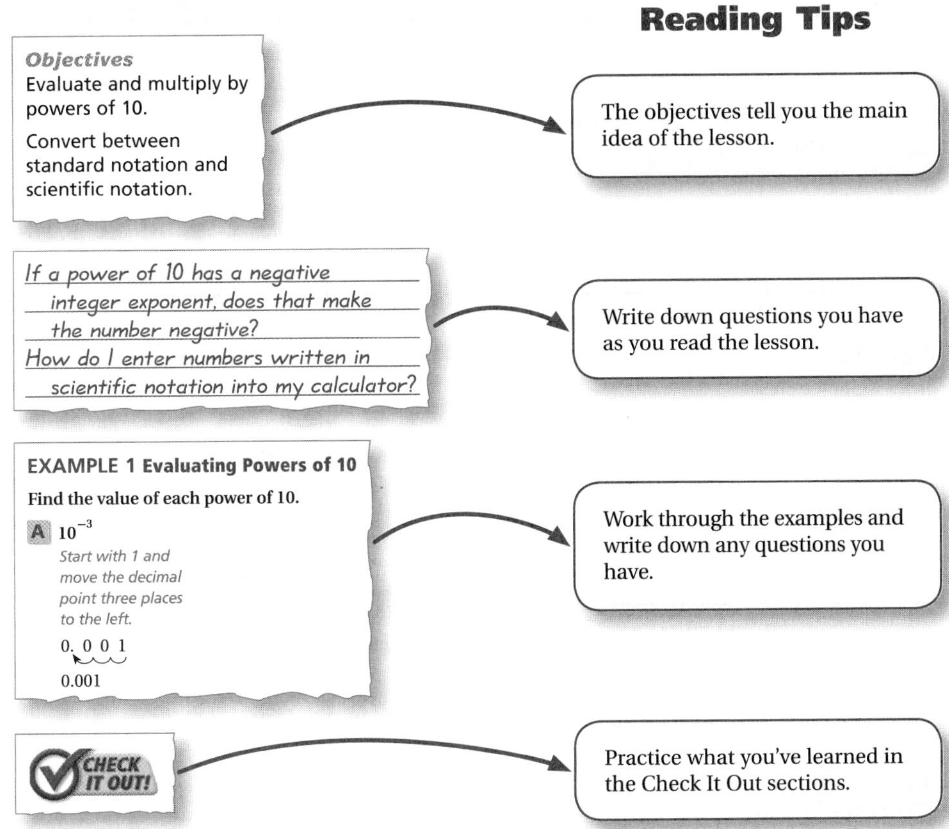

Try This

Read Lesson 8-1 prior to your next class. Then answer the questions below.

1. What are the lesson objectives?
2. What vocabulary, formulas, and symbols are new?
3. Which examples, if any, are unclear?
4. What questions do you have about the lesson?

Reading and Writing Math

Organizer

Objective: Help students apply strategies to understand and retain key concepts.

English Language Learners

Reading Strategy: Read a Lesson for Understanding

Discuss Discuss with students what options they have if there is not enough time during class to ask a question. Students may need to ask a classmate or talk to the teacher after class or after school.

Extend Before each lesson in Chapter 8, students should read the lesson and make notes similar to those shown on this page. Tell students to make sure that all their questions are answered before they start their homework.

Answers to *Try This*

1. Write the prime factorization of numbers. Find the GCF of monomials.
2. prime factorization, greatest common factor
3. Check students' work.
4. Check students' work.

Reading Connection

***Secrets of Mental Math* by Arthur Benjamin and Michael Shermer**

Quick: What's the fifth root of 11,881,376? Easy: 26! This book is a fascinating guide to rapid mental calculation, which has practical use as a check on calculator work.

Activity Ask students to choose and practice a mental math technique from the book. Have each student teach the technique to a partner, and learn his or her partner's technique.

SECTION **8A** Factoring Methods

One-Minute Section Planner

Lesson	Lab Resources	Materials
Lesson 8-1 Factors and Greatest Common Factors • Write the prime factorization of numbers. • Find the GCF of monomials. ☐ SAT-10 ☑ NAEP ☑ ACT ☑ SAT ☐ SAT Subject Tests		**Optional** colored counters (MK)
8-2 Algebra Lab Model Factoring • Use algebra tiles to model and factor polynomials. ☐ SAT-10 ☐ NAEP ☑ ACT ☐ SAT ☐ SAT Subject Tests	***Algebra Lab Activities*** 8-2 Lab Recording Sheet	**Required** algebra tiles (MK)
Lesson 8-2 Factoring by GCF • Factor polynomials by using the greatest common factor. ☐ SAT-10 ☑ NAEP ☑ ACT ☑ SAT ☑ SAT Subject Tests		**Optional** algebra tiles (MK)
8-3 Algebra Lab Model Factorization of Trinomials • Use algebra tiles to model and factor trinomials. ☐ SAT-10 ☐ NAEP ☑ ACT ☐ SAT ☐ SAT Subject Tests	***Algebra Lab Activities*** 8-3 Lab Recording Sheet	**Required** algebra tiles (MK) **Optional** transparency mat, transparency algebra tiles (MK)
Lesson 8-3 Factoring $x^2 + bx + c$ • Factor quadratic trinomials of the form $x^2 + bx + c$. ☐ SAT-10 ☑ NAEP ☑ ACT ☑ SAT ☑ SAT Subject Tests		
Lesson 8-4 Factoring $ax^2 + bx + c$ • Factor quadratic trinomials of the form $ax^2 + bx + c$. ☐ SAT-10 ☑ NAEP ☑ ACT ☑ SAT ☑ SAT Subject Tests		**Optional** algebra tiles (MK)
8-4 Technology Lab Use a Graph to Factor Polynomials • Use a graphing calculator to factor a polynomial. ☐ SAT-10 ☑ NAEP ☐ ACT ☐ SAT ☐ SAT Subject Tests	***Technology Lab Activities*** 8-4 Lab Recording Sheet	**Required** graphing calculator

Note: If NAEP is checked, the content is tested on either the Grade 8 or the Grade 12 NAEP assessment.

MK = *Manipulatives Kit*

Math Background

FACTORING NUMBERS

Lesson 8-1

Understanding factoring begins with an understanding of prime numbers. We define a *prime number* as a whole number greater than 1 that has exactly two whole numbers as factors, itself and 1. The first few prime numbers form the familiar sequence 2, 3, 5, 7, 11, ...

More than 2000 years ago, Euclid proved that there are infinitely many prime numbers. His proof went as follows: Suppose there were a finite number of primes. Then they could be listed in their entirety as $p_1, p_2, ..., p_n$. Consider the number that is the product of all the primes plus one; that is, $p_1 \cdot p_2 \cdot ... \cdot p_n + 1$. This number is not divisible by any of the primes in the list since division by any of these primes would result in a remainder of 1. This means that the number itself must be prime. However, it is greater than any of the primes in the list, so it cannot be one of the primes in the list. This contradicts the assumption that the list includes all of the primes. Thus, the original assumption that there is a finite number of primes must be false.

THE FUNDAMENTAL THEOREM OF ARITHMETIC

Lesson 8-1

The Fundamental Theorem of Arithmetic (also known as the Unique Factorization Theorem) states that every whole number greater than 1 is either a prime number or may be written as a unique product of prime numbers. For example, the number 495 may be written as the product $3 \cdot 3 \cdot 5 \cdot 11$ (or $3^2 \cdot 5 \cdot 11$), and the Fundamental Theorem of Arithmetic asserts that this is the *only* prime factorization, with the exception of different orderings of the factors. One result of this theorem is that when finding the prime factorization of the same number, two students may use very different methods, but in the end they will always arrive at the same prime factors.

The proof of the theorem has two parts: showing that every whole number greater than 1 may be written as a product of primes and showing that this factorization is unique.

The first part is straightforward. Suppose there were one or more whole numbers greater than 1 that could not be written as a product of prime numbers. Let k be the least of all such numbers. Then k cannot be prime, since every prime number is the product of a single prime (namely, itself). Thus, k must be composite and so $k = ab$ where a and b are whole numbers less than k. Since k was taken to be the least whole number that cannot be written as a product of primes, we know that a and b can be written as a product of primes: $a = p_1 \cdot p_2 \cdot ... \cdot p_m$ and $b = q_1 \cdot q_2 \cdot ... \cdot q_n$. So $k = p_1 \cdot p_2 \cdot ... \cdot p_m \cdot q_1 \cdot q_2 \cdot ... \cdot q_n$, which contradicts the initial assumption that k cannot be written as a product of prime numbers. Thus, every whole number greater than 1 must have a prime factorization.

The proof that the prime factorization is unique requires some basic number theory and will not be provided here, but it is worth noting that the standard proof is once again a proof by contradiction.

Students sometimes wonder why 1 is not considered prime. One reason is the fact that including 1 among the prime numbers would mean that prime factorizations are no longer unique. For example, we could write $495 = 1 \cdot 3^2 \cdot 5 \cdot 11$, $495 = 1^2 \cdot 3^2 \cdot 5 \cdot 11$, and so on.

However, it *is* possible to consider negative factors, and in fact, students must consider negative factors when factoring polynomials. From this perspective, a prime number p has exactly four factors (p, $-p$, 1, and -1) and integers such as -5 and -17 would be considered prime. The Fundamental Theorem of Arithmetic would no longer hold, however. For example, the number 18 could be written as a product of primes as $2 \cdot 3^2$ or $2 \cdot (-3)^2$.

Finally, prime factorization gives a convenient method of identifying *all* whole number factors of a number. For example, any factor of 495 must have the form $3^k \cdot 5^m \cdot 11^n$, where $k = 0$, 1, or 2, $m = 0$ or 1, and $n = 0$ or 1. Taking the various combinations shows that the whole number factors of 495 are 1, 3, 5, 9, 11, 15, 33, 45, 55, 99, 165, and 495.

8-1 Organizer

Pacing: Traditional 1 day
Block $\frac{1}{2}$ day

Objectives: Write the prime factorization of numbers.

Find the GCF of monomials.

Online Edition
Tutorial Videos

Countdown Week 17

Power Presentations with PowerPoint®

Warm Up

Tell whether the second number is a factor of the first number.

1. 50, 6 no **2.** 105, 7 yes

3. List the factors of 28. ±1, ±2, ±4, ±7, ±14, ±28

Tell whether each number is prime or composite. If the number is composite, write it as the product of two numbers.

4. 11 prime

5. 98 composite; 49 • 2

Also available on transparency

Math Humor

Q: Why couldn't 2 get along with the odd numbers?

A: They had nothing in common.

8-1 Factors and Greatest Common Factors

Objectives
Write the prime factorization of numbers.

Find the GCF of monomials.

Vocabulary
prime factorization
greatest common factor

Who uses this?
Web site designers who sell electronic greeting cards can use the greatest common factor of numbers to design their Web sites. (See Example 4.)

The numbers that are multiplied to find a product are called *factors* of that product. A number is divisible by its factors.

You can use the factors of a number to write the number as a product. The number 12 can be factored several ways.

Remember!
A prime number is a whole number that has exactly two positive factors, itself and 1. The number 1 is not prime because it only has one positive factor.

Factorizations of 12

1 · 12 2 · 6 3 · 4 1 · 4 · 3 (2 · 2 · 3)

The order of the factors does not change the product, but there is only one example above that cannot be factored further. The circled factorization is the **prime factorization** because all the factors are prime numbers. The prime factors can be written in any order, and, except for changes in the order, there is only one way to write the prime factorization of a number.

EXAMPLE 1 Writing Prime Factorizations

Write the prime factorization of 60.

Method 1 Factor tree
Choose any two factors of 60 to begin. Keep finding factors until each branch ends in a prime factor.

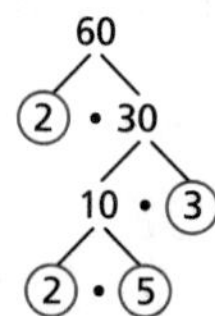

$60 = 2 \cdot 2 \cdot 5 \cdot 3$

Method 2 Ladder diagram
Choose a prime factor of 60 to begin. Keep dividing by prime factors until the quotient is 1.

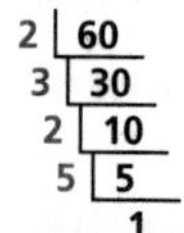

$60 = 2 \cdot 3 \cdot 2 \cdot 5$

The prime factorization of 60 is $2 \cdot 2 \cdot 3 \cdot 5$ or $2^2 \cdot 3 \cdot 5$.

Write the prime factorization of each number.

1a. 40 $2^3 \cdot 5$ **1b.** 33 $3 \cdot 11$ **1c.** 49 7^2 **1d.** 19 19

State Resources

go.hrw.com
State Resources Online
KEYWORD: MA7 Resources

1 Introduce

EXPLORATION

8-1 Factors and Greatest Common Factors

An artist is planning to create two large rectangular paintings for the lobby of a museum.

1. One of the paintings is to have an area of 24 ft². The height and width of the painting will be whole numbers. List all the possible heights and widths. (You may not need all of the columns of the table.)

Height (ft)	1	2						
Width (ft)	24	12						

2. The other painting is to have an area of 18 ft². The height and width of the painting will be whole numbers. List all the possible heights and widths. (You may not need all of the columns of the table.)

Height (ft)								
Width (ft)								

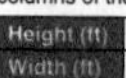

3. The artist wants the two paintings to have the same height. What are the possible heights?
4. The artist decides to make the two paintings the same height and as tall as possible. What should the height of the paintings be?

THINK AND DISCUSS

5. **Explain** how the heights in the tables are related to the areas of the paintings.
6. **Explain** whether it is possible to make both paintings 12 feet

Motivate

Ask students what it means for two people to have something in common (e.g., to have the same hair color, belong to the same club, etc.). Then ask students what it means for two numbers to have a common factor. What would the greatest common factor of two numbers be? Tell students that in this lesson, they will learn how to find the greatest common factor of numbers and monomials.

Explorations and answers are provided in *Alternate Openers: Explorations Transparencies.*

Factors that are shared by two or more whole numbers are called *common factors.* The greatest of these common factors is called the **greatest common factor**, or GCF.

> Factors of 12: 1, 2, 3, 4, 6, 12
> Factors of 32: 1, 2, 4, 8, 16, 32
> Common factors: 1, 2, (4)
> The greatest of the common factors is 4.

EXAMPLE 2 Finding the GCF of Numbers

Find the GCF of each pair of numbers.

A **24 and 60**

Method 1 List the factors.

factors of 24: 1, 2, 3, 4, 6, 8, (12), 24 — *List all the factors.*
factors of 60: 1, 2, 3, 4, 5, 6, 10, (12), 15, 20, 30, 60 — *Circle the GCF.*

The GCF of 24 and 60 is 12.

B **18 and 27**

Method 2 Use prime factorization.

$18 = 2 \cdot \boxed{3} \cdot \boxed{3}$ — *Write the prime factorization of each number.*
$27 = \boxed{3} \cdot \boxed{3} \cdot 3$ — *Align the common factors.*

$3 \cdot 3 = 9$

The GCF of 18 and 27 is 9.

Find the GCF of each pair of numbers.

2a. 12 and 16 **4** **2b.** 15 and 25 **5**

You can also find the GCF of monomials that include variables. To find the GCF of monomials, write the prime factorization of each coefficient and write all powers of variables as products. Then find the product of the common factors.

EXAMPLE 3 Finding the GCF of Monomials

Find the GCF of each pair of monomials.

A $3x^3$ **and** $6x^2$

$3x^3 = \boxed{3} \cdot \boxed{x} \cdot \boxed{x} \cdot x$ — *Write the prime factorization of each coefficient and write powers as products.*
$6x^2 = 2 \cdot \boxed{3} \cdot \boxed{x} \cdot \boxed{x}$ — *Align the common factors.*

$3 \cdot x \cdot x = 3x^2$ — *Find the product of the common factors.*

The GCF of $3x^3$ and $6x^2$ is $3x^2$.

B $4x^2$ **and** $5y^3$

$4x^2 = 2 \cdot 2 \cdot x \cdot x$ — *Write the prime factorization of each coefficient and write powers as products.*
$5y^3 = 5 \cdot y \cdot y \cdot y$ — *Align the common factors.*

There are no common factors other than 1.

The GCF of $4x^2$ and $5y^3$ is 1.

Helpful Hint

If two terms contain the same variable raised to different powers, the GCF will contain that variable raised to the lower power.

Find the GCF of each pair of monomials.

3a. $18g^2$ and $27g^3$ $9g^2$ **3b.** $16a^6$ and $9b$ **1** **3c.** $8x$ and $7v^2$ **1**

2 Teach

Guided Instruction

Review prime and composite numbers. Show students that different factor trees can be drawn for some numbers, but they all give the same prime factorization. Show that the GCF of two numbers or monomials is the largest term that divides into both of the numbers or monomials.

Reaching All Learners

Through Number Sense

Discuss with students how to quickly find the GCF of two numbers. If one number is a factor of the other number, it is the GCF of the two numbers. If not, then check the factors of the smaller number from largest to smallest until one is a factor of the greater number. This is the GCF of the two numbers.

COMMON ERROR ALERT

In **Example 1,** when using a ladder diagram to find the prime factorization of a number, students might include 1 as a prime factor. Remind students that 1 is not a prime number.

Power Presentations with PowerPoint®

Additional Examples

Example 1

Write the prime factorization of 98. $2 \cdot 7^2$

Example 2

Find the GCF of each pair of numbers.

A. 100 and 60 20

B. 26 and 52 26

Example 3

Find the GCF of each pair of monomials.

A. $15x^3$ and $9x^2$ $3x^2$

B. $8x^2$ and $7y^3$ 1

INTERVENTION

Questioning Strategies

EXAMPLE 1

- Is the order of the prime factors important?
- How can you check your answer?

EXAMPLE 2

- How can you determine whether you have found all the factors of a number when using Method 1?
- Can the GCF of two numbers be one of the numbers? Explain.

EXAMPLE 3

- If two terms contain the same variable raised to different powers, what power of the variable will the GCF include? Explain.
- What happens if the monomials do not contain the same variable?

Power Presentations with PowerPoint®

Additional Examples

Example 4

A cafeteria has 18 chocolate-milk cartons and 24 regular-milk cartons. The cook wants to arrange the cartons with the same number of cartons in each row. Chocolate and regular milk will not be in the same row. How many rows will there be if the cook puts the greatest possible number of cartons in each row?

7

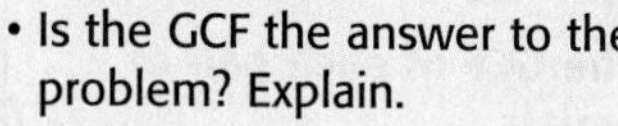

Questioning Strategies

EXAMPLE 4

- Is the GCF the answer to the problem? Explain.

Kinesthetic Suggest that students use different colored counters to model the items in **Example 4.** These can be found in the Manipulatives Kit (MK).

EXAMPLE 4 Technology Application

Garrison is creating a Web page that offers electronic greeting cards. He has 24 special occasion designs and 42 birthday designs. The cards will be displayed with the same number of designs in each row. Special occasion and birthday designs will not appear in the same row. How many rows will there be if Garrison puts the greatest possible number of designs in each row?

The 24 special occasion designs and 42 birthday designs must be divided into groups of equal size. The number of designs in each row must be a common factor of 24 and 42.

factors of 24: 1, 2, 3, 4, (6), 8, 12, 24
factors of 42: 1, 2, 3, (6), 7, 14, 21, 42

Find the common factors of 24 and 42.

The GCF of 24 and 42 is 6.

The greatest possible number of designs in each row is 6. Find the number of rows of each group of designs when there are 6 designs in each row.

$$\frac{24 \text{ special occasion designs}}{6 \text{ designs per row}} = 4 \text{ rows}$$

$$\frac{42 \text{ birthday designs}}{6 \text{ designs per row}} = 7 \text{ rows}$$

When the greatest possible number of designs is in each row, there are 11 rows in total.

4. Adrianne is shopping for a CD storage unit. She has 36 CDs by pop music artists and 48 CDs by country music artists. She wants to put the same number of CDs on each shelf without putting pop music and country music CDs on the same shelf. If Adrianne puts the greatest possible number of CDs on each shelf, how many shelves does her storage unit need? 7

THINK AND DISCUSS

1. Describe two ways you can find the prime factorization of a number.
2. **GET ORGANIZED** Copy and complete the graphic organizer. Show how to write the prime factorization of $100x^2$ by filling in each box.

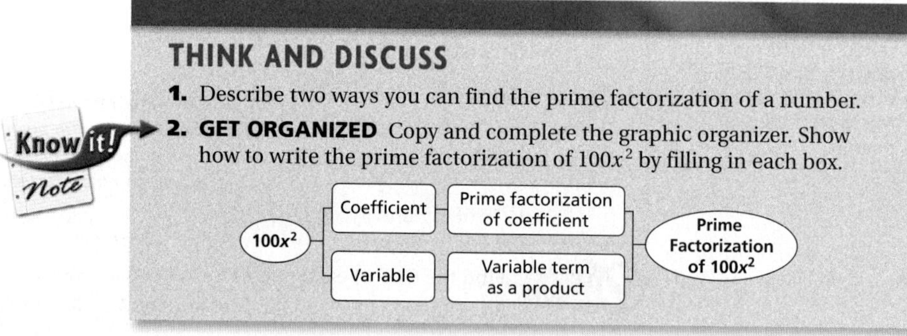

3 Close

Summarize

Have students find the GCF of the following.

56 and 70 14
15 and 30 15
35 and 24 1
$36x^3$ and $50x$ $2x$
$10x^2$ and $25x^4y^2$ $5x^2$

ONGOING ASSESSMENT and INTERVENTION

***Diagnose Before* the Lesson**
8-1 Warm Up, TE p. 544

***Monitor During* the Lesson**
Check It Out! Exercises, SE pp. 544–546
Questioning Strategies, TE pp. 545–546

***Assess After* the Lesson**
8-1 Lesson Quiz, TE p. 549
Alternative Assessment, TE p. 549

Answers to *Think and Discuss*

1. Use a factor tree or divide the number by prime factors until the quotient is 1.
2. See p. A7.

8-1 Exercises

go.hrw.com
Homework Help Online
KEYWORD: MA7 8-1
Parent Resources Online
KEYWORD: MA7 Parent

GUIDED PRACTICE

1. **Vocabulary** Define the term *greatest common factor* in your own words.
Possible answer: the greatest number that is a factor of two or more given numbers

SEE EXAMPLE 1 p. 544

Write the prime factorization of each number.

2. 20 $2^2 \cdot 5$
3. 36 $3^2 \cdot 2^2$
4. 27 3^3
5. 54 $3^3 \cdot 2$
6. 96 $2^5 \cdot 3$
7. 7 **7**
8. 100 $2^2 \cdot 5^2$
9. 75 $3 \cdot 5^2$

SEE EXAMPLE 2 p. 545

Find the GCF of each pair of numbers.

10. 12 and 60 **12**
11. 14 and 49 **7**
12. 55 and 121 **11**

SEE EXAMPLE 3 p. 545

Find the GCF of each pair of monomials.

13. $6x^2$ and $5x^2$ x^2
14. $15y^3$ and $-20y$ $5y$
15. $13q^4$ and $2p^2$ **1**

SEE EXAMPLE 4 p. 546

16. Samantha is making beaded necklaces using 54 glass beads and 18 clay beads. She wants each necklace to have the same number of beads, but each necklace will have only one type of bead. If she puts the greatest possible number of beads on each necklace, how many necklaces can she make? **4**

PRACTICE AND PROBLEM SOLVING

Independent Practice

For Exercises	See Example
17–24	1
25–27	2
28–30	3
31	4

Extra Practice
Skills Practice p. S18
Application Practice p. S35

Write the prime factorization of each number.

17. 18 $2 \cdot 3^2$
18. 64 2^6
19. 12 $2^2 \cdot 3$
20. 150 $2 \cdot 3 \cdot 5^2$
21. 17 **17**
22. 226 $2 \cdot 113$
23. 49 7^2
24. 63 $3^2 \cdot 7$

Find the GCF of each pair of numbers.

25. 36 and 63 **9**
26. 14 and 15 **1**
27. 30 and 40 **10**

Find the GCF of each pair of monomials.

28. $8a^2$ and 11 **1**
29. $9s$ and $63s^3$ $9s$
30. $-64n^4$ and $24n^2$ $8n^2$

31. José is making fruit-filled tart shells for a party. He has 72 raspberries and 108 blueberries. The tarts will each have the same number of berries. Raspberries and blueberries will not be in the same tart. If he puts the greatest possible number of fruits in each tart, how many tarts can he make? **5**

Find the GCF of each pair of products.

32. $3 \cdot 5 \cdot t$ and $2 \cdot 2 \cdot 5 \cdot t \cdot t$ $5t$
33. $-1 \cdot 2 \cdot 2 \cdot x \cdot x$ and $2 \cdot 2 \cdot 7 \cdot x \cdot x \cdot x$ $4x^2$
34. $2 \cdot 2 \cdot 2 \cdot 11 \cdot x \cdot x \cdot x$ and $3 \cdot 11$ **11**
35. $2 \cdot 5 \cdot n \cdot n \cdot n$ and $-1 \cdot 2 \cdot 3 \cdot n$ $2n$

36. **Write About It** The number 2 is even and is prime. Explain why all other prime numbers are odd numbers. **Possible answer: Even numbers greater than 2 all have 2 as a factor and thus are not prime.**

8-1 Exercises

Assignment Guide

Assign *Guided Practice* exercises as necessary.

If you finished Examples **1–2**
Basic 17–27, 40–45, 47–55
Average 17–27, 40–46, 50–55, 68
Advanced 17–27, 40–46, 50–55, 68

If you finished Examples **1–4**
Basic 17–35, 38–59, 69–75
Average 17–46, 56–59, 60–68 even, 69–75
Advanced 17–39, 40–46 even, 56–75

Homework Quick Check
Quickly check key concepts.
Exercises: 20, 26, 30, 31, 32, 38

State Resources

Teaching Tip **Multiple Representations** Suggest to students that they put the information in **Exercise 38** in a table to better organize their work, listing the lengths in increasing order.

ℓ	w	P
1	84	170
2		
3		

Answers

59.

24 ft

1 ft

$P = 50$ ft;

12 ft

2 ft

$P = 28$ ft;

8 ft

3 ft

$P = 22$ ft;

6 ft

4 ft

$P = 20$ ft;

Patricia should make the pen 4 ft × 6 ft because these dimensions give the shortest perimeter and she will need to buy the least fencing.

38a. 1 × 84, 2 × 42, 3 × 28, 4 × 21, 6 × 14, 7 × 12

37. Critical Thinking The GCF of two numbers is 1. Explain whether this means the two numbers must be prime. **No; 2 comp. numbers could share no common factors other than 1.**

38. Multi-Step Angelo is making a rectangular floor for a clubhouse with an area of 84 square feet. The length of each side of the floor is a whole number of feet.

a. What are the possible lengths and widths for Angelo's clubhouse floor?

b. What is the minimum perimeter for the clubhouse floor? **38 ft**

c. What is the maximum perimeter for the clubhouse floor? **170 ft**

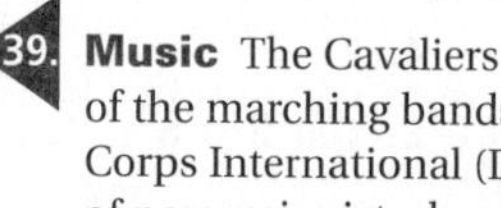

Music

DCI is a nonprofit organization that oversees drum and bugle corps performances and competitions for youths between the ages of 14 and 21.

39. Music The Cavaliers and the Blue Devils are two of the marching bands that are members of Drum Corps International (DCI). DCI bands are made up of percussionists, brass players, and color guard members who use flags and other props.

In 2004, there were 35 color guard members in the Cavaliers and 40 in the Blue Devils. The two color guards will march in rows with the same number of people in each row without mixing the guards together. If the greatest possible number of people are in each row, how many rows will there be? **15 rows**

For each set of numbers, determine which two numbers have a GCF greater than 1, and find that GCF.

40. 11, 12, 14 **12 and 14; 2**
41. 8, 20, 63 **8 and 20; 4**
42. 16, 21, 27 **21 and 27; 3**
43. 32, 63, 105 **63 and 105; 21**
44. 25, 35, 54 **25 and 35; 5**
45. 35, 54, 72 **54 and 72; 18**

46. Number Sense The prime factorization of 24 is $2^3 \cdot 3$. Without using a diagram, write the prime factorization of 48. Explain your reasoning. **$2^4 \cdot 3$; possible answer: because $48 = 2 \cdot 24$ and $24 = 2^3 \cdot 3$, $48 = 2 \cdot 2^3 \cdot 3 = 2^4 \cdot 3$.**

Fill in each diagram. Then write the prime factorization of the number.

47. **$2^3 \cdot 3^2$**

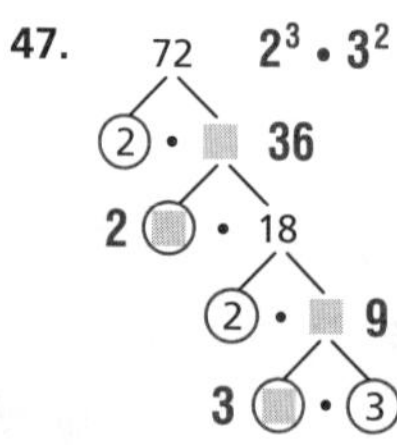

48. **3^4**

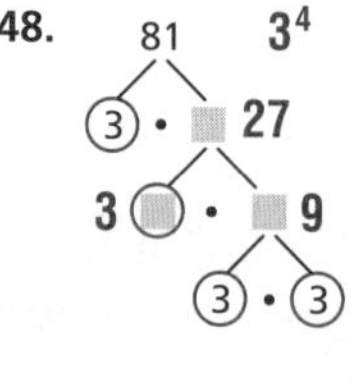

49. **$2 \cdot 3 \cdot 5 \cdot 7$**

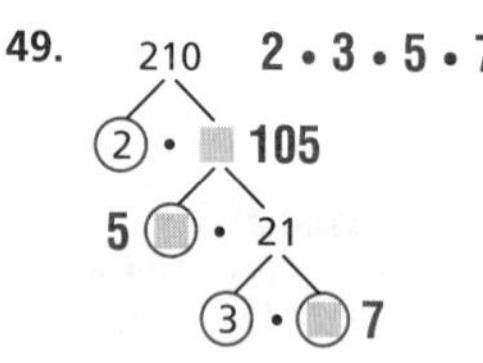

50. **$2^3 \cdot 7$**

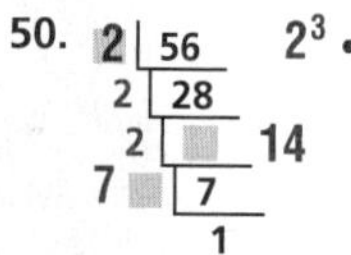

51. 2 | 108, 2 | 54, 3 | 27, 3 | 9, 3 | 3, 1 **$2^2 \cdot 3^3$**

52. 2 | 136, 2 | 68, 2 | 34, 17 | 17, 1 **$2^3 \cdot 17$**

53. 2 | 48, 2 | 24, 2 | 12, 2 | 6, 3 | 3, 1 **$2^4 \cdot 3$**

54. 2 | 140, 2 | 70, 5 | 35, 7 | 7, 1 **$2^2 \cdot 5 \cdot 7$**

55. 2 | 40, 2 | 20, 2 | 10, 5 | 5, 1 **$2^3 \cdot 5$**

8-1 PRACTICE A
8-1 PRACTICE C
8-1 PRACTICE B

Write the prime factorization of each number.

1. 18 **$2 \cdot 3^2$**
2. 120 **$2^3 \cdot 3 \cdot 5$**
3. 56 **$2^3 \cdot 7$**
4. 390 **$2 \cdot 3 \cdot 5 \cdot 13$**
5. 144 **$2^4 \cdot 3^2$**
6. 153 **$3^2 \cdot 17$**

Find the GCF of each pair of numbers.

7. 16 and 20 **4**
8. 9 and 36 **9**
9. 15 and 28 **1**
10. 35 and 42 **7**
11. 33 and 66 **33**
12. 100 and 120 **20**
13. 78 and 30 **6**
14. 84 and 42 **42**

Find the GCF of each pair of monomials.

15. $15x^4$ and $35x^2$ **$5x^2$**
16. $12p^2$ and $30q^5$ **6**
17. $-6t^3$ and $9t$ **$3t$**
18. $27y^3z$ and $45x^2y$ **$9y$**
19. $12ab$ and 12 **12**
20. $-8d^3$ and $14d^4$ **$2d^3$**
21. $-m^8n^4$ and $3m^6n$ **m^6n**
22. $10gh^2$ and $5h$ **$5h$**

23. Kirstin is decorating her bedroom wall with photographs. She has 36 photographs of family and 28 photographs of friends. She wants to arrange the photographs in rows so that each row has the same number of photographs, and photographs of family and photographs of friends do not appear in the same row.

a. How many rows will there be if Kirstin puts the greatest possible number of photographs in each row? **16**

b. How many photographs will be in each row? **4**

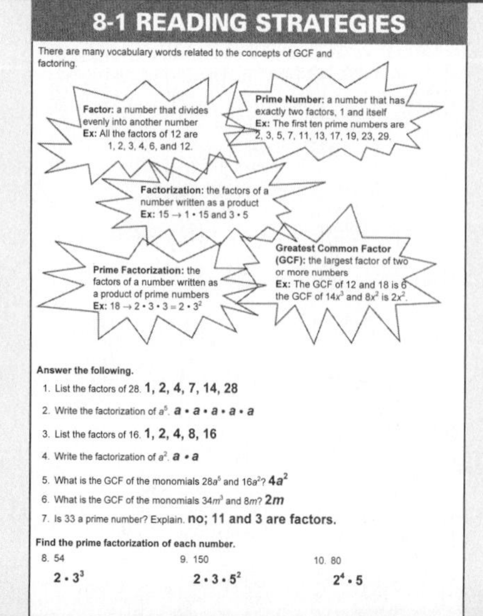

8-1 READING STRATEGIES

There are many vocabulary words related to the concepts of GCF and factoring.

Factor: a number that divides evenly into another number
Ex: All the factors of 12 are 1, 2, 3, 4, 6, and 12.

Prime Number: a number that has exactly two factors, 1 and itself
Ex: The first ten prime numbers are 2, 3, 5, 7, 11, 13, 17, 19, 23, 29.

Factorization: the factors of a number written as a product
Ex: $15 \rightarrow 1 \cdot 15$ and $3 \cdot 5$

Prime Factorization: the factors of a number written as a product of prime numbers
Ex: $18 \rightarrow 2 \cdot 3 \cdot 3 = 2 \cdot 3^2$

Greatest Common Factor (GCF): the largest factor of two or more numbers
Ex: The GCF of 12 and 18 is 6; the GCF of $14x^3$ and $8x^2$ is $2x^2$.

Answer the following.

1. List the factors of 28. **1, 2, 4, 7, 14, 28**
2. Write the factorization of a^5. **$a \cdot a \cdot a \cdot a \cdot a$**
3. List the factors of 16. **1, 2, 4, 8, 16**
4. Write the factorization of a^2. **$a \cdot a$**
5. What is the GCF of the monomials $28a^5$ and $16a^2$? **$4a^2$**
6. What is the GCF of the monomials $34m^3$ and $8m$? **$2m$**
7. Is 33 a prime number? Explain. **no; 11 and 3 are factors.**

Find the prime factorization of each number.

8. 54 **$2 \cdot 3^3$**
9. 150 **$2 \cdot 3 \cdot 5^2$**
10. 80 **$2^4 \cdot 5$**

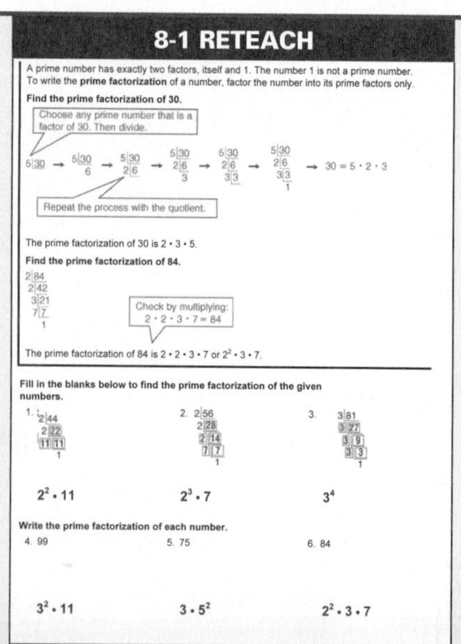

8-1 RETEACH

A prime number has exactly two factors, itself and 1. The number 1 is not a prime number. To write the **prime factorization** of a number, factor the number into its prime factors only.

Find the prime factorization of 30.

Choose any prime number that is a factor of 30. Then divide.

5 | 30 → 5 | 30, 6 → 5 | 30, 2 | 6 → 5 | 30, 2 | 6, 3 → 5 | 30, 2 | 6, 3 | 3 → 5 | 30, 2 | 6, 3 | 3, 1 → $30 = 5 \cdot 2 \cdot 3$

Repeat the process with the quotient.

The prime factorization of 30 is $2 \cdot 3 \cdot 5$.

Find the prime factorization of 84.

2 | 84
2 | 42
3 | 21
7 | 7
1

Check by multiplying: $2 \cdot 2 \cdot 3 \cdot 7 = 84$

The prime factorization of 84 is $2 \cdot 2 \cdot 3 \cdot 7$ or $2^2 \cdot 3 \cdot 7$.

Fill in the blanks below to find the prime factorization of the given numbers.

1. 2 | 44, 2 | 22, 11 | 11, 1 **$2^2 \cdot 11$**
2. 2 | 56, 2 | 28, 2 | 14, 7 | 7, 1 **$2^3 \cdot 7$**
3. 3 | 81, 3 | 27, 3 | 9, 3 | 3, 1 **3^4**

Write the prime factorization of each number.

4. 99 **$3^2 \cdot 11$**
5. 75 **$3 \cdot 5^2$**
6. 84 **$2^2 \cdot 3 \cdot 7$**

56. This problem will prepare you for the Multi-Step Test Prep on page 576.

The equation for the motion of an object with constant acceleration is $d = vt + \frac{1}{2}at^2$ where d is distance traveled in feet, v is starting velocity in ft/s, a is acceleration in ft/s², and t is time in seconds.

a. A toy car begins with a velocity of 2 ft/s and accelerates at 2 ft/s². Write an expression for the distance the toy car travels after t seconds. $2t + t^2$

b. What is the GCF of the terms in your expression from part **a**? t

MULTI-STEP TEST PREP Exercise 56 involves finding the GCF of terms in an expression for constant acceleration. This exercise prepares students for the Multi-Step Test Prep on page 576.

57. Which set of numbers has a GCF greater than 6?

Ⓐ 18, 24, 36 Ⓑ 30, 35, 40 Ⓒ 11, 29, 37 **Ⓓ 16, 24, 48**

58. The slope of a line is the GCF of 48 and 12. The y-intercept is the GCF of the slope and 8. Which equation describes the line?

Ⓕ $y = 12x + 4$ Ⓖ $y = 6x + 2$ Ⓗ $y = 4x + 4$ Ⓙ $y = 3x + 1$

59. Extended Response Patricia is making a dog pen in her back yard. The pen will be rectangular and have an area of 24 square feet. Draw and label a diagram that shows all possible whole-number dimensions for the pen. Find the perimeter of each rectangle you drew. Which dimensions should Patricia use in order to spend the least amount of money on fencing materials? Explain your reasoning.

TEST PREP DOCTOR In **Exercise 57,** choice **C** can be eliminated because it lists only prime numbers.

CHALLENGE AND EXTEND

Find the GCF of each set.

60. $4n^3, 16n^2, 8n$ $4n$

61. $27y^3, 18y^2, 81y$ $9y$

62. $100, 25s^5, 50s$ 25

63. $2p^4r, 8p^3r^2, 16p^2r^3$ $2p^2r$

64. $2x^3y, 8x^2y^2, 17xy^3$ xy

65. $8a^4b^3, 4a^3b^3, 12a^2b^3$ $4a^2b^3$

66. Geometry The area of a triangle is 10 in². What are the possible whole-number dimensions for the base and height of the triangle?
1×20; 2×10; 4×5; 20×1; 10×2; 5×4

67. Number Sense The GCF of three different numbers is 7. The sum of the three numbers is 105. What are the three numbers? **Possible answer: 21, 35, 49**

68. Critical Thinking Find three different *composite* numbers whose GCF is 1. (*Hint:* A composite number has factors other than 1 and itself.) **Possible answer: 6, 35, 143**

Journal

Have students explain how to use the prime factorization of 36 to find *all* of the factors of 36.

SPIRAL REVIEW

Use dimensional analysis to convert each measure. *(Lesson 2-7)*

69. 11,232 s to h **3.12 h**

70. 9 gal to pt **72 pt**

71. 18 in./day to mi/yr **≈ 0.10 mi/yr**

Find each value. Round to the nearest tenth if necessary. *(Lesson 2-9)*

72. 40% of 60 **24**

73. 250% of 16 **40**

74. What percent of 80 is 20? **25%**

75. Write a simplified polynomial expression for the perimeter of the triangle. *(Lesson 7-7)* $3x^2 + 14x - 3$

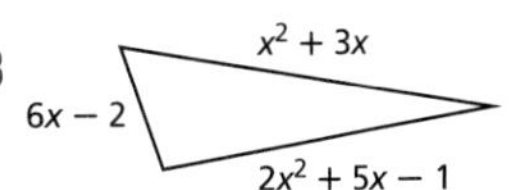

ALTERNATIVE ASSESSMENT

Have students create pairs of numbers or monomials that have the following GCFs: 15, 1, 7, $3x^2$, $2xy$, and $8b$.

Power Presentations with PowerPoint®

8-1 Lesson Quiz

Write the prime factorization of each number.

1. 50 $2 \cdot 5^2$
2. 84 $2^2 \cdot 3 \cdot 7$

Find the GCF of each pair of numbers.

3. 18 and 75 3
4. 20 and 36 4

Find the GCF of each pair of monomials.

5. $12x$ and $28x^3$ $4x$
6. $27x^2$ and $45x^3y^2$ $9x^2$
7. Cindi is planting a rectangular flower bed with 40 orange flowers and 28 yellow flowers. She wants to plant them so that each row will have the same number of plants but of only one color. How many rows will Cindi need if she puts the greatest possible number of plants in each row? 17

Also available on transparency

8-1 PROBLEM SOLVING

Write the correct answer.

1. Eloise saved all her awards from school. She has 18 athletic awards and 27 academic awards. Eloise wants to display the two types separately but in rows of equal length. Determine the greatest number of awards Eloise can put in each row. Then determine the total number of rows.
   9 awards in each row; total of 5 rows
2. Parker is preparing snacks for the children at a day camp. He has 48 carrot sticks and 36 apple slices. Find the number of identical snacks he can prepare if he puts as much food into each snack as possible without any leftovers. Then describe the snack.
   12 snacks of 4 carrot sticks and 3 apple slices
3. Matías and Hannah are responsible for the centerpieces on the buffet tables at the school dance. They have 6 dozen carnations, 80 lilies, and 64 rosebuds. All the centerpieces must be identical. Determine the greatest number of centerpieces Matías and Hannah can make if they use all the flowers. Then describe the centerpiece.
   8 centerpieces; 9 carnations, 10 lilies, 8 rosebuds
4. Ms. Thompson has 120 same-sized tiles with which to make a rectangular design on her patio floor. 54 of the tiles are green; the rest are blue. To keep the rectangular shape, all rows must have the same number of tiles. If she wants each row to have the same number of blue and green tiles, how many rows will there be if she wants to use all the tiles and wants the rows to be as long as possible?
   6 rows

Part of an ad for interlocking foam squares is shown below. Use it to answer questions 5–7. Select the best answer.

Each package comes with 36 foam squares that interlock for a safe, colorful floor mat! You can make a ... square rectangle or any shape you want!

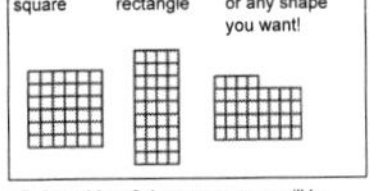

5. A class arranges one package into a rectangle with dimensions other than those shown. Which could have been the dimensions?
   A 2 × 18 C 4 × 8
   B 3 × 16 D 5 × 6
6. A teacher has 2 packages of red, 6 packages of blue, and half a package of yellow squares. He wants to build a rectangle so that each row is the same color. What can be the maximum number of squares per row?
   F 2 **H 18**
   G 6 J 36
7. In problem 6, how many rows will be blue?
   A 2 C 6
   B 3 **D 12**

8-1 CHALLENGE

There are many reasons why you might need to factor a number. Small numbers are easily factorable, and you can write their factors with a small amount of work. For large numbers, such as 180, you can use the method shown at right. Notice that the method is based on successive division by small prime numbers. First try 2 as a divisor, then try 3, and so on. From the division shown at right, you can write the prime factorization of 180 as follows.

2 | 180
2 | 90
3 | 45
3 | 15
5 | 5
1

$$180 = 2 \times 2 \times 3 \times 3 \times 5 = 2^2 3^2 5$$

Using the method shown above, find the prime factorization of each number.

1. 825 $3^1 5^2 11^1$
2. 1575 $3^2 5^2 7^1$
3. 1024 2^{10}
4. 25,200 $2^4 3^2 5^2 7^1$

Once you have written two large numbers by using their prime factorization, you can easily find their common factors.

List the distinct prime-number factors of each pair of numbers. If the numbers have no common factors other than 1, write *relatively prime*.

5. $2^2 3^2 5^2 7^2$ and $2^1 3^3 5^9 7^4$ **2, 3, 5, and 7**
6. $2^5 3^2 11^2 13^5$ and $2^1 11^3 19^9$ **2 and 11**
7. $2^{10} 5^8 23^2 53^2$ and $3^1 7^3 17^9 19^4$ **relatively prime**
8. $5^5 3^2 17^2 31^5$ and $2^1 11^3 5^5 3^2 17^2 31^5$ **3, 5, 17, and 31**

Once you have identified which prime numbers are common factors of two numbers, then find the highest powers of those prime factors that are common factors. The product of such powers gives the greatest common factor (GCF) of the two numbers.

Find the greatest common factor of each pair of numbers.

9. the pair in Exercise 5 $2^1 3^2 5^2 7^2$
10. the pair in Exercise 6 $2^1 11^2$
11. the pair in Exercise 7 1
12. the pair in Exercise 8 $3^2 5^5 17^2 31^5$
13. 3,293,136 and 3,778,488 $2^3 3^4 7^1$
14. 2,662,000 and 26,159,679 1

Organizer

Use with Lesson 8-2

Pacing:
Traditional $\frac{1}{2}$ day
Block $\frac{1}{4}$ day

Objective: Use algebra tiles to model and factor polynomials.

Materials: algebra tiles

Resources

Algebra Lab Activities
8-2 Lab Recording Sheet

Teach

Discuss

If the algebra tiles (MK) modeling a polynomial cannot be arranged into a rectangle, then the polynomial cannot be factored.

Ask students if they see another way to make a rectangle for $4x + 8$.

Close

Key Concept

You can factor polynomials by arranging tiles into a rectangle and finding expressions for the rectangle's length and width.

Assessment

Journal Have students explain how to model and factor polynomials with algebra tiles.

State Resources

Model Factoring

You can use algebra tiles to write a polynomial as the product of its factors. This process is called *factoring*. Factoring is the reverse of multiplying.

Use with Lesson 8-2

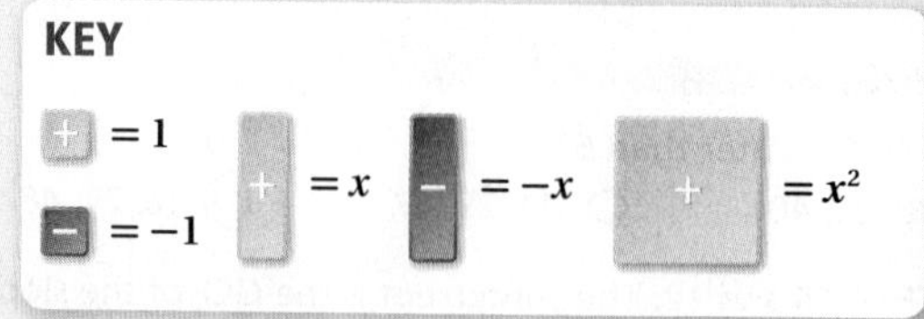

Activity

Use algebra tiles to factor $4x + 8$.

MODEL	ALGEBRA
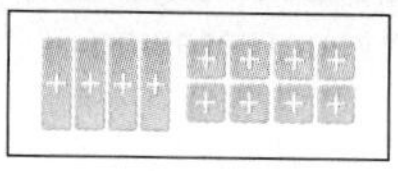 *Model $4x + 8$.*	$4x + 8$
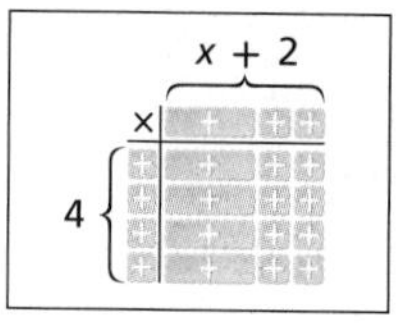 (tiles: $x + 2$, 4) *Arrange the tiles into a rectangle. The total area represents $4x + 8$. The length and width represent the factors. The rectangle has a width of $x + 2$ and a length of 4.*	$4x + 8 = 4(x + 2)$

Use algebra tiles to factor $x^2 - 2x$.

MODEL	ALGEBRA
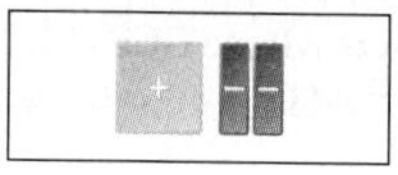 *Model $x^2 - 2x$.*	$x^2 - 2x$
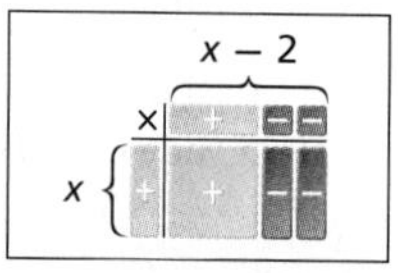 (tiles: $x - 2$, x) *Arrange the tiles into a rectangle. The total area represents $x^2 - 2x$. The length and width represent the factors. The rectangle has a width of $x - 2$ and a length of x.*	$x^2 - 2x = x(x - 2)$

Try This

Use algebra tiles to factor each polynomial.

1. $3x + 9$ **$3(x + 3)$**
2. $2x + 8$ **$2(x + 4)$**
3. $4x - 12$ **$4(x - 3)$**
4. $3x - 12$ **$3(x - 4)$**
5. $2x^2 + 2x$ **$2x(x + 1)$**
6. $x^2 + 4x$ **$x(x + 4)$**
7. $x^2 - 3x$ **$x(x - 3)$**
8. $2x^2 - 4x$ **$2x(x - 2)$**

8-2 Factoring by GCF

Objective
Factor polynomials by using the greatest common factor.

Why learn this?
You can determine the dimensions of a solar panel by factoring an expression representing the panel's area. (See Example 2.)

Recall that the Distributive Property states that $ab + ac = a(b + c)$. The Distributive Property allows you to factor out the GCF of the terms in a polynomial to write a factored form of the polynomial.

A polynomial is in its factored form when it is written as a product of monomials and polynomials that cannot be factored further. The expression $2(3x - 4x)$ is not fully factored because the terms in the parentheses have a common factor of x.

EXAMPLE 1 Factoring by Using the GCF

Writing Math
Aligning common factors can help you find the greatest common factor of two or more terms.

Factor each polynomial. Check your answer.

A $4x^2 - 3x$

$4x^2 = 2 \cdot 2 \cdot \boxed{x} \cdot x$
$3x = 3 \cdot \boxed{x}$
x — *Find the GCF.*

The GCF of $4x^2$ and $3x$ is x.

$4x(x) - 3(x)$ — *Write terms as products using the GCF as a factor.*

$x(4x - 3)$ — *Use the Distributive Property to factor out the GCF.*

Check $x(4x - 3)$ — *Multiply to check your answer.*
$4x^2 - 3x$ ✓ — *The product is the original polynomial.*

B $10y^3 + 20y^2 - 5y$

$10y^3 = 2 \cdot \boxed{5} \cdot \boxed{y} \cdot y \cdot y$ — *Find the GCF.*
$20y^2 = 2 \cdot 2 \cdot \boxed{5} \cdot \boxed{y} \cdot y$
$5y = \boxed{5} \cdot \boxed{y}$
$5 \cdot y = 5y$ — *The GCF of $10y^3$, $20y^2$, and $5y$ is $5y$.*

$2y^2(5y) + 4y(5y) - 1(5y)$ — *Write terms as products using the GCF as a factor.*

$5y(2y^2 + 4y - 1)$ — *Use the Distributive Property to factor out the GCF.*

Check $5y(2y^2 + 4y - 1)$ — *Multiply to check your answer.*
$10y^3 + 20y^2 - 5y$ ✓ — *The product is the original polynomial.*

8-2 Organizer

Pacing: Traditional 1 day
Block $\frac{1}{2}$ day

Objective: Factor polynomials by using the greatest common factor.

Online Edition
Tutorial Videos

Countdown Week 18

Power Presentations with PowerPoint®

Warm Up

Simplify.

1. $2(w + 1)$ $2w + 2$

2. $3x(x^2 - 4)$ $3x^3 - 12x$

Find the GCF of each pair of monomials.

3. $4h^2$ and $6h$ $2h$

4. $13p$ and $26p^5$ $13p$

Also available on transparency

Math Fact !!!

Around 300 B.C.E., Euclid developed a way of finding the GCF of two numbers by writing the smaller number and the difference of the two numbers as a pair and repeating this process until the two numbers are equal. The GCF of 36 and 60 is found by writing (36, 60); (36, 24); (24, 12); (12, 12). The GCF is 12.

1 Introduce

EXPLORATION

8-2 Factoring by GCF

In this Exploration, you will need to use the Distributive Property. Recall that the Distributive Property states that $a(b + c) = ab + ac$.

1. The table shows the factored form of several polynomials. Use the Distributive Property to multiply the factors and write the resulting polynomial in the middle column of the table.

Factored Form	Polynomial	GCF of Terms
$3(x + 2)$		
$x^2(x - 5)$		
$ab(a + 2b)$		
$5y^2(y^3 - 8)$		
$3a(a^2 + b + 1)$		

2. For each polynomial in the table, find the GCF of the terms. Write the GCF of the terms in the right-hand column of the table.

THINK AND DISCUSS

3. **Describe** what you notice about the GCF of the terms and the factored form of each polynomial.
4. **Explain** whether you think $2(x^2 + x)$ is the factored form of the polynomial $2x^2 + 2x$.

Motivate

Write 6 + 8 on the board. Ask students what the greatest common factor of 6 and 8 is. 2 Then rewrite 6 + 8 with 6 and 8 expressed as products of 2 and one other factor: $2 \cdot 3 + 2 \cdot 4$. Show how to use the Distributive Property to write $2(3 + 4)$.

Explorations and answers are provided in *Alternate Openers: Explorations Transparencies.*

State Resources

Power Presentations with PowerPoint®

Additional Examples

Example 1

Factor each polynomial. Check your answer.

A. $2x^2 - 4$ $2(x^2 - 2)$

B. $8x^3 - 4x^2 - 16x$ $4x(2x^2 - x - 4)$

C. $-14x - 12x^2$ $-2x(7 + 6x)$

D. $3x^3 + 2x^2 - 10$ cannot be factored

Example 2

The area of a court for the game squash is $(9x^2 + 6x)$ m². Factor this polynomial to find possible expressions for the dimensions of the squash court. Possible answer: $3x$ m and $(3x + 2)$ m

INTERVENTION

Questioning Strategies

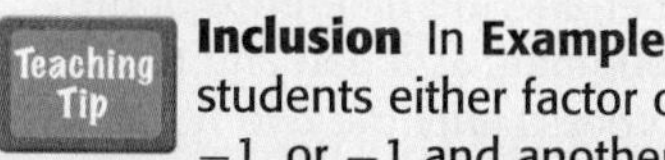

- How do you find a common factor?

EXAMPLE 2

- How could factoring a binomial help you with a problem about area?

Teaching Tip **Inclusion** In **Example 1C,** students either factor out −1, or −1 and another positive factor. Remind them that in either case, they need to change the sign of the terms in the parentheses.

When you factor out −1 as the first step, be sure to include it in all the other steps as well.

Factor each polynomial. Check your answer.

C $-12x - 8x^2$

$-1(12x + 8x^2)$ *Both coefficients are negative. Factor out −1.*

$12x = \boxed{2} \cdot \boxed{2} \cdot 3 \cdot \boxed{x}$ *Find the GCF.*

$8x^2 = \boxed{2} \cdot \boxed{2} \cdot 2 \cdot \boxed{x} \cdot x$

$2 \cdot 2 \cdot \quad x = 4x$ *The GCF of 12x and 8x² is 4x.*

$-1[3(4x) + 2x(4x)]$ *Write each term as a product using the GCF.*

$-1[4x(3 + 2x)]$ *Use the Distributive Property to factor out the GCF.*

$-1(4x)(3 + 2x)$

$-4x(3 + 2x)$

Check

$-4x(3 + 2x) = -12x - 8x^2$ ✓ *Multiply to check your answer.*

D $5x^2 + 7$

$5x^2 = 5 \quad \cdot x \cdot x$ *Find the GCF.*

$7 = \quad 7$

$5x^2 + 7$ *There are no common factors other than 1.*

The polynomial cannot be factored.

CHECK IT OUT! Factor each polynomial. Check your answer.

1a. $5b + 9b^3$ $b(5 + 9b^2)$ **1b.** $9d^2 - 8^2$ **cannot be factored**

1c. $-18y^3 - 7y^2$ $-y^2(18y + 7)$ **1d.** $8x^4 + 4x^3 - 2x^2$ $2x^2(4x^2 + 2x - 1)$

To write expressions for the length and width of a rectangle whose area is expressed as a polynomial, you need to write the polynomial as a product. You can write a polynomial as a product by factoring it.

EXAMPLE 2 ***Science Application***

Mandy's calculator is powered by solar energy. The area of the solar panel is $(7x^2 + x)$ cm². Factor this polynomial to find possible expressions for the dimensions of the solar panel.

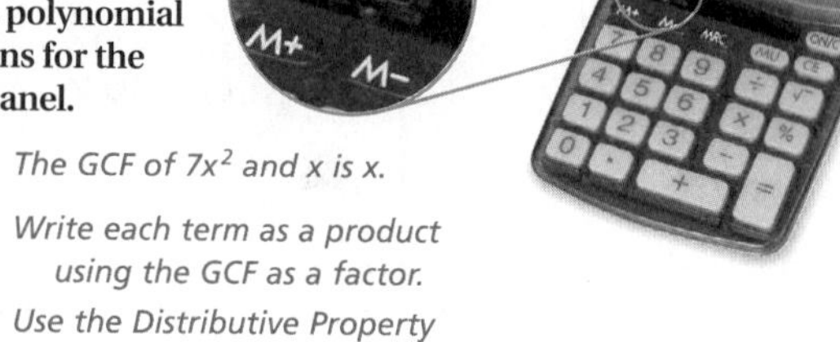

$A = 7x^2 + x$ *The GCF of 7x² and x is x.*

$= 7x(x) + 1(x)$ *Write each term as a product using the GCF as a factor.*

$= x(7x + 1)$ *Use the Distributive Property to factor out the GCF.*

Possible expressions for the dimensions of the solar panel are x cm and $(7x + 1)$ cm.

2. What if...? The area of the solar panel on another calculator is $(2x^2 + 4x)$ cm². Factor this polynomial to find possible expressions for the dimensions of the solar panel. **2x cm; (x + 2) cm**

2 Teach

Guided Instruction

Show students how the Distributive Property can be used to write $a(b + c)$ as $ab + ac$ and $ab + ac$ as $a(b + c)$. When factoring out common monomials and determining the remaining factors, have students determine the coefficient part first and then the variable part. Encourage students to check their work at each step, mentally "redistributing" the common factor to see if it matches the line in the previous step.

Reaching All Learners

Through Cognitive Strategies

In **Example 5,** students learn to factor with opposites. To help students learn to recognize opposite binomials, work through the first row of the following chart with students. Then have students complete the chart on their own.

	Opposites		
$x - 3$	$-1(x - 3)$ →	$-x + 3$ →	$3 - x$
$8 - a$	$-1(8 - a)$	$-8 + a$	$a - 8$
$m - n$	$-1(m - n)$	$-m + n$	$n - m$
$y^2 - 6$	$-1(y^2 - 6)$	$-y^2 + 6$	$6 - y^2$

Sometimes the GCF of terms is a binomial. This GCF is called a *common binomial factor*. You factor out a common binomial factor the same way you factor out a monomial factor.

EXAMPLE 3 Factoring Out a Common Binomial Factor

Factor each expression.

A $7(x-3)-2x(x-3)$

$7(x-3)-2x(x-3)$ — *$(x-3)$ is a common binomial factor.*

$(x-3)(7-2x)$ — *Factor out $(x-3)$.*

B $-t(t^2+4)+(t^2+4)$

$-t(t^2+4)+(t^2+4)$ — *(t^2+4) is a common binomial factor.*

$-t(t^2+4)+1(t^2+4)$ — *$(t^2+4)=1(t^2+4)$*

$(t^2+4)(-t+1)$ — *Factor out (t^2+4).*

C $9x(x+4)-5(4+x)$

$9x(x+4)-5(4+x)$ — *$(x+4)=(4+x)$, so $(x+4)$ is a common binomial factor.*

$9x(x+4)-5(x+4)$

$(x+4)(9x-5)$ — *Factor out $(x+4)$.*

D $-3x^2(x+2)+4(x-7)$

$-3x^2(x+2)+4(x-7)$ — *There are no common factors.*

The expression cannot be factored.

Factor each expression.

3a. $4s(s+6)-5(s+6)$ — $(4s-5)(s+6)$

3b. $7x(2x+3)+(2x+3)$ — $(7x+1)(2x+3)$

3c. $3x(y+4)-2y(x+4)$ — cannot be factored

3d. $5x(5x-2)-2(5x-2)$ — $(5x-2)^2$

You may be able to factor a polynomial by grouping. When a polynomial has four terms, you can make two groups and factor out the GCF from each group.

EXAMPLE 4 Factoring by Grouping

Factor each polynomial by grouping. Check your answer.

A $12a^3-9a^2+20a-15$

$(12a^3-9a^2)+(20a-15)$ — *Group terms that have a common number or variable as a factor.*

$3a^2(4a-3)+5(4a-3)$ — *Factor out the GCF of each group.*

$3a^2(4a-3)+5(4a-3)$ — *$(4a-3)$ is a common factor.*

$(4a-3)(3a^2+5)$ — *Factor out $(4a-3)$.*

Check $(4a-3)(3a^2+5)$ — *Multiply to check your solution.*

$4a(3a^2)+4a(5)-3(3a^2)-3(5)$

$12a^3+20a-9a^2-15$

$12a^3-9a^2+20a-15$ ✓ — *The product is the original polynomial.*

COMMON ERROR ALERT

Students may forget that a binomial written without a coefficient actually has a coefficient of 1. Suggest that students write in the coefficient of 1 so that they don't forget it is there.

Power Presentations with PowerPoint®

Additional Examples

Example 3

Factor each expression.

A. $5(x+2)+3x(x+2)$
$(x+2)(5+3x)$

B. $-2b(b^2+1)+(b^2+1)$
$(b^2+1)(-2b+1)$

C. $4z(z^2-7)+9(2z^3+1)$
cannot be factored

Example 4

Factor each polynomial by grouping. Check your answer.

A. $6h^4-4h^3+12h-8$
$(3h-2)(2h^3+4)$

B. $5y^4-15y^3+y^2-3y$
$(y-3)(5y^3+y)$

INTERVENTION
Questioning Strategies

EXAMPLE 3

- How is the Distributive Property used in these examples?

EXAMPLE 4

- How do you determine which terms to group?
- How can you check your answer?

Power Presentations with PowerPoint®

Additional Examples

Example 5

Factor $2x^3 - 12x^2 + 18 - 3x$ by grouping. $(x - 6)(2x^2 - 3)$

INTERVENTION

Questioning Strategies

EXAMPLE 5

- How can you recognize opposite binomials?
- Does it matter which pair of terms has -1 as a factor? Explain.

Visual Cues Students can check their answers using algebra tiles (MK). If an expression is not factored fully, each row of the model can be rearranged into a smaller rectangle.

If $4x + 8$ is factored as $2(2x + 4)$, then each row can still form another rectangle:

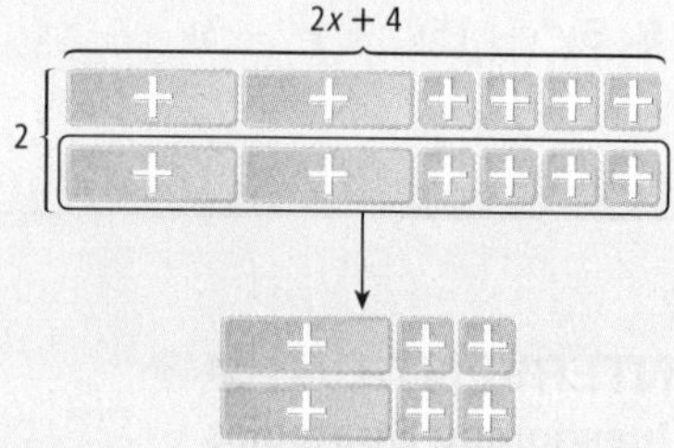

When $4x + 8$ is completely factored as $4(x + 2)$, the rows cannot form another rectangle:

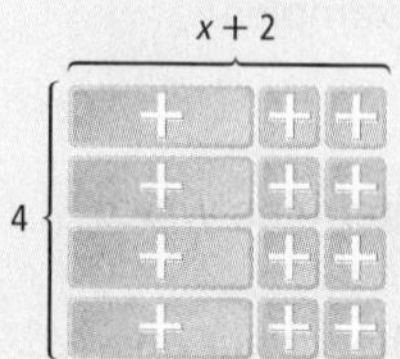

Factor each polynomial by grouping. Check your answer.

B $9x^3 + 18x^2 + x + 2$

$(9x^3 + 18x^2) + (x + 2)$	*Group terms.*
$9x^2(x + 2) + 1(x + 2)$	*Factor out the GCF of each group.*
$9x^2(x + 2) + 1(x + 2)$	*$(x + 2)$ is a common factor.*
$(x + 2)(9x^2 + 1)$	*Factor out $(x + 2)$.*
Check $(x + 2)(9x^2 + 1)$	*Multiply to check your solution.*
$x(9x^2) + x(1) + 2(9x^2) + 2(1)$	
$9x^3 + x + 18x^2 + 2$	
$9x^3 + 18x^2 + x + 2$ ✓	*The product is the original polynomial.*

Factor each polynomial by grouping. Check your answer.

4a. $6b^3 + 8b^2 + 9b + 12$ $(2b^2 + 3)(3b + 4)$

4b. $4r^3 + 24r + r^2 + 6$ $(4r + 1)(r^2 + 6)$

Helpful Hint

If two quantities are opposites, their sum is 0.

$(5 - x) + (x - 5)$
$5 - x + x - 5$
$(-x + x) + (5 - 5)$
$0 + 0$
0

Recognizing opposite binomials can help you factor polynomials. The binomials $(5 - x)$ and $(x - 5)$ are opposites. Notice $(5 - x)$ can be written as $-1(x - 5)$.

$-1(x - 5) = (-1)(x) + (-1)(-5)$	*Distributive Property*
$= -x + 5$	*Simplify.*
$= 5 - x$	*Commutative Property of Addition*

So, $(5 - x) = -1(x - 5)$.

EXAMPLE 5 Factoring with Opposites

Factor $3x^3 - 15x^2 + 10 - 2x$ by grouping.

$3x^3 - 15x^2 + 10 - 2x$	
$(3x^3 - 15x^2) + (10 - 2x)$	*Group terms.*
$3x^2(x - 5) + 2(5 - x)$	*Factor out the GCF of each group.*
$3x^2(x - 5) + 2(-1)(x - 5)$	*Write $(5 - x)$ as $-1(x - 5)$.*
$3x^2(x - 5) - 2(x - 5)$	*Simplify. $(x - 5)$ is a common factor.*
$(x - 5)(3x^2 - 2)$	*Factor out $(x - 5)$.*

Factor each polynomial by grouping. Check your answer.

5a. $15x^2 - 10x^3 + 8x - 12$ $(5x^2 - 4)(3 - 2x)$

5b. $8y - 8 - x + xy$ $(8 + x)(y - 1)$

THINK AND DISCUSS

1. Explain how finding the GCF of monomials helps you factor a polynomial.

2. GET ORGANIZED Copy and complete the graphic organizer.

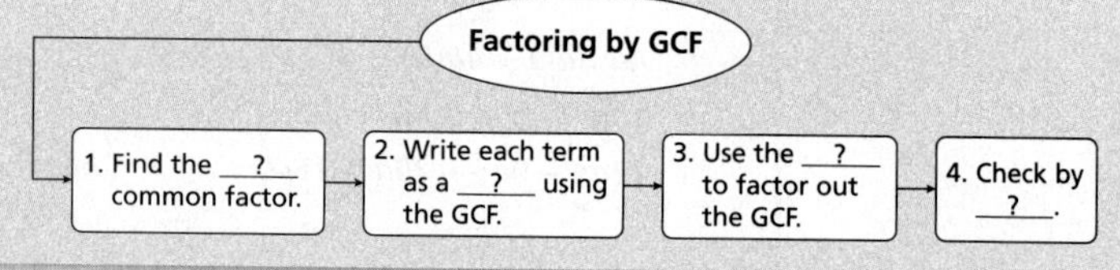

3 Close

Summarize

Ask students whether each of the following can be factored further. If yes, have them factor the polynomial.

$2x^5 - 7x^3$ yes; $x^3(2x^2 - 7)$

$3x^4 + 13y^4 + 3z^4$ no

$p(2p - 1) - 2(p - 1)$ no

$g^2(g - 8) + 6(8 - g)$ yes; $(g - 8)(g^2 - 6)$

$14y^5 + 21$ yes; $7(2y^5 + 3)$

ONGOING ASSESSMENT and INTERVENTION

***Diagnose Before* the Lesson**
8-2 Warm Up, TE p. 551

***Monitor During* the Lesson**
Check It Out! Exercises, SE pp. 552–554
Questioning Strategies, TE pp. 552–554

***Assess After* the Lesson**
8-2 Lesson Quiz, TE p. 557
Alternative Assessment, TE p. 557

Answers to *Think and Discuss*

Possible answers:

1. When you know the GCF of the monomials in a polynomial, you can factor out the GCF from each monomial to factor the polynomial.
2. See p. A7.

Multiple Representations Some factorizations may be written differently but still be correct. For instance, **Check It Out 5a** could also be written as $(4 - 5x^2)(2x - 3)$.

8-2 Exercises

go.hrw.com
Homework Help Online
KEYWORD: MA7 8-2
Parent Resources Online
KEYWORD: MA7 Parent

GUIDED PRACTICE

SEE EXAMPLE 1 p. 551

Factor each polynomial. Check your answer.

1. $15a - 5a^2$ $5a(3 - a)$
2. $10g^3 - 3g$ $g(10g^2 - 3)$
3. $-35x + 42$ $7(-5x + 6)$
4. $-4x^2 - 6x$ $-2x(2x + 3)$
5. $12h^4 + 8h^2 - 6h$
6. $3x^2 - 9x + 3$
7. $9m^2 + m$
8. $14n^3 + 7n + 7n^2$
9. $36f + 18f^2 + 3$
10. $-15b^2 + 7b$

SEE EXAMPLE 2 p. 552

11. **Physics** A model rocket is fired vertically into the air at 320 ft/s. The expression $-16t^2 + 320t$ gives the rocket's height after t seconds. Factor this expression. $16t(-t + 20)$

SEE EXAMPLE 3 p. 553

Factor each expression.

12. $5(m - 2) - m(m - 2)$ $(5 - m)(m - 2)$
13. $2b(b + 3) + 5(b + 3)$ $(2b + 5)(b + 3)$
14. $4(x - 3) - x(y + 2)$ cannot be factored

Factor each polynomial by grouping. Check your answer.

SEE EXAMPLE 4 p. 553

15. $x^3 + 4x^2 + 2x + 8$
16. $6x^3 + 4x^2 + 3x + 2$
17. $4b^3 - 6b^2 + 10b - 15$
18. $2m^3 + 4m^2 + 6m + 12$
19. $7r^3 - 35r^2 + 6r - 30$
20. $10a^3 + 4a^2 + 5a + 2$

SEE EXAMPLE 5 p. 554

21. $2r^2 - 6r + 12 - 4r$
22. $6b^2 - 3b + 4 - 8b$
23. $14q^2 - 21q + 6 - 4q$
24. $3r - r^2 + 2r - 6$
25. $2m^3 - 6m^2 + 9 - 3m$
26. $6a^3 - 9a^2 - 12 + 8a$

PRACTICE AND PROBLEM SOLVING

Independent Practice

For Exercises	See Example
27–35	1
36	2
37–42	3
43–48	4
49–54	5

Extra Practice
Skills Practice p. S18
Application Practice p. S35

37. cannot be factored

Factor each polynomial. Check your answer.

27. $9y^2 + 45y$ $9y(y + 5)$
28. $36d^3 + 24$ $12(3d^3 + 2)$
29. $-14x^4 + 5x^2$ $x^2(-14x^2 + 5)$
30. $-15f - 10f^2$
31. $-4d^4 + d^3 - 3d^2$
32. $14x^3 + 63x^2 - 7x$
33. $21c^2 + 14c$
34. $33d^3 + 22d + 11$
35. $-5g^3 - 15g^2$
36. **Finance** After t years, the amount of money in a savings account that earns simple interest is $P + Prt$, where P is the starting amount and r is the yearly interest rate. Factor this expression. $P(1 + rt)$

Factor each expression.

37. $6a(a - 2) - 5b(b + 4)$
38. $-4x(x + 2) + 9(x + 2)$ $(-4x + 9)(x + 2)$
39. $6y(y - 7) + (y - 7)$ $(6y + 1)(y - 7)$
40. $a(x - 3) + 2b(x - 3)$ $(a + 2b)(x - 3)$
41. $-3(2 + b) + 4b(b + 2)$ $(-3 + 4b)(b + 2)$
42. $5(3x - 2) + x(3x - 2)$ $(5 + x)(3x - 2)$

Factor each polynomial by grouping. Check your answer.

43. $2a^3 - 8a^2 + 3a - 12$
44. $x^3 + 3x^2 + 5x + 15$
45. $6x^3 + 18x^2 + x + 3$
46. $7x^3 + 2x^2 + 28x + 8$
47. $n^3 - 2n^2 + 5n - 10$
48. $10b^3 - 16b^2 + 25b - 40$
49. $2m^3 - 2m^2 + 3 - 3m$
50. $2d^3 - d^2 - 3 + 6d$
51. $6f^3 - 8f^2 + 20 - 15f$
52. $5k^2 - k^3 + 3k - 15$
53. $b^3 - 2b - 8 + 4b^2$
54. $20 - 15x - 6x^2 + 8x$

8-2 Exercises

Assignment Guide

Assign *Guided Practice* exercises as necessary.

If you finished Examples **1–3**
Basic 27–42, 55–58
Average 27–42, 55, 57, 74, 76
Advanced 27–42, 55, 57, 74, 76

If you finished Examples **1–5**
Basic 27–54, 55–62, 66, 68, 70–73, 81–85
Average 27–39, 40–54 even, 55–76, 81–85
Advanced 28–32 even, 39, 40–54 even, 55–69, 71–85

Homework Quick Check
Quickly check key concepts.
Exercises: 28, 39, 40, 44, 54, 66

Answers

5. $2h(6h^3 + 4h - 3)$
6. $3(x^2 - 3x + 1)$
7. $m(9m + 1)$
8. $7n(2n^2 + 1 + n)$
9. $3(12f + 6f^2 + 1)$
10. $b(-15b + 7)$
15. $(x^2 + 2)(x + 4)$
16. $(2x^2 + 1)(3x + 2)$
17. $(2b^2 + 5)(2b - 3)$
18. $2(m + 2)(m^2 + 3)$
19. $(7r^2 + 6)(r - 5)$
20. $(2a^2 + 1)(5a + 2)$
21. $2(r - 2)(r - 3)$
22. $(3b - 4)(2b - 1)$
23. $(7q - 2)(2q - 3)$
24. $(2 - r)(r - 3)$
25. $(2m^2 - 3)(m - 3)$
26. $(3a^2 + 4)(2a - 3)$
30. $-5f(3 + 2f)$
31. $-d^2(4d^2 - d + 3)$
32. $7x(2x^2 + 9x - 1)$
33. $7c(3c + 2)$
34. $11(3d^3 + 2d + 1)$
35. $-5g^2(g + 3)$
43. $(2a^2 + 3)(a - 4)$
44. $(x^2 + 5)(x + 3)$
45. $(6x^2 + 1)(x + 3)$
46. $(x^2 + 4)(7x + 2)$
47. $(n^2 + 5)(n - 2)$
48. $(2b^2 + 5)(5b - 8)$
49. $(2m^2 - 3)(m - 1)$
50. $(d^2 + 3)(2d - 1)$
51. $(2f^2 - 5)(3f - 4)$
52. $(k^2 - 3)(5 - k)$
53. $(b^2 - 2)(b + 4)$
54. $(5 + 2x)(4 - 3x)$

State Resources

go.hrw.com
State Resources Online
KEYWORD: MA7 Resources

MULTI-STEP TEST PREP Exercise 68 involves discovering the Zero Product Property. This exercise prepares students for the Multi-Step Test Prep on page 576.

Answers

63b. $100x^3 + 200x^2 + 400x + 800$

65. $(3a - 3b) - (4a - 4b)$
$3(a - b) - 4(a - b)$
$(3 - 4)(a - b)$
$-1(a - b)$
$(b - a)$;
$(3a - 4a) - (3b - 4b)$
$a(3 - 4) - b(3 - 4)$
$(a - b)(3 - 4)$
$(a - b)(-1)$
$(b - a)$

68a. Either a, b, or both must equal 0.

b. The product of t and $3 - t$ is 0, so at least one of the factors must be 0.

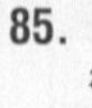

85.

Fill in the missing part of each factorization.

55. $16v + 12v^2 = 4v(4 + \mathbf{3v})$

56. $15x - 25x^2 = 5x(3 - \mathbf{5x})$

57. $-16k^3 - 24k^2 = -8k^2(\mathbf{2k} + 3)$

58. $-x - 10 = -1(\mathbf{x} + 10)$

Copy and complete the table.

	Polynomial	Number of Terms	Name	Completely Factored Form
	$3y + 3x + 9$	3	trinomial	$3(y + x + 3)$
59.	$x^2 + 5x$	**2**	**binomial**	$x(x + 5)$
60.	$28c^2 - 49c$	**2**	**binomial**	$7c(4c - 7)$
61.	$a^4 + a^3 + a^2$	**3**	**trinomial**	$a^2(a^2 + a + 1)$
62.	$36 + 99r - 40r^2 - 110r^3$	**4**	**polynomial**	$(11r + 4)(-10r^2 + 9)$

63. **Personal Finance** The final amount of money earned by a certificate of deposit (CD) after n years is $P(1 + r)^n$, where P is the original amount contributed and r is the interest rate as a decimal.

Year	Amount of CD
2004	$100.00
2005	$200.00
2006	$400.00

Justin's aunt purchased three CDs with the same interest rate to help him pay for college. The table shows the amount of the CD she purchased each year. In 2007, she paid $800.00 directly to the college.

a. Let $x = 1 + r$. Write expressions in terms of x for the value of the CDs purchased in 2004, 2005, and 2006 when Justin started college in 2007. **$100x^3$; $200x^2$; $400x$**

b. Write a polynomial in terms of x to represent the total value of the CDs purchased in 2004, 2005, and 2006 plus the amount paid to the college in 2007.

c. Factor the polynomial in part **b** by grouping. Evaluate the factored form of the polynomial when the interest rate is 9%. (*Hint*: Remember that $x = 1 +$ the interest rate expressed as a decimal.) **$100(x^2 + 4)(x + 2)$; $1603.12**

64. **Write About It** Describe how to find the area of the figure shown. Show each step and write your answer in factored form. **$5x(x + 4)$**

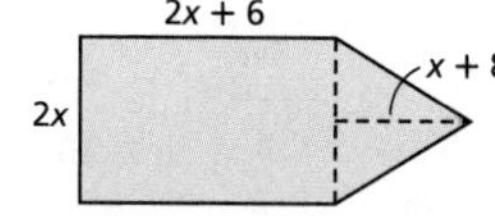

65. **Critical Thinking** Show two methods of factoring the expression $3a - 3b - 4a + 4b$.

66. **Geometry** The area of a triangle is $\frac{1}{2}(x^3 - 2x + 2x^2 - 4)$. The height h is $x + 2$. Write an expression for the base b of the triangle. (*Hint:* Area of a triangle $= \frac{1}{2}bh$) **$x^2 - 2$**

67. **Write About It** Explain how you know when two binomials are opposites. **The sum of opposite binomials is 0.**

MULTI-STEP TEST PREP

68. This problem will prepare you for the Multi-Step Test Prep on page 576.

a. The Multiplication Property of Zero states that the product of any number and 0 is 0. What must be true about either a or b to make $ab = 0$?

b. A toy car's distance in feet from the starting point is given by the equation $d = t(3 - t)$. Explain why $t(3 - t) = 0$ means that either $t = 0$ or $3 - t = 0$.

c. When $d = 0$, the car is at the starting point. Use the fact that $t = 0$ or $3 - t = 0$ when $d = 0$ to find the two times when the car is at the starting point. **$t = 0$ and $t = 3$**

8-2 PRACTICE A

8-2 PRACTICE C

8-2 PRACTICE B

Factor each polynomial. Check your answer.

1. $8c^2 + 7c$ — **$c(8c + 7)$**
2. $3n^3 + 12n^2$ — **$3n^2(n + 4)$**
3. $15x^5 - 18x$ — **$3x(5x^4 - 6)$**
4. $-8s^4 + 20t^3 - 28$ — **$6(-2s^4 + 5t^3 - 7)$**
5. $6n^6 + 18n^4 - 24n$ — **$6n(n^5 + 3n^3 - 4)$**
6. $-5m^4 - 5m^3 + 5m^2$ — **$5m^2(-m^2 - m + 1)$**
7. A ball is hit vertically into the air using a paddle at a speed of 32 ft/sec. The expression $-16t^2 + 32t$ gives the ball's height after t seconds. Factor this expression. **$16t(-t + 2)$**
8. The area of Margo's laptop computer screen is $12x^2 + 3x$ in^2. Factor this polynomial to find expressions for the dimensions of her computer screen. **$3x$ and $4x + 1$**

Factor each expression.

9. $3m(m + 5) + 4(m + 5)$ — **$(m + 5)(3m + 4)$**
10. $16b(b - 3) + (b - 3)$ — **$(b - 3)(16b + 1)$**

Factor each polynomial by grouping.

11. $2x^3 + 8x^2 + 3x + 12$ — **$(x + 4)(2x^2 + 3)$**
12. $4n^3 + 3n^2 + 4n + 3$ — **$(4n + 3)(n^2 + 1)$**
13. $10d^2 - 6d + 35d - 21$ — **$(5d - 3)(2d + 7)$**
14. $12n^3 - 15n^2 - 8n + 10$ — **$(4n - 5)(3n^2 - 2)$**
15. $5b^4 - 15b^3 + 3 - b$ — **$(b - 3)(5b^3 + 1)$**
16. $t^3 - 5t^2 + 10 - 2t$ — **$(t^2 - 2)(t - 5)$**

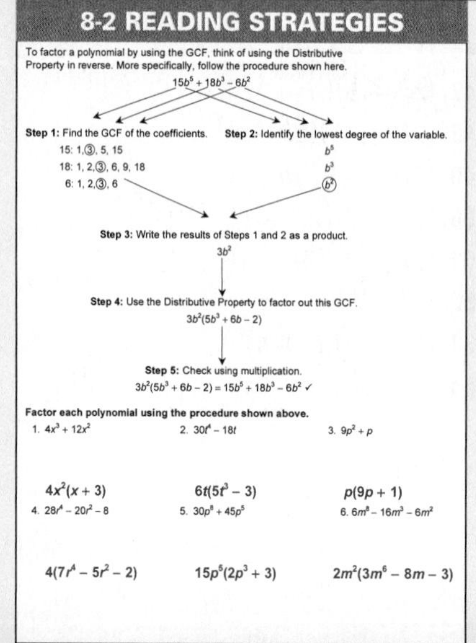

8-2 READING STRATEGIES

To factor a polynomial by using the GCF, think of using the Distributive Property in reverse. More specifically, follow the procedure shown here.

$15b^5 + 18b^3 - 6b^2$

Step 1: Find the GCF of the coefficients.
15: 1, ③, 5, 15
18: 1, 2, ③, 6, 9, 18
6: 1, 2, ③, 6

Step 2: Identify the lowest degree of the variable.
b^5
b^3
(b^2)

Step 3: Write the results of Steps 1 and 2 as a product.
$3b^2$

Step 4: Use the Distributive Property to factor out this GCF.
$3b^2(5b^3 + 6b - 2)$

Step 5: Check using multiplication.
$3b^2(5b^3 + 6b - 2) = 15b^5 + 18b^3 - 6b^2$ ✓

Factor each polynomial using the procedure shown above.

1. $4x^3 + 12x^2$ — **$4x^2(x + 3)$**
2. $30t^4 - 18t$ — **$6t(5t^3 - 3)$**
3. $9p^2 + p$ — **$p(9p + 1)$**
4. $28r^4 - 20r^2 - 8$ — **$4(7r^4 - 5r^2 - 2)$**
5. $30p^8 + 45p^5$ — **$15p^5(2p^3 + 3)$**
6. $6m^8 - 16m^3 - 6m^2$ — **$2m^2(3m^6 - 8m - 3)$**

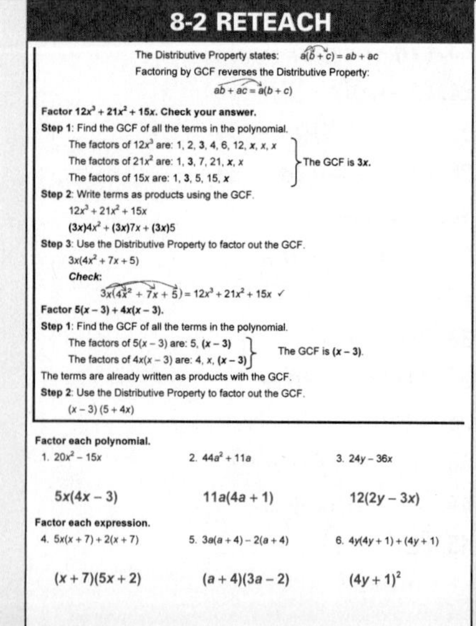

8-2 RETEACH

The Distributive Property states: $a(b + c) = ab + ac$
Factoring by GCF reverses the Distributive Property:
$ab + ac = a(b + c)$

Factor $12x^3 + 21x^2 + 15x$. Check your answer.

Step 1: Find the GCF of all the terms in the polynomial.
The factors of $12x^3$ are: 1, 2, **3**, 4, 6, 12, **x**, x, x
The factors of $21x^2$ are: 1, **3**, 7, 21, **x**, x
The factors of $15x$ are: 1, **3**, 5, 15, **x**
The GCF is **3x**.

Step 2: Write terms as products using the GCF.
$12x^3 + 21x^2 + 15x$
$(3x)4x^2 + (3x)7x + (3x)5$

Step 3: Use the Distributive Property to factor out the GCF.
$3x(4x^2 + 7x + 5)$
Check:
$3x(4x^2 + 7x + 5) = 12x^3 + 21x^2 + 15x$ ✓

Factor $5(x - 3) + 4x(x - 3)$.

Step 1: Find the GCF of all the terms in the polynomial.
The factors of $5(x - 3)$ are: 5, **(x − 3)**
The factors of $4x(x - 3)$ are: 4, x, **(x − 3)**
The GCF is **(x − 3)**.
The terms are already written as products with the GCF.

Step 2: Use the Distributive Property to factor out the GCF.
$(x - 3)(5 + 4x)$

Factor each polynomial.

1. $20x^2 - 15x$ — **$5x(4x - 3)$**
2. $44a^2 + 11a$ — **$11a(4a + 1)$**
3. $24y - 36x$ — **$12(2y - 3x)$**

Factor each expression.

4. $5x(x + 7) + 2(x + 7)$ — **$(x + 7)(5x + 2)$**
5. $3a(a + 4) - 2(a + 4)$ — **$(a + 4)(3a - 2)$**
6. $4y(4y + 1) + (4y + 1)$ — **$(4y + 1)^2$**

Fill in each blank with a property or definition that justifies the step.

69a. Comm. Prop. of Add.
b. Assoc. Prop. of Add.
c. Dist. Prop.
d. Dist. Prop.

69. $7x^3 + 2x + 21x^2 + 6 = 7x^3 + 21x^2 + 2x + 6$ a. ___?___
$= (7x^3 + 21x^2) + (2x + 6)$ b. ___?___
$= 7x^2(x + 3) + 2(x + 3)$ c. ___?___
$= (x + 3)(7x^2 + 2)$ d. ___?___

70. **/// ERROR ANALYSIS ///** Which factorization of $3n^3 - n^2$ is incorrect? Explain.

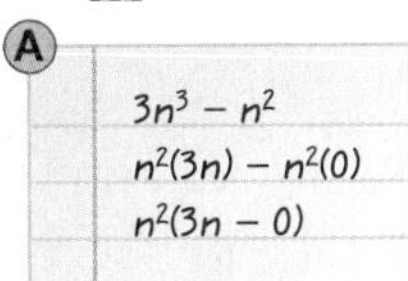

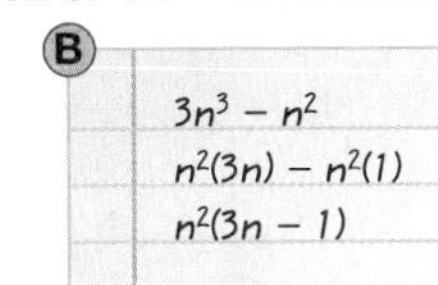

A is incorrect because $n^2 \neq n^2(0)$.

71. Which is the complete factorization of $24x^3 - 12x^2$?
Ⓐ $6(4x^3 - 2x^2)$ Ⓑ $12(2x^3 - x^2)$ Ⓒ $12x(2x^2 - x)$ **Ⓓ** $12x^2(2x - 1)$

72. Which is NOT a factor of $18x^2 + 36x$?
Ⓕ 1 **Ⓖ** $4x$ Ⓗ $x + 2$ Ⓙ $18x$

73. The area of a rectangle is represented by the polynomial $x^2 + 3x - 6x - 18$. Which of the following could represent the length and width of the rectangle?
Ⓐ Length: $x + 3$; width: $x + 6$
Ⓒ Length: $x + 3$; width: $x - 6$
Ⓑ Length: $x - 3$; width: $x - 6$
Ⓓ Length: $x - 3$; width: $x + 6$

CHALLENGE AND EXTEND

Factor each polynomial.

74. $6a(b^2 - 4a)$
77. $(a + c)(b + d)$

74. $6ab^2 - 24a^2$ **75.** $-72a^2b^2 - 45ab$ $-9ab(8ab + 5)$ **76.** $-18a^2b^2 + 21ab$ $-3ab(6ab - 7)$

77. $ab + bc + ad + cd$ **78.** $4y^2 + 8ay - y - 2a$ **79.** $x^3 - 4x^2 + 3x - 12$

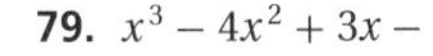

78. $(4y - 1)(y + 2a)$
79. $(x^2 + 3)(x - 4)$

80. **Geometry** The area between two concentric circles is called an *annulus*. The formula for area of an annulus is $A = \pi R^2 - \pi r^2$, where R is the radius of the larger circle and r is the radius of the smaller circle. $A = \pi(R^2 - r^2)$

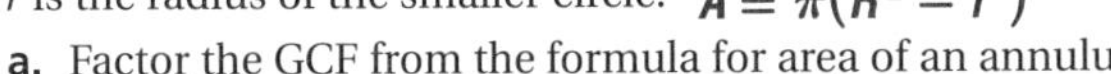

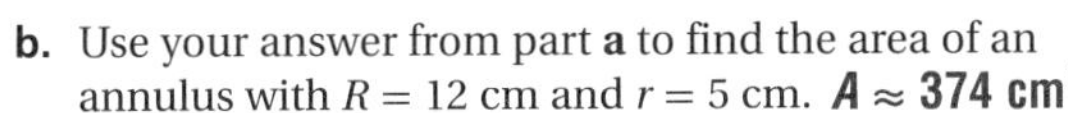

a. Factor the GCF from the formula for area of an annulus.
b. Use your answer from part **a** to find the area of an annulus with $R = 12$ cm and $r = 5$ cm. $A \approx 374\ \text{cm}^2$

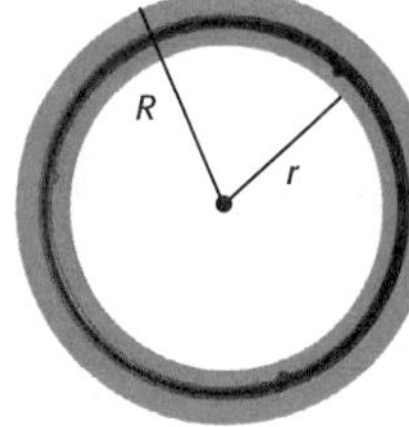

SPIRAL REVIEW

Solve each equation. *(Lesson 2-4)*

81. $4(x + 1) = 3(2x - 6)$ **11** **82.** $-20 + 8n = n + 29$ **7** **83.** $8\left(n + \frac{3}{4}\right) = 10n - 4$ **5**

84. The coordinates of the vertices of a quadrilateral are $A(-2, 5)$, $B(6, 5)$, $C(4, -3)$, and $D(-4, -3)$. Use slope to show that $ABCD$ is a parallelogram. *(Lesson 5-9)*

84. $\overline{AB}$ and $\overline{CD}$ are both horiz., so they have the same slope and are par. The slope of both $\overline{AD}$ and $\overline{BC}$ is 4, so they are par. Two pairs of par. sides define a parallelogram.

85. Graph the data in the table and show the rates of change. *(Lesson 5-3)*

Time (yr)	1998	1999	2002	2004	2005
Profit (million $)	0.6	0.8	1.3	1.9	2.4

TEST PREP DOCTOR + If students have difficulty with **Exercise 71,** remind them that a complete factorization means that the terms *inside* the parentheses have no common factors. That eliminates all options except **D.**

If students chose **H** for **Exercise 72,** they may have forgotten that a binomial can be a factor of a binomial. Remind them that $ab + ac = a(b + c)$. Then point out that 4 is not a factor of 18, which means that **G** is the correct answer.

Journal

Have students use examples to describe how to determine whether a polynomial with four terms can be factored into two binomial expressions.

ALTERNATIVE ASSESSMENT

Have students write three polynomial expressions such that one expression cannot be factored, another has a monomial GCF, and the third has a binomial GCF.

Power Presentations with PowerPoint®

8-2 Lesson Quiz

Factor each polynomial. Check your answer.

1. $16x + 20x^3$ $4x(4 + 5x^2)$

2. $4m^4 - 12m^2 + 8m$
$4m(m^3 - 3m + 2)$

Factor each expression.

3. $7k(k - 3) + 4(k - 3)$
$(k - 3)(7k + 4)$

4. $3y(2y + 3) - 5(2y + 3)$
$(2y + 3)(3y - 5)$

Factor each polynomial by grouping. Check your answer.

5. $2x^3 + x^2 - 6x - 3$
$(2x + 1)(x^2 - 3)$

6. $7p^4 - 2p^3 + 63p - 18$
$(7p - 2)(p^3 + 9)$

7. A rocket is fired vertically into the air at 40 m/s. The expression $-5t^2 + 40t + 20$ gives the rocket's height after t seconds. Factor this expression.
$-5(t^2 - 8t - 4)$

Also available on transparency

8-2 PROBLEM SOLVING

Write the correct answer.

1. The area of a rug, which is shaped like a rectangle, is $4x^2 + 4x$ square feet. Factor this polynomial to find expressions for the 17imensions of the rug.
$4x$ ft; $(x + 1)$ ft

2. The number of customers visiting a local museum since the year 2000 can be modeled by the expression $-3x^2 - 27x + 825$, where x is the number of years since 2000. Factor this polynomial.
$-3(x^2 + 9x - 275)$

3. The perimeter of a rhombus is $12x + 28$ feet. Factor this expression. Then find the length of one side if $x = 8$. (*Hint:* A rhombus is a parallelogram with four congruent sides.)
$4(3x + 7)$; 31 feet

4. The foundation for a new high school building is rectangular in shape, and the area is $5x^3 + 4x^2 - 10x - 8$ square meters. Factor by grouping to find expressions for the dimensions of the building.
$(5x + 4)$ m; $(x^2 - 2)$ m

The diagram shows four sections of an herb garden. Use the figure to answer questions 5–8. Select the best answer.

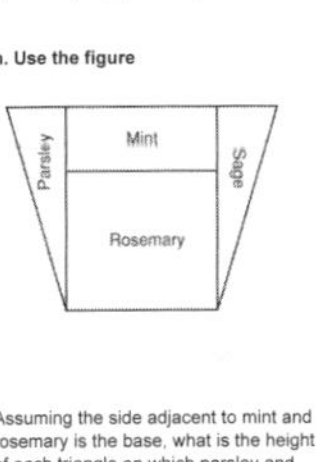

5. The section where rosemary grows is square and has an area of $4x^2$ square feet. What is the length of one side?
A x feet **C** $2x$ feet
B x^2 feet D $4x$ feet

6. Rosemary and mint cover $6x^2 - 2x$ square feet. Assuming the length is adjacent to rosemary, what is the width of the mint section?
F $2x$ feet H $2x - 2$ feet
G $x - 1$ feet J $3x - 1$ feet

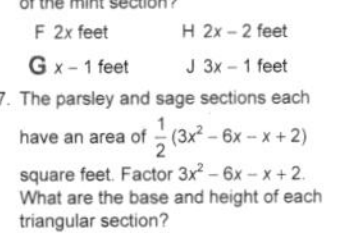

7. The parsley and sage sections each have an area of $\frac{1}{2}(3x^2 - 6x - x + 2)$ square feet. Factor $3x^2 - 6x - x + 2$. What are the base and height of each triangular section?
A $2x - 3$ feet; $x + 1$ feet
B $2x - 3$ feet; $x^2 + 1$ feet
C $3x - 1$ feet; $x - 2$ feet
D $3x - 1$ feet; $x^2 - 2$ feet

8. Assuming the side adjacent to mint and rosemary is the base, what is the height of each triangle on which parsley and sage grow?
F $x - 2$ feet
G $x + 1$ feet
H $x^2 + 1$ feet
J $2x$ feet

8-2 CHALLENGE

Factoring by grouping requires 4 or more terms. When a polynomial has 3 terms, it is possible to divide the middle term into two terms and factor by grouping. When deciding on which two terms to use, think of terms that will have a common factor with the first and last terms. If that pair doesn't work, change the order of the pairs, or try another pair.

$x^2 + \mathbf{10x} + 21$
$x^2 + \mathbf{3x} + \mathbf{7x} + 21$
$(x^2 + 3x) + (7x + 21)$
$x(x + 3) + 7(x + 3)$
$(x + 3)(x + 7)$

Divide the *b* term into two separate terms. Then factor by grouping.

1. $x^2 + 8x + 12$ **$(x + 6)(x + 2)$**
2. $x^2 - 13x + 42$ **$(x - 6)(x - 7)$**
3. $2x^2 + 13x + 21$ **$(2x + 7)(x + 3)$**
4. $10x^2 + 19x + 6$ **$(5x + 2)(2x + 3)$**
5. $5x^2 + 19x + 12$ **$(5x + 4)(x + 3)$**
6. $4x^2 - 16x + 15$ **$(2x - 5)(2x - 3)$**

When a polynomial has more than 4 terms, it is sometimes possible to factor by grouping.

$(x^3 + 4x^2) + (x^2 + 4x) + (3x + 12)$
$x^2(x + 4) + x(x + 4) + 3(x + 4)$
$(x + 4)(x^2 + x + 3)$

Factor by grouping.

7. $(x^3 + x^2) + (x^2 + x) + (x + 1)$ **$(x + 1)(x^2 + x + 1)$**
8. $(3x^3 - 6x^2) + (4x^2 - 8x) + (5x - 10)$ **$(x - 2)(3x^2 + 4x + 5)$**

Factor by grouping in groups of three. You may need to rearrange the terms.

9. $x^6 + 5x^5 + 7x^4 + 3x^2 + 15x + 21$
$(x^4 + 3)(x^2 + 5x + 7)$

10. $6x^{10} + 24x^9 + 48x^8 + 7x^6 + 28x^5 + 56x^4 + 3x^2 + 12x + 24$
$(6x^8 + 7x^4 + 3)(x^2 + 4x + 8)$

Organizer

Use with Lesson 8-3

Pacing:

Traditional $\frac{1}{2}$ day

Block $\frac{1}{4}$ day

Objective: Model and factor trinomials.

Materials: algebra tiles

Resources

Algebra Lab Activities

8-3 Lab Recording Sheet

Teach

Discuss

Remind students that a square is a rectangle, so their algebra tile (MK) arrangements may form a square.

In **Activity 2,** additional *x*-tiles were used because there were originally not enough to fill the empty spaces.

Alternative Approach

Use the transparency mat and transparency algebra tiles (MK).

Use with Lesson 8-3

Model Factorization of Trinomials

You can use algebra tiles to write a trinomial as a product of two binomials. This is called *factoring a trinomial.*

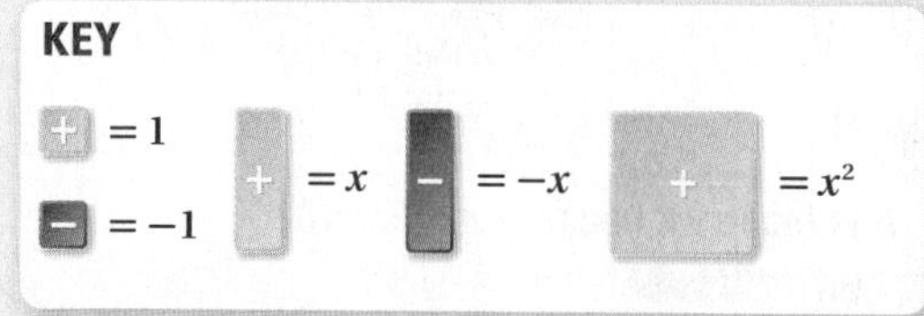

Activity 1

Use algebra tiles to factor $x^2 + 7x + 6$.

MODEL		ALGEBRA
	Model $x^2 + 7x + 6$.	$x^2 + 7x + 6$
	Try to arrange all of the tiles in a rectangle. Start by placing the x^2-tile in the upper left corner. *Arrange the unit tiles in a rectangle so that the top left corner of this rectangle touches the bottom right corner of the x^2-tile.* *Arrange the x-tiles so that all the tiles together make one large rectangle.* *This arrangement does not work because two x-tiles are left over.*	$x^2 + 7x + 6 \neq (x + 2)(x + 3)$
	Rearrange the unit tiles to form another rectangle. *Fill in the empty spaces with x-tiles. All 7 x-tiles fit. This is the correct arrangement.* *The total area represents the trinomial. The length and width represent the factors.*	$x^2 + 7x + 6 = (x + 1)(x + 6)$

The rectangle has width $x + 1$ and length $x + 6$. So $x^2 + 7x + 6 = (x + 1)(x + 6)$.

Answers to *Try This*

1. $(x + 1)(x + 1)$
2. $(x + 1)(x + 2)$
3. $(x + 1)(x + 5)$
4. $(x + 3)(x + 3)$
5. $(x + 1)(x + 4)$
6. $(x + 2)(x + 4)$
7. $(x + 2)(x + 3)$
8. $(x + 2)(x + 6)$

Try This

Use algebra tiles to factor each trinomial.

1. $x^2 + 2x + 1$ **2.** $x^2 + 3x + 2$ **3.** $x^2 + 6x + 5$ **4.** $x^2 + 6x + 9$

5. $x^2 + 5x + 4$ **6.** $x^2 + 6x + 8$ **7.** $x^2 + 5x + 6$ **8.** $x^2 + 8x + 12$

Activity 2

Use algebra tiles to factor $x^2 + x - 2$.

MODEL	ALGEBRA
Model $x^2 + x - 2$.	$x^2 + x - 2$
Start by placing the x^2-tile in the upper left corner. *Arrange the unit tiles in a rectangle so that the top left corner of this rectangle touches the bottom right corner of the x^2-tile.* *To make a rectangle, you need to fill in the empty spaces, but there aren't enough x-tiles to fill in the empty spaces.*	
Add a zero pair. Arrange the x-tiles to complete the rectangle. *Remember that the product of two positive values is positive and the product of a positive and a negative value is negative.*	
The total area represents the trinomial. The length and width represent the factors.	$x^2 + x - 2 = (x - 1)(x + 2)$

The rectangle has width $x - 1$ and length $x + 2$. So, $x^2 + x - 2 = (x - 1)(x + 2)$.

Try This

9. Why can you add one red $-x$-tile and one yellow x-tile?

Use algebra tiles to factor each trinomial.

10. $x^2 - x - 2$ **11.** $x^2 - 2x - 3$ **12.** $x^2 - 5x + 4$ **13.** $x^2 - 7x + 10$

14. $x^2 - 2x + 1$ **15.** $x^2 - 6x + 5$ **16.** $x^2 + 5x - 6$ **17.** $x^2 + 3x - 4$

18. $x^2 - x - 6$ **19.** $x^2 + 3x - 10$ **20.** $x^2 - 2x - 8$ **21.** $x^2 + x - 12$

Close

Key Concept

You can factor trinomials by arranging the tiles into a rectangle such that the x^2-tile is in the upper left, the unit tiles are in the lower right, and the x-tiles fill in the remaining spaces. The dimensions of the rectangle are the factors.

Assessment

Journal Have students explain how to model and factor trinomial expressions. Explanations should include what to do when there are not enough x-tiles to fill the empty spaces.

Answers to *Try This*

9. Adding $-x$ and x gives you 0, so if you add both tiles, you don't change the value of the polynomial.
10. $(x - 2)(x + 1)$
11. $(x - 3)(x + 1)$
12. $(x - 1)(x - 4)$
13. $(x - 2)(x - 5)$
14. $(x - 1)(x - 1)$
15. $(x - 1)(x - 5)$
16. $(x - 1)(x + 6)$
17. $(x - 1)(x + 4)$
18. $(x - 3)(x + 2)$
19. $(x - 2)(x + 5)$
20. $(x - 4)(x + 2)$
21. $(x - 3)(x + 4)$

Teacher to Teacher

I have found that using algebra tiles really helps students achieve success with algebraic concepts. Since students are already familiar with the area of rectangles, connecting the factors of a trinomial with the dimensions of a rectangle provides a comfortable introduction to factoring trinomials.

Make sure that everyone knows what to call each tile so that students can discuss the ideas constructively in class and with each other outside of class.

Vicki Petty
Murfreesboro, TN

8-3 Organizer

Pacing: Traditional 1 day
Block $\frac{1}{2}$ day

Objective: Factor quadratic trinomials of the form $x^2 + bx + c$.

Online Edition
Tutorial Videos, Interactivity

Countdown Week 18

Power Presentations with PowerPoint®

Warm Up

1. Which pair of factors of 8 has a sum of 9? 1 and 8
2. Which pair of factors of 30 has a sum of −17? −2 and −15

Multiply.

3. $(x + 2)(x + 3)$ $x^2 + 5x + 6$
4. $(r + 5)(r - 9)$ $r^2 - 4r - 45$

Also available on transparency

Math Humor

Q: What did the two binomials say when they were multiplied?

A: Curses! FOILed again!

8-3 Factoring $x^2 + bx + c$

Objective
Factor quadratic trinomials of the form $x^2 + bx + c$.

Why learn this?
Factoring polynomials will help you find the dimensions of rectangular shapes, such as a fountain. (See Exercise 71.)

In Chapter 7, you learned how to multiply two binomials using the Distributive Property or the FOIL method. In this lesson, you will learn how to factor a trinomial into two binomials.

Notice that when you multiply $(x + 2)(x + 5)$, the constant term in the trinomial is the product of the constants in the binomials.

$$(x + 2)(x + 5) = x^2 + 7x + 10$$

You can use this fact to factor a trinomial into its binomial factors. Look for two numbers that are factors of the constant term in the trinomial. Write two binomials with those numbers, and then multiply to see if you are correct.

Remember!
When you multiply two binomials, multiply:
First terms
Outer terms
Inner terms
Last terms

EXAMPLE 1 Factoring Trinomials by Guess and Check

Factor $x^2 + 19x + 60$ by guess and check.

$(\blacksquare + \blacksquare)(\blacksquare + \blacksquare)$ *Write two sets of parentheses.*

$(x + \blacksquare)(x + \blacksquare)$ *The first term is x^2, so the variable terms have a coefficient of 1.*

The constant term in the trinomial is 60.

Try factors of 60 for the constant terms in the binomials.

$(x + 1)(x + 60) = x^2 + 61x + 60$ ✗

$(x + 2)(x + 30) = x^2 + 32x + 60$ ✗

$(x + 3)(x + 20) = x^2 + 23x + 60$ ✗

$(x + 4)(x + 15) = x^2 + 19x + 60$ ✓

The factors of $x^2 + 19x + 60$ are $(x + 4)$ and $(x + 15)$.

$x^2 + 19x + 60 = (x + 4)(x + 15)$

Factor each trinomial by guess and check.

1a. $x^2 + 10x + 24$ **1a.** $(x + 4)(x + 6)$

1b. $x^2 + 7x + 12$ $(x + 4)(x + 3)$

State Resources

go.hrw.com
State Resources Online
KEYWORD: MA7 Resources

1 Introduce

EXPLORATION

8-3 Factoring $x^2 + bx + c$

Look for patterns as you multiply binomials. The patterns that you discover will help you factor trinomials.

1. Complete the table by multiplying the binomial factors. Be sure to write the products as trinomials in the form $x^2 + bx + c$.

Factors	Product
$(x + 2)(x + 4)$	
$(x + 5)(x + 3)$	
$(x + 3)(x - 7)$	
$(x - 5)(x + 2)$	
$(x - 5)(x - 9)$	

2. Look at the constant terms of the trinomials. How are these related to the constant terms of the binomial factors?
3. Look at the coefficients of the middle terms of the trinomials. How are these related to the constant terms of the binomial factors?

THINK AND DISCUSS

4. **Discuss** what you know about the constant terms of the binomial factors of $x^2 + 10x + 24$.
5. **Explain** how you know that $(x + 12)(x + 2)$ is not a correct factorization of $x^2 + 10x + 24$.

Motivate

Ask students when they have seen inverse operations—for example, addition and subtraction, multiplication and division, squaring a number and finding its square root. Tell students that in this lesson, they will learn how to undo binomial multiplication by factoring.

Explorations and answers are provided in *Alternate Openers: Explorations Transparencies.*

The guess and check method is usually not the most efficient method of factoring a trinomial. Look at the product of $(x + 3)$ and $(x + 4)$.

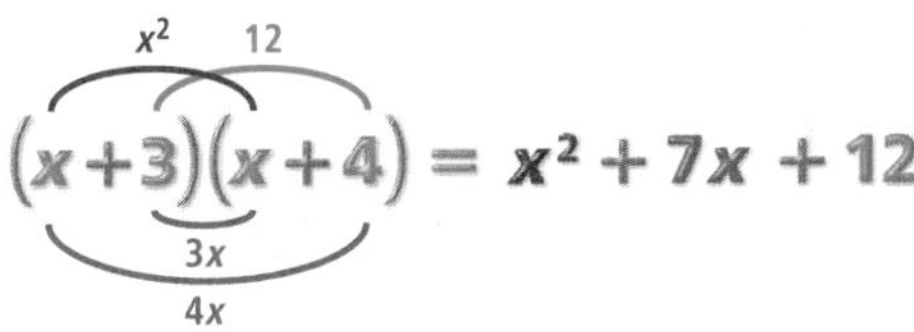

The coefficient of the middle term is the sum of 3 and 4. The third term is the product of 3 and 4.

Factoring $x^2 + bx + c$

WORDS	EXAMPLE
To factor a quadratic trinomial of the form $x^2 + bx + c$, find two factors of c whose sum is b. If no such integers exist, the trinomial is not factorable.	To factor $x^2 + 9x + 18$, look for factors of 18 whose sum is 9.

Factors of 18	Sum	
1 and 18	19 ✗	
2 and 9	11 ✗	
3 and 6	9 ✓	$x^2 + 9x + 18 = (x + 3)(x + 6)$

When c is positive, its factors have the same sign. The sign of b tells you whether the factors are positive or negative. When b is positive, the factors are positive, and when b is negative, the factors are negative.

EXAMPLE 2 Factoring $x^2 + bx + c$ When c Is Positive

Factor each trinomial. Check your answer.

A $x^2 + 6x + 8$

$(x + \blacksquare)(x + \blacksquare)$ *$b = 6$ and $c = 8$; look for factors of 8 whose sum is 6.*

Factors of 8	Sum	
1 and 8	9	✗
2 and 4	6	✓

The factors needed are 2 and 4.

$(x + 2)(x + 4)$

Check $(x + 2)(x + 4) = x^2 + 4x + 2x + 8$ *Use the FOIL method.*

$= x^2 + 6x + 8$ ✓ *The product is the original polynomial.*

B $x^2 + 5x + 6$

$(x + \blacksquare)(x + \blacksquare)$ *$b = 5$ and $c = 6$; look for factors of 6 whose sum is 5.*

Factors of 6	Sum	
1 and 6	7	✗
2 and 3	5	✓

The factors needed are 2 and 3.

$(x + 2)(x + 3)$

Use the FOIL method.

Check $(x + 2)(x + 3) = x^2 + 3x + 2x + 6$

$= x^2 + 5x + 6$ ✓ *The product is the original polynomial.*

Power Presentations with PowerPoint®

Additional Examples

Example 1

Factor $x^2 + 15x + 36$.
$(x + 3)(x + 12)$

Example 2

Factor each trinomial. Check your answer.

A. $x^2 + 6x + 5$ $(x + 1)(x + 5)$

B. $x^2 + 6x + 9$ $(x + 3)(x + 3)$

C. $x^2 - 8x + 15$ $(x - 3)(x - 5)$

INTERVENTION

Questioning Strategies

EXAMPLE 1

- For which number do you try different pairs of factors?

EXAMPLE 2

- What does the sign of c tell you about the factors?
- What does the sign of b tell you about the factors?

Visual Suggest that students write down what the product of the two constants in the binomials should be and what their sum should be. They can write "P": and "S": next to the trinomial as a reminder to themselves.

$x^2 + 13x + 36$ P: 36
S: 13

2 Teach

Guided Instruction

Review the FOIL method before factoring any trinomials. Remind students that the FOIL method is an application of the Distributive Property. Have students examine the product of two binomials, such as $(x + 2)(x + 3) = x^2 + 5x + 6$, and discuss where each term in the trinomial came from. Lead them to see that $5x$ came from the sum of like terms $2x$ and $3x$ and that 6 came from the product of constants 2 and 3.

Reaching All Learners

Through Graphic Organizers

Have students make a chart like the one below, filling in their own examples. Then have students factor each example.

b	c	Example	Sign of Factors	Factors
+	+	$x^2 + 5x + 4$	Both positive	$(x + 1)(x + 4)$
–	+	$n^2 - 6n + 8$	Both negative	$(n - 2)(n - 4)$
–	–	$t^2 - t - 6$	Factor with greater abs. val. is negative.	$(t - 3)(t + 2)$
+	–	$q^2 + 3q - 18$	Factor with greater abs. val. is positive.	$(q + 6)(q - 3)$

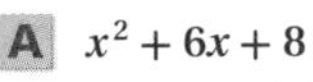

Power Presentations with PowerPoint®

Additional Examples

Example 3

Factor each trinomial.

A. $x^2 + x - 20$ $(x + 5)(x - 4)$

B. $x^2 - 3x - 18$ $(x - 6)(x + 3)$

INTERVENTION

Questioning Strategies

EXAMPLE 3

- How are these problems like those in **Example 2**?
- How do you know which factor will be positive and which will be negative?

Teaching Tip **Inclusion** As students begin to factor trinomials in which c is negative, remind them that the absolute value of a number is the number's distance from 0 on a number line.

Factor each trinomial. Check your answer.

C $x^2 - 10x + 16$

$(x + \square)(x + \square)$ — *$b = -10$ and $c = 16$; look for factors of 16 whose sum is -10.*

Factors of 16	Sum	
-1 and -16	-17	✗
-2 and -8	-10	✓

The factors needed are -2 and -8.

$(x - 2)(x - 8)$

Check $(x - 2)(x - 8) = x^2 - 8x - 2x + 16$ — *Use the FOIL method.*

$= x^2 - 10x + 16$ ✓ — *The product is the original polynomial.*

Factor each trinomial. Check your answer.

2a. $x^2 + 8x + 12$ $(x + 6)(x + 2)$ **2b.** $x^2 - 5x + 6$ $(x - 2)(x - 3)$

2c. $x^2 + 13x + 42$ $(x + 6)(x + 7)$ **2d.** $x^2 - 13x + 40$ $(x - 8)(x - 5)$

When c is negative, its factors have opposite signs. The sign of b tells you which factor is positive and which is negative. The factor with the greater absolute value has the same sign as b.

EXAMPLE 3 Factoring $x^2 + bx + c$ When c Is Negative

Factor each trinomial.

A $x^2 + 7x - 18$

$(x + \square)(x + \square)$ — *$b = 7$ and $c = -18$; look for factors of -18 whose sum is 7. The factor with the greater absolute value is positive.*

Factors of -18	Sum	
-1 and 18	17	✗
-2 and 9	7	✓

The factors needed are -2 and 9.

$(x - 2)(x + 9)$

B $x^2 - 5x - 24$

$(x + \square)(x + \square)$ — *$b = -5$ and $c = -24$; look for factors of -24 whose sum is -5. The factor with the greater absolute value is negative.*

Factors of -24	Sum	
1 and -24	-23	✗
2 and -12	-10	✗
3 and -8	-5	✓

The factors needed are 3 and -8.

$(x + 3)(x - 8)$

Helpful Hint

If you have trouble remembering the rules for which factor is positive and which is negative, you can try all the factor pairs and check their sums.

Factor each trinomial. Check your answer.

3a. $x^2 + 2x - 15$ **3b.** $x^2 - 6x + 8$ **3c.** $x^2 - 8x - 20$ $(x - 10)(x + 2)$

3a. $(x + 5)(x - 3)$

3b. $(x - 4)(x - 2)$

Answer to *Check It Out*

4.

n	$n^2 - 7n + 10$	$(n - 5)(n - 2)$
0	$0^2 - 7(0) + 10 = 10$	$(0 - 5)(0 - 2) = 10$
1	$1^2 - 7(1) + 10 = 4$	$(1 - 5)(1 - 2) = 4$
2	$2^2 - 7(2) + 10 = 0$	$(2 - 5)(2 - 2) = 0$
3	$3^2 - 7(3) + 10 = -2$	$(3 - 5)(3 - 2) = -2$
4	$4^2 - 7(4) + 10 = -2$	$(4 - 5)(4 - 2) = -2$

A polynomial and the factored form of the polynomial are equivalent expressions. When you evaluate these two expressions for the same value of the variable, the results are the same.

EXAMPLE 4 Evaluating Polynomials

Factor $n^2 + 11n + 24$. Show that the original polynomial and the factored form have the same value for $n = 0, 1, 2, 3,$ and 4.

$n^2 + 11n + 24$

$(n + \square)(n + \square)$ — *$b = 11$ and $c = 24$; look for factors of 24 whose sum is 11.*

Factors of 24	Sum	
1 and 24	25	✗
2 and 12	14	✗
3 and 8	11	✓

The factors needed are 3 and 8.

$(n + 3)(n + 8)$

Evaluate the original polynomial and the factored form for $n = 0, 1, 2, 3,$ and 4.

n	$n^2 + 11n + 24$
0	$0^2 + 11(0) + 24 = 24$
1	$1^2 + 11(1) + 24 = 36$
2	$2^2 + 11(2) + 24 = 50$
3	$3^2 + 11(3) + 24 = 66$
4	$4^2 + 11(4) + 24 = 84$

n	$(n + 3)(n + 8)$
0	$(0 + 3)(0 + 8) = 24$
1	$(1 + 3)(1 + 8) = 36$
2	$(2 + 3)(2 + 8) = 50$
3	$(3 + 3)(3 + 8) = 66$
4	$(4 + 3)(4 + 8) = 84$

The original polynomial and the factored form have the same value for the given values of n.

4. Factor $n^2 - 7n + 10$. Show that the original polynomial and the factored form have the same value for $n = 0, 1, 2, 3,$ and 4. $(n - 5)(n - 2)$

THINK AND DISCUSS

1. Explain in your own words how to factor $x^2 + 9x + 14$. Show how to check your answer.

2. Explain how you can determine the signs of the factors of c when factoring a trinomial of the form $x^2 + bx + c$.

3. GET ORGANIZED Copy and complete the graphic organizer. In each box, write an example of a trinomial with the given properties and factor it.

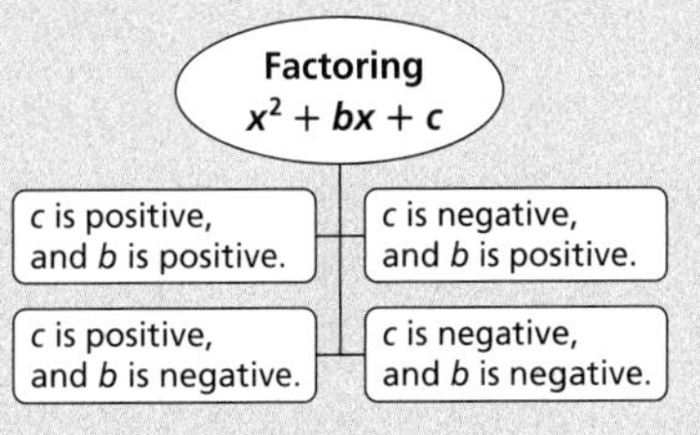

COMMON ERROR ALERT

When factoring a trinomial with a negative c, students may write a minus sign in the binomial factor with the greater constant term. Remind students that the binomial factor with the greater constant term should have the same sign as b.

Power Presentations with PowerPoint®

Additional Examples

Example 4

Factor $y^2 + 10y + 21$. Show that the original polynomial and the factored form have the same value for $y = 0, 1, 2, 3,$ and 4. $(y + 7)(y + 3)$

y	$y^2 + 10y + 21$
0	$0^2 + 10(0) + 21 = 21$
1	$1^2 + 10(1) + 21 = 32$
2	$2^2 + 10(2) + 21 = 45$
3	$3^2 + 10(3) + 21 = 60$
4	$4^2 + 10(4) + 21 = 77$

y	$(y + 7)(y + 3)$
0	$(0 + 7)(0 + 3) = 21$
1	$(1 + 7)(1 + 3) = 32$
2	$(2 + 7)(2 + 3) = 45$
3	$(3 + 7)(3 + 3) = 60$
4	$(4 + 7)(4 + 3) = 77$

INTERVENTION

Questioning Strategies

EXAMPLE 4

- How would you know if the trinomial was not factored correctly?

3 Close

Summarize

Review with students how to factor trinomials of all four types: two cases when c is positive and two cases when c is negative.

ONGOING ASSESSMENT and INTERVENTION

***Diagnose Before* the Lesson**
8-3 Warm Up, TE p. 560

***Monitor During* the Lesson**
Check It Out! Exercises, SE pp. 560–563
Questioning Strategies, TE pp. 561–563

***Assess After* the Lesson**
8-3 Lesson Quiz, TE p. 567
Alternative Assessment, TE p. 567

Answers to *Think and Discuss*

Possible answers:

1. Find the 2 factors of 14 that have a sum of 9: 2 and 7. Then use these numbers as the constants in the factors: $(x + 2)(x + 7)$.
2. For $x^2 + bx + c = (x + m)(x + n)$, if $c > 0$ and $b > 0$, $m > 0$ and $n > 0$. If $c > 0$ and $b < 0$, $m < 0$ and $n < 0$. If $c < 0$ and $b > 0$, the greater of m and n is positive and the lesser is negative. If $c < 0$ and $b < 0$, the greater of m and n is negative and the lesser is positive.
3. See p. A7.

8-3 Exercises

Assignment Guide

Assign *Guided Practice* exercises as necessary.

If you finished Examples **1–2**
Basic 17–25, 52, 55, 60, 70
Average 17–25, 60, 70, 71, 77
Advanced 17–25, 70, 71, 77, 83

If you finished Examples **1–4**
Basic 17–36, 51–66, 73–76, 86–94
Average 17–50, 53, 62–76, 77–83 odd, 86–94
Advanced 17–32, 37, 51–57 odd, 62–94

Homework Quick Check
Quickly check key concepts.
Exercises: 18, 22, 30, 32, 53, 60

Answers

4. $(x + 1)(x + 3)$
5. $(x + 2)(x + 8)$
6. $(x + 4)(x + 11)$
7. $(x - 1)(x - 6)$
8. $(x - 2)(x - 7)$
9. $(x - 3)(x - 8)$
10. $(x - 7)(x + 1)$
11. $(x + 9)(x - 3)$
12. $(x + 6)(x - 5)$
13. $(x - 2)(x + 1)$
14. $(x - 6)(x + 3)$
15. $(x - 9)(x + 5)$
16. $(n + 7)(n - 1)$; for table see p. A28.
20. $(x + 1)(x + 11)$
21. $(x + 2)(x + 14)$

22–32, 38–50. See p. A28.

State Resources

go.hrw.com
State Resources Online
KEYWORD: MA7 Resources

8-3 Exercises

go.hrw.com
Homework Help Online
KEYWORD: MA7 8-3
Parent Resources Online
KEYWORD: MA7 Parent

GUIDED PRACTICE

SEE EXAMPLE 1 p. 560

Factor each trinomial by guess and check.

1. $x^2 + 13x + 36$ $(x + 4)(x + 9)$
2. $x^2 + 11x + 24$ $(x + 3)(x + 8)$
3. $x^2 + 14x + 40$ $(x + 4)(x + 10)$

SEE EXAMPLE 2 p. 561

Factor each trinomial. Check your answer.

4. $x^2 + 4x + 3$
5. $x^2 + 10x + 16$
6. $x^2 + 15x + 44$
7. $x^2 - 7x + 6$
8. $x^2 - 9x + 14$
9. $x^2 - 11x + 24$

SEE EXAMPLE 3 p. 562

10. $x^2 - 6x - 7$
11. $x^2 + 6x - 27$
12. $x^2 + x - 30$
13. $x^2 - x - 2$
14. $x^2 - 3x - 18$
15. $x^2 - 4x - 45$

SEE EXAMPLE 4 p. 563

16. Factor $n^2 + 6n - 7$. Show that the original polynomial and the factored form have the same value for $n = 0, 1, 2, 3,$ and 4.

PRACTICE AND PROBLEM SOLVING

Independent Practice

For Exercises	See Example
17–19	1
20–25	2
26–31	3
32	4

Extra Practice
Skills Practice p. S18
Application Practice p. S35

Factor each trinomial by guess and check.

17. $x^2 + 13x + 30$ $(x + 3)(x + 10)$
18. $x^2 + 11x + 28$ $(x + 4)(x + 7)$
19. $x^2 + 16x + 48$ $(x + 4)(x + 12)$

Factor each trinomial. Check your answer.

20. $x^2 + 12x + 11$
21. $x^2 + 16x + 28$
22. $x^2 + 15x + 36$
23. $x^2 - 6x + 5$
24. $x^2 - 9x + 18$
25. $x^2 - 12x + 32$
26. $x^2 + x - 12$
27. $x^2 + 4x - 21$
28. $x^2 + 9x - 36$
29. $x^2 - 12x - 13$
30. $x^2 - 10x - 24$
31. $x^2 - 2x - 35$
32. Factor $n^2 - 12n - 45$. Show that the original polynomial and the factored form have the same value for $n = 0, 1, 2, 3,$ and 4.

Match each trinomial with its correct factorization.

33. $x^2 + 3x - 10$ **C**
34. $x^2 - 7x + 10$ **A**
35. $x^2 - 9x - 10$ **D**
36. $x^2 + 11x + 10$ **B**

A. $(x - 2)(x - 5)$
B. $(x + 1)(x + 10)$
C. $(x - 2)(x + 5)$
D. $(x + 1)(x - 10)$

37. **Write About It** Compare multiplying binomials with factoring polynomials into binomial factors. **They are inverse operations.**

Factor each trinomial. Check your answer.

38. $x^2 + x - 20$
39. $x^2 - 11x + 18$
40. $x^2 - 4x - 21$
41. $x^2 + 10x + 9$
42. $x^2 - 12x + 32$
43. $x^2 + 13x + 42$
44. $x^2 - 7x + 12$
45. $x^2 + 11x + 18$
46. $x^2 - 6x - 27$
47. $x^2 + 5x - 24$
48. $x^2 - 10x + 21$
49. $x^2 + 4x - 45$
50. Factor $n^2 + 11n + 28$. Show that the original polynomial and the factored form have the same value for $n = 0, 1, 2, 3,$ and 4.

51. **Estimation** The graph shows the areas of rectangles with dimensions $(x + 1)$ yards and $(x + 2)$ yards. Estimate the value of x for a rectangle with area 9 square yards. **approximately 1.5**

52. **Geometry** The area of a rectangle in square feet can be represented by $x^2 + 8x + 12$. The length is $(x + 6)$ ft. What is the width of the rectangle? $\mathbf{(x + 2)}$ **ft**

Area (yd²) vs. x-values graph: Area axis 0, 10, 20, 30, 40; x-values 1, 2, 3, 4.

53. **Remodeling** A homeowner wants to enlarge a rectangular closet that has an area of $(x^2 + 3x + 2)$ ft². The length is $(x + 2)$ ft. After construction, the area will be $(x^2 + 8x + 15)$ ft² with a length of $(x + 3)$ ft.

a. Find the dimensions of the closet before construction.

b. Find the dimensions of the closet after construction.

c. By how many feet will the length and width increase after construction? **The length will increase by 1 ft. The width will increase by 4 ft.**

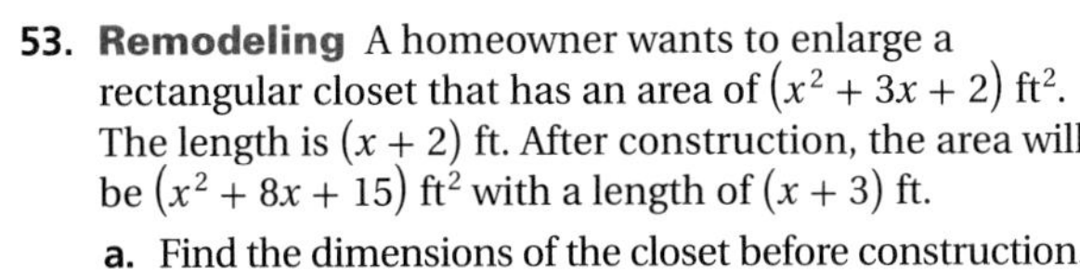

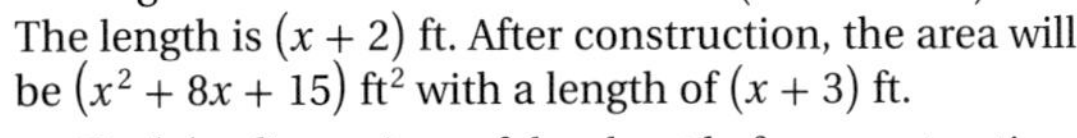

LINK **Art**

The Dutch painter Theo van Doesburg (1883–1931) is most famous for his paintings composed of lines and rectangles, such as the one shown above.

Art Write the polynomial modeled and then factor.

54. 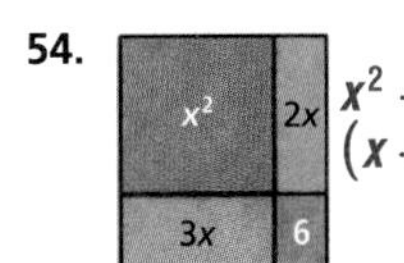

$x^2 + 5x + 6$; $(x + 3)(x + 2)$

55. 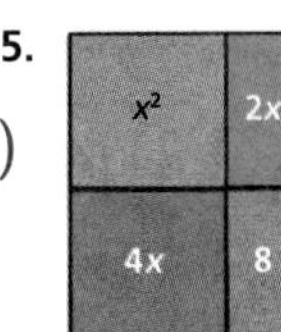

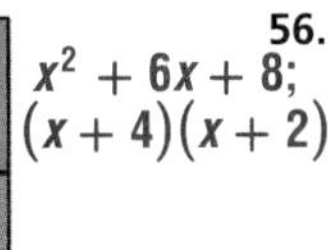
$x^2 + 6x + 8$; $(x + 4)(x + 2)$

56. 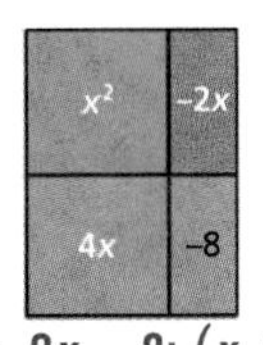

$x^2 + 2x - 8$; $(x + 4)(x - 2)$

Copy and complete the table.

	$x^2 + bx + c$	Sign of c	Binomial Factors	Signs of Numbers in Binomials
	$x^2 + 4x + 3$	Positive	$(x + 1)(x + 3)$	Both positive
57.	$x^2 - 4x + 3$	**Pos.**	$(x - 1)(x - 3)$	**Both neg.**
58.	$x^2 + 2x - 3$	**Neg.**	$(x - 1)(x + 3)$	**Neg.; pos.**
59.	$x^2 - 2x - 3$	**Neg.**	$(x + 1)(x - 3)$	**Pos.; neg.**

60. **Geometry** A rectangle has area $x^2 + 6x + 8$. The length is $x + 4$. Find the width of the rectangle. Could the rectangle be a square? Explain why or why not. $\mathbf{x + 2}$**; no; Possible answer:** $\mathbf{2 \neq 4}$ **so** $\mathbf{x + 2 \neq x + 4}$

61. This problem will prepare you for the Multi-Step Test Prep on page 576.

The equation for the motion of an object with constant acceleration is $d = vt + \frac{1}{2}at^2$ where d is distance traveled in feet, v is starting velocity in feet per second, a is acceleration in feet per second squared, and t is time in seconds.

a. Janna has two toy race cars on a track. One starts with a velocity of 0 ft/s and accelerates at 2 ft/s². Write an equation for the distance the car travels in time t. **a.** $\mathbf{d = t^2}$

b. The second car travels at a constant speed of 4 ft/s. Write an equation for the distance the second car travels in time t. (*Hint:* When speed is constant, the acceleration is 0 ft/s².) $\mathbf{d = 4t}$

c. By setting the equations equal to each other you can determine when the cars have traveled the same distance: $t^2 = 4t$. This can be written as $t^2 - 4t = 0$. Factor the left side of the equation. $\mathbf{t(t - 4)}$

COMMON ERROR ALERT

Students might assign the larger value to length in part **b** of **Exercise 53.** This would yield a remodeled length of $x + 5$. Students may then carry the error over into part **c,** answering that length changed by 3 and width changed by 2. Tell students to read the problem carefully. Draw their attention to the last line. The problem clearly states that the new length is $x + 3$, so the new *width* is $x + 5$.

Answers

53a. length: $(x + 2)$ ft; width: $(x + 1)$ ft

b. length: $(x + 3)$ ft; width: $(x + 5)$ ft

Exercise 61 involves using the equation $d = vt + \frac{1}{2}at^2$ to calculate when two moving objects will be at the same location. This exercise prepares students for the Multi-Step Test Prep on page 576.

8-3 PRACTICE A

8-3 PRACTICE C

8-3 PRACTICE B

Factor each trinomial.

1. $x^2 + 7x + 10$ — $(x + 2)(x + 5)$
2. $x^2 + 9x + 8$ — $(x + 1)(x + 8)$
3. $x^2 + 13x + 36$ — $(x + 4)(x + 9)$
4. $x^2 + 9x + 14$ — $(x + 7)(x + 2)$
5. $x^2 + 7x + 12$ — $(x + 3)(x + 4)$
6. $x^2 + 9x + 18$ — $(x + 6)(x + 3)$
7. $x^2 - 9x + 18$ — $(x - 6)(x - 3)$
8. $x^2 - 5x + 4$ — $(x - 4)(x - 1)$
9. $x^2 - 9x + 20$ — $(x - 5)(x - 4)$
10. $x^2 - 12x + 20$ — $(x - 2)(x - 10)$
11. $x^2 - 11x + 18$ — $(x - 9)(x - 2)$
12. $x^2 - 12x + 32$ — $(x - 8)(x - 4)$
13. $x^2 + 7x - 18$ — $(x + 9)(x - 2)$
14. $x^2 + 10x - 24$ — $(x + 12)(x - 2)$
15. $x^2 + 2x - 3$ — $(x + 3)(x - 1)$
16. $x^2 + 2x - 15$ — $(x + 5)(x - 3)$
17. $x^2 + 5x - 6$ — $(x + 6)(x - 1)$
18. $x^2 + 5x - 24$ — $(x + 8)(x - 3)$
19. $x^2 - 5x - 6$ — $(x + 1)(x - 6)$
20. $x^2 - 2x - 35$ — $(x + 5)(x - 7)$
21. $x^2 - 7x - 30$ — $(x + 3)(x - 10)$
22. $x^2 - x - 56$ — $(x + 7)(x - 8)$
23. $x^2 - 2x - 8$ — $(x + 2)(x - 4)$
24. $x^2 - x - 20$ — $(x + 4)(x - 5)$

25. Factor $n^2 + 5n - 24$. Show that the original polynomial and the factored form describe the same sequence of numbers for $n = 0, 1, 2, 3$, and 4. $(n + 8)(n - 3)$

n	$n^2 + 5n - 24$
0	$0^2 + 5(0) - 24 = -24$
1	$1^2 + 5(1) - 24 = -18$
2	$2^2 + 5(2) - 24 = -10$
3	$3^2 + 5(3) - 24 = 0$
4	$4^2 + 5(4) - 24 = 12$

n	$(n + 8)(n - 3)$
0	$(0 + 8)(0 - 3) = -24$
1	$(1 + 8)(1 - 3) = -18$
2	$(2 + 8)(2 - 3) = -10$
3	$(3 + 8)(3 - 3) = 0$
4	$(4 + 8)(4 - 3) = 12$

Test Prep Doctor Some students will be drawn to choice **A** for **Exercise 73** because $-4 + -6 = -10$. Remind them that the product of two negative numbers is positive.

Critical Thinking Have students substitute a single variable for the common binomial expression in **Exercises 80** and **82**. Then, when they have factored the trinomial, they can substitute the binomial expression back in for the single variable.

Answers

64. The correct factorization is $(x-1)(x+2)$.
65. The correct factorization is $(x-4)(x+1)$.
66. Many trinomials cannot be factored.
77. $(x^2+9)(x^2+9)$
78. $(y^2-8)(y^2+3)$
79. $(d^2+21)(d^2+1)$
80. $(u+v+3)(u+v-1)$
81. $(de-5)(de+4)$
82. $(m-n-9)(m-n+5)$

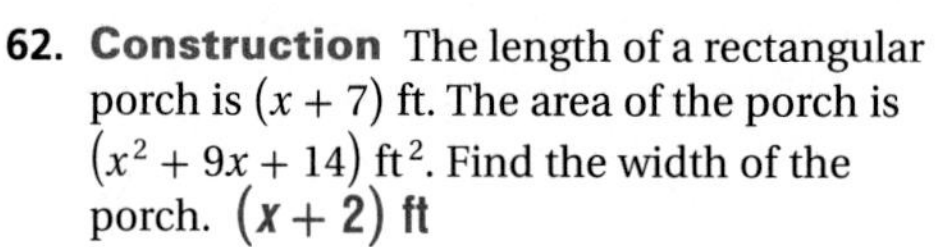

62. **Construction** The length of a rectangular porch is $(x+7)$ ft. The area of the porch is $(x^2+9x+14)$ ft^2. Find the width of the porch. **$(x+2)$ ft**

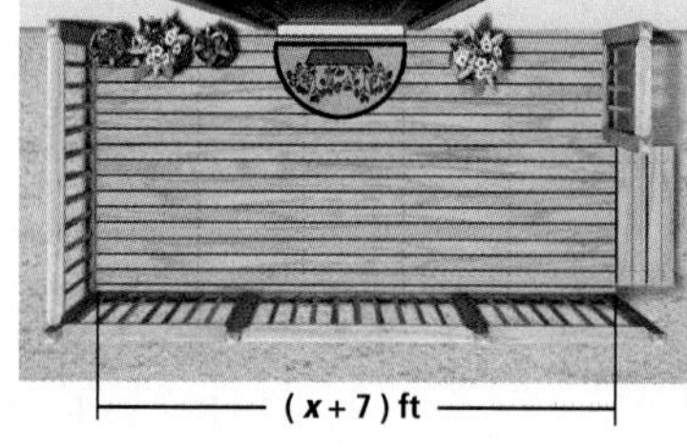

Tell whether each statement is true or false. If false, explain.

63. The third term in a factorable trinomial is equal to the product of the constants in its binomial factors. **true**
64. The constants in the binomial factors of x^2+x-2 are both negative. **false**
65. The correct factorization of x^2-3x-4 is $(x+4)(x-1)$. **false**
66. All trinomials of the form x^2+bx+c can be factored. **false**

Fill in the missing part of each factorization.

67. $x^2-6x+8=(x-2)(x-\boxed{4})$
68. $x^2-2x-8=(x+2)(x-\boxed{4})$
69. $x^2+2x-8=(x-2)(x+\boxed{4})$
70. $x^2+6x+8=(x+2)(x+\boxed{4})$

71. **Construction** The area of a rectangular fountain is $(x^2+12x+20)$ ft^2. The width is $(x+2)$ ft.
    a. Find the length of the fountain. **$(x+10)$ ft**
    b. A 2-foot walkway is built around the fountain. Find the dimensions of the outside border of the walkway. **$\ell=(x+14)$ ft; $w=(x+6)$ ft**
    c. Find the total area covered by the fountain and walkway. **$A=(x^2+20x+84)$ ft^2**

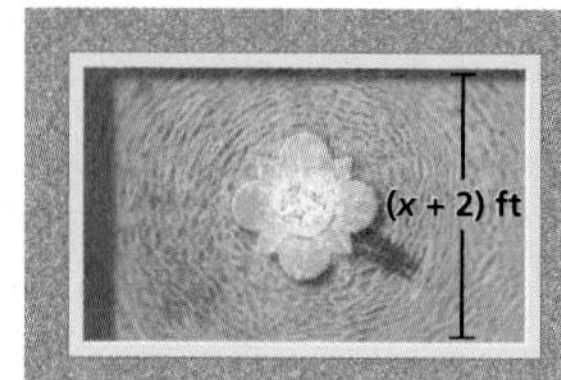

72. **Critical Thinking** Find all possible values of b so that x^2+bx+6 can be factored into binomial factors. **7, 5, −7, −5**

Test Prep

73. Which is the correct factorization of $x^2-10x-24$?
    (A) $(x-4)(x-6)$ (B) $(x+4)(x-6)$ (C) $(x-2)(x+12)$ **(D) $(x+2)(x-12)$**
74. Which value of b would make $x^2+bx-20$ factorable?
    (F) 9 (G) 12 **(H) 19** (J) 21
75. Which value of b would NOT make $x^2+bx-36$ factorable?
    (A) 5 (B) 9 **(C) 15** (D) 16
76. **Short Response** What are the factors of $x^2+2x-24$? Show and explain each step of factoring the polynomial. **$(x+6)(x-4)$**

Challenge and Extend

Factor each expression.

77. x^4+18x^2+81
78. y^4-5y^2-24
79. d^4+22d^2+21
80. $(u+v)^2+2(u+v)-3$
81. $(de)^2-(de)-20$
82. $(m-n)^2-4(m-n)-45$

566 *Chapter 8 Factoring Polynomials*

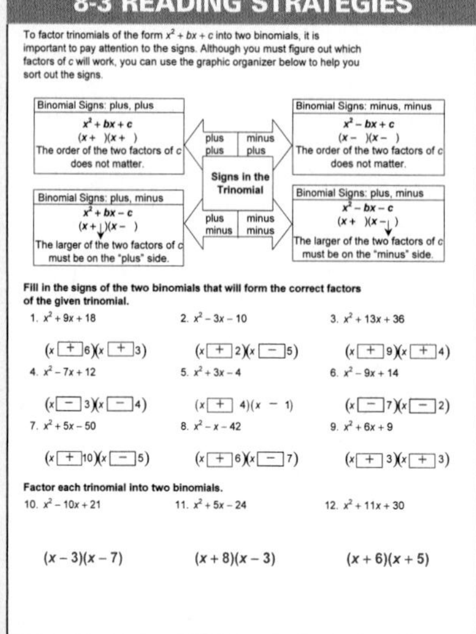

8-3 Reading Strategies

To factor trinomials of the form x^2+bx+c into two binomials, it is important to pay attention to the signs. Although you must figure out which factors of c will work, you can use the graphic organizer below to help you sort out the signs.

Binomial Signs: plus, plus
x^2+bx+c
$(x+\ )(x+\ )$
The order of the two factors of c does not matter.

Binomial Signs: minus, minus
x^2-bx+c
$(x-\ )(x-\ )$
The order of the two factors of c does not matter.

Signs in the Trinomial: plus plus | minus plus | plus minus | minus minus

Binomial Signs: plus, minus
x^2+bx-c
$(x+\ )(x-\ )$
The larger of the two factors of c must be on the "plus" side.

Binomial Signs: plus, minus
x^2-bx-c
$(x+\ )(x-\ )$
The larger of the two factors of c must be on the "minus" side.

Fill in the signs of the two binomials that will form the correct factors of the given trinomial.

1. $x^2+9x+18$ $(x\boxed{+}6)(x\boxed{+}3)$
2. $x^2-3x-10$ $(x\boxed{+}2)(x\boxed{-}5)$
3. $x^2+13x+36$ $(x\boxed{+}9)(x\boxed{+}4)$
4. $x^2-7x+12$ $(x\boxed{-}3)(x\boxed{-}4)$
5. x^2+3x-4 $(x\boxed{+}4)(x-1)$
6. $x^2-9x+14$ $(x\boxed{-}7)(x\boxed{-}2)$
7. $x^2+5x-50$ $(x\boxed{+}10)(x\boxed{-}5)$
8. x^2-x-42 $(x\boxed{+}6)(x\boxed{-}7)$
9. x^2+6x+9 $(x\boxed{+}3)(x\boxed{+}3)$

Factor each trinomial into two binomials.

10. $x^2-10x+21$ $(x-3)(x-7)$
11. $x^2+5x-24$ $(x+8)(x-3)$
12. $x^2+11x+30$ $(x+6)(x+5)$

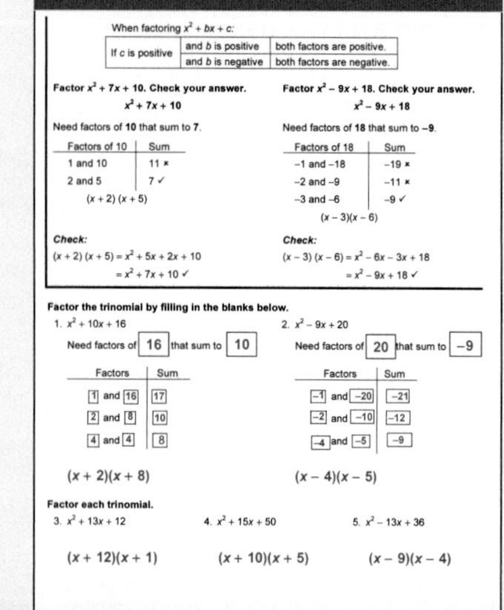

8-3 Reteach

When factoring x^2+bx+c:

If c is positive	and b is positive	both factors are positive.
	and b is negative	both factors are negative.

Factor $x^2+7x+10$. Check your answer.

$x^2+7x+10$

Need factors of **10** that sum to **7**.

Factors of 10	Sum
1 and 10	11 ×
2 and 5	7 ✓

$(x+2)(x+5)$

Check:
$(x+2)(x+5)=x^2+5x+2x+10$
$=x^2+7x+10$ ✓

Factor $x^2-9x+18$. Check your answer.

$x^2-9x+18$

Need factors of **18** that sum to **−9**.

Factors of 18	Sum
−1 and −18	−19 ×
−2 and −9	−11 ×
−3 and −6	−9 ✓

$(x-3)(x-6)$

Check:
$(x-3)(x-6)=x^2-6x-3x+18$
$=x^2-9x+18$ ✓

Factor the trinomial by filling in the blanks below.

1. $x^2+10x+16$
Need factors of $\boxed{16}$ that sum to $\boxed{10}$

Factors	Sum
1 and 16	17
2 and 8	10
4 and 4	8

$(x+2)(x+8)$

2. $x^2-9x+20$
Need factors of $\boxed{20}$ that sum to $\boxed{-9}$

Factors	Sum
−1 and −20	−21
−2 and −10	−12
−4 and −5	−9

$(x-4)(x-5)$

Factor each trinomial.

3. $x^2+13x+12$ $(x+12)(x+1)$
4. $x^2+15x+50$ $(x+10)(x+5)$
5. $x^2-13x+36$ $(x-9)(x-4)$

83. Find all possible values of b such that, when $x^2 + bx + 28$ is factored, both constants in the binomials are positive. **16; 11; 29**

84. Find all possible values of b such that, when $x^2 + bx + 32$ is factored, both constants in the binomials are negative. **−33; −18; −12**

85. The area of Beth's rectangular garden is $(x^2 + 13x + 42)$ ft². The width is $(x + 6)$ ft.

Item	Cost
Fertilizer	0.28 ($/ft²)
Fencing	2.00 ($/ft)

a. What is the length of the garden? **$(x + 7)$ ft**
b. Find the perimeter in terms of x. **$(4x + 26)$ ft**
c. Find the cost to fence the garden when x is 5. **$92.00**
d. Find the cost of fertilizer when x is 5. **$36.96**
e. Find the total cost to fence and fertilize Beth's garden when x is 5. **$128.96**

SPIRAL REVIEW

86. Choose the situation that best describes the graph. *(Lesson 4-1)*
A. An object increases speed, stops, and then moves in reverse.
(B.) An object starts at rest, increases speed steadily, maintains constant speed, and then comes to an immediate stop.
C. An object increases speed quickly, then increases speed slowly, and then comes to an immediate stop.

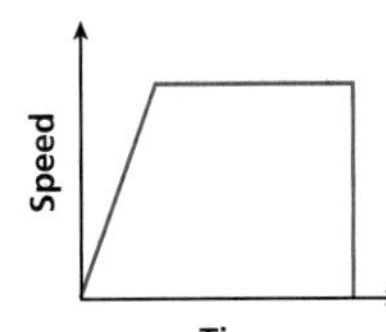

Simplify. *(Lesson 7-3)*

87. x^3x^2 **x^5**
88. $m^8n^3m^{-12}$ **$\frac{n^3}{m^4}$**
89. $(t^4)^3$ **t^{12}**
90. $(-2xy^3)^5$ **$-32x^5y^{15}$**

Factor each polynomial by grouping. *(Lesson 8-2)*

91. $x^3 + 2x^2 + 5x + 10$ **$(x + 2)(x^2 + 5)$**
92. $2n^3 - 8n^2 - 3n + 12$ **$(n - 4)(2n^2 - 3)$**
93. $2p^4 - 4p^3 + 7p - 14$ **$(p - 2)(2p^3 + 7)$**
94. $x^3 - 4x^2 + x - 4$ **$(x - 4)(x^2 + 1)$**

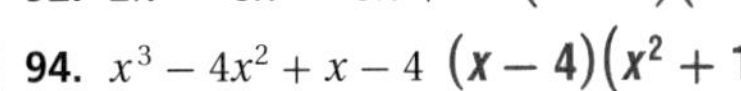

Career Path

Career Resources Online
KEYWORD: MA7 Career

Jessica Rubino
Environmental Sciences major

Q: What math classes did you take in high school?
A: Algebra 1, Algebra 2, and Geometry

Q: What college math classes have you taken?
A: I took several computer modeling and programming classes as well as Statistics and Probability.

Q: How is math used in some of your projects?
A: Computer applications help me analyze data collected from a local waste disposal site. I used my mathematical knowledge to make recommendations on how to preserve surrounding water supplies.

Q: What plans do you have for the future?
A: I enjoy my studies in the area of water pollution. I would also like to research more efficient uses of natural energy resources.

Journal

Have students compare factoring a trinomial when c is negative and b is positive with factoring a trinomial when c is negative and b is negative.

ALTERNATIVE ASSESSMENT

Have students write four trinomials by multiplying four pairs of binomials. In two of the trinomials, c should be positive. Have students trade papers and factor the trinomials they received.

Power Presentations with PowerPoint®

8-3 Lesson Quiz

Factor each trinomial.

1. $x^2 - 11x + 30$
$(x - 5)(x - 6)$
2. $x^2 + 10x + 9$
$(x + 1)(x + 9)$
3. $x^2 - 6x - 27$
$(x - 9)(x + 3)$
4. $x^2 + 14x - 32$
$(x + 16)(x - 2)$
5. Factor $n^2 + n - 6$. Show that the original polynomial and the factored form have the same value for $n = 0, 1, 2, 3,$ and 4. $(n + 3)(n - 2)$

n	$n^2 + n - 6$
0	$0^2 + 0 - 6 = -6$
1	$1^2 + 1 - 6 = -4$
2	$2^2 + 2 - 6 = 0$
3	$3^2 + 3 - 6 = 6$
4	$4^2 + 4 - 6 = 14$

n	$(n + 3)(n - 2)$
0	$(0 + 3)(0 - 2) = -6$
1	$(1 + 3)(1 - 2) = -4$
2	$(2 + 3)(2 - 2) = 0$
3	$(3 + 3)(3 - 2) = 6$
4	$(4 + 3)(4 - 2) = 14$

Also available on transparency

8-3 PROBLEM SOLVING

Write the correct answer.

1. A plot of land is rectangular and has an area of $x^2 - 5x - 24$ m². The length is $x + 3$ m. Find the width of the plot.
$x - 8$ m

2. An antique Persian carpet has an area of $(x^2 + x - 20)$ ft² and a length of $(x + 5)$ feet. The rug is displayed on a wall in a museum. The wall has a width of $(x + 2)$ feet and an area of $(x^2 + 17x + 30)$ ft². Write expressions for the length and width of both the rug and wall. Then find the dimensions of the rug and the wall if $x = 20$ feet.

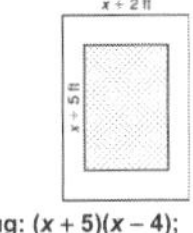

rug: $(x + 5)(x - 4)$;
wall. $(x + 2)(x + 15)$;
rug: 16 ft by 25 ft,
wall: 22 ft by 35 ft

3. The area of a poster board is $x^2 + 3x - 10$ inches. The width is $x - 2$ inches.
a. Write an expression for the length of the poster board.
$x + 5$
b. Find the dimensions of the poster board when $x = 14$.
12 in. by 19 in.
c. Write a polynomial for the area of the poster board if one inch is removed from each side.
$x^2 + x - 12$

The figure shows the plans for an addition on the back of a house. Use the figure to answer questions 4–6. Select the best answer.

Addition
Original House
x − 10
x + 10

4. The area of the addition is $(x^2 + 10x - 200)$ ft². What is its length?
A $(x - 20)$ feet
B $(x - 2)$ feet
C $(x + 2)$ feet
D $(x + 20)$ feet

5. What is the area of the original house?
F $(x^2 - 10x - 200)$ ft²
G $(x^2 + 8x - 20)$ ft²
H $(x^2 + 12x + 200)$ ft²
J $(x^2 + 30x + 200)$ ft²

6. The homeowners decide to extend the addition. The area with the addition is now $(x^2 + 12x - 160)$ ft². By how many feet was the addition extended?
A 1 foot
B 2 feet
C 3 feet
D 4 feet

8-3 CHALLENGE

One day, Denise's mathematics teacher, Ms. Dolenze, asked her to factor $6x^2 + 5x + 1$. After puzzling over the problem for a while, Denise told Ms. Dolenze that the expression could not be factored. Amazed, Ms. Dolenze asked Denise why. "I could not find two binomials in x with integer coefficients whose product is $6x^2 + 5x + 1$," replied Denise. Then Ms. Dolenze quickly responded, "Why should that stop you?"

In the exercises that follow, you will see how to push back the boundaries of factoring.

In Exercise 1–4, answer each question in order to help Denise factor $6x^2 + 5x + 1$.

1. By what property of real numbers, can you justify $6x^2 + 5x + 1 = 6\left(x^2 + \frac{5}{6}x + \frac{1}{6}\right)$?
Distributive Property

2. Show that $\left(\frac{1}{2}\right)\left(\frac{1}{3}\right) = \frac{1}{6}$ and that $\frac{1}{2} + \frac{1}{3} = \frac{5}{6}$.
$\left(\frac{1}{2}\right)\left(\frac{1}{3}\right) = \frac{1\times1}{2\times3} = \frac{1}{6}$. $\frac{1}{2} + \frac{1}{3} = \frac{1}{2}\times\frac{3}{3} + \frac{1}{3}\times\frac{2}{2} = \frac{3+2}{2\times3} = \frac{5}{6}$

3. Show that $6\left(x + \frac{1}{2}\right)\left(x + \frac{1}{3}\right) = 6x^2 + 5x + 1$.
$6\left(x + \frac{1}{2}\right)\left(x + \frac{1}{3}\right) = 2\left(x + \frac{1}{2}\right) \times 3\left(x + \frac{1}{3}\right) = (2x + 1)(3x + 1)$
$= 6x^2 + 3x + 2x + 1 = 6x^2 + 5x + 1$

4. Is the product in Exercise 3 a factorization of $6x^2 + 5x + 1$? Is it necessary to find integers in order to factor a quadratic trinomial? Explain your response.
Yes; the given polynomial expression is written as a product of polynomials of lower degree. There is no requirement that the coefficients be integers.

Factor each quadratic trinomial as a number times a product of two linear binomials in x, each having rational numbers among the coefficients. Use Exercises 1–3 above as a model.

5. $15x^2 + 8x + 1$
$15\left(x + \frac{1}{5}\right)\left(x + \frac{1}{3}\right)$

6. $28x^2 + 11x + 1$
$28\left(x + \frac{1}{7}\right)\left(x + \frac{1}{4}\right)$

7. $6x^2 - 23x + 20$
$6\left(x - \frac{4}{3}\right)\left(x - \frac{5}{2}\right)$

8. $12x^2 + x - 35$
$12\left(x - \frac{5}{3}\right)\left(x + \frac{7}{4}\right)$

8-4 Organizer

Pacing: Traditional $1\frac{1}{2}$ days
Block $\frac{3}{4}$ day

Objective: Factor quadratic trinomials of the form $ax^2 + bx + c$.

Online Edition
Tutorial Videos

Countdown Week 18

Power Presentations with PowerPoint®

Warm Up

Find each product.

1. $(x - 2)(2x + 7)$ $2x^2 + 3x - 14$
2. $(3y + 4)(2y + 9)$ $6y^2 + 35y + 36$
3. $(3n - 5)(n - 7)$ $3n^2 - 26n + 35$

Factor each trinomial.

4. $x^2 + 4x - 32$ $(x - 4)(x + 8)$
5. $z^2 + 15z + 36$ $(z + 3)(z + 12)$
6. $h^2 - 17h + 72$ $(h - 8)(h - 9)$

Also available on transparency

Math Humor

Q: What is the hidden math term?

NOMIAL
NOMIAL

A: Binomial.

8-4 Factoring $ax^2 + bx + c$

Objective
Factor quadratic trinomials of the form $ax^2 + bx + c$.

Why learn this?
The height of a football that has been kicked can be modeled by a factored polynomial. (See Exercise 69.)

In the previous lesson you factored trinomials of the form $x^2 + bx + c$. Now you will factor trinomials of the form $ax^2 + bx + c$, where $a \neq 0$ or 1.

When you multiply $(3x + 2)(2x + 5)$, the coefficient of the x^2-term is the product of the coefficients of the x-terms. Also, the constant term in the trinomial is the product of the constants in the binomials.

$$(3x + 2)(2x + 5) = 6x^2 + 19x + 10$$

To factor a trinomial like $ax^2 + bx + c$ into its binomial factors, write two sets of parentheses: $(\square x + \square)(\square x + \square)$.

Write two numbers that are factors of a next to the x's and two numbers that are factors of c in the other blanks. Then multiply to see if the product is the original trinomial. If there are not two such integers, the trinomial is unfactorable.

EXAMPLE 1 Factoring $ax^2 + bx + c$ by Guess and Check

Factor $4x^2 + 16x + 15$ by guess and check.

$(\square + \square)(\square + \square)$ *Write two sets of parentheses.*

$(\square x + \square)(\square x + \square)$ *The first term is $4x^2$, so at least one variable term has a coefficient other than 1.*

The coefficient of the x^2-term is 4. The constant term in the trinomial is 15.

Try factors of 4 for the coefficients and factors of 15 for the constant terms.

$(1x + 15)(4x + 1) = 4x^2 + 61x + 15$ ✗
$(1x + 5)(4x + 3) = 4x^2 + 23x + 15$ ✗
$(1x + 3)(4x + 5) = 4x^2 + 17x + 15$ ✗
$(1x + 1)(4x + 15) = 4x^2 + 19x + 15$ ✗
$(2x + 15)(2x + 1) = 4x^2 + 32x + 15$ ✗
$(2x + 5)(2x + 3) = 4x^2 + 16x + 15$ ✓

The factors of $4x^2 + 16x + 15$ are $(2x + 5)$ and $(2x + 3)$.

$4x^2 + 16x + 15 = (2x + 5)(2x + 3)$

CHECK IT OUT! **Factor each trinomial by guess and check.**

1a. $6x^2 + 11x + 3$ **1b.** $3x^2 - 2x - 8$

1a. $(3x + 1)(2x + 3)$
1b. $(3x + 4)(x - 2)$

State Resources

go.hrw.com
State Resources Online
KEYWORD: MA7 Resources

1 Introduce

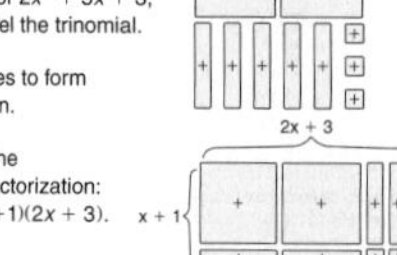

EXPLORATION

8-4 Factoring $ax^2 + bx + c$

You will need algebra tiles for this Exploration.

You can use algebra tiles to factor trinomials in the form $ax^2 + bx + c$.

For example, to factor $2x^2 + 5x + 3$, first use tiles to model the trinomial.

Then arrange the tiles to form a rectangle as shown.

The dimensions of the rectangle give the factorization: $2x^2 + 5x + 3 = (x + 1)(2x + 3)$.

Use algebra tiles to factor each of the following trinomials.

1. $2x^2 + 7x + 3$ 2. $2x^2 + 9x + 10$ 3. $4x^2 + 4x + 1$

THINK AND DISCUSS

4. **Explain** how the coefficients of the x-terms in the binomial factors are related to the coefficient of the x^2-term in the trinomial.
5. **Describe** one way in which factoring a trinomial in the form $ax^2 + bx + c$, where $a \neq 0$, is similar to factoring a trinomial in the form $x^2 + bx + c$.

Motivate

Write $6x^2 + 7x + 2$ on the board. Ask students how it is different from the trinomials they factored in Lesson 8-3. The x^2-term has a coefficient that is not 1.

Tell students that because b depends on both a and c, this means that more factors, and their placements, will need to be tested.

Explorations and answers are provided in *Alternate Openers: Explorations Transparencies.*

So, to factor $ax^2 + bx + c$, check the factors of a and the factors of c in the binomials. The sum of the products of the outer and inner terms should be b.

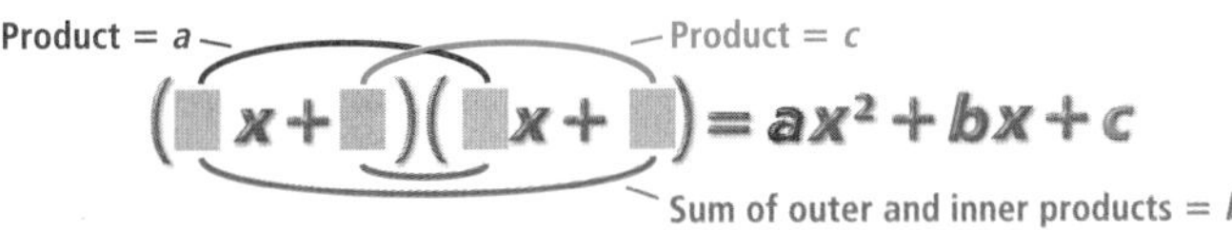

Since you need to check all the factors of a and all the factors of c, it may be helpful to make a table. Then check the products of the outer and inner terms to see if the sum is b. You can multiply the binomials to check your answer.

EXAMPLE 2 Factoring $ax^2 + bx + c$ When c Is Positive

Factor each trinomial. Check your answer.

A $2x^2 + 11x + 12$

$(\square x + \square)(\square x + \square)$ *$a = 2$ and $c = 12$; Outer + Inner = 11*

Factors of 2	Factors of 12	Outer + Inner	
1 and 2	1 and 12	$1(12) + 2(1) = 14$	✗
1 and 2	12 and 1	$1(1) + 2(12) = 25$	✗
1 and 2	2 and 6	$1(6) + 2(2) = 10$	✗
1 and 2	6 and 2	$1(2) + 2(6) = 14$	✗
1 and 2	3 and 4	$1(4) + 2(3) = 10$	✗
1 and 2	4 and 3	$1(3) + 2(4) = 11$	✓

$(x + 4)(2x + 3)$

Check $(x + 4)(2x + 3) = 2x^2 + 3x + 8x + 12$ *Use the FOIL method.*
$= 2x^2 + 11x + 12$ ✓

B $5x^2 - 14x + 8$

$(\square x + \square)(\square x + \square)$ *$a = 5$ and $c = 8$; Outer + Inner = −14*

Factors of 5	Factors of 8	Outer + Inner	
1 and 5	−1 and −8	$1(-8) + 5(-1) = -13$	✗
1 and 5	−8 and −1	$1(-1) + 5(-8) = -41$	✗
1 and 5	−2 and −4	$1(-4) + 5(-2) = -14$	✓

$(x - 2)(5x - 4)$

Check $(x - 2)(5x - 4) = 5x^2 - 4x - 10x + 8$ *Use the FOIL method.*
$= 5x^2 - 14x + 8$ ✓

Remember!
When b is negative and c is positive, the factors of c are both negative.

Factor each trinomial. Check your answer.

2a. $6x^2 + 17x + 5$ $(2x + 5)(3x + 1)$ **2b.** $9x^2 - 15x + 4$ $(3x - 4)(3x - 1)$ **2c.** $3x^2 + 13x + 12$ $(3x + 4)(x + 3)$

When c is negative, one factor of c will be positive and the other factor will be negative. Only some of the factors are shown in the examples, but you may need to check all of the possibilities.

Power Presentations with PowerPoint®

Additional Examples

Example 1

Factor $6x^2 + 11x + 4$.
$(3x + 4)(2x + 1)$

Example 2

Factor each trinomial. Check your answer.

A. $2x^2 + 17x + 21$
$(2x + 3)(x + 7)$

B. $3x^2 - 16x + 16$
$(x - 4)(3x - 4)$

INTERVENTION
Questioning Strategies

EXAMPLE 1

- How is factoring a trinomial in the form $ax^2 + bx + c$ similar to factoring a trinomial in the form $x^2 + bx + c$? How is it different?

EXAMPLE 2

- What is true about the signs of the factors of the last term if the middle term is positive? negative?
- What should the sum of the inner and outer products be?

Inclusion Confident students may have been able to factor the trinomials in the previous lesson in their heads. Remind students that careless errors are easy to make. To factor the trinomials in this lesson, these students may need to write out their work.

2 Teach

Guided Instruction

Review factoring trinomials of the form $x^2 + bx + c$. Then have students factor trinomials of the form $ax^2 + bx + c$ by the guess-and-check method. For **Examples 2, 3,** and **4,** use a table when teaching, and encourage students to use a table when working on their own. This will allow students to see what factors they have already checked and prevent them from trying the same sets of factors more than once.

Reaching All Learners
Through Critical Thinking

Present students with the following trinomials. Challenge students to find values of k for each trinomial that will make the trinomial factorable.

1. $x^2 + kx + 81$ $\pm 82, \pm 30, \pm 18$
2. $x^2 + 14x + k$ 13, 24, 33, ..., $n(14 - n)$
3. $kx^2 + 10x + 1$ 9, 16, 21, 24, 25

Power Presentations with PowerPoint®

Additional Examples

Example 3

Factor each trinomial. Check your answer.

A. $3n^2 + 11n - 4$
$(n + 4)(3n - 1)$

B. $2x^2 + 9x - 18$
$(x + 6)(2x - 3)$

C. $4x^2 - 15x - 4$
$(x - 4)(4x + 1)$

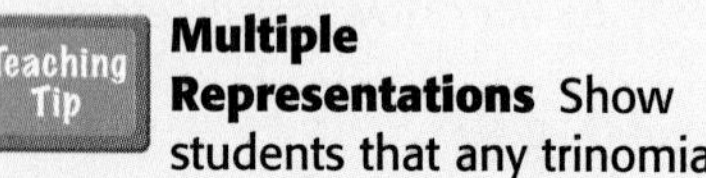

Questioning Strategies

EXAMPLE 3

- What do you know about the binomials in the factored expression when the constant term in the trinomial is negative?

Teaching Tip **Multiple Representations** Show students that any trinomial can be written as a polynomial with four terms. It can then be factored by grouping. To factor $6x^2 + 19x + 15$, find ac and factors of ac that sum to b. Rewrite the trinomial using those factors: $6x^2 + 10x + 9x + 15$. Then factor by grouping.

$(6x^2 + 10x) + (9x + 15)$
$= 2x(3x + 5) + 3(3x + 5)$
$= (3x + 5)(2x + 3)$

EXAMPLE 3 Factoring $ax^2 + bx + c$ When c Is Negative

Factor each trinomial. Check your answer.

A $4y^2 + 7y - 2$

$(\blacksquare y + \blacksquare)(\blacksquare y + \blacksquare)$ *$a = 4$ and $c = -2$; Outer + Inner = 7*

Factors of 4	Factors of −2	Outer + Inner
1 and 4	1 and −2	$1(-2) + 4(1) = 2$ ✗
1 and 4	−1 and 2	$1(2) + 4(-1) = -2$ ✗
1 and 4	2 and −1	$1(-1) + 4(2) = 7$ ✓

$(y + 2)(4y - 1)$

Check $(y + 2)(4y - 1) = 4y^2 - y + 8y - 2$ *Use the FOIL method.*
$= 4y^2 + 7y - 2$ ✓

B $4x^2 + 19x - 5$

$(\blacksquare x + \blacksquare)(\blacksquare x + \blacksquare)$ *$a = 4$ and $c = -5$; Outer + Inner = 19*

Factors of 4	Factors of −5	Outer + Inner
1 and 4	1 and −5	$1(-5) + 4(1) = -1$ ✗
1 and 4	−1 and 5	$1(5) + 4(-1) = 1$ ✗
1 and 4	5 and −1	$1(-1) + 4(5) = 19$ ✓

$(x + 5)(4x - 1)$

Check $(x + 5)(4x - 1) = 4x^2 - x + 20x - 5$ *Use the FOIL method.*
$= 4x^2 + 19x - 5$ ✓

C $2x^2 - 7x - 15$

$(\blacksquare x + \blacksquare)(\blacksquare x + \blacksquare)$ *$a = 2$ and $c = -15$; Outer + Inner = −7*

Factors of 2	Factors of −15	Outer + Inner
1 and 2	1 and −15	$1(-15) + 2(1) = -13$ ✗
1 and 2	−1 and 15	$1(15) + 2(-1) = 13$ ✗
1 and 2	3 and −5	$1(-5) + 2(3) = 1$ ✗
1 and 2	−3 and 5	$1(5) + 2(-3) = -1$ ✗
1 and 2	5 and −3	$1(-3) + 2(5) = 7$ ✗
1 and 2	−5 and 3	$1(3) + 2(-5) = -7$ ✓

$(x - 5)(2x + 3)$

Check $(x - 5)(2x + 3) = 2x^2 + 3x - 10x - 15$ *Use the FOIL method.*
$= 2x^2 - 7x - 15$ ✓

Factor each trinomial. Check your answer.

3a. $6x^2 + 7x - 3$ $(3x - 1)(2x + 3)$

3b. $4n^2 - n - 3$ $(4n + 3)(n - 1)$

Student to Student

Factoring $ax^2 + bx + c$

Reggie Wilson
Franklin High School

When a, b, and c are positive, I like to use a box to help me factor. I look for factors of ac that add to b. Then I arrange the terms in a box and factor.

To factor $6x^2 + 7x + 2$, first I find the factors I need.

$ac = 2(6) = 12 \quad b = 7$

Factors of 12	Sum
1 and 12	13
2 and 6	8
3 and 4	7

Then I rewrite the trinomial as $6x^2 + 3x + 4x + 2$.

Now I arrange $6x^2 + 3x + 4x + 2$ in a box and factor out the common factors from each row and column.

$6x^2$	$3x$	→ $3x$
$4x$	2	→ 2
↓ $2x$	↓ 1	

The factors are $(2x + 1)$ and $(3x + 2)$.

When the leading coefficient is negative, factor out −1 from each term before using other factoring methods.

EXAMPLE 4 Factoring $ax^2 + bx + c$ When a Is Negative

Caution!

When you factor out −1 in an early step, you must carry it through the rest of the steps.

Factor $-2x^2 - 15x - 7$.

$-1(2x^2 + 15x + 7)$ *Factor out −1.*

$-1(\square x + \square)(\square x + \square)$ *a = 2 and c = 7; Outer + Inner = 15*

Factors of 2	Factors of 7	Outer + Inner	
1 and 2	1 and 7	$1(7) + 2(1) = 9$	✗
1 and 2	7 and 1	$1(1) + 2(7) = 15$	✓

$(x + 7)(2x + 1)$

$-1(x + 7)(2x + 1)$

CHECK IT OUT! Factor each trinomial. Check your answer.

4a. $-6x^2 - 17x - 12$ $\quad -1(2x + 3)(3x + 4)$

4b. $-3x^2 - 17x - 10$ $\quad -1(3x + 2)(x + 5)$

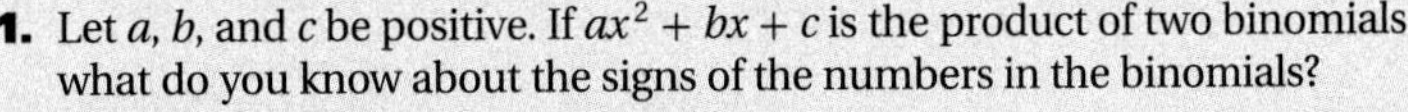

THINK AND DISCUSS

1. Let a, b, and c be positive. If $ax^2 + bx + c$ is the product of two binomials, what do you know about the signs of the numbers in the binomials?

2. **GET ORGANIZED** Copy and complete the graphic organizer. Write each of the following trinomials in the appropriate box and factor each one.
$3x^2 + 10x - 8 \quad 3x^2 + 10x + 8$
$3x^2 - 10x + 8 \quad 3x^2 - 10x - 8$

Factoring $ax^2 + bx + c$	
$c > 0$	
$b > 0$	$b < 0$
$c < 0$	
$b < 0$	$b > 0$

COMMON ERROR ALERT

Students sometimes forget that every number has 1 and itself as two of its factors. When students are making their lists of factors, remind them to try all possible factors.

Power Presentations with PowerPoint®

Additional Examples

Example 4

Factor $-2x^2 - 5x - 3$.
$-1(x + 1)(2x + 3)$

INTERVENTION
Questioning Strategies

EXAMPLE 4

- How do you know which term is the leading coefficient?
- What is the advantage to factoring out −1 in the first step?

3 Close

Summarize

Tell students that to factor a trinomial in the form $ax^2 + bx + c$, they should make a table, such that each row has two factors of a, two factors of c, and the sum of the inner and outer products. Remind them that if they factor out −1, they need to remember to put it in the factored form. It doesn't just disappear.

ONGOING ASSESSMENT and INTERVENTION

Diagnose **Before** the Lesson
8-4 Warm Up, TE p. 568

Monitor **During** the Lesson
Check It Out! Exercises, SE pp. 568–571
Questioning Strategies, TE pp. 569–571

Assess **After** the Lesson
8-4 Lesson Quiz, TE p. 574
Alternative Assessment, TE p. 574

Answers to *Think and Discuss*

1. They are all positive.
2. See p. A7.

8-4 Exercises

Assignment Guide

Assign *Guided Practice* exercises as necessary.

If you finished Examples **1–2**
- **Basic** 25–39, 52, 55, 58–64 even
- **Average** 25–39, 58–64 even, 81, 83
- **Advanced** 25–39, 58–64 even, 81, 83

If you finished Examples **1–4**
- **Basic** 25–64, 68–74, 76–80, 90–96
- **Average** 25–70, 75–81, 83, 90–96
- **Advanced** 25–51, 52–62 even, 64–69, 75–96

Homework Quick Check
Quickly check key concepts.
Exercises: 30, 35, 48, 50, 58, 64

Answers

1. $(2x + 5)(x + 2)$
2. $(x + 6)(5x + 1)$
3. $(5x - 3)(x + 2)$
4. $(x + 6)(6x + 1)$
5. $(3x + 4)(x - 6)$
6. $(2x - 1)(3x + 2)$
7. $(x + 2)(5x + 1)$
8. $(x + 5)(2x + 1)$
9. $(4x - 5)(x - 1)$
10. $(2y - 7)(y - 2)$
11. $(5x + 4)(x + 1)$
12. $(x + 2)(3x + 1)$

13–63. See pp. A28–A29.

State Resources

8-4 Exercises

go.hrw.com
Homework Help Online
KEYWORD: MA7 8-4
Parent Resources Online
KEYWORD: MA7 Parent

GUIDED PRACTICE

SEE EXAMPLE 1 p. 568

Factor each trinomial by guess and check.

1. $2x^2 + 9x + 10$
2. $5x^2 + 31x + 6$
3. $5x^2 + 7x - 6$
4. $6x^2 + 37x + 6$
5. $3x^2 - 14x - 24$
6. $6x^2 + x - 2$

Factor each trinomial. Check your answer.

SEE EXAMPLE 2 p. 569

7. $5x^2 + 11x + 2$
8. $2x^2 + 11x + 5$
9. $4x^2 - 9x + 5$
10. $2y^2 - 11y + 14$
11. $5x^2 + 9x + 4$
12. $3x^2 + 7x + 2$

SEE EXAMPLE 3 p. 570

13. $4a^2 + 8a - 5$
14. $15x^2 + 4x - 3$
15. $2x^2 + x - 6$
16. $6n^2 - 11n - 10$
17. $10x^2 - 9x - 1$
18. $7x^2 - 3x - 10$

SEE EXAMPLE 4 p. 571

19. $-2x^2 + 5x + 12$
20. $-4n^2 - 16n + 9$
21. $-5x^2 + 7x + 6$
22. $-6x^2 + 13x - 2$
23. $-4x^2 - 8x + 5$
24. $-5x^2 + x + 18$

PRACTICE AND PROBLEM SOLVING

Independent Practice

For Exercises	See Example
25–33	1
34–42	2
43–48	3
49–51	4

Extra Practice
Skills Practice p. S19
Application Practice p. S35

Factor each trinomial by guess and check.

25. $9x^2 + 9x + 2$
26. $2x^2 + 7x + 5$
27. $3n^2 + 8n + 4$
28. $10d^2 + 17d + 7$
29. $4c^2 - 17c + 15$
30. $6x^2 + 14x + 4$
31. $8x^2 + 22x + 5$
32. $6x^2 - 13x + 6$
33. $5x^2 + 9x - 18$

Factor each trinomial. Check your answer.

34. $6x^2 + 23x + 7$
35. $10n^2 - 17n + 7$
36. $3x^2 + 11x + 6$
37. $7x^2 + 15x + 2$
38. $3n^2 + 4n + 1$
39. $3x^2 - 19x + 20$
40. $6x^2 + 11x + 4$
41. $4x^2 - 31x + 21$
42. $10x^2 + 31x + 15$
43. $12y^2 + 17y - 5$
44. $3x^2 + 10x - 8$
45. $4x^2 + 4x - 3$
46. $2n^2 - 7n - 4$
47. $3x^2 - 4x - 15$
48. $3n^2 - n - 4$
49. $-4x^2 - 4x + 15$
50. $-3x^2 + 16x - 16$
51. $-3x^2 - x + 2$

Geometry For Exercises 52–54, write the polynomial modeled and then factor.

52.

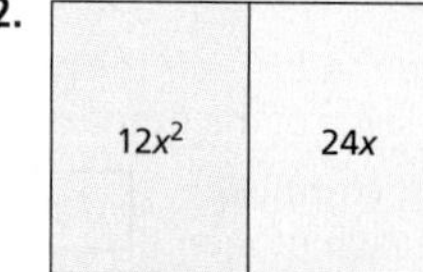

53.

$2x^2$	$-x$
$-4x$	2

54.

$5x^2$	$-4x$
$35x$	-28

Factor each trinomial, if possible.

55. $9n^2 + 17n + 8$
56. $2x^2 - 7x - 4$
57. $4x^2 - 12x + 5$
58. $5x^2 - 4x + 12$
59. $3x^2 + 14x + 16$
60. $-3x^2 - 11x + 4$
61. $6x^2 - x - 12$
62. $10a^2 + 11a + 3$
63. $4x^2 - 12x + 9$

8-4 READING STRATEGIES

Most people factor trinomials of the form $ax^2 + bx + c$ using a sort of organized guess-and-check method. Look at the model below.

Factor the trinomial $4x^2 - 17x - 15$ into two binomials.

- **Recall:** The acronym FOIL stands for First, Outer, Inner, Last.
- **Signs:** This trinomial requires a "plus" and a "minus" binomial.
- **Setup:** (F + L) (F – L) → (x +) (x –)
- **"First":** The factorizations of 4 are: 1 • 4 and 2 • 2.
- **"Last":** The factorizations of 15 are: 1 • 15 and 3 • 5.
- **"Outer" and "Inner":** Guess-and-check these values in the binomials. The goal is to multiply the "Outer" terms and the "Inner" terms, and get a sum of –17.

(	x +	)(	x –	)	Outer	+	Inner	=		
1	1	4	–15		1 • –15	+	1 • 4	=	–11	No
1	15	4	–1		1 • –1	+	15 • 4	=	59	No
1	5	4	–3		1 • –3	+	5 • 4	=	–7	No
1	3	4	–5		1 • –5	+	3 • 4	=	7	No
4	1	1	–15		4 • –15	+	1 • 1	=	–59	No
4	15	1	–1		4 • –1	+	15 • 1	=	11	No
4	5	1	–3		4 • –3	+	5 • 1	=	–7	No
4	**3**	**1**	**–5**		4 • –5	+	3 • 1	=	–17	Yes

- **Answer:** $4x^2 - 17x - 15$ factors into (**4**x + **3**) (**1**x – **5**), or just (4x + 3) (x – 5).

Complete the following to guide you in factoring $3x^2 - 20x + 12$.

1. What are the factorizations of 3? **1 • 3**
2. What are the factorizations of 12? **1 • 12; 2 • 6; 3 • 4**
3. What signs are needed in each of the two binomials? **minus, minus**
4. Set up the binomials for factoring this polynomial. **(x –)(x –)**
5. Guess-and-check the factors that will result in the correct middle term coefficient of 20.
Possible answer:

(	x –	)(	x –	)	Outer	+	Inner	=		
3	–1	1	–12		3 • –12	+	–1 • 1	=	–37	No
3	–12	1	–1		3 • –1	+	–12 • 1	=	–15	No
3	–4	1	–3		3 • –3	+	–4 • 1	=	–13	No
3	–3	1	–4		3 • –4	+	–3 • 1	=	–15	No
3	–6	1	–2		3 • –2	+	–6 • 1	=	–12	No
3	–2	1	–6		3 • –6	+	–2 • 1	=	–20	Yes

6. What is the final answer for factoring $3x^2 - 20x + 12$? **(3x – 2)(x – 6)**

8-4 RETEACH

When factoring $ax^2 + bx + c$, first find factors of *a* and *c*. Then check the products of the inner and outer terms to see if the sum is *b*.

Factor $2x^2 + 11x + 15$. Check your answer.

$2x^2 + 11x + 15 = (\ x + \ )(\ x + \ )$

Factors of 2	Factors of 15	Outer + Inner
1 and 2	1 and 15	1 • 15 + 2 • 1 = 17 ×
1 and 2	15 and 1	1 • 1 + 2 • 15 = 31 ×
1 and 2	5 and 3	1 • 3 + 2 • 5 = 13 ×
1 and 2	3 and 5	1 • 5 + 2 • 3 = 11 ✓

(x + 3) (2x + 5)

Check:
(x + 3) (2x + 5) = $2x^2 + 5x + 6x + 15$
$= 2x^2 + 11x + 15$ ✓

Factor $3x^2 - 23x + 14$. Check your answer.

$3x^2 - 23x + 14 = (\ x + \ )(\ x + \ )$

Factors of 3	Factors of 14	Outer + Inner
1 and 3	–1 and –14	1 • (–14) + 3 • (–1) = –17 ×
1 and 3	–14 and –1	1 • (–1) + 3 • (–14) = –42 ×
1 and 3	–2 and –7	1 • (–7) + 3 • (–2) = –13 ×
1 and 3	–7 and –2	1 • (–2) + 3 • (–7) = –23 ✓

(x – 7) (3x – 2)

Check:
(x – 7) (3x – 2) = $3x^2 - 2x - 21x + 14$
$= 3x^2 + 23x + 14$ ✓

1. Factor $5x^2 + 12x + 4$ by filling in the blanks below.

Factors	Factors	Outer + Inner
1 and 5	1 and 4	1 • 4 + 5 • 1 = 9
1 and 5	4 and 1	1 • 1 + 5 • 4 = 21
1 and 5	2 and 2	1 • 2 + 5 • 2 = 12

(x + 2)(5x + 2)

Factor each trinomial.

2. $3x^2 + 7x + 4$ **(3x + 4)(x + 1)**
3. $2x^2 - 13x + 21$ **(2x – 7)(x – 3)**
4. $4x^2 + 8x + 3$ **(2x + 3)(2x + 1)**

64. **Geometry** The area of a rectangle is $(6x^2 + 11x + 5)$ cm^2. The width is $(x + 1)$ cm. What is the length of the rectangle? **$(6x + 5)$ cm**

$(x + 1)$ cm

65. **Write About It** Write a paragraph describing how to factor $6x^2 + 13x + 6$. Show each step you would take and explain your steps. **$(2x + 3)(3x + 2)$; Check students' work.**

Complete each factorization.

66.
$$8x^2 + 18x - 5$$
$$8x^2 + 20x - 2x - 5$$
$$(8x^2 + 20x) - (2x + 5)$$
$$\mathbf{4x}(\mathbf{2x} + \mathbf{5}) - \mathbf{1}(2x + 5)$$
$$(\mathbf{4x} - \mathbf{1})(2x + 5)$$

67.
$$4x^2 + 9x + 2$$
$$4x^2 + 8x + x + 2$$
$$(4x^2 + 8x) + (x + 2)$$
$$\mathbf{4x}(\mathbf{x} + \mathbf{2}) + \mathbf{1}(x + 2)$$
$$(\mathbf{4x} + \mathbf{1})(x + 2)$$

68. width increased by 2 yd; length increased by 3 yd

68. **Gardening** The length of Rebecca's rectangular garden was two times the width w. Rebecca increased the length and width of the garden so that the area of the new garden is $(2w^2 + 7w + 6)$ square yards. By how much did Rebecca increase the length and the width?

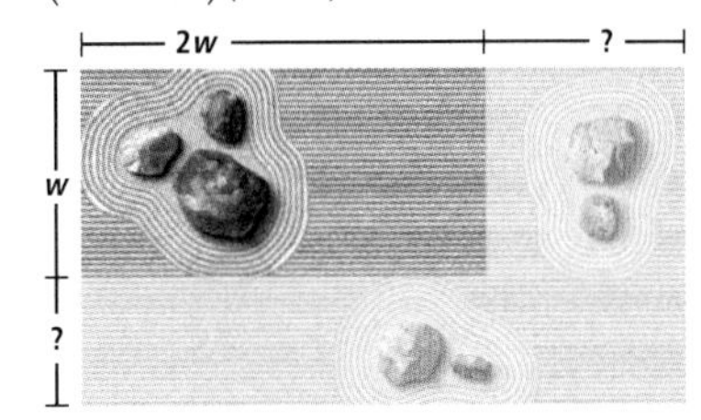

69. **Physics** The height of a football that has been thrown or kicked can be described by the expression $-16t^2 + vt + h$ where t is the time in seconds, v is the initial upward velocity, and h is the initial height in feet.
   a. Write an expression for the height of a football at time t when the initial upward velocity is 20 feet per second and the initial height is 6 feet. **$-16t^2 + 20t + 6$**
   b. Factor your expression from part **a.** **$-2(4t + 1)(2t - 3)$**
   c. Find the height of the football after 1 second. **10 ft**

70. **/// ERROR ANALYSIS ///** A student attempted to factor $2x^2 + 11x + 12$ as shown. Find and explain the error.

Possible answer: The student tried factors of 12, but forgot to try factors of 2 also.

$2x^2 + 11x + 12$

Factors of 12	Sum	
1 and 12	13	✓
2 and 6	8	x
3 and 4	7	x

$(2x + 1)(x + 12)$

MULTI-STEP TEST PREP

71. This problem will prepare you for the Multi-Step Test Prep on page 576.
The equation $d = 2t^2$ gives the distance from the start point of a toy boat that starts at rest and accelerates at 4 cm/s^2. The equation $d = 10t - 8$ gives the distance from the start point of a second boat that starts at rest 8 cm behind the first boat and travels at a constant rate of 10 cm/s. **a. $2t^2 - 10t + 8 = 0$**
   a. By setting the equations equal to each other, you can determine when the cars are the same distance from the start point: $2t^2 = 10t - 8$. Use properties of algebra to collect all terms on the left side of the equation, leaving 0 on the right side.
   b. Factor the expression on the left side of the equation. **$2(t - 1)(t - 4)$**
   c. The boats are the same distance from the start point at $t = 1$ and $t = 4$. Explain how the factors you found in part **b** were used to find these two times. **$2(t - 4)(t - 1) = 0$ so $t - 4 = 0$ or $t - 1 = 0$**

Teaching Tip

Geometry Link In **Exercise 68,** have students draw a rectangle and label it with the original dimensions of the garden: w and $2w$. This will make it easier for them to see which factor of the factored expression is the length and which is the width.

MULTI-STEP TEST PREP **Exercise 71** involves solving a quadratic equation by factoring. This exercise prepares students for the Multi-Step Test Prep on page 576.

8-4 PROBLEM SOLVING

Write the correct answer.

1. A rectangular painting has an area of $(2x^2 + 8x + 6)$ cm^2. Its length is $(2x + 2)$ cm. Find the width of the painting.
   $(x + 3)$ cm
2. A ball is kicked straight up into the air. The height of the ball in feet is given by the expression $-16t^2 + 12t + 4$, where t is time in seconds. Factor the expression. Then find the height of the ball after 1 second.
   $-1(4t - 4)(4t + 1)$ or $-4(4t + 1)(t - 1)$; 0 feet
3. Instructors led an exercise class from a raised rectangular platform at the front of the room. The width of the platform was $(3x - 1)$ feet and the area was $(9x^2 + 6x - 3)$ ft^2. Find the length of this platform. After the exercise studio is remodeled, the area of the platform will be $(9x^2 + 12x + 3)$ ft^2. By how many feet will the width of the platform change?
   $(3x + 3)$ ft; increase of 2 ft
4. A clothing store has a rectangular clearance section with a length that is twice the width w. During a sale, the section is expanded to an area of $(2w^2 + 19w + 35)$ ft^2. Find the amount of the increase in the length and width of the clearance section.
   length increased by 5 ft, width increased by 7 ft

Select the best answer.

5. The area of a soccer field is $(24x^2 + 100x + 100)$ m^2. The width of the field is $(4x + 10)$ m. What is the length?
   A $(3x + 10)$ m **C** $(6x + 10)$ m
   B $(6x + 1)$ m D $(8x + 2)$ m
6. A square parking lot has an area of $(4x^2 + 20x + 25)$ ft^2. What is the length of one side of the parking lot?
   F $(2x + 5)$ ft H $(5x + 4)$ ft
   G $(2x + 10)$ ft J $(5x + 2)$ ft
7. For a certain college, the number of applications received after x recruiting seminars is modeled by the polynomial $3x^2 + 490x + 6000$. What is this expression in factored form?
   A $(3x - 40)(x - 150)$
   B $(3x + 40)(x + 150)$
   C $(3x - 30)(x - 200)$
   D $(3x - 30)(x + 200)$
8. Jin needs to fence in his rectangular backyard. The fence will have one long section away from, but parallel to, the length of his house and two shorter sides connecting that section to the house. The length of Jin's house is $(3x + 4)$ yd and the area of his backyard is $(9x^2 + 15x + 4)$ yd^2. How many yards of fencing will Jin need?
   F $(6x + 2)$ yd H $(9x + 9)$ yd
   G $(9x + 6)$ yd J $(12x + 10)$ yd

8-4 CHALLENGE

Synthetic division is a quick way to divide a polynomial by a binomial in the form $x - a$ yielding another factor of the polynomial.

$(x - 5)$ is a factor of $2x^2 - 3x - 35$. Use synthetic division to find the other factor.

$x - 5$ | $2x^2 - 3x - 35$

```
5 | 2   -3   -35
        10    35
    ------------
    2    7     0
```

Step 1: Write the coefficients of the polynomial (in standard form). Write a in a box to the left. Draw a line below the coefficients.

Step 2: Write the first coefficient below the line.

Step 3: Multiply that coefficient by the value of a and write the product under the next coefficient.

Step 4: Add the numbers in the second column.

Step 5: Repeat until all additions are completed.

The other factor is $2x + 7$.

If done correctly, the last sum will be zero. The numbers under the bar are the coefficients of the quotient, in decreasing degree.

A polynomial and one factor is given. Use synthetic division to find the other factor.

1. $4x^2 - 7x - 15$; $(x - 3)$

```
3 | 4   -7   -15
        12    15
    ------------
    4    5     0
```

   $(5x + 5)$

2. $3x^2 + 4x - 32$; $(x + 4)$

```
-4 | 3    4   -32
         -12    32
     -------------
     3   -8     0
```

   $(3x - 8)$

3. $6x^2 - 29x - 5$; $(x - 5)$
   $(6x + 1)$
4. $8x^2 + 11x - 10$; $(x + 2)$
   $(8x - 5)$

Some polynomials have three factors.

$(x - 2)$ is a factor of $x^3 - 3x^2 - 10x + 24$. Factor completely.

```
2 | 1   -3   -10    24
         2    -2   -24
    ------------------
    1   -1   -12     0
```

Now factor $x^2 - x - 12$ using a method you know.
$x^2 - x - 12 = (x + 3)(x - 4)$
The factors are: $(x - 2)(x + 3)(x - 4)$.

A polynomial and one factor is given. Factor completely.

5. $x^3 + 7x^2 + 7x - 15$; $(x - 1)$
   $(x - 1)(x + 3)(x + 5)$
6. $2x^3 - 3x^2 - 39x + 20$; $(x + 4)$
   $(x + 4)(2x - 1)(x - 5)$

8-4 PRACTICE A
8-4 PRACTICE C
8-4 PRACTICE B

Factor each trinomial.

1. $2x^2 + 13x + 15$ **$(2x + 3)(x + 5)$**
2. $3x^2 + 10x + 8$ **$(3x + 4)(x + 2)$**
3. $4x^2 + 24x + 27$ **$(2x + 9)(2x + 3)$**
4. $5x^2 + 21x + 4$ **$(5x + 1)(x + 4)$**
5. $4x^2 + 11x + 7$ **$(4x + 7)(x + 1)$**
6. $6x^2 - 23x + 20$ **$(3x - 4)(2x - 5)$**
7. $7x^2 - 59x + 24$ **$(7x - 3)(x - 8)$**
8. $3x^2 - 14x + 15$ **$(3x - 5)(x - 3)$**
9. $8x^2 - 73x + 9$ **$(8x - 1)(x - 9)$**
10. $2x^2 + 11x - 13$ **$(2x + 13)(x - 1)$**
11. $3x^2 + 2x - 16$ **$(3x + 8)(x - 2)$**
12. $2x^2 + 17x - 30$ **$(x + 10)(2x - 3)$**
13. $8x^2 + 29x - 12$ **$(x + 4)(8x - 3)$**
14. $11x^2 + 25x - 24$ **$(x + 3)(11x - 8)$**
15. $9x^2 - 3x - 2$ **$(3x + 1)(3x - 2)$**
16. $12x^2 - 7x - 12$ **$(4x + 3)(3x - 4)$**
17. $9x^2 - 49x - 30$ **$(9x + 5)(x - 6)$**
18. $6x^2 + x - 40$ **$(3x + 8)(2x - 5)$**
19. $-12x^2 - 35x - 18$ **$-1(4x + 9)(3x + 2)$**
20. $-20x^2 + 29x - 6$ **$-1(5x - 6)(4x - 1)$**
21. $-2x^2 + 5x + 42$ **$-1(2x + 7)(x - 6)$**
22. The area of a rectangle is $20x^2 - 27x - 8$. The length is $4x + 1$. What is the width? **$5x - 8$**

TEST PREP DOCTOR In **Exercise 78,** 1 and 5 are the only choices for the factors of a. Choices **F** and **J** can be eliminated.

Tell students that they can immediately eliminate **C** and **D** in **Exercise 79.** Because b is negative and c is positive, the constants will be subtracted in both binomials.

Answers

81. $(2x + 1)(2x + 1)$
82. $(7x - 1)(7x - 1)$
83. $(9x + 1)(9x + 1)$
84. $(3x + 5)(3x + 5)$
85. $(5x + 2)(5x + 2)$
86. $(3x - 2)(3x - 2)$
90. Archie's Earnings

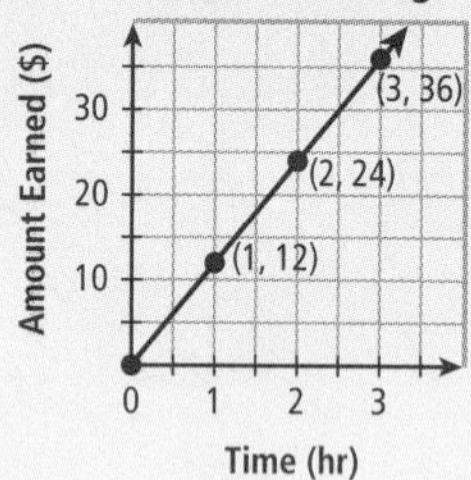

Journal

Have students explain how to factor a trinomial of the form $ax^2 + bx + c$ when a is negative.

ALTERNATIVE ASSESSMENT

Have students write binomials of the form $(x + a)$, $(x - a)$, $(ax + b)$, and $(ax - b)$ and then make six trinomials by multiplying each different pair. Have students give their trinomials to another student to factor.

Power Presentations with PowerPoint®

8-4 Lesson Quiz

Factor each trinomial. Check your answer.

1. $5x^2 + 17x + 6$
   $(5x + 2)(x + 3)$
2. $2x^2 + 5x - 12$
   $(2x - 3)(x + 4)$
3. $6x^2 - 23x + 7$
   $(3x - 1)(2x - 7)$
4. $-4x^2 + 11x + 20$
   $(-x + 4)(4x + 5)$
5. $-2x^2 + 7x - 3$
   $(-2x + 1)(x - 3)$
6. $8x^2 + 27x + 9$
   $(8x + 3)(x + 3)$

Also available on transparency

Match each trinomial with its correct factorization.

72. $6x^2 - 29x - 5$ **D**   **A.** $(x + 5)(6x + 1)$
73. $6x^2 - 31x + 5$ **B**   **B.** $(x - 5)(6x - 1)$
74. $6x^2 + 31x + 5$ **A**   **C.** $(x + 5)(6x - 1)$
75. $6x^2 + 29x - 5$ **C**   **D.** $(x - 5)(6x + 1)$
76. **Critical Thinking** The quadratic trinomial $ax^2 + bx + c$ has $a > 0$ and can be factored into the product of two binomials.
    a. Explain what you know about the signs of the constants in the factors if $c > 0$.
    b. Explain what you know about the signs of the constants in the factors if $c < 0$.

76a. Both signs are pos., or both signs are neg.
b. One sign is pos., and the other is neg.

TEST PREP

77. What value of b would make $3x^2 + bx - 8$ factorable?
    Ⓐ 3   Ⓑ 10 (circled)   Ⓒ 11   Ⓓ 25
78. Which product of binomials is represented by the model?
    Ⓕ $(x + 4)(3x + 5)$ Ⓗ $(x + 3)(5x + 4)$ (circled)
    Ⓖ $(x + 4)(5x + 3)$ Ⓙ $(x + 5)(3x + 4)$

$5x^2$	$4x$
$15x$	12

79. Which binomial is a factor of $24x^2 - 49x + 2$?
    Ⓐ $x - 2$ (circled)   Ⓑ $x - 1$ Ⓒ $x + 1$ Ⓓ $x + 2$
80. Which value of c would make $2x^2 + x + c$ NOT factorable?
    Ⓕ -15 Ⓖ -9 (circled)   Ⓗ -6 Ⓙ -1

CHALLENGE AND EXTEND

Factor each trinomial. Check your answer.

81. $1 + 4x + 4x^2$
82. $1 - 14x + 49x^2$
83. $1 + 18x + 81x^2$
84. $25 + 30x + 9x^2$
85. $4 + 20x + 25x^2$
86. $4 - 12x + 9x^2$
87. Find all possible values of b such that $3x^2 + bx + 2$ can be factored. **−7; −5; 5; 7**
88. Find all possible values of b such that $3x^2 + bx - 2$ can be factored. **−5; −1; 1; 5**
89. Find all possible values of b such that $5x^2 + bx + 1$ can be factored. **−6; 6**

SPIRAL REVIEW

90. Archie makes \$12 per hour. The function $f(x) = 12x$ gives the amount of money that Archie makes in x hours. Graph this function and give its domain and range. *(Lesson 5-1)*
    D: $x \geq 0$; R: $y \geq 0$

Graph each system of linear inequalities. Give two ordered pairs that are solutions and two that are not solutions. *(Lesson 6-6)*

91. $\begin{cases} y < -2x + 1 \\ y > 3x - 5 \end{cases}$
92. $\begin{cases} y \geq -x + 2 \\ y \leq x - 3 \end{cases}$
93. $\begin{cases} y \leq -4x \\ y > 2x - 6 \end{cases}$

Factor each trinomial. Check your answer. *(Lesson 8-3)*

94. $x^2 + 6x + 8$
    $(x + 2)(x + 4)$
95. $x^2 - 8x - 9$
    $(x + 1)(x - 9)$
96. $x^2 - 8x + 12$
    $(x - 2)(x - 6)$

Answers

91. Possible answer: solutions: $(-10, 0)$, $(-20, 0)$; not solutions: $(10, 0)$, $(20, 0)$

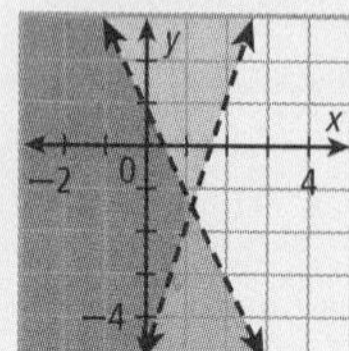

92. Possible answer: solutions: $(4, 0)$, $(5, 0)$; not solutions: $(-4, 0)$, $(-5, 0)$

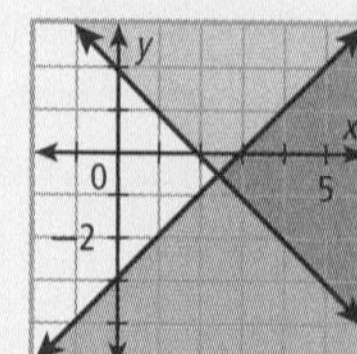

93. Possible answer: solutions: $(-1, 0)$, $(-2, 0)$; not solutions: $(4, 0)$, $(5, 0)$

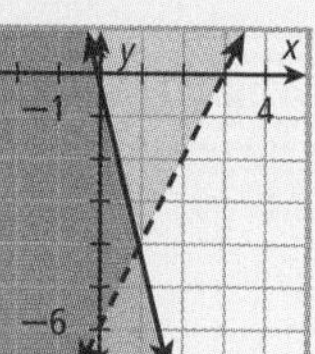

Use a Graph to Factor Polynomials

You can use a graphing calculator to help factor polynomials.

Use with Lesson 8-4

go.hrw.com
Lab Resources Online
KEYWORD: MA7 Lab8

Activity

Factor $x^2 - 3x - 4$ using algebra and check your factorization using a graphing calculator.

1. $x^2 - 3x - 4$

   $(x + \square)(x + \square)$ *$b = -3$ and $c = -4$; look for factors of -4 whose sum is -3.*

   $(x - 4)(x + 1)$ *$-4(1) = -4$; $-4 + 1 = -3$*

2. Press Y= and enter $x^2 - 3x - 4$ for **Y1**.

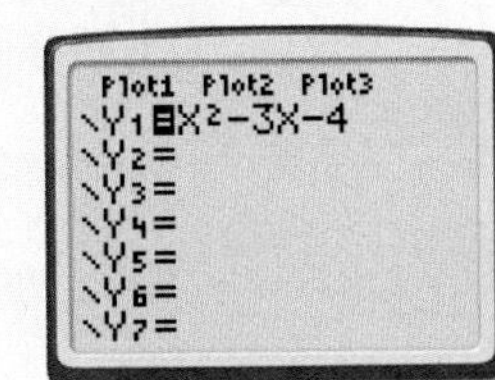

3. Press GRAPH to view the graph of the equation.
4. Press TRACE and use the left and right buttons to move the cursor along the graph. The graph appears to cross the x-axis at $x = -1$ and $x = 4$.

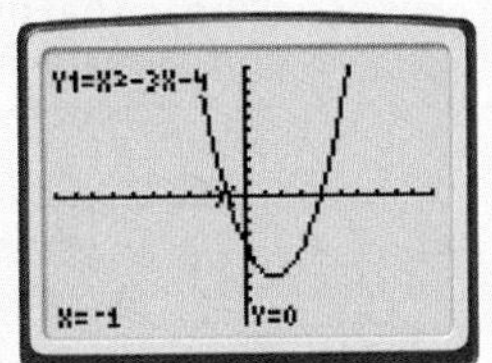

5. To find the value of y at $x = -1$, enter -1 and press ENTER while in *Trace* mode. The calculator gives you a value for y. Then enter 4 to find the value of y at $x = 4$.

   The calculator tells you that $y = 0$ at $x = -1$ and at $x = 4$.

   Notice that for a function with a binomial factor of the form $(x - a)$, it appears that a is an x-intercept.

Y1=X²-3X-4
X=-1 Y=0

Try This

Graph each trinomial and use the graph to predict the factors. Then factor each trinomial using algebra.

1. $x^2 - x - 2$
2. $x^2 + 5x + 6$
3. $x^2 + x - 12$
4. $x^2 + 12x - 64$
5. $x^2 - 4x - 5$
6. $3x^2 + 16x - 12$

Answers to *Try This*

1. $(x - 2)(x + 1)$

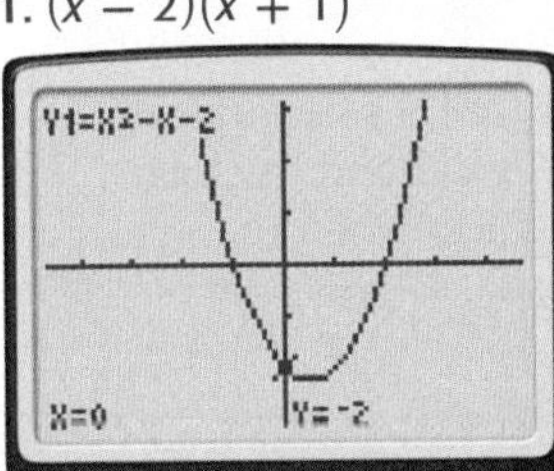

2. $(x + 3)(x + 2)$

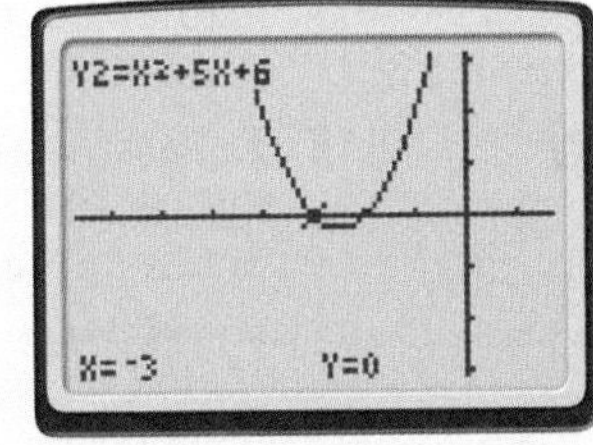

3. $(x + 4)(x - 3)$

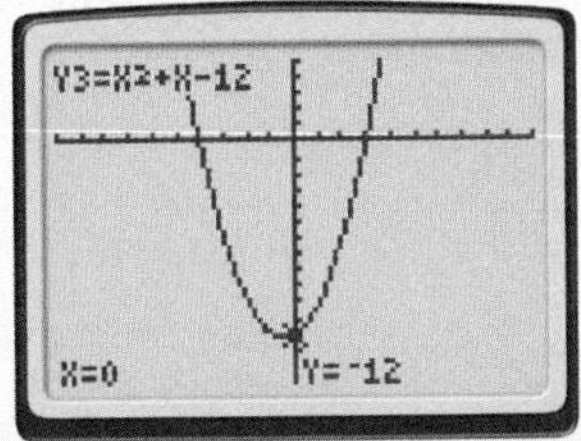

4. $(x + 16)(x - 4)$

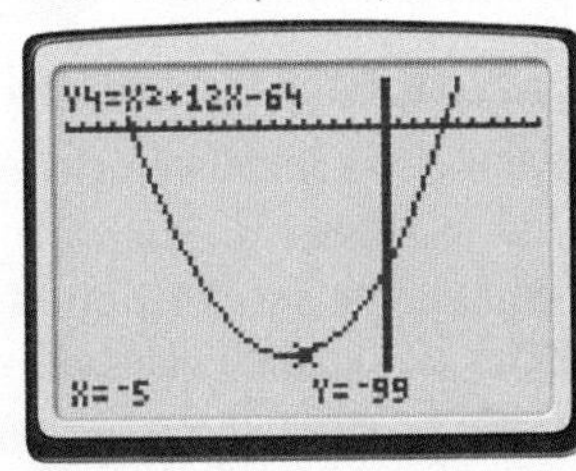

5–6. See p. A29.

Technology LAB Organizer

Use with Lesson 8-4

Pacing:
Traditional $\frac{1}{2}$ day
Block $\frac{1}{4}$ day

Objective: Use a graphing calculator to factor a polynomial by studying its graph.

Materials: graphing calculator

PREMIER **Online Edition**
Graphing Calculator, TechKeys

Resources

Technology Lab Activities
8-4 Lab Recording Sheet

Teach

Discuss

The factors of c are the opposites of the x-intercepts. Students can graph both the factored and original form of a polynomial and determine whether they have the same graph.

Alternative Approach

Students can use the TABLE feature to find the x-intercepts.

Close

Key Concept

If a is an x-intercept, then $(x - a)$ is a factor of the graphed polynomial.

Assessment

Journal Have students explain how to factor a polynomial by using a graphing calculator.

State Resources

Organizer

Objective: Assess students' ability to apply concepts and skills in Lessons 8-1 through 8-4 in a real-world format.

 **Online Edition**

Resources

www.mathtekstoolkit.org

Problem	Text Reference
1	Lesson 8-1
2	Lesson 8-1
3	Lessons 8-2 and 8-3
4	Lessons 8-2 and 8-3
5	Lesson 8-1
6	Lesson 8-4

State Resources

CHAPTER 8

MULTI-STEP TEST PREP

SECTION 8A

Factoring

Red Light, Green Light The equation for the motion of an object with constant acceleration is $d = vt + \frac{1}{2}at^2$ where d is distance traveled in meters, v is starting velocity in m/s, a is acceleration in m/s^2, and t is time in seconds.

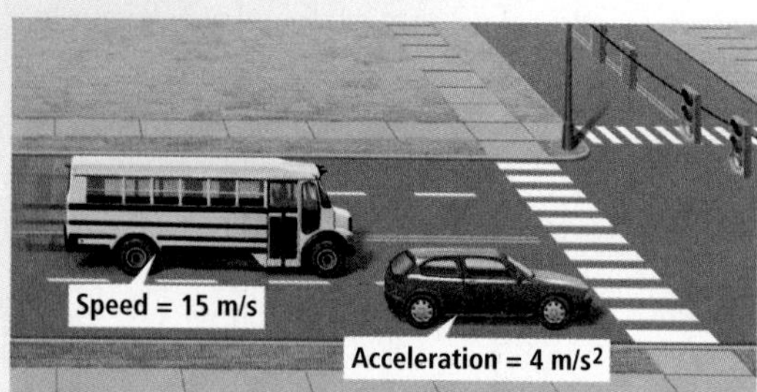

1. A car is stopped at a traffic light. The light changes to green and the driver starts to drive, accelerating at a rate of 4 m/s^2. Write an equation for the distance the car travels in time t. $d = 2t^2$
2. A bus is traveling at a speed of 15 m/s. The driver approaches the same traffic light in another traffic lane. He does not brake, and continues at the same speed. Write an equation for the distance the bus travels in time t. (*Hint:* At a constant speed, the acceleration is 0 m/s^2.) $d = 15t$
3. Set the equations equal to each other so you can determine when the car and bus are the same distance from the intersection. Collect all the terms on the left side of this new equation, leaving 0 on the right side. Factor the expression on the left side of the equation. $2t^2 - 15t = 0$; $t(2t - 15)$
4. Let $t = 0$ be the point at which the car is just starting to drive and the bus is even with the car. Find the other time when the vehicles will be the same distance from the intersection. $t = 7.5$ s
5. What distance will the two vehicles have traveled when they are again at the same distance from the intersection? $d = 112.5$ m
6. A truck traveling at 16 m/s is 24 meters behind the bus at $t = 0$. The equation $d = -24 + 16t$ gives the position of the truck. At what time will the truck be the same distance from the intersection as the bus? What will that distance be? $t = 24$ s; $d = 360$ m

INTERVENTION

Scaffolding Questions

1. What is the initial velocity of an object that is stopped? zero m/s
2. What is the acceleration of an object that does not change velocity? zero m/s^2
3. If the product of two numbers is zero, why is at least one of the numbers zero? Zero multiplied by any number is zero.
4. Explain why one solution to the equation for the car and bus is $t = 0$. The car and bus both start at the intersection with the traffic light.
5. How can you determine the distance traveled by the car? Substitute the time from Problem 4 in the equation from Problem 1.
6. Explain why $t = 0$ is not a solution for the car and truck. The car and truck are not at the same position when the light changes.

Extension

During what period of time is the truck ahead of the car? between $t = 2$ s and $t = 6$ s

Quiz for Lessons 8-1 Through 8-4

8-1 Factors and Greatest Common Factors

Write the prime factorization of each number.

1. 54 $2 \cdot 3^3$
2. 42 $2 \cdot 3 \cdot 7$
3. 50 $2 \cdot 5^2$
4. 120 $2^3 \cdot 3 \cdot 5$
5. 44 $2^2 \cdot 11$
6. 78 $2 \cdot 3 \cdot 13$

Find the GCF of each pair of monomials.

7. $6p^3$ and $2p$ $2p$
8. $12x^3$ and $18x^4$ $6x^3$
9. -15 and $20s^4$ 5
10. $3a$ and $4b^2$ 1
11. Brent is making a wooden display case for his baseball collection. He has 24 balls from American League games and 30 balls from National League games. He wants to display the same number of baseballs in each row and does not want to put American League baseballs in the same row as National League baseballs. How many rows will Brent need in the display case to put the greatest number of baseballs possible in each row? 9

8-2 Factoring by GCF

Factor each polynomial. Check your answer.

12. $2d^3 + 4d$ $2d(d^2 + 2)$
13. $m^2 - 8m^5$ $m^2(1 - 8m^3)$
14. $12x^4 - 8x^3 - 4x^2$ $4x^2(3x^2 - 2x - 1)$
15. $3k^2 + 6k - 3$ $3(k^2 + 2k - 1)$
16. The surface area of a cone can be found using the expression $s\pi r + \pi r^2$, where s represents the slant height and r represents the radius of the base. Factor this expression. $\pi r(s + r)$

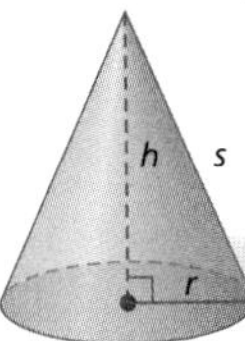

Factor each polynomial by grouping. Check your answer.

17. $w^3 - 4w^2 + w - 4$ $(w^2 + 1)(w - 4)$
18. $3x^3 + 6x^2 - 4x - 8$ $(3x^2 - 4)(x + 2)$
19. $2p^3 - 6p^2 + 15 - 5p$ $(2p^2 - 5)(p - 3)$
20. $n^3 - 6n^2 + 5n - 30$ $(n^2 + 5)(n - 6)$

8-3 Factoring $x^2 + bx + c$

Factor each trinomial. Check your answer.

21. $n^2 + 9n + 20$
22. $d^2 - 6d - 7$
23. $x^2 - 6x + 8$
24. $y^2 + 7y - 30$
25. $k^2 - 6k + 5$
26. $c^2 - 10c + 24$
27. Simplify and factor the expression $n(n + 3) - 4$. Show that the original expression and the factored form have the same value for $n = 0, 1, 2, 3,$ and 4.

8-4 Factoring $ax^2 + bx + c$

Factor each trinomial. Check your answer.

28. $2x^2 + 11x + 5$
29. $3n^2 + 16n + 21$
30. $5y^2 - 7y - 6$
31. $4g^2 - 10g + 6$
32. $6p^2 - 18p - 24$
33. $12d^2 + 7d - 12$
34. The area of a rectangle is $(8x^2 + 8x + 2)$ cm². The width is $(2x + 1)$ cm. What is the length of the rectangle? $(4x + 2)$ cm

READY TO GO ON? SECTION 8A

Organizer

Objective: Assess students' mastery of concepts and skills in Lessons 8-1 through 8-4.

Resources

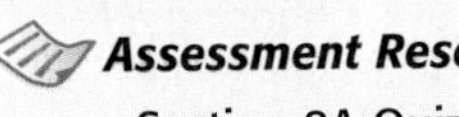

Section 8A Quiz

Teacher One Stop™

Test & Practice Generator

INTERVENTION

Resources

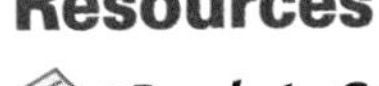

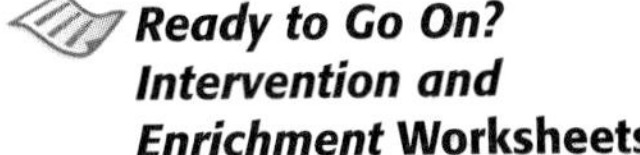

my.hrw.com

Answers

21–33. See p. A29.

READY TO GO ON? Diagnose and Prescribe

NO INTERVENE

Ready to Go On? Intervention	Worksheets	CD-ROM	Online
	Ready to Go On? Intervention, Section 8A		
Lesson 8-1	8-1 Intervention	Activity 8-1	Diagnose and Prescribe Online
Lesson 8-2	8-2 Intervention	Activity 8-2	
Lesson 8-3	8-3 Intervention	Activity 8-3	
Lesson 8-4	8-4 Intervention	Activity 8-4	

YES ENRICH

SECTION **8B**

Applying Factoring Methods

One-Minute Section Planner

Lesson	Lab Resources	Materials
Lesson 8-5 Factoring Special Products • Factor perfect-square trinomials. • Factor the difference of two squares ☐ SAT-10 ☑ NAEP ☑ ACT ☑ SAT ☑ SAT Subject Tests	***Algebra Lab Activities*** 8-5 Algebra Lab	**Optional** algebra tiles (MK)
Lesson 8-6 Choosing a Factoring Method • Choose an appropriate method for factoring a polynomial. • Combine methods for factoring a polynomial. ☐ SAT-10 ☑ NAEP ☑ ACT ☑ SAT ☑ SAT Subject Tests		

Note: If NAEP is checked, the content is tested on either the Grade 8 or the Grade 12 NAEP assessment.

MK = *Manipulatives Kit*

FACTORING POLYNOMIALS

Lessons 8-5 and 8-6

Algebra is an extension of arithmetic. As such, there are many parallels between the two. For example, the arithmetic idea of factoring a number can be extended into the realm of algebra by considering factorizations of polynomials.

Factoring polynomials is an essential algebraic skill. As students will see in Chapter 9, it provides a powerful method for solving quadratic equations. However, students must first develop an arsenal of techniques for factoring.

FACTORING METHODS

Lesson 8-6

The simplest factoring methods are direct applications of the Distributive Property. In particular, the Distributive Property makes it possible to factor out the greatest common factor (GCF) of the terms of a polynomial.

For example, to factor the polynomial $3x^2 + 12x^3$, we may rewrite it as $3 \cdot x \cdot x + 2 \cdot 2 \cdot 3 \cdot x \cdot x \cdot x$, where the integer coefficients have been written in their prime factorizations. This form of the polynomial makes it easy to see that the GCF of the terms is $3x^2$, and by the Distributive Property, $3x^2 + 12x^3 = 3x^2(1 + 4x)$.

The Distributive Property is also at work when students use more general methods to factor binomials. To factor the polynomial $x^2 + 7x + 12$, students will look for two factors of 12 whose sum is 7. This leads to the factorization $(x + 4)(x + 3)$. However, it is instructive to look at the intermediate steps. Once the correct factors of 12 have been identified, we can write

1. $x^2 + 7x + 12 = x^2 + 3x + 4x + 12$
2. $= x(x + 3) + 4(x + 3)$
3. $= (x + 4)(x + 3)$

The Distributive Property has been used twice to go from Step 1 to Step 2 and has been applied again to go from Step 2 to Step 3. It is also useful to recognize that the polynomial on the right side of the equation in Step 1 consists of precisely the set of terms that result from multiplying $(x + 4)(x + 3)$ by using the FOIL method taught in Chapter 7. In other words, multiplying polynomials and factoring polynomials are inverse processes based on the Distributive Property.

UNFACTORABLE POLYNOMIALS

Lesson 8-6

Students should understand that some polynomials cannot be factored. For example, the trinomials $x^2 + x + 1$ and $2x^2 + 5x + 4$ are unfactorable. We call these polynomials *prime polynomials*.

Note that when we say a polynomial is unfactorable in an Algebra 1 course, this generally means that it cannot be factored *over the integers*. In other words, the polynomial cannot be written as a product of polynomials of lesser degree whose terms have integer coefficients. However, it may be possible to factor the polynomial over other sets of numbers.

For example, consider the binomial $x^2 - 2$. This binomial is unfactorable over the integers, but it can be factored over the real numbers as $(x + \sqrt{2})(x - \sqrt{2})$. Furthermore, the binomial $x^2 + 4$ cannot be factored over the integers or over the real numbers, but it can be factored over the complex numbers as $(x + 2i)\ (x - 2i)$, where $i = \sqrt{-1}$. (Students will be introduced to the set of complex numbers in Algebra 2.)

To take this a step further, the Fundamental Theorem of Algebra asserts that every polynomial of degree $n \geq 1$ has n roots in the complex numbers. As a result, every polynomial can be completely factored (that is, written as a product of linear factors) in a unique way over the complex numbers, with the exception of different orderings of the factors. Thus, the Fundamental Theorem of Algebra is analogous to the Fundamental Theorem of Arithmetic, demonstrating once again that algebra is an extension of arithmetic.

8-5 Organizer

Pacing: Traditional 1 day
Block $\frac{1}{2}$ day

Objectives: Factor perfect-square trinomials.

Factor the difference of two squares.

Algebra Lab
In *Algebra Lab Activities*

Online Edition
Tutorial Videos, Interactivity

Countdown Week 18

Power Presentations with PowerPoint®

Warm Up

Determine whether the following are perfect squares. If so, find the positive square root.

1. 64 yes; 8 **2.** 36 yes; 6

3. 45 no **4.** x^2 yes; x

5. y^8 yes; y^4 **6.** $4x^6$ yes; $2x^3$

7. $9y^7$ no **8.** $49p^{10}$ yes; $7p^5$

Also available on transparency

Math Humor

Q: What did Polly Nomial call her spoiled triplets?

A: The perfect Tri Nomials.

8-5 Factoring Special Products

Objectives
Factor perfect-square trinomials.

Factor the difference of two squares.

Who uses this?
Urban planners can use the area of a square park to find its length and width. (See Example 2.)

You studied the patterns of some special products of binomials in Chapter 7. You can use those patterns to factor certain polynomials.

A trinomial is a perfect square if:

- The **first** and **last** terms are perfect squares.
- The **middle** term is two times one factor from the first term and one factor from the last term.

$$9x^2 + 12x + 4$$
$$3x \cdot 3x \quad 2(3x \cdot 2) \quad 2 \cdot 2$$

Know it! Note

Perfect-Square Trinomials

PERFECT-SQUARE TRINOMIAL	EXAMPLES
$a^2 + 2ab + b^2 = (a + b)(a + b) = (a + b)^2$	$x^2 + 6x + 9 = (x + 3)(x + 3) = (x + 3)^2$
$a^2 - 2ab + b^2 = (a - b)(a - b) = (a - b)^2$	$x^2 - 2x + 1 = (x - 1)(x - 1) = (x - 1)^2$

EXAMPLE 1 **Recognizing and Factoring Perfect-Square Trinomials**

Determine whether each trinomial is a perfect square. If so, factor. If not, explain.

A $x^2 + 12x + 36$

$$x^2 + 12x + 36$$
$$x \cdot x \quad 2(x \cdot 6) \quad 6 \cdot 6$$

The trinomial is a perfect square. Factor.

Method 1 Factor.

$x^2 + 12x + 36$

Factors of 36	Sum	
1 and 36	37	✗
2 and 18	20	✗
3 and 12	15	✗
4 and 9	13	✗
6 and 6	12	✓

$(x + 6)(x + 6)$

Method 2 Use the rule.

$x^2 + 12x + 36$ *$a = x$, $b = 6$*

$x^2 + 2(x)(6) + 6^2$ *Write the trinomial as $a^2 + 2ab + b^2$.*

$(x + 6)^2$ *Write the trinomial as $(a + b)^2$.*

1 Introduce

EXPLORATION

8-5 Factoring Special Products

In this Exploration, you will look for patterns as you find the squares of binomials.

1. Complete the table by writing each square as a product of two factors. Then find the product of the two factors and express the result as a trinomial.

Square	Factors	Product
$(x + 2)^2$	$(x + 2)(x + 2)$	$x^2 + 4x + 4$
$(x + 3)^3$		
$(x + 5)^2$		
$(x - 4)^2$		
$(2x + 5)^2$		
$(3x - 7)^2$		
$(5x + 1)^2$		

2. Look at the constant terms of the trinomials in your table. What do you notice?
3. Look at the x^2-terms of the trinomials in your table. What do you notice?

THINK AND DISCUSS

4. **Explain** whether it is possible for the constant term of a trinomial to be negative if the trinomial can be written as the square of a binomial.
5. **Discuss** whether you think $x^2 + 6x + 24$ can be written as the square of a binomial.

Motivate

Have students write all the steps for multiplying $(2x + 3)(2x - 3)$ using the FOIL method.

$(2x)(2x) + (2x)(-3) + (3)(2x) + (3)(-3)$
$= 4x^2 - 6x + 6x - 9$
$= 4x^2 - 9$

Ask students why there is no middle term in the final step. The sum of the inner product and the outer product is zero.

Explorations and answers are provided in *Alternate Openers: Explorations Transparencies.*

State Resources

go.hrw.com
State Resources Online
KEYWORD: MA7 Resources

Determine whether each trinomial is a perfect square. If so, factor. If not, explain.

Helpful Hint

You can check your answer by using the FOIL method.

For Example 1B,
$(2x - 3)^2 =$
$(2x - 3)(2x - 3) =$
$4x^2 - 6x - 6x + 9 =$
$4x^2 - 12x + 9$

B $4x^2 - 12x + 9$

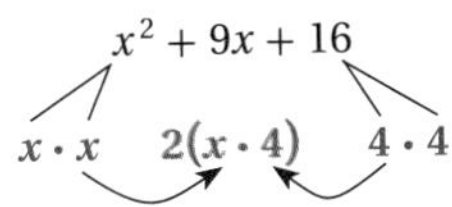

$4x^2 - 12x + 9$

$2x \cdot 2x \quad 2(2x \cdot 3) \quad 3 \cdot 3$ *The trinomial is a perfect square. Factor.*

$4x^2 - 12x + 9$ — $a = 2x,\ b = 3$

$(2x)^2 - 2(2x)(3) + 3^2$ — $a^2 - 2ab + b^2$

$(2x - 3)^2$ — $(a - b)^2$

C $x^2 + 9x + 16$

$x^2 + 9x + 16$

$x \cdot x \quad 2(x \cdot 4) \quad 4 \cdot 4$ — $2(x \cdot 4) \neq 9x$

$x^2 + 9x + 16$ is not a perfect-square trinomial because $9x \neq 2(x \cdot 4)$.

CHECK IT OUT! Determine whether each trinomial is a perfect square. If so, factor. If not, explain.

1a. $x^2 + 4x + 4$ yes; $(x + 2)^2$

1b. $x^2 - 14x + 49$ yes; $(x - 7)^2$

1c. $9x^2 - 6x + 4$ no; $-6x \neq 2(3x)(2)$

EXAMPLE 2 *Problem-Solving Application*

PROBLEM SOLVING

The park in the center of the Place des Vosges in Paris, France, is in the shape of a square. The area of the park is $(25x^2 + 70x + 49)$ ft². The side length of the park is in the form $cx + d$, where c and d are whole numbers. Find an expression in terms of x for the perimeter of the park. Find the perimeter when $x = 8$ ft.

1 Understand the Problem

The **answer** will be an expression for the perimeter of the park and the value of the expression when $x = 8$.

List the **important information:**

- The park is a square with area $(25x^2 + 70x + 49)$ ft².
- The side length of the park is in the form $cx + d$, where c and d are whole numbers.

2 Make a Plan

The formula for the area of a square is area = $(\text{side})^2$.

Factor $25x^2 + 70x + 49$ to find the side length of the park. Write a formula for the perimeter of the park, and evaluate the expression for $x = 8$.

COMMON ERROR ALERT

When checking the answer for **Example 1A,** students might multiply $(x + 6)^2$ as $x^2 + 6^2 = x^2 + 36$. Encourage students to write $(x + 6)^2$ as $(x + 6)(x + 6)$ and then use the FOIL method.

Power Presentations with PowerPoint®

Additional Examples

Example 1

Determine whether each trinomial is a perfect square. If so, factor. If not, explain.

A. $9x^2 - 15x + 64$
no; $-15x \neq 2(3x \cdot 8)$

B. $81x^2 + 90x + 25$
yes; $(9x + 5)^2$

C. $36x^2 - 10x + 14$
No; 14 is not a perfect square.

Example 2

A square piece of cloth must be cut to make a tablecloth. The area needed is $(16x^2 - 24x + 9)$ in². The dimensions of the cloth are of the form $cx - d$, where c and d are whole numbers. Find an expression for the perimeter of the cloth. Find the perimeter when $x = 11$ inches.
$16x - 12$; 164 in.

INTERVENTION 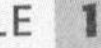

Questioning Strategies

EXAMPLE 1

- Identify the steps for determining whether a trinomial is a perfect-square trinomial.
- When factoring a perfect-square trinomial, do you think it is easier to list the factors or use the pattern? Explain your reasoning.

EXAMPLE 2

- What must be true about the factors of a rectangular area for that area to be a square? Explain.

2 Teach

Guided Instruction

Before beginning this lesson, review factoring trinomials and identifying perfect squares. Point out that perfect-square trinomials can be factored using the methods from the previous sections. Because these polynomials contain perfect-square numbers, easier methods are shown. Emphasize that factoring the difference of two squares is possible only for the difference. The sum of two squares cannot be factored.

Reaching All Learners

Through Number Sense

Show students a quick way to rule out the possibility of a trinomial being a perfect-square trinomial. Remind them that if $ax^2 + bx + c$ is a perfect-square trinomial, then b must be an even number. This is because in a perfect-square trinomial, $b = 2 \cdot \sqrt{a} \cdot \sqrt{c}$. If b is even, then the trinomial *might* be a perfect square.

Inclusion After completing Step 3 of **Example 2,** show that the numerical value of the perimeter could be found by first substituting $x = 8$ into $5x + 7$ to find the length of one side. The length of one side is 47 ft, and the perimeter is 47×4, or 188, ft.

Solve

$25x^2 + 70x + 49$ — *$a = 5x$, $b = 7$*

$(5x)^2 + 2(5x)(7) + 7^2$ — *Write the trinomial as $a^2 + 2ab + b^2$.*

$(5x + 7)^2$ — *Write the trinomial as $(a + b)^2$.*

$$25x^2 + 70x + 49 = (5x + 7)(5x + 7)$$

The side length of the park is $(5x + 7)$ ft.

Write a formula for the perimeter of the park.

$P = 4s$ — *Write the formula for the perimeter of a square.*

$= 4(5x + 7)$ — *Substitute the side length for s.*

$= 20x + 28$ — *Distribute 4.*

An expression for the perimeter of the park in feet is $20x + 28$.

Evaluate the expression when $x = 8$.

$P = 20x + 28$

$= 20(8) + 28$ — *Substitute 8 for x.*

$= 188$

When $x = 8$ ft, the perimeter of the park is 188 ft.

Look Back

For a square with a perimeter of 188 ft, the side length is $\frac{188}{4} = 47$ ft and the area is $47^2 = 2209$ ft^2.

Evaluate $25x^2 + 70x + 49$ for $x = 8$:

$25(8)^2 + 70(8) + 49$

$1600 + 560 + 49$

2209 ✓

CHECK IT OUT!

2. **What if...?** A company produces square sheets of aluminum, each of which has an area of $(9x^2 + 6x + 1)$ m^2. The side length of each sheet is in the form $cx + d$, where c and d are whole numbers. Find an expression in terms of x for the perimeter of a sheet. Find the perimeter when $x = 3$ m. **$4(3x + 1)$ m; 40 m**

In Chapter 7 you learned that the difference of two squares has the form $a^2 - b^2$. The difference of two squares can be written as the product $(a + b)(a - b)$. You can use this pattern to factor some polynomials.

A polynomial is a difference of two squares if:

- There are two terms, one subtracted from the other.
- Both terms are perfect squares.

$$4x^2 - 9$$
$$2x \cdot 2x \quad 3 \cdot 3$$

Know it! Note

Difference of Two Squares

DIFFERENCE OF TWO SQUARES	EXAMPLE
$a^2 - b^2 = (a + b)(a - b)$	$x^2 - 9 = (x + 3)(x - 3)$

Reaching All Learners

Through Modeling

Recall modeling the factors of trinomials with algebra tiles (MK). The tiles must be arranged in a rectangle. When the factors of a perfect-square trinomial are modeled with algebra tiles, the tiles will be arranged in a square.

EXAMPLE 3 Recognizing and Factoring the Difference of Two Squares

Determine whether each binomial is a difference of two squares. If so, factor. If not, explain.

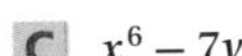

Reading Math

Recognize a difference of two squares: the coefficients of variable terms are perfect squares, powers on variable terms are even, and constants are perfect squares.

A $x^2 - 81$

$x^2 - 81$

$x \cdot x \quad 9 \cdot 9$ — *The polynomial is a difference of two squares.*

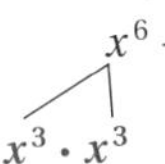

$x^2 - 9^2$ — *$a = x$, $b = 9$*

$(x + 9)(x - 9)$ — *Write the polynomial as $(a + b)(a - b)$.*

$x^2 - 81 = (x + 9)(x - 9)$

B $9p^4 - 16q^2$

$9p^4 - 16q^2$

$3p^2 \cdot 3p^2 \quad 4q \cdot 4q$ — *The polynomial is a difference of two squares.*

$(3p^2)^2 - (4q)^2$ — *$a = 3p^2$, $b = 4q$*

$(3p^2 + 4q)(3p^2 - 4q)$ — *Write the polynomial as $(a + b)(a - b)$.*

$9p^4 - 16q^2 = (3p^2 + 4q)(3p^2 - 4q)$

C $x^6 - 7y^2$

$x^6 - 7y^2$

$x^3 \cdot x^3$ — *$7y^2$ is not a perfect square.*

$x^6 - 7y^2$ is not the difference of two squares because $7y^2$ is not a perfect square.

CHECK IT OUT! Determine whether the binomial is a difference of two squares. If so, factor. If not, explain.

3a. $1 - 4x^2$ — yes; $(1 - 2x)(1 + 2x)$

3b. $p^8 - 49q^6$ — yes; $(p^4 + 7q^3)(p^4 - 7q^3)$

3c. $16x^2 - 4y^5$ — No; $4y^5$ is not a perfect square.

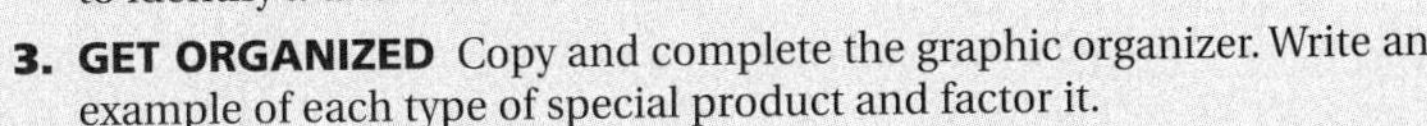

THINK AND DISCUSS

1. The binomial $1 - x^4$ is a difference of two squares. Use the rule to identify a and b in $1 - x^4$.
2. The polynomial $x^2 + 8x + 16$ is a perfect-square trinomial. Use the rule to identify a and b in $x^2 + 8x + 16$.
3. **GET ORGANIZED** Copy and complete the graphic organizer. Write an example of each type of special product and factor it.

Know it! Note

Special Product	Factored Form
Perfect-square trinomial with positive coefficient of middle term	
Perfect-square trinomial with negative coefficient of middle term	
Difference of two squares	

Power Presentations with PowerPoint®

Additional Examples

Example 3

Determine whether the binomial is a difference of two squares. If so, factor. If not, explain.

A. $3p^2 - 9q^4$ No; $3p^2$ is not a perfect square.

B. $100x^2 - 4y^2$ yes; $(10x + 2y)(10x - 2y)$

C. $x^4 - 25y^6$ yes; $(x^2 + 5y^3)(x^2 - 5y^3)$

INTERVENTION

Questioning Strategies

EXAMPLE 3

- Explain why the product of binomials of the form $(a + b)(a - b)$ is not a trinomial.

Teaching Tip **Math Background** In **Example 3C,** students might think that x^6 is not a perfect square because the number 6 is not a perfect square. Remind them of the Product of Powers Property, which states that $a^m \cdot a^n = a^{m+n}$. Thus, x^6 is a perfect square because it can be written as $x^3 \cdot x^3$.

3 Close

Summarize

Have students name the characteristics of

- a perfect-square trinomial of the form $ax^2 + bx + c$. 1) a and c must be perfect squares. 2) $b = 2\sqrt{ac}$
- a difference of squares of the form $a^2 - b^2$. 1) Both terms must be perfect squares. 2) It must be a difference.

ONGOING ASSESSMENT and INTERVENTION

***Diagnose Before* the Lesson**
8-5 Warm Up, TE p. 578

***Monitor During* the Lesson**
Check It Out! Exercises, SE pp. 579–581
Questioning Strategies, TE pp. 579, 581

***Assess After* the Lesson**
8-5 Lesson Quiz, TE p. 584
Alternative Assessment, TE p. 584

Answers to *Think and Discuss*

1. $a = 1$; $b = x^2$
2. $a = x$; $b = 4$
3. See p. A7.

8-5 Exercises

Assignment Guide

Assign *Guided Practice* exercises as necessary.

If you finished Examples **1–2**
Basic 14–20, 27–29
Average 14–20, 27, 29, 38
Advanced 14–20, 27, 29, 38

If you finished Examples **1–3**
Basic 14–36, 38–49, 55–64,
Average 14–40, 46–50, 55–64
Advanced 14–29, 30–34 even, 36–40, 47–64

Homework Quick Check
Quickly check key concepts.
Exercises: 14, 16, 20, 22, 26, 38

Answers

14. yes; $(2x-1)^2$
15. No; the last term must be pos.
16. yes; $(6x-1)^2$
17. no; $10x \neq 2(5x)(2)$
18. yes; $(3x+3)^2$
19. yes; $(4x-5)^2$
30. $(x-4)^2$; perf.-square trinomial
31. $(10x+9y)(10x-9y)$; diff. of 2 squares
32. $(6x+2)^2$; perf.-square trinomial
33. $(2r^3+5s^3)(2r^3-5s^3)$; diff. of 2 squares
34. $(7x-5)^2$; perf.-square trinomial
35. $(x^7+12)(x^7-12)$; diff. of 2 squares
36–37. See p. A29.

State Resources

8-5 Exercises

go.hrw.com
Homework Help Online
KEYWORD: MA7 8-5
Parent Resources Online
KEYWORD: MA7 Parent

GUIDED PRACTICE

SEE EXAMPLE 1 p. 578

Determine whether each trinomial is a perfect square. If so, factor. If not, explain.

1. x^2-4x+4 **yes; $(x-2)^2$**
2. x^2-4x-4 **No; the last term must be pos.**
3. $9x^2-12x+4$ **yes; $(3x-2)^2$**
4. x^2+2x+1 **yes; $(x+1)^2$**
5. x^2-6x+9 **yes; $(x-3)^2$**
6. x^2-6x-9 **No; the last term must be pos**

SEE EXAMPLE 2 p. 579

7. **City Planning** A city purchases a square plot of land with an area of $(x^2+24x+144)$ yd² for a park. The dimensions of the plot are of the form $ax+b$, where a and b are whole numbers. Find an expression for the perimeter of the park. Find the perimeter when $x = 10$ yd. **$4(x+12)$; 88 yd**

SEE EXAMPLE 3 p. 581

Determine whether each binomial is a difference of two squares. If so, factor. If not, explain.

8. $1-4x^2$ **yes; $(1+2x)(1-2x)$**
9. s^2-4^2 **yes; $(s+4)(s-4)$**
10. $81x^2-1$ **yes; $(9x+1)(9x-1)$**
11. $4x^4-9y^2$ **yes; $(2x^2+3y)(2x^2-3y)$**
12. x^8-50 **No; 50 is not a perf. square.**
13. x^6-9 **yes; $(x^3+3)(x^3-3)$**

PRACTICE AND PROBLEM SOLVING

Independent Practice	
For Exercises	See Example
14–19	1
20	2
21–26	3

Extra Practice
Skills Practice p. S19
Application Practice p. S35

Determine whether the trinomial is a perfect square. If so, factor. If not, explain.

14. $4x^2-4x+1$
15. $4x^2-4x-1$
16. $36x^2-12x+1$
17. $25x^2+10x+4$
18. $9x^2+18x+9$
19. $16x^2-40x+25$

20. **Measurement** You are given a sheet of paper and told to cut out a square piece with an area of $(4x^2-44x+121)$ mm². The dimensions of the square have the form $ax-b$, where a and b are whole numbers. Find an expression for the perimeter of the square you cut out. Find the perimeter when $x = 41$ mm. **$4(2x-11)$; 284 mm**

Determine whether each binomial is a difference of two squares. If so, factor. If not, explain.

21. 1^2-4x^2 **yes; $(1+2x)(1-2x)$**
22. $25m^2-16n^2$ **yes; $(5m-4n)(5m+4n)$**
23. $4x-9y$ **No; $4x$ and $9y$ are not perf. squares.**
24. $49p^{12}-9q^6$ **yes; $(7p^6-3q^3)(7p^6+3q^3)$**
25. 9^2-100x^4 **yes; $(9-10x^2)(9+10x^2)$**
26. x^3-y^3 **No; x^3 and y^3 are not perf. squares.**

Find the missing term in each perfect-square trinomial.

27. x^2+14x+ **49**
28. $9x^2+$ **$30x$** $+25$
29. **$4y^2$** $-36y+81$

Factor each polynomial using the rule for perfect-square trinomials or the rule for a difference of two squares. Tell which rule you used.

30. $x^2-8x+16$
31. $100x^2-81y^2$
32. $36x^2+24x+4$
33. $4r^6-25s^6$
34. $49x^2-70x+25$
35. $x^{14}-144$

36. **Write About It** What is similar about a perfect-square trinomial and a difference of two squares? What is different?
37. **Critical Thinking** Describe two ways to create a perfect-square trinomial.
38. For what value of b would $(x+b)(x+b)$ be the factored form of $x^2-22x+121$? **$b=-11$**
39. For what value of c are the factors of $x^2+cx+256$ the same? **$c=32$**

8-5 READING STRATEGIES

The chart below shows how to recognize and factor two special products.

Perfect Square Trinomial Ex: x^2+6x+9	Contrast	Difference of Squares Ex: $4x^2-25$
3	Number of Terms	2
+ + or − +	Sign(s)	always −
x^2+6x+9: $x \cdot x$, $2(x \cdot 3)$, $3 \cdot 3$	Pattern	$4x^2-25$: $2x \cdot 2x$, $5 \cdot 5$
binomial squared $(x+3)(x+3) = (x+3)^2$	Factored Form	two binomials, opposite signs $(2x+5)(2x-5)$

Compare

The first term and last term of both special products are perfect squares.

Identify each of the following as a perfect square trinomial (P), a difference of squares (D), or neither (N).

1. x^2-16 **D**
2. $x^2-14x+49$ **P**
3. $100x^2-36$ **D**
4. $4x^2-12x-9$ **N**
5. $x^2+14x+49$ **P**
6. $25x^2+64$ **N**

Factor each special product.

7. $16x^2-9$ **$(4x+3)(4x-3)$**
8. $121x^2-44x+4$ **$(11x-2)^2$**
9. $81x^2-1$ **$(9x+1)(9x-1)$**

8-5 RETEACH

If a polynomial is a perfect square trinomial, the polynomial can be factored using a pattern.

$$a^2+2ab+b^2=(a+b)^2$$
$$a^2-2ab+b^2=(a-b)^2$$

Determine whether $4x^2+20x+25$ is a perfect square trinomial. If so, factor it. If not, explain why.

Step 1: Find a, b, then $2ab$.

$a=\sqrt{4x^2}=2x$ — *The first term is a perfect square.*
$b=\sqrt{25}=5$ — *The last term is a perfect square.*
$2ab=2(2x)(5)=20x$ — *Middle term $(20x)=2ab$.*

Therefore, $4x^2+20x+25$ is a perfect square trinomial.

Step 2: Substitute expressions for a and b into $(a+b)^2$.

$(2x+5)^2$

Determine whether $9x^2+25x+36$ is a perfect square trinomial. If so, factor it. If not, explain why.

Step 1: Find a, b, then $2ab$.

$a=\sqrt{9x^2}=3x$ — *The first term is a perfect square.*
$b=\sqrt{36}=6$ — *The last term is a perfect square.*
$2ab=2(3x)(6)=36x$ — *Middle term $(25x) \neq 2ab$.*

STOP
Because $25x$ does not equal $2ab$, $9x^2-25x+36$ is not a perfect square trinomial.

Determine whether each trinomial is a perfect square. If so, factor it. If not, explain why.

1. $9x^2+30x+100$
   $a=$ **$3x$**
   $b=$ **10**
   $2ab=$ **$60x$**
   Factor or explain: **$30x \neq 2ab$**
2. $x^2-14x+49$
   $a=$ **x**
   $b=$ **7**
   $2ab=$ **$14x$**
   Factor or explain: **$(x-7)^2$**
3. $25x^2+20x+4$
   $a=$ **$5x$**
   $b=$ **2**
   $2ab=$ **$20x$**
   Factor or explain: **$(5x+2)^2$**

40. This problem will prepare you for the Multi-Step Test Prep on page 592.

Juanita designed a vegetable garden in the shape of a square and purchased fencing for that design. Then she decided to change the design to a rectangle. $(x - 5)(x + 5)$

a. The square garden had an area of x^2 ft². The area of the rectangular garden is $(x^2 - 25)$ ft². Factor this expression.

b. The rectangular garden must have the same perimeter as the square garden, so Juanita added a number of feet to the length and subtracted the same number of feet from the width. Use your factors from part **a** to determine how many feet were added to the length and subtracted from the width.

c. If the original length of the square garden was 8 feet, what are the length and width of the new garden? $\ell = 13$ ft; $w = 3$ ft

40b. ℓ: added 5 ft; w: subtracted 5 ft

41. **Multi-Step** The area of a square is represented by $25z^2 - 40z + 16$.

a. What expression represents the length of a side of the square? $5z - 4$

b. What expression represents the perimeter of the square? $20z - 16$

c. What are the length of a side, the perimeter, and the area of the square when $z = 3$? 11; 44; 121

42. **Multi-Step** A small rectangle is drawn inside a larger rectangle as shown.

3x

x

y

3y

a. What is the area of each rectangle? $3x^2$; $3y^2$

b. What is the area of the green region? $3x^2 - 3y^2$

c. Factor the expression for the area of the green region. (*Hint:* First factor out the common factor of 3 and then factor the binomial.) $3(x + y)(x - y)$

43. Evaluate each expression for the values of x.

	x	$x^2 + 10x + 25$	$(x + 5)^2$	$(x - 5)^2$	$x^2 - 10x + 25$	$x^2 - 25$
a.	−5	0	0	100	100	0
b.	−1	16	16	36	36	−24
c.	0	25	25	25	25	−25
d.	1	36	36	16	16	−24
e.	5	100	100	0	0	0

44. In the table above, which columns have equivalent values? Explain why.

45. **Geometry** A model for the difference of two squares is shown below. Copy and complete the second figure by writing the missing labels.

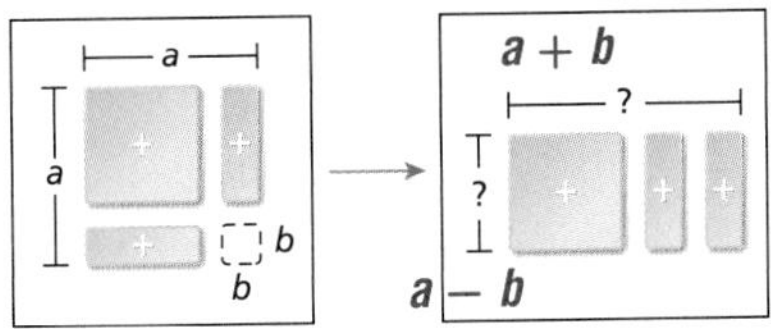

46. **ERROR ANALYSIS** Two students factored $25x^4 - 9y^2$. Which is incorrect? Explain the error.

Student A; $(5x)(5x) \neq 25x^4$ and $(-3)(3) \neq 9y^2$.

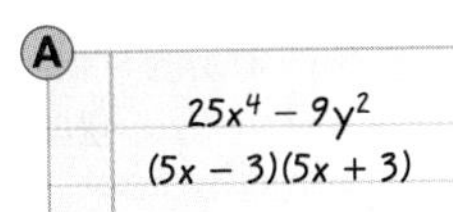

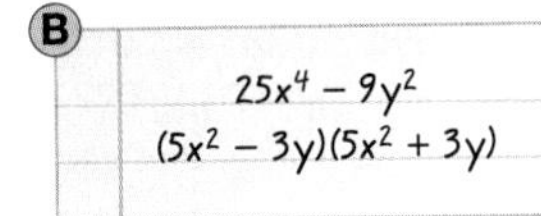

Exercise 40 involves using factoring to find dimensions of squares and rectangles. This exercise prepares students for the Multi-Step Test Prep on page 592.

Answers

44. The first and second columns and the third and fourth columns have the same values; the second column is the factored form of the first column. The third column is the factored form of the fourth column.

8-5 PROBLEM SOLVING

Write the correct answer.

1. A rectangular fountain has an area of $(16x^2 + 8x + 1)$ ft². The dimensions of the rectangle have the form $ax + b$, where a and b are whole numbers. Write an expression for the perimeter of the fountain. Then find the perimeter when $x = 2$ feet.

$16x + 4$;
36 feet

2. A square tabletop has an area of $(9x^2 - 90x + 225)$ cm². The dimensions of the tabletop have the form $cx - d$, where c and d are whole numbers. Write an expression for the perimeter of the tabletop. Then find the perimeter when $x = 25$ centimeters.

$12x - 60$;
240 cm

3. The floor plan of a daycare center is shown.

x
x
2y
2y

The arts and crafts area in the lower right corner is not carpeted. The rest of the center is carpeted. Write an expression, in factored form, for the area of the floor that is carpeted.

$(x + 2y)(x - 2y)$

4. A plate with a decorative border is shown.

6
x

Write an expression, in factored form, for the area of the border. (*Hint:* First factor out the GCF.)

$\pi(x + 6)(x - 6)$

Nelson is making open top boxes by cutting out corners from a sheet of cardboard, folding the edges up, and then taping them together. Select the best answer.

x
x

5. Nelson cut corners so that each corner was a square with side lengths of 4. What is the total area of the remaining piece of cardboard?

A $x^2 - 8x + 16$
B $x^2 + 8x + 16$
C $x^2 - 16x + 64$
D $x^2 + 16x + 64$

6. What are the dimensions of the square corners if the total remaining area is $x^2 - 4x + 4$?

F 1 by 1
G 2 by 2
H 4 by 4
J 8 by 8

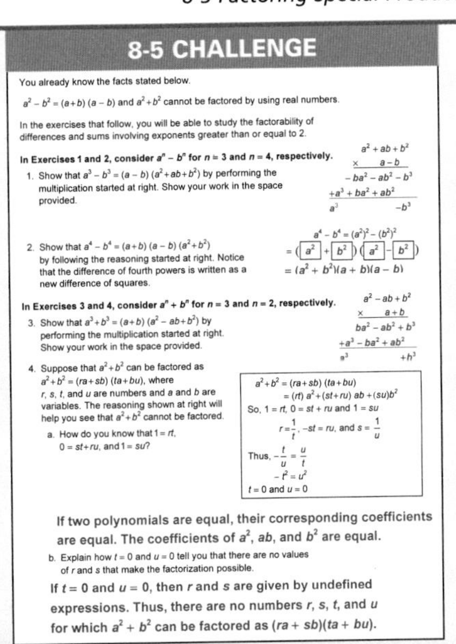

8-5 CHALLENGE

You already know the facts stated below.

$a^2 - b^2 = (a+b)(a-b)$ and $a^2 + b^2$ cannot be factored by using real numbers.

In the exercises that follow, you will be able to study the factorability of differences and sums involving exponents greater than or equal to 2.

In Exercises 1 and 2, consider $a^n - b^n$ for $n = 3$ and $n = 4$, respectively.

1. Show that $a^3 - b^3 = (a - b)(a^2 + ab + b^2)$ by performing the multiplication started at right. Show your work in the space provided.

$$\begin{array}{r} a^2 + ab + b^2 \\ \times \quad a - b \\ \hline -ba^2 - ab^2 - b^3 \\ +a^3 + ba^2 + ab^2 \quad \\ \hline a^3 \qquad\qquad -b^3 \end{array}$$

2. Show that $a^4 - b^4 = (a+b)(a-b)(a^2+b^2)$ by following the reasoning started at right. Notice that the difference of fourth powers is written as a new difference of squares.

$$a^4 - b^4 = (a^2)^2 - (b^2)^2$$
$$= (\boxed{a^2} + \boxed{b^2})(\boxed{a^2} - \boxed{b^2})$$
$$= (a^2 + b^2)(a + b)(a - b)$$

In Exercises 3 and 4, consider $a^n + b^n$ for $n = 3$ and $n = 2$, respectively.

3. Show that $a^3 + b^3 = (a+b)(a^2 - ab + b^2)$ by performing the multiplication started at right. Show your work in the space provided.

$$\begin{array}{r} a^2 - ab + b^2 \\ \times \quad a + b \\ \hline ba^2 - ab^2 + b^3 \\ +a^3 - ba^2 + ab^2 \quad \\ \hline a^3 \qquad\qquad +b^3 \end{array}$$

4. Suppose that $a^2 + b^2$ can be factored as $a^2 + b^2 = (ra + sb)(ta + bu)$, where r, s, t, and u are numbers and a and b are variables. The reasoning shown at right will help you see that $a^2 + b^2$ cannot be factored.

$a^2 + b^2 = (ra + sb)(ta + bu)$
$= (rt)a^2 + (st + ru)ab + (su)b^2$
So, $1 = rt$, $0 = st + ru$ and $1 = su$
$r = \frac{1}{t}$, $-st = ru$, and $s = \frac{1}{u}$
Thus, $-\frac{t}{u} = \frac{u}{t}$
$-t^2 = u^2$
$t = 0$ and $u = 0$

a. How do you know that $1 = rt$, $0 = st + ru$, and $1 = su$?

If two polynomials are equal, their corresponding coefficients are equal. The coefficients of a^2, ab, and b^2 are equal.

b. Explain how $t = 0$ and $u = 0$ tell you that there are no values of r and s that make the factorization possible.

If $t = 0$ and $u = 0$, then r and s are given by undefined expressions. Thus, there are no numbers r, s, t, and u for which $a^2 + b^2$ can be factored as $(ra + sb)(ta + bu)$.

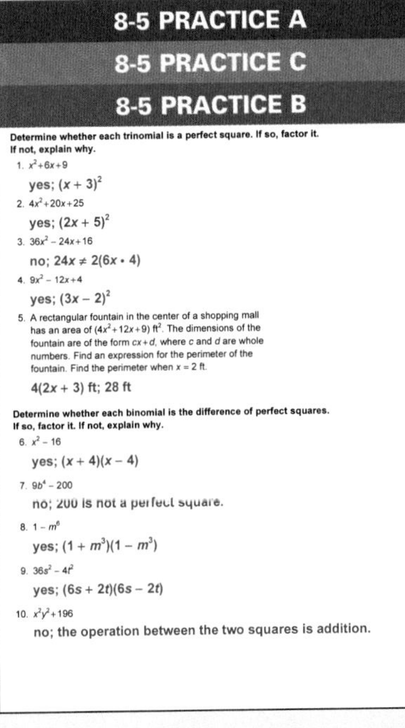

8-5 PRACTICE A

8-5 PRACTICE C

8-5 PRACTICE B

Determine whether each trinomial is a perfect square. If so, factor it. If not, explain why.

1. $x^2 + 6x + 9$
yes; $(x + 3)^2$

2. $4x^2 + 20x + 25$
yes; $(2x + 5)^2$

3. $36x^2 - 24x + 16$
no; $24x \neq 2(6x \cdot 4)$

4. $9x^2 - 12x + 4$
yes; $(3x - 2)^2$

5. A rectangular fountain in the center of a shopping mall has an area of $(4x^2 + 12x + 9)$ ft². The dimensions of the fountain are of the form $cx + d$, where c and d are whole numbers. Find an expression for the perimeter of the fountain. Find the perimeter when $x = 2$ ft.
$4(2x + 3)$ ft; 28 ft

Determine whether each binomial is the difference of perfect squares. If so, factor it. If not, explain why.

6. $x^2 - 16$
yes; $(x + 4)(x - 4)$

7. $9b^4 - 200$
no; 200 is not a perfect square.

8. $1 - m^6$
yes; $(1 + m^3)(1 - m^3)$

9. $36s^2 - 4t^2$
yes; $(6s + 2t)(6s - 2t)$

10. $x^2y^2 + 196$
no; the operation between the two squares is addition.

TEST PREP DOCTOR For **Exercise 47,** encourage students to write each expression in factored form before substituting values for x and y.

In **Exercise 48,** the trinomial contains only positive numbers. Therefore, the factored answer must contain only positive numbers, so **F, G,** and **H** can be eliminated.

Journal

Explain how you can find the missing term in the perfect-square trinomial $100x^2 + 120x + \square$.

ALTERNATIVE ASSESSMENT

Create one trinomial that is a perfect-square trinomial and one that is not. Factor the first trinomial. Explain why the second trinomial is not a perfect square. Repeat for the difference of two squares.

Power Presentations with PowerPoint®

8-5 Lesson Quiz

Determine whether each trinomial is a perfect square. If so, factor. If not, explain.

1. $64x^2 - 40x + 25$
   no; $-40x \neq 2(8x \cdot 5)$
2. $121x^2 - 44x + 4$
   yes; $(11x - 2)^2$
3. $49x^2 + 140x + 100$
   yes; $(7x^2 + 10)^2$
4. A fence will be built around a square garden with an area of $(49x^2 + 56x + 16)$ ft². The dimensions of the garden are in the form $cx + d$, where c and d are whole numbers. Find an expression for the perimeter of the garden. Find the perimeter when $x = 5$ feet.
   $P = 28x + 16$; 156 ft

Determine whether the binomial is a difference of two squares. If so, factor. If not, explain.

5. $9x^2 - 144y^4$
   yes; $(3x + 12y^2)(3x - 12y^2)$
6. $30x^2 - 64y^2$ No; $30x^2$ is not a perfect square.
7. $121x^2 - 4y^8$
   yes; $(11x + 2y^4)(11x - 2y^4)$

Also available on transparency

TEST PREP

47. A polynomial expression is evaluated for the x- and y-values shown in the table. Which expression could have been evaluated to give the values shown in the third column?

x	y	Value of Expression
0	0	0
−1	−1	0
1	1	0
1	−1	4

Ⓐ $x^2 - y^2$
Ⓑ $x^2 + 2xy + y^2$
Ⓒ $x^2 - 2xy + y^2$ (circled)
Ⓓ None of the above

48. The area of a square is $4x^2 + 20x + 25$. Which expression can also be used to model the area of the square?

Ⓕ $(2x - 5)(5 - 2x)$　Ⓗ $(2x - 5)^2$
Ⓖ $(2x + 5)(2x - 5)$　Ⓙ $(2x + 5)^2$ (circled)

49. **Gridded Response** Evaluate the polynomial expression $x^2 - 18x + 81$ for $x = 10$. 1

CHALLENGE AND EXTEND

50. The binomial $81x^4 - 16$ can be factored using the rule for a difference of two squares.
   a. Fill in the factorization: $81x^4 - 16$
      $(9x^2 + \blacksquare)(\blacksquare - \blacksquare)$ 4; $9x^2$; 4
   b. One binomial from part **a** can be further factored. Identify the binomial and factor it. $9x^2 - 4 = (3x + 2)(3x - 2)$
   c. Write your own binomial that can be factored twice as the difference of two squares. Possible answer: $x^4 - 1 = (x^2 + 1)(x^2 - 1) = (x^2 + 1)(x + 1)(x - 1)$

51. The expression $4 - (v + 2)^2$ is the difference of two squares, because it fits the rule $a^2 - b^2$.
   a. Identify a and b in the expression. $a = 2$; $b = v + 2$
   b. Factor and simplify $4 - (v + 2)^2$.
      $[2 + (v + 2)][2 - (v + 2)] = (v + 4)(-v) = -v^2 - 4v$

The *difference of cubes* is an expression of the form $a^3 - b^3$. It can be factored according to the rule $a^3 - b^3 = (a - b)(a^2 + ab + b^2)$. For each binomial, identify a and b, and factor using the rule.

52. $x^3 - 1$
   $a = x$; $b = 1$; $(x - 1)(x^2 + x + 1)$
53. $27y^3 - 64$
   $a = 3y$; $b = 4$; $(3y - 4)(9y^2 + 12y + 16)$
54. $n^6 - 8$
   $a = n^2$; $b = 2$; $(n^2 - 2)(n^4 + 2n + 4)$

SPIRAL REVIEW

Find the domain and range for each relation and tell whether the relation is a function. *(Lesson 4-2)*

55. $\{(5, 2), (4, 1), (3, 0), (2, -1)\}$
   D: {5, 4, 3, 2}; R: {2, 1, 0, −1}; yes
56. $\{(-3, 6), (-1, 6), (1, 6), (3, 6)\}$
   D: {−3, −1, 1, 3}; R: {6}; yes
57. $\{(2, -8), (2, -2), (2, 4), (2, 10)\}$
   D: {2}; R: {−8, −2, 4, 10}; no
58. $\{(-2, 4), (-1, 1), (0, 0), (1, 1)\}$
   D: {−2, −1, 0, 1}; R: {0, 1, 4}; yes

Multiply. *(Lesson 7-8)*

59. $2a(3a^2 + 7a - 5)$ $6a^3 + 14a^2 - 10a$
60. $(x + 3)(x - 8)$ $x^2 - 5x - 24$
61. $(t - 4)^2$ $t^2 - 8t + 16$

Find the GCF of each pair of monomials. *(Lesson 8-1)*

62. $9m^2$ and $3m^2$ $3m^2$
63. $8c^2$ and $8d^2$ 8
64. $-12x^3y$ and $16y^2$ $4y$

Mental Math

Recognizing patterns of special products can help you perform multiplication mentally.

Remember these special products that you studied in Chapters 7 and 8.

Patterns of Special Products	
Difference of Two Squares	$(a+b)(a-b)=a^2-b^2$
Perfect-Square Trinomial	$(a+b)^2=a^2+2ab+b^2$ $(a-b)^2=a^2-2ab+b^2$

Example 1

Simplify 17^2-7^2.

This expression is a difference of two squares with $a = 17$ and $b = 7$.

$a^2-b^2=(a+b)(a-b)$ *Write the rule for a difference of two squares.*

$17^2-7^2=(17+7)(17-7)$ *Substitute 17 for a and 7 for b.*

$=(24)(10)$ *Simplify.*

$=240$

Example 2

Simplify $14^2+2(14)(6)+6^2$.

This expression is a perfect-square trinomial with $a = 14$ and $b = 6$.

$a^2+2ab+b^2=(a+b)^2$ *Write the rule for a perfect-square trinomial.*

$14^2+2(14)(6)+6^2=(14+6)^2$ *Substitute 14 for a and 6 for b.*

$=(20)^2$ *Simplify.*

$=400$

Try This

Simplify each expression using the rules for special products.

1. 18^2-12^2
2. $11^2+2(11)(14)+14^2$
3. 22^2-18^2
4. $38^2-2(38)(27)+27^2$
5. $29^2-2(29)(17)+17^2$
6. $55^2+2(55)(45)+45^2$
7. 14^2-9^2
8. 13^2-12^2
9. $14^2+2(14)(16)+16^2$

Answers to *Try This*

1. $(18+12)(18-12)=30(6)=180$
2. $(11+14)^2=25^2=625$
3. $(22+18)(22-18)=40(4)=160$
4. $(38-27)^2=11^2=121$
5. $(29-17)^2=12^2=144$
6. $(55+45)^2=100^2=10{,}000$
7. $(14+9)(14-9)=23(5)=115$
8. $(13+12)(13-12)=25(1)=25$
9. $(14+16)^2=30^2=900$

Organizer

Pacing:
Traditional 1 day
Block $\frac{1}{2}$ day

Objective: Apply patterns of special products to performing multiplication mentally.

Teach

Remember

Students review and apply mental math techniques.

Close

Assess

Have students explain how to use patterns of special products and mental math to simplify Try This **Problems 4** and **8.**

State Resources

8-6 Organizer

Pacing: Traditional 1 day
Block $\frac{1}{2}$ day

Objectives: Choose an appropriate method for factoring a polynomial.

Combine methods for factoring a polynomial.

Online Edition
Tutorial Videos

Countdown Week 18

Power Presentations with PowerPoint®

Warm Up

Factor each trinomial.

1. $x^2 + 13x + 40$
$(x + 5)(x + 8)$

2. $5x^2 - 18x - 8$
$(5x + 2)(x - 4)$

3. Factor the perfect-square trinomial $16x^2 + 40x + 25$.
$(4x + 5)(4x + 5)$

4. Factor $9x^2 - 25y^2$ using the difference of two squares.
$(3x + 5y)(3x - 5y)$

Also available on transparency

Math Humor

Q: Where do math teachers buy their products?

A: From the factor-*y*.

8-6 Choosing a Factoring Method

Objectives
Choose an appropriate method for factoring a polynomial.

Combine methods for factoring a polynomial.

Why learn this?
You will need to factor polynomials to solve quadratic equations, which have many applications in physics. (See Exercise 42.)

The height of a leaping ballet dancer can be modeled by a quadratic polynomial. Solving an equation that contains that polynomial may require factoring the polynomial.

Recall that a polynomial is in its fully factored form when it is written as a product that cannot be factored further.

EXAMPLE 1 Determining Whether an Expression Is Completely Factored

Tell whether each expression is completely factored. If not, factor it.

A $2x(x^2 + 4)$

$2x(x^2 + 4)$ *Neither 2x nor $x^2 + 4$ can be factored further.*
$2x(x^2 + 4)$ is completely factored.

B $(2x + 6)(x + 5)$

$(2x + 6)(x + 5)$ *2x + 6 can be further factored.*
$2(x + 3)(x + 5)$ *Factor out 2, the GCF of 2x and 6.*
$2(x + 3)(x + 5)$ is completely factored.

Caution!
$x^2 + 4$ is a *sum* of squares, and cannot be factored.

Tell whether each expression is completely factored. If not, factor it.

1a. $5x^2(x - 1)$ **yes** **1b.** $(4x + 4)(x + 1)$ **no; $4(x + 1)^2$**

To factor a polynomial completely, you may need to use more than one factoring method. Use the steps below to factor a polynomial completely.

Factoring Polynomials	
Step 1	Check for a greatest common factor.
Step 2	Check for a pattern that fits the difference of two squares or a perfect-square trinomial.
Step 3	To factor $x^2 + bx + c$, look for two numbers whose sum is b and whose product is c. To factor $ax^2 + bx + c$, check factors of a and factors of c in the binomial factors. The sum of the products of the outer and inner terms should be b.
Step 4	Check for common factors.

State Resources

go.hrw.com
State Resources Online
KEYWORD: MA7 Resources

1 Introduce

EXPLORATION

8-6 Choosing a Factoring Method

You now know several methods for factoring polynomials. This Exploration will help you see how some of the methods can be used in combination with each other.

1. Factor out the GCF of each polynomial in the table. Write the result in the middle column of the table. Then look at the remaining factor. Identify its type and write this in the right-hand column of the table.

Polynomial	Factor Out the GCF	Type of Factor That Remains
$2x^3 + 12x^2 + 18x$	$2x(x^2 + 6x + 9)$	Perfect-square trinomial
$12a^3b + 60a^2b + 75ab$		
$x^5 - 36x^3$		
$2xy^3 - 20xy^2 + 50xy$		
$3y^2 - 48y$		

2. Explain what you would do to continue factoring $2x^3 + 12x^2 + 18x$ after factoring out the GCF, $2x$.
3. Explain what you would do to continue factoring $x^5 - 36x^3$ after factoring out the GCF.

THINK AND DISCUSS

4. **Describe** the advantages of first factoring out the GCF when factoring a polynomial.
5. **Explain** how factoring out the GCF can be helpful even if the remaining factor is not one of the types that you

Motivate

Have students describe characteristics of the following polynomials. Possible answers:

$9x^2 - 25y^2$ first and last terms are perfect squares; difference of two terms

$3x + 6$ common factor in each term; binomial

$2x^3 + 6x^2 - 5x - 15$ four terms; common factor in first two terms; common factor in last two terms.

Explorations and answers are provided in *Alternate Openers: Explorations Transparencies.*

EXAMPLE 2 Factoring by GCF and Recognizing Patterns

Factor $-2xy^2 + 16xy - 32x$ completely. Check your answer.

$-2xy^2 + 16xy - 32x$

$-2x(y^2 - 8y + 16)$ *Factor out the GCF. $y^2 - 8y + 16$ is a perfect-square trinomial of the form $a^2 - 2ab + b^2$.*

$-2x(y - 4)^2$ *$a = y, b = 4$*

Check $-2x(y-4)^2 = -2x(y^2 - 8y + 16)$
$= -2xy^2 + 16xy - 32x$ ✓

Factor each polynomial completely. Check your answer.

2a. $4x^3 + 16x^2 + 16x$ **$4x(x+2)^2$**

2b. $2x^2y - 2y^3$ **$2y(x-y)(x+y)$**

If none of the factoring methods work, the polynomial is unfactorable.

EXAMPLE 3 Factoring by Multiple Methods

Factor each polynomial completely.

A $2x^2 + 5x + 4$

$2x^2 + 5x + 4$ *The GCF is 1 and there is no pattern.*

$(\square x + \square)(\square x + \square)$ *$a = 2$ and $c = 4$; Outer + Inner = 5*

Factors of 2	Factors of 4	Outer + Inner	
1 and 2	1 and 4	$1(4) + 2(1) = 6$	✗
1 and 2	4 and 1	$1(1) + 2(4) = 9$	✗
1 and 2	2 and 2	$1(2) + 2(2) = 6$	✗

$2x^2 + 5x + 4$ is unfactorable.

Remember!

For a polynomial of the form $ax^2 + bx + c$, if there are no integers whose sum is b and whose product is ac, then the polynomial is unfactorable.

B $3n^4 - 15n^3 + 12n^2$

$3n^2(n^2 - 5n + 4)$ *Factor out the GCF. There is no pattern.*

$(n + \square)(n + \square)$ *$b = -5$ and $c = 4$; look for factors of 4 whose sum is -5.*

Factors of 4	Sum	
−1 and −4	−5	✓

The factors needed are −1 and −4.

$3n^2(n-1)(n-4)$

C $4x^3 + 18x^2 + 20x$

$2x(2x^2 + 9x + 10)$ *Factor out the GCF. There is no pattern.*

$(\square x + \square)(\square x + \square)$ *$a = 2$ and $c = 10$; Outer + Inner = 9*

Factors of 2	Factors of 10	Outer + Inner	
1 and 2	1 and 10	$1(10) + 2(1) = 12$	✗
1 and 2	10 and 1	$1(11) + 2(10) = 21$	✗
1 and 2	2 and 5	$1(5) + 2(2) = 9$	✓

$(x+2)(2x+5)$

$2x(x+2)(2x+5)$

COMMON ERROR ALERT

Students often think the factoring is complete after using one factoring method. Remind students to continue to look for common factors and factoring patterns until the polynomial is completely factored.

Power Presentations with PowerPoint®

Additional Examples

Example 1

Tell whether each expression is completely factored. If not, factor it.

A. $3x^2(6x - 4)$ no; $6x^2(3x - 2)$

B. $(x^2 + 1)(x - 4)$ completely factored

Example 2

Factor each polynomial completely. Check your answer.

A. $10x^2 + 48x + 32$
$2(5x + 4)(x + 4)$

B. $8x^6y^2 - 18x^2y^2$
$2x^2y^2(2x^2 - 3)(2x^2 + 3)$

INTERVENTION

Questioning Strategies

EXAMPLE 1

- How do you check that a polynomial has been completely factored?

EXAMPLE 2

- What are the benefits of looking for the GCF first when factoring a polynomial?

2 Teach

Guided Instruction

Be sure that students are comfortable with all methods of factoring before beginning this section. Encourage them to first look for the GCF, then look for a pattern (for difference of squares or perfect-square trinomial), and lastly begin checking factors for a and c. Remind students that some polynomials cannot be factored. Have students check their answers to determine whether they have factored correctly.

Reaching All Learners

Through Graphic Organizers

Have groups of students create flowcharts for factoring polynomials. Include:

- Look for GCF.
- If binomial, then difference of squares OR cannot factor
- If trinomial, then perfect-square trinomial OR find factors of a and c OR cannot factor.
- If four or more terms, then factor by grouping OR cannot factor.
- Can it be factored more?

Power Presentations with PowerPoint®

Additional Examples

Example 3

Factor each polynomial completely.

A. $9x^2 + 3x - 2$
$(3x - 1)(3x + 2)$

B. $12b^3 + 48b^2 + 48b$
$12b(b + 2)^2$

C. $4y^2 + 12y - 72$
$4(y + 6)(y - 3)$

D. $(x^4 - x^2)$
$x^2(x + 1)(x - 1)$

INTERVENTION
Questioning Strategies

EXAMPLE 3

- For what type of polynomials do you consider factoring by grouping?
- What methods of factoring do you consider when factoring a trinomial?

Teaching Tip **Math Background** Remind students that because of the Commutative Property of Multiplication, $(a + b)(a - b) = (a - b)(a + b)$. Thus the factors can be written in any order.

D $p^5 - p$

$p(p^4 - 1)$	Factor out the GCF.
$p(p^2 + 1)(p^2 - 1)$	$p^4 - 1$ is a difference of two squares.
$p(p^2 + 1)(p + 1)(p - 1)$	$p^2 - 1$ is a difference of two squares.

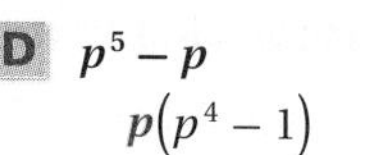

CHECK IT OUT! Factor each polynomial completely. Check your answer.

3a. $3x^2 + 7x + 4$ **3b.** $2p^5 + 10p^4 - 12p^3$

3c. $9q^6 + 30q^5 + 24q^4$ **3d.** $2x^4 + 18$

3a. $(3x + 4)(x + 1)$ **3b.** $2p^3(p + 6)(p - 1)$

3c. $3q^4(3q + 4)(q + 2)$ **3d.** $2(x^4 + 9)$

Know it! Note

Methods to Factor Polynomials

Any Polynomial—Look for the greatest common factor.

$ab - ac = a(b - c)$	$6x^2y + 10xy^2 = 2xy(3x + 5y)$

Binomials—Look for a difference of two squares.

$a^2 - b^2 = (a + b)(a - b)$	$x^2 - 9y^2 = (x + 3y)(x - 3y)$

Trinomials—Look for perfect-square trinomials and other factorable trinomials.

$a^2 + 2ab + b^2 = (a + b)^2$ $a^2 - 2ab + b^2 = (a - b)^2$	$x^2 + 4x + 4 = (x + 2)^2$ $x^2 - 2x + 1 = (x - 1)^2$
$x^2 + bx + c = (x + \square)(x + \square)$ $ax^2 + bx + c = (\square x + \square)(\square x + \square)$	$x^2 + 3x + 2 = (x + 1)(x + 2)$ $6x^2 + 7x + 2 = (2x + 1)(3x + 2)$

Polynomials of Four or More Terms—Factor by grouping.

$ax + bx + ay + by = x(a + b) + y(a + b)$ $= (x + y)(a + b)$	$2x^3 + 4x^2 + x + 2 = (2x^3 + 4x^2) + (x + 2)$ $= 2x^2(x + 2) + 1(x + 2)$ $= (x + 2)(2x^2 + 1)$

THINK AND DISCUSS

1. Give an expression that includes a polynomial that is not completely factored.

2. Give an example of an unfactorable binomial and an unfactorable trinomial.

Know it! Note

3. GET ORGANIZED Copy the graphic organizer. Draw an arrow from each expression to the method you would use to factor it.

Factoring Methods	
Polynomial	**Method**
1. $16x^4 - 25y^8$	A. Factoring out the GCF
2. $x^2 + 10x + 25$	B. Factoring by grouping
3. $9t^2 + 27t + 18t^4$	C. Unfactorable
4. $a^2 + 3a - 7a - 21$	D. Difference of two squares
5. $100b^2 + 81$	E. Perfect-square trinomial

3 Close

Summarize

Ask students to state the method they would use **first** to factor the following polynomials.

$16x^2 - 25$ difference of squares

$3x^2 + 12x + 27$ GCF

$4x^3 + 20x^2 + x + 5$ factor by grouping

$8x^2 - 32$ GCF

$x^2 + x - 12$ find factors for -12

Point out that no matter what the first step is, the resulting factorization is the same.

ONGOING ASSESSMENT and INTERVENTION

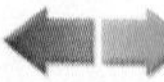

Diagnose Before **the Lesson**
8-6 Warm Up, TE p. 586

Monitor During **the Lesson**
Check It Out! Exercises, SE pp. 586–588
Questioning Strategies, TE pp. 587–588

Assess After **the Lesson**
8-6 Lesson Quiz, TE p. 591
Alternative Assessment, TE p. 591

Answers to *Think and Discuss*

Possible answers:

1. $x^2 - 1$
2. $x^2 + 1$; $x^2 + x + 1$
3. See p. A8.

go.hrw.com
Homework Help Online
KEYWORD: MA7 8-6
Parent Resources Online
KEYWORD: MA7 Parent

GUIDED PRACTICE

SEE EXAMPLE 1 p. 586

Tell whether each expression is completely factored. If not, factor it.

1. $3x(9x^2 + 1)$ **yes**
2. $2(4x^3 - 3x^2 - 8x)$
3. $2k^2(4 - k^3)$ **yes**
4. $(2x + 3)(3x - 5)$ **yes**
5. $4(4p^4 - 1)$
6. $a(a^3 + 2ab + b^2)$ **yes**

Factor each polynomial completely. Check your answer.

SEE EXAMPLE 2 p. 587

7. $3x^5 - 12x^3$
8. $4x^3 + 8x^2 + 4x$
9. $8pq^2 + 8pq + 2p$
10. $18rs^2 - 2r$
11. $mn^5 - m^3n$
12. $2x^2y - 20xy + 50y$

SEE EXAMPLE 3 p. 587

13. $6x^4 - 3x^3 - 9x^2$
14. $3y^2 + 14y + 4$
15. $p^5 + 3p^3 + p^2 + 3$
16. $7x^5 + 21x^4 - 28x^3$ **$7x^3(x + 4)(x - 1)$**
17. $2z^2 + 11z + 6$ **unfactorable**
18. $9p^2 - q^2 + 3p$ **unfactorable**

PRACTICE AND PROBLEM SOLVING

Independent Practice

For Exercises	See Example
19–24	1
25–30	2
31–36	3

Extra Practice
Skills Practice p. S19
Application Practice p. S35

Tell whether each expression is completely factored. If not, factor it.

19. $2x(y^3 - 4y^2 + 5y)$
20. $2r(25r^6 - 36)$
21. $3n^2(n^2 - 25)$
22. $2m(m + 1)(m + 4)$ **yes**
23. $2y^2(4x^2 + 9)$ **yes**
24. $4(7g + 9h^2)$ **yes**

Factor each polynomial completely. Check your answer.

25. $-4x^3 + 24x^2 - 36x$
26. $24r^2 - 6r^4$
27. $5d^2 - 60d + 135$
28. $4y^8 + 36y^7 + 81y^6$
29. $98x^3 - 50xy^2$
30. $4x^3y - 4x^2y - 8xy$
31. $5x^2 - 10x + 14$
32. $121x^2 + 36y^2$
33. $p^4 - 16$
34. $4m^6 - 30m^5 + 36m^4$ **$2m^4(m - 6)(2m - 3)$**
35. $2k^3 + 3k^2 + 6k + 9$ **$(k^2 + 3)(2k + 3)$**
36. $ab^4 - 16a$ **$a(b^2 + 4)(b + 2)(b - 2)$**

Write an expression for each situation. Factor your expression.

37. the square of Ella's age plus 12 times Ella's age plus 36 **$x^2 + 12x + 36 = (x + 6)^2$**
38. the square of the distance from point A to point B minus 81 **$d^2 - 81 = (d - 9)(d + 9)$**
39. the square of the number of seconds Bob can hold his breath minus 16 times the number of seconds plus 28 **$s^2 - 16s + 28 = (s - 2)(s - 14)$**
40. three times the square of the number of apples on a tree minus 22 times the number of apples plus 35 **$3a^2 - 22a + 35 = (a - 5)(3a - 7)$**
41. the square of Beth's score minus 49 **$b^2 - 49 = (b + 7)(b - 7)$**
42. **Physics** The height in meters of a ballet dancer's center of mass when she leaps can be modeled by the polynomial $-5t^2 + 30t + 1$, where t is time in seconds after the jump. Tell whether the polynomial is fully factored when written as $-1(5t^2 - 30t - 1)$. Explain. **Yes; $5t^2 - 30t - 1$ is unfactorable.**

43. **Write About It** When asked to factor a polynomial completely, you first determine that the terms in the polynomial do not share any common factors. What would be your next step? **Check for a pattern such as a perfect-square trinomial or a difference of 2 squares.**

Factor and simplify each expression.

44. $12(x + 1)^2 + 60(x + 1) + 75$ **$3(2x + 7)^2$**
45. $(2x + 3)^2 - (x - 4)^2$ **$(3x - 1)(x + 7)$**
46. $45x(x - 2)^2 + 60x(x - 2) + 20x$ **$5x(3x - 4)^2$**
47. $(3x - 5)^2 - (y + 2)^2$ **$(3x + y - 3)(3x - y - 7)$**

Answers

2. no; $2x(4x^2 - 3x - 8)$
5. no; $4(2p^2 + 1)(2p^2 - 1)$
7. $3x^3(x + 2)(x - 2)$
8. $4x(x + 1)^2$
9. $2p(2q + 1)^2$
10. $2r(3s + 1)(3s - 1)$
11. $mn(n^2 + m)(n^2 - m)$
12. $2y(x - 5)^2$
13. $3x^2(2x - 3)(x + 1)$
14. unfactorable
15. $(p^3 + 1)(p^2 + 3)$
19. no; $2xy(y^2 - 4y + 5)$
20. no; $2r(5r^3 + 6)(5r^3 - 6)$
21. no; $3n^2(n + 5)(n - 5)$
25. $-4x(x - 3)^2$
26. $-1(6r^2)(r - 2)(r + 2)$
27. $5(d - 3)(d - 9)$
28. $y^6(2y + 9)^2$
29. $2x(7x + 5y)(7x - 5y)$
30. $4xy(x - 2)(x + 1)$
31. unfactorable
32. unfactorable
33. $(p^2 + 4)(p + 2)(p - 2)$

8-6 Exercises

Assignment Guide

Assign *Guided Practice* exercises as necessary.

If you finished Examples **1–3**
Basic 19–48, 50–58, 65–72
Average 19–42, 44–58, 65–72
Advanced 19–36, 40, 42, 44–72

Homework Quick Check

Quickly check key concepts.
Exercises: 20, 22, 28, 32, 36, 42

Teaching Tip

Inclusion For **Exercises 25–36,** have students count the number of terms in the polynomial when deciding which factoring method to use. Four or more terms could indicate factoring by grouping, three terms could indicate the pattern for a perfect-square trinomial, and two terms could indicate the pattern for the difference of two squares.

State Resources

go.hrw.com
State Resources Online
KEYWORD: MA7 Resources

MULTI-STEP TEST PREP Exercise 48 involves factoring a polynomial to find the dimensions of a rectangle. This exercise prepares students for the Multi-Step Test Prep on page 592.

TEST PREP DOCTOR + In **Exercise 56,** students who chose **F** may have factored out the GCF but forgotten to factor by using the difference of squares. Students who chose **G** may have factored by using the difference of squares but forgotten to factor out the GCF.

Students who chose **B** in **Exercise 57** may have forgotten to keep the subtraction sign with the 1 when using the Distributive Property.

Answers

48b.

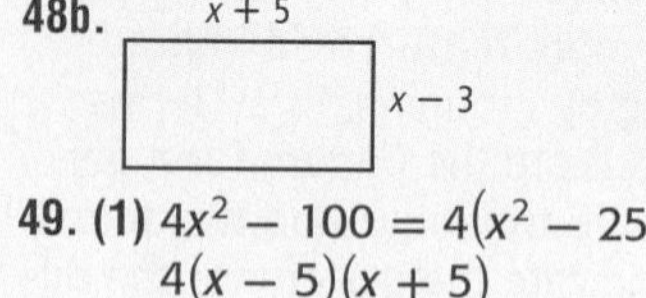

49. (1) $4x^2 - 100 = 4(x^2 - 25) = 4(x-5)(x+5)$

(2) $4x^2 - 100 = (2x+10)(2x-10) = 2(x+5)(2(x-5)) = 4(x+5)(x-5)$

MULTI-STEP TEST PREP

48. This problem will prepare you for the Multi-Step Test Prep on page 588.

a. The area of a Marci's rectangular flower garden is $(x^2 + 2x - 15)$ ft². Factor this expression. $(x+5)(x-3)$

b. Draw a diagram of the garden and label the length and width with your factors from part **a.**

c. Find the length and width of the flower garden if $x = 7$ ft. $\ell = 12$ ft; $w = 4$ ft

49. Critical Thinking Show two methods of factoring $4x^2 - 100$.

50. Estimation Estimate the value of $2x^2 + 5xy + 3y^2$ when $x = -10.1$ and $y = 10.05$. (*Hint:* Factor the expression first.) **approx. 0**

51. ///ERROR ANALYSIS/// Examine the factorization shown. Explain why the factorization is incorrect. **Possible answer:** $(2x-1)^2 \neq 4x^2 - 4x - 1$

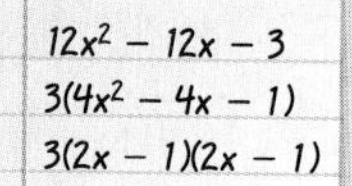

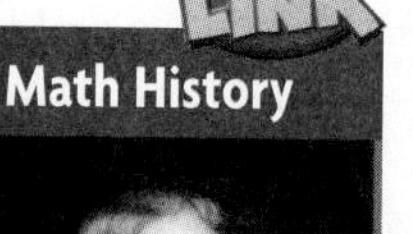

Math History

Blaise Pascal was a French mathematician who lived in the 1600s.

Math History **Use the following information for Exercises 52–54.**

The triangle at right is called *Pascal's Triangle.* The triangle starts with 1 and each of the other numbers in the triangle is the sum of the two numbers in the row above it.

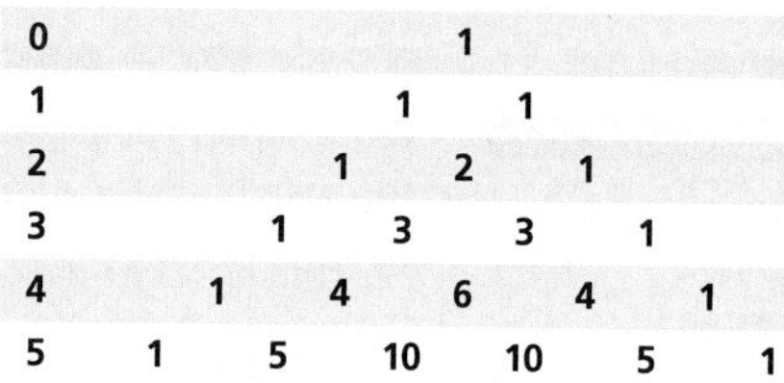

Row						
0	1					
1	1	1				
2	1	2	1			
3	1	3	3	1		
4	1	4	6	4	1	
5	1	5	10	10	5	1

Pascal's Triangle can be used to write the product of a binomial raised to an integer power. The numbers in each row give you the coefficients of each term in the product.

$$(a+b)^3 = a^3 + 3a^2b + 3ab^2 + b^3$$

The numbers in row 3 are 1, 3, 3, 1. These are the coefficients of the terms in the product $(a+b)^3$. The power of a decreases in each term and the power of b increases in each term.

Use the patterns you see in Pascal's Triangle to write the power of the binomial $a + b$ given by each polynomial.

52. $a^6 + 6a^5b + 15a^4b^2 + 20a^3b^3 + 15a^2b^4 + 6ab^5 + b^6 = (a+b)^{\mathbf{6}}$

53. $a^8 + 8a^7b + 28a^6b^2 + 56a^5b^3 + 70a^4b^4 + 56a^3b^5 + 28a^2b^6 + 8ab^7 + b^8 = (a+b)^{\mathbf{8}}$

54. $a^7 + 7a^6b + 21a^5b^2 + 35a^4b^3 + 35a^3b^4 + 21a^2b^5 + 7ab^6 + b^7 = (a+b)^{\mathbf{7}}$

TEST PREP

55. Which expression equals $6x^2 + 7x - 10$?

Ⓐ $(6x+2)(x-5)$　　Ⓒ $(x+2)(6x-5)$ (circled)

Ⓑ $(2x+5)(3x-2)$　　Ⓓ $(3x+2)(2x-5)$

56. What is the complete factorization of $16x^{12} - 256$?

Ⓕ $16(x^6+4)(x^6-4)$　　Ⓗ $16(x^6+4)(x^3+2)(x^3-2)$ (circled)

Ⓖ $(4x^6+16)(4x^6-16)$　　Ⓙ $(4x^6+16)(2x^3+4)(2x^3-4)$

8-6 PRACTICE A
8-6 PRACTICE C
8-6 PRACTICE B

Tell whether each polynomial is completely factored. If not, factor it.

1. $6(t^2 + 12)$ — yes
2. $5(m^2 + 9m)$ — no; $5m(m+9)$
3. $2p(p^4 - 9)$ — no; $2p(p^2+3)(p^2-3)$
4. $(x-8)(2x+3)$ — yes
5. $3k^3(5k^2 + 19)$ — yes
6. $7(14g^4 - 4g + 10)$ — no; $14(7g^4 - 2g + 5)$

Factor each polynomial completely.

7. $24x + 40$ — $8(3x+5)$
8. $5r^3 - 10r$ — $5r(r^2 - 2)$
9. $3x^3y + x^2y^2$ — $x^2y(3x+y)$
10. $-3a^2b + 12ab - 12b$ — $-3b(a-2)^2$
11. $5t^3 - 45t + 3t^2 - 27$ — $(5t+3)(t+3)(t-3)$
12. $2y^2 - 6y - 56$ — $2(y+4)(y-7)$
13. $6a^3 + 39a^2 + 45a$ — $3a(2a+3)(a+5)$
14. $x^3 - 9x$ — $x(x-3)(x+3)$
15. $12n^3 - 48$ — $12(n^3 - 4)$
16. $3c^4 + 24c^3 + 48c^2$ — $3c^2(c+4)^2$
17. $3d^3 + 4d - 2$ — unfactorable
18. $10w^6 - 160w^2$ — $10w^2(w^2+4)(w-2)(w+2)$

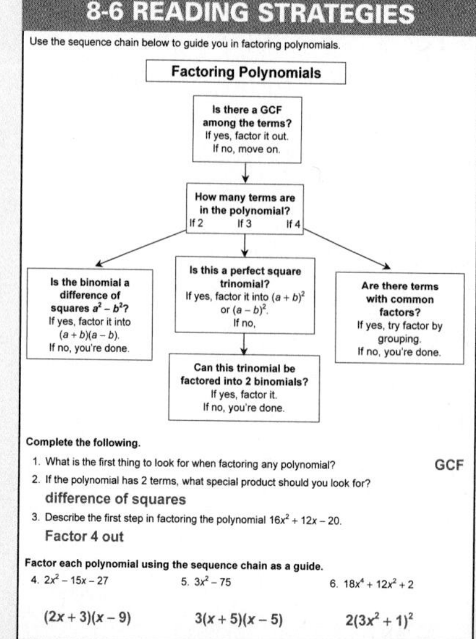

8-6 READING STRATEGIES

Use the sequence chain below to guide you in factoring polynomials.

Factoring Polynomials

Is there a GCF among the terms? If yes, factor it out. If no, move on.

How many terms are in the polynomial? If 2 / If 3 / If 4

Is the binomial a difference of squares $a^2 - b^2$? If yes, factor it into $(a+b)(a-b)$. If no, you're done.

Is this a perfect square trinomial? If yes, factor it into $(a+b)^2$ or $(a-b)^2$. If no,

Can this trinomial be factored into 2 binomials? If yes, factor it. If no, you're done.

Are there terms with common factors? If yes, try factor by grouping. If no, you're done.

Complete the following.

1. What is the first thing to look for when factoring any polynomial? GCF
2. If the polynomial has 2 terms, what special product should you look for? difference of squares
3. Describe the first step in factoring the polynomial $16x^2 + 12x - 20$. Factor 4 out

Factor each polynomial using the sequence chain as a guide.

4. $2x^2 - 15x - 27$ — $(2x+3)(x-9)$
5. $3x^2 - 75$ — $3(x+5)(x-5)$
6. $18x^4 + 12x^2 + 2$ — $2(3x^2+1)^2$

8-6 RETEACH

Use the following table to help you choose a factoring method.

First factor out a GCF if possible. Then,

If binomial,	check for difference of squares.	yes →	Use $(a+b)(a-b)$.
		no →	If no GCF, it cannot be factored.
If trinomial,	check for perfect square trinomial.	yes →	Factor using $(a+b)^2$ or $(a-b)^2$.
		no →	If $a = 1$, check factors of c that sum to b. If $a \neq 1$, check inner plus outer factors of a and c that sum to b.
If 4 or more terms,	→		Try to factor by grouping.

Explain how to choose a factoring method for $x^2 - x - 30$. Then state the method.

- There is no GCF.
- $x^2 - x - 30$ is a trinomial.
- The terms a and b are not perfect squares, therefore this is not a perfect square trinomial.
- $a = 1$

Method: Factor by checking factors of c that sum to b.

Explain how to choose a factoring method for $2x^2 - 50$. Then state the method.

- Factor out the GCF: $2(x^2 - 25)$
- $x^2 - 25$ is a binomial.
- a and b are perfect squares. This is a difference of squares.

Method: Factor out GCF. Then use $(a+b)(a-b)$.

Explain how to choose a factoring method for each polynomial. Then state the method.

1. $x^2 + 14x + 49$ — no GCF; $x^2 + 14x + 49$ is a trinomial; This is a perfect square trinomial. Method: use $(a+b)^2$.
2. $4x^2 - 40$ — factor out the GCF: $4(x^2 - 10)$; $x^2 - 10$ is a binomial; This is not a difference of squares. Method: Factor out GCF.
3. $2x^2 + 8x + 6$ — factor out the GCF: $2(x^2 + 4x + 3)$; $x^2 + 4x + 3$ is a trinomial; This is not a perfect square trinomial; $a = 1$; Method: Factor out GCF. Then find factors of c that sum to b.

57. Which of the expressions below represents the fifth step of the factorization?

Step 1: $40a^3 - 60a^2 - 10a + 15$

Step 2: $5(8a^3 - 12a^2 - 2a + 3)$

Step 3: $5[(8a^3 - 12a^2) - (2a - 3)]$

Step 4: $5[4a^2(2a - 3) - 1(2a - 3)]$

Step 5:

Step 6: $5(2a - 3)(2a + 1)(2a - 1)$

(A) $5(2a - 3)(2a + 3)(4a^2 - 1)$ **(C)** $5(2a - 3)(4a^2 - 1)$

(B) $5(2a - 3)(4a^2 + 1)$ (D) $5(2a - 3)(2a - 3)(4a^2 - 1)$

58. **Short Response** Use the polynomial $8x^3 + 24x^2 + 18x$ for the following.

a. Factor the polynomial. Explain each step and tell whether you used any rules for special products.

b. Explain another set of steps that could be used to factor the polynomial.
The polynomial could be factored by finding factors of 8 and factors of 18 that would result in 24 as the sum of the outer and inner products. Then one binomial would need to be factored again.

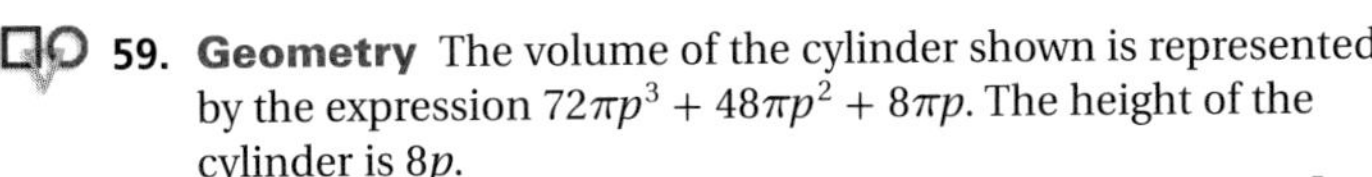

CHALLENGE AND EXTEND

59. **Geometry** The volume of the cylinder shown is represented by the expression $72\pi p^3 + 48\pi p^2 + 8\pi p$. The height of the cylinder is $8p$.

a. Factor the expression for volume. $\mathbf{V = 8p[\pi(3p + 1)^2]}$

b. What expression represents the radius of the cylinder? $\mathbf{r = (3p + 1)}$ **cm**

c. If the radius is 4 cm, what are the height and volume of the cylinder? $\mathbf{h = 8}$ **cm;** $\mathbf{V = 128\pi}$ **cm**^{3}

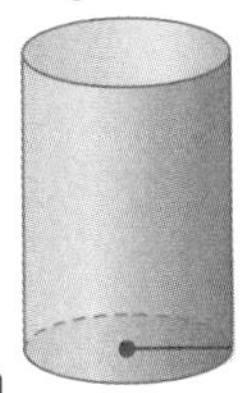

Factor.

60. $g^7 + g^3 + g^5 + g^4$ $\mathbf{g^3(g^4 + g^2 + g + 1)}$

61. $h^2 + h^8 + h^6 + h^4$ $\mathbf{h^2(h^4 + 1)(h^2 + 1)}$

62. $x^{n+2} + x^{n+1} + x^n$ $\mathbf{x^n(x^2 + x + 1)}$

63. $x^{n+5} + x^{n+4} + x^{n+3}$ $\mathbf{x^{n+3}(x^2 + x + 1)}$

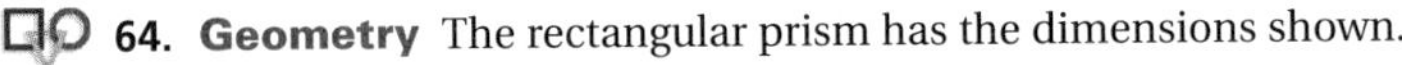

64. **Geometry** The rectangular prism has the dimensions shown.

a. Write expressions for the height and length of the prism using w. $\mathbf{h = w + 5;\ \ell = w + 9}$

b. Write a polynomial that represents the volume of the prism using w. $\mathbf{V = w^3 + 14w^2 + 45w}$

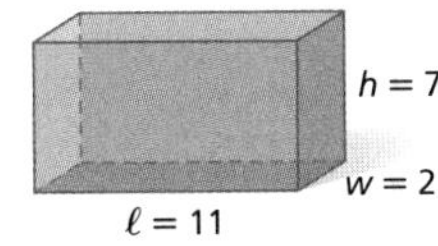

SPIRAL REVIEW

Simplify each expression by combining like terms. *(Lesson 1-7)*

65. $-6n + 4n$ $\mathbf{-2n}$

66. $5x^2 - 8x + 4x^2$ $\mathbf{9x^2 - 8x}$

67. $2.6r + 9.7r$ $\mathbf{12.3r}$

Write and solve a proportion to answer each question. *(Lesson 2-7)*

68. The ratio of fiction to nonfiction books on Jessika's shelf is 3 to 4. Jessika has 12 nonfiction books. How many fiction books does she have? $\mathbf{\frac{3}{4} = \frac{x}{12}}$**; 9 fiction books**

69. The scale of a model car is 23:2. The steering wheel on the model car has a diameter of 3 cm. What is the diameter of the steering wheel on the actual car? $\mathbf{\frac{23}{2} = \frac{x}{3}}$**; 34.5 cm**

Factor each trinomial. *(Lesson 8-4)*

70. $2x^2 + 13x + 15$ $\mathbf{(2x + 3)(x + 5)}$

71. $4x^2 + 4x - 3$ $\mathbf{(2x - 1)(2x + 3)}$

72. $6x^2 - 11x - 10$ $\mathbf{(3x + 2)(2x - 5)}$

Teaching Tip

Geometry In **Exercise 59,** students must factor an expression that represents the volume of a cylinder. Remind students that π is a number and can be factored out just like any other number.

Answers

58a. $8x^3 + 24x^2 + 18x = 2x(4x^2 + 12x + 9) = 2x(2x + 3)^2$; first I factored out the GCF, $2x$, and then I used the pattern for a perfect-square trinomial.

Journal

Explain what you think is the easiest type of polynomial to factor. Use an example to demonstrate.

ALTERNATIVE ASSESSMENT

Pair students. Have each student work backward to create three different polynomials that require at least two different factoring methods. Then have students switch papers and factor their partner's polynomials.

Power Presentations with PowerPoint®

8-6 Lesson Quiz

Tell whether each expression is completely factored. If not, factor it.

1. $(x + 3)(5x + 10)$
   no; $5(x + 3)(x + 2)$

2. $3x^2(x^2 + 9)$
   yes

Factor each polynomial completely. Check your answer.

3. $x^3 + 4x^2 + 3x + 12$
   $(x + 4)(x^2 + 3)$

4. $4x^2 + 16x - 48$
   $4(x + 6)(x - 2)$

5. $18x^2 - 3x - 3$
   $3(3x + 1)(2x - 1)$

6. $18x^2 - 50y^2$
   $2(3x + 5y)(3x - 5y)$

7. $5x - 20x^3 + 7 - 28x^2$
   $(1 + 2x)(1 - 2x)(5x + 7)$

Also available on transparency

8-6 PROBLEM SOLVING

Write the correct answer.

1. A rectangular stage set up in a theater has an area of $(15x^2 + 3x - 12)$ square feet. Factor the polynomial completely.
   $3(5x - 4)(x + 1)$

2. The area of a circular rug is $(16\pi k^2 - 16\pi k + 4\pi)$ m^2. Factor the expression completely. Then find the area of the rug if $k = 1$ meter.
   $4\pi(2k - 1)^2$; $4\pi m^2$

3. An artist framed a picture. The dimensions of the picture and frame are shown below.

Completely factor the expression for the area of the frame.
   $4(2x + y)(2x - y)$

4. The attendance for a team's basketball game can be approximated with the polynomial $-5x^2 + 80x + 285$, where x is the number of wins the team had in the previous month. Factor the polynomial completely. Then estimate the attendance when the team won 4 games in the previous month.
   $-5(x - 19)(x + 3)$; 525 attendees

Select the best answer.

5. The volume of a box can be modeled by the expression $7x^4 - 28$. Which shows this expression completely factored?
   A $7(x^4 - 4)$
   B $7(x^2 - 2)^2$
   C $(7x^2 + 4)(x^2 - 7)$
   D $7(x^2 + 2)(x^2 - 2)$

6. The area of a Japanese rock garden is $(30x^2 + 3x - 6)$ square feet. Factor the polynomial completely.
   F $3(10x^2 + x - 2)$
   G $3(2x + 1)(5x - 2)$
   H $(6x + 3)(5x - 2)$
   J $(15x - 6)(2x + 1)$

7. The money made from the sales of x mountain bikes is approximated by $20x^2 + 10x + 90$. Factor the expression completely.
   A $2(10x + 9)(x + 5)$
   B $5(4x^2 + 2x + 18)$
   C $10(2x^2 + x + 9)$
   D The expression cannot be factored.

8. Kyle stood on a bridge and threw a rock up and over the side. The height of the rock, in meters, can be approximated by $-5t^2 + 5t + 24$, where t is the time in seconds after Kyle threw it. Completely factor the expression.
   F $-5(t^2 + t + 24)$
   G $(-5t + 3)(t + 8)$
   H $-1(5t + 8)(t + 3)$
   J The expression cannot be factored.

8-6 CHALLENGE

A sum of cubes can be factored using: $a^3 + b^3 = (a + b)(a^2 - ab + b^2)$.

Factor $x^3 + 125y^3$.

$(x)^3 + (5y)^3$ $a = x, b = 5y$

$(x + 5y)(x^2 - 5xy + 25y^2)$ *Substitute into $(a + b)(a^2 - ab + b^2)$.*

Factor each polynomial.

1. $x^3 + 8$ **$(x + 2)(x^2 - 2x + 4)$**
2. $64x^3 + y^3$ **$(4x + y)(16x^2 - 4xy + y^2)$**
3. $125x^3 + 216$ **$(5x + 6)(25x^2 - 30x + 36)$**

A difference of cubes can be factored using: $a^3 - b^3 = (a - b)(a^2 + ab + b^2)$.

Factor $8x^3 - 27$.

$(2x)^3 - (3)^3$ $a = 2x, b = 3$

$(2x - 3)(4x^2 + 6x + 9)$ *Substitute into $(a - b)(a^2 + ab + b^2)$.*

Factor each polynomial.

4. $x^3 - 64$ **$(x - 4)(x^2 + 4x + 16)$**
5. $343x^3 - y^3$ **$(7x - y)(49x^2 + 7xy + y^2)$**
6. $729x^3 - 1000$ **$(9x - 10)(81x^2 + 90x + 100)$**

You can use the sum and difference of cubes with other factoring methods to completely factor a polynomial.

Factor each polynomial completely.

7. $2x^3 - 54$ **$2(x - 3)(x^2 + 3x + 9)$**
8. $216x^3 + 8y^3$ **$8(3x + y)(9x^2 - 3xy + y^2)$**
9. $x^6 + 12x^3 + 32$ **$(x + 2)(x^2 + 2x + 4)(x^3 + 4)$**
10. $3x^6 + 18x^3 + 15$ **$3(x^3 + 5)(x + 1)(x^2 - x + 1)$**
11. $x^5 - 27x^2 - 9x^3 + 243$ **$(x + 3)(x - 3)^2(x^2 + 3x + 9)$**

Use difference of squares to factor each binomial. Then factor completely.

12. $729x^6 - 64$ **$(3x + 2)(3x - 2)(9x^2 - 6x + 4)(9x^2 + 6x + 4)$**
13. $64x^6 - y^6$ **$(2x + y)(2x - y)(4x^2 - 2xy + y^2)(4x^2 + 2xy + y^2)$**

SECTION 8B MULTI-STEP TEST PREP

Organizer

Objective: Assess students' ability to apply concepts and skills in Lessons 8-5 through 8-6 in a real-world format.

 Online Edition

Resources

 ***Algebra I Assessments***

www.mathtekstoolkit.org

Problem	Text Reference
1	Lesson 8-5
2	Lesson 2-1
3	Lesson 8-3
4	Lesson 8-6
5	Lesson 1-1
6	Lesson 1-1

Answers

1. $\ell = (x + 6)$ ft; $w = (x + 6)$ ft
2. $w = 12$ ft; $x = 6$; $A = 144$ ft^2
3. $\ell = (x + 12)$ ft; $w = (x + 2)$ ft

State Resources

go.hrw.com
State Resources Online
KEYWORD: MA7 Resources

CHAPTER 8

MULTI-STEP TEST PREP

SECTION 8B

Factoring

Shaping the Environment The Environmental Awareness Club is going to plant a garden on the front lawn of the school. Henry suggests a garden in the shape of a square. Theona suggests a rectangular shape.

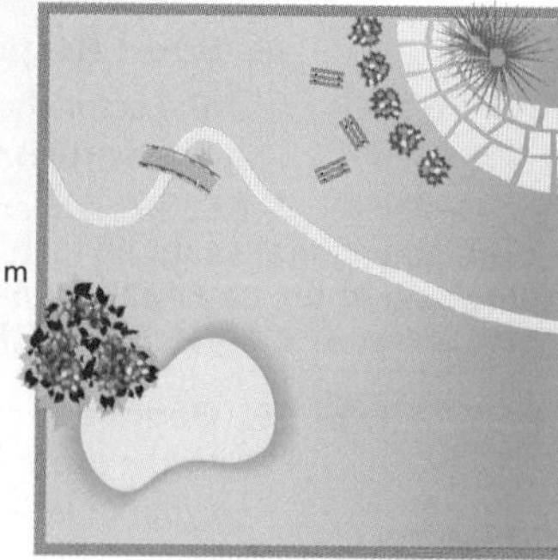

1. Henry's plans include a square garden with an area of $(x^2 + 12x + 36)$ m^2. Write expressions for the length and width of the square garden.
2. A drawing of the square garden shows a length of 12 m. What is the width of the square garden? What is the value of x? What is the total area of the square garden?
3. Theona's plans include a rectangular garden with an area of $(x^2 + 14x + 24)$ m^2. Write expressions for the length and width of the rectangular garden.

4. A drawing of the rectangular garden shows that the length is 6 m longer than the length of the square garden. What is the width of the rectangular garden? How much shorter is the width of the rectangular garden than the square garden? **$w = 8$ m; 4 m**
5. Find the perimeter of each garden in terms of x.
6. Which plan should the club choose if they want the garden that covers the most area? Which plan should the club choose if they want the garden that requires the least fencing around it? Explain your reasoning.

5. square garden: $4(x + 6)$ m; rectangular garden: $4(x + 7)$ m

6. Area of square garden: 144 m^2; area of rectangular garden: 144 m^2; the gardens have the same area; the perimeter of the square

INTERVENTION 

Scaffolding Questions

1. When given the area, how can you find the length and width? Factor the area.
2. What values of x are reasonable? x must be positive.
3. Will the length and width be equal if the rectangle is not a square? no
4. Does it matter which side of the square garden you label as the width? No; the sides are all the same length.
5. What does perimeter describe? the distance around a figure
6. How do you know which garden requires the least fencing? The garden with the smaller perimeter requires less fencing.

Extension

Do you think the perimeter of two gardens with the same area will be larger for a square or rectangle? The perimeter will be larger for the rectangle.

Quiz for Lessons 8-5 Through 8-6

8-5 Factoring Special Products

Determine whether each trinomial is a perfect square. If so, factor. If not, explain.

1. $x^2 + 8x + 16$ **yes; $(x + 4)^2$**
2. $4x^2 - 20x + 25$ **yes; $(2x - 5)^2$**
3. $x^2 + 3x + 9$ **no; $3x \neq 2(x)(3)$**
4. $2x^2 - 4x + 4$
5. $9x^2 - 12x + 4$
6. $x^2 - 12x - 36$
7. An architect is designing square windows with an area of $(x^2 + 20x + 100)$ ft^2. The dimensions of the windows are of the form $ax + b$, where a and b are whole numbers. Find an expression for the perimeter of the windows. Find the perimeter of a window when $x = 4$ ft. **$4(x + 10)$ ft; 56 ft**

Determine whether each trinomial is a difference of two squares. If so, factor. If not, explain.

8. $x^2 - 121$
9. $4t^2 - 20$
10. $1 - 9y^4$
11. $25m^2 - 4m^6$
12. $16x^2 + 49$
13. $r^4 - t^2$
14. The area of a square is $(36d^2 - 36d + 9)$ in^2.
    a. What expression represents the length of a side of the square? **$\ell = (6d - 3)$ in.**
    b. What expression represents the perimeter of the square? **$4(6d - 3)$ in.**
    c. What are the length of a side, the perimeter, and the area of the square when $d = 2$ in.? **9 in.; 36 in.; 81 in^2**

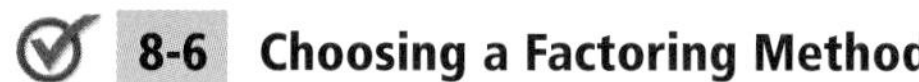

8-6 Choosing a Factoring Method

Tell whether each expression is completely factored. If not, factor it.

15. $5(x^2 + 3x + 1)$ **yes**
16. $6x(5x^2 - x)$ **no; $6x^2(5x - 1)$**
17. $3t(t^4 - 9)$ **no; $3t(t^2 - 3)(t^2 + 3)$**
18. $2(m^2 - 10m + 25)$ **no; $2(m - 5)^2$**
19. $3(2y^2 - 5)(y + 1)$ **yes**
20. $(2n + 6)(n - 4)$ **no; $2(n + 3)(n - 4)$**

Factor each polynomial completely. Check your answer.

21. $3x^3 - 12x^2 + 12x$
22. $16m^3 - 4m$
23. $5x^3y - 45xy$
24. $3t^2 + 5t - 1$
25. $3c^2 + 12c - 63$
26. $x^5 - 81x$

Write an expression for each situation. Then factor your expression.

27. the difference of the square of a board's length and 36
28. the square of Michael's age minus 8 times Michael's age plus 16
29. two times the square of a car's speed plus 2 times the car's speed minus 12
30. three times the cube of Jessie's height plus 3 times the square of Jessie's height minus 6 times Jessie's height
31. Write an expression for the area of the shaded region. Then factor the expression.

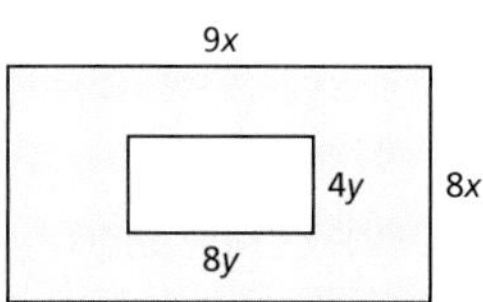

READY TO GO ON? SECTION 8B

Organizer

Objective: Assess students' mastery of concepts and skills in Lessons 8-5 through 8-6.

Resources

 ***Assessment Resources***
Section 8B Quiz

Teacher One Stop™
Test & Practice Generator

INTERVENTION

Resources

 ***Ready to Go On? Intervention and Enrichment* Worksheets**

 ***Ready to Go On?* CD-ROM**

***Ready to Go On?* Online**

my.hrw.com

Answers

4–6, 8–13, 21–31. See p. A29.

READY TO GO ON? Diagnose and Prescribe

NO INTERVENE

Ready to Go On? Intervention	*Ready to Go On? Intervention,* Section 8B Worksheets	CD-ROM	Online
Lesson 8-5	8-5 Intervention	Activity 8-5	Diagnose and Prescribe Online
Lesson 8-6	8-6 Intervention	Activity 8-6	

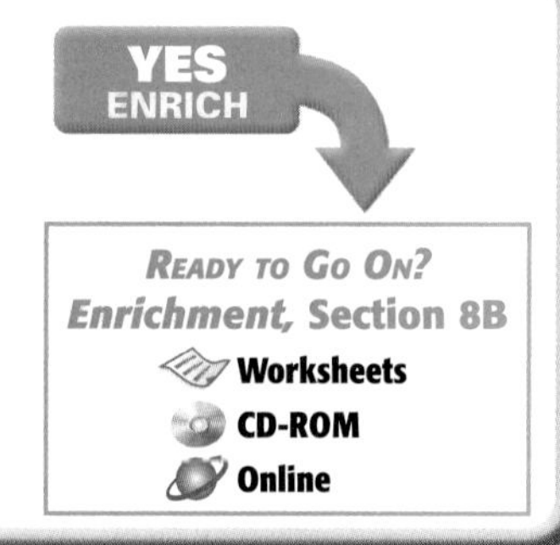

CHAPTER 8 Study Guide: Review

Organizer

Objective: Help students organize and review key concepts and skills presented in Chapter 8.

Online Edition
Multilingual Glossary

Resources

Teacher One Stop™
PuzzleView
Test & Practice Generator

***Multilingual Glossary* Online**
go.hrw.com
KEYWORD: MA7 Glossary

Lesson Tutorial Videos
CD-ROM

Answers

1. prime factorization
2. greatest common factor
3. $2^2 \cdot 3$
4. $2^2 \cdot 5$
5. 2^5
6. prime
7. $2^3 \cdot 5$
8. 2^6
9. $2 \cdot 3 \cdot 11$
10. $2 \cdot 3 \cdot 19$
11. 5
12. 12
13. 1
14. 27
15. 4
16. 3
17. $2x$
18. $9b^2$
19. $25r$
20. 6 boxes; 13 rows

CHAPTER 8 Study Guide: Review

Vocabulary

greatest common factor 544

prime factorization 544

Complete the sentences below with vocabulary words from the list above.

1. A number written as a product so that each of its factors has no factors other than 1 and itself is the ___?___.
2. The ___?___ of two monomials is the greatest of the factors that the monomials share.

8-1 Factors and Greatest Common Factors *(pp. 544–549)*

EXAMPLES

■ **Write the prime factorization of 84.**

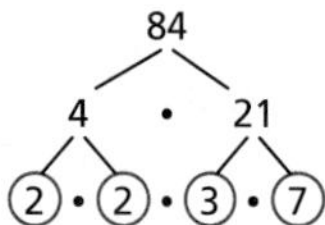

Write as a product. Continue until all factors are prime.

■ **Write the prime factorization of 75.**

3	75
5	25
5	5
	1

Keep dividing by prime factors until the quotient is 1.

$75 = 3 \cdot 5 \cdot 5 = 3 \cdot 5^2$

■ **Find the GCF of 36 and 90.**

$36 = 2 \cdot \boxed{2} \cdot \boxed{3} \cdot \boxed{3}$
$90 = \boxed{2} \cdot \boxed{3} \cdot \boxed{3} \cdot 5$

$2 \cdot 3 \cdot 3 = 18$

The GCF of 36 and 90 is 18.

Write the prime factorization of each number. Find the product of the common factors.

■ **Find the GCF of $10x^5$ and $4x^2$.**

$10x^5 = \boxed{2} \cdot 5 \cdot \boxed{x} \cdot \boxed{x} \cdot x \cdot x \cdot x$
$4x^2 = \boxed{2} \cdot 2 \cdot \boxed{x} \cdot \boxed{x}$

$2 \cdot x \cdot x = 2x^2$

The GCF of $10x^5$ and $4x^2$ is $2x^2$.

Write the prime factorization of each coefficient. Write powers as products. Find the product of the common factors.

EXERCISES

Write the prime factorization of each number.

3. 12
4. 20
5. 32
6. 23
7. 40
8. 64
9. 66
10. 114

Find the GCF of each pair of numbers.

11. 15 and 50
12. 36 and 132
13. 29 and 30
14. 54 and 81
15. 20 and 48

Find the GCF of each pair of monomials.

16. $9m$ and 3
17. $4x$ and $2x^2$
18. $-18b^4$ and $27b^2$
19. $100r$ and $25r^5$
20. A hardware store carries 42 types of boxed nails and 36 types of boxed screws. The store manager wants to build a rack so that he can display the hardware in rows. He wants to put the same number of boxes in each row, but he wants no row to contain both nails and screws. What is the greatest number of boxes that he can display in one row? How many rows will there be if the manager puts the greatest number of boxes in each row?

8-2 Factoring by GCF *(pp. 551–557)*

EXAMPLES

- **Factor $3t^3 - 9t^2$. Check your answer.**

$3t^3 = 3 \cdot t \cdot t \cdot t$
$9t^2 = 3 \cdot 3 \cdot t \cdot t$ *Find the GCF.*

GCF: $3 \cdot t \cdot t = 3t^2$

$3t^3 - 9t^2 = 3t^2(t) - 3t^2(3)$
$= 3t^2(t - 3)$ *Factor out the GCF.*

Check $3t^2(t - 3) = 3t^3 - 9t^2$ ✓

- **Factor $-12s - 6s^3$. Check your answer.**

$-1(12s + 6s^3)$ *Factor out −1.*

$12s = 2 \cdot 2 \cdot 3 \cdot s$
$6s^3 = 2 \cdot \quad 3 \cdot s \cdot s \cdot s$ *Find the GCF.*

GCF: $2 \cdot 3 \cdot s = 6s$

$-1(12s + 6s^3)$
$-1[(6s)(2) + (6s)(s^2)]$
$-1[(6s)(2 + s^2)]$
$-6s(2 + s^2)$ *Factor out the GCF.*

Check $-6s(2 + s^2) = -12s - 6s^3$ ✓

- **Factor $5(x - 7) + 3x(x - 7)$ by grouping.**

$5(x - 7) + 3x(x - 7)$ *(x − 7) is a common factor.*

$(x - 7)(5 + 3x)$ *Factor out (x − 7).*

- **Factor $6b^3 + 8b + 15b^2 + 20$ by grouping.**

$(6b^3 + 8b) + (15b^2 + 20)$ *Group terms that have a common factor.*

$2b(3b^2 + 4) + 5(3b^2 + 4)$ *Factor each group.*

$(3b^2 + 4)(2b + 5)$ *Factor out $(3b^2 + 4)$.*

- **Factor $2m^3 - 6m^2 + 15 - 5m$. Check your answer.**

$(2m^3 - 6m^2) + (15 - 5m)$ *Group terms.*
$2m^2(m - 3) + 5(3 - m)$ *Factor each group.*
$2m^2(m - 3) + 5(-1)(m - 3)$ *Rewrite (3 − m) as (−1)(m − 3).*
$2m^2(m - 3) - 5(m - 3)$ *Simplify.*
$(m - 3)(2m^2 - 5)$ *Factor out (m − 3).*

Check $(m - 3)(2m^2 - 5)$
$2m^3 - 5m - 6m^2 + 15$
$2m^3 - 6m^2 + 15 - 5m$ ✓

EXERCISES

Factor each polynomial. Check your answer.

21. $5x - 15x^3$ **22.** $-16b + 32$

23. $-14v - 21$ **24.** $4a^2 - 12a - 8$

25. $5g^5 - 10g^3 - 15g$ **26.** $40p^2 - 10p + 30$

27. A civil engineer needs the area of a rectangular lot to be $(6x^2 + 5x)$ ft². Factor this polynomial to find possible expressions for the dimensions of the lot.

Factor each expression.

28. $2x(x - 4) + 9(x - 4)$

29. $t(3t + 5) - 6(3t + 5)$

30. $5(6 - n) - 3n(6 - n)$

31. $b(b + 4) + 2(b + 4)$

32. $x^2(x - 3) + 7(x - 3)$

Factor each polynomial. Check your answer.

33. $n^3 + n - 4n^2 - 4$

34. $6b^2 - 8b + 15b - 20$

35. $2h^3 - 7h + 14h^2 - 49$

36. $3t^2 + 18t + t + 6$

37. $10m^3 + 15m^2 - 2m - 3$

38. $8p^3 + 4p - 6p^2 - 3$

39. $5r - 10 + 2r - r^2$

40. $b^3 - 5b + 15 - 3b^2$

41. $6t - t^3 - 4t^2 + 24$

42. $12h - 3h^2 + h - 4$

43. $d - d^2 + d - 1$

44. $6b - 5b^2 + 10b - 12$

45. $5t - t^2 - t + 5$

46. $8b^2 - 2b^3 - 5b + 20$

47. $3r - 3r^2 - 1 + r$

48. Write an expression for the area of each of the two rectangles shown. Then write and factor an expression for the combined area.

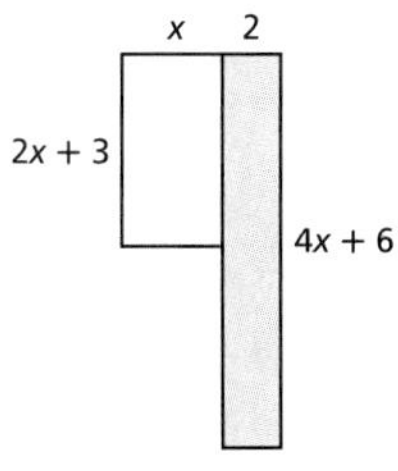

Answers

21. $5x(1 - 3x^2)$
22. $16(-b + 2)$
23. $-7(2v + 3)$
24. $4(a^2 - 3a - 2)$
25. $5g(g^2 - 3)(g^2 + 1)$
26. $10(4p^2 - p + 3)$
27. $(6x + 5)$ ft by x ft
28. $(2x + 9)(x - 4)$
29. $(t - 6)(3t + 5)$
30. $(5 - 3n)(6 - n)$
31. $(b + 2)(b + 4)$
32. $(x^2 + 7)(x - 3)$
33. $(n^2 + 1)(n - 4)$
34. $(2b + 5)(3b - 4)$
35. $(2h^2 - 7)(h + 7)$
36. $(3t + 1)(t + 6)$
37. $(5m^2 - 1)(2m + 3)$
38. $(4p - 3)(2p^2 + 1)$
39. $-1(r - 5)(r - 2)$
40. $(b^2 - 5)(b - 3)$
41. $(t + 4)(-t^2 + 6)$
42. $-1(3h - 1)(h - 4)$
43. $-1(d - 1)^2$
44. $(2 - b)(5b - 6)$
45. $(t + 1)(5 - t)$
46. $(2b^2 + 5)(4 - b)$
47. $-1(3r - 1)(r - 1)$
48. left rectangle: $2x^2 + 3x$; right rectangle: $8x + 12$; combined: $2x^2 + 8x + 3x + 12$; $(2x + 3)(x + 4)$

Answers

49. $(x+1)(x+5)$
50. $(x+2)(x+4)$
51. $(x+3)(x+5)$
52. $(x-6)(x-2)$
53. $(x+5)^2$
54. $(x-2)(x-11)$
55. $(x+4)(x+20)$
56. $(x-6)(x-20)$
57. $(x+12)(x-7)$
58. $(x+3)(x-8)$
59. $(x+4)(x-7)$
60. $(x-1)(x+5)$
61. $(x+3)(x-2)$
62. $(x+5)(x-4)$
63. $(x-8)(x+6)$
64. $(x-9)(x+4)$
65. $(x-12)(x+6)$
66. $(x-10)(x+7)$
67. $(x+20)(x-6)$
68. $(x+7)(x-1)$
69. $(y+3)$ m
70. $(2x+1)(x+5)$
71. $(3x+7)(x+1)$
72. $(2x-1)(x-1)$
73. $(3x+2)(x+2)$
74. $(5x+3)(x+5)$
75. $(2x-3)(3x-5)$
76. $(4x+5)(x+2)$
77. $(3x+4)(x+2)$
78. $(7x-2)(x-5)$
79. $(3x+2)(3x+4)$
80. $(2x+1)(x-1)$
81. $(3x+1)(x-4)$
82. $(2x-1)(x-5)$
83. $(7x+2)(x-3)$
84. $(5x+1)(x-2)$
85. $-1(2x-1)(3x+2)$
86. $(6x+5)(x-1)$
87. $(3x-2)(2x+7)$
88. $-1(2x+1)(2x-5)$
89. $-1(2x-3)(5x+2)$
90. $12x^2-11x-5$; $(4x-5)(3x+1)$

8-3 Factoring $x^2 + bx + c$ *(pp. 560–567)*

EXAMPLES

Factor each trinomial. Check your answer.

■ $x^2 + 14x + 45$

$(x + \square)(x + \square)$ — *Look for factors of 45 whose sum is 14.*

$(x+9)(x+5)$

Check $(x+9)(x+5) = x^2 + 5x + 9x + 45$
$= x^2 + 14x + 45$ ✓

■ $x^2 + 6x - 27$

$(x + \square)(x - \square)$ — *Look for factors of −27 whose sum is 6.*

$(x+9)(x-3)$

Check $(x+9)(x-3) = x^2 - 3x + 9x - 27$
$= x^2 + 6x - 27$ ✓

EXERCISES

Factor each trinomial. Check your answer.

49. $x^2 + 6x + 5$
50. $x^2 + 6x + 8$
51. $x^2 + 8x + 15$
52. $x^2 - 8x + 12$
53. $x^2 + 10x + 25$
54. $x^2 - 13x + 22$
55. $x^2 + 24x + 80$
56. $x^2 - 26x + 120$
57. $x^2 + 5x - 84$
58. $x^2 - 5x - 24$
59. $x^2 - 3x - 28$
60. $x^2 + 4x - 5$
61. $x^2 + x - 6$
62. $x^2 + x - 20$
63. $x^2 - 2x - 48$
64. $x^2 - 5x - 36$
65. $x^2 - 6x - 72$
66. $x^2 - 3x - 70$
67. $x^2 + 14x - 120$
68. $x^2 + 6x - 7$
69. The rectangle shown has an area of $(y^2 + 8y + 15)$ m². What is the width of the rectangle?

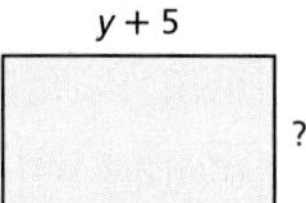

8-4 Factoring $ax^2 + bx + c$ *(pp. 568–574)*

EXAMPLES

Factor each trinomial.

■ $6x^2 + 17x + 5$

$(\square x + \square)(\square x + \square)$ — *$a = 6$ and $c = 5$; Outer + Inner = 17*

Factors of 6	Factors of 5	Outer + Inner	
1 and 6	5 and 1	$1(1) + 6(5) = 31$	✗
2 and 3	1 and 5	$2(5) + 3(1) = 13$	✗
2 and 3	5 and 1	$1(1) + 3(5) = 17$	✓

$(2x+5)(3x+1)$

■ $2n^2 - n - 10$

$(\square n + \square)(\square n + \square)$ — *$a = 2$ and $c = -10$; Outer + Inner = −1*

Factors of 2	Factors of −10	Outer + Inner	
1 and 2	1 and −10	$1(-10) + 2(1) = -8$	✗
1 and 2	−1 and 10	$1(10) + 2(-1) = 8$	✗
1 and 2	2 and −5	$1(-5) + 2(2) = -1$	✓

$(1n+2)(2n-5) = (n+2)(2n-5)$

EXERCISES

Factor each trinomial. Check your answer.

70. $2x^2 + 11x + 5$
71. $3x^2 + 10x + 7$
72. $2x^2 - 3x + 1$
73. $3x^2 + 8x + 4$
74. $5x^2 + 28x + 15$
75. $6x^2 - 19x + 15$
76. $4x^2 + 13x + 10$
77. $3x^2 + 10x + 8$
78. $7x^2 - 37x + 10$
79. $9x^2 + 18x + 8$
80. $2x^2 - x - 1$
81. $3x^2 - 11x - 4$
82. $2x^2 - 11x + 5$
83. $7x^2 - 19x - 6$
84. $5x^2 - 9x - 2$
85. $-6x^2 - x + 2$
86. $6x^2 - x - 5$
87. $6x^2 + 17x - 14$
88. $-4x^2 + 8x + 5$
89. $-10x^2 + 11x + 6$
90. Write the polynomial modeled and then factor.

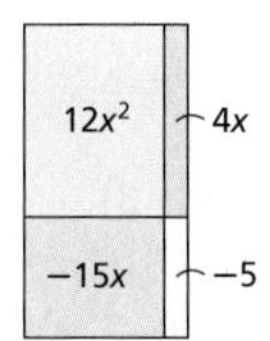

8-5 Factoring Special Products *(pp. 578–584)*

EXAMPLES

- Determine whether $x^2 + 18x + 81$ is a perfect square. If so, factor. If not, explain.

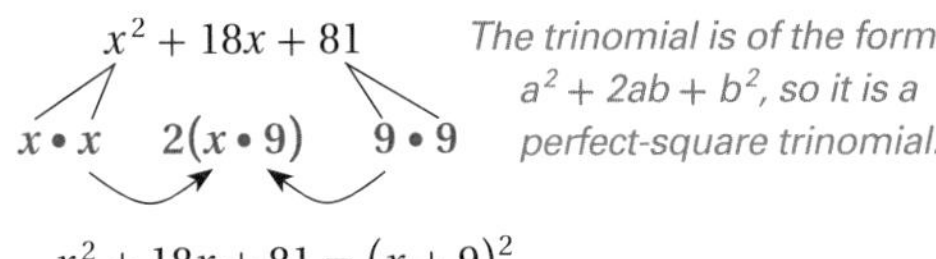

The trinomial is of the form $a^2 + 2ab + b^2$, so it is a perfect-square trinomial.

$x^2 + 18x + 81 = (x + 9)^2$

- Determine whether $49x^4 - 25y^6$ is a difference of two squares. If so, factor. If not, explain.

$49x^4 - 25y^6$

$7x^2 \cdot 7x^2 \quad 5y^3 \cdot 5y^3$ — *The binomial is a difference of two squares.*

$(7x^2)^2 - (5y^3)^2$ — *$a = 7x^2$, $b = 5x^3$*

$(7x^2 + 5y^3)(7x^2 - 5y^3)$ — *Write the binomial as $(a + b)(a - b)$.*

$49x^4 - 25y^6 = (7x^2 + 5y^3)(7x^2 - 5y^3)$

EXERCISES

Determine whether each trinomial is a perfect square. If so, factor. If not, explain.

91. $x^2 + 12x + 36$ **92.** $x^2 + 5x + 25$

93. $4x^2 - 2x + 1$ **94.** $9x^2 + 12x + 4$

95. $16x^2 + 8x + 4$ **96.** $x^2 + 14x + 49$

Determine whether each binomial is a difference of two squares. If so, factor. If not, explain.

97. $100x^2 - 81$ **98.** $x^2 - 2$

99. $5x^4 - 10y^6$ **100.** $(-12)^2 - (x^3)^2$

101. $121b^2 + 9c^8$ **102.** $100p^2 - 25q^2$

Factor each polynomial using the rule for perfect-square trinomials or the rule for a difference of two squares. Tell which rule you used.

103. $x^2 - 25$ **104.** $x^2 + 20x + 100$

105. $j^2 - k^4$ **106.** $9x^2 - 42x + 49$

107. $81x^2 + 144x + 64$ **108.** $16b^4 - 121c^6$

8-6 Choosing a Factoring Method *(pp. 586–591)*

EXAMPLES

- Tell whether $(3x - 9)(x + 4)$ is completely factored. If not, factor it.

$(3x - 9)(x + 4)$ — *$3x - 9$ can be factored.*

$3(x - 3)(x + 4)$ — *Factor out 3, the GCF of $3x$ and 9.*

- $3ab^2 - 48a$

$3a(b^2 - 16)$ — *Factor out the GCF.*

$3a(b + 4)(b - 4)$ — *Factor the difference of two squares.*

Check $3a(b + 4)(b - 4) = 3a(b^2 - 16)$

$= 3ab^2 - 48a$ ✓

- $2m^3 + 4m^2 - 48m$

$2m(m^2 + 2m - 24)$ — *Factor out the GCF.*

$2m(m - 4)(m + 6)$ — *Factor the trinomial.*

Check $2m(m - 4)(m + 6)$

$2m(m^2 + 2m - 24)$

$2m^3 + 4m^2 - 48m$ ✓

EXERCISES

Tell whether each polynomial is completely factored. If not, factor it.

109. $4x^2 + 10x + 6 = (4x + 6)(x + 1)$

110. $3y^2 + 75 = 3(y^2 + 25)$

111. $b^4 - 81 = (b^2 + 9)(b^2 - 9)$

112. $x^2 - 6x + 9 = (x - 3)^2$

Factor each polynomial completely. Check your answer.

113. $4x^2 - 64$ **114.** $3b^5 - 6b^4 - 24b^3$

115. $a^4b^3 - a^2b^5$ **116.** $t^{20} - t^4$

117. $5x^2 + 20x + 15$ **118.** $2x^4 - 50x^2$

119. $8t + 32 + 2st + 8s$

120. $25m^3 - 90m^2 - 40m$

121. $32x^4 - 48x^3 + 8x^2 - 12x$

122. $6s^4t + 12s^3t^2 + 6s^2t^3$

123. $10m^3 + 4m^2 - 90m - 36$

Answers

91. yes; $(x + 6)^2$
92. no; $5x \neq 2(x)(5)$
93. no; $-2x \neq 2(2x)(1)$
94. yes; $(3x + 2)^2$
95. no; $8x \neq 2(4x)(2)$
96. yes; $(x + 7)^2$
97. yes; $(10x - 9)(10x + 9)$
98. No; 2 is not a perfect square.
99. No; 5 and 10 are not perfect squares.
100. yes; $(-12 + x^3)(-12 - x^3)$
101. no; not a difference
102. yes; $(10p - 5q)(10p + 5q)$
103. $(x - 5)(x + 5)$; difference of 2 squares
104. $(x + 10)^2$; perfect-square trinomial
105. $(j - k^2)(j + k^2)$; difference of 2 squares
106. $(3x - 7)^2$; perfect-square trinomial
107. $(9x + 8)^2$; perfect-square trinomial
108. $(4b^2 - 11c^3)(4b^2 + 11c^3)$; difference of 2 squares
109. no; $2(2x + 3)(x + 1)$
110. yes
111. no; $(b^2 + 9)(b - 3)(b + 3)$
112. yes
113. $4(x - 4)(x + 4)$
114. $3b^3(b - 4)(b + 2)$
115. $a^2b^3(a - b)(a + b)$
116. $t^4(t^8 + 1)(t^4 + 1)(t^2 + 1)(t + 1)(t - 1)$
117. $5(x + 3)(x + 1)$
118. $2x^2(x - 5)(x + 5)$
119. $2(s + 4)(t + 4)$
120. $5m(5m + 2)(m - 4)$
121. $4x(4x^2 + 1)(2x - 3)$
122. $6s^2t(s + t)^2$
123. $2(m + 3)(m - 3)(5m + 2)$

Organizer

Objective: Assess students' mastery of concepts and skills in Chapter 8.

 **Online Edition**

Resources

 ***Assessment Resources***

Chapter 8 Tests
- Free Response (Levels A, B, C)
- Multiple Choice (Levels A, B, C)
- Performance Assessment

Teacher One Stop™
Test & Practice Generator

Answers

9. $(3 + 4c)(c - 5)$
10. $(5x^2 + 2)(2x - 5)$
11. $(y - 1)(4y^2 + 3)$
29. $8x(x + 4)(x + 5)$

State Resources

Find the GCF of each pair of monomials.

1. $3t^4$ and $8t^2$ **t^2**
2. $2y^3$ and $-12y$ **$2y$**
3. $15n^5$ and $9n^4$ **$3n^4$**
4. Write the prime factorization of 360. **$2^3 \cdot 3^2 \cdot 5$**
5. A coin collector is arranging a display of three types of nickels. The types of nickels and number of each type are shown in the table. The collector wants to arrange them in rows with the same number in each row without having different types in the same row. How many rows will she need if she puts the greatest possible number of nickels in each row? **10 rows**

Type of Nickel	Number of Nickels
Liberty	16
Buffalo	24
Jefferson	40

Factor each expression.

6. $24m^2 + 4m^3$ **$4m^2(6 + m)$**
7. $9x^5 - 12x$ **$3x(3x^4 - 4)$**
8. $-2r^4 - 6$ **$-2(r^4 + 3)$**
9. $3(c - 5) + 4c(c - 5)$
10. $10x^3 + 4x - 25x^2 - 10$
11. $4y^3 - 4y^2 - 3 + 3y$
12. A model rocket is shot vertically from a deck into the air at a speed of 50 m/s. The expression $-5t^2 + 50t + 5$ gives the approximate height of the rocket after t seconds. Factor this expression. **$-5(t^2 - 10t - 1)$**

Factor each trinomial.

13. $x^2 + 6x + 5$ **$(x + 5)(x + 1)$**
14. $x^2 - 4x - 21$ **$(x - 7)(x + 3)$**
15. $x^2 - 8x + 15$ **$(x - 5)(x - 3)$**
16. $2x^2 + 9x + 7$ **$(2x + 7)(x + 1)$**
17. $2x^2 + 9x - 18$ **$(2x - 3)(x + 6)$**
18. $-3x^2 - 2x + 8$ **$-1(3x - 4)(x + 2)$**

Determine whether each trinomial is a perfect square. If so, factor. If not, explain.

19. $a^2 + 14a + 49$ **yes; $(a + 7)^2$**
20. $2x^2 + 10x + 25$ **No; $2x^2$ is not a perf. square.**
21. $9t^2 - 6t + 1$ **yes; $(3t - 1)^2$**

Determine whether each binomial is a difference of two squares. If so, factor. If not, explain.

22. $b^2 - 16$ **yes; $(b - 4)(b + 4)$**
23. $25y^2 - 10$ **No; 10 is not a perf. square.**
24. $9a^2 - b^{10}$ **yes; $(3a - b^5)(3a + b^5)$**
25. A company is producing square sheets of plastic. Each has an area of $(9x^2 + 30x + 25)$ ft². The dimensions of each sheet are of the form $ax + b$, where a and b are whole numbers. Find an expression for the perimeter of a sheet. Find the perimeter when $x = 4$ ft. **$P = 4(3x + 5)$ ft; 68 ft**

Tell whether each expression is completely factored. If not, factor it.

26. $(6x - 3)(x + 5)$ **no; $3(2x - 1)(x + 5)$**
27. $(v^5 + 10)(v^5 - 10)$ **yes**
28. $(2b + 3)(3b - 2)$ **yes**

Factor each polynomial completely.

29. $8x^3 + 72x^2 + 160x$
30. $3x^5 - 27x^3$ **$3x^3(x - 3)(x + 3)$**
31. $8x^3 + 64x^2 - 20x - 160$ **$4(2x^2 - 5)(x + 8)$**
32. $cd^4 - c^7d^6$ **$cd^4(1 - c^3d)(1 + c^3d)$**
33. $100x^2 - 80x + 16$ **$4(5x - 2)^2$**
34. $7m^8 - 7$ **$7(m^4 + 1)(m^2 + 1)(m + 1)(m - 1)$**

COLLEGE ENTRANCE EXAM PRACTICE

CHAPTER 8

FOCUS ON ACT

The ACT Mathematics test booklet usually has writing space for scratch work. You may not bring your own scratch paper to the testing center. Remember that any scratch work done in the test booklet is for your use only and will not be scored. Be sure to transfer your final answer to the answer sheet.

If you are unsure how to solve a problem, look through the answer choices. They may provide you with a clue to the solution method. It may take longer to work backward from the answer choices, so make sure you monitor your time.

You may want to time yourself as you take this practice test. It should take you about 6 minutes to complete.

1. What is the value of $c^2 - d^2$ if $c + d = 7$ and $c - d = -2$?
   (A) -14
   (B) -5
   (C) 5
   (D) 14
   (E) 45

2. Which of the following is the complete factorization of $6a^3b + 3a^2b^3$?
   (F) $6a^3b^3$
   (G) $9a^5b^4$
   (H) $3ab(2a^2 + ab^2)$
   (J) $3a^2b(2a + b^2)$
   (K) $(6a^3b)(3a^2b^3)$

3. Which of the following is a factor of $x^2 + 3x - 18$?
   (A) $x + 2$
   (B) $x + 3$
   (C) $x + 6$
   (D) $x + 9$
   (E) $x + 18$

4. The binomial $x - 3$ is NOT a factor of which of the following trinomials?
   (F) $2x^2 - x - 3$
   (G) $2x^2 - 5x - 3$
   (H) $2x^2 - 8x + 6$
   (J) $3x^2 - 6x - 9$
   (K) $3x^2 - 10x + 3$

5. For what value of n is $4x^2 + 20x + n^2 = (2x + n)^2$ true for any real number x?
   (A) 4
   (B) 5
   (C) 8
   (D) 10
   (E) 25

6. What is the factored form of $x^2 + \frac{2x}{3} + \frac{x}{2} + \frac{2}{6}$?
   (F) $\left(x + \frac{1}{3}\right)\left(x + \frac{1}{2}\right)$
   (G) $\left(x + \frac{1}{2}\right)\left(x + \frac{2}{3}\right)$
   (H) $\left(x + \frac{2}{3}\right)\left(x + \frac{1}{6}\right)$
   (J) $(x + 2)\left(x + \frac{1}{3}\right)$
   (K) $\left(x + \frac{1}{3}\right)\left(x + \frac{2}{3}\right)$

COLLEGE ENTRANCE EXAM PRACTICE

CHAPTER 8

Organizer

Objective: Provide practice for college entrance exams such as the ACT.

Online Edition

Resources

College Entrance Exam Practice

Questions on the ACT represent the following content areas:

Pre-Algebra, 23%
Elementary Algebra, 17%
Intermediate Algebra, 15%
Coordinate Geometry, 15%
Plane Geometry, 23%
Trigonometry, 7%

Items on this page focus on:
- Elementary Algebra

Text References:

Item	1	2	3	4	5	6
Lesson	8-5	8-1	8-3	8-4	8-5	8-2

TEST PREP DOCTOR

1. Students who chose **B** may have added the values of the factors instead of multiplying them. Students who chose **E** squared the value of each factor and subtracted the results.
2. Students who chose **H** found a factored form of the expression but did not find the greatest common factor to obtain the complete factorization. Remind students to check for any remaining common factors once they think they are done factoring.
3. Students who chose **B** may have factored the polynomial with the correct numerical values but the incorrect signs, i.e., as $(x + 3)(x - 6)$.
4. Students may spend too much time on this item if they try to factor each answer choice. Suggest that students start by considering the form of the unknown factor, given the coefficient of the x^2-term in each choice, and then use the constant term of the trinomial to find a possible constant term of the unknown factor.
5. Students who chose **E** found the value of n^2 instead of n. Students who chose **D** may have mistakenly thought that the middle term is twice the product of the terms of the squared binomial.
6. Students who did not choose **G** should check their work by multiplying the factors and seeing whether their answer matches the given expression.

Organizer

Objective: Provide opportunities to learn and practice common test-taking strategies.

This Test Tackler describes how to use key words and context clues to translate a word problem into a mathematical equation or expression. Encourage students to refer to the table as they answer the questions.

Any Question Type: Translate Words to Math

When reading a word problem, look for key words and context clues to help you translate the words into a mathematical equation or expression.

Some key words, such as those shown in this table, represent certain mathematical operations.

Action	Math Operation
Combining, increasing	Addition
Decreasing, reducing	Subtraction
Increasing or decreasing by a factor	Multiplication
Separating	Division

EXAMPLE

Short Response **The polynomial $x^2 + 7x + 12$ represents the area of a rectangle in square meters. The width is $(x + 3)$ meters. Find the combined measure of the length and the width.**

Use action words and context clues to translate the words into equations.

$x^2 + 7x + 12$ represents the **area of a rectangle** in square meters.
$x^2 + 7x + 12 \quad = \quad A$

The width is $(x + 3)$ meters.
$w = (x + 3)$

Find the **combined measure** of the length and the width.
$m = \ell + w$

Now use the equations to solve the problem.

$A = \ell w$	*Write the formula for area of a rectangle.*
$x^2 + 7x + 12 = \ell(x + 3)$	*Substitute $x^2 + 7x + 12$ for A and $(x + 3)$ for w.*
$(x + \boxed{?})(x + 3)$	*Factor $x^2 + 7x + 12$ to find an expression for the length.*
$(x + 4)(x + 3)$	*$3(4) = 12$; $3 + 4 = 7$*

The length is $(x + 4)$.

$m = \ell + w$	*Write the equation for the combined measure of the length and width.*
$m = (x + 4) + (x + 3)$	*Substitute $(x + 4)$ for ℓ and $(x + 3)$ for w.*
$m = 2x + 7$	*Combine like terms.*

The combined measure of the length and width is $(2x + 7)$ meters.

Sometimes you cannot write an expression or equation in the order that the key words appear. For example, the expression "4 years younger than Maria" is written mathematically as $m - 4$.

Read each test item and answer the questions that follow.

Item A
Short Response The width of Alvin's rectangular mural is 6 times the length x. Alvin plans to make a new mural with an area of $(6x^2 - 24x + 24)$ square meters. By how much did Alvin decrease the area of the mural? Show your work.

1. What key words or context clues are in the first sentence of the test item? Use these clues to write an expression that represents the width of the rectangle.
2. Write an equation to represent the area of Alvin's first mural.
3. What math operation does the key word *decrease* represent?

Item B
Multiple Choice Which factored expression represents the phrase shown below?

the square of the number of hours it takes to empty a cistern minus 20 times the number of hours plus 64

Ⓐ $(h - 16)(h - 4)$
Ⓑ $(h^2 - 20)(h - 64)$
Ⓒ $(h - 8)(h - 8)$
Ⓓ $(h - 16)(h + 4)$

4. Which word in the phrase tells you to use an exponent in your expression?
5. What is the unknown value in the expression? Define a variable to represent this value.
6. Identify other key words and the mathematical operation phrase each one represents.

Item C
Multiple Choice A company owns two packaging plants. The polynomial $0.05x^2 + 16x - 9400$ models one plant's profit, where x is the number of units packaged. The polynomial $-0.01x^2 + 17x - 5400$ models the other plant's profit. If x is 25,000, what is the total profit of both plants?

Ⓐ −$5,830,300
Ⓑ $25,810,200
Ⓒ $31,640,500
Ⓓ $37,471,000

7. What mathematical symbol does the word *models* represent?
8. Write an equation for each plant that can be used to determine its profit P.
9. What mathematical operation does the term "total profit" represent?

Item D
Gridded Response One of the bases of a trapezoid is 12 meters greater than its height. The other base is 4 meters less than its height. Find the area of the trapezoid when the height is 6 meters.

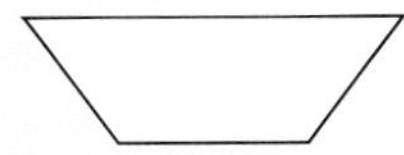

10. Identify the unknown dimension, and assign it a variable.
11. A student is unsure how many bases a trapezoid has. Identify the context clues that can help this student.
12. Make a list of the key words in the problem, and link each word to its mathematical meaning.
13. Write an expression for each base of the trapezoid.

Answers

1. *is, times*; $w = 6x$
2. $A = 6x^2$
3. subtraction
4. *square*
5. the number of hours; h
6. *minus* represents subtraction; *plus* represents addition
7. equal sign
8. $P_1 = 0.05x^2 + 16x - 9400$; $P_2 = -0.01x^2 + 17x - 5400$
9. addition
10. height; h
11. "One of the bases"; "the other base"; these clues show that there are 2 bases.
12. *Is* means "equals." *Greater than* represents addition. *Less than* represents subtraction.
13. $b_1 = h + 12$; $b_2 = h - 4$

Answers to Test Items

A. $(24x - 24)$ m^2
B. A
C. B
D. 60 m^2

State Resources

go.hrw.com
State Resources Online
KEYWORD: MA7 Resources

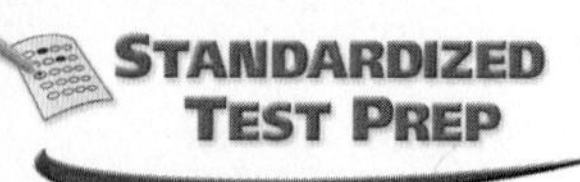

Organizer

Objective: Provide review and practice for Chapters 1–8 and standardized tests.

Online Edition

Resources

Assessment Resources

Chapter 8 Cumulative Test

State Resources

CUMULATIVE ASSESSMENT, CHAPTERS 1–8

Multiple Choice

1. A rectangle has an area of $(x^2 + 5x - 24)$ square units. Which of the following are possible expressions for the length and the width of the rectangle?

Ⓐ Length: $(x - 24)$ units; width: $(x + 1)$ units

Ⓑ Length: $(x - 4)$ units; width: $(x + 6)$ units

Ⓒ Length: $(x - 3)$ units; width: $(x + 8)$ units

Ⓓ Length: $(x + 12)$ units; width: $(x - 2)$ units

2. Which property of real numbers is used to transform the equation in Step 1 into the equation in Step 2?

Step 1: $4(x - 5) + 8 = 88$
Step 2: $4x - 20 + 8 = 88$
Step 3: $4x - 12 = 88$
Step 4: $4x = 100$
Step 5: $4x = 25$

Ⓕ Commutative Property of Multiplication

Ⓖ Associative Property of Multiplication

Ⓗ Multiplication Property

Ⓙ Distributive Property

3. If $\frac{2}{3}x - 9 = 3$, what is the value of the expression $8x - 3$?

Ⓐ -75 Ⓒ 61

Ⓑ -35 Ⓓ 141

4. Carlos and Bonita were just hired at a manufacturing plant. Carlos will earn \$12.50 per hour. He will receive a hiring bonus of \$300. Bonita will not get a hiring bonus, but she will earn \$14.50 per hour. Which equation can you use to determine the number of hours h when both employees will have earned the same total amount?

Ⓕ $300 + 14.50h = 12.50h$

Ⓖ $14.50h + 300 = 12.50h$

Ⓗ $14.50h + 12.50h = 300$

Ⓙ $300 + 12.50h = 14.50h$

5. Which of the following expressions is equivalent to $x^2 - 8x + 16$?

Ⓐ $(x + 4)^2$ Ⓒ $(x + 8)(x + 2)$

Ⓑ $(x + 4)(x - 4)$ Ⓓ $(x - 4)^2$

6. An amusement park has two jumping attractions called moonbounces in the shape of similar cubes. The larger moonbounce has a volume of 4800 cubic feet. The smaller moonbounce is half the length of the larger one. What is the volume of the smaller moonbounce?

Ⓕ 300 cubic feet

Ⓖ 600 cubic feet

Ⓗ 1200 cubic feet

Ⓙ 2400 cubic feet

7. What is the value of y if the line through $(1, -1)$ and $(2, 2)$ is parallel to the line through $(-2, 1)$ and $(-1, y)$?

Ⓐ -8 Ⓒ 3

Ⓑ -2 Ⓓ 4

8. Which of the following shows the complete factorization of $2x^3 + 4x^2 - 6x$?

Ⓕ $(2x^2 - 2x)(x + 3)$

Ⓖ $2x(x^2 + 2x - 3)$

Ⓗ $2x(x - 1)(x + 3)$

Ⓙ $2(x^3 + 2x^2 - 3x)$

9. Which graph shows the solution set of the compound inequality $-9 \le 5 - 2x \le 13$?

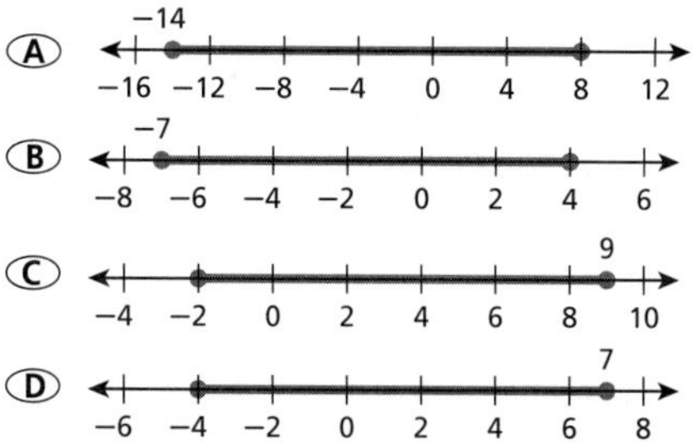

Ⓐ −14
−16 −12 −8 −4 0 4 8 12

Ⓑ −7
−8 −6 −4 −2 0 2 4 6

Ⓒ 9
−4 −2 0 2 4 6 8 10

Ⓓ 7
−6 −4 −2 0 2 4 6 8

Answers

1. C
2. J
3. D
4. J
5. D
6. G
7. D
8. H
9. D
10. F
11. D
12. G
13. C
14. 3
15. $\frac{1}{4}$
16. 29.40
17. 10

Many standardized test booklets have a page listing commonly used formulas and basic measurement facts. Before the test begins, ask if you can remove the page from the booklet. If allowed, place the page nearby for easy reference.

10. Which point lies on the graph of both functions?

$f(x) = 2x - 10$
$g(x) = 10 - 2x$

Ⓕ (5, 0) Ⓗ (0, 0)
Ⓖ (1, −8) Ⓙ (2, 6)

11. Hayley plans to solve the system of equations below.

$$\begin{cases} x + 3y = 8 \\ 5x - y = 8 \end{cases}$$

Which of the following does NOT show an equation Hayley can use to solve the system of equations?

Ⓐ $x + 3(5x - 8) = 8$
Ⓑ $5(8 - 3y) - y = 8$
Ⓒ $x = 8 - 3y$
Ⓓ $5x - (-x + 8) = 8$

12. Which value of b would make $x^2 + bx - 2$ factorable?

Ⓕ −2 Ⓗ 0
Ⓖ −1 Ⓙ 3

13. Which expression is equivalent to $5(x - 2) + 4x$?

Ⓐ $5x - 10$ Ⓒ $9x - 10$
Ⓑ $9x - 2$ Ⓓ $20x - 2$

Gridded Response

14. The complete factorization of $-12x^3 + 14x^2 + 6x$ is $-2x(ax + 1)(2x - 3)$. What is the value of a?

15. The expression $x^2 + x + b$ is a perfect-square trinomial. What is the value of b?

16. Margaret is buying a \$35 sweater that is on sale for 20% off. What is the total price of the sweater, in dollars, when 5% sales tax is added?

17. A car is traveling at a constant speed. In 4 hours, the car travels 220 miles. How many hours will it take the car to travel 550 miles?

Short Response

18. The area of a certain circle is $\pi(9x^2 + 6x + 1)$ square centimeters. Find an expression for the length of the circle's radius. Explain how you found your answer.

19. A rectangle has an area of $(x^2 - 25)$ square feet.

a. Use factoring to write possible expressions for the length and width of the rectangle.

b. Use your expressions from part **a** to write an expression for the perimeter of the rectangle. Simplify the expression.

c. Use your expressions from parts **a** and **b** to find the perimeter and the area of the rectangle when $x = 10$ feet. Show your work.

20. Write the numbers 57,000,000,000 and 19,000 in scientific notation. Then show how to divide 57,000,000,000 by 19,000 using properties of exponents.

21. Show that you can factor the expression $x^2y - 12 + 3y - 4x^2$ by grouping in two different ways.

Extended Response

22. The diagram below can be used to show that the expression $(a + b)^2$ is equivalent to the expression $a^2 + 2ab + b^2$.

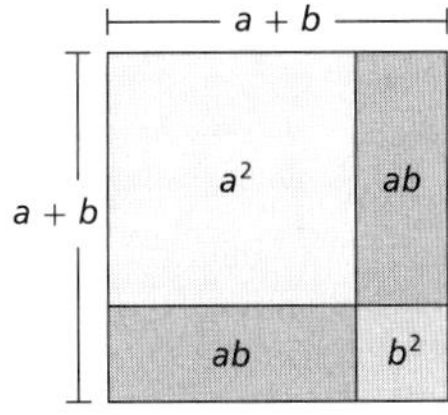

a. Make a diagram similar to the one above to model the expression $(a + b + c)^2$. Label each distinct area.

b. Use the labels from your diagram to write an expression equivalent to $(a + b + c)^2$.

c. Show that your expression in part **b** is equivalent to $(a + b + c)^2$ by evaluating each expression for $a = 4$, $b = 2$, and $c = 1$.

d. Factor $x^2 + y^2 + 9 + 2xy + 6x + 6y$. Show or explain how you found your answer.

Short-Response Rubric

Items 18–21

2 Points = The student's answer is an accurate and complete execution of the task or tasks.

1 Point = The student's answer contains attributes of an appropriate response but is flawed.

0 Points = The student's answer contains no attributes of an appropriate response.

Extended-Response Rubric

Item 22

4 Points = The student correctly draws and labels a diagram in part **a,** writes a correct expression in part **b,** correctly evaluates the expression in part **c,** and correctly factors in part **d** with an explanation.

3 Points = The student correctly draws and labels **a** diagram in part a and writes a correct expression in part **b** but does not show any work or give an explanation for part **c** or part **d.**

2 Points = The student answers all parts correctly but does not show any work or explanation, or the student correctly answers parts **a** and **b** but does not correctly answer parts **c** and **d.**

1 Point = The student draws and labels a diagram in part **a** but does not correctly answer other parts of the problem, or the student attempts to answer all parts of the problem but does not correctly answer any part.

0 Points = The student does not answer correctly or does not attempt all parts of the problem.

Answers

18. $A = \pi r^2 = (9x^2 + 6x + 1)\pi = (3x + 1)^2\pi$, so $r = (3x + 1)$ cm

19a. $\ell = (x + 5)$ ft; $w = (x - 5)$ ft

b. $P = 4x$ ft

c. $P = 40$ ft; $A = 75$ ft²

20. 5.7×10^{10}; 1.9×10^4; $\dfrac{5.7 \times 10^{10}}{1.9 \times 10^4} = \left(\dfrac{5.7}{1.9}\right) \times 10^{10-4} = 3 \times 10^6$

21. (1) $x^2y - 12 + 3y - 4x^2 =$
$(x^2y - 4x^2) + (3y - 12) =$
$x^2(y - 4) + 3(y - 4) =$
$(x^2 + 3)(y - 4)$

(2) $x^2y - 12 + 3y - 4x^2 =$
$(x^2y + 3y) + (-4x^2 - 12) =$
$y(x^2 + 3) - 4(x^2 + 3) =$
$(y - 4)(x^2 + 3)$

22a.

←a→	←b→	←c→	
a^2	ab	ac	a
ab	b^2	bc	b
ac	bc	c^2	c

b. $a^2 + 2ab + b^2 + 2ac + 2bc + c^2$

c. Both expressions should equal 49.

d. $(x + y + 3)^2$; check students' work.

Organizer

Objective: Choose appropriate problem-solving strategies and use them with skills from Chapters 7 and 8 to solve real-world problems.

PREMIER **Online Edition**

Alligator Adventure

Reading Strategies

In **Problem 2,** ask students what other question could be inserted before the actual question to make the problem easier. Possible answer: How many baby alligators would be in the nest?

Problem-Solving Focus

In **Problem 3,** students should recognize that $y = 3x - 4$ is a linear function and that its graph forms a line. Therefore, they need to use only the Guess and Test strategy with the other two functions. Students may use the Find a Pattern strategy once they notice that the graphs are symmetric about the y-axis.

Discuss with students the importance of substituting both positive and negative values for x because a portion of $y = |x^2 - 4|$ may appear to be linear.

State Resources

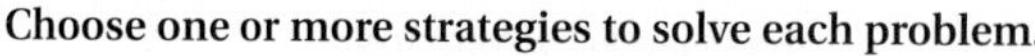

Alligator Adventure

Alligator Adventure is a tourist attraction in North Myrtle Beach, South Carolina. Its exhibits feature alligators, snakes, Galapagos tortoises, bears, frogs, lizards, tropical birds, and crocodiles.

Choose one or more strategies to solve each problem.

1. At birth, alligators are about 8 inches long. Adult male alligators can grow up to 18 feet long. How many times as long as a newborn alligator is an alligator that measures 18 feet? **27 times**
2. Alligators build their nests out of dirt, grass, and leaves. The female alligator will deposit 40 to 50 eggs in her nest. Suppose there were 40 eggs in a nest and 80 percent of them hatched. The baby alligators each weigh 3 ounces. What is the total weight of the hatched alligators? **96 oz**
3. Most alligators have U-shaped snouts while most crocodiles have V-shaped snouts. Which of the equations below has a graph that could model the shape of an alligator's snout? Explain.

$y = 3x - 4$

$y = x^2 - 12$

$y = |x^2 - 4|$

3. $y = x^2 - 12$; when several points generated by this equation are graphed, they form a U shape.

Melton Memorial Observatory

Melton Memorial Observatory is run by the University of South Carolina in Columbia, South Carolina. The table lists some of the stars that can be seen from the observatory.

A light-year is the distance light can travel in one year, which is 9,500,000,000,000 kilometers.

Eight of the Brightest Stars as Seen from Earth

Name	Rank	Apparent Magnitude	Distance from Earth (light-years)	Temperature (kelvins)
Sirius	1	−1.46	8.6	9,400
Arcturus	4	−0.04	34	4,290
Vega	5	0.03	25	9,600
Procyon	8	0.38	11.4	6,500
Altair	12	0.77	16	7,550
Spica	14	0.98	220	22,400
Deneb	20	1.25	1500	8,400
Regulus	25	1.35	69	12,000

Choose one or more strategies and use the table to solve each problem.

1. Write 1 light-year as a distance in kilometers in scientific notation. Write the distance in kilometers of each star from Earth in scientific notation.
2. Order the stars from closest to Earth to farthest from Earth.
3. Identify which star is farthest from and which is closest to Earth. Approximate how many times as far as the closest star the farthest star is.
Deneb is farthest, and Sirius is closest; about 175 times

Apparent magnitude is a measure of how bright a star (or other object) appears from Earth. The lower the apparent magnitude of a star, the brighter the star appears.

4. Describe the correlation between apparent magnitude and distance from Earth in light-years. Make a scatter plot to support your answer.
A star's distance from Earth does not determine its apparent magnitude.

Real-World Connections

Melton Memorial Observatory

Reading Strategies

ENGLISH LANGUAGE LEARNERS

Tell students that in everyday life, *magnitude* refers to the extent or importance of something. For instance, if someone is describing the *magnitude of a problem,* they are discussing how serious it is.

Using Data Ask students to compare the second and third columns of the table. What do they notice? The magnitudes get larger as the ranks increase. Have students find the median magnitude. 0.575

Problem-Solving Focus

Encourage students to use the four-step problem-solving process for **Problem 4.** Focus on the second step: **(2) Make a Plan.** Have students determine a reasonable scale and interval for each axis. Possible answer: magnitude: −1.5 to 1.5 by 0.25, distance: 0 to 1650 by 150

Answers

1. 9.5×10^{12} km; 8.17×10^{13} km; 3.23×10^{14} km; 2.375×10^{14} km; 1.083×10^{14} km; 1.52×10^{14} km; 2.09×10^{15} km; 1.425×10^{16} km; 6.555×10^{14} km
2. Sirius, Procyon, Altair, Vega, Arcturus, Regulus, Spica, Deneb
4. 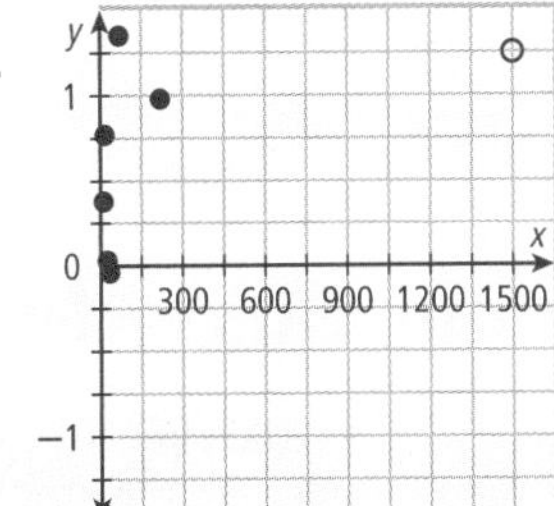

Quadratic Functions and Equations

Section 9A
Quadratic Functions

- 9-1 **Identifying Quadratic Functions**
- 9-2 **Algebra Lab** Explore the Axis of Symmetry
- 9-2 **Characteristics of Quadratic Functions**
- 9-3 **Graphing Quadratic Functions**
- 9-4 **Technology Lab** The Family of Quadratic Functions
- 9-4 **Transforming Quadratic Functions**

Section 9B
Solving Quadratic Equations

- 9-5 **Solving Quadratic Equations by Graphing**
- 9-5 **Technology Lab** Explore Roots, Zeros, and *x*-Intercepts
- 9-6 **Solving Quadratic Equations by Factoring**
- 9-7 **Solving Quadratic Equations by Using Square Roots**
- 9-8 **Algebra Lab** Model Completing the Square
- 9-8 **Completing the Square**
- 9-9 **The Quadratic Formula and the Discriminant**
- EXTENSION **Cubic Functions and Equations**

Pacing Guide for 45-Minute Classes

Teacher One Stop™
Calendar Planner®

Chapter 9

Countdown Weeks 19, 20, 21

DAY 1	DAY 2	DAY 3	DAY 4	DAY 5
9-1 Lesson	9-2 Algebra Lab 9-2 Lesson	9-2 Lesson	9-3 Lesson	9-4 Technology Lab 9-4 Lesson
DAY 6	**DAY 7**	**DAY 8**	**DAY 9**	**DAY 10**
9-4 Lesson Multi-Step Test Prep	Ready to Go On? 9-5 Lesson	9-5 Lesson 9-5 Technology Lab	9-6 Lesson	9-7 Lesson
DAY 11	**DAY 12**	**DAY 13**	**DAY 14**	**DAY 15**
9-8 Algebra Lab	9-8 Lesson	9-9 Lesson	Multi-Step Test Prep Ready to Go On?	EXTENSION
DAY 16	**DAY 17**			
Chapter 9 Review	Chapter 9 Test			

Pacing Guide for 90-Minute Classes

Teacher One Stop™
Calendar Planner®

Chapter 9

DAY 1	DAY 2	DAY 3	DAY 4	DAY 5
9-1 Lesson 9-2 Algebra Lab 9-2 Lesson	9-2 Lesson 9-3 Lesson	9-4 Technology Lab 9-4 Lesson Multi-Step Test Prep	Ready to Go On? 9-5 Lesson 9-5 Technology Lab	9-6 Lesson 9-7 Lesson
DAY 6	**DAY 7**	**DAY 8**	**DAY 9**	
9-8 Algebra Lab 9-8 Lesson	9-9 Lesson Multi-Step Test Prep Ready to Go On?	EXTENSION Chapter 9 Review	Chapter 9 Test	

ONGOING ASSESSMENT and INTERVENTION

DIAGNOSE | **PRESCRIBE**

Assess Prior Knowledge

Before Chapter 9

Diagnose readiness for the chapter.

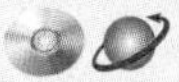 **Are You Ready?** SE p. 607

Prescribe intervention.

Are You Ready? Intervention

Formative Assessment

Before Every Lesson

Diagnose readiness for the lesson.

Warm Up TE

Prescribe intervention.

Reteach CRB

During Every Lesson

Diagnose understanding of lesson concepts.

Check It Out! SE
Questioning Strategies TE
Think and Discuss SE
Write About It SE
Journal TE

Prescribe intervention.

Reading Strategies CRB
Success for Every Learner
Lesson Tutorial Videos

After Every Lesson

Diagnose mastery of lesson concepts.

Lesson Quiz TE
Test Prep SE
Test and Practice Generator

Prescribe intervention.

Reteach CRB
Test Prep Doctor TE
Homework Help Online

Before Chapter 9 Testing

Diagnose mastery of concepts in chapter.

Ready to Go On? SE pp. 641, 679
Multi-Step Test Prep SE pp. 640, 678
Section Quizzes AR
Test and Practice Generator

Prescribe intervention.

Ready to Go On? Intervention
Scaffolding Questions TE pp. 640, 678
Reteach CRB
 ***Lesson Tutorial Videos***

Before High Stakes Testing

Diagnose mastery of benchmark concepts.

College Entrance Exam Practice SE p. 689
Standardized Test Prep SE pp. 692–693

Prescribe intervention.

College Entrance Exam Practice

Summative Assessment

After Chapter 9

Check mastery of chapter concepts.

Multiple-Choice Tests (Forms A, B, C)
Free-Response Tests (Forms A, B, C)
Performance Assessment AR
Cumulative Test AR
Test and Practice Generator

Prescribe intervention.

Reteach CRB
Lesson Tutorial Videos

KEY: **SE** = *Student Edition* **TE** = *Teacher's Edition* **CRB** = *Chapter Resource Book* **AR** = *Assessment Resources*  Available online Available on CD- or DVD-ROM

Lesson Resources

Before the Lesson

Prepare ***Teacher One Stop*** 
- Editable lesson plans
- Calendar Planner
- Easy access to all chapter resources

Lesson Transparencies
- Teacher Tools

Teach the Lesson

Introduce ***Alternate Openers: Explorations***

Lesson Transparencies
- Warm Up
- Problem of the Day

Teach ***Lesson Transparencies***
- Teaching Transparencies

Know-It Notebook™
- Vocabulary
- Key Concepts

Power Presentations

Lesson Tutorial Videos 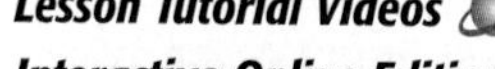 

Interactive Online Edition
- Lesson Activities
- Lesson Tutorial Videos

Lab Activities

Lab Resources Online

Online Interactivities  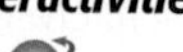

TechKeys 

Practice the Lesson

Practice ***Chapter Resources***
- Practice A, B, C

Practice and Problem Solving Workbook SPANISH

IDEA Works!® Modified Worksheets and Tests

ExamView Test and Practice Generator 

Homework Help Online

Online Interactivities 

Interactive Online Edition 
- Homework Help

Apply ***Chapter Resources***
- Problem Solving SPANISH

Practice and Problem Solving Workbook 

Interactive Online Edition
- Chapter Project

Project Teacher Support

After the Lesson

Reteach ***Chapter Resources***
- Reteach
- Reading Strategies ELL

Success for Every Learner

Review ***Interactive Answers and Solutions***

Solutions Key

Know-It Notebook™
- Big Ideas
- Chapter Review

Extend ***Chapter Resources***
- Challenge

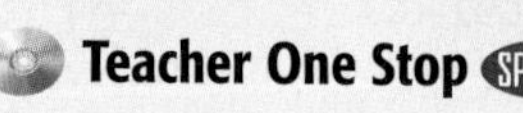

Technology Highlights for the Teacher

Power Presentations

Dynamic presentations to engage students. Complete PowerPoint® presentations for every lesson in Chapter 9.

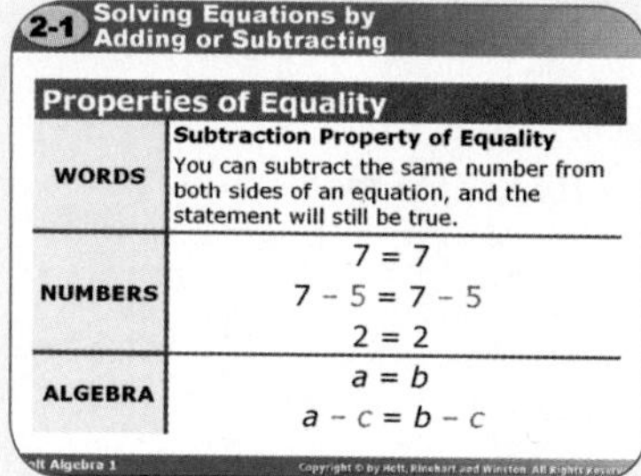

Teacher One Stop SPANISH

Easy access to Chapter 9 resources and assessments. Includes lesson planning, test generation, and puzzle creation software.

Premier Online Edition SPANISH

Chapter 9 includes Tutorial Videos, Lesson Activities, Lesson Quizzes, Homework Help, and Chapter Project.

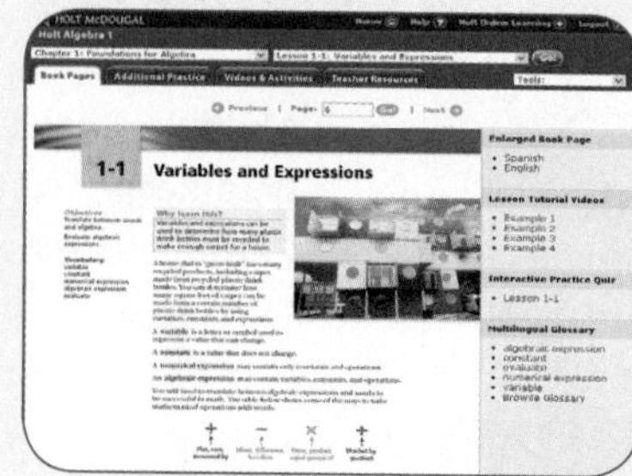

KEY: **SE** = *Student Edition* **TE** = *Teacher's Edition*  English Language Learners  Spanish version available  Available online  Available on CD- or DVD-RO

Reaching All Learners

Teaching tips to help all learners appear throughout the chapter. A few that target specific students are included in the lists below.

All Learners

Lab Activities
Practice and Problem Solving Workbook SPANISH
Know-It Notebook

Special Needs Students

Practice A	CRB
Reteach	CRB
Reading Strategies	CRB
Are You Ready?	SE p. 607
Inclusion	TE pp. 616, 622, 630, 634, 635, 665, 674

IDEA Works!® Modified Worksheets and Tests
Ready to Go On? Intervention SPANISH
Know-It Notebook
Online Interactivities SPANISH
Lesson Tutorial Videos SPANISH

Developing Learners

Practice A	CRB
Reteach	CRB
Reading Strategies	CRB
Are You Ready?	SE p. 607
Vocabulary Connections	SE p. 608
Questioning Strategies	TE

Ready to Go On? Intervention SPANISH
Know-It Notebook
Homework Help Online
Online Interactivities SPANISH
Lesson Tutorial Videos SPANISH

On-Level Learners

Practice B	CRB
Problem Solving	CRB
Vocabulary Connections	SE p. 608
Questioning Strategies	TE

Ready to Go On? Intervention SPANISH
Know-It Notebook
Homework Help Online
Online Interactivities SPANISH

Advanced Learners

Practice C	CRB
Challenge	CRB
Challenge Exercises	SE
Reading and Writing Math *Extend*	TE p. 609
Critical Thinking	TE pp. 643, 644, 651, 658, 665

Are You Ready? Enrichment SPANISH
Ready To Go On? Enrichment SPANISH

English Language Learners

ENGLISH LANGUAGE LEARNERS

Reading Strategies	CRB
Are You Ready? Vocabulary	SE p. 607
Vocabulary Connections	SE p. 608
Vocabulary Review	SE p. 684
English Language Learners	TE pp. 609, 612

Success for Every Learner
Know-It Notebook
Multilingual Glossary
Lesson Tutorial Videos SPANISH

Technology Highlights for Reaching All Learners

Lesson Tutorial Videos SPANISH

Starring Holt authors Ed Burger and Freddie Renfro! Live tutorials to support every lesson in Chapter 9.

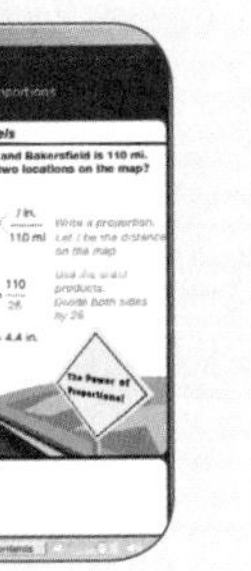

Multilingual Glossary

Searchable glossary includes definitions in English, Spanish, Vietnamese, Chinese, Hmong, Korean, and 4 other languages.

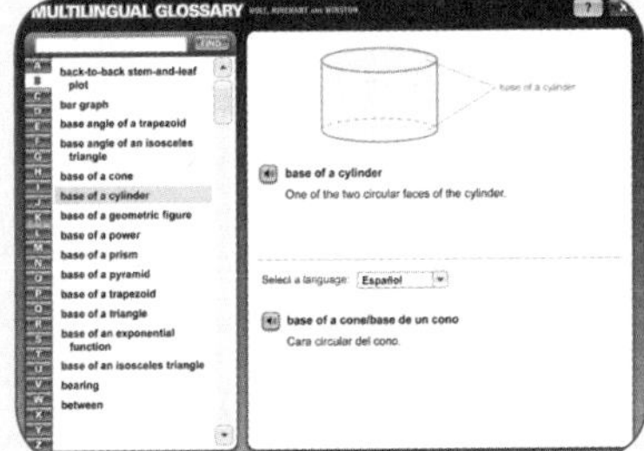

Online Interactivities

Interactive tutorials provide visually engaging alternative opportunities to learn concepts and master skills.

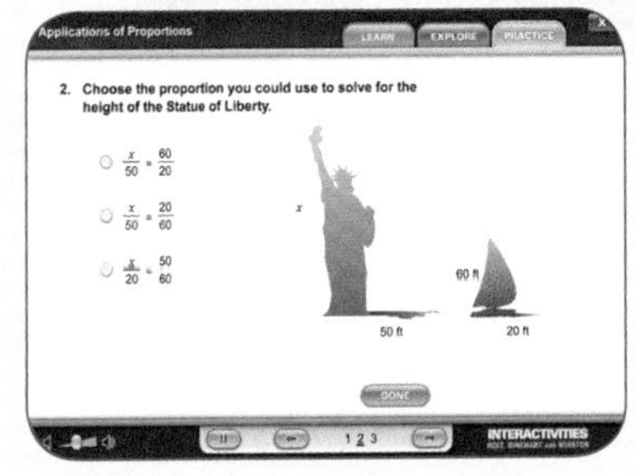

KEY: **SE** = *Student Edition* **TE** = *Teacher's Edition* **CRB** = *Chapter Resource Book* SPANISH Spanish version available  Available online Available on CD- or DVD-ROM

Ongoing Assessment

Assessing Prior Knowledge

Determine whether students have the prerequisite concepts and skills for success in Chapter 9.

Are You Ready? SPANISH .... SE p. 607
Warm Up .... TE

Test Preparation

Provide review and practice for Chapter 9 and standardized tests.

Multi-Step Test Prep .... SE pp. 640, 678
Study Guide: Review .... SE pp. 684–687
Test Tackler .... SE pp. 690–691
Standardized Test Prep .... SE pp. 692–693
College Entrance Exam Practice .... SE p. 689
Countdown to Testing .... SE pp. C4–C27
IDEA Works!® Modified Worksheets and Tests

Alternative Assessment

Assess students' understanding of Chapter 9 concepts and combined problem-solving skills.

Chapter 9 Project .... SE p. 606
Alternative Assessment .... TE
Performance Assessment SPANISH .... AR
Portfolio Assessment SPANISH .... AR

Lesson Assessment

Provide formative assessment for each lesson of Chapter 9.

Questioning Strategies .... TE
Think and Discuss .... SE
Check It Out! Exercises .... SE
Write About It .... SE
Journal .... TE
Lesson Quiz .... TE
Alternative Assessment .... TE
IDEA Works!® Modified Worksheets and Tests

Weekly Assessment

Provide formative assessment for each section of Chapter 9.

Multi-Step Test Prep .... SE pp. 640, 678
Ready to Go On? SPANISH .... SE pp. 641, 679
Section Quizzes SPANISH .... AR
Test and Practice Generator SPANISH .... *Teacher One Stop*

Chapter Assessment

Provide summative assessment of Chapter 9 mastery.

Chapter 9 Test .... SE p. 688
Chapter Test (Levels A, B, C) SPANISH .... AR
- Multiple Choice
- Free Response

Cumulative Test SPANISH .... AR
Test and Practice Generator SPANISH .... *Teacher One Stop*
IDEA Works!® Modified Worksheets and Tests

Technology Highlights for Assessment

Automatically assess readiness and prescribe intervention for Chapter 9 prerequisite skills.

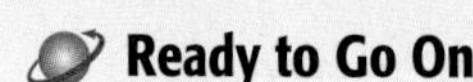

Automatically assess understanding of and prescribe intervention for Sections 9A and 9B.

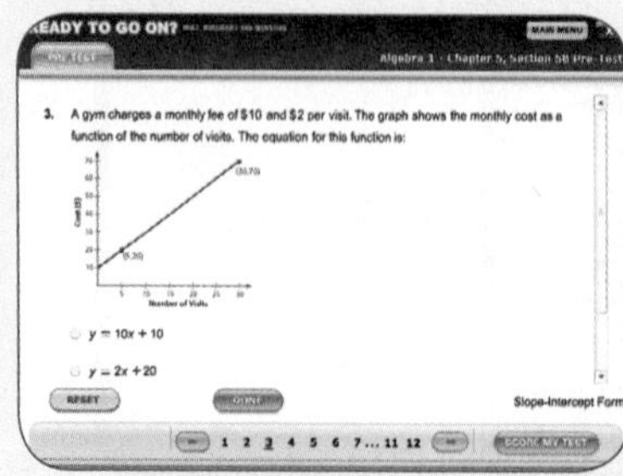

Test and Practice Generator SPANISH

Use Chapter 9 problem banks to create assessments and worksheets to print out or deliver online. Includes dynamic problems.

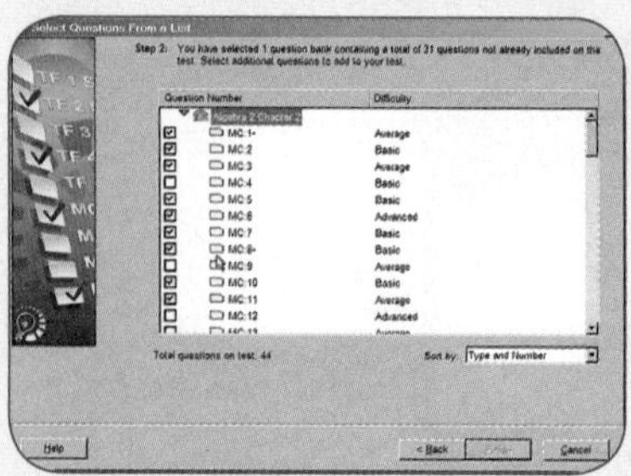

KEY: **SE** = *Student Edition* **TE** = *Teacher's Edition* **AR** = *Assessment Resources*  SPANISH Spanish version available · Available online · Available on CD- or DVD-ROM

CHAPTER 9

Formal Assessment

Three levels (A, B, C) of multiple-choice and free-response chapter tests, along with a performance assessment, are available in the *Assessment Resources*.

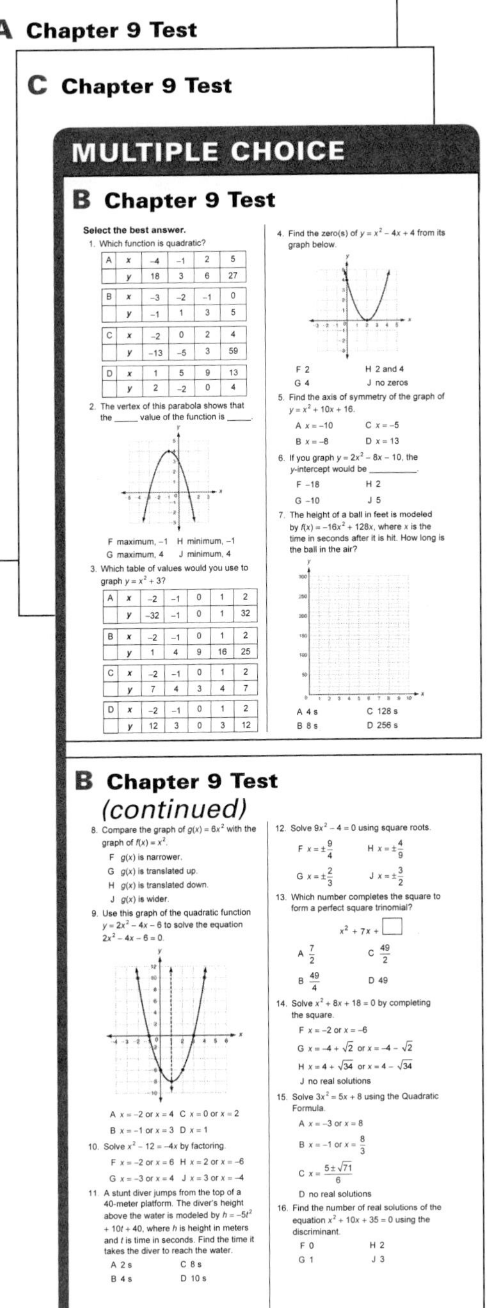

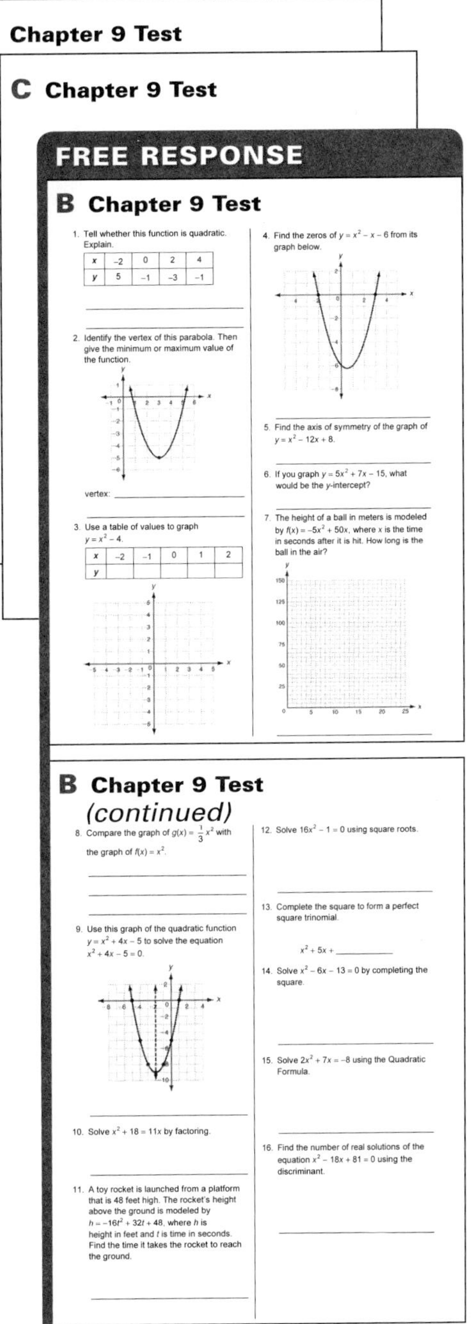

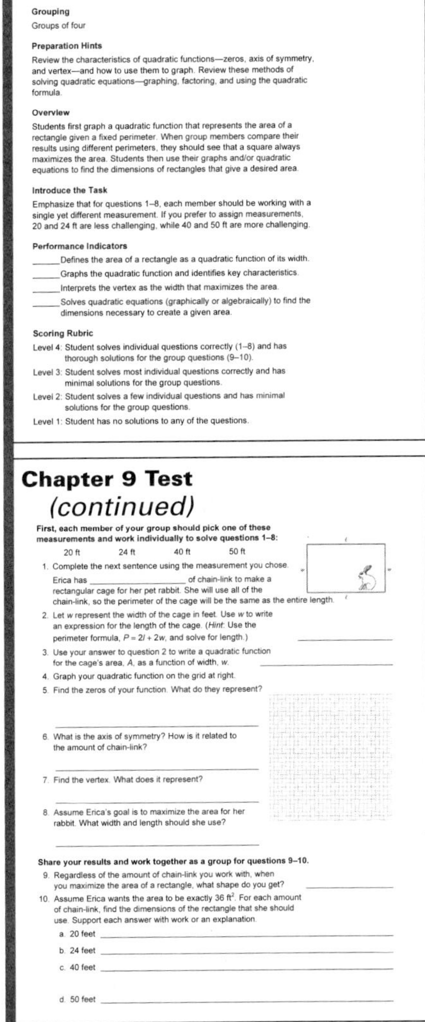

Teacher One Stop™ 

Test & Practice Generator

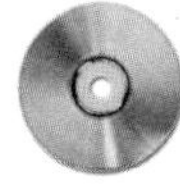

Create and customize Chapter 9 Tests. Instantly generate multiple test versions, answer keys, and Spanish versions of test items.

Modified chapter tests that address special learning needs are available in *IDEA Works!® Modified Worksheets and Tests.*

CHAPTER 9

SECTION 9A

Quadratic Functions

On page 640, students write, solve, and graph equations to model real-world rocket-flight situations.

Exercises designed to prepare students forsuccess on the Multi-Step Test Prep can be found in each lesson.

SECTION 9B

Solving Quadratic Equations

On page 678, students write, solve, and graph equations to model a real-world situation involving the motion of a golf ball.

Exercises designed to prepare students for success on the Multi-Step Test Prep can be found in each lesson.

Interactivities Online ▶

Lessons 9-4, 9-9

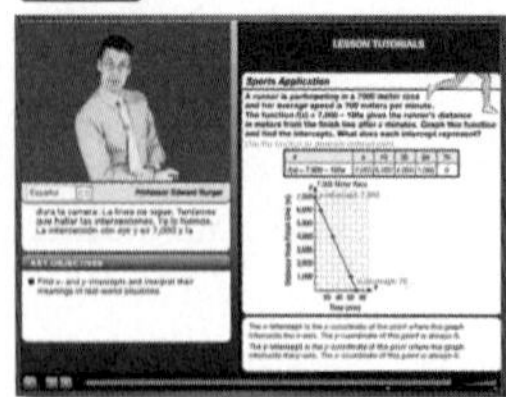

Lesson Tutorial Videos are available for EVERY example.

CHAPTER 9

Quadratic Functions and Equations

Chapter Focus

- Graph quadratic functions.
- Solve quadratic equations.
- Use quadratic functions and equations to solve real-world problems.

FREE *Falling*

Physicists use quadratic equations to describe the motion of falling objects, such as water over a waterfall.

Free Falling

About the Project

In the Chapter Project, students use a motion detector to collect data about falling objects. Students organize the height-time data, graph a function model, analyze the function, and then use the function model to make predictions.

Project Resources

All project resources for teachers and students are provided online.

Materials:

- an electronic data collection device, such as CBL or CBR, with a motion detector
- graphing calculator

ARE YOU READY?

Vocabulary

Match each term on the left with a definition on the right.

1. factoring **A**
2. quadratic **D**
3. trinomial **C**
4. x-intercept **B**

A. the process of writing a number or an algebraic expression as a product

B. the x-coordinate(s) of the point(s) where a graph intersects the x-axis

C. a polynomial with three terms

D. a polynomial with degree 2

E. the first number of an ordered pair of numbers that describes the location of a point on the coordinate plane

Graph Functions

Graph each function for the given domain.

5. $y = -2x + 8$; D: $\{-4, -2, 0, 2, 4\}$
6. $y = (x+1)^2$; D: $\{-3, -2, -1, 0, 1\}$
7. $y = x^2 + 3$; D: $\{-2, -1, 0, 1, 2\}$
8. $y = 2x^2$; D: all real numbers

Multiply Binomials

Find each product.

9. $(m+2)(m+5)$ **9.** $m^2 + 7m + 10$
10. $(y-7)(y+2)$ **10.** $y^2 - 5y - 14$
11. $(2a+4)(5a+6)$ $10a^2 + 32a + 24$
12. $(x+1)(x+1)$ $x^2 + 2x + 1$
13. $(t+5)(t+5)$ $t^2 + 10t + 25$
14. $(3n-8)(3n-8)$ $9n^2 - 48n + 64$

Factor Trinomials

Factor each polynomial completely.

15. $x^2 - 2x + 1$ $(x-1)^2$
16. $x^2 - x - 2$ $(x-2)(x+1)$
17. $x^2 - 6x + 5$ $(x-5)(x-1)$
18. $x^2 - x - 12$ $(x-4)(x+3)$
19. $x^2 - 9x + 18$ $(x-6)(x-3)$
20. $x^2 - 7x - 18$ $(x-9)(x+2)$

Squares and Square Roots

Find each square root.

21. $\sqrt{36}$ **6**
22. $\sqrt{121}$ **11**
23. $-\sqrt{64}$ **−8**
24. $\sqrt{16}\sqrt{81}$ **36**
25. $\sqrt{\frac{9}{25}}$ $\frac{3}{5}$
26. $-\sqrt{6(24)}$ **−12**

Solve Multi-Step Equations

Solve each equation.

27. $3m + 5 = 11$ $m = 2$
28. $3t + 4 = 10$ $t = 2$
29. $5n + 13 = 28$ $n = 3$
30. $2(k-4) + k = 7$ $k = 5$
31. $10 = \frac{r}{3} + 8$ $r = 6$
32. $2(y-6) = 8.6$ $y = 10.3$

ARE YOU READY?

Organizer

Objective: Assess students' understanding of prerequisite skills.

Assessing Prior Knowledge

INTERVENTION

Diagnose and Prescribe

Use this page to determine whether intervention is necessary or whether enrichment is appropriate.

Resources

 ***Are You Ready? Intervention and Enrichment*** **Worksheets**

 ***Are You Ready?*** **CD-ROM**

 ***Are You Ready?*** **Online**

my.hrw.com

Answers

5–8. See pp. A29–A30.

ARE YOU READY?

Diagnose and Prescribe

Prerequisite Skill	*Are You Ready? Intervention,* Chapter 9: Worksheets	CD-ROM	Online
Graph Functions	Skill 80	Activity 80	Diagnose and Prescribe Online
Multiply Binomials	Skill 64	Activity 64	
Factor Trinomials	Skill 67	Activity 67	
Squares and Square Roots	Skill 6	Activity 6	
Solve Multi-Step Equations	Skill 69	Activity 69	

Are You Ready? Enrichment, Chapter 9

Worksheets

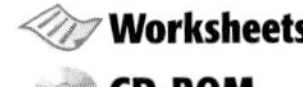 CD-ROM

 Online

CHAPTER 9 Study Guide: Preview

Organizer

Objective: Help students organize the new concepts they will learn in Chapter 9.

Online Edition
Multilingual Glossary

Resources

Teacher One Stop™
PuzzleView

Multilingual Glossary **Online**

go.hrw.com
KEYWORD: MA7 Glossary

Possible answers to *Vocabulary Connections*

1. It will be a polynomial of degree 2.
2. a curve
3. a point on a graph of a curve with the greatest *y*-coordinate
4. an imaginary line that splits a figure such that one side of the figure is a mirror image of the other

CHAPTER 9

Study Guide: Preview

Where You've Been

Previously, you

- identified and graphed linear functions.
- transformed linear functions.
- solved linear equations.
- factored quadratic polynomials, including perfect-square trinomials.

In This Chapter

You will study

- identifying and graphing quadratic functions.
- transforming quadratic equations.
- solving quadratic equations.
- using factoring to graph quadratic functions and solve quadratic equations.

Where You're Going

You can use the skills in this chapter

- to determine the maximum height of a ball thrown into the air.
- to graph higher-degree polynomials in future math classes, including Algebra 2.
- to solve problems about the height of launched or thrown objects in Physics.

Key Vocabulary/Vocabulario

axis of symmetry	eje de simetría
completing the square	completar el cuadrado
maximum	máximo
minimum	mínimo
parabola	parábola
quadratic equation	ecuación cuadrática
quadratic function	función cuadrática
vertex	vértice
zero of a function	cero de una función

Vocabulary Connections

To become familiar with some of the vocabulary terms in the chapter, consider the following. You may refer to the chapter, the glossary, or a dictionary if you like.

1. The value of a function is determined by its rule. The rule is an algebraic expression. What is true about the algebraic expression that determines a **quadratic function** ?
2. The shape of a **parabola** is similar to the shape of an open parachute. Predict the shape of a *parabola*.
3. A **minimum** is a point on the graph of a curve with the least *y*-coordinate. How might a **maximum** be described?
4. An axis is an imaginary line. Use this information and your understanding of symmetry to define the term **axis of symmetry** .

608 Chapter 9

Study Strategy: Learn Vocabulary

Mathematics has a vocabulary all its own. Many new terms appear on the pages of your textbook. Learn these new terms as they are introduced. They will give you the necessary tools to understand new concepts.

Some tips to learning new vocabulary include:

- Look at the **context** in which a new word appears.
- Use **prefixes** or **suffixes** to figure out the word's meaning.
- Relate the new term to familiar **everyday words.** Keep in mind that a word's mathematical meaning may not exactly match its everyday meaning.

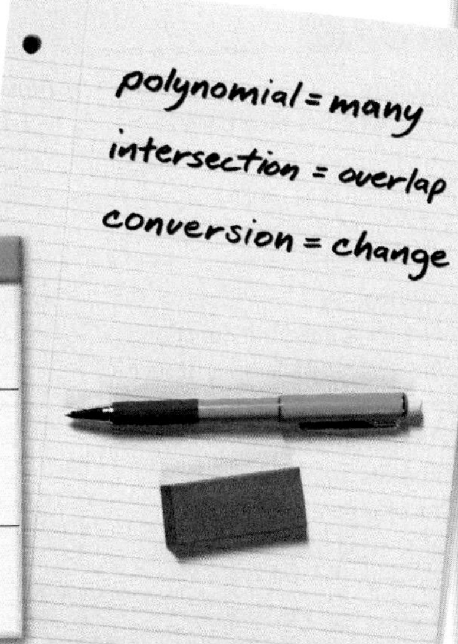

Vocabulary Word	Study Tip	Definition
Polynomial	The prefix "poly-" means many.	One monomial or the sum or the difference of monomials
Intersection	Relate it to the meaning of the "intersection of two roads".	The overlapping region that shows the solution to a system of inequalities
Conversion Factor	Relate it to the word "convert", which means change or alter.	Used to convert a measurement to different units

Try This

Complete the chart.

	Vocabulary Word	Study Tips	Definition
1.	Trinomial	■	■
2.	Independent system	■	■
3.	Variable	■	■

Use the context of each sentence to define the underlined word. Then relate the word to everyday words.

4. If two linear equations in a system have the same graph, the graphs are called <u>coincident</u> lines, or simply the same line.
5. In the formula $d = rt$, d is <u>isolated</u>.

Reading and Writing Math

Organizer

Objective: Help students apply strategies to understand and retain key concepts.

ENGLISH LANGUAGE LEARNERS

Study Strategy: Learn Vocabulary

When trying to determine the meaning of a new word based on the context, students should not look only at the sentence in which it appears. Remind them to consider the preceding and following sentences as well.

Extend As students work through Chapter 9, have them find the vocabulary words on the lesson pages and figure out their meanings based on any of the strategies shown on this page.

Answers to *Try This*

Possible answers:

1. The prefix *tri-* means "three"; a polynomial with only 3 terms.
2. Relate it to the word *independent*, which means "alone" or "by itself"; a system that has exactly one solution.

3–5. See p. A30.

Reading Connection

Women in Mathematics
by Lynn M. Osen

Osen tells inspiring stories of women mathematicians who overcame enormous obstacles to make major contributions in their fields.

Activity Have students read the chapter about Hypatia, who studied both quadratic equations and Diophantine equations, which allow only integer solutions. Pose this problem: Goldfish cost $3. Guppies cost $5. Joe spent $27 on goldfish and guppies. Ask students to explain why the equation $3x + 5y = 27$, which has an infinite number of solutions, has only one solution when used to solve this problem. The solution must be positive integers.

SECTION 9A

Quadratic Functions

One-Minute Section Planner

Lesson	Lab Resources	Materials
Lesson 9-1 Identifying Quadratic Functions • Identify quadratic functions and determine whether they have a minimum or maximum. • Graph a quadratic function and give its domain and range. ☐ SAT-10 ☑ NAEP ☑ ACT ☑ SAT ☑ SAT Subject Tests	***Algebra Lab Activities*** 9-1 Algebra Lab	**Optional** graphing calculator, index cards, sticky notes
9-2 Algebra Lab Explore the Axis of Symmetry • Find the equation of the axis of symmetry for a quadratic function. ☑ SAT-10 ☑ NAEP ☐ ACT ☑ SAT ☐ SAT Subject Tests	***Algebra Lab Activities*** 9-2 Lab Recording Sheet	
Lesson 9-2 Characteristics of Quadratic Functions • Find the zeros of a quadratic function from its graph. • Find the axis of symmetry and the vertex of a parabola. ☑ SAT-10 ☑ NAEP ☑ ACT ☑ SAT ☑ SAT Subject Tests	***Algebra Lab Activities*** 9-2 Algebra Lab	**Optional** graphing calculator, jump rope
Lesson 9-3 Graphing Quadratic Functions • Graph a quadratic function in the form $y = ax^2 + bx + c$. ☐ SAT-10 ☑ NAEP ☑ ACT ☑ SAT ☑ SAT Subject Tests	***Algebra Lab Activities*** 9-3 Algebra Lab	**Optional** graphing calculator
9-4 Technology Lab The Family of Quadratic Functions • Use a graphing calculator to explore how the value of a affects the graph of $y = ax^2$. ☐ SAT-10 ☑ NAEP ☐ ACT ☑ SAT ☑ SAT Subject Tests	***Technology Lab Activities*** 9-4 Lab Recording Sheet	**Required** graphing calculator
Lesson 9-4 Transforming Quadratic Functions • Graph and transform quadratic functions. ☐ SAT-10 ☑ NAEP ☑ ACT ☑ SAT ☑ SAT Subject Tests	***Algebra Lab Activities*** 9-4 Algebra Lab ***Technology Lab Activities*** 9-4 Technology Lab	**Optional** graphing calculator

Note: If NAEP is checked, the content is tested on either the Grade 8 or the Grade 12 NAEP assessment.

MK = *Manipulatives Kit*

QUADRATIC FUNCTIONS

Lesson 9-1

A *quadratic function* is any function that can be written in the form $y = ax^2 + bx + c$, where a, b, and c are real numbers and $a \neq 0$. This is called the *standard form* of a quadratic function.

Lesson 9-1 shows several ways to identify a quadratic function. One of these is to use a table of values. Recall that linear functions have a constant rate of change. Therefore, in a table of values for a linear function, a constant change in the x-values corresponds to a constant change in the y-values. For quadratic functions, it is the rate of change itself that has a constant rate of change. In other words, when there is a constant change in x-values, a quadratic function has *constant second differences.* The table illustrates this for the quadratic function $y = x^2 + 3$.

x	2	3	4	5	6
y	7	12	19	28	39

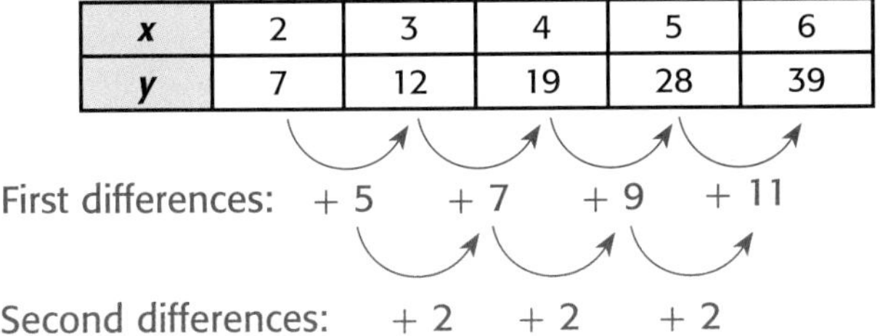

DEVELOPING QUADRATIC FUNCTIONS

LESSONS 9-1 to 9-4

The simplest quadratic function is $y = x^2$. Its graph is a *parabola* that opens upward, has its vertex at the origin, and is symmetric about the y-axis. The graphs of all other quadratic functions may be built by performing a series of transformations on the graph of $y = x^2$.

For functions in the form $y = ax^2$ $(a \neq 0)$, the value of a determines the direction and shape of the parabola. If $a > 0$, the parabola opens upward; if $a < 0$, the parabola opens downward. If $|a| > 1$, the parabola is narrower than the graph of $y = x^2$; if $|a| < 1$, the parabola is wider than the graph of $y = x^2$.

The graph of a function in the form $y = a(x - h)^2$ is a horizontal translation of the graph of $y = ax^2$. For example, the graph of $y = 2(x - 3)^2$ is identical to the graph of $y = 2x^2$, but shifted 3 units to the right.

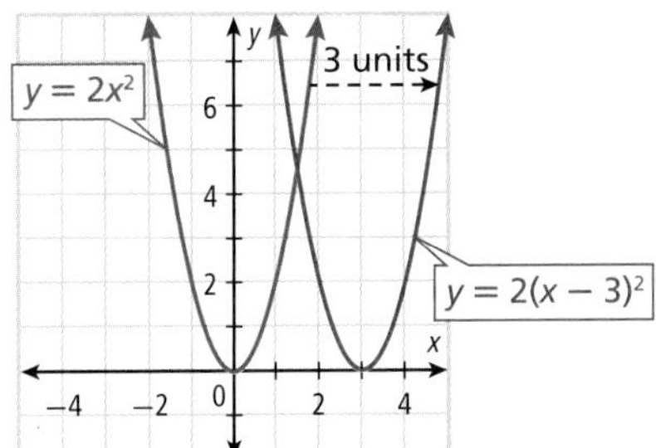

Finally, the constant k in $y = a(x - h)^2 + k$ represents a vertical translation of the graph of $y = a(x - h)^2$. The translation is k units upward if $k > 0$ and $|k|$ units downward if $k < 0$.

The equation $y = a(x - h)^2 + k$ is called the *vertex form* of a quadratic function. This form makes it easy to identify the vertex of the parabola, (h, k), and the axis of symmetry, $x = h$. (Students will study vertex form in Algebra 2.)

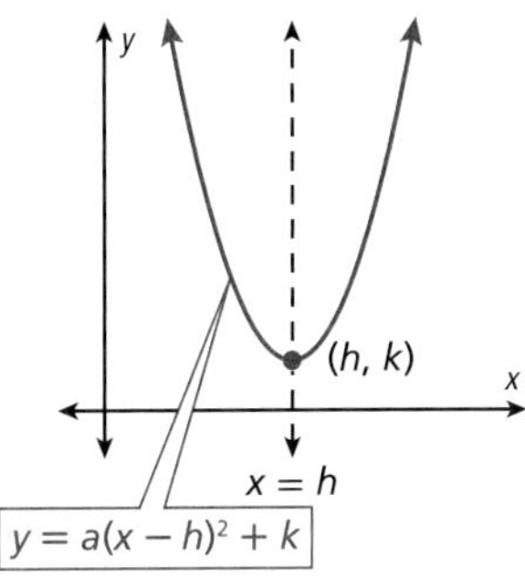

One way to find the formula for the axis of symmetry of a parabola $\left(x = -\frac{b}{2a}\right)$ is by using vertex form. As shown below, the basic idea is to transform vertex form into standard form and then write the equation of the axis of symmetry, $x = h$, in terms of a, b, and c.

$$y = a(x - h)^2 + k$$
$$y = a(x^2 - 2hx + h^2) + k$$
$$y = ax^2 - 2ahx + ah^2 + k$$

In standard form, the value of b is the coefficient of x, so $b = -2ah$. Solving for h gives $h = -\frac{b}{2a}$. Thus, the axis of symmetry is the vertical line $x = -\frac{b}{2a}$.

9-1 Organizer

Pacing: Traditional 1 day
Block $\frac{1}{2}$ day

Objectives: Identify quadratic functions and determine whether they have a minimum or maximum.

Graph a quadratic function and give its domain and range.

Algebra Lab
In *Algebra Lab Activities*

Online Edition
Tutorial Videos

Countdown Week 19

Power Presentations with PowerPoint®

Warm Up

1. Evaluate $x^2 + 5x$ for $x = 4$ and $x = -3$. 36; −6
2. Generate ordered pairs for the function $y = x^2 + 2$ with the given domain.
   D: {−2, −1, 0, 1, 2}

x	−2	−1	0	1	2
y	6	3	2	3	6

Also available on transparency

Math Humor

Q: Why can't quadratics ever be considered cool?

A: One of their terms is always a square.

9-1 Identifying Quadratic Functions

Objectives
Identify quadratic functions and determine whether they have a minimum or maximum.

Graph a quadratic function and give its domain and range.

Vocabulary
quadratic function
parabola
vertex
minimum
maximum

Why learn this?

The height of a soccer ball after it is kicked into the air can be described by a quadratic function. (See Exercise 51.)

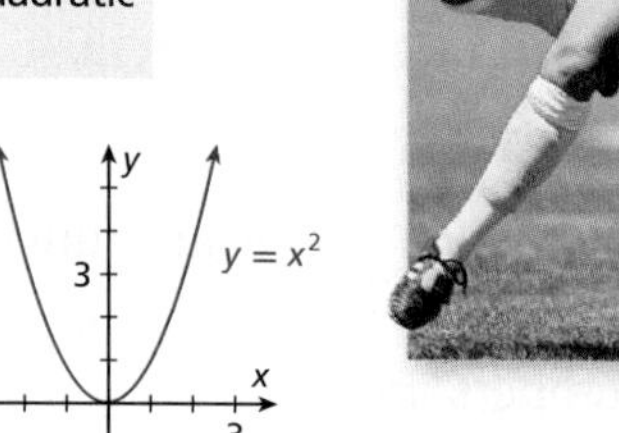

The function $y = x^2$ is shown in the graph. Notice that the graph is not linear. This function is a *quadratic function*. A **quadratic function** is any function that can be written in the standard form $y = ax^2 + bx + c$, where a, b, and c are real numbers and $a \neq 0$. The function $y = x^2$ can be written as $y = 1x^2 + 0x + 0$, where $a = 1$, $b = 0$, and $c = 0$.

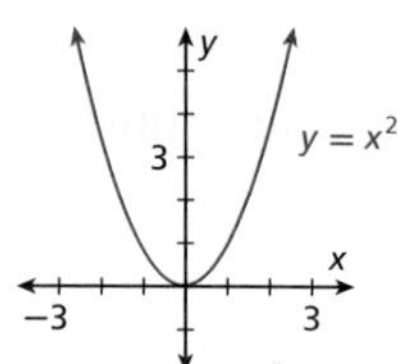

In Lesson 5-1, you identified linear functions by finding that a constant change in x corresponded to a constant change in y. The differences between y-values for a constant change in x-values are called *first differences*.

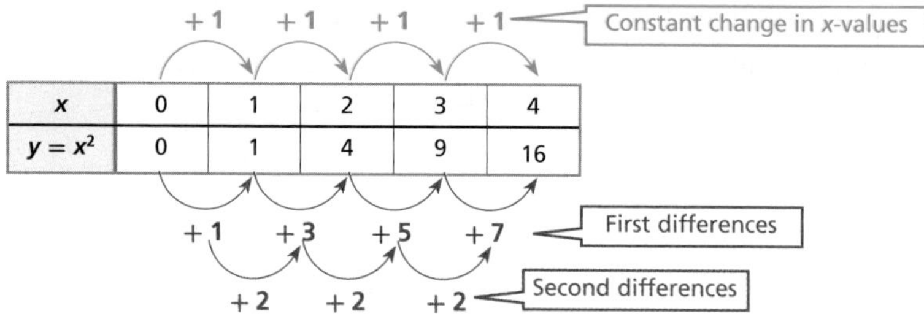

x	0	1	2	3	4
$y = x^2$	0	1	4	9	16

Notice that the quadratic function $y = x^2$ does not have constant first differences. It has constant *second differences*. This is true for all quadratic functions.

Caution!
Be sure there is a constant change in x-values before you try to find first or second differences.

EXAMPLE 1 Identifying Quadratic Functions

Tell whether each function is quadratic. Explain.

A

	x	y		
	−4	8		
+2	−2	2	−6	
+2	0	0	−2	+4
+2	2	2	+2	+4
+2	4	8	+6	+4

Since you are given a table of ordered pairs with a constant change in x-values, see if the second differences are constant.

Find the first differences, then find the second differences.

The function is quadratic. The second differences are constant.

B $y = -3x + 20$ *Since you are given an equation, use $y = ax^2 + bx + c$.*

This is not a quadratic function because the value of a is 0.

State Resources

go.hrw.com
State Resources Online
KEYWORD: MA7 Resources

1 Introduce

EXPLORATION

9-1 Identifying Quadratic Functions

The following pattern is formed by square tiles.

Figure 1 2 tiles
Figure 2 5 tiles
Figure 3 10 tiles

1. Continue the pattern to complete the table.

Figure x	1	2	3	4	5	6
Number of tiles y						

2. Find the differences between consecutive y-values in the table.
3. Recall that for a linear function, a constant change in x-values corresponds to a constant change in y-values. Is the function in the table a linear function?
4. Now find the differences between the consecutive differences found in Problem 1. What do you notice?

THINK AND DISCUSS

5. **Show** how you can write an equation relating x and y.
6. **Explain** how you know that the graph of the equation will

Motivate

Remind students that data representing a linear relationship will have constant first differences. Then explain that data representing a quadratic relationship can also be identified from a table of values that shows constant second differences.

Explorations and answers are provided in *Alternate Openers: Explorations Transparencies.*

Helpful Hint

In a quadratic function, only a cannot equal 0. It is okay for the values of b and c to be 0.

Tell whether each function is quadratic. Explain.

C $y + 3x^2 = -4$

$$\begin{aligned} -3x^2 \quad & -3x^2 \\ y &= -3x^2 - 4 \end{aligned}$$

Try to write the function in the form $y = ax^2 + bx + c$ by solving for y. Subtract $3x^2$ from both sides.

This is a quadratic function because it can be written in the form $y = ax^2 + bx + c$ where $a = -3$, $b = 0$, and $c = -4$.

1a. Yes; the second differences are constant.

1b. Yes; the function can be written in the form $y = ax^2 + bx + c$.

Tell whether each function is quadratic. Explain.

1a. $\{(-2, 4), (-1, 1), (0, 0), (1, 1), (2, 4)\}$ **1b.** $y + x = 2x^2$

The graph of a quadratic function is a curve called a **parabola**. To graph a quadratic function, generate enough ordered pairs to see the shape of the parabola. Then connect the points with a smooth curve.

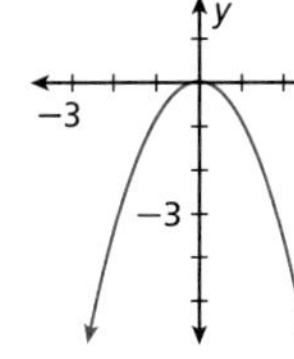

EXAMPLE 2 Graphing Quadratic Functions by Using a Table of Values

Use a table of values to graph each quadratic function.

A $y = 2x^2$

x	$y = 2x^2$
−2	8
−1	2
0	0
1	2
2	8

Make a table of values. Choose values of x and use them to find values of y.

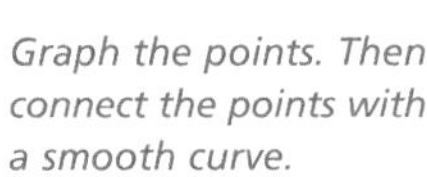

Graph the points. Then connect the points with a smooth curve.

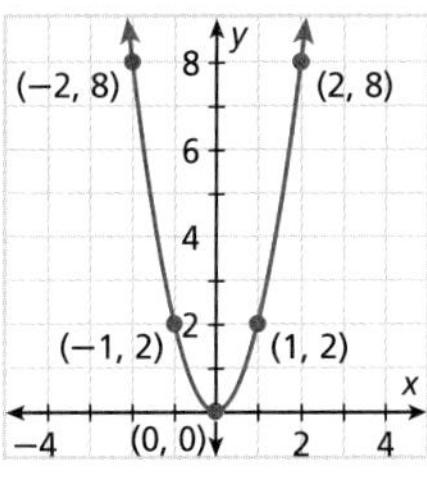

2a.

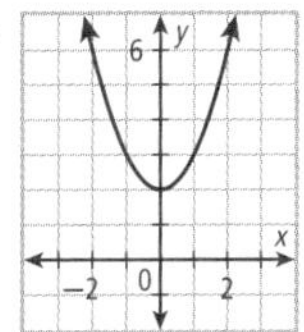

2b.

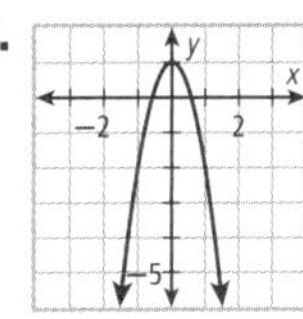

B $y = -2x^2$

x	$y = -2x^2$
−2	−8
−1	−2
0	0
1	−2
2	−8

Make a table of values. Choose values of x and use them to find values of y.

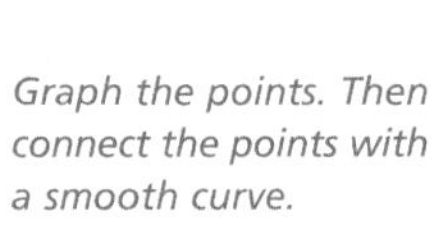

Graph the points. Then connect the points with a smooth curve.

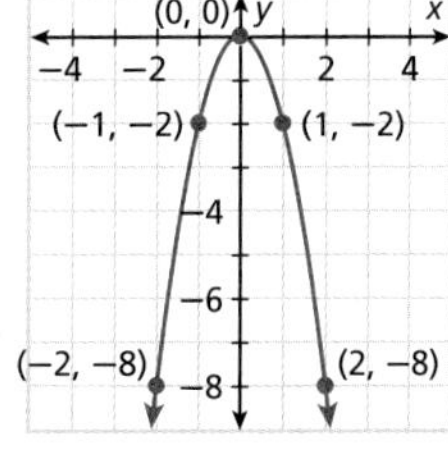

Use a table of values to graph each quadratic function.

2a. $y = x^2 + 2$ **2b.** $y = -3x^2 + 1$

As shown in the graphs in Examples 2A and 2B, some parabolas open upward and some open downward. Notice that the only difference between the two equations is the value of a. When a quadratic function is written in the form $y = ax^2 + bx + c$, the value of a determines the direction a parabola opens.

- A parabola opens **upward** when $a > 0$.
- A parabola opens **downward** when $a < 0$.

COMMON ERROR ALERT

Students might think a function rule needs three terms to be quadratic. Remind them that the values of b and c can equal 0; only a cannot be 0.

Power Presentations with PowerPoint®

Additional Examples

Example 1

Tell whether each function is quadratic. Explain.

A. $\{(-2, -9), (-1, -2), (0, -1), (1, 0), (2, 7)\}$ No; the second differences are not constant.

B. $y = 7x + 3$ No; there is no x^2-term, so $a = 0$.

C. $y - 10x^2 = 9$ Yes; it can be written in the form $y = ax^2 + bx + c$, where $a = 10$, $b = 0$, and $c = 9$.

Example 2

Use a table of values to graph each quadratic function.

A. $y = \frac{1}{3}x^2$

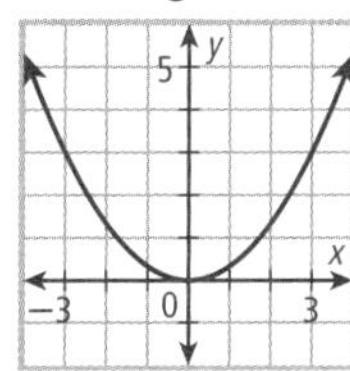

B. $y = -4x^2$

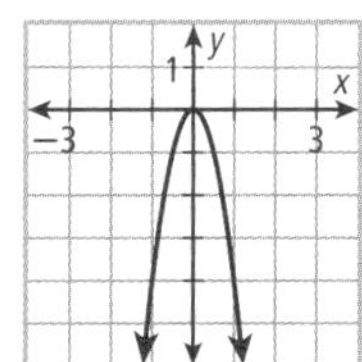

2 Teach

Guided Instruction

Show students how to identify quadratic functions given a table of values or a function rule. Explain that the graph of a quadratic function is a parabola. Point out the parabolic shape, the symmetrical features, and the vertex of the graph.

Explain that the value of a in $y = ax^2 + bx + c$ determines whether the function has a minimum or a maximum value. This minimum or maximum value determines the range of the function.

Reaching All Learners

Through Kinesthetic Experience

Display each function below one at a time. Have students discuss, in pairs, whether to lift their arms up in the shape of a U if the graph opens upward or down in a shape of an upside-down U if the graph opens downward. Then have students demonstrate their decision.

$y = -3x^2 + 18$	down
$y = 5x + 8 - \frac{1}{5}x^2$	down
$-2x^2 + y = -5$	up
$y - \frac{1}{2}x^2 + 10 - x = 0$	up
$3x - y = -x^2$	up

INTERVENTION

Questioning Strategies

EXAMPLE 1

- How do you find the second differences of a set of ordered pairs with a constant change in x-values?
- How can you tell by looking at an equation whether the value of a is 0?

EXAMPLE 2

- How do you know when you have enough values in the table to graph the parabola?

Power Presentations with PowerPoint®

Additional Examples

Example 3

Tell whether the graph of each quadratic function opens upward or downward. Explain.

A. $y - \frac{1}{4}x^2 = x - 3$ upward; $a > 0$

B. $y = 5x - 3x^2$ downward; $a < 0$

Example 4

Identify the vertex of each parabola. Then give the minimum or maximum value of the function.

A.

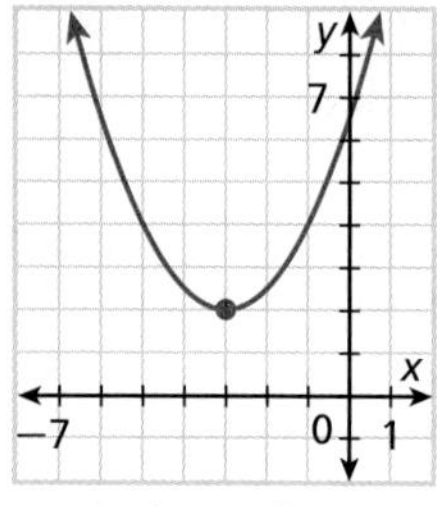

vertex: $(-3, 2)$; minimum: 2

B.

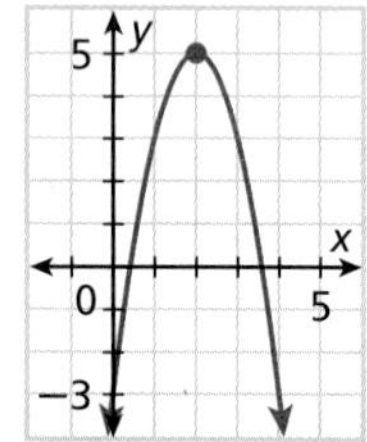

vertex: $(2, 5)$; maximum: 5

INTERVENTION

Questioning Strategies

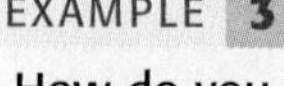

EXAMPLE 3

- How do you determine from an equation of a quadratic function whether the graph will open upward or downward?
- Why is it necessary that the function be in the form $y = ax^2 + bx + c$ before determining whether the graph opens upward or downward?

EXAMPLE 4

- Are minimums and maximums x-values or y-values?

EXAMPLE 3 Identifying the Direction of a Parabola

Tell whether the graph of each quadratic function opens upward or downward. Explain.

A $y = 4x^2$

$y = 4x^2$

$a = 4$ *Identify the value of a.*

Since $a > 0$, the parabola opens upward.

B $2x^2 + y = 5$

$$\begin{aligned} 2x^2 + y &= 5 \\ -2x^2 \qquad &-2x^2 \\ y &= -2x^2 + 5 \end{aligned}$$

Write the function in the form $y = ax^2 + bx + c$ by solving for y. Subtract $2x^2$ from both sides.

$a = -2$ *Identify the value of a.*

Since $a < 0$, the parabola opens downward.

CHECK IT OUT! Tell whether the graph of each quadratic function opens upward or downward. Explain.

3a. $f(x) = -4x^2 - x + 1$ **3b.** $y - 5x^2 = 2x - 6$

3a. Because $a < 0$, the parabola opens downward.

3b. Because $a > 0$, the parabola opens upward.

The highest or lowest point on a parabola is the **vertex**. If a parabola opens upward, the vertex is the lowest point. If a parabola opens downward, the vertex is the highest point.

Know it! Note

Minimum and Maximum Values

WORDS	If $a > 0$, the parabola opens upward, and the y-value of the vertex is the **minimum** value of the function.	If $a < 0$, the parabola opens downward, and the y-value of the vertex is the **maximum** value of the function.
GRAPHS	$y = x^2 + 6x + 9$ 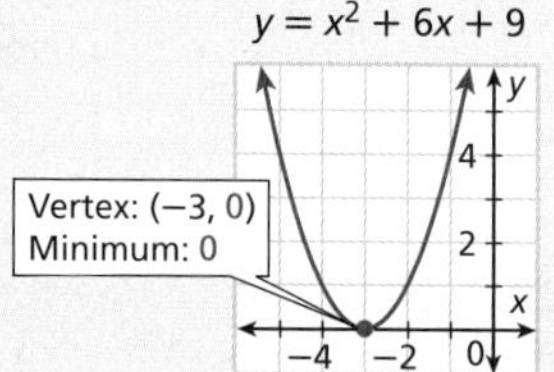	$y = -x^2 + 6x - 4$ 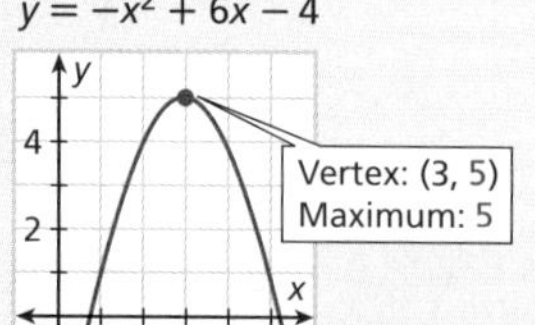

EXAMPLE 4 Identifying the Vertex and the Minimum or Maximum

Identify the vertex of each parabola. Then give the minimum or maximum value of the function.

A

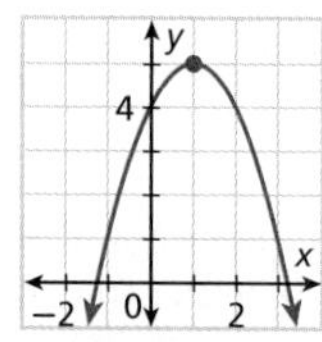

The vertex is $(1, 5)$, and the maximum is 5.

B

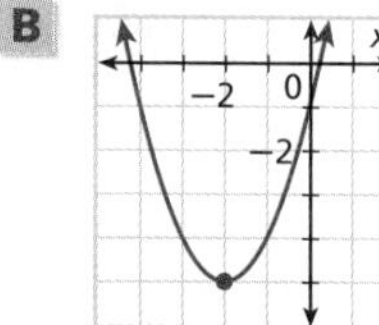

The vertex is $(-2, -5)$, and the minimum is -5.

Teaching Tip **Multiple Representations** Have students graph several quadratic functions using a graphing calculator, and make a conjecture about whether a graph opens upward or downward prior to viewing the graph.

Teaching Tip **Reading Math** Discuss with students the meanings of *minimum* and *maximum* in common usage. Connect these everyday meanings with those that are used with parabolas by associating them with the maximum value or minimum value of a quadratic function. **English Language Learners**

Identify the vertex of each parabola. Then give the minimum or maximum value of the function.

4a.

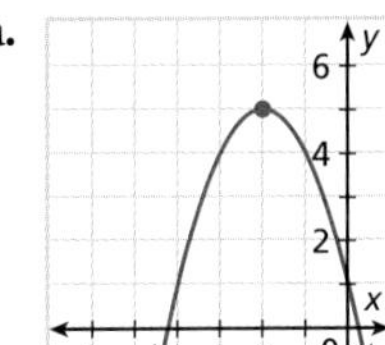

vertex: $(-2, 5)$; maximum: 5

4b.

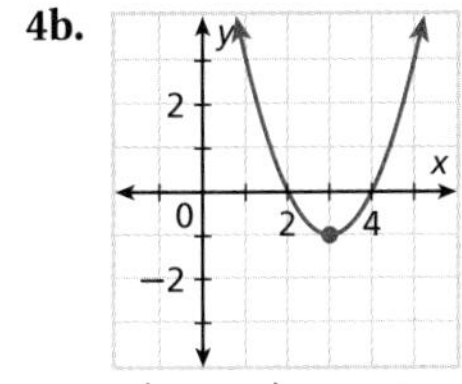

vertex: $(3, -1)$; minimum: -1

Caution!

You may not be able to see the entire graph, but that does not mean the graph stops. Remember that the arrows indicate that the graph continues.

Unless a specific domain is given, you may assume that the domain of a quadratic function is all real numbers. You can find the range of a quadratic function by looking at its graph.

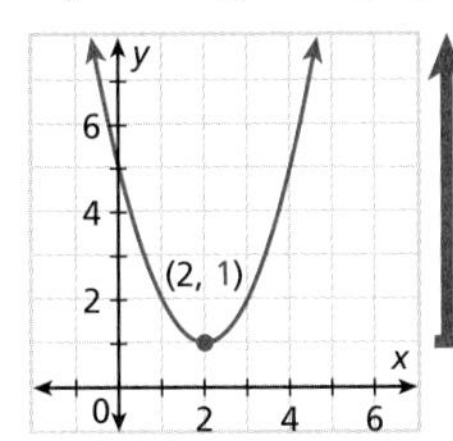

For the graph of $y = x^2 - 4x + 5$, the range begins at the minimum value of the function, where $y = 1$. All the y-values of the function are greater than or equal to 1. So the range is $y \geq 1$.

EXAMPLE 5 Finding Domain and Range

Find the domain and range.

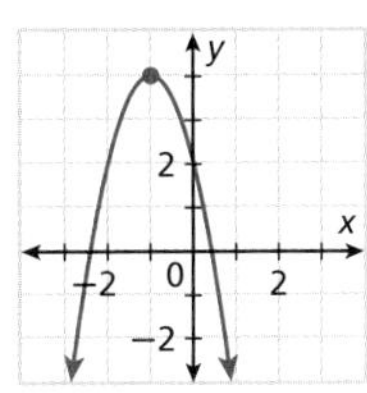

Step 1 The graph opens downward, so identify the maximum.

The vertex is $(-1, 4)$, so the maximum is 4.

Step 2 Find the domain and range.

D: all real numbers

R: $y \leq 4$

Find the domain and range.

5a.

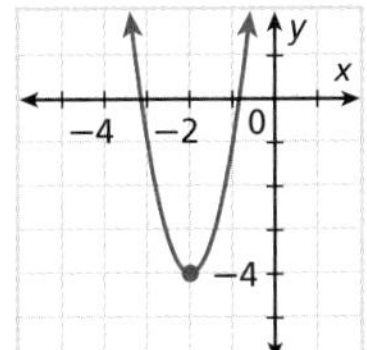

5b.

5a. D: all real numbers; R: $y \geq -4$

5b. D: all real numbers; R: $y \leq 3$

THINK AND DISCUSS

1. How can you identify a quadratic function from ordered pairs? from looking at the function rule?

2. GET ORGANIZED Copy and complete the graphic organizer below. In each box, describe a way of identifying quadratic functions.

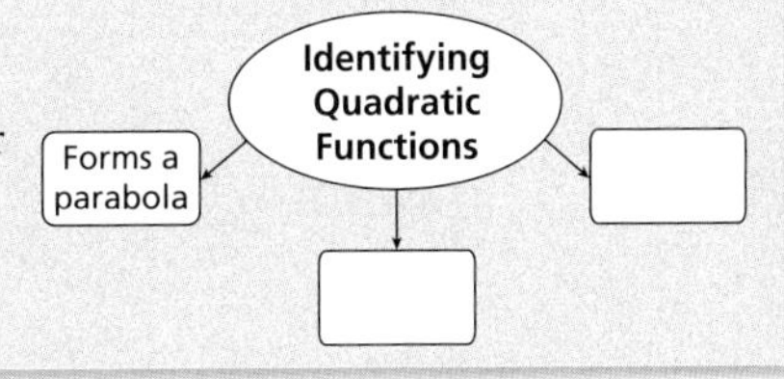

COMMON ERROR ALERT

Some students may automatically say that the function has a minimum when a parabola opens downward, and maximum when a parabola opens upward because of the word association. Tell students to visualize the graph before determining whether it has a minimum or maximum.

Power Presentations with PowerPoint®

Additional Examples

Example 5

Find the domain and range.

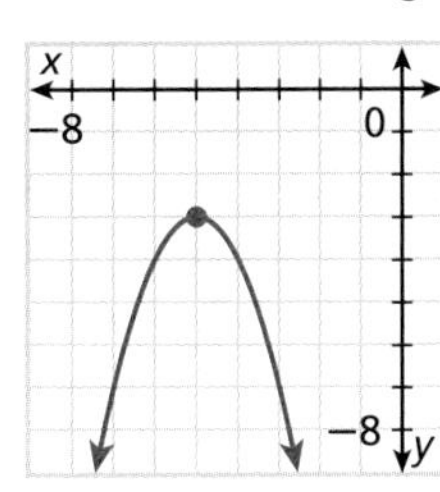

D: all real numbers

R: $y \leq -3$

INTERVENTION

Questioning Strategies

EXAMPLE 5

- Is the set of all real numbers the domain or the range? Is this true for all quadratic functions?

3 Close

Summarize

Write $y = 3x^2$ on the board. Ask students for the values of a, b, and c. Then have students list five ordered pairs for this function and find the second differences. Ask whether the graph would open upward or downward and whether the parabola would have a minimum or maximum. Graph the function by plotting the ordered pairs. Continue with other quadratic equations as time allows.

ONGOING ASSESSMENT

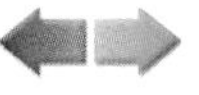

and INTERVENTION

***Diagnose Before* the Lesson**
9-1 Warm Up, TE p. 610

***Monitor During* the Lesson**
Check It Out! Exercises, SE pp. 611–613
Questioning Strategies, TE pp. 611–613

***Assess After* the Lesson**
9-1 Lesson Quiz, TE p. 617
Alternative Assessment, TE p. 617

Answers to *Think and Discuss*

1. If the second differences are constant, the function is quadratic. If the function can be written in the form $y = ax^2 + bx + c$, where $a \neq 0$, it is quadratic.
2. See p. A8.

Assignment Guide

Assign *Guided Practice* exercises as necessary.

If you finished Examples **1–3**

Basic	22–32, 45–50, 53–60
Average	22–32, 45–50, 53–60
Advanced	22–32, 45–50, 53–60, 68

If you finished Examples **1–5**

Basic	22–50, 53–60, 61–67, 70–75
Average	22–75
Advanced	22–75

Homework Quick Check

Quickly check key concepts.
Exercises: 24, 26, 30, 34, 38

Answers

6.

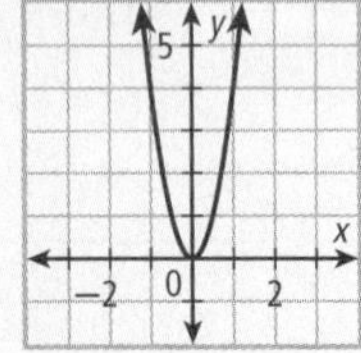

7.

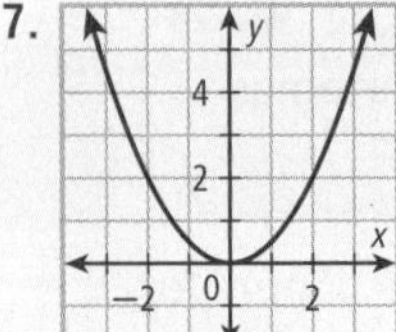

State Resources

State Resources Online
KEYWORD: MA7 Resources

go.hrw.com
Homework Help Online
KEYWORD: MA7 9-1
Parent Resources Online
KEYWORD: MA7 Parent

GUIDED PRACTICE

1. **Vocabulary** The y-value of the vertex of a parabola that opens upward is the ___?___ value of the function. (*maximum* or *minimum*) **minimum**

SEE EXAMPLE 1 p. 610

Tell whether each function is quadratic. Explain.

2. $y + 6x = -14$ **2. No; $a = 0$**
3. $2x^2 + y = 3x - 1$ **3. Yes; the function can be written in the form $y = ax^2 + bx + c$.**
4.

x	−4	−3	−2	−1	0
y	39	18	3	−6	−9

Yes; the second differences are constant.

5. $\{(-10, 15), (-9, 17), (-8, 19), (-7, 21), (-6, 23)\}$
No; the first differences are constant, so the function is linear.

SEE EXAMPLE 2 p. 611

Use a table of values to graph each quadratic function.

6. $y = 4x^2$
7. $y = \frac{1}{2}x^2$
8. $y = -x^2 + 1$
9. $y = -5x^2$

SEE EXAMPLE 3 p. 612

Tell whether the graph of each quadratic function opens upward or downward. Explain.

10. $y = -3x^2 + 4x$ **10. downward; $a < 0$**
11. $y = 1 - 2x + 6x^2$ **11. $a > 0$; upward**
12. $y + x^2 = -x - 2$ **12. downward; $a < 0$**
13. $y + 2 = x^2$ **upward; $a > 0$**
14. $y - 2x^2 = -3$ **upward; $a > 0$**
15. $y + 2 + 3x^2 = 1$ **downward; $a < 0$**

SEE EXAMPLE 4 p. 612

Identify the vertex of each parabola. Then give the minimum or maximum value of the function.

16.

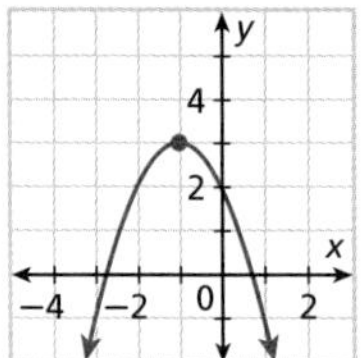

$(-1, 3)$; maximum: 3

17. **$(-3, -4)$; minimum: −4**

SEE EXAMPLE 5 p. 613

Find the domain and range.

18.

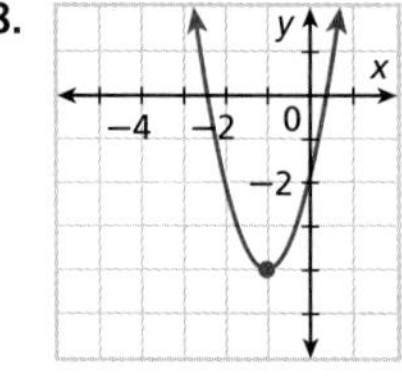

D: all real numbers; R: $y \geq -4$

19.

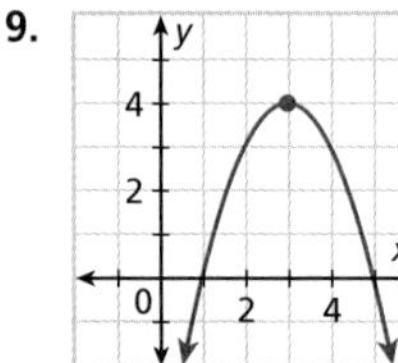

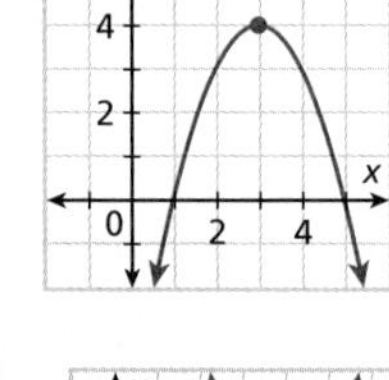

D: all real numbers; R: $y \leq 4$

20.

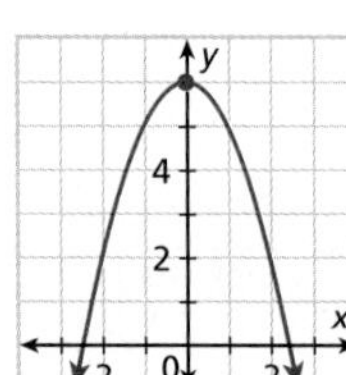

D: all real numbers; R: $y \leq 6$

21. **D: all real numbers; R: $y \geq -4$**

9-1 READING STRATEGIES

Study the information about the example below to better understand quadratic functions.

Quadratic functions are written in the form $y = ax^2 + bx + c$, where $a \neq 0$.

$y = -\frac{1}{2}x^2 + 3$

$a = -\frac{1}{2}$, $b = 0$ and $c = 3$

You can create a table of values to graph a quadratic function.

x	y
−4	−5
−2	1
0	3
2	1
4	−5

The graph of a quadratic function is a *parabola*.

vertex: (0, 3); *maximum*: 3

The graph of $y = -\frac{1}{2}x^2 + 3$ opens downward because $a < 0$.

Recall that the domain is the set of x-values and the range is the set of y-values for a function.

D: all real numbers
R: $y \leq 3$

Complete the following.

1. Identify the values of a, b, and c in the quadratic function $y = 3x^2 - 5x + 2$.
$a = 3$, $b = -5$, $c = 2$
2. Does the graph of the function $y = 3x^2 - 5x + 2$ open upward or downward?
upward
3. Identify the domain and range for a function whose graph opens upward with vertex (0, −5).
D: all real numbers; R: $y \geq -5$

Answer the following about the function $y = 2x^2$.

4. Create a table of values for the function.
5. Graph the function.
6. What is the vertex of the graph?
(0, 0)
7. Does the graph open upward or or downward? Why?
upward; because $a > 0$.

x	y
−2	8
−1	2
0	0
1	2
2	8

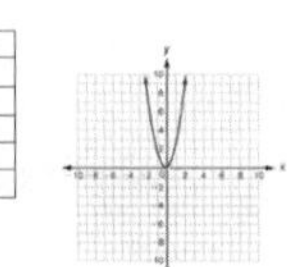

9-1 RETEACH

There are three steps to identify a quadratic function from a table of ordered pairs.

Tell whether this function is quadratic. Explain.

x	y
−5	−191
−3	−59
−1	1
1	−11
3	−95

$-3 - (-5) = +2$
$-1 - (-3) = +2$
$1 - (-1) = +2$
$3 - 1 = +2$

$-59 - (-191) = +132$
$1 - (-59) = +60$
$-11 - 1 = -12$
$-95 - (-11) = -84$

$60 - 132 = -72$
$-12 - 60 = -72$
$-84 - (-12) = -72$

Step 1: Check for a constant change in x-values. Calculate the second value minus the first.

Step 2: Find the first differences in y-values. If they are constant, the function is linear.

Step 3: Find the second differences in y-values. If the second differences are constant, then the function is quadratic.

This function is quadratic because the second differences are constant.

Tell whether each function is quadratic. Explain.

1.

x	y
−4	43
−1	16
2	7
5	16
8	43

$-1 - (-4) = +3$
$2 - (-1) = +3$
$5 - 2 = +3$
$8 - 5 = +3$

$16 - 43 = -27$
$7 - 16 = -9$
$16 - 7 = +9$
$43 - 16 = +27$

$-9 - (-27) = +18$
$9 - (-9) = +18$
$27 - (9) = +18$

quadratic; the second difference are constant.

2. 3.

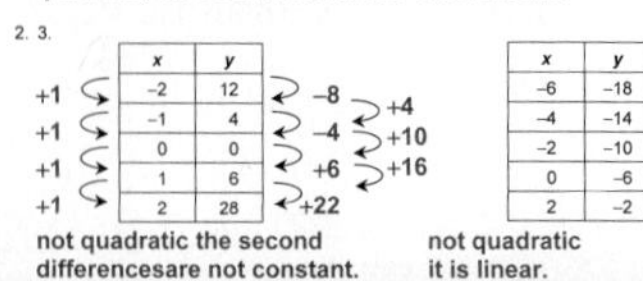

x	y
−2	12
−1	4
0	0
1	6
2	28

+1, +1, +1, +1

−8, −4, +6, +22

+4, +10, +16

not quadratic the second differencesare not constant.

x	y
−6	−18
−4	−14
−2	−10
0	−6
2	−2

not quadratic it is linear.

PRACTICE AND PROBLEM SOLVING

Independent Practice

For Exercises	See Example
22–25	1
26–29	2
30–32	3
33–34	4
35–38	5

Extra Practice

Skills Practice p. S20

Application Practice p. S36

22. No; the second differences are not constant.

Tell whether each function is quadratic. Explain.

22.

x	−2	−1	0	1	2
y	−1	0	4	9	15

23. $-3x^2 + x = y - 11$ **Yes; the function can be written in the form $y = ax^2 + bx + c$.**

24. $\{(0, -3), (1, -2), (2, 1), (3, 6), (4, 13)\}$ **Yes; the second differences are constant.**

25. $y = \frac{2}{3}x - \frac{4}{9} + \frac{1}{6}x^2$ **Yes; the function can be written in the form $y = ax^2 + bx + c$.**

Use a table of values to graph each quadratic function.

26. $y = x^2 - 5$ 27. $y = -\frac{1}{2}x^2$ 28. $y = -2x^2 + 2$ 29. $y = 3x^2 - 2$

Tell whether the graph of each quadratic function opens upward or downward. Explain.

30. $y = 7x^2 - 4x$ **upward; $a > 0$**

31. $x - 3x^2 + y = 5$ **upward; $a > 0$**

32. $y = -\frac{2}{3}x^2$ **downward; $a < 0$**

Identify the vertex of each parabola. Then give the minimum or maximum value of the function.

33. 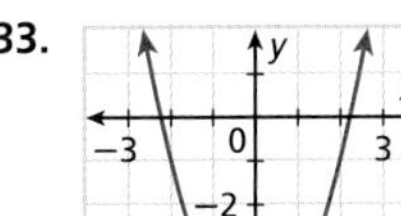

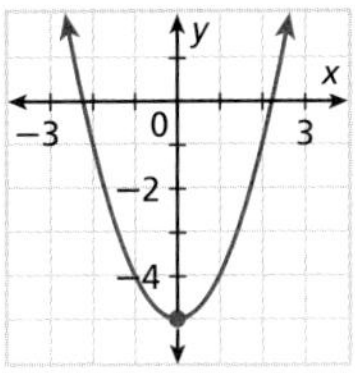

vertex: $(0, -5)$; minimum: -5

34. 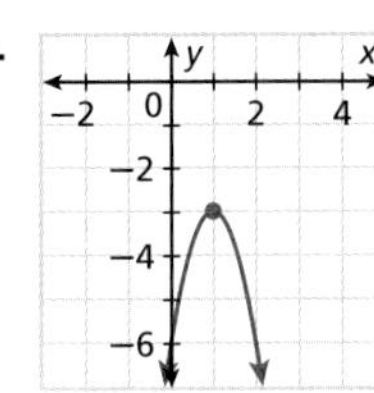

vertex: $(1, -3)$; maximum: -3

Find the domain and range.

35. 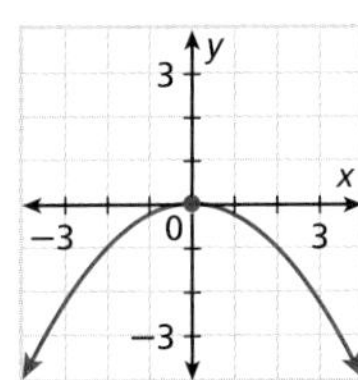

D: all real numbers; R: $y \leq 0$

36. **D: all real numbers; R: $y \geq 2$**

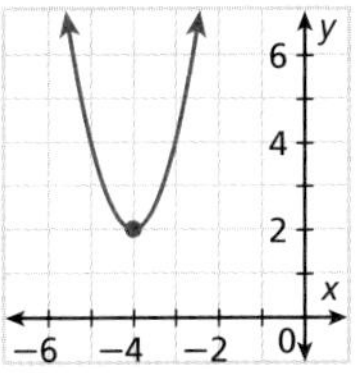

37. 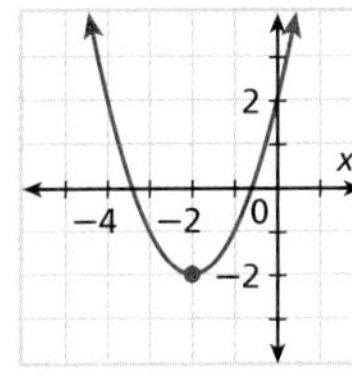

D: all real numbers; R: $y \geq -2$

38. 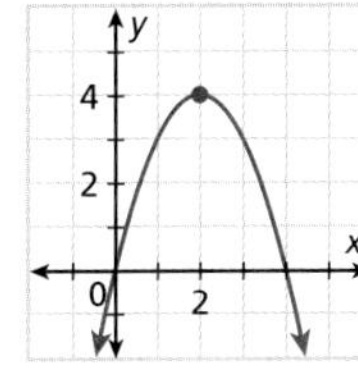

D: all real numbers; R: $y \leq 4$

Tell whether each statement is sometimes, always, or never true.

39. The graph of a quadratic function is a straight line. **never**

40. The range of a quadratic function is the set of all real numbers. **never**

41. The highest power of the independent variable in a quadratic function is 2. **always**

42. The graph of a quadratic function contains the point $(0, 0)$. **sometimes**

43. The vertex of a parabola occurs at the minimum value of the function. **sometimes**

44. The graph of a quadratic function that has a minimum opens upward. **always**

Answers

8. 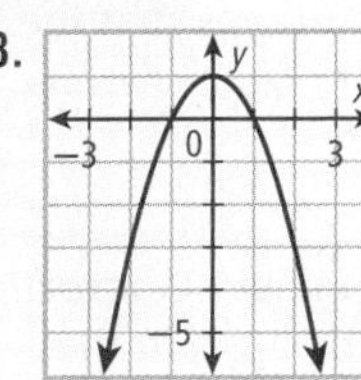

9. 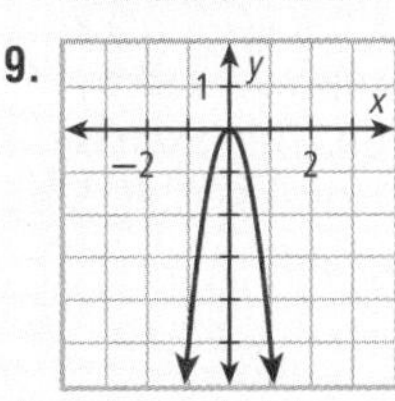

26. 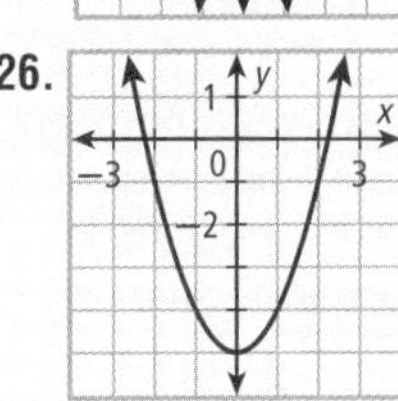

27. 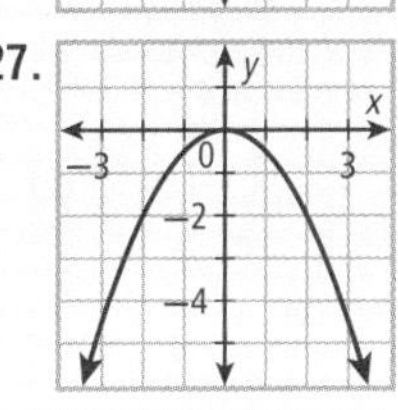

28. 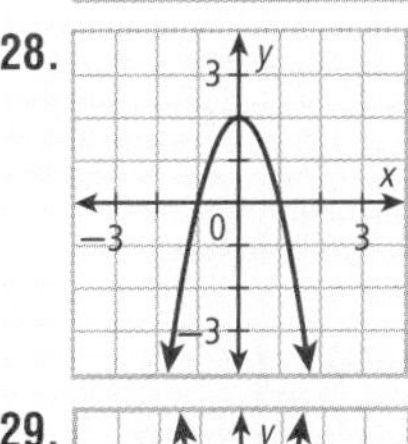

29. 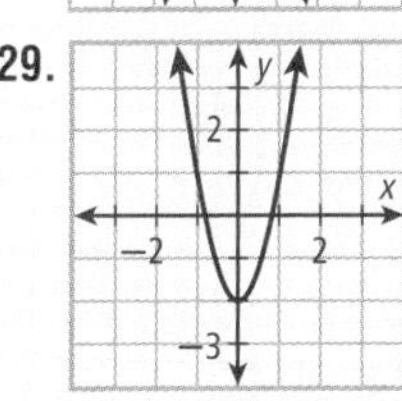

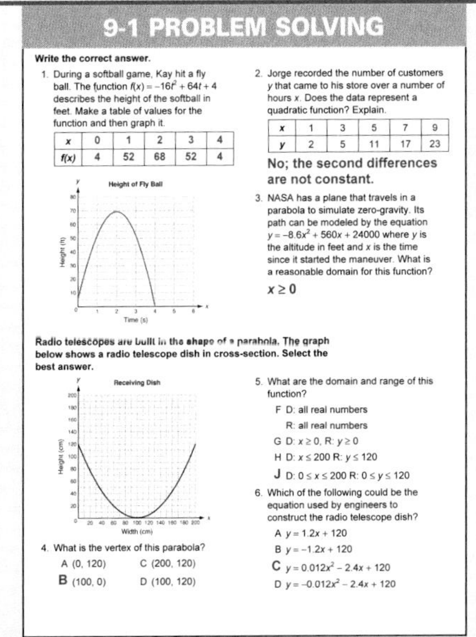

9-1 PROBLEM SOLVING

Write the correct answer.

1. During a softball game, Kay hit a fly ball. The function $f(x) = -16t^2 + 64t + 4$ describes the height of the softball in feet. Make a table of values for the function and then graph it.

x	0	1	2	3	4
$f(x)$	4	52	68	52	4

2. Jorge recorded the number of customers y that came to his store over a number of hours x. Does the data represent a quadratic function? Explain.

x	1	3	5	7	9
y	2	5	11	17	23

No; the second differences are not constant.

3. NASA has a plane that travels in a parabola to simulate zero-gravity. Its path can be modeled by the equation $y = -8.6x^2 + 560x + 24000$ where y is the altitude in feet and x is the time since it started the maneuver. What is a reasonable domain for this function? **$x \geq 0$**

Radio telescopes are built in the shape of a parabola. The graph below shows a radio telescope dish in cross-section. Select the best answer.

4. What is the vertex of this parabola?
A (0, 120) C (200, 120)
B (100, 0) D (100, 120)

5. What are the domain and range of this function?
F D: all real numbers R: all real numbers
G D: $x \geq 0$, R: $y \geq 0$
H D: $x \leq 200$ R: $y \leq 120$
J D: $0 \leq x \leq 200$ R: $0 \leq y \leq 120$

6. Which of the following could be the equation used by engineers to construct the radio telescope dish?
A $y = 1.2x + 120$
B $y = -1.2x + 120$
C $y = 0.012x^2 - 2.4x + 120$
D $y = -0.012x^2 - 2.4x + 120$

9-1 CHALLENGE

In Lesson 9-1 you saw that quadratic functions have constant ***second differences*** between y-values when there is a constant change between the x-values. You can use the form $y = ax^2 + bx + c$ to prove this.

Use this table to organize your work as you follow the steps provided below.

x	y	first differences	second differences
n	$an^2 + bn + c$		
$n + 1$	$a(n+1)^2 + b(n+1) + c =$ $a(n^2 + 2n + 1) + b(n+1) + c =$ $an^2 + 2an + a + bn + b + c$	$an^2 + 2an + a + bn + b + c$ $-(an^2 + bn + c)$ $2an + a + b$	
$n + 2$	$a(n+2)^2 + b(n+2) + c =$ $a(n^2 + 4n + 4) + b(n+2) + c =$ $an^2 + 4an + 4a + bn + 2b + c$	$an^2 + 4an + 4a + bn + 2b + c$ $-(an^2 + 2an + a + bn + b + c)$ $2an + 3a + b$	$2an + 3a + b$ $-(2an + a + b)$ $2a$
$n + 3$	$a(n+3)^2 + b(n+3) + c =$ $a(n^2 + 6n + 9) + b(n+3) + c =$ $an^2 + 6an + 9a + bn + 3b + c$	$an^2 + 6an + 9a + bn + 3b + c$ $-(an^2 + 4an + 4a + bn + 2b + c)$ $2an + 5a + b$	$2an + 5a + b$ $-(2an + 3a + b)$ $2a$

1. You want to prove that the second differences between y-values are constant regardless of the x-values, so let the variable n represent the first x-value, and let the constant change between x-values be 1. Write the next three x-values in the table.
2. In the y-column of the table, substitute each x-value into the expression $ax^2 + bx + c$. Multiply and combine like terms to simplify each polynomial.
3. Subtract polynomials to find the first differences.
4. Are the first differences constant? Explain. **No, the middle terms (a, $3a$, $5a$) are different.**
5. Subtract polynomials to find the second differences.
6. Are the second differences constant? Explain. **Yes, the second differences are $2a$.**
7. In general, for any quadratic function of the form $y = ax^2 + bx + c$, when the change between x-values is 1, what will be the second differences between y-values? **$2a$**
8. If you make a table of coordinates for these quadratic functions, and use a constant change of 1 between x-values, what will be the second differences? (Don't actually make a table of values!)
 a. $y = 5x^2 + 7x - 8$ **$2(5) = 10$**
 b. $y = -3x^2 + 12$ **$2(-3) = -6$**

9-1 PRACTICE A

9-1 PRACTICE C

9-1 PRACTICE B

Tell whether each function is quadratic. Explain.

1. (0, 6), (1, 12), (2, 20), (3, 30) **yes; the second differences are constant.**

2. $3x + 2y = 8$ **no; it cannot be written in the form $y = ax^2 + bx + c$.**

Use a table of values to graph each quadratic function.

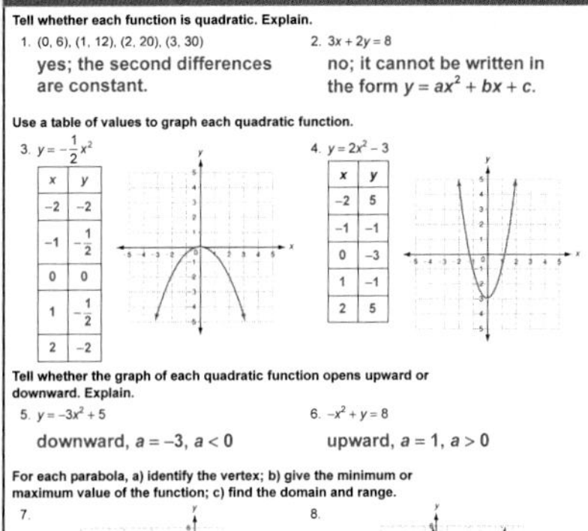

3. $y = -\frac{1}{2}x^2$

x	y
−2	−2
−1	$-\frac{1}{2}$
0	0
1	$-\frac{1}{2}$
2	−2

4. $y = 2x^2 - 3$

x	y
−2	5
−1	−1
0	−3
1	−1
2	5

Tell whether the graph of each quadratic function opens upward or downward. Explain.

5. $y = -3x^2 + 5$ **downward, $a = -3$, $a < 0$**

6. $-x^2 + y = 8$ **upward, $a = 1$, $a > 0$**

For each parabola, a) identify the vertex; b) give the minimum or maximum value of the function; c) find the domain and range.

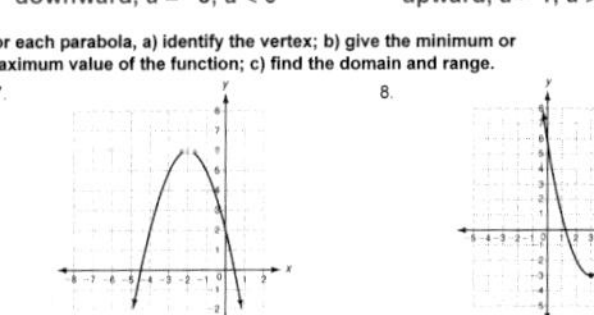

7. a. **(−2, 6)** b. **maximum: 6** c. **D: all real numbers; R: $y \leq 6$**

8. a. **(3, −3)** b. **minimum: −3** c. **D: all real numbers; R: $y \geq -3$**

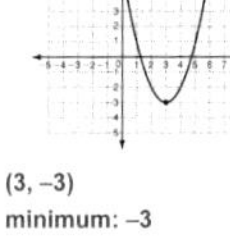

Inclusion In **Exercise 47,** remind students that the quantity $(x + 1)^2$ means $(x + 1)(x + 1)$, not $x^2 + 1$.

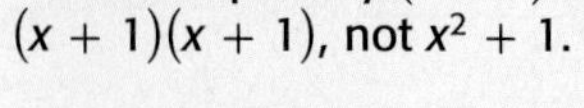

Exercise 63 involves showing that the height of a rocket over time can be represented by a quadratic function. This exercise prepares students for the Multi-Step Test Prep on page 640.

Answers

51c. The independent variable x represents the time since the volleyball is served, so this makes sense only for nonnegative numbers.

52a.

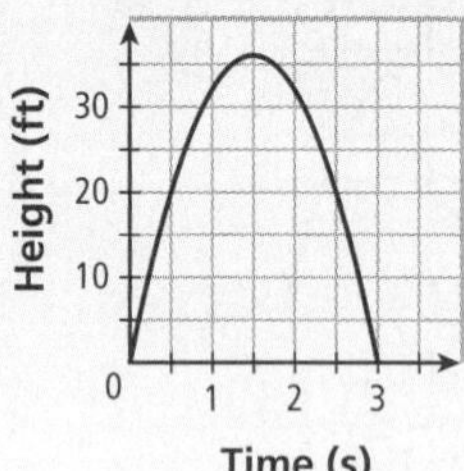

61a.

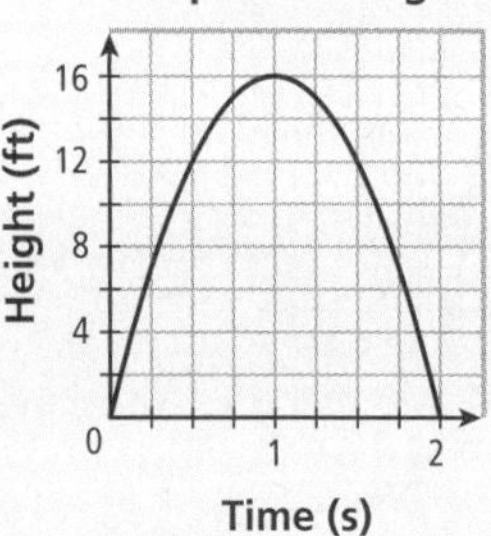

62a. For a linear function, the first differences will be constant for a constant change in x. For a quadratic function, the second differences will be constant for a constant change in x.

b. A linear function can be written in the form $y = mx + b$. A quadratic function can be written in the form $y = ax^2 + bx + c$, where a, b, and c are real numbers and a is not equal to 0.

c. The graph of a linear function is a line. The graph of a quadratic function is a parabola.

45. No; the value of a is 0.

46. yes; $y = 2x^2 + 3x - 5$

47. yes; $y = x^2 + 2x + 1$

48. yes; $y = -x^2 + 2x + 4$

49. yes; $y = 3x^2 + 0x - 9$

50. No; the function has a power of x greater than 2.

Tell whether each function is quadratic. If it is, write the function in standard form. If not, explain why not.

45. $y = 3x - 1$ **46.** $y = 2x^2 - 5 + 3x$ **47.** $y = (x + 1)^2$

48. $y = 5 - (x - 1)^2$ **49.** $y = 3x^2 - 9$ **50.** $y = (x + 1)^3 - x^2$

51. Estimation The graph shows the approximate height y in meters of a volleyball x seconds after it is served.

a. Estimate the time it takes for the volleyball to reach its greatest height. **about 0.375 s**

b. Estimate the greatest height that the volleyball reaches. **about 2.25 m**

c. **Critical Thinking** If the domain of a quadratic function is all real numbers, why is the domain of this function limited to nonnegative numbers?

Volleyball's Height

Height (m): 0.5, 1, 1.5, 2, 2.5, 3; Time (s): 0, 0.5, 1

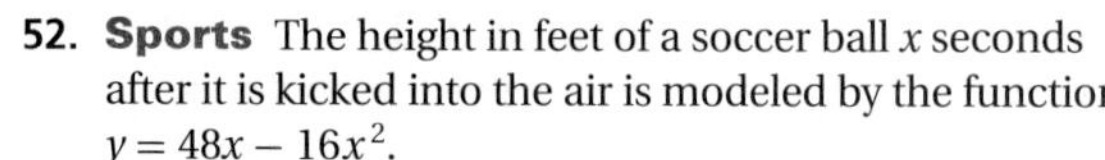

52. Sports The height in feet of a soccer ball x seconds after it is kicked into the air is modeled by the function $y = 48x - 16x^2$.

a. Graph the function.

b. In this situation, what values make sense for the domain? $x \geq 0$

c. Does the soccer ball ever reach a height of 50 ft? How do you know? **No; the maximum y-value on the parabola is less than 50.**

Tell whether each function is linear, quadratic, or neither.

53. $y = \frac{1}{2}x - x^2$ **quadratic** **54.** $y = \frac{1}{2}x - 3$ **linear** **55.** $y + 3 = -x^2$ **quadratic** **56.** $y - 2x^2 = 0$ **quadratic**

57. $y = \frac{1}{2}x(x^2)$ **neither** **58.** $y = \frac{3}{x^2}$ **neither** **59.** $y = \frac{3}{2}x$ **linear** **60.** $x^2 + 2x + 1 = y$ **quadratic**

61. Marine Biology A scientist records the motion of a dolphin as it jumps from the water. The function $h(t) = -16t^2 + 32t$ models the dolphin's height in feet above the water after t seconds.

a. Graph the function.

b. What domain makes sense for this situation? $t \geq 0$

c. What is the dolphin's maximum height above the water? **16 ft**

d. How long is the dolphin out of the water? **2 s**

62. Write About It Explain how to tell the difference between a linear function and a quadratic function when given each of the following:

a. ordered pairs b. the function rule c. the graph

MULTI-STEP TEST PREP

63. This problem will prepare you for the Multi-Step Test Prep on page 640.

A rocket team is using simulation software to create and study water bottle rockets. The team begins by simulating the launch of a rocket without a parachute. The table gives data for one rocket design.

a. Show that the data represent a quadratic function.

b. Graph the function.

c. The acceleration due to gravity is 9.8 m/s^2. How is this number related to the data for this water bottle rocket?

Time (s)	Height (m)
0	0
1	34.3
2	58.8
3	73.5
4	78.4
5	73.5
6	58.8
7	34.3
8	0

63a.

Time (s)	Height (m)	First differences	Second differences
0	0		
1	34.3	+34.3	−9.8
2	58.8	+24.5	−9.8
3	73.5	+14.7	−9.8
4	78.4	+4.9	−9.8
5	73.5	−4.9	−9.8
6	58.8	−14.7	−9.8
7	34.3	−24.5	−9.8
8	0	−34.3	

The second differences are constant.

b. Bottle Rocket Launch

Height (m): 20, 40, 60; Times (s): 0, 2, 4, 6

c. The acceleration is the absolute value of the second differences.

64. **Critical Thinking** Given the function $-3 - y = x^2 + x$, why is it incorrect to state that the parabola opens upward and has a minimum?
After the equation is solved for y, x^2 will be negative. This means the parabola opens downward and has a maximum.

65. Which of the following is the graph of a quadratic function?

Ⓐ
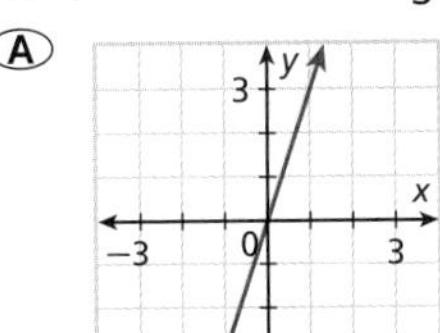

Ⓒ (circled)
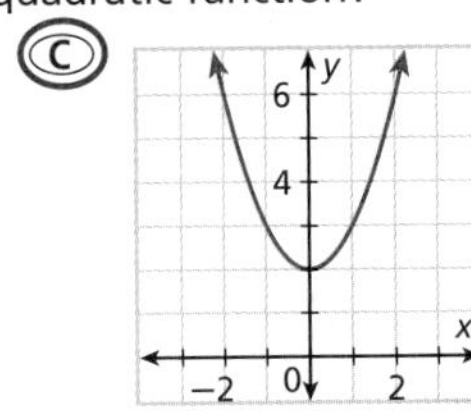

Ⓑ
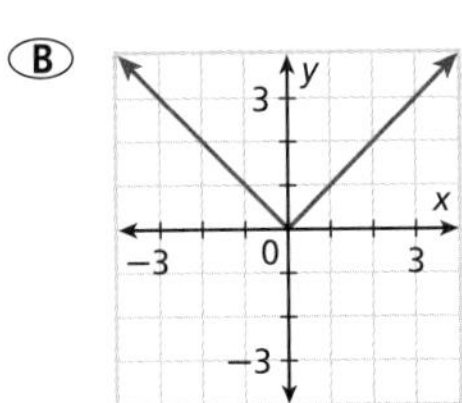

Ⓓ
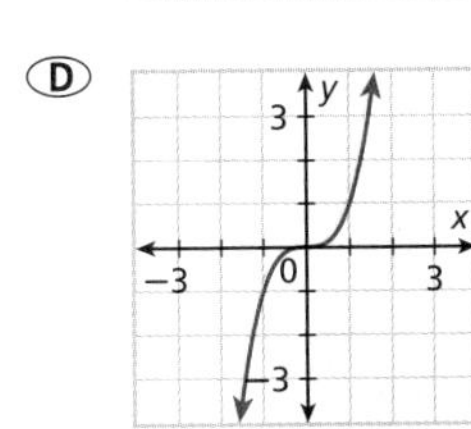

66. Which of the following quadratic functions has a maximum?
- Ⓕ $2x^2 - y = 3x - 2$
- Ⓖ $y = x^2 + 4x + 16$
- Ⓗ $y - x^2 + 6 = 9x$
- Ⓙ (circled) $y + 3x^2 = 9$

67. **Short Response** Is the function $f(x) = 5 - 2x^2 + 3x$ quadratic? Explain your answer by using two different methods of identification. **Yes; the function can be written in the form $y = ax^2 + bx + c$, and the graph forms a parabola.**

67. (graph: y-axis label 6; x-axis labels −2, 0, 4)

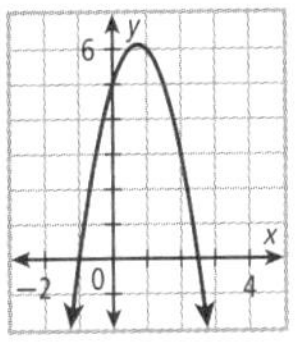

CHALLENGE AND EXTEND

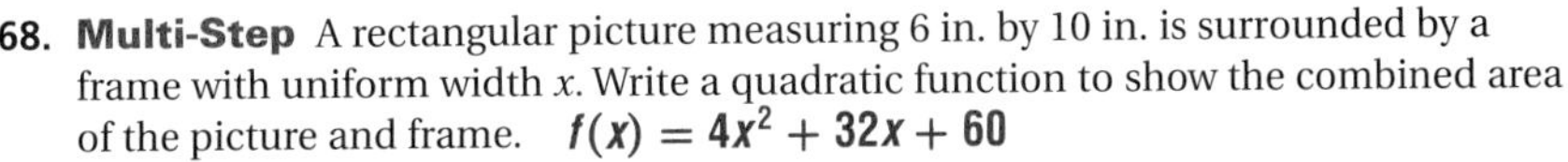

68. **Multi-Step** A rectangular picture measuring 6 in. by 10 in. is surrounded by a frame with uniform width x. Write a quadratic function to show the combined area of the picture and frame. **$f(x) = 4x^2 + 32x + 60$**

69. **Graphing Calculator** Use a graphing calculator to find the domain and range of the quadratic functions $y = x^2 - 4$ and $y = -(x + 2)^2$. **$f(x) = x^2 - 4 \rightarrow$ D: all real numbers; R: $y \geq -4$; $f(x) = -(x + 2)^2 \rightarrow$ D: all real numbers; R: $y \leq 0$**

SPIRAL REVIEW

Write each number as a power of the given base. *(Lesson 1-4)*

70. 10,000; base 10 **10^4**

71. 16; base −2 **$(-2)^4$**

72. $\frac{8}{27}$; base $\frac{2}{3}$ **$\left(\frac{2}{3}\right)^3$**

73. A map shows a scale of 1 inch:3 miles. On the map, the distance from Lin's home to the park is $14\frac{1}{4}$ inches. What is the actual distance? *(Lesson 2-7)* **$42\frac{3}{4}$ mi**

Write a function to describe the situation. Find the reasonable domain and range for the function. *(Lesson 4-3)*

74. Camp Wildwood has collected \$400 in registration fees. It can enroll another 3 campers for \$25 each.

75. Sal works between 30 and 35 hours per week. He earns \$9 per hour.

Answers

74. $r(c) = 25c + 400$, where r is the total registration money in dollars and c is the number of additional campers;
D: {0, 1, 2, 3}; R: {400, 425, 450, 475}

75. $p(h) = 9h$, where p is Sal's pay in dollars and h is the number of hours worked;
D: $30 \leq x \leq 35$; R: $270 \leq y \leq 315$

If students chose **H** in **Exercise 66,** they may not have written the equation in the form $y = ax^2 + bx + c$. Students who chose **F** may not have divided both sides by −1 when solving for y.

Journal

Have students describe relationships between a minimum or maximum, the vertex, and the range of a quadratic function.

ALTERNATIVE ASSESSMENT

Have students choose two of the quadratic functions from **Exercises 53–60,** write each in the form $y = ax^2 + bx + c$, and identify a, b, and c. Also have them identify the vertex, the minimum or maximum, the domain, and the range for each function.

Power Presentations with PowerPoint®

9-1 Lesson Quiz

1. Is $y = -x - 1$ quadratic? Explain. No; there is no x^2-term, so $a = 0$.
2. Use a table of values to graph $y = 1.5x^2$.

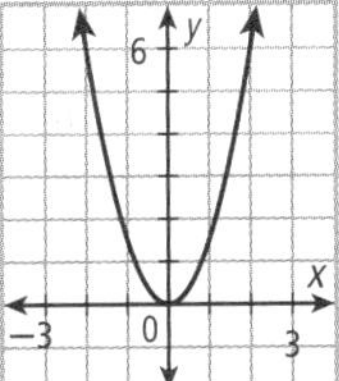

Use the graph for Problems 3–5.

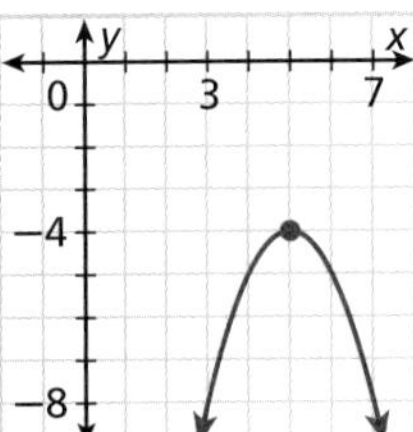

3. Identify the vertex. (5, −4)
4. Does the function have a minimum or maximum? What is it? max.; −4
5. Find the domain and range. D: all real numbers; R: $y \leq -4$

Also available on transparency

Organizer

Use with Lesson 9-2

Pacing:

Traditional $\frac{1}{2}$ day
Block $\frac{1}{4}$ day

Objective: Find the equation of the axis of symmetry for the graph of a quadratic function.

Online Edition

Countdown Week 19

Resources

Algebra Lab Activities
9-2 Lab Recording Sheet

Teach

Discuss

When there is no x-term in a quadratic function, then $b = 0$. Because 0 divided by any nonzero number is 0, the equation of the axis of symmetry for the graph of this type of function is always $x = 0$, which is the y-axis. When there is an x-term, the axis of symmetry is *not* $x = 0$.

Close

Key Concept

The equation of the axis of symmetry for the graph of a quadratic function of the form $y = ax^2 + bx + c$ is $x = -\frac{b}{2a}$.

Assessment

Journal Have students explain how to find the equation of the axis of symmetry for the graph of a quadratic function.

State Resources

Use with Lesson 9-2

Explore the Axis of Symmetry

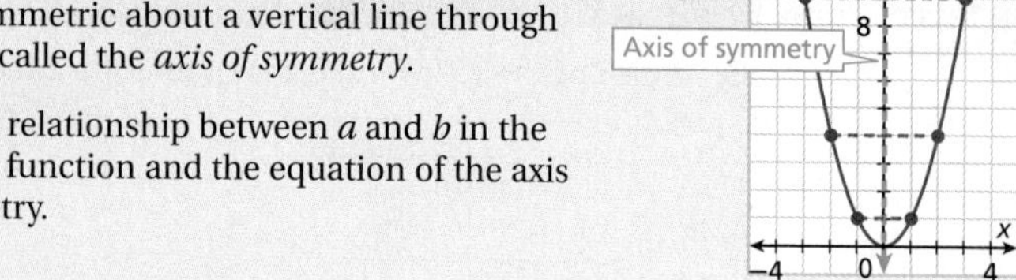

Every graph of a quadratic function is a parabola that is symmetric about a vertical line through its vertex called the *axis of symmetry*.

There is a relationship between a and b in the quadratic function and the equation of the axis of symmetry.

Activity

1 Copy and complete the table.

Function	$y = 1x^2 - 2x - 3$	$y = -2x^2 - 8x - 6$	$y = -1x^2 + 4x$
Graph			
a	1	−2	−1
b	−2	−8	4
$\frac{b}{a}$	−2	4	−4
Axis of Symmetry (from graph)	$x = 1$	$x = -2$	$x = 2$

2 Compare the axis of symmetry with $\frac{b}{a}$ in your chart. What can you multiply $\frac{b}{a}$ by to get the number in the equation of the axis of symmetry? (*Hint:* Write and solve an equation to find the value.) Check your answer for each function. $-\frac{1}{2}$

3 Use your answer from Problem 2 to complete the equation of the axis of symmetry of a quadratic function. $x =$ ___?___ $x = -\frac{1}{2}\left(\frac{b}{a}\right) = \frac{-b}{2a}$

Try This

For the graph of each quadratic function, find the equation of the axis of symmetry.

1. $y = 2x^2 + 12x - 7$ $x = -3$
2. $y = 4x^2 + 8x - 12$ $x = -1$
3. $y = 5x^2 - 20x + 10$ $x = 2$
4. $y = -3x^2 + 9x + 1$ $x = \frac{3}{2}$
5. $y = x^2 - 7$ $x = 0$
6. $y = 3x^2 + x + 4$ $x = -\frac{1}{6}$

9-2 Characteristics of Quadratic Functions

Objectives
Find the zeros of a quadratic function from its graph.

Find the axis of symmetry and the vertex of a parabola.

Vocabulary
zero of a function
axis of symmetry

Who uses this?

Engineers can use characteristics of quadratic functions to find the height of the arch supports of bridges. (See Example 5.)

Recall that an x-intercept of a function is a value of x when $y = 0$. A **zero of a function** is an x-value that makes the function equal to 0. So a zero of a function is the same as an x-intercept of a function. Since a graph intersects the x-axis at the point or points containing an x-intercept these intersections are also at the zeros of the function. A quadratic function may have one, two, or no zeros.

EXAMPLE 1 Finding Zeros of Quadratic Functions From Graphs

Find the zeros of each quadratic function from its graph. Check your answer.

A $y = x^2 - x - 2$

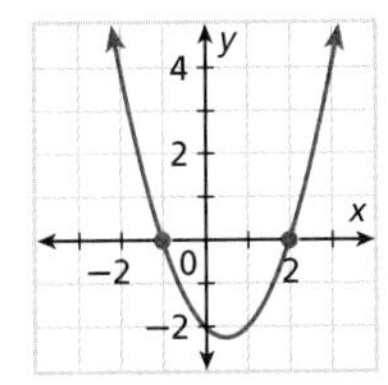

The zeros appear to be −1 and 2.

Check

$y = x^2 - x - 2$

$y = (-1)^2 - (-1) - 2$

$= 1 + 1 - 2 = 0$ ✓

$y = 2^2 - 2 - 2$

$= 4 - 2 - 2 = 0$ ✓

B $y = -2x^2 + 4x - 2$

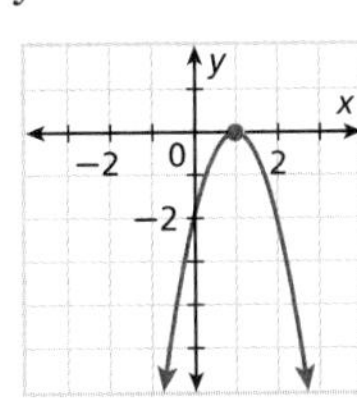

The only zero appears to be 1.

Check

$y = -2x^2 + 4x - 2$

$y = -2(1)^2 + 4(1) - 2$

$= -2(1) + 4 - 2$

$= -2 + 4 - 2$

$= 0$ ✓

C $y = \frac{1}{4}x^2 + 1$

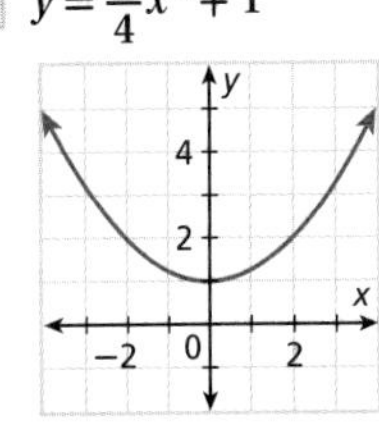

The graph does not cross the x-axis, so there are no zeros of this function.

Helpful Hint

Notice that if a parabola has only one zero, the zero is the x-coordinate of the vertex.

CHECK IT OUT! Find the zeros of each quadratic function from its graph. Check your answer.

1a. $y = -4x^2 - 2$ **no zeros**

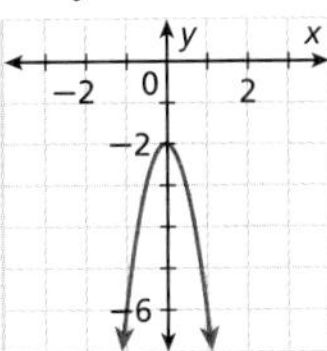

1b. $y = x^2 - 6x + 9$ **3**

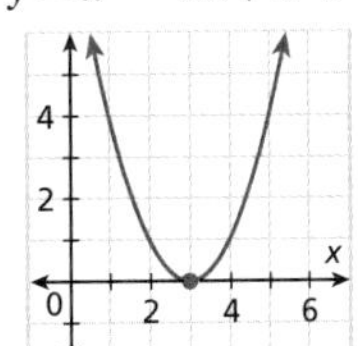

9-2 Organizer

Pacing: Traditional $1\frac{1}{2}$ days
Block $\frac{3}{4}$ day

Objectives: Find the zeros of a quadratic function from its graph.

Find the axis of symmetry and the vertex of a parabola.

Algebra Lab
In *Algebra Lab Activities*

Online Edition
Tutorial Videos

Countdown Week 19

Power Presentations with PowerPoint®

Warm Up

Find the *x*-intercept of each linear function.

1. $y = 2x - 3$ $\frac{3}{2}$
2. $y = -\frac{2}{3}x + \frac{7}{3}$ $\frac{7}{2}$
3. $y = 3x + 6$ -2

Evaluate each quadratic function for the given input values.

4. $y = -3x^2 + x - 2$, when $x = 2$ -12
5. $y = x^2 + 2x + 3$, when $x = -1$ 2

Also available on transparency

Math Humor

Q: What do functions use to take their babies out for a walk?

A: A parabolator! (A *perambulator* is a baby carriage.)

State Resources

1 Introduce

EXPLORATION

9-2 Characteristics of Quadratic Functions

In this Exploration, you will use a graphing calculator to investigate quadratic functions.

1. Enter the function $y = x^2 - 2x - 8$ as **Y1**.
2. Press [2nd] [GRAPH] to view a table of values for the function. Use the arrow keys to scroll up and down the table. For which x-values does $y = 0$?

3. Press [GRAPH] to graph the function. At which points does the graph intersect the x-axis?
4. Now enter the function $y = x^2 - x + 3$ as **Y1**.

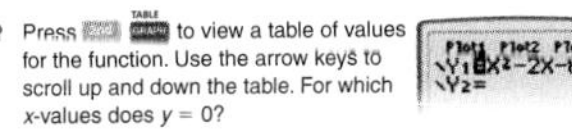

5. View a table for this function. For which x-values does $y = 0$?
6. View a graph of the function. At which points does the graph intersect the x-axis?

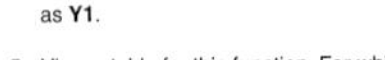

THINK AND DISCUSS

7. **Discuss** what you could conclude about the graph of a quadratic function that has only one value of x for which $y = 0$.

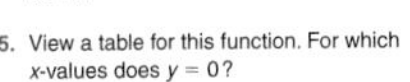

Motivate

Present students with some shapes, such as those below, and discuss lines of symmetry. Ask which shapes have a vertical line of symmetry and which have a horizontal line of symmetry.

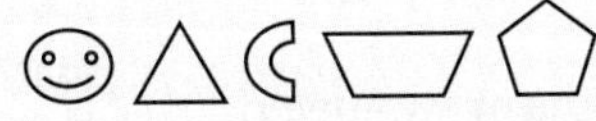

Vertical: face, triangle, trapezoid, pentagon
Horizontal: arch

Explorations and answers are provided in *Alternate Openers: Explorations Transparencies*.

go.hrw.com
State Resources Online
KEYWORD: MA7 Resources

Power Presentations with PowerPoint®

Additional Examples

Example 1

Find the zeros of each quadratic function from its graph. Check your answer.

A. $y = x^2 - 2x - 3$ −1, 3

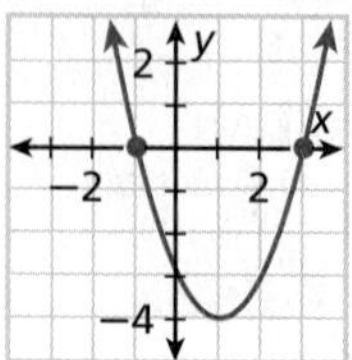

B. $y = x^2 + 8x + 16$ −4

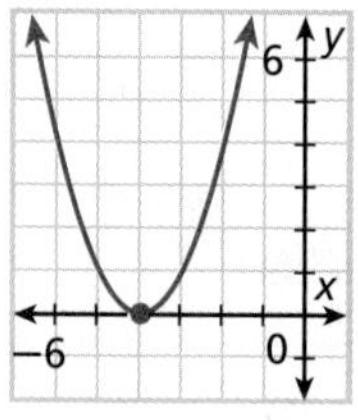

C. $y = -2x^2 - 2$ no zeros

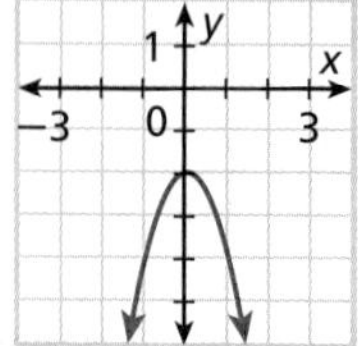

INTERVENTION

Questioning Strategies

EXAMPLE 1

- Which intercepts do you look for when looking for the zeros of a function?
- How are the zeros of a quadratic function related to the vertex of its graph?

A vertical line that divides a parabola into two symmetrical halves is the **axis of symmetry**. The axis of symmetry always passes through the vertex of the parabola. You can use the zeros to find the axis of symmetry.

Finding the Axis of Symmetry by Using Zeros

WORDS	NUMBERS	GRAPH
One Zero		
If a function has one zero, use the x-coordinate of the vertex to find the axis of symmetry.	Vertex: $(3, 0)$ Axis of symmetry: $x = 3$	$x = 3$; $(3, 0)$
Two Zeros		
If a function has two zeros, use the average of the two zeros to find the axis of symmetry.	$\frac{-4 + 0}{2} = \frac{-4}{2} = -2$ Axis of symmetry: $x = -2$	$x = -2$; $(-4, 0)$; $(0, 0)$

EXAMPLE 2 Finding the Axis of Symmetry by Using Zeros

Find the axis of symmetry of each parabola.

A

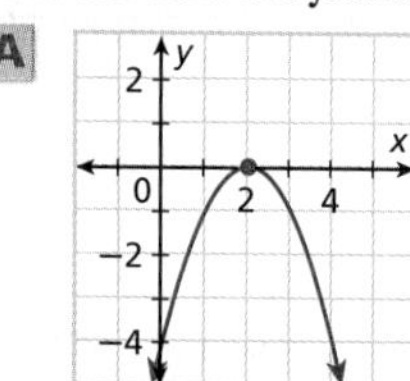

$(2, 0)$ *Identify the x-coordinate of the vertex.*

The axis of symmetry is $x = 2$.

B

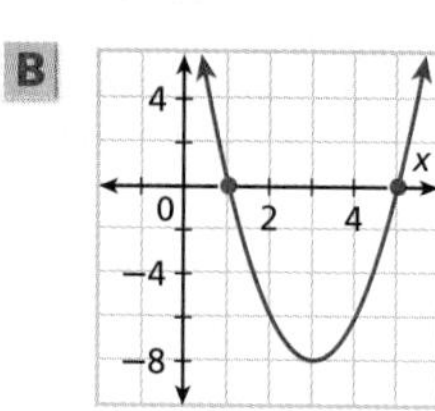

$\frac{1 + 5}{2} = \frac{6}{2} = 3$ *Find the average of the zeros.*

The axis of symmetry is $x = 3$.

Find the axis of symmetry of each parabola.

2a.

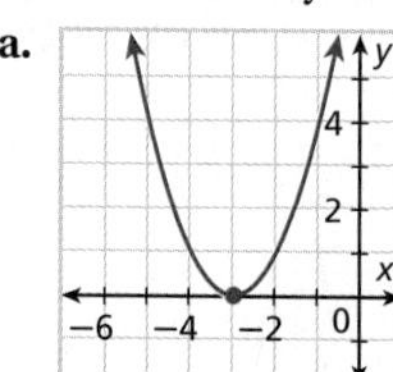

$x = -3$

2b.

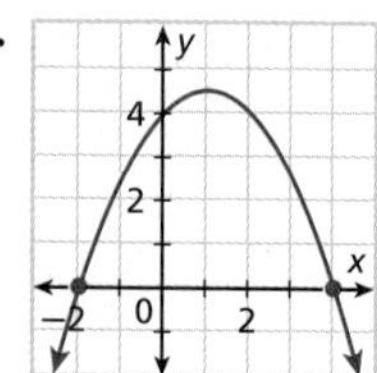

$x = 1$

2 Teach

Guided Instruction

Tell students that the zeros of a function can also be called the x-intercepts, or the x-values when $y = 0$. Explain that the x-value of the vertex is the arithmetic mean (average) of the zeros.

Geometry The axis of symmetry is a line of reflection because the figure on the left is a reflection of the figure on the right.

Reaching All Learners

Through Kinesthetic Experience

Have two students hold the ends of a jump rope at the same height from the ground. Use a measuring tape to place the students 4 feet, 6 feet, and 8 feet apart. Point out that the lowest point of the jump rope is always halfway between the students. If there is space in the room, have the two students swing the rope. Show the class that when the rope is overhead, its highest point is also halfway between the two students.

If a function has no zeros or they are difficult to identify from a graph, you can use a formula to find the axis of symmetry. The formula works for all quadratic functions.

Finding the Axis of Symmetry by Using the Formula

FORMULA	EXAMPLE
For a quadratic function $y = ax^2 + bx + c$, the axis of symmetry is the vertical line $x = -\frac{b}{2a}$.	$y = 2x^2 + 4x + 5$ $x = -\frac{b}{2a}$ $= -\frac{4}{2(2)} = -1$ The axis of symmetry is $x = -1$.

EXAMPLE 3 Finding the Axis of Symmetry by Using the Formula

Find the axis of symmetry of the graph of $y = x^2 + 3x + 4$.

Step 1 Find the values of a and b.
$y = 1x^2 + 3x + 4$
$a = 1, b = 3$

Step 2 Use the formula $x = -\frac{b}{2a}$.
$x = -\frac{3}{2(1)} = -\frac{3}{2} = -1.5$

The axis of symmetry is $x = -1.5$.

3. Find the axis of symmetry of the graph of $y = 2x^2 + x + 3$.

$x = -\frac{1}{4}$

Once you have found the axis of symmetry, you can use it to identify the vertex.

Finding the Vertex of a Parabola
Step 1 To find the x-coordinate of the vertex, find the axis of symmetry by using zeros or the formula.
Step 2 To find the corresponding y-coordinate, substitute the x-coordinate of the vertex into the function.
Step 3 Write the vertex as an ordered pair.

EXAMPLE 4 Finding the Vertex of a Parabola

Find the vertex.

A $y = -x^2 - 2x$

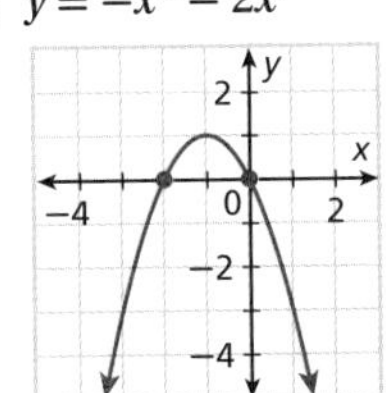

Step 1 Find the x-coordinate.
The zeros are −2 and 0.
$x = \frac{-2 + 0}{2} = \frac{-2}{2} = -1$

Step 2 Find the corresponding y-coordinate.
$y = -x^2 - 2x$ *Use the function rule.*
$= -(-1)^2 - 2(-1) = 1$ *Substitute −1 for x.*

Step 3 Write the ordered pair.
$(-1, 1)$

The vertex is $(-1, 1)$.

Caution!
In Example 4A Step 2, use the order of operations to simplify.
$-(-1)^2 = -(1) = -1$

Power Presentations with PowerPoint®

Additional Examples

Example 2

Find the axis of symmetry of each parabola.

A.

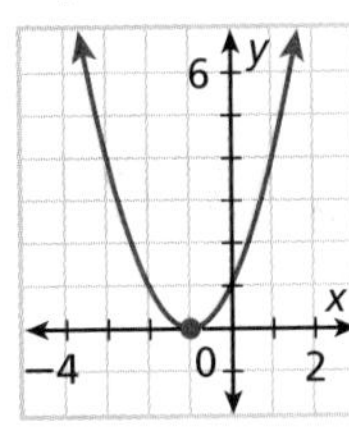

$x = -1$

B.

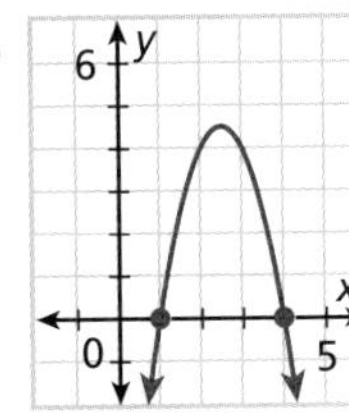

$x = 2.5$

Example 3

Find the axis of symmetry of the graph of $y = -3x^2 + 10x + 9$.

$x = \frac{5}{3}$

INTERVENTION

Questioning Strategies

EXAMPLE 2

- What does the axis of symmetry tell you about the graph?

EXAMPLE 3

- What values are used in the formula for the axis of symmetry?

Teaching Tip **Multiple Representations** Encourage students to use the formula to find the axis of symmetry when the zeros do not appear to be integers.

Teaching Tip

Inclusion Remind students that when there appears to be no coefficient for a variable term, the coefficient is 1, and when there is a term missing, the coefficient of the term or the constant is 0.

Power Presentations with PowerPoint®

Additional Examples

Example 4

Find the vertex.

A. $y = 0.25x^2 + 2x + 3$ $(-4, -1)$

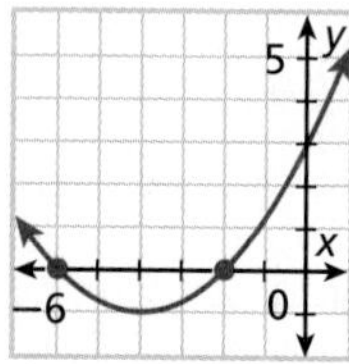

B. $y = -3x^2 + 6x - 7$ $(1, -4)$

Example 5

The graph of $f(x) = -0.06x^2 + 0.6x + 10.26$ can be used to model the height in meters of an arch support for a bridge, where x represents the horizontal distance in meters from where the arch support enters the water. Can a sailboat that is 14 meters tall pass under the bridge? Explain. Since the highest point of the support is 11.76 m above the water, the sailboat cannot pass under the bridge.

INTERVENTION

Questioning Strategies

EXAMPLE 4

- What is the relationship between the vertex and axis of symmetry?

EXAMPLE 5

- What do the zeros represent?
- What part of the graph do you need to find?

Find the vertex.

B $y = 5x^2 - 10x + 3$

Step 1 Find the x-coordinate.

$a = 5, b = -10$ *Identify a and b.*

$x = -\frac{b}{2a}$

$= -\frac{-10}{2(5)} = -\frac{-10}{10} = 1$ *Substitute 5 for a and −10 for b.*

The x-coordinate of the vertex is 1.

Step 2 Find the corresponding y-coordinate.

$y = 5x^2 - 10x + 3$ *Use the function rule.*

$= 5(1)^2 - 10(1) + 3$ *Substitute 1 for x.*

$= 5 - 10 + 3$

$= -2$

Step 3 Write the ordered pair.

The vertex is $(1, -2)$.

4. Find the vertex of the graph of $y = x^2 - 4x - 10$. **(2, −14)**

EXAMPLE 5 *Architecture Application*

The height above water level of a curved arch support for a bridge can be modeled by $f(x) = -0.007x^2 + 0.84x + 0.8$, where x is the distance in feet from where the arch support enters the water. Can a sailboat that is 24 feet tall pass under the bridge? Explain.

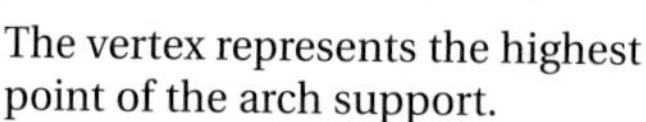

The vertex represents the highest point of the arch support.

Step 1 Find the x-coordinate.

$a = -0.007, b = 0.84$ *Identify a and b.*

$x = -\frac{b}{2a}$

$= -\frac{0.84}{2(-0.007)} = 60$ *Substitute −0.007 for a and 0.84 for b.*

Step 2 Find the corresponding y-coordinate.

$f(x) = -0.007x^2 + 0.84x + 0.8$ *Use the function rule.*

$= -0.007(60)^2 + 0.84(60) + 0.8$ *Substitute 60 for x.*

$= 26$

Since the height of the arch support is 26 feet, the sailboat can pass under the bridge.

5. The height of a small rise in a roller coaster track is modeled by $f(x) = -0.07x^2 + 0.42x + 6.37$, where x is the horizontal distance in feet from a support pole at ground level. Find the greatest height of the rise. **7 ft**

3 Close

Summarize

Review how to find the zeros of a function, the vertex, and the axis of symmetry from the graph. Remind students that there may not always be two zeros. Review how to find the axis of symmetry using the formula and how to determine the y-value of the vertex by substituting the value for x in the quadratic function.

ONGOING ASSESSMENT and INTERVENTION

***Diagnose Before* the Lesson**
9-2 Warm Up, TE p. 619

***Monitor During* the Lesson**
Check It Out! Exercises, SE pp. 619–622
Questioning Strategies, TE pp. 620–622

***Assess After* the Lesson**
9-2 Lesson Quiz, TE p. 625
Alternative Assessment, TE p. 625

THINK AND DISCUSS

1. How do you find the zeros of a function from its graph?
2. Describe how to find the axis of symmetry of a quadratic function if its graph does not cross the x-axis
3. **GET ORGANIZED** Copy and complete the graphic organizer. In each box, sketch a graph that fits the given description.

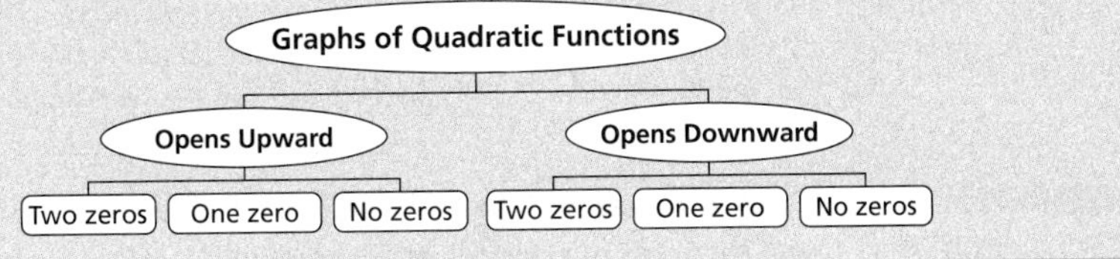

Answers to *Think and Discuss*

Possible answers:

1. Find the point(s) where the graph intersects the x-axis. The values of the x-coordinates are the zeros.
2. Using the quadratic function, $y = ax^2 + bx + c$, find the values of a, b, and c. Then use the formula $x = -\frac{b}{2a}$ to find the equation of the axis of symmetry.
3. See p. A8.

9-2 Exercises

GUIDED PRACTICE

Vocabulary Apply the vocabulary from this lesson to answer each question.

1. Why is the *zero of a function* the same as an x-intercept of a function?
2. Where is the *axis of symmetry* of a parabola located?

SEE EXAMPLE 1 p. 619

Find the zeros of each quadratic function from its graph. Check your answer.

3. $y = x^2 + 2x + 1$

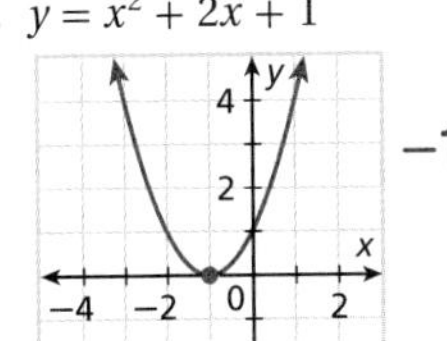

−1

4. $y = 9 - x^2$

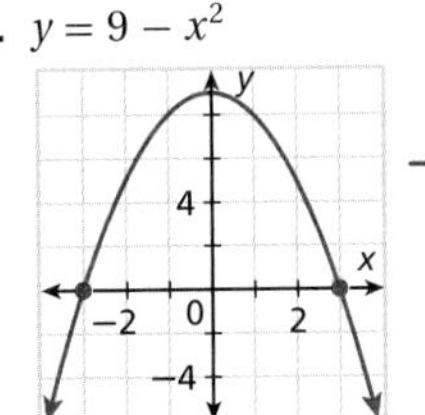

−3, 3

5. $y = -x^2 - x - 4$

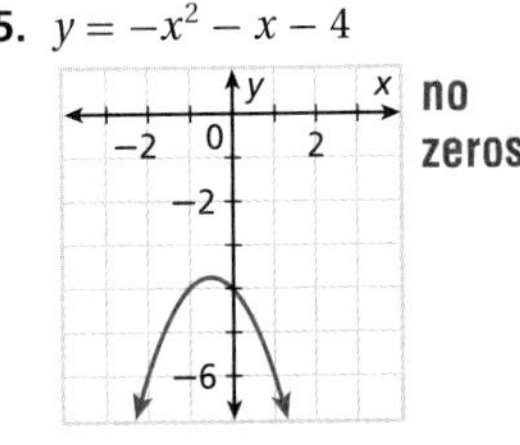

no zeros

SEE EXAMPLE 2 p. 620

Find the axis of symmetry of each parabola.

6.

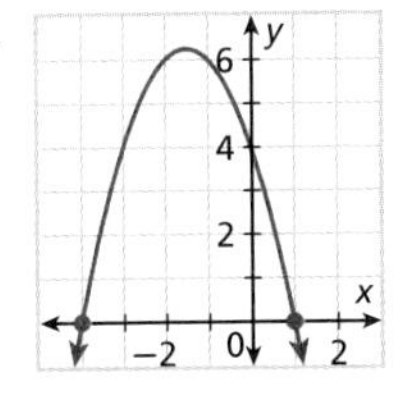

$\mathbf{x = -\frac{3}{2}}$

7.

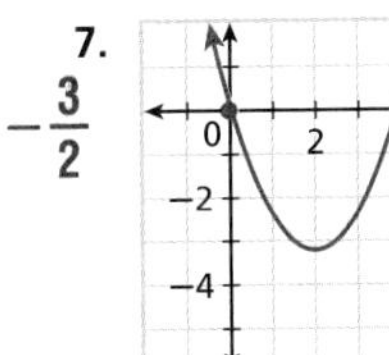

$\mathbf{x = 2}$

8.

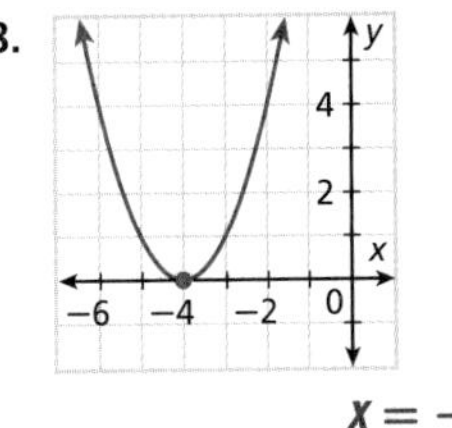

$\mathbf{x = -4}$

SEE EXAMPLE 3 p. 621

For each quadratic function, find the axis of symmetry of its graph.

9. $y = x^2 + 4x - 7$ $\mathbf{x = -2}$
10. $y = 3x^2 - 18x + 1$ $\mathbf{x = 3}$
11. $y = 2x^2 + 3x - 4$ $\mathbf{x = -\frac{3}{4}}$
12. $y = -3x^2 + x + 5$ $\mathbf{x = \frac{1}{6}}$

Answers

1. An x-intercept is a value of x where $f(x) = 0$.
2. The axis of symmetry is the vertical line passing through the vertex that divides the parabola into 2 symmetric halves.

9-2 Exercises

Assignment Guide

Assign *Guided Practice* exercises as necessary.

If you finished Examples **1–3**
- **Basic** 19–28, 37–39
- **Average** 19–28, 37–39, 44
- **Advanced** 19–28, 37–39, 44

If you finished Examples **1–5**
- **Basic** 19–34, 36–43, 46–52
- **Average** 19–44, 46–52
- **Advanced** 19–52

Homework Quick Check
Quickly check key concepts.
Exercises: 20, 22, 26, 30, 34

State Resources

go.hrw.com
State Resources Online
KEYWORD: MA7 Resources

MULTI-STEP TEST PREP Exercise 36 involves finding the vertex of a parabola and telling what it represents. This exercise prepares students for the Multi-Step Test Prep on page 640.

SEE EXAMPLE 4 p. 621

Find the vertex.

13. $y = -5x^2 + 10x + 3$ **(1, 8)**
14. $y = x^2 + 4x - 7$ **(−2, −11)**
15. $y = \frac{1}{2}x^2 + 2x$ **(−2, −2)**
16. $y = -x^2 + 6x + 1$ **(3, 10)**
17. $y = x^2 + 4x - 5$ **(−2, −9)**

SEE EXAMPLE 5 p. 622

18. **Archery** The height in feet above the ground of an arrow after it is shot can be modeled by $y = -16t^2 + 63t + 4$. Can the arrow pass over a tree that is 68 feet tall? Explain. **No; the highest the arrow will go is about 66 feet.**

PRACTICE AND PROBLEM SOLVING

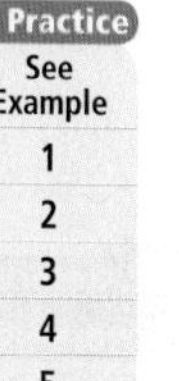

Independent Practice

For Exercises	See Example
19–21	1
22–24	2
25–28	3
29–33	4
34	5

Extra Practice
Skills Practice p. S20
Application Practice p. S36

Find the zeros of each quadratic function from its graph. Check your answer.

19. $y = \frac{1}{4}x^2 - x + 3$

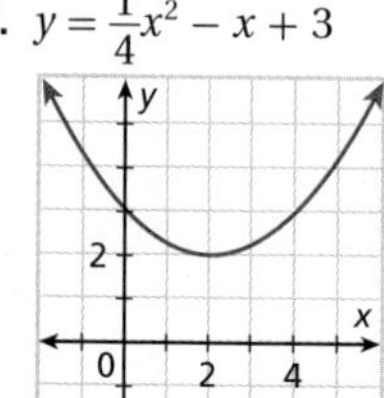

no zeros

20. $y = -\frac{1}{3}x^2$

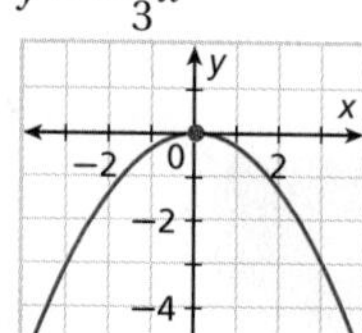
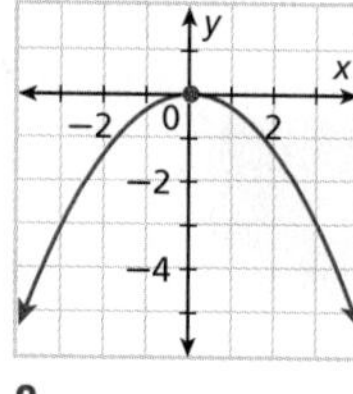

0

21. $y = x^2 + 10x + 16$

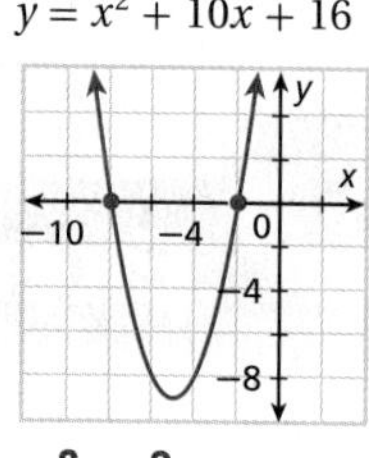

−8, −2

Find the axis of symmetry of each parabola.

22.

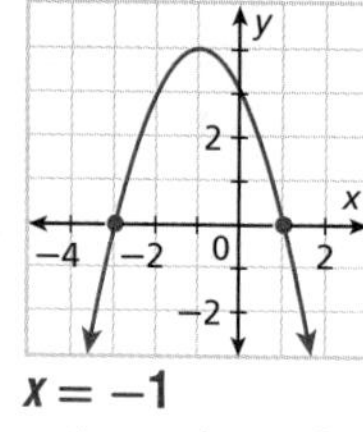

$x = -1$

23.

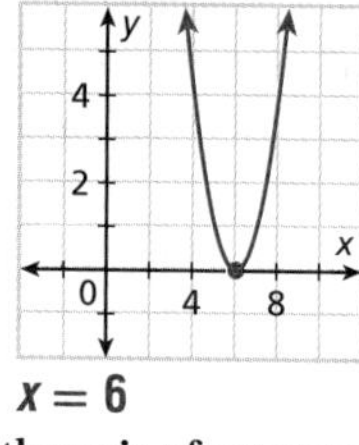

$x = 6$

24.

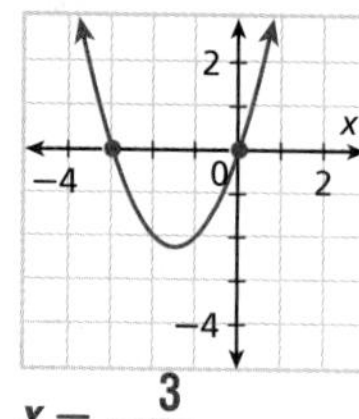

$x = -\frac{3}{2}$

For each quadratic function, find the axis of symmetry of its graph.

25. $y = x^2 + x + 2$ **$x = -\frac{1}{2}$**
26. $y = 3x^2 - 2x - 6$ **$x = \frac{1}{3}$**
27. $y = \frac{1}{2}x^2 - 5x + 4$ **$x = 5$**
28. $y = -2x^2 + \frac{1}{3}x - \frac{3}{4}$ **$x = \frac{1}{12}$**

Find the vertex.

29. $y = x^2 + 7x$ **(−3.5, −12.25)**
30. $y = -x^2 + 8x + 16$ **(4, 32)**
31. $y = -2x^2 - 8x - 3$ **(−2, 5)**
32. $y = -x^2 + \frac{1}{2}x + 2$ **$\left(\frac{1}{4}, 2\frac{1}{16}\right)$**
33.

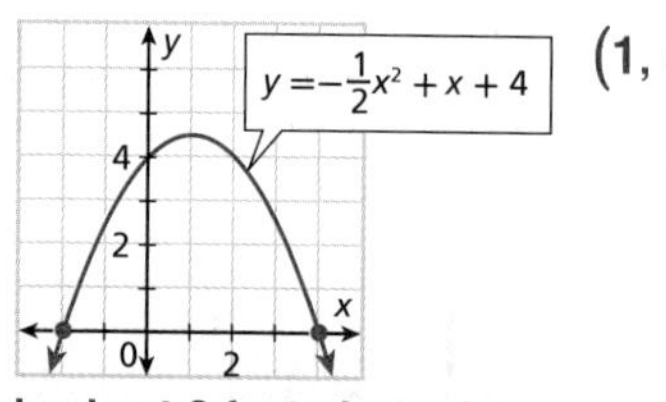

(1, 4.5)

LINK Engineering

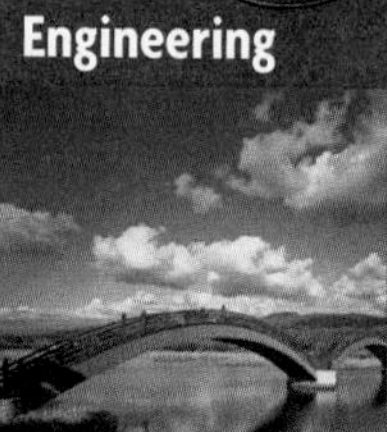

This arched bridge spans a river near the city of Yokote in northwestern Japan.

34. **Engineering** The height in feet of the curved arch support for a bridge over a creek can be modeled by $f(x) = -0.628x^2 + 4.5x$, where x is the horizontal distance in feet from where the arch support enters the water. If there is a flood that raises the level of the creek by 5.5 feet, will the top of the arch support be above the water? Explain. **Yes; the highest point of the arch support is about 8 feet above the creek.**

35. **Critical Thinking** What conclusion can be drawn about the axis of symmetry of any quadratic function for which $b = 0$? **The axis of symmetry is the y-axis or $x = 0$.**

9-2 PRACTICE A
9-2 PRACTICE C
9-2 PRACTICE B

Find the zeros of each quadratic function from its graph.

1. −6 and 1
2. no zeros
3. 5

Find the axis of symmetry of each parabola.

4. $x = \frac{7}{2}$
5. $x = 3$
6. $x = -1$

For each quadratic function, find the axis of symmetry of its graph.

7. $y = 3x^2 - 6x + 4$ $x = 1$
8. $y = -x^2 + 4x$ $x = 2$
9. $y = 4x^2 + \frac{1}{2}x + 3$ $x = -\frac{1}{16}$

Find the vertex of each parabola.

10. $y = 3x^2 - 6x - 2$ (1, −5)
11. $y = 3x^2 + 12x - 10$ (−2, −22)
12. $y = x^2 + 2x - 35$ (−1, −36)

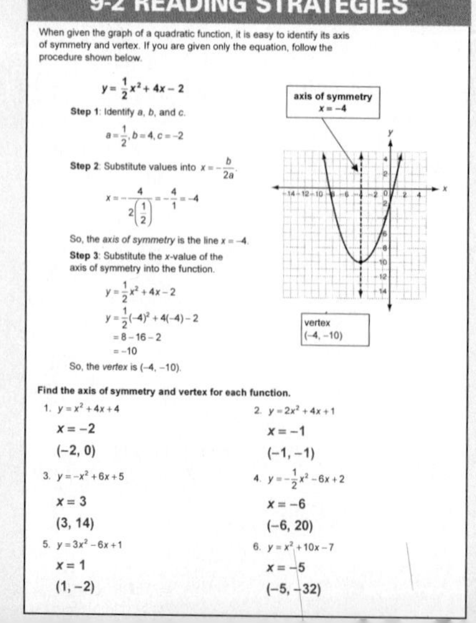

9-2 READING STRATEGIES

When given the graph of a quadratic function, it is easy to identify its axis of symmetry and vertex. If you are given only the equation, follow the procedure shown below.

$y = \frac{1}{2}x^2 + 4x - 2$

Step 1: Identify a, b, and c. $a = \frac{1}{2}, b = 4, c = -2$

Step 2: Substitute values into $x = -\frac{b}{2a}$. $x = -\frac{4}{2\left(\frac{1}{2}\right)} = -\frac{4}{1} = -4$

So, the axis of symmetry is the line $x = -4$.

Step 3: Substitute the x-value of the axis of symmetry into the function.

$y = \frac{1}{2}x^2 + 4x - 2$
$y = \frac{1}{2}(-4)^2 + 4(-4) - 2$
$= 8 - 16 - 2$
$= -10$

So, the vertex is (−4, −10).

axis of symmetry $x = -4$
vertex (−4, −10)

Find the axis of symmetry and vertex for each function.

1. $y = x^2 + 4x + 4$ $x = -2$ (−2, 0)
2. $y = 2x^2 + 4x + 1$ $x = -1$ (−1, −1)
3. $y = -x^2 + 6x + 5$ $x = 3$ (3, 14)
4. $y = -\frac{1}{2}x^2 - 6x + 2$ $x = -6$ (−6, 20)
5. $y = 3x^2 - 6x + 1$ $x = 1$ (1, −2)
6. $y = x^2 + 10x - 7$ $x = -5$ (−5, −32)

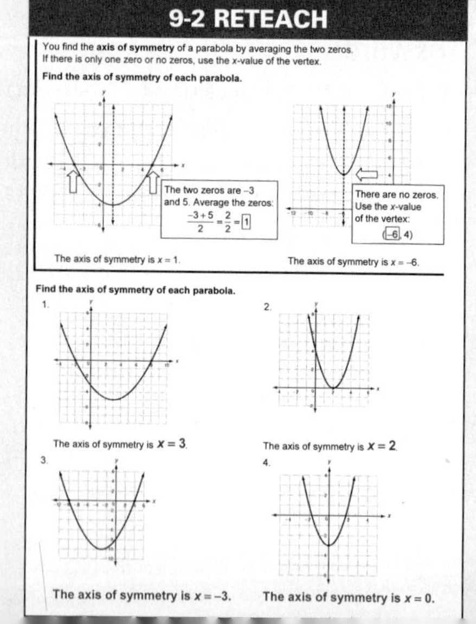

9-2 RETEACH

You find the **axis of symmetry** of a parabola by averaging the two zeros. If there is only one zero or no zeros, use the x-value of the vertex.

Find the axis of symmetry of each parabola.

The two zeros are −3 and 5. Average the zeros: $\frac{-3+5}{2} = \frac{2}{2} = 1$

The axis of symmetry is $x = 1$.

There are no zeros. Use the x-value of the vertex: (−6, 4)

The axis of symmetry is $x = -6$.

Find the axis of symmetry of each parabola.

1. The axis of symmetry is $x = 3$.
2. The axis of symmetry is $x = 2$.
3. The axis of symmetry is $x = -3$.
4. The axis of symmetry is $x = 0$.

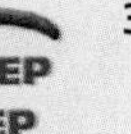

MULTI-STEP TEST PREP

36. This problem will prepare you for the Multi-Step Test Prep on page 640.
    a. Use the graph of the height of a water bottle rocket to estimate the coordinates of the parabola's vertex.
    b. What does the vertex represent?
    c. Find the zeros of the function. What do they represent?
    d. Find the axis of symmetry. How is it related to the vertex and the zeros?

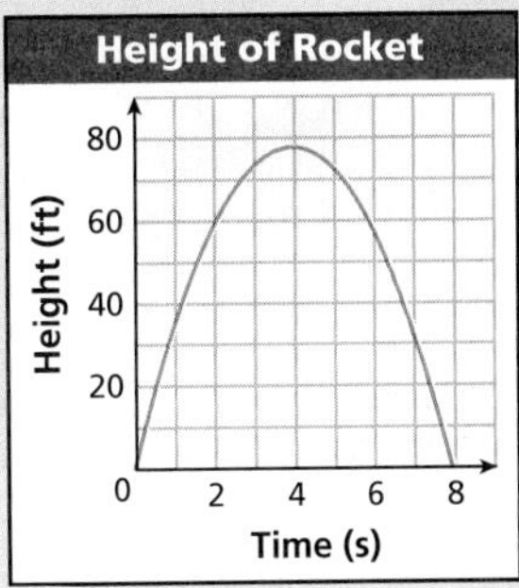

Graphing Calculator Tell how many zeros each quadratic function has.

37. $y = 8x^2 - 4x + 2$ **0**
38. $0 = y + 16x^2$ **1**
39. $\frac{1}{4}x^2 - 7x - 12 = y - 4$ **2**

40. **Write About It** If you are given the axis of symmetry of a quadratic function and know that the function has two zeros, how would you describe the location of the two zeros? **The two zeros are on either side of the axis of symmetry and are equidistant from it.**

TEST PREP

41. Which function has the zeros shown in the graph?
    Ⓐ $y = x^2 + 2x + 8$
    Ⓑ $y = x^2 - 2x - 8$ (circled)
    Ⓒ $y = x^2 + 2x - 8$
    Ⓓ $y = 2x^2 - 2x + 8$

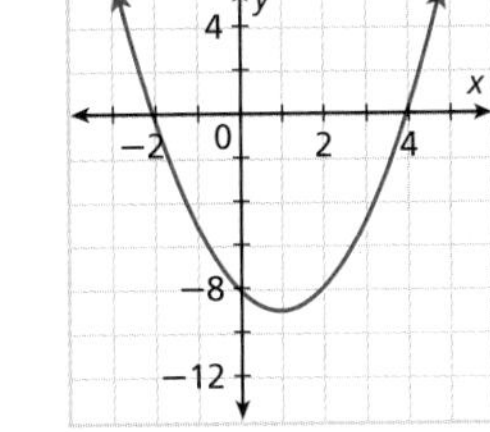

42. Which of the following functions has a graph with an axis of symmetry of $x = -\frac{1}{2}$?
    Ⓕ $y = 2x^2 - 2x + 5$
    Ⓖ $2x + 5 = 2x^2 - y$
    Ⓗ $2x^2 + y = 2x + 5$
    Ⓙ $2x - y = 5 - 2x^2$ (circled)

43. **Gridded Response** For the graph of $f(x) = -3 + 20x - 5x^2$, what is the x-coordinate of its vertex? **2**

CHALLENGE AND EXTEND

44. The domain is all real numbers, and the range is $y \leq 0$.

44. Describe the domain and range of a quadratic function that has exactly one zero and whose graph opens downward.

45. **Graphing Calculator** The height in feet of a parabolic bridge support is modeled by $f(x) = -0.01x^2 + 20$, where $y = -5$ represents ground level and the x-axis represents the middle of the bridge. Find the height and the width of the bridge support. **25 ft; 100 ft**

50. No; $a = 0$.

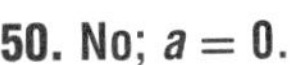

SPIRAL REVIEW

51. Yes; the function can be written in the form $y = ax^2 + bx + c$.

52. Yes; the function can be written in the form $y = ax^2 + bx + c$.

46. The value of y varies directly with x, and $y = -4$ when $x = 2$. Find y when $x = 6$. **−12** *(Lesson 5-6)*

Write each equation in slope-intercept form. *(Lesson 5-7)*

47. $2x + y = 3$ **$y = -2x + 3$**
48. $4y = 12x - 8$ **$y = 3x - 2$**
49. $10 - 5y = 20x$ **$y = -4x + 2$**

Tell whether each function is quadratic. Explain. *(Lesson 9-1)*

50. $y = 5x - 7$
51. $x^2 - 5x = 2 + y$
52. $y = -x^2 - 6x$

TEST PREP DOCTOR + In Exercise 41, remind students that they can determine the y-intercept by substituting 0 for x. Students can immediately eliminate **A** and **D** because the graphs of those functions cross the y-axis at 8, not −8.

Answers

36a. about (4, 78)
b. the time and height at the moment when the rocket was at its highest point
c. 0 and 8; the starting and ending times in seconds
d. $x = 4$; the x-value of the axis of symmetry is the average of the two zeros; it is also the x-coordinate of the vertex.

Journal

Have students explain how the vertex and the axis of symmetry are related graphically and algebraically.

ALTERNATIVE ASSESSMENT

Have students create two quadratic functions: one with one zero and the other with two zeros. Have them state the zeros, the axis of symmetry, and the vertex for each.

Power Presentations with PowerPoint®

9-2 Lesson Quiz

1. Find the zeros and the axis of symmetry of the parabola.

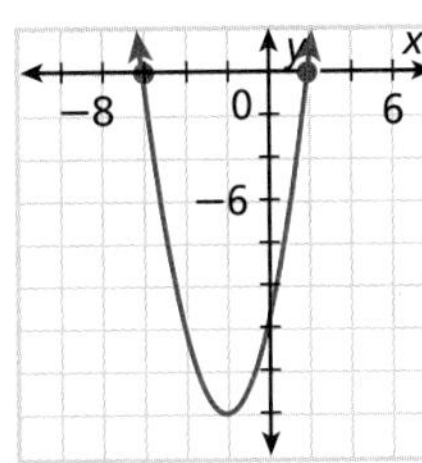

zeros: −6, 2; $x = -2$

2. Find the axis of symmetry and the vertex of the graph of $y = 3x^2 + 12x + 8$. $x = -2$; $(-2, -4)$
3. The graph of $f(x) = -0.01x^2 + x$ can be used to model the height in feet of a curved arch support for a bridge, where x represents the horizontal distance in feet from where the arch support enters the water. Find the height of the highest point of the support. 25 ft

Also available on transparency

9-2 PROBLEM SOLVING

Write the correct answer.

1. A superhero is trying to leap over a tall building. The function $f(x) = -16x^2 + 200x$ gives the superhero's height in feet as a function of time. The building is 612 feet high. Will the superhero make it over the building? Explain.
   Yes; the vertex is (6.25, 625) and 625 > 612
2. The graph shows the height of an arch support for a pedestrian bridge.

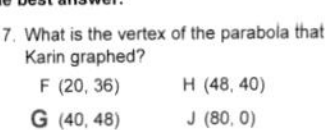

   Find the zeros (if any) and axis of symmetry of this parabola.
   0 and 50
   $x = 25$
3. The distance between the cables suspending a bridge and the water below is given by the function $y = 0.02x^2 - 2x + 80$. Find the vertex of the graph.
   (50, 30)

After a heavy snowfall, Joe and Karin made an igloo. The dome of the igloo is in the shape of a parabola and the height of the igloo in inches is given by $f(x) = -0.03x^2 + 2.4x$. Select the best answer.

4. Joe wants to place a support in the middle of the igloo, along the axis of symmetry. How far from the edge of the igloo should he place the support?
   A 24 in. C 48 in.
   B 40 in. D 80 in.
5. Neither Joe nor Karin can stand up inside the igloo. How tall is the center of the igloo? (*Hint:* the top of the igloo is the vertex of the parabola.)
   F 24 in. **H** 48 in.
   G 40 in. J 80 in.
6. Karin graphs the parabola and looks at the zeros to see how wide the igloo is. What are the zeros of this parabola?
   A −80 and 80 **C** 0 and 80
   B −40 and 40 D 40 and 80
7. What is the vertex of the parabola that Karin graphed?
   F (20, 36) H (48, 40)
   G (40, 48) J (80, 0)
8. Which graph below is the graph that Karin made?

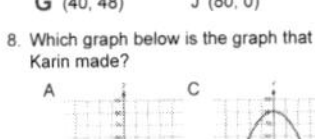

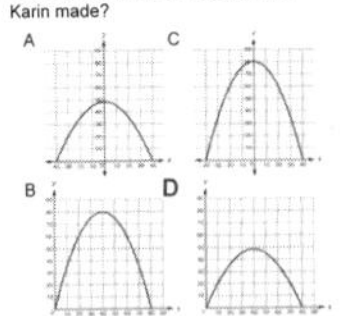

9-2 CHALLENGE

You may recall from Chapter 5 that for any *two* points, there is exactly one *line* that contains both. You used this property to find the equation of a line that passes through two given points.

A similar property exists for parabolas — for any *three* points, there is exactly one *parabola* that contains all three. You'll use this property to find the quadratic function that passes through three given points.

Follow these steps to find the quadratic function for this graph.

1. Name the coordinates of the two x-intercepts and the vertex.
   (−6, 0) **(−3, −9)** **(0, 0)**
2. Substitute each pair of coordinates into the general quadratic function $y = ax^2 + bx + c$, and simplify. You will get three *linear* equations with the variables a, b, and c.
   $0 = 36a - 6b + c$
   $-9 = 9a - 3b + c$
   $0 = c$
3. Treat the three linear equations in question 2 as a system. Use substitution and elimination to find the values of a, b, and c.
   $a =$ **1**, $b =$ **6**, $c =$ **0**
4. Substitute the values of a, b, and c into the general function $y = ax^2 + bx + c$. What is the specific quadratic function for the graph above? **$y = x^2 + 6x$**

Use a similar process to find these quadratic functions.

5. The quadratic function for the graph at right.
   $0 = 9a - 3b + c$; $18 = c$; $0 = 9a + 3b + c$; $y = -2x^2 + 18$

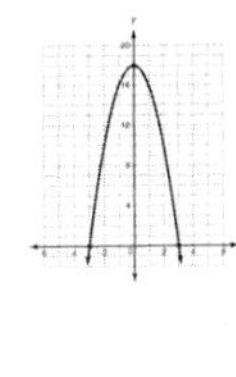

6. The quadratic function that passes through the points (−5, 0), (2, 0), and (−1.5, −12.25).
   $0 = 25a - 5b + c$; $0 = 4a + 2b + c$; $-12.25 = 2.25a - 1.5b + c$; $y = x^2 + 3x - 10$

9-3 Organizer

Pacing: Traditional 1 day
Block $\frac{1}{2}$ day

Objective: Graph a quadratic function in the form $y = ax^2 + bx + c$.

Algebra Lab
In *Algebra Lab Activities*

Online Edition
Tutorial Videos

Countdown Week 19

Power Presentations with PowerPoint®

Warm Up

Find the axis of symmetry.

1. $y = 4x^2 - 7$ $\quad x = 0$
2. $y = x^2 - 3x + 1$ $\quad x = \frac{3}{2}$
3. $y = -2x^2 + 4x + 3$ $\quad x = 1$
4. $y = -2x^2 + 3x - 1$ $\quad x = \frac{3}{4}$

Find the vertex.

5. $y = x^2 + 4x + 5$ $\quad (-2, 1)$
6. $y = 3x^2 + 2$ $\quad (0, 2)$
7. $y = 2x^2 + 2x - 8$ $\quad \left(-\frac{1}{2}, -\frac{17}{2}\right)$

Also available on transparency

Math Humor

Q: What do you call a tough old quadratic equation?

A: A battle-ax².

9-3 Graphing Quadratic Functions

Objective
Graph a quadratic function in the form $y = ax^2 + bx + c$.

Why use this?
Graphs of quadratic functions can help you determine how high an object is tossed or kicked. (See Exercise 14.)

Recall that a y-intercept is the y-coordinate of the point where a graph intersects the y-axis. The x-coordinate of this point is always 0. For a quadratic function written in the form $y = ax^2 + bx + c$, when $x = 0$, $y = c$. So the y-intercept of a quadratic function is c.

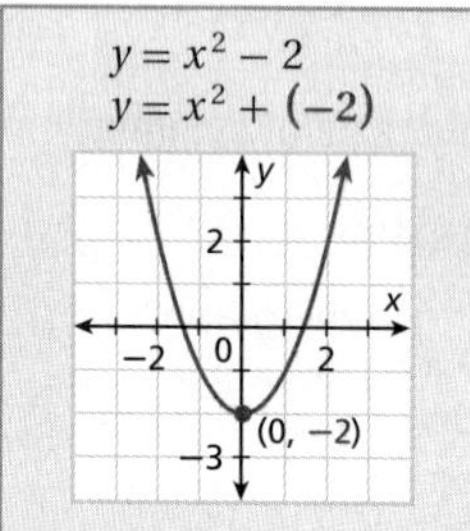

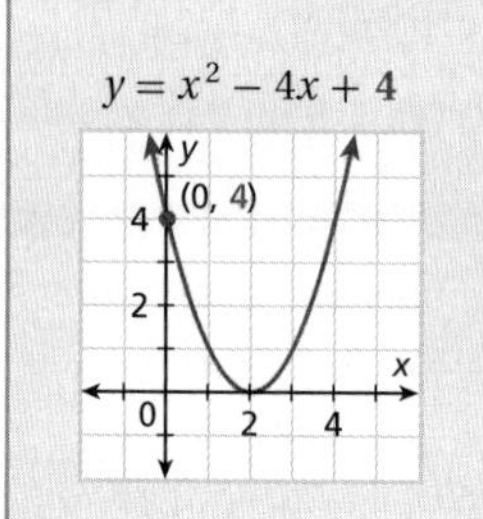

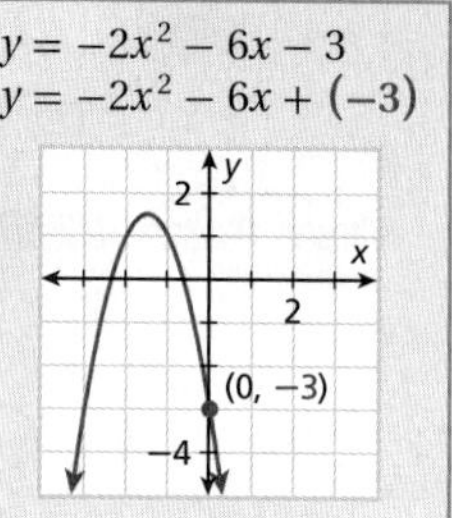

In the previous lesson, you found the axis of symmetry and vertex of a parabola. You can use these characteristics, the y-intercept, and symmetry to graph a quadratic function.

EXAMPLE 1 Graphing a Quadratic Function

Graph $y = x^2 - 4x - 5$.

Step 1 Find the axis of symmetry.

$x = -\frac{-4}{2(1)}$ *Use $x = -\frac{b}{2a}$. Substitute 1 for a and −4 for b.*

$= 2$ *Simplify.*

The axis of symmetry is $x = 2$.

Step 2 Find the vertex.

$y = x^2 - 4x - 5$

$= 2^2 - 4(2) - 5$ *The x-coordinate of the vertex is 2. Substitute 2 for x.*

$= 4 - 8 - 5$ *Simplify.*

$= -9$ *The y-coordinate is −9.*

The vertex is $(2, -9)$.

Step 3 Find the y-intercept.

$y = x^2 - 4x - 5$

$y = x^2 - 4x + (-5)$ *Identify c.*

The y-intercept is -5; the graph passes through $(0, -5)$.

1 Introduce

EXPLORATION

9-3 Graphing Quadratic Functions

Recall that a y-intercept is the y-coordinate of a point where a graph intersects the y-axis. Use a graphing calculator to explore the y-intercepts of some quadratic functions.

1. Use your calculator to graph each of the quadratic functions in the table. For each function, use the graph to identify the y-intercept.

Function	y-intercept
$y = x^2 - 2x + 3$	
$y = x^2 + x - 6$	
$y = -2x^2 + 3x + 4$	
$y = -\frac{1}{2}x^2 - x - 2$	
$y = 3x^2 - 5x$	

2. Look for a pattern in your table. In general, what can you say about the y-intercept of a quadratic function written in the form $y = ax^2 + bx + c$?
3. Without graphing the function, determine the y-intercept of $y = 4x^2 - 7x - 8$.

THINK AND DISCUSS

4. **Explain** how knowing the y-intercept of a quadratic function can help you sketch its graph.

Motivate

Discuss with students how the more they know about the properties of a geometric figure, the easier it is for them to sketch an accurate drawing of it. For example, if you know the length of a rectangle, you have only part of the information you need to draw it accurately. If you also know the width of the rectangle, then you can make an accurate drawing. Tell students that in this lesson they will learn to use the properties of parabolas to graph them.

Explorations and answers are provided in *Alternate Openers: Explorations Transparencies*.

State Resources

go.hrw.com
State Resources Online
KEYWORD: MA7 Resources

Step 4 Find two more points on the same side of the axis of symmetry as the point containing the y-intercept.

Since the axis of symmetry is $x = 2$, choose x-values less than 2.

Let $x = 1$.		Let $x = -1$.
$y = 1^2 - 4(1) - 5$	*Substitute x-coordinates.*	$y = (-1)^2 - 4(-1) - 5$
$= 1 - 4 - 5$	*Simplify.*	$= 1 + 4 - 5$
$= -8$		$= 0$

Two other points are $(1, -8)$ and $(-1, 0)$.

Helpful Hint

Because a parabola is symmetrical, each point is the same number of units away from the axis of symmetry as its reflected point.

Step 5 Graph the axis of symmetry, the vertex, the point containing the y-intercept, and two other points.

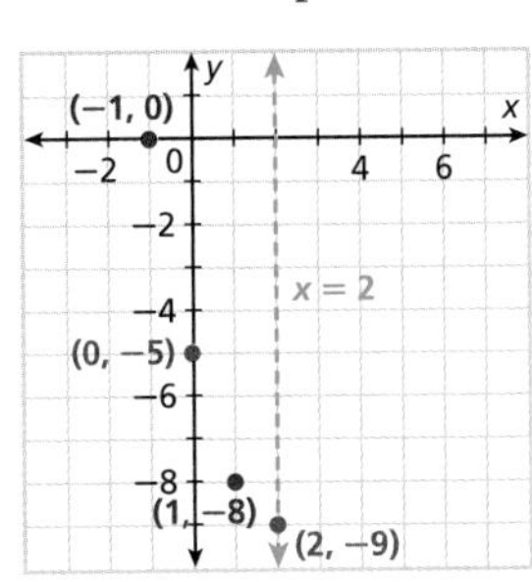

Step 6 Reflect the points across the axis of symmetry. Connect the points with a smooth curve.

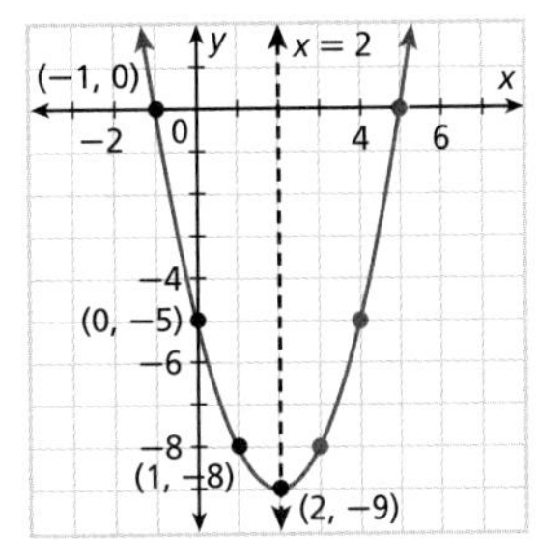

Graph each quadratic function.

1a. $y = 2x^2 + 6x + 2$ **1b.** $y + 6x = x^2 + 9$

1a.

1b.

EXAMPLE 2 *Problem-Solving Application*

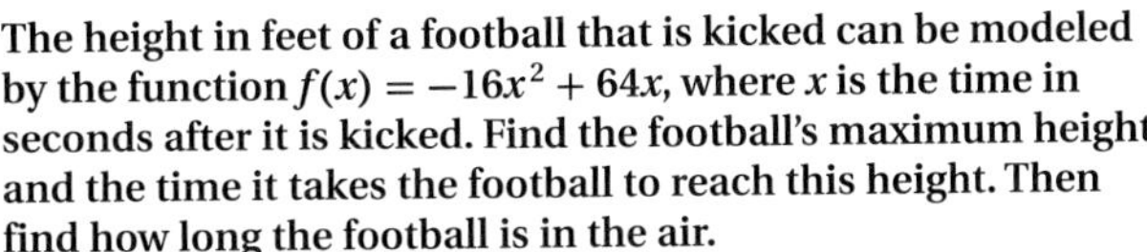

The height in feet of a football that is kicked can be modeled by the function $f(x) = -16x^2 + 64x$, where x is the time in seconds after it is kicked. Find the football's maximum height and the time it takes the football to reach this height. Then find how long the football is in the air.

1 Understand the Problem

The **answer** includes three parts: the maximum height, the time to reach the maximum height, and the time to reach the ground.

List the important information:

- The function $f(x) = -16x^2 + 64x$ models the approximate height of the football after x seconds.

Remember!

The vertex is the highest or lowest point on a parabola. Therefore, in the example, it gives the maximum height of the football.

2 Make a Plan

Find the vertex of the graph because the maximum height of the football and the time it takes to reach it are the coordinates of the vertex. The football will hit the ground when its height is 0, so find the zeros of the function. You can do this by graphing.

COMMON ERROR ALERT

Some students get confused by multiple negative signs when using the formula to find the axis of symmetry. Encourage them to write the expression as $-\left(\frac{b}{2a}\right)$.

Power Presentations with PowerPoint®

Additional Examples

Example 1

Graph $y = 3x^2 - 6x + 1$.

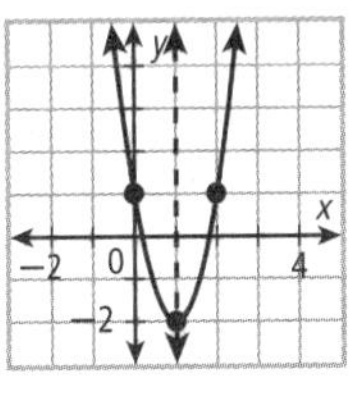

INTERVENTION

Questioning Strategies

EXAMPLE 1

- How do you know whether the parabola opens upward or downward?
- Can you have points both above and below the vertex?
- What does the axis of symmetry tell you about the graph?

2 Teach

Guided Instruction

Review the characteristics of a parabola with students. Show students how to use these characteristics to graph the parabola. Then show how to interpret the graph of a quadratic function when it models a real-world relationship such as height over time.

Reaching All Learners

Through Modeling

Have students in small groups create a scenario that could be represented by a quadratic function (see examples). Have them create a graph of their function using realistic labels and scales on the axes (they do not need to create a function rule) and present it to the class. They should tell the class what scenario is modeled by the graph, what the vertex and zeros represent, and what a reasonable domain and range are.

Power Presentations with PowerPoint®

Additional Examples

Example 2

The height in feet of a soccer ball can be modeled by $f(x) = -16x^2 + 32x$, where x is the time in seconds after it is kicked. Find the soccer ball's maximum height and the time it takes the soccer ball to reach this height. Then find how long the soccer ball is in the air. 16 ft; 1 s; 2 s

INTERVENTION
Questioning Strategies

EXAMPLE 2

- What do the zeros represent in the problem?
- What is a reasonable domain and range in this situation?

Reading Math Emphasize that the quadratic model in **Example 2** models height over time, whereas the quadratic models in Example 5 of Lesson 9-2 modeled height over distance. Point out that a height-over-time model does not represent the shape of the projectile's path and that the units on the axes are not both measures of length.

3 Solve

Step 1 Find the axis of symmetry.

$x = -\frac{64}{2(-16)}$ *Use $x = -\frac{b}{2a}$. Substitute −16 for a and 64 for b.*

$= -\frac{64}{-32} = 2$ *Simplify.*

The axis of symmetry is $x = 2$.

Step 2 Find the vertex.

$y = -16x^2 + 64x$

$= -16(2)^2 + 64(2)$ *The x-coordinate of the vertex is 2. Substitute 2 for x.*

$= -16(4) + 128$ *Simplify.*

$= -64 + 128$

$= 64$ *The y-coordinate is 64.*

The vertex is $(2, 64)$.

Step 3 Find the y-intercept.

$y = -16x^2 + 64x + 0$ *Identify c.*

The y-intercept is **0**; the graph passes through $(0, 0)$.

Step 4 Find another point on the same side of the axis of symmetry as the point containing the y-intercept.

Since the axis of symmetry is $x = 2$, choose an x-value that is less than 2. Let $x = 1$.

$y = -16(1)^2 + 64(1)$ *Substitute 1 for x.*

$= -16 + 64$ *Simplify.*

$= 48$

Another point is $(1, 48)$.

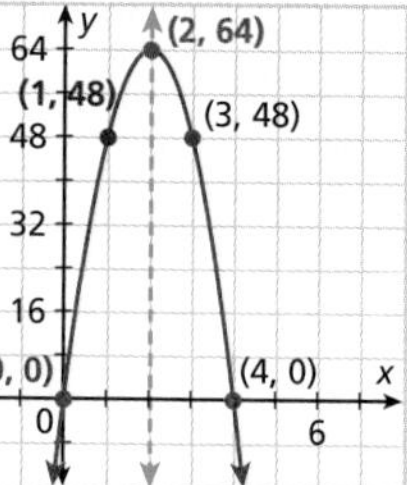

Step 5 Graph the **axis of symmetry**, the **vertex**, the point containing the **y-intercept**, and the **other point**. Then **reflect** the points across the axis of symmetry. Connect the points with a smooth curve.

The vertex is (2, 64). So at 2 seconds, the football has reached its maximum height of 64 feet. The graph shows the zeros of the function are 0 and 4. At 0 seconds the football has not yet been kicked, and at 4 seconds it reaches the ground. The football is in the air for 4 seconds.

4 Look Back

Check by substituting $(2, 64)$ and $(4, 0)$ into the function.

$64 = -16(2)^2 + 64(2)$	$0 = -16(4)^2 + 64(4)$
$64 = -64 + 128$	$0 = -256 + 256$
$64 = 64$ ✓	$0 = 0$ ✓

CHECK IT OUT!

2. As Molly dives into her pool, her height in feet above the water can be modeled by the function $f(x) = -16x^2 + 16x + 12$ where x is the time in seconds after she begins diving. Find the maximum height of her dive and the time it takes Molly to reach this height. Then find how long it takes her to reach the pool. **maximum height: 16 ft at 0.5 s; time it takes to reach the pool: 1.5 s**

Multiple Representations Students can check the reasonableness of their graph by choosing a reflected point and substituting the ordered pair into the function. If it satisfies the function, the point was reflected correctly and the graph is reasonable.

3 Close

Summarize

Have students identify the vertex of each function. Then have them tell whether the parabola opens upward or downward.

$y = 4x^2 - 4$ $(0, -4)$; upward

$y = 2x^2 + 2x + 1$ $\left(-\frac{1}{2}, \frac{1}{2}\right)$; upward

$y = -x^2 + 6x - 7$ $(3, 2)$; downward

ONGOING ASSESSMENT and INTERVENTION

***Diagnose Before* the Lesson**
9-3 Warm Up, TE p. 626

***Monitor During* the Lesson**
Check It Out! Exercises, SE pp. 627–628
Questioning Strategies, TE pp. 627–628

***Assess After* the Lesson**
9-3 Lesson Quiz, TE p. 631
Alternative Assessment, TE p. 631

THINK AND DISCUSS

1. Explain how to find the y-intercept of a quadratic function that is written in the form $ax^2 - y = bx + c$.
2. Explain how to graph a quadratic function.
3. What do the vertex and zeros of the function represent in the situation in the Check It Out for Example 2?

4. **GET ORGANIZED** Copy and complete the graphic organizer using your own quadratic function.

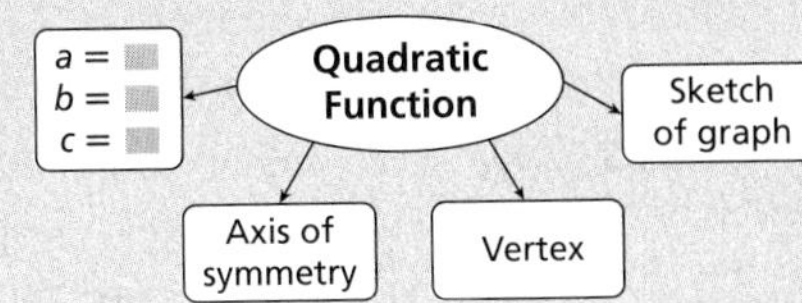

Answers to *Think and Discuss*

Possible answers:

1. Solve the equation for y. The resulting value of the constant term is the y-intercept.
2. Find the axis of symmetry, the vertex, the point containing the y-intercept, and several other points on the graph. Draw a curved line that passes through the points and is symmetrical about the axis of symmetry.
3. The vertex shows the maximum height of Molly's dive and the time at which she reached this height. The zero shows the time when she reaches the pool.
4. See p. A8.

9-3 Exercises

GUIDED PRACTICE

SEE EXAMPLE 1 p. 626

Graph each quadratic function.

1. $y = x^2 - 2x - 3$
2. $-y - 3x^2 = -3$
3. $y = 2x^2 + 2x - 4$
4. $y = x^2 + 4x - 8$
5. $y + x^2 + 5x + 2 = 0$
6. $y = 4x^2 + 2$

SEE EXAMPLE 2 p. 627

7. **Multi-Step** The height in feet of a golf ball that is hit from the ground can be modeled by the function $f(x) = -16x^2 + 96x$, where x is the time in seconds after the ball is hit. Find the ball's maximum height and the time it takes the ball to reach this height. Then find how long the ball is in the air.
maximum height: 144 ft at 3 s; time in the air: 6 s

PRACTICE AND PROBLEM SOLVING

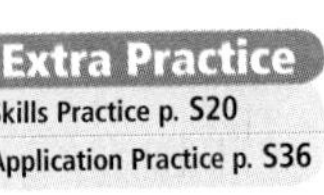

For Exercises	See Example
8–13	1
14	2

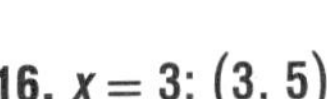

Skills Practice p. S20
Application Practice p. S36

Graph each quadratic function.

8. $y = -4x^2 + 12x - 5$
9. $y = 3x^2 + 12x + 9$
10. $y - 7x^2 - 14x = 3$
11. $y = -x^2 + 2x$
12. $y - 1 = 4x^2 + 8x$
13. $y = -2x^2 - 3x + 4$
14. **Multi-Step** A juggler tosses a ring into the air. The height of the ring in feet above the juggler's hands can be modeled by the function $f(x) = -16x^2 + 16x$, where x is the time in seconds after the ring is tossed. Find the ring's maximum height above the juggler's hands and the time it takes the ring to reach this height. Then find how long the ring is in the air. **4 ft at 0.5 s; 1 s**

For each quadratic function, find the axis of symmetry and the vertex of its graph.

15. $y = x^2 - 8x$ **15.** $x = 4$; $(4, -16)$
16. $y = -x^2 + 6x - 4$ **16.** $x = 3$; $(3, 5)$
17. $y = 4 - 3x^2$ $x = 0$; $(0, 4)$
18. $y = -2x^2 - 4$ $x = 0$; $(0, -4)$
19. $y = -x^2 - x - 4$ **19.** $x = -\frac{1}{2}$; $\left(-\frac{1}{2}, -\frac{15}{4}\right)$
20. $y = x^2 + 8x + 16$ $x = -4$; $(-4, 0)$

5.
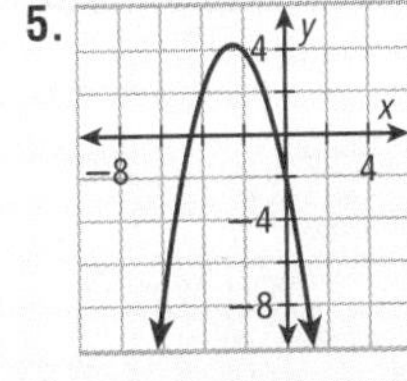

6.
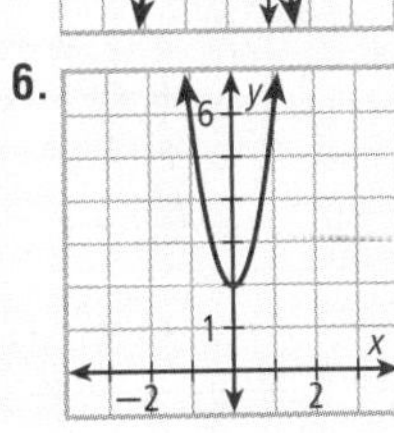

8.
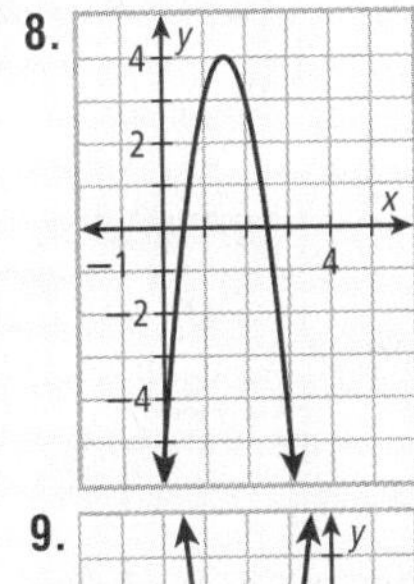

9.
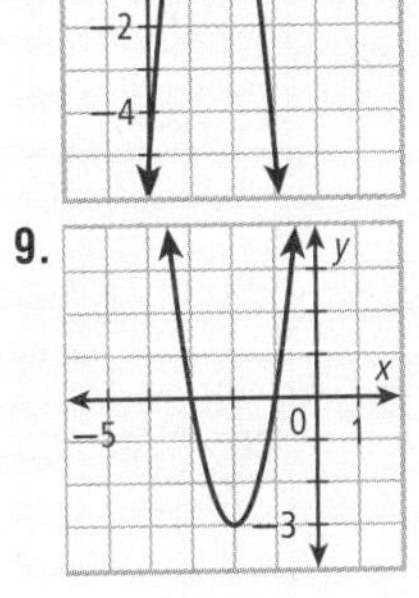

10.
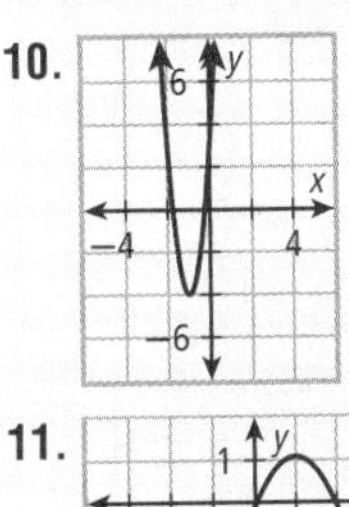

11.
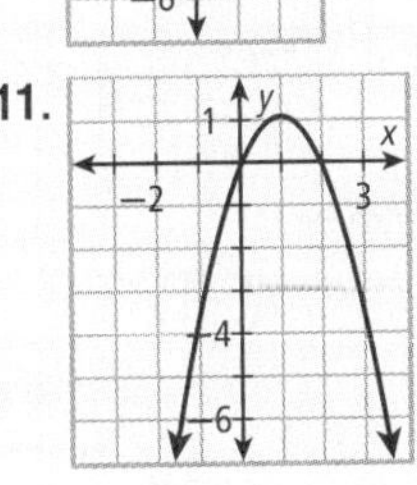

12.
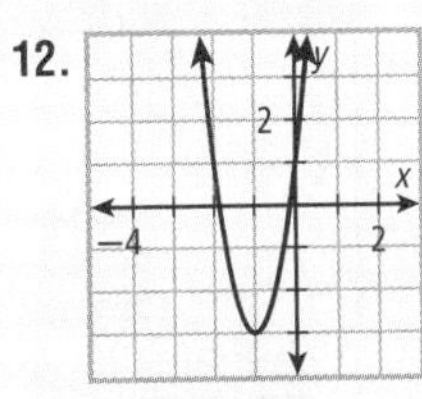

13.
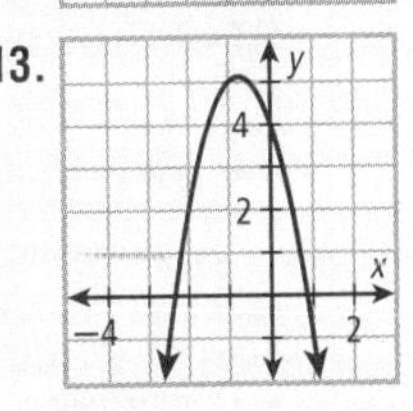

9-3 Exercises

Assignment Guide

Assign *Guided Practice* exercises as necessary.

If you finished Examples **1–2**

Basic 8–28, 35–40, 43–51
Average 8–41, 43–51
Advanced 8–51

Homework Quick Check
Quickly check key concepts.
Exercises: 8, 10, 14, 16, 24, 27

Answers

1. 3.
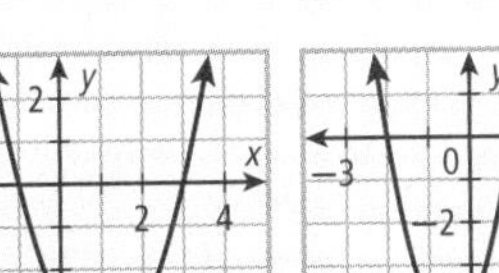

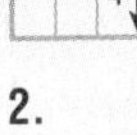

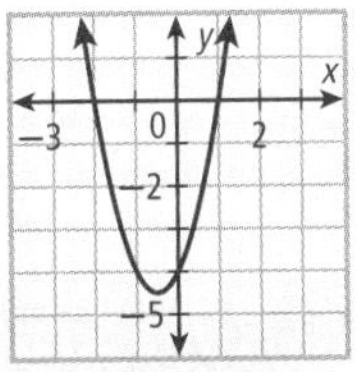

2. 4.
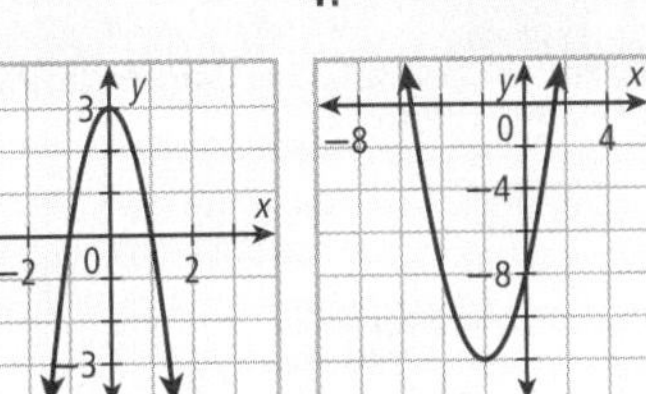

MULTI-STEP TEST PREP **Exercise 35** involves writing and using a quadratic model for projectile motion. This exercise prepares students for the Multi-Step Test Prep on page 640.

Inclusion Students may be overwhelmed by the number of variables used in **Exercise 35.** Help them understand what each variable represents: h is the dependent variable, and t is the independent variable. Then help students relate v_i to the coefficient b and h_i to the constant c. Show them that $-\frac{1}{2}a$ is the leading coefficient.

Answers

21–27a. See p. A30.

33. (−1, 6); the axis of symmetry is a vertical line through the vertex. So its equation is $x = 0$. Reflect the point (1, 6) across the axis of symmetry.

34. The x-coordinate of the vertex gives the axis of symmetry. If the range includes values greater than the y-coordinate of the vertex, then the parabola opens upward. If the range includes values less than the y-coordinate of the vertex, then the parabola opens downward.

35c–d. See p. A30.

LINK Travel

Building began on the Tower of Pisa, located in Pisa, Italy, in 1173. The tower started leaning after the third story was added. At the fifth story, attempts were made to correct the leaning. The tower was finally complete in 1350.

Graph each quadratic function. On your graph, label the coordinates of the vertex. Draw and label the axis of symmetry.

21. $y = -x^2$ **22.** $y = -x^2 + 4x$ **23.** $y = x^2 - 6x + 4$

24. $y = x^2 - x$ **25.** $y = 3x^2 - 4$ **26.** $y = -2x^2 - 16x - 25$

27. Travel While on a vacation in Italy, Rudy visited the Leaning Tower of Pisa. When he leaned over the railing to look down from the tower, his sunglasses fell off. The height in meters of the sunglasses as they fell can be approximated by the function $y = -5x^2 + 50$, where x is the time in seconds.

a. Graph the function. (*Hint:* Use a graphing calculator.)

b. What is a reasonable domain and range? **27b. D: $0 \le x \le 3.16$; R: $0 \le y \le 50$**

c. How long did it take for the glasses to reach the ground? **about 3.16 s**

28. ///ERROR ANALYSIS/// Two students found the equation of the axis of symmetry for the graph of $f(x) = -x^2 - 2x + 1$. Who is incorrect? Explain the error.

28. Student A is incorrect; the student incorrectly identified the values a and b.

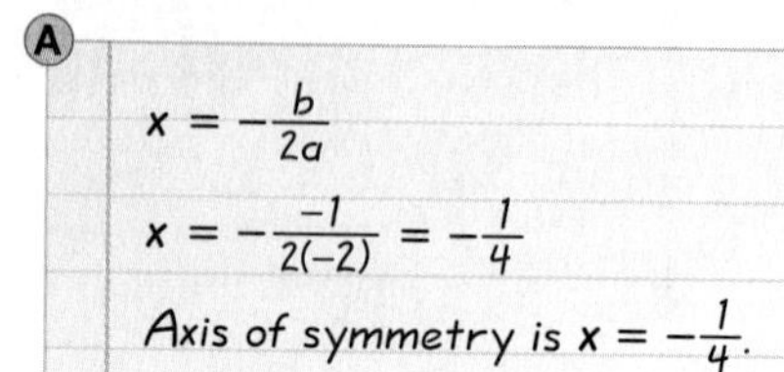

Ⓐ

$x = -\frac{b}{2a}$

$x = -\frac{-1}{2(-2)} = -\frac{1}{4}$

Axis of symmetry is $x = -\frac{1}{4}$.

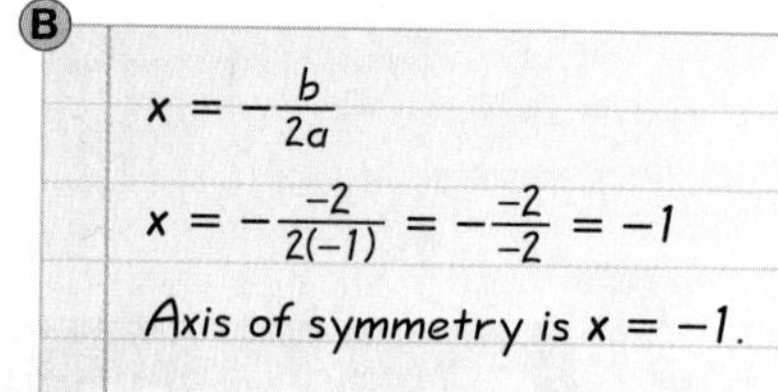

Ⓑ

$x = -\frac{b}{2a}$

$x = -\frac{-2}{2(-1)} = -\frac{-2}{-2} = -1$

Axis of symmetry is $x = -1$.

29. Critical Thinking The point (5, 4) lies on the graph of a quadratic function whose axis of symmetry is $x = 2$. Find another point on the graph. Explain how you found the point.

29. (−1, 4); reflect the given point across the axis of symmetry.

Engineering **Use the graph for Exercises 30–32. The velocity v in centimeters per second of a fluid flowing in a pipe varies according to the radius r of the pipe.**

Velocity of a Fluid Through a Pipe

30. Find the radius of the pipe when the velocity is 7 cm/s. **3 cm**

31. Find the velocity of the fluid when the radius is 2 cm. **12 cm/s**

32. What is a reasonable domain for this function? Explain.

32. $0 \le x \le 4$; when x is greater than 4, the velocity would be negative, which does not make sense.

33. Critical Thinking The graph of a quadratic function has the vertex (0, 5). One point on the graph is (1, 6). Find another point on the graph. Explain how you found the point.

34. Write About It Explain how the vertex and the range can help you graph a quadratic function.

MULTI-STEP TEST PREP

35. This problem will prepare you for the Multi-Step Test Prep on page 640.

A water bottle rocket is shot upward with an initial velocity of $v_i = 45$ ft/s from the roof of a school, which is at h_i, 50 ft above the ground. The equation $h = -\frac{1}{2}at^2 + v_i t + h_i$ models the rocket's height as a function of time. The acceleration due to gravity a is 32 ft/s². **$h(t) = -16t^2 + 45t + 50$**

a. Write the equation for height as a function of time for this situation.

b. Find the vertex of this parabola. **approximately (1.4, 81.6)**

c. Sketch the graph of this parabola and label the vertex.

d. What do the coordinates of the vertex represent in terms of time and height?

9-3 PRACTICE A

9-3 PRACTICE C

9-3 PRACTICE B

Graph each quadratic function.

1. $y = x^2 + 4x - 4$

axis of symmetry: **$x = -2$**

vertex: **(−2, −8)**

y-intercept: **−4**

two other points: **Possible answers: (1, 1) and (2, 8)**

2. $y + 2x^2 - 4x - 6 = 0$

axis of symmetry: **$x = 1$**

vertex: **(1, 8)**

y-intercept: **6**

two other points: **Possible answers: (−1, 0) and (−2, −10)**

3. The height in feet of a soccer ball that is kicked can be modeled by the function $f(x) = -8x^2 + 24x$, where x is the time in seconds after it is kicked. Graph this function. Find the soccer ball's maximum height and the time it takes the ball to reach this height. Then find how long the soccer ball is in the air.

maximum height: **18 feet**

time to reach maximum height: **1.5 seconds**

time in the air: **3 seconds**

Soccer Kick (Height (ft) vs. Time (s))

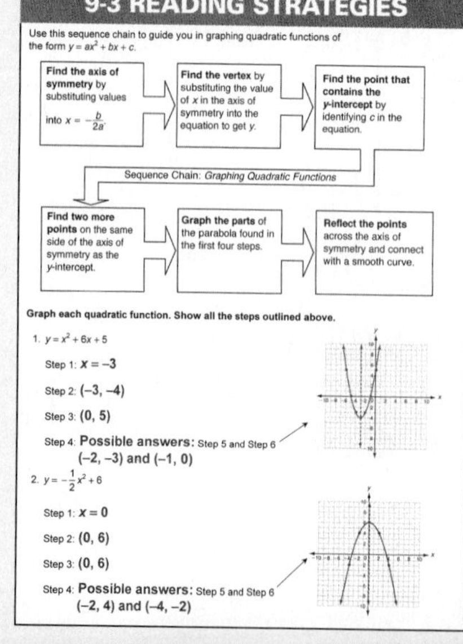

9-3 READING STRATEGIES

Use this sequence chain to guide you in graphing quadratic functions of the form $y = ax^2 + bx + c$.

Sequence Chain: *Graphing Quadratic Functions*

1. **Find the axis of symmetry** by substituting values into $x = -\frac{b}{2a}$.
2. **Find the vertex** by substituting the value of x in the axis of symmetry into the equation to get y.
3. **Find the point that contains the y-intercept** by identifying c in the equation.
4. **Find two more points** on the same side of the axis of symmetry as the y-intercept.
5. **Graph the parts** of the parabola found in the first four steps.
6. **Reflect the points** across the axis of symmetry and connect with a smooth curve.

Graph each quadratic function. Show all the steps outlined above.

1. $y = x^2 + 6x + 5$

Step 1: **$x = -3$**

Step 2: **(−3, −4)**

Step 3: **(0, 5)**

Step 4: **Possible answers: (−2, −3) and (−1, 0)** Step 5 and Step 6

2. $y = -\frac{1}{2}x^2 + 6$

Step 1: **$x = 0$**

Step 2: **(0, 6)**

Step 3: **(0, 6)**

Step 4: **Possible answers: (−2, 4) and (−4, −2)** Step 5 and Step 6

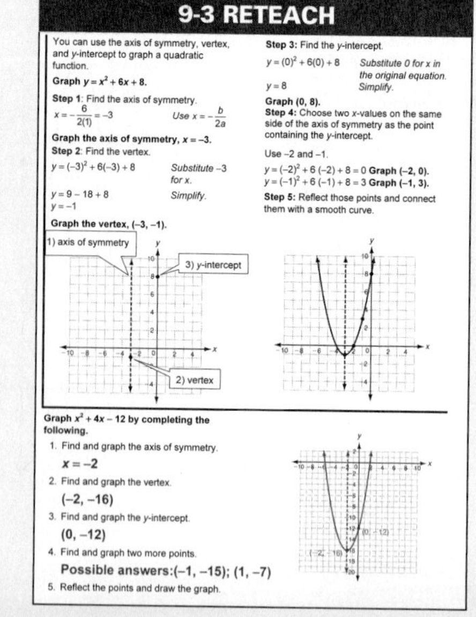

9-3 RETEACH

You can use the axis of symmetry, vertex, and y-intercept to graph a quadratic function.

Graph $y = x^2 + 6x + 8$.

Step 1: Find the axis of symmetry.

$x = -\frac{6}{2(1)} = -3$ *Use $x = -\frac{b}{2a}$*

Graph the axis of symmetry, $x = -3$.

Step 2: Find the vertex.

$y = (-3)^2 + 6(-3) + 8$ *Substitute −3 for x.*

$y = 9 - 18 + 8$ *Simplify.*

$y = -1$

Graph the vertex, (−3, −1).

Step 3: Find the y-intercept.

$y = (0)^2 + 6(0) + 8$ *Substitute 0 for x in the original equation.*

$y = 8$ *Simplify.*

Graph (0, 8).

Step 4: Choose two x-values on the same side of the axis of symmetry as the point containing the y-intercept.

Use −2 and −1.

$y = (-2)^2 + 6(-2) + 8 = 0$ **Graph (−2, 0).**

$y = (-1)^2 + 6(-1) + 8 = 3$ **Graph (−1, 3).**

Step 5: Reflect those points and connect them with a smooth curve.

Graph $x^2 + 4x - 12$ by completing the following.

1. Find and graph the axis of symmetry.
$x = -2$
2. Find and graph the vertex.
(−2, −16)
3. Find and graph the y-intercept.
(0, −12)
4. Find and graph two more points.
Possible answers: (−1, −15); (1, −7)
5. Reflect the points and draw the graph.

36. Copy and complete the table for each function.

Function	Graph Opens	Axis of Symmetry	Vertex	Zeros	Domain and Range
$y = x^2 + 4$	Upward	$x = 0$	$(0, 4)$	None	D: See R: left
$y = -x^2 + 4$	Down-ward	$x = 0$	$(0, 4)$	$-2, 2$	D: margin. R:
$y + 8 - x^2 = -2x$	Upward	$x = 1$	$(1, -9)$	$-2, 4$	D: R:

D: all real numbers
R: $y \geq 4$

D: all real numbers
R: $y \leq 4$

D: all real numbers
R: $y \geq -9$

TEST PREP

37. Which is the axis of symmetry for the graph of $f(x) = 6 - 5x + \frac{1}{2}x^2$?

(A) $x = 5$ (B) $x = \frac{1}{20}$ (C) $x = -5$ (D) $x = -\frac{1}{20}$

38. What are the coordinates of the vertex for the graph of $f(x) = x^2 - 5x + 6$?

(F) $\left(-\frac{5}{2}, -\frac{1}{4}\right)$ (G) $\left(-\frac{5}{2}, \frac{1}{4}\right)$ (H) $\left(\frac{5}{2}, \frac{1}{4}\right)$ (J) $\left(\frac{5}{2}, -\frac{1}{4}\right)$

39. Which function's graph has an axis of symmetry of $x = 1$ and a vertex of $(1, 8)$?

(A) $y = -x^2 + x + 8$
(B) $y = x^2 + 8x + 1$
(C) $y = 2x^2 - 4x - 8$
(D) $y = -3x^2 + 6x + 5$

40. Short Response Graph $y = x^2 + 3x + 2$. What are the zeros, the axis of symmetry, and the coordinates of the vertex? Show your work.

CHALLENGE AND EXTEND

41. The graph of a quadratic function has its vertex at $(1, -4)$ and one zero of the function is 3. Find the other zero. Explain how you found the other zero.

42. The x-intercepts of a quadratic function are 3 and -3. The y-intercept is 6. What are the coordinates of the vertex? Does the function have a maximum or a minimum? Explain.

42. $(0, 6)$; maximum; the parabola opens downward because the zeros are below the vertex, so the vertex is a maximum.

SPIRAL REVIEW

Find the x- and y-intercepts. *(Lesson 5-2)*

43. 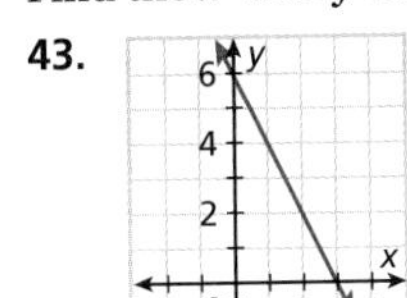

x-int.: 3; y-int.: 6

44. 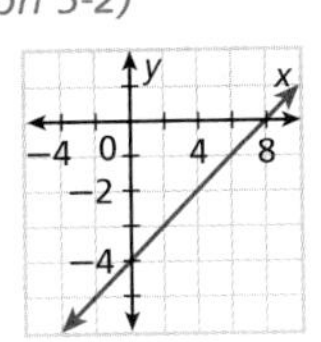

x-int.: 8; y-int.: -4

45. 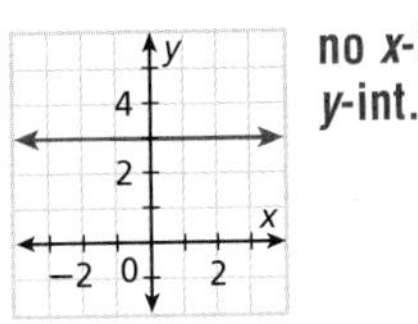

no x-int.; y-int.: 3

Solve each system by using any method. *(Lessons 6-1, 6-2, and 6-3)*

46. $\begin{cases} 3x - y = 2 \\ x + 4y = 18 \end{cases}$ $(2, 4)$

47. $\begin{cases} 2x + 3y = 3 \\ 4x - y = 13 \end{cases}$ $(3, -1)$

48. $\begin{cases} -2x + 3y = 12 \\ 6x + y = 4 \end{cases}$ $(0, 4)$

Find the vertex. *(Lesson 9-2)*

49. $y = x^2 + 2x - 15$ $(-1, -16)$

50. $y = -3x^2 + 12x - 4$ $(2, 8)$

51. $y = -2x - x^2 + 3$ $(-1, 4)$

TEST PREP DOCTOR Suggest that students rewrite the function in **Exercise 37** in standard form as a first step.

In **Exercise 38,** students can eliminate choices **F** and **G** before finding the axis of symmetry by counting the negative signs of $-\frac{b}{2a}$.

Answers

40. 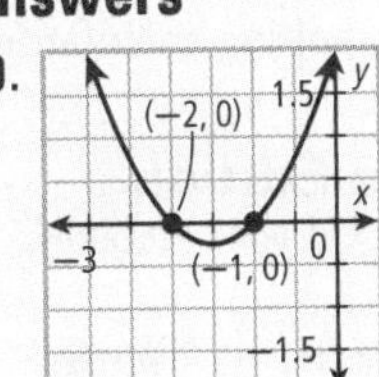

zeros: $-2, -1$

axis of symmetry: $x = -\frac{3}{2}$

vertex: $\left(-\frac{3}{2}, -\frac{1}{4}\right)$

41. -1; the axis of symmetry is $x = 1$. The given zero is 2 units right of the axis of symmetry. The other zero is 2 units left of the axis of symmetry.

Journal

Have students compare and contrast the process for graphing a linear function with the process for graphing a quadratic function.

ALTERNATIVE ASSESSMENT

Have students write and graph a quadratic function in the form $y = ax^2 + bx + c$, where a, b, and c are not zero. Have students give the domain and range of the function.

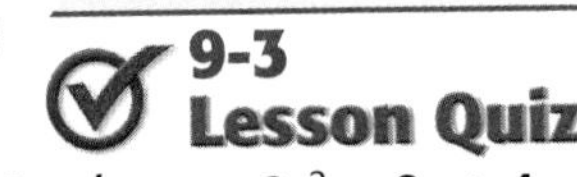

9-3 Lesson Quiz

1. Graph $y = -2x^2 - 8x + 4$.

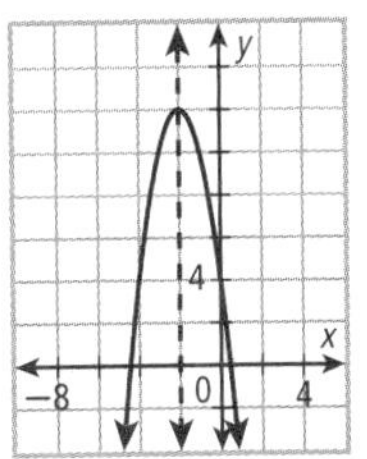

2. The height in feet of a fireworks shell can be modeled by $h(t) = -16t^2 + 224t$, where t is the time in seconds after it is fired. Find the maximum height of the shell, the time it takes to reach its maximum height, and the length of time the shell is in the air if it does not explode. 784 ft; 7 s; 14 s

Also available on transparency

9-3 PROBLEM SOLVING

Write the correct answer.

1. An Olympic diver is competing for a medal. His height in feet above the water can be modeled by the function $f(x) = -3x^2 + 6x + 24$, where x is the time in seconds after he begins the dive. Graph the function. Then find how long it takes the diver to reach the water.

Height During Dive

4 seconds

2. Tanisha kicks a soccer ball during a game. The height of the ball, in feet, can be modeled by the function $f(x) = -16x^2 + 48x$, where x is the time in seconds after she kicks the ball. Graph the function. Find the maximum height of the ball and how long it takes the ball to reach that height.

Height of Soccer Ball

36 ft; 1.5 seconds

A model rocket is launched from a platform into the air. Keona records its height at different times until it reaches its peak at 259 ft. Her graph of these points is shown below. Use this graph to answer questions 3-5.

Rocket Flight

3. Keona wants to complete her graph by plotting the heights of the rocket as it descended. Which of the following points will she graph?

F (4, 180) H (6, 200)
G (5, 150) J (10, 0)

4. How long will the rocket be in the air?

A 4 seconds C 8 seconds
B 6 seconds D 10 seconds

5. Which of the following equations models the flight of the ball where x is the time in seconds and y is the height in feet?

A $16x^2 + 15x + 125$
B $16x^2 + 125x + 15$
C $-16x^2 + 125x + 15$
D $-16x^2 + 15x + 125$

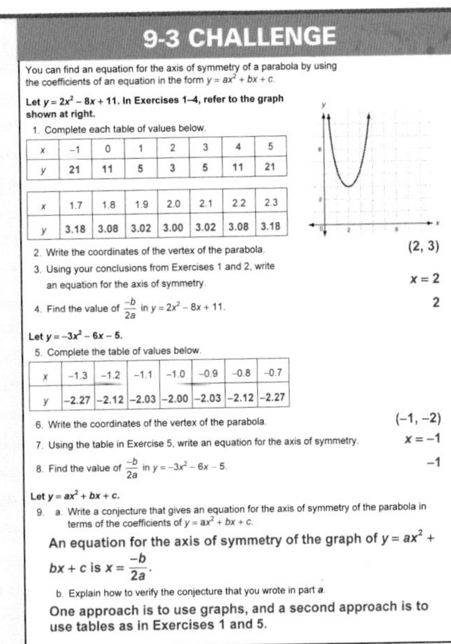

9-3 CHALLENGE

You can find an equation for the axis of symmetry of a parabola by using the coefficients of an equation in the form $y = ax^2 + bx + c$.

Let $y = 2x^2 - 8x + 11$. In Exercises 1–4, refer to the graph shown at right.

1. Complete each table of values below.

x	−1	0	1	2	3	4	5
y	21	11	5	3	5	11	21

x	1.7	1.8	1.9	2.0	2.1	2.2	2.3
y	3.18	3.08	3.02	3.00	3.02	3.08	3.18

2. Write the coordinates of the vertex of the parabola. (2, 3)

3. Using your conclusions from Exercises 1 and 2, write an equation for the axis of symmetry. $x = 2$

4. Find the value of $\frac{-b}{2a}$ in $y = 2x^2 - 8x + 11$. 2

Let $y = -3x^2 - 6x - 5$.

5. Complete the table of values below.

x	−1.3	−1.2	−1.1	−1.0	−0.9	−0.8	−0.7
y	−2.27	−2.12	−2.03	−2.00	−2.03	−2.12	−2.27

6. Write the coordinates of the vertex of the parabola. (−1, −2)

7. Using the table in Exercise 5, write an equation for the axis of symmetry. $x = -1$

8. Find the value of $\frac{-b}{2a}$ in $y = -3x^2 - 6x - 5$. −1

Let $y = ax^2 + bx + c$.

9. a. Write a conjecture that gives an equation for the axis of symmetry of the parabola in terms of the coefficients of $y = ax^2 + bx + c$.

An equation for the axis of symmetry of the graph of $y = ax^2 + bx + c$ is $x = \frac{-b}{2a}$.

b. Explain how to verify the conjecture that you wrote in part **a**.

One approach is to use graphs, and a second approach is to use tables as in Exercises 1 and 5.

Organizer

Use with Lesson 9-4

Pacing:

Traditional $\frac{1}{2}$ day
Block $\frac{1}{4}$ day

Objective: Use a graphing calculator to explore how the value of a affects the graph of $y = ax^2$.

Materials: graphing calculator

Online Edition
Graphing Calculator, TechKeys

Countdown Week 19

Resources

Technology Lab Activities
9-4 Lab Recording Sheet

Teach

Discuss

Encourage students to test other values for a, such as 0.1, 0.2, and 0.3.

Close

Key Concept

The absolute value of a affects the width of the graph of $y = ax^2$. The sign of a affects whether the graph opens upward or downward.

Assessment

Journal Have students explain how the graphs of $y = 5x^2$ and $y = \frac{1}{5}x^2$ compare with the graph of $y = x^2$.

State Resources

go.hrw.com
State Resources Online
KEYWORD: MA7 Resources

9-4

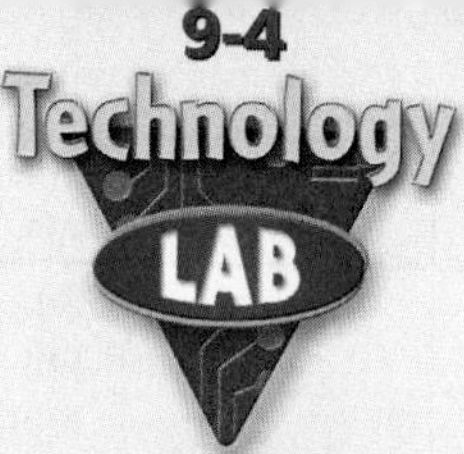

The Family of Quadratic Functions

Use with Lesson 9-4

In Chapter 5, you learned that functions whose graphs share the same basic characteristics form a *family of functions.* All quadratic functions form a family because their graphs are all parabolas. You can use a graphing calculator to explore the family of quadratic functions.

go.hrw.com
Lab Resources Online
KEYWORD: MA7 Lab9

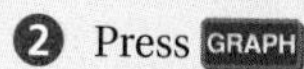

Activity

Describe how the value of a affects the graph of $y = ax^2$.

1. Press Y=. Enter Y_1 through Y_4 as shown.

   Notice that Y_2 represents the parent function $y = x^2$. To make it stand out from the other functions, change its line style. When you enter Y_2, move the cursor to the line style indicator by pressing ◄. Then press ENTER to cycle through the choices until a thicker line appears.

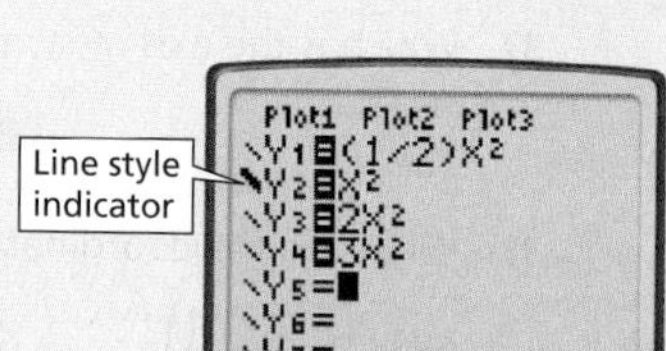

2. Press GRAPH.

   Keep in mind the values of a as the functions are graphed. The graphing calculator will graph the functions in order.

   Notice that the graph of $y = \frac{1}{2}x^2$ is wider than the graph of the parent function. The graphs of $y = 2x^2$ and $y = 3x^2$ are narrower than the graph of the parent function.

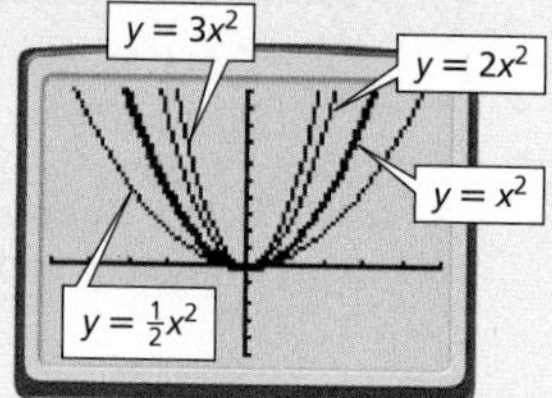

Try This

1. How would the graph of $y = 6x^2$ compare with the graph of the parent function? **much narrower**
2. How would the graph of $y = \frac{1}{5}x^2$ compare with the graph of the parent function? **much wider**
3. **Make a Conjecture** Make a conjecture about the effect of a on the graph of $y = ax^2$.

Consider the graphs of $y = -\frac{1}{2}x^2$, $y = -x^2$, $y = -2x^2$, and $y = -3x^2$.

4. Describe the differences in the graphs.
5. How would the graph of $y = -8x^2$ compare with the graph of $y = -x^2$? **much narrower**
6. How do these results affect your conjecture from Problem 3?
   When a is negative, the parabolas open downward. Otherwise the conjecture is the same.

Consider the graphs of $y = x^2 - 1$, $y = x^2$, $y = x^2 + 2$, and $y = x^2 + 4$.

7. Describe the differences in the graphs.
8. How would the graph of $y = x^2 - 7$ compare with the graph of the parent function? **8. lower, with a vertex at (0, −7)**
9. **Make a Conjecture** Make a conjecture about the effect of c on the graph of $y = x^2 + c$.
   The value of c causes the parabola to move up if $c > 0$ and down if $c < 0$.

Answers to *Try This*

3. The closer the value of a to 0, the wider the parabola. The greater the value of a, the narrower the parabola.
4. All the graphs open downward. The graph of $y = -\frac{1}{2}x^2$ is the widest. The graphs of $y = -2x^2$ and $y = -3x^2$ are narrower than the parent function.
7. The graph of $y = x^2 - 1$ is lower than the parent function. The graphs of $y = x^2 + 2$ and $y = x^2 + 4$ are higher.

9-4 Transforming Quadratic Functions

Objective
Graph and transform quadratic functions.

Why learn this?
You can compare how long it takes raindrops to reach the ground from different heights. (See Exercise 18.)

Remember!
You saw in Lesson 5-10 that the graphs of all linear functions are transformations of the linear parent function, $f(x) = x$.

The quadratic parent function is $f(x) = x^2$. The graph of all other quadratic functions are transformations of the graph of $f(x) = x^2$.

For the parent function $f(x) = x^2$:

- The axis of symmetry is $x = 0$, or the y-axis.
- The vertex is $(0, 0)$.
- The function has only one zero, 0.

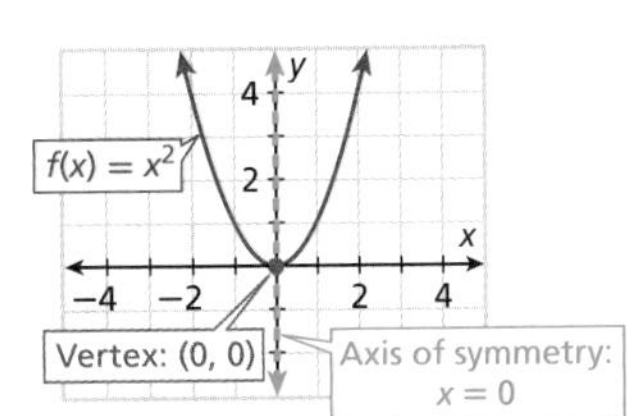

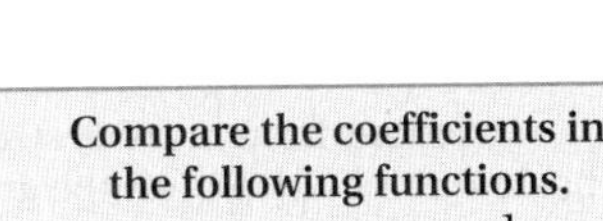

Compare the coefficients in the following functions.

$f(x) = x^2 \qquad g(x) = \frac{1}{2}x^2$

$h(x) = -3x^2$

$f(x) = 1x^2 + 0x + 0$
$g(x) = \frac{1}{2}x^2 + 0x + 0$
$h(x) = -3x^2 + 0x + 0$

Same	Different
• $b = 0$ • $c = 0$	• Value of a

Compare the graphs of the same functions.

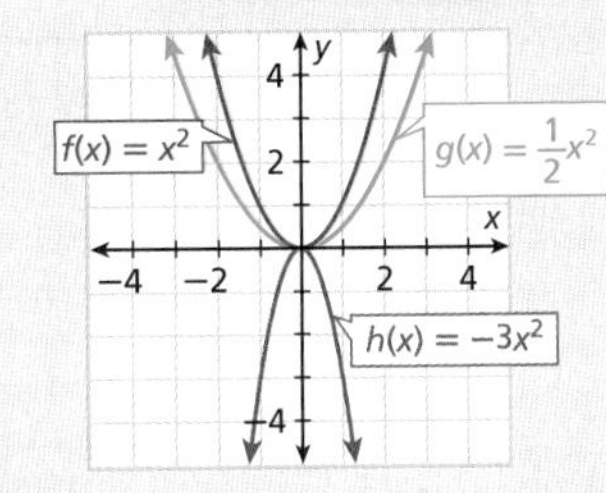

Same	Different
• Axis of symmetry is $x = 0$. • Vertex is $(0, 0)$.	• Widths of parabolas

The value of a in a quadratic function determines not only the direction a parabola opens, but also the width of the parabola.

Know it! Note

Width of a Parabola

WORDS	EXAMPLES
The graph of $f(x) = ax^2$ is narrower than the graph of $f(x) = x^2$ if $\lvert a\rvert > 1$ and wider if $\lvert a\rvert < 1$.	Compare the graphs of $g(x)$ and $h(x)$ with the graph of $f(x)$. $\lvert -2\rvert \,?\, 1$ $\quad$ $\left\lvert \frac{1}{4}\right\rvert \,?\, 1$ $2 > 1$ $\quad$ $\frac{1}{4} < 1$ narrower $\quad$ wider (graph: $f(x) = x^2$, $h(x) = \frac{1}{4}x^2$, $g(x) = -2x^2$)

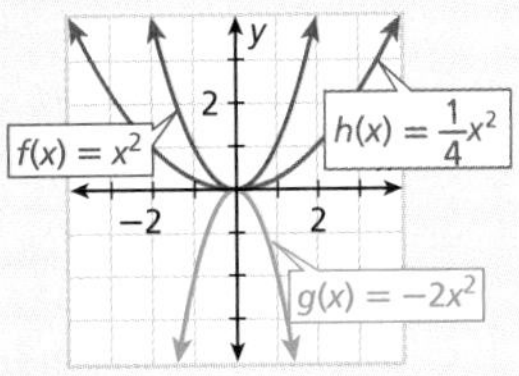

9-4 Organizer

Pacing: Traditional $1\frac{1}{2}$ days
Block $\frac{3}{4}$ day

Objective: Graph and transform quadratic functions.

Algebra Lab
In *Algebra Lab Activities*

Technology Lab
In *Technology Lab Activities*

Online Edition
Tutorial Videos, Interactivity

Countdown Week 20

Power Presentations with PowerPoint®

Warm Up

For each quadratic function, find the axis of symmetry and vertex, and state whether the function opens upward or downward.

1. $y = x^2 + 3$ $\quad x = 0; (0, 3);$ upward
2. $y = 2x^2$ $\quad x = 0; (0, 0);$ upward
3. $y = -0.5x^2 - 4$ $\quad x = 0; (0, -4);$ downward

Also available on transparency

Math Humor

Sales Clerk: May I help you?

Math Student: Yes, I would like to order $f(x) = 4x^2$ and $g(x) = 3x^2$.

Sales Clerk: What are you talking about?

Math Student: My teacher told me to order my quadratic functions.

1 Introduce

EXPLORATION

9-4 Transforming Quadratic Functions

Look for patterns as you use a graphing calculator to graph quadratic functions.

1. Enter $y = x^2$ in your calculator as **Y1**. Then graph the function.
2. For each quadratic function in the table, enter the function as **Y2** and then graph the function in the same window as the graph of $y = x^2$. Find the vertex of the function and describe how the graph of the function compares to the graph of $y = x^2$.

Function	Vertex	How does the graph compare to the graph of $y = x^2$?
$y = x^2 + 2$		
$y = x^2 + 5$		
$y = x^2 - 6$		
$y = x^2 - 10$		

3. Explain how the value of c determines how the graph of $y = x^2 + c$ is related to the graph of $y = x^2$.

THINK AND DISCUSS

4. **Explain** how you can sketch the graph of $y = x^2 + 11$ without using your calculator.

Motivate

Have students graph $f(x) = x^2$, $g(x) = x^2 + 3$, and $h(x) = x^2 - 2$ on the same coordinate plane. Ask students to name one similarity among the graphs. Possible answers: all open upward, same axis of symmetry, same shape

Ask students to name one difference among the graphs. Possible answer: they intersect the y-axis in different places.

Tell students that in this lesson they will learn to determine the effects of many parameter changes on the graph of a quadratic function.

Explorations and answers are provided in *Alternate Openers: Explorations Transparencies.*

State Resources

Inclusion When ordering the functions in **Example 1,** have students write the absolute value of a for each function, order these values from greatest to least, and then write the functions in order from narrowest to widest.

Power Presentations with PowerPoint®

Additional Examples

Example 1

Order the functions from narrowest graph to widest.

A. $f(x) = 3x^2$, $g(x) = 0.5x^2$ $f(x), g(x)$

B. $f(x) = x^2$, $g(x) = \frac{1}{2}x^2$, $h(x) = -2x^2$ $h(x), f(x), g(x)$

INTERVENTION

Questioning Strategies

EXAMPLE 1

- What two properties of the graph of $y = ax^2$ can be determined from the value of a?

Visual Students may not think the parabolas at the bottom of page 634 look like they have the same width. Have them compare the widths at specific locations above the vertex. For example, at 1 unit above the vertex, each parabola is 2 units wide.

EXAMPLE 1 Comparing Widths of Parabolas

Order the functions from narrowest graph to widest.

A $f(x) = -2x^2, g(x) = \frac{1}{3}x^2, h(x) = 4x^2$

Step 1 Find $|a|$ for each function.

$|-2| = 2$ $\quad \left|\frac{1}{3}\right| = \frac{1}{3}$ $\quad |4| = 4$

Step 2 Order the functions.

$h(x) = 4x^2$

$f(x) = -2x^2$

$g(x) = \frac{1}{3}x^2$

The function with the narrowest graph has the greatest value for $|a|$.

Check Use a graphing calculator to compare the graphs.

$h(x) = 4x^2$ has the narrowest graph, and $g(x) = \frac{1}{3}x^2$ has the widest graph. ✓

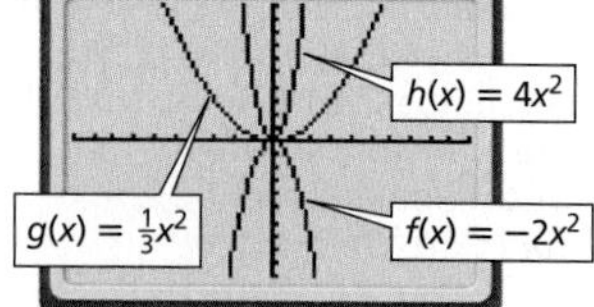

B $f(x) = 2x^2, g(x) = -2x^2$

Step 1 Find $|a|$ for each function.

$|2| = 2$ $\quad |-2| = 2$

Step 2 Order the functions from narrowest graph to widest.

Since the absolute values are equal, the graphs are the same width.

Order the functions from narrowest graph to widest.

1a. $f(x) = -x^2, g(x) = \frac{2}{3}x^2$ **$f(x)$, $g(x)$**

1b. $f(x) = -4x^2, g(x) = 6x^2, h(x) = 0.2x^2$ **$g(x)$, $f(x)$, $h(x)$**

Compare the coefficients in the following functions.

$f(x) = x^2 \quad g(x) = x^2 - 4$

$h(x) = x^2 + 3$

$f(x) = 1x^2 + 0x + 0$

$g(x) = 1x^2 + 0x + (-4)$

$h(x) = 1x^2 + 0x + 3$

Same	Different
• $a = 1$ • $b = 0$	• Value of c

Compare the graphs of the same functions.

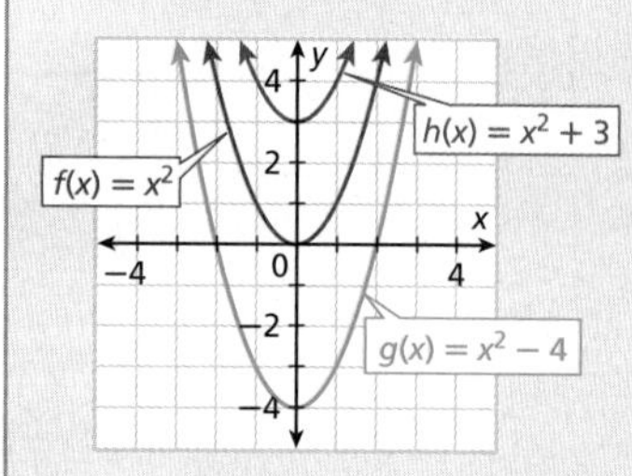

Same	Different
• Axis of symmetry is $x = 0$. • Width of parabola	• Vertex of parabola

The value of c makes these graphs look different. The value of c in a quadratic function determines not only the value of the y-intercept but also a vertical translation of the graph of $f(x) = ax^2$ up or down the y-axis.

2 Teach

Guided Instruction

Review how to find the axis of symmetry and vertex of a parabola. Introduce the quadratic parent function, $f(x) = x^2$. Remind students that in Lesson 5-10, they studied transformations of linear functions from the parent function $f(x) = x$. Encourage students to compare the effects of each parameter change on the graphs of quadratic functions to the effects of the corresponding parameter change on the graphs of linear functions.

Reaching All Learners

Through Visual Cues

Have students create a design made of transformed parabolas and keep a record of each parabola's function. Encourage students to use their imagination with colors and patterns. Allow students to use graphing calculators to check their work. Some students will be motivated to explore additional types of transformations.

Vertical Translations of a Parabola

The graph of the function $f(x) = x^2 + c$ is the graph of $f(x) = x^2$ translated vertically.

- If $c > 0$, the graph of $f(x) = x^2$ is translated c units **up**.
- If $c < 0$, the graph of $f(x) = x^2$ is translated c units **down**.

EXAMPLE 2 Comparing Graphs of Quadratic Functions

Compare the graph of each function with the graph of $f(x) = x^2$.

A $g(x) = -\frac{1}{3}x^2 + 2$

Helpful Hint

When comparing graphs, it is helpful to draw them on the same coordinate plane.

Method 1 Compare the graphs.

- The graph of $g(x) = -\frac{1}{3}x^2 + 2$ is **wider** than the graph of $f(x) = x^2$.
- The graph of $g(x) = -\frac{1}{3}x^2 + 2$ opens **downward**, and the graph of $f(x) = x^2$ opens **upward**.
- The axis of symmetry is the same.
- The vertex of $f(x) = x^2$ is $(0, 0)$. The vertex of $g(x) = -\frac{1}{3}x^2 + 2$ is translated **2 units up** to $(0, 2)$.

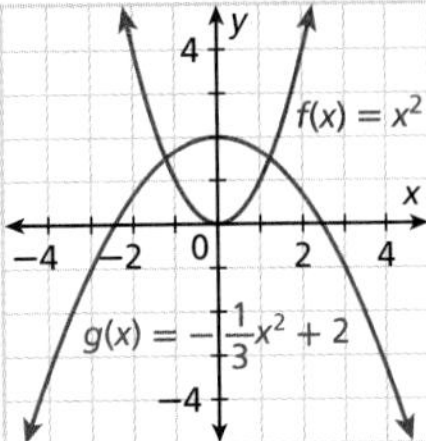

B $g(x) = 2x^2 - 3$

Method 2 Use the functions.

- Since $|2| > |1|$, the graph of $g(x) = 2x^2 - 3$ is **narrower** than the graph of $f(x) = x^2$.
- Since $-\frac{b}{2a} = 0$ for both functions, the axis of symmetry is the same.
- The vertex of $f(x) = x^2$ is $(0, 0)$. The vertex of $g(x) = 2x^2 - 3$ is translated **3 units down** to $(0, -3)$.

Check Use a graph to verify all comparisons.

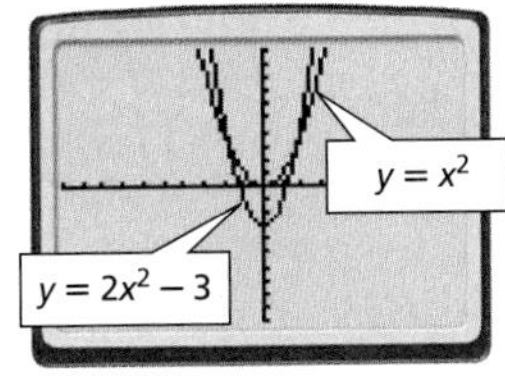

CHECK IT OUT! Compare the graph of each function with the graph of $f(x) = x^2$.

2a. $g(x) = -x^2 - 4$ **2b.** $g(x) = 3x^2 + 9$ **2c.** $g(x) = \frac{1}{2}x^2 + 2$

2a. The graph of $g(x)$ is the same width, has the same axis of symmetry, opens downward, and its vertex is translated 4 units down to $(0, -4)$.

2b. The graph of $g(x)$ is narrower, has the same axis of symmetry, and also opens upward, and its vertex is translated 9 units up to $(0, 9)$.

2c. The graph of $g(x)$ is wider, has the same axis of symmetry, and also opens upward, and its vertex is translated 2 units up to $(0, 2)$.

The quadratic function $h(t) = -16t^2 + c$ can be used to approximate the height h in feet above the ground of a falling object t seconds after it is dropped from a height of c feet. This model is used only to approximate the height of falling objects because it does not account for air resistance, wind, and other real-world factors.

COMMON ERROR ALERT

Some students mistakenly associate a greater absolute value of a with a wider parabola. Encourage students to associate the absolute value of a with the rate at which the graph rises or falls. The greater the absolute value of a, the faster the graph rises or falls and the narrower it is.

Power Presentations with PowerPoint®

Additional Examples

Example 2

Compare the graph of each function with the graph of $f(x) = x^2$.

A. $g(x) = -\frac{1}{4}x^2 + 3$

- The graph of $g(x)$ is wider than the graph of $f(x)$.
- The graph of $g(x)$ opens downward, and the graph of $f(x)$ opens upward.
- Both have the axis of symmetry $x = 0$.
- The vertex of $g(x)$ is $(0, 3)$, and the vertex of $f(x)$ is $(0, 0)$.

B. $g(x) = 3x^2$

- The graph of $g(x)$ is narrower than the graph of $f(x)$.
- Both graphs open upward.
- Both have the axis of symmetry $x = 0$.
- Both have the vertex at $(0, 0)$.

INTERVENTION

Questioning Strategies

EXAMPLE 2

- What does each term in the function rule tell you about the graph?
- Does shifting the graph up or down change the axis of symmetry?
- What shifts the graph up or down?

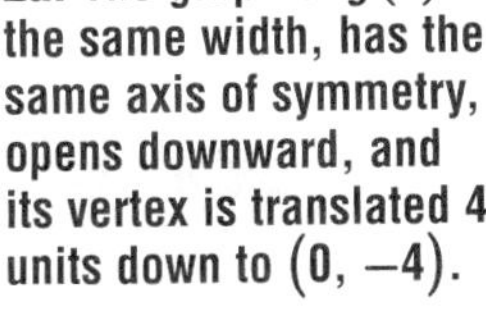

Teaching Tip

Inclusion To help students remember how a affects the width of a parabola, compare $|a|$ to $|m|$, where m is the slope of a line. As $|a|$ increases, the parabola narrows (gets steeper), just as when $|m|$ increases, the line gets steeper. For example, $y = 10x^2$ is a very narrow parabola and $y = 10x$ is a very steep line. Also, $y = \frac{1}{10}x^2$ is a very wide parabola and $y = \frac{1}{10}x$ is an almost horizontal line.

Power Presentations with PowerPoint®

Additional Examples

Example 3

Two identical softballs are dropped. The first is dropped from a height of 400 feet and the second is dropped from a height of 324 feet.

a. Write the two height functions and compare their graphs. The graph of $h_1(t) = -16t^2 + 400$ is a vertical translation of the graph of $h_2(t) = -16t^2 + 324$; the y-intercept of h_1 is 76 units higher than that of h_2.

b. Use the graphs to tell when each softball reaches the ground. 5 s from 400 ft; 4.5 s from 324 ft

INTERVENTION
Questioning Strategies

EXAMPLE 3

- What are reasonable domain and range values for these functions?
- How can you find the number of units that the graph of h_2 was translated from the graph of h_1?

Teaching Tip **Technology** Have students set **Ymin** = 0 and **Xmin** = 0 when graphing **Example 3** on a graphing calculator. **Ymax** should be set to the greater height.

EXAMPLE 3 Physics Application

Two identical water balloons are dropped from different heights as shown in the diagram.

a. Write the two height functions and compare their graphs.

Step 1 Write the height functions.
The y-intercept c represents the original height.

$h_1(t) = -16t^2 + 64$ *Dropped from 64 feet*
$h_2(t) = -16t^2 + 144$ *Dropped from 144 feet*

Step 2 Use a graphing calculator.
Since time and height cannot be negative, set the window for nonnegative values.

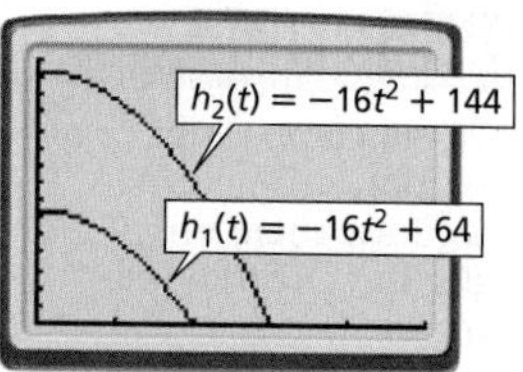

The graph of h_2 is a vertical translation of the graph of h_1. Since the balloon in h_2 is dropped from 80 feet higher than the one in h_1, the y-intercept of h_2 is 80 units higher.

Caution!
Remember that the graphs shown here represent the *height* of the objects over time, not the *paths* of the objects.

b. Use the graphs to tell when each water balloon reaches the ground.

The zeros of each function are when the water balloons reach the ground.

The water balloon dropped from 64 feet reaches the ground in 2 seconds. The water balloon dropped from 144 feet reaches the ground in 3 seconds.

Check These answers seem reasonable because the water balloon dropped from a greater height should take longer to reach the ground.

3. Two tennis balls are dropped, one from a height of 16 feet and the other from a height of 100 feet.
   a. Write the two height functions and compare their graphs.
   b. Use the graphs to tell when each tennis ball reaches the ground.

3a. $h_1(t) = -16t^2 + 16$, $h_2(t) = -16t^2 + 100$; The graph of the ball that is dropped from a height of 100 ft is a vertical translation of the graph of the ball that is dropped from a height of 16 ft. The y-intercept of the graph of the ball that is dropped from 100 ft is 84 units higher.

3b. The ball that is dropped from 16 ft reaches the ground in 1 s. The ball that is dropped from 100 ft reaches the ground in 2.5 s.

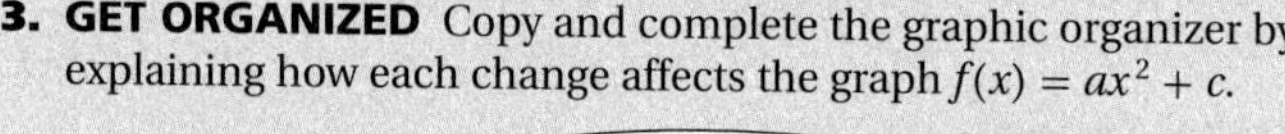

THINK AND DISCUSS

1. Describe how the graph of $f(x) = x^2 + c$ differs from the graph of $f(x) = x^2$ when the value of c is positive and when the value of c is negative.
2. Tell how to determine whether a graph of a function is wider or narrower than the graph of $f(x) = x^2$.
3. **GET ORGANIZED** Copy and complete the graphic organizer by explaining how each change affects the graph $f(x) = ax^2 + c$.

Know it! Note

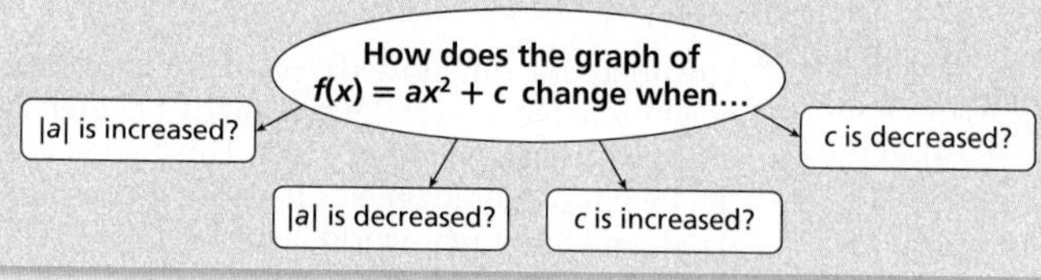

3 Close

Summarize

Have students write a function to describe each of the following situations.

The graph of $f(x) = x^2$ is

- translated 3 units down. $g(x) = x^2 - 3$
- narrowed. Possible answer: $g(x) = 5x^2$
- widened and translated 2 units up. Possible answer: $g(x) = 0.25x^2 + 2$
- the same width and location but opens downward. $g(x) = -x^2$

ONGOING ASSESSMENT and INTERVENTION

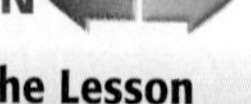

Diagnose Before **the Lesson**
9-4 Warm Up, TE p. 633

Monitor During **the Lesson**
Check It Out! Exercises, SE pp. 634–636
Questioning Strategies, TE pp. 634–636

Assess After **the Lesson**
9-4 Lesson Quiz, TE p. 639
Alternative Assessment, TE p. 639

Answers to *Think and Discuss*

1. When c is positive, the graph of $y = x^2 + c$ is a translation c units up of the graph of $y = x^2$. When c is negative, the graph of $y = x^2 + c$ is a translation c units down of the graph of $y = x^2$.
2. The graph of $g(x) = ax^2$ is narrower than the graph of $f(x) = x^2$ if $|a| > 1$, and wider if $|a| < 1$.
3. See p. A8.

go.hrw.com
Homework Help Online
KEYWORD: MA7 9-4
Parent Resources Online
KEYWORD: MA7 Parent

GUIDED PRACTICE

SEE EXAMPLE 1 p. 634

Order the functions from narrowest graph to widest.

1. $f(x) = 3x^2$, $g(x) = 2x^2$ **f(x), g(x)**
2. $f(x) = 5x^2$, $g(x) = -5x^2$ **The graphs have the same width.**
3. $f(x) = \frac{3}{4}x^2$, $g(x) = -2x^2$, $h(x) = -8x^2$ **h(x), g(x), f(x)**
4. $f(x) = x^2$, $g(x) = -\frac{4}{5}x^2$, $h(x) = 3x^2$ **h(x), f(x), g(x)**

SEE EXAMPLE 2 p. 635

Compare the graph of each function with the graph of $f(x) = x^2$.

5. $g(x) = x^2 + 6$
6. $g(x) = -2x^2 + 5$
7. $g(x) = \frac{1}{3}x^2$
8. $g(x) = -\frac{1}{4}x^2 - 2$

SEE EXAMPLE 3 p. 636

9. **Multi-Step** Two baseballs are dropped, one from a height of 16 feet and the other from a height of 256 feet.
   a. Write the two height functions and compare their graphs.
   b. Use the graphs to tell when each baseball reaches the ground.

PRACTICE AND PROBLEM SOLVING

Independent Practice	
For Exercises	See Example
10–13	1
14–17	2
18	3

Extra Practice
Skills Practice p. S20
Application Practice p. S36

Order the functions from narrowest graph to widest.

10. $f(x) = x^2$, $g(x) = 4x^2$ **g(x), f(x)**
11. $f(x) = -2x^2$, $g(x) = \frac{1}{2}x^2$ **f(x), g(x)**
12. $f(x) = -x^2$, $g(x) = -\frac{5}{8}x^2$, $h(x) = \frac{1}{2}x^2$ **f(x), g(x), h(x)**
13. $f(x) = -5x^2$, $g(x) = -\frac{3}{8}x^2$, $h(x) = 3x^2$ **f(x), h(x), g(x)**

Compare the graph of each function with the graph of $f(x) = x^2$.

14. $g(x) = \frac{1}{2}x^2 - 10$
15. $g(x) = -4x^2 - 2$
16. $g(x) = \frac{2}{3}x^2 - 9$
17. $g(x) = -\frac{1}{5}x^2 + 1$

18. **Multi-Step** A raindrop falls from a cloud at an altitude of 10,000 ft. Another raindrop falls from a cloud at an altitude of 14,400 ft.
    a. Write the two height functions and compare their graphs.
    b. Use the graphs to tell when each raindrop reaches the ground.

18a. $h_1(t) = -16t^2 + 10{,}000$, $h_2(t) = -16t^2 + 14{,}400$; The graph of h_2 is a vertical translation of the graph of h_1. The y-intercept of h_2 is 4400 units higher.

Tell whether each statement is sometimes, always, or never true.

19. The graphs of $f(x) = ax^2$ and $g(x) = -ax^2$ have the same width. **always**
20. The function $f(x) = ax^2 + c$ has three zeros. **never**
21. The graph of $y = ax^2 + 1$ has its vertex at the origin. **never**
22. The graph of $y = -x^2 + c$ intersects the x-axis. **sometimes**
23. **Data Collection** Use a graphing calculator and a motion detector to graph the height of a falling object over time. **Check students' work.**
    a. Find a function to model the height of the object while it is in motion.
    b. **Critical Thinking** Explain why the value of a in your function is not -16.

23b. Possible answer: Air resistance or wind may have affected the fall of the object.

9-4 Exercises

Assignment Guide

Assign *Guided Practice* exercises as necessary.

If you finished Examples **1–3**
Basic 10–32, 35, 34, 38–40, 44–49
Average 10–42, 44–49
Advanced 10–49

Homework Quick Check
Quickly check key concepts.
Exercises: 12, 16, 18, 35

Data Collection To help students complete **Exercise 23,** see *Technology Lab Activities.*

Answers

5. The graph of $g(x)$ is the same width, has the same axis of symmetry, and also opens upward; its vertex is translated 6 units up to (0, 6).
6. The graph of $g(x)$ is narrower, has the same axis of symmetry, and opens downward; its vertex is translated 5 units up to (0, 5).
7. The graph of $g(x)$ is wider, has the same axis of symmetry, also opens upward, and has the same vertex.
8. The graph of $g(x)$ is wider, has the same axis of symmetry, and opens downward; its vertex is translated 2 units down to (0, –2.)

9a. $h_1(t) = -16t^2 + 16$, $h_2(t) = -16t^2 + 256$; the graph of h_2 is a vertical translation of the graph of h_1. The y-intercept of the graph h_2 is 240 units higher.
   b. The baseball that is dropped from 256 ft reaches the ground in 4 s. The baseball that is dropped from 16 ft reaches the ground in 1 s.

14. The graph of $g(x)$ is wider, has the same axis of symmetry, and also opens upward; its vertex is translated 10 units down to (0, –10).
15. The graph of $g(x)$ is narrower, has the same axis of symmetry, and opens downward; its vertex is translated 2 units down to (0, –2).
16. The graph of $g(x)$ is wider, has the same axis of symmetry, also opens upward, and its vertex is translated 9 units down to (0, –9).
17. The graph of $g(x)$ is wider, has the same axis of symmetry, and opens downward; its vertex is translated 1 unit up to (0, 1).

18b. 10,000 ft: 25 s;
14,400 ft: 30 s

State Resources

MULTI-STEP TEST PREP Exercise 38 involves finding the height of an object as a function of time. This exercise prepares students for the Multi-Step Test Prep on page 640.

Answers

37. The graph of $f(x) = \frac{1}{10}x^2 - 5$ will look like the graph of $f(x) = x^2$, except that it will be wider (because $\frac{1}{10} < 1$) and it will be translated 5 units down (because $c = -5$).

38a. 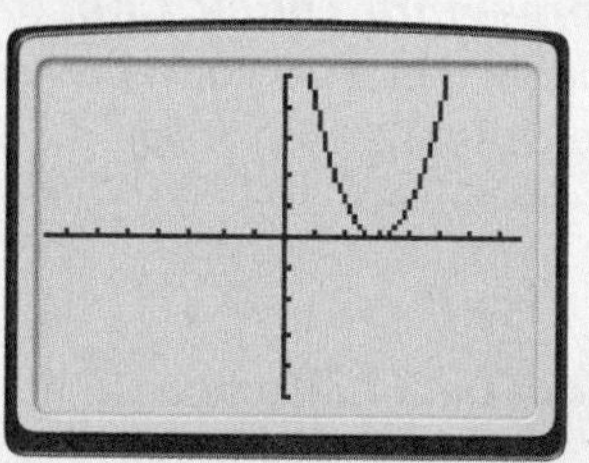

$y = (x - 3)^2$ and $y = x^2 - 3$ have the same width as $y = x^2$, and all of these parabolas open upward. $y = (x - 3)^2$ is translated 3 units right of $y = x^2$, has an axis of symmetry of $x = 3$, and has 1 zero (like $y = x^2$). $y = x^2 - 3$ has 2 zeros and is translated 3 units down from $y = x^2$.

b. 64 ft; 4 s

c. The x-coordinate of the vertex is the amount subtracted from x in the quantity that is squared, and the y-coordinate is the constant term in the equation. On the graph, find the greatest value of y, and then find the x-coordinate that corresponds to this y-coordinate.

27. Possible answer: $f(x) = -10x^2 + 2$

28. Possible answer: $f(x) = \frac{1}{2}x^2 + 1$

34a. 50 ft and 75 ft

b. $h(t) = -16t^2 + 75$

35. Possible answers:

a. $f(x) = x^2 + 2$

b. $f(x) = -x^2 + 2$

c. $f(x) = 5x^2 + 2$

36. c is the y-intercept of $y = x^2 + c$, and b is the y-intercept of $y = x + b$.

Write a function to describe each of the following.

24. The graph of $f(x) = x^2 + 10$ is translated 10 units down. $f(x) = x^2$

25. The graph of $f(x) = 3x^2 - 2$ is translated 4 units down. $f(x) = 3x^2 - 6$

26. The graph of $f(x) = 0.5x^2$ is narrowed. **Possible answer:** $f(x) = x^2$

27. The graph of $f(x) = -5x^2$ is narrowed and translated 2 units up.

28. The graph of $f(x) = x^2 - 7$ is widened and has no x-intercept.

Match each function to its graph.

29. $f(x) = 4x^2 - 3$ **B** 30. $f(x) = \frac{1}{4}x^2 - 3$ **D** 31. $f(x) = 4x^2 + 3$ **A** 32. $f(x) = -\frac{1}{4}x^2 - 3$ **C**

A. 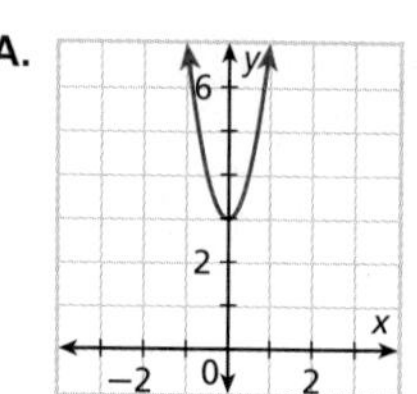

B. 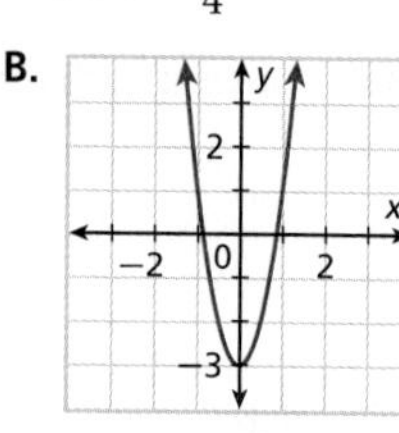

C. 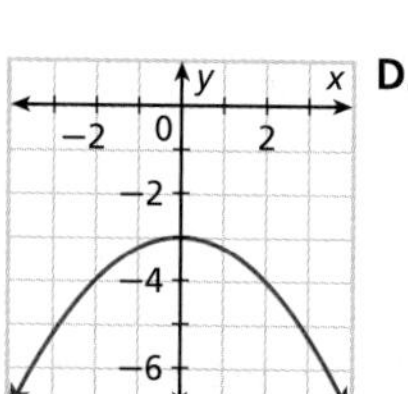

D. 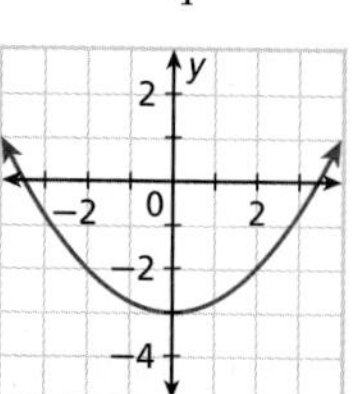

33. **Critical Thinking** For what values of a and c will $f(x) = ax^2 + c$ have one zero? $c = 0$ **and** $a \neq 0$

34. **Physics** The graph compares the heights of two identical coconuts that fell from different trees.
    a. What are the starting heights of each coconut?
    b. What is a possible function for the blue graph?
    c. Estimate the time for each coconut to reach the ground. **about 1.8 s and 2.2 s**

Coconuts' Heights

Height (ft): 0, 10, 20, 30, 40, 50, 60, 70, 80

Time (s): 1, 2, 3

35. Give an example of a quadratic function for each description.
    a. Its graph opens upward.
    b. Its graph has the same width as in part **a**, but the graph opens downward.
    c. Its graph is narrower than the graph in part **a**.

36. **Critical Thinking** Describe how the effect that the value of c has on the graph of $y = x^2 + c$ is similar to the effect that the value of b has on the graph of $y = x + b$.

37. **Write About It** Explain how you know, without graphing, what the graph of $f(x) = \frac{1}{10}x^2 - 5$ looks like.

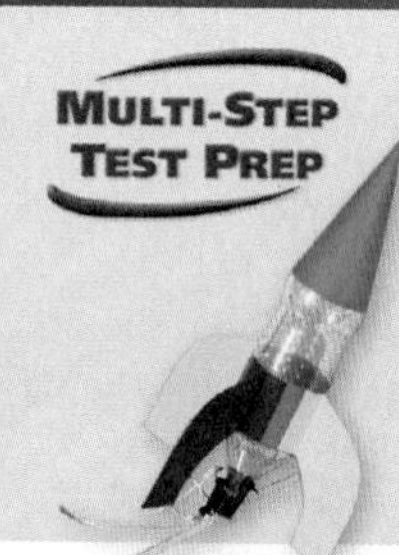

MULTI-STEP TEST PREP

38. This problem will prepare you for the Multi-Step Test Prep on page 640.
    a. Use a graphing calculator to graph $y = (x - 3)^2$. Compare this graph to the graph of $y = x^2$. How does this differ from $y = x^2 - 3$?
    b. The equation $h = -16(x - 2)^2 + 64$ describes the height in feet of a water bottle rocket as a function of time. What is the highest point that the rocket will reach? When will it return to the ground?
    c. How can the vertex be located from the equation? from the graph?

9-4 PRACTICE A

9-4 PRACTICE C

9-4 PRACTICE B

Order the functions from narrowest graph to widest.

1. $f(x) = 3x^2$; $g(x) = -2x^2$ **$f(x)$, $g(x)$**

2. $f(x) = \frac{1}{2}x^2$; $g(x) = 5x^2$; $h(x) = x^2$ **$g(x)$, $h(x)$, $f(x)$**

3. $f(x) = 4x^2$; $g(x) = -3x^2$; $h(x) = \frac{1}{4}x^2$ **$f(x)$, $g(x)$, $h(x)$**

4. $f(x) = 0.5x^2$; $g(x) = \frac{1}{4}x^2$; $h(x) = \frac{1}{3}x^2$ **$f(x)$, $h(x)$, $g(x)$**

Compare the graph of each function with the graph of $f(x) = x^2$.

5. $g(x) = 5x^2 + 10$ **The graph of $g(x)$ is narrower. Both graphs open upward. The vertex of $g(x)$, (0, 10), is translated 10 units up from the vertex of $f(x)$ at (0, 0).**

6. $g(x) = \frac{1}{8}x^2 - 3$ **The graph of $g(x)$ is wider. Both graphs open upward. The vertex of $g(x)$, (0, –3), is translated 3 units down from the vertex of $f(x)$ at (0, 0).**

7. $g(x) = -3x^2 + 8$ **The graph of g(x) is narrower. $g(x)$ opens downward and $f(x)$ opens upward. The vertex of $g(x)$, (0, 8), is translated 8 units up from the vertex of $f(x)$ at (0, 0).**

8. $g(x) = -\frac{3}{4}x^2 + \frac{1}{4}$ **The graph of $g(x)$ is wider. $g(x)$ opens downward and $f(x)$ opens upward. The vertex of $g(x)$, $(0, \frac{1}{4})$, is translated $\frac{1}{4}$ units up from the vertex of $f(x)$ at (0, 0).**

9. Two sandbags are dropped from a hot air balloon, one from a height of 400 feet and the other from a height of 1600 feet.
    a. Write the two height functions.
    $h_1(t) = -16t^2 + 400$ $h_2(t) = -16t^2 + 1600$
    b. Sketch and compare their graphs.
    The graph of h_2 is a vertical translation of the graph of h_1: 1200 units up.
    c. Tell when each sandbag reaches the ground.
    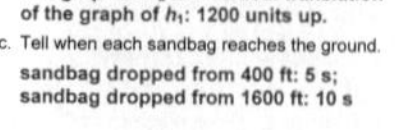
    sandbag dropped from 400 ft: 5 s; sandbag dropped from 1600 ft: 10 s

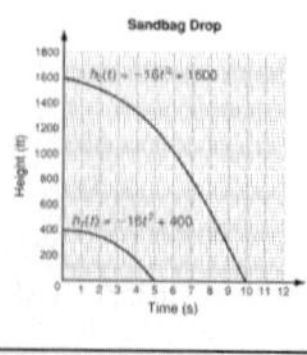

9-4 READING STRATEGIES

The table shows how changing the values of a and c affect the shape and location of a parabola. All the functions are in the form $f(x) = ax^2 + c$.

$f(x) = x^2$ $g(x) = 4x^2$	$f(x) = x^2$ $g(x) = \frac{1}{2}x^2$	$f(x) = x^2$ $g(x) = x^2 + 5$	$f(x) = x^2$ $g(x) = x^2 - 7$
When $\lvert a\rvert$ increases, the parabola becomes narrower.	When $\lvert a\rvert$ decreases, the parabola becomes wider.	When c increases, the parabola is translated up.	When c decreases, the parabola is translated down.

Use the functions above to answer the following questions.

1. Which is wider: $g(x) = 4x^2$ or $g(x) = \frac{1}{2}x^2$? **$g(x) = \frac{1}{2}x^2$**
   How would you be able to tell without looking at their graphs?
   The absolute value of $\frac{1}{2}$ is less than the absolute value of 4.

2. Why would $g(x) = 4x^2$ and $h(x) = -4x^2$ have the same width?
   4 and –4 have the same absolute value: 4.
   How would their graphs be different? **$g(x)$ will open upward, $h(x)$ will open downward.**

3. Order the graphs of the following functions from narrowest (1) to widest (4) by numbering.
   $f(x) = -2x^2$ **2** $g(x) = \frac{1}{4}x^2$ **4** $h(x) = 3x^2$ **1** $j(x) = -x^2$ **3**

4. Which has its vertex below the x-axis: $g(x) = x^2 + 5$ or $g(x) = x^2 - 7$? **$g(x) = x^2 - 7$**
   How would you be able to tell without looking at their graphs?
   c is negative, so it was translated down from the origin.

5. How many vertical units separate the y-intercepts of $g(x) = x^2 + 5$ or $g(x) = x^2 - 7$?
   12 How would you be able to tell without looking at their graphs?
   $g(x) = x^2 + 5$ is translated up 5 units and $g(x) = x^2 - 7$ is translated down 7 units so they are 5 + 7, or 12, units apart.

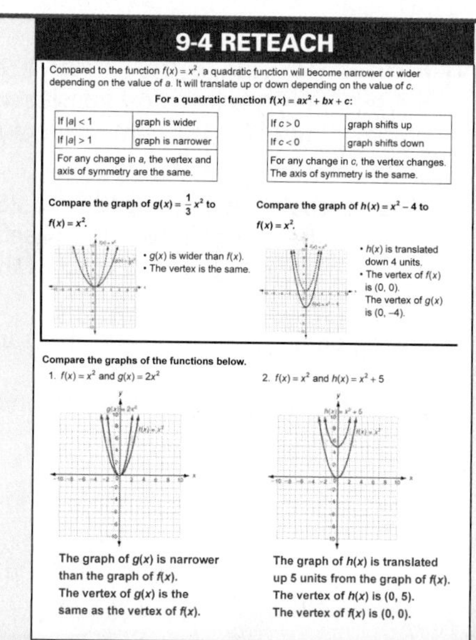

9-4 RETEACH

Compared to the function $f(x) = x^2$, a quadratic function will become narrower or wider depending on the value of a. It will translate up or down depending on the value of c.

For a quadratic function $f(x) = ax^2 + bx + c$:

If $\lvert a\rvert < 1$	graph is wider
If $\lvert a\rvert > 1$	graph is narrower
For any change in a, the vertex and axis of symmetry are the same.	

If $c > 0$	graph shifts up
If $c < 0$	graph shifts down
For any change in c, the vertex changes. The axis of symmetry is the same.	

Compare the graph of $g(x) = \frac{1}{3}x^2$ to $f(x) = x^2$.

- $g(x)$ is wider than $f(x)$.
- The vertex is the same.

Compare the graph of $h(x) = x^2 - 4$ to $f(x) = x^2$.

- $h(x)$ is translated down 4 units.
- The vertex of $f(x)$ is (0, 0). The vertex of $g(x)$ is (0, –4).

Compare the graphs of the functions below.

1. $f(x) = x^2$ and $g(x) = 2x^2$
   The graph of $g(x)$ is narrower than the graph of $f(x)$. The vertex of $g(x)$ is the same as the vertex of $f(x)$.

2. $f(x) = x^2$ and $h(x) = x^2 + 5$
   The graph of $h(x)$ is translated up 5 units from the graph of $f(x)$. The vertex of $h(x)$ is (0, 5). The vertex of $f(x)$ is (0, 0).

TEST PREP

39. Which function's graph is the result of shifting the graph of $f(x) = -x^2 - 4$ 3 units down?

Ⓐ $g(x) = -x^2 - 1$ Ⓒ $g(x) = -4x^2 - 4$
Ⓑ $g(x) = -\frac{1}{3}x^2 - 4$ Ⓓ $g(x) = -x^2 - 7$ (circled)

40. Which of the following is true when the graph of $f(x) = x^2 + 4$ is transformed into the graph of $g(x) = 2x^2 + 4$?

Ⓕ The new function has more zeroes than the old function.
Ⓖ Both functions have the same vertex. (circled)
Ⓗ The function is translated up.
Ⓙ The axis of symmetry changes.

41. **Gridded Response** For what value of c will $f(x) = x^2 + c$ have one zero? **0**

CHALLENGE AND EXTEND

42. **Graphing Calculator** Graph the functions $f(x) = (x + 1)^2$, $g(x) = (x + 4)^2$, $h(x) = (x - 2)^2$, and $k(x) = (x - 5)^2$. Make a conjecture about the result of transforming the graph of $f(x) = x^2$ into the graph of $f(x) = (x - h)^2$.

42. The graph of $f(x) = (x - h)^2$ is the result of translating the graph of $f(x) = x^2$ by h units along the x-axis.

43. Using the function $f(x) = x^2$, write each new function:
    a. The graph is translated 7 units down. $\mathbf{f(x) = x^2 - 7}$
    b. The graph is reflected across the x-axis and translated 2 units up. $\mathbf{f(x) = -x^2 + 2}$
    c. Each y-value is halved, and then the graph is translated 1 unit up. $\mathbf{f(x) = \frac{1}{2}x^2 + 1}$

SPIRAL REVIEW

44. Justify each step. *(Lesson 1-7)*

Procedure	Justification
$5x - 2(4 - x)$	
$5x - 2(4 - x) = 5x - 8 + 2x$	a. **Distributive Property**
$= 5x + 2x - 8$	b. **Commutative Property of Addition**
$= (5x + 2x) - 8$	c. **Associative Property of Addition**
$= 7x - 8$	d. **Combine like terms.**

Describe the correlation illustrated by each scatter plot. *(Lesson 4-5)*

45. **no correlation**

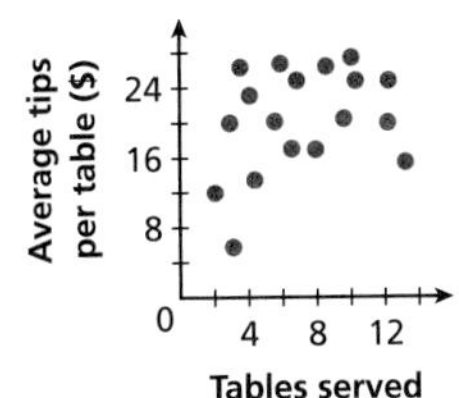

46. **positive**

Test Scores and Sleep
Test Score: 40, 60, 80, 100
Sleep (h): 0, 4, 6, 8, 10

Graph each quadratic function. *(Lesson 9-3)*

47. $y = 2x^2 - 1$ 48. $y = x^2 - 2x - 2$ 49. $y = -3x^2 - x + 6$

47.

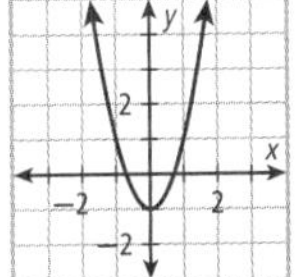

48.

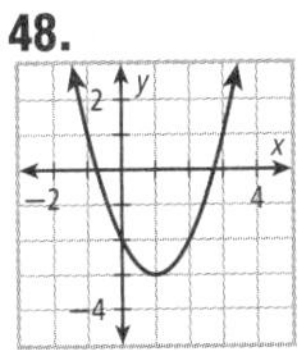

49.

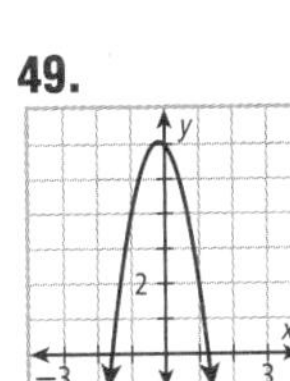

9-4 PROBLEM SOLVING

Write the correct answer.

1. Two construction workers working at different heights on a skyscraper dropped their hammers at the same time. The first was working at a height of 400 ft, the second at a height of 160 ft. Write the two functions that describe the heights of the hammers.
$y = -16x^2 + 400$
$y = -16x^2 + 160$

2. Graph the two functions you found in problem 1 on the grid below.

Dropping Hammers

3. Based on the graphs you drew in problem 2, how long will it take each hammer to reach the ground?
3.2 seconds
5 seconds

The pull of gravity varies from planet to planet. The graph shows the height of objects dropped from 500 ft on the surface of four planets. Use this graph to answer questions 4–6. Select the best answer.

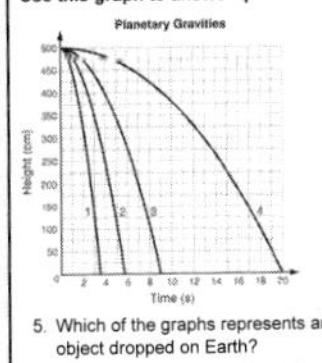

4. Of the four planets, Jupiter has the strongest gravity. Which of the four graphs represents the height of the object dropped on Jupiter?
F Graph 1   H Graph 3
G Graph 2   J Graph 4

5. Which of the graphs represents an object dropped on Earth?
A Graph 1   C Graph 3
B Graph 2   D Graph 4

6. Due to its small size, Pluto has a very weak pull of gravity. Which of the equations below represents the graph of the object dropped on Pluto?
A $h(t) = -41x^2 + 500$
B $h(t) = -16x^2 + 500$
C $h(t) = -6x^2 + 500$
D $h(t) = -1.25x^2 + 500$

9-4 CHALLENGE

You've learned that any quadratic function can be written in the form $f(x) = ax^2 + bx + c$. This form is called **standard form.**

Any quadratic function can also be written in **vertex form,** $\mathbf{f(x) = a(x - h)^2 + k}$, where a, h, and k are real numbers and $a \neq 0$.

1. Use a graphing calculator to compare these functions.
$f(x) = x^2$ $g(x) = (x - 3)^2$ $h(x) = (x - 6)^2$ $j(x) = (x + 4)^2$
    a. Which parameter, a, h, or k, changes in each function? **h**
    b. What is the value of that parameter in each function? **0, 3, 6, –4**
    c. What characteristic of the graphs changes each time? **vertex moves horizontally**
    d. In terms of transformations, describe the effect of this parameter.
    The parameter h determines a horizontal translation.

2. Use a graphing calculator to compare these functions.
$f(x) = x^2$ $g(x) = x^2 + 2$ $h(x) = x^2 + 5$ $j(x) = x^2 - 3$
    a. Which parameter changes in each function? **k**
    b. What is the value of that parameter in each function? **0, 2, 5, –3**
    c. What characteristic of the graphs changes each time? **vertex moves vertically**
    d. In terms of transformations, describe the effect of this parameter.
    The parameter k determines a vertical translation.

3. Use a graphing calculator to compare these functions.
$f(x) = (x - 3)^2 + 5$ $g(x) = 2(x - 3)^2 + 5$ $h(x) = -1(x - 3)^2 + 5$ $j(x) = \left(\frac{1}{5}\right)(x - 3)^2 + 5$
    a. Which parameter changes in each function? **a**
    b. What is the value of that parameter in each function? **1, 2, –1, $\frac{1}{5}$**
    c. What characteristic of the graphs changes each time? **width and direction**
    d. In terms of transformations, describe the effect of this parameter.
    The parameter a makes the parabola narrower or wider and makes the parabola open up or down.

4. Why do you think $f(x) = a(x - h)^2 + k$ is called vertex form?
The coordinates of the vertex are (h, k).

5. Without graphing, find the vertex of $f(x) = 6(x + 18)^2 + 24$. **(–18, 24)**

TEST PREP DOCTOR + Shifting the quadratic function in **Exercise 39** will change only the value of c. Eliminate choices **B** and **C.**

Answers

42.

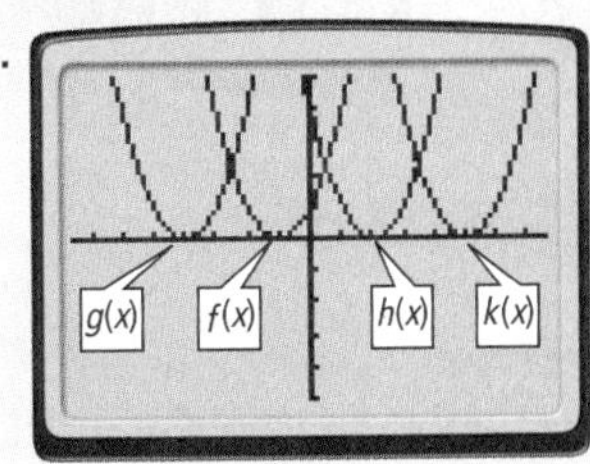

Journal

Describe the effects that a and c have on the graph of $y = ax^2 + c$.

ALTERNATIVE ASSESSMENT

Write a quadratic function that is wider than $f(x) = x^2$ and translated 3 units down. Write a second function that is narrower and translated 2 units up. Then compare each graph to $f(x) = x^2$.

Power Presentations with PowerPoint®

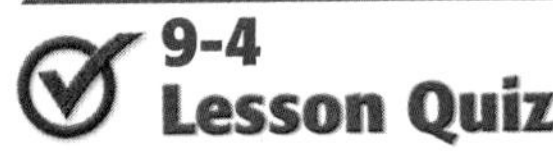

9-4 Lesson Quiz

1. Order the functions $f(x) = 4x^2$, $g(x) = -5x^2$, and $h(x) = 0.8x^2$ from narrowest graph to widest. $g(x)$, $f(x)$, $h(x)$

2. Compare the graph of $g(x) = 0.5x^2 - 2$ with the graph of $f(x) = x^2$.
    - The graph of $g(x)$ is wider.
    - Both graphs open upward.
    - Both have the axis of symmetry $x = 0$.
    - The vertex of $g(x)$ is $(0, -2)$; the vertex of $f(x)$ is $(0, 0)$.

Two identical soccer balls are dropped. The first is dropped from a height of 100 feet and the second is dropped from a height of 196 feet.

3. Write the two height functions and compare their graphs. The graph of $h_1(t) = -16t^2 + 100$ is a vertical translation of the graph of $h_2(t) = -16t^2 + 196$; the y-intercept of h_1 is 96 units lower than that of h_2.

4. Use the graphs to tell when each soccer ball reaches the ground. 2.5 s from 100 ft; 3.5 from 196 ft

Also available on transparency

Organizer

Objective: Assess students' ability to apply concepts and skills in Lessons 9-1 through 9-4 in a real-world format.

Online Edition

Resources

Algebra I Assessments
www.mathtekstoolkit.org

Problem	Text Reference
1	Lesson 9-1
2	Lessons 9-1, 9-3
3	Lessons 9-2, 9-3, 9-4
4	Lessons 9-2, 9-3
5	Lesson 9-2

Answers

2. See p. A30.
4. The x-coordinate represents the time when the water bottle rocket reaches its maximum height, which is represented by the y-coordinate.
5. 1.775 s; for $y = 110$ the corresponding x-coordinate is 1.775.

State Resources

CHAPTER 9

MULTI-STEP TEST PREP

SECTION 9A

Quadratic Functions

The Sky's the Limit The Physics Club is using computer simulation software to design a water bottle rocket that doesn't have a parachute. The data for their current design are shown in the table.

Time (s)	Height (ft)
0	0
1	80
2	128
3	144
4	128
5	80

1. Tell whether the data satisfy a quadratic function. **yes**
2. Graph the function from Problem 1.
3. Find and label the zeros, axis of symmetry, and vertex. **0 and 6; $x = 3$; $(3,144)$**
4. Explain what the x- and y-coordinates of the vertex represent in the context of the problem.
5. Estimate how many seconds it will take the rocket to reach 110 feet. Explain.

INTERVENTION

Scaffolding Questions

1. How can you tell from a table of data whether the data is linear or quadratic? linear: constant first differences quadratic: constant second differences
2. Do you need to graph negative x- or y-values? Explain. No; neither time nor height can be negative.
3. Which points do you look for when finding the zeros of a function from its graph? points that contain the x-intercepts
4. Does this graph have a maximum or a minimum? maximum What are the labels on the axes of your graph? vertical axis: Height (ft), horizontal axis: Time (s)
5. Between what two heights given in the table would 110 ft belong? between 80 ft and 128 ft What are the times associated with those two heights? 1 s and 2 s

Extension

If the function that models the height of a rocket is $h(t) = -16t^2 + 96t$, what equation would you solve to find the time it takes the rocket to reach 130 ft? How many answers are there? Explain. $130 = -16t^2 + 96t$; 2; there are 2 zeros.

READY TO GO ON?

CHAPTER 9

SECTION 9A

Quiz for Lessons 9-1 Through 9-4

9-1 Identifying Quadratic Functions

Tell whether each function is quadratic. Explain.

1. $y + 2x^2 = 3x$
2. $x^2 + y = 4 + x^2$
3. $\{(2, 12), (-1, 3), (0, 0), (1, 3)\}$

1. Yes; the equation can be written in the form $y = ax^2 + bx + c$.
2. No; $a = 0$
3. Yes; the second differences are constant.

Tell whether the graph of each quadratic function opens upward or downward and whether the parabola has a maximum or a minimum.

4. $y = -x^2 - 7x + 18$ **downward; maximum**
5. $y - 2x^2 = 4x + 3$ **upward; minimum**
6. $y = 5x - 0.5x^2$ **downward; maximum**
7. Graph the function $y = \frac{1}{2}x^2 - 2$ and give the domain and range.

9-2 Characteristics of Quadratic Functions

Find the zeros of each quadratic function from its graph. Then find the axis of symmetry.

8\. 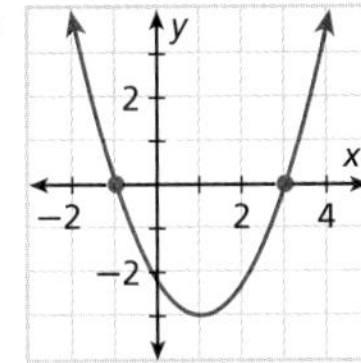

−1 and 3; $x = 1$

9\.  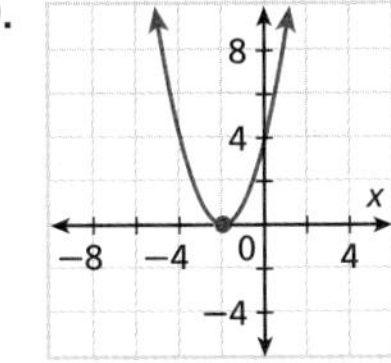

−2; $x = -2$

10\.  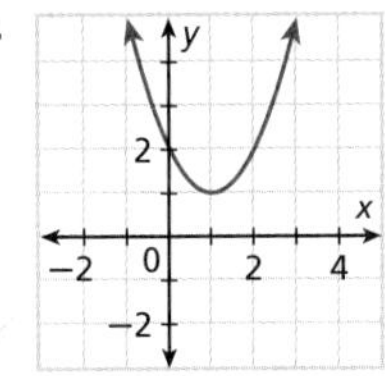

no zeros; $x = 1$

Fnd the vertex.

11. $y = x^2 + 6x + 2$ **(−3, −7)**
12. $y = 3 + 4x - 2x^2$ **(1, 5)**
13. $y = 3x^2 + 12x - 12$ **(−2, −24)**
14. The height in feet of the curved roof of an aircraft hangar can be modeled by $y = -0.02x^2 + 1.6x$, where x is the horizontal distance in feet from one wall at ground level. What is the greatest height of the hangar? **32 ft**

9-3 Graphing Quadratic Functions

Graph each quadratic function.

15. $y = x^2 + 3x + 9$
16. $y = x^2 - 2x - 15$
17. $y = x^2 - 2x - 8$
18. $y = 2x^2 - 6$
19. $y = 4x^2 + 8x - 2$
20. $y = 2x^2 + 10x + 1$

9-4 Transforming Quadratic Functions

Compare the graph of each function with the graph of $f(x) = x^2$.

21. $g(x) = x^2 - 2$
22. $g(x) = \frac{2}{3}x^2$
23. $g(x) = 5x^2 + 3$
24. $g(x) = -x^2 + 4$
25. The pilot of a hot-air balloon drops a sandbag onto a target from a height of 196 feet. Later, he drops an identical sandbag from a height of 676 feet.
    a. Write the two height functions and compare their graphs. Use $h(t) = -16t^2 + c$, where c is the height of the balloon. **$h_1(t) = -16t^2 + 196$; $h_2(t) = -16t^2 + 676$**
    b. Use the graphs to tell when each sandbag will reach the ground. **3.5 s; 6.5 s**

READY TO GO ON? SECTION 9A

Organizer

Objective: Assess students' mastery of concepts and skills in Lessons 9-1 through 9-4.

Resources

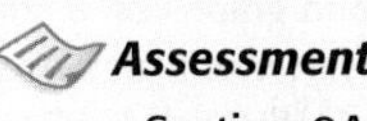

Assessment Resources
Section 9A Quiz

Teacher One Stop™
Test & Practice Generator

INTERVENTION

Resources

Ready to Go On? Intervention and Enrichment **Worksheets**

Ready to Go On? **CD-ROM**

Ready to Go On? **Online**

my.hrw.com

Answers

7, 15–24. See pp. A30–A31.

READY TO GO ON?
Diagnose and Prescribe

Ready to Go On? Intervention	*Ready to Go On? Intervention*, Section 9A Worksheets	CD-R.OM	Online
Lesson 9-1	9-1 Intervention	Activity 9-1	Diagnose and Prescribe Online
Lesson 9-2	9-2 Intervention	Activity 9-2	
Lesson 9-3	9-3 Intervention	Activity 9-3	
Lesson 9-4	9-4 Intervention	Activity 9-4	

Ready to Go On? Enrichment**, Section 9A**

Worksheets
CD-ROM
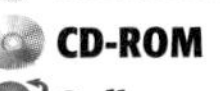
Online

SECTION **9B**

Solving Quadratic Equations

One-Minute Section Planner

Lesson	Lab Resources	Materials
Lesson 9-5 Solving Quadratic Equations by Graphing • Solve quadratic equations by graphing. ☑ SAT-10 ☑ NAEP ☑ ACT ☑ SAT ☑ SAT Subject Tests		**Required** graphing calculator
9-5 Technology Lab Explore Roots, Zeros, and *x*-Intercepts • Use tables and graphs on a graphing calculator to explore the relationships between zeros, roots, and *x*-intercepts. ☑ SAT-10 ☑ NAEP ☑ ACT ☑ SAT ☑ SAT Subject Tests	***Technology Lab Activities*** 9-5 Lab Recording Sheet	**Required** graphing calculator
Lesson 9-6 Solving Quadratic Equations by Factoring • Solve quadratic equations by factoring. ☑ SAT-10 ☑ NAEP ☑ ACT ☑ SAT ☑ SAT Subject Tests		**Optional** graphing calculator
Lesson 9-7 Solving Quadratic Equations by Using Square Roots • Solve quadratic equations by factoring. ☑ SAT-10 ☑ NAEP ☑ ACT ☑ SAT ☑ SAT Subject Tests		
9-8 Algebra Lab Model Completing the Square • Use algebra tiles to model completing the square. ☐ SAT-10 ☑ NAEP ☐ ACT ☐ SAT ☐ SAT Subject Tests	***Algebra Lab Activities*** 9-8 Lab Recording Sheet	**Required** algebra tiles (MK)
Lesson 9-8 Completing the Square • Solve quadratic equations by completing the square. ☑ SAT-10 ☑ NAEP ☐ ACT ☑ SAT ☐ SAT Subject Tests		**Required** graphing calculator **Optional** algebra tiles (MK)
Lesson 9-9 The Quadratic Formula and the Discriminant • Solve quadratic equations by using the Quadratic Formula. • Determine the number of solutions of a quadratic equation by using the discriminant. ☑ SAT-10 ☑ NAEP ☑ ACT ☑ SAT ☑ SAT Subject Tests		**Optional** graphing calculator
Extension Cubic Functions and Equations • Recognize and graph cubic functions. • Solve cubic equations. ☐ SAT-10 ☐ NAEP ☐ ACT ☐ SAT ☑ SAT Subject Tests		

Note: If NAEP is checked, the content is tested on either the Grade 8 or the Grade 12 NAEP assessment.

MK = *Manipulatives Kit*

Math Background

Professional Learning

QUADRATIC EQUATIONS

Lesson 9-5

A *quadratic equation* is an equation that can be written in the form $ax^2 + bx + c = 0$, where a, b, and c are real numbers and $a \neq 0$. This is the *standard form* of a quadratic equation. Every quadratic equation written in this form has a related quadratic function $y = ax^2 + bx + c$.

Just as with the solutions of all equations, a solution of a quadratic equation is a value of the variable that makes the equation true. One way to solve a quadratic equation in standard form is to graph the related quadratic function and find its x-intercepts.

For example, for the quadratic equation $x^2 + x - 6 = 0$, the graph of the related function $y = x^2 + x - 6$ is the set of all ordered pairs of the form $(x, x^2 + x - 6)$. It must be true that at any point where the graph intersects the x-axis, the y-coordinate is 0; that is, $x^2 + x - 6 = 0$. In other words, the x-intercepts of the graph are precisely the solutions of the quadratic equation.

Students should understand that this is a general method that works for any equation set equal to 0 whose related function can be graphed. For example, the linear equation $\frac{1}{2}x - 2 = 0$ may be solved by graphing the related linear function $y = \frac{1}{2}x - 2$ and noticing that the graph intersects the x-axis at $x = 4$.

SOLUTION METHODS

Lessons 9-5 to 9-9

Although graphing has the advantage of being a fairly intuitive solution method, it is often inefficient and imprecise. These drawbacks motivate the need for other solution techniques.

The method of solving a quadratic equation by factoring springs from the *Zero Product Property*: If the product of two real numbers is zero, then at least one of the numbers is zero. This property justifies solving quadratic equations by factoring. For example, to solve $x^2 + x - 6 = 0$, note that $x^2 + x - 6 = (x - 2)(x + 3)$. By the Zero Product Property, it must be true that $x - 2 = 0$ or $x + 3 = 0$, which gives the solutions 2 and -3.

Some quadratic equations do not lend themselves to factoring, so still more methods are needed. The techniques of completing the square and using the Quadratic Formula work for *any* quadratic equation. It is essential for students to realize that graphing, factoring, and the Quadratic Formula can be used to solve quadratic equations only when one side of the quadratic equation is equal to zero (i.e., the equation is written in standard form).

THE DISCRIMINANT

Lesson 9-9

Given a quadratic equation in standard form, the discriminant, $b^2 - 4ac$, offers an efficient means of determining the number of real solutions. If the discriminant is positive, there are two real solutions. If the discriminant is zero, there is one real solution. If the discriminant is negative, there are no real solutions.

According to the Fundamental Theorem of Algebra, every polynomial function of degree $n \geq 1$ has exactly n zeros. This means that all quadratic equations, whose related functions are polynomials of degree 2, have exactly two solutions. This may seem to contradict the previous discussion about the discriminant, but there are two important points.

If there is only one real solution, it has *multiplicity* 2. For example, the factored form of $x^2 - 2x + 1 = 0$ is $(x - 1)^2 = 0$, so $x = 1$ is the only solution. It is called a solution of multiplicity 2, meaning it is counted twice, since the factor $x - 1$ occurs twice. (An example of the analogous situation when dealing with numbers is $9 = 3^2$. Even though 3 is the only prime factor, we say that the prime factorization of 9 contains two factors.)

If there are no real solutions, the quadratic equation has two *complex* solutions. Complex numbers have the form $a + bi$, where a and b are real numbers and $i = \sqrt{-1}$. Students will study complex numbers in Algebra 2.

9-5 Organizer

Pacing: Traditional 1 day
Block $\frac{1}{2}$ day

Objective: Solve quadratic equations by graphing.

Online Edition
Tutorial Videos

Countdown Week 20

Power Presentations with PowerPoint®

Warm Up

1. Graph $y = x^2 + 4x + 3$.

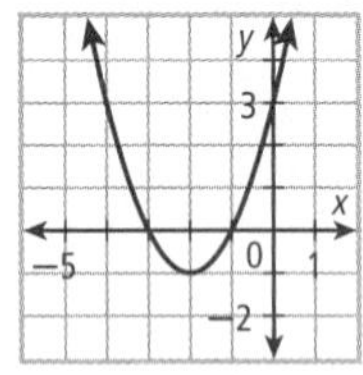

2. Identify the vertex and zeros of the function above. vertex: $(-2, -1)$; zeros: $-3, -1$

Also available on transparency

Math Humor

Q: What does a person have if they can easily find solutions to quadratic equations?

A: Zero visibility.

9-5 Solving Quadratic Equations by Graphing

Objective
Solve quadratic equations by graphing.

Vocabulary
quadratic equation

Who uses this?
Dolphin trainers can use solutions of quadratic equations to plan the choreography for their shows. (See Example 2.)

Every quadratic function has a related *quadratic equation*. A **quadratic equation** is an equation that can be written in the standard form $ax^2 + bx + c = 0$, where a, b, and c are real numbers and $a \neq 0$.

When writing a quadratic function as its related quadratic equation, you replace y with 0.

$$y = ax^2 + bx + c$$
$$0 = ax^2 + bx + c$$
$$ax^2 + bx + c = 0$$

One way to solve a quadratic equation in standard form is to graph the related function and find the x-values where $y = 0$. In other words, find the zeros of the related function. Recall that a quadratic function may have two, one, or no zeros.

Solving Quadratic Equations by Graphing
Step 1 Write the related function.
Step 2 Graph the related function.
Step 3 Find the zeros of the related function.

EXAMPLE 1 **Solving Quadratic Equations by Graphing**

Solve each equation by graphing the related function.

A $2x^2 - 2 = 0$

Step 1 Write the related function.
$2x^2 - 2 = y$, or $y = 2x^2 + 0x - 2$

Step 2 Graph the function.

- The axis of symmetry is $x = 0$.
- The vertex is $(0, -2)$.
- Two other points are $(1, 0)$ and $(2, 6)$.
- Graph the points and **reflect** them across the axis of symmetry.

Step 3 Find the zeros.
The zeros appear to be -1 and 1.

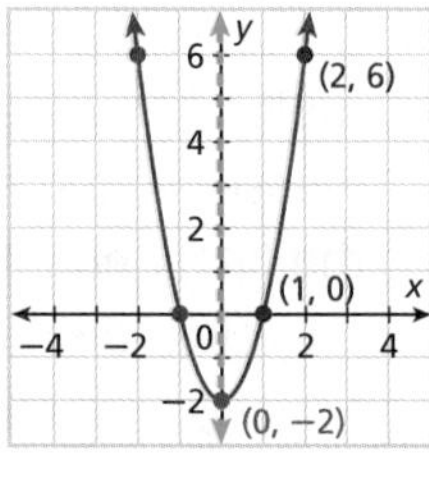

Check

$2x^2 - 2 = 0$	
$2(-1)^2 - 2$	0
$2(1) - 2$	0
$2 - 2$	0
0	0 ✓

Substitute −1 and 1 for x in the quadratic equation.

$2x^2 - 2 = 0$	
$2(1)^2 - 2$	0
$2(1) - 2$	0
$2 - 2$	0
0	0 ✓

State Resources

1 Introduce

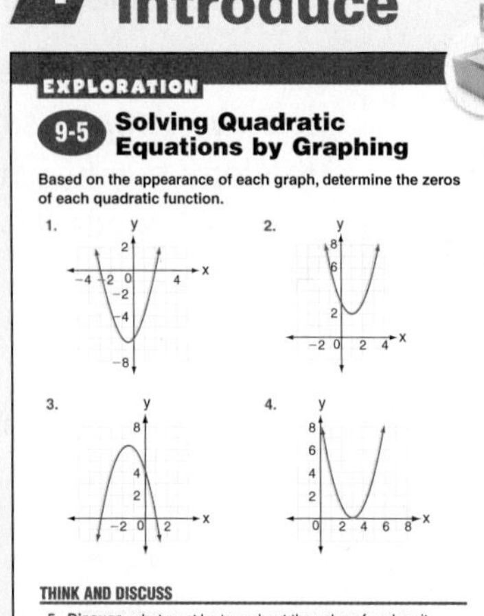
EXPLORATION

9-5 Solving Quadratic Equations by Graphing

Based on the appearance of each graph, determine the zeros of each quadratic function.

1. 2. 3. 4.

THINK AND DISCUSS

5. **Discuss** what must be true about the value of y when it corresponds to a zero of a function.

6. **Explain** the connection between the zeros of a function and the intersection of its graph with the line $y = 0$.

Motivate

Display the graph of a quadratic function with integer zeros, such as $y = 2x^2 + 14x + 24$. Point out that the zeros of the function are the x-values that correspond to a y-value of 0. Remind students that a quadratic function can have two, one, or no real zeros. Have students find the zeros of the function displayed. −3 and −4 Tell students that in this lesson they will learn to solve quadratic equations by graphing.

Explorations and answers are provided in *Alternate Openers: Explorations Transparencies.*

go.hrw.com
State Resources Online
KEYWORD: MA7 Resources

Solve each equation by graphing the related function.

B $-x^2 - 4x - 4 = 0$

Step 1 Write the related function.

$y = -x^2 - 4x - 4$

Step 2 Graph the function.

- The axis of symmetry is $x = -2$.
- The vertex is $(-2, 0)$.
- The y-intercept is -4.
- Another point is $(-1, -1)$.
- Graph the points and reflect them across the axis of symmetry.

Step 3 Find the zeros.

The only zero appears to be -2.

Check

$-x^2 - 4x - 4 = 0$	
$-(-2)^2 - 4(-2) - 4$	0
$-(4) + 8 - 4$	0
$4 - 4$	0
0	0 ✓

You can also confirm the solution by using the **Table** function. Enter the equation and press  TABLE GRAPH. When $y = 0$, $x = -2$. The x-intercept is -2.

X	Y1
-4	-4
-3	-1
-2	0
-1	-1
0	-4
1	-9
2	-16

X=-2

C $x^2 + 5 = 4x$

Step 1 Write the related function.

$x^2 - 4x + 5 = 0$

$y = x^2 - 4x + 5$

Step 2 Graph the function.

Use a graphing calculator.

Step 3 Find the zeros.

The function appears to have no zeros.

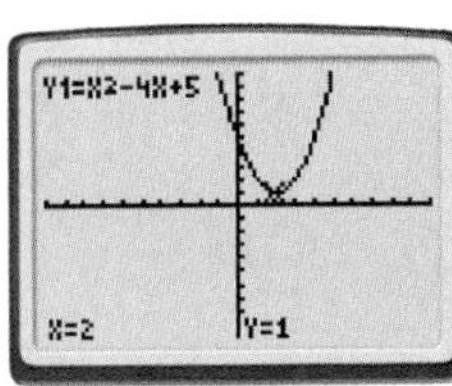

The equation has no real-number solutions.

Check reasonableness Use the table function.

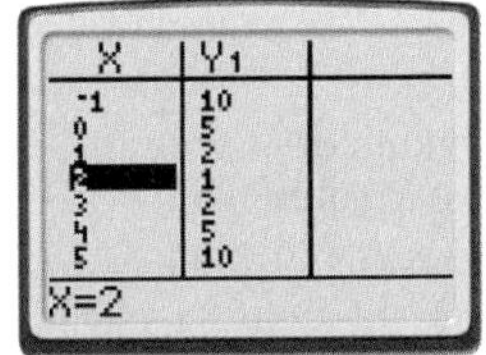

X	Y1
-1	10
0	5
1	2
2	1
3	2
4	5
5	10

X=2

There are no zeros in the Y1 column. Also, the signs of the values in this column do not change. The function appears to have no zeros.

CHECK IT OUT! Solve each equation by graphing the related function.

1a. $x^2 - 8x - 16 = 2x^2$ -4

1b. $6x + 10 = -x^2$ no real solutions

1c. $-x^2 + 4 = 0$ $-2, 2$

COMMON ERROR ALERT

Students may try to identify a, b, and c without first writing the equation in the form $ax^2 + bx + c = 0$. Remind students to rewrite the equation in the form $ax^2 + bx + c = 0$ so that the correct signs of each coefficient are identified.

Power Presentations with PowerPoint®

Additional Examples

Example 1

Solve each equation by graphing the related function.

A. $2x^2 - 18 = 0$ 3, −3

B. $-12x + 18 = -2x^2$ 3

C. $2x^2 + 4x = -3$ no real solutions

INTERVENTION

Questioning Strategies

EXAMPLE 1

- If the vertex has a y-coordinate of 0, what does that tell you about the number of zeros of the function?
- Can a quadratic equation have more than two solutions?

Critical Thinking Explain to students how to determine that the equation in **Example 1C** has no real solutions without a graphing calculator. First find the vertex. The vertex, $(2, 1)$, is above the x-axis, and because $a > 0$, the parabola opens upward. This means that the parabola never touches the x-axis and there are no real solutions.

Reading Math Be sure that students understand that a quadratic equation in *standard form* means a quadratic equation in the form $ax^2 + bx + c = 0$. This is the first lesson in which that phrase is used.

2 Teach

Guided Instruction

Emphasize to students that solving an equation by graphing may not always yield exact solutions. Although graphing calculators can do much of the graphing work, the student will need to be familiar with what the function should look like and how many zeros it will have before using a graphing calculator. Tell students that later in this chapter they will learn methods for finding precise solutions and that they may use graphing as a way to support their solutions found by those methods.

Reaching All Learners

Through Multiple Representations

Show students how the equation $x^2 + x = 6$ can also be solved by graphing both sides of the equation as $y = x^2 + x$ and $y = 6$. By looking at where the two graphs intersect, you can find the x-values for which $y = 6$. 2, −3

Discuss with students how solving $x^2 + x = 6$ by finding the zeros of the related function $f(x) = x^2 + x - 6$ is the same as finding the points where the function intersects with the x-axis, or $y = 0$.

Power Presentations with PowerPoint®

Additional Examples

Example 2

A frog jumps straight up from the ground. The quadratic function $f(t) = -16t^2 + 12t$ models the frog's height in feet above the ground after t seconds. About how long is the frog in the air?
0.75 s

INTERVENTION
Questioning Strategies

EXAMPLE 2

- What are the reasonable domain and range values for this function?
- How do you know which zero is the answer to the question?

Critical Thinking Have students solve $x^2 + x - 6 = 0$ by graphing the related function. The solutions are 2 and -3. Ask students to predict what the graph of $-x^2 - x + 6 = 0$ will look like. The graph will be a reflection across the x-axis. Then have students solve $-x^2 - x + 6 = 0$ by graphing the function. Are the solutions the same? yes What is the conclusion to be drawn, and why is it important? The opposite of a function will have the same solutions and will be a reflection across the x-axis.

EXAMPLE 2 Aquatics Application

A dolphin jumps out of the water. The quadratic function $y = -16x^2 + 20x$ models the dolphin's height above the water after x seconds. How long is the dolphin out of the water?

When the dolphin leaves the water, its height is 0, and when the dolphin reenters the water, its height is 0. So solve $0 = -16x^2 + 20x$ to find the times when the dolphin leaves and reenters the water.

Step 1 Write the related function.

$0 = -16x^2 + 20x$

$y = -16x^2 + 20x$

Step 2 Graph the function.

Use a graphing calculator.

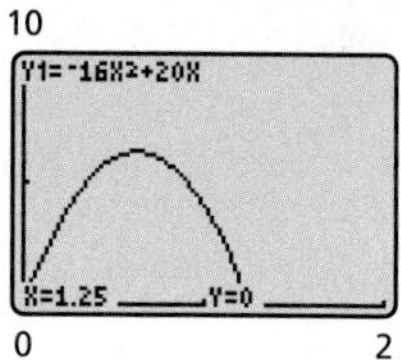

Step 3 Use 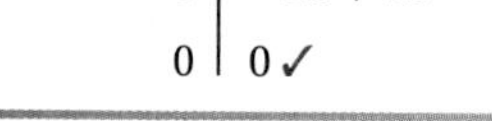 TRACE to estimate the zeros.

The zeros appear to be 0 and 1.25.

The dolphin leaves the water at 0 seconds and reenters the water at 1.25 seconds.

The dolphin is out of the water for 1.25 seconds.

Check $0 = -16x^2 + 20x$

0	$-16(1.25)^2 + 20(1.25)$
0	$-16(1.5625) + 25$
0	$-25 + 25$
0	0 ✓

Substitute 1.25 for x in the quadratic equation.

2. What if...? Another dolphin jumps out of the water. The quadratic function $y = -16x^2 + 32x$ models the dolphin's height above the water after x seconds. How long is the dolphin out of the water? 2 s

THINK AND DISCUSS

1. Describe the graph of a quadratic function whose related quadratic equation has only one solution.
2. Describe the graph of a quadratic function whose related quadratic equation has no real solutions.
3. Describe the graph of a quadratic function whose related quadratic equation has two solutions.

4. **GET ORGANIZED** Copy and complete the graphic organizer. In each of the boxes, write the steps for solving quadratic equations by graphing.

3 Close

Summarize

Review with students the steps for solving quadratic equations by graphing.

1. Write the equation in the form $ax^2 + bx + c = 0$.
2. Write the related function.
3. Graph the function.
4. Find the x-intercepts.

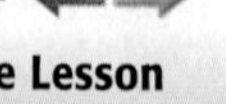

ONGOING ASSESSMENT and INTERVENTION

***Diagnose Before* the Lesson**
9-5 Warm Up, TE p. 642

***Monitor During* the Lesson**
Check It Out! Exercises, SE pp. 643–644
Questioning Strategies, TE pp. 643–644

***Assess After* the Lesson**
9-5 Lesson Quiz, TE p. 647
Alternative Assessment, TE p. 647

Answers to *Think and Discuss*

1. The vertex is on the x-axis.
2. Either the vertex is above the x-axis and the graph opens upward, or the vertex is below the x-axis and the graph opens downward.
3. Either the vertex is above the x-axis and the graph opens downward, or the vertex is below the x-axis and the graph opens upward.
4. See p. A8.

9-5 Exercises

go.hrw.com
Homework Help Online
KEYWORD: MA7 9-5
Parent Resources Online
KEYWORD: MA7 Parent

GUIDED PRACTICE

1. **Vocabulary** Write two words related to the graph of a quadratic function that can be used to find the solution of the related *quadratic equation*. **zeros, x-intercepts**

SEE EXAMPLE 1 p. 642

Solve each equation by graphing the related function.

2. $x^2 - 4 = 0$ **−2, 2**
3. $x^2 = 16$ **−4, 4**
4. $-2x^2 - 6 = 0$ **no real solutions**
5. $-x^2 + 12x - 36 = 0$ **6**
6. $-x^2 = -9$ **−3, 3**
7. $2x^2 = 3x^2 - 2x - 8$ **−2, 4**
8. $x^2 - 6x + 9 = 0$ **3**
9. $8x = -4x^2 - 4$ **−1**
10. $x^2 + 5x + 4 = 0$ **−4, −1**
11. $x^2 + 2 = 0$ **no real solutions**
12. $x^2 - 6x = 7$ **−1, 7**
13. $x^2 + 5x = -8$ **no real solutions**

SEE EXAMPLE 2 p. 644

14. **Sports** A baseball coach uses a pitching machine to simulate pop flies during practice. The quadratic function $y = -16x^2 + 80x$ models the height of the baseball after x seconds. How long is the baseball in the air? **5 s**

PRACTICE AND PROBLEM SOLVING

Independent Practice	
For Exercises	See Example
15–23	1
24	2

Skills Practice p. S21
Application Practice p. S36

Solve each equation by graphing the related function.

15. $-x^2 + 16 = 0$ **−4, 4**
16. $3x^2 = -7$ **no real solutions**
17. $5x^2 - 12x + 10 = x^2 + 10x$ **$\frac{1}{2}$, 5**
18. $x^2 + 10x + 25 = 0$ **−5**
19. $-4x^2 - 24x = 36$ **−3**
20. $-9x^2 + 10x - 9 = -8x$ **1**
21. $-x^2 - 1 = 0$ **no real solutions**
22. $3x^2 - 27 = 0$ **−3, 3**
23. $4x^2 - 4x + 5 = 2x^2$ **no real solutions**
24. **Geography** Yosemite Falls in California is made of three smaller falls. The upper fall drops 1450 feet. The height h in feet of a water droplet falling from the upper fall to the next fall is modeled by $h(t) = -16t^2 + 1450$, where t is the time in seconds after the initial fall. Estimate the time it takes for the droplet to reach the next cascade.

24. about 9.5 s

Tell whether each statement is always, sometimes, or never true.

25. If the graph of a quadratic function has its vertex at the origin, then the related quadratic equation has exactly one solution. **always**
26. If the graph of a quadratic function opens upward, then the related quadratic equation has two solutions. **sometimes**
27. If the graph of a quadratic function has its vertex on the x-axis, then the related quadratic equation has exactly one solution. **always**
28. If the graph of a quadratic function has its vertex in the first quadrant, then the related quadratic equation has two solutions. **sometimes**
29. A quadratic equation in the form $ax^2 - c = 0$, where $a < 0$ and $c > 0$, has two solutions. **never**

30. **Graphing Calculator** A fireworks shell is fired from a mortar. Its height is modeled by the function $h(t) = -16(t - 7)^2 + 784$, where t is the time in seconds and h is the height in feet.
    a. Graph the function.
    b. If the shell is supposed to explode at its maximum height, at what height should it explode? **784 ft**
    c. If the shell does not explode, how long will it take to return to the ground? **14 s**

9-5 Exercises

Assignment Guide

Assign *Guided Practice* exercises as necessary.

If you finished Examples **1–2**

Basic 15–36, 40–43, 48–61
Average 15–31, 37–43, 48–61
Advanced 15–31, 37–61

Homework Quick Check
Quickly check key concepts.
Exercises: 18, 20, 22, 24, 30, 31

Answers

30a.

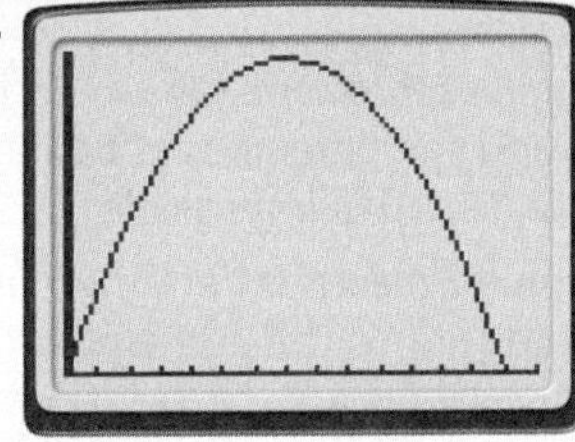

State Resources

MULTI-STEP TEST PREP **Exercise 40** involves solving a quadratic equation by graphing to determine the amount of time an object is in the air and then analyzing the graph to find other information. This exercise prepares students for the Multi-Step Test Prep on page 678.

Answers

31c. Possible answer: According to the graph, $x = 4$ is a solution to the related equation, but $x = 4$ is not a solution of $0 = -5x^2 + 10x$.

37a. $x - 4$, $x - 8$

b. $0 = x^2 - 24x + 80$

c. 4 and 20

d. Two possible lengths for the hypotenuse; no; if $x = 4$, then the length of one leg would be 0 and the other would be negative, which is impossible.

38. Look for places where the output values are 0. The corresponding input values are the solutions of the related quadratic equation. If there are no output values equal to 0, then look for sign changes. The solution is between the input values that correspond to the y-values with the sign change.

39. The graph of $y = ax^2 - c$, where $a > 0$ and $c > 0$, will always have two solutions because it is a parabola that opens upward whose vertex is below the origin. So it will always cross the x-axis in two places. By contrast, the graph of $y = ax^2 + c$, where $a > 0$ and $c > 0$, opens upward but its vertex is above the origin. Therefore, it will never cross the x-axis.

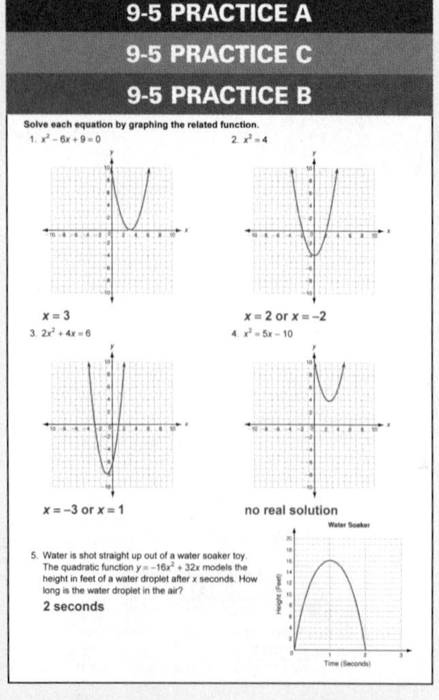

9-5 PRACTICE A

9-5 PRACTICE C

9-5 PRACTICE B

Solve each equation by graphing the related function.

1. $x^2 - 6x + 9 = 0$

$x = 3$

2. $x^2 = 4$

$x = 2$ or $x = -2$

3. $2x^2 + 4x = 6$

$x = -3$ or $x = 1$

4. $x^2 = 5x - 10$

no real solution

5. Water is shot straight up out of a water soaker toy. The quadratic function $y = -16x^2 + 32x$ models the height in feet of a water droplet after x seconds. How long is the water droplet in the air?

2 seconds

31. Athletics The graph shows the height y in feet of a gymnast jumping off a vault after x seconds.

a. How long does the gymnast stay in the air? **4 s**

b. What is the maximum height that the gymnast reaches? **10 ft**

c. Explain why the function $y = -5x^2 + 10x$ cannot accurately model the gymnast's motion.

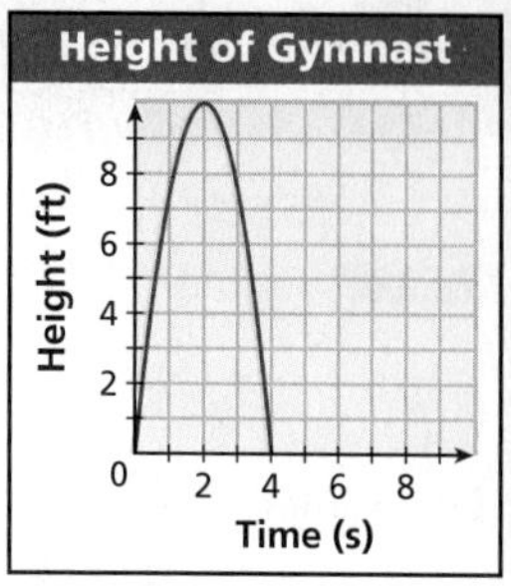

Height of Gymnast

Height (ft) vs. Time (s)

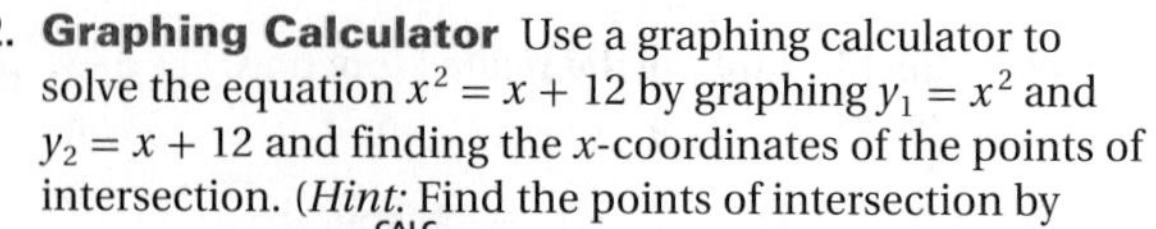

32. Graphing Calculator Use a graphing calculator to solve the equation $x^2 = x + 12$ by graphing $y_1 = x^2$ and $y_2 = x + 12$ and finding the x-coordinates of the points of intersection. (*Hint:* Find the points of intersection by using the 2nd CALC TRACE function after graphing.) **−3, 4**

LINK Biology

Some species of kangaroos are able to jump 30 feet in distance and 6 feet in height.

33. Biology The quadratic function $y = -5x^2 + 7x$ approximates the height y in meters of a kangaroo x seconds after it has jumped. How long does it take the kangaroo to return to the ground? **1.4 s**

For Exercises 34–36, use the table to determine the solutions of the related quadratic equation.

34. **−1**

x	y
−2	−1
−1	0
0	−1
1	−4
2	−9

35. **−1, 1**

x	y
−2	−6
−1	0
0	2
1	0
2	−6

36. **no real solutions**

x	y
−2	6
−1	3
0	2
1	3
2	6

40d. 84 ft; yes, at 1.5 s; 3.5 is 1 unit right of the axis of symmetry ($x = 2.5$). The ball will have the same height at the time represented by the point 1 unit left of the axis of symmetry.

37. Geometry The hypotenuse of a right triangle is 4 cm longer than one leg and 8 cm longer than the other leg. Let x represent the length of the hypotenuse.

a. Write an expression for the length of each leg in terms of x.

b. Use the Pythagorean Theorem to write an equation that can be solved for x.

c. Find the solutions of your equation from part **b**.

d. **Critical Thinking** What do the solutions of your equation represent? Are both solutions reasonable? Explain.

38. Write About It Explain how to find solutions of a quadratic equation by analyzing a table of values.

39. Critical Thinking Explain why a quadratic equation in the form $ax^2 - c = 0$, where $a > 0$ and $c > 0$, will always have two solutions. Explain why a quadratic equation in the form $ax^2 + c = 0$, where $a > 0$ and $c > 0$, will never have any real-number solutions.

MULTI-STEP TEST PREP

40. This problem will prepare you for the Multi-Step Test Prep on page 640.

The quadratic equation $0 = -16t^2 + 80t$ gives the time t in seconds when a golf ball is at height 0 feet.

a. How long is the golf ball in the air? **5 s**

b. What is the maximum height of the golf ball? **100 ft**

c. After how many seconds is the ball at its maximum height? **2.5 s**

d. What is the height of the ball after 3.5 seconds? Is there another time when the ball reaches that height? Explain. **See margin above.**

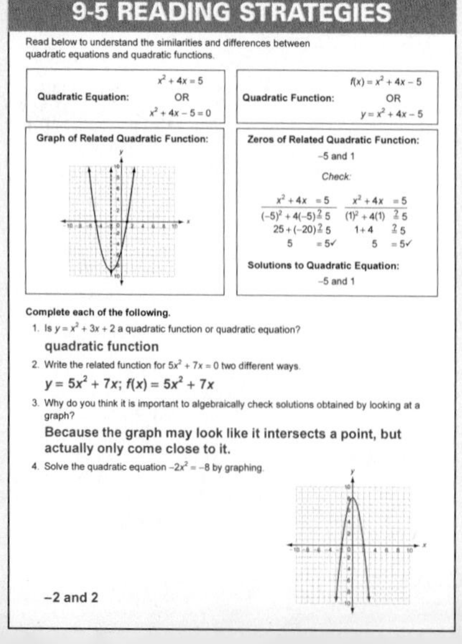

9-5 READING STRATEGIES

Read below to understand the similarities and differences between quadratic equations and quadratic functions.

Quadratic Equation: $x^2 + 4x = 5$ OR $x^2 + 4x - 5 = 0$

Quadratic Function: $f(x) = x^2 + 4x - 5$ OR $y = x^2 + 4x - 5$

Graph of Related Quadratic Function:

Zeros of Related Quadratic Function: −5 and 1

Check:

$x^2 + 4x = 5$	$x^2 + 4x = 5$
$(-5)^2 + 4(-5) \stackrel{?}{=} 5$	$(1)^2 + 4(1) \stackrel{?}{=} 5$
$25 + (-20) \stackrel{?}{=} 5$	$1 + 4 \stackrel{?}{=} 5$
$5 = 5$ ✓	$5 = 5$ ✓

Solutions to Quadratic Equation: −5 and 1

Complete each of the following.

1. Is $y = x^2 + 3x + 2$ a quadratic function or quadratic equation?

quadratic function

2. Write the related function for $5x^2 + 7x = 0$ two different ways.

$y = 5x^2 + 7x$; $f(x) = 5x^2 + 7x$

3. Why do you think it is important to algebraically check solutions obtained by looking at a graph?

Because the graph may look like it intersects a point, but actually only come close to it.

4. Solve the quadratic equation $-2x^2 = -8$ by graphing.

−2 and 2

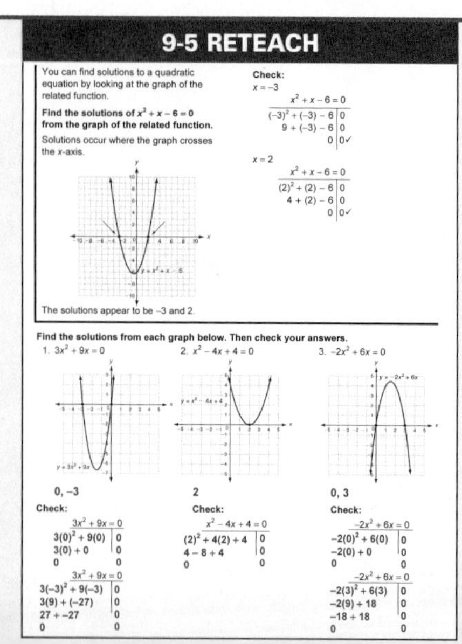

9-5 RETEACH

You can find solutions to a quadratic equation by looking at the graph of the related function.

Find the solutions of $x^2 + x - 6 = 0$ from the graph of the related function.

Solutions occur where the graph crosses the x-axis.

The solutions appear to be −3 and 2.

Check:

$x = -3$

$x^2 + x - 6 = 0$	
$(-3)^2 + (-3) - 6$	0
$9 + (-3) - 6$	0
0	0 ✓

$x = 2$

$x^2 + x - 6 = 0$	
$(2)^2 + (2) - 6$	0
$4 + (2) - 6$	0
0	0 ✓

Find the solutions from each graph below. Then check your answers.

1. $3x^2 + 9x = 0$

0, −3

Check:

$3x^2 + 9x = 0$	
$3(0)^2 + 9(0)$	0
$3(0) + 0$	0
0	0

$3x^2 + 9x = 0$	
$3(-3)^2 + 9(-3)$	0
$3(9) + (-27)$	0
$27 + -27$	0
0	0

2. $x^2 - 4x + 4 = 0$

2

Check:

$x^2 - 4x + 4 = 0$	
$(2)^2 + 4(2) + 4$	0
$4 - 8 + 4$	0
0	0

3. $-2x^2 + 6x = 0$

0, 3

Check:

$-2x^2 + 6x = 0$	
$-2(0)^2 + 6(0)$	0
$-2(0) + 0$	0
0	0

$-2x^2 + 6x = 0$	
$-2(3)^2 + 6(3)$	0
$-2(9) + 18$	0
$-18 + 18$	0
0	0

TEST PREP

41. Use the graph to find the number of solutions of $-2x^2 + 2 = 0$.

(A) 0 **(C) 2**
(B) 1 (D) 3

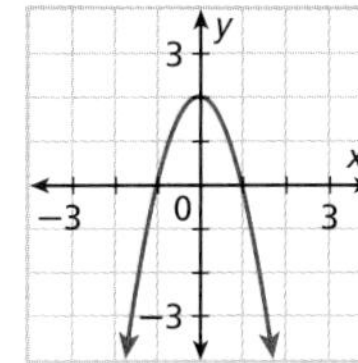

42. Which graph could be used to find the solutions of $x^2 = -4x + 12$?

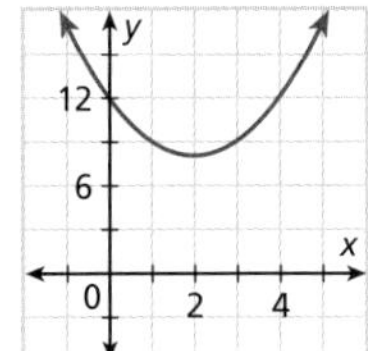

(H)

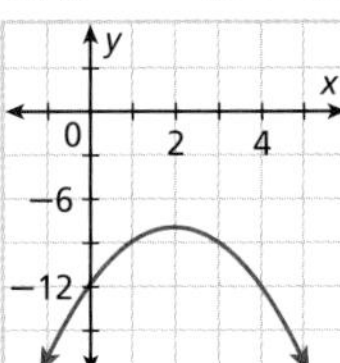

(G)

y
x
−4
0
4
−6
−12

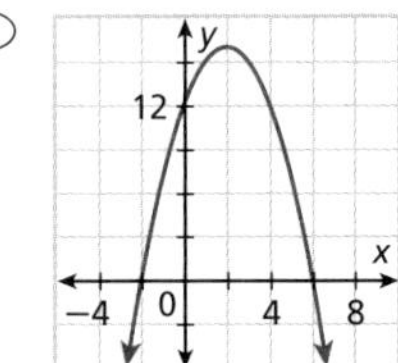

43.

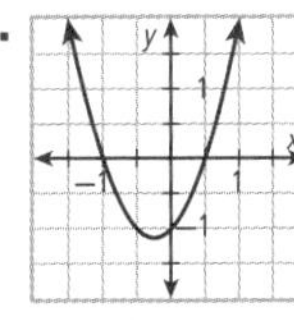

−1 and $\frac{1}{2}$; the x-intercepts are the solutions of the equation.

43. **Short Response** Find the solutions of $2x^2 + x - 1 = 0$ by graphing. Explain how the graph of the related function shows the solutions of the equation.

CHALLENGE AND EXTEND

Graphing Calculator Use a graphing calculator to approximate the solutions of each quadratic equation.

44. $\frac{5}{16}x + \frac{1}{4}x^2 = \frac{3}{5}$ **$x \approx -2.3$ or $x \approx 1$**

45. $1200x^2 - 650x - 100 = -200x - 175$ **no real solutions**

46. $\frac{1}{5}x + \frac{3}{4}x^2 = \frac{7}{12}$ **$x \approx -1$ or $x \approx 0.75$**

47. $400x^2 - 100 = -300x + 456$ **$x \approx -1.6$ or $x \approx 0.86$**

SPIRAL REVIEW

Write an equation in point-slope form for the line with the given slope that contains the given point. *(Lesson 5-8)*

48. $y - 3 = \frac{1}{2}(x - 2)$

48. slope $= \frac{1}{2}$; (2, 3)

49. slope $= -3$; $(-2, 4)$ **$y - 4 = -3(x + 2)$**

50. slope $= 0$; (2, 1) **$y - 1 = 0(x - 2)$**

Simplify. *(Lesson 7-4)*

51. $\frac{3^4}{3}$ **27**

52. $\frac{5^2 \cdot 2^4}{5 \cdot 2^2}$ **20**

53. $\frac{(x^4)^5}{(x^3)^3}$ **x^{11}**

54. $\left(\frac{x^3}{y^2}\right)^{-3}$ **$\frac{y^6}{x^9}$**

57. $\frac{27b^2}{8a^6}$

55. $\left(\frac{a^2b^3}{ab^2}\right)^3$ **a^3b^3**

56. $\left(\frac{4s}{3t}\right)^{-2}$ **$\frac{9t^2}{16s^2}$**

57. $\left(\frac{2}{3}\right)^{-3} \cdot \left(\frac{a^3}{b}\right)^{-2}$

58. $\left(\frac{-k^2}{5k^3}\right)^{-3}$ **$-125k^3$**

Compare the graph of each function with the graph of $f(x) = x^2$. *(Lesson 9-4)*

59. $g(x) = 3x^2$

60. $g(x) = x^2 - 8$

61. $g(x) = \frac{3}{4}x^2 + 2$

TEST PREP DOCTOR + In **Exercise 42,** remind students to consider the equation in the form $ax^2 + bx + c = 0$. Because $a > 0$, the graph opens upward, so **H** and **J** can be eliminated. By finding that the *y*-intercept of the related function is −12, **F** can also be eliminated.

Answers

59. The parabola is narrower, and has the same vertex and the same zero.

60. The parabola is the same width, has a vertex translated 8 units down from $f(x)$, and has 2 zeros.

61. The parabola is wider than $f(x)$, has a vertex translated 2 units up from $f(x)$, and has no zeros.

Journal

Have students explain how to find solutions to a quadratic equation by graphing the related function.

ALTERNATIVE ASSESSMENT

Have students write a quadratic equation with two solutions. They should then solve by graphing. Then have them change either *a*, *b*, or *c* so that the equation has no solutions.

Power Presentations with PowerPoint®

9-5 Lesson Quiz

Solve each equation by graphing the related function.

1. $3x^2 - 12 = 0$ 2, −2

2. $x^2 + 2x = 8$ −4, 2

3. $3x - 5 = x^2$ no real solutions

4. $3x^2 + 3 = 6x$ 1

5. A rocket is shot straight up from the ground. The quadratic function $f(t) = -16t^2 + 96t$ models the rocket's height in feet above the ground after *t* seconds. How long does it take for the rocket to return to the ground? 6 s

Also available on transparency

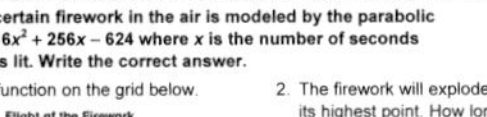

9-5 PROBLEM SOLVING

The path of a certain firework in the air is modeled by the parabolic function $y = -16x^2 + 256x - 624$ where x is the number of seconds after the fuse is lit. Write the correct answer.

1. Graph the function on the grid below.

Flight of the Firework

Height (ft)
Time (s)

2. The firework will explode when it reaches its highest point. How long after the fuse is lit will the firework explode and how high will the firework be?

8 seconds

400 feet

3. Based on the graph of the firework, what are the two zeros of this function?

$x = 3$

$x = 13$

4. What is the meaning of each of the zeros you found in problem 3?

The firework launches at 3s; The firework lands at 13s

Select the best answer.

5. The quadratic function $f(x) = -16x^2 + 90x$ models the height of a baseball in feet after x seconds. How long is the baseball in the air?

A 2.8125 s C 11.25 s
B 5.625 s D 126.5625 s

6. The height of a football y in feet is given by the function $y = -16x^2 + 56x + 2$ where x is the time in seconds after the ball was kicked. This function is graphed below. How long was the football in the air?

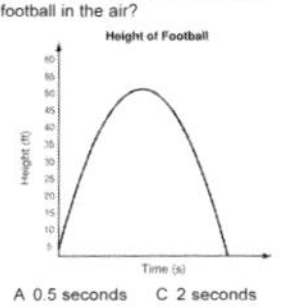

A 0.5 seconds C 2 seconds
B 1.75 seconds **D** 3.5 seconds

7. The function $y = -0.04x^2 + 2x$ models the height of an arch support for a bridge, where x is the distance in feet from where the arch supports enter the water. How many real solutions does this function have?

F 0 **H** 2
G 1 J 3

9-5 CHALLENGE

A parabolic tunnel is to be built for a two-lane road. The Department of Transportation (DOT) wants the tunnel to be wide enough for the two lanes and a walkway on either side. An architect proposes a design that uses $y = -0.08x^2 + 2.88x$ to model the height of the ceiling in feet at a distance x feet from the bottom left. Your task is to determine whether the design will satisfy all of the DOT's requirements.

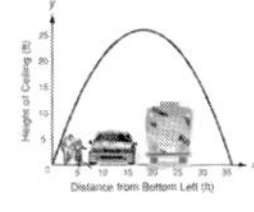

Use a graphing calculator as necessary.

1. What is the width of the tunnel from the bottom left to the bottom right? Explain how you solved this problem. **36 ft**

Solve $0 = -0.08x^2 + 2.88x$ by graphing on a graphing calculator. The zeros are 0 and 36.

2. According to state law, the maximum height of any vehicle is 13.5 ft. To the nearest foot, how close to the bottom left or bottom right could the tallest vehicle drive? Explain how you found your answer. **6 ft**

Solve $13.5 = -0.08x^2 + 2.88x$ by graphing $y = -0.08x^2 + 2.88x - 13.5$. The zeros are approximately 6 and 30.

3. According to state law, the standard width for one lane of road is 12 ft. Is the tunnel wide enough for two lanes? Is it wide enough for three lanes? Explain. **yes; no**

Two lanes require 24 ft, which is exactly the width that is taller than 13.5 ft. Three lanes require 36 ft; the cars in the outside lanes would hit the tunnel walls.

4. For the safety of pedestrians on the walkways, a 2-ft-wide wall will be built between the outside edges of the road and the walkways. If only two lanes are put in the middle of the tunnel, how much room is left on either side for the walkway? **4 ft**

5. Considering your answer to problem 4, will the ceiling of the walkways be tall enough for an "average" pedestrian to walk through? Explain. **Yes**

Evaluate $y = -0.08x^2 + 2.88x$ when $x = 4$ to find $y = 10.24$. Because an "average" pedestrian is shorter than 10 ft, the walkway will be tall enough.

6. Should the DOT accept or reject the architect's design? **accept**

Technology LAB Organizer

Use with Lesson 9-5

Pacing:
Traditional $\frac{1}{2}$ day
Block $\frac{1}{4}$ day

Objective: Use tables and graphs on a graphing calculator to explore the relationships between roots, zeros, and *x*-intercepts.

Materials: graphing calculator

Online Edition
Graphing Calculator, TechKeys

Countdown Week 20

Resources

Technology Lab Activities
9-5 Lab Recording Sheet

Teach

Discuss

Discuss how to use sign changes in *y*-values to approximate the zeros from a table when 0 does not appear in the *y*-column.

Close

Key Concept

A quadratic equation can be solved by using a table of values for the related function and locating the zeros of the function, which are the solutions, or roots, of the equation.

Assessment

Journal Have students explain how to use a table to solve a quadratic equation with noninteger solutions.

State Resources

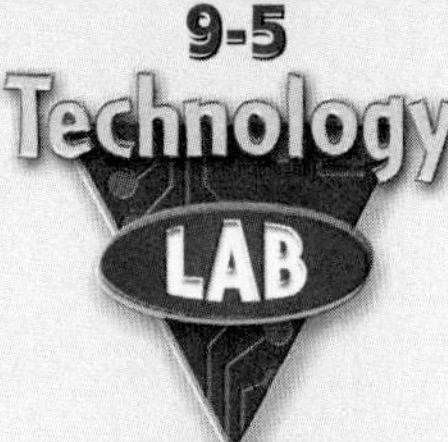

9-5 Technology LAB

Use with Lesson 9-5

Explore Roots, Zeros, and *x*-Intercepts

The solutions, or *roots*, of a quadratic equation are the *x*-intercepts, or zeros, of the related quadratic function. You can use tables or graphs on a graphing calculator to understand the connections between zeros, roots, and *x*-intercepts.

Activity 1

Solve $5x^2 + 8x - 4 = 0$ by using a table.

1. Enter the related function in $\mathbf{Y_1}$.

2. Press 2nd GRAPH (TABLE) to use the **TABLE** function.

3. Scroll through the values by using ▲ and ▼. Look for values of 0 in the $\mathbf{Y_1}$ column. The corresponding *x*-value is a zero of the function. There is one zero at −2.

   Also look for places where the signs of nonzero *y*-values change. There is a zero between the corresponding *x*-values. So there is another zero somewhere between 0 and 1.

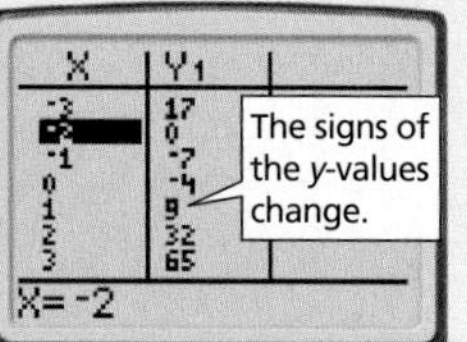

4. To get a better estimate of the zero, change the table settings. Press 2nd WINDOW (TBLSET) to view the **TABLE SETUP** screen. Set **TblStart = 0** and the step value **△Tbl = .1**. Press 2nd GRAPH (TABLE) to see the table again. The table will show you more *x*-values between 0 and 1.

5. Scroll through the values by using ▲ and ▼. The second zero is at 0.4.

   The zeros of the function, −2 and 0.4, are the solutions, or roots, of the equation $5x^2 + 8x - 4 = 0$. Check the solutions algebraically.

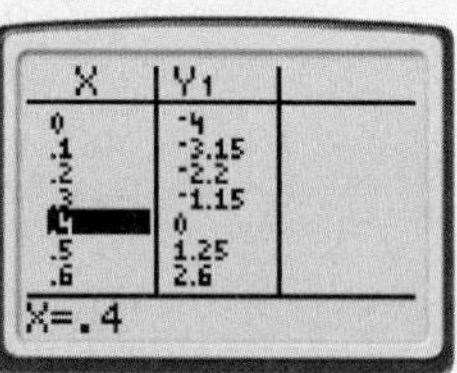

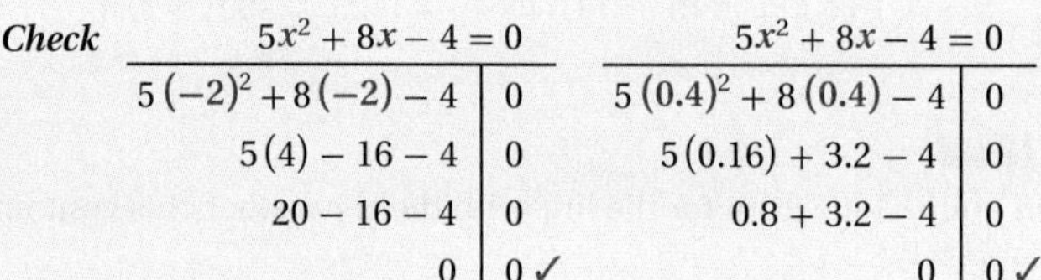

Check

$5x^2 + 8x - 4 = 0$	
$5(-2)^2 + 8(-2) - 4$	0
$5(4) - 16 - 4$	0
$20 - 16 - 4$	0
0	0 ✓

$5x^2 + 8x - 4 = 0$	
$5(0.4)^2 + 8(0.4) - 4$	0
$5(0.16) + 3.2 - 4$	0
$0.8 + 3.2 - 4$	0
0	0 ✓

Try This

Solve each equation by using a table.

1. $x^2 - 4x - 5 = 0$ **−1, 5**
2. $x^2 - x - 6 = 0$ **−2, 3**
3. $2x^2 + x - 1 = 0$ **−1, 0.5**
4. $5x^2 - 6x - 8 = 0$ **−0.8, 2**
5. **Critical Thinking** How would you find the zero of a function that showed a sign change in the *y*-values between the *x*-values 1.2 and 1.3?
6. **Make a Conjecture** If you scrolled up and down the list and found only positive *y*-values, what might you conclude?

Teaching Tip

Technology When changing the increments of *x* with the **TBLSET** function in **Activity 1,** consider also changing the *x*-value at which the table starts. This can reduce excess scrolling when locating sign changes in *y*. For instance, if you know there is a zero between 1 and 2, start the table at 1.

Answers to *Try This*

5. Possible answer: Change **TblStart** to 1.2 and **△Tbl** to 0.01 and scroll until I found the zero.
6. Possible answer: The function has no zeros, and the equation has no real solutions.

Activity 2

Solve $5x^2 + x - 8.4 = 0$ by using a table and a graph.

1. Enter the related function in $\mathbf{Y_1}$.

2. To view both the table and the graph at the same time, set your calculator to the Graph-Table mode. Press MODE and select **G-T**.

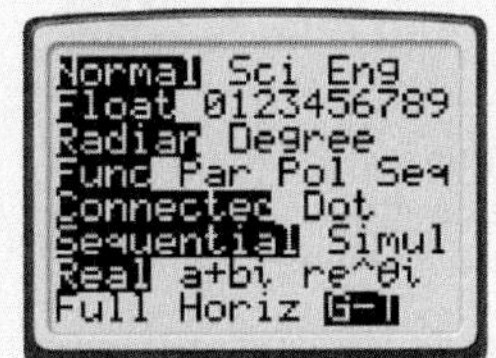

3. Press GRAPH. You should see the graph and the table. Notice that the function appears to have one negative zero and one positive zero near the y-axis.

4. To get a closer view of the graph, press ZOOM and select **4:ZDecimal**.

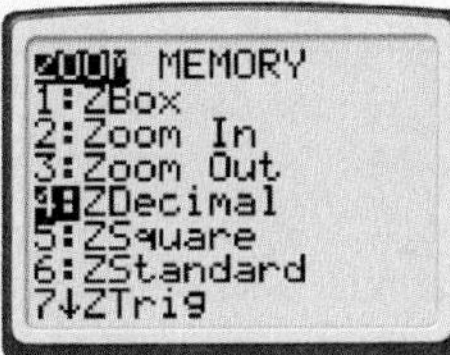

5. Press TRACE. Use ◀ to scroll to find the negative zero. The graph and the table show that the zero is −1.4.

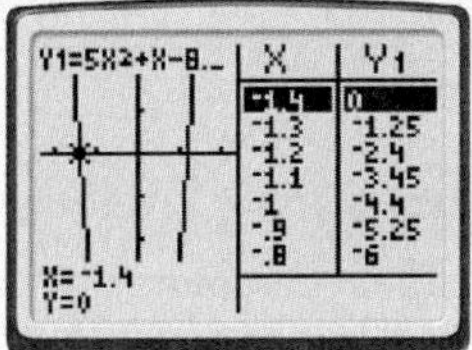

6. Use ▶ to scroll and find the positive zero. The graph and the table show that the zero is 1.2.

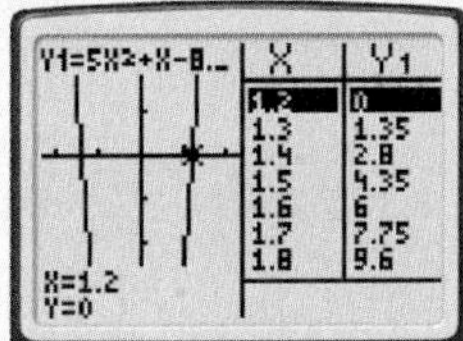

The solutions are −1.4 and 1.2. Check the solutions algebraically.

$5x^2 + x - 8.4$	0
$5(-1.4)^2 + (-1.4) - 8.4$	0
$5(1.96) - 1.4 - 8.4$	0
$9.8 - 1.4 - 8.4$	0
0	0 ✓

$5x^2 + x - 8.4$	0
$5(1.2)^2 + (1.2) - 8.4$	0
$5(1.44) + 1.2 - 8.4$	0
$7.2 + 1.2 - 8.4$	0
0	0 ✓

Try This

Solve each equation by using a table and a graph.

7. $2x^2 - x - 3 = 0$ **−1, 1.5**
8. $5x^2 + 13x + 6 = 0$ **−2, −0.6**
9. $10x^2 - 3x - 4 = 0$ **−0.5, 0.8**
10. $x^2 - 2x - 0.96 = 0$ **−0.4, 2.4**

11. **Critical Thinking** Suppose that when you graphed a quadratic function, you could see only one side of the graph and one zero. What methods would you use to try to find the other zero? **Possible answer: Set the window dimensions wider to see both zeros, and then trace to find the other zero.**

9-5 Technology Lab 649

9-6 Organizer

Pacing: Traditional 1 day
Block $\frac{1}{2}$ day

Objective: Solve quadratic equations by factoring.

Online Edition
Tutorial Videos

Countdown Week 20

Power Presentations with PowerPoint®

Warm Up

Find each product.

1. $(x + 2)(x + 7)$ $x^2 + 9x + 14$
2. $(x - 11)(x + 5)$ $x^2 - 6x - 55$
3. $(x - 10)^2$ $x^2 - 20x + 100$

Factor each polynomial.

4. $x^2 + 12x + 35$ $(x + 5)(x + 7)$
5. $x^2 + 2x - 63$ $(x - 7)(x + 9)$
6. $x^2 - 10x + 16$ $(x - 2)(x - 8)$
7. $2x^2 - 16x + 32$ $2(x - 4)^2$

Also available on transparency

Citizen: Why is that quadratic equation lurking about our town?
Sheriff: He's searching for his roots.

9-6 Solving Quadratic Equations by Factoring

Objective
Solve quadratic equations by factoring.

Who uses this?
In order to determine how many seconds she will be in the air, a high diver can use a quadratic equation. (See Example 3.)

You have solved quadratic equations by graphing. Another method used to solve quadratic equations is to factor and use the Zero Product Property.

Zero Product Property

For all real numbers *a* and *b*,

WORDS	NUMBERS	ALGEBRA
If the product of two quantities equals zero, at least one of the quantities equals zero.	$3(0) = 0$ $0(4) = 0$	If $ab = 0$, then $a = 0$ or $b = 0$.

EXAMPLE 1 Using the Zero Product Property

Use the Zero Product Property to solve each equation. Check your answer.

A $(x - 3)(x + 7) = 0$

$x - 3 = 0$ or $x + 7 = 0$ *Use the Zero Product Property.*
$x = 3$ or $x = -7$ *Solve each equation.*

The solutions are 3 and -7.

Check

$(x - 3)(x + 7) = 0$	
$(3 - 3)(3 + 7)$	0
$(0)(10)$	0
0	0 ✓

Substitute each solution for x into the original equation.

$(x - 3)(x + 7) = 0$	
$(-7 - 3)(-7 + 7)$	0
$(-10)(0)$	0
0	0 ✓

B $(x)(x - 5) = 0$

$x = 0$ or $x - 5 = 0$ *Use the Zero Product Property.*
$x = 5$ *Solve the second equation.*

The solutions are 0 and 5.

Check

$(x)(x - 5) = 0$	
$(0)(0 - 5)$	0
$(0)(-5)$	0
0	0 ✓

Substitute each solution for x into the original equation.

$(x)(x - 5) = 0$	
$(5)(5 - 5)$	0
$(5)(0)$	0
0	0 ✓

CHECK IT OUT! Use the Zero Product Property to solve each equation. Check your answer.

1a. $(x)(x + 4) = 0$ **0, −4**
1b. $(x + 4)(x - 3) = 0$ **−4, 3**

State Resources

1 Introduce

EXPLORATION

9-6 Solving Quadratic Equations by Factoring

You will need a graphing calculator for this Exploration.

1. Graph each function listed in the table, and use the graph to find the zeros of the function. Record the zeros and the number of zeros.

Function	Zeros	Number of Zeros
$y = (x - 2)(x + 1)$		
$y = (x + 3)(x + 7)$		
$y = (x + 6)(x - 1)$		
$y = (x - 2.5)(x - 5)$		
$y = (x - 4)^2$		
$y = (x + 3)^2$		

2. Predict the zeros of the function $y = (x - 7)(x + 10)$ without graphing.
3. Predict the zeros of the function $y = (x + 8)^2$ without graphing.

THINK AND DISCUSS

4. **Explain** how you predicted the zeros of the functions in Problems 2 and 3.
5. **Describe** any patterns you notice in your table.

Motivate

Display the linear equation $4x = x + 12$ and the quadratic equation $4x = x^2 + 12$. Ask students why they cannot solve for x in the quadratic equation as they would in the linear equation. Possible answer: The variable terms are not like terms and cannot be combined to isolate x.
Tell them that another method is needed to solve quadratic equations algebraically.

Explorations and answers are provided in *Alternate Openers: Explorations Transparencies.*

If a quadratic equation is written in standard form, $ax^2 + bx + c = 0$, you may need to factor before using the Zero Product Property to solve the equation.

EXAMPLE 2 Solving Quadratic Equations by Factoring

Solve each quadratic equation by factoring. Check your answer.

Helpful Hint

To review factoring techniques, see Lessons 8-3 through 8-5.

A $x^2 + 7x + 10 = 0$

$(x + 5)(x + 2) = 0$ *Factor the trinomial.*

$x + 5 = 0$ or $x + 2 = 0$ *Use the Zero Product Property.*

$x = -5$ or $x = -2$ *Solve each equation.*

The solutions are -5 and -2.

Check

$x^2 + 7x + 10$	$= 0$
$(-5)^2 + 7(-5) + 10$	0
$25 - 35 + 10$	0
0	0 ✓

$x^2 + 7x + 10$	$= 0$
$(-2)^2 + 7(-2) + 10$	0
$4 - 14 + 10$	0
0	0 ✓

B $x^2 + 2x = 8$

$x^2 + 2x = 8$ *The equation must be written in standard form. So subtract 8 from both sides.*

$\quad -8 \quad -8$

$x^2 + 2x - 8 = 0$

$(x + 4)(x - 2) = 0$ *Factor the trinomial.*

$x + 4 = 0$ or $x - 2 = 0$ *Use the Zero Product Property.*

$x = -4$ or $x = 2$ *Solve each equation.*

The solutions are -4 and 2.

Check Graph the related quadratic function. The zeros of the related function should be the same as the solutions from factoring.

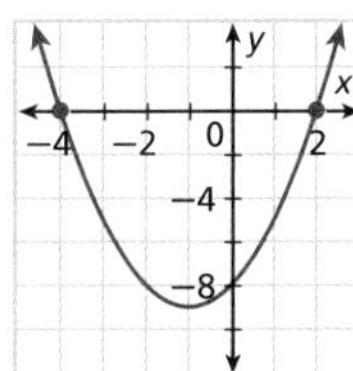

The graph of $y = x^2 + 2x - 8$ shows two zeros that appear to be -4 and 2, the same as the solutions from factoring. ✓

C $x^2 + 2x + 1 = 0$

$(x + 1)(x + 1) = 0$ *Factor the trinomial.*

$x + 1 = 0$ or $x + 1 = 0$ *Use the Zero Product property.*

$x = -1$ or $x = -1$ *Solve each equation.*

Both factors result in the same solution, so there is one solution, -1.

Check Use a graphing calculator to graph the related function.

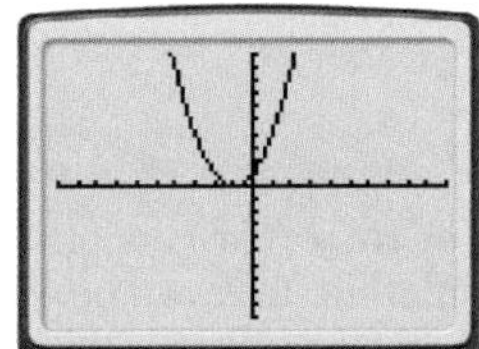

The graph of $y = x^2 + 2x + 1$ shows one zero that appears to be -1, the same as the solution from factoring. ✓

COMMON ERROR ALERT

When solving quadratic equations by factoring, students sometimes choose the constants in the binomial factors as the solutions. For example, students might say that the solutions of $(x + 3)(x + 5) = 0$ are 3 and 5. Remind students to find the value of x that would make each factor equal 0.

$x + 3 = 0$ or $x + 5 = 0$

$x = -3$ $\quad x = -5$

Power Presentations with PowerPoint®

Additional Examples

Example 1

Use the Zero Product Property to solve each equation. Check your answer.

A. $(x - 7)(x + 2) = 0$ 7, −2

B. $(x - 2)(x) = 0$ 0, 2

Example 2

Solve each quadratic equation by factoring. Check your answer.

A. $x^2 - 6x + 8 = 0$ 4, 2

B. $x^2 + 4x = 21$ −7, 3

C. $x^2 - 12x + 36 = 0$ 6

D. $-2x^2 = 20x + 50$ −5

2 Teach

Guided Instruction

Review multiplying binomials and factoring trinomials, including how to recognize perfect-square trinomials. Remind students that the first step in factoring is always to look for a GCF. Emphasize the importance of not using the Zero Product Property until one side of the equation is zero. Encourage students to substitute solutions into the original equations to check their answers.

Reaching All Learners

Through Critical Thinking

Show students how to create quadratic equations with given solutions by working backward. For example, if the solutions are −2 and 5, then:

$$x = -2 \text{ or } x = 5$$
$$(x + 2)(x - 5) = 0$$
$$x^2 - 3x - 10 = 0$$

Explain that there are infinitely many equivalent equations that can be generated by performing the same operation on both sides.

INTERVENTION

Questioning Strategies

EXAMPLE 1

- Why do you set each factor equal to zero?
- How can you tell whether an expression is quadratic when it is written in factored form?

EXAMPLE 2

- Why must one side of the equation be equal to zero?
- What types of quadratic equations have only one real solution?
- When the graph of a function crosses the x-axis, what is the value of y?

Power Presentations with PowerPoint®

Additional Examples

Example 3

The height in feet above the water of a diver can be modeled by $h(t) = -16t^2 + 8t + 8$, where t is time in seconds after the diver jumps off a platform. Find the time it takes for the diver to reach the water. 1 s

INTERVENTION

Questioning Strategies

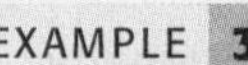

EXAMPLE 3

- What equation do you need to solve?
- What is a reasonable domain and range for this situation?

Helpful Hint

$(x - 3)(x - 3)$ is a perfect square. Since both factors are the same, you solve only one of them.

Solve each quadratic equation by factoring. Check your answer.

D $-2x^2 = 18 - 12x$

$-2x^2 + 12x - 18 = 0$ *Write the equation in standard form.*

$-2(x^2 - 6x + 9) = 0$ *Factor out the GCF, −2.*

$-2(x - 3)(x - 3) = 0$ *Factor the trinomial.*

$-2 \neq 0$ or $x - 3 = 0$ *Use the Zero Product Property. −2 cannot equal 0.*

$x = 3$ *Solve the remaining equation.*

The only solution is 3.

Check $-2x^2 = 18 - 12x$

$-2(3)^2$	$18 - 12(3)$
-18	$18 - 36$
-18	-18 ✓

Substitute 3 into the original equation.

Solve each quadratic equation by factoring. Check your answer.

2a. $x^2 - 6x + 9 = 0$ **3**

2b. $x^2 + 4x = 5$ **1, −5**

2c. $30x = -9x^2 - 25$ $-\frac{5}{3}$

2d. $3x^2 - 4x + 1 = 0$ $\frac{1}{3}$, 1

EXAMPLE 3 *Sports Application*

The height of a diver above the water during a dive can be modeled by $h = -16t^2 + 8t + 48$, where h is height in feet and t is time in seconds. Find the time it takes for the diver to reach the water.

48 ft

$h = -16t^2 + 8t + 48$

$0 = -16t^2 + 8t + 48$ *The diver reaches the water when h = 0.*

$0 = -8(2t^2 - t - 6)$ *Factor out the GCF, −8.*

$0 = -8(2t + 3)(t - 2)$ *Factor the trinomial.*

$-8 \neq 0,\ 2t + 3 = 0$ or $t - 2 = 0$ *Use the Zero Product Property.*

$2t = -3$ or $t = 2$ *Solve each equation.*

$t = -\frac{3}{2}$ ✗ *Since time cannot be negative, $-\frac{3}{2}$ does not make sense in this situation.*

It takes the diver 2 seconds to reach the water.

Check $0 = -16t^2 + 8t + 48$

0	$-16(2)^2 + 8(2) + 48$
0	$-64 + 16 + 48$
0	0 ✓

Substitute 2 into the original equation.

3. What if...? The equation for the height above the water for another diver can be modeled by $h = -16t^2 + 8t + 24$. Find the time it takes this diver to reach the water. **1.5 s**

3 Close

Summarize

Have students state the first step in solving each equation.

- $(x + 1)(x - 2) = 0$
  Set each factor equal to zero.
- $x^2 + 8x + 7 = 0$
  Factor the left side.
- $2x^2 - 16x + 30 = 0$
  Factor out 2 from each term in the trinomial.
- $x^2 - 9x - 10 = -18$
  Add 18 to each side.

ONGOING ASSESSMENT and INTERVENTION

***Diagnose Before* the Lesson**
9-6 Warm Up, TE p. 650

***Monitor During* the Lesson**
Check It Out! Exercises, SE pp. 650–652
Questioning Strategies, TE pp. 651–652

***Assess After* the Lesson**
9-6 Lesson Quiz, TE p. 655
Alternative Assessment, TE p. 655

THINK AND DISCUSS

1. Explain two ways to solve $x^2 + x - 6 = 0$. How are these two methods similar?
2. Describe the relationships among the solutions of $x^2 - 4x - 12 = 0$, the zeros and x-intercepts of $y = x^2 - 4x - 12$, and the factors of $x^2 - 4x - 12$.

3. **GET ORGANIZED** Copy and complete the graphic organizer. In each box, write a step used to solve a quadratic equation by factoring.

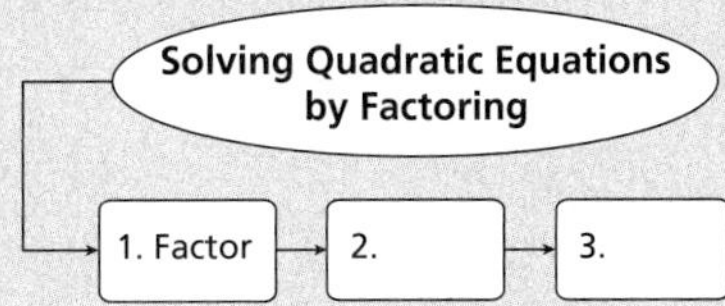

9-6 Exercises

GUIDED PRACTICE

SEE EXAMPLE 1 p. 650

Use the Zero Product Property to solve each equation. Check your answer.

1. $(x + 2)(x - 8) = 0$ **−2, 8**
2. $(x - 6)(x - 5) = 0$ **6, 5**
3. $(x + 7)(x + 9) = 0$ **−7, −9**
4. $(x)(x - 1) = 0$ **0, 1**
5. $(x)(x + 11) = 0$ **−11, 0**
6. $(3x + 2)(4x - 1) = 0$ **$-\frac{2}{3}, \frac{1}{4}$**

SEE EXAMPLE 2 p. 651

Solve each quadratic equation by factoring. Check your answer.

7. $x^2 + 4x - 12 = 0$ **−6, 2**
8. $x^2 - 8x - 9 = 0$ **−1, 9**
9. $x^2 - 5x + 6 = 0$ **2, 3**
10. $x^2 - 3x = 10$ **−2, 5**
11. $x^2 + 10x = -16$ **−8, −2**
12. $x^2 + 2x = 15$ **−5, 3**
13. $x^2 - 8x + 16 = 0$ **4**
14. $-3x^2 = 18x + 27$ **−3**
15. $x^2 + 36 = 12x$ **6**
16. $2x^2 + 5x - 3 = 0$ **$-3, \frac{1}{2}$**
17. $2x^2 + 7x + 6 = 0$ **$-2, -\frac{3}{2}$**
18. $2x^2 + 6x = -18$ **no real solutions**

SEE EXAMPLE 3 p. 652

19. **Games** A group of friends tries to keep a beanbag from touching the ground. On one kick, the beanbag's height can be modeled by $h = -16t^2 + 14t + 2$, where h is the height in feet above the ground and t is the time in seconds. Find the time it takes the beanbag to reach the ground. **1 s**

PRACTICE AND PROBLEM SOLVING

Independent Practice

For Exercises	See Example
20–25	1
26–31	2
32	3

Extra Practice
Skills Practice p. S21
Application Practice p. S36

Use the Zero Product Property to solve each equation. Check your answer.

20. $(x - 8)(x + 6) = 0$ **−6, 8**
21. $(x + 4)(x + 7) = 0$ **−4, −7**
22. $(x - 2)(x - 5) = 0$ **2, 5**
23. $(x - 9)(x) = 0$ **9, 0**
24. $(x)(x + 25) = 0$ **0, −25**
25. $(2x + 1)(3x - 1) = 0$ **$-\frac{1}{2}, \frac{1}{3}$**

Solve each quadratic equation by factoring. Check your answer.

26. $x^2 + 8x + 15 = 0$ **−3, −5**
27. $x^2 - 2x - 8 = 0$ **−2, 4**
28. $x^2 - 4x + 3 = 0$ **1, 3**
29. $3x^2 - 2x - 1 = 0$ **$-\frac{1}{3}, 1$**
30. $4x^2 - 9x + 2 = 0$ **$\frac{1}{4}, 2$**
31. $-x^2 = 4x + 4$ **−2**

Answers to *Think and Discuss*

1. Possible answer: One method would be to factor and set each factor equal to 0. Another method would be to graph and find the x-intercepts of the graph. In both methods, 0 is important. In the factoring method, one side of the equation must be 0. In the graphing method, you identify values of x where $f(x) = 0$.
2. Possible answer: The solutions of the equation are $x = -2$ and $x = 6$. These solutions indicate both the zeros and the x-intercepts of the related function (−2 and 6). The factors of $x^2 - 4x - 12$ are $x - 6$ and $x + 2$. When each of these factors is set equal to 0 and solved for x, the solutions are the same as the solutions of $x^2 - 4x - 12 = 0$.
3. See p. A8.

9-6 Exercises

Assignment Guide

Assign *Guided Practice* exercises as necessary.

If you finished Examples **1–2**
Basic 20–31, 33–39, 46
Average 20–31, 33–39, 45–46
Advanced 20–31, 33–38, 45

If you finished Examples **1–3**
Basic 20–39, 41–43, 46–49, 62–71
Average 20–39, 40–44, 46–50, 62–71
Advanced 20–38, 40–45, 47–71

Homework Quick Check
Quickly check key concepts.
Exercises: 20, 24, 26, 30, 32, 44

State Resources

Exercise 47 involves solving a quadratic equation by factoring to determine the amount of time an object is in the air. This exercise prepares students for the Multi-Step Test Prep on page 678.

Answers

40. $x(x + 2) = 24$; 4 and 6 or −6 and −4

45. No; by the Zero Product Property, you can solve $(x - 2)(x + 3) = 0$ by solving $x - 2 = 0$ and $x + 3 = 0$. There is no "Five" Product Property, however, so you cannot solve $(x - 2)(x + 3) = 5$ by solving $x - 2 = 5$ and $x + 3 = 5$.

46. The Zero Product Property states that if the product of two numbers is 0, then at least one of the numbers must be 0. When you factor a quadratic and the product of the factors is 0, at least one of the factors must be 0.

32. Multi-Step The height of a flare can be approximated by the function $h = -16t^2 + 95t + 6$, where h is the height in feet and t is the time in seconds. Find the time it takes the flare to hit the ground. **6 s**

Determine the number of solutions of each equation.

33. $(x + 8)(x + 8) = 0$ **1** **34.** $(x - 3)(x + 3) = 0$ **2** **35.** $(x + 7)^2 = 0$ **1**

36. $3x^2 + 12x + 9 = 0$ **2** **37.** $x^2 + 12x + 40 = 4$ **1** **38.** $(x - 2)^2 = 9$ **2**

39. ERROR ANALYSIS Which solution is incorrect? Explain the error.

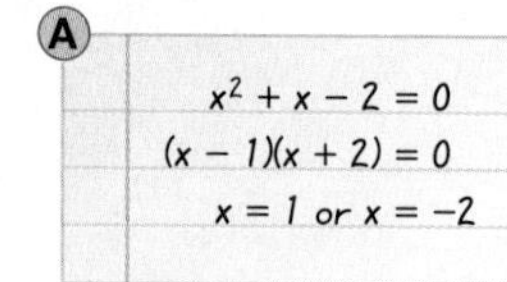

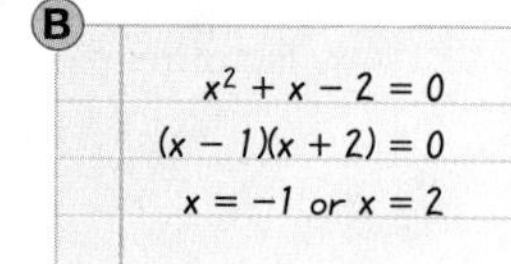

39. B; after factoring the polynomial, you should solve the equations $x - 1 = 0$ and $x + 2 = 0$. The correct solutions are 1 and −2.

40. Number Theory Write an equation that could be used to find two consecutive even integers whose product is 24. Let x represent the first integer. Solve the equation and give the two integers.

41. Geometry The photo shows a traditional thatched house as found in Santana, Madeira, in Portugal. The front of the house is in the shape of a triangle. Suppose the base of the triangle is 1 m less than its height and the area of the triangle is 15 m^2. Find the height of the triangle. (*Hint:* Use $A = \frac{1}{2}bh$.) **6 m**

42. Multi-Step The length of a rectangle is 1 ft less than 3 times the width. The area is 310 ft^2. Find the dimensions of the rectangle. **$10\frac{1}{3}$ ft by 30 ft**

43. Physics The height of a fireworks rocket in meters can be approximated by $h = -5t^2 + 30t$, where h is the height in meters and t is time in seconds. Find the time it takes the rocket to reach the ground after it has been launched. **6 s**

44. Geometry One base of a trapezoid is the same length as the height of the trapezoid. The other base is 4 cm more than the height. The area of the trapezoid is 48 cm^2. Find the length of the shorter base. (*Hint:* Use $A = \frac{1}{2}h(b_1 + b_2)$.) **6 cm**

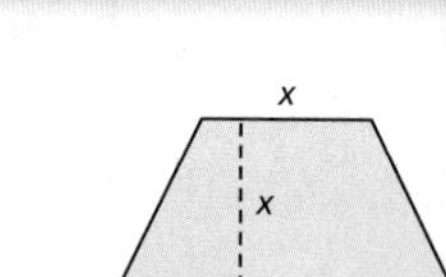

45. Critical Thinking Can you solve $(x - 2)(x + 3) = 5$ by solving $x - 2 = 5$ and $x + 3 = 5$? Why or why not?

46. Write About It Explain why you set each factor equal to zero when solving a quadratic equation by factoring.

47. This problem will prepare you for the Multi-Step Test Prep on page 678.

A tee box is 48 feet above its fairway. When a golf ball is hit from the tee box with an initial vertical velocity of 32 ft/s, the quadratic equation $0 = -16t^2 + 32t + 48$ gives the time t in seconds when a golf ball is at height 0 feet on the fairway.

a. Solve the quadratic equation by factoring to see how long the ball is in the air. **3 s**

b. What is the height of the ball at 1 second? **64 ft**

c. Is the ball at its maximum height at 1 second? Explain. **Yes; the vertex is (1, 64), which represents the ball's maximum height of 64 ft after 1 s in the air.**

9-6 PRACTICE A

9-6 PRACTICE C

9-6 PRACTICE B

Use the Zero Product Property to solve each equation. Check your answers.

1. $(x - 1)(x - 5) = 0$
   $x - 1 = 0$ or $x - 5 = 0$
   $x = 1$ or $x = 5$
2. $(x - 2)(x - 9) = 0$
   $x - 2 = 0$ or $x - 9 = 0$
   $x = 2$ or $x = 9$
3. $(x - 2)(x + 4) = 0$
   2; −4
4. $(2x + 1)(x - 6) = 0$
   $-\frac{1}{2}$; −6

Solve each quadratic equation by factoring.

5. $x^2 - 3x = 0$ 0; 3
6. $x^2 + 4x + 3 = 0$ −3; −1
7. $x^2 + 5x - 6 = 0$ 1; −6
8. $x^2 + 11x + 24 = 0$ −3; −8
9. $x^2 - 12x + 11 = 0$ 1; 11
10. $x^2 + 18x + 65 = 0$ −13; −5
11. $x^2 - 4x - 12 = 0$ 6; −2
12. $x^2 + 11x + 10 = 0$ −1; −10
13. $x^2 + 12x + 35 = 0$ −5; −7
14. $2x^2 - 3x - 5 = 0$ $\frac{5}{2}$; −1
15. $3x^2 - 5x - 2 = 0$ $-\frac{1}{3}$; 2
16. $x^2 = 3x + 40$ 8; −5
17. $x^2 - 14 = 5x$ 7; −2
18. $2x - 1 = -8x^2$ $\frac{1}{4}$; $-\frac{1}{2}$
19. $x = 10x^2 - 2$ $-\frac{2}{5}$; $\frac{1}{2}$
20. $2x^2 = 13x + 7$ 7; $-\frac{1}{2}$
21. $6x^2 + x = 5$ −1; $\frac{5}{6}$
22. $x^2 = 5x$ 0; 5
23. The height of a flare fired from the deck of a ship in distress can be modeled by $h = -16t^2 + 104t + 56$, where h is the height of the flare above water and t is the time in seconds. Find the time it takes the flare to hit the water. 7 seconds

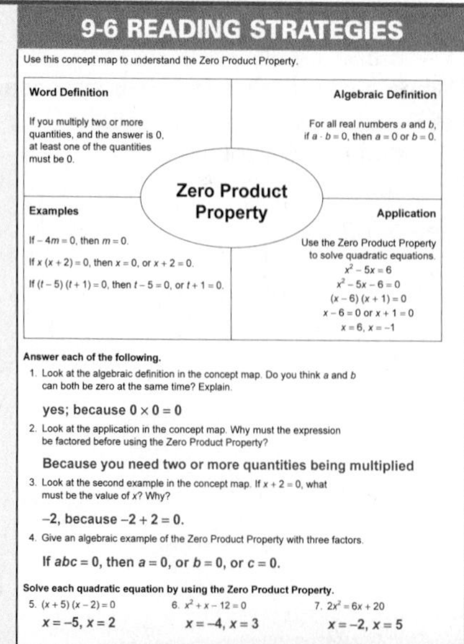

9-6 READING STRATEGIES

Use this concept map to understand the Zero Product Property.

Zero Product Property

Word Definition
If you multiply two or more quantities, and the answer is 0, at least one of the quantities must be 0.

Algebraic Definition
For all real numbers a and b, if $a \cdot b = 0$, then $a = 0$ or $b = 0$.

Examples
If $-4m = 0$, then $m = 0$.
If $x(x + 2) = 0$, then $x = 0$, or $x + 2 = 0$.
If $(t - 5)(t + 1) = 0$, then $t - 5 = 0$, or $t + 1 = 0$.

Application
Use the Zero Product Property to solve quadratic equations.
$x^2 - 5x = 6$
$x^2 - 5x - 6 = 0$
$(x - 6)(x + 1) = 0$
$x - 6 = 0$ or $x + 1 = 0$
$x = 6, x = -1$

Answer each of the following.

1. Look at the algebraic definition in the concept map. Do you think a and b can both be zero at the same time? Explain.
   yes; because $0 \times 0 = 0$
2. Look at the application in the concept map. Why must the expression be factored before using the Zero Product Property?
   Because you need two or more quantities being multiplied
3. Look at the second example in the concept map. If $x + 2 = 0$, what must be the value of x? Why?
   −2, because $-2 + 2 = 0$.
4. Give an algebraic example of the Zero Product Property with three factors.
   If $abc = 0$, then $a = 0$, or $b = 0$, or $c = 0$.

Solve each quadratic equation by using the Zero Product Property.

5. $(x + 5)(x - 2) = 0$ $x = -5, x = 2$
6. $x^2 + x - 12 = 0$ $x = -4, x = 3$
7. $2x^2 = 6x + 20$ $x = -2, x = 5$

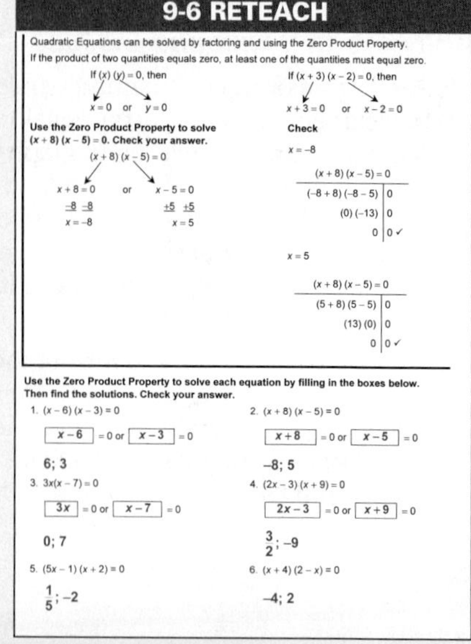

9-6 RETEACH

Quadratic Equations can be solved by factoring and using the Zero Product Property.
If the product of two quantities equals zero, at least one of the quantities must equal zero.

If $(x)(y) = 0$, then $x = 0$ or $y = 0$

If $(x + 3)(x - 2) = 0$, then $x + 3 = 0$ or $x - 2 = 0$

Use the Zero Product Property to solve $(x + 8)(x - 5) = 0$. Check your answer.

$(x + 8)(x - 5) = 0$

$x + 8 = 0$ or $x - 5 = 0$
$\underline{-8}\ \underline{-8}$ $\underline{+5}\ \underline{+5}$
$x = -8$ $x = 5$

Check

$x = -8$

$(x + 8)(x - 5) = 0$	
$(-8 + 8)(-8 - 5)$	0
$(0)(-13)$	0
0	0 ✓

$x = 5$

$(x + 8)(x - 5) = 0$	
$(5 + 8)(5 - 5)$	0
$(13)(0)$	0
0	0 ✓

Use the Zero Product Property to solve each equation by filling in the boxes below. Then find the solutions. Check your answer.

1. $(x - 6)(x - 3) = 0$
   [$x - 6$] = 0 or [$x - 3$] = 0
   6; 3
2. $(x + 8)(x - 5) = 0$
   [$x + 8$] = 0 or [$x - 5$] = 0
   −8; 5
3. $3x(x - 7) = 0$
   [$3x$] = 0 or [$x - 7$] = 0
   0; 7
4. $(2x - 3)(x + 9) = 0$
   [$2x - 3$] = 0 or [$x + 9$] = 0
   $\frac{3}{2}$; −9
5. $(5x - 1)(x + 2) = 0$
   $\frac{1}{5}$; −2
6. $(x + 4)(2 - x) = 0$
   −4; 2

48. What are the solutions to $(x - 1)(2x + 5) = 0$?

(A) -1 and $\frac{5}{2}$ (C) 1 and $-\frac{5}{2}$

(B) -1 and $\frac{2}{5}$ (D) 1 and $-\frac{2}{5}$

49. Which graph could be used to solve the equation $(x - 3)(x - 2) = 0$?

(F)
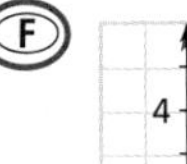
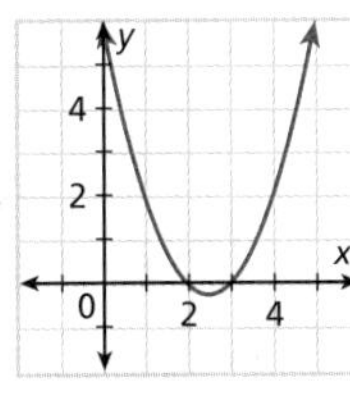

(H)
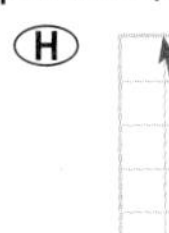

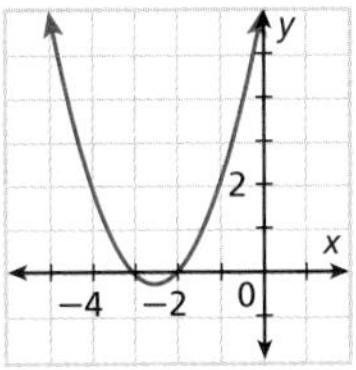

(G)
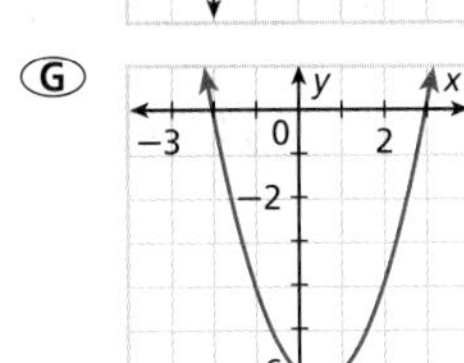

(J)
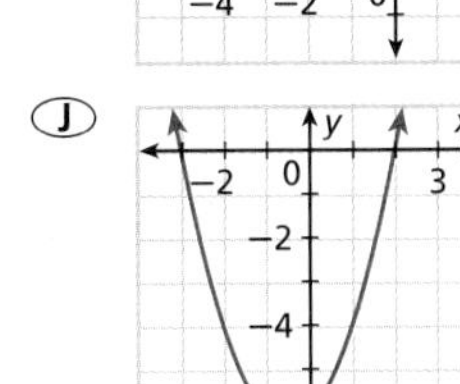

CHALLENGE AND EXTEND

Solve each equation by factoring.

50. $6x^2 + 11x = 10$ **$-\frac{5}{2}, \frac{2}{3}$**
51. $0.2x^2 + 1 = -1.2x$ **$-5, -1$**
52. $\frac{1}{3}x^2 = 2x - 3$ **3**
53. $75x - 45 = -30x^2$ **$\frac{1}{2}, -3$**
54. $x^2 = -4(2x + 3)$ **$-6, -2$**
55. $\frac{x(x - 3)}{2} = 5$ **$-2, 5$**
56. $x(x - 10)(x - 3) = 0$ **0, 3, 10**
57. $x^3 + 2x^2 + x = 0$ **$-1, 0$**
58. $x^3 + 4x^2 = 0$ **$-4, 0$**

Geometry Use the diagram for Exercises 59–61.

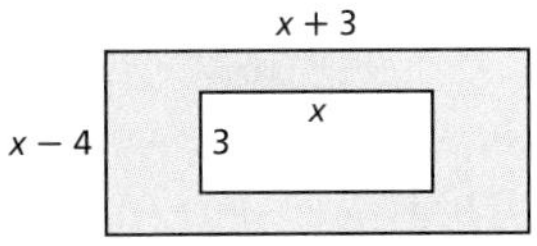

$x + 3$ (width of larger rectangle), $x - 4$ (height of larger rectangle); x (width of smaller rectangle), 3 (height of smaller rectangle)

59. Write a polynomial to represent the area of the larger rectangle. **$x^2 - x - 12$**
60. Write a polynomial to represent the area of the smaller rectangle. **$3x$**
61. Write a polynomial to represent the area of the shaded region. Then solve for x given that the area of the shaded region is 48 square units. **$x^2 - 4x - 12 = 48$; $x = 10$**

SPIRAL REVIEW

Find each root. *(Lesson 1-5)*

62. $\sqrt{121}$ **11**
63. $-\sqrt{64}$ **-8**
64. $-\sqrt{100}$ **-10**
65. $\sqrt[4]{16}$ **2**

Solve each system by using substitution. *(Lesson 6-2)*

66. $\begin{cases} 2x + 2y = 10 \\ y = x - 3 \end{cases}$ **(4, 1)**
67. $\begin{cases} 4x - 3y = 12 \\ x - y = 7 \end{cases}$ **$(-9, -16)$**
68. $\begin{cases} x - 2y = 6 \\ 10x + y = 18 \end{cases}$ **$(2, -2)$**

Solve each equation by graphing the related function. *(Lesson 9-5)*

69. $x^2 - 49 = 0$ **± 7**
70. $x^2 = x + 12$ **$4, -3$**
71. $-x^2 + 8x = 15$ **3, 5**

9-6 PROBLEM SOLVING

Write the correct answer.

1. The height of an acorn falling out of a tree is $h = -16t^2 + 25$ where h is height in feet and t is time in seconds. Determine how long it takes the acorn to reach the ground. Check your answer by graphing the function.

Height of Acorn

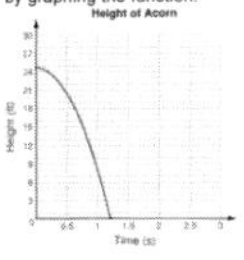

1.25 seconds

2. An architect is designing a building with a right triangular footprint.

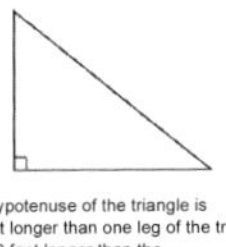

The hypotenuse of the triangle is 80 feet longer than one leg of the triangle and 40 feet longer than the other leg. Use the Pythagorean Theorem to find the dimensions of the footprint of the building.

200 ft, 120 ft, 160 ft

3. Robert threw a rock off a bridge into the river. The distance from the rock to the river is modeled by the equation $h = -16t^2 - 16t + 60$, where h is the height in feet and t is the time in seconds. Find how long it took the rock to enter the water.

1.5 seconds

4. During a game of golf, Kayley hits her ball out of a sand trap. The equation $h = -16t^2 + 20t - 4$ models the height of the golf ball in feet in relation to the number of t seconds since it was hit. Find how long it takes Kayley's golf ball to reach to green.

1 second

A new store is being built in the shape of a rectangle with a parking lot in the shape of an isosceles trapezoid. The parking lot and the store will share a side as shown. Select the best answer.

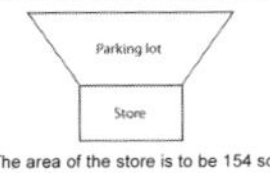

5. The parking lot will have an area of 160 square meters. The shorter base is 4 m longer than the height of the trapezoid, and the longer base is 8 m longer than the height. What is the length of the shorter base?

F 10 meters H 18 meters
G 14 meters J 20 meters

6. The area of the store is to be 154 square meters. If the depth is given as $\frac{1}{14}x^2 + \frac{15}{14}x$, what is the value of x?

A 7 C 14
B 11 D 28

7. What is the depth of the store in meters?

F 7 H 14
G 11 J 28

9-6 CHALLENGE

In Chapter 8 you learned methods for factoring polynomials that are *not* quadratic. By using these methods and by extending the Zero Product Property to more than two factors, you can solve some higher-degree polynomial equations. Here's an example:

Solve $2x^3 + 3x^2 - 2x = 3$ by factoring.

$2x^3 + 3x^2 - 2x - 3 = 0$	*Write the equation in standard form.*
$(2x^3 + 3x^2) + (-2x - 3) = 0$	*Group terms.*
$x^2(2x + 3) - 1(2x + 3) = 0$	*Factor out the GCF of each group.*
$(2x + 3)(x^2 - 1) = 0$	*Factor out the common binomial.*
$(2x + 3)(x + 1)(x - 1) = 0$	*Factor the difference of two squares.*
$2x + 3 = 0$ or $x + 1 = 0$ or $x - 1 = 0$	*Use the Zero Product Property.*
$x = -\frac{3}{2}$ or $x = -1$ or $x = 1$	*Solve each equation.*

Check

$2x^3 + 3x^2 - 2x = 3$		$2x^3 + 3x^2 - 2x = 3$		$2x^3 + 3x^2 - 2x = 3$	
$2\left(-\frac{3}{2}\right)^3 + 3\left(-\frac{3}{2}\right)^2 - 2\left(-\frac{3}{2}\right)$	3	$2(-1)^3 + 3(-1)^2 - 2(-1)$	3	$2(1)^3 + 3(1)^2 - 2(1)$	3
$-\frac{27}{4} + \frac{27}{4} + 3$	3	$-2 + 3 + 2$	3	$2 + 3 - 2$	3
3	3 ✓	3	3 ✓	3	3 ✓

Solve each polynomial equation by factoring.

1. $x^3 + 3x^2 - 25x - 75 = 0$ **$-3, -5, 5$**
2. $8x^3 - 20x^2 = 18x - 45$ **$\frac{5}{2}, \frac{3}{2}, -\frac{3}{2}$**
3. $x^3 + 63 = 7x^2 + 9x$ **$-3, 3, 7$**
4. $3x^3 - 6x^2 - 72x = 0$ **$0, -4, 6$**
5. $-39x^2 = 18x^3 + 15x$ **$0, -\frac{1}{2}, -\frac{5}{3}$**
6. $-8x^3 - 44x^2 = -32x - 176$ **$2, -2, -\frac{11}{2}$**

TEST PREP DOCTOR In **Exercise 49,** students can examine the equation to see that the zeros of the related function must be 3 and 2. Only **F** shows a function with these zeros.

Journal

Explain why you must have 0 on one side of the equation in order to apply the Zero Product Property to solve an equation.

ALTERNATIVE ASSESSMENT

Have students use binomial factors to work backward to create two equivalent quadratic equations with given solutions.

Power Presentations with PowerPoint®

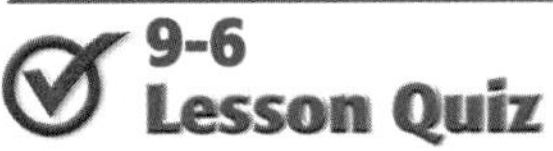

9-6 Lesson Quiz

Use the Zero Product Property to solve each equation. Check your answer.

1. $(x - 10)(x + 5) = 0$ 10, −5
2. $(x + 5)(x) = 0$ −5, 0

Solve each quadratic equation by factoring. Check your answer.

3. $x^2 + 16x + 48 = 0$ −4, −12
4. $x^2 - 11x = -24$ 3, 8
5. $2x^2 + 12x - 14 = 0$ 1, −7
6. $x^2 + 18x + 81 = 0$ −9
7. $-4x^2 = 16x + 16$ −2
8. The height of a rocket launched upward from a 160-foot cliff is modeled by the function $h(t) = -16t^2 + 48t + 160$, where h is height in feet and t is time in seconds. Find the time it takes the rocket to reach the ground at the bottom of the cliff. 5 s

Also available on transparency

9-7 Organizer

Pacing: Traditional 1 day
Block $\frac{1}{2}$ day

Objective: Solve quadratic equations by using square roots.

Online Edition
Tutorial Videos

Countdown Week 20

Power Presentations with PowerPoint®

Warm Up

Find each square root.

1. $\sqrt{36}$ 6
2. $\sqrt{121}$ 11
3. $-\sqrt{625}$ −25
4. $\sqrt{\frac{4}{25}}$ $\frac{2}{5}$

Solve each equation.

5. $-6x = -60$ 10
6. $\frac{1}{5}x = 16$ 80
7. $2x - 40 = 0$ 20
8. $5x = 3$ $\frac{3}{5}$

Also available on transparency

Math Humor

Mother: Why did you rip up my garden?

Student: My math assignment is to find roots.

State Resources

go.hrw.com
State Resources Online
KEYWORD: MA7 Resources

9-7 Solving Quadratic Equations by Using Square Roots

Objective
Solve quadratic equations by using square roots.

Why learn this?
Square roots can be used to find how much fencing is needed for a pen at a zoo. (See Example 4.)

Some quadratic equations cannot be easily solved by factoring. Square roots can be used to solve some of these quadratic equations. Recall from Lesson 1-5 that every positive real number has two square roots, one positive and one negative.

$$3(3) = 3^2 = 9 \longrightarrow \sqrt{9} = 3 \leftarrow \text{Positive square root of 9}$$

$$(-3)(-3) = (-3)^2 = 9 \longrightarrow -\sqrt{9} = -3 \leftarrow \text{Negative square root of 9}$$

Reading Math
The expression ± 3 is read "plus or minus three."

When you take the square root of a positive real number and the sign of the square root is not indicated, you must find both the positive and negative square root. This is indicated by $\pm\sqrt{\ }$.

$$\pm\sqrt{9} = \pm 3 \leftarrow \text{Positive and negative square roots of 9}$$

Know it! Note

Square-Root Property

WORDS	NUMBERS	ALGEBRA
To solve a quadratic equation in the form $x^2 = a$, take the square root of both sides.	$x^2 = 15$ $x = \pm\sqrt{15}$	If $x^2 = a$ and a is a positive real number, then $x = \pm\sqrt{a}$.

EXAMPLE 1 Using Square Roots to Solve $x^2 = a$

Solve using square roots.

A $x^2 = 16$

$x = \pm\sqrt{16}$ — *Solve for x by taking the square root of both sides. Use ± to show both square roots.*

$x = \pm 4$

The solutions are 4 and −4.

Check

$x^2 = 16$	
$(4)^2$	16
16	16 ✓

Substitute 4 and −4 into the original equation.

$x^2 = 16$	
$(-4)^2$	16
16	16 ✓

1 Introduce

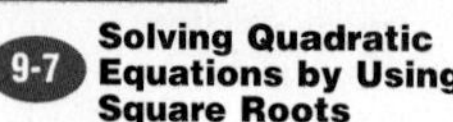

EXPLORATION

9-7 Solving Quadratic Equations by Using Square Roots

In this activity, you will use what you already know about squares to solve some simple quadratic equations.

1. Complete the table.

x	1	2	3	4	5	6	7	8	9	10
x^2										

2. Complete the table.

x	−1	−2	−3	−4	−5	−6	−7	−8	−9	−10
x^2										

3. Suppose $x^2 = 36$. What can you say about the value of x?
4. Suppose $x^2 = 100$. What can you say about the value of x?
5. In general, if a is a positive real number, how many solutions are there to the equation $x^2 = a$?

THINK AND DISCUSS

6. **Explain** how to find the solutions of $x^2 = 144$.
7. **Describe** how you can use your tables from Problems 1 and 2 to estimate the solutions of the equation $x^2 = 20$.

Motivate

Have students translate the following sentence into an algebraic equation: The sum of the square of a number and ten is forty-six. $x^2 + 10 = 46$

Have students use guess-and-check to find the values of x that make the sentence true. 6 and −6

Tell students that in this lesson they will learn algebraic methods for solving these types of equations.

Explorations and answers are provided in *Alternate Openers: Explorations Transparencies*.

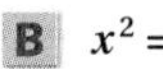

Solve using square roots.

B $x^2 = -4$

$x = \pm\sqrt{-4}$ *There is no real number whose square is negative.*

There is no real solution.

Solve using square roots. Check your answer.

1a. $x^2 = 121$ ± 11 **1b.** $x^2 = 0$ 0 **1c.** $x^2 = -16$ no real solutions

If necessary, use inverse operations to isolate the squared part of a quadratic equation before taking the square root of both sides.

EXAMPLE 2 Using Square Roots to Solve Quadratic Equations

Helpful Hint

0 is neither positive nor negative.

Solve using square roots.

A $x^2 + 5 = 5$

$$x^2 + 5 = 5$$

$$\underline{-5 \quad -5}$$ *Subtract 5 from both sides.*

$$x^2 = 0$$

$$x = \pm\sqrt{0} = 0$$ *Take the square root of both sides.*

The solution is 0.

B $4x^2 - 25 = 0$

$$4x^2 - 25 = 0$$

$$\underline{+25 \quad +25}$$ *Add 25 to both sides.*

$$\frac{4x^2}{4} = \frac{25}{4}$$ *Divide both sides by 4.*

$$x^2 = \frac{25}{4}$$

$$x = \pm\sqrt{\frac{25}{4}} = \pm\frac{5}{2}$$ *Take the square root of both sides. Use ± to show both square roots.*

The solutions are $\frac{5}{2}$ and $-\frac{5}{2}$.

C $(x + 2)^2 = 9$

$$(x + 2)^2 = 9$$

$$x + 2 = \pm\sqrt{9}$$ *Take the square root of both sides. Use ± to show both square roots.*

$$x + 2 = \pm 3$$

$$x + 2 = 3 \text{ or } x + 2 = -3$$ *Write two equations, using both the positive and negative square roots, and solve each equation.*

$$\underline{-2 \quad -2} \qquad \underline{-2 \quad -2}$$

$$x = 1 \text{ or } x = -5$$

The solutions are 1 and −5.

Check

$(x + 2)^2$	$= 9$
$(1 + 2)^2$	9
3^2	9
9	9 ✓

$(x + 2)^2$	$= 9$
$(-5 + 2)^2$	9
$(-3)^2$	9
9	9 ✓

Solve by using square roots. Check your answer.

2a. $100x^2 + 49 = 0$ no real solutions **2b.** $(x - 5)^2 = 16$ 9, 1

When solving quadratic equations by using square roots, you may need to find the square root of a number that is not a perfect square. In this case, the answer is an irrational number. You can approximate the solutions.

COMMON ERROR ALERT

For equations like $4x^2 = 25$, students sometimes mentally stack the smaller number on top of the larger number and get $x^2 = \frac{4}{25}$. Remind students that the goal is to isolate x^2, so both sides will be divided by the coefficient of x^2.

Power Presentations with PowerPoint®

Additional Examples

Example 1

Solve using square roots.

A. $x^2 = 169$ ± 13

B. $x^2 = -49$ no real solutions

Example 2

Solve using square roots. Check your answer.

A. $x^2 + 7 = 7$ 0

B. $16x^2 - 49 = 0$ $\pm\frac{7}{4}$

INTERVENTION

Questioning Strategies

EXAMPLES **1–2**

- Are there any real numbers whose square is negative?
- When does a quadratic equation of the form $x^2 = a$ have one solution?
- How do you take the square root of a fraction?

2 Teach

Guided Instruction

Discuss with students that squaring and finding square roots are inverse operations and can be used to isolate a variable in an equation. Remind students that if you take the square root of one side of the equation, you must also take the square root of the other side to maintain the balance.

Reaching All Learners

Through Visual Cues

Encourage students to circle on their own paper what is to be isolated in each step of solving the equations in this lesson.

1. Circle the entire x^2-term and think of how it can be isolated.
2. Circle only x^2 and think of how it can be isolated.
3. Circle the x in x^2, showing that the last operation to be undone is the square.

Power Presentations with PowerPoint®

Additional Examples

Example 3

Solve. Round to the nearest hundredth.

A. $x^2 = 15$ ± 3.87

B. $-3x^2 + 90 = 0$ ± 5.48

Example 4

Ms. Pirzada is building a retaining wall along one of the long sides of her rectangular garden. The garden is twice as long as it is wide. It also has an area of 578 square feet. What will be the length of the retaining wall? 34 ft

INTERVENTION

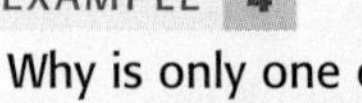

Questioning Strategies

EXAMPLE 3

- Describe a method to approximate the solution without a calculator.

EXAMPLE 4

- Why is only one of the solutions to the equation used to answer the question?

Critical Thinking Ask students what is wrong with solving the equation $x^2 = 3x$ by dividing both sides by x. If they divide by x, the equation is $x = 3$, and they have lost the solution $x = 0$. Also, be sure they realize that if $x = 0$, division of both sides by x is undefined.

EXAMPLE 3 **Solve the equation $0 = -2x^2 + 80$. Round to the nearest hundredth.**

$0 = -2x^2 + 80$

$\underline{-80 \qquad -80}$ — *Subtract 80 from both sides.*

$\frac{-80}{-2} = \frac{-2x^2}{-2}$ — *Divide both sides by −2.*

$40 = x^2$

$\pm\sqrt{40} = x$ — *Take the square root of both sides.*

$x \approx \pm 6.32$ — *Find $\sqrt{40}$ on a calculator.*

The approximate solutions are 6.32 and −6.32.

Check Use a graphing calculator to support your answer.

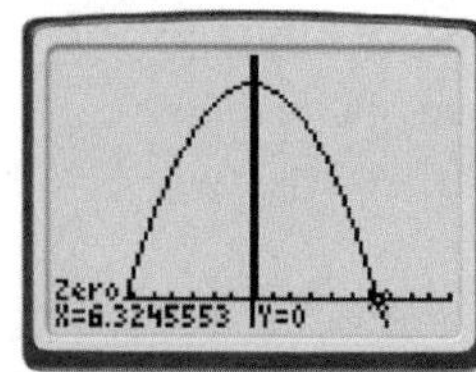

Use the zero function. The approximate solutions are 6.32 and −6.32. ✓

CHECK IT OUT! Solve. Round to the nearest hundredth.

3a. $0 = 90 - x^2$ **±9.49** **3b.** $2x^2 - 64 = 0$ **±5.66** **3c.** $x^2 + 45 = 0$ **no real solutions**

EXAMPLE 4 ***Career Application***

A zookeeper is buying fencing to enclose a pen at the zoo. The pen is an isosceles right triangle. There is already a fence on the side that borders a path. The area of the pen will be 4500 square feet. The zookeeper can buy the fencing in whole feet only. How many feet of fencing should he buy?

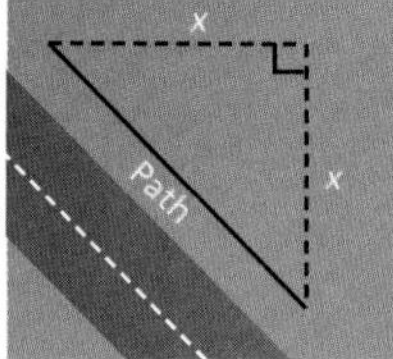

Remember!

An isosceles triangle has at least two sides of the same length.

Let x represent the length of one of the sides.

$\frac{1}{2}bh = A$ — *Use the formula for area of a triangle.*

$\frac{1}{2}x(x) = 4500$ — *Substitute x for both b and h and 4500 for A.*

$(2)\frac{1}{2}x^2 = 4500(2)$ — *Simplify. Multiply both sides by 2.*

$x^2 = 9000$

$x = \pm\sqrt{9000}$ — *Take the square root of both sides.*

$x \approx \pm 94.9$ — *Find $\sqrt{9000}$ on a calculator.*

Negative numbers are not reasonable for length, so $x \approx 94.9$ is the only solution that makes sense. Therefore, the zookeeper needs 95 + 95, or 190, feet of fencing.

CHECK IT OUT! **4.** A house is on a lot that is shaped like a trapezoid. The solid lines show the boundaries, where x represents the width of the front yard. Find the width of the front yard, given that the area is 6000 square feet. Round to the nearest foot. (*Hint:* Use $A = \frac{1}{2}h(b_1 + b_2)$.) **45 ft**

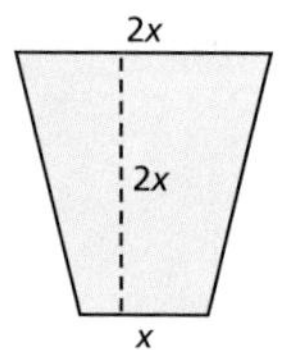

3 Close

Summarize

Review the steps for solving quadratic equations, by using square roots, comparing them to steps for solving linear equations: undo the operations performed on the variable. For quadratic equations, the last step is to take the square root of each side.

Have students state the steps they would use to solve $5x^2 - 18 = 27$.

Add 18 to each side. Divide both sides by 5. Take the square root of both sides.

ONGOING ASSESSMENT and INTERVENTION

***Diagnose Before** the Lesson*
9-7 Warm Up, TE p. 656

***Monitor During** the Lesson*
Check It Out! Exercises, SE pp. 657–658
Questioning Strategies, TE pp. 657–658

***Assess After** the Lesson*
9-7 Lesson Quiz, TE p. 661
Alternative Assessment, TE p. 661

THINK AND DISCUSS

1. Explain why there are no solutions to the quadratic equation $x^2 = -9$.
2. Describe how to estimate the solutions of $4 = x^2 - 16$. What are the approximate solutions?
3. **GET ORGANIZED** Copy and complete the graphic organizer. In each box, write an example of a quadratic equation with the given number of solutions. Solve each equation.

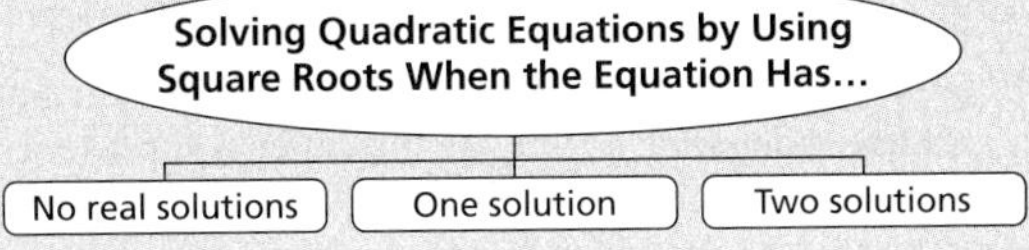

Answers to *Think and Discuss*

Possible answers:

1. There is no real number whose square is negative.
2. The equation is equivalent to $x^2 = 20$, so $x = \pm\sqrt{20}$. $\sqrt{20}$ is between 4 and 5, so x is approximately ± 4.5.
3. See p. A8.

9-7 Exercises

GUIDED PRACTICE

Solve using square roots. Check your answer.

SEE EXAMPLE 1 p. 656

1. $x^2 = 225$ **±15**
2. $x^2 = 49$ **±7**
3. $x^2 = -100$ **no real solutions**
4. $x^2 = 400$ **±20**
5. $-25 = x^2$ **no real solutions**
6. $36 = x^2$ **±6**

SEE EXAMPLE 2 p. 657

7. $3x^2 - 75 = 0$ **±5**
8. $0 = 81x^2 - 25$ **$\pm\frac{5}{9}$**
9. $49x^2 + 64 = 0$ **no real solutions**
10. $16x^2 + 10 = 131$ **$\pm\frac{11}{4}$**
11. $(x - 3)^2 = 64$ **11, −5**
12. $(x - 9)^2 = 25$ **4, 14**

SEE EXAMPLE 3 p. 658

Solve. Round to the nearest hundredth.

13. $3x^2 = 81$ **±5.20**
14. $0 = x^2 - 60$ **±7.75**
15. $100 - 5x^2 = 0$ **±4.47**

SEE EXAMPLE 4 p. 658

16. **Geometry** The length of a rectangle is 3 times its width. The area of the rectangle is 170 square meters. Find the width. Round to the nearest tenth of a meter. (*Hint:* Use $A = \ell w$.) **7.5 m**

PRACTICE AND PROBLEM SOLVING

Independent Practice

For Exercises	See Example
17–22	1
23–28	2
29–34	3
35	4

Extra Practice
Skills Practice p. S21
Application Practice p. S36

Solve using square roots. Check your answer.

17. $x^2 = 169$ **±13**
18. $x^2 = 25$ **±5**
19. $x^2 = -36$ **no real solutions**
20. $x^2 = 10{,}000$ **±100**
21. $-121 = x^2$ **no real solutions**
22. $625 = x^2$ **±25**
23. $4 - 81x^2 = 0$ **$\pm\frac{2}{9}$**
24. $(2x + 1)^2 = 25$ **2, −3**
25. $64x^2 - 5 = 20$ **$\pm\frac{5}{8}$**
26. $(x - 7)^2 = 1$ **6, 8**
27. $49x^2 + 1 = 170$ **$\pm\frac{13}{7}$**
28. $81x^2 + 17 = 81$ **$\pm\frac{8}{9}$**

Solve. Round to the nearest hundredth.

29. $4x^2 = 88$ **±4.69**
30. $x^2 - 29 = 0$ **±5.39**
31. $x^2 + 40 = 144$ **±10.20**
32. $3x^2 - 84 = 0$ **±5.29**
33. $50 - x^2 = 0$ **±7.07**
34. $2x^2 - 10 = 64$ **±6.08**

9-7 Exercises

Assignment Guide

Assign *Guided Practice* Exercises as necessary.

If you finished Examples **1–2**
Basic 17–28, 43, 53
Average 17–28, 43, 44, 53
Advanced 17–28, 39, 44, 53

If you finished Examples **1–4**
Basic 17–35, 42, 43, 46–49, 54–56, 61–65
Average 17–38, 40–52, 54–58, 61–65
Advanced 17–42, 44–65,

Homework Quick Check
Quickly check key concepts.
Exercises: 22, 24, 32, 35, 46,

State Resources

go.hrw.com
State Resources Online
KEYWORD: MA7 Resources

Teacher to Teacher

Throughout the lesson and as students work through the exercises, it is important to remind them that the graph of the related function can be used to confirm each of their answers. This reminds students again of the relationship between the solutions of an algebraic equation, the zeros of the related function, and the points containing the x-intercepts of the function's graph.

Jill Springer
Henderson, KY

Teaching Tip **Geometry** In **Exercise 40**, students find a geometric mean. The geometric mean of two positive numbers a and b can be thought of the side length of a square whose area is equal to that of a rectangle with side lengths a and b. In other words, the geometric mean of a and b is $\sqrt{ab}$.

MULTI-STEP TEST PREP **Exercise 48** involves solving a quadratic equation related to the height of a falling golf ball over time. This exercise prepares students for the Multi-Step Test Prep on page 678.

Answers

48b.

t	$d = 16t^2$
0	0
1	16
2	64
3	144
4	256

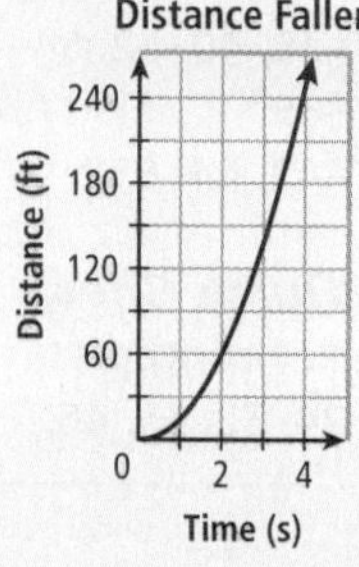

35. **Entertainment** For a scene in a movie, a sack of money is dropped from the roof of a 600 ft skyscraper. The height of the sack above the ground is given by $h = -16t^2 + 600$, where t is the time in seconds. How long will it take the sack to reach the ground? Round to the nearest tenth of a second. **6.1 s**

Solve for the indicated variable. Assume all values are positive.

36. $A = \pi r^2$ for r $\quad r = \sqrt{\frac{A}{\pi}}$
37. $d = \frac{1}{2}at^2$ for t $\quad t = \sqrt{\frac{2d}{a}}$
38. $F = \frac{mv^2}{r}$ for v $\quad v = \sqrt{\frac{Fr}{m}}$

39. **Number Theory** If $a = 2b$ and $2ab = 36$, find all possible solutions for a and b. **$a = -6$ and $b = -3$ or $a = 6$ and $b = 3$**

40. **Geometry** The geometric mean of two positive numbers a and b is the positive number x such that $\frac{a}{x} = \frac{x}{b}$. Find the geometric mean of 2 and 18. **6**

LINK **Physics**

The first pendulum clock was invented by Christian Huygens, a Dutch physicist and mathematician, around 1656. Early pendulum clocks swung about 50° to the left and right. Modern pendulum clocks swing only 10° to 15°.

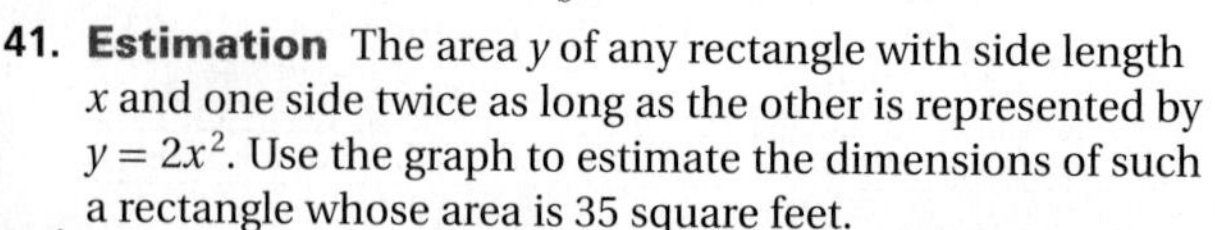

41. **Estimation** The area y of any rectangle with side length x and one side twice as long as the other is represented by $y = 2x^2$. Use the graph to estimate the dimensions of such a rectangle whose area is 35 square feet. **about 4.2 ft by 8.4 ft**

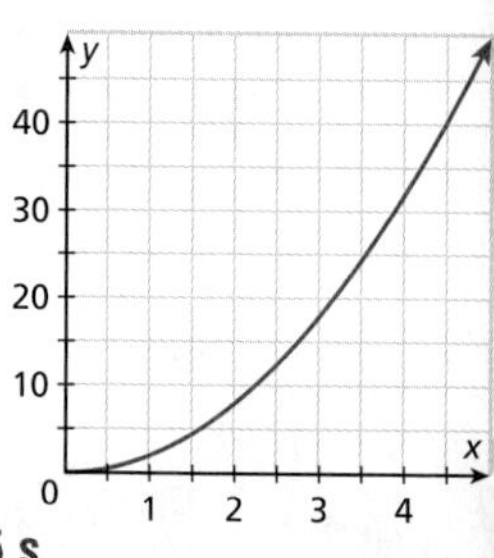

42. **Physics** The period of a pendulum is the amount of time it takes to swing back and forth one time. The relationship between the length of the pendulum L in inches and the length of the period t in seconds can be approximated by $L = 9.78t^2$. Find the period of a pendulum whose length is 60 inches. Round to the nearest tenth of a second. **about 2.5 s**

43. **///ERROR ANALYSIS///** Which solution is incorrect? Explain the error.

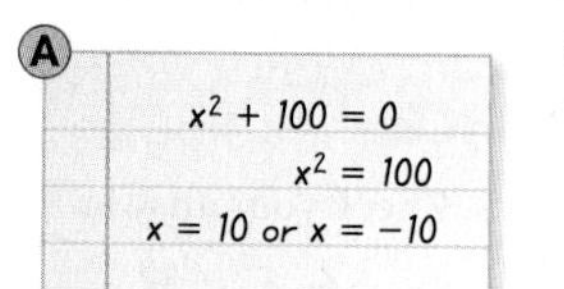

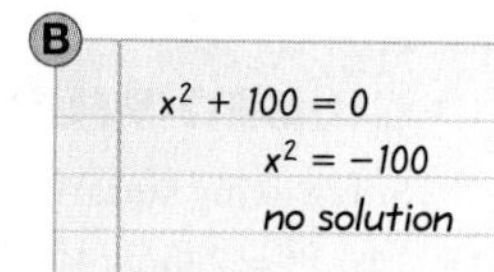

A; 100 was added to the right side of the equation instead of subtracted.

Determine whether each statement is always, sometimes, or never true.

44. There are two solutions to $x^2 = n$ when n is positive. **always**

45. If n is a rational number, then the solutions to $x^2 = n$ are rational numbers. **sometimes**

46. **Multi-Step** The height in feet of a soccer ball kicked upward from the ground with initial velocity 60 feet per second is modeled by $h = -16t^2 + 60t$, where t is the time in seconds. Find the time it takes for the ball to return to the ground. **3.75 s**

47. **Critical Thinking** For the equation $x^2 = a$, describe the values of a that will result in each of the following.
    a. two solutions **$a > 0$**
    b. one solution **$a = 0$**
    c. no solution **$a < 0$**

MULTI-STEP TEST PREP

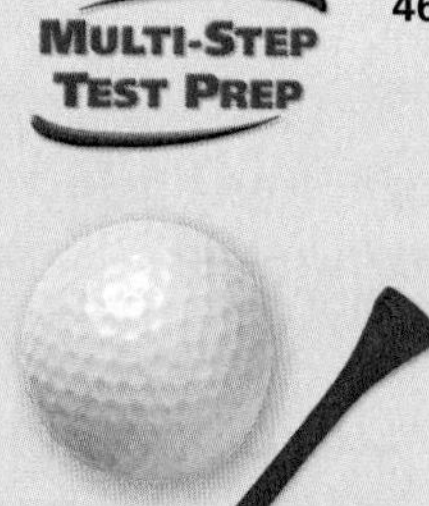

48. This problem will prepare you for the Multi-Step Test Prep on page 678.

The equation $d = 16t^2$ describes the distance d in feet that a golf ball falls in relation to the number of seconds t that it falls.

a. How many seconds will it take a golf ball to drop to the ground from a height of 4 feet? **$\frac{1}{2}$ s**
b. Make a table and graph the function.
c. How far will the golf ball drop in 1 second? **16 ft**
d. How many seconds will it take the golf ball to drop 64 feet? **2 s**

9-7 PRACTICE A
9-7 PRACTICE C
9-7 PRACTICE B

Solve using square roots. Check your answer.

1. $x^2 = 81$
   $x = \pm\sqrt{81}$
   $x = \pm 9$
   The solutions are **9** and **−9**.
2. $x^2 = 100$
   $x = \pm\sqrt{100}$
   $x = \pm 10$
   The solutions are **10** and **−10**.
3. $x^2 = 225$
   $x = \pm\sqrt{225}$
   $x = \pm 15$
4. $441 = x^2$
   $\pm\sqrt{441} = x$
   $\pm 21 = x$
5. $x^2 = -400$
   no real solutions
6. $3x^2 = 108$ **−4, 8**
7. $100 = 4x^2$ **±5**
8. $x^2 = 7 \pm 71$ **±8**
9. $49x^2 - 64 = 0$ **$\pm\frac{8}{7}$**
10. $-2x^2 = -162$ **±9**
11. $9x^2 + 100 = 0$ **no real solutions**
12. $0 = 81x^2 - 121$ **$\pm\frac{11}{9}$**
13. $100x^2 = 25$ **$\pm\frac{1}{2}$**
14. $100x^2 = 121$ **−14, 8**

Solve. Round to the nearest hundredth.

15. $8x^2 = 56$ **±2.65**
16. $5 - x^2 = 20$ **no real solutions**
17. $x^2 + 35 = 105$ **±8.37**
18. The height of a skydiver jumping out of an airplane is given by $h = -16t^2 + 3200$. How long will it take the skydiver to reach the ground? Round to the nearest tenth of a second. **14.1 seconds**
19. The height of a triangle is twice the length of its base. The area of the triangle is 50 m². Find the height and base to the nearest tenth of a meter. **height: 14.2 m, base: 7.1 m**
20. The height of an acorn falling out of a tree is given by $h = -16t^2 + b$. If an acorn takes 1 second to fall to the ground. What is the value of b? **$b = 16$**

9-7 READING STRATEGIES

You've learned to solve quadratic equations by graphing. Equations that are in the form $ax^2 + c = 0$ (where $b = 0$) can also be solved by using square roots. Study the examples below to make the connection between solving quadratic equations by graphing and solving by using square roots.

Example 1: The equation $x^2 = 9$ has **2 solutions.**

Solve by using square roots:	Solve by graphing:
$x^2 = 9$	$x^2 = 9$
$x = \pm\sqrt{9}$	$x^2 - 9 = 0$
$x = \pm 3$	$x^2 - 9 = y$
$x = 3$ and $x = -3$	$y = x^2 - 9$
The solutions are 3 and −3.	The graph has zeros at 3 and −3.

Example 2: The equation $x^2 = -9$ has **no real solutions.**

Solve by using square roots:	Solve by graphing:
$x^2 = -9$	$x^2 = -9$
$x = \pm\sqrt{-9}$	$x^2 + 9 = 0$
There is no real number	$x^2 + 9 = y$
whose square is negative.	$y = x^2 + 9$
There are no solutions.	The graph does not cross the x-axis

Example 3: The equation $x^2 + 9 = 9$ has **1 solution.**

Solve by using square roots:	Solve by graphing:
$x^2 + 9 = 9$	$x^2 + 9 = 9$
$x^2 = 0$	$x^2 + 0 = 0$
$x = \pm\sqrt{0}$	$x^2 = x$
$x = 0$	$y = x^2$
The solutions is 0.	The graph has a zero at 0.

Complete the following.

1. Solve $x^2 = 25$ by using square roots. **$x = \pm 5$**
2. Sketch a graph of the related function $y = x^2 - 25$ to show that you get the same solution(s).
3. How many solutions does $x^2 = -36$ have? **zero**
   a. Explain, in terms of the graph: **The parabola does not cross the x-axis.**
   b. Explain, in terms of square roots: **There is no real number whose square is negative.**

9-7 RETEACH

If a quadratic equation is in the form $x^2 = a$, you must take the square root of both sides to find the solutions. Remember to find both the positive and negative square roots.

Solve $x^2 = 36$ using square roots.

$x^2 = 36$
$\sqrt{x^2} = \pm\sqrt{36}$ *Take the square root of both sides.*
$x = \pm 6$
The solutions are 6 and −6.

Check:

$x = 6$	$x = -6$
$x^2 = 36$	$x^2 = 36$
$(6)^2 \stackrel{?}{=} 36$	$(-6)^2 \stackrel{?}{=} 36$
$36 \stackrel{?}{=} 36$ ✓	$36 \stackrel{?}{=} 36$ ✓

Solve $2x^2 + 7 = 207$ using square roots.

$2x^2 + 7 = 207$
$\underline{-7} \quad \underline{-7}$ *Add −7 to both sides.*
$2x^2 = 200$
$\frac{2x^2}{2} = \frac{200}{2}$ *Divide both sides by 2.*
$\sqrt{x^2} = \pm\sqrt{100}$ *Take the square root of both sides.*
$x = \pm 10$
The solutions are 10 and −10.

Check:

$x = 10$	$x = -10$
$2x^2 + 7 \stackrel{?}{=} 207$	$2x^2 + 7 \stackrel{?}{=} 207$
$2(10)^2 + 7 \stackrel{?}{=} 207$	$2(-10)^2 + 7 \stackrel{?}{=} 207$
$2(100) + 7 \stackrel{?}{=} 207$	$2(100) + 7 \stackrel{?}{=} 207$
$200 + 7 \stackrel{?}{=} 207$	$200 + 7 \stackrel{?}{=} 207$
$207 \stackrel{?}{=} 207$ ✓	$207 \stackrel{?}{=} 207$ ✓

Solve using square roots.

1. $x^2 = 81$ **±9**
2. $x^2 = 9$ **±3**
3. $x^2 = -64$ **no solution**
4. $x^2 + 44 = 188$ **±12**
5. $x^2 - 12 = 37$ **±7**
6. $x^2 + 10 = 131$ **±11**
7. $3x^2 + 25 = 73$ **±4**
8. $5x^2 - 9 = 116$ **±5**
9. $-4x^2 + 42 = -102$ **±6**
10. $4x^2 - 11 = 25$ **±3**
11. $x^2 - 13 = 87$ **±10**
12. $-3x^2 + 200 = 8$ **±8**

49. no; $x = \pm\sqrt{\frac{1}{2}}$, irrational

For the quadratic equation $x^2 + a = 0$, determine whether each value of a will result in two rational solutions. Explain.

49. $-\frac{1}{2}$ **50.** $\frac{1}{2}$ **51.** $-\frac{1}{4}$ **52.** $\frac{1}{4}$

53. Write About It Explain why the quadratic equation $x^2 + 4 = 0$ has no real solutions but the quadratic equation $x^2 - 4 = 0$ has two solutions.

TEST PREP

54. The formula for finding the approximate volume of a cylinder is $V = 3.14r^2h$, where r is the radius and h is the height. The height of a cylinder is 100 cm, and the approximate volume is 1256 cm^3. Find the radius of the cylinder.

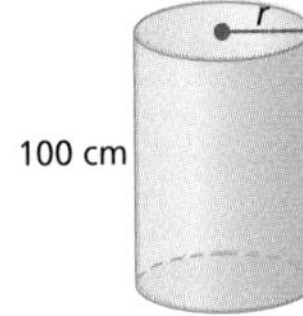

Ⓐ 400 cm Ⓒ 4 cm
Ⓑ 20 cm **Ⓓ 2 cm**

55. Which best describes the positive solution of $\frac{1}{2}x^2 = 20$?

Ⓕ Between 4 and 5 **Ⓗ Between 6 and 7**
Ⓖ Between 5 and 6 Ⓙ Between 7 and 8

56. Which best describes the solutions of $81x^2 - 169 = 0$?

Ⓐ Two rational solutions Ⓒ No solution
Ⓑ Two irrational solutions Ⓓ One solution

CHALLENGE AND EXTEND

Find the solutions of each equation without using a calculator.

57. $288x^2 - 19 = -1$ $\pm\frac{1}{4}$ **58.** $-75x^2 = -48$ $\pm\frac{4}{5}$ **59.** $x^2 = \frac{128}{242}$ $\pm\frac{8}{11}$

60. Geometry The Pythagorean Theorem states that $a^2 + b^2 = c^2$ if a and b represent the lengths of the legs of a right triangle and c represents the length of the hypotenuse.

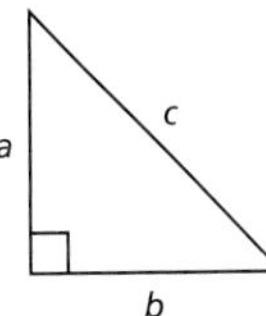

a. Find the length of the hypotenuse if the lengths of the legs are 9 cm and 12 cm. **15 cm**

b. Find the length of each leg of an isosceles right triangle whose hypotenuse is 10 cm. Round to the nearest tenth of a centimeter. **7.1 cm**

SPIRAL REVIEW

61. The figures shown have the same perimeter. What is the value of x? *(Lesson 2-4)* **13**

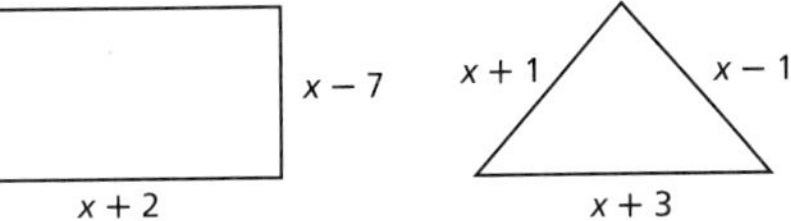

62. Identify which of the following lines are parallel: $y = -2x + 3$, $2x - y = 8$, $6x - 2y = 10$, and $y + 4 = 2(3 - x)$. *(Lesson 5-9)* **$y = -2x + 3$ and $y + 4 = 2(3 - x)$**

Solve each quadratic equation by factoring. Check your answer. *(Lesson 9-6)*

63. $x^2 - 6x + 8 = 0$ **2, 4** **64.** $x^2 + 5x - 6 = 0$ **−6, 1** **65.** $x^2 - 5x = 14$ **−2, 7**

9-7 PROBLEM SOLVING

A furniture maker has designed a bookcase with the proportions shown in the diagram below. Write the correct answer.

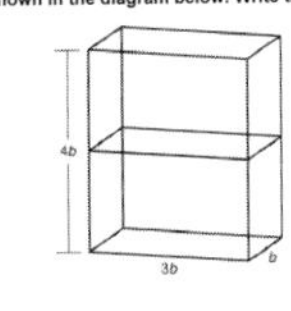

1. A customer has requested a bookcase with the two shelves having a total area of 864 square inches. What should b equal to meet the customer's specifications? **12 inches**

2. Barnard has a stain on his wall and would like to cover it up with a bookcase. What should b equal in order for the back of the bookcase to cover an area of 4800 square inches? **20 inches**

3. Bria would like to display her collection of soap carvings on top of her bookcase. The collection takes up an area of 400 square inches. What should b equal for the top of the bookcase to have the correct area? Round your answer to the nearest tenth of an inch. **11.5 inches**

4. Eliana would like to cover the side panels with silk. She has 1600 square inches of silk. What should b equal so that she can use all of her silk to completely cover the sides? Round your answer to the nearest tenth of an inch. **14.1 inches**

Select the best answer.

5. Carter plans to wallpaper the longest wall in his living room. The wall is twice as long as it is high and has an area of 162 square feet. What is the height of the wall?
A 8 feet C 12 feet
B 9 feet D 18 feet

6. An apple drops off the apple tree from a height of 8 feet. How long does it take the apple to reach the ground? Use the function $f(x) = -16x^2 + c$, where c is the initial height of a falling object, to find the answer.
F 0.5 seconds H 1 second
G 0.71 seconds J 2.23 seconds

7. Trinette cut a square tablecloth into 4 equal pieces that she used to make two pillow covers. The area of the tablecloth was 3600 square inches. What is the side length of each piece Trinette used to make the pillow covers?
A 20 inches C 60 inches
B 30 inches D 90 inches

8. Elton earns x dollars per hour at the bookstore. His mother, Evelyn, earns x^2 dollars per hour as a career counselor. Twice Evelyn's wage equals \$84.50. What is Elton's hourly wage? Round your answer to the nearest cent.
F \$4.60 H \$9.19
G \$6.50 J \$13.00

9-7 CHALLENGE

You know that $\sqrt{9} = 3$ because if 3 is squared, the result is 9. In other words, $3^2 = 9$.

This is helpful as long as you take the square root of a number that is a perfect square.

perfect squares: 0, 1, 4, 9, 16, 25, 36, 49, . . .

But what does something like $\sqrt{12}$ mean?

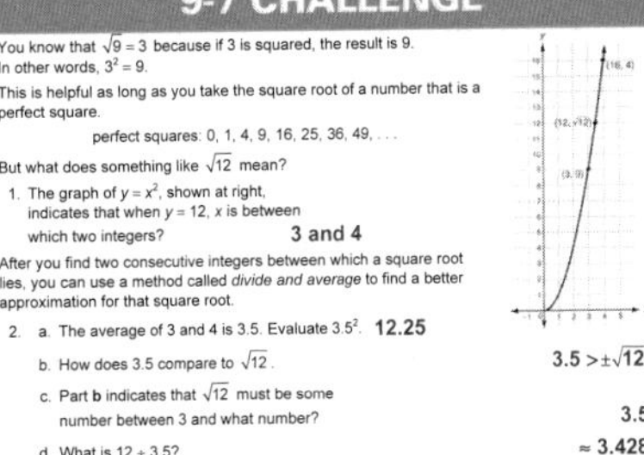

1. The graph of $y = x^2$, shown at right, indicates that when $y = 12$, x is between which two integers? **3 and 4**

After you find two consecutive integers between which a square root lies, you can use a method called *divide and average* to find a better approximation for that square root.

2. a. The average of 3 and 4 is 3.5. Evaluate 3.5^2. **12.25**
b. How does 3.5 compare to $\sqrt{12}$. **$3.5 > \pm\sqrt{12}$**
c. Part **b** indicates that $\sqrt{12}$ must be some number between 3 and what number? **3.5**
d. What is $12 \div 3.5$? **≈ 3.428**
e. Average 3.5 and your answer to part **d**. **≈ 3.464**

3. For how many places past the decimal does your answer to part **e** of Exercise 2 match the calculator value for $\sqrt{12}$. **up to 3 places, depending on how the numbers were rounded**

Using the procedure outlined in Exercise 2, approximate each square root to the nearest tenth.

4. $\sqrt{13}$ **≈3.6** 5. $\sqrt{20}$ **≈4.5**

6. If you use this process on a number that is not a perfect square, will you ever get an exact answer? Explain your response.
No; the square root will be an irrational number which cannot be written as a terminating decimal.

TEST PREP DOCTOR For **Exercise 56,** remind students that rational numbers are numbers that can be written in the form $\frac{a}{b}$, where a and b are both integers and b is not zero. For students who change the fraction to a decimal, remind them that repeating decimals are also rational numbers.

Answers

50. no; $x = \pm\sqrt{-\frac{1}{2}}$, no real solutions
51. yes; $x = \pm\frac{1}{2}$, rational
52. no; $x = \pm\sqrt{-\frac{1}{4}}$, no real solutions
53. See p. A31.

Journal

Have students explain how to solve an equation of the form $ax^2 + c = 0$ by using square roots.

ALTERNATIVE ASSESSMENT

Have students create and solve quadratic equations in the form $ax^2 + c = 0$ where 1) a and c are both positive, 2) a and c are both negative, and 3) a is positive and c is negative.

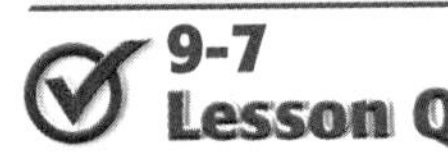

Power Presentations with PowerPoint®

9-7 Lesson Quiz

Solve using square roots. Check your answer.

1. $x^2 - 195 = 1$ ± 14
2. $4x^2 - 18 = -9$ $\pm\frac{3}{2}$
3. $(x + 7)^2 = 81$ $-16, 2$
4. Solve $0 = -5x^2 + 225$. Round to the nearest hundredth. ± 6.71
5. A community swimming pool is in the shape of a trapezoid. The height of the trapezoid is twice as long as the shorter base and the longer base is twice as long as the height.

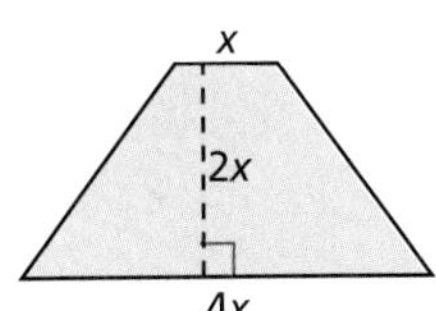

The area of the pool is 3675 square feet. What is the length of the longer base? Round to the nearest foot. (*Hint:* Use $A = \frac{1}{2}h(b_1 + b_2)$.) 108 feet

Also available on transparency

Organizer

Use with Lesson 9-8

Pacing:

Traditional $\frac{1}{2}$ day

Block $\frac{1}{4}$ day

Objective: Use algebra tiles to model completing the square.

Materials: algebra tiles

Online Edition

Countdown Week 21

Resources

Algebra Lab Activities

9-8 Lab Recording Sheet

Teach

Discuss

In the second step of the activity, discuss why 9 unit-tiles are added to the mat. Explain that the goal is to make a perfect square by adding one-tiles.

Close

Key Concept

You can use algebra tiles to model completing the square to form a perfect-square trinomial. Algebra tiles can be found in the Manipulatives Kit (MK). Note that completing the square results in an expression that is not equivalent to the original expression.

Assessment

Journal Have students explain how to use algebra tiles to complete the square for $x^2 + 20x$. Have them write the new expression in factored form. $x^2 + 20x + 100$; $(x + 10)^2$

State Resources

Use with Lesson 9-8

Model Completing the Square

One way to solve a quadratic equation is by using a procedure called *completing the square.* In this procedure, you add something to a quadratic expression to make it a perfect-square trinomial. This procedure can be modeled with algebra tiles.

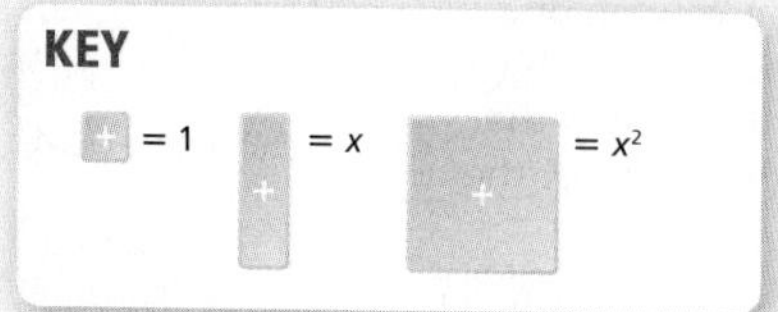

Activity

Use algebra tiles to model $x^2 + 6x$. Add unit tiles to complete a perfect-square trinomial. Then write the new expression in factored form.

MODEL		ALGEBRA
	Arrange the tiles to form part of a large square. *Part of the square is missing. How many one-tiles do you need to complete it?*	$x^2 + 6x$
	Complete the square by placing 9 one-tiles on the mat. *$x^2 + 6x + 9$ is a perfect-square trinomial.*	$x^2 + 6x + 9$
$x + 3$, $x + 3$	*Use the length and the width of the square to rewrite the area expression in factored form.*	$(x + 3)^2$

Try This

Use algebra tiles to model each expression. Add unit tiles to complete a perfect-square trinomial. Then write the new expression in factored form.

1. $x^2 + 4x$
2. $x^2 + 2x$
3. $x^2 + 10x$
4. $x^2 + 8x$
5. **Make a Conjecture** Examine the pattern in Problems 1–4. How many unit tiles would you have to add to make $x^2 + 12x$ a perfect-square trinomial? **36**

Answers to *Try This*

1. $x^2 + 4x + 4 = (x + 2)^2$
2. $x^2 + 2x + 1 = (x + 1)^2$
3. $x^2 + 10x + 25 = (x + 5)^2$
4. $x^2 + 8x + 16 = (x + 4)^2$

9-8 Completing the Square

Objective
Solve quadratic equations by completing the square.

Vocabulary
completing the square

Who uses this?
Landscapers can solve quadratic equations to find dimensions of patios. (See Example 4.)

In the previous lesson, you solved quadratic equations by isolating x^2 and then using square roots. This method works if the quadratic equation, when written in standard form, is a perfect square.

When a trinomial is a perfect square, there is a relationship between the coefficient of the x-term and the constant term.

$$x^2 + 6x + 9 \qquad x^2 - 8x + 16$$

$$\left(\frac{6}{2}\right)^2 = 9 \qquad \left(\frac{-8}{2}\right)^2 = 16$$

Divide the coefficient of the x-term by 2, then square the result to get the constant term.

An expression in the form $x^2 + bx$ is not a perfect square. However, you can use the relationship shown above to add a term to $x^2 + bx$ to form a trinomial that is a perfect square. This is called **completing the square**.

Completing the Square

WORDS	NUMBERS	ALGEBRA
To complete the square of $x^2 + bx$, add $\left(\frac{b}{2}\right)^2$ to the expression. This will form a perfect-square trinomial.	$x^2 + 6x + \square$ $x^2 + 6x + \left(\frac{6}{2}\right)^2$ $x^2 + 6x + 9$ $(x + 3)^2$	$x^2 + bx + \square$ $x^2 + bx + \left(\frac{b}{2}\right)^2$ $\left(x + \frac{b}{2}\right)^2$

EXAMPLE 1 Completing the Square

Complete the square to form a perfect-square trinomial.

A $x^2 + 10x + \square$

$x^2 + 10x$ — *Identify b.*

$\left(\frac{10}{2}\right)^2 = 5^2 = 25$ — *Find $\left(\frac{b}{2}\right)^2$.*

$x^2 + 10x + 25$ — *Add $\left(\frac{b}{2}\right)^2$ to the expression.*

B $x^2 - 9x + \square$

$x^2 + -9x$

$\left(\frac{-9}{2}\right)^2 = \frac{81}{4}$

$x^2 - 9x + \frac{81}{4}$

Complete the square to form a perfect-square trinomial.

1a. $x^2 + 12x +$ **36** **1b.** $x^2 - 5x + \frac{25}{4}$ **1c.** $8x + x^2 +$ **16**

To solve a quadratic equation in the form $x^2 + bx = c$, first complete the square of $x^2 + bx$. Then you can solve using square roots.

9-8 Organizer

Pacing: Traditional 1 day
Block $\frac{1}{2}$ day

Objective: Solve quadratic equations by completing the square.

Online Edition
Tutorial Videos

Countdown Week 21

Power Presentations with PowerPoint®

Warm Up

Simplify.

1. $\left(\frac{7}{2}\right)^2$ $\frac{49}{4}$ **2.** $\left(\frac{10}{2}\right)^2 - 6$ 19

3. $\left(\frac{-9}{2}\right)^2$ $\frac{81}{4}$ **4.** $\left(\frac{3}{2}\right)^2 + 3$ $\frac{21}{4}$

Solve each quadratic equation by factoring.

5. $x^2 + 8x + 16 = 0$ −4

6. $x^2 - 22x + 121 = 0$ 11

7. $x^2 - 12x + 36 = 0$ 6

Also available on transparency

Math Humor

Q: What did the quadratic binomial say when he proposed to the constant?

A: You complete me.

1 Introduce

Recall that you can square a binomial by using the following rule:

$$(a + b)^2 = (a + b)(a + b) = a^2 + 2ab + b^2.$$

1. Complete the table by squaring the binomials.

Binomial Squared	Trinomial
$(x + 2)^2$	$x^2 + 4x + 4$
$(x - 5)^2$	
$(x + 3)^2$	
$(x - 4)^2$	
$(x - 7)^2$	
$(x + 9)^2$	

2. The trinomials in the table are perfect-square trinomials. In each of them, how is the constant term related to the coefficient of the x-term?

3. Suppose you know that $x^2 - 12x + \square$ is a perfect-square trinomial. What must be the value of the constant term?

4. What binomial was squared in order to get the perfect-square trinomial in Problem 3?

THINK AND DISCUSS

5. **Explain** how you found the constant term of the perfect-square trinomial in Problem 3.

Motivate

Display $x^2 + 8x + \square$. Have students find four numbers that make the trinomial factorable.
Possible answer: 7, 12, 15, 16
Which makes it a perfect-square trinomial? 16

Explorations and answers are provided in *Alternate Openers: Explorations Transparencies*.

go.hrw.com
State Resources Online
KEYWORD: MA7 Resources

Power Presentations with PowerPoint®

Additional Examples

Example 1

Complete the square to form a perfect-square trinomial.

A. $x^2 + 2x +$ ▭ 1

B. $x^2 - 6x +$ ▭ 9

Example 2

Solve by completing the square. Check your answer.

A. $x^2 + 16x = -15$ $-1, -15$

B. $x^2 - 4x - 6 = 0$
$2 \pm \sqrt{10}$

INTERVENTION

Questioning Strategies

EXAMPLE 1

- Can the number added to complete the square ever be negative? Explain.

EXAMPLE 2

- In what form should the equation be before you find $\left(\frac{b}{2}\right)^2$?
- When will solutions be irrational? Give an example.

Math Background When the solution of a quadratic equation involves the square root of a negative number, we say it has no real solutions. In fact, these types of quadratic equations have nonreal solutions, called *complex numbers*. Students will study complex numbers in Algebra 2.

Solving a Quadratic Equation by Completing the Square

Step 1	Write the equation in the form $x^2 + bx = c$.
Step 2	Find $\left(\frac{b}{2}\right)^2$.
Step 3	Complete the square by adding $\left(\frac{b}{2}\right)^2$ to both sides of the equation.
Step 4	Factor the perfect-square trinomial.
Step 5	Take the square root of both sides.
Step 6	Write two equations, using both the positive and negative square root, and solve each equation.

EXAMPLE 2 Solving $x^2 + bx = c$ by Completing the Square

Solve by completing the square. Check your answer.

Helpful Hint

$(x + 7)(x + 7) = (x + 7)^2$. So the square root of $(x + 7)^2$ is $x + 7$.

A $x^2 + 14x = 15$

Step 1 $x^2 + 14x = 15$ *The equation is in the form $x^2 + bx = c$.*

Step 2 $\left(\frac{14}{2}\right)^2 = 7^2 = 49$ *Find $\left(\frac{b}{2}\right)^2$.*

Step 3 $x^2 + 14x + 49 = 15 + 49$ *Complete the square.*

Step 4 $(x + 7)^2 = 64$ *Factor and simplify.*

Step 5 $x + 7 = \pm 8$ *Take the square root of both sides.*

Step 6 $x + 7 = 8$ or $x + 7 = -8$ *Write and solve two equations.*
$x = 1$ or $x = -15$

The solutions are 1 and −15.

Check

$x^2 + 14x = 15$	
$(1)^2 + 14(1)$	15
$1 + 14$	15
15	15 ✓

$x^2 + 14x = 15$	
$(-15)^2 + 14(-15)$	15
$225 - 210$	15
15	15 ✓

B $x^2 - 2x - 2 = 0$

Step 1 $x^2 + (-2)x = 2$ *Write in the form $x^2 + bx = c$.*

Step 2 $\left(\frac{-2}{2}\right)^2 = (-1)^2 = 1$ *Find $\left(\frac{b}{2}\right)^2$.*

Step 3 $x^2 - 2x + 1 = 2 + 1$ *Complete the square.*

Step 4 $(x - 1)^2 = 3$ *Factor and simplify.*

Step 5 $x - 1 = \pm\sqrt{3}$ *Take the square root of both sides.*

Step 6 $x - 1 = \sqrt{3}$ or $x - 1 = -\sqrt{3}$ *Write and solve two equations.*
$x = 1 + \sqrt{3}$ or $x = 1 - \sqrt{3}$

Writing Math

The expressions $1 + \sqrt{3}$ and $1 - \sqrt{3}$ can be written as one expression: $1 \pm \sqrt{3}$, which is read as "1 plus or minus the square root of 3."

The solutions are $1 + \sqrt{3}$ and $1 - \sqrt{3}$.

Check Use a graphing calculator to check your answer.

Solve by completing the square. Check your answer.

2a. $x^2 + 10x = -9$ **−9, −1** **2b.** $t^2 - 8t - 5 = 0$ **$4 \pm \sqrt{21}$**

2 Teach

Guided Instruction

Review how to factor perfect-square trinomials and how to solve quadratic equations by using square roots. Stress that the equation must be in the form $x^2 + bx = c$ before $\left(\frac{b}{2}\right)^2$ is added to both sides.

Visual Use algebra tiles (MK) as shown on page 662 to help students see how they are forming a perfect square.

Reaching All Learners

Through Communication

Have students work in small groups to make a poster showing how to apply the six steps for solving quadratic equations by factoring. Give each group a different equation to solve. Then have each group present their posters to the rest of the class, explaining each step.

EXAMPLE 3 Solving $ax^2 + bx = c$ by Completing the Square

Solve by completing the square.

A $-2x^2 + 12x - 20 = 0$

Step 1 $\frac{-2x^2}{-2} + \frac{12x}{-2} - \frac{20}{-2} = \frac{0}{-2}$ *Divide by −2 to make a = 1.*

$x^2 - 6x + 10 = 0$ *Write in the form $x^2 + bx = c$.*

$x^2 - 6x = -10$

$x^2 + (-6)x = -10$

Step 2 $\left(\frac{-6}{2}\right)^2 = (-3)^2 = 9$ *Find $\left(\frac{b}{2}\right)^2$.*

Step 3 $x^2 - 6x + 9 = -10 + 9$ *Complete the square.*

Step 4 $(x-3)^2 = -1$ *Factor and simplify.*

There is no real number whose square is negative, so there are no real solutions.

B $3x^2 - 10x = -3$

Step 1 $\frac{3x^2}{3} - \frac{10}{3}x = \frac{-3}{3}$ *Divide by 3 to make a = 1.*

$x^2 - \frac{10}{3}x = -1$

$x^2 + \left(-\frac{10}{3}\right)x = -1$ *Write in the form $x^2 + bx = c$.*

Step 2 $\left(-\frac{10}{3} \cdot \frac{1}{2}\right)^2 = \left(-\frac{10}{6}\right)^2 = \frac{100}{36} = \frac{25}{9}$ *Find $\left(\frac{b}{2}\right)^2$.*

Step 3 $x^2 - \frac{10}{3}x + \frac{25}{9} = -1 + \frac{25}{9}$ *Complete the square.*

$x^2 - \frac{10}{3}x + \frac{25}{9} = -\frac{9}{9} + \frac{25}{9}$ *Rewrite using like denominators.*

Step 4 $\left(x - \frac{5}{3}\right)^2 = \frac{16}{9}$ *Factor and simplify.*

Step 5 $x - \frac{5}{3} = \pm\frac{4}{3}$ *Take the square root of both sides.*

Step 6 $x - \frac{5}{3} = \frac{4}{3}$ or $x - \frac{5}{3} = -\frac{4}{3}$ *Write and solve two equations.*

$x = 3$ or $x = \frac{1}{3}$

The solutions are 3 and $\frac{1}{3}$.

Remember!

Dividing by 2 is the same as multiplying by $\frac{1}{2}$.

CHECK IT OUT! Solve by completing the square.

3a. $3x^2 - 5x - 2 = 0$ $-\frac{1}{3}$, 2

3b. $4t^2 - 4t + 9 = 0$ no real solutions

EXAMPLE 4 *Problem-Solving Application*

A landscaper is designing a rectangular brick patio. She has enough bricks to cover 144 square feet. She wants the length of the patio to be 10 feet greater than the width. What dimensions should she use for the patio?

1 Understand the Problem

The **answer** will be the length and width of the patio.

COMMON ERROR ALERT

In **Example 3B,** students may have difficulty finding $\left(\frac{b}{2}\right)^2$ when b is a fraction. Remind them that dividing by 2 is the same as multiplying by $\frac{1}{2}$. For $b = -\frac{10}{3}$, $\left(\frac{b}{2}\right)^2$ becomes $\left[\frac{1}{2} \cdot \left(-\frac{10}{3}\right)\right]^2$, or $\left(-\frac{10}{6}\right)^2$. Let students practice with a few examples and lead them to see that dividing a fraction by 2 is the same as doubling the denominator.

Power Presentations with PowerPoint®

Additional Examples

Example 3

Solve by completing the square.

A. $-3x^2 + 12x - 15 = 0$ no real solutions

B. $5x^2 + 19x = 4$ $-4, \frac{1}{5}$

INTERVENTION

Questioning Strategies

EXAMPLE 3

- When will there be no real solutions?

Critical Thinking Students can save time by checking that an equation has real solutions by first finding the vertex of the related function and using the value of a to see how the graph opens. In **Example 3A,** the related function has the vertex at (3, −2), below the x-axis, and opens downward.

Inclusion Remind students to always check their answers either by graphing the related function or by direct substitution.

Power Presentations with PowerPoint®

Additional Examples

Example 4

A rectangular room has an area of 195 square feet. Its width is 2 feet shorter than its length. Find the dimensions of the room.

13 ft by 15 ft

INTERVENTION 
Questioning Strategies

EXAMPLE 4

- How do you know which of the two solutions to use?
- How would the equation be different if the area were triangular?

List the important information:

- There are enough bricks to cover 144 square feet.
- One edge of the patio is to be 10 feet longer than the other edge.

2 Make a Plan

Set the formula for the area of a rectangle equal to 144, the area of the patio. Solve the equation.

3 Solve

Let x be the width.
Then $x + 10$ is the length.

Use the formula for area of a rectangle.

ℓ	$\cdot$	w	$=$	A
length	times	width	=	area of patio
$(x + 10)$	$\cdot$	x	$=$	144

Step 1	$x^2 + 10x = 144$	*Simplify.*
Step 2	$\left(\frac{10}{2}\right)^2 = 5^2 = 25$	*Find* $\left(\frac{b}{2}\right)^2$.
Step 3	$x^2 + 10x + 25 = 144 + 25$	*Complete the square by adding 25 to both sides.*
Step 4	$(x + 5)^2 = 169$	*Factor the perfect-square trinomial.*
Step 5	$x + 5 = \pm 13$	*Take the square root of both sides.*
Step 6	$x + 5 = 13$ or $x + 5 = -13$	*Write and solve two equations.*
	$x = 8$ or $x = -18$	

Negative numbers are not reasonable for length, so $x = 8$ is the only solution that makes sense.

The width is 8 feet, and the length is $8 + 10$, or 18, feet.

4 Look Back

The length of the patio is 10 feet greater than the width. Also, $8(18) = 144$.

4. An architect designs a rectangular room with an area of 400 ft^2. The length is to be 8 ft longer than the width. Find the dimensions of the room. Round your answers to the nearest tenth of a foot. **16.4 ft by 24.4 ft**

THINK AND DISCUSS

1. Tell how to solve a quadratic equation in the form $x^2 + bx + c = 0$ by completing the square.

2. **GET ORGANIZED** Copy and complete the graphic organizer. In each box, write and solve an example of the given type of quadratic equation.

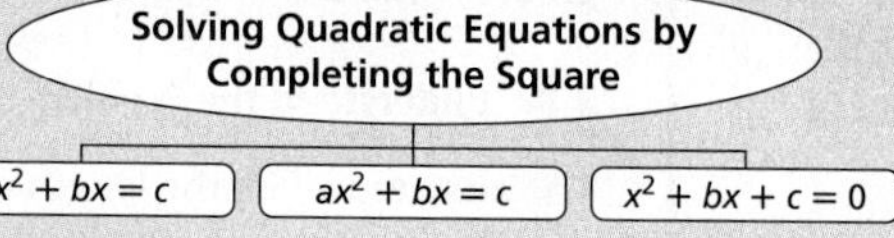

3 Close

Summarize

Review with students the steps for solving a quadratic equation by completing the square. Remind students that when they check their answers algebraically, they should substitute the values for x in the original equation, not in the equation with the value added for a perfect-square trinomial. For irrational solutions, students can approximate the solutions and check their answers on a graphing calculator.

ONGOING ASSESSMENT and INTERVENTION 

Diagnose Before the Lesson
9-8 Warm Up, TE p. 663

Monitor During the Lesson
Check It Out! Exercises, SE pp. 663–666
Questioning Strategies, TE pp. 664–666

Assess After the Lesson
9-8 Lesson Quiz, TE p. 669
Alternative Assessment, TE p. 669

Answers to *Think and Discuss*

1. Possible answer: Subtract c from both sides. Then add $\left(\frac{b}{2}\right)^2$ to both sides. Factor the perfect-square trinomial. Take the square root of both sides. Write two equations, using both the positive and negative square roots, and solve each equation.
2. See p. A8.

go.hrw.com
Homework Help Online
KEYWORD: MA7 9-8
Parent Resources Online
KEYWORD: MA7 Parent

GUIDED PRACTICE

1. **Vocabulary** Describe in your own words how to *complete the square* for the equation $1 = x^2 + 4x$.

SEE EXAMPLE 1 p. 663

Complete the square to form a perfect-square trinomial.

2. $x^2 + 14x +$ **49**
3. $x^2 - 4x +$ **4**
4. $x^2 - 3x +$ $\mathbf{\frac{9}{4}}$

SEE EXAMPLE 2 p. 664

Solve by completing the square.

5. $x^2 + 6x = -5$ **−5, −1**
6. $x^2 - 8x = 9$ **−1, 9**
7. $x^2 + x = 30$ **−6, 5**
8. $x^2 + 2x = 21$ $\mathbf{-1 \pm \sqrt{22}}$
9. $x^2 - 10x = -9$ **1, 9**
10. $x^2 + 16x = 91$ $\mathbf{-8 \pm \sqrt{155}}$

SEE EXAMPLE 3 p. 665

11. $-x^2 - 5x = -5$
12. $-x^2 - 3x + 2 = 0$
13. $-6x = 3x^2 + 9$ **no real solutions**
14. $2x^2 - 6x = -10$ **no real solutions**
15. $-x^2 + 8x - 6 = 0$ $\mathbf{4 \pm \sqrt{10}}$
16. $4x^2 + 16 = -24x$ $\mathbf{-3 \pm \sqrt{5}}$

SEE EXAMPLE 4 p. 665

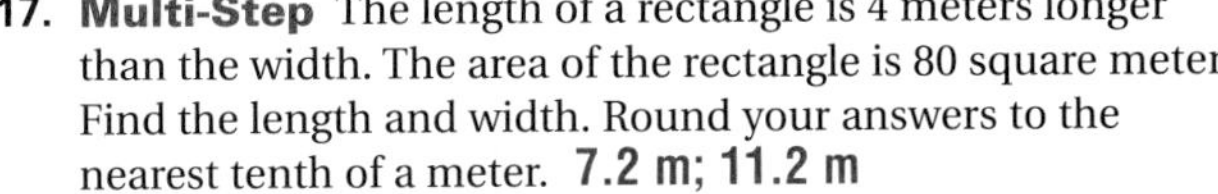

17. **Multi-Step** The length of a rectangle is 4 meters longer than the width. The area of the rectangle is 80 square meters. Find the length and width. Round your answers to the nearest tenth of a meter. **7.2 m; 11.2 m**

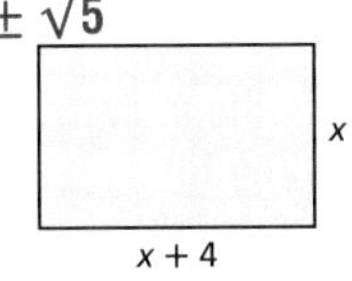

PRACTICE AND PROBLEM SOLVING

Independent Practice

For Exercises	See Example
18–20	1
21–26	2
27–32	3
33	4

Extra Practice
Skills Practice p. S21
Application Practice p. S36

Complete the square to form a perfect-square trinomial.

18. $x^2 - 16x +$ **64**
19. $x^2 - 2x +$ **1**
20. $x^2 + 11x +$ $\mathbf{\frac{121}{4}}$

Solve by completing the square.

21. $x^2 - 10x = 24$ **−2, 12**
22. $x^2 - 6x = -9$ **3**
23. $x^2 + 15x = -26$ **−13, −2**
24. $x^2 + 6x = 16$ **−8, 2**
25. $x^2 - 2x = 48$ **−6, 8**
26. $x^2 + 12x = -36$ **−6**
27. $-x^2 + x + 6 = 0$ **−2, 3**
28. $2x^2 = -7x - 29$ **no real solutions**
29. $-x^2 - x + 1 = 0$
30. $3x^2 - 6x - 9 = 0$ **3, −1**
31. $-x^2 = 15x + 30$
32. $2x^2 + 20x - 10 = 0$

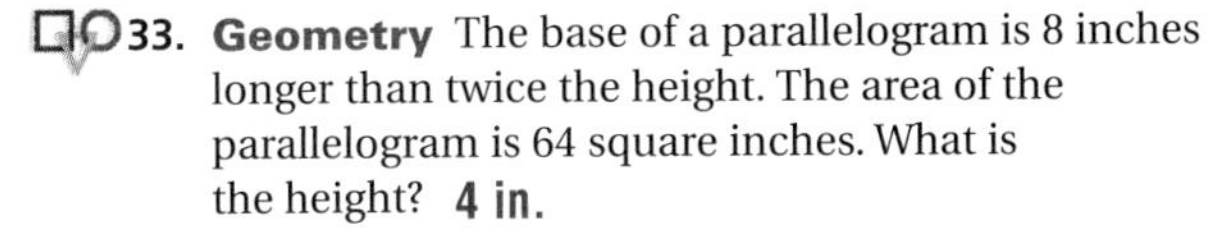
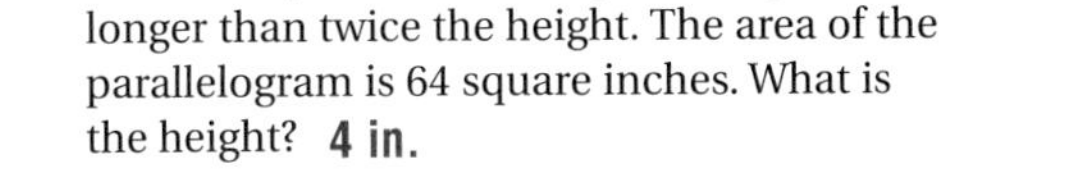

33. **Geometry** The base of a parallelogram is 8 inches longer than twice the height. The area of the parallelogram is 64 square inches. What is the height? **4 in.**

Solve each equation by completing the square.

34. $3x^2 + x = 10$ $\mathbf{-2, \frac{5}{3}}$
35. $x^2 = 2x + 6$ $\mathbf{1 \pm \sqrt{7}}$
36. $2a^2 = 5a + 12$ $\mathbf{-\frac{3}{2}, 4}$
37. $2x^2 + 5x = 3$ $\mathbf{-3, \frac{1}{2}}$
38. $4x = 7 - x^2$ $\mathbf{-2 \pm \sqrt{11}}$
39. $8x = -x^2 + 20$ **−10, 2**

40. **Hobbies** The height in feet h of a water bottle rocket launched from a rooftop is given by the equation $h = -16t^2 + 320t + 32$, where t is the time in seconds. After the rocket is fired, how long will it take to return to the ground? Solve by completing the square. Round your answer to the nearest tenth of a second. **20.1 s**

Complete each trinomial so that it is a perfect square.

41. $x^2 + 18x +$ **81**
42. $x^2 - 100x +$ **2500**
43. $x^2 - 7x +$ $\mathbf{\frac{49}{4}}$
44. $x^2 +$ **4** $x + 4$
45. $x^2 -$ **9** $x + \frac{81}{4}$
46. $x^2 +$ $\mathbf{\frac{1}{3}}$ $x + \frac{1}{36}$

29. $x = \frac{-1 \pm \sqrt{5}}{2}$

31. $x = \frac{-15 \pm \sqrt{105}}{2}$

32. $x = \frac{-10 \pm \sqrt{120}}{2} = -5 \pm \sqrt{30}$

Assignment Guide

Assign *Guided Practice* exercises as necessary.

If you finished Examples **1–2**
Basic 18–26, 41–43, 47
Average 18–26, 35, 41–47
Advanced 18–26, 35, 41–47, 60

If you finished Examples **1–4**
Basic 18–43, 47–58, 61–66, 73–94
Average 18–46, 48–67, 73–94
Advanced 18–46, 48–94

Homework Quick Check
Quickly check key concepts.
Exercises: 18, 24, 28, 33, 48

Kinesthetic For **Exercise 1,** students can use a model such as algebra tiles in their descriptions.

Answers

1. Divide 4 by 2 and square the result: $\left(\frac{4}{2}\right)^2 = 4$. Add 4 to both sides of the equation: $5 = x^2 + 4x + 4$.

11. $x = \frac{-5 \pm \sqrt{45}}{2} = \frac{-5 \pm 3\sqrt{5}}{2}$

12. $x = \frac{-3 \pm \sqrt{17}}{2}$

State Resources

go.hrw.com
State Resources Online
KEYWORD: MA7 Resources

Kinesthetic To determine the width and length of the combined area in **Exercise 47,** suggest that students run their finger horizontally across the diagram from left to right. The distance is x, then 10, then x again, so the expression for width is $x + 10 + x$, or $2x + 10$. Then have students repeat for the length.

Exercise 61 involves writing and solving a quadratic equation to solve a projectile problem. This exercise prepares students for the Multi-Step Test Prep on page 678.

Answers

48a. $-\frac{1}{2}, 2$

b.

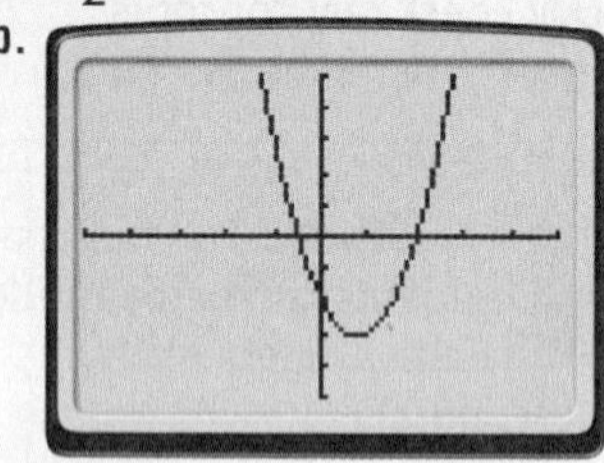

c. Use the zero feature to find where the graph crosses the x-axis.

d. Possible answer: Completing the square takes several steps, but it produces the exact solutions. Creating the graph with a graphing calculator is fast, but you may get only approximate solutions.

59. Possible answer: Completing the square to solve $x^2 + 11x + 18 = 0$ involves fractions, whereas completing the square to solve $x^2 + 20x - 21 = 0$ does not.

60. Add $2xy$. The perfect-square trinomial of $(x + y)(x + y)$ simplifies to $x^2 + xy + xy + y^2$, or $x^2 + 2xy + y^2$. This is the equivalent of $x^2 + y^2 + 2xy$.

47. **Multi-Step** A roped-off area of width x is created around a 34-by-10-foot rectangular museum display of Egyptian artifacts, as shown. The combined area of the display and the roped-off area is 640 square feet.
    a. Write an equation for the combined area. **$(10 + 2x)(34 + 2x) = 640$**
    b. Find the width of the roped-off area. **3 ft**

10 ft
34 ft
x
x

48. **Graphing Calculator** Compare solving a quadratic equation by completing the square with finding the solutions on a graphing calculator.
    a. Complete the square to solve $2x^2 - 3x - 2 = 0$.
    b. Use your graphing calculator to graph $y = 2x^2 - 3x - 2$.
    c. Explain how to use this graph to find the solutions of $2x^2 - 3x - 2 = 0$.
    d. Compare the two methods of solving the equation. What are the advantages and disadvantages of each?

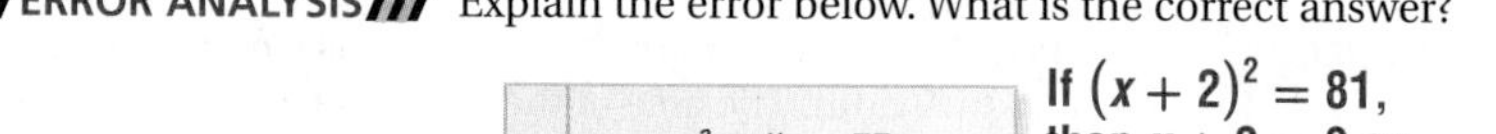

49. **///ERROR ANALYSIS///** Explain the error below. What is the correct answer?

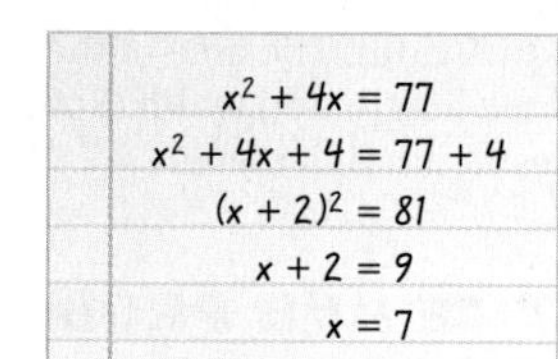

If $(x + 2)^2 = 81$, then $x + 2 = 9$ or $x + 2 = -9$. The correct answer is $x = 7$ or $x = -11$.

Solve each equation by completing the square.

50. $5x^2 - 50x = 55$ **−1, 11**
51. $3x^2 + 36x = -30$ **$-6 \pm \sqrt{26}$**
52. $28x - 2x^2 = 26$ **1, 13**
53. $-36x = 3x^2 + 108$ **−6**
54. $0 = 4x^2 + 32x + 44$ **$-4 \pm \sqrt{5}$**
55. $16x + 40 = -2x^2$ **no real solutions**
56. $x^2 + 5x + 6 = 10x$ **2, 3**
57. $x^2 + 3x + 18 = -3x$ **no real solutions**
58. $4x^2 + x + 1 = 3x^2$ **no real solutions**
59. **Write About It** Jamal prefers to solve $x^2 + 20x - 21 = 0$ by completing the square. Heather prefers to solve $x^2 + 11x + 18 = 0$ by factoring. Explain their reasoning.
60. **Critical Thinking** What should be done to the binomial $x^2 + y^2$ to make it a perfect-square trinomial? Explain.

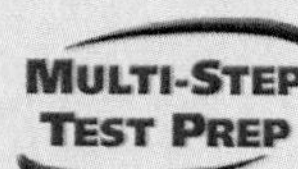

61. This problem will prepare you for the Multi-Step Test Prep on page 678.

    The function $h(t) = -16t^2 + vt + c$ models the height in feet of a golf ball after t seconds when it is hit with initial vertical velocity v from initial height c feet. A golfer stands on a tee box that is 32 feet above the fairway. He hits the golf ball from the tee at an initial vertical velocity of 64 feet per second.
    a. Write an equation that gives the time t when the golf ball lands on the fairway at height 0. **$-16t^2 + 64t + 32 = 0$**
    b. What number would be added to both sides of the equation in part **a** to complete the square while solving for t? **4**
    c. Solve the equation from part **a** by completing the square to find the time it takes the ball to reach the fairway. Round to the nearest tenth of a second. **4.4 s**

9-8 PRACTICE A
9-8 PRACTICE C
9-8 PRACTICE B

Complete the square to form a perfect square trinomial.

1. $x^2 + 4x +$ **4**
2. $x^2 - 16x +$ **64**
3. $x^2 + 7x +$ **$\frac{49}{4}$**

Solve each equation by completing the square.

4. $x^2 + 6x = -8$ **−2, −4**
5. $x^2 + 4x = 12$ **−6, 2**
6. $x^2 - 2x = 15$ **−3, 5**
7. $x^2 - 8x + 13 = 0$ **$4 + \sqrt{3}, 4 - \sqrt{3}$**
8. $x^2 + 6x + 34 = 0$ **no real solutions**
9. $x^2 - 2x - 35 = 0$ **−5, 7**
10. $2x^2 + 16x + 42 = 0$ **no real solutions**
11. $4x^2 - 7x - 2 = 0$ **$-\frac{1}{4}, 2$**
12. $2x^2 + 9x + 4 = 0$ **$-\frac{1}{2}, -4$**
13. A rectangular pool has an area of 880 ft^2. The length is 10 feet longer than the width. Find the dimensions of the pool. Solve by completing the square. Round answers to the nearest tenth of a foot. **width = 25.1 feet; length = 35.1 feet**
14. A small painting has an area of 400 cm^2. The length is 4 more than 2 times the width. Find the dimensions of the painting. Solve by completing the square. Round answers to the nearest tenth of a centimeter. **width = 13.2 cm; length = 30.4 cm**

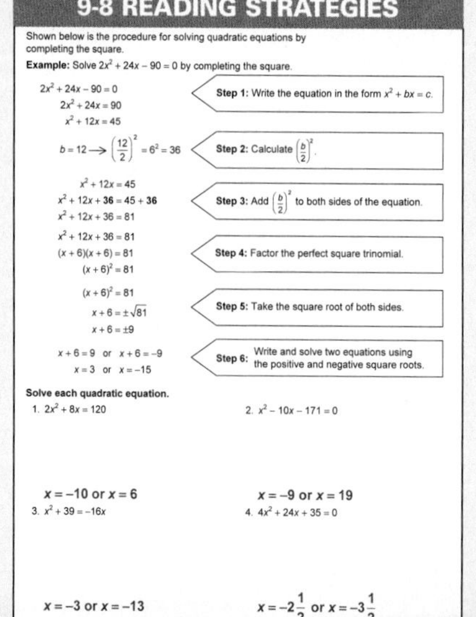

9-8 READING STRATEGIES

Shown below is the procedure for solving quadratic equations by completing the square.

Example: Solve $2x^2 + 24x - 90 = 0$ by completing the square.

$2x^2 + 24x - 90 = 0$, $2x^2 + 24x = 90$, $x^2 + 12x = 45$ — **Step 1:** Write the equation in the form $x^2 + bx = c$.

$b = 12 \rightarrow \left(\frac{12}{2}\right)^2 = 6^2 = 36$ — **Step 2:** Calculate $\left(\frac{b}{2}\right)^2$.

$x^2 + 12x = 45$, $x^2 + 12x + \mathbf{36} = 45 + \mathbf{36}$, $x^2 + 12x + 36 = 81$ — **Step 3:** Add $\left(\frac{b}{2}\right)^2$ to both sides of the equation.

$x^2 + 12x + 36 = 81$, $(x + 6)(x + 6) = 81$, $(x + 6)^2 = 81$ — **Step 4:** Factor the perfect square trinomial.

$(x + 6)^2 = 81$, $x + 6 = \pm\sqrt{81}$, $x + 6 = \pm 9$ — **Step 5:** Take the square root of both sides.

$x + 6 = 9$ or $x + 6 = -9$, $x = 3$ or $x = -15$ — **Step 6:** Write and solve two equations using the positive and negative square roots.

Solve each quadratic equation.

1. $2x^2 + 8x = 120$ **$x = -10$ or $x = 6$**
2. $x^2 - 10x - 171 = 0$ **$x = -9$ or $x = 19$**
3. $x^2 + 39 = -16x$ **$x = -3$ or $x = -13$**
4. $4x^2 + 24x + 35 = 0$ **$x = -2\frac{1}{2}$ or $x = -3\frac{1}{2}$**

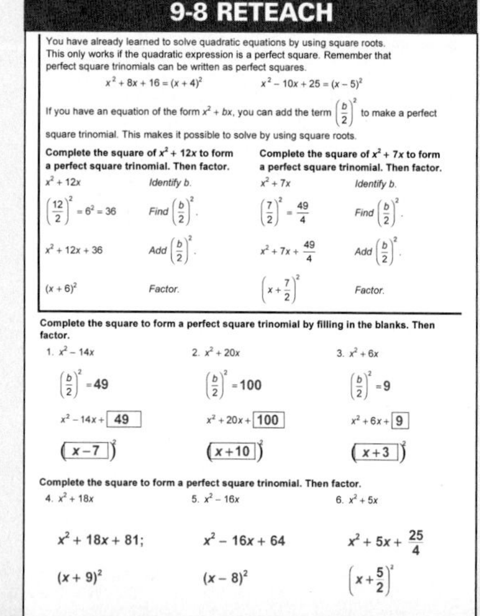

9-8 RETEACH

You have already learned to solve quadratic equations by using square roots. This only works if the quadratic expression is a perfect square. Remember that perfect square trinomials can be written as perfect squares.

$x^2 + 8x + 16 = (x + 4)^2$ $x^2 - 10x + 25 = (x - 5)^2$

If you have an equation of the form $x^2 + bx$, you can add the term $\left(\frac{b}{2}\right)^2$ to make a perfect square trinomial. This makes it possible to solve by using square roots.

Complete the square of $x^2 + 12x$ to form a perfect square trinomial. Then factor.

$x^2 + 12x$	*Identify b.*
$\left(\frac{12}{2}\right)^2 = 6^2 = 36$	*Find $\left(\frac{b}{2}\right)^2$.*
$x^2 + 12x + 36$	*Add $\left(\frac{b}{2}\right)^2$.*
$(x + 6)^2$	*Factor.*

Complete the square of $x^2 + 7x$ to form a perfect square trinomial. Then factor.

$x^2 + 7x$	*Identify b.*
$\left(\frac{7}{2}\right)^2 = \frac{49}{4}$	*Find $\left(\frac{b}{2}\right)^2$.*
$x^2 + 7x + \frac{49}{4}$	*Add $\left(\frac{b}{2}\right)^2$.*
$\left(x + \frac{7}{2}\right)^2$	*Factor.*

Complete the square to form a perfect square trinomial by filling in the blanks. Then factor.

1. $x^2 - 14x$: $\left(\frac{b}{2}\right)^2 =$ **49**; $x^2 - 14x +$ **49**; $($**$x - 7$**$)^2$
2. $x^2 + 20x$: $\left(\frac{b}{2}\right)^2 =$ **100**; $x^2 + 20x +$ **100**; $($**$x + 10$**$)^2$
3. $x^2 + 6x$: $\left(\frac{b}{2}\right)^2 =$ **9**; $x^2 + 6x +$ **9**; $($**$x + 3$**$)^2$

Complete the square to form a perfect square trinomial. Then factor.

4. $x^2 + 18x$ **$x^2 + 18x + 81$; $(x + 9)^2$**
5. $x^2 - 16x$ **$x^2 - 16x + 64$; $(x - 8)^2$**
6. $x^2 + 5x$ **$x^2 + 5x + \frac{25}{4}$; $\left(x + \frac{5}{2}\right)^2$**

62. **Write About It** Compare solving an equation of the form $x^2 + bx + c = 0$ by completing the square and solving an equation of the form $ax^2 + bx + c = 0$ by completing the square. **When solving an equation of the form $ax^2 + bx + c = 0$, you must first divide the equation by the coefficient a.**

63. What value of c will make $x^2 + 16x + c$ a perfect-square trinomial?
   Ⓐ 32 **Ⓑ 64** Ⓒ 128 Ⓓ 256

64. What value of b will make $x^2 + b + 25$ a perfect-square trinomial?
   Ⓕ 5 Ⓖ 5x Ⓗ 10 **Ⓙ 10x**

65. Which of the following is closest to a solution of $3x^2 + 2x - 4 = 0$?
   Ⓐ 0 **Ⓑ 1** Ⓒ 2 Ⓓ 3

66. **Short Response** Solve $x^2 - 8x - 20 = 0$ by completing the square. Explain each step in your solution. **−2, 10**

CHALLENGE AND EXTEND

Solve each equation by completing the square.

67. $6x^2 + 5x = 6$ $\mathbf{-\frac{3}{2}, \frac{2}{3}}$
68. $7x + 3 = 6x^2$ $\mathbf{-\frac{1}{3}, \frac{3}{2}}$
69. $4x = 1 - 3x^2$ $\mathbf{-\frac{2}{3} \pm \frac{\sqrt{7}}{3}}$
70. What should be done to the binomial $ax^2 + bx$ to obtain a perfect-square trinomial?
71. Solve $ax^2 + bx = 0$ for x. $\mathbf{0, -\frac{b}{a}}$
72. **Geometry** The hypotenuse of a right triangle is 20 cm. One of the legs is 4 cm longer than the other leg. Find the area of the triangle. (*Hint:* Use the Pythagorean Theorem.) **96 cm²**

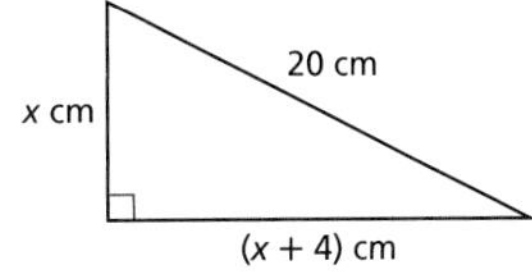

SPIRAL REVIEW

Graph the line with the given slope and y-intercept. (Lesson 5-7)

73. slope = 4, y-intercept = −3
74. slope = $-\frac{2}{3}$, y-intercept = 4
75. slope = −2, y-intercept = −2
76. slope = $-\frac{4}{3}$, y-intercept = 0

73.
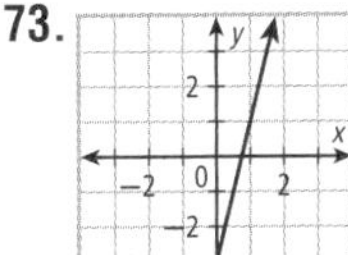

74.

75.

Multiply. (Lesson 7-9)

77. $(x - 4)^2$ $\mathbf{x^2 - 8x + 16}$
78. $(x - 4)(x + 4)$ $\mathbf{x^2 - 16}$
79. $(4 - t)^2$ $\mathbf{t^2 - 8t + 16}$
80. $(2z + 3)^2$ $\mathbf{4z^2 + 12z + 9}$
81. $(8b^2 - 2)(8b^2 + 2)$ $\mathbf{64b^4 - 4}$
82. $(2x - 6)(2x + 6)$ $\mathbf{4x^2 - 36}$

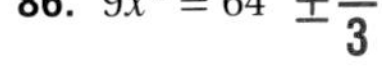

Solve using square roots. (Lesson 9-7)

83. $5x^2 = 5$ $\mathbf{\pm 1}$
84. $x^2 + 3 = 12$ $\mathbf{\pm 3}$
85. $5x^2 = 80$ $\mathbf{\pm 4}$
86. $9x^2 = 64$ $\mathbf{\pm \frac{8}{3}}$
87. $25 + x^2 = 250$ $\mathbf{\pm 15}$
88. $64x^2 + 3 = 147$ $\mathbf{\pm \frac{3}{2}}$

Solve. Round to the nearest hundredth. (Lesson 9-7)

89. $12 = 5x^2$ $\mathbf{\pm 1.55}$
90. $3x^2 - 4 = 15$ $\mathbf{\pm 2.52}$
91. $x^2 - 7 = 19$ $\mathbf{\pm 5.10}$
92. $6 + x^2 = 72$ $\mathbf{\pm 8.12}$
93. $10x^2 - 10 = 12$ $\mathbf{\pm 1.48}$
94. $2x^2 + 2 = 33$ $\mathbf{\pm 3.94}$

TEST PREP DOCTOR In **Exercise 64,** explain to students that in this equation, b stands for the x-term, not the coefficient of x.

Explain that the correct answer to **Exercise 65** is the value of x that makes the left side of the equation closest to zero.

Answers

70. Divide both terms by a:
$x^2 + \frac{b}{a}x$.
Then add half of $\frac{b}{a}$ squared:
$x^2 + \frac{b}{a}x + \left(\frac{b}{2a}\right)^2$.

76.
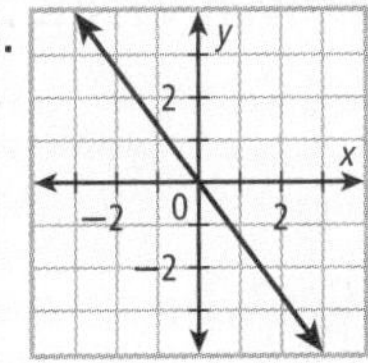

Journal

Have students explain what it means to complete the square.

ALTERNATIVE ASSESSMENT

Have students write an equation of the form $x^2 + bx = c$ that cannot be solved by factoring. Have them solve the equation by completing the square and justify each step.

Power Presentations with PowerPoint®

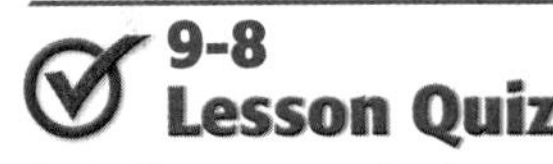

9-8 Lesson Quiz

Complete the square to form a perfect-square trinomial.

1. $x^2 + 11x +$ ▢ $\frac{121}{4}$
2. $x^2 - 18x +$ ▢ 81

Solve by completing the square.

3. $x^2 - 2x - 1 = 0$
   $\frac{2 \pm \sqrt{8}}{2} = 1 \pm \sqrt{2}$
4. $3x^2 + 6x = 144$ 6, −8
5. $4x^2 + 44x = 23$ $\frac{1}{2}, -\frac{23}{2}$
6. Dymond is painting a rectangular banner for a football game. She has enough paint to cover 120 ft². She wants the length of the banner to be 7 ft longer than the width. What dimensions should Dymond use for the banner?
   8 ft by 15 ft

Also available on transparency

9-8 PROBLEM SOLVING

The Ward family is redecorating several rooms of their house. Write the correct answer.

1. The Wards decided to use carpet tiles in the family room. The room has an area of 176 square feet and is 5 feet longer than it is wide. Find the dimensions of the family room.
   11 ft by 16 ft
2. Angelique wants to have a rug that is 9 feet long and 7 feet wide in her bedroom. The rug will cover the whole floor except a border that is x feet wide. The area of her room is 167 square feet.
   Find the width of the border, x. Round your answer to the nearest tenth of a foot.
   2.5 ft
3. Giselle is going to frame a portrait of the family and place it on the mantle in the family room. The portrait is 10 inches longer than it is tall and will take up a total area of 1344 square inches once it is inside the 2 inch thick frame. Find the dimensions and area of the unframed portrait.
   38 in. by 28 in.
   1064 square in.

Select the best answer.

4. The landing for the steps leading up to a county courthouse is shaped like a trapezoid. The area of the landing is 1500 square feet. The shorter base of the trapezoid is 15 feet longer than the height. The longer base is 5 feet longer than 3 times the height. What is the length of the longer base?
   A 25 feet **C 80 feet**
   B 40 feet D 95 feet
5. The height of a pumpkin launched from a cannon is given by the function $h = -16t^2 + 240t + 16$ where t is the time in seconds. How many seconds is the pumpkin in the air? Round your answer to the nearest tenth of a second.
   F 7.5 seconds H 16 seconds
   G 15.1 seconds J 32 seconds
6. Georgia works part-time at a daycare while she is going to college. She earned $160 last week. Georgia worked 12 more hours than the amount she is paid per hour. What is Georgia's hourly pay rate?
   A $6.00 C $12.00
   B $8.00 D $20.00
7. Part of the set for a play is a triangular piece of plywood. The area of the triangle is 20 square feet. The base is 3 feet longer than the height. What is the height of the triangle? Round your answer to the nearest tenth of a foot.
   F 3 feet H 3.9 feet
   G 3.2 feet **J 5 feet**

9-8 CHALLENGE

To write $y = x^2 - 7x + 3$ in the form $y = (x - h)^2 + k$, you could follow these steps.

$y = x^2 - 7x + 3$

$y = x^2 - 7x + \left(\frac{-7}{2}\right)^2 + 3 - \left(\frac{-7}{2}\right)^2$

$y = \left(x - \frac{7}{2}\right)^2 + 3 - \frac{7^2}{4}$

Notice that the number outside the parentheses has not been simplified; leaving it in this form will help you to see a pattern in the following exercises.

Use the method shown above to rewrite each function in the form $y = (x - h)^2 + k$.

1. $y = x^2 + 5x - 1$
   $y = \left(x + \frac{5}{2}\right)^2 - 1 - \frac{5^2}{4}$
2. $y = x^2 - 11x + 6$
   $y = \left(x - \frac{11}{2}\right)^2 + 6 - \frac{11^2}{4}$
3. $y = x^2 + bx + c$
   $y = \left(x + \frac{b}{2}\right)^2 + c - \frac{b^2}{4}$
4. Recall that the vertex of the graph of $y = (x - h)^2 + k$ is at (h, k). Use your answer to Exercise 3 to give the coordinates of the vertex of the graph of $y = x^2 + bx + c$ in terms of b and c. $\left(\frac{-b}{2}, c - \frac{b^2}{4}\right)$

For Exercises 5–7, consider the parabola whose equation is $y = ax^2 + bx + c$.

5. How do you know that the graph of this parabola opens upward? $a > 0$
6. How does the y-coordinate of the vertex show whether the parabola crosses the x-axis?
   If the parabola opens upward and the y-coordinate of the vertex is greater than 0, then the parabola is completely above the x-axis. If it is less than 0, then the parabola crosses the x-axis at two points. If it is equal to 0, then the parabola touches the x-axis at one point.
7. How many x-intercepts does the graph of $y = x^2 + bx + c$ have if you know that
   a. $c - \frac{b^2}{4} > 0$? 0
   b. $c - \frac{b^2}{4} = 0$? 1
   c. $c - \frac{b^2}{4} < 0$? 2

Use your answers to Exercises 4 and 7 to determine (a) the coordinates of the vertex and (b) the number of x-intercepts for each of the following functions.

8. $y = x^2 + 2x - 8$
   a. (−1, −9)
   b. 2
9. $y = x^2 - 9x + 18$
   a. (4.5, −2.25)
   b. 2

9-9 Organizer

Pacing: Traditional 1 day
Block $\frac{1}{2}$ day

Objectives: Solve quadratic equations by using the Quadratic Formula.

Determine the number of solutions of a quadratic equation by using the discriminant.

Online Edition
Tutorial Videos, Interactivity

Countdown Week 21

Power Presentations with PowerPoint®

Warm Up

Evaluate for $x = -2$, $y = 3$, and $z = -1$.

1. x^2 4 **2.** xyz 6

3. $x^2 - yz$ 7 **4.** $y - xz$ 1

5. $-x$ 2 **6.** $z^2 - xy$ 7

Also available on transparency

Math Humor

Q: What do you call a person who is crazy about solving quadratic equations?

A: A quadratic fanatic.

9-9 The Quadratic Formula and the Discriminant

Objectives
Solve quadratic equations by using the Quadratic Formula.

Determine the number of solutions of a quadratic equation by using the discriminant.

Vocabulary
discriminant

Why learn this?
You can use the discriminant to determine whether the weight in a carnival strength test will reach a certain height. (See Exercise 4.)

In the previous lesson, you completed the square to solve quadratic equations. If you complete the square of $ax^2 + bx + c = 0$, you can derive the *Quadratic Formula*. The Quadratic Formula can be used to solve *any* quadratic equation.

Numbers		Algebra
$2x^2 + 6x + 1 = 0$		$ax^2 + bx + c = 0,\ a \neq 0$
$\frac{2}{2}x^2 + \frac{6}{2}x + \frac{1}{2} = \frac{0}{2}$	*Divide both sides by a.*	$\frac{a}{a}x^2 + \frac{b}{a}x + \frac{c}{a} = \frac{0}{a}$
$x^2 + 3x + \frac{1}{2} = 0$		$x^2 + \frac{b}{a}x + \frac{c}{a} = 0$
$x^2 + 3x = -\frac{1}{2}$	*Subtract $\frac{c}{a}$ from both sides.*	$x^2 + \frac{b}{a}x = -\frac{c}{a}$
$x^2 + 3x + \left(\frac{3}{2}\right)^2 = -\frac{1}{2} + \left(\frac{3}{2}\right)^2$	*Complete the square.*	$x^2 + \frac{b}{a}x + \left(\frac{b}{2a}\right)^2 = -\frac{c}{a} + \left(\frac{b}{2a}\right)^2$
$\left(x + \frac{3}{2}\right)^2 = \frac{9}{4} - \frac{1}{2}$	*Factor and simplify.*	$\left(x + \frac{b}{2a}\right)^2 = \frac{b^2}{4a^2} - \frac{c}{a}$
$\left(x + \frac{3}{2}\right)^2 = \frac{9}{4} - \frac{2}{4}$	*Use common denominators.*	$\left(x + \frac{b}{2a}\right)^2 = \frac{b^2}{4a^2} - \frac{4ac}{4a^2}$
$\left(x + \frac{3}{2}\right)^2 = \frac{7}{4}$	*Simplify.*	$\left(x + \frac{b}{2a}\right)^2 = \frac{b^2 - 4ac}{4a^2}$
$x + \frac{3}{2} = \pm\frac{\sqrt{7}}{2}$	*Take square roots.*	$x + \frac{b}{2a} = \pm\frac{\sqrt{b^2 - 4ac}}{2a}$
$x = -\frac{3}{2} \pm \frac{\sqrt{7}}{2}$	*Subtract $\frac{b}{2a}$ from both sides.*	$x = -\frac{b}{2a} \pm \frac{\sqrt{b^2 - 4ac}}{2a}$
$x = \frac{-3 \pm \sqrt{7}}{2}$	*Simplify.*	$x = \frac{-b \pm \sqrt{b^2 - 4ac}}{2a}$

Remember!
To add fractions, you need a common denominator.

$$\frac{b^2}{4a^2} - \frac{c}{a} = \frac{b^2}{4a^2} - \frac{c}{a}\left(\frac{4a}{4a}\right) = \frac{b^2}{4a^2} - \frac{4ac}{4a^2} = \frac{b^2 - 4ac}{4a^2}$$

The Quadratic Formula

The solutions of $ax^2 + bx + c = 0$, where $a \neq 0$, are $x = \frac{-b \pm \sqrt{b^2 - 4ac}}{2a}$.

State Resources

go.hrw.com
State Resources Online
KEYWORD: MA7 Resources

1 Introduce

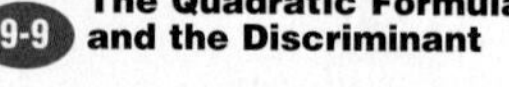

EXPLORATION

9-9 The Quadratic Formula and the Discriminant

Use a graphing calculator to explore quadratic equations of the form $ax^2 + bx + c = 0$.

1. Graph the related function for each of the quadratic equations in the table to determine how many real solutions each equation has. Then complete the table as shown.

Quadratic Equation	Number of Real Solutions	a	b	c	$b^2 - 4ac$	Is $b^2 - 4ac$ positive, negative, or zero?
$x^2 + 2x - 8 = 0$	2	1	2	−8	36	Positive
$x^2 - 8x + 16 = 0$						
$x^2 + 6x + 11 = 0$						
$2x^2 + 3x + 3 = 0$						
$4x^2 - 8x + 3 = 0$						
$4x^2 + 4x + 1 = 0$						

2. Look for a relationship between the number of real solutions and the value of $b^2 - 4ac$. What do you notice?

THINK AND DISCUSS

3. **Discuss** what you can conclude about a quadratic equation for which $b^2 - 4ac > 0$.
4. **Explain** what you know about the value of $b^2 - 4ac$ for a

Motivate

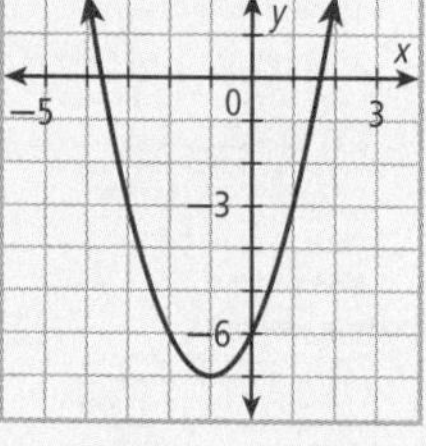

Have students graph $y = x^2 + 2x - 6$.

Show students that the solutions of the related quadratic equation are not integers. Tell students they can find exact solutions to any quadratic equation by using the Quadratic Formula.

Explorations and answers are provided in *Alternate Openers: Explorations Transparencies.*

EXAMPLE 1 Using the Quadratic Formula

Solve using the Quadratic Formula.

A $2x^2 + 3x - 5 = 0$

$2x^2 + 3x + (-5) = 0$ *Identify a, b, and c.*

$x = \dfrac{-b \pm \sqrt{b^2 - 4ac}}{2a}$ *Use the Quadratic Formula.*

$x = \dfrac{-3 \pm \sqrt{3^2 - 4(2)(-5)}}{2(2)}$ *Substitute 2 for a, 3 for b, and −5 for c.*

$x = \dfrac{-3 \pm \sqrt{9 - (-40)}}{4}$ *Simplify.*

$x = \dfrac{-3 \pm \sqrt{49}}{4} = \dfrac{-3 \pm 7}{4}$ *Simplify.*

$x = \dfrac{-3 + 7}{4}$ or $x = \dfrac{-3 - 7}{4}$ *Write as two equations.*

$x = 1$ or $x = -\dfrac{5}{2}$ *Simplify.*

B $2x = x^2 - 3$

$1x^2 + (-2)x + (-3) = 0$ *Write in standard form. Identify a, b, and c.*

$x = \dfrac{-(-2) \pm \sqrt{(-2)^2 - 4(1)(-3)}}{2(1)}$ *Substitute 1 for a, −2 for b, and −3 for c.*

$x = \dfrac{2 \pm \sqrt{4 - (-12)}}{2}$ *Simplify.*

$x = \dfrac{2 \pm \sqrt{16}}{2} = \dfrac{2 \pm 4}{2}$ *Simplify.*

$x = \dfrac{2 + 4}{2}$ or $x = \dfrac{2 - 4}{2}$ *Write as two equations.*

$x = 3$ or $x = -1$ *Simplify.*

Helpful Hint

You can graph the related quadratic function to see if your solutions are reasonable.

CHECK IT OUT! Solve using the Quadratic Formula.

1a. $-3x^2 + 5x + 2 = 0$ $2, -\dfrac{1}{3}$ **1b.** $2 - 5x^2 = -9x$ $2, -\dfrac{1}{5}$

Many quadratic equations can be solved by graphing, factoring, taking the square root, or completing the square. Some cannot be easily solved by any of these methods, but you can use the Quadratic Formula to solve any quadratic equation.

EXAMPLE 2 Using the Quadratic Formula to Estimate Solutions

Solve $x^2 - 2x - 4 = 0$ using the Quadratic Formula.

$x = \dfrac{-(-2) \pm \sqrt{(-2)^2 - 4(1)(-4)}}{2(1)}$

$x = \dfrac{2 \pm \sqrt{4 - (-16)}}{2} = \dfrac{2 \pm \sqrt{20}}{2}$

$x = \dfrac{2 + \sqrt{20}}{2}$ or $x = \dfrac{2 - \sqrt{20}}{2}$

Use a calculator: $x \approx 3.24$ or $x \approx -1.24$.

Check reasonableness

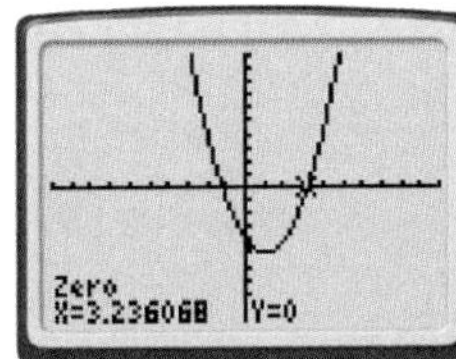

2. $\dfrac{8 - \sqrt{56}}{4} \approx 0.13$, $\dfrac{8 + \sqrt{56}}{4} \approx 3.87$

CHECK IT OUT! **2.** Solve $2x^2 - 8x + 1 = 0$ using the Quadratic Formula.

COMMON ERROR ALERT

Students might make sign errors in finding $-b$ when b is negative. Encourage students to use parentheses and to write down every step.

Power Presentations with PowerPoint®

Additional Examples

Example 1

Solve using the Quadratic Formula.

A. $6x^2 + 5x - 4 = 0$ $-\dfrac{4}{3}, \dfrac{1}{2}$

B. $x^2 = x + 20$ $-4, 5$

Example 2

Solve $x^2 + 3x - 7 = 0$ by using the Quadratic Formula.

$\dfrac{-3 + \sqrt{37}}{2} \approx 1.54$, $\dfrac{-3 - \sqrt{37}}{2} \approx -4.54$

INTERVENTION
Questioning Strategies

EXAMPLES **1–2**

- How can you check your answer?
- Why is the symbol $\pm$ in the Quadratic Formula?
- Where does the Quadratic Formula come from?

Communicating Math Make sure that students know what an exact answer is. In **Example 2,** $\frac{2 + \sqrt{20}}{2}$ is an exact solution; 3.24 is an approximation.

2 Teach

Guided Instruction

Let students know that any quadratic equation can be solved by using the Quadratic Formula and that it will always give exact solutions, but it may not always be the quickest method. Caution students to pay attention to signs when using the Quadratic Formula to avoid simple mistakes. Point out the benefit of finding the discriminant first so that students will be aware of the number of real solutions.

Reaching All Learners
Through Auditory Cues

Help students remember the Quadratic Formula by singing it to the tune of "Row, Row, Row Your Boat" or "Pop Goes the Weasel."

x equals negative *b*
plus or minus square root
of *b* squared minus four *a c*
all over two *a*.

Power Presentations with PowerPoint®

Additional Examples

Example 3

Find the number of real solutions of each equation using the discriminant.

A. $3x^2 - 2x + 2 = 0$ 0

B. $2x^2 + 11x + 12 = 0$ 2

C. $x^2 + 8x + 16 = 0$ 1

INTERVENTION

Questioning Strategies

EXAMPLE 3

- What part of the Quadratic Formula does the discriminant come from?
- Explain why the value of the discriminant indicates the number of solutions.

If the quadratic equation is in standard form, the **discriminant** of a quadratic equation is $b^2 - 4ac$, the part of the equation under the radical sign. Recall that quadratic equations can have two, one, or no real solutions. You can determine the number of solutions of a quadratic equation by evaluating its discriminant.

Equation	$x^2 - 4x + 3 = 0$	$x^2 + 2x + 1 = 0$	$x^2 - 2x + 2 = 0$
Discriminant	$a = 1, b = -4, c = 3$ $b^2 - 4ac$ $(-4)^2 - 4(1)(3)$ $16 - 12$ 4 The discriminant is positive.	$a = 1, b = 2, c = 1$ $b^2 - 4ac$ $2^2 - 4(1)(1)$ $4 - 4$ 0 The discriminant is zero.	$a = 1, b = -2, c = 2$ $b^2 - 4ac$ $(-2)^2 - 4(1)(2)$ $4 - 8$ -4 The discriminant is negative.
Graph of Related Function	Notice that the related function has two x-intercepts. (1, 0) (3, 0)	Notice that the related function has one x-intercept. (−1, 0)	Notice that the related function has no x-intercepts.
Number of Solutions	two real solutions	one real solution	no real solutions

The Discriminant of Quadratic Equation $ax^2 + bx + c = 0$

If $b^2 - 4ac > 0$, the equation has two real solutions.
If $b^2 - 4ac = 0$, the equation has one real solution.
If $b^2 - 4ac < 0$, the equation has no real solutions.

EXAMPLE 3 Using the Discriminant

Find the number of real solutions of each equation using the discriminant.

A $3x^2 + 10x + 2 = 0$

$a = 3, b = 10, c = 2$
$b^2 - 4ac$
$10^2 - 4(3)(2)$
$100 - 24$
76
$b^2 - 4ac$ is positive.
There are two real solutions.

B $9x^2 - 6x + 1 = 0$

$a = 9, b = -6, c = 1$
$b^2 - 4ac$
$(-6)^2 - 4(9)(1)$
$36 - 36$
0
$b^2 - 4ac$ is zero.
There is one real solution.

C $x^2 + x + 1 = 0$

$a = 1, b = 1, c = 1$
$b^2 - 4ac$
$1^2 - 4(1)(1)$
$1 - 4$
-3
$b^2 - 4ac$ is negative.
There are no real solutions.

Find the number of real solutions of each equation using the discriminant.

3a. $2x^2 - 2x + 3 = 0$ **0** **3b.** $x^2 + 4x + 4 = 0$ **1** **3c.** $x^2 - 9x + 4 = 0$ **2**

Reaching All Learners

Through Communication

Discuss with students why each type of discriminant indicates the number of real solutions that it does.

If the discriminant is negative, you cannot take its square root, so there are no real solutions.

Have students give explanations for the number of real solutions when the discriminant is positive or 0.

The height h in feet of an object shot straight up with initial velocity v in feet per second is given by $h = -16t^2 + vt + c$, where c is the beginning height of the object above the ground.

EXAMPLE 4 Physics Application

Helpful Hint

If the object is shot straight up from the ground, the initial height of the object above the ground equals 0.

A weight 1 foot above the ground on a carnival strength test is shot straight up with an initial velocity of 35 feet per second. Will it ring the bell at the top of the pole? Use the discriminant to explain your answer.

$h = -16t^2 + vt + c$

$20 = -16t^2 + 35t + 1$ — *Substitute 20 for h, 35 for v, and 1 for c.*

$0 = -16t^2 + 35t + (-19)$ — *Subtract 20 from both sides.*

$b^2 - 4ac$ — *Evaluate the discriminant.*

$35^2 - 4(-16)(-19) = 9$ — *Substitute −16 for a, 35 for b, and −19 for c.*

The discriminant is positive, so the equation has two solutions. The weight will reach a height of 20 feet so it will ring the bell.

4. What if...? Suppose the weight is shot straight up with an initial velocity of 20 feet per second. Will it ring the bell? Use the discriminant to explain your answer.

No; the discriminant is negative so the weight will not ring the bell.

There is no one correct way to solve a quadratic equation. Many quadratic equations can be solved using several different methods.

EXAMPLE 5 Solving Using Different Methods

Solve $x^2 + 7x + 6 = 0$.

Method 1 Solve by graphing.

$y = x^2 + 7x + 6$ — *Write the related quadratic function and graph it.*

The solutions are the x-intercepts, −6 and −1.

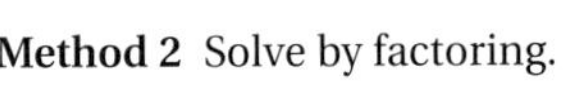

Method 2 Solve by factoring.

$x^2 + 7x + 6 = 0$

$(x + 6)(x + 1) = 0$ — *Factor.*

$x + 6 = 0$ or $x - 1 = 0$ — *Use the Zero Product Property.*

$x = -6$ or $x = -1$ — *Solve each equation.*

Method 3 Solve by completing the square.

$x^2 + 7x + 6 = 0$

$x^2 + 7x = -6$

$x^2 + 7x + \frac{49}{4} = -6 + \frac{49}{4}$ — *Add $\left(\frac{b}{2}\right)^2$ to both sides.*

$\left(x + \frac{7}{2}\right)^2 = \frac{25}{4}$ — *Factor and simplify.*

$x + \frac{7}{2} = \pm\frac{5}{2}$ — *Take the square root of both sides.*

$x + \frac{7}{2} = \frac{5}{2}$ or $x + \frac{7}{2} = -\frac{5}{2}$ — *Solve each equation.*

$x = -1$ or $x = -6$

COMMON ERROR ALERT

When solving problems like **Example 4,** students may forget to write the equation in standard form after they substitute the value for height. Remind them that the quadratic equation must be in the form $ax^2 + bx + c = 0$ before they can begin to use the Quadratic Formula.

Power Presentations with PowerPoint®

Additional Examples

Example 4

The height h in feet of an object shot straight up with initial velocity v in feet per second is given by $h = -16t^2 + vt + c$, where c is the initial height of the object above the ground. The ringer on a carnival strength test is 2 feet off the ground and is shot upward with an initial velocity of 30 feet per second. Will it reach a height of 20 feet? Use the discriminant to explain your answer. The discriminant of $20 = -16t^2 + 30t + 2$ is negative, so there are no real solutions. The ringer will not reach a height of 20 feet.

Example 5

Solve $x^2 - 9x + 20 = 0$. 4, 5

INTERVENTION

Questioning Strategies

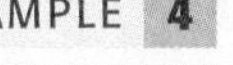

EXAMPLE 4

- What would a positive discriminant indicate in this situation?
- What would a negative discriminant indicate?

EXAMPLE 5

- Which of the methods for solving a quadratic equation give an exact answer every time? Explain.
- What are the advantages and disadvantages of each of the methods?
- Which method do you like best? Why?

Inclusion To help prevent computational errors, some students find it helpful to circle everything after b^2, calculate that, and then add that answer to b^2.

For example,

$\sqrt{7^2 \boxed{- 4(2)(-3)}}$

$= \sqrt{49 + 24}$

$= \sqrt{73}$

Method 4 Solve using the Quadratic Formula.

$1x^2 + 7x + 6 = 0$	*Identify a, b, and c.*
$x = \dfrac{-7 \pm \sqrt{7^2 - 4(1)(6)}}{2(1)}$	*Substitute 1 for a, 7 for b, and 6 for c.*
$x = \dfrac{-7 \pm \sqrt{49 - 24}}{2} = \dfrac{-7 \pm \sqrt{25}}{2} = \dfrac{-7 \pm 5}{2}$	*Simplify.*
$x = \dfrac{-7 + 5}{2}$ or $x = \dfrac{-7 - 5}{2}$	*Write as two equations.*
$x = -1$ or $x = -6$	*Solve each equation.*

CHECK IT OUT! **Solve.**

5a. $x^2 + 7x + 10 = 0$ **−2, −5** **5b.** $-14 + x^2 = 5x$ **−2, 7** **5c.** $2x^2 + 4x - 21 = 0$

5c. $\dfrac{-4 - \sqrt{184}}{4} \approx -4.39$, $\dfrac{-4 + \sqrt{184}}{4} \approx 2.39$

Notice that all of the methods in Example 5 produce the same solutions, −1 and −6. The only method you cannot use to solve $x^2 + 7x + 6 = 0$ is using square roots. Sometimes one method is better for solving certain types of equations. The table below gives some advantages and disadvantages of the different methods.

Know it! Note

Methods of Solving Quadratic Equations

METHOD	ADVANTAGES	DISADVANTAGES
Graphing	• Always works to give approximate solutions • Can quickly see the number of solutions	• Cannot always get an exact solution
Factoring	• Good method to try first • Straightforward if the equation is factorable	• Complicated if the equation is not easily factorable • Not all quadratic equations are factorable.
Using square roots	• Quick when the equation has no *x*-term	• Cannot easily use when there is an *x*-term
Completing the square	• Always works	• Sometimes involves difficult calculations
Using the Quadratic Formula	• Always works • Can always find exact solutions	• Other methods may be easier or less time consuming.

Student to Student

Solving Quadratic Equations

Binh Pham
Johnson High School

No matter what method I use, I like to check my answers for reasonableness by graphing.

I used the Quadratic Formula to solve $2x^2 - 7x - 10 = 0$. I found that $x \approx -1.09$ and $x \approx 4.59$. Then I graphed $y = 2x^2 - 7x - 10$. The x-intercepts appeared to be close to −1 and 4.5, so I knew my solutions were reasonable.

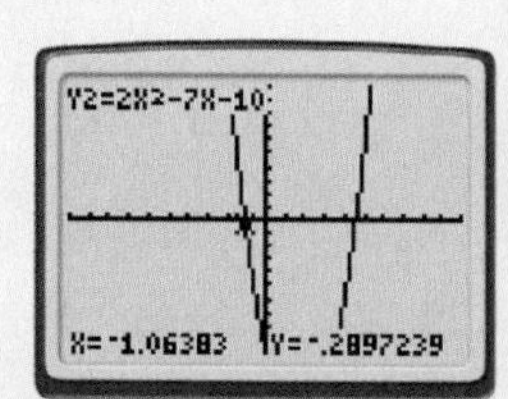

3 Close

Summarize

Ask students to give *a*, *b*, and *c* for the following quadratic equations. Then use the discriminant to find the number of real solutions.

$x^2 + 3x = -7$ $a = 1, b = 3, c = 7$; no real solutions

$3x^2 = 5x + 10$ $a = 3, b = -5, c = -10$; two real solutions

$12x + 2 = -18x^2$ $a = 18, b = 12, c = 2$; one real solution

ONGOING ASSESSMENT and INTERVENTION

***Diagnose Before* the Lesson**
9-9 Warm Up, TE p. 670

***Monitor During* the Lesson**
Check It Out! Exercises, SE pp. 671–674
Questioning Strategies, TE pp. 671–673

***Assess After* the Lesson**
9-9 Lesson Quiz, TE p. 677
Alternative Assessment, TE p. 677

THINK AND DISCUSS

1. Describe how to use the discriminant to find the number of real solutions to a quadratic equation.
2. Choose a method to solve $x^2 + 5x + 4 = 0$ and explain why you chose that method.
3. Describe how the discriminant can be used to determine if an object will reach a given height.

4. **GET ORGANIZED** Copy and complete the graphic organizer. In each box, write the number of real solutions.

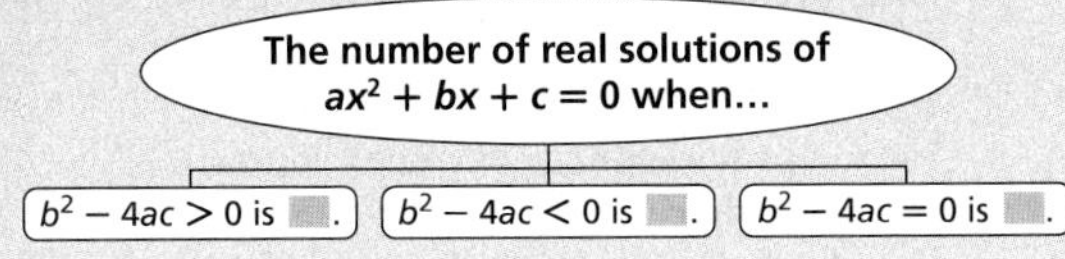

Answers to *Think and Discuss*

Possible answers:

1. If $b^2 - 4ac > 0$, there are 2 real solutions. If $b^2 - 4ac = 0$, there is 1 real solution. If $b^2 - 4ac < 0$, there are no real solutions.
2. $x = -1$ or $x = -4$; factoring method; least number of steps
3. If the discriminant of the equation describing the object's height is negative, there are no real solutions and the object will not reach the given height. If the discriminant is 0 or positive, there are 1 or 2 solutions and the object will reach the given height.
4. See p. A9.

9-9 Exercises

GUIDED PRACTICE

1. **Vocabulary** If the *discriminant* is negative, the quadratic equation has ___?___ real solution(s). (*no*, *one*, or *two*) **no**

SEE EXAMPLE 1 p. 671

Solve using the Quadratic Formula.

2. $x^2 - 5x + 4 = 0$ **1, 4**
3. $2x^2 = 7x - 3$ $\frac{1}{2}$, **3**
4. $x^2 - 6x - 7 = 0$ **−1, 7**
5. $x^2 = -14x - 40$ **−4, −10**
6. $3x^2 - 2x = 8$ $-\frac{4}{3}$, **2**
7. $4x^2 - 4x - 3 = 0$ $-\frac{1}{2}, \frac{3}{2}$

SEE EXAMPLE 2 p. 671

8. $2x^2 - 6 = 0$
9. $x^2 + 6x + 3 = 0$
10. $x^2 - 7x + 2 = 0$
11. $3x^2 = -x + 5$
12. $x^2 - 4x - 7 = 0$
13. $2x^2 + x - 5 = 0$

SEE EXAMPLE 3 p. 672

Find the number of real solutions of each equation using the discriminant.

14. $2x^2 + 4x + 3 = 0$ **0**
15. $x^2 + 4x + 4 = 0$ **1**
16. $2x^2 - 11x + 6 = 0$ **2**
17. $x^2 + x + 1 = 0$ **0**
18. $3x^2 = 5x - 1$ **2**
19. $-2x + 3 = 2x^2$ **2**
20. $2x^2 + 12x = -18$ **1**
21. $5x^2 + 3x = -4$ **0**
22. $8x = 1 - x^2$ **2**

SEE EXAMPLE 4 p. 673

23. **Hobbies** The height above the ground in meters of a model rocket on a particular launch can be modeled by the equation $h = -4.9t^2 + 102t + 100$, where t is the time in seconds after its engine burns out 100 m above the ground. Will the rocket reach a height of 600 m? Use the discriminant to explain your answer. **Yes; the discriminant of $600 = -4.9t^2 + 102t + 100$ is positive so the rocket will reach the given height.**

SEE EXAMPLE 5 p. 673

Solve.

24. $x^2 + x - 12 = 0$ **−4, 3**
25. $x^2 + 6x + 9 = 0$ **−3**
26. $2x^2 - x - 1 = 0$ **1,** $-\frac{1}{2}$
27. $4x^2 + 4x + 1 = 0$ $-\frac{1}{2}$
28. $2x^2 + x - 7 = 0$
29. $9 = 2x^2 + 3x$ **−3,** $\frac{3}{2}$

Assignment Guide

Assign *Guided Practice* exercises as necessary.

If you finished Examples **1–3**
Basic 30–38, 43–52, 56
Average 30–38, 43–52, 56
Advanced 30–38, 43–52, 55

If you finished Examples **1–5**
Basic 30–54, 56–59, 62–69
Average 30–59, 62–69
Advanced 30–51, 53–55, 57–69

Homework Quick Check
Quickly check key concepts.
Exercises: 30, 34, 38, 39, 42, 53

State Resources

Answers

8. $x = \pm\sqrt{3} \approx \pm 1.73$
9. $x = \frac{-6 - \sqrt{24}}{2} \approx -5.45$, $x = \frac{-6 + \sqrt{24}}{2} \approx -0.55$
10. $x = \frac{7 - \sqrt{41}}{2} \approx 0.30$, $x = \frac{7 + \sqrt{41}}{2} \approx 6.70$
11. $x = \frac{-1 - \sqrt{61}}{6} \approx -1.47$, $x = \frac{-1 + \sqrt{61}}{6} \approx -1.14$
12. $x = \frac{4 - \sqrt{44}}{2} \approx -1.32$, $x = \frac{4 + \sqrt{44}}{2} \approx 5.32$
13. $x = \frac{-1 - \sqrt{41}}{4} \approx -1.85$, $x = \frac{-1 + \sqrt{41}}{4} \approx 1.35$
28. $x = \frac{-1 - \sqrt{57}}{4} \approx -2.14$, $x = \frac{-1 + \sqrt{57}}{4} \approx 1.64$

go.hrw.com
State Resources Online
KEYWORD: MA7 Resources

Exercise 56 involves evaluating a discriminant to determine whether a given height is possible. This exercise prepares students for the Multi-Step Test Prep on page 678.

Answers

33. $x = \frac{4 - \sqrt{12}}{2} \approx 0.27$, $x = \frac{4 + \sqrt{12}}{2} \approx 3.73$

34. $x = \pm\frac{\sqrt{60}}{6} \approx \pm 1.29$

35. $x = \frac{-7 - \sqrt{17}}{4} \approx -2.78$, $x = \frac{-7 + \sqrt{17}}{4} \approx -0.72$

54. 2; 0; 1; $x^2 = k$ in standard form is $1x^2 + 0x - k = 0$, so $a = 1$, $b = 0$, $c = -k$ and $b^2 - 4ac = 4k$. $k > 0$: positive discriminant; $k < 0$: negative discriminant; $k = 0$: 0 discriminant.

55. The discriminant tells how many real solutions there are. If an equation looks difficult to solve, first use the discriminant to find out if it has any real solutions. If it doesn't, stop right there.

44. 2 solutions; $\frac{2 - \sqrt{40}}{2} \approx -2.16$, $\frac{2 + \sqrt{40}}{2} \approx 4.16$

45. 2 solutions; $-2, \frac{1}{4}$

49. 2 x-intercepts; $\frac{7}{2}, -3$

PRACTICE AND PROBLEM SOLVING

Independent Practice

For Exercises	See Example
30–32	1
33–35	2
36–38	3
39	4
40–42	5

Extra Practice

Skills Practice p. S21

Application Practice p. S36

Solve using the Quadratic Formula.

30. $3x^2 = 13x - 4$ **$\frac{1}{3}, 4$**
31. $x^2 - 10x + 9 = 0$ **1, 9**
32. $1 = 3x^2 + 2x$ **$-1, \frac{1}{3}$**
33. $x^2 - 4x + 1 = 0$
34. $3x^2 - 5 = 0$
35. $2x^2 + 7x = -4$

Find the number of real solutions of each equation using the discriminant.

36. $3x^2 - 6x + 3 = 0$ **1**
37. $x^2 - 3x - 8 = 0$ **2**
38. $7x^2 + 6x + 2 = 0$ **0**

39. **Multi-Step** A gymnast who can stretch her arms up to reach 6 feet jumps straight up on a trampoline. The height of her feet above the trampoline can be modeled by the equation $h = -16x^2 + 12x$, where x is the time in seconds after her jump. Do the gymnast's hands reach a height of 10 feet above the trampoline? Use the discriminant to explain. (*Hint:* Let $h = 10 - 6$, or 4.)
No; the discriminant of $4 = -16x^2 + 12x$ is negative.

Solve.

40. $x^2 + 4x + 3 = 0$ **−3, −1**
41. $x^2 + 2x = 15$ **−5, 3**
42. $x^2 - 12 = -x$ **−4, 3**

Write each equation in standard form. Use the discriminant to determine the number of solutions. Then find any real solutions.

43. $2x = 3 + 2x^2$ **no real solutions**
44. $x^2 = 2x + 9$
45. $2 = 7x + 4x^2$
46. $-7 = x^2$ **no real solutions**
47. $-12x = -9x^2 - 4$ **1 solution; $\frac{2}{3}$**
48. $x^2 - 14 = 0$ **2 solutions; $\pm\sqrt{14} \approx \pm 3.7$**

Multi-Step **Use the discriminant to determine the number of x-intercepts. Then find them.**

49. $y = 2x^2 - x - 21$
50. $y = 5x^2 + 12x + 8$ **no x-intercepts**
51. $y = x^2 - 10x + 25$ **1 x-intercept; 5**

52. Copy and complete the table.

Quadratic Equation	Discriminant	Number of Real Solutions
$x^2 + 12x - 20 = 0$	**224**	**2**
$8x + x^2 = -16$	**0**	**1**
$0.5x^2 + x - 3 = 0$	**7**	**2**
$-3x^2 - 2x = 1$	**−8**	**0**

53. **Sports** A diver begins on a platform 10 meters above the surface of the water. The diver's height is given by the equation $h(t) = -4.9t^2 + 3.5t + 10$, where t is the time in seconds after the diver jumps.
    a. How long does it take the diver to reach a point 1 meter above the water? **about 1.76 s**
    b. How many solutions does the equation you used in part **a** have? **2 solutions**
    c. Do all of the solutions to the equation make sense in the situation? Explain. **No; negative solutions do not make sense because the variable represents time.**

54. **Critical Thinking** How many real solutions does the equation $x^2 = k$ have when $k > 0$, when $k < 0$, and when $k = 0$? Use the discriminant to explain.

55. **Write About It** How can you use the discriminant to save time?

9-9 PRACTICE A
9-9 PRACTICE C
9-9 PRACTICE B

Solve using the quadratic formula.

1. $x^2 + x = 12$ **3, −4**
2. $4x^2 - 17x - 15 = 0$ **$5, -\frac{3}{4}$**
3. $2x^2 - 5x = 3$ **$3, -\frac{1}{2}$**
4. $3x^2 + 14x - 5 = 0$ **$\frac{1}{3}, -5$**

Find the number of real solutions of each equation using the discriminant.

5. $x^2 + 25 = 0$ **no real solutions**
6. $x^2 - 11x + 28 = 0$ **2**
7. $x^2 + 8x + 16 = 0$ **1**

Solve using any method.

8. $x^2 + 8x + 15 = 0$ **−3, −5**
9. $x^2 - 49 = 0$ **7, −7**
10. $6x^2 + x - 1 = 0$ **$\frac{1}{3}, -\frac{1}{2}$**
11. $x^2 + 8x - 20 = 0$ **−10, 2**
12. In the past, professional baseball was played at the Astrodome in Houston, Texas. The Astrodome has a maximum height of 63.4 m. The height of a baseball t seconds after it is hit straight up in the air with a velocity of 45 ft/s is given by $h = -9.8t^2 + 45t + 1$. Will a baseball hit straight up with this velocity hit the roof of the Astrodome? Use the discriminant to explain your answer.
No; the discriminant is negative so it will never reach the given height.

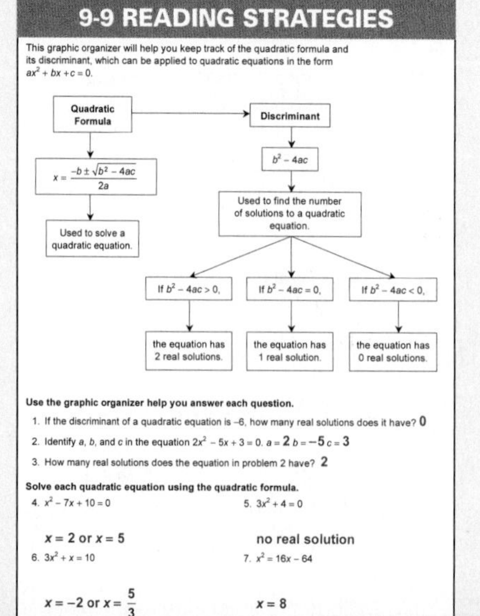

9-9 READING STRATEGIES

This graphic organizer will help you keep track of the quadratic formula and its discriminant, which can be applied to quadratic equations in the form $ax^2 + bx + c = 0$.

Use the graphic organizer help you answer each question.

1. If the discriminant of a quadratic equation is −6, how many real solutions does it have? **0**
2. Identify a, b, and c in the equation $2x^2 - 5x + 3 = 0$. $a =$ **2** $b =$ **−5** $c =$ **3**
3. How many real solutions does the equation in problem 2 have? **2**

Solve each quadratic equation using the quadratic formula.

4. $x^2 - 7x + 10 = 0$ **$x = 2$ or $x = 5$**
5. $3x^2 + 4 = 0$ **no real solution**
6. $3x^2 + x = 10$ **$x = -2$ or $x = \frac{5}{3}$**
7. $x^2 = 16x - 64$ **$x = 8$**

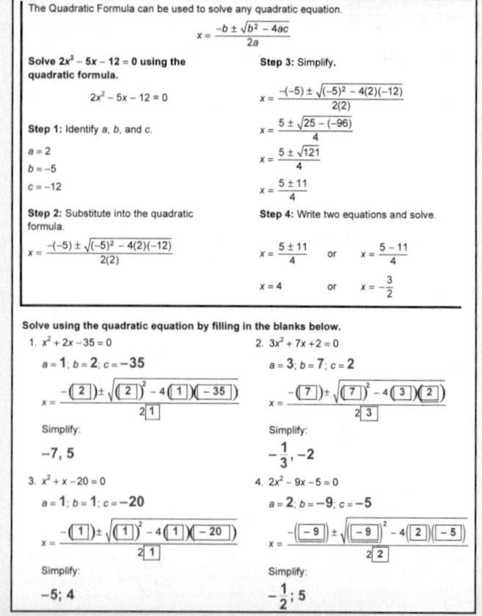

9-9 RETEACH

The Quadratic Formula can be used to solve any quadratic equation.

$$x = \frac{-b \pm \sqrt{b^2 - 4ac}}{2a}$$

Solve $2x^2 - 5x - 12 = 0$ using the quadratic formula.

$2x^2 - 5x - 12 = 0$

Step 1: Identify a, b, and c.

$a = 2$
$b = -5$
$c = -12$

Step 2: Substitute into the quadratic formula.

$x = \frac{-(-5) \pm \sqrt{(-5)^2 - 4(2)(-12)}}{2(2)}$

Step 3: Simplify.

$x = \frac{-(-5) \pm \sqrt{(-5)^2 - 4(2)(-12)}}{2(2)}$

$x = \frac{5 \pm \sqrt{25 - (-96)}}{4}$

$x = \frac{5 \pm \sqrt{121}}{4}$

$x = \frac{5 \pm 11}{4}$

Step 4: Write two equations and solve.

$x = \frac{5 + 11}{4}$ or $x = \frac{5 - 11}{4}$

$x = 4$ or $x = -\frac{3}{2}$

Solve using the quadratic equation by filling in the blanks below.

1. $x^2 + 2x - 35 = 0$
   $a =$ **1**; $b =$ **2**; $c =$ **−35**
   $x = \frac{-(2) \pm \sqrt{(2)^2 - 4(1)(-35)}}{2(1)}$
   Simplify: **−7, 5**
2. $3x^2 + 7x + 2 = 0$
   $a =$ **3**; $b =$ **7**; $c =$ **2**
   $x = \frac{-(7) \pm \sqrt{(7)^2 - 4(3)(2)}}{2(3)}$
   Simplify: **$-\frac{1}{3}, -2$**
3. $x^2 + x - 20 = 0$
   $a =$ **1**; $b =$ **1**; $c =$ **−20**
   $x = \frac{-(1) \pm \sqrt{(1)^2 - 4(1)(-20)}}{2(1)}$
   Simplify: **−5; 4**
4. $2x^2 - 9x - 5 = 0$
   $a =$ **2**; $b =$ **−9**; $c =$ **−5**
   $x = \frac{-(-9) \pm \sqrt{(-9)^2 - 4(2)(-5)}}{2(2)}$
   Simplify: **$-\frac{1}{2}; 5$**

MULTI-STEP TEST PREP

56. This problem will prepare you for the Multi-Step Test Prep on page 678.

The equation $0 = -16t^2 + 80t + 20$ gives the time t in seconds when a golf ball is at height 0 feet.

a. Will the height of the ball reach 130 feet? Explain.

b. Will the golf ball reach a height of 116 feet? If so, when? **yes; 2 s and 3 s**

c. Solve the given quadratic equation using the Quadratic Formula. **≈ 5.24 s**

TEST PREP

57. How many real solutions does $4x^2 - 3x + 1 = 0$ have?

(A) 0   (B) 1   (C) 2   (D) 4

58. For which of the following conditions does $ax^2 + bx + c = 0$ have two real solutions?

I. $b^2 = 4ac$

II. $b^2 > 4ac$

III. $a = b, c = b$

(F) I only   (G) II only   (H) III only   (J) II and III

59. Extended Response Use the equation $0 = x^2 + 2x + 1$ to answer the following.

a. How many solutions does the equation have? **1**

b. Solve the equation by graphing. **−1**

c. Solve the equation by factoring. **−1**

d. Solve the equation by using the Quadratic Formula. **−1**

e. Explain which method was easiest for you. Why?

59e. Possible answer: The easiest was solving by factoring: $0 = (x+1)(x+1)$ because the equation includes a perfect-square trinomial.

CHALLENGE AND EXTEND

60. Agriculture A rancher has 80 yards of fencing to build a rectangular pen. Let w be the width of the pen. Write an equation giving the area of the pen. Find the dimensions of the pen when the area is 400 square yards.

60. Area of pen $= 40w - w^2$; the width and length are each 20 yd.

61. Agriculture A farmer wants to fence a four-sided field using an existing fence along the south side of the field. He has 1000 feet of fencing. He makes the northern boundary perpendicular to and twice as long as the western boundary. The eastern and western boundaries have to be parallel, but the northern and southern ones do not.

a. Can the farmer enclose an area of 125,000 square feet? Explain why or why not. (*Hint:* Use the formula for the area of a trapezoid, $A = \frac{1}{2}h(b_1 + b_2)$.)

b. What geometric shape will the field be? **rectangle**

61a. Yes; the three boundaries can be represented by x, $2x$, and $1000 - 3x$. The area is represented by $\frac{1}{2}(2x)(x + 1000 - 3x)$, or $-2x^2 + 1000x$. So $-2x^2 + 1000x = 125{,}000$. Rewrite this in standard form: $2x^2 - 1000x + 125{,}000 = 0$. The discriminant is 0, so there is exactly one solution.

SPIRAL REVIEW

Solve each equation by completing the square. *(Lesson 9-8)*

62. $x^2 - 2x - 24 = 0$ **−4, 6**

63. $x^2 + 6x = 40$ **−10, 4**

64. $-3x^2 + 12x = 15$ **no real solutions**

Factor each polynomial by grouping. *(Lesson 8-2)*

65. $s^2r^3 + 5r^3 + 5t + s^2t$ **$(r^3 + t)(s^2 + 5)$**

66. $b^3 - 4b^2 + 2b - 8$ **$(b^2 + 2)(b - 4)$**

67. $n^5 - 6n^4 - 2n + 12$ **$(n^4 - 2)(n - 6)$**

Order the functions from narrowest graph to widest. *(Lesson 9-4)*

68. $f(x) = 0.2x^2$, $g(x) = 1.5x^2 + 4$, $h(x) = x^2 - 8$ **$g(x)$, $h(x)$, $f(x)$**

69. $f(x) = -\frac{1}{5}x^2 + 5$, $g(x) = \frac{1}{6}x^2$ **$f(x)$, $g(x)$**

TEST PREP DOCTOR In **Exercise 58,** students can write $b^2 - 4ac > 0$ and rearrange it, yielding $b^2 > 4ac$. Thus, **II** is true and choices **F** and **H** can be eliminated. To find out whether **III** is true, substitute b for a and c in $b^2 > 4ac$. This yields $b^2 > 4b^2$, which simplifies to $1 > 4$, so **III** is false, and **J** can be eliminated.

Answers

56a. No; the discriminant of $130 = -16t^2 + 80t + 20$ is negative, so the equation has no real solutions.

Journal

Have students write about their preferred method of solving quadratic equations. Have them describe its advantages and disadvantages.

ALTERNATIVE ASSESSMENT

Have students write a quadratic equation and use the discriminant to find the number of real solutions. Have them use the Quadratic Formula to find the real solution(s), if any exist. If there are no real solutions, have them explain what this means.

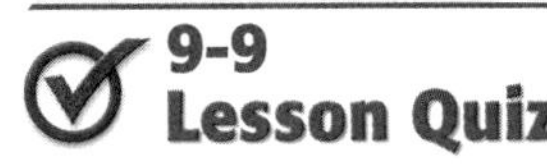

Power Presentations with PowerPoint®

9-9 Lesson Quiz

1. Solve $-3x^2 + 5x = 1$ by using the Quadratic Formula.
$\frac{5 - \sqrt{13}}{6} \approx 0.23$, $\frac{5 + \sqrt{13}}{6} \approx 1.43$

2. Find the number of real solutions of $5x^2 - 10x - 8 = 0$ by using the discriminant. 2

3. The height h in feet of an object shot straight up is modeled by $h = -16t^2 + vt + c$, where c is the beginning height of the object above the ground. An object is shot up from 4 feet off the ground with an initial velocity v of 48 feet per second. Will it reach a height of 40 feet? Use the discriminant to explain your answer.
The discriminant is zero. The object will reach a height of 40 feet once.

4. Solve $8x^2 - 13x - 6 = 0$.
$2, -\frac{3}{8}$

Also available on transparency

9-9 PROBLEM SOLVING

Write the correct answer.

1. Theo's flying disc got stuck in a tree 14 feet from the ground. Theo threw his shoe up at the disc to dislodge it. The height in feet h of the shoe is given by the equation $h = -16t^2 + 25t + 6$, where t is the time in seconds. Determine whether the shoe hit the disc. Use the discriminant to explain your answer.
Yes; the discriminant (113) is positive.

2. A picture frame holds a 4-in. by 6-in. photograph. The frame adds a border x inches wide around three sides of the photo. On the fourth side the frame forms a border that is $3x - 0.5$ in. wide.

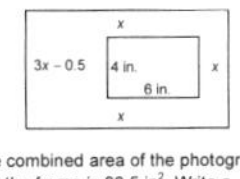

x; 3x − 0.5; 4 in.; 6 in.; x; x

The combined area of the photograph and the frame is 80.5 in². Write a quadratic equation for the combined area. Then use the quadratic formula to find x.
$8x^2 + 27x + 22 = 80.5$
$x = 1.5$

3. The manager of a park enclosed an area for small dogs to play. He made the length 15 feet longer than the width and enclosed an area covering 1350 square feet. What are the dimensions of the dogs' play area?
30 ft by 45 ft

The equation $-5x^2 + 72x + 378$ models the number of students enrolled in a school where x is the number of years since the school first opened in 1990. Select the best answer.

4. How many students did the school have when it opened?
A 68
B 72
C 378
D 445

5. Which equation can be used to find the year in which 502 students were enrolled?
F $-5x^2 + 72x + 502 = 0$
G $-5x^2 + 72x - 124 = 0$
H $-5x^2 + 72x - 502 = 0$
J $-5x^2 + 72x + 124 = 0$

6. In which year were 502 students enrolled?
A 1992   C 1998
B 1996   D 2002

7. In which year were 598 students enrolled?
F 1995   **H** 2000
G 1998   J 2010

8. Which statement is true?
A Enrollment exceeded 650 students at one point.
B Enrollment never exceeded 650 students.
C The highest enrollment of any year was exactly 650 students.
D There were two years where 650 students were enrolled.

9-9 CHALLENGE

The general form of a quadratic equation is $ax^2 + bx + 5 = 0$, where $a \neq 0$.

Identify a, b, and c for each of the following quadratic equations.

1. $2x^2 - 5x - 8 = 0$ **$a = 2$; $b = -5$; $c = -8$**
2. $7x^2 - 56 = 0$ **$a = 7$; $b = 0$; $c = -56$**
3. $12x^2 - 16x = 0$ **$a = 12$; $b = -16$; $c = 0$**
4. Why is $5x - 15 = 0$ not a quadratic equation? **$a = 0$; there is no x^2 – term**

Three methods for solving quadratic equations are taking square roots, factoring, and using the quadratic formula. Although the quadratic formula can be used to solve any quadratic equation, often one of the other methods is more efficient.

Use Exercises 1–3 to answer the following questions:

5. For which exercise would *taking square roots* be the quickest way to find a solution? **2**
6. For which exercise would *factoring* be the quickest way to find a solution? **3**
7. For which exercise would *using the quadratic formula* be the quickest way to find a solution? **1**

Complete the following table to help you organize the results from the above exercises:

		Example	Method
	if $b = 0$ and $c = 0$	$5x^2 = 0$	none; $x = 0$
8.	if $b = 0$ and $c \neq 0$	answers may vary	answers may vary
9.	if $b \neq 0$ and $c = 0$	answers may vary	answers may vary
10.	if $b \neq 0$ and $c \neq 0$	answers may vary	answers may vary

11. Solve $ax^2 = 0$ for x. **$x = 0$**
12. Solve $ax^2 - c = 0$ for x in terms of a and c. **$x = \pm\sqrt{\frac{c}{a}}$**
13. Solve $ax^2 + bx = 0$ for x in terms of a and b. **$x = \frac{-b}{a}$ or $x = 0$**
14. Solve $ax^2 + bx + c = 0$ for x in terms of a, b and c. **$x = \frac{-b \pm \sqrt{b^2 - 4ac}}{2a}$**
15. What is the name of the formula you found in Exercise 14? **the quadratic formula**

Organizer

Objective: Assess students' ability to apply concepts and skills in Lessons 9-5 through 9-9 in a real-world format.

Online Edition

Resources

Algebra I Assessments

www.mathtekstoolkit.org

For additional assessment activities, see www.utdanacenter.org

Problem	Text Reference
1	Lesson 9-5
2	Lesson 9-5
3	Lesson 9-5
4	Lessons 9-5, 9-6
5	Lesson 9-9

State Resources

MULTI-STEP TEST PREP

Solving Quadratic Equations

Seeing Green A golf player hits a golf ball from a tee with an initial vertical velocity of 80 feet per second. The height of the golf ball t seconds after it is hit is given by $h = -16t^2 + 80t$.

1. How long is the golf ball in the air? **5 s**
2. What is the maximum height of the golf ball? **100 ft**
3. How long after the golf ball is hit does it reach its maximum height? **2.5 s**
4. What is the height of the golf ball after 3.5 seconds? **84 ft**
5. At what times is the golf ball 64 feet in the air? Explain.

At 1 s and 4 s; using the table function in a graphing calculator, X = 1 and 4 when $Y_1 = 64$.

INTERVENTION

Scaffolding Questions

1. What is a reasonable domain for this situation? $0 \le t \le 5$
2. What is a reasonable range for this situation? $0 \le h \le 100$
3. What point represents the maximum height? the vertex
4. Does this problem ask for the value of an independent or dependent variable? dependent
5. What equation could you solve in order to answer this question? $64 = -16t^2 + 80t$

Extension

How would the function change if the golfer hit the ball with an initial velocity of 60 ft/s? How would the graph and the reasonable domain and range change? $h = -16t^2 + 60t$; the graph in the first quadrant would be shorter and not as wide; reasonable domain: $0 \le t \le 3.75$; reasonable range: $0 \le h \le 56.25$.

CHAPTER 9

SECTION 9B

Quiz for Lessons 9-5 Through 9-9

9-5 Solving Quadratic Equations by Graphing

Solve each equation by graphing the related function.

1. $x^2 - 9 = 0$ **3, −3**
2. $x^2 + 3x - 4 = 0$ **1, −4**
3. $4x^2 + 8x = 32$ **2, −4**
4. The height of a fireworks rocket launched from a platform 35 meters above the ground can be approximated by $h = -5t^2 + 30t + 35$, where h is the height in meters and t is the time in seconds. Find the time it takes the rocket to reach the ground after it is launched. **7 s**

9-6 Solving Quadratic Equations by Factoring

Use the Zero Product Property to solve each equation.

5. $(x + 1)(x + 3) = 0$ **−1, −3**
6. $(x - 6)(x - 3) = 0$ **6, 3**
7. $(x + 6)(x - 3) = 0$ **−6, 3**
8. $(x + 7)(x - 10) = 0$ **−7, 10**

Solve each quadratic equation by factoring.

9. $x^2 - 4x - 32 = 0$ **8, −4**
10. $x^2 - 8x + 15 = 0$ **3, 5**
11. $x^2 + x = 6$ **2, −3**
12. $-8x - 33 = -x^2$ **11, −3**
13. The height of a soccer ball kicked from the ground can be approximated by the function $h = -16t^2 + 64t$, where h is the height in feet and t is the time in seconds. Find the time it takes for the ball to return to the ground. **4 s**

9-7 Solving Quadratic Equations by Using Square Roots

Solve using square roots.

14. $3x^2 = 48$ **4, −4**
15. $36x^2 - 49 = 0$ **$\frac{7}{6}, -\frac{7}{6}$**
16. $-12 = x^2 - 21$ **3, −3**
17. Solve $3x^2 + 5 = 21$. Round to the nearest hundredth. **2.31, −2.31**

9-8 Completing the Square

Complete the square to form a perfect-square trinomial.

18. $x^2 - 12x +$ **36**
19. $x^2 + 4x +$ **4**
20. $x^2 + 9x +$ **$\frac{81}{4}$**

Solve by completing the square.

21. $x^2 + 2x = 3$ **1, −3**
22. $x^2 - 5 = 2x$ **$1 \pm \sqrt{6}$**
23. $x^2 + 7x = 8$ **1, −8**
24. The width of a rectangle is 4 feet shorter than its length. The area of the rectangle is 42 square feet. Find the length and width. Round your answer to the nearest tenth of a foot. **length: 8.8 ft; width: 4.8 ft**

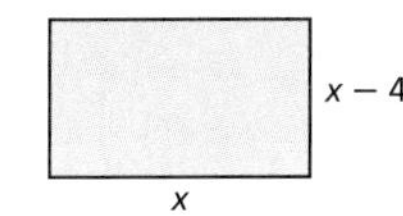

9-9 Using the Quadratic Formula and the Discriminant

Solve using the Quadratic Formula. Round your answer to the nearest hundredth.

25. $x^2 + 5x + 1 = 0$ **−0.21, −4.79**
26. $3x^2 + 1 = 2x$ **no real solutions**
27. $5x + 8 = 3x^2$ **−1, 2.67**

Find the number of real solutions of each equation using the discriminant.

28. $2x^2 - 3x + 4 = 0$ **no real solutions**
29. $x^2 + 1 + 2x = 0$ **1 real solution**
30. $x^2 - 5 + 4x = 0$ **2 real solutions**

READY TO GO ON? SECTION 9B

Organizer

Objective: Assess students' mastery of concepts and skills in Lessons 9-5 through 9-9.

Resources

Assessment Resources
Section 9B Quiz

Teacher One Stop™
Test & Practice Generator

INTERVENTION

Resources

Ready to Go On? Intervention and Enrichment **Worksheets**

Ready to Go On? **CD-ROM**

Ready to Go On? **Online**

my.hrw.com

READY TO GO ON? Diagnose and Prescribe

Ready to Go On? Intervention	*Ready to Go On? Intervention,* Section 9B Worksheets	CD-ROM	Online
Lesson 9-5	9-5 Intervention	Activity 9-5	Diagnose and Prescribe Online
Lesson 9-6	9-6 Intervention	Activity 9-6	
Lesson 9-7	9-7 Intervention	Activity 9-7	
Lesson 9-8	9-8 Intervention	Activity 9-8	
Lesson 9-9	9-9 Intervention	Activity 9-9	

Ready to Go On? Enrichment, Section 9B
Worksheets

CD-ROM

Online

CHAPTER 9
Organizer

Pacing: Traditional 1 day
Block $\frac{1}{2}$ day

Objectives: Recognize and graph cubic functions.

Solve cubic equations.

Online Edition

Countdown Week 21

Using the Extension

In Chapter 9, students learned to graph quadratic functions and solve quadratic equations. In this lesson, students apply similar techniques to graphing cubic functions and solving cubic equations.

State Resources

EXTENSION Cubic Functions and Equations

Objectives
Recognize and graph cubic functions.

Solve cubic equations.

Vocabulary
cubic function
cubic equation

A **cubic function** is a function that can be written in the form $f(x) = ax^3 + bx^2 + cx + d$, where $a \neq 0$. The parent cubic function is $f(x) = x^3$. To graph this function, choose several values of x and find ordered pairs.

x	f(x)
2	8
1	1
0	0
−1	−1
−2	−8

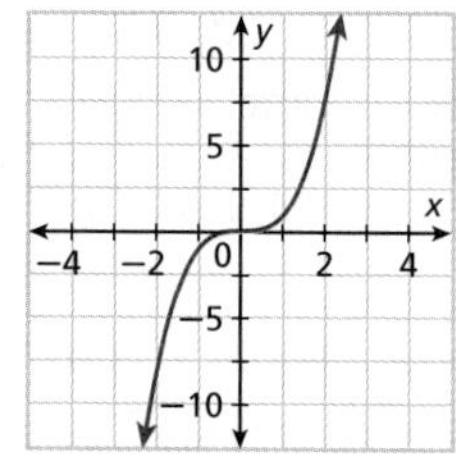

From the graph of $f(x) = x^3$, you can see

- the general shape of a cubic function.
- that the domain and the range are all real numbers.
- that the x-intercept and the y-intercept are both 0.

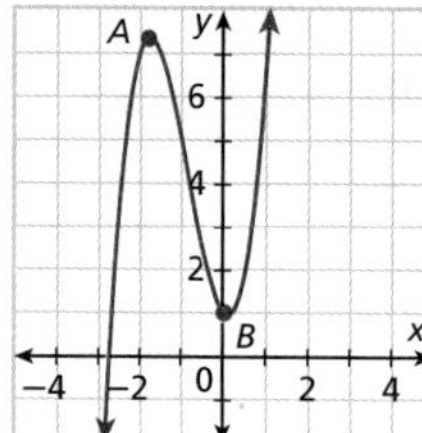

The graph of $f(x) = 2x^3 + 5x^2 - x + 1$ illustrates another characteristic of the graphs of cubic functions. Points A and B are called *turning points.* In general, the graph of a cubic function will have two turning points.

EXAMPLE 1 Graphing Cubic Functions

Graph $f(x) = -2x^3 + 3x^2 + x - 4$. Identify the intercepts and give the domain and range.

x	$f(x) = -2x^3 + 3x^2 + x - 4$	f(x)
−1	$-2(-1)^3 + 3(-1)^2 - 1 - 4$	0
0	$-2(0)^3 + 3(0)^2 + 0 - 4$	−4
1	$-2(1)^3 + 3(1)^2 + 1 - 4$	−2
2	$-2(2)^3 + 3(2)^2 + 2 - 4$	−6

Choose positive, negative, and zero values for x, and find ordered pairs.

1 Introduce

Motivate

Show students the formulas for the volume of a sphere and a cube.

cube: $V = s^3$

sphere: $V = \frac{4}{3}\pi r^3$

Help students recognize that both of these are cubic functions.

2 Teach

Guided Instruction

There are three basic strategies for solving cubic equations. One strategy is to graph the related function. The x-intercepts of the function are the solutions of the equation. A second strategy is to rewrite the equation so that one side is equal to 0, factor the cubic polynomial into a linear factor and a quadratic factor, and apply the techniques for solving linear and quadratic equations. A third strategy is to rewrite the equation in the form *cubed expression = constant* and to take the cube root of both sides.

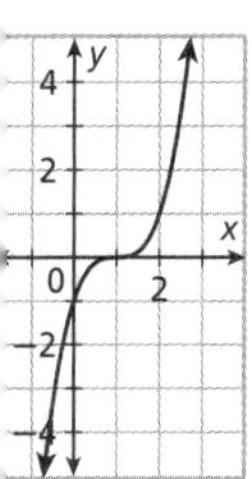

-int.: 1; *y*-int.: –1;
: all real numbers;
: all real numbers

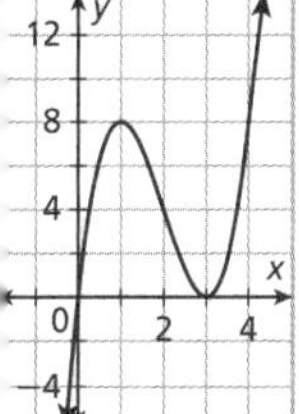

-int.: 0, 3; *y*-int.: 0;
: all real numbers;
: all real numbers

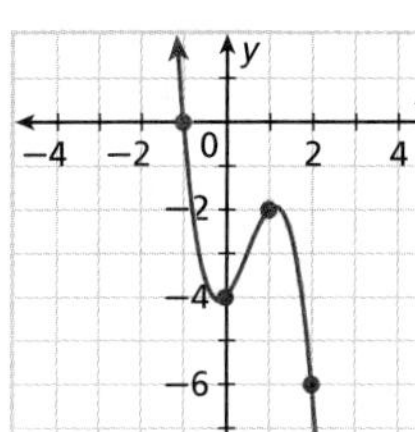

Plot the ordered pairs and connect them with a smooth curve.

Notice that, in general, this graph falls from left to right. This is because the value of a is negative.

The x-intercept is –1. The y-intercept is –4. The domain and range are all real numbers.

Graph each cubic function. Identify the intercepts and give the domain and range.

1a. $f(x) = (x-1)^3$ **1b.** $f(x) = 2x^3 - 12x^2 + 18x$

Previously, you saw that every quadratic function has a related quadratic equation. Cubic functions also have related *cubic equations.* A **cubic equation** is an equation that can be written in the form $ax^3 + bx^2 + cx + d = 0$, where $a \neq 0$.

One way to solve a cubic equation is by graphing the related function and finding its zeros.

EXAMPLE 2 Solving Cubic Equations by Graphing

Solve $x^3 - 2x^2 - x = -2$ by graphing. Check your answer.

Step 1 Rewrite the equation in the form $ax^3 + bx^2 + cx + d = 0$.

$x^3 - 2x^2 - x = -2$

$x^3 - 2x^2 - x + 2 = 0$ *Add 2 to both sides of the equation.*

Step 2 Write and graph the related function: $f(x) = x^3 - 2x^2 - x + 2$

x	$f(x) = x^3 - 2x^2 - x + 2$	$f(x)$
–1	$(-1)^3 - 2(-1)^2 - (-1) + 2$	0
0	$(0)^3 - 2(0)^2 - 0 + 2$	2
1	$(1)^3 - 2(1)^2 - 1 + 2$	0
2	$(2)^3 - 2(2)^2 - 2 + 2$	0
3	$(3)^3 - 2(3)^2 - 3 + 2$	8

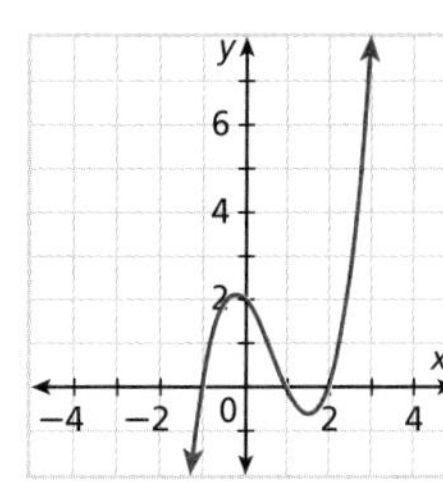

Step 3 Find the zeros.

The zeros appear to be –1, 1, and 2. Check these values in the original equation.

$x^3 - 2x^2 - x$	$= -2$
$(-1)^3 - 2(-1)^2 - (-1)$	-2
$(-1) - 2 + 1$	-2
-2	-2 ✓

$x^3 - 2x^2 - x$	$= -2$
$1^3 - 2(1)^2 - 1$	-2
$1 - 2 - 1$	-2
-2	-2 ✓

$x^3 - 2x^2 - x$	$= -2$
$2^3 - 2(2)^2 - 2$	-2
$8 - 8 - 2$	-2
-2	-2 ✓

Power Presentations with PowerPoint®

Additional Examples

Example 1

Graph $f(x) = 2x^3 - x^2 + 4x + 7$. Identify the intercepts and give the domain and range.

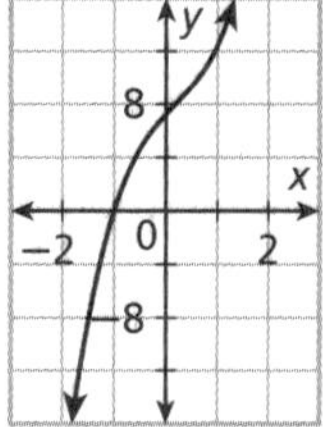

x-int.: –1; y-int.: 7; D: all real numbers; R: all real numbers

Example 2

Solve each equation by graphing. Check your answer.

A. $x^3 - 13x + 12 = 0$ –4, 1, 3

B. $3x^3 - 15x^2 - 12x = -60$ –2, 2, 5

INTERVENTION

Questioning Strategies

EXAMPLE 1

- What is the shape of the graph of a cubic function?

EXAMPLE 2

- Why must you write the cubic equation so that one side is equal to 0?
- Can a cubic equation have no real solutions?

Power Presentations with PowerPoint®

Additional Examples

Example 3

Solve each equation. Check your answer.

A. $4x^3 - 5x^2 + 2x = 3$ $0, \frac{5 \pm \sqrt{57}}{8}$

B. $5x^3 = 20x$ 0, 2, −2

C. $(2x + 1)^3 = -125$ −3

INTERVENTION

Questioning Strategies

EXAMPLE 3

- When can you solve a cubic equation by taking the cube root of both sides of the equation?

Solve each equation by graphing. Check your answer.

2a. $x^3 - 2x^2 - 25x = -50$ **−5, 2, 5** **2b.** $2x^3 + 12x^2 = 30x + 200$ **−5, 4**

Cubic equations can also be solved algebraically. Many of the methods used to solve quadratic equations can be applied to cubic equations as well.

EXAMPLE 3 **Solving Cubic Equations Algebraically**

Solve each equation. Check your answer.

A $(x + 5)^3 = 27$

$\sqrt[3]{(x + 5)^3} = \sqrt[3]{27}$ *Take the cube root of both sides.*

$x + 5 = 3$

$x = -2$ *Subtract 5 from both sides.*

Check

$(x + 5)^3 = 27$	
$(-2 + 5)^3$	27
3^3	27
27	27 ✓

Substitute −2 for x in the original equation.

B $x^3 + 3x^2 = -2x$

$x^3 + 3x^2 + 2x = 0$ *Add 2x to both sides.*

$x(x^2 + 3x + 2) = 0$ *Factor out x on the left side.*

$x(x + 1)(x + 2) = 0$ *Factor the quadratic trinomial.*

$x = 0$ or $x + 1 = 0$ or $x + 2 = 0$ *Zero Product Property*

$x = -1$ or $x = -2$ *Solve each equation.*

The solutions are 0, −1, and −2.

Check

$x^3 + 3x^2 = -2x$	
$0^3 + 3(0)^2$	$-2(0)$
$0 + 0$	0
0	0 ✓

$x^3 + 3x^2 = -2x$	
$(-1)^3 + 3(-1)^2$	$-2(-1)$
$-1 + 3(1)$	2
$-1 + 3$	2
2	2 ✓

$x^3 + 3x^2 = -2x$	
$(-2)^3 + 3(-2)^2$	$-2(-2)$
$-8 + 3(4)$	4
$-8 + 12$	4
4	4 ✓

Remember!

The factored expression must equal zero to use the Zero Product Property.

C $x^3 - 3.125x = -1.25x^2$

$x^3 + 1.25x^2 - 3.125x = 0$ *Add $1.25x^2$ to both sides.*

$x(x^2 + 1.25x - 3.125) = 0$ *Factor out x on the left side.*

$x = 0$ or $x^2 + 1.25x - 3.125 = 0$ *Zero Product Property*

$x = \frac{-1.25 \pm \sqrt{(1.25)^2 - 4(1)(-3.125)}}{2(1)}$ *Quadratic Formula*

$x = \frac{-1.25 \pm 3.75}{2}$ *Simplify.*

$x = -2.5$ or $x = 1.25$

The solutions are −2.5, 0, and 1.25.

3 Close

Summarize

Ask one group of students to solve $2x^3 - 14x^2 + 24x = 0$ by graphing. Ask another group to solve the same equation algebraically. Have the groups present their solutions. 0, 3, 4

Check Use a graphing calculator.

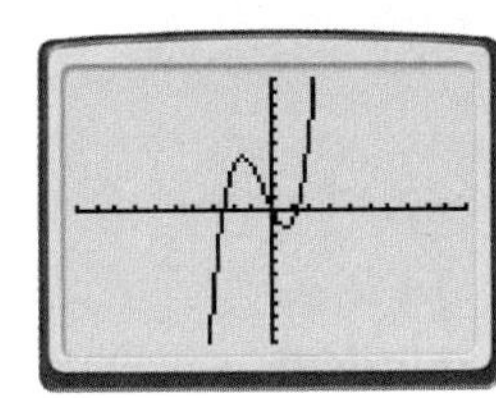

Graph the related function and look for the zeros.

The solutions look reasonable.

Solve each equation. Check your answer.

3a. $(x + 2)^3 = 64$ **2** **3b.** $4x^3 - 12x^2 + 4x = 0$ **3c.** $x^3 + 3x^2 = 10x$ **−5, 0, 2**

3b. $0, \frac{3+\sqrt{5}}{2} \approx 2.62, \frac{3-\sqrt{5}}{2} \approx 0.38$

EXTENSION

Exercises

Graph each cubic function. Identify the intercepts and give the domain and range.

1. $f(x) = x^3 - 2x^2 + 3x + 6$
2. $g(x) = -4x^3 + 2x - 2$

Solve each equation by graphing. Check your answer.

3. $2x^3 - 6x = -4x^2$ **−3, 0, 1**
4. $-3x^3 + 12x^2 + 12x = 48$ **−2, 2, 4**

Solve each equation. Check your answer.

5. $(x - 9)^3 = 64$ **13**
6. $8x + 4x^2 = 4x^3$ **2, −1, 0**
7. $5x^3 + 3x^2 = 4x$

7. $0, \frac{3+\sqrt{89}}{2} \approx 6.22, \frac{3-\sqrt{89}}{2} \approx -3.22$

8. The Send-It Store uses shipping labels that are x in. tall and $2x$ in. wide. Six labels fit on the front of the store's standard shipping box with an area of $3x$ in^2 left over. Three labels fit on the side of the box. The volume of the box is $108x$ in^3. What is the area of one label? **8 in^2**

9. **a.** Graph the functions $f(x) = x^3$, $f(x) = x^3 + 1$, and $f(x) = x^3 + 2$ on the same coordinate plane. Describe any patterns you observe. Predict the shape of the graph of $f(x) = x^3 + c$.

   b. Graph the functions $g(x) = x^3$, $g(x) = (x - 1)^3$, and $g(x) = (x - 2)^3$ on the same coordinate plane. Describe any patterns you observe. Predict the shape of the graph of $g(x) = (x - c)^3$.

Use a graphing calculator to find the approximate solution(s) of each cubic equation. Round to the nearest hundredth.

10. $100x^3 - 40x^2 = 6x$ **−0.12, 0, 0.52**
11. $2x^3 - 5x^2 + 4x = -3$ **−0.45**
12. $-1.32x^3 - 3.65x^2 = -0.43x$ **−2.88, 0, 0.11**
13. $\frac{3}{5}x^3 + x^2 - \frac{1}{2}x = 9$ **2.12**
14. **Critical Thinking** How many zeros can a cubic function have? What does this tell you about the number of real solutions possible for a cubic equation?

14. 1, 2, or 3; a cubic equation will have 1, 2, or 3 real solutions.

Answers

1. x-int.: −1; y-int.: 6; D: all real numbers; R: all real numbers

2. 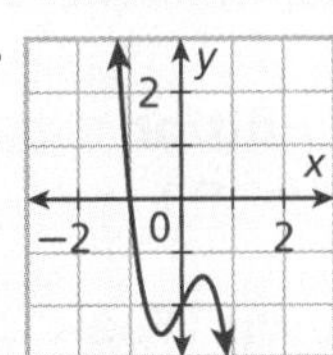

x-int.: −1; y-int.: −2; D: all real numbers; R: all real numbers

9a.

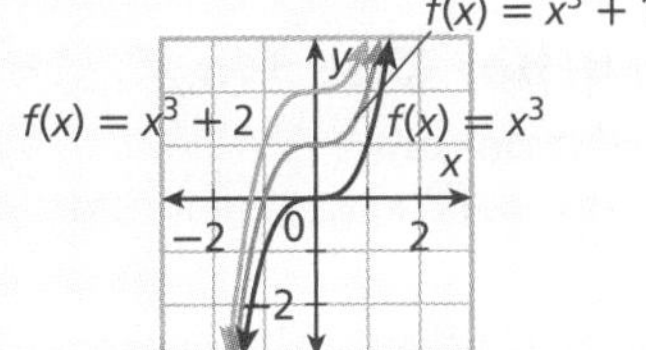

The graphs are the same shape, but each is a vertical translation of the others. The graph of $f(x) = x^3 + c$ will be the graph of $f(x) = x^3$ translated c units vertically.

b.

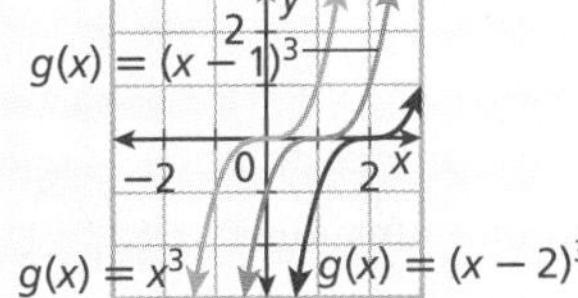

The graphs are the same shape, but each is a horizontal translation of the others. The graph of $g(x) = (x - c)^3$ will be the graph of $g(x) = x^3$ translated c units horizontally.

CHAPTER 9 Study Guide: Review

Organizer

Objective: Help students organize and review key concepts and skills presented in Chapter 9.

Online Edition
Multilingual Glossary

Countdown Week 21

Resources

Teacher One Stop™
PuzzleView
Test & Practice Generator

Multilingual Glossary **Online**
go.hrw.com
KEYWORD: MA7 Glossary

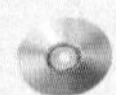

Lesson Tutorial Videos
CD-ROM

Answers

1. vertex
2. minimum; maximum
3. zero of a function
4. discriminant
5. completing the square
6. Yes; it is in standard form.
7. No; $a = 0$
8. Yes; it is in standard form.
9. No; a quadratic function does not have a power of x greater than 2.
10. 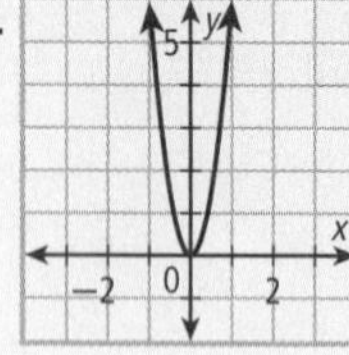
11. 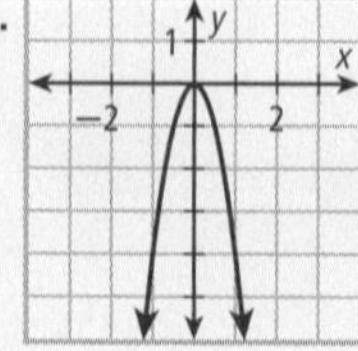

CHAPTER 9

Study Guide: Review

Vocabulary

Complete the sentences below with vocabulary words from the list above.

1. The ___?___ is the highest or lowest point on a parabola.
2. A quadratic function has a ___?___ if its graph opens upward and a ___?___ if its graph opens downward.
3. A ___?___ can also be called an x-intercept of the function.
4. Finding the ___?___ can tell you how many real-number solutions a quadratic equation has.
5. ___?___ is a process that results in a perfect-square trinomial.

9-1 Identifying Quadratic Functions *(pp. 610–617)*

EXAMPLE

■ **Use a table of values to graph $y = -5x^2 + 40x$.**

Step 1 Make a table of values.
Choose values of x and use them to find values of y.

x	0	1	3	4	6	7	8
y	0	35	75	80	60	35	0

Step 2 Plot the points and connect them with a smooth curve.

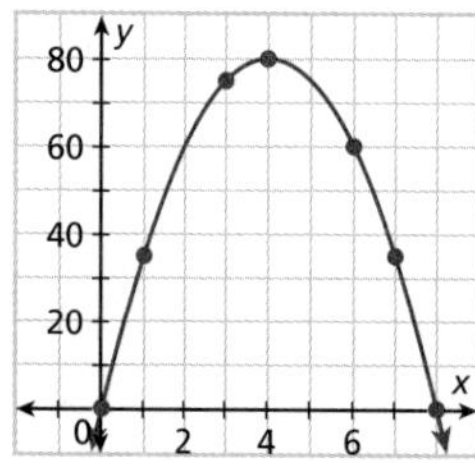

EXERCISES

Tell whether each function is quadratic. Explain.

6. $y = 2x^2 + 9x - 5$
7. $y = -4x + 3$
8. $y = -\frac{1}{2}x^2$
9. $y = 5x^3 + 8$

Use a table of values to graph each quadratic function.

10. $y = 6x^2$
11. $y = -4x^2$
12. $y = \frac{1}{4}x^2$
13. $y = -3x^2$

Tell whether the graph of each function opens upward or downward. Explain.

14. $y = 5x^2 - 12$
15. $y = -x^2 + 3x - 7$
16. Identify the vertex of the parabola. Then give the minimum or maximum value of the function.

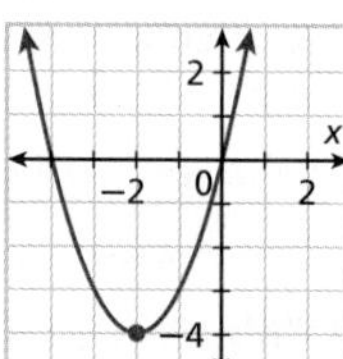

12. 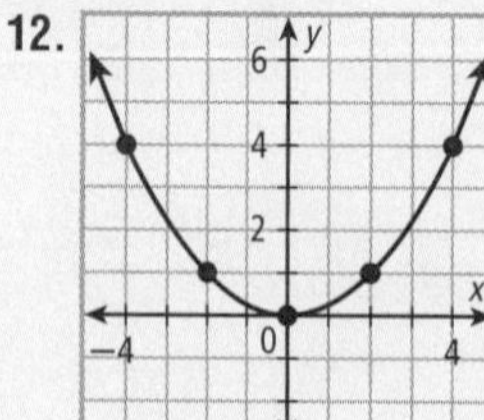

13. 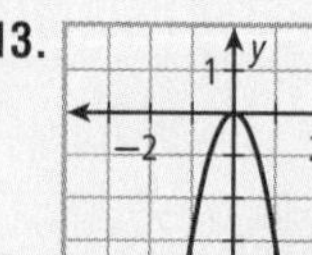

14. Upward; the value of a is positive.
15. Downward; the value of a is negative.
16. $(-2, -4)$; minimum: -4

9-2 Characteristics of Quadratic Functions *(pp. 619–625)*

EXAMPLE

■ **Find the zeros of $y = 2x^2 - 4x - 6$ from its graph. Then find the axis of symmetry and the vertex.**

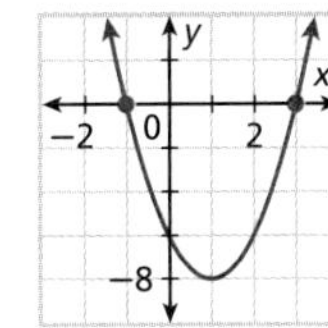

Step 1 Use the graph to find the zeros.
The zeros are −1 and 3.

Step 2 Find the axis of symmetry.

$x = \frac{-1+3}{2} = \frac{2}{2} = 1$ *Find the average of the zeros.*

The axis of symmetry is the vertical line $x = 1$.

Step 3 Find the vertex.

$y = 2x^2 - 4x - 6$
$y = 2(1)^2 - 4(1) - 6$ *Substitute 1 for x to find the y-value of the vertex.*
$y = -8$

The vertex is $(1, -8)$.

EXERCISES

Find the zeros of each quadratic function from its graph. Check your answer.

17. $y = x^2 + 3x - 10$

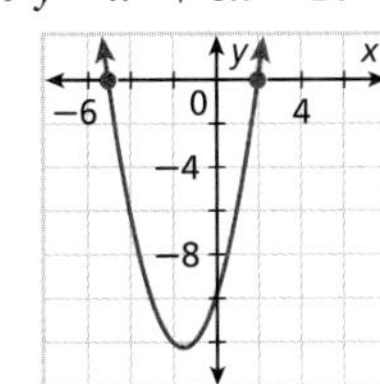

18. $y = x^2 - x - 2$

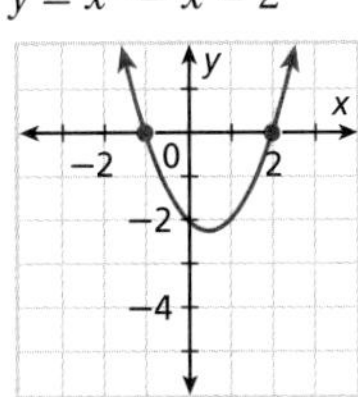

Find the axis of symmetry and vertex of each parabola.

19. $y = -x^2 + 12x - 32$

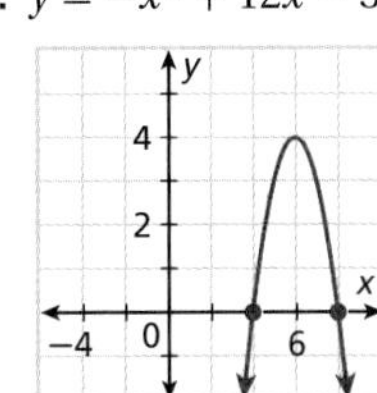

20. $y = 2x^2 + 4x - 16$

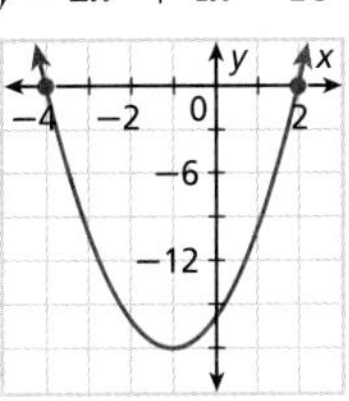

9-3 Graphing Quadratic Functions *(pp. 626–631)*

EXAMPLE

■ **Graph $y = 2x^2 - 8x - 10$.**

Step 1 Find the axis of symmetry.

$x = \frac{-b}{2a} = \frac{-(-8)}{2(2)} = \frac{8}{4} = 2$

The axis of symmetry is $x = 2$.

Step 2 Find the vertex.

$y = 2x^2 - 8x - 10$
$y = 2(2)^2 - 8(2) - 10$
$y = -18$

The vertex is $(2, -18)$.

Step 3 Find the y-intercept.
$c = -10$

Step 4 Find one more point on the graph.

$y = 2(-1)^2 - 8(-1) - 10 = 0$ *Let x = −1.*
Use $(-1, 0)$.

Step 5 Graph the axis of symmetry and the points. **Reflect** the points and connect with a smooth curve.

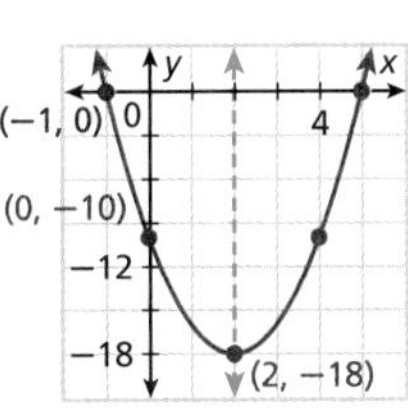

EXERCISES

Graph each quadratic function.

21. $y = x^2 + 6x + 6$

22. $y = x^2 - 4x - 12$

23. $y = x^2 - 8x + 7$

24. $y = 2x^2 - 6x - 8$

25. $3x^2 + 6x = y - 3$

26. $2 - 4x^2 + y = 8x - 10$

27. Water that is sprayed upward from a sprinkler with an initial velocity of 20 m/s can be approximated by the function $y = -5x^2 + 20x$, where y is the height of a drop of water x seconds after it is released. Graph this function. Find the time it takes a drop of water to reach its maximum height, the water's maximum height, and the time it takes the water to reach the ground.

Answers

17. −5, 2

18. −1, 2

19. $x = 6$; $(6, 4)$

20. $x = -1$; $(-1, -18)$

21.

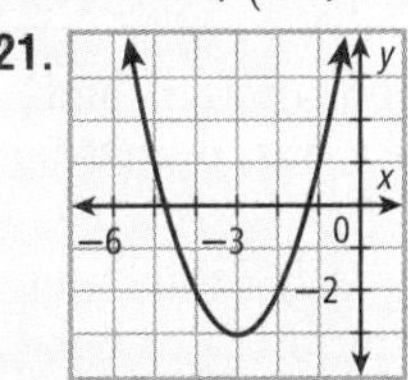

22.

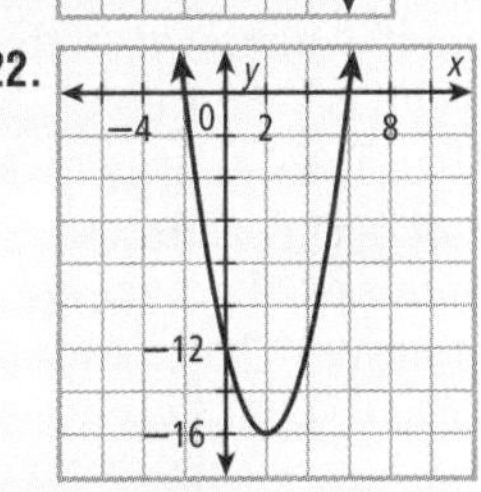

23.

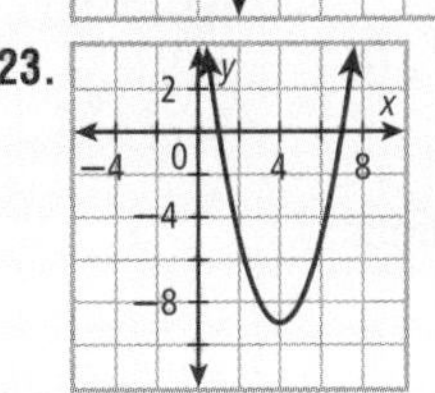

24.

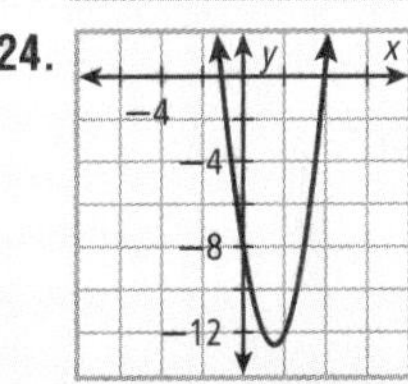

25.

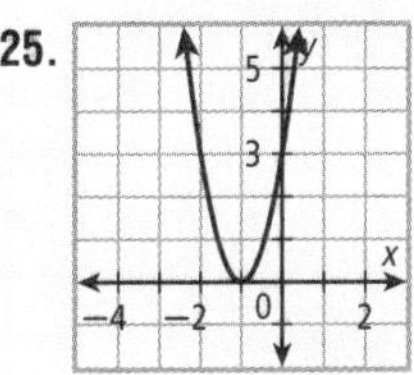

26.

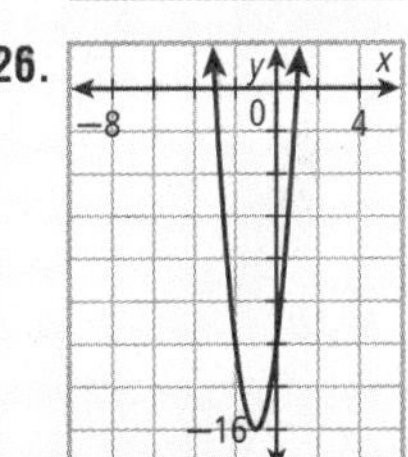

27.

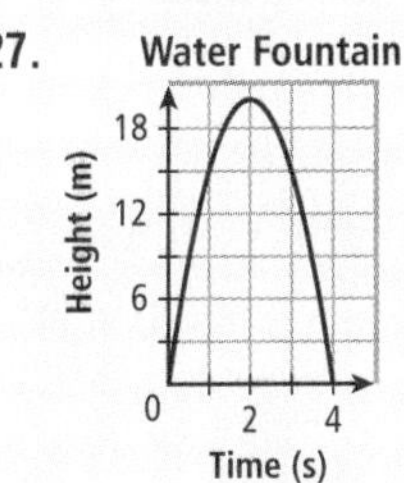

In 2 seconds, the water reaches its maximum height of 20 meters. It takes a total of 4 seconds for the water to reach the ground.

Answers

28. $g(x)$, $f(x)$
29. The graphs have the same width.
30. $h(x)$, $f(x)$, $g(x)$
31. The graph of $g(x)$ has the same width, has the same axis of symmetry, also opens upward, and its vertex is translated 5 units up to $(0, 5)$.
32. The graph of $g(x)$ has the same axis of symmetry, and also opens upward, but it is narrower, and its vertex is translated 1 unit down to $(0, -1)$.
33. The graph of $g(x)$ is narrower, has the same axis of symmetry, also opens upward, and its vertex is translated 3 units up to $(0, 3)$.
34. $x = -3$ or $x = -1$
35. $x = -3$
36. no real solutions
37. $x = 1$ or $x = 5$
38. $x = 4$
39. $x = \pm 1$
40. no real solutions
41. $x = -5$ or $x = -1$
42. $x = -7$ or $x = -2$
43. $x = -3$ or $x = 5$
44. $x = -1$ or $x = 2$
45. $x = -5$
46. $x = 4.5$
47. $x^2 + 2x = 48$; 6 ft

9-4 Transforming Quadratic Functions *(pp. 633–639)*

EXAMPLE

- **Compare the graph of $g(x) = 3x^2 - 4$ with the graph of $f(x) = x^2$. Use the functions.**
  - Both graphs open upward because $a > 0$.
  - The axis of symmetry is the same, $x = 0$, because $b = 0$ in both functions.
  - The graph of $g(x)$ is narrower than the graph of $f(x)$ because $|3| > |1|$.
  - The vertex of $f(x)$ is $(0, 0)$. The vertex of $g(x)$ is translated 4 units down to $(0, -4)$.
  - $f(x)$ has one zero at the origin. $g(x)$ has two zeros because the vertex is below the origin and the parabola opens upward.

EXERCISES

Compare the widths of the graphs of the given quadratic functions. Order functions with different widths from narrowest graph to widest.

28. $f(x) = 2x^2$, $g(x) = 4x^2$
29. $f(x) = 6x^2$, $g(x) = -6x^2$
30. $f(x) = x^2$, $g(x) = \frac{1}{3}x^2$, $h(x) = 3x^2$

Compare the graph of each function with the graph of $f(x) = x^2$.

31. $g(x) = x^2 + 5$
32. $g(x) = 3x^2 - 1$
33. $g(x) = 2x^2 + 3$

9-5 Solving Quadratic Equations by Graphing *(pp. 642–647)*

EXAMPLE

- **Solve $-4 = 4x^2 - 8x$ by graphing the related function.**

Step 1 Write the equation in standard form.

$$0 = 4x^2 - 8x + 4$$

Step 2 Graph the related function.

$$y = 4x^2 - 8x + 4$$

Step 3 Find the zeros.
The only zero is 1. The solution is $x = 1$.

EXERCISES

Solve each equation by graphing the related function.

34. $0 = x^2 + 4x + 3$
35. $0 = x^2 + 6x + 9$
36. $-4x^2 = 3$
37. $x^2 + 5 = 6x$
38. $-4x^2 = 64 - 32x$
39. $9 = 9x^2$
40. $-3x^2 + 2x = 5$

9-6 Solving Quadratic Equations by Factoring *(pp. 650–655)*

EXAMPLE

- **Solve $3x^2 - 6x = 24$ by factoring.**

$3x^2 - 6x = 24$	*Write the equation in standard form.*
$3x^2 - 6x - 24 = 0$	
$3(x^2 - 2x - 8) = 0$	*Factor out 3.*
$3(x + 2)(x - 4) = 0$	*Factor the trinomial.*
$3 \neq 0$, $x + 2 = 0$ or $x - 4 = 0$	*Zero Product Property*
$x = -2$ or $x = 4$	*Solve each equation.*

EXERCISES

Solve each quadratic equation by factoring.

41. $x^2 + 6x + 5 = 0$
42. $x^2 + 9x + 14 = 0$
43. $x^2 - 2x - 15 = 0$
44. $2x^2 - 2x - 4 = 0$
45. $x^2 + 10x + 25 = 0$
46. $4x^2 - 36x = -81$
47. A rectangle is 2 feet longer than it is wide. The area of the rectangle is 48 square feet. Write and solve an equation that can be used to find the width of the rectangle.

9-7 Solving Quadratic Equations by Using Square Roots (pp. 656–661)

EXAMPLE

■ **Solve $2x^2 = 98$ using square roots.**

$\frac{2x^2}{2} = \frac{98}{2}$ *Divide both sides of the equation by 2 to isolate x^2.*

$x^2 = 49$

$x = \pm\sqrt{49}$ *Take the square root of both sides.*

$x = \pm 7$ *Use ± to show both roots.*

The solutions are −7 and 7.

EXERCISES

Solve using square roots.

48. $5x^2 = 320$

49. $-x^2 + 144 = 0$

50. $x^2 = -16$

51. $x^2 + 7 = 7$

52. $2x^2 = 50$

53. $4x^2 = 25$

54. A rectangle is twice as long as it is wide. The area of the rectangle is 32 square feet. Find the rectangle's width.

9-8 Completing the Square (pp. 663–669)

EXAMPLE

■ **Solve $x^2 - 6x = -5$ by completing the square.**

$\left(\frac{-6}{2}\right)^2 = 9$ *Find $\left(\frac{b}{2}\right)^2$.*

$x^2 - 6x + 9 = -5 + 9$ *Complete the square by adding $\left(\frac{b}{2}\right)^2$ to both sides.*

$x^2 - 6x + 9 = 4$

$(x-3)^2 = 4$ *Factor the trinomial.*

$x - 3 = \pm\sqrt{4}$ *Take the square root of both sides.*

$x - 3 = \pm 2$ *Use the ± symbol.*

$x - 3 = 2$ or $x - 3 = -2$ *Solve each equation.*

$x = 5$ or $x = 1$

The solutions are 5 and 1.

EXERCISES

Solve by completing the square.

55. $x^2 + 2x = 48$

56. $x^2 + 4x = 21$

57. $2x^2 - 12x + 10 = 0$

58. $x^2 - 10x = -20$

59. A homeowner is planning an addition to her house. She wants the new family room to be a rectangle with an area of 192 square feet. The contractor says that the length needs to be 4 more feet than the width. What will the dimensions of the new room be?

9-9 The Quadratic Formula and the Discriminant (pp. 670–677)

EXAMPLE

■ **Solve $x^2 + 4x + 4 = 0$ using the Quadratic Formula.**

The equation $x^2 + 4x + 4 = 0$ is in standard form with $a = 1$, $b = 4$, and $c = 4$.

$x = \frac{-b \pm \sqrt{b^2 - 4ac}}{2a}$ *Write the Quadratic Formula.*

$= \frac{-4 \pm \sqrt{4^2 - 4(1)(4)}}{2(1)}$ *Substitute for a, b, and c.*

$= \frac{-4 \pm \sqrt{16 - 16}}{2}$ *Simplify.*

$= \frac{-4 \pm \sqrt{0}}{2} = \frac{-4}{2} = -2$

The solution is $x = -2$.

EXERCISES

Solve using the Quadratic Formula.

60. $x^2 - 5x - 6 = 0$

61. $2x^2 - 9x - 5 = 0$

62. $4x^2 - 8x + 4 = 0$

63. $x^2 - 6x = -7$

Find the number of real solutions of each equation using the discriminant.

64. $x^2 - 12x + 36 = 0$

65. $3x^2 + 5 = 0$

66. $2x^2 - 13x = -20$

67. $6x^2 - 20 = 15x + 1$

Answers

48. $x = \pm 8$
49. $x = \pm 12$
50. no real solutions
51. $x = 0$
52. $x = \pm 5$
53. $x = \pm\frac{5}{2}$
54. 4 ft
55. $x = -8$ or $x = 6$
56. $x = -7$ or $x = 3$
57. $x = 1$ or $x = 5$
58. $x = 5 \pm \sqrt{5}$
59. 16 ft by 12 ft
60. $x = -1$ or $x = 6$
61. $x = -\frac{1}{2}$ or $x = 5$
62. $x = 1$
63. $x = \frac{6 \pm \sqrt{8}}{2}$
64. 1
65. 0
66. 2
67. 2

Study Guide: Review 687

Organizer

Objective: Assess students' mastery of concepts and skills in Chapter 9.

Online Edition

Resources

Assessment Resources

Chapter 9 Tests

- Free Response (Levels A, B, C)
- Multiple Choice (Levels A, B, C)
- Performance Assessment

Teacher One Stop™
Test & Practice Generator

State Resources

Tell whether each function is quadratic. Explain.

1. $\{(10, 50), (11, 71), (12, 94), (13, 119), (14, 146)\}$
2. $3x^2 + y = 4 + 3x^2$ **No; $a = 0$**
3. Tell whether the graph of $y = -2x^2 + 7x - 5$ opens upward or downward and whether the parabola has a maximum or a minimum. **downward; maximum**
4. Estimate the zeros of the quadratic function.

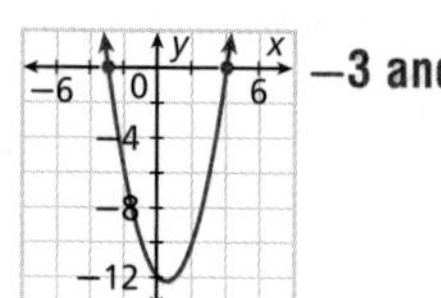

−3 and 4

5. Find the axis of symmetry of the parabola.

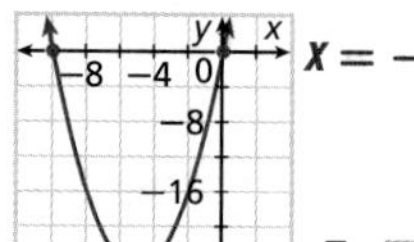

$x = -5$

6. Find the vertex of the graph of $y = x^2 + 6x + 8$. **(−3, −1)**
7. Graph the quadratic function $y = x^2 - 4x + 2$.

Compare the graph of each function with the graph of $f(x) = x^2$.

8. $g(x) = -x^2 - 2$
9. $h(x) = \frac{1}{3}x^2 + 1$
10. $g(x) = 3x^2 - 4$
11. A hammer is dropped from a 40-foot scaffold. Another one is dropped from a 60-foot scaffold.
    a. Write the two height functions and compare their graphs. Use $h(t) = -16t^2 + c$, where c is the height of the scaffold.
    b. Use the graphs to estimate when each hammer will reach the ground. **about 1.6 s and about 1.9 s**
12. A rocket is launched with an initial vertical velocity of 110 m/s. The height of the rocket in meters is approximated by the quadratic equation $h = -5t^2 + 110t$ where t is the time after launch in seconds. About how long does it take for the rocket to return to the ground? **about 22 s**

Solve each quadratic equation by factoring.

13. $x^2 + 6x + 5 = 0$ **−5, −1**
14. $x^2 - 12x = -36$ **6**
15. $x^2 - 81 = 0$ **−9, 9**

Solve by using square roots.

16. $-2x^2 = -72$ **± 6**
17. $9x^2 - 49 = 0$ **$\pm\frac{7}{3}$**
18. $3x^2 + 12 = 0$ **no real solutions**

Solve by completing the square.

19. $x^2 + 10x = -21$ **−7, −3**
20. $x^2 - 6x + 4 = 0$ **$3 \pm \sqrt{5}$**
21. $2x^2 + 16x = 0$ **−8, 0**
22. A landscaper has enough cement to make a rectangular patio with an area of 150 square feet. The homeowner wants the length to be 6 feet longer than the width. What dimensions should be used for the patio? Round to the nearest tenth of a foot. **9.6 ft by 15.6 ft**

Solve each quadratic equation. Round to the nearest hundredth if necessary.

23. $x^2 + 3x - 40 = 0$ **−8, 5**
24. $2x^2 + 7x = -5$ **$-\frac{5}{2}, -1$**
25. $8x^2 + 3x - 1 = 0$ **$\approx -0.59, \approx 0.21$**

Find the number of real solutions of each equation using the discriminant.

26. $4x^2 - 4x + 1 = 0$ **1**
27. $2x^2 + 5x - 25 = 0$ **2**
28. $\frac{1}{2}x^2 + 8 = 0$ **no real solutions**

Answers

1. Yes; the second differences of the y-coordinates are constant.
8. The graph of $g(x)$ is the same width, has the same axis of symmetry, opens downward, and its vertex is translated 2 units down to (0, −2.)
9. The graph of $h(x)$ is wider, has the same axis of symmetry, opens upward, and its vertex is translated 1 unit up.
10. The graph of $g(x)$ is narrower, has the same axis of symmetry, opens upward, and its vertex is translated 4 units down.

11a. $h_1(t) = -16t^2 + 40$; $h_2(t) = -16t^2 + 60$; The graph of h_2 is a vertical translation of h_1. The y-intercept of the graph of h_2 is 20 units higher.

COLLEGE ENTRANCE EXAM PRACTICE

FOCUS ON SAT SUBJECT TESTS

In addition to the SAT, some colleges require the SAT Subject Tests for admission. Colleges that don't require the SAT Subject Tests may still use the scores to learn about your academic background and to place you in the appropriate college math class.

Take the SAT Subject Test in mathematics while the material is still fresh in your mind. You are not expected to be familiar with all of the test content, but you should have completed at least three years of college-prep math.

You may want to time yourself as you take this practice test. It should take you about 6 minutes to complete.

1. The graph below corresponds to which of the following quadratic functions?

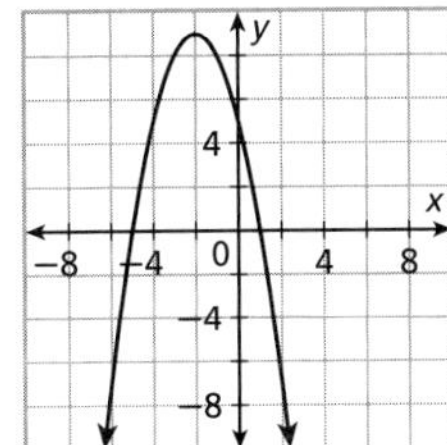

(A) $f(x) = x^2 + 4x - 5$

(B) $f(x) = -x^2 - 4x + 3$

(C) $f(x) = -x^2 + 5x - 4$

(D) $f(x) = -x^2 - 4x + 5$

(E) $f(x) = -x^2 - 3x + 5$

2. What is the sum of the solutions to the equation $9x^2 - 6x = 8$?

(A) $\frac{4}{3}$

(B) $\frac{2}{3}$

(C) $\frac{1}{3}$

(D) $-\frac{2}{3}$

(E) $-\frac{8}{3}$

3. If $h(x) = ax^2 + bx + c$, where $b^2 - 4ac < 0$ and $a < 0$, which of the following statements must be true?

   I. The graph of $h(x)$ has no points in the first or second quadrants.

   II. The graph of $h(x)$ has no points in the third or fourth quadrants.

   III. The graph of $h(x)$ has points in all quadrants.

(A) I only

(B) II only

(C) III only

(D) I and II only

(E) None of the statements are true.

4. What is the axis of symmetry for the graph of a quadratic function whose zeros are −2 and 4?

(A) $x = -2$

(B) $x = 0$

(C) $x = 1$

(D) $x = 2$

(E) $x = 6$

5. How many real-number solutions does $0 = x^2 - 7x + 1$ have?

(A) None

(B) One

(C) Two

(D) All real numbers

(E) It is impossible to determine.

Organizer

Objective: Provide practice for college entrance exams such as the SAT Mathematics Subject Tests.

Resources

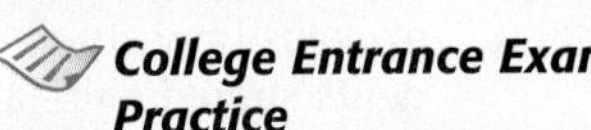

College Entrance Exam Practice

Questions on the SAT Mathematics Subject Tests Levels 1 and 2 represent the following math content areas:

	Level	
	1	2
Number and Operations	10–14%	10–14%
Algebra and Functions	38–42%	48–52%
Geometry and Measurement	38–42%	28–32%
Plane Euclidean	18–22%	0%
Coordinate	8–12%	10–14%
Three-dimensional	4–6%	4–6%
Trigonometry	6–8%	12–16%
Data Analysis, Statistics, and Probability	6–10%	6–10%

Items on this page focus on:

- Algebra and Functions

Text References:

Item	1	2	3	4	5
Lesson	9-3	9-8	9-9	9-2	9-9

TEST PREP DOCTOR

1. Students who chose **B** found the correct axis of symmetry but not the correct vertex or *y*-intercept. Students who chose **E** found the correct *y*-intercept but did not find the correct axis of symmetry.
2. Students who chose **A** or **D** found just one of the solutions of the equation. Students who chose **E** may have tried to find the product of the solutions of the equation.
3. Students who chose **B** did not use the fact that $a < 0$. Students who chose **D** may not realize that if statements I and II are both true, then the graph of $h(x)$ is restricted to the axes.
4. Students who chose **E** found the distance between $x = -2$ and $x = 4$, not the vertical line halfway between them. Students who chose **A** might not understand the meaning of the axis of symmetry.
5. Students who chose **E** did not realize that the graph or the discriminant could be used to determine the answer. Students who chose **A** or **B** may have made a computational error in finding the discriminant or may not have applied it correctly.

Organizer

Objective: Provide opportunities to learn and practice common test-taking strategies.

Online Edition

This Test Tackler explains how students should write an explanation to an extended-response test item. Students need to be aware that even if their calculations are correct, the item will not receive full credit if their explanation does not clearly support their work.

Give students a problem from the chapter. Once students work through the problem, have them explain out loud to a partner how they determined their answer. When students are comfortable doing this, have them write it down in paragraph form. Guide students to use complete sentences.

As students rewrite the response in **Problem 5,** encourage them to write neatly. If students are struggling with forming complete sentences, have them list their thought process in bulleted form.

Extended Response: Explain Your Reasoning

Extended response test items often include multipart questions that evaluate your understanding of a math concept. To receive full credit, you must answer the problem correctly, show all of your work, and explain your reasoning. Use complete sentences and show your problem-solving method clearly.

EXAMPLE 1

Extended Response **Given $\frac{1}{2}x^2 + y = 4x - 3$ and $y = 2x - 12x$, identify which is a quadratic function. Provide an explanation for your decision. For the quadratic function, tell whether the graph of the function opens upward or downward and whether the parabola has a maximum or a minimum. Explain your reasoning.**

Read the solutions provided by two different students.

Student A

The quadratic function is $\frac{1}{2}x^2 + y = 4x - 3$ because it can be written in standard form, $y = -\frac{1}{2}x^2 + 4x - 3$, where a, b, and c are real numbers and $a \neq 0$. The other function, $y = 2x - 12x$, is not quadratic because there is no x^2- term.

The graph of this function will open downward because a, which is equal to $-\frac{1}{2}$, is less than 0. Because the parabola opens downward, the graph will have a maximum.

Excellent explanation

The response includes the correct answers along with a detailed explanation for each part of the problem. The explanation is written using complete sentences and is presented in an order that is easy to follow and to understand. It is obvious that this student knows how to determine and interpret a quadratic function.

Student B

$\frac{1}{2}x^2 + y = 4x - 3$ There is an x^2.

When I graphed the function on my calculator, I saw a parabola that opened downward.

It had a maximum.

Poor explanation

The response includes the correct answers, but the explanation does not include details. The reason for defining the function as quadratic does not show knowledge of the concept. The student shows a lack of understanding of how to write and interpret a quadratic function in standard form.

Include as many details as possible to support your reasoning. This increases the chance of getting full credit for your response.

Read each test item and answer the questions that follow.

Item A
The height y in feet of a tennis ball x seconds after it is ejected from a serving machine is given by the ordered pairs $\{(0, 10), (0.5, 9), (1, 7), (1.5, 4), (2, 0)\}$. Determine whether the function is quadratic. Find its domain and range. Explain your answers.

1. What should a student include in the explanation to receive full credit?
2. Read the two explanations below. Which explanation is better? Why?

Student A

Range: $0 \le y \le 10$ Domain: $0 \le x \le 2$
Second differences are -1 : quadratic

Student B

The function is quadratic because the second differences are constant: -1. The domain and range are determined by the points $(0, 10)$ and $(2, 0)$. The range is $0 \le y \le 10$, and the domain is $0 \le x \le 2$.

Item B
The height of a golf ball can be approximated by the function $y = -5x^2 + 20x + 8$, where y is the height in meters above the ground and x is the time in seconds after the ball is hit. What is the maximum height of the ball? How long does it take for the ball to reach its maximum height? Explain.

3. A student correctly found the following answers. Use this information to write a clear and concise explanation.

Axis of symmetry is the vertical line at $x = 2$.
Vertex is at $(2, 28)$.
28 meters; 2 seconds

Item C
A science teacher set off a bottle rocket as part of a lab experiment. The function $h = -16t^2 + 96t$ represents the height in feet of a rocket that is shot out of a bottle with an initial vertical velocity of 96 feet per second. Find the time that the rocket is in the air. Explain how you found your answer.

4. Read the two responses below.
   a. Which student provided the better explanation? Why?
   b. What advice would you give the other student to improve his or her explanation?

Student C

Graph the function $h = -16t^2 + 96t$, and then find the zeros. The first zero is when $t = 0$, when the rocket is launched. The second zero is when the rocket hits the ground: $t = 6$. The difference between 6 and 0 is the time that the rocket is in the air: 6 seconds.

Student D

6 seconds.
Graph the function to find how long the rocket is in the air, and find the values where it crosses the x-axis.

Item D
The base of a parallelogram is 12 centimeters more than its height. The area of the parallelogram is 13 square centimeters. Explain how to determine the height and base of the figure. What is the height? What is the base?

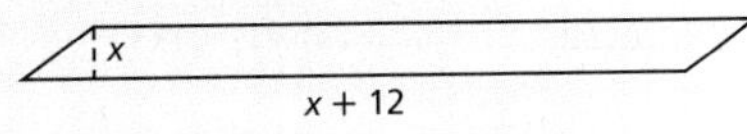

5. Read the following response. Identify any areas that need improvement. Rewrite the response so that it will receive full credit.

$x^2 + 12x + 36 = 49$ Complete the square.
$(x+6)^2 = 49$
$x + 6 = \sqrt{49}$
$x + 6 = \pm 7$; $x = 1$ or -13

base = 13, height = 1

Answers

Possible answers:

1. A student should include whether the function is quadratic, a table supporting the claim with 1st and 2nd differences in the y-values, the values of the domain and range, and an explanation of what the domain and range represent.
2. Student B gave the better explanation. It is written in complete sentences, and the thought process is clear. All parts of the question are explained thoroughly. Student A's explanation is out of order, it is not in complete sentences, and there is not enough support for the answers.
3. To find the axis of symmetry, substitute -5 for a and 20 for b in the formula $x = -\frac{b}{2a}$.
   $x = -\frac{20}{2(-5)}$
   $x = 2$
   To find the y-coordinate of the vertex, find the value of y when $x = 2$.
   $y = -5(2)^2 + 20(2) + 8$
   $y = 28$
   The vertex is $(2, 28)$. The ball reaches its maximum height of 28 m in 2 s.

4a. Student C provided the better explanation. This student used complete sentences and gave specific information about the solution of the problem.

b. I would advise student D to give more details to ensure that the answer could be found using his or her explanation. Also, I would advise student D to mention graphing the function and what the zeros of the function relate to.

State Resources

5. The response should include an explanation of how to determine the height and base of the figure. Units should be included. Use the area formula to write an equation.
   $A = bh = (x + 12)x = 13 \rightarrow x^2 + 12x = 13$. Solve for x, the height, by completing the square.
   $x^2 + 12x + 36 = 49$
   $(x + 6)^2 = 49$
   $x + 6 = \pm\sqrt{49}$
   $x + 6 = \pm 7$; $x = 1$ or $x = -13$
   The height is 1 cm and the base is $x + 12$, or 13 cm. The value of -13 for x can be eliminated because the height cannot be negative.

Answers to Test Items

A. yes; D: $0 \le x \le 2$; R: $0 \le y \le 10$
B. 28 m; 2 s
C. 6 s
D. $h = 1$ cm; $b = 13$ cm

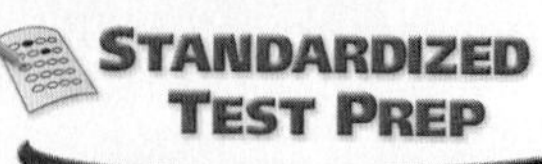

Organizer

Objective: Provide review and practice for Chapters 1–9 and standardized tests.

Resources

Assessment Resources

Chapter 9 Cumulative Test

go.hrw.com
KEYWORD: MA7 TestPrep

State Resources

CUMULATIVE ASSESSMENT, CHAPTERS 1–9

Multiple Choice

1. Which expression is NOT equal to the other three?

Ⓐ 0^1 Ⓒ 1^0
Ⓑ 1^1 Ⓓ $(-1)^0$

2. Which function's graph is a translation of the graph of $f(x) = 3x^2 + 4$ seven units down?

Ⓕ $f(x) = -4x^2 + 4$
Ⓖ $f(x) = 10x^2 + 4$
Ⓗ $f(x) = 3x^2 - 3$
Ⓙ $f(x) = 3x^2 + 11$

3. The area of a circle in square units is $\pi(9x^2 + 42x + 49)$. Which expression represents the circumference of the circle in units?

Ⓐ $\pi(3x + 7)$
Ⓑ $2\pi(3x + 7)$
Ⓒ $2\pi(3x + 7)^2$
Ⓓ $6x + 14$

4. CyberCafe charges a computer station rental fee of \$5, plus \$0.20 for each quarter-hour spent surfing. Which expression represents the total amount Carl will pay to use a computer station for three and a half hours?

Ⓕ $5 + 0.20(3.5)$
Ⓖ $5 + 0.20(3.5)(4)$
Ⓗ $5 + \frac{0.20}{3.5 \div 4}$
Ⓙ $5 + \frac{1}{4} \cdot \frac{0.20}{3.5}$

5. What is the numerical solution to the equation *five less than three times a number equals four more than eight times the number?*

Ⓐ $-\frac{9}{5}$ Ⓒ $\frac{1}{11}$
Ⓑ $-\frac{1}{5}$ Ⓓ $\frac{1}{5}$

6. Which is a possible situation for the graph?

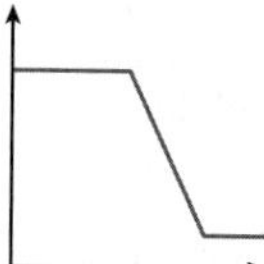

Ⓕ A car travels at a steady speed, slows down in a school zone, and then resumes its previous speed.
Ⓖ A child climbs the ladder of a slide and then slides down.
Ⓗ A person flies in an airplane for a while, parachutes out, and gets stuck in a tree.
Ⓙ The number of visitors increases in the summer, declines in the fall, and levels off in the winter.

7. Which of the following is the graph of $f(x) = -x^2 + 2$?

Ⓐ
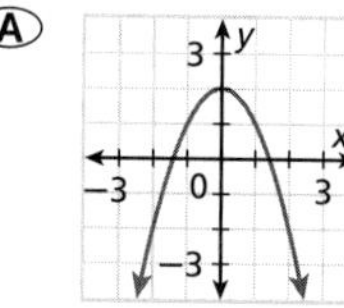

Ⓒ
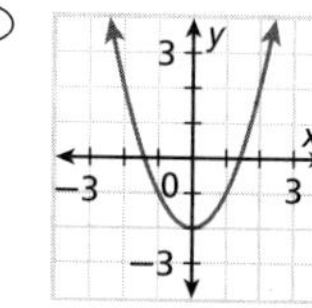

Ⓑ
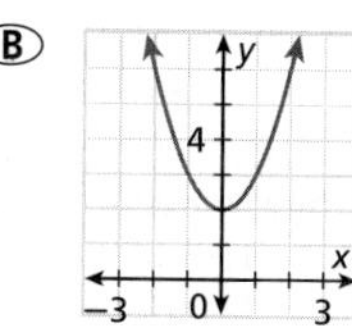

Ⓓ
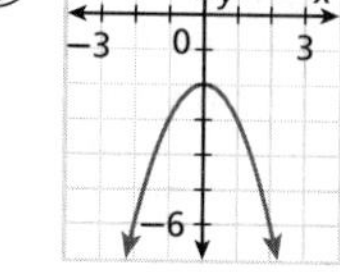

8. The value of y varies directly with x, and $y = 40$ when $x = -5$. Find y when $x = 8$.

Ⓕ 25 Ⓗ −8
Ⓖ −1 Ⓙ −64

9. What is the slope of the line that passes through the points $(4, 7)$ and $(5, 3)$?

Ⓐ 4 Ⓒ $-\frac{1}{4}$
Ⓑ $\frac{1}{4}$ Ⓓ −4

Answers

1. A
2. H
3. B
4. G
5. A
6. H
7. A
8. J
9. D
10. H
11. D
12. G
13. 4
14. 41
15. 2.69
16. 1

The problems on many standardized tests are ordered from least to most difficult, but all items are usually worth the same amount of points. If you are stuck on a question near the end of the test, your time may be better spent rechecking your answers to earlier questions.

10. Putting Green Mini Golf charges a $4 golf club rental fee plus $1.25 per game. Good Times Golf charges a $1.25 golf club rental fee plus $3.75 per game. Which system of equations could be solved to determine for how many games the cost is the same at both places?

(F) $\begin{cases} y = 4x + 1.25 \\ y = 3.75 + 1.25x \end{cases}$

(G) $\begin{cases} y = 4 - 1.25x \\ y = -3.75 + 1.25x \end{cases}$

(H) $\begin{cases} y = 1.25x + 4 \\ y = 3.75x + 1.25 \end{cases}$

(J) $\begin{cases} y = 1.25x - 4 \\ y = 1.25x + 3.75 \end{cases}$

11. The graph of which quadratic function has an axis of symmetry of $x = -2$?

(A) $y = 2x^2 - x + 3$

(B) $y = 4x^2 + 2x + 3$

(C) $y = x^2 - 2x + 3$

(D) $y = x^2 + 4x + 3$

12. Which polynomial is the product of $x - 4$ and $x^2 - 4x + 1$?

(F) $-4x^2 + 17x - 4$

(G) $x^3 - 8x^2 + 17x - 4$

(H) $x^3 + 17x - 4$

(J) $x^3 - 15x + 4$

Gridded Response

13. The length of a rectangle is 2 units greater than the width. The area of the rectangle is 24 square units. What is its width in units?

14. Find the value of the discriminant of the equation $0 = -2x^2 + 3x + 4$.

15. What is the positive solution of $4x^2 = 10x + 2$? Round your answer to the nearest hundredth if necessary.

Short Response

16. The data in the table shows ordered pair solutions to a linear function. Find the missing y-value. Show your work.

x	y
−2	−7
−1	−3
0	
1	5
2	9

17. Answer the following questions using the function $f(x) = 2x^2 + 4x - 1$.

a. Make a table of values and give five points on the graph.

b. Find the axis of symmetry and vertex. Show all calculations.

18. a. Show how to solve $x^2 - 2x - 8 = 0$ by graphing the related function. Show all your work.

b. Show another way to solve the equation in part **a**. Show all your work.

19. What can you say about the value of a if the graph of $y = ax^2 - 8$ has no x-intercepts? Explain.

Extended Response

20. The graph shows the quadratic function $f(x) = ax^2 + bx + c$.

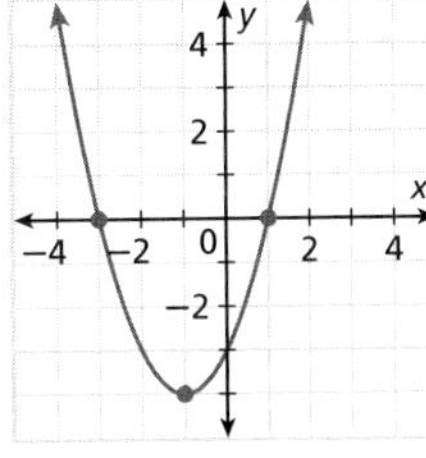

a. What are the solutions of the equation $0 = ax^2 + bx + c$? Explain how you know.

b. If the point $(-5, 12)$ lies on the graph of $f(x)$, the point $(a, 12)$ also lies on the graph. Find the value of a.

c. What do you know about the relationship between the values of a and b? Use the coordinates of the vertex in your explanation.

d. Use what you know about solving quadratic equations by factoring to make a conjecture about the values of a, b, and c in the function $f(x) = ax^2 + bx + c$.

Short-Response Rubric

Items 17–19

2 Points = The student's answer is an accurate and complete execution of the task or tasks.

1 Point = The student's answer contains attributes of an appropriate response but is flawed.

0 Points = The student's answer contains no attributes of an appropriate response.

Extended-Response Rubric

Item 20

4 Points = The student writes the correct solutions and an explanation in part **a,** gives a correct x-value and correct explanation in part **b,** explains the relationship between a and b and uses the vertex in the explanation in part **c,** and uses solutions to find factors and the values for a, b, and c in part **d.**

3 Points = The student writes the correct solutions and an explanation in part **a,** gives a correct x-value and some explanation in part **b,** explains the relationship between a and b with minor errors and uses the vertex in the explanation in part **c,** and uses solutions to find factors and the values for a, b, and c in part **d.**

2 Points = The student writes one correct solution with some explanation in part **a,** gives a correct x-value and some explanation in part **b,** explains the relationship between a and b with minor errors and does not use the vertex in the explanation in part **c,** and uses solutions to find only one factor and does not find the values for a, b, and c in part **d;** or the student attempts to answer all parts of the problem and answers two correctly.

1 Point = The student answers one part correctly but does not attempt all parts, or the student attempts to answer all parts of the problem but does not correctly answer any part.

0 Points = The student does not answer correctly and does not attempt all parts of the problem.

Answers

17a. Possible answer:

x	−3	−1	0	1	2
y	5	−3	−1	5	15

b. $x = -1$; $(-1, -3)$

18a. −2, 4

b. Check students' work.

19. $a < 0$

20a. −3, 1

b. $a = 3$

c. $b = 2a$

d. If the solutions are −3 and 1, then $(x + 3)(x - 1) = 0$. So the equation is $x^2 + 2x - 3 = 0$, and $a = 1$, $b = 2$, and $c = -3$.

Data Analysis and Probability

Section 10A	
Data Analysis	
Connecting Algebra to Data Analysis	Bar and Circle Graphs
10-1	**Organizing and Displaying Data**
10-2	**Frequency and Histograms**
10-3	**Data Distributions**
10-3	**Technology Lab** Use Technology to Make Graphs
10-4	**Misleading Graphs and Statistics**
Connecting Algebra to Data Analysis	Sampling and Bias

Section 10B	
Probability	
10-5	**Algebra Lab** Simulations
10-5	**Experimental Probability**
10-5	**Technology Lab** Use Random Numbers
10-6	**Theoretical Probability**
10-7	**Independent and Dependent Events**
10-7	**Algebra Lab** Compound Events
10-8	**Combinations and Permutations**
EXTENSION	**Matrices**

Pacing Guide for 45-Minute Classes

Teacher One Stop™
Calendar Planner®

Chapter 10

Countdown Weeks 22, 23, 24

DAY 1	DAY 2	DAY 3	DAY 4	DAY 5
Connecting Algebra to Data Analysis	10-1 Lesson	10-2 Lesson	10-3 Lesson	10-3 Technology Lab 10-4 Lesson
DAY 6	**DAY 7**	**DAY 8**	**DAY 9**	**DAY 10**
10-4 Lesson Connecting Algebra to Data Analysis	Multi-Step Test Prep Ready to Go On?	10-5 Algebra Lab 10-5 Lesson	10-5 Lesson 10-5 Technology Lab	10-6 Lesson
DAY 11	**DAY 12**	**DAY 13**	**DAY 14**	**DAY 15**
10-7 Lesson	10-7 Algebra Lab 10-8 Lesson	10-8 Lesson	Multi-Step Test Prep Ready to Go On?	EXTENSION
DAY 16	**DAY 17**			
Chapter 10 Review	Chapter 10 Test			

Pacing Guide for 90-Minute Classes

Teacher One Stop™
Calendar Planner®

Chapter 10

DAY 1	DAY 2	DAY 3	DAY 4	DAY 5
Chapter 9 Test Connecting Algebra to Data Analysis	10-1 Lesson 10-2 Lesson	10-3 Lesson 10-3 Technology Lab 10-4 Lesson	10-4 Lesson Connecting Algebra to Data Analysis Multi-Step Test Prep Ready to Go On?	10-5 Algebra Lab 10-5 Lesson 10-5 Technology Lab
DAY 6	**DAY 7**	**DAY 8**	**DAY 9**	
10-6 Lesson 10-7 Lesson	10-7 Algebra Lab 10-8 Lesson	Multi-Step Test Prep Ready to Go On? EXTENSION	Chapter 10 Review Chapter 10 Test	

ONGOING ASSESSMENT and INTERVENTION

	DIAGNOSE	PRESCRIBE
Assess Prior Knowledge	**Before Chapter 10**	
	Diagnose readiness for the chapter.	Prescribe intervention.
	Are You Ready? SE p. 695	***Are You Ready? Intervention***
Formative Assessment	**Before Every Lesson**	
	Diagnose readiness for the lesson.	Prescribe intervention.
	Warm Up TE	**Reteach** CRB
	During Every Lesson	
	Diagnose understanding of lesson concepts.	Prescribe intervention.
	Check It Out! SE	**Reading Strategies** CRB
	Questioning Strategies TE	***Success for Every Learner***
	Think and Discuss SE	***Lesson Tutorial Videos***
	Write About It SE	
	Journal TE	
	After Every Lesson	
	Diagnose mastery of lesson concepts.	Prescribe intervention.
	Lesson Quiz TE	**Reteach** CRB
	Test Prep SE	**Test Prep Doctor** TE
	Test and Practice Generator	***Homework Help* Online**
	Before Chapter 10 Testing	
	Diagnose mastery of concepts in chapter.	Prescribe intervention.
	Ready to Go On? SE pp. 735, 769	***Ready to Go On? Intervention***
	Multi-Step Test Prep SE pp. 734, 768	**Scaffolding Questions** TE pp. 734, 768
	Section Quizzes AR	**Reteach** CRB
	Test and Practice Generator	***Lesson Tutorial Videos***
	Before High Stakes Testing	
	Diagnose mastery of benchmark concepts.	Prescribe intervention.
	College Entrance Exam Practice SE p. 779	***College Entrance Exam Practice***
	Standardized Test Prep SE pp. 782–783	
Summative Assessment	**After Chapter 10**	
	Check mastery of chapter concepts.	Prescribe intervention.
	Multiple-Choice Tests (Forms A, B, C)	**Reteach** CRB
	Free-Response Tests (Forms A, B, C)	***Lesson Tutorial Videos***
	Performance Assessment AR	
	Cumulative Test AR	
	Test and Practice Generator	

KEY: **SE** = *Student Edition* **TE** = *Teacher's Edition* **CRB** = *Chapter Resource Book* **AR** = *Assessment Resources*  Available online · Available on CD- or DVD-ROM

Lesson Resources

Before the Lesson

Prepare ***Teacher One Stop*** SPANISH
- Editable lesson plans
- Calendar Planner
- Easy access to all chapter resources

Lesson Transparencies
- Teacher Tools

Teach the Lesson

Introduce ***Alternate Openers: Explorations***

Lesson Transparencies
- Warm Up
- Problem of the Day

Teach ***Lesson Transparencies***
- Teaching Transparencies

Know-It Notebook™
- Vocabulary
- Key Concepts

Power Presentations 

Lesson Tutorial Videos SPANISH

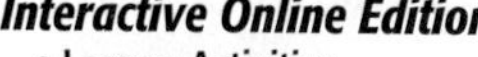
Interactive Online Edition

- Lesson Activities
- Lesson Tutorial Videos

Lab Activities

Lab Resources Online

Online Interactivities 

TechKeys

Practice the Lesson

Practice ***Chapter Resources***
- Practice A, B, C

Practice and Problem Solving Workbook SPANISH

IDEA Works!® Modified Worksheets and Tests

ExamView Test and Practice Generator 

Homework Help Online

Online Interactivities 

Interactive Online Edition
- Homework Help

Apply ***Chapter Resources***
- Problem Solving SPANISH

Practice and Problem Solving Workbook SPANISH

Interactive Online Edition 
- Chapter Project

Project Teacher Support

After the Lesson

Reteach ***Chapter Resources***
- Reteach
- Reading Strategies ELL

Success for Every Learner

Review ***Interactive Answers and Solutions***

Solutions Key

Know-It Notebook™
- Big Ideas
- Chapter Review

Extend ***Chapter Resources***
- Challenge

Technology Highlights for the Teacher

 **Power Presentations**

Dynamic presentations to engage students. Complete PowerPoint® presentations for every lesson in Chapter 10.

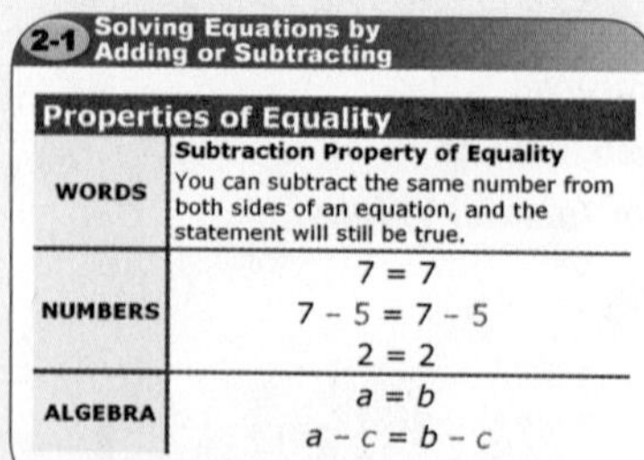

 **Teacher One Stop** SPANISH

Easy access to Chapter 10 resources and assessments. Includes lesson planning, test generation, and puzzle creation software.

 **Premier Online Edition** SPANISH

Chapter 10 includes Tutorial Videos, Lesson Activities, Lesson Quizzes, Homework Help, and Chapter Project.

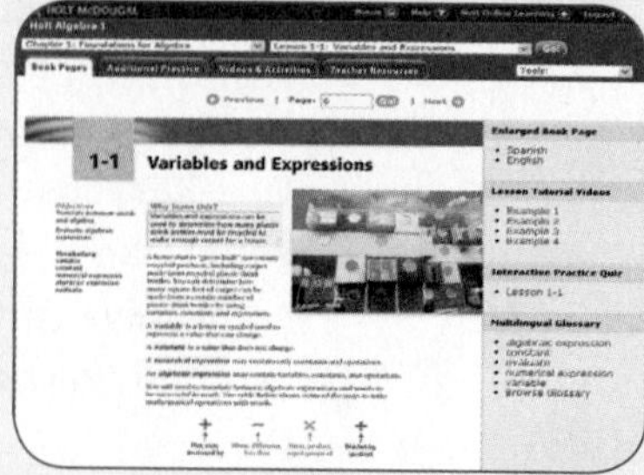

KEY: **SE** = *Student Edition* **TE** = *Teacher's Edition*  English Language Learners SPANISH Spanish version available — Available online — Available on CD- or DVD-RO

Reaching All Learners

Teaching tips to help all learners appear throughout the chapter. A few that target specific students are included in the lists below.

All Learners

Lab Activities
Practice and Problem Solving Workbook SPANISH
Know-It Notebook

Special Needs Students

Practice A .... CRB
Reteach .... CRB
Reading Strategies .... CRB
Are You Ready? .... SE p. 695
Inclusion .... TE pp. 704, 713, 721, 722, 727, 740, 751
IDEA Works!® Modified Worksheets and Tests
Ready to Go On? Intervention SPANISH
Know-It Notebook
Online Interactivities 
Lesson Tutorial Videos SPANISH

Developing Learners

Practice A .... CRB
Reteach .... CRB
Reading Strategies .... CRB
Are You Ready? .... SE p. 695
Vocabulary Connections .... SE p. 696
Questioning Strategies .... TE
Ready to Go On? Intervention SPANISH
Know-It Notebook
Homework Help Online
Online Interactivities SPANISH
Lesson Tutorial Videos 

On-Level Learners

Practice B .... CRB
Problem Solving .... CRB
Vocabulary Connections .... SE p. 696
Questioning Strategies .... TE
Ready to Go On? Intervention SPANISH
Know-It Notebook
Homework Help Online
Online Interactivities SPANISH

Advanced Learners

Practice C .... CRB
Challenge .... CRB
Challenge Exercises .... SE
Reading and Writing Math *Extend* .... TE p. 697
Critical Thinking .... TE pp. 752, 763
Are You Ready? Enrichment SPANISH
Ready To Go On? Enrichment SPANISH

English Language Learners

ENGLISH LANGUAGE LEARNERS

Reading Strategies .... CRB
Are You Ready? Vocabulary .... SE p. 695
Vocabulary Connections .... SE p. 696
Vocabulary Review .... SE p. 774
English Language Learners .... TE p. 785
Success for Every Learner
Know-It Notebook
Multilingual Glossary
Lesson Tutorial Videos  

Technology Highlights for Reaching All Learners

Lesson Tutorial Videos SPANISH

Starring Holt authors Ed Burger and Freddie Renfro! Live tutorials to support every lesson in Chapter 10.

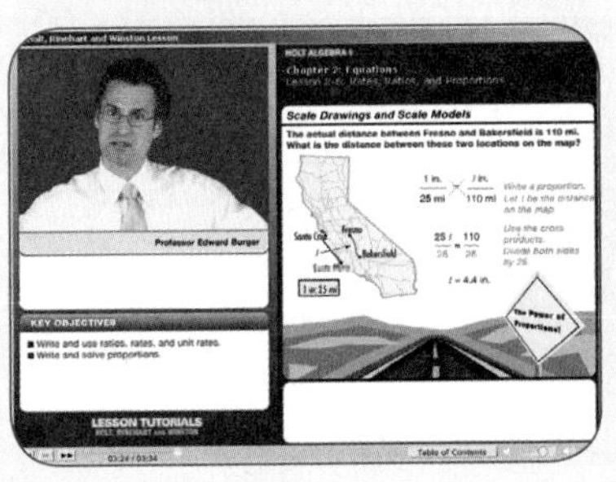

Multilingual Glossary

Searchable glossary includes definitions in English, Spanish, Vietnamese, Chinese, Hmong, Korean, and 4 other languages.

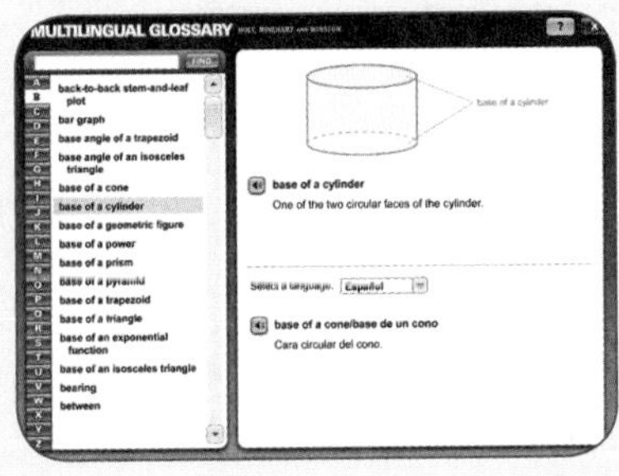

Online Interactivities

Interactive tutorials provide visually engaging alternative opportunities to learn concepts and master skills.

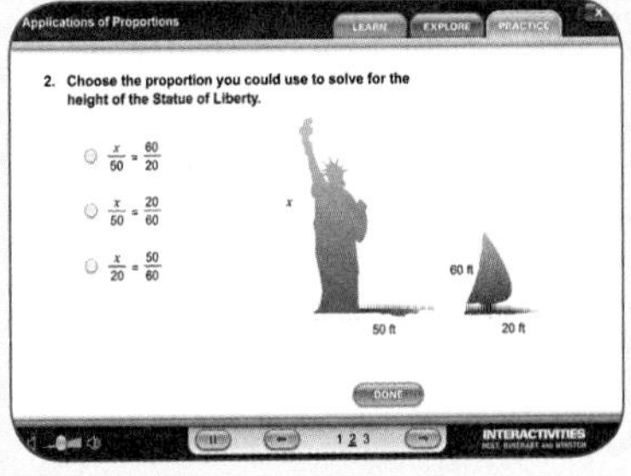

KEY: **SE** = *Student Edition* **TE** = *Teacher's Edition* **CRB** = *Chapter Resource Book* SPANISH Spanish version available  Available online Available on CD- or DVD-ROM

Ongoing Assessment

Assessing Prior Knowledge

Determine whether students have the prerequisite concepts and skills for success in Chapter 10.

Are You Ready? SPANISH .... SE p. 695
Warm Up .... TE

Test Preparation

Provide review and practice for Chapter 10 and standardized tests.

Multi-Step Test Prep .... SE pp. 734, 768
Study Guide: Review .... SE pp. 774–777
Test Tackler .... SE pp. 780–781
Standardized Test Prep .... SE pp. 782–783
College Entrance Exam Practice .... SE p. 779
Countdown to Testing .... SE pp. C4-C27
IDEA Works!® Modified Worksheets and Tests

Alternative Assessment

Assess students' understanding of Chapter 10 concepts and combined problem-solving skills.

Chapter 10 Project .... SE p. 694
Alternative Assessment .... TE
Performance Assessment SPANISH .... AR
Portfolio Assessment SPANISH .... AR

Lesson Assessment

Provide formative assessment for each lesson of Chapter 10.

Questioning Strategies .... TE
Think and Discuss .... SE
Check It Out! Exercises .... SE
Write About It .... SE
Journal .... TE
Lesson Quiz .... TE
Alternative Assessment .... TE
IDEA Works!® Modified Worksheets and Tests

Weekly Assessment

Provide formative assessment for each section of Chapter 10.

Multi-Step Test Prep .... SE pp. 734, 768
Ready to Go On? SPANISH .... SE pp. 735, 769
Section Quizzes SPANISH .... AR
Test and Practice Generator SPANISH .... *Teacher One Stop*

Chapter Assessment

Provide summative assessment of Chapter 10 mastery.

Chapter 10 Test .... SE p. 778
Chapter Test (Levels A, B, C) SPANISH .... AR
• Multiple Choice • Free Response
Cumulative Test SPANISH .... AR
Test and Practice Generator SPANISH .... *Teacher One Stop*
IDEA Works!® Modified Worksheets and Tests

Technology Highlights for Assessment

 **Are You Ready?** SPANISH

Automatically assess readiness and prescribe intervention for Chapter 10 prerequisite skills.

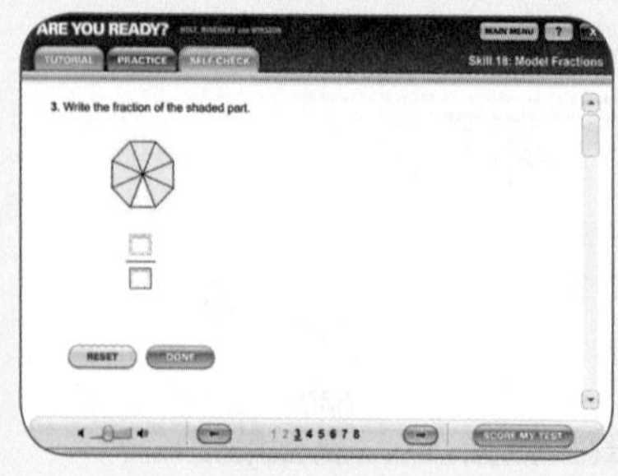

 **Ready to Go On?**

Automatically assess understanding of and prescribe intervention for Sections 10A and 10B.

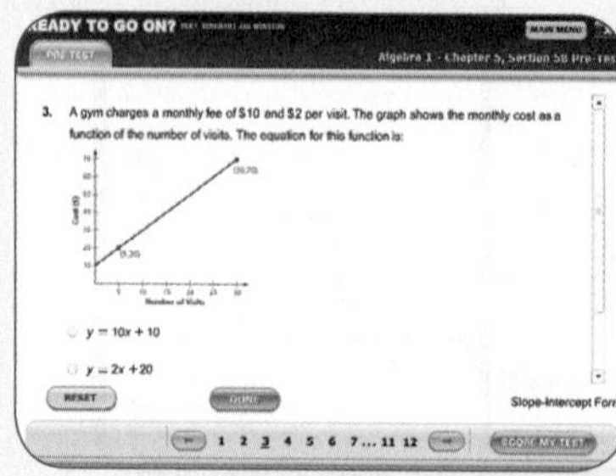

 **Test and Practice Generator** SPANISH

Use Chapter 10 problem banks to create assessments and worksheets to print out or deliver online. Includes dynamic problems.

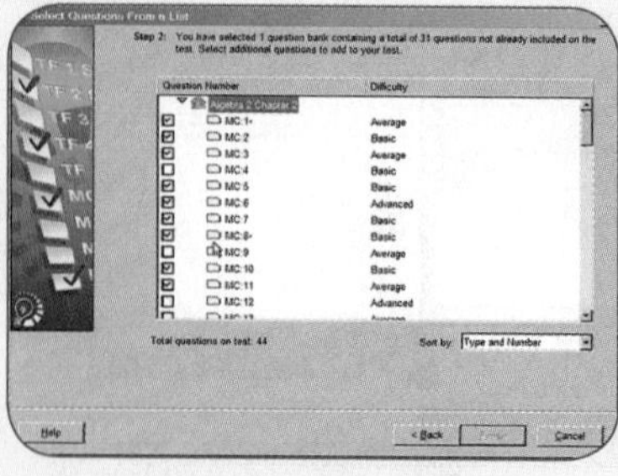

KEY: **SE** = *Student Edition* **TE** = *Teacher's Edition* **AR** = *Assessment Resources* SPANISH Spanish version available Available online  Available on CD- or DVD-ROM

Formal Assessment

Three levels (A, B, C) of multiple-choice and free-response chapter tests, along with a performance assessment, are available in the *Assessment Resources.*

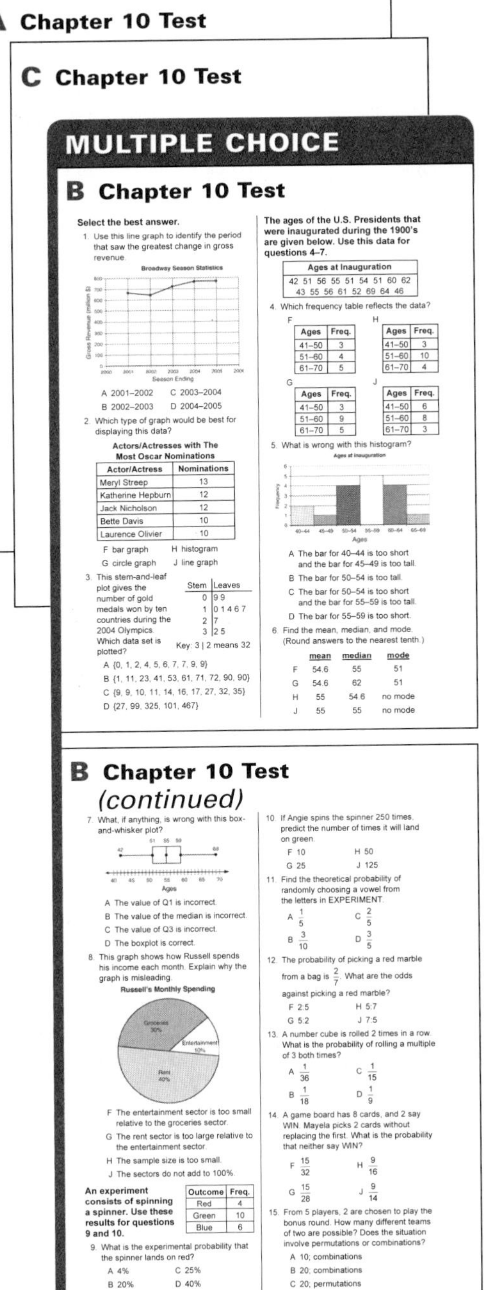

A Chapter 10 Test

C Chapter 10 Test

MULTIPLE CHOICE

B Chapter 10 Test

B Chapter 10 Test (continued)

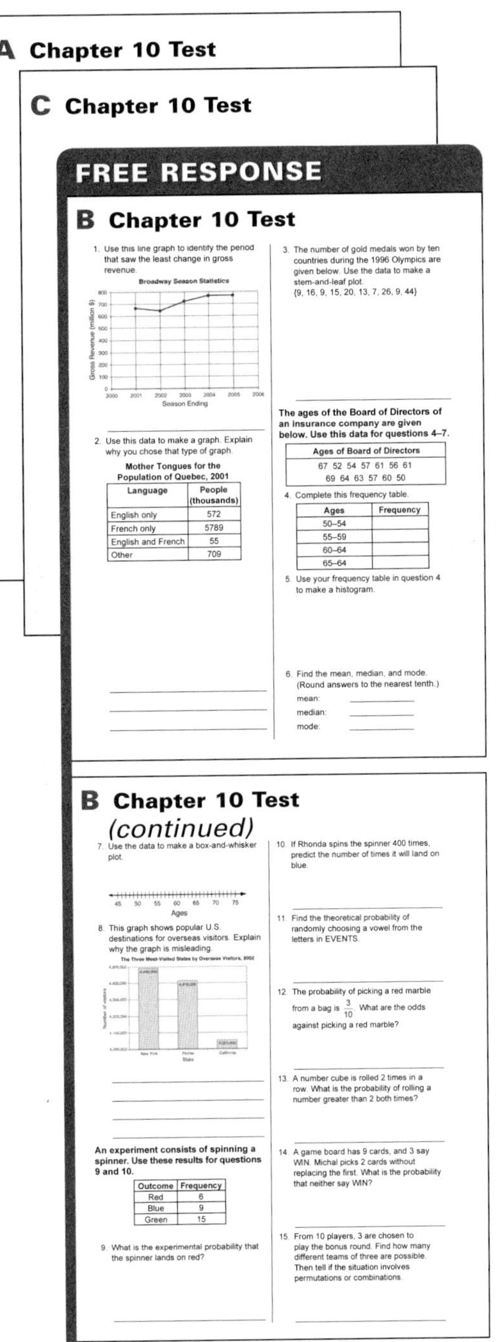

A Chapter 10 Test

C Chapter 10 Test

FREE RESPONSE

B Chapter 10 Test

B Chapter 10 Test (continued)

PERFORMANCE ASSESSMENT

Chapter 10 Test

Purpose
This performance task assesses the student's ability to solve problems involving combinations and to find the theoretical probability of an event.

Time
30–55 minutes

Grouping
Pairs

Preparation Hints
Divide the students into pairs and have them play *Hangman* using vocabulary from the chapter. After one or two rounds, ask whether anyone won a game with no wrong letters or lost a game with no correct letters. Ask students how likely they think these two situations are.

Overview
In this activity, students first use combinations to count the number of outcomes possible when letters are randomly guessed in a game of *Hangman*. The students combine these counts to find the theoretical probabilities of winning by guessing all of the correct letters and losing by guessing all incorrect letters. The activity concludes with a game show scenario in which frequently used letters are automatically given.

Introduce the Task
Distribute the activity and review the scenario outlined in the opening paragraphs. Make sure students understand that 7 correct letters are required to win and 6 wrong letters are required to lose. Also emphasize that the activity calculates theoretical probabilities based on random guessing; for simplicity the influences of strategy and skill are ignored.

Performance Indicators
______ Identifies that *Hangman* is a situation involving combinations.
______ Uses combinations to find the number of ways you can randomly guess letters.
______ Determines theoretical probabilities by finding the ratio of favorable outcomes to total outcomes.
______ Recognizes an impossible event and understands the probability is 0.

Scoring Rubric
Level 4: Student solves problems correctly and gives good explanations.
Level 3: Student solves problems but does not give satisfactory explanations.
Level 2: Student solves some problems but does not give satisfactory explanations.
Level 1: Student is not able to solve any of the problems.

Chapter 10 Test (continued)

In the game called *Hangman*, your opponent thinks of a mystery word and draws blanks to represent each letter in the word. You then try to fill in the blanks by guessing letters, but the order of your guesses does not matter. For each correct guess, your opponent fills the letter into all of the blanks where it belongs. For each wrong guess, your opponent draws part of a hangman diagram. In one variation of the game, you lose after guessing 6 wrong letters.

For each wrong letter, one of these 6 body parts is drawn.

For 1–6, assume that the mystery word is UNLIKELY. Also assume that you randomly guess letters. (That is, you don't use any strategies such as guessing vowels first.)

1. Does playing *Hangman* involve combinations or permutations? Explain.
2. How many ways can you guess any 7 letters, regardless of whether they are right or wrong? Support your answer.
3. What is the *probability* that you correctly guess all 7 letters without a single wrong guess?
4. How many ways can you lose without getting a single correct letter? Support your answer.
5. What is the *probability* of losing without getting a single correct letter? (*Hint:* The denominator is not the same as for question 3.)
6. The bonus round of a popular television game show is similar to *Hangman* except the letters R, S, T, L, N, and E are automatically revealed. You get to guess 3 more consonants and 1 more vowel. What is the probability of correctly guessing all of the remaining letters? Support your answer.

Modified chapter tests that address special learning needs are available in *IDEA Works!*® *Modified Worksheets and Tests.*

Teacher One Stop™ 

Test & Practice Generator

Create and customize Chapter 10 Tests. Instantly generate multiple test versions, answer keys, and Spanish versions of test items.

CHAPTER 10

SECTION 10A
Data Analysis

On page 734, students use graphs and statistics to model real-world situations at the Olympics.

Exercises designed to prepare students for success on the Multi-Step Test Prep can be found in each lesson.

SECTION 10B
Probability

On page 768, students use probability and counting methods to model real-world games.

Exercises designed to prepare students for success on the Multi-Step Test Prep can be found in each lesson.

Interactivities Online ▶

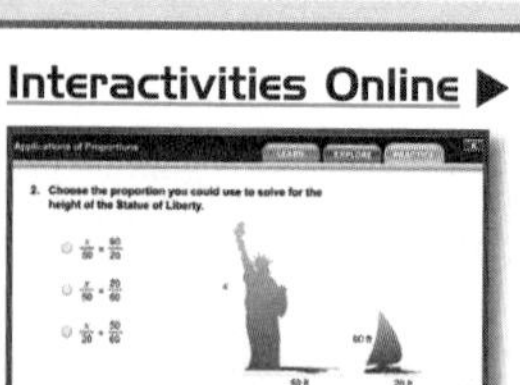

Lessons 10-4, 10-8

Video Lesson Tutorials Online

Lesson Tutorial Videos are available for EVERY example.

CHAPTER 10

Data Analysis and Probability

Chapter Focus

- Organize and display data to answer questions.
- Use descriptive statistics to summarize data sets.
- Understand experimental probability and theoretical probability.
- Use probability to make appropriate predictions.

You're *the Designer*

Research studies are designed to gather and analyze data in order to answer questions. The results are displayed in tables and graphs.

go.hrw.com
Chapter Project Online
KEYWORD: MA7 ChProj

694 *Chapter 10*

You're the Designer

About the Project

In the Chapter Project, students choose a question to research and answer it by collecting and analyzing data. Then students design a simulation to model an experimental situation.

Project Resources

All project resources for teachers and students are provided online.

ARE YOU READY?

Vocabulary

Match each term on the left with a definition on the right.

1. difference **D**
2. factor **B**
3. natural numbers **F**
4. ratio **E**
5. sum **A**

A. the result of an addition
B. a whole number that is multiplied by another whole number to get a product
C. numbers that can be expressed in the form $\frac{a}{b}$, where a and b are both integers and $b \neq 0$
D. the result of a subtraction
E. a comparison of two quantities by division
F. the counting numbers: 1, 2, 3, ...

Solve Proportions

Solve each proportion.

6. $\frac{3}{4} = \frac{x}{12}$ **9**
7. $\frac{15}{9} = \frac{3}{x}$ **1.8**
8. $\frac{10}{20} = \frac{x}{100}$ **50**
9. $\frac{250}{1500} = \frac{x}{100}$ **$16\frac{2}{3}$**

Compare and Order Real Numbers

Compare. Write <, >, or =.

10. 20 **>** 13
11. $\frac{2}{3}$ **>** $\frac{1}{2}$
12. $\frac{3}{4}$ **<** $\frac{7}{9}$
13. 0.75 **=** $\frac{9}{12}$

Order the numbers from least to greatest.

14. $\frac{1}{2}, \frac{4}{5}, \frac{1}{8}, \frac{3}{4}, \frac{2}{3}$ **$\frac{1}{8}, \frac{1}{2}, \frac{2}{3}, \frac{3}{4}, \frac{4}{5}$**
15. $0.12, \frac{2}{5}, \frac{3}{4}, 0.3, \frac{1}{3}$ **$0.12, 0.3, \frac{1}{3}, \frac{2}{5}, \frac{3}{4}$**

Multiply Decimals

Multiply.

16. 0.25×300 **75**
17. 0.5×4000 **2000**
18. 0.05×200 **10**
19. 0.125×9600 **1200**

Divide Decimals

Divide.

20. $435 \div 10$ **43.5**
21. $32 \div 100$ **0.32**
22. $777 \div 1000$ **0.777**
23. $295 \div 10{,}000$ **0.0295**

Fractions, Decimals, and Percents

Write the equivalent decimal.

24. $\frac{3}{5}$ **0.6**
25. 45% **0.45**
26. $\frac{3}{4}$ **0.75**
27. 8% **0.08**

Write the equivalent percent.

28. $\frac{1}{4}$ **25%**
29. 0.2 **20%**
30. 0.36 **36%**
31. $\frac{1}{10}$ **10%**

ARE YOU READY?

Organizer

Objective: Assess students' understanding of prerequisite skills.

Assessing Prior Knowledge

INTERVENTION

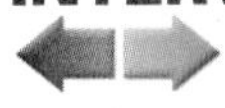

Diagnose and Prescribe

Use this page to determine whether intervention is necessary or whether enrichment is appropriate.

Resources

 ***Are You Ready? Intervention and Enrichment*** **Worksheets**

 ***Are You Ready?*** **CD-ROM**

 ***Are You Ready?*** **Online**

my.hrw.com

ARE YOU READY?

Diagnose and Prescribe

Prerequisite Skill	*Are You Ready? Intervention,* Chapter 10: Worksheets	CD-ROM	Online
Solve Proportions	Skill 77	Activity 77	Diagnose and Prescribe Online
Compare and Order Real Numbers	Skill 16	Activity 16	
Multiply Decimals	Skill 45	Activity 45	
Divide Decimals	Skill 46	Activity 46	
Fractions, Decimals, and Percents	Skill 14	Activity 14	

***Are You Ready? Enrichment,* Chapter 10**

Worksheets

CD-ROM

Online

Organizer

Objective: Help students organize the new concepts they will learn in Chapter 10.

Online Edition
Multilingual Glossary

Resources

Teacher One Stop™
PuzzleView

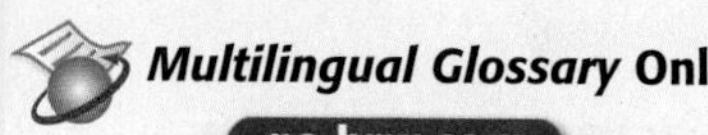
***Multilingual Glossary* Online**
go.hrw.com
KEYWORD: MA7 Glossary

Possible answers to *Vocabulary Connections*

1. the middle value that divides a set of data into 2 equal parts
2. Quarter, quarterly, quartet; they all refer to something with 4 parts.
3. Experimental probability describes the likelihood that something will happen based on trials and experiences. Theoretical probability describes the likelihood that something will happen based on formulas and theorems.
4. 2 or more events

CHAPTER 10 Study Guide: Preview

Where You've Been

Previously, you

- read information from tables and graphs.
- added, subtracted, multiplied, and divided real numbers.
- worked with ratios and percents.

In This Chapter

You will study

- how to organize data in tables, graphs, and plots.
- how to find the central tendency of a data set by calculating mean, median, and mode.
- writing experimental and theoretical probability as ratios, percents, and decimals.
- combinations, permutations, and factorials as extensions of multiplication.

Where You're Going

You can use the skills in this chapter

- to present your findings from science laboratory experiments in an appropriate and accurate graphical form.
- to be more informed about statistical information in the news and not to be misled by how it is presented.

Key Vocabulary/Vocabulario

combination	combinación
compound event	suceso compuesto
dependent events	sucesos dependientes
experimental probability	probabilidad experimental
frequency	frecuencia
independent events	sucesos independientes
median	mediana
outlier	valor extremo
permutation	permutación
probability	probabilidad
quartile	cuartil
theoretical probability	probabilidad teórica

Vocabulary Connections

To become familiar with some of the vocabulary terms in the chapter, consider the following. You may refer to the chapter, the glossary, or a dictionary if you like.

1. The *median strip* is the middle region that divides a highway in half. Use this knowledge to define **median** as it relates to a set of data.
2. The word **quartile** starts with the prefix *quart-*. What are some other words that start with the prefix *quart-*? What do they all have in common?
3. **Probability** is the chance something will happen. Based on your understanding of the words *experiment* and *theory*, compare and contrast the terms **experimental probability** and **theoretical probability**.
4. A *compound word* is made up of two or more words. What do you think makes up a **compound event**?

Reading Strategy: Read and Interpret Graphics

Knowing how to interpret figures, diagrams, charts, and graphs will help you gather the information you need to get the correct answer.

What You See

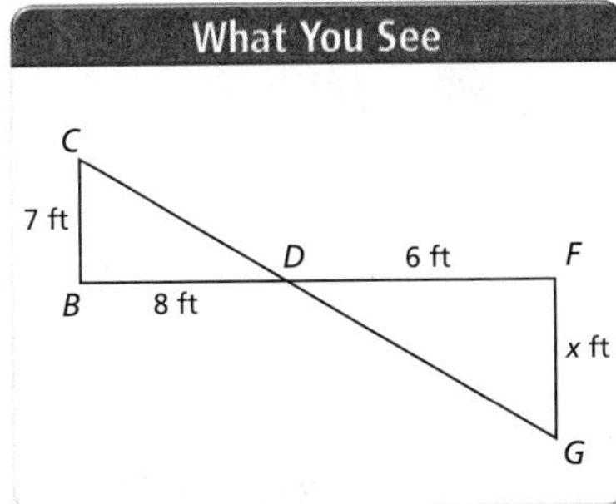

How to Interpret

✔ **Read all labels.**
$CB = 7$ ft; $BD = 8$ ft;
$DF = 6$ ft; $FG = x$ ft

✘ **Do not assume anything.**

It appears that $\overline{DF}$ is longer than $\overline{BD}$, but the labels indicate that it is shorter.

$\angle B$ and $\angle F$ appear to be 90°, but the diagram does not indicate this.

What You See

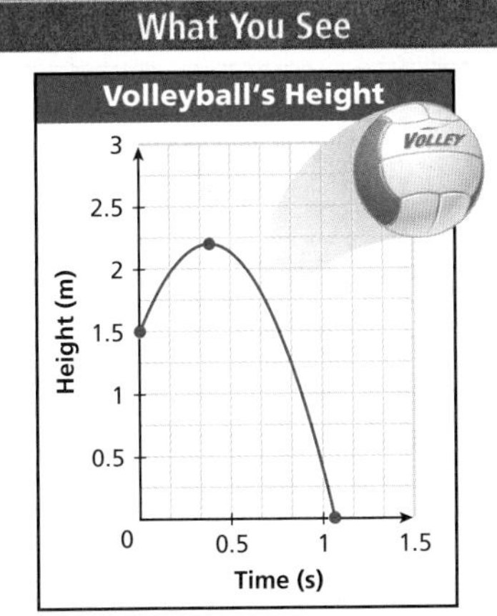

How to Interpret

✔ **Read the title.**
"Volleyball's Height"

✔ **Read each axis label.**

x-axis Indicates **time** measured in seconds

y-axis Indicates **height** measured in meters

✔ **Determine what information is represented.**

Each point on the graph gives the **height** of the ball at that **time**.

Try This

Look up each exercise in the text and answer the corresponding questions.

1. Lesson 2-7 Exercise 42: What is the title of the table? What is the record for the 200-meter run?
2. Lesson 7-8 Exercise 69: What does x represent in the diagram? Make a list of the information you know from the diagram.
3. Lesson 8-3 Exercise 51: What is represented by the y-axis? What is the y-value when x equals 3.5? Is the graph linear? How do you know?
4. Lesson 9-8 Exercise 33: What does the dashed line represent? What facts about the parallelogram are given from the diagram?

Reading and Writing Math

CHAPTER 10

Organizer

Objective: Help students apply strategies to understand and retain key concepts.

Reading Strategy: Read and Interpret Graphics

Discuss When a word problem includes a graph, tell students to look at the graph before reading the problem. Knowing what data the graph displays may help them make more sense of the problem.

Extend As you learn about different graphs in Chapter 10, discuss with students what information can and cannot be assumed from them.

Answers

1. Women's Olympic Records; 21.3 s
2. the width of the prism; length $= x + 5$, height $= x + 2$
3. Area; 25 square units; no; it is not a straight line.
4. height of the parallelogram; height $= x$; base $= 2x + 8$

Reading Connection

Innumeracy
by John Allen Paulos

The word *innumeracy* refers to a person's inability to make sense of the numbers he or she encounters in daily life. Paulos popularized the term in this enormously readable book, which provides scores of examples of the misuse of numbers, particularly as they relate to statistics and probability.

Activity Have students read Chapter 2 of *Innumeracy* and then describe the amazing birthday paradox. Is it true that in a group of 23 randomly chosen people, the probability that two will have the same birthday is greater than 50%? Have students test the proposition using randomly chosen people or lists of birthdays of presidents, celebrities, etc. Ask students to describe their results.

SECTION

10A Data Analysis

One-Minute Section Planner

Lesson	Lab Resources	Materials
Lesson 10-1 Organizing and Displaying Data • Organize data in tables and graphs. • Choose a table or graph to display data. ☐ SAT-10 ☑ NAEP ☐ ACT ☑ SAT ☑ SAT Subject Tests	***Algebra Lab Activities*** 10-1 Algebra Lab	**Optional** magazines, newspapers
Lesson 10-2 Frequency and Histograms • Create stem-and-leaf plots. • Create frequency tables and histograms. ☐ SAT-10 ☑ NAEP ☐ ACT ☐ SAT ☐ SAT Subject Tests		**Optional** coins (MK), sticky notes
Lesson 10-3 Data Distributions • Describe the central tendency of a data set. • Create and interpret box-and-whisker plots. ☑ SAT-10 ☑ NAEP ☑ ACT ☑ SAT ☑ SAT Subject Tests		**Optional** colored pencils (MK)
Lesson 10-3 Technology Lab Use Technology to Make Graphs • Use a spreadsheet or graphing calculator to create graphs. ☐ SAT-10 ☐ NAEP ☐ ACT ☐ SAT ☐ SAT Subject Tests	***Technology Lab Activities*** 10-3 Lab Recording Sheet	**Required** spreadsheet program, graphing calculator
Lesson 10-4 Misleading Graphs and Statistics • Recognize misleading graphs. • Recognize misleading statistics. ☐ SAT-10 ☑ NAEP ☐ ACT ☐ SAT ☐ SAT Subject Tests		

Note: If NAEP is checked, the content is tested on either the Grade 8 or Grade 12 NAEP assessment.

MK = *Manipulatives Kit*

MEAN, MEDIAN, AND MODE

Lesson 10-3

The *measures of central tendency,* mean, median, and mode, are three ways of summarizing a data set by using a single value. With this goal in mind, students may wonder which measure best represents a particular set of data. Although there is no definitive answer to this question, there are cases in which one measure is clearly more effective at describing a data set than the others. Some general guidelines for choosing a measure to describe a data set can be established.

Mean: The mean (or average) takes every data value into account, is easy to calculate, and works well for describing data sets that are normally distributed. (In a data set that is normally distributed, the graph of the distribution is a bell-shaped curve with the mean at the center.) The mean is not as useful for sets that contain outliers because the outliers can have a large effect on the mean.

Median: The median is also easy to calculate. The median is useful for describing data sets that are not normally distributed because it is much less affected by outliers than the mean.

Mode: The mode is useful when the frequency of data values is important or when the data cluster around multiple values. Among the mean, median, and mode, only the mode can be used to summarize a set of non-numerical data, such as favorite colors.

Each measure provides a slightly different perspective on a data set. The clearest understanding of a data set is generally obtained when all three measures are considered as a group.

Students should recognize that the mean of a data set need not be one of the data values. The same is true of the median. For example, the data set {10, 20} has a mean and median of 15. On the other hand, the mode, if it exists, must be one of the values in the data set.

VARIABILITY

Lesson 10-3

The mean, median, and mode are all ways to describe the "typical" value in a data set. It is also useful to describe the *variability,* or spread, of a data set. The simplest way to quantify variability is with the range.

The *range* of a data set is the difference between the greatest and least values in the set. Consider the two data sets shown below. Both have a mean, median, and mode of 5. However, the values in data set *B* are more spread out, and this is reflected in the fact that the data set has a greater range. The range of data set *B* is 6, as compared to a range of 2 for data set *A*.

Data Set *A*

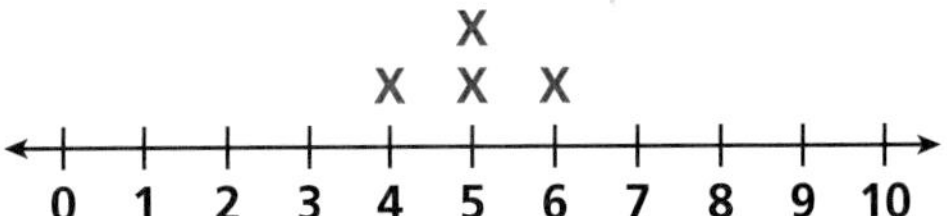

Data Set *B*

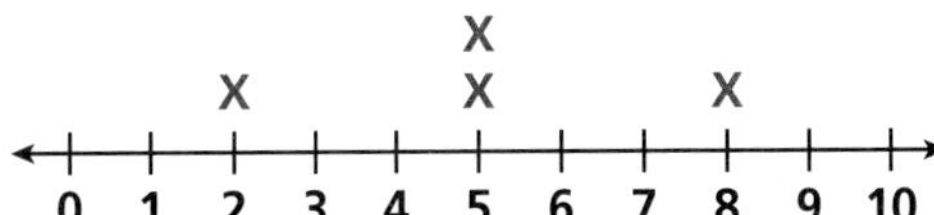

In future math courses, students will learn more sophisticated ways to measure variability. Two of the most useful measures in statistics are the variance and the standard deviation.

The *variance,* denoted σ^2, is the average square deviation of each value from the mean. For data set *A*, the variance is

$$\sigma^2 = \frac{(4-5)^2 + (5-5)^2 + (5-5)^2 + (6-5)^2}{4} = 0.5.$$

For data set *B*, the variance is

$$\sigma^2 = \frac{(2-5)^2 + (5-5)^2 + (5-5)^2 + (8-5)^2}{4} = 4.5.$$

The *standard deviation,* σ, is the square root of the variance. For data set *A*, the standard deviation is $\sigma = \sqrt{0.5} \approx 0.7$. For data set *B*, the standard deviation is $\sigma = \sqrt{4.5} \approx 2.1$.

As the examples show, a greater variance and a greater standard deviation indicate a greater spread of data.

Organizer

Pacing:
Traditional 1 day
Block $\frac{1}{2}$ day

Objective: Students use data presented in bar graphs and circle graphs to solve equations.

Online Edition

Countdown Week 22

Teach

Remember

Students review and apply writing equations.

Visual Cues Direct students' attention to the bar graph in **Example 1.** Point out that the top of the second bar is missing because it has been torn off. Ask for ideas for how the missing information could be found.

State Resources

go.hrw.com
State Resources Online
KEYWORD: MA7 Resources

Bar and Circle Graphs

Data displayed in bar graphs and circle graphs can be used to solve equations. In these problems, parts of the graphs are missing.

Example 1

The top part of this graph was torn off. If Warren received 15% of the votes, how many votes did Adams receive?

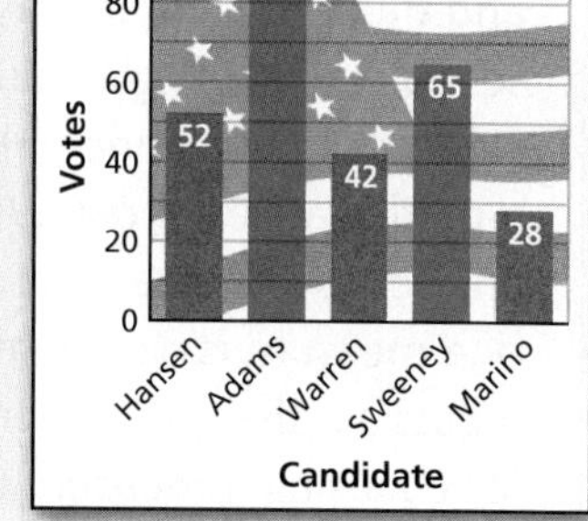

Step 1 Find the total number of votes. Let t represent the total.

15%	of	the total votes	is	42 votes.
0.15	•	t	=	42

$$0.15t = 42$$

$$t = 280 \text{ votes}$$

Step 2 Find the number of votes Adams received.

Let a represent the number of votes received by Adams. Let h, w, s, and m represent the number of votes received by Hansen, Warren, Sweeney, and Marino.

$$t = a + h + w + s + m$$

$280 = a + 52 + 42 + 65 + 28$ *Substitute the numbers shown on the graph.*

$280 = a + 187$ *Simplify the right side of the equation.*

$\underline{-187} \quad \underline{-187}$ *Subtract 187 from both sides.*

$93 = a$

Adams received 93 votes.

Try This

1. The missing bar is twice as tall as the bar for week 2. How many total miles did Kim bike in these five weeks? **122 mi**

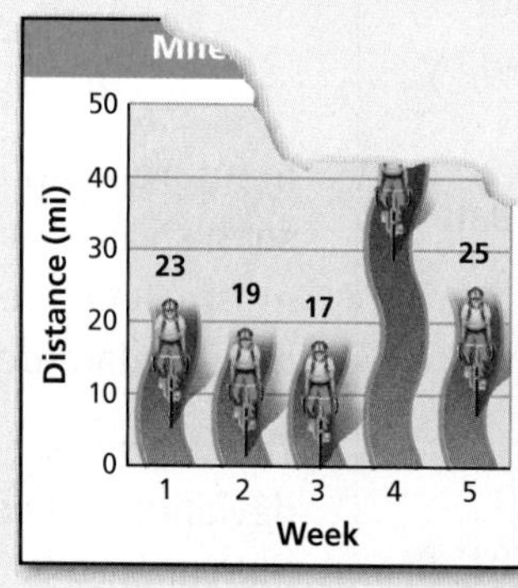

2. People aged 20–29 years walked 275 more miles than the oldest age group. Find the total miles walked by all age groups. **1268 mi**

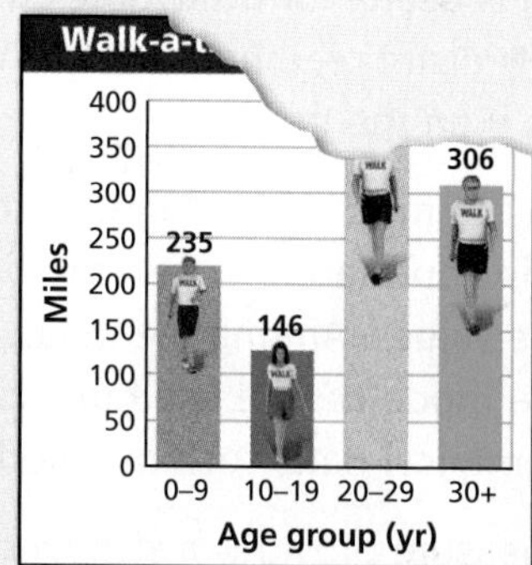

Remember that a circle graph represents all the data in a data set. The percent represented by each section is a part of the whole data set, so the sum of all the percents must be 100%.

Example 2

A survey asked people in a neighborhood to agree or disagree with the following statement:

"We need a traffic light at Jefferson Avenue and Third Street."

If 35% of the people disagreed with the statement, how many people had no opinion?

Opinion Survey

Strongly agree 36
Strongly disagree 45
Agree 27
Disagree 63
No opinion ?

The number of people who answered "no opinion" is missing from the graph.

Step 1 Find the total number of people who answered the survey. Let t represent the total number of people.

35%	of	the total number of people	is	63 people.
0.35	•	t	=	63

$$0.35t = 63$$
$$t = 180 \text{ people}$$

Step 2 Find the number of people who answered "no opinion."

Let n represent the number of "no opinion" answers. Let d, s, g, and a represent the number of "disagree," "strongly disagree," "strongly agree," and "agree" answers.

$$t = n + d + s + g + a$$
$$180 = n + 63 + 45 + 36 + 27 \quad \textit{Substitute the numbers shown on the graph.}$$
$$180 = n + 171 \quad \textit{Simplify the right side of the equation.}$$
$$\underline{-171} \quad \underline{-171} \quad \textit{Subtract 171 from both sides.}$$
$$9 = n$$

There were 9 people who had no opinion.

Try This

3. The students in a junior high school voted on their choice for a field trip. Sixteen students voted for the natural history museum. How many students voted for the winning choice? **28**

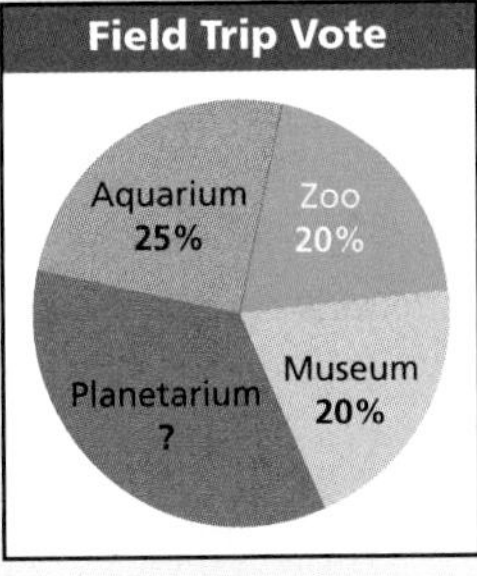

4. At the fall dance recital, 40% of the tickets were sold to adults. What percent of the sales were to seniors? **10%**

Ticket Sales

Students 105
Children 70
Seniors ?
Adults 140

Close

Assess

After students have solved the problems, have them make a circle graph for the data in **Example 1** and a bar graph for the data in **Example 2.** Discuss when data should be displayed in a bar graph and when a circle graph is a better display.

10-1 Organizer

Pacing: Traditional 1 day
Block $\frac{1}{2}$ day

Objectives: Organize data in tables and graphs.

Choose a table or graph to display data.

Algebra Lab
In *Algebra Lab Activities*

Online Edition
Tutorial Videos

Countdown Week 22

Power Presentations with PowerPoint®

Warm Up

Write the equivalent percent.

1. $\frac{4}{16}$ 25%
2. $\frac{12}{60}$ 20%
3. $\frac{35}{280}$ 12.5%

Find each value.

4. 20% of 360 72
5. 75% of 360 270
6. $\frac{1}{15}$ of 360 24

Also available on transparency

Math Humor

Scout Leader: I think we're lost. Someone hand me a compass.

Scout: How is a circle graph going to help us?

10-1 Organizing and Displaying Data

Objectives
Organize data in tables and graphs.

Choose a table or graph to display data.

Vocabulary
bar graph
line graph
circle graph

Who uses this?
Nutritionists can display health information about food in bar graphs.

Bar graphs, line graphs, and *circle graphs* can be used to present data in a visual way.

A **bar graph** displays data with vertical or horizontal bars. Bar graphs are a good way to display data that can be organized into categories. Using a bar graph, you can quickly compare the categories.

EXAMPLE 1 Reading and Interpreting Bar Graphs

Use the graph to answer each question.

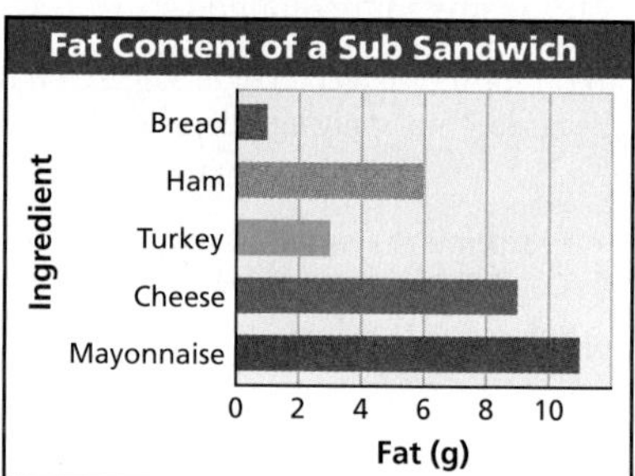

A Which ingredient contains the most fat?
mayonnaise — *The bar for mayonnaise is the longest.*

B How many more grams of fat are in ham than in turkey?
$6 - 3 = 3$ — *There are 6 grams of fat in ham and 3 grams of fat in turkey.*

C How many total fat grams are in this sandwich?
$1 + 6 + 3 + 9 + 11 = 30$ — *Add the number of fat grams for each ingredient.*

D What percent of the total fat grams in this sandwich are from turkey?
$\frac{3}{30} = \frac{1}{10} = 10\%$ — *Out of 30 total fat grams, 3 fat grams are from turkey.*

Use the graph to answer each question.

1a. Which ingredient contains the least amount of fat? **bread**

1b. Which ingredients contain at least 8 grams of fat?

1b. cheese and mayonnaise

State Resources

1 Introduce

EXPLORATION

10-1 Organizing and Displaying Data

A company makes yogurt-covered raisins in several flavors. The percentage of each flavor manufactured is shown here in three different ways.

Version 1

Color	Percentage
Blueberry	10
Strawberry	35
Banana	30
Cherry	5
Orange	20

Version 2 (bar graph: Flavor A–E; Percentage 0 10 20 30 40)

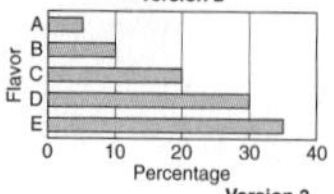

1. In version 2 of the data, which bar represents which flavor?

Version 3 (circle graph: sectors V, W, X, Y, Z)

2. In version 3 of the data, which sector of the circle represents which flavor?

THINK AND DISCUSS

3. **Describe** the advantages of representing the data as shown in version 2.
4. **Describe** the advantages of representing the data as shown in version 3.

Motivate

Find examples of data displays such as bar graphs, line graphs, and circle graphs in news magazines or newspapers. Show them to students and discuss some of the many ways that graphs are used in the real world. Have students list careers in which analyzing data is important, such as science, market research, finance, and politics.

Explorations and answers are provided in *Alternate Openers: Explorations Transparencies*.

A double-bar graph can be used to compare two data sets. A double-bar graph has a key to distinguish between the two sets of data.

EXAMPLE 2 Reading and Interpreting Double Bar Graphs

Use the graph to answer each question.

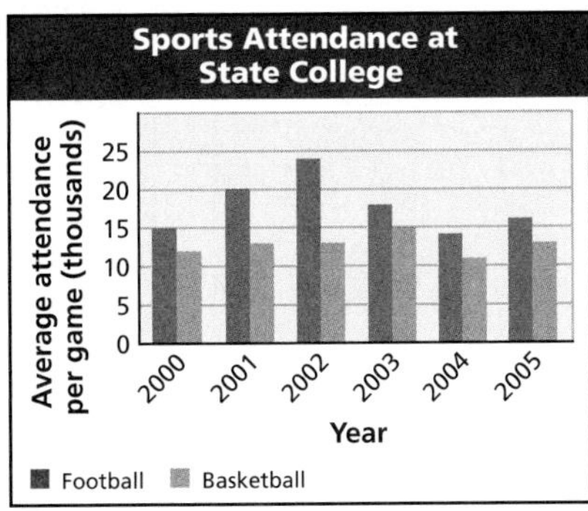

A **In which year did State College have the greatest average attendance for basketball?**

2003

Find the tallest orange bar.

B **On average, how many more people attended a football game than a basketball game in 2001?**

20,000 − 13,000 = 7000

Find the height of each bar for 2001 and subtract.

2. Use the graph to determine which years had the same average basketball attendance. What was the average attendance for those years? **2001, 2002, and 2005; about 13,000**

A **line graph** displays data using line segments. Line graphs are a good way to display data that changes over a period of time.

EXAMPLE 3 Reading and Interpreting Line Graphs

Use the graph to answer each question.

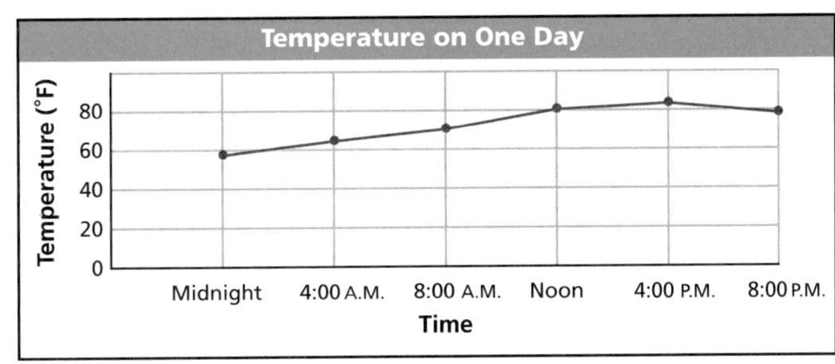

A **At what time was the temperature the warmest?**

4:00 P.M. *Identify the highest point.*

B **During which 4-hour time period did the temperature increase the most?**

From 8:00 A.M. to noon *Look for the segment with the greatest positive slope.*

3. Use the graph to estimate the difference in temperature between 4:00 A.M. and noon. **about 18 °F**

2 Teach

Guided Instruction

Show the importance of labeling the axes. In **Example 2** the interval on the vertical axis is marked in increments of 5, but the axis label shows that each increment represents 5000. In **Example 4,** it may seem obvious that the price is in dollars, but that might not be clear if the graph appeared in an international magazine.

Visual Cues To help find values on bar and line graphs, use a straightedge to line up the bars and points with the axes.

Reaching All Learners

Through Cognitive Strategies

Have students copy and use this chart to help with reading the word problems. Encourage them to add rows for other actions such as divide, subtract, and multiply.

Cue Words	Action
most, least, -est	Look for extremes.
same	Look for equal values.
more, less/fewer	Make a comparison.
total, altogether	Add.

Power Presentations with PowerPoint®

Additional Examples

Example 1

Use the graph to answer each question.

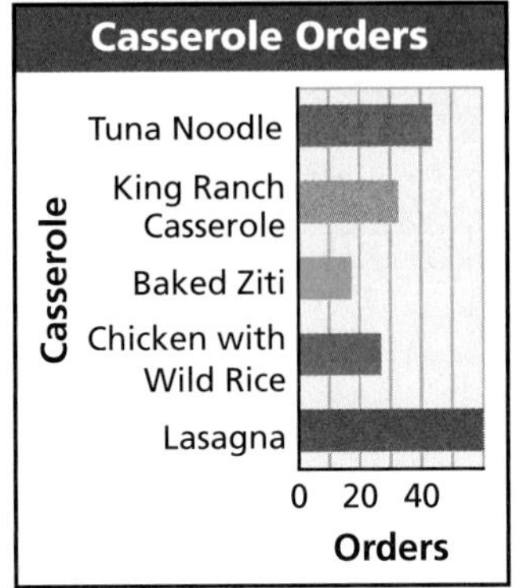

A. Which casserole was ordered the most? lasagna

B. About how many total orders were placed? 180

C. About how many more tuna noodle casseroles were ordered than king ranch casseroles? 10

D. About what percent of the total orders were for baked ziti? 10%

Example 2

Use the graph to answer each question.

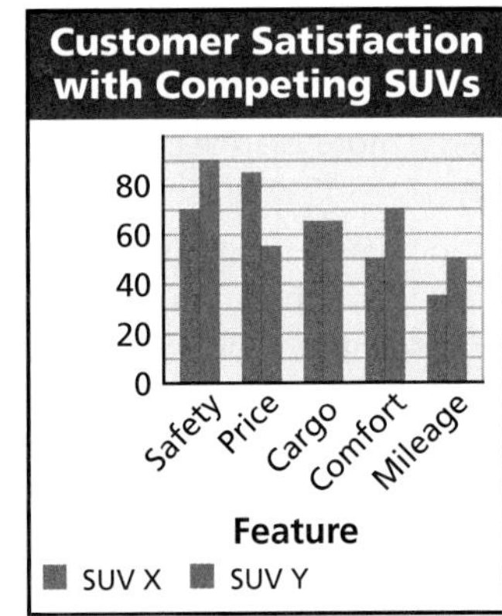

A. Which feature received the same satisfaction rating for each SUV? cargo

B. Which SUV received a better rating for mileage? SUV Y

INTERVENTION

Questioning Strategies

EXAMPLES 1–2

- Why is the data displayed in these particular graphs?

Power Presentations with PowerPoint®

Additional Examples

Example 3

Use the graph to answer each question.

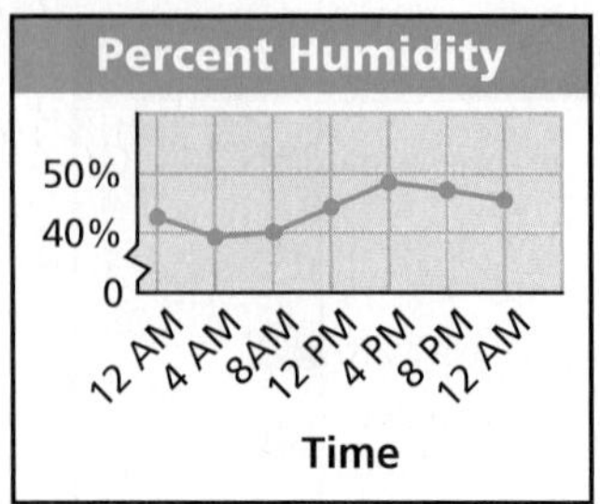

A. At what time was the humidity the lowest? 4 A.M.

B. During which 4-hour time period did the humidity increase the most? 12 to 4 P.M.

Example 4

Use the graph to answer each question.

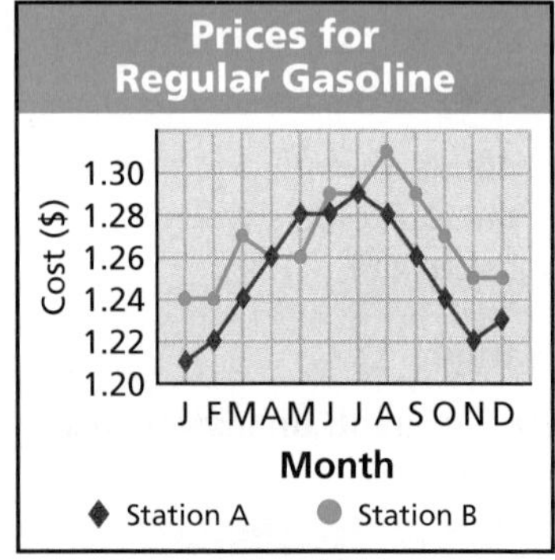

A. In which month did station A charge more than station B? May

B. During which month(s) did the stations charge the same for gasoline? April, July

Example 5

Use the graph to answer the question.

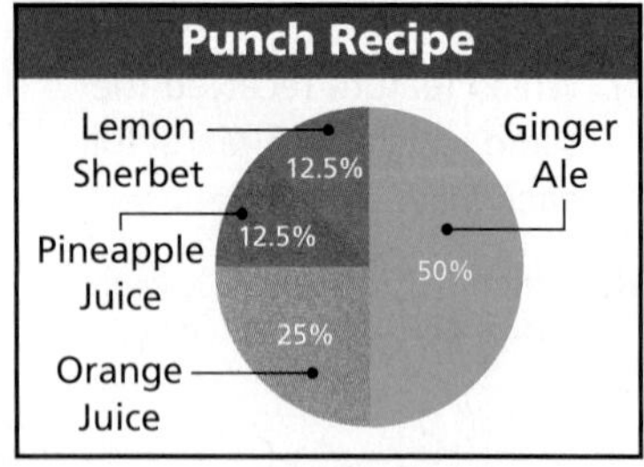

Which ingredients are present in equal amounts? lemon sherbet and pineapple juice

A double-line graph can be used to compare how two related data sets change over time. A double-line graph has a key to distinguish between the two sets of data.

EXAMPLE 4 Reading and Interpreting Double-Line Graphs

Use the graph to answer each question.

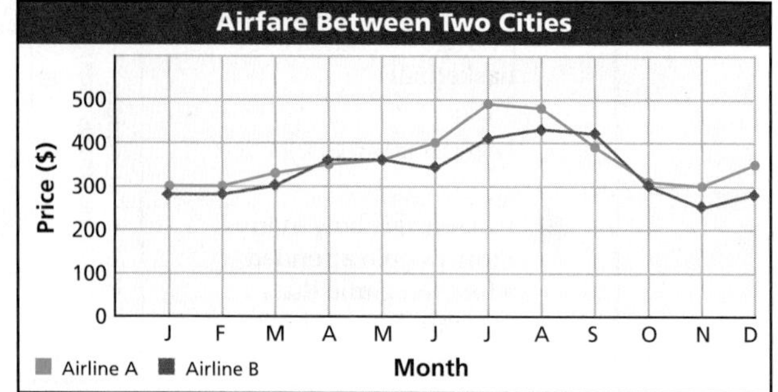

A **In which month(s) did airline B charge more than airline A?**

April and September — *Identify the points when the purple line is higher than the blue line.*

B **During which month(s) did the airlines charge the same airfare?**

May — *Look for the point where the data points overlap.*

4. Use the graph to describe the general trend of the data. **Prices increased from Jan through Jul or Aug, and then prices decreased through Nov.**

A **circle graph** shows parts of a whole. The entire circle represents 100% of the data and each sector represents a percent of the total. Circle graphs are good for comparing each category of data to the whole set.

EXAMPLE 5 Reading and Interpreting Circle Graphs

Use the graph to answer each question.

Reading Math

The sections of a circle graph are called *sectors*.

A **Which two fruits together make up half of the fruit salad?**

bananas and strawberries

Look for two fruits that together make up half of the circle.

B **Which fruit is used more than any other?**

cantaloupe

Look for the largest sector of the graph.

5. Use the graph to determine what percent of the fruit salad is cantaloupe. **31.25%**

INTERVENTION

Questioning Strategies

EXAMPLES 3–4

- Why is the data in **Example 3** displayed in a line graph?
- Why do the graphs in **Examples 2** and **4** have a key? Do the graphs in **Examples 1** and **3** need a key?

EXAMPLE 5

- What does the size of each sector indicate?
- When would you use a circle graph instead of a bar graph?

EXAMPLE 6 Choosing and Creating an Appropriate Display

Use the given data to make a graph. Explain why you chose that type of graph.

A

Livestock Show Entries	
Animal	Number
Chicken	38
Goat	10
Horse	32
Pig	12
Sheep	25

A bar graph is appropriate for this data because it will be a good way to compare categories.

Step 1 Determine an appropriate scale and interval. The scale must include all of the data values. The scale is separated into equal parts, called intervals.

Step 2 Use the data to determine the lengths of the bars. Draw bars of equal width. The bars should not touch.

Step 3 Title the graph and label the horizontal and vertical scales.

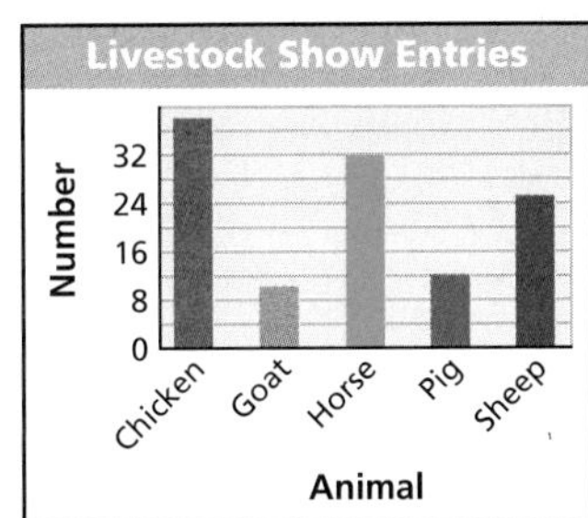

B

Division of Crops	
Crop	Area (acres)
Corn	70
Fallow	50
Mixed vegetables	10
Soybeans	40
Wheat	30

A circle graph is appropriate for this data because it shows categories as parts of a whole.

Step 1 Calculate the percent of the total represented by each category.

Corn: $\frac{70}{200} = 0.35 = 35\%$

Soybeans: $\frac{40}{200} = 0.2 = 20\%$

Fallow: $\frac{50}{200} = 0.25 = 25\%$

Wheat: $\frac{30}{200} = 0.15 = 15\%$

Mixed vegetables: $\frac{10}{200} = 0.05 = 5\%$

Step 2 Find the angle measure for each sector of the graph. Since there are 360° in a circle, multiply each percent by 360°.

Corn: $0.35 \times 360° = 126°$

Fallow: $0.25 \times 360° = 90°$

Mixed vegetables: $0.05 \times 360° = 18°$

Soybeans: $0.2 \times 360° = 72°$

Wheat: $0.15 \times 360° = 54°$

Step 3 Use a compass to draw a circle. Mark the center and use a straightedge to draw one radius. Then use a protractor to draw each central angle.

Step 4 Title the graph and label each sector.

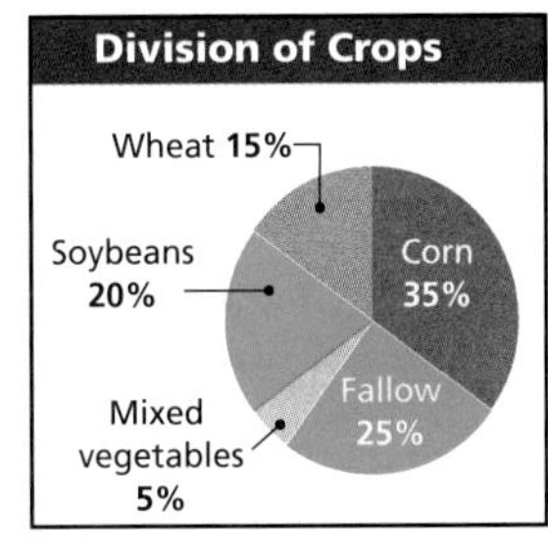

COMMON ERROR ALERT

Students may have trouble deciding whether to display data in a bar or circle graph. If the data represents a whole, a circle graph is probably a better choice. If the data displays several categories that do not make up a whole, a bar graph is probably a better choice.

Power Presentations with PowerPoint®

Additional Examples

Example 6

Use the given data to make a graph. Explain why you chose that type of graph.

A.

Flower	Number
Roses	6
Lilies	4
Agapanthus	6
Peonies	3

A bar graph is good for displaying categories that do not make up a whole.

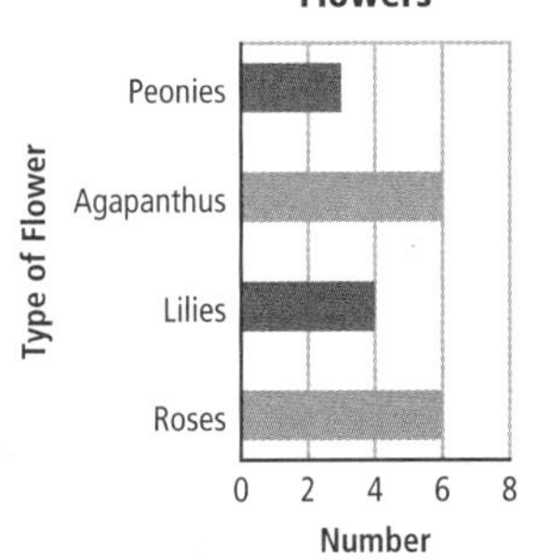

B.

Degree Held	Faculty Members
PhD	6
Master's	24
Bachelor's	31

A circle graph is good for displaying categories that make up a whole.

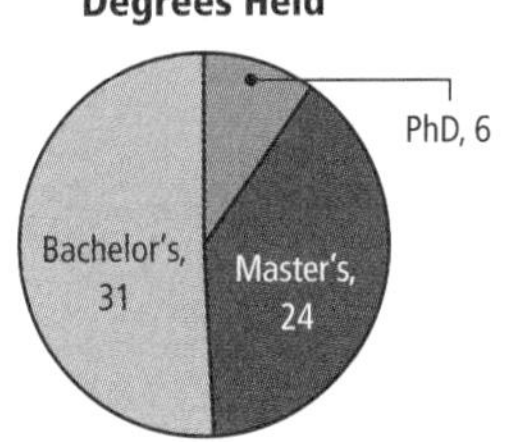

Power Presentations with PowerPoint®

Additional Examples

Example 6

Use the given data to make a graph. Explain why you chose that type of graph.

C.

Year	Farms
1880	265
1920	238
1960	124
2000	53

A line graph is good for displaying how something changes over time.

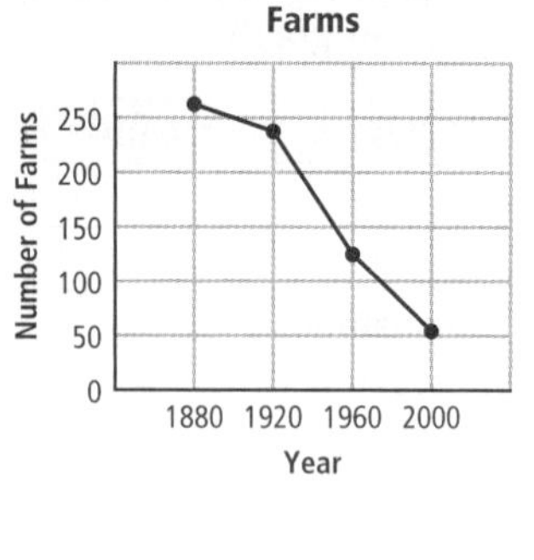

INTERVENTION

Questioning Strategies

EXAMPLE 6

- How do you determine the interval to use on a bar or line graph?
- How do you determine the angle measurements for a circle graph?

Inclusion Axis labels should describe the data and the units of measurement if applicable. The title of a graph should quickly summarize what the graph displays.

Use the given data to make a graph. Explain why you chose that type of graph.

Chinnick College Enrollment	
Year	**Students**
1930	586
1955	2,361
1980	15,897
2005	21,650

A line graph is appropriate for this data because it will show the change in enrollment over a period of time.

Step 1 Determine the scale and interval for each set of data. Time should be plotted on the horizontal axis because it is independent.

Step 2 Plot a point for each pair of values. Connect the points using line segments.

Step 3 Title the graph and label the horizontal and vertical scales.

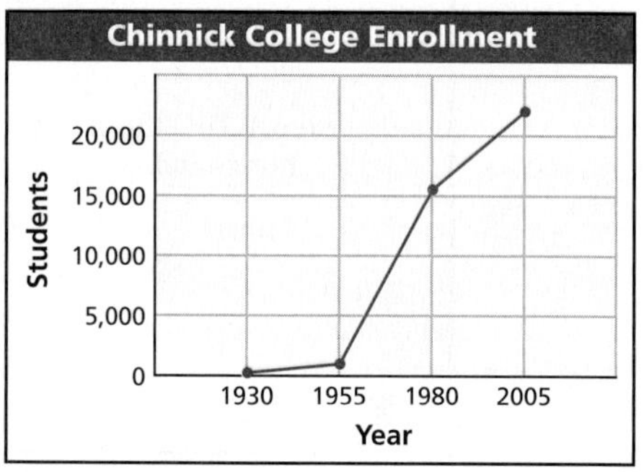

6.

Vera's Day

Homework, 10; Other, 17; Sleeping, 45; Sports, 10; School, 30; Eating, 8

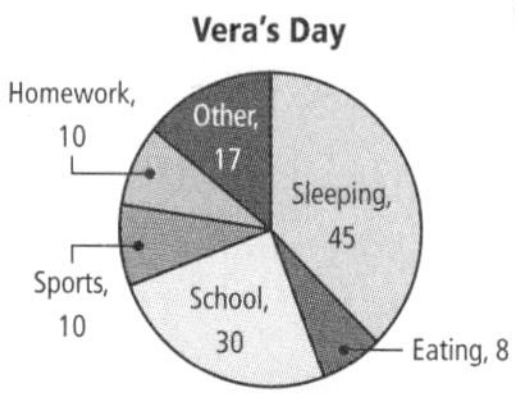

A circle graph shows parts of a whole.

CHECK IT OUT! **6. Use the given data to make a graph. Explain why you chose that type of graph.**

The data below shows how Vera spends her time during a typical 5-day week during the school year.

Vera's Schedule						
Activity	Sleeping	Eating	School	Sports	Homework	Other
Time (h)	45	8	30	10	10	17

THINK AND DISCUSS

1. What are some comparisons you can make by looking at a bar graph?

2. Name some key components of a good line graph.

3. GET ORGANIZED Copy and complete the graphic organizer. In each box, tell which kind of graph is described.

Know it! Note

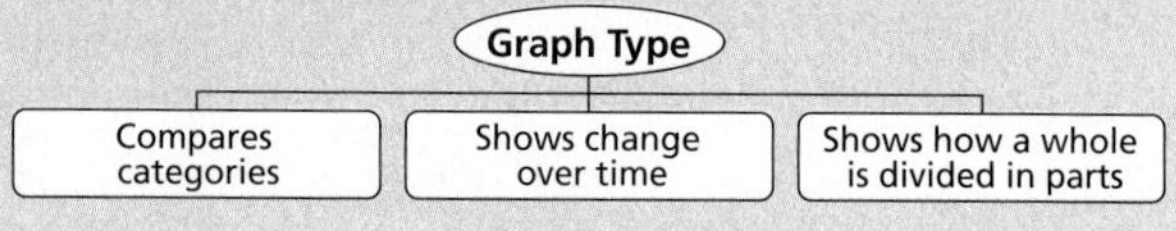

Graph Type

- Compares categories
- Shows change over time
- Shows how a whole is divided in parts

3 Close

Summarize

Review the characteristics of each type of graph.

Bar/Double-Bar Graph: data organized into categories for the purpose of comparing categories

Line/Double-Line Graph: data that changes over a period of time

Circle Graph: data organized into categories for the purpose of comparing each category to the whole set

ONGOING ASSESSMENT and INTERVENTION

***Diagnose Before* the Lesson**
10-1 Warm Up, TE p. 700

***Monitor During* the Lesson**
Check It Out! Exercises, SE pp. 700–704
Questioning Strategies, TE pp. 701–704

***Assess After* the Lesson**
10-1 Lesson Quiz, TE p. 708
Alternative Assessment, TE p. 708

Answers to *Think and Discuss*

Possible answers:

1. You can compare quantities.
2. The horizontal and vertical scales start at 0, time is placed on the horizontal axis, and even intervals are used between items on the horizontal axis.
3. See p. A9.

10-1 Exercises

go.hrw.com
Homework Help Online
KEYWORD: MA7 10-1
Parent Resources Online
KEYWORD: MA7 Parent

GUIDED PRACTICE

2. As the steepness of the line increases, the rate of change increases.

Vocabulary Use the vocabulary from this lesson to answer the following questions.

1. In a *circle graph,* what does each sector represent? **one part of a whole**
2. In a *line graph,* how does the slope of a line segment relate to the rate of change?

SEE EXAMPLE 1 p. 700

Use the bar graph for Exercises 3 and 4.

3. Estimate the total number of animals at the shelter. **82 animals**
4. There are 3 times as many ___?___ as ___?___ at the animal shelter. **cats; rabbits**

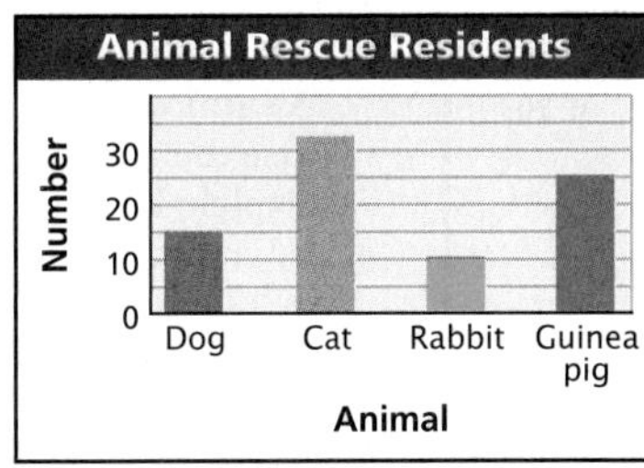

SEE EXAMPLE 2 p. 701

Use the double-bar graph for Exercises 5–7.

5. About how much more is a club level seat at stadium A than at stadium B? **$15**
6. Which type of seat is the closest in price at the two stadiums? **box seats**
7. Describe one relationship between the ticket prices at stadium A and stadium B. **Prices at stadium A are greater than prices at stadium B.**

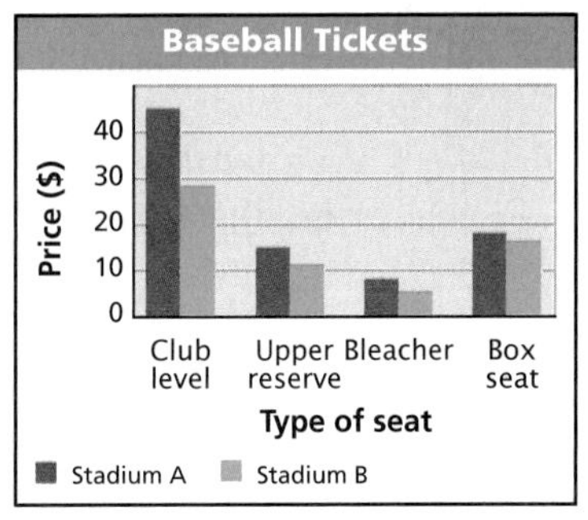

SEE EXAMPLE 3 p. 701

Use the line graph for Exercises 8 and 9.

8. Estimate the number of tickets sold during the week of the greatest sales. **34,000 tickets**
9. Which one-week period of time saw the greatest change in sales? **between weeks 4 and 5**

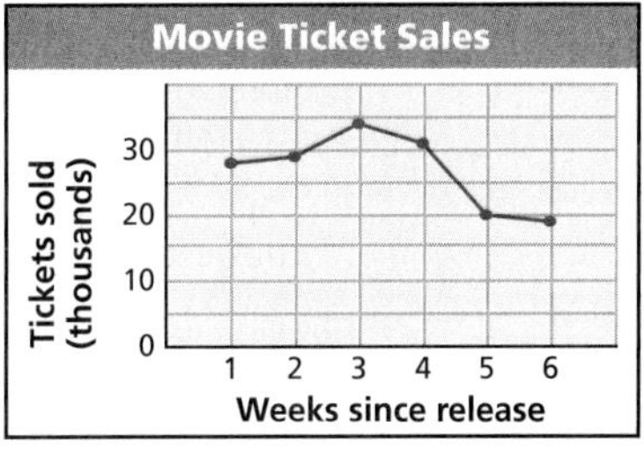

SEE EXAMPLE 4 p. 702

Use the double-line graph for Exercises 10–12.

10. When was the support for the two candidates closest? **1 week before the election**
11. Estimate the difference in voter support for the two candidates five weeks before the election. **18%**
12. Describe the general trend(s) of voter support for the two candidates.

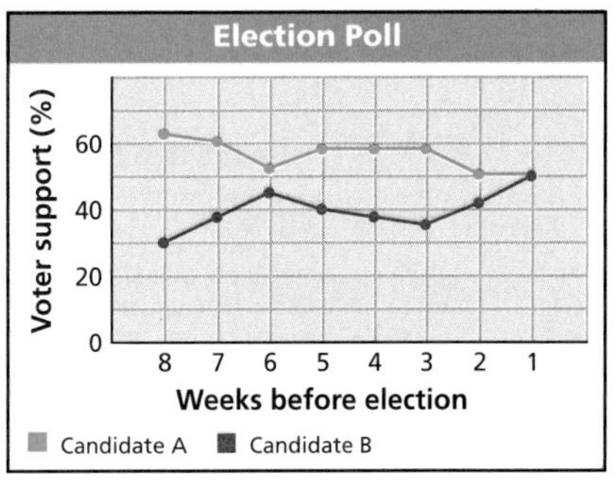

10-1 Exercises

Assignment Guide

Assign *Guided Practice* exercises as necessary.

If you finished Examples **1–4**
Basic 17–26
Average 17–26
Advanced 17–26

If you finished Examples **1–6**
Basic 17–35, 37–39, 43–48
Average 17–29, 34–48
Advanced 17–29, 34–48

Homework Quick Check
Quickly check key concepts.
Exercises: 18, 20, 22, 24, 28, 29, 32

Answers

12. Support for candidate B generally increased. Support for candidate A generally decreased.

State Resources

Social Studies Link **Exercises 17 and 18** show populations of Native American tribes. The Cherokee now live mostly in Oklahoma, while the Chippewa, also called Ojibwe or Ojibwa, live primarily in the Great Lakes area. Some Choctaw live in Mississippi and Alabama as well as in Oklahoma. The Navajo Nation is located on the borders of the states of Arizona, New Mexico, and Utah, and the Sioux tribes, also called Lakota, live mostly in the Dakotas.

Reading Math Tell students that the word *overall* in **Exercise 19** indicates a sum. Students will need to add the number of customers for lunch and dinner to answer the question. Although Saturday had the most dinner customers, there were relatively few lunch customers.

Answers

16. **Karim's Budget**

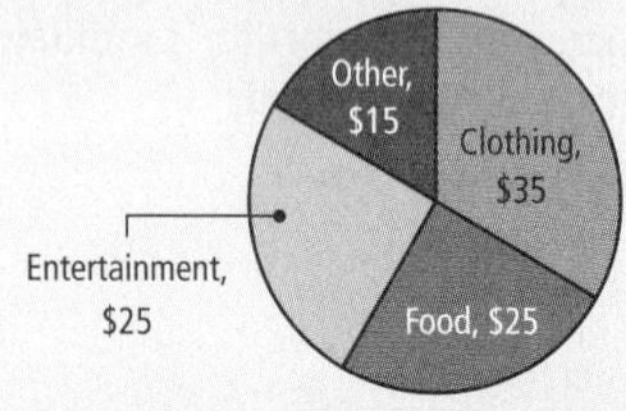

SEE EXAMPLE 5 p. 702

Use the circle graph for Exercises 13–15.

13. Which color is least represented in the ball playpen? **purple**
14. There are 500 balls in the playpen. How many are yellow? **120**
15. Which two colors are approximately equally represented in the ball playpen? **blue and green**

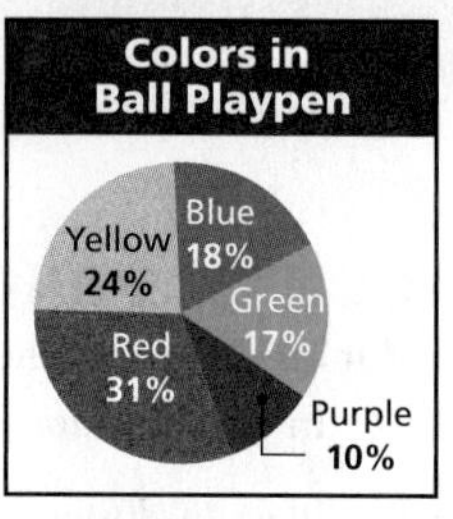

SEE EXAMPLE 6 p. 703

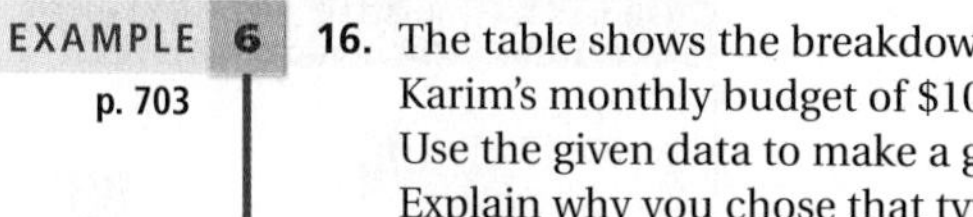

16. The table shows the breakdown of Karim's monthly budget of $100. Use the given data to make a graph. Explain why you chose that type of graph.
A circle graph compares how much of Karim's total budget is spent in each category.

Item/Activity	Spending ($)
Clothing	35
Food	25
Entertainment	25
Other	15

PRACTICE AND PROBLEM SOLVING

Independent Practice

For Exercises	See Example
17–18	1
19–21	2
22–23	3
24–26	4
27–28	5
29	6

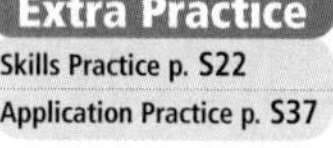

Extra Practice
Skills Practice p. S22
Application Practice p. S37

Use the bar graph for Exercises 17 and 18.

17. Estimate the difference in population between the tribes with the largest and the smallest population. **225,000**
18. Approximately what percent of the total population shown in the table is Cherokee? **about 35%**

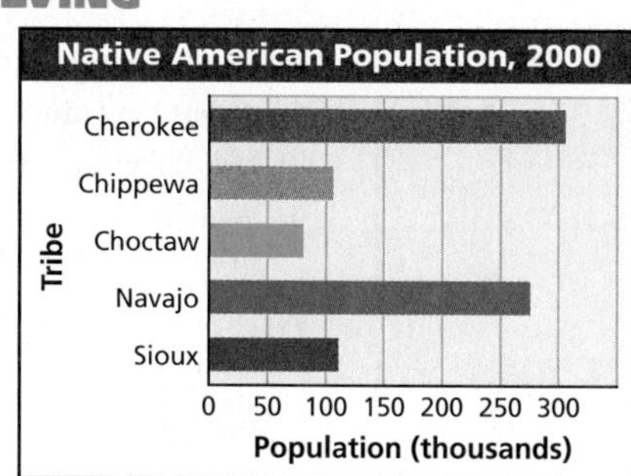

Source: U.S. Census Bureau

Use the double bar graph for Exercises 19–21.

19. On what day did Ray do the most overall business? **Fri**
20. On what day did Ray have the busiest lunch? **Wed**
21. On Sunday, about how many times as great was the number of dinner customers as the number of lunch customers? **3.5 times**

Ray's Restaurant
Customers: 0, 50, 100, 150, 200, 250
S M T W T F S
Day of the week
Lunch ■ Dinner

Use the line graph for Exercises 22 and 23.

22. Between which two games did Marlon's score increase the most? **games 1 and 2**
23. Between which three games did Marlon's score increase by about the same amount? **games 3, 4, and 5**

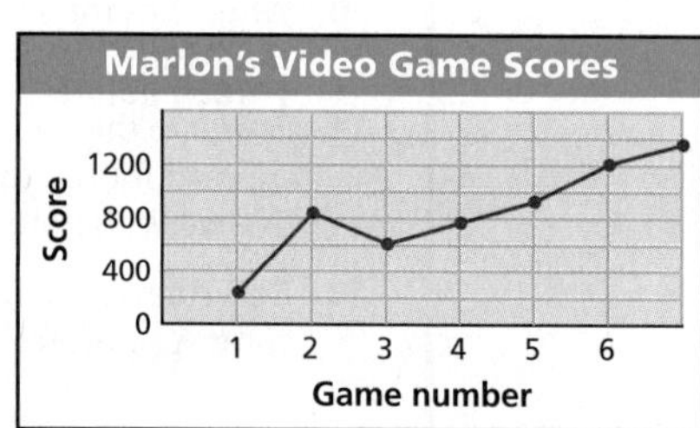

10-1 PRACTICE A

10-1 PRACTICE C

10-1 PRACTICE B

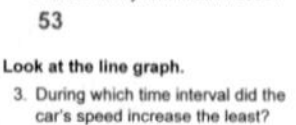

Look at the double bar graph.
1. Which was the first year that the Barnes rented more DVDs than VHS tapes? **2005**
2. About how many videos did the Barnes family rent in all in 2003? **53**

Look at the line graph.
3. During which time interval did the car's speed increase the least? **1 to 2 s**
4. Describe how the speed changed over time. **It always increased, but from 0–6 s, the speed increased by growing amounts.**

Look at the circle graph.
5. There were 5 times the number of orders for **chocolate** as there were for strawberry.
6. What percent of the orders for ice cream were for mint chip or vanilla? **60%**
7. The table shows the number of customers who pumped 4 types of fuel at a gas station in a given time period. Use the given data to make a graph. Explain why you chose that type of graph.

87 Octane	89 Octane	93 Octane	Diesel
12	1	5	2

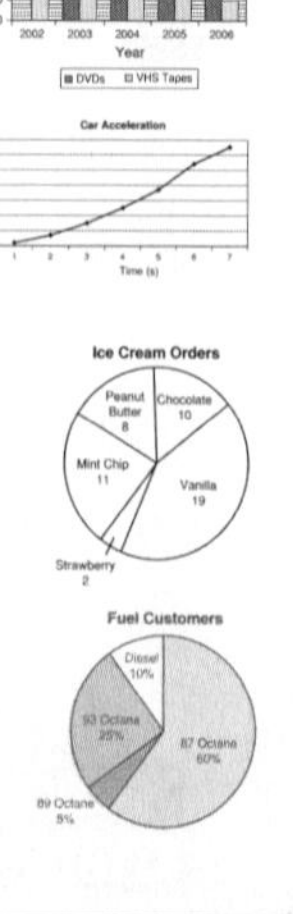

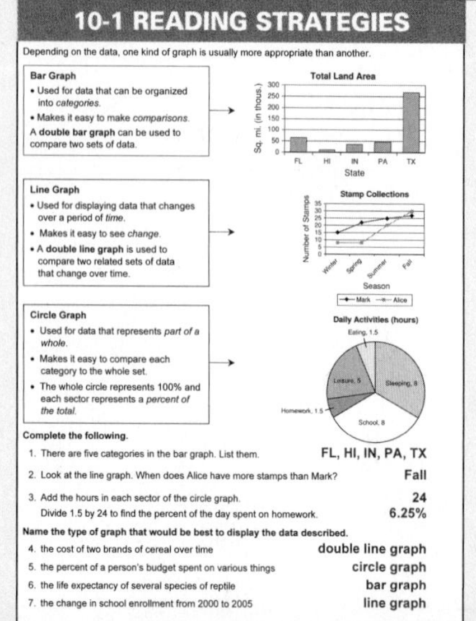

10-1 READING STRATEGIES

Depending on the data, one kind of graph is usually more appropriate than another.

Bar Graph
- Used for data that can be organized into *categories*.
- Makes it easy to make *comparisons*.

A **double bar graph** can be used to compare two sets of data.

Line Graph
- Used for displaying data that changes over a period of *time*.
- Makes it easy to see *change*.
- A **double line graph** is used to compare two related sets of data that change over time.

Circle Graph
- Used for data that represents *part of a whole*.
- Makes it easy to compare each category to the whole set.
- The whole circle represents 100% and each sector represents a *percent of the total*.

Complete the following.
1. There are five categories in the bar graph. List them. **FL, HI, IN, PA, TX**
2. Look at the line graph. When does Alice have more stamps than Mark? **Fall**
3. Add the hours in each sector of the circle graph. **24**
Divide 1.5 by 24 to find the percent of the day spent on homework. **6.25%**

Name the type of graph that would be best to display the data described.
4. the cost of two brands of cereal over time **double line graph**
5. the percent of a person's budget spent on various things **circle graph**
6. the life expectancy of several species of reptile **bar graph**
7. the change in school enrollment from 2000 to 2005 **line graph**

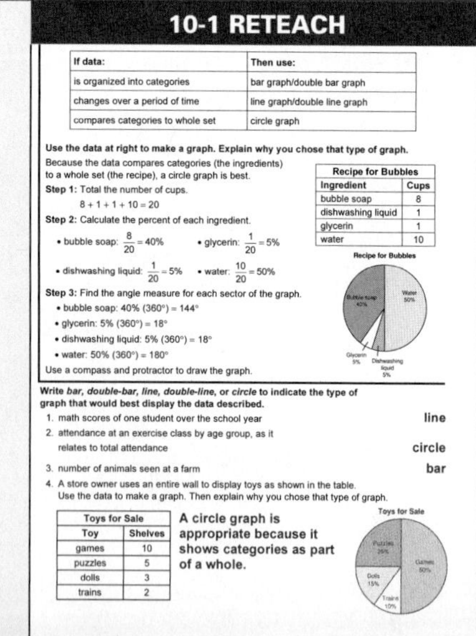

10-1 RETEACH

If data:	Then use:
is organized into categories	bar graph/double bar graph
changes over a period of time	line graph/double line graph
compares categories to whole set	circle graph

Use the data at right to make a graph. Explain why you chose that type of graph.
Because the data compares categories (the ingredients) to a whole set (the recipe), a circle graph is best.

Recipe for Bubbles	
Ingredient	Cups
bubble soap	8
dishwashing liquid	1
glycerin	1
water	10

Step 1: Total the number of cups.
8 + 1 + 1 + 10 = 20
Step 2: Calculate the percent of each ingredient.
- bubble soap: $\frac{8}{20} = 40\%$ • glycerin: $\frac{1}{20} = 5\%$
- dishwashing liquid: $\frac{1}{20} = 5\%$ • water: $\frac{10}{20} = 50\%$

Step 3: Find the angle measure for each sector of the graph.
- bubble soap: 40% (360°) = 144°
- glycerin: 5% (360°) = 18°
- dishwashing liquid: 5% (360°) = 18°
- water: 50% (360°) = 180°

Use a compass and protractor to draw the graph.

Write *bar, double-bar, line, double-line,* or *circle* to indicate the type of graph that would best display the data described.
1. math scores of one student over the school year **line**
2. attendance at an exercise class by age group, as it relates to total attendance **circle**
3. number of animals seen at a farm **bar**
4. A store owner uses an entire wall to display toys as shown in the table. Use the data to make a graph. Then explain why you chose that type of graph.

Toys for Sale	
Toy	Shelves
games	10
puzzles	5
dolls	3
trains	2

A circle graph is appropriate because it shows categories as part of a whole.

Use the double-line graph for Exercises 24–26.

Juan's Stock Values

Value per share ($): 0, 10, 20, 30
Date: Jan 2004, Apr 2004, Jul 2004, Oct 2004, Jan 2005
■ Stock X ■ Stock Y

24. What was the average value per share of Juan's two stocks in July 2004? **$32.50**

25. Which stock's value changed the most over any time period?

25. Stock Y changed the most between Apr. and Jul. of 2004.

26. Describe the trend of the values of both stocks. **Both generally increased.**

Use the circle graph for Exercises 27 and 28.

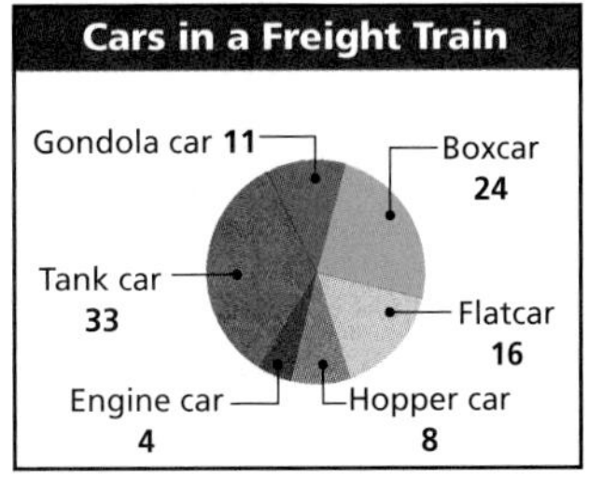

27. About what percent of the total number of cars are hopper cars? $8\frac{1}{3}\%$

28. About what percent of the total number of cars are gondola or tank cars? **about 46%**

29. The table shows the weight of twin babies at various times from birth to four weeks old. Use the given data to make a graph. Explain why you chose that type of graph.

A double-line graph shows the change over time for 2 things. It also allows you to compare the 2 things.

Age (days)	Boy's Weight (lb)	Girl's Weight (lb)
1	5.3	5.7
3	5.0	5.2
7	5.5	5.9
14	6.2	6.8
28	7.9	7.5

Write *bar, double-bar, line, double-line,* or *circle* to indicate the type of graph that would best display the data described.

30. attendance at a carnival each year over a ten-year period **line**

31. attendance at two different carnivals each year over a ten-year period **double line**

32. attendance at five different carnivals during the same year **bar**

33. attendance at a carnival by age group as it relates to total attendance **circle**

34. **Critical Thinking** Give an example of real-world data that would best be displayed by each type of graph: line graph, circle graph, double-bar graph.

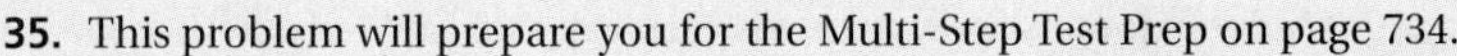

MULTI-STEP TEST PREP

35. This problem will prepare you for the Multi-Step Test Prep on page 734.

The first modern Olympic Games took place in 1896 in Athens, Greece. The circle graph shows the total number of medals won by several countries at the Olympic Games of 1896.

a. Which country won the most medals? Estimate the percent of the medals won by this country. **Greece; about 40%**

b. Which country won the second most medals? Estimate the percent of the medals won by this country. **United States; about 15%**

MULTI-STEP TEST PREP Exercise **35** involves reading a circle graph. This exercise prepares students for the Multi-Step Test Prep on page 734.

Answers

29.

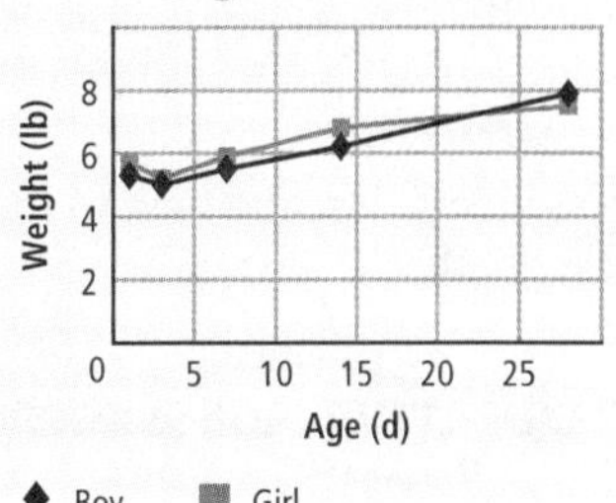

A double-line graph shows the change over time for 2 things. It also allows you to compare the 2 things.

34. Possible answer: line graph: your height over time; circle graph: your CD collection divided into categories; double-bar graph: number of hours you spend on homework or sports each day of the week

10-1 PROBLEM SOLVING

The table below gives the top five ringtone genres reported during a survey of cell phone subscribers in August, 2005.

Ringtone genre	Males (millions)	Females (millions)
Hip Hop or Rap	2.232	2.472
Rock or Alternative	2.219	2.082
Pop	1.044	2.069
TV/Movie/Game Themes	1.161	1.371
Classic Rock	0.949	0.918

Top Five Ringtone Genres

1. Use the data to make a graph below. Explain why you chose that type of graph.
   A double-bar graph compares the number of males and females that prefer each of the five categories.

2. From the graph (*not* the table), explain how you can tell that the Pop genre is nearly twice as popular with females as males.
   In the category of Pop, the bar for females is twice as tall as the bar for males.

In 2000, there were approximately 27 million people 18–24 years old in the United States. The circle graph below shows the highest level of education for that population. Use the graph to select the best answers for questions 3–5.

Educational Attainment of the Population 18–24 Years Old, 2000

3. Which level of education was least represented?
   A Less than high school graduate
   B Some college or associate degree
   C High school graduate
   D Bachelor's degree or higher

4. How many 18–24 year-olds had attained a bachelor's degree or higher?
   F 2.16 million H 10.26 million
   G 8 million J 12.42 million

5. How many 18–24 year-olds never attended college?
   A 6.75 million C 12.42 million
   B 7.83 million **D** 14.58 million

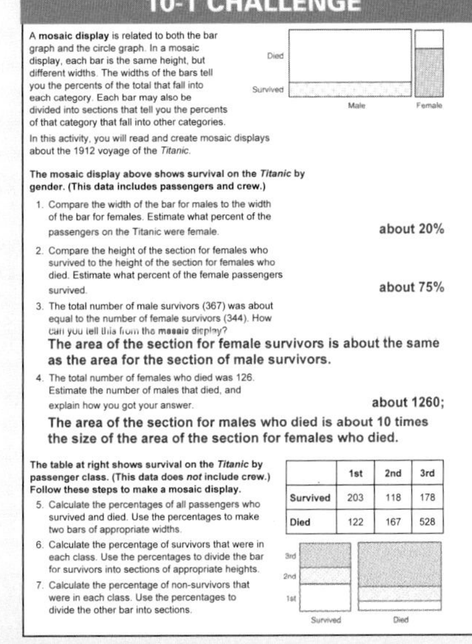

10-1 CHALLENGE

A **mosaic display** is related to both the bar graph and the circle graph. In a mosaic display, each bar is the same height, but different widths. The widths of the bars tell you the percents of the total that fall into each category. Each bar may also be divided into sections that tell you the percents of that category that fall into other categories.

In this activity, you will read and create mosaic displays about the 1912 voyage of the *Titanic*.

The mosaic display above shows survival on the *Titanic* by gender. (This data includes passengers and crew.)

1. Compare the width of the bar for males to the width of the bar for females. Estimate what percent of the passengers on the Titanic were female. **about 20%**

2. Compare the height of the section for females who survived to the height of the section for females who died. Estimate what percent of the female passengers survived. **about 75%**

3. The total number of male survivors (367) was about equal to the number of female survivors (344). How can you tell this from the mosaic display?
   The area of the section for female survivors is about the same as the area for the section of male survivors.

4. The total number of females who died was 126. Estimate the number of males that died, and explain how you got your answer. **about 1260;**
   The area of the section for males who died is about 10 times the size of the area of the section for females who died.

The table at right shows survival on the *Titanic* by passenger class. (This data does *not* include crew.) Follow these steps to make a mosaic display.

	1st	2nd	3rd
Survived	203	118	178
Died	122	167	528

5. Calculate the percentages of all passengers who survived and died. Use the percentages to make two bars of appropriate widths.

6. Calculate the percentage of survivors that were in each class. Use the percentages to divide the bar for survivors into sections of appropriate heights.

7. Calculate the percentage of non-survivors that were in each class. Use the percentages to divide the other bar into sections.

In **Exercise 37,** the words *contribution* and *each* show that the focus is on the *parts* of the team's *total* points, so a circle graph is most appropriate.

Students who chose **J** in **Exercise 38** found 75% of 4 but did not add that amount to 4.

Journal

Have students describe how to make a circle graph.

ALTERNATIVE ASSESSMENT

Have students collect real-world data and display it in an appropriate graph.

Power Presentations with PowerPoint®

10-1 Lesson Quiz

1. Which two apartments are about the same size?

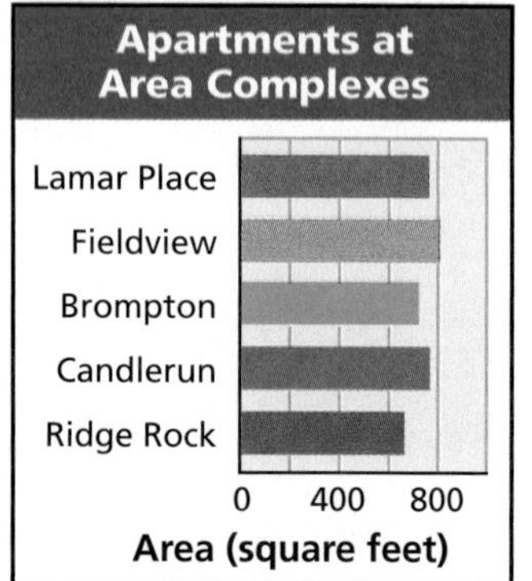

2. In which week(s) did store B charge more than store A?

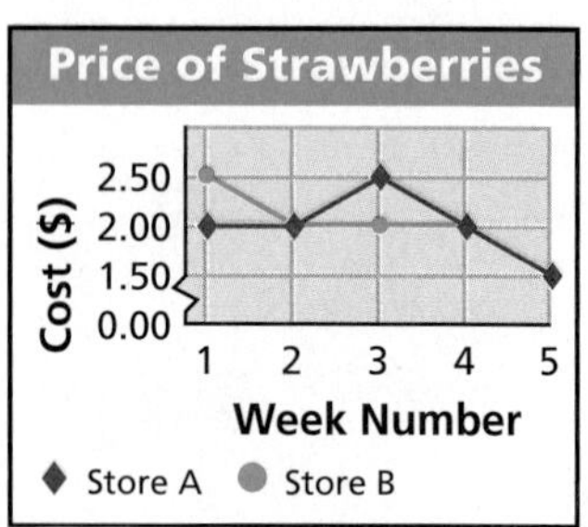

3. The table shows how many orders were placed for each type of muffin at a bakery in one week. Use the data to make a graph. Explain why you chose that type of graph.

Type	Number
Banana nut	69
Blueberry	20
Cinnamon chip	25
Lemon poppy seed	11

For answers, see p. A31.

Also available on transparency

36. **Write About It** Explain how you could use a line graph to make predictions.
If the graph is generally increasing, you can predict that the value in the future will increase.

TEST PREP

37. Which type of graph would best display the contribution of each high school basketball player to the team, in terms of points scored?
Ⓐ Bar graph Ⓑ Line graph Ⓒ Double-line graph Ⓓ Circle graph

38. At what age did Marianna have 75% more magazine subscriptions than she did at age 40?
Ⓕ 25
Ⓖ 30
Ⓗ 35
Ⓙ 45

Marianna's Magazines
Subscriptions: 0 2 4 6 8
Marianna's age (yr): 15 20 25 30 35 40 45

39. **Short Response** The table shows the number of students in each algebra class. Make a graph to display the data. Explain why you chose that type of graph.

Teacher	Students
Mr. Abrams	34
Ms. Belle	29
Mr. Marvin	25
Ms. Swanson	27

CHALLENGE AND EXTEND

Students and teachers at Lauren's school went on one of three field trips.

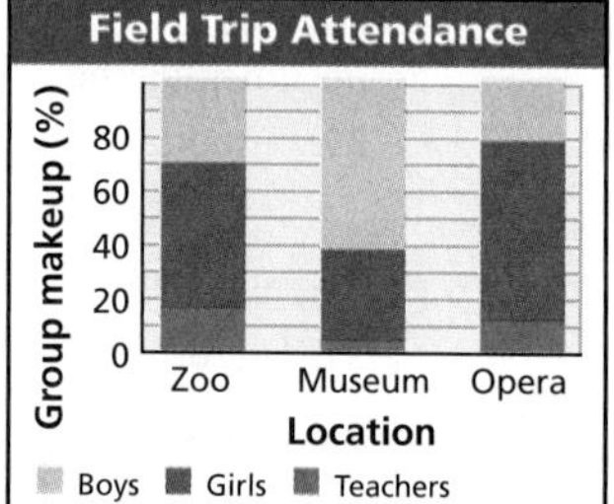

40. On which trip were there more boys than girls? **museum**

41. A total of 60 people went to the museum. Estimate the number of girls who went to the museum. **19 girls**

42. Explain why it is not possible to determine whether fewer teachers went to the museum than to the zoo or the opera.
The graph shows only the percentages of each group made up of teachers, boys, and girls. It does not tell how many people went on each trip.

SPIRAL REVIEW

Find the domain and range for each relation and tell whether the relation is a function. *(Lesson 4-2)*

43. $\{(-3, 3), (-1, 1), (0, 0), (1, 1), (3, 3)\}$ **D: $\{-3, -1, 0, 1, 3\}$; R: $\{0, 1, 3\}$; yes**

44.

x	1	2	3	4	5
y	2	4	6	8	10

D: $\{1, 2, 3, 4, 5\}$; R: $\{2, 4, 6, 8, 10\}$; yes

45. Triangle ABC has vertices on a coordinate plane as follows: $A = (0, 5)$, $B = (3, 0)$, $C = (8, 3)$. Show that $\triangle ABC$ is a right triangle. *(Lesson 5-9)*

Classify each polynomial according to its degree and number of terms. *(Lesson 7-6)*

46. $24y$ **linear monomial**

47. $3x^2 + 6$ **quadratic binomial**

48. $4m - 18m^2 - 45m^3 + 120$ **cubic polynomial**

Answers

39. **Algebra Classrooms**
Students: 0 10 20 30
Teacher: Mr. Abrams, Ms. Belle, Mr. Marvin, Ms. Swanson

A bar graph allows you to compare categories.

45. Slope of $\overline{AB} = \frac{0-5}{3-0} = -\frac{5}{3}$; slope of $\overline{BC} = \frac{3-0}{8-3} = \frac{3}{5}$; $\overline{AB}$ is perpendicular to $\overline{BC}$ because $\left(-\frac{5}{3}\right)\left(\frac{3}{5}\right) = -1$; ABC is a right triangle because it contains a right angle.

10-2 Frequency and Histograms

Objectives
Create stem-and-leaf plots.

Create frequency tables and histograms.

Vocabulary
stem-and-leaf plot
frequency
frequency table
histogram
cumulative frequency

Why learn this?
Stem-and-leaf plots can be used to organize data, like the number of students in elective classes. (See Example 1.)

A **stem-and-leaf plot** arranges data by dividing each data value into two parts. This allows you to see each data value.

The digits other than the last digit of each value are called a stem. → **2|3** ← The last digit of a value is called a leaf.

Key: 2|3 means 23 ← The key tells you how to read each value.

EXAMPLE 1 Making a Stem-and-Leaf Plot

A The numbers of students in each of the elective classes at a school are given below. Use the data to make a stem-and-leaf plot.

24, 14, 12, 25, 32, 18, 23, 24, 9, 18, 34, 28, 24, 27

Number of Students in Elective Classes

Stem	Leaves
0	9
1	2 4 8 8
2	3 4 4 4 5 7 8
3	2 4

Key: 2|3 means 23

The tens digits are the stems.
The ones digits are the leaves. List the leaves from least to greatest within each row.
Title the graph and add a key.

B Marty's and Bill's scores for ten games of bowling are given below. Use the data to make a back-to-back stem-and-leaf plot.

Marty: 137, 149, 167, 134, 121, 127, 143, 123, 168, 162
Bill: 129, 138, 141, 124, 139, 160, 149, 145, 128, 130

Bowling Scores

Marty		Bill
7 3 1	12	4 8 9
7 4	13	0 8 9
9 3	14	1 5 9
	15	
8 7 2	16	0

Key: |14|1 means 141
3|14| means 143

The first two digits are the stems.
The ones digits are the leaves.
Put Marty's scores on the left side and Bill's scores on the right.
Title the graph and add a key.
The graph shows that three of Marty's scores were higher than Bill's highest score.

Writing Math
Stems are always consecutive numbers. In Example 1B, neither player has scores that start with 15, so there are no leaves in that row.

CHECK IT OUT! 1. The temperatures in degrees Celsius for two weeks are given below. Use the data to make a stem-and-leaf plot.
7, 32, 34, 31, 26, 27, 23, 19, 22, 29, 30, 36, 35, 31

1. Temperature (°C)

Stem	Leaves
0	7
1	9
2	2 3 6 7 9
3	0 1 1 2 4 5 6

Key: 1|9 means 19

10-2 Organizer

Pacing: Traditional 1 day
Block $\frac{1}{2}$ day

Objectives: Create stem-and-leaf plots.
Create frequency tables and histograms.

Online Edition
Tutorial Videos

Countdown Week 22

Power Presentations with PowerPoint®

Warm Up

Identify the least and greatest value in each data set.

1. 34, 62, 45, 35, 75, 23, 35, 65, 23 23, 75

2. 1.6, 3.4, 2.6, 4.8, 1.3, 3.5, 4.0 1.3, 4.8

Order the data from least to greatest.

3. 2.4, 5.1, 3.7, 2.1, 3.6, 4.0, 2.9
2.1, 2.4, 2.9, 3.6, 3.7, 4.0, 5.1

4. 5, 5, 6, 8, 7, 4, 6, 5, 9, 3, 6, 6, 9
3, 4, 5, 5, 5, 6, 6, 6, 6, 7, 8, 9, 9

Also available on transparency

Q: What did the investigator say when he collected more data?
A: The stem-and-leaf plot thickens!

1 Introduce

EXPLORATION

10-2 Frequency and Histograms

A teacher is analyzing the scores from the last exam he gave. The scores are shown here.
65, 73, 99, 94, 68, 52, 69, 72, 97, 88, 72, 88, 84, 95, 97, 97, 91, 85, 77, 74

1. How many students took the exam?
2. Order the scores from least to greatest.
3. Complete the table by counting the number of scores that lie in each interval.
4. In which interval do the greatest number of scores lie?
5. Add the values in the right-hand column of the table. What is the sum? Why does this make sense?

Scores	Number of Scores in This Interval
90–99	
80–89	
70–79	
60–69	
50–59	

THINK AND DISCUSS
6. Describe one conclusion that the teacher might make from looking at the table.

Motivate

Give students a set of two-digit numbers. Ask students to group the numbers by tens and then to order each group from least to greatest. Explain that these are the first steps in making a stem-and-leaf plot. Show students a histogram of the same data set. Ask students how they could use their groups of numbers to make a histogram. Line up the numbers in each group vertically.

Explorations and answers are provided in *Alternate Openers: Explorations Transparencies.*

State Resources

The **frequency** of a data value is the number of times it occurs. A **frequency table** shows the frequency of each data value. If the data is divided into intervals, the table shows the frequency of each interval.

EXAMPLE 2 Making a Frequency Table

The final scores for each golfer in a tournament are given below. Use the data to make a frequency table with intervals.

77, 71, 70, 82, 75, 76, 72, 70, 77, 74, 71, 75, 68, 72, 75, 74

Step 1 Identify the least and greatest values.

The least value is 68. The greatest value is 82.

Step 2 Divide the data into equal intervals.

For this data set, use an interval of 3.

Step 3 List the intervals in the first column of the table. Count the number of data values in each interval and list the count in the last column. Give the table a title.

Golf Tournament Scores

Scores	Frequency
68–70	3
71–73	4
74–76	6
77–79	2
80–82	1

2. The numbers of days of Maria's last 15 vacations are listed below. Use the data to make a frequency table with intervals.

4, 8, 6, 7, 5, 4, 10, 6, 7, 14, 12, 8, 10, 15, 12

2.

Days	Frequency
4–6	5
7–9	4
10–12	4
13–15	2

A **histogram** is a bar graph used to display the frequency of data divided into equal intervals. The bars must be of equal width and should touch, but not overlap.

EXAMPLE 3 Making a Histogram

Use the frequency table in Example 2 to make a histogram.

Step 1 Use the scale and interval from the frequency table.

Step 2 Draw a bar for the number of scores in each interval.

All bars should be the same width. The bars should touch, but not overlap.

Step 3 Title the graph and label the horizontal and vertical scales.

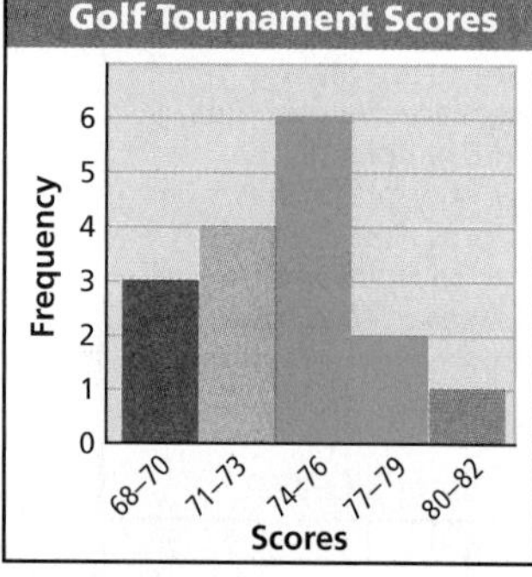

Helpful Hint

The intervals in a histogram must be of equal size.

3. Make a histogram for the number of days of Maria's last 15 vacations.

4, 8, 6, 7, 5, 4, 10, 6, 7, 14, 12, 8, 10, 15, 12

3. Vacation

Number: 0, 1, 2, 3, 4, 5

Length: 4–6, 7–9, 10–12, 13–15

Power Presentations with PowerPoint®

Additional Examples

Example 1

A. The numbers of defective widgets in batches of 1000 are given below. Use the data to make a stem-and-leaf plot.
14, 12, 8, 9, 13, 20, 15, 9, 21, 8, 13, 19

Defective Widgets per Batch

Stem	Leaves
0	8 8 9 9
1	2 3 3 4 5 9
2	0 1

Key: 1|2 means 12

B. The season's scores for the football teams going to the state championship are given below. Use the data to make a back-to-back stem-and-leaf plot.
Team A: 65, 42, 56, 49, 58, 42, 61, 55, 45, 72
Team B: 57, 60, 48, 49, 52, 61, 58, 37, 63, 48

Football State Championship Scores

Team A		Team B
	3	7
9 5 2 2	4	8 8 9
8 6 5	5	2 7 8
5 1	6	0 1 3
2	7	

Key: |4|8 means 48
2|4| means 42

Example 2

The numbers of students enrolled in Western Civilization classes at a university are given below. Use the data to make a frequency table with intervals.
12, 22, 18, 9, 25, 31, 28, 19, 22, 27, 32, 14

Enrollment in Western Civilization Classes

Number Enrolled	Frequency
1–10	1
11–20	4
21–30	5
31–40	2

INTERVENTION
Questioning Strategies

EXAMPLES 1–3

- How do you decide what the stems should be for a stem-and-leaf plot?
- How can a stem-and-leaf plot help you make a frequency table?

2 Teach

Guided Instruction

Tell students that whether they are creating stem-and-leaf plots or frequency tables, it is helpful to first arrange the data from least to greatest. In **Example 2,** point out that frequency tables should have between four and seven intervals and that each interval should have at least two pieces of data.

Visual A stem-and-leaf plot, rotated 90° counterclockwise, resembles a histogram.

Reaching All Learners

Through Kinesthetic Experience

Allow each student to grab a handful of integer chips. These can be found in the Manipulatives Kit (MK). Each student should count the number of integer chips he or she holds and write that number on a sticky note. Write intervals of 5 across the board and have students place their number above the correct interval. Numbers within the same interval should be lined up vertically. The result resembles a histogram.

Cumulative frequency shows the frequency of all data values less than or equal to a given value. You could just count the number of values, but if the data set has many values, you might lose track. Recording the data in a cumulative frequency table can help you keep track of the data values as you count.

EXAMPLE 4 Making a Cumulative Frequency Table

The heights in inches of the players on a school basketball team are given below.

72, 68, 71, 70, 73, 69, 79, 76, 72, 75, 72, 74, 68, 70, 69, 75, 72, 71, 73, 76

a. Use the data to make a cumulative frequency table.

Step 1 Choose intervals for the first column of the table.

Step 2 Record the frequency of values in each interval for the second column.

Step 3 Add the frequency of each interval to the frequencies of all the intervals before it. Put that number in the third column of the table.

Step 4 Title the table.

Basketball Players' Heights

Height (in.)	Frequency	Cumulative Frequency
68–70	6	6
71–73	8	14
74–76	5	19
77–79	1	20

b. How many players have heights under 74 in?

All heights under 74 in. are displayed in the first two rows of the table, so look at the cumulative frequency shown in the second row.

There are 14 players with heights under 74 in.

4. The numbers of vowels in each sentence of a short essay are listed below.

33, 36, 39, 37, 34, 35, 43, 35, 28, 32, 36, 35, 29, 40, 33, 41, 37

a. Use the data to make a cumulative frequency table.

b. How many sentences contain 35 vowels or fewer? **9**

THINK AND DISCUSS

1. In a stem-and-leaf plot, the number of ______?______ is always the same as the number of data values. (*stems* or *leaves*)
2. Explain how to make a histogram from a stem-and-leaf plot.
3. **GET ORGANIZED** Copy and complete the graphic organizer.

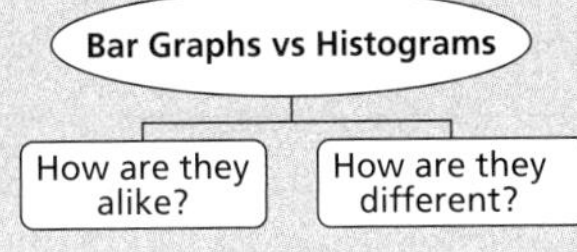

Power Presentations with PowerPoint®

Additional Examples

Example 3

Use the frequency table in **Additional Example 2** to make a histogram.

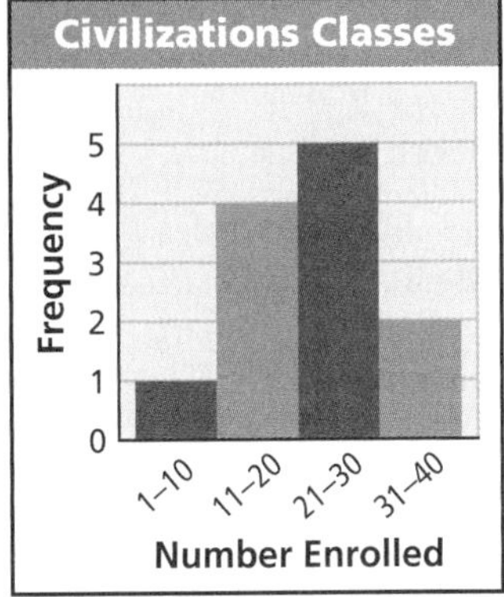

Example 4

The weights (in ounces) of packages of pork chops are given below.

19, 20, 26, 18, 25, 29, 18, 18, 22, 24, 27, 26, 24, 21, 29, 19

A. Use the data to make a cumulative frequency table.

Pork Chops

Weight (oz)	Frequency	Cumulative Frequency
18–20	6	6
21–23	2	8
24–26	5	13
27–29	3	16

B. How many packages weigh less than 24 ounces? 8

Answer to *Check It Out!*

4a. See p. A31.

3 Close

Summarize

Remind students that stem-and-leaf plots, frequency tables, and histograms all show how often a data value, or range of data values, occurs. A benefit of a stem-and-leaf plot is that it shows what the individual data values are. A histogram gives a quick visual representation of where most of the data lie, but it does not reveal the individual data values.

ONGOING ASSESSMENT and INTERVENTION

***Diagnose Before* the Lesson**
10-2 Warm Up, TE p. 709

***Monitor During* the Lesson**
Check It Out! Exercises, SE pp. 709–711
Questioning Strategies, TE pp. 710–711

***Assess After* the Lesson**
10-2 Lesson Quiz, TE p. 715
Alternative Assessment, TE p. 715

INTERVENTION
Questioning Strategies

EXAMPLE 

- What does the last number in the cumulative frequency column represent? Explain.

Answers to *Think and Discuss*

1. leaves
2. The stems are the intervals, and the number of leaves for each stem gives the height of the bar.
3. See p. A9.

10-2 Exercises

Assignment Guide

Assign *Guided Practice* exercises as necessary.

If you finished Examples **1–2**
Basic 7–9
Average 7–9, 21
Advanced 7–9, 21

If you finished Examples **1–4**
Basic 7–16, 18–20, 22–28
Average 7–11, 13–20, 22–28
Advanced 7–11, 13, 15–28

Homework Quick Check
Quickly check key concepts.
Exercises: 7, 8, 9, 10, 11, 16

Answers

2.

Stem	Leaves
1	8 9
2	0 1 1 1 1 2 2 2 3 4

Key: 1|8 means 18

3.

Austin		New York
9 9 9	1	
4 3 2 1	2	
6 5 3 2 0	3	1 3 3 3 6 6 7 9
	4	1 1 2 2

Key: |3|1 means 3.1
9|1| means 1.9

4–6a, 7. See p. A31.

State Resources

10-2 Exercises

go.hrw.com
Homework Help Online
KEYWORD: MA7 10-2
Parent Resources Online
KEYWORD: MA7 Parent

GUIDED PRACTICE

1. **Vocabulary** A(n) ___?___ is a data display that shows individual data values. (*stem-and-leaf plot* or *histogram*) **stem-and-leaf plot**

SEE EXAMPLE 1 p. 709

2. **Sports** The ages of professional basketball players at the time the players were recruited are given. Use the data to make a stem-and-leaf plot.

Ages When Recruited											
21	23	21	18	22	19	24	22	21	22	20	21

3. **Weather** The average monthly rainfall for two cities (in inches) is given below. Use the data to make a back-to-back stem-and-leaf plot.

Average Monthly Rainfall (in.)												
Austin, TX	1.9	2.4	1.9	3.0	3.6	3.3	1.9	2.1	3.2	3.5	2.2	2.3
New York, NY	3.3	3.1	3.9	3.7	4.2	3.3	4.1	4.1	3.6	3.3	4.2	3.6

SEE EXAMPLE 2 p. 710

4. **Sports** The finishing times of runners in a 5K race, to the nearest minute, are given. Use the data to make a frequency table with intervals.

Finishing Times in 5K Race (to the nearest minute)								
19	25	23	29	32	30	21	22	24
19	28	26	31	34	30	28	25	24

SEE EXAMPLE 3 p. 710

5. **Biology** The breathing intervals of gray whales are given. Use the frequency table to make a histogram for the data.

Breathing Intervals (min)	
Interval	Frequency
5–7	4
8–10	7
11–13	7
14–16	8

SEE EXAMPLE 4 p. 711

6. The scores made by a group of eleventh-grade students on the mathematics portion of the SAT are given.
   a. Use the data to make a cumulative frequency table.
   b. How many students scored 650 or higher on the mathematics portion of the SAT? **5**

Scores on Mathematics Portion of SAT							
520	560	720	690	540	630	790	540
600	580	710	500	540	660	630	

PRACTICE AND PROBLEM SOLVING

7. The numbers of people who visited a park each day over two weeks during different seasons are given below. Use the data to make a back-to-back stem-and-leaf plot.

Visitors to a Park														
Summer	25	25	26	27	27	57	59	22	23	29	22	23	54	53
Winter	11	12	13	9	30	27	4	19	14	19	21	33	35	9

Independent Practice	
For Exercises	See Example
7–8	1
9	2
10	3
11	4

Extra Practice
Skills Practice p. S22
Application Practice p. S37

8. **Weather** The daily high temperatures in degrees Fahrenheit in a town during one month are given. Use the data to make a stem-and-leaf plot.

Daily High Temperatures (°F)									
68	72	79	77	70	72	75	71	64	64
68	62	70	71	78	83	83	87	91	89
87	75	73	70	69	69	62	58	71	76

9. The overall GPAs of several high school seniors are given. Use the data to make a frequency table with intervals.

Overall GPAs								
3.6	2.9	3.1	3.0	2.5	2.6	3.8	2.9	
2.2	2.9	3.1	3.3	3.6	3.0	2.3	2.8	2.9

10. **Chemistry** The atomic masses of the nonmetal elements are given in the table. Use the frequency table to make a histogram for the data.

Atomic Masses of Nonmetal Elements					
Interval	0–49.9	50–99.9	100–149.9	150–199.9	200–249.9
Frequency	11	3	2	0	2

11. The numbers of pretzels found in several samples of snack mix are given in the table.
    a. Use the data to make a cumulative frequency table.
    b. How many samples of snack mix had fewer than 42 pretzels? **10**

Numbers of Pretzels				
42	39	39	38	40
41	44	42	38	44
47	36	40	40	43	38

LINK
Automobiles

Solar cars usually weigh between 330 and 880 pounds. A conventional car weighs over 4000 pounds.

12. **Automobiles** The table shows gas mileage for the most economical cars in July 2004, including three hybrids.

Gas Mileage of Economical Cars									
Mileage in City (mi/gal)	32	60	48	38	36	60	35	38	32
Mileage on Highway (mi/gal)	38	51	47	46	47	66	43	46	40

Make a back-to-back stem-and-leaf plot for the data.

13. Damien's math test scores are given in the table:
    a. Make a stem-and-leaf plot of Damien's test scores.
    b. Make a histogram of the test scores using intervals of 5.
    c. Make a histogram of the test scores using intervals of 10.
    d. Make a histogram of the test scores using intervals of 20.
    e. How does the size of the interval affect the appearance of the histogram?
    f. **Write About It** Which histogram makes Damien's grades look highest? Explain.

Damien's Math Test Scores		
75	84	68
72	59	88
72	77	81
84	60	70

14. **///ERROR ANALYSIS///** Two students made stem-and-leaf plots for the following data: 530, 545, 550, 555, 570. Which is incorrect? Explain the error. **A; there is no stem for 56.**

(A)

Stem	Leaves
53	0
54	5
55	0 5
57	0

Key: 52|5 means 525

(B)

Stem	Leaves
53	0
54	5
55	0 5
56	
57	0

Key: 52|5 means 525

COMMON ERROR ALERT

Students might choose whole number intervals for **Exercise 9,** which are too large. Explain that intervals can be as small or as large as necessary.

Inclusion Remind students that each value must be in only one interval. For instance, they should use 10–19 and 20–29 instead of 10–20 and 20–30.

Answers

8.

Stem	Leaves
5	8
6	2 2 4 4 8 8 9 9
7	0 0 0 1 1 1 2 2 3 5 5 6 7 8 9
8	3 3 7 7 9
9	1

Key: 5|8 means 58

9.

Interval	Frequency
2.0–2.4	2
2.5–2.9	7
3.0–3.4	5
3.5–3.9	3

10.

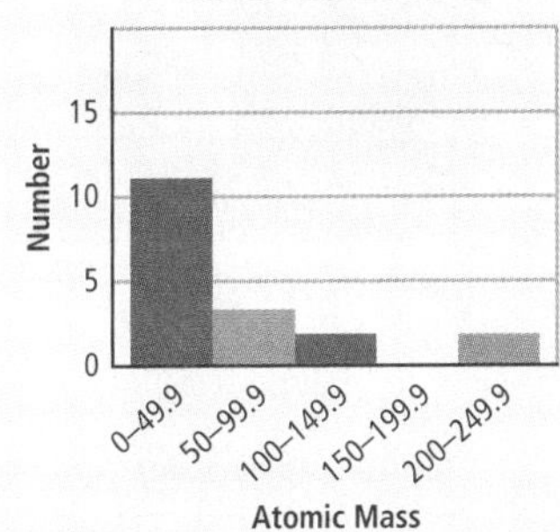

10-2 PRACTICE A
10-2 PRACTICE C
10-2 PRACTICE B

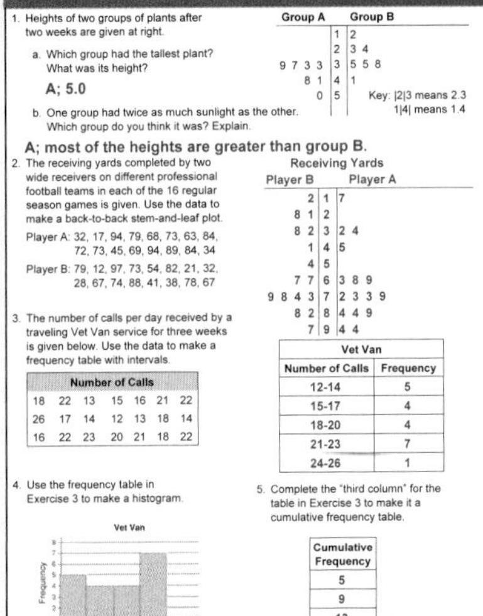

11a.

Interval	Frequency	Cumulative Frequency
36–38	4	4
39–41	6	10
42–44	5	15
45–47	1	16

12.

City Driving		Highway Driving
8 8 6 5 2 2	3	8
8	4	0 3 6 6 7 7
	5	1
0 0	6	6

Key: |3|8 means 38
8|4| means 48

13. See p. A31.

Exercise 15 involves organizing data for display in a graph. This exercise prepares students for the Multi-Step Test Prep on page 734.

If students answered **Exercise 18** incorrectly, draw their attention to the key. Remind them that in this plot, the stem is the ones place and the leaf is the tenths place of a data value. The only number that is expressed in tenths is 4.7, choice **B.**

Students who chose **F** for **Exercise 19** probably referred to the cumulative frequency column instead of the frequency column.

Answers

15a.

Interval	Frequency
160–169.9	2
170–179.9	4
180–189.9	3
190–199.9	1
200–209.9	2
210–219.9	1

b.

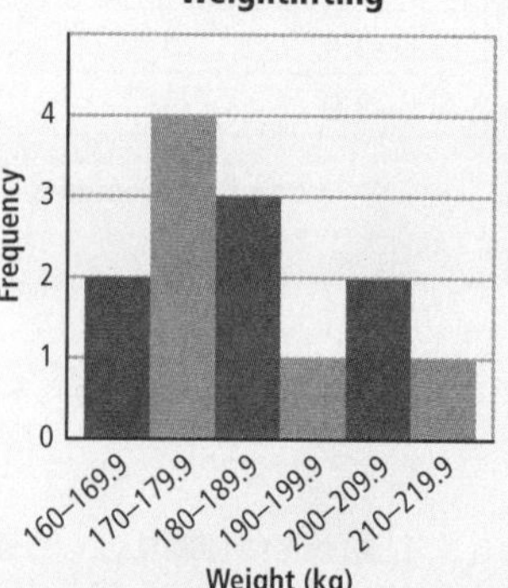

16.

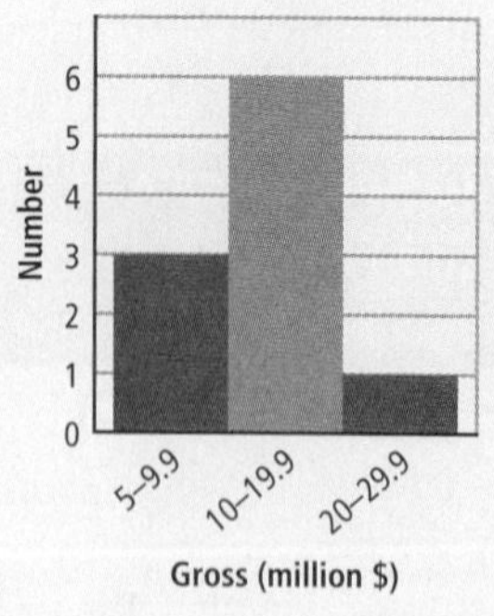

15. This problem will prepare you for the Multi-Step Test Prep on page 734.

The 2004 Olympic results for women's weightlifting in the 48 kg weight class are 210, 205, 200, 190, 187.5, 182.5, 180, 177.5, 175, 172.5, 170, 167.5, and 165, measured in kilograms. Medals are awarded to the athletes who can lift the most weight.

   a. Create a frequency table beginning at 160 and using intervals of 10 kg.
   b. Create a histogram of the data.
   c. Tara Cunningham from the United States lifted 172.5 kg. Did she win a medal? How do you know? **No; she did not lift 1 of the 3 greatest weights.**

16. **Entertainment** The top ten movies in United States theaters for the weekend of June 25–27, 2004, grossed the following amounts (in millions of dollars). Create a histogram for the data. Make the first interval 5–9.9.

Ticket Sales (million $)				
23.9	19.7	18.8	13.5	13.1
11.2	10.2	7.5	6.1	5.1

17. **Critical Thinking** Margo's homework assignment is to make a data display of some data she finds in a newspaper. She found a frequency table with the given intervals.

Explain why Margo must be careful when drawing the bars of the histogram.

17. The intervals are not the same size, so the histogram may not accurately represent ages under 18 or over 55.

Age
Under 18
18–30
31–54
55 and older

18. What data value occurs most often in the stem-and-leaf plot?

   Ⓐ 7 　 **Ⓑ 4.7** 　 Ⓒ 47 　 Ⓓ 777

Stem	Leaves
3	2 3 4 4 7 9
4	0 1 5 7 7 7 8
5	1 2 2 3

Key: 3|2 means 3.2

19. The table shows the results of a survey about time spent on the Internet each month. Which statement is NOT supported by the data in the table?

Time Spent on the Internet per Month		
Time (h)	Frequency	Cumulative Frequency
0–4	4	4
5–9	6	10
10–14	3	13
15–19	16	29
20–24	12	41
25–29	7	48
30–34	2	50

   Ⓕ The interval of 30 to 34 h/mo has the lowest frequency.
   Ⓖ More than half of those who responded spend more than 20 h/mo on the Internet.
   Ⓗ Only four people responded that they spend less than 5 h/mo on the Internet.
   Ⓙ Sixteen people responded that they spend less than 20 h/mo on the Internet.

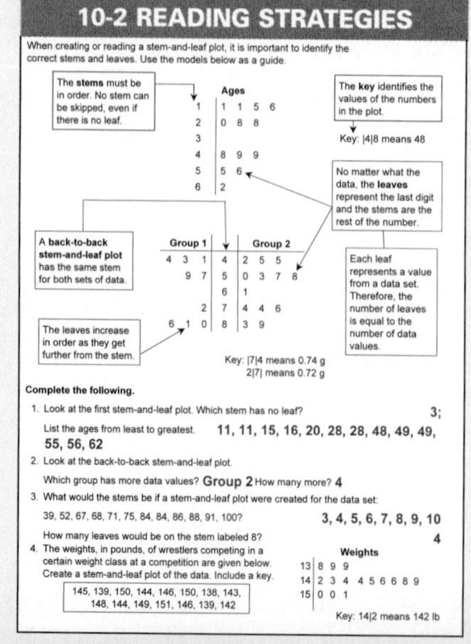

10-2 READING STRATEGIES

When creating or reading a stem-and-leaf plot, it is important to identify the correct stems and leaves. Use the models below as a guide.

The **stems** must be in order. No stem can be skipped, even if there is no leaf.

	Ages
1	1 1 5 6
2	0 8 8
3	
4	8 9 9
5	5 6
6	2

The **key** identifies the values of the numbers in the plot.

Key: |4|8 means 48

No matter what the data, the **leaves** represent the last digit and the stems are the rest of the number.

A **back-to-back stem-and-leaf plot** has the same stem for both sets of data.

Group 1		Group 2
4 3 1	4	2 5 5
9 7	5	0 3 7 8
	6	1
2	7	4 4 6
6 1 0	8	3 9

Key: |7|4 means 0.74 g
2|7| means 0.72 g

The leaves increase in order as they get further from the stem.

Each leaf represents a value from a data set. Therefore, the number of leaves is equal to the number of data values.

Complete the following.

1. Look at the first stem-and-leaf plot. Which stem has no leaf? **3;**
   List the ages from least to greatest. **11, 11, 15, 16, 20, 28, 28, 48, 49, 49, 55, 56, 62**
2. Look at the back-to-back stem-and-leaf plot.
   Which group has more data values? **Group 2** How many more? **4**
3. What would the stems be if a stem-and-leaf plot were created for the data set:
   39, 52, 67, 68, 71, 75, 84, 84, 86, 88, 91, 100? **3, 4, 5, 6, 7, 8, 9, 10**
   How many leaves would be on the stem labeled 8? **4**
4. The weights, in pounds, of wrestlers competing in a certain weight class at a competition are given below. Create a stem-and-leaf plot of the data. Include a key.

   145, 139, 150, 144, 146, 150, 138, 143, 148, 144, 149, 151, 146, 139, 142

	Weights
13	8 9 9
14	2 3 4 4 5 6 6 8 9
15	0 0 1

Key: 14|2 means 142 lb

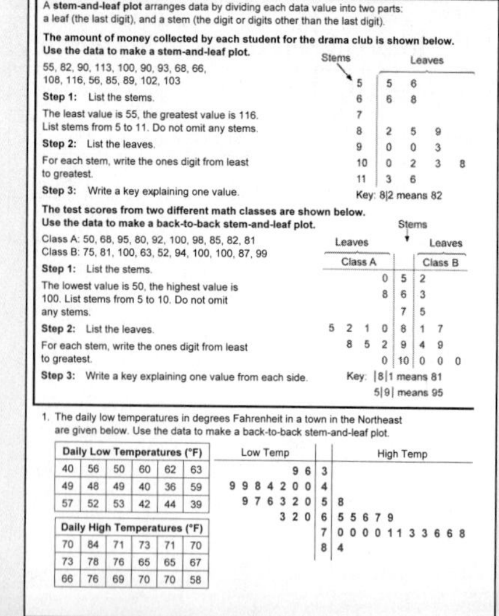

10-2 RETEACH

A **stem-and-leaf plot** arranges data by dividing each data value into two parts: a leaf (the last digit), and a stem (the digit or digits other than the last digit).

The amount of money collected by each student for the drama club is shown below. Use the data to make a stem-and-leaf plot.

55, 82, 90, 113, 100, 90, 93, 68, 66, 108, 116, 56, 85, 89, 102, 103

Step 1: List the stems.

The least value is 55, the greatest value is 116. List stems from 5 to 11. Do not omit any stems.

Step 2: List the leaves.

For each stem, write the ones digit from least to greatest.

Step 3: Write a key explaining one value.

Stems	Leaves
5	5 6
6	6 8
7	
8	2 5 9
9	0 0 3
10	0 2 3 8
11	3 6

Key: 8|2 means 82

The test scores from two different math classes are shown below. Use the data to make a back-to-back stem-and-leaf plot.

Class A: 50, 68, 95, 80, 92, 100, 98, 85, 82, 81
Class B: 75, 81, 100, 63, 52, 94, 100, 100, 87, 99

Step 1: List the stems.

The lowest value is 50, the highest value is 100. List stems from 5 to 10. Do not omit any stems.

Step 2: List the leaves.

For each stem, write the ones digit from least to greatest.

Step 3: Write a key explaining one value from each side.

Leaves: Class A	Stems	Leaves: Class B
0	5	2
8	6	3
	7	5
5 2 1 0	8	1 7
8 5 2	9	4 9
0	10	0 0 0

Key: |8|1 means 81
5|9| means 95

1. The daily low temperatures in degrees Fahrenheit in a town in the Northeast are given below. Use the data to make a back-to-back stem-and-leaf plot.

Daily Low Temperatures (°F)					
40	56	50	60	62	63
49	48	49	40	36	59
57	52	53	42	44	39

Daily High Temperatures (°F)					
70	84	71	73	71	70
73	78	76	65	65	67
66	76	69	70	70	58

Low Temp		High Temp
9 6	3	
9 9 8 4 2 0 0	4	
9 7 6 3 2 0	5	8
3 2 0	6	5 5 6 7 9
	7	0 0 0 0 1 1 3 3 6 6 8
	8	4

20. The frequencies of starting salary ranges for college graduates are noted in the table. Which histogram best reflects the data?

Starting Salaries	
Salary Range ($)	**Frequency**
20,000–29,000	𝍸 𝍸 𝍸 𝍸 II
30,000–39,000	𝍸 𝍸 𝍸 𝍸 𝍸 𝍸
40,000–49,000	𝍸 𝍸 𝍸 I
50,000–59,000	I

Ⓐ
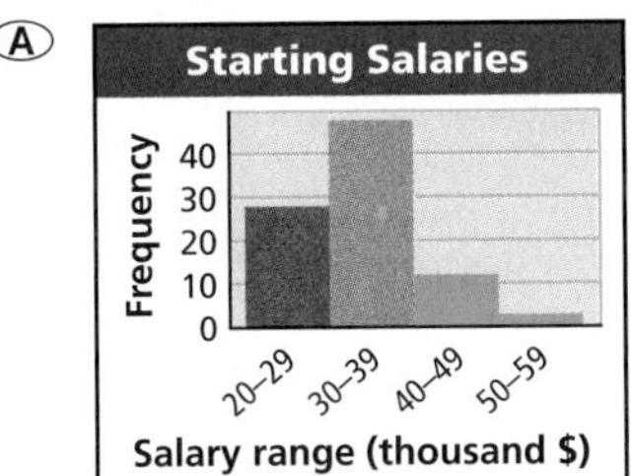

Ⓒ
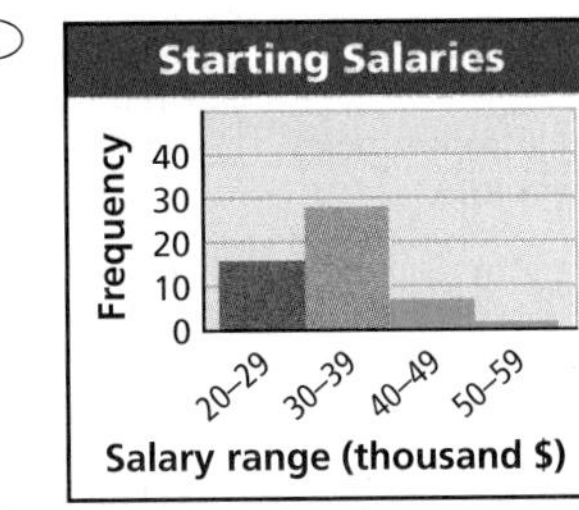

Ⓑ
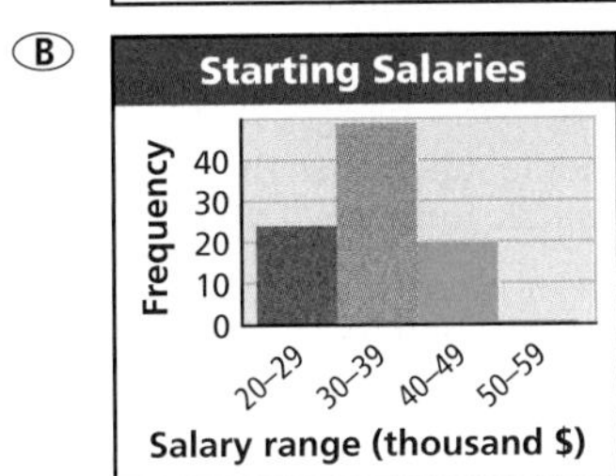

Ⓓ
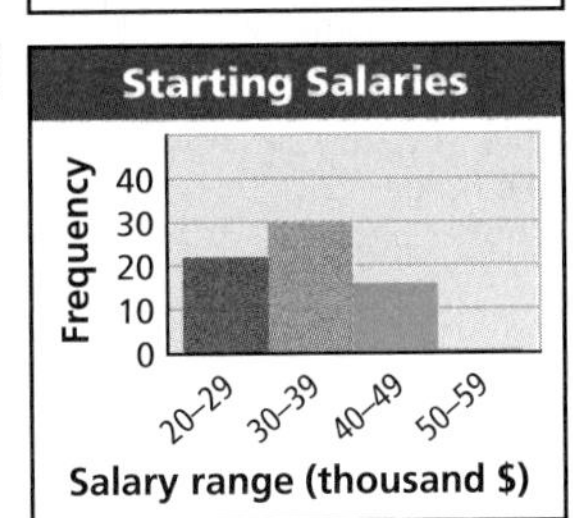

CHALLENGE AND EXTEND

21. The cumulative frequencies of each interval have been given. Use this information to complete the frequency column.

Interval	Frequency	Cumulative Frequency
13–16	**8**	8
17–20	**8**	16
21–24	**41**	57
25–28	**66**	123

SPIRAL REVIEW

Solve each equation. *(Lessons 2-3 and 2-4)*

22. $19 = -2c + 5$ **−7**

23. $4(m + 2) = -1.2$ **−2.3**

24. $2(x - 3) + 7 = 3x - 9$ **10**

25. The U.S. standard railroad gauge is 56.5 inches, which is the distance between the track's rails. Charles has a model train whose scale is 113:1. What is the distance between the rails on his model train track? *(Lesson 2-7)* **0.5 in.**

Use the circle graph for Exercises 26–28. *(Lesson 10-1)*

26. Which two types of gifts make up just over half of the donated gifts? **clothes and books**

27. Which type of gift represents $\frac{1}{5}$ of the total donated gifts? **books**

28. If there were 160 gifts donated, how many were books? **32**

Journal

Have students explain why it is important for a stem-and-leaf plot to have a key.

ALTERNATIVE ASSESSMENT

Have students create or collect a set of data and use that data to make a stem-and-leaf plot, frequency table, and histogram. Encourage students to collect real data.

Power Presentations with PowerPoint®

10-2 Lesson Quiz

1. The numbers of miles on the new cars in a car lot are given below. Use the data to make a stem-and-leaf plot.
35, 21, 15, 51, 39, 41, 46, 22, 28, 16, 12, 40, 34, 56, 25, 14

New Car Mileage

Stem	Leaves
1	2 4 5 6
2	1 2 5 8
3	4 5 9
4	0 1 6
5	1 6

Key: 1|2 means 12

2. The numbers of pounds of laundry in the washers at a laundromat are given below. Use the data to make a cumulative frequency table.
2, 12, 4, 8, 5, 8, 11, 3, 6, 9, 8

Weight of Laundry in Washers		
Pounds	**Freq.**	**Cum. Freq.**
2–4	3	3
5–7	2	5
8–10	4	9
11–13	2	11

3. Use the frequency table from **Problem 2** to make a histogram.

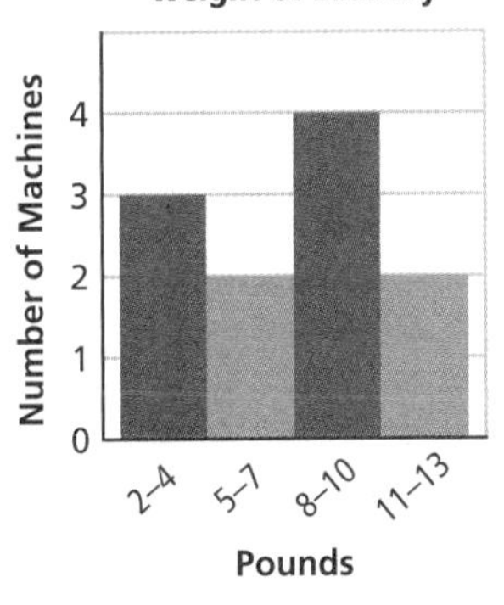

10-2 PROBLEM SOLVING

The heights in inches of the 2005 NBA All-Star Game players are given below.

Players' Heights (in.)											
75	78	80	87	72	80	81	83	85	78	76	81
77	78	83	83	78	82	79	80	75	84	82	90

1. Use the data to make a frequency table with intervals. Use an interval of 5.

Players' Heights	
Heights (in.)	**Frequency**
72-76	4
77-81	11
82-86	7
87-91	2

2. Use your frequency table to make a histogram for the data.

Player's Heights

Select the best answer.

3. The stem-and-leaf plot below gives the file sizes of the songs on two albums after being converted to mp3 files. What is the largest file size for Album 1?

MP3 File Sizes (megabytes)

Album 1		Album 2
0	5	0 1 2 4 5 5 8
6 6 5 3 1	6	0 6 7
7 3 0	7	3 6 8
3 1	8	6
8 7 2 0	9	9

Key: |8|6 means 8.6 MB
1|8| means 8.1 MB

A 6.6 MB
B 8.9 MB
C 9.8 MB
D 9.9 MB

4. The cumulative frequency table below gives the scores of 100 students on a standardized mathematics test. How many students scored between 400 and 499?

Standardized Test Scores	
Scores	**Cumulative Frequency**
200–299	1
300–399	3
400–499	19
500–599	50
600–699	85
700–799	100

F 15
G 16
H 19
J 31

10-2 CHALLENGE

You have learned how to create a cumulative frequency table. A graph of a cumulative frequency table is called an **ogive**. Ogives are often presented in terms of percentage.

The test scores of 280 schools are shown. Use the graph to estimate your answers below.

1. What percent of schools had scores less than 1000? **55%**
2. How many schools had scores less than 1000? **154**
3. What percent of schools scored less than 850? **18%**
4. What is the median score? **980**
5. Seventy-five percent of schools scored less than what score? **1075**
6. A survey was taken of 546 students with jobs. They were asked how many hours they worked per week, on average. Complete the table. Round to the nearest whole percent.

Average Weekly Hours	Frequency	Cumulative Frequency	Cumulative Percentage
0-4	22	**22**	**4%**
5-9	40	**62**	**11%**
10-14	78	**140**	**26%**
15-19	85	**225**	**41%**
20-24	90	**315**	**58%**
25-29	83	**398**	**73%**
30-34	88	**486**	**89%**
35-39	52	**538**	**99%**
40-44	8	**546**	**100%**

7. Draw the ogive.

Use the ogive to answer the following.

8. In which interval does the rate of change increase by the least amount? **40–44**
9. Give the range of hours in which the rate of increase appears constant. **10–34**

10-3 Organizer

Pacing: Traditional 1 day
Block $\frac{1}{2}$ day

Objectives: Describe the central tendency of a data set.

Create and interpret box-and-whisker plots.

Online Edition
Tutorial Videos

Countdown Week 22

Power Presentations with PowerPoint®

Warm Up

Identify the least and greatest value in each set.

1. 34, 62, 45, 35, 75, 23, 35, 65
   23, 75
2. 1.6, 3.4, 2.6, 4.8, 1.3, 3.5, 4.0
   1.3, 4.8
3. Use the data below to make a stem-and-leaf plot.
   7, 8, 10, 18, 24, 15, 17, 9, 12, 20, 25, 18, 21, 12

Stem	Leaves
0	7 8 9
1	0 2 2 5 7 8 8
2	0 1 4 5

Key: 1|2 means 12

Also available on transparency

Math Humor

Q: Why would you use the median to describe an average politician?

A: Because he or she is middle-of-the-road.

10-3 Data Distributions

Objectives
Describe the central tendency of a data set.
Create and interpret box-and-whisker plots.

Vocabulary
mean
median
mode
range
outlier
first quartile
third quartile
interquartile range (IQR)
box-and-whisker plot

Who uses this?
Sports analysts examine data distributions to make predictions. (See Example 4.)

A *measure of central tendency* describes the center of a set of data. Measures of central tendency include the *mean*, *median*, and *mode*.

- The **mean** is the average of the data values, or the sum of the values in the set divided by the number of values in the set.
- The **median** is the middle value when the values are in numerical order, or the mean of the two middle numbers if there are an even number of values.
- The **mode** is the value or values that occur most often. A data set may have one mode or more than one mode. If no value occurs more often than another, the data set has no mode.

The **range** of a set of data is the difference between the greatest and least values in the set. The range is one measure of the spread of a data set.

EXAMPLE 1 Finding Mean, Median, Mode, and Range of a Data Set

The numbers of hours Isaac did homework on six days are 3, 8, 4, 6, 5, and 4. Find the mean, median, mode, and range of the data set.

3, 4, 4, 5, 6, 8 — *Write the data in numerical order.*

mean: $\frac{3 + 4 + 4 + 5 + 6 + 8}{6} = \frac{30}{6} = 5$ — *Add all the values and divide by the number of values.*

median: 3, 4, (4, 5), 6, 8
The median is 4.5. — *There is an even number of values. Find the mean of the two middle values.*

mode: 4 — *4 occurs more than any other value.*

range: $8 - 3 = 5$ — *Subtract the least value from the greatest value.*

1. mean: 14 lb; median: 14 lb; modes: 12 lb and 16 lb; range: 4 lb

1. The weights in pounds of five cats are 12, 14, 12, 16, and 16. Find the mean, median, mode, and range of the data set.

A value that is very different from the other values in a data set is called an **outlier**. In the data set below, one value is much greater than the other values.

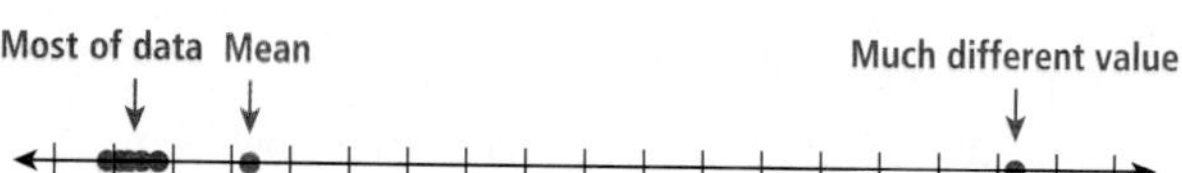

State Resources

State Resources Online
KEYWORD: MA7 Resources

1 Introduce

Tori recorded the times, in minutes, it took for her to complete various mazes on her computer.

Times: 10, 15, 13, 23, 80, 19, 17, 15, 15

1. Order the values from least to greatest.
2. Determine the difference between the longest time and the shortest time.
3. What time was the most common for Tori to take to complete a maze?
4. When viewing your ordered list from Problem 1, what number appears in the middle of the list?
5. What is Tori's average time for completing a maze?
6. If you had to describe Tori's times with a single number, what number would you choose? Why?

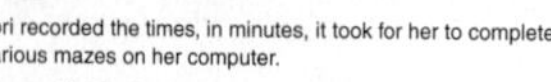

THINK AND DISCUSS

7. **Discuss** how Tori's average time would change if the time of 80 minutes was removed from the list.
8. **Explain** how to predict the number of minutes it will take Tori to complete her next maze.

Motivate

Read the following test scores aloud and ask students what value they think should be given as the score of a typical student: 70, 70, 70, 70, 100. Tell students that there are three ways to describe a "typical" score: the value that occurs most frequently, the value in the middle, and the average of the values.

Explorations and answers are provided in the *Alternate Openers: Explorations Transparencies.*

EXAMPLE 2 Determining the Effects of Outliers

Identify the outlier in the data set {7, 10, 54, 9, 12, 8, 5}, and determine how the outlier affects the mean, median, mode, and range of the data.

5, 7, 8, 9, 10, 12, 54 — *Write the data in numerical order.*

The outlier is 54. — *Look for a value much greater or less than the rest.*

With the Outlier:

mean: $\frac{5 + 7 + 8 + 9 + 10 + 12 + 54}{7} = 15$

median: 5, 7, 8, (9), 10, 12, 54
The median is 9.

mode: Each value occurs once.
There is no mode.

range: $54 - 5 = 49$

Without the Outlier:

mean: $\frac{5 + 7 + 8 + 9 + 10 + 12}{6} = 8.5$

median: 5, 7, (8, 9), 10, 12
The median is 8.5.

mode: Each value occurs once.
There is no mode.

range: $12 - 5 = 7$

The outlier increases the mean by 6.5, the median by 0.5, and the range by 42. It has no effect on the mode.

2. Identify the outlier in the data set {21, 24, 3, 27, 30, 24}, and determine how the outlier affects the mean, median, mode, and range of the data. **3; the outlier decreases the mean by 3.7 and increases the range by 18. It has no effect on the median and mode.**

As you can see in Example 2, an outlier can strongly affect the mean of a data set, while having little or no impact on the median and mode. Therefore, the mean may not be the best measure to describe a data set that contains an outlier. In such cases, the median or mode may better describe the center of the data set.

EXAMPLE 3 Choosing a Measure of Central Tendency

Niles scored 70, 74, 72, 71, 73, and 96 on his six geography tests. For each question, choose the mean, median, or mode, and give its value.

A **Which measure gives Niles's test average?**

The average of Niles's scores is the mean.

mean: $\frac{70 + 74 + 72 + 71 + 73 + 96}{6} = 76$

B **Which measure best describes Niles's typical score? Explain.**

The outlier of 96 causes the mean to be greater than all but one of the test scores, so it is not the best measure in this situation.

The data set has no mode.

The median best describes the typical score.

median: 70, 71, (72, 73), 74, 96 — *Find the mean of the two middle values.*
The median is 72.5.

Josh scored 75, 75, 81, 84, and 85 on five tests. For each question, choose the mean, median, or mode, and give its value.

3a. Which measure describes the score Josh received most often?

3b. Which measure should Josh use to convince his parents that he is doing well in school? Explain.

3a. mode: 75

3b. Median: 81; the median is greater than either the mean or the mode.

Power Presentations with PowerPoint®

Additional Examples

Example 1

The weights in pounds of six members of a basketball team are 161, 156, 150, 156, 150, and 163. Find the mean, median, mode, and range of the data set.
mean: 156 lb; median: 156 lb; mode: 150 lb, 156 lb; range: 13 lb

Example 2

Identify the outlier in the data set {16, 23, 21, 18, 75, 21}, and determine how the outlier affects the mean, median, mode, and range of the data.
75; the outlier increases the mean by 9.2 and the range by 52. It has no effect on the median and mode.

Example 3

Rico scored 74, 73, 80, 75, 67, and 54 on his six history tests. For each question, choose the mean, median, or mode, and give its value.

A. Which measure best describes Rico's typical score? Explain.
Median: 73.5; the outlier of 54 lowers the mean, and there is no mode.

B. Which measure should Rico use to describe his test scores to his parents? Explain.
Median: 73.5; the median is greater than the mean, and there is no mode.

2 Teach

Guided Instruction

Discuss mean, median, mode, and range. Show how an outlier can drastically change the mean and range of a data set, while having little or no effect on the median and mode. Discuss how the presence or lack of an outlier can be used to determine whether a mean or median should be reported as a typical value. Then show how to find first and third quartiles and how to make a box-and-whisker plot.

Reaching All Learners

Through Modeling

Bring 4 students to the front of the class. Give one student 5 pencils, one 2 pencils, one 1 pencil, and one no pencils. Have the students put their pencils in one group and then take turns taking one pencil until none are left. They should now each have 2 pencils, which is the mean. Ask students how this activity connects with the definition of *mean*. The number of pencils each student has at the end is the total number of pencils divided by the number of students.

INTERVENTION

Questioning Strategies

EXAMPLE 1

- When is the median a member of the data set?

EXAMPLE 2

- How can you tell without calculating whether a mean will increase or decrease due to an outlier?
- Why will an outlier always have an effect on the range?

EXAMPLE 3

- How does an outlier affect which measure of central tendency you choose?

Power Presentations with PowerPoint®

Additional Examples

Example 4

The numbers of runs scored by a baseball team in 19 games are given. Use the data to make a box-and-whisker plot.

3, 8, 10, 12, 4, 9, 13, 20, 12, 15, 10, 5, 11, 5, 10, 6, 7, 6, 11

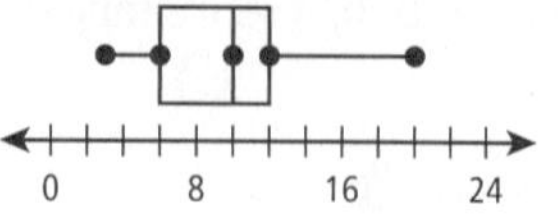

Example 5

The box-and-whisker plots show the number of mugs sold per student in two different grades.

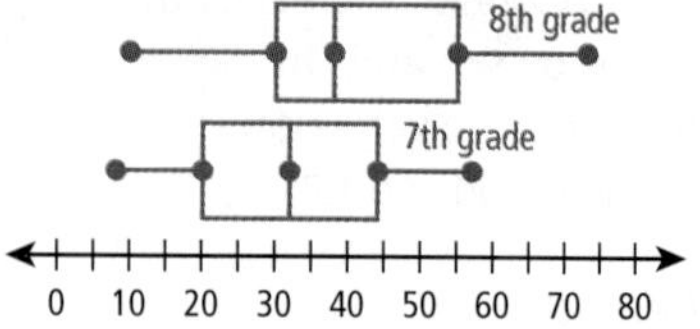

A. About how much greater was the median number of mugs sold by the 8th grade than the median number of mugs sold by the 7th grade? about 6

B. Which data set has a greater maximum? Explain. The data set for the 8th grade; the point representing the maximum is farther to the right for the 8th grade than for the 7th grade.

INTERVENTION
Questioning Strategies

EXAMPLE 4

- What five values do you need to construct a box-and-whisker plot?
- Why must the median be found before the first and third quartiles?

EXAMPLE 5

- What is the benefit of using just one number line for both box-and-whisker plots?

Measures of central tendency describe how data cluster around one value. Another way to describe a data set is by its spread—how the data values are spread out from the center.

Quartiles divide a data set into four equal parts. Each quartile contains one-fourth of the values in the set. The **first quartile** is the median of the lower half of the data set. The second quartile is the median of the data set, and the **third quartile** is the median of the upper half of the data set.

Reading Math

The first quartile is sometimes called the lower quartile, and the third quartile is sometimes called the upper quartile.

The **interquartile range (IQR)** of a data set is the difference between the third and first quartiles. It represents the range of the middle half of the data.

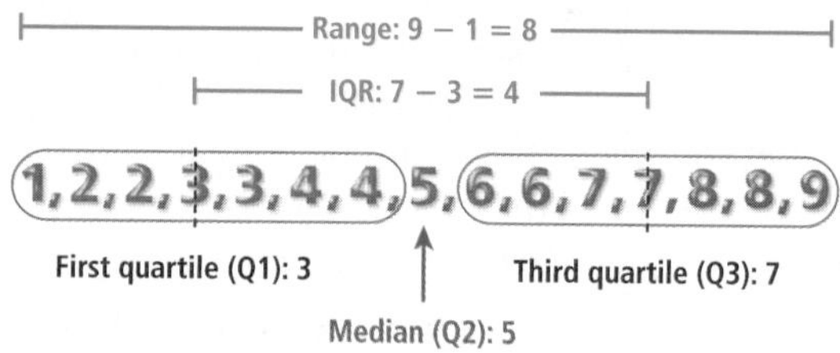

A **box-and-whisker plot** can be used to show how the values in a data set are distributed. You need five values to make a box-and-whisker plot: the minimum (or least value), first quartile, median, third quartile, and maximum (or greatest value).

EXAMPLE 4 *Sports Application*

The numbers of runs scored by a softball team in 20 games are given. Use the data to make a box-and-whisker plot.

3, 4, 8, 12, 7, 5, 4, 12, 3, 9, 11, 4, 14, 8, 2, 10, 3, 10, 9, 7

Step 1 Order the data from least to greatest.

2, 3, 3, 3, 4, 4, 4, 5, 7, 7, 8, 8, 9, 9, 10, 10, 11, 12, 12, 14

Step 2 Identify the five needed values.

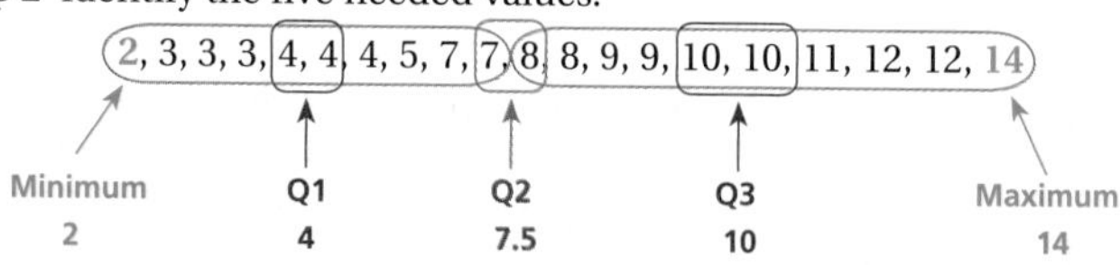

Step 3 Draw a number line and plot a point above each of the five needed values. Draw a box through the first and third quartiles and a vertical line through the median. Draw lines from the box to the minimum and maximum.

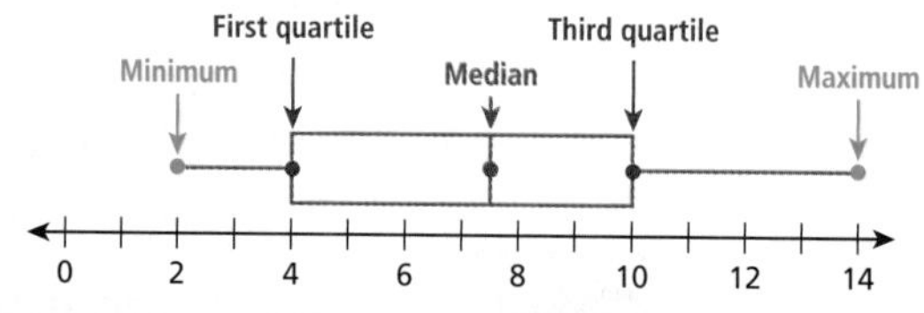

4.

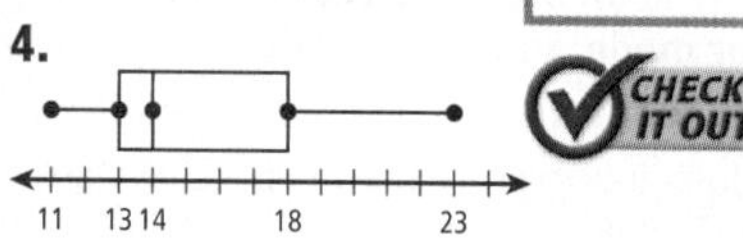

CHECK IT OUT! **4.** Use the data to make a box-and-whisker plot.

13, 14, 18, 13, 12, 17, 15, 12, 13, 19, 11, 14, 14, 18, 22, 23

Teaching Tip **Math Background** One definition of an outlier is any data value that is at least 1.5(IQR) less than the first quartile or at least 1.5(IQR) more than the third quartile.

EXAMPLE 5 Reading and Interpreting Box-and-Whisker Plots

The box-and-whisker plots show the ticket sales, in millions of dollars, of the top 25 movies in 2000 and 2007 (for the United States only).

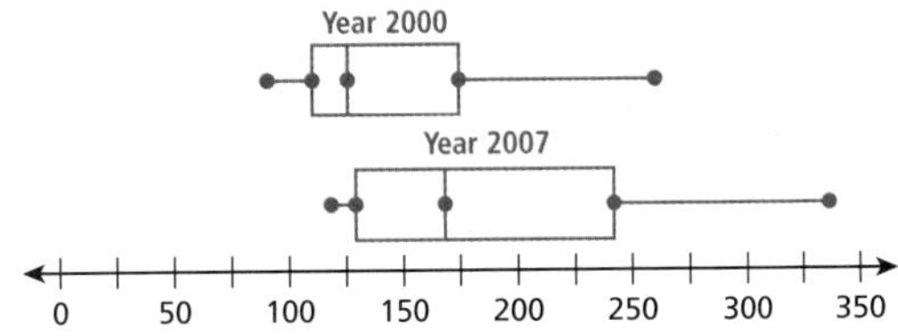

A Which data set has a greater median? Explain.

The vertical line in the box for 2007 is farther to the right than the vertical line in the box for 2000.

The data set for 2007 has a greater median.

B Which data set has a greater interquartile range? Explain.

The length of the box for 2007 is greater than the length of the box for 2000.

The data set for 2007 has a greater interquartile range.

C About how much more were the ticket sales for the top movie in 2007 than for the top movie in 2000?

2007 maximum: **about \$335 million** — *Read the maximum values from*

2000 maximum: **about \$260 million** — *the box-and-whisker plots.*

$335 - 260 = 75$ — *Subtract the maximum values.*

The ticket sales for the top movie in 2007 were about \$75 million more than for the top movie in 2000.

5a. The data set for 2000; the distance between the points for the least and greatest values is less for 2000 than for 2007.

5b. about \$40 million

CHECK IT OUT! **Use the box-and-whisker plots above to answer each question.**

5a. Which data set has a smaller range? Explain.

5b. About how much more was the median ticket sales for the top 25 movies in 2007 than in 2000?

THINK AND DISCUSS

1. Explain when the median is a value in the data set.
2. Give an example of a data set for which the mean is twice the median. Explain how you determined your answer.
3. Suppose the minimum in a data set is the same as the first quartile. How would this affect a box-and-whisker plot of the data?

4. **GET ORGANIZED** Copy and complete the graphic organizer. Tell which measure of central tendency answers each question.

Measures of Central Tendency	
Measure	**Used to Answer**
	What is the average?
	What is the halfway point of the data?
	What is the most common value?

Students may include the median in the upper and lower halves of the data set when finding Q1 and Q3. Tell them that the median is never included in these halves.

Technology Students can use a graphing calculator to find the five numbers needed to make a box-and-whisker plot. First enter the data values into a list. Then press **STAT** and select **1:1-Var Stats** from the **CALC** menu.

Visual If one side of a box-and-whisker plot is longer than the other, it does not mean there are more values on that side. It means that the data values are farther apart from each other on that side.

Answers to *Think and Discuss*

1. Either the data set has an odd number of values, or the data set has an even number of values and the two middle values are the same.
2. Possible answer: 1, 2, 9; start with two numbers and a variable, where the variable is the greatest number in the set: 1, 2, x. The median of this set is 2, so the mean must be 4. Write an equation for the mean: $\frac{1+2+x}{3} = 4$. Solving yields $x = 9$.
3. Because the minimum and the first quartile are the same, the box-and-whisker plot would have no whisker on the left side.
4. See p. A9.

3 Close

Summarize

Review the steps for creating a box-and-whisker plot.

- Order the data.
- Find the median and the first and third quartiles.
- Draw a number line. Plot the minimum, first quartile, median, third quartile, and maximum, and draw the box and whiskers.

ONGOING ASSESSMENT and INTERVENTION

***Diagnose Before* the Lesson**
10-3 Warm Up, TE p. 716

***Monitor During* the Lesson**
Check It Out! Exercises, SE pp. 716–719
Questioning Strategies, TE pp. 717–718

***Assess After* the Lesson**
10-3 Lesson Quiz, TE p. 723
Alternative Assessment, TE p. 723

Assignment Guide

Assign *Guided Practice* Exercises as necessary.

If you finished Examples **1–3**
- **Basic** 14–21, 27–35, 41–43, 48, 49, 53
- **Average** 14–21, 31–43, 48–53, 58
- **Advanced** 14–21, 28–34 even, 48–53, 58

If you finished Examples **1–5**
- **Basic** 14–35, 41–49, 53–57, 61–67
- **Average** 14–26, 28–34 even, 36–58, 61–67
- **Advanced** 14–34 even, 36–67

Homework Quick Check
Quickly check key concepts.
Exercises: 16, 18, 20, 22, 24, 30

Answers

2. mean: 83.75; median: 84; mode: 85; range: 3
3. mean: 31.5; median: 33.5; mode: 44; range: 32

4–8, 10–12, 14–19, 22, 23. See pp. A31–A32.

State Resources

go.hrw.com
State Resources Online
KEYWORD: MA7 Resources

10-3 Exercises

go.hrw.com
Homework Help Online
KEYWORD: MA11 10-3
Parent Resources Online
KEYWORD: MA7 Parent

GUIDED PRACTICE

1. **Vocabulary** What is the difference between the *range* and the *interquartile range* of a data set? **The range is the difference between the greatest and least values. The interquartile range is the difference between the third and first quartile**

SEE EXAMPLE 1 p. 716

Find the mean, median, mode, and range of each data set.

2. 85, 83, 85, 82
3. 12, 22, 33, 34, 44, 44
4. 10, 26, 25, 10, 20, 22, 25, 20
5. 71, 73, 75, 78, 78, 80, 85, 86

SEE EXAMPLE 1 p. 717

Identify the outlier in each data set, and determine how the outlier affects the mean, median, mode, and range of the data.

6. 10, 96, 12, 17, 15
7. 64, 75, 72, 13, 64

SEE EXAMPLE 3 p. 717

Adrienne scored 82, 54, 85, 91, and 83 on her last five science tests. For each question, choose the mean, median, or mode, and give its value.

8. Which measure best describes Adrienne's typical score? Explain.
9. Which measure should Adrienne use to convince her soccer coach she is doing well in science? Explain. **median: 83; the median is greater than the mean, and there is no mode.**

SEE EXAMPLE 4 p. 718

Use the data to make a box-and-whisker plot.

10. 21, 31, 26, 24, 28, 26
11. 12, 13, 42, 62, 62, 82

SEE EXAMPLE 5 p. 719

The box-and-whisker plots show the scores, in thousands of points, of two players on a video game. Use the box-and-whisker plots to answer each question.

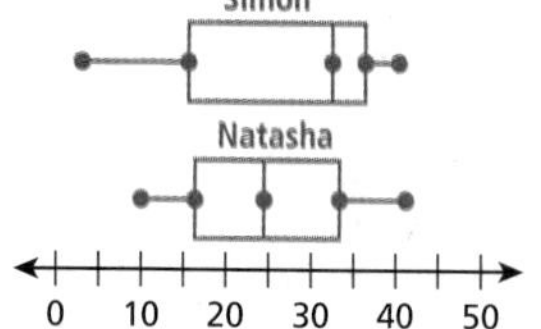

12. Which player has a higher median score? Explain.
13. Which player had the lowest score? Estimate this score. **Simon; about 3000 points**

PRACTICE AND PROBLEM SOLVING

Independent Practice	
For Exercises	See Example
14–17	1
18–19	2
20–21	3
22–23	4
24-26	5

Extra Practice
Skills Practice p. S22
Application Practice p. S37

Find the mean, median, mode, and range of each data set.

14. 75, 63, 89, 91
15. 1, 2, 2, 2, 3, 3, 3, 4
16. 19, 25, 31, 19, 34, 22, 31, 34
17. 58, 58, 60, 60, 60, 61, 63

Identify the outlier in each data set, and determine how the outlier affects the mean, median, mode, and range of the data.

18. 42, 8, 54, 37, 29
19. 3, 8, 3, 3, 23, 8

Lamont bowled 153, 145, 148, and 166 in four games. For each question, choose the mean, median, or mode, and give its value.

20. Which measure gives Lamont's average score? **mean: 153**
21. Which measure should Lamont use to convince his parents to let him join a bowling league? Explain.
mean: 153; the mean is greater than the median, and there is no mode.

Use the data to make a box-and-whisker plot.

22. 62, 63, 62, 64, 68, 62, 62
23. 85, 90, 81, 100, 92, 85

The box-and-whisker plots show the prices, in dollars, of athletic shoes at two sports apparel stores. Use the box-and-whisker plots to answer each question.

Jump N Run

Sneaks R Us

0 25 50 75 100 125 150 175 200

24. Which store has the greater median price? About how much greater? **Sneaks R Us, about $10**

25. Sneaks R Us; the middle half of the data doesn't vary as much at Sneaks R Us as at Jump N Run.

25. Which store has the smaller interquartile range? What does this tell you about the data sets?

26. Estimate the difference in price between the most expensive shoe type at Jump N Run and the most expensive shoe at Sneaks R Us. **about $32**

Find the mean, median, mode, and range of each data set.

27. 1, 2, 3, 4, 5, 6, 7, 8, 9, 10

28. 5, 6, 6, 5, 5

29. 2.1, 4.3, 6.5, 1.2, 3.4

30. $0, \frac{1}{4}, \frac{1}{2}, \frac{3}{4}, 1$

31. 23, 25, 26, 25, 23

32. –3, –3, –3, –2, –2, –1

33. 1, 4, 9, 16, 25, 36

34. 1, 0, 0, 1, 1, 4

35. **Estimation** Estimate the mean of $16\frac{7}{8}$, $12\frac{1}{4}$, $22\frac{1}{10}$, $18\frac{5}{7}$, $19\frac{1}{3}$, $13\frac{8}{11}$, and $13\frac{8}{11}$. **Possible answer: 17**

Tell whether each statement is sometimes, always, or never true.

36. The mean is a value in the data set. **sometimes**

37. The median is a value in the data set. **sometimes**

38. If a data set has one mode, the mode is a value in the data set. **always**

39. The mean is affected by including an outlier. **always**

40. The mode is affected by including an outlier. **never**

41. **Sports** The table shows the attendance at six football games at Jefferson High School. Which measure of central tendency best indicates the typical attendance at a football game? Why?

Attendance at Football Games	
Eagles vs. Bulldogs	743
Eagles vs. Panthers	768
Eagles vs. Coyotes	835
Eagles vs. Bears*	1218
Eagles vs. Colts	797
Eagles vs. Mustangs	854

*Homecoming Game

42. **Weather** The high temperatures in degrees Fahrenheit on 11 consecutive days were 68, 71, 75, 74, 75, 71, 73, 71, 72, 74, and 79. Find the mean, median, mode, and range of the temperatures. Describe the effect on the mean, median, mode, and range if the next day's temperature was 70 °F.

43. **Advertising** A home-decorating store sells five types of candles, which are priced at $3, $2, $2, $2, and $15. If the store puts an ad in the paper titled "Best Local Candle Prices," which measure of central tendency should it advertise? Justify your answer.

Use the data to make a box-and-whisker plot.

44. 25, 28, 26, 16, 18, 15, 25, 28, 26, 16

45. 2, 3, 5, 7, 11, 13, 17, 19, 23, 29, 31

46. 1, 1, 1, 1, 2, 2, 2, 2, 3, 3, 4, 4, 4, 4, 4

47. 50, 52, 45, 62, 36, 55, 40, 50, 65, 33

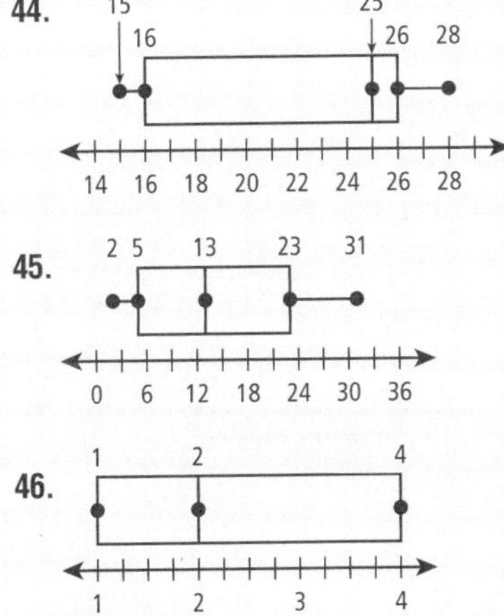

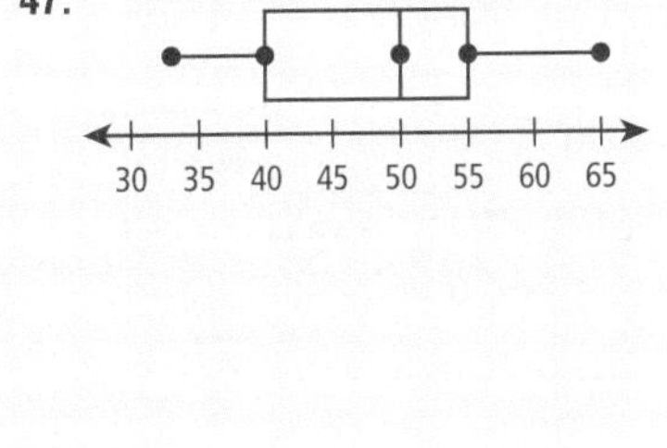

Inclusion In Exercise 32, students may expect the range to be a negative number. Use the formula maximum – minimum: $-1 - (-3) = -1 + 3 = 2$.

Answers

27. mean: 5.5; median: 5.5; mode: none; range: 9

28. mean: 5.4; median: 5; mode: 5; range: 1

29. mean: 3.5; median: 3.4; mode: none; range: 5.3

30. mean: $\frac{1}{2}$; median: $\frac{1}{2}$; mode: none; range: 1

31. mean: 24.4; median: 25; modes: 23 and 25; range: 3

32. mean: $-2\frac{1}{3}$; median: $-2\frac{1}{2}$; mode: –3; range: 2

33. mean: $15\frac{1}{6}$; median: $12\frac{1}{2}$; mode: none; range: 35

34. mean: $1\frac{1}{6}$; median: 1; mode: 1; range: 4

41. Median; the mean is affected by the outlier of 1218, and there is no mode.

42. Mean: 73 °F; median: 73 °F; mode: 71 °F; range: 11 °F; the mean would decrease by 0.25 °F, the median would decrease by 0.5 °F, and the mode and range would not change.

43. Median or mode; the store wants their prices to appear low, and the median and mode are both $2.80 less than the mean.

10-3 PRACTICE A

10-3 PRACTICE C

10-3 PRACTICE B

Find the mean, median, mode, and range of each data set.

1. 22, 45, 30, 18, 22
mean: 27.4 median: 22
mode: 22 range: 27

2. 8, 10, 8, 14, 8, 15
mean: 10.5 median: 9
mode: 8 range: 7

3. 1.25, 0.5, 3.25, 0.75, 1.75
mean: 1.5 median: 1.25
mode: none range: 2.75

4. 95, 92, 96, 93, 94, 95, 93
mean: 94 median: 94
modes: 93, 95 range: 4

Identify the outlier in each data set, and determine how the outlier affects the mean, median, mode, and range of the data.

5. 31, 35, 41, 40, 40, 98
outlier: 98, increases mean by 10.1 and range by 57, no effect on median or mode

6. 82, 24, 100, 96, 79, 93, 86
outlier: 24, decreases mean by $9\frac{1}{3}$, median by 3.5, increases range by 55, no effect on mode

7. The amounts of Cathy's last six clothing purchases were $109, $72, $99, $15, $99, and $89. For each question, choose the mean, median, or mode, and give its value.

a. Which value describes the average of Cathy's purchases? mean: $80.50

b. Which value would Cathy tell her parents to convince them that she is not spending too much money on clothes? Explain.
mean, because it is the lowest of the three measures, lower because of the outlier $15

c. Which value would Cathy tell her parents to convince them that she needs an increase in her allowance? Explain.
mode, $99, because it is the greatest of the three measures

Use the data to make a box-and-whisker plot.

8. 71, 79, 56, 24, 35, 37, 81, 63, 75

20 30 40 50 60 70 80 90

9. 210, 195, 350, 250, 260, 300

175 200 225 250 275 300 325 350

The finishing times of two runners for several one-mile races, in minutes, are shown in the box-and-whisker plots.

Jamal

Tim

5 6 7

10. Who has the faster median time? Tim

11. Who has the slowest time? Jamal

12. Overall, who is the faster runner? Explain.
Tim, his box is to the left of Jamal's.

Exercise 48 involves finding measures of central tendency, including the median. This exercise prepares students for the Multi-Step Test Prep on page 734.

Number Sense For **Exercise 49**, ask students if the data seem reasonable and why. If needed, prompt them to think about the manager of the company.

Inclusion Use **Exercise 52** to show the difference between a mode of 0 and no mode.

Tell students who answered **D** in **Exercise 54** that **B** is the *best* answer because, while the range can be found by subtracting, the median is readily available.

Answers

48a. mean: 5.66; median: 5.70; mode: 5.70; range: 0.51

b. 5.96 m

49. Mean: \$32,000, median: \$25,000; median; the outlier of \$78,000 increases the mean significantly.

52. 20.75; possible answer: No, Earth's number of moons is much less than either the mean or median number of moons per planet.

53. increase the mean; decrease the mean

MULTI-STEP TEST PREP

48. This problem will prepare you for the Multi-Step Test Prep on page 734.

The results in Olympic pole-vaulting are given as heights in meters. In the 2008 Olympic Games in Beijing, the following results occurred for the men's pole-vault finals: 5.96, 5.85, 5.70, 5.70, 5.70, 5.70, 5.60, 5.60, 5.60, 5.45, 5.45.

a. Find the mean, median, mode, and range of this data set. Round to the nearest hundredth if needed.

b. The gold medal was won by Steve Hooker of Australia. What was his height in the pole-vault finals?

49. Business The salaries for the eight employees at a small company are shown in the stem-and-leaf plot. Find the mean and median of the salaries. Which measure better describes the typical salary of an employee at this company? Explain.

Salaries ($1000)

Stem	Leaves
2	0 0 3 5 5
3	0 5
4	
5	
6	
7	8

Key: 2|0 means \$20,000

50. Critical Thinking Use the data set {1, 2, 3, 5, 8, 13, 21, 34} to complete the following.

a. Find the mean of the data set. **10.875**

b. What happens to the mean of the data set if every number is increased by 2? **The mean increases by 2.**

c. What happens to the mean of the data set if every number is multiplied by 2? **The mean is multiplied by 2.**

51. Allison has taken 5 tests worth 100 points each. Her scores are shown in the grade book below. What score does she need on her next test to have a mean of 90%? **96**

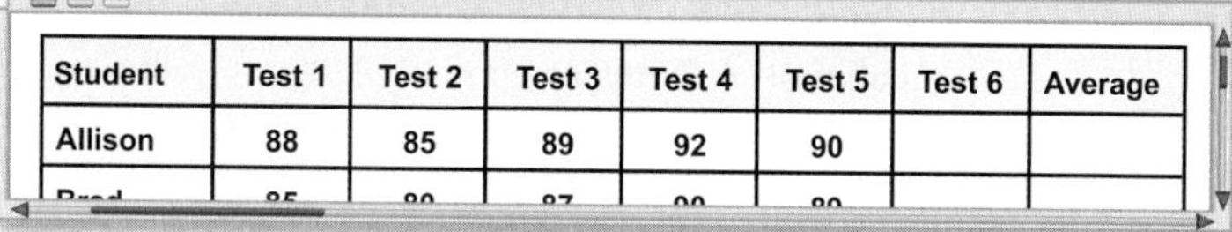

Student	Test 1	Test 2	Test 3	Test 4	Test 5	Test 6	Average
Allison	88	85	89	92	90		

52. Astronomy The table shows the number of moons of the planets in our solar system. What is the mean number of moons per planet? Is Earth's value of one moon typical for the solar system? Explain.

Planet	Mercury	Venus	Earth	Mars	Jupiter	Saturn	Uranus	Neptune
Moons	0	0	1	2	63	60	27	13

53. Write About It Explain how an outlier with a large value will affect the mean. Explain how an outlier with a small value will affect the mean.

TEST PREP

54. Which value is always represented on a box-and-whisker plot?

Ⓐ Mean　Ⓑ Median　Ⓒ Mode　Ⓓ Range

55. The lengths in feet of the alligators at a zoo are 9, 7, 12, 6, and 10. The lengths in feet of the crocodiles at the zoo are 13, 10, 8, 19, 18, and 16. What is the difference between the mean length of the crocodiles and the mean length of the alligators?

Ⓕ 0.5 foot　Ⓖ 5.2 feet　Ⓗ 8 feet　Ⓙ 11.4 feet

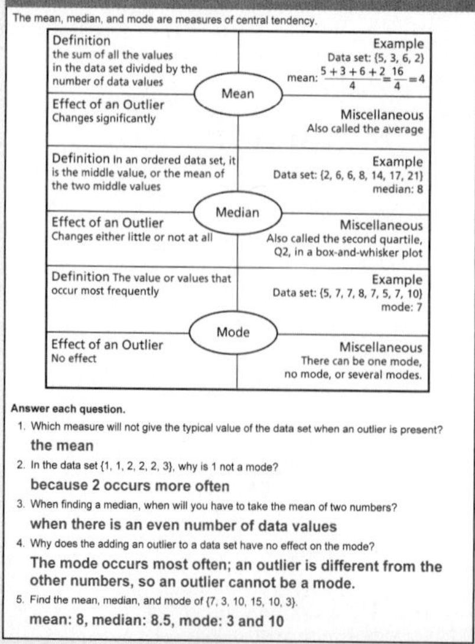

10-3 READING STRATEGIES

The mean, median, and mode are measures of central tendency.

	Mean	
Definition the sum of all the values in the data set divided by the number of data values		**Example** Data set: {5, 3, 6, 2} mean: $\frac{5+3+6+2}{4}=\frac{16}{4}=4$
Effect of an Outlier Changes significantly		**Miscellaneous** Also called the average

	Median	
Definition In an ordered data set, it is the middle value, or the mean of the two middle values		**Example** Data set: {2, 6, 6, 8, 14, 17, 21} median: 8
Effect of an Outlier Changes either little or not at all		**Miscellaneous** Also called the second quartile, Q2, in a box-and-whisker plot

	Mode	
Definition The value or values that occur most frequently		**Example** Data set: {5, 7, 7, 8, 7, 5, 7, 10} mode: 7
Effect of an Outlier No effect		**Miscellaneous** There can be one mode, no mode, or several modes.

Answer each question.

1. Which measure will not give the typical value of the data set when an outlier is present?
   the mean
2. In the data set {1, 1, 2, 2, 2, 3}, why is 1 not a mode?
   because 2 occurs more often
3. When finding a median, when will you have to take the mean of two numbers?
   when there is an even number of data values
4. Why does the adding an outlier to a data set have no effect on the mode?
   The mode occurs most often; an outlier is different from the other numbers, so an outlier cannot be a mode.
5. Find the mean, median, and mode of {7, 3, 10, 15, 10, 3}.
   mean: 8, median: 8.5, mode: 3 and 10

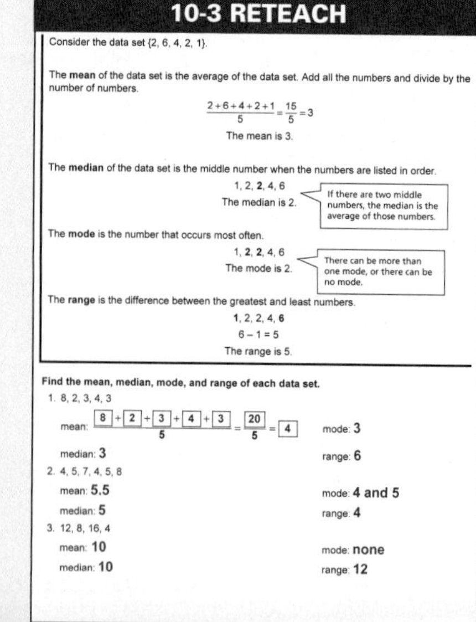

10-3 RETEACH

Consider the data set {2, 6, 4, 2, 1}.

The **mean** of the data set is the average of the data set. Add all the numbers and divide by the number of numbers.

$$\frac{2+6+4+2+1}{5}=\frac{15}{5}=3$$

The mean is 3.

The **median** of the data set is the middle number when the numbers are listed in order.

1, 2, **2**, 4, 6
The median is 2.

If there are two middle numbers, the median is the average of those numbers.

The **mode** is the number that occurs most often.

1, **2**, **2**, 4, 6
The mode is 2.

There can be more than one mode, or there can be no mode.

The **range** is the difference between the greatest and least numbers.

1, 2, 2, 4, **6**
6 − 1 = 5
The range is 5.

Find the mean, median, mode, and range of each data set.

1. 8, 2, 3, 4, 3
   mean: $\frac{8+2+3+4+3}{5}=\frac{20}{5}=4$　mode: **3**
   median: **3**　range: **6**
2. 4, 5, 7, 4, 5, 8
   mean: **5.5**　mode: **4 and 5**
   median: **5**　range: **4**
3. 12, 8, 16, 4
   mean: **10**　mode: **none**
   median: **10**　range: **12**

56. The mean score on a test is 50. Which CANNOT be true?

(A) Half the scores are 0, and half the scores are 100.

(B) The range is 50.

(C) Half the scores are 25, and half the scores are 50.

(D) Every score is 50.

57. **Short Response** The table shows the weights in pounds of six dogs. How does the mean weight of the dogs change if Rex's weight is not included in the data set? **The mean decreases by 6.6 lb.**

Weights of Dogs (lb)			
Duffy	23	Rex	62
Rocky	15	Skipper	34
Pepper	21	Sunny	19

CHALLENGE AND EXTEND

58. List a set of data values with the following measures of central tendency:
mean: 8 median: 7 mode: 6 **Possible answer: 6, 6, 7, 9, 12**

59. Collect a set of data about your classmates or your school. For example, you might collect data about the number of points per game scored by your school's basketball team. Use the data you collect to make a box-and-whisker plot. **Check students' work.**

60. A *weighted average* is an average in which each data value has an importance, or weight, assigned to it. A teacher uses the following weights when determining course grades: homework 25%, tests 30%, and final exam 45%. The table shows Nathalie's scores in the class.

Homework	78, 83, 95, 82, 79, 93
Tests	88, 92, 81
Final exam	90

a. Find the mean of Nathalie's homework scores and the mean of her test scores. **85; 87**

b. Find Nathalie's weighted average for the class. To do so, multiply the homework mean, the test mean, and the final exam score by their corresponding weights. Then add the products. **87.85**

c. **What if...?** What would Nathalie's mean score for the class be if her teacher did not use a weighted average? **86.1**

SPIRAL REVIEW

Find the slope of each line. Then tell what the slope represents. *(Lesson 5-4)*

61. 32; typing speed is 32 words per minute.

62. 4; diesel fuel costs $4 per gallon.

61.

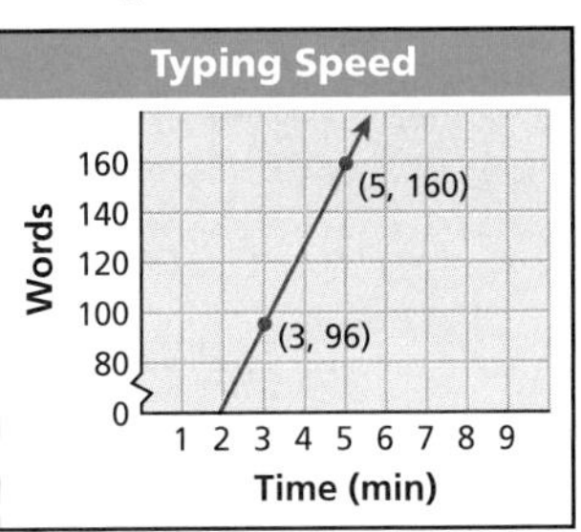

62.

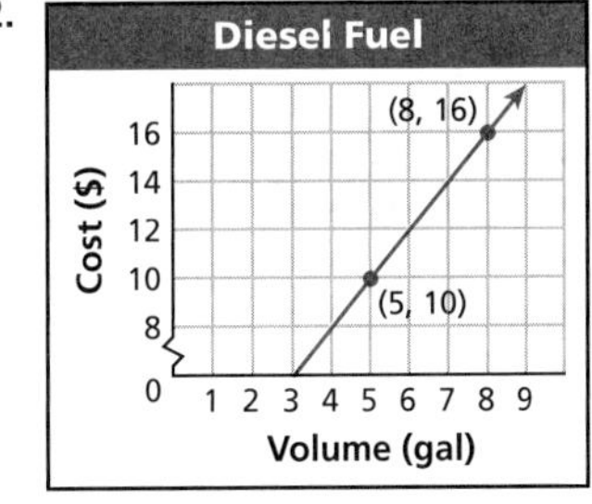

Simplify each expression. *(Lesson 7-5)*

63. $32^{\frac{1}{5}}$ **2**　64. $81^{\frac{1}{4}}$ **3**　65. $125^{\frac{1}{3}}$ **5**　66. $64^{\frac{1}{3}}$ **4**

67. length: 5 yd; width: 3 yd

67. The length of a rectangle is 1 yard less than two times the width. The area is 15 square yards. What are the dimensions of the rectangle? *(Lesson 9-9)*

10-3 PROBLEM SOLVING

Write the correct answer.

1. While window shopping, Sandra recorded the prices of shoes she would like to try on. The prices were $48, $63, $52, $99, and $58. Find the mean, median, and mode of the prices. Which best represents the typical shoe she looked at? Why?
mean: $64, median: $58, mode: none; The median because only one price is above the mean.

2. The number of cans Xavier recycled each week for eight weeks is 24, 33, 76, 42, 35, 33, 45, and 33. Find the mean, median, and mode of the numbers of cans. How do the mean and median change when the outlier is removed?
mean: 40.125, median: 34, mode: 33; The mean decreases by 5.125, median decreases by 1.

3. The amounts due on the Harvey's electric bill, rounded to the nearest dollar, for the past six months were $64, $83, $76, $134, $76, and $71. Find the mean, median, and mode of the amounts. Which value should Mr. Harvey tell his family to convince them to cut down on electric use?
mean: 84, median: 76, mode: 76; the mean

4. A manager at a bowling alley surveys adult patrons about their shoes sizes. He records sizes 11, 12, 8, 4, 8, 5, 8, 7, 9, 10, 8, 9, 8, and 10. Find the mean, median, and mode of the sizes. Which is most important to the manager when ordering new rental shoes?
mean: ≈8.4, median: 8, mode: 8; the mode

The number of traffic citations given daily by two police departments over a two-week period is shown in the box-and-whisker plots. Choose the letter of the best answer.

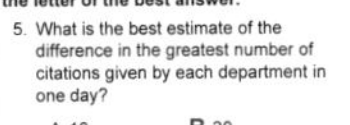

West
East
80 100 120 140 160 180 200 220

5. What is the best estimate of the difference in the greatest number of citations given by each department in one day?
A 10　**B 20**
C 30　D 35

6. What is the difference in the median number of citations between the two departments?
F about 8
G about 15
H about 22
J about 40

7. Which statement is NOT true?
A The East department gave the greatest number of citations in one day.
B The East department gave the least number of citations in one day.
C The East department has a greater IQR than the West department.
D The East department has the greater median number of citations in one day.

10-3 CHALLENGE

Box-and-whisker plots can be misleading if either the minimum or maximum value is an outlier. The fair options are either to not use box-and-whisker plots for data with outliers or to show them as individual points.

Mathematically, a value is accepted as an outlier if it is at least 1.5(IQR) below Q1 or 1.5(IQR) above Q3.

For the data set {46, 22, 19, 2, 17, 23, 31, 42, 73, 16, 22, 26, 28}:

1. Find Q1. **18**
2. Find Q3. **36.5**
3. Find the IQR. **18.5**
4. Find 1.5(IQR). **27.75**
5. Find Q1 – 1.5(IQR). **–9.75**
6. Find Q3 + 1.5(IQR). **64.25**
7. Using the rule of being 1.5(IQR) away from Q1 or Q3, what is the outlier in the data set above? **73**

Outliers can be mild or extreme. A **mild outlier** is more than 1.5(IQR) from Q1 or Q3, but less than 3(IQR) from them. An **extreme outlier** is more than 3(IQR) from Q1 or Q3.

8. Classify the outlier identified in question 7. **mild**

To draw a box-and-whisker plot that has outliers, first plot Q1, the median, and Q3 as usual. Draw the box. Plot the minimum and maximum points that are not outliers. Draw the whiskers to these points. Then plot mild outliers with a closed dot and extreme outliers with an open dot.

9. Draw a box-and-whisker plot, displaying the outlier, for the data set above.
0 10 20 30 40 50 60 70 80

Draw box-and-whisker plots, displaying outliers, for each data set.

10. 41, 43, 30, 42, 29, 42, 41, 51, 43, 41, 43, 48
25 30 35 40 45 50 55

11. 30, 28, 27, 29, 33, 10, 21, 32, 27, 29
5 10 15 20 25 30 35

12. 124, 135, 83, 140, 210, 144
80 100 120 140 160 180 200 220

Journal

Have students describe what information a box-and-whisker plot can convey.

ALTERNATIVE ASSESSMENT

Ask students to make up a data set with at least ten values and find the mean, median, mode, and range of the set. Then have them add an outlier and explain the effect that the outlier has on each measure.

Power Presentations with PowerPoint®

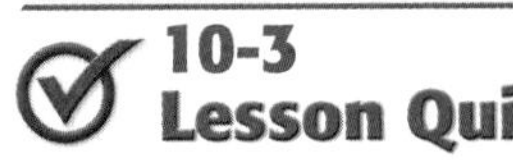

10-3 Lesson Quiz

1. Find the mean, median, mode, and range of the data set {7, 3, 5, 4, 5}.
mean: 4.8; median: 5; mode: 5; range: 4

2. Identify the outlier in the data set {12, 15, 20, 44, 18, 20}, and determine how the outlier affects the mean, median, mode, and range of the data.
44; the mean increases by 4.5, median by 1, and range by 24; no effect on mode.

3. The data set {12, 23, 13, 14, 13} gives the times of Tara's one-way ride to school (in minutes) for one week. For each question, choose the mean, median, or mode, and give its value.

a. Which value describes the time that occurred most often? mode, 13

b. Which value best describes Tara's ride time? Explain.
Median, 13 or mode, 13; there is an outlier, so the mean is strongly affected.

4. The amounts of snow (in inches) that fell during the last 8 winters in one city are given. Use the data to make a box-and-whisker plot.
25, 17, 14, 27, 20, 11, 29, 32
See p. A32.

Also available on transparency

Organizer

Use with Lesson 10-3

Pacing:
Traditional $\frac{1}{2}$ day
Block $\frac{1}{4}$ day

Objective: Use a spreadsheet or graphing calculator to create graphs.

Materials: spreadsheet program, graphing calculator

Online Edition
TechKeys, Graphing Calculator

Countdown Week 22

Resources

Technology Lab Activities
10-3 Lab Recording Sheet

Teach

Discuss

In **Activity 1,** the spreadsheet program will automatically choose a reasonable scale and interval for the data. However, these can be changed by clicking on the vertical axis of the bar graph and selecting the Scale tab.

The legend was turned off to create a bar graph. The legend should be turned on for double-bar graphs and double-line graphs. The legend should also be turned on when the sectors of a circle graph are not individually labeled.

10-3

Use Technology to Make Graphs

Use with Lesson 10-3

You can use a spreadsheet program to create bar graphs, line graphs, and circle graphs. You can also use a graphing calculator to make a box-and-whisker plot.

Activity 1

Many colors are used on the flags of the 50 United States. The table shows the number of flags that use each color. Use a spreadsheet program to make a bar graph to display the data.

Color	Black	Blue	Brown	Gold	Green	Purple	Red	White
Number	27	46	20	36	24	4	34	42

1. Enter the data from the table in the first two columns of the spreadsheet.

2. Select the cells containing the titles and the data.
   Then click the Chart Wizard icon, . Click Column from the list on the left, and then choose the small picture of a vertical bar graph. Click Next.

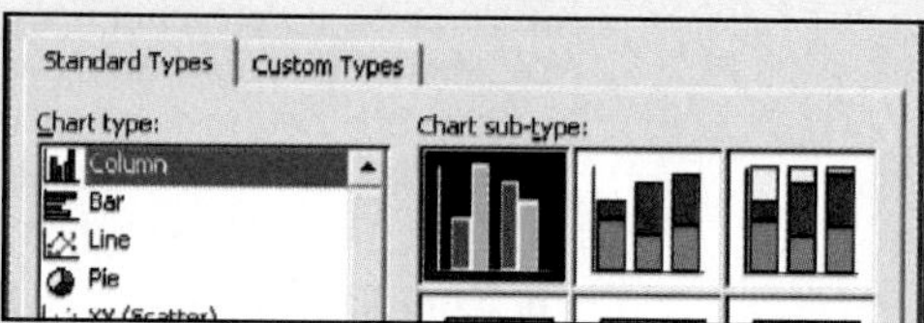

3. The next screen shows the range of cells used to make the graph. Click Next.

4. Give the chart a title and enter titles for the *x*-axis and *y*-axis. Click the Legend tab, and then click the box next to Show Legend to turn off the key. (A key is needed when making a double-bar graph.) Click Next.

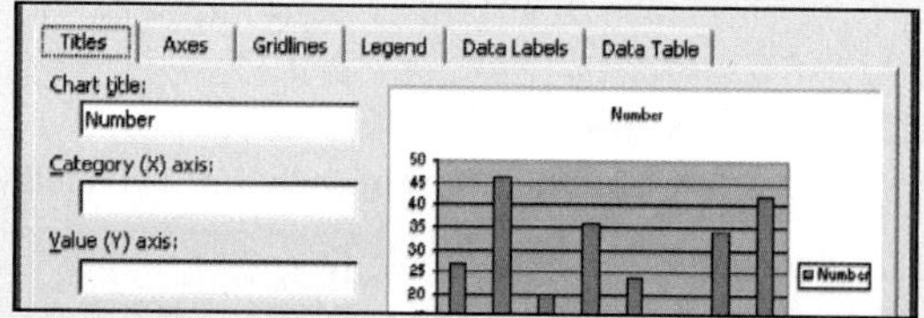

5. Click Finish to place the chart in the spreadsheet.

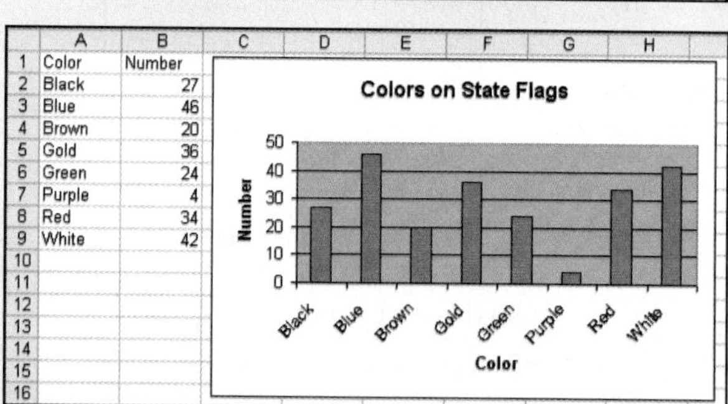

	A	B
1	Color	Number
2	Black	27
3	Blue	46
4	Brown	20
5	Gold	36
6	Green	24
7	Purple	4
8	Red	34
9	White	42

Alternative Approach

In **Activity 2,** have students select the fourth type of graph, which will show marks at outliers. Discuss why there are outliers in the data set and how they affect the five important values.

Try This

1. The table shows the average number of hours of sleep people at different ages get each night. Use a spreadsheet program to make a bar graph to display the data.

Age (yr)	3–9	10–13	14–18	19–30	31–45	46–50	51+
Sleep (h)	11	10	9	8	7.5	6	5.5

Activity 2

Adrianne is a waitress at a restaurant. The amounts Adrianne made in tips during her last 15 shifts are listed below. Use a graphing calculator to make a box-and-whisker plot to display the data. Give the minimum, first quartile, median, third quartile, and maximum values.

$58, $63, $40, $44, $57, $59, $61, $53, $54, $58, $57, $57, $58, $58, $56

1. To make a list of the data, press STAT, select **Edit**, and enter the values in List 1 (**L1**). Press ENTER after each value.

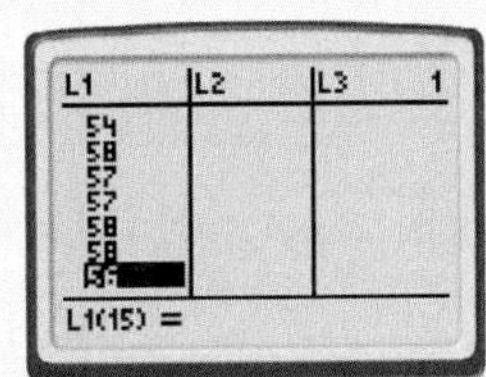

2. To use the **STAT PLOT** editor to set up the box-and-whisker plot, press 2nd Y= (STAT PLOT), and then ENTER.

   Press ENTER to select **Plot 1**.

3. Select **On**. Then use the arrow keys to choose the fifth type of graph, a box-and-whisker plot.

   Xlist should be **L1** and **Freq:** should be 1.

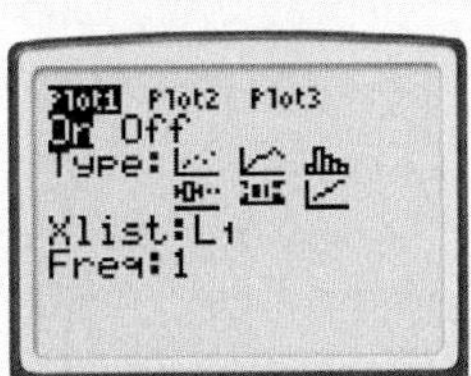

4. Press ZOOM and select **9: ZoomStat** to see the graph in the statistics window.

5. Use TRACE and the arrow keys to move the cursor along the graph to the five important values: minimum (**MinX**), first quartile (**Q1**), median (**MED**), third quartile (**Q3**), and maximum (**MaxX**).

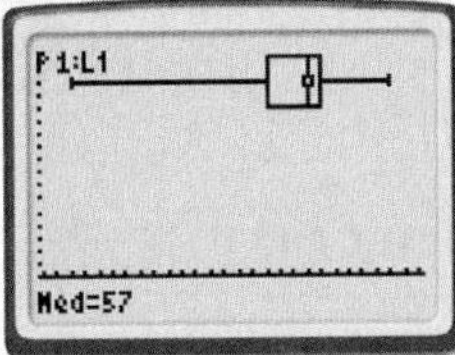

   minimum: 40

   first quartile: 54

   median: 57

   third quartile: 58

   maximum: 63

Try This

2. The average length in inches of the ten longest bones in the human body are listed. Use a graphing calculator to make a box-and-whisker plot to display the data. What are the minimum, first quartile, median, third quartile, and maximum values of the data set?

   19.88, 16.94, 15.94, 14.35, 11.10, 10.40, 9.45, 9.06, 7.28, 6.69

Close

Key Concept

Spreadsheets can be used to quickly create several types of data displays, including bar graphs, line graphs, and circle graphs. Box-and-whisker plots can be created on a graphing calculator.

Assessment

Journal Have students explain how to create and interpret a box-and-whisker plot on a graphing calculator.

Answers to *Try This*

1.

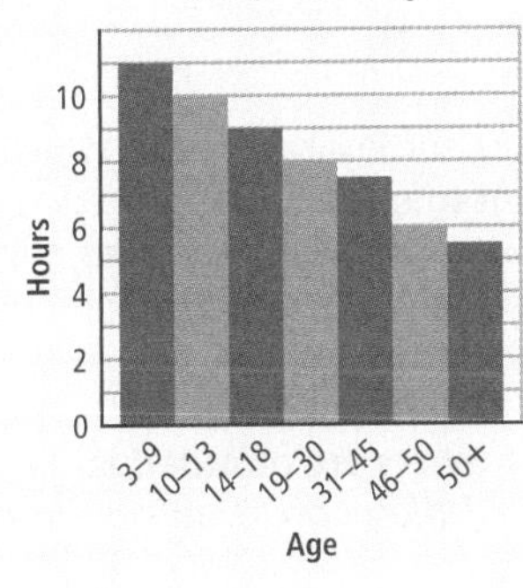

2.

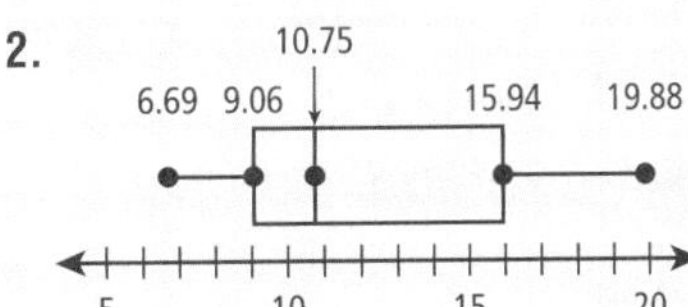

min.: 6.69; Q1: 9.06; med.: 10.75; Q3: 15.94; max.: 19.88

10-4 Organizer

Pacing: Traditional 1 day
Block $\frac{1}{2}$ day

Objectives: Recognize misleading graphs.

Recognize misleading statistics.

Online Edition
Interactivity, Tutorial Videos

Countdown Week 23

Power Presentations with PowerPoint®

Warm Up

Determine the measure of central tendency that best describes each set of data.

1. home team scores for basketball games: 56, 61, 75, 49, 69, 91, 87, 54, 79, 62 mean
2. number of scouts in the city's scouting troops: 10, 8, 21, 11, 9, 7, 5, 10, 6, 9 median
3. number of apricots in bags of mixed dried fruit: 3, 3, 3, 4, 3, 3, 2, 0, 3, 3, 4, 6, 3, 2, 3, 3 mode

Also available on transparency

Math Humor

Q: What is the most misleading type of graph?

A: A lyin' graph.

10-4 Misleading Graphs and Statistics

GUARANTEED NOT TO BREAK DOWN (while parked)

Objectives
Recognize misleading graphs.

Recognize misleading statistics.

Vocabulary
random sample

Why learn this?
A misleading graph can be used to distort the results of a student council election. (See Example 3.)

Graphs can be used to influence what people believe. The way a data set is displayed can influence how the data are interpreted.

EXAMPLE 1 Misleading Bar Graphs

The graph shows the size of tomatoes on plants that were treated with different fertilizers.

A **Explain why the graph is misleading.**
The scale on the vertical axis begins at 80. This exaggerates the differences between the sizes of the bars.

B **What might someone believe because of the graph?**
Someone might believe that the tomato treated with fertilizer D is much larger than the other tomatoes. It is only 3.3 grams larger than the tomato treated with fertilizer B.

1. Who might want to use the graph above? Explain.
Company D; the fertilizer from company D appears to be more effective than the other fertilizers.

EXAMPLE 2 Misleading Line Graphs

The graph shows the average price of gasoline in the U.S. in September.

Average Gas Price in September
$1.60, $1.40, $1.20, $1.18, $1.16, $1.14, $1.12, $1.10, $1.00
1.08/gal, 1.10/gal, 1.24/gal, 1.26/gal, 1.43/gal
1993 1995 1997 1999 2001

A **Explain why the graph is misleading.**
The intervals on the vertical axis are not equal.

B **What might people be influenced to believe by the graph?**
Someone might believe that the price of gasoline increased the most between 1995 and 1997. However, the change between 1995 and 1997 was only \$0.14/gal while the change between 1999 and 2001 was \$0.17/gal.

2. Who might want to use the graph above? Explain.

2. Possible answer: taxi drivers; the drivers could justify charging higher rates by using this graph, which seems to show that gas prices have increased dramatically.

State Resources

State Resources Online
KEYWORD: MA7 Resources

1 Introduce

EXPLORATION

10-4 Misleading Graphs and Statistics

The table shows the number of games won by four baseball teams over the course of a season.

Team	Games Won
Cougars	50
Stars	55
Whales	90
Redwoods	60

1. Use the grid shown to make a bar graph of the data.

2. Use this grid to make a bar graph of the same data.

THINK AND DISCUSS

3. Describe how the second graph could be misleading.

Motivate

Discuss with students some situations in which someone might want to make a graph that suggests an incorrect conclusion. Examples might include companies who want to sell their product, candidates who want votes, and so on.

Explorations and answers are provided in *Alternate Openers: Explorations Transparencies.*

A circle graph compares each category of a data set to the whole. When any category is not represented in the graph, it may appear that another category represents a greater percentage of the total than it should.

EXAMPLE 3 Misleading Circle Graphs

The graph shows what percent of the total votes were received by three candidates for student council president.

Student Council Election

Atkins 10%
Smith 20%
Napier 5%

A Explain why the graph is misleading.

The sections of the graph do not add to 100%, so the votes for at least one of the candidates is not represented.

B What might people be influenced to believe by the graph?

Someone might believe that Smith won the election.

3. Who might want to use the graph above? Explain.
Possible answer: Smith; Smith might want to show that he or she got many more votes than Atkins or Napier.

Statistics can be misleading because of the way the data is collected or the way the results are reported. A sufficiently large *random sample* is a good way to collect unbiased data. In a **random sample** , all members of the group being surveyed have an equal chance of being selected.

EXAMPLE 4 Misleading Statistics

A researcher surveys people leaving a basketball game about what they like to watch on TV. Explain why the following statement is misleading: "80% of people like to watch sports on TV."

The sample is biased because people who attend sporting events are more likely to watch sports on TV than people who watch TV but do not attend sporting events.

4. A researcher asks 4 people if they have seasonal allergies. Three people respond yes. Explain why the following statement is misleading: "75% of people have seasonal allergies."
The sample size is much too small.

THINK AND DISCUSS

1. Give an example of a situation in which someone might intentionally try to make a graph misleading.
2. **GET ORGANIZED** Copy and complete the graphic organizer. Add more boxes if needed.

Know it! Note

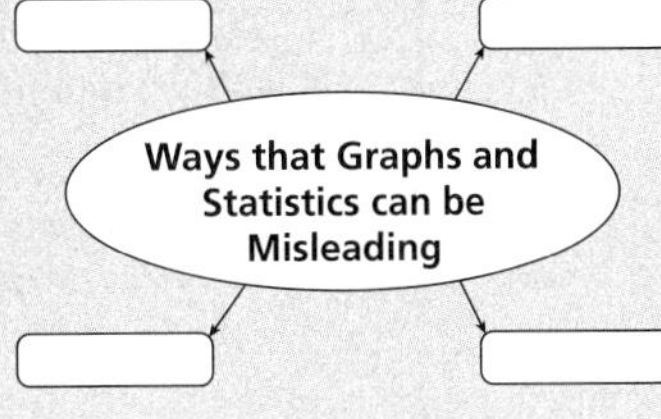

Power Presentations with PowerPoint®

Additional Examples

Examples 1–3

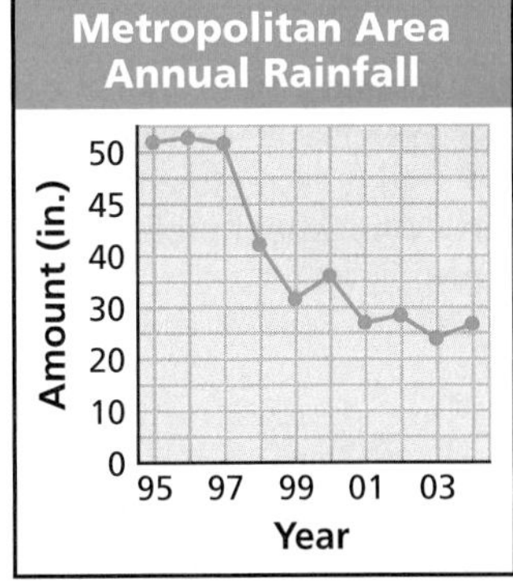

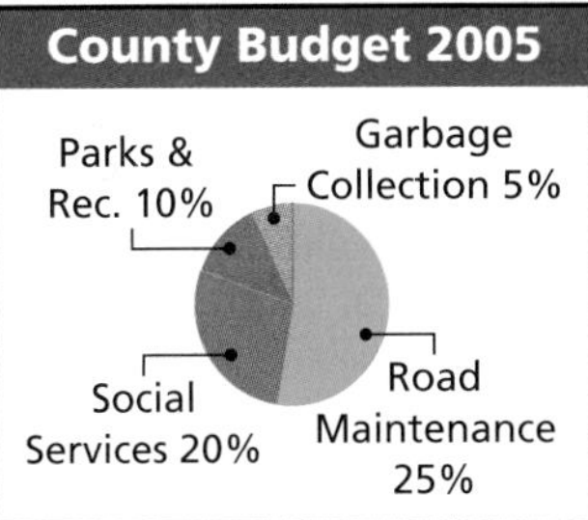

A. Explain why each graph is misleading.

B. What might someone believe because of each graph?

Example 4

A study of 5 households found the following number of pets per household: 2, 1, 1, 9, and 2. Explain why the following statement is misleading: "The average household has 3 pets."

For answers, see p. A32.

2 Teach

Guided Instruction

Review the characteristics of line, bar, and circle graphs. In **Example 3,** tell students that another way for circle graphs to be misleading is if the sectors are not drawn to scale. If a sector representing 20% of the data is larger than a sector representing 50% of the data, the graph is misleading, even if the percents add to 100%.

Inclusion Have students redraw each of the graphs in the examples so that they are no longer misleading. (Have them create more data for the circle graph.)

3 Close

Summarize

A misleading graph may cause a certain interpretation of the data. Tell students to check that the scale fits the data so that relationships are not exaggerated or minimized. The scale should also have evenly spaced intervals.

Answers to *Think and Discuss*

1. Possible answer: Someone selling a product might want to make the product appear better than other similar products.
2. See p. A9.

INTERVENTION

Questioning Strategies

EXAMPLES 1–3

- How can an accurate graph or statement about data be misleading?

EXAMPLE 4

- Why is a random sample the best way to collect accurate data?

10-4 Exercises

Assignment Guide

Assign *Guided Practice* exercises as necessary.

If you finished Examples **1–4**
Basic 7–12, 15, 16, 19–25
Average 7–17, 19–25
Advanced 7–11, 13–25

Homework Quick Check
Quickly check key concepts.
Exercises: 7–10, 13

Reading Math In part **c** of **Exercises 2–4,** students may find it easier to answer the question, "Who would profit from this graph?"

Answers

1. No member of a group is more likely to be picked for the sample than any other member of the group.

2a. The vert. scale does not start at 0. This exaggerates the differences in heights of the bars.

b. Someone might believe that employees at company Y make about twice as much as employees at company Z.

3c. Possible answer: someone who wants to increase spending on promoting tourism in San Francisco; the graph makes it appear that San Francisco is becoming a less popular travel destination.

State Resources

10-4 Exercises

GUIDED PRACTICE

1. **Vocabulary** Explain in your own words what the term *random sample* means.

SEE EXAMPLE 1 p. 726

2. The graph shows the average salaries of employees at three companies.
   a. Explain why the graph is misleading.
   b. What might someone believe because of the graph?
   c. Who might want to use this graph? Explain.
   Possible answer: company Y; the graph makes it appear that company Y pays high salaries.

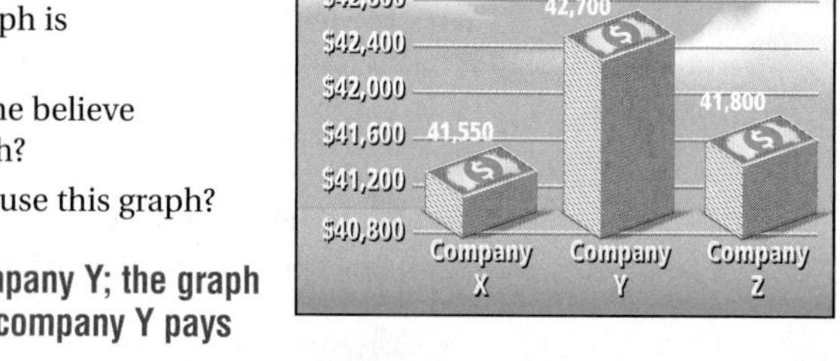

SEE EXAMPLE 2 p. 726

3a. The vert. scale does not start at 0, and the categories on the horiz. scale are not at equal time intervals.

3. The graph shows hotel occupancy in San Francisco over four years.
   a. Explain why the graph is misleading.
   b. What might someone believe because of the graph?
   c. Who might want to use this graph? Explain.
   3b. Tourism is decreasing rapidly.

SEE EXAMPLE 3 p. 727

4a. The sectors of the graph do not add to 100%.
b. Possible answer: The granola bar is almost half protein.

4. The graph shows the nutritional information for a granola bar.
   a. Explain why the graph is misleading.
   b. What might someone believe because of the graph?
   c. Who might want to use this graph? Explain.
   Possible answer: the granola bar company; they might want their product to look healthful.

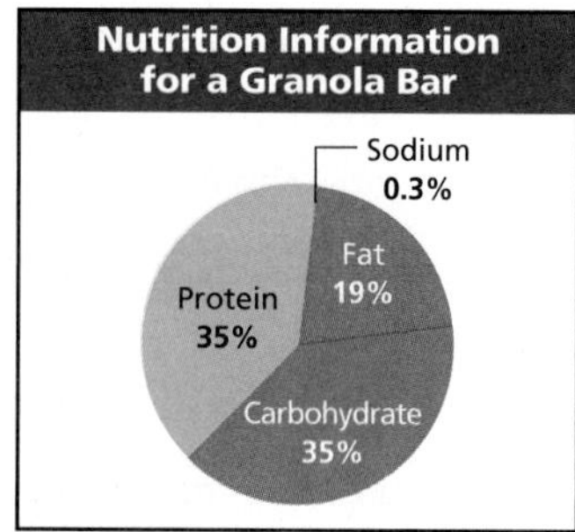

SEE EXAMPLE 4 p. 727

5. Three students were surveyed about their favorite teacher. Two students answer Mr. Gregory, and one answers Mr. Blaine. Explain why the following statement is misleading: "Mr. Gregory is the favorite teacher of a majority of the students." **The sample size is too small.**

6. A researcher surveys people at a shopping mall about whether they favor enlarging the size of the mall parking lot. Explain why the following statement is misleading: "85% of the community is in favor of enlarging the parking lot."
   People shopping at the mall are more likely to favor a larger parking lot.

ONGOING ASSESSMENT and INTERVENTION

***Diagnose Before* the Lesson**
10-4 Warm Up, TE p. 726

***Monitor During* the Lesson**
Check It Out! Exercises, SE pp. 726–727
Questioning Strategies, TE p. 727

***Assess After* the Lesson**
10-4 Lesson Quiz, TE p. 731
Alternative Assessment, TE p. 731

PRACTICE AND PROBLEM SOLVING

Independent Practice

For Exercises	See Example
7	1
8	2
9	3
10	4

Extra Practice

Skills Practice p. S22
Application Practice p. S37

7a. The vert. scale does not start at 0.

b. Possible answer: Single men pay significantly more than single women.

8a. The vert. scale extends beyond what is needed.

b. Possible answer: The price has not changed very much at all.

9a. The sectors of the graph do not add to 100%.

b. Possible answer: Nearly half of the state's spending was for welfare.

7. The graph shows the median rent for men and women in a metropolitan area.
   a. Explain why the graph is misleading.
   b. What might someone believe because of the graph?
   c. Who might want to use this graph? Explain.
   Possible answer: single men looking for apartments who want to negotiate a lower rent; the graph makes it appear that single men are overcharged.

Metropolitan Area Median Rent 2000

$620, $610, $600, $590, $580, $570; $612 Single man; $601 Single woman

8. The graph shows the export prices of Colombian arabica coffee over nine years.
   a. Explain why the graph is misleading.
   b. What might someone believe because of the graph?
   c. Who might want to use this graph? Explain.
   Possible answer: coffee growers; the graph makes it appear that coffee prices are low.

Colombian Arabica Coffee
Export Price/lb

$5.56, $4.60, $3.64, $2.68, $1.72, $0.49, $0; 1994, 1996, 1998, 2000, 2002

9. The graph shows how the state spent tax dollars during 1999 and 2000.
   a. Explain why the graph is misleading.
   b. What might someone believe because of the graph?
   c. Who might want to use this graph? Explain.

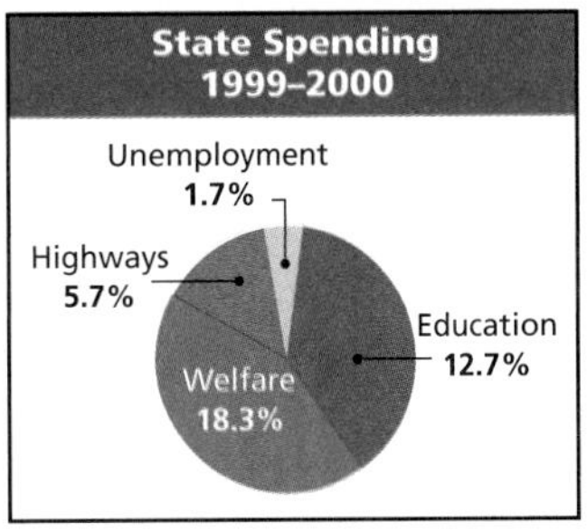

10. A college math course has one section with 240 students and 8 sections with 30 students. Explain why the following statement is misleading: "The average class size for the course is 53 students."
    Most of the classes have fewer than 53 students. The mean is not a good descriptor.

11. This problem will prepare you for the Multi-Step Test Prep on page 734.
    The table shows scores from the women's gymnastics finals in the floor exercise at the 2004 Summer Olympic Games.
    a. Find the average score for the women in the finals. **9.339**
    b. Would it be misleading to describe the data using the average score? Explain.
    c. Make a graph for this data that could convince someone that the difference between the first place score and the eighth place score was very small.

Rank	Name	Score
1	Catalina Ponor	9.750
2	Nicoleta Sofronie	9.562
3	Patricia Moreno	9.487
4	Fei Cheng	9.412
5	Daiane dos Santos	9.375
6	Mohini Bhardwaj	9.312
7	Kate Richardson	9.312
8	Alina Kozich	8.500

b. Yes; the lowest score, 8.500, brings the mean lower than most of the scores.

In **Exercise 3,** students may look only at the vertical scale. Point out that the graph shows data for months that are not evenly spaced on the horizontal scale. Also, measuring hotel occupancy at different times of the year may not be an accurate way to gauge tourism.

Exercise 11 involves finding the mean of a data set and determining whether it is the best statistic to describe the data set. This exercise prepares students for the Multi-Step Test Prep on page 734.

Answers

9c. Possible answer: someone who wants to justify cutting spending on welfare; the graph makes it appear that a large part of the spending was for welfare.

11c.

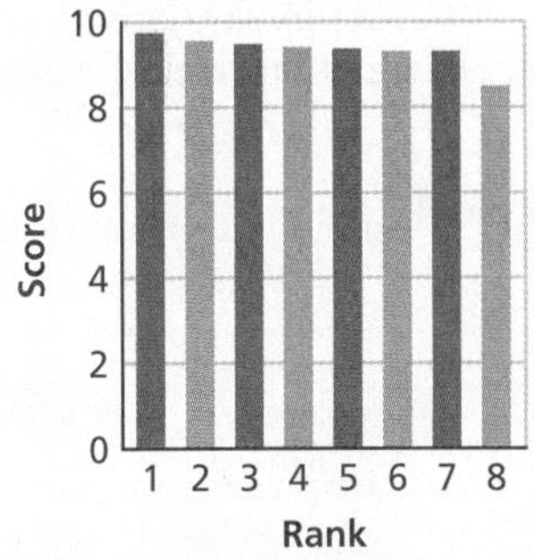

10-4 PRACTICE A

10-4 PRACTICE C

10-4 PRACTICE B

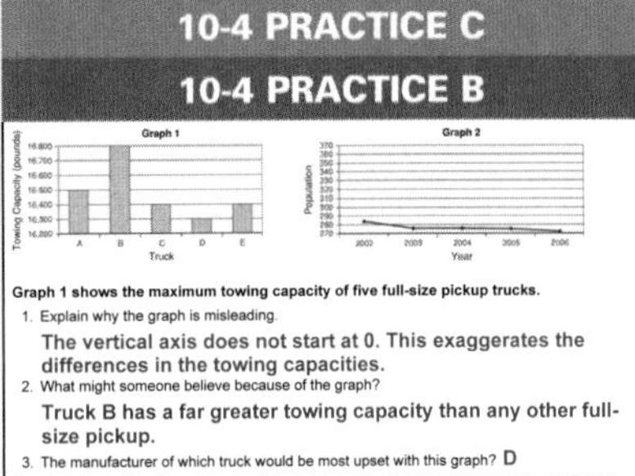

Graph 1 shows the maximum towing capacity of five full-size pickup trucks.
1. Explain why the graph is misleading.
   The vertical axis does not start at 0. This exaggerates the differences in the towing capacities.
2. What might someone believe because of the graph?
   Truck B has a far greater towing capacity than any other full-size pickup.
3. The manufacturer of which truck would be most upset with this graph? D

Graph 2 shows the change in population of a certain animal species in a wooded area.
4. Explain why the graph is misleading.
   The vertical axis does not start at 0 and extends beyond what is needed for this data.
5. What might someone believe because of the graph?
   Someone might believe that the population of this animal species is very low and nearly extinct.
6. Who might want to use this graph?
   someone advocating for support of this animal

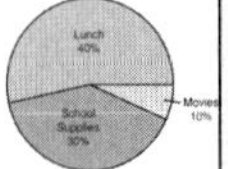

The circle graph shows how a school distributed money.
7. Explain why the graph is misleading.
   The sectors do not add to 100%.
8. What might someone believe because of the graph?
   The art classes get very little money and the math and computer classes get far more money than the other departments.
9. Who might want to use this graph?
   art teachers or other supporters of the arts
10. Sue surveyed people at a baseball stadium about their leisure activities. Explain why her statement is misleading: "85% of this town prefers sports over music."
    People attending a baseball game are more likely to prefer sports.

Teaching Tip **Technology** For **Exercise 13,** students can easily change the scale of the vertical axis with graph-making software or a spreadsheet program. The defaults for these programs usually generate relatively accurate graphs. By adjusting the preferences for the vertical scale, students can generate graphs for parts **b** and **c.**

TEST PREP DOCTOR + Students who answered **C** for **Exercise 15** may have seen that the mortality rate greatly decreased over time. Point out that most of the decrease occurred before the vaccine was introduced in 1963.

Teaching Tip **Social Studies** **Exercise 16** is about voting in the United States and France. Some students may not have a strong understanding of the political process in either country. Explain that in both countries, adults who meet certain basic requirements (citizenship, for example) may register to vote in elections. Both countries are democracies.

Answers

13a. Internet Service

Connection Speed (kbps): 850, 900, 950

Speedy Online 954; TelQuick 914; Alacrity 858

Provider

b. Internet Service

Connection Speed (kbps): 0, 500, 1000

Speedy Online 954; TelQuick 914; Alacrity 858

Provider

c. Possible answer: an objective report or Alacrity advertising materials. Someone who has no reason to make one company look better than another might make this graph. Alacrity might make this graph to show that they are very similar to the other companies.

17. See p. A32.

22–24. For graphs, see p. A32.

25. See p. A32.

12. B; the vert. scale extends beyond what is needed, so it appears that the pop. grew slowly; however, the pop. is several times the size that it started.

12. ***///ERROR ANALYSIS///*** The graph shows the population of a city over time. Which conclusion is incorrect? Explain why the conclusion is incorrect and how the graph was misleading.

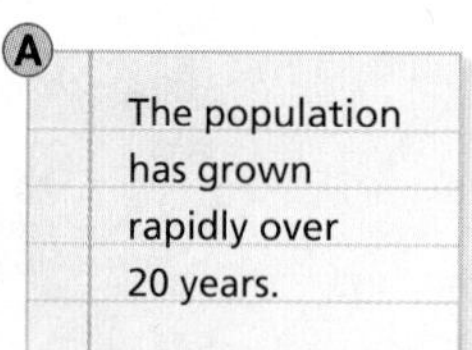

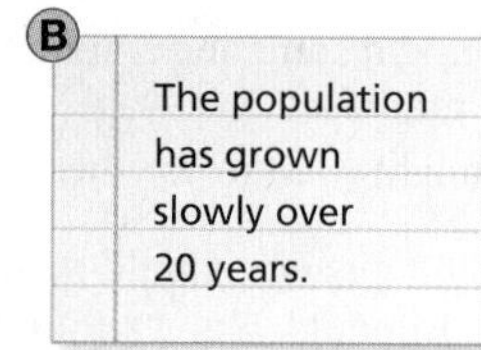

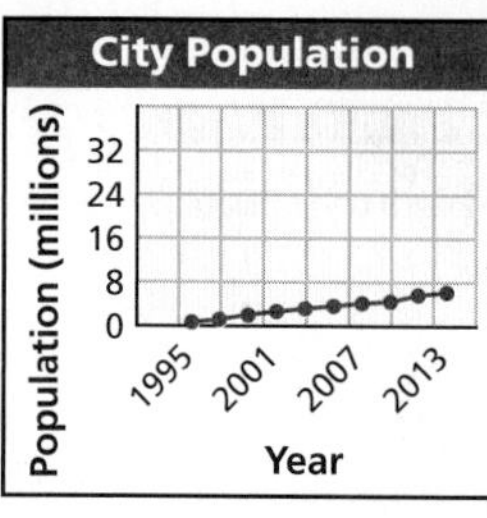

13. The table shows the average connection speeds of some broadband Internet service providers.

Provider	Connection Speed (Kbps)
Speedy Online	954
TelQuick	914
Alacrity	858

a. Construct a display that suggests that Speedy Online is much faster than the other services.

b. Construct a display that suggests that all of the services offer about the same connection speeds.

c. **Write About It** Where might you expect to see your graph from part **b**? Explain.

14. Critical Thinking Explain how a graph can show truthful data but still be misleading. **Possible answer: The scale of a graph can exaggerate the differences in the heights of bars or the slopes of lines. The data may be accurate, but the display encourages an inaccurate interpretation.**

TEST PREP

15. What might someone be influenced to believe because of the graph?

Ⓐ The measles vaccine was introduced when the mortality rate was at its highest.

Ⓑ The measles vaccine was unnecessary. (circled)

Ⓒ The measles vaccine dramatically decreased the mortality rate.

Ⓓ The measles vaccine increased the mortality rate.

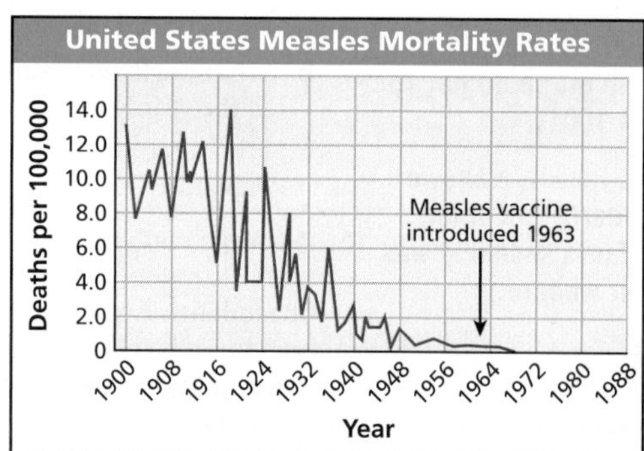

Source: www.healthsentinel.com

16. The table shows the number of votes cast in the 2000 U.S. presidential election and in the 2002 French presidential election. What additional information is needed to determine whether the following statement is misleading?

Country	Votes Cast
United States	105,405,100
France	29,497,272

"American voters are more likely to vote than French voters."

Ⓕ The number of candidates in each election

Ⓖ The legal voting age in France

Ⓗ The number of registered voters in the United States in 2000 and France in 2002 (circled)

Ⓙ The number of polling locations in the United States in 2000 and France in 2002

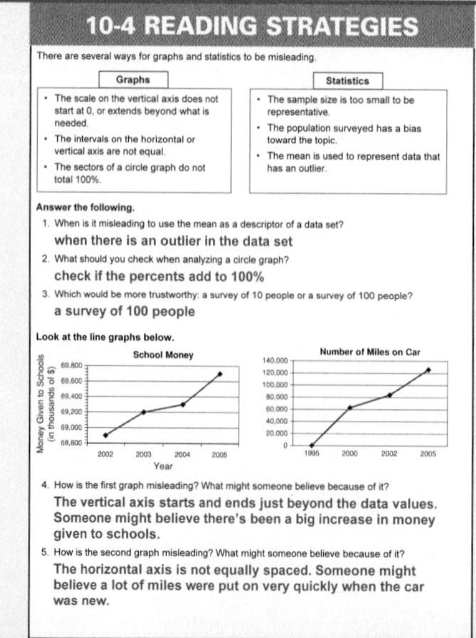

10-4 READING STRATEGIES

There are several ways for graphs and statistics to be misleading.

Graphs
- The scale on the vertical axis does not start at 0, or extends beyond what is needed.
- The intervals on the horizontal or vertical axis are not equal.
- The sectors of a circle graph do not total 100%.

Statistics
- The sample size is too small to be representative.
- The population surveyed has a bias toward the topic.
- The mean is used to represent data that has an outlier.

Answer the following.

1. When is it misleading to use the mean as a descriptor of a data set?
when there is an outlier in the data set
2. What should you check when analyzing a circle graph?
check if the percents add to 100%
3. Which would be more trustworthy: a survey of 10 people or a survey of 100 people?
a survey of 100 people

Look at the line graphs below.

4. How is the first graph misleading? What might someone believe because of it?
The vertical axis starts and ends just beyond the data values. Someone might believe there's been a big increase in money given to schools.
5. How is the second graph misleading? What might someone believe because of it?
The horizontal axis is not equally spaced. Someone might believe a lot of miles were put on very quickly when the car was new.

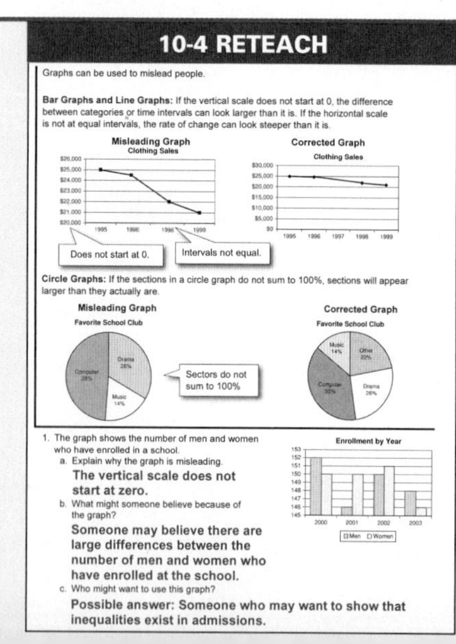

10-4 RETEACH

Graphs can be used to mislead people.

Bar Graphs and Line Graphs: If the vertical scale does not start at 0, the difference between categories or time intervals can look larger than it is. If the horizontal scale is not at equal intervals, the rate of change can look steeper than it is.

Circle Graphs: If the sections in a circle graph do not sum to 100%, sections will appear larger than they actually are.

1. The graph shows the number of men and women who have enrolled in a school.
a. Explain why the graph is misleading.
The vertical scale does not start at zero.
b. What might someone believe because of the graph?
Someone may believe there are large differences between the number of men and women who have enrolled at the school.
c. Who might want to use this graph?
Possible answer: Someone who may want to show that inequalities exist in admissions.

CHALLENGE AND EXTEND

17. **Logic** A fingerprint analyst is studying a fingerprint that was found in the chemistry lab. He reports that the fingerprint belongs to Dr. Arenson. Below are two questions the analyst was asked and the answers he gave.

Question 1: What are the chances that the fingerprint belongs to someone else who has the same fingerprint as Dr. Arenson? **Answer:** One in several billion.	**Question 2:** What are the chances that the fingerprint was wrongly identified? **Answer:** About 1 in 100.

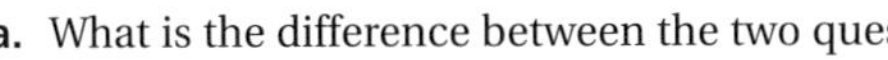

a. What is the difference between the two questions?
b. What does the answer to question 1 lead you to believe?
c. Who do you think might have asked question 1?
d. What does the answer to question 2 lead you to believe?
e. Who do you think might have asked question 2?

LINK History

Florence Nightingale (1820–1910) served as a nurse in the Crimean War. In 1854, she brought the first female nurses to military hospitals.

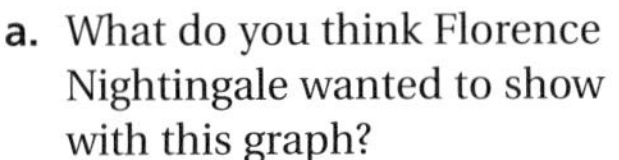

18. **History** Graphs like the one at right were created by Florence Nightingale. Nightingale served as a nurse during the Crimean War and was concerned with the unsanitary conditions the soldiers lived in. Each "wedge" of the circle represents a month between April 1854 and March 1855.

a. What do you think Florence Nightingale wanted to show with this graph?
b. Who do you think Nightingale showed the graph to?

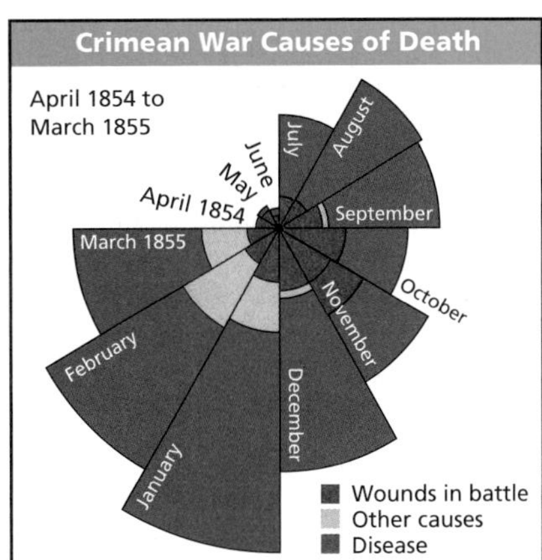

Source: The Florence Nightingale Museum

18a. Possible answer: Most deaths during the Crimean War were due to unclean conditions.
b. Possible answer: military officials who could control the conditions of military hospitals

SPIRAL REVIEW

Write an inequality for each situation. *(Lesson 3-1)*

19. The maximum weight for a certain truck load is 1500 pounds. $w \leq 1500$
20. Isaac's research paper must be at least 12 pages. $p \geq 12$
21. A moving company will transport up to 20 boxes for no fee. $b \leq 20$

Solve each inequality and graph the solutions. *(Lesson 3-4)*

22. $2x - 3 < 7$ $x < 5$
23. $3(t - 1) \geq -15$ $t \geq -4$
24. $6 - n < 2n + 9$ $n > -1$

25. The table shows the weight of a golden retriever at different ages. Choose a type of graph to display the given data. Make the graph, and explain why you chose that type of graph. *(Lesson 10-1)*

Age (mo)	1	3	6	12
Weight (lb)	8	23	45	66

Journal

Have students write four questions they could ask themselves to determine whether a graph or description of data is misleading.

ALTERNATIVE ASSESSMENT

Have students create misleading bar, line, and circle graphs. Then have them explain why their graphs are misleading and draw accurate representations.

Power Presentations with PowerPoint®

10-4 Lesson Quiz

Explain why each graph is misleading.

1.

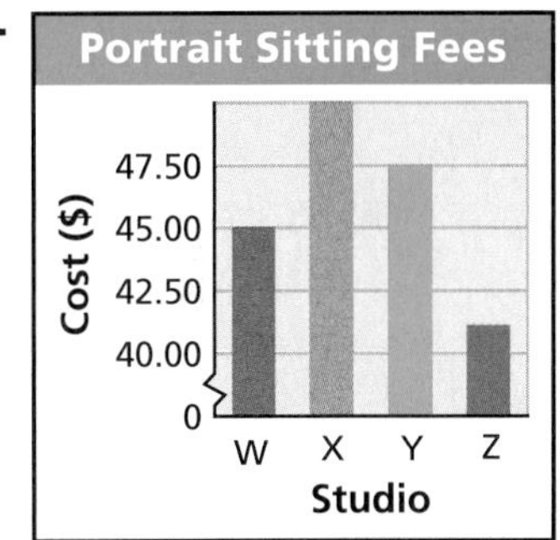

2.

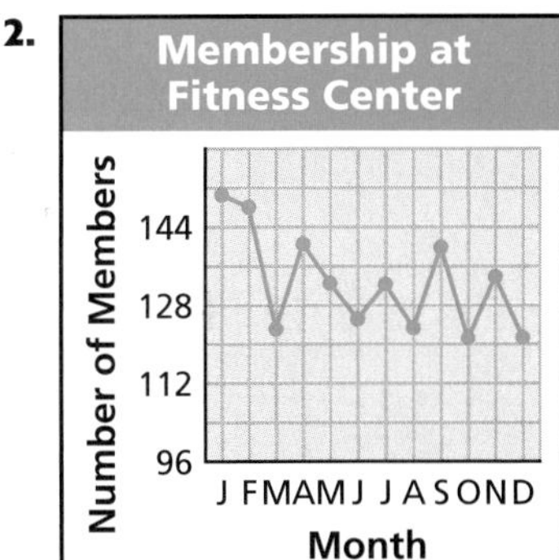

3.

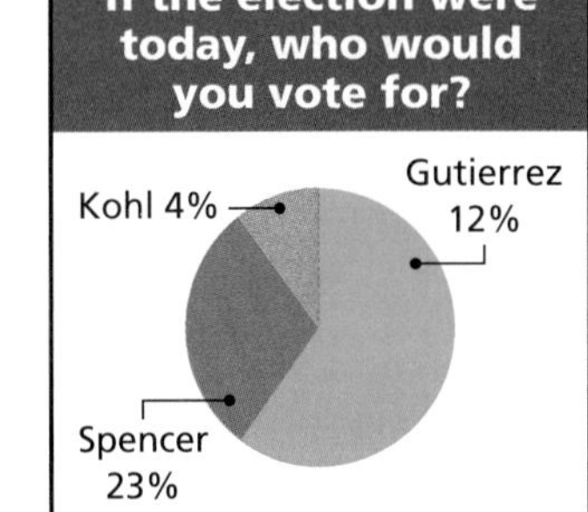

4. A researcher asks 5 people if they like to snow ski. Four people respond yes. Explain why the following statement is misleading: "80% of people like to snow ski."

For answers, see p. A32.

Also available on transparency

10-4 PROBLEM SOLVING

Analyze these misleading graphs.

1. This graph shows the years in which the world population reached, or is projected to reach, integer multiples of 1 billion people.

World Population Milestones — Billions of People — Year: 1804, 1927, 1960, 1974, 1987, 1999, 2013, 2028, 2054

a. Explain why the graph is misleading.
The years are not at equal time intervals.

b. What might someone believe because of the graph?
that world population is increasing in a linear fashion

2. This graph shows dog registrations with the American Kennel Club.

Dog Breeds Registered with the American Kennel Club, 2004

Beagle 5%; German Shepherd 5%; Golden Retriever 5%; Labrador Retriever 15%

a. Explain why the graph is misleading.
The sectors of the graph do not add to 100% because several dog breeds are omitted.

b. Who might want to use this graph, and why?
A breeder of labrador retrievers might use the graph to overemphasize the popularity of the breed.

Use the graph to select the best answer.

3. The graph is misleading because of which scale(s)?
A horizontal only
B vertical only
C both
D neither

4. Which statement is certainly true?
F The average house price increased every year between 1995 and 2004.
G The average house prices have increased $80,000 between 1995 and 2004.
H The average house price in 2001 was about $160,000.
J None of the above.

Average House Prices — Price ($) — Year

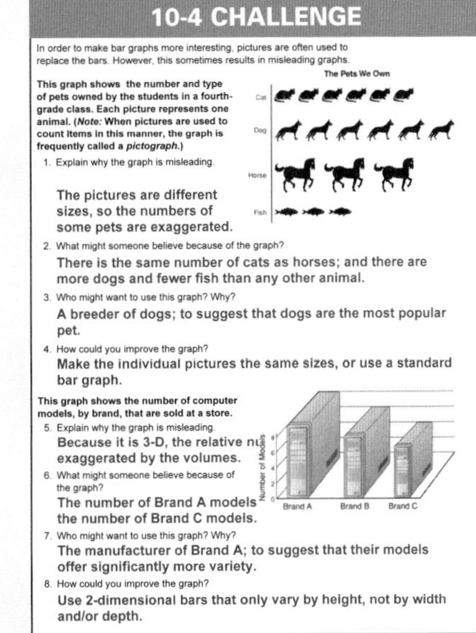

10-4 CHALLENGE

In order to make bar graphs more interesting, pictures are often used to replace the bars. However, this sometimes results in misleading graphs.

This graph shows the number and type of pets owned by the students in a fourth-grade class. Each picture represents one animal. (*Note:* When pictures are used to count items in this manner, the graph is frequently called a *pictograph*.)

The Pets We Own — Cat, Dog, Horse, Fish

1. Explain why the graph is misleading.
The pictures are different sizes, so the numbers of some pets are exaggerated.
2. What might someone believe because of the graph?
There is the same number of cats as horses; and there are more dogs and fewer fish than any other animal.
3. Who might want to use this graph? Why?
A breeder of dogs; to suggest that dogs are the most popular pet.
4. How could you improve the graph?
Make the individual pictures the same sizes, or use a standard bar graph.

This graph shows the number of computer models, by brand, that are sold at a store.

Number of Models — Brand A, Brand B, Brand C

5. Explain why the graph is misleading.
Because it is 3-D, the relative numbers are exaggerated by the volumes.
6. What might someone believe because of the graph?
The number of Brand A models is ... the number of Brand C models.
7. Who might want to use this graph? Why?
The manufacturer of Brand A; to suggest that their models offer significantly more variety.
8. How could you improve the graph?
Use 2-dimensional bars that only vary by height, not by width and/or depth.

Organizer

Pacing:
Traditional $\frac{1}{2}$ day
Block $\frac{1}{4}$ day

Objective: Examine different sampling methods and sources of bias.

Teach

Remember

Students review random samples.

Teaching Tip **Science** In science classes, students learn about how Earth is divided into stratified layers. Explain that in a stratified random sample, the population is divided into groups, or layers.

Sampling and Bias

If you wanted to collect data about a very large group of people, you would most likely need to survey a smaller group. The large group that contains all the people you could survey is called a *population.* The smaller group is called a *sample.*

You have learned that a random sample is a good way of collecting data that is unbiased. There are different ways of selecting a random sample.

Random Samples		
Type	**Definition**	**Example**
Simple Random Sample	Every member of the population has an equal chance of being chosen for the sample.	The names of all students in your class are placed in a hat and three names are chosen at random.
Stratified Random Sample	The population is divided into similar groups. Then a simple random sample is chosen from each group.	Your class is divided into boys and girls and two students are chosen at random from each group.
Systematic Random Sample	A member of the population is chosen for the sample at a regular interval.	Every third student who comes into the classroom is chosen.

Example 1

In each situation, identify the population and the sample. Tell whether each sample is a simple, stratified, or systematic random sample.

A **For one week, the manager of a pet supplies store asks every tenth customer what brand of pet food they buy.**

population: all customers at the pet supplies store during one week

sample: every tenth customer during that same week

The sample is systematic because one member of the population is chosen for the sample at a regular interval.

B **Every person who enters a theater one evening places their ticket stub in a bowl. The theater owner chooses five ticket stubs to award prizes.**

population: all people who put their ticket stub in the bowl

sample: five ticket stubs chosen from the bowl

The sample is simple because every member of the population has the same chance of being chosen.

C **One student from each classroom at a school is chosen at random for a committee.**

population: all students at a school

sample: one student from each classroom

The sample is stratified because the population is divided into similar groups and one member is chosen at random from each group.

Try This

1. Choose a topic to research. Describe the population, why you need to choose a sample, and the sample.
2. Choose whether to use a simple, stratified, or systematic random sample. Explain your choice and the process you would use to choose your sample.

A random sample is not biased because no part of the population is favored over another. In a biased sample, one or more parts of the population have an advantage for being chosen for the sample.

There are two main types of biased samples.

Biased Samples		
Type	**Definition**	**Example**
Convenience Sample	Those members of the population that are easily accessed are chosen for the sample.	A reporter questions people he personally knows.
Voluntary Response Sample	Members of the population who want to participate make up the sample.	A reporter questions people who fill out comment cards and indicate that they would like to be contacted.

Example 2

In each situation, identify the population and the sample. Tell whether each sample is a convenience or voluntary response sample. Explain why the sample is biased.

A **A website asks visitors to complete a survey about Internet usage.**

population: all visitors to the website

sample: those visitors who choose to complete the survey

The sample is a voluntary response sample because visitors to the website chose whether to complete the survey. The sample is biased because those visitors who choose to complete the survey may not be representative of all visitors to the website.

B **A reporter asks people leaving a shopping center through one door about their shopping habits.**

population: all people at the shopping center

sample: people who leave from one door at the shopping center

The sample is a convenience sample because the people leaving through the chosen door are easily accessed. The sample is biased because people leaving through another door do not have an opportunity to be chosen.

Try This

3. Choose a topic to research. Describe the population, why you need to choose a sample, and the sample.
4. Assume that you want an unbiased sample. Choose whether to use a simple, stratified, or systematic random sample. Explain your choice and the process you would use to choose your sample.
5. Describe how a biased sample could be chosen for this same situation.

Close

Assess

After students have described how they would choose a random sample for their given topic, discuss how sources of bias could be avoided.

Answers to *Try This*

1–2. Check students' work.

3–5. Check students' work.

Organizer

Objective: Assess students' ability to apply concepts and skills in Lessons 10-1 through 10-4 in a real-world format.

Online Edition

Resources

Algebra I Assessments

www.mathtekstoolkit.org

Problem	Text Reference
1	Lesson 10-1
2	Lessons 10-1 and 10-2
3	Lesson 10-3
4	Lesson 10-3

State Resources

CHAPTER 10

MULTI-STEP TEST PREP

SECTION 10A

Data Analysis

USA! USA! USA! In 708 B.C.E., the Olympic Games included the pentathlon. This event included the discus, javelin, long jump, running, and wrestling. The winner of the pentathlon was considered a "super athlete." The modern pentathlon of the Olympic Games includes five disciplines: target shooting, fencing, swimming, horseback riding, and cross-country running.

1. The pentathlon includes five events. What type of graph should be used to show what percent of this event is made up of each discipline? **circle graph**
2. Do you think the winner of the modern pentathlon must win each of the five events? Explain.
3. Thirty-two men competed in the modern pentathlon in the 2004 Olympic Games. The chart shows the total points for the competitors.

Pentathlon Scores
5480 5428 5392 5356 5340
5332 5320 5295 5276 5252 5200 5196
5192 5184 5180 5172 5144 5132 5084
5084 5068 5016 4976 4936 4932 4916
4904 4848 4732 4676 4420 4388

Find the mean, median, and mode of this data set. Which value best describes the data? Explain.

4. Find the minimum, first quartile, third quartile, and maximum values of the data set above. Use these values and the median to make a box-and-whisker plot of the data. **min.: 4388; Q1: 4934; Q3: 5285.5; max.: 5480**

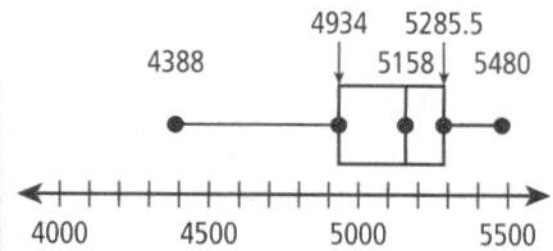

2. No; an athlete could score very well in 1 event but have low scores in the other 4 events. Another athlete with 4 high scores and 1 low score would have a better total score.

3. Mean: 5089.09375; median: 5158; mode: 5084; the mean best describes the data because there are no outliers.

INTERVENTION

Scaffolding Questions

1. What type of graph compares the parts to the whole? circle graph
2. What if an athlete wins one event but has low scores in the other four events? Another athlete might win four events but have a low score in one event. This athlete could have the highest total score.
3. Are there any outliers? yes How does an outlier affect the mean? A very small outlier makes the mean smaller, and a very large outlier makes the mean greater.
4. How do you show an outlier on a box-and-whisker plot? Draw a dot and do not connect it to the rest of the graph.

Extension

How would you display the data if you wanted to show the number of athletes who had total scores within a certain interval? a frequency table or a histogram

Quiz for Lessons 10-1 Through 10-4

10-1 Organizing and Displaying Data

Use the circle graph for 1–3.

1. Which material represents over 50% of Don's recyclables? **paper/cardboard**
2. How many pounds of materials does Don recycle? **20**
3. What percent of Don's recyclables are glass? **25%**
4. The table shows the total proceeds for a fund-raiser at various times during the day. Choose a type of graph to display the given data. Make the graph, and explain why you chose that type of graph.

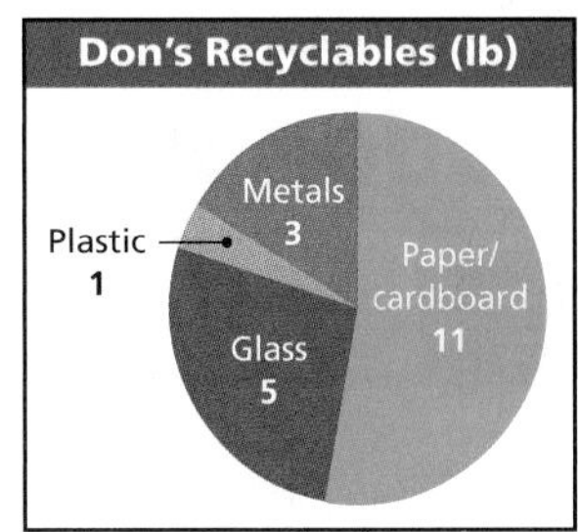

Time	Total Proceeds (thousand $)	Time	Total Proceeds (thousand $)
3:00 P.M.	1.5	6:00 P.M.	6.5
4:00 P.M.	2	7:00 P.M.	8
5:00 P.M.	4	8:00 P.M.	9.5

10-2 Frequency and Histograms

5. The Miller family is going to buy a new car. The approximate prices of the cars they are considering are given. Use the data to make a stem-and-leaf plot.
   $24,000, $28,000, $26,000, $32,000, $30,000, $41,000, $27,000, $22,000, $26,000, $33,000
6. The number of people at a caterer's last 12 parties are given below.
   16, 18, 17, 19, 15, 25, 18, 17, 18, 16, 17, 19
   a. Use the data to make a frequency table with intervals.
   b. Use your frequency table from part **a** to make a histogram.

10-3 Data Distributions

7. The daily high temperatures on 14 consecutive days in one city were 59 °F, 49 °F, 48 °F, 46 °F, 47 °F, 51 °F, 49 °F, 43 °F, 45 °F, 52 °F, 51 °F, 51 °F, 51 °F, and 38 °F.
   a. Find the mean, median, and mode of the temperatures. **mean: 48.57; med.: 49; mode: 51**
   b. Which value describes the average high temperature for the 14 days? **mean**
   c. Which value best describes the high temperatures? Explain.
8. Use the temperature data above to make a box-and-whisker plot.

10-4 Misleading Graphs and Statistics

9. The graph shows the value of a company's stock over time. Explain why the graph is misleading. What might people be influenced to believe because of the graph? Who might want to use this graph?
10. The results of an online survey of 230 people showed that 92% of the population felt very comfortable using technology. Explain why this statistic is misleading.

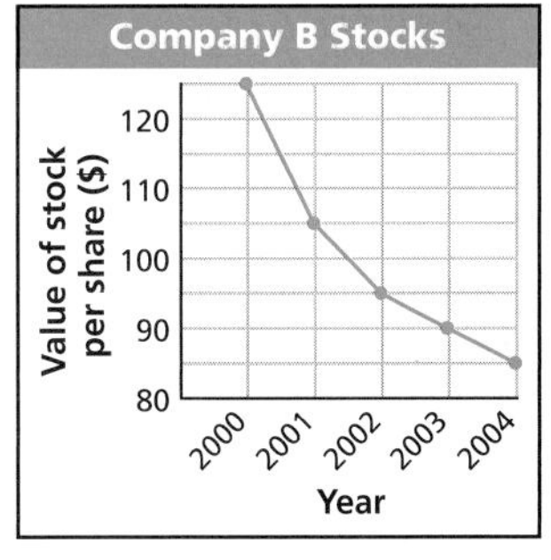

READY TO GO ON? SECTION 10

Organizer

Objective: Assess students' mastery of concepts and skills in Lessons 10-1 through 10-4.

Resources

 ***Assessment Resources***
Section 10A Quiz

Teacher One Stop™
Test & Practice Generator

INTERVENTION

Resources

 ***Ready to Go On? Intervention and Enrichment* Worksheets**

 ***Ready to Go On?* CD-ROM**

***Ready to Go On?* Online**

my.hrw.com

Answers

4–6, 7c–10. See p. A32.

READY TO GO ON? Diagnose and Prescribe

NO INTERVENE

Ready to Go On? Intervention	*Ready to Go On? Intervention,* Section 10A Worksheets	CD-ROM	Online
Lesson 10-1	10-1 Intervention	Activity 10-1	Diagnose and Prescribe Online
Lesson 10-2	10-2 Intervention	Activity 10-2	
Lesson 10-3	10-3 Intervention	Activity 10-3	
Lesson 10-4	10-4 Intervention	Activity 10-4	

YES ENRICH

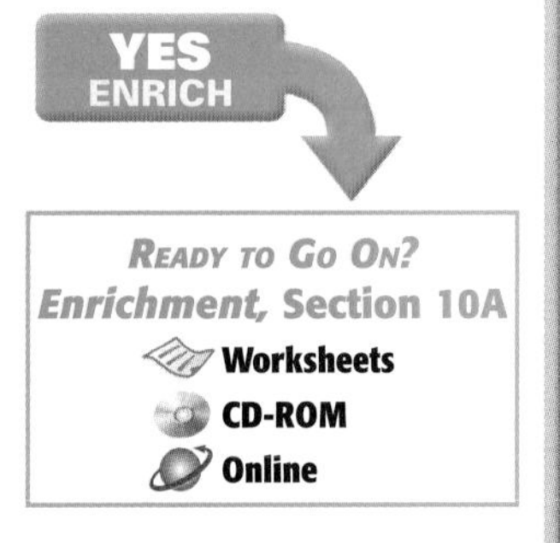

SECTION
10B Probability

One-Minute Section Planner

Lesson	Lab Resources	Materials
10-5 Algebra Lab Simulations • Use a number cube to simulate a probability experiment. ☐ SAT-10 ☑ NAEP ☐ ACT ☐ SAT ☐ SAT Subject Tests	***Algebra Lab Activities*** 10-5 Lab Recording Sheet	**Required** number cube (MK)
Lesson 10-5 Experimental Probability • Determine the experimental probability of an event. • Use experimental probability to make predictions. ☑ SAT-10 ☑ NAEP ☑ ACT ☑ SAT ☑ SAT Subject Tests	***Algebra Lab Activities*** 10-5 Algebra Lab	**Optional** number cube (MK)
10-5 Technology Lab Use Random Numbers • Use a graphing calculator to find experimental probabilities by generating random numbers. ☐ SAT-10 ☑ NAEP ☐ ACT ☑ SAT ☑ SAT Subject Tests	***Technology Lab Activities*** 10-5 Lab Recording Sheet	**Required** graphing calculator
Lesson 10-6 Theoretical Probability • Determine the theoretical probability of an event. • Convert between probabilities and odds. ☑ SAT-10 ☑ NAEP ☑ ACT ☑ SAT ☑ SAT Subject Tests		**Optional** number cube (MK), spinner (MK)
Lesson 10-7 Independent and Dependent Events • Find the probability of independent events. • Find the probability of dependent events. ☑ SAT-10 ☑ NAEP ☑ ACT ☑ SAT ☑ SAT Subject Tests	***Algebra Lab Activities*** 10-7 Algebra Lab	**Optional** red and black marbles, checkers, playing cards
10-7 Algebra Lab Compound Events • Find the probability of compound events. ☑ SAT-10 ☑ NAEP ☑ ACT ☑ SAT ☑ SAT Subject Tests	***Technology Lab Activities*** 10-7 Lab Recording Sheet	
Lesson 10-8 Combinations and Permutations • Solve problems involving permutations. • Solve problems involving combinations. ☑ SAT-10 ☑ NAEP ☑ ACT ☑ SAT ☑ SAT Subject Tests	***Algebra Lab Activities*** 10-8 Algebra Lab	
Extension Matrices • Organize data in a matrix. • Add and subtract matrices and multiply a matrix by a scalar. ☐ SAT-10 ☐ NAEP ☑ ACT ☑ SAT ☑ SAT Subject Tests		

Note: If NAEP is checked, the content is tested on either the Grade 8 or Grade 12 NAEP assessment.

MK = *Manipulatives Kit*

Math Background

Professional Learning

PROBABILITY

Lessons 10-5 to 10-7

A *probability* is a number between 0 and 1 inclusive that measures the likelihood of an event. When an event consists of finitely many equally likely outcomes, the *theoretical probability* of the event is the ratio of the number of outcomes in the event to the total number of possible outcomes. The probability of an impossible event is 0; the probability of a certain event is 1. When the set of all possible outcomes is finite, the converses of these statements are also true.

Probabilities may also be found by experimental means. The *experimental probability* of an event is the ratio of the number of times the event occurs to the total number of trials. For example, if you toss a coin 100 times and it comes up heads 54 times, the experimental probability of heads is $\frac{54}{100}$, or 0.54.

The *Law of Large Numbers* states that the experimental probability of an event approaches the theoretical probability as the number of trials becomes arbitrarily large. In the above examples, as the number of coin tosses increases, the experimental probability of heads will tend to approach the theoretical probability, 0.5.

Two events are *independent* if the occurrence of one does not affect the probability of the other. If A and B are independent, then $P(A \text{ and } B)$, also written $P(A \cap B)$, is $P(A) \cdot P(B)$. More generally, events A_1, A_2, ..., A_n are *mutually independent* if the occurrence of any one does not affect the probability of any other. Then, $P(A_1 \cap A_2 \cap \ldots \cap A_n) = P(A_1) \cdot P(A_2) \cdot \ldots \cdot P(A_n)$.

Mutually exclusive events cannot occur in the same trial. For example, a coin cannot simultaneously show heads and tails. If A and B are mutually exclusive, then $P(A \text{ or } B)$, also written $P(A \cup B)$, is $P(A) + P(B)$. This addition rule is generally used when finding probability for a single trial, while the multiplication rule for independent events is usually applied to two or more separate trials, performed either simultaneously or in succession.

COMBINATORICS

LESSON 10-8

Combinatorics is the branch of mathematics that deals with arranging and counting finite collections of items. One of the earliest known uses of combinatorial reasoning is in a medical text from India that dates from the 6th century B.C.E. The author asserts that six basic tastes—salty, sour, bitter, sweet, hot, and astringent—may be combined to form 63 different taste combinations (6 individual tastes, 15 combinations of two tastes, 20 combinations of three tastes, 15 combinations of four tastes, 6 combinations of five tastes, and 1 combination using all six tastes.)

This is an example of a combination. A *combination* is a grouping of items in which the order does not matter. In a *permutation,* the order of the items does matter. For a permutation of n items taken r items at a time $({}_nP_r)$, there are

n choices for the 1st item
$n - 1$ choices for the 2nd item
$n - 2$ choices for the 3rd item

.
.
.

$n - (r + 1)$ choices for the last item

The total number of permutations is the product $n(n-1)(n-2)\ldots\big(n-(r+1)\big)$, or $\frac{n!}{(n-r)!}$.

For combinations, the order does not matter. Consider permutations of 4 numbers taken 3 at a time, shown in the array below. Each row shows six distinct permutations that are equivalent combinations.

123	132	213	231	312	321
124	142	214	241	412	421
134	143	314	341	413	431
234	243	324	342	423	432

In general, for a combination of n items taken r at a time $({}_nC_r)$, each combination appears $r!$ times in the corresponding list of permutations. In other words, ${}_nC_r = \frac{{}_nP_r}{r!} = \frac{n!}{r!(n-r)!}$.

Organizer

Use with Lesson 10-5

Pacing:
Traditional $\frac{1}{2}$ day
Block $\frac{1}{4}$ day

Objective: Use a number cube to simulate a probability experiment.

Materials: number cube

Online Edition
TechKeys

Countdown Week 23

Resources

Algebra Lab Activities
10-5 Lab Recording Sheet

Teach

Discuss

To *simulate* means to pretend to experience something. It is a word also used outside of mathematics.

A number cube (MK) is only one way to create the simulation in the activity. A spinner with six equal sections would also work.

Close

Key Concept

A simulation can replace the need for actually performing an experiment. This is particularly helpful if the experiment would be difficult or inconvenient to perform.

Assessment

Journal Have students explain when and how a simulation is used.

State Resources

go.hrw.com
State Resources Online
KEYWORD: MA7 Resources

10-5

Simulations

A simulation can be used to model an experiment that would be difficult or inconvenient to actually perform. In this lab, you will conduct simulations.

Use with Lesson 10-5

Activity

The local movie theater is offering an opportunity for customers to win a free night at the movies. To win, you must collect six different letters to spell CINEMA. Each movie ticket sold during this promotion will have one of the six letters stamped on the back of the ticket. An equal number of tickets will be stamped with each of the letters.

1 Since there are six different letters that appear on the tickets an equal number of times, you can use a number cube to simulate collecting the six letters. Each of the numbers on the number cube will represent a letter. Each roll of the number cube will represent purchasing one movie ticket, and the number rolled will represent the letter stamped on the ticket.

2 The table shows the results of rolling the number cube until each number has been rolled once.

a. Based on the results shown in the table, how many rolls did it take to get all six numbers?

b. Based on the results in the table, how many movie tickets would you expect to have to buy to get all six letters? If you purchased this number of tickets, would you be sure to win? Explain.

Number on Cube	Letter on Ticket	Frequency
1	C	I
2	I	~~IIII~~ I
3	N	IIII
4	E	II
5	M	II
6	A	III

Try This

1. Repeat the simulation four more times and record the results. **Check students' work.**
2. Find the average number of rolls from all five simulations $\left(\frac{\text{total number of rolls from 5 simulations}}{5}\right)$. **Possible answer:** $\frac{18 + 15 + 9 + 12 + 27}{5} = 16.2$
3. Based on your answer to Problem 2, how many movie tickets would you expect to have to buy to get all six letters? Is this number different from the answer you gave based on the results in the table above? **Check students' work.**
4. Would any of your answers have been different if you had used a different correspondence between the numbers and letters? Explain. **No; if 1 number corresponds to 1 letter, the results should be about the same.**

Answers to Activity

2a. 18 rolls

b. No; a simulation is just a model and there may be different results each time the simulation is performed.

10-5 Experimental Probability

Objectives

Determine the experimental probability of an event.

Use experimental probability to make predictions.

Vocabulary

experiment
trial
outcome
sample space
event
probability
experimental probability
prediction

Why learn this?

Experimental probability can be used by manufacturers for quality control. (See Example 4.)

An **experiment** is an activity involving chance. Each repetition or observation of an experiment is a **trial**, and each possible result is an **outcome**. The **sample space** of an experiment is the set of all possible outcomes.

Experiment	Rolling a number cube	Tossing a coin	Spinning a game spinner
Sample Space	{1, 2, 3, 4, 5, 6}	{heads, tails}	{red, blue, green, yellow}

EXAMPLE 1 Identifying Sample Spaces and Outcomes

Identify the sample space and the outcome shown for each experiment.

A tossing two coins
Sample space: {HH, HT, TH, TT}
Outcome shown: heads, tails (H, T)

B spinning a game spinner
Sample space: {yellow, red, blue, green}
Outcome shown: green

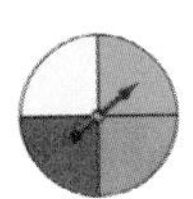

1. Identify the sample space and the outcome shown for the experiment: rolling a number cube.

sample space: {1, 2, 3, 4, 5, 6}; outcome shown: 3

An **event** is an outcome or set of outcomes in an experiment. **Probability** is the measure of how likely an event is to occur. Probabilities are written as fractions or decimals from 0 to 1, or as percents from 0% to 100%.

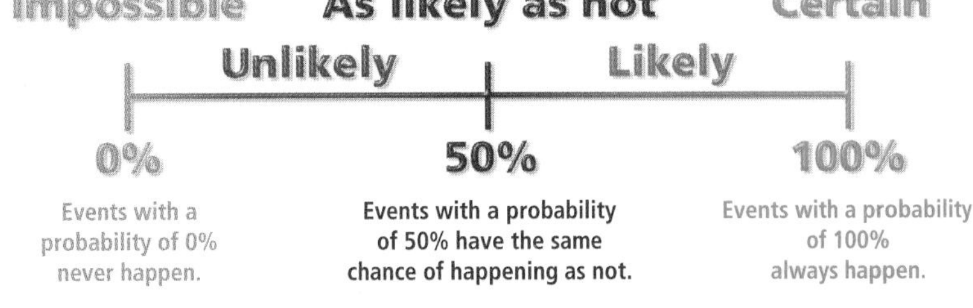

10-5 Organizer

Pacing: Traditional 1 day
Block $\frac{1}{2}$ day

Objectives: Determine the experimental probability of an event.

Use experimental probability to make predictions.

Algebra Lab
In *Algebra Lab Activities*

Online Edition
Tutorial Videos

Countdown Week 23

Power Presentations with PowerPoint®

Warm Up

Write the equivalent percent.

1. $\frac{3}{10}$ 30%
2. $\frac{1}{4}$ 25%
3. $\frac{18}{90}$ 20%
4. $\frac{88}{550}$ 16%

Write the equivalent fraction.

5. 50% $\frac{1}{2}$
6. 10% $\frac{1}{10}$
7. 40% $\frac{2}{5}$
8. 35% $\frac{7}{20}$

Write the equivalent decimal.

9. 18% 0.18
10. 50% 0.5
11. $\frac{1}{5}$ 0.2
12. $\frac{9}{10}$ 0.9

Also available on transparency

Math Fact !!

South African mathematician John Kerrich tossed a coin 10,000 times. The coin landed with heads showing 5067 times.

1 Introduce

10-5 Experimental Probability

You can use a graphing calculator to simulate tossing a coin. In this simulation, a result of 0 represents tails, and a result of 1 represents heads.

1. Press [MATH] and use the arrow keys to move to the **PRB** menu. Then choose the random integer function by selecting **5:randInt(**.

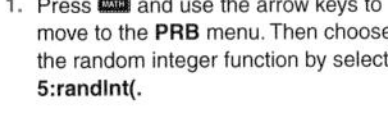

2. Press 0 [,] 1 [)] to give the range of integers. Press [ENTER] to simulate tossing a coin.

3. You can press [ENTER] repeatedly to simulate multiple coin tosses.
4. Simulate tossing a coin 10 times. How many of the tosses resulted in heads?
5. Combine your results with those of other students. What is the total number of coin tosses? How many of the tosses resulted in heads?

THINK AND DISCUSS

6. Explain how many times you would expect the result to be heads if you tossed a coin 1000 times.

Motivate

Roll a number cube (MK) several times and record the results on the board. Tell students that you have just performed a probability experiment. Tell students they will learn about experimental probability, which is used to make predictions about the stock market, sports, and the behavior of humans and animals.

Explorations and answers are provided in *Alternate Openers: Explorations Transparencies.*

State Resources

Power Presentations with PowerPoint®

Additional Examples

Example 1

Identify the sample space and the outcome shown for each experiment.

A. rolling a number cube

sample space: {1, 2, 3, 4, 5, 6}; outcome shown: 4

B. spinning a spinner

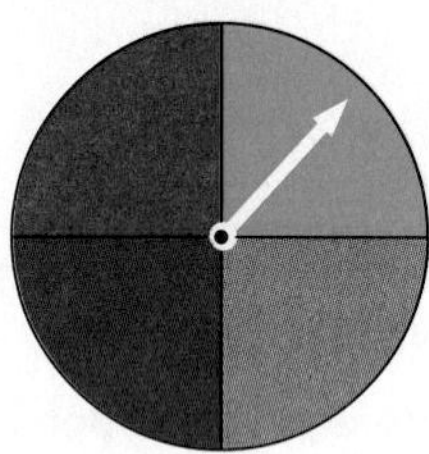

sample space: {red, green, purple, orange}; outcome shown: green

Example 2

Write *impossible, unlikely, as likely as not, likely,* or *certain* to describe each event.

A. A shoe selected from a pair of shoes fits the right foot. as likely as not

B. Katrina correctly guesses the last digit of a phone number. unlikely

C. Max pulls a green marble from a bag of all green marbles. certain

D. A randomly selected month contains the letter R. likely

Example 3

An experiment consists of spinning a spinner. Use the results in the table to find the experimental probability of each event.

Outcome	Frequency
Green	15
Orange	10
Purple	8
Pink	7

A. The spinner lands on orange. $\frac{1}{4}$

B. The spinner does not land on green. $\frac{5}{8}$

EXAMPLE 2 Estimating the Likelihood of an Event

Write *impossible, unlikely, as likely as not, likely,* or *certain* to describe each event.

A There are 31 days in August.

August always has 31 days. This event is *certain.*

B Carlos correctly guesses a number between 1 and 1000.

Carlos must pick one outcome out of 1000 possible outcomes. This event is *unlikely.*

C A coin lands heads up.

Heads is one of two possible outcomes. This event is *as likely as not.*

D Cecilia rolls a 10 on a standard number cube.

A standard number cube is numbered 1 through 6. This event is *impossible.*

CHECK IT OUT! 2. Write *impossible, unlikely, as likely as not, likely,* or *certain* to describe the event: Anthony rolls a number less than 7 on a standard number cube. **certain**

You can estimate the probability of an event by performing an experiment. The **experimental probability** of an event is the ratio of the number of times the event occurs to the number of trials. The more trials performed, the more accurate the estimate is likely to be.

Know it! Note

Experimental Probability

$$\text{experimental probability} = \frac{\text{number of times the event occurs}}{\text{number of trials}}$$

EXAMPLE 3 Finding Experimental Probability

An experiment consists of spinning a spinner. Use the results in the table to find the experimental probability of each event.

Outcome	Frequency
Red	7
Blue	8
Green	5

Helpful Hint

Probabilities can be expressed as fractions, decimals, or percents. For Example 3, the probabilities are:

3A: $\frac{2}{5} = 0.4 = 40\%$

3B: $\frac{3}{4} = 0.75 = 75\%$

A spinner lands on blue

$$\frac{\text{number of times the event occurs}}{\text{number of trials}} = \frac{8}{7+8+5} = \frac{8}{20} = \frac{2}{5}$$

B spinner does not land on green

When the spinner does not land on green, it must land on red or blue.

$$\frac{\text{number of times the event occurs}}{\text{number of trials}} = \frac{7+8}{7+8+5} = \frac{15}{20} = \frac{3}{4}$$

INTERVENTION

Questioning Strategies

EXAMPLES 1–2

- If an event is impossible, what is the relationship between the event and the sample space? What if the event is certain?

EXAMPLE 3

- How do you find the experimental probability of an event not occurring?

2 Teach

Guided Instruction

Introduce an experiment as a process that leads to outcomes. Practice listing the sample spaces for several experiments. Refer to the continuum on page 737 when working through **Example 2.** Mention that many people say *fifty-fifty* instead of *as likely as not.*

Cognitive Strategies Reinforce definitions by using the vocabulary in the lesson when discussing the lesson.

Use the information in Example 3 to find the experimental probability of each event.

3a. spinner lands on red **$\frac{7}{20}$**

3b. spinner does not land on red **$\frac{13}{20}$**

You can use experimental probability to make *predictions.* A **prediction** is an estimate or guess about something that has not yet happened.

EXAMPLE 4 *Quality Control Application*

A manufacturer inspects 800 light bulbs and finds that 796 of them have no defects.

A **What is the experimental probability that a light bulb chosen at random has no defects?**

Find the experimental probability that a light bulb has no defects.

$$\frac{\text{number of times the event occurs}}{\text{number of trials}} = \frac{796}{800}$$

$$= 99.5\%$$

The experimental probability that a light bulb has no defects is 99.5%.

B **The manufacturer sent a shipment of 2400 light bulbs to a retail store. Predict the number of light bulbs in the shipment that are likely to have no defects.**

Find 99.5% of 2400.

$0.995(2400) = 2388$

The manufacturer predicts that 2388 light bulbs have no defects.

4. A manufacturer inspects 1500 electric toothbrush motors and finds that 1497 of them have no defects.
   a. What is the experimental probability that a motor chosen at random will have no defects? **99.8%**
   b. There are 35,000 motors in a warehouse. Predict the number of motors that are likely to have no defects. **34,930**

THINK AND DISCUSS

1. Explain the difference between an outcome and an event.
2. Is the experimental probability of an event always the same? Explain why or why not.

3. **GET ORGANIZED** Copy and complete the graphic organizer. In each box, write an example of an event that has the given likelihood.

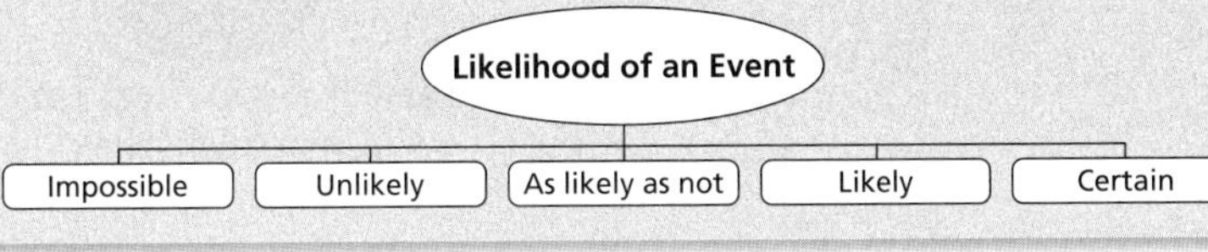

COMMON ERROR ALERT

Students might list extremely unlikely events as impossible and extremely likely events as certain. Remind students that if an event is impossible, then there is absolutely no way it could ever happen. If an event is certain, there is absolutely no way it could not happen.

Power Presentations with PowerPoint®

Additional Examples

Example 4

A manufacturer inspects 500 strollers and finds that 498 have no defects.

a. What is the experimental probability that a stroller chosen at random has no defects? 99.6%

b. The manufacturer shipped 3500 strollers to a distribution center. Predict the number of strollers that are likely to have no defects. 3486

INTERVENTION 

Questioning Strategies

EXAMPLE 4

- How do you use experimental probability to make a prediction?

Multiple Representations Students can use proportions in part **b** of **Example 4:**

$$\frac{\text{no. w/o defects}}{\text{no. inspected}} = \frac{x}{\text{no. in shipment}}.$$

3 Close

Summarize

Tell students that to determine the experimental probability of an event, they need to count the number of trials in the experiment. Then they should count the number of times the event occurred and divide by the number of trials. Predictions can be made by using experimental probabilities.

ONGOING ASSESSMENT and INTERVENTION

***Diagnose Before* the Lesson**
10-5 Warm Up, TE p. 737

***Monitor During* the Lesson**
Check It Out! Exercises, SE pp. 737–739
Questioning Strategies, TE pp. 738–739

***Assess After* the Lesson**
10-5 Lesson Quiz, TE p. 742
Alternative Assessment, TE p. 742

Answers to *Think and Discuss*

Possible answers:

1. An outcome is 1 possible result of an experiment. An event is a set of outcomes.
2. No; different outcomes may occur with different frequencies each time the experiment is carried out. The more trials performed, the more accurate the estimate is likely to be.
3. See p. A9.

10-5 Exercises

Assignment Guide

Assign *Guided Practice* exercises as necessary.

If you finished Examples **1–2**

Basic	12–17, 23, 26, 27
Average	12–17, 23, 26, 27
Advanced	12–16 even, 26, 27, 34–37

If you finished Examples **1–4**

Basic	12–23, 25–32, 38–45
Average	12–22, 24–36, 38–45
Advanced	12–20 even, 21, 22, 24–45

Homework Quick Check
Quickly check key concepts.
Exercises: 12, 16, 20, 21, 26, 28

Teaching Tip

Inclusion Some students may benefit from noting that the answer to **Exercise 8** plus the answer to **Exercise 10** equals 1.

State Resources

10-5 Exercises

go.hrw.com
Homework Help Online
KEYWORD: MA7 10-5
Parent Resources Online
KEYWORD: MA7 Parent

GUIDED PRACTICE

1. **Vocabulary** Give an example of an *event* that has two possible *outcomes*. **Possible answer: picking a shoe at random from a pair of shoes**

SEE EXAMPLE 1 p. 737

Identify the sample space and the outcome shown for each experiment.

2. rolling a number cube

2. sample space: {1, 2, 3, 4, 5, 6}; outcome shown: 2

3. spinning a spinner

sample space: {blue, red, yellow, green}; outcome shown: red

4. tossing 3 coins

sample space: {HHH, HHT, HTH, THH, HTT, THT, TTH, TTT}; outcome shown: THT

SEE EXAMPLE 2 p. 738

Write *impossible, unlikely, as likely as not, likely,* or *certain* to describe each event.

5. Peter was born in January. Thomas was born in June. Peter and Thomas have the same birthday. **impossible**
6. The football team won 9 of its last 10 games. The team will win the next game. **likely**
7. A board game has a rule that if you roll the game cube and get a 6, you get an extra turn. You get an extra turn on your first roll. **unlikely**

SEE EXAMPLE 3 p. 738

An experiment consists of rolling a number cube. Use the results in the table to find the experimental probability of each event.

Outcome	1	2	3	4	5	6
Frequency	5	6	2	2	3	7

8. rolling a 6 $\frac{7}{25}$
9. rolling an even number $\frac{3}{5}$
10. not rolling a 6 $\frac{18}{25}$

SEE EXAMPLE 4 p. 739

11. **Sports** One game of bowling consists of ten frames. Elyse usually rolls 3 strikes in each game.
    a. What is the experimental probability that Elyse will roll a strike on any frame? **30%**
    b. Predict the number of strikes Elyse will roll in 18 games. **54**

PRACTICE AND PROBLEM SOLVING

Independent Practice

For Exercises	See Example
12–14	1
15–17	2
18–20	3
21	4

Extra Practice
Skills Practice p. S23
Application Practice p. S37

Identify the sample space and the outcome shown for each experiment.

12. tossing two coins

sample space: {HH, HT, TH, TT}; outcome shown: TT

13. spinning a spinner

sample space: {blue, red, yellow}; outcome shown: blue

14. selecting a marble

14. sample space: {blue, yellow, green, red}; outcome shown: green

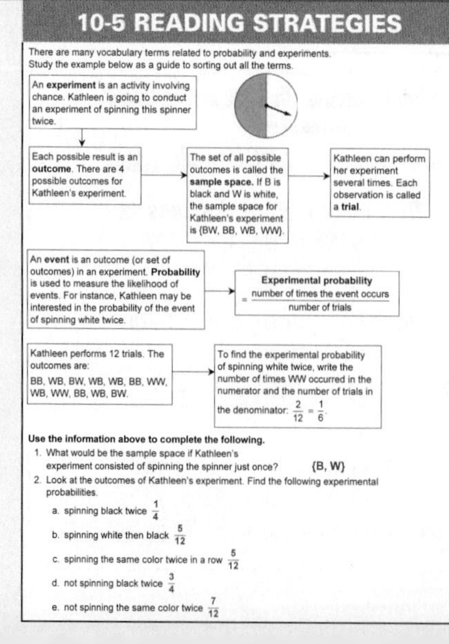

10-5 READING STRATEGIES

There are many vocabulary terms related to probability and experiments. Study the example below as a guide to sorting out all the terms.

An **experiment** is an activity involving chance. Kathleen is going to conduct an experiment of spinning this spinner twice.

Each possible result is an **outcome**. There are 4 possible outcomes for Kathleen's experiment. → The set of all possible outcomes is called the **sample space.** If B is black and W is white, the sample space for Kathleen's experiment is {BW, BB, WB, WW}. → Kathleen can perform her experiment several times. Each observation is called a **trial**.

An **event** is an outcome (or set of outcomes) in an experiment. **Probability** is used to measure the likelihood of events. For instance, Kathleen may be interested in the probability of the event of spinning white twice. → **Experimental probability** $= \frac{\text{number of times the event occurs}}{\text{number of trials}}$

Kathleen performs 12 trials. The outcomes are: BB, WB, BW, WB, WB, BB, WW, WB, WW, BB, WB, BW. → To find the experimental probability of spinning white twice, write the number of times WW occurred in the numerator and the number of trials in the denominator: $\frac{2}{12} = \frac{1}{6}$.

Use the information above to complete the following.

1. What would be the sample space if Kathleen's experiment consisted of spinning the spinner just once? **{B, W}**
2. Look at the outcomes of Kathleen's experiment. Find the following experimental probabilities.
   a. spinning black twice $\frac{1}{4}$
   b. spinning white then black $\frac{5}{12}$
   c. spinning the same color twice in a row $\frac{5}{12}$
   d. not spinning black twice $\frac{3}{4}$
   e. not spinning the same color twice $\frac{7}{12}$

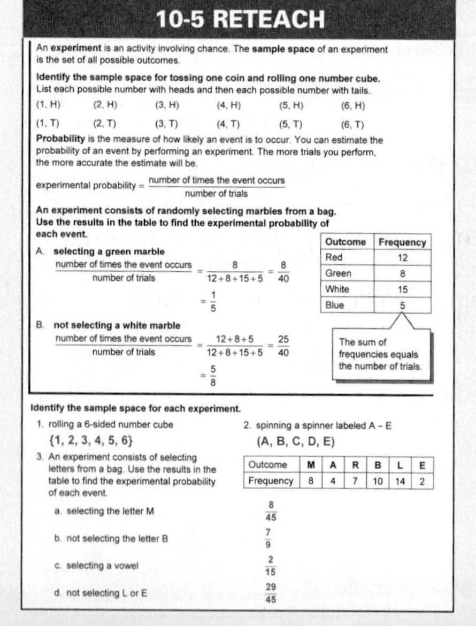

10-5 RETEACH

An **experiment** is an activity involving chance. The **sample space** of an experiment is the set of all possible outcomes.

Identify the sample space for tossing one coin and rolling one number cube.
List each possible number with heads and then each possible number with tails.

(1, H) (2, H) (3, H) (4, H) (5, H) (6, H)

(1, T) (2, T) (3, T) (4, T) (5, T) (6, T)

Probability is the measure of how likely an event is to occur. You can estimate the probability of an event by performing an experiment. The more trials you perform, the more accurate the estimate will be.

experimental probability $= \frac{\text{number of times the event occurs}}{\text{number of trials}}$

An experiment consists of randomly selecting marbles from a bag. Use the results in the table to find the experimental probability of each event.

Outcome	Frequency
Red	12
Green	8
White	15
Blue	5

The sum of frequencies equals the number of trials.

A. **selecting a green marble**

$$\frac{\text{number of times the event occurs}}{\text{number of trials}} = \frac{8}{12+8+15+5} = \frac{8}{40} = \frac{1}{5}$$

B. **not selecting a white marble**

$$\frac{\text{number of times the event occurs}}{\text{number of trials}} = \frac{12+8+5}{12+8+15+5} = \frac{25}{40} = \frac{5}{8}$$

Identify the sample space for each experiment.

1. rolling a 6-sided number cube **{1, 2, 3, 4, 5, 6}**
2. spinning a spinner labeled A – E **(A, B, C, D, E)**
3. An experiment consists of selecting letters from a bag. Use the results in the table to find the experimental probability of each event.

Outcome	M	A	R	B	L	E
Frequency	8	4	7	10	14	2

   a. selecting the letter M $\frac{8}{45}$
   b. not selecting the letter B $\frac{7}{9}$
   c. selecting a vowel $\frac{2}{15}$
   d. not selecting L or E $\frac{29}{45}$

Write *impossible, unlikely, as likely as not, likely,* or *certain* to describe each event.

15. Marlo purchased a new pair of shoes. She takes one shoe out of the box. The shoe is for the left foot. **as likely as not**
16. Sam takes the bus to school. The bus came late twice in the last two weeks. The bus will be late today. **unlikely**
17. Tammy dropped two quarters on the floor. At least one of them lands heads up. **likely**

An experiment consists of randomly choosing a marble from a bag. Use the results in the table to find the experimental probability of each event.

Outcome	Frequency
Red	4
Blue	6
Green	6
Yellow	9

18. choosing a yellow marble $\frac{9}{25}$
19. choosing a blue marble $\frac{6}{25}$
20. not choosing a green marble $\frac{19}{25}$
21. **Sports** A ski lodge inspects 80 skis and finds 4 to be defective.
    a. What is the experimental probability that a ski chosen at random will be defective? **5%**
    b. The lodge has 420 skis. Predict the number of skis that are likely to be defective. **21**
22. The table shows the results of a survey asking students the season of their birthday. What is the experimental probability that a student has a birthday during the summer? $\frac{17}{50}$

Season	Birthdays
Fall	39
Winter	27
Spring	33
Summer	51

23. You and your friend can either go swimming or to a movie on Thursday. The weather forecast says there is a 70% chance of rain on Thursday. Should you plan on going swimming or to a movie? Explain.

23. A 70% chance of rain means that it is likely to rain on Thu., so you should plan to go to a movie.

24. An unlikely event may occur in any single experiment. Repeating the experiment many times gives a more accurate picture of exp. probabilities.

24. **Critical Thinking** Tell why it is important to repeat an experiment many times.
25. **Write About It** Explain what it means for an event to have a 50-50 chance of happening. **The event is as likely to happen as not.**
26. How many outcomes are in the sample space for an experiment consisting of rolling two standard number cubes? **36**
27. **Estimation** A manufacturing company produced 986 units in one day. Of those, 9 units were found to be defective. Estimate the experimental probability that a unit produced that day was defective. Then predict approximately how many units will be defective when 5680 units are produced in one week. **about 1%; about 57**

MULTI-STEP TEST PREP

28. This problem will prepare you for the Multi-Step Test Prep on page 768.

    In a standard deck of cards, there are 13 cards in each of four suits: hearts, diamonds, clubs, and spades. The hearts and diamonds are red and the clubs and spades are black. Ricardo randomly drew cards from a standard deck of 52 cards. The table shows the results.

Outcome	Frequency
Hearts	7
Diamonds	7
Clubs	8
Spades	6

    a. Find the experimental probability of drawing a club. $\frac{2}{7}$
    b. Find the experimental probability of drawing a black suit. $\frac{1}{2}$

MULTI-STEP TEST PREP Exercise 28 involves finding the probability of an event involving a standard deck of cards. This exercise prepares students for the Multi-Step Test Prep on page 768.

10-5 PROBLEM SOLVING

Write the correct answer.

1. A manufacturer of bottled juices has a contest where prizes are printed on the inside of the bottle caps. 2 million caps are printed with "Sorry"; 1.5 million say "Free Bottle"; 0.4 million say "T-Shirt"; and 0.1 million say "CD."
   a. Identify the sample space.
   {Sorry, Free Bottle, T-Shirt, CD}
   b. If Tammy buys one bottle, is it impossible, unlikely, as likely as not, likely, or certain that she will get a cap that says "Sorry"?
   as likely as not
   c. If Eagle buys one bottle, is it impossible, unlikely, as likely as not, likely, or certain that he will get a cap that says "CD"?
   unlikely
2. At the end of the 2005 season, Major League Baseball player Andruw Jones had 1408 hits out of 5271 times at bat during his entire career.
   a. What is the experimental probability that Andruw Jones will have a hit during any time at bat? (This statistic is called his *batting average* and is usually stated as a decimal rounded to the thousandths.)
   0.267 or 26.7%
   b. If Andruw has 570 at-bats during a season, predict the number of hits he will have during the season.
   152 hits

A pharmaceutical company tests the effectiveness of a diabetes screening test by administering it to several volunteers who actually know whether or not they have diabetes. The results are summarized in the table below. Select the best answer.

3. What is the experimental probability that this screening test will *not* identify someone who actually does have diabetes? (This type of result is called a false negative.)

   A 2.9 % **B** 16.6% C 20% D 28.6%

4. If this test is used on 1000 patients who do not know whether or not they have diabetes, about how many patients would the test predict *do* have diabetes?

   F 66 G 79 **H** 92 J 101

		Volunteer ____ have diabetes.	
		does	does not
Test predicts that the person ____ have diabetes.	does	10	4
	does not	2	136

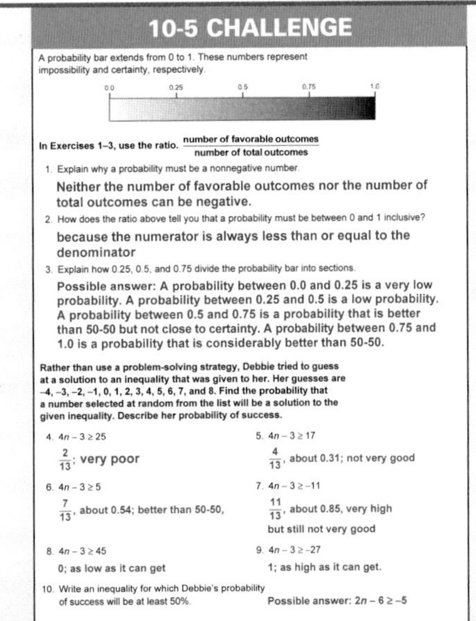

10-5 CHALLENGE

A probability bar extends from 0 to 1. These numbers represent impossibility and certainty, respectively.

In Exercises 1–3, use the ratio. $\frac{\text{number of favorable outcomes}}{\text{number of total outcomes}}$

1. Explain why a probability must be a nonnegative number.
   Neither the number of favorable outcomes nor the number of total outcomes can be negative.
2. How does the ratio above tell you that a probability must be between 0 and 1 inclusive?
   because the numerator is always less than or equal to the denominator
3. Explain how 0.25, 0.5, and 0.75 divide the probability bar into sections.
   Possible answer: A probability between 0.0 and 0.25 is a very low probability. A probability between 0.25 and 0.5 is a low probability. A probability between 0.5 and 0.75 is a probability that is better than 50-50 but not close to certainty. A probability between 0.75 and 1.0 is a probability that is considerably better than 50-50.

Rather than use a problem-solving strategy, Debbie tried to guess at a solution to an inequality that was given to her. Her guesses are −4, −3, −2, −1, 0, 1, 2, 3, 4, 5, 6, 7, and 8. Find the probability that a number selected at random from the list will be a solution to the given inequality. Describe her probability of success.

4. $4n - 3 \geq 25$
   $\frac{2}{13}$; very poor
5. $4n - 3 \geq 17$
   $\frac{4}{13}$, about 0.31; not very good
6. $4n - 3 \geq 5$
   $\frac{7}{13}$, about 0.54; better than 50-50,
7. $4n - 3 \geq -11$
   $\frac{11}{13}$, about 0.85, very high but still not very good
8. $4n - 3 \geq 45$
   0; as low as it can get
9. $4n - 3 \geq -27$
   1; as high as it can get.
10. Write an inequality for which Debbie's probability of success will be at least 50%.
    Possible answer: $2n - 6 \geq -5$

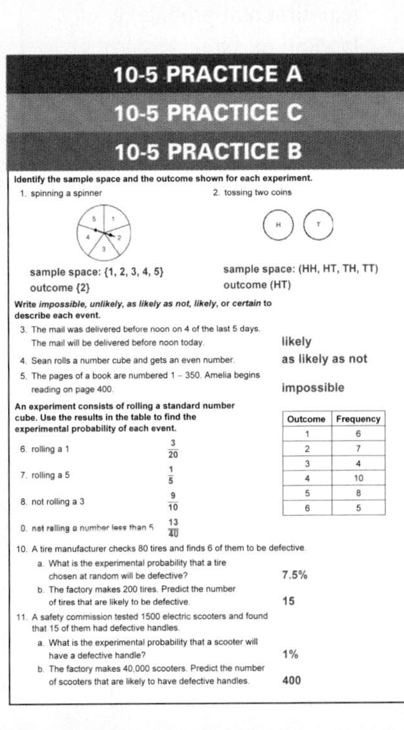

10-5 PRACTICE A

10-5 PRACTICE C

10-5 PRACTICE B

Identify the sample space and the outcome shown for each experiment.

1. spinning a spinner

   sample space: {1, 2, 3, 4, 5}
   outcome {2}
2. tossing two coins

   sample space: (HH, HT, TH, TT)
   outcome (HT)

Write *impossible, unlikely, as likely as not, likely,* or *certain* to describe each event.

3. The mail was delivered before noon on 4 of the last 5 days. The mail will be delivered before noon today. **likely**
4. Sean rolls a number cube and gets an even number. **as likely as not**
5. The pages of a book are numbered 1 – 350. Amelia begins reading on page 400. **impossible**

An experiment consists of rolling a standard number cube. Use the results in the table to find the experimental probability of each event.

Outcome	Frequency
1	6
2	7
3	4
4	10
5	8
6	5

6. rolling a 1 $\frac{3}{20}$
7. rolling a 5 $\frac{1}{5}$
8. not rolling a 3 $\frac{9}{10}$
9. not rolling a number less than 5 $\frac{13}{40}$
10. A tire manufacturer checks 80 tires and finds 6 of them to be defective.
    a. What is the experimental probability that a tire chosen at random will be defective? **7.5%**
    b. The factory makes 200 tires. Predict the number of tires that are likely to be defective. **15**
11. A safety commission tested 1500 electric scooters and found that 15 of them had defective handles.
    a. What is the experimental probability that a scooter will have a defective handle? **1%**
    b. The factory makes 40,000 scooters. Predict the number of scooters that are likely to have defective handles. **400**

TEST PREP DOCTOR + Students who chose C for **Exercise 29** may have been considering the probability of rolling a number less than 4 on only one number cube.

If students need help starting **Exercise 32,** have them write the number of tails as x and the number of heads as $x + 6$.

Journal

Have students explain how to use experimental probability to make a prediction.

ALTERNATIVE ASSESSMENT

Have students roll a number cube 20 times and record their results in a table as in **Example 3.** Then have them use their results to find the experimental probability of rolling a 5 and use it to make a prediction about how many times they would roll a 5 in 100 trials.

Power Presentations with PowerPoint®

10-5 Lesson Quiz

1. Identify the sample space and the outcome shown for selecting a marble.

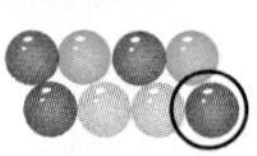

sample space: {red, green, yellow}; outcome shown: red

2. An experiment consists of spinning a spinner. Use the results in the table to find the experimental probability of landing on blue. $\frac{3}{10}$

Outcome	Frequency
Red	9
Blue	6
Yellow	5

3. The neighbors' dog barked at Tana the last 4 out of 5 times she walked by their house.
   a. What is the experimental probability that the dog barks at Tana when she walks past the house? 80%
   b. Predict the number of times the dog will bark at Tana if she walks past the house 45 times. 36

Also available on transparency

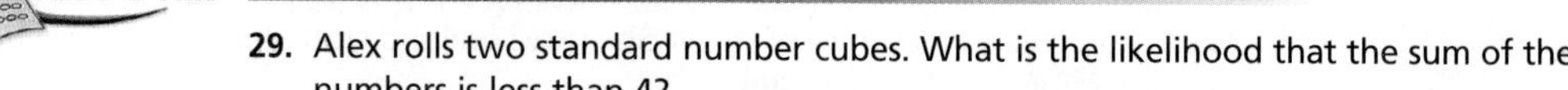

TEST PREP

29. Alex rolls two standard number cubes. What is the likelihood that the sum of the numbers is less than 4?
    (A) Impossible (B) Unlikely (C) As likely as not (D) Likely

30. A community reported that $\frac{2}{3}$ of the residents had a pet and $\frac{1}{2}$ of the pet owners had a dog. If there are 84 residents in the community, how many residents are likely to have a dog?
    (F) 14 (G) 28 (H) 42 (J) 56

31. What is the probability that a number chosen at random from the list below will be a solution of the inequality $3x + 2 \le 23$?

    −8, −7, −6, −5, −4, −3, −2, −1, 0, 1, 2, 3, 4, 5, 6, 7, 8, 9

    (A) $\frac{17}{18}$ (B) $\frac{8}{9}$ (C) $\frac{1}{9}$ (D) $\frac{1}{18}$

32. **Short Response** A coin was tossed 50 times. It landed showing heads 6 more times than it landed showing tails. What is the experimental probability of the coin landing on heads? Show your work. $\frac{14}{25}$; **check students' work.**

CHALLENGE AND EXTEND

A coin is tossed 3 times. Use the sample space for this experiment to describe each event below as *impossible, unlikely, as likely as not, likely,* or *certain.* Justify each answer.

33. At least 2 heads
34. 2 heads and 1 tail
35. 2 tails and 1 head
36. 3 tails

35. Unlikely; there are 3 outcomes in this event (TTH, THT, HTT) among 8 outcomes in the sample space.

36. Unlikely; there is 1 outcome in this event (TTT) among 8 outcomes in the sample space.

37. One coin is tossed 20 times.
    a. The experimental probability of the coin showing heads is 65%. How many times did the coin show tails? **7**
    b. If the coin is tossed ten more times, how many more times must the coin land showing tails for the experimental probability of tails to be 50%? **8**

SPIRAL REVIEW

38. A sales representative earns 4.5% commission on sales. Find the commission earned when the total sales are $124,000. *(Lesson 2-10)* **$5580**

39. Estimate the tax on a $255 printer when the tax rate is 5.5%. *(Lesson 2-10)* **$14**

Compare the graph of each function to the graph of $f(x) = x^2$. *(Lesson 9-4)*

40. $g(x) = \frac{1}{3}x^2$ **wider**
41. $g(x) = -x^2$ **reflected across the x-axis**
42. $g(x) = x^2 - 12$ **translated 12 units down**

The data shows the number of books read by seven students over the summer: 5, 5, 14, 2, 5, 5, 6. *(Lesson 10-3)*

43. Give the mean, median, and mode of the data. **mean: 6; median: 5; mode 5**
44. Which measure of central tendency best describes the data? Explain.
45. Create a box-and-whisker plot of the data.

44. the median (or mode), since 4 out of the 7 students read 5 books

Answers

33. As likely as not; there are 4 outcomes in this event (HHH, HHT, HTH, THH) among 8 outcomes in the sample space.

34. Unlikely; there are 3 outcomes in this event (HHT, HTH, THH) among 8 outcomes in the sample space.

45.

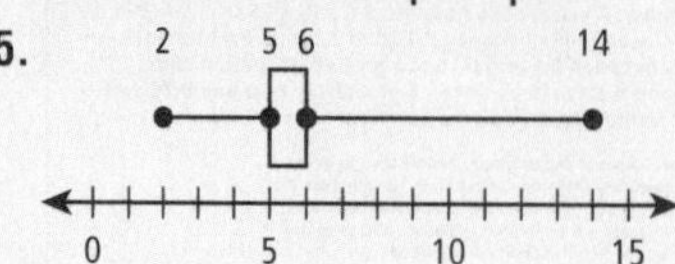

Use Random Numbers

A calculator can be used to model an experiment that would be difficult or inconvenient to perform. To do this, you will use random numbers.

Use with Lesson 10-5

Activity

You can use a calculator to explore the experimental probability that at least 2 people in a group of 6 people were born in the same month. Assume that all months are equally likely to be a person's birth month.

```
MATH NUM CPX PRB
1:rand
2:nPr
3:nCr
4:!
5:randInt(
6:randNorm(
7:randBin(
```

1. Represent each month with an integer. Since there are 12 months, use the numbers 1–12.

   To set your calculator up to generate random numbers, press MATH. Then use the arrow keys to highlight **PRB**. Select **5: randInt(**.

2. Now give the start number, 1, press **,** , and give the end number, 12.

   Each time you press ENTER the calculator will return an integer from 1 to 12.

3. You are considering a group of 6 people. This means you need 6 random numbers.

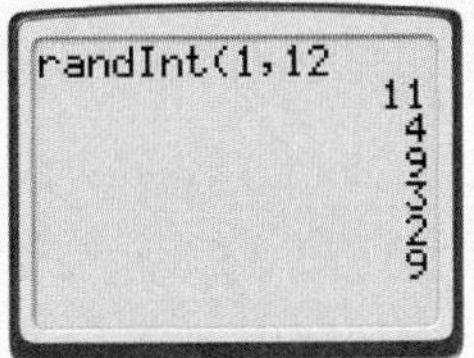

	Person					
	1	2	3	4	5	6
Trial 1	11	4	9	3	2	9
Trial 2	3	8	10	12	6	2

In the first trial, the number 9 appears twice. This means that two people have a birth day in the ninth month, September.

In the second trial, no number appears more than once. This means that none of the people were born in the same month.

Try This

1. Repeat the experiment until you have 10 trials of the experiment. Count the number of trials in which a number appears more than once. Divide this number by the number of trials, 10, to find the experimental probability that at least 2 people in a group of 6 people will have the same birth month. **Check students' work.**
2. Gather the results from at least 100 trials of the experiment. (Either perform all of the trials yourself or combine data with your classmates.) Using your results, what is the experimental probability that at least 2 people in a group of 6 people will have the same birth month? Compare the results from 100 trials to the results of 10 trials. **Check students' work; as the number of trials increases, the result should approach 78%.**
3. How could you set up the experiment to find the experimental probability that at least 2 people in a group of 6 people will have the same birthday (same month and same date)? **Generate 6 random numbers from 1 to 365 for each trial.**

Math Background Discuss with students that a greater number of trials leads to more accurate results.

Teaching Tip

Technology The "random" numbers generated by a graphing calculator are determined by a "seed." Calculators of the same model return the same sequence of numbers for any given seed value, so it is possible for two or more students to generate the same "random" number sequence. The seed can be changed by storing a number for **rand.**

Organizer

Use with Lesson 10-5

Pacing:
Traditional $\frac{1}{2}$ day
Block $\frac{1}{4}$ day

Objective: Use a graphing calculator to find experimental probabilities by generating random numbers.

Materials: graphing calculator

Online Edition
Graphing Calculator, TechKeys

Countdown Week 23

Resources

Technology Lab Activities
10-5 Lab Recording Sheet

Teach

Discuss

The number of possible outcomes determines the interval after **randInt(**. The number of people determines the number of times ENTER is pressed.

Close

Key Concept

Experiments can be modeled by using the random integer function on a calculator.

Assessment

Journal Have students explain how to use the random integer function to find the experimental probability that at least 3 people out of 5 were born in the same season.

State Resources

10-6 Organizer

Pacing: Traditional 1 day
Block $\frac{1}{2}$ day

Objectives: Determine the theoretical probability of an event.

Convert between probabilities and odds.

Online Edition
Tutorial Videos

Countdown Week 23

Power Presentations with PowerPoint®

Warm Up

An experiment consists of spinning a spinner 8 times. The spinner lands on red 4 times, yellow 3 times, and green once. Find the experimental probability of each event.

1. The spinner lands on red. $\frac{1}{2}$
2. The spinner does not land on green. $\frac{7}{8}$
3. The spinner lands on yellow. $\frac{3}{8}$

Also available on transparency

Math Humor

Q: What is the probability of a coin landing on heads 20 times out of 100 trials?

A: A lot higher than the probability that I'll stand around to find out.

10-6 Theoretical Probability

Objectives
Determine the theoretical probability of an event.

Convert between probabilities and odds.

Vocabulary
equally likely
theoretical probability
fair
complement
odds

Why learn this?
Theoretical probability can be used to determine the likelihood of different weather conditions. (See Example 2.)

A developing tornado near Amarillo, Texas.

When the outcomes in the sample space of an experiment have the same chance of occurring, the outcomes are said to be **equally likely**.

Equally likely outcomes

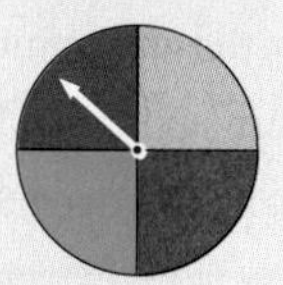

There is the same chance that the spinner will land on any of the colors.

Not equally likely outcomes

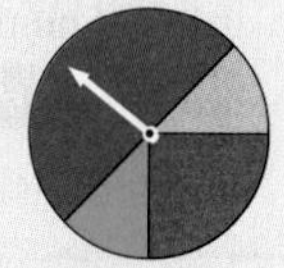

There is a greater chance that the spinner will land on blue than on any other color.

The **theoretical probability** of an event is the ratio of the number of ways the event can occur to the total number of equally likely outcomes.

Theoretical Probability

$$\text{theoretical probability} = \frac{\text{number of ways the event can occur}}{\text{total number of equally likely outcomes}}$$

An experiment in which all outcomes are equally likely is said to be **fair**. You can usually assume that experiments involving coins and number cubes are fair.

Caution!
The use of the word *experiment* does not necessarily mean you are looking for experimental probability.

EXAMPLE 1 Finding Theoretical Probability

An experiment consists of rolling a number cube. Find the theoretical probability of each outcome.

A **rolling a 3**

$$\frac{\text{number of ways the event can occur}}{\text{total number of equally likely outcomes}} = \frac{1}{6}$$

There is one 3 on a number cube.

$$= 0.1\overline{6}$$

$$= 16\frac{2}{3}\%$$

State Resources

go.hrw.com
State Resources Online
KEYWORD: MA7 Resources

1 Introduce

EXPLORATION

10-6 Theoretical Probability

At a school carnival, visitors have a chance to win a prize by spinning one of these spinners.

Spin to Win

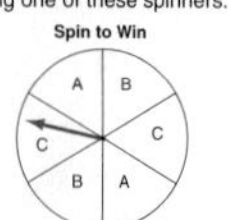

Spin-A-Rama

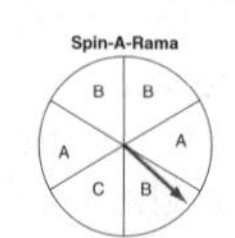

1. Complete the tables. For each spinner, count the number of sectors labeled with each letter. Then find the fraction of the spinner labeled with each letter.

Spin to Win		
Sector Label	Number of Sectors	Fraction of Spinner
A	2	$\frac{2}{6} = \frac{1}{3}$
B		
C		

Spin-A-Rama		
Sector Label	Number of Sectors	Fraction of Spinner
A		
B		
C		

2. For Spin to Win, is the spinner equally likely to land on A, B, and C? How about for Spin-A-Rama?

THINK AND DISCUSS

3. **Discuss** which result is most likely when you spin Spin-A-Rama.

Motivate

Have students pretend they are entering a contest in which the odds of winning are 3 to 1. Ask students to guess whether this means it will be impossible, unlikely, as likely as not, likely, or certain that they will win. Have students discuss what they think *odds* means. Tell students that in this section they will learn how to convert odds to probability to determine the likelihood of winning the contest.

Explorations and answers are provided in *Alternate Openers: Explorations Transparencies.*

An experiment consists of rolling a number cube. Find the theoretical probability of each outcome.

B rolling a number greater than 3

$$\frac{\text{number of ways the event can occur}}{\text{total number of equally likely outcomes}} = \frac{3}{6} = \frac{1}{2}$$ *There are 3 numbers greater than 3.*

$$= 0.5 = 50\%$$

An experiment consists of rolling a number cube. Find the theoretical probability of each outcome.

1a. rolling an even number **50%**

1b. rolling a multiple of 3 $33\frac{1}{3}\%$

When you toss a coin, there are two possible outcomes, heads or tails. The table below shows the theoretical probabilities and experimental results of tossing a coin 10 times.

	P(heads)	P(tails)	P(heads) + P(tails)
Experimental Probability	$\frac{3}{10}$	$\frac{7}{10}$	$\frac{3}{10} + \frac{7}{10} = \frac{10}{10} = 1$
Theoretical Probability	$\frac{1}{2}$	$\frac{1}{2}$	$\frac{1}{2} + \frac{1}{2} = \frac{2}{2} = 1$

Reading Math

The probability of an event can be written as *P*(event). *P*(heads) means "the probability that heads will be the outcome."

The sum of the probability of heads and the probability of tails is 1, or 100%. This is because it is certain that one of the two outcomes will always occur.

$$P(\text{event happening}) + P(\text{event not happening}) = 1$$

The **complement** of an event is all the outcomes in the sample space that are not included in the event. The sum of the probabilities of an event and its complement is 1, or 100%, because the event will either happen or not happen. Two events are *complementary events* if the sum of their probabilities equals 1 and if one event occurs if and only if the other does not.

$$P(\text{event}) + P(\text{complement of event}) = 1$$

EXAMPLE 2 **Finding Probability by Using the Complement**

The weather forecaster predicts a 20% chance of snow. What is the probability that it will not snow?

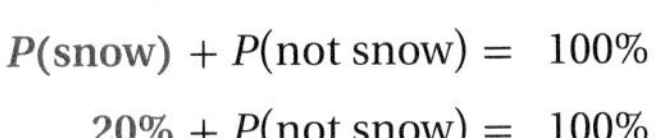

$P(\text{snow}) + P(\text{not snow}) = 100\%$		*Either it will snow or it will not snow.*
$20\% + P(\text{not snow}) = 100\%$		
-20%	-20%	*Subtract 20% from both sides.*
$P(\text{not snow}) = 80\%$		

2. A jar has green, blue, purple, and white marbles. The probability of choosing a green marble is 0.2, the probability of choosing blue is 0.3, and the probability of choosing purple is 0.1. What is the probability of choosing white? **0.4**

COMMON ERROR ALERT

In **Example 1A,** some students may automatically write that the probability of rolling a 3 is $\frac{3}{6}$, instead of $\frac{1}{6}$. Remind them that the numerator is found by counting the number of ways to get a 3.

Power Presentations with PowerPoint®

Additional Examples

Example 1

An experiment consists of rolling a number cube. Find the theoretical probability of each outcome.

A. rolling a 5 $16\frac{2}{3}\%$

B. rolling an odd number 50%

C. rolling a number less than 3 $33\frac{1}{3}\%$

Example 2

A box contains only red, black, and white blocks. The probability of choosing a red block is $\frac{1}{4}$, the probability of choosing a black block is $\frac{1}{2}$. What is the probability of choosing a white block? $\frac{1}{4}$

INTERVENTION

Questioning Strategies

EXAMPLE 1

- When will the numerator and denominator of a probability be the same number?
- Why is it impossible for a probability to be an improper fraction?

EXAMPLE 2

- Why do you subtract from 1, or 100%, to find the complement?
- How are complements in probability similar to complements in geometry?

2 Teach

Guided Instruction

Emphasize that the formula for theoretical probability in this lesson applies to equally likely outcomes, while experimental probability depends on the frequency of a particular outcome and the number of trials. When converting between probabilities and odds, show that the sum of the two numbers in the odds ratio equals the total number of outcomes, which is the denominator in the probability fraction.

Reaching All Learners

Through Home Connection

Have students find advertisements for contests and sweepstakes. For each, have students use the odds (usually found in the small print at the end of the rules) to calculate the probability of winning.

Have students discuss their findings. Remind them that some prizes state "win up to...." For these, the odds of winning usually refer to the smallest amount possible.

Power Presentations with PowerPoint®

Additional Examples

Example 3

A. The probability of rolling a 2 on a number cube is $\frac{1}{6}$. What are the odds of rolling a 2? 1:5

B. The odds in favor of winning a contest are 1:9. What is the probability of winning the contest? $\frac{1}{10}$

C. The odds against a spinner landing on red are 2:3. What is the probability of the spinner landing on red? $\frac{3}{5}$

INTERVENTION
Questioning Strategies

EXAMPLE 3

- How do you find the odds against an event if you know the odds in favor of the event?
- How do you find the probability of an event if you know the odds in favor of the event?

Odds are another way to indicate the likelihood of an event. **Odds** express likelihood by comparing the number of ways an event can happen to the number of ways an event can fail to happen. The *odds in favor of an event* describe the likelihood that the event will occur. The *odds against an event* describe the likelihood that the event will not occur.

Odds are usually written with a colon in the form $a:b$, but can also be written as a to b or $\frac{a}{b}$.

Know it! Note — Odds

ODDS IN FAVOR OF AN EVENT WITH EQUALLY LIKELY OUTCOMES

$$\text{odds in favor} = \frac{\text{number of ways an event can happen}}{\text{number of ways an event can fail to happen}} = a:b$$

ODDS AGAINST AN EVENT WITH EQUALLY LIKELY OUTCOMES

$$\text{odds against} = \frac{\text{number of ways an event can fail to happen}}{\text{number of ways an event can happen}} = b:a$$

a represents the number of ways an event can occur.
b represents the number of ways an event can fail to occur.

The two numbers given as the odds will add up to the total number of possible outcomes. You can use this relationship to convert between odds and probabilities.

EXAMPLE 3 Converting Between Odds and Probabilities

A **The probability of choosing a red card from a standard deck of playing cards is 50%. What are the odds of choosing a red card?**

The probability of choosing a red card is 50%, so the probability of not drawing a red card is 100% − 50% = 50%.

Odds in favor = 50:50, or 1:1

The odds in favor of choosing a red card are 1:1.

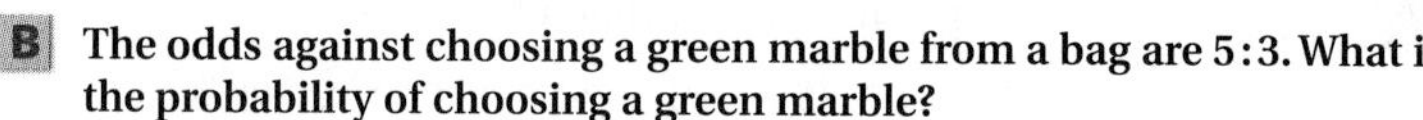

B **The odds against choosing a green marble from a bag are 5:3. What is the probability of choosing a green marble?**

The odds against green are 5:3, so the odds in favor of green are 3:5. This means there are 3 favorable outcomes and 5 unfavorable outcomes for a total of 8 possible outcomes.

$$\frac{\text{number of ways event can happen}}{\text{total possible outcomes}} = \frac{3}{8}$$

The probability of choosing a green marble is $\frac{3}{8}$.

Reading Math

You may see an outcome called "favorable." This does not mean that the outcome is good or bad. A favorable outcome is the outcome you are looking for in a probability experiment.

CHECK IT OUT! 3. The odds in favor of winning a free drink are 1:24. What is the probability of winning a free drink?

3. $\frac{1}{25}$

3 Close

Summarize

A bag of marbles holds 3 red, 4 blue, 5 yellow, and 6 white marbles. If one marble is drawn at random, find:

- P(blue) $\frac{2}{9}$
- P(not white) $\frac{2}{3}$
- odds in favor of yellow marble 5:13
- odds against red marble 5:1

ONGOING ASSESSMENT and INTERVENTION

***Diagnose Before* the Lesson**
10-6 Warm Up, TE p. 744

***Monitor During* the Lesson**
Check It Out! Exercises, SE pp. 745–746
Questioning Strategies, TE pp. 745–746

***Assess After* the Lesson**
10-6 Lesson Quiz, TE p. 749
Alternative Assessment, TE p. 749

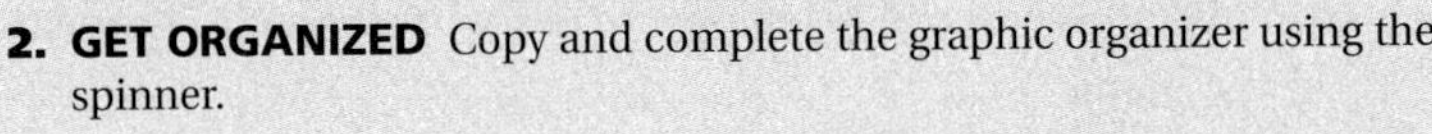

THINK AND DISCUSS

1. Tell how to find the probability of the complement of an event.
2. **GET ORGANIZED** Copy and complete the graphic organizer using the spinner.

Know it! Note

Probabilities on Spinner	
P(gray)	
P(not gray)	
Odds in favor of gray	
Odds against gray	

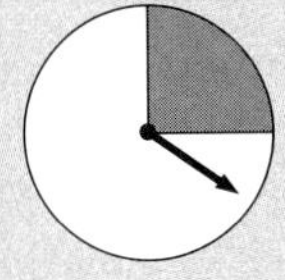

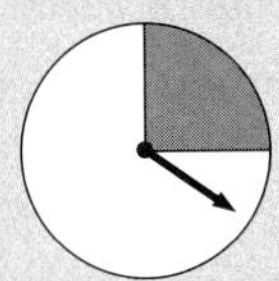

Answers to *Think and Discuss*

1. Subtract the probability of the event from 1.
2. See p. A9.

10-6 Exercises

go.hrw.com
Homework Help Online
KEYWORD: MA7 10-6
Parent Resources Online
KEYWORD: MA7 Parent

GUIDED PRACTICE

1. **Vocabulary** All of the outcomes in the sample space that are not included in the event are called the ___?___. (*theoretical probability*, *complement*, or *odds*) **complement**

SEE EXAMPLE 1 p. 744

Find the theoretical probability of each outcome.

2. rolling a number divisible by 3 on a number cube **$33\frac{1}{3}$%**
3. tossing 2 coins and both landing with tails showing **25%**
4. randomly choosing the letter S from the letters in STARS **40%**
5. rolling a prime number on a number cube **$\frac{1}{2}$**

STARS

SEE EXAMPLE 2 p. 745

6. A spinner is green, red, and blue. The probability that the spinner will land on green is 15% and red is 35%. What is the probability the spinner will land on blue? **50%**
7. The probability of choosing a red marble from a bag is $\frac{1}{3}$. What is the probability of not choosing a red marble? **$\frac{2}{3}$**
8. You have a $\frac{1}{50}$ chance of winning. What is the probability you will not win? **$\frac{49}{50}$**
9. There is a $\frac{1}{10}$ chance that you will be chosen as class representative. What is the probability that you will not be chosen? **$\frac{9}{10}$**

SEE EXAMPLE 3 p. 746

10. The odds against a spinner landing on blue are 3 : 1. What is the probability of the spinner landing on blue? **$\frac{1}{4}$**
11. The probability of choosing an ace from a deck of cards is $\frac{1}{13}$. What are the odds of choosing an ace? **1 : 12**
12. The probability of not winning a game is 80%. What are the odds of winning? **1 : 4**
13. The odds in favor of a spinner landing on blue are 1 : 3. What is the probability of landing on blue? **$\frac{1}{4}$**

10-6 Exercises

Assignment Guide

Assign *Guided Practice* exercises as necessary.

If you finished Examples **1–3**
Basic 14–28, 32–37, 39–45
Average 14–22, 24–34 even, 35–45
Advanced 14–22, 23–29, 31–45

Homework Quick Check
Quickly check key concepts.
Exercises: 16, 18, 22, 26, 34

State Resources

go.hrw.com
State Resources Online
KEYWORD: MA7 Resources

Teaching Tip **Math Background** For **Exercise 29,** remind students that "less than 3" does not include 3. Likewise, the sample space for "greater than 3" is 4, 5, and 6.

MULTI-STEP TEST PREP **Exercise 32** involves finding theoretical probabilities. This exercise prepares students for the Multi-Step Test Prep on page 768.

PRACTICE AND PROBLEM SOLVING

Independent Practice

For Exercises	See Example
14–16	1
17–19	2
20–22	3

Extra Practice

Skills Practice p. S23

Application Practice p. S37

Find the theoretical probability of each outcome.

14. rolling a 5 on a number cube **$16\frac{2}{3}$%**
15. tossing 2 coins and 1 landing with heads showing, the other with tails showing **50%**
16. randomly choosing a blue marble from a bag of 5 blue marbles, 8 red marbles, and 7 yellow marbles **25%**
17. The probability of a spinner landing on yellow is $\frac{4}{9}$. What is the probability of it not landing on yellow? **$\frac{5}{9}$**
18. There is a 3% probability of winning a game. Find the probability of not winning the game. **97%**
19. There is a 15% chance it will snow and a 15% chance it will rain. What is the probability that it will neither snow nor rain? **70%**
20. The odds against winning a contest are 99 : 1. What is the probability of not winning the contest? **$\frac{99}{100}$**
21. The odds of choosing a white marble from a bag are 1 : 9. Find the probability of not choosing a white marble. **$\frac{9}{10}$**
22. The probability of a spinner landing on green is 25%. What are the odds of the spinner not landing on green? **3 : 1**

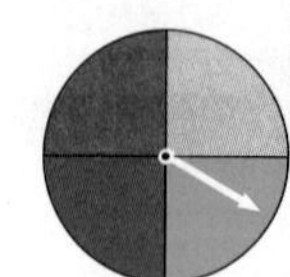

Use the spinner for Exercises 23–28.

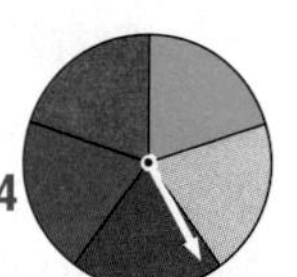

23. P(red) **$\frac{1}{5}$**
24. P(green) **$\frac{1}{5}$**
25. P(not blue) **$\frac{4}{5}$**
26. odds in favor of yellow **1 : 4**
27. odds against red **4 : 1**
28. odds against green **4 : 1**

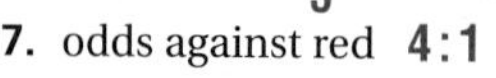

29. **Write About It** A number cube is rolled. Which event has a greater theoretical probability: rolling a number less than 3 or rolling a number greater than three? Explain.
30. **ERROR ANALYSIS** The odds in favor of an event are 1 : 4. Two students converted these odds into the probability of the event NOT happening. Which is incorrect? Explain the error.

A

Odds in favor of event	1:4
Probability that event will not happen	$\frac{1}{5}$

B

Odds in favor of event	1:4
Probability that event will not happen	$\frac{4}{5}$

31. **Critical Thinking** The odds in favor of a certain event are the same as the odds against that event. What is the probability of the event occurring? **$\frac{1}{2}$**

29. Rolling a number greater than 3 because there are 3 outcomes in this event (4, 5, 6), whereas rolling a number less than 3 has 2 outcomes (1, 2).

30. Student A; since the odds in favor are 1 : 4, there is 1 way the event can happen and 4 ways the event can fail to happen. So the probability of the event not happening is $\frac{4}{5}$.

MULTI-STEP TEST PREP

32. This problem will prepare you for the Multi-Step Test Prep on page 768.

Chutes and Ladders is a children's game that uses a spinner with the numbers 1 through 6.

a. What is the probability of spinning a 3? **$\frac{1}{6}$**
b. What is the probability of spinning an odd number? **$\frac{1}{2}$**
c. What is the probability of spinning a number that is less than or equal to 4? **$\frac{2}{3}$**

10-6 PRACTICE A

10-6 PRACTICE C

10-6 PRACTICE B

Find the theoretical probability of each outcome.

1. rolling a number less than 4 on a standard number cube **50%**
2. randomly choosing a day of the week and it is a weekend **$28\frac{4}{7}$%**
3. spinning red on a spinner with equal sections of red, blue, and green **$33\frac{1}{3}$%**
4. randomly choosing the letter N from the letters in NUMBER **$16\frac{2}{3}$%**
5. The probability it will snow is 60%. What is the probability it will not snow? **40%**
6. The probability of tossing two coins and having them land heads up is $\frac{1}{4}$. What is the probability the coins will not land heads up? **$\frac{3}{4}$**
7. A spinner has red, green, blue, and yellow. The probability of spinning a red is 0.4, the probability of spinning a blue is 0.05 and the probability of spinning a yellow is 0.25. What is the probability of spinning a green? **0.3**
8. Miguel entered a contest offering prizes to the top 3 finishers. The probability of winning 1st is 12%, the probability of winning 2nd is 18% and probability of winning 3rd is 20%. What is the probability that Miguel will not win any prize? **50%**
9. The odds of winning a contest are 1:50. What is the probability of winning the contest? **$\frac{1}{51}$**
10. The odds against a spinner landing on yellow are 3:1. What is the probability the spinner will not land on yellow? **$\frac{3}{4}$**
11. The probability of a thunderstorm is 80%. What are the odds that there will be a thunderstorm? **4:1**
12. The odds of selecting a red card from a box of cards are 2:5. What is the probability of not selecting a red card from a box? **$\frac{5}{7}$**

The table shows how many of each letter are in a bag. Use the table for 13–16. Find the following.

Letter	How Many in Bag
A	5
B	4
C	6
D	2
E	8

13. P(A) **20%**
14. P(B) **16%**
15. odds in favor of C **6:19**
16. odds against E **17:8**

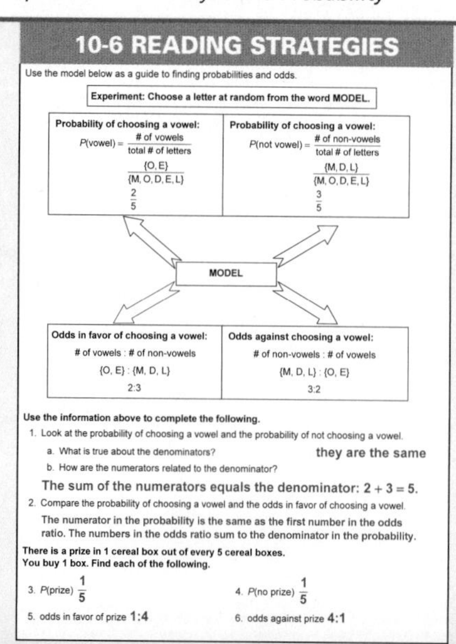

10-6 READING STRATEGIES

Use the model below as a guide to finding probabilities and odds.

Experiment: Choose a letter at random from the word MODEL.

Probability of choosing a vowel:	**Probability of choosing a vowel:**
$P(\text{vowel}) = \frac{\text{\# of vowels}}{\text{total \# of letters}}$	$P(\text{not vowel}) = \frac{\text{\# of non-vowels}}{\text{total \# of letters}}$
$\frac{\{O, E\}}{\{M, O, D, E, L\}}$	$\frac{\{M, D, L\}}{\{M, O, D, E, L\}}$
$\frac{2}{5}$	$\frac{3}{5}$

MODEL

Odds in favor of choosing a vowel:	**Odds against choosing a vowel:**
# of vowels : # of non-vowels	# of non-vowels : # of vowels
{O, E} : {M, D, L}	{M, D, L} : {O, E}
2:3	3:2

Use the information above to complete the following.

1. Look at the probability of choosing a vowel and the probability of not choosing a vowel.
   a. What is true about the denominators? **they are the same**
   b. How are the numerators related to the denominator?
   The sum of the numerators equals the denominator: 2 + 3 = 5.
2. Compare the probability of choosing a vowel and the odds in favor of choosing a vowel.
   The numerator in the probability is the same as the first number in the odds ratio. The numbers in the odds ratio sum to the denominator in the probability.

There is a prize in 1 cereal box out of every 5 cereal boxes. You buy 1 box. Find each of the following.

3. P(prize) **$\frac{1}{5}$**
4. P(no prize) **$\frac{1}{5}$**
5. odds in favor of prize **1:4**
6. odds against prize **4:1**

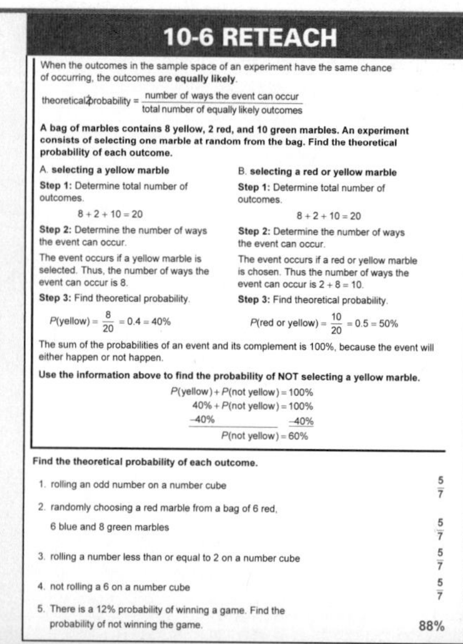

10-6 RETEACH

When the outcomes in the sample space of an experiment have the same chance of occurring, the outcomes are **equally likely**.

$$\text{theoretical probability} = \frac{\text{number of ways the event can occur}}{\text{total number of equally likely outcomes}}$$

A bag of marbles contains 8 yellow, 2 red, and 10 green marbles. An experiment consists of selecting one marble at random from the bag. Find the theoretical probability of each outcome.

A. **selecting a yellow marble**

Step 1: Determine total number of outcomes.

$8 + 2 + 10 = 20$

Step 2: Determine the number of ways the event can occur.

The event occurs if a yellow marble is selected. Thus, the number of ways the event can occur is 8.

Step 3: Find theoretical probability.

$P(\text{yellow}) = \frac{8}{20} = 0.4 = 40\%$

B. **selecting a red or yellow marble**

Step 1: Determine total number of outcomes.

$8 + 2 + 10 = 20$

Step 2: Determine the number of ways the event can occur.

The event occurs if a red or yellow marble is chosen. Thus the number of ways the event can occur is 2 + 8 = 10.

Step 3: Find theoretical probability.

$P(\text{red or yellow}) = \frac{10}{20} = 0.5 = 50\%$

The sum of the probabilities of an event and its complement is 100%, because the event will either happen or not happen.

Use the information above to find the probability of NOT selecting a yellow marble.

$$P(\text{yellow}) + P(\text{not yellow}) = 100\%$$
$$40\% + P(\text{not yellow}) = 100\%$$
$$-40\% \qquad -40\%$$
$$P(\text{not yellow}) = 60\%$$

Find the theoretical probability of each outcome.

1. rolling an odd number on a number cube **$\frac{5}{7}$**
2. randomly choosing a red marble from a bag of 6 red, 6 blue and 8 green marbles **$\frac{5}{7}$**
3. rolling a number less than or equal to 2 on a number cube **$\frac{5}{7}$**
4. not rolling a 6 on a number cube **$\frac{5}{7}$**
5. There is a 12% probability of winning a game. Find the probability of not winning the game. **88%**

33. **Write About It** Explain how to convert odds to probability.

34. **Geometry** The radius of each circle in the diagram is given. Find the probability that a point chosen at random will lie in the red area of the diagram. (*Hint:* Find the ratio of the red area to the total area of the diagram.) $\frac{1}{9}$

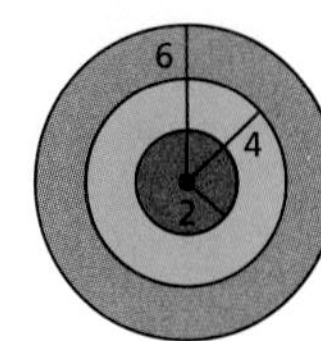

TEST PREP

35. Two coins are tossed. What is the probability that at least one of the coins lands with heads showing?

Ⓐ 25%   Ⓑ $33\frac{1}{3}\%$ Ⓒ 50%   Ⓓ 75%

36. A standard number cube is rolled. Which has the greatest probability?

Ⓕ P(even)   Ⓖ P(less than 5)   Ⓗ P(not 2)   Ⓙ P(greater than 3)

37. Find the probability that a point chosen at random would fall in the yellow area.

Ⓐ $\frac{1}{6}$ Ⓒ $\frac{4}{9}$

Ⓑ $\frac{2}{9}$ Ⓓ $\frac{2}{3}$

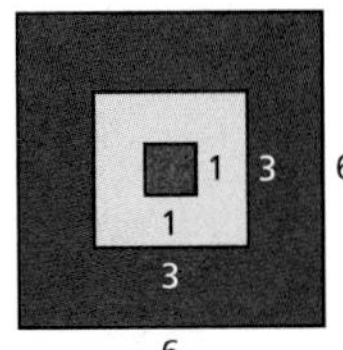

CHALLENGE AND EXTEND

Use the results of 3 coin-tossing experiments in the table for Exercise 38.

38. Find the experimental probability of the coin showing heads for

a. experiment 1. **0.4**

b. experiment 2. **0.48**

c. experiment 3. **0.502**

d. Find the theoretical probability of the coin showing heads. **0.5**

e. **Write About It** How do the experimental probabilities of each experiment compare to the theoretical probability? **The exp. prob. is closer to the theor. prob. in the experiments with more tosses.**

	Experiment		
	1	2	3
Number of Tosses	10	100	1000
Heads	4	48	502

SPIRAL REVIEW

39. The table shows the volume of water in an office water cooler over time. Find the rate of change for each time period. For which time period did the volume of water decrease at the slowest rate? *(Lesson 5-3)*

Time of day	7:00 A.M.	9:00 A.M.	1:00 P.M.	4:00 P.M.	5:00 P.M.
Volume (gal)	4.2	3.8	2.7	1.2	0.8

39. 7 A.M. to 9 A.M.: −0.2 gal/h; 9 A.M. to 1 P.M.: −0.275 gal/h; 1 P.M. to 4 P.M.: −0.5 gal/h; 4 P.M. to 5 P.M.: −0.4 gal/h; slowest rate of decrease: 7 A.M. to 9 A.M.

Factor each trinomial. *(Lesson 8-4)*

40. $2x^2 + x - 21$ **$(2x + 7)(x - 3)$**

41. $4x^2 - 7x + 3$ **$(4x - 3)(x - 1)$**

42. $6x^2 + 23x + 20$ **$(2x + 5)(3x + 4)$**

An experiment consists of choosing a card out of a deck and recording the results. Use the table to find the experimental probability of each event. *(Lesson 10-5)*

Outcome	Frequency
Hearts	2
Diamonds	6
Spades	5
Clubs	7

43. choosing a heart $\frac{1}{10}$

44. choosing a heart or a diamond $\frac{2}{5}$

45. not choosing a club $\frac{13}{20}$

TEST PREP DOCTOR + For **Exercise 35,** encourage students to write the sample space as (HH, HT, TH, TT). Also remind students that *at least one head* means either one or two heads.

Answers

33. If the odds in favor of an event are $a:b$, then there are a total of $a + b$ outcomes, where a is the number of ways the event can occur. So the probability of the event is $\frac{a}{a+b}$.

Journal

Have students explain the difference between theoretical and experimental probability.

ALTERNATIVE ASSESSMENT

Have students write a probability problem using a number cube (MK) or a fair spinner (MK) with four different colors. Have students choose an outcome, give the probability of the outcome, and convert the probability to odds in favor of the event.

Power Presentations with PowerPoint®

10-6 Lesson Quiz

Find the theoretical probability of each outcome.

1. randomly choosing *B* from the letters in **ALGEBRA** $\frac{1}{7}$
2. rolling a factor of 10 on a number cube $\frac{1}{2}$
3. The probability that it will be sunny is 15%. What is the probability that it will not be sunny? 85%
4. The probability of choosing a red marble out of a bag of marbles is $\frac{3}{10}$. What are the odds in favor of choosing a red marble? 3:7
5. A spinner has only blue and red sections. The odds against the spinner landing on blue are 7:5. What is the probability of the spinner landing on red? $\frac{5}{12}$

Also available on transparency

10-6 PROBLEM SOLVING

Mahjong is a classic Chinese game frequently played with tiles. Each tile has numbers, pictures, or characters on them. Similar to a deck of playing cards, most of the tiles can be grouped into suits. From a certain set of mahjong tiles, the odds *in favor* of selecting a tile from the bamboo suit is 1:3.

1. What is the probability of selecting a tile from the bamboo suit? $\frac{1}{4}$
2. What is the probability of selecting a tile that is *not* from the bamboo suit? $\frac{3}{4}$
3. Any set of mahjong tiles has 36 tiles in the bamboo suit. How many tiles are in the entirety of this set? (*Hint:* Set up a proportion using your answer from question 1.) 144 tiles
4. This set of mahjong tiles also has 8 special tiles that represent flowers or seasons. What are the odds *against* selecting a tile that represents a flower or a season? 17:1

At a carnival game, you drop a ball into the top of the machine shown below. As the ball falls, it goes either left or right as it hits each peg. In total, the ball can follow 16 different paths. (See if you can find all 16 paths.) The ball eventually lands in one of the bins at the bottom and you win that amount of money. (One path to $0 is shown.) Select the best answer.

5. What is the probability of wining $2?

A $\frac{1}{16}$ C $\frac{1}{4}$

B $\frac{1}{8}$ D $\frac{1}{2}$

6. What is the probability of wining $1?

F $\frac{1}{8}$ H $\frac{1}{4}$

G $\frac{3}{16}$ **J** $\frac{3}{8}$

7. What are the odds in favor of winning nothing ($0)?

A 1:1   C 1:3

B 1:2   D 1:4

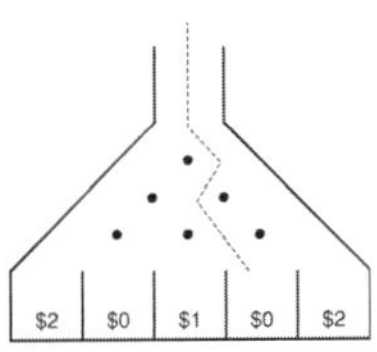

$2 | $0 | $1 | $0 | $2

10-6 CHALLENGE

The wheel shown at right is similar to those used on game shows.

Consider a game-show function that has as its domain the dollar amounts that you could win with one spin of the wheel.

1. Write the domain of the function. {100, 250, 500, 1000, 5000}

This game-show function will assign a number to the probability of landing on each dollar amount. For example, since 6 out of 16 spins are labeled with $100, the theoretical probability of landing on a space marked with $100 is $\frac{6}{16}$ or $\frac{3}{8}$. Thus, $P(100) = \frac{3}{8}$.

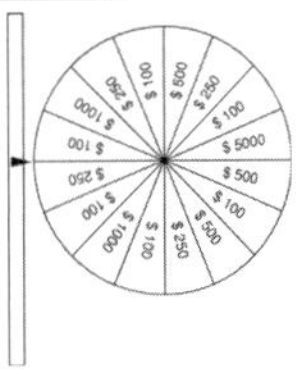

$100, $500, $250, $100, $5000, $500, $100, $500, $250, $100, $1000, $100, $250, $100, $1000, $250

Complete each of the following.

2. $P(250) = \frac{1}{4}$ 3. $P(500) = \frac{3}{16}$ 4. $P(1000) = \frac{1}{8}$ 5. $P(5000) = \frac{1}{16}$

6. What is the range of this function? $\left\{\frac{1}{16}, \frac{1}{8}, \frac{3}{16}, \frac{1}{4}, \frac{3}{8}\right\}$

This function has a special property.

7. What is the sum of all the range elements for this function? 1
8. Why does the sum have to be the number that you found in Exercise 7? The total of the probabilities for all possible events must be 1.
9. Is the sum of the range elements for any function always this number? Explain your response. No; the range of functions can vary widely. A sum of 1 is only required for a probability function such as the one used here.

For this game-show function, find each of the following probabilities.

10. P(100 or 500) $\frac{9}{16}$
11. P(500 or 1000) $\frac{5}{16}$
12. P(more than 500) $\frac{3}{16}$
13. P(at least 500) $\frac{3}{8}$
14. P(less than 500) $\frac{5}{8}$
15. P(10,000) 0

10-7 Organizer

Pacing: Traditional 1 day
Block $\frac{1}{2}$ day

Objectives: Find the probability of independent events.

Find the probability of dependent events.

Algebra Lab
In *Algebra Lab Activities*

Online Edition
Tutorial Videos

Countdown Week 24

Power Presentations with PowerPoint®

Warm Up

Find the theoretical probability of each outcome.

1. rolling a 6 on a number cube $\frac{1}{6}$
2. rolling an odd number on a number cube $\frac{1}{2}$
3. tossing a coin and it landing heads up $\frac{1}{2}$

Also available on transparency

Math Humor

Q: What do you call two unrelated activities scheduled on July 4th?

A: Independence events.

10-7 Independent and Dependent Events

Objectives
Find the probability of independent events.

Find the probability of dependent events.

Vocabulary
independent events
dependent events

Why learn this?
You may need to understand independent and dependent events to determine the number of reading selections available.

Adam's teacher gives the class two lists of titles and asks each student to choose two of them to read. Adam can choose one title from each list or two titles from the same list.

One title from each list

Animal Farm (circled)	*Never Cry Wolf*
Ethan Frome	*Night*
Frankenstein	*Things Fall Apart*
Great Expectations	*Wish You Well*
Jane Eyre	*Wuthering Heights* (circled)

Choosing a title from one list does not affect the number of titles to choose from on the other list. The events are *independent.*

Two titles from the same list

First choice	Second choice
Animal Farm (circled)	~~*Animal Farm*~~
Ethan Frome	*Ethan Frome*
Frankenstein	*Frankenstein* (circled)
Great Expectations	*Great Expectations*
Jane Eyre	*Jane Eyre*

Choosing a title from one of the lists changes the number of titles that can be chosen from the same list. The events are *dependent.*

Events are **independent events** if the occurrence of one event does not affect the probability of the other. Events are **dependent events** if the occurrence of one event does affect the probability of the other.

EXAMPLE 1 Classifying Events as Independent or Dependent

Tell whether each set of events is independent or dependent. Explain your answer.

A **A dime lands heads up and a nickel lands heads up.**
The result of tossing a dime does not affect the result of tossing a nickel, so the events are independent.

B **You choose a colored game piece in a board game, and then your sister picks another color.**
Your sister cannot pick the same color you picked, and there are fewer game pieces for your sister to choose from after you choose, so the events are dependent.

Tell whether each set of events is independent or dependent. Explain your answer.

1a. A number cube lands showing an odd number. It is rolled a second time and lands showing 6.

1b. One student in your class is chosen for a project. Then another student in the class is chosen.

1a. Indep.; the result of rolling the number cube the 1st time does not affect the result of the 2nd roll.

1b. Dep.; choosing the 1st student leaves fewer students to choose from the 2nd time.

State Resources

1 Introduce

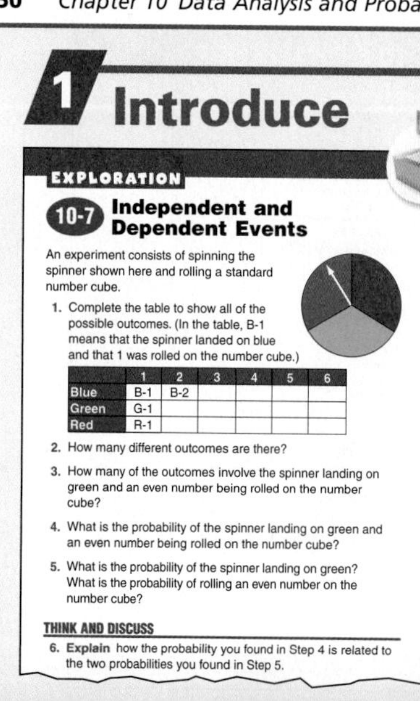
EXPLORATION

10-7 Independent and Dependent Events

An experiment consists of spinning the spinner shown here and rolling a standard number cube.

1. Complete the table to show all of the possible outcomes. (In the table, B-1 means that the spinner landed on blue and that 1 was rolled on the number cube.)

	1	2	3	4	5	6
Blue	B-1	B-2				
Green	G-1					
Red	R-1					

2. How many different outcomes are there?
3. How many of the outcomes involve the spinner landing on green and an even number being rolled on the number cube?
4. What is the probability of the spinner landing on green and an even number being rolled on the number cube?
5. What is the probability of the spinner landing on green? What is the probability of rolling an even number on the number cube?

THINK AND DISCUSS

6. **Explain** how the probability you found in Step 4 is related to the two probabilities you found in Step 5.

Motivate

Ask students for ideas about how to find the probability that three coins land showing heads. Have students find the sample space. HHH, HHT, HTH, THH, TTH, THT, HTT, TTT Then have them find the probability of all three coins showing heads. $\frac{1}{8}$

Show students that writing the entire sample space for some events can take time. Explain that in this section they will learn to find the probability of events without writing out the sample space.

Explorations and answers are provided in *Alternate Openers: Explorations Transparencies.*

Student to Student — *Independent and Dependent Events*

Lydia Delgado
Northridge High School

I use the everyday meanings of independent and dependent to remember their mathematical meanings.

The math class I take next year depends on which math classes I have already taken.	*The history class I take next year is independent from (does not depend on) which math classes I have taken.*
For dependent events, the occurrence of one affects the probability of the other.	*For independent events, the occurrence of one does not affect the occurrence of the other.*

Suppose an experiment involves tossing two fair coins. The sample space of outcomes is shown by the tree diagram. Determine the theoretical probability of both coins landing heads up.

1st Coin — **2nd Coin**

H → H, T
T → H, T

There are four possible outcomes in the sample space: $\{(H, H), (H, T), (T, H), (T, T)\}$

Only one outcome includes both coins landing heads up.

The theoretical probability of both coins landing heads up is $\frac{1}{4}$.

Now look back at the separate theoretical probabilities of each coin landing heads up. The theoretical probability in each case is $\frac{1}{2}$. The product of these two probabilities is $\frac{1}{4}$, the same probability shown by the tree diagram.

To determine the probability of two independent events, multiply the probabilities of the two events.

Probability of Independent Events

If A and B are independent events, then $P(A \text{ and } B) = P(A) \cdot P(B)$.

EXAMPLE 2 Finding the Probability of Independent Events

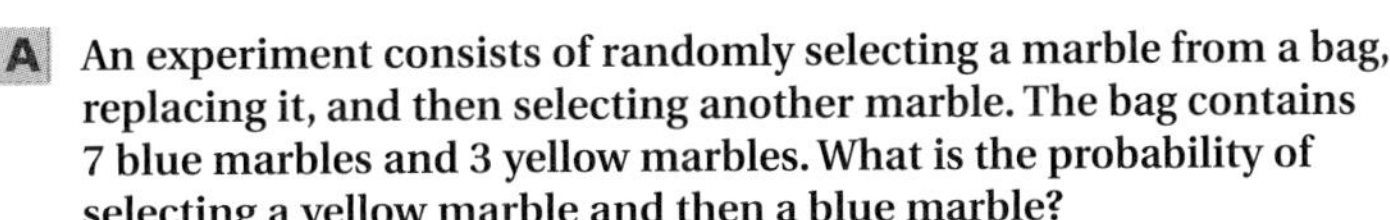

A **An experiment consists of randomly selecting a marble from a bag, replacing it, and then selecting another marble. The bag contains 7 blue marbles and 3 yellow marbles. What is the probability of selecting a yellow marble and then a blue marble?**

Because the first marble is replaced after it is selected, the sample space for each selection is the same. The events are independent.

$$P(\text{yellow, blue}) = P(\text{yellow}) \cdot P(\text{blue})$$

$$= \frac{3}{10} \cdot \frac{7}{10}$$ *The probability of selecting yellow is $\frac{3}{10}$, and the probability of selecting blue is $\frac{7}{10}$.*

$$= \frac{21}{100}$$

Power Presentations with PowerPoint®

Additional Examples

Example 1

Tell whether each set of events is independent or dependent. Explain your answer.

A. You select a card from a standard deck of cards and hold it. A friend selects another card from the same deck. Dependent; your friend cannot pick the card you picked and has fewer cards to choose from.

B. You toss a coin and it lands heads up. You toss the same coin and it lands heads up again. Independent; the result of the first toss does not affect the sample space for the second toss.

Example 2

A. An experiment consists of randomly selecting a marble from a bag, replacing it, and then selecting another marble. The bag contains 3 red marbles and 12 green marbles. What is the probability of selecting a red marble and then a green marble? $\frac{4}{25}$

B. A coin is tossed 4 times. What is the probability of getting 4 heads in a row? $\frac{1}{16}$

INTERVENTION

Questioning Strategies

EXAMPLE 1

- How are independent events different from dependent events?

EXAMPLE 2

- Does the probability of independent events change if the order of the occurrence of the events changes? Explain.

Inclusion Explain that choosing two items with replacement represents independent events. Choosing without replacement represents dependent events.

2 Teach

Guided Instruction

Tell students that in Lesson 10-6 they found the probability of one event. For two or more events, they have to know whether the events are independent or dependent. Emphasize that independent events have the same probability each time, regardless of past events. Thus, a coin that lands heads up 10 times in a row still has a 50% probability of landing heads up on the next toss. Coins can't "remember" what they did on previous tosses.

Reaching All Learners

Through Concrete Manipulatives

To help show the difference between dependent and independent events give each student (or pair of students) two red and two black marbles (or checker pieces or playing cards). Instruct them to choose two objects at random without replacing the first object, and record the results of ten trials. Then have them do the same with replacement. Find the experimental probability of selecting two red marbles with and without replacement. Discuss which probability is higher and why.

Critical Thinking Use **Example 2B** to show students that probabilities can be calculated for more than two events. For three independent events, the equation becomes $P(A \text{ and } B \text{ and } C) = P(A) \cdot P(B) \cdot P(C)$.

B **When a person rolls 2 number cubes and they land showing the same number, we say the person rolled doubles. What is the probability of rolling doubles 3 times in a row?**

The result of one roll does not affect any following rolls. The events are independent.

When you roll 2 number cubes, there are 36 possible outcomes, six of which are doubles:

So, the probability of rolling doubles once is $P(\text{double}) = \frac{6}{36} = \frac{1}{6}$.

$$P(\text{double, double, double}) = P(\text{double}) \cdot P(\text{double}) \cdot P(\text{double})$$
$$= \frac{1}{6} \cdot \frac{1}{6} \cdot \frac{1}{6}$$
$$= \frac{1}{216}$$

2. An experiment consists of spinning the spinner twice. What is the probability of spinning two odd numbers? $\frac{1}{4}$

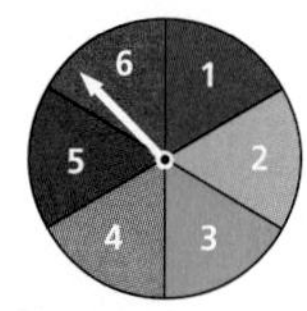

Suppose an experiment involves drawing marbles from a bag. Determine the theoretical probability of drawing a red marble and then drawing a second red marble *without replacing the first one.*

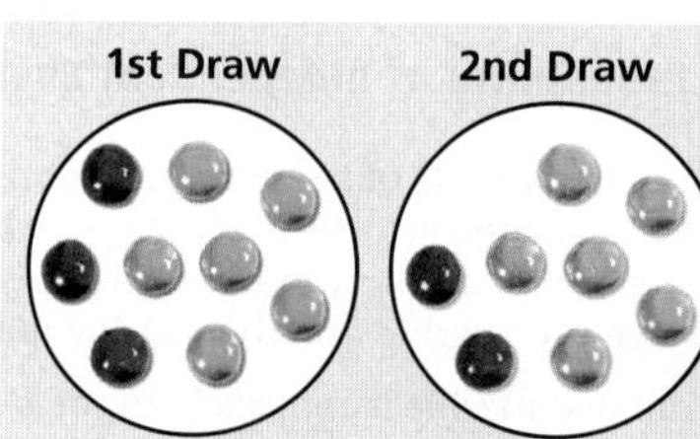

The sample space for the second draw is not the same as the sample space for the first draw. There are fewer marbles in the bag for the second draw.

This means the events are dependent.

Probability of drawing a red marble on the first draw $= \frac{3}{9} = \frac{1}{3}$

Probability of drawing a red marble on the second draw $= \frac{2}{8} = \frac{1}{4}$

To determine the probability of two dependent events, multiply the probability of the first event times the probability of the second event after the first event has occurred.

Probability of Dependent Events

If A and B are dependent events, then $P(A \text{ and } B) = P(A) \cdot P(B \text{ after } A)$.

EXAMPLE 3 ***Problem-Solving Application***

PROBLEM SOLVING

There are 7 pink flowers and 5 yellow flowers in a bunch. Jane selects a flower at random, and then Leah selects a flower at random from the remaining flowers. What is the probability that Jane selects a pink flower and Leah selects a yellow flower?

1 Understand the Problem

The **answer** will be the probability that a yellow flower is chosen after a pink flower is chosen.

List the **important information:**

- Jane chooses a pink flower from 7 pink flowers and 5 yellow flowers.
- Leah chooses a yellow flower from 6 pink flowers and 5 yellow flowers.

2 Make a Plan

Draw a diagram.

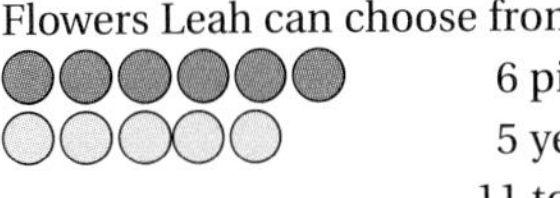

Flowers Jane can choose from:		Flowers Leah can choose from:	
●●●●●●●	7 pink	●●●●●●	6 pink
○○○○○	5 yellow	○○○○○	5 yellow
	12 total		11 total

After Jane selects a flower, the sample space changes. So the events are dependent.

3 Solve

$P(\text{pink and yellow}) = P(\text{pink}) \cdot P(\text{yellow after pink})$

$= \frac{7}{12} \cdot \frac{5}{11}$ *Jane selects one of 7 pink flowers from 12 total flowers. Then Leah selects one of 5 yellow flowers from the 11 flowers left.*

$= \frac{35}{132}$

The probability that Jane selects a pink flower and Leah selects a yellow flower is $\frac{35}{132}$.

4 Look Back

Drawing a diagram helps you see how the sample space changes. This means the events are dependent, so you can use the formula for probability of dependent events.

3. A bag has 10 red marbles, 12 white marbles, and 8 blue marbles. Two marbles are randomly drawn from the bag. What is the probability of drawing a blue marble and then a red marble? $\frac{8}{87}$

COMMON ERROR ALERT

When finding the probability of dependent events in **Example 3,** students often forget that the denominator of the second fraction will be different from the first. Remind them that after the first event has occurred, there are fewer possible outcomes.

Power Presentations with PowerPoint®

Additional Examples

Example 3

A snack cart has 6 bags of pretzels and 10 bags of chips. Grant selects a bag at random, and then Iris selects a bag at random. What is the probability that Grant will select a bag of pretzels and Iris will select a bag of chips? $\frac{1}{4}$

INTERVENTION

Questioning Strategies

EXAMPLE 3

- Why are the denominators different when calculating probability for dependent events?
- What is the meaning of $P(B \text{ after } A)$?

3 Close

Summarize

Have students find the probability for the following. A bag has 2 green, 4 red, and 3 white marbles.

1) Probability of choosing one green, replacing it, and choosing one red $\frac{8}{81}$

2) Probability of choosing one green and then one red, without replacement $\frac{1}{9}$

Discuss why the second situation has the higher probability.

ONGOING ASSESSMENT and INTERVENTION

***Diagnose Before* the Lesson**
10-7 Warm Up, TE p. 750

***Monitor During* the Lesson**
Check It Out! Exercises, SE pp. 750–753
Questioning Strategies, TE pp. 751, 753

***Assess After* the Lesson**
10-7 Lesson Quiz, TE p. 757
Alternative Assessment, TE p. 757

Answers to *Think and Discuss*

1. Possible answer: Choosing an ace from a deck of cards and then choosing a king; the events are dependent because the sample space changes after the first card is selected.
2. See p. A9.

THINK AND DISCUSS

1. Give an example of two events that are dependent. Explain why the events are dependent.

Know it! Note

2. **GET ORGANIZED** Copy and complete the graphic organizer.

	Example	Probability
Dependent Events	$A =$ $B =$	$P(A \text{ and } B) =$
Independent Events	$A =$ $B =$	$P(A \text{ and } B) =$

10-7 Exercises

10-7 Exercises

Assignment Guide

Assign *Guided Practice* exercises as necessary.

If you finished Examples **1–3**

Basic 14–22, 29, 35–38, 45–51

Average 14–21, 23–39, 45–51

Advanced 14–20 even, 23–51

Homework Quick Check

Quickly check key concepts.

Exercises: 16, 18, 20, 26, 32

Answers

2. Dep.; the choice of the 1st card affects the sample space for the choice of the 2nd card.
3. Indep.; the guess for the 1st question does not affect the sample space for the 2nd question.
4. Dep.; after you have selected your kitten, there are fewer kittens for your friend to choose from.

5–6. See p. A32.

State Resources

GUIDED PRACTICE

1. **Vocabulary** Two events are ___?___ if the occurrence of one event affects the probability of the other event. (*independent* or *dependent*) **dependent**

SEE EXAMPLE 1 p. 750

Tell whether each set of events is independent or dependent. Explain your answers.

2. You draw a heart from a deck of cards and set it aside. Then you draw a club from the deck of cards.
3. You guess "true" on two true-false questions.
4. You select a kitten to adopt from an animal shelter. Then your friend selects a kitten to adopt.
5. You order from a menu, and then your friend orders.
6. A doctors' office schedules several patients. Then you make an appointment.

SEE EXAMPLE 2 p. 751

7. A coin is tossed three times. What is the probability of the coin landing heads up three times? $\frac{1}{8}$
8. Seven cards are numbered from 1 to 7 and placed in a box. One card is selected at random and replaced. Another card is randomly selected. What is the probability of selecting two odd numbers? $\frac{16}{49}$
9. Stacey rolls two number cubes. What is the probability that the sum of the numbers on the two number cubes is 7? $\frac{1}{6}$
10. A number cube is rolled twice and a coin is tossed once. What is the probability of the coin landing heads up and the number cube landing with 2 showing both times? $\frac{1}{72}$
11. A spinner with four equal sections of red, yellow, green, and blue is spun twice. What is the probability that it lands on yellow and then on green? $\frac{1}{16}$

SEE EXAMPLE 3
p. 753

12. A bag contains 4 red marbles, 3 white marbles, and 6 blue marbles. What is the probability of randomly selecting a red marble, setting it aside, and then randomly selecting a white marble from the bag? $\frac{1}{13}$

13. Seven cards are numbered from 1 to 7 and placed in a box. One card is selected at random and not replaced. Another card is randomly selected. What is the probability of selecting two odd numbers? $\frac{2}{7}$

14. There are 15 boys and 14 girls in a room. Two of them are selected at random to take a survey. What is the probability that the two people selected will be girls? $\frac{13}{58}$

COMMON ERROR ALERT

In **Exercise 23,** students might write $\frac{1}{64}$ for both **a** and **b.** Remind students that the numerator in a probability fraction represents the number of ways that the event can occur. With four possible answers, there are three ways to choose the wrong answer and one way to choose the right answer.

PRACTICE AND PROBLEM SOLVING

Independent Practice	
For Exercises	See Example
15–16	1
17–19	2
20–22	3

Extra Practice
Skills Practice p. S23
Application Practice p. S37

Tell whether each set of events is independent or dependent. Explain your answer.

15. The teacher randomly selects two students from the class.

16. You roll a 3 on a number cube and choose a 3 from a deck of cards.

17. A number cube is rolled three times. What is the probability of rolling three even numbers? $\frac{1}{8}$

18. Ten cards are numbered from 1 to 10 and placed in a box. One card is selected at random and replaced. Another card is randomly selected. What is the probability of selecting two even numbers? $\frac{1}{4}$

19. Stacey rolls a number cube and tosses a coin. What is the probability that she rolls a 5 and the coin lands heads up? $\frac{1}{12}$

20. A bag contains 5 red marbles, 3 white marbles, and 4 blue marbles. What is the probability of randomly selecting a red marble, setting it aside, and then randomly selecting another red marble from the bag? $\frac{5}{33}$

21. Ten cards are numbered from 1 to 10 and placed in a box. One card is selected at random and not replaced. Another card is randomly selected. What is the probability of selecting two even numbers? $\frac{2}{9}$

22. A game has 6 colored playing pieces. They are red, yellow, green, blue, purple, and white. You and a friend each pick a game piece without looking. What is the probability that your friend picks the blue piece and then you pick the yellow piece? $\frac{1}{30}$

LINK School

On some standardized tests, there is no penalty for a wrong answer. On these tests, it is better to guess than to leave the answer blank, especially if some choices can be eliminated.

23. **School** On a multiple-choice test, each question has 4 possible answers. A student does not know the answers to three questions, so the student guesses.
    a. What is the probability that the student gets all three questions wrong? $\frac{27}{64}$
    b. What is the probability that the student gets all three questions right? $\frac{1}{64}$

Tell whether each set of events is independent or dependent. Explain your answer.

24. Pick "Joe" from a box of names, replace it, and then pick "Craig."

25. Pick "Joe" from a box of names, set it aside, and then pick "Craig."

26. Roll a prime number on a number cube and get tails when tossing a coin.

27. Roll an even number, then an odd number, and then a 1 on a number cube.

Answers

15. Dependent; the choice of the first student affects the sample space for the choice of the second student.

16. Independent; the result of rolling the number cube does not affect the sample space of the deck of cards.

24. Independent; the choice of the first name does not affect the sample space for the choice of the second name.

25. Dependent; the choice of the first name affects the sample space for the choice of the second name.

26. Independent; the roll of the number cube does not affect the sample space for tossing the coin.

27. Independent; each roll does not affect the sample space for the next roll.

State Resources

MULTI-STEP TEST PREP Exercise 28 involves finding the probability of independent events. This exercise prepares students for the Multi-Step Test Prep on page 768.

MULTI-STEP TEST PREP

28. This problem will prepare you for the Multi-Step Test Prep on page 768.

    Yahtzee is a game that involves rolling five dice. On his or her turn, a player can roll up to three times to try to score points in various categories. Rolling a "Yahtzee" means rolling five of a kind, or five of the same number.

    a. Juan has rolled twice and has three 5's showing. He rolls the remaining two dice. What is the probability that both dice will land showing 5? $\frac{1}{36}$

    b. Shauna has two 3's showing. She has one more roll with the remaining three dice. What is the probability that all three dice will land showing 3? $\frac{1}{216}$

    c. Mike rolls all five number cubes and all of them land showing 6. What is the probability of getting five 6's in one roll? $\frac{1}{7776}$

29. A bag contains 3 red, 5 blue, and 2 white marbles.

    a. Find the probability of randomly picking a red marble, replacing it, and then picking a blue marble. $\frac{3}{20}$

    b. Find the probability of randomly picking a red marble, setting it aside, and then picking a blue marble. $\frac{1}{6}$

    c. Find the probability of randomly picking a red marble, replacing it, and then picking another red marble. $\frac{9}{100}$

    d. Find the probability of randomly picking a red marble, setting it aside, and then picking another red marble. $\frac{1}{15}$

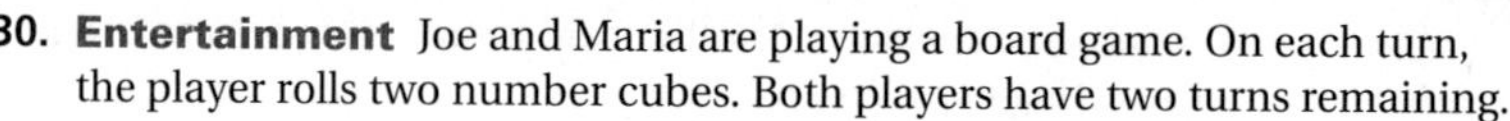

30. **Entertainment** Joe and Maria are playing a board game. On each turn, the player rolls two number cubes. Both players have two turns remaining.

    a. Joe will win if he rolls double 6's on both turns. What is the probability that Joe will roll double 6's on both turns? $\frac{1}{1296}$

    b. Maria will win if she rolls 2 on the first turn and 12 on the second turn. What is the probability that Maria will roll 2 on the first turn and 12 on the second turn?

    c. **Write About It** Who has the better probability of winning? Explain.

30b. $\frac{1}{1296}$

c. The players have the same prob. of winning.

31. Tamika has $2.50 in quarters in her pocket, including four state quarters. She reaches into her pocket and takes out two quarters, one at a time. What is the probability that they are both state quarters? $\frac{2}{15}$

32. Ten cards are numbered 1 through 10 and placed in a bag. You draw a card, set it aside, and draw another card. What is the probability that you will draw two numbers that are divisible by 3? $\frac{1}{15}$

33. **Critical Thinking** What is the probability of a coin landing heads up on two tosses if it lands tails up on the first toss? Explain.

33. The prob. is 0 because it is impossible for the coin to land heads up on both tosses.

34. **Write About It** Explain what it means for two events to be independent.

    2 events are indep. if the occurrence of 1 event does not affect the prob. of the other.

TEST PREP

35. A number cube is rolled twice. What is the probability of getting a 2 on both rolls?

    Ⓐ $\frac{1}{3}$ Ⓑ $\frac{1}{4}$ Ⓒ $\frac{1}{9}$ **Ⓓ $\frac{1}{36}$**

36. In baseball, Julio averages 3 hits in every 10 at bats. What is the probability that he will get hits in both of his next two at bats?

    Ⓕ 0.03 **Ⓖ 0.09** Ⓗ 0.3 Ⓙ 0.9

10-7 PRACTICE A

10-7 PRACTICE C

10-7 PRACTICE B

Tell whether each set of events is independent or dependent. Explain your answer.

1. You roll a die and flip a coin. independent
   the result of the die does not affect the result of the coin.
2. You select one marble, do not replace it, then select another marble. dependent
   selecting one marble without replacing it will change the number to choose from.
3. A number cube is rolled three times. What is the probability of rolling a 2 each time? $\frac{1}{216} \approx 0.5\%$
4. The numbers 1 – 40 are written on pieces of paper and put in a box. Two pieces of paper are randomly selected. What is the probability both numbers will be multiples of 4? $\frac{3}{52} \approx 5.8\%$
5. A coin is tossed 4 times. What is the probability of getting 4 tails? $\frac{1}{16} \approx 6.25\%$
6. **A bag contains 2 yellow, 12 red, and 6 green marbles.**
   a. What is the probability of selecting a red marble, replacing it, then selecting another red marble? $\frac{9}{25} \approx 36\%$
   b. What is the probability of selecting a red marble, not replacing it, then selecting another red marble? $\frac{33}{95} \approx 34.7\%$
   c. What is the probability of selecting 1 yellow marble, not replacing it, then selecting a green marble? $\frac{3}{95} \approx 3.2\%$
7. **There are 7 girls and 3 boys in a class. Two students are to be randomly chosen for a special project.**
   a. What is the probability both students will be girls? $\frac{7}{15} \approx 46.7\%$
   b. What is the probability both students will be boys? $\frac{1}{15} \approx 6.7\%$
   c. What is the probability of selecting a boy and a girl? $\frac{7}{30} \approx 23.3\%$

A music class consists of 9th and 10th graders as shown in the table. Two students will be selected at the same time.

Music Class		
	9th	10th
male	9	8
female	12	11

8. What is the probability both students are male? $\frac{34}{195} \approx 17.4\%$
9. What is the probability both students are 9th graders? $\frac{7}{26} \approx 26.9\%$
10. What is the probability one student is female and the second student is male? $\approx 25.1\%$

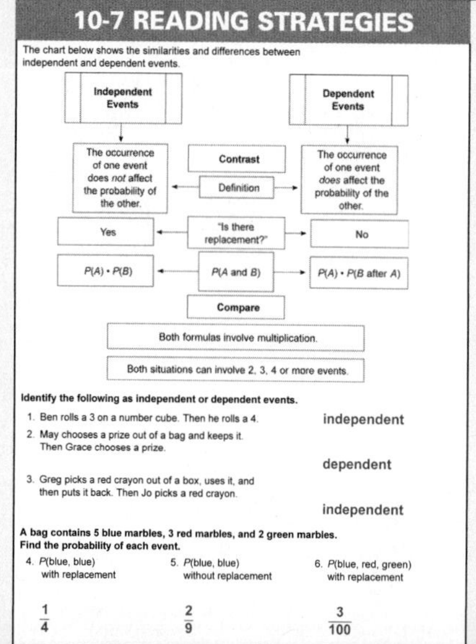

10-7 READING STRATEGIES

The chart below shows the similarities and differences between independent and dependent events.

Independent Events	Contrast	Dependent Events
The occurrence of one event does *not* affect the probability of the other.	← Definition →	The occurrence of one event *does* affect the probability of the other.
Yes	← "Is there replacement?" →	No
$P(A) \cdot P(B)$	← $P(A \text{ and } B)$ →	$P(A) \cdot P(B \text{ after } A)$

Compare

Both formulas involve multiplication.

Both situations can involve 2, 3, 4 or more events.

Identify the following as independent or dependent events.

1. Ben rolls a 3 on a number cube. Then he rolls a 4. independent
2. May chooses a prize out of a bag and keeps it. Then Grace chooses a prize. dependent
3. Greg picks a red crayon out of a box, uses it, and then puts it back. Then Jo picks a red crayon. independent

A bag contains 5 blue marbles, 3 red marbles, and 2 green marbles. Find the probability of each event.

4. $P(\text{blue, blue})$ with replacement $\frac{1}{4}$
5. $P(\text{blue, blue})$ without replacement $\frac{2}{9}$
6. $P(\text{blue, red, green})$ with replacement $\frac{3}{100}$

10-7 RETEACH

Events are **independent** if the occurrence of one event does not affect the probability of the other.

If A and B are independent events, then $P(A \text{ and } B) = P(A) \cdot P(B)$.

In other words, if two or more events are independent, multiply their individual probabilities.

An experiment consists of rolling a number cube twice. What is the probability of rolling a 3 the first time and a 2 the second time?

Step 1: Determine if the two events are independent.

The first roll of a number cube will not affect the second roll. Therefore, the two rolls are independent events.

Step 2: Find the probability.

$$P(A \text{ and } B) = P(A) \cdot P(B)$$
$$P(3, 2) = P(3) \cdot P(2) = \frac{1}{6} \cdot \frac{1}{6} = \frac{1}{36}$$

An experiment consists of randomly selecting a marble from a bag, replacing it, and then selecting another marble. The bag contains 2 red marbles, 1 white marble, and 7 yellow marbles. What is the probability of selecting a white marble and then a yellow marble?

Step 1: Determine if the two events are independent.

Because the first marble is replaced, the probability of getting a certain color on the second selection is not affected by which color was selected first. The events are independent.

Step 2: Find the probability.

$$P(A \text{ and } B) = P(A) \cdot P(B)$$
$$P(\text{white, yellow}) = P(\text{white}) \cdot P(\text{yellow}) = \frac{1}{10} \cdot \frac{7}{10} = \frac{7}{100}$$

1. Six cards are numbered 1 to 6 and placed in a box. One card is selected at random and replaced. Another card is selected at random. What is the probability of selecting a 1 and then a 6?
   $P(1)$ $\frac{1}{6}$; $P(6)$ $\frac{1}{6}$; $P(1 \text{ and } 6)$ $\frac{1}{36}$
2. A coin is tossed three times. What is the probability of the coin landing heads all three times? $\frac{1}{8}$
3. A bag contains 5 red marbles, 8 white marbles, and 7 green marbles. What is the probability of randomly selecting a white marble, replacing it, then randomly selecting another white marble? $\frac{4}{25}$
4. Ten cards are numbered from 1 to 10 and placed in a box. One card is selected at random and replaced. Another card is selected at random. What is the probability of selecting a multiple of 3, then a multiple of 2? $\frac{3}{20}$

37. Two people from a group of 30 will be selected at random for a prize. Twenty people in the group are women. What is the probability that both people selected will be men?

Ⓐ $\frac{3}{29}$ (circled)   Ⓑ $\frac{38}{87}$ Ⓒ $\frac{56}{87}$ Ⓓ $\frac{1}{10}$

38. Ravi has 10 pairs of socks in a drawer, but none of the pairs are matched up. Each pair is a different color, and one pair is blue. Ravi has to pick his socks in the dark so he does not wake his brother. Which expression can be used to find the probability that Ravi will choose a blue sock and then the matching sock?

Ⓕ $\frac{1}{20}+\frac{1}{20}$ Ⓖ $\frac{1}{10}\cdot\frac{1}{20}$ Ⓗ $\frac{1}{20}+\frac{1}{19}$ Ⓙ $\frac{1}{10}\cdot\frac{1}{19}$ (circled)

CHALLENGE AND EXTEND

39. Basketball Terrance has made 90% of the free throws he has attempted at basketball practice. What is the probability that he will make the next three free throws he attempts? **72.9%**

40. A number cube is rolled three times. What is the probability of rolling a 5 at least once? $\frac{91}{216}$

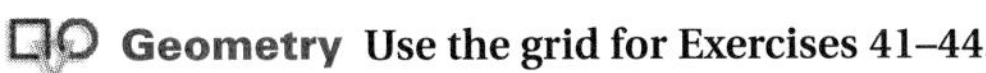

Geometry **Use the grid for Exercises 41–44.**

On the grid at right, one small square represents 1% probability.

The shaded rows represent the probability that event *A* occurs.

The shaded columns represent the probability that event *B* occurs.

The area where the shaded rows and columns overlap represents the probability that both events occur.

Use the grid to find each probability.

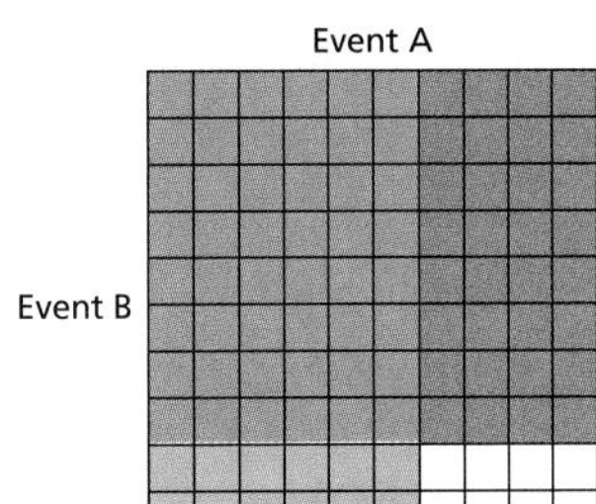

41. Event *A* occurs. **80%**

42. Event *B* occurs. **60%**

43. Event *A* occurs AND event *B* occurs. **48%**

44. Neither event *A* nor event *B* occurs. **8%**

SPIRAL REVIEW

45. A tennis player serves 2 aces (unreturned serves) for every 17 serves. If the player serves 204 times in the next match, how many serves would you expect to be aces? *(Lesson 2-7)* **24**

46. narrower and translated 1 unit down

47. wider

48. reflected across x-axis and translated 3 units up

Compare the graph of each function to the graph of $f(x) = x^2$. *(Lesson 9-4)*

46. $g(x) = 4x^2 - 1$ **47.** $g(x) = \frac{1}{5}x^2$ **48.** $g(x) = -x^2 + 3$

Find the theoretical probability of each outcome. *(Lesson 10-6)*

49. Randomly selecting a blue marble out of a bag with 6 red and 9 blue marbles $\frac{3}{5}$

50. Rolling a number less than 10 on a number cube **1**

51. Randomly selecting A, E, I, O, or U from all letters of the alphabet $\frac{5}{26}$

10-7 PROBLEM SOLVING

Janeesa's backpack has 4 pens and 6 pencils in the front pocket. She reaches in, grabs one, and removes it. Then she reaches in again, grabs another, and removes it. Write the correct answer.

1. Are these two events independent or dependent? Explain.
   dependent; the item removed first affects the sample space for the second item.
2. What is the probability that Janeesa removes two pens?
   $\frac{2}{15}$
3. What is the probability that Janeesa removes two pencils?
   $\frac{1}{3}$
4. What is the probability that Janessa removes a pencil and then a pen?
   $\frac{4}{15}$
5. What is the probability that she removes a pen and then a pencil?
   $\frac{4}{15}$
6. Your answers to questions 4 and 5 should be numerically identical. Does that mean that the events are identical? Explain.
   no; the events are different because the order in which the items are removed is different.

On a game show, a contestant tries to win a car by randomly picking tiles from a bag. Some of the tiles are printed with the digits in the price of the car and some are printed with strikes (red X's). Select the best answer.

7. When the prices of cars only had four digits, the game was played with 7 tiles—4 digits and 3 strikes. Whenever you picked a strike, it was removed from the bag. In this old version of the game, what was the probability of picking three strikes in a row?

   A $\frac{1}{343}$ C $\frac{6}{343}$
   B $\frac{1}{210}$ **D** $\frac{1}{35}$

8. When the prices of cars began to have five digits, the game was modified to use 6 tiles—5 digits and 1 strike. Whenever you picked a strike, it was put back in the bag. In this new version of the game, what is the probability of picking three strikes in a row?

   F $\frac{1}{216}$ H $\frac{1}{36}$
   G $\frac{1}{120}$ J $\frac{1}{20}$

10-7 CHALLENGE

It is dark when you stumble out of bed and you are not ready to turn on the light. You pick socks out of the sock drawer at random. The wash has just been done, so you know that there are 8 blue, 4 tan, and 12 white socks in the drawer.

1. What is the probability that the first sock that you pick is blue? $\frac{1}{3}$
2. If the first sock that you picked was blue, and you hold onto it, what is the probability that the second sock that you pick will also be blue? $\frac{7}{23}$
3. What is the probability that you picked 2 blue socks? $\frac{7}{69}$
4. Using the same process that you used for Exercises 1–3 and starting over with a full drawer of socks, what is the probability of picking 2 socks, without replacement, that both are white? $\frac{11}{46}$

Suppose that there are n socks in another drawer and that 6 of them are brown. (Assume that there are more than 6 socks in the drawer.)

5. What is the probability of picking 1 brown sock? $\frac{6}{n}$
6. If the first sock that you picked was brown, and you hold onto it, what is the probability that the second sock that you picked will also be brown? $\frac{5}{n-1}$
7. What is the probability of picking 2 brown socks if the first one is not replaced? $\frac{30}{n(n-1)}$

There are tryouts for seating positions in band. To determine the order of the n students trying out, slips of paper numbered 1 through n are placed in the bag, and each student draws a number.

8. What is the probability that the first number drawn is 8? (Assume that there are at least 8 students.) $\frac{6}{n}$
9. If the first student draws position 8, what is the probability that the next student will draw 5. $\frac{1}{n-1}$
10. If the slips with 8 and 5 have been drawn, what is the probability that the number 4 will be drawn next? $\frac{1}{n-2}$
11. Find the probability that the slips with 8, 5, and 4 are selected in this order. $\frac{1}{n(n-1)(n-2)}$
12. Suppose you want to draw the number 1 so that you can play first. As other students draw other numbers, what happens to your chances of getting the 1? Use math to explain.
    Your chances of drawing a 1 get better until the 1 is drawn. This happens because the number in the denominator of the probability fraction keeps getting lesser, and the value of the fraction gets closer to 1.

TEST PREP DOCTOR For **Exercise 37,** students who chose **D** did not change the sample space for the second probability.

Journal

Explain why selecting two objects at the same time can be considered the same as selecting two objects without replacement.

ALTERNATIVE ASSESSMENT

Have students write a set of independent events, explain why they are independent, and then find the probability. Have them repeat the task for dependent events.

Power Presentations with PowerPoint®

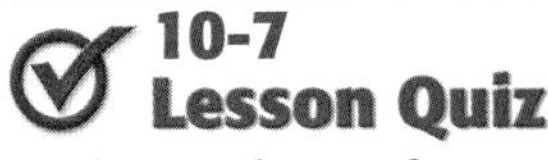

10-7 Lesson Quiz

Tell whether each set of events is independent or dependent. Explain your answer.

1. tossing two coins and each coin landing showing heads Independent; the toss of the first coin does not affect the sample space for the toss of the second coin.
2. drawing a red card from a standard deck of cards and not replacing it; then drawing a black card from the same deck of cards Dependent; there are fewer cards to choose from when drawing the black card.
3. Eight cards are numbered from 1 to 8 and placed in a box. One card is selected at random and not replaced. Another card is randomly selected. What is the probability that both cards are greater than 5? $\frac{3}{28}$
4. An experiment consists of randomly selecting a marble from a bag, replacing it, and then selecting another marble. The bag contains 3 yellow marbles and 2 white marbles. What is the probability of selecting a white marble and then a yellow marble? $\frac{6}{25}$
5. A number cube is rolled two times. What is the probability of rolling an even number first and then a number less than 3? $\frac{1}{6}$

Also available on transparency

Organizer

Use with Lesson 10-7

Pacing:
Traditional $\frac{1}{2}$ day
Block $\frac{1}{4}$ day

Objective: Find the probability of compound events.

Online Edition

Countdown Week 24

Resources

Algebra Lab Activities
10-7 Lab Recording Sheet

Teach

Discuss

Students may find it easier to discover the rules if they do not reduce the fractions. That is, keep a denominator of 36.

The symbol ∪ is sometimes used for the word OR and the symbol ∩ is sometimes used for the word AND. Using these symbols, the rule can also be written as $P(A \cup B) = P(A) + P(B) - P(A \cap B)$, where $P(A \cap B) = 0$ for mutually exclusive events.

Use with Lesson 10-7

Compound Events

When two events cannot happen at the same time, they are called *mutually exclusive* events. When two events can happen at the same time, they are called *inclusive* events. You can use sample spaces to determine the probabilities of mutually exclusive events and inclusive events.

When finding the probablity of a compound event, you should first determine whether the simple events involved are dependent or independent.

Activity 1

Suppose you are playing Monopoly and are "just visiting" the Jail. If you roll 7 on your next turn, you will land on Community Chest. If you roll 12, you will land on Chance. What is the probability that on your next roll you land on either Community Chest or Chance?

You cannot land on Community Chest and Chance at the same time, so the events are mutually exclusive. You cannot roll 7 and 12 at the same time, so those events are also mutually exclusive.

The table shows some of the totals when rolling two fair dice. Copy and complete the table. Use one color to circle all rolls with a total of 7. Use a second color to circle all rolls with a total of 12.

+	1	2	3	4	5	6
1	2	3	4	5	6	7
2	3	4	5	6	7	8
3	4	5	6	7	8	9
4	5	6	7	8	9	10
5	6	7	8	9	10	11
6	7	8	9	10	11	12

Try This

1. What is the total number of possible rolls? **36**
2. What is the probability that the total will be 7? $\frac{1}{6}$
3. What is the probability that the total will be 12? $\frac{1}{36}$
4. What is the probability that the total will be 7 or 12? $\frac{7}{36}$
5. What do you notice about the probabilities in Problems 2, 3, and 4?
The sum of the probabilities in Problems 2 and 3 is equal to the probability in Problem 4.

Suppose you are three spaces away from Community Chest and eight spaces away from Chance.

6. What is the probability that on your next roll the total will be 3? $\frac{1}{18}$
7. What is the probability that on your next roll the total will be 8? $\frac{5}{36}$
8. What is the probability that on your next roll the total will be 3 or 8? $\frac{7}{36}$
9. Complete the following statement:
The probability that one of two mutually exclusive events will occur is the ___?___ of the probabilities of the individual events. **sum**

In this lab, you discovered this rule: If A and B are mutually exclusive events, then $P(A \text{ or } B) = P(A) + P(B)$.

Teacher to Teacher

You can make this activity come alive by having students in groups find the probabilities while playing the actual game.

Students can find theoretical probabilities and compare them with the actual ratios of the number of times certain events occurred.

Students will learn to identify the types of probabilities and determine how to find them.

Dr. Katherine Staltare
Yonkers, NY

Suppose you are playing Yahtzee and on the last roll of your turn, you roll two of the five dice. You need to roll either a 1 or a 5 to make what is called a "small straight" (four consecutive numbers).

What is the probability that you will make a small straight?

You can roll a 1 and a 5 at the same time on different dice. These events are inclusive.

(If you roll a 1 and a 5, you will need to look at only four of the dice to make a small straight.)

There are three outcomes that involve rolling a 1 or rolling a 5.

Case 1	Case 2	Case 3
⚀ ?	? ⚄	⚀ ⚄
At least one 1	At least one 5	Both a 1 and a 5

Try This

10. Find the probability of Case 1, rolling at least one 1.

a. What is the probability of rolling ⚀ on the first die and any number on the second die? $\frac{1}{6}$

b. What is the probability of rolling any number on the first die and ⚀ on the second die? $\frac{1}{6}$

c. What is the probability of rolling ⚀ on the first die and ⚀ on the second die? $\frac{1}{36}$

d. Parts **a** and **b** both include rolling ⚀ on the first die and ⚀ on the second die. You need to count this outcome only once, so subtract the probability from part **c** from the sum of parts **a** and **b.** $\frac{11}{36}$

11. Find the probability of Case 2, rolling at least one 5. (*Hint:* Repeat the steps in Problem 10.) $\frac{11}{36}$

12. Find the probability of Case 3, rolling a 1 and a 5. $\frac{1}{18}$

13. The probability of rolling a small straight, is the probability of rolling ⚀ *or* ⚄.

Subtract the probability of rolling both ⚀ *and* ⚄ from the sum of the probabilities of rolling ⚀ on one of the dice (Problem 10) and rolling ⚄ on one of the dice (Problem 11). $\frac{5}{9}$

14. Complete the following statement:

The probability that one of two inclusive events will occur is the ___?___ of the probabilities of the individual events ___?___ the probability of the intersection of the two events. **sum; minus**

In this lab, you discovered this rule:

If A and B are inclusive events, then $P(A \text{ or } B) = P(A) + P(B) - P(A \text{ and } B)$.

Close

Key Concept

To find the probability of a compound event, add the individual probabilities. If the events are mutually exclusive, subtract the probability of both occurring at the same time.

Assessment

Journal Have students explain the difference between mutually exclusive events and inclusive events.

10-8 Organizer

Pacing: Traditional $1\frac{1}{2}$ days
Block $\frac{3}{4}$ day

Objectives: Solve problems involving permutations.

Solve problems involving combinations.

Algebra Lab
In *Algebra Lab Activities*

Online Edition
Interactivity, Tutorial Videos

Countdown Week 24

Power Presentations with PowerPoint®

Warm Up

For a main dish, you can choose steak or chicken; your side dish can be rice or a baked potato; and your drink can be tea or water. Make a tree diagram to show the number of possible meals if you have one of each.

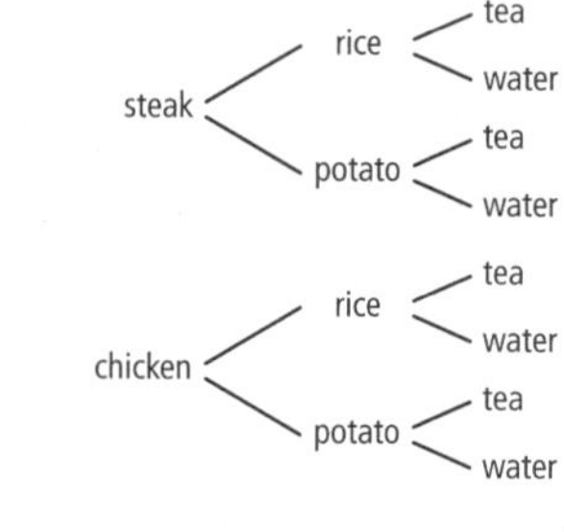

Also available on transparency

Q: What do you call a hairstyle gone bad?

A: A perm mutation.

State Resources

10-8 Combinations and Permutations

Objectives
Solve problems involving permutations.
Solve problems involving combinations.

Vocabulary
compound event
combination
permutation

Who uses this?
Security companies use permutations to create many security codes using a limited number of digits or letters. (See Exercise 8.)

Sometimes there are too many possible outcomes to make a tree diagram or a list. The *Fundamental Counting Principle* is one method of finding the number of possible outcomes.

Know it! Note

Fundamental Counting Principle

If there are m ways to choose a first item and n ways to choose a second item after the first item has been chosen, then there are $m \cdot n$ ways to choose both items.

The Fundamental Counting Principle can also be used when there are more than two items to choose.

EXAMPLE 1 **Using the Fundamental Counting Principle**

A florist is arranging centerpieces that include 1 flower, 1 plant, and 1 vase. The florist has 2 kinds of vases, 2 kinds of plants, and 3 kinds of flowers to choose from. How many different centerpieces are possible?

Method 1 Use a tree diagram. *Follow each branch of the tree diagram to find all of the possible centerpieces.*

There are 12 possible centerpieces.

Method 2 Use the Fundamental Counting Principle.

$2 \cdot 2 \cdot 3$ *There are 2 choices for the first item, 2 choices for the second item, and 3 choices for the third item.*

12

There are 12 possible centerpieces.

1. A voicemail system password is 1 letter followed by a 3-digit number less than 600. How many different voicemail passwords are possible? **15,600**

1 Introduce

EXPLORATION

10-8 Combinations and Permutations

You can solve the following problems by making an organized list or by making a tree diagram.

1. Kathryn wears a uniform to school. She must choose a shirt and a skirt from the color choices that are shown.
   a. List all the possible combinations of shirts and skirts that Kathryn can wear.
   b. How many different outfits are there?

Shirt Colors
Red
White
Blue

Skirt Colors
Navy
Khaki

2. Jason is choosing his lunch at the cafeteria. He will choose 1 sandwich and 1 drink from the menu.
   a. List all the possible combinations of sandwiches and drinks.
   b. How many different lunch choices are there?

Sandwiches
Ham
Turkey
Cheese

Drinks
Water
Milk
Juice

THINK AND DISCUSS

3. **Describe** how the total number of choices in each problem is related to the number of choices in each category.
4. **Explain** how you can predict the number of different outfits Juanita can make if she has 3 different pairs of jeans and

Motivate

Select seven students to come to the front of the class. Then ask the remaining students: "If I list how many ways I could arrange these seven students in seven seats, would I have a list of

- about 50?
- about 500?
- about 5000? about 5000 (exact answer 5040)

Explorations and answers are provided in *Alternate Openers: Explorations Transparencies.*

A **compound event** consists of two or more simple events, such as a rolled number cube landing with 3 showing and a tossed coin landing heads up. (A simple event has only one outcome, such as rolling a 3 on a number cube.) For some compound events, the order in which the simple events occur is important.

A **combination** is a grouping of outcomes in which the order does not matter. A **permutation** is an arrangement of outcomes in which the order does matter.

EXAMPLE 2 Finding Combinations and Permutations

Tell whether each situation involves combinations or permutations. Then give the number of possible outcomes.

A **A street vendor sells cashews, peanuts, and almonds. How many different ways are there to mix two kinds of nuts?**

List all of the possible groupings:

cashews and peanuts	peanuts and almonds	almonds and cashews
peanuts and cashews	almonds and peanuts	cashews and almonds

The order of the outcomes is not important, so this situation involves combinations. Eliminate the groupings that are duplicates.

cashews and peanuts	peanuts and almonds	almonds and cashews
~~peanuts and cashews~~	~~almonds and peanuts~~	~~cashews and almonds~~

There are 3 different ways to mix two kinds of nuts.

B **Karen is painting her bedroom. She has orange, green, blue, and purple paint. She plans to use one color as a base coat and stencil a design with another color. How many different ways can she do this?**

List all of the possible groupings:

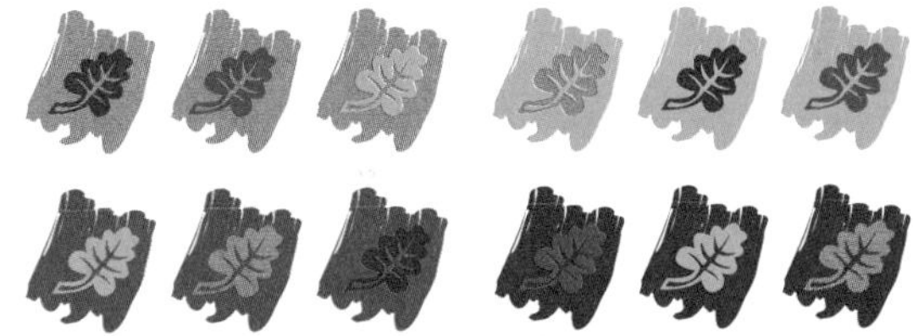

The order of the outcomes is important, because one color is painted on top of the other. This situation involves permutations.

There are 12 different ways for Karen to paint her room.

Tell whether each situation involves combinations or permutations. Then give the number of possible outcomes.

2a. Ingrid is stringing three different types of beads on a bracelet. How many ways can she use one bead of each type to string the next three beads? **perm.; 6**

2b. Nathan wants to order a sandwich with two of the following ingredients: mushroom, eggplant, tomato, and avocado. How many different sandwiches can Nathan choose? **comb.; 6**

2 Teach

Guided Instruction

Review tree diagrams before introducing the Fundamental Counting Principle. Have students first find permutations and combinations by writing lists. Then give them a situation with more permutations than could reasonably be listed. When students realize this, introduce and use the formula for permutations. Show that *n* permutations taken *n* at a time is the same as *n* factorial. Then introduce and use the formula for combinations.

Reaching All Learners

Through Home Connection

Have students research the types of license plates or driver's license numbers in different states. Students should find out whether there are any letters, numbers, or combinations of letters or numbers that are not allowed. Have students calculate how many license plate or driver's license numbers are possible.

COMMON ERROR ALERT

Students often have difficulty determining whether order will matter. Encourage them to ask themselves questions such as, "Is a peanut butter and jelly sandwich the same as a jelly and peanut butter sandwich?"

Power Presentations with PowerPoint®

Additional Examples

Example 1

A sandwich can be made with 3 different types of bread, 5 different meats, and 2 types of cheese. How many types of sandwiches can be made if each sandwich consists of one bread, one meat, and one cheese? 30

Example 2

Tell whether each situation involves combinations or permutations. Then give the number of possible outcomes.

A. An English test contains 5 different essay questions labeled A, B, C, D, and E. You are supposed to choose 2 to answer. How many different ways are there to do this? combinations; 10

B. A family of 3 plans to sit in the same row at a movie theater. How many ways can the family be seated in 3 seats? permutations; 6

INTERVENTION

Questioning Strategies

EXAMPLE 1

- What is the benefit of using the Fundamental Counting Principle over drawing a tree diagram?
- When would you use a tree diagram rather than the Fundamental Counting Principle?
- How can you "see" the Fundamental Counting Principle in a tree diagram?

EXAMPLE 2

- Are there more possible outcomes with a combination or with a permutation? Why?

Power Presentations with PowerPoint®

Additional Examples

Example 3

A group of 8 swimmers are swimming in a race. Prizes are given for first, second, and third place. How many different outcomes can there be? 336

INTERVENTION

Questioning Strategies

EXAMPLE 3

- What does the denominator represent?
- What will the denominator equal if $n = r$? What does this mean?

Auditory Cues To help remember that order matters in a permutation, tell students a **per**mutation must be in a **par**ticular order.

Helpful Hint

The factorial of 0 is defined to be 1.
$0! = 1$

The factorial of a number is the product of the number and all the natural numbers less than the number. The factorial of 5 is written 5! and is read "five factorial." $5! = 5 \cdot 4 \cdot 3 \cdot 2 \cdot 1 = 120$. Factorials can be used to find the number of combinations and permutations that can be made from a set of choices.

Suppose you want to make a five-letter password from the letters *A, B, C, D,* and *E* without repeating a letter. You have 5 choices for the first letter, but only 4 choices for the second letter. You have one fewer choice for each letter of the password.

First letter | Second letter | Third letter | Fourth letter | Fifth letter

5 choices × 4 choices × 3 choices × 2 choices × 1 choice = 120 permutations

Suppose you want to make a three-letter password from the 5 letters *A, B, C, D,* and *E* without repeating a letter. Again, you have one fewer choice for each letter of the password.

First letter | Second letter | Third letter

There are 5 choices (A, B, C, D, E), and you are choosing 3 of them.

5 choices × 4 choices × 3 choices = 60 permutations

The number of permutations is $\frac{5!}{2!}$, or $\frac{5 \cdot 4 \cdot 3 \cdot \cancel{2} \cdot \cancel{1}}{\cancel{2} \cdot \cancel{1}} = 5 \cdot 4 \cdot 3 = 60$.

Permutations

FORMULA	The number of permutations of n things chosen r at a time:	${}_nP_r = \frac{n!}{(n-r)!}$
EXAMPLE	A club will choose a president, a vice president, and a secretary from a list of 8 people. How many ways can the club choose the 3 officers? The position that each person takes matters, so this situation involves permutations.	
	Think: There are 8 people, and the club will choose 3 of them.	${}_8P_3 = \frac{8!}{(8-3)!} = \frac{8!}{5!} = 336$

EXAMPLE 3 Finding Permutations

Lee brings 7 CDs numbered 1–7 to a party. How many different ways can he choose the first 4 CDs to play?

The order in which the CDs are played matters, so use the formula for permutations.

$${}_7P_4 = \frac{7!}{(7-4)!} = \frac{7!}{3!}$$

n = 7 and r = 4.

$$= \frac{7 \cdot 6 \cdot 5 \cdot 4 \cdot \cancel{3} \cdot \cancel{2} \cdot \cancel{1}}{\cancel{3} \cdot \cancel{2} \cdot \cancel{1}}$$

A number divided by itself is 1, so you can divide out common factors in the numerator and denominator.

$$= 7 \cdot 6 \cdot 5 \cdot 4 = 840$$

There are 840 different ways Lee can choose to play the 4 CDs.

3. How many different ways can 9 people line up for a picture? **362,880**

The formula for combinations also involves factorials.

Combinations

FORMULA	The number of combinations of n things chosen r at a time: $_nC_r = \frac{n!}{r!(n-r)!}$.
EXAMPLE	A club will form a 3-person committee from a list of 8 people. How many ways can the club choose the 3 people? The position that each person takes does not matter, so this situation involves combinations. Think: There are 8 people, and the club will choose 3 of them. $_8C_3 = \frac{8!}{3!(8-3)!} = \frac{8!}{3!5!} = 56$

EXAMPLE 4 Finding Combinations

There are 11 different cereals for sale at a grocery store. How many different ways can a shopper select 4 different cereals?

The order in which the cereals are selected does not matter, so use the formula for combinations.

Method 1 Use the formula for combinations.

$$_{11}C_4 = \frac{11!}{4!(11-4)!} = \frac{11!}{4!7!} \quad n = 11 \text{ and } r = 4.$$

$$= \frac{11 \cdot 10 \cdot 9 \cdot 8 \cdot \cancel{7} \cdot \cancel{6} \cdot \cancel{5} \cdot \cancel{4} \cdot \cancel{3} \cdot \cancel{2} \cdot \cancel{1}}{(4 \cdot 3 \cdot 2 \cdot 1)(\cancel{7} \cdot \cancel{6} \cdot \cancel{5} \cdot \cancel{4} \cdot \cancel{3} \cdot \cancel{2} \cdot \cancel{1})}$$

$$= \frac{7920}{24} = 330$$

Method 2 Use the **nCr** function of a calculator.

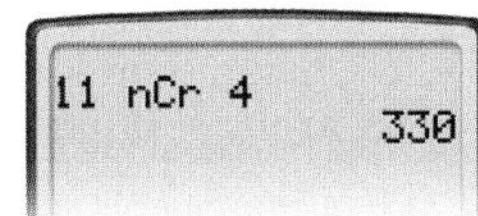

There are 330 different ways the shopper can choose 4 different cereals.

Helpful Hint

You can also use a calculator to find permutations. Look for the **nPr** function on your calculator.

4. A basketball team has 12 members who can play any position. How many different ways can the coach choose 5 starting players? **792**

THINK AND DISCUSS

1. Explain how to find $\frac{10!}{9!}$ without a calculator.

2. GET ORGANIZED Copy and complete the graphic organizer.

	Fundamental Counting Principle	Permutation	Combination
When to Use			
Formula			

COMMON ERROR ALERT

Students might mistakenly believe that factorials can be multiplied while in factorial form. That is, they might think that $(2!)(3!) = 6!$. Write out the factorials to show this is not true.

$(2!)(3!) = (2 \cdot 1) \cdot (3 \cdot 2 \cdot 1) = 12$
$6! = 6 \cdot 5 \cdot 4 \cdot 3 \cdot 2 \cdot 1 = 720$

Power Presentations with PowerPoint®

Additional Examples

Example 4

Four people need to be selected from a class of 15 to help clean up the campus. How many different ways can the 4 people be chosen? 1365

INTERVENTION
Questioning Strategies

EXAMPLE 4

- How are the formulas for combinations and permutations similar? How are they different?

Teaching Tip **Critical Thinking** Both $_5P_1$ and $_5C_1$ equal 5. Discuss with students that this is true because order is not relevant when choosing only 1 item.

3 Close

Summarize

Have students state whether each situation involves combinations or permutations.

Choose 3 types of appetizers from a tray of 8. combinations

Choose 4 books out of 8 to arrange on a bookshelf. permutations

Choose 2 people out of 6 to be the secretary and the treasurer. permutations

ONGOING ASSESSMENT and INTERVENTION

***Diagnose Before* the Lesson**
10-8 Warm Up, TE p. 760

***Monitor During* the Lesson**
Check It Out! Exercises, SE pp. 760–763
Questioning Strategies, TE pp. 761–763

***Assess After* the Lesson**
10-8 Lesson Quiz, TE p. 767
Alternative Assessment, TE p. 767

Answers to *Think and Discuss*

1. Writing the expression as $\frac{10 \cdot 9 \cdot 8 \cdot 7 \cdot 6 \cdot 5 \cdot 4 \cdot 3 \cdot 2 \cdot 1}{9 \cdot 8 \cdot 7 \cdot 6 \cdot 5 \cdot 4 \cdot 3 \cdot 2 \cdot 1}$ shows that it equals 10.
2. See p. A9.

10-8 Exercises

Assignment Guide

Assign *Guided Practice* exercises as necessary.

If you finished Examples **1–2**
Basic 12–15, 20
Average 12–15, 20
Advanced 12–15, 20, 30

If you finished Examples **1–4**
Basic 12–20, 24–29, 36–42
Average 12–29, 34, 36–42
Advanced 12–20 even, 21–42

Homework Quick Check
Quickly check key concepts.
Exercises: 12, 14, 16, 18, 20

State Resources

go.hrw.com
State Resources Online
KEYWORD: MA7 Resources

10-8 Exercises

go.hrw.com
Homework Help Online
KEYWORD: MA7 10-8
Parent Resources Online
KEYWORD: MA7 Parent

GUIDED PRACTICE

1. **Vocabulary** A ___?___ is an arrangement of outcomes in which the order does not matter. (*compound event, permutation,* or *combination*) **combination**

SEE EXAMPLE 1 p. 760

2. The menu for a restaurant is shown. How many different meals with one salad, one soup, one entree, and one dessert are possible? **72**

3. You have 4 colors of wrapping paper and 2 kinds of ribbon. How many different ways are there to use one color of paper and one type of ribbon to wrap a package? **8**

SEE EXAMPLE 2 p. 761

Tell whether each situation involves combinations or permutations. Then give the number of possible outcomes.

4. How many different ways can 4 people be seated in a row of 4 seats? **perm.; 24**
5. How many different kinds of punch can be made from 2 of the following: cranberry juice, apple juice, orange juice, and grape juice? **comb.; 6**

SEE EXAMPLE 3 p. 762

6. An airport identification code is made up of three letters, like the examples shown. How many different airport identification codes are possible? (Assume any letter can be repeated and can appear in any position.) **17,576**

Albuquerque International Airport, New Mexico

Dallas/Fort Worth International Airport, Texas

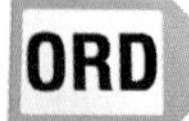

John F. Kennedy International Airport, New York

LAX
Los Angeles International Airport, California

ORD
O'Hare International Airport, Illinois

7. A manager is scheduling interviews for job applicants. She has 8 time slots and 6 applicants to interview. How many different interview schedules are possible? **20,160**
8. An e-mail server password must be 6 different lowercase letters. How many different e-mail server passwords are possible? **165,765,600**

SEE EXAMPLE 4 p. 763

9. Francine is deciding which after-school clubs to join. She has time to participate in 3. How many different ways can Francine choose which 3 clubs to join? **35**

Join a Club!
Science Club
Math Club
Drama Club
Dance Club
Chess Club
Spanish Club
Student Government

10. Laura is making gift baskets. Each basket has 2 gifts, and she has 5 gifts to choose from. How many different gift baskets can Laura make? **10**
11. How many different ways can a contest judge select 5 finalists from 20 contestants? **15,504**

PRACTICE AND PROBLEM SOLVING

Independent Practice

For Exercises	See Example
12–13	1
14–15	2
16–17	3
18–19	4

Extra Practice

Skills Practice p. S23
Application Practice p. S37

12. Maria looks in her closet and exclaims, "I have nothing to wear!" How many different outfits of one shirt, one pair of shorts, and one pair of sandals are possible using the items shown? **30**

13. When a customer buys tickets for a concert, the ticket office assigns a confirmation code that is made up of 2 lowercase consonants, followed by a 3-digit number from 000 to 999. A letter or digit may be repeated. How many different confirmation codes are possible? **441,000**

For Exercises 14 and 15, tell whether each situation involves combinations or permutations. Then give the number of possible outcomes.

14. A team of archeologists divides a dig site into 3 areas. They dig one area at a time. How many different ways can they order the 3 areas? **perm.; 6**
15. To decide which team will lead the class discussion, a teacher writes the names of 5 students on slips of paper and puts them in a hat. Then she draws 2 names. How many teams of two are possible? **comb.; 10**
16. The code for a bicycle lock is made up of 4 digits from 0 through 9. How many different codes are possible? **10,000**
17. A television station has 5 different commercials to play during the news. In how many different ways can they order the commercials? **120**

LINK

History

Telephone "numbers" used to be made up of two letters and several digits. Calls were made by speaking the telephone number to a central operator, who then connected the call by hand.

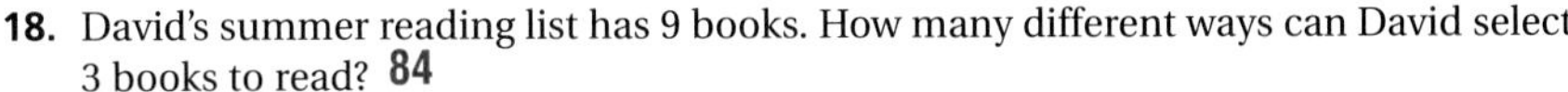

18. David's summer reading list has 9 books. How many different ways can David select 3 books to read? **84**
19. Steve draws a hand of 7 cards from a deck of 52 different cards. How many different hands are possible? **133,784,560**
20. **History** The North American Numbering Plan (NANP) was first used in 1947. It is a system for assigning telephone numbers and area codes.
    a. Originally, the NANP allowed only 3-digit area codes whose first digit was not 0 or 1, and whose second digit was always 0 or 1. How many different area codes were possible under this system? **160**
    b. In 1995, because of increased demand, the NANP removed the restriction that the second digit of the area code must be 0 or 1. How many more area codes did this make possible? **640**
21. **Critical Thinking** For $n = 6$ and $r = 2$, which is larger: ${}_nP_r$ or ${}_nC_r$? Explain why this is true.
22. **Write About It** Explain why a "combination lock" should be called a "permutation lock."
23. **Write About It** You roll a number cube 6 times. Explain how to determine the number of possible outcomes. Would a tree diagram be useful in solving this problem? Explain why or why not.

22. The lock's code is a permutation of numbers because the order of the numbers matters.

Teaching Tip

Social Studies Link For **Exercise 20,** you may wish to point out to students that according to the NANP (North American Numbering Plan), not all area code possibilities are available for use as area codes. Area codes with 11 as the last two digits are designated as service codes. Examples are 411 (information) and 911 (emergency).

Answers

21. ${}_nP_r$ is larger. This is true because the permutations take the order of the objects into account, so there are more possible arrangements.

23. The number of possible outcomes is 6^6. A tree diagram would not be useful because it would be too large to be practical.

10-8 PRACTICE A

10-8 PRACTICE C

10-8 PRACTICE B

1. A code consists of 3 letters and then 3 digits. Any of the letters and numbers can be repeated. How many different codes are there? 17,576,000
2. A restaurant is having a breakfast special. The choices are shown in the table. How many different breakfasts with one of each item are possible? 24

Eggs	Meat	Bread	Juice
fried	bacon	biscuits	apple
scrambled	sausage	toast	orange
	ham		

3. A movie on DVD comes with different viewing options as shown in the table. How many different ways can the movie be watched? 12

Audio	Commentary	Language
on	on	English
off	off	Spanish
		French

Write C for combinations or P for permutations. Then answer the question.

4. A coach must pick 5 players out of 30 to go on a trip. How many ways can the 5 players be chosen? C; 142,506
5. Jenn has 5 types of flowers in her garden. How many ways can she make a bouquet consisting of 2 types of flowers? C; 10
6. How many different ways can the letters in MUSIC be arranged? P; 120
7. A grocery store carries 15 different types of cereals. Only 4 of the cereals can be displayed on the middle shelf. How many different ways can the 4 cereals be displayed? P; 32,760

Answer each question.

8. A science fair awards prizes to the first, second and third place winners. There are 48 people entered in the science fair. How many ways can the winners be selected? 103,776
9. A 3-digit computer password consists only of odd numbers that cannot be repeated. How many different 3-digit passwords are possible? 60
10. In a lottery, 6 different numbers are selected from a set of 50 numbers. A winner can have the numbers in any order. How many sets of winning numbers are there? 15,890,700
11. A band competition awards prizes to the top 3 schools. If 12 schools are entered, how many ways can 3 schools be chosen? 220

MULTI-STEP TEST PREP **Exercise 24** involves finding the number of possible outcomes for an arrangement of numbers. This exercise prepares students for the Multi-Step Test Prep on page 768.

TEST PREP DOCTOR + Students who chose **C** or **D** in **Exercise 26** did not recognize that the situation involves permutations. Students who chose **A** did not recognize that the situation does not involve choosing 4 things from a group of 10.

Exercise 29 asks for the number of ways Maria can choose the elements. It does not ask for the number of ways in which she can present them (which would involve order, and therefore permutations).

Answers

42. The sample space is too small.

MULTI-STEP TEST PREP

24. This problem will prepare you for the Multi-Step Test Prep on page 768.
    Many states have lotteries to raise money. In one lottery, the players choose 6 different numbers from the numbers 1–49. The order of the numbers does not matter.
    a. How many combinations are there? **13,983,816**
    b. The probability that your first number is on the winning ticket is $\frac{6}{49}$. The probability that your second number matches is $\frac{5}{48}$. The probabilities of the third, fourth, fifth, and sixth numbers matching are $\frac{4}{47}$, $\frac{3}{46}$, $\frac{2}{45}$, and $\frac{1}{44}$. The product of these probabilities is the probability of winning the lottery with one ticket. Find that probability. How does it relate to the number of combinations shown in part **a**? $\frac{1}{13,983,816}$**; the prob. is the reciprocal of the number of combinations.**

25. **Technology** Nancy's password for her online banking program is made up of 6 letters. It does not matter whether the letters are uppercase or lowercase and any letter may be repeated.
    a. What is the probability of someone correctly guessing Nancy's password? $\frac{1}{308,915,776}$
    b. How many hours would it take for someone to try all the possible passwords if the person could guess one password each second? **about 85,810 h**
    c. **Write About It** Explain why you think some Internet companies require that passwords be at least 6 characters long.
    If a password is at least 6 characters long it is not feasible for a person to guess the password by trying various permutations.

TEST PREP
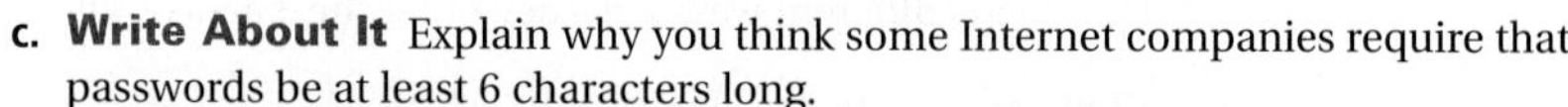

26. Which situation is best modeled by the expression ${}_{10}C_4$?
    Ⓐ Lisa's salon offers 10 kinds of shampoo and 4 kinds of conditioner. How many different ways can she shampoo and condition a client's hair?
    Ⓑ Sara has a box of 10 colored pencils. How many different ways can she choose 4 colored pencils from the box? (circled)
    Ⓒ A personal identification number (PIN) is a 4-digit number. Digits can be repeated in a PIN. How many different PINs are possible?
    Ⓓ There are 10 chairs placed around a table. How many different ways can 4 people seat themselves around the table?

27. Which of the following is equal to 4!?
    Ⓕ $10! - 6!$ Ⓖ $\frac{8!}{2!}$ Ⓗ $(2!)(2!)$ Ⓙ $\frac{24!}{23!}$ (circled)

28. Which table represents the values of ${}_xC_4$ for the given values of x?

Ⓐ

x	${}_xC_4$
5	5
6	30
7	210
8	1680

Ⓑ

x	${}_xC_4$
5	120
6	360
7	840
8	1680

Ⓒ (circled)

x	${}_xC_4$
5	5
6	15
7	35
8	70

Ⓓ

x	${}_xC_4$
5	30
6	90
7	210
8	240

29. **Short Response** The periodic table of the elements is a chart listing 117 different elements. Maria must give a presentation on 3 different elements from the periodic table. How many ways can she choose which elements to present? Show your work and explain each step. **260,130; check students' work.**

10-8 READING STRATEGIES

This concept map will help you understand combinations and permutations.

Definition	**Formula**	**Example**
A *combination* is a grouping of outcomes in which the order does not matter.	The number of *combinations* of n things chosen r at a time is found using ${}_nC_r = \frac{n!}{r!(n-r)!}$.	How many pairs can be made from a group of 6 people? (Jin and Tom are the same pair as Tom and Jin) ${}_6C_2 = \frac{6!}{2!(6-2)!} = \frac{720}{2(24)} = 15$
	Combinations	
Definition	**Permutations**	**Example**
A *permutation* is an arrangement of outcomes in which the order does matter.	**Formula** The number of *permutations* of n things chosen r at a time is found using ${}_nP_r = \frac{n!}{(n-r)!}$.	6 people are in a contest. How many ways can 1st and 2nd place be awarded? (Jin first and Tom second is different than Tom first and Jin second) ${}_6P_2 = \frac{6!}{(6-2)!} = \frac{720}{24} = 30$

Tell whether each situation involves combinations or permutations. Then find the number of possible outcomes.

1. For her birthday, Marianna may choose 3 DVDs from the 5 that her mother picked out. How many ways can Marianna choose her DVDs?
   combinations
   10
2. A box has 8 hats. A group of 5 children playing dress up each choose a hat from the box. How many ways can the children choose their hats?
   permutations
   6720
3. Six students tried out for 3 different roles in a school play. How many ways could the director fill the roles?
   permutations
   120
4. Fiona is going to order bunches of balloons for a party. In each bunch she wants 4 different colored balloons. The store offers 7 colors. How many ways could Fiona make one bunch?
   combinations
   35

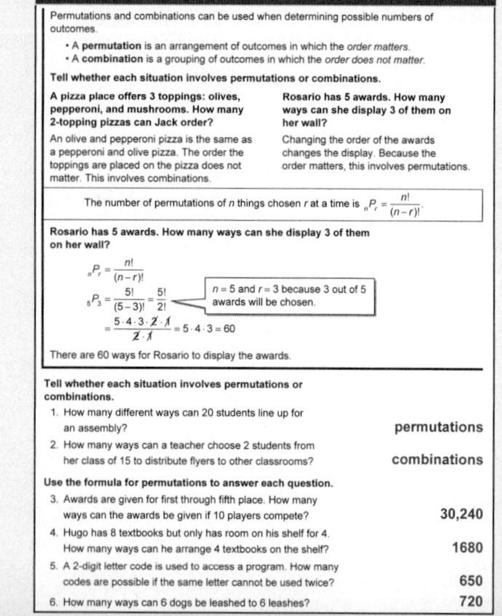
10-8 RETEACH

Permutations and combinations can be used when determining possible numbers of outcomes.

- A **permutation** is an arrangement of outcomes in which the *order matters.*
- A **combination** is a grouping of outcomes in which the *order does not matter.*

Tell whether each situation involves permutations or combinations.

A pizza place offers 3 toppings: olives, pepperoni, and mushrooms. How many 2-topping pizzas can Jack order?

An olive and pepperoni pizza is the same as a pepperoni and olive pizza. The order the toppings are placed on the pizza does not matter. This involves combinations.

Rosario has 5 awards. How many ways can she display 3 of them on her wall?

Changing the order of the awards changes the display. Because the order matters, this involves permutations.

The number of permutations of n things chosen r at a time is ${}_nP_r = \frac{n!}{(n-r)!}$.

Rosario has 5 awards. How many ways can she display 3 of them on her wall?

$${}_nP_r = \frac{n!}{(n-r)!}$$
$${}_5P_3 = \frac{5!}{(5-3)!} = \frac{5!}{2!}$$
$$= \frac{5 \cdot 4 \cdot 3 \cdot 2 \cdot 1}{2 \cdot 1} = 5 \cdot 4 \cdot 3 = 60$$

$n = 5$ and $r = 3$ because 3 out of 5 awards will be chosen.

There are 60 ways for Rosario to display the awards.

Tell whether each situation involves permutations or combinations.

1. How many different ways can 20 students line up for an assembly? **permutations**
2. How many ways can a teacher choose 2 students from her class of 15 to distribute flyers to other classrooms? **combinations**

Use the formula for permutations to answer each question.

3. Awards are given for first through fifth place. How many ways can the awards be given if 10 players compete? **30,240**
4. Hugo has 8 textbooks but only has room on his shelf for 4. How many ways can he arrange 4 textbooks on the shelf? **1680**
5. A 2-digit letter code is used to access a program. How many codes are possible if the same letter cannot be used twice? **650**
6. How many ways can 6 dogs be leashed to 6 leashes? **720**

CHALLENGE AND EXTEND

Simplify each expression.

30. $\frac{8!}{3!}$ **6720** **31.** $\frac{7!4!}{6!}$ **168** **32.** $\frac{{}_7P_5}{{}_7P_3}$ **12**

33. The chart shows the different toppings offered by a pizza shop.

a. How many different pizzas with 2 toppings are possible? **28**

b. How many different pizzas with 6 toppings are possible? **28**

c. What do you notice about your answers to parts **a** and **b**? Explain why you think this is.

33c. They are equal. This makes sense because choosing 2 toppings is equivalent to choosing the 6 that you don't want.

Pizza Ingredients	
•Extra Cheese	•Green Peppers
•Mushrooms	•Pepperoni
•Sausage	•Onions
•Pineapple	•Green Olives

34. Use the permutation and combination formulas you learned in this lesson.

a. What is the number of permutations when $n = r$? **$n!$**

b. What is the number of combinations when $n = r$? **1**

35. You roll a number cube six times in a row. What is the probability that you roll the numbers 1 through 6 in order? $\frac{1}{46,656}$

SPIRAL REVIEW

Simplify each expression. *(Lesson 1-7)*

36. $4.9m + 3.8 - 2.1m - 3.9$ **$2.8m - 0.1$** **37.** $4(2x - 1) + 9 - 3x$ **$5x + 5$** **38.** $3a^2 - 5a - 7a^2$ **$-4a^2 - 5a$**

Identify the independent and dependent variables. Write an equation in function notation for each situation. *(Lesson 4-3)*

39. A bathtub fills at a rate of 15 gallons per minute.

40. About 5 seeds should be planted per square inch.

41. A snow removal company charges a contract fee of \$300 plus \$80 per hour.

42. Five people responded that they spend the following amounts for haircuts during one year: \$150, \$120, \$135, \$0, and \$145. A researcher concluded that "people spend an average of \$110 per year on haircuts." Why is this statistic misleading? *(Lesson 10-4)*

39. ind.: minutes; dep.: volume of water in tub; $f(x) = 15x$

40. ind.: square inches; dep.: seeds; $f(x) = 5x$

41. ind.: hours; dep.: total fee; $f(x) = 300 + 80x$

Career Path

go.hrw.com
Career Resources Online
KEYWORD: MA7 Career

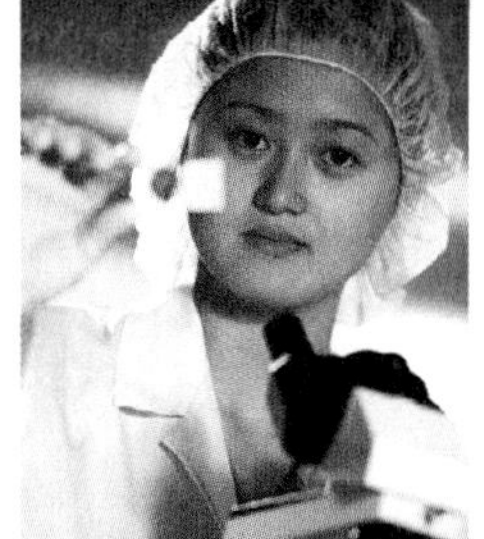

Erika Sheehan
Biostatistics major

Q: What math classes did you take in high school?

A: Algebra, Geometry, Precalculus, Calculus

Q: What math classes have you taken in college?

A: Statistics, Linear Algebra, Problem Solving

Q: What do Biostatisticians do?

A: Biostatisticians apply statistical methods to research scientific questions relating to health and medicine.

Q: What are your plans for the future?

A: After graduating, I would like to get a job at a pharmaceutical company testing the safety and effectiveness of new medicines.

Journal

Have students use a real-life example to explain why a situation involving combinations will always have fewer possibilities than a situation involving permutations.

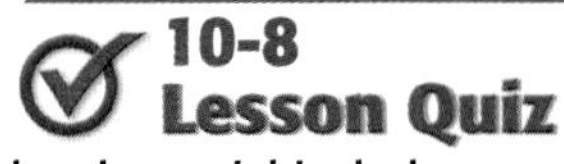

ALTERNATIVE ASSESSMENT

Have students write and solve a problem involving permutations in which 3 objects are chosen from a group of 10. Then have them do the same for a problem involving combinations.

Power Presentations with PowerPoint®

10-8 Lesson Quiz

1. A lunch special includes one main item, one side, and one drink.

Main Item	Side	Drink
Hamburger	Chips	Juice
Hot dog	Apple	Water
Pizza	Crackers	Milk
Salad		

How many different meals can you choose? 36

For Problems 2–3, tell whether each situation involves combinations or permutations. Then give the number of possible outcomes.

2. When ordering a pizza, you can choose 2 toppings from the following: mushrooms, olives, pepperoni, pineapple, and sausage. How many different types of pizza can you order? combinations; 10

3. Three people in a writing contest are competing for first, second and third prize. How many ways can the 3 people be chosen? permutations; 6

4. You are ordering a triple-scoop ice-cream cone. There are 18 flavors to choose from and you don't care which flavor is on the top, middle, or bottom. How many different ways can you select a triple-scoop ice-cream cone? 816

5. An art gallery has 12 paintings in storage. They have room to display 4 of them, with each painting in a different room. How many possible ways can they display the 4 additional paintings? 11,880

Also available on transparency

10-8 PROBLEM SOLVING

Write the correct answer.

1. In 1963, the United States Postal Service started using ZIP (Zone Improvement Plan) codes. Each ZIP code is a sequence of five digits. How many different U.S. ZIP codes are possible?

100,000

2. In the early 1970's, Canada Post started using six-character postal codes. Each postal code uses three letters and three digits in an alternating pattern. How many different Canadian postal codes are possible?

17,576,000

3. A band's new album contains 12 songs. The record company decides to promote the album at a music festival by giving away CD samplers that contain 3 songs from the album.
   a. Does this situation involve combinations or permutations? Explain.
   permutations; the tracks on a CD are in a specific order.
   b. How many different ways can the band select songs for the sampler?
   1320

4. A 12-person jury is being selected for a court trial. After lengthy interviews, the attorney's have narrowed the candidates down to 14 people that they both think are fair and unbiased.
   a. Does this situation involve combinations or permutations? Explain.
   combinations; the members of a jury have no particular order.
   b. How many different ways can the attorneys select the jury?
   91

Select the best answer.

5. Myra works Monday to Thursday as a waitress. She has 6 short-sleeve shirts that are appropriate for her to wear as part of her uniform. If she doesn't wear the same shirt twice, how many different ways can she wear her shirts during a 4-day work week?

A 15 **C** 360
B 24 D 720

6. At Cold Marble Ice Cream, you create your own ice cream flavor by choosing from a list of 10 "add-ins" that can be mixed into vanilla ice-cream. If you can pick one add-in, any combination of two add-ins, or any combination of three add-ins, how many different flavors are possible?

F 120 H 210
G 175 J 820

10-8 CHALLENGE

Three siblings, Aliyah, Bentley, and Chris, go out for an evening with their parents. Use permutations to answer these questions.

1. The family first goes out for dinner. A large booth is available. Mom and Dad sit on one side and the kids sit on the other side. How many different arrangements of the siblings are there?

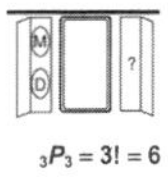

$_3P_3 = 3! = 6$

2. After dinner, the family goes to an ice cream shop for dessert. The shop has little round tables, so Mom and Dad sit at one table and the siblings sit at another. How many different arrangements of the siblings are there?

Note: When objects are arranged in a circle, any arrangement that is merely a rotation of another is considered to be the same. For example, all three of the arrangements at right are the same.

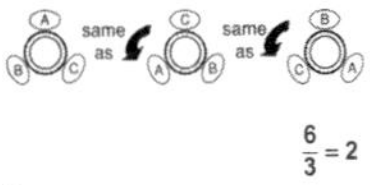

$\frac{6}{3} = 2$

3. In Lesson 10-8, you learned that the number of *linear* permutations (arrangements in a line) of n things chosen r at a time is represented by $_nP_r$. If those r items are arranged in a circle, what expression represents the number of *circular* permutations?

$\frac{_nP_r}{r}$

4. The family then goes to the mall, where Mom buys a bracelet (without a clasp) and three charms with her children's names on them. How many different ways can Mom hang the charms on her bracelet?

Note: When objects are arranged in a ring that can be flipped upside down, any arrangement that is a mirror reflection of another is considered to be the same arrangement. But, remember that a ring is also a circle!

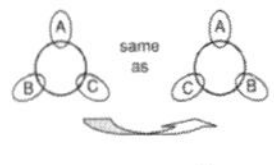

$\frac{6}{2 \cdot 3} = 1$

5. If the number of linear permutations of n things chosen r at a time is represented by $_nP_r$, what expression represents the number of *ring* permutations of those r items?

$\frac{_nP_r}{2 \cdot r}$

Organizer

Objective: Assess students' ability to apply concepts and skills from Lessons 10-5 through 10-8 in a real-world format.

Resources

 ***Algebra I Assessments***

www.mathtekstoolkit.org

Problem	Text Reference
1	Lesson 10-7
2	Lesson 10-6
3	Lesson 10-6
4	Lesson 10-8

State Resources

MULTI-STEP TEST PREP

Probability

The Games People Play Probability is involved in most board and card games.

1. There are 108 cards in a deck for the game Uno. The table shows the number of each type of card found in an Uno deck. What is the probability of randomly selecting a red card from a complete deck of Uno cards? $\frac{25}{108}$

Type of Card	Number in Deck
Blue cards, 0–9	19
Green cards, 0–9	19
Red cards, 0–9	19
Yellow cards, 0–9	19
Draw Two	8 (2 in each color)
Reverse	8 (2 in each color)
Skip	8 (2 in each color)
Wild	4
Wild Draw Four	4

2. Robert is playing Monopoly. He starts the game on the GO space. He wants to avoid the Income Tax space, which he will land on if he rolls a 4 with the two dice. What is the probability that he will land on the Income Tax space? $\frac{1}{12}$
3. In the game Battleship, each player chooses locations for small ships on a 10-by-10 grid. Each player guesses grid spaces to try to locate the other player's ships. A correct guess equals a hit, and by hitting each space occupied by a ship, the ship is sunk. The battleship piece occupies four grid spaces. What is the probability that a player randomly guesses a correct grid space and hits the other player's battleship? $\frac{1}{25}$
4. In the game Set, each card can be characterized in four ways. Cards are either red, green, or purple. The design on each card is either an oval, a squiggle, or a diamond. There are either one, two, or three of the design on the card. The designs are either solid, empty, or striped. How many different cards are possible? **81**

INTERVENTION

Scaffolding Questions

1. How many possible outcomes are there when rolling 2 dice? 36 How many ways can Robert roll a total of 4? 3
2. How many red cards are in a complete deck? 26
3. How many groups of 4 grid spaces are in a straight line? 140
4. How could you draw a diagram to help you find the number of possible cards? Draw a tree diagram.

Extension

In Battleship, the submarine ship piece occupies 3 grid spaces. What is the probability that a player randomly guesses a correct grid space and hits the other player's submarine? $\frac{3}{100}$

Quiz for Lessons 10-5 Through 10-8

10-5 Experimental Probability

An experiment consists of pushing the random select button on a CD player for a disc with five tracks. Use the results in the table to find the experimental probability of each event.

Outcome	Frequency
Track 1	4
Track 2	6
Track 3	2
Track 4	5
Track 5	3

1. Selecting track 4 **25%**
2. Selecting track 3 **10%**
3. Not selecting track 2 **70%**
4. Selecting an odd numbered track **45%**
5. Selecting one of the first 3 tracks **60%**
6. Ms. Bleakman checks 32 papers and finds 2 with no name. What is the experimental probability that a paper chosen at random will have no name? Ms. Bleakman has the papers of 176 students. Predict the number of papers she will find with no name. **6.25%; 11 papers**

10-6 Theoretical Probability

Find the theoretical probability of each outcome.

7. Landing on an odd number when spinning a spinner with 4 equal spaces marked 1, 4, 6, 8 **25%**
8. Randomly selecting a vowel from all the letters in the word VOWELS $\frac{1}{3}$
9. Picking a red marble out of a bag with 3 green, 5 blue, 2 red, and 6 yellow marbles **12.5%**
10. The probability of winning a certain prize is 5%. What are the odds of winning the prize? **1:19**
11. The odds of choosing a winning ticket are 2:8. What is the probability of choosing a winning ticket? **20%**
12. The probability of snow is 70%. What are the odds of it not snowing? **3:7**

10-7 Independent and Dependent Events

13. A physical education class has 12 boys and 18 girls. Each day, the teacher randomly selects a team captain. Assume that no student is absent. What is the probability that the team captain is a girl two days in a row? **36%**
14. After reading to a kindergarten class at the library, Tobey gives out stickers. He has 9 zoo animal stickers and 16 scratch-n-sniff stickers. If Tobey gives the stickers out at random, what is the probability that the first child gets a scratch-n-sniff sticker and the second child gets a zoo animal sticker? **24%**

10-8 Combinations and Permutations

15. Luisa is choosing a line-up of CDs to play from beginning to end at her party. She has 12 CDs from which to choose and time to play only 5. How many ways are there for Luisa to arrange the musical line-up? **95,040**
16. Gavin is shopping for school clothes with his father. After trying on several shirts, Gavin has identified 8 shirts that he likes. His father says Gavin must narrow it down to 5 shirts. How many ways can Gavin choose 5 shirts from the 8 he likes? **56**

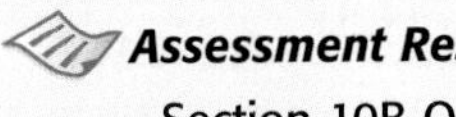

SECTION 10B

Organizer

Objective: Assess students' mastery of concepts and skills in Lessons 10-5 through 10-8.

Resources

Assessment Resources
Section 10B Quiz

Teacher One Stop™
Test & Practice Generator

INTERVENTION

Resources

Ready to Go On? Intervention and Enrichment **Worksheets**

Ready to Go On? **CD-ROM**

Ready to Go On? **Online**

my.hrw.com

READY TO GO ON? Diagnose and Prescribe

Ready to Go On? Intervention	*Ready to Go On? Intervention,* Section 10B — Worksheets	CD-ROM	Online
Lesson 10-5	10-5 Intervention	Activity 10-5	Diagnose and Prescribe Online
Lesson 10-6	10-6 Intervention	Activity 10-6	
Lesson 10-7	10-7 Intervention	Activity 10-7	
Lesson 10-8	10-8 Intervention	Activity 10-8	

Ready to Go On? Enrichment, **Section 10B**
Worksheets
CD-ROM
Online

CHAPTER **10** # Organizer

Pacing: Traditional 1 day
Block $\frac{1}{2}$ day

Objectives: Organize data in a matrix.

Add and subtract matrices and multiply a matrix by a scalar.

Online Edition
Tutorial Videos

Countdown Week 24

Using the Extension

In Chapter 10, students learn various ways to organize data. In this extension, students learn that data displayed in a table can also be displayed in a matrix, allowing for ease of basic math operations.

Power Presentations with PowerPoint®

Additional Examples

Example 1

The table shows the number of yearbooks sold to students at two high schools. Arrange the data in a matrix. Give the dimensions of the matrix. 2 × 4

	9th	10th	11th	12th
West Hills	98	108	110	121
College Park	86	95	105	132

$$\begin{array}{c} \\ WH \\ CP \end{array}\begin{array}{c} \begin{array}{cccc} 9th & 10th & 11th & 12th \end{array} \\ \begin{bmatrix} 98 & 108 & 110 & 121 \\ 86 & 95 & 105 & 132 \end{bmatrix} \end{array}$$

State Resources

EXTENSION

Matrices

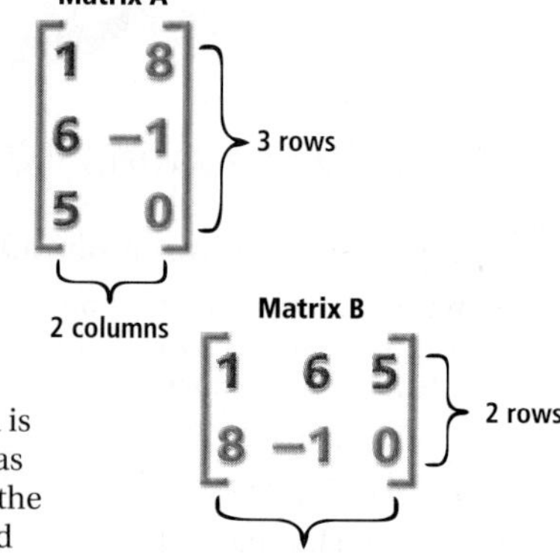

Objectives
Organize data in a matrix.
Add and subtract matrices and multiply a matrix by a scalar.

Vocabulary
matrix
entry
scalar

A **matrix** is a rectangular arrangement of numbers in rows and columns. Each number in the matrix is called an **entry**.

Matrices are described by the number of rows and columns in the matrix. Matrix A is called a 3 × 2 (3 by 2) matrix because it has 3 rows and 2 columns. Matrix B contains the same data, but it is arranged in 2 rows and 3 columns, so it is called a 2 × 3 (2 by 3) matrix.

EXAMPLE 1 **Organizing Data in a Matrix**

The table shows the number of members in each section of two marching bands. Arrange the data in a matrix. Give the dimensions of the matrix.

Table

	Percussion	Brass	Woodwinds
Northmount High	14	23	16
Western High	19	36	41

Matrix

$$\begin{array}{c} \\ \text{North} \\ \text{West} \end{array}\begin{array}{c} \begin{array}{ccc} P & B & W \end{array} \\ \begin{bmatrix} 14 & 23 & 16 \\ 19 & 36 & 41 \end{bmatrix} \end{array}$$

The matrix has 2 rows and 3 columns, so its dimensions are 2 × 3.

1. $\begin{array}{c} \\ P \\ B \\ W \end{array}\begin{array}{c} \begin{array}{cc} \text{North} & \text{West} \end{array} \\ \begin{bmatrix} 14 & 19 \\ 23 & 36 \\ 16 & 41 \end{bmatrix} \end{array}$

CHECK IT OUT! **1.** Use the information above to make a 3 × 2 matrix.

If two matrices have the same dimensions, they can be added or subtracted by finding the sum or difference of the corresponding entries.

EXAMPLE 2 **Adding and Subtracting Matrices**

The matrices show the enrollment by grade level at two high schools during the same year.

Washington

$$\begin{array}{c} \\ 10th \\ 11th \\ 12th \end{array}\begin{array}{c} \begin{array}{cc} \text{Boys} & \text{Girls} \end{array} \\ \begin{bmatrix} 141 & 148 \\ 132 & 115 \\ 105 & 128 \end{bmatrix} \end{array}$$

Central

$$\begin{array}{c} \\ 10th \\ 11th \\ 12th \end{array}\begin{array}{c} \begin{array}{cc} \text{Boys} & \text{Girls} \end{array} \\ \begin{bmatrix} 139 & 127 \\ 141 & 136 \\ 112 & 98 \end{bmatrix} \end{array}$$

A Add the two matrices to find the total enrollment of girls in the tenth grade.

Total

$$\begin{bmatrix} 141 & 148 \\ 132 & 115 \\ 105 & 128 \end{bmatrix} + \begin{bmatrix} 139 & 127 \\ 141 & 136 \\ 112 & 98 \end{bmatrix} = \begin{bmatrix} 141+139 & 148+127 \\ 132+141 & 115+136 \\ 105+112 & 128+98 \end{bmatrix} = \begin{array}{c} \\ 10th \\ 11th \\ 12th \end{array}\begin{array}{c} \begin{array}{cc} \text{Boys} & \text{Girls} \end{array} \\ \begin{bmatrix} 280 & 275 \\ 273 & 251 \\ 217 & 226 \end{bmatrix} \end{array}$$

The total enrollment of girls in the tenth grade was 275.

1 Introduce

Motivate

Have students organize the following information in a table:

During the fall, the Art Club raised $500 and the Music Club raised $350. During the winter, the Music Club raised $250 and the Art Club raised $100. During the spring, the Art Club raised $200 while the Music Club raised $275. Possible answer:

	Fall	Winter	Spring
Art	$500	$100	$200
Music	$350	$250	$275

2 Teach

Guided Instruction

Clarify the difference between rows and columns, stressing that a 2 × 4 matrix is not the same as a 4 × 2 matrix. Show how data displayed in a table can be arranged into a matrix. Stress that matrices can be added or subtracted only when they have the same dimensions.

Communicating Math A matrix with the same number of rows and columns is called a square matrix. A 3 by 3 matrix can be called a square matrix of order 3.

The matrices show the enrollment by grade level at two high schools during the same year.

B Subtract the two matrices to find how many more eleventh-grade boys were enrolled at Washington High than at Central High.

Washington

	Boys	Girls
10th	141	148
11th	141	136
12th	112	128

Central

	Boys	Girls
10th	139	127
11th	132	115
12th	105	98

$$\begin{bmatrix} 141 & 148 \\ 141 & 136 \\ 112 & 128 \end{bmatrix} - \begin{bmatrix} 139 & 127 \\ 132 & 115 \\ 105 & 98 \end{bmatrix} = \begin{bmatrix} 141-139 & 148-127 \\ 141-132 & 136-115 \\ 112-105 & 128-98 \end{bmatrix} = \begin{matrix} 10\text{th} \\ 11\text{th} \\ 12\text{th} \end{matrix}\begin{bmatrix} 2 & 21 \\ 9 & 21 \\ 7 & 30 \end{bmatrix}$$

Total (Boys, Girls)

There were 9 more eleventh-grade boys enrolled at Washington High than at Central High.

Use the information above to answer the following.

2a. What was the total enrollment of boys in the twelfth grade that year? **217**

2b. How many more tenth-grade girls were enrolled at Washington High than at Central High that year? **21**

To multiply a matrix by a number, multiply each entry in the matrix by the number. This kind of multiplication is called *scalar* multiplication. The **scalar** is the number by which the matrix is multiplied.

EXAMPLE 3 Scalar Multiplication of a Matrix

The matrix shows the number of field goals (FG) and touchdowns (TD) scored by a football team in each quarter of last week's game. This week they scored twice as many field goals and touchdowns in each quarter of the game. Multiply the matrix by 2 to show the number of scores from this week's game.

Points per Quarter

	1st	2nd	3rd	4th
FG	1	0	2	1
TD	0	0	1	1

$$2\begin{bmatrix} 1 & 0 & 2 & 1 \\ 0 & 0 & 1 & 1 \end{bmatrix} = \begin{bmatrix} 2(1) & 2(0) & 2(2) & 2(1) \\ 2(0) & 2(0) & 2(1) & 2(1) \end{bmatrix}$$

Multiply each entry in the matrix by the scalar 2.

Points per Quarter

	1st	2nd	3rd	4th
FG	2	0	4	2
TD	0	0	2	2

3. The matrix shows the number of short sleeve and long sleeve T-shirts a store has in its inventory. A second store has 3 times as many shirts in inventory. How many of each shirt and size does the second store have in its inventory?

Inventory

	Short sleeve	Long sleeve
Small	42	52
Medium	76	43
Large	19	26

3.

	Short sleeve	Long sleeve
Small	126	156
Medium	228	129
Large	57	78

Power Presentations with PowerPoint®

Additional Examples

Example 2

The matrices show the sales, in thousands of dollars, of two companies for the first three months of each year.

Year 1

	Jan	Feb	Mar
A	75	70	89
B	46	55	97

Year 2

	Jan	Feb	Mar
A	58	62	76
B	35	48	82

A. Add the two matrices to find company A's total sales, in thousands of dollars, for March. $165,000

B. Subtract the two matrices to find by how many thousands of dollars February's sales declined for company B in year 2. $7000

Example 3

The matrices show the ticket prices by age at two movie theaters. Ticket prices are going to increase by 25%. Multiply the matrix by 1.25 to show the new ticket prices.

	Royal	Cove
Adult	7.00	8.00
Child	5.00	6.00
Senior	4.00	5.00

	Royal	Cove
Adult	8.75	10.00
Child	6.25	7.50
Senior	5.00	6.25

Kinesthetic Break students into groups of six and have each group arrange themselves into a 1×6, 2×3, 3×2, and 6×1 matrix. Alter the group sizes and dimensions as class size permits.

3 Close

Summarize

Remind students that when adding and subtracting matrices, they must add or subtract every corresponding entry in the two matrices. Similarly, with scalar multiplication, every entry in the matrix is multiplied by the given number. Caution students that two matrices cannot be multiplied the way they are added or subtracted. It is a more complex process that they will learn in a later algebra course.

INTERVENTION

Questioning Strategies

EXAMPLE 1

- In an $m \times n$ matrix, what does m represent?

EXAMPLE 2

- Is matrix addition commutative? Is matrix subtraction commutative? Explain.

EXAMPLE 3

- How is scalar multiplication similar to the Distributive Property?

Answers

1.
$$\begin{array}{r} \\ \text{Tetrahedron} \\ \text{Cube} \\ \text{Octahedron} \\ \text{Icosahedron} \end{array}\begin{array}{c} \begin{array}{ccc} \text{F} & \text{V} & \text{E} \end{array} \\ \begin{bmatrix} 4 & 4 & 6 \\ 6 & 8 & 12 \\ 8 & 6 & 12 \\ 20 & 12 & 30 \end{bmatrix} \end{array}$$

2.
$$\begin{array}{r} \\ \text{Europe} \\ \text{N. America} \\ \text{Asia} \\ \text{Africa} \end{array}\begin{array}{c} \text{Visitors} \\ \begin{bmatrix} 52{,}790 \\ 13{,}041 \\ 126{,}441 \\ 354 \end{bmatrix} \end{array}$$

3.
$$\begin{array}{r} \\ \text{Johnson} \\ \text{Crabtree} \\ \text{Aguirre} \end{array}\begin{array}{c} \begin{array}{cc} \text{At bats} & \text{Hits} \end{array} \\ \begin{bmatrix} 69 & 22 \\ 108 & 31 \\ 47 & 13 \end{bmatrix} \end{array}$$

4.
$$\begin{array}{r} \\ \text{New Releases} \\ \text{Weekly Rentals} \end{array}\begin{array}{c} \begin{array}{ccc} \text{Comedy} & \text{Drama} & \text{Horror} \end{array} \\ \begin{bmatrix} 16 & 19 & 8 \\ 57 & 62 & 39 \end{bmatrix} \end{array}$$

10. Subtract the expenses matrix from the revenue matrix. The entries of the resulting matrix will show the profit for each product during each month. Then add the entries in each column to find the total profit for each product over the 2-month period.

EXTENSION

Exercises

Arrange the data in each table in a matrix.

1.

Polyhedra			
	Faces	Vertices	Edges
Tetrahedron	4	4	6
Cube	6	8	12
Octahedron	8	6	12
Icosahedron	20	12	30

2.

Tourism in Burma, 1998–99	
	Number of Visitors
From Europe	52,790
From N. America	13,041
From Asia	126,441
From Africa	354

3.

Batting Statistics		
	At Bats	Hits
Johnson	69	22
Crabtree	108	31
Aguirre	47	13

4.

Video Inventory			
	Comedy	Drama	Horror
New Releases	16	19	8
Weekly Rentals	57	62	39

Give the dimensions of each matrix.

5. $\begin{bmatrix} -6 \end{bmatrix}$ **1 × 1**

6. $\begin{bmatrix} -1 & 0 \\ 0 & -1 \end{bmatrix}$ **2 × 2**

7. $\begin{bmatrix} 9 & 11 & 7 & 6 \\ 2 & -3 & 4 & 6 \end{bmatrix}$ **2 × 4**

8. $\begin{bmatrix} 0 \\ 15 \\ 22 \end{bmatrix}$ **3 × 1**

9. $\begin{bmatrix} 2 & 1 & 1 \\ 1 & 2 & 1 \\ 1 & 1 & 2 \end{bmatrix}$ **3 × 3**

10. **Write About It** The matrices show the revenue and expenses, in millions of dollars, generated by the three different products that a company sells during two months of the year. Explain how to find the company's total profit for each of the products for those two months. (*Hint:* Profit is revenue minus expenses.)

$$\textbf{Revenue}\quad \begin{array}{r} \\ \text{Month 1} \\ \text{Month 2} \end{array}\begin{array}{c} \begin{array}{ccc} \text{A} & \text{B} & \text{C} \end{array} \\ \begin{bmatrix} 2.3 & 0.7 & 3.0 \\ 2.1 & 1.1 & 2.8 \end{bmatrix} \end{array} \qquad \textbf{Expenses}\quad \begin{array}{r} \\ \text{Month 1} \\ \text{Month 2} \end{array}\begin{array}{c} \begin{array}{ccc} \text{A} & \text{B} & \text{C} \end{array} \\ \begin{bmatrix} 1.8 & 1.6 & 2.1 \\ 1.9 & 1.2 & 2.0 \end{bmatrix} \end{array}$$

Add or subtract.

11. $\begin{bmatrix} -1 & 4 \\ -3 & 6 \end{bmatrix} + \begin{bmatrix} 4 & 6 \\ 2 & -4 \end{bmatrix}$ **$\begin{bmatrix} 3 & 10 \\ -1 & 2 \end{bmatrix}$**

12. $\begin{bmatrix} 5 & 7 & 3 \\ -4 & 6 & -2 \end{bmatrix} - \begin{bmatrix} 9 & 19 & 6 \\ -3 & 7 & 2 \end{bmatrix}$ **12.** **$\begin{bmatrix} -4 & -12 & -3 \\ -1 & -1 & -4 \end{bmatrix}$**

13. $\begin{bmatrix} 1.4 \\ -0.6 \end{bmatrix} - \begin{bmatrix} 2.8 \\ -1.3 \end{bmatrix}$ **$\begin{bmatrix} -1.4 \\ 0.7 \end{bmatrix}$**

14. $\begin{bmatrix} \frac{3}{5} & \frac{1}{3} & \frac{4}{5} \end{bmatrix} - \begin{bmatrix} \frac{1}{5} & \frac{5}{6} & \frac{3}{10} \end{bmatrix}$ **14.** **$\begin{bmatrix} \frac{2}{5} & -\frac{1}{2} & \frac{1}{2} \end{bmatrix}$**

15. **Hiking** The matrix shows the number of miles hiked on each day of a three-day hiking trip.

$$\begin{array}{r} \\ \text{Day 1} \\ \text{Day 2} \\ \text{Day 3} \end{array}\begin{array}{c} \text{Miles} \\ \begin{bmatrix} 10.2 \\ 18.6 \\ 4.3 \end{bmatrix} \end{array}$$

a. Use scalar multiplication to convert the distances to kilometers. Write your answer as a matrix. (*Hint:* A mile is about 1.6 kilometers.)

b. What is the total length of the hiking trip in kilometers? **52.96 km**

15a.
$$\begin{array}{r} \\ \textbf{Day 1} \\ \textbf{Day 2} \\ \textbf{Day 3} \end{array}\begin{array}{c} \textbf{km} \\ \begin{bmatrix} 16.32 \\ 29.76 \\ 6.88 \end{bmatrix} \end{array}$$

Multiply.

16. $6\begin{bmatrix}3 & 2\\ -2 & -9\end{bmatrix}$ $\begin{bmatrix}\mathbf{18} & \mathbf{12}\\ \mathbf{-12} & \mathbf{-54}\end{bmatrix}$

17. $-4\begin{bmatrix}1 & 0 & -4\\ 3 & -3 & 5\\ 0 & 6 & -1\end{bmatrix}$ $\begin{bmatrix}\mathbf{-4} & \mathbf{0} & \mathbf{16}\\ \mathbf{-12} & \mathbf{12} & \mathbf{-20}\\ \mathbf{0} & \mathbf{-24} & \mathbf{4}\end{bmatrix}$

18. $2.7\begin{bmatrix}1.9 & 2.7\\ -0.8 & -3.6\\ 1.4 & 4.2\end{bmatrix}$ $\begin{bmatrix}\mathbf{5.13} & \mathbf{7.29}\\ \mathbf{-2.16} & \mathbf{-9.72}\\ \mathbf{3.78} & \mathbf{11.34}\end{bmatrix}$

19. $-0.6\begin{bmatrix}8.2 & 10 & -2.8\end{bmatrix}$ $\begin{bmatrix}\mathbf{-4.92} & \mathbf{-6} & \mathbf{1.68}\end{bmatrix}$

20. $\frac{2}{3}\begin{bmatrix}\frac{1}{4} & -6\\ -4 & \frac{3}{2}\end{bmatrix}$ $\begin{bmatrix}\mathbf{\frac{1}{6}} & \mathbf{-4}\\ \mathbf{-\frac{8}{3}} & \mathbf{1}\end{bmatrix}$

21. $-2\frac{1}{2}\begin{bmatrix}-5 & 3 & \frac{4}{5}\\ \frac{1}{5} & -4 & 2\end{bmatrix}$ $\begin{bmatrix}\mathbf{12\frac{1}{2}} & \mathbf{-7\frac{1}{2}} & \mathbf{-2}\\ \mathbf{-\frac{1}{2}} & \mathbf{10} & \mathbf{-5}\end{bmatrix}$

22. Entertainment Two teams are competing in a scavenger hunt. Each item on the list is worth 1, 5, or 10 points. The matrix shows the number of items of each point value that was found by the two teams.

	Red team	Blue team
1-point	22	7
5-point	13	18
10-point	4	6

a. How many items did the red team find? **39**

b. How many total points were scored by the red team? **127**

c. How many items did the blue team find? **31**

d. How many total points were scored by the blue team? **157**

e. What is the total number of 5-point items found by the two teams? **31**

f. How many more 1-point items did the red team find than the blue team? **15**

LINK Technology

Computer-animated films, like *Robots*, are made of a series of images. Animators use a coordinate system to program the movement we see in the final product.

23. Technology Computer animation programs store data in matrices. The data may describe how a figure moves across the screen. Matrix A represents the coordinates of the vertices of a polygon. Matrices E and F represent translations of the polygon.

Matrix A: $\begin{bmatrix}0 & 0\\ 4 & 1\\ 2 & 5\\ -2 & 3\end{bmatrix}$ (columns x, y)

Matrix E: $\begin{bmatrix}0 & 3\\ 0 & 3\\ 0 & 3\\ 0 & 3\end{bmatrix}$ (columns x, y)

Matrix F: $\begin{bmatrix}-2 & 0\\ -2 & 0\\ -2 & 0\\ -2 & 0\end{bmatrix}$ (columns x, y)

a. Graph the ordered pairs given by matrix A and connect them in the order they are listed. Connect the last point to the first point.

b. Add matrices A and E and graph the new ordered pairs. Connect the points as in part **a** and describe how the graph is different from part **a.**

c. Subtract matrix F from matrix A and graph the new ordered pairs. Connect the points and describe how the graph is different from part **a.**

d. Multiply matrix A by 2 and graph the new ordered pairs. Connect the points and describe how the graph is different from part **a.**

e. Add matrices A and F, and then multiply the result by $\frac{1}{2}$. Graph the new ordered pairs and connect the points. Describe how the graph is different from part **a.**

f. **Challenge** Use the following information to write matrix G: Matrices A and G are added and the new ordered pairs are graphed. The points are connected as in part **a.** The graph looks like the graph from part **a** has been shifted down 2 units and to the right 3 units.

COMMON ERROR ALERT

Students might subtract incorrectly in **Exercise 13** if they do not distribute the negative to each number in the second matrix. Encourage students to change the subtraction to addition and to change the sign of every number in the second matrix to its opposite.

Transformations **Exercise 23** involves transformations. Parts **b** and **c** are translations. Parts **d** and **e** are dilations, which are enlargements and reductions (stretching and shrinking) created by multiplication.

Answers

23a.

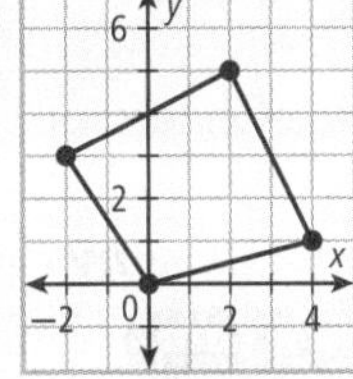

b. The graph is translated 3 units up.

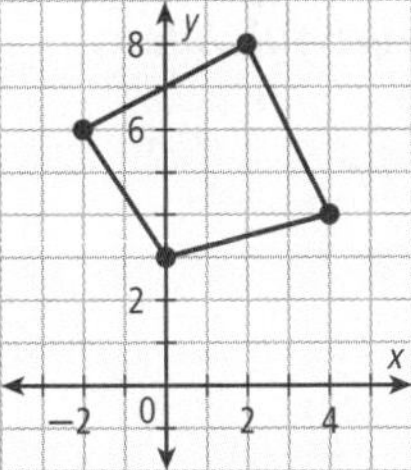

c. The graph is translated 2 units right.

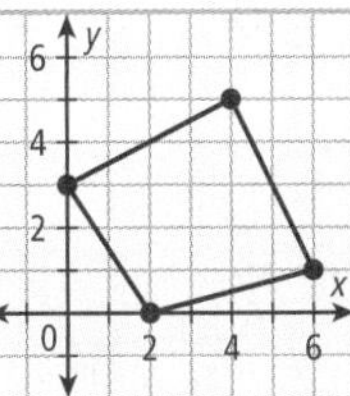

d. The graph has the same shape as the graph in part **a,** but it is twice as big.

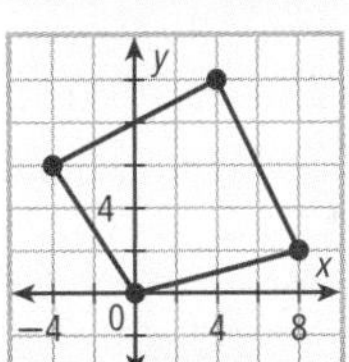

23e. The graph has been translated 2 units left and then reduced to half its original size.

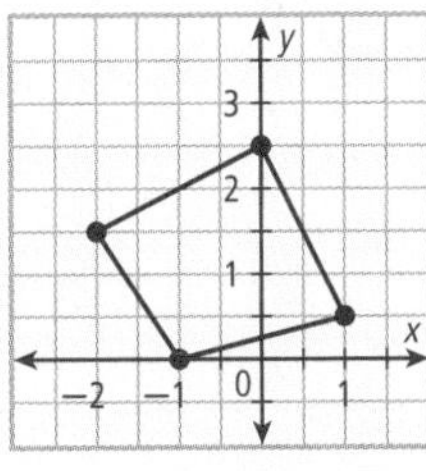

f. **Matrix G** (columns x, y)

$\begin{bmatrix}3 & -2\\ 3 & -2\\ 3 & -2\\ 3 & -2\end{bmatrix}$

CHAPTER 10 Study Guide: Review

Organizer

Objective: Help students organize and review key concepts and skills presented in Chapter 10.

Online Edition Multilingual Glossary

Countdown Week 24

Resources

Teacher One Stop™

PuzzleView
Test & Practice Generator

***Multilingual Glossary* Online**

go.hrw.com
KEYWORD: MA7 Glossary

***Lesson Tutorial Videos* CD-ROM**

Answers

1. outcome
2. interquartile range
3. independent events
4. 2003
5. 14 more boys

CHAPTER 10

Study Guide: Review

Vocabulary

Complete the sentences below with vocabulary words from the list above.

1. A(n) ___?___ is one possible result of an experiment.
2. The ___?___ is the difference between the third and first quartiles.
3. Two events are ___?___ if the occurrence of one event does not affect the probability of the other.

10-1 Organizing and Displaying Data *(pp. 700–708)*

EXAMPLE

The circle graph shows the post-graduation plans for a high school's 500 graduating seniors.

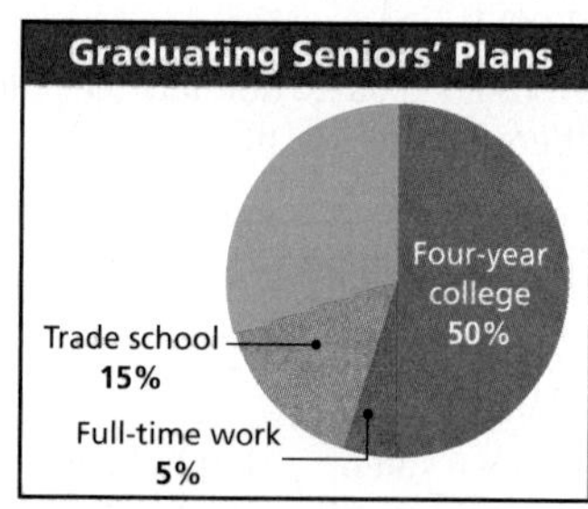

- How many seniors plan to attend a four-year college?
  50% of 500 *Find the percentage.*
  $0.50 \times 500 = 250$
  250 students plan to attend a four-year college.

EXERCISES

Use the double-bar graph for Exercises 4 and 5.

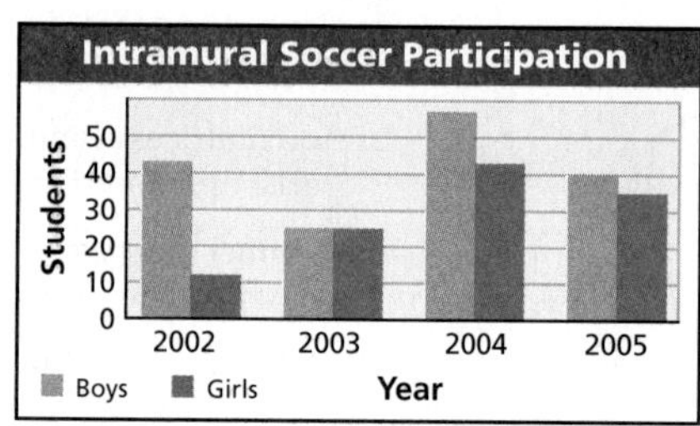

4. In which year did the same number of boys and girls participate?
5. How many more boys than girls participated during 2004?

10-2 Frequency and Histograms *(pp. 709–715)*

EXAMPLE

- **The lives (in hours) of each light bulb in a test are given below. Use the data to make a frequency table and a histogram.**

  22, 28, 25, 21, 19, 21, 25,
  21, 22, 18, 20, 29, 25, 26

Identify the least and greatest values. Divide the data into equal intervals.

Light Bulb Life (h)	
Life	**Frequency**
18–20	3
21–23	5
24–26	4
27–29	2

Draw a bar for the number of hours in each interval. The bars touch, but do not overlap.

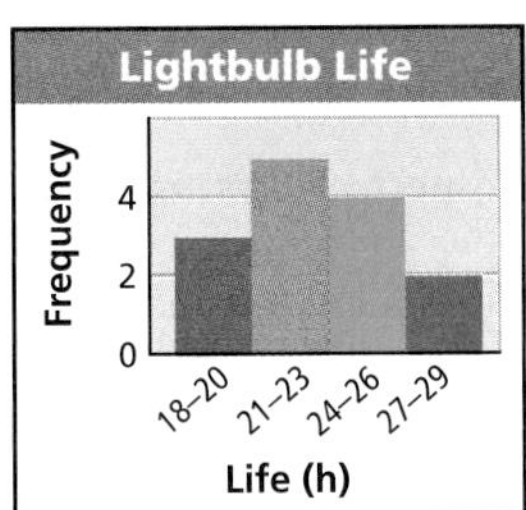

EXERCISES

6. The weights of packages shipped by an online retailer are given below. Use the data to make a stem-and-leaf plot.

Package Weight (lb)										
14	9	22	24	7	1	19	22	28	18	12

7. The numbers of people who attended two different plays are shown in the table below. Make a back-to-back stem-and-leaf plot.

Play Attendance	
Comedy Camp	**Days and Days**
104 62 83 102 104 120 81 126 122	103 105 80 135 109 128 82 132 139

8. The capacities of the gas tanks on several new vehicles are shown below. Use the data to make a frequency table with intervals.

Gas Tank Capacity (gal)										
15	12	12	15	18	26	25	12	15	18	11
10	12	16	15	16	18	25	21	18	20	21

9. Use your frequency table from Exercise 9 to make a histogram.

10-3 Data Distributions *(pp. 716–723)*

EXAMPLE

- **Consider the following ages of the winners of an art contest: 13, 15, 14, 18, 12, 10, 11, 13. Find the mean and mode of the data.**

mean:

$$\frac{10 + 11 + 12 + 13 + 13 + 14 + 15 + 18}{8}$$

$$= \frac{106}{8}$$

$= 13.25$

mode: 13 *13 occurs most often.*

EXERCISES

Find the mean, median, mode, and range of each data set.

10. Years of playing experience of the members of a musical ensemble:

    5, 14, 25, 7, 8, 10, 12, 33, 12

Herman has five pairs of cowboy boots. The prices were $120, $137, $120, $145, and $482.
mean: $200.80 median: $137 mode: $120

11. Which value best describes the price Herman paid? Explain.

Use the data to make a box-and-whisker plot.

12. 25, 28, 2, 24, 28, 21, 18, 29, 31, 12, 6, 19, 27, 3

Answers

6.

Stem	Leaves
0	1 7 9
1	2 4 8 9
2	2 2 4 8

Key: 1|2 means 12

7.

Comedy Camp		Days and Days
2	6	
	7	
3 1	8	0 2
	9	
4 4 2	10	3 5 9
	11	
6 2 0	12	8
	13	2 5 9

Key: |12|8 means 128
4|10| means 104

8.

Gas Tank Capacities		
Capacity	**Tally**	**Frequency**
10 – 14	~~IIII~~ I	6
15 – 19	~~IIII~~ ~~IIII~~	10
20 – 24	III	3
25 – 29	III	3

9. **Gas Tank Capacities**

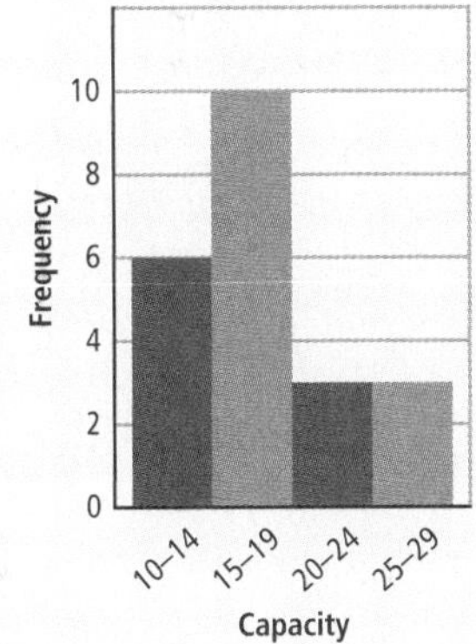

10. mean: 14; median: 12; mode: 12; range: 28
11. Median; the mean is higher than 4 of the 5 prices; the mode is the lowest price.
12.

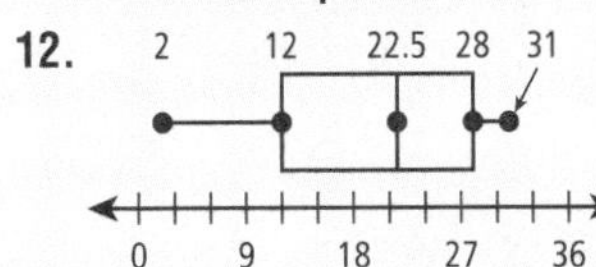

Study Guide: Review 775

Answers

13. The scale on the vertical axis is too large. This makes the slopes of the segments less steep.
14. Someone might believe that the price has been relatively stable, when in fact it has doubled.
15. 99.5%
16. 24,875
17. 250
18. $\frac{1}{2}$
19. $\frac{1}{4}$
20. $\frac{5}{8}$

10-4 Misleading Graphs and Statistics *(pp. 726–731)*

EXAMPLE

- **Explain why the graph is misleading.**

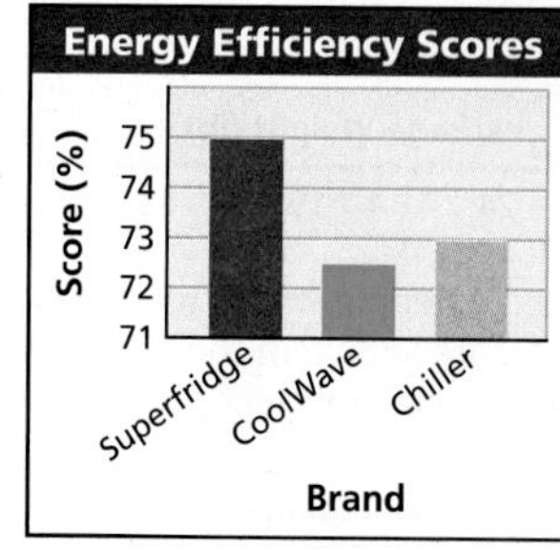

The vertical axis begins at 71. This exaggerates the difference in the heights of the bars.

EXERCISES

The graph shows the cost of admission to an amusement park over 20 years.

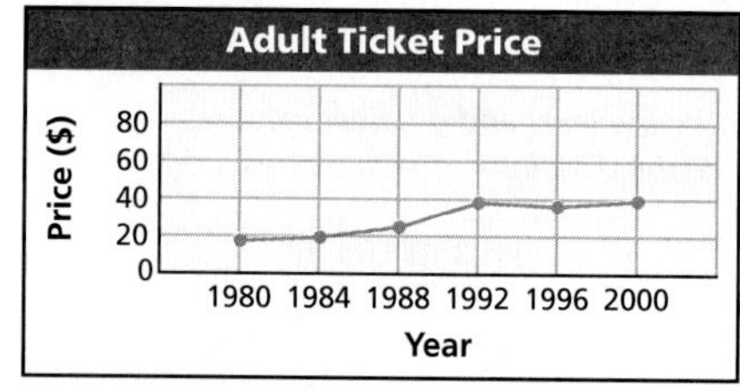

13. Explain why the graph is misleading.
14. What might someone believe because of the graph?

10-5 Experimental Probability *(pp. 737–742)*

EXAMPLES

The manager of a photo processing lab inspects 500 photos and finds that 4 have flaws.

- What is the experimental probability that a photo is flawed?

$$\frac{\text{number of times the event occurs}}{\text{number of trials}} = \frac{4}{500} = 0.8\%$$

- In one month, the lab processes 13,000 photos. Predict the number that are likely to be flawed.

$0.008 \cdot 13{,}000 = 104$ *Find 0.8% of 13,000.*

104 photos are likely to be flawed.

EXERCISES

A manufacturer inspects 800 batteries and finds that 796 have no defects.

15. What is the experimental probability that a battery chosen at random has no defects?
16. There are 25,000 batteries in storage. How many batteries are likely to have no defects?
17. Another storage area holds 50,000 batteries. How many batteries are likely to have a defect?

10-6 Theoretical Probability *(pp. 744–749)*

EXAMPLE

- **A jar contains red, green, brown, and blue marbles. The probability of choosing red is 0.30, of choosing green is 0.20, and of choosing brown is 0.25. Find the probability of choosing blue.**

$$P(\text{blue}) + P(\text{not blue}) = 1$$
$$P(\text{blue}) + P(\text{red, green, or brown}) = 1$$
$$P(\text{blue}) + (0.30 + 0.20 + 0.25) = 1$$
$$P(\text{blue}) + 0.75 = 1$$
$$P(\text{blue}) = 0.25$$

EXERCISES

Find the theoretical probability of each outcome.

18. Rolling a number less than 4 on a standard number cube
19. Randomly selecting a month that starts with "J" from all month names
20. Randomly selecting a vowel from the letters in EQUATION

10-7 Independent and Dependent Events *(pp. 750–757)*

EXAMPLES

A hardware store shelf holds 12 cans of red paint, 4 cans of yellow paint, and 6 cans of black paint.

- Syd selects one can at random and replaces it. Then she selects another can at random. What is the probability that Syd selects a red can and then a yellow can?

$$P(\text{red, yellow}) = P(\text{red}) \cdot P(\text{yellow})$$
$$= \frac{12}{22} \cdot \frac{4}{22} \quad \textit{Independent events}$$
$$= \frac{48}{484} = \frac{12}{121}$$

- Gene selects one can at random and then selects another can at random from the remaining cans. What is the probability that Gene selects two cans of black paint?

$$P(\text{black, black}) = P(\text{black}) \cdot P(\text{black after black})$$
$$= \frac{6}{22} \cdot \frac{5}{21} \quad \textit{Dependent events}$$
$$= \frac{30}{462} = \frac{5}{77}$$

EXERCISES

Tell whether each set of events is independent or dependent. Explain your answers.

21. A computer generates a random number and then generates another random number.

22. You roll two number cubes. One is a 6 and the other is a 1.

23. Two audience members are called to the stage.

A lottery machine contains different-colored balls. There are 64 green, 128 yellow, 1 golden, and 3 silver balls. Find the probability of each event.

24. A yellow ball is drawn and set aside. Then a green ball is drawn.

25. A golden ball is drawn and set aside. Then another golden ball is drawn.

26. A green ball is drawn and replaced. Then another green ball is drawn.

10-8 Combinations and Permutations *(pp. 760–767)*

EXAMPLES

A sporting goods store carries sweatshirts for 8 local high school football teams.

- How many different packages of 4 different high school sweatshirts are possible?

Use a combination. The order does not matter.

$${}_8C_4 = \frac{8!}{4!(8-4)!} = \frac{8!}{4!(4)!}$$
$$= \frac{8 \cdot 7 \cdot 6 \cdot 5 \cdot \cancel{4} \cdot \cancel{3} \cdot \cancel{2} \cdot \cancel{1}}{(4 \cdot 3 \cdot 2 \cdot 1)(\cancel{4} \cdot \cancel{3} \cdot \cancel{2} \cdot \cancel{1})} = \frac{1680}{24} = 70$$

Seventy different packages are possible.

- Three different high school sweatshirts will be hung in a row. How many displays are possible?

Use a permutation. The order matters.

$${}_8P_3 = \frac{8!}{(8-3)!} = \frac{8!}{5!} =$$
$$\frac{8 \cdot 7 \cdot 6 \cdot \cancel{5} \cdot \cancel{4} \cdot \cancel{3} \cdot \cancel{2} \cdot \cancel{1}}{\cancel{5} \cdot \cancel{4} \cdot \cancel{3} \cdot \cancel{2} \cdot \cancel{1}} = 336$$

There are 336 different possible displays.

EXERCISES

27. A catering hall offers 4 different plates, 3 different silverware patterns, and 5 different types of glassware. How many place settings of one plate, one silverware pattern, and one type of glassware are possible?

Tell whether each situation involves combinations or permutations. Then give the number of possible outcomes.

28. Shelly is making up a 7-digit phone number to use in a play. She can choose any digit from 0–9 but does not want to repeat a number. How many different phone numbers are possible?

29. A restaurant offers 12 different appetizers. How many ways can a group of friends share 3 different appetizers?

30. A group of 15 friends is at an amusement park. In how many ways can a group be chosen to ride in a four-person gondola?

Answers

21. The result of the first random number does not affect the result of the second random number, so the events are independent.

22. The result of the first roll does not affect the result of the second, so the events are independent.

23. There are fewer people to choose from after the first person is called, so the events are dependent.

24. $\frac{2048}{9555}$

25. 0

26. $\frac{256}{2401}$

27. 60

28. permutation; 604,800

29. combination; 220

30. combination; 1365

Organizer

Objective: Assess students' mastery of concepts and skills in Chapter 10.

Online Edition

Resources

Assessment Resources

Chapter 10 Tests
- Free Response (Levels A, B, C)
- Multiple Choice (Levels A, B, C)
- Performance Assessment

Teacher One Stop™
Test & Practice Generator

Answers

1.

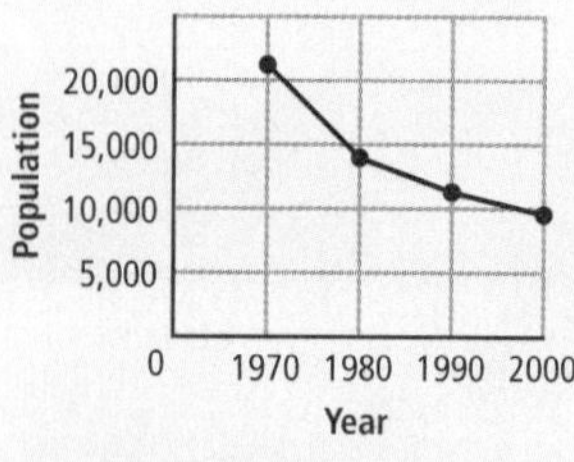

A line graph is appropriate for this data because it will show the change in population over a period of time.

State Resources

Population of Oakville	
Year	**Population**
1970	20,851
1980	14,229
1990	11,198
2000	9,579

1. The table shows the population of Oakville. Use the data to make a graph. Explain why you chose that type of graph.
2. Which ten-year period saw the greatest change in population? **from 1970 to 1980**
3. Describe the trend in Oakville's population. **The pop. is decreasing, but by smaller amounts as time passes.**

The high temperatures in degrees Fahrenheit for two weeks are given: 64, 66, 63, 58, 59, 55, 51, 54, 61, 62, 68, 70, 63, 63.

4. Use the data to make a stem-and-leaf plot.
5. Use the data to make a frequency table with intervals.
6. Use your frequency table from Problem 5 to make a histogram.

The lengths of statements during a town council meeting are given.

Length of Statement (min)						
6	25	12	14	2	13	38
22	21	14	3	8	5	17

7. Find the mean, median, mode, and range of the data.
8. Use the data to make a box-and-whisker plot.

A manufacturer inspects 500 watches and finds that 498 have no defects.

9. What is the experimental probability that a watch chosen at random has no defects? **99.6%**
10. There are 30,000 watches in a warehouse. Predict the number of watches that are likely to have no defects. **29,880**

The graph shows how the money raised by a charity is spent.

Charity Spending
Administrative costs 4%
Postage costs 1%
Charitable causes 15%

11. Explain why the graph is misleading.
12. What might someone believe because of the graph?
13. Who might want to use this graph?
14. A bag contains 12 cards, each with a different month of the year printed on it. A card is selected at random. What is the probability that the month begins with *A*? $\frac{1}{6}$
15. The odds of spinning red on a spinner are 2:7. What is the probability of not spinning red? $\frac{7}{9}$
16. A bag has 14 red marbles and 10 white marbles. Rosa randomly picks two marbles from the bag, one at a time. What is the probability that Rosa picks two white marbles? $\frac{15}{92}$

Tell whether each situation involves combinations or permutations. Then give the number of possible outcomes.

17. Sara is ordering a deli platter for a party. The deli offers 9 kinds of meats. Sara must select 4 kinds for the platter. How many different platters can Sara choose? **comb.; 126**
18. Armando has 12 antique books. He will select 3 books and put one up for auction each day for three days. How many different ways can he do this? **perm.; 1320**

4. **High Temperatures for Two Weeks**

Stem	Leaves
5	1 4 5 8 9
6	1 2 3 3 3 4 6 8
7	0

Key: 5|1 means 51

5.

High Temperature for Two Weeks		
Temperatures (°F)	**Tally**	**Frequency**
51–54	II	2
55–58	II	2
59–62	III	3
63–66	~~IIII~~	5
67–70	II	2

6.

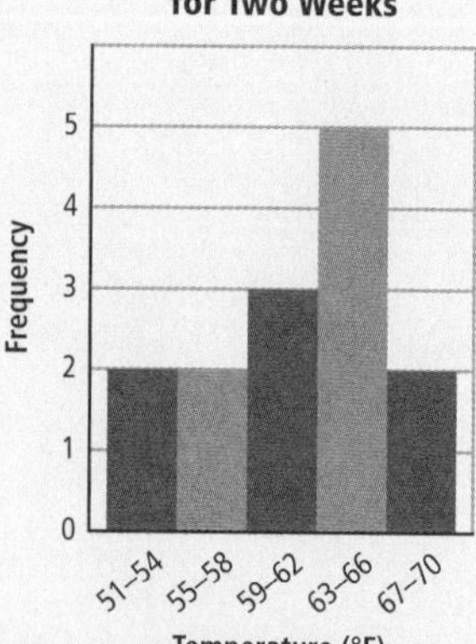

7, 8, 11–13. See p. A33.

COLLEGE ENTRANCE EXAM PRACTICE

FOCUS ON SAT MATHEMATICS SUBJECT TEST

There are two levels of SAT Subject Tests: Mathematics Level 1 and Mathematics Level 2. Each test has 50 multiple-choice questions. The content of each test is very different. Getting a high score on one test does not mean you will get a high score on the other test.

You can write all over the test book to sketch figures, do scratch work, or cross out incorrect answers to help you eliminate choices. Remember to mark your final answer on the answer sheet because the test book is not used for scoring.

You may want to time yourself as you take this practice test. It should take you about 6 minutes to complete.

1. Which of the following represents the number of ways 6 committee members can be selected from a group of 25 teachers?

(A) ${}_6C_{25}$

(B) ${}_{19}C_6$

(C) ${}_{25}C_6$

(D) ${}_6P_{25}$

(E) ${}_{25}P_6$

2. Your friend randomly selects 2 movies from your collection to borrow. Your collection includes 9 comedies, 5 dramas, 3 mysteries, 1 musical, and 2 horror movies. What is the probability that both movies are comedies?

(A) $\frac{1}{36}$

(B) $\frac{18}{95}$

(C) $\frac{81}{400}$

(D) $\frac{2}{9}$

(E) $\frac{331}{380}$

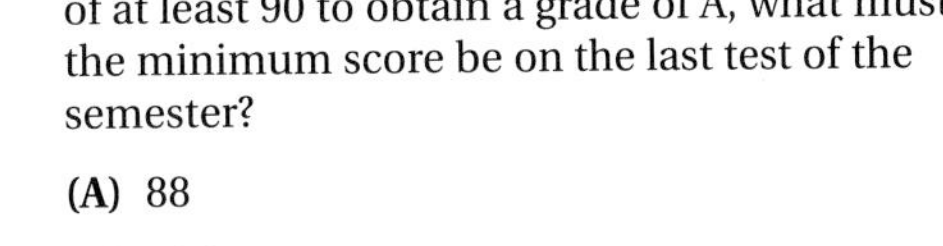

3. A student's test scores are 88, 87, 82, 95, and 89. If the student needs an average test score of at least 90 to obtain a grade of A, what must the minimum score be on the last test of the semester?

(A) 88

(B) 88.2

(C) 91

(D) 99

(E) 100

4. What is the probability of not getting a 2 on the spinner?

(A) 0.10

(B) 0.25

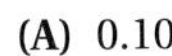

(C) 0.50

(D) 0.75

(E) 1

5. What is the value of $\frac{(n+1)!}{(n-1)!}$?

(A) $n^2 + n$

(B) $2n + 1$

(C) $n!$

(D) $n^2 - 1$

(E) -1

COLLEGE ENTRANCE EXAM PRACTICE

Organizer

Objective: Provide practice for college entrance exams such as the SAT Mathematics Subject Tests.

PREMIER Online Edition

Resources

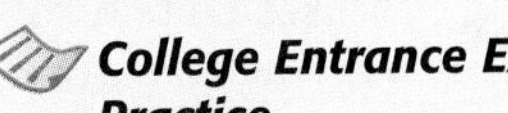

College Entrance Exam Practice

Questions on the SAT Mathematics Subject Tests Levels 1 and 2 represent the following math content areas:

	Level	
	1	2
Number and Operations	10–14%	10–14%
Algebra and Functions	38–42%	48–52%
Geometry and Measurement	38–42%	28–32%
Plane Euclidean	18–22%	0%
Coordinate	8–12%	10–14%
Three-dimensional	4–6%	4–6%
Trigonometry	6–8%	12–16%
Data Analysis, Statistics, and Probability	6–10%	6–10%

Items on this page focus on:

- Data Analysis, Statistics, and Probability

Text References:

Item	1	2	3	4	5
Lesson	10-8	10-7	10-3	10-6	10-8

TEST PREP DOCTOR

1. Students who chose **A** reversed the numbers in the formula for combinations. Students who chose **E** incorrectly believed that the order of the committee members mattered and used the permutations formula.

2. Students who chose **C** used the formula for independent events instead of the formula for dependent events. Students who chose **A** found the probability of selecting 2 movies from the 9 comedies.

3. Students who chose **A** found the median of the given test scores. Students who chose **B** found the mean of the given test scores.

4. Students who chose **B** found the probability of getting a 2 on the spinner.

5. Students who chose **B** may have simplified the expression to $n + 1$ plus n instead of $n + 1$ times n. Remind students of the definition of the factorial symbol and suggest that they write out the first few factors of the numerator and denominator.

Organizer

Objective: Provide opportunities to learn and practice common test-taking strategies.

Online Edition

TEST PREP DOCTOR + This Test Tackler focuses on how to use spatial reasoning to answer questions that require visualization of a solid figure. Before you begin, show students, using a three-dimensional model, the different views of a solid figure.

Standardized Test Strategies

Any Question Type: Spatial Reasoning

Some test questions include a three-dimensional figure. You must use spatial reasoning to correctly interpret the figure.

EXAMPLE 1

Which of the following shows the top view of the solid figure?

Ⓐ 
Ⓑ 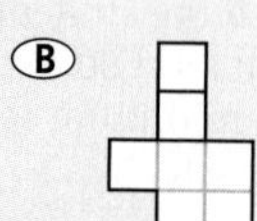
Ⓒ 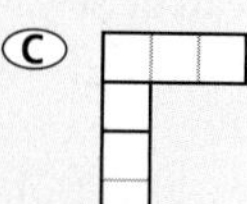
Ⓓ 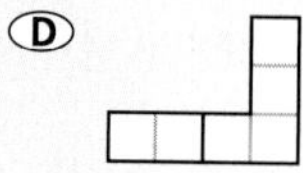

Notice that the isometric drawing shows three sides of the figure: the top, front, and right side. Use the isometric drawing to make a foundation plan of the figure.

Count the number of cubes at the widest part of the figure and at the longest part of the figure.

The widest part is 3 cubes across.
The longest part is 4 cubes deep.

Draw a 3-by-4 grid.

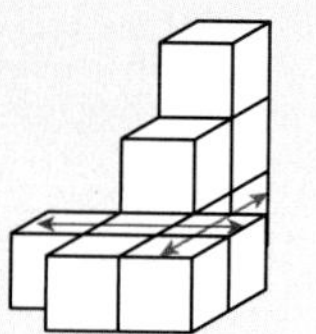
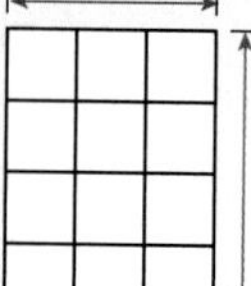

Each cube on the bottom level of the figure corresponds to a square on the grid.

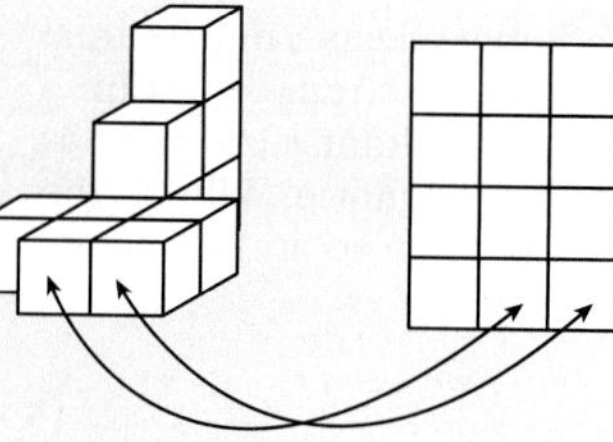

Start at the front of the figure. Shade in each square of the grid that corresponds to a cube on the bottom level of the figure.

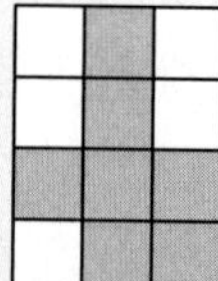

Using the foundation plan, you can see that choice B shows the top view of the solid.

Imagine that you are stacking blocks to help you to visualize the solid figure. Each square shown in the drawing represents a face of one block.

Read each test item and answer the questions that follow.

Item A

Multiple Choice Which solid is represented by these top, side, and front views?

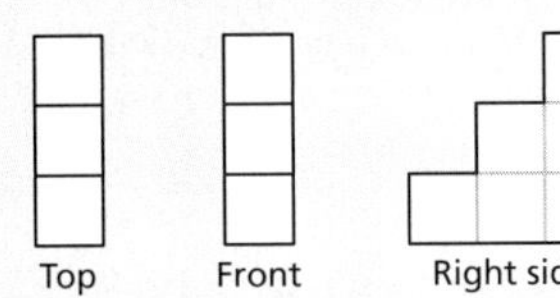

Ⓐ 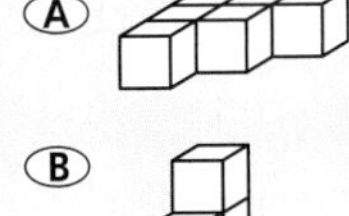

Ⓑ

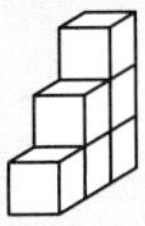

Ⓒ 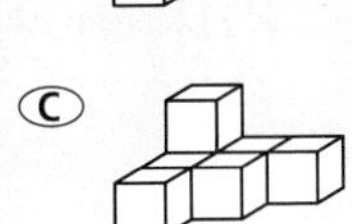

Ⓓ 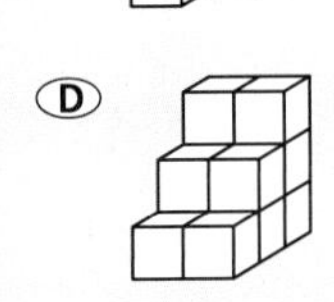

1. How many cubes can you see if you are looking down on the figure? How do you know?
2. How many cubes can you see if you are looking at the front of the figure? How do you know?
3. How many cubes high is the highest stack of the figure? Explain how you know.
4. Using your answers from Problems 1–3, what is the correct answer choice?

Item B

Short Response The drawing shows a foundation plan of a solid figure made of stacked cubes. The numbers in the squares identify the number of cubes in each stack. Draw a three-dimensional view of this solid figure.

2	4	6
2	2	3
2	1	1

5. Draw the top view of the figure.
6. If you were to look at the figure from the right or from the front, how many cubes high is the highest stack? Explain how you know.
7. A student drew this figure as his response. Do you agree that this is the correct drawing? If so, explain how you know. If not, what did the student do wrong?

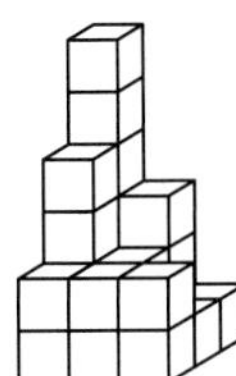

Item C

Short Response Draw the top view and front view of the solid figure.

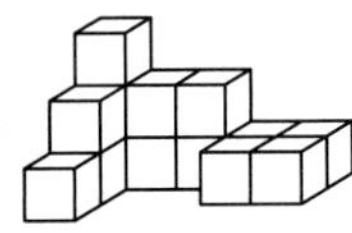

8. If you look down on the figure, how many cubes do you see?
9. Create a base plan or foundation plan for the figure.
10. Nolan drew his version of the top view of the figure. Is he correct? If not, show how you would change his drawing so that it is correct.

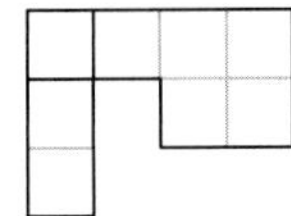

11. If you look at the figure from the front, how tall is the highest stack of cubes and how short is the shortest stack of cubes?
12. Draw the front view of the figure.

Answers

1. 3 cubes; the top view shows 3 squares.
2. 3 cubes; the front view shows 3 squares.
3. 3 cubes; the front view and the right side view both show a maximum of 3 cubes stacked.
4. B
5. 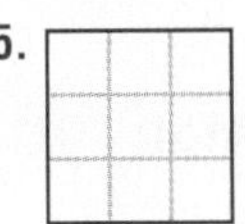
6. 6 cubes; the greatest number in the foundation drawing is 6.
7. No; the drawing should be rotated so that the highest stack is at the back right corner of the figure.
8. 9 cubes
9. 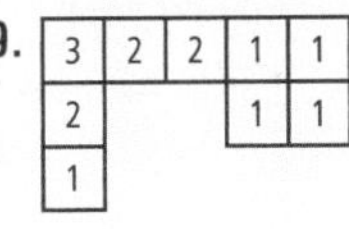

10. No; I would place another square between the column with 3 squares and the column with 1 square.
11. The tallest is 3 cubes high and the shortest is 1 cube high.
12. 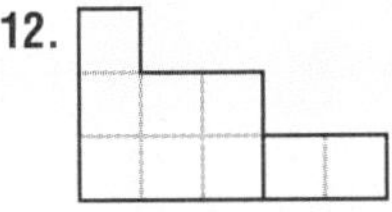

State Resources

Answers to Test Items

A. B

B. See answer to Problem 7.

C. See answers to Problems 10 and 12.

go.hrw.com
State Resources Online
KEYWORD: MA7 Resources

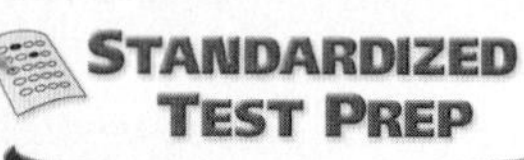

Organizer

Objective: Provide review and practice for Chapters 1–10 and standardized tests.

 Online Edition

Resources

 ***Assessment Resources***

Chapter 10 Cumulative Test

go.hrw.com
KEYWORD: MA7 TestPrep

CUMULATIVE ASSESSMENT, CHAPTERS 1–10

Multiple Choice

1. Josephine has 9 cousins. Her friend Summer has s more cousins. Which expression can be used to show the number of cousins Summer has?
   - (A) $9 \div s$
   - (B) $9s$
   - (C) $9 + s$
   - (D) $9 - s$

2. A negative number raised to an exponent is positive. Which of the following is NOT true?
   - (F) The number could be even.
   - (G) The number could be odd.
   - (H) The exponent could be even.
   - (J) The exponent could be odd.

3. A computer game normally sells for \$40. Niko bought it when it went on sale for 25% off. The sales tax was 6%. How much did Niko pay for the game?
   - (A) \$10.60
   - (B) \$12.40
   - (C) \$31.80
   - (D) \$32.40

4. The graph shows the profit made at a family yard sale that lasted 8 hours. Between which hours did the profit increase at the slowest rate?

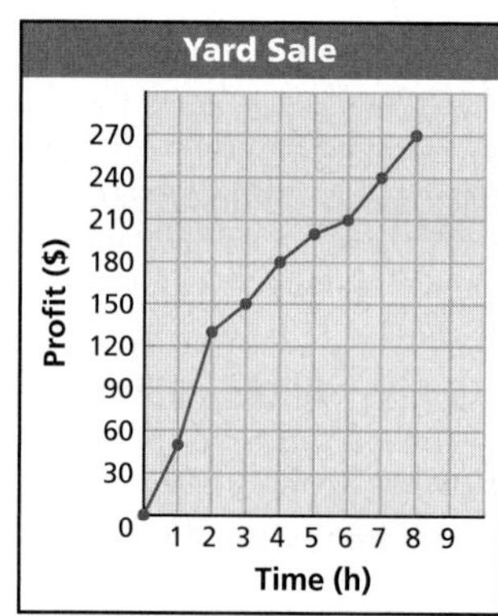

   - (F) 0–1
   - (G) 1–2
   - (H) 5–6
   - (J) 7–8

5. Which of the following is one of the five values needed to make a box-and-whisker plot?
   - (A) Mean
   - (B) Median
   - (C) Mode
   - (D) Average

6. Which value is a solution of $2(1 - x) < 12$?
   - (F) −7
   - (G) −6
   - (H) −5
   - (J) −4

7. What is the median of the data presented in this stem-and-leaf plot?

Stem	Leaves
6	0 2 2 2 5 8
7	3 4 4 6 7
8	2 5 8 9

Key: 8 | 2 means 0.82

   - (A) 0.62
   - (B) 0.74
   - (C) 6.2
   - (D) 7.4

8. Which of the following does NOT represent a function?
   - (F) $\{(-4, 3), (-2, 1), (-2, -1), (-4, -3)\}$
   - (G)

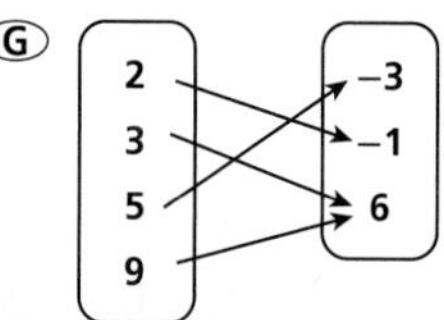

   - (H)

x	−4	−3	−2	−1	0	1
y	4	3	2	1	0	−1

   - (J)

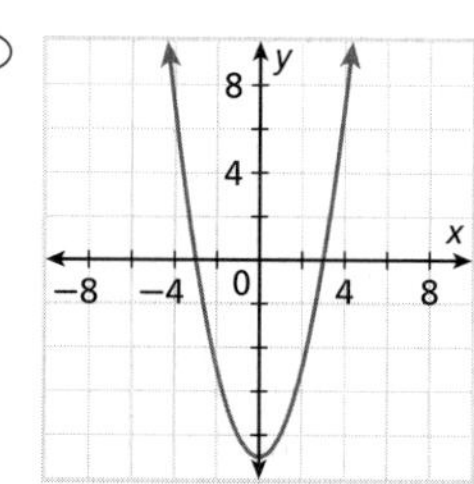

State Resources

go.hrw.com
State Resources Online
KEYWORD: MA7 Resources

Answers

1. C
2. J
3. C
4. H
5. B
6. J
7. B
8. F
9. B
10. J
11. C
12. G
13. 2
14. 0.64
15. 2600

16a. {HHH, HHT, HTH, HTT, TTT, TTH, THT, THH}

b. $\frac{3}{8} = 37.5\%$

If you are allowed to write in your test booklet, you may want to add additional information to a given diagram. Be sure to mark your answer on the answer sheet since your marks on the test booklet will not be graded.

9. Which of these equations describes a line parallel to $x + 2y = 6$?

Ⓐ $y = \frac{1}{2}x$

Ⓑ $y = -\frac{1}{2}x + 4$

Ⓒ $y = -2x + 6$

Ⓓ $y = 2x + 3$

10. What is the probability that the spinner will NOT land on white?

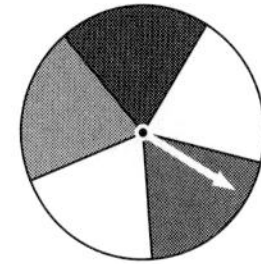

Ⓕ 20%

Ⓖ 40%

Ⓗ 50%

Ⓙ 60%

11. A CD-ROM is storing 4.2×10^8 bytes of information. What is this number in standard form?

Ⓐ 0.0000000042

Ⓑ 0.00000042

Ⓒ 420,000,000

Ⓓ 4,200,000,000

12. Which is a factor of $4x^2 + 24x + 36$?

Ⓕ $x + 12$

Ⓖ $2x + 6$

Ⓗ $2x + 18$

Ⓙ $4x + 18$

Gridded Response

13. Yvette is choosing between two stores to get her family pictures taken. Say Cheese charges a $20 sitting fee and $14 per sheet of pictures. Picture Me charges a $12 sitting fee and $18 per sheet of pictures. For how many sheets will the total cost be the same at both stores?

14. Brian plays basketball. In the past, he has made 4 out of every 5 free throws. What is the probability, as a decimal, that Brian will make the next two free throws?

15. A password for a security system must consist of a letter followed by two digits. How many possible passwords are there?

Short Response

16. An experiment consists of tossing 3 coins at the same time.

a. Identify the sample space.

b. What is the probability of tossing 2 tails and 1 head?

c. Which is more likely to occur: tossing exactly 1 tail or tossing at least 2 heads? Explain.

17. If 8% of a number is 4, what is 12% of the number? Explain your reasoning.

18. Nat surveyed 30 twelfth-grade students and found that 27 of them were in favor of allowing seniors to leave campus for lunch. As a result, Nat reported that "90% of the student body supports off-campus lunch privileges for seniors." Was Nat's statistic misleading? Explain.

19. A service technician is scheduling house calls to make repairs. He has 9 time slots in his work day. He has 7 house calls to make. How many different schedules of his day are possible? Show and explain your work.

20. For her scrapbook page, Denise has 5 different background colors, 4 different framing styles, and 2 different accents. How many possible scrapbook layouts can Denise create with the available materials? Show and explain your work.

Extended Response

21. The ages of the first 15 people to enter a community center for bingo one evening are 77, 85, 76, 73, 69, 70, 84, 82, 76, 74, 89, 83, 68, 91, and 88.

a. Find the mean, median, mode, and range of the data.

b. Create a box-and-whisker plot of the data.

c. The sixteenth person to enter the center is 39 years old. Calculate the mean, median, mode, and range of the data with the 16 people.

d. Create a box-and-whisker plot with the 16 people.

e. When the sixteenth person was added, which measure of central tendency changed the most? Which measure changed the least? Explain.

f. How did the addition of the sixteenth person affect the box-and-whisker plot?

Short-Response Rubric

Items 16–20

2 Points = The student's answer is an accurate and complete execution of the task or tasks.

1 Point = The student's answer contains attributes of an appropriate response but is flawed.

0 Points = The student's answer contains no attributes of an appropriate response.

Extended-Response Rubric

Item 21

4 Points = The student correctly answers parts **a** and **c** and draws correct graphs in parts **b** and **d.** The student provides explanations in parts **e** and **f.**

3 Points = The student correctly answers parts **a** and **c** and draws correct graphs in parts **b** and **d** but does not provide explanations in parts **e** and **f.**

2 Points = The student correctly answers parts **a** and **c.** The student draws incorrect graphs in parts **b** and **d** or gives an incorrect explanation in parts **e** or **f.**

1 Point = The student incorrectly answers parts **a** and **c** but draws correct graphs from that information in parts **b** and **d,** or the student attempts to answer all parts of the problem but does not correctly answer any part.

0 Points = The student does not answer correctly and does not attempt all parts of the problem.

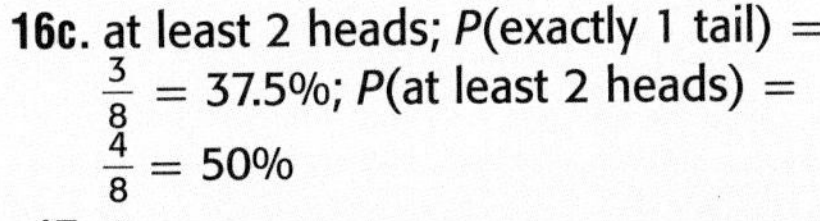

16c. at least 2 heads; $P(\text{exactly 1 tail}) = \frac{3}{8} = 37.5\%$; $P(\text{at least 2 heads}) = \frac{4}{8} = 50\%$

17. 6

18. The sample is biased and small. Nat surveyed only 30 students out of the entire student body. Also, those surveyed were seniors, who are naturally going to be in favor of an action that benefits seniors.

19. 181,440

20. 40

21a. mean: 79; median: 77; mode: 76; range: 23

b. **Bingo Ages, 15 People**

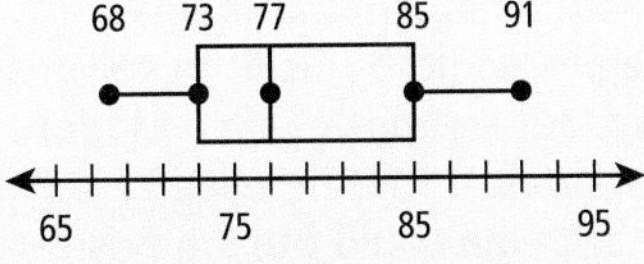

c. mean: 76.5, median: 76.5, mode: 76, range: 52

d. **Bingo Ages, 16 People**

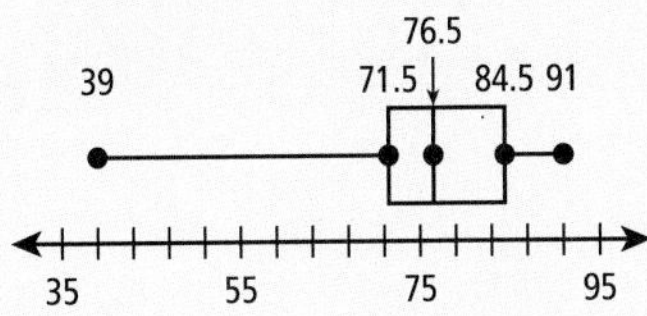

e. Mean; mode; the mean decreased because the 16th person was much younger than the other people. The mode remained unchanged.

f. stretched out the left "whisker"

Organizer

Objective: Choose appropriate problem-solving strategies and use them with skills from Chapters 9 and 10 to solve real-world problems.

PREMIER **Online Edition**

Roadside America Indoor Miniature Village

Reading Strategies

In **Problem 1,** ask students what measurement is represented by the 180 one-inch cubes. the volume Remind students that the base of a geometric figure is the bottom face.

Using Data Have students find how many square miles of land are shown in the grid.

State Resources

Roadside America Indoor Miniature Village

The Roadside America Indoor Miniature Village in Shartlesville, Pennsylvania, is sometimes referred to as the World's Greatest Indoor Miniature Village. The exhibit uses miniature buildings and realistic landscaping to show what life was like in the 1700s, 1800s, and 1900s. Laurence Gieringer built the village using a $\frac{3}{8}$-inch-to-1-foot scale.

Choose one or more strategies to solve each problem.

1. Suppose a model of a building is made of 180 one-inch cubes. The area of the base of the model is 15 in^2. How tall is the miniature building? Using a scale of $\frac{3}{8}$ inch to 1 foot, how tall is the actual building? **12 in.; 32 ft**
2. There are about 4000 miniature people in the village. This number is about 100 more than thirteen times the number of buildings in the village. Estimate the number of miniature buildings in the village. **300**

For 3, use the map.

3. It might be helpful to use a coordinate grid when designing a miniature village. Suppose you decide to arrange it as shown. About how far is it from the school to the post office along a straight line? **about 8 mi**

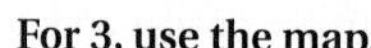

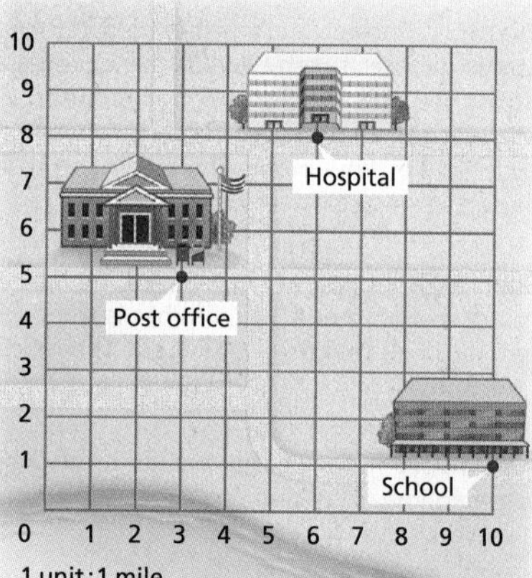

Problem-Solving Focus

Discuss with students what problem-solving strategies could be used to solve each problem. For example, Use a Model and Work Backward could be used to solve **Problem 1.** Students could build a prism-shaped model of a building with a base that has an area of 15 in^2.

The National Aviary

The National Aviary is located on the north side of Pittsburgh. It is America's only independent indoor nonprofit bird zoo. The aviary is home to more than 600 birds of over 200 species, many of which are threatened or endangered in the wild. Visitors can see birds from almost every continent. Visitors can even feed the birds flying around in a 200,000-cubic-foot indoor rainforest where it actually rains every 15 minutes.

Choose one or more strategies to solve each problem.

For 1 and 2, use the circle graph.

Location of Red-crowned Cranes in the World

South Korea 14%
North Korea 16%
China 40%
Japan 30%

1. 600 **1.** The red-crowned crane is the second rarest crane species. The total population of red-crowned cranes in the wild is about 2000 birds. The circle graph shows the approximate percent of this population in four countries where they are found. About how many red-crowned cranes live in Japan?

2. About how many of the total population of red-crowned cranes living in the wild do not live in North Korea or South Korea? **1400**

3. One exhibit at the aviary contains bald eagles. An eagle can see a rabbit from about one mile away. The average person must be 1650 feet away to see the same rabbit. Do humans or eagles see farther? How many times as far? **eagles; 3.2 times as far**

4. It is estimated that only one of every 18 attempts by an eagle to hunt for food is successful. Because of this, eagles use a great deal of energy hunting and have to spend a lot of time resting quietly. According to this information, if you observe an eagle diving for a fish, what is the probability that he is not going to catch the fish on the first try? $\frac{17}{18}$

Real-World Connections

The National Aviary

Reading Strategies

ENGLISH LANGUAGE LEARNERS

Ask students if they know what *aviators* do. They fly planes. Then ask how this knowledge is related to an *aviary*, which is a large building which houses birds. Both aviators and birds fly.

Remind students that information needed for one problem may be given in a previous problem. Such is the case with **Problem 2.**

Using Data Have students check that the sum of the percents in the circle graph is 100.

Problem-Solving Focus

Encourage students to use the four-step problem-solving process for **Problem 2.** Focus on the second and fourth steps: **(2) Make a Plan:** Ask students for two different ways to solve the problem. You could add the percents for China and Japan and multiply that percent by the total, or you could add the percents for North and South Korea, multiply that percent by the total, and then subtract that number from the total. **(4) Look Back:** Ask students how they can use the circle graph to check their answer for reasonableness. Over half of the shaded area is not for North and South Korea, so the answer should be greater than half of 2000. 1400 is greater than 1000, so the answer is reasonable.

Exponential and Radical Functions

Section 11A: Exponential Functions	Section 11B: Radical Functions and Equations
11-1 Geometric Sequences	**11-5 Square-Root Functions**
11-2 Exponential Functions	**11-5 Technology Lab** Graph Radical Functions
Connecting Algebra to Geometry Changing Dimensions	**11-6 Radical Expressions**
11-3 Algebra Lab Model Growth and Decay	**11-7 Adding and Subtracting Radical Expressions**
11-3 Exponential Growth and Decay	**11-8 Multiplying and Dividing Radical Expressions**
11-4 Linear, Quadratic, and Exponential Models	**11-9 Solving Radical Equations**

Pacing Guide for 45-Minute Classes

Teacher One Stop™
Calendar Planner®

Chapter 11

DAY 1	DAY 2	DAY 3	DAY 4	DAY 5
11-1 Lesson	11-2 Lesson	Connecting Algebra to Geometry	11-3 Algebra Lab	11-3 Lesson
DAY 6	**DAY 7**	**DAY 8**	**DAY 9**	**DAY 10**
11-4 Lesson	Multi-Step Test Prep Ready to Go On?	11-5 Lesson	11-5 Technology Lab	11-6 Lesson
DAY 11	**DAY 12**	**DAY 13**	**DAY 14**	**DAY 15**
11-7 Lesson	11-8 Lesson	11-9 Lesson	Multi-Step Test Prep Ready to Go On?	Chapter 11 Review
DAY 16				
Chapter 11 Test				

Pacing Guide for 90-Minute Classes

Teacher One Stop™
Calendar Planner®

Chapter 11

DAY 1	DAY 2	DAY 3	DAY 4	DAY 5
11-1 Lesson 11-2 Lesson	Connecting Algebra to Geometry 11-3 Algebra Lab	11-3 Lesson 11-4 Lesson	Multi-Step Test Prep Ready to Go On? 11-5 Lesson	11-5 Technology Lab 11-6 Lesson
DAY 6	**DAY 7**	**DAY 8**		
11-7 Lesson 11-8 Lesson	11-9 Lesson Multi-Step Test Prep Ready to Go On?	Chapter 11 Review Chapter 11 Test		

ONGOING ASSESSMENT and INTERVENTION

	DIAGNOSE	PRESCRIBE
Assess Prior Knowledge	**Before Chapter 11**	
	Diagnose readiness for the chapter.	Prescribe intervention.
	Are You Ready? SE p. 787	***Are You Ready? Intervention***
Formative Assessment	**Before Every Lesson**	
	Diagnose readiness for the lesson.	Prescribe intervention.
	Warm Up TE	**Reteach** CRB
	During Every Lesson	
	Diagnose understanding of lesson concepts.	Prescribe intervention.
	Check It Out! SE	**Reading Strategies** CRB
	Questioning Strategies TE	***Success for Every Learner***
	Think and Discuss SE	***Lesson Tutorial Videos***
	Write About It SE	
	Journal TE	
	After Every Lesson	
	Diagnose mastery of lesson concepts.	Prescribe intervention.
	Lesson Quiz TE	**Reteach** CRB
	Test Prep SE	**Test Prep Doctor** TE
	Test and Practice Generator	***Homework Help*** **Online**
	Before Chapter 11 Testing	
	Diagnose mastery of concepts in chapter.	Prescribe intervention.
	Ready to Go On? SE pp. 821, 855	***Ready to Go On? Intervention***
	Multi-Step Test Prep SE pp. 820, 854	**Scaffolding Questions** TE pp. 820, 854
	Section Quizzes AR	**Reteach** CRB
	Test and Practice Generator	***Lesson Tutorial Videos***
	Before High Stakes Testing	
	Diagnose mastery of benchmark concepts.	Prescribe intervention.
	College Entrance Exam Practice SE p. 861	***College Entrance Exam Practice***
	Standardized Test Prep SE pp. 864–865	
Summative Assessment	**After Chapter 11**	
	Check mastery of chapter concepts.	Prescribe intervention.
	Multiple-Choice Tests (Forms A, B, C)	**Reteach** CRB
	Free-Response Tests (Forms A, B, C)	***Lesson Tutorial Videos***
	Performance Assessment AR	
	Cumulative Test AR	
	Test and Practice Generator	

KEY: **SE** = *Student Edition* **TE** = *Teacher's Edition* **CRB** = *Chapter Resource Book* **AR** = *Assessment Resources* Available online 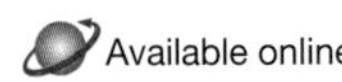 Available on CD- or DVD-ROM

Lesson Resources

Before the Lesson

Prepare

Teacher One Stop 
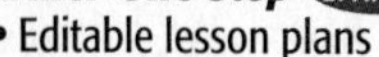
- Editable lesson plans
- Calendar Planner
- Easy access to all chapter resources

Lesson Transparencies
- Teacher Tools

Teach the Lesson

Introduce

Alternate Openers: Explorations

Lesson Transparencies
- Warm Up
- Problem of the Day

Teach

Lesson Transparencies
- Teaching Transparencies

Know-It Notebook™
- Vocabulary
- Key Concepts

Power Presentations

Lesson Tutorial Videos SPANISH

Interactive Online Edition 
- Lesson Activities
- Lesson Tutorial Videos

Lab Activities

Lab Resources Online

Online Interactivities 

TechKeys 

Practice the Lesson

Practice

Chapter Resources
- Practice A, B, C

Practice and Problem Solving Workbook SPANISH

IDEA Works!® Modified Worksheets and Tests

ExamView Test and Practice Generator SPANISH 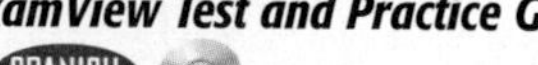

Homework Help Online

Online Interactivities SPANISH

Interactive Online Edition 
- Homework Help

Apply

Chapter Resources
- Problem Solving SPANISH

Practice and Problem Solving Workbook SPANISH

Interactive Online Edition
- Chapter Project

Project Teacher Support

After the Lesson

Reteach

Chapter Resources
- Reteach
- Reading Strategies ELL

Success for Every Learner

Review

Interactive Answers and Solutions

Solutions Key

Know-It Notebook™
- Big Ideas
- Chapter Review

Extend

Chapter Resources
- Challenge

Technology Highlights for the Teacher

 **Power Presentations**

Dynamic presentations to engage students. Complete PowerPoint® presentations for every lesson in Chapter 11.

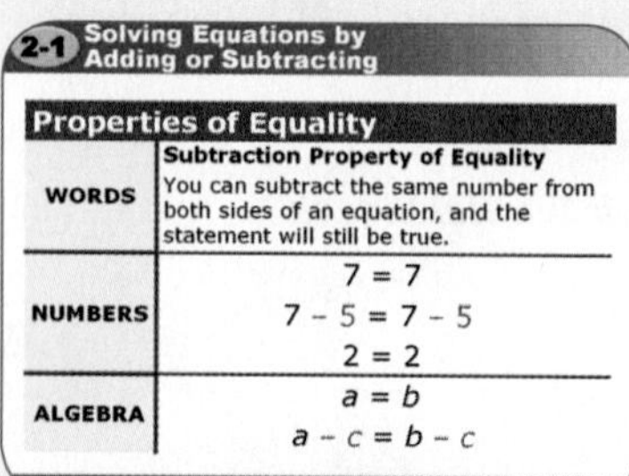

 **Teacher One Stop** SPANISH

Easy access to Chapter 11 resources and assessments. Includes lesson planning, test generation, and puzzle creation software.

 **Premier Online Edition** SPANISH

Chapter 11 includes Tutorial Videos, Lesson Activities, Lesson Quizzes, Homework Help, and Chapter Project.

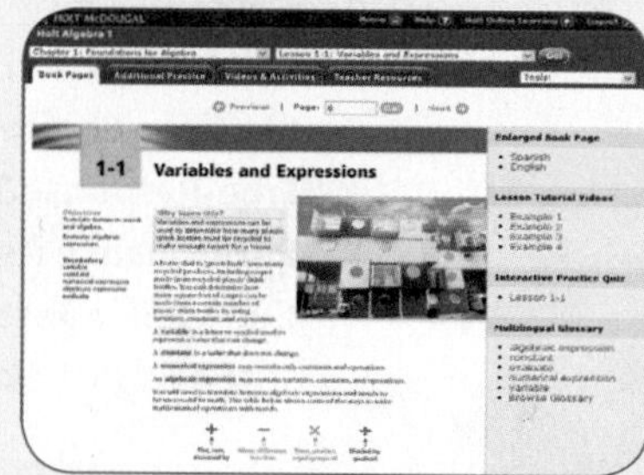

KEY: **SE** = *Student Edition* **TE** = *Teacher's Edition*  English Language Learners  Spanish version available  Available online Available on CD- or DVD-ROM

Reaching All Learners

Teaching tips to help all learners appear throughout the chapter. A few that target specific students are included in the lists below.

All Learners

Lab Activities
Practice and Problem Solving Workbook SPANISH
Know-It Notebook

Special Needs Students

Practice A	CRB
Reteach	CRB
Reading Strategies	CRB
Are You Ready?	SE p. 787
Inclusion	TE pp. 798, 814, 817, 825, 831

IDEA Works!® Modified Worksheets and Tests
Ready to Go On? Intervention SPANISH
Know-It Notebook
Online Interactivities  SPANISH
Lesson Tutorial Videos  SPANISH

Developing Learners

Practice A	CRB
Reteach	CRB
Reading Strategies	CRB
Are You Ready?	SE p. 787
Vocabulary Connections	SE p. 788
Questioning Strategies	TE

Ready to Go On? Intervention SPANISH
Know-It Notebook
Homework Help Online
Online Interactivities   SPANISH
Lesson Tutorial Videos  SPANISH

On-Level Learners

Practice B	CRB
Problem Solving	CRB
Vocabulary Connections	SE p. 788
Questioning Strategies	TE

Ready to Go On? Intervention SPANISH
Know-It Notebook
Homework Help Online
Online Interactivities SPANISH

Advanced Learners

Practice C	CRB
Challenge	CRB
Challenge Exercises	SE
Reading and Writing Math *Extend*	TE p. 789
Critical Thinking	TE pp. 791, 807, 814

Are You Ready? Enrichment SPANISH
Ready To Go On? Enrichment  SPANISH

English Language Learners

ENGLISH LANGUAGE LEARNERS

Reading Strategies	CRB
Are You Ready? Vocabulary	SE p. 787
Vocabulary Connections	SE p. 788
Vocabulary Review	SE p. 856
English Language Learners	TE pp. 806, 842, 849

Success for Every Learner
Know-It Notebook
Multilingual Glossary
Lesson Tutorial Videos  SPANISH 

Technology Highlights for Reaching All Learners

Lesson Tutorial Videos SPANISH

Starring Holt authors Ed Burger and Freddie Renfro! Live tutorials to support every lesson in Chapter 11.

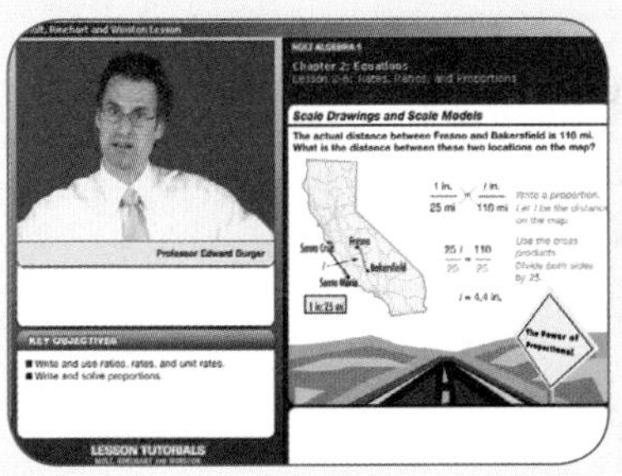

Multilingual Glossary

Searchable glossary includes definitions in English, Spanish, Vietnamese, Chinese, Hmong, Korean, and 4 other languages.

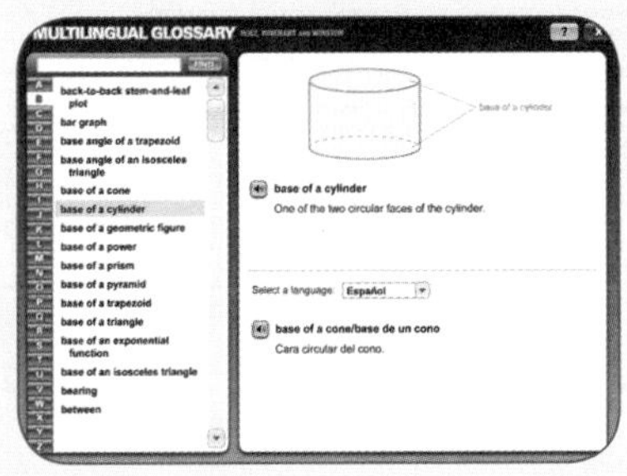

Online Interactivities

Interactive tutorials provide visually engaging alternative opportunities to learn concepts and master skills.

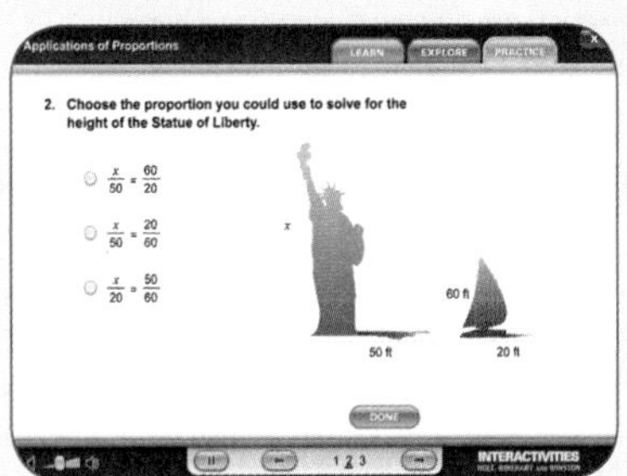

KEY: **SE** = *Student Edition* **TE** = *Teacher's Edition* **CRB** = *Chapter Resource Book* SPANISH Spanish version available · Available online · Available on CD- or DVD-ROM

Ongoing Assessment

Assessing Prior Knowledge

Determine whether students have the prerequisite concepts and skills for success in Chapter 11.

Are You Ready? SPANISH .... SE p. 787
Warm Up .... TE

Test Preparation

Provide review and practice for Chapter 11 and standardized tests.

Multi-Step Test Prep .... SE pp. 820, 854
Study Guide: Review .... SE pp. 856–859
Test Tackler .... SE pp. 862–863
Standardized Test Prep .... SE pp. 864–865
College Entrance Exam Practice .... SE p. 861
Countdown to Testing .... SE pp. C4–C27
IDEA Works!® Modified Worksheets and Tests

Alternative Assessment

Assess students' understanding of Chapter 11 concepts and combined problem-solving skills.

Chapter 11 Project .... SE p. 786
Alternative Assessment .... TE

Performance Assessment SPANISH .... AR
Portfolio Assessment SPANISH .... AR

Lesson Assessment

Provide formative assessment for each lesson of Chapter 11.

Questioning Strategies .... TE
Think and Discuss .... SE
Check It Out! Exercises .... SE
Write About It .... SE
Journal .... TE
Lesson Quiz .... TE
Alternative Assessment .... TE
IDEA Works!® Modified Worksheets and Tests

Weekly Assessment

Provide formative assessment for each section of Chapter 11.

Multi-Step Test Prep .... SE pp. 820, 854
Ready to Go On? SPANISH .... SE pp. 821, 855
Section Quizzes SPANISH .... AR
Test and Practice Generator SPANISH .... *Teacher One Stop*

Chapter Assessment

Provide summative assessment of Chapter 11 mastery.

Chapter 11 Test .... SE p. 860
Chapter Test (Levels A, B, C) SPANISH .... AR
- Multiple Choice
- Free Response

Cumulative Test SPANISH .... AR
Test and Practice Generator SPANISH .... *Teacher One Stop*
IDEA Works!® Modified Worksheets and Tests

Technology Highlights for Assessment

Are You Ready? SPANISH

Automatically assess readiness and prescribe intervention for Chapter 11 prerequisite skills.

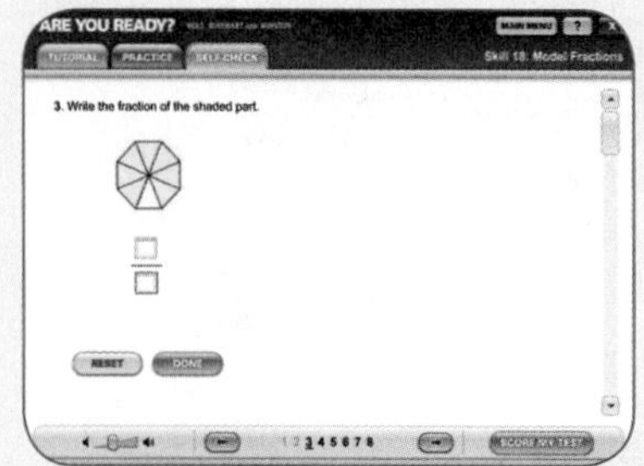

Ready to Go On?

Automatically assess understanding of and prescribe intervention for Sections 11A and 11B.

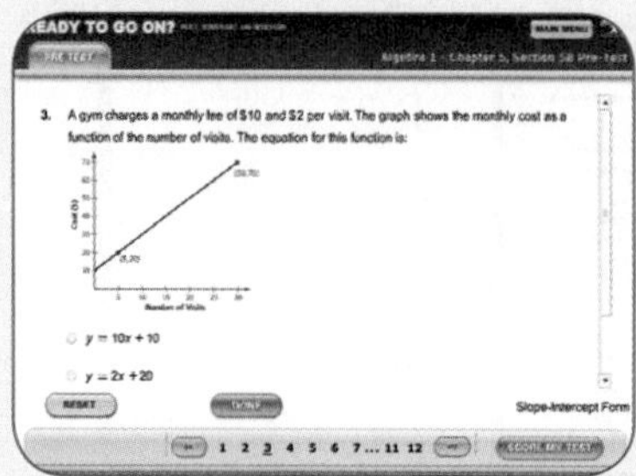

Test and Practice Generator SPANISH

Use Chapter 11 problem banks to create assessments and worksheets to print out or deliver online. Includes dynamic problems.

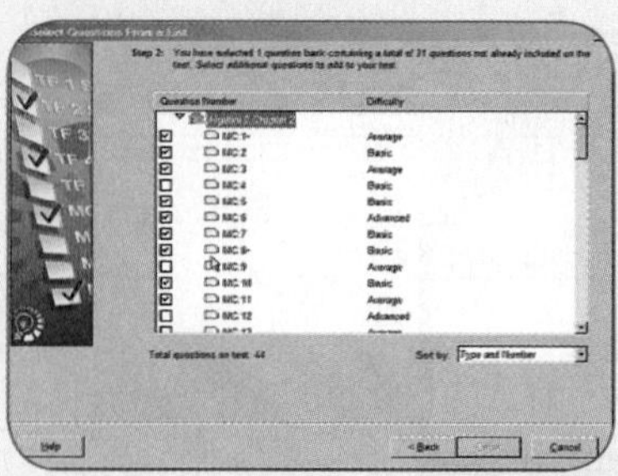

KEY: **SE** = *Student Edition* **TE** = *Teacher's Edition* **AR** = *Assessment Resources*  Spanish version available 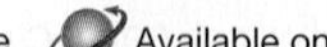  

Formal Assessment

Three levels (A, B, C) of multiple-choice and free-response chapter tests, along with a performance assessment, are available in the *Assessment Resources.*

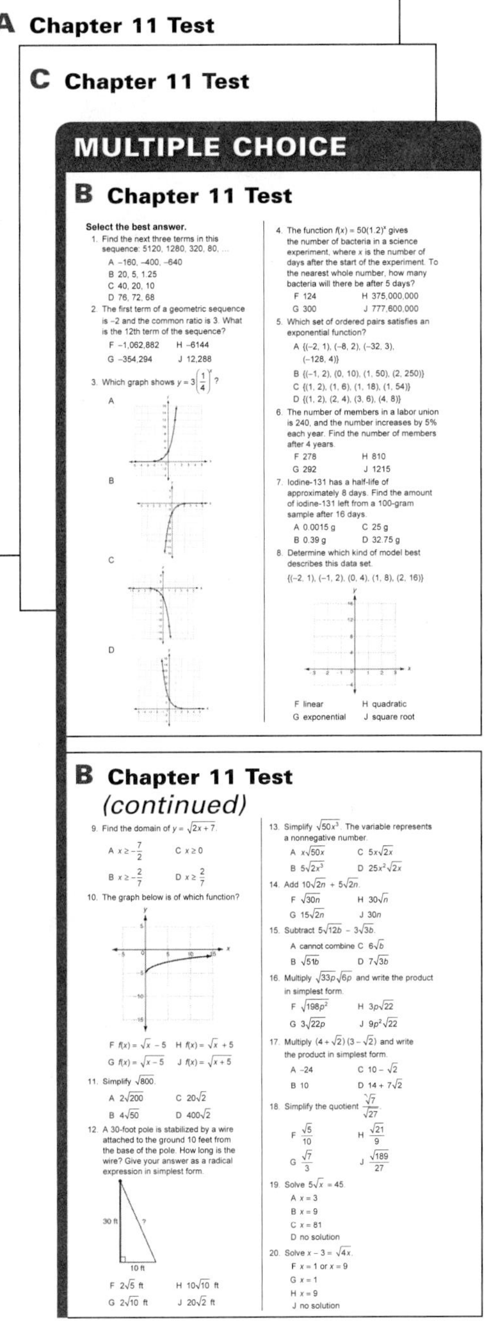

A Chapter 11 Test

C Chapter 11 Test

MULTIPLE CHOICE

B Chapter 11 Test

Select the best answer.

1. Find the next three terms in this sequence: 5120, 1280, 320, 80, ...
   A −160, −400, −640
   B 20, 5, 1.25
   C 40, 20, 10
   D 76, 72, 68

2. The first term of a geometric sequence is −2 and the common ratio is 3. What is the 12th term of the sequence?
   F −1,062,882 H −6144
   G −354,294 J 12,288

3. Which graph shows $y = 3\left(\frac{1}{4}\right)^x$?
   A B C D

4. The function $f(x) = 50(1.2)^x$ gives the number of bacteria in a science experiment, where x is the number of days after the start of the experiment. To the nearest whole number, how many bacteria will there be after 5 days?
   F 124 H 375,000,000
   G 300 J 777,600,000

5. Which set of ordered pairs satisfies an exponential function?
   A {(−2, 1), (−8, 2), (−32, 3), (−128, 4)}
   B {(−1, 2), (0, 10), (1, 50), (2, 250)}
   C {(1, 2), (1, 6), (1, 18), (1, 54)}
   D {(1, 2), (2, 4), (3, 6), (4, 8)}

6. The number of members in a labor union is 240, and the number increases by 5% each year. Find the number of members after 4 years.
   F 278 H 810
   G 292 J 1215

7. Iodine-131 has a half-life of approximately 8 days. Find the amount of iodine-131 left from a 100-gram sample after 16 days.
   A 0.0015 g C 25 g
   B 0.39 g D 32.75 g

8. Determine which kind of model best describes this data set.
   {(−2, 1), (−1, 2), (0, 4), (1, 8), (2, 16)}
   F linear H quadratic
   G exponential J square root

B Chapter 11 Test *(continued)*

9. Find the domain of $y = \sqrt{2x + 7}$.
   A $x \geq -\frac{7}{2}$ C $x \geq 0$
   B $x \geq -\frac{2}{7}$ D $x \geq \frac{2}{7}$

10. The graph below is of which function?
   F $f(x) = \sqrt{x} - 5$ H $f(x) = \sqrt{x} + 5$
   G $f(x) = \sqrt{x - 5}$ J $f(x) = \sqrt{x + 5}$

11. Simplify $\sqrt{800}$.
   A $2\sqrt{200}$ C $20\sqrt{2}$
   B $4\sqrt{50}$ D $400\sqrt{2}$

12. A 30-foot pole is stabilized by a wire attached to the ground 10 feet from the base of the pole. How long is the wire? Give your answer as a radical expression in simplest form.
   30 ft ? 10 ft
   F $2\sqrt{5}$ ft H $10\sqrt{10}$ ft
   G $2\sqrt{10}$ ft J $20\sqrt{2}$ ft

13. Simplify $\sqrt{50x^3}$. The variable represents a nonnegative number.
   A $x\sqrt{50x}$ C $5x\sqrt{2x}$
   B $5\sqrt{2x^3}$ D $25x^2\sqrt{2x}$

14. Add $10\sqrt{2n} + 5\sqrt{2n}$.
   F $\sqrt{30n}$ H $30\sqrt{n}$
   G $15\sqrt{2n}$ J $30n$

15. Subtract $5\sqrt{12b} - 3\sqrt{3b}$.
   A cannot combine C $6\sqrt{b}$
   B $\sqrt{51b}$ D $7\sqrt{3b}$

16. Multiply $\sqrt{33p}\sqrt{6p}$ and write the product in simplest form.
   F $\sqrt{198p^2}$ H $3p\sqrt{22}$
   G $3\sqrt{22p}$ J $9p^2\sqrt{22}$

17. Multiply $(4 + \sqrt{2})(3 - \sqrt{2})$ and write the product in simplest form.
   A −24 C $10 - \sqrt{2}$
   B 10 D $14 + 7\sqrt{2}$

18. Simplify the quotient $\frac{\sqrt{7}}{\sqrt{27}}$.
   F $\frac{\sqrt{5}}{10}$ H $\frac{\sqrt{21}}{9}$
   G $\frac{\sqrt{7}}{3}$ J $\frac{\sqrt{189}}{27}$

19. Solve $5\sqrt{x} = 45$.
   A $x = 3$
   B $x = 9$
   C $x = 81$
   D no solution

20. Solve $x - 3 = \sqrt{4x}$.
   F $x = 1$ or $x = 9$
   G $x = 1$
   H $x = 9$
   J no solution

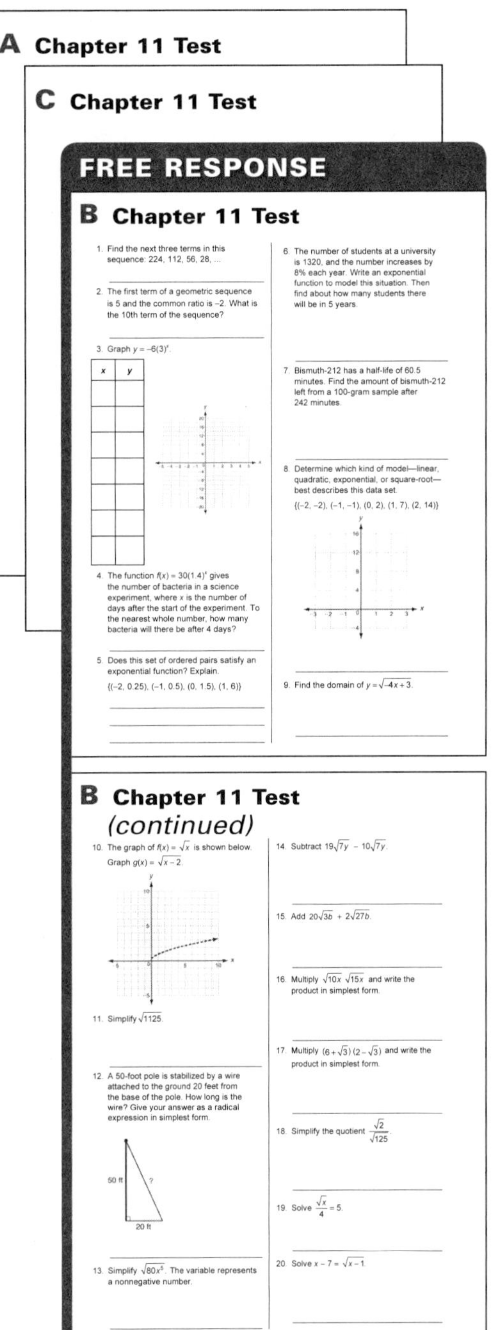

A Chapter 11 Test

C Chapter 11 Test

FREE RESPONSE

B Chapter 11 Test

1. Find the next three terms in this sequence: 224, 112, 56, 28, ...

2. The first term of a geometric sequence is 5 and the common ratio is −2. What is the 10th term of the sequence?

3. Graph $y = -6(3)^x$.

x	y

4. The function $f(x) = 30(1.4)^x$ gives the number of bacteria in a science experiment, where x is the number of days after the start of the experiment. To the nearest whole number, how many bacteria will there be after 4 days?

5. Does this set of ordered pairs satisfy an exponential function? Explain.
   {(−2, 0.25), (−1, 0.5), (0, 1.5), (1, 6)}

6. The number of students at a university is 1320, and the number increases by 8% each year. Write an exponential function to model this situation. Then find about how many students there will be in 5 years.

7. Bismuth-212 has a half-life of 60.5 minutes. Find the amount of bismuth-212 left from a 100-gram sample after 242 minutes.

8. Determine which kind of model—linear, quadratic, exponential, or square-root—best describes this data set.
   {(−2, −2), (−1, −1), (0, 2), (1, 7), (2, 14)}

9. Find the domain of $y = \sqrt{-4x + 3}$.

B Chapter 11 Test *(continued)*

10. The graph of $f(x) = \sqrt{x}$ is shown below. Graph $g(x) = \sqrt{x - 2}$.

11. Simplify $\sqrt{1125}$.

12. A 50-foot pole is stabilized by a wire attached to the ground 20 feet from the base of the pole. How long is the wire? Give your answer as a radical expression in simplest form.
   50 ft ? 20 ft

13. Simplify $\sqrt{80x^5}$. The variable represents a nonnegative number.

14. Subtract $19\sqrt{7y} - 10\sqrt{7y}$.

15. Add $20\sqrt{3b} + 2\sqrt{27b}$.

16. Multiply $\sqrt{10x}\,\sqrt{15x}$ and write the product in simplest form.

17. Multiply $(6 + \sqrt{3})(2 - \sqrt{3})$ and write the product in simplest form.

18. Simplify the quotient $\frac{\sqrt{2}}{\sqrt{125}}$.

19. Solve $\frac{\sqrt{x}}{4} = 5$.

20. Solve $x - 7 = \sqrt{x - 1}$.

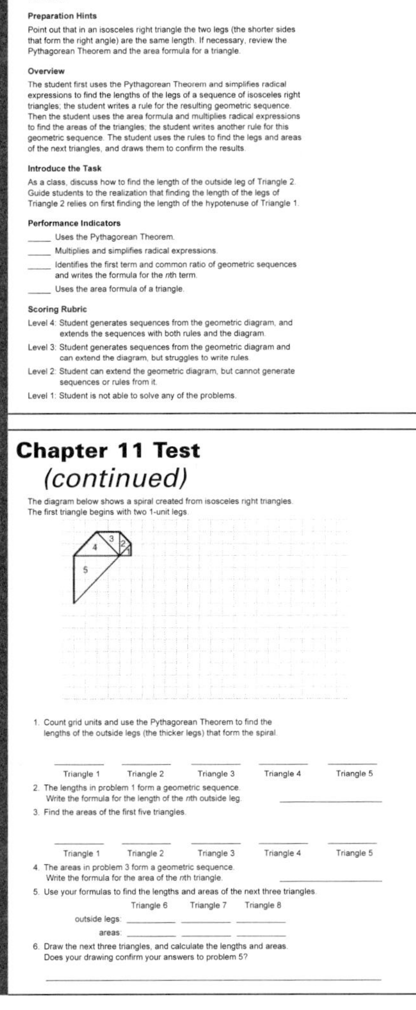

PERFORMANCE ASSESSMENT

Chapter 11 Test

Purpose
This performance task assesses the student's ability to find the *n*th term of a geometric sequence and to multiply and simplify radical expressions.

Time
20–40 minutes

Grouping
Individuals

Preparation Hints
Point out that in an isosceles right triangle the two legs (the shorter sides that form the right angle) are the same length. If necessary, review the Pythagorean Theorem and the area formula for a triangle.

Overview
The student first uses the Pythagorean Theorem and simplifies radical expressions to find the lengths of the legs of a sequence of isosceles right triangles; the student writes a rule for the resulting geometric sequence. Then the student uses the area formula and multiplies radical expressions to find the areas of the triangles; the student writes another rule for this geometric sequence. The student uses the rules to find the legs and areas of the next triangles, and draws them to confirm the results.

Introduce the Task
As a class, discuss how to find the length of the outside leg of Triangle 2. Guide students to the realization that finding the length of the legs of Triangle 2 relies on first finding the length of the hypotenuse of Triangle 1.

Performance Indicators
_____ Uses the Pythagorean Theorem.
_____ Multiplies and simplifies radical expressions.
_____ Identifies the first term and common ratio of geometric sequences and writes the formula for the *n*th term.
_____ Uses the area formula of a triangle.

Scoring Rubric
Level 4: Student generates sequences from the geometric diagram, and extends the sequences with both rules and the diagram.
Level 3: Student generates sequences from the geometric diagram and can extend the diagram, but struggles to write rules.
Level 2: Student can extend the geometric diagram, but cannot generate sequences or rules from it.
Level 1: Student is not able to solve any of the problems.

Chapter 11 Test *(continued)*

The diagram below shows a spiral created from isosceles right triangles. The first triangle begins with two 1-unit legs.

1. Count grid units and use the Pythagorean Theorem to find the lengths of the outside legs (the thicker legs) that form the spiral.
   Triangle 1 Triangle 2 Triangle 3 Triangle 4 Triangle 5
2. The lengths in problem 1 form a geometric sequence. Write the formula for the length of the *n*th outside leg.
3. Find the areas of the first five triangles.
   Triangle 1 Triangle 2 Triangle 3 Triangle 4 Triangle 5
4. The areas in problem 3 form a geometric sequence. Write the formula for the area of the *n*th triangle.
5. Use your formulas to find the lengths and areas of the next three triangles.

	Triangle 6	Triangle 7	Triangle 8
outside legs:			
areas:			

6. Draw the next three triangles, and calculate the lengths and areas. Does your drawing confirm your answers to problem 5?

Teacher One Stop™ 

Test & Practice Generator

Create and customize Chapter 11 Tests. Instantly generate multiple test versions, answer keys, and Spanish versions of test items.

Modified chapter tests that address special learning needs are available in *IDEA Works!® Modified Worksheets and Tests.*

CHAPTER 11

SECTION 11A

Exponential Functions

On page 820, students write and graph functions to model real-world college tuition situations.

Exercises designed to prepare students for success on the Multi-Step Test Prep can be found in each lesson.

SECTION 11B

Radical Functions and Equations

On page 854, students solve radical equations to model real-world velocity and distance situations.

Exercises designed to prepare students for success on the Multi-Step Test Prep can be found in each lesson.

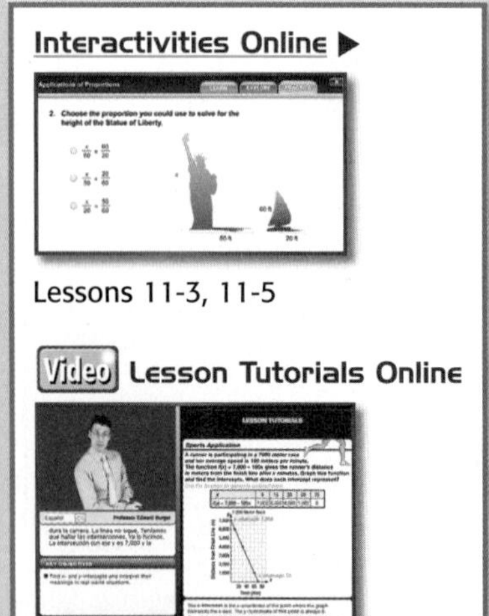

Interactivities Online ▶

Lessons 11-3, 11-5

Video Lesson Tutorials Online

Lesson Tutorial Videos are available for EVERY example.

CHAPTER 11

Exponential and Radical Functions

Chapter Focus

- Graph and use exponential functions to model real-world problems.
- Simplify radical expressions.
- Use radical equations to solve real-world problems.

Population Explosion

The concepts in this chapter are used to model many real-world phenomena, such as changes in wildlife populations.

go.hrw.com
Chapter Project Online
KEYWORD: MA7 ChProj

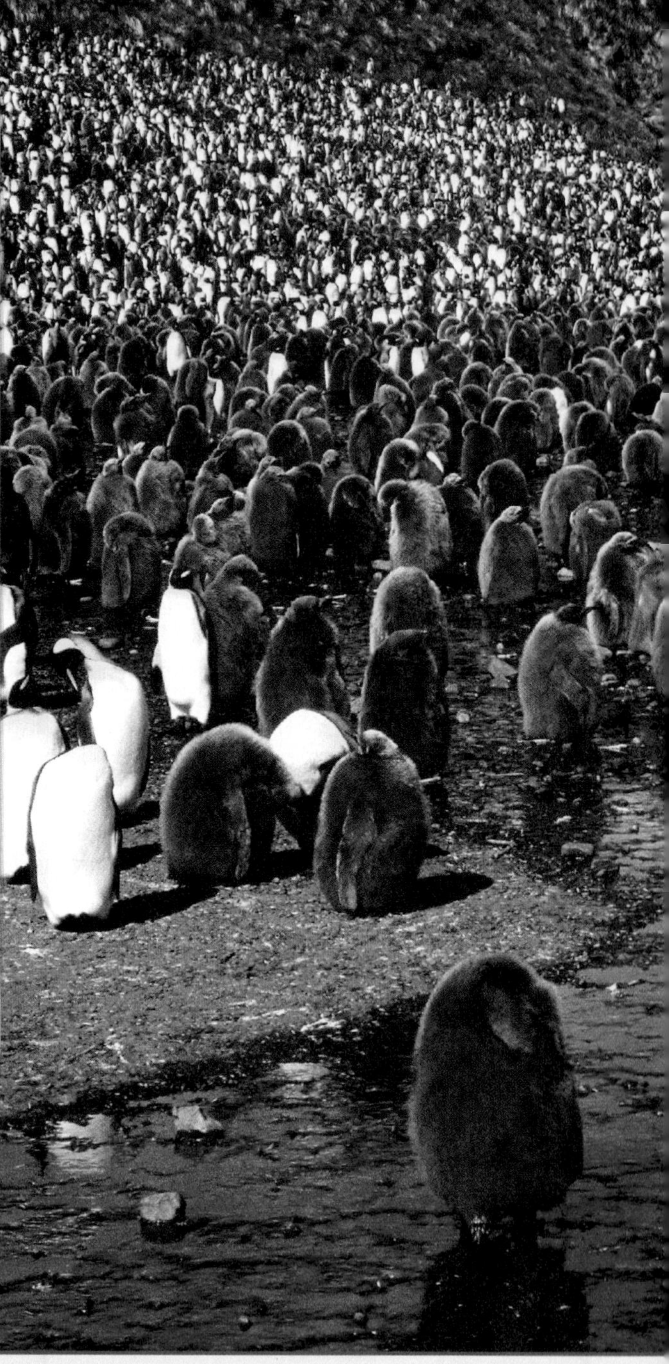

Population Explosion

About the Project

Students research population data, model the growth or decay two ways, and predict the population for the next 10 years using both models. Students decide which model is the more reasonable model and justify their reasoning.

Students also conduct a pendulum experiment to determine how the length of the string impacts the time it takes for one complete swing.

Project Resources

All project resources for teachers and students are provided online.

Materials:

- graphing calculator
- washer, string, centimeter tape measure, stopwatch

Match each term on the left with a definition on the right.

1. like terms **B**
2. square root **F**
3. domain **C**
4. perfect square **E**
5. exponent **D**

A. the set of second elements of a relation
B. terms that contain the same variables raised to the same powers
C. the set of first elements of a relation
D. a number that tells how many times a base is used as a factor
E. a number whose positive square root is a whole number
F. one of two equal factors of a number

Evaluate Powers

Find the value of each expression.

6. 2^4 **16**
7. 5^0 **1**
8. $7 \cdot 3^2$ **63**
9. $3 \cdot 5^3$ **375**
10. 3^5 **243**
11. $-6^2 + 8^1$ **−28**
12. $40 \cdot 2^3$ **320**
13. $7^2 \cdot 3^1$ **147**

Graph Functions

Graph each function.

14. $y = 8$
15. $y = x + 3$
16. $y = x^2 - 4$
17. $y = x^2 + 2$

Fractions, Decimals, and Percents

Write each percent as a decimal.

18. 50% **0.5**
19. 25% **0.25**
20. 15.2% **0.152**
21. 200% **2.0**
22. 1.9% **0.019**
23. 0.3% **0.003**
24. 0.1% **0.001**
25. 1.04% **0.0104**

Squares and Square Roots

Find each square root.

26. $\sqrt{36}$ **6**
27. $\sqrt{81}$ **9**
28. $\sqrt{25}$ **5**
29. $\sqrt{64}$ **8**

Pythagorean Theorem

Find the length of the hypotenuse in each right triangle.

30. **5 cm**

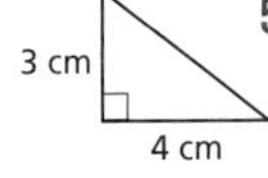

31. **13 in.**

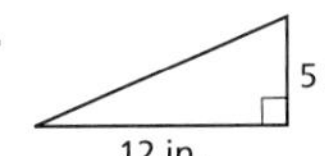

32. **10 ft**

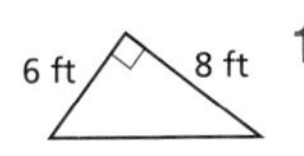

Multiply Monomials and Polynomials

Multiply.

33. $5(2m - 3)$ **$10m - 15$**
34. $3x(8x + 9)$ **$24x^2 + 27x$**
35. $2t(3t - 1)$ **$6t^2 - 2t$**
36. $4r(4r - 5)$ **$16r^2 - 20r$**

CHAPTER 11

ARE YOU READY?

Organizer

Objective: Assess students' understanding of prerequisite skills.

Assessing Prior Knowledge

INTERVENTION

Diagnose and Prescribe

Use this page to determine whether intervention is necessary or whether enrichment is appropriate.

Resources

***Are You Ready? Intervention and Enrichment* Worksheets**

***Are You Ready?* CD-ROM**

***Are You Ready?* Online**

my.hrw.com

Answers

14–17. See p. A33.

ARE YOU READY?

Diagnose and Prescribe

Prerequisite Skill	*Are You Ready? Intervention*, Chapter 11		
	Worksheets	CD-ROM	Online
Evaluate Powers	Skill 8	Activity 8	Diagnose and Prescribe Online
Graph Functions	Skill 80	Activity 80	
Fractions, Decimals, and Percents	Skill 14	Activity 14	
Squares and Square Roots	Skill 6	Activity 6	
Pythagorean Theorem	Skill 31	Activity 31	
Multiply Monomials and Polynomials	Skill 62	Activity 62	

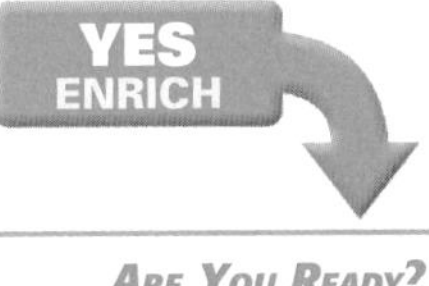

Are You Ready? Enrichment, Chapter 11
- Worksheets
- CD-ROM
- Online

Study Guide: Preview

Organizer

Objective: Help students organize the new concepts they will learn in Chapter 11.

Online Edition
Multilingual Glossary

Resources

Teacher One Stop™
Puzzle View

Multilingual Glossary **Online**
go.hrw.com
KEYWORD: MA7 Glossary

Answers to *Vocabulary Connections*

1. There is something about them that is the same; a comparison of two numbers by division; when you divide the terms, the resulting values will be the same.
2. 16
3. an expression with a square root; an equation with a square root
4. an extra solution that does not make the equation true

CHAPTER 11

Study Guide: Preview

Where You've Been

Previously, you

- identified and extended arithmetic sequences.
- identified and graphed linear functions and quadratic functions.
- solved linear and quadratic equations.

In This Chapter

You will study

- another type of sequence—geometric sequences.
- two more types of functions—exponential functions and square-root functions.
- radical equations.

Where You're Going

You can use the skills in this chapter

- to analyze more complicated functions in later math courses, such as Calculus.
- to explore exponential growth and decay models that are used in science.
- to make informed decisions about finances.

Key Vocabulary/Vocabulario

common ratio	razón común
compound interest	interés compuesto
exponential decay	decrecimiento exponencial
exponential function	función exponencial
exponential growth	crecimiento exponencial
extraneous solution	solución extraña
geometric sequence	sucesión geométrica
like radicals	radicales semejantes
radical equation	ecuación radical
radical expression	expresión radical
radicand	radicando
square-root function	función de raíz cuadrada

Vocabulary Connections

To become familiar with some of the vocabulary terms in the chapter, consider the following. You may refer to the chapter, the glossary, or a dictionary if you like.

1. What does it mean when several items have something "in common"? What is a ratio? What do you think **common ratio** means?
2. In the division problem $2\overline{)50}$ with quotient 25, the *dividend* is 50. If a *radicand* is similar to a dividend, then what is the **radicand** in $\sqrt{16} = 4$?
3. A square-root sign is also known as a *radical.* Use this knowledge to define **radical expression** and **radical equation** .
4. The root word of *extraneous* is *extra. Extraneous* means *irrelevant* or *unrelated.* Use this information to define **extraneous solution** .

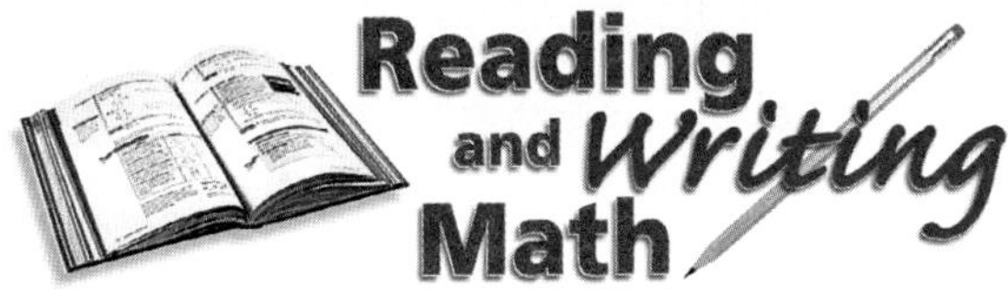

Study Strategy: Remember Formulas

In math, there are many formulas, properties, and rules that you should commit to memory.

To memorize a formula, create flash cards. Write the name of the formula on one side of a card. Write the formula on the other side of the card. You might also include a diagram or an example if helpful. Study your flash cards on a regular basis.

Sample Flash Card

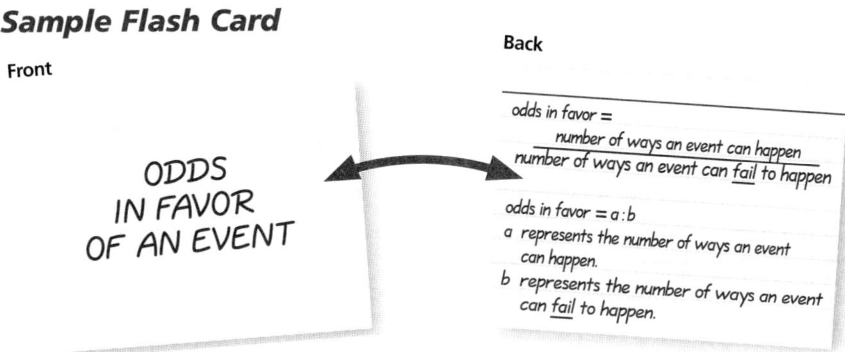

Knowing when and how to apply a mathematical formula is as important as memorizing the formula itself.

To know what formula to apply, read the problem carefully and look for key words.

From Lesson 10-6

> The **probability** of choosing an ace from a deck of cards is $\frac{1}{13}$.
> What are the **odds of choosing an ace**?

The key words have been highlighted. The probability is given, and you are asked to find the odds. You should use the formula for *odds in favor of an event.*

Try This

Read each problem. Then write the formula(s) needed to solve it. What key words helped you identify the formula?

1. A manufacturer inspects 450 computer chips and finds that 22 are defective. What is the experimental probability that a chip chosen at random is defective?
2. The area of a rectangular pool is 120 square feet. The length is 1 foot less than twice the width. What is the perimeter of the pool?

Reading and Writing Math CHAPTER 11

Organizer

Objective: Help students apply strategies to understand and retain key concepts.

Online Edition

Study Strategy: Remember Formulas

Discuss Remind students to be careful with units when using formulas. For instance, if t stands for time in years and the time is 6 months, the value of t is 0.5, not 6. Also consider forms of numbers. If r stands for rate as a decimal and the rate is 25%, the value of r is 0.25, not 25.

Extend There are several formulas in the first section of Chapter 11. Have students make and use flashcards to quiz each other each day.

Answers to *Try This*

Possible answers:

1. experimental probability = $\frac{\text{number of times the event occurs}}{\text{number of trials}}$, experimental probability
2. $A = \ell w$; $P = 2\ell + 2w$; area, rectangular, perimeter

Reading Connection

***Marvels of Math* by Kendall F. Haven**

Haven describes 16 fascinating episodes in the history of mathematics. He introduces each with a short discussion of key terms; tells the stories in short-story form, complete with imagined conversations; and follows each story with questions and exploratory activities.

Activity After students have studied radical expressions, have them read Chapter 1, *Numbers in the Sand.* Ask them to write about the discovery made by the followers of Pythagoras, and to explain how this discovery contradicted Pythagoras's teachings. Pythagoras believed that all numbers could be expressed as a ratio of whole numbers. His followers discovered $\sqrt{2}$, which cannot be expressed in this way.

SECTION

11A Exponential Functions

One-Minute Section Planner

Lesson	Lab Resources	Materials
Lesson 11-1 Geometric Sequences • Recognize and extend geometric sequences. • Find the *n*th term of a geometric sequence. ☐ SAT-10 ☑ NAEP ☑ ACT ☑ SAT ☑ SAT Subject Tests		**Required** graphing calculator
Lesson 11-2 Exponential Functions • Evaluate exponential functions. • Identify and graph exponential functions. ☐ SAT-10 ☑ NAEP ☐ ACT ☑ SAT ☑ SAT Subject Tests		**Required** graphing calculator
11-3 Algebra Lab Model Growth and Decay • Fold and cut paper to model exponential growth and decay. ☐ SAT-10 ☐ NAEP ☐ ACT ☑ SAT ☑ SAT Subject Tests	***Algebra Lab Activities*** 11-3 Lab Recording Sheet	**Required** notebook paper, scissors
Lesson 11-3 Exponential Growth and Decay • Solve problems involving exponential growth and decay. ☐ SAT-10 ☑ NAEP ☐ ACT ☑ SAT ☑ SAT Subject Tests	***Algebra Lab Activities*** 11-3 Algebra Lab	**Required** graphing calculator
Lesson 11-4 Linear, Quadratic, and Exponential Models • Compare linear, quadratic, and exponential models. • Given a set of data, decide which type of function models the data and write an equation to describe the function. ☑ SAT-10 ☑ NAEP ☑ ACT ☑ SAT ☑ SAT Subject Tests		**Optional** graphing calculator

Note: If NAEP is checked, the content is tested on either the Grade 8 or the Grade 12 NAEP assessment.

MK = *Manipulatives Kit*

Math Background

Professional Learning

GEOMETRIC SEQUENCES AND EXPONENTIAL FUNCTIONS

Lessons 11-1 and 11-2

To understand the connection between geometric sequences and exponential functions, we begin with the definition of *exponential function:* a function of the form $y = ab^x$, where $a \neq 0$, $b > 0$, and $b \neq 1$. At this point, students have seen b^x defined for limited x-values only (namely, rational numbers), but the domain of an exponential function is all real numbers. Students will fill in this gap in future courses and can be assured in the meantime that they may draw a smooth, continuous curve when graphing an exponential function.

For $a > 0$, the range of an exponential function is all positive real numbers, as illustrated in the graph of $y = 3(2)^x$.

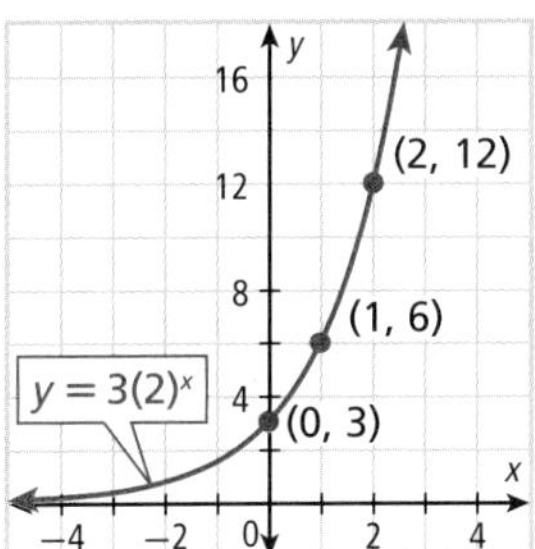

When the domain is restricted to the whole numbers, the graph becomes a set of discrete points, the first few of which are shown above. The points' y-values are 3, 6, 12, ... ; this is precisely the *geometric sequence* $a_n = 3(2)^{n-1}$. In other words, a geometric sequence is simply an exponential function with a restricted domain. (Note that the domain is usually restricted to the natural numbers, so that the first term of the sequence corresponds to the input value 1 rather than 0.)

EXPONENTIAL GROWTH AND DECAY

Lesson 11-3

Exponential growth and decay are important applications of exponential functions.

Exponential growth occurs when a quantity increases by the same rate in each time period. Thus, exponential growth can be understood as an extension of percent change in which a percent increase is repeatedly applied. *Exponential decay* occurs when a quantity decreases by the same rate in each time period, and, similar to exponential growth, can be understood as an extension of percent change in which a percent decrease is repeatedly applied.

In an exponential growth situation with initial amount a ($a > 0$) and rate of growth r expressed as a decimal, after one time period, the new amount is $a + ar$, or $a(1 + r)$. After the second time period, the new amount is $a(1 + r)(1 + r)$, or $a(1 + r)^2$. Continuing in this way shows that after t time periods, the final amount y is given by $y = a(1 + r)^t$. For exponential decay, a similar argument shows that the final amount y after t time periods is given by $y = a(1 - r)^t$.

An important attribute of exponential growth and decay is the fact that the amount added or subtracted in each time period is proportional to the amount already present. For exponential growth, this means that as the amount becomes greater, the amount of increase in each time period also becomes greater. Contrast this to linear growth, in which the amount of increase remains constant.

COMPOUND INTEREST

Lesson 11-3

Compound interest is closely related to exponential growth. In fact, for interest compounded once per year, the formula is analogous to that for exponential growth: $A = P(1 + r)^t$, where P represents the principal and A represents the total balance after t years. If interest is compounded n times per year, then the rate must be divided by n, and because there are nt periods in t years, the formula becomes $A = P\left(1 + \frac{r}{n}\right)^{nt}$.

As n increases, we approach a situation in which interest is compounded continuously. In future courses, students will study continuously compounded interest, which is given by $A = Pe^{rt}$ where $e \approx 2.71828$.

11-1 Organizer

Pacing: Traditional 1 day
Block $\frac{1}{2}$ day

Objectives: Recognize and extend geometric sequences.

Find the *n*th term of a geometric sequence.

Online Edition
Tutorial Videos

Power Presentations with PowerPoint®

Warm Up

Find the value of each expression.

1. 2^5 32 **2.** 2^{-5} $\frac{1}{32}$

3. -3^4 -81 **4.** $(-3)^4$ 81

5. $(0.2)^3$ 0.008 **6.** $7(-4)^2$ 112

7. $15\left(\frac{1}{3}\right)^3$ $\frac{5}{9}$

8. $12(-0.4)^3$ -0.768

Also available on transparency

Math Humor

Q: What type of dress did the rectangle wear to the prom?
A: A dress with geometric sequins.

11-1 Geometric Sequences

Objectives
Recognize and extend geometric sequences.

Find the *n*th term of a geometric sequence.

Vocabulary
geometric sequence
common ratio

Who uses this?
Bungee jumpers can use geometric sequences to calculate how high they will bounce.

The table shows the heights of a bungee jumper's bounces.

Bounce	1	2	3
Height (ft)	200	80	32

The height of the bounces shown in the table form a *geometric sequence.* In a **geometric sequence**, the ratio of successive terms is the same number *r*, called the **common ratio**.

Writing Math

The variable *a* is often used to represent terms in a sequence. The variable a_4 (read "*a* sub 4") is the fourth term in a sequence.

Geometric sequences can be thought of as functions. The term number, or position in the sequence, is the input, and the term itself is the output.

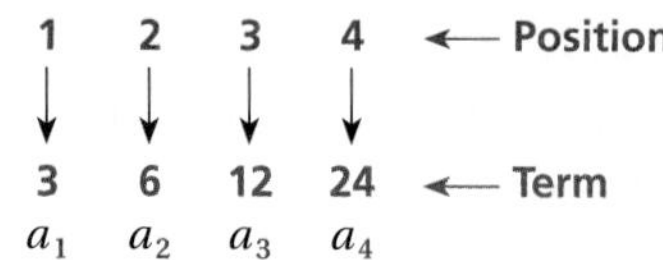

To find a term in a geometric sequence, multiply the previous term by *r*.

Finding a Term of a Geometric Sequence

The *n*th term of a geometric sequence with common ratio *r* is

$$a_n = a_{n-1}r$$

EXAMPLE 1 **Extending Geometric Sequences**

Find the next three terms in each geometric sequence.

A 1, 3, 9, 27, ...

Step 1 Find the value of *r* by dividing each term by the one before it.

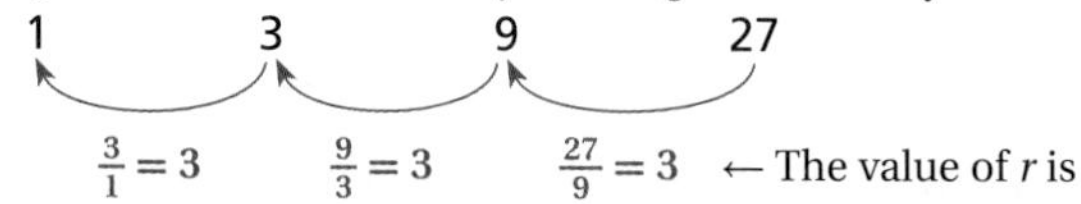

Step 2 Multiply each term by 3 to find the next three terms.

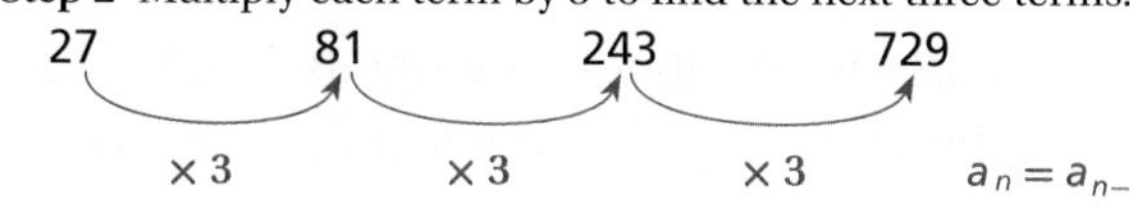

The next three terms are 81, 243, and 729.

State Resources

State Resources Online
KEYWORD: MA7 Resources

1 Introduce

EXPLORATION

11-1 Geometric Sequences

Marcella's grandmother wants to begin saving for Marcella's college education. She decides that the first year she will save \$1 and that each year thereafter she will save twice as much as the previous year.

1. Complete the table.

Year	1	2	3	4	5	6	7
Amount (\$)	1	2	4				

2. Look at the amounts in the table above. What is the ratio of any amount to the one before it?
3. Rewrite the amounts as powers of 2.

Year	1	2	3	4	5	6	7
Amount (\$)	2^0	2^1					

4. How is the exponent in each rewritten amount related to the year?

THINK AND DISCUSS

5. **Show** how to write a rule that you can use to predict the amount of money saved in year *n*.
6. **Explain** how you can use your rule to find the amount of money saved in year 10.

Motivate

Have students solve the following problem:

You are given 1 cent on the first of 20 days. Each day you will receive twice the amount as the previous day. How much will you receive on the 20th day? \$5242.88

Ask students how they figured out the answer. Possible answer: I wrote the amount received for the first day and then doubled the amount for the next 19 days.

Explorations and answers are provided in *Alternate Openers: Explorations Transparencies.*

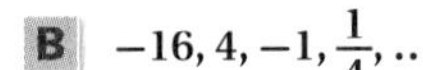

Helpful Hint

When the terms in a geometric sequence alternate between positive and negative, the value of r is negative.

B $-16, 4, -1, \frac{1}{4}, \ldots$

Step 1 Find the value of r by dividing each term by the one before it.

$-16 \quad 4 \quad -1 \quad \frac{1}{4}$

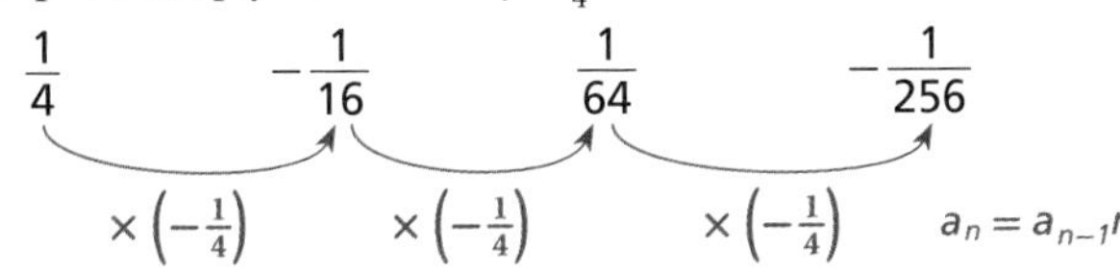

$\frac{4}{-16} = -\frac{1}{4} \quad \frac{-1}{4} = -\frac{1}{4} \quad \frac{\frac{1}{4}}{-1} = -\frac{1}{4}$ ← The value of r is $-\frac{1}{4}$.

Step 2 Multiply each term by $-\frac{1}{4}$ to find the next three terms.

$\frac{1}{4} \quad -\frac{1}{16} \quad \frac{1}{64} \quad -\frac{1}{256}$

$\times\left(-\frac{1}{4}\right) \quad \times\left(-\frac{1}{4}\right) \quad \times\left(-\frac{1}{4}\right) \quad a_n = a_{n-1}r$

The next three terms are $-\frac{1}{16}$, $\frac{1}{64}$, and $-\frac{1}{256}$.

CHECK IT OUT! **Find the next three terms in each geometric sequence.**

1a. 5, −10, 20, −40, ... **80, −160, 320**

1b. 512, 384, 288, ... **216, 162, 121.5**

To find the output a_n of a geometric sequence when n is a large number, you need an equation, or function rule.

The pattern in the table shows that to get the nth term, multiply the first term by the common ratio raised to the power $n - 1$.

Words	Numbers	Algebra
1st term	3	a_1
2nd term	$3 \cdot 2^1 = 6$	$a_1 \cdot r^1$
3rd term	$3 \cdot 2^2 = 12$	$a_1 \cdot r^2$
4th term	$3 \cdot 2^3 = 24$	$a_1 \cdot r^3$
nth term	$3 \cdot 2^{n-1}$	$a_1 \cdot r^{n-1}$

If the first term of a geometric sequence is a_1, the nth term is a_n, and the common ratio is r, then

$$a_n = a_1 r^{n-1}$$

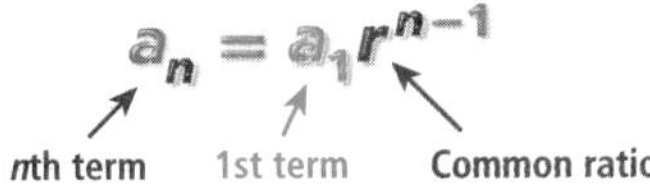

EXAMPLE 2 Finding the nth Term of a Geometric Sequence

A **The first term of a geometric sequence is 128, and the common ratio is 0.5. What is the 10th term of the sequence?**

$a_n = a_1 r^{n-1}$ *Write the formula.*

$a_{10} = 128(0.5)^{10-1}$ *Substitute 128 for a_1, 10 for n, and 0.5 for r.*

$= 128(0.5)^9$ *Simplify the exponent.*

$= 0.25$ *Use a calculator.*

B **For a geometric sequence, $a_1 = 8$ and $r = 3$. Find the 5th term of this sequence.**

$a_n = a_1 r^{n-1}$ *Write the formula.*

$a_5 = 8(3)^{5-1}$ *Substitute 8 for a_1, 5 for n, and 3 for r.*

$= 8(3)^4$ *Simplify the exponent.*

$= 648$ *Use a calculator.*

COMMON ERROR ALERT

When finding a common ratio, students might divide in the wrong order. For instance, in **Example 1B,** students might divide −16 by 4 and so on to get a common ratio of −4. Tell them they are really finding what each term is being *multiplied* by to get the next term, so the inverse operation (division), used in reverse, will produce r.

Power Presentations with PowerPoint®

Additional Examples

Example 1

Find the next three terms in each geometric sequence.

A. 1, 4, 16, 64,... 256, 1024, 4096

B. $-9, 3, -1, \frac{1}{3}, -\frac{1}{9}, \ldots$ $\frac{1}{27}, -\frac{1}{81}, \frac{1}{243}$

Example 2

A. The first term of a geometric sequence is 500 and the common ratio is 0.2. What is the 7th term of the sequence? 0.032

B. For a geometric sequence, $a_1 = 5$ and $r = 2$. Find the 6th term of this sequence. 160

C. What is the 9th term of the sequence 2, −6, 18, −54, ...? 13,122

INTERVENTION

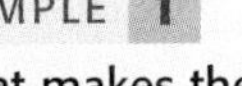

Questioning Strategies

EXAMPLE 1

- What makes the terms in some geometric sequences alternate signs?
- How do you find r when given part of a geometric sequence?

EXAMPLE 2

- When finding the nth term of a geometric sequence, why is r raised to $n - 1$, not n?
- How are geometric sequences and arithmetic sequences alike? How are they different?

Teaching Tip **Visual** Write the formula for a geometric sequence as *term wanted = first term × common ratio* $^{(\text{number of term wanted}) - 1}$.

2 Teach

Guided Instruction

After reviewing operations with exponents, show students a geometric sequence and how it can be extended with continued multiplication by r. Remind them that an arithmetic sequence is extended with continued addition by d. Choose a sequence from **Example 1** and show how each term is the product of the first term and the common ratio raised to an increasing power (starting with r^0).

Reaching All Learners

Through Critical Thinking

Display the following sequence: 3, 9, 27, 81, 243,...

Under each term, write a_1, a_2, a_3, a_4, and a_5. Write a_n directly below a_1 and ask how a_2 can be written in terms of n. a_{n+1} Then write the rule for finding the common ratio, r: divide each term by the one before it. Ask how the rule can be written algebraically. $r = \frac{a_{n+1}}{a_n}$ Show students that any two consecutive terms can be used; it can be the third and fourth terms or the fifth and sixth terms.

Power Presentations with PowerPoint®

Additional Examples

Example 3

A ball is dropped from a tower. The table shows the heights of the ball's bounces, which form a geometric sequence. What is the height of the 6th bounce?

9.375 cm

Bounce	Height (cm)
1	300
2	150
3	75

INTERVENTION

Questioning Strategies

EXAMPLE 3

- How can you tell whether the common ratio will be greater than one or less than one?
- How do you expect the sequence to continue? Why?

Teaching Tip **Math Background** The box on page 790 shows the recursive definition of a geometric sequence; in this form, the nth term is determined using the terms that precede it. The formula on page 791 is the iterative definition of a geometric sequence.

Caution!

When writing a function rule for a sequence with a negative common ratio, remember to enclose r in parentheses.

$-2^{12} \neq (-2)^{12}$

C What is the 13th term of the geometric sequence 8, −16, 32, −64, ... ?

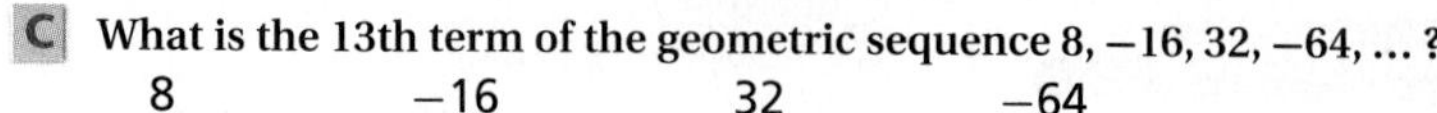

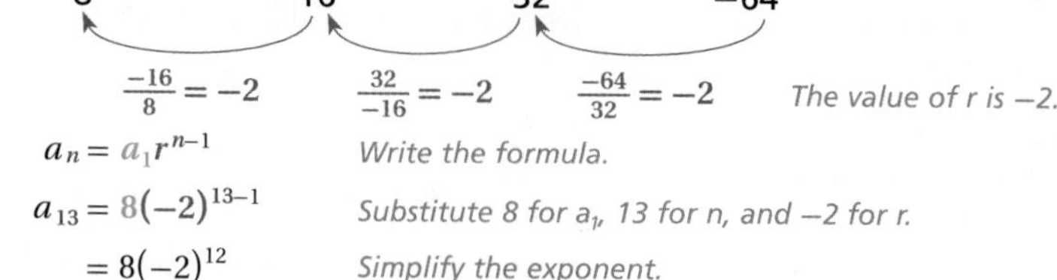

8, −16, 32, −64

$\frac{-16}{8} = -2$ $\quad \frac{32}{-16} = -2$ $\quad \frac{-64}{32} = -2$ *The value of r is −2.*

$a_n = a_1 r^{n-1}$ *Write the formula.*

$a_{13} = 8(-2)^{13-1}$ *Substitute 8 for a_1, 13 for n, and −2 for r.*

$= 8(-2)^{12}$ *Simplify the exponent.*

$= 32,768$ *Use a calculator.*

2. What is the 8th term of the sequence 1000, 500, 250, 125, ... ?

7.8125

EXAMPLE 3 ***Sports Application***

A bungee jumper jumps from a bridge. The diagram shows the bungee jumper's height above the ground at the top of each bounce. The heights form a geometric sequence. What is the bungee jumper's height at the top of the 5th bounce?

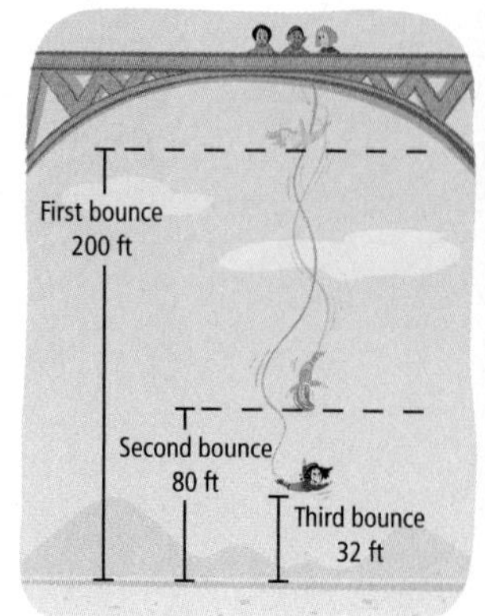

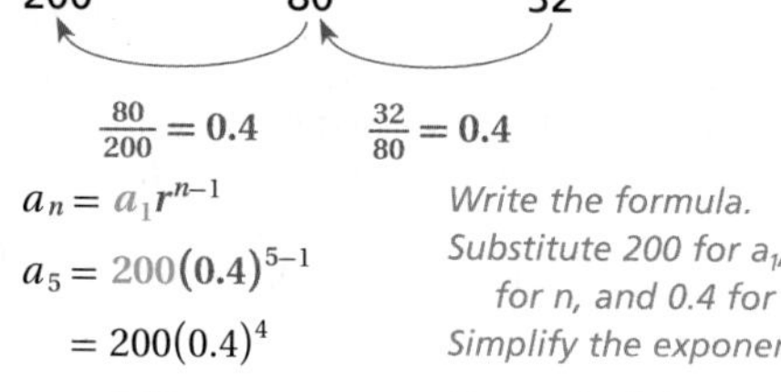

200, 80, 32

$\frac{80}{200} = 0.4$ $\quad \frac{32}{80} = 0.4$

$a_n = a_1 r^{n-1}$ *Write the formula.*

$a_5 = 200(0.4)^{5-1}$ *Substitute 200 for a_1, 5 for n, and 0.4 for r.*

$= 200(0.4)^4$ *Simplify the exponent.*

$= 5.12$ *Use a calculator.*

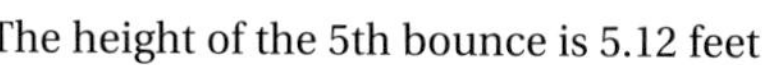

The height of the 5th bounce is 5.12 feet.

3. The table shows a car's value for 3 years after it is purchased. The values form a geometric sequence. How much will the car be worth in the 10th year?

$1342.18

Year	Value ($)
1	10,000
2	8,000
3	6,400

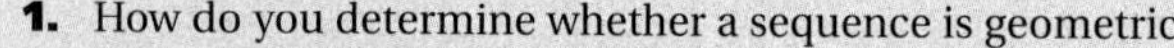

THINK AND DISCUSS

1. How do you determine whether a sequence is geometric?

2. GET ORGANIZED Copy and complete the graphic organizer. In each box, write a way to represent the geometric sequence.

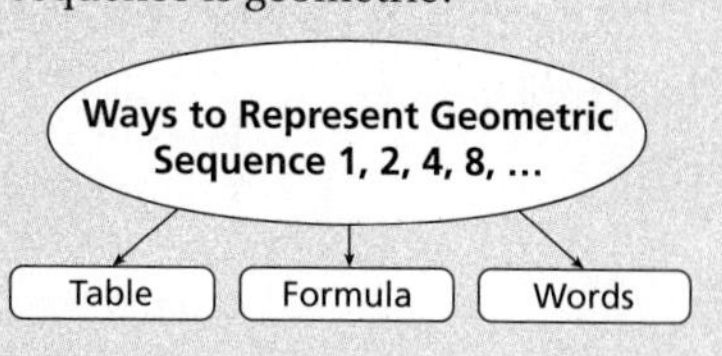

3 Close

Summarize

Tell students that they have learned about two kinds of sequences in this course: arithmetic and geometric. Arithmetic sequences have common differences and geometric sequences have common ratios. Common ratios are found by dividing each term by the term before it. Have students state in their own words how to find any term in a geometric sequence.

ONGOING ASSESSMENT and INTERVENTION

***Diagnose Before* the Lesson**
11-1 Warm Up, TE p. 790

***Monitor During* the Lesson**
Check It Out! Exercises, SE pp. 791–792
Questioning Strategies, TE pp. 791–792

***Assess After* the Lesson**
11-1 Lesson Quiz, TE p. 795
Alternative Assessment, TE p. 795

Answers to *Think and Discuss*

1. Possible answer: Divide each term after the first by the preceding term. If the quotients are all the same, the sequence is geometric.
2. See p. A10.

11-1 Exercises

go.hrw.com
Homework Help Online
KEYWORD: MA7 11-1
Parent Resources Online
KEYWORD: MA7 Parent

GUIDED PRACTICE

1. **Vocabulary** What is the *common ratio* of a geometric sequence? **the value that each term is multiplied by to get the next term**

SEE EXAMPLE 1 p. 790

Find the next three terms in each geometric sequence.

2. 2, 4, 8, 16, ... **32, 64, 128**
3. 400, 200, 100, 50, ... **25, 12.5, 6.25**
4. 4, −12, 36, −108, ... **324, −972, 2916**

SEE EXAMPLE 2 p. 791

5. The first term of a geometric sequence is 1, and the common ratio is 10. What is the 10th term of the sequence? **1,000,000,000**
6. What is the 11th term of the geometric sequence 3, 6, 12, 24, ... ? **3072**

SEE EXAMPLE 3 p. 792

7. **Sports** In the NCAA men's basketball tournament, 64 teams compete in round 1. Fewer teams remain in each following round, as shown in the graph, until all but one team have been eliminated. The numbers of teams in each round form a geometric sequence. How many teams compete in round 5? **4**

NCAA Men's Basketball Tournament

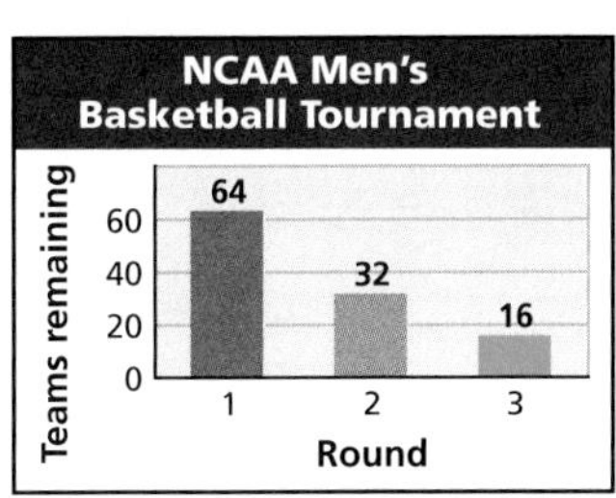

PRACTICE AND PROBLEM SOLVING

Independent Practice

For Exercises	See Example
8–13	1
14–15	2
16	3

Extra Practice
Skills Practice p. S24
Application Practice p. S38

Find the next three terms in each geometric sequence.

8. −2, 10, −50, 250, ...
9. 32, 48, 72, 108, ...
10. 625, 500, 400, 320, ...
11. 6, 42, 294, ...
12. 6, −12, 24, −48, ...
13. 40, 10, $\frac{5}{2}$, $\frac{5}{8}$, ...
14. The first term of a geometric sequence is 18 and the common ratio is 3.5. What is the 5th term of the sequence? **2701.125**
15. What is the 14th term of the geometric sequence 1000, 100, 10, 1, ... ? **0.0000000001, or 1×10^{-10}**
16. **Physical Science** A ball is dropped from a height of 500 meters. The table shows the height of each bounce, and the heights form a geometric sequence. How high does the ball bounce on the 8th bounce? Round your answer to the nearest tenth of a meter. **83.9 m**

Bounce	Height (m)
1	400
2	320
3	256

Find the missing term(s) in each geometric sequence.

17. 20, 40, **80**, **160**, ...
18. **2**, 6, 18, **54**, ...
19. 9, 3, 1, **$\frac{1}{3}$**, ...
20. 3, 12, **48**, 192, **768**, ...
21. 7, 1, **$\frac{1}{7}$**, **$\frac{1}{49}$**, $\frac{1}{343}$, ...
22. **400**, 100, 25, **$\frac{25}{4}$**, $\frac{25}{16}$, ...
23. −3, **6**, −12, 24, **−48**, ...
24. **$\frac{1}{9}$**, ▒, 1, −3, 9, ... **$-\frac{1}{3}$**
25. 1, 17, 289, ▒, ... **4913**

Determine whether each sequence could be geometric. If so, give the common ratio.

26. 2, 10, 50, 250, ... **yes; 5**
27. 15, 5, $\frac{5}{3}$, $\frac{5}{9}$, ... **yes; $\frac{1}{3}$**
28. 6, 18, 24, 38, ... **no**
29. 9, 3, −1, −5, ... **no**
30. 7, 21, 63, 189, ... **yes; 3**
31. 4, 1, −2, −4, ... **no**

11-1 Exercises

Assignment Guide

Assign *Guided Practice* exercises as necessary.

If you finished Examples **1–3**
Basic 8–33, 34–39, 43–46, 55–62
Average 8–40, 42–46, 54–62
Advanced 8–16 even, 17–62

Homework Quick Check
Quickly check key concepts.
Exercises: 8, 14, 16, 24, 32, 36

Diversity Exercise 7 is about a basketball tournament. Have students discuss the different types of tournaments they have participated in that have a similar type of elimination system.

Answers

8. −1250, 6250, −31,250
9. 162, 243, 364.5
10. 256, 204.8, 163.84
11. 2058, 14,406, 100,842
12. 96, −192, 384
13. $\frac{5}{32}$, $\frac{5}{128}$, $\frac{5}{512}$

State Resources

Exercise 43 involves using a common ratio to find terms in a geometric sequence. This exercise prepares students for the Multi-Step Test Prep on page 820.

Answers

39. 12, 3, $\frac{3}{4}$, $\frac{3}{16}$

40. Each term is multiplied by 2^{n-1}, where n is the term number. For example, begin with the geometric sequence 4, 12, 36, 108, ..., where $r = 3$. If r is doubled to 6, the sequence becomes 4, 24, 144, 864, ...

41a, 41b. See p. A33.

42. Divide each term by the term before it to find the value of r. Then use the formula $a_n = a_1r^{n-1}$, where a_1 is the first term of the sequence.

54, 58–60. See p. A33.

32a. Yes, it is a geom. seq. with $r = 2$.

b. Possible answer: Plan 1; Under Plan 2, the cost for the 10th week alone is \$512, which is more than the cost for the entire summer under Plan 1.

32. Multi-Step Billy earns money by mowing lawns for the summer. He offers two payment plans, as shown at right.

a. Do the payments for plan 2 form a geometric sequence? Explain.

b. If you were one of Billy's customers, which plan would you choose? (Assume that the summer is 10 weeks long.) Explain your choice.

Billy's Better Lawns
Weekly Lawn Care Service
TWO WAYS TO PAY!
Plan 1: Pay \$150 for the entire summer.
Plan 2: Pay \$1 the 1ST week, \$2 the 2ND week, \$4 the 3RD week, \$8 the 4TH week, and so on.

33. Measurement When you fold a piece of paper in half, the thickness of the folded piece is twice the thickness of the original piece. A piece of copy paper is about 0.1 mm thick.

a. How thick is a piece of copy paper that has been folded in half 7 times? **1.28 cm**

b. Suppose that you could fold a piece of copy paper in half 12 times. How thick would it be? Write your answer in centimeters. **40.96 cm**

List the first four terms of each geometric sequence.

34. $a_1 = 3, a_n = 3(2)^{n-1}$ **3, 6, 12, 24**

35. $a_1 = -2, a_n = -2(4)^{n-1}$ **−2, −8, −32, −128**

36. $a_1 = 5, a_n = 5(-2)^{n-1}$ **5, −10, 20, −40**

37. $a_1 = 2, a_n = 2(2)^{n-1}$ **2, 4, 8, 16**

38. $a_1 = 2, a_n = 2(5)^{n-1}$ **2, 10, 50, 250**

39. $a_1 = 12, a_n = 12\left(\frac{1}{4}\right)^{n-1}$

40. Critical Thinking What happens to the terms of a geometric sequence when r is doubled? Use an example to support your answer.

41. Geometry The steps below describe how to make a geometric figure by repeating the same process over and over on a smaller and smaller scale.

Step 1 (stage 0) Draw a large square.

Step 2 (stage 1) Divide the square into four equal squares.

Step 3 (stage 2) Divide each small square into four equal squares.

Step 4 Repeat Step 3 indefinitely.

a. Draw stages 0, 1, 2, and 3.

b. How many small squares are in each stage? Organize your data relating stage and number of small squares in a table.

c. Does the data in part **b** form a geometric sequence? Explain. **yes; $r = 4$**

d. Write a rule to find the number of small squares in stage n. **$a_n = 4(4)^{n-1}$, or 4^n**

42. Write About It Write a series of steps for finding the nth term of a geometric sequence when you are given the first several terms.

43. This problem will prepare you for the Multi-Step Test Prep on page 820.

a. Three years ago, the annual tuition at a university was \$3000. The following year, the tuition was \$3300, and last year, the tuition was \$3630. If the tuition has continued to grow in the same manner, what is the tuition this year? What do you expect it to be next year? **\$3993; \$4392.30**

b. What is the common ratio? **1.1**

c. What would you predict the tuition was 4 years ago? How did you find that value? **\$2727.27; divide tuition 3 years ago (\$3000) by 1.1 (the common ratio).**

11-1 PRACTICE A
11-1 PRACTICE C
11-1 PRACTICE B

Find the next three terms in each geometric sequence.

1. −5, −10, −20, −40, ... **−80; −160; −320**
2. 7, 56, 448, 3584... **28,672; 229,376; 1,835,008**
3. −10, 40, −160, 640, ... **−2560, −10,240, −40,960**
4. 40, 10, $\frac{5}{2}$, $\frac{5}{8}$, ... **$\frac{5}{32}$, $\frac{5}{128}$, $\frac{5}{512}$**
5. The first term of a geometric sequence is 6 and the common ratio is −8. Find the 7th term. **1,572,864**
6. The first term of a geometric sequence is −3 and the common ratio is $\frac{1}{2}$. Find the 6th term. **$-\frac{3}{32}$**
7. The first term of a geometric sequence is −0.25 and the common ratio is −3. Find the 10th term. **4920.75**
8. What is the 12th term of the geometric sequence −4, −12, −36, ...? **−708,588**
9. What is the 10th term of the geometric sequence 2, −6, 18, ...? **−39,366**
10. What is the 6th term of the geometric sequence 50, 10, 2, ...? **0.016**
11. A shoe store is discounting shoes each month. A pair of shoes cost \$80. The table shows the discount prices for several months. Find the cost of the shoes after 8 months. Round your answer to the nearest cent. **\$38.26**

Month	Price
1	\$80.00
2	\$72.00
3	\$64.80

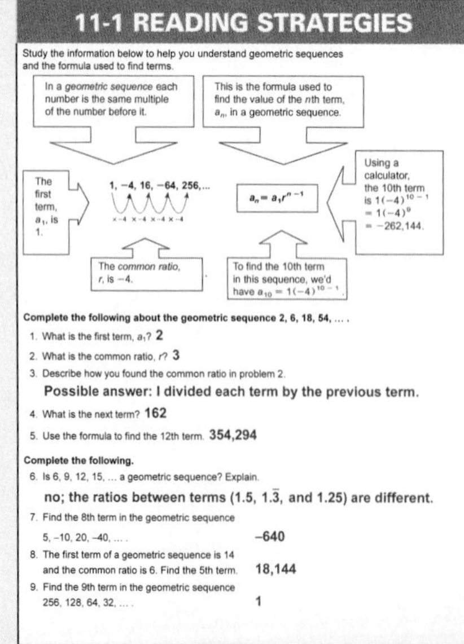

11-1 READING STRATEGIES

Study the information below to help you understand geometric sequences and the formula used to find terms.

In a *geometric sequence* each number is the same multiple of the number before it.

This is the formula used to find the value of the nth term, a_n, in a geometric sequence.

The first term, a_1, is 1.

1, −4, 16, −64, 256,...
×−4 ×−4 ×−4 ×−4

$a_n = a_1r^{n-1}$

Using a calculator, the 10th term is $1(-4)^{10-1} = 1(-4)^9 = -262{,}144$.

The *common ratio*, r, is −4.

To find the 10th term in this sequence, we'd have $a_{10} = 1(-4)^{10-1}$.

Complete the following about the geometric sequence 2, 6, 18, 54, ...

1. What is the first term, a_1? **2**
2. What is the common ratio, r? **3**
3. Describe how you found the common ratio in problem 2. **Possible answer: I divided each term by the previous term.**
4. What is the next term? **162**
5. Use the formula to find the 12th term. **354,294**

Complete the following.

6. Is 6, 9, 12, 15, ... a geometric sequence? Explain. **no; the ratios between terms (1.5, $1.\overline{3}$, and 1.25) are different.**
7. Find the 8th term in the geometric sequence 5, −10, 20, −40, ... **−640**
8. The first term of a geometric sequence is 14 and the common ratio is 6. Find the 5th term. **18,144**
9. Find the 9th term in the geometric sequence 256, 128, 64, 32, ... **1**

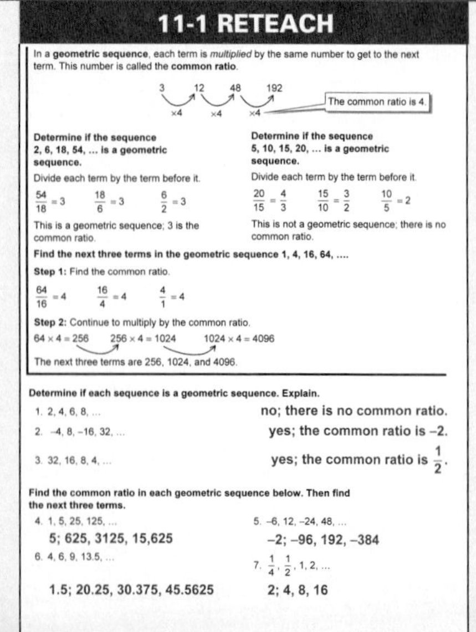

11-1 RETEACH

In a **geometric sequence**, each term is *multiplied* by the same number to get to the next term. This number is called the **common ratio**.

3 → 12 → 48 → 192 (×4 ×4 ×4) The common ratio is 4.

Determine if the sequence 2, 6, 18, 54, ... is a geometric sequence.

Divide each term by the term before it.

$\frac{54}{18} = 3$ $\frac{18}{6} = 3$ $\frac{6}{2} = 3$

This is a geometric sequence; 3 is the common ratio.

Determine if the sequence 5, 10, 15, 20, ... is a geometric sequence.

Divide each term by the term before it.

$\frac{20}{15} = \frac{4}{3}$ $\frac{15}{10} = \frac{3}{2}$ $\frac{10}{5} = 2$

This is not a geometric sequence; there is no common ratio.

Find the next three terms in the geometric sequence 1, 4, 16, 64, ...

Step 1: Find the common ratio.

$\frac{64}{16} = 4$ $\frac{16}{4} = 4$ $\frac{4}{1} = 4$

Step 2: Continue to multiply by the common ratio.

$64 \times 4 = 256$ $256 \times 4 = 1024$ $1024 \times 4 = 4096$

The next three terms are 256, 1024, and 4096.

Determine if each sequence is a geometric sequence. Explain.

1. 2, 4, 6, 8, ... **no; there is no common ratio.**
2. −4, 8, −16, 32, ... **yes; the common ratio is −2.**
3. 32, 16, 8, 4, ... **yes; the common ratio is $\frac{1}{2}$.**

Find the common ratio in each geometric sequence below. Then find the next three terms.

4. 1, 5, 25, 125, ... **5; 625, 3125, 15,625**
5. −6, 12, −24, 48, ... **−2; −96, 192, −384**
6. 4, 6, 9, 13.5, ... **1.5; 20.25, 30.375, 45.5625**
7. $\frac{1}{4}$, $\frac{1}{2}$, 1, 2, ... **2; 4, 8, 16**

TEST PREP

44. Which of the following is a geometric sequence?

(A) $\frac{1}{2}, 1, \frac{3}{2}, 2, \ldots$ (C) 3, 8, 13, 18, …
(B) −2, −6, −10, −14, … **(D)** 5, 10, 20, 40, …

45. Which equation represents the *n*th term in the geometric sequence 2, −8, 32, −128, …?

(F) $a_n = (-4)^n$ (G) $a_n = (-4)^{n-1}$ (H) $a_n = 2(-4)^n$ **(J)** $a_n = 2(-4)^{n-1}$

46. The frequency of a musical note, measured in hertz (Hz), is called its pitch. The pitches of the A keys on a piano form a geometric sequence, as shown.

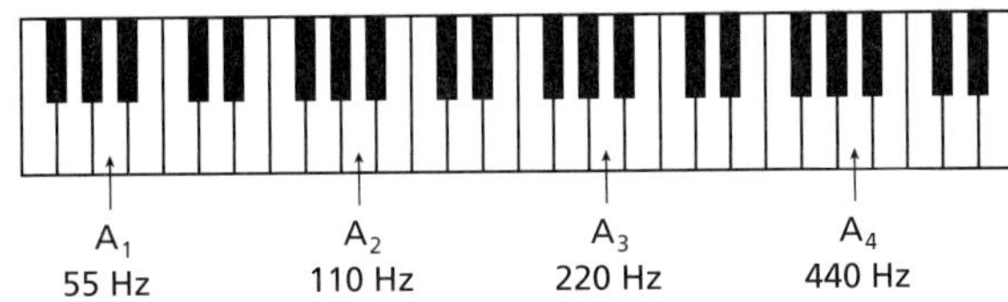

What is the frequency of A_7?

(A) 880 Hz (B) 1760 Hz **(C)** 3520 Hz (D) 7040 Hz

CHALLENGE AND EXTEND

Find the next three terms in each geometric sequence. **50.** $x + 1, (x + 1)^2, (x + 1)^3$

47. $x, x^2, x^3, \ldots$ **x^4, x^5, x^6**

48. $2x^2, 6x^3, 18x^4, \ldots$ **$54x^5, 162x^6, 486x^7$**

49. $\frac{1}{y^3}, \frac{1}{y^2}, \frac{1}{y}, \ldots$ **$1, y, y^2$**

50. $\frac{1}{(x+1)^2}, \frac{1}{x+1}, 1, \ldots$

51. The 10th term of a geometric sequence is 0.78125. The common ratio is −0.5. Find the first term of the sequence. **−400**

52. The first term of a geometric sequence is 12 and the common ratio is $\frac{1}{2}$. Is 0 a term in this sequence? Explain.

52. No; each term of the seq. is found by multiplying the prev. term by the common ratio $\frac{1}{2}$. $\frac{1}{2}$ of any pos. number is always another pos. number.

53. A geometric sequence starts with 14 and has a common ration of 0.4. Colin finds that another number in the sequence is 0.057344. Which term in the sequence did Colin find? **the 7th term**

54. The first three terms of a sequence are 1, 2, and 4. Susanna said the 8th term of this sequence is 128. Paul said the 8th term is 29. Explain how the students found their answers. Why could these both be considered correct answers?

SPIRAL REVIEW

Solve each inequality and graph the solutions. *(Lesson 3-2)*

55. $b - 4 > 6$ **$b > 10$**

−5 0 5 10 15 20 25 30

56. $-12 + x \le -8$ **$x \le 4$**

−8 −6 −4 −2 0 2 4 6 8

57. $c + \frac{2}{3} < \frac{1}{3}$ **$c < -\frac{1}{3}$**

−6 −4 −2 0 2

Graph the solutions of each linear inequality. *(Lesson 6-5)*

58. $y < 2x - 4$

59. $3x + y > 6$

60. $-y \le 2x + 1$

Write a function to describe each of the following graphs. *(Lesson 9-4)*

61. The graph of $f(x) = x^2 - 3$ translated 7 units up **$f(x) = x^2 + 4$**

62. The graph of $f(x) = 2x^2 + 6$ narrowed and translated 2 units down **Possible answer: $f(x) = 3x^2 + 4$**

TEST PREP DOCTOR The incorrect choices, **A, B,** and **C,** in **Exercise 44** are arithmetic sequences. They have common differences, not common ratios.

In **Exercise 45,** choices **F** and **G** can be quickly eliminated because they do not include the first term, 2. To help distinguish between **H** and **J,** have students substitute 1 for *n*, which will result in the first term.

Journal

Have students explain the difference between the rules used to create the following sequences:

3, 6, 9, 12, 15,…

3, 6, 12, 24, 48,…

ALTERNATIVE ASSESSMENT

Have students write the first five terms of a geometric sequence for which *r* is greater than one. Then have them write the first five terms of a geometric sequence for which *r* is less than one. Last, have them find the 10th and 20th terms of each of their sequences by using the formula taught in the lesson.

Power Presentations with PowerPoint®

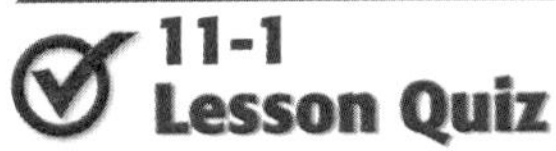

11-1 Lesson Quiz

Find the next three terms in each geometric sequence.

1. 3, 15, 75, 375,…
1875, 9375, 46,875

2. $5, -1, \frac{1}{5}, -\frac{1}{25}, \frac{1}{125}, \ldots$
$-\frac{1}{625}, \frac{1}{3125}, -\frac{1}{15{,}625}$

3. The first term of a geometric sequence is 300 and the common ratio is 0.6. What is the 7th term of the sequence?
13.9968

4. What is the 15th term of the sequence 4, −8, 16, −32, 64,…? 65,536

5. The table shows a car's value for 3 years after it is purchased. The values form a geometric sequence. How much will the car be worth after 8 years? $5770.39

Year	Value ($)
1	18,000
2	15,300
3	13,005

Also available on transparency

11-1 PROBLEM SOLVING

Write the correct answer.

1. A ball is dropped from 400 feet. The table shows the height of each bounce.

Bounce	Height (ft)
1	280
2	196
3	137.2

Find the height of the ball on the 6th bounce. Round your answer to the nearest tenth of a foot.
47.1 feet

2. A plant starts with 1 branch. Every year, each branch becomes 3 branches. A sketch of the plant for the first 3 years is shown. How many branches will the plant have in year 10?
Year 1 Year 2 Year 3
19,683 branches
How many branches would the plant have in year 10 if the plant had 5 branches the first year? (Each branch still becomes 3 branches every year.)
98,415 branches

3. Jeanette started selling bagels to offices in her area. Her sales for the first 3 months are shown in the table.

Month	Sales ($)
1	$200.00
2	$230.00
3	$264.50

If this trend continues, find the amount of Jeanette's sales in Month 8.
$532

The table shows the number of houses in a new subdivision. Use the table to answer questions 4–7. Select the best answer.

Month	Houses
1	3
2	6
3	12
4	24

4. The number of houses forms a geometric sequence. What is *r*?
A 0.5 C 3
B 2 D 6

5. Assuming that the trend continues, how many houses would be in the subdivision in Month 6?
F 36 H 60
G 48 **J** 96

6. Management decides the subdivision is complete when the number of houses reaches 48. When will this happen?
A Month 5 C Month 7
B Month 6 D Month 8

7. Suppose the number of houses tripled every month. How many more houses would be in the subdivision in Month 4? (The number of houses in Month 1 is still 3.)
F 48 H 72
G 57 J 81

11-1 CHALLENGE

A **sequence** is a list of numbers that often forms a pattern. You have worked with arithmetic sequences and geometric sequences.

A **series** is the sum of the terms of a sequence. You can either find a *partial sum* of a few terms or determine what happens when you sum infinitely many terms. (You'll look at infinite series in Algebra 2.)

The Greek capital letter sigma (Σ) is often used to represent summation in mathematics. Numbers above and below sigma tell you which terms to sum.

For example, $\sum_{n=1}^{5}$ represents the partial sum of the 1st to 5th terms.

Find the partial sums of these arithmetic series.

1. $\sum_{n=1}^{5} 4 + (n-1)(3) = \underbrace{4}_{n=1} + \underbrace{7}_{n=2} + \underbrace{10}_{n=3} + \underbrace{13}_{n=4} + \underbrace{16}_{n=5} = 50$

2. $\sum_{n=1}^{8} -10 + (n-1)(2) = \underbrace{-10}_{n=1} + \underbrace{-8}_{n=2} + \underbrace{-6}_{n=3} + \underbrace{-4}_{n=4} + \underbrace{-2}_{n=5} + \underbrace{0}_{n=6} + \underbrace{2}_{n=7} + \underbrace{4}_{n=8} = -24$

3. $\sum_{n=1}^{6} 23 + (n-1)(-5) = 23 + 18 + 13 + 8 + 3 + (-2) = 63$

4. $\sum_{n=1}^{4} \frac{1}{2} + (n-1)\left(\frac{1}{8}\right) = \frac{1}{2} + \frac{5}{8} + \frac{3}{4} + \frac{7}{8} = \frac{11}{4}$ or $2\frac{3}{4}$

5. $\sum_{n=5}^{10} -7 + (n-1)(-1.2) = -11.8 + (-13) + (-14.2) + (-15.4) + (-16.6) + (-17.8) = -88.8$ Caution!

Find the partial sums of these geometric series.

6. $\sum_{n=1}^{5} 4(3)^{n-1} = \underbrace{4}_{n=1} + \underbrace{12}_{n=2} + \underbrace{36}_{n=3} + \underbrace{108}_{n=4} + \underbrace{324}_{n=5} = 484$

7. $\sum_{n=1}^{8} -10(2)^{n-1} = \underbrace{-10}_{n=1} + \underbrace{-20}_{n=2} + \underbrace{-40}_{n=3} + \underbrace{-80}_{n=4} + \underbrace{-160}_{n=5} + \underbrace{-320}_{n=6} + \underbrace{-640}_{n=7} + \underbrace{-1280}_{n=8} = -2550$

8. $\sum_{n=1}^{6} 3(-2)^{n-1} = 3 + (-6) + 12 + (-24) + 48 + (-96) = -63$

9. $\sum_{n=1}^{4} 16\left(\frac{1}{4}\right)^{n-1} = 16 + 4 + 1 + \frac{1}{4} = \frac{85}{4}$ or $21\frac{1}{4}$

10. $\sum_{n=5}^{10} -6\left(-\frac{2}{3}\right)^{n-1} = -\frac{32}{27} + \frac{64}{81} + \left(-\frac{128}{243}\right) + \frac{256}{729}\left(-\frac{512}{2187}\right) + \frac{1024}{6561} = \frac{-4256}{6561} = -0.649$

11-2 Organizer

Pacing: Traditional 1 day
Block $\frac{1}{2}$ day

Objectives: Evaluate exponential functions.

Identify and graph exponential functions.

Power Presentations with PowerPoint®

Warm Up

Simplify each expression. Round to the nearest whole number if necessary.

1. 3^2 9 **2.** 5^4 625

3. $2(3)^3$ 54 **4.** $\frac{2}{3}(3)^4$ 54

5. $-5(2)^5$ −160 **6.** $-\frac{1}{2}(4)^3$ −32

7. $100(0.5)^2$ 25

8. $3000(0.95)^8$ 1990

Also available on transparency

Math Humor

Exponential Function: Why is my energy level falling?

Doctor: Your common ratio is below one. Your energy levels will rise if your common ratio is above one.

11-2 Exponential Functions

Objectives
Evaluate exponential functions.

Identify and graph exponential functions.

Vocabulary
exponential function

Who uses this?
Scientists model populations with exponential functions.

The table and the graph show an insect population that increases over time.

Time (days)	Population
0	2
1	6
2	18
3	54

(Each population value is × 3 the previous.)

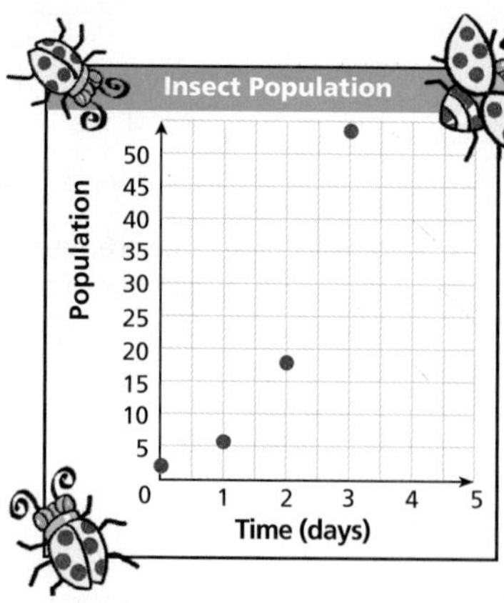

A function rule that describes the pattern above is $f(x) = 2(3)^x$. This type of function, in which the independent variable appears in an exponent, is an **exponential function**. Notice that 2 is the starting population and 3 is the amount by which the population is multiplied each day.

Know it! Note

Exponential Functions

An exponential function has the form $f(x) = ab^x$, where $a \neq 0$, $b \neq 1$, and $b > 0$.

EXAMPLE 1 Evaluating an Exponential Function

A **The function $f(x) = 2(3)^x$ models an insect population after x days. What will the population be on the 5th day?**

$f(x) = 2(3)^x$ *Write the function.*

$f(5) = 2(3)^5$ *Substitute 5 for x.*

$= 2(243)$ *Evaluate 3^5.*

$= 486$ *Multiply.*

There will be 486 insects on the 5th day.

B **The function $f(x) = 1500(0.995)^x$, where x is the time in years, models a prairie dog population. How many prairie dogs will there be in 8 years?**

$f(x) = 1500(0.995)^x$

$f(8) = 1500(0.995)^8$ *Substitute 8 for x.*

≈ 1441 *Use a calculator. Round to the nearest whole number.*

There will be about 1441 prairie dogs in 8 years.

Helpful Hint

In Example 1B, round your answer to the nearest whole number because there can only be a whole number of prairie dogs.

1. The function $f(x) = 8(0.75)^x$ models the width of a photograph in inches after it has been reduced by 25% x times. What is the width of the photograph after it has been reduced 3 times? **3.375 in.**

State Resources

1 Introduce

11-2 Exponential Functions

A biologist is studying bacteria growth. He begins with 10 bacteria in a Petri dish. The number of bacteria doubles each hour.

1. Complete the middle column of the table to show the rate of bacteria growth.

Hour	Bacteria	Exponential Form
0	10	$10(2)^0$
1	20	$10(2)^1$
2		
3		
4		
5		

2. Complete the right-hand column of the table, which shows the number of bacteria written as a power of 2.
3. Look for a pattern in the table to help you write an equation for the number of bacteria B in terms of the number of hours h.

THINK AND DISCUSS

4. **Explain** how to use your equation to find the number of bacteria after 15 hours.
5. **Describe** how your equation would be different if the biologist had started with 12 bacteria.

Motivate

Write 6, 12, 24, 48 . . . on the board. Remind students that this is a geometric sequence with a common ratio of 2. Tell students that in this lesson they will study functions very similar to geometric sequences. But unlike geometric sequences, which have discrete terms, these new functions will be continuous. The graphs of these new functions will be unbroken.

Explorations and answers are provided in *Alternate Openers: Explorations Transparencies.*

Remember that linear functions have constant first differences and quadratic functions have constant second differences. Exponential functions do not have constant differences, but they do have *constant ratios.*

As the x-values increase by a constant amount, the y-values are multiplied by a constant amount. This amount is the constant ratio and is the value of b in $f(x) = ab^x$.

x	$f(x) = 2(3)^x$
1	6
2	18
3	54
4	162

(+1 for each step in x; ×3 for each step in $f(x)$)

EXAMPLE 2 Identifying an Exponential Function

Tell whether each set of ordered pairs satisfies an exponential function. Explain your answer.

A $\{(-1, 1.5), (0, 3), (1, 6), (2, 12)\}$

x	y
−1	1.5
0	3
1	6
2	12

(+1, +1, +1; ×2, ×2, ×2)

This is an exponential function. As the x-values increase by a constant amount, the y-values are multiplied by a constant amount.

B $\{(-1, -9), (1, 9), (3, 27), (5, 45)\}$

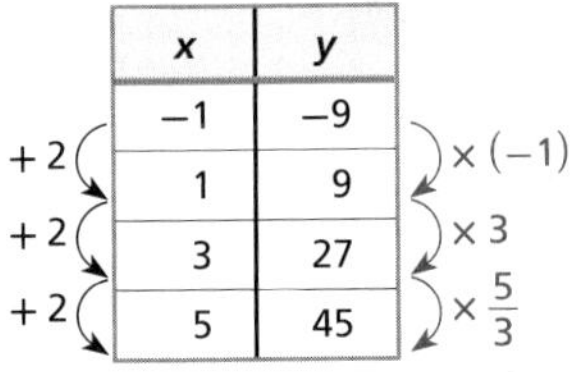

x	y
−1	−9
1	9
3	27
5	45

(+2, +2, +2; ×(−1), ×3, ×$\frac{5}{3}$)

This is *not* an exponential function. As the x-values increase by a constant amount, the y-values are *not* multiplied by a constant amount.

2a. No; as the x-values change by a constant amount, the y-values are not multiplied by a constant amount.

2b. Yes; as the x-values change by a constant amount, the y-values are multiplied by a constant amount.

CHECK IT OUT! **Tell whether each set of ordered pairs satisfies an exponential function. Explain your answer.**

2a. $\{(-1, 1), (0, 0), (1, 1), (2, 4)\}$ **2b.** $\{(-2, 4), (-1, 2), (0, 1), (1, 0.5)\}$

To graph an exponential function, choose several values of x (positive, negative, and 0) and generate ordered pairs. Plot the points and connect them with a smooth curve.

EXAMPLE 3 Graphing $y = ab^x$ with $a > 0$ and $b > 1$

3a.

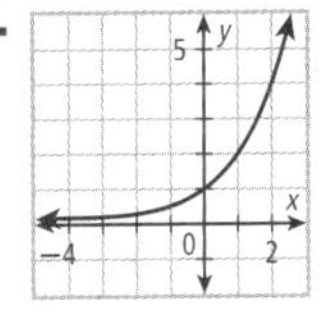

3b.

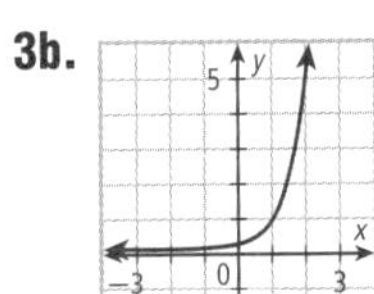

Graph $y = 3(4)^x$.

Choose several values of x and generate ordered pairs.

x	$y = 3(4)^x$
−1	0.75
0	3
1	12
2	48

Graph the ordered pairs and connect with a smooth curve.

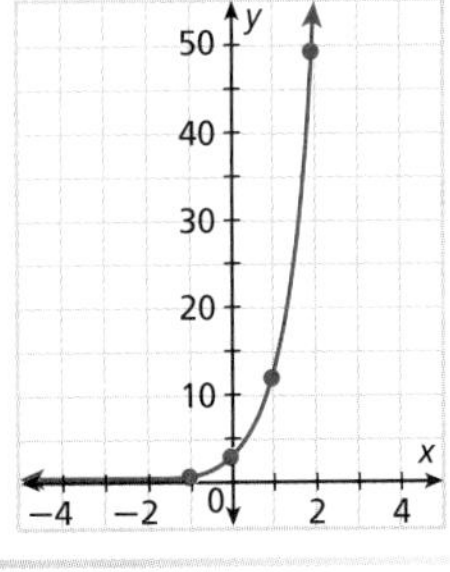

CHECK IT OUT! **3a.** Graph $y = 2^x$. **3b.** Graph $y = 0.2(5)^x$.

COMMON ERROR ALERT

When generating ordered pairs for exponential functions, students may multiply a by b and then raise that product to x. Remind students to use the correct order of operations.

Power Presentations with PowerPoint®

Additional Examples

Example 1

A. The function $f(x) = 500(1.035)^x$ models the amount of money in a certificate of deposit after x years. How much money will there be in 6 years? $614.63

B. The function $f(x) = 200{,}000(0.98)^x$, where x is the time in years, models the population of a city. What will the population be in 7 years? about 173,625

Example 2

Tell whether each set of ordered pairs satisfies an exponential function. Explain your answer.

A. $\{(0, 4), (1, 12), (2, 36), (3, 108)\}$ Yes; as the x-values change by a constant amount, the y-values are multiplied by a constant amount.

B. $\{(-1, -64), (0, 0), (1, 64), (2, 128)\}$ No; as the x-values change by a constant amount, the y-values are not multiplied by a constant amount.

Example 3

Graph $y = 0.5(2)^x$.

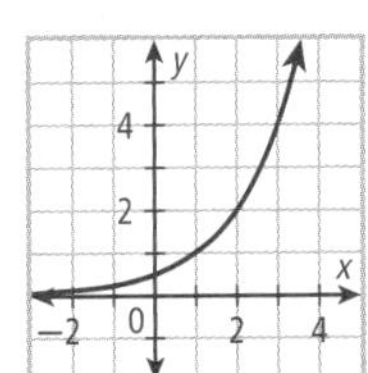

2 Teach

Guided Instruction

In **Example 1,** point out that b in an exponential function corresponds to r in a geometric sequence. Explain that these predictions are accurate only if all conditions remain the same throughout the given time period.

When graphing exponential functions, explain that $b = 1$ represents no change (no growth or decline—the graph is linear), so $b > 1$ represents growth and $b < 1$ represents decline.

Reaching All Learners

Through Graphic Organizers

To show why the exponent in a geometric sequence has 1 subtracted from the variable but an exponential function does not, create the following chart, which corresponds to **Example 1A.**

1st Term	2nd Term	3rd Term	4th Term	5th Term	6th Term
2	6	18	54	162	486
After 0 days	After 1 day	After 2 days	After 3 days	After 4 days	After 5 days

INTERVENTION

Questioning Strategies

EXAMPLES **1–2**

- How do you know the exponent applies to b and not ab?

EXAMPLE **3**

- What are the domain and range of an exponential function if both a and b are positive?

Transformations The graph of $y = -ab^x$ is a reflection of $y = ab^x$ over the x-axis.

Power Presentations with PowerPoint®

Additional Examples

Example 4

Graph $y = -\frac{1}{4}(2)^x$.

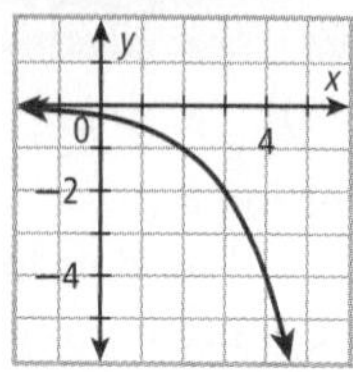

Example 5

Graph each exponential function.

A. $y = -1\left(\frac{1}{4}\right)^x$

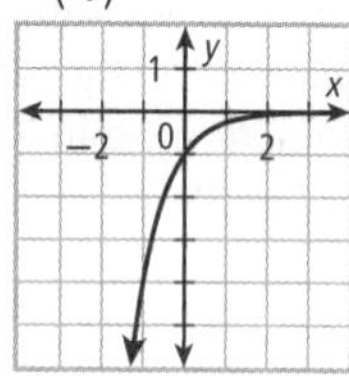

B. $y = 4(0.6)^x$

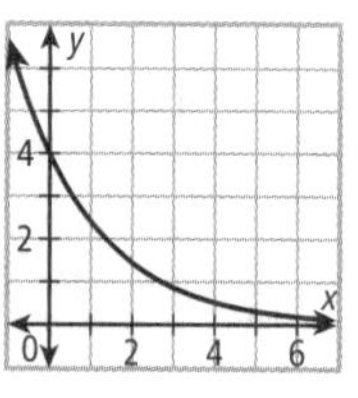

INTERVENTION

Questioning Strategies

EXAMPLES 4–5

- How can the values of a and b tell you which direction the graph takes and in which quadrants the graph is located?

Teaching Tip

Inclusion Point out to students that, unlike linear functions, b in an exponential function is not the y-intercept.

EXAMPLE 4 Graphing $y = ab^x$ with $a < 0$ and $b > 1$

Graph $y = -5(2)^x$.

Choose several values of x and generate ordered pairs.

x	$y = -5(2)^x$
−1	−2.5
0	−5
1	−10
2	−20

Graph the ordered pairs and connect with a smooth curve.

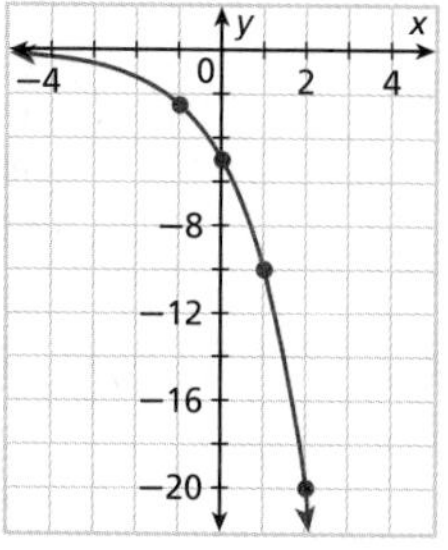

4a. Graph $y = -6^x$.

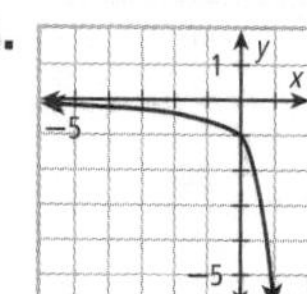

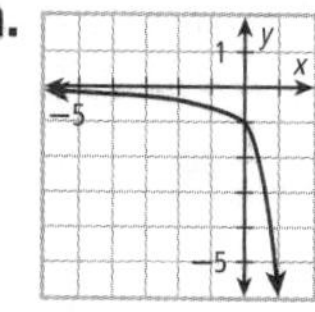

4b. Graph $y = -3(3)^x$.

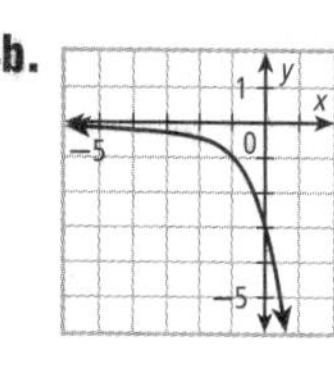

EXAMPLE 5 Graphing $y = ab^x$ with $0 < b < 1$

Graph each exponential function.

A $y = 3\left(\frac{1}{2}\right)^x$

Choose several values of x and generate ordered pairs.

x	$y = 3\left(\frac{1}{2}\right)^x$
−1	6
0	3
1	1.5
2	0.75

Graph the ordered pairs and connect with a smooth curve.

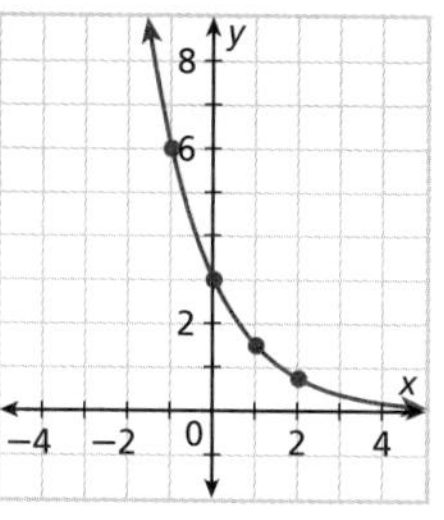

B $y = -2(0.4)^x$

Choose several values of x and generate ordered pairs.

x	$y = -2(0.4)^x$
−2	−12.5
−1	−5
0	−2
1	−0.8

Graph the ordered pairs and connect with a smooth curve.

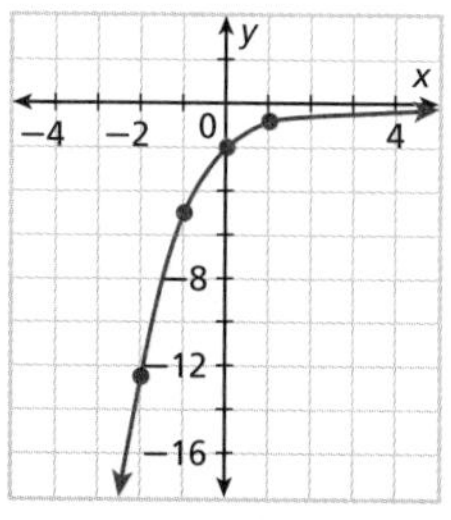

CHECK IT OUT! Graph each exponential function.

5a. $y = 4\left(\frac{1}{4}\right)^x$ **5b.** $y = -2(0.1)^x$

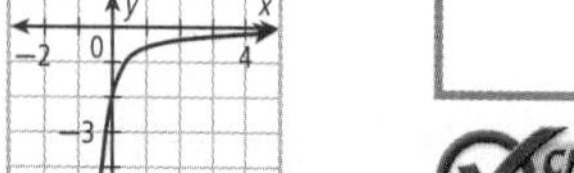

Teacher to Teacher

As students study exponential functions, it is critical that they understand why the base $b > 1$ makes the graph of $y = ab^x$ (where a is positive) increase while the base $0 < b < 1$ makes it decrease.

Students need plenty of real-world examples to help them understand the connection between the common ratio and the base b. For example, you can discuss what happens if you multiply something over and over by 5, as in $y = 5^x$, versus multiplying it over and over by $\frac{1}{5}$, as in $y = \left(\frac{1}{5}\right)^x$.

Once students understand how the base b affects the graph of $y = ab^x$, where $a > 0$, they can more easily remember how $a < 0$ affects the graph of $y = ab^x$ by thinking of it as a reflection across the x-axis.

Jennifer Bauer
East Haven, CT

The box summarizes the general shapes of exponential function graphs.

Graphs of Exponential Functions

For $y = ab^x$, if $b > 1$, then the graph will have one of these shapes.	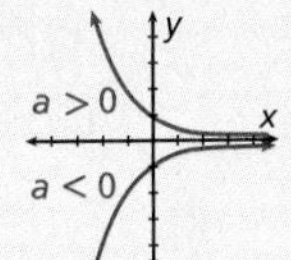 For $y = ab^x$, if $0 < b < 1$, then the graph will have one of these shapes.

EXAMPLE 6 *Statistics Application*

In the year 2000, the world population was about 6 billion, and it was growing by 1.21% each year. At this growth rate, the function $f(x) = 6(1.0121)^x$ gives the population, in billions, x years after 2000. Using this model, in about what year does the population reach 7 billion?

Enter the function into the Y= editor of a graphing calculator.

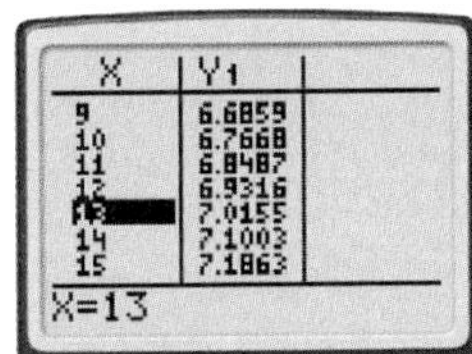

Press 2nd GRAPH (TABLE). Use the arrow keys to find a y-value as close to 7 as possible. The corresponding x-value is 13.

The world population reaches 7 billion in about 2013.

Caution!
The function values give the population *in billions*, so a y-value of 7 means 7 billion.

6. An accountant uses $f(x) = 12{,}330(0.869)^x$, where x is the time in years since the purchase, to model the value of a car. When will the car be worth \$2000? **after about 13 yr**

THINK AND DISCUSS

1. How can you find the constant ratio of a set of exponential data?
2. **GET ORGANIZED** Copy and complete the graphic organizer. In each box, give an example of an appropriate exponential function and sketch its graph.

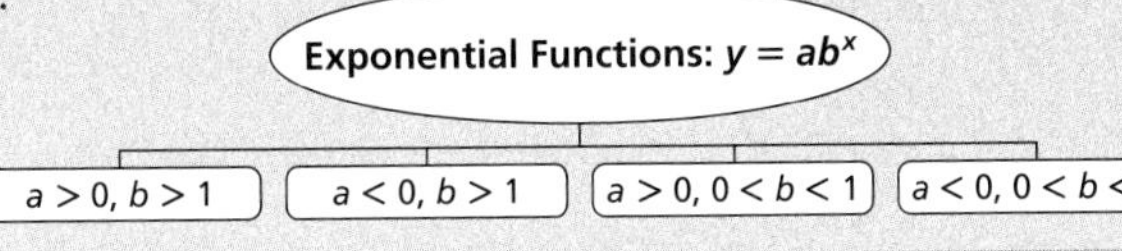

COMMON ERROR ALERT

Students might use the word *slope* when describing exponential functions. Remind them that slope, when referring to linear functions, refers to a constant rate of change.

Teaching Tip **Multiple Representations** In **Example 6,** students could also graph the function and trace as close to $y = 7$ as possible.

Power Presentations with PowerPoint®

Additional Examples

Example 6

In 2000, each person in India consumed an average of 13 kg of sugar. Sugar consumption in India is projected to increase by 3.6% per year. At this growth rate, the function $f(x) = 13(1.036)^x$ gives the average yearly amount of sugar, in kilograms, consumed per person x years after 2000. Using this model, in about what year does sugar consumption average about 18 kg per person? 2009

INTERVENTION
Questioning Strategies

EXAMPLE 6

- Why is the x-value not the answer to the question?
- What types of conditions could change this prediction?

3 Close

Summarize

Write $f(x) = ab^x$ on the board. Point out the initial amount a, the common ratio b, and the independent variable x. Remind students that the independent variable always serves as the exponent in an exponential function. Then review the different shapes of exponential graphs. If a is positive, then the range is all positive numbers greater than 0, with an increasing graph for values of b greater than one. If a is negative, the graph is reflected across the x-axis.

ONGOING ASSESSMENT and INTERVENTION

***Diagnose Before* the Lesson**
11-2 Warm Up, TE p. 796

***Monitor During* the Lesson**
Check It Out! Exercises, SE pp. 796–799
Questioning Strategies, TE pp. 797–799

***Assess After* the Lesson**
11-2 Lesson Quiz, TE p. 802
Alternative Assessment, TE p. 802

Answers to *Think and Discuss*

1. Possible answer: Make a table of values. Use x-values that change by the same amount each time as you move down the column. Then divide each y-value, starting with the second row, by the y-value before it. The quotient is the common ratio.
2. See p. A10.

11-2 Exercises

Assignment Guide

Assign *Guided Practice* exercises as necessary.

If you finished Examples **1–2**
- **Basic** 18–24, 38–42
- **Average** 18–24, 35, 38–42
- **Advanced** 18–24, 35, 38–42

If you finished Examples **1–6**
- **Basic** 18–34, 38–43, 45–47, 52–56
- **Average** 18–34 even, 35–47, 51–56
- **Advanced** 18–34 even, 35–56

Homework Quick Check
Quickly check key concepts.
Exercises: 18, 22, 26, 28, 32, 34, 40

Answers

3. As the *x*-values change by a constant amount, the *y*-values are not multiplied by a constant amount.
4. As the *x*-values change by a constant amount, the *y*-values are multiplied by a constant amount.
5. 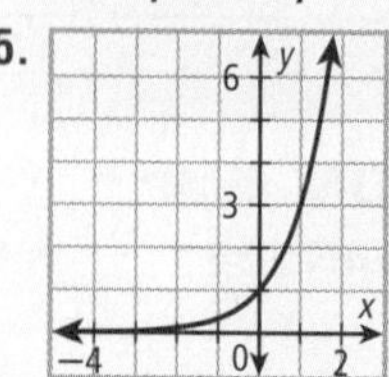

6–16. See p. A33.

21–24. For explanations, see p. A33.

State Resources

11-2 Exercises

go.hrw.com
Homework Help Online
KEYWORD: MA7 11-2
Parent Resources Online
KEYWORD: MA7 Parent

GUIDED PRACTICE

1. **Vocabulary** Tell whether $y = 3x^4$ is an *exponential function*. Explain your answer. **No; there is no variable in the exponent.**

SEE EXAMPLE 1 p. 796

2. **Physics** The function $f(x) = 50{,}000(0.975)^x$, where x represents the underwater depth in meters, models the intensity of light below the water's surface in lumens per square meter. What is the intensity of light 200 meters below the surface? Round your answer to the nearest whole number. **316 lumens/m²**

SEE EXAMPLE 2 p. 797

Tell whether each set of ordered pairs satisfies an exponential function. Explain your answer.

3. $\{(-1, -1), (0, 0), (1, -1), (2, -4)\}$ **no**
4. $\{(0, 1), (1, 4), (2, 16), (3, 64)\}$ **yes**

Graph each exponential function.

SEE EXAMPLE 3 p. 797

5. $y = 3^x$
6. $y = 5^x$
7. $y = 10(3)^x$
8. $y = 5(2)^x$

SEE EXAMPLE 4 p. 798

9. $y = -2(3)^x$
10. $y = -4(2)^x$
11. $y = -3(2)^x$
12. $y = 2(3)^x$

SEE EXAMPLE 5 p. 798

13. $y = -\left(\frac{1}{4}\right)^x$
14. $y = \left(\frac{1}{3}\right)^x$
15. $y = 2\left(\frac{1}{4}\right)^x$
16. $y = -2(0.25)^x$

SEE EXAMPLE 6 p. 799

17. The function $f(x) = 57.8(1.02)^x$ gives the number of passenger cars, in millions, in the United States x years after 1960. Using this model, in about what year does the number of passenger cars reach 200 million? **about 2023**

PRACTICE AND PROBLEM SOLVING

Independent Practice	
For Exercises	See Example
18–20	1
21–24	2
25–27	3
28–30	4
31–33	5
34	6

Extra Practice
Skills Practice p. S24
Application Practice p. S38

18. **Sports** If a golf ball is dropped from a height of 27 feet, the function $f(x) = 27\left(\frac{2}{3}\right)^x$ gives the height in feet of each bounce, where x is the bounce number. What will be the height of the 4th bounce? $5\frac{1}{3}$ **ft**
19. Suppose the depth of a lake can be described by the function $y = 334(0.976)^x$, where x represents the number of weeks from today. Today, the depth of the lake is 334 ft. What will the depth be in 6 weeks? Round your answer to the nearest whole number. **289 ft**
20. **Physics** A ball rolling down a slope travels continuously faster. Suppose the function $y = 1.3(1.41)^x$ describes the speed of the ball in inches per minute. How fast will the ball be rolling in 15 minutes? Round your answer to the nearest hundredth. **225.02 in./min**

Tell whether each set of ordered pairs satisfies an exponential function. Explain your answer.

21. $\left\{(-2, 9), (-1, 3), (0, 1), \left(1, \frac{1}{3}\right)\right\}$ **yes**
22. $\{(-1, 0), (0, 1), (1, 4), (2, 9)\}$ **no**
23. $\{(-1, -5), (0, -3), (1, -1), (2, 1)\}$ **no**
24. $\{(-3, 6.25), (-2, 12.5), (-1, 25), (0, 50)\}$ **yes**

11-2 READING STRATEGIES

An *exponential function* is always in the form $f(x) = ab^x$. And the graph of an exponential function is always the same general shape. But the values of a and b determine the quadrants the graph is in, and the "direction" in which the graph is facing. Analyze the information in the examples below.

$y = ab^x$

- $y = 2(3)^x$: $a > 0$, $b > 1$
- $y = -2(3)^x$: $a < 0$, $b < 1$
- $y = 2\left(\frac{1}{3}\right)^x$: $a > 0$, $0 < b < 1$
- $y = -2\left(\frac{1}{3}\right)^x$: $a < 0$, $0 < b < 1$

Respond to each statement by writing *sometimes*, *always*, or *never*.

1. When a is negative, the graph of $y = ab^x$ is contained entirely in quadrants III and IV. **always**
2. When b is a fraction, the graph of $y = ab^x$ is contained entirely in quadrants I and II. **sometimes**
3. The y-intercept of $y = ab^x$ is at a. **always**
4. The graph of $y = ab^x$ is a straight line. **never**
5. Complete the table of values and sketch the graph of $y = -3(2)^x$.

x	y
–1	$-\frac{3}{2}$
0	–3
1	–6
2	–12

11-2 RETEACH

An **exponential function** has the independent variable as the exponent.

$y = 3^x$ and $y = -2(0.5)^x$ are exponential functions.

A set of ordered pairs satisfies an exponential function if the y–values are multiplied by a constant amount as the x–values change by a constant amount.

Tell whether the following ordered pairs satisfy an exponential function.

x	y
3	4
5	12
7	36
9	108

Think 4 × ? = 12.
Think 12 × ? = 36.
Think 36 × ? = 108.

The x-values increase by the constant amount 2.
Each y-value is multiplied by the constant amount 3.
This is an exponential function.

x	y
1	2
2	4
3	6
4	8

Think 2 × ? = 4.
Think 4 × ? = 6.
Think 6 × ? = 8.

The x-values increase by the constant amount 1.
The y-value is multiplied by 2, then 1.5, Then $1.\bar{3}$. There is no constant ratio.
This is not an exponential function.

The population of a school can be described by the function $f(x) = 1500(1.02)^x$, where x represents the number of years since the school was built. What will be the population of the school in 12 years?

$f(x) = 1500(1.02)^x$
$f(12) = 1500(1.02)^{12}$ *Substitute 12 for x.*
≈ 1902 *Round number of people to the nearest whole number.*

Tell whether the ordered pairs satisfy an exponential function.

1.

x	y
–1	1.5
–2	3
–3	6
–4	12

yes

2.

x	y
1	1
2	2
3	6
4	24

no

3.

x	y
–2	–2
–1	–10
0	–50
1	–250

yes

4. If a rubber ball is dropped from a height of 10 feet, the function $f(x) = 20(0.6)^x$ gives the height in feet of each bounce, where x is the bounce number. What will be the height of the 5th bounce? Round to the nearest tenth of a foot. **1.6 feet**
5. A population of pigs is expected to increase at a rate of 4% each year. If the original population is 1000, the function $f(x) = 1000(1.04)^x$ gives the population in x years. What will be the population in 12 years? **≈1601**

Graph each exponential function.

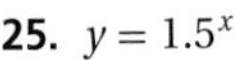

25. $y = 1.5^x$
26. $y = \frac{1}{3}(3)^x$
27. $y = 100(0.7)^x$
28. $y = -2(4)^x$
29. $y = -1(5)^x$
30. $y = -\frac{1}{2}(4)^x$
31. $y = 4\left(\frac{1}{2}\right)^x$
32. $y = -2\left(\frac{1}{3}\right)^x$
33. $y = 0.5(0.25)^x$

LINK Technology

Early silicon chips were about the size of your pinky finger and held one transistor. Today, chips the size of a baby's fingernail hold over 100 million transistors.

34. **Technology** Moore's law states that the maximum number of transistors that can fit on a silicon chip doubles every two years. The function $f(x) = 42(1.41)^x$ models the number of transistors, in millions, that can fit on a chip, where x is the number of years since 2000. Using this model, in what year can a chip hold 1 billion transistors? **about 2009**

35. **Multi-Step** A computer randomly creates three different functions. The functions are $y = (3.1x + 7)^2$, $y = 4.8(2)^x$, and $y = \frac{1}{5}(6)^x$. The computer then generates the y value 38.4. Given the three different functions, determine which one is exponential *and* produces the generated number. **$y = 4.8(2)^x$**

36. **Contests** As a promotion, a clothing store draws the name of one of its customers each week. The prize is a coupon for the store. If the winner is not present at the drawing, he or she cannot claim the prize, and the amount of the coupon increases for the following week's drawing. The function $f(x) = 20(1.2)^x$ gives the amount of the coupon in dollars after x weeks of the prize going unclaimed.

Clothes for everyone!
Math Apparel
Win Valuable Store Coupon
Must be present to win!

a. What is the amount of the coupon after 2 weeks of the prize going unclaimed? **$28.80**
b. After how many weeks of the prize going unclaimed will the amount of the coupon be greater than $100?
c. What is the original amount of the coupon? **$20**
d. Find the percent increase each week. **20%**

36b. after 9 weeks

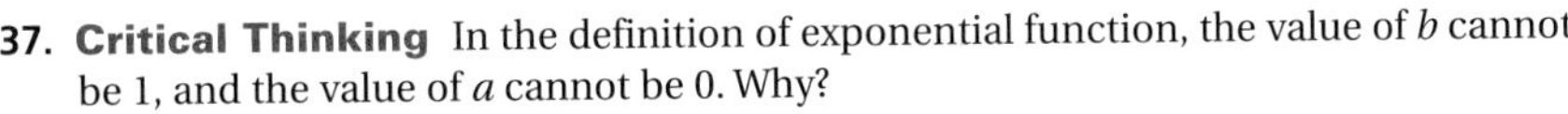

37. **Critical Thinking** In the definition of exponential function, the value of b cannot be 1, and the value of a cannot be 0. Why?

37. If the value of b were 1, the function would be constant. If the value of a were 0, the function would be the constant function $y = 0$.

Graphing Calculator Graph each group of functions on the same screen. How are their graphs alike? How are they different?

38. $y = 2^x, y = 3^x, y = 4^x$
39. $y = \left(\frac{1}{2}\right)^x, y = \left(\frac{1}{3}\right)^x, y = \left(\frac{1}{4}\right)^x$

Evaluate each of the following for the given value of x.

40. $f(x) = 4^x; x = 3$ **64**
41. $f(x) = -(0.25)^x; x = 1.5$ **−0.125**
42. $f(x) = 0.4(10)^x; x = -3$ **0.0004, or 4×10^{-4}**

MULTI-STEP TEST PREP

43. This problem will prepare you for the Multi-Step Test Prep on page 820.
a. The annual tuition at a community college since 2001 is modeled by the equation $C = 2000(1.08)^n$, where C is the tuition cost and n is the number of years since 2001. What was the tuition cost in 2001? **$2000**
b. What is the annual percentage of tuition increase? **8%**
c. Find the tuition cost in 2006. **$2938.66**

Exercise 43 involves evaluating exponential functions. This exercise prepares students for the Multi-Step Test Prep on page 820.

Answers

25.

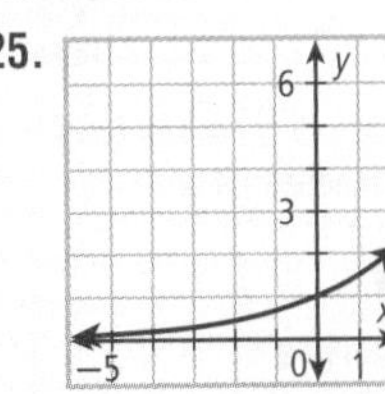

26.

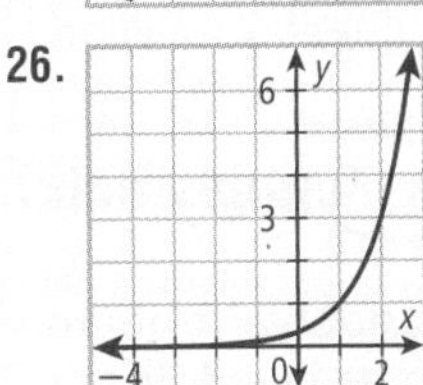

27.

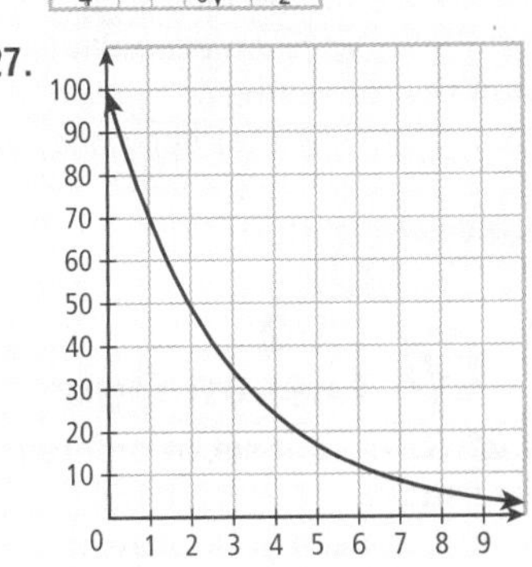

28.

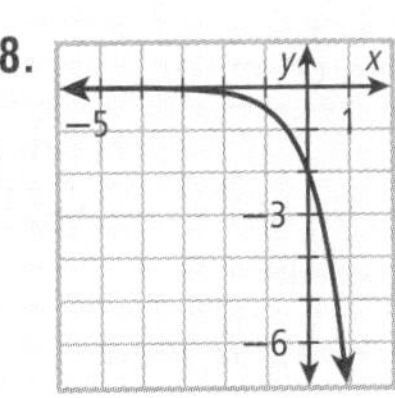

29–33, 38–39. See pp. A33–A34.

11-2 PROBLEM SOLVING

Write the correct answer.

1. The function $f(x) = 6(1.5)^x$ models the length of a photograph in inches after the photo has been enlarged by 50% x times.
a. What is the length of the photograph after it has been enlarged 4 times?
30.375 in.
b. Graph the function.

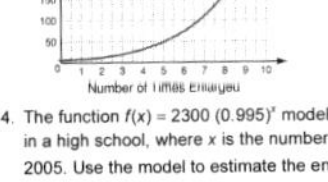

2. A population of 550 rabbits is increasing by 2.5% each year. The function $y = 5.5(1.025)^x$ gives the population of rabbits, in hundreds, x years from now. About how long will it take the population to reach 600 rabbits? 1200 rabbits?
4 years
32 years

3. The function $y = 200(1.0004)^x$ models the balance on a customer's line of credit x days after the end of the grace period (the time when no interest accumulates). If Jack does not make any payments, determine Jack's balance 30 days after the grace period ends.
$202.41

4. The function $f(x) = 2300(0.995)^x$ models enrollment in a high school, where x is the number of years after 2005. Use the model to estimate the enrollment in 2013. **2210**

A lake was stocked with fish in early April. Select the best answer.

5. The function $f(x) = 300(0.85)^x$ models the number of landlocked salmon in the lake x months after the lake was stocked. Which is the best estimate of the number of landlocked salmon in early July?
A 157
C 217
B 184
D 255

6. The function $f(x) = 75(1.2)^x$ models the number of rainbow trout in the lake x years after 2005. Likewise, the function $f(x) = 105(1.08)^x$ models the number of perch in the lake for the same time period. Which statement is NOT true?
A The population of perch will reach 120 before the population of rainbow trout does.
B In 2009, the number of rainbow trout will exceed the number of perch.
C In 2007, the number of rainbow trout will be less than 100.
D In 10 years, there will be at least twice as many rainbow trout as perch.

7. The function $f(x) = 400(1.05)^x$ models the number of bass x months after the lake was stocked. During what month will the population reach 600?
F September
H November
G October
J December

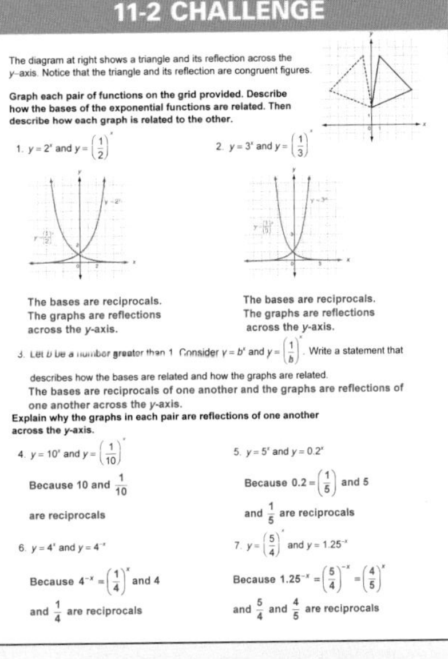

11-2 CHALLENGE

The diagram at right shows a triangle and its reflection across the y-axis. Notice that the triangle and its reflection are congruent figures.

Graph each pair of functions on the grid provided. Describe how the bases of the exponential functions are related. Then describe how each graph is related to the other.

1. $y = 2^x$ and $y = \left(\frac{1}{2}\right)^x$
The bases are reciprocals. The graphs are reflections across the y-axis.

2. $y = 3^x$ and $y = \left(\frac{1}{3}\right)^x$
The bases are reciprocals. The graphs are reflections across the y-axis.

3. Let b be a number greater than 1. Consider $y = b^x$ and $y = \left(\frac{1}{b}\right)^x$. Write a statement that describes how the bases are related and how the graphs are related.
The bases are reciprocals of one another and the graphs are reflections of one another across the y-axis.

Explain why the graphs in each pair are reflections of one another across the y-axis.

4. $y = 10^x$ and $y = \left(\frac{1}{10}\right)^x$
Because 10 and $\frac{1}{10}$ are reciprocals

5. $y = 5^x$ and $y = 0.2^x$
Because $0.2 = \left(\frac{1}{5}\right)$ and 5 and $\frac{1}{5}$ are reciprocals

6. $y = 4^x$ and $y = 4^{-x}$
Because $4^{-x} = \left(\frac{1}{4}\right)^x$ and 4 and $\frac{1}{4}$ are reciprocals

7. $y = \left(\frac{5}{4}\right)^x$ and $y = 1.25^{-x}$
Because $1.25^{-x} = \left(\frac{5}{4}\right)^{-x} = \left(\frac{4}{5}\right)^x$ and $\frac{5}{4}$ and $\frac{4}{5}$ are reciprocals

11-2 PRACTICE A
11-2 PRACTICE C
11-2 PRACTICE B

1. If a basketball is bounced from a height of 15 feet, the function $f(x) = 15(0.75)^x$ gives the height of the ball in feet of each bounce, where x is the bounce number. What will be the height of the 5th bounce? Round to the nearest tenth of a foot. **3.6 feet**

Tell whether each set of ordered pairs satisfies an exponential function. Explain your answer.

2. {(2, 4), (4, 8), (6, 16), (8, 32)} **yes, as the x-values increase by 2, the y values are multiplied by 2.**
3. {(−2, 5), (−1, 10), (0, 15), (1, 20)} **no, as the x-values increase by 1, the y-values are not multiplied by a constant amount.**
4. {(1, 750), (2, 150), (3, 30), (4, 6)} **yes, as the x-values increase by 1, the y-values are multiplied by $\frac{1}{5}$**
5. $\left\{\left(-5, \frac{1}{3}\right), (0, 1), (5, 3), (10, 9)\right\}$ **yes, as the x-values increase by 5, the y-values are multiplied by 3.**

Graph each exponential function.

6. $y = 5(2)^x$
7. $y = -2(3)^x$
8. $y = 3\left(\frac{1}{2}\right)^x$

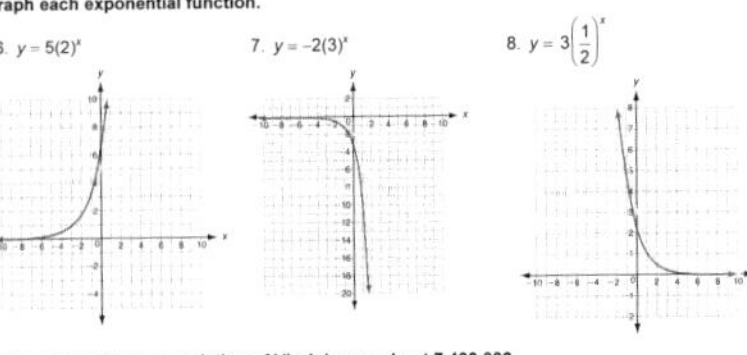

In the year 2000, the population of Virginia was about 7,400,000. Between the years 2000 and 2004, the population in Virginia grew at a rate of 5.4%. At this growth rate, the function $f(x) = 7,400,000(1.054)^x$ gives the population x years after 2000.

9. In what year will the population reach 15,000,000? **2014**
10. In what year will the population reach 20,000,000? **2019**

TEST PREP DOCTOR + Students who chose **A** or **B** in **Exercise 45** may have forgotten that the range of an exponential function is restricted to either values greater than 0 or values less than 0. Students who chose **D** may have forgotten that the domain of an exponential function is all real numbers.

Students who chose **H** in **Exercise 46** raised 1.4 to the power of $x - 1$.

Journal

Have students describe two ways of identifying an exponential function.

ALTERNATIVE ASSESSMENT

Sketch the four basic shapes of exponential graphs on the board. Then have students write an exponential function that would have a graph with a similar shape for each one.

Power Presentations with PowerPoint®

11-2 Lesson Quiz

Tell whether each set of ordered pairs satisfies an exponential function. Explain your answer.

1. $\{(0, 0), (1, -2), (2, -16), (3, -54)\}$ No; for a constant change in x, y is not multiplied by the same value.
2. $\{(0, -5), (1, -2.5), (2, -1.25), (3, -0.625)\}$ Yes; for a constant change in x, y is multiplied by the same value.
3. Graph $y = -0.5(3)^x$.

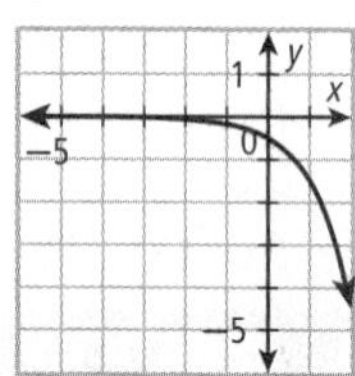

4. The function $y = 11.6(1.009)^x$ models residential energy consumption in quadrillion Btu where x is the number of years after 2003. What will residential energy consumption be in 2013? ≈12.7 quadrillion Btu
5. In 2000, the population of Texas was about 21 million, and it was growing by about 2% per year. At this growth rate, the function $f(x) = 21(1.02)^x$ gives the population, in millions, x years after 2000. Using this model, in about what year will the population reach 30 million? 2018

Also available on transparency

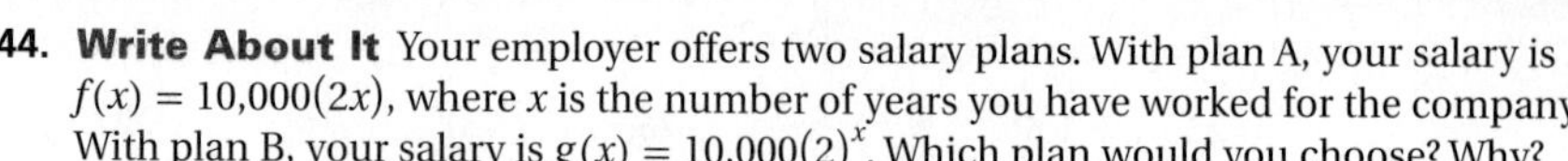

44. **Write About It** Your employer offers two salary plans. With plan A, your salary is $f(x) = 10{,}000(2x)$, where x is the number of years you have worked for the company. With plan B, your salary is $g(x) = 10{,}000(2)^x$. Which plan would you choose? Why?

TEST PREP

45. Which graph shows an exponential function?

Ⓐ 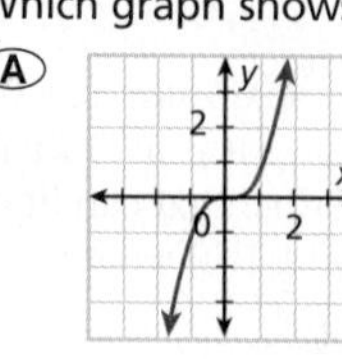

Ⓒ (circled) 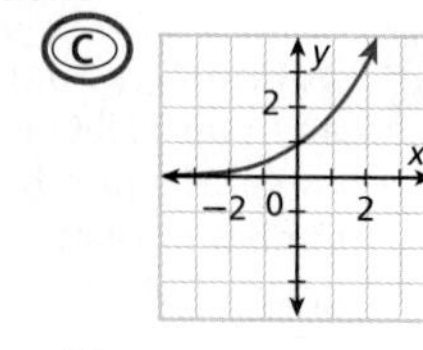

Ⓑ

Ⓓ 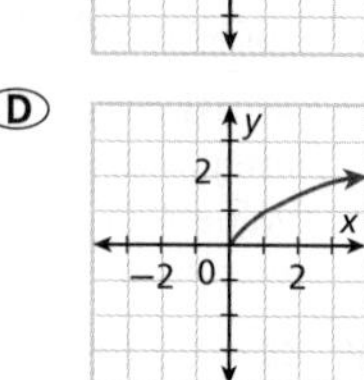

46. The function $f(x) = 15(1.4)^x$ represents the area in square inches of a photograph after it has been enlarged x times by a factor of 140%. What is the area of the photograph after it has been enlarged 4 times?

Ⓕ 5.6 square inches Ⓗ 41.16 square inches

Ⓖ (circled) 57.624 square inches Ⓙ 560 square inches

47. Look at the pattern. How many squares will there be in the nth stage?

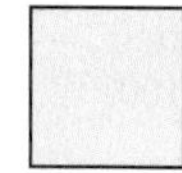
Stage 0

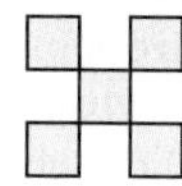
Stage 1

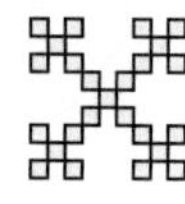
Stage 2

Ⓐ $5n$ Ⓑ $2.5 \cdot 2^n$ Ⓒ 25^{n-1} Ⓓ (circled) 5^n 

CHALLENGE AND EXTEND

Solve each equation.

48. $4^x = 64$ **3**

49. $\left(\frac{1}{3}\right)^x = \frac{1}{27}$ **3**

50. $2^x = \frac{1}{16}$ **−4**

51. Graph the following functions: $y = 2(2)^x$, $y = 3(2)^x$, $y = -2(2)^x$. Then make a conjecture about the relationship between the value of a and the y-intercept of $y = ab^x$.

SPIRAL REVIEW

52. The average of Roger's three test scores must be at least 90 to earn an A in his science class. Roger has scored 88 and 89 on his first two tests. Write and solve an inequality to find what he must score on the third test to earn an A. *(Lesson 3-4)*

52. $\frac{88 + 89 + x}{3} \geq 90$; $x \geq 93$

Find the missing term in each perfect-square trinomial. *(Lesson 8-5)*

53. $x^2 + 10x + \blacksquare$ **25**

54. $4x^2 + \blacksquare + 64$ **32x**

55. $\blacksquare + 42x + 49$ **9x²**

56. What is the 12th term of the sequence 4, 12, 36, 108, …? *(Lesson 11-1)* **708,588**

Answers

44. Possible answer: The following table shows how much money you could earn with each plan.

Year	Salary w/ Plan A ($)	Salary w/ Plan B ($)
0	0	10,000
1	20,000	20,000
2	40,000	40,000
3	60,000	80,000

I would choose plan B because plan A doesn't pay you anything for the first year and because after 3 years, plan B pays more money.

51.

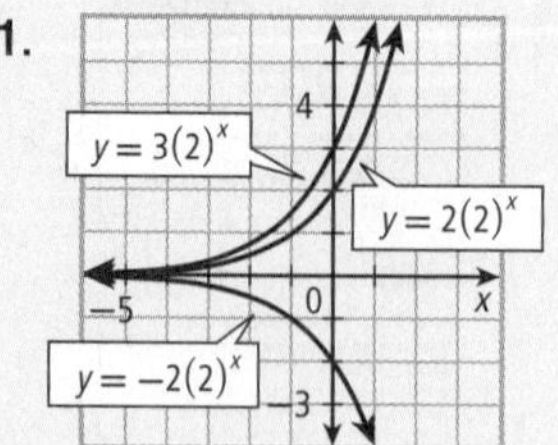

The value of a is the y-intercept.

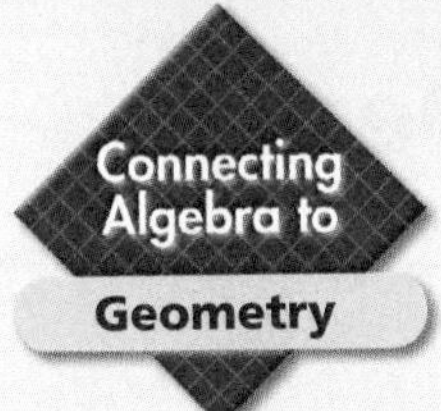

Changing Dimensions

What happens to the volume of a three-dimensional figure when you repeatedly double the dimensions?

Recall these formulas for the volumes of common three-dimensional figures.

Cube $V = s^3$ **Rectangular Prism** $V = \ell wh$ **Pyramid** $V = \frac{1}{3}(\text{area of base}) \cdot h$

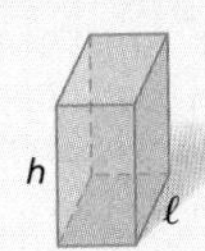

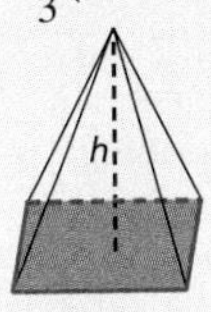

Changing the dimensions of three-dimensional figures results in geometric sequences.

Example

Find the volume of a cube with a side length of 3 cm. Double the side length and find the new volume. Repeat two more times. Show the patterns for the side lengths and volumes as geometric sequences. Identify the common ratios.

Cube	Side Length (cm)	Volume (cm^3)
1	3	27
2	6 (×2)	216 (×8)
3	12 (×2)	1,728 (×8)
4	24 (×2)	13,824 (×8)

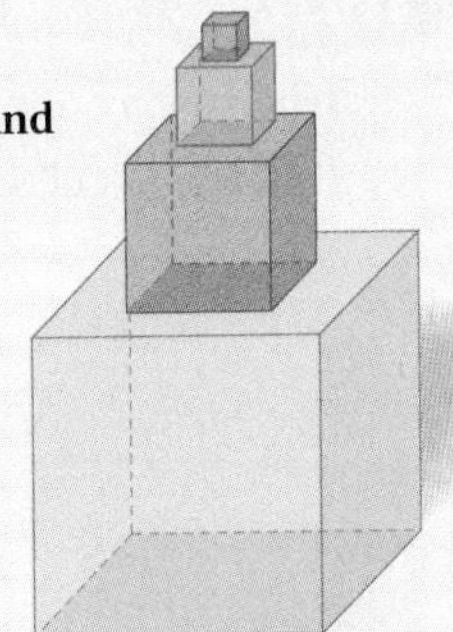

The side lengths and the volumes form geometric sequences. The sequence of the side lengths has a common ratio of 2. The sequence of the volumes has a common ratio of 2^3, or 8.

The patterns in the example above are a specific instance of a general rule.

> When the dimensions of a solid figure are multiplied by x, the volume of the figure is multiplied by x^3.

Try This

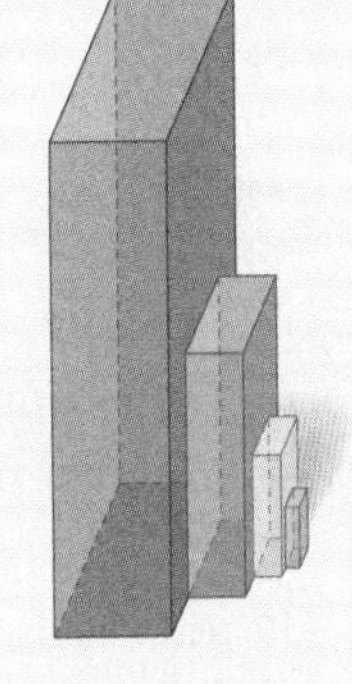

1. The large rectangular prism at right is 8 in. wide, 16 in. long, and 32 in. tall. The dimensions are multiplied by $\frac{1}{2}$ to create each next smaller prism. Show the patterns for the dimensions and the volumes as geometric sequences. Identify the common ratios.
2. A pyramid has a height of 8 cm and a square base of 3 cm on each edge. Triple the dimensions two times. Show the patterns for the dimensions and the volumes as geometric sequences. Identify the common ratios.

Organizer

Pacing:
Traditional $\frac{1}{2}$ day
Block $\frac{1}{4}$ day

Objective: Express with geometric sequences how the changing dimensions of solid figures affects volume.

Online Edition

Teach

Remember

Students review and apply volume formulas for common solids.

Visual Ask students what they notice about the sets of figures on the lesson pages. If no one realizes it, point out that each set shows a group of similar figures.

Close

Assess

The edges of a cube are multiplied by 5. What happens to the volume of the cube? The volume is multiplied by $5^3 = 125$.

State Resources

Answers

1. widths: 8, 4, 2, 1; common ratio: $\frac{1}{2}$; lengths: 16, 8, 4, 2; common ratio: $\frac{1}{2}$ heights: 32, 16, 8, 4; common ratio: $\frac{1}{2}$, volumes: 4096, 512, 64, 8; common ratio: $\frac{1}{8}$
2. heights: 8, 24, 72; common ratio: 3 edge of bases: 3, 9, 27; common ratio: 3 volumes: 24, 648, 17,496; common ratio: 27

Organizer

Use with Lesson 11-3

Pacing:
Traditional $\frac{1}{2}$ day
Block $\frac{1}{4}$ day

Objective: Fold and cut paper to model exponential growth and decay.

Materials: notebook paper, scissors

Resources

Algebra Lab Activities
11-3 Lab Recording Sheet

Teach

Discuss

Remind students that $2^0 = 1$ and $2^{-n} = \frac{1}{2^n}$.

In **Activity 1,** the exponent equals the number of folds. In **Activity 2,** the exponent equals the opposite of the number of cuts.

Close

Key Concept

Multiplying repeatedly by numbers greater than 1 causes a quantity to increase, while multiplying repeatedly by numbers between 0 and 1 causes a quantity to decrease.

Assessment

Journal For each activity, have students explain what b represents in the exponential function $f(x) = b^x$.

State Resources

Model Growth and Decay

You can fold and cut paper to model quantities that increase or decrease exponentially.

Use with Lesson 11-3

Activity 1

1. Copy the table at right.
2. Fold a piece of notebook paper in half. Then open it back up. Count the number of regions created by the fold. Record your answer in the table.
3. Now fold the paper in half twice. Record the number of regions created by the folds in the table.
4. Repeat this process for 3, 4, and 5 folds.

Folds	Regions
0	1
1	**2**
2	**4**
3	**8**
4	**16**
5	**32**

Try This

1. When the number of folds increases by 1, the number of regions ___?___. **doubles**
2. For each row of the table, write the number of regions as a power of 2. $2^0, 2^1, 2^2, 2^3, 2^4, 2^5$
3. Write an exponential expression for the number of regions formed by n folds. 2^n
4. If you could fold the paper 8 times, how many regions would be formed? **256**
5. How many times would you have to fold the paper to make 512 regions? **9**

Activity 2

1. Copy the table at right.
2. Begin with a square piece of paper. The area of the paper is 1 square unit. Cut the paper in half. Each piece has an area of $\frac{1}{2}$ square unit. Record the result in the table.
3. Cut one of those pieces in half again, and record the area of one of the new, smaller pieces in the table.
4. Repeat this process for 3, 4, and 5 cuts.

Cuts	Area
0	1
1	$\frac{1}{2}$
2	$\frac{1}{4}$
3	$\frac{1}{8}$
4	$\frac{1}{16}$
5	$\frac{1}{32}$

Try This

6. When the number of cuts increases by 1, the area ___?___. **is divided in half**
7. For each row of the table, write the area as a power of 2. $2^0, 2^{-1}, 2^{-2}, 2^{-3}, 2^{-4}, 2^{-5}$
8. Write an exponential expression for the area after n cuts. 2^{-n}
9. What would be the area after 7 cuts? $\frac{1}{128}$
10. How many cuts would you have to make to get an area of $\frac{1}{256}$ square unit? **8**

11-3 Exponential Growth and Decay

Objective
Solve problems involving exponential growth and decay.

Vocabulary
exponential growth
compound interest
exponential decay
half-life

Why learn this?
Exponential growth and decay describe many real-world situations, such as the value of artwork. (See Example 1.)

Exponential growth occurs when a quantity increases by the same rate r in each time period t. When this happens, the value of the quantity at any given time can be calculated as a function of the rate and the original amount.

Exponential Growth

An exponential growth function has the form $y = a(1 + r)^t$, where $a > 0$.

- y represents the final amount.
- a represents the original amount.
- r represents the rate of growth expressed as a decimal.
- t represents time.

EXAMPLE 1 Exponential Growth

The original value of a painting is \$1400, and the value increases by 9% each year. Write an exponential growth function to model this situation. Then find the value of the painting in 25 years.

In Example 1, round to the nearest hundredth because the problem deals with money. This means you are rounding to the nearest cent.

Step 1 Write the exponential growth function for this situation.

$y = a(1 + r)^t$	*Write the formula.*
$= 1400(1 + 0.09)^t$	*Substitute 1400 for a and 0.09 for r.*
$= 1400(1.09)^t$	*Simplify.*

Step 2 Find the value in 25 years.

$y = 1400(1.09)^t$	
$= 1400(1.09)^{25}$	*Substitute 25 for t.*
$\approx 12{,}072.31$	*Use a calculator and round to the nearest hundredth.*

The value of the painting in 25 years is \$12,072.31.

1. A sculpture is increasing in value at a rate of 8% per year, and its value in 2000 was \$1200. Write an exponential growth function to model this situation. Then find the sculpture's value in 2006. $y = 1200(1.08)^t$; **\$1904.25**

11-3 Organizer

Pacing: Traditional 1 day
Block $\frac{1}{2}$ day

Objective: Solve problems involving exponential growth and decay.

Algebra Lab
In *Algebra Lab Activities*

Online Edition
Tutorial Videos, Interactivity

Power Presentations with PowerPoint®

Warm Up

Simplify each expression.

1. $(4 + 0.05)^2$ 16.4025
2. $25(1 + 0.02)^3$ 26.5302
3. $1 + \frac{0.03}{4}$ 1.0075
4. The first term of a geometric sequence is 3 and the common ratio is 2. What is the 5th term of the sequence? 48
5. The function $f(x) = 2(4)^x$ models an insect population after x days. What is the insect population after 3 days? 128 insects

Also available on transparency

Q: Why was the banker's son sent to the principal's office?

A: He had an interest in another student's test paper.

1 Introduce

EXPLORATION

11-3 Exponential Growth and Decay

Kendrick puts \$200 in a savings account that earns 4% interest each year.

1. How much interest will Kendrick earn in the first year?
2. What is the total amount of money that Kendrick will have at the end of the first year?
3. In the second year, Kendrick will receive 4% interest on the total amount of money you found in Problem 2. How much interest will that be?
4. Complete the table.

Year	Process: Beginning Amount × 1.04	Exponential Form	Total (\$)
1	200(1.04)	200(1.04)	
2	[200(1.04)](1.04)	$200(1.04)^2$	
3			
4			
5			

THINK AND DISCUSS

5. **Describe** any patterns you see in the table.
6. **Show** how to write an equation for the total amount of money A that Kendrick will have in year t.

Motivate

Review the formula for simple interest I: $I = Prt$, where P is the principal, or original amount, r is the interest rate, and t is time.

Have students compute the simple interest on \$200 invested at 4% for 20 years. \$160

Explorations and answers are provided in *Alternate Openers: Explorations Transparencies.*

State Resources

Power Presentations with PowerPoint®

Additional Examples

Example 1

The original value of a painting is \$9000 and the value increases by 7% each year. Write an exponential growth function to model this situation. Then find the painting's value in 15 years.

$y = 9000(1.07)^t$; \$24,831.28

Example 2

Write a compound interest function to model each situation. Then find the balance after the given number of years.

A. \$1200 invested at a rate of 2% compounded quarterly; 3 years $A = 1200(1.005)^{4t}$; \$1274.01

B. \$15,000 invested at a rate of 4.8% compounded monthly; 2 years. $A = 15{,}000(1.004)^{12t}$; \$16,508.22

INTERVENTION

Questioning Strategies

EXAMPLE 1

- How is the formula for exponential growth similar to the standard form of an exponential function?
- How is this formula like that for finding the nth term of a geometric sequence?

EXAMPLE 2

- How is compound interest different from simple interest?
- In the formula for compound interest, why is r divided by n? Why is t multiplied by n?

Reading Math Have students find different definitions of *compound*. Examples may include a substance formed by two or more ingredients, to combine, or to make stronger and more intense. Relate these definitions to the meaning of *compound interest*.

ENGLISH LANGUAGE LEARNERS

A common application of exponential growth is *compound interest*. Recall that simple interest is earned or paid only on the principal. **Compound interest** is interest earned or paid on *both* the principal and previously earned interest.

Know it! Note — **Compound Interest**

$$A = P\left(1 + \frac{r}{n}\right)^{nt}$$

A represents the balance after t years.
P represents the principal, or original amount.
r represents the annual interest rate expressed as a decimal.
n represents the number of times interest is compounded per year.
t represents time in years.

EXAMPLE 2 *Finance Application*

Write a compound interest function to model each situation. Then find the balance after the given number of years.

A **\$1000 invested at a rate of 3% compounded quarterly; 5 years**

Step 1 Write the compound interest function for this situation.

$A = P\left(1 + \frac{r}{n}\right)^{nt}$ — *Write the formula.*

$= 1000\left(1 + \frac{0.03}{4}\right)^{4t}$ — *Substitute 1000 for P, 0.03 for r, and 4 for n.*

$= 1000(1.0075)^{4t}$ — *Simplify.*

Step 2 Find the balance after 5 years.

$A = 1000(1.0075)^{4(5)}$ — *Substitute 5 for t.*

$= 1000(1.0075)^{20}$

≈ 1161.18 — *Use a calculator and round to the nearest hundredth.*

The balance after 5 years is \$1161.18.

B **\$18,000 invested at a rate of 4.5% compounded annually; 6 years**

Step 1 Write the compound interest function for this situation.

$A = P\left(1 + \frac{r}{n}\right)^{nt}$ — *Write the formula.*

$= 18{,}000\left(1 + \frac{0.045}{1}\right)^{t}$ — *Substitute 18,000 for P, 0.045 for r, and 1 for n.*

$= 18{,}000(1.045)^{t}$ — *Simplify.*

Step 2 Find the balance after 6 years.

$A = 18{,}000(1.045)^{6}$ — *Substitute 6 for t.*

$\approx 23{,}440.68$ — *Use a calculator and round to the nearest hundredth.*

The balance after 6 years is \$23,440.68.

For compound interest,
- *annually* means "once per year" ($n = 1$).
- *quarterly* means "4 times per year" ($n = 4$).
- *monthly* means "12 times per year" ($n = 12$).

CHECK IT OUT! **Write a compound interest function to model each situation. Then find the balance after the given number of years.**

2a. \$1200 invested at a rate of 3.5% compounded quarterly; 4 years

2b. \$4000 invested at a rate of 3% compounded monthly; 8 years

2a. $A = 1200(1.00875)^{4t}$; **\$1379.49**
2b. $A = 4000(1.0025)^{12t}$; **\$5083.47**

2 Teach

Guided Instruction

Show that the formulas for exponential growth and decay are just variations of $y = ab^x$ with either $1 + r$ or $1 - r$ replacing b. Point out also the similarities between $y = ab^x$ and the compound interest formula: P is the original amount a, and $1 + \frac{r}{n}$ is b. Explain that the exponent must be the number of time periods nt and that the common ratio must correspond with it. Because r is always given as an annual rate, it must be divided by n when n is not 1.

Exponential decay occurs when a quantity decreases by the same rate r in each time period t. Just like exponential growth, the value of the quantity at any given time can be calculated by using the rate and the original amount.

Exponential Decay

An exponential decay function has the form $y = a(1 - r)^t$, where $a > 0$.

y represents the final amount.

a represents the original amount.

r represents the rate of decay as a decimal.

t represents time.

Notice an important difference between exponential growth functions and exponential decay functions. For exponential growth, the value inside the parentheses will be greater than 1 because r is added to 1. For exponential decay, the value inside the parentheses will be less than 1 because r is subtracted from 1.

EXAMPLE 3 Exponential Decay

The population of a town is decreasing at a rate of 1% per year. In 2000 there were 1300 people. Write an exponential decay function to model this situation. Then find the population in 2008.

Helpful Hint

In Example 3, round your answer to the nearest whole number because there can only be a whole number of people.

Step 1 Write the exponential decay function for this situation.

$y = a(1 - r)^t$ *Write the formula.*

$= 1300(1 - 0.01)^t$ *Substitute 1300 for a and 0.01 for r.*

$= 1300(0.99)^t$ *Simplify.*

Step 2 Find the population in 2008.

$y = 1300(0.99)^8$ *Substitute 8 for t.*

≈ 1200 *Use a calculator and round to the nearest whole number.*

The population in 2008 is approximately 1200 people.

CHECK IT OUT!

3. The fish population in a local stream is decreasing at a rate of 3% per year. The original population was 48,000. Write an exponential decay function to model this situation. Then find the population after 7 years. $y = 48{,}000(0.97)^t$; **38,783**

A common application of exponential decay is *half-life*. The **half-life** of a substance is the time it takes for one-half of the substance to decay into another substance.

Half-life

$A = P(0.5)^t$

A represents the final amount.

P represents the original amount.

t represents the number of half-lives in a given time period.

COMMON ERROR ALERT

When writing compound interest functions, students may forget to multiply t by n. Remind students that the exponent is the number of times the interest is compounded, which is not necessarily the number of years.

Power Presentations with PowerPoint®

Additional Examples

Example 3

The population of a town is decreasing at a rate of 3% per year. In 2000, there were 1700 people. Write an exponential decay function to model this situation. Then find the population in 2012. $y = 1700(0.97)^t$; 1180

INTERVENTION

Questioning Strategies

EXAMPLE 3

- How is the formula for exponential decay similar to the formula for exponential growth? How is it different?

Reaching All Learners

Through Modeling

Have students complete the table for 80 g of a substance for 45 h, given that the half-life of the substance is 15 h.

Time passed (h)	Substance left (g)
15	half of 80 = 40
30	half of 40 = 20
45	half of 20 = 10

Then show the formula: $y = 80(0.5)^3$. Point out that the exponent 3 represents the number of rows in the table.

Through Critical Thinking

Have students complete the following:

$800 \times (1 - 0.55) = 800 \times 0.45 = 360$

$800 \times (1 - 0.05) = 800 \times 0.95 = 760$

$800 \times 1 = 800$

$800 \times (1 + 0.45) = 800 \times 1.45 = 1160$

$800 \times (1 + 0.95) = 800 \times 1.95 = 1560$

Point out that answers are less than 800 for $1 - r$ and greater than 800 for $1 + r$. Therefore, r is added to 1 in growth problems and subtracted from 1 in decay problems.

Power Presentations with PowerPoint®

Additional Examples

Example 4

Astatine-218 has a half-life of 2 seconds.

a. Find the amount left from a 500-gram sample of astatine-218 after 10 seconds. 15.625 g

b. Find the amount left from a 500-gram sample of astatine-218 after 1 minute. 0.00000047 g

INTERVENTION

Questioning Strategies

EXAMPLE 4

- How does the formula for half-life compare to $y = ab^x$? Why is b always 0.5?
- How do you find the value of t in the half-life formula?

EXAMPLE 4 ***Science Application***

Fluorine-20 has a half-life of 11 seconds.

A **Find the amount of fluorine-20 left from a 40-gram sample after 44 seconds.**

Step 1 Find t, the number of half-lives in the given time period.

$\frac{44 \text{ s}}{11 \text{ s}} = 4$ *Divide the time period by the half-life. The value of t is 4.*

Step 2 $A = P(0.5)^t$ *Write the formula.*

$= 40(0.5)^4$ *Substitute 40 for P and 4 for t.*

$= 2.5$ *Use a calculator.*

There are 2.5 grams of fluorine-20 remaining after 44 seconds.

B **Find the amount of fluorine-20 left from a 40-gram sample after 2.2 minutes. Round your answer to the nearest hundredth.**

Step 1 Find t, the number of half-lives in the given time period.

$2.2(60) = 132$ *Find the number of seconds in 2.2 minutes.*

$\frac{132 \text{ s}}{11 \text{ s}} = 12$ *Divide the time period by the half-life. The value of t is $\frac{132}{11} = 12$.*

Step 2 $A = P(0.5)^t$ *Write the formula.*

$= 40(0.5)^{12}$ *Substitute 40 for P and 12 for t.*

≈ 0.01 *Use a calculator. Round to the nearest hundredth.*

There is about 0.01 gram of fluorine-20 remaining after 2.2 minutes.

4a. Cesium-137 has a half-life of 30 years. Find the amount of cesium-137 left from a 100-milligram sample after 180 years. **1.5625 mg**

4b. Bismuth-210 has a half-life of 5 days. Find the amount of bismuth-210 left from a 100-gram sample after 5 weeks. (*Hint:* Change 5 weeks to days.) **0.78125 g**

THINK AND DISCUSS

1. Describe three real-world situations that can be described by exponential growth or exponential decay functions.
2. The population of a town after t years can be modeled by $P = 1000(1.02)^t$. Is the population increasing or decreasing? By what percentage rate?
3. An exponential function is a function of the form $y = ab^x$. Explain why both exponential growth functions and exponential decay functions are exponential functions.

4. **GET ORGANIZED** Copy and complete the graphic organizer.

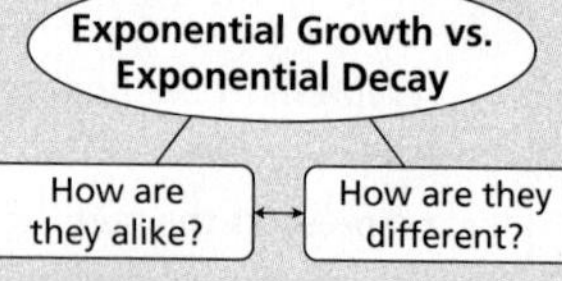

3 Close

Summarize

Write $y = ab^x$ on the board. Below it, write and identify by name the four formulas covered in the lesson. Have students compare each one with the standard form of an exponential function, identifying a and b. Have them also identify each as growth or decay.

and INTERVENTION

***Diagnose Before* the Lesson**
11-3 Warm Up, TE p. 805

***Monitor During* the Lesson**
Check It Out! Exercises, SE pp. 805–808
Questioning Strategies, TE pp. 806–808

***Assess After* the Lesson**
11-3 Lesson Quiz, TE p. 812
Alternative Assessment, TE p. 812

Answers to *Think and Discuss*

1. Possible answers: interest earned on an investment, population growth or decline, radioactive decay
2. increasing; by 2% per year
3. An exponential growth function has the form $y = a(1 + r)^t$. The base $(1 + r)$ corresponds to the base b. The exponent t corresponds to the exponent x. An exponential decay function has the form $y = a(1 - r)^t$. The base $(1 - r)$ corresponds to the base b. The exponent t corresponds to the exponent x.
4. See p. A10.

go.hrw.com
Homework Help Online
KEYWORD: MA7 11-3
Parent Resources Online
KEYWORD: MA7 Parent

GUIDED PRACTICE

1. **Vocabulary** The function $y = 0.68(2)^x$ is an example of ___?___. (*exponential growth* or *exponential decay*) **exponential growth**

SEE EXAMPLE 1 p. 805

Write an exponential growth function to model each situation. Then find the value of the function after the given amount of time.

2. The cost of tuition at a college is \$12,000 and is increasing at a rate of 6% per year; 4 years. $y = 12{,}000(1.06)^t$; \$15,149.72
3. The number of student-athletes at a local high school is 300 and is increasing at a rate of 8% per year; 5 years. $y = 300(1.08)^t$; 441

SEE EXAMPLE 2 p. 806

Write a compound interest function to model each situation. Then find the balance after the given number of years.

4. \$1500 invested at a rate of 3.5% compounded annually; 4 years $A = 1500(1.035)^t$; \$1721.28
5. \$4200 invested at a rate of 2.8% compounded quarterly; 6 years $A = 4200(1.007)^{4t}$; \$4965.43

SEE EXAMPLE 3 p. 807

Write an exponential decay function to model each situation. Then find the value of the function after the given amount of time.

6. The value of a car is \$18,000 and is depreciating at a rate of 12% per year; 10 years. $y = 18{,}000(0.88)^t$; \$5013.02
7. The amount (to the nearest hundredth) of a 10-mg dose of a certain antibiotic decreases in your bloodstream at a rate of 16% per hour; 4 hours. $y = 10(0.84)^t$; 4.98 mg

SEE EXAMPLE 4 p. 808

8. Bismuth-214 has a half-life of approximately 20 minutes. Find the amount of bismuth-214 left from a 30-gram sample after 1 hour. **3.75 g**
9. Mendelevium-258 has a half-life of approximately 52 days. Find the amount of mendelevium-258 left from a 44-gram sample after 156 days. **5.5 g**

PRACTICE AND PROBLEM SOLVING

Independent Practice	
For Exercises	See Example
10–13	1
14–17	2
18–19	3
20	4

Extra Practice
Skills Practice p. S24
Application Practice p. S38

Write an exponential growth function to model each situation. Then find the value of the function after the given amount of time.

10. Annual sales for a company are \$149,000 and are increasing at a rate of 6% per year; 7 years. $y = 149{,}000(1.06)^t$; \$224,040.91
11. The population of a small town is 1600 and is increasing at a rate of 3% per year; 10 years. $y = 1600(1.03)^t$; 2150
12. A new savings account starts at \$700 and increases at 1.2% yearly; 8 years. $A = 700(1.012)^t$; \$770.09
13. Membership of a local club grows at a rate of 7.8% yearly and currently has 30 members; 6 years. $A = 30(1.078)^t$; 47 members

Write a compound interest function to model each situation. Then find the balance after the given number of years.

14. \$28,000 invested at a rate of 4% compounded annually; 5 years $A = 28{,}000(1.04)^t$; \$34,066.28
15. \$7000 invested at a rate of 3% compounded quarterly; 10 years $A = 7000(1.0075)^{4t}$; \$9438.44
16. \$3500 invested at a rate of 1.8% compounded monthly; 4 years $A = 3500(1.0015)^{12t}$; \$3761.09
17. \$12,000 invested at a rate of 2.6% compounded annually; 15 years

17. $A = 12{,}000(1.026)^t$; \$17,635.66

Assignment Guide

Assign *Guided Practice* exercises as necessary.

If you finished Examples **1–2**
Basic 10–17, 29, 30
Average 10–17, 29, 30
Advanced 10–17, 29, 37

If you finished Examples **1–4**
Basic 10–20, 29–33, 35, 38, 39, 41, 45–48, 55–60
Average 10–20, 22–34 even, 35–48, 50–54 even, 55–60
Advanced 10–20, 22–34 even, 36–60

Homework Quick Check
Quickly check key concepts.
Exercises: 11, 15, 19, 20, 25, 31, 40

State Resources

Teaching Tip **Communicating Math** In **Exercise 34,** help students find t by writing the exponent as $\frac{\text{time period}}{\text{half-life}}$. Then they can substitute 3500 for the numerator and 5700 for the denominator. Show students that the answer is reasonable by considering that one half-life is not yet finished. Therefore, half of the 15 grams is not yet gone.

Teaching Tip **Science Link Exercise 34** involves carbon-14 dating, one common method of dating ancient objects. Scientists also use other isotopes to date objects. Some isotopes' half-lives are millions of years!

18. $y = 18{,}000(0.98)^t$; 15,945

19. $y = 58(0.9)^t$; $24.97

23. decay; $33\frac{1}{3}\%$

24. growth; 50%

Write an exponential decay function to model each situation. Then find the value of the function after the given amount of time.

18. The population of a town is 18,000 and is decreasing at a rate of 2% per year; 6 years.
19. The value of a book is $58 and decreases at a rate of 10% per year; 8 years.
20. The half-life of bromine-82 is approximately 36 hours. Find the amount of bromine-82 left from an 80-gram sample after 6 days. **$y = 80(0.5)^t$; 5 g**

Identify each of the following functions as exponential growth or decay. Then give the rate of growth or decay as a percent.

21. $y = 3(1.61)^t$ **growth; 61%**
22. $y = 39(0.098)^t$ **decay; 90.2%**
23. $y = a\left(\frac{2}{3}\right)^t$
24. $y = a\left(\frac{3}{2}\right)^t$
25. $y = a(1.1)^t$ **growth; 10%**
26. $y = a(0.8)^t$ **decay; 20%**
27. $y = a\left(\frac{5}{4}\right)^t$ **growth; 25%**
28. $y = a\left(\frac{1}{2}\right)^t$ **decay; 50%**

Write an exponential growth or decay function to model each situation. Then find the value of the function after the given amount of time.

29. The population of a country is 58,000,000 and grows by 0.1% per year; 3 years. **$y = 58{,}000{,}000(1.001)^t$; 58,174,174**
30. An antique car is worth $32,000, and its value grows by 7% per year; 5 years. **$y = 32{,}000(1.07)^t$; $44,881.66**
31. An investment of $8200 loses value at a rate of 2% per year; 7 years. **$y = 8200(0.98)^t$; $7118.63**
32. A new car is worth $25,000, and its value decreases by 15% each year; 6 years. **$y = 25{,}000(0.85)^t$; $9428.74**
33. The student enrollment in a local high school is 970 students and increases by 1.2% per year; 5 years. **$y = 970(1.012)^t$; 1030**

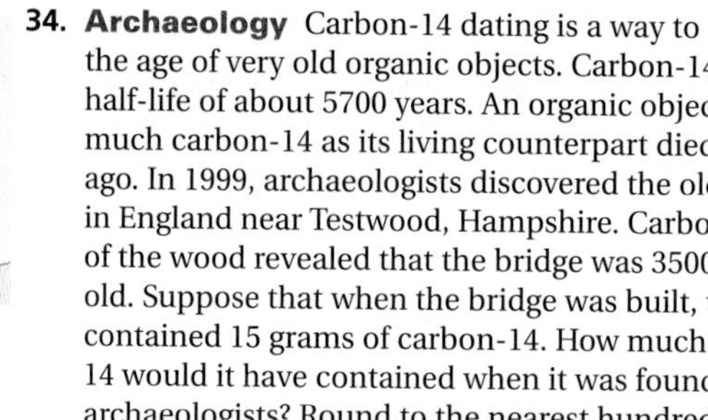

34. **Archaeology** Carbon-14 dating is a way to determine the age of very old organic objects. Carbon-14 has a half-life of about 5700 years. An organic object with $\frac{1}{2}$ as much carbon-14 as its living counterpart died 5700 years ago. In 1999, archaeologists discovered the oldest bridge in England near Testwood, Hampshire. Carbon dating of the wood revealed that the bridge was 3500 years old. Suppose that when the bridge was built, the wood contained 15 grams of carbon-14. How much carbon-14 would it have contained when it was found by the archaeologists? Round to the nearest hundredth. **9.80 g**

A computer-generated image of w[hat] the bridge at Testwood might hav[e] looked like

35. **ERROR ANALYSIS** Two students were asked to find the value of a $1000-item after 3 years. The item was depreciating (losing value) at a rate of 40% per year. Which is incorrect? Explain the error.

B; possible answer: student B did not subtract the rate from 1.

A
$1000(0.6)^3$
$216

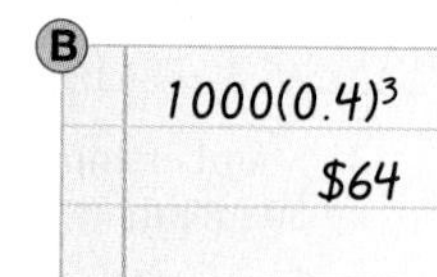

B
$1000(0.4)^3$
$64

36. **Critical Thinking** The value of a certain car can be modeled by the function $y = 20{,}000(0.84)^t$, where t is time in years. Will the value ever be zero? Explain.

36. No; possible answer: there is no value for t that would make $(0.84)^t$ equal 0.

37. The value of a rare baseball card increases every year at a rate of 4%. Today, the card is worth $300. The owner expects to sell the card as soon as the value is over $600. How many years will the owner wait before selling the card? Round your answer to the nearest whole number. **18 years**

11-3 PRACTICE A
11-3 PRACTICE C
11-3 PRACTICE B

Write an exponential growth function to model each situation. Then find the value of the function after the given amount of time.

1. Annual sales for a fast food restaurant are $650,000 and are increasing at a rate of 4% per year; 5 years **$y = 650{,}000(1.04)^x$ ≈$790,824.39**
2. The population of a school is 800 students and is increasing at a rate of 2% per year; 6 years **$y = 800(1.02)^x$ ≈901**
3. During a certain period of time, about 70 northern sea otters had an annual growth rate of 18%; 4 years **$y = 70(1.18)^x$ ≈136**

Write a compound interest function to model each situation. Then find the balance after the given number of years.

4. $50,000 invested at a rate of 3% compounded monthly; 6 years **$y = 50{,}000(1.0025)^{12t}$ ≈$59,847.42**
5. $43,000 invested at a rate of 5% compounded annually; 3 years **$y = 43{,}000(1.05)^t$ ≈$49,777.88**
6. $65,000 invested at a rate of 6% compounded quarterly; 12 years **$y = 65{,}000(1.015)^{4t}$ ≈$132,826.09**

Write an exponential decay function to model each situation. Then find the value of the function after the given amount of time.

7. The population of a town is 2500 and is decreasing at a rate of 3% per year; 5 years **$y = 2500(0.97)^x$ ≈2147**
8. The value of a company's equipment is $25,000 and decreases at a rate of 15% per year; 8 years **$y = 25{,}000(0.85)^x$ ≈$6812.26**
9. The half-life of Iodine-131 is approximately 8 days. Find the amount of Iodine-131 left from a 35 gram sample after 32 days. **2.1875 grams**

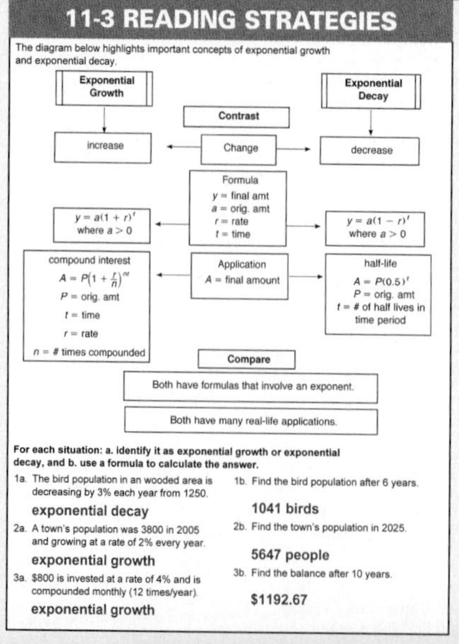

11-3 READING STRATEGIES

The diagram below highlights important concepts of exponential growth and exponential decay.

For each situation: a. identify it as exponential growth or exponential decay, and b. use a formula to calculate the answer.

1a. The bird population in an wooded area is decreasing by 3% each year from 1250. **exponential decay**
1b. Find the bird population after 6 years. **1041 birds**
2a. A town's population was 3800 in 2005 and growing at a rate of 2% every year. **exponential growth**
2b. Find the town's population in 2025. **5647 people**
3a. $800 is invested at a rate of 4% and is compounded monthly (12 times/year). **exponential growth**
3b. Find the balance after 10 years. **$1192.67**

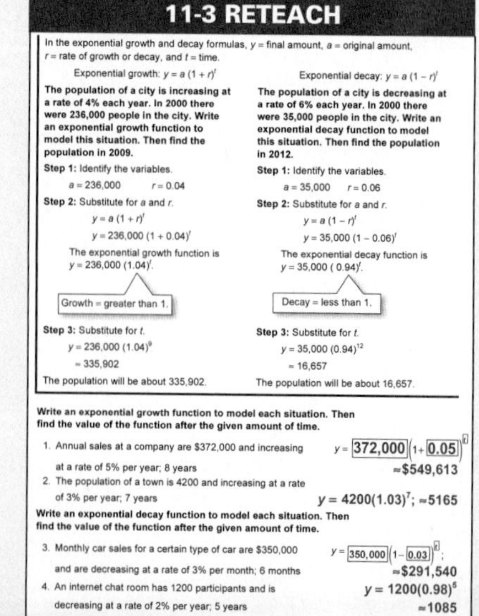

11-3 RETEACH

In the exponential growth and decay formulas, y = final amount, a = original amount, r = rate of growth or decay, and t = time.

Exponential growth: $y = a(1 + r)^t$

The population of a city is increasing at a rate of 4% each year. In 2000 there were 236,000 people in the city. Write an exponential growth function to model this situation. Then find the population in 2009.

Step 1: Identify the variables.
$a = 236{,}000$ $r = 0.04$

Step 2: Substitute for a and r.
$y = a(1 + r)^t$
$y = 236{,}000(1 + 0.04)^t$
The exponential growth function is $y = 236{,}000(1.04)^t$.

Growth = greater than 1.

Step 3: Substitute for t.
$y = 236{,}000(1.04)^9$
$\approx 335{,}902$
The population will be about 335,902.

Exponential decay: $y = a(1 - r)^t$

The population of a city is decreasing at a rate of 6% each year. In 2000 there were 35,000 people in the city. Write an exponential decay function to model this situation. Then find the population in 2012.

Step 1: Identify the variables.
$a = 35{,}000$ $r = 0.06$

Step 2: Substitute for a and r.
$y = a(1 - r)^t$
$y = 35{,}000(1 - 0.06)^t$
The exponential decay function is $y = 35{,}000(0.94)^t$.

Decay = less than 1.

Step 3: Substitute for t.
$y = 35{,}000(0.94)^{12}$
$\approx 16{,}657$
The population will be about 16,657.

Write an exponential growth function to model each situation. Then find the value of the function after the given amount of time.

1. Annual sales at a company are $372,000 and increasing at a rate of 5% per year; 8 years $y =$ **372,000** $(1 +$ **0.05**$)^{t}$ **≈$549,613**
2. The population of a town is 4200 and increasing at a rate of 3% per year; 7 years **$y = 4200(1.03)^7$; ≈5165**

Write an exponential decay function to model each situation. Then find the value of the function after the given amount of time.

3. Monthly car sales for a certain type of car are $350,000 and are decreasing at a rate of 3% per month; 6 months $y =$ **350,000** $(1 -$ **0.03**$)^{t}$; **≈$291,540**
4. An internet chat room has 1200 participants and is decreasing at a rate of 2% per year; 5 years **$y = 1200(0.98)^5$ ≈1085**

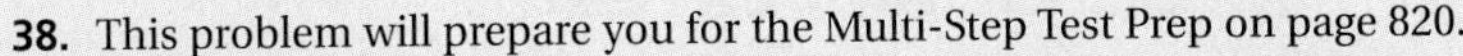

38. This problem will prepare you for the Multi-Step Test Prep on page 820.

a. The annual tuition at a prestigious university was \$20,000 in 2002. It generally increases at a rate of 9% each year. Write a function to describe the cost as a function of the number of years since 2002. Use 2002 as year zero when writing the function rule. **$y = 20{,}000(1.09)^t$**

b. What do you predict the cost of tuition will be in 2008? **\$33,542**

c. Use a table of values to find the first year that the cost of the tuition is more than twice the cost in 2002. **2011**

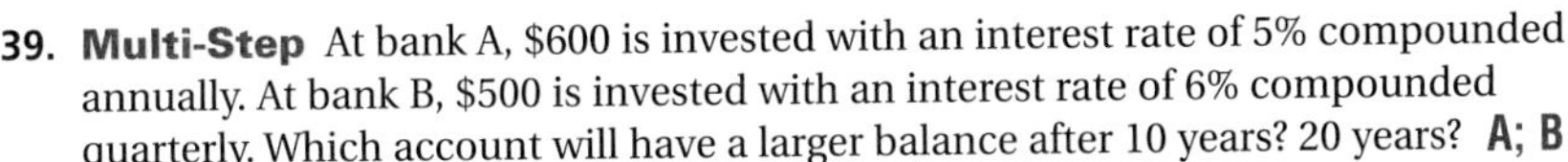

39. Multi-Step At bank A, \$600 is invested with an interest rate of 5% compounded annually. At bank B, \$500 is invested with an interest rate of 6% compounded quarterly. Which account will have a larger balance after 10 years? 20 years? **A; B**

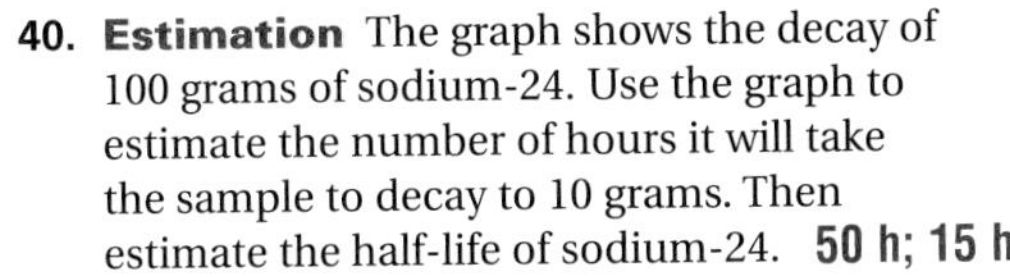

40. Estimation The graph shows the decay of 100 grams of sodium-24. Use the graph to estimate the number of hours it will take the sample to decay to 10 grams. Then estimate the half-life of sodium-24. **50 h; 15 h**

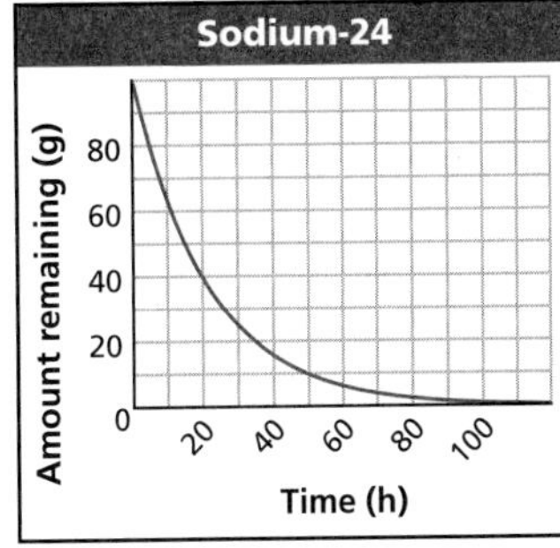

41. Graphing Calculator Use a graphing calculator to graph $y = 10(1 + r)^x$ for $r = 10\%$ and $r = 20\%$. Compare the two graphs. How does the value of r affect the graphs?

42. Write About It Write a real-world situation that could be modeled by $y = 400(1.08)^t$.

42. Possible answer: \$400 is invested at a rate of 8% compounded annually.

43. Write About It Write a real-world situation that could be modeled by $y = 800(0.96)^t$. **Possible answer: The population is 800 and decreasing at a rate of 4% per year.**

44. Critical Thinking The amount of water in a container doubles every minute. After 6 minutes, the container is full. Your friend says it was half full after 3 minutes. Do you agree? Why or why not? **No; possible answer: the sample doubles every minute, so the container is half full 1 min before it is full. This would be after 5 min.**

Test Prep

45. A population of 500 is decreasing by 1% per year. Which function models this situation?

Ⓐ $y = 500(0.01)^t$ Ⓑ $y = 500(0.1)^t$ Ⓒ $y = 500(0.9)^t$ **Ⓓ** $y = 500(0.99)^t$

46. Which function is NOT an exponential decay model?

Ⓕ $y = 5\left(\frac{1}{3}\right)^x$ **Ⓖ** $y = -5\left(\frac{1}{3}\right)^x$ Ⓗ $y = 5(3)^{-x}$ Ⓙ $y = 5(3^{-1})^x$

47. Stephanie wants to save \$1000 for a down payment on a car that she wants to buy in 3 years. She opens a savings account that pays 5% interest compounded annually. About how much should Stephanie deposit now to have enough money for the down payment in 3 years?

Ⓐ \$295 Ⓑ \$333 Ⓒ \$500 **Ⓓ** \$865

48. Short Response In 2000, the population of a town was 1000 and was growing at a rate of 5% per year.

a. Write an exponential growth function to model this situation. **$y = 1000(1.05)^t$**

b. In what year is the population 1300? Show how you found your answer.

48b. about 2005; check students' work.

Multi-Step Test Prep **Exercise 38** involves writing an exponential function and using it to make a prediction. This exercise prepares students for the Multi-Step Test Prep on page 820.

Test Prep Doctor In **Exercise 45,** the value of a is the same for each function. Only the value of b is different. Students who chose **A** may have forgotten to subtract the rate of decay from 1.

In **Exercise 46,** students should be looking for a value of b that is greater than 1. Students who chose **J** may have forgotten how to simplify expressions with negative exponents.

Students can solve **Exercise 47** by writing the compound interest formula, substituting the given numbers, and solving for A. After simplifying, the equation to be solved is $1000 = 1.157625A$.

Answers

38c.

Year	Tuition (\$)
2002	20,000
2003	21,800
2004	23,762
2005	25,900.58
2006	28,231.63
2007	30,772.48
2008	33,542.00
2009	36,560.78
2010	39,851.25
2011	43,437.87

41.

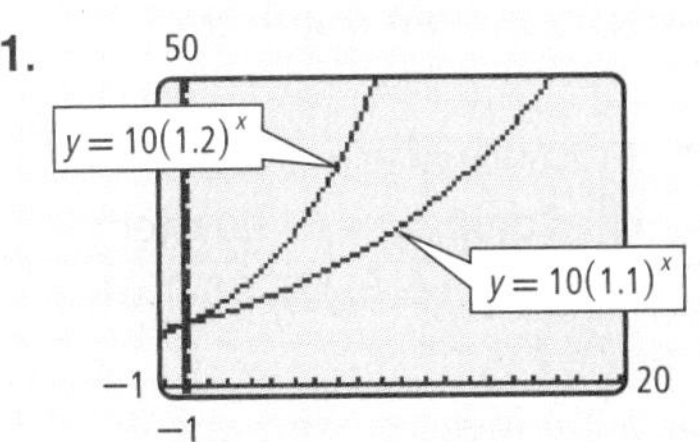

The graph when r is 20% rises faster than when r is 10%. The greater the value of r, the faster the graph will rise.

11-3 PROBLEM SOLVING

Write the correct answer.

1. A condo in Austin, Texas, was worth \$80,000 in 1990. The value of the condo increased by an average of 3% each year. Write an exponential growth function to model this situation. Then find the value of the condominium in 2005.

   $y = 80{,}000(1.03)^t$

   \$124,637

2. Markiya deposited \$500 in a savings account. The annual interest rate is 2%, and the interest is compounded monthly. Write a compound interest function to model this situation. Then find the balance in Markiya's account after 4 years.

   $y = 500\left(1 + \frac{0.02}{12}\right)^{12t}$

   \$541.61

3. The population of a small Midwestern town is 4500. The population is decreasing at a rate of 1.5% per year. Write an exponential decay function to model this situation. Then find the number of people in the town after 25 years.

   $y = 4500(0.985)^t$

   3084

4. Twelve students at a particular high school passed an advanced placement test in 2000. The number of students who passed the test increased by 16.4% each year thereafter. Find the number of students who passed the test in 2004.

   22

Half-lives range from less than a second to billions of years. The table below shows the half-lives of several substances. Select the best answer.

Half-Lives	
Nitrogen-16	7 s
Technetium-99	6 h
Sulfur-35	87 days
Tritium	12.3 yr
Uranium-238	4.5 billion yrs

5. About how many grams of a 500 g sample of Technetium-99 is left after 2 days?

   A 1.95 g C 31.25 g
   B 7.81 g D 62.5 g

6. Which equation can be used to find how much of a 50 g sample of Nitrogen-16 is left after 7 minutes?

   F $A = 50(0.5)^1$ H $A = 50(0.5)^{42}$
   G $A = 50(0.5)^7$ **J** $A = 50(0.5)^{60}$

7. How many billions of years will it take 1000 grams of Uranium-238 to decay to just 125 grams?

   A 0.125 C 9
   B 3 **D** 13.5

8. A researcher had 37.5 g left from a 600 g sample of Sulfer-35. How many half-lives passed during that time?

   F 4 H 7
   G 5 J 16

9. Look at problem 8. How many days passed during that time?

   A 7 **C** 348
   B 16 D 435

11-3 CHALLENGE

Some of the parents of the students in a mathematics class invest money in accounts that pay compound interest. Their hope is to have their investments grow so that, at some time in the future, they can use the money that has accumulated to help the local Boys and Girls Club. The compound interest that they need for their financial planning is shown at right.

$A = P(1+r)^t =$ P represents the inital amount. r represents the rate as a decimal. t represents time in years. A represents the final amount.

Suppose that \$10,000 is invested into an account that pays 5.65% interest compounded annually. Give answers rounded to the nearest cent.

1. Write a function that will give A as a function of t. **$A = 10{,}000(1.0565)^t$**

2. Complete the table below.

t	0	1	2	3	4	5	6	7
A	10,000	10,565	11,161.92	11,792.57	12,458.85	13,162.78	13,906.47	14,692.19

3. a. When will the value of the account exceed \$12,000?

   sometime after the end of the third year but before the end of the fourth year

   b. When will the value of the account exceed \$12,000 but be less than \$14,000?

   sometime after the end of the third year but before the end of the seventh year

4. The group of parents wants their initial deposit amount to grow to \$15,000. Use guess-and-check to approximate the number of years that it will take for this to happen. Give your answer to the nearest tenth of a year. **7.4 years**

5. The group wants their initial deposit amount to grow to \$18,000 within 10 years. After that time, they want to make an \$18,000 donation to the local club. Will they achieve their goal? Explain your response.

   No; after 10 years, they will have \$17,325.87, which is less than \$18,000.

Use guess-and-check to approximate the time that it takes the given investment to grow to the target goal. Round answers to the nearest tenth of a year.

6. \$12,500 at 4.5% compounded yearly; target goal: \$18,000 **8.3 years**

7. \$15,500 at 6.5% compounded yearly; target goal: \$20,000 **4.1 years**

8. \$5 at 5.5% compounded yearly; target goal: \$18,000 **153 years**

Journal

Have students explain what each number represents in the population decay function $P = 6000(0.99)^4$.

ALTERNATIVE ASSESSMENT

Have students write and solve four different word problems, one for each of the four formulas taught in the lesson.

Power Presentations with PowerPoint®

11-3 Lesson Quiz

1. The number of employees at a certain company is 1440 and is increasing at a rate of 1.5% per year. Write an exponential growth function to model this situation. Then find the number of employees in the company after 9 years. $y = 1440(1.015)^t$; 1646

Write a compound interest function to model each situation. Then find the balance after the given number of years.

2. \$12,000 invested at a rate of 6% compounded quarterly; 15 years $A = 12{,}000(1.015)^{4t}$; \$29,318.64
3. \$500 invested at a rate of 2.5% compounded annually; 10 years $A = 500(1.025)^t$; \$640.04
4. The deer population of a game preserve is decreasing by 2% per year. The original population was 1850. Write an exponential decay function to model the situation. Then find the population after 4 years. $y = 1850(0.98)^t$; 1706
5. Iodine-131 has a half-life of about 8 days. Find the amount left from a 30-gram sample of iodine-131 after 40 days. 0.9375 g

Also available on transparency

CHALLENGE AND EXTEND

49. You invest \$700 at a rate of 6% compounded quarterly. Use a graph to estimate the number of years it will take for your investment to increase to \$2300. **about 20 yr**
50. Omar invested \$500 at a rate of 4% compounded annually. How long will it take for Omar's money to double? How long would it take if the interest were 8% compounded annually? **18 yr; 9 yr**
51. An 80-gram sample of a radioactive substance decayed to 10 grams after 300 minutes. Find the half-life of the substance. **100 min, or 1 h 40 min**
52. Praseodymium-143 has a half-life of 2 weeks. The original measurement for the mass of a sample was lost. After 6 weeks, 15 grams of praseodymium-143 remain. How many grams was the original sample? **120 g**
53. Phillip invested some money in a business 8 years ago. Since then, his investment has grown at an average rate of 1.3% compounded quarterly. Phillip's investment is now worth \$250,000. How much was his original investment? Round your answer to the nearest dollar. **\$225,344**
54. **Personal Finance** Anna has a balance of \$200 that she owes on her credit card. She plans to make a \$30 payment each month. There is also a 1.5% finance charge (interest) on the remaining balance each month. Copy and complete the table to answer the questions below. You may add more rows to the table as necessary.

Month	Balance (\$)	Monthly Payment (\$)	Remaining Balance (\$)	1.5% Finance Charge (\$)	New Balance (\$)
1	200	30	170	2.55	172.55
2	172.55	30	**142.55**	**2.14**	**144.69**
3	**144.69**	30	**114.69**	**1.72**	**116.41**
4	**116.41**	30	**86.41**	**1.30**	**87.71**

a. How many months will it take Anna to pay the entire balance? **7 mo**

b. By the time Anna pays the entire balance, how much total interest will she have paid? **\$9.01**

SPIRAL REVIEW

Write and solve a proportion for each situation. *(Lesson 2-8)*

55. A daffodil that is 1.2 feet tall casts a shadow that is 1.5 feet long. At the same time, a nearby lamppost casts a shadow that is 20 feet long. What is the height of the lamppost? **16 ft**
56. A green rectangular throw pillow measures 20 inches long by 10 inches wide. A proportionally similar yellow throw pillow is 12 inches long. What is the width of the yellow pillow? **6 in.**

Graph each function. *(Lesson 4-4)*

57. $f(x) = 2x + 1$ 58. $f(x) = |x - 4|$ 59. $f(x) = x^2 - 1$

60. The function $f(x) = 0.10(2)^x$ describes the total cost in dollars of a library book fine, where x is the number of days that the book is overdue. What is the amount of the fine if a book is 4 days overdue? How many days overdue is a book if the fine is \$12.80? *(Lesson 11-2)* **\$1.60; 7 days**

Answers

54.

5	87.71	30	57.71	0.87	58.58
6	58.58	30	28.58	0.43	29.01
7	29.01	29.01	0	0	0

57.

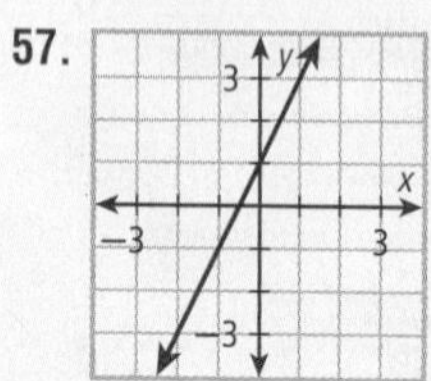

58.

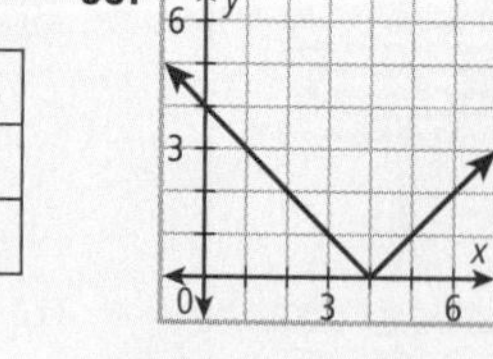

59.

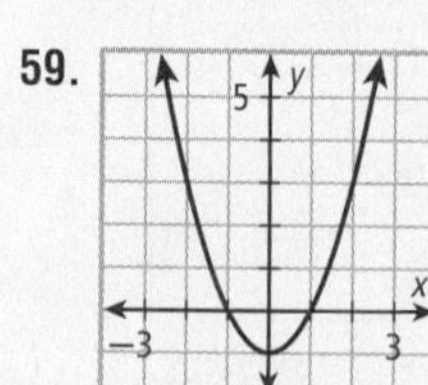

11-4 Linear, Quadratic, and Exponential Models

Objectives

Compare linear, quadratic, and exponential models.

Given a set of data, decide which type of function models the data and write an equation to describe the function.

Why learn this?

Different situations in sports can be described by linear, quadratic, or exponential models.

Look at the tables and graphs below. The data show three ways you have learned that variable quantities can be related. The relationships shown are linear, quadratic, and exponential.

Linear

Training Heart Rate	
Age (yr)	Beats/min
20	170
30	161.5
40	153
50	144.5

Quadratic

Volleyball Height	
Time (s)	Height (ft)
0.4	10.44
0.8	12.76
1	12
1.2	9.96

Exponential

Volleyball Tournament	
Round	Teams Left
1	16
2	8
3	4
4	2

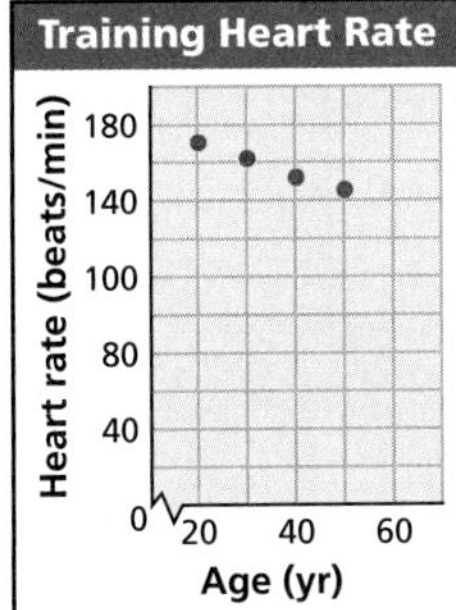

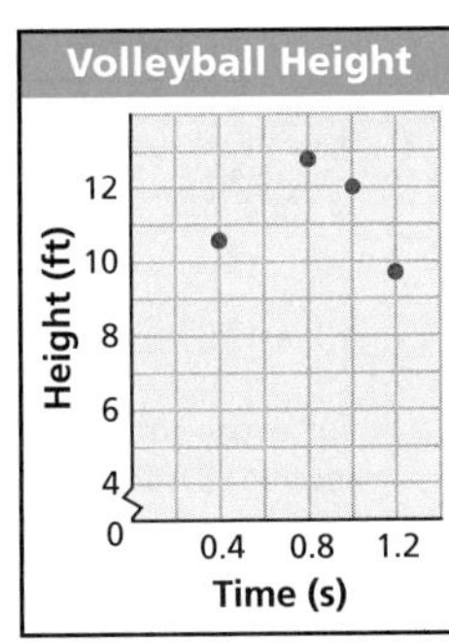

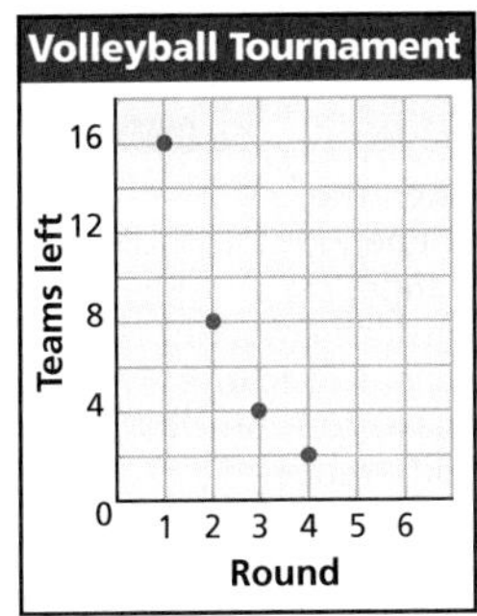

In the real world, people often gather data and then must decide what kind of relationship (if any) they think best describes their data.

EXAMPLE 1 Graphing Data to Choose a Model

Graph each data set. Which kind of model best describes the data?

A

Time (h)	0	1	2	3
Bacteria	10	20	40	80

Plot the data points and connect them.

The data appear to be exponential.

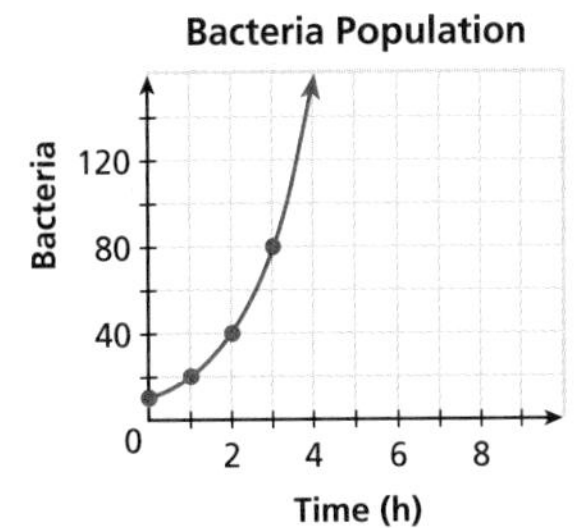

11-4 Organizer

Pacing: Traditional 1 day
Block $\frac{1}{2}$ day

Objectives: Compare linear, quadratic, and exponential models.

Given a set of data, decide which type of function models the data and write an equation to describe the function.

Online Edition
Tutorial Videos

Power Presentations with PowerPoint®

Warm Up

1. Find the slope and the y-intercept of the line that passes through (4, 20) and (20, 24). $\frac{1}{4}$; 19

The population of a town is decreasing at a rate of 1.8% per year. In 1990, there were 4600 people.

2. Write an exponential decay function to model this situation. $y = 4600(0.982)^t$
3. Find the population in 2010. 3199

Also available on transparency

Teacher: Why are you so dressed up?
Student: You said we'd be modeling today.

1 Introduce

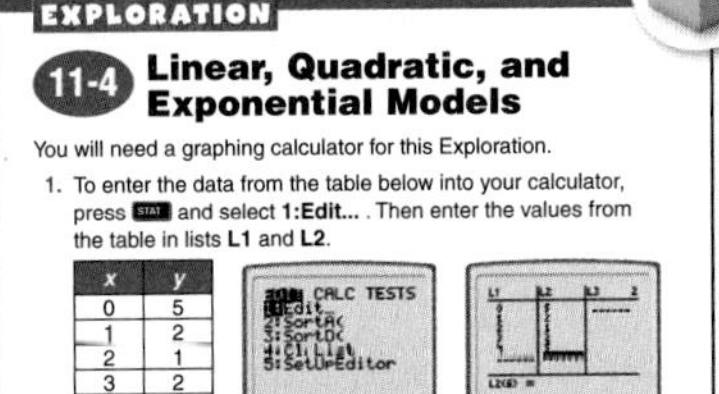

EXPLORATION

11-4 Linear, Quadratic, and Exponential Models

You will need a graphing calculator for this Exploration.

1. To enter the data from the table below into your calculator, press STAT and select **1:Edit...** . Then enter the values from the table in lists **L1** and **L2**.

x	y
0	5
1	2
2	1
3	2
4	5

2. To plot the data points, press Y= and select **Plot 1** at the top of the screen. Then press GRAPH.
3. Based on the shape of the graph, what type of function do you think models the data? Why?
4. Repeat the process for the data in this table.

x	y
1	7.2
2	5.8
3	4.6
4	3.7
5	2.9

THINK AND DISCUSS

5. Explain what type of function you think models the data in Problem 4.

Motivate

Display the following table and have students list information they remember about each type of function.

Linear	Quadratic	Exponential
Possible answers: graph is a line, has a slope	Possible answers: graph is a parabola, opens up or down	Possible answers: graph is a curve, variable is in exponent

Explorations and answers are provided in *Alternate Openers: Explorations Transparencies.*

State Resources

Power Presentations with PowerPoint®

Additional Examples

Example 1

Graph each data set. Which kind of model best describes the data?

A.

Time (h)	Bacteria
0	24
1	96
2	384
3	1536
4	6144

exponential

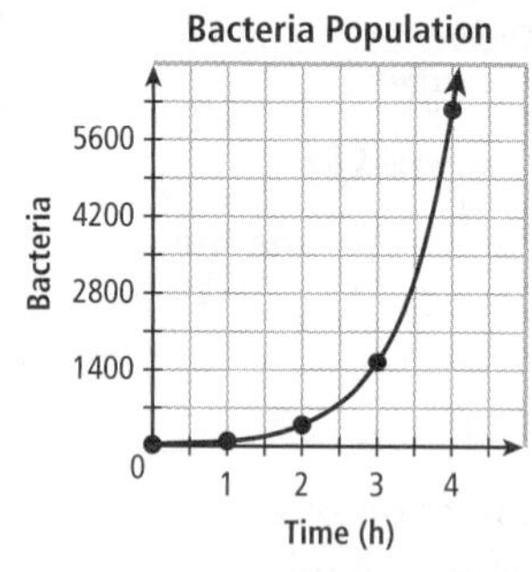

B.

Boxes	Reams of Paper
1	10
5	50
20	200
50	500

linear

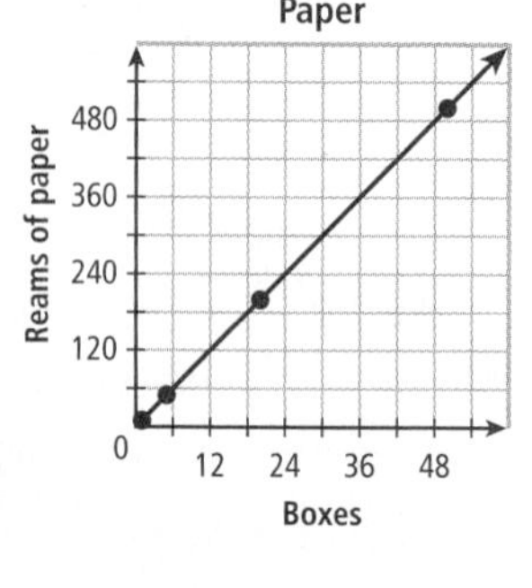

1a.

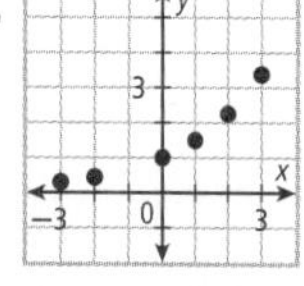

exponential

1b.

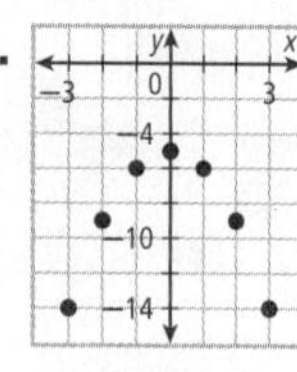

quadratic

Graph each data set. Which kind of model best describes the data?

B

°C	0	5	10	15	20
°F	32	41	50	59	68

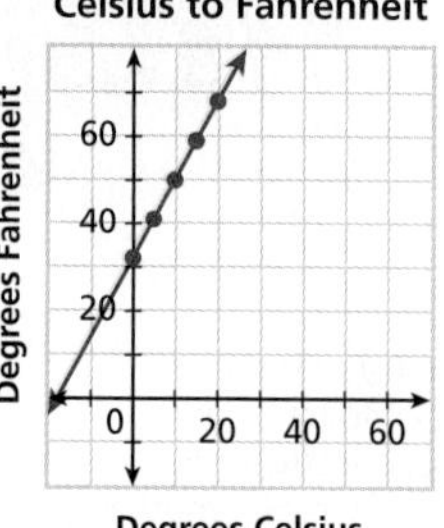

Plot the data points and connect them.

The data appear to be linear.

CHECK IT OUT! Graph each data set. Which kind of model best describes the data?

1a. $\{(-3, 0.30), (-2, 0.44), (0, 1), (1, 1.5), (2, 2.25), (3, 3.38)\}$

1b. $\{(-3, -14), (-2, -9), (-1, -6), (0, -5), (1, -6), (2, -9), (3, -14)\}$

Another way to decide which kind of relationship (if any) best describes a data set is to use patterns.

EXAMPLE 2 Using Patterns to Choose a Model

Look for a pattern in each data set to determine which kind of model best describes the data.

A

Height of Bridge Suspension Cables	
Cable's Distance from Tower (ft)	Cable's Height (ft)
0	400
100	256
200	144
300	64

Distance: +100, +100, +100. Height first differences: −144, −112, −80; second differences: +32, +32.

For every constant change in distance of +100 feet, there is a constant second difference of +32.

The data appear to be quadratic.

B

Value of a Car	
Car's Age (yr)	Value ($)
0	20,000
1	17,000
2	14,450
3	12,282.50

Age: +1, +1, +1. Value: × 0.85, × 0.85, × 0.85.

For every constant change in age of +1 year, there is a constant ratio of 0.85.

The data appear to be exponential.

Remember!

When the independent variable changes by a constant amount,
- linear functions have constant first differences.
- quadratic functions have constant second differences.
- exponential functions have a constant ratio.

CHECK IT OUT! **2.** Look for a pattern in the data set $\{(-2, 10), (-1, 1), (0, -2), (1, 1), (2, 10)\}$ to determine which kind of model best describes the data. **quadratic**

INTERVENTION Questioning Strategies

EXAMPLE 1

- What does the graph of a linear function look like?
- How are the graphs of quadratic and exponential functions similar? How are they different?

2 Teach

Guided Instruction

Show how to choose a model graphically and then by looking at patterns. **Check It Out Problem 3** involves finding the slope and *y*-intercept of a linear function. These skills may need to be reviewed. This lesson does not include finding a function to model quadratic data; that is beyond the scope of this book. Interested or advanced students can find the function for **Example 2A** on a graphing calculator by entering the data into two lists and using the **QuadReg** feature.

Teaching Tip **Inclusion** When graphing, students might choose the wrong model if their graph is sloppy or if they do not graph all the points. For example, points that appear to be parabolic may actually be exponential. Tell students that when in doubt, they should look for patterns.

Teaching Tip **Critical Thinking** Remind students that $y \neq 0$ in an exponential function. If the data set includes $y = 0$, then the function must be linear or quadratic.

After deciding which model best fits the data, you can write a function. Recall the general forms of linear, quadratic, and exponential functions.

General Forms of Functions

LINEAR	QUADRATIC	EXPONENTIAL
$y = mx + b$	$y = ax^2 + bx + c$	$y = ab^x$

EXAMPLE 3 Problem-Solving Application

Use the data in the table to describe how the ladybug population is changing. Then write a function that models the data. Use your function to predict the ladybug population after one year.

Ladybug Population	
Time (mo)	Ladybugs
0	10
1	30
2	90
3	270

1 Understand the Problem

The **answer** will have three parts—a description, a function, and a prediction.

2 Make a Plan

Determine whether the data is linear, quadratic, or exponential. Use the general form to write a function. Then use the function to find the population after one year.

3 Solve

Step 1 Describe the situation in words.

Ladybug Population		
Time (mo)	Ladybugs	
0	10	
1 (+1)	30	×3
2 (+1)	90	×3
3 (+1)	270	×3

Each month, the ladybug population is multiplied by 3. In other words, the population triples each month.

Step 2 Write the function.

There is a constant ratio of 3. The data appear to be exponential.

$y = ab^x$ *Write the general form of an exponential function.*

$y = a(3)^x$ *Substitute the constant ratio, 3, for b.*

$10 = a(3)^0$ *Choose an ordered pair from the table, such as (0, 10). Substitute for x and y.*

$10 = a(1)$ *Simplify. $3^0 = 1$*

$10 = a$ *The value of a is 10.*

$y = 10(3)^x$ *Substitute 10 for a in $y = a(3)^x$.*

Helpful Hint

You can choose any given ordered pair to substitute for x and y. However, it is often easiest to choose an ordered pair that contains 0.

Power Presentations with PowerPoint®

Additional Examples

Example 2

Look for a pattern in each data set to determine which kind of model best describes the data.

A.

Height of Golf Ball	
Time (s)	Height (ft)
0	4
1	68
2	100
3	100
4	68

quadratic

B.

Money in CD	
Time (yr)	Amount ($)
0	1000.00
1	1169.86
2	1368.57
3	1601.04

exponential

Example 3

Use the data in the table to describe how the number of people changes. Then write a function that models the data. Use your function to predict the number of people who received the e-mail after one week.

E-mail Forwarding	
Time (days)	Number of People Who Received the E-mail
0	8
1	56
2	392
3	2744

increasing by a factor of 7 each day; $y = 8(7)^x$; 6,588,344

Reaching All Learners

Through Cooperative Learning

Break students into small groups. Assign each group one of the following kinds of models: linear, quadratic, or exponential. Tell students to prepare a 5-minute presentation that covers:

- characteristics of their model
- how to recognize when their model best describes a set of data
- examples of real-life situations that tend to fit their model

INTERVENTION

Questioning Strategies

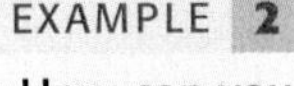

EXAMPLE 2

- How can you use the pattern in the table to predict the contents of the next row?

EXAMPLE 3

- How can you use the function to predict other data values?
- How accurate is this prediction?

Teaching Tip **Visual** Students may get a better understanding of exponential functions if they attempt to draw a tree diagram of the situation. For the data in **Example 3,** they should start by drawing 10 circles for 10 bugs and then draw 3 circles for each of those 10 circles, and so on.

Step 3 Predict the ladybug population after one year.

$y = 10(3)^x$ *Write the function.*

$= 10(3)^{12}$ *Substitute 12 for x (1 year = 12 mo).*

$= 5{,}314{,}410$ *Use a calculator.*

There will be 5,314,410 ladybugs after one year.

4 Look Back

You chose the ordered pair (0, 10) to write the function. Check that every other ordered pair in the table satisfies your function.

$y = 10(3)^x$	
30	$10(3)^1$
30	$10(3)$
30	30 ✓

$y = 10(3)^x$	
90	$10(3)^2$
90	$10(9)$
90	90 ✓

$y = 10(3)^x$	
270	$10(3)^3$
270	$10(27)$
270	270 ✓

CHECK IT OUT! **3.** Use the data in the table to describe how the oven temperature is changing. Then write a function that models the data. Use your function to predict the temperature after 1 hour.

The oven temperature decreases by 50 °F every 10 min; $y = -5x + 375$; 75 °F

Oven Temperature				
Time (min)	0	10	20	30
Temperature (°F)	375	325	275	225

Student to Student *Checking Units*

Michael Gambhir
Warren High School

I used to get a lot of answers wrong because of the units. If a question asked for the value of something after 1 year, I would always just substitute 1 into the function.

I finally figured out that you have to check what x is. If x represents months and you're trying to find the value after 1 year, then you have to substitute 12, not 1, because there are 12 months in a year.

THINK AND DISCUSS

1. Do you think that every data set will be able to be modeled by a linear, quadratic, or exponential function? Why or why not?
2. In Example 3, is it certain that there will be 5,314,410 ladybugs after one year? Explain.
3. **GET ORGANIZED** Copy and complete the graphic organizer. In each box, list some characteristics and sketch a graph of each type of model.

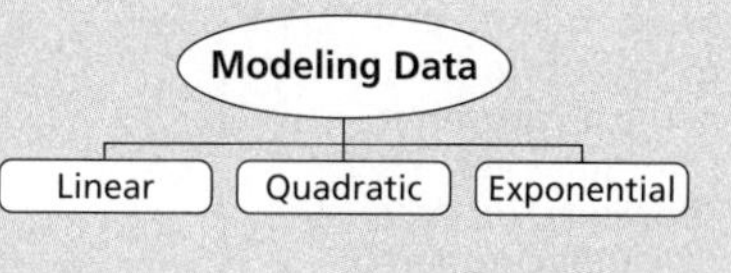

3 Close

Summarize

Ask students which model best fits each of the following situations:

- With a constant change in x, the differences between the first differences are constant. quadratic
- With a constant change in x, there is a constant ratio in the y-values. exponential
- The graph forms a parabola. quadratic
- With a constant change in x, the second differences are zero. linear

ONGOING ASSESSMENT and INTERVENTION

***Diagnose Before* the Lesson**
11-4 Warm Up, TE p. 813

***Monitor During* the Lesson**
Check It Out! Exercises, SE pp. 814, 816
Questioning Strategies, TE pp. 814–815

***Assess After* the Lesson**
11-4 Lesson Quiz, TE p. 819
Alternative Assessment, TE p. 819

Answers to *Think and Discuss*

Possible answers:

1. No; most real-world data probably will not fit exactly into one of these patterns.
2. No; this is just a prediction based on the assumption that the observed trends will continue, which they may or may not do.
3. See p. A10.

11-4 Exercises

go.hrw.com
Homework Help Online
KEYWORD: MA7 11-4
Parent Resources Online
KEYWORD: MA7 Parent

GUIDED PRACTICE

SEE EXAMPLE 1 p. 813

Graph each data set. Which kind of model best describes the data?

1. $\{(-1, 4), (-2, 0.8), (0, 20), (1, 100), (-3, 0.16)\}$ **exponential**
2. $\{(0, 3), (1, 9), (2, 11), (3, 9), (4, 3)\}$ **quadratic**
3. $\{(2, -7), (-2, -9), (0, -8), (4, -6), (6, -5)\}$ **linear**

SEE EXAMPLE 2 p. 814

Look for a pattern in each data set to determine which kind of model best describes the data.

4. $\{(-2, 1), (-1, 2.5), (0, 3), (1, 2.5), (2, 1)\}$ **quadratic**
5. $\{(-2, 0.75), (-1, 1.5), (0, 3), (1, 6), (2, 12)\}$ **exponential**
6. $\{(-2, 2), (-1, 4), (0, 6), (1, 8), (2, 10)\}$ **linear**

SEE EXAMPLE 3 p. 815

7. **Consumer Economics** Use the data in the table to describe the cost of grapes. Then write a function that models the data. Use your function to predict the cost of 6 pounds of grapes.

Total Cost of Grapes

Amount (lb)	1	2	3	4
Cost ($)	1.79	3.58	5.37	7.16

Grapes cost \$1.79/lb; $y = 1.79x$; \$10.74

PRACTICE AND PROBLEM SOLVING

Independent Practice

For Exercises	See Example
8–10	1
11–13	2
14	3

Extra Practice

Skills Practice p. S24
Application Practice p. S38

Graph each data set. Which kind of model best describes the data?

8. $\{(-3, -5), (-2, -8), (-1, -9), (0, -8), (1, -5), (2, 0), (3, 7)\}$ **quadratic**
9. $\{(-3, -1), (-2, 0), (-1, 1), (0, 2), (1, 3), (2, 4), (3, 5)\}$ **linear**
10. $\{(0, 0.1), (2, 0.9), (3, 2.7), (4, 8.1)\}$ **exponential**

Look for a pattern in each data set to determine which kind of model best describes the data.

11. $\{(-2, 5), (-1, 4), (0, 3), (1, 2), (2, 1)\}$ **linear**
12. $\{(-2, 12), (-1, 15), (0, 16), (1, 15), (2, 12)\}$ **quadratic**
13. $\{(-2, 8), (-1, 4), (0, 2), (1, 1), (2, 0.5)\}$ **exponential**

14. **Business** Use the data in the table to describe how the company's sales are changing. Then write a function that models the data. Use your function to predict the amount of sales after 10 years.

14. The company's sales are increasing by 20% each year; $y = 25{,}000(1.2)^x$; \$154,793.41.

Company Sales

Year	0	1	2	3
Sales ($)	25,000	30,000	36,000	43,200

15. **Multi-Step** Jay's hair grows about 6 inches each year. Write a function that describes the length ℓ in inches that Jay's hair will grow for each year k. Which kind of model best describes the function? **$\ell = 6k$; linear**

11-4 Exercises

Assignment Guide

Assign *Guided Practice* exercises as necessary.

If you finished Examples **1–2**
Basic 8–13, 16–18, 21, 22
Average 8–13, 16–18, 21, 22
Advanced 8–13, 16–18, 21, 22

If you finished Examples **1–3**
Basic 8–21, 24, 26–29, 32–40
Average 8–19, 23–29, 32–40,
Advanced 8–19, 23, 25–40

Homework Quick Check
Quickly check key concepts.
Exercises: 8, 10, 12, 14, 18, 20

Teaching Tip

Inclusion In **Exercise 10,** there is not a constant change in *x*. Have students focus on the last three points and then use that to find *y* when *x* is 1. Students should then check whether the pattern works for all four points.

Answers

1. 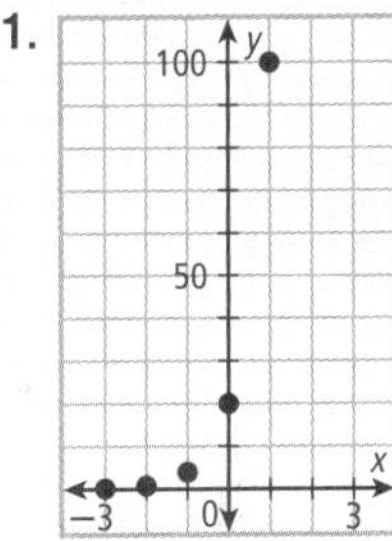

2. 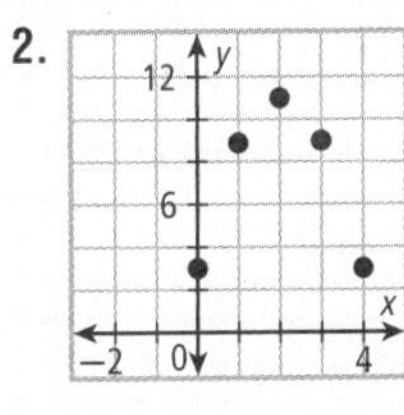

3. 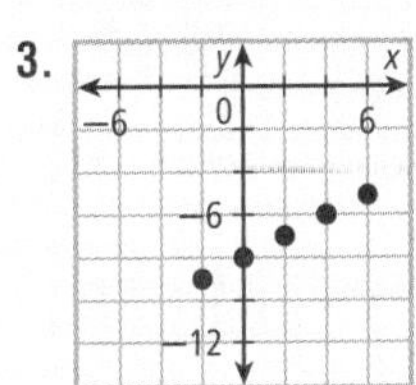

8. 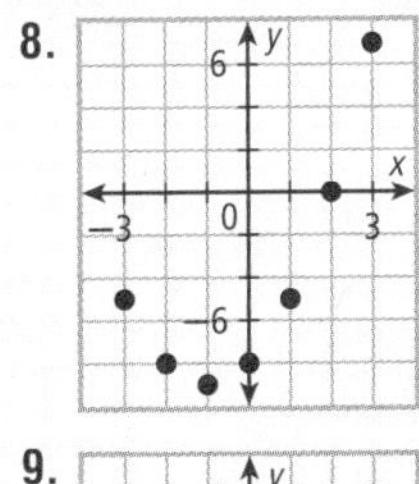

9. 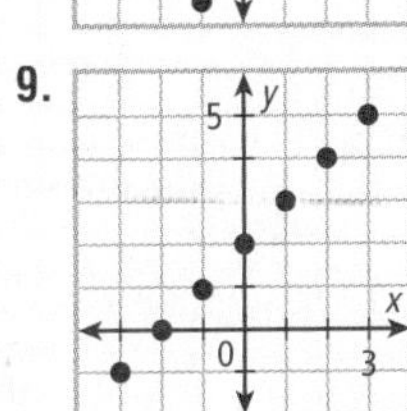

10. 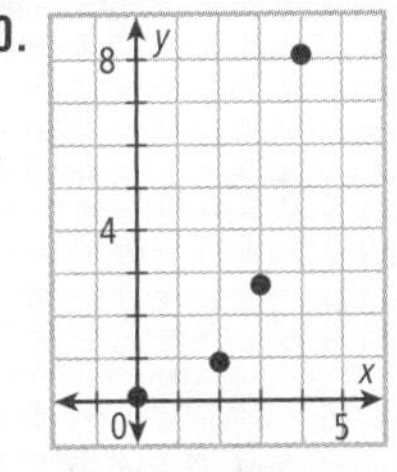

go.hrw.com
State Resources Online
KEYWORD: MA7 Resources

Exercise 26 involves writing a function rule to describe data. This exercise prepares students for the Multi-Step Test Prep on page 820.

Answers

26a. college 1: linear; college 2: exponential

b. college 1: $y = 200x + 2000$; college 2: $y = 2000(1.1)^x$

c. Both have the same tuition ($2000) in 2000.

d. For college 1, $200 is added each year, so 2000 + 200 = 2200. For college 2, 10% is added each year, so 2000 + (0.1)(2000) = 2200.

38. 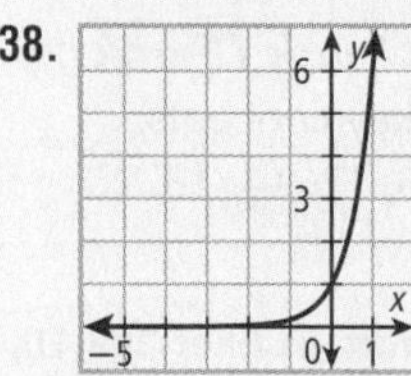

39. 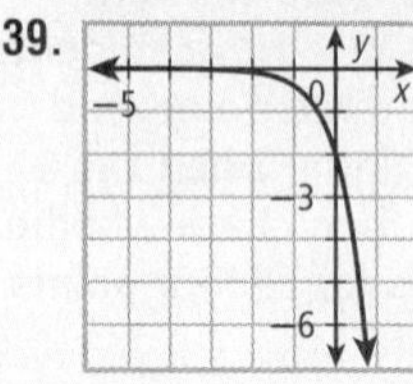

40. 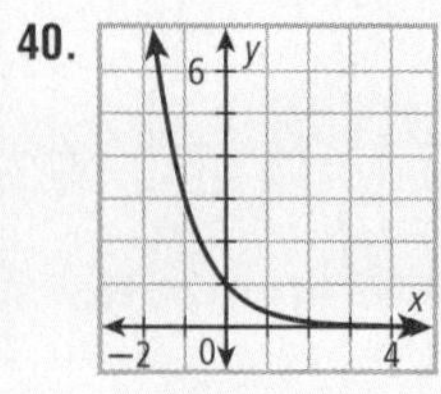

19. $y = 0.2(4)^x$

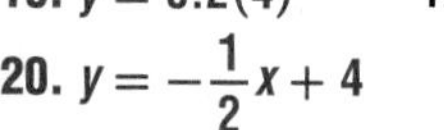

20. $y = -\frac{1}{2}x + 4$

21. linear

22. quadratic

23. Possible answer: (0, 3), (1, 6), (2, 12), (3, 24); for a constant change in x of +1, there is a common ratio of 2.

24. Possible answer: The first differences are constant, so there is no need to check the second differences. A linear function would best model the data.

Tell which kind of model best describes each situation.

16. The height of a plant at weekly intervals over the last 6 weeks was 1 inches, 1.5 inches, 2 inches, 2.5 inches, 3 inches., and 3.5 inches. **linear**

17. The number of games a baseball player played in the last four years was 162, 162, 162, and 162. **linear**

18. The height of a ball in a certain time interval was recorded as 30.64 feet, 30.96 feet, 31 feet, 30.96 feet, and 30.64 feet. **quadratic**

Write a function to model each set of data.

19.

x	−1	0	1	2	4
y	0.05	0.2	0.8	3.2	51.2

20.

x	−2	0	2	4	8
y	5	4	3	2	0

Tell which kind of model best describes each graph.

21. 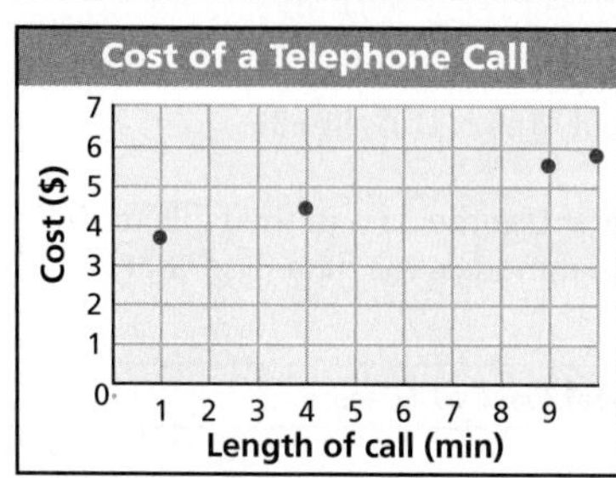

22. 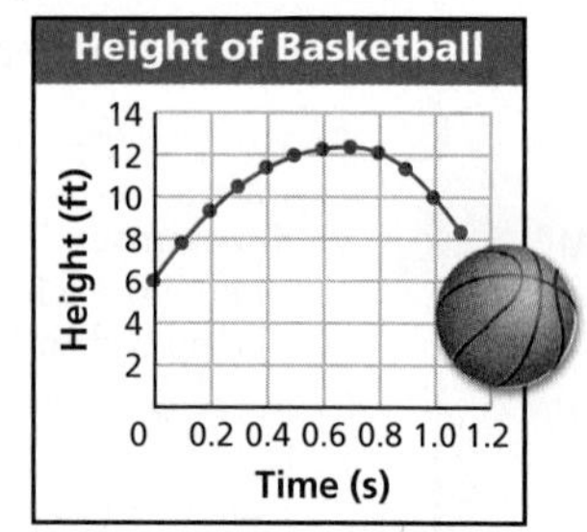

23. **Write About It** Write a set of data that you could model with an exponential function. Explain why the exponential model would work.

24. **/// ERROR ANALYSIS ///** A student concluded that the data set would best be modeled by a quadratic function. Explain the student's error.

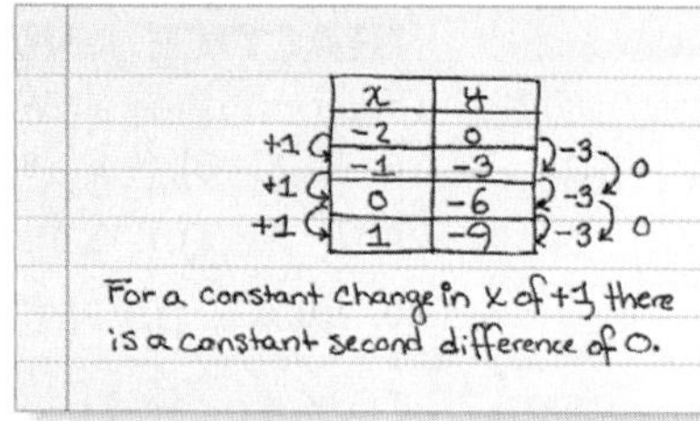

25. **Critical Thinking** Sometimes the graphs of quadratic data and exponential data can look very similar. Describe how you can tell them apart.
Possible answer: Make a table of ordered pairs and see whether the y-values show a pattern of constant second differences or constant ratios.

26. This problem will prepare you for the Multi-Step Test Prep on page 820.

a. Examine the two models that represent annual tuition for two colleges. Describe each model as linear, quadratic, or exponential.

b. Write a function rule for each model.

c. Both models have the same values for 2004. What does this mean?

d. Why do both models have the same value for year 1?

Years After 2004	Tuition at College 1 ($)	Tuition at College 2 ($)
0	2000.00	2000.00
1	2200.00	2200.00
2	2400.00	2420.00
3	2600.00	2662.00
4	2800.00	2928.20

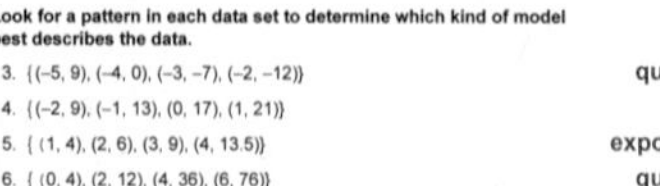

Graph each data set. Which kind of model best describes the data?

1. {(−2, 0), (−1, −3), (0, −4), (1, −3), (2, 0)} **quadratic**

2. {(0, 3), (1, 6), (2, 12), (3, 24), (4, 48)} **exponential**

Look for a pattern in each data set to determine which kind of model best describes the data.

3. {(−5, 9), (−4, 0), (−3, −7), (−2, −12)} **quadratic**

4. {(−2, 9), (−1, 13), (0, 17), (1, 21)} **linear**

5. {(1, 4), (2, 6), (3, 9), (4, 13.5)} **exponential**

6. {(0, 4), (2, 12), (4, 36), (6, 76)} **quadratic**

7. $\left\{(1, 17), \left(3, 8\frac{1}{2}\right), \left(5, 4\frac{1}{4}\right), \left(7, 2\frac{1}{8}\right)\right\}$ **exponential**

8. Use the data in the table to describe how the restaurant's sales are changing. Then write a function that models the data. Use your function to predict the amount of sales after 8 years.

Restaurant				
Year	0	1	2	3
Sales ($)	20,000	19,000	18,050	17,147.50

The sales decrease by 5% each month; $y = 20{,}000(0.95)^x$; ≈$13,268.41

9. Use the data in the table to describe how the clothing store's sales are changing. Then write a function that models the data. Use your function to predict the amount of sales after 10 years.

Clothing Store				
Year	0	1	2	3
Sales ($)	15,000	15,750	16,500	17,250

The sales increase by $750 every year; $y = 750x + 15{,}000$; $22,500

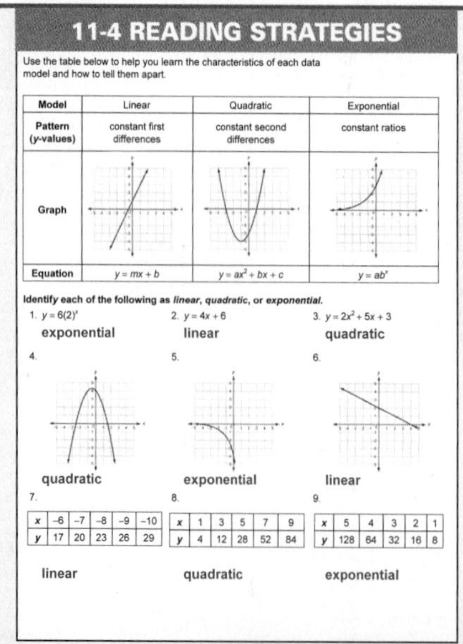

11-4 READING STRATEGIES

Use the table below to help you learn the characteristics of each data model and how to tell them apart.

Model	Linear	Quadratic	Exponential
Pattern (y-values)	constant first differences	constant second differences	constant ratios
Graph			
Equation	$y = mx + b$	$y = ax^2 + bx + c$	$y = ab^x$

Identify each of the following as *linear*, *quadratic*, or *exponential*.

1. $y = 6(2)^x$ **exponential**

2. $y = 4x + 6$ **linear**

3. $y = 2x^2 + 5x + 3$ **quadratic**

4. **quadratic**

5. **exponential**

6. **linear**

7.

x	−6	−7	−8	−9	−10
y	17	20	23	26	29

linear

8.

x	1	3	5	7	9
y	4	12	28	52	84

quadratic

9.

x	5	4	3	2	1
y	128	64	32	16	8

exponential

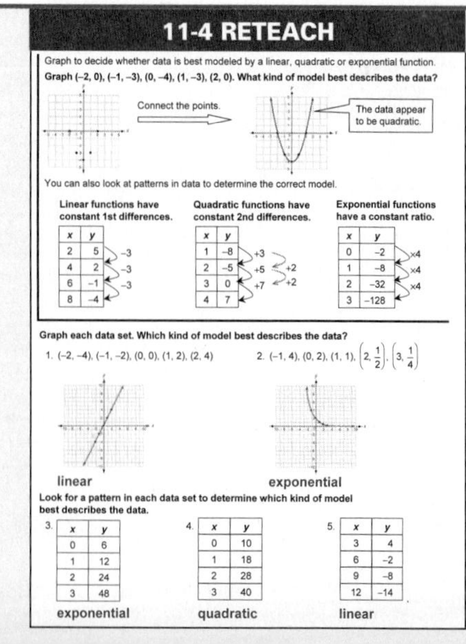

11-4 RETEACH

Graph to decide whether data is best modeled by a linear, quadratic or exponential function.

Graph (−2, 0), (−1, −3), (0, −4), (1, −3), (2, 0). What kind of model best describes the data?

Connect the points.

The data appear to be quadratic.

You can also look at patterns in data to determine the correct model.

Linear functions have constant 1st differences.

x	y
2	5
4	2
6	−1
8	−4

−3, −3, −3

Quadratic functions have constant 2nd differences.

x	y
1	−8
2	−5
3	0
4	7

+3, +5, +7; +2, +2

Exponential functions have a constant ratio.

x	y
0	−2
1	−8
2	−32
3	−128

×4, ×4, ×4

Graph each data set. Which kind of model best describes the data?

1. (−2, −4), (−1, −2), (0, 0), (1, 2), (2, 4) **linear**

2. (−1, 4), (0, 2), (1, 1), $\left(2, \frac{1}{2}\right)$, $\left(3, \frac{1}{4}\right)$ **exponential**

Look for a pattern in each data set to determine which kind of model best describes the data.

3.

x	y
0	6
1	12
2	24
3	48

exponential

4.

x	y
0	10
1	18
2	28
3	40

quadratic

5.

x	y
3	4
6	−2
9	−8
12	−14

linear

TEST PREP

27. Which function best models the data: $\{(-4, -2), (-2, -1), (0, 0), (2, 1), (4, 2)\}$?

Ⓐ $y = \left(\frac{1}{2}\right)^x$ Ⓑ $y = \frac{1}{2}x^2$ **Ⓒ** $y = \frac{1}{2}x$ Ⓓ $y = \left(\frac{1}{2}x\right)^2$

28. A city's population is increasing at a rate of 2% per year. Which type of model describes this situation?

Ⓕ Exponential Ⓖ Quadratic Ⓗ Linear Ⓙ None of these

29. Which data set is best modeled by a linear function?

Ⓐ $\{(-2, 0), (-1, 2), (0, -4), (1, -1), (2, 2)\}$

Ⓑ $\{(-2, 2), (-1, 4), (0, 6), (1, 16), (2, 32)\}$

Ⓒ $\{(-2, 2), (-1, 4), (0, 6), (1, 8), (2, 10)\}$

Ⓓ $\{(-2, 0), (-1, 5), (0, 7), (1, 5), (2, 0)\}$

CHALLENGE AND EXTEND

30. **Finance** An accountant estimates that a certain new automobile worth \$18,000 will lose value at a rate of 16% per year.

a. Make a table that shows the worth of the car for years 0, 1, 2, 3, and 4. What is the real-world meaning of year 0? **the year when the car is new**

b. Which type of model best represents the data in your table? Explain. **exponential**

c. Write a function for your data. $\mathbf{y = 18{,}000(0.84)^x}$

d. What is the value of the car after $5\frac{1}{2}$ years? **\$6899.36**

e. What is the value of the car after 8 years? **\$4461.77**

30a.

Year	Value (\$)
0	18,000
1	15,120
2	12,700.80
3	10,668.67
4	8961.68

31. **Pet Care** The table shows general guidelines for the weight of a Great Dane at various ages.

Great Dane	
Age (mo)	Weight (kg)
2	12
4	23
6	33
8	40
10	45

a. None of the three models in this lesson—linear, quadratic, or exponential—fits this data exactly. Which of these is the *best* model for the data? Explain your choice.

b. What would you predict for the weight of a Great Dane who is 1 year old? **about 48 kg**

c. Do you think you could use your model to find the weight of a Great Dane at any age? Why or why not?

31a. Possible answer: quadratic; the second differences are approximately constant at −2.

No; this quadratic model will begin to decrease although the dog's weight will either continue to grow or eventually remain constant.

SPIRAL REVIEW

Write an algebraic expression for each situation. *(Lesson 1-1)*

32. the total number of kilometers run by Helen in n 5-kilometer races **$5n$**

33. the average gas mileage of a car that travels 145 miles on g gallons of gasoline $\frac{145}{g}$

34. Lorraine's height if she is b inches shorter than Gene, who is 74 inches tall **$74 - b$**

Solve by using square roots. *(Lesson 9-7)*

35. $4x^2 = 100$ **5, −5**

36. $10 - x^2 = 10$ **0**

37. $16x^2 + 5 = 86$ $\frac{9}{4}, -\frac{9}{4}$

Graph each exponential function. *(Lesson 11-2)*

38. $y = 6^x$

39. $y = -2(5)^x$

40. $y = \left(\frac{1}{3}\right)^x$

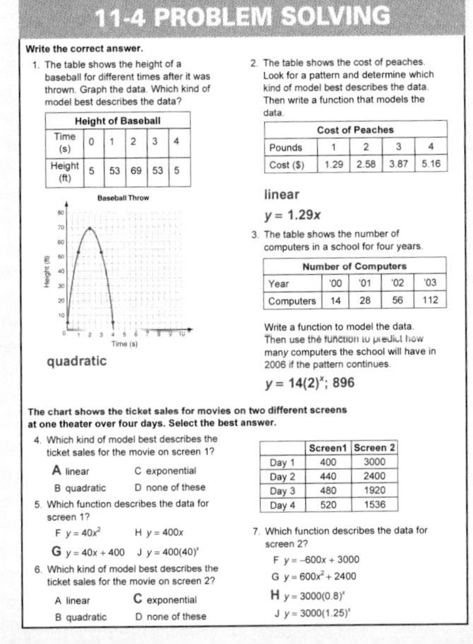

11-4 PROBLEM SOLVING

Write the correct answer.

1. The table shows the height of a baseball for different times after it was thrown. Graph the data. Which kind of model best describes the data?

Height of Baseball					
Time (s)	0	1	2	3	4
Height (ft)	5	53	69	53	5

Baseball Throw

quadratic

2. The table shows the cost of peaches. Look for a pattern and determine which kind of model best describes the data. Then write a function that models the data.

Cost of Peaches				
Pounds	1	2	3	4
Cost (\$)	1.29	2.58	3.87	5.16

linear

$y = 1.29x$

3. The table shows the number of computers in a school for four years.

Number of Computers				
Year	'00	'01	'02	'03
Computers	14	28	56	112

Write a function to model the data. Then use the function to predict how many computers the school will have in 2006 if the pattern continues.

$y = 14(2)^x$; 896

The chart shows the ticket sales for movies on two different screens at one theater over four days. Select the best answer.

	Screen1	Screen 2
Day 1	400	3000
Day 2	440	2400
Day 3	480	1920
Day 4	520	1536

4. Which kind of model best describes the ticket sales for the movie on screen 1?

A linear C exponential
B quadratic D none of these

5. Which function describes the data for screen 1?

F $y = 40x^2$ H $y = 400x$
G $y = 40x + 400$ J $y = 400(40)^x$

6. Which kind of model best describes the ticket sales for the movie on screen 2?

A linear **C** exponential
B quadratic D none of these

7. Which function describes the data for screen 2?

F $y = -600x + 3000$
G $y = 600x^2 + 2400$
H $y = 3000(0.8)^x$
J $y = 3000(1.25)^x$

11-4 CHALLENGE

If you've ridden in a car on a highway, you've probably noticed that the speed of traffic slows down when there are more cars on the road. The data at right was gathered to research this phenomenon.

None of the models you have studied fits this data exactly. Furthermore, the values of the independent variable don't change by a constant amount, so you can't check for constant differences or constant ratios. You'll use a graphing calculator to find models instead.

Traffic Density (vehicles/mi)	Average Speed (mi/h)
20.4	38.8
26.5	34.0
29.5	31.8
30.0	28.8
97.0	12.3
106.2	10.6
106.7	11.4
107.2	10.3
121.7	8.5
123.9	9.8
130.5	8.6
141.3	7.7

1. Enter the data into lists **L1** and **L2** on your calculator, and make a scatter plot. (Review Technology Lab 4-5 on page 262 of your textbook if you forget how.) Sketch the scatter plot below.
2. Based on the shape of the scatter plot, which kind of model do you think will best describe the data?
exponential or quadratic
3. Press STAT and select the **CALC** menu. Select **LinReg(ax + b)** and press ENTER to find a linear model. Write the equation here, rounding to the thousandths.
$y = -0.251x + 39.469$
4. Press Y=, enter the equation for the linear model, and press GRAPH. Sketch the line on your graph above.
5. Repeat step 3, but select **QuadReg** to find a quadratic model. Write the equation here. **$y = 0.002x^2 - 0.547x + 46.625$**
6. Graph the quadratic equation, and sketch it above.
7. Repeat step 3, but select **ExpReg** to find an exponential model. Write the equation here. **$y = 46.700(0.987)^x$**
8. Graph the exponential equation, and sketch it above.
9. From the graphs of the three models, which model(s) seems to fit best? Explain your choice(s).
Exponential or quadratic; either model is a good fit for the curvature of the scatter plot.
10. Use each model to predict the average speed of traffic when the traffic density is 180 vehicles per mile.
linear: **−5.711 mi/h** quadratic: **12.965 mi/h** exponential: **4.430 mi/h**
11. From your answers to question 10, which model(s) seems to fit best? Explain your choice(s).
The exponential model fits best because it gives decreasing speeds as traffic density increases; the linear model gives negative speeds and the quadratic model gives increasing speeds.

TEST PREP DOCTOR In **Exercise 27,** remind students that a variable in a linear function, like the variable in choice **C,** has an exponent of one, which is usually not written.

Journal

Have students write a data set that could be modeled by an exponential function. Then have them explain how to write the function rule and how to use it to make predictions.

ALTERNATIVE ASSESSMENT

Have students create a data set that can best be modeled by a quadratic function. Have them explain why a quadratic model fits their data better than either a linear or exponential model.

Power Presentations with PowerPoint®

11-4 Lesson Quiz

Which kind of model best describes each set of data?

1.

Time (s)	Height of Ball (ft)
0	200
1	184
2	136
3	56

quadratic

2.

Value of Townhouse	
Age (yr)	Value (\$)
0	100,000
1	102,000
2	104,040
3	106,121

exponential

3. Use the data in the table to describe how the amount of water is changing. Then write a function that models the data. Use your function to predict the amount of water in the pool after 3 hours.

Water in a Swimming Pool	
Time (min)	Amount of Water (gal)
10	327
20	342
30	357
40	372

increasing by 15 gal every 10 min; $y = 1.5x + 312$; 582 gal

Also available on transparency

Organizer

Objective: Assess students' ability to apply concepts and skills in Lessons 11-1 through 11-4 in a real-world format.

 Online Edition

Resources

 ***Algebra I Assessments***
www.mathtekstoolkit.org

Problem	Text Reference
1	Lesson 11-4
2	Lessons 11-2, 11-3
3	Lessons 11-2, 11-3
4	Lessons 11-2, 11-3
5	Lessons 11-2, 11-3

For additional assessment activities, see www.utdanacenter.org.

Answers

2, 4, 5. For tables and graphs, see p. A34.

State Resources

State Resources Online
KEYWORD: MA7 Resources

CHAPTER 11

SECTION 11A

Exponential Functions

1. $y = 350(1.09)^x$; $y =$ tuition (dep.); $x =$ years since 1980 (indep.)

Dollars for Scholars In 1980, the average annual tuition at two-year colleges was $350. Since then, the cost of tuition has increased by an average of 9% each year.

1. Write a function rule that models the annual growth in tuition at two-year colleges since 1980. Let 1980 be year zero in your function. Identify the variables, and tell which is independent and which is dependent.
2. Use your function to determine the average annual tuition in 2006. Use a table and a graph to support your answer. **$3289.71**
3. Use your function to predict the average annual tuition at two-year colleges for the year you plan to graduate from high school. **Answers will vary.**
4. In what year is the average annual tuition twice as much as in 1980? Use a table and a graph to support your answer. **about 1988**
5. In what year does the average annual tuition reach $1000? Use a table and a graph to support your answer. **1993**

INTERVENTION 

Scaffolding Questions

1. Explain why it is best to use 1980 as year zero. This is the first year with given data.
2. What is the annual growth factor as a decimal? 1.09
3. How do you find your x-value? the year I graduate from high school minus 1980
4. What is the starting value for tuition? $350
5. Describe how the tuition amounts change with each additional year. Each year the cost is 9% more than the previous year.

Extension

How would the function change if the annual growth rate were 12%? The function would be $y = 350(1.12)^x$.

How would the graph change with this growth rate? It would increase more rapidly.

CHAPTER 11

SECTION 11A

Quiz for Lessons 11-1 Through 11-4

11-1 Geometric Sequences

Find the next three terms in each geometric sequence.

1. 3, 6, 12, 24, ... **48, 96, 192**
2. −1, 2, −4, 8, ... **−16, 32, −64**
3. −2400, −1200, −600, −300, ... **−150, −75, −37.5**
4. The first term of a geometric sequence is 2 and the common ratio is 3. What is the 8th term of the sequence? **4374**
5. The table shows the distance swung by a pendulum during its first three swings. The values form a geometric sequence. What will be the length of the 7th swing? **262.144 cm**

Swing	Length (cm)
1	1000
2	800
3	640

11-2 Exponential Functions

6. The function $f(x) = 3(1.1)^x$ gives the length (in inches) of an image after being enlarged by 10% x times. What is the length of the image after it has been enlarged 4 times? Round your answer to the nearest hundredth. **4.39 in.**

Graph each exponential function.

7. $y = 3^x$
8. $y = 2(2)^x$
9. $y = -2(4)^x$
10. $y = -(0.5)^x$
11. The function $f(x) = 40(0.8)^x$ gives the amount of a medication in milligrams present in a patient's system x hours after taking a 40-mg dose. In how many hours will there be less than 2 mg of the drug in a patient's system? **14 h**

11-3 Exponential Growth and Decay

Write a function to model each situation. Then find the value of the function after the given amount of time.

12. Fiona's salary is $30,000, and she expects to receive a 3% raise each year; 10 years.
13. $2000 is invested at a rate of 4.5% compounded monthly; 3 years.
14. A $1200 computer is losing value at a rate of 20% per year; 4 years.
15. Strontium-90 has a half-life of 29 years. About how much strontium-90 will be left from a 100-mg sample after 290 years? Round your answer to the nearest thousandth. **0.098 mg**

11-4 Linear, Quadratic, and Exponential Models

Graph each data set. Which kind of model best describes the data?

16. $\{(-2, 5), (3, 10), (0, 1), (1, 2), (0.5, 1.25)\}$ **quadratic**
17. $\{(0, 3), (2, 12), (-1, 1.5), (-3, 0.375), (4, 48)\}$ **exponential**

Look for a pattern in each data set to determine which kind of model best describes the data.

18. $\{(-2, -6), (-1, -5), (0, -4), (1, -3), (2, -2)\}$ **linear**
19. $\{(-2, -24), (-1, -12), (0, -6), (1, -3)\}$ **exponential**
20. Use the data in the table to describe how the value of the stamp is changing. Then write a function that models the data. Use your function to predict the value of the stamp in 11 years.
The value of the stamp is increasing by 20% each year; $y = 5(1.2)^x$; $37.15.

Value of Collectible Stamp				
Year	0	1	2	3
Value ($)	5.00	6.00	7.20	8.64

READY TO GO ON?

SECTION 11A

Organizer

Objective: Assess students' mastery of concepts and skills in Lessons 11-1 through 11-4.

Resources

 ***Assessment Resources***
Section 11A Quiz

Teacher One Stop™
Test & Practice Generator

INTERVENTION

Resources

 ***Ready to Go On? Intervention and Enrichment*** **Worksheets**

 ***Ready to Go On?*** **CD-ROM**

 ***Ready to Go On?*** **Online**

my.hrw.com

Answers

7–10, 12–14. See p. A34.
16, 17. For graphs, see p. A34.

READY TO GO ON? Diagnose and Prescribe

NO INTERVENE

Ready to Go On? Intervention	READY TO GO ON? *Intervention,* Section 11A: Worksheets	CD-ROM	Online
Lesson 11-1	11-1 Intervention	Activity 11-1	Diagnose and Prescribe Online
Lesson 11-2	11-2 Intervention	Activity 11-2	
Lesson 11-3	11-3 Intervention	Activity 11-3	
Lesson 11-4	11-4 Intervention	Activity 11-4	

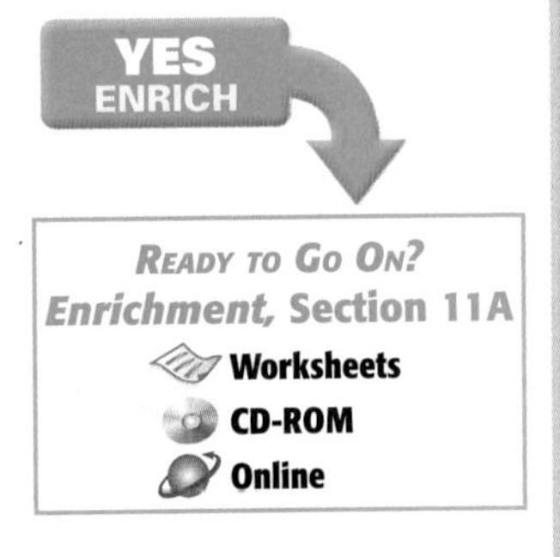

SECTION

11B Radical Functions and Equations

One-Minute Section Planner

Lesson	Lab Resources	Materials
Lesson 11-5 Square-Root Functions • Identify square-root functions and their domains and ranges. • Graph square-root functions. ☐ SAT-10 ☑ NAEP ☐ ACT ☐ SAT ☑ SAT Subject Tests		**Required** graphing calculator
11-5 Technology Lab Graph Radical Functions • Use a graphing calculator to graph radical functions. ☐ SAT-10 ☐ NAEP ☐ ACT ☐ SAT ☐ SAT Subject Tests	***Technology Lab Activities*** 11-5 Lab Recording Sheet	**Required** graphing calculator
Lesson 11-6 Radical Expressions • Simplify radical expressions. ☑ SAT-10 ☑ NAEP ☑ ACT ☑ SAT ☑ SAT Subject Tests		**Optional** graphing calculator
Lesson 11-7 Adding and Subtracting Radical Expressions • Add and subtract radical expressions. ☑ SAT-10 ☑ NAEP ☑ ACT ☑ SAT ☑ SAT Subject Tests	***Algebra Lab Activities*** 11-7 Algebra Lab	**Optional** graphing calculator
Lesson 11-8 Multiplying and Dividing Radical Expressions • Multiply and divide radical expressions. • Rationalize denominators. ☑ SAT-10 ☑ NAEP ☑ ACT ☑ SAT ☑ SAT Subject Tests		**Optional** graphing calculator
Lesson 11-9 Solving Radical Equations • Solve radical equations. ☑ SAT-10 ☑ NAEP ☑ ACT ☑ SAT ☑ SAT Subject Tests		**Optional** graphing calculator

Note: If NAEP is checked, the content is tested on either the Grade 8 or the Grade 12 NAEP assessment.

MK = *Manipulatives Kit*

RADICAL FUNCTIONS

Lessons 11-5 to 11-9

A *radical function* is a function whose rule contains a variable within a radical. For example, $y = \sqrt[3]{x^5}$ is a radical function. In this course, the emphasis is on square-root functions, which are a particular kind of radical functions. A *square-root function* is a function whose rule contains a variable under a square-root sign, such as $y = \sqrt{3x + 5}$. The simplest square-root function is $y = \sqrt{x}$. (Students may need to be reminded that the symbol $\sqrt{}$ indicates a principal, or nonnegative, square root.)

Because the square root of a negative number is undefined in the real numbers, the domains of square-root functions are restricted to those values of the variable for which the expression under the radical sign is nonnegative. The domain of $y = \sqrt{x}$ is $x \geq 0$; the domain of $y = \sqrt{3x + 5}$ of is $x \geq -\frac{5}{3}$.

THE FUNCTION $y = \sqrt{x}$

Lesson 11-5

When dealing with square roots and square-root functions, it is useful to understand the inverse relationship between $y = x^2$ and $y = \sqrt{x}$. In general, given a relation defined by a set of ordered pairs (x, y), the *inverse relation* is the set of all ordered pairs (y, x). The graph of an inverse relation is the reflection of the original relation over the line $y = x$. The following graph shows that $y = \pm\sqrt{x}$ is the inverse relation of $y = x^2$ because its graph is the reflection of the graph of $y = x^2$ over the line $y = x$.

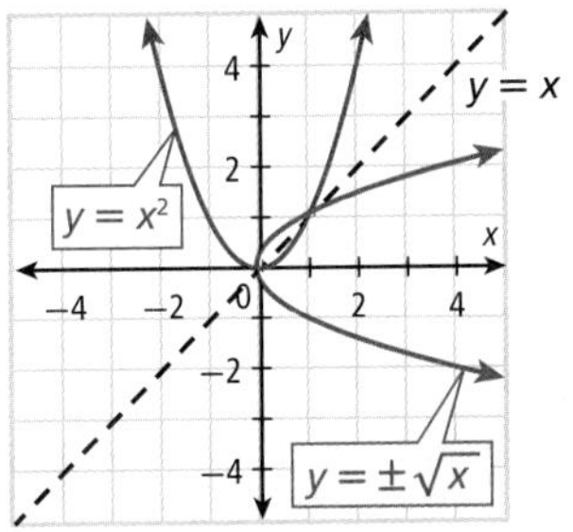

Given a rule for a relation, you can find the rule for the inverse relation by exchanging x and y in the original rule and then solving for y. For the function $y = x^2$, exchanging x and y gives $x = y^2$. To solve for y, take the square root of both sides. This shows that the inverse relation of $y = x^2$ is described by $y = \pm\sqrt{x}$.

The inverse of a function may or may not be a function. For example, $y = \pm\sqrt{x}$, which is the inverse of the function $y = x^2$, is not itself a function; we can see from the graph that every domain value is paired with two range values. However, the relation becomes a function when the range is restricted to the principal square root of x; that is, $y = \sqrt{x}$. Note that this corresponds to the portion of the graph of $y = \pm\sqrt{x}$ that lies above the x-axis.

GRAPHING SQUARE-ROOT FUNCTIONS

Lesson 11-5

Most of the square-root functions that students graph in this chapter are transformations of the graph of $y = \sqrt{x}$. For example, the graph of $y = \sqrt{x} + c$ is a vertical translation of the graph of $y = \sqrt{x}$. The graph is translated c units up if $c > 0$ and $|c|$ units down if $c < 0$. Similarly, the graph of $y = \sqrt{x - a}$ is a horizontal translation of the graph of $y = \sqrt{x}$. The graph is translated a units to the right if $a > 0$ and $|a|$ units to the left if $a < 0$.

This approach offers a convenient way to graph a square-root function. To graph $y = \sqrt{x + 4} - 3$, begin with the graph of $y = \sqrt{x}$, translate it 4 units to the left (since, in this case, $a = -4$) and then 3 units down.

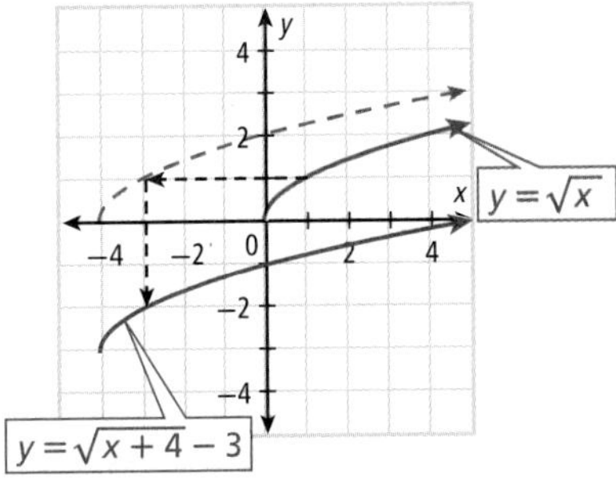

Notice how the transformations affect the domain and range.

This concept can in fact be extended to all functions. In general, the graph of $y = f(x - a) + c$ is the graph of $y = f(x)$ translated $|a|$ units horizontally (left or right, depending on the sign of a) and $|c|$ units vertically (up or down, depending on the sign of c).

11-5 Organizer

Pacing: Traditional 1 day
Block $\frac{1}{2}$ day

Objectives: Identify square-root functions and their domains and ranges.

Graph square-root functions.

Online Edition
Tutorial Videos, Interactivity

Power Presentations with PowerPoint®

Warm Up

Find each square root.

1. $\sqrt{36}$ 6 **2.** $\sqrt{144}$ 12

3. $-\sqrt{400}$ -20 **4.** $\sqrt{-196}$ undef.

Solve each inequality.

5. $x + 5 \geq 0$ $x \geq -5$

6. $0 \leq 4x - 8$ $x \geq 2$

7. $0 \leq 3x$ $x \geq 0$

8. $10 - 3x \geq 0$ $x \leq \frac{10}{3}$

Compare. Write $<$, $>$, or $=$.

9. $\sqrt{45}$ ▪ 7 $<$

10. $\sqrt{12}$ ▪ 3 $>$

Also available on transparency

Math Humor

Q: Why did the square-root function lose the singing competition?

A: He didn't have a full range.

11-5 Square-Root Functions

Objectives
Identify square-root functions and their domains and ranges.
Graph square-root functions.

Vocabulary
square-root function

Who uses this?
Astronauts can use square-root functions to calculate their speed in free fall.

Astronauts at NASA practice living in the weightlessness of space by training in the KC-135, also known as the "Vomit Comet." This aircraft flies to a certain altitude and then free falls for a period of time, simulating a zero-gravity environment.

The function $y = 8\sqrt{x}$ gives the speed in feet per second of an object in free fall after falling x feet. This function is different from others you have seen so far. It contains a variable under the square-root sign, $\sqrt{\ }$.

Know it! Note

Square-Root Function

WORDS	EXAMPLES	NONEXAMPLES
A **square-root function** is a function whose rule contains a variable under a square-root sign.	$y = \sqrt{x}$ $y = \sqrt{2x + 1}$ $y = 3\sqrt{\frac{x}{2}} - 6$	$y = x^2$ $y = \frac{2}{x + 1}$ $y = \sqrt{3}x$

EXAMPLE 1 Evaluating Square-Root Functions

A **Find the speed of an object in free fall after it has fallen 4 feet.**

$y = 8\sqrt{x}$ *Write the speed function.*
$= 8\sqrt{4}$ *Substitute 4 for x.*
$= 8(2)$ *Simplify.*
$= 16$

After an object has fallen 4 feet, its speed is 16 ft/s.

B **Find the speed of an object in free fall after it has fallen 50 feet. Round your answer to the nearest tenth.**

$y = 8\sqrt{x}$ *Write the speed function.*
$= 8\sqrt{50}$ *Substitute 50 for x.*
≈ 56.6 *Use a calculator.*

After an object has fallen 50 feet, its speed is about 56.6 ft/s.

Helpful Hint
Check that your answer is reasonable. In Example 1B, $8\sqrt{49} = 8(7) = 56$, so $8\sqrt{50} \approx 56.6$ is reasonable.

1a. Find the speed of an object in free fall after it has fallen 25 feet.

1b. Find the speed of an object in free fall after it has fallen 15 feet. Round your answer to the nearest hundredth.

1a. 40 ft/s
1b. 30.98 ft/s

State Resources

1 Introduce

EXPLORATION

11-5 Square-Root Functions

The figure shows a square with side length *s*.

1. Write an equation that expresses the area *A* of the square as a function of *s*.
2. Solve the equation for *s*.
3. Use the equation to help you complete the table.

A	1	4	16	36	64	81	100
s							

4. Plot the points in your table on the coordinate plane.

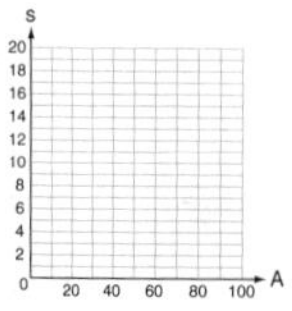

THINK AND DISCUSS

5. **Explain** how you could add additional points to your graph.
6. **Describe** the domain of the function you graphed.

Motivate

Have students find ordered-pair solutions of $y = \sqrt{x}$ using x-values of $-9, -4, -1, 0, 1, 4,$ and 9. $\{(0, 0), (1, 1), (4, 2), (9, 3)\}$ Ask students what happened when they used a negative number for x. Possible answer: There is no y-value because the square root of a negative number is undefined.

Explorations and answers are provided in *Alternate Openers: Explorations Transparencies.*

Recall that the square root of a negative number is not a real number. The domain (x-values) of a square-root function is restricted to numbers that make the value under the radical sign greater than or equal to 0.

EXAMPLE 2 Finding the Domain of Square-Root Functions

Find the domain of each square-root function.

A $y = \sqrt{x + 4} - 3$

$x + 4 \geq 0$ *The expression under the radical sign must be greater than or equal to 0.*

$\underline{-4 \quad -4}$ *Solve the inequality. Subtract 4 from both sides.*

$x \geq -4$

The domain is the set of all real numbers greater than or equal to -4.

B $y = \sqrt{3(x - 2)}$

$3(x - 2) \geq 0$ *The expression under the radical sign must be greater than or equal to 0.*

$3x - 6 \geq 0$ *Solve the inequality. Distribute 3 on the left side.*

$\underline{+6 \quad +6}$ *Add 6 to both sides.*

$3x \geq 6$

$x \geq 2$ *Divide both sides by 3.*

The domain is the set of all real numbers greater than or equal to 2.

Find the domain of each square-root function.

2a. $y = \sqrt{2x - 1}$ $x \geq \frac{1}{2}$ **2b.** $y = \sqrt{3x - 5}$ $x \geq \frac{5}{3}$

The parent function for square-root functions, $f(x) = \sqrt{x}$, is graphed at right. Notice there are no x-values to the left of 0 because the domain is $x \geq 0$.

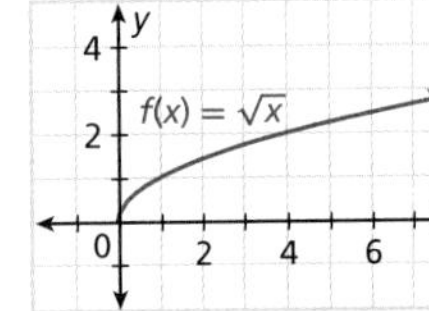

Know it! Note

Translations of the Graph of $f(x) = \sqrt{x}$

The graph of $f(x) = \sqrt{x} + c$ is a vertical translation of the graph of $f(x) = \sqrt{x}$.	The graph of $f(x) = \sqrt{x - a}$ is a horizontal translation of the graph of $f(x) = \sqrt{x}$.
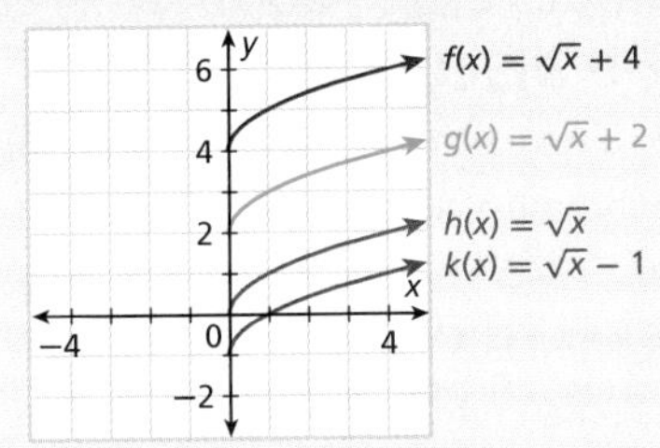	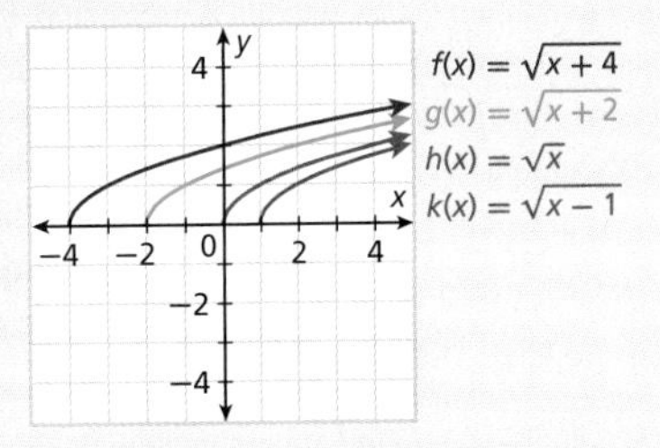
The graph is translated c units up for $c > 0$ and c units down for $c < 0$.	The graph is translated a units right for $a > 0$ and a units left for $a < 0$.

If a square-root function is given in one of these forms, you can graph the parent function $f(x) = \sqrt{x}$ and translate it vertically or horizontally.

2 Teach

Guided Instruction

First review square roots, perfect squares, and estimating square roots that are not perfect squares. In **Example 2,** remind students that radical signs are used as grouping symbols in the order of operations. Tell students that it is necessary to know the domain of a square-root function so that appropriate x-values are chosen when graphing such functions.

Reaching All Learners

Through Visual Cues

On separate transparencies, graph and label the following with students by generating and connecting ordered pairs:

$y = \sqrt{x} - 3$, $y = \sqrt{x} - 1$, $y = \sqrt{x}$, $y = \sqrt{x} + 4$

Then place the transparencies on top of each other and have students discuss what they see. Have a volunteer sketch $y = \sqrt{x} + 7$ without creating a table of values. Repeat the activity for $y = \sqrt{x - 3}$, $y = \sqrt{x - 1}$, $y = \sqrt{x}$, and $y = \sqrt{x + 4}$.

COMMON ERROR ALERT

When finding the domain of a square-root function, students might write an equation, rather than an inequality. Show students how several different values can make the expression under the radical sign positive.

Power Presentations with PowerPoint®

Additional Examples

Example 1

The function $y = 8\sqrt{x}$ gives the speed in feet per second of an object in free fall after falling x feet.

A. Find the speed of an object in free fall after it has fallen 16 feet. 32 ft/s

B. Find the speed of an object in free fall after it has fallen 20 feet. Round your answer to the nearest tenth. 35.8 ft/s

Example 2

Find the domain of each square-root function.

A. $y = 1 + \sqrt{x - 4}$ $x \geq 4$

B. $y = \sqrt{4(x + 3)}$ $x \geq -3$

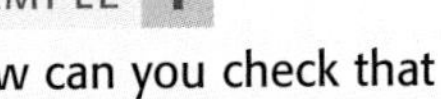

INTERVENTION

Questioning Strategies

EXAMPLE 1

- How can you check that your answer is reasonable when the square root is not a perfect square?
- Why is $y = \sqrt{2}x$ not a square-root function?

EXAMPLE 2

- How do you choose which expression should be set greater than or equal to zero?
- How can you find the range of each function?

Power Presentations with PowerPoint®

Additional Examples

Example 3

Graph each square-root function.

A. $f(x) = \sqrt{x - 3}$

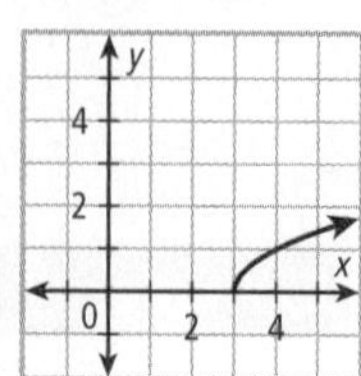

B. $f(x) = 3\sqrt{x} + 4$

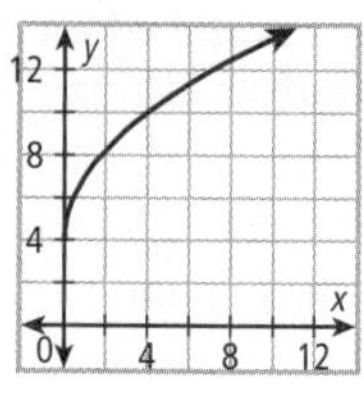

INTERVENTION
Questioning Strategies

EXAMPLE 3

- How is the graph of a square-root function similar to the graph of an exponential function? How is it different?
- How do you pick x-values for the table?

EXAMPLE 3 Graphing Square-Root Functions

A Graph $f(x) = \sqrt{x - 4}$.

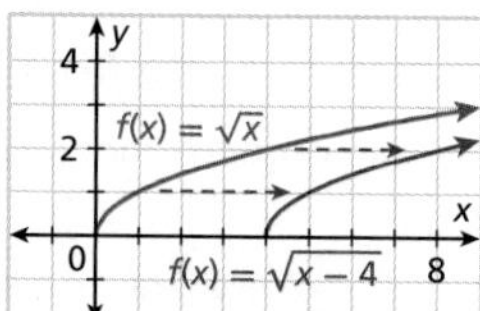

Since this function is in the form $f(x) = \sqrt{x - a}$, you can graph it as a horizontal translation of the graph of $f(x) = \sqrt{x}$.

Graph $f(x) = \sqrt{x}$ and then shift the graph 4 units to the right.

Helpful Hint

In Example 3B, when generating ordered pairs, choose x-values that make the expression under the radical sign a perfect square.

B Graph $f(x) = \sqrt{2x} + 3$.

This is not a horizontal or vertical translation of the graph of $f(x) = \sqrt{x}$.

Step 1 Find the domain of the function.

$2x \geq 0$ *The expression under the radical sign must be greater than or equal to 0.*

$x \geq 0$ *Solve the inequality by dividing both sides by 2.*

The domain is the set of all real numbers greater than or equal to 0.

Step 2 Choose x-values greater than or equal to 0 and generate ordered pairs.

x	$f(x) = \sqrt{2x} + 3$
0	3
2	5
8	7
18	9
32	11

Step 3 Plot the points. Then connect them with a smooth curve.

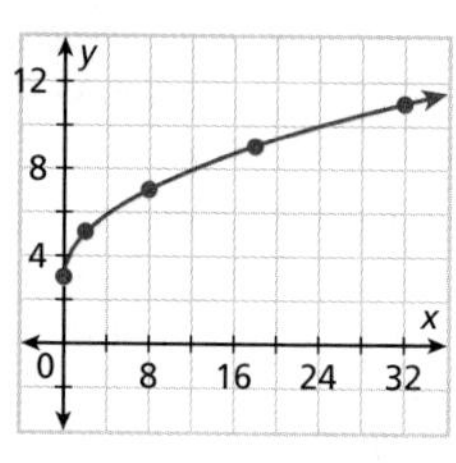

3a.

3b.

Graph each square-root function.

3a. $f(x) = \sqrt{x} + 2$ **3b.** $f(x) = 2\sqrt{x} + 3$

THINK AND DISCUSS

1. How do you find the domain of a square-root function?
2. Compare the graph of $f(x) = \sqrt{x + 8}$ with the graph of $f(x) = \sqrt{x}$.
3. Compare the graph of $f(x) = \sqrt{x + 8}$ with the graph of $f(x) = \sqrt{x} + 8$.

4. **GET ORGANIZED** Copy and complete the graphic organizer. In each box, graph the function and give its domain.

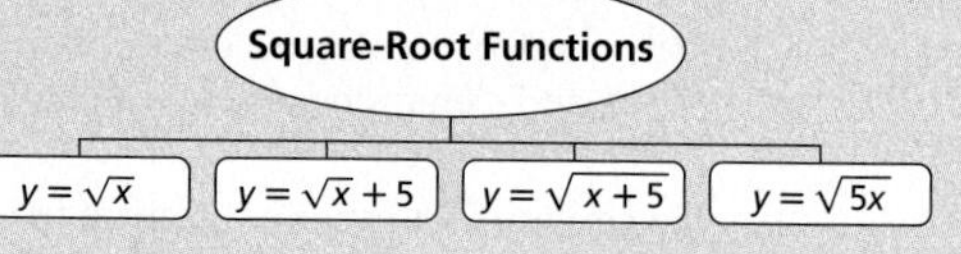

3 Close

Summarize

Tell students that to find the domain of a square-root function, they need to set the expression under the radical sign greater than or equal to 0 and solve for x.

Remind students that when the function is in the form $f(x) = \sqrt{x - a}$, the graph will be translated to the left or right of $f(x) = \sqrt{x}$. When the function is in the form $f(x) = \sqrt{x} + c$, the graph will be translated up or down.

ONGOING ASSESSMENT and INTERVENTION

***Diagnose Before* the Lesson**
11-5 Warm Up, TE p. 822

***Monitor During* the Lesson**
Check It Out! Exercises, SE pp. 822–824
Questioning Strategies, TE pp. 823–824

***Assess After* the Lesson**
11-5 Lesson Quiz, TE p. 827
Alternative Assessment, TE p. 827

Answers to *Think and Discuss*

Possible answers:

1. Set the expression under the square-root sign greater than or equal to zero and solve.
2. The graph of $f(x) = \sqrt{x + 8}$ is the graph of $f(x) = \sqrt{x}$ translated 8 units to the left.
3. The graph of $f(x) = \sqrt{x + 8}$ is the graph of $f(x) = \sqrt{x}$ translated 8 units to the left, while the graph of $f(x) = \sqrt{x} + 8$ is the graph of $f(x) = \sqrt{x}$ translated 8 units up.
4. See p. A10.

11-5 Exercises

go.hrw.com
Homework Help Online
KEYWORD: MA7 11-5
Parent Resources Online
KEYWORD: MA7 Parent

GUIDED PRACTICE

1. There is no variable under the square-root sign.

1. **Vocabulary** Explain why $y = x + \sqrt{3}$ is not a *square-root function.*

SEE EXAMPLE 1 p. 822

2. **Geometry** In a right triangle, $c = \sqrt{a^2 + b^2}$, where c is the length of the hypotenuse (the longest side) and a and b are the lengths of the other two sides, called the legs. What is the length of the hypotenuse of a right triangle if its legs measure 14 cm and 8 cm? Round your answer to the nearest hundredth. **16.12 cm**

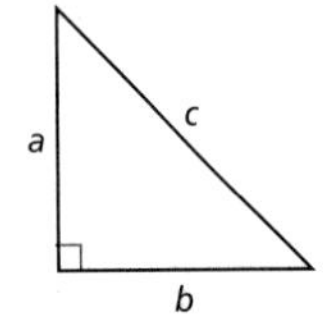

SEE EXAMPLE 2 p. 823

Find the domain of each square-root function.

3. $y = \sqrt{x + 6}$ **$x \geq -6$**
4. $y = 4 - \sqrt{3 - x}$ **$x \leq 3$**
5. $y = \sqrt{2x} - 5$ **$x \geq 0$**
6. $y = \sqrt{x + 2}$ **$x \geq -2$**
7. $y = \sqrt{3x + 9}$ **$x \geq -3$**
8. $y = x + \sqrt{x - 5}$ **$x \geq 5$**

SEE EXAMPLE 3 p. 824

Graph each square-root function.

9. $f(x) = \sqrt{x - 1}$
10. $f(x) = -\sqrt{2x}$
11. $f(x) = \sqrt{x} + 1$
12. $f(x) = \sqrt{x} - 12$
13. $f(x) = \sqrt{4 - x}$
14. $f(x) = \sqrt{x + 4}$

PRACTICE AND PROBLEM SOLVING

Independent Practice

For Exercises	See Example
15	1
16–27	2
28–33	3

Extra Practice
Skills Practice p. S25
Application Practice p. S38

15. **Law Enforcement** At the scene of a car accident, police measure the length of the skid marks to estimate the speed that the car was traveling. On dry concrete, $f(x) = \sqrt{24x}$ gives the speed in mi/h when the length of the skid mark is x feet. Find the speed that a car was traveling if it left a skid mark that was 104 ft long. Round your answer to the nearest hundredth. **49.96 mi/h**

Find the domain of each square-root function.

16. $y = \sqrt{8 - 2x}$ **$x \leq 4$**
17. $y = 4 - \sqrt{\frac{x}{2}}$ **$x \geq 0$**
18. $y = \sqrt{3x + 2}$ **$x \geq -\frac{2}{3}$**
19. $y = \sqrt{-2x + 3}$ **$x \leq \frac{3}{2}$**
20. $y = 2\sqrt{x + 1} - 2$ **$x \geq -1$**
21. $y = \sqrt{3(x + 2)} - 1$ **$x \geq -\frac{5}{3}$**
22. $y = \sqrt{2(x + 4)} - 3$ **$x \geq -4$**
23. $y = 7\sqrt{\frac{x}{5} - 8}$ **$x \geq 40$**
24. $y = \sqrt{2(3x - 6)}$ **$x \geq 2$**
25. $y = \sqrt{\frac{1}{3}(x - 9)}$ **$x \geq 9$**
26. $y = \sqrt{2(x + 7)} - 6$ **$x \geq -4$**
27. $y = 4 + \sqrt{3x + 2}$ **$x \geq -\frac{2}{3}$**

Graph each square-root function.

28. $f(x) = \sqrt{x - 5}$
29. $f(x) = \sqrt{2x} - 4$
30. $f(x) = -1 - \sqrt{x}$
31. $f(x) = \sqrt{x} - 4$
32. $f(x) = 3\sqrt{x - 6}$
33. $f(x) = \frac{1}{2}\sqrt{x + 4}$

34. **Geometry** If you know a circle's area, you can use the formula $r = \sqrt{\frac{A}{\pi}}$ to find the radius. What is the radius of a circle whose area is 60 cm²? Use 3.14 for π. Round your answer to the nearest hundredth of a centimeter. **4.37 cm**

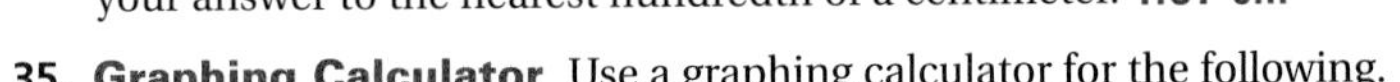

35d. Possible answer: It has a min. value of 0 and curves to the right. As *a* increases, the curve becomes steeper.

35. **Graphing Calculator** Use a graphing calculator for the following.
    a. Graph $y = \sqrt{x}$, $y = \frac{1}{2}\sqrt{x}$, $y = 2\sqrt{x}$, $y = 3\sqrt{x}$, and $y = 4\sqrt{x}$ on the same screen.
    b. What is the domain of each function? **$x \geq 0$**
    c. What is the range of each function? **$y \geq 0$**
    d. Describe the characteristics of $y = a\sqrt{x}$ for $a > 0$.

11-5 Exercises

Assignment Guide

Assign *Guided Practice* exercises as necessary.

If you finished Examples **1–2**
Basic 15–27, 34, 37
Average 15–27, 34, 37
Advanced 15–27, 34, 37, 49–51

If you finished Examples **1–3**
Basic 15–34, 37–40, 44–48, 58–68
Average 15–41, 44–48, 57–68
Advanced 15, 16–40 even, 41–68

Homework Quick Check
Quickly check key concepts.
Exercises: 15, 16, 20, 28, 30, 34

Teaching Tip

Inclusion For **Exercises 4, 13,** and **16,** remind students that the direction of an inequality symbol is switched when both sides of the inequality are multiplied or divided by a negative number.

Answers

9. (graph)

10.
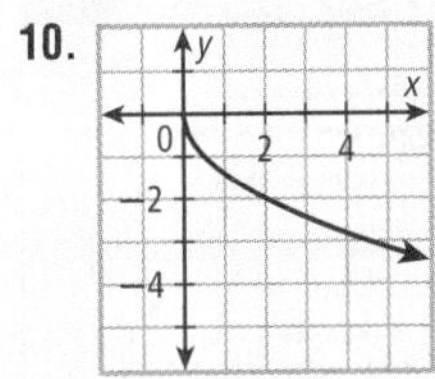
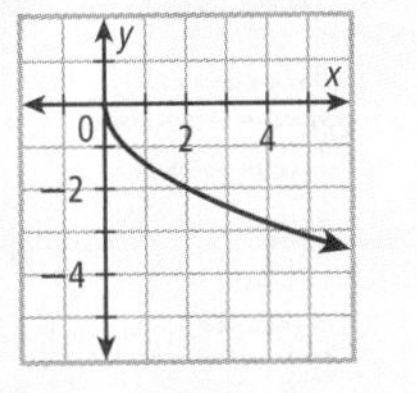

11.
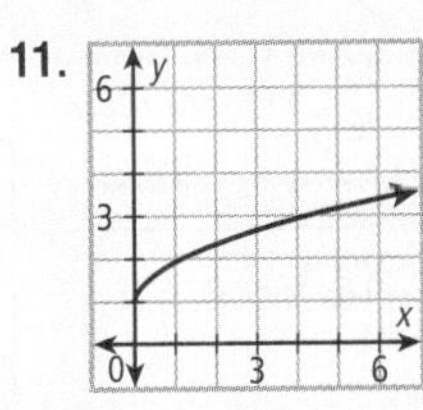

12.
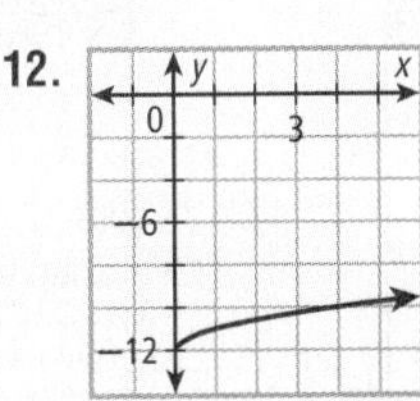

13.
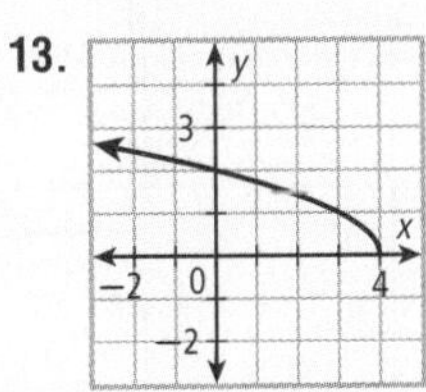

14.
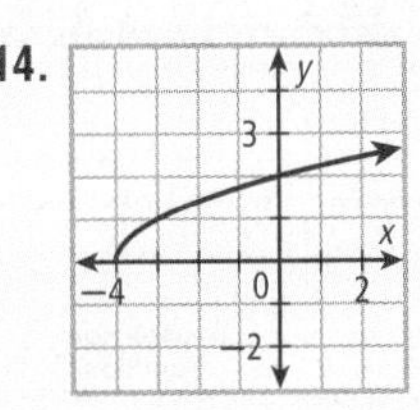

28–33. See p. A34.

35a.
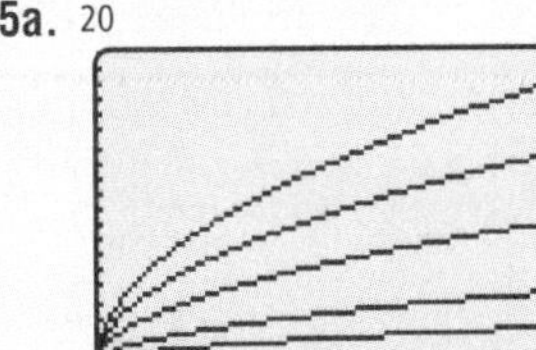

Teaching Tip **Science Link** Escape velocity is discussed in **Exercise 39.** Explain that if you throw an object up, it falls back down because of gravity. But if you could throw it up fast enough, gravity would not be able to pull it back down. From the surface of Earth, the escape velocity is about 25,000 miles per hour.

Exercise 44 involves evaluating square-root functions. This exercise prepares students for the Multi-Step Test Prep on page 854.

Answers

36a.

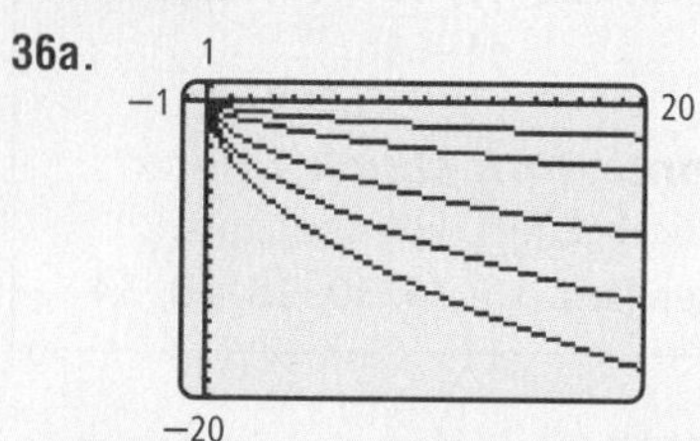

38. For graph, see p. A34.

43. No; the domain of a square-root function is limited to values that make the value under the square-root sign nonnegative. A function with a limited domain cannot have a range of all real numbers.

44c. See p. A34.

LINK Geology

In December 2004, devastating tsunamis struck south and southeast Asia and eastern Africa. A worldwide relief effort ensued. Aid from the United States, both public and private, totaled over $2 billion in the year following the disaster.

36. Graphing Calculator Use a graphing calculator for the following.

a. Graph $y = -\sqrt{x}$, $y = -\frac{1}{2}\sqrt{x}$, $y = -2\sqrt{x}$, $y = -3\sqrt{x}$, and $y = -4\sqrt{x}$ on the same screen.

b. What is the domain of each function? **$x \geq 0$**

c. What is the range of each function? **$y \leq 0$**

d. Describe the characteristics of $y = a\sqrt{x}$ for $a < 0$.

36d. Possible answer: It has a max. value of 0 and curves to the right. As a decreases, the curve becomes steeper.

37. The distance d between two points (x, y) and (w, z) in the coordinate plane can be found by using the formula $d = \sqrt{(w - x)^2 + (z - y)^2}$. What is the distance between the points $(2, 1)$ and $(5, 3)$? Round your answer to the nearest hundredth. **3.61 units**

38. Geology Tsunamis are large waves that move across deep oceans at high speeds. When tsunamis hit shallow water, their energy moves them upward into a destructive force. The speed of a tsunami in meters per second can be found using the function $f(x) = \sqrt{9.8x}$, where x is the depth of the water in meters. Graph this function. Then find the speed of a tsunami when the water depth is 500 meters. **70 m/s**

39. Astronomy A planet's *escape velocity* is the initial velocity that an object must have to escape the planet's gravity. Escape velocity v in meters per second can be found by using the formula $v = \sqrt{2gr}$, where g is the planet's surface gravity and r is the planet's radius. Find the escape velocity for each planet in the table. Round your answers to the nearest whole number. **Mercury: 4214 m/s; Venus: 10,361 m/s; Earth: 11,200 m/s; Mars: 5016 m/s**

Planet	g (m/s²)	r (m)
Mercury	3.7	2.4×10^6
Venus	8.8	6.1×10^6
Earth	9.8	6.4×10^6
Mars	3.7	3.4×10^6

40. Geometry The volume V of a cylinder can be found by using the formula $V = \pi r^2 h$, where r represents the radius of the cylinder and h represents its height. Find the radius of a cylinder whose volume is 1212 in³ and whose height is 10 inches. Use 3.14 for π. **6.21 in.**

41. Write About It Explain how to find the domain of a square-root function. Why is the domain not all real numbers?

41. Set the expression under the square root sign ≥ 0; because the square root of a neg. number is not a real number.

42. Multi-Step For the function $y = \sqrt{3(x - 5)}$, find the value of y that corresponds to the least possible value for x. **0**

43. Critical Thinking Can the range of a square-root function be all real numbers? Explain.

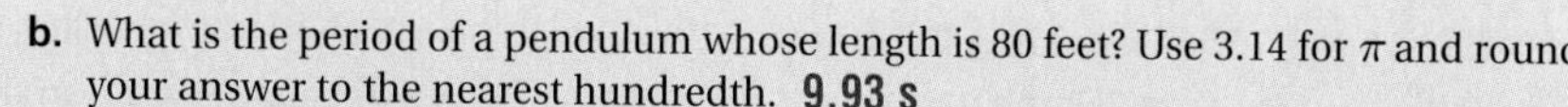

MULTI-STEP TEST PREP

44. This problem will prepare you for the Multi-Step Test Prep on page 854.

a. The Ocean Motion ride at Ohio's Cedar Point amusement park is a giant ship that swings like a pendulum. If a pendulum is under the influence of gravity only, then the time in seconds that it takes for one complete swing back and forth (called the pendulum's period) is $T = 2\pi\sqrt{\frac{\ell}{32}}$, where ℓ is the length of the pendulum in feet. What is the domain of this function? **$\ell \geq 0$**

b. What is the period of a pendulum whose length is 80 feet? Use 3.14 for π and round your answer to the nearest hundredth. **9.93 s**

c. The length of the Ocean Motion pendulum is about 80 feet. Do you think your answer to part **b** is its period? Explain why or why not.

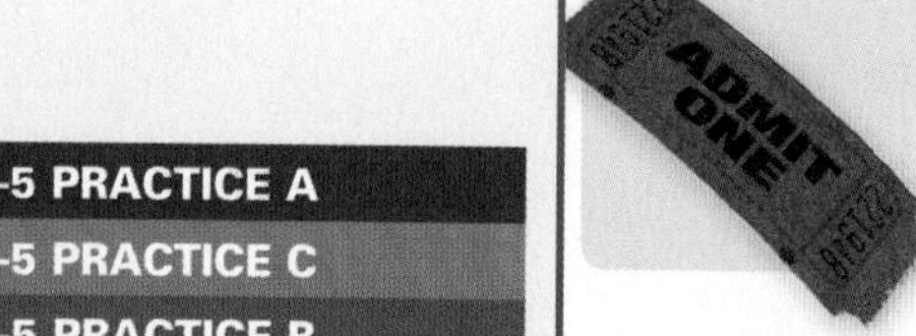

11-5 PRACTICE A

11-5 PRACTICE C

11-5 PRACTICE B

1. An apartment manager needs to order wallpaper border for the remodeled bathrooms. The function $y = 640\sqrt{x}$ gives the amount of border needed, in feet, if x is the square footage of each bathroom. Find the amount of border needed if each bathroom is 100 ft². **6400 feet**
2. The current I, in amps, flowing through a household appliance is given by $I = \sqrt{\frac{P}{R}}$, where P is the power required in watts and R is the resistance in ohms. What is the current in an electric skillet when the power required is 1500 watts and the resistance is 75 ohms? Round your answer to the nearest tenth. **≈4.5 amps**

Find the domain of each square-root function.

3. $y = \sqrt{x + 6}$ **$x \geq -6$**
4. $y = \sqrt{-3x}$ **$x \leq 0$**
5. $y = \sqrt{2x + 8}$ **$x \geq -4$**
6. $y = \sqrt{\frac{2}{3}x - 6}$ **$x \geq 9$**
7. $y = -2\sqrt{10 - 5x}$ **$x \leq 2$**
8. $y = \sqrt{7(x - 3)}$ **$x \geq 3$**

Complete each function table. Then graph each square-root function.

9. $f(x) = \sqrt{4x}$

x	$f(x)$
0	0
$\frac{1}{4}$	1
1	2
4	4
9	6

10. $f(x) = \sqrt{-x} + 3$

x	$f(x)$
0	3
−1	4
−4	5
−9	6
−16	7

11. $f(x) = \frac{1}{2}\sqrt{x - 2}$

x	$f(x)$
2	0
3	$\frac{1}{2}$
6	1
11	$\frac{3}{2}$
18	2

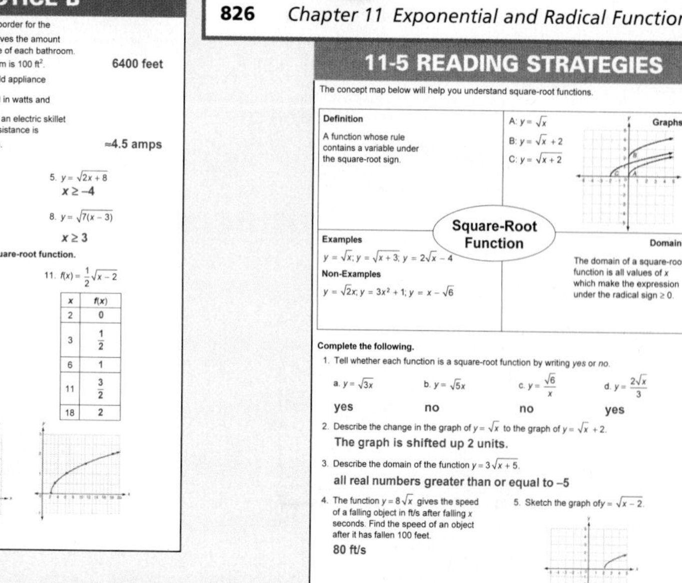

11-5 READING STRATEGIES

The concept map below will help you understand square-root functions.

Square-Root Function

Definition
A function whose rule contains a variable under the square-root sign.

Graphs
A: $y = \sqrt{x}$
B: $y = \sqrt{x} + 2$
C: $y = \sqrt{x + 2}$

Examples
$y = \sqrt{x}$; $y = \sqrt{x + 3}$; $y = 2\sqrt{x} - 4$

Non-Examples
$y = \sqrt{2}x$; $y = 3x^2 + 1$; $y = x - \sqrt{6}$

Domain
The domain of a square-root function is all values of x which make the expression under the radical sign ≥ 0.

Complete the following.

1. Tell whether each function is a square-root function by writing *yes* or *no*.

a. $y = \sqrt{3x}$ **yes** b. $y = \sqrt{5}x$ **no** c. $y = \frac{\sqrt{6}}{x}$ **no** d. $y = \frac{2\sqrt{x}}{3}$ **yes**

2. Describe the change in the graph of $y = \sqrt{x}$ to the graph of $y = \sqrt{x} + 2$. **The graph is shifted up 2 units.**
3. Describe the domain of the function $y = 3\sqrt{x + 5}$. **all real numbers greater than or equal to −5**
4. The function $y = 8\sqrt{x}$ gives the speed of a falling object in ft/s after falling x seconds. Find the speed of an object after it has fallen 100 feet. **80 ft/s**
5. Sketch the graph of $y = \sqrt{x - 2}$.

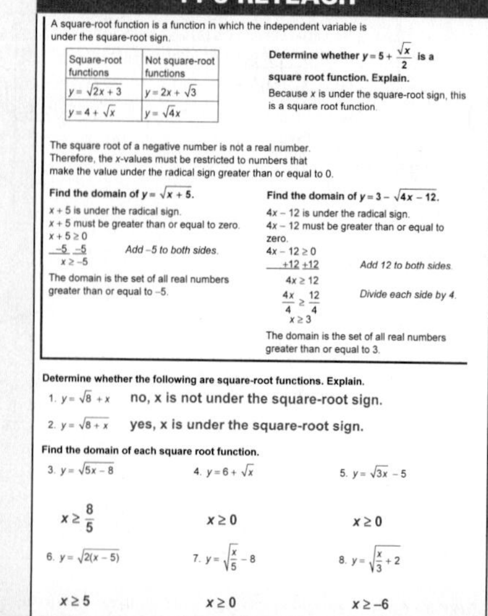

11-5 RETEACH

A square-root function is a function in which the independent variable is under the square-root sign.

Square-root functions	Not square-root functions
$y = \sqrt{2x + 3}$	$y = 2x + \sqrt{3}$
$y = 4 + \sqrt{x}$	$y = \sqrt{4}x$

Determine whether $y = 5 + \frac{\sqrt{x}}{2}$ is a square root function. Explain.

Because x is under the square-root sign, this is a square root function.

The square root of a negative number is not a real number. Therefore, the x-values must be restricted to numbers that make the value under the radical sign greater than or equal to 0.

Find the domain of $y = \sqrt{x + 5}$.

$x + 5$ is under the radical sign.
$x + 5$ must be greater than or equal to zero.
$x + 5 \geq 0$
$-5 \ \ -5$ *Add −5 to both sides.*
$x \geq -5$
The domain is the set of all real numbers greater than or equal to −5.

Find the domain of $y = 3 - \sqrt{4x - 12}$.

$4x - 12$ is under the radical sign.
$4x - 12$ must be greater than or equal to zero.
$4x - 12 \geq 0$
$+12 \ +12$ *Add 12 to both sides.*
$4x \geq 12$
$\frac{4x}{4} \geq \frac{12}{4}$ *Divide each side by 4.*
$x \geq 3$
The domain is the set of all real numbers greater than or equal to 3.

Determine whether the following are square-root functions. Explain.

1. $y = \sqrt{8} + x$ **no, x is not under the square-root sign.**
2. $y = \sqrt{8 + x}$ **yes, x is under the square-root sign.**

Find the domain of each square root function.

3. $y = \sqrt{5x - 8}$ **$x \geq \frac{8}{5}$**
4. $y = 6 + \sqrt{x}$ **$x \geq 0$**
5. $y = \sqrt{3x} - 5$ **$x \geq 0$**
6. $y = \sqrt{2(x - 5)}$ **$x \geq 5$**
7. $y = \sqrt{\frac{x}{5}} - 8$ **$x \geq 0$**
8. $y = \sqrt{\frac{x}{3} + 2}$ **$x \geq -6$**

TEST PREP

45. Which function is graphed at right?

(A) $f(x) = \sqrt{x+3}$ (C) $f(x) = \sqrt{x-3}$

(B) $f(x) = \sqrt{x} + 3$ (D) $f(x) = \sqrt{x} - 3$

46. Which function has domain $x \geq 2$?

(F) $y = \sqrt{2x}$ (H) $y = \sqrt{\frac{x}{2}}$

(G) $y = \sqrt{x+2}$ (J) $y = \sqrt{x-2}$

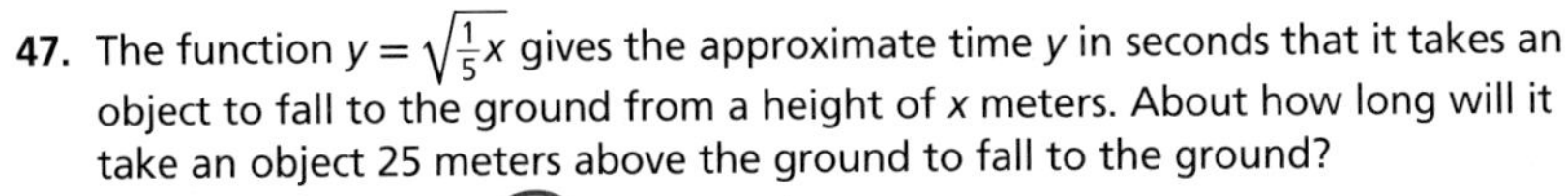

47. The function $y = \sqrt{\frac{1}{5}x}$ gives the approximate time y in seconds that it takes an object to fall to the ground from a height of x meters. About how long will it take an object 25 meters above the ground to fall to the ground?

(A) 11.2 seconds (C) 2.2 seconds

(B) 5 seconds (D) 0.4 seconds

48. **Gridded Response** If $g(x) = \sqrt{4x} - 1$, what is $g(9)$? **5**

CHALLENGE AND EXTEND

Find the domain of each function.

49. $y = \sqrt{x^2 - 25}$ **$x \leq -5$ OR $x \geq 5$**

50. $y = \sqrt{x^2 + 5x + 6}$ **$x \leq -3$ OR $x \geq -2$**

51. $y = \sqrt{2x^2 + 5x - 12}$ **$x \leq -4$ OR $x \geq \frac{3}{2}$**

Find the domain and range of each function.

52. $y = 2 - \sqrt{x+3}$ **D: $x \geq -3$; R: $y \leq 2$**

53. $y = 4 - \sqrt{3-x}$ **D: $x \leq 3$; R: $y \leq 4$**

54. $y = 6 - \sqrt{\frac{x}{2}}$ **D: $x \geq 0$; R: $y \leq 6$**

55. Give an example of a square-root function whose graph is above the x-axis.

55. Possible answer: $y = \sqrt{x} + 6$

56. Give an example of a square-root function whose graph is in Quadrant IV.

56. Possible answer: $y = -\sqrt{x-1} - 1$

57. **Multi-Step** Justin is given the function $y = 3 - \sqrt{2(x-5)}$ and $x = 2, 4, 5,$ and 7. He notices that two of these values are not in the function's domain.

a. Which two values are not in the domain? How do you know?

57a. 2, 4; when $x = 2$ or $x = 4$, the expression under the square root sign is neg.

b. What are the values of y for the two given x-values that are in the domain? **3, 1**

SPIRAL REVIEW

Write each equation in slope-intercept form, and then graph. *(Lesson 5-7)*

58. $2y = 4x - 8$

59. $3x + 6y = 12$

60. $2x = -y - 9$

58. $y = 2x - 4$

59. $y = -\frac{1}{2}x + 2$

60. $y = -2x - 9$

Find each product. *(Lesson 7-9)*

61. $(3x-1)^2$ **$9x^2 - 6x + 1$**

62. $(2x-5)(2x+5)$ **$4x^2 - 25$**

63. $(a - b^2c)^2$ **$a^2 - 2ab^2c + b^4c^2$**

64. $(x^2 + 2y)^2$

65. $(3r - 2s)(3r + 2s)$

66. $(a^3b^2 - c^4)(a^3b^2 + c^4)$

64. $x^4 + 4x^2y + 4y^2$

65. $9r^2 - 4s^2$

66. $a^6b^4 - c^8$

67. Blake invested $42,000 at a rate of 5% compounded quarterly. Write a function to model this situation. Then find the value of Blake's investment after 3 years. *(Lesson 11-3)* **$A = 42{,}000(1.0125)^{4t}$; $48,751.69**

68. Lead-209 has a half-life of about 3.25 hours. Find the amount of lead-209 left from a 230-mg sample after 1 day. Round your answer to the nearest hundredth. *(Lesson 11-3)* **1.38 g**

11-5 PROBLEM SOLVING

Write the correct answer.

1. Use the formula $r = \sqrt{\frac{A}{\pi}}$ to find the radius of a circular fountain with an area of 200 square feet. Use 3.14 for π. Round your answer to the nearest foot.

8 ft

2. The manager of a magazine gives a rating to each article written using $y = \sqrt{10x}$ where x is the number of positive responses received about that article. What rating would the manager give an article if it received 21 positive responses? (Round to the nearest tenth.)

14.5

3. The distance to the horizon (in km) from an aircraft can be roughly approximated using $y = 4\sqrt{x}$ where x is the aircraft's altitude in meters. Graph this function.

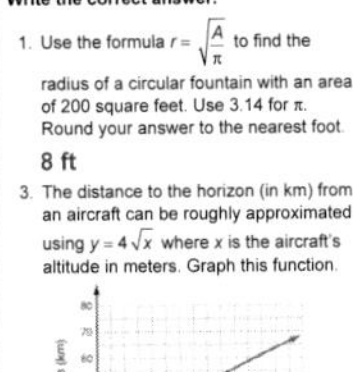

4. The amount of water flowing through a hose in gallons per minute is given by $y = 35\sqrt{x}$ where x is the nozzle pressure in pounds per square inch. What is the water flow in the hose if the pressure is 25 pounds per square inch?

175 gal/min

Select the best answer.

5. The diameter of a can of tuna is found by $d = 2\sqrt{\frac{V}{\pi h}}$ where V is volume and h is height. To the nearest cm, what is the radius of a tuna can with a volume of 150 cm³ and a height of 3 cm?

A 2 cm C 8 cm

B 4 cm D 16 cm

6. The side length of the base of a square pyramid can be found by $s = \sqrt{\frac{3V}{h}}$ where V is volume and h is height. To the nearest meter, what is the side length of the base of a square pyramid if its volume is 13,653 m³ and its height is 40 m?

F 3 m **H** 32 m

G 18 m J 55 m

7. The radius of a ball is found by $r = \sqrt{\frac{S}{4\pi}}$ where S is surface area. To the nearest tenth of an inch, what is the radius of a ball with a surface area of 154 in²?

A 3.5 in. C 7.0 in.

B 6.2 in. D 12.3 in.

11-5 CHALLENGE

If you start with 5 and add 2, you get 7. Then if you take 7 and subtract 2, you get 5 again. That's because addition and subtraction are *inverse operations* that "undo" each other. Notice that what you start with and what you end with flip-flop.

Start with 5. $5 + 2 = 7$ End with 7.
Start with 7. $7 - 2 = 5$ End with 5.

Relations also have inverses that undo each other. Two **inverse relations** will flip-flop inputs and outputs.

$y = 2x + 3 \mapsto y = 2(5) + 3 = 10 + 3 = 13$ (Input 5, Output 13)

So, one way to find the inverse of a relation is to flip-flop the input (x) and the output (y).

$y = \frac{x-3}{2} \mapsto y = \frac{13 - 3}{2} = \frac{10}{2} = 5$ (Input 13, Output 5)

Find the inverse of $y = x - 6$.

$x = y - 6$ *Flip-flop x and y.*

$+6 \quad +6$ *Use inverse operations.*

$x + 6 = y$ *Solve for y.*

The inverse relation is $y = x + 6$.

Flip-flop x and y to find the inverse of each relation.

1. $y = x + 10$ **$y = x - 10$**

2. $y = \frac{x}{5}$ **$y = 5x$**

3. $y = -3x + 6$ **$y = -\frac{1}{3}x + 2$**

4. $y = x^2$ (*Hint:* Review Lesson 9-7.) **$y = \pm\sqrt{x}$**

5. $y = (x+2)^2$ **$y = \pm\sqrt{x} - 2$**

6. $y = \frac{1}{4}x^2 - 2$ **$y = \pm\sqrt{4x + 8}$**

7. On a graphing calculator, enter each relation into **Y1** and its inverse into **Y2**, and graph in a square window (**Zsquare**). (For 4–6, enter each inverse as two halves in **Y2** and **Y3**.) Describe any patterns.

The line or curve of each original relation is reflected across the line $y = x$ to create the line or curve of the inverse relation.

8. Notice that all of the original relations in 1–6 are functions. For which are the inverses also functions? **1, 2, and 3**

9. In Lesson 11–5, you may have noticed that the graph of the function $f(x) = \sqrt{x}$ looks like half of a sideways parabola. Explain why this is.

The graph of $y = x^2$ is a parabola, and the inverse relation $y = \pm\sqrt{x}$ is the same parabola reflected across the line $y = x$. The graph of $f(x) = \sqrt{x}$ is the top (positive) half of $y = \pm\sqrt{x}$.

TEST PREP DOCTOR The graph in **Exercise 45** is a horizontal translation of the parent graph $f(x) = \sqrt{x}$. Students can immediately eliminate choices **B** and **D** because they would be vertical translations.

Students who chose **B** in **Exercise 47** may have forgotten to take the square root after taking one-fifth of x.

Answers

58–60. For graphs, see p. A34.

Journal

Have students describe the graph of $f(x) = \sqrt{x}$ and compare it to the graph of $f(x) = -\sqrt{x}$.

ALTERNATIVE ASSESSMENT

Have students graph $f(x) = \sqrt{2(x+1)} - 6$ by generating at least five ordered pairs. Then have them state the domain and range of the function.

Power Presentations with PowerPoint®

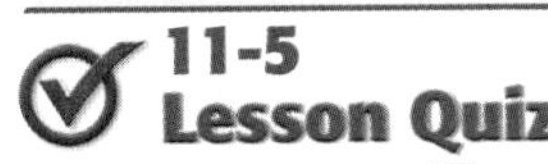

11-5 Lesson Quiz

1. Use the formula $r = \sqrt{\frac{A}{\pi}}$ to find the radius of a circle whose area is 28 in². Use 3.14 for π. Round your answer to the nearest tenth of an inch. 3.0 in.

Find the domain of each square-root function.

2. $y = \sqrt{3x} - 1$ $x \geq 0$

3. $y = -\sqrt{2x + 1}$ $x \geq -\frac{1}{2}$

4. $y = \sqrt{2(x-5)}$ $x \geq 5$

Graph each square-root function.

5. $f(x) = 2 + \sqrt{3x}$

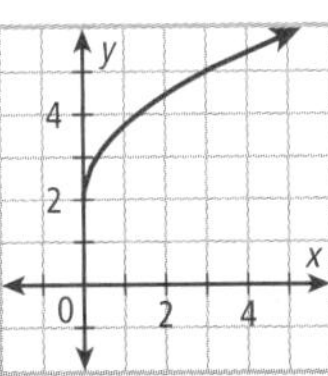

6. $f(x) = \sqrt{x+1}$

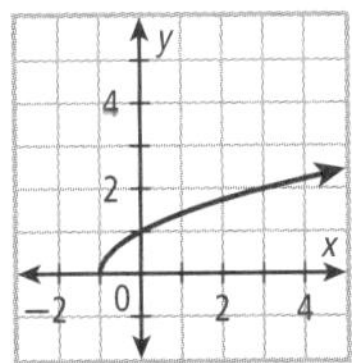

Also available on transparency

Organizer

Use with Lesson 11-5

Pacing:
Traditional 1 day
Block $\frac{1}{2}$ day

Objective: Use a graphing calculator to graph radical functions.

Materials: graphing calculator

Online Edition
Graphing Calculator, TechKeys

Resources

Technology Lab Activities
11-5 Lab Recording Sheet

Teach

Discuss

On a graphing calculator, parentheses are used to indicate what goes under the radical sign. When the square-root symbol is entered, the left parenthesis may automatically appear.

Close

Key Concept

You can use a graphing calculator to verify conjectures about transformations on the graph of $y = \sqrt{x}$.

Assessment

Journal Have students explain how to enter $y = 2\sqrt{x-1} - 3$ into the Y= editor on a graphing calculator.

State Resources

11-5

Graph Radical Functions

You can use a graphing calculator to graph radical functions or to quickly check that a graph drawn by hand is reasonable.

Use with Lesson 11-5

Activity

Graph $f(x) = \sqrt{x-1}$ without using a graphing calculator. Then graph the same function on a graphing calculator and compare.

1. The graph will be a shift of the graph of the parent function $f(x) = \sqrt{x}$ one unit right. Graph $f(x) = \sqrt{x}$ and then shift the graph one unit right.

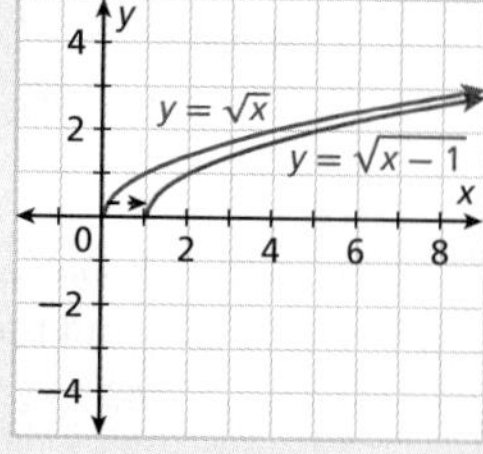

2. Enter the function into the **Y=** editor.

Press WINDOW and enter −1 for **Xmin**, 9 for **Xmax**, −5 for **Ymin**, and 5 for **Ymax**.

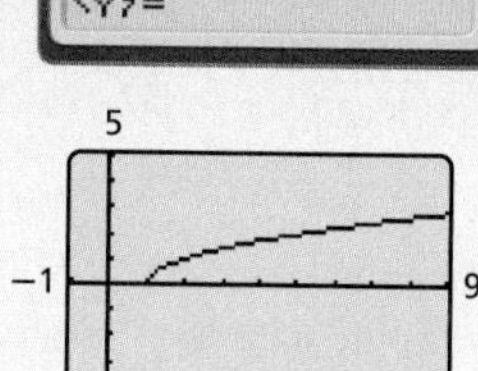

Press GRAPH and compare the graph on the screen to the graph done by hand.

The graph on the screen indicates that the graph done by hand is reasonable.

5
−1
9
−5

Try This

1. Graph $f(x) = \sqrt{x+3}$ without using a graphing calculator. Then graph the same function on a graphing calculator and compare.
2. Graph $f(x) = \sqrt{x} - 2$ without using a graphing calculator. Then graph the same function on a graphing calculator and compare.
3. **Make a Conjecture** How do you think the graph of $f(x) = \sqrt{x+1} + 4$ compares to the graph of $f(x) = \sqrt{x}$? Use a graphing calculator to check your conjecture.
4. **Make a Conjecture** How do you think the graph of $f(x) = 2\sqrt{x}$ compares to the graph of $f(x) = \sqrt{x}$? Use a graphing calculator to check your conjecture.

Answers

1.

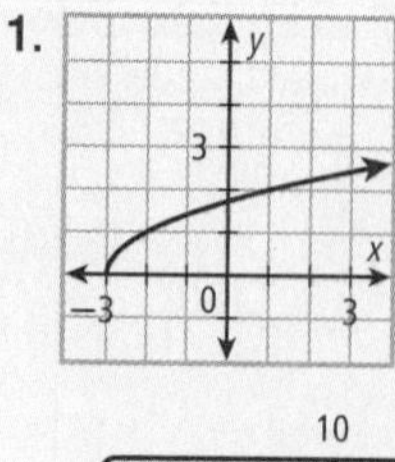

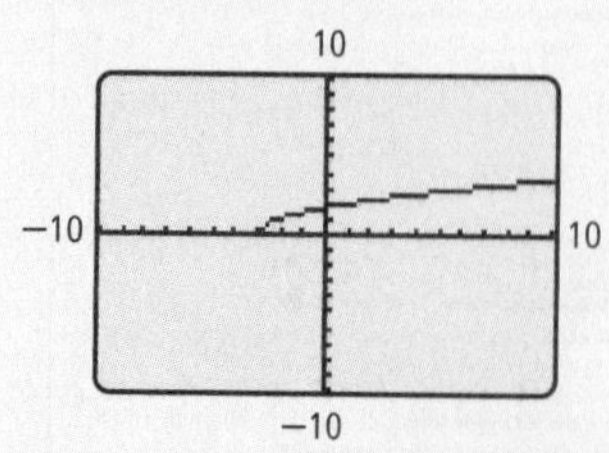

2.

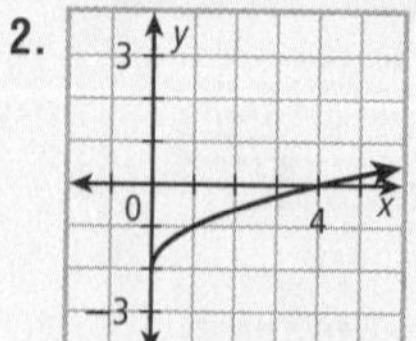

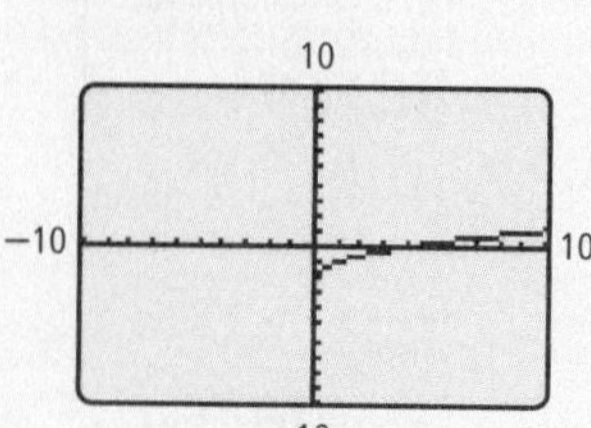

3, 4. See p. A34.

11-6 Radical Expressions

Objective
Simplify radical expressions.

Vocabulary
radical expression
radicand

Why learn this?
You can use a radical expression to find the length of a throw in baseball. (See Example 5.)

An expression that contains a radical sign ($\sqrt{}$) is a **radical expression**. There are many different types of radical expressions, but in this chapter, you will only study radical expressions that contain square roots.

Examples of radical expressions:

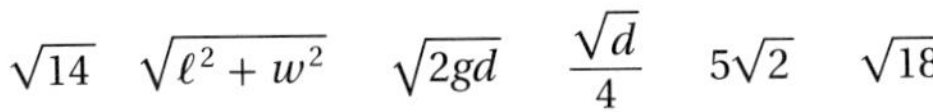

$\sqrt{14}$ $\sqrt{\ell^2 + w^2}$ $\sqrt{2gd}$ $\frac{\sqrt{d}}{4}$ $5\sqrt{2}$ $\sqrt{18}$

The expression under a radical sign is the **radicand**. A radicand may contain numbers, variables, or both. It may contain one term or more than one term.

Simplest Form of a Square-Root Expression

An expression containing square roots is in simplest form when
- the radicand has no perfect square factors other than 1.
- the radicand has no fractions.
- there are no square roots in any denominator.

Remember that positive numbers have two square roots, one positive and one negative. However, $\sqrt{}$ indicates a nonnegative square root. When you simplify, be sure that your answer is not negative. To simplify $\sqrt{x^2}$, you should write $\sqrt{x^2} = |x|$, because you do not know whether x is positive or negative.

Below are some simplified square-root expressions:

$\sqrt{x^2} = |x|$ $\sqrt{x^3} = x\sqrt{x}$ $\sqrt{x^4} = x^2$ $\sqrt{x^5} = x^2\sqrt{x}$ $\sqrt{x^6} = |x^3|$

EXAMPLE 1 Simplifying Square-Root Expressions

Simplify each expression.

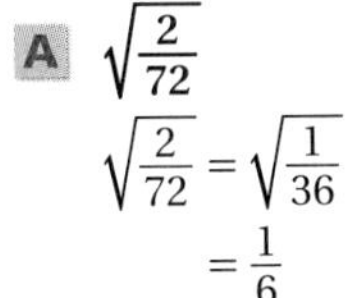

A $\sqrt{\frac{2}{72}}$

$\sqrt{\frac{2}{72}} = \sqrt{\frac{1}{36}}$
$= \frac{1}{6}$

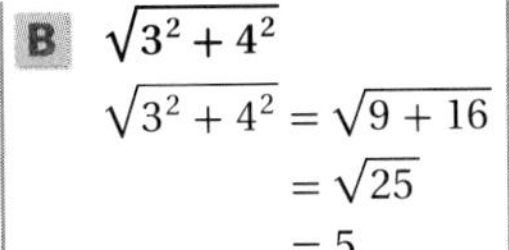

B $\sqrt{3^2 + 4^2}$

$\sqrt{3^2 + 4^2} = \sqrt{9 + 16}$
$= \sqrt{25}$
$= 5$

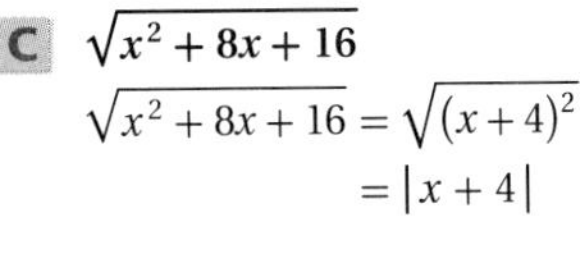

C $\sqrt{x^2 + 8x + 16}$

$\sqrt{x^2 + 8x + 16} = \sqrt{(x+4)^2}$
$= |x + 4|$

Simplify each expression.

1a. $\sqrt{\frac{256}{4}}$ **1b.** $\sqrt{40 + 9}$ **1c.** $\sqrt{5^2 + 12^2}$ **1d.** $\sqrt{(3 - x)^2}$

1a. 8
1b. 7
1c. 13
1d. $|3 - x|$

11-6 Organizer

Pacing: Traditional 1 day
Block $\frac{1}{2}$ day

Objective: Simplify radical expressions.

Power Presentations with PowerPoint®

Warm Up

Identify the perfect square in each set.

1. 45 81 27 111   81
2. 156 99 8 25   25
3. 256 84 12 1000   256
4. 35 216 196 72   196

Write each number as a product of prime numbers.

5. 36   2 • 2 • 3 • 3
6. 64   2 • 2 • 2 • 2 • 2 • 2
7. 196   2 • 2 • 7 • 7
8. 24   2 • 2 • 2 • 3

Also available on transparency

Math Fact !!!

The symbol ℞ was used as a square-root symbol in the thirteenth century. The symbol used today was not introduced until the seventeenth century and is thought to have evolved from a single dot and a diagonal pen stroke.

1 Introduce

EXPLORATION

11-6 Radical Expressions

You will need a calculator for this Exploration.

1. Use your calculator to find a decimal approximation for each expression in the table. Round to the nearest thousandth.

Expression	Decimal Approximation	Expression	Decimal Approximation
$\sqrt{3}\sqrt{6}$		$\sqrt{18}$	
$\sqrt{2}\sqrt{17}$		$\sqrt{34}$	
$\sqrt{50}\sqrt{3}$		$\sqrt{150}$	
$\sqrt{5}\sqrt{2}\sqrt{3}$		$\sqrt{30}$	

2. What do you notice in the table?
3. Use your calculator to find a decimal approximation for each expression in the table. Round to the nearest thousandth.

Expression	Decimal Approximation	Expression	Decimal Approximation
$\frac{\sqrt{10}}{\sqrt{2}}$		$\sqrt{5}$	
$\frac{\sqrt{38}}{\sqrt{19}}$		$\sqrt{2}$	
$\frac{\sqrt{30}}{\sqrt{5}}$		$\sqrt{6}$	

4. What do you notice in the table?

THINK AND DISCUSS

5. Describe any conjectures that you can make based on your

Motivate

Have students list pairs of numbers whose product is 48. 1 • 48, 2 • 24, 3 • 16, 4 • 12, 6 • 8

Which pairs include a number that is a perfect square? 3 • 16, 4 • 12

Tell students that factoring numbers so that one number is a perfect square is an essential skill in this lesson.

Explorations and answers are provided in *Alternate Openers: Explorations Transparencies.*

State Resources

Product Property of Square Roots

WORDS	NUMBERS	ALGEBRA
For any nonnegative real numbers a and b, the square root of ab is equal to the square root of a times the square root of b.	$\sqrt{4(25)} = \sqrt{100} = 10$ $\sqrt{4(25)} = \sqrt{4}\sqrt{25} = 2(5) = 10$	$\sqrt{ab} = \sqrt{a}\sqrt{b}$, where $a \ge 0$ and $b \ge 0$

EXAMPLE 2 Using the Product Property of Square Roots

Simplify. All variables represent nonnegative numbers.

A $\sqrt{18}$

$\sqrt{18} = \sqrt{9(2)}$ — *Factor the radicand using perfect squares.*

$= \sqrt{9}\sqrt{2}$ — *Product Property of Square Roots*

$= 3\sqrt{2}$ — *Simplify.*

B $\sqrt{x^4y^3}$

$\sqrt{x^4y^3} = \sqrt{x^4}\sqrt{y^3}$ — *Product Property of Square Roots*

$= \sqrt{x^4}\sqrt{y^2}\sqrt{y}$ — *Product Property of Square Roots*

$= x^2y\sqrt{y}$ — *Since y is nonnegative, $\sqrt{y^2} = y$.*

Helpful Hint

When factoring the radicand, use factors that are perfect squares. In Example 2A, you could have factored 18 as 6 • 3, but this contains no perfect squares.

CHECK IT OUT! Simplify. All variables represent nonnegative numbers.

2a. $\sqrt{128}$ $8\sqrt{2}$ **2b.** $\sqrt{x^3y^2}$ $xy\sqrt{x}$ **2c.** $\sqrt{48a^2b}$ $4a\sqrt{3b}$

Quotient Property of Square Roots

WORDS	NUMBERS	ALGEBRA
For any real numbers a and b ($a \ge 0$ and $b > 0$), the square root of $\frac{a}{b}$ is equal to the square root of a divided by the square root of b.	$\sqrt{\frac{36}{4}} = \sqrt{9} = 3$ $\sqrt{\frac{36}{4}} = \frac{\sqrt{36}}{\sqrt{4}} = \frac{6}{2} = 3$	$\sqrt{\frac{a}{b}} = \frac{\sqrt{a}}{\sqrt{b}}$, where $a \ge 0$ and $b > 0$

EXAMPLE 3 Using the Quotient Property of Square Roots

Simplify. All variables represent nonnegative numbers.

A $\sqrt{\frac{5}{9}}$

$\sqrt{\frac{5}{9}} = \frac{\sqrt{5}}{\sqrt{9}}$ — *Quotient Property of Square Roots*

$= \frac{\sqrt{5}}{3}$ — *Simplify.*

B $\sqrt{\frac{a^5}{81a}}$

$\sqrt{\frac{a^5}{81a}} = \sqrt{\frac{a^4}{81}}$ — *Simplify.*

$= \frac{\sqrt{a^4}}{\sqrt{81}}$ — *Quotient Property of Square Roots*

$= \frac{a^2}{9}$ — *Simplify.*

Power Presentations with PowerPoint®

Additional Examples

Example 1

Simplify each expression.

A. $\sqrt{\frac{2}{50}}$ $\frac{1}{5}$ **B.** $\sqrt{8^2 + 15^2}$ 17

C. $\sqrt{x^2 - 6x + 9}$ $|x - 3|$

Example 2

Simplify. All variables represent nonnegative numbers.

A. $\sqrt{24}$ $2\sqrt{6}$ **B.** $\sqrt{x^3y^4}$ $xy^2\sqrt{x}$

Example 3

Simplify. All variables represent nonnegative numbers.

A. $\sqrt{\frac{5}{4}}$ $\frac{\sqrt{5}}{2}$ **B.** $\sqrt{\frac{m^3}{9m}}$ $\frac{m}{3}$

Example 4

Simplify. All variables represent nonnegative numbers.

A. $\sqrt{\frac{108}{25}}$ $\frac{6\sqrt{3}}{5}$ **B.** $\sqrt{\frac{9x^3}{16}}$ $\frac{3x\sqrt{x}}{4}$

INTERVENTION

Questioning Strategies

EXAMPLE 1

- How do you know when a radical expression is simplified?
- When do radical expressions require absolute-value signs in the simplified answer? Why?

EXAMPLE 2

- How do you choose the factors when using the Product Property of Square Roots?

EXAMPLES 3–4

- When would you simplify a fraction before using the Quotient Property of Square Roots?
- How is the Quotient Property of Square Roots similar to the Product Property of Square Roots?

2 Teach

Guided Instruction

Introduce radical expressions and give some examples that are simplified and some that are not simplified, explaining why they aren't simplified. Show students how to simplify radical expressions, stressing that they must read the direction lines carefully. If it is not stated that all variables represent nonnegative numbers, as in **Example 1,** students must use absolute-value symbols for expressions containing variables in order to show that the answer is not negative.

Reaching All Learners

Through Cognitive Strategies

Show students how to simplify a radical expression by completely factoring the radicand. Every pair can be "pulled out" and written outside the radical one time.

$\sqrt{108}$	$\sqrt{x^3y^4}$
$\sqrt{(2 \cdot 2) \cdot (3 \cdot 3) \cdot 3}$	$\sqrt{(x \cdot x) \cdot x \cdot (y \cdot y) \cdot (y \cdot y)}$
$2 \cdot 3\sqrt{3}$	$x \cdot y \cdot y\sqrt{x}$
$6\sqrt{3}$	$xy^2\sqrt{x}$

Simplify. All variables represent nonnegative numbers.

3a. $\sqrt{\frac{12}{27}}$ $\frac{2}{3}$ 3b. $\sqrt{\frac{36}{x^4}}$ $\frac{6}{x^2}$ 3c. $\sqrt{\frac{y^6}{4}}$ $\frac{y^3}{2}$

EXAMPLE 4 Using the Product and Quotient Properties Together

Simplify. All variables represent nonnegative numbers.

A $\sqrt{\frac{80}{25}}$

$\frac{\sqrt{80}}{\sqrt{25}}$ *Quotient Property of Square Roots*

$\frac{\sqrt{16(5)}}{\sqrt{25}}$ *Write 80 as 16(5).*

$\frac{\sqrt{16}\sqrt{5}}{\sqrt{25}}$ *Product Property of Square Roots*

$\frac{4\sqrt{5}}{5}$ *Simplify.*

B $\sqrt{\frac{4x^5}{9}}$

$\frac{\sqrt{4x^5}}{\sqrt{9}}$ *Quotient Property of Square Roots*

$\frac{\sqrt{4}\sqrt{x^5}}{\sqrt{9}}$ *Product Property of Square Roots*

$\frac{\sqrt{4}\sqrt{x^4}\sqrt{x}}{\sqrt{9}}$

$\frac{2x^2\sqrt{x}}{3}$ *Simplify.*

In the expression $\frac{4\sqrt{5}}{5}$, $\sqrt{5}$ and 5 are not common factors. $\frac{4\sqrt{5}}{5}$ is completely simplified.

Simplify. All variables represent nonnegative numbers.

4a. $\sqrt{\frac{20}{49}}$ $\frac{2\sqrt{5}}{7}$ 4b. $\sqrt{\frac{z^5}{25y^2}}$ $\frac{z^2\sqrt{z}}{5y}$ 4c. $\sqrt{\frac{p^6}{q^{10}}}$ $\frac{p^3}{q^5}$

EXAMPLE 5 *Sports Application*

A baseball diamond is a square with sides of 90 feet. How far is a throw from third base to first base? Give the answer as a radical expression in simplest form. Then estimate the length to the nearest tenth of a foot.

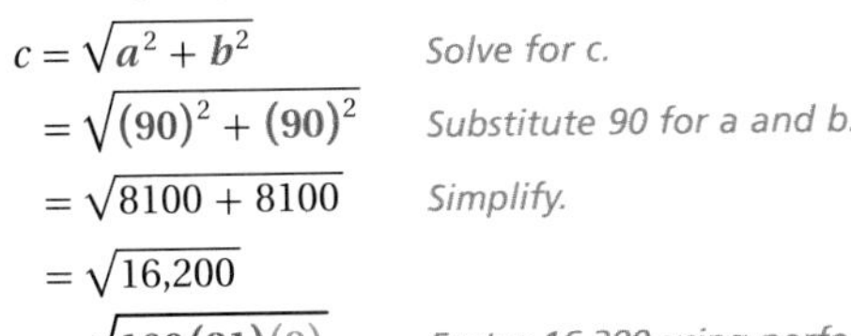

The distance from third base to first base is the hypotenuse of a right triangle. Use the Pythagorean Theorem: $c^2 = a^2 + b^2$.

$c = \sqrt{a^2 + b^2}$ *Solve for c.*

$= \sqrt{(90)^2 + (90)^2}$ *Substitute 90 for a and b.*

$= \sqrt{8100 + 8100}$ *Simplify.*

$= \sqrt{16{,}200}$

$= \sqrt{100(81)(2)}$ *Factor 16,200 using perfect squares.*

$= \sqrt{100}\sqrt{81}\sqrt{2}$ *Use the Product Property of Square Roots.*

$= 10(9)\sqrt{2}$

$= 90\sqrt{2}$ *Simplify.*

≈ 127.3 *Use a calculator and round to the nearest tenth.*

The distance is $90\sqrt{2}$, or about 127.3, feet.

5. A softball diamond is a square with sides of 60 feet. How long is a throw from third base to first base in softball? Give the answer as a radical expression in simplest form. Then estimate the length to the nearest tenth of a foot. $60\sqrt{2}$ ft; 84.9 ft

COMMON ERROR ALERT

Students might write the square root of a sum as the sum of the square roots. For example, they may write $\sqrt{3^2 + 4^2} = 3 + 4 = 7$ instead of $\sqrt{3^2 + 4^2} = \sqrt{9 + 16} = \sqrt{25} = 5$. Remind students that the radical sign acts as a grouping symbol in determining the order of operations.

Inclusion While $\sqrt{72} = \sqrt{9 \cdot 8}$ is a true statement, $\sqrt{72} = \sqrt{36 \cdot 2}$ is easier to simplify. Students struggling with choosing factors may benefit from looking at a chart of perfect squares. Students should quickly learn that using the largest perfect-square factor is "easier" and leads to the simplified form more quickly.

Geometry The diagonal of a square divides the square into two isosceles right triangles. The diagonal is the hypotenuse of each. It is always equal to $\sqrt{2}$ times the length of a leg.

Power Presentations with PowerPoint®

Additional Examples

Example 5

A quadrangle on a college campus is a square with sides of 250 feet. If a student takes a shortcut by walking diagonally across the quadrangle, how far does he walk? Give the answer as a radical expression in simplest form. Then estimate the length to the nearest tenth of a foot. $250\sqrt{2}$ ft; about 353.6 ft

INTERVENTION
Questioning Strategies

EXAMPLE 5

- Why is the Pythagorean Theorem used?

3 Close

Summarize

Have students list the three criteria that must be satisfied in order for a radical expression to be simplified.
no perfect square factors other than 1, no fractions in radicand, no square roots in any denominator

Tell students that when the radicand is a constant, they should write factors that are perfect squares.

ONGOING ASSESSMENT and INTERVENTION

***Diagnose Before* the Lesson**
11-6 Warm Up, TE p. 829

***Monitor During* the Lesson**
Check It Out! Exercises, SE pp. 829–831
Questioning Strategies, TE pp. 830–831

***Assess After* the Lesson**
11-6 Lesson Quiz, TE p. 834
Alternative Assessment, TE p. 834

Answers to *Think and Discuss*

1. $\sqrt{144} = 12$; $(\sqrt{16})(\sqrt{9}) = 4 \times 3 = 12$
2. $\sqrt{25} = 5$; $\sqrt{\frac{100}{4}} = \frac{10}{2} = 5$
3. See p. A10.

11-6 Exercises

Assignment Guide

Assign *Guided Practice* exercises as necessary.

If you finished Examples **1–3**
Basic 24–39
Average 24–39
Advanced 24–39, 70

If you finished Examples **1–5**
Basic 24–65, 67–69, 74–78
Average 24–78
Advanced 24–78

Homework Quick Check
Quickly check key concepts.
Exercises: 26, 30, 34, 38, 40, 44

Teaching Tip **Number Sense** Remind students of divisibility rules. If the number formed by the last two digits of a number is divisible by 4, as in **Exercises 17–19, 34,** and **35,** then the number is divisible by 4. If the sum of the digits of a number is divisible by 9, as in **Exercises 7, 17, 22,** and **34,** the number is divisible by 9.

State Resources

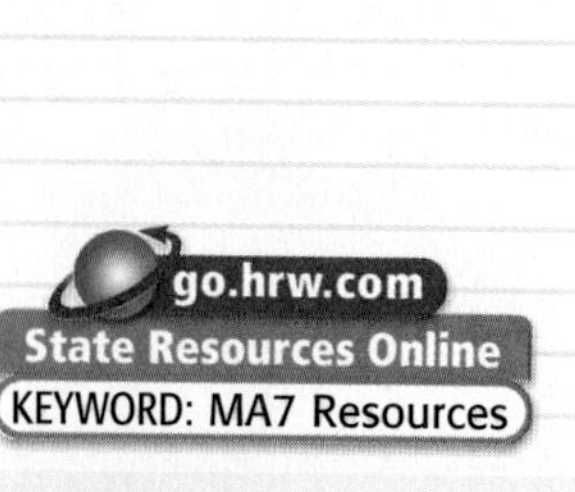

THINK AND DISCUSS

1. Show two ways to evaluate $\sqrt{16(9)}$.
2. Show two ways to evaluate $\sqrt{\frac{100}{4}}$.

3. **GET ORGANIZED** Copy and complete the graphic organizer. In each box, write the property and give an example.

	Product Property of Square Roots	Quotient Property of Square Roots
Words		
Example		

11-6 Exercises

GUIDED PRACTICE

1. **Vocabulary** In the expression $\sqrt{3x - 6} + 7$, what is the *radicand*? **3x − 6**

SEE EXAMPLE 1 p. 829

Simplify each expression.

2. $\sqrt{81}$ **9**
3. $\sqrt{\frac{98}{2}}$ **7**
4. $\sqrt{(a+7)^2}$ $|a+7|$

Simplify. All variables represent nonnegative numbers.

SEE EXAMPLE 2 p. 830

5. $\sqrt{180}$ $6\sqrt{5}$
6. $\sqrt{40}$ $2\sqrt{10}$
7. $\sqrt{648}$ $18\sqrt{2}$
8. $\sqrt{m^5n^3}$ $m^2n\sqrt{mn}$
9. $\sqrt{32x^4y^3}$ $4x^2y\sqrt{2y}$
10. $\sqrt{200a^2b}$ $10a\sqrt{2b}$

SEE EXAMPLE 3 p. 830

11. $\sqrt{\frac{17}{25}}$ $\frac{\sqrt{17}}{5}$
12. $\sqrt{\frac{7}{16}}$ $\frac{\sqrt{7}}{4}$
13. $\sqrt{\frac{6}{49}}$ $\frac{\sqrt{6}}{7}$
14. $\sqrt{\frac{b}{c^2}}$ $\frac{\sqrt{b}}{c}$
15. $\sqrt{\frac{4x^2}{36x}}$ $\frac{\sqrt{x}}{3}$
16. $\sqrt{\frac{7a^4}{9a^3}}$ $\frac{\sqrt{7a}}{3}$

SEE EXAMPLE 4 p. 831

17. $\sqrt{\frac{108}{49}}$ $\frac{6\sqrt{3}}{7}$
18. $\sqrt{\frac{204}{25}}$ $\frac{2\sqrt{51}}{5}$
19. $\sqrt{\frac{512}{81}}$ $\frac{16\sqrt{2}}{9}$
20. $\sqrt{\frac{1}{36x^2}}$ $\frac{1}{6x}$
21. $\sqrt{\frac{50x^2}{169}}$ $\frac{5x\sqrt{2}}{13}$
22. $\sqrt{\frac{72x^7}{4x^4}}$ $3x\sqrt{2x}$

SEE EXAMPLE 5 p. 831

23. **Recreation** Your boat is traveling due north from a dock. Your friend's boat left at the same time from the same dock and is headed due east. After an hour, your friend calls and tells you that he has just stopped because of engine trouble. How far must you travel to meet your friend? Give your answer as a radical expression in simplest form. Then estimate the distance to the nearest mile. $5\sqrt{41}$ **mi; 32 mi**

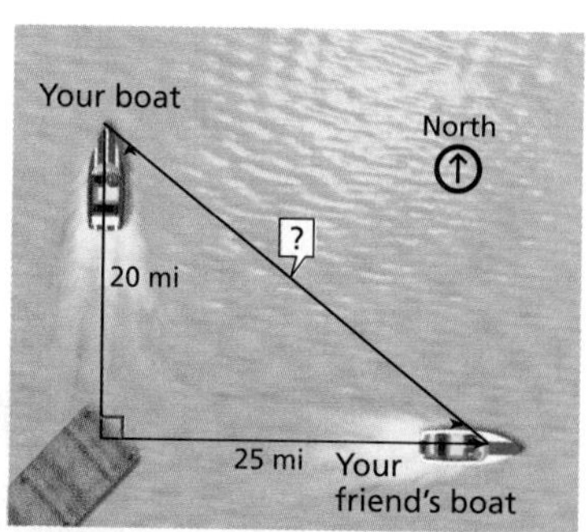

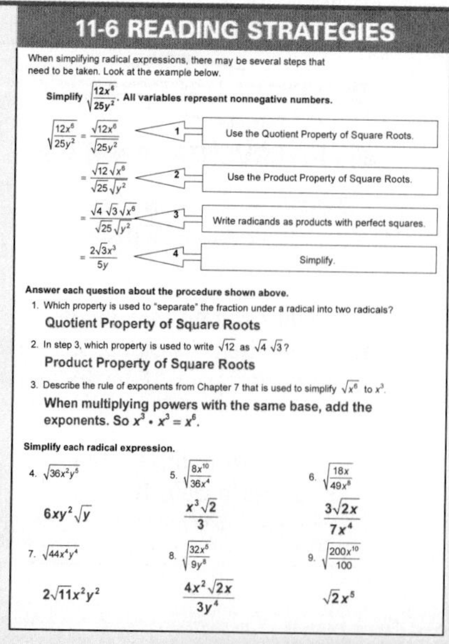

11-6 READING STRATEGIES

When simplifying radical expressions, there may be several steps that need to be taken. Look at the example below.

Simplify $\sqrt{\frac{12x^6}{25y^2}}$. All variables represent nonnegative numbers.

$\sqrt{\frac{12x^6}{25y^2}} = \frac{\sqrt{12x^6}}{\sqrt{25y^2}}$ — 1 Use the Quotient Property of Square Roots.

$= \frac{\sqrt{12}\sqrt{x^6}}{\sqrt{25}\sqrt{y^2}}$ — 2 Use the Product Property of Square Roots.

$= \frac{\sqrt{4}\sqrt{3}\sqrt{x^6}}{\sqrt{25}\sqrt{y^2}}$ — 3 Write radicands as products with perfect squares.

$= \frac{2\sqrt{3}x^3}{5y}$ — 4 Simplify.

Answer each question about the procedure shown above.

1. Which property is used to "separate" the fraction under a radical into two radicals?
Quotient Property of Square Roots
2. In step 3, which property is used to write $\sqrt{12}$ as $\sqrt{4}\sqrt{3}$?
Product Property of Square Roots
3. Describe the rule of exponents from Chapter 7 that is used to simplify $\sqrt{x^6}$ to x^3.
When multiplying powers with the same base, add the exponents. So $x^3 \cdot x^3 = x^6$.

Simplify each radical expression.

4. $\sqrt{36x^2y^5}$ $6xy^2\sqrt{y}$
5. $\sqrt{\frac{8x^{10}}{36x^4}}$ $\frac{x^3\sqrt{2}}{3}$
6. $\sqrt{\frac{18x}{49x^8}}$ $\frac{3\sqrt{2x}}{7x^4}$
7. $\sqrt{44x^4y^4}$ $2\sqrt{11}x^2y^2$
8. $\sqrt{\frac{32x^5}{9y^8}}$ $\frac{4x^2\sqrt{2x}}{3y^4}$
9. $\sqrt{\frac{200x^{10}}{100}}$ $\sqrt{2}x^5$

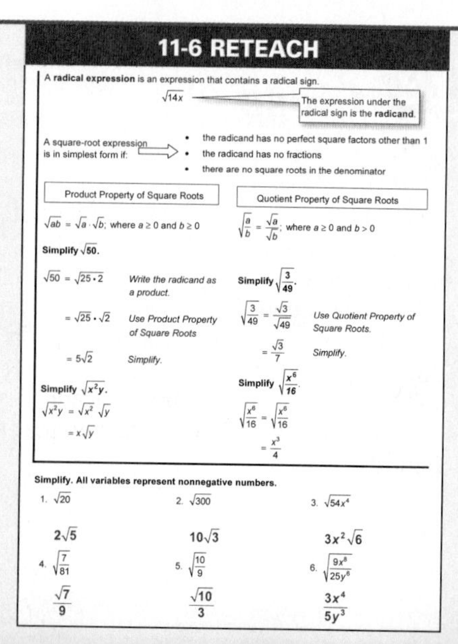

11-6 RETEACH

A **radical expression** is an expression that contains a radical sign.

$\sqrt{14x}$ — The expression under the radical sign is the **radicand**.

A square-root expression is in simplest form if:
- the radicand has no perfect square factors other than 1
- the radicand has no fractions
- there are no square roots in the denominator

Product Property of Square Roots	Quotient Property of Square Roots
$\sqrt{ab} = \sqrt{a} \cdot \sqrt{b}$; where $a \ge 0$ and $b \ge 0$	$\sqrt{\frac{a}{b}} = \frac{\sqrt{a}}{\sqrt{b}}$; where $a \ge 0$ and $b > 0$

Simplify $\sqrt{50}$.

$\sqrt{50} = \sqrt{25 \cdot 2}$ *Write the radicand as a product.*
$= \sqrt{25} \cdot \sqrt{2}$ *Use Product Property of Square Roots*
$= 5\sqrt{2}$ *Simplify.*

Simplify $\sqrt{\frac{3}{49}}$.

$\sqrt{\frac{3}{49}} = \frac{\sqrt{3}}{\sqrt{49}}$ *Use Quotient Property of Square Roots.*
$= \frac{\sqrt{3}}{7}$ *Simplify.*

Simplify $\sqrt{x^2y}$.

$\sqrt{x^2y} = \sqrt{x^2}\sqrt{y}$
$= x\sqrt{y}$

Simplify $\sqrt{\frac{x^6}{16}}$.

$\sqrt{\frac{x^6}{16}} = \sqrt{\frac{x^6}{16}}$
$= \frac{x^3}{4}$

Simplify. All variables represent nonnegative numbers.

1. $\sqrt{20}$ $2\sqrt{5}$
2. $\sqrt{300}$ $10\sqrt{3}$
3. $\sqrt{54x^4}$ $3x^2\sqrt{6}$
4. $\sqrt{\frac{7}{81}}$ $\frac{\sqrt{7}}{9}$
5. $\sqrt{\frac{10}{9}}$ $\frac{\sqrt{10}}{3}$
6. $\sqrt{\frac{9x^8}{25y^6}}$ $\frac{3x^4}{5y^3}$

PRACTICE AND PROBLEM SOLVING

Independent Practice

For Exercises	See Example
24–31	1
32–35	2
36–39	3
40–43	4
44	5

Extra Practice
Skills Practice p. S25
Application Practice p. S38

Simplify.

24. $\sqrt{100}$ **10**
25. $\sqrt{\frac{800}{2}}$ **20**
26. $\sqrt{3^2+4^2}$ **5**
27. $\sqrt{3 \cdot 27}$ **9**
28. $\sqrt{a^4}$ a^2
29. $\sqrt{(x+1)^2}$ $|x+1|$
30. $\sqrt{(5-x)^2}$ $|5-x|$
31. $\sqrt{(x-3)^2}$ $|x-3|$

Simplify. All variables represent nonnegative numbers.

32. $\sqrt{125}$ $5\sqrt{5}$
33. $\sqrt{4000}$ $20\sqrt{10}$
34. $\sqrt{216a^2b^2}$ $6ab\sqrt{6}$
35. $\sqrt{320r^2s^2}$ $8rs\sqrt{5}$
36. $\sqrt{\frac{15}{64}}$ $\frac{\sqrt{15}}{8}$
37. $\sqrt{\frac{45}{4}}$ $\frac{3\sqrt{5}}{2}$
38. $\sqrt{\frac{64a^4}{4a^6}}$ $\frac{4}{a}$
39. $\sqrt{\frac{14z^3}{9z^3}}$ $\frac{\sqrt{14}}{3}$
40. $\sqrt{\frac{128}{81}}$ $\frac{8\sqrt{2}}{9}$
41. $\sqrt{\frac{x^3}{y^6}}$ $\frac{x\sqrt{x}}{y^3}$
42. $\sqrt{\frac{150}{196x^2}}$ $\frac{5\sqrt{6}}{14x}$
43. $\sqrt{\frac{192s^3}{49s}}$ $\frac{8s\sqrt{3}}{7}$

44. **Amusement Parks** A thrill ride at an amusement park carries riders 160 feet straight up and then releases them for a free fall. The time t in seconds that it takes an object in free fall to reach the ground is $t = \sqrt{\frac{d}{16}}$, where d is the distance in feet that it falls. How long does it take the riders to reach the ground? Give your answer as a radical expression in simplest form. Then estimate the answer to the nearest tenth of a second. $\sqrt{10}$ **s; 3.2 s**

Simplify. All variables represent nonnegative numbers.

45. $-4\sqrt{75}$ $-20\sqrt{3}$
46. $-\sqrt{80}$ $-4\sqrt{5}$
47. $5x\sqrt{63}$ $15x\sqrt{7}$
48. $3\sqrt{48x}$ $12\sqrt{3x}$
49. $2\sqrt{\frac{x^2}{4}}$ x
50. $\frac{1}{2}\sqrt{\frac{1}{25}}$ $\frac{1}{10}$
51. $3x\sqrt{\frac{x^5}{81}}$ $\frac{x^3\sqrt{x}}{3}$
52. $\frac{12}{x}\sqrt{\frac{x^2y}{36}}$ $2\sqrt{y}$

Use the Product Property or the Quotient Property of Square Roots to write each expression as a single square root. Then simplify if possible.

53. $\sqrt{12}\sqrt{3}$ $\sqrt{36}$; 6
54. $\sqrt{18}\sqrt{8}$ $\sqrt{144}$; 12
55. $\sqrt{10}\sqrt{5}$
56. $\sqrt{8}\sqrt{14}$
57. $\frac{\sqrt{33}}{\sqrt{11}}$ $\sqrt{3}$
58. $\frac{\sqrt{24}}{\sqrt{2}}$ $\sqrt{12}$; $2\sqrt{3}$
59. $\frac{\sqrt{60}}{\sqrt{3}}$ $\sqrt{20}$; $2\sqrt{5}$
60. $\frac{\sqrt{72}}{\sqrt{9}}$ $\sqrt{8}$; $2\sqrt{2}$

55. $\sqrt{50}$; $5\sqrt{2}$
56. $\sqrt{112}$; $4\sqrt{7}$
61. 42 ft; length of missing side ≈ 17.2 ft, which will need to be rounded up to 18. $10 + 14 + 18 = 42$ ft

61. **Multi-Step** How many whole feet of fencing would be needed to enclose the triangular garden that is sketched at right? Explain your answer.

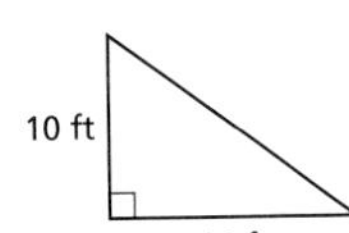

62. **Write About It** Write a series of steps that you could use to simplify $\sqrt{\frac{28}{49}}$.

63. This problem will prepare you for the Multi-Step Test Prep on page 854.
a. The vertical component of a roller coaster's speed in feet per second at the bottom of a hill is $v = \sqrt{64h}$, where h is the hill's height in feet. Simplify this expression. Then estimate the velocity at the bottom of a 137-foot hill.
b. The distance along the track of a hill is $d = \sqrt{x^2 + h^2}$, where x is the horizontal distance along the ground and h is the hill's height. Where does this equation come from?
c. For the hill in part a, the horizontal distance along the ground is 103 feet. What is the distance along the track? Round your answer to the nearest tenth. **171.4 ft**

a. $v = 8\sqrt{h}$; 93.6 ft/s
b. Pythagorean Theorem

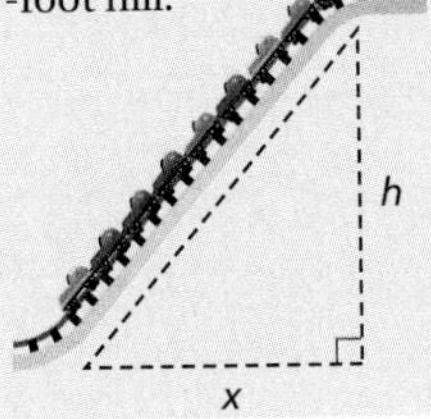

Teaching Tip

Communicating Math Not all denominators are perfect squares as in **Exercises 36–43.** Lesson 11-8 addresses denominators that are not perfect squares.

Exercise 63 involves using formulas with radical expressions. This exercise prepares students for the Multi-Step Test Prep on page 854.

Answers

62. Possible answer: Use the Quotient Property of Square Roots:
$\sqrt{\frac{28}{49}} = \frac{\sqrt{28}}{\sqrt{49}}$.
Then use the Product Property of Square Roots in the numerator:
$\frac{\sqrt{28}}{\sqrt{49}} = \frac{\sqrt{4 \cdot 7}}{\sqrt{49}} = \frac{\sqrt{4}\sqrt{7}}{\sqrt{49}}$.
Then simplify by taking the square roots of the perfect squares:
$\frac{\sqrt{4}\sqrt{7}}{\sqrt{49}} = \frac{2\sqrt{7}}{7}$.

11-6 PROBLEM SOLVING

Write the correct answer.

1. Annalise walks 200 meters from her house, turns a corner, and then walks another 100 meters to the bus stop. She wants to know how much shorter her walk would be if she cut across the field. Find the distance across the field from Annalise's house to the bus stop. Give your answer as a radical expression in simplest form. Then find the difference in the two routes to the nearest meter.

100 m
200 m

$100\sqrt{5}$ m; 76 m

2. A construction worker drops a nail from some scaffolding 192 feet from the ground. The nail is in freefall. The time t in seconds for an object in freefall to reach the ground is $t = \sqrt{\frac{d}{16}}$, where d is the distance in feet that it falls. The speed v in feet per second of an object in freefall is modeled by $v = 8\sqrt{d}$. Determine how long it takes the nail to reach the ground. Also find the speed the nail is traveling at 192 feet. Give your answers as radical expressions in simplest form. Then estimate the time to the nearest second and the speed to the nearest foot per second.

time: $2\sqrt{3}$ s, 3s;
speed: $64\sqrt{3}$ ft/s, 111 ft/s

Police officers determine the speed a car was traveling when the driver slammed on the brakes by measuring the length of skid marks left by the tires. On dry concrete, $f(x) = \sqrt{24x}$ gives the speed in mi/h when the length of the skid marks is x feet. The graph shows lengths of skid marks from several cars. Select the best answer.

Length of Skid Marks
Car A 140, Car B 52, Car C 90, Car D 110
Length (feet); Car

3. Which shows the speed of car A in simplest radical form?
A $\sqrt{3360}$ mi/h
C $4\sqrt{210}$ mi/h
B $2\sqrt{840}$ mi/h
D $16\sqrt{210}$ mi/h

4. Which shows the speed of car B in simplest radical form?
F $2\sqrt{78}$ mi/h
H $8\sqrt{78}$ mi/h
G $4\sqrt{78}$ mi/h
J $16\sqrt{78}$ mi/h

5. Which shows the speed of car C in simplest radical form?
A $2\sqrt{540}$ mi/h
C $12\sqrt{15}$ mi/h
B $4\sqrt{135}$ mi/h
D $16\sqrt{135}$ mi/h

6. The driver of car D claims his skid marks were really only 60% as long as officers claim they were. If the driver is telling the truth, what was his speed in simplest radical form?
F $\sqrt{66}$ mi/h
H $2\sqrt{396}$ mi/h
G $\sqrt{1584}$ mi/h
J $12\sqrt{11}$ mi/h

11-6 CHALLENGE

The diagram below is the beginning of a square-root spiral. It begins with an isosceles right triangle (A) that has two 1-inch legs. Then another right triangle (B) with a 1-inch leg is constructed on the hypotenuse, and then another (C), and another (D), and so on.

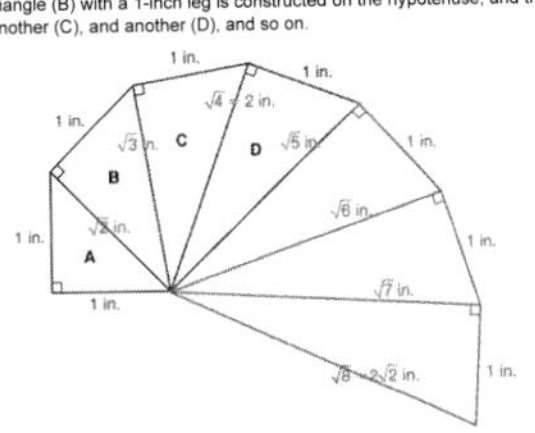

1. Use the Pythagorean Theorem to calculate the length of the hypotenuse of each triangle above. Give each answer as a radical expression. Label the lengths on the diagram as well.
a. Triangle A $\sqrt{2}$ in.
b. Triangle B $\sqrt{4} = 2$ in.
c. Triangle C $\sqrt{3}$ in.
d. Triangle D $\sqrt{5}$ in.

2. Describe any patterns you see in the lengths of the hypotenuses.
The length of each hypotenuse is a square root expression in which the radicand increases by 1 from the previous hypotenuse.

3. Use a ruler, protractor, and/or compass to draw the next three right triangles in the spiral. Extend the pattern in the lengths of the hypotenuses to label the sides of each new triangle.

4. How could you draw a segment that represents $\sqrt{13}$?
Continue the spiral until you have 12 triangles; the length of the hypotenuse of the 12th triangle will be $\sqrt{13}$ in.

5. In general, what is the length of the hypotenuse of the nth triangle in the spiral? $\sqrt{n+1}$ in.

11-6 PRACTICE A
11-6 PRACTICE C
11-6 PRACTICE B

Simplify each expression.

1. $\sqrt{225} = 15$
2. $\sqrt{\frac{75}{3}} = \sqrt{25} = 5$
3. $\sqrt{7^2 + 24^2} = 25$
4. $\sqrt{(x+8)^2} = |x+8|$
5. $\sqrt{\frac{4}{100}} = \frac{1}{5}$
6. $\sqrt{x^2 + 8x + 16} = |x+4|$

Simplify. All variables represent nonnegative numbers.

7. $\sqrt{32}$ $4\sqrt{2}$
8. $\sqrt{28}$ $2\sqrt{7}$
9. $\sqrt{x^4y^3}$ $x^2y\sqrt{y}$
10. $\sqrt{147}$ $7\sqrt{3}$
11. $\sqrt{45}$ $3\sqrt{5}$
12. $\sqrt{36x^4y^5}$ $6x^2y^2\sqrt{y}$
13. $\sqrt{\frac{7}{25}}$ $\frac{\sqrt{7}}{5}$
14. $\sqrt{\frac{3b^2}{27b^4}}$ $\frac{1}{3b}$
15. $\sqrt{\frac{m^3}{121n^4}}$ $\frac{m\sqrt{m}}{11n^2}$
16. $\sqrt{\frac{10b^4}{2b^3}}$ $\sqrt{5b}$
17. $\sqrt{\frac{9y^6}{36y^2}}$ $\frac{y^2}{2}$
18. $\sqrt{\frac{40m^3}{10n^4}}$ $\frac{2m\sqrt{m}}{n^2}$
19. $\sqrt{\frac{128}{25}}$ $\frac{8\sqrt{2}}{5}$
20. $\sqrt{\frac{4}{81x^8}}$ $\frac{2}{9x^4}$
21. $\sqrt{\frac{250q^{10}}{5q^4}}$ $5q^3\sqrt{2}$

22. Two hikers leave a ranger station at noon. Tom heads due south at 5 mi/h and Kyle heads due east at 3 mi/h. How far apart are the hikers at 4 PM? Give your answer as a radical expression in simplest form. Then estimate the distance to the nearest tenth of a mile.

$4\sqrt{34}$ mi; 23.3 mi

In **Exercise 67,** choices **A** and **D** are easily eliminated because the radicands are perfect squares. Students who chose **B** probably did not see that 16 is a factor of 48.

In **Exercise 69,** students need to first take the square root of 100 to get the side length of the square. Then they can use the Pythagorean Theorem to determine the length of the diagonal.

Journal

Have students explain the Product and Quotient Properties of Square Roots, using examples as needed.

ALTERNATIVE ASSESSMENT

Write $\sqrt{\frac{800x^5}{25x}}$ on the board. Have students simplify the expression and explain when the variable needs an absolute-value symbol.

Power Presentations with PowerPoint®

11-6 Lesson Quiz

Simplify each expression.

1. $\sqrt{31+5}$ 6
2. $\sqrt{x^2+10x+25}$ $|x+5|$

Simplify. All variables represent nonnegative numbers.

3. $\sqrt{50}$ $5\sqrt{2}$
4. $\sqrt{\frac{28}{81}}$ $\frac{2\sqrt{7}}{9}$
5. $\sqrt{a^3b^5}$ $ab^2\sqrt{ab}$
6. $\sqrt{\frac{27x^3}{48}}$ $\frac{3x\sqrt{x}}{4}$
7. Two archaeologists leave from the same campsite. One travels 10 miles due north and the other travels 6 miles due west. How far apart are the archaeologists? Give the answer as a radical expression in simplest form. Then estimate the distance to the nearest tenth of a mile. $2\sqrt{34}$ mi; 11.7 mi

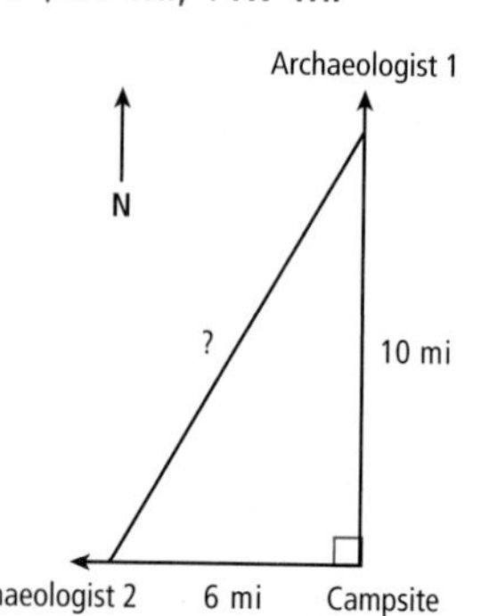

Also available on transparency

64. **Critical Thinking** The Product Property of Square Roots states that $\sqrt{ab}=\sqrt{a}\sqrt{b}$, where $a \geq 0$ and $b \geq 0$. Why must a and b be greater than or equal to zero?
Possible answer: The square root of a neg. number is not a real number.

65. **Architecture** The formula $d=\frac{\sqrt{6h}}{3}$ estimates the distance d in miles that a person can see to the horizon from h feet above the ground. Find the distance you could see to the horizon from the top of each building in the graph. Give your answers as radical expressions in simplest form and as estimates to the nearest tenth of a mile.

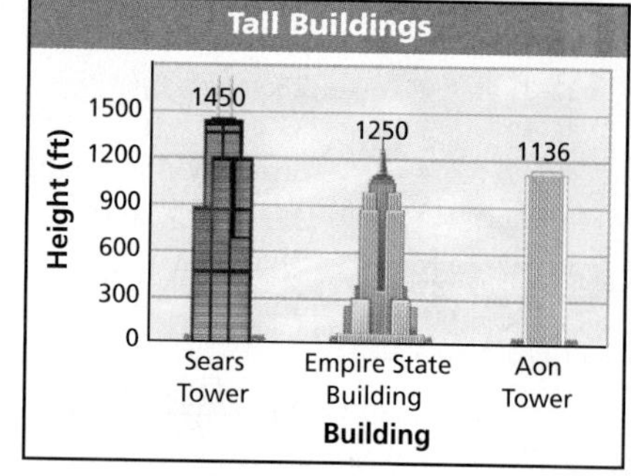

LINK Math History

Heron of Alexandria, Egypt, also called Hero, lived around 60 C.E. Heron's formula for the area of a triangle can be found in Book I of his *Metrica*.

66. **Math History** Heron's formula for the area A of a triangle is $A=\sqrt{s(s-a)(s-b)(s-c)}$, where a, b, and c are the side lengths and $s=\frac{1}{2}(a+b+c)$. Find the area of a triangle with side lengths of 7 m, 9 m, and 12 m. Give your answer as a radical expression in simplest form and as an estimate to the nearest tenth. **$14\sqrt{5}$ m²; 31.3 m²**

TEST PREP

67. Which expression is in simplest form?
Ⓐ $\sqrt{49}$ Ⓑ $\sqrt{48}$ **Ⓒ $\sqrt{35}$** Ⓓ $\sqrt{36}$

68. Which expression is equal to $\sqrt{60}$?
Ⓕ $2\sqrt{15}$ Ⓖ $6\sqrt{10}$ Ⓗ $15\sqrt{2}$ Ⓙ $10\sqrt{60}$

69. How long is the diagonal of a square whose area is 100 square feet?
Ⓐ $2\sqrt{10}$ feet Ⓑ 10 feet **Ⓒ $10\sqrt{2}$ feet** Ⓓ 20 feet

CHALLENGE AND EXTEND

Simplify. All variables represent nonnegative numbers.

70. $\sqrt{4x+16}$ **$2\sqrt{x+4}$**
71. $\sqrt{x^3+x^2}$ **$x\sqrt{x+1}$**
72. $\sqrt{9x^3-18x^2}$ **$3x\sqrt{x-2}$**
73. Let x represent any real number (including negative numbers). Simplify each of the following expressions, using absolute-value symbols when necessary.
a. $\sqrt{x^2}$ **$|x|$** b. $\sqrt{x^4}$ **x^2** c. $\sqrt{x^6}$ **$|x^3|$** d. $\sqrt{x^8}$ **x^4** e. $\sqrt{x^{10}}$ **$|x^5|$**
f. For any nonnegative integer n, $\sqrt{x^{2n}}$ = **x^n** if n is even, and $\sqrt{x^{2n}}$ = **$|x^n|$** if n is odd.

SPIRAL REVIEW

Tell whether each relationship is a direct variation. Explain. *(Lesson 5-6)*

74. **yes**

x	2	3	4
y	12	18	24

75. **no**

x	2	3	4
y	−6	−5	−4

76. Write an equation in slope-intercept form for the line through (3, 1) and (2, −5). *(Lesson 5-7)* **$y=6x-17$**

Graph each data set. Which kind of model best describes the data? *(Lesson 11-4)*

77. $\{(-3,16),(-2,8),(0,2),(1,1),(3,0.25)\}$ **exponential**
78. $\{(-5,15),(-2,-6),(0,-10),(3,-1),(4,6)\}$ **quadratic**

Answers

65. Sears: $\frac{10\sqrt{87}}{3}$ mi; 31.1 mi
Empire: $\frac{50\sqrt{3}}{3}$ mi; 28.9 mi
Aon: $\frac{4\sqrt{426}}{3}$ mi; 27.5 mi
74. Possible answer: Its rule can be written in the form $y=kx$, where $k=6$.
75. Possible answer: The value of $\frac{y}{x}$ is not the same for each ordered pair.

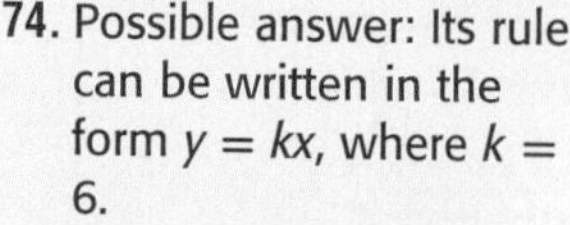

77.
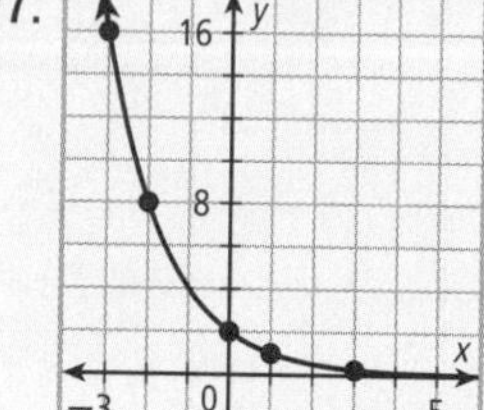

78.
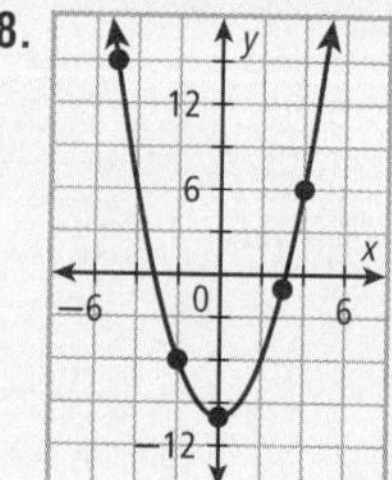

11-7 Adding and Subtracting Radical Expressions

Objective
Add and subtract radical expressions.

Vocabulary
like radicals

Why learn this?
You can add or subtract radical expressions to find perimeter. (See Example 3.)

Square-root expressions with the same radicand are examples of **like radicals**.

Like Radicals	$2\sqrt{5}$ and $4\sqrt{5}$	$6\sqrt{x}$ and $-2\sqrt{x}$	$3\sqrt{4t}$ and $\sqrt{4t}$
Unlike Radicals	2 and $\sqrt{15}$	$6\sqrt{x}$ and $\sqrt{6x}$	$3\sqrt{2}$ and $2\sqrt{3}$

Like radicals can be combined by adding or subtracting. You can use the Distributive Property to show how this is done:

$$2\sqrt{5} + 4\sqrt{5} = (2 + 4)\sqrt{5} = 6\sqrt{5}$$

$$6\sqrt{x} - 2\sqrt{x} = (6 - 2)\sqrt{x} = 4\sqrt{x}$$

Notice that you can combine like radicals by adding or subtracting the numbers multiplied by the radical and keeping the radical the same.

Helpful Hint

Combining like radicals is similar to combining like terms.
$2\sqrt{5} + 4\sqrt{5} = 6\sqrt{5}$
$2x + 4x = 6x$

EXAMPLE 1 Adding and Subtracting Square-Root Expressions

Add or subtract.

A $3\sqrt{7} + 8\sqrt{7}$
$3\sqrt{7} + 8\sqrt{7}$ — *The terms are like radicals.*
$11\sqrt{7}$

B $9\sqrt{y} - \sqrt{y}$
$9\sqrt{y} - 1\sqrt{y}$ — *$\sqrt{y} = 1\sqrt{y}$; the terms are like radicals.*
$8\sqrt{y}$

C $12\sqrt{2} - 4\sqrt{11}$
$12\sqrt{2} - 4\sqrt{11}$ — *The terms are unlike radicals. Do not combine.*

D $-8\sqrt{3d} + 6\sqrt{2d} + 10\sqrt{3d}$
$-8\sqrt{3d} + 6\sqrt{2d} + 10\sqrt{3d}$ — *Identify like radicals.*
$2\sqrt{3d} + 6\sqrt{2d}$ — *Combine like radicals.*

Add or subtract.

1a. $5\sqrt{7} - 6\sqrt{7}$ **$-\sqrt{7}$**
1b. $8\sqrt{3} - 5\sqrt{3}$ **$3\sqrt{3}$**
1c. $4\sqrt{n} + 4\sqrt{n}$ **$8\sqrt{n}$**
1d. $\sqrt{2s} - \sqrt{5s} + 9\sqrt{5s}$ **$\sqrt{2s} + 8\sqrt{5s}$**

Sometimes radicals do not appear to be like until they are simplified. Simplify all radicals in an expression before trying to identify like radicals.

11-7 Organizer

Pacing: Traditional 1 day
Block $\frac{1}{2}$ day

Objective: Add and subtract radical expressions.

Algebra Lab
In *Algebra Lab Activities*

Online Edition
Tutorial Videos

Power Presentations with PowerPoint®

Warm Up

Simplify each expression.

1. $14x + 15y - 12y + x$ $15x + 3y$

2. $9xy + 2xy - 8xy$ $3xy$

3. $-3(a + b) + 5\left(2 + \frac{2}{5}b\right)$ $-3a - b + 10$

Simplify. All variables represent nonnegative numbers.

4. $\sqrt{96}$ $4\sqrt{6}$

5. $\sqrt{x^9y^{10}}$ $x^4y^5\sqrt{x}$

6. $\sqrt{\frac{72a^5}{81}}$ $\frac{2a^2\sqrt{2a}}{3}$

Also available on transparency

Q: What did the surfer say when he saw the square root of two?
A: Radical, dude!

1 Introduce

EXPLORATION

11-7 Adding and Subtracting Radical Expressions

You will need a calculator for this Exploration.

1. Find a decimal approximation for each expression in the table. Round to the nearest thousandth.

Expression	Decimal Approximation	Expression	Decimal Approximation
$2\sqrt{3} + 3\sqrt{3}$		$5\sqrt{3}$	
$8\sqrt{2} - 5\sqrt{2}$		$3\sqrt{2}$	
$4\sqrt{7} + 11\sqrt{7}$		$15\sqrt{7}$	

2. What do you notice in the table?
3. Find a decimal approximation for each expression in the table. Round to the nearest thousandth.

Expression	Decimal Approximation	Expression	Decimal Approximation
$\sqrt{7} + \sqrt{3}$		$\sqrt{10}$	
$\sqrt{25} + \sqrt{9}$		$\sqrt{34}$	
$\sqrt{17} - \sqrt{5}$		$\sqrt{12}$	

THINK AND DISCUSS

4. **Describe** a conjecture you can make based on your findings in the first table.
5. **Discuss** whether $\sqrt{a} + \sqrt{b} = \sqrt{a + b}$ and whether $\sqrt{a} - \sqrt{b} = \sqrt{a - b}$.

Motivate

Write the following on the board. $3a + 8a =$ ___

Ask students to simplify this expression by filling in the blank. After they have written $3a + 8a = \underline{11a}$, substitute $\sqrt{7}$ for a and have them simplify $3\sqrt{7} + 8\sqrt{7} =$ ___ by filling in the blank.
$3\sqrt{7} + 8\sqrt{7} = \underline{11\sqrt{7}}$

Ask students how many terms are in the simplified expression. 1

Explorations and answers are provided in *Alternate Openers: Explorations Transparencies.*

State Resources

EXAMPLE 2 Simplifying Before Adding or Subtracting

Simplify each expression.

A $\sqrt{12} + \sqrt{27}$

$\sqrt{4(3)} + \sqrt{9(3)}$	*Factor the radicands using perfect squares.*
$\sqrt{4}\sqrt{3} + \sqrt{9}\sqrt{3}$	*Product Property of Square Roots*
$2\sqrt{3} + 3\sqrt{3}$	*Simplify.*
$5\sqrt{3}$	*Combine like radicals.*

B $3\sqrt{8} + \sqrt{45}$

$3\sqrt{4(2)} + \sqrt{9(5)}$	*Factor the radicands using perfect squares.*
$3\sqrt{4}\sqrt{2} + \sqrt{9}\sqrt{5}$	*Product Property of Square Roots*
$3(2)\sqrt{2} + 3\sqrt{5}$	*Simplify.*
$6\sqrt{2} + 3\sqrt{5}$	*The terms are unlike radicals. Do not combine.*

C $5\sqrt{28x} - 8\sqrt{7x}$

$5\sqrt{4(7x)} - 8\sqrt{7x}$	*Factor 28x using a perfect square.*
$5\sqrt{4}\sqrt{7x} - 8\sqrt{7x}$	*Product Property of Square Roots*
$5(2)\sqrt{7x} - 8\sqrt{7x}$	*Simplify.*
$10\sqrt{7x} - 8\sqrt{7x}$	
$2\sqrt{7x}$	*Combine like radicals.*

D $\sqrt{125b} + 3\sqrt{20b} - \sqrt{45b}$

$\sqrt{25(5b)} + 3\sqrt{4(5b)} - \sqrt{9(5b)}$	*Factor the radicands using perfect squares.*
$\sqrt{25}\sqrt{5b} + 3\sqrt{4}\sqrt{5b} - \sqrt{9}\sqrt{5b}$	*Product Property of Square Roots*
$5\sqrt{5b} + 3(2)\sqrt{5b} - 3\sqrt{5b}$	*Simplify.*
$5\sqrt{5b} + 6\sqrt{5b} - 3\sqrt{5b}$	
$8\sqrt{5b}$	*Combine like radicals.*

Remember!

When you write a radicand as a product, make at least one factor a perfect square.

Simplify each expression.

2a. $\sqrt{54} + \sqrt{24}$ **$5\sqrt{6}$** **2b.** $4\sqrt{27} - \sqrt{18}$ **$12\sqrt{3} - 3\sqrt{2}$** **2c.** $\sqrt{12y} + \sqrt{27y}$ **$5\sqrt{3y}$**

EXAMPLE 3 *Geometry Application*

Find the perimeter of the triangle. Give your answer as a radical expression in simplest form.

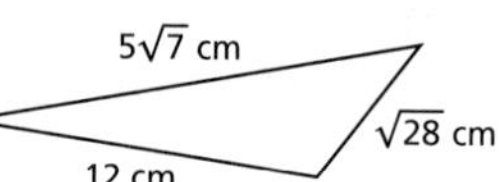

$12 + 5\sqrt{7} + \sqrt{28}$	*Write an expression for perimeter.*
$12 + 5\sqrt{7} + \sqrt{4(7)}$	*Factor 28 using a perfect square.*
$12 + 5\sqrt{7} + \sqrt{4}\sqrt{7}$	*Product Property of Square Roots*
$12 + 5\sqrt{7} + 2\sqrt{7}$	*Simplify.*
$12 + 7\sqrt{7}$	*Combine like radicals.*

The perimeter is $(12 + 7\sqrt{7})$ cm.

3. Find the perimeter of a rectangle whose length is $2\sqrt{b}$ inches and whose width is $3\sqrt{b}$ inches. Give your answer as a radical expression in simplest form. **$10\sqrt{b}$ in.**

Power Presentations with PowerPoint®

Additional Examples

Example 1

Add or subtract.

A. $9\sqrt{3} - 4\sqrt{3}$ $5\sqrt{3}$

B. $6\sqrt{x} + 8\sqrt{y}$ $6\sqrt{x} + 8\sqrt{y}$

C. $\sqrt{m} - 7\sqrt{m}$ $-6\sqrt{m}$

D. $2\sqrt{xy} + 2\sqrt{y} + 9\sqrt{xy}$ $11\sqrt{xy} + 2\sqrt{y}$

Example 2

Simplify each expression.

A. $\sqrt{45} - \sqrt{20}$ $\sqrt{5}$

B. $9\sqrt{75} + 2\sqrt{50}$ $45\sqrt{3} + 10\sqrt{2}$

C. $\sqrt{75y} - 2\sqrt{27y} + \sqrt{48y}$ $3\sqrt{3y}$

Example 3

Find the perimeter of the triangle. Give the answer as a radical expression in simplest form.

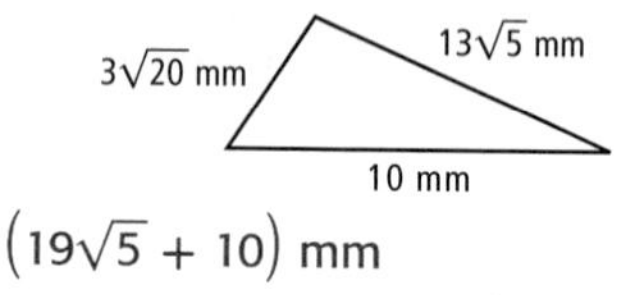

$(19\sqrt{5} + 10)$ mm

INTERVENTION

Questioning Strategies

EXAMPLES 1–3

- How do you know which terms can be combined?
- How do you decide which numbers to use when you write a radicand as a product?

2 Teach

Guided Instruction

Students can use their calculators to check numerical problems by comparing the values of the original and simplified expressions. Students can check algebraic problems by substituting a number for the variable in the original and simplified expressions and then comparing their values. Calculator displays show only the first part of an irrational number. Show students how to type in expressions involving radicals all at once, avoiding the need to write down partial calculations.

3 Close

Summarize

Tell students that terms with like radicals can be combined by adding or subtracting the coefficients and keeping the radical the same. As a first step, all radicals should be simplified until the expressions under the radical signs have no perfect square factors.

ONGOING ASSESSMENT and INTERVENTION

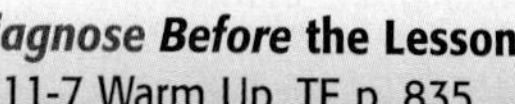

***Diagnose Before* the Lesson**
11-7 Warm Up, TE p. 835

***Monitor During* the Lesson**
Check It Out! Exercises, SE pp. 835–836
Questioning Strategies, TE p. 836

***Assess After* the Lesson**
11-7 Lesson Quiz, TE p. 839
Alternative Assessment, TE p. 839

THINK AND DISCUSS

1. Rearrange the following into two groups of like radicals: $2\sqrt{6}$, $6\sqrt{5}$, $\sqrt{600}$, $\sqrt{150}$, $-\sqrt{20}$, $\sqrt{5}$.
2. Tell why you should simplify radicals when adding and subtracting expressions with radicals.

3. **GET ORGANIZED** Copy and complete the graphic organizer.

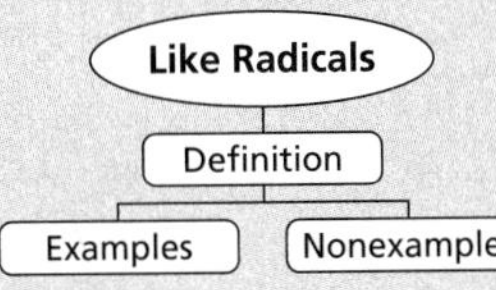

Answers to *Think and Discuss*

1. $2\sqrt{6}$, $\sqrt{600}$, $\sqrt{150}$; $6\sqrt{5}$, $-\sqrt{20}$, $\sqrt{5}$
2. Possible answer: Without simplifying, you cannot tell which terms are like radicals.
3. See p. A10.

11-7 Exercises

GUIDED PRACTICE

1. **Vocabulary** Give an example of *like radicals*. **Possible answer: $4\sqrt{6}$ and $-2\sqrt{6}$**

SEE EXAMPLE 1 p. 835

Add or subtract.

2. $14\sqrt{3} - 6\sqrt{3}$ **$8\sqrt{3}$**
3. $9\sqrt{5} + \sqrt{5}$ **$10\sqrt{5}$**
4. $6\sqrt{2} + 5\sqrt{2} - 15\sqrt{2}$ **$-4\sqrt{2}$**
5. $3\sqrt{7} + 5\sqrt{2}$ **$3\sqrt{7} + 5\sqrt{2}$**
6. $5\sqrt{a} - 9\sqrt{a}$ **$-4\sqrt{a}$**
7. $9\sqrt{6a} + 6\sqrt{5a} - 4\sqrt{6a}$ **$5\sqrt{6a} + 6\sqrt{5a}$**

SEE EXAMPLE 2 p. 836

Simplify each expression.

8. $\sqrt{32} - \sqrt{8}$ **$2\sqrt{2}$**
9. $4\sqrt{12} + \sqrt{75}$ **$13\sqrt{3}$**
10. $2\sqrt{3} + 5\sqrt{12} - \sqrt{27}$ **$9\sqrt{3}$**
11. $\sqrt{20x} - \sqrt{45x}$ **$-\sqrt{5x}$**
12. $\sqrt{28c} + 9\sqrt{24c}$ **$2\sqrt{7c} + 18\sqrt{6c}$**
13. $\sqrt{50t} - 2\sqrt{12t} + 3\sqrt{2t}$ **$8\sqrt{2t} - 4\sqrt{3t}$**

SEE EXAMPLE 3 p. 836

14. **Geometry** Find the perimeter of the trapezoid shown. Give your answer as a radical expression in simplest form. **$12\sqrt{2}$ in.**

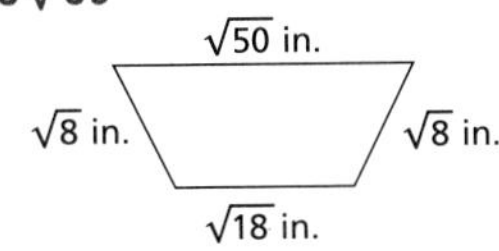

Assignment Guide

Assign *Guided Practice* exercises as necessary.

If you finished Examples **1–3**

Basic	15–56, 59–61, 71–76
Average	15–30, 32–38 even, 39, 40–48 even, 49–63, 71–78
Advanced	16–30 even, 31–47, 49–76

Homework Quick Check
Quickly check key concepts.
Exercises: 16, 20, 22, 26, 30, 40

PRACTICE AND PROBLEM SOLVING

Independent Practice

For Exercises	See Example
15–20	1
21–29	2
30	3

Extra Practice
Skills Practice p. S25
Application Practice p. S38

Add or subtract.

15. $4\sqrt{3} + 2\sqrt{3}$ **$6\sqrt{3}$**
16. $\frac{1}{2}\sqrt{72} - 12$ **$3\sqrt{2} - 12$**
17. $2\sqrt{11} + \sqrt{11} - 6\sqrt{11}$ **$-3\sqrt{11}$**
18. $6\sqrt{7} + 7\sqrt{6}$ **$6\sqrt{7} + 7\sqrt{6}$**
19. $-3\sqrt{n} - \sqrt{n}$ **$-4\sqrt{n}$**
20. $2\sqrt{2y} + 3\sqrt{2y} - 2\sqrt{3y}$ **$5\sqrt{2y} - 2\sqrt{3y}$**

Simplify each expression.

21. $\sqrt{175} + \sqrt{28}$ **$7\sqrt{7}$**
22. $2\sqrt{80} - \sqrt{20}$ **$6\sqrt{5}$**
23. $5\sqrt{8} - \sqrt{32} + 2\sqrt{18}$ **$12\sqrt{2}$**
24. $\sqrt{150r} + \sqrt{54r}$ **$8\sqrt{6r}$**
25. $\sqrt{63x} - 4\sqrt{27x}$
26. $\sqrt{48p} + 3\sqrt{18p} - 2\sqrt{27p}$
27. $\sqrt{180j} - \sqrt{45j}$ **$3\sqrt{5j}$**
28. $3\sqrt{90c} - \sqrt{40c}$ **$7\sqrt{10c}$**
29. $2\sqrt{75m} - \sqrt{12m} - \sqrt{108m}$

Answers

25. $3\sqrt{7x} - 12\sqrt{3x}$
26. $9\sqrt{2p} - 2\sqrt{3p}$
29. $2\sqrt{3m}$

State Resources

Teaching Tip **Math Background** Remind students that radical expressions can be written as exponential expressions. For instance, $\sqrt{x} = x^{\frac{1}{2}}$. Therefore, the like radicals $18\sqrt{ab}$ and $10\sqrt{ab}$ in **Exercise 32** are like terms because they are terms that contain the same variable to the same power, $18a^{\frac{1}{2}}b^{\frac{1}{2}}$ and $10a^{\frac{1}{2}}b^{\frac{1}{2}}$.

Exercise 56 involves using the radius and diameter of a circle. This exercise prepares students for the Multi-Step Test Prep on page 854.

Answers

39c. Because the areas found in parts **a** and **b** must be equal, the model shows that $3\sqrt{11} + 2\sqrt{11} + 5\sqrt{11} = (3 + 2 + 5)\sqrt{11} = 10\sqrt{11}$.

49. Possible answer: Like radicals have the same radicands; examples: $\sqrt{2}$ and $3\sqrt{2}$; nonexamples: $\sqrt{5}$ and $\sqrt{3}$.

11-7 PRACTICE A

11-7 PRACTICE C

11-7 PRACTICE B

Add or subtract.

1. $9\sqrt{7} + 4\sqrt{7} = \mathbf{13\sqrt{7}}$
2. $-10\sqrt{5} + 2\sqrt{5} = \mathbf{-8\sqrt{5}}$
3. $4\sqrt{y} + 6\sqrt{y} = \mathbf{10\sqrt{y}}$
4. $-2\sqrt{3b} + 10\sqrt{3b} = \mathbf{8\sqrt{3b}}$
5. $6\sqrt{15} - \sqrt{15} + \sqrt{15} = \mathbf{6\sqrt{15}}$
6. $5\sqrt{2} - 3\sqrt{2x} - 4\sqrt{2} = \mathbf{\sqrt{2} - 3\sqrt{2x}}$

Simplify each expression.

7. $\sqrt{108} + \sqrt{75}$ **$11\sqrt{3}$**
8. $\sqrt{63} + \sqrt{175} + \sqrt{112}$ **$12\sqrt{7}$**
9. $\sqrt{28x} + \sqrt{63x}$ **$5\sqrt{7x}$**
10. $\sqrt{45} + \sqrt{180}$ **$9\sqrt{5}$**
11. $\sqrt{52} - \sqrt{1300}$ **$-8\sqrt{13}$**
12. $5\sqrt{98} - 3\sqrt{32}$ **$23\sqrt{2}$**
13. $\sqrt{32} + \sqrt{128}$ **$12\sqrt{2}$**
14. $\sqrt{147} + 6\sqrt{3}$ **$13\sqrt{3}$**
15. $\sqrt{168} + \sqrt{42}$ **$3\sqrt{42}$**
16. $5\sqrt{17} + 17\sqrt{5}$ **$5\sqrt{17} + 17\sqrt{5}$**
17. $6\sqrt{3} + \sqrt{300}$ **$16\sqrt{3}$**
18. $-2\sqrt{3b} + \sqrt{27b}$ **$\sqrt{3b}$**
19. $4\sqrt{2m} + 6\sqrt{3m} - 4\sqrt{2m}$ **$6\sqrt{3m}$**
20. $\sqrt{50m} + \sqrt{72m}$ **$11\sqrt{2m}$**
21. $\sqrt{16z} + 2\sqrt{8z} - 3\sqrt{z}$ **$\sqrt{z} + 4\sqrt{2z}$**
22. $\sqrt{216t} + \sqrt{96t}$ **$10\sqrt{6t}$**
23. $4\sqrt{52x} + \sqrt{117x} - 2\sqrt{13}$ **$11\sqrt{13x} - 2\sqrt{13}$**
24. $3\sqrt{96k} + 2\sqrt{180}$ **$12\sqrt{6k} + 12\sqrt{5}$**
25. Write the numbers $3\sqrt{8}$, $4\sqrt{2}$ and $\sqrt{50}$ in order from least to greatest. **$4\sqrt{2}, \sqrt{50}3, \sqrt{8}$**
26. The map at right shows the path traveled by a delivery person on his afternoon route. Write the total distance traveled as a simplified radical expression. **$5 + 8\sqrt{7}$ miles**

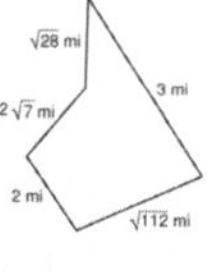

30. **Fitness** What is the total length of the jogging path? Give your answer as a radical expression in simplest form. **$2 + 4\sqrt{2}$ mi**

Simplify each expression.

31. $5\sqrt{7} + 7\sqrt{7}$ **$12\sqrt{7}$**
32. $18\sqrt{ab} - 10\sqrt{ab}$ **$8\sqrt{ab}$**
33. $-3\sqrt{3} + 3\sqrt{3}$ **0**
34. $\sqrt{98} + \sqrt{128}$ **$15\sqrt{2}$**
35. $\sqrt{300} - \sqrt{27}$ **$7\sqrt{3}$**
36. $\sqrt{45x} + \sqrt{500x}$ **$13\sqrt{5x}$**
37. $\frac{5}{2}\sqrt{8} + \frac{\sqrt{32}}{2}$ **$7\sqrt{2}$**
38. $\frac{1}{6}\sqrt{18} - \frac{\sqrt{2}}{2}$ **0**

39. **Geometry** Use the diagram to answer the following:
    a. What is the area of section A? section B? section C? **$3\sqrt{11}$; $2\sqrt{11}$; $5\sqrt{11}$**
    b. What is the combined area of the three sections?
    c. Explain how this model relates to adding like radicals.

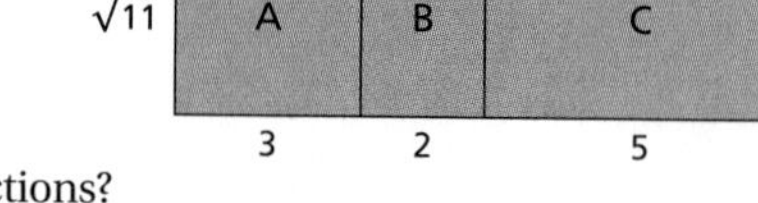

39b. $10\sqrt{11}$

Simplify each expression.

40. $\sqrt{450ab} - \sqrt{50ab}$ **$10\sqrt{2ab}$**
41. $\sqrt{12} + \sqrt{125} + \sqrt{25}$ **$2\sqrt{3} + 5\sqrt{5} + 5$**
42. $\sqrt{338} - \sqrt{18}$ **$10\sqrt{2}$**
43. $\sqrt{700x} - \sqrt{28x} - \sqrt{70x}$ **$8\sqrt{7x} - \sqrt{70x}$**
44. $-3\sqrt{90} - 3\sqrt{160}$ **$-21\sqrt{10}$**
45. $7\sqrt{80k} + 2\sqrt{20k} + \sqrt{45k}$ **$35\sqrt{5k}$**
46. $\sqrt{24abc} + \sqrt{600abc}$ **$12\sqrt{6abc}$**
47. $\sqrt{12} + \sqrt{20} + \sqrt{27} + \sqrt{45}$ **$5\sqrt{3} + 5\sqrt{5}$**

48. **///ERROR ANALYSIS///** Which expressions are simplified incorrectly? Explain the error in each incorrect simplification.

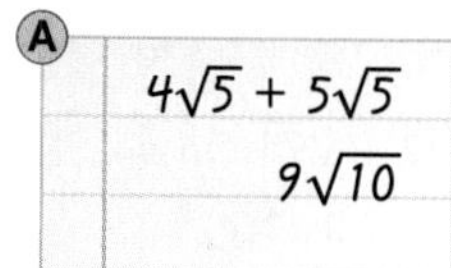

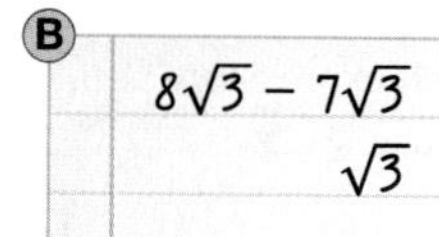

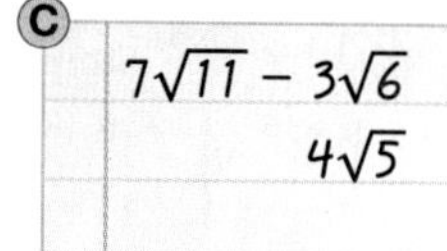

48. A and C are incorrect. In A, the radicands were added. In C, the radicals were not like radicals but they were incorrectly combined by subtracting the radicands.

49. **Write About It** Tell how to identify like radicals. Give examples and nonexamples of like radicals in your answer.

Complete each box to make a true statement.

50. $5\sqrt{ab} + 2\sqrt{\mathbf{ab}} - 3\sqrt{a} = 7\sqrt{ab} - 3\sqrt{a}$
51. $4\sqrt{x} - \sqrt{\mathbf{9}\,x} = \sqrt{x}$
52. $5\sqrt{2} - \sqrt{\mathbf{8}} + \sqrt{2} = 4\sqrt{2}$
53. $\sqrt{\mathbf{18}} + 8\sqrt{2} = 11\sqrt{2}$
54. $3\sqrt{3} + 2\sqrt{3} + \sqrt{\mathbf{48}} = 9\sqrt{3}$
55. $2x - \sqrt{\square} = -4x$ **$36x^2$**

56. This problem will prepare you for the Multi-Step Test Prep on page 854.
    a. The first Ferris wheel was designed by George W. Ferris and introduced at the 1893 Chicago World's Fair. Its diameter was 250 feet. What was its radius? **125 ft**
    b. For a rider halfway up on the ride, the distance from the boarding point can be found by using the equation $d = \sqrt{2r^2}$, where r is the radius of the wheel. Explain where this equation comes from. (*Hint:* Draw a picture.) **Pythagorean Theorem**

11-7 READING STRATEGIES

The process for adding and subtracting radical expressions is similar to the process for simplifying algebraic expressions. Look at the connections below.

Simplify $9x^2 + 8x - 4x^2$.	**Simplify $5\sqrt{6} + 2\sqrt{5} - 3\sqrt{6}$.**
$9x^2 + 8x - 4x^2$	$5\sqrt{6} + 2\sqrt{5} - 3\sqrt{6}$
Step 1: Identify like terms/like radicals.	
$9x^2$ and $-4x^2$	$5\sqrt{6}$ and $-3\sqrt{6}$
Step 2: Rearrange so like terms/like radicals are together.	
$9x^2 - 4x^2 + 8x$	$5\sqrt{6} - 3\sqrt{6} + 2\sqrt{5}$
Step 3: Combine like terms/like radicals.	
$5x^2 + 8x$	$2\sqrt{6} + 2\sqrt{5}$

Complete the following based on the examples above.

1. What makes $5\sqrt{6}$ and $-3\sqrt{6}$ like radicals? **They have the same radicand, 6.**
2. Describe how to combine the radicals $5\sqrt{6}$ and $-3\sqrt{6}$. **Keep $\sqrt{6}$ and subract 5 – 3.**
3. What extra step would need to be done first if the problem was $5\sqrt{6} + 2\sqrt{54} - 3\sqrt{6}$? **Write $2\sqrt{54}$ as $6\sqrt{6}$.**
4. Simplify the radical expression given in problem 3. **$8\sqrt{6}$**

Simplify each expression.

5. $7\sqrt{5} + 2\sqrt{5} - 12\sqrt{5}$ **$-3\sqrt{5}$**
6. $7\sqrt{3x} + 2\sqrt{10x} - \sqrt{3x}$ **$6\sqrt{3x} + 2\sqrt{10x}$**
7. $9\sqrt{2} - \sqrt{8} + 13\sqrt{2}$ **$20\sqrt{2}$**
8. $3\sqrt{28y} + 5\sqrt{63y}$ **$21\sqrt{7y}$**

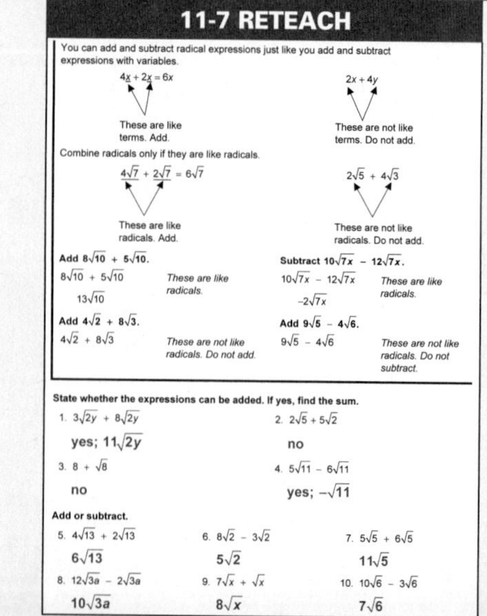

11-7 RETEACH

You can add and subtract radical expressions just like you add and subtract expressions with variables.

$4x + 2x = 6x$ — These are like terms. Add.

$2x + 4y$ — These are not like terms. Do not add.

Combine radicals only if they are like radicals.

$4\sqrt{7} + 2\sqrt{7} = 6\sqrt{7}$ — These are like radicals. Add.

$2\sqrt{5} + 4\sqrt{3}$ — These are not like radicals. Do not add.

Add $8\sqrt{10} + 5\sqrt{10}$.
$8\sqrt{10} + 5\sqrt{10}$
$13\sqrt{10}$
These are like radicals.

Subtract $10\sqrt{7x} - 12\sqrt{7x}$.
$10\sqrt{7x} - 12\sqrt{7x}$
$-2\sqrt{7x}$
These are like radicals.

Add $4\sqrt{2} + 8\sqrt{3}$.
$4\sqrt{2} + 8\sqrt{3}$
These are not like radicals. Do not add.

Add $9\sqrt{5} - 4\sqrt{6}$.
$9\sqrt{5} - 4\sqrt{6}$
These are not like radicals. Do not subtract.

State whether the expressions can be added. If yes, find the sum.

1. $3\sqrt{2y} + 8\sqrt{2y}$ **yes; $11\sqrt{2y}$**
2. $2\sqrt{5} + 5\sqrt{2}$ **no**
3. $8 + \sqrt{8}$ **no**
4. $5\sqrt{11} - 6\sqrt{11}$ **yes; $-\sqrt{11}$**

Add or subtract.

5. $4\sqrt{13} + 2\sqrt{13}$ **$6\sqrt{13}$**
6. $8\sqrt{2} - 3\sqrt{2}$ **$5\sqrt{2}$**
7. $5\sqrt{5} + 6\sqrt{5}$ **$11\sqrt{5}$**
8. $12\sqrt{3a} - 2\sqrt{3a}$ **$10\sqrt{3a}$**
9. $7\sqrt{x} + \sqrt{x}$ **$8\sqrt{x}$**
10. $10\sqrt{6} - 3\sqrt{6}$ **$7\sqrt{6}$**

57. **Multi-Step** A square has an area of 48 in^2. Another square has an area of 12 in^2. Write a simplified radical expression for the perimeter of each square. Then write a simplified radical expression for the combined perimeters of the two squares. **$16\sqrt{3}$ in.; $8\sqrt{3}$ in.; $24\sqrt{3}$ in.**

58. **Critical Thinking** How are like radicals similar to like terms? **The radical is similar to a variable. To add or subtract, combine coefficients.**

TEST PREP

59. Which of the following expressions CANNOT be simplified?
 A $3\sqrt{5} + 4\sqrt{5}$ C $2\sqrt{8} + 3\sqrt{2}$
 (B) $5\sqrt{6} + 6\sqrt{5}$ D $3\sqrt{12} + \sqrt{27}$

60. What is $-5\sqrt{7x} + 6\sqrt{7x}$?
 (F) $\sqrt{7x}$ G $\sqrt{14x^2}$ H $\sqrt{14x}$ J $7x$

61. What is $\sqrt{18} - \sqrt{2}$?
 (A) $2\sqrt{2}$ B 4 C $4\sqrt{2}$ D $8\sqrt{2}$

CHALLENGE AND EXTEND

Simplify. All radicands represent nonnegative numbers.

62. $5\sqrt{x-5} + 2\sqrt{x-5}$ **$7\sqrt{x-5}$**

63. $x\sqrt{x} + 2\sqrt{x}$ **$\sqrt{x}\,(x+2)$**

64. $4\sqrt{x-3} + \sqrt{25x-75}$ **$9\sqrt{x-3}$**

65. $2\sqrt{x+7} - \sqrt{4x+28}$ **0**

66. $\sqrt{4x^3 + 24x^2} + \sqrt{x^3 + 6x^2}$ **$3x\sqrt{x+6}$**

67. $\sqrt{x^3 - x^2} + \sqrt{4x-4}$ **$(x+2)\sqrt{x-1}$**

68. $\sqrt{x^3 + 2x^2} - \sqrt{x+2}$ **$(x-1)\sqrt{x+2}$**

69. $\sqrt{9x+9} - \sqrt{x^3 + 2x^2}$

69. $3\sqrt{x+1} - x\sqrt{x+2}$

70. **Geometry** Find the area of the trapezoid. Use the formula $A = \frac{1}{2}h(b_1 + b_2)$. **50 cm^2**

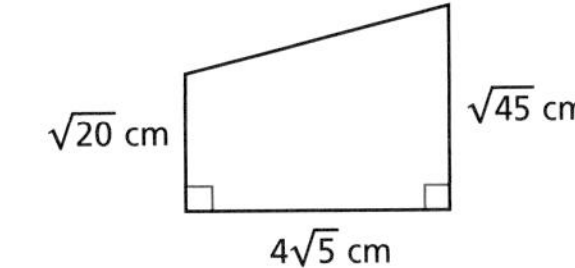

SPIRAL REVIEW

71. Use slope to show that $ABCD$ is a parallelogram. *(Lesson 5-9)*

71. $m_{AB} = 1$, $m_{BC} = \frac{1}{6}$, $m_{CD} = 1$, $m_{AD} = \frac{1}{6}$. Since $m_{AB} = m_{CD}$, $\overline{AB} \parallel \overline{CD}$. Since $m_{BC} = m_{AD}$, $\overline{BC} \parallel \overline{AD}$. Since both pairs of opp. sides are par., $ABCD$ is a parallelogram.

72. Use slope to show that XYZ is a right triangle. *(Lesson 5-9)*

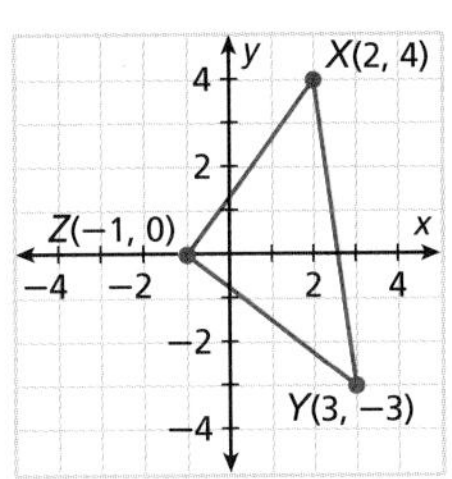

72. $m_{XZ} = \frac{4}{3}$; $m_{YZ} = -\frac{3}{4}$; since the prod. of the slopes is −1, $\overline{XZ} \perp \overline{YZ}$, making XYZ a rt. triangle.

73. A number cube is rolled and a coin is tossed. What is the probability of rolling a 6 and tossing heads? *(Lesson 10-7)* **$\frac{1}{12}$**

Find the domain of each square-root function. *(Lesson 11-5)*

74. $y = \sqrt{4x-2}$ **$x \geq \frac{1}{2}$**

75. $y = -2\sqrt{x+3}$ **$x \geq -3$**

76. $y = 1 + \sqrt{x+6}$ **$x \geq -6$**

COMMON ERROR ALERT

With so much focus on looking for perfect squares, students might accidentally take the square root of a number that is not under a radical sign. For example, in **Exercise 30,** they might write $4\sqrt{2}$ as $2\sqrt{2}$. Remind them to take square roots only of numbers under the radical sign.

TEST PREP DOCTOR In **Exercise 61,** students who chose **B** probably subtracted the numbers under each radical sign and then took the square root. Students who chose **C** may have added the simplified terms. Students who chose **D** likely did not take the square root of 9 after writing 18 as a product.

Journal

Have students explain how to combine $3\sqrt{f} + 10\sqrt{f} + 5\sqrt{f}$ by using the Distributive Property.

ALTERNATIVE ASSESSMENT

Have students simplify $\sqrt{1200x} + \sqrt{300x} + \sqrt{9x}$ step by step, writing the justification for each step as they go.

Power Presentations with PowerPoint®

11-7 Lesson Quiz

Add or subtract.

1. $18\sqrt{6} + 22\sqrt{6}$ $40\sqrt{6}$
2. $3\sqrt{x} + 3\sqrt{3x}$ $3\sqrt{x} + 3\sqrt{3x}$
3. $-4\sqrt{11y} - 14\sqrt{10y} + 2\sqrt{10y} + \sqrt{11y}$ $-3\sqrt{11y} - 12\sqrt{10y}$

Simplify each expression.

4. $\sqrt{242} - \sqrt{128}$ $3\sqrt{2}$
5. $\sqrt{108yz} + 3\sqrt{98yz} + 2\sqrt{75yz}$ $16\sqrt{3yz} + 21\sqrt{2yz}$
6. Find the perimeter of the trapezoid. Give the answer as a radical expression in simplest form. $(10\sqrt{6} + 2)$ ft

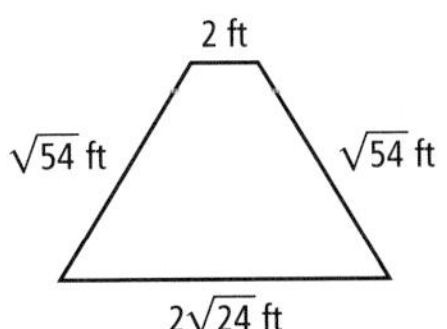

Also available on transparency

11-7 PROBLEM SOLVING

Write the correct answer as a radical expression in simplest form.

1. The parks department is installing a fence along a scenic overlook. The area to be fenced has 3 sides measuring $4\sqrt{5}$ feet, $3\sqrt{5}$ feet, and $5\sqrt{5}$ feet. Find the total amount of fencing that needs to be installed.
 $12\sqrt{5}$ ft

2. A rectangular laundry room has a length of $\sqrt{54}$ feet and a width of $\sqrt{48}$ feet. Find the perimeter of the laundry room.
 $6\sqrt{6} + 8\sqrt{3}$ ft

3. Mr. Lansberry bought four watermelons for a family reunion. The watermelons weighed $\sqrt{75}$ pounds, $\sqrt{108}$ pounds, $\sqrt{125}$ pounds, and $\sqrt{80}$ pounds. How many pounds of watermelon did Mr. Lansberry bring to the reunion?
 $11\sqrt{3} + 9\sqrt{5}$ lbs

4. Travon is hanging the same wallpaper border in two rooms. One room is a perfect square with an area of 120 square feet. The other room, a rectangle, has a width of $\sqrt{30}$ feet and a length of 8 feet. How much wallpaper border does Travon need to go around the perimeter of the two rooms?
 $10\sqrt{30} + 16$ ft

Select the best answer.

5. A cafeteria tray is shaped like an isosceles trapezoid. The bases measure $\sqrt{180}$ in. and $\sqrt{320}$ in. The legs measure $\sqrt{80}$ in. Find the perimeter of the tray.
 A $2\sqrt{145}$ in. C $18\sqrt{5}$ in.
 B $2\sqrt{165}$ in. **D** $22\sqrt{5}$ in.

6. Jack, Aislinn, Mercedes, and Dae are a team participating in a relay at a fall festival. Jack's time was $7\sqrt{2}$ seconds, Aislinn's was $12\sqrt{2}$ seconds, Mercedes's was $6\sqrt{2}$ seconds, and Dae's was $9\sqrt{2}$ seconds. What was the team's total time?
 F 24 s **H** $34\sqrt{2}$ s
 G $24\sqrt{2}$ s J 68 s

7. Lily has two picture frames she is replacing. The first frame is shaped like a regular octagon, and all sides measure $\sqrt{12}$ in. The second frame is shaped like a rectangle; the length and width are $\sqrt{60}$ in. and $\sqrt{12}$ in. respectively. How much total framing will she need?
 A $2\sqrt{6} + 2\sqrt{15}$ in.
 B $4\sqrt{3} + 2\sqrt{15}$ in.
 C $16\sqrt{3} + 4\sqrt{15}$ in.
 D $20\sqrt{3} + 4\sqrt{15}$ in.

8. A triangular pennant has two sides that measure $28\sqrt{3}$ centimeters and a third side that measures $7\sqrt{3}$ centimeters. Mrs. Kwan is sewing 2 rows of gold ribbon around the perimeter of the pennant. How much ribbon does she need?
 F $63\sqrt{3}$ cm **H** $126\sqrt{3}$ cm
 G $70\sqrt{3}$ cm J 189 cm

11-7 CHALLENGE

This game is for 2 players. Each should have paper and a pencil.

Preparation:

- Cut out the 16 game cards below. You can make the cards sturdier and not see-through by mounting them on cardboard with glue or tape.
- Put all of the game cards upside-down on a table and mix them up. Keeping the cards upside-down, arrange them into a 4-by-4 grid.

Game Play:

- Player 1 picks any two cards and turns them right-side up. The player identifies whether the two expressions can simplify to be like radicals.
  - If the expressions *can* be like radicals, then Player 1 adds them. Player 2 checks the opponent's addition. If the sum is correct, Player 1 removes and keeps the two cards.
  - If the expressions are *not* like radicals, or Player 1 adds incorrectly, the cards remain and are turned upside-down again.
- Players alternate, repeating the process described above. To improve their chances of winning, both players should remember what expressions have been revealed and where they are located.
- After all cards are removed, the winner is the player with the most cards.

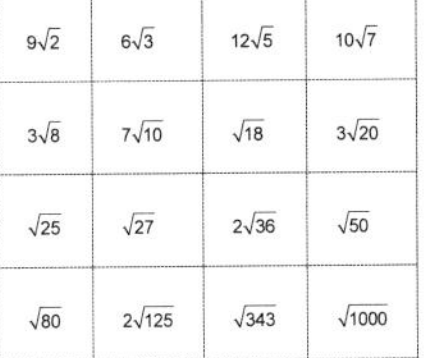

$9\sqrt{2}$	$6\sqrt{3}$	$12\sqrt{5}$	$10\sqrt{7}$
$3\sqrt{8}$	$7\sqrt{10}$	$\sqrt{18}$	$3\sqrt{20}$
$\sqrt{25}$	$\sqrt{27}$	$2\sqrt{36}$	$\sqrt{50}$
$\sqrt{80}$	$2\sqrt{125}$	$\sqrt{343}$	$\sqrt{1000}$

11-8 Organizer

Pacing: Traditional 1 day
Block $\frac{1}{2}$ day

Objectives: Multiply and divide radical expressions.

Rationalize denominators.

Online Edition
Tutorial Videos

Power Presentations with PowerPoint®

Warm Up

Simplify each expression.

1. $\sqrt{72}$ $6\sqrt{2}$
2. $\sqrt{x^5}$ $x^2\sqrt{x}$
3. $\sqrt{\frac{24}{9}}$ $\frac{2\sqrt{6}}{3}$
4. $\sqrt{\frac{18}{x^2}}$ $\frac{3\sqrt{2}}{|x|}$

Also available on transparency

Math Humor

Q: Why did the troublemaker keep failing his test on radical expressions?

A: He kept trying to rationalize his behavior instead of the denominators.

11-8 Multiplying and Dividing Radical Expressions

Objectives
Multiply and divide radical expressions.

Rationalize denominators.

Who uses this?
Electricians can divide radical expressions to find how much current runs through an appliance. (See Exercise 64.)

Off the Mark. Cartoon copyrighted by Mark Parisi, printed with permission.

You can use the Product and Quotient Properties of square roots you have already learned to multiply and divide expressions containing square roots.

EXAMPLE 1 Multiplying Square Roots

Multiply. Write each product in simplest form.

A $\sqrt{3}\sqrt{6}$

$\sqrt{3(6)}$	*Product Property of Square Roots*
$\sqrt{18}$	*Multiply the factors in the radicand.*
$\sqrt{9(2)}$	*Factor 18 using a perfect-square factor.*
$\sqrt{9}\sqrt{2}$	*Product Property of Square Roots*
$3\sqrt{2}$	*Simplify.*

B $(5\sqrt{3})^2$

$5\sqrt{3}\cdot 5\sqrt{3}$	*Expand the expression.*
$5(5)\sqrt{3}\sqrt{3}$	*Commutative Property of Multiplication*
$25\sqrt{3(3)}$	*Product Property of Square Roots*
$25\sqrt{9}$	*Simplify the radicand.*
$25(3)$	*Simplify the square root.*
75	*Multiply.*

C $2\sqrt{8x}\sqrt{4x}$

$2\sqrt{8x(4x)}$	*Product Property of Square Roots*
$2\sqrt{32x^2}$	*Multiply the factors in the radicand.*
$2\sqrt{16(2)x^2}$	*Factor 32 using a perfect-square factor.*
$2\sqrt{16}\sqrt{2}\sqrt{x^2}$	*Product Property of Square Roots*
$2(4)\sqrt{2}(x)$	
$8x\sqrt{2}$	

Helpful Hint

In Example 1C, $\sqrt{8x}$ and $\sqrt{4x}$ represent real numbers only if $x \geq 0$, so, in this case, $\sqrt{x^2} = x$.

CHECK IT OUT! **Multiply. Write each product in simplest form.**

1a. $\sqrt{5}\sqrt{10}$ $5\sqrt{2}$ **1b.** $(3\sqrt{7})^2$ 63 **1c.** $\sqrt{2m}\sqrt{14m}$ $2m\sqrt{7}$

State Resources

go.hrw.com
State Resources Online
KEYWORD: MA7 Resources

1 Introduce

EXPLORATION

11-8 Multiplying and Dividing Radical Expressions

You will need a graphing calculator for this Exploration.

1. Press and enter the expression $\sqrt{3x}\sqrt{2x}$ for **Y1** as follows:
2. Press .
3. Describe the graph of the function.
4. Enter the expression $x\sqrt{6}$ for **Y2**.
5. Press .
6. Describe the graph of this function.

THINK AND DISCUSS

7. **Compare** the graph of $y = \sqrt{3x}\sqrt{2x}$ with the graph of $y = x\sqrt{6}$.
8. **Discuss** whether $\sqrt{3x}\sqrt{2x} = x\sqrt{6}$.

Motivate

Display the two expressions $8(\sqrt{2})$ and $\sqrt{8(2)}$. Ask students if the two expressions are equivalent. No, $8(\sqrt{2}) \approx 11.31$ and $\sqrt{8(2)} = 4$. Tell students that when multiplying radical expressions, they must pay attention to whether the numbers are outside or inside the radical sign.

Explorations and answers are provided in *Alternate Openers: Explorations Transparencies.*

EXAMPLE 2 Using the Distributive Property

Multiply. Write each product in simplest form.

A $\sqrt{2}\left(5+\sqrt{12}\right)$

$\sqrt{2}\left(5+\sqrt{12}\right)$	
$\sqrt{2}(5)+\sqrt{2}\sqrt{12}$	*Distribute $\sqrt{2}$.*
$5\sqrt{2}+\sqrt{2(12)}$	*Product Property of Square Roots*
$5\sqrt{2}+\sqrt{24}$	*Multiply the factors in the second radicand.*
$5\sqrt{2}+\sqrt{4(6)}$	*Factor 24 using a perfect-square factor.*
$5\sqrt{2}+\sqrt{4}\sqrt{6}$	*Product Property of Square Roots*
$5\sqrt{2}+2\sqrt{6}$	*Simplify.*

B $\sqrt{3}\left(\sqrt{3}-\sqrt{5}\right)$

$\sqrt{3}\left(\sqrt{3}-\sqrt{5}\right)$	
$\sqrt{3}\sqrt{3}-\sqrt{3}\sqrt{5}$	*Distribute $\sqrt{3}$.*
$\sqrt{3(3)}-\sqrt{3(5)}$	*Product Property of Square Roots*
$\sqrt{9}-\sqrt{15}$	*Simplify the radicands.*
$3-\sqrt{15}$	*Simplify.*

Multiply. Write each product in simplest form.

2a. $\sqrt{6}\left(\sqrt{8}-3\right)$ **$4\sqrt{3}-3\sqrt{6}$** **2b.** $\sqrt{5}\left(\sqrt{10}+4\sqrt{3}\right)$ **$5\sqrt{2}+4\sqrt{15}$**

2c. $\sqrt{7k}\left(\sqrt{7}-5\right)$ **$7\sqrt{k}-5\sqrt{7k}$** **2d.** $5\sqrt{5}\left(-4+6\sqrt{5}\right)$ **$150-20\sqrt{5}$**

Remember!

First terms
Outer terms
Inner terms
Last terms
See Lesson 7-8.

In Chapter 7, you learned to multiply binomials by using the FOIL method. The same method can be used to multiply square-root expressions that contain two terms.

$$\left(4+\sqrt{3}\right)\left(5+\sqrt{3}\right)=\underset{F}{4(5)}+\underset{O}{4\sqrt{3}}+\underset{I}{5\sqrt{3}}+\underset{L}{\sqrt{3}\sqrt{3}}$$
$$=20\quad+9\sqrt{3}\quad+3\quad=\quad 23+9\sqrt{3}$$

EXAMPLE 3 Multiplying Sums and Differences of Radicals

Multiply. Write each product in simplest form.

A $\left(4+\sqrt{5}\right)\left(3-\sqrt{5}\right)$

$12-4\sqrt{5}+3\sqrt{5}-5$	*Use the FOIL method.*
$7-\sqrt{5}$	*Simplify by combining like terms.*

B $\left(\sqrt{7}-5\right)^2$

$\left(\sqrt{7}-5\right)\left(\sqrt{7}-5\right)$	*Expand the expression.*
$7-5\sqrt{7}-5\sqrt{7}+25$	*Use the FOIL method.*
$32-10\sqrt{7}$	*Simplify by combining like terms.*

Multiply. Write each product in simplest form.

3a. $\left(3+\sqrt{3}\right)\left(8-\sqrt{3}\right)$ **$21+5\sqrt{3}$** **3b.** $\left(9+\sqrt{2}\right)^2$ **$83+18\sqrt{2}$**

3c. $\left(3-\sqrt{2}\right)^2$ **$11-6\sqrt{2}$** **3d.** $\left(4-\sqrt{3}\right)\left(\sqrt{3}+5\right)$ **$17-\sqrt{3}$**

COMMON ERROR ALERT

When distributing in **Example 2A,** students may mistakenly think that $\sqrt{2}(5)=\sqrt{10}$. Suggest to students that they check answers on their calculators to see that $\sqrt{2}(5)\approx 7.07$, while $\sqrt{10}\approx 3.16$. Also emphasize that $\sqrt{2}(5)=5\sqrt{2}$ by the Commutative Property of Multiplication.

Power Presentations with PowerPoint®

Additional Examples

Example 1

Multiply. Write each product in simplest form.

A. $\sqrt{8}\sqrt{6}$ $4\sqrt{3}$

B. $\left(2\sqrt{5}\right)^2$ 20

C. $\sqrt{3y}\sqrt{12y}$ $6y$

Example 2

Multiply. Write each product in simplest form.

A. $\sqrt{3}\left(7-\sqrt{8}\right)$ $7\sqrt{3}-2\sqrt{6}$

B. $\sqrt{2}\left(\sqrt{8}+\sqrt{18}\right)$ 10

Example 3

Multiply. Write each product in simplest form.

A. $\left(3-\sqrt{8}\right)\left(2+\sqrt{8}\right)$ $-2+2\sqrt{2}$

B. $\left(4+\sqrt{3}\right)^2$ $19+8\sqrt{3}$

INTERVENTION

Questioning Strategies

EXAMPLES 1–2

- When is a product of radicals in simplest form?

EXAMPLE 3

- How is **Example 3B** similar to squaring a binomial?
- Why are there only two terms in the product instead of three?

2 Teach

Guided Instruction

Review the Product Property of Square Roots as it was used in Lessons 11-6 and 11-7: $\sqrt{ab}=\sqrt{a}\sqrt{b}$. In **Example 4,** point out that rationalizing the denominator does not change the value of the quotient. For all examples, show that the simplified answers are equivalent to the original expressions by finding each value on a calculator.

Reaching All Learners

Through Communication

Show students 2 different ways to begin simplifying $\frac{5}{\sqrt{8}}$ (shown below). Discuss the pros and cons of each method.

1. Multiply by $\frac{\sqrt{8}}{\sqrt{8}}$.
2. Simplify $\sqrt{8}$ to $2\sqrt{2}$. Then multiply by $\frac{\sqrt{2}}{\sqrt{2}}$.

Power Presentations with PowerPoint®

Additional Examples

Example 4

Simplify each quotient.

A. $\frac{\sqrt{11}}{\sqrt{3}}$ $\frac{\sqrt{33}}{3}$

B. $\frac{\sqrt{13m}}{\sqrt{20}}$ $\frac{\sqrt{65m}}{10}$

INTERVENTION
Questioning Strategies

EXAMPLE 4

- When is it necessary to rationalize the denominator?
- Why does the process of rationalizing the denominator not change the value of the expression?

Teaching Tip **Communicating Math** Explain the phrase *rationalizing the denominator*. The square root of a nonperfect square is an irrational number. The number below the fraction bar is the denominator. So rationalizing the denominator means making the number below the fraction bar a rational number. ENGLISH LANGUAGE LEARNERS

A quotient with a square root in the denominator is **not** simplified. To simplify these expressions, multiply by a form of 1 to get a perfect-square radicand in the denominator. This is called *rationalizing the denominator*.

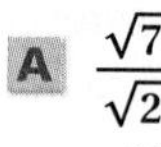

EXAMPLE 4 Rationalizing the Denominator

Simplify each quotient.

A $\frac{\sqrt{7}}{\sqrt{2}}$

$\frac{\sqrt{7}}{\sqrt{2}}\left(\frac{\sqrt{2}}{\sqrt{2}}\right)$ *Multiply by a form of 1 to get a perfect-square radicand in the denominator.*

$\frac{\sqrt{14}}{\sqrt{4}}$ *Product Property of Square Roots*

$\frac{\sqrt{14}}{2}$ *Simplify the denominator.*

Helpful Hint

Use the square root in the denominator to find the appropriate form of 1 for multiplication.

B $\frac{\sqrt{7}}{\sqrt{8n}}$

$\frac{\sqrt{7}}{\sqrt{4(2n)}}$ *Write 8n using a perfect-square factor.*

$\frac{\sqrt{7}}{2\sqrt{2n}}$ *Simplify the denominator.*

$\frac{\sqrt{7}}{2\sqrt{2n}}\left(\frac{\sqrt{2n}}{\sqrt{2n}}\right)$ *Multiply by a form of 1 to get a perfect-square radicand in the denominator.*

$\frac{\sqrt{14n}}{2\sqrt{4n^2}}$ *Product Property of Square Roots*

$\frac{\sqrt{14n}}{2(2n)}$ *Simplify the square root in the denominator.*

$\frac{\sqrt{14n}}{4n}$ *Simplify the denominator.*

CHECK IT OUT! Simplify each quotient.

4a. $\frac{\sqrt{13}}{\sqrt{5}}$ $\frac{\sqrt{65}}{5}$ **4b.** $\frac{\sqrt{7a}}{\sqrt{12}}$ $\frac{\sqrt{21a}}{6}$ **4c.** $\frac{2\sqrt{80}}{\sqrt{7}}$ $\frac{8\sqrt{35}}{7}$

THINK AND DISCUSS

1. Explain why multiplying $\frac{\sqrt{6}}{\sqrt{5}}$ by $\frac{\sqrt{5}}{\sqrt{5}}$ does not change the value of $\frac{\sqrt{6}}{\sqrt{5}}$.

2. **GET ORGANIZED** Copy and complete the graphic organizer. In each box, give an example and show how to simplify it.

Multiplying Radical Expressions
- Multiplying two square roots
- Using the Distributive Property
- Using FOIL

3 Close

Summarize

Have students multiply and write each product in simplest form.

$\sqrt{6}\sqrt{10}$ $2\sqrt{15}$

$(2+\sqrt{7})(3+\sqrt{5})$ $6+2\sqrt{5}+3\sqrt{7}+\sqrt{35}$

Have students simplify the quotient below.

$\frac{2\sqrt{3}}{\sqrt{18}}$ $\frac{\sqrt{6}}{3}$

ONGOING ASSESSMENT and INTERVENTION

Diagnose Before the Lesson
11-8 Warm Up, TE p. 840

Monitor During the Lesson
Check It Out! Exercises, SE pp. 840–842
Questioning Strategies, TE pp. 841–842

Assess After the Lesson
11-8 Lesson Quiz, TE p. 845
Alternative Assessment, TE p. 845

Answers to *Think and Discuss*

1. $\frac{\sqrt{5}}{\sqrt{5}}$ is equal to 1, so multiplying by $\frac{\sqrt{5}}{\sqrt{5}}$ does not change the value of the original expression.
2. See p. A10.

11-8 Exercises

GUIDED PRACTICE

Multiply. Write each product in simplest form.

SEE EXAMPLE 1 p. 840

1. $\sqrt{2}\sqrt{3}$ $\sqrt{6}$
2. $\sqrt{3}\sqrt{8}$ $2\sqrt{6}$
3. $(5\sqrt{5})^2$ 125
4. $(4\sqrt{2})^2$ 32
5. $3\sqrt{3a}\sqrt{10}$ $3\sqrt{30a}$
6. $2\sqrt{15p}\sqrt{3p}$ $6p\sqrt{5}$

SEE EXAMPLE 2 p. 841

7. $\sqrt{6}(2+\sqrt{7})$ $2\sqrt{6}+\sqrt{42}$
8. $\sqrt{3}(5-\sqrt{3})$ $5\sqrt{3}-3$
9. $\sqrt{7}(\sqrt{5}-\sqrt{3})$
10. $\sqrt{2}(\sqrt{10}+8\sqrt{2})$
11. $\sqrt{5y}(\sqrt{15}+4)$
12. $\sqrt{2t}(\sqrt{6t}-\sqrt{2t})$

SEE EXAMPLE 3 p. 841

13. $(2+\sqrt{2})(5+\sqrt{2})$
14. $(4+\sqrt{6})(3-\sqrt{6})$
15. $(\sqrt{3}-4)(\sqrt{3}+2)$
16. $(5+\sqrt{3})^2$ $28+10\sqrt{3}$
17. $(\sqrt{6}-5\sqrt{3})^2$ $81-30\sqrt{2}$
18. $(6+3\sqrt{2})^2$ $54+36\sqrt{2}$

SEE EXAMPLE 4 p. 842

Simplify each quotient.

19. $\frac{\sqrt{13}}{\sqrt{2}}$ $\frac{\sqrt{26}}{2}$
20. $\frac{\sqrt{20}}{\sqrt{8}}$ $\frac{\sqrt{10}}{2}$
21. $\frac{\sqrt{11}}{6\sqrt{3}}$ $\frac{\sqrt{33}}{18}$
22. $\frac{\sqrt{28}}{\sqrt{3s}}$ $\frac{2\sqrt{21s}}{3s}$
23. $\frac{2}{\sqrt{7}}$ $\frac{2\sqrt{7}}{7}$
24. $\frac{3}{\sqrt{6}}$ $\frac{\sqrt{6}}{2}$
25. $\frac{1}{\sqrt{5x}}$ $\frac{\sqrt{5x}}{5x}$
26. $\frac{\sqrt{3}}{\sqrt{x}}$ $\frac{\sqrt{3x}}{x}$

PRACTICE AND PROBLEM SOLVING

Independent Practice

For Exercises	See Example
27–32	1
33–38	2
39–44	3
45–52	4

Extra Practice
Skills Practice p. S25
Application Practice p. S38

Multiply. Write each product in simplest form.

27. $\sqrt{3}\sqrt{5}\sqrt{6}$ $3\sqrt{10}$
28. $3\sqrt{6}(5\sqrt{6})$ 90
29. $(2\sqrt{2})^2$ 8
30. $(3\sqrt{6})^2$ 54
31. $\sqrt{21d}(2\sqrt{3d})$ $6d\sqrt{7}$
32. $4\sqrt{5n}(2\sqrt{5n})(3\sqrt{3n})$
33. $\sqrt{5}(4-\sqrt{10})$
34. $\sqrt{2}(\sqrt{6}+2)$
35. $\sqrt{2}(\sqrt{6}-\sqrt{10})$
36. $3\sqrt{3}(\sqrt{8}-2\sqrt{6})$
37. $\sqrt{3f}(\sqrt{3}+12)$
38. $\sqrt{8m}(\sqrt{10}+\sqrt{2m})$
39. $(15+\sqrt{15})(4+\sqrt{15})$
40. $(\sqrt{6}+4)(\sqrt{2}-7)$
41. $(3-\sqrt{2})(4+\sqrt{2})$
42. $(\sqrt{5}-5)^2$ $30-10\sqrt{5}$
43. $(\sqrt{3}+8)^2$ $67+16\sqrt{3}$
44. $(2\sqrt{3}+4\sqrt{5})^2$ $92+16\sqrt{15}$

Simplify each quotient.

45. $\frac{\sqrt{75}}{\sqrt{2}}$ $\frac{5\sqrt{6}}{2}$
46. $\frac{\sqrt{5}}{4\sqrt{8}}$ $\frac{\sqrt{10}}{16}$
47. $\frac{\sqrt{27}}{3\sqrt{x}}$ $\frac{\sqrt{3x}}{x}$
48. $\frac{\sqrt{48k}}{\sqrt{5}}$ $\frac{4\sqrt{15k}}{5}$
49. $\frac{\sqrt{49x}}{\sqrt{2}}$ $\frac{7\sqrt{2x}}{2}$
50. $\frac{3\sqrt{27}}{\sqrt{b}}$ $\frac{9\sqrt{3b}}{b}$
51. $\frac{\sqrt{12y}}{\sqrt{3}}$ $2\sqrt{y}$
52. $\frac{\sqrt{12t}}{\sqrt{6}}$ $\sqrt{2t}$

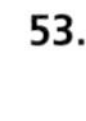

Geometry Find the area of each figure. Give your answer as a radical expression in simplest form.

53. 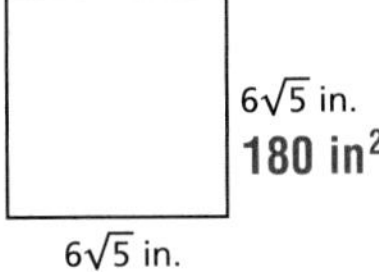

180 in^2

54. 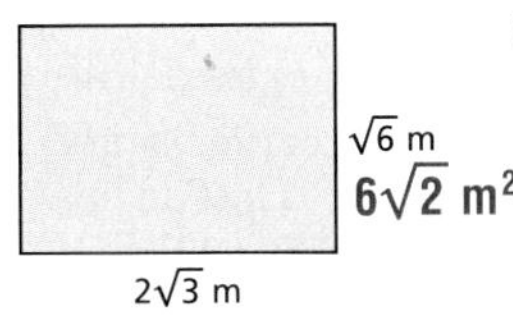

$6\sqrt{2}$ m^2

55. 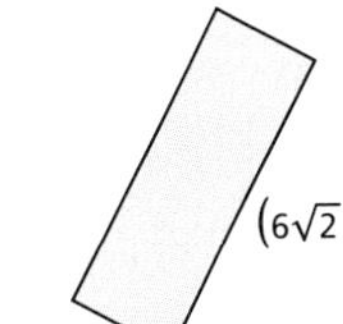

$(6\sqrt{10}-2\sqrt{5})$ cm^2

11-8 Exercises

Assignment Guide

Assign *Guided Practice* exercises as necessary.

If you finished Examples **1–2**
Basic 27–38, 53–55
Average 27–38, 53–55
Advanced 27–38, 53–55

If you finished Examples **1–4**
Basic 27–72, 74–77, 87–98
Average 27–77, 78–84 even, 87–98
Advanced 27–69, 74–98

Homework Quick Check
Quickly check key concepts.
Exercises: 28, 32, 36, 38, 42, 46

Answers

9. $\sqrt{35}-\sqrt{21}$
10. $2\sqrt{5}+16$
11. $5\sqrt{3y}+4\sqrt{5y}$
12. $2t\sqrt{3}-2t$
13. $12+7\sqrt{2}$
14. $6-\sqrt{6}$
15. $-5-2\sqrt{3}$
32. $120n\sqrt{3n}$
33. $4\sqrt{5}-5\sqrt{2}$
34. $2\sqrt{3}+2\sqrt{2}$
35. $2\sqrt{3}-2\sqrt{5}$
36. $6\sqrt{6}-18\sqrt{2}$
37. $3\sqrt{f}+12\sqrt{3f}$
38. $4\sqrt{5m}+4m$
39. $75+19\sqrt{15}$
40. $2\sqrt{3}-7\sqrt{6}+4\sqrt{2}-28$
41. $10-\sqrt{2}$

State Resources

go.hrw.com
State Resources Online
KEYWORD: MA7 Resources

Multiple Representations In **Exercise 69,** students could rewrite the expression as $\frac{\pi\sqrt{2\ell}}{4}$ before substituting 3 for ℓ.

Exercise 74 involves evaluating radical expressions. This exercise prepares students for the Multi-Step Test Prep on page 854.

Answers

73. Possible answer: $\frac{1}{\sqrt{3}}$; multiply the fraction by $\frac{\sqrt{3}}{\sqrt{3}}$. This will rationalize the denominator, since $\sqrt{3}\sqrt{3} = 3$.

74b. 5.6 s; it takes more than twice as long to go up the tower as it does to come down.

LINK Electricity

People began using wind to generate electricity in the early twentieth century. A modern wind turbine is 120–180 feet tall and, depending on its construction, can generate up to 1 megawatt of power.

Simplify.

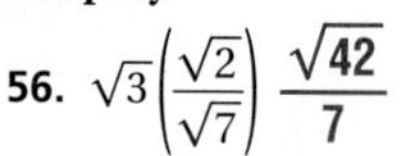

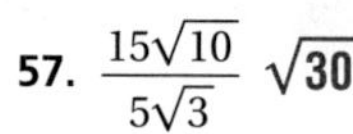

56. $\sqrt{3}\left(\frac{\sqrt{2}}{\sqrt{7}}\right)$ **$\frac{\sqrt{42}}{7}$**
57. $\frac{15\sqrt{10}}{5\sqrt{3}}$ **$\sqrt{30}$**
58. $\frac{6+\sqrt{18}}{3}$ **$2+\sqrt{2}$**
59. $(\sqrt{3}-4)(\sqrt{3}+2)$ **$-5-2\sqrt{3}$**
60. $\sqrt{2}(6+\sqrt{12})$ **$6\sqrt{2}+2\sqrt{6}$**
61. $\frac{\sqrt{1}+\sqrt{25}}{\sqrt{2}}$ **$3\sqrt{2}$**
62. $\frac{\sqrt{15}+\sqrt{10}}{\sqrt{5}}$ **$\sqrt{3}+\sqrt{2}$**
63. $\sqrt{12}(\sqrt{3}+8)^2$ **$134\sqrt{3}+96$**
64. $\sqrt{3}(4-2\sqrt{5})$ **$4\sqrt{3}-2\sqrt{15}$**
65. $(\sqrt{x}-\sqrt{y})^2$ **$x-2\sqrt{xy}+y$**
66. $(\sqrt{x}-5)(3\sqrt{x}+7)$ **$3x-8\sqrt{x}-35$**
67. $(\sqrt{3}+\sqrt{x})^2$ **$3+2\sqrt{3x}+x$**

68. **Electricity** Electrical current in amps can be represented by $\frac{\sqrt{W}}{\sqrt{R}}$, where W is power in watts and R is resistance in ohms. How much electrical current is running through a microwave oven that has 850 watts of power and 5 ohms of resistance? Give the answer as a radical expression in simplest form. Then estimate the amount of current to the nearest tenth. **$\sqrt{170}$ amps $\approx$ 13.0 amps**

69. **Physics** The *period* of a pendulum is the amount of time it takes the pendulum to make one complete swing and return to its starting point. The period of a pendulum in seconds can be represented by $2\pi\sqrt{\frac{\ell}{32}}$, where ℓ is the length of the pendulum in feet. What is the period of a pendulum whose length is 3 feet? Give the answer as a radical expression in simplest form. Then estimate the period to the nearest tenth. **$\frac{\pi\sqrt{6}}{4}$ s $\approx$ 1.9 s**

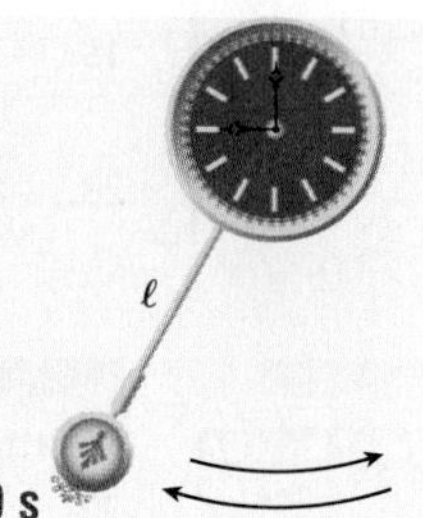

Geometry **Find the area of each triangle. Give the exact answer in simplest form. (*Hint:* The formula for the area of a triangle is $A = \frac{1}{2}bh$.)**

70. 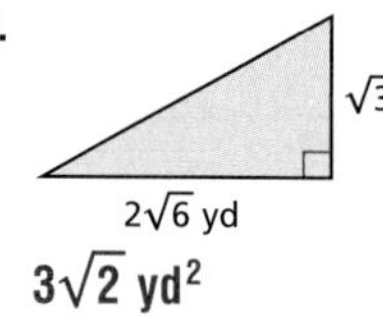

$3\sqrt{2}$ yd^2

71.
269.5 ft^2

72. 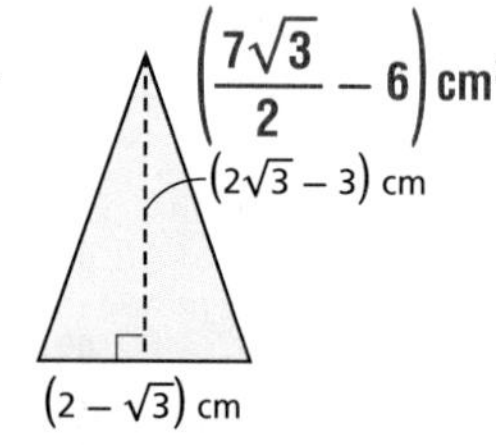

$\left(\frac{7\sqrt{3}}{2}-6\right)$ cm^2

73. **Write About It** Describe an expression for which you would have to rationalize the denominator. How would you do it? Include an explanation of how you would choose what to multiply the original expression by.

MULTI-STEP TEST PREP

74. This problem will prepare you for the Multi-Step Test Prep on page 854.
   a. Many amusement parks have free-fall rides in which cars travel straight up a tower and then are allowed to fall back to the ground. The time in seconds for any object in free fall is $t = \sqrt{\frac{d}{16}}$, where d is the distance that the object falls in feet. On a particular free-fall ride, the cars are in free fall for 100 feet. How long does free fall last on this ride? **2.5 s**
   b. The cars in the ride from part **a** travel up the tower at a speed of 18 feet per second. How long does this trip take? Round your answer to the nearest tenth. How does this time compare with the time spent in free fall?

11-8 PRACTICE A
11-8 PRACTICE C
11-8 PRACTICE B

Multiply. Write each product in simplest form.

1. $\sqrt{15}\cdot\sqrt{6}$ — $\sqrt{15\cdot 6}$ — **$3\sqrt{10}$**
2. $(3\sqrt{6})^2$ — $3\sqrt{6}\cdot 3\sqrt{6}$ — **54**
3. $4\sqrt{7x}\cdot\sqrt{20x}$ — $4\cdot\sqrt{(7x)(20x)}$ — **$8x\sqrt{35}$**
4. $\sqrt{12}\cdot\sqrt{5}$ **$2\sqrt{15}$**
5. $(2\sqrt{7})^2$ **28**
6. $-2\sqrt{5b}\cdot\sqrt{10b}$ **$-10b\sqrt{2}$**
7. $3\sqrt{10y}\,\sqrt{6y}$ **$6y\sqrt{15}$**
8. $\sqrt{8}(\sqrt{12}-\sqrt{2})$ **$4\sqrt{6}-4$**
9. $\sqrt{2x}(\sqrt{5}+\sqrt{2x})$ **$\sqrt{10x}+2x$**
10. $\sqrt{2}(\sqrt{7}-5)$ **$\sqrt{14}-5\sqrt{2}$**
11. $\sqrt{10}(\sqrt{5m}-\sqrt{4})$ **$5\sqrt{2m}-2\sqrt{10}$**
12. $(4+\sqrt{3})(2-\sqrt{3})$ **$5-2\sqrt{3}$**
13. $\sqrt{3}(\sqrt{8}-6)$ **$2\sqrt{6}-6\sqrt{3}$**
14. $\sqrt{5}(\sqrt{2}+\sqrt{8})$ **$3\sqrt{10}$**
15. $(5+\sqrt{2})(6-\sqrt{2})$ **$28+\sqrt{2}$**
16. $\sqrt{5}(\sqrt{2}-\sqrt{6})$ **$\sqrt{10}-\sqrt{30}$**
17. $(3-\sqrt{2})(5+\sqrt{2})$ **$13-2\sqrt{2}$**
18. $(7+\sqrt{3})(7-\sqrt{3})$ **46**

Simplify each quotient.

19. $\frac{\sqrt{2}}{\sqrt{6}}$ **$\frac{\sqrt{3}}{3}$**
20. $\frac{\sqrt{10}}{\sqrt{11}}$ **$\frac{\sqrt{110}}{11}$**
21. $\frac{\sqrt{13}}{\sqrt{50t}}$ **$\frac{\sqrt{26t}}{10t}$**
22. $\frac{\sqrt{7}}{\sqrt{15}}$ **$\frac{\sqrt{105}}{15}$**
23. $\frac{\sqrt{2}}{\sqrt{17}}$ **$\frac{\sqrt{34}}{17}$**
24. $\frac{\sqrt{32}}{\sqrt{48z}}$ **$\frac{\sqrt{6z}}{3z}$**
25. $\frac{\sqrt{3}}{\sqrt{3a}}$ **$\frac{\sqrt{a}}{a}$**
26. $\frac{\sqrt{8x}}{\sqrt{5}}$ **$\frac{2\sqrt{10x}}{5}$**
27. $-\frac{\sqrt{75k}}{10\sqrt{2k}}$ **$-\frac{\sqrt{6}}{4}$**

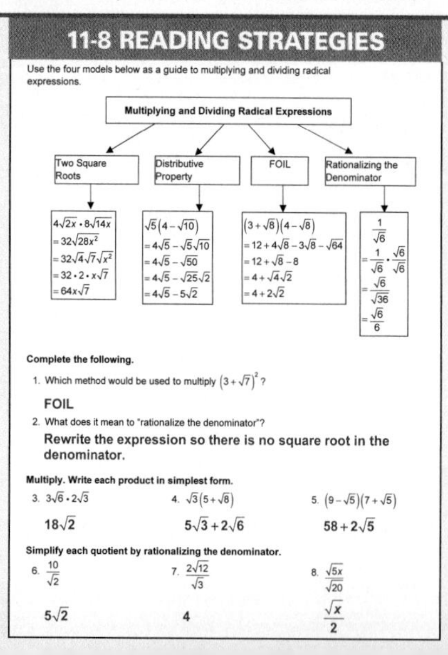

11-8 READING STRATEGIES

Use the four models below as a guide to multiplying and dividing radical expressions.

Multiplying and Dividing Radical Expressions

Two Square Roots: $4\sqrt{2x}\cdot 8\sqrt{14x} = 32\sqrt{28x^2} = 32\sqrt{4}\sqrt{7}\sqrt{x^2} = 32\cdot 2\cdot x\sqrt{7} = 64x\sqrt{7}$

Distributive Property: $\sqrt{5}(4-\sqrt{10}) = 4\sqrt{5}-\sqrt{5}\sqrt{10} = 4\sqrt{5}-\sqrt{50} = 4\sqrt{5}-\sqrt{25}\sqrt{2} = 4\sqrt{5}-5\sqrt{2}$

FOIL: $(3+\sqrt{8})(4-\sqrt{8}) = 12+4\sqrt{8}-3\sqrt{8}-\sqrt{64} = 12+\sqrt{8}-8 = 4+\sqrt{4}\sqrt{2} = 4+2\sqrt{2}$

Rationalizing the Denominator: $\frac{1}{\sqrt{6}} = \frac{1}{\sqrt{6}}\cdot\frac{\sqrt{6}}{\sqrt{6}} = \frac{\sqrt{6}}{\sqrt{36}} = \frac{\sqrt{6}}{6}$

Complete the following.

1. Which method would be used to multiply $(3+\sqrt{7})^2$?
   FOIL
2. What does it mean to "rationalize the denominator"?
   Rewrite the expression so there is no square root in the denominator.

Multiply. Write each product in simplest form.

3. $3\sqrt{6}\cdot 2\sqrt{3}$ **$18\sqrt{2}$**
4. $\sqrt{3}(5+\sqrt{8})$ **$5\sqrt{3}+2\sqrt{6}$**
5. $(9-\sqrt{5})(7+\sqrt{5})$ **$58+2\sqrt{5}$**

Simplify each quotient by rationalizing the denominator.

6. $\frac{10}{\sqrt{2}}$ **$5\sqrt{2}$**
7. $\frac{2\sqrt{12}}{\sqrt{3}}$ **4**
8. $\frac{\sqrt{5x}}{\sqrt{20}}$ **$\frac{\sqrt{x}}{2}$**

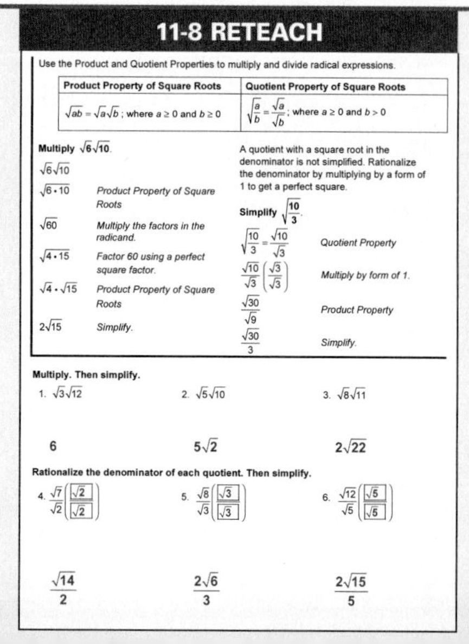

11-8 RETEACH

Use the Product and Quotient Properties to multiply and divide radical expressions.

Product Property of Square Roots	Quotient Property of Square Roots
$\sqrt{ab}=\sqrt{a}\sqrt{b}$; where $a \ge 0$ and $b \ge 0$	$\sqrt{\frac{a}{b}}=\frac{\sqrt{a}}{\sqrt{b}}$; where $a \ge 0$ and $b > 0$

Multiply $\sqrt{6}\sqrt{10}$.

$\sqrt{6}\sqrt{10}$
$\sqrt{6\cdot 10}$ — *Product Property of Square Roots*
$\sqrt{60}$ — *Multiply the factors in the radicand.*
$\sqrt{4\cdot 15}$ — *Factor 60 using a perfect square factor.*
$\sqrt{4}\cdot\sqrt{15}$ — *Product Property of Square Roots*
$2\sqrt{15}$ — *Simplify.*

A quotient with a square root in the denominator is not simplified. Rationalize the denominator by multiplying by a form of 1 to get a perfect square.

Simplify $\sqrt{\frac{10}{3}}$.

$\sqrt{\frac{10}{3}}=\frac{\sqrt{10}}{\sqrt{3}}$ — *Quotient Property*
$\frac{\sqrt{10}}{\sqrt{3}}\left(\frac{\sqrt{3}}{\sqrt{3}}\right)$ — *Multiply by form of 1.*
$\frac{\sqrt{30}}{\sqrt{9}}$ — *Product Property*
$\frac{\sqrt{30}}{3}$ — *Simplify.*

Multiply. Then simplify.

1. $\sqrt{3}\sqrt{12}$ **6**
2. $\sqrt{5}\sqrt{10}$ **$5\sqrt{2}$**
3. $\sqrt{8}\sqrt{11}$ **$2\sqrt{22}$**

Rationalize the denominator of each quotient. Then simplify.

4. $\frac{\sqrt{7}}{\sqrt{2}}\left(\frac{\sqrt{2}}{\sqrt{2}}\right)$ **$\frac{\sqrt{14}}{2}$**
5. $\frac{\sqrt{8}}{\sqrt{3}}\left(\frac{\sqrt{3}}{\sqrt{3}}\right)$ **$\frac{2\sqrt{6}}{3}$**
6. $\frac{\sqrt{12}}{\sqrt{5}}\left(\frac{\sqrt{5}}{\sqrt{5}}\right)$ **$\frac{2\sqrt{15}}{5}$**

TEST PREP

75. What is the product of $3\sqrt{5}$ and $\sqrt{15}$?

(A) $5\sqrt{3}$ (B) $15\sqrt{3}$ (C) $15\sqrt{15}$ (D) $45\sqrt{5}$

76. Which of the following is the result of rationalizing the denominator in the expression $\frac{4}{3\sqrt{2}}$?

(F) $\frac{\sqrt{2}}{3}$ (G) $2\sqrt{2}$ (H) $\frac{2\sqrt{2}}{3}$ (J) $\frac{3\sqrt{2}}{2}$

77. Which of the following is equivalent to $\left(5\sqrt{10}\right)^2$?

(A) 50 (B) 100 (C) 125 (D) 250

CHALLENGE AND EXTEND

The expressions $\sqrt{a}+\sqrt{b}$ and $\sqrt{a}-\sqrt{b}$ are called *conjugates.* When a and b are nonnegative, you can use the FOIL method to multiply conjugates as follows:

$$\left(\sqrt{a}-\sqrt{b}\right)\left(\sqrt{a}+\sqrt{b}\right) = a+\sqrt{ab}-\sqrt{ab}-b = a-b$$

$$\left(\sqrt{3}-\sqrt{5}\right)\left(\sqrt{3}+\sqrt{5}\right) = 3+\sqrt{15}-\sqrt{15}-5 = 3-5 = -2$$

Notice that the product does not contain any square roots. This means that you can use conjugates to rationalize denominators that contain sums or differences of square roots:

$$\frac{\sqrt{2}}{\sqrt{7}+\sqrt{2}}\left(\frac{\sqrt{7}-\sqrt{2}}{\sqrt{7}-\sqrt{2}}\right) = \frac{\sqrt{2}\left(\sqrt{7}-\sqrt{2}\right)}{\left(\sqrt{7}+\sqrt{2}\right)\left(\sqrt{7}-\sqrt{2}\right)} = \frac{\sqrt{14}-\sqrt{4}}{7-2} = \frac{\sqrt{14}-2}{5}$$

Simplify.

78. $\frac{4}{\sqrt{3}-\sqrt{2}}$ **$4\sqrt{3}+4\sqrt{2}$**

79. $\frac{8}{\sqrt{3}+\sqrt{5}}$ **$-4\sqrt{3}+4\sqrt{5}$**

80. $\frac{\sqrt{5}}{\sqrt{10}+\sqrt{3}}$ **$\frac{5\sqrt{2}-\sqrt{15}}{7}$**

81. $\frac{\sqrt{2}+\sqrt{3}}{\sqrt{2}-\sqrt{3}}$ **$-5-2\sqrt{6}$**

82. $\frac{\sqrt{3}}{\sqrt{2}+\sqrt{3}}$ **$3-\sqrt{6}$**

83. $\frac{\sqrt{2}}{\sqrt{8}+\sqrt{6}}$ **$2-\sqrt{3}$**

84. $\frac{6}{\sqrt{2}+\sqrt{3}}$ **$6\sqrt{3}-6\sqrt{2}$**

85. $\frac{2}{\sqrt{6}-\sqrt{5}}$ **$2\sqrt{6}+2\sqrt{5}$**

86. **Geometry** One rectangle is $4\sqrt{6}$ feet long and $\sqrt{2}$ feet wide. Another rectangle is $8\sqrt{2}$ feet long and $2\sqrt{6}$ feet wide. How much more area does the larger rectangle cover than the smaller rectangle? (*Hint:* The formula for the area of a rectangle is $A = \ell w$.) **$24\sqrt{3}$ ft^2**

SPIRAL REVIEW

Describe the transformation(s) from the graph of $f(x)$ to the graph of $g(x)$. (Lesson 5-10)

87. $f(x) = -2x+3$; $g(x) = -2x-1$ **trans. 4 units down**

88. $f(x) = 4x$; $g(x) = 5x$ **rot. about (0, 0) (steeper)**

Factor each polynomial completely. Check your answer. (Lesson 8-6)

89. $x^2+7x-30$

90. $6x^2+11x+3$

91. x^2-16

92. $3x^2+30x+75$ **$3(x+5)^2$**

93. $2x^4-18$ **$2(x^2+3)(x^2-3)$**

94. $8x^3-20x^2-12x$ **$4x(2x+1)(x-3)$**

89. $(x-3)(x+10)$
90. $(3x+1)(2x+3)$
91. $(x+4)(x-4)$

Simplify. All variables represent nonnegative numbers. (Lesson 11-6)

95. $\sqrt{360}$ **$6\sqrt{10}$**

96. $\sqrt{\frac{72}{16}}$ **$\frac{3\sqrt{2}}{2}$**

97. $\sqrt{\frac{49x^2}{64y^4}}$ **$\frac{7x}{8y^2}$**

98. $\sqrt{\frac{50a^7}{9a^3}}$ **$\frac{5a^2\sqrt{2}}{3}$**

TEST PREP DOCTOR Students choosing **A** in **Exercise 75** chose the simplified form of $\sqrt{75}$.

Students who chose **A** in **Exercise 77** most likely forgot to square the 5 outside the radical sign. Remind them to square every factor inside the parentheses:

$\left(5\sqrt{10}\right)^2 = 5^2\left(\sqrt{10}\right)^2 = 25 \cdot 10 = 250$

Journal

Have students explain how to multiply and simplify the product of $3\sqrt{5}$ and $2\sqrt{10}$.

ALTERNATIVE ASSESSMENT

Have students write a square-root expression that contains two terms. Then have them write the simplified form of the square of their expression. Next, have students write a fraction with a denominator that is a square root whose radicand is not a perfect square. Have them simplify their fractions.

Power Presentations with PowerPoint®

11-8 Lesson Quiz

Multiply. Write each product in simplest form.

1. $\sqrt{5}\sqrt{10}$ $5\sqrt{2}$
2. $3\sqrt{6x}\sqrt{8x}$ $12x\sqrt{3}$
3. $\sqrt{2}\left(\sqrt{7}+\sqrt{2}\right)$ $\sqrt{14}+2$
4. $\left(2+\sqrt{5}\right)^2$ $9+4\sqrt{5}$
5. $\left(3\sqrt{6}\right)^2$ 54
6. $\sqrt{3}\left(5-\sqrt{18}\right)$ $5\sqrt{3}-3\sqrt{6}$
7. $\left(6+\sqrt{3}\right)\left(2-\sqrt{3}\right)$ $9-4\sqrt{3}$

Simplify each quotient.

8. $\frac{\sqrt{5}}{\sqrt{6}}$ $\frac{\sqrt{30}}{6}$
9. $\frac{\sqrt{3x}}{\sqrt{18}}$ $\frac{\sqrt{6x}}{6}$

Also available on transparency

11-8 PROBLEM SOLVING

Write each correct answer as a radical expression in simplest form.

1. The expression $\sqrt{\frac{W}{R}}$ models the electrical current in amperes, where W is power in watts and R is resistance in ohms. How much electrical current is running through an appliance with 500 watts of power and 16 ohms of resistance?

$\frac{5\sqrt{5}}{2}$ amps

2. The diagram shows the dimensions of a dining table. With a leaf in place, the table expands to seat eight people.

[Diagram: rectangle $28\sqrt{10}$ in. by $8\sqrt{6}$ in.]

Find the area of the table.

$448\sqrt{15}$ in^2

Find the area of the table with the addition of a leaf that measures $8\sqrt{6}$ inches by $18\sqrt{3}$ inches.

$448\sqrt{15}+432\sqrt{2}$ in^2

3. Riley's new bedroom is a perfect square. Each side measures $2\sqrt{3}$ meters. Find the area and perimeter of Riley's bedroom.

area: 12 m^2; perimeter: $8\sqrt{3}$ m

Select the best answer.

4. R.J. lives in a studio apartment. The apartment is rectangular with a width of $10+4\sqrt{2}$ feet and a length of $20+11\sqrt{2}$ feet. What is the area of R.J.'s apartment?

A 60 ft^2
B 288 ft^2
C $200+190\sqrt{2}$ ft^2
D $288+190\sqrt{2}$ ft^2

5. The volume of water in a lake, in gallons, can be represented by $x\sqrt{2}$. Heavy rains are forecast. The volume of water is expected to increase $\sqrt{2}$ times. How many gallons of water are expected in the lake after the rain?

F $\frac{x}{2}$ gallons
G x gallons
H $x\sqrt{2}$ gallons
J $2x$ gallons

6. The area of a rectangular window is 40 square feet. The length is $\sqrt{20}$ feet. What is the width of the window?

A $\sqrt{2}$ feet
B 2 feet
C $4\sqrt{5}$ feet
D $4\sqrt{10}$ feet

7. The height of a triangle can be found using $h = \frac{2A}{b}$ where A is the area and b is the base of the triangle. Which shows the height of a triangle with an area of $\sqrt{90}$ cm^2 and a base of $\sqrt{5}$ cm written in simplest form?

F $2\sqrt{18}$ cm
G $3\sqrt{18}$ cm
H $6\sqrt{2}$ cm
J $18\sqrt{2}$ cm

11-8 CHALLENGE

The solutions of a quadratic equation are sometimes called *roots*, but that has nothing to do with whether or not the solution contains a square root. If a solution does contain a square root, it is called an *irrational root.*

1. Is $x = -5+\sqrt{3}$ an irrational root of $0 = x^2+10x+22$? Substitute and simplify to find out.

Yes; $(-5+\sqrt{3})^2+10(-5+\sqrt{3})+22 =$
$(28-10\sqrt{3})+(-50+10\sqrt{3})+22 = 0$

2. Use the Quadratic Formula to find all roots of $0 = x^2+10x+22$. Does this support your answer to question 1?

$x = -5\pm\sqrt{3}$; yes, $x = -5+\sqrt{3}$ is one of the two roots.

3. Is $x = 1-3\sqrt{2}$ an irrational root of $0 = 4x^2-4x-17$? Substitute and simplify to find out.

No; $4(1-3\sqrt{2})^2-4(1-3\sqrt{2})-17 =$
$(76-24\sqrt{2})-(4-12\sqrt{2})-17 =$
$55-12\sqrt{2} \neq 0$

4. Use the Quadratic Formula to find all roots of $0 = 4x^2-4x-17$. Does this support your answer to question 3?

$x = \frac{1\pm3\sqrt{2}}{2} = \frac{1}{2}\pm\frac{3}{2}\sqrt{2}$; yes, $x = 1-3\sqrt{2}$ is *not* one of the two roots.

5. Look at the roots that you found in questions 2 and 4. Based on these few examples, complete these conjectures about the irrational roots of quadratic equations that have rational coefficients:

a. In general, the irrational roots are **conjugates** of each other.

b. If one root is $m+n\sqrt{p}$, then the other root is **$m-n\sqrt{p}$**

6. Explain how the Quadratic Formula guarantees that your conjectures in question 5 will hold true any time a quadratic equation has irrational roots.

The quadratic formula includes ± square root; irrational roots will always be conjugates.

7. Recall that when the discriminant (b^2-4ac) is greater than zero, there are two real solutions. What must be true about the discriminant for there to be two irrational solutions?

b^2-4ac would have to be greater than zero and *not* a perfect square.

11-9 Organizer

Pacing: Traditional 1 day
Block $\frac{1}{2}$ day

Objective: Solve radical equations.

Warm Up

Solve each equation.

1. $3x + 5 = 17$ 4
2. $4x + 1 = 2x - 3$ -2
3. $\frac{x}{7} = 5$ 35
4. $(x + 7)(x - 4) = 0$ $-7, 4$
5. $x^2 - 11x + 30 = 0$ 6, 5
6. $x^2 = 2x + 15$ 5, -3

Also available on transparency

Math Humor

Q: What did Mr. and Mrs. Square find when they were researching their family history?

A. Square roots.

11-9 Solving Radical Equations

Objective
Solve radical equations.

Vocabulary
radical equation
extraneous solution

Who uses this?
Meteorologists can use radical equations to estimate the size of a storm. (See Exercise 76.)

A **radical equation** is an equation that contains a variable within a radical. In this course, you will only study radical equations that contain square roots.

Recall that you use inverse operations to solve equations. For nonnegative numbers, squaring and taking the square root are inverse operations. When an equation contains a variable within a square root, square both sides of the equation to solve.

Know it! Note

Power Property of Equality

WORDS	NUMBERS	ALGEBRA
You can square both sides of an equation, and the resulting equation is still true.	$3 = 1 + 2$ $(3)^2 = (1 + 2)^2$ $9 = 9$	If a and b are real numbers and $a = b$, then $a^2 = b^2$.

EXAMPLE 1 Solving Simple Radical Equations

Solve each equation. Check your answer.

A $\sqrt{x} = 8$

$(\sqrt{x})^2 = (8)^2$ *Square both sides.*

$x = 64$

Check $\sqrt{x} = 8$

$\sqrt{64}$ | 8 *Substitute 64 for x in the original equation.*

8 | 8 ✓ *Simplify.*

B $6 = \sqrt{4x}$

$(6)^2 = (\sqrt{4x})^2$ *Square both sides.*

$36 = 4x$

$9 = x$ *Divide both sides by 4.*

Check $6 = \sqrt{4x}$

6 | $\sqrt{4(9)}$ *Substitute 9 for x in the original equation.*

6 | $\sqrt{36}$ *Simplify.*

6 | 6 ✓

Solve each equation. Check your answer.

1a. $\sqrt{x} = 6$ **36** **1b.** $9 = \sqrt{27x}$ **3** **1c.** $\sqrt{3x} = 1$ $\mathbf{\frac{1}{3}}$

State Resources

1 Introduce

11-9 Solving Radical Equations

You will need a graphing calculator for this Exploration.

1. To solve the equation $\sqrt{x+3} = 3$, press [Y=] and enter $\sqrt{x+3}$ for **Y1** and 3 for **Y2**.

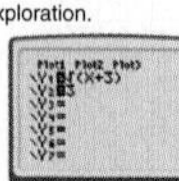

2. Press [GRAPH].

3. The solution of the equation is the x-value where the graphs intersect. To find this value, use the calculator's Intersect feature by pressing [2nd] [TRACE] and selecting **5:intersect**.

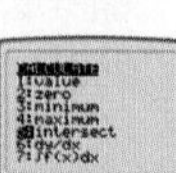

Use the arrow keys to move the cursor to the graph of the first function and press [ENTER]. Then move the cursor to the graph of the second function and press [ENTER]. Finally, move the cursor near the intersection and press [ENTER]. The coordinates of the point of intersection will be displayed.

4. What is the solution of the equation?

5. Use the same method to solve $\sqrt{3x+1} = 4$.

THINK AND DISCUSS

6. **Describe** how you could check your solutions.

7. **Discuss** what you think would happen if you tried to use this

Motivate

Have students use guess and check to find the correct value of x in $8 = \sqrt{2x}$. $x = 32$

Have students use guess and check to solve $\sqrt{7x + 4} - 9 = 0$. $x = 11$

Tell students that in this lesson they will learn methods to help them solve more complicated radical equations such as the second type.

Explorations and answers are provided in *Alternate Openers: Explorations Transparencies.*

Some square-root equations do not have the square root isolated. To solve these equations, you may have to isolate the square root before squaring both sides. You can do this by using one or more inverse operations.

EXAMPLE 2 Solving Radical Equations by Adding or Subtracting

Solve each equation. Check your answer.

A $\sqrt{x} + 3 = 10$

$\sqrt{x} = 7$ *Subtract 3 from both sides.*

$(\sqrt{x})^2 = (7)^2$ *Square both sides.*

$x = 49$

Check

$\sqrt{x} + 3$	$= 10$
$\sqrt{49} + 3$	10
$7 + 3$	10
10	10 ✓

B $\sqrt{x - 5} = 4$

$(\sqrt{x-5})^2 = (4)^2$ *Square both sides.*

$x - 5 = 16$

$x = 21$ *Add 5 to both sides.*

Check

$\sqrt{x - 5}$	$= 4$
$\sqrt{21 - 5}$	4
$\sqrt{16}$	4
4	4 ✓

C $\sqrt{2x - 1} + 4 = 7$

$\sqrt{2x-1} = 3$ *Subtract 4 from both sides.*

$(\sqrt{2x-1})^2 = (3)^2$ *Square both sides.*

$2x - 1 = 9$

$2x = 10$ *Add 1 to both sides.*

$x = 5$ *Divide both sides by 2.*

Check

$\sqrt{2x - 1} + 4$	$= 7$
$\sqrt{2(5) - 1} + 4$	7
$\sqrt{10 - 1} + 4$	7
$\sqrt{9} + 4$	7
$3 + 4$	7
7	7 ✓

Solve each equation. Check your answer.

2a. $\sqrt{x} - 2 = 1$ **9** **2b.** $\sqrt{x + 7} = 5$ **18** **2c.** $\sqrt{3x + 7} - 1 = 3$ **3**

EXAMPLE 3 Solving Radical Equations by Multiplying or Dividing

Solve each equation. Check your answer.

A $3\sqrt{x} = 21$

Method 1

$3\sqrt{x} = 21$

$\sqrt{x} = 7$ *Divide both sides by 3.*

$(\sqrt{x})^2 = (7)^2$ *Square both sides.*

$x = 49$

Method 2

$3\sqrt{x} = 21$

$(3\sqrt{x})^2 = 21^2$ *Square both sides.*

$9x = 441$

$x = 49$ *Divide both sides by 9.*

Check

$3\sqrt{x}$	$= 21$	
$3\sqrt{49}$	21	*Substitute 49 for x in the original equation.*
$3(7)$	21	*Simplify.*
21	21 ✓	

2 Teach

Guided Instruction

Tell students that the goal in solving a radical equation is the same as it was for linear equations: to isolate the variable by using inverse operations. Students might try to square both sides of an equation before moving a term to the other side. Explain that, while this is not incorrect, if they make that choice, they must square the entire left side, which would require using FOIL and many algebraic steps. Encourage students to move one term to the other side to reduce the number of steps and the possibility of error.

Reaching All Learners

Through Multiple Representations

Show students how to use a graphing calculator to determine how many solutions a radical equation has. First rewrite the equation so that one side is 0. Then substitute y for 0 and check the graph for x-intercepts. For $11 + \sqrt{5x} = 6$ in **Check It Out 5A,** graph $y = \sqrt{5x} + 5$. It does not cross the x-axis; it has no solution. You can also graph $y = 11 + \sqrt{5x}$ and $y = 6$ and see that they do not intersect.

COMMON ERROR ALERT

When squaring the product of a constant and a radical, students might forget to square the constant. For example, they might write $(3\sqrt{x})^2$ as $3x$. Show students that $(3\sqrt{x})^2 = (3\sqrt{x})(3\sqrt{x}) = 9x$.

Power Presentations with PowerPoint®

Additional Examples

Example 1

Solve each equation. Check your answer.

A. $\sqrt{x} = 5$ 25

B. $10 = \sqrt{2x}$ 50

Example 2

Solve each equation. Check your answer.

A. $\sqrt{x} - 4 = 5$ 81

B. $\sqrt{x + 3} = 7$ 46

C. $\sqrt{5x + 1} + 6 = 10$ 3

Example 3

Solve each equation. Check your answer.

A. $4\sqrt{x} = 32$ 64

B. $6 = \frac{\sqrt{x}}{2}$ 144

INTERVENTION

Questioning Strategies

EXAMPLE 1

- What inverse operation isolates the variable in a radical equation?

EXAMPLE 2

- How do you choose whether to square both sides or to add or subtract for your first step?

EXAMPLE 3

- How are the two methods similar? How are they different?

Power Presentations with PowerPoint®

Additional Examples

Example 4

Solve each equation. Check your answer.

A. $\sqrt{2x-1} = \sqrt{x+7}$ 8

B. $\sqrt{5x-4} - \sqrt{6} = 0$ 2

INTERVENTION
Questioning Strategies

EXAMPLE 4

- Why is it more efficient to have only one radical term on each side when solving a radical equation?

Multiple Representations Solutions to equations like those in **Example 4B** can be checked by graphing the related function and finding the zero.

Solve each equation. Check your answer.

B $\frac{\sqrt{x}}{3} = 5$

Method 1

$\sqrt{x} = 15$ *Multiply both sides by 3.*

$(\sqrt{x})^2 = (15)^2$ *Square both sides.*

$x = 225$

Method 2

$\left(\frac{\sqrt{x}}{3}\right)^2 = (5)^2$ *Square both sides.*

$\frac{x}{9} = 25$

$x = 225$ *Multiply both sides by 9.*

Check $\frac{\sqrt{x}}{3} = 5$

$\frac{\sqrt{225}}{3}$	5
$\frac{15}{3}$	5
5	5 ✓

Substitute 225 for x in the original equation.

Simplify.

Solve each equation. Check your answer.

3a. $2\sqrt{x} = 22$ **121** **3b.** $2 = \frac{\sqrt{x}}{4}$ **64** **3c.** $\frac{2\sqrt{x}}{5} = 4$ **100**

EXAMPLE 4 Solving Radical Equations with Square Roots on Both Sides

Solve each equation. Check your answer.

A $\sqrt{x+1} = \sqrt{3}$

$(\sqrt{x+1})^2 = (\sqrt{3})^2$ *Square both sides.*

$x + 1 = 3$

$x = 2$ *Subtract 1 from both sides.*

Check $\sqrt{x+1} = \sqrt{3}$

$\sqrt{2+1}$	$\sqrt{3}$
$\sqrt{3}$	$\sqrt{3}$ ✓

B $\sqrt{x+8} - \sqrt{3x} = 0$

$\sqrt{x+8} = \sqrt{3x}$ *Add $\sqrt{3x}$ to both sides.*

$(\sqrt{x+8})^2 = (\sqrt{3x})^2$ *Square both sides.*

$x + 8 = 3x$

$8 = 2x$ *Subtract x from both sides.*

$4 = x$ *Divide both sides by 2.*

Check $\sqrt{x+8} - \sqrt{3x} = 0$

$\sqrt{4+8} - \sqrt{3(4)}$	0
$\sqrt{12} - \sqrt{12}$	0
0	0 ✓

Solve each equation. Check your answer.

4a. $\sqrt{3x+2} = \sqrt{x+6}$ **2** **4b.** $\sqrt{2x-5} - \sqrt{6} = 0$ $\mathbf{\frac{11}{2}}$

Squaring both sides of an equation may result in an **extraneous solution**—a number that is not a solution of the original equation.

Suppose your original equation is $x = 3$. $x = 3$

Square both sides. Now you have a new equation. $x^2 = 9$

Solve this new equation for x by taking the square root of both sides. $\sqrt{x^2} = \sqrt{9}$; $x = 3$ or $x = -3$

Now there are two solutions of the new equation. One ($x = 3$) is a solution of the original equation. The other ($x = -3$) is extraneous—it is not a solution of the original equation. Because of extraneous solutions, it is important to check your answers.

EXAMPLE 5 Extraneous Solutions

Solve $\sqrt{6-x}=x$. Check your answer.

$$\left(\sqrt{6-x}\right)^2=(x)^2 \quad \textit{Square both sides.}$$
$$6-x=x^2$$
$$x^2+x-6=0 \quad \textit{Write in standard form.}$$
$$(x-2)(x+3)=0 \quad \textit{Factor.}$$
$$x-2=0 \text{ or } x+3=0 \quad \textit{Zero-Product Property}$$
$$x=2 \text{ or } x=-3 \quad \textit{Solve for x.}$$

Helpful Hint

The equation in Example 5 has one solution. When all of the solutions of an equation are extraneous, the original equation has no solutions.

Check $\sqrt{6-x}=x$

$\sqrt{6-2}$	2	*Substitute 2 for x in the equation.*
$\sqrt{4}$	2	
2	2 ✓	

$\sqrt{6-x}=x$

$\sqrt{6-(-3)}$	-3	*Substitute −3 for x in the equation.*
$\sqrt{9}$	-3	
3	-3 ✗	

-3 does not check; it is extraneous. The only solution is 2.

Solve each equation. Check your answer.

5a. $11+\sqrt{5x}=6$ **no solution** **5b.** $x=\sqrt{-3x-2}$ **no solution** **5c.** $x-2=\sqrt{x}$ **4**

EXAMPLE 6 *Geometry Application*

Geometry

A rectangle has an area of 52 square feet. Its length is 13 feet, and its width is $\sqrt{x}$ feet. What is the value of x? What is the width of the rectangle?

$A = 52\text{ ft}^2$ | $\sqrt{x}$ ft | 13 ft

$$A=\ell w \quad \textit{Use the formula for area of a rectangle.}$$
$$52=13\sqrt{x} \quad \textit{Substitute 52 for A, 13 for } \ell \textit{, and } \sqrt{x} \textit{ for w.}$$
$$\frac{52}{13}=\frac{13\sqrt{x}}{13} \quad \textit{Divide both sides by 13.}$$
$$4=\sqrt{x}$$
$$4^2=\left(\sqrt{x}\right)^2 \quad \textit{Square both sides.}$$
$$16=x$$

Check $A=\ell w$

$52=13\sqrt{x}$

52	$13\sqrt{16}$	*Substitute 16 for x in the equation.*
52	$13(4)$	
52	52 ✓	

The value of x is 16. The width of the rectangle is $\sqrt{16}=4$ feet.

6. A rectangle has an area of 15 cm². Its width is 5 cm, and its length is $\left(\sqrt{x+1}\right)$ cm. What is the value of x? What is the length of the rectangle? **8; 3 cm**

Reading Math Explain that sometimes *extra* is good, like extra credit, but in math, the *extra* in *extraneous* refers to something that is not valid or that is irrelevant and not wanted. **English Language Learners**

Power Presentations with PowerPoint®

Additional Examples

Example 5

Solve each equation. Check your answer.

A. $12+\sqrt{6x}=6$ no solution

B. $x=\sqrt{2x+3}$ 3

Example 6

A triangle has an area of 36 square feet. Its base is 8 feet, and its height is $\sqrt{x-1}$ feet. What is the value of x? What is the height of the triangle? 82; 9 ft

INTERVENTION

Questioning Strategies

EXAMPLE 5

- Why is it necessary to check your answers when solving radical equations?

EXAMPLE 6

- Is it necessary to find the value of x in order to determine the width of the rectangle? Explain.

3 Close

Summarize

Have students state the first step they would take to solve each equation.

$15=\sqrt{x}$ Square both sides.

$\sqrt{3x}+1=6$ Subtract 1 from both sides.

$\sqrt{3x+1}=6$ Square both sides.

$\frac{\sqrt{x}}{5}=8$ Multiply both sides by 5, or square both sides.

$\sqrt{x+2}-\sqrt{2x}=0$ Add $\sqrt{2x}$ to both sides.

Ongoing Assessment and INTERVENTION 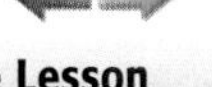

***Diagnose Before* the Lesson**
11-9 Warm Up, TE p. 846

***Monitor During* the Lesson**
Check It Out! Exercises, SE pp. 846–849
Questioning Strategies, TE pp. 847–849

***Assess After* the Lesson**
11-9 Lesson Quiz, TE p. 853
Alternative Assessment, TE p. 853

Answers to *Think and Discuss*

1. Possible answer: Method 1 is preferable because 21 is easily divided by 3 and dividing by 3 first keeps the numbers small.
2. Subtract 3 from both sides. After doing this, you can square both sides to eliminate the radical.
3. See p. A10.

THINK AND DISCUSS

1. Compare the two methods used in Example 3A. Which method do you prefer? Why?
2. What is the first step to solve $\sqrt{x-2}+3=8$? Why?

3. **GET ORGANIZED** Copy and complete the graphic organizer. Write and solve a radical equation, using the boxes to show each step.

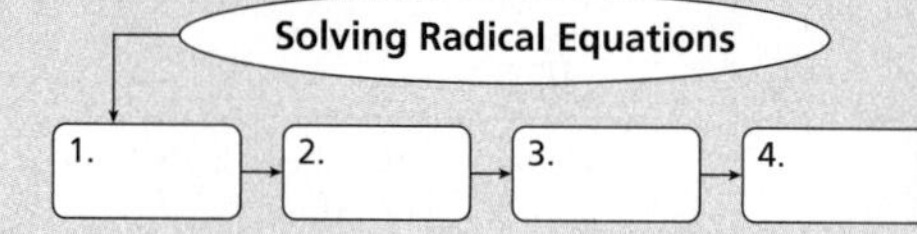

11-9 Exercises

11-9 Exercises

Assignment Guide

Assign *Guided Practice* exercises as necessary.

If you finished Examples **1–3**
Basic 41–52, 69, 70, 74
Average 41–52, 69, 70, 74, 80
Advanced 41–52, 69, 70, 74, 80

If you finished Examples **1–6**
Basic 41–74, 76, 78, 83, 84, 86–91, 101–107
Average 42–76 even, 78–82, 84–91, 98, 99, 101–107
Advanced 42–66 even, 67–82, 84–107

Homework Quick Check
Quickly check key concepts.
Exercises: 42, 48, 50, 56, 64, 67

GUIDED PRACTICE

1. **Vocabulary** Is $x=\sqrt{3}$ a *radical equation*? Why or why not? **No; it does not contain a variable under the radical sign.**

SEE EXAMPLE 1 p. 846

Solve each equation. Check your answer.

2. $\sqrt{x}=7$ **49**
3. $4=\sqrt{-2y}$ **−8**
4. $\sqrt{20a}=10$ **5**
5. $12=\sqrt{-x}$ **−144**

SEE EXAMPLE 2 p. 847

6. $\sqrt{x}+6=11$ **25**
7. $\sqrt{2x-5}=7$ **27**
8. $\sqrt{2-a}=3$ **−7**
9. $\sqrt{2x}-3=7$ **50**
10. $\sqrt{x-2}=3$ **11**
11. $\sqrt{x+3}=1$ **−2**
12. $\sqrt{x-1}=2$ **5**
13. $\sqrt{4y+13}-1=6$ **9**

SEE EXAMPLE 3 p. 847

14. $-2\sqrt{x}=-10$ **25**
15. $\frac{\sqrt{a}}{2}=4$ **64**
16. $5\sqrt{-x}=20$ **−16**
17. $\frac{3\sqrt{x}}{4}=3$ **16**
18. $\frac{5\sqrt{x}}{6}=10$ **144**
19. $2\sqrt{x}=8$ **16**
20. $\frac{\sqrt{x}}{3}=3$ **81**
21. $\frac{3\sqrt{x}}{2}=1$ $\mathbf{\frac{4}{9}}$
22. $13\sqrt{2x}=26$ **2**
23. $\frac{\sqrt{x}}{5}=2$ **100**
24. $\frac{\sqrt{x-7}}{3}=1$ **16**
25. $4\sqrt{2x-1}=12$ **5**

SEE EXAMPLE 4 p. 848

Solve each equation. Check your answer.

26. $\sqrt{5-x}=\sqrt{6x-2}$ **1**
27. $\sqrt{x+7}=\sqrt{3x-19}$ **13**
28. $0=\sqrt{2x}-\sqrt{x+3}$ **3**
29. $\sqrt{x-5}=\sqrt{7-x}$ **6**
30. $\sqrt{-x}=\sqrt{2x+1}$ $\mathbf{-\frac{1}{3}}$
31. $\sqrt{3x+1}-\sqrt{2x+3}=0$ **2**

SEE EXAMPLE 5 p. 849

Solve each equation. Check your answer.

32. $\sqrt{x-5}+5=0$
33. $\sqrt{3x}+5=3$
34. $\sqrt{2-7x}=2x$
35. $x=\sqrt{12+x}$
36. $6+\sqrt{x-1}=4$
37. $\sqrt{6-3x}+2=x$
38. $\sqrt{x-2}=2-x$
39. $10+\sqrt{x}=5$

SEE EXAMPLE 6 p. 849

40. **Geometry** A trapezoid has an area of 14 cm^2. The length of one base is 4 cm and the length of the other base is 10 cm. The height is $(\sqrt{2x+3})$ cm. What is the value of x? What is the height of the trapezoid? (*Hint:* The formula for the area of a trapezoid is $A=\frac{1}{2}(b_1+b_2)h$.) $\mathbf{x=\frac{1}{2}}$**; 2 cm**

State Resources

PRACTICE AND PROBLEM SOLVING

Independent Practice

For Exercises	See Example
41–44	1
45–48	2
49–52	3
53–58	4
59–66	5
67	6

Extra Practice
Skills Practice p. S25
Application Practice p. S38

Solve each equation. Check your answer.

41. $\sqrt{3x} = 12$ **48**
42. $2 = \sqrt{-2x}$ **−2**
43. $\sqrt{-a} = 5$ **−25**
44. $11 = \sqrt{c}$ **121**
45. $\sqrt{x-7} = 8$ **71**
46. $\sqrt{x} - 4 = 0$ **16**
47. $\sqrt{1-3x} = 5$ **−8**
48. $\sqrt{5x+1} + 2 = 6$ **3**
49. $5\sqrt{x} = 30$ **36**
50. $\dfrac{\sqrt{2x}}{2} = 4$ **32**
51. $5\sqrt{-x} = 20$ **−16**
52. $3\sqrt{3p} = 9$ **3**

Solve each equation. Check your answer.

53. $\sqrt{3x-13} = \sqrt{x+3}$ **8**
54. $\sqrt{x} - \sqrt{6-x} = 0$ **3**
55. $\sqrt{x+5} = \sqrt{2x-4}$ **9**
56. $\sqrt{4x-2} = \sqrt{3x+4}$ **6**
57. $\sqrt{5x-6} = \sqrt{16-6x}$ **2**
58. $\sqrt{12x-3} = \sqrt{4x+93}$ **12**

Solve each equation. Check your answer.

59. $\sqrt{x+6} = 1$ **−5**
60. $-2\sqrt{x} = 6$
61. $x = \sqrt{2x+15}$ **5**
62. $\sqrt{6x} + 9 = 2$
63. $\sqrt{4-3x} = x$ **1**
64. $\sqrt{5x+4} = x - 4$
65. $\sqrt{2x+2} = 2x$ **1**
66. $\sqrt{x+3} + 10 = 7$

60. no solution
62. no solution
64. 12
66. no solution

67. **Geometry** A triangle has an area of 60 in^2. Its base is 10 inches and its height is $\sqrt{x}$ inches. What is the value of x? What is the height of the triangle? (*Hint:* The formula for the area of a triangle is $A = \frac{1}{2}bh$.) **$x = 144$; 12 in.**

Translate each sentence into an equation. Then solve the equation and check your answer.

68. The square root of three times a number is nine. **$\sqrt{3x} = 9$; 27**
69. The difference of the square root of a number and three is four. **$\sqrt{x} - 3 = 4$; 49**
70. The square root of the difference of a number and three is four. **$\sqrt{x-3} = 4$; 19**
71. A number is equal to the square root of the sum of that number and six. **$x = \sqrt{x+6}$; 3**

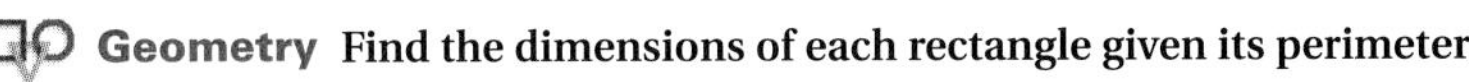

Geometry **Find the dimensions of each rectangle given its perimeter.**

72.
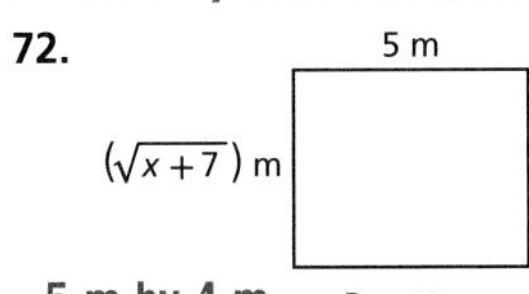

5 m by 4 m

73.
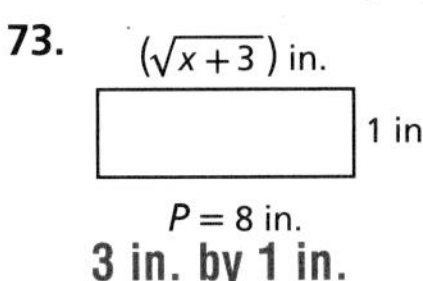

3 in. by 1 in.

74.
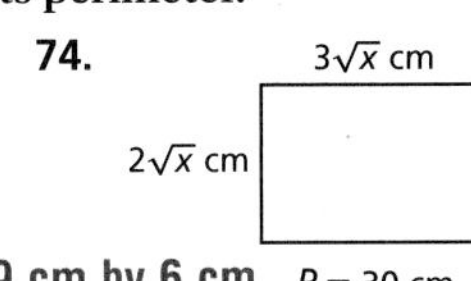

9 cm by 6 cm

75. **Physics** The formula $v = \dfrac{\sqrt{2Em}}{m}$ describes the relationship between an object's mass m in kilograms, its velocity v in meters per second, and its kinetic energy E in joules.
    a. A baseball with a mass of 0.14 kg is thrown with a velocity of 28 m/s. How much kinetic energy does the baseball have? **54.88 joules**
    b. What is the kinetic energy of an object at rest ($v = 0$)? **0 joules**

76. **Meteorology** The formula $t = \sqrt{\dfrac{d^2}{216}}$ gives the time t in hours that a storm with diameter d miles will last. What is the diameter of a storm that lasts 1 hour? Round your answer to the nearest hundredth. **14.70 mi**

77. **Transportation** A sharp curve may require a driver to slow down to avoid going off the road. The equation $v = \sqrt{2.5r}$ describes the relationship between the radius r in feet of an unbanked curve and the maximum velocity v in miles per hour that a car can safely go around the curve. An engineer is designing a highway with a maximum speed limit of 65 mi/h. What is the radius of an unbanked curve for which this is the maximum safe speed? **1690 ft**

LINK Meteorology

This color-enhanced satellite image is from the National Hurricane Center. Images such as this one show the size of a storm and the area that it covers.

COMMON ERROR ALERT

In **Exercise 16,** students may think there is no solution because there is a negative in the radicand. Remind students that there is no real solution if the radical expression, in this case $-x$, is equal to a negative number. However, if x is negative, then $-x$ is positive and can therefore appear in a radicand and there will be a real solution.

Answers

32. no solution
33. no solution
34. $\frac{1}{4}$
35. 4
36. no solution
37. 2
38. 2
39. no solution

11-9 PRACTICE A
11-9 PRACTICE C
11-9 PRACTICE B

Solve each equation. Check your answer.

1. $\sqrt{x} = 11$
   $(\sqrt{x})^2 = (11)^2$
   $x = $ **121**
2. $\dfrac{\sqrt{x}}{3} = 5$
   $\sqrt{x} = 15$
   $x = $ **225**
3. $\sqrt{3x} + 5 = 11$
   $\sqrt{3x} = $ **6**
   $3x = $ **36**
   $x = $ **12**
4. $2\sqrt{x} = 16$ **64**
5. $\dfrac{\sqrt{4x}}{2} = 4$ **16**
6. $\dfrac{3\sqrt{20x+4}}{4} = 6$ **3**
7. $\sqrt{x+5} = 9$ **76**
8. $\dfrac{\sqrt{x}}{4} = 1$ **16**
9. $\dfrac{3\sqrt{2x}}{4} = 12$ **128**
10. $\dfrac{\sqrt{2x}}{4} = 2$ **32**
11. $\dfrac{\sqrt{x+5}}{3} = 4$ **139**
12. $3\sqrt{6-x} = 6$ **2**
13. $\sqrt{10-x} = \sqrt{x-2}$ **6**
14. $\sqrt{x+2} = \sqrt{2x-1}$ **3**
15. $\sqrt{2x+10} - \sqrt{x+13} = 0$ **3**
16. $\sqrt{-x} = \sqrt{x+128}$ **−64**
17. $\sqrt{4+x} = 5\sqrt{x-20}$ **21**
18. $4 + x = \sqrt{x+4}$ **−4; −3**
19. $-3\sqrt{x} = 8$ **no solution**
20. $x = \sqrt{2x+15}$ **5**
21. According to Heron's formula, the area of a triangle is given by $A = \sqrt{s(s-a)(s-b)(s-c)}$, where s is equal to one half its perimeter, and a, b, and c are the lengths of its sides. If a triangle has area 20 m^2, $s = 10$ m, $a = 5$ m and $b = 2$ m, what is c? **9 m**

Exercise 86 involves solving radical equations. This exercise prepares students for the Multi-Step Test Prep on page 854.

Answers

82. Sometimes; for the equation $\sqrt{2x} = \sqrt{x^2 - 3}$, the value of x must be nonnegative in order for the left side to be defined, so the statement is true. For the equation $\sqrt{7 - x} = 3$, the solution is -2 and the statement is false.

78. **Write About It** Explain why it is important to check solutions when solving radical equations. **Radical equations may have extraneous solutions.**

79. **Multi-Step** Solve for x and y in the equations $\sqrt{x} + \sqrt{y} = \sqrt{81}$ and $6\sqrt{y} = 24$. (*Hint:* Solve for y first, and then use substitution to solve for x.) $x = 25$; $y = 16$

Tell whether the following statements are *always, sometimes,* or *never* true. If the answer is *sometimes,* give one example that is true and one that is false.

80. If $a = b$, then $a^2 = b^2$. **always**

81. If $a^2 = b^2$, then $a = b$. **Sometimes; for $a = b = 2$, the statement is true. For $a = 2$ and $b = -2$, the statement is false.**

82. When solving radical equations, the value of the variable is nonnegative.

83. **ERROR ANALYSIS** Two students solved $\sqrt{5 - x} = \sqrt{x + 9}$. Which is incorrect? Explain the error.

83. Student B made an error in going from $5 - x = x + 9$ to $4 = 2x$. The student should have added x to both sides and subtracted 9 from both sides to get $-4 = 2x$.

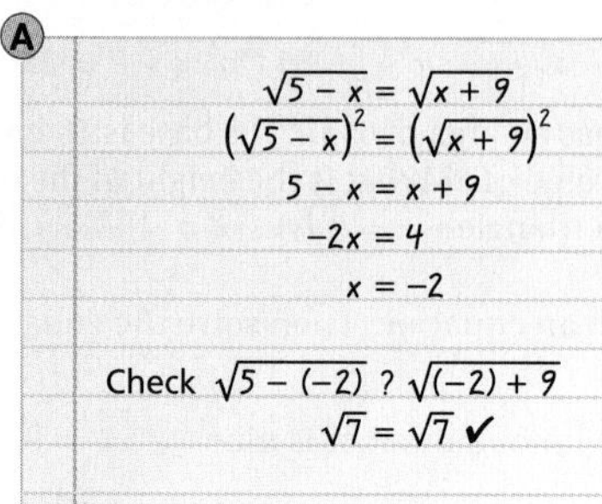

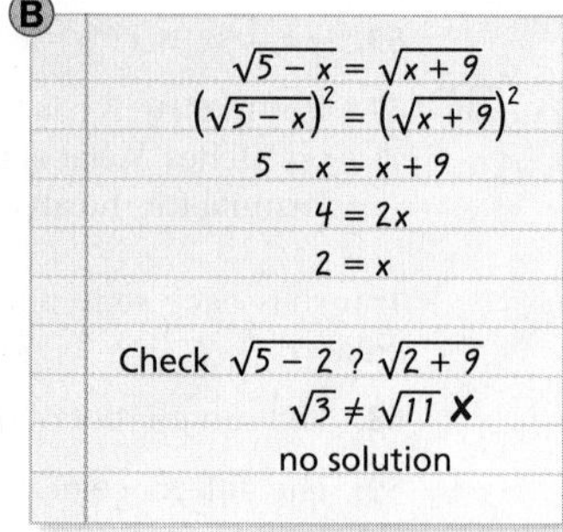

84. **Estimation** The relationship between a circle's radius and its area can be modeled by $r = \sqrt{\frac{A}{\pi}}$, where r is the radius and A is the area. Solutions to this equation are graphed at right. Use the graph to estimate the radius of a circle with an area of 29 m^2. **3 m**

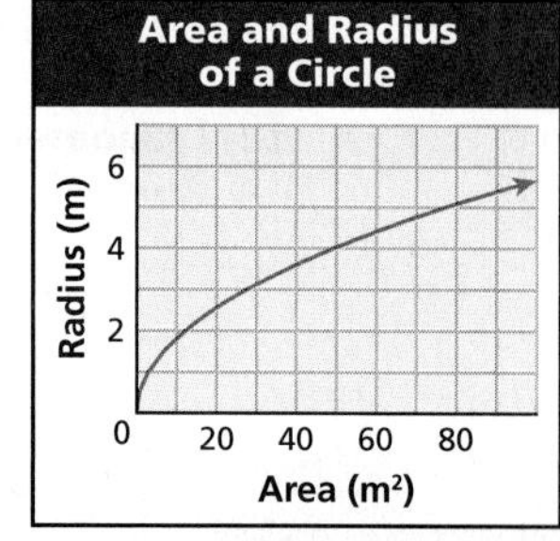

85. **Critical Thinking** Suppose that the equation $\sqrt{-x} = k$ has a solution. What does that tell you about the value of x? the value of k? Explain.

85. $x \le 0$ since the square root is only defined for nonneg. values. $k \ge 0$ since the value of the square root must be nonneg.

MULTI-STEP TEST PREP

86. This problem will prepare you for the Multi-Step Test Prep on page 854.
    a. The Demon Drop is a free-fall ride at Ohio's Cedar Point amusement park. The maximum speed on the Demon Drop is 42 miles per hour. Convert this speed to feet per second. (*Hint:* There are 5280 feet in a mile.) **61.6 ft/s**
    b. The Demon Drop is 131 feet tall. Most of the drop is a vertical free fall, but near the bottom, the track curves so that the cars slow down gradually. The velocity of any object in free fall is $v = 8\sqrt{d}$, where v is the velocity in feet per second and d is the distance the object has fallen in feet. Use this equation and your answer to part **a** to estimate the free-fall distance. **≈59.29 ft**

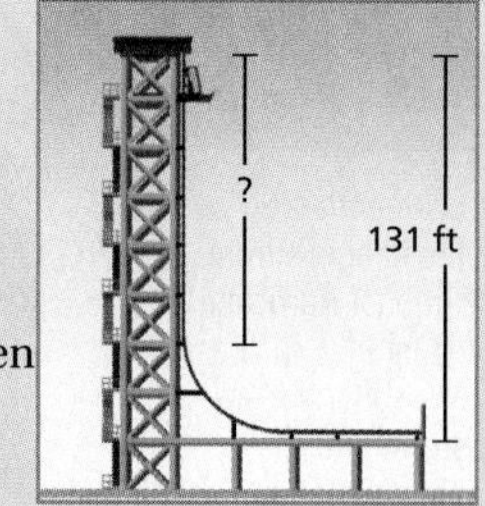

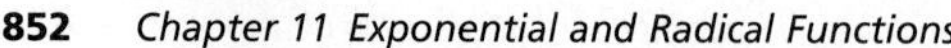

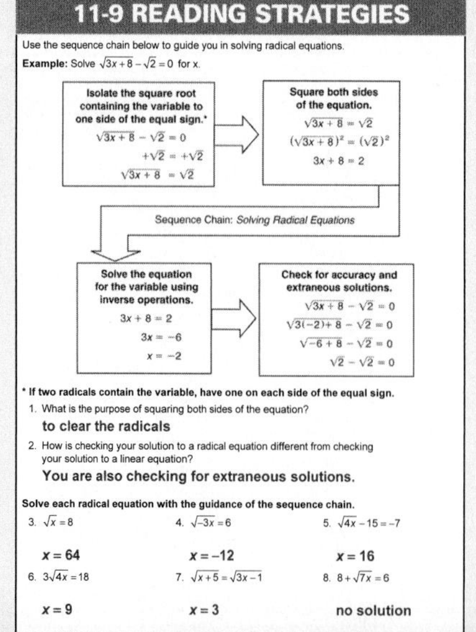

11-9 READING STRATEGIES

Use the sequence chain below to guide you in solving radical equations.

Example: Solve $\sqrt{3x + 8} - \sqrt{2} = 0$ for x.

Isolate the square root containing the variable to one side of the equal sign.*
$\sqrt{3x + 8} - \sqrt{2} = 0$
$+\sqrt{2} = +\sqrt{2}$
$\sqrt{3x + 8} = \sqrt{2}$

Square both sides of the equation.
$\sqrt{3x + 8} = \sqrt{2}$
$(\sqrt{3x + 8})^2 = (\sqrt{2})^2$
$3x + 8 = 2$

Sequence Chain: *Solving Radical Equations*

Solve the equation for the variable using inverse operations.
$3x + 8 = 2$
$3x = -6$
$x = -2$

Check for accuracy and extraneous solutions.
$\sqrt{3x + 8} - \sqrt{2} = 0$
$\sqrt{3(-2) + 8} - \sqrt{2} = 0$
$\sqrt{-6 + 8} - \sqrt{2} = 0$
$\sqrt{2} - \sqrt{2} = 0$

*** If two radicals contain the variable, have one on each side of the equal sign.**

1. What is the purpose of squaring both sides of the equation?
   to clear the radicals
2. How is checking your solution to a radical equation different from checking your solution to a linear equation?
   You are also checking for extraneous solutions.

Solve each radical equation with the guidance of the sequence chain.

3. $\sqrt{x} = 8$ — $x = 64$
4. $\sqrt{-3x} = 6$ — $x = -12$
5. $\sqrt{4x} - 15 = -7$ — $x = 16$
6. $3\sqrt{4x} = 18$ — $x = 9$
7. $\sqrt{x + 5} = \sqrt{3x - 1}$ — $x = 3$
8. $8 + \sqrt{7x} = 6$ — no solution

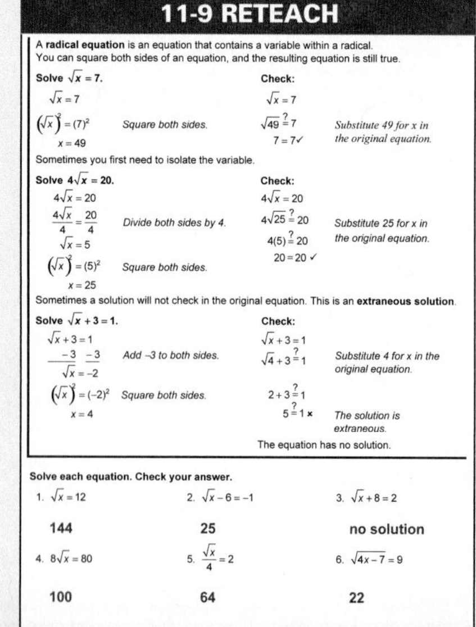

11-9 RETEACH

A **radical equation** is an equation that contains a variable within a radical.
You can square both sides of an equation, and the resulting equation is still true.

Solve $\sqrt{x} = 7$.
$\sqrt{x} = 7$
$(\sqrt{x})^2 = (7)^2$ *Square both sides.*
$x = 49$

Check:
$\sqrt{x} = 7$
$\sqrt{49} \stackrel{?}{=} 7$ *Substitute 49 for x in the original equation.*
$7 = 7$ ✓

Sometimes you first need to isolate the variable.

Solve $4\sqrt{x} = 20$.
$4\sqrt{x} = 20$
$\frac{4\sqrt{x}}{4} = \frac{20}{4}$ *Divide both sides by 4.*
$\sqrt{x} = 5$
$(\sqrt{x})^2 = (5)^2$ *Square both sides.*
$x = 25$

Check:
$4\sqrt{x} = 20$
$4\sqrt{25} \stackrel{?}{=} 20$ *Substitute 25 for x in the original equation.*
$4(5) \stackrel{?}{=} 20$
$20 = 20$ ✓

Sometimes a solution will not check in the original equation. This is an **extraneous solution**.

Solve $\sqrt{x} + 3 = 1$.
$\sqrt{x} + 3 = 1$
$-3\ \ -3$ *Add −3 to both sides.*
$\sqrt{x} = -2$
$(\sqrt{x})^2 = (-2)^2$ *Square both sides.*
$x = 4$

Check:
$\sqrt{x} + 3 = 1$
$\sqrt{4} + 3 \stackrel{?}{=} 1$ *Substitute 4 for x in the original equation.*
$2 + 3 \stackrel{?}{=} 1$
$5 \stackrel{?}{=} 1$ ✗ *The solution is extraneous.*
The equation has no solution.

Solve each equation. Check your answer.

1. $\sqrt{x} = 12$ — 144
2. $\sqrt{x} - 6 = -1$ — 25
3. $\sqrt{x} + 8 = 2$ — no solution
4. $8\sqrt{x} = 80$ — 100
5. $\frac{\sqrt{x}}{4} = 2$ — 64
6. $\sqrt{4x} - 7 = 9$ — 22

TEST PREP

87. Which of the following is the solution of $\sqrt{8-2x}-2=2$?

(A) -4 (B) -2 (C) 2 (D) 4

88. For which of the following values of k does the equation $\sqrt{x+1}+k=0$ have no real solution?

(F) -2 (G) -1 (H) 0 (J) 1

89. Which of the following is the solution of $x=\sqrt{12-x}$?

(A) -4 (B) -3 (C) 3 (D) 4

90. Which of the following is the solution of $\sqrt{x+13}=5\sqrt{x-11}$?

(F) 9 (G) 12 (H) 16 (J) 17

91. Which of the following is an extraneous solution of $\sqrt{3x-2}=x-2$?

(A) 1 (B) 2 (C) 3 (D) 6

CHALLENGE AND EXTEND

Solve each equation. Check your answer.

92. $\sqrt{x+3}=x+1$ **1**
93. $\sqrt{x-1}=x-1$ **1, 2**
94. $x-1=\sqrt{2x+6}$ **5**
95. $\sqrt{x^2+5x+11}=x+3$ **2**
96. $\sqrt{x^2+9x+14}=x+4$ **2**
97. $x+2=\sqrt{x^2+5x+4}$ **0**

98b. The equation has no solution. This is clear from the graphs since they do not intersect.

98. **Graphing Calculator** Solve $\sqrt{2x-2}=-\sqrt{x}$ and check your answer. Then use your graphing calculator for the following:
   a. Graph $y=\sqrt{2x-2}$ and $y=-\sqrt{x}$ on the same screen. Make a sketch of the graphs.
   b. Use the graphs in part **a** to explain your solution to $\sqrt{2x-2}=-\sqrt{x}$.

99b. The solution is $x=3$, which is where the graphs intersect.

99. **Graphing Calculator** Solve $x=\sqrt{x+6}$ and check your answer. Then use your graphing calculator for the following:
   a. Graph $y=x$ and $y=\sqrt{x+6}$ on the same screen. Make a sketch of the graphs.
   b. Use the graphs in part **a** to explain your solution to $x=\sqrt{x+6}$.

100. Find the domain for the function $y=\frac{4}{\sqrt{x-2}}$. Is the domain for this function different from the domain for the function $y=\sqrt{x-2}$? Why or why not?
$x>2$; x cannot equal 2 because the denom. cannot equal 0.

SPIRAL REVIEW

101. On a map, the distance between two towns is 3.2 inches. If the map uses the scale 2.5 in:40 mi, what is the actual distance between the towns? *(Lesson 2-7)* **51.2 mi**

102. In model railroading, O-scale trains use the scale 1:48. An O-scale boxcar measures 12.5 inches. How many feet long is the boxcar that it models? *(Lesson 2-7)* **50 ft**

103. The personal identification number (PIN) for a debit card is made up of four numbers. How many PINs are possible? *(Lesson 10-8)* **10,000**

104. A dessert menu offers 6 different selections. The restaurant offers a dessert sampler that includes small portions of any 4 different choices from the dessert menu. How many different dessert samplers are possible? *(Lesson 10-8)* **15**

Graph each square-root function. *(Lesson 11-5)*

105. $f(x)=\sqrt{x+3}$
106. $f(x)=\sqrt{3x-6}$
107. $f(x)=2\sqrt{x}+1$

TEST PREP DOCTOR A radical equation has no real solution if the radical expression is equal to a negative number. In **Exercise 88,** moving k to the other side yields $-k$ on the right side. The only way to obtain a negative number on the right side is to substitute a number greater than zero for k.

Answers

98a.

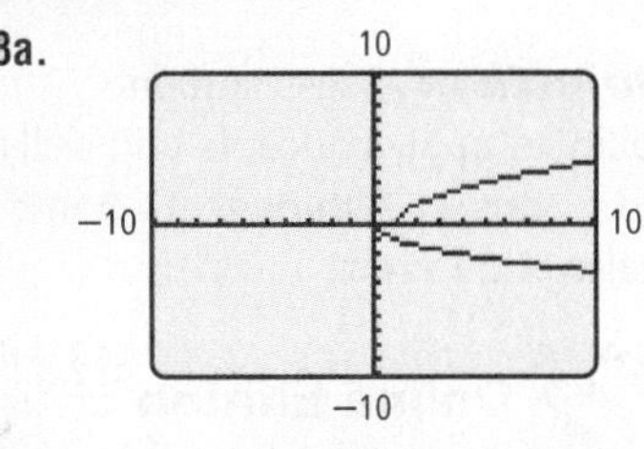

99a.

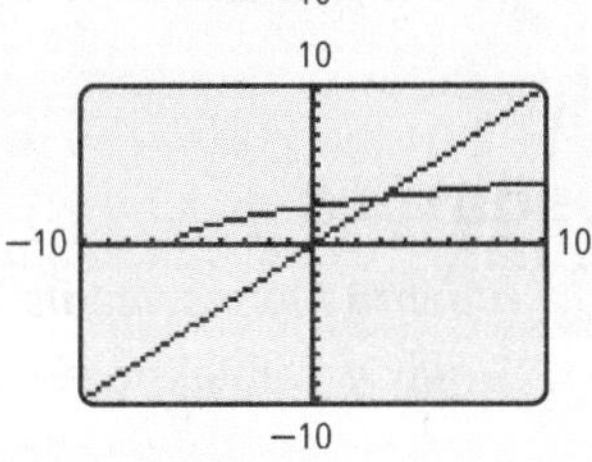

105–107. See p. A35.

Journal

Explain how the process of solving radical equations sometimes generates extraneous solutions.

ALTERNATIVE ASSESSMENT

Have students solve the following equations, justifying each step along the way. Solutions must include answer checking.

1. $\sqrt{-2x+3}=\sqrt{x}$
2. $\sqrt{-2x+3}=x$

Power Presentations with PowerPoint®

11-9 Lesson Quiz

Solve each equation. Check your answer.

1. $\frac{2\sqrt{x}}{3}=4$ 36
2. $\sqrt{5x}=15$ 45
3. $\sqrt{5x}+8=3$ no solution
4. $\sqrt{4x+5}-2=5$ 11
5. $\sqrt{3x+1}-\sqrt{2x+5}=0$ 4
6. $x=\sqrt{2x+8}$ 4
7. A triangle has an area of 48 square feet. Its base is 6 feet, and its height is $\sqrt{x+3}$ feet. What is the value of x? What is the height of the triangle? 253; 16 ft

Also available on transparency

11-9 PROBLEM SOLVING

Write the correct answer.

1. The perimeter of the marching band's practice field is 360 yards. Its length and width are shown in the diagram.

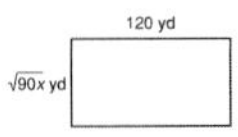

120 yd; $\sqrt{90x}$ yd

Find the value of x and the width of the field. Then calculate the area of the field.
$x=40$; width $=60$ yd; Area $=7200$ yd^2

2. The formula $v=\frac{\sqrt{2Em}}{m}$ describes the relationship between an object's mass m in kilograms, its velocity v in meters per second, and its kinetic energy E in joules. A bowling ball with a mass of 5 kg is thrown with a velocity of 8 meters per second. Determine the kinetic energy of the bowling ball.
160 joules

3. An office has a storage closet with an area of 48 square feet. The length of the closet is 8 feet. The width is $2\sqrt{11-x}$ feet. Find the value of x and the width of the closet.
$x=2$; 6 feet

Select the best answer.

4. The equation $v=\sqrt{2.5r}$ describes the relationship between the radius r in feet of an unbanked curve and the maximum velocity v in miles per hour that a car can safely go around the curve. A primary road with a speed limit of 35 miles per hour curves through a residential area. What is the radius of the unbanked curve?

A 14 feet C 450 feet
B 49 feet **D** 490 feet

5. The remains of a structure on an archeological site are laid out in the shape of a rectangle. The area of the rectangle is 12 square meters. The width is 3 meters and the length is $\sqrt{x+6}$ meters. What is the value of x?

F 4 H 12
G 10 J 16

6. A building sits on a lot that is shaped like a triangle with a base of 120 feet and a height of $\sqrt{5000x}$ feet. The area of the lot is 12,000 square feet. Which length represents the height of the triangle?

A 8 feet **C** 200 feet
B 100 feet D 400 feet

7. Gretchen mixes her own bubble bath using essential oils. She uses a jar that holds $\sqrt{33}$ ounces. Gretchen fills the jar with $\sqrt{x-4}$ ounces of bubble solution and oils. What is the value of x?

F 37 H 1089
G 39 J 1093

11-9 CHALLENGE

The function $y=\sqrt{x}$ is the parent function from which you can write each of the functions below.

$y=\sqrt{x}+2$ $y=\sqrt{x}+4$ $y=\sqrt{x}+6$
$y=\sqrt{x-2}$ $y=\sqrt{x-4}$ $y=\sqrt{x-6}$

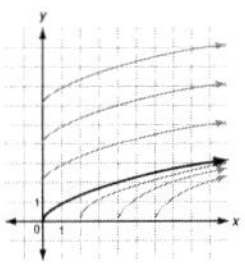

All six functions are graphed at right along with the parent function, which is darker than the other graphs.

The graphs of $y=\sqrt{x}+2$, $y=\sqrt{x}+4$, and $y=\sqrt{x}+6$ are the three curves directly above the graph of $y=\sqrt{x}$. Use the graphs to explain why the equations below have no solution.

1. $\sqrt{x}+2=\sqrt{x}+4$ **Their graphs do not intersect.**
2. $\sqrt{x}+2=\sqrt{x}+6$ **Their graphs do not intersect.**
3. $\sqrt{x}+4=\sqrt{x}+6$ **Their graphs do not intersect.**

The graphs of $y=\sqrt{x-2}$, $y=\sqrt{x-4}$, and $y=\sqrt{x-6}$ are the three curves below the graph of $y=\sqrt{x}$. Show algebraically that each equation below has no solution.

4. $\sqrt{x-2}=\sqrt{x-4}$ **$x-2\neq x-4$ for all values of x**
5. $\sqrt{x-2}=\sqrt{x-6}$ **$x-2\neq x-6$ for all values of x**
6. $\sqrt{x-4}=\sqrt{x-6}$ **$x-4\neq x-6$ for all values of x**

The diagram above suggests that the graphs of $y=\sqrt{x-2}$, $y=\sqrt{x-4}$, and $y=\sqrt{x-6}$ get closer to the graph of $y=\sqrt{x}$ as x gets larger.

7. Complete the table below. Round values to the nearest thousandth.

x	10	20	50	100	200	500	1000	5000
$\sqrt{x}$	3.162	4.472	7.071	10	14.142	22.361	31.623	70.711
$\sqrt{x-2}$	2.828	4.243	6.928	9.899	14.071	22.316	31.591	70.697
$\sqrt{x}-\sqrt{x-2}$	0.334	0.229	0.143	0.101	0.071	0.045	0.032	0.014

8. Let n be a positive integer. Write and justify a conjecture about $\sqrt{x}-\sqrt{x-n}$.
In the expression $\sqrt{x}-\sqrt{x-n}$, as n remains constant and x becomes larger, the expression gets closer to 0 in value.

Organizer

Objective: Assess students' ability to apply concepts and skills in Lessons 11-5 through 11-9 in a real-world format.

 Online Edition

Resources

Algebra I Assessments
www.mathtekstoolkit.org

Problem	Text Reference
1	Previous course
2	Lesson 11-6
3	Lesson 1-3
4	Previous course
5	Lesson 11-7
6	Lesson 11-7

State Resources

go.hrw.com
State Resources Online
KEYWORD: MA7 Resources

CHAPTER 11

MULTI-STEP TEST PREP

SECTION 11B

Radical Functions and Equations

Eye in the Sky The London Eye is a giant observation wheel in London, England. It carries people in enclosed capsules around its circumference. Opened on December 31, 1999, to welcome the new millennium, its diameter is 135 meters. On the London Eye, riders can see a distance of 40 kilometers.

1. What is the circumference of the London Eye? Use 3.14 for π. **423.9 m**
2. The London Eye's velocity in meters per second can be found using the equation $v = \sqrt{0.001r}$, where r is the radius of the wheel in meters. Find the velocity in meters per second. Round to the nearest hundredth. **0.26 m/s**
3. Another way to find the velocity is to divide the distance around the wheel by the time for the ride. A ride on the London Eye lasts 30 minutes. Use this method to find the velocity of the wheel in meters per second to the nearest hundredth. **0.24 m/s**
4. Are your answers to problems 2 and 3 the same? If not, explain any differences. **Differences are due to rounding.**
5. When a rider is at the highest point on the London Eye, how far is he from the bottom of the ride? Explain. **135 m; the required dist. is the diam. of the wheel.**
6. When a rider is at half the maximum height, her distance from the bottom of the ride can be found using the equation $d = \sqrt{2r^2}$. Explain where this equation comes from. Then find this distance. Round to the nearest hundredth. **Pythagorean Theorem; $d \approx 95.46$ m**

INTERVENTION

Scaffolding Questions

1. What is the circumference of a circle? distance around the outside of the circle
2. What formula is used to calculate the circumference of a circle? $C = \pi d$ or $C = 2\pi r$
3. How do we calculate the speed of an object moving at a constant speed? Speed is distance divided by time.
4. How would this apply to an object moving around the edge of a circle? Speed is circumference divided by time.
5. How do you find the distance between two points? Use the distance formula, which is the Pythagorean Theorem.

Extension

If the diameter increases and the time for the ride remains the same, what happens to the velocity? increases Explain. If the diameter increases, the distance traveled increases. To travel a greater distance in the same time, velocity must increase.

READY TO GO ON?

Quiz for Lessons 11-5 Through 11-9

11-5 Square-Root Functions

1. The distance in kilometers that a person can see to the horizon can be approximated by the formula $D = 113\sqrt{h}$, where h is the person's height in kilometers above sea level. What is the distance to the horizon observed by a mountain climber who is 0.3 km above sea level? **61.9 km**

Find the domain of each square-root function.

2. $y = \sqrt{3x} - 7$ **$x \geq 0$**
3. $y = \sqrt{x - 5}$ **$x \geq 5$**
4. $y = \sqrt{2x - 6}$ **$x \geq 3$**

Graph each square-root function.

5. $f(x) = \sqrt{x - 6}$
6. $f(x) = \sqrt{x} + 5$
7. $f(x) = \sqrt{8 - 4x}$

11-6 Radical Expressions

Simplify. All variables represent nonnegative numbers.

8. $\sqrt{75}$ **$5\sqrt{3}$**
9. $\sqrt{\frac{300}{3}}$ **10**
10. $\sqrt{a^2b^3}$ **$ab\sqrt{b}$**
11. $\sqrt{98xy^2}$ **$7y\sqrt{2x}$**
12. $\sqrt{\frac{32}{25}}$ **$\frac{4\sqrt{2}}{5}$**
13. $\sqrt{\frac{128}{121}}$ **$\frac{8\sqrt{2}}{11}$**
14. $\sqrt{\frac{4b^2}{81}}$ **$\frac{2b}{9}$**
15. $\sqrt{\frac{75a^9}{49a^3}}$ **$\frac{5a^3\sqrt{3}}{7}$**
16. How long is the diagonal of a rectangular television screen that is 19.2 inches long and 14.4 inches high? **24 in.**

11-7 Adding and Subtracting Radical Expressions

Simplify each expression.

17. $12\sqrt{7} - 5\sqrt{7}$ **$7\sqrt{7}$**
18. $3\sqrt{x} + 3\sqrt{x}$ **$6\sqrt{x}$**
19. $\sqrt{12} + \sqrt{75}$ **$7\sqrt{3}$**
20. $5\sqrt{50} + \sqrt{98}$ **$32\sqrt{2}$**
21. $4\sqrt{3} - 3\sqrt{4}$ **$4\sqrt{3} - 6$**
22. $\sqrt{98x} + \sqrt{18x} - \sqrt{200x}$ **0**

11-8 Multiplying and Dividing Radical Expressions

Multiply. Write each product in simplest form.

23. $\sqrt{6}\sqrt{11}$ **$\sqrt{66}$**
24. $\sqrt{3}\sqrt{8}$ **$2\sqrt{6}$**
25. $4\sqrt{12x}\sqrt{3x}$ **$24x$**
26. $(3 - \sqrt{3})(5 + \sqrt{3})$ **$12 - 2\sqrt{3}$**

Simplify each quotient.

27. $\frac{\sqrt{19}}{\sqrt{3}}$ **$\frac{\sqrt{57}}{3}$**
28. $\frac{\sqrt{14}}{\sqrt{8}}$ **$\frac{\sqrt{7}}{2}$**
29. $\frac{\sqrt{6b}}{\sqrt{8}}$ **$\frac{\sqrt{3b}}{2}$**
30. $\frac{\sqrt{27}}{\sqrt{3t}}$ **$\frac{3\sqrt{t}}{t}$**

11-9 Solving Radical Equations

Solve each equation. Check your answer.

31. $\sqrt{x} - 4 = 21$ **625**
32. $-3\sqrt{x} = -12$ **16**
33. $\frac{5\sqrt{x}}{2} = 40$ **256**
34. $\sqrt{4x - 2} - \sqrt{43 - x} = 0$ **9**
35. $\sqrt{20 + x} = x$ **5**
36. $\sqrt{4x} + 12 = 10$ **no solution**

READY TO GO ON? SECTION 11B

Organizer

Objective: Assess students' mastery of concepts and skills in Lessons 11-5 through 11-9.

Resources

Assessment Resources
Section 11B Quiz

Teacher One Stop™
Test & Practice Generator

INTERVENTION

Resources

***Ready to Go On? Intervention and Enrichment* Worksheets**

***Ready to Go On?* CD-ROM**

***Ready to Go On?* Online**

my.hrw.com

Answers

5–7. See p. A35.

READY TO GO ON?

Diagnose and Prescribe

Ready to Go On? Intervention	*Ready to Go On? Intervention*, Section 11B		
	Worksheets	CD-ROM	Online
Lesson 11-5	11-5 Intervention	Activity 11-5	Diagnose and Prescribe Online
Lesson 11-6	11-6 Intervention	Activity 11-6	
Lesson 11-7	11-7 Intervention	Activity 11-7	
Lesson 11-8	11-8 Intervention	Activity 11-8	
Lesson 11-9	11-9 Intervention	Activity 11-9	

***Ready to Go On? Enrichment*, Section 11B**
Worksheets
CD-ROM
Online

Organizer

Objective: Help students organize and review key concepts and skills presented in Chapter 11.

Resources

Teacher One Stop™
PuzzleView
Test & Practice Generator

***Multilingual Glossary* Online**
go.hrw.com
KEYWORD: MA7 Glossary

***Lesson Tutorial Videos* CD-ROM**

Answers

1. square-root function
2. exponential decay
3. common ratio
4. exponential function
5. 81, 243, 729
6. 48, −96, 192
7. 5, 2.5, 1.25
8. −256, −1024, −4096
9. 7,812,500
10. 19,131,876
11. Yes; as the *x*-values change by a const. amt., the *y*-values are multiplied by a const. amt.
12. No; as the *x*-values change by a const. amt., the *y*-values are not multiplied by a const. amt.
13. 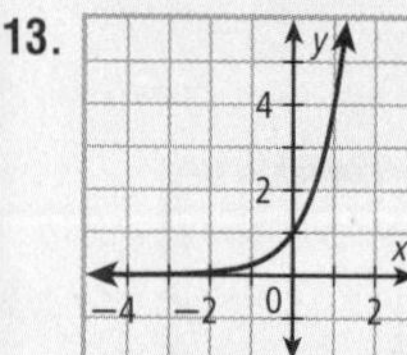
14. 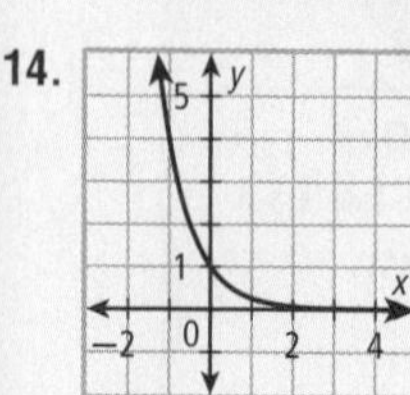

CHAPTER 11 Study Guide: Review

Vocabulary

Complete the sentences below with vocabulary words from the list above.

1. $f(x) = \sqrt{2x}$ is an example of a(n) ___?___.
2. A(n) ___?___ function has the form $y = a(1 - r)^t$, where $a > 0$.
3. In the formula $a_n = a_1r^{n-1}$, the variable r represents the ___?___.
4. $f(x) = 2^x$ is an example of a(n) ___?___.

11-1 Geometric Sequences *(pp. 790–795)*

EXAMPLE

■ **What is the 10th term of the geometric sequence −6400, 3200, −1600, 800, ...?**

Find the common ratio by dividing consecutive terms.

$\frac{3200}{-6400} = -0.5 \quad \frac{-1600}{3200} = -0.5$

$a_n = a_1r^{n-1}$ *Write the formula.*

$a_{10} = -6400(-0.5)^{10-1}$ *Substitute.*

$= -6400(-0.5)^9$ *Simplify.*

$= 12.5$

EXERCISES

Find the next three terms in each geometric sequence.

5. 1, 3, 9, 27, ...
6. 3, −6, 12, −24, ...
7. 80, 40, 20, 10, ...
8. −1, −4, −16, −64, ...
9. The first term of a geometric sequence is 4 and the common ratio is 5. What is the 10th term?
10. What is the 15th term of the geometric sequence 4, 12, 36, 108, ...?

11-2 Exponential Functions *(pp. 796–802)*

EXAMPLE

■ **Tell whether the ordered pairs $\{(1,4), (2,16), (3,36), (4,64)\}$ satisfy an exponential function. Explain.**

x	y
1	4
2	16
3	36
4	64

As the x-values increase by a constant amount, the y-values are not multiplied by a constant amount. This function is not exponential.

EXERCISES

Tell whether each set of ordered pairs satisfies an exponential function. Explain.

11. $\{(0, 1), (2, 9), (4, 81), (6, 729)\}$
12. $\{(-2, -8), (-1, -4), (0, 0), (1, 4)\}$

Graph each exponential function.

13. $y = 4^x$
14. $y = \left(\frac{1}{4}\right)^x$

11-3 Exponential Growth and Decay *(pp. 805–812)*

EXAMPLE

- **The value of a piece of antique furniture has been increasing at a rate of 2% per year. In 1990, its value was \$800. Write an exponential growth function to model the situation. Then find the value of the furniture in the year 2010.**

Step 1	$y = a(1 + r)^t$	*Write the formula.*
	$y = 800(1 + 0.02)^t$	*Substitute.*
	$y = 800(1.02)^t$	*Simplify.*
Step 2	$y = 800(1.02)^{20}$	*Substitute 20 for t.*
	≈ 1188.76	*Simplify and round.*

The furniture's value will be \$1188.76.

EXERCISES

15. The number of students in the book club is increasing at a rate of 15% per year. In 2001, there were 9 students in the book club. Write an exponential growth function to model the situation. Then find the number of students in the book club in the year 2008.

16. The population of a small town is decreasing at a rate of 4% per year. In 1970, the population was 24,500. Write an exponential decay function to model the situation. Then find the population in the year 2020.

11-4 Linear, Quadratic, and Exponential Models *(pp. 813–819)*

EXAMPLE

- **Use the data in the table to describe how Jasmin's debt is changing. Then write a function that models the data. Use your function to predict Jasmin's debt after 8 years.**

Jasmin's Debt	
Years	Debt (\$)
1	130
2	260
3	520
4	1040

(+1 between successive years; ×2 between successive debts)

Jasmin's debt doubles every year.

For a constant change in time $(+1)$, there is a constant ratio of 2, so the data is exponential.

$y = ab^x$	*Write the general form.*
$y = a(2)^x$	*Substitute 2 for b.*
$130 = a(2)^1$	*Substitute (1, 130) for x and y.*
$a = 65$	*Solve for a.*
$y = 65(2)^x$	*Replace a and b in $y = ab^x$.*
$y = 65(2)^8$	*Substitute 8 for x.*
$y = 16{,}640$	*Simplify with a calculator.*

Jasmin's debt in 8 years will be \$16,640.

EXERCISES

Graph each data set. Which kind of model best describes the data?

17. $\{(-2, -12), (-1, -3), (0, 0), (1, -3), (2, -12)\}$

18. $\{(-2, -2), (-1, 2), (0, 6), (1, 10), (2, 14)\}$

19. $\left\{\left(-2, -\frac{1}{4}\right), \left(-1, -\frac{1}{2}\right), (0, -1), (1, -2), (2, -4)\right\}$

Look for a pattern in each data set to determine which kind of model best describes the data.

20. $\{(0, 2), (1, 6), (2, 18), (3, 54), (4, 162)\}$

21. $\{(0, 0), (2, -20), (4, -80), (6, -180), (8, -320)\}$

22. $\{(-8, 5), (-4, 3), (0, 1), (4, -1), (8, -3)\}$

23. Write a function that models the data. Then use your function to predict how long the humidifier will produce steam with 10 quarts of water.

Input and Output of a Humidifier	
Water Volume (qt)	Steam Time (h)
3	4.5
4	6
5	7.5
6	9

Answers

15. $y = 9(1.15)^t$; 24
16. $y = 24{,}500(0.96)^t$; 3182
17. 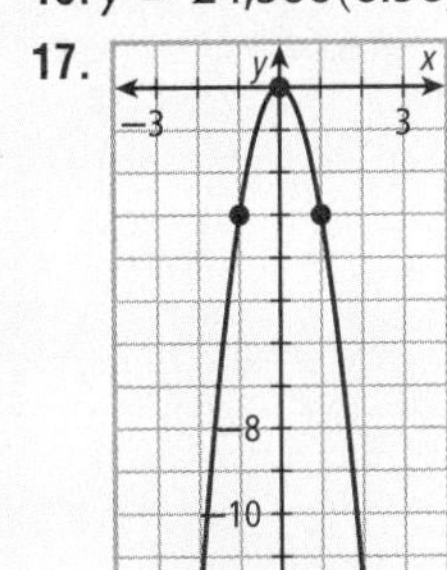

quadratic
18. 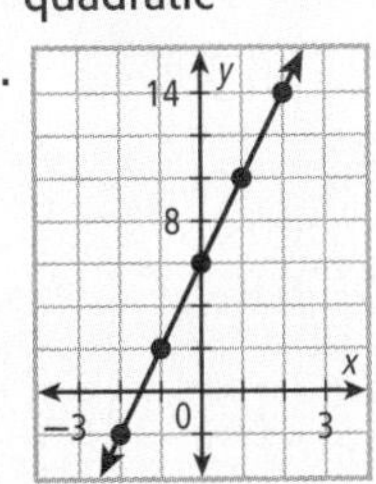

linear
19. 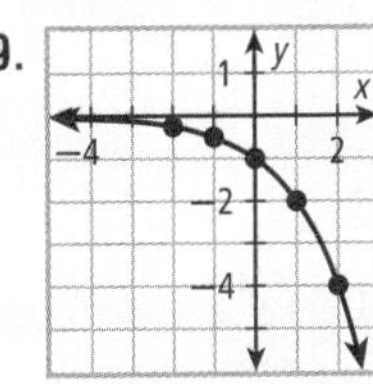

exponential
20. exponential
21. quadratic
22. linear
23. $y = 1.5x$; 15 h

Study Guide: Review 857

Answers

24. 4.74 cm
25. $x \geq 0$
26. $x \geq -4$
27. $x \geq 0$
28. $x \geq -2$
29. $x \geq \frac{4}{3}$
30. $x \geq -3$
31. $x \geq \frac{7}{2}$
32. $x \geq -\frac{18}{5}$
33. $x \geq \frac{3}{4}$
34. $x \geq 1$

35.
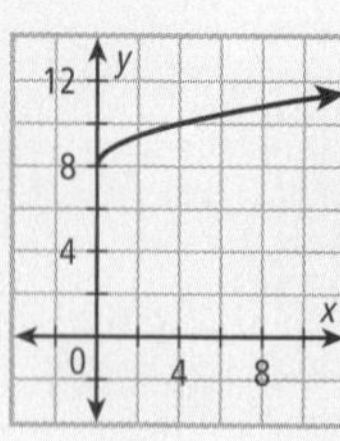

36.
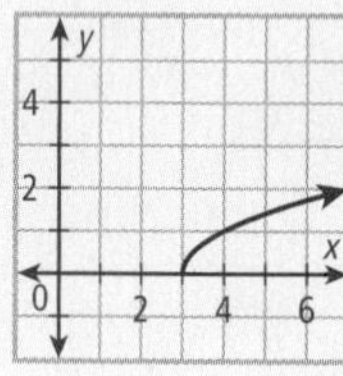

37.
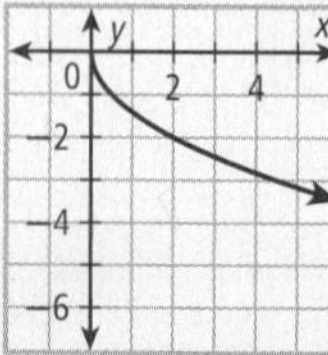

38.
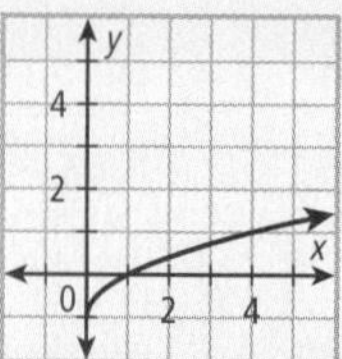

39.
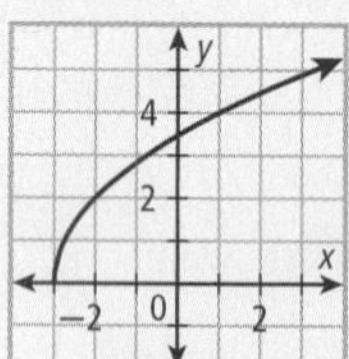

40.
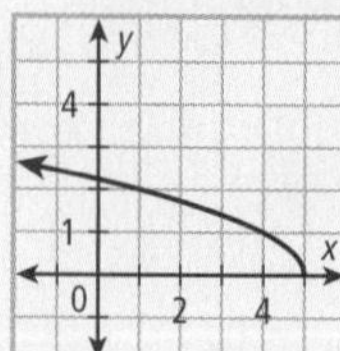

41.
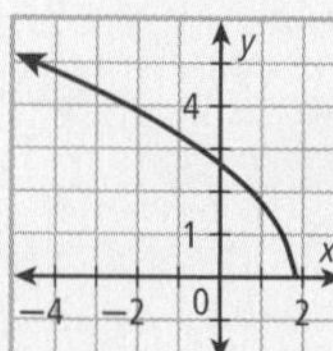

42.
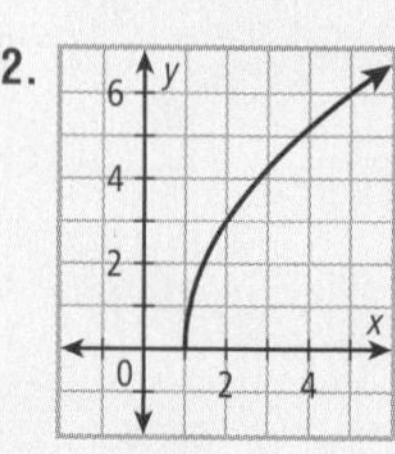

11-5 Square-Root Functions *(pp. 822–827)*

EXAMPLE

■ **Graph $f(x) = 3\sqrt{x-2}$.**

Step 1 Find the domain of the function.

$x - 2 \geq 0$ *The radicand must be greater*
$x \geq 2$ *than or equal to 0.*

Step 2 Generate ordered pairs.

x	$f(x) = 3\sqrt{x-2}$
2	0
3	3
6	6
11	9
18	12

Choose x-values greater than or equal to 2 that form a perfect square under the radical sign.

Step 3 Plot and connect the points.

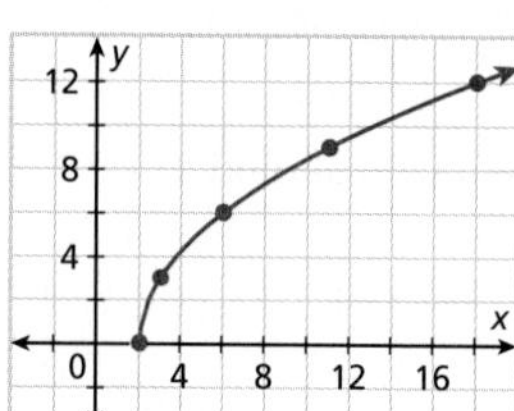

EXERCISES

24. If you know the surface area S of a cube, you can use the formula $\ell = \sqrt{\frac{S}{6}}$ to find the length ℓ of a side. What is the side length of a cube whose surface area is 135 cm^2? Round your answer to the nearest hundredth of a centimeter.

Find the domain of each square-root function.

25. $y = \sqrt{x} + 5$
26. $y = \sqrt{x+4}$
27. $y = 8 - \sqrt{3x}$
28. $y = 2\sqrt{x+2}$
29. $y = 1 + \sqrt{3x-4}$
30. $y = \sqrt{2x+6}$
31. $y = \sqrt{2x-7}$
32. $y = \sqrt{5x+18}$
33. $y = \sqrt{4x-3}$
34. $y = 3\sqrt{x-1}$

Graph each square-root function.

35. $f(x) = \sqrt{x} + 8$
36. $f(x) = \sqrt{x-3}$
37. $f(x) = -\sqrt{2x}$
38. $f(x) = \sqrt{x} - 1$
39. $f(x) = 2\sqrt{x+3}$
40. $f(x) = \sqrt{5-x}$
41. $f(x) = \sqrt{7-4x}$
42. $f(x) = 3\sqrt{x-1}$
43. $f(x) = 1 + \sqrt{x+1}$
44. $f(x) = \frac{1}{2}\sqrt{x-2}$

11-6 Radical Expressions *(pp. 829–834)*

EXAMPLES

Simplify. All variables represent nonnegative numbers.

■ $\sqrt{50x^4}$

$\sqrt{(25)(2)x^4}$ *Factor the radicand.*
$\sqrt{25}\sqrt{2}\sqrt{x^4}$ *Use the Product Property.*
$5x^2\sqrt{2}$ *Simplify.*

■ $\sqrt{\frac{16m^6}{64m^3}}$

$\sqrt{\frac{m^3}{4}}$ *Simplify the radicand.*
$\frac{\sqrt{m^3}}{\sqrt{4}}$ *Use the Quotient Property of Square Roots.*
$\frac{\sqrt{m^2}\sqrt{m}}{\sqrt{4}}$ *Use the Product Property of Square Roots.*
$\frac{m\sqrt{m}}{2}$ *Simplify.*

EXERCISES

Simplify. All variables represent nonnegative numbers.

45. $\sqrt{121}$
46. $\sqrt{n^4}$
47. $\sqrt{(x+3)^2}$
48. $\sqrt{\frac{75}{3}}$
49. $\sqrt{36d^2}$
50. $\sqrt{y^6x}$
51. $\sqrt{12}$
52. $\sqrt{32ab^5}$
53. $\sqrt{\frac{5}{4}}$
54. $\sqrt{\frac{t^3}{100t}}$
55. $\sqrt{\frac{8}{18}}$
56. $\sqrt{\frac{32p^4}{49}}$
57. $\sqrt{\frac{s^2t^9}{s^4}}$
58. $\sqrt{\frac{72b^6}{225}}$

43.
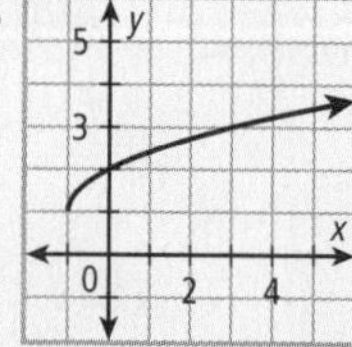

44.
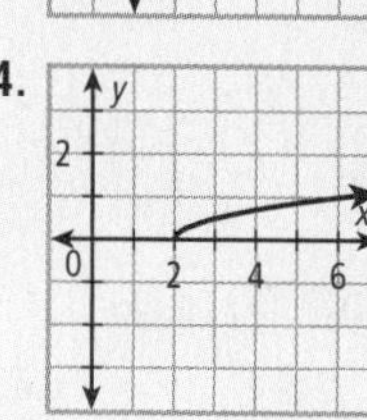

45. 11
46. n^2
47. $x + 3$
48. 5
49. $6d$
50. $y^3\sqrt{x}$
51. $2\sqrt{3}$
52. $4b^2\sqrt{2ab}$
53. $\frac{\sqrt{5}}{2}$
54. $\frac{t}{10}$
55. $\frac{2}{3}$
56. $\frac{4p^2\sqrt{2}}{7}$
57. $\frac{t^4\sqrt{t}}{s}$
58. $\frac{2b^3\sqrt{2}}{5}$

11-7 Adding and Subtracting Radical Expressions *(pp. 835–839)*

EXAMPLE

- Simplify $\sqrt{50x} - \sqrt{2x} + \sqrt{12x}$.

$\sqrt{50x} - 1\sqrt{2x} + \sqrt{12x}$

$\sqrt{(25)(2)x} - 1\sqrt{2x} + \sqrt{(4)(3)x}$

$\sqrt{25}\sqrt{2x} - 1\sqrt{2x} + \sqrt{4}\sqrt{3x}$

$5\sqrt{2x} - 1\sqrt{2x} + 2\sqrt{3x}$

$4\sqrt{2x} + 2\sqrt{3x}$

EXERCISES

Simplify each expression.

59. $6\sqrt{7} + 3\sqrt{7}$
60. $4\sqrt{3} - \sqrt{3}$
61. $3\sqrt{2} + 2\sqrt{3}$
62. $9\sqrt{5t} - 8\sqrt{5t}$
63. $\sqrt{50} - \sqrt{18}$
64. $\sqrt{12} + \sqrt{20}$
65. $\sqrt{20x} - \sqrt{80x}$
66. $4\sqrt{54} - \sqrt{24}$

11-8 Multiplying and Dividing Radical Expressions *(pp. 840–845)*

EXAMPLES

- Multiply $(\sqrt{3} + 6)^2$. Write the product in simplest form.

$(\sqrt{3} + 6)^2$

$(\sqrt{3} + 6)(\sqrt{3} + 6)$ — *Expand the expression.*

$3 + 6\sqrt{3} + 6\sqrt{3} + 36$ — *Use the FOIL method.*

$39 + 12\sqrt{3}$ — *Simplify.*

- Simplify the quotient $\frac{\sqrt{5}}{\sqrt{3}}$.

$\frac{\sqrt{5}}{\sqrt{3}}\left(\frac{\sqrt{3}}{\sqrt{3}}\right) = \frac{\sqrt{15}}{3}$ — *Rationalize the denominator.*

EXERCISES

Multiply. Write each product in simplest form.

67. $\sqrt{2}\sqrt{7}$
68. $\sqrt{3}\sqrt{6}$
69. $3\sqrt{2x}\sqrt{14}$
70. $(5\sqrt{6})^2$
71. $\sqrt{2}(4 - \sqrt{8})$
72. $(8 + \sqrt{7})^2$

Simplify each quotient.

73. $\frac{4}{\sqrt{5}}$
74. $\frac{a\sqrt{9}}{\sqrt{2}}$
75. $\frac{\sqrt{8}}{2\sqrt{6}}$
76. $\frac{\sqrt{5}}{\sqrt{2n}}$
77. $\frac{\sqrt{18}}{\sqrt{12}}$
78. $\frac{-3}{\sqrt{3}}$

11-9 Solving Radical Equations *(pp. 846–853)*

EXAMPLE

- Solve $\sqrt{4x + 1} - 8 = -3$. Check your answer.

$\sqrt{4x + 1} - 8 = -3$

$\sqrt{4x + 1} = 5$ — *Add 8 to both sides.*

$(\sqrt{4x + 1})^2 = (5)^2$ — *Square both sides.*

$4x + 1 = 25$

$4x = 24$ — *Subtract 1 from both sides.*

$x = 6$ — *Divide both sides by 4.*

Check $\sqrt{4x + 1} - 8 = -3$

$\sqrt{4(6) + 1} - 8$	-3
$\sqrt{25} - 8$	-3
$5 - 8$	-3
-3	-3 ✓

EXERCISES

Solve each equation. Check your answer.

79. $\sqrt{x} = 8$
80. $\sqrt{2x} = 4$
81. $\sqrt{x + 6} = 3$
82. $-3\sqrt{x} = -15$
83. $3\sqrt{-x} = 27$
84. $\frac{4\sqrt{x}}{5} = 8$
85. $\sqrt{x + 1} = \sqrt{3x - 5}$
86. $\sqrt{x - 2} + 4 = 3$
87. $12 = 4\sqrt{2x + 1}$
88. $\sqrt{x - 5} = \sqrt{7 - x}$
89. $\sqrt{x + 2} = 3$
90. $\sqrt{2x - 3} = 4$
91. $4\sqrt{x - 3} = 12$
92. $\sqrt{x + 6} = x$
93. $\sqrt{3x + 4} = x$
94. $\sqrt{2x + 6} = x - 1$

Answers

59. $9\sqrt{7}$
60. $3\sqrt{3}$
61. $3\sqrt{2} + 2\sqrt{3}$
62. $\sqrt{5t}$
63. $2\sqrt{2}$
64. $2\sqrt{3} + 2\sqrt{5}$
65. $-2\sqrt{5x}$
66. $10\sqrt{6}$
67. $\sqrt{14}$
68. $3\sqrt{2}$
69. $6\sqrt{7x}$
70. 150
71. $4\sqrt{2} - 4$
72. $71 + 16\sqrt{7}$
73. $\frac{4\sqrt{5}}{5}$
74. $\frac{3a\sqrt{2}}{2}$
75. $\frac{\sqrt{3}}{3}$
76. $\frac{\sqrt{10n}}{2n}$
77. $\frac{\sqrt{6}}{2}$
78. $-\sqrt{3}$
79. 64
80. 8
81. 3
82. 25
83. −81
84. 100
85. 3
86. no solution
87. $x = 4$
88. $x = 6$
89. $x = 7$
90. $x = \frac{19}{2}$
91. $x = 12$
92. $x = 3$
93. $x = 4$
94. $x = 5$

Organizer

Objective: Assess students' mastery of concepts and skills in Chapter 11.

Online Edition

Resources

Assessment Resources

Chapter 11 Tests

- Free Response (Levels A, B, C)
- Multiple Choice (Levels A, B, C)
- Performance Assessment

Teacher One Stop™

Test & Practice Generator

Answers

5\.

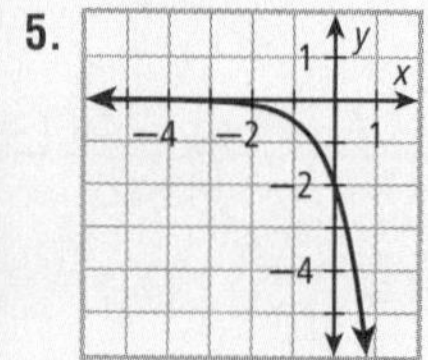

State Resources

Find the next three terms in each geometric sequence.

1. 2, 6, 18, 54, ... **162, 486, 1458**
2. 4800, 2400, 1200, 600, ... **300, 150, 75**
3. −4, 20, −100, 500, ... **−2500, 12,500, −62,500**

4. **Communication** If school is cancelled, the school secretary calls 2 families. Each of those families calls 2 other families. In the third round of calls, each of the 4 families calls 2 more families. If this pattern continues, how many families are called in the seventh round of calls? **128**

Graph each exponential function.

5. $y = -2(4)^x$
6. $y = 3(2)^x$
7. $y = 4\left(\frac{1}{2}\right)^x$
8. $-\left(\frac{1}{3}\right)^x$

9. A teacher is repeatedly enlarging a diagram on a photocopier. The function $f(x) = 3(1.25)^x$ represents the length of the diagram, in centimeters, after x enlargements. What is the length after 5 enlargements? Round to the nearest centimeter. **9 cm**
10. Chelsea invested \$5600 at a rate of 3.6% compounded quarterly. Write a compound interest function to model the situation. Then find the balance after 6 years. $\mathbf{A = 5600(1.009)^{4t}}$**; \$6943.46**
11. The number of trees in a forest is decreasing at a rate of 5% per year. The forest had 24,000 trees 15 years ago. Write an exponential decay function to model the situation. Then find the number of trees now. $\mathbf{y = 24{,}000(0.95)^t}$**; 11,119 trees**

Look for a pattern in each data set to determine which kind of model best describes the data.

12. $\{(-10, -17), (-5, -7), (0, 3), (5, 13), (10, 23)\}$ **linear**
13. $\{(1, 3), (2, 9), (3, 27), (4, 81), (5, 243)\}$ **exponential**

14. Use the data in the table to describe how the bacteria population is changing. Then write a function that models the data. Use your function to predict the bacteria population after 10 hours. **The bacteria pop. is tripling every hour;** $\mathbf{y = 6(3)^x}$**; 354,294**

Bacteria Population				
Time (h)	0	1	2	3
Bacteria	6	18	54	162

Find the domain of each square-root function.

15. $y = 6 + \sqrt{x}$ $\mathbf{x \geq 0}$
16. $y = -2\sqrt{x + 9}$ $\mathbf{x \geq -9}$
17. $y = x + \sqrt{3x - 3}$ $\mathbf{x \geq 1}$

Graph each square-root function.

18. $f(x) = \sqrt{x} + 2$
19. $f(x) = \sqrt{x - 1}$
20. $f(x) = -3\sqrt{2x}$

Simplify. All variables represent nonnegative numbers.

21. $\sqrt{27}$ $\mathbf{3\sqrt{3}}$
22. $\sqrt{75m^4}$ $\mathbf{5m^2\sqrt{3}}$
23. $\sqrt{\frac{x^6}{y^2}}$ $\mathbf{\frac{x^3}{y}}$
24. $\sqrt{\frac{p^9}{144p}}$ $\mathbf{\frac{p^4}{12}}$
25. $4\sqrt{10} - 2\sqrt{10}$ $\mathbf{2\sqrt{10}}$
26. $5\sqrt{3y} + \sqrt{3y}$ $\mathbf{6\sqrt{3y}}$
27. $\sqrt{8} - \sqrt{50}$ $\mathbf{-3\sqrt{2}}$
28. $2\sqrt{75} - \sqrt{32} + \sqrt{48}$ $\mathbf{14\sqrt{3} - 4\sqrt{2}}$
29. $\sqrt{2}\sqrt{3m}$ $\mathbf{\sqrt{6m}}$
30. $\frac{\sqrt{128d}}{\sqrt{5}}$ $\mathbf{\frac{8\sqrt{10d}}{5}}$
31. $\sqrt{3}(\sqrt{21} - 2)$ $\mathbf{3\sqrt{7} - 2\sqrt{3}}$
32. $(\sqrt{3} - 2)(\sqrt{3} + 4)$ $\mathbf{-5 + 2\sqrt{3}}$

Solve each equation. Check your answer.

33. $\sqrt{2x} = 6$ **18**
34. $\sqrt{3x + 4} - 2 = 5$ **15**
35. $\frac{2\sqrt{x}}{3} = 8$ **144**
36. $\sqrt{5x + 1} = \sqrt{2x - 2}$ **no solution**

6\.

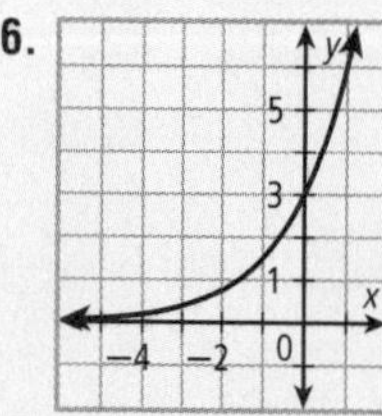

7\.

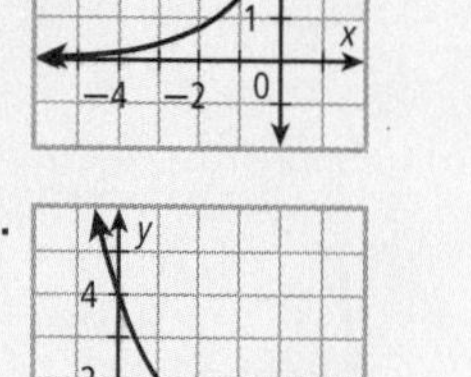

8\.

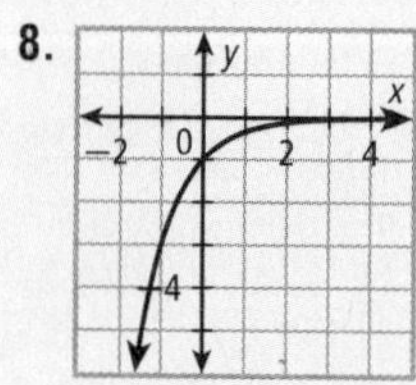

18\.

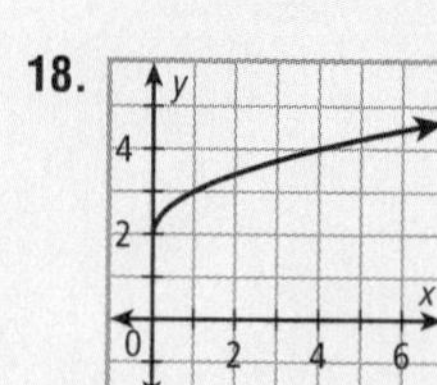

19\.

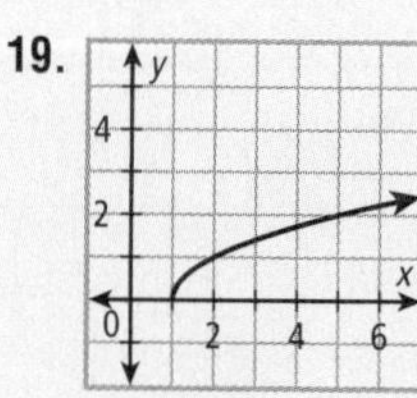

20\.

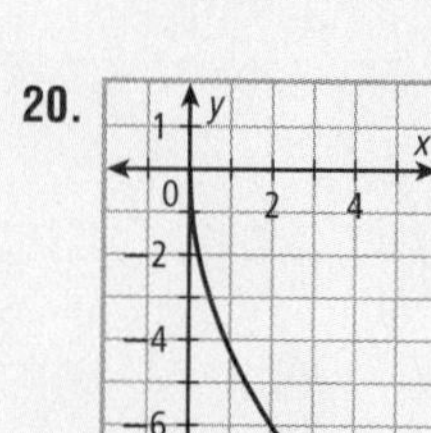

COLLEGE ENTRANCE EXAM PRACTICE

CHAPTER 11

FOCUS ON SAT MATHEMATICS SUBJECT TESTS

Colleges use standardized test scores to confirm what your academic record indicates. Because courses and instruction differ from school to school, standardized tests are one way in which colleges try to compare students fairly when making admissions decisions.

You will need to use a calculator on the SAT Mathematics Subject Tests. If you do not already have a graphing calculator, consider getting one because it may give you an advantage when solving some problems. Spend time getting used to your calculator before the test.

You may want to time yourself as you take this practice test. It should take you about 6 minutes to complete.

1. What is the domain of $y = \sqrt{x - 4}$?
   (A) $x \geq -2$
   (B) $x \geq 2$
   (C) $x \geq -4$
   (D) $x \geq 4$
   (E) $x > 4$

2. $\frac{\sqrt{8}\sqrt{3}}{\sqrt{5}} =$
   (A) $2\sqrt{3}$
   (B) $\frac{2\sqrt{3}}{5}$
   (C) $\sqrt{12}$
   (D) $\frac{4\sqrt{30}}{5}$
   (E) $\frac{2\sqrt{30}}{5}$

3. If $\frac{\sqrt{6 - 3x}}{5} = 3$, what is the value of x?
   (A) -3
   (B) -13
   (C) -73
   (D) -77
   (E) -89

4. The third term of a geometric sequence is 32 and the fifth term is 512. What is the eighth term of the sequence?
   (A) 544
   (B) 1232
   (C) 8192
   (D) 32,768
   (E) 2,097,152

5. A band releases a new CD and tracks its sales. The table shows the number of copies sold each week (in thousands). Which type of function best models this data?

CD Sales	
Week	**Copies Sold (thousands)**
1	129.5
2	155
3	179.5
4	203
5	225.5
6	247

   (A) Linear function
   (B) Quadratic function
   (C) Exponential function
   (D) Square-root function
   (E) Absolute-value function

COLLEGE ENTRANCE EXAM PRACTICE — CHAPTER 11

Organizer

Objective: Provide practice for college entrance exams such as the SAT Mathematics Subject Tests.

Online Edition

Resources

College Entrance Exam Practice

Questions on the SAT Mathematics Subject Tests (Levels 1 and 2) represent the following math content areas:

	Level	
	1	**2**
Number and Operations	10–14%	10–14%
Algebra and Functions	38–42%	48–52%
Geometry and Measurement	38–42%	28–32%
Plane Euclidean	18–22%	0%
Coordinate	8–12%	10–14%
Three-dimensional	4–6%	4–6%
Trigonometry	6–8%	12–16%
Data Analysis, Statistics, and Probability	6–10%	6–10%

Items on this page focus on:
- Algebra and Functions

Text References:

Item	1	2	3	4	5
Lesson	11-5	11-8	11-9	11-1	11-4

TEST PREP DOCTOR +

1. Students who chose **E** may not know that 0 can be a value of the radicand. Students who chose **A** may have mistakenly simplified the function as $\sqrt{x} - 2$ and confused domain values and range values.
2. Students who chose **D** may have incorrectly found $\sqrt{8}$ to be $4\sqrt{2}$.
3. Students who chose **B** may have squared both sides of the equation first but forgot to square the denominator. Remind students to check their solutions to radical equations, not only because there might be extraneous roots but to avoid simple mistakes like this.
4. Students who chose **B** found the eighth term of the arithmetic sequence with the same third and fifth terms. Students who chose **E** found the ratio of a_5 to a_3 and used that as the common ratio for the sequence.
5. Students who chose **A** may have thought the first differences were close enough to being the same that a linear model would fit. However, there is a constant second difference of 1, so a quadratic model is the best fit.

Organizer

Objective: Provide opportunities to learn and practice common test-taking strategies.

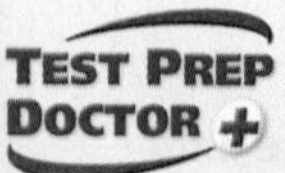

TEST PREP DOCTOR + This Test Tackler focuses on choosing the best answer when there are multiple correct answers or no correct answers. Remind students that they must check *all* of the answers if the answer is "all of the above." Encourage students to combine the strategies for all of the above and none of the above with other strategies they have learned, such as eliminating answer choices and working backward from the answer.

Standardized Test Strategies

Multiple Choice: *None of the Above* or *All of the Above*

In some multiple-choice test items, one of the options is *None of the above* or *All of the above.* To answer these types of items, first determine whether each of the other options is true or false. If you find that more than one option is true, then the correct choice is likely to be *All of the above.* If none of the options are true, the correct choice is *None of the above.*

If you do not know how to solve the problem and have to guess, *All of the above* is most often correct, and *None of the above* is usually incorrect.

EXAMPLE

There are 8 players on the chess team. Which of the following expressions gives the number of ways in which the coach can choose 2 players to start the game?

Ⓐ ${}_8C_2$

Ⓑ $\frac{8!}{2!(6!)}$

Ⓒ 28

Ⓓ All of the above

Notice that choice D is All of the above. *This means that you must look at each option. As you consider each option, mark it true or false in your test booklet.*

A Because order does not matter, this is a combination problem. The number of combinations of 8 players, taken 2 at a time, is given by ${}_nC_r$, where $n = 8$ and $r = 2$, so ${}_8C_2$ is a correct model of the combination. Choice A is true.

B The number of combinations of 8 players, taken 2 at a time, is given by ${}_nC_r = \frac{n!}{r!(n-r)!}$, where $n = 8$ and $r = 2$.

$${}_nC_r = \frac{n!}{r!(n-r)!} = \frac{8!}{2!(8-2)!} = \frac{8!}{2!(6)!}$$

Choice B is a correct model of the combination. Choice B is also true. The answer is likely to be choice D, *All of the above*, but you should also check whether choice C is true.

C The number of combinations of 8 players, taken 2 at a time, is given by ${}_nC_r = \frac{n!}{r!(n-r)!}$, where $n = 8$ and $r = 2$.

$${}_nC_r = \frac{n!}{r!(n-r)!} = \frac{8!}{2!(8-2)!} = \frac{8!}{2!(6)!} = 28$$

Choice C is a correct model of the combination. Choice C is true as well.

Because A, B, and C are all true, the correct response is D, *All of the above.*

Be careful of problems that contain more than one negative word, such as *no, not,* or *never.* Read the problem and each option twice before selecting an answer.

Read each test item and answer the questions that follow.

Item A
The mean score on a test is 68. Which CANNOT be true?

Ⓐ Every score is 68.

Ⓑ Half of the scores are 68, and half of the scores are 0.

Ⓒ Half of the scores are 94, and half of the scores are 42.

Ⓓ None of the above

1. What is the definition of *mean*?
2. If you find that an option is true, is that the correct response? Explain.
3. Willie determined that A and C could both be true, so he chose D as his response. Do you agree? Why or why not?

Item B
What is the probability of rolling a 2 on a number cube?

Ⓕ $16.\overline{6}\%$

Ⓖ $1 - P(\text{rolling } 1, 3, 4, 5, \text{ or } 6)$

Ⓗ $\frac{1}{6}$

Ⓙ All of the above

4. What is the complement of rolling a 2? Is choice G correct? Explain.
5. If you roll a number cube, how many possible outcomes are there? How does this information help you solve this problem?
6. Is the value given in choice H equivalent to any other choice? If so, which one(s)?
7. How many choices are true? What is the correct response to the test item?

Item C
Suppose that a dart lands at a random point on the circular dartboard. Find the probability that the dart does NOT land inside the center circle.

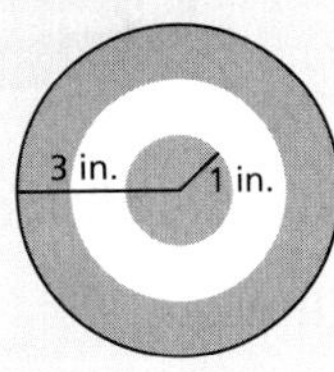

Ⓐ $\frac{1}{9}$ Ⓒ $\frac{8}{9}$

Ⓑ 8π Ⓓ None of the above

8. Kyle finds that choices A and B are both false. To save time, he selects choice D as his answer because he figures it is likely that choice C will also be false. Do you think Kyle made a wise decision? Why or why not?
9. What is the formula for the area of a circle? What is the total area of this dartboard? How can you determine the area of the dartboard outside the center circle?
10. Determine whether choices A, B, and C are true, and then give the correct response to this test item.

Item D
Each gym member receives a 3-digit locker combination. Digits are from 0–9 and may repeat. What is the probability that you will receive a code consisting of three identical numbers?

Ⓕ $\frac{1}{100}$ Ⓗ ${}_{10}P_3 = \frac{10!}{7!}$

Ⓖ $\frac{10}{{}_{10}C_3}$ Ⓙ All of the above

11. How can you determine whether choice J is the correct response to the test item?
12. Are the values given in choices F, G, and H equivalent? What does this tell you about choice J?

Answers

Possible answers:

1. the sum of all the values in the set divided by the number of values in the set
2. No; the question asks which statements cannot be true.
3. No; "None of the above" would mean that all of the statements must be true, but choice **B** is not true.
4. Not rolling a 2, or rolling a 1, 3, 4, 5, or 6; yes; the probability of an event is 1 minus the probability of the complement of that event.
5. 6; the probability of rolling a 2 will be 1 outcome out of 6, so choice **H** is correct.
6. yes; **F**
7. 3 (**F, G,** and **H**); **J**
8. No; choice **C** is correct.
9. $A = \pi r^2$; 9π; area outside center circle $= 9\pi - \pi = 8\pi$
10. Only choice **C** is true; the correct response is **C.**
11. Determine whether or not the values in choices **G, F,** and **H** are equivalent.
12. No; choice **J** cannot be the correct choice.

Answers to Test Items

A. B
B. J
C. C
D. F

State Resources

go.hrw.com
State Resources Online
KEYWORD: MA7 Resources

Organizer

Objective: Provide review and practice for Chapters 1–11 and standardized tests.

Online Edition

Resources

Assessment Resources

Chapter 11 Cumulative Test

go.hrw.com
KEYWORD: MA7 TestProp

State Resources

go.hrw.com
State Resources Online
KEYWORD: MA7 Resources

go.hrw.com
State Test Practice Online
KEYWORD: MA7 TestPrep

CUMULATIVE ASSESSMENT, CHAPTERS 1–11

Multiple Choice

1. A sequence is defined by the rule $a_n = -3(2)^{n-1}$. What is the 5th term of the sequence?

Ⓐ 5
Ⓑ −30
Ⓒ −48
Ⓓ −216

2. Which could be the graph of $y = -2^x$?

Ⓕ
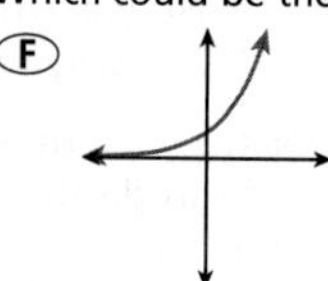

Ⓖ
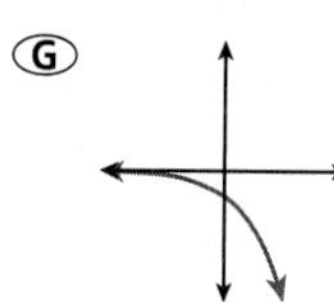

Ⓗ
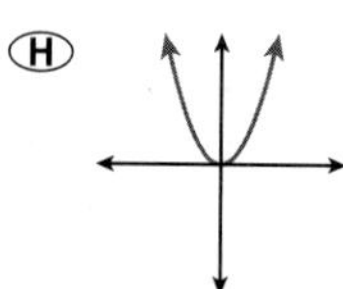

Ⓙ
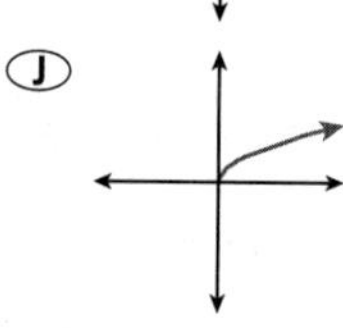

3. What is the slope of the line described by $4x - 3y = 12$?

Ⓐ 4
Ⓑ 3
Ⓒ $\frac{4}{3}$
Ⓓ $-\frac{3}{4}$

4. The odds in favor of a spinner landing on blue are 2:7. What is the probability of the spinner NOT landing on blue?

Ⓕ $\frac{7}{9}$
Ⓗ $\frac{2}{7}$
Ⓖ $\frac{5}{7}$
Ⓙ $\frac{2}{9}$

5. Which rule can be used to find any term in the sequence 8, 4, 2, 1, ...?

Ⓐ $a_n = 8\left(\frac{1}{2}\right)^n$
Ⓒ $a_n = \left(\frac{1}{2}\right)^{n-1}$
Ⓑ $a_n = 2(1)^n$
Ⓓ $a_n = 8\left(\frac{1}{2}\right)^{n-1}$

6. Jerome walked on a treadmill for 45 minutes at a speed of 4.2 miles per hour. Approximately how far did Jerome walk?

Ⓕ 1.89 miles
Ⓖ 2.1 miles
Ⓗ 3.15 miles
Ⓙ 5.6 miles

7. What is the solution to the system of equations below?

$$\begin{cases} 2x - y = 2 \\ y = 3x - 5 \end{cases}$$

Ⓐ (4, 6)
Ⓒ (2, 1)
Ⓑ (3, 4)
Ⓓ (0, 2)

8. What is the complete factorization of $2x^3 + 18x$?

Ⓕ $2x(x^2 + 9)$
Ⓖ $2x(x + 3)^2$
Ⓗ $2x(x + 3)(x - 3)$
Ⓙ $2(x^3 + 18)$

9. Which ordered pair lies on the graph of $y = 3(2)^{x+1}$?

Ⓐ (−1, 0)
Ⓒ (1, 12)
Ⓑ (0, 9)
Ⓓ (3, 24)

Answers

1. C
2. G
3. C
4. F
5. D
6. H
7. B
8. F
9. C
10. G
11. A
12. 5033
13. 2
14. 272
15. 19.21

16a. exponential; $y = 3^{x-1}$

b. 19,683

When a test item gives an equation to be solved, it may be quicker to work backward from the answer choices by substituting them into the equation. If time remains, check your answer by solving the equation.

10. Which shows the product of 5.1×10^4 and 3×10^9 written in scientific notation?

(F) 1.53×10^{12}

(G) 1.53×10^{14}

(H) 15.3×10^{12}

(J) 15.3×10^{13}

11. Which is an arithmetic sequence?

I 3, 6, 9, 12, 15, ...
II 1, 10, 100, 1000, ...
III 4000, −2000, 1000, −500, ...

(A) I only

(B) II and III

(C) I and III

(D) III only

Gridded Response

12. The function $f(x) = 30{,}000(0.8)^x$ gives the value of a vehicle, where x is the number of years after purchase. According to the function, what will be the value of the car in dollars 8 years after purchase? Round your answer to the nearest whole dollar.

13. The graph of $f(x)$ is shown below. How many zeros does $f(x)$ have?

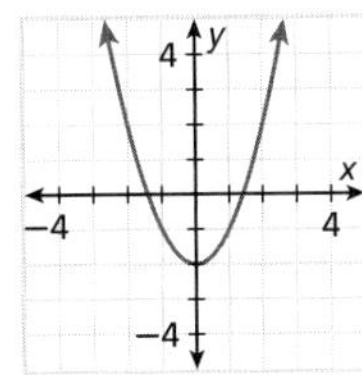

14. Rosalind purchased a sewing machine at a 20%-off sale. The original selling price of the machine was $340. What was the sale price in dollars?

15. Two planes leave an airport, one heading due north and the other heading due west. After several minutes, the first plane is 12 miles north of the airport, and the second plane is 15 miles west of the airport. Estimate the distance between the two planes to the nearest hundredth of a mile.

Short Response

16. The table shows the number of people newly infected by a certain virus with one person as the original source.

Week	1	2	3	4	5	6	7
Newly Infected People	1	3	9	27	81	243	729

a. Is the data set best described by a linear function, a quadratic function, or an exponential function? Write a function to model the data.

b. Use the function to predict the number of people that will become infected in the 10th week. Show your work.

17. Ella and Mia went on a camping trip. The total cost for their trip was $124, which the girls divided evenly. Ella paid for 4 nights at the campsite and $30 for supplies. Mia paid for 2 nights at the campsite and $46 for supplies.

a. Write an equation that could be used to find the cost of one night's stay at the campsite. Explain what each variable in your equation represents.

b. Solve your equation from part **a** to find the cost of one night's stay at the campsite. Show your work.

Extended Response

18. Regina is beginning a training program to prepare for a race. In week 1, she will run 3 miles during each workout. Each week thereafter, she plans to increase the distance of her runs by 20%.

a. Write an equation to show the number of miles Regina plans to run during her workouts each week. Use the variable n to represent the week number.

b. Make a table of values to show the distances of the runs in Regina's workouts for the first 6 weeks. Round each distance to the nearest hundredth of a mile. Then graph the points.

c. Explain how to use your equation from part **a** to determine how many miles Regina will run during each workout in week 8. Then find this number.

d. Explain how to the use your graph from part **b** to determine how many miles Regina will run during each workout in week 8. How does the graph verify the answer you found in part **c**?

Short-Response Rubric

Items 16–17

2 Points = The student's answer is an accurate and complete execution of the task or tasks.

1 Point = The student's answer contains attributes of an appropriate response but is flawed.

0 Points = The student's answer contains no attributes of an appropriate response.

Extended-Response Rubric

Item 18

4 Points = The student writes the correct equation in part **a,** creates the correct table of values and graphs the points correctly in part **b,** explains how to use the equation and finds correct answer in part **c,** and explains how to use the graph to verify the algebraic answer in part **d.**

3 Points = The student writes the correct equation in part **a,** creates the correct table of values and graphs the points in part **b,** finds the correct answer in part **c** but does not explain how to use the equation, and somewhat explains how to use the graph to verify the algebraic answer in part **d.**

2 Points = The student writes the equation with a minor error in part **a,** creates a table of values and graphs the points (wrong, but correct for their equation) in part **b,** explains how to use the equation and finds an answer in part **c,** and explains how to use the graph to verify their answer in part **d.**

1 Point = The student writes a completely incorrect equation in part **a** and attempts to answer all parts, but struggles because part of their equation doesn't make sense.

0 Points = The student does not attempt all parts of the problem.

Answers

17a. $4n + 30 = 2n + 46$; n represents the cost of one night's stay at the campsite.

b. $8.00

18a. $y = 3(1.2)^{n-1}$

b.

Week	1	2	3	4	5	6
Length of Run (mi)	3.00	3.60	4.32	5.18	6.22	7.46

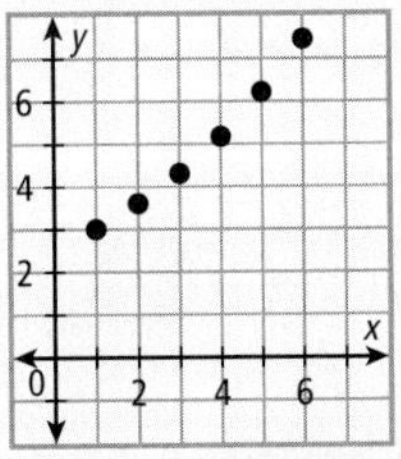

c. Use $n = 8$ in the equation from part **a;** 10.75 mi

d. Draw a smooth curve through the points. Use the curve to estimate the y-value when $n = 8$. This y-value is between 10 and 11, which verifies the answer to part **c.**

Rational Functions and Equations

Section 12A

Rational Functions and Expressions

- 12-1 **Algebra Lab** Model Inverse Variation
- 12-1 **Inverse Variation**
- 12-2 **Rational Functions**
- 12-3 **Simplifying Rational Expressions**
- 12-3 **Technology Lab** Graph Rational Functions
- **Connecting Algebra to Geometry** Representing Solid Figures

Section 12B

Operations with Rational Expressions

- 12-4 **Multiplying and Dividing Rational Expressions**
- 12-5 **Adding and Subtracting Rational Expressions**
- 12-6 **Algebra Lab** Model Polynomial Division
- 12-6 **Dividing Polynomials**
- 12-7 **Solving Rational Equations**
- EXTENSION **Trigonometric Ratios**

Pacing Guide for 45-Minute Classes

Teacher One Stop™
Calendar Planner®

Chapter 12

Countdown Weeks 28, 29, 30

DAY 1	DAY 2	DAY 3	DAY 4	DAY 5
12-1 Algebra Lab 12-1 Lesson	12-1 Lesson 12-2 Lesson	12-2 Lesson 12-3 Lesson	12-3 Lesson 12-3 Technology Lab	Connecting Algebra to Geometry Multi-Step Test Prep
DAY 6	**DAY 7**	**DAY 8**	**DAY 9**	**DAY 10**
Ready to Go On? 12-4 Lesson	12-4 Lesson 12-5 Lesson	12-5 Lesson 12-6 Algebra Lab	12-6 Lesson	12-7 Lesson
DAY 11	**DAY 12**	**DAY 13**	**DAY 14**	
Multi-Step Test Prep Ready to Go On?	EXTENSION	Chapter 12 Review	Chapter 12 Test	

Pacing Guide for 90-Minute Classes

Teacher One Stop™
Calendar Planner®

Chapter 12

DAY 1	DAY 2	DAY 3	DAY 4	DAY 5
12-1 Algebra Lab 12-1 Lesson 12-2 Lesson	12-2 Lesson 12-3 Lesson 12-3 Technology Lab	Connecting Algebra to Geometry Multi-Step Test Prep Ready to Go On? 12-4 Lesson	12-4 Lesson 12-5 Lesson 12-6 Algebra Lab	12-6 Lesson 12-7 Lesson
DAY 6	**DAY 7**			
Multi-Step Test Prep Ready to Go On? EXTENSION	Chapter 12 Review Chapter 12 Test			

ONGOING ASSESSMENT and INTERVENTION

	DIAGNOSE	PRESCRIBE
Assess Prior Knowledge	**Before Chapter 12**	
	Diagnose readiness for the chapter.	Prescribe intervention.
	Are You Ready? SE p. 867	***Are You Ready? Intervention***
Formative Assessment	**Before Every Lesson**	
	Diagnose readiness for the lesson.	Prescribe intervention.
	Warm Up TE	**Reteach** CRB
	During Every Lesson	
	Diagnose understanding of lesson concepts.	Prescribe intervention.
	Check It Out! SE	**Reading Strategies** CRB
	Questioning Strategies TE	***Success for Every Learner***
	Think and Discuss SE	***Lesson Tutorial Videos***
	Write About It SE	
	Journal TE	
	After Every Lesson	
	Diagnose mastery of lesson concepts.	Prescribe intervention.
	Lesson Quiz TE	**Reteach** CRB
	Test Prep SE	**Test Prep Doctor** TE
	Test and Practice Generator	***Homework Help Online***
	Before Chapter 12 Testing	
	Diagnose mastery of concepts in chapter.	Prescribe intervention.
	Ready to Go On? SE pp. 897, 927	***Ready to Go On? Intervention***
	Multi-Step Test Prep SE pp. 896, 926	**Scaffolding Questions** TE pp. 896, 926
	Section Quizzes AR	**Reteach** CRB
	Test and Practice Generator	***Lesson Tutorial Videos***
	Before High Stakes Testing	
	Diagnose mastery of benchmark concepts.	Prescribe intervention.
	College Entrance Exam Practice SE p. 935	***College Entrance Exam Practice***
	Standardized Test Prep SE pp. 938–939	
Summative Assessment	**After Chapter 12**	
	Check mastery of chapter concepts.	Prescribe intervention.
	Multiple-Choice Tests (Forms A, B, C)	**Reteach** CRB
	Free-Response Tests (Forms A, B, C)	***Lesson Tutorial Videos***
	Performance Assessment AR	
	Cumulative Test AR	
	Test and Practice Generator	

KEY: **SE** = *Student Edition* **TE** = *Teacher's Edition* **CRB** = *Chapter Resource Book* **AR** = *Assessment Resources* Available online  Available on CD- or DVD-ROM

Lesson Resources

Before the Lesson

Prepare ***Teacher One Stop*** SPANISH
- Editable lesson plans
- Calendar Planner
- Easy access to all chapter resources

Lesson Transparencies
- Teacher Tools

Teach the Lesson

Introduce ***Alternate Openers: Explorations***

Lesson Transparencies
- Warm Up
- Problem of the Day

Teach ***Lesson Transparencies***
- Teaching Transparencies

Know-It Notebook™
- Vocabulary
- Key Concepts

Power Presentations 

Lesson Tutorial Videos SPANISH

Interactive Online Edition

- Lesson Activities
- Lesson Tutorial Videos

Lab Activities

Lab Resources Online 

Online Interactivities SPANISH 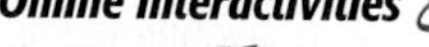

TechKeys 

Practice the Lesson

Practice ***Chapter Resources***
- Practice A, B, C

Practice and Problem Solving Workbook SPANISH

IDEA Works!® Modified Worksheets and Tests

ExamView Test and Practice Generator

Homework Help Online 

Online Interactivities SPANISH

Interactive Online Edition
- Homework Help

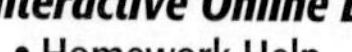

Apply ***Chapter Resources***
- Problem Solving SPANISH

Practice and Problem Solving Workbook SPANISH

Interactive Online Edition 
- Chapter Project

Project Teacher Support 

After the Lesson

Reteach ***Chapter Resources***
- Reteach
- Reading Strategies ELL

Success for Every Learner

Review ***Interactive Answers and Solutions***

Solutions Key

Know-It Notebook™
- Big Ideas
- Chapter Review

Extend ***Chapter Resources***
- Challenge

Technology Highlights for the Teacher

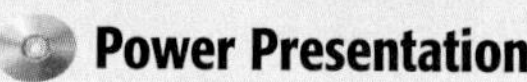

Power Presentations

Dynamic presentations to engage students. Complete PowerPoint® presentations for every lesson in Chapter 12.

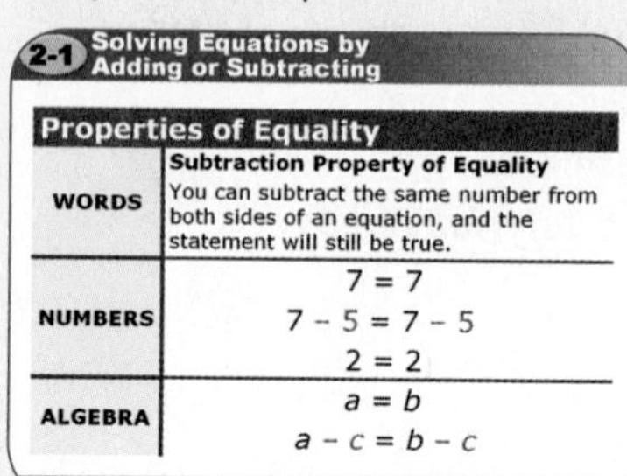

Teacher One Stop SPANISH 

Easy access to Chapter 12 resources and assessments. Includes lesson planning, test generation, and puzzle creation software.

Premier Online Edition SPANISH 

Chapter 12 includes Tutorial Videos, Lesson Activities, Lesson Quizzes, Homework Help, and Chapter Project.

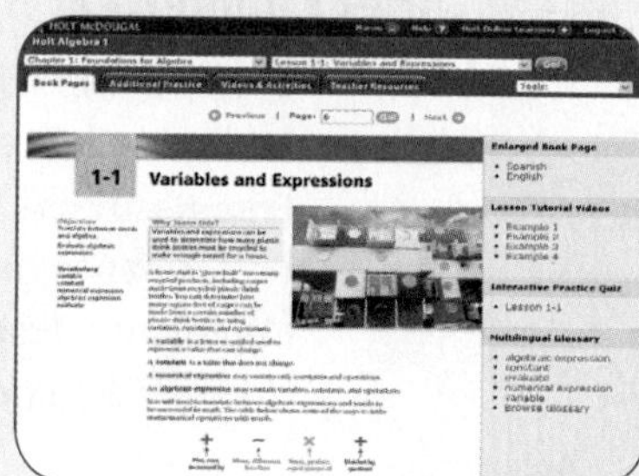

KEY: **SE** = *Student Edition* **TE** = *Teacher's Edition*  English Language Learners  Spanish version available  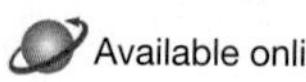 Available online  Available on CD- or DVD-ROM

CHAPTER 12

Reaching All Learners

Teaching tips to help all learners appear throughout the chapter. A few that target specific students are included in the lists below.

All Learners

Lab Activities
Practice and Problem Solving Workbook SPANISH
Know-It Notebook

Special Needs Students

Practice A .... CRB
Reteach .... CRB
Reading Strategies .... CRB
Are You Ready? .... SE p. 867
Inclusion .... TE pp. 888, 900, 906, 915, 923, 924
IDEA Works!® Modified Worksheets and Tests
Ready to Go On? Intervention 
Know-It Notebook
Online Interactivities 
Lesson Tutorial Videos SPANISH

Developing Learners

Practice A .... CRB
Reteach .... CRB
Reading Strategies .... CRB
Are You Ready? .... SE p. 867
Vocabulary Connections .... SE p. 868
Questioning Strategies .... TE
Ready to Go On? Intervention SPANISH
Know-It Notebook
Homework Help Online 
Online Interactivities 
Lesson Tutorial Videos  SPANISH

On-Level Learners

Practice B .... CRB
Problem Solving .... CRB
Vocabulary Connections .... SE p. 868
Questioning Strategies .... TE
Ready to Go On? Intervention 
Know-It Notebook
Homework Help Online
Online Interactivities SPANISH

Advanced Learners

Practice C .... CRB
Challenge .... CRB
Challenge Exercises .... SE
Reading and Writing Math *Extend* .... TE p. 869
Critical Thinking .... TE pp. 907, 914
Are You Ready? Enrichment 
Ready To Go On? Enrichment SPANISH

English Language Learners

ENGLISH LANGUAGE LEARNERS

Reading Strategies .... CRB
Are You Ready? Vocabulary .... SE p. 867
Vocabulary Connections .... SE p. 868
Vocabulary Review .... SE p. 930
English Language Learners .... TE pp. 873, 879, 906, 940
Success for Every Learner
Know-It Notebook
Multilingual Glossary 
Lesson Tutorial Videos 

Technology Highlights for Reaching All Learners

Lesson Tutorial Videos 

Starring Holt authors Ed Burger and Freddie Renfro! Live tutorials to support every lesson in Chapter 12.

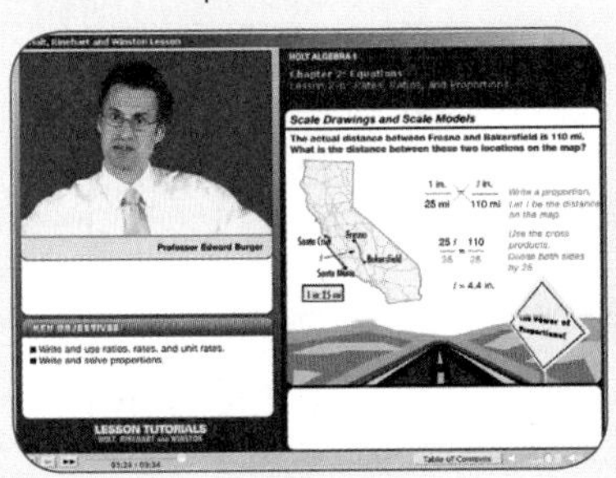

Multilingual Glossary

Searchable glossary includes definitions in English, Spanish, Vietnamese, Chinese, Hmong, Korean, and 4 other languages.

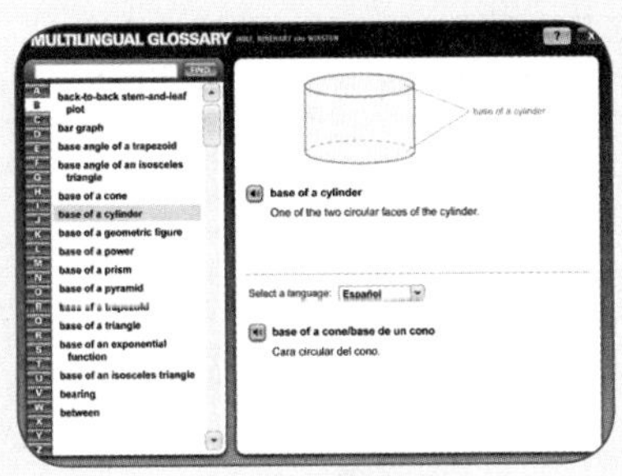

Online Interactivities

Interactive tutorials provide visually engaging alternative opportunities to learn concepts and master skills.

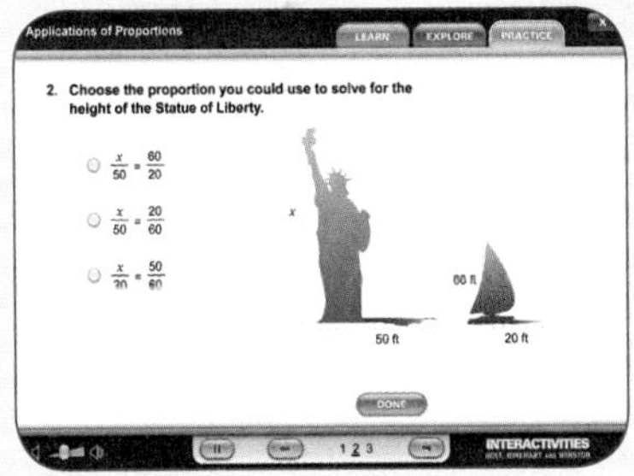

KEY: **SE** = *Student Edition* **TE** = *Teacher's Edition* **CRB** = *Chapter Resource Book* SPANISH Spanish version available 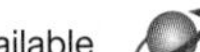 Available online  Available on CD- or DVD-ROM

Ongoing Assessment

Assessing Prior Knowledge

Determine whether students have the prerequisite concepts and skills for success in Chapter 12.

Are You Ready? SPANISH .... SE p. 867
Warm Up .... TE

Test Preparation

Provide review and practice for Chapter 12 and standardized tests.

Multi-Step Test Prep .... SE pp. 896, 926
Study Guide: Review .... SE pp. 930–933
Test Tackler .... SE pp. 936–937
Standardized Test Prep .... SE pp. 938–939
College Entrance Exam Practice .... SE p. 935
Countdown to Testing .... SE pp. C4-C27
IDEA Works!® Modified Worksheets and Tests

Alternative Assessment

Assess students' understanding of Chapter 12 concepts and combined problem-solving skills.

Chapter 12 Project .... SE p. 866
Alternative Assessment .... TE
Performance Assessment SPANISH .... AR
Portfolio Assessment SPANISH .... AR

Lesson Assessment

Provide formative assessment for each lesson of Chapter 12.

Questioning Strategies .... TE
Think and Discuss .... SE
Check It Out! Exercises .... SE
Write About It .... SE
Journal .... TE
Lesson Quiz .... TE
Alternative Assessment .... TE
IDEA Works!® Modified Worksheets and Tests

Weekly Assessment

Provide formative assessment for each section of Chapter 12.

Multi-Step Test Prep .... SE pp. 896, 926
Ready to Go On? SPANISH .... SE pp. 897, 927
Section Quizzes SPANISH .... AR
Test and Practice Generator SPANISH .... *Teacher One Stop*

Chapter Assessment

Provide summative assessment of Chapter 12 mastery.

Chapter 12 Test .... SE p. 934
Chapter Test (Levels A, B, C) SPANISH .... AR
• Multiple Choice • Free Response
Cumulative Test SPANISH .... AR
Test and Practice Generator SPANISH .... *Teacher One Stop*
IDEA Works!® Modified Worksheets and Tests

Technology Highlights for Assessment

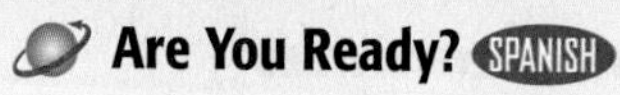

Automatically assess readiness and prescribe intervention for Chapter 12 prerequisite skills.

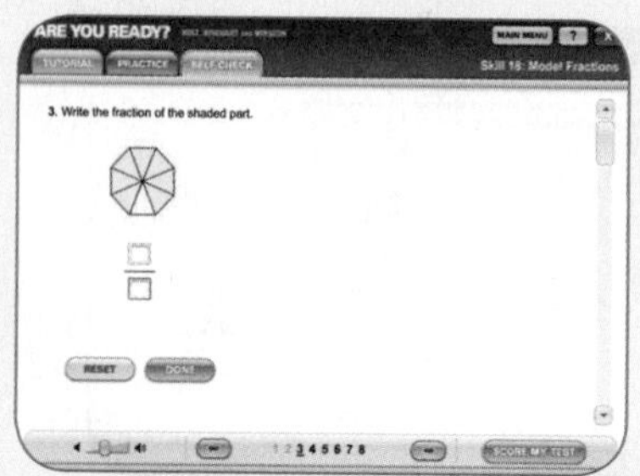

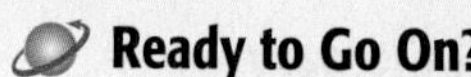

Automatically assess understanding of and prescribe intervention for Sections 12A and 12B.

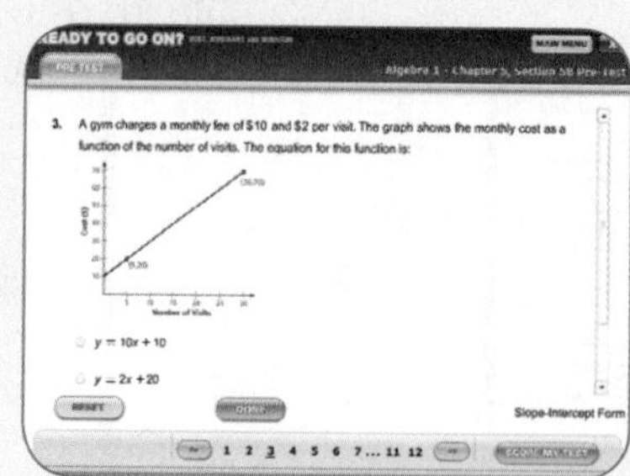

 **Test and Practice Generator** SPANISH

Use Chapter 12 problem banks to create assessments and worksheets to print out or deliver online. Includes dynamic problems.

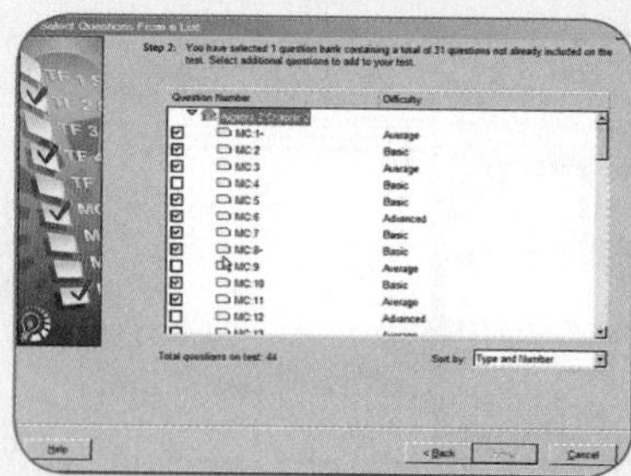

KEY: **SE** = *Student Edition* **TE** = *Teacher's Edition* **AR** = *Assessment Resources* SPANISH Spanish version available · Available online · Available on CD- or DVD-ROM

Formal Assessment

Three levels (A, B, C) of multiple-choice and free-response chapter tests, along with a performance assessment, are available in the *Assessment Resources.*

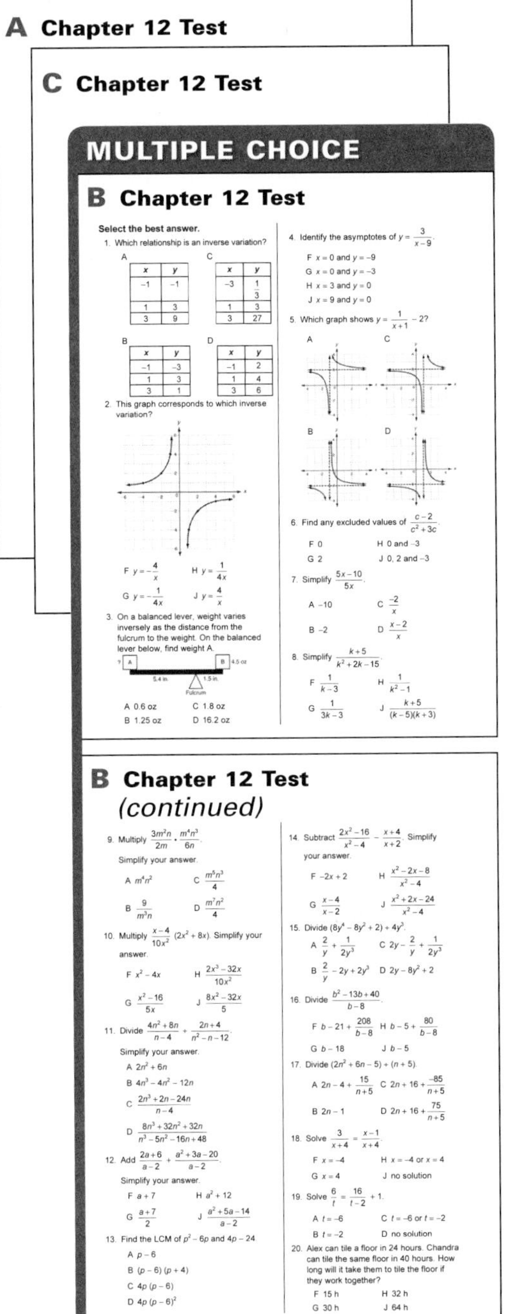

A Chapter 12 Test

C Chapter 12 Test

MULTIPLE CHOICE

B Chapter 12 Test

Select the best answer.

1. Which relationship is an inverse variation?

A

x	y
−1	−1
1	3
3	9

C

x	y
−3	1
1	3
3	27

B

x	y
−1	−3
1	3
3	1

D

x	y
−1	2
1	4
3	6

2. This graph corresponds to which inverse variation?

F $y = -\frac{4}{x}$ H $y = \frac{1}{4x}$

G $y = -\frac{1}{4x}$ J $y = \frac{4}{x}$

3. On a balanced lever, weight varies inversely as the distance from the fulcrum to the weight. On the balanced lever below, find weight A.

A 0.6 oz C 1.8 oz

B 1.25 oz D 16.2 oz

4. Identify the asymptotes of $y = \frac{3}{x-9}$.

F $x = 0$ and $y = -9$

G $x = 0$ and $y = -3$

H $x = 3$ and $y = 0$

J $x = 9$ and $y = 0$

5. Which graph shows $y = \frac{1}{x+1} - 2$?

6. Find any excluded values of $\frac{c-2}{c^2+3c}$.

F 0 H 0 and −3

G 2 J 0, 2 and −3

7. Simplify $\frac{5x-10}{5x}$.

A −10 C $\frac{-2}{x}$

B −2 D $\frac{x-2}{x}$

8. Simplify $\frac{k+5}{k^2+2k-15}$.

F $\frac{1}{k-3}$ H $\frac{1}{k^2-1}$

G $\frac{1}{3k-3}$ J $\frac{k+5}{(k-5)(k+3)}$

B Chapter 12 Test (continued)

9. Multiply $\frac{3m^2n}{2m} \cdot \frac{m^4n^3}{6n}$. Simplify your answer.

A m^4n^2 C $\frac{m^6n^3}{4}$

B $\frac{9}{m^2n}$ D $\frac{m^7n^2}{4}$

10. Multiply $\frac{x-4}{10x^2}(2x^2+8x)$. Simplify your answer.

F $x^2 - 4x$ H $\frac{2x^3-32x}{10x^2}$

G $\frac{x^2-16}{5x}$ J $\frac{8x^2-32x}{5}$

11. Divide $\frac{4n^2+8n}{n-4} \div \frac{2n+4}{n^2-n-12}$. Simplify your answer.

A $2n^2+6n$

B $4n^3-4n^2-12n$

C $\frac{2n^3+2n-24n}{n-4}$

D $\frac{8n^3+32n^2+32n}{n^3-5n^2-16n+48}$

12. Add $\frac{2a+6}{a-2} + \frac{a^2+3a-20}{a-2}$. Simplify your answer.

F $a+7$ H a^2+12

G $\frac{a+7}{2}$ J $\frac{a^2+5a-14}{a-2}$

13. Find the LCM of $p^2 - 6p$ and $4p - 24$.

A $p - 6$

B $(p-6)(p+4)$

C $4p(p-6)$

D $4p(p-6)^2$

14. Subtract $\frac{2x^2-16}{x^2-4} - \frac{x+4}{x+2}$. Simplify your answer.

F $-2x+2$ H $\frac{x^2-2x-8}{x^2-4}$

G $\frac{x-4}{x-2}$ J $\frac{x^2+2x-24}{x^2-4}$

15. Divide $(8y^4 - 8y^2 + 2) \div 4y^2$.

A $\frac{2}{y} + \frac{1}{2y^3}$ C $2y - \frac{2}{y} + \frac{1}{2y^3}$

B $\frac{2}{y} - 2y + 2y^3$ D $2y - 8y^2 + 2$

16. Divide $\frac{b^2-13b+40}{b-8}$.

F $b-21+\frac{208}{b-8}$ H $b-5+\frac{80}{b-8}$

G $b-18$ J $b-5$

17. Divide $(2n^3 + 6n - 5) \div (n+5)$.

A $2n-4+\frac{15}{n+5}$ C $2n+16+\frac{-85}{n+5}$

B $2n-1$ D $2n+16+\frac{75}{n+5}$

18. Solve $\frac{3}{x+4} = \frac{x-1}{x+4}$.

F $x = -4$ H $x = -4$ or $x = 4$

G $x = 4$ J no solution

19. Solve $\frac{6}{t} = \frac{16}{t-2} + 1$.

A $t = -6$ C $t = -6$ or $t = -2$

B $t = -2$ D no solution

20. Alex can tile a floor in 24 hours. Chandra can tile the same floor in 40 hours. How long will it take them to tile the floor if they work together?

F 15 h H 32 h

G 30 h J 64 h

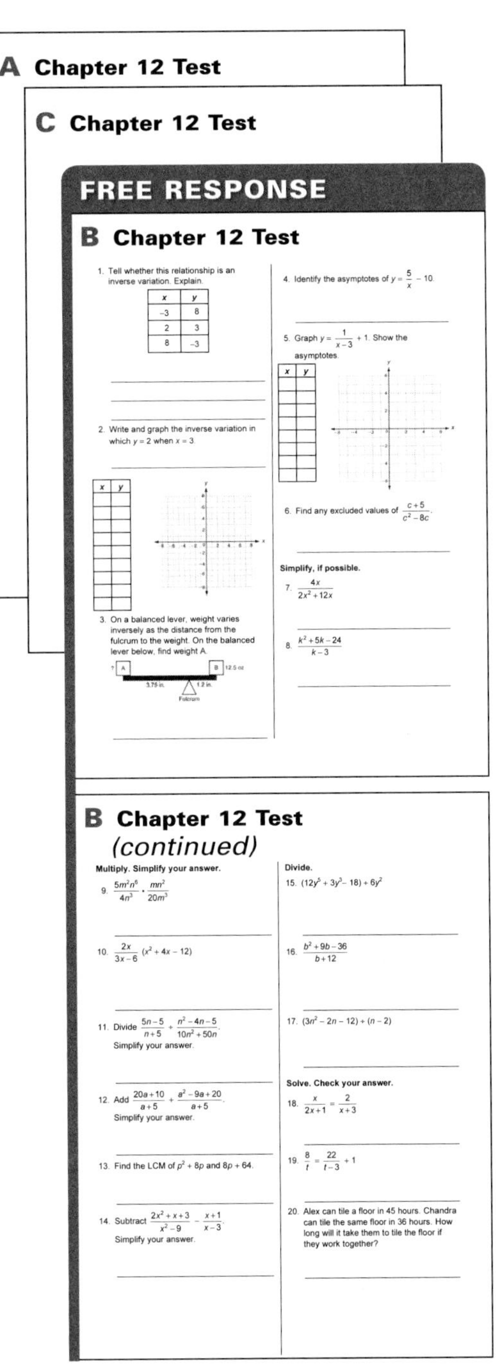

A Chapter 12 Test

C Chapter 12 Test

FREE RESPONSE

B Chapter 12 Test

1. Tell whether this relationship is an inverse variation. Explain.

x	y
−3	8
2	3
8	−3

2. Write and graph the inverse variation in which $y = 2$ when $x = 3$.

3. On a balanced lever, weight varies inversely as the distance from the fulcrum to the weight. On the balanced lever below, find weight A.

4. Identify the asymptotes of $y = \frac{5}{x} - 10$.

5. Graph $y = \frac{1}{x-3} + 1$. Show the asymptotes.

6. Find any excluded values of $\frac{c+5}{c^2-8c}$.

Simplify, if possible.

7. $\frac{4x}{2x^2+12x}$

8. $\frac{k^2+5k-24}{k-3}$

B Chapter 12 Test (continued)

Multiply. Simplify your answer.

9. $\frac{5m^2n^6}{4n^3} \cdot \frac{mn^2}{20m^3}$

10. $\frac{2x}{3x-6}(x^2+4x-12)$

11. Divide $\frac{5n-5}{n+5} \div \frac{n^2-4n-5}{10n^2+50n}$. Simplify your answer.

12. Add $\frac{20a+10}{a+5} + \frac{a^2-9a+20}{a+5}$. Simplify your answer.

13. Find the LCM of $p^2 + 8p$ and $8p + 64$.

14. Subtract $\frac{2x^2+x+3}{x^2-9} - \frac{x+1}{x-3}$. Simplify your answer.

Divide.

15. $(12y^5 + 3y^3 - 18) \div 6y^2$

16. $\frac{b^2+9b-36}{b+12}$

17. $(3n^2 - 2n - 12) \div (n-2)$

Solve. Check your answer.

18. $\frac{x}{2x+1} = \frac{2}{x+3}$

19. $\frac{8}{t} = \frac{22}{t-3} + 1$

20. Alex can tile a floor in 45 hours. Chandra can tile the same floor in 36 hours. How long will it take them to tile the floor if they work together?

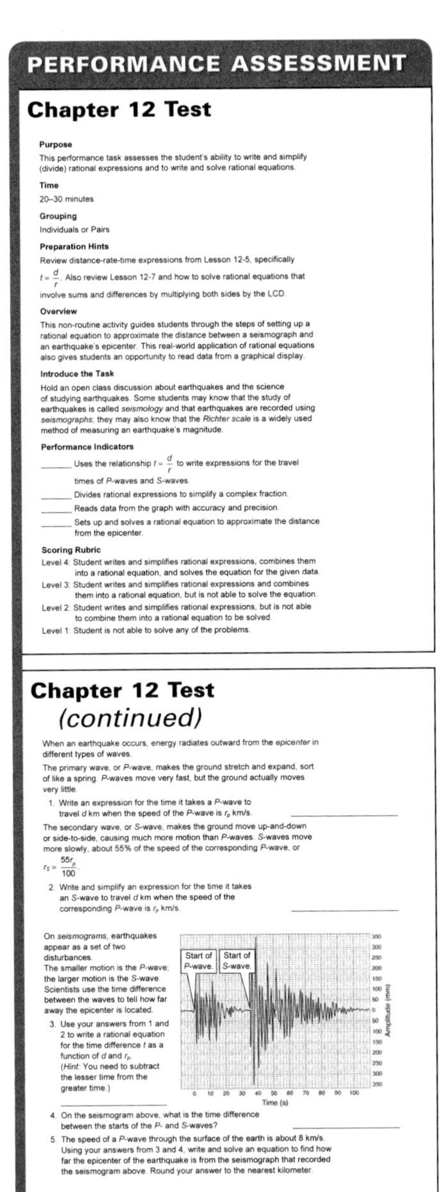

PERFORMANCE ASSESSMENT

Chapter 12 Test

Purpose
This performance task assesses the student's ability to write and simplify (divide) rational expressions and to write and solve rational equations.

Time
20–30 minutes

Grouping
Individuals or Pairs

Preparation Hints
Review distance-rate-time expressions from Lesson 12-5, specifically $t = \frac{d}{r}$. Also review Lesson 12-7 and how to solve rational equations that involve sums and differences by multiplying both sides by the LCD.

Overview
This non-routine activity guides students through the steps of setting up a rational equation to approximate the distance between a seismograph and an earthquake's epicenter. This real-world application of rational equations also gives students an opportunity to read data from a graphical display.

Introduce the Task
Hold an open class discussion about earthquakes and the science of studying earthquakes. Some students may know that the study of earthquakes is called *seismology* and that earthquakes are recorded using *seismographs*; they may also know that the *Richter scale* is a widely used method of measuring an earthquake's magnitude.

Performance Indicators

_____ Uses the relationship $t = \frac{d}{r}$ to write expressions for the travel times of P-waves and S-waves.

_____ Divides rational expressions to simplify a complex fraction.

_____ Reads data from the graph with accuracy and precision.

_____ Sets up and solves a rational equation to approximate the distance from the epicenter.

Scoring Rubric

Level 4: Student writes and simplifies rational expressions, combines them into a rational equation, and solves the equation for the given data.

Level 3: Student writes and simplifies rational expressions and combines them into a rational equation, but is not able to solve the equation.

Level 2: Student writes and simplifies rational expressions, but is not able to combine them into a rational equation to be solved.

Level 1: Student is not able to solve any of the problems.

Chapter 12 Test (continued)

When an earthquake occurs, energy radiates outward from the epicenter in different types of waves.

The primary wave, or P-wave, makes the ground stretch and expand, sort of like a spring. P-waves move very fast, but the ground actually moves very little.

1. Write an expression for the time it takes a P-wave to travel d km when the speed of the P-wave is r_p km/s.

The secondary wave, or S-wave, makes the ground move up-and-down or side-to-side, causing much more motion than P-waves. S-waves move more slowly, about 55% of the speed of the corresponding P-wave, or $r_S = \frac{55r_p}{100}$.

2. Write and simplify an expression for the time it takes an S-wave to travel d km when the speed of the corresponding P-wave is r_p km/s.

On *seismograms*, earthquakes appear as a set of two disturbances. The smaller motion is the P-wave; the larger motion is the S-wave. Scientists use the time difference between the waves to tell how far away the epicenter is located.

3. Use your answers from 1 and 2 to write a rational equation for the time difference t as a function of d and r_p. (*Hint:* You need to subtract the lesser time from the greater time.)

4. On the seismogram above, what is the time difference between the starts of the P- and S-waves?

5. The speed of a P-wave through the surface of the earth is about 8 km/s. Using your answers from 3 and 4, write and solve an equation to find how far the epicenter of the earthquake is from the seismograph that recorded the seismogram above. Round your answer to the nearest kilometer.

Teacher One Stop™

Test & Practice Generator

Create and customize Chapter 12 Tests. Instantly generate multiple test versions, answer keys, and Spanish versions of test items.

Modified chapter tests that address special learning needs are available in *IDEA Works!®* *Modified Worksheets and Tests.*

CHAPTER 12

SECTION 12A
Rational Functions and Expressions

On page 896, students write, solve, and graph functions to model real-world construction situations.

Exercises designed to prepare students for success on the Multi-Step Test Prep can be found in each lesson.

SECTION 12B
Operations with Rational Expressions

On page 926, students write, solve, and graph functions to model a real-world projection situation.

Exercises designed to prepare students for success on the Multi-Step Test Prep can be found in each lesson.

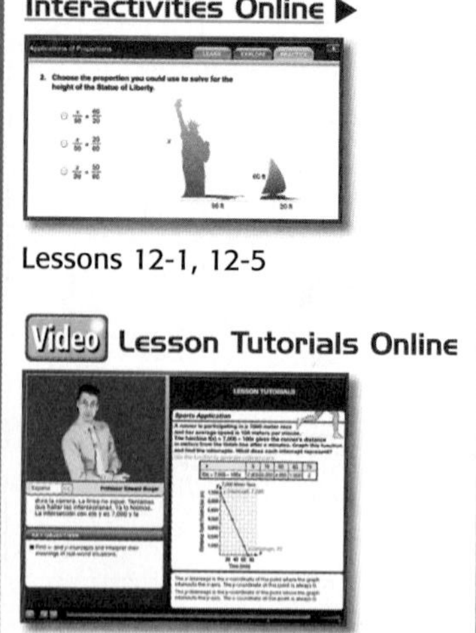

Interactivities Online ▶

Lessons 12-1, 12-5

Video Lesson Tutorials Online

Lesson Tutorial Videos are available for EVERY example.

CHAPTER 12

Rational Functions and Equations

Chapter

- Graph and use rational functions to solve real-world problems.
- Simplify rational expressions.
- Use rational equations to solve real-world problems.

By Design

Ratios and rational expressions can be used to explore perspective in art and dimensions in package design. Try your hand at both.

go.hrw.com
Chapter Project Online
KEYWORD: MA7 ChProj

By Design

About the Project

In the first activity, students investigate linear perspective—how objects appear smaller when farther away. In the second activity, students design a new yogurt drink container that comfortably fits in an eight-year-old child's hand and that minimizes the cost of producing the container.

Project Resources

All project resources for teachers and students are provided online.

Materials:

- ruler
- customary tape measure
- metric tape measure
- cylindrical containers, such as water bottles, soda cans, juice cans, and soup cans

ARE YOU READY?

Vocabulary

Match each term on the left with a definition on the right.

1. perfect-square trinomial **F**
2. greatest common factor **A**
3. monomial **B**
4. polynomial **E**
5. reciprocals **C**

A. the greatest factor that is shared by two or more terms
B. a number, a variable, or a product of numbers and variables with whole-number exponents
C. two numbers whose product is 1
D. a polynomial with three terms
E. the sum or difference of monomials
F. a trinomial that is the result of squaring a binomial

Simplify Fractions

Simplify.

6. $\frac{12}{4}$ **3** 7. $\frac{100}{36}$ $\mathbf{2\frac{7}{9}}$ 8. $\frac{240}{18}$ $\mathbf{13\frac{1}{3}}$ 9. $\frac{121}{66}$ $\mathbf{1\frac{5}{6}}$

Add and Subtract Fractions

Add or subtract.

10. $\frac{1}{3}+\frac{1}{2}$ $\mathbf{\frac{5}{6}}$ 11. $\frac{7}{8}-\frac{1}{6}$ $\mathbf{\frac{17}{24}}$ 12. $\frac{3}{4}+\frac{2}{3}+\frac{1}{2}$ $\mathbf{1\frac{11}{12}}$ 13. $\frac{5}{9}+\frac{1}{12}-\frac{1}{3}$ $\mathbf{\frac{11}{36}}$

Factor GCF from Polynomials

Factor each polynomial.

14. x^2+2x $\mathbf{x(x+2)}$ 15. x^2+x $\mathbf{x(x+1)}$ 16. $2x^2+x$ $\mathbf{x(2x+1)}$ 17. x^2-x $\mathbf{x(x-1)}$

18. $3x^2+2x$ $\mathbf{x(3x+2)}$ 19. $4x^2-4$ $\mathbf{4(x+1)(x-1)}$ 20. $3x^2-6x$ $\mathbf{3x(x-2)}$ 21. x^3-x^2 $\mathbf{x^2(x-1)}$

Properties of Exponents

Simplify each expression.

22. $4x\cdot 3x^2$ $\mathbf{12x^3}$ 23. $-5\cdot 2jk$ $\mathbf{-10jk}$ 24. $-2a^3\cdot 3a^4$ $\mathbf{-6a^7}$ 25. $3ab\cdot 4a^2b$ $\mathbf{12a^3b^2}$

26. $2x\cdot 3y\cdot xy$ $\mathbf{6x^2y^2}$ 27. $a^2b\cdot 3ab^3$ $\mathbf{3a^3b^4}$ 28. $3rs\cdot 3rs^3$ $\mathbf{9r^2s^4}$ 29. $5m^2n^2\cdot 4mn^2$ $\mathbf{20m^3n^4}$

Simplify Polynomial Expressions

Simplify each expression.

30. $4x-2y-8y$ $\mathbf{4x-10y}$ 31. $2r-4s+3s-8r$ $\mathbf{-6r-s}$

32. $ab^2-ab+4ab^2+2a^2b+a^2b^2$ $\mathbf{5ab^2-ab+2a^2b+a^2b^2}$ 33. $3g(g-4)+g^2+g$ $\mathbf{4g^2-11g}$

CHAPTER 12

ARE YOU READY?

Organizer

Objective: Assess students' understanding of prerequisite skills.

Assessing Prior Knowledge

INTERVENTION

Diagnose and Prescribe

Use this page to determine whether intervention is necessary or whether enrichment is appropriate.

Resources

***Are You Ready? Intervention and Enrichment* Worksheets**

***Are You Ready?* CD-ROM**

***Are You Ready?* Online**

my.hrw.com

ARE YOU READY?

Diagnose and Prescribe

Prerequisite Skill	*Are You Ready? Intervention*, Chapter 12 Worksheets	CD-ROM	Online
Simplify Fractions	Skill 10	Activity 10	Diagnose and Prescribe Online
Add and Subtract Fractions	Skill 48	Activity 48	
Factor GCF from Polynomials	Skill 66	Activity 66	
Properties of Exponents	Skill 59	Activity 59	
Simplify Polynomial Expressions	Skill 63	Activity 63	

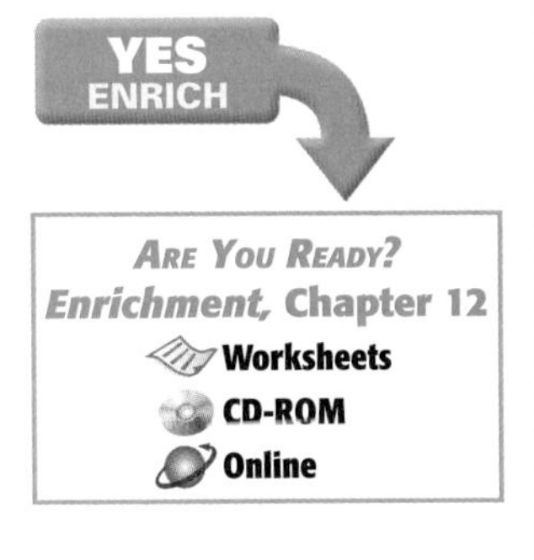

Organizer

Objective: Help students organize the new concepts they will learn in Chapter 12.

Online Edition
Multilingual Glossary

Resources

Teacher One Stop™
PuzzleView

***Multilingual Glossary* Online**

go.hrw.com
KEYWORD: MA7 Glossary

Answers to *Vocabulary Connections*

1. Possible answer: Smooth, connected, uninterrupted. The graph of a discontinuous function might have breaks in it.
2. Possible answer: Included: belonging to the group; having similar characteristics to the others in the group; excluded: not part of the group; unlike those in the group; excluded values are values for which the function is undefined.
3. $y = k \cdot \frac{1}{x}$ or $y = \frac{k}{x}$, where k is a nonzero constant
4. Possible answer: A rational expression is an expression that contains variable(s), number(s), and operation(s) and can be written in the form of a fraction; $\frac{5}{x+2}$.

CHAPTER 12 Study Guide: Preview

Where You've Been

Previously you
- identified, wrote, and graphed equations of direct variation.
- identified and graphed quadratic, exponential, and square-root functions.
- used factoring to solve quadratic equations.
- simplified radical expressions and solved radical equations.

In This Chapter

You will study
- how to identify, write, and graph equations of inverse variation.
- how to graph rational functions and simplify rational expressions.
- how to solve rational equations.

Where You're Going

You can use the skills in this chapter
- to build upon your knowledge of graphing and transforming various types of functions.
- to solve problems involving inverse variation in classes such as Physics and Chemistry.
- to calculate costs when working with a fixed budget.

Key Vocabulary/Vocabulario

asymptote	asíntota
discontinuous function	función discontinua
excluded values	valores excluidos
inverse variation	variación inversa
rational equation	ecuación racional
rational expression	expresión racional
rational function	función racional

Vocabulary Connections

To become familiar with some of the vocabulary terms in the chapter, consider the following. You may refer to the chapter, the glossary, or a dictionary if you like.

1. What are some other words that mean the same as *continuous*? The prefix *dis-* generally means "not." Describe what the graph of a **discontinuous function** might look like.
2. What does it mean for someone or something to be *included* in a group? What about *excluded*? What might it mean for some values to be **excluded values** for a particular function?
3. A *direct variation* is a relationship between two variables, x and y, that can be written in the form $y = kx$ where k is a nonzero constant. The inverse of a number x is $\frac{1}{x}$. Use this information to write the form of an **inverse variation**.
4. You learned in Chapter 1 that an *algebraic expression* is an expression that contains one or more variables, numbers, or operations. You also learned that a *rational number* is a number that can be written in the form of a fraction. Combine these terms to define **rational expression**. Give an example.

868 Chapter 12

Study Strategy: Prepare for Your Final Exam

Math is a cumulative subject, so your final exam will probably cover all of the material you have learned since the beginning of the course. Preparation is essential for you to be successful on your final exam. It may help you to make a study timeline like the one below.

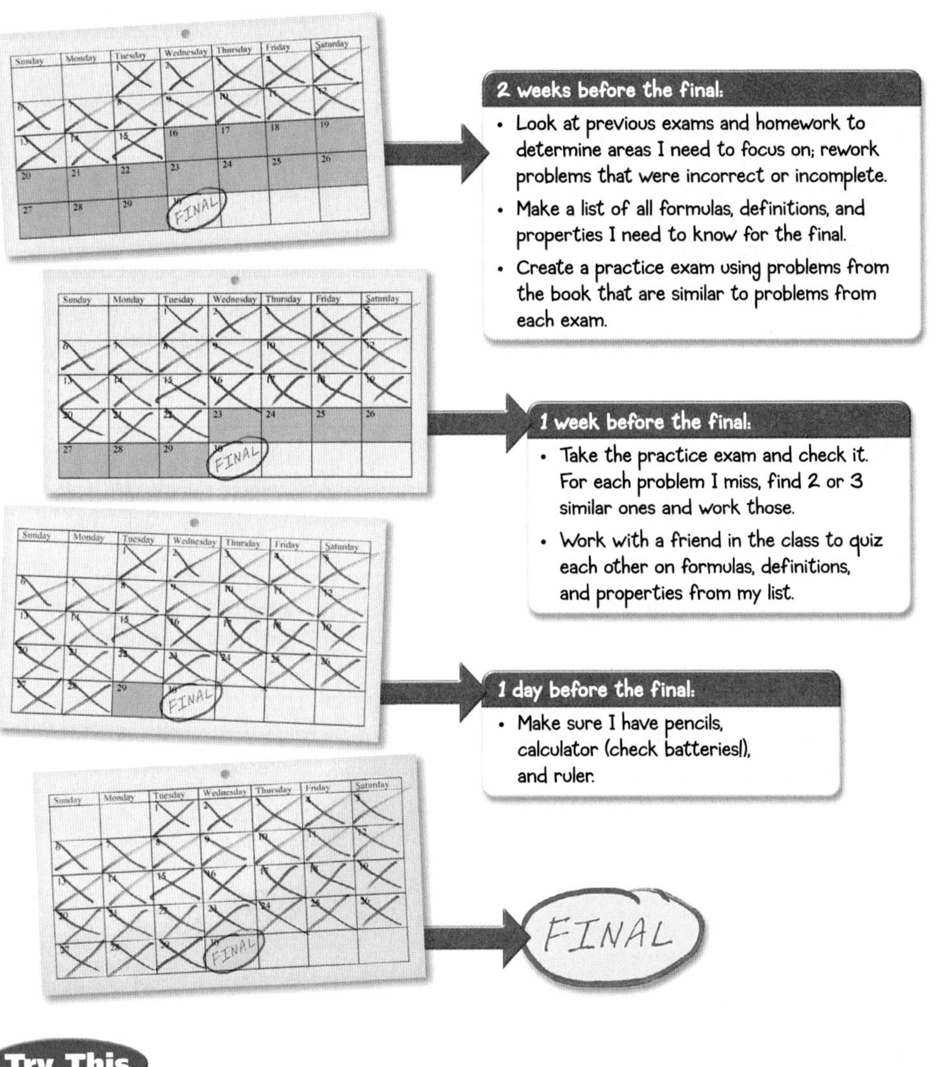

Try This

1. Create a timeline that you will use to study for your final exam.

Organizer

Objective: Help students apply strategies to understand and retain key concepts.

Study Strategy: Prepare for Your Final Exam

Discuss For the two weeks before the final exam, students can place each of the chapter numbers into a block on a calendar, using those days to review previous exams, homework, formulas, properties, and vocabulary from that chapter.

Extend Have students work in small groups to list strategies they have used to study for exams in this or other courses. Students can make posters describing their most effective strategies. Display the posters in the weeks leading up to the final exam.

Answer to *Try This*

1. Check students' work.

Reading Connection

The Great Equations
by Robert P. Crease

From $1 + 1 = 2$ to $E = mc^2$, several equations stand out in the history of mathematics and science. The author discusses ten such equations, making clear that each was not the result of a sudden brainstorm, but instead was the long, painstaking work of a succession of thinkers. Newton's Law of Universal Gravitation is an example of the "inverse-square" relationship, which has countless applications in science and industry.

Activity After students read Chapter 3, ask them to explain how the equation describing the force of gravity illustrates both direct and inverse variation. The force of gravity varies directly with the product of the masses of two objects and inversely with the square of the distance between them.

SECTION

12A Rational Functions and Expressions

One-Minute Section Planner

Lesson	Lab Resources	Materials
12-1 Algebra Lab Model Inverse Variation • Use square tiles or grid paper to model inverse variation. ☐ SAT-10 ☐ NAEP ☐ ACT ☐ SAT ☐ SAT Subject Tests	***Algebra Lab Activities*** 12-1 Lab Recording Sheet	**Required** square tiles (MK) or grid paper
Lesson 12-1 Inverse Variation • Identify, write, and graph inverse variations. ☐ SAT-10 ☑ NAEP ☐ ACT ☐ SAT ☐ SAT Subject Tests		**Optional** cylindrical containers
Lesson 12-2 Rational Functions • Identify excluded values of rational functions. • Graph rational functions. ☐ SAT-10 ☐ NAEP ☐ ACT ☑ SAT ☑ SAT Subject Tests		**Optional** graphing calculator
Lesson 12-3 Simplifying Rational Expressions • Simplify rational expressions. • Identify excluded values of rational expressions. ☐ SAT-10 ☑ NAEP ☑ ACT ☑ SAT ☑ SAT Subject Tests		**Optional** colored pencils (MK)
12-3 Technology Lab Graph Rational Functions • Use a graphing calculator to explore rational functions. ☐ SAT-10 ☐ NAEP ☐ ACT ☑ SAT ☑ SAT Subject Tests	***Technology Lab Activities*** 12-3 Lab Recording Sheet	**Required** graphing calculator

Note: If NAEP is checked, the content is tested on either the Grade 8 or the Grade 12 NAEP assessment.

MK = *Manipulatives Kit*

Math Background

Professional Learning

RATIONAL FUNCTIONS

Lessons 12-1 and 12-2

The focus of this section is rational functions. In a general sense, many functions may be considered to be rational functions since a function may be written as a fraction with a denominator of 1. The linear and quadratic functions that students have already studied are rational functions. In this chapter, however, we limit rational functions to functions that are a quotient of polynomials in which the denominator has a degree of at least 1. In other words, these rational functions have a variable in the denominator.

INVERSE VARIATION

Lesson 12-1

The simplest rational functions are those given by inverse variations. These functions have the form $y = \frac{k}{x}$, where k is a nonzero constant and $x \neq 0$. In this case, the numerator is a polynomial of degree 0 (a constant) and the denominator is a polynomial of degree 1.

In an inverse variation with a positive value of k, the value of y increases as the value of x decreases. More generally, in any inverse variation, the absolute value of one variable increases while the absolute value of the other variable decreases.

The inverse relationship between the two variables can also be seen by rewriting the function in the form $xy = k$. This form shows that the product of x and y is a fixed, nonzero constant. Therefore, when one variable changes, the other variable must change accordingly to preserve the constant product. For example, when x is doubled, y must be halved. When x is halved, y is doubled.

The graph of an inverse variation is a *hyperbola.* Unlike other graphs students have seen up to this point, a hyperbola consists of two distinct "branches." When $k > 0$, the hyperbola lies in Quadrants I and III. When $k < 0$, the hyperbola lies in Quadrants II and IV. The x- and y-axes are *asymptotes.* That is, the curve approaches the axes arbitrarily closely, but never intersects the axes.

It is also worth noting that the graph of an inverse variation is a *discontinuous* graph. Informally speaking, this means that the complete graph cannot be drawn without lifting your pencil. The graphs of inverse variations are likely to be the first discontinuous graphs that students encounter.

Finally, the absolute value of k determines the shape of the hyperbola. The smaller the absolute value of k, the closer the curve is to the origin. This is illustrated in the graphs of $y = \frac{k}{x}$ for $k = 1, 6$, and 20.

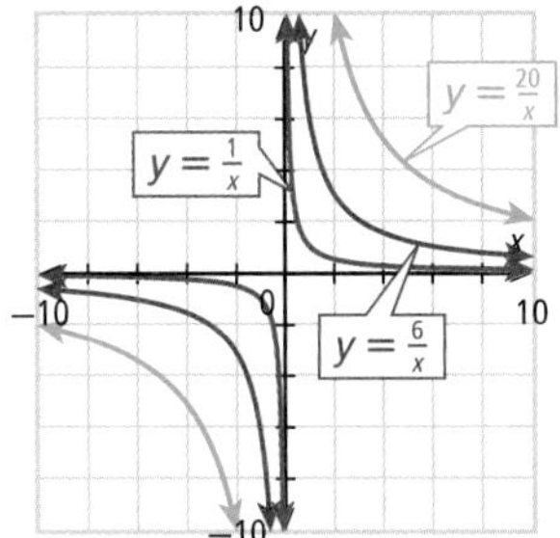

BASIC RATIONAL FUNCTIONS

Lesson 12-2

Although there are many different types of rational functions, in Lesson 12-2 the focus is on rational functions of the form $y = \frac{a}{x - b} + c$, where a, b, and c are real numbers and $a \neq 0$. These are indeed rational functions (that is, a quotient of polynomials) because they may be written equivalently as

$$\begin{aligned} y &= \frac{a}{x - b} + c \\ &= \frac{a}{x - b} + c \cdot \frac{x - b}{x - b} \\ &= \frac{a + c(x - b)}{x - b} \\ &= \frac{a + cx - cb}{x - b} \text{ for all } x \neq b. \end{aligned}$$

An inverse variation is a special case of this basic type of rational function. In an inverse variation, $b = c = 0$. Like graphs of inverse variations, the graph of any rational function that has the form $y = \frac{a}{x - b} + c$ is a hyperbola.

Organizer

Use with Lesson 12-1

Pacing:

Traditional $\frac{1}{2}$ day

Block $\frac{1}{4}$ day

Objective: Use square tiles or grid paper to model the area of a rectangle as an inverse variation.

Materials: Square tiles or grid paper

Resources

Algebra Lab Activities

12-1 Lab Recording Sheet

Teach

Discuss

The area of a rectangle will never equal zero because each dimension must be greater than zero. Caution students against extending the graphs all the way to either axis.

Close

Key Concept

In an inverse-variation relationship, one value increases as the other decreases.

Assessment

Journal Have students list the characteristics they discovered about inverse-variation relationships.

Model Inverse Variation

Use with Lesson 12-1

The relationship between the width and the length of a rectangle with a constant area is an inverse variation. In this activity, you will study this relationship by modeling rectangles with square tiles or grid paper.

Activity

Use 12 square tiles to form a rectangle with an area of 12 square units, or draw the rectangle on grid paper. Use a width of 1 unit and a length of 12 units.

Your rectangle should look like the one shown.

Using the same 12 square tiles, continue forming rectangles by changing the width and length until you have formed all the different rectangles you can that have an area of 12 square units. Copy and complete the table as you form each rectangle.

Width (x)	Length (y)	Area (xy)
1	12	12
2	6	12
3	4	12
4	3	12
6	2	12
12	1	12

Plot the ordered pairs from the table on a graph. Draw a smooth curve through the points.

Try This

1. Look at the table and graph above. What happens to the length as the width increases? Why? **Length decreases as width increases because the product of the length and width must always be 12.**
2. This type of relationship is called an *inverse variation.* Why do you think it is called that? **The value of one variable increases as the other decreases, so the variables move in opposite (inverse) directions.**
3. For each point, what does xy equal? Complete the equation $xy = \blacksquare$. Solve this equation for y. **At each point, xy equals 12; $xy = 12$; $y = \frac{12}{x}$.**
4. Form all the different rectangles that have an area of 24 square units. Record their widths and lengths in a table. Graph your results. Write an equation relating the width x and length y. $xy = 24$ **or** $y = \frac{24}{x}$
5. **Make a Conjecture** Using the equations you wrote in 3 and 4, what do you think the equation of any inverse variation might look like when solved for y? $y = \frac{k}{x}$

Answers to *Activity*

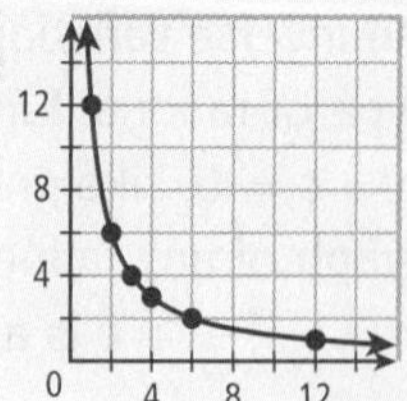

Answers to *Try This*

4.

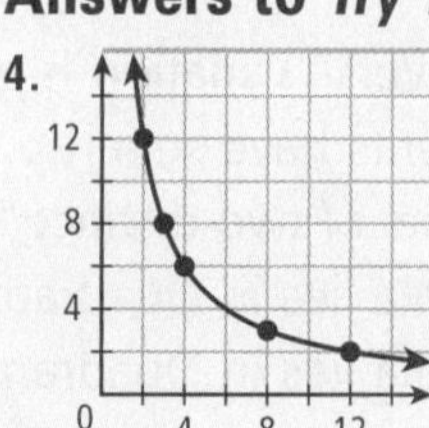

12-1 Inverse Variation

Objective
Identify, write, and graph inverse variations.

Vocabulary
inverse variation

Remember!
A direct variation is an equation that can be written in the form $y = kx$, where k is a nonzero constant.

Why learn this?
Inverse variation can be used to find the frequency at which a guitar string vibrates. (See Example 3.)

A relationship that can be written in the form $y = \frac{k}{x}$, where k is a nonzero constant and $x \neq 0$, is an **inverse variation**. The constant k is the constant of variation.

Multiplying both sides of $y = \frac{k}{x}$ by x gives $xy = k$. So, for any inverse variation, the product of x and y is a nonzero constant.

Inverse Variations

WORDS	NUMBERS	ALGEBRA
y varies inversely as x.	$y = \frac{3}{x}$	$y = \frac{k}{x}$
y is inversely proportional to x.	$xy = 3$	$xy = k (k \neq 0)$

There are two methods to determine whether a relationship between data is an inverse variation. You can write a function rule in $y = \frac{k}{x}$ form, or you can check whether xy is constant for each ordered pair.

EXAMPLE 1 **Identifying an Inverse Variation**

Tell whether each relationship is an inverse variation. Explain.

A

x	y
1	20
2	10
4	5

Method 1 Write a function rule.

$y = \frac{20}{x}$ *Can write in $y = \frac{k}{x}$ form.*

The relationship is an inverse variation.

Method 2 Find xy for each ordered pair.

$1(20) = 20, 2(10) = 20, 4(5) = 20$

The product xy is constant, so the relationship is an inverse variation.

B

x	y
2	6
3	9
6	18

Method 1 Write a function rule.

$y = 3x$ *Cannot write in $y = \frac{k}{x}$ form.*

The relationship is not an inverse variation.

Method 2 Find xy for each ordered pair.

$2(6) = 12, 3(9) = 27, 6(18) = 108$

The product xy is not constant, so the relationship is not an inverse variation.

12-1 Organizer

Pacing: Traditional 1 day
Block $\frac{1}{2}$ day

Objective: Identify, write, and graph inverse variations.

Online Edition
Tutorial Videos, Interactivity

Power Presentations with PowerPoint®

Warm Up

Solve each proportion.

1. $\frac{2}{5} = \frac{4}{y}$ 10
2. $\frac{14}{9} = \frac{x}{2.7}$ 4.2
3. $\frac{3}{8} = \frac{x}{7}$ 2.625
4. $\frac{2y}{15} = \frac{1}{3}$ 2.5
5. The value of y varies directly with x, and $y = -6$ when $x = 3$. Find y when $x = -4$. 8
6. The value of y varies directly with x, and $y = 6$ when $x = 30$. Find y when $x = 45$. 9

Also available on transparency

Math Humor

Student: My love life is like inverse variation!

Friend: What do you mean?

Student: The more I'm interested in someone, the less they're interested in me!

1 Introduce

EXPLORATION

12-1 Inverse Variation

Jennifer's piano teacher tells her that she must practice for 12 hours in order to prepare for an upcoming recital.

1. Jennifer wants to practice for the same number of hours on each day that she practices. For example, if she practices on 6 days, she would have to practice 2 hours each day. Jennifer makes a table to consider her options. Complete the table.

Days	1	2			6	12
Hours per day		6	4	3		
Total Hours of Practice		12				

2. Make a graph of the number of hours per day as a function of the number of days.
3. Write an equation describing this relationship. Let x represent the number of days, and let y represent the number of hours per day.

Hours per day: 0, 2, 4, 6, 8, 10, 12
Number of Days: 0, 2, 4, 6, 8, 10, 12

THINK AND DISCUSS

4. **Explain** what happens to the number of hours per day as the number of days increases.

Motivate

Display three cylinders with the same height but increasing diameter. Tell students that the first cylinder is full of water. Have volunteers mark where they think the water height on the other cylinders will be if the water from the first cylinder is poured into them. Tell students that the amount of water remains constant, and as the diameter of the cylinders increase, the height of the water decreases.

Explorations and answers are provided in *Alternate Openers: Explorations Transparencies.*

State Resources

State Resources Online
KEYWORD: MA7 Resources

Power Presentations with PowerPoint®

Additional Examples

Example 1

Tell whether each relationship is an inverse variation. Explain.

A.

x	y
1	30
2	15
3	10

Yes; the product *xy* is constant.

B.

x	y
1	5
2	10
4	20

No; the product *xy* is not constant.

C. $2xy = 28$ Yes; the equation can be written in the form $y = \frac{k}{x}$.

Example 2

Write and graph the inverse variation in which $y = 0.5$ when $x = -12$. $y = \frac{-6}{x}$

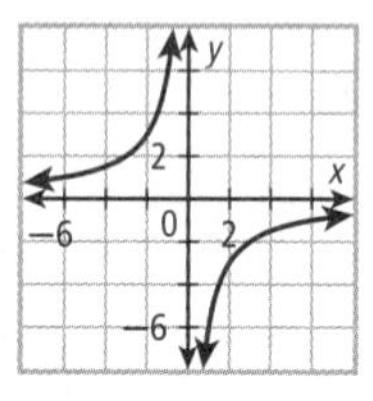

INTERVENTION

Questioning Strategies

EXAMPLE 1

- In an inverse variation, what does the product *xy* represent?

EXAMPLE 2

- How do you determine *k*?
- How do you use *k* to determine the rule for the inverse variation?
- Should you use zero as a value for *x*?

1a. No; the product *xy* is not constant.

1b. Yes; the product *xy* is constant.

1c. No; the equation cannot be written in the form $y = \frac{k}{x}$.

Tell whether each relationship is an inverse variation. Explain.

C $5xy = -21$

$\frac{5xy}{5} = \frac{-21}{5}$ *Find xy. Since xy is multiplied by 5, divide both sides by 5 to undo the multiplication.*

$xy = \frac{-21}{5}$ *Simplify.*

xy equals the constant $\frac{-21}{5}$, so the relationship is an inverse variation.

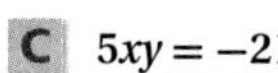

Tell whether each relationship is an inverse variation. Explain.

1a.

x	y
−12	24
1	−2
8	−16

1b.

x	y
3	3
9	1
18	0.5

1c. $2x + y = 10$

Helpful Hint

Since *k* is a nonzero constant, $xy \neq 0$. Therefore, neither *x* nor *y* can equal 0, and no solution points will be on the *x*- or *y*-axes.

An inverse variation can also be identified by its graph. Some inverse variation graphs are shown. Notice that each graph has two parts that are not connected.

Also notice that none of the graphs contain (0, 0). This is because (0, 0) can never be a solution of an inverse variation equation.

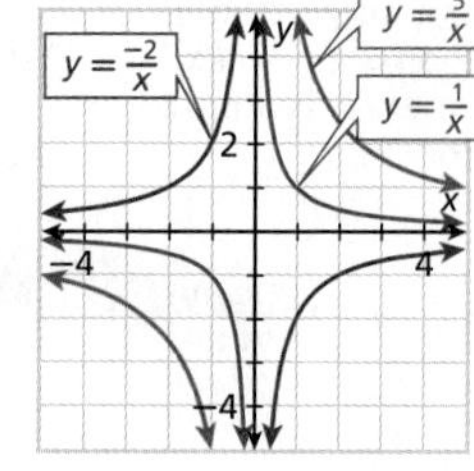

EXAMPLE 2 **Graphing an Inverse Variation**

Write and graph the inverse variation in which $y = 2$ when $x = 4$.

Step 1 Find *k*.

$k = xy$ *Write the rule for constant of variation.*

$= 4(2)$ *Substitute 4 for x and 2 for y.*

$= 8$

Step 2 Use the value of *k* to write an inverse variation equation.

$y = \frac{k}{x}$ *Write the rule for inverse variation.*

$y = \frac{8}{x}$ *Substitute 8 for k.*

Step 3 Use the equation to make a table of values.

x	−4	−2	−1	0	1	2	4
y	−2	−4	−8	undef.	8	4	2

Step 4 Plot the points and connect them with smooth curves.

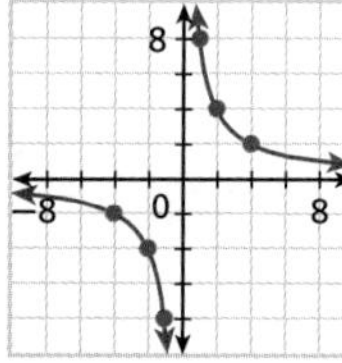

2.

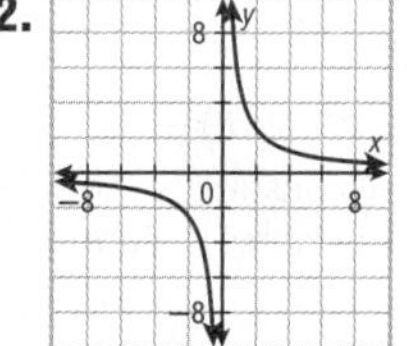

2. Write and graph the inverse variation in which $y = \frac{1}{2}$ when $x = 10$. $y = \frac{5}{x}$

2 Teach

Guided Instruction

Remind students that a direct variation is in the form $y = kx$ and means that as one variable increases, so does the other. Then show students that $y = \frac{k}{x}$ is the form of an inverse variation, which means that as one variable increases, the other decreases. When graphing inverse variations, show that the domain is all real numbers except zero and that the range is also all real numbers except zero.

Reaching All Learners

Through Multiple Representations

Show students that the Product Rule for Inverse Variation can be seen from ordered pairs in a table. Display the following table and have students write a new table for values when $k = 12$.

$y = \frac{k}{x}$	
x_1	y_1
x_2	y_2

$y = \frac{12}{x}$	
2	6
4	3

Point out that the product of each row is 12, so the product of each *xy* pair is *k*.

EXAMPLE 3 Music Application

The inverse variation $xy = 2400$ relates the vibration frequency y in hertz (Hz) to the length x in centimeters of a guitar string. Determine a reasonable domain and range and then graph this inverse variation. Use the graph to estimate the frequency of vibration when the string length is 100 centimeters.

Step 1 Solve the function for y so you can graph it.

$xy = 2400$

$y = \frac{2400}{x}$ *Divide both sides by x.*

Step 2 Decide on a reasonable domain and range.

$x > 0$ *Length is never negative and $x \neq 0$.*

$y > 0$ *Because x and xy are both positive, y is also positive.*

Step 3 Use values of the domain to generate reasonable ordered pairs.

x	20	40	60	120
y	120	60	40	20

Step 4 Plot the points. Connect them with a smooth curve.

Step 5 Find the y-value where $x = 100$. When the string length is 100 cm, the frequency of vibration is about 24 Hz.

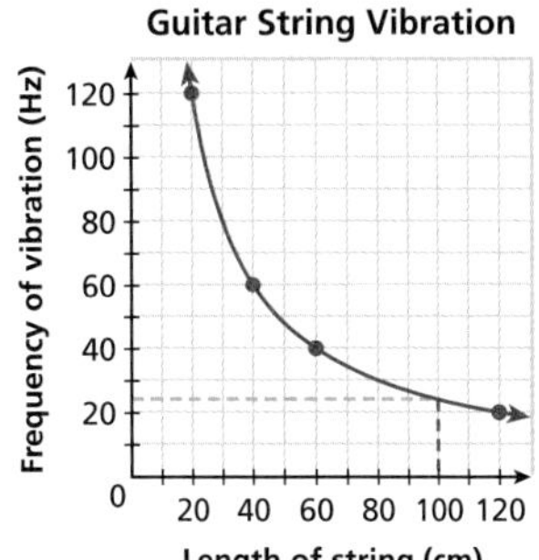

Remember!

Recall that sometimes domain and range are restricted in real-world situations.

3.

3. The inverse variation $xy = 100$ represents the relationship between the pressure x in atmospheres (atm) and the volume y in mm^3 of a certain gas. Determine a reasonable domain and range and then graph this inverse variation. Use the graph to estimate the volume of the gas when the pressure is 40 atmospheric units.

D: $x > 0$; R: $y > 0$; 2.5 mm^3

The fact that $xy = k$ is the same for every ordered pair in any inverse variation can help you find missing values in the relationship.

Product Rule for Inverse Variation

If (x_1, y_1) and (x_2, y_2) are solutions of an inverse variation, then $x_1y_1 = x_2y_2$.

EXAMPLE 4 Using the Product Rule

Let $x_1 = 3$, $y_1 = 2$, and $y_2 = 6$. Let y vary inversely as x. Find x_2.

$x_1y_1 = x_2y_2$ *Write the Product Rule for Inverse Variation.*

$(3)(2) = x_2(6)$ *Substitute 3 for x_1, 2 for y_1, and 6 for y_2.*

$6 = 6x_2$ *Simplify.*

$\frac{6}{6} = \frac{6x_2}{6}$ *Solve for x_2 by dividing both sides by 6.*

$1 = x_2$ *Simplify.*

Reading Math Remind students that *reciprocal* is another word for multiplicative inverse. Thus, for inverse variation, y equals k times the reciprocal of x.

ENGLISH LANGUAGE LEARNERS

COMMON ERROR ALERT

Because the form of an inverse variation contains a fraction, students might divide x by y, or y by x, to find k. Encourage students to start each problem by writing one of the given formulas.

Power Presentations with PowerPoint®

Additional Examples

Example 3

The inverse variation $xy = 350$ relates the constant speed x in mi/h to the time y in hours that it takes to travel 350 miles. Determine a reasonable domain and range and then graph this inverse variation. Use the graph to estimate how long it will take to travel 350 miles driving 55 mi/h. $x > 0$, $y > 0$; 6 h

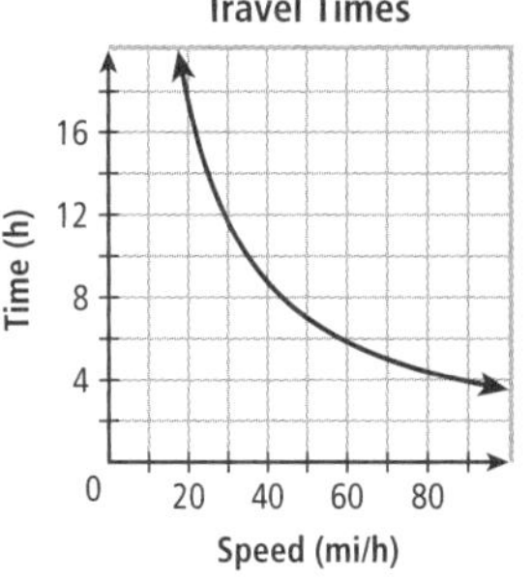

Example 4

Let $x_1 = 5$, $x_2 = 3$, and $y_2 = 10$. Let y vary inversely as x. Find y_1. 6

INTERVENTION

Questioning Strategies

EXAMPLE 3

- How can you use the equation to check your estimate?
- Why is this graph only in Quadrant I?

EXAMPLE 4

- How does the Product Rule for Inverse Variation relate to the methods used to determine whether a relationship between data is an inverse variation?

Teaching Tip **Science Link** The abbreviation psi stands for *pounds per square inch*.

Power Presentations with PowerPoint®

Additional Examples

Example 5

Boyle's law states that the pressure of a quantity of gas x varies inversely as the volume of the gas y. The volume of a gas inside a container is 400 in^3 and the pressure is 25 psi. What is the pressure when the volume is compressed to 125 in^3? 80 psi

INTERVENTION

Questioning Strategies

EXAMPLE 5

- How do you determine x_1y_1 and x_2y_2?
- How can you tell whether your answer is reasonable?

4. Let $x_1 = 2$, $y_1 = -6$, and $x_2 = -4$. Let y vary inversely as x. Find y_2. **3**

EXAMPLE 5 Physics Application

Reading Math

In Example 5, x_1 and y_1 represent volume and pressure **before** the handle is pushed in, and x_2 and y_2 represent volume and pressure **after** the handle is pushed in.

Boyle's law states that the pressure of a quantity of gas x varies inversely as the volume of the gas y. The volume of air inside a bicycle pump is 5.2 in^3, and the pressure is 15.5 psi. Assuming no air escapes, what is the pressure of the air inside the pump after the handle is pushed in, and the air is compressed to a volume of 2.6 in^3?

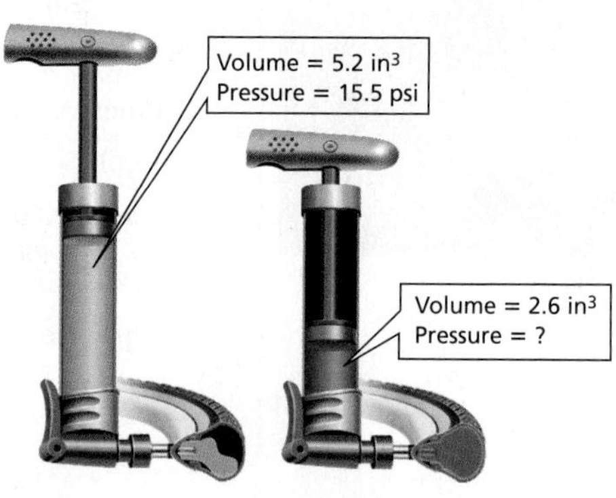

$x_1y_1 = x_2y_2$ *Use the Product Rule for Inverse Variation.*

$(5.2)(15.5) = (2.6)y_2$ *Substitute 5.2 for x_1, 15.5 for y_1, and 2.6 for x_2.*

$80.6 = 2.6y_2$ *Simplify.*

$\frac{80.6}{2.6} = \frac{2.6y_2}{2.6}$ *Solve for y_2 by dividing both sides by 2.6.*

$31 = y_2$ *Simplify.*

The pressure after the handle is pushed in is 31 psi.

5. On a balanced lever, weight varies inversely as the distance from the fulcrum to the weight. The diagram shows a balanced lever. How much does the child weigh? **80.625 lb**

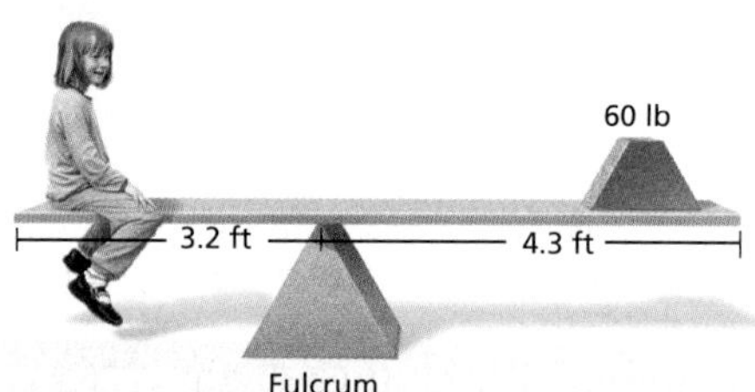

THINK AND DISCUSS

Know it! Note

1. Name two ways you can identify an inverse variation.

2. **GET ORGANIZED** Copy and complete the graphic organizer. In each box, write an example of the parts of the given inverse variation.

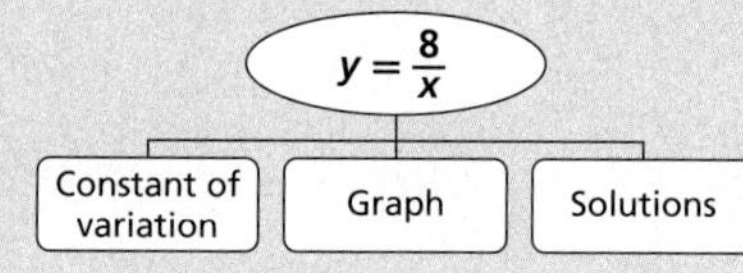

3 Close

Summarize

Remind students that in an inverse variation, $xy = k$ is the same for every ordered pair. Because k is constant, x and y must vary such that if one increases, the other decreases. An inverse variation can also be written in the form $y = \frac{k}{x}$. The variation can be graphed by generating ordered pairs. Have students describe the characteristics of inverse-variation graphs.

ONGOING ASSESSMENT and INTERVENTION

***Diagnose Before* the Lesson**
12-1 Warm Up, TE p. 871

***Monitor During* the Lesson**
Check It Out! Exercises, SE pp. 872–874
Questioning Strategies, TE pp. 872–874

***Assess After* the Lesson**
12-1 Lesson Quiz, TE p. 877
Alternative Assessment, TE p. 877

Answers to *Think and Discuss*

Possible answers:

1. Check that the function rule has the form $y = \frac{k}{x}$, or check that xy is the same nonzero constant for each ordered pair.
2. See p. A11.

go.hrw.com
Homework Help Online
KEYWORD: MA7 12-1
Parent Resources Online
KEYWORD: MA7 Parent

GUIDED PRACTICE

1. **Vocabulary** Describe the graph of an *inverse variation.*
The graph of an inverse variation consists of 2 disconnected branches.

SEE EXAMPLE 1 p. 871

Tell whether each relationship is an inverse variation. Explain.

2.

x	y
1	8
4	2
2	4

Yes; the product *xy* is constant.

3.

x	y
$\frac{1}{6}$	1
$\frac{1}{3}$	2
2	12

No; the product *xy* is not constant.

4. $x + y = 8$ No; the equation cannot be written in the form $y = \frac{k}{x}$.

5. $4xy = 3$ Yes; *xy* equals the constant $\frac{3}{4}$.

SEE EXAMPLE 2 p. 872

6. Write and graph the inverse variation in which $y = 2$ when $x = 2$. $y = \frac{4}{x}$

7. Write and graph the inverse variation in which $y = 6$ when $x = -1$. $y = \frac{-6}{x}$

SEE EXAMPLE 3 p. 873

8. **Travel** The inverse variation $xy = 30$ relates the constant speed x in mi/h to the time y in hours that it takes to travel 30 miles. Determine a reasonable domain and range and then graph this inverse variation. Use the graph to estimate how many hours it would take traveling 4 mi/h.

SEE EXAMPLE 4 p. 873

9. Let $x_1 = 3$, $y_1 = 12$, and $x_2 = 9$. Let y vary inversely as x. Find y_2. 4

10. Let $x_1 = 1$, $y_1 = 4$, and $y_2 = 16$. Let y vary inversely as x. Find x_2. $\frac{1}{4}$

SEE EXAMPLE 5 p. 874

11. **Mechanics** The rotational speed of a gear varies inversely as the number of teeth on the gear. A gear with 12 teeth has a rotational speed of 60 rpm. How many teeth are on a gear that has a rotational speed of 45 rpm? 16 teeth

PRACTICE AND PROBLEM SOLVING

Independent Practice

For Exercises	See Example
12–15	1
16–17	2
18	3
19–20	4
21	5

Extra Practice
Skills Practice p. S26
Application Practice p. S39

Tell whether each relationship is an inverse variation. Explain.

12.

x	y
3	−3
−5	5
7	−7

No; the product *xy* is not constant.

13.

x	y
2	5
0.5	20
8	1.25

Yes; the product *xy* is constant.

14. $x = \frac{13}{y}$ yes; can be written in the form $y = \frac{k}{x}$

15. $y = 5x$ no; cannot be written in the form $y = \frac{k}{x}$

16. Write and graph the inverse variation in which $y = -2$ when $x = 5$.

17. Write and graph the inverse variation in which $y = -6$ when $x = -\frac{1}{3}$.

18. **Engineering** The inverse variation $xy = 12$ relates the current x in amps to the resistance y in ohms of a circuit attached to a 12-volt battery. Determine a reasonable domain and range and then graph this inverse variation. Use the graph to estimate the resistance of a circuit when the current is 5 amps.

19. Let $x_1 = -3$, $y_1 = -4$, and $y_2 = 6$. Let y vary inversely as x. Find x_2. 2

20. Let $x_1 = 7$, $y_1 = 9$, and $x_2 = 6$. Let y vary inversely as x. Find y_2. 10.5

16. $y = \frac{-10}{x}$

17. $y = \frac{2}{x}$

8. D: $x > 0$; R: $y > 0$;

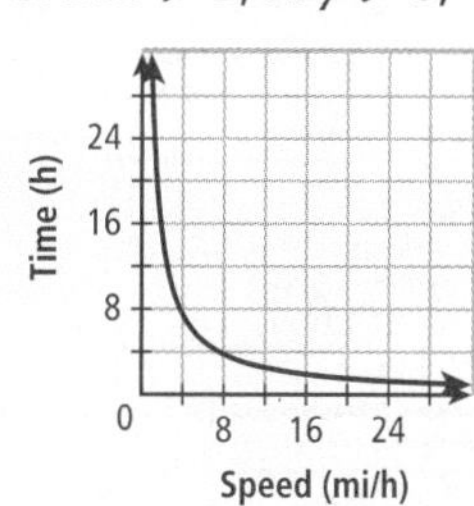

7.5 hr

16.

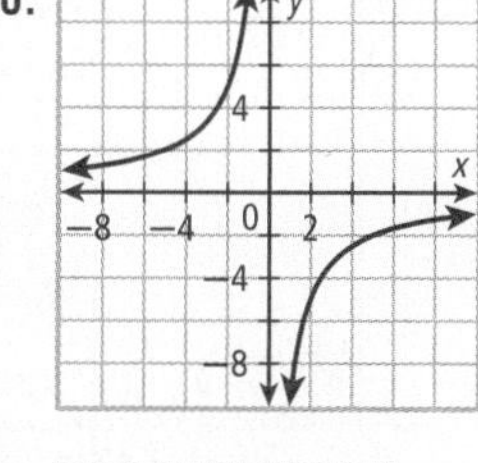

17.

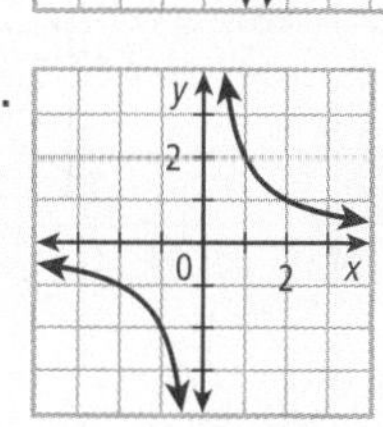

18. D: $x > 0$; R: $y > 0$;

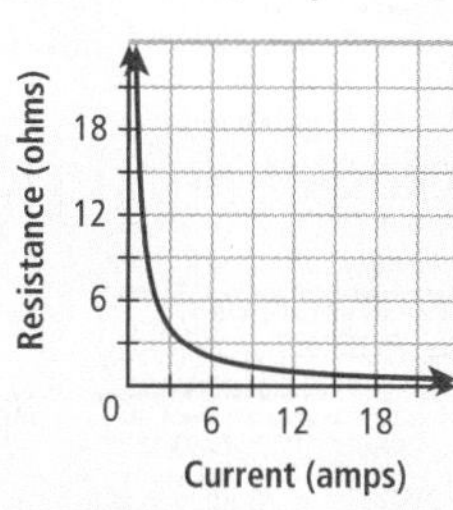

2.4 ohms

Assignment Guide

Assign *Guided Practice* exercises as necessary.

If you finished Examples **1–3**
Basic 12–18, 22–27
Average 12–18, 22–27, 35
Advanced 12–18, 22–27, 35

If you finished Examples **1–5**
Basic 12–34, 39–44, 48–53
Average 12–31, 38–46, 48–53
Advanced 12–22, 31–53

Homework Quick Check
Quickly check key concepts.
Exercises: 12, 14, 16, 18, 20, 22

Answers

6.

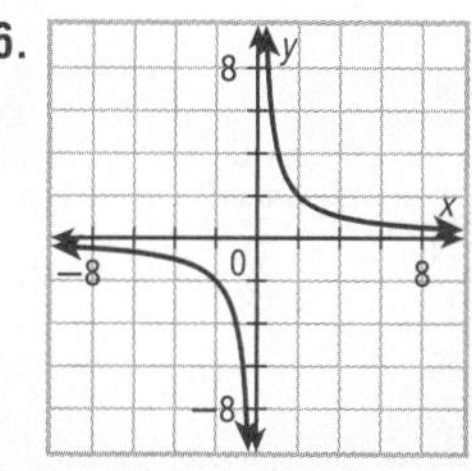

7.

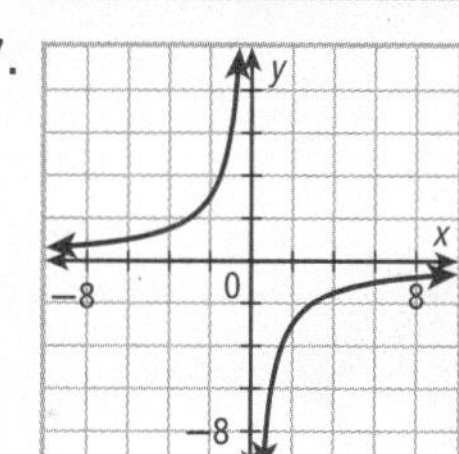

State Resources

go.hrw.com
State Resources Online
KEYWORD: MA7 Resources

Exercise 40 involves writing an inverse-variation function. This exercise prepares students for the Multi-Step Test Prep on page 896.

Answers

35. $y = \frac{2000}{x}$; D: natural numbers; R: $y > 0$

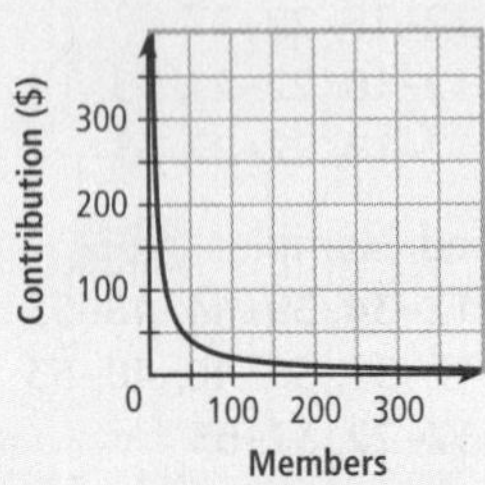

38. Substitute the known values of x and y into $y = \frac{k}{x}$ and solve for k. Use this value of k in the equation $y = \frac{k}{x}$.

40c.

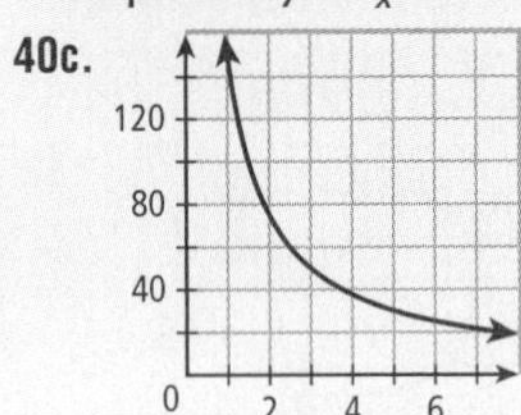

LINK Winter Sports

Snowshoes were originally made of wooden frames strung with animal intestines. Modern snowshoes are made with steel frames and may have cleats for gripping the snow.

21. **Home Economics** The length of fabric that June can afford varies inversely as the price per yard of the fabric. June can afford exactly 5 yards of fabric that costs $10.50 per yard. How many yards of fabric that costs $4.25 per yard can June buy? (Assume that she can only buy whole yards.) **12 yd**

22. **Winter Sports** When a person is snowshoeing, the pressure on the top of the snow in psi varies inversely as the area of the bottom of the snowshoe in square inches. The constant of variation is the weight of the person wearing the snowshoes in pounds.
    a. Helen weighs 120 pounds. About how much pressure does she put on top of the snow if she wears snowshoes that cover 360 in^2? **$\frac{1}{3}$ psi**
    b. Max weighs 207 pounds. If he exerts 0.4 psi of pressure on top of the snow, what is the area of the bottom of his snowshoes in square inches? **517.5 in^2**

Determine if each equation represents a direct variation, an inverse variation, or neither. Find the constant of variation when one exists.

23. $y = 8x$ **direct; 8**
24. $y = \frac{14}{x}$ **inverse; 14**
25. $y = \frac{1}{3}x - 2$ **neither**
26. $y = \frac{1}{5}x$ **direct; $\frac{1}{5}$**
27. $y = 4\frac{3}{x}$ **inverse; 12**
28. $y = \frac{x}{2} + 7$ **neither**
29. $y = \frac{15}{x}$ **inverse; 15**
30. $y = 5x$ **direct; 5**
31. **Multi-Step** A track team is competing in a 10 km race. The distance will be evenly divided among the team members. Write an equation that represents the distance d each runner will run if there are n runners. Does this represent a direct variation, inverse variation, or neither? **$d = \frac{10}{n}$; inverse**

Determine whether each data set represents a direct variation, an inverse variation, or neither.

32.

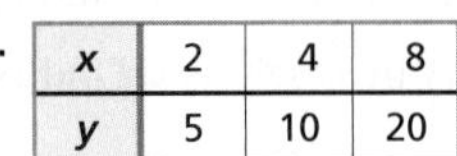

x	2	4	8
y	5	10	20

direct

33.

x	6	12	15
y	6	8	9

neither

34.

x	1	2	3
y	12	6	4

inverse

35. **Multi-Step** Your club awards one student a $2000 scholarship each year, and each member contributes an equal amount. Your contribution y depends on the number of members x. Write and graph an inverse variation equation that represents this situation. What are a reasonable domain and range?

36. **Estimation** Estimate the value of y if y is inversely proportional to x, $x = 4$, and the constant of variation is 6π. **4.5**

37. **Critical Thinking** Why will the point $(0, 0)$ never be a solution to an inverse variation? **An inverse variation function, $y = \frac{k}{x}$, is not defined at $x = 0$.**

38. **Write About It** Explain how to write an inverse variation equation of the form $y = \frac{k}{x}$ when values of x and y are known.

39. **Write About It** List all the mathematical terms you know that contain the word *inverse*. How are these terms all similar? How is *inverse variation* similar to these terms?

39. Inverse function, inverse operations, additive inverse, etc.; all of the terms involve moving in opposite directions; inverse variation describes a relationship in which the magnitudes of the variables move in opposite directions (one increases while the other decreases).

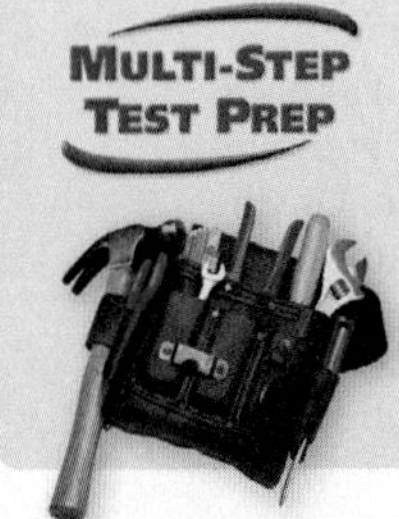

MULTI-STEP TEST PREP

40. This problem will prepare you for the Multi-Step Test Prep on page 896. The total number of workdays it takes to build the frame of a house varies inversely as the number of people working in a crew. Let x be the number of people in the crew and let y be the number of workdays.
    a. Find the constant of variation when $y = 75$ and $x = 2$. **$k = 150$**
    b. Write the rule for the inverse of variation equation. **$y = \frac{150}{x}$**
    c. Graph the equation of this inverse variation.

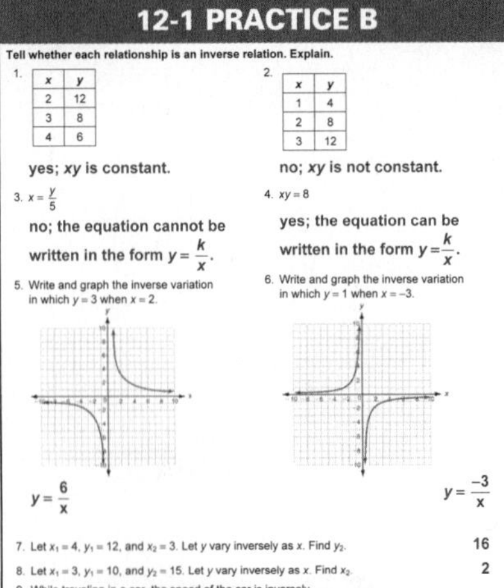

12-1 PRACTICE A
12-1 PRACTICE C
12-1 PRACTICE B

Tell whether each relationship is an inverse relation. Explain.

1.

x	y
2	12
3	8
4	6

yes; xy is constant.

2.

x	y
1	4
2	8
3	12

no; xy is not constant.

3. $x = \frac{y}{5}$ no; the equation cannot be written in the form $y = \frac{k}{x}$.

4. $xy = 8$ yes; the equation can be written in the form $y = \frac{k}{x}$.

5. Write and graph the inverse variation in which $y = 3$ when $x = 2$. $y = \frac{6}{x}$

6. Write and graph the inverse variation in which $y = 1$ when $x = -3$. $y = \frac{-3}{x}$

7. Let $x_1 = 4$, $y_1 = 12$, and $x_2 = 3$. Let y vary inversely as x. Find y_2. 16

8. Let $x_1 = 3$, $y_1 = 10$, and $y_2 = 15$. Let y vary inversely as x. Find x_2. 2

9. While traveling in a car, the speed of the car is inversely proportional to the time it takes to travel a certain distance. At 25 mi/h, it takes 15 minutes to travel to work. How many minutes would it take traveling 30 mi/h? 12.5 minutes

10. The amount of pizza that Kirby can buy varies inversely as the price of the pizza increases. Kirby can afford to buy 3 pizzas that cost $15.00 each. How many pizzas that cost $9.00 each can Kirby buy? 5 pizzas

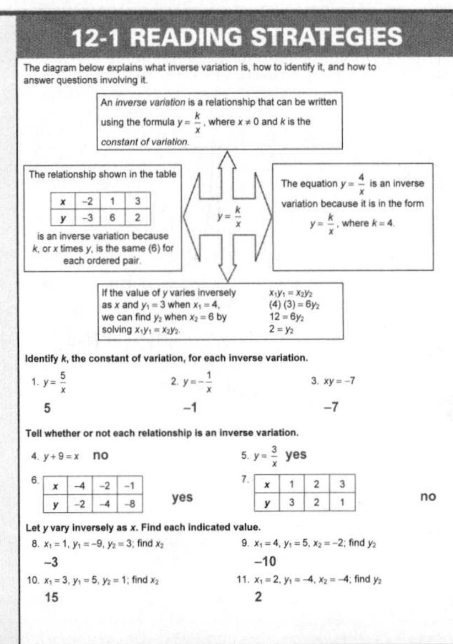

12-1 READING STRATEGIES

The diagram below explains what inverse variation is, how to identify it, and how to answer questions involving it.

An *inverse variation* is a relationship that can be written using the formula $y = \frac{k}{x}$, where $x \neq 0$ and k is the *constant of variation*.

The relationship shown in the table

x	-2	1	3
y	-3	6	2

is an inverse variation because k, or x times y, is the same (6) for each ordered pair.

$y = \frac{k}{x}$

The equation $y = \frac{4}{x}$ is an inverse variation because it is in the form $y = \frac{k}{x}$, where $k = 4$.

If the value of y varies inversely as x and $y_1 = 3$ when $x_1 = 4$, we can find y_2 when $x_2 = 6$ by solving $x_1y_1 = x_2y_2$.
$x_1y_1 = x_2y_2$
$(4)(3) = 6y_2$
$12 = 6y_2$
$2 = y_2$

Identify k, the constant of variation, for each inverse variation.

1. $y = \frac{5}{x}$ 5
2. $y = -\frac{1}{x}$ −1
3. $xy = -7$ −7

Tell whether or not each relationship is an inverse variation.

4. $y + 9 = x$ no
5. $y = \frac{3}{x}$ yes

6.

x	-4	-2	-1
y	-2	-4	-8

yes

7.

x	1	2	3
y	3	2	1

no

Let y vary inversely as x. Find each indicated value.

8. $x_1 = 1$, $y_1 = -9$, $y_2 = 3$; find x_2 −3
9. $x_1 = 4$, $y_1 = 5$, $x_2 = -2$; find y_2 −10
10. $x_1 = 3$, $y_1 = 5$, $y_2 = 1$; find x_2 15
11. $x_1 = 2$, $y_1 = -4$, $x_2 = -4$; find y_2 2

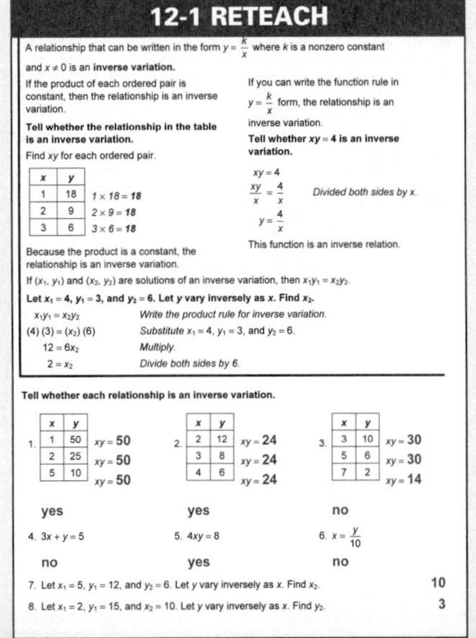

12-1 RETEACH

A relationship that can be written in the form $y = \frac{k}{x}$ where k is a nonzero constant and $x \neq 0$ is an **inverse variation.**

If the product of each ordered pair is constant, then the relationship is an inverse variation.

If you can write the function rule in $y = \frac{k}{x}$ form, the relationship is an inverse variation.

Tell whether the relationship in the table is an inverse variation.
Find xy for each ordered pair.

x	y	
1	18	$1 \times 18 = 18$
2	9	$2 \times 9 = 18$
3	6	$3 \times 6 = 18$

Because the product is a constant, the relationship is an inverse variation.

Tell whether $xy = 4$ is an inverse variation.
$xy = 4$
$\frac{xy}{x} = \frac{4}{x}$ Divided both sides by x.
$y = \frac{4}{x}$
This function is an inverse relation.

If (x_1, y_1) and (x_2, y_2) are solutions of an inverse variation, then $x_1y_1 = x_2y_2$.

Let $x_1 = 4$, $y_1 = 3$, and $y_2 = 6$. Let y vary inversely as x. Find x_2.
$x_1y_1 = x_2y_2$ *Write the product rule for inverse variation.*
$(4)(3) = (x_2)(6)$ *Substitute $x_1 = 4$, $y_1 = 3$, and $y_2 = 6$.*
$12 = 6x_2$ *Multiply.*
$2 = x_2$ *Divide both sides by 6.*

Tell whether each relationship is an inverse variation.

1.

x	y	
1	50	$xy = 50$
2	25	$xy = 50$
5	10	$xy = 50$

yes

2.

x	y	
2	12	$xy = 24$
3	8	$xy = 24$
4	6	$xy = 24$

yes

3.

x	y	
3	10	$xy = 30$
5	6	$xy = 30$
7	2	$xy = 14$

no

4. $3x + y = 5$ no
5. $4xy = 8$ yes
6. $x = \frac{y}{10}$ no

7. Let $x_1 = 5$, $y_1 = 12$, and $y_2 = 6$. Let y vary inversely as x. Find x_2. 10
8. Let $x_1 = 2$, $y_1 = 15$, and $x_2 = 10$. Let y vary inversely as x. Find y_2. 3

TEST PREP

41. Which equation best represents the graph?

Ⓐ $y = -\frac{1}{4}x$ **Ⓒ** $y = -\frac{4}{x}$

Ⓑ $y = \frac{1}{4}x$ Ⓓ $y = \frac{4}{x}$

42. Determine the constant of variation if y varies inversely as x and $y = 2$ when $x = 7$.

Ⓕ $\frac{2}{7}$ Ⓖ $\frac{7}{2}$ Ⓗ 3.5   **Ⓙ** 14

43. Which of the following relationships does NOT represent an inverse variation?

Ⓐ

x	2	4	5
y	10	5	4

Ⓒ

x	2	4	5
y	8	16	20

Ⓑ $y = \frac{17.5}{x}$ Ⓓ $\frac{11}{2} = xy$

44. Gridded Response At a carnival, the number of tickets Brad can buy is inversely proportional to the price of the tickets. He can afford 12 tickets that cost \$2.50 each. How many tickets can Brad buy if each costs \$3.00? **10**

CHALLENGE AND EXTEND

45. The definition of inverse variation says that k is a nonzero constant. What function would $y = \frac{k}{x}$ represent if $k = 0$? **the constant function $y = 0$**

46. Mechanics A part of a car's braking system uses a lever to multiply the force applied to the brake pedal. The force at the end of a lever varies inversely with the distance from the fulcrum. Point P is the end of the lever. A force of 2 lb is applied to the brake pedal. What is the force created at the point P? **12 lb**

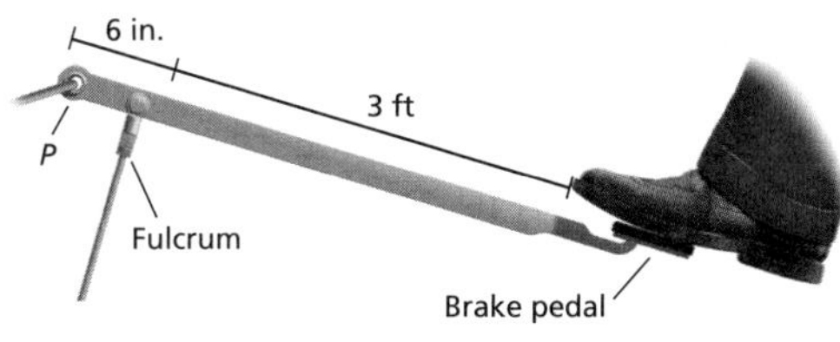

47. Communication The strength of a radio signal varies inversely with the square of the distance from the transmitter. A signal has a strength of 2000 watts when it is 4 kilometers from the transmitter. What is the strength of the signal 6 kilometers from the transmitter? **approx. 888.9 watts**

SPIRAL REVIEW

Find the domain and range for each relation. Tell whether the relation is a function. *(Lesson 4-2)*

48. $\{(-2, -4), (-2, -2), (-2, 0), (-2, 2)\}$ **D: {−2}; R: {−4, −2, 0, 2}; no**

49. $\{(-4, 5), (-2, 3), (0, 1), (2, 3), (4, 5)\}$ **D: {−4, −2, 0, 2, 4}; R: {1, 3, 5}; yes**

Solve by completing the square. *(Lesson 9-8)*

50. $x^2 + 12x = 45$ **3, −15**

51. $d^2 - 6d - 7 = 0$ **−1, 7**

52. $2y^2 + 6y = -\frac{5}{2}$ **$-\frac{5}{2}, -\frac{1}{2}$**

53. A rectangle has a length of 6 cm and a width of 2 cm. Find the length of the diagonal and write it as a simplified radical expression. *(Lesson 11-6)* **$2\sqrt{10}$ cm**

TEST PREP DOCTOR Choices **A** and **B** in **Exercise 41** are functions whose graphs are lines because they can be written in the form $y = mx + b$.

For **Exercise 42,** remind students that $xy = k$, so the answer is found by multiplying 2 and 7.

Journal

Have students explain the difference between the graphs of $y = \frac{x}{2}$ and $y = \frac{2}{x}$.

ALTERNATIVE ASSESSMENT

Have students find x_1 when $y_1 = 4$, $x_2 = 2$, $y_2 = 8$, and y varies inversely as x. Then have students write and graph the inverse variation.

Power Presentations with PowerPoint®

12-1 Lesson Quiz

1. Write and graph the inverse variation in which $y = 0.25$ when $x = 12$. $y = \frac{3}{x}$

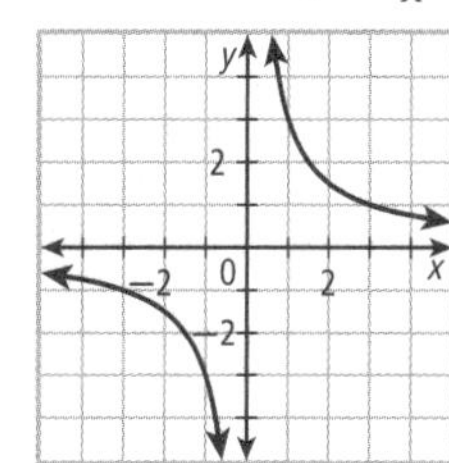

2. The inverse variation $xy = 210$ relates the length y in cm to the width x in cm of a rectangle with an area of 210 cm². Determine a reasonable domain and range and then graph this inverse variation. Use the graph to estimate the length when the width is 14 cm.
$x > 0, y > 0$; 15 cm

Rectangle Dimensions

3. Let $x_1 = 12$, $y_1 = -4$, and $y_2 = 6$, and let y vary inversely as x. Find x_2. −8

Also available on transparency

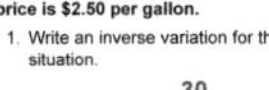

12-1 PROBLEM SOLVING

The number of gallons of gasoline that Isaac can afford y varies inversely as the price per gallon x. Isaac can afford 12 gal when the price is \$2.50 per gallon.

1. Write an inverse variation for this situation.
   $xy = 30$ or $y = \frac{30}{x}$
2. Determine a reasonable domain and range.
   $x > 0$ and $y > 0$
3. Complete this table of ordered pairs and graph the inverse variation.

x	1.50	2.50	3.00	5.00	10.00
y	20	12	10	6	3

4. Use the graph to estimate the number of gallons Isaac can afford when the price is \$3.49 per gallon.
   8.6 gal

Select the best answer.

5. The inverse variation $xy = 9$ relates the current x in amps to the resistance y in ohms of a circuit attached to a 9-volt battery. What is the resistance of the circuit when the current is 1.8 amps?
   A 0.2 ohms   C 10.8 ohms
   B 5 ohms   D 16.2 ohms
6. Boyle's law states that the pressure of a quantity of gas x varies inversely as the volume of the gas y. The volume of air inside a bicycle pump is 6.1 in³, and the pressure is 18.3 psi. Which equation represents this situation?
   F $y = 3x$ H $y = 111.63x$
   G $y = \frac{3}{x}$ **J** $y = \frac{111.63}{x}$
7. The time it takes to drive between two cities varies inversely as speed. Dolores can drive between Houston, Texas, and San Antonio, Texas, in 3.5 h at 60 mi/h. How long will the trip take if she drives 70 mi/h? (Round your answer to the nearest tenth.)
   A 2.3 h   **C** 3 h
   B 2.6 h   D 4.1 h
8. On a balanced lever, weight varies inversely as the distance from the fulcrum. Angie weighs 120 lb. When she sits $2\frac{1}{2}$ ft from the fulcrum of a seesaw, she balances with her brother, who weighs 80 lb. How far is her brother from the fulcrum of the seesaw?
   F $\frac{4}{15}$ ft   H $1\frac{2}{3}$ ft
   G $\frac{3}{5}$ ft   **J** $3\frac{3}{4}$ ft

12-1 CHALLENGE

When two children of different weights sit on a seesaw that is joined to the pivot at its midpoint, one child sits higher than the pivot point, and the other child sits lower than it. They achieve balance and reverse who is higher and who is lower by exerting a downward force on the ground.

The diagram at right shows two different weights positioned at different distances from the pivot point of a seesaw. The equation indicates that weight and distance have an inverse variation. w_1 and w_2 represent weight, and d_1 and d_2 represent distance.

$w_1 d_1 = w_2 d_2$

In Exercises 1–3, the total length of a seesaw is 12 feet, and boxes A and B are balanced.

1. Boxes A and B weigh 60 pounds and 80 pounds, respectively. How far from the pivot point is box A if box B is 4 feet from the pivot point? $5\frac{1}{3}$ feet
2. Box A weighs 100 pounds and is 5 feet from the pivot point of the seesaw. How much does box B weigh if it is 6 feet from the pivot point? $83\frac{1}{3}$ pounds
3. Boxes A and B weigh 120 pounds and 150 pounds, respectively. How far is each box from the pivot point of the seesaw? (Hint: Let x represent the distance between box A and the pivot point. Then write and solve an equation for x.) Box A: $6\frac{2}{3}$ feet, Box B: $5\frac{1}{3}$ feet

In Exercises 4 and 5, solve each seesaw problem. The length of the board used to balance boxes A and B is 20 feet.

4. Boxes A and B weigh 60 pounds and 80 pounds, respectively. John wants to put box A at the left end of the board and to position the pivot point 5 feet to the right of box A. How far from the right end of the board should he place box B? $11\frac{1}{4}$ feet
5. Boxes A and B weigh 60 pounds and 80 pounds, respectively. John wants to put box A at the left end of the board and to position the pivot point 15 feet to the right of box A. Is it possible to put box B on the seesaw so that the boxes balance? Explain your response.
   No; box B would have to be $11\frac{1}{4}$ feet from the pivot point. The board is not long enough.
6. A board is L feet long. Boxes A and B weigh 60 pounds and 80 pounds, respectively. Box A is placed x feet from the pivot point.
   a. Write and solve an equation for L in terms of x. $L = \frac{7}{4}x$
   b. Write and solve an equation for x in terms of L. $x = \frac{4}{7}L$

12-2 Organizer

Pacing: Traditional 1 day
Block $\frac{1}{2}$ day

Objectives: Identify excluded values of rational functions.

Graph rational functions.

Online Edition
Tutorial Videos

Power Presentations with PowerPoint®

Warm Up

The inverse variation $xy = 8$ relates the constant speed x in mi/h to the time y in hours that it takes to travel 8 miles. Graph this inverse variation. Then use the graph to estimate how many hours it would take to travel 8 miles jogging at a speed of 4.5 mi/h.

Possible answer: 1 h 45 min

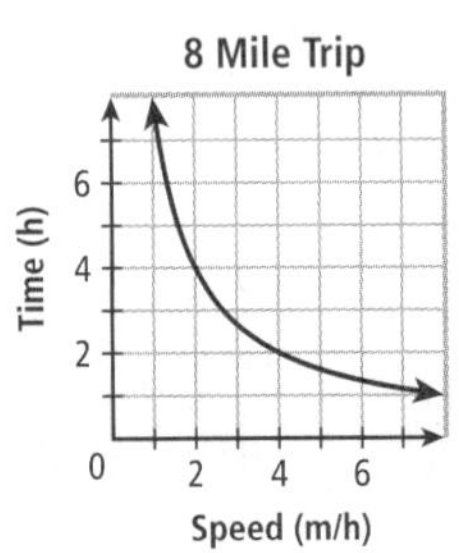

Also available on transparency

Q: What do math teachers carry their math books in?

A: Asymp-tote bags

12-2 Rational Functions

Objectives
Identify excluded values of rational functions.

Graph rational functions.

Vocabulary
rational function
excluded value
discontinuous function
asymptote

Who uses this?
Gemologists can use rational functions to maximize reflected light. (See Example 4.)

A **rational function** is a function whose rule is a quotient of polynomials. The inverse variations you studied in the previous lesson are a special type of rational function.

Rational functions: $y = \frac{2}{x}$, $y = \frac{3}{4 - 2x}$, $y = \frac{1}{x^2}$

For any function involving x and y, an **excluded value** is any x-value that makes the function value y undefined. For a rational function, an excluded value is any value that makes the denominator equal 0.

EXAMPLE 1 Identifying Excluded Values

Identify the excluded value for each rational function.

A $y = \frac{8}{x}$

$x = 0$ *Set the denominator equal to 0.*

The excluded value is 0.

B $y = \frac{3}{x + 3}$

$x + 3 = 0$ *Set the denominator equal to 0.*

$x = -3$ *Solve for x.*

The excluded value is -3.

Identify the excluded value for each rational function.

1a. $y = \frac{10}{x}$ **0** **1b.** $y = \frac{4}{x - 1}$ **1** **1c.** $y = -\frac{5}{x + 4}$ **−4**

Most rational functions are **discontinuous functions**, meaning their graphs contain one or more jumps, breaks, or holes. This occurs at an excluded value.

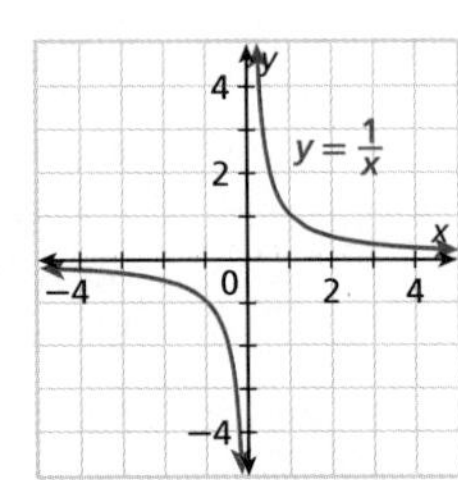

One place that a graph of a rational function is discontinuous is at an *asymptote*. An **asymptote** is a line that a graph gets closer to as the absolute value of a variable increases. In the graph shown, both the x- and y-axes are asymptotes. The graphs of rational functions will get closer and closer to but never touch the asymptotes.

State Resources

go.hrw.com
State Resources Online
KEYWORD: MA7 Resources

1 Introduce

EXPLORATION

12-2 Rational Functions

You can use a graphing calculator to explore rational functions.

Enter the function $y = \frac{1}{x}$ into your graphing calculator. Graph the function in the standard decimal window by pressing [ZOOM], selecting **6:ZStandard**, pressing [ZOOM] again, and selecting **4:ZDecimal**. Press [TRACE]. Use the left and right arrow keys to move the cursor along the graph.

1. What happens to the y-values as the x-values increase from 0?
2. What happens when $x = 0$? Why?
3. Press [2nd] [GRAPH] to view a table of values for the function. What y-value does the table show at $x = 0$?
4. Now graph $y = \frac{1}{x - 1}$. For what value of x is there no y-value?

THINK AND DISCUSS

5. **Discuss** how the graph of $y = \frac{1}{x - 1}$ is related to the graph of $y = \frac{1}{x}$.
6. **Explain** what you think would happen if you graphed $y = \frac{1}{\ }$. For what x-value would there be no y-value?

Motivate

Have students give values they would choose for x when graphing $y = \sqrt{x}$. Possible answers: 1, 4, 9

Ask why they did not choose a negative value for x. A negative in the radicand of a square root does not yield a real number.

Tell students that the functions they will be graphing in this lesson are undefined for certain values of x.

Explorations and answers are provided in *Alternate Openers: Explorations Transparencies.*

For rational functions, vertical asymptotes will occur at excluded values.

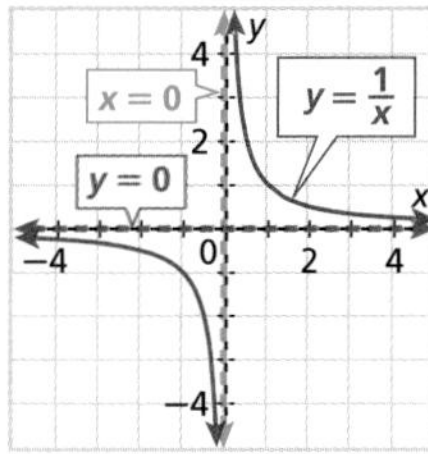

Look at the graph of $y = \frac{1}{x}$. The denominator is 0 when $x = 0$ so 0 is an excluded value. This means there is a vertical asymptote at $x = 0$. Notice the horizontal asymptote at $y = 0$.

Writing Math

Vertical lines are written in the form $x = b$, and horizontal lines are written in the form $y = c$.

Look at the graph of $y = \frac{1}{x-3} + 2$. Notice that the graph of the parent function $y = \frac{1}{x}$ has been translated **3 units right** and there is a vertical asymptote at $x = 3$. The graph has also been translated **2 units up** and there is a horizontal asymptote at $y = 2$.

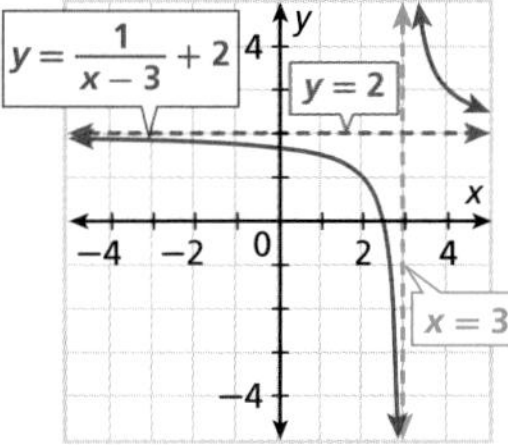

These translations lead to the following formulas for identifying asymptotes in rational functions.

Identifying Asymptotes

WORDS	EXAMPLES	
A rational function in the form $y = \frac{a}{x-b} + c$ has a vertical asymptote at the excluded value, or $x = b$, and a horizontal asymptote at $y = c$.	$y = \frac{2}{x}$ $= \frac{2}{x-0} + 0$ Vertical asymptote: $x = 0$ Horizontal asymptote: $y = 0$	$y = \frac{1}{x+2} + 4$ $= \frac{1}{x-(-2)} + 4$ Vertical asymptote: $x = -2$ Horizontal asymptote: $y = 4$

EXAMPLE 2 Identifying Asymptotes

Identify the asymptotes.

A $y = \frac{1}{x-6}$

Step 1 Write in $y = \frac{1}{x-b} + c$ form.

$$y = \frac{1}{x-6} + 0$$

Step 2 Identify the asymptotes.

vertical: $x = 6$

horizontal: $y = 0$

B $y = \frac{2}{3x-10} - 7$

Step 1 Identify the vertical asymptote.

$3x - 10 = 0$ *Find the excluded value. Set the denominator equal to 0.*

$\underline{+10 \quad +10}$ *Add 10 to both sides.*

$3x = 10$

$x = \frac{10}{3}$ *Solve for x. $\frac{10}{3}$ is an excluded value.*

COMMON ERROR ALERT

Students might use the value of $-b$, rather than b, in the vertical asymptote. Remind students that the vertical asymptote is at the excluded value, which is found by setting the denominator equal to 0 and solving.

Power Presentations with PowerPoint®

Additional Examples

Example 1

Identify the excluded value for each rational function.

A. $y = \frac{2}{x}$ 0

B. $y = \frac{6}{x-2}$ 2

Example 2

Identify the asymptotes.

A. $y = \frac{3}{x+7}$ $x = -7; y = 0$

B. $y = \frac{1}{2x-3} + 8$ $x = \frac{3}{2}; y = 8$

INTERVENTION

Questioning Strategies

EXAMPLE 1

- How do you determine the excluded value?

EXAMPLE 2

- What is the difference between the vertical and horizontal asymptotes?

Reading Math Ask students what it means if they are *included* in a group. Tell them that *excluded* is the opposite of included. Students can also think of an *excluded* value as an *exception*.

ENGLISH LANGUAGE LEARNERS

2 Teach

Guided Instruction

Introduce examples of rational functions. (Rational functions with variables in both the numerator and denominator will be studied in Algebra 2.) Remind students that a number cannot be divided by zero, so a fraction with a zero in the denominator is undefined. After identifying excluded values, identify vertical asymptotes, show how they are related to the excluded value, and then identify horizontal asymptotes. Then show how to graph either by generating ordered pairs or by using translations.

Reaching All Learners

Through Multiple Representations

Help students understand why a horizontal asymptote occurs at c in $y = \frac{a}{x+b} + c$ by having them fill in a table with ordered pairs for the function $y = \frac{2}{x+1} + 4$. Have students choose larger and larger values for x. Ask what happens to the fraction as x gets larger. gets closer to 0 Ask what happens to the value of y as the fraction gets closer to zero. gets closer to 4 Do the same for smaller and smaller values for x.

Power Presentations with PowerPoint®

Additional Examples

Example 3

Graph each function.

A. $y = \dfrac{2}{x-3}$

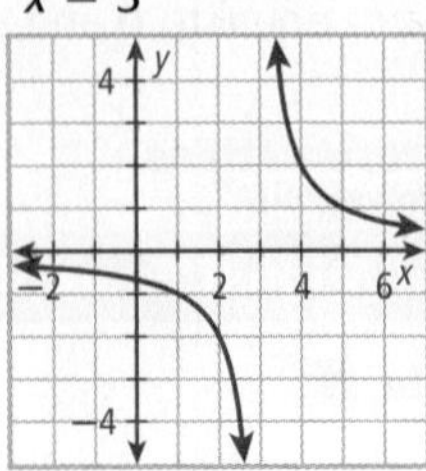

B. $y = \dfrac{1}{x+4} - 2$

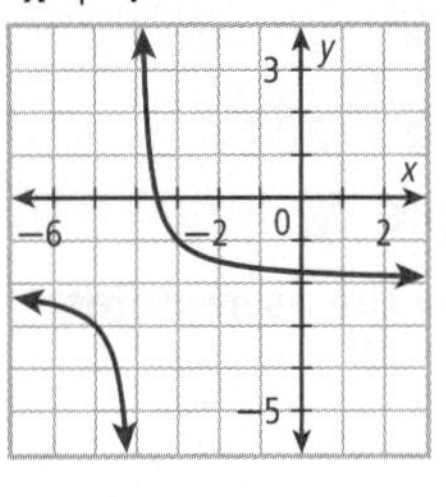

INTERVENTION

Questioning Strategies

EXAMPLE 3

- When do you use a translation and when do you use a table of values to graph?
- How do you know whether the graph should be translated left or right? up or down?

Answers to *Check It Out*

3a.

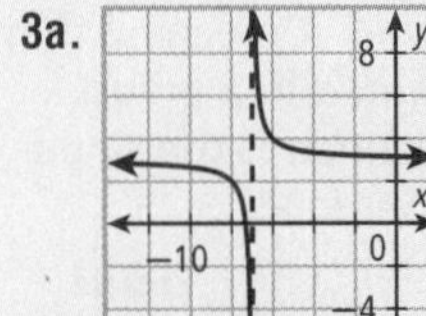

3b.

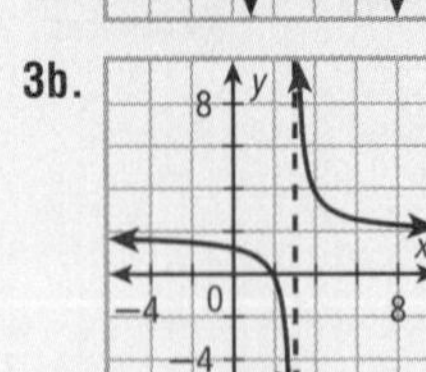

Step 2 Identify the horizontal asymptote.

$c = -7$ *−7 can be written as + (−7)*

$y = -7$ *y = c*

vertical asymptote: $x = \frac{10}{3}$; horizontal asymptote: $y = -7$

CHECK IT OUT! **Identify the asymptotes.**

2a. $y = \dfrac{2}{x-5}$ **2b.** $y = \dfrac{1}{4x+16} + 5$ **2c.** $y = \dfrac{3}{x+77} - 15$

x = 5; y = 0   **x = −4; y = 5**   **x = −77; y = −15**

To graph a rational function in the form $y = \frac{a}{x-b} + c$ when $a = 1$, you can graph the asymptotes and then translate the parent function $y = \frac{1}{x}$. However, if $a \neq 1$, the graph is not a translation of the parent function. In this case, you can use the asymptotes and a table of values.

EXAMPLE 3 Graphing Rational Functions Using Asymptotes

Graph each function.

A $y = \dfrac{2}{x+1}$

Since the numerator is not 1, use the asymptotes and a table of values.

Step 1 Identify the vertical and horizontal asymptotes.

vertical: $x = -1$ *Use x = b. x + 1 = x − (−1), so b = −1.*

horizontal : $y = 0$ *Use y = c. c = 0*

Step 2 Graph the asymptotes using dashed lines.

Step 3 Make a table of values. Choose x-values on both sides of the vertical asymptote.

x	−3	−2	$-\frac{3}{2}$	$-\frac{1}{2}$	0	1
y	−1	−2	−4	4	2	1

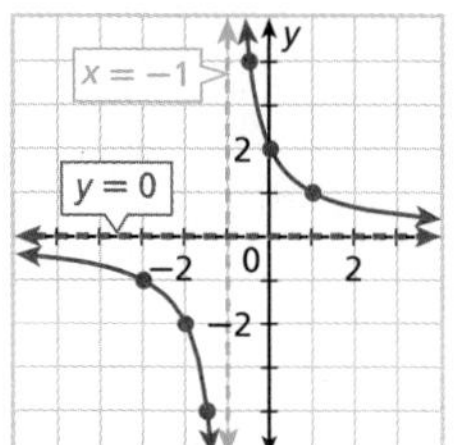

Step 4 Plot the points and connect them with smooth curves. The curves will get very close to the asymptotes, but will not touch them.

B $y = \dfrac{1}{x-2} - 4$

Since the numerator is 1, use the asymptotes and translate $y = \frac{1}{x}$.

Step 1 Identify the vertical and horizontal asymptotes.

vertical: $x = 2$ *Use x = b. b = 2*

horizontal: $y = -4$ *Use y = c. c = −4*

Step 2 Graph the asymptotes using dashed lines.

Step 3 Draw smooth curves to show the translation.

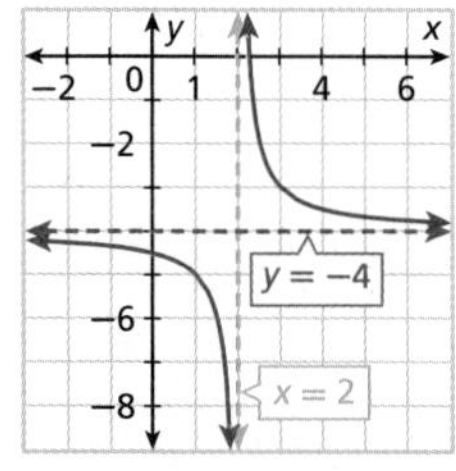

CHECK IT OUT! **Graph each function.**

3a. $y = \dfrac{1}{x+7} + 3$ **3b.** $y = \dfrac{2}{x-3} + 2$

Reaching All Learners

Through Modeling

Help students understand how a change in the numerator affects the graph of a rational function by having them graph the following on their graphing calculators:

$y = \frac{1}{x}$; $y = \frac{5}{x}$; $y = \frac{10}{x}$

Then have students make predictions about the shapes of $y = \frac{25}{x}$ and $y = \frac{50}{x}$.

EXAMPLE 4 *Gemology Application*

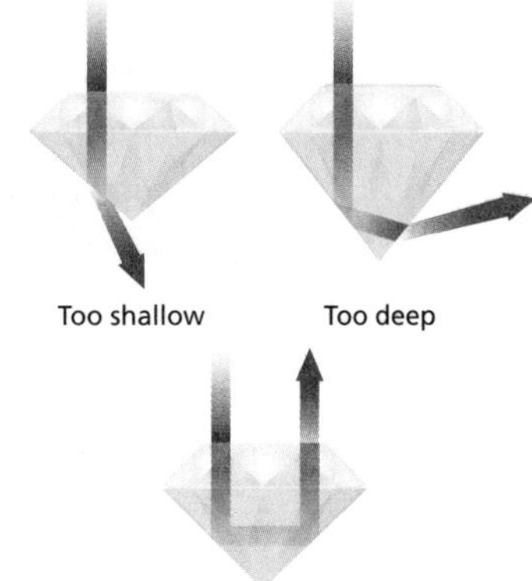

Some diamonds are cut using ratios calculated by a mathematician, Marcel Tolkowsky, in 1919. The amount of light reflected up through the top of a diamond (brilliancy) can be maximized using the ratio between the width of the diamond and the depth of the diamond. A gemologist has a diamond with a width of 90 millimeters. If x represents the depth of the diamond, then $y = \frac{90}{x}$ represents the brilliancy ratio y.

a. **Describe the reasonable domain and range values.**
   Both the depth of the diamond and the brilliancy ratio will be nonnegative, so nonnegative values are reasonable for the domain and range.

b. **Graph the function.**

Step 1 Identify the vertical and horizontal asymptotes.

vertical: $x = 0$ *Use $x = b$. $b = 0$*
horizontal: $y = 0$ *Use $y = c$. $c = 0$*

Step 2 Graph the asymptotes.
The asymptotes will be the x- and y-axes.

Step 3 Since the domain is restricted to nonnegative values, only choose x-values on the right side of the vertical asymptote.

Depth of Diamond (mm)	2	10	20	45
Brilliancy Ratio	45	9	4.5	2

Step 4 Plot the points and connect them with smooth curves.

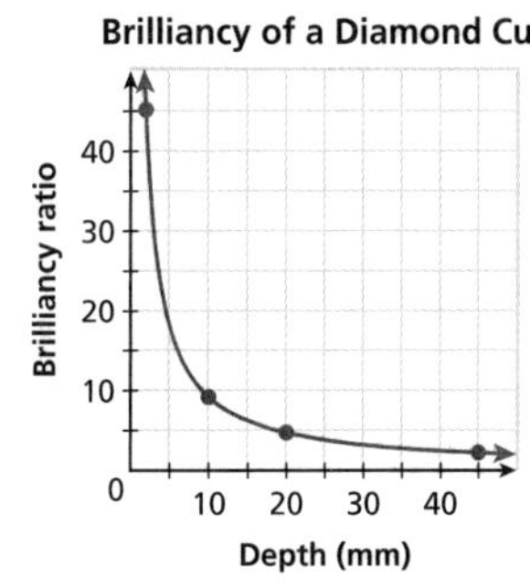

4. A librarian has a budget of $500 to buy copies of a software program. She will receive 10 free copies when she sets up an account with the supplier. The number of copies y of the program that she can buy is given by $y = \frac{500}{x} + 10$, where x is the price per copy. **D: $x > 0$; R: natural numbers > 10**

a. Describe the reasonable domain and range values.

b. Graph the function.

Power Presentations with PowerPoint®

Additional Examples

Example 4

Your club has $75 with which to purchase snacks to sell at an afterschool game. The number of snacks y that you can buy, if the average price of the snacks is x dollars, is given by $y = \frac{75}{x}$.

a. Describe the reasonable domain and range values.
D: $x > 0$; R: $y > 0$

b. Graph the function.

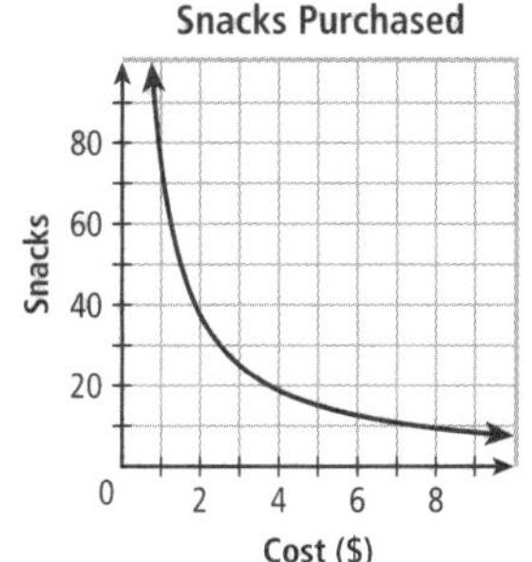

INTERVENTION

Questioning Strategies

EXAMPLE 4

- How can the asymptotes help you determine a reasonable domain and range?

Answers to *Check It Out*

4b.

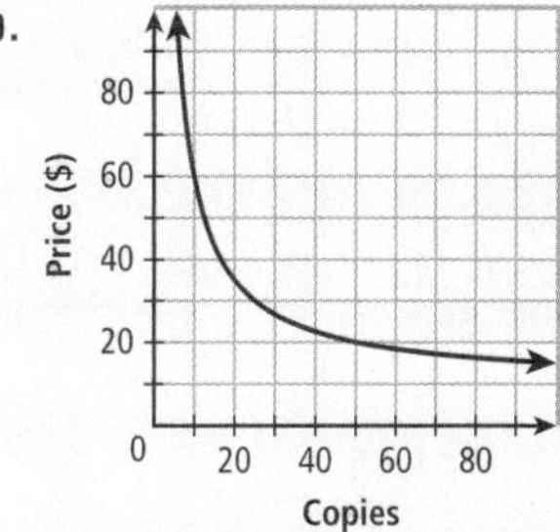

The table shows some of the properties of the four families of functions you have studied and their graphs.

Know it! Note

Families of Functions

LINEAR FUNCTION	QUADRATIC FUNCTION
$y = mx + b$ • Parent function: $y = x$ • m is the slope. It rotates the graph about $(0, b)$. • b is the y-intercept. It translates the graph of $y = x$ vertically. 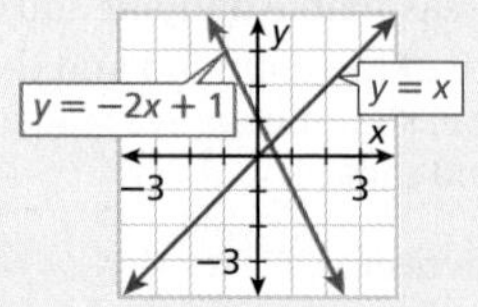 	$y = ax^2 + bx + c$ • Parent function: $y = x^2$ • a determines the width of the parabola and the direction it opens. • c translates the graph of $y = ax^2$ vertically. • The axis of symmetry is the vertical line $x = -\frac{b}{2a}$. 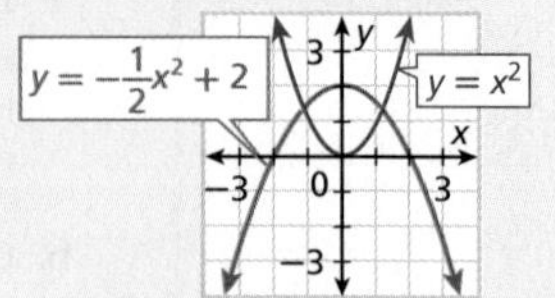
SQUARE-ROOT FUNCTION	**RATIONAL FUNCTION**
$y = \sqrt{x - a} + b$ • Parent function: $y = \sqrt{x}$ • a translates the graph of $y = \sqrt{x}$ horizontally. • b translates the graph of $y = \sqrt{x}$ vertically. 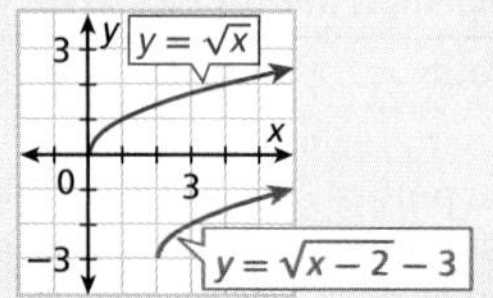 	$y = \frac{a}{x - b} + c$ • Parent function: $y = \frac{1}{x}$ • b translates the graph $y = \frac{1}{x}$ horizontally. • c translates the graph of $y = \frac{1}{x}$ vertically. 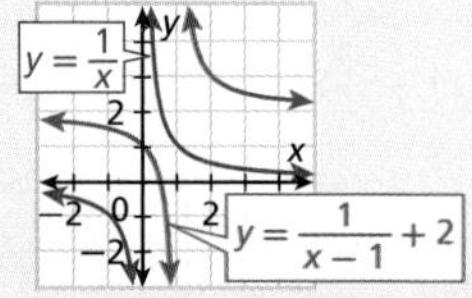

THINK AND DISCUSS

1. Does $y = \frac{1}{x-5}$ have any excluded values? Explain.
2. Tell how to find the vertical and horizontal asymptotes of $y = \frac{1}{x+9} - 5$.
3. **GET ORGANIZED** Copy and complete the graphic organizer. In each box, find the asymptotes for the given rational function.

Know it! Note

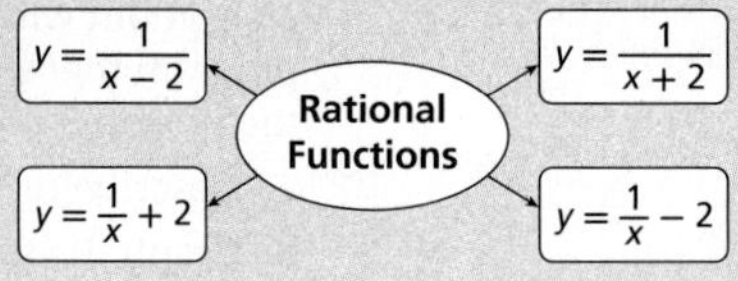

3 Close

Summarize

Tell students that the first step to graphing a rational function is graphing the asymptotes. Then the function can be sketched from a table of values or by a translation of $y = \frac{1}{x}$. Have students name the asymptotes for $y = \frac{2}{x+7} + 8$. $x = -7$; $y = 8$ Then ask them if they would use a table of values or a translation of $y = \frac{1}{x}$ to graph the function. table of values

ONGOING ASSESSMENT and INTERVENTION

***Diagnose Before* the Lesson**
12-2 Warm Up, TE p. 878

***Monitor During* the Lesson**
Check It Out! Exercises, SE pp. 878–881
Questioning Strategies, TE pp. 879–881

***Assess After* the Lesson**
12-2 Lesson Quiz, TE p. 885
Alternative Assessment, TE p. 885

Answers to *Think and Discuss*

1. Yes; the function is undefined at $x = 5$.
2. To find the vertical asymptote, set $x + 9$ equal to 0 and solve for x. The vertical asymptote is $x = -9$. To find the horizontal asymptote, look at the constant term. The horizontal asymptote is $y = -5$.
3. See p. A11.

12-2 Exercises

go.hrw.com
Homework Help Online
KEYWORD: MA7 12-2
Parent Resources Online
KEYWORD: MA7 Parent

GUIDED PRACTICE

1. **Vocabulary** An x-value that makes a function undefined is a(n) ___?___. (*asymptote* or *excluded value*) **excluded value**

SEE EXAMPLE 1 p. 878

Identify the excluded value for each rational function.

2. $y = \frac{4}{x}$ **0**
3. $y = \frac{2}{x+3}$ **−3**
4. $y = -\frac{2}{x}$ **0**
5. $y = \frac{16}{x-4}$ **4**

SEE EXAMPLE 2 p. 879

Identify the asymptotes.

6. $y = \frac{1}{x-3}$ **$x = 3$; $y = 0$**
7. $y = \frac{4}{3x+15}$ **$x = -5$; $y = 0$**
8. $y = \frac{2}{3x-5} + 2$ **$x = \frac{5}{3}$; $y = 2$**
9. $y = \frac{1}{x+9} - 10$ **$x = -9$; $y = -10$**

SEE EXAMPLE 3 p. 880

Graph each function.

10. $y = \frac{2}{x+6}$
11. $y = \frac{1}{x-2} - 6$
12. $y = \frac{1}{x} + 2$
13. $y = \frac{1}{x-3} - 2$

SEE EXAMPLE 4 p. 881

14. **Catering** A caterer has $100 in her budget for fruit. Slicing and delivery of each pound of fruit costs $5. If x represents the cost per pound of the fruit itself, then $y = \frac{100}{x+5}$ represents the number of pounds y she can buy.
    a. Describe the reasonable domain and range values. **D: $x > 0$; R: $0 < y < 20$**
    b. Graph the function.

PRACTICE AND PROBLEM SOLVING

Independent Practice	
For Exercises	See Example
15–18	1
19–22	2
23–26	3
27	4

Extra Practice
Skills Practice p. S26
Application Practice p. S39

Identify the excluded value for each rational function.

15. $y = \frac{7}{x}$ **0**
16. $y = \frac{1}{x-4}$ **4**
17. $y = -\frac{15}{x}$ **0**
18. $y = \frac{12}{x-5}$ **5**

Identify the asymptotes.

19. $y = \frac{9}{x-4}$ **$x = 4$; $y = 0$**
20. $y = \frac{2}{x+4}$ **$x = -4$; $y = 0$**
21. $y = \frac{7}{4x-12} + 4$ **$x = 3$; $y = 4$**
22. $y = \frac{7}{3x+5} - 9$ **$x = -\frac{5}{3}$; $y = -9$**

Graph each function.

23. $y = \frac{5}{x-5}$
24. $y = \frac{1}{x+5} - 6$
25. $y = \frac{1}{x+4}$
26. $y = \frac{1}{x-4} + 2$

27. **Business** A wholesaler is buying auto parts. He has $200 to spend. He receives 5 parts free with the order. The number of parts y he can buy, if the average price of the parts is x dollars, is $y = \frac{200}{x} + 5$.
    a. Describe the reasonable domain and range values. **D: $x > 0$; R: natural numbers > 5**
    b. Graph the function.

Find the excluded value for each rational function.

28. $y = \frac{4}{x}$ **0**
29. $y = \frac{1}{x-7}$ **7**
30. $y = \frac{2}{x+4}$ **−4**
31. $y = \frac{3}{2x+1}$ **$-\frac{1}{2}$**

Graph each rational function. Show the asymptotes.

32. $y = \frac{1}{x-2}$
33. $y = \frac{2}{x} + 3$
34. $y = \frac{3}{x+1} + 2$
35. $y = \frac{1}{x-4} - 1$

36. **Multi-Step** The function $y = \frac{60}{x^2}$ relates the luminescence in lumens y of a 60-watt lightbulb viewed from a distance of x ft. Graph the function. Use the graph to find the luminescence of a 60-watt lightbulb viewed from a distance of 6 ft.

12-2 Exercises

Assignment Guide

Assign *Guided Practice* exercises as necessary.

If you finished Examples **1–2**
Basic 15–22, 28–31
Average 15–22, 28–31
Advanced 15–22, 28–31, 59

If you finished Examples **1–4**
Basic 15–45, 51–60, 64–70
Average 15–50, 55–61, 64–70
Advanced 15–36, 44–70

Homework Quick Check
Quickly check key concepts.
Exercises: 18, 20, 22, 24, 27, 36

Number Sense When the denominator of a rational expression is x as in **Exercises 2, 4, 15,** and **17,** the excluded value is 0 regardless of whether the expression is positive or negative.

Answers

10–13. See p. A35.

14b.

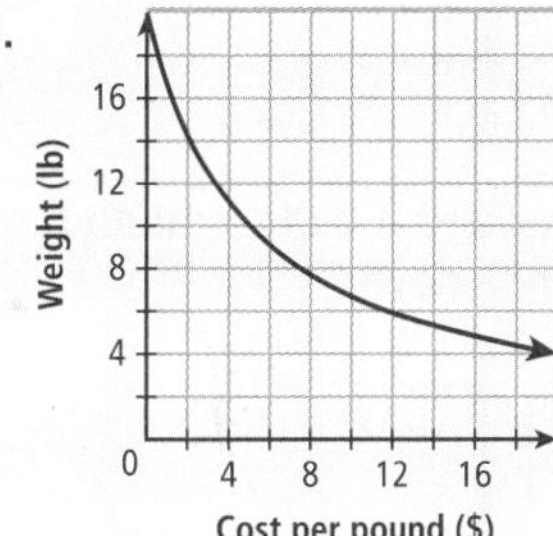

23–26, 27b, 32–36. See p. A35.

State Resources

Teacher to Teacher

At the end of this lesson, there is a summary chart of parent functions. At this point, I like to include a real-world application for each type of function.

I give a worksheet with four columns: Name of Function, Equation, Graph, and Real-World Connection. I fill in one blank, and students fill in the other three. This is a great way to wrap up the course at the end of the year.

Connie Johnsen
Harker Heights, TX

go.hrw.com
State Resources Online
KEYWORD: MA7 Resources

Exercise 56 involves writing a rational function and finding the asymptotes. This exercise prepares students for the Multi-Step Test Prep on page 896.

Answers

44. Student B is incorrect. The student identified the value at which there is a vertical asymptote ($x = -2$).

45–46a. See p. A35.

47. translated 6 units right

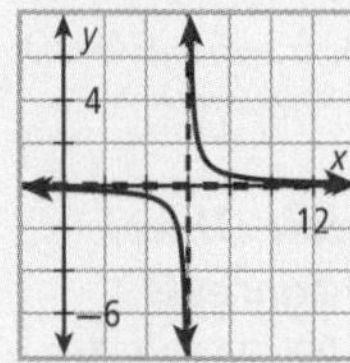

48. translated 7 units left

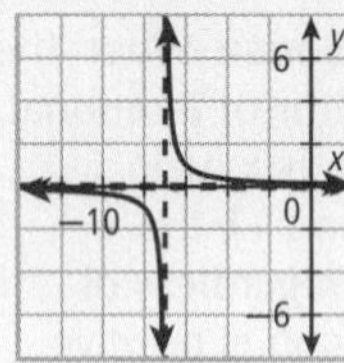

49. translated 4 units up

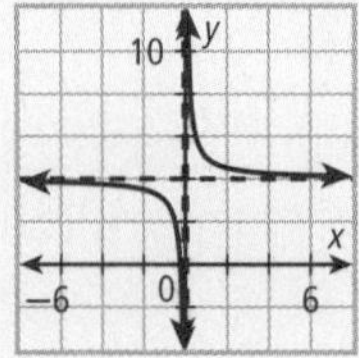

50. translated 2 units right and 9 units down

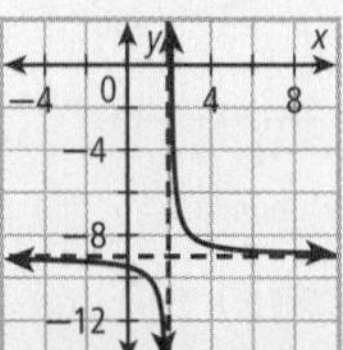

56c–57. See p. A36.

12-2 PRACTICE A

12-2 PRACTICE C

12-2 PRACTICE B

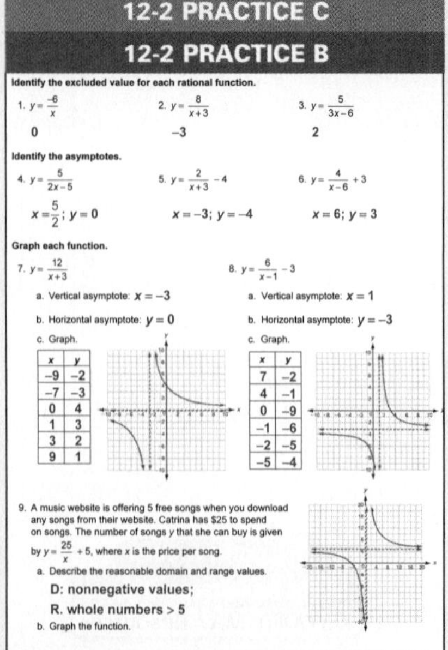

Identify the excluded value for each rational function.

1. $y = \frac{-6}{x}$ 0
2. $y = \frac{8}{x+3}$ −3
3. $y = \frac{5}{3x-6}$ 2

Identify the asymptotes.

4. $y = \frac{5}{2x-5}$ $x = \frac{5}{2}$; $y = 0$
5. $y = \frac{2}{x+3} - 4$ $x = -3$; $y = -4$
6. $y = \frac{4}{x-6} + 3$ $x = 6$; $y = 3$

Graph each function.

7. $y = \frac{12}{x+3}$
   a. Vertical asymptote: $x = -3$
   b. Horizontal asymptote: $y = 0$
   c. Graph.

x	y
−9	−2
−7	−3
0	4
1	3
3	2
9	1

8. $y = \frac{6}{x-1} - 3$
   a. Vertical asymptote: $x = 1$
   b. Horizontal asymptote: $y = -3$
   c. Graph.

x	y
7	−2
4	−1
0	−9
−1	−6
−2	−5
−5	−4

9. A music website is offering 5 free songs when you download any songs from their website. Catrina has $25 to spend on songs. The number of songs y that she can buy is given by $y = \frac{25}{x} + 5$, where x is the price per song.
   a. Describe the reasonable domain and range values.
   D: nonnegative values;
   R. whole numbers > 5
   b. Graph the function.

Identify the asymptotes of each rational function.

37. $y = \frac{7}{x+1}$ **$x = -1$; $y = 0$**
38. $y = \frac{1}{x} - 5$ **$x = 0$; $y = -5$**
39. $y = \frac{12}{x-2} + 5$ **$x = 2$; $y = 5$**
40. $y = \frac{18}{x+3} - 9$ **$x = -3$; $y = -9$**

Match each graph with one of the following functions.

A. $y = \frac{1}{x+1} + 2$ B. $y = \frac{1}{x+2} - 1$ C. $y = \frac{1}{x-2} + 1$

41. **B**

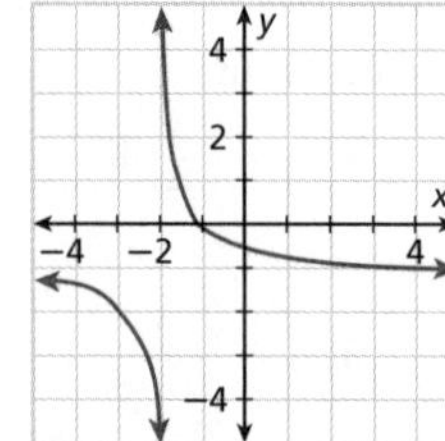

42. **A**

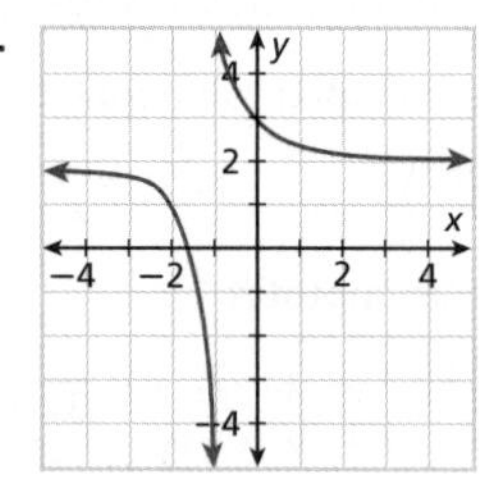

43. **C**

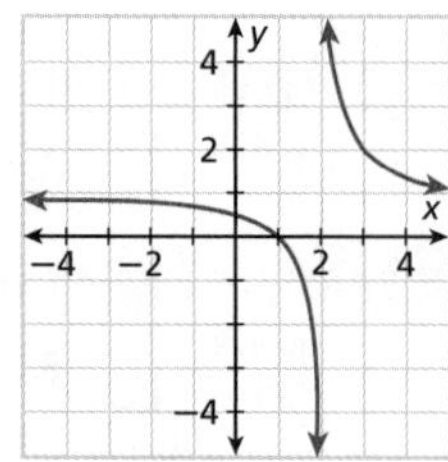

44. **ERROR ANALYSIS** In finding the horizontal asymptote of $y = \frac{1}{x+2} - 3$, student A said the asymptote is at $y = -3$, and student B said it is at $y = -2$. Who is incorrect? Explain the error.

45. **Finance** The time in months y that it will take to pay off a bill of $1200, when x dollars are paid each month and the finance charge is $15 per month, is $y = \frac{1200}{x-15}$. Describe the reasonable domain and range values and graph the function.

46. The table shows how long it takes different size landscaping teams to complete a project.
   a. Graph the data.
   b. Write a rational function to represent the data. **$y = \frac{60}{x}$**
   c. How many hours would it take 12 landscapers to complete the project? **5 h**

Landscapers	Time (h)
2	30
4	15
5	12
10	6

Graph each function. Compare its graph to the graph of $y = \frac{1}{x}$.

47. $y = \frac{1}{x-6}$
48. $y = \frac{1}{x+7}$
49. $y = \frac{1}{x} + 4$
50. $y = \frac{1}{x-2} - 9$

Find the domain that makes the range positive.

51. $y = \frac{10}{x-2}$ **D: $x > 2$**
52. $y = \frac{10}{x+2}$ **D: $x > -2$**
53. $y = \frac{5}{5x+1}$ **D: $x > -\frac{1}{5}$**
54. $y = \frac{4}{3x-7}$ **D: $x > \frac{7}{3}$**

55. **Critical Thinking** In which quadrants would you find the graph of $y = \frac{a}{x}$ when a is positive? when a is negative? **I and III; II and IV**

MULTI-STEP TEST PREP

56. This problem will prepare you for the Multi-Step Test Prep on page 896.

It takes a total of 250 workdays to build a house for charity. For example, if 2 workers build the house, it takes them 125 actual construction days. If 10 workers are present, it takes 25 construction days to build the house.

a. Write a function that represents the number of construction days to build as a function of the number of workers. **$y = \frac{250}{x}$**
b. What is the domain of this function? **D: natural numbers**
c. Sketch a graph of the function.

12-2 READING STRATEGIES

The concept map below will help you understand rational functions.

Definitions: A *rational function* is a function whose rule has a variable in the denominator. An *excluded value* for a rational function is any value that makes the denominator equal to 0.

Graphs: $y = \frac{1}{x-1} + 2$

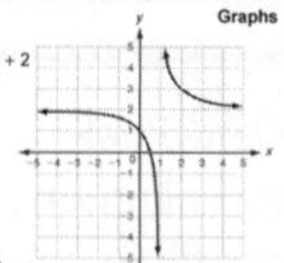

Rational Function

Examples: $y = \frac{4}{x}$; $y = \frac{1}{x^2}$; $y = \frac{2}{x-5} + 3$

Non-Examples: $y = \frac{x}{6}$; $y = x + \frac{1}{2}$; $y = 3x^2$

Asymptotes: A rational function in the form $y = \frac{a}{x+b} + c$ has a *vertical asymptote* at the excluded value $x = -b$, and a *horizontal asymptote* at $y = c$.

Complete the following.

1. Tell whether or not each of the following is a rational function.
   a. $y = \frac{x}{3} + 2$ no
   b. $y = \frac{3}{x^2} - 1$ yes
   c. $y = \frac{1}{x+8}$ yes
2. Explain why $y = x + \frac{1}{2}$ is not a rational function.
   It has no variable in the denominator.
3. Describe how to find the excluded value of the rational function $y = \frac{3}{x-5}$. Then find it.
   Find what value makes $x - 5 = 0$; 5
4. Identify the asymptotes for the rational function $y = \frac{1}{x-1} + 2$ graphed above.
   vertical: $x = 1$
   horizontal: $y = 2$

12-2 RETEACH

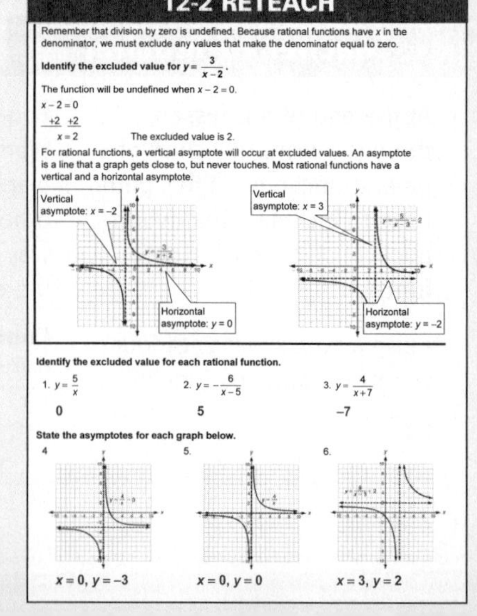

Remember that division by zero is undefined. Because rational functions have x in the denominator, we must exclude any values that make the denominator equal to zero.

Identify the excluded value for $y = \frac{3}{x-2}$.

The function will be undefined when $x - 2 = 0$.

$x - 2 = 0$
$+2 \ \ +2$
$x = 2$ The excluded value is 2.

For rational functions, a vertical asymptote will occur at excluded values. An asymptote is a line that a graph gets close to, but never touches. Most rational functions have a vertical and a horizontal asymptote.

Identify the excluded value for each rational function.

1. $y = \frac{5}{x}$ 0
2. $y = -\frac{6}{x-5}$ 5
3. $y = \frac{4}{x+7}$ −7

State the asymptotes for each graph below.

4. $x = 0$, $y = -3$
5. $x = 0$, $y = 0$
6. $x = 3$, $y = 2$

57. Write About It Graph each pair of functions on a graphing calculator. Then make a conjecture about the relationship between the graphs of the rational functions $y = \frac{k}{x}$ and $y = \frac{-k}{x}$.

a. $y = \frac{1}{x}; y = \frac{-1}{x}$ b. $y = \frac{3}{x}; y = \frac{-3}{x}$ c. $y = \frac{5}{x}; y = \frac{-5}{x}$

TEST PREP

58. Which function is graphed?

(A) $y = \frac{2}{x+3} - 4$ (C) $y = \frac{2}{x-3} + 4$

(B) $y = \frac{2}{x+4} - 3$ (D) $y = \frac{2}{x-4} + 3$

59. Which rational function has a graph with the horizontal asymptote $y = -1$?

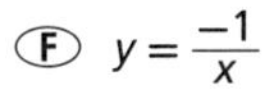

(F) $y = \frac{-1}{x}$ (H) $y = \frac{1}{x+1}$

(G) $y = \frac{1}{x-1}$ (J) $y = \frac{1}{x} - 1$

60. **Short Response** Write a rational function whose graph is the same shape as the graph of $f(x) = \frac{1}{x}$, but is translated 2 units left and 3 units down. Graph the function. $f(x) = \frac{1}{x+2} - 3$

CHALLENGE AND EXTEND

61. Graph the equation $y = \frac{1}{x^2+1}$.

a. Does this equation represent a rational function? Explain. **Yes; the function is a quotient of polynomials.**

b. What is the domain of the function? **D: all real numbers**

c. What is the range of the function? **R: $0 < y \leq 1$**

d. Is the graph discontinuous? **no**

62. **Graphing Calculator** Are the graphs of $f(x) = \frac{(x-3)(x-1)}{x-3}$ and $g(x) = x - 1$ identical? Explain. (*Hint:* Are there any excluded values?)

63. **Critical Thinking** Write the equation of the rational function that has a horizontal asymptote at $y = 3$ and a vertical asymptote at $x = -2$ and contains the point $(1, 4)$. $y = \frac{3}{x+2} + 3$

SPIRAL REVIEW

Solve each equation by graphing the related function. *(Lesson 9-5)*

64. $4 - x^2 = 0$ **±2** 65. $3x^2 = x^2 + 2x + 12$ **−2, 3** 66. $-x^2 = -6x + 9$ **3**

67. In the first five stages of a fractal design, a line segment has the following lengths, in centimeters: 240, 120, 60, 30, 15. Use this pattern and your knowledge of geometric sequences to determine the length of the segment in the tenth stage. *(Lesson 11-1)* **0.46875 cm**

Determine whether each function represents an inverse variation. Explain. *(Lesson 12-1)*

68. $x + y = 12$ **No; the function cannot be written in the form $y = \frac{k}{x}$.**

69. **No; the product xy is not constant.**

x	30	60	90	120
y	10	20	30	40

70. $xy = -4$ **Yes; the product of xy is the constant −4.**

TEST PREP DOCTOR Students who chose H in Exercise 59 chose a function with a vertical asymptote at $x = -1$.

Answers

60–61. For graphs, see p. A36.

62. No; the graph of $f(x)$ has an excluded value at $x = 3$. The graph of $g(x)$ has no excluded values.

Journal

Have students explain the steps for graphing a rational function.

ALTERNATIVE ASSESSMENT

Create a rational function with a vertical asymptote at 4 and horizontal asymptote at −3. Then graph the function.

Power Presentations with PowerPoint®

12-2 Lesson Quiz

Identify the excluded value for each rational function.

1. $y = \frac{12}{x}$ 0 2. $y = \frac{7}{x-5}$ 5

3. Identify the asymptotes of $y = \frac{6}{x+4}$ and then graph the function. $x = -4; y = 0$

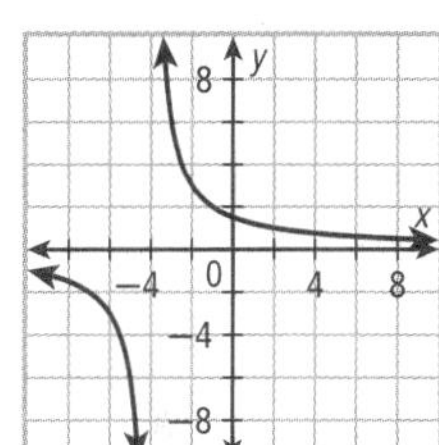

4. You have $100 to spend on CDs. A CD club advertises 6 free CDs for anyone who becomes a member. The number of CDs y that you can receive is given by $y = \frac{100}{x} + 6$, where x is the average price per CD.

a. Describe the reasonable domain and range values. D: $x > 0$; R: natural numbers > 6

b. Graph the function.

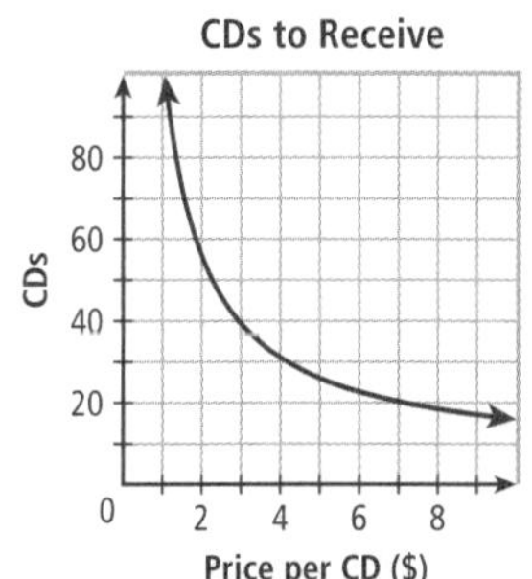

Also available on transparency

12-2 PROBLEM SOLVING

Gabrielle saves $100 and decides to join a CD Club. As a member, she gets 12 CDs free and then must buy the rest at the regular price of x dollars. The number of CDs y she can buy is $y = \frac{100}{x} + 12$.

1. Determine a reasonable domain and range.
D: $x > 0$; R: natural numbers greater than 12

2. Identify the vertical and horizontal asymptotes.
$x = 0$ and $y = 12$

3. Complete this table of ordered pairs and graph the rational function.

x	5	10	20	25
y	32	22	17	16

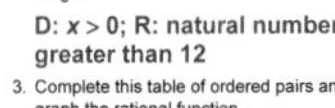

4. Gabrielle learns that the regular price of a CD is $17.90. How many CDs can she buy through the Club with $100?
17

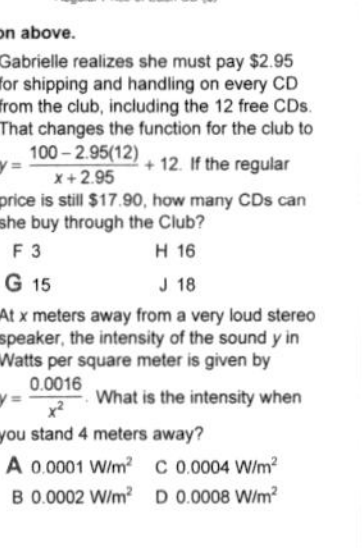

Select the best answer. For 5–6, refer to the situation above.

5. Before joining the CD Club, Gabrielle learns about the Student Savings Card. If she buys a card for $20, she gets $5 off every CD she buys at the local record store. If each CD costs x dollars at the local record store, then the number of CDs y she can buy is $y = \frac{100-20}{x-5}$. The average price of each CD at the local record store is $14.95. How many CDs can she buy with the Card and $100?

A 4 C 10
B 8 D 12

6. Gabrielle realizes she must pay $2.95 for shipping and handling on every CD from the club, including the 12 free CDs. That changes the function for the club to $y = \frac{100 - 2.95(12)}{x + 2.95} + 12$. If the regular price is still $17.90, how many CDs can she buy through the Club?

F 3 H 16
G 15 J 18

7. At x meters away from a very loud stereo speaker, the intensity of the sound y in Watts per square meter is given by $y = \frac{0.0016}{x^2}$. What is the intensity when you stand 4 meters away?

A 0.0001 W/m² C 0.0004 W/m²
B 0.0002 W/m² D 0.0008 W/m²

12-2 CHALLENGE

The function $f(x) = x$ is a polynomial function. The function $g(x) = \frac{1}{x}$ is a rational function. The diagram at right shows the graphs of $f(x) = x$ and $g(x) = \frac{1}{x}$.

Notice that the graph of f is a continuous and straight line. The graph of g is neither continuous nor straight. Taking the reciprocal of x has the effect of breaking a straight line into two curved branches, each extending indefinitely. Notice also that the break occurs at $x = 0$, the only real number that has no reciprocal.

In Exercises 1 and 2, graph f and g on the same coordinate grid. For what value of x does the break occur?

1. $f(x) = x + 1$ and $g(x) = \frac{1}{x+1}$
break at $x = -1$

2. $f(x) = x - 1$ and $g(x) = \frac{1}{x-1}$
break at $x = 1$

Graph each function and its reciprocal on the same coordinate grid.

3. $y = x - 2.5$
$y = x - 2.5$ and $y = \frac{1}{x - 2.5}$

4. $y = x - 3$
$y = x - 3$ and $y = \frac{1}{x - 3}$

5. $y = x + 3$
$y = x + 3$ and $y = \frac{1}{x + 3}$

12-3 Organizer

Pacing: Traditional 1 day
Block $\frac{1}{2}$ day

Objectives: Simplify rational expressions.

Identify excluded values of rational expressions.

Power Presentations with PowerPoint®

Warm Up

Simplify each expression.

1. $\frac{12}{40}$ $\frac{3}{10}$ **2.** $\frac{24}{60}$ $\frac{2}{5}$

Factor each expression.

3. $x^2 + 5x + 6$ $(x + 2)(x + 3)$

4. $4x^2 - 64$ $4(x + 4)(x - 4)$

5. $2x^2 + 3x + 1$ $(2x + 1)(x + 1)$

6. $9x^2 + 60x + 100$ $(3x + 10)^2$

Also available on transparency

Math Humor

Q: Why was the number so happy to get accepted into the Rational Expression Club?

A: It didn't want to be excluded.

State Resources

12-3 Simplifying Rational Expressions

Objectives
Simplify rational expressions.

Identify excluded values of rational expressions.

Vocabulary
rational expression

Why learn this?
The shapes and sizes of plants and animals are partly determined by the ratio of surface area to volume.

If an animal's body is small and its surface area is large, the rate of heat loss will be high. Hummingbirds must maintain a high metabolism to compensate for the loss of body heat due to having a high surface-area-to-volume ratio. Formulas for surface-area-to-volume ratios are *rational expressions.*

A **rational expression** is an algebraic expression whose numerator and denominator are polynomials. The value of the polynomial expression in the denominator cannot be zero since division by zero is undefined. This means that rational expressions may have excluded values.

EXAMPLE 1 Identifying Excluded Values

Find any excluded values of each rational expression.

A $\frac{5}{8r}$

$8r = 0$ *Set the denominator equal to 0.*

$r = \frac{0}{8} = 0$ *Solve for r by dividing both sides by 8.*

The excluded value is 0.

B $\frac{9d + 1}{d^2 - 2d}$

$d^2 - 2d = 0$ *Set the denominator equal to 0.*

$d(d - 2) = 0$ *Factor.*

$d = 0$ or $d - 2 = 0$ *Use the Zero Product Property.*

$d = 2$ *Solve for d.*

The excluded values are 0 and 2.

Remember!
To review the Zero Product Property, see Lesson 9-6.
To review factoring trinomials, see Chapter 8.

C $\frac{x + 4}{x^2 + 5x + 6}$

$x^2 + 5x + 6 = 0$ *Set the denominator equal to 0.*

$(x + 3)(x + 2) = 0$ *Factor.*

$x + 3 = 0$ or $x + 2 = 0$ *Use the Zero Product Property.*

$x = -3$ or $x = -2$ *Solve each equation for x.*

The excluded values are -3 and -2.

Find any excluded values of each rational expression.

1a. $\frac{12}{t + 5}$ **−5** **1b.** $\frac{3b}{b^2 + 5b}$ **0, −5** **1c.** $\frac{3k^2}{k^2 + 7k + 12}$ **−3, −4**

1 Introduce

EXPLORATION

12-3 Simplifying Rational Expressions

You will need a graphing calculator for this Exploration.

1. Consider the functions $y = \frac{2x^2 + 6x}{2x^2}$ and $y = \frac{x + 3}{x}$. What are the excluded values for these functions?
2. Evaluate each function for the x-values in the table.

x	$y = \frac{2x^2 + 6x}{2x^2}$	$y = \frac{x + 3}{x}$
1		
3		
6		

3. Enter the functions into your calculator as shown. Press GRAPH. What do you notice?
4. Press 2nd GRAPH to view a table of values for the functions. What do you notice?

THINK AND DISCUSS

5. Explain what you can conclude about the expressions $\frac{2x^2 + 6x}{2x^2}$ and $\frac{x + 3}{x}$.
6. Describe how the numerator and denominator of $\frac{2x^2 + 6x}{2x^2}$

Motivate

Review with students that $\frac{24}{50}$ can be written as $\frac{2 \cdot 2 \cdot 2 \cdot 3}{2 \cdot 5 \cdot 5}$ and that when the common factor of 2 is divided out, the expression equals $\frac{2 \cdot 2 \cdot 3}{5 \cdot 5} = \frac{12}{25}$. Ask students to conjecture about how to simplify rational expressions.

Explorations and answers are provided in *Alternate Openers: Explorations Transparencies.*

A rational expression is in its simplest form when the numerator and denominator have no common factors except 1. Remember that to simplify fractions you can divide out common factors that appear in both the numerator and the denominator. You can do the same to simplify rational expressions.

EXAMPLE 2 Simplifying Rational Expressions

Simplify each rational expression, if possible. Identify any excluded values.

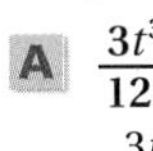

A $\dfrac{3t^3}{12t}$

$\dfrac{3t^3}{3 \cdot 4t}$ — *Factor 12.*

$\dfrac{{}^{1}\cancel{3}\cancel{t^3}^{t^2}}{{}_{1}\cancel{3} \cdot 4\cancel{t}^{1}}$ — *Divide out common factors. Note that if t = 0, the expression is undefined.*

$\dfrac{t^2}{4};\ t \neq 0$ — *Simplify. The excluded value is 0.*

B $\dfrac{3x^2 - 9x}{x - 3}$

$\dfrac{3x(x-3)}{x-3}$ — *Factor the numerator.*

$\dfrac{3x\cancel{(x-3)}^{1}}{\cancel{x-3}^{1}}$ — *Divide out common factors. Note that if x = 3, the expression is undefined.*

$3x;\ x \neq 3$ — *Simplify. The excluded value is 3.*

C $\dfrac{c}{c+5}$

$\dfrac{c}{c+5};\ c \neq -5$ — *The numerator and denominator have no common factors. The excluded value is −5.*

Caution!

Be sure to use the original denominator when finding excluded values. The excluded values may not be "seen" in the simplified denominator.

CHECK IT OUT! Simplify each rational expression, if possible. Identify any excluded values.

2a. $\dfrac{5m^2}{15m}$ $\quad \dfrac{m}{3};\ m \neq 0$ **2b.** $\dfrac{6p^3 + 12p}{p^2 + 2}$ $\quad 6p$ **2c.** $\dfrac{3n}{n-2}$ $\quad \dfrac{3n}{n-2};\ n \neq 2$

From now on in this chapter, you may assume that the values of the variables that make the denominator equal to 0 are excluded values. You do not need to include excluded values in your answers unless they are asked for.

EXAMPLE 3 Simplifying Rational Expressions with Trinomials

Simplify each rational expression, if possible.

A $\dfrac{k+1}{k^2 - 4k - 5}$

$\dfrac{k+1}{(k+1)(k-5)}$ — *Factor the numerator and the denominator when possible.*

$\dfrac{\cancel{k+1}^{1}}{\cancel{(k+1)}^{1}(k-5)}$ — *Divide out common factors.*

$\dfrac{1}{k-5}$ — *Simplify.*

B $\dfrac{y^2 - 16}{y^2 - 8y + 16}$

$\dfrac{(y+4)(y-4)}{(y-4)(y-4)}$

$\dfrac{(y+4)\cancel{(y-4)}^{1}}{(y-4)\cancel{(y-4)}^{1}}$

$\dfrac{y+4}{y-4}$

COMMON ERROR ALERT

When identifying excluded values, students might forget to include zero for the monomial variable factor in expressions like $d(d-2)$. Remind them of the Zero Product Property: If $ab = 0$, then $a = 0$ or $b = 0$. So, if $d(d-2) = 0$, then $d = 0$ or $d - 2 = 0$.

Power Presentations with PowerPoint®

Additional Examples

Example 1

Find any excluded values of each rational expression.

A. $\dfrac{6}{g+4}$ $\quad -4$

B. $\dfrac{2x+1}{x^2 - 15x}$ $\quad 0, 15$

C. $\dfrac{y-2}{y^2 + 5y + 4}$ $\quad -1, -4$

Example 2

Simplify each rational expression, if possible. Identify any excluded values.

A. $\dfrac{2r^4}{14r}$ $\quad \dfrac{r^3}{7};\ r \neq 0$

B. $\dfrac{6n^2 + 3n}{2n + 1}$ $\quad 3n;\ n \neq -\dfrac{1}{2}$

C. $\dfrac{12p}{3p - 2}$ $\quad \dfrac{12p}{3p-2};\ p \neq \dfrac{2}{3}$

INTERVENTION

Questioning Strategies

EXAMPLE 1

- Why are some values excluded?

EXAMPLE 2

- How can a simplified rational expression have an excluded value when its denominator has no variables?

2 Teach

Guided Instruction

Review factoring using the GCF, factorable trinomials, perfect-square trinomials, difference of squares, and grouping. Tell students that finding excluded values for rational expressions is the same process as finding excluded values for rational functions: find values that make the denominator equal to zero. As you work through each example, stress that *factors* are divided out. Terms that are added or subtracted are not.

Reaching All Learners

Through Number Sense

Ask students whether $\frac{x+5}{x+7}$ can be simplified to $\frac{5}{7}$. no Tell students that whenever they are not sure if a step in simplifying an expression is correct, they can substitute real numbers, as demonstrated in Student to Student on p. 888. For example, since $\frac{4+5}{4+7} \neq \frac{5}{7}$, then $\frac{x+5}{x+7}$ cannot be simplified to $\frac{5}{7}$.

Inclusion Before introducing **Example 4,** help students understand that when the numerator and denominator are opposites, the expression is equal to −1. For example, $\frac{5-3}{3-5} = \frac{2}{-2} = -1$.

Power Presentations with PowerPoint®

Additional Examples

Example 3

Simplify each rational expression, if possible.

A. $\frac{x+2}{x^2+5x+6}$ $\quad \frac{1}{x+3}$

B. $\frac{w^2-4}{w^2-8w+12}$ $\quad \frac{w+2}{w-6}$

Example 4

Simplify each rational expression, if possible.

A. $\frac{5x-10}{4-x^2}$ $\quad -\frac{5}{2+x}$

B. $\frac{18-6r}{2r^2+8r-42}$ $\quad -\frac{3}{r+7}$

INTERVENTION

Questioning Strategies

EXAMPLE 3

- How is simplifying a rational expression similar to simplifying a fraction? How is it different?

EXAMPLE 4

- How is −1 used to simplify opposite binomials?

Simplify each rational expression, if possible.

3a. $\frac{r+2}{r^2+7r+10}$ $\quad \mathbf{\frac{1}{r+5}}$ **3b.** $\frac{b^2-25}{b^2+10b+25}$ $\quad \mathbf{\frac{b-5}{b+5}}$

Recall from Chapter 8 that opposite binomials can help you factor polynomials. Recognizing opposite binomials can also help you simplify rational expressions.

Consider $\frac{x-3}{3-x}$. The numerator and denominator are opposite binomials. Therefore,

$$\frac{x-3}{3-x} = \frac{x-3}{-x+3} = \frac{\cancel{x-3}^1}{-1\cancel{(x-3)}^1} = \frac{1}{-1} = -1.$$

EXAMPLE 4 **Simplifying Rational Expressions Using Opposite Binomials**

Simplify each rational expression, if possible.

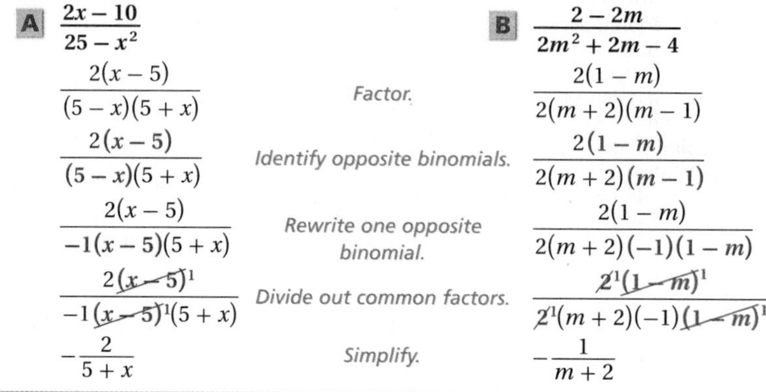

A $\frac{2x-10}{25-x^2}$

$\frac{2(x-5)}{(5-x)(5+x)}$ *Factor.*

$\frac{2(x-5)}{(5-x)(5+x)}$ *Identify opposite binomials.*

$\frac{2(x-5)}{-1(x-5)(5+x)}$ *Rewrite one opposite binomial.*

$\frac{2\cancel{(x-5)}^1}{-1\cancel{(x-5)}^1(5+x)}$ *Divide out common factors.*

$-\frac{2}{5+x}$ *Simplify.*

B $\frac{2-2m}{2m^2+2m-4}$

$\frac{2(1-m)}{2(m+2)(m-1)}$ *Factor.*

$\frac{2(1-m)}{2(m+2)(m-1)}$ *Identify opposite binomials.*

$\frac{2(1-m)}{2(m+2)(-1)(1-m)}$ *Rewrite one opposite binomial.*

$\frac{\cancel{2}^1\cancel{(1-m)}^1}{\cancel{2}^1(m+2)(-1)\cancel{(1-m)}^1}$ *Divide out common factors.*

$-\frac{1}{m+2}$ *Simplify.*

Simplify each rational expression, if possible.

4a. $\frac{3x-12}{16-x^2}$ $\quad \mathbf{-\frac{3}{4+x}}$ **4b.** $\frac{6-2x}{2x^2-4x-6}$ $\quad \mathbf{-\frac{1}{x+1}}$ **4c.** $\frac{3x-33}{x^2-121}$ $\quad \mathbf{\frac{3}{x+11}}$

Student to Student

Simplifying Rational Expressions

Tanika Brown, Washington High School

When I can't tell if I'm allowed to divide out part of an expression, I substitute a number into the original expression and simplify it. Then I simplify the original expression by dividing out the term in question. I check by seeing if the results are the same.

For example, I'll use x = 2 to see if I can divide out 4x in $\frac{4x}{4x-7}$.

Substitute x = 2.	*Divide out 4x.*
$\frac{4x}{4x-7}$	$\frac{\cancel{4}^1\cancel{x}^1}{\cancel{4}^1\cancel{x}^1-7}$
$\frac{4(2)}{4(2)-7}$	$\frac{1}{1-7}$
$\frac{8}{8-7} = \frac{8}{1} = 8$	$\frac{1}{-6}$

4x cannot be divided out because $8 \neq \frac{1}{-6}$.

Visual When dividing out common factors, encourage students to use a different colored pencil (MK) to strike out each matching pair of factors. Some students will find it helpful to circle the remaining factors before writing the simplified answer.

EXAMPLE 5 Biology Application

Desert plants must conserve water. Water evaporates from the surface of a plant. The volume determines how much water is in a plant. So the greater the surface-area-to-volume ratio, the less likely a plant is to survive in the desert. A barrel cactus is a desert plant that is close to spherical in shape.

a. What is the surface-area-to-volume ratio of a spherical barrel cactus? (*Hint:* For a sphere, $S = 4\pi r^2$ and $V = \frac{4}{3}\pi r^3$.)

$\frac{4\pi r^2}{\frac{4}{3}\pi r^3}$ *Write the ratio of surface area to volume.*

$\frac{4\pi^1 r^2}{\frac{4}{3}\pi^1 r^3}$ *Divide out common factors.*

$\frac{4r^{2^1}}{\frac{4}{3}r^{3^r}}$ *Use properties of exponents.*

$\frac{4}{r} \cdot \frac{3}{4}$ *Multiply by the reciprocal of $\frac{4}{3}$.*

$\frac{4^1}{r} \cdot \frac{3}{4^1}$ *Divide out common factors.*

$\frac{3}{r}$ *Simplify.*

b. Which barrel cactus has a greater chance of survival in the desert, one with a radius of 4 inches or one with a radius of 7 inches? Explain.

$\frac{3}{r} = \frac{3}{4}$ $\frac{3}{r} = \frac{3}{7}$ *Write the ratio of surface area to volume twice. Substitute 4 and 7 for r.*

$\frac{3}{4} > \frac{3}{7}$ *Compare the ratios.*

The barrel cactus with a radius of 7 inches has a greater chance of survival. Its surface-area-to-volume ratio is less than for a cactus with a radius of 4 inches.

Remember!

For two fractions with the same numerator, the value of the fraction with a greater denominator is less than the value of the other fraction.

$9 > 3$

$\frac{2}{9} < \frac{2}{3}$

CHECK IT OUT! 5. Which barrel cactus has less of a chance to survive in the desert, one with a radius of 6 inches or one with a radius of 3 inches? Explain. **The barrel cactus with a radius of 3 inches has less of a chance to survive. Its surface-area-to-volume ratio is greater than for a cactus with a radius of 6 inches.**

THINK AND DISCUSS

1. Write a rational expression that has an excluded value that cannot be identified when the expression is in its simplified form.

2. **GET ORGANIZED** Copy and complete the graphic organizer. In each box, write and simplify one of the given rational expressions using the most appropriate method. $\frac{x-3}{x^2-6x+9}, \frac{5x^4}{x^2}, \frac{4-x}{x-4}, \frac{4x^2-4x}{8x}$

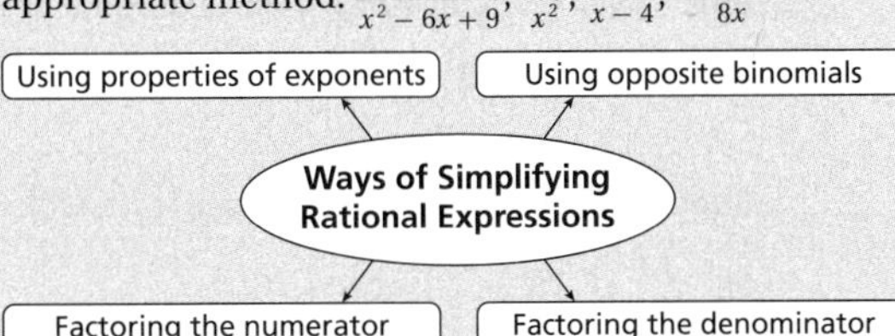

Power Presentations with PowerPoint®

Additional Examples

Example 5

A theater at an amusement park is shaped like a sphere. The sphere is held up with support rods.

a. What is the ratio of the theater's volume to its surface area? (*Hint:* For a sphere, $V = \frac{4}{3}\pi r^3$ and $S = 4\pi r^2$.) $\frac{r}{3}$

b. Use this ratio to find the ratio of the theater's volume to its surface area when the radius is 45 feet. 15

INTERVENTION Questioning Strategies

EXAMPLE 5

- How do you know which expression is written in the numerator and which is written in the denominator?

3 Close

Summarize

Remind students that they must use the original, not simplified, denominator of a rational expression when finding excluded values.

Ask students why x and 2 in $\frac{x^2+2}{x+4}$ cannot be divided out. They are not factors.

ONGOING ASSESSMENT and INTERVENTION

***Diagnose Before* the Lesson**
12-3 Warm Up, TE p. 886

***Monitor During* the Lesson**
Check It Out! Exercises, SE pp. 886–889
Questioning Strategies, TE pp. 887–889

***Assess After* the Lesson**
12-3 Lesson Quiz, TE p. 892
Alternative Assessment, TE p. 892

Answers to *Think and Discuss*

1. Possible answer: The expression $\frac{x+2}{x^2+5x+6}$ has the excluded values −2 and −3, but −2 cannot be identified as an excluded value in the simplified form, $\frac{1}{x+3}$.
2. See p. A11.

12-3 Exercises

Assignment Guide

Assign *Guided Practice* exercises as necessary.

If you finished Examples **1–3**
Basic 24–37, 43–45
Average 24–37, 43–45
Advanced 24–37, 43–45, 59–61

If you finished Examples **1–5**
Basic 24–52, 54–58, 68–73
Average 24–61, 68–73
Advanced 24–42, 49–73

Homework Quick Check
Quickly check key concepts.
Exercises: 26, 28, 34, 38, 41

Teaching Tip **Multiple Representations** For the formula of the area of a trapezoid in **Exercise 23**, the 2 in the denominator can be written as a coefficient of $\frac{1}{2}$, so the area of a trapezoid can be expressed as $\frac{1}{2}(b_1 + b_2)h$ or $\frac{1}{2}h(b_1 + b_2)$.

State Resources

12-3 Exercises

go.hrw.com
Homework Help Online
KEYWORD: MA7 12-3
Parent Resources Online
KEYWORD: MA7 Parent

GUIDED PRACTICE

1. **Vocabulary** What is true about both the numerator and denominator of rational expressions? **Both the numerator and denominator are polynomials.**

SEE EXAMPLE 1 p. 886

Find any excluded values of each rational expression.

2. $\frac{5}{m}$ **0**
3. $\frac{x+2}{x^2-8x}$ **0, 8**
4. $\frac{p^2}{p^2-2p-15}$ **−3, 5**

SEE EXAMPLE 2 p. 887

Simplify each rational expression, if possible. Identify any excluded values.

5. $\frac{4a^2}{8a}$ $\mathbf{\frac{a}{2}; a \neq 0}$
6. $\frac{2d^2+12d}{d+6}$ $\mathbf{2d; d \neq -6}$
7. $\frac{2}{y+3}$ $\mathbf{\frac{2}{y+3}; y \neq -3}$
8. $\frac{10}{5-y}$ $\mathbf{\frac{10}{5-y}; y \neq 5}$
9. $\frac{2h}{2h+4}$ $\mathbf{\frac{h}{h+2}; h \neq -2}$
10. $\frac{3(x+4)}{6x}$ $\mathbf{\frac{x+4}{2x}; x \neq 0}$

Simplify each rational expression, if possible.

SEE EXAMPLE 3 p. 887

19. not possible

11. $\frac{b+4}{b^2+5b+4}$ $\mathbf{\frac{1}{b+1}}$
12. $\frac{s^2-4}{s^2+4s+4}$ $\mathbf{\frac{s-2}{s+2}}$
13. $\frac{c^2+5c+6}{(c+3)(c-4)}$ $\mathbf{\frac{c+2}{c-4}}$
14. $\frac{(x-2)(x+1)}{x^2+4x+3}$ $\mathbf{\frac{x-2}{x+3}}$
15. $\frac{j^2-25}{j^2+2j-15}$ $\mathbf{\frac{j-5}{j-3}}$
16. $\frac{p+1}{p^2-4p-5}$ $\mathbf{\frac{1}{p-5}}$

SEE EXAMPLE 4 p. 888

17. $\frac{2n-16}{64-n^2}$ $\mathbf{-\frac{2}{8+n}}$
18. $\frac{8-4x}{2x^2-12x+16}$ $\mathbf{-\frac{2}{x-4}}$
19. $\frac{10-5r}{r^2-4r-12}$
20. $\frac{2x-14}{49-x^2}$ $\mathbf{-\frac{2}{7+x}}$
21. $\frac{5q-50}{100-q^2}$ $\mathbf{-\frac{5}{10+q}}$
22. $\frac{36-12a}{a^2+2a-15}$ $\mathbf{-\frac{12}{a+5}}$

SEE EXAMPLE 5 p. 889

23. **Construction** The side of a triangular roof will have the same height h and base b_2 as the side of a trapezoidal roof.

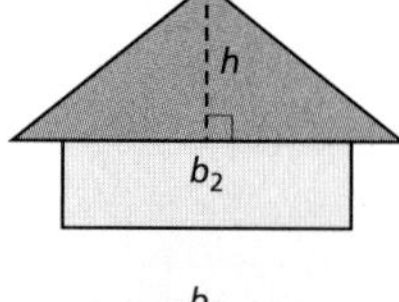

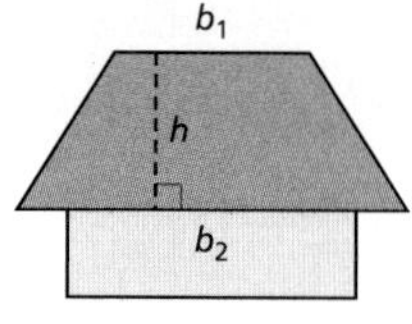

a. What is the ratio of the area of the triangular roof to the area of the trapezoidal roof? $\mathbf{\frac{b_2}{b_1+b_2}}$
($Hint:$ For a triangle, $A = \frac{1}{2}b_2h$. For a trapezoid, $A = \frac{b_1+b_2}{2}h$.)

b. Compare the ratio from part **a** to what the ratio will be if b_1 is doubled for the trapezoidal roof and b_2 is doubled for both roofs. **They will be the same:** $\mathbf{\frac{b_2}{b_1+b_2}}$.

PRACTICE AND PROBLEM SOLVING

Find any excluded values of each rational expression.

24. $\frac{c}{c^2+c}$ **−1, 0**
25. $\frac{2}{-3x}$ **0**
26. $\frac{4}{x^2-3x-10}$ **−2, 5**
27. $\frac{n^2-1}{2n^2-7n-4}$ $\mathbf{-\frac{1}{2}, 4}$

Simplify each rational expression, if possible. Identify any excluded values.

28. $\frac{4d^3+4d^2}{d+1}$ $\mathbf{4d^2; d \neq -1}$
29. $\frac{3m^2}{m-4}$ **already simplified;** $\mathbf{m \neq 4}$
30. $\frac{10y^4}{2y}$ $\mathbf{5y^3; y \neq 0}$
31. $\frac{2t^2}{16t}$ $\mathbf{\frac{t}{8}; t \neq 0}$

12-3 READING STRATEGIES

The table below shows examples of the many ways that rational expressions can be simplified.

Use Properties of Exponents	Factor out Common Monomials	Factor Trinomials & Special Products	Use Opposite Binomials
$\frac{4m^5}{24m^2}$	$\frac{2b^2-18b}{b-9}$	$\frac{x^2-9}{x^2+2x-15}$	$\frac{6t-t^2}{t^2-4t-12}$
$\frac{m^3}{6}$	$\frac{2b(b-9)}{b-9}$	$\frac{(x+3)(x-3)}{(x+5)(x-3)}$	$\frac{t(6-t)}{(t+2)(t-6)}$
	$2b$	$\frac{x+3}{x+5}$	$\frac{t(-1)(t-6)}{(t+2)(t-6)}$
			$-\frac{t}{(t+2)}$

Use the table to answer the following.

1. Look at the first column. Explain how $\frac{4m^5}{24m^2}$ was simplified to $\frac{m^2}{6}$.
   $\frac{4}{24}$ simplified to $\frac{1}{6}$ and the exponents were subtracted, making $\frac{m^5}{m^2} = m^3$.
2. Look at the second column. What expression was divided out of the numerator and denominator? $b - 9$
3. Look at the third column. What type of special product was in the numerator? difference of squares
4. Look at the fourth column. What happened in the numerator? $(6 - t)$ became $(-1)(t - 6)$

Simplify each rational expression.

5. $\frac{3t^4}{9t^6}$ $\frac{1}{3t^2}$
6. $\frac{n^4+3n^3}{2n^2+6n}$ $\frac{n^2}{2}$
7. $\frac{4c+4}{2c^2-5c-7}$ $\frac{4}{2c-7}$
8. $\frac{18-2x}{x^2-81}$ $-\frac{2}{x+9}$

12-3 RETEACH

A **rational expression** is an algebraic expression whose numerator and denominator are polynomials.

Exclude any values from a rational expression that make the denominator equal zero.

Find any excluded values of $\frac{6x}{x^2-5x}$.

$\frac{6x}{x^2-5x}$

$x^2 - 5x = 0$ *Set denominator = 0.*

$x(x-5) = 0$ *Factor.*

$x = 0$ or $x - 5 = 0$ *Zero Product Property*
$+5 \quad +5$
$x = 5$

The excluded values are 0 and 5.

Simplify $\frac{x+4}{2x^2+8x}$, **if possible. Identify any excluded values.**

$\frac{x+4}{2x^2+8x}$

$\frac{x+4}{2x(x+4)}$ Factor the denominator.

Find excluded values here.

$\frac{(x+4)^1}{2x(x+4)^1}$ Divide out common factors.

$\frac{1}{2x}$ Simplify.

Remember to find the excluded value from the original equation (not the simplified one).
The excluded values are 0 and −4.

Identify any excluded values.

1. $\frac{3}{4x}$ 0
2. $\frac{5x}{3x^2+15x}$ 0; −5
3. $\frac{6}{x^2-5x-14}$ −2, 7

Simplify each rational expression, if possible. Identify any excluded values.

4. $\frac{4x}{20x^3}$ $\frac{1}{5x^2}; x \neq 0$
5. $\frac{x+3}{x-4}$ $\frac{x+3}{x-4}; x \neq 4$
6. $\frac{27x}{3x^2}$ $\frac{9}{x}; x \neq 0$
7. $\frac{6}{3x+9}$ $\frac{2}{x+3}; x \neq -3$
8. $\frac{x+4}{2x^2+8x}$ $\frac{1}{2x}; x \neq 0, x \neq -4$
9. $\frac{5x^2-20x}{x-4}$ $5x; x \neq 4$

Independent Practice

For Exercises	See Example
24–27	1
28–31	2
32–37	3
38–40	4
41	5

Extra Practice
Skills Practice p. S26
Application Practice p. S39

Multi-Step Test Prep Exercise 52 involves writing a rational function. This exercise prepares students for the Multi-Step Test Prep on page 896.

Answers

41a. $\dfrac{2(\ell w + \ell h + wh)}{\ell wh}$

b. Box A; the surface area of box A is 184 in^2 and the surface area of box B is 232 in^2. The volumes are the same, so the company should use the box with less surface area, box A.

Simplify each rational expression, if possible.

32. $\dfrac{q-6}{q^2-9q+18}$ $\quad \dfrac{1}{q-3}$

33. $\dfrac{z^2-2z+1}{z^2-1}$ $\quad \dfrac{z-1}{z+1}$

34. $\dfrac{t-3}{t^2-5t+6}$ $\quad \dfrac{1}{t-2}$

35. $\dfrac{p^2-6p-7}{p^2-4p-5}$ $\quad \dfrac{p-7}{p-5}$

36. $\dfrac{x^2-1}{x^2+4x+3}$ $\quad \dfrac{x-1}{x+3}$

37. $\dfrac{2x-4}{x^2-6x+8}$ $\quad \dfrac{2}{x-4}$

38. $\dfrac{20-4x}{x^2-25}$ $\quad -\dfrac{4}{x+5}$

39. $\dfrac{3-3b}{3b^2+18b-21}$ $\quad -\dfrac{1}{b+7}$

40. $\dfrac{3v-36}{144-v^2}$ $\quad -\dfrac{3}{12+v}$

LINK Biology

As a result of a nationwide policy of protection and reintroduction, the population of bald eagles in the lower 48 states grew from 417 nesting pairs in 1963 to more than 6400 nesting pairs in 2000.

Source: U.S. Fish and Wildlife Service

41. **Geometry** When choosing package sizes, a company wants a package that uses the least amount of material to hold the greatest volume of product.
   a. What is the surface-area-to-volume ratio for a rectangular prism? (*Hint:* For a rectangular prism, $S = 2\ell w + 2\ell h + 2wh$ and $V = \ell wh$.)
   b. Which box should the company choose? Explain.

42. **Biology** The table gives information on two populations of animals that were released into the wild. Suppose 16 more predators and 20 more prey are released into the area. Write and simplify a rational expression to show the ratio of predator to prey. $\dfrac{4x+16}{5x+20}$; $\dfrac{4}{5}$

	Predator	Prey
Original Population	x	x
Population 5 Years Later	$4x$	$5x$

Simplify each rational expression, if possible.

43. $\dfrac{p^2+12p+36}{12p+72}$ $\quad \dfrac{p+6}{12}$

44. $\dfrac{3n^3+33n^2+15n}{3n^3+15n}$ $\quad \dfrac{n^2+11n+5}{n^2+5}$

45. $\dfrac{a}{2a+a}$ $\quad \dfrac{1}{3}$

46. $\dfrac{j-5}{j^2-25}$ $\quad \dfrac{1}{j+5}$

47. $\dfrac{6w^2+11w-7}{6w-3}$ $\quad \dfrac{3w+7}{3}$

48. $\dfrac{n^2-n-56}{n^2-16n+64}$ $\quad \dfrac{n+7}{n-8}$

49. $\dfrac{(x+1)^2}{x^2+2x+1}$ $\quad 1$

50. $\dfrac{5}{(x+5)^2}$ $\quad$ not possible

51. $\dfrac{25-x^2}{x^2-3x-10}$ $\quad -\dfrac{5+x}{x+2}$

52. This problem will prepare you for the Multi-Step Test Prep on page 896.

It takes 250 workdays to build a house. The number of construction days is determined by the size of the crew. The crew includes one manager who supervises workers and checks for problems, but does not do any building.

   a. The table shows the number of construction days as a function of the number of workers. Copy and complete the table.
   b. Use the table to write a function that represents the number of construction days. $y = \dfrac{250}{x-1}$
   c. Identify the excluded values of the function. $x = 1$

Crew Size (x)	$\dfrac{\text{Workdays}}{\text{Workers}}$	Construction Days (y)
2	$\dfrac{250}{2-1}$	250
3	$\dfrac{250}{3-1}$	125
6	$\dfrac{250}{6-1}$	50
11	$\dfrac{250}{11-1}$	25

12-3 PROBLEM SOLVING

A food company is considering two types of cylindrical cans for a new trail mix. The company wants a can that uses the least material for the greatest volume. For a cylinder, $S = 2\pi r^2 + 2\pi rh$ and $V = \pi r^2 h$.

1. What is the surface-area-to-volume ratio for any cylinder? $\dfrac{2(r+h)}{rh}$

2. Can A has radius 2 in. and height 3 in. What is the surface-area-to-volume ratio for Can A? $\dfrac{10}{6} = 1.\overline{6}$

3. Can B has radius 1.5 in. and height 4 in. What is the surface-area-to-volume ratio for Can B? $\dfrac{11}{6} = 1.8\overline{3}$

4. Which can should the company choose? Explain. **Can A; the ratio is lesser, Can A uses less material for each unit of volume.**

Select the best answer.

5. For any circle with radius r, $P = 2\pi r$ and $A = \pi r^2$. Which expression represents the perimeter-to-area ratio?

A $2r$ C $\dfrac{r}{2}$
B $\dfrac{2}{r}$ D $\dfrac{1}{2r}$

6. Tyrone takes an 8-by-8 square piece of cardboard and cuts x-by-x squares out of each corner. (All units are inches.) He then folds up the sides to form a box with no top. Which expression represents the surface-area-to-volume ratio? (*Hint:* For the surface area, find the area of the entire piece of cardboard and subtract the squares that were removed.)

8, x, $8-2x$, There is no top

F $\dfrac{1}{x}$ H $\dfrac{8}{x(4-x)}$
G $\dfrac{1}{2x(1-16x)}$ **J** $\dfrac{4+x}{x(4-x)}$

7. In 2000, there are x mountain lions (predators) and x deer (prey) in a wildlife preserve. In 2005, the populations level off at $3x$ mountain lions and $4x$ deer, for a predator-to-prey ratio of $\dfrac{3}{4}$. If the wildlife preserve adds 12 more deer in 2007, how many mountain lions should also be added to keep the predator-to-prey ratio equivalent to $\dfrac{3}{4}$?

A 9 C 16
B 12 D 20

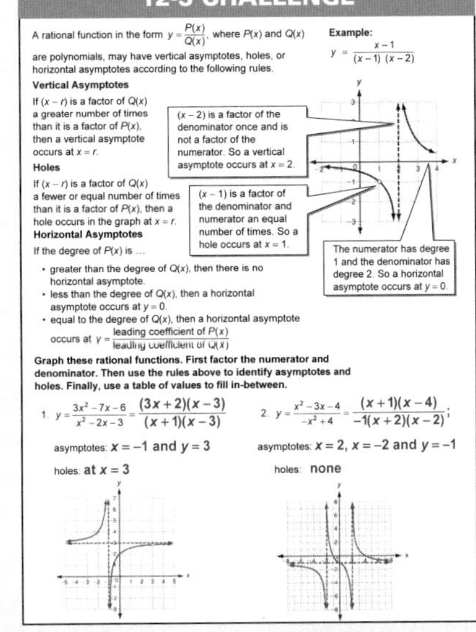

12-3 CHALLENGE

A rational function in the form $y = \dfrac{P(x)}{Q(x)}$, where $P(x)$ and $Q(x)$ are polynomials, may have vertical asymptotes, holes, or horizontal asymptotes according to the following rules.

Vertical Asymptotes
If $(x-r)$ is a factor of $Q(x)$ a greater number of times than it is a factor of $P(x)$, then a vertical asymptote occurs at $x = r$.

Holes
If $(x-r)$ is a factor of $Q(x)$ a fewer or equal number of times than it is a factor of $P(x)$, then a hole occurs in the graph at $x = r$.

Horizontal Asymptotes
If the degree of $P(x)$ is ...
- greater than the degree of $Q(x)$, then there is no horizontal asymptote.
- less than the degree of $Q(x)$, then a horizontal asymptote occurs at $y = 0$.
- equal to the degree of $Q(x)$, then a horizontal asymptote occurs at $y = \dfrac{\text{leading coefficient of } P(x)}{\text{leading coefficient of } Q(x)}$

Example: $y = \dfrac{x-1}{(x-1)(x-2)}$

$(x-2)$ is a factor of the denominator once and is not a factor of the numerator. So a vertical asymptote occurs at $x = 2$.

$(x-1)$ is a factor of the denominator and numerator an equal number of times. So a hole occurs at $x = 1$.

The numerator has degree 1 and the denominator has degree 2. So a horizontal asymptote occurs at $y = 0$.

Graph these rational functions. First factor the numerator and denominator. Then use the rules above to identify asymptotes and holes. Finally, use a table of values to fill in-between.

1. $y = \dfrac{3x^2-7x-6}{x^2-2x-3} = \dfrac{(3x+2)(x-3)}{(x+1)(x-3)}$
asymptotes: $x = -1$ and $y = 3$
holes: at $x = 3$

2. $y = \dfrac{x^2-3x-4}{-x^2+4} = \dfrac{(x+1)(x-4)}{-1(x+2)(x-2)}$;
asymptotes: $x = 2$, $x = -2$ and $y = -1$
holes: none

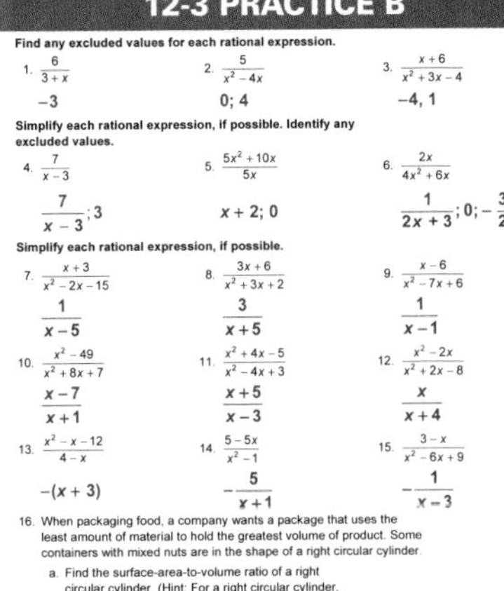

12-3 PRACTICE A

12-3 PRACTICE C

12-3 PRACTICE B

Find any excluded values for each rational expression.

1. $\dfrac{6}{3+x}$ $\quad -3$

2. $\dfrac{5}{x^2-4x}$ $\quad 0; 4$

3. $\dfrac{x+6}{x^2+3x-4}$ $\quad -4, 1$

Simplify each rational expression, if possible. Identify any excluded values.

4. $\dfrac{7}{x-3}$ $\quad \dfrac{7}{x-3}; 3$

5. $\dfrac{5x^2+10x}{5x}$ $\quad x+2; 0$

6. $\dfrac{2x}{4x^2+6x}$ $\quad \dfrac{1}{2x+3}; 0; -\dfrac{3}{2}$

Simplify each rational expression, if possible.

7. $\dfrac{x+3}{x^2-2x-15}$ $\quad \dfrac{1}{x-5}$

8. $\dfrac{3x+6}{x^2+3x+2}$ $\quad \dfrac{3}{x+5}$

9. $\dfrac{x-6}{x^2-7x+6}$ $\quad \dfrac{1}{x-1}$

10. $\dfrac{x^2-49}{x^2+8x+7}$ $\quad \dfrac{x-7}{x+1}$

11. $\dfrac{x^2+4x-5}{x^2-4x+3}$ $\quad \dfrac{x+5}{x-3}$

12. $\dfrac{x^2-2x}{x^2+2x-8}$ $\quad \dfrac{x}{x+4}$

13. $\dfrac{x^2-x-12}{4-x}$ $\quad -(x+3)$

14. $\dfrac{5-5x}{x^2-1}$ $\quad -\dfrac{5}{x+1}$

15. $\dfrac{3-x}{x^2-6x+9}$ $\quad -\dfrac{1}{x-3}$

16. When packaging food, a company wants a package that uses the least amount of material to hold the greatest volume of product. Some containers with mixed nuts are in the shape of a right circular cylinder.
   a. Find the surface-area-to-volume ratio of a right circular cylinder. (Hint: For a right circular cylinder, $S = 2\pi rh + 2\pi r^2$ and $V = \pi r^2 h$.) $\quad \dfrac{2(r+h)}{rh}$
   b. Container A has a radius of 2 in. and a height of 5 in. Container B has a radius of 4 in. and a height of 8 in. Which container should the company choose? Explain.
   ratio for A: $\dfrac{7}{5}$; ratio for B: $\dfrac{3}{4}$; The company wants the smallest surface-area-to-volume ratio, so it should choose container B.

Geometry In **Exercise 53,** the area of a square is s^2, where s is the length of one side. Because a cube has 6 sides, the surface area is $6s^2$.

In **Exercise 56,** students who chose **C** may have factored incorrectly. Students who chose **A** may have simply matched the numbers given in the problem.

Journal

Have students compare and contrast simplifying fractions and simplifying rational expressions.

ALTERNATIVE ASSESSMENT

Write $\frac{(x+a)(x+a)}{(x+a)(x+b)}$ and $\frac{c(x-d)}{(x+c)(d-x)}$ on the board. Have students replace a, b, c, and d with positive integers and then multiply the factors. Have students then exchange those two expressions with a partner. Tell students to simplify their partner's expressions and identify the excluded values.

Power Presentations with PowerPoint®

12-3 Lesson Quiz

Find any excluded values of each rational expression.

1. $\frac{3}{4x}$ 0
2. $\frac{4h^2}{3h^2 - 6h}$ 0, 2

Simplify each rational expression, if possible.

3. $\frac{5t^3}{10t^2 + 15t}$ $\frac{t^2}{2t+3}$
4. $\frac{m+2}{m^2 - 3m - 10}$ $\frac{1}{m-5}$
5. $\frac{n^2 - 1}{1 - n}$ $-n - 1$
6. Calvino is building a rectangular tree house. The length is 10 feet longer than the width. His friend Fabio is building a square tree house. The sides of Fabio's tree house are equal to the width of Calvino's tree house.
   a. What is the ratio of the area of Calvino's tree house to the area of Fabio's tree house? $\frac{x+10}{x}$
   b. Use this ratio to find the ratio of the areas if the width of Calvino's tree house is 14 feet. $\frac{12}{7}$

Also available on transparency

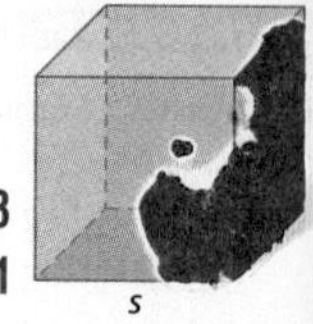

53. **Geometry** Let s represent the length of an edge of a cube.
    a. Write the ratio of a cube's surface area to volume in simplified form. (*Hint:* For a cube, $S = 6s^2$.) $\frac{6}{s}$
    b. What is the ratio of the cube's surface area to volume when $s = 2$? **3**
    c. What is the ratio of the cube's surface area to volume when $s = 6$? **1**

54. **Write About It** Explain how to find excluded values for a rational expression. **Set the denominator equal to 0 and solve for the variable.**
55. **Critical Thinking** Give an example of a rational expression that has x in both the numerator and denominator, but cannot be simplified. **Possible answer:** $\frac{x}{x+1}$

TEST PREP

56. Which expression is undefined for $x = 4$ and $x = -1$?
    Ⓐ $\frac{x-1}{x+4}$ Ⓑ $\frac{x-4}{x+4}$ Ⓒ $\frac{x}{x^2+3x-4}$ **Ⓓ** $\frac{x}{x^2-3x-4}$
57. Which expression is the ratio of the area of a triangle to the area of a rectangle that has the same base and height?
    Ⓕ $\frac{1}{2}$ Ⓖ $\frac{bh}{2}$ Ⓗ $\frac{(bh)^2}{2}$ Ⓙ 2
58. **Gridded Response** What is the excluded value for $\frac{x-4}{x^2-8x+16}$? **4**

CHALLENGE AND EXTEND

Tell whether each statement is sometimes, always, or never true. Explain.

59. A rational expression has an excluded value.
60. A rational expression has a variable in a square root in the numerator. **Never; the numerator must be a polynomial.**
61. The graph of a rational function has at least one asymptote.

Simplify each rational expression.

62. $\frac{9v - 6v^2}{4v^2 - 4v - 3}$ $-\frac{3v}{2v+1}$
63. $\frac{2a^2 - 7a + 3}{2a^2 + 9a - 5}$ $\frac{a-3}{a+5}$
64. $\frac{0.25y - 0.10}{0.25y^2 - 0.04}$ $\frac{5}{5y+2}$

Identify any excluded values of each rational expression.

65. $\frac{\frac{1}{4}x^2 - 7x + 49}{\frac{1}{4}x^2 - 49}$ ± 14
66. $\frac{-80x + 40x^2 + 40}{-30 - 30x^2 + 60x}$ 1
67. $\frac{6x + 12}{12x + 6x^2}$ $-2, 0$

SPIRAL REVIEW

68. A rectangle has an area of 24 square feet. Every dimension is multiplied by a scale factor, and the new rectangle has an area of 864 square feet. What is the scale factor? *(Lesson 2-8)* **6**

Use intercepts to graph the line described by each equation. *(Lesson 5-2)*

69. $5x - 3y = -15$
70. $y = 8x - 8$
71. $\frac{1}{2}x + y = 2$

For each of the following, let y vary inversely as x. *(Lesson 12-1)*

72. $x_1 = 2$, $y_1 = 4$, and $x_2 = 1$. Find y_2. **8**
73. $x_1 = 2$, $y_1 = -1$, and $y_2 = \frac{1}{3}$. Find x_2. **−6**

Answers

59. Sometimes; the rational expression $\frac{1}{x+1}$ has -1 as an excluded value, but the rational expression $\frac{1}{x^2+1}$ has no excluded values.
61. Sometimes; the rational function $y = \frac{1}{x+1}$ has $x = -1$ as an asymptote, but the rational function $y = \frac{x^3}{x^2+1}$ has no asymptotes.

69.

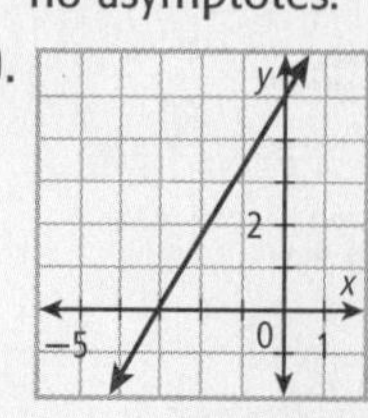

70.

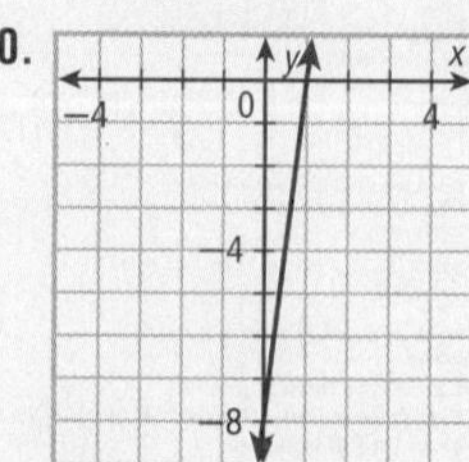

71.

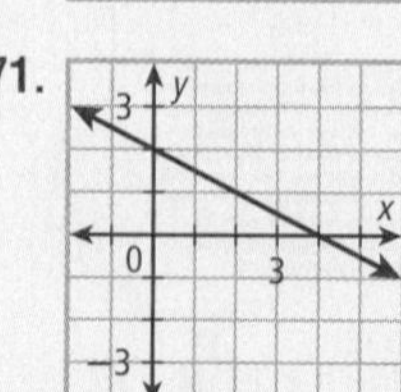

Graph Rational Functions

You can use a graphing calculator to graph rational functions and to compare graphs of rational functions before and after they are simplified.

Use with Lesson 12-3

go.hrw.com
Lab Resources Online
KEYWORD: MA7 Lab12

Activity

Simplify $y = \frac{x-1}{x^2-5x+4}$ and give any excluded values. Then graph both the original function and the simplified function and compare the graphs.

1. Simplify the function and find the excluded values.
$\frac{x-1}{x^2-5x+4} = \frac{x-1}{(x-1)(x-4)} = \frac{1}{x-4}$; excluded values: 4, 1
2. Enter $y = \frac{x-1}{x^2-5x+4}$ and $y = \frac{1}{x-4}$ into your calculator as shown and press GRAPH.

3. To compare the graphs, press TRACE. At the top of the screen, you can see which graph the cursor is on. To change between graphs, press ▲ and ▼.
4. The graphs appear to be the same, but check the excluded values, 4 and 1. While on **Y1**, press 4 ENTER. Notice that there is no *y*-value at $x = 4$. The function is undefined.

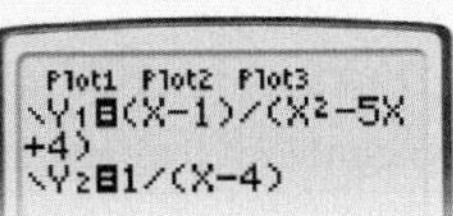
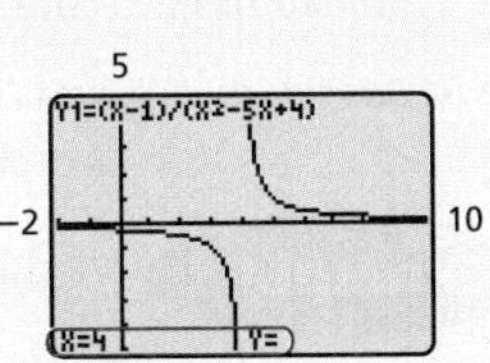

5. Press ▼ to switch to **Y2** and press 4 ENTER. This function is also undefined at $x = 4$. The graphs are the same at this excluded value.
6. Return to **Y1** and press 1 ENTER. This function is undefined at $x = 1$. However, this is not a vertical asymptote. Instead, this graph has a "hole" at $x = 1$.

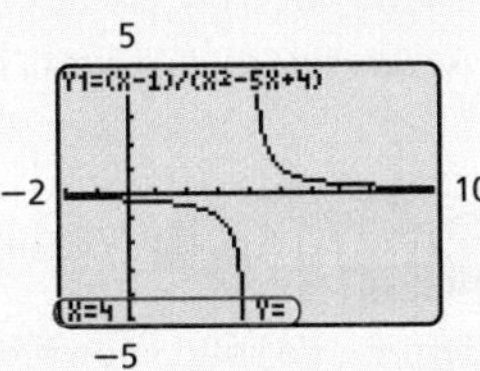
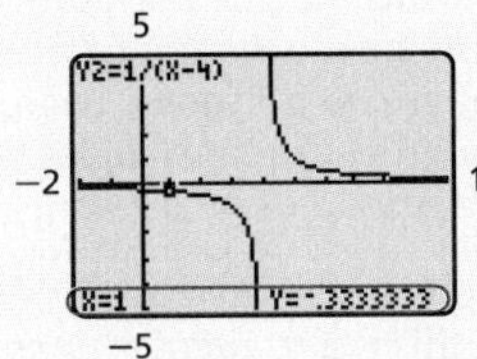

7. Switch to **Y2** and press 1 ENTER. This function is defined at $x = 1$. So the two graphs are the same except at $x = 1$.

Try This

1. Why is $x = 1$ an excluded value for one function but not for the other?
2. Are the functions $y = \frac{x-1}{x^2-5x+4}$ and $y = \frac{1}{x-4}$ truly equivalent for all values of *x*? Explain.
3. **Make a Conjecture** Complete each statement.
   a. If a value of *x* is excluded from a function and its simplified form, it appears on the graph as a(n) ___?___. **asymptote**
   b. If a value of *x* is excluded from a function but not its simplified form, it appears on the graph as a ___?___. **hole**

Technology Lab Organizer

Use with Lesson 12-3

Pacing:
Traditional $\frac{1}{2}$ day
Block $\frac{1}{4}$ day

Objective: Use a graphing calculator to explore rational functions.

Materials: graphing calculator

Resources

Technology Lab Activities
12-3 Lab Recording Sheet

Teach

Discuss

Tell students they can use the TABLE feature to compare the excluded values for each expression.

Close

Key Concept

Graphing calculators offer support for problems involving rational functions and expressions.

Assessment

Journal Have students explain how to show support for an algebraic simplification of a rational expression with a graphing calculator.

State Resources

Answers to *Try This*

1. When the denominator of $y = \frac{x-1}{(x-1)(x-4)}$ is set equal to 0 and solved for *x*, then *x* equals 1 or 4. However, when the denominator of $y = \frac{1}{x-4}$ is set equal to 0, the excluded value seems to be only 4.
2. No; for the value of $x = 1$, $y = \frac{x-1}{x^2-5x+4}$ is undefined, while $y = \frac{1}{x-4}$ is defined as $-\frac{1}{3}$.

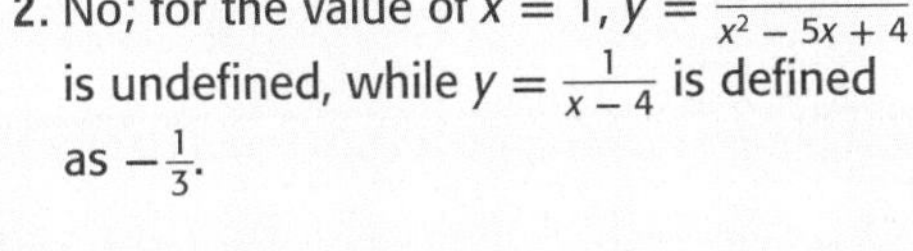

Organizer

Pacing:
Traditional $\frac{1}{2}$ day
Block $\frac{1}{4}$ day

Objective: Identify geometric solids represented by nets.

Teach

Remember

Students review prisms and pyramids and name them by the shapes of their bases.

Teaching Tip **Multiple Representations** Solid figures are three-dimensional figures. Discuss with students the differences between two-dimensional and three-dimensional figures.

Teaching Tip **Kinesthetic** If students have no prior experience with foundation plans, provide unit cubes (MK) so that they can explore building solids and relating their figures to the foundation plans.

State Resources

Representing Solid Figures

Connecting Algebra to Geometry

A *net* is a flat pattern that can be folded to make a solid figure. The net shows all of the faces and surfaces of the solid.

To identify the solid shown by a net, remember these properties of solids.

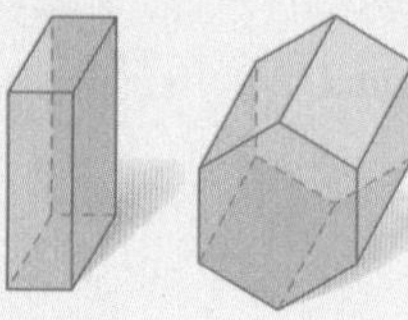

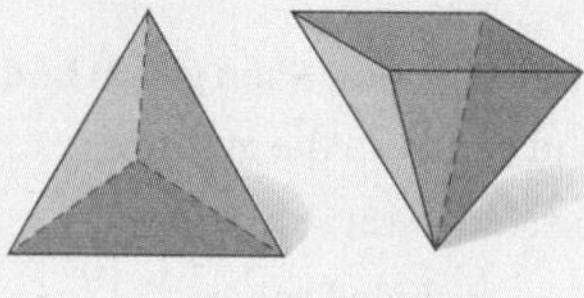

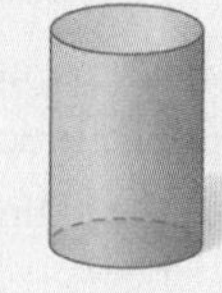

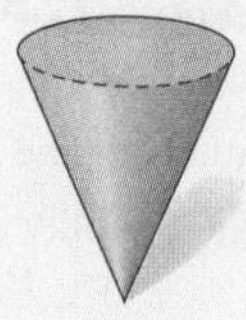

Prisms Pyramids Cylinder Cone

- A ***prism*** has two parallel, congruent bases that are polygons. The other faces are rectangles or parallelograms.
- A base of a ***pyramid*** is a polygon. The other faces are triangles.
- A ***cylinder*** has two congruent circles as its bases.
- A ***cone*** has one circle as its base.

Example 1

Identify the solid shown by this net.

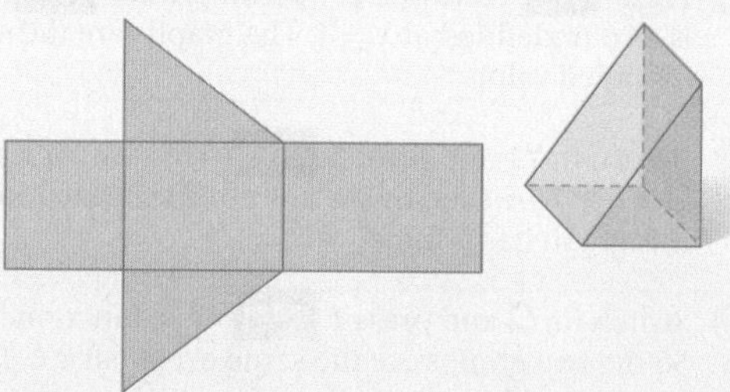

The faces are all polygons, so this is either a prism or a pyramid. Look for a pair of congruent polygons. There are two congruent right triangles. The solid is a *prism*.

A prism is named by the shape of its bases, so this is a *triangular prism*.

Try This

Identify the solid shown by each net.

1. cone

2.

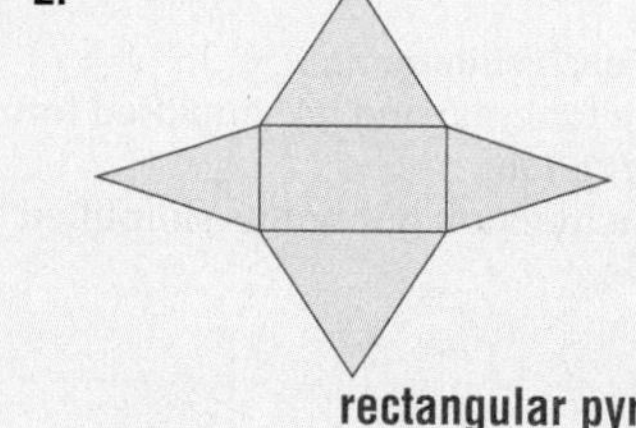

rectangular pyramid

3.

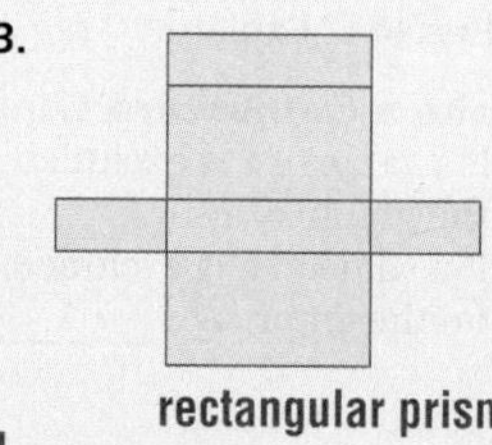

rectangular prism

Identify the solid shown by each net.

4.

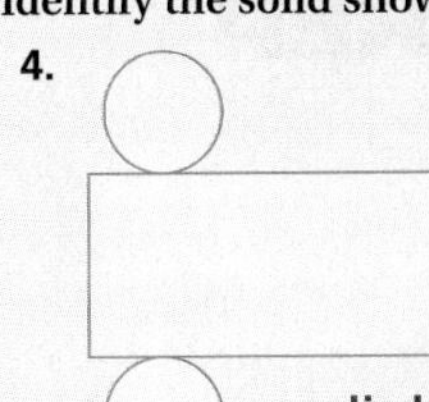

cylinder

5.

triangular pyramid

6.

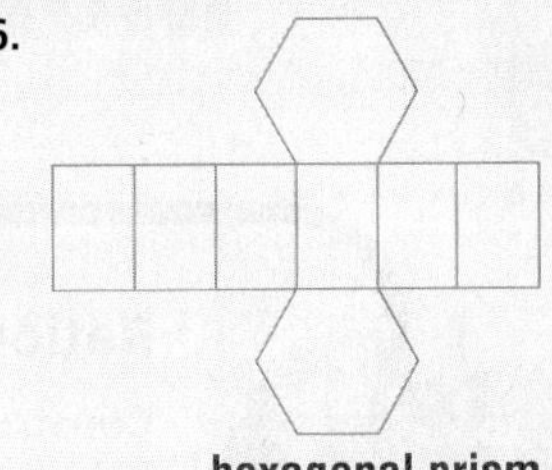

hexagonal prism

A foundation plan is a drawing that represents a solid made from cubes. The squares in the foundation plan are a top view of the solid. The number in each square shows the height of the solid at that point. The foundation plan shown is like a set of instructions for building the solid next to it.

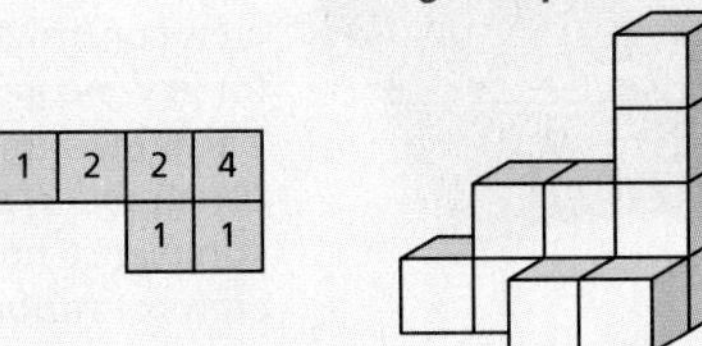

Example 2

Draw a foundation plan for this solid figure.

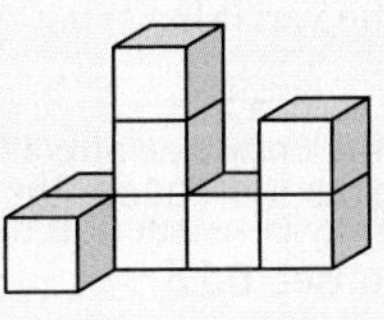

Use squares to show a top view of the solid.

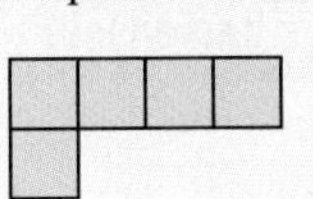

Put a number in each square to show the height at that point.

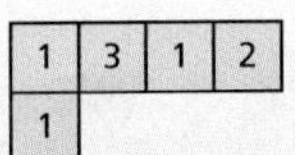

Try This

Draw a foundation plan for each solid figure.

7.

8.

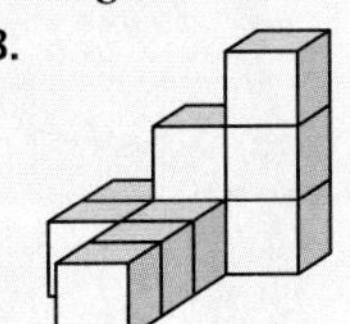

9.

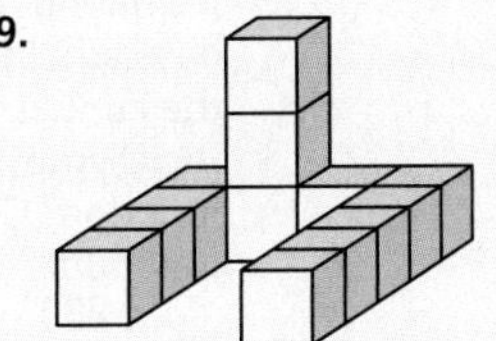

10.

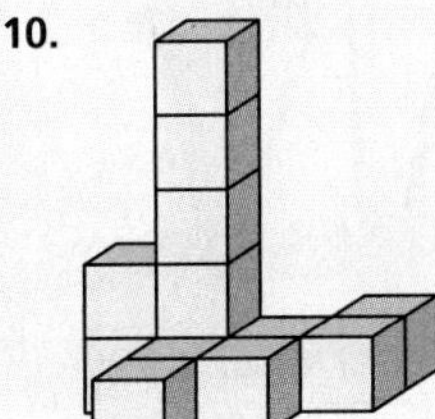

11.

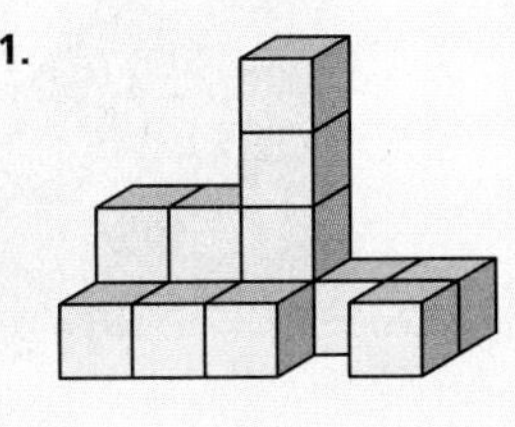

12.

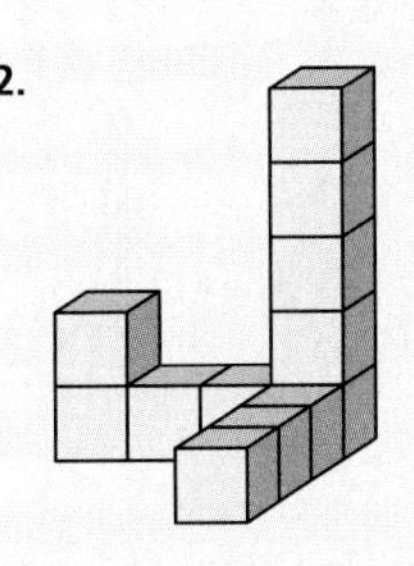

Close

Assess

How are a net and a foundation plan alike? How are they different?
Possible answer: They both are 2-D ways of showing 3-D figures. The foundation plan is only useful if the figure is built from cubes.

Answers

7.

3	2	1	1
			1
			1

8.

1	2	3
1	1	
	1	
	1	

9.

1	3	1	1
1			1
1			1
1			1
			1

10.

			1
2	5	1	1
	1	1	
	1		

11.

2	2	4	1	1
1	1	1		1

12.

2	1	1	5
			1
			1
			1

SECTION 12A MULTI-STEP TEST PREP

Organizer

Objective: Assess students' ability to apply concepts and skills from Lessons 12-1 through 12-3 in a real-world format.

Online Edition

Resources

Algebra I Assessments
www.mathtekstoolkit.org

For additional assessment activities, see www.utdanacenter.org

Problem	Text Reference
1	Lesson 12-2
2	Lessons 12-1, 12-2, 12-3
3	Lesson 12-1
4–6	Lesson 12-2
7	Lessons 12-1, 12-2, 12-3

Answers

2. $y = \frac{200}{x}$; x = the number of people in the crew; y = the number of construction days; inverse variation

State Resources

go.hrw.com
State Resources Online
KEYWORD: MA7 Resources

CHAPTER 12

MULTI-STEP TEST PREP

SECTION 12A

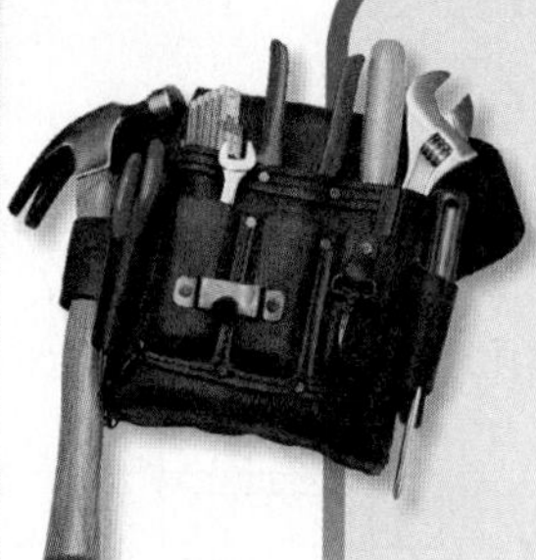

Rational Functions and Expressions

Construction Daze

Robert is part of a volunteer crew constructing houses for low-income families. The table shows how many construction days it takes to complete a house for work crews of various sizes.

Crew Size	Construction Days	Workdays
2	100	200
4	50	200
8	25	200
10	20	200
20	10	200

1. Working at the same rate, how many construction days should it take a crew of 40 people to build the house? **5**
2. Express the number of construction days as a function of the crew size. Define the variables. What type of relationship is formed in the situation?
3. Explain how the crew size affects the number of construction days. **As the crew size increases, the number of construction days decreases.**
4. About how many construction days would it take a crew of 32 to complete a house? **6.25**
5. If a crew can complete a house in 12.5 days, how many people are in the crew? **16**
6. What are a reasonable domain and range of the function? **D: natural numbers; R: $y > 0$**
7. Suppose there are two managers that do not contribute to the work of building the house, yet are counted as part of the crew. Express the number of construction days as a function of the crew size. What are the asymptotes of this function? Graph the function.
$y = \frac{200}{x-2}$; $x = 2$ and $y = 0$

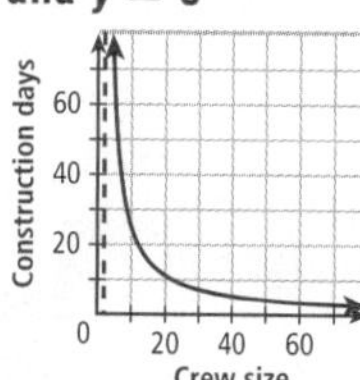

INTERVENTION

Scaffolding Questions

1. What is the pattern in the table? As the crew doubles, workdays halve.

2–3. What is the constant? construction units

4–5. What do the variables represent in the function you wrote for **Problem 2**? crew size and workdays

6. Does it make sense to have a negative number of people or days? no

7. What is the new variable expression for crew size? $x - 2$

Extension

Assuming that crew size varies inversely as workdays, how long would it take 12 workers to complete a house that requires 250 construction tasks?

$y = \frac{250}{12} = 20\frac{5}{6}$, or almost 21 days

CHAPTER 12

SECTION 12A

Quiz for Lessons 12-1 Through 12-3

12-1 Inverse Variation

Tell whether each relationship represents an inverse variation. Explain.

1.

x	−5	−4	−3
y	10	−8	6

No; the product xy is not constant.

2.

x	18	9	6
y	2	4	6

Yes; the product xy is constant.

3. $y = \frac{3}{x}$ yes
4. $y + x = \frac{3}{4}$ no
5. $xy = -2$ yes
6. $y = \frac{x}{5}$ no
7. Write and graph the inverse variation in which $y = 3$ when $x = 2$. $y = \frac{6}{x}$
8. Write and graph the inverse variation in which $y = 4$ when $x = -1$. $y = \frac{-4}{x}$
9. The number of calculators Mrs. Hopkins can buy for the classroom varies inversely as the cost of each calculator. She can buy 24 calculators that cost \$60 each. How many calculators can she buy if they cost \$80 each? 18 calculators

12-2 Rational Functions

Identify the excluded value and the vertical and horizontal asymptotes for each rational function. Then graph each function.

10. $y = \frac{12}{x}$
11. $y = \frac{6}{x + 2}$
12. $y = \frac{4}{x - 1}$
13. $y = \frac{2}{x + 1} - 3$
14. Jeff builds model train layouts. He has \$75 to spend on packages of miniature landscape items. He receives 6 free packages with each order. The number of packages y that Jeff can buy is given by $y = \frac{75}{x} + 6$, where x represents the cost of each package in dollars. Describe the reasonable domain and range values and graph the function. D: $x > 0$; R: natural numbers > 6

12-3 Simplifying Rational Expressions

Find any excluded values of each rational expression.

15. $\frac{15}{n}$ 0
16. $\frac{p}{p - 8}$ 8
17. $\frac{x + 2}{x^2 + 6x + 8}$ −4, −2
18. $\frac{t - 1}{t^2 + t}$ −1, 0

Simplify each rational expression, if possible. Identify any excluded values.

19. $\frac{3x^2}{6x^3}$ $\frac{1}{2x}$; $x \neq 0$
20. $\frac{2n}{n^2 - 3n}$
21. $\frac{s + 1}{s^2 - 4s - 5}$
22. $\frac{12 - 3x}{x^2 - 8x + 16}$
23. Suppose a cone and a cylinder have the same radius and that the slant height ℓ of the cone is the same as the height h of the cylinder. Find the ratio of the cone's surface area to the cylinder's surface area. $\frac{1}{2}$

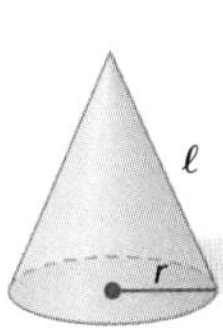
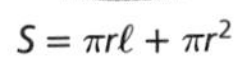

$S = \pi r\ell + \pi r^2$

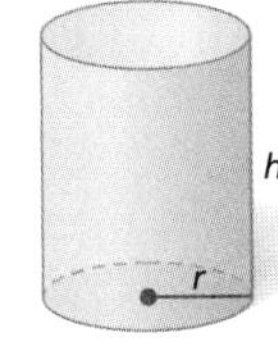

$S = 2\pi rh + 2\pi r^2$

20. $\frac{2}{n - 3}$; $n \neq 0$ and $n \neq 3$

21. $\frac{1}{s - 5}$; $s \neq -1$ and $s \neq 5$

22. $-\frac{3}{x - 4}$; $x \neq 4$

READY TO GO ON? SECTION 12A

Organizer

Objective: Assess students' mastery of concepts and skills in Lessons 12-1 through 12-3.

Resources

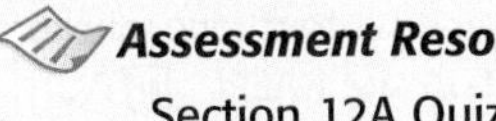

Assessment Resources
Section 12A Quiz

Teacher One Stop™
Test & Practice Generator

INTERVENTION

Resources

Ready to Go On? Intervention and Enrichment **Worksheets**

Ready to Go On? **CD-ROM**

Ready to Go On? **Online**

my.hrw.com

Answers

3. $xy = 3$
4. cannot be written in the form $y = \frac{k}{x}$

5–6. For explanations, see p. A36.
7–8. For graphs, see p. A36.
10–13. See p. A36.
14. For graph, see p. A36.

READY TO GO ON?

Diagnose and Prescribe

NO INTERVENE

Ready to Go On? Intervention	*Ready to Go On? Intervention*, Section 12A: Worksheets	CD-ROM	Online
Lesson 12-1	12-1 Intervention	Activity 12-1	Diagnose and Prescribe Online
Lesson 12-2	12-2 Intervention	Activity 12-2	
Lesson 12-3	12-3 Intervention	Activity 12-3	

YES ENRICH

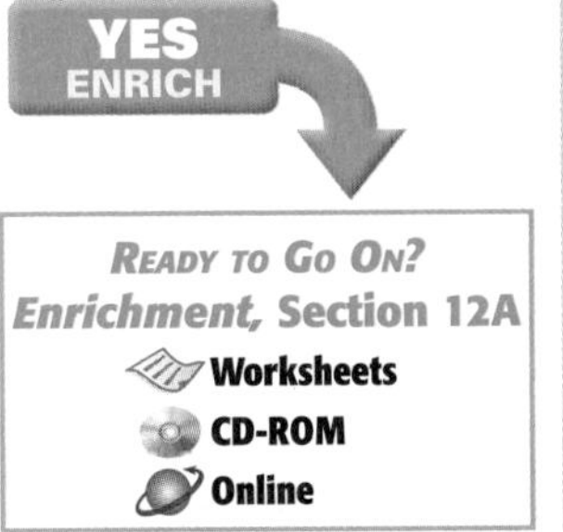

Ready to Go On? Enrichment, Section 12A
Worksheets
CD-ROM
Online

SECTION

12B Operations with Rational Expressions

One-Minute Section Planner

Lesson	Lab Resources	Materials
Lesson 12-4 Multiplying and Dividing Rational Expressions • Multiply and divide rational expressions. ☐ SAT-10 ☑ NAEP ☑ ACT ☑ SAT ☑ SAT Subject Tests		
Lesson 12-5 Adding and Subtracting Rational Expressions • Add and subtract rational expressions with like denominators. • Add and subtract rational expressions with unlike denominators. ☐ SAT-10 ☑ NAEP ☑ ACT ☑ SAT ☐ SAT Subject Tests		
12-6 Algebra Lab Model Polynomial Division • Use algebra tiles to model polynomial division. ☐ SAT-10 ☐ NAEP ☐ ACT ☐ SAT ☐ SAT Subject Tests	***Algebra Lab Activities*** 12-6 Lab Recording Sheet	**Required** algebra tiles (MK)
Lesson 12-6 Dividing Polynomials • Divide a polynomial by a monomial or binomial. ☐ SAT-10 ☑ NAEP ☑ ACT ☑ SAT ☐ SAT Subject Tests		**Optional** grid paper
Lesson 12-7 Solving Rational Equations • Solve rational equations. • Identify extraneous solutions. ☐ SAT-10 ☑ NAEP ☑ ACT ☑ SAT ☑ SAT Subject Tests		**Optional** 2 containers with different size pouring spouts, 1 bowl
Extension Trigonometric Ratios • Find the three basic trigonometric ratios in a right triangle. • Use trigonometric ratios to find missing lengths. ☑ SAT-10 ☑ NAEP ☑ ACT ☑ SAT ☑ SAT Subject Tests		**Required** scientific calculator **Optional** graphing calculator

MK = *Manipulatives Kit*

RATIONAL EXPRESSIONS

Lessons 12-3 to 12-5

A *rational expression* is an expression whose numerator and denominator are polynomials. In the same way that a fraction cannot have a denominator of zero, a rational expression is not defined for values of the variable that make the polynomial in the denominator equal to zero. These values of the variable are called *excluded values.*

Students should understand that not all rational expressions have excluded values. For example, the rational expression $\frac{1}{x^2 + 1}$ has the polynomial $x^2 + 1$ as its denominator. This polynomial is not equal to zero for any real value of x. Thus, the rational expression has no excluded values; it is defined for all values of x. Equivalently, one can say that the domain of the rational function $y = \frac{1}{x^2 + 1}$ is all real numbers.

SIMPLIFYING RATIONAL EXPRESSIONS

Lesson 12-3

Simplifying a rational expression is analogous to simplifying a fraction. Common factors that appear in both the numerator and the denominator may be divided out. However, it is important to be careful when there are excluded values. Once a rational expression has been simplified, it may no longer be possible to identify the excluded values; however, the expression remains undefined for these values.

For example, students may be quick to state that the expression $\frac{x^2}{x}$ "is the same as x." To decide whether this is true, it is instructive to consider the related functions. The function $y = x$ is defined for all real values of x, and its graph is a straight line through the origin. On the other hand, the rational expression $\frac{x^2}{x}$ has an excluded value at $x = 0$. Therefore, the rational function $y = \frac{x^2}{x}$ is not defined at $x = 0$, and its graph is a straight line with a "hole" at the origin.

Comparing the two graphs shows that $\frac{x^2}{x} = x$ for all values of x except $x = 0$. In other words, the expressions are equal except at the excluded value.

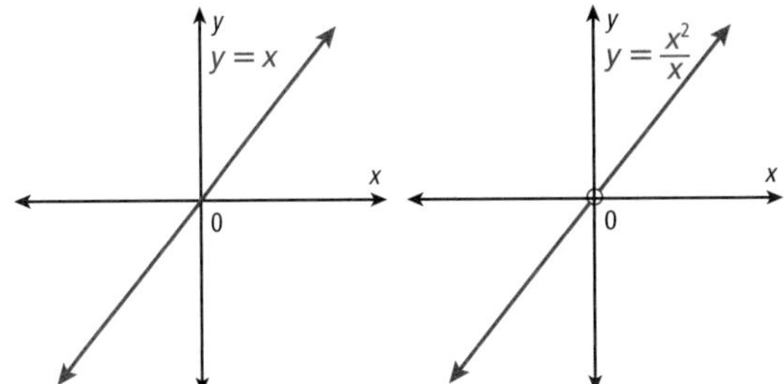

OPERATIONS ON RATIONAL EXPRESSIONS

Lessons 12-4 and 12-5

In general, operations on rational expressions are similar to operations on fractions, as long as excluded values are identified. The table below summarizes these similarities. In the table, $a(x)$, $b(x)$, $c(x)$, and $d(x)$ are polynomials.

Fractions	Rational Expressions
Addition and Subtraction	
$\frac{a}{b} \pm \frac{c}{d} = \frac{ad \pm bc}{bd}$ $(b, d \neq 0)$	$\frac{a(x)}{b(x)} \pm \frac{c(x)}{d(x)} = \frac{a(x)d(x) \pm b(x)c(x)}{b(x)d(x)}$ (except where $b(x), d(x) = 0$)
Multiplication	
$\frac{a}{b} \cdot \frac{c}{d} = \frac{ac}{bd}$ $(b, d \neq 0)$	$\frac{a(x)}{b(x)} \cdot \frac{c(x)}{d(x)} = \frac{a(x)c(x)}{b(x)d(x)}$ (except where $b(x), d(x) = 0$)
Division	
$\frac{a}{b} \div \frac{c}{d} = \frac{a}{b} \cdot \frac{d}{c} = \frac{ad}{bc}$ $(b, c, d \neq 0)$	$\frac{a(x)}{b(x)} \div \frac{c(x)}{d(x)} = \frac{a(x)}{b(x)} \cdot \frac{d(x)}{c(x)}$ $= \frac{a(x)d(x)}{b(x)c(x)}$ (except where $b(x), c(x)\ d(x) = 0$)

Note also that the Cross Products Property holds for rational expressions. That is, if $\frac{a(x)}{b(x)} = \frac{c(x)}{d(x)}$, then $a(x)d(x) = b(x)c(x)$, except where $b(x), d(x) = 0$.

12-4 Organizer

Pacing: Traditional 1 day
Block $\frac{1}{2}$ day

Objective: Multiply and divide rational expressions.

Online Edition
Tutorial Videos

Power Presentations with PowerPoint®

Warm Up

Multiply.

1. $2x^2(x+3)$ $2x^3 + 6x^2$
2. $(x-5)(3x+7)$ $3x^2 - 8x - 35$
3. $3x(x^2+2x+2)$ $3x^3 + 6x^2 + 6x$
4. Simplify $\frac{12x^{12}y^{10}}{40x^5y^{15}}$. $\frac{3x^7}{10y^5}$

Divide. Simplify your answer.

5. $\frac{2}{3} \div \frac{1}{2}$ $\frac{4}{3}$ 6. $\frac{3}{5} \div \frac{11}{3}$ $\frac{9}{55}$
7. $\frac{2}{5} \div \frac{7}{15}$ $\frac{6}{7}$ 8. $\frac{3}{4} \div \frac{9}{16}$ $\frac{4}{3}$

Also available on transparency

Math Humor

Q: What do you call a rational expression when it enlists in the military?

A: A national rational.

12-4 Multiplying and Dividing Rational Expressions

Objective
Multiply and divide rational expressions.

Why learn this?
You can multiply rational expressions to determine the probabilities of winning prizes at carnivals. (See Example 5.)

The rules for multiplying rational expressions are the same as the rules for multiplying fractions. You multiply the numerators, and you multiply the denominators.

Multiplying Rational Expressions

If a, b, c, and d are nonzero polynomials, then $\frac{a}{b} \cdot \frac{c}{d} = \frac{ac}{bd}$.

EXAMPLE 1 Multiplying Rational Expressions

Multiply. Simplify your answer.

A $\frac{a+3}{2} \cdot \frac{6}{3a+9}$

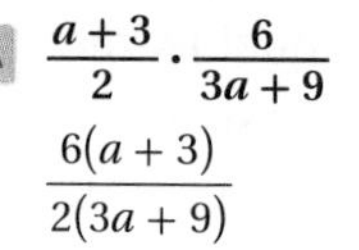

$\frac{6(a+3)}{2(3a+9)}$ *Multiply the numerators and denominators.*

$\frac{6(a+3)}{2 \cdot 3(a+3)}$ *Factor.*

$\frac{\cancel{6}^1\cancel{(a+3)}^1}{\cancel{6}^1\cancel{(a+3)}^1}$ *Divide out the common factors.*

1 *Simplify.*

Remember!
See the Quotient of Powers Property in Lesson 7-4.
$\frac{a^m}{a^n} = a^{m-n}$

B $\frac{12b^3c^2}{5ac} \cdot \frac{15a^2b}{3b^2c}$

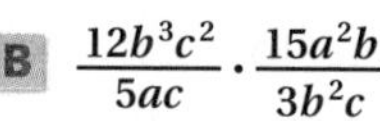

$\frac{(12)(15)a^2(b^3 \cdot b)c^2}{(5)(3)ab^2(c \cdot c)}$ *Multiply the numerators and the denominators. Arrange the expression so like variables are together.*

$\frac{180a^2b^4c^2}{15ab^2c^2}$ *Simplify.*

$12a^1b^2c^0$ *Divide out common factors. Use properties of exponents.*

$12ab^2$ *Simplify. Remember that $c^0 = 1$.*

C $\frac{5x^2}{2y^3} \cdot \frac{3x}{2y^2}$

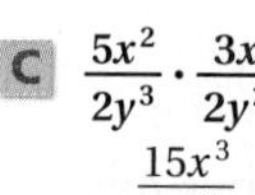

$\frac{15x^3}{4y^5}$ *Multiply. There are no common factors, so the product cannot be simplified.*

State Resources

go.hrw.com
State Resources Online
KEYWORD: MA7 Resources

1 Introduce

EXPLORATION

12-4 Multiplying and Dividing Rational Expressions

You can compare expressions by evaluating them for different values of the variables.

1. Complete the table. Evaluate each expression for the given values of the variables.

x	y	$\frac{x}{2y} \cdot \frac{3x}{y}$	$\frac{3x^2}{2y^2}$
1	1		
1	3		
2	4		

2. What do you notice in the table?
3. Complete the table. Evaluate each expression for the given values of the variables.

m	n	$\frac{3}{m^2} \cdot \frac{2n}{m}$	$\frac{6n}{m^3}$
1	2		
2	2		
3	1		

4. What do you notice in the table?

THINK AND DISCUSS

5. **Explain** how you can multiply $\frac{a}{b} \cdot \frac{c}{d}$, where a, b, c, and d are nonzero polynomials.

Motivate

Write $\frac{4}{5} \cdot \frac{3}{10}$ on the board. Review with students two different ways to find the simplified product. (1) Multiply the numerators and then denominators, and then divide out a factor of 2. (2) Divide out 2 from 4 and 10, and then multiply the remaining numerators and denominators. Explain that the same procedures apply to multiplying rational expressions.

Explorations and answers are provided in *Alternate Openers: Explorations Transparencies.*

Multiply. Simplify your answer.

1a. $\frac{(c-4)}{5} \cdot \frac{45}{(-4c+16)}$ $-\frac{9}{4}$ **1b.** $\frac{5y^5z}{3xy^2z} \cdot \frac{2x^4y^2}{4xy}$ $\frac{5x^2y^4}{6}$

EXAMPLE 2 Multiplying a Rational Expression by a Polynomial

Remember!

Just as you can write an integer as a fraction, you can write any expression as a rational expression by writing it with a denominator of 1.

Multiply $(x^2+8x+15)\frac{4}{2x+6}$. Simplify your answer.

$\frac{x^2+8x+15}{1} \cdot \frac{4}{2x+6}$ *Write the polynomial over 1.*

$\frac{(x+3)(x+5)}{1} \cdot \frac{4}{2(x+3)}$ *Factor the numerator and denominator.*

$\frac{(x+3)^1(x+5)4^2}{2^1(x+3)^1}$ *Divide out common factors.*

$2x+10$ *Multiply remaining factors.*

2. Multiply $\frac{m-5}{m^2-4m-12} \cdot (3m+6)$. Simplify your answer. $\frac{3m-15}{m-6}$

There are two methods for simplifying rational expressions. You can **simplify first** by dividing out common factors and **then multiply** the remaining factors. You can also **multiply first** and **then simplify**. Using either method will result in the same answer.

EXAMPLE 3 Multiplying Rational Expressions Containing Polynomials

Multiply $\frac{4d^3+4d}{16f} \cdot \frac{2f}{7d^2f+7f}$. Simplify your answer.

Method 1 Simplify first.

$\frac{4d^3+4d}{16f} \cdot \frac{2f}{7d^2f+7f}$

$\frac{4d(d^2+1)}{16f} \cdot \frac{2f}{7f(d^2+1)}$ *Factor.*

$\frac{4^1d(d^2+1)^1}{16^2f^1} \cdot \frac{2^1f^1}{7f(d^2+1)^1}$ *Divide out common factors.*

Then multiply.

$\frac{d}{14f}$ *Simplify.*

Method 2 Multiply first.

$\frac{4d^3+4d}{16f} \cdot \frac{2f}{7d^2f+7f}$

$\frac{(4d^3+4d)2f}{16f(7d^2f+7f)}$ *Multiply.*

$\frac{8d^3f+8df}{112d^2f^2+112f^2}$ *Distribute.*

Then simplify.

$\frac{8df(d^2+1)}{112f^2(d^2+1)}$ *Factor.*

$\frac{8^1df^1(d^2+1)^1}{112^{14}f^{2f}(d^2+1)^1}$ *Divide out common factors.*

$\frac{d}{14f}$ *Simplify.*

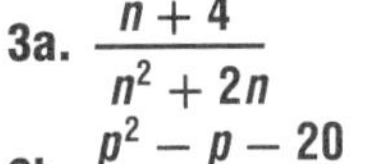

3a. $\frac{n+4}{n^2+2n}$

3b. $\frac{p^2-p-20}{p^3+16p}$

Multiply. Simplify your answer.

3a. $\frac{n-5}{n^2+4n} \cdot \frac{n^2+8n+16}{n^2-3n-10}$ **3b.** $\frac{p+4}{p^2+2p} \cdot \frac{p^2-3p-10}{p^2+16}$

COMMON ERROR ALERT

Students might divide out common factors in a division problem before the division is rewritten as multiplication. For example, $\frac{1}{2} \div \frac{2}{3} \cdot \frac{1}{2} \div \frac{2}{3} = \frac{1}{1} \cdot \frac{3}{1} = 3$. The correct solution is $\frac{1}{2} \div \frac{2}{3} = \frac{1}{2} \cdot \frac{3}{2} = \frac{3}{4}$. Have students use a calculator to see that the second method is correct.

Power Presentations with PowerPoint®

Additional Examples

Example 1

Multiply. Simplify your answer.

A. $\frac{c-1}{2} \cdot \frac{4}{3c-3}$ $\frac{2}{3}$

B. $\frac{8x^2y^3}{5yz^2} \cdot \frac{10y^2z^2}{16y^3}$ x^2y

C. $\frac{6r^2}{5s^3} \cdot \frac{3r^2}{7s}$ $\frac{18r^4}{35s^4}$

Example 2

Multiply $(x^2-6x+9) \cdot \frac{2x}{6x-18}$.

Simplify your answer. $\frac{x^2-3x}{3}$

Example 3

Multiply $\frac{3a^2+6a}{12b^2} \cdot \frac{2b^3}{3ab+6b}$.

Simplify your answer. $\frac{a}{6}$

INTERVENTION

Questioning Strategies

EXAMPLE 1

- How do you find common factors?

EXAMPLE 2

- What does it mean to divide out common factors?

EXAMPLE 3

- Which method do you prefer? Why?

2 Teach

Guided Instruction

Review multiplying and dividing fractions. Then show how to multiply and divide rational expressions.

Before **Example 5,** review independent and dependent events. In **Example 5,** the events are dependent because there is no replacement between the two picks.

Communicating Math Have students go to the board to demonstrate different methods of multiplying and simplifying.

Reaching All Learners

Through Visual Cues

Encourage students to align like factors in the numerator and denominator. Students can even draw lines to separate the factors. When a factor isn't in the numerator or denominator, use 1. For **Example 3 Method 2,** the second step can be written as:

8	d	f	d^2+1
112	1	f^2	d^2+1

Then simplify:

1	d	1	1
14	1	f	1

$= \frac{d}{14f}$

Power Presentations with PowerPoint®

Additional Examples

Example 4

Divide. Simplify your answer.

A. $\frac{2}{g} \div \frac{g+4}{g^2}$ $\quad \frac{2g}{g+4}$

B. $\frac{1-n^2}{n} \div \frac{n-1}{n^2-4n}$

$-n^2+3n+4$

C. $\frac{4xy^2}{y} \div (2x^2+6x)$ $\quad \frac{2y}{x+3}$

INTERVENTION

Questioning Strategies

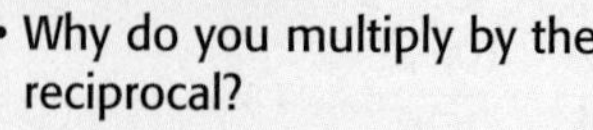

EXAMPLE 4

- Why do you multiply by the reciprocal?

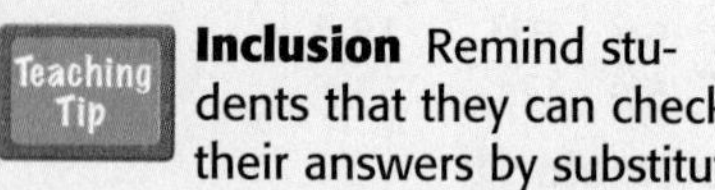

Inclusion Remind students that they can check their answers by substituting a user-friendly number into both the original and simplified expressions.

The rules for dividing rational expressions are the same as the rules for dividing fractions. To divide by a rational expression, multiply by its reciprocal.

Dividing Rational Expressions

If a, b, c, and d are nonzero polynomials, then $\frac{a}{b} \div \frac{c}{d} = \frac{a}{b} \cdot \frac{d}{c} = \frac{ad}{bc}$.

EXAMPLE 4 Dividing by Rational Expressions and Polynomials

Divide. Simplify your answer.

A $\frac{1}{x} \div \frac{x-2}{2x}$

$\frac{1}{x} \cdot \frac{2x}{x-2}$ — *Write as multiplication by the reciprocal.*

$\frac{1(2x)}{x(x-2)}$ — *Multiply the numerators and the denominators.*

$\frac{2\cancel{x}^1}{\cancel{x}^1(x-2)}$ — *Divide out common factors.*

$\frac{2}{x-2}$ — *Simplify.*

B $\frac{x^2-2x}{x} \div \frac{2-x}{x^2+2x+1}$

$\frac{x^2-2x}{x} \cdot \frac{x^2+2x+1}{2-x}$ — *Write as multiplication by the reciprocal.*

$\frac{x(x-2)}{x} \cdot \frac{(x+1)(x+1)}{2-x}$ — *Factor.*

$\frac{x(x-2)}{x} \cdot \frac{(x+1)(x+1)}{-1(x-2)}$ — *Rewrite one opposite binomial.*

$\frac{\cancel{x}^1\cancel{(x-2)}^1}{\cancel{x}^1} \cdot \frac{(x+1)(x+1)}{-1\cancel{(x-2)}^1}$ — *Divide out common factors.*

$-(x+1)^2$ — *Multiply.*

C $\frac{3a^2b}{b} \div (3a^2+6a)$

$\frac{3a^2b}{b} \div \frac{3a^2+6a}{1}$ — *Write the binomial over 1.*

$\frac{3a^2b}{b} \cdot \frac{1}{3a^2+6a}$ — *Write as multiplication by the reciprocal.*

$\frac{3a^2b}{b(3a^2+6a)}$ — *Multiply the numerators and the denominators.*

$\frac{\cancel{3}^1\cancel{a^2}^a\cancel{b}^1}{\cancel{b}^1[\cancel{3}^1\cancel{a}^1(a+2)]}$ — *Factor. Divide out common factors.*

$\frac{a}{a+2}$ — *Simplify.*

Divide. Simplify your answer.

4a. $\frac{3}{x^2} \div \frac{x^3}{x-5}$ $\quad \frac{3x-15}{x^5}$

4b. $\frac{18vw^2}{6v} \div \frac{3v^2x^4}{2w^4x}$ $\quad \frac{2w^6}{v^2x^3}$

4c. $\frac{x^2-x}{x+2} \div (x^2+2x-3)$ $\quad \frac{x}{x^2+5x+6}$

EXAMPLE 5 Probability Application

Marty is playing a carnival game. He needs to pick two items out of a bag without looking. The bag has red and blue items. There are three more red items than blue items.

a. Write and simplify an expression that represents the probability that Marty will pick two blue items without replacing the first item.

Let x = the number of blue items.

Blue + Red = Total	
$x + x + 3 = 2x + 3$	*Write expressions for the number of each color item and for the total number of items.*

The probability of picking a blue item and then another blue item is the product of the probabilities of the individual events.

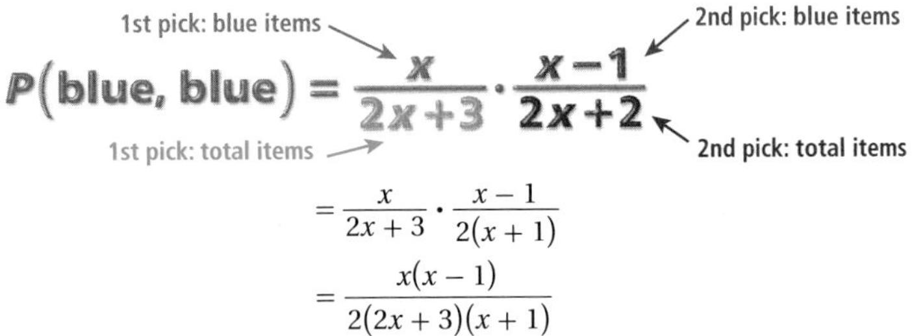

$$P(\text{blue, blue}) = \frac{x}{2x+3} \cdot \frac{x-1}{2x+2}$$

$$= \frac{x}{2x+3} \cdot \frac{x-1}{2(x+1)}$$

$$= \frac{x(x-1)}{2(2x+3)(x+1)}$$

b. What is the probability that Marty picks two blue items if there are 10 blue items in the bag before his first pick?

Use the probability of picking two blue items. Since x represents the number of blue items, substitute 10 for x.

$$P(\text{blue, blue}) = \frac{10(10-1)}{2(2 \cdot 10 + 3)(10+1)} \quad \textit{Substitute.}$$

$$= \frac{10(9)}{2(23)(11)} = \frac{90}{506} \approx 0.18 \quad \textit{Use the order of operations to simplify.}$$

The probability of picking two blue items if there are 10 blue items in the bag before the first pick is approximately 0.18.

CHECK IT OUT! **5. What if...?** There are 50 blue items in the bag before Marty's first pick. What is the probability that Marty picks two blue items? **approximately 0.23**

> **Remember!**
> For a review of probability topics, see Chapter 10.

THINK AND DISCUSS

1. Explain how to divide by a polynomial.

Know it! Note

2. GET ORGANIZED Copy and complete the graphic organizer. In each box, describe how to perform the operation with rational expressions.

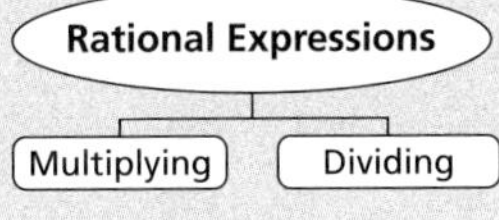

Power Presentations with PowerPoint®

Additional Examples

Example 5

Tanya is playing a carnival game. She needs to pick 2 cards out of a deck without looking. The deck has cards with numbers and cards with letters. There are 6 more letter cards than number cards.

a. Write and simplify an expression that represents the probability that Tanya will pick 2 number cards. $\frac{x(x-1)}{2(x+3)(2x+5)}$

b. What is the probability that Tanya picks 2 number cards if there are 25 number cards in the deck before her first pick? Round your answer to the nearest hundredth. 0.19

INTERVENTION Questioning Strategies

EXAMPLE 5

- How do you find the total number of items?
- Why are the numerator and the denominator of the second expression different from the first expression?
- For what type of situation would the first and second fractions be the same?

3 Close

Summarize

Remind students that the methods for multiplying and dividing rational expressions are similar to those for multiplying and dividing fractions. They need to look for common factors that divide out to simplify the product or quotient. Tell students to write their work carefully, using the lines in their notebooks and completely crossing out simplified terms, to avoid careless errors.

ONGOING ASSESSMENT and INTERVENTION

***Diagnose Before* the Lesson**
12-4 Warm Up, TE p. 898

***Monitor During* the Lesson**
Check It Out! Exercises, SE pp. 899–901
Questioning Strategies, TE pp. 899–901

***Assess After* the Lesson**
12-4 Lesson Quiz, TE p. 904
Alternative Assessment, TE p. 904

Answers to *Think and Discuss*

1. Possible answer: Dividing by a polynomial is the same as multiplying by the reciprocal of the polynomial.
2. See p. A11.

Assignment Guide

Assign *Guided Practice* exercises as necessary.

If you finished Examples **1–3**
Basic 23–31, 38, 40
Average 23–31, 38, 40
Advanced 23–31, 38, 40

If you finished Examples **1–5**
Basic 23–36, 38–49, 56–66
Average 23–51, 56–66
Advanced 23–35, 37–66

Homework Quick Check
Quickly check key concepts.
Exercises: 24, 28, 30, 32, 35

Number Sense Exercise 33 contains opposite binomials $a - 4$ and $4 - a$. Remind students that the quotient of opposite binomials is -1. For example, $\frac{6-3}{3-6} = \frac{3}{-3} = -1$.

Answers

8. $\dfrac{5x^2 + 20x + 20}{6x^2}$
9. $\dfrac{m^2 - 10m}{2}$
16. $\dfrac{3p^2q^3 + 12q^4 - 4p^2 - 16q}{q}$
20. $\dfrac{m-1}{2m-4}$
21. $\dfrac{1}{3x-15}$

State Resources

12-4 Exercises

go.hrw.com
Homework Help Online
KEYWORD: MA7 12-4
Parent Resources Online
KEYWORD: MA7 Parent

GUIDED PRACTICE

Multiply. Simplify your answer.

SEE EXAMPLE 1 p. 898

1. $\dfrac{4hj^2}{10j^3} \cdot \dfrac{3h^3k}{h^3k^3}$ $\mathbf{\dfrac{6h}{5jk^2}}$
2. $\dfrac{4y}{x^5} \cdot \dfrac{2yz^2}{9x^2}$ $\mathbf{\dfrac{8y^2z^2}{9x^7}}$
3. $\dfrac{x-2}{x+3} \cdot \dfrac{4x+12}{6}$ $\mathbf{\dfrac{2x-4}{3}}$
4. $\dfrac{ab}{c} \cdot \dfrac{2a^2}{3c}$ $\mathbf{\dfrac{2a^3b}{3c^2}}$
5. $\dfrac{7c^4d}{10c} \cdot \dfrac{5a}{21c^3d}$ $\mathbf{\dfrac{a}{6}}$
6. $\dfrac{12p^2q}{5p} \cdot \dfrac{15p^4q^3}{12q}$ $\mathbf{3p^5q^3}$

SEE EXAMPLE 2 p. 899

7. $\dfrac{12}{4y+8}(y^2-4)$ $\mathbf{3y-6}$
8. $\dfrac{x+2}{6x^2}(5x+10)$
9. $\dfrac{3m}{6m+18}(m^2-7m-30)$
10. $\dfrac{4p}{8p+16}(p^2-5p-14)$ $\mathbf{\dfrac{p^2-7p}{2}}$
11. $\dfrac{a^2}{a}(a^2+10a+25)$ $\mathbf{a^3+10a^2+25a}$
12. $\dfrac{-c}{4c+4}(c^2-c-2)$ $\mathbf{\dfrac{-c^2+2c}{4}}$

SEE EXAMPLE 3 p. 899

13. $\dfrac{a^2+6ab}{b} \cdot \dfrac{5+3a}{3a^2b+5ab}$ $\mathbf{\dfrac{a+6b}{b^2}}$
14. $\dfrac{x^2+5x+4}{x-4} \cdot \dfrac{x^2-2x-8}{x^2+6x+8}$ $\mathbf{x+1}$
15. $\dfrac{j-1}{j^2-4j+3} \cdot \dfrac{j^2-5j+6}{2j-4}$ $\mathbf{\dfrac{1}{2}}$
16. $\dfrac{p^3+4pq}{p} \cdot \dfrac{6q^3-8}{2q}$
17. $\dfrac{r^2+15r+14}{r^2-16} \cdot \dfrac{2r+8}{r+1}$ $\mathbf{\dfrac{2r+28}{r-4}}$
18. $\dfrac{y-8}{y^2-1} \cdot \dfrac{y+2}{y^2-49}$ $\mathbf{\dfrac{y^2-6y-16}{y^4-50y^2+49}}$

SEE EXAMPLE 4 p. 900

Divide. Simplify your answer.

19. $\dfrac{3a^4b}{2a^2c^3} \div \dfrac{12a^2c}{8c^4}$ $\mathbf{b}$
20. $\dfrac{2m^3+2m}{m^2-2m} \div \dfrac{4m^2+4}{m-1}$
21. $\dfrac{x^2+4x-5}{3x-3} \div (x^2-25)$

SEE EXAMPLE 5 p. 901

22. **Probability** While playing a game, Rachel pulls two tiles out of a bag without looking and without replacing the first tile. The bag has two colors of tiles—black and white. There are 10 more white tiles than black tiles.
    a. Write and simplify an expression that represents the probability that Rachel will pick a black tile, then a white tile.
    b. What is the probability that Rachel pulls a black tile and then a white tile if there are 5 black tiles in the bag before her first pick? **approximately 0.20**

22a. $\mathbf{\dfrac{x(x+10)}{(2x+10)(2x+9)}}$

PRACTICE AND PROBLEM SOLVING

Independent Practice	
For Exercises	See Example
23–25	1
26–28	2
29–31	3
32–34	4
35	5

Extra Practice
Skills Practice p. S27
Application Practice p. S39

Multiply. Simplify your answer.

23. $\dfrac{p^6q^2}{7r^3} \cdot \dfrac{-3p^2}{r}$ $\mathbf{-\dfrac{3p^8q^2}{7r^4}}$
24. $\dfrac{3r^2t}{6st^3} \cdot \dfrac{2r^2s^3t^2}{8r^4s^2}$ $\mathbf{\dfrac{1}{8}}$
25. $\dfrac{10}{y+5} \cdot \dfrac{y+2}{3}$ $\mathbf{\dfrac{10y+20}{3y+15}}$
26. $\dfrac{3}{2a+6}(a^2+4a+3)$ $\mathbf{\dfrac{3a+3}{2}}$
27. $\dfrac{4m^2-8m}{m^2+6m-16}(m^2+7m-8)$ $\mathbf{4m^2-4m}$
28. $\dfrac{x}{2x^2-12x+18}(2x^2-4x-6)$ $\mathbf{\dfrac{x^2+x}{x-3}}$
29. $\dfrac{6n^2+18n}{n^2+9n+8} \cdot \dfrac{n^2-1}{2n+6}$ $\mathbf{\dfrac{3n^2-3n}{n+8}}$
30. $\dfrac{3a^2b}{5a^3+10a^2b} \cdot \dfrac{2a+4b}{6a^3b+6a^2b^2}$ $\mathbf{\dfrac{1}{5a^3+5a^2b}}$
31. $\dfrac{t^2-100}{5t+50} \cdot \dfrac{5}{t-10}$ $\mathbf{1}$

Divide. Simplify your answer.

32. $\dfrac{6j^2k^5}{5j} \div \dfrac{4j^3k^3}{3j}$ $\mathbf{\dfrac{9k^2}{10j}}$
33. $\dfrac{a-4}{a^2} \div (8a-2a^2)$ $\mathbf{-\dfrac{1}{2a^3}}$
34. $\dfrac{x^2-9}{x^2+6x+9} \div \dfrac{4x^2-12x}{16x}$ $\mathbf{\dfrac{4}{x+3}}$

12-4 READING STRATEGIES

The rules for multiplying and dividing rational expressions are the same as the rules for multiplying and dividing fractions. Look at the connections below.

FRACTIONS | RATIONAL EXPRESSIONS

Rule 1: $\frac{a}{b} \cdot \frac{c}{d} = \frac{ac}{bd}$

$\frac{8}{9} \cdot \frac{3}{5} = \frac{8 \cdot 3}{9 \cdot 5} = \cdots$

$\frac{m+2}{4} \cdot \frac{8}{3m+6} = \frac{8(m+2)}{4(3m+6)} = \cdots$

Rule 2: $\frac{a}{b} \cdot c = \frac{a}{b} \cdot \frac{c}{1}$ and $\frac{a}{b} \div c = \frac{a}{b} \div \frac{c}{1}$

$\frac{3}{4} \cdot 16 = \frac{3}{4} \cdot \frac{16}{1} = \cdots$

$\frac{6}{2x+10} \cdot (x^2+3x-10) = \frac{6}{2x+10} \cdot \frac{x^2+3x-10}{1} = \cdots$

Rule 3: $\frac{a}{b} \div \frac{c}{d} = \frac{a}{b} \cdot \frac{d}{c}$

$\frac{1}{12} \div \frac{2}{3} = \frac{1}{12} \cdot \frac{3}{2} = \cdots$

$\frac{3ab^4}{a^3} \div \frac{3ab}{ab^2} = \frac{3ab^4}{a^3} \cdot \frac{ab^2}{3ab} = \cdots$

Finish multiplying and dividing the rational expressions given above so that each is simplified completely.

1. Rule 1 $\quad \frac{2}{3}$
2. Rule 2 $\quad 3(x-2)$
3. Rule 3 $\quad \frac{b^5}{a^2}$

Multiply or divide. Simplify your answer.

4. $\frac{3}{t+2} \cdot (t^2-4)$ $\quad 3t-6$
5. $\frac{m+5}{4} \div (3m+15)$ $\quad \frac{1}{12}$
6. $\frac{x^2y^3}{8y} \cdot \frac{10x^4}{xy^2}$ $\quad \frac{5x^5}{4}$

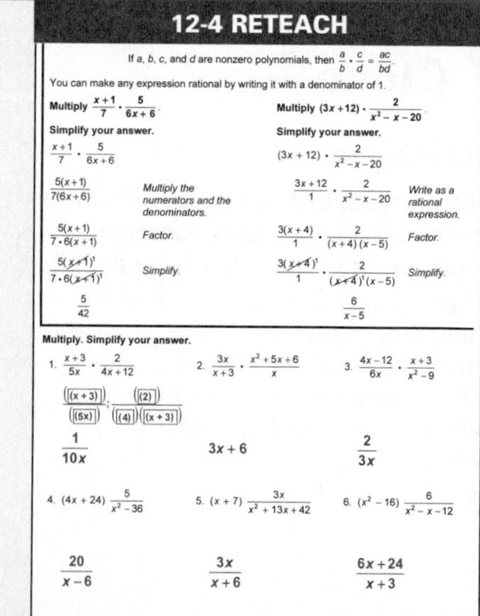

12-4 RETEACH

If a, b, c, and d are nonzero polynomials, then $\frac{a}{b} \cdot \frac{c}{d} = \frac{ac}{bd}$.

You can make any expression rational by writing it with a denominator of 1.

Multiply $\frac{x+1}{7} \cdot \frac{5}{6x+6}$. **Simplify your answer.**

$\frac{x+1}{7} \cdot \frac{5}{6x+6}$

$\frac{5(x+1)}{7(6x+6)}$ *Multiply the numerators and the denominators.*

$\frac{5(x+1)}{7 \cdot 6(x+1)}$ *Factor.*

$\frac{5(x+1)^1}{7 \cdot 6(x+1)^1}$ *Simplify.*

$\frac{5}{42}$

Multiply $(3x+12) \cdot \frac{2}{x^2-x-20}$. **Simplify your answer.**

$(3x+12) \cdot \frac{2}{x^2-x-20}$

$\frac{3x+12}{1} \cdot \frac{2}{x^2-x-20}$ *Write as a rational expression.*

$\frac{3(x+4)}{1} \cdot \frac{2}{(x+4)(x-5)}$ *Factor.*

$\frac{3(x+4)^1}{1} \cdot \frac{2}{(x+4)^1(x-5)}$ *Simplify.*

$\frac{6}{x-5}$

Multiply. Simplify your answer.

1. $\frac{x+3}{5x} \cdot \frac{2}{4x+12}$ $\quad \frac{(x+3)}{(5x)} \cdot \frac{(2)}{(4)(x+3)}$ $\quad \frac{1}{10x}$
2. $\frac{3x}{x+3} \cdot \frac{x^2+5x+6}{x}$ $\quad 3x+6$
3. $\frac{4x-12}{6x} \cdot \frac{x+3}{x^2-9}$ $\quad \frac{2}{3x}$
4. $(4x+24)\,\frac{5}{x^2-36}$ $\quad \frac{20}{x-6}$
5. $(x+7)\,\frac{3x}{x^2+13x+42}$ $\quad \frac{3x}{x+6}$
6. $(x^2-16)\,\frac{6}{x^2-x-12}$ $\quad \frac{6x+24}{x+3}$

35. **Entertainment** A carnival game board is covered completely in small balloons. You throw darts at the board and try to pop the balloons.

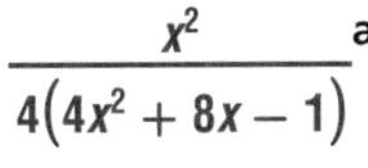

a. Write and simplify an expression describing the probability that the next two balloons popped are red and then blue. (*Hint:* Write the probabilities as ratios of the areas of rectangles.)

$\frac{x^2}{4(4x^2 + 8x - 1)}$

b. What is the probability that the next two balloons popped are red and then blue if $x = 3$? $\frac{9}{236}$

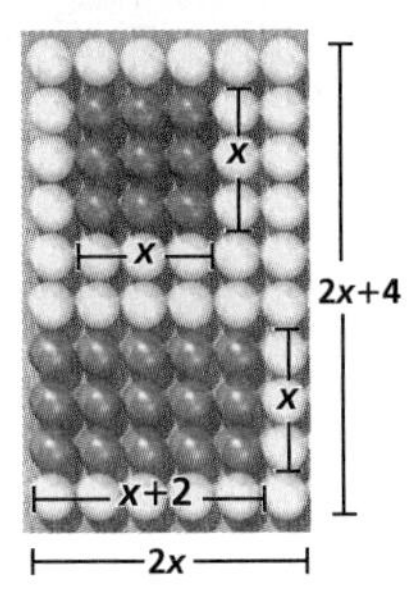

36. **///ERROR ANALYSIS///** Which is incorrect? Explain the error.

Student A is incorrect because individual terms (rather than factors) were canceled.

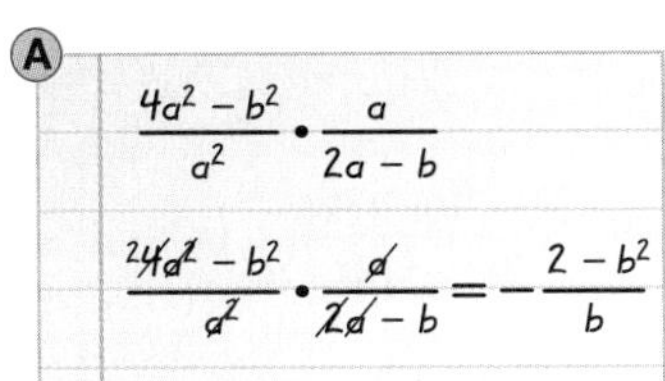

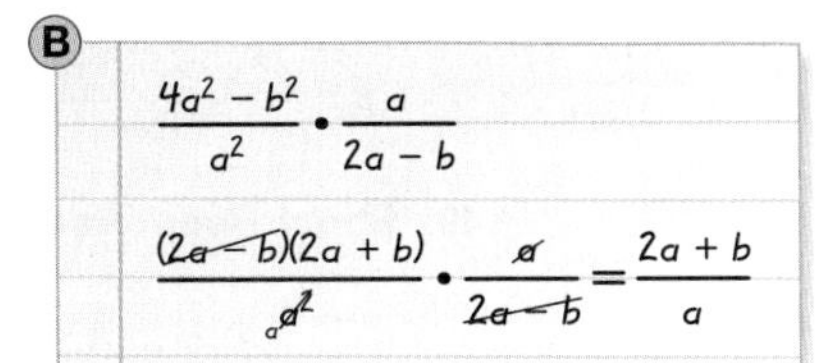

37. **Critical Thinking** Which of the following expressions is NOT equivalent to the other three? Explain why.

a. $\frac{4x^2}{x^2 - 3x} \cdot \frac{2x - 6}{8y^2}$

b. $\frac{6xy^2}{x^2} \div \frac{3y^4}{2x^2}$

c. $\frac{10x^4y}{5xy^2} \div 2x^2y$

d. $\frac{4x}{xy^2 + 2y^2} \cdot \frac{x^2 - 4}{4x - 8}$

b; the other 3 expressions are all equivalent to $\frac{x}{y^2}$, but b simplifies to $\frac{4x}{y^2}$.

Multiply or divide. Simplify your answer.

38. $\frac{5p^3}{p^2q} \cdot \frac{2q^3}{p^2}$ $\frac{10q^2}{p}$

39. $\frac{6m^2 - 18m}{12m^3 + 12m^2} \div \frac{m^2 - 9}{m^2 + 4m + 3}$ $\frac{1}{2m}$

40. $\frac{2x^2}{4x - 8} \cdot \frac{x^2 - 5x + 6}{x^5}$ $\frac{x - 3}{2x^3}$

41. $\frac{x^2 - 9}{4x} \div (4x^2 - 36)$ $\frac{1}{16x}$

42. $\frac{33m - 3m^2}{-2m - 4} \div \frac{6m - 66}{m^2 - 4m}$ $\frac{m^3 - 4m^2}{4m + 8}$

43. $\frac{12w^4x^7}{3w^3} \cdot \frac{w^{-1}x^{-7}}{4}$ 1

44. **Write About It** Explain how to divide $\frac{1}{m} \div \frac{3}{4m}$.

Multiply $\frac{1}{m}$ by $\frac{4m}{3}$. Then divide out the common factor m to get a final answer of $\frac{4}{3}$.

45. This problem will prepare you for the Multi-Step Test Prep on page 926.

The size of an image projected on a screen depends on how far the object is from the lens, the magnification of the lens, and the distance between the image and the lens. Magnification of a lens is $M = \frac{I}{O} = \frac{y}{x}$ where I is the height of the image, O is the height of the object, x is the distance of the object from the lens, and y is the distance of the image from the lens.

a. If an object 16 cm high is placed 15 cm from the lens, it forms an image 60 cm from the lens. What is the height of the image? **64 cm**

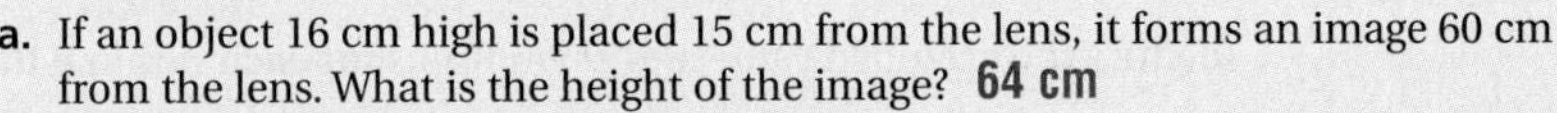

b. Marie moves the same object to a distance of 20 cm from the lens. If the image is the same size as part **a**, what is the distance between the image and the lens? **80 cm**

c. What is the magnification of the lens? **4**

MULTI-STEP TEST PREP Exercise 45 involves a variation function that describes magnification. This exercise prepares students for the Multi-Step Test Prep on page 926.

12-4 PROBLEM SOLVING

A bag contains 5 more red marbles than blue marbles. Janis is going to pick two marbles out of the bag without looking, and without replacing the first marble. Let x represent the number of blue marbles.

1. Write and simplify an expression that represents the probability that Janis will pick two blue marbles.

$\frac{x(x-1)}{(2x+5)(2x+4)}$

2. Is the probability that Janis picks a red marble and then a blue marble the same as the probability that she picks a blue and then a red? Explain.

Yes; P(red then blue) $= \frac{x+5}{2x+5} \cdot \frac{x}{2x+4}$ and P(blue then red) $= \frac{x}{2x+5} \cdot \frac{x+5}{2x+4}$; both $= \frac{x(x+5)}{(2x+5)(2x+4)}$.

3. Write and simplify an expression that represents the probability that Janis will pick two red marbles. Then find the probability of picking two red marbles if the bag contains 20 blue marbles.

$\frac{(x+5)(x+4)}{(2x+5)(2x+4)}$; $\frac{10}{33} \approx 0.3$;

A square dart board has three regions, A, B, and C, as shown. Units are in inches. Select the best answer.

2x + 4, x + 4, x, A, B, C

4. Which expression represents the probability of throwing two darts that land in region A and then region B?

A $\frac{2x^2}{x+2}$ C $\frac{(x+4)^2}{16(x+2)^4}$

B $\frac{x^2}{2(x+2)^3}$ D $\frac{x^2(x+4)^2}{4(x+2)^2}$

5. Divide two rational expressions to find how many times greater the probability of a dart landing in region C is than the probability of a dart landing in region A.

F $\frac{3x+8}{x}$ H $\frac{4(x+2)^2}{x^2}$

G $\frac{x}{2(x+1)}$ J $\frac{x(3x+8)}{8(x+2)}$

6. Which expression represents the probability of throwing two darts that both land in region B?

A $\frac{4}{(x+2)^2}$

B $\frac{x^2}{(x+4)^2}$

C $\frac{(x+4)^4}{16(x+2)^4}$

D $\frac{64(x+2)^2}{x^2(3x+8)^2}$

7. If $x = 2$ in., what is the probability of throwing two darts that both land in region A?

F $\frac{1}{4}$ H $\frac{1}{32}$

G $\frac{1}{16}$ **J** $\frac{1}{256}$

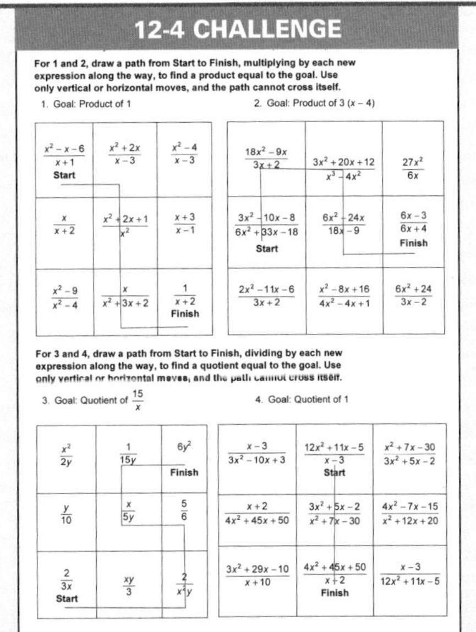

12-4 CHALLENGE

For 1 and 2, draw a path from Start to Finish, multiplying by each new expression along the way, to find a product equal to the goal. Use only vertical or horizontal moves, and the path cannot cross itself.

1. Goal: Product of 1

$\frac{x^2-x-6}{x+1}$ Start	$\frac{x^2+2x}{x-3}$	$\frac{x^2-4}{x-3}$
$\frac{x}{x+2}$	$\frac{x^2+2x+1}{x^2}$	$\frac{x+3}{x-1}$
$\frac{x^2-9}{x^2-4}$	$\frac{x}{x^2+3x+2}$	$\frac{1}{x+2}$ Finish

2. Goal: Product of 3 $(x - 4)$

$\frac{18x^2-9x}{3x+2}$	$\frac{3x^2+20x+12}{x^3-4x^2}$	$\frac{27x^2}{6x}$
$\frac{3x^2-10x-8}{6x^2+33x-18}$ Start	$\frac{6x^2-24x}{18x-9}$	$\frac{6x-3}{6x+4}$ Finish
$\frac{2x^2-11x-6}{3x+2}$	$\frac{x^2-8x+16}{4x^2-4x+1}$	$\frac{6x^2+24}{3x-2}$

For 3 and 4, draw a path from Start to Finish, dividing by each new expression along the way, to find a quotient equal to the goal. Use only vertical or horizontal moves, and the path cannot cross itself.

3. Goal: Quotient of $\frac{15}{x}$

$\frac{x^2}{2y}$	$\frac{1}{15y}$	$6y^2$ Finish
$\frac{y}{10}$	$\frac{x}{5y}$	$\frac{5}{6}$
$\frac{2}{3x}$ Start	$\frac{xy}{3}$	$\frac{2}{x^2y}$

4. Goal: Quotient of 1

$\frac{x-3}{3x^2-10x+3}$	$\frac{12x^2+11x-5}{x-3}$ Start	$\frac{x^2+7x-30}{3x^2+5x-2}$
$\frac{x+2}{4x^2+45x+50}$	$\frac{3x^2+5x-2}{x^2+7x-30}$	$\frac{4x^2-7x-15}{x^2+12x+20}$
$\frac{3x^2+29x-10}{x+10}$	$\frac{4x^2+45x+50}{x+2}$ Finish	$\frac{x-3}{12x^2+11x-5}$

12-4 PRACTICE A

12-4 PRACTICE C

12-4 PRACTICE B

Multiply. Simplify your answer.

1. $\frac{8a^2b^5}{a^3} \cdot \frac{3a^2}{4b^9}$ $\frac{6a}{b^4}$

2. $\frac{4x+8}{3} \cdot \frac{6x}{x+2}$ $8x$

3. $\frac{7}{2t-6} \cdot (t^2 + t - 12)$ $\frac{7t+28}{2}$

4. $\frac{3x^2+xy^3}{y^3} \cdot \frac{2xy+8y}{4x+x^2}$ $\frac{6x+2y^3}{y^2}$

Divide. Simplify your answer.

5. $\frac{5j^2k^2}{3jk^5} \div \frac{10j^2k}{9j^3}$ $\frac{3j^2}{2k^4}$

6. $\frac{3c^2+24c}{c^2-2c+1} \div \frac{c^2+9c+8}{9c-9}$ $\frac{27c}{c^2-1}$

7. Ramon is playing a game in which he must pull two blocks out of a bag containing red and yellow blocks. He cannot look, and he cannot replace the block. The bag has 4 more red blocks than yellow blocks.

a. Write and simplify an expression that represents Ramon's probability of picking a red block, then a yellow block. $\frac{x(x+4)}{2(x+2)(2x+3)}$

b. What is the probability that Ramon pulls a red block then a yellow block if there are 6 yellow blocks in the bag before his first pick? 25%

c. What is the probability that Ramon pulls two yellow blocks if there are 6 yellow blocks in the bag before his first pick? 12.5%

TEST PREP DOCTOR Students who chose **B** for **Exercise 46** may not have found the middle term of the trinomial in the numerator. Remind them to use FOIL to multiply two binomials. Students who chose **C** may have written the reciprocal of the second expression and then multiplied.

Factoring is the best first step to take in **Exercise 49.** However, dividing out common terms cannot occur until the division is written as a multiplication.

Journal

Explain how to multiply a rational expression by a polynomial.

Have students write a multiplication problem and a division problem that have the same rational expression as a solution.

Power Presentations with PowerPoint®

12-4 Lesson Quiz

Multiply. Simplify your answer.

1. $\frac{b-2}{3} \cdot \frac{12}{2b-4}$ 2
2. $\frac{3m^2}{n} \cdot \frac{m^3}{2n^2}$ $\frac{3m^5}{2n^3}$
3. $\frac{3x^2+3x}{6y} \cdot \frac{12y^2}{7x^2y+7xy}$ $\frac{6}{7}$

Divide. Simplify your answer.

4. $\frac{3}{b} \div \frac{b+1}{2b}$ $\frac{6}{b+1}$
5. $\frac{4gh^3}{h} \div (2g^2-8g)$ $\frac{2h^2}{g-4}$
6. A bag contains purple and green toy cars. There are 9 more purple cars than green cars.
   a. Write and simplify an expression to represent the probability that someone will pick a purple car and a green car. $\frac{x(x+9)}{2(x+4)(2x+9)}$
   b. What is the probability of someone picking a purple car and a green car if there are 12 green cars before the first pick? Round to the nearest hundredth. 0.24

Also available on transparency

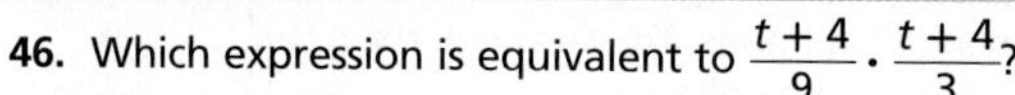

TEST PREP

46. Which expression is equivalent to $\frac{t+4}{9} \cdot \frac{t+4}{3}$?
    (A) $\frac{(t+4)^2}{27}$ (B) $\frac{t^2+16}{27}$ (C) $\frac{1}{3}$ (D) $\frac{1}{27}$

47. Identify the product $-\frac{20b^2}{a^2} \cdot \frac{3ab}{15b}$.
    (F) $-\frac{a}{4b^2}$ (G) $-4b^2$ (H) $-\frac{4b^2}{a}$ (J) $-\frac{b^2}{4a}$

48. Which of the following is equivalent to $\frac{2x}{x+5}$?
    (A) $\frac{x-2}{8x} \cdot \frac{4}{x^2+3x-10}$ (C) $\frac{x-2}{4} \div \frac{x^2+3x-10}{8x}$
    (B) $\frac{x^2-3x-10}{8x} \cdot \frac{4}{x-2}$ (D) $\frac{x^2-3x-10}{4} \div \frac{x-2}{8x}$

49. **Short Response** Simplify $\frac{x^2-10x+24}{3x^2-12x} \div (x^2-3x-18)$. Show your work. $\frac{1}{3x^2+9x}$

CHALLENGE AND EXTEND

Simplify.

50. $\frac{x-3}{3x-6} \cdot \frac{3x+12}{x+1} \cdot \frac{2x-4}{x^2+x-12}$ $\frac{2}{x+1}$
51. $\frac{x^2-1}{x+2} \div \frac{3x+3}{x+2} \div (x-1)$ $\frac{1}{3}$

A *complex fraction* is a fraction that contains one or more fractions in the numerator or the denominator. Simplify each complex fraction.

$\left(\textit{Hint:} \text{ Use the rule } \frac{\frac{a}{b}}{\frac{c}{d}} = \frac{a}{b} \div \frac{c}{d}.\right)$

52. $\frac{\frac{c+5}{c^2-4}}{\frac{c^2+6c+5}{c+2}}$ $\frac{1}{c^2-c-2}$
53. $\frac{\frac{x^2y}{xz^3}}{\frac{x^2y}{x^2z}}$ $\frac{x}{z^2}$
54. $\frac{\frac{x^2}{2} \cdot \frac{x}{3}}{\frac{x}{6}}$ x^2
55. $\frac{\frac{a+1}{a^2+6a+5}}{\frac{2a+2}{a+5}}$ $\frac{1}{2a+2}$

SPIRAL REVIEW

56. Jillian's mother told her to preheat the oven to at least 325 °F. When Jillian went into the kitchen, the oven was already set to 200 °F. Write and solve an inequality to determine how many more degrees Jillian should increase the temperature. *(Lesson 3-2)* $200 + x \geq 325$; $x \geq 125$

57. Pierce has \$30 to spend on a night out. He already spent \$12 on dinner and \$9 on a movie ticket. He will spend some money m on snacks. Write and solve an inequality that will show all the values of m that Pierce can spend on snacks. *(Lesson 3-2)* $12 + 9 + m \leq 30$; $m \leq 9$

Simplify each radical. Then add or subtract, if possible. *(Lesson 11-7)*

58. $\sqrt{18} - \sqrt{8}$ $\sqrt{2}$
59. $\sqrt{3t} + 5\sqrt{3t} + \sqrt{12t}$ $8\sqrt{3t}$
60. $\sqrt{20} - \sqrt{80} + \sqrt{3}$ $-2\sqrt{5} + \sqrt{3}$

Identify the excluded value and asymptotes for each rational function. *(Lesson 12-2)*

61. $y = \frac{4}{x-3}$ $x \neq 3$; $x = 3$ and $y = 0$
62. $y = \frac{1}{2x+4}$ $x \neq -2$; $x = -2$ and $y = 0$
63. $y = -\frac{1}{x} + 3$ $x \neq 0$; $x = 0$ and $y = 3$
64. $y = -\frac{2}{x+5}$ $x \neq -5$; $x = -5$ and $y = 0$
65. $y = \frac{12}{4x}$ $x \neq 0$; $x = 0$ and $y = 0$
66. $y = -\frac{1}{3x-2}$ $x \neq \frac{2}{3}$; $x = \frac{2}{3}$ and $y = 0$

12-5 Adding and Subtracting Rational Expressions

Objectives
Add and subtract rational expressions with like denominators.
Add and subtract rational expressions with unlike denominators.

Who uses this?
Kayakers can use rational expressions to figure out travel time for different river trips. (See Example 5.)

The rules for adding rational expressions are the same as the rules for adding fractions. If the denominators are the same, you add the numerators and keep the common denominator.

$$\frac{3}{8} + \frac{2}{8} = \frac{3+2}{8} = \frac{5}{8}$$

Know it! Note

Adding Rational Expressions with Like Denominators

If a, b, and c represent polynomials and $c \neq 0$, then $\frac{a}{c} + \frac{b}{c} = \frac{a+b}{c}$.

EXAMPLE 1 Adding Rational Expressions with Like Denominators

Add. Simplify your answer.

A $\frac{3b}{b^2} + \frac{5b}{b^2}$

$\frac{3b+5b}{b^2} = \frac{8\cancel{b}^1}{\cancel{b^2}_b}$ *Combine like terms in the numerator. Divide out common factors.*

$= \frac{8}{b}$ *Simplify.*

B $\frac{x^2-8x}{x-4} + \frac{2x+8}{x-4}$

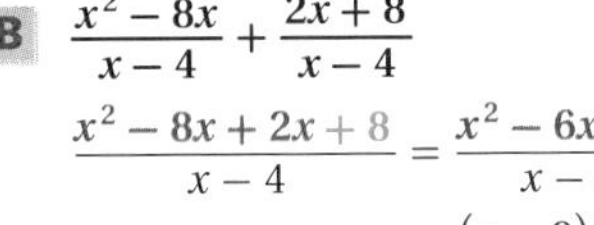

$\frac{x^2-8x+2x+8}{x-4} = \frac{x^2-6x+8}{x-4}$ *Combine like terms in the numerator.*

$= \frac{(x-2)\cancel{(x-4)}^1}{\cancel{x-4}_1}$ *Factor. Divide out common factors.*

$= x - 2$ *Simplify.*

C $\frac{2m+4}{m^2-9} + \frac{2}{m^2-9}$

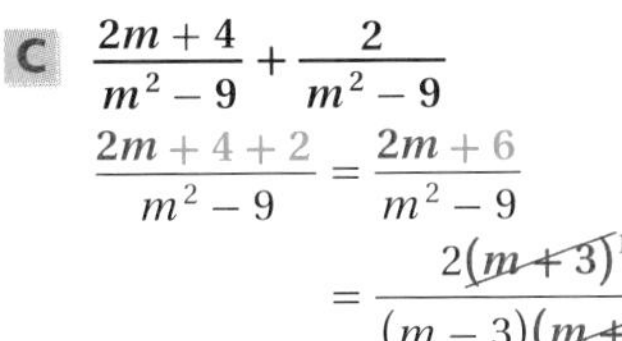

$\frac{2m+4+2}{m^2-9} = \frac{2m+6}{m^2-9}$ *Combine like terms in the numerator.*

$= \frac{2\cancel{(m+3)}^1}{(m-3)\cancel{(m+3)}_1}$ *Factor. Divide out common factors.*

$= \frac{2}{m-3}$ *Simplify.*

CHECK IT OUT! Add. Simplify your answer.

1a. $\frac{n}{2n} + \frac{3n}{2n}$ **2** **1b.** $\frac{3y^2}{y+1} + \frac{3y}{y+1}$ **3y**

12-5 Organizer

Pacing: Traditional 1 day
Block $\frac{1}{2}$ day

Objectives: Add and subtract rational expressions with like denominators.

Add and subtract rational expressions with unlike denominators.

Online Edition
Tutorial Videos, Interactivity

Power Presentations with PowerPoint®

Warm Up

Add. Simplify your answer.

1. $\frac{3}{4} + \frac{3}{4}$ $\frac{3}{2}$ **2.** $\frac{5}{6} + \frac{1}{6}$ 1

3. $\frac{1}{4} + \frac{2}{3}$ $\frac{11}{12}$ **4.** $\frac{1}{2} + \frac{2}{5}$ $\frac{9}{10}$

Subtract. Simplify your answer.

5. $\frac{5}{8} - \frac{1}{8}$ $\frac{1}{2}$ **6.** $\frac{4}{3} - \left(-\frac{1}{3}\right)$ $\frac{5}{3}$

7. $\frac{7}{9} - \frac{1}{5}$ $\frac{26}{45}$ **8.** $\frac{2}{5} - 1$ $-\frac{3}{5}$

Also available on transparency

Q: Why is the common denominator absent?

A: He's home with a common cold.

1 Introduce

EXPLORATION

12-5 Adding and Subtracting Rational Expressions

You can compare expressions by evaluating them for different values of the variables.

1. Complete the table. Evaluate each expression for the given x-values.

x	$\frac{x^2}{x+1} + \frac{2x^2}{x+1}$	$\frac{3x^2}{x+1}$
1		
2		
3		

2. What do you notice in the table?

3. Complete the table. Evaluate each expression for the given p-values.

p	$\frac{p+2}{p^2} + \frac{p+1}{p^2}$	$\frac{2p+3}{p^2}$
1		
3		
5		

4. What do you notice in the table?

THINK AND DISCUSS

Motivate

Review with students how to add fractions with like and unlike denominators. Explain that adding rational expressions requires the same steps—adding numerators when denominators are common.

Explorations and answers are provided in *Alternate Openers: Explorations Transparencies.*

State Resources

go.hrw.com
State Resources Online
KEYWORD: MA7 Resources

Power Presentations with PowerPoint®

Additional Examples

Example 1

Add. Simplify your answer.

A. $\frac{2x}{x^4} + \frac{4x}{x^4}$ $\frac{6}{x^3}$

B. $\frac{m^2 + 2m}{m + 4} + \frac{3m + 4}{m + 4}$ $m + 1$

C. $\frac{3k - 18}{k^2 - 16} + \frac{6}{k^2 - 16}$ $\frac{3}{k + 4}$

Example 2

Subtract. Simplify your answer.

$\frac{6y - 6}{y^2 + 4y - 12} - \frac{y + 4}{y^2 + 4y - 12}$

$\frac{5}{y + 6}$

Example 3

Find the LCM of the given expressions.

A. $12x^2y$, $9xy^3$ $36x^2y^3$

B. $c^2 + 8c + 15$, $3c^2 + 18c + 27$
$3(c + 3)^2(c + 5)$

INTERVENTION

Questioning Strategies

EXAMPLE 1

- How are these examples similar to adding fractions?
- Why should the numerator be factored when possible?

EXAMPLE 2

- How do you combine numerators?
- How does subtracting expressions affect the numerator of the second fraction?

EXAMPLE 3

- What does LCM mean?
- How is finding the LCM of two whole numbers similar to or different from finding the LCM of two expressions?

Inclusion When identifying the LCM of two expressions, tell students that each expression must divide into the LCM. Therefore, the LCM must be equal to or greater than each individual expression.

To subtract rational expressions with like denominators, remember to add the opposite of *each* term in the second numerator.

EXAMPLE 2 Subtracting Rational Expressions with Like Denominators

Caution!

Make sure you add the opposite of all the terms in the numerator of the second expression when subtracting rational expressions.

Subtract. Simplify your answer.

$$\frac{3m - 6}{m^2 + m - 6} - \frac{-m + 2}{m^2 + m - 6}$$

$$\frac{3m - 6 - (-m + 2)}{m^2 + m - 6} = \frac{3m - 6 + m - 2}{m^2 + m - 6}$$ *Subtract numerators.*

$$= \frac{4m - 8}{m^2 + m - 6}$$ *Combine like terms.*

$$= \frac{4(m - 2)^1}{(m + 3)(m - 2)^1}$$ *Factor. Divide out common factors.*

$$= \frac{4}{m + 3}$$ *Simplify.*

Subtract. Simplify your answer.

2a. $\frac{5a + 2}{a^2 - 4} - \frac{2a - 4}{a^2 - 4}$ $\frac{3}{a - 2}$

2b. $\frac{2b + 14}{b^2 + 3b - 4} - \frac{-2b + 2}{b^2 + 3b - 4}$ $\frac{4b + 12}{b^2 + 3b - 4}$

As with fractions, rational expressions must have a common denominator before they can be added or subtracted. If they do not have a common denominator, you can use the least common multiple, or LCM, of the denominators to find one.

To find the LCM, write the prime factorization of both expressions. Use each factor the greatest number of times it appears in either expression.

$6x^2 = 2 \cdot 3 \cdot x \cdot x$
$8x = 2 \cdot 2 \cdot 2 \cdot x$
$\text{LCM} = 2 \cdot 2 \cdot 2 \cdot 3 \cdot x \cdot x = 24x^2$

$5x + 15 = 5(x + 3)$
$x^2 - 9 = (x + 3)(x - 3)$
$\text{LCM} = 5(x + 3)(x - 3)$

EXAMPLE 3 Identifying the Least Common Multiple

Find the LCM of the given expressions.

A $24a^3, 4a$

$24a^3 = 2 \cdot 2 \cdot 2 \cdot 3 \cdot a \cdot a \cdot a$
$4a = 2 \cdot 2 \cdot a$
$\text{LCM} = 2 \cdot 2 \cdot 2 \cdot 3 \cdot a \cdot a \cdot a = 24a^3$

Write the prime factorization of each expression. Use every factor of both expressions the greatest number of times it appears in either expression.

B $2d^2 + 10d + 12, d^2 + 7d + 12$

$2d^2 + 10d + 12 = 2(d^2 + 5d + 6)$ *Factor each expression.*
$= 2(d + 3)(d + 2)$
$d^2 + 7d + 12 = (d + 3)(d + 4)$
$\text{LCM} = 2(d + 3)(d + 2)(d + 4)$

Use every factor of both expressions the greatest number of times it appears in either expression.

Find the LCM of the given expressions.

3a. $5f^2h$, $15fh^2$ $15f^2h^2$

3b. $x^2 - 4x - 12$, $(x - 6)(x + 5)$ $(x - 6)(x + 2)(x + 5)$

2 Teach

Guided Instruction

After adding and subtracting with like denominators, review how to find the LCM of two numbers, such as 12 and 20, and then find the LCM of expressions with just one variable, such as $12x^2$ and $20x^5$, and then more than one variable, such as $12x^2y^3$ and $20x^6y$. Then include expressions with binomial factors. Show how the LCD is used to add and subtract rational expressions with unlike denominators.

ENGLISH LANGUAGE LEARNERS

Reaching All Learners

Through Number Sense

Sometimes students get confused about how to find the LCM because the word *least* causes them to choose the least number of different common factors. Emphasize that *least* in LCM describes the common multiples, not the common factors. Remind students to check that the LCM they find is really a multiple, not just a factor, of both expressions.

The LCM of the denominators of fractions or rational expressions is also called the least common denominator, or LCD. You use the same method to add or subtract rational expressions.

Adding or Subtracting Rational Expressions
Step 1 Identify the LCD.
Step 2 Multiply each expression by an appropriate form of 1 so that each term has the LCD as its denominator.
Step 3 Write each expression using the LCD.
Step 4 Add or subtract the numerators, combining like terms as needed.
Step 5 Factor.
Step 6 Simplify as needed.

EXAMPLE  4 Adding and Subtracting with Unlike Denominators

Add or subtract. Simplify your answer.

A $\frac{3x}{6x^2} + \frac{2x}{4x}$

$6x^2 = 2 \quad \cdot 3 \cdot x \cdot x$

Step 1 $4x = 2 \cdot 2 \quad \cdot x$ *Identify the LCD.*

$\text{LCD} = 2 \cdot 2 \cdot 3 \cdot x \cdot x = 12x^2$

Step 2 $\frac{3x}{6x^2}\left(\frac{2}{2}\right) + \frac{2x}{4x}\left(\frac{3x}{3x}\right)$ *Multiply each expression by an appropriate form of 1.*

Step 3 $\frac{6x}{12x^2} + \frac{6x^2}{12x^2}$ *Write each expression using the LCD.*

Step 4 $\frac{6x + 6x^2}{12x^2}$ *Add the numerators.*

Step 5 $\frac{\cancel{6}^1\cancel{x}^1(1 + x)}{\cancel{6}^1 \cdot 2\cancel{x^2}^x}$ *Factor and divide out common factors.*

Step 6 $\frac{1 + x}{2x}$ *Simplify.*

B $\frac{1}{m - 3} - \frac{5}{3 - m}$

Step 1 The denominators are **opposite binomials.** The LCD can be either $m - 3$ or $3 - m$. *Identify the LCD.*

Step 2 $\frac{1}{m - 3} - \frac{5}{3 - m}\left(\frac{-1}{-1}\right)$ *Multiply the second expression by $\frac{-1}{-1}$ to get an LCD of $m - 3$.*

Step 3 $\frac{1}{m - 3} - \frac{-5}{m - 3}$ *Write each expression using the LCD.*

Step 4 $\frac{1 - (-5)}{m - 3}$ *Subtract the numerators.*

Steps 5, 6 $\frac{6}{m - 3}$ *No factoring is needed, so just simplify.*

Remember!

Expressions like $m - 3$ and $3 - m$ are opposite binomials.

$3 - m = -1(m - 3)$

and

$m - 3 = -1(3 - m)$

Add or subtract. Simplify your answer.

4a. $\frac{4}{3d} - \frac{2d}{2d^3}$ **4b.** $\frac{a^2 + 4a}{a^2 + 2a - 8} + \frac{8}{a - 2}$ $\frac{a + 8}{a - 2}$

4a. $\frac{4d - 3}{3d^2}$

COMMON ERROR ALERT

When the denominators are opposite binomials, students might multiply only the denominator by -1. Remind students that the only way the expression remains equivalent is to multiply both the numerator and denominator by -1.

Power Presentations with PowerPoint®

Additional Examples

Example 4

Add or subtract. Simplify your answer.

A. $\frac{2n}{5n^3} + \frac{4n}{2n^2}$ $\frac{10n + 2}{5n^2}$

B. $\frac{2}{5 - w} - \frac{5}{w - 5}$ $-\frac{7}{w - 5}$

INTERVENTION
Questioning Strategies

EXAMPLE 4

- How do you determine the common denominator for two expressions?
- Would simplifying the expressions before finding the LCD change the LCD? Would it change the final answer?

Reaching All Learners
Through Critical Thinking

Show students that a negative sign can be distributed to the numerator or denominator. The resulting equivalent expressions can look very different.

$$-\frac{x + 3}{x - 7} = \frac{-(x + 3)}{x - 7} = \frac{-x - 3}{x - 7}$$

$$-\frac{x + 3}{x - 7} = \frac{x + 3}{-(x - 7)} = \frac{x + 3}{-x + 7}$$

Have students practice writing expressions in various equivalent ways.

Power Presentations with PowerPoint®

Additional Examples

Example 5

Roland needs to take supplies by canoe to some friends camping 2 miles upriver and then return to his own campsite. Roland's average paddling rate is about twice the speed of the river's current.

a. Write and simplify an expression for how long it will take Roland to canoe round trip. $\frac{8}{3x}$

b. If the speed of the river's current is 2.5 miles per hour, about how long will it take Roland to make the round trip? 64 minutes

INTERVENTION

Questioning Strategies

EXAMPLE 5

- Why are the numerators in the two expressions the same?
- Why are the denominators in the two expressions different?
- How do you change the fractional answer to minutes?

Diversity Canoes are open boats with paddles that are single-ended. Most kayaks have a closed top, and their paddles are usually double-ended.

EXAMPLE 5 Recreation Application

Katy wants to find out how long it will take to kayak 1 mile up a river and return to her starting point. Katy's average padding rate is 4 times the speed of the river's current.

a. Write and simplify an expression for the time it will take Katy to kayak the round-trip in terms of the rate of the river's current.

Step 1 Write expressions for the distances and rates in the problem.

The distance in both directions is 1 mile.

Let x represent the rate of the current, and let $4x$ represent Katy's paddling rate.

Katy's **rate against the current** is $4x - x$, or $3x$.

Katy's **rate with the current** is $4x + x$, or $5x$.

Step 2 Use a table to write expressions for time.

Direction	Distance (mi)	Rate (mi/h)	Time (h) = $\frac{\text{distance}}{\text{rate}}$
Upstream (against current)	1	$3x$	$\frac{1}{3x}$
Downstream (with current)	1	$5x$	$\frac{1}{5x}$

Helpful Hint

To write expressions for time in terms of distance and rate, solve $d = rt$ for t.

$t = \frac{d}{r}$

Step 3 Write and simplify an expression for the total time.

total time = time upstream + time downstream

total time $= \frac{1}{3x} + \frac{1}{5x}$ *Substitute known values.*

$= \frac{1}{3x}\left(\frac{5}{5}\right) + \frac{1}{5x}\left(\frac{3}{3}\right)$ *Multiply each fraction by an appropriate form of 1.*

$= \frac{5}{15x} + \frac{3}{15x}$ *Write each expression using the LCD, 15x.*

$= \frac{8}{15x}$ *Add the numerators.*

b. If the rate of the river is 2 miles per hour, how long will it take Katy to kayak round trip?

$\frac{8}{15(2)} = \frac{4}{15}$ *Substitute 2 for x. Simplify.*

It will take Katy $\frac{4}{15}$ of an hour, or 16 minutes, to kayak the round-trip.

5. What if?... Katy's average paddling rate increases to 5 times the speed of the current. Now how long will it take Katy to kayak the round trip? $\frac{5}{24}$ h or 12.5 min

THINK AND DISCUSS

1. Explain how to find the least common denominator of rational expressions.

2. GET ORGANIZED Copy and complete the graphic organizer. In each box, compare and contrast operations with fractions and rational expressions.

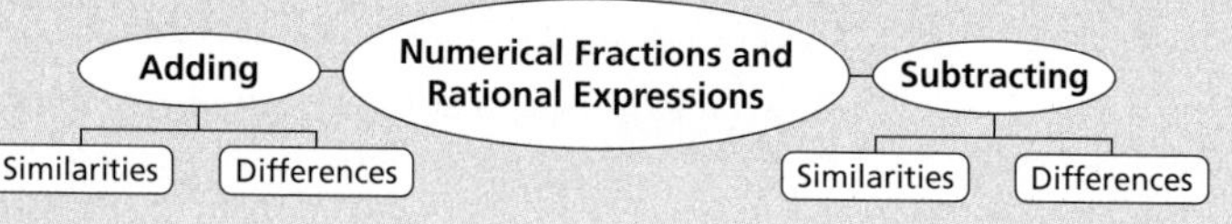

3 Close

Summarize

Tell students that rational expressions, like fractions, can be added or subtracted only if they have a common denominator. The easiest way is to use the LCD, which is the LCM of the denominators, although any common multiple will work (it just means more simplifying later in the problem). For example, $\frac{1}{x^2} + \frac{1}{x^3}$ can be written as $\frac{x}{x^3} + \frac{1}{x^3}$ or $\frac{x^3}{x^5} + \frac{x^2}{x^5}$. Both simplify to $\frac{x+1}{x^3}$.

ONGOING ASSESSMENT and INTERVENTION

***Diagnose Before* the Lesson**
12-5 Warm Up, TE p. 905

***Monitor During* the Lesson**
Check It Out! Exercises, SE pp. 905–908
Questioning Strategies, TE pp. 906–908

***Assess After* the Lesson**
12-5 Lesson Quiz, TE p. 911
Alternative Assessment, TE p. 911

Answers to *Think and Discuss*

1. Possible answer: Factor the denominators. Then write each factor the greatest number of times it appears in either denominator.
2. See p. A11.

go.hrw.com
Homework Help Online
KEYWORD: MA7 12-5
Parent Resources Online
KEYWORD: MA7 Parent

GUIDED PRACTICE

SEE EXAMPLE 1 p. 905

Add. Simplify your answer.

1. $\frac{y}{3y^2} + \frac{5y}{3y^2}$ $\mathbf{\frac{2}{y}}$

2. $\frac{4m + 30}{m + 5} + \frac{m^2 + 8m + 5}{m + 5}$ $\mathbf{m + 7}$

3. $\frac{x}{x^2 - 16} + \frac{4}{x^2 - 16}$ $\mathbf{\frac{1}{x - 4}}$

SEE EXAMPLE 2 p. 906

Subtract. Simplify your answer.

4. $\frac{7}{2x^3} - \frac{3}{2x^3}$ $\mathbf{\frac{2}{x^3}}$

5. $\frac{7a - 2}{a^2 + 3a + 2} - \frac{5a - 6}{a^2 + 3a + 2}$ $\mathbf{\frac{2}{a + 1}}$

6. $\frac{3x^2 + 1}{2x + 2} - \frac{2x^2 - 2x}{2x + 2}$ $\mathbf{\frac{x + 1}{2}}$

SEE EXAMPLE 3 p. 906

Find the LCM of the given expressions.

7. $3xy^2, 6x^3yz$ $\mathbf{6x^3y^2z}$

8. $x^2 + 9x + 20, (x + 5)(x - 4)$ $\mathbf{(x + 5)(x + 4)(x - 4)}$

9. $y^2 - 16, (y + 9)(y - 4)$ $\mathbf{(y + 4)(y - 4)(y + 9)}$

SEE EXAMPLE 4 p. 907

Add or subtract. Simplify your answer.

10. $\frac{3}{c} - \frac{4}{3c}$ $\mathbf{\frac{5}{3c}}$

11. $\frac{x^2 + x}{x^2 + 3x + 2} + \frac{3}{x + 2}$ $\mathbf{\frac{x + 3}{x + 2}}$

12. $\frac{2x}{x - 5} + \frac{x}{5 - x}$ $\mathbf{\frac{x}{x - 5}}$

SEE EXAMPLE 5 p. 908

13. **Travel** The Escobar family went on a car trip. They drove 100 miles on country roads and 240 miles on the highway. They drove 50% faster on the highway than on the country roads. Let r represent their rate on country roads in miles per hour.

    a. Write and simplify an expression that represents the number of hours it took the Escobar family to complete their trip in terms of r. (*Hint:* 50% faster means 150% of the original rate.) $\mathbf{\frac{260}{r}}$

    b. Find their total travel time if they drove the posted speed limit. $\mathbf{6\frac{1}{2}}$ **h**

PRACTICE AND PROBLEM SOLVING

Independent Practice	
For Exercises	See Example
14–16	1
17–19	2
20–25	3
26–31	4
32	5

Extra Practice
Skills Practice p. S27
Application Practice p. S39

Add. Simplify your answer.

14. $\frac{4y}{y^3} + \frac{4y}{y^3}$ $\mathbf{\frac{8}{y^2}}$

15. $\frac{a^2 - 3}{a + 3} + \frac{2a}{a + 3}$ $\mathbf{a - 1}$

16. $\frac{4x - 13}{x^2 - 5x + 6} + \frac{1}{x^2 - 5x + 6}$ $\mathbf{\frac{4}{x - 2}}$

Subtract. Simplify your answer.

17. $\frac{m^2}{m - 6} - \frac{6m}{m - 6}$ $\mathbf{m}$

18. $\frac{c + 3}{4c^2 - 25} - \frac{-c + 8}{4c^2 - 25}$ $\mathbf{\frac{1}{2c + 5}}$

19. $\frac{-2a^2 - 9a}{a - 2} - \frac{-5a^2 - 4a + 2}{a - 2}$ $\mathbf{3a + 1}$

Find the LCM of the given expressions.

20. $4jk^4m, 25jm$ $\mathbf{100jk^4m}$

21. $12a^2 + 4a, 27a + 9$ $\mathbf{36a(3a + 1)}$

22. $p^2 - 3p, pqr^2$ $\mathbf{pqr^2(p - 3)}$

23. $5xy^2z, 10y^3$ $\mathbf{10xy^3z}$

24. $5x^2, 7x - 14$ $\mathbf{35x^2(x - 2)}$

25. $y^2 + 7y + 10, y^2 + 9y + 20$ $\mathbf{(y + 5)(y + 2)(y + 4)}$

Add or subtract. Simplify your answer.

26. $\frac{2x}{5x} + \frac{10x}{3x^2}$ $\mathbf{\frac{6x + 50}{15x}}$

27. $\frac{y^2 - y}{y^2 - 4y + 3} - \frac{2y - 2}{3y - 9}$

28. $\frac{-3t}{t - 4} - \frac{2t + 4}{4 - t}$ $\mathbf{-1}$

29. $\frac{z}{3z^2} + \frac{4}{7z}$ $\mathbf{\frac{19}{21z}}$

30. $\frac{5x}{2x - 6} + \frac{x + 2}{3 - x}$

31. $\frac{3m}{4m - 8} - \frac{m^2}{m^2 - 4m + 4}$

27. $\mathbf{\frac{y + 2}{3(y - 3)}}$

Assignment Guide

Assign *Guided Practice* exercises as necessary.

If you finished Examples **1–2**
Basic 14–19, 34–35
Average 14–19, 34–35
Advanced 14–19, 34–35

If you finished Examples **1–5**
Basic 14–32, 34–43, 46, 49–52, 57–65
Average 14–43, 46–52, 57–65
Advanced 14–33, 43–65

Homework Quick Check
Quickly check key concepts.
Exercises: 16, 18, 22, 27, 28, 32

Number Sense In **Exercise 13,** students may write $0.50r$ for the rate of highway driving. Remind students to add 50% to 100% of the rate of the country-road driving:
$(100\%)r + (50\%)r = (150\%)r = 1.5r$

Answers

30. $\frac{3x - 4}{2(x - 3)}$

31. $\frac{-m^2 - 6m}{4(m - 2)^2}$

State Resources

go.hrw.com
State Resources Online
KEYWORD: MA7 Resources

Exercise 46 involves subtracting rational expressions. This exercise prepares students for the Multi-Step Test Prep on page 926.

Answers

40. $\frac{y^2+9}{4y^3}$

41. $\frac{8x+20}{(x+4)(x+2)}$

42. $\frac{2y^2+3y-3}{3(y+3)(y-3)}$

45. Possible answer: $\frac{3x}{x+1} + \frac{-2x}{x+1}$

46a. He subtracted $\frac{1}{x}$ from both sides of the equation.

b. He subtracted $\frac{1}{x}$ from $\frac{1}{12}$ by finding a common denominator $(12x)$.

57.

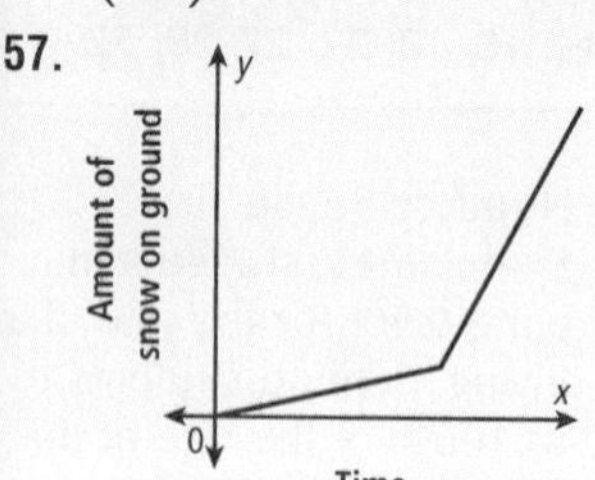

58.

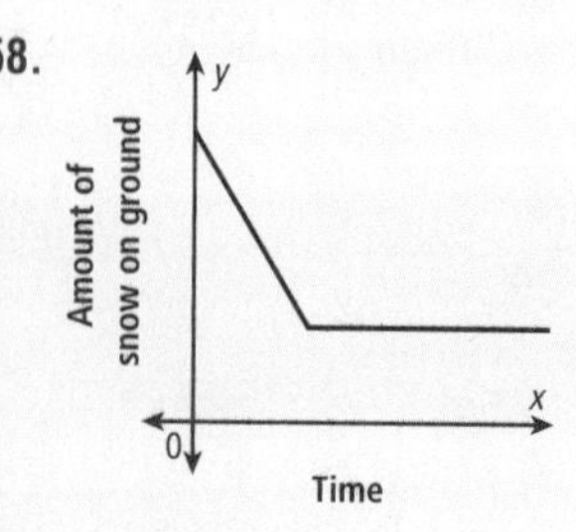

59.

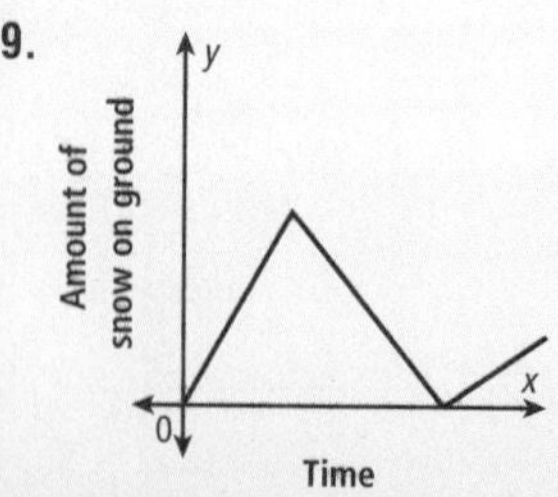

32. Fitness Ira walks one mile from his house to the recreation center. After playing basketball, he walks home at only 85% of his normal walking speed. Let w be Ira's normal rate of walking.

a. Write an expression to represent Ira's round-trip walking time. $\frac{37}{17w}$

b. If Ira's normal rate of walking is 3 miles per hour, how long did it take for him to complete his walking? $\frac{37}{51}$ **h or ≈ 44 min**

The first transcontinental railroad was completed in Utah on May 10, 1869. The occasion was commemorated with a golden spike that connected the eastern and western tracks.

33. Travel A train travels 500 miles across the Midwest—50 miles through cities and 450 miles through open country. As it passes through cities, it slows to one-fifth the speed it travels through open country. Let r represent the rate in open country in miles per hour.

a. Write and simplify an expression in terms of r that represents the number of hours it takes the train to travel 500 miles. $\frac{700}{r}$

b. Find the total travel time if the train's rate through open country is 50 miles per hour. **14 h**

c. **Critical Thinking** If you knew the time it took the train to make the trip, how could you find its average rate? **Divide the total distance (500 mi) by the total time.**

Add or subtract. Simplify your answer.

34. $\frac{10}{5+y} + \frac{2y}{5+y}$ **2**

35. $\frac{7}{49-c^2} - \frac{c}{49-c^2}$ $\frac{1}{7+c}$

36. $\frac{6a}{a-12} + \frac{4}{12-a}$ $\frac{6a-4}{a-12}$

37. $\frac{b}{2b^3} + \frac{3}{3b^2}$ $\frac{3}{2b^2}$

38. $\frac{r^2+2r}{r+3} - \frac{2r+9}{r+3}$ $r-3$

39. $\frac{x^2-2x}{3x-15} - \frac{8x-25}{3x-15}$ $\frac{x-5}{3}$

40. $\frac{2y}{8y^2} + \frac{9}{4y^3}$

41. $\frac{2}{x+2} + \frac{6}{x+4}$

42. $\frac{2y}{3y-9} - \frac{y+1}{y^2-9}$

43. Student A is incorrect. The student may have subtracted and then simplified before setting the denominator equal to 0. 4 is also an excluded value.

43. **ERROR ANALYSIS** Two students were asked to find the excluded values of the expression $\frac{p}{p^2-p-12} - \frac{4}{p^2-p-12}$. Student A identified the excluded value as $p=-3$. Student B identified the excluded values as $p=-3$ and $p=4$. Who is incorrect? What is the error?

44. **Multi-Step** At the spring fair there is a square Velcro target as shown. A player tosses a ball, which will stick to the target in some random spot. If the ball sticks to a spot in either the small square or the circle, the player wins a prize. What is the probability that a player will win a prize, assuming the ball sticks somewhere on the target? Round your answer to the nearest hundredth. **0.46**

x 3x x 3x x

45. **Critical Thinking** Write two expressions whose sum is $\frac{x}{x+1}$.

46. This problem will prepare you for the Multi-Step Test Prep on page 926.

Jonathan is studying light in his science class. He finds that a magnifying glass can be used to project upside-down images onto a piece of paper. The equation $\frac{1}{f} = \frac{1}{x} + \frac{1}{y}$ relates the focal length of the lens f, the distance of the object from the lens x, and the distance of the image from the lens y. The focal length of Jonathan's lens is 12 cm.

a. Jonathan wants to write y, the distance of the image from the lens, as a function of x, the distance of the object from the lens. To begin, he rewrote the equation above as $\frac{1}{y} = \frac{1}{12} - \frac{1}{x}$. Explain how he did this.

b. Explain how Jonathan simplified the equation in part **a** to $\frac{1}{y} = \frac{x-12}{12x}$.

12-5 PRACTICE A
12-5 PRACTICE C
12-5 PRACTICE B

Add or subtract. Simplify your answer.

1. $\frac{3m}{8m^3} + \frac{m}{8m^3}$ $\frac{1}{2m^2}$

2. $\frac{x^2-6x}{x+3} + \frac{4x-15}{x+3}$ $x-5$

3. $\frac{c^2+c}{c^2-25} - \frac{c^2+5}{c^2-25}$ $\frac{1}{c+5}$

4. $\frac{6a-1}{a^2+7a+10} - \frac{2a-9}{a^2+7a+10}$ $\frac{4}{a+5}$

Find the LCM of the given expressions.

5. $4a^2b$, $6a$, $10b^3$ $60a^2b^3$

6. x^2+5x+6, $(x+3)(x-1)$ $(x+2)(x+3)(x-1)$

Add or subtract. Simplify your answer.

7. $\frac{5}{3n} - \frac{2}{2n}$ $\frac{2}{3n}$

8. $\frac{y^2+4y}{y^2+6y+8} + \frac{3}{y+2}$ $\frac{y+3}{y+2}$

9. $\frac{x+2}{x^2-9} - \frac{1}{9-x^2}$ $\frac{1}{x-3}$

10. $\frac{1}{6y^2+24y} - \frac{3}{y^2-y-20}$ $\frac{-17y-5}{6y^3-6y^2-120y}$

11. Kendrick walked 1 mile, and then jogged 5 miles. His jogging speed was 4 times his walking speed w in mi/h.

a. Write and simplify an expression that represents Kendrick's total exercise time. $\frac{9}{4w}$

b. How many minutes did Kendrick exercise if his walking speed was 3 mi/h? **45 min**

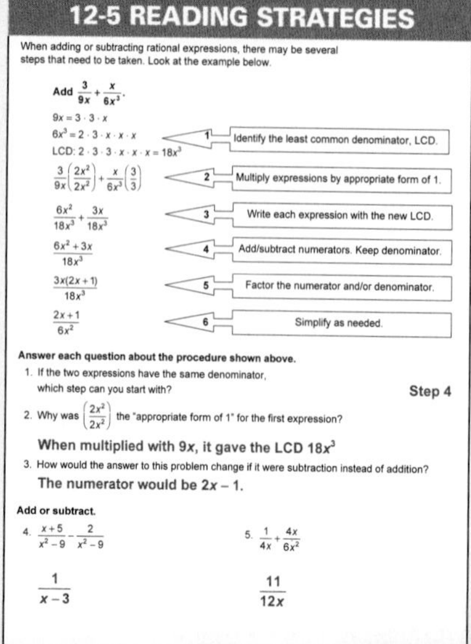

12-5 READING STRATEGIES

When adding or subtracting rational expressions, there may be several steps that need to be taken. Look at the example below.

Add $\frac{3}{9x} + \frac{x}{6x^3}$.

$9x = 3 \cdot 3 \cdot x$
$6x^3 = 2 \cdot 3 \cdot x \cdot x \cdot x$
LCD: $2 \cdot 3 \cdot 3 \cdot x \cdot x \cdot x = 18x^3$ — 1 Identify the least common denominator, LCD.

$\frac{3}{9x}\left(\frac{2x^2}{2x^2}\right) + \frac{x}{6x^3}\left(\frac{3}{3}\right)$ — 2 Multiply expressions by appropriate form of 1.

$\frac{6x^2}{18x^3} + \frac{3x}{18x^3}$ — 3 Write each expression with the new LCD.

$\frac{6x^2+3x}{18x^3}$ — 4 Add/subtract numerators. Keep denominator.

$\frac{3x(2x+1)}{18x^3}$ — 5 Factor the numerator and/or denominator.

$\frac{2x+1}{6x^2}$ — 6 Simplify as needed.

Answer each question about the procedure shown above.

1. If the two expressions have the same denominator, which step can you start with? **Step 4**

2. Why was $\left(\frac{2x^2}{2x^2}\right)$ the "appropriate form of 1" for the first expression?

When multiplied with $9x$, it gave the LCD $18x^3$

3. How would the answer to this problem change if it were subtraction instead of addition?

The numerator would be $2x-1$.

Add or subtract.

4. $\frac{x+5}{x^2-9} - \frac{2}{x^2-9}$ $\frac{1}{x-3}$

5. $\frac{1}{4x} + \frac{4x}{6x^2}$ $\frac{11}{12x}$

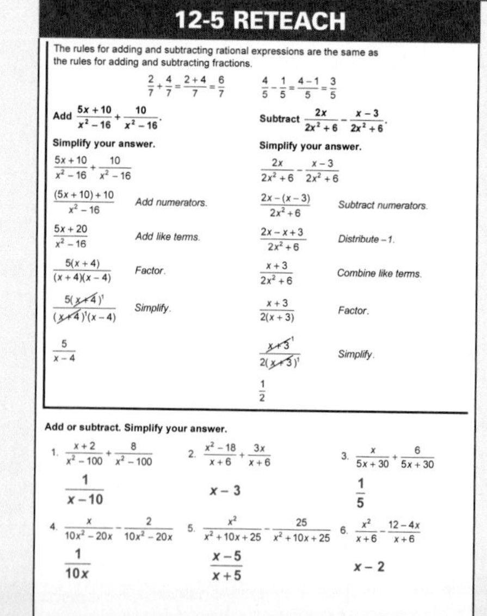

12-5 RETEACH

The rules for adding and subtracting rational expressions are the same as the rules for adding and subtracting fractions.

$\frac{2}{7} + \frac{4}{7} = \frac{2+4}{7} = \frac{6}{7}$ $\frac{4}{5} - \frac{1}{5} = \frac{4-1}{5} = \frac{3}{5}$

Add $\frac{5x+10}{x^2-16} + \frac{10}{x^2-16}$.

Simplify your answer.

$\frac{5x+10}{x^2-16} + \frac{10}{x^2-16}$

$\frac{(5x+10)+10}{x^2-16}$ *Add numerators.*

$\frac{5x+20}{x^2-16}$ *Add like terms.*

$\frac{5(x+4)}{(x+4)(x-4)}$ *Factor.*

$\frac{5(x+4)^1}{(x+4)^1(x-4)}$ *Simplify.*

$\frac{5}{x-4}$

Subtract $\frac{2x}{2x^2+6} - \frac{x-3}{2x^2+6}$.

Simplify your answer.

$\frac{2x}{2x^2+6} - \frac{x-3}{2x^2+6}$

$\frac{2x-(x-3)}{2x^2+6}$ *Subtract numerators.*

$\frac{2x-x+3}{2x^2+6}$ *Distribute −1.*

$\frac{x+3}{2x^2+6}$ *Combine like terms.*

$\frac{x+3}{2(x+3)}$ *Factor.*

$\frac{x+3^1}{2(x+3)^1}$ *Simplify.*

$\frac{1}{2}$

Add or subtract. Simplify your answer.

1. $\frac{x+2}{x^2-100} + \frac{8}{x^2-100}$ $\frac{1}{x-10}$

2. $\frac{x^2-18}{x+6} + \frac{3x}{x+6}$ $x-3$

3. $\frac{x}{5x+30} + \frac{6}{5x+30}$ $\frac{1}{5}$

4. $\frac{x}{10x^2-20x} - \frac{2}{10x^2-20x}$ $\frac{1}{10x}$

5. $\frac{x^2}{x^2+10x+25} - \frac{25}{x^2+10x+25}$ $\frac{x-5}{x+5}$

6. $\frac{x^2}{x+6} - \frac{12-4x}{x+6}$ $x-2$

47. **Critical Thinking** Identify three common denominators that could be used to add $\frac{3}{2x^2}$ to $\frac{3}{4x}$. **$4x^2$; $8x^2$; $8x^3$**

48. **Write About It** Explain how to find the least common denominator of two rational expressions when the denominators are opposite binomials.
In this case, either binomial can be used as the least common denominator. After selecting the binomial for the denominator, change the other binomial to match by multiplying it by −1.

TEST PREP

49. What is the LCD of $\frac{6}{3p+3}$ and $\frac{4}{p+1}$?

Ⓐ $p + 1$ (circled)   Ⓑ 12   Ⓒ $3p + 1$ Ⓓ $3p + 3$

50. Simplify $\frac{4}{2x} - \frac{1}{x}$.

Ⓕ $\frac{1}{x}$ (circled)   Ⓖ $\frac{3}{x}$ Ⓗ $\frac{5}{x}$ Ⓙ $\frac{3}{2x}$

51. Which of the following is equivalent to $\frac{2x}{x-2}$?

Ⓐ $\frac{x}{x+2} + \frac{x}{x-2}$ Ⓒ $\frac{x^2+4x}{x^2-4} + \frac{x}{x+2}$

Ⓑ $\frac{2x}{x^2-4} + \frac{4}{x-2}$ Ⓓ $\frac{x}{x+2} + \frac{x^2+6x}{x^2-4}$ (circled)

52. **Extended Response** Andrea biked 3 miles to the post office and 5 miles to the library. The rate at which she biked to the library was three times faster than her rate to the post office r.

a. Write an expression that represents Andrea's total biking time in hours. Explain what each part of your expression means in the situation.

52a. $\frac{3}{r} + \frac{5}{3r}$; time to post office: $\frac{3}{r}$; time to library: $\frac{5}{3r}$

b. Simplify the expression. **$\frac{14}{3r}$**

c. How long did it take Andrea to bike the 8 miles if her biking rate to the post office was 3 miles per hour? **$\frac{14}{9}$ h or ≈ 1 h 33 min**

CHALLENGE AND EXTEND

Add or subtract and simplify. Find the excluded values.

53. $\frac{3}{x+y} - \frac{2x+y}{x^2-y^2}$ 54. $\frac{3}{2m} + \frac{4}{m^2} + \frac{2}{5m}$ 55. $\frac{a}{xy} + \frac{b}{xz} + \frac{c}{yz}$

53. $\frac{x-4y}{(x+y)(x-y)}$; $x \neq y$ and $x \neq -y$

54. $\frac{19m+40}{10m^2}$; $m \neq 0$

55. $\frac{az+by+cx}{xyz}$; $x \neq 0$, $y \neq 0$, and $z \neq 0$

56. Simplify the complex fraction $\dfrac{\frac{1}{x} - \frac{1}{y}}{\frac{x}{xy} - \frac{1}{x}}$. (*Hint:* Simplify the numerator and denominator of the complex fraction first.) **−1**

SPIRAL REVIEW

Sketch a graph for each situation. *(Lesson 4-1)*

57. Snow falls lightly at first, then falls heavily at a steady rate.

58. Snow melts quickly during the afternoon, then stops melting at night.

59. Snow falls heavily, is shoveled away, and then a light snow falls.

Solve each quadratic equation by factoring. *(Lesson 9-6)*

60. $d^2 - 4d - 12 = 0$ **−2, 6**   61. $2g^2 - 9g = -4$ **$\frac{1}{2}$, 4**   62. $9x^2 + 6x + 1 = 0$ **$-\frac{1}{3}$**

Simplify each rational expression, if possible. Identify any excluded values. *(Lesson 12-3)*

63. $\frac{2t^2-8}{t^2-4}$ **2; $t \neq \pm 2$**   64. $\frac{n^2+5n}{n^2+3n-10}$ 65. $\frac{4-x}{x^2-16}$ **$-\frac{1}{x+4}$; $x \neq \pm 4$**

64. $\frac{n}{n-2}$; −5, 2

TEST PREP DOCTOR Students who chose **C** for **Exercise 49** may have identified 3 and $p + 1$ as factors but forgot to distribute when finding their product.

Students who chose **G** for **Exercise 50** may have either added the expressions or subtracted both the numerator and the denominator.

Journal

Have students explain how to find the least common multiple of $6x^2y$ and $9x$.

ALTERNATIVE ASSESSMENT

Have students select and answer one addition or subtraction problem with unlike denominators from the exercises. Tell them to show and explain each step of their work as if they were explaining it to someone who was seeing it for the first time.

Power Presentations with PowerPoint®

12-5 Lesson Quiz

Add or subtract. Simplify your answer.

1. $\frac{3h}{h^2} + \frac{2h}{h^2}$ $\frac{5}{h}$

2. $\frac{x+4}{x^2} - \frac{2x+4}{x^2}$ $-\frac{1}{x}$

3. $\frac{5}{2fh^3} + \frac{g}{f^2h}$ $\frac{5f+2gh^2}{2f^2h^3}$

4. $\frac{7}{h-5} - \frac{4}{5-h}$ $\frac{11}{h-5}$

5. $\frac{5x-30}{x^2-13x+42} + \frac{11}{x^2-6x-7}$ $\frac{5x+16}{x^2-6x-7}$

6. Vong drove 98 miles on interstate highways and 80 miles on state roads. He drove 25% faster on the interstate highways than on the state roads. Let r represent his rate on the state roads in miles per hour.

a. Write and simplify an expression that represents the number of hours Vong drove in terms of r. $\frac{198}{1.25r}$

b. Find Vong's driving time if he averaged 55 miles per hour on the state roads. about 2 h 53 min

Also available on transparency

12-5 PROBLEM SOLVING

Adib is kayaking on the Peconic River in Long Island, New York. He paddles his kayak at an average rate of 3 mi/h, but does not know the rate of the river's current. Adib plans to kayak upstream 2 mi and then back downstream to his starting point.

1. Let x represent the rate of the current in the Peconic River in miles per hour. Write and simplify an expression for the total time of Adib's round trip.
$\frac{12}{(3-x)(3+x)}$

2. If the rate of the river's current is 2 mi/h, how long will it take Adib to kayak round trip?
$\frac{12}{5}$ h, or 2.4 h, or 2 h 24 min

3. If the rate of the river's current is 3 mi/h, how long will it take Adib to kayak round trip? Explain what your answer could mean in this context.
$\frac{12}{0}$ = undefined; because the rate of the current is equal to Adib's rate of paddling, he remains stationary and is never able to kayak upstream.

Select the best answer.

4. Terry drives 2 mi on city streets, and 20 mi on the highway. Her speed on the highway is three times her speed on the city streets r, in miles per hour. Write and simplify and expression that represents the length of Terry's trip in hours.

A $\frac{13}{3r}$ C $\frac{26}{3r}$
B $\frac{22}{4r}$ D $\frac{62}{3r}$

5. Nahuel walks 1 km to school at a rate of w km/h. When he gets to school, he realizes that he forgot his math book, so he jogs back home and back to school at a rate 4 km/h faster than his walking rate. Write and simplify an expression that represents the length of Nahuel's entire trip to school in hours.

F $\frac{3}{2w}$ H $\frac{2(w+1)}{w(w+2)}$
G $\frac{3}{2(w+2)}$ **J** $\frac{3w+4}{w(w+4)}$

6. A test consists of 4 free response questions and 50 multiple choice questions. The test's writers assume an average student can do x free response questions per hour, and four times as many multiple choice questions per hour. If an average student can do 6 free response questions per hour, how long is the test?

A $1\frac{4}{5}$ h   C $3\frac{3}{8}$ h
B $2\frac{3}{4}$ h   D $5\frac{2}{3}$ h

7. In a carnival game, Beth runs 100 m to a table, picks up water balloons, and runs back to the starting line. Beth originally runs to the table at a rate of y m/s, but runs 1 m/s slower when she carries the balloons. If Beth originally runs 5 m/s, how long, to the nearest second, does it take her to finish?

F 10 s   H 37 s
G 22 s   **J** 45 s

12-5 CHALLENGE

At 8 A.M., Mr. Varhalla drives from home to work. Because of rush-hour traffic, he is only able to drive 40 mi/h.
At 3 P.M. he leaves work early to drive back home. Because he avoids rush-hour traffic, he is able to drive the same distance at 65 mi/h.

1. Let d represent the distance in miles between home and work. What is the total distance of Mr. Varhalla's round trip? **$2d$**

2. Write an expression for the time in hours that it takes Mr. Varhalla to drive from home to work. **$\frac{d}{40}$**

3. Write an expression for the time in hours that it takes him to drive from work back home. **$\frac{d}{45}$**

4. Write (but don't simplify) an addition expression for the total time in hours of Mr. Varhalla's round trip. **$\frac{d}{40} + \frac{d}{65}$**

5. Because $d = rt$, you can find average speed for the entire round trip by dividing the total distance by the total time, or $r = \frac{d}{t}$. Write a complex fraction that represents Mr. Varhalla's average speed in miles per hour. **$\dfrac{2d}{\frac{d}{40} + \frac{d}{65}}$**

6. Simplify the complex fraction to find Mr. Varhalla's average speed in miles per hour. Round to the nearest tenth. **≈49.5 mi/h**

7. Is the average speed for the round trip the same as the average of the speeds 40 mi/h and 65 mi/h?
No; the average of 40 mi/h and 65 mi/h is $\frac{40+65}{2}$ = 52.5 mi/h.

Use what you have learned in questions 1–7 to solve these problems. For each, first write a complex fraction that represents average speed and then simplify it to find the average speed. Round your answers to the nearest tenth.

8. Teri drives 30 mi/h from home to the hardware store. After loading her truck with lumber, she drives 15 mi/h back home. What is Teri's average speed in miles per hour for the entire round trip? **20 mi/h**

9. Kevin runs four laps around Piedmont Park at 10 mi/h. Then, to cool down, he walks one more lap at 3 mi/h. What is Kevin's average speed for the entire workout? (*Hint:* Let d represent the distance of one lap.) **6.8 mi/h**

Organizer

Use with Lesson 12-6

Pacing:

Traditional $\frac{1}{2}$ day

Block $\frac{1}{4}$ day

Objective: Use algebra tiles to model polynomial division.

Materials: algebra tiles

Resources

Algebra Lab Activities

12-6 Lab Recording Sheet

Teach

Discuss

Students need to add zero pairs to their polynomial model when the required tiles for filling the rectangle are not available.

Close

Key Concept

After modeling the polynomial and placing tiles for the length, the width can be found by completing the rectangle and reading the width.

Assessment

Journal Have students choose one expression from the Try This exercise and explain in detail how to find the quotient by using algebra tiles.

12-6

Model Polynomial Division

Some polynomial divisions can be modeled by algebra tiles. If a polynomial can be modeled by a rectangle, then its factors are represented by the length and width of the rectangle. If one factor is a divisor, then the other factor is a quotient.

Use with Lesson 12-6

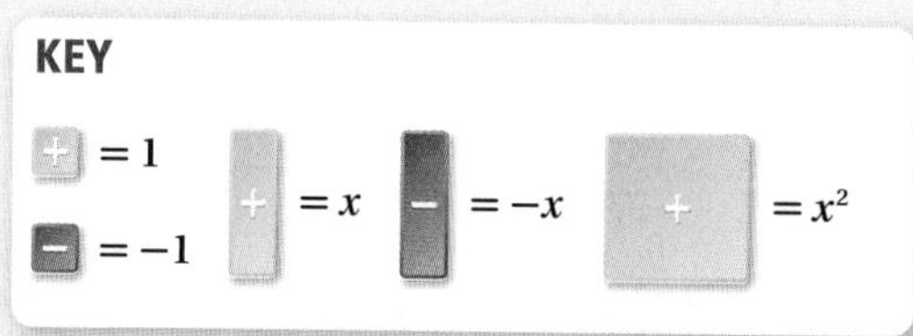

Activity 1

Use algebra tiles to find the quotient $(x^2 + 5x + 6) \div (x + 2)$.

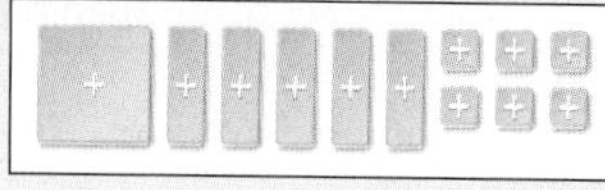

Model $x^2 + 5x + 6$.

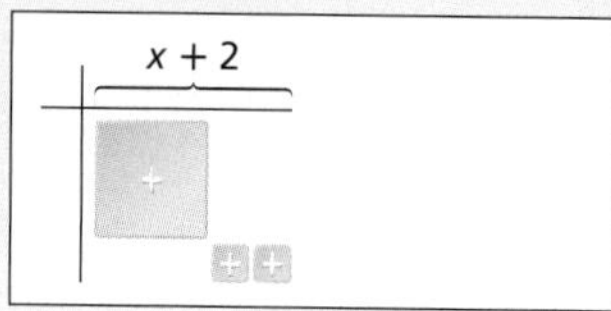

Try to form a rectangle with a length of $x + 2$.

Place the x^2-tile in the upper-left corner. Then place two unit tiles in a row at the lower-right corner.

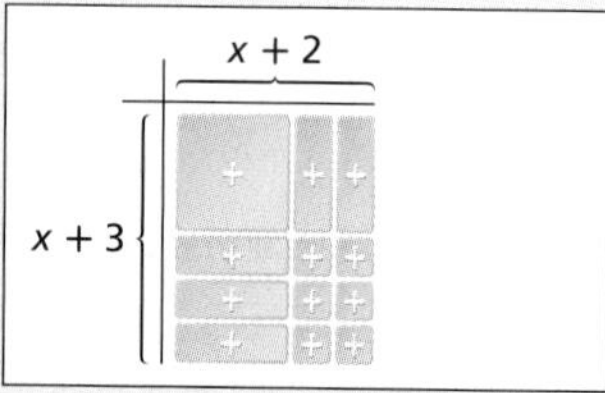

Try to use all the remaining tiles to complete a rectangle.

If you can complete a rectangle, then the width of the rectangle is the quotient.

The rectangle has length $x + 2$ and width $x + 3$. So, $(x^2 + 5x + 6) \div (x + 2) = x + 3$.

You can check your answer by multiplying.	$(x + 3)(x + 2)$ $x^2 + 2x + 3x + 6$ $x^2 + 5x + 6$ ✓	*Use the FOIL method.*

Try This

Use algebra tiles to find each quotient.

1. $(x^2 + 5x + 4) \div (x + 1)$ **$x + 4$**
2. $(x^2 + 7x + 10) \div (x + 5)$ **$x + 2$**
3. $(x^2 + 4x - 5) \div (x - 1)$ **$x + 5$**
4. $(2x^2 + 5x + 2) \div (x + 2)$ **$2x + 1$**
5. $(x^2 - 6x + 8) \div (x - 2)$ **$x - 4$**
6. $(2x^2 - x - 3) \div (x + 1)$ **$2x - 3$**
7. Describe what happens when you try to model $(x^2 - 4x + 3) \div (x + 1)$.

Answers to *Try This*

7. There is no arrangement of tiles that will form a rectangle with a side length of $x + 1$ because $x + 1$ is not a factor of $x^2 - 4x + 3$.

State Resources

12-6 Dividing Polynomials

Objective
Divide a polynomial by a monomial or binomial.

Why learn this?
Division of polynomials can be used to compare the energy produced by solar panels. (See Exercise 51.)

The electrical power (in watts) produced by a solar panel is directly proportional to the surface area of the solar panel. Division of polynomials can be used to compare energy production by solar panels of different sizes.

To divide a polynomial by a monomial, you can first write the division as a rational expression. Then divide each term in the polynomial by the monomial.

EXAMPLE 1 Dividing a Polynomial by a Monomial

Divide $(6x^3 + 8x^2 - 4x) \div 2x$.

$\dfrac{6x^3 + 8x^2 - 4x}{2x}$ *Write as a rational expression.*

$\dfrac{6x^3}{2x} + \dfrac{8x^2}{2x} - \dfrac{4x}{2x}$ *Divide each term in the polynomial by the monomial 2x.*

$\dfrac{\cancel{6}^3 \cancel{x^3}^{x^2}}{\cancel{2}^1 \cancel{x}^1} + \dfrac{\cancel{8}^4 \cancel{x^2}^{x}}{\cancel{2}^1 \cancel{x}^1} - \dfrac{\cancel{4}^2 \cancel{x}^1}{\cancel{2}^1 \cancel{x}^1}$ *Divide out common factors.*

$3x^2 + 4x - 2$ *Simplify.*

CHECK IT OUT! Divide.

1a. $(8p^3 - 4p^2 + 12p) \div (-4p^2)$ $-2p + 1 - \dfrac{3}{p}$

1b. $(6x^3 + 2x - 15) \div 6x$ $x^2 + \dfrac{1}{3} - \dfrac{5}{2x}$

Division of a polynomial by a binomial is similar to division of whole numbers.

Know it! Note — Dividing Polynomials

	WORDS	NUMBERS	POLYNOMIALS
Step 1	Factor the numerator and/or denominator if possible.	$\dfrac{168}{3} = \dfrac{56 \cdot 3}{3}$	$\dfrac{r^2 + 3r + 2}{r + 2} = \dfrac{(r+2)(r+1)}{(r+2)}$
Step 2	Divide out any common factors.	$\dfrac{56 \cdot \cancel{3}}{\cancel{3}}$	$\dfrac{\cancel{(r+2)}(r+1)}{\cancel{(r+2)}}$
Step 3	Simplify.	56	$r + 1$

12-6 Organizer

Pacing: Traditional 1 day
Block $\frac{1}{2}$ day

Objective: Divide a polynomial by a monomial or binomial.

PREMIER Online Edition
Tutorial Videos

Power Presentations with PowerPoint®

Warm Up

Divide.

1. $m^2n \div mn^4$ $\dfrac{m}{n^3}$

2. $2x^3y^2 \div 6xy$ $\dfrac{x^2y}{3}$

3. $(3a + 6a^2) \div 3a^2b$ $\dfrac{1 + 2a}{ab}$

Factor each expression.

4. $5x^2 + 16x + 12$ $(5x + 6)(x + 2)$

5. $16p^2 - 72p + 81$ $(4p - 9)^2$

Also available on transparency

Math Humor

Q: What do math teachers train their parrots to say?

A: Polly want to factor?

1 Introduce

EXPLORATION

12-6 Dividing Polynomials

Recall that multiplication and division are inverse operations. If you know that $ab = c$, you can also write $\frac{c}{a} = b$, where $a \neq 0$.

1. Multiply to show that $4x(3x^2 - 2x + 5) = 12x^3 - 8x^2 + 20x$.
2. Based on the equation in Problem 1, complete the following: $\dfrac{12x^3 - 8x^2 + 20x}{4x} = $ ___?___
3. Use this idea to help you complete the table. In each row, first multiply to find the product of the polynomials. Then write a related quotient.

Product	Related Quotient
$2y(y^2 + 3y - 1) =$ ___?___	$\dfrac{?}{2y} =$ ___?___
$4m^2(m^2 + 2m + 9) =$ ___?___	$\dfrac{?}{4m^2} =$ ___?___
$3c(c^3 - c^2 - 2) =$ ___?___	$\dfrac{?}{3c} =$ ___?___

THINK AND DISCUSS

4. **Describe** a rule for dividing a polynomial by a monomial.
5. **Show** how you can use your rule to find the quotient $\dfrac{x^3 + x^2 + x}{x}$.

Motivate

Have students solve $14\overline{)186{,}509}$ using long division. 13,322 R 1, or $13{,}322\frac{1}{14}$

Ask how they can check their answer. Multiply 13,322 by 14 and add 1.

Tell students they will learn to use long division to divide polynomials.

Explorations and answers are provided in *Alternate Openers: Explorations Transparencies.*

State Resources

go.hrw.com
State Resources Online
KEYWORD: MA7 Resources

Power Presentations with PowerPoint®

Additional Examples

Example 1

Divide $(5x^3 - 20x^2 + 30x) \div 5x$. $x^2 - 4x + 6$

Example 2

Divide.

A. $\dfrac{x^2 + 2x - 15}{x - 3}$ $x + 5$

B. $\dfrac{2x^2 - 7x - 4}{x^2 - x - 12}$ $\dfrac{2x + 1}{x + 3}$

INTERVENTION
Questioning Strategies

EXAMPLE 1

- How are common factors divided out?

EXAMPLE 2

- Why would writing each term of the numerator over the denominator not be a good first step in this type of problem?
- Why should you factor the numerator?

EXAMPLE 2 Dividing a Polynomial by a Binomial

Divide.

A $\dfrac{c^2 + 4c - 5}{c - 1}$

$\dfrac{(c+5)(c-1)}{c-1}$ *Factor the numerator.*

$\dfrac{(c+5)\cancel{(c-1)}^1}{\cancel{(c-1)}^1}$ *Divide out common factors.*

$c + 5$ *Simplify.*

B $\dfrac{3x^2 - 10x - 8}{4 - x}$

$\dfrac{(3x+2)(x-4)}{4-x}$ *Factor the numerator.*

$\dfrac{(3x+2)(x-4)}{-1(x-4)}$ *Factor one opposite binomial.*

$\dfrac{(3x+2)\cancel{(x-4)}^1}{-1\cancel{(x-4)}^1}$ *Divide out common factors.*

$-3x - 2$ *Simplify.*

Helpful Hint

Put each term of the numerator over the denominator only when the denominator is a monomial. If the denominator is a polynomial, try to factor first.

CHECK IT OUT! Divide.

2a. $\dfrac{10 + 7k + k^2}{k + 2}$ $k + 5$ **2b.** $\dfrac{b^2 - 49}{b + 7}$ $b - 7$ **2c.** $\dfrac{s^2 + 12s + 36}{s + 6}$ $s + 6$

Recall how you used long division to divide whole numbers as shown at right. You can also use long division to divide polynomials. An example is shown below.

$$\begin{array}{r} 15 \\ 23\overline{)345} \\ \underline{-23} \\ 115 \\ \underline{-115} \\ 0 \end{array}$$

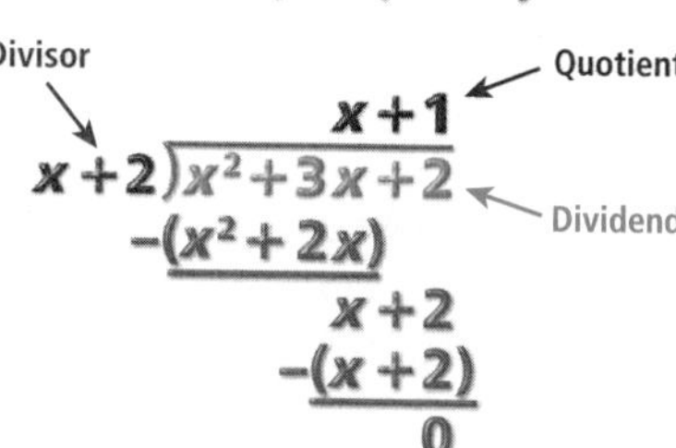

Using Long Division to Divide a Polynomial by a Binomial	
Step 1	Write the binomial and polynomial in long division form.
Step 2	Divide the first term of the dividend by the first term of the divisor. This is the first term of the quotient.
Step 3	Multiply this first term of the quotient by the binomial divisor and place the product under the dividend, aligning like terms.
Step 4	Subtract the product from the dividend.
Step 5	Bring down the next term in the dividend.
Step 6	Repeat Steps 2–5 as necessary until you get 0 or until the degree of the remainder is less than the degree of the binomial.

2 Teach

Guided Instruction

Review the process of long division with numbers. Also review the standard form of a polynomial: terms are written in order from highest to lowest degree. Stress the importance of writing polynomials in standard form and using a zero as a placeholder for a missing term, when necessary.

Reaching All Learners
Through Visual Cues

Some students may have more success with their long division by using centimeter grid paper to help align like terms. Show students how to put each term and operation symbol of the long division problem into a separate box of the grid paper. For example:

x	+	3	$2x^2$	+	$9x$	+	14

Teaching Tip

Critical Thinking Show students how to check their answers for long division with remainders by multiplying the divisor by each term of the quotient. For example:

$(3x^2 + 11x + 16) \div (x + 2) = 3x + 5 + \dfrac{6}{x+2}$

Check: $(x + 2)\left(3x + 5 + \dfrac{6}{x+2}\right)$

$= 3x(x + 2) + 5(x + 2) + \left(\dfrac{6}{x+2}\right)(x + 2)$

$= 3x^2 + 6x + 5x + 10 + 6 = 3x^2 + 11x + 16$

EXAMPLE 3 Polynomial Long Division

Divide using long division.

A $(x^2 + 2 + 3x) \div (x + 2)$

Step 1 $x + 2\overline{)x^2 + 3x + 2}$ — *Write in long division form with expressions in standard form.*

Step 2 $x + 2\overline{)x^2 + 3x + 2}$, quotient x — *Divide the first term of the dividend by the first term of the divisor to get the first term of the quotient.*

Step 3 $x + 2\overline{)x^2 + 3x + 2}$, quotient x; $x^2 + 2x$ — *Multiply the first term of the quotient by the binomial divisor. Place the product under the dividend, aligning like terms.*

Step 4 $x + 2\overline{)x^2 + 3x + 2}$, quotient x

$$\begin{array}{r} -(x^2 + 2x) \\ \hline 0 + x \end{array}$$

Subtract the product from the dividend.

Step 5 $x + 2\overline{)x^2 + 3x + 2}$, quotient x

$$\begin{array}{r} -(x^2 + 2x)\downarrow \\ \hline x + 2 \end{array}$$

Bring down the next term in the dividend.

Step 6 $x + 2\overline{)x^2 + 3x + 2}$, quotient $x + 1$

$$\begin{array}{r} -(x^2 + 2x) \\ \hline x + 2 \\ -(x + 2) \\ \hline 0 \end{array}$$

Repeat Steps 2–5 as necessary.
The remainder is 0.

Check Multiply the answer and the divisor.

$$\begin{aligned} &(x + 2)(x + 1) \\ &x^2 + x + 2x + 2 \\ &x^2 + 3x + 2 ✓ \end{aligned}$$

B $\dfrac{x^2 + 4x + 3}{x + 1}$

$x + 1\overline{)x^2 + 4x + 3}$ — *Write in long division form.*

$x + 1\overline{)x^2 + 4x + 3}$, quotient $x + 3$

$$\begin{array}{rl} -(x^2 + x)\downarrow & x^2 \div x = x \\ & \text{Multiply } x \cdot (x + 1)\text{. Subtract.} \\ \hline 3x + 3 & \text{Bring down the 3. } 3x \div x = 3 \\ -(3x + 3) & \text{Multiply } 3(x + 1)\text{. Subtract.} \\ \hline 0 & \text{The remainder is 0.} \end{array}$$

Check Multiply the answer and the divisor.

$$\begin{aligned} &(x + 1)(x + 3) \\ &x^2 + 3x + 1x + 3 \\ &x^2 + 4x + 3 ✓ \end{aligned}$$

Helpful Hint

You can check your simplified answer by multiplying it by the divisor. When the remainder is 0, the product should be the numerator.

CHECK IT OUT! Divide using long division.

3a. $(2y^2 - 5y - 3) \div (y - 3)$ **$2y + 1$**

3b. $(a^2 - 8a + 12) \div (a - 6)$ **$a - 2$**

COMMON ERROR ALERT

In Step 4 of **Example 3A,** subtracting the product can be thought of as adding the opposite of the product. Tell students to change the sign of each term and then add.

Teaching Tip **Inclusion** In Step 3 of **Example 3A,** students might multiply the first term of the quotient only by the first term of the divisor. Remind students to use the Distributive Property in this step.

Power Presentations with PowerPoint®

Additional Examples

Example 3

Divide using long division.

A. $(x^2 + 10x + 21) \div (x + 3)$ $x + 7$

B. $\dfrac{x^2 - 2x - 8}{x - 4}$ $x + 2$

INTERVENTION

Questioning Strategies

EXAMPLE 3

- What does it mean to divide by a binomial?
- When would you choose long division instead of factoring and dividing out? Why?

Teaching Tip **Math Connections** Introduce long division of polynomials by having students work some numerical problems that require long division. Then show how polynomial long division parallels this process.

Power Presentations with PowerPoint®

Additional Examples

Example 4

Divide $(3x^2 + 19x + 26) \div (x + 5)$.

$3x + 4 + \frac{6}{x + 5}$

Example 5

Divide $(x^3 - 7 - 4x) \div (x - 3)$.

$x^2 + 3x + 5 + \frac{8}{x - 5}$

INTERVENTION

Questioning Strategies

EXAMPLE 4

- What does having a remainder mean?
- Is it possible to check the answer when the answer contains a remainder? Explain.

EXAMPLE 5

- When dividing polynomials, in what form should the dividend be written?
- How is a placeholder created when dividing polynomials?

Sometimes the divisor is not a factor of the dividend, so the remainder is not 0. Then the remainder can be written as a rational expression.

EXAMPLE 4 Long Division with a Remainder

Divide $(2x^2 + 3x - 6) \div (x - 2)$.

$$x - 2\overline{)2x^2 + 3x - 6}$$ *Write in long division form.*

$$\begin{array}{r} 2x + 7 \\ x - 2\overline{)2x^2 + 3x - 6} \\ \underline{-(2x^2 - 4x)} \quad\downarrow \\ 7x - 6 \\ \underline{-(7x - 14)} \\ 8 \end{array}$$

$2x^2 \div x = 2x$

Multiply $2x(x - 2)$. Subtract.

Bring down the -6. $7x \div x = 7$

Multiply $7(x - 2)$. Subtract.

The remainder is 8.

$\frac{8}{x - 2}$ *Write the remainder as a rational expression using the divisor as the denominator.*

$2x + 7 + \frac{8}{x - 2}$ *Write the quotient with the remainder.*

Divide.

4a. $(3m^2 + 4m - 2) \div (m + 3)$ **4b.** $(y^2 + 3y + 2) \div (y - 3)$

$3m - 5 + \frac{13}{m + 3}$ $y + 6 + \frac{20}{y - 3}$

Sometimes you need to write a placeholder for a term using a zero coefficient. This is best seen if you write the polynomials in standard form.

Remember!

Recall from Chapter 7 that a polynomial in one variable is written in standard form when the degrees of the terms go from greatest to least.

EXAMPLE 5 Dividing Polynomials That Have a Zero Coefficient

Divide $(3x - 4x^3 - 15) \div (2x + 3)$.

$(-4x^3 + 3x - 15) \div (2x + 3)$ *Write the polynomials in standard form.*

$2x + 3\overline{)-4x^3 + 0x^2 + 3x - 15}$ *Write in long division form. Use $0x^2$ as a placeholder for the x^2 term.*

$$\begin{array}{r} -2x^2 + 3x - 3 \\ 2x + 3\overline{)-4x^3 + 0x^2 + 3x - 15} \\ \underline{-(-4x^3 - 6x^2)} \quad\downarrow \qquad \\ 6x^2 + 3x \qquad \\ \underline{-(6x^2 + 9x)} \quad\downarrow \\ -6x - 15 \\ \underline{-(-6x - 9)} \\ -6 \end{array}$$

$-4x^3 \div 2x = -2x^2$

Multiply $-2x^2(2x + 3)$. Subtract.

Bring down $3x$. $6x^2 \div 2x = 3x$

Multiply $3x(2x + 3)$. Subtract.

Bring down -15. $-6x \div 2x = -3$

Multiply $-3(2x + 3)$. Subtract.

The remainder is -6.

$(3x - 4x^3 - 15) \div (2x + 3) = -2x^2 + 3x - 3 + \frac{-6}{2x + 3}$.

Divide.

5a. $(1 - 4x^2 + x^3) \div (x - 2)$ $x^2 - 2x - 4 + \frac{-7}{x - 2}$

5b. $(4p - 1 + 2p^3) \div (p + 1)$ $2p^2 - 2p + 6 + \frac{-7}{p + 1}$

3 Close

Summarize

Tell students that long division always results in the correct answer, but for sake of time, they should try to factor the polynomials first and see whether any factors divide out. When using long division, remind students to write the dividend in standard form, using a placeholder with a coefficient of zero for any missing terms. Also remind students that in Step 4 (*subtract the product from the dividend*) they must change the sign of each term in the product.

ONGOING ASSESSMENT and INTERVENTION

***Diagnose Before* the Lesson**
12-6 Warm Up, TE p. 913

***Monitor During* the Lesson**
Check It Out! Exercises, SE pp. 913–916
Questioning Strategies, TE pp. 914–916

***Assess After* the Lesson**
12-6 Lesson Quiz, TE p. 919
Alternative Assessment, TE p. 919

THINK AND DISCUSS

1. When dividing a polynomial by a binomial, what does it mean when the remainder is 0?
2. Suppose that the final answer to a polynomial division problem is $x - 5 + \frac{3}{x+2}$. Find an excluded value. Justify your answer.

3. **GET ORGANIZED** Copy and complete the graphic organizer. In each box, show an example.

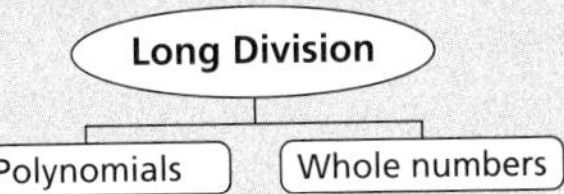

Answers to *Think and Discuss*

Possible answers:

1. It means the binomial is a factor of the polynomial.
2. $x \neq -2$; the denominator of the remainder cannot equal zero.
3. See p. A11.

12-6 Exercises

go.hrw.com
Homework Help Online
KEYWORD: MA7 12-6
Parent Resources Online
KEYWORD: MA7 Parent

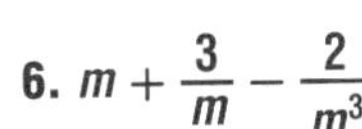

GUIDED PRACTICE

Divide.

SEE EXAMPLE 1 p. 913

1. $(4x^2 - x) \div 2x$ **$2x - \frac{1}{2}$**
2. $(16a^4 - 4a^3) \div 4a$ **$4a^3 - a^2$**
3. $(21b^2 - 14b + 24) \div 3b$ **$7b - \frac{14}{3} + \frac{8}{b}$**
4. $(18r^2 - 12r + 6) \div (-6r)$ **$-3r + 2 - \frac{1}{r}$**
5. $(6x^3 + 12x^2 + 9x) \div 3x^2$ **$2x + 4 + \frac{3}{x}$**
6. $(5m^4 + 15m^2 - 10) \div 5m^3$

SEE EXAMPLE 2 p. 914

7. $\frac{2x^2 - x - 3}{x + 1}$ **$2x - 3$**
8. $\frac{a^2 - a - 12}{a - 4}$ **$a + 3$**
9. $\frac{6y^2 + 11y - 10}{3y - 2}$ **$2y + 5$**
10. $\frac{t^2 - 6t + 8}{t - 4}$ **$t - 2$**
11. $\frac{x^2 + 16x + 15}{x + 15}$ **$x + 1$**
12. $\frac{p^2 - p - 20}{p + 4}$ **$p - 5$**

Divide using long division.

SEE EXAMPLE 3 p. 915

13. $(c^2 + 7c + 12) \div (c + 4)$ **$c + 3$**
14. $(3s^2 - 12s - 15) \div (s - 5)$ **$3s + 3$**
15. $\frac{x^2 + 5x - 14}{x + 7}$ **$x - 2$**
16. $\frac{x^2 + 4x - 12}{x - 2}$ **$x + 6$**

SEE EXAMPLE 4 p. 916

17. $(a^2 + 4a + 3) \div (a + 2)$ **$a + 2 + \frac{-1}{a + 2}$**
18. $(2r^2 + 11r + 5) \div (r - 3)$ **$2r + 17 + \frac{56}{r - 3}$**
19. $(n^2 + 8n + 15) \div (n + 4)$ **$n + 4 + \frac{-1}{n + 4}$**
20. $(2t^2 - t + 4) \div (t - 1)$ **$2t + 1 + \frac{5}{t - 1}$**
21. $(8n^2 - 6n - 7) \div (2n + 1)$
22. $(b^2 - b + 1) \div (b + 2)$

SEE EXAMPLE 5 p. 916

23. $(3x - 2x^3 - 10) \div (3 + x)$
24. $(3p^3 - 2p^2 - 4) \div (p - 2)$
25. $(m^2 + 2) \div (m - 1)$
26. $(3x^2 + 4x^3 - 5) \div (5 + x)$
27. $(4k^3 - 2k - 8) \div (k + 1)$ **$4k^2 - 4k + 2 + \frac{-10}{k + 1}$**
28. $(j^3 + 6j + 2) \div (j + 4)$

28. **$j^2 - 4j + 22 + \frac{-86}{j + 4}$**

PRACTICE AND PROBLEM SOLVING

Divide.

29. $(9t^3 + 12t^2 - 6t) \div 3t^2$ **$3t + 4 - \frac{2}{t}$**
30. $(5n^3 - 10n + 15) \div (-5n)$ **$-n^2 + 2 - \frac{3}{n}$**
31. $(-16p^4 + 4p^3 + 8) \div 4p^3$

31. **$-4p + 1 + \frac{2}{p^3}$**

32. $\frac{4r^2 - 9r + 2}{r - 2}$ **$4r - 1$**
33. $\frac{8t^2 + 2t - 3}{2t - 1}$ **$4t + 3$**
34. $\frac{3g^2 + 7g - 6}{g + 3}$ **$3g - 2$**

12-6 Exercises

Assignment Guide

Assign *Guided Practice* exercises as necessary.

If you finished Examples **1–2**
Basic 29–34, 46, 48
Average 29–34, 46, 48
Advanced 29–34, 46, 48

If you finished Examples **1–5**
Basic 29–48, 52–54, 57–60, 67–73
Average 29–62, 67–73
Advanced 29–45, 49–73

Homework Quick Check
Quickly check key concepts.
Exercises: 30, 32, 38, 40, 44

State Resources

Answers

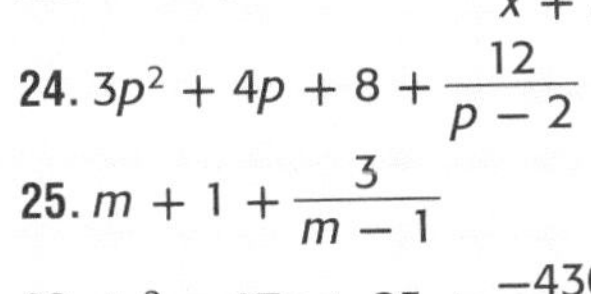

21. $4n - 5 + \frac{-2}{2n + 1}$
22. $b - 3 + \frac{7}{b + 2}$
23. $-2x^2 + 6x - 15 + \frac{35}{x + 3}$
24. $3p^2 + 4p + 8 + \frac{12}{p - 2}$
25. $m + 1 + \frac{3}{m - 1}$
26. $4x^2 - 17x + 85 + \frac{-430}{x + 5}$

MULTI-STEP TEST PREP Exercise 53 involves writing and graphing a rational function. This exercise prepares students for the Multi-Step Test Prep on page 926.

Answers

40. $2m + 3 + \frac{5}{m+1}$

41. $3x + 1 + \frac{-2}{2x-1}$

42. $m^2 + 5m + 23 + \frac{200}{2m-10}$

43. $2t^2 - 6t + 25 + \frac{-216}{3t+9}$

44. $p^3 + 3p^2 + 2p + 7 + \frac{22}{p-3}$

49a. The values of y are negative and decreasing.

b. The values of y are positive and decreasing.

53b.

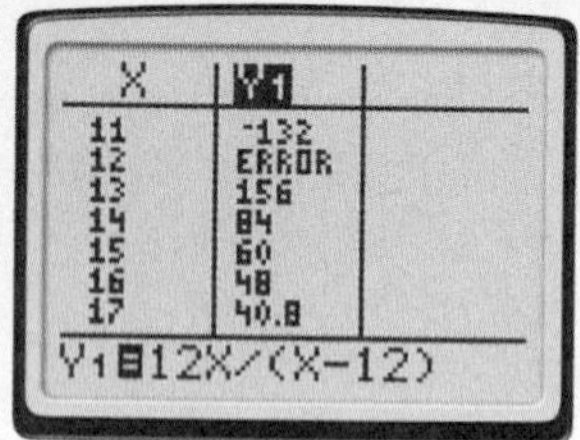

Independent Practice	
For Exercises	See Example
29–31	1
32–34	2
35–38	3
39–41	4
42–44	5

Extra Practice

Skills Practice p. S27

Application Practice p. S39

Divide using long division.

35. $(x^2 - 5x + 6) \div (x - 2)$ **$x - 3$**

36. $(2m^2 + 8m + 8) \div (m + 2)$ **$2m + 4$**

37. $(6a^2 + 7a - 3) \div (2a + 3)$ **$3a - 1$**

38. $(3x^2 - 10x - 8) \div (x - 4)$ **$3x + 2$**

39. $(3x^2 - 2x + 6) \div (x - 2)$ **$3x + 4 + \frac{14}{x-2}$**

40. $(2m^2 + 5m + 8) \div (m + 1)$

41. $(6x^2 - x - 3) \div (2x - 1)$

42. $(2m^3 - 4m - 30) \div (2m - 10)$

43. $(6t^3 + 21t + 9) \div (3t + 9)$

44. $(p^4 - 7p^2 + p + 1) \div (p - 3)$

45. **Multi-Step** Find the value of n, so that $x - 4$ is a factor of $x^2 + x + n$. **-20**

Geometry The area of each of three rectangles is $2x^2 - 3x - 2$ cm². Below are the different widths of the rectangles. Find each corresponding length.

46. $x - 2$ **$2x + 1$**

47. $x + 1$ **$2x - 5 + \frac{3}{x+1}$**

48. $2x + 1$ **$x - 2$**

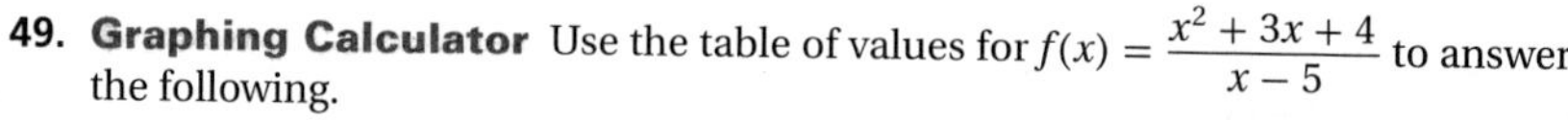

49. **Graphing Calculator** Use the table of values for $f(x) = \frac{x^2 + 3x + 4}{x - 5}$ to answer the following.

a. Describe what is happening to the values of y as x increases from 2 to 4.

b. Describe what is happening to the values of y as x increases from 6 to 8.

c. Explain why there is no value in the y column when x is 5. **The function is not defined at $x = 5$.**

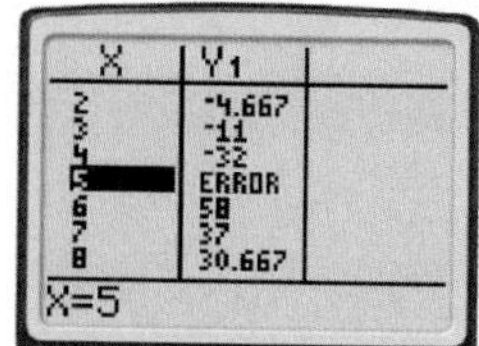

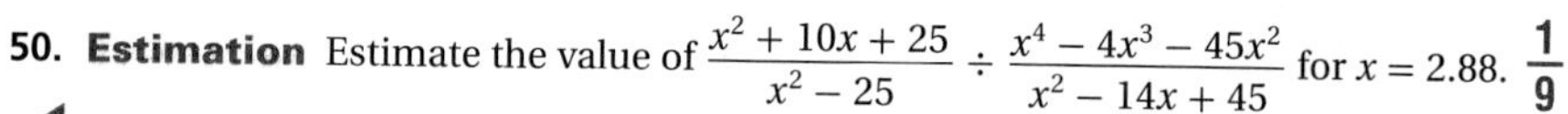

50. **Estimation** Estimate the value of $\frac{x^2 + 10x + 25}{x^2 - 25} \div \frac{x^4 - 4x^3 - 45x^2}{x^2 - 14x + 45}$ for $x = 2.88$. **$\frac{1}{9}$**

51. **Solar Energy** The greater the area of a solar panel, the greater the number of watts of energy produced. The area of two solar panels A and B, in square meters, can be represented by $A = m^2 + 3m + 2$ and $B = 2m + 2$. Divide the polynomials to find an expression that represents the ratio of the area of A to the area of B. **$0.5m + 1$**

LINK **Solar Energy**

NASA is researching unmanned solar-powered aircraft. In the future, these aircraft may be able to stay in the air indefinitely.

52. **ERROR ANALYSIS** Two students attempted to divide $\frac{4x^2 - 6x + 12}{-2x}$. Which is incorrect? Explain the error.

Student B is incorrect. The second term should be positive.

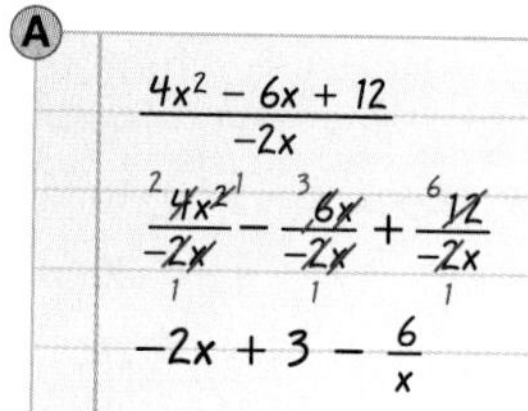

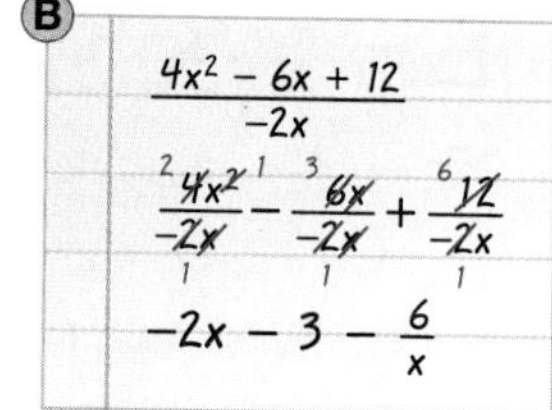

MULTI-STEP TEST PREP

53. This problem will prepare you for the Multi-Step Test Prep on page 926.

Jonathan continues to study lenses and uses the equation $\frac{1}{y} = \frac{x-12}{12x}$.

a. Jonathan wants to write y, the distance of the image from the lens, as a function of x, the distance of the object from the lens. What is the equation solved for y? **$y = \frac{12x}{x-12}$**

b. Use a graphing calculator to create a table of values for the function $y(x)$. For which value of x is the function undefined? **The function is undefined at $x = 12$.**

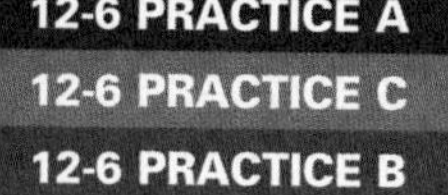

12-6 PRACTICE A

12-6 PRACTICE C

12-6 PRACTICE B

Divide.

1. $(15c^3 + 3c^2) \div 3c$ **$5c^2 + c$**

2. $(20b^4 - 12b + 4) \div 4b$ **$5b^3 - 3 + \frac{1}{b}$**

3. $(27q^6 - 3q^3 + 18) \div 9q^5$ **$3q - \frac{1}{3q^2} + \frac{2}{q^5}$**

4. $(15t^4 - 30t^2 + 6) \div 15t^3$ **$t - \frac{2}{t} + \frac{2}{5t^3}$**

5. $(d^2 - 4d - 77) \div (d - 11)$ **$d + 7$**

6. $(x^2 - 12x + 27) \div (x - 3)$ **$x - 9$**

7. $(9p^2 + 6p + 1) \div (3p + 1)$ **$3p + 1$**

8. $(4b^2 + b - 3) \div (b + 1)$ **$4b - 3$**

Divide using long division.

9. $\frac{m^2 + 4m - 12}{m + 6}$ **$m - 2$**

10. $(12y^2 + 31y + 14) \div (y + 2)$ **$12y + 7$**

11. $(t^2 + t - 6) \div (t - 1)$ **$t + 2 + \frac{-4}{t-1}$**

12. $(3p^3 + 4p - 6) \div (p + 2)$ **$3p^2 - 6p + 16 + \frac{-38}{p+2}$**

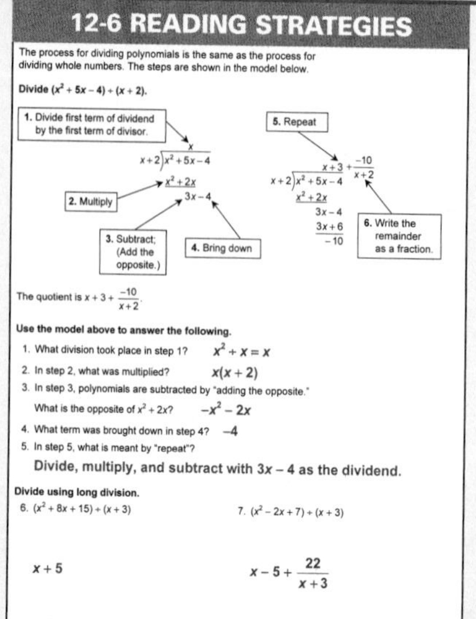

12-6 READING STRATEGIES

The process for dividing polynomials is the same as the process for dividing whole numbers. The steps are shown in the model below.

Divide $(x^2 + 5x - 4) \div (x + 2)$.

The quotient is $x + 3 + \frac{-10}{x+2}$.

Use the model above to answer the following.

1. What division took place in step 1? **$x^2 \div x = x$**
2. In step 2, what was multiplied? **$x(x + 2)$**
3. In step 3, polynomials are subtracted by "adding the opposite." What is the opposite of $x^2 + 2x$? **$-x^2 - 2x$**
4. What term was brought down in step 4? **-4**
5. In step 5, what is meant by "repeat"? **Divide, multiply, and subtract with $3x - 4$ as the dividend.**

Divide using long division.

6. $(x^2 + 8x + 15) \div (x + 3)$ **$x + 5$**

7. $(x^2 - 2x + 7) \div (x + 3)$ **$x - 5 + \frac{22}{x+3}$**

12-6 RETEACH

To divide a polynomial by a monomial, first write the division as a rational expression.

Divide $(12x^2 + 9x) \div 3x$.

$\frac{12x^2 + 9x}{3x}$ *Rewrite as a rational expression.*

$\frac{12x^2}{3x} + \frac{9x}{3x}$ *Divide each term by 3x.*

$\frac{{}_4\cancel{12}\,x^{\cancel{2}}}{{}_1\cancel{3}\,\cancel{x}_1} + \frac{\cancel{9}^3\,\cancel{x}^1}{{}_1\cancel{3}\,\cancel{x}_1}$ *Divide out common factors.*

$4x + 3$ *Simplify.*

To divide a polynomial by a binomial, try to factor and divide out common factors.

Divide $\frac{x^2 + 6x + 5}{x + 1}$.

$\frac{x^2 + 6x + 5}{x + 1}$

$\frac{(x + 1)(x + 5)}{x + 1}$ *Factor the numerator.*

$\frac{\cancel{(x + 1)}^1(x + 5)}{\cancel{x + 1}^1}$ *Divide out common factors.*

$x + 5$ *Simplify.*

You may find that a rational expression does not divide evenly.

Divide $(5x^2 + 10x + 3) \div 5x$.

$\frac{5x^2 + 10x + 3}{5x}$ *Rewrite as a rational expression.*

$\frac{5x^2}{5x} + \frac{10x}{5x} + \frac{3}{5x}$ *Divide each term by 5x.*

$x + 2 + \frac{3}{5x}$

Divide.

1. $(14x^3 + 6x) \div 2x$ **$7x^2 + 3$**

2. $(6x^4 + 12x^2 + 18x) \div 6x^2$ **$x^2 + 2 + \frac{3}{x}$**

3. $(10x^3 + 12x^2 + 2x) \div 2x$ **$5x^2 + 6x + 1$**

4. $(x^2 - 49) \div (x + 7)$ **$x - 7$**

5. $(3x^2 - 15x) \div (x - 5)$ **$3x$**

6. $(x^2 - 5x - 24) \div (x - 8)$ **$x + 3$**

54. **Write About It** When dividing a polynomial by a binomial, what does it mean when there is a remainder? **The binomial is not a factor of the polynomial.**

55. **Critical Thinking** Divide $2x + 3\overline{)2x^2 + 7x + 6}$. Find a value for each expression by substituting 10 for x in the original problem. Repeat the division. Compare the results of each division.
$x + 2$; $276 \div 23 = 12$; when $x = 10$, $x + 2 = 12$, so the results are equal.

56. **Write About It** Is $3x + 2$ a factor of $3x^2 + 14x + 8$? Explain.
Yes; there is no remainder when you divide $3x^2 + 14x + 8$ by $3x + 2$, so $3x + 2$ must be a factor of $3x^2 + 14x + 8$.

TEST PREP

57. Which expression has an excluded value of $-\frac{1}{2}$?

Ⓐ $\frac{4x^2 - 2x - 2}{4x - 2}$ Ⓑ $\frac{4x^2 - 2x - 2}{2x - 4}$ **Ⓒ** $\frac{4x^2 - 2x - 2}{4x + 2}$ Ⓓ $\frac{4x^2 - 2x - 2}{2x + 4}$

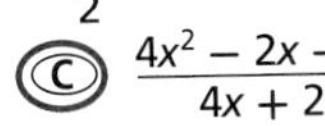

58. Find $(x^2 - 1) \div (x + 2)$.

Ⓕ $x - 2 + \frac{-5}{x + 2}$ **Ⓖ** $x - 2 + \frac{3}{x + 2}$ Ⓗ $x + 2 + \frac{-5}{x - 2}$ Ⓙ $x + 2 + \frac{3}{x - 2}$

59. Which expression is a factor of $x^2 - 4x - 5$?

Ⓐ $x - 1$ **Ⓑ** $x + 1$ Ⓒ $x - 4$ Ⓓ $x + 5$

60. Which of the following expressions is equivalent to $(x^3 + 2x^2 + 3x + 1) \div (x - 1)$?

Ⓕ $x^2 + 3x + 6 + \frac{7}{x - 1}$ Ⓗ $x^2 + 3x + 6 + \frac{-5}{x - 1}$

Ⓖ $x^2 + x + 2 + \frac{-1}{x - 1}$ Ⓙ $x^2 + x + 2 + \frac{3}{x - 1}$

CHALLENGE AND EXTEND

Divide. Simplify your answer.

61. $(6x^3y - x^2 + 4xy^2) \div (2x^2y)$ **$3x - \frac{1}{2y} + \frac{2y}{x}$**
62. $(x^3 - 1) \div (x - 1)$ **$x^2 + x + 1$**
63. $(x^3 + 2x^2 - x - 2) \div (x^2 - 1)$ **$x + 2$**
64. $(x^3 + 8) \div (x + 2)$ **$x^2 - 2x + 4$**

65. **Geometry** The base of a triangle is $2x + 4$ m and the area is $2x^2 + 5x + 2$ m^2. How much longer is the base than the height? **3 m**

66. **Geometry** The formula for finding the volume of a cylinder is $V = BH$, where B is the area of the base of the cylinder and H is the height.
 a. Find the height of the cylinder given that $V = \pi(x^3 + 4x^2 + 5x + 2)$ and $B = \pi(x^2 + 2x + 1)$. **$x + 2$**
 b. Find an expression for the radius of the base. **$x + 1$**

SPIRAL REVIEW

67. Find the probability that a point within the boundaries of the larger rectangle is in the shaded region. Express your answer as a simplified radical expression. *(Lesson 11-8)* **$\frac{\sqrt{15}}{15}$**

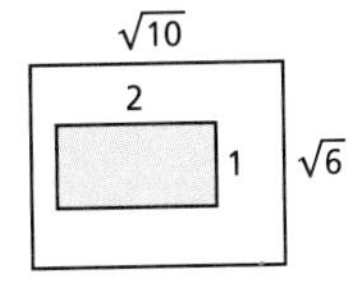

Multiply. Write each product in simplest form. *(Lesson 11-8)*

68. $3\sqrt{3} \cdot \sqrt{6}$ **$9\sqrt{2}$**
69. $\sqrt{5}(6 - \sqrt{10})$ **$6\sqrt{5} - 5\sqrt{2}$**
70. $(\sqrt{3} + 2)(\sqrt{3} + 5)$ **$13 + 7\sqrt{3}$**

Multiply. Simplify your answer. *(Lesson 12-4)*

71. $(x^2 + 4x + 3) \cdot \frac{8}{2(x + 3)}$ **$4(x + 1)$**
72. $\frac{9xy^2}{2x^3} \cdot \frac{8y}{3x^4}$ **$\frac{12y^3}{x^6}$**
73. $\frac{2k^2 + 4k^3}{k + 1} \cdot \frac{k^2 + 3k + 2}{2k^2}$ **$2k^2 + 5k + 2$**

TEST PREP DOCTOR + Remind students that in **Exercise 57,** an excluded value occurs when the denominator equals zero. Because the excluded value is negative, the possible choices are **C** and **D;** the denominators involve addition, and subtraction is the inverse operation.

In long division, a remainder is written over the divisor. Therefore, choices **H** and **J** in **Exercise 58** can be eliminated.

Journal

Have students explain the difference between dividing by a monomial and dividing by a binomial. Have them give an example of each.

ALTERNATIVE ASSESSMENT

Have students divide $(2x^2 + 5x + 3) \div (x + 1)$ by factoring and then by long division.

Power Presentations with PowerPoint®

12-6 Lesson Quiz

Divide.

1. $(12x^3 - 4x^2 + 20x) \div 4x$ **$3x^2 - x + 5$**
2. $\frac{2x^2 - 7x - 15}{x - 5}$ **$2x + 3$**
3. $\frac{x^2 + 3x - 10}{x + 5}$ **$x - 2$**
4. $\frac{x^2 - 6x - 27}{x - 9}$ **$x + 3$**

Divide using long division.

5. $(x^2 + 4x + 7) \div (x + 1)$ **$x + 3 + \frac{4}{x + 1}$**
6. $(8x^2 + 2x^3 + 7) \div (x + 3)$ **$2x^2 + 2x - 6 + \frac{25}{x + 3}$**

Also available on transparency

12-6 PROBLEM SOLVING

Write the correct answer.

1. The area of a rectangle is $x^2 + 2x - 8$ m^2, and the width is $x - 2$ m. Find the length.
 $x + 4$ m

2. On the dartboard below, the area of the outside ring is the difference between the area of the two largest circles, or $\pi(x + 4)^2 - \pi(x + 2)^2$ in^2. The area of the bull's-eye is πx^2 in^2. Expand and divide $[\pi(x + 4)^2 - \pi(x + 2)^2] \div \pi x^2$ to find the ratio of the area of the outside ring to the bull's-eye.

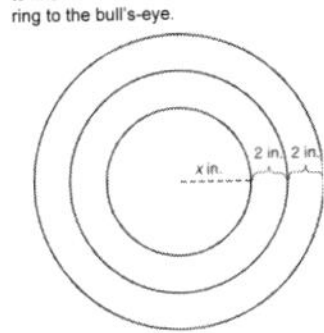
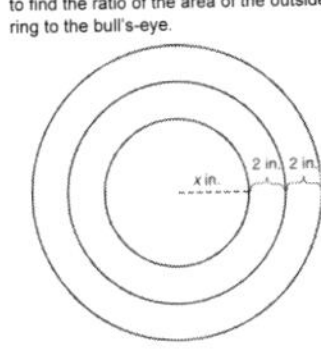

 $\frac{4}{x} + \frac{12}{x^2}$

3. The area of a rectangular piece of paper is $4n^2 - 4n - 9$ cm^2. Then a triangle with area $2n + 6$ cm^2 is cut from one corner of the paper. What is the ratio of the area of the paper that remains to the area of the triangle that was removed? (*Hint:* First subtract to find the area of the paper that remains.)
 $2n - 9 + \frac{39}{2n + 6}$

Select the best answer.

4. The area of a triangle is $8a^2 - 10a$ ft^2, and the height is $4a$ ft. Find the base. (*Hint:* Solve $A = \frac{1}{2}bh$ for b.)
 A $a - \frac{5a}{4}$ ft C $4a - \frac{5a}{2}$ ft
 B $2a - \frac{5a}{2}$ ft **D** $4a - 5$ ft

5. The volume of a rectangular prism is $2x^3 + 9x^2 - 11x - 30$ cm^3, and the height is $x + 5$ cm. Find the area of the base. ($V = BH$, where B is the area of the base and H is the height.)
 F $2x^2 - x - 6$ cm^2
 G $2x^2 - x - 16 + \frac{-110}{x + 5}$ cm^2
 H $2x^2 - 4x - 16 + \frac{-35}{x + 5}$ cm^2
 J $2x^2 + 19x + 84 + \frac{390}{x + 5}$ cm^2

6. The volume of a cylinder is $V = \pi r^2 h$, where r is the radius and h is the height. The volume of a certain cylinder is $\pi(n^3 - 6n^2 - 36n + 216)$ in^3, and the radius is $n - 6$ in. Find the height. (*Hint:* To divide by r^2, divide by r twice.)
 A n in. **C** $n + 6$ in.
 B $n - 6$ in. D $n^2 - 36$ in.

12-6 CHALLENGE

For 1–5, use the polynomial $P(x) = 2x^2 + 3x - 5$.

1. Use long division to divide $P(x) \div (x - 2)$.
 a. What value do you get for the remainder? **9**
 b. Now evaluate $P(2)$. What value do you get? **9**
2. Use long division to divide $P(x) \div (x - 1)$.
 a. What value do you get for the remainder? **0**
 b. Now evaluate $P(1)$. What value do you get? **0**
3. Use long division to divide $P(x) \div x$.
 a. What value do you get for the remainder? **−5**
 b. Now evaluate $P(0)$. What value do you get? **−5**
4. Use long division to divide $P(x) \div (x + 1)$.
 a. What value do you get for the remainder? **−6**
 b. Now evaluate $P(-1)$. What value do you get? **−6**
5. Use long division to divide $P(x) \div (x + 2)$.
 a. What value do you get for the remainder? **−3**
 b. Now evaluate $P(-2)$. What value do you get? **−3**
6. Look for a pattern in your results and complete this theorem.
 Polynomial Remainder Theorem: If a polynomial $P(x)$ is divided by $(x - r)$, then the remainder is a constant given by **$P(r)$**
7. Your results in question 2 are unique. What do they tell you about the binomial $(x - 1)$?
 Because the remainder is zero, $(x - 1)$ is a factor of $2x^2 + 3x - 5$: $(x - 1)(2x + 5)$.
8. Given $Q(x) = 6x^4 - 31x^3 - 49x^2 + 104x + 60$, explain how you could determine whether a binomial of the form $(x - r)$ is a factor of $Q(x)$ without doing long division.
 Evaluate $Q(r)$; if $Q(r) = 0$, then the binomial $(x - r)$ is a factor.
9. a. Is $(x - 1)$ a factor of $Q(x)$? Justify.
 No; $Q(1) = 6(1)^4 - 31(1)^3 - 49(1)^2 + 104(1) + 60 = 90 \neq 0$
 b. Is $(x + 2)$ a factor of $Q(x)$? Justify.
 Yes; $Q(-2) = 6(-2)^4 - 31(-2)^3 - 49(-2)^2 + 104(-2) + 60 = 0$

12-7 Organizer

Pacing: Traditional 1 day
Block $\frac{1}{2}$ day

Objectives: Solve rational equations.

Identify extraneous solutions.

Warm Up

1. Find the LCM of x, $2x^2$, and 6. $6x^2$
2. Find the LCM of $p^2 - 4p$ and $p^2 - 16$. $p(p-4)(p+4)$

Multiply. Simplify your answer.

3. $\frac{5x}{3y} \cdot \frac{2x^2}{7}$ $\quad \frac{10x^3}{21y}$
4. $(x^2 - 9) \cdot \frac{4}{x+3}$ $\quad 4x - 12$
5. $\frac{x^2 - x - 30}{x - 1} \cdot \frac{x^2 - 1}{4x^2 - 20x - 24}$ $\quad \frac{x+5}{4}$

Also available on transparency

Math Humor

Q: How do you know when a math teacher is insane?

A: The teacher can no longer solve rational equations.

State Resources

12-7 Solving Rational Equations

Objectives
Solve rational equations.

Identify extraneous solutions.

Vocabulary
rational equation

Why learn this?
Rational equations can be used to find how much time it takes two or more people working together to complete a job. (See Example 3.)

A **rational equation** is an equation that contains one or more rational expressions. If a rational equation is a proportion, it can be solved using the Cross Product Property.

EXAMPLE 1 Solving Rational Equations by Using Cross Products

Solve $\frac{3}{t-3} = \frac{2}{t}$. Check your answer.

$\frac{3}{t-3} = \frac{2}{t}$ *Use cross products.*

$3t = (t-3)(2)$

$3t = 2t - 6$ *Distribute 2 on the right side.*

$t = -6$ *Subtract 2t from both sides.*

Check

$\frac{3}{t-3}$	$=$ $\frac{2}{t}$
$\frac{3}{-6-3}$	$\frac{2}{-6}$
$\frac{3}{-9}$	$\frac{2}{-6}$
$-\frac{1}{3}$	$-\frac{1}{3}$ ✓

Solve. Check your answer.

1a. $\frac{1}{n} = \frac{3}{n+4}$ **2** **1b.** $\frac{4}{h+1} = \frac{2}{h}$ **1** **1c.** $\frac{21}{x-7} = \frac{3}{x}$ $-\frac{7}{6}$

Some rational equations contain sums or differences of rational expressions. To solve these, you must find the LCD of all the rational expressions in the equation.

EXAMPLE 2 Solving Rational Equations by Using the LCD

Solve $\frac{1}{c} + \frac{3}{2c} = \frac{2}{c+1}$.

Step 1 Find the LCD.

$2c(c+1)$ *Include every factor of the denominators.*

Step 2 Multiply both sides by the LCD.

$$2c(c+1)\left(\frac{1}{c} + \frac{3}{2c}\right) = 2c(c+1)\left(\frac{2}{c+1}\right)$$

$$2c(c+1)\left(\frac{1}{c}\right) + 2c(c+1)\left(\frac{3}{2c}\right) = 2c(c+1)\left(\frac{2}{c+1}\right)$$ *Distribute on the left side.*

1 Introduce

EXPLORATION

12-7 Solving Rational Equations

You can use a graphing calculator to help you solve equations.

To solve the equation $\frac{5}{x+2} = 2$, enter each side of the equation into your calculator as a separate function.

Graph the functions in the standard decimal window by pressing [ZOOM], selecting **6:ZStandard**, pressing [ZOOM] again, and selecting **4:ZDecimal**.

1. Find the intersection of the graphs by pressing [TRACE] and using the arrow keys to move to the point of intersection. What is the x-value of the point of intersection?
2. Use substitution to verify that this value of x is a solution.
3. Use the same method to solve the equation $\frac{2}{x-1} = x$.

THINK AND DISCUSS

4. **Describe** how the solution of $\frac{2}{x-1} = x$ differs from the solution of $\frac{5}{x+2} = 2$.
5. **Explain** how you could solve $\frac{2}{x-1} = x$ using a table of values.

Motivate

Have students use cross products to solve the following proportion:

$\frac{x}{4} = \frac{12}{8}$ $\quad 6$

Tell students that in this lesson they will learn to use cross products to solve rational equations that are proportions.

Explorations and answers are provided in *Alternate Openers: Explorations Transparencies.*

Step 3 Simplify and solve.

$$2\cancel{c}^1(c+1)\left(\frac{1}{\cancel{c}^1}\right) + \cancel{2c}^1(c+1)\left(\frac{3}{\cancel{2c}^1}\right) = 2c\cancel{(c+1)}^1\left(\frac{2}{\cancel{c+1}^1}\right)$$ *Divide out common factors.*

$2(c+1) + (c+1)3 = (2c)2$ *Simplify.*

$2c + 2 + 3c + 3 = 4c$ *Distribute and multiply.*

$5c + 5 = 4c$ *Combine like terms.*

$c + 5 = 0$ *Subtract 4c from both sides.*

$c = -5$ *Subtract 5 from both sides.*

Check Verify that your solution is not extraneous.

$\frac{1}{c} + \frac{3}{2c}$	$=$	$\frac{2}{c+1}$
$\frac{1}{-5} + \frac{3}{2(-5)}$		$\frac{2}{-5+1}$
$\frac{2}{-10} + \frac{3}{-10}$		$\frac{2}{-4}$
$-\frac{5}{10}$		$-\frac{1}{2}$
$-\frac{1}{2}$		$-\frac{1}{2}$ ✓

Solve each equation. Check your answer.

2a. $\frac{2}{a+1} + \frac{1}{a+1} = \frac{4}{a}$ **−4**

2b. $\frac{6}{j+2} - \frac{10}{j} = \frac{4}{2j}$ **−4**

2c. $\frac{8}{t+3} = \frac{1}{t} + 1$ **1, 3**

EXAMPLE 3 *Problem-Solving Application*

Greg can clean a house in 5 hours. It takes Armin 7 hours to clean the same house. How long will it take them to clean the house if they work together?

Armin 7 hours

Greg 5 hours

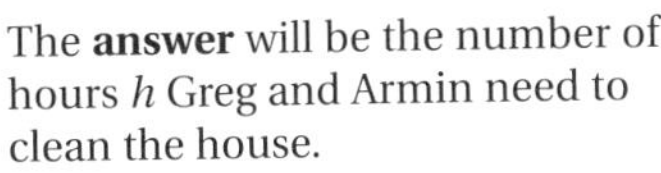

1 Understand the Problem

The **answer** will be the number of hours h Greg and Armin need to clean the house.

List the important information:

- Greg cleans the house in 5 hours, so he cleans $\frac{1}{5}$ of the house per hour.
- Armin cleans the house in 7 hours, so he cleans $\frac{1}{7}$ of the house per hour.

2 Make a Plan

The part of the house Greg cleans plus the part of the house Armin cleans equals the complete job. Greg's rate times the number of hours worked plus Armin's rate times the number of hours worked will give the complete time to clean the house. Let h represent the number of hours worked.

(Greg's rate) h + **(Armin's rate)** h = **complete job**

$$\frac{1}{5}h + \frac{1}{7}h = 1$$

COMMON ERROR ALERT

After multiplying both sides of an equation by the LCD, students might think they should still have something in the denominator. Remind students that correctly multiplying by the LCD eliminates the denominators.

Power Presentations with PowerPoint®

Additional Examples

Example 1

Solve $\frac{5}{x-2} = \frac{3}{x}$. Check your answer. −3

Example 2

Solve each equation. Check your answer.

A. $\frac{2}{x+1} + \frac{3}{x} = \frac{5}{2x}$ $-\frac{1}{5}$

B. $\frac{4}{x} - \frac{3}{x^2} = 1$ 3, 1

Example 3

Copy machine A can make 200 copies in 60 minutes. Copy machine B can make 200 copies in 10 minutes. How long will it take both machines working together to make 200 copies?

$8\frac{4}{7}$ min

INTERVENTION

Questioning Strategies

EXAMPLES **1–2**

- When can you use cross products to solve a rational equation?
- What is the purpose of multiplying both sides by the LCD?

EXAMPLE **3**

- Why is the equation always equal to 1 in a "working together" problem?

2 Teach

Guided Instruction

Review finding the LCM of rational expressions. Although **Example 1** can be solved by multiplying both sides of the equation by the LCD, as in **Example 2,** it is easier to solve most proportions by using cross products. Point out that the "working together" problems can apply to either people or machines that are working together to complete a task. They can also be stated with any unit of time (seconds, minutes, hours, etc.). Emphasize the importance of checking solutions to rule out extraneous solutions.

Reaching All Learners

Through Modeling

Obtain two containers with different-sized pouring spouts and one bowl so that students can create their own "working together" experiment. Fill each container with water (or sand) and have students count the number of seconds it takes to fill the bowl from each container individually. Then have students write and solve the equation for the amount of time it takes to fill the bowl using both containers simultaneously. Have students "check" their answer by filling the bowl using both containers simultaneously.

Power Presentations with PowerPoint®

Additional Examples

Example 4

Solve $\frac{2}{x+1} = \frac{x-6}{x^2-1}$. Identify any extraneous solutions.

-4; -1 is extraneous.

INTERVENTION

Questioning Strategies

EXAMPLE 4

- How are the extraneous solutions related to the denominators in the equation?
- Are excluded values always extraneous solutions?

Solve

$$35\left(\frac{1}{5}h + \frac{1}{7}h\right) = 35(1) \qquad \textit{Multiply both sides by the LCD, 35.}$$

$$7h + 5h = 35 \qquad \textit{Distribute 35 on the left side.}$$

$$12h = 35 \qquad \textit{Combine like terms.}$$

$$h = \frac{35}{12} = 2\frac{11}{12} \qquad \textit{Divide by 12 on both sides.}$$

Greg and Armin working together can clean the house in $2\frac{11}{12}$ hours, or 2 hours 55 minutes.

Look Back

Greg cleans $\frac{1}{5}$ of the house per hour and Armin cleans $\frac{1}{7}$ of the house per hour. So, in $2\frac{11}{12}$ hours, Greg cleans $\frac{35}{12} \cdot \frac{1}{5} = \frac{7}{12}$ of the house and Armin cleans $\frac{35}{12} \cdot \frac{1}{7} = \frac{5}{12}$ of the house. Together, they clean $\frac{7}{12} + \frac{5}{12} = 1$ house.

CHECK IT OUT! **3.** Cindy mows a lawn in 50 minutes. It takes Sara 40 minutes to mow the same lawn. How long will it take them to mow the lawn if they work together? $22\frac{2}{9}$ min

When you multiply each side of an equation by the LCD, you may get an extraneous solution. Recall from Chapter 11 that an extraneous solution is a solution to a resulting equation that is not a solution to the original equation.

EXAMPLE 4 Extraneous Solutions

Solve $\frac{x-9}{x^2-9} = \frac{-3}{x-3}$. **Identify any extraneous solutions.**

Step 1 Solve.

$(x-9)(x-3) = -3(x^2-9)$	*Use cross products.*
$x^2 - 12x + 27 = -3x^2 + 27$	*Multiply the left side. Distribute −3 on the right side.*
$4x^2 - 12x + 27 = 27$	*Add $3x^2$ to both sides.*
$4x^2 - 12x = 0$	*Subtract 27 from both sides.*
$4x(x-3) = 0$	*Factor the quadratic expression.*
$4x = 0$ or $x - 3 = 0$	*Use the Zero Product Property.*
$x = 0$ or $x = 3$	*Solve for x.*

Helpful Hint

Extraneous solutions may be introduced by squaring both sides of an equation or by multiplying both sides of an equation by a variable expression.

Step 2 Find extraneous solutions.

$\frac{x-9}{x^2-9}$	$\frac{-3}{x-3}$
$\frac{0-9}{0^2-9}$	$\frac{-3}{0-3}$
$\frac{-9}{-9}$	$\frac{-3}{-3}$
1	1 ✓

$\frac{x-9}{x^2-9}$	$\frac{-3}{x-3}$
$\frac{3-9}{3^2-9}$	$\frac{-3}{3-3}$
$\frac{-6}{0}$	$\frac{-3}{0}$

Because both $\frac{-6}{0}$ and $\frac{-3}{0}$ are undefined, 3 is not a solution.

The only solution is 0, so 3 is an extraneous solution.

4a. 5; 7 is extraneous.

4b. 1 and 5; no extraneous solutions

4c. 4; 0 is extraneous.

CHECK IT OUT! **Solve. Identify any extraneous solutions.**

4a. $\frac{3}{x-7} = \frac{x-2}{x-7}$ **4b.** $\frac{x+1}{x-2} = \frac{4}{x-3}$ **4c.** $\frac{9}{x^2+2x} = \frac{6}{x^2}$

3 Close

Summarize

Tell students that if a rational equation is a proportion, they can solve the equation by using cross products. Otherwise, they need to multiply every term on both sides by the LCD to eliminate the denominators. Remind students that they need to check their answers because some may be extraneous. Have students solve the following equations and check their answers:

$\frac{5}{x} = \frac{6}{x+2}$ 10 $\quad \frac{7}{x} + \frac{4}{x^2} = 2 - \frac{1}{2}$; 4

ONGOING ASSESSMENT

and INTERVENTION

***Diagnose Before* the Lesson**
12-7 Warm Up, TE p. 920

***Monitor During* the Lesson**
Check It Out! Exercises, SE pp. 920–922
Questioning Strategies, TE pp. 921–922

***Assess After* the Lesson**
12-7 Lesson Quiz, TE p. 925
Alternative Assessment, TE p. 925

THINK AND DISCUSS

1. Why is it important to check your answers to rational equations?
2. For what values of x are the rational expressions in the equation $\frac{x}{x-3} = \frac{2}{x+3}$ undefined?
3. Explain why some rational equations, such as $\frac{x}{x-4} = \frac{4}{x-4}$, have no solutions.

4. **GET ORGANIZED** Copy and complete the graphic organizer. In each box, write the solution and check.

Solving Rational Equations

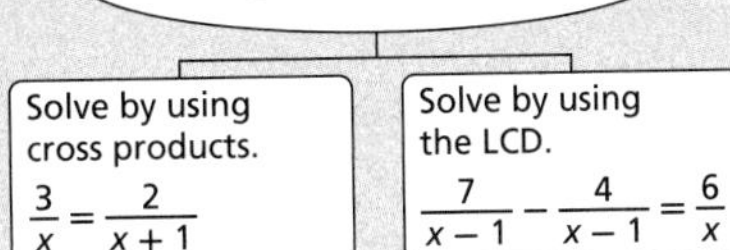

Answers to *Think and Discuss*

1. Some solutions may be extraneous.
2. 3 and −3
3. Because the denominators are the same, the expressions would only be equal when $x = 4$, but 4 is an excluded value, so there is no solution.
4. See p. A11.

12-7 Exercises

GUIDED PRACTICE

1. **Vocabulary** A(n) ___?___ contains one or more rational expressions. (*extraneous solution* or *rational equation*) **rational equation**

Solve. Check your answer.

SEE EXAMPLE 1 p. 920

2. $\frac{3}{x+4} = \frac{2}{x}$ **8**
3. $\frac{5}{s-6} = \frac{4}{s}$ **−24**
4. $\frac{20}{p+100} = \frac{-10}{2p}$ **−20**
5. $\frac{4}{j} = \frac{1}{j+2}$ $-\frac{8}{3}$
6. $\frac{3}{x-4} = \frac{9}{x-2}$ **5**
7. $\frac{6}{2x-1} = 3$ $\frac{3}{2}$

SEE EXAMPLE 2 p. 920

8. $\frac{6}{x} - \frac{5}{x} = \frac{1}{3}$ **3**
9. $\frac{a}{9} + \frac{1}{3} = \frac{2}{5}$ $\frac{3}{5}$
10. $\frac{3}{x+1} = \frac{2}{x} + \frac{3}{x}$ $-\frac{5}{2}$
11. $\frac{8}{d} = \frac{1}{d+2} - \frac{3}{d}$ $-\frac{11}{5}$
12. $\frac{3}{s-6} = \frac{4}{s} + \frac{1}{2s}$ **18**
13. $\frac{7}{r} + \frac{2}{r-1} = \frac{-1}{2r}$ $\frac{15}{19}$
14. $\frac{3}{a-4} = \frac{a}{a-2}$ **1, 6**
15. $\frac{r}{2} - \frac{2}{r} = \frac{5}{6}$ **3,** $-\frac{4}{3}$
16. $\frac{6}{n} = \frac{7}{n^2} - 1$ **−7, 1**
17. $\frac{4}{x+1} = x - 2$ **−2, 3**
18. $\frac{5}{a^2} = \frac{-4}{a} + 1$ **−1, 5**
19. $\frac{1}{p} = \frac{-3}{p^2} + 2$ **−1,** $\frac{3}{2}$

23. $-\frac{4}{3}$**; 1 is extraneous.**

24. −6; 5 is extraneous.

SEE EXAMPLE 3 p. 921

20. **Painting** Summer can paint a room in 3 hours. Louise can paint the room in 5 hours. How many hours will it take to paint the room if they work together? $1\frac{7}{8}$ **h**
21. **Technology** Lawrence's old robotic vacuum can clean his apartment in $1\frac{1}{2}$ hours. His new robotic vacuum can clean his apartment in 45 minutes. How long will it take both vacuums, working together, to clean his apartment?

21. $\frac{1}{2}$ **h, or 30 min**

SEE EXAMPLE 4 p. 922

Solve. Identify any extraneous solutions. **22. No solution; 4 is extraneous.**

22. $\frac{3}{c-4} = \frac{c-1}{c-4}$
23. $\frac{w+3}{w^2-1} - \frac{2w}{w-1} = 1$
24. $\frac{3x-7}{x-5} + \frac{x}{2} = \frac{8}{x-5}$

12-7 Exercises

Assignment Guide

Assign *Guided Practice* exercises as necessary.

If you finished Examples **1–2**
- **Basic** 25–36, 42
- **Average** 25–36, 42
- **Advanced** 25–36, 42

If you finished Examples **1–4**
- **Basic** 25–45, 48–50, 54–63
- **Average** 25–41, 43–50, 54–63
- **Advanced** 25–41, 43–63

Homework Quick Check
Quickly check key concepts.
Exercises: 26, 30, 36, 37, 40

Teaching Tip

Inclusion Remind students that the right side of the equation in **Exercise 7** can be written as $\frac{3}{1}$. The equation can then be solved using cross products.

State Resources

Inclusion The rational expressions on the left side of the equations in **Exercises 29** and **31** have common denominators. Students can subtract the expressions and then solve the resulting proportion with cross products.

Exercise **45** involves solving a problem about focal length by writing and solving a rational equation. This exercise prepares students for the Multi-Step Test Prep on page 926.

Answers

61.

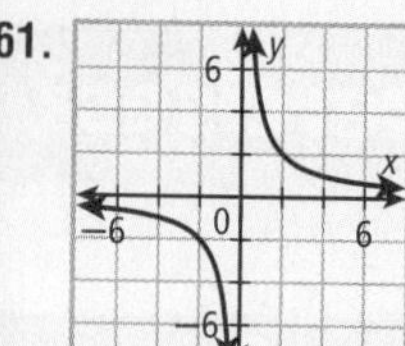

62.

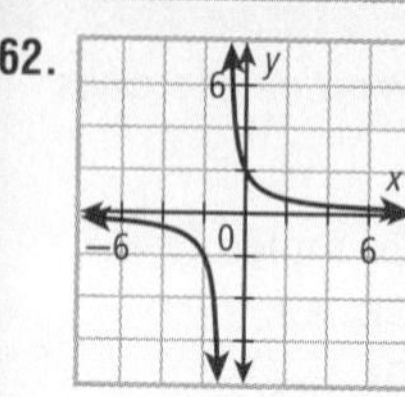

63.

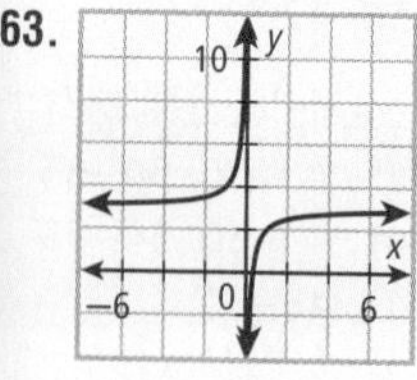

PRACTICE AND PROBLEM SOLVING

Independent Practice	
For Exercises	See Example
25–28	1
29–36	2
37	3
38–41	4

Extra Practice
Skills Practice p. S27
Application Practice p. S39

30. no solution

32. no solution

33. $\frac{3}{2}$

42a. $86\frac{2}{3}\%$

b. $\frac{39+f}{45+f} = 0.9$; 15 free throws

Solve. Check your answer.

25. $\frac{8}{x-2} = \frac{2}{x+1}$ **−2**
26. $\frac{12}{3n-1} = \frac{3}{n}$ **−1**
27. $\frac{x}{x+4} = \frac{x}{x-1}$ **0**
28. $\frac{9}{x+5} = \frac{4}{x}$ **4**
29. $\frac{6}{s} - \frac{2}{s} = 5$ $\mathbf{\frac{4}{5}}$
30. $\frac{1}{2x} + \frac{1}{4x} = \frac{7}{8x}$
31. $\frac{7}{c} - \frac{2}{c} = \frac{4}{c-1}$ **5**
32. $\frac{9}{m} - \frac{3}{2m} = \frac{15}{m}$
33. $\frac{3}{x^2} = \frac{2}{x}$
34. $\frac{r}{3} - 3 = -\frac{6}{r}$ **3, 6**
35. $\frac{6}{x^2} = \frac{1}{2} + \frac{1}{2x}$ **−4, 3**
36. $\frac{8}{3x^2} = \frac{2}{x} - \frac{1}{3}$ **2, 4**
37. Mel can carpet a floor in 10 hours. Sandy can carpet the same floor in 15 hours. How many hours will it take them to carpet the floor if they work together? **6 h**

Solve. Identify any extraneous solutions.

38. $\frac{5x}{x-3} = 8 + \frac{15}{x-3}$ **No solution; 3 is extraneous.**
39. $\frac{3t}{t-3} = \frac{t+4}{t-3}$ **2; 3 is extraneous.**
40. $\frac{2}{x} = \frac{x+1}{x^2-1}$ **2; −1 is extraneous.**
41. $\frac{1}{x} = \frac{x-4}{x^2-16}$ **No solution; 4 is extraneous.**

42. **Multi-Step** Clancy has been keeping his free throw statistics. Use his data to write the ratio of the number of free throws Clancy has made to the number of attempts.
    a. What percentage has he made?
    b. Write and solve an equation to find how many free throws *f* Clancy would have to make in a row to improve his free-throw percentage to 90%. (*Hint:* Clancy needs to make *f* more free throws in *f* more attempts.)

Clancy's Free Throws	
Attempts	Made
45	39

43. **Travel** A passenger train travels 20 mi/h faster than a freight train. It took the passenger train 2 hours less time than the freight train to travel 240 miles. The freight train took *t* hours. Copy and complete the chart. Then find the rate of the freight train. **40 mi/h**

	Distance	Rate	Time
Passenger train	240	$\frac{240}{t-2}$	$t - 2$
Freight train	240	$\frac{240}{t}$	t

Suspecting that just such a word problem might be on the algebra midterm, Gary came prepared.

44. Pipe A fills a storage tank with a certain chemical in 12 hours. Pipe B fills the tank in 18 hours. How long would it take both pipes to fill the tank? $\mathbf{7\frac{1}{5}}$ **h**

MULTI-STEP TEST PREP

45. This problem will prepare you for the Multi-Step Test Prep on page 926.
    Blanca sets up a lens with a focal length *f* of 15 cm and places a candle 24 cm from the lens. She knows that $\frac{1}{f} = \frac{1}{x} + \frac{1}{y}$ where *x* is the distance of the object from the lens and *y* is the distance of the image from the lens.
    a. Write the equation using the given values. $\mathbf{\frac{1}{15} = \frac{1}{24} + \frac{1}{y}}$
    b. For the values of *f* and *x* given above, how far will the image appear from the lens? **b. 40 cm**
    c. How will distance between the image and the lens be affected if Blanca uses a lens with a focal length of 18 cm? **It will increase to 72 cm.**

12-7 PRACTICE A
12-7 PRACTICE C
12-7 PRACTICE B

olve. Check your answer.

1. $\frac{6}{t+3} = \frac{4}{t}$ **6**
2. $\frac{3}{m} = \frac{4}{m-2}$ **−6**
3. $\frac{a}{4} + \frac{1}{2} = \frac{2}{3}$ $\mathbf{\frac{2}{3}}$
4. $\frac{3}{2x} - \frac{3}{x-2} = \frac{1}{2x}$ **−1**
5. $\frac{3}{2x} + \frac{5}{x} = \frac{13}{x+4}$ **4**
6. $\frac{3}{x} + \frac{3x+1}{x^2} = \frac{13}{x^2}$ **2**

lve. Identify any extraneous solutions.

7. $\frac{8}{x-2} = \frac{x+3}{x-2}$ **5; 2 is an extraneous solution.**
8. $\frac{-2}{x-1} = \frac{x-8}{x+1}$ **5 and 2; no extraneous solutions**

Caroline can paint a fence in 6 hours. Her sister Lily can paint the same fence in 4 hours. How long will it take them to paint the fence if they work together? $\mathbf{2\frac{2}{5}}$ **h or 2h 24 min**

Jalon bicycled against the wind for 10 miles in the same time he bicycled with the wind for 25 miles. The wind speed was 4 mi/h. What was Jalon's average bicycling speed? (*Hint:* Use $t = \frac{d}{r}$.) $\mathbf{9\frac{1}{3}}$ **mi/h**

There are two positive numbers. The second number is 6 less than the first number. When the reciprocal of the second number is subtracted from the reciprocal of the first, the difference is $-\frac{3}{8}$. Find the first number. **11**

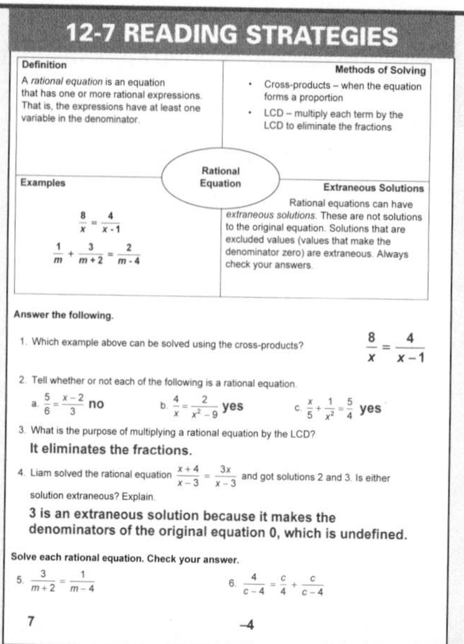

12-7 READING STRATEGIES

Definition
A *rational equation* is an equation that has one or more rational expressions. That is, the expressions have at least one variable in the denominator.

Methods of Solving
- Cross-products – when the equation forms a proportion
- LCD – multiply each term by the LCD to eliminate the fractions

Rational Equation

Examples
$\frac{8}{x} = \frac{4}{x-1}$
$\frac{1}{m} + \frac{3}{m+2} = \frac{2}{m-4}$

Extraneous Solutions
Rational equations can have *extraneous solutions*. These are not solutions to the original equation. Solutions that are excluded values (values that make the denominator zero) are extraneous. Always check your answers.

Answer the following.

1. Which example above can be solved using the cross-products? $\mathbf{\frac{8}{x} = \frac{4}{x-1}}$
2. Tell whether or not each of the following is a rational equation.
   a. $\frac{5}{6} = \frac{x-2}{3}$ **no** b. $\frac{4}{x} = \frac{2}{x^2-9}$ **yes** c. $\frac{x}{5} + \frac{1}{x^2} = \frac{5}{4}$ **yes**
3. What is the purpose of multiplying a rational equation by the LCD?
   It eliminates the fractions.
4. Liam solved the rational equation $\frac{x+4}{x-3} = \frac{3x}{x-3}$ and got solutions 2 and 3. Is either solution extraneous? Explain.
   3 is an extraneous solution because it makes the denominators of the original equation 0, which is undefined.

Solve each rational equation. Check your answer.

5. $\frac{3}{m+2} = \frac{1}{m-4}$ **7**
6. $\frac{4}{c-4} = \frac{c}{4} + \frac{c}{c-4}$ **−4**

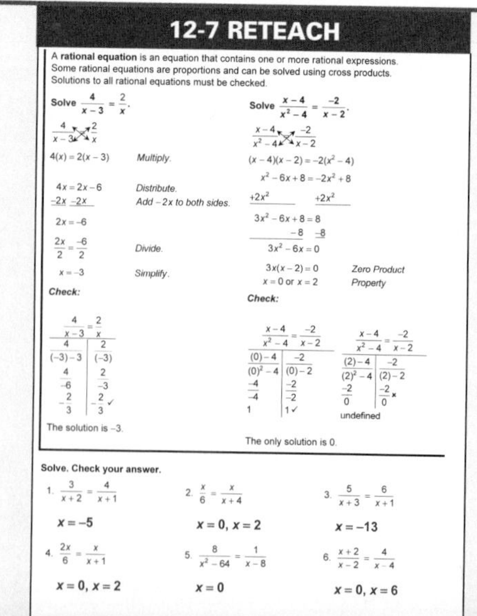

12-7 RETEACH

A **rational equation** is an equation that contains one or more rational expressions. Some rational equations are proportions and can be solved using cross products. Solutions to all rational equations must be checked.

Solve $\frac{4}{x-3} = \frac{2}{x}$.

$4(x) = 2(x-3)$ *Multiply.*
$4x = 2x - 6$ *Distribute.*
$-2x \; -2x$ *Add −2x to both sides.*
$2x = -6$
$\frac{2x}{2} = \frac{-6}{2}$ *Divide.*
$x = -3$ *Simplify.*

Check:
$\frac{4}{(-3)-3} = \frac{2}{(-3)}$; $\frac{4}{-6} = \frac{2}{-3}$; $-\frac{2}{3} = -\frac{2}{3}$ ✓

The solution is −3.

Solve $\frac{x-4}{x^2-4} = \frac{-2}{x-2}$.

$(x-4)(x-2) = -2(x^2-4)$
$x^2 - 6x + 8 = -2x^2 + 8$
$+2x^2 \qquad +2x^2$
$3x^2 - 6x + 8 = 8$
$-8 \quad -8$
$3x^2 - 6x = 0$
$3x(x-2) = 0$ *Zero Product Property*
$x = 0$ or $x = 2$

Check:
$\frac{(0)-4}{(0)^2-4} = \frac{-2}{(0)-2}$; $\frac{-4}{-4} = \frac{-2}{-2}$; $1 = 1$ ✓
$\frac{(2)-4}{(2)^2-4} = \frac{-2}{(2)-2}$; $\frac{-2}{0} = \frac{-2}{0}$ ✗ undefined

The only solution is 0.

Solve. Check your answer.

1. $\frac{3}{x+2} = \frac{4}{x+1}$ $\mathbf{x = -5}$
2. $\frac{x}{6} = \frac{x}{x+4}$ $\mathbf{x = 0, x = 2}$
3. $\frac{5}{x+3} = \frac{6}{x+1}$ $\mathbf{x = -13}$
4. $\frac{2x}{6} = \frac{x}{x+1}$ $\mathbf{x = 0, x = 2}$
5. $\frac{8}{x^2-64} = \frac{1}{x-8}$ $\mathbf{x = 0}$
6. $\frac{x+2}{x-2} = \frac{4}{x-4}$ $\mathbf{x = 0, x = 6}$

46. **Critical Thinking** Can you cross multiply to solve all rational equations? If so, explain. If not, how do you identify which ones can be solved using cross products?

47. **Write About It** Solve $\frac{1}{x} + \frac{3}{x} = \frac{3}{x-1}$. Explain each step and why you chose the method you used. **4; possible answer: first add the fractions on the left to get $\frac{4}{x} = \frac{3}{x-1}$. Then cross multiply and solve to find that $x = 4$. This method may be easier than finding the LCM.**

46. No; you can only use cross multiplication if the equation is in the form of a proportion.

TEST PREP

48. Which value is an extraneous solution to $\frac{x}{x+4} - \frac{4}{x-4} = \frac{x^2+16}{x^2-16}$?

Ⓐ -16 Ⓑ -4 (circled) Ⓒ 4 Ⓓ 16

49. Which is a solution to $\frac{x+2}{x-3} - \frac{1}{x} = \frac{3}{x^2-3x}$?

Ⓕ -1 (circled) Ⓖ 0 Ⓗ 1 Ⓙ 3

50. What are the solutions of $\frac{5}{x^2} = \frac{1}{3} + \frac{2}{3x}$?

Ⓐ -3 and 5 Ⓑ -3 and 2 Ⓒ 2 and 3 Ⓓ 3 and -5 (circled)

CHALLENGE AND EXTEND

51. Below is a solution to a rational equation. Use an algebraic property to justify each step.

Solve $\frac{3}{x} = \frac{6}{x+4}$.

Statements	Reasons
a. $3(x+4) = 6x$	**Cross Products Property**
b. $3x + 12 = 6x$	**Distributive Property**
c. $12 = 3x$	**Subtraction Property of Equality**
d. $4 = x$	**Division Property of Equality**

52. For what value of a will the equation $\frac{x+4}{x-a} = \frac{7}{x-a}$ have no solution? **3**

53. Luke, Eddie, and Ryan can do a job in 1 hour and 20 minutes if they work together. Working alone, it takes Ryan 1 hour more to do the job than it takes Luke, and Luke does the job twice as fast as Eddie. How much time would it take each to do the job working alone? **Eddie: 6 h; Luke: 3 h; Ryan: 4 h**

SPIRAL REVIEW

Identify which lines are parallel and which lines are perpendicular. *(Lesson 5-9)*

54. $y = \frac{1}{3}x$; $y = 3x + 1$; $y = 3x - 1$

55. $y = -2x$; $y = 2x - 2$; $y = \frac{1}{2}x + 4$

56. $y = -x - 3$; $y = x - 2$; $y = x + 3$

57. $y = -\frac{2}{3}x + 2$; $y = \frac{3}{2}x + 3$; $y = -\frac{3}{2}x - 1$

54. $y = 3x + 1$ and $y = 3x - 1$ are parallel.

55. $y = -2x$ and $y = \frac{1}{2}x + 4$ are perpendicular.

56. $y = x - 2$ and $y = x + 3$ are parallel; $y = -x - 3$ is perpendicular to both $y = x - 2$ and $y = x + 3$.

57. $y = -\frac{2}{3}x + 2$ and $y = \frac{3}{2}x + 3$ are perpendicular.

Solve each equation. Check your answer. *(Lesson 11-9)*

58. $2\sqrt{x} = 24$ **144**

59. $\sqrt{x+15} = \sqrt{4x}$ **5**

60. $\sqrt{2-x} = x$ **1**

Graph each rational function. *(Lesson 12-2)*

61. $y = \frac{4}{x}$

62. $y = \frac{2}{x+1}$

63. $y = -\frac{1}{x} + 3$

TEST PREP DOCTOR + In **Exercise 49,** choices **G** and **J** are excluded values and cannot be solutions. These can be eliminated. Students could then substitute either 1 or -1 for x in the equation. If it makes a true statement, it's the answer. If it makes a false statement, the other choice is the answer.

Journal

Suppose that it takes Mark 20 minutes to wash the car and it takes Amanda 30 minutes to wash the same car. Explain how you would set up an equation to find how long it would take them working together.

ALTERNATIVE ASSESSMENT

Solve the following equations:

$\frac{4}{x+2} = \frac{3}{x}$

$\frac{4}{x+2} + \frac{3}{x} = 1$

Explain your method for solving each equation.

Power Presentations with PowerPoint®

12-7 Lesson Quiz

Solve each equation. Check your answer.

1. $\frac{x-4}{5} = \frac{x}{6}$ 24
2. $\frac{12}{x^2} = \frac{1}{x} + 1$ $-4, 3$
3. $\frac{3}{4x} + \frac{2}{x+6} = \frac{5}{8}$ $-3\frac{3}{5}, 2$
4. Pipe A can fill a tank with water in 4 hours. Pipe B can fill the same tank in 5 hours. How long will it take both pipes working together to fill the tank? $2\frac{2}{9}$ hours
5. Solve $\frac{1}{x+1} + \frac{x}{x-3} = \frac{12}{x^2-2x-3}$. Identify any extraneous solutions. -5; 3 is extraneous.

Also available on transparency

12-7 PROBLEM SOLVING

Write the correct answer.

1. Alex can remodel a bathroom in 2 days. Abraham can remodel the same bathroom in 4 days. How long will it take them to remodel the bathroom if they work together?

$1\frac{1}{3}$ days

2. When only the cold faucet is fully turned on, a bathtub fills in 8 minutes. When only the hot faucet is fully turned on, the same bathtub fills in 12 minutes. If both the cold and hot faucets are fully turned on, how long will it take to fill the bathtub?

$4\frac{4}{5}$ min

3. 100 mL of a solution contains 30 mL of acid; this is called a 30% acid solution because $\frac{\text{part}}{\text{whole}} = \frac{30}{100} = 0.30$. How many milliliters of acid x would need to be added to the solution to turn it into a 50% acid solution? (*Hint:* Adding acid increases both the volume of acid and the volume of the complete solution.)

40 mL

4. Markus jogs 4 mi around a track at an average rate of r mi/h. Then he cools down by walking 1 mi at a rate 3 mi/h slower. His whole workout lasts 1 h. At what rates did Markus jog and walk?

jog: 6 mi/h; walk: 3 mi/h

Select the best answer.

5. Ms. Spinoni can prepare a mass-mailing of 500 letters in 10 hours. Mr. Harris can prepare a mass-mailing of 500 letters in 15 hours. How long will it take them to prepare a mass-mailing of 1000 letters if they work together? (*Hint:* The complete job is twice as big.)

A 6 h C $12\frac{1}{2}$ h
B 12 h D 25 h

6. At a cafeteria, the automatic ice machine can completely fill itself in 20 minutes. During lunch time, customers can completely empty the ice machine in 30 minutes. At the start of lunch time, the ice machine is completely empty and it starts making ice at the same time that customers start taking ice. How long will it take for the machine to be completely full? (*Hint:* The customers *take away* ice.)

F 12 min H 30 min
G 20 min **J** 60 min

7. To attend a family reunion, Beth drives 100 mi from Fresno and Clara drives 220 mi from San Jose. Both women drive the same speed in miles per hour, but Clara's drive takes 2 h longer than Beth's. Find the length of Beth's drive.

A 1 h C $2\frac{1}{5}$ h
B $1\frac{2}{3}$ h D $3\frac{2}{3}$ h

12-7 CHALLENGE

In Lesson 12.7, you learned how to solve rational equations in one variable. Each equation below is a rational equation in two variables, x and y.

$\frac{1}{x} + \frac{1}{y} = 1$ $\frac{1}{x} + \frac{1}{y} = 2$ $\frac{1}{x} + \frac{1}{y} = \frac{1}{2}$

In the exercises on this page, assume that x and y are positive integers.

Find one solution to each equation of the form $\frac{1}{x} + \frac{1}{y} = \frac{1}{n}$, where n is a positive integer.

1. $\frac{1}{x} + \frac{1}{y} = 1$ **$x = 2, y = 2$**
2. $\frac{1}{x} + \frac{1}{y} = \frac{1}{2}$ **Possible answer: $x = 4, y = 4$**
3. $\frac{1}{x} + \frac{1}{y} = \frac{1}{4}$ **Possible answer: $x = 8, y = 8$**
4. $\frac{1}{x} + \frac{1}{y} = \frac{1}{6}$ **Possible answer: $x = 12, y = 12$**
5. $\frac{1}{x} + \frac{1}{y} = \frac{1}{8}$ **Possible answer: $x = 16, y = 16$**
6. $\frac{1}{x} + \frac{1}{y} = \frac{1}{100}$ **Possible answer: $x = 200, y = 200$**
7. Suppose that you are given $\frac{1}{x} + \frac{1}{y} = \frac{1}{n}$, where n is an even positive integer. Based on your work in Exercises 1–6, write formulas in terms of n for x and for y. **$x = 2n, y = 2n$**
8. a. Let $\frac{1}{x} + \frac{1}{y} = 2$. Show that $x = 1$ and $y = 1$ are solutions to the equation by using substitution. **$\frac{1}{1} + \frac{1}{1} = 2$**

b. If x and y are positive integers other than 1, then $0 < \frac{1}{x} < 1$ and $0 < \frac{1}{y} < 1$. Explain how this fact helps you show that there are no positive integer solutions to $\frac{1}{x} + \frac{1}{y} = 2$ other than $x = 1$ and $y = 1$.

If x and y are integers with $0 < \frac{1}{x} < 1$ and $0 < \frac{1}{y} < 1$, then $0 < \frac{1}{x} + \frac{1}{y} < 2$. Therefore, $\frac{1}{x} + \frac{1}{y} = 2$ is only true when $x = 1$ and $y = 1$.

c. How does the reasoning in Part b help you show that, when n is an integer greater than 2 and x and y are positive integers, the equation $\frac{1}{x} + \frac{1}{y} = n$ has no integer solutions? **Since $0 < \frac{1}{x} + \frac{1}{y} < 2$, there are no positive integers x and y for $n > 2$.**

Use trial and error to help you decide whether the given equation has any integer solutions. If so, state one solution.

9. $\frac{1}{x} + \frac{1}{y} = \frac{1}{3}$ **Possible answer: $x = 6, y = 6$**
10. $\frac{1}{x} + \frac{1}{y} = \frac{1}{5}$ **Possible answer: $x = 10, y = 10$**

Organizer

Objective: Assess students' ability to apply concepts and skills from Lessons 12-4 through 12-7 in a real-world format.

 **Online Edition**

Resources

 ***Algebra I Assessments***

www.mathtekstoolkit.org

Problem	Text Reference
1	Lesson 12-5
2	Lesson 12-2
3	Lesson 12-2
4	Lesson 12-1
5	Lesson 12-1

Answers

2. For table, see p. A36.
3. See p. A36.
5. Magnification decreases.

State Resources

go.hrw.com
State Resources Online
KEYWORD: MA7 Resources

MULTI-STEP TEST PREP

SECTION 12B

Operations with Rational Expressions and Equations

An Upside-Down World Jamal is studying lenses and their images for a science project. He finds in a science book that a magnifying glass can be used to project upside-down images on a screen. The equation $\frac{1}{f} = \frac{1}{x} + \frac{1}{y}$ relates the focal length of the lens f, the distance of the object from the lens x, and the distance of the image from the lens y. The focal length of Jamal's lens is 10 cm.

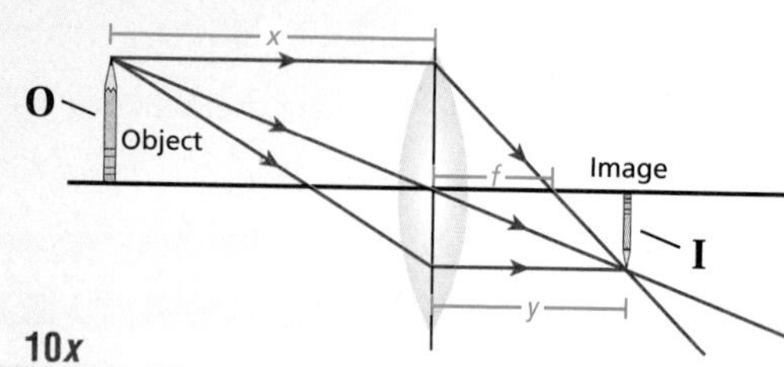

1. Solve the given equation for y using the given value of f. $y = \frac{10x}{x - 10}$
2. Jamal experiments with a candle, the lens, and a screen. Given that the focal length remains constant, use a table for the x-values 0, 2, 4, 6, 8, 10, 12, 14, and 16 cm. For which x-values are the y-values positive? **The y-values are positive for $x > 10$.**
3. Graph the function $y(x)$. Label the axes.

Magnification for images is the ratio of the height of the image to the height of the object. This is also equal to the ratio of the distance between the image and the lens and the distance between the object and the lens: $M = \frac{I}{O} = \frac{y}{x}$. I is the height of the image, O is the height of the object, y is the distance of the image from the lens, and x is the distance of the object from the lens.

4. If the height of a candle is 15 cm and the projected image of that candle is 37.5 cm, what is the magnification of the lens? **2.5**
5. As Jamal moves the candle further from the lens (increases x), and the distance between the lens and the screen decreases (y decreases), does the magnification M stay the same, increase, or decrease?

INTERVENTION

Scaffolding Questions

1. What is the first step in solving for y? Subtract $\frac{1}{x}$ from both sides.

2–3. What values are excluded? 10 What are the asymptotes? $y = 0, x = 10$

4. What variable represents the height of the candle? O

5. Which is greater, $\frac{1}{5}$ or $\frac{1}{6}$? $\frac{1}{5}$

Extension

Use the magnification equation to find the image height I as a function of the object distance x for an object 5 cm tall and a focal length of 10 cm.

$I = \frac{50x}{x(x - 10)}$

CHAPTER 12

SECTION 12B

Quiz for Lessons 12-4 Through 12-7

12-4 Multiplying and Dividing Rational Expressions

Multiply. Simplify your answer.

1. $\frac{n+3}{n-5}\cdot(n^2-5n)$ n^2+3n
2. $\frac{8}{2x+6}\cdot(x^2+6x+9)$ $4x+12$
3. $\frac{5a^2b^3}{ab^5}\cdot\frac{2a^4bc^5}{20c}$ $\frac{a^5c^4}{2b}$
4. $\frac{6xy^2}{2x^2y^6}\cdot\frac{6x^4y^4}{9x^3}$ 2
5. $\frac{3h^3-6h}{10g^2}\cdot\frac{4g}{gh^2-2g}$ $\frac{6h}{5g^2}$
6. $\frac{m^2+m-2}{m^2-2m-8}\cdot\frac{m^2-8m+16}{3m-3}$ $\frac{m-4}{3}$

Divide. Simplify your answer.

7. $\frac{2}{n^3}\div\frac{n-6}{n^5}$ $\frac{2n^2}{n-6}$
8. $\frac{2x^2+8x+6}{x}\div\frac{2x^2+2x}{x^3-x^2}$ x^2+2x-3
9. $\frac{8b^3c}{b^2c}\div(4b^2+4b)$ $\frac{2}{b+1}$

12-5 Adding and Subtracting Rational Expressions

Add or subtract. Simplify your answer.

10. $\frac{15}{2p}-\frac{13}{2p}$ $\frac{1}{p}$
11. $\frac{3m^2}{4m^5}+\frac{5m^2}{4m^5}$ $\frac{2}{m^3}$
12. $\frac{x^2+8x}{x-2}-\frac{3x+14}{x-2}$ $x+7$
13. $\frac{2t}{4t^2}+\frac{2}{t}$ $\frac{5}{2t}$
14. $\frac{m^2-m-2}{m^2+6m+5}-\frac{2}{m+5}$ $\frac{m-4}{m+5}$
15. $\frac{4x}{x-2}+\frac{3x}{2-x}$ $\frac{x}{x-2}$
16. Julianne competes in a biathlon that consists of a 25-mile running leg and a 45-mile biking leg. Julianne averages 3 times the rate of speed on her bike that she does on her feet. Let *r* represent Julianne's running rate of speed. Write and simplify an expression, in terms of *r*, that represents the time it takes for Julianne to complete both legs of the race. Then determine how long it will take Julianne to complete the race if she runs an average of 10 mi/h. $\frac{25}{r}+\frac{45}{3r}=\frac{40}{r}$; 4 h

12-6 Dividing Polynomials

Divide.

17. $(6d^2+4d)\div 2d$ $3d+2$
18. $(15x^4+3x^3-x)\div(-3x^2)$ $-5x^2-x+\frac{1}{3x}$
19. $(2x^2-7x-4)\div(2x+1)$ $x-4$

Divide using long division.

20. $(a^2+3a-10)\div(a-2)$ $a+5$
21. $(4y^2-9)\div(2y-3)$ $2y+3$
22. $(2x^2+5x-8)\div(x+2)$ $2x+1+\frac{-10}{x+2}$

12-7 Solving Rational Equations

Solve. Identify any extraneous solutions.

23. $\frac{3}{x}=\frac{4}{x-1}$ -3
24. $\frac{1}{x}=\frac{2}{x^2}$ 2; 0 is extraneous.
25. $\frac{2}{t}+\frac{4}{3t}=\frac{4}{t+2}$ 10
26. $\frac{4}{n^2}=\frac{7}{n}+2$
27. $\frac{d+2}{d+8}=\frac{-6}{d+8}$
28. $\frac{x-6}{x^2-6}=\frac{-4}{x-4}$
29. It takes Dustin 2 hours to shovel the snow from his driveway and sidewalk. It takes his sister 3 hours to shovel the same area. How long will it take them to shovel the walk if they work together? $1\frac{1}{5}$ h

READY TO GO ON?

SECTION 12B

Organizer

Objective: Assess students' mastery of concepts and skills in Lessons 12-4 through 12-7.

Resources

 *Assessment Resources*
Section 12B Quiz

Teacher One Stop™
Test & Practice Generator

INTERVENTION

Resources

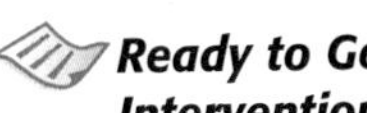 *Ready to Go On? Intervention and Enrichment* Worksheets

Ready to Go On? CD-ROM

Ready to Go On? Online

 my.hrw.com

Answers

26. $-4, \frac{1}{2}$
27. No solution; -8 is extraneous.
28. 2, 0

READY TO GO ON? Diagnose and Prescribe

Ready to Go On? Intervention	READY TO GO ON? Intervention, Section 12B: Worksheets	CD-ROM	Online
Lesson 12-4	12-4 Intervention	Activity 12-4	Diagnose and Prescribe Online
Lesson 12-5	12-5 Intervention	Activity 12-5	
Lesson 12-6	12-6 Intervention	Activity 12-6	
Lesson 12-7	12-7 Intervention	Activity 12-7	

READY TO GO ON? Enrichment, Section 12B
Worksheets
CD-ROM
Online

CHAPTER 12 **Organizer**

Pacing: Traditional 1 day
Block $\frac{1}{2}$ day

Objectives: Find the three basic trigonometric ratios in a right triangle.

Use trigonometric ratios to find missing lengths.

Using the Extension

In Lesson 12-7, students learned that if a rational equation is a proportion, they can solve it by using cross products. In this extension, students learn that they can use proportions to solve problems involving trigonometric ratios.

Teaching Tip **Auditory Cues** To help students remember which sides go with each name and in which order, abbreviate the trigonometric ratios as follows:

Sin = **O**pp divided by **H**yp

Cos = **A**dj divided by **H**yp

Tan = **O**pp divided by **A**dj.

Then combine to form the mnemonic **SOHCAHTOA** (pronounced "soak a toe ah").

Technology Have students put calculators in degree mode by pressing MODE and selecting **Degree**.

State Resources

EXTENSION Trigonometric Ratios

Objectives
Find the three basic trigonometric ratios in a right triangle.

Use trigonometric ratios to find missing lengths.

Vocabulary
trigonometric ratios
sine
cosine
tangent

A **trigonometric ratio** is a ratio of the lengths of two sides in a right triangle. Three basic trigonometric ratios are *sine*, *cosine*, and *tangent*, abbreviated *sin*, *cos*, and *tan*, respectively.

Trigonometric Ratios

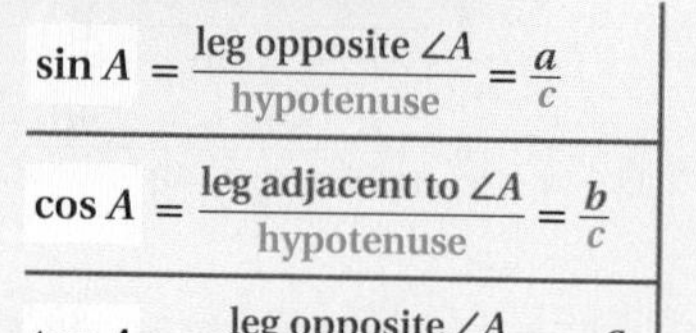

$\sin A = \frac{\text{leg opposite } \angle A}{\text{hypotenuse}} = \frac{a}{c}$

$\cos A = \frac{\text{leg adjacent to } \angle A}{\text{hypotenuse}} = \frac{b}{c}$

$\tan A = \frac{\text{leg opposite } \angle A}{\text{side adjacent to } \angle A} = \frac{a}{b}$

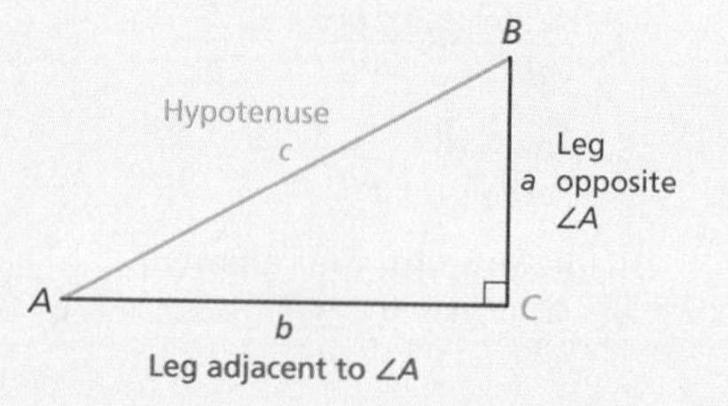

EXAMPLE **1** **Finding the Value of a Trigonometric Ratio**

Find each trigonometric ratio to the nearest thousandth.

A $\sin A$

$\sin A = \frac{\text{opposite}}{\text{hypotenuse}} = \frac{3}{5} = 0.600$

B $\cos A$

$\cos A = \frac{\text{adjacent}}{\text{hypotenuse}} = \frac{4}{5} = 0.800$

C $\tan A$

$\tan A = \frac{\text{opposite}}{\text{adjacent}} = \frac{3}{4} = 0.750$

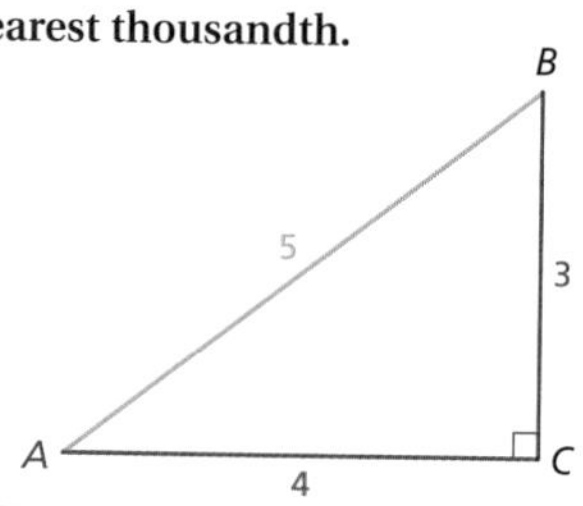

(Figure: right triangle ABC with hypotenuse 5, BC = 3, AC = 4.)

1. Use the figure above to find $\sin B$, $\cos B$ and $\tan B$.

$\frac{4}{5} = 0.800$; $\frac{3}{5} = 0.600$; $\frac{4}{3} \approx 1.333$

EXAMPLE **2** ***Aviation Application***

A plane takes off with a 9° angle of ascent. What is the plane's altitude when it has covered a horizontal distance of 184,800 feet? Round your answer to the nearest foot.

Helpful Hint

To find trigonometric ratios on a graphing calculator, press SIN, COS, or TAN and then the value of the degree. Be sure your calculator is in Degree mode.

Draw a diagram to model the problem.

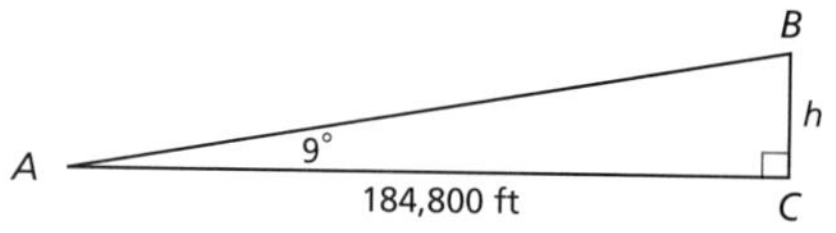

(Figure: right triangle ABC, angle A = 9°, AC = 184,800 ft, BC = h.)

$\tan A = \frac{\text{opposite}}{\text{adjacent}}$

$\tan 9° = \frac{h}{184{,}800}$

$184{,}800(\tan 9°) = h$ *Multiply both sides by 184,800.*

$29{,}269.4 \approx h$ *Simplify the left side with a calculator.*

The plane's altitude is about 29,269 feet.

1 Introduce

Motivate

Ask students to guess the height of the flagpole (or a tree) on their campus.

Then ask students how the flagpole could be measured. What obstacles might there be?

Tell students that they learned how to measure objects indirectly with similar triangles in Chapter 2. This extension will show them another method of indirect measurement.

2 Teach

Guided Instruction

Be sure students can identify the hypotenuse of any right triangle before beginning this extension. Have students use the fact that the hypotenuse is always the longest side to check the reasonableness of their answers. Help students determine whether to use sin, cos, or tan by having them identify the two sides of the triangle marked with either a number or a variable. Then find the angle being referred to. Point out that the angle being referred to in a trigonometric ratio is never the right angle.

2. **Construction** A 14-foot ladder is leaning against a building. The ladder makes a 70° angle with the ground. How far is the base of the ladder from the building? Round your answer to the nearest tenth of a foot. **4.8 ft**

EXTENSION

Exercises

Use the diagram for Exercises 1 and 2.

1. Find sin A, cos A, and tan A to the nearest thousandth. **0.923; 0.385; 2.400**
2. Find sin B, cos B, and tan B to the nearest thousandth. **0.385; 0.923; 0.417**

A, B, C, 13, 5, 12

Find the value of x. Round answers to the nearest tenth.

3. **5.0**

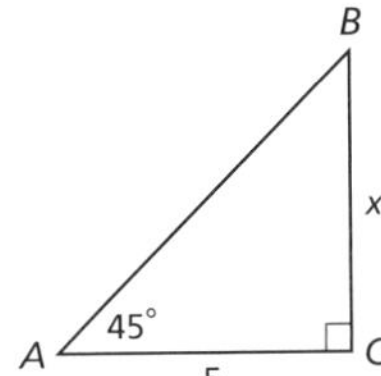

4. **5.1**

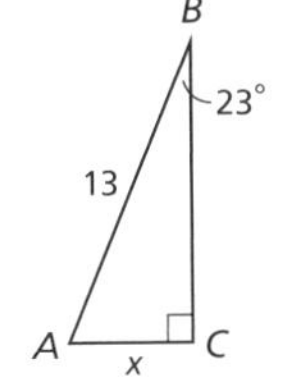

5. **8.0**

B, 16, 60°, A, x, C

6. **Diving** If a submarine travels 3 miles while rising to the surface at a 9° angle, how deep was the submarine when it started? Round your answer to the nearest tenth of a mile. **0.5 mi**

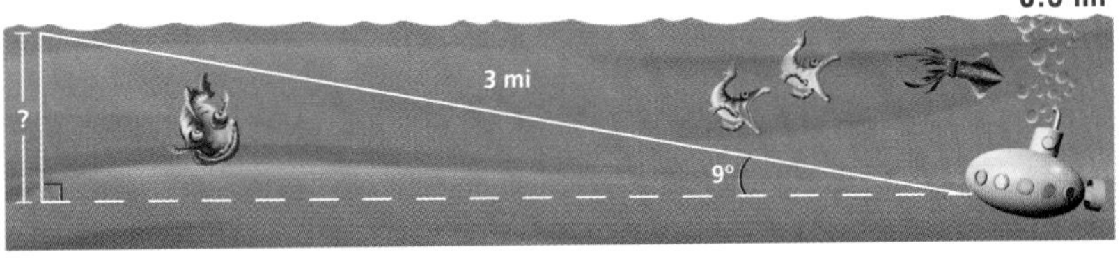

7. **Construction** A wheelchair ramp is to have an angle of 4.5° with the ground. The deck at the top of the ramp is 20 inches above ground level.
   a. Draw a diagram to illustrate the situation.
   b. How long should the ramp be? Round your answer to the nearest tenth of an inch. **254.9 in.**
   c. How far from the deck should the ramp begin? Round your answer to the nearest tenth of an inch. **254.1 in.**

7a.

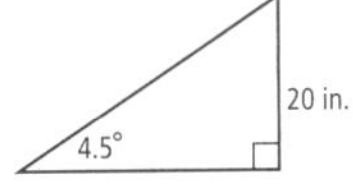

8. **Navigation** The top of a lighthouse is 40 meters above sea level. The angle of elevation from a fishing boat to the top of the lighthouse is 20°. How far is the fishing boat from the base of the lighthouse? Round your answer to the nearest tenth of a meter. **109.9 m**

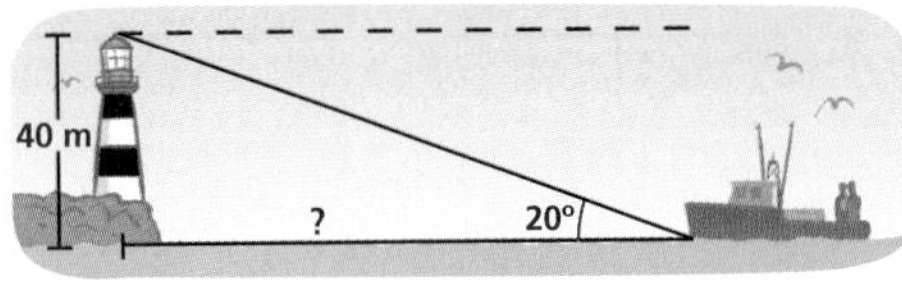

9. **Write About It** What would have to be true about the legs of a right triangle for an angle to have a tangent of 1? What would be the measure of that angle?

COMMON ERROR ALERT

Students often confuse sine and cosine because they can't distinguish between the adjacent and opposite sides. Have students first determine the hypotenuse (across from right angle) and then the opposite side (across from angle referred to). The remaining side is the adjacent side.

Power Presentations with PowerPoint®

Additional Examples

Example 1

Find sin A, cos A, and tan A to the nearest thousandth.

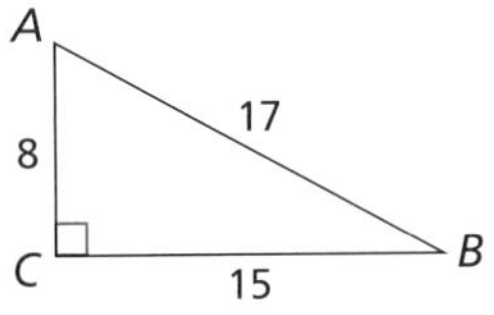

0.882; 0.471; 1.875

Example 2

A ladder is leaning against a wall. The base of the ladder makes a 60° angle with the ground. The base of the ladder is 17 feet from the wall. What is the length of the ladder? 34 feet

INTERVENTION

Questioning Strategies

EXAMPLE 1

- How do you determine the hypotenuse of a right triangle?
- How do you determine the adjacent or opposite side of a right triangle?
- Which trigonometric ratio does not involve the hypotenuse?

EXAMPLE 2

- How can you write the equation as a proportion?
- Explain why the variable could be in either the numerator or denominator. For which would you use cross products as your first step in solving? Why?

3 Close

Summarize

Draw the following triangle on the board:

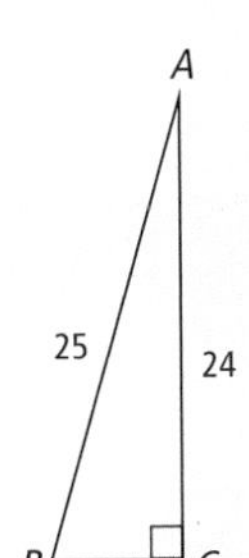

Have students find sin B, cos B, and tan B to the nearest thousandth.
0.960; 0.280; 3.429

Answers

9. The legs would have to be of equal length. The angle would measure 45°.

Organizer

Objective: Help students organize and review key concepts and skills presented in Chapter 12.

Online Edition
Multilingual Glossary

Resources

Teacher One Stop™
PuzzleView
Test & Practice Generator

***Multilingual Glossary* Online**
go.hrw.com
KEYWORD: MA7 Glossary

Lesson Tutorial Videos
CD-ROM

Answers

1. rational expression
2. rational function
3. rational equation
4. inverse variation
5. discontinuous function
6. Yes; the product xy is constant.
7. No; the product xy is not constant.
8. $y = -\frac{4}{x}$

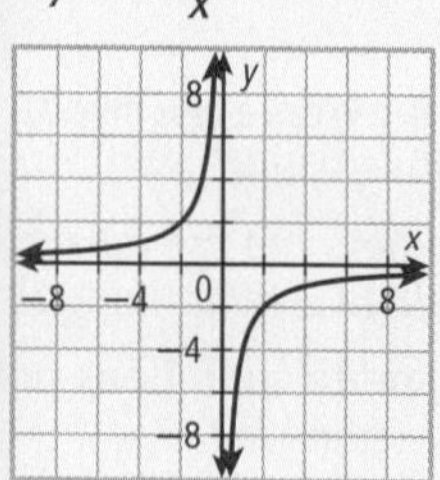

9. $y = \frac{1}{x}$

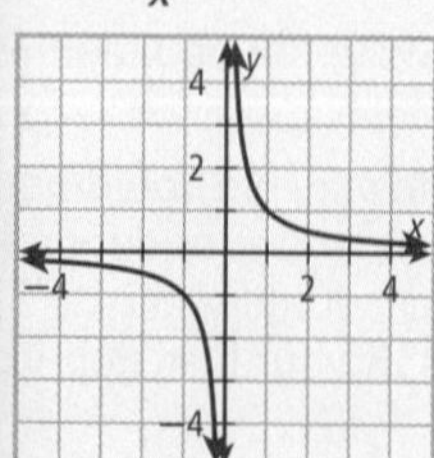

0. −15
1. $13,200

CHAPTER 12 Study Guide: Review

Vocabulary

Complete the sentences below with vocabulary words from the list above.

1. A(n) ___?___ is an algebraic expression whose numerator and denominator are polynomials.
2. A function whose rule is a quotient of polynomials in which the denominator has a degree of at least 1 is a(n) ___?___ .
3. A(n) ___?___ is an equation that contains one or more rational expressions.
4. A(n) ___?___ is a relationship that can be written in the form $y = \frac{k}{x}$, where k is a nonzero constant.
5. A function is a ___?___ if its graph contains one or more jumps, breaks, or holes.

12-1 Inverse Variation *(pp. 871–877)*

EXAMPLE

■ **Write and graph the inverse variation in which $y = 2$ when $x = 3$.**

$y = \frac{k}{x}$ *Use the form $y = \frac{k}{x}$.*

$2 = \frac{k}{3}$ *Substitute known values.*

$6 = k$ *Multiply by 3 to find the value of k.*

$y = \frac{6}{x}$ *Substitute 6 for k in $y = \frac{k}{x}$.*

x	−6	−3	−2	−1	0	1	2	3	6
y	−1	−2	−3	−6	und.	6	3	2	1

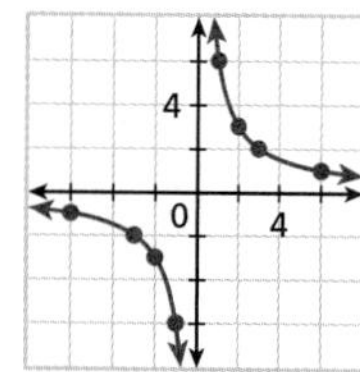

Make a table of values and plot the points.

EXERCISES

Tell whether each relationship represents an inverse variation. Explain.

6.

x	y
4	−3
−12	1
6	−2

7.

x	y
2	4
6	8
10	12

8. Write and graph the inverse variation in which $y = 4$ when $x = -1$.
9. Write and graph the inverse variation in which $y = \frac{1}{2}$ when $x = 2$.
10. Let $x_1 = 5$, $y_1 = -6$, and $x_2 = 2$. Let y vary inversely as x. Find y_2.
11. The number of fleet vehicles a town can afford to buy varies inversely as the price of each car. If the town can afford 3 cars priced at $22,000 each, what must the price of a car be in order for the town to purchase 5 of them?

12-2 Rational Functions *(pp. 878–885)*

EXAMPLE

- **Graph the function $y = \frac{1}{x+1} + 3$.**

Since the numerator is 1, use the asymptotes and translate $y = \frac{1}{x}$.

Find the asymptotes.

$x = -1$ *$b = -1$*

$y = 3$ *$c = 3$*

Graph the asymptotes. Draw smooth curves to show the translation.

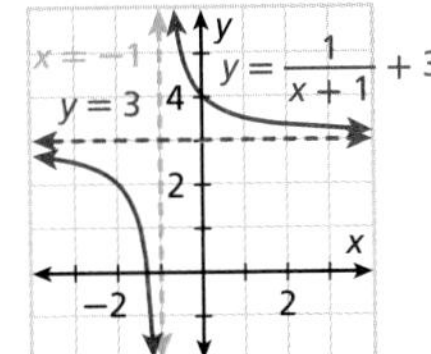

EXERCISES

Identify the excluded values and the vertical and horizontal asymptotes for each rational function.

12. $y = \frac{1}{x+4}$

13. $y = \frac{1}{x+1} + 3$

14. $y = \frac{-5}{2x+6} - 4$

15. $y = \frac{2}{4x-7} + 5$

Graph each function.

16. $y = \frac{3}{x}$

17. $y = \frac{4}{x+5}$

18. $y = \frac{1}{x+4} - 2$

19. $y = \frac{1}{x-6} + 2$

20. A rectangle has an area of 24 cm². If x represents the width, then $y = \frac{24}{x}$ represents the length y. Describe the reasonable domain and range values and graph the function.

12-3 Simplifying Rational Expressions *(pp. 886–892)*

EXAMPLE

Simplify the rational expression, if possible. Identify any excluded values.

- $\frac{x-1}{x^2+2x-3}$

$\frac{x-1}{(x+3)(x-1)}$ *Factor the denominator.*

$\frac{\cancel{x-1}^1}{(x+3)\cancel{(x-1)}^1}$ *Divide out common factors.*

$\frac{1}{x+3}$ *Simplify.*

Identify the excluded values.

$x^2 + 2x - 3 = 0$ *To find excluded values, set the denominator equal to 0.*

$(x+3)(x-1) = 0$ *Factor.*

$x + 3 = 0$ or $x - 1 = 0$ *Use the Zero Product Property.*

$x = -3$ or $x = 1$ *Solve each equation for x.*

The excluded values are −3 and 1.

EXERCISES

Find any excluded values of each rational expression.

21. $\frac{3}{5p}$

22. $\frac{-2}{r-7}$

23. $\frac{t}{t^2-t}$

24. $\frac{-4}{x^2-4x-5}$

25. $\frac{x-1}{x^2-25}$

26. $\frac{x+4}{x^2-11x+28}$

Simplify each rational expression, if possible. Identify any excluded values.

27. $\frac{7r^2}{21r^3}$

28. $\frac{3k^2}{6k^3-9k^2}$

29. $\frac{x+6}{x^2+4x-12}$

30. $\frac{2x-6}{9-x^2}$

31. $\frac{3x+15}{x^2+4x-5}$

32. $\frac{x^2+9x+18}{x^2+x-30}$

33. What is the ratio of the area of the square to the area of the circle?

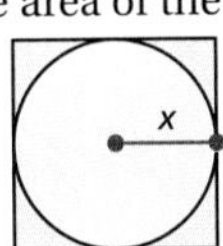

Answers

12. $-4; x = -4; y = 0$
13. $-1; x = -1; y = 3$
14. $-3; x = -3; y = -4$
15. $\frac{7}{4}; x = \frac{7}{4}; y = 5$
16.

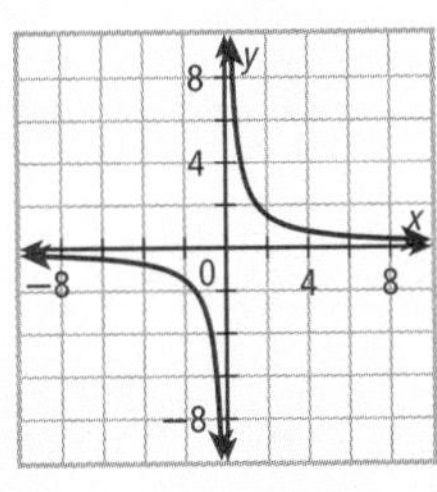

17.

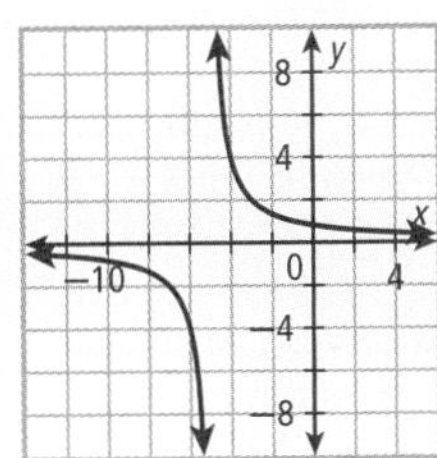

18.

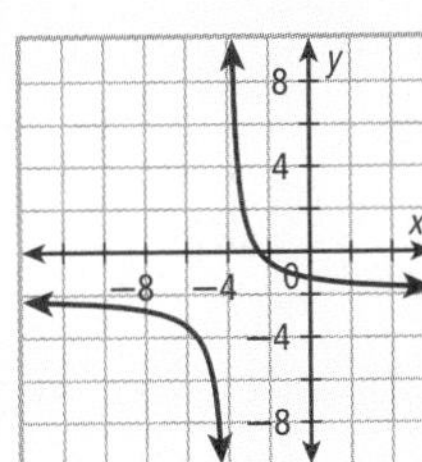

19.

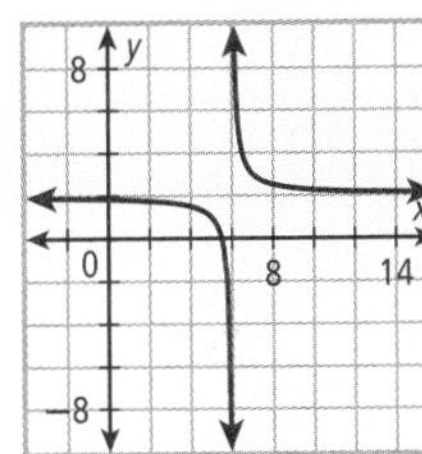

20. D: $x > 0$; R: $y > 0$

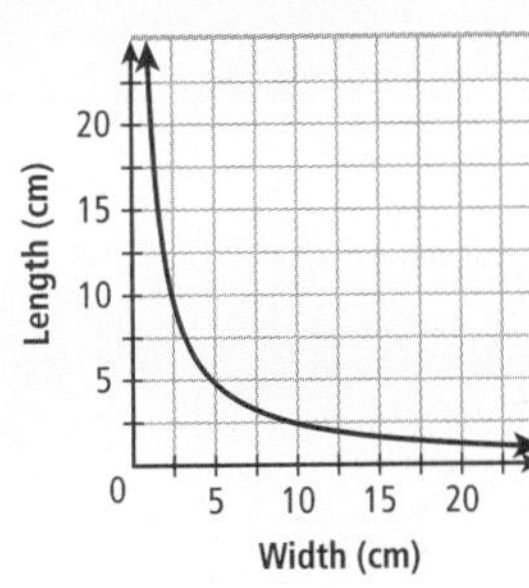

Answers

21. 0
22. 7
23. 0, 1
24. −1, 5
25. 5, −5
26. 4, 7
27. $\frac{1}{3r}; r \neq 0$
28. $\frac{1}{2k-3}; k \neq 0$ and $k \neq \frac{3}{2}$
29. $\frac{1}{x-2}; x \neq -6$ and $x \neq 2$
30. $\frac{-2}{x+3}; x \neq \pm 3$
31. $\frac{3}{x-1}; x \neq -5$ and $x \neq 1$
32. $\frac{x+3}{x-5}; x \neq -6$ and $x \neq 5$
33. $\frac{4}{\pi}$

Answers

34. $\dfrac{2b^2 + 2b}{3}$

35. $\dfrac{4x^2 - 12x}{3}$

36. $\dfrac{15b^2}{2}$

37. $-\dfrac{3c^3}{4d^2}$

38. $\dfrac{b + 2}{2b^2 + 8b}$

39. $\dfrac{n^2 + 3n + 2}{n^2 - n - 42}$

40. $\dfrac{1}{b - 3}$

41. $\dfrac{y^2}{3}$

42. $\dfrac{12n^3}{m}$

43. $\dfrac{x^2 + 2x - 3}{4x^2 - 16}$

44. $\dfrac{(b + 8)(b + 7)}{2(b + 4)(2b + 7)}$

45. $10a^2b^2$

46. $10x(x - 3)$

47. $\dfrac{b^2 + 8}{2b}$

48. $\dfrac{3x^2 + 2x - 4}{x^2 - 2}$

49. $\dfrac{8p - 2}{p^2 - 4p + 2}$

50. $\dfrac{5b - 1}{7 - b}$

51. $\dfrac{-10}{n^2 - 1}$

52. $\dfrac{7m + 2}{10m^2}$

53. $\dfrac{h^2 + 5h - 1}{h - 5}$

54. $\dfrac{40}{3r}$

12-4 Multiplying and Dividing Rational Expressions *(pp. 898–904)*

EXAMPLES

- **Multiply. Simplify your answer.**

$$\frac{5x^3 - 10x}{4x} \cdot \frac{6x^2}{7x^4 - 14x^2}$$

$$\frac{5x(x^2 - 2)}{4x} \cdot \frac{6x^2}{7x^2(x^2 - 2)} \quad \text{Factor.}$$

$$\frac{5x^1 (x^2 - 2)^1}{{}^2 4\, x^1} \cdot \frac{{}^3 6\, x^{2\,1}}{7x^{2\,1}(x^2 - 2)^1} \quad \text{Divide out common factors.}$$

$$\frac{15}{14} \quad \text{Simplify.}$$

- **Divide. Simplify your answer.**

$$\frac{32x^2y^2}{7z} \div \frac{2xy^2}{28xz^3}$$

$$\frac{32x^2y^2}{7z} \cdot \frac{28xz^3}{2xy^2} \quad \text{Multiply by the reciprocal.}$$

$$\frac{32^{16}\, x^2 y^{2\,1}}{7^1 z^1} \cdot \frac{28^4 x^1 z^{3\,2}}{2^1 x^1 y^{2\,1}} \quad \text{Divide out common factors.}$$

$$64x^2z^2 \quad \text{Simplify.}$$

EXERCISES

Multiply. Simplify your answer.

34. $\dfrac{2b}{3b - 6} \cdot (b^2 - b - 2)$

35. $\dfrac{4x}{3x + 9} \cdot (x^2 - 9)$

36. $\dfrac{5ab^2}{2ab} \cdot \dfrac{3a^2b^2}{a^2b}$

37. $\dfrac{3c}{2d} \cdot \dfrac{-4c^2d}{8d^2}$

38. $\dfrac{b + 2}{2b^2 + 12b} \cdot \dfrac{b^2 + 2b - 24}{b^2 - 16}$

39. $\dfrac{n^2 - n - 12}{n^2 + 2n - 24} \cdot \dfrac{n^2 + 3n + 2}{n^2 - 4n - 21}$

Divide. Simplify your answer.

40. $\dfrac{3b + b^2}{b + 3b^2} \div \dfrac{b^2 - 9}{3b + 1}$

41. $\dfrac{7}{y} \div \dfrac{21}{y^3}$

42. $16n^3 \div \dfrac{4m^2n}{3mn}$

43. $\dfrac{x^2 + 2x - 3}{4x} \div \dfrac{x^2 - 4}{x}$

44. A bag contains red and blue marbles. It has 8 more red marbles than blue marbles. Veronica reaches into the bag and selects one marble at random. She sets the marble aside and then selects another. What is the probability that she selects two red marbles?

12-5 Adding and Subtracting Rational Expressions *(pp. 905–911)*

EXAMPLES

Add or subtract. Simplify your answer.

- $\dfrac{7x}{3xy} - \dfrac{x^2 - 3x}{3xy}$

$$\frac{7x - (x^2 - 3x)}{3xy} \quad \text{Subtract numerators.}$$

$$\frac{7x - x^2 + 3x}{3xy} \quad \text{Distribute.}$$

$$\frac{10x - x^2}{3xy} \quad \text{Simplify.}$$

- $\dfrac{3w}{w - 5} + \dfrac{4}{w^2 - 2w - 15}$

$$\frac{3w}{w - 5} + \frac{4}{(w - 5)(w + 3)} \quad \text{Factor to find the LCD.}$$

$$\frac{3w(w + 3)}{(w - 5)(w + 3)} + \frac{4}{(w - 5)(w + 3)} \quad \text{Write each expression using the LCD.}$$

$$\frac{3w^2 + 9w}{(w - 5)(w + 3)} + \frac{4}{(w - 5)(w + 3)}$$

$$\frac{3w^2 + 9w + 4}{(w - 5)(w + 3)} \quad \text{Add and simplify.}$$

EXERCISES

Find the LCM of the given expressions.

45. $5a^2b$, $10ab^2$

46. $2x^2 - 6x$, $5x - 15$

Add or subtract. Simplify your answer.

47. $\dfrac{b^2}{2b} + \dfrac{8}{2b}$

48. $\dfrac{3x^2 - 4}{x^2 - 2} + \dfrac{2x}{x^2 - 2}$

49. $\dfrac{8p}{p^2 - 4p + 2} - \dfrac{2}{p^2 - 4p + 2}$

50. $\dfrac{3b + 4}{7 - b} - \dfrac{5 - 2b}{7 - b}$

51. $\dfrac{n - 5}{n^2 - 1} - \dfrac{n + 5}{n^2 - 1}$

52. $\dfrac{3}{5m} + \dfrac{m + 2}{10m^2}$

53. $\dfrac{h^2 + 2h}{h - 5} - \dfrac{3h - 1}{5 - h}$

54. A scout troop hikes 10 miles to the top of a mountain. Because the return trip is downhill, the troop is able to hike 3 times faster on their way down. Let r represent the troop's rate to the mountaintop. Write and simplify an expression for the round-trip hiking time in terms of r.

12-6 Dividing Polynomials *(pp. 913–919)*

EXAMPLES

Divide.

■ $\left(6x^4 - 9x^3 + 3x^2\right) \div 3x$

$\frac{6x^4 - 9x^3 + 3x^2}{3x}$ *Write as a rational expression.*

$\frac{6x^4}{3x} - \frac{9x^3}{3x} + \frac{3x^2}{3x}$ *Divide each term separately.*

$\frac{\not{6}^2 x^{\not{4} x^3}}{\not{3}^1 \not{x}^1} - \frac{\not{9}^3 x^{\not{3} x^2}}{\not{3}^1 \not{x}^1} + \frac{\not{3}^1 x^{\not{2} x}}{\not{3}^1 \not{x}^1}$ *Divide out common factors.*

$2x^3 - 3x^2 + x$ *Simplify.*

■ $\left(4x^3 - 2x^2 + 5x - 1\right) \div (x - 2)$

$$
\begin{array}{r}
4x^2 + 6x + 17 \\
x - 2 \overline{)\,4x^3 - 2x^2 + 5x - 1} \\
-\left(4x^3 - 8x^2\right) \\
\hline
6x^2 + 5x \\
-\left(6x^2 - 12x\right) \\
\hline
17x - 1 \\
-\left(17x - 34\right) \\
\hline
33
\end{array}
$$

$4x^2 + 6x + 17 + \frac{33}{x - 2}$

EXERCISES

Divide.

55. $\left(4n^3 - 6n^2 - 10n\right) \div 2n$

56. $\left(-5x^3 + 10x - 25\right) \div \left(-5x^2\right)$

57. $\frac{x^2 - 8x - 20}{x - 10}$

58. $\frac{6n^2 - 13n - 5}{2n - 5}$

59. $\frac{h^2 - 144}{h - 12}$

60. $\frac{9x^2 + 12x + 4}{3x + 2}$

61. $\frac{m^2 - 2m - 24}{m + 4}$

62. $\frac{3m^2 + m - 4}{m - 1}$

Divide using long division.

63. $\left(x^2 + 5x + 6\right) \div (x + 3)$

64. $\left(x^2 + x - 30\right) \div (x - 5)$

65. $\left(p^2 + 2p - 8\right) \div (p + 4)$

66. $\left(2x^2 + 3x - 5\right) \div (x + 2)$

67. $\left(2n^2 - 3n + 1\right) \div (n - 5)$

68. $\left(3b^3 - 4b + 2\right) \div (b - 2)$

69. $\left(2x^2 - 4x^3 + 3x\right) \div (x + 2)$

12-7 Solving Rational Equations *(pp. 920–925)*

EXAMPLE

Solve. Identify any extraneous solutions.

■ $\frac{3}{x + 3} - 4 = \frac{2}{x}$

$x(x + 3)\left(\frac{3}{x + 3} - 4\right) = x(x + 3)\frac{2}{x}$

$x(x + 3)\left(\frac{3}{x + 3}\right) - x(x + 3)4 = x(x + 3)\frac{2}{x}$

$x\cancel{(x + 3)}^1\left(\frac{3}{\cancel{x + 3}^1}\right) - x(x + 3)4 = \cancel{x}^1(x + 3)\frac{2}{\cancel{x}^1}$

$3x - 4x(x + 3) = 2(x + 3)$

$3x - 4x^2 - 12x = 2x + 6$

$0 = 4x^2 + 11x + 6$

$0 = (4x + 3)(x + 2)$

$4x + 3 = 0$ or $x + 2 = 0$

$x = -\frac{3}{4}$ or $x = -2$ *$x \neq -3$ or 0, so there are no extraneous solutions.*

EXERCISES

Solve. Identify any extraneous solutions.

70. $-4 = \frac{3}{r}$

71. $\frac{6}{7} = \frac{x}{2}$

72. $\frac{6}{b} = \frac{-5}{3 + b}$

73. $\frac{7}{3y^2} = \frac{-2}{y}$

74. $\frac{2}{x - 1} = \frac{3x}{1 - x}$

75. $\frac{2x}{x^2} + \frac{1}{x^2} = 3$

76. $\frac{2}{3} + \frac{4}{x} = \frac{6}{3x}$

77. $-\frac{1}{3x} + \frac{x}{4} = -\frac{1}{12x}$

78. $\frac{2}{3b} + 4 = \frac{1}{3b}$

79. $\frac{4}{x - 4} = \frac{8}{x^2 - 16}$

80. $\frac{5x - 10}{x + 1} = \frac{x}{2}$

81. $\frac{2x}{x + 3} + \frac{x}{4} = \frac{3}{x + 3}$

82. $\frac{9m}{m - 5} = 7 - \frac{3}{m - 5}$

83. $\frac{x - 4}{x^2 - 4} = \frac{-2}{x - 2}$

Answers

55. $2n^2 - 3n - 5$
56. $x - \frac{2}{x} + \frac{5}{x^2}$
57. $x + 2$
58. $3n + 1$
59. $h + 12$
60. $3x + 2$
61. $m - 6$
62. $3m + 4$
63. $x + 2$
64. $x + 6$
65. $p - 2$
66. $2x - 1 + \frac{-3}{x + 2}$
67. $2n + 7 + \frac{36}{n - 5}$
68. $3b^2 + 6b + 8 + \frac{18}{b - 2}$
69. $-4x^2 + 10x - 17 + \frac{34}{x + 2}$
70. $-\frac{3}{4}$
71. $\frac{12}{7}$
72. $-\frac{18}{11}$
73. $-\frac{7}{6}$; 0 is extraneous.
74. $-\frac{2}{3}$; 1 is extraneous.
75. $-\frac{1}{3}$, 1
76. -3
77. ± 1
78. $-\frac{1}{12}$
79. -2; 4 is extraneous.
80. 4, 5
81. -12, 1
82. -19
83. 0; 2 is extraneous.

Organizer

Objective: Assess students' mastery of concepts and skills presented in Chapter 12.

Online Edition

Resources

Assessment Resources

Chapter 12 Tests

- Free Response (Levels A, B, C)
- Multiple Choice (Levels A, B, C)
- Performance Assessment

Teacher One Stop™

Test & Practice Generator

State Resources

CHAPTER TEST

1. Write and graph the inverse variation in which $y = -4$ when $x = 2$. $y = -\frac{8}{x}$
2. The number of posters the Spanish Club can buy varies inversely as the cost of each poster. The club can buy 15 posters that cost \$2.60 each. How many posters can the club buy if they cost \$3.25 each? **12**

Identify the excluded values and the vertical and horizontal asymptotes for each rational function.

3. $y = \frac{3}{x+1}$ $x \neq -1$; $x = -1$ and $y = 0$
4. $y = \frac{1}{2x-1} + 5$ $x \neq \frac{1}{2}$; $x = \frac{1}{2}$ and $y = 5$
5. $y = \frac{1}{x+3} - 3$ $x \neq -3$; $x = -3$ and $y = -3$

Simplify each rational expression, if possible. Identify any excluded values.

6. $\frac{2b}{4b^2}$ $\frac{1}{2b}$; $b \neq 0$
7. $\frac{x^2 - 16}{x^2 + 3x - 4}$ $\frac{x-4}{x-1}$; $x \neq -4$ and $x \neq 1$
8. $\frac{b^2 - 2b - 15}{5 - b}$ $-b - 3$; $b \neq 5$
9. $\frac{x^2 + 4x - 5}{x^2 - 25}$ $\frac{x-1}{x-5}$; $x \neq \pm 5$

Multiply. Simplify your answer.

10. $\frac{-4}{x^2 - 9} \cdot (x - 3)$ $\frac{-4}{x+3}$
11. $\frac{2a^2b^2}{5b^3} \cdot \frac{15a^2b}{8a^4}$ $\frac{3}{4}$
12. $\frac{x^2 - x - 12}{x^2 - 16} \cdot \frac{x^2 + x - 12}{x^2 + 3x + 2}$ $\frac{x^2 - 9}{x^2 + 3x + 2}$

Divide. Simplify your answer.

13. $\frac{4x^2y^4}{3xy^2} \div \frac{12xy}{15x^3y^2}$ $\frac{5x^3y^3}{3}$
14. $\frac{3b^2 - 6b}{2b^3 + 3b^2} \div \frac{2b - 4}{8b + 12}$ $\frac{6}{b}$
15. $\frac{x^2 + 2x - 15}{x^2 - 9} \div \frac{x^2 - 25}{x^2 + 3x + 2}$ $\frac{x^2 + 3x + 2}{x^2 - 2x - 15}$

Add or subtract. Simplify your answer.

16. $\frac{b^2 + 3}{5b} + \frac{4}{5b}$ $\frac{b^2 + 7}{5b}$
17. $\frac{5x - 2}{x^2 + 2} - \frac{2x}{x^2 + 2}$ $\frac{3x - 2}{x^2 + 2}$
18. $\frac{2}{3x^2} - \frac{5 - 2x}{3x^2}$ $\frac{-3 + 2x}{3x^2}$
19. $\frac{3m}{2m^2} + \frac{1}{2m}$ $\frac{2}{m}$
20. $\frac{3x}{2x + 4} - \frac{1}{x + 2}$ $\frac{3x - 2}{2x + 4}$
21. $\frac{y^2 + 4}{y - 3} + \frac{y^2}{3 - y}$ $\frac{4}{y - 3}$

Divide.

22. $(8t^2 - 2t) \div 2t$ $4t - 1$
23. $\frac{3x^2 + 2x - 8}{x + 2}$ $3x - 4$
24. $\frac{k^2 - 2k - 35}{k + 5}$ $k - 7$

Divide using long division.

25. $(2w^2 + 5w - 12) \div (w + 4)$ $2w - 3$
26. $(x^2 - 4x + 9) \div (x + 2)$ $x - 6 + \frac{21}{x + 2}$
27. The area of a rectangle can be modeled by $A(x) = x^3 - 1$. The length is $x - 1$.
    a. Find a polynomial to represent the width of the rectangle. $x^2 + x + 1$
    b. Find the width when x is 6 cm. **43 cm**

Solve. Identify any extraneous solutions.

28. $\frac{2}{x - 1} = \frac{9}{2x - 3}$ $\frac{3}{5}$
29. $\frac{3}{n - 1} = \frac{n}{n + 4}$ $-2, 6$
30. $\frac{2}{n + 2} = \frac{n - 4}{n^2 - 4}$ 0; -2 is extraneous.
31. Julio can wash and wax the family car in 2 hours. It takes Leo 4 hours to wash and wax the same car. How long will it take them to wash and wax the car if they work together? $1\frac{1}{3}$ h

Answers

1.

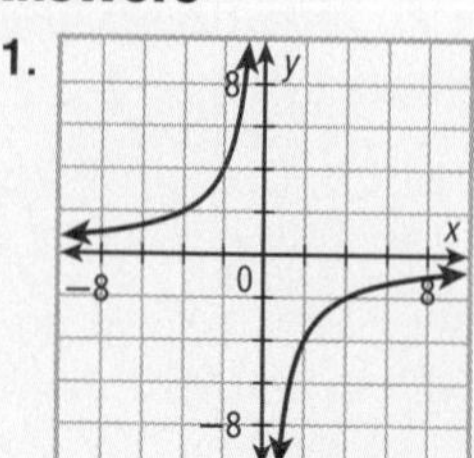

COLLEGE ENTRANCE EXAM PRACTICE

FOCUS ON SAT MATHEMATICS SUBJECT TESTS

The topics covered on each SAT Mathematics Subject Test vary only slightly each time the test is given. Find out the general distribution of test items across topics, and then identify the areas you need to concentrate on while studying.

HOT TIP! To prepare for the SAT Math Subject Tests, start reviewing material several months before your test date. Take sample tests to find the areas you need to focus on. You are not expected to have studied all topics on the test.

You may want to time yourself as you take this practice test. It should take you about 6 minutes to complete.

1. Which set of ordered pairs satisfies an inverse variation?

(A) $(6, 3)$ and $(8, 4)$

(B) $(2, -3)$ and $(4, 5)$

(C) $(4, -2)$ and $(-5, 10)$

(D) $(2, 6)$ and $(-3, -4)$

(E) $\left(4, \frac{1}{4}\right)$ and $\left(-4, \frac{1}{4}\right)$

2. If $\frac{3}{x+3} = \frac{7x}{x^2-9}$, what is x?

(A) -12

(B) -3

(C) $-\frac{9}{4}$

(D) $\frac{9}{4}$

(E) 3

3. What is h if $(x^3 + 2x^2 - 4x + h) \div (x + 1)$ has a remainder of 15?

(A) -10

(B) -5

(C) 5

(D) 10

(E) 20

4. The graph of which function is shown?

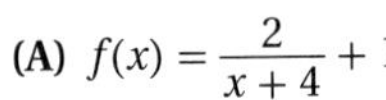

(A) $f(x) = \frac{2}{x+4} + 1$

(B) $f(x) = \frac{4}{x+2} - 1$

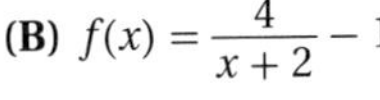

(C) $f(x) = \frac{4}{x-2} + 1$

(D) $f(x) = \frac{4}{x-2} - 1$

(E) $f(x) = \frac{2}{x-4} + 1$

5. Which function has the same graph as $f(x) = \frac{x^2 - 4x - 5}{x^2 - 3x - 10}$ except at $x = 5$?

(A) $g(x) = \frac{x-1}{x-2}$

(B) $g(x) = \frac{x+1}{x+2}$

(C) $g(x) = \frac{x+1}{(x-5)(x+2)}$

(D) $g(x) = \frac{(x+5)(x-1)}{x+2}$

(E) $g(x) = \frac{(x-5)(x+1)}{x-2}$

COLLEGE ENTRANCE EXAM PRACTICE

Organizer

Objective: Provide practice for college entrance exams such as the SAT Mathematics Subject Tests.

PREMIER **Online Edition**

Resources

College Entrance Exam Practice

Questions on the SAT Mathematics Subject Tests Levels 1 and 2 represent the following math content areas:

	Level	
	1	**2**
Number and Operations	10–14%	10–14%
Algebra and Functions	38–42%	48–52%
Geometry and Measurement	38–42%	28–32%
Plane Euclidean	18–22%	0%
Coordinate	8–12%	10–14%
Three-dimensional	4–6%	4–6%
Trigonometry	6–8%	12–16%
Data Analysis, Statistics, and Probability	6–10%	6–10%

Items on this page focus on:

- Algebra and Functions

Text References:

Item	1	2	3	4	5
Lesson	12-1	12-7	12-6	12-2	12-3

TEST PREP DOCTOR

1. Students who chose **A** might think that if (x_1, y_1) and (x_2, y_2) are solutions of an inverse variation, then $x_1y_2 = x_2y_1$. Students who chose **C** might think that if (x_1, y_1) and (x_2, y_2) are solutions of an inverse variation, then $x_1x_2 = y_1y_2$.

2. Students who chose **B** did not check their answer. This choice is an extraneous solution and an excluded value.

3. Students who chose **E** may not have distributed signs correctly in the process of long division. Remind students to check their work if they have time.

4. Students who chose **B** may have thought that the numerator should be $x + 2$ because the graph is shifted 2 units to the right. Students who chose **C** did not recognize that the graph has a horizontal asymptote of $y = -1$.

5. Students who chose **A** may have factored $f(x)$ incorrectly as $\frac{(x+5)(x-1)}{(x+5)(x-2)}$ and then cancelled the common factor. Students who chose **C** may have factored $f(x)$ correctly but did not cancel the common factor from both the numerator and denominator.

Organizer

Objective: Provide opportunities to learn and practice common test-taking strategies.

Standardized Test Strategies

Multiple Choice: Choose Combinations of Answers

Some multiple-choice test items require selecting a combination of correct answers. The correct response is the most complete option available. To solve this type of test item, determine if each statement is true or false. Then choose the option that includes each correct statement.

EXAMPLE

Which of the following has an excluded value of −5?

I. $\frac{5}{x-5}$ **III.** $\frac{x^2-10}{5x+25} \cdot \frac{5}{x+10}$

II. $\frac{8x^2+36x-20}{2(x+5)}$ **IV.** $\frac{2(x+2)}{2x^2+12x+10}$

(A) I only (C) II, III, and IV

(B) II and III (D) III and IV

Look at each statement separately and determine whether it is true. You can keep track of which statements are true in a table.

Statement	True/False
I	False
II	True
III	True
IV	True

Statement I
The denominator, $x - 5$, equals 0 when $x = 5$.

Statement I does not answer the question, so it is false.

Statement II
The denominator, $2(x + 5)$, equals 0 when $x = -5$.

Statement II does answer the question, so it is true.

Statement III
The denominator, $(5x + 25)(x + 10)$, equals 0 when $x = -5$ or $x = -10$.

Statement III does answer the question, so it is true.

Statement IV
The denominator, $2x^2 + 12x + 10$, can be factored as $2(x + 5)(x + 1)$. This expression equals 0 when $x = -5$ or $x = -1$.

Statement IV does answer the question, so it is true.

Statements II, III, and IV are all true. Option C is the correct response because it includes all the true statements.

Options B and D contain some of the true statements, but option C is the **most complete** answer.

Evaluate all of the statements before deciding on an answer choice. Make a table to keep track of whether each statement is true or false.

Read each test item and answer the questions that follow.

Item A
Which dimensions represent a rectangle that has an area equivalent to the expression $2x^2 + 18x + 16$?

I. $\ell = x + 8$

$w = 2(x + 1)$

II. $\ell = 2x + 2$

$w = \dfrac{x^2 + 3x - 40}{x - 5}$

III. $\ell = x + 2$

$w = \dfrac{(2x + 2)(x + 4)}{1} \cdot \dfrac{3x - 1}{3x^2 - 11x - 4}$

Ⓐ I only Ⓒ I and II

Ⓑ III only Ⓓ I, II, and III

1. How do you determine the area of a rectangle?
2. Daisy realized that the area of rectangle I was equivalent to the given area and selected option A as her response. Do you agree? Explain your reasoning.
3. Write a simplified expression for the width of rectangle II.
4. Explain each step for determining the area of rectangle III.
5. If rectangle II has an area equivalent to the given expression, then which options can you eliminate?

Item B
Which expression is undefined for $x = 3$ or $x = -2$?

I. $2x + 12 \cdot \dfrac{4}{2(x - 3)(x + 6)}$ **III.** $\dfrac{x - 2}{(x + 2)(x - 1)}$

II. $\dfrac{9x - 1}{x^2 + 3}$ **IV.** $\dfrac{14}{x^2 - x - 6}$

Ⓕ I, III, and IV Ⓗ III and IV

Ⓖ I and II Ⓙ I and IV

6. When is an expression undefined?
7. Henry determined that statement I is undefined when $x = 3$. He decides it is an incorrect answer because the expression is defined when $x = -2$. Should he select option H by process of elimination? Explain your reasoning.
8. Make a table to determine the correct response.

Item C
Which rational function has a graph with a horizontal asymptote of $y = 4$?

I. $y = \dfrac{-4}{x}$ **III.** $y = \dfrac{1}{x - 4}$

II. $y = \dfrac{1}{x} + 4$ **IV.** $y = -\dfrac{1}{x} + 4$

Ⓐ I and III Ⓒ I and II

Ⓑ II only Ⓓ II and IV

9. Where does the horizontal asymptote of the function in statement I occur?
10. Using your answer from Problem 9, which option(s) can you eliminate? Explain your reasoning.
11. Look at the options remaining. Which statement would be best to check next? Explain your reasoning.

Answers to Test Items

A. C
B. F
C. D

Answers

Possible answers:

1. $A = \ell w$
2. No; she should have checked to see if the other rectangles also have an area that is equivalent to the given expression.
3. $x + 8$
4. Simplify the width by factoring the denominator of the second expression. Then divide out common factors and multiply. Then multiply the length and the width and simplify the result.
5. **A** and **B**
6. when the value of the denominator is zero
7. No; the problem asks for expressions that are undefined for $x = 3$ or $x = -2$, not necessarily both.
8. **F** is the correct response.

Statement	True/False
I	True
II	False
III	True
IV	True

9. $y = 0$
10. **A** and **C** can be eliminated because the function in statement I does not have a horizontal asymptote of $y = 4$.
11. Statement **IV** should be checked next. If it is false, then by elimination, the correct response is **B.**

State Resources

go.hrw.com
State Resources Online
KEYWORD: MA7 Resources

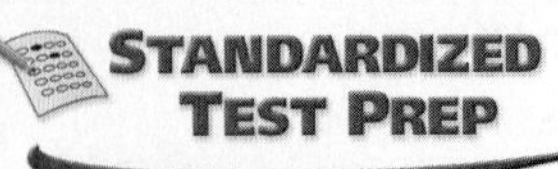

Organizer

Objective: Provide review and practice for Chapters 1–12 and standardized tests.

Resources

Assessment Resources

Chapter 12 Cumulative Test

go.hrw.com
KEYWORD: MA7 TestPrep

CUMULATIVE ASSESSMENT, CHAPTERS 1–12

Multiple Choice

1. Simplify the expression $4(2d - 1) - 6d$.
   - (A) $2d$
   - (B) $2d - 4$
   - (C) $-4d + 3$
   - (D) $2d - 1$

2. Which equation is the result of solving $3x + 2y = 8$ for y?
   - (F) $y = \frac{3}{2}x - 4$
   - (G) $y = 3x + 4$
   - (H) $y = -3x + 8$
   - (J) $y = -\frac{3}{2}x + 4$

3. Which function is shown in the graph?
   - (A) $y = 3x$
   - (B) $y = \frac{x}{3}$
   - (C) $y = \sqrt{x} + 3$
   - (D) $y = \frac{1}{x} + 3$

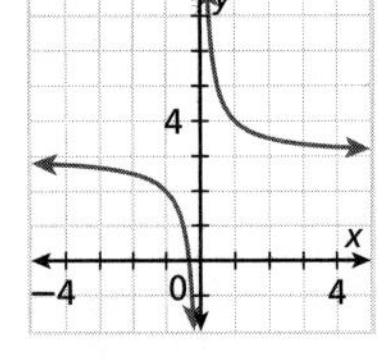

4. The drama club needs to raise at least \$1400 for a field trip. The club was given \$150 by the school administration. Club members are selling key chains for \$5 each. Which inequality represents the number of key chains k that the drama club needs to sell to go on its field trip?
   - (F) $150 + 5k \geq 1400$
   - (G) $5k - 150 \geq 1400$
   - (H) $5k + 150 \leq 1400$
   - (J) $150 \leq 5k + 1400$

5. Which expression is NOT equivalent to $\frac{3}{x-1}$?
   - (A) $\frac{3x+6}{x^2+x-2}$
   - (B) $\frac{3x-3}{x^2-2x+1}$
   - (C) $\frac{3x+3}{x^2-1}$
   - (D) $\frac{3x-3}{x-1}$

6. Which situation best describes a negative correlation?
   - (F) The intensity level of an exercise and the number of Calories burned per minute
   - (G) The amount of time that an electronic game is on and the amount of power remaining in the game's batteries
   - (H) The height of a tree and the amount of ink in a ballpoint pen
   - (J) The daytime temperature and the number of people at an ice cream stand

7. Which expression is equivalent to $\frac{3m^2n}{5m} \cdot \frac{20mn}{n^6}$?
   - (A) $\frac{12m^2}{n^4}$
   - (B) $\frac{12m^3}{n^3}$
   - (C) $12m^2n^3$
   - (D) $\frac{12m}{n}$

8. Simplify $\frac{3}{x} + \frac{3}{5x}$.
   - (F) $\frac{1}{x}$
   - (G) $\frac{9}{5x}$
   - (H) $\frac{18}{5x}$
   - (J) $\frac{1}{2x}$

9. Which of the following has a slope of -3?

(A)

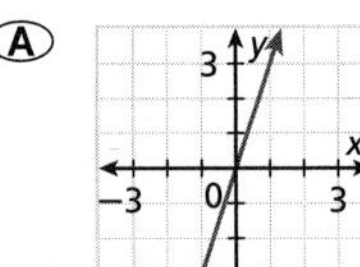

(C)

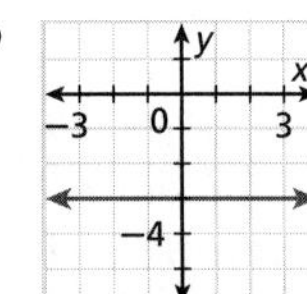

(B)

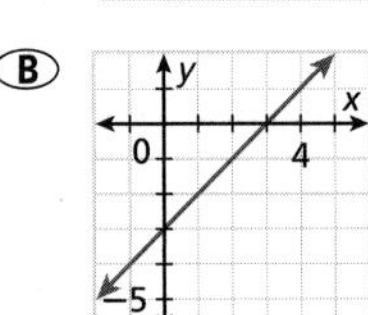

(D)

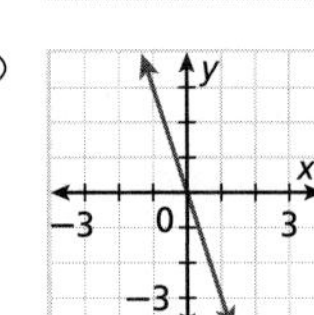

10. What is $(-12x^6 + x) \div (-4x^2)$?
    - (F) $3x^3 - \frac{1}{4x}$
    - (G) $3x^4 - \frac{1}{4x}$
    - (H) $3x^5$
    - (J) $3x^4 + x$

State Resources

go.hrw.com
State Resources Online
KEYWORD: MA7 Resources

Answers

1. B
2. J
3. D
4. F
5. D
6. G
7. A
8. H
9. D
10. G
11. B
12. F
13. A
14. H
15. 2
16. 819.2
17. 18
18. $\frac{7}{8}$
19. 2

11. Abe flips two coins. What is the probability of both coins landing heads up?

Ⓐ $\frac{1}{2}$ Ⓒ $\frac{1}{8}$

Ⓑ $\frac{1}{4}$ Ⓓ $\frac{1}{16}$

12. Which is a solution to $\frac{n}{n+2} = \frac{-8}{n}$?

Ⓕ -4 Ⓗ 2

Ⓖ -2 Ⓙ 4

13. Which of the following is equivalent to $\left(\frac{2x^5y^2}{8x}\right)^{-2}$?

Ⓐ $\frac{16}{x^8y^4}$ Ⓒ $\frac{4}{x^4y^2}$

Ⓑ $\frac{x^8}{16y^4}$ Ⓓ $\frac{x^5}{16}$

14. What situation can be modeled by the function $y = \frac{140}{x}$?

Ⓕ The cost of attending a ski trip is $140 for each person who attends.

Ⓖ The area of a rectangle with a width of 140 meters varies directly as its length.

Ⓗ The cost per person of a boat rental is $140 divided by the number of people.

Ⓙ Attendance at this year's concert was 140 people more than at last year's concert.

Know the rules for writing gridded-response answers. For example, can you write the fraction $\frac{2}{3}$ as 0.6666 or as 0.67? Different tests may have different rules, so pay close attention to the directions.

Gridded Response

15. What is the excluded value for the rational expression $\frac{x^2-4}{3x-6}$?

16. What is the next term in the geometric sequence 2000, 1600, 1280, 1024,...?

17. What is the constant of variation if y varies inversely as x and $y = 3$ when $x = 6$?

18. What is the value of $4^0 - (2^{-3})$?

19. Identify the excluded value for $y = \frac{x-4}{x-2}$.

Short Response

20. Mr. Lui wrote $\frac{15-5x}{x^2-9x+18}$ on the board.

a. Explain what kind of expression it is.

b. Simplify the expression. Show your work.

c. Identify any excluded values.

21. Describe the similarities and differences between the graph of $f(x) = x^2 + 4$ and the graph of $g(x) = \frac{1}{2}x^2 + 3$.

22. What are 2 values of b that will make $2x^2 - bx - 20$ factorable? Explain your answer.

23. Brandee makes an hourly wage. In the last pay period, she earned $800 for regular hours and $240 for overtime hours. Her overtime rate of pay is 50% more per hour than her regular rate of pay r. Write and simplify an expression, in terms of r, that represents the number of hours h Brandee worked in the pay period. Show your work.

Extended Response

24. Principal Farley has $200 to pay for some teachers to attend a technology conference. The company hosting the conference is allowing 2 teachers to attend for free. The number of teachers y that can be sent to the conference is given by the function $y = \frac{200}{x} + 2$, where x is the cost per teacher.

a. Describe the reasonable domain and range values for this function.

b. Identify the vertical and horizontal asymptotes.

c. Graph the function.

d. Give two whole-number solutions to the equation and describe what they mean in the context of this situation.

Short-Response Rubric

Items 20–23

2 Points = The student's answer is an accurate and complete execution of the task or tasks.

1 Point = The student's answer contains attributes of an appropriate response but is flawed.

0 Points = The student's answer contains no attributes of an appropriate response.

Extended-Response Rubric

Item 24

4 Points = The student gives a reasonable domain and range in part **a,** identifies the vertical and horizontal asymptotes correctly in part **b,** graphs the function correctly in part **c,** and gives the two whole-number solutions and describes what they mean in part **d.**

3 Points = The student gives a reasonable domain and range in part **a,** identifies the vertical and horizontal asymptotes correctly in part **b,** graphs the function in part **c,** and gives two whole-number solutions but only partially describes what they mean in part **d.**

2 Points = The student gives a reasonable domain and range with a minor error in part **a,** identifies the vertical and horizontal asymptotes in part **b,** graphs the function in part **c,** and gives one whole-number solution and describes what it means in part **d** or gives two whole-number solutions but does not explain what they mean.

1 Point = The student answers one part correctly but does not attempt all parts, or the student attempts to answer all parts of the problem but does not correctly answer any part.

0 Points = The student does not answer correctly and does not attempt all parts of the problem.

Answers

20a. rational expression

b. $-\frac{5}{x-6}$

c. 3, 6

21. Both graphs have the parabola $y = x^2$ as the parent function. To get the graph of $f(x)$, the parent function is translated 4 units up. The graph of $g(x)$ is wider than that of $f(x)$ and is translated only 3 units up.

22. Possible answers: ±3, ±6, ±18

23. $h(r) = \frac{800}{r} + \frac{240}{1.5r}$;

regular hours: $\frac{\$800}{r \text{ dollars per hour}}$;

overtime hours: $\frac{\$240}{1.50(r \text{ dollars per hour})}$

24a. D: $x > 0$; R: natural numbers > 2

b. $x = 0$ and $y = 2$

c.

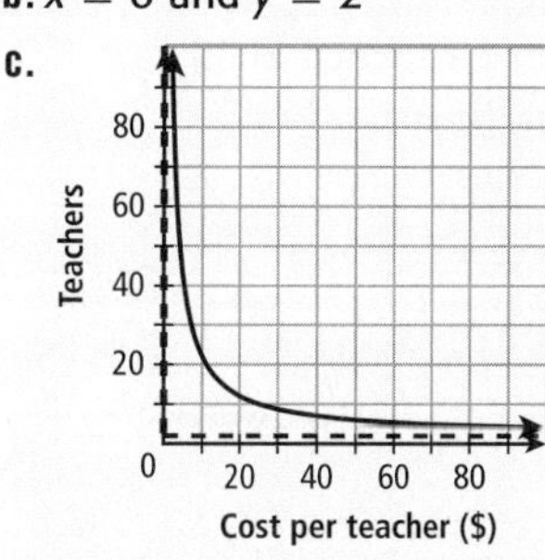

d. (50, 6) and (100, 4); at a cost of $50 per teacher, 6 teachers attend; at a cost of $100 per teacher, 4 teachers attend.

CONNECTIONS

Organizer

Objective: Choose appropriate problem-solving strategies and use them with skills from Chapters 11 and 12 to solve real-world problems.

Cincinnati Reds

Reading Strategies

ENGLISH LANGUAGE LEARNERS

For a long word problem, such as **Problem 4,** encourage students to read through the entire question once for understanding. Then have them write down important information as they read through the second time.

Using Data Remind students that when they divide data values to find the percent increase, the result will be a decimal greater than 1. Remind them that the percent increase is only the portion of the number after the decimal expressed as a percent.

Problem-Solving Focus

"Make an organized list" may be a helpful problem-solving strategy for **Problem 3.** "Make a table" may be a useful way to organize the information given in **Problem 2.**

State Resources

Cincinnati Reds

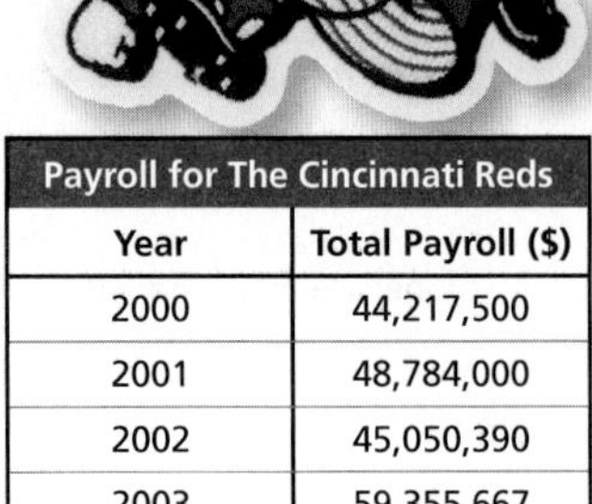

Organized in 1866, the Cincinnati Reds, known then as the Cincinnati Red Stockings, were the first major league baseball team. They now play in a stadium built in 2003 called the Great American Ballpark.

Choose one or more strategies to solve each problem.

1. The table shows the total payroll for the Reds from 2000 to 2005. What percent did the total payroll increase from 2000 to 2005? **about 40%**
2. Assume the payroll percent increase for the next x years is the same as from 2004 to 2005. Write an exponential growth function to model this situation.
3. Using the function found in Problem 2, what is the expected total payroll for the Reds in the year 2010?
4. Suppose that at a Cincinnati Reds game, tickets in the blue zone average \$28 and tickets in the green zone average \$20. Suppose twice as many tickets were sold to fans in the green zone as in the blue zone and the total ticket sales for these two zones was \$204,000. Fans bought 14,197 tickets in other zones and sections. How many people had tickets to the game? **23,197**

Payroll for The Cincinnati Reds

Year	Total Payroll (\$)
2000	44,217,500
2001	48,784,000
2002	45,050,390
2003	59,355,667
2004	46,615,250
2005	61,892,583

Answers

2. $y \approx 61{,}892{,}583(1.33)^x$, where x is the number of years since 2005
3. $\approx$ \$257,570,910

✪ Bicycle Museum of America

The Bicycle Museum of America in New Bremen, Ohio, is home to one of the largest private collections of bicycles and bicycle memorabilia in the world. The collection represents every era, including antique bicycles from the 1800s, balloon-tire classics of the 1940s and 1950s, and banana-seat bikes with high-rise handlebars from the 1960s.

Choose one or more strategies to solve each problem.

1. Alfred Letourner was one of the top racers of his era. On May 17, 1941, at an event sponsored by Schwinn, Letourner rode a bike similar to the one in the photo with a gear ratio of $9\frac{1}{2}$ to 1. The bike only weighed 20 pounds. At this event, Letourner shattered speed records when he rode a mile in 33.05 seconds. At this pace, about how many miles per hour was Letourner riding? **108.9 mi/h**

The diagram shows the relationship between the number of teeth on the pedal gear and the number of teeth on the wheel gear of a bicycle. This relationship affects the speed and effort of pedaling. For example, if the pedal gear has 39 teeth and the wheel gear has 17 teeth, then the gear ratio is $\frac{39}{17} = 2.294$. This number represents the number of turns of the wheel for every full turn of the pedal.

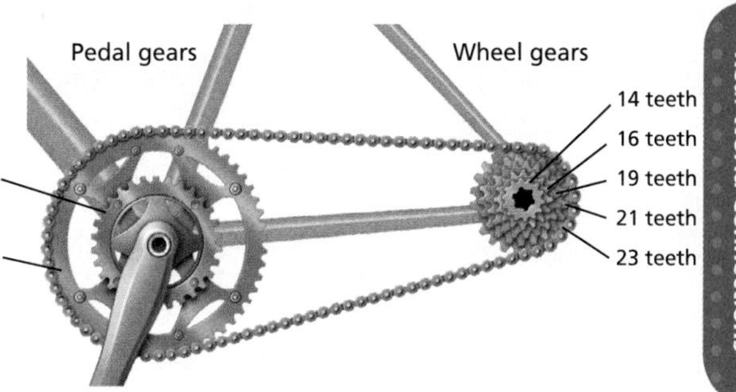

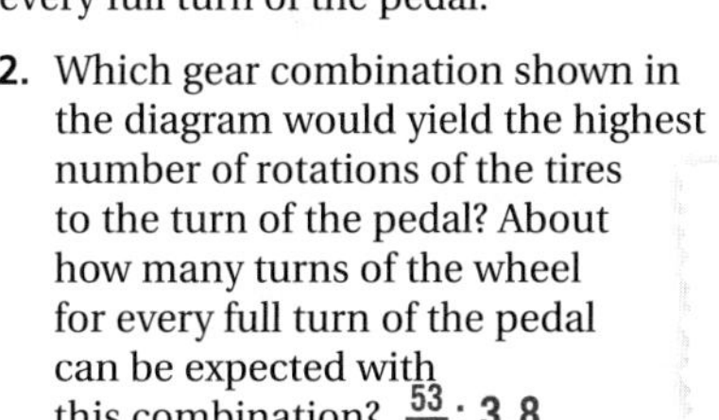

2. Which gear combination shown in the diagram would yield the highest number of rotations of the tires to the turn of the pedal? About how many turns of the wheel for every full turn of the pedal can be expected with this combination? $\frac{53}{14}$; **3.8**
3. If a mountain bike has tires with a diameter of 26 inches, how far, in feet, will a rider travel for each full turn of the pedal if the pedal gear has 39 teeth and the wheel gear has 14 teeth? **18.96 ft**

Real-World Connections

✪ Bicycle Museum of America

Reading Strategies

Problems appear harder than they really are when they contain unfamiliar words or concepts. Encourage students to ask other students or their teacher for help with new terms when needed.

Using Data Have students use the diagram to find the greatest number of teeth on a wheel gear and the greatest number of teeth on any type of gear. 23; 53

Problem-Solving Focus

Encourage students to use the four-step problem-solving process for **Problem 1.** Focus on the first and second steps: **(1) Understand the problem:** Ask students what information is not needed. the gear ratio and weight of the bike

(2) Make a plan: The answer should be in miles per hour. Ask students how they could find the time in miles per minute. Find $\frac{60}{33.05}$. Ask what they should do from there. Convert miles per minute to miles per hour by writing a proportion with the correct conversion factor.

Discuss how estimation can be used in **Problem 1.** Letourner took about $\frac{1}{2}$ of a minute to ride 1 mile, or 2 miles per minute. This estimated rate is equivalent to 120 mph. Discuss with students that because the time, 33.05 seconds, was rounded down, the estimated speed is an overestimate.

Real-World Connections **941**

Additional Topics

ADDITIONAL TOPIC

A-1 Organizer

Objective: Analyze the characteristics of power functions.

Warm Up

Identify the leading coefficient and degree of each polynomial.

1. $2x^3 - 5x^2 + 6x - 7$
   2; 3
2. $-3x^4 + 5x - 7$
   −3; 4
3. $x^6 - 2x^3 + 4x$
   1; 6
4. $-0.5x^2 + 12x + 6$
   −0.5; 2

State Resources

go.hrw.com
State Resources Online
KEYWORD: MA7 Resources

ADDITIONAL TOPIC

A-1 Introduction to Power Functions

Objective
Analyze the characteristics of power functions.

Vocabulary
power function

A **power function** is a function that can be written in the form $f(x) = ax^n$, where a and n are real numbers and $a \neq 0$. This lesson will only address power functions for which n is a positive integer.

Power Functions

$n = 1$	$n = 2$	$n = 3$	$n = 4$	$n = 5$
$y = ax$	$y = ax^2$	$y = ax^3$	$y = ax^4$	$y = ax^5$

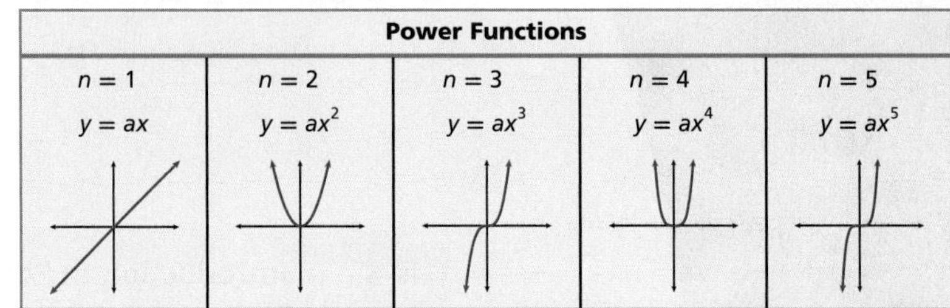

EXAMPLE 1 Graphing Power Functions

Graph the power function $y = x^5$, and then describe the graph.

Step 1 Make a table of values.

x	$x^5 = y$
−2	$(-2)^5 = -32$
−1	$(-1)^5 = -1$
0	$0^5 = 0$
1	$1^5 = 1$
2	$2^5 = 32$

The ordered pairs (−2, −32), (−1, −1), (0, 0), (1, 1) and (2, 32) lie on the graph.

Step 2 Sketch the graph by plotting the ordered pairs from the table.

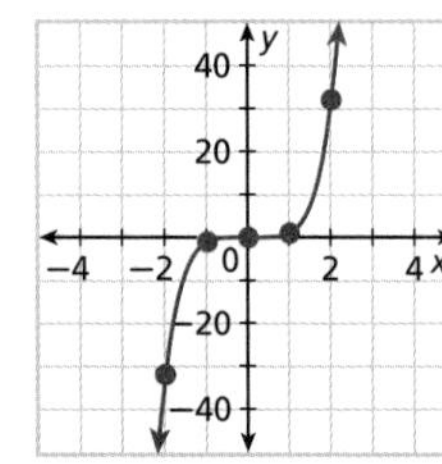

From left to right, the graph increases. It crosses the x-axis once, at the origin.

CHECK IT OUT! **1.** Graph the power function $y = x^4$, and then describe the graph.

1. The graph decreases from left to right for $x < 0$, and it increases from left to right for $x > 0$. It intersects the x-axis once, at the origin.

1 Introduce

Motivate

Ask students to name some of the families of functions that they have already studied. linear, quadratic, exponential, etc.
Tell students that this lesson focuses on another family of functions, known as power functions. Point out that some quadratic and cubic functions can also be classified as power functions.

2 Teach

Guided Instruction

Emphasize that for $n \geq 2$, the graph of a power function has one of two basic shapes. If n is odd, the shape of the graph is similar to that of $y = x^3$, and the domain and range are all real numbers. If n is even, the graph has a U shape, similar to that of $y = x^4$, and the graph has either a maximum or minimum value.

Substituting any real value of x into a power function results in a real number. Therefore, the domain of any power function is all real numbers. The range of a power function depends on the *degree* of the function. The degree of the power function $f(x) = ax^n$ is n.

The table summarizes the possibilities for the range and the maximum and minimum values of a power function.

Range, Maximum Value, and Minimum Value

Odd Degree	Even Degree, $a > 0$	Even Degree , $a < 0$
The range is all real numbers. There is no maximum or minimum value.	The graph opens upward. The minimum value is 0. The range is $y \geq 0$.	The graph opens downward. The maximum value is 0. The range is $y \leq 0$.

EXAMPLE 2 Finding Maximum or Minimum Values

Give the domain and range of each power function. Then give the minimum or maximum value, if any.

A $f(x) = -0.5x^7$

The degree, 7, is odd.

The domain is all real numbers. The range is all real numbers. There is no minimum or maximum value.

B $f(x) = -2x^4$

The degree, 4, is even, and $a < 0$.

The domain is all real numbers.

The range is $y \leq 0$.

The maximum value is 0.

Check The graph supports the answer.

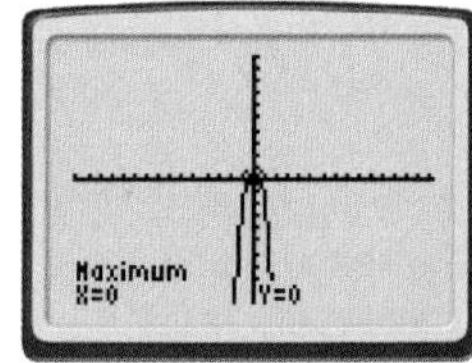

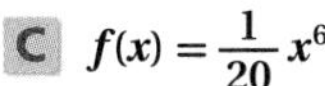

C $f(x) = \frac{1}{20}x^6$

The degree, 6, is even, and $a > 0$.

The domain is all real numbers.

The range is $y \geq 0$.

The minimum value is 0.

Check The graph supports the answer.

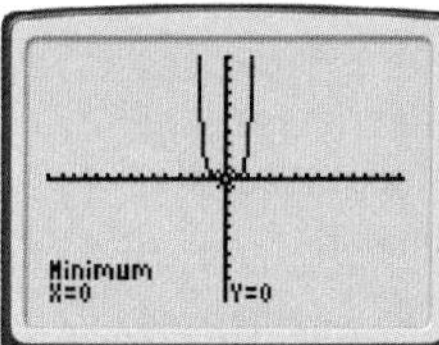

2a. D: all real numbers; R: $y \leq 0$; maximum value: 0

2b. D: all real numbers; R: all real numbers; no minimum or maximum value

2c. D: all real numbers; R: $y \geq 0$; minimum value: 0

Give the domain and range of each power function. Then give the minimum or maximum value, if any.

2a. $f(x) = -x^8$ **2b.** $f(x) = -2.5x^5$ **2c.** $f(x) = \frac{1}{4}x^{10}$

Additional Examples

Example 1

Graph the power function $y = x^6$, and then describe the graph.

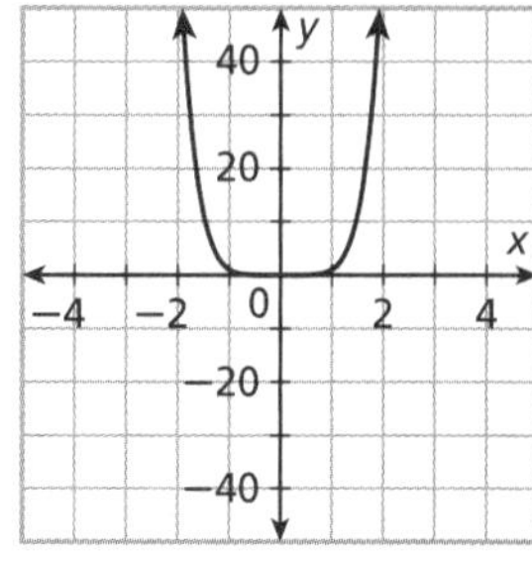

The graph decreases from left to right for $x < 0$, and it increases from left to right for $x > 0$. It intersects the x-axis once, at the origin.

Example 2

Give the domain and range of each power function. Then give the minimum or maximum value, if any.

A. $f(x) = -4x^5$
D: all real numbers; R: all real numbers; no minimum or maximum value

B. $f(x) = 0.3x^8$
D: all real numbers; R: $y \geq 0$; minimum value: 0

C. $f(x) = -\frac{1}{2}x^4$
D: all real numbers; R: $y \leq 0$; minimum value: 0

INTERVENTION

Questioning Strategies

EXAMPLE 1

- How is the shape of the graph of a power function related to the degree of its function rule?

EXAMPLE 2

- Why is the domain of any power function all real numbers?
- What are the possibilities for the range of a power function?
- For the function $f(x) = ax^n$, how can you use the values of a and n to decide whether the function has a minimum or maximum value?

3 Close

Summarize

Ask students to state as many facts as they can about the power function $y = -3x^{11}$.

Possible answer: The degree is 11; from left to right, the graph decreases; the graph crosses the x-axis at the origin; the domain and range are all real numbers.

A-1 Exercises

Graph each power function, and then describe the graph.

1. $y = x^3$
2. $y = x^6$
3. $y = x^7$

Give the domain and range of each power function. Then give the minimum or maximum value, if any. **4. D, R: all real numbers; no minimum or maximum value**

4. $f(x) = -2x^{11}$
5. $f(x) = -\frac{1}{8}x^{16}$ **5. D: all real numbers; R: $y \leq 0$; maximum value: 0**
6. $f(x) = 0.05x^8$ **6. D: all real numbers; R: $y \geq 0$; minimum value: 0**
7. **Geometry** A cube has sides of length x.
   a. Write a power function f that gives the area of each face of the cube. $\mathbf{f(x) = x^2}$
   b. Write a power function g that gives the surface area of the cube. $\mathbf{g(x) = 6x^2}$

x

8. **Geometry** The volume V of a sphere of radius x is given by the power function $V(x) = \frac{4}{3}\pi x^3$. Use a graphing calculator to determine the radius of a sphere that has a volume of 100 cm^3. Round your answer to the nearest tenth of a centimeter and explain your method.

Determine whether each statement is always, sometimes, or never true. Explain.

9. A power function has two x-intercepts. **never**
10. A power function has a minimum value of 1. **never**
11. The graph of a power function that passes through the point (a, b) also passes through the point $(-a, -b)$. **sometimes**
12. A power function that has a minimum value has an even degree. **always**

The *end behavior* of a function is a description of the function's values as x increases or decreases. For example, you can describe the end behavior of $f(x) = x^3$ as follows: As x increases, $f(x)$ increases. As x decreases, $f(x)$ decreases.

Describe the end behavior of each power function.

13. $f(x) = -4x^4$
14. $f(x) = \frac{1}{3}x^7$
15. $f(x) = -2x^9$

13. As x decreases, $f(x)$ decreases, and as x increases, $f(x)$ decreases.

14. As x decreases, $f(x)$ decreases, and as x increases, $f(x)$ increases.

15. As x decreases, $f(x)$ increases, and as x increases, $f(x)$ decreases.

16. **Physics** A certain metal sphere sinks in a lake according to the function $d(t) = 2.1t^2$ where t is the time in seconds and $d(t)$ is the depth of the sphere in meters. Sketch a graph of the function. Then give a reasonable domain and range for the function when the sphere is dropped in a lake with a maximum depth of 100 meters.
17. Determine whether the power function $f(x) = -3x^3$ is increasing or decreasing on the interval $-5 \leq x \leq -1$. **decreasing**
18. **Critical Thinking** Is a direct variation a power function? Explain why or why not.
19. Graph $f(x) = x^3$, $g(x) = x^3 + 1$, and $h(x) = x^3 - 2$. Make a conjecture, in terms of a transformation, about the effect of b on the graph of $f(x) = ax^3 + b$.

18. Yes; a direct variation has the form $y = kx$, and this is a power function of degree 1.

Answers

1.

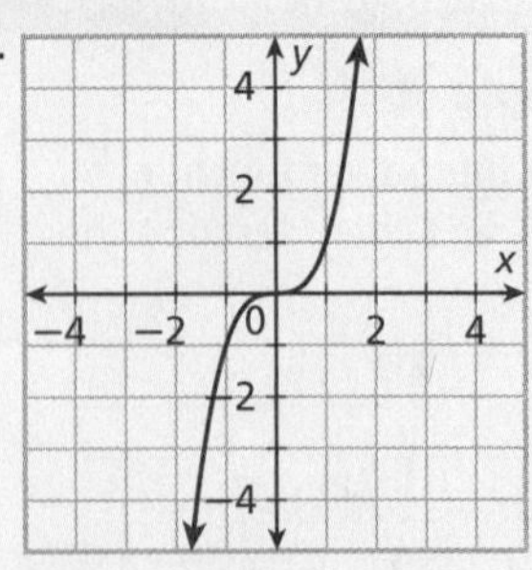

From left to right, the graph increases. It crosses the x-axis once, at the origin.

2.

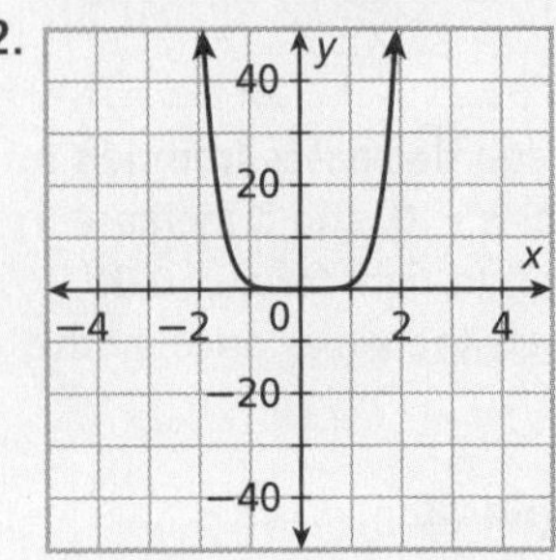

The graph decreases from left to right for $x < 0$, and it increases from left to right for $x > 0$. It intersects the x-axis once, at the origin.

3.

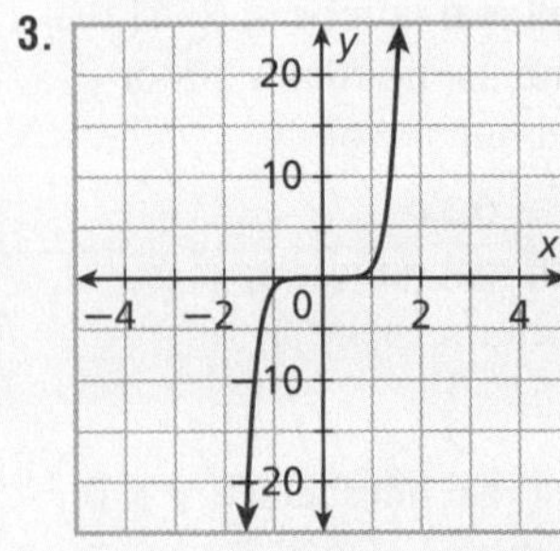

From left to right, the graph increases. It crosses the x-axis once, at the origin.

8. ≈ 2.9 cm; possible answer: Graph $y = \frac{4}{3}\pi x^3$ and $y = 100$, and use the calculator's intersect feature to find the point of intersection of the graphs.
9. Every power function has exactly one x-intercept at $x = 0$.
10. The minimum or maximum value of a power function is always 0.
11. Possible answer: the statement is true for $y = x^3$ but false for $y = x^4$.
12. Power functions with odd degrees have no minimum or maximum value.

16.

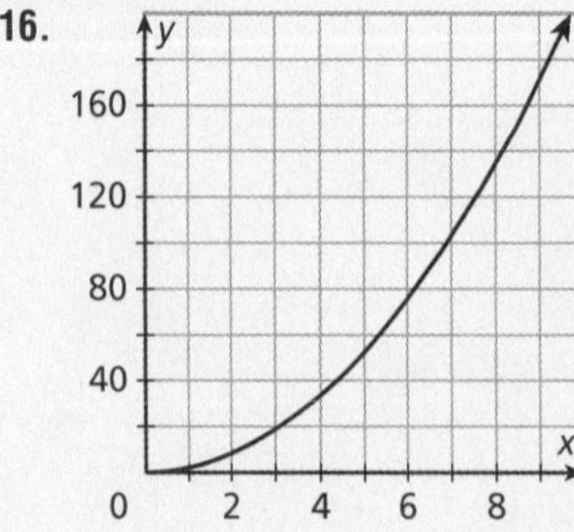

D: $0 \leq x < 7.1$; R: $0 \leq y \leq 100$

19.

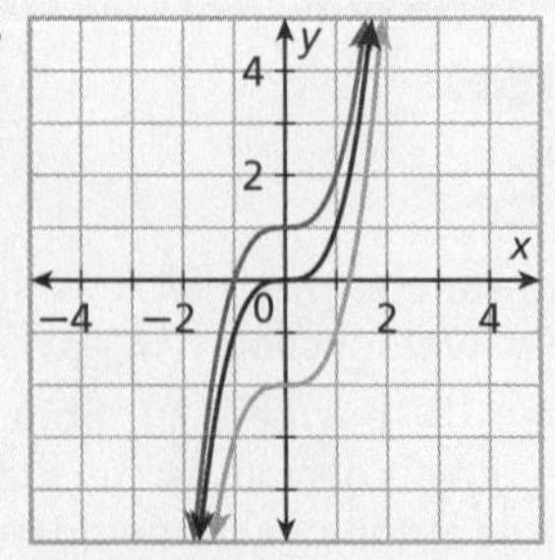

A change in the value of b translates the graph up or down.

AT4 Additional Topics

ADDITIONAL TOPIC

A-2 Piecewise and Step Functions

Objective
Recognize, identify, and graph piecewise and step functions.

Vocabulary
piecewise function
step function
greatest-integer function

A **piecewise function** is a function that is a combination of one or more functions. The rule for a piecewise function may be different for different parts of the function's domain.

For example, the absolute value function $y = |x|$ is a piecewise function and can be defined by the following rule:

$$y = \begin{cases} -x \text{ if } x < 0 \\ x \quad \text{if } x \geq 0 \end{cases}$$

To evaluate a piecewise function for a given input value, find the interval of the domain that contains the input value and apply the rule for that interval.

EXAMPLE 1 Evaluating a Piecewise Function

For $f(x) = \begin{cases} x^2 + 1 & \text{if } x < 2 \\ -3x + 4 & \text{if } x \geq 2 \end{cases}$, evaluate $f(x)$ for $x = -3$ and $x = 6$.

$f(-3) = (-3)^2 + 1 = 10$ *Because $-3 < 2$, use the rule for $x < 2$.*

$f(6) = -3(6) + 4 = -14$ *Because $6 \geq 2$, use the rule for $x \geq 2$.*

CHECK IT OUT! **1.** For $g(x) = \begin{cases} 3x - 3 & \text{if } x < -1 \\ -x^2 & \text{if } x \geq -1 \end{cases}$, evaluate $g(x)$ for $x = -4$ and $x = -1$.

−15; −1

EXAMPLE 2 Graphing a Piecewise Function

Graph $f(x) = \begin{cases} -3 & \text{if } x < 0 \\ x^2 + 1 & \text{if } x \geq 0 \end{cases}$.

This function is composed of two pieces.

For $x < 0$, the function is the constant function $f(x) = -3$. Draw a horizontal ray to the left of (0, −3). Draw an open circle at (0, −3) to show that this point is not part of the graph.

For $x \geq 0$, the function is the quadratic function $f(x) = x^2 + 1$. Draw half of a parabola to the right of (0, 1). Draw a solid circle at (0, 1) to show that this point is part of the graph.

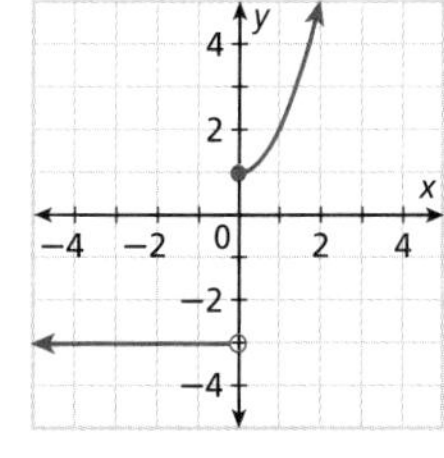

2.

2. Graph $g(x) = \begin{cases} 2x & \text{if } x < 1 \\ x - 1 & \text{if } x \geq 1 \end{cases}$.

ADDITIONAL TOPIC

A-2 Organizer

Objective: Recognize, identify, and graph piecewise and step functions.

Warm Up

1. For $f(x) = \frac{2}{3}x - 5$, find $f(x)$ when $x = -6$ and when $x = 9$. −9, 1

2. For $f(x) = x^2 + 2x + 4$, find $f(x)$ when $x = -2$ and when $x = 5$. 4, 39

3. For $f(x) = -0.5x^2 + 2$, find $f(x)$ when $x = -4$ and when $x = 10$. −6, −48

Additional Examples

Example 1

For $g(x) = \begin{cases} -3 & \text{if } x \leq -1 \\ 2x^2 & \text{if } x > -1 \end{cases}$, evaluate $g(x)$ for $x = -2$ and $x = 3$. −3; 18

INTERVENTION

Questioning Strategies

EXAMPLE 1

- How do you decide which rule to use when evaluating the function for a given value of x?

State Resources

1 Introduce

Motivate

Ask students if they know how postage is determined by the weight of a letter. If necessary, explain that the cost of first-class postage is the same for any weight up to 1 ounce. For letters that weigh more than 1 ounce and no more than 2 ounces, there is a different postage rate. Tell students that in this lesson they will learn that the function that gives the cost of postage is an example of a piecewise function.

2 Teach

Guided Instruction

As you teach the lesson, emphasize that a piecewise function has different rules for different parts of the function's domain. Point out that piecewise functions often have discontinuous graphs. That is, the graph may consist of unconnected segments or curves. However, students should understand that a piecewise function can also have a continuous graph. The absolute-value function, for example, is a piecewise function with a continuous graph.

Additional Examples

Example 2

Graph $g(x) = \begin{cases} 2x \text{ if } x \le 0 \\ -2 \text{ if } x > 0 \end{cases}$.

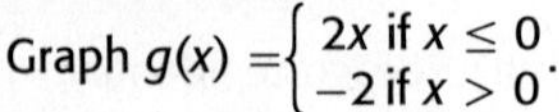

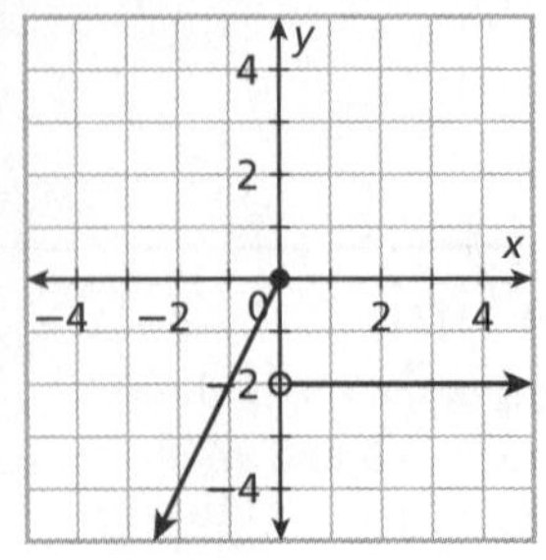

Example 3

The graph shows the bonus points that a customer earns for each purchase at J-Mart. Create a table and a verbal description for the graph.

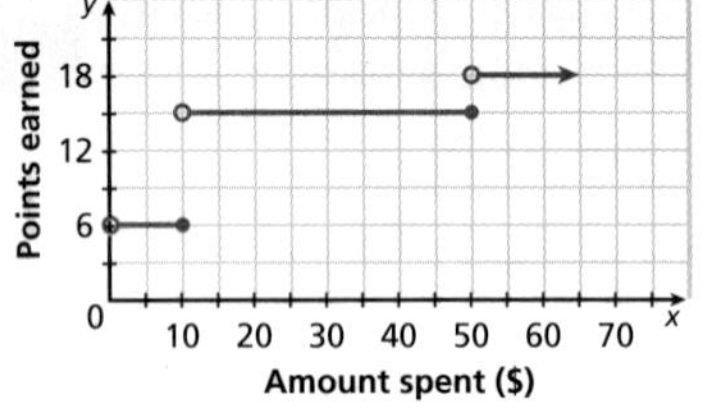

Amount Spent ($)	Points
$0 < x \le 10$	6
$10 < x \le 50$	15
$x > 50$	18

For any amount up to $10, 6 points are earned. For more than $10 and no more than $50, 15 points are earned. For more than $50, 18 points are earned.

INTERVENTION
Questioning Strategies

EXAMPLE 2

- How can you make a table of values to help you graph a piecewise function?

EXAMPLE 3

- What do the open circles and closed circles in the graph tell you?

The graph and table at right give the price of admission to a theme park. The function is defined differently over different domain intervals (age groups), so the function is a piecewise function.

Theme Park Admission Prices	
Regular admission	$25
Youth (under 15)	$10
Seniors (55 and older)	$20

The function that describes the theme park admission prices is a *step function*. A **step function** is a piecewise function that is constant over each interval in its domain.

Theme Park Admission Prices

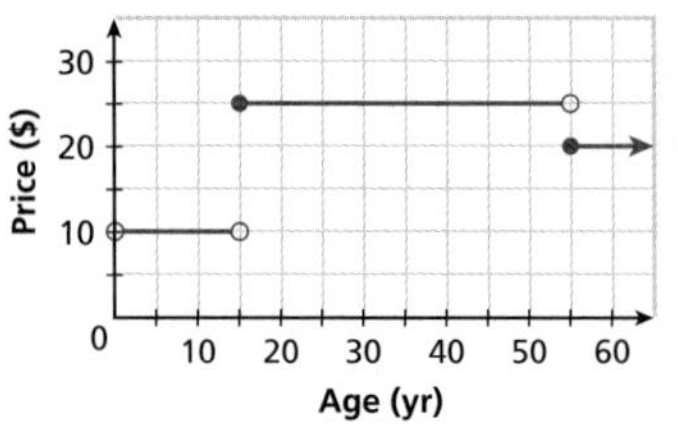

EXAMPLE 3 Step Functions

The graph shows parking fees at a garage. Create a table and a verbal description to represent the graph.

Parking Fees

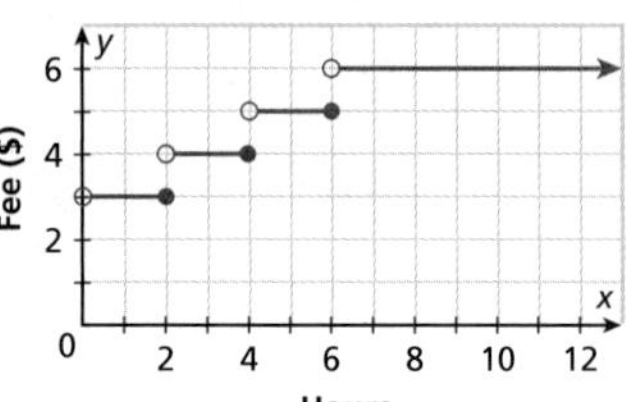

Step 1 Create a table.

Use the endpoints of the segments of the graph to identify the intervals of the domain.

Parking Fees	
Hours x	Fee y ($)
$0 < x \le 2$	3
$2 < x \le 4$	4
$4 < x \le 6$	5
$x > 6$	6

On the graph, an open circle means that a value is not included in the interval. A solid circle means that a value is included in the interval.

Step 2 Write a verbal description.

For any amount of time up to 2 hours, the parking fee is $3. For more than 2 hours and no more than 4 hours, the fee is $4. For more than 4 hours and no more than 6 hours, the fee is $5. For more than 6 hours, the fee is $6.

3. The graph shows the shipping costs for books that are ordered online. Create a table and a verbal description to represent the graph.

Shipping Costs

3.

Shipping Costs	
Weight x (oz)	Cost y ($)
$0 < x \le 6$	2
$6 < x \le 16$	4
$x > 16$	6

For any weight up to 6 oz, the shipping cost is $2. For more than 6 oz and no more than 16 oz, the cost is $4. For more than 16 oz, the cost is $6.

3 Close

Summarize

Review the definitions of piecewise, step, and greatest-integer functions. Ask students to give an example of each kind of function and have a volunteer graph each example for the class.

The **greatest-integer function** is a piecewise function, written $f(x) = \lfloor x \rfloor$, in which the number x is rounded down to the greatest integer that is less than or equal to x. For example, $f(3.14) = \lfloor 3.14 \rfloor = 3$. The graph of the greatest-integer function shows that it is a step function.

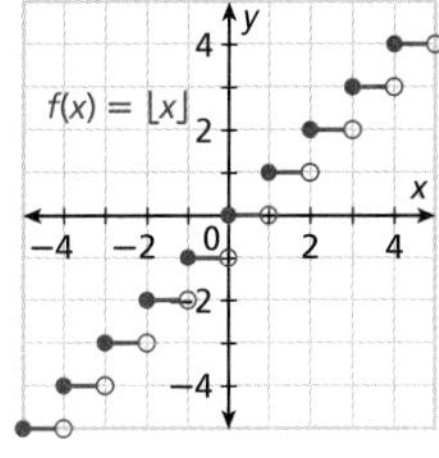

EXAMPLE 4 **Using the Greatest-Integer Function**

Write a function that gives the number of magazines that you can buy with x dollars if a magazine costs \$3.75. Then use the function to find the number of magazines you can buy with \$20.

The number of magazines you can buy with x dollars is $\frac{x}{3.75}$, rounded down to the greatest integer that is less than or equal to this quotient.

The function is $f(x) = \left\lfloor \frac{x}{3.75} \right\rfloor$.

To find how many magazines you can buy with \$20, evaluate $f(x)$ for $x = 20$.

$$f(20) = \left\lfloor \frac{20}{3.75} \right\rfloor = \lfloor 5.\overline{3} \rfloor = 5$$

You can buy 5 magazines with \$20.

4. Write a function that gives the number of movie tickets that you can buy with x dollars if a movie ticket costs \$10.95. Then use the function to find the number of movie tickets you can buy with \$50.

$f(x) = \left\lfloor \frac{x}{10.95} \right\rfloor$; 4 tickets

A-2 Exercises

Evaluate each function for $x = -2$ and $x = 3$.

1. $f(x) = \begin{cases} 2x + 1 & \text{if } x < 0 \\ -x + 2 & \text{if } x \ge 0 \end{cases}$ **−3; −1**

2. $g(x) = \begin{cases} -x^2 & \text{if } x \le -1 \\ 5x & \text{if } x > -1 \end{cases}$ **−4; 15**

3. $h(x) = \begin{cases} x^2 + 1 & \text{if } x < -3 \\ 2x - 5 & \text{if } x \ge -3 \end{cases}$ **−9; 1**

4. $f(x) = \begin{cases} -5 & \text{if } x < 3 \\ 3x^2 + 1 & \text{if } x \ge 3 \end{cases}$ **−5; 28**

Evaluate each function for $x = -1$ and $x = 2$.

5. $f(x) = \begin{cases} 4x - 1 & \text{if } x < -1 \\ -x + 5 & \text{if } -1 \le x < 2 \\ 3x & \text{if } x \ge 2 \end{cases}$ **6; 6**

6. $f(x) = \begin{cases} x^2 & \text{if } x \le -2 \\ 4x + 6 & \text{if } -2 \le x \le 1 \\ \frac{1}{2}x & \text{if } x \ge 1 \end{cases}$ **2; 1**

Graph each function.

7. $f(x) = \begin{cases} x - 1 & \text{if } x < 0 \\ 4 & \text{if } x \ge 0 \end{cases}$

8. $f(x) = \begin{cases} -1 & \text{if } x \le -1 \\ 2x & \text{if } -1 < x \le 2 \\ x - 4 & \text{if } x > 2 \end{cases}$

COMMON ERROR ALERT

In **Example 4,** students may think of the greatest-integer function as a rounding function and make errors such as $\lfloor 4.99 \rfloor = 5$. Remind students that the greatest-integer function always rounds *down,* so that $\lfloor 4.99 \rfloor = 4$.

Additional Examples

Example 4

Write a function that gives the number of birthday cards that can be bought with x dollars if a birthday card costs \$1.69. Then use the function to find the number of birthday cards you can buy with \$10. $f(x) = \left\lfloor \frac{x}{1.69} \right\rfloor$; 5

INTERVENTION

Questioning Strategies

EXAMPLE 4

- Why do you use the greatest-integer function instead of simply writing the quotient of x and the price?

Answers

7.

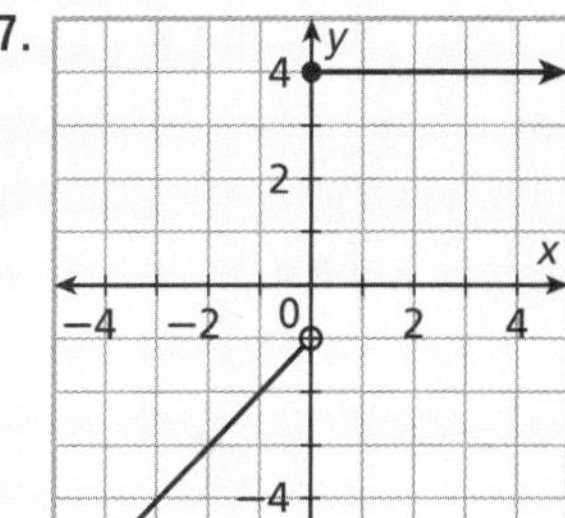

8.

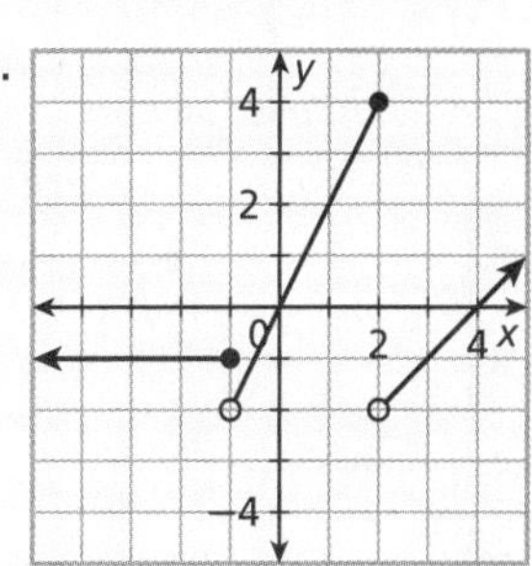

A-2 Piecewise and Step Functions **AT7**

Answers

9.

Admission Prices	
Age x (yr)	Price y ($)
$0 < x \le 4$	0
$4 < x \le 12$	2
$x > 12$	6

For any age up to 4 yr, admission is free. For any age greater than 4 yr and no more than 12 yr, admission is $2. For any age greater than 12 yr, admission is $6.

10.

Weeks of Paid Vacation	
Years of Employment x	Weeks of Vacation y
$0 < x < 4$	2
$4 \le x < 6$	3
$x \ge 6$	4

For less than 4 years of employment, there are 2 weeks of paid vacation. For at least 4 years of employment and less than 6 years, there are 3 weeks of vacation. For 6 or more years of employment, there are 4 weeks of vacation.

13. $f(x) = \begin{cases} 2 & \text{if } x \le -2 \\ -2 & \text{if } -2 < x \le 3 \\ 4 & \text{if } x > 3 \end{cases}$

14. $f(x) = \begin{cases} -3 & \text{if } x < 0 \\ x & \text{if } x \ge 0 \end{cases}$

15. $f(x) = \begin{cases} -2x-2 & \text{if } x < 0 \\ x-2 & \text{if } x \ge 0 \end{cases}$

16a. $f(x) = \begin{cases} 4 & \text{if } 0 < x < 12 \\ 8 & \text{if } x \ge 12 \end{cases}$

b.

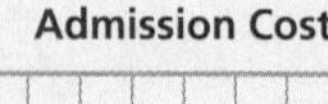

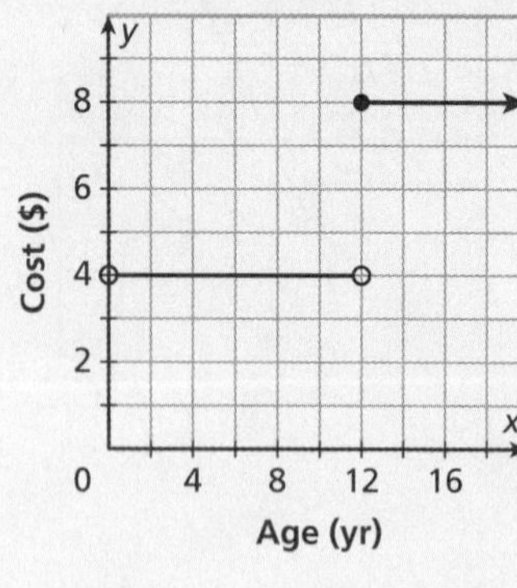

Create a table and a verbal description to represent each graph.

9. 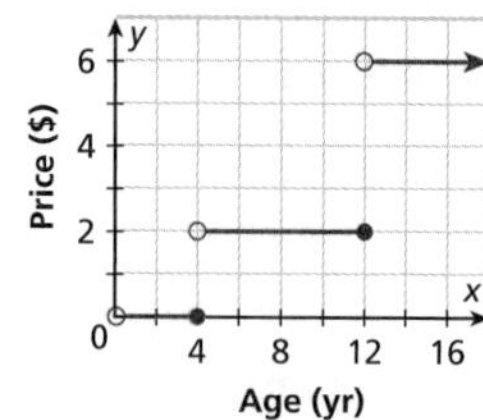

10. 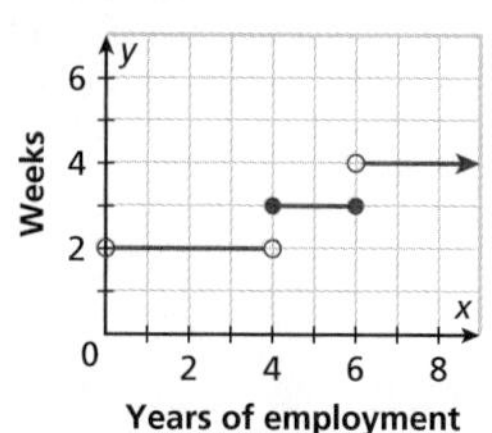

11. Write a function that gives the number of energy bars that you can buy with x dollars if an energy bar costs $1.35. Then use the function to find the number of energy bars you can buy with $10. **$f(x) = \left\lfloor \frac{x}{1.35} \right\rfloor$; 7 energy bars**

12. The function $g(x) = \left\lfloor \frac{x}{3.95} \right\rfloor$ gives the number of gel pens you can buy with x dollars. What is the price of one gel pen? How many gel pens can you buy with $15? **$3.95; 3 pe**

Write a piecewise function for each graph.

13. 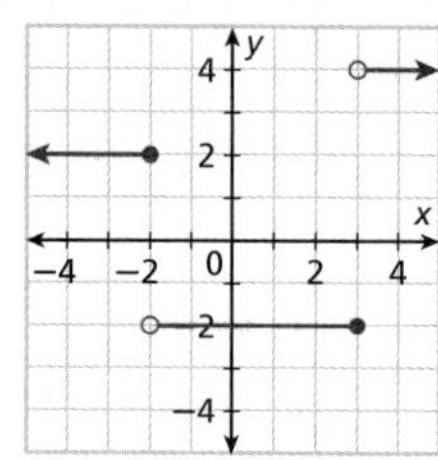

14. 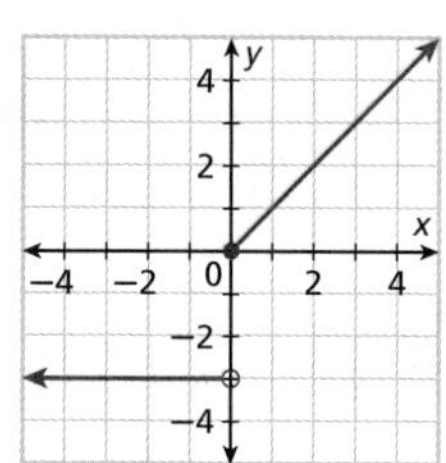

15. 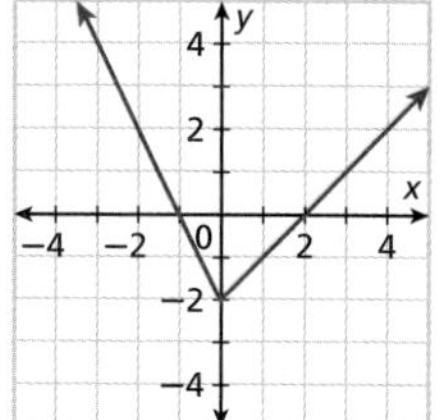

16. **Entertainment** The cost of admission to a state fair is $4 for children less than 12 years old and $8 for everyone 12 or older.

a. Write a function that gives the cost of admission for a person who is x years old.

b. Graph the function.

17. **Pet Care** The table shows the recommended amount of dog food based on a dog's weight.

Recommended Amount of Dog Food	
Weight of dog (lb)	Amount of food (c)
Less than 10	$\frac{1}{2}$
At least 10 and no more than 20	1
More than 20	$1\frac{1}{2}$

a. Write a function that gives the amount of dog food in cups for a dog that weighs x pounds.

b. Graph the function.

18. **Travel** Carolyn leaves her house and drives for 3 hours at a constant rate of 60 mi/h. Then she stops for 1 hour to have lunch. After lunch, she continues to drive away from her house at a constant rate of 60 mi/h for another 2 hours. Graph a piecewise function that gives Carolyn's distance in miles from her house after x hours.

19. **Critical Thinking** What are the domain and range of the piecewise function $f(x) = \begin{cases} x & \text{if } x < 0 \\ x^2 & \text{if } x \ge 0 \end{cases}$? **D: all real numbers; R: all real numbers**

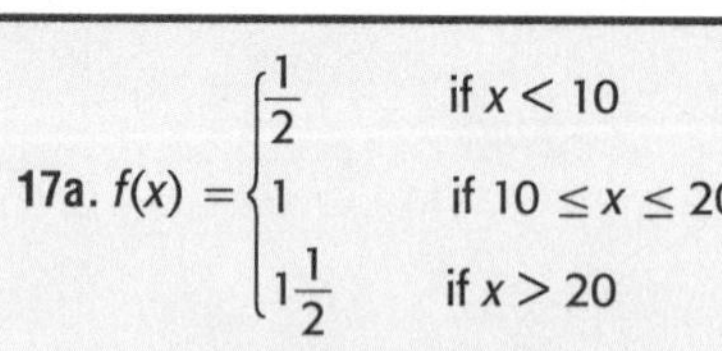

17a. $f(x) = \begin{cases} \frac{1}{2} & \text{if } x < 10 \\ 1 & \text{if } 10 \le x \le 20 \\ 1\frac{1}{2} & \text{if } x > 20 \end{cases}$

b. Amount of Dog Food

y; Amount (c): 0.5, 1, 1.5; x; 0, 10, 20, 30; Weight (lb)

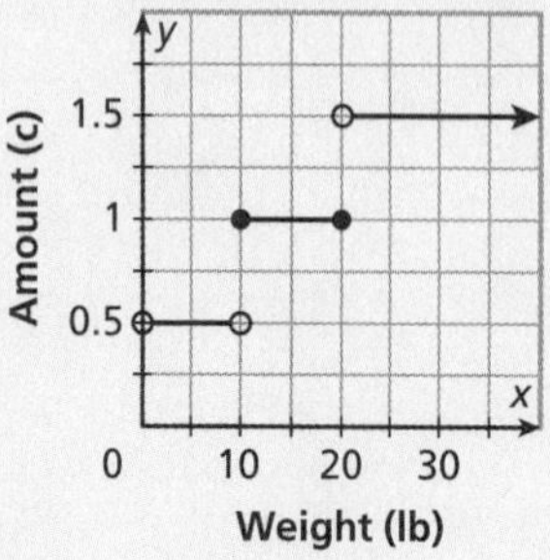

18.

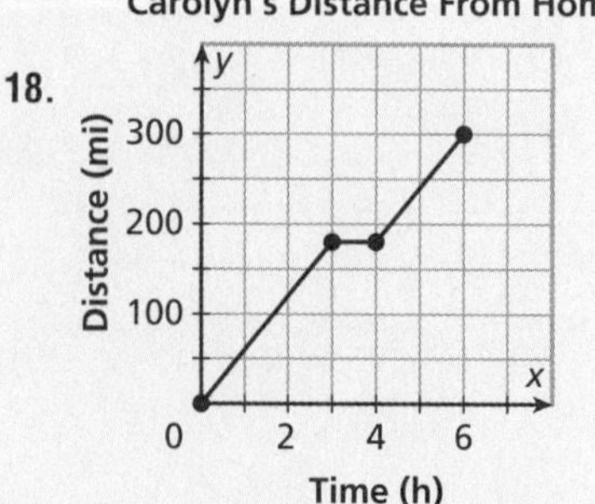

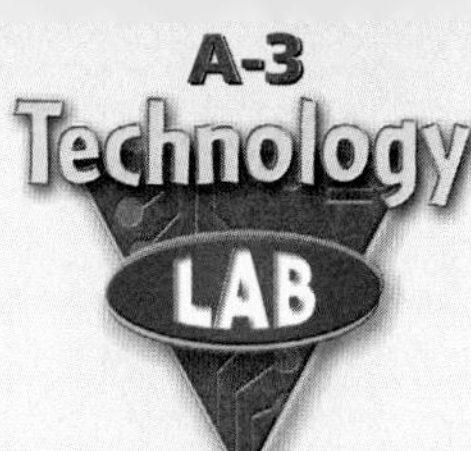

Graphing to Solve Nonlinear Equations

You can use a graphing calculator to solve nonlinear equations, including quadratic and exponential equations.

Use a graph to solve $x^2 - x - 5 = -3$.

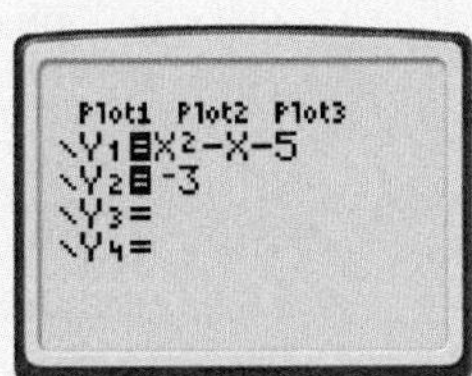

Enter the left side of the equation as **Y1** and the right side as **Y2**.

Press GRAPH. The x-values of the points where the graphs intersect (where **Y1** = **Y2**) are the solutions of the equation. Notice that there is more than one solution.

To find the coordinates of an intersection point:

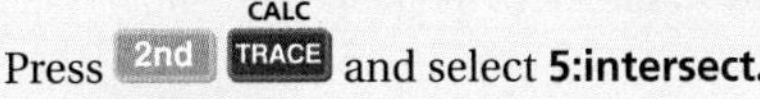

Press 2nd CALC TRACE and select **5:intersect.**

Press ENTER to select **Y1**.

Press ENTER again to select **Y2**.

Use ◀ and ▶ to move the cursor close to the intersection point.

Press ENTER.

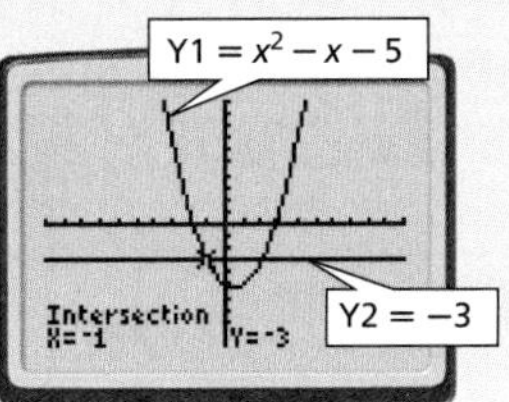

One point of intersection is (–1, –3), so one solution is $x = -1$.

Repeat these steps to find the coordinates of the second intersection point. This point is (2, –3), so the second solution is $x = 2$.

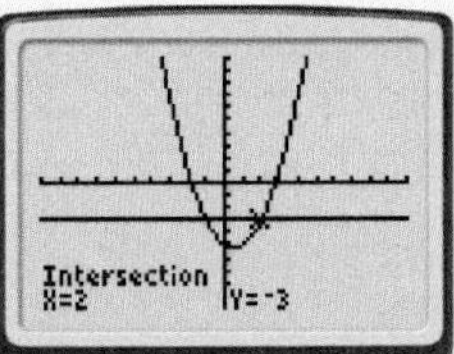

The solutions of $x^2 - x - 5 = -3$ are –1 and 2.

Check

$x^2 - x - 5$	$= -3$
$(-1)^2 - (-1) - 5$	-3
$1 + 1 - 5$	-3
-3	-3 ✓

$x^2 - x - 5$	$= -3$
$(2)^2 - 2 - 5$	-3
$4 - 2 - 5$	-3
-3	-3 ✓

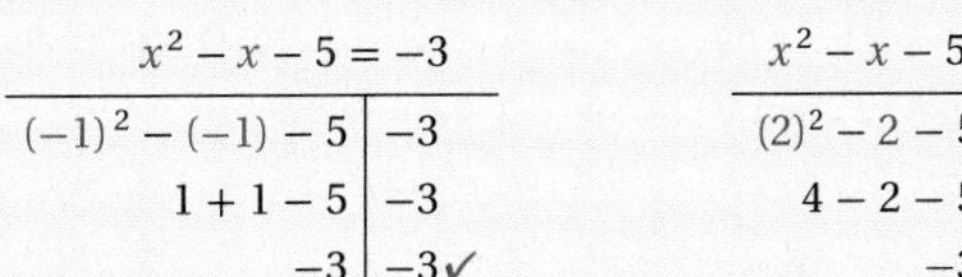

Use a graph to solve each equation.

1. $x^2 + 6x + 9 = 1$ **−4, −2**
2. $1.5(2)^x = 6$ **2**
3. $-x^2 + 3x - 4 = -4$ **0, 3**
4. $2\left(\frac{1}{2}\right)^x = 4$ **−1**
5. $2x^2 + 2x - 12 = -8$ **−2, 1**
6. $\frac{2}{3}\left(\frac{1}{3}\right)^x = 6$ **−2**
7. **Critical Thinking** Explain how you could use a graphing calculator to show that the equation $x^2 - 2x + 4 = 1$ has no real solutions.
8. **Critical Thinking** Could you use the method described in the activity to solve an equation like $x^2 + 4x = x + 4$? Explain.

Answers

7. Possible answer: Graph Y1 = $x^2 - 2x + 4$ and Y2 = 1. Since the graphs do not intersect, there are no real solutions to the equation.
8. Possible answer: Yes; graph Y1 = $x^2 + 4x$ and Y2 = $x + 4$, and find the x-values of any intersection points.

Teaching Tip **Multiple Representations** Show students how to use the table feature of a graphing calculator to verify solutions found by graphing. For example, after viewing the graph in the Activity, students can view a table of **Y1** and **Y2** values by pressing 2nd TABLE GRAPH.

Objective: Use a graphing calculator to solve nonlinear equations.

Materials: graphing calculator

Online Edition
Graphing Calculator

Teach

Discuss

Review the general procedure for solving equations by graphing: (1) set each side of the equation equal to y, (2) graph the resulting functions, and (3) find the x-values of any points where the graphs intersect. Those x-values are solutions of the original equation.

With nonlinear functions, it is important for students to understand that an equation may have more than one solution. Encourage students to use large windows to be sure that they get a good overview of the graphs before focusing on a single point of intersection.

Close

Key Concept

You can solve a nonlinear equation by graphing both sides of the equation on a graphing calculator.

Assessment

Journal Have students explain how they would use a graphing calculator to solve $x^2 - 2x = 2$.

State Resources

go.hrw.com
State Resources Online
KEYWORD: MA7 Resources

ADDITIONAL TOPIC

A-4 Organizer

Objective: Identify and extend patterns using recursion.

Warm Up

Find the next three terms in each arithmetic or geometric sequence.

1. 12, 9.5, 7, 4.5, ... 2, −0.5, −3
2. −1, 3, −9, 27, ... −81, 243, −729
3. −9, −4, 1, 6, ... 11, 16, 21
4. 81, 54, 36, 24, ... 16, $\frac{32}{3}$, $\frac{64}{9}$

State Resources

ADDITIONAL TOPIC

A-4 Patterns and Recursion

Objective
Identify and extend patterns using recursion.

Vocabulary
recursive pattern

In a **recursive pattern** or *recursive sequence*, each term is defined using one or more previous terms. For example, the sequence 1, 4, 7, 10, 13, ... can be defined recursively as follows: The first term is 1 and each term after the first is equal to the preceding term plus 3.

You can use recursive techniques to identify patterns. The table summarizes the characteristics of four types of patterns.

Using Recursive Techniques to Identify Patterns	
Type of Pattern	**Characteristics**
Linear	First differences are constant.
Quadratic	Second differences are constant.
Cubic	Third differences are constant.
Exponential	Ratios between successive terms are constant.

EXAMPLE 1 Identifying and Extending a Pattern

Helpful Hint

You may need to use trial and error when identifying a pattern. If first, second, and third differences are not constant, check for constant ratios.

Identify the type of pattern. Then find the next three numbers in the pattern.

A **4, 6, 10, 16, 24, ...**

Find first, second, and, if necessary, third differences.

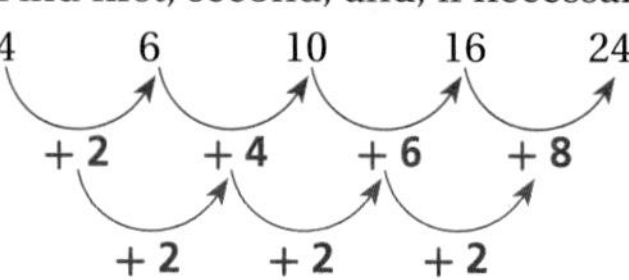

Second differences are constant, so the pattern is quadratic.

Extend the pattern by continuing the sequence of first and second differences.

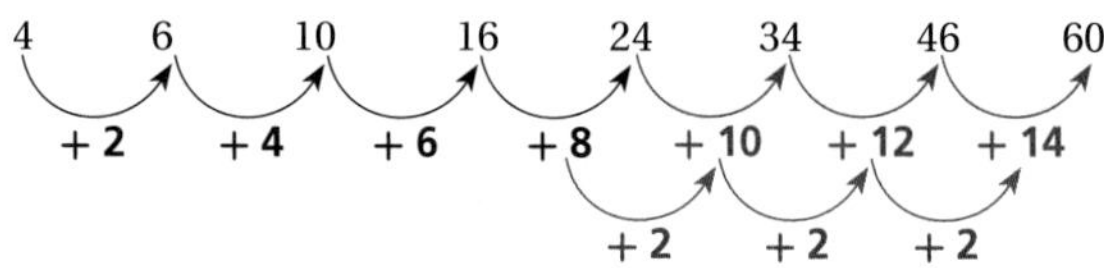

The next three numbers in the pattern are 34, 46, and 60.

B $\frac{1}{8}$, $\frac{1}{2}$, **2, 8, 32**

Find the ratio between successive terms.

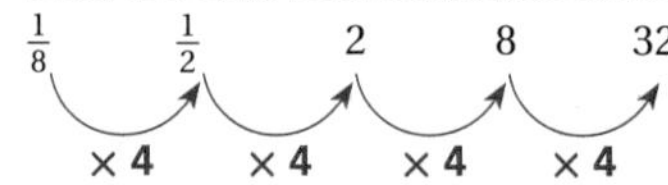

Ratios between terms are constant, so the pattern is exponential.

Extend the pattern by continuing the sequence of ratios.

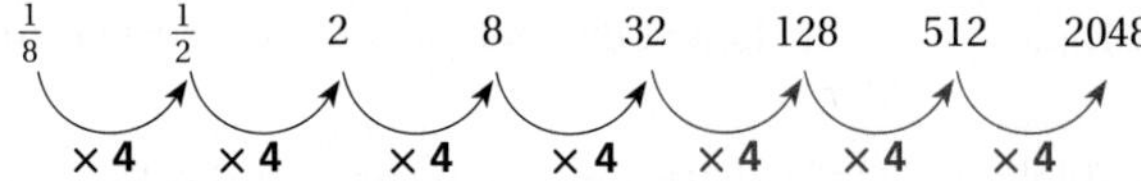

The next three numbers in the pattern are 128, 512, and 2048.

1 Introduce

Motivate

Write the sequence 5, 10, 15, 20, 25, ... on the board. Ask students to describe the pattern. In particular, ask them to give a rule that they could use to find the next few numbers in the pattern. Possible answer: Add 5 to each term to get the next term. Explain that there are different ways to describe the pattern and give a rule for the pattern. Point out that the method in which each term is found by doing something to a previous term is called *recursion*.

2 Teach

Guided Instruction

Remind students that they have already worked with first differences, second differences, and ratios between successive terms. Tell them that this lesson pulls these ideas together for identifying and describing both patterns and functions. When you discuss **Example 2,** be sure to emphasize that the method of looking for constant differences or ratios in the *y*-values only works when the *x*-values are evenly spaced.

Identify the type of pattern. Then find the next three numbers in the pattern.

1a. 56, 47, 38, 29, 20, ...
linear; 11, 2, −7

1b. 1, 8, 27, 64, 125, ...
cubic; 216, 343, 512

You can use a similar process to determine whether a function is linear, quadratic, cubic, or exponential. Note that before comparing *y*-values, you must first make sure there is a constant change in the corresponding *x*-values.

Using Recursive Techniques to Identify Functions

Type of Function	Characteristics (Given a Constant Change in *x*-values)
Linear	First differences of *y*-values are constant.
Quadratic	Second differences of *y*-values are constant.
Cubic	Third differences of *y*-values are constant.
Exponential	Ratios between successive *y*-values are constant.

EXAMPLE 2 Identifying a Function

The ordered pairs {(−4, −4), (0, 0), (4, 4), (8, 32), (12, 108)} satisfy a function. Determine whether the function is linear, quadratic, cubic, or exponential. Then find three additional ordered pairs that satisfy the function.

Make a table. Check for a constant change in the *x*-values. Then find first, second, and third differences of *y*-values.

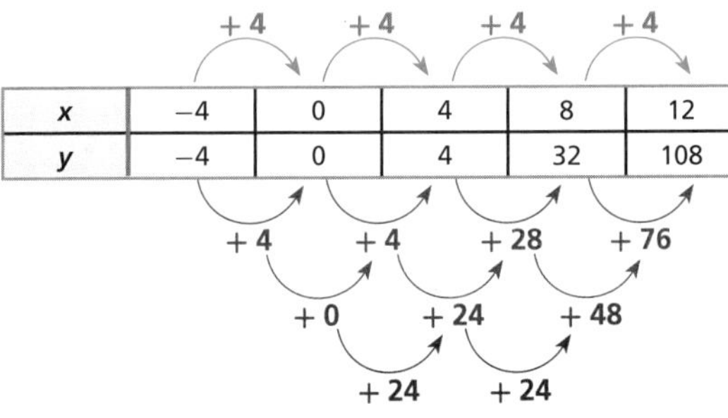

x	−4	0	4	8	12
y	−4	0	4	32	108

There is a constant change in the *x*-values. Third differences are constant. The function is a cubic function.

To find additional ordered pairs, extend the pattern by working backward from the constant third differences.

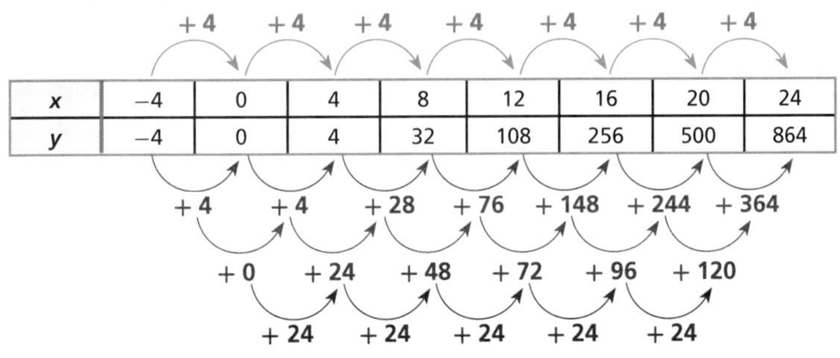

x	−4	0	4	8	12	16	20	24
y	−4	0	4	32	108	256	500	864

Three additional ordered pairs that satisfy this function are (16, 256), (20, 500), and (24, 864).

elpful Hint

Example 2, the
nstant third
fferences are 24. To
tend the pattern,
st find each second
fference by adding
to the previous
cond difference.
en find each
st difference by
lding the second
fference below
the previous first
fference.

Additional Examples

Example 1

Identify the type of pattern. Then find the next three numbers in the pattern.

A. 16, 54, 128, 250, 432, ...
cubic; 686, 1024, 1458

B. 800, 400, 200, 100, 50, ...
exponential; 25, 12.5, 6.25

Example 2

Determine whether each function is linear, quadratic, or exponential.

A.

x	0	2	4	6	8
y	2	5	17	38	68

quadratic

B.

x	−3	1	5	9	13
y	2	4	8	16	32

exponential

INTERVENTION
Questioning Strategies

EXAMPLE 1

- To find first differences, in which order should you subtract consecutive terms?
- Is it possible for first differences to be positive? negative? zero?

EXAMPLE 2

- What is the first thing you should do when trying to determine what type of function is shown in a table?
- How is identifying a function from a table similar to identifying a pattern from a sequence of numbers? How is it different?

3 Close

Summarize

Ask students to summarize in their own words how they can recognize a linear, quadratic, cubic, or exponential pattern or function.
Possible answer:
Linear: constant first differences
Quadratic: constant second differences
Cubic: constant third differences
Exponential: constant ratios

Teaching Tip

Multiple Representations A quick demonstration can connect the ideas of this lesson to what students know about equations. Starting with a quadratic equation, such as $y = x^2 + 1$, generate a table of values with evenly spaced *x*-values. Then check that the second differences of the *y*-values are constant.

Answers

15a. Linear; for a constant change in the number of months, first differences of costs are constant.

b. 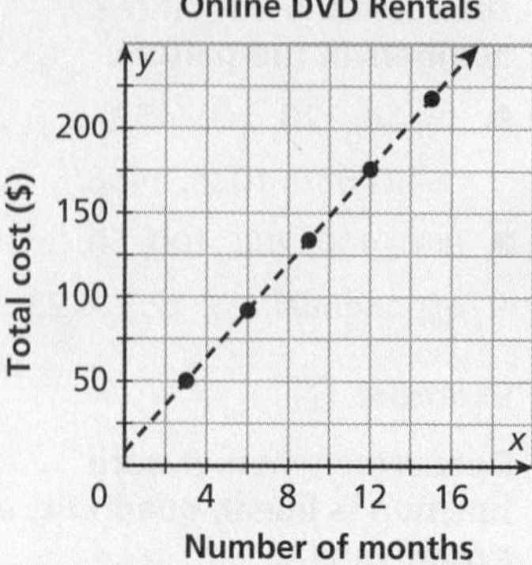

c. The data lie on a line; the function is linear.

d. $260

Several ordered pairs that satisfy a function are given. Determine whether the function is linear, quadratic, cubic, or exponential. Then find three additional ordered pairs that satisfy the function.

2a. {(0, 1), (1, 3), (2, 9), (3, 19), (4, 33)} **quad.; (5, 51), (6, 73), (7, 99)**

2b. $\left\{\left(1, \frac{1}{2}\right), \left(3, \frac{1}{6}\right), \left(5, \frac{1}{18}\right), \left(7, \frac{1}{54}\right), \left(9, \frac{1}{162}\right)\right\}$

2b. exp.; $\left(11, \frac{1}{486}\right), \left(13, \frac{1}{1458}\right), \left(15, \frac{1}{4374}\right)$

A-4 Exercises

Identify the type of pattern. Then find the next three numbers in the pattern.

1. 25, 28, 31, 34, 37, ... **linear; 40, 43, 46**
2. 20, 45, 80, 125, 180, ... **quad.; 245, 320, 405**
3. 128, 64, 32, 16, 8, ... **exp.; 4, 2, 1**
4. 4, 32, 108, 256, 500, ... **cubic; 864, 1372, 2048**
5. $\frac{1}{2}, \frac{3}{4}, 1, 1\frac{1}{4}, 1\frac{1}{2}, \ldots$ **linear; $1\frac{3}{4}$, 2, $2\frac{1}{4}$**
6. 0.3, 0.03, 0.003, 0.0003, 0.00003, ... **exp.; 0.000003, 0.0000003, 0.00000003**
7. 127, 66, 29, 10, 3, ... **cubic; 2, 1, −6**
8. 2, 8, 18, 32, 50, ... **quad.; 72, 98, 128**

Several ordered pairs that satisfy a function are given. Determine whether the function is linear, quadratic, cubic, or exponential. Then find three additional ordered pairs that satisfy the function.

9. {(3, 1), (5, −3), (7, −7), (9, −11), (11, −15)} **linear; (13, −19), (15, −23), (17, −27)**
10. {(−1, −2), (2, 7), (5, 124), (8, 511), (11, 1330)} **cubic; (14, 2743), (17, 4912), (20, 7999)**
11. $\left\{\left(2, \frac{1}{4}\right), \left(3, \frac{1}{8}\right), \left(4, \frac{1}{16}\right), \left(5, \frac{1}{32}\right), \left(6, \frac{1}{64}\right)\right\}$ **exp.; $\left(7, \frac{1}{128}\right), \left(8, \frac{1}{256}\right), \left(9, \frac{1}{512}\right)$**
12. {(−3, −7), (0, 2), (3, −7), (6, −34), (9, −79)} **quad.; (12, −142), (15, −223), (18, −322)**
13. {(0, 600), (10, 480), (20, 384), (30, 307.2), (40, 245.76)}
14. {(−8, 2), (−5, 7), (−2, 12), (1, 17), (4, 22)} **linear; (7, 27), (10, 32), (13, 37)**

13. exp.; (50, 196.608), (60, 157.2864), (70, 125.82912)

15. **Entertainment** The table shows the cost of using an online DVD rental service for different numbers of months.
    a. Determine whether the function that models the data is linear, quadratic, cubic, or exponential. Explain.
    b. Graph the data in the table.
    c. What do you notice about your graph? Why does this make sense?
    d. Predict the cost of the service for 18 months.

Online DVD Rentals

Months	Cost ($)
3	50
6	92
9	134
12	176
15	218

16. A student claimed that the function shown in the table is a quadratic function. Do you agree or disagree? Explain.

x	3	7	10	14	17
y	2	6	12	20	30

+4 +6 +8 +10

+2 +2 +2

Disagree; the table does not show a constant change in *x*-values.

17. **Business** The table shows the annual sales for a small company.

Annual Sales	
Year	Sales ($)
2006	513,000
2007	516,000
2008	521,000
2009	528,000
2010	537,000

a. Determine whether the function that models the data is linear, quadratic, cubic, or exponential. Explain.

b. Suppose sales continue to grow according to the pattern in the table. Predict the annual sales for 2011, 2012, and 2013.

c. If the pattern continues, in what year will annual sales be $17,000 greater than the previous year's sales?

18. **Critical Thinking** Use the table for the following problems.

x	0	1	2	3	4
y	3	6			

a. Copy and complete the table so that the function is a linear function.

b. Copy and complete the table so that the function is a quadratic function.

c. Copy and complete the table so that the function is an exponential function.

d. For which of these three types of functions is there more than one correct way to complete the table? Explain.

Use the description to write the first five terms in each numerical pattern.

19. The first term is 8. Each following term is 11 less than the term before it. **8, −3, −14, −25, −36**

20. The first term is 1000. Each following term is 40% of the term before it. **1000, 400, 160, 64, 25.6**

21. The first two terms are 1 and 2. Each following term is the sum of the two terms before it. **1, 2, 3, 5, 8**

Make a table for a function that has the given characteristics. Include at least five ordered pairs.

22. The function is linear. The first differences are −3.

23. The function is quadratic. The second differences are 6.

24. The function is cubic. The third differences are 1.

A *recursive formula* for a sequence shows how to find the value of a term from one or more terms that come before it. For example, the recursive formula $a_n = a_{n-1} + 3$ tells you that each term is equal to the preceding term plus 3. Given that $a_1 = 5$, you can use the formula to generate the sequence 5, 8, 11, 14, ...

Write the first four terms of each sequence.

25. $a_n = a_{n-1} + 2$; $a_1 = 12$ **12, 14, 16, 18**

26. $a_n = a_{n-1} - 7$; $a_1 = 16$ **16, 9, 2, −5**

27. $a_n = 2a_{n-1}$; $a_1 = 4$ **4, 8, 16, 32**

28. $a_n = 0.6a_{n-1}$; $a_1 = 100$ **100, 60, 36, 21.6**

29. $a_n = 5a_{n-1} - 2$; $a_1 = 0$ **0, −2, −12, −62**

30. $a_n = (a_{n-1})^2$; $a_1 = -2$ **−2, 4, 16, 256**

31. A *recursive function* defines a function for whole numbers by referring to the value of the function at previous whole numbers. Consider the recursive function $f(n) = f(n-1) + 5$ with $f(0) = 1$.

a. According to the formula, $f(1) = f(0) + 5$. What is the value of $f(1)$? **6**

b. Use the formula to find $f(2)$, $f(3)$, $f(4)$, and $f(5)$. **11, 16, 21, 26**

c. Graph $f(n)$ by plotting points at $x = 0$, $x = 1$, $x = 2$, $x = 3$, $x = 4$, and $x = 5$.

d. What do you notice about your graph? What does this tell you about $f(n)$?

Answers

17a. Quadratic; for a constant change in years, second differences of sales are constant.

b. $548,000; $561,000; $576,000

c. 2014

18a.

x	0	1	2	3	4
y	3	6	9	12	15

b. Possible answer:

x	0	1	2	3	4
y	3	6	11	18	27

c.

x	0	1	2	3	4
y	3	6	12	24	48

d. Quadratic; you can choose any value for the constant second difference.

22-24. Possible answers given.

22.

x	0	1	2	3	4
y	4	1	−2	−5	−8

23.

x	−2	−1	0	1	2
y	1	5	15	31	53

24.

x	1	2	3	4	5
y	7	4	6	14	29

31c.

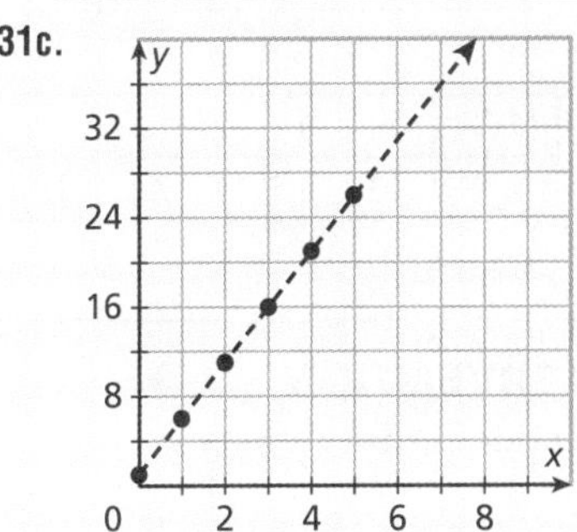

d. The points lie on a line; the function is linear.

ADDITIONAL TOPIC

A-5 Organizer

Objectives: Identify linear and nonlinear rates of change.

Compare rates of change.

Warm Up

Find the slope of each line.

1. $y = \frac{1}{4}x - \frac{1}{2}$ $\frac{1}{4}$

2. $3x - y = 6$ 3

3. $x + 5y = 12$ $-\frac{1}{5}$

Additional Examples

Example 1

Determine whether each function has a constant or variable rate of change.

A.

x	0	2	6	8	12
y	1	2	4	5	7

constant

B.

x	−1	0	2	3	6
y	−2	0	4	8	11

variable

INTERVENTION
Questioning Strategies

EXAMPLE 1

- In the table, which variable is the dependent variable? Which variable is the independent variable?
- Can a rate of change be positive? negative? zero?

State Resources

ADDITIONAL TOPIC **A-5**

Linear and Nonlinear Rates of Change

Objectives
Identify linear and nonlinear rates of change.

Compare rates of change.

Recall that a *rate of change* is a ratio that compares the amount of change in a dependent variable to the amount of change in an independent variable.

$$\text{rate of change} = \frac{\text{change in dependent variable}}{\text{change in independent variable}}$$

The table shows the price of one ounce of gold in 2005 and 2008. The year is the independent variable and the price is the dependent variable. The rate of change is $\frac{870-513}{2008-2005} = \frac{357}{3} = 119$, or \$119 per year.

Price of Gold	
Year	**Price (\$/oz)**
2005	513
2008	870

EXAMPLE 1 Identifying Constant and Variable Rates of Change

Determine whether each function has a constant or variable rate of change.

A $\{(0, 0), (1, 4), (3, 8), (6, 8), (8, 6)\}$

Find the ratio of the amount of change in the dependent variable *y* to the corresponding amount of change in the independent variable *x*.

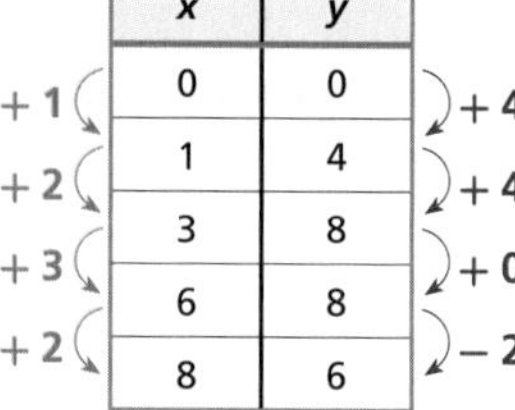

x	*y*
0	0
1	4
3	8
6	8
8	6

The rates of change are $\frac{4}{1} = 4$, $\frac{4}{2} = 2$, $\frac{0}{3} = 0$, and $\frac{-2}{2} = -1$. The function has a variable rate of change.

B $\{(0, 1), (1, 2), (4, 5), (6, 7), (7, 8)\}$

Find the ratio of the amount of change in the dependent variable *y* to the corresponding amount of change in the independent variable *x*.

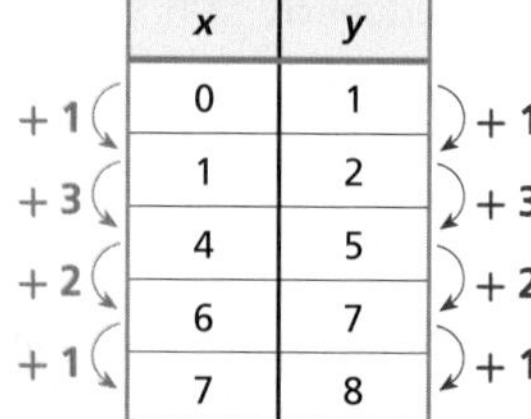

x	*y*
0	1
1	2
4	5
6	7
7	8

The rates of change are $\frac{1}{1} = 1$, $\frac{3}{3} = 1$, $\frac{2}{2} = 1$, and $\frac{1}{1} = 1$. The function has a constant rate of change.

Determine whether each function has a constant or variable rate of change.

1a. $\{(-3, 10), (0, 7), (1, 6), (4, 3), (7, 0)\}$ **constant**

1b. $\{(-2, -3), (2, 5), (3, 7), (5, 9), (8, 12)\}$ **variable**

1 Introduce

Motivate

Remind students that they have already worked with rates of change. Ask students to give a real-world example of a rate of change. Possible answer: a tank that fills with water at the rate of 10 gallons per minute Explain that a function may have a constant rate of change or a variable rate of change.

2 Teach

Guided Instruction

As you teach the lesson, emphasize the connection between rate of change and slope. In particular, point out that for a nonlinear function, the rate of change between two points on the graph is the slope of the line segment connecting the points. The different slopes of the different line segments illustrate why a nonlinear function has a variable rate of change.

The functions in Examples 1A and 1B are graphed below.

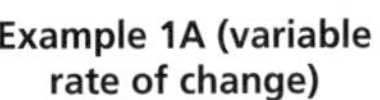

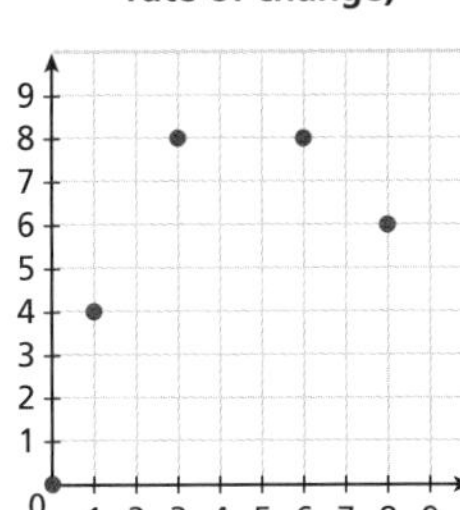

Example 1B (constant rate of change)

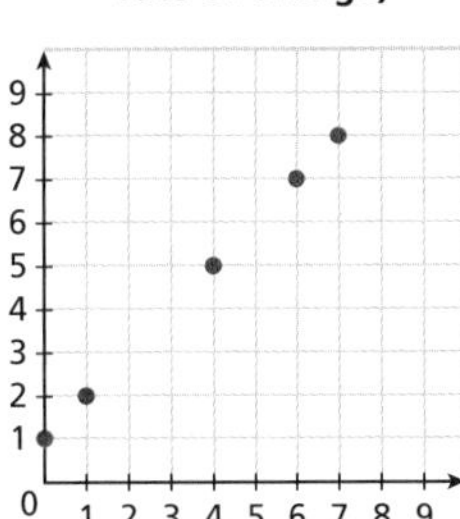

Recall from Chapter 5 that a function is a *linear function* if and only if the function has a constant rate of change. The graph of such a function is a straight line and the rate of change is the slope of the line, as in Example 1B.

A function with a variable rate of change, as in Example 1A, is a *nonlinear function*. Examples of nonlinear functions include quadratic functions and exponential functions.

EXAMPLE 2 Identifying Linear and Nonlinear Functions

Use rates of change to determine whether each function is linear or nonlinear.

A

x	y
−2	0
0	1
1	1.5
4	3
10	6

Changes in x: +2, +1, +3, +6; changes in y: +1, +0.5, +1.5, +3

Find the rates of change.

$\frac{1}{2}$ $\quad \frac{0.5}{1} = \frac{1}{2} \quad \frac{1.5}{3} = \frac{1}{2} \quad \frac{3}{6} = \frac{1}{2}$

There is a constant rate of change, $\frac{1}{2}$, so this function is linear.

B

x	y
−6	18
−2	2
2	2
0	0
4	8

Changes in x: +4, +4, −2, +4; changes in y: −16, +0, −2, +8

Find the rates of change.

$\frac{-16}{4} = -4 \quad \frac{0}{4} = 0 \quad \frac{-2}{-2} = 1 \quad \frac{8}{4} = \frac{1}{2}$

The rates of change are not constant, so this function is nonlinear.

Use rates of change to determine whether each function is linear or nonlinear.

2a. nonlinear

x	y
−2	$\frac{1}{4}$
−1	$\frac{1}{2}$
0	1
3	8
4	16

2b. linear

x	y
−5	3
−1	3
1	3
3	3
7	3

When you are given a verbal description of a function, you can determine whether the function is linear or nonlinear by making a table of values and examining the rates of change. You can compare two functions by comparing their rates of change.

COMMON ERROR ALERT

When students calculate rates of change from a table, they may calculate the ratio of the change in the independent variable to the change in the dependent variable. Students may make this error because the independent variable is usually shown above the dependent variable in a horizontal table. Remind students that the change in the dependent variable goes in the numerator.

Additional Examples

Example 2

Use rates of change to determine whether each function is linear or nonlinear.

A.

x	y
−1	1
1	1
2	−2
4	−14
5	−23

nonlinear

B.

x	y
−3	20
0	11
1	8
5	−4
10	−19

linear

INTERVENTION
Questioning Strategies

EXAMPLE 2

- Can a linear function have a variable rate of change? Why or why not?

Teaching Tip

Reading Math Be sure students realize that the word *variable* is used in two different ways in this lesson. In the terms *dependent variable* and *independent variable*, the word *variable* refers to a letter or symbol that is used to represent a value. In the term *variable rate of change*, the word *variable* means "changing."

Additional Examples

Example 3

Two auction Web sites start with 100 members each. At site A, the number of members doubles each month. At site B, 500 new members are added each month. Describe the functions that give the number of members for each site as linear or nonlinear. Which web site is growing more quickly from month 3 to month 4? site A: nonlinear; site B: linear; site A

INTERVENTION
Questioning Strategies

EXAMPLE 3

- How can you use a verbal description of a function to tell whether the function is linear or nonlinear?
- What should you compare in order to determine which function is increasing more quickly?

EXAMPLE 3 ***Physical Science Application***

Two water tanks contain 512 gallons of water each. Tank A begins to drain, losing half of its volume of water every hour. Tank B begins to drain at the same time and loses 40 gallons of water every hour. Identify the function that gives the volume of water in each tank as linear or nonlinear. Which tank loses water more quickly between hour 4 and hour 5?

Use the verbal descriptions to make a table for the volume of water in each tank.

Time (h)	0	1	2	3	4	5
Water in Tank A (gal)	512	256	128	64	32	16

Time (h)	0	1	2	3	4	5
Water in Tank B (gal)	512	472	432	392	352	312

For tank A, the rates of change are –256, –128, –64, –32, and –16, so the rate of change is variable and the function is nonlinear.

For tank B, the rates of change are all –40, so the rate of change is constant and the function is linear.

Between hours 4 and 5, the volume of water in tank A decreases at a rate of 16 gallons per hour. The volume of water in tank B decreases at a rate of 40 gallons per hour. Tank B loses water more quickly.

3. Reka and Charlotte each invest $500. Each month, Charlotte's investment grows by $25, while Reka's investment grows by 5% of the previous month's amount. Identify the function that gives the value of each investment as linear or nonlinear. Who is earning money more quickly between month 3 and month 4?
Reka: nonlinear; Charlotte: linear; Reka

A-5 Exercises

Use rates of change to determine whether each function is linear or nonlinear.

1.

x	4	5	7	10	12
y	–2	–1	1	4	6

linear

2.

x	–2	3	4	6	8
y	–4	6	8	14	20

nonlinear

3.

x	0	3	9	12	18
y	14	12	8	6	2

linear

4.

x	–8	–6	–4	–2	0
y	–3	1	3	5	9

nonlinear

3 Close

Summarize

Help students make a table like the one below to summarize the main ideas of this lesson.

Type of Function	Rate of Change	Graph
Linear	constant	line
Nonlinear	variable	not a line

5. Caitlin: linear; Greg: nonlinear; Caitlin's collection

5. **Hobbies** Caitlin and Greg collect stamps. Each starts with a collection of 50 stamps. Caitlin adds 15 stamps to her collection each week. Greg adds 1 stamp to his collection the first week, 3 stamps the second week, 5 stamps the third week, and so on. Identify the function that gives the number of stamps in each collection as linear or nonlinear. Which collection is growing more quickly between week 5 and week 6?

Determine whether each function has a constant or variable rate of change.

6. variable
7. constant
8. variable

6.

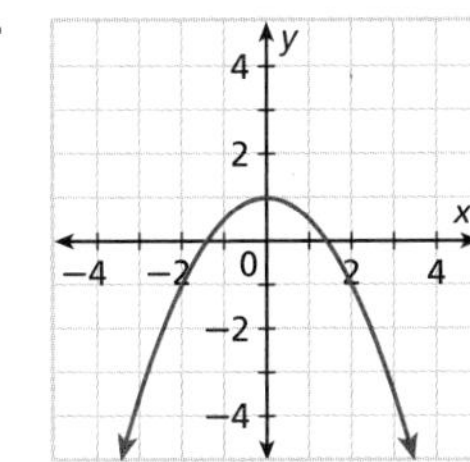

7.

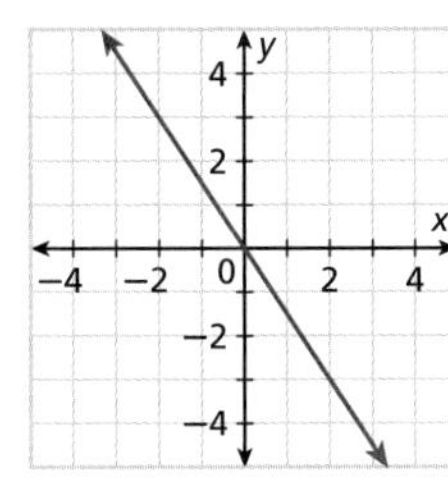

8.

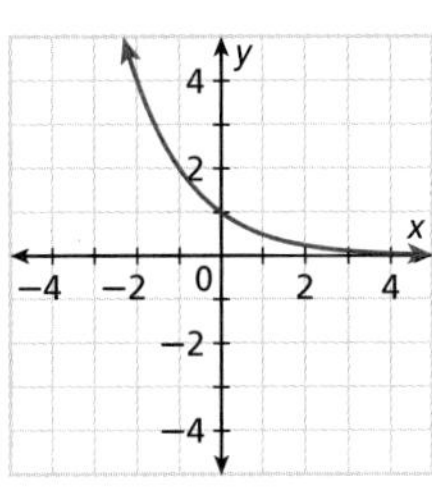

9. $y = 2x^2$ **variable**
10. $y + 1 = 3x$ **constant**
11. $y = -7$ **constant**
12. $y = \frac{1}{5}x$ **constant**
13. $y = 5^x$ **variable**
14. $y = x^2 + 1$ **variable**
15. $y = 3\sqrt{x}$ **variable**
16. $y = \frac{x-3}{2x}$ **variable**
17. $x + y = 6.25$ **constant**

Determine whether each statement is sometimes, always, or never true.

18. A function whose graph is a straight line has a variable rate of change. **never**
19. A quadratic function has a constant rate of change. **never**
20. The rate of change of a linear function is negative. **sometimes**
21. The rate of change between two points on the graph of a nonlinear function is 0. **sometimes**
22. **Critical Thinking** The figure shows the graph of the exponential function $y = \left(\frac{1}{2}\right)^x$.

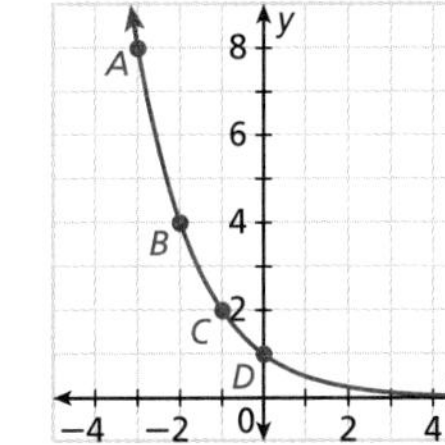

   a. Find the rates of change between points *A* and *B*, between points *B* and *C*, and between points *A* and *D*. **-4; -2; $-\frac{7}{3}$**

   b. What do you notice about the rates of change you found in part **a**? Do you think this would be true for the rate of change between any two points on the graph?

   c. How do your findings about the rates of change relate to the shape of the graph?

22b. All of the rates of change are negative; yes.

c. Since the graph moves downward from left to right, it makes sense that the rate of change between any two points is negative.

23. A model rocket is launched from the ground. The graph shows the height of the rocket at various times.

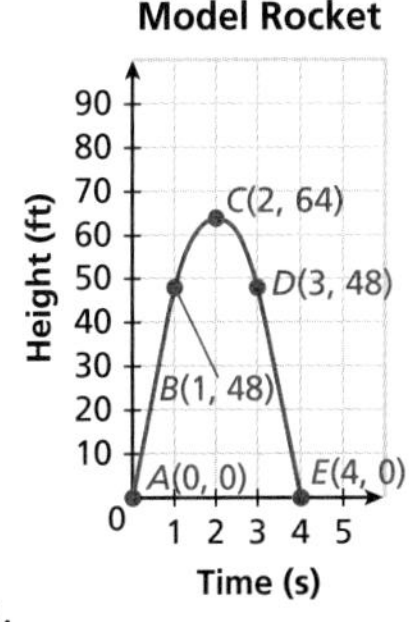

   a. Find the rates of change between points *A* and *B* and between points *B* and *C*. **48; 16**

   b. Which rate of change is greater? What does this tell you about the motion of the rocket?

   c. Find the rates of change between points *C* and *D* and between points *D* and *E*. **-16; -48**

   d. What does the sign of the rates of change you found in part **c** tell you about the motion of the rocket? Explain.

23b. Between *A* and *B*; the rocket is rising more quickly between 0 s and 1 s (48 ft/s) than between 1 s and 2 s (16 ft/s).

d. The rocket is falling; the height is decreasing.

Teaching Tip **Multiple Representations** If students have difficulty finding the rate of change between two points on the graph of a nonlinear function, encourage them to draw a line through the two points. This will help them visualize the slope and quickly determine whether the rate of change is positive or negative.

A-5 Linear and Nonlinear Rates of Change AT17

ADDITIONAL TOPIC

A-6 Organizer

Objectives: Use inductive reasoning to make conjectures.

Use deductive reasoning to prove conjectures, and find counterexamples to disprove conjectures.

Warm Up

Determine whether each statement is sometimes, always, or never true.

1. A quadratic function has two x-intercepts. sometimes
2. A linear function has exactly two x-intercepts. never
3. A direct variation has a single x-intercept at 0. always

Additional Examples

Example 

Use inductive reasoning to make a conjecture about the 50th term in the sequence 4, 12, 20, 28, 36, … . 396

INTERVENTION

Questioning Strategies

EXAMPLE 1

- How is each number in a sequence related to its position in the sequence?
- When you write a rule for a sequence, what is the input? What is the output?

State Resources

ADDITIONAL TOPIC

A-6 Reasoning and Counterexamples

Objectives

Use inductive reasoning to make conjectures.

Use deductive reasoning to prove conjectures, and find counterexamples to disprove conjectures.

Vocabulary

inductive reasoning
conjecture
counterexample
deductive reasoning

Inductive reasoning is the process of concluding that a general rule or statement is true because specific cases are true. A statement based on inductive reasoning is called a **conjecture**.

Row 1 ★
Row 2 ★★★
Row 3 ★★★★★

When several numbers or geometric figures form a pattern and you assume the pattern will continue, you are using inductive reasoning. For example, you might use inductive reasoning to make the conjecture that the fourth row of the pattern at right will contain seven stars.

EXAMPLE 1 Using Inductive Reasoning

Use inductive reasoning to make a conjecture about the value of the 100th term in the sequence 5, 9, 13, 17, 21, … .

Make a table. Examine the values and look for a pattern.

Term	1st	2nd	3rd	4th	5th
Value	5	9	13	17	21
Pattern	4(1) + 1	4(2) + 1	4(3) + 1	4(4) + 1	4(5) + 1

Each value in the sequence is 4 times its position in the sequence, plus 1. The rule $4n + 1$ can be used to find the nth term. A reasonable conjecture for the value of the 100th term is $4(100) + 1 = 401$.

1. Use inductive reasoning to make a conjecture about the value of the 45th term in the sequence 1, 4, 9, 16, 25, … . **2025**

A **counterexample** is a case that proves that a conjecture or statement is false. One counterexample is enough to disprove a statement.

Counterexamples	
Statement	**Counterexample**
No month has fewer than 30 days.	February has fewer than 30 days, so the statement is false.
All prime numbers are odd.	The number 2 is a prime number, but it is not odd. This example shows that the statement is false.
Every integer that is divisible by 2 is also divisible by 4.	The integer 18 is divisible by 2, but it is not divisible by 4. This example shows that the statement is false.

Recall that the Commutative and Associative Properties are true for addition and multiplication. The following example shows how you can use a counterexample to demonstrate that those properties are not true for other operations.

1 Introduce

Motivate

Ask students to look at the page numbers of the right-hand pages in their textbook. Ask them what they notice. The right-hand page numbers are always odd. Have students check other books to see if this observation holds. yes Ask students what they can conclude. In every book, the right-hand page numbers are odd. Tell students that this is an example of a conjecture and that they made this conjecture by using inductive reasoning.

2 Teach

Guided Instruction

Be sure students understand the connections among inductive reasoning, deductive reasoning, and counterexamples. Explain that mathematicians use a combination of inductive and deductive reasoning in their work. Inductive reasoning is often used to formulate a conjecture. Once the conjecture has been stated, deductive reasoning is used to prove that it is true. If the conjecture is not true, a single counterexample is sufficient to demonstrate that it is false.

EXAMPLE 2 **Finding a Counterexample**

Find a counterexample to disprove the statement "The Associative Property is true for subtraction."

Find three real numbers a, b, and c such that $a - (b - c) \neq (a - b) - c$.
Try $a = 10$, $b = 7$, and $c = 2$.

$a - (b - c)$	$(a - b) - c$
$10 - (7 - 2)$	$(10 - 7) - 2$
$10 - 5 = 5$	$3 - 2 = 1$

Since $10 - (7 - 2) \neq (10 - 7) - 2$, this is a counterexample that shows that the statement is false.

2. Find a counterexample to disprove the statement "The Commutative Property is true for division."

Possible answer: $6 \div 2 \neq 2 \div 6$

Inductive reasoning can be used to make conjectures, but it cannot be used to prove a statement. To prove a statement, you must use *deductive reasoning.* **Deductive reasoning** is the process of drawing conclusions from given facts, definitions, and properties.

You may not realize it, but you use deductive reasoning every time you solve an equation. In fact, solving an equation can be thought of as a proof.

EXAMPLE 3 **Using Deductive Reasoning**

Use deductive reasoning to prove each statement.

Writing Math

Notice that each step of a proof is justified with a definition, a property, an operation, or a piece of given information.

A **If $3x + 4 = 19$, then $x = 5$.**

Statements	Reasons
1. $3x + 4 = 19$	Given
2. $3x + 4 - 4 = 19 - 4$	Subtraction Property of Equality
3. $3x = 15$	Subtraction
4. $\frac{3x}{3} = \frac{15}{3}$	Division Property of Equality
5. $x = 5$	Division

B **If $5(x - 3) = -20$, then $x = -1$.**

Statements	Reasons
1. $5(x - 3) = -20$	Given
2. $5x - 5(3) = -20$	Distributive Property
3. $5x - 15 = -20$	Multiplication
4. $5x - 15 + 15 = -20 + 15$	Addition Property of Equality
5. $5x = -5$	Addition
6. $\frac{5x}{5} = \frac{-5}{5}$	Division Property of Equality
7. $x = -1$	Division

Use deductive reasoning to prove each statement.

3a. If $\frac{x}{2} - 1 = 7$, then $x = 16$.

3b. If $4(x + 2) = 8$, then $x = 0$.

Answers to Check it Out

3a.

Statements	Reasons
1. $\frac{x}{2} - 1 = 7$	Given
2. $\frac{x}{2} - 1 + 1 = 7 + 1$	Add. Prop. of Eq.
3. $\frac{x}{2} = 8$	Add.
4. $2 \cdot \frac{x}{2} = 2 \cdot 8$	Mult. Prop. of Eq.
5. $x = 16$	Mult.

3a.

Statements	Reasons
1. $4(x + 2) = 8$	Given
2. $4 \cdot x + 4 \cdot 2 = 8$	Dist. Prop.
3. $4x + 8 = 8$	Mult.
4. $4x + 8 - 8 = 8 - 8$	Subt. Prop. of Eq.
5. $4x = 0$	Subt.
6. $\frac{4x}{4} = \frac{0}{4}$	Div. Prop. of Eq.

3 Close

Summarize

Ask students to explain in their own words the difference between inductive reasoning and deductive reasoning.

Additional Examples

Example 2

Find a counterexample to disprove the statement "The Commutative Property is true for subtraction."

Possible answer: $7 - 4 \neq 4 - 7$

Example 3

Use deductive reasoning to prove each statement.

A. If $2x - 7 = 9$, then $x = 8$.

Statements	Reasons
1. $2x - 7 = 9$	Given
2. $2x - 7 + 7 = 9 + 7$	Add. Prop. of Eq.
3. $2x = 16$	Add.
4. $\frac{2x}{2} = \frac{16}{2}$	Div. Prop. of Eq.
5. $x = 8$	Div.

B. If $4(x + 5) = -24$, then $x = -11$.

Statements	Reasons
1. $4(x + 5) = -24$	Given
2. $4 \cdot x + 4 \cdot 5 = -24$	Dist. Prop.
3. $4x + 20 = -24$	Mult.
4. $4x + 20 - 20 = -24 - 20$	Subt. Prop. of Eq.
5. $4x = -44$	Subt.
6. $\frac{4x}{4} = \frac{-44}{4}$	Div. Prop. of Eq.
7. $x = -11$	Div.

INTERVENTION

Questioning Strategies

EXAMPLE 2

- How do you know which numbers to test when you look for a counterexample?

EXAMPLE 3

- How do you decide the sequence of steps in a proof?

Language Arts Students may already be familiar with deductive reasoning from detective novels. In these stories, the detective often uses a series of clues and logical reasoning to solve a mystery.

A-6 Reasoning and Counterexamples **AT19**

Answers

24. $x - 16 = 41$ (Given); $x - 16 + 16 = 41 + 16$ (Add. Prop. of Eq.); $x = 57$ (Add.)

25. $3x - 17 = 13$ (Given); $3x - 17 + 17 = 13 + 17$ (Add. Prop. of Eq.); $3x = 30$ (Add.); $\frac{3x}{3} = \frac{30}{3}$ (Div. Prop. of Eq.); $x = 10$ (Div.)

26. $7(x - 2) = 21$ (Given); $7 \cdot x - 7 \cdot 2 = 21$ (Dist. Prop.); $7x - 14 = 21$ (Mult.); $7x - 14 + 14 = 21 + 14$ (Add. Prop. of Eq.); $7x = 35$ (Add.); $\frac{7x}{7} = \frac{35}{7}$ (Div. Prop. of Eq.); $x = 5$ (Div.)

27. $3(x + 1) = -9$ (Given); $3 \cdot x + 3 \cdot 1 = -9$ (Dist. Prop.); $3x + 3 = -9$ (Mult.); $3x + 3 - 3 = -9 - 3$ (Subt. Prop. of Eq.); $3x = -12$ (Subt.); $\frac{3x}{3} = \frac{-12}{3}$ (Div. Prop. of Eq.); $x = -4$ (Div.)

A-6 Exercises

Use inductive reasoning to make a conjecture about the value of the 40th term in each sequence.

1. 7, 8, 9, 10, 11, ... **46**
2. 4, 7, 10, 13, 16, ... **121**
3. 5, 10, 15, 20, 25, 30, ... **200**
4. 0, 3, 6, 9, 12, ... **117**
5. 3, 5, 3, 5, 3, ... **5**
6. 1, 2, 3, 1, 2, 3, 1, ... **1**

Use inductive reasoning to make a conjecture about the next item in each pattern.

7. d, e, f, d, e, f, ... **d**
8. $\frac{1}{2}, \frac{3}{4}, \frac{7}{8}, \frac{15}{16}, \ldots$ **$\frac{31}{32}$**
9. 0.1, 0.02, 0.003, ... **0.0004**
10. 66, 57, 48, 39, ... **30**
11. −1, 5, −3, 5, −5, 5, ... **−7**
12. △, □, ⬠, ... **⬡**

Find a counterexample to disprove each statement.

13. The Associative Property is true for division.
14. The Commutative Property is true for subtraction.

13. Possible answer: $12 \div (6 \div 2) \neq (12 \div 6) \div 2$

14. Possible answer: $5 - 3 \neq 3 - 5$

Use deductive reasoning to fill in each missing term.

15. The Red-Q company makes only red clothes. This shirt is made by Red-Q. Therefore, this shirt is ___?___. **red**
16. Lance goes to the library every ___?___. Today is Wednesday. Therefore, Lance went to the library today. **Wednesday**

Tell whether each statement is true or false. If the statement is false, give a counterexample to disprove the statement.

17. If n is an even number, then $3n$ is also an even number. **true**
18. The sum of two odd numbers is also an odd number. **false**
19. If a number is divisible by 6, then it is divisible by 12. **false**
20. The product of two odd numbers is an odd number. **true**
21. Every number that is a multiple of 4 is a multiple of 2. **true**
22. If m is a multiple of 3 and n is a multiple of 4, then $m + n$ is a multiple of 7. **false**

18. Possible answer: $3 + 3 = 6$

19. Possible answer: 18 is divisible by 6 but not by 12.

22. Possible answer: Let $m = 6$ and $n = 4$. Then $m + n = 10$, which is not a multiple of 7.

23. Fill in the missing statement or reason to complete the proof of the following statement: If $-2(x + 6) = -18$, then $x = 3$.

Statements	Reasons
1. $-2(x + 6) = -18$	Given
2. $(-2)x + (-2)6 = -18$	Distributive Property
3. a. **$-2x - 12 = -18$**	Multiplication
4. $-2x - 12 + 12 = -18 + 12$	b. **Add. Prop. of Eq.**
5. $-2x = -6$	Addition
6. $\frac{-2x}{-2} = \frac{-6}{-2}$	c. **Div. Prop. of Eq.**
7. $x = 3$	Division

Use deductive reasoning to prove each statement.

24. If $x - 16 = 41$, then $x = 57$.
25. If $3x - 17 = 13$, then $x = 10$.
26. If $7(x - 2) = 21$, then $x = 5$.
27. If $3(x + 1) = -9$, then $x = -4$.

AT20 *Additional Topics*

28. **Geometry** A student drew the set of figures shown below. Then the student made the following conjecture: Given three points in a plane, it is possible to draw exactly three distinct lines through the points. Do you agree or disagree? Explain.

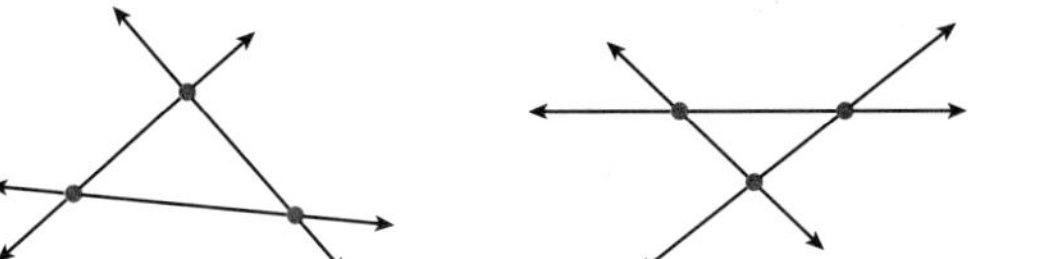

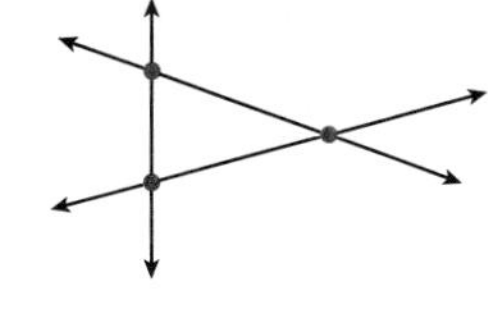

29. **Geometry** An *exterior angle* of a triangle is the angle formed by extending one side of the triangle. An exterior angle of a triangle has two *remote interior angles.* In the figure, $\angle 4$ is an exterior angle. Its remote interior angles are $\angle 1$ and $\angle 2$.

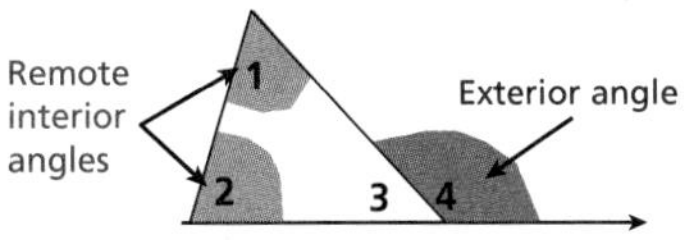

    a. Draw a triangle and an exterior angle. Use a protractor to measure the exterior angle and its remote interior angles. What do you notice about the sum of the measures of the remote interior angles?

    b. Repeat the process in part **a** several more times. Make a conjecture.

    c. What type of reasoning did you use to make your conjecture? Explain.

Determine whether inductive or deductive reasoning was used in each situation. Explain.

30. Christine visited San Diego four times. Each time it was raining. Christine concludes, "San Diego is a very rainy city."

31. Stephanie knows that her cousin's new pet is a lizard. She also knows that every lizard is a reptile and that every reptile has scales. Stephanie concludes that her cousin's new pet has scales.

32. According to Aaron's textbook, the sum of the angle measures in any triangle is 180°. Aaron finds that two angles of a triangle measure 50° and 60°. Aaron concludes that the third angle must measure 70°.

33. Looking at the sequence 3, 9, 27, 81, ..., David concludes that the next number must be 243 because each term is 3 times the previous term.

A *conditional statement* is a statement that can be written in the form "If *p*, then *q*." The *contrapositive* of a conditional statement is the statement "If not *q*, then not *p*." The contrapositive of a true conditional statement is also true. Use the contrapositive to make a true conjecture based on each conditional statement.

34. If today is Tuesday, then tomorrow is Wednesday.

35. If Sam lives in Detroit, then Sam lives in Michigan.

36. If n is an even number, then $n + 1$ is an odd number.

37. If $8x + 3 = 19$, then $x = 2$. **If $x \neq 2$, then $8x + 3 \neq 19$.**

38. **Logic** The mockingbird, the cardinal, the goldfinch, and the grouse are the state birds of Illinois, New Jersey, Pennsylvania, and Tennessee, but not necessarily in that order. Use deductive reasoning and the following clues to match each bird with its state.

    - The cardinal is not the state bird of Tennessee. **mockingbird: TN; cardinal: IL; goldfinch: NJ; grouse: PA**
    - The state bird of Pennsylvania begins with the same letter as the state bird of New Jersey.
    - The state whose capital is Trenton has the goldfinch as its state bird.

28. Disagree; a counterexample is three collinear pts.

29a. The sum of the measures of the remote int. angles equals the measure of the ext. angle.

b. Given an ext. angle of any triangle, the sum of the measures of the remote int. angles equals the measure of the ext. angle.

c. Ind.; the conclusion is based on several observations.

30. Ind.; the conclusion is based on several observations.

31. Ded.; the conclusion is based on a sequence of logical steps.

32. Ded.; the conclusion is based on a sequence of logical steps.

33. Ind.; the conclusion is based on several observations.

34. If tomorrow is not Wed, then today is not Tue.

35. If Sam does not live in Michigan, then Sam does not live in Detroit.

36. If $n + 1$ is not an odd number, then n is not an even number.

In **Exercises 17–23,** students may think that if the statement is true for a single example, then it is true for all examples. Make sure students understand that to be true, a statement must be valid for all examples and that a single counterexample proves a statement false.

A-6 Reasoning and Counterexamples AT21

Student Handbook

Student Handbook

Extra Practice

Extra Practice

Chapter 1 ■ Skills Practice

Lesson 1-1 Give two ways to write each algebraic expression in words. **1–4. See p. A36.**

1. $x + 8$ 2. $6(y)$ 3. $g - 4$ 4. $\frac{12}{h}$

Evaluate each expression for $a = 4$, $b = 2$, and $c = 5$.

5. $b + c$ **7** 6. $\frac{a}{b}$ **2** 7. $c - a$ **1** 8. ab **8**

Write an algebraic expression for each verbal expression. Then evaluate the algebraic expression for the given values of y.

	Verbal	Algebraic	$y = 9$	$y = 6$
9.	y reduced by 4	$y - 4$	5	2
10.	the quotient of y and 3	$y \div 3$	3	2
11.	5 more than y	$y + 5$	14	11
12.	the sum of y and 2	$y + 2$	11	8

Lesson 1-2 Add or subtract using a number line.

13. $-7 - 9$ **−16** 14. $-2.2 + 4.3$ **2.1** 15. $-5\frac{1}{2} - 2\frac{1}{2}$ **−8** 16. $3.4 - 6.5$ **−3.1**

Subtract.

17. $12 - 47$ **−35** 18. $1.3 - 9.2$ **−7.9** 19. $1\frac{1}{3} - 4\frac{2}{3}$ $-3\frac{1}{3}$

Compare. Write <, >, or =.

20. $-5 - (-8)$ **>** $-4 - 9$ 21. $|-6 - (-2)|$ **>** $7 - 4$ 22. $-2 - 5$ **=** $7 - 14$

Evaluate the expression $g - (-7)$ for each value of g.

23. $g = 121$ **128** 24. $g = 1.25$ **8.25** 25. $g = -\frac{2}{5}$ $6\frac{3}{5}$ 26. $g = -8\frac{1}{3}$ $-1\frac{1}{3}$

Lesson 1-3 Find the value of each expression.

27. $-24 \div (-8)$ **3** 28. $5(-9)$ **−45** 29. $-5.2 \div (-1.3)$ **4**

30. $\frac{2}{7} \div \left(-\frac{6}{7}\right)$ $-\frac{1}{3}$ 31. $0 \div \left(-\frac{4}{5}\right)$ **0** 32. $\frac{9}{10} \div 0$ **undefined**

Evaluate each expression for $x = -8$, $y = 6$, and $z = -4$.

33. xy **−48** 34. yz **−24** 35. $\frac{y}{z}$ $-1\frac{1}{2}$ 36. $\frac{z}{x}$ $\frac{1}{2}$

Let a represent a positive number, b represent a negative number, and z represent zero. Tell whether each expression is positive, negative, zero, or undefined.

37. ab **negative** 38. $-bz$ **zero** 39. $-\frac{a}{b}$ **positive** 40. $\frac{ab}{z}$ **undefined**

Lesson 1-4 Write each expression as repeated multiplication. Then simplify the expression.

41. 3^3 **3 • 3 • 3; 27** 42. -2^4 **−(2 • 2 • 2 • 2); −16** 43. $(-5)^3$ **−5 • (−5) • (−5); −125** 44. $(-1)^5$ **44. See p. A36.**

Write each expression using a base and an exponent.

45. $5 \cdot 5 \cdot 5 \cdot 5 \cdot 5$ 5^5 46. $4 \cdot 4 \cdot 4$ 4^3 47. $2 \cdot 2 \cdot 2 \cdot 2$ 2^4

Write the exponent that makes each equation true.

48. $2^{■} = 16$ **4** 49. $4^{■} = 256$ **4** 50. $(-3)^{■} = 81$ **4** 51. $-5^{■} = -125$ **3**

Chapter 1 ■ Skills Practice

Lesson 1-5 Find each root.

52. $-\sqrt{64}$ **−8** 53. $\sqrt{144}$ **12** 54. $\sqrt[3]{\frac{8}{125}}$ $\frac{2}{5}$

Compare. Write <, >, or =.

55. $\sqrt{118}$ **<** 11 56. 6 **>** $\sqrt{35}$ 57. 14 **=** $\sqrt{196}$ 58. $\sqrt{50}$ **>** 7

Write all classifications that apply to each real number.

59. −44 **term. dec., int., rat.** 60. $\sqrt{49}$ **nat., whole, term. dec., int., rat.** 61. 15.982 **rat., term. dec.** 62. $\frac{1}{9}$ **rat., rep. dec.**

Lesson 1-6 Evaluate each expression for the given value of the variable.

63. $22 - 3g + 5$ for $g = 4$ **15** 64. $12 - 30 \div h$ for $h = 6$ **7** 65. $\sqrt{(11j + j)} + 6$ for $j = 3$ **12**

Simplify each expression.

66. $4 + 12 \div |3 - 9|$ **6** 67. $-36 - \sqrt{4 + 15 \div 3}$ **−39** 68. $\frac{5 - \sqrt{12(3)}}{-4 + \sqrt{2(8)}}$ **undef.**

Translate each word phrase into an algebraic expression.

69. the quotient of 8 and the difference of a and 5 $8 \div (a - 5)$

70. the sum of −9 and the square root of the product of 7 and c $-9 + \sqrt{7c}$

Lesson 1-7 Simplify each expression.

71. $-5 + 38 + 5 + 62$ **100** 72. $2\frac{1}{3} - 42 + 7\frac{2}{3}$ **−32** 73. $\frac{1}{5} \cdot 4 \cdot 25$ **20**

Write each product using the Distributive Property. Then simplify. **74–76. See p. A36.**

74. $12(108)$ 75. $7(89)$ 76. $11(33)$

Simplify each expression by combining like terms.

77. $7a - 3a$ $4a$ 78. $-2b - 12b$ $-14b$ 79. $4c + 5c^2 - c$ $3c + 5c^2$

Simplify each expression. Justify each step with an operation or property. **80–86. See pp. A36–A37.**

80. $6(p - 2) + 3p$ 81. $8q - 3 + 5q(2 + q)$ 82. $-4 + 3r - 7(2s - r)$

Lesson 1-8 Graph each point.

83. $A(2, 3)$ 84. $B(-4, 1)$ 85. $C(0, -2)$ 86. $D(-4, -1)$

Name the quadrant in which each point lies.

87. J **none** 88. K **Q IV** 89. L **Q II**

90. M **Q II** 91. N **Q III** 92. P **Q I**

Generate ordered pairs for each function for $x = -2, -1, 0, 1,$ and 2. Graph the ordered pairs and describe the pattern. **93–98. See p. A37.**

93. $y = x - 3$ 94. $y = -2x$ 95. $y = -x^2$ 96. $y = |3x|$

Write an equation for each rule. Use the given values for x to generate ordered pairs. Graph the ordered pairs and describe the pattern.

97. y is equal to the sum of one-third of x and −2; $x = -6, -3, 0, 3,$ and 6.

98. y is equal to 4 less than x squared; $x = -2, -1, 0, 1,$ and 2.

Chapter 2 ■ Skills Practice

Lesson 2-1 Solve each equation. Check your answer.

1. $x - 9 = 5$ **14** 2. $4 = y - 12$ **16** 3. $a + \frac{3}{5} = 7$ $6\frac{2}{5}$

4. $7.3 = b + 3.4$ **3.9** 5. $-6 + j = 5$ **11** 6. $-1.7 = -6.1 + k$ **4.4**

Write an equation to represent each relationship. Then solve the equation.

7. A number decreased by 7 is equal to 10. $x - 7 = 10; x = 17$ 8. The sum of 6 and a number is −3. $6 + x = -3; x = -9$

Lesson 2-2 Solve each equation. Check your answer.

9. $\frac{h}{5} = 15$ **75** 10. $-6 = \frac{k}{4}$ **−24** 11. $\frac{r}{2.6} = 5$ **13**

12. $3b = 27$ **9** 13. $56 = -7d$ **−8** 14. $-3.6 = -2f$ **1.8**

15. $\frac{1}{4}z = 3$ **12** 16. $12 = \frac{4}{5}g$ **15** 17. $\frac{1}{3}a = -5$ **−15**

Write an equation to represent each relationship. Then solve the equation.

18. A number multiplied by 4 is −20. $4x = -20; x = -5$ 19. The quotient of a number and 5 is 7. $\frac{x}{5} = 7; x = 35$

Lesson 2-3 Solve each equation. Check your answer.

20. $2k + 7 = 15$ **4** 21. $11 - 5m = -4$ **3** 22. $23 = 9 - 2d$ **−7**

23. $\frac{2}{5}b + 6 = 10$ **10** 24. $\frac{f}{3} - 4 = 2$ **18** 25. $6n + 4 = 22$ **3**

Write an equation to represent each relationship. Solve each equation.

26. The difference of 11 and 4 times a number equals 3. $11 - 4x = 3; x = 2$

27. Thirteen less than 5 times a number is equal to 7. $5x - 13 = 7; x = 4$

Lesson 2-4 Solve each equation. Check your answer.

28. $5b - 3 = 4b + 1$ **4** 29. $3g + 7 = 11g - 17$ **3**

30. $-8 + 4y = y - 6 + 3y - 2$ **all real numbers** 31. $7 + 3d - 5 = -1 + 2d - 12 + d$ **no solutions**

Write an equation to represent each relationship. Then solve the equation. **32, 33. See p. A37.**

32. Three more than one-half a number is the same as 17 minus three times the number.

33. Two times the difference of a number and 4 is the same as 5 less than the number.

Lesson 2-5 Solve each equation for the indicated variable.

34. $q - 3r = 2$ for r $r = \frac{2 - q}{-3}$ 35. $\frac{5 - c}{6} = d - 7$ for c $c = -6d + 47$

36. $2x + 3\frac{y}{4} = 5$ for y $y = \frac{20 - 8x}{3}$ 37. $2fgh - 3g = 10$ for h $h = \frac{10 + 3g}{2fg}$

Lesson 2-6 Solve each equation. Check your answer.

38. $|a| = 13$ ± 13 39. $|x| - 16 = 3$ ± 19 40. $|g + 5| = 11$ **−16, 6**

41. $|7s| - 6 = 8$ ± 2 42. $\left|\frac{f}{2} + 1\right| = 15$ **−32, 28** 43. $|p - 5| - 12 = -9$ **2, 8**

44. $500 = 25|z| + 200$ ± 12 45. $|7j + 14| - 5 = 16$ **−5, 1** 46. $\frac{|p - 2| - 15}{5} = -1$ **−8, 12**

Chapter 2 ■ Skills Practice

Lesson 2-7

47. A long-distance runner ran 9000 meters in 30 minutes. Find the unit rate in meters per minute. **300 m/min**

48. A hummingbird flapped its wings 770 times in 14 seconds. Find the unit rate in flaps per second. **55 flaps/s**

49. A car traveled 210 miles in 3 hours. Find the unit rate in miles per hour. **70 mi/h**

50. A printer printed 60 pages in 5 minutes. Find the unit rate in pages per minute. **12 pages/min**

Solve each proportion.

51. $\frac{h}{4} = \frac{5}{6}$ $\frac{10}{3}$ 52. $\frac{5}{m} = \frac{2}{5}$ $\frac{25}{2}$ 53. $\frac{r}{3} = \frac{10}{7}$ $\frac{30}{7}$

54. $\frac{2}{3} = \frac{2x}{8}$ $\frac{8}{3}$ 55. $\frac{5}{x - 3} = \frac{3}{10}$ $\frac{59}{3}$ 56. $\frac{b - 2}{4} = \frac{7}{12}$ $\frac{13}{3}$

Lesson 2-8 Find the value of x in each diagram.

57. $ABCD \sim EFGH$ **25** 58. $\triangle JKL \sim \triangle MNO$ **10.5**

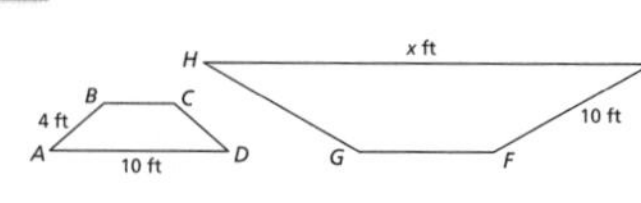

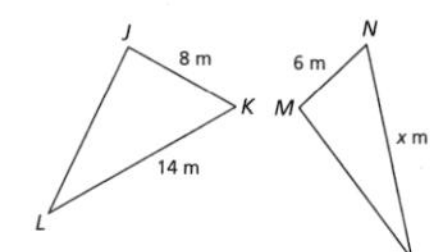

Lesson 2-9

59. Find 25% of 60. **15** 60. Find 40% of 95. **38**

61. What percent of 75 is 15? **20%** 62. What percent of 60 is 33? **55%**

63. 91 is what percent of 65? **140%** 64. 35% of what number is 24.5? **70**

Write each decimal or fraction as a percent.

65. $\frac{4}{5}$ **80%** 66. 0.55 **55%** 67. $\frac{9}{6}$ **150%** 68. 0.0375 **3.75%**

Write each percent as a decimal and as a fraction.

69. 32% $0.32; \frac{8}{25}$ 70. 24% $0.24; \frac{6}{25}$ 71. 37.5% $0.375; \frac{3}{8}$ 72. 118.75% $1.1875; \frac{19}{16}$

Write each list in order from least to greatest.

73. $\frac{2}{17}$, 0.28, 1.9%, $\frac{6}{25}$, 0.19 **1.9%, $\frac{2}{17}$, 0.19, $\frac{6}{25}$, 0.28** 74. $\frac{5}{3}$, 9.2, 117%, $\frac{9}{11}$, 8.8% **8.8%, $\frac{9}{11}$, 117%, $\frac{5}{3}$, 9.2**

Lesson 2-10

75. Estimate the tax on a $2438.00 clarinet when the sales tax is 7.9%. **about $200.00**

76. Estimate the tip on a $21.32 check using a tip rate of 20%. **about $4.00**

Lesson 2-11 Find each percent change. Tell whether it is a percent increase or decrease.

77. 10 to 25 **150%; increase** 78. 40 to 2 **95%; decrease** 79. 800 to 160 **80%; decrease**

80. 4 to 14 **250%; increase** 81. 8 to 30 **275%; increase** 82. 60 to 36 **40%; decrease**

83. Find the result when 45 is increased by 40%. **63**

84. Find the result when 120 is decreased by 70%. **36**

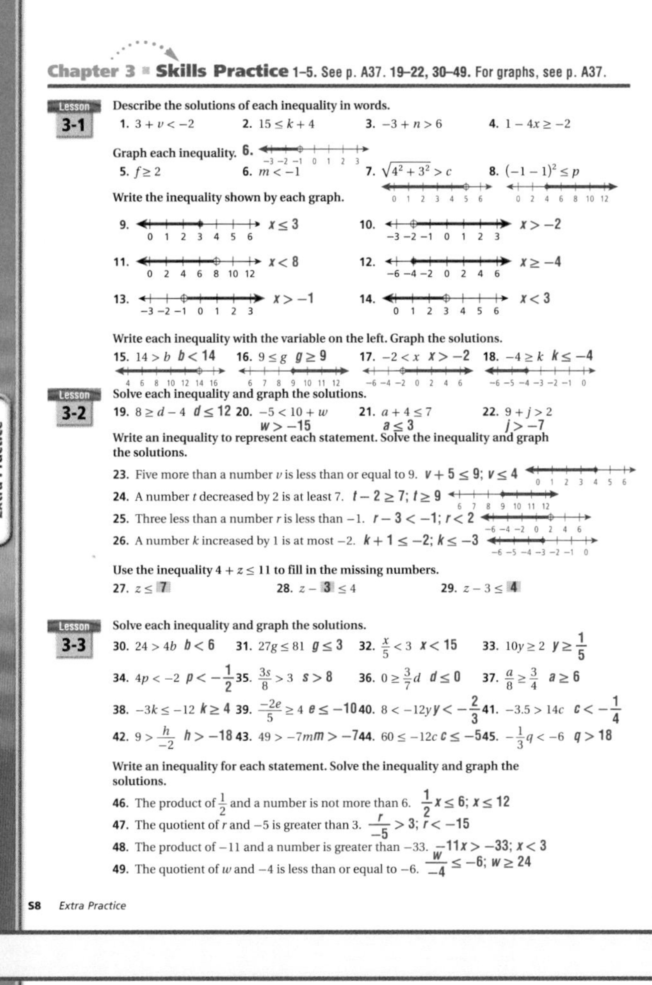

Chapter 3 ■ Skills Practice 1–5. See p. A37. 19–22, 30–49. For graphs, see p. A37.

Lesson 3-1

Describe the solutions of each inequality in words.

1. $3 + v < -2$ 2. $15 \le k + 4$ 3. $-3 + n > 6$ 4. $1 - 4x \ge -2$

Graph each inequality.

5. $f \ge 2$ 6. $m < -1$ 7. $\sqrt{4^2 + 3^2} > c$ 8. $(-1 - 1)^2 \le p$

Write the inequality shown by each graph.

9. $x \le 3$ 10. $x > -2$ 11. $x < 8$ 12. $x \ge -4$ 13. $x > -1$ 14. $x < 3$

Write each inequality with the variable on the left. Graph the solutions.

15. $14 > b$ $b < 14$ 16. $9 \le g$ $g \ge 9$ 17. $-2 < x$ $x > -2$ 18. $-4 \ge k$ $k \le -4$

Lesson 3-2

Solve each inequality and graph the solutions.

19. $8 \ge d - 4$ $d \le 12$ 20. $-5 < 10 + w$ $w > -15$ 21. $a + 4 \le 7$ $a \le 3$ 22. $9 + j > 2$ $j > -7$

Write an inequality to represent each statement. Solve the inequality and graph the solutions.

23. Five more than a number v is less than or equal to 9. $v + 5 \le 9$; $v \le 4$
24. A number t decreased by 2 is at least 7. $t - 2 \ge 7$; $t \ge 9$
25. Three less than a number r is less than -1. $r - 3 < -1$; $r < 2$
26. A number k increased by 1 is at most -2. $k + 1 \le -2$; $k \le -3$

Use the inequality $4 + z \le 11$ to fill in the missing numbers.

27. $z \le$ **7** 28. $z -$ **3** ≤ 4 29. $z - 3 \le$ **4**

Lesson 3-3

Solve each inequality and graph the solutions.

30. $24 > 4b$ $b < 6$ 31. $27g \le 81$ $g \le 3$ 32. $\frac{x}{5} < 3$ $x < 15$ 33. $10y \ge 2$ $y \ge \frac{1}{5}$
34. $4p < -2$ $p < -\frac{1}{2}$ 35. $\frac{3s}{8} > 3$ $s > 8$ 36. $0 \ge \frac{3}{7}d$ $d \le 0$ 37. $\frac{a}{8} \ge \frac{3}{4}$ $a \ge 6$
38. $-3k \le -12$ $k \ge 4$ 39. $\frac{-2e}{5} \ge 4$ $e \le -10$ 40. $8 < -12y$ $y < -\frac{2}{3}$ 41. $-3.5 > 14c$ $c < -\frac{1}{4}$
42. $9 > \frac{h}{-2}$ $h > -18$ 43. $49 > -7m$ $m > -7$ 44. $60 \le -12c$ $c \le -5$ 45. $-\frac{1}{3}q < -6$ $q > 18$

Write an inequality for each statement. Solve the inequality and graph the solutions.

46. The product of $\frac{1}{2}$ and a number is not more than 6. $\frac{1}{2}x \le 6$; $x \le 12$
47. The quotient of r and -5 is greater than 3. $\frac{r}{-5} > 3$; $r < -15$
48. The product of -11 and a number is greater than -33. $-11x > -33$; $x < 3$
49. The quotient of w and -4 is less than or equal to -6. $\frac{w}{-4} \le -6$; $w \ge 24$

Chapter 3 ■ Skills Practice 50–58, 63–67, 73–76, 79–86, 90, 91. For graphs, see p. A38.

Lesson 3-4

Solve each inequality and graph the solutions.

50. $3t - 2 < 5$ $t < \frac{7}{3}$ 51. $-6 < 5b - 4$ $b > -\frac{2}{5}$ 52. $4 < \frac{2f + 3}{2}$ $f > \frac{5}{2}$
53. $10 \le 3(4 - r)$ $r \le \frac{2}{3}$ 54. $\frac{2}{3} + \frac{3}{4}h < \frac{4}{3}$ $h < \frac{8}{9}$ 55. $\frac{1}{5}(10k - 2) > 1$ $k > \frac{7}{10}$
56. $-n - 3 < -2^3$ $n > 5$ 57. $37 - 4d \le \sqrt{3^2 + 4^2}$ $d \ge 8$ 58. $-\frac{3}{4}(8q - 2^2) < -3$ $q > 1$

Use the inequality $-6 - 2w \ge 10$ to fill in the missing numbers.

59. $w \le$ **−8** 60. $w - 3 \le$ **−11** 61. **9** $+ w \le 1$

62. See p. A38.

Write an inequality for each statement. Solve the inequality and graph the solutions.

62. Twelve is less than or equal to the product of 6 and the difference of 5 and a number.
63. The difference of one-third a number and 8 is more than -4. $\frac{1}{3}x - 8 > -4$; $x > 12$
64. One-fourth of the sum of $2x$ and 4 is more than 5. $\frac{1}{4}(2x + 4) > 5$; $x > 8$

Lesson 3-5

Solve each inequality and graph the solutions.

65. $4v - 2 \le 3v$ $v \le 2$ 66. $2(7 - s) > 4(s + 2)$ $s < 1$ 67. $\frac{1}{3}u - \frac{5}{2} \ge \frac{1}{6}u$ $u \ge 15$

Solve each inequality.

68. $3 + 3c < 6 + 3c$ all real numbers 69. $4(k + 2) \ge 4k + 5$ all real numbers 70. $2(5 - b) \le 3 - 2b$ no solutions

Write an inequality to represent each relationship. Solve your inequality.

71. The difference of three times a number and 5 is more than the number times 4. $3x - 5 > 4x$; $x < -5$
72. One less than a number is greater than the product of 3 and the difference of 5 and the number. $x - 1 > 3(5 - x)$; $x > 4$

Lesson 3-6

Solve each compound inequality and graph the solutions.

73. $6 < 3 + x < 8$ $3 < x < 5$ 74. $-1 \le b + 4 \le 3$ $-5 \le b \le -1$
75. $k + 5 \le -3$ OR $k + 5 \ge 1$ $k < -8$ OR $k > -4$ 76. $r - 3 > 2$ OR $r + 1 < 4$ $r > 5$ OR $r < 3$

Write the compound inequality shown by each graph.

77. $x < -1$ OR $x \ge 1$ 78. $-4 \le x < 0$

Write and graph a compound inequality for the numbers described.

79. all real numbers less than 2 and greater than or equal to -1 $-1 \le x < 2$
80. all real numbers between -3 and 1 $-3 < x < 1$

Lesson 3-7

Solve each inequality and graph the solutions.

81. $|n + 5| \le 26$ $-31 \le n \le 21$ 82. $|x| + 6 < 13$ $-7 < x < 7$ 83. $4|k| \le 12$ $-3 \le k \le 3$
84. $|c - 8| > 18$ $c < -10$ OR $c > 26$ 85. $6|p| \ge 48$ $p \le -8$ OR $p \ge 8$ 86. $|3 + t| - 1 \ge 5$ $t \le -9$ OR $t \ge 3$

Solve each inequality.

87. $|a| - 2 \le -5$ no solutions 88. $2|w| + 5 < 3$ no solutions 89. $|s| + 12 > 8$ all real numbers

Write and solve an absolute-value inequality for each expression. Graph the solutions on a number line.

90. All numbers whose absolute value is greater than 14. $|x| > 14$; $x < -14$ OR $x > 14$
91. All numbers whose absolute value multiplied by 3 is less than 27. $3|x| < 27$; $-9 < x < 9$

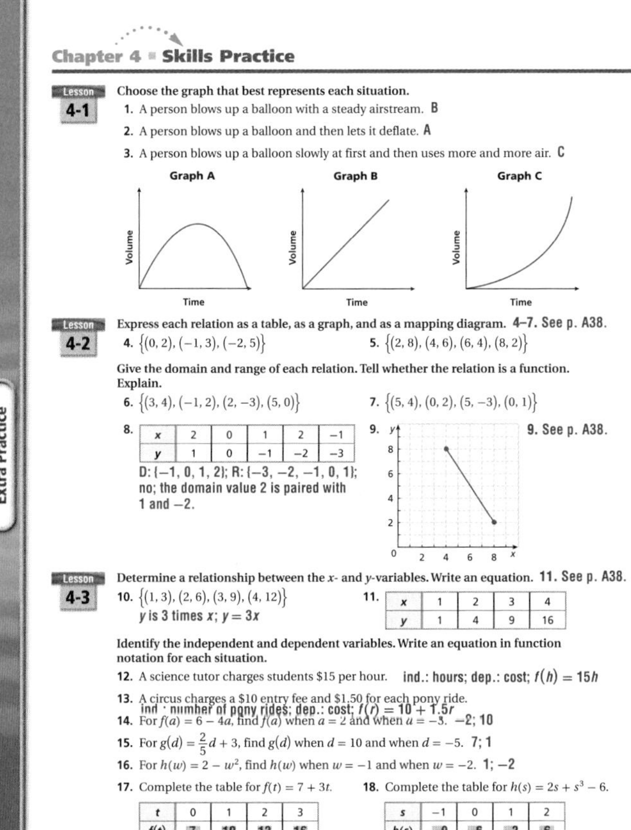

Chapter 4 ■ Skills Practice

Lesson 4-1

Choose the graph that best represents each situation.

1. A person blows up a balloon with a steady airstream. B
2. A person blows up a balloon and then lets it deflate. A
3. A person blows up a balloon slowly at first and then uses more and more air. C

Lesson 4-2

Express each relation as a table, as a graph, and as a mapping diagram. 4–7. See p. A38.

4. $\{(0, 2), (-1, 3), (-2, 5)\}$ 5. $\{(2, 8), (4, 6), (6, 4), (8, 2)\}$

Give the domain and range of each relation. Tell whether the relation is a function. Explain.

6. $\{(3, 4), (-1, 2), (2, -3), (5, 0)\}$ 7. $\{(5, 4), (0, 2), (5, -3), (0, 1)\}$

8.

x	2	0	1	2	−1
y	1	0	−1	−2	−3

D: {−1, 0, 1, 2}; R: {−3, −2, −1, 0, 1}; no; the domain value 2 is paired with 1 and −2.

9. 9. See p. A38.

Lesson 4-3

Determine a relationship between the x- and y-variables. Write an equation. 11. See p. A38.

10. $\{(1, 3), (2, 6), (3, 9), (4, 12)\}$ y is 3 times x; $y = 3x$

11.

x	1	2	3	4
y	1	4	9	16

Identify the independent and dependent variables. Write an equation in function notation for each situation.

12. A science tutor charges students $15 per hour. ind.: hours; dep.: cost; $f(h) = 15h$
13. A circus charges a $10 entry fee and $1.50 for each pony ride. ind.: number of pony rides; dep.: cost; $f(r) = 10 + 1.5r$
14. For $f(a) = 6 - 4a$, find $f(a)$ when $a = 2$ and when $a = -3$. -2; 10
15. For $g(d) = \frac{2}{5}d + 3$, find $g(d)$ when $d = 10$ and when $d = -5$. 7; 1
16. For $h(w) = 2 - w^2$, find $h(w)$ when $w = -1$ and when $w = -2$. 1; -2
17. Complete the table for $f(t) = 7 + 3t$.

t	0	1	2	3
f(t)	7	10	13	16

18. Complete the table for $h(s) = 2s + s^3 - 6$.

s	−1	0	1	2
h(s)	−9	−6	−3	6

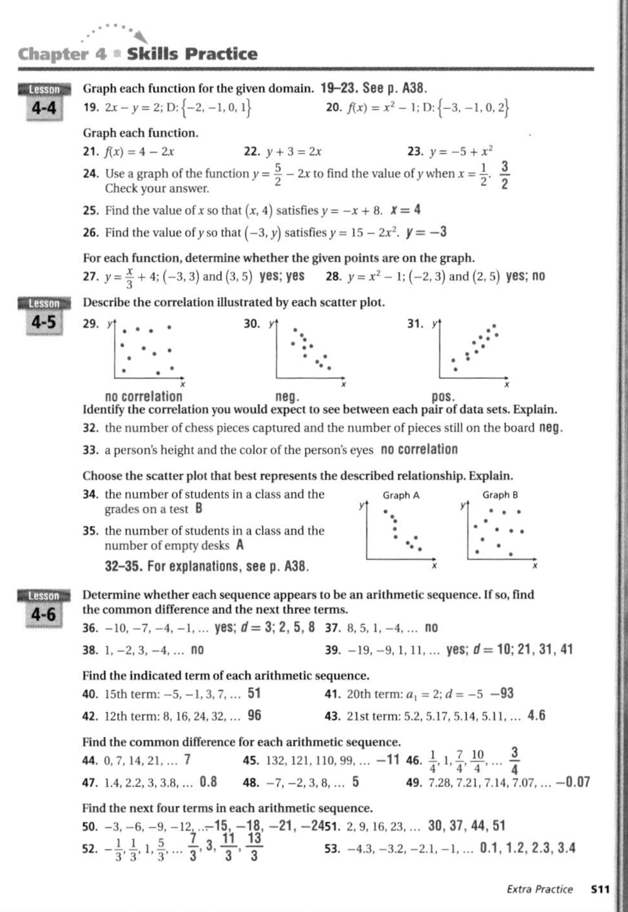

Chapter 4 ■ Skills Practice

Lesson 4-4

Graph each function for the given domain. 19–23. See p. A38.

19. $2x - y = 2$; D: $\{-2, -1, 0, 1\}$ 20. $f(x) = x^2 - 1$; D: $\{-3, -1, 0, 2\}$

Graph each function.

21. $f(x) = 4 - 2x$ 22. $y + 3 = 2x$ 23. $y = -5 + x^2$
24. Use a graph of the function $y = \frac{5}{2} - 2x$ to find the value of y when $x = \frac{1}{2}$. Check your answer. $\frac{3}{2}$
25. Find the value of x so that $(x, 4)$ satisfies $y = -x + 8$. $x = 4$
26. Find the value of y so that $(-3, y)$ satisfies $y = 15 - 2x^2$. $y = -3$

For each function, determine whether the given points are on the graph.

27. $y = \frac{x}{3} + 4$; $(-3, 3)$ and $(3, 5)$ yes; yes 28. $y = x^2 - 1$; $(-2, 3)$ and $(2, 5)$ yes; no

Lesson 4-5

Describe the correlation illustrated by each scatter plot.

29. no correlation 30. neg. 31. pos.

Identify the correlation you would expect to see between each pair of data sets. Explain.

32. the number of chess pieces captured and the number of pieces still on the board neg.
33. a person's height and the color of the person's eyes no correlation

Choose the scatter plot that best represents the described relationship. Explain.

34. the number of students in a class and the grades on a test B
35. the number of students in a class and the number of empty desks A

32–35. For explanations, see p. A38.

Lesson 4-6

Determine whether each sequence appears to be an arithmetic sequence. If so, find the common difference and the next three terms.

36. $-10, -7, -4, -1, \ldots$ yes; $d = 3$; 2, 5, 8 37. $8, 5, 1, -4, \ldots$ no
38. $1, -2, 3, -4, \ldots$ no 39. $-19, -9, 1, 11, \ldots$ yes; $d = 10$; 21, 31, 41

Find the indicated term of each arithmetic sequence.

40. 15th term: $-5, -1, 3, 7, \ldots$ 51 41. 20th term: $a_1 = 2$; $d = -5$ -93
42. 12th term: $8, 16, 24, 32, \ldots$ 96 43. 21st term: $5.2, 5.17, 5.14, 5.11, \ldots$ 4.6

Find the common difference for each arithmetic sequence.

44. $0, 7, 14, 21, \ldots$ 7 45. $132, 121, 110, 99, \ldots$ -11 46. $\frac{1}{4}, 1, \frac{7}{4}, \frac{10}{4}, \ldots$ $\frac{3}{4}$
47. $1.4, 2.2, 3, 3.8, \ldots$ 0.8 48. $-7, -2, 3, 8, \ldots$ 5 49. $7.28, 7.21, 7.14, 7.07, \ldots$ -0.07

Find the next four terms in each arithmetic sequence.

50. $-3, -6, -9, -12, \ldots$ $-15, -18, -21, -24$ 51. $2, 9, 16, 23, \ldots$ 30, 37, 44, 51
52. $-\frac{1}{3}, \frac{1}{3}, 1, \frac{5}{3}, \ldots$ $\frac{7}{3}, 3, \frac{11}{3}, \frac{13}{3}$ 53. $-4.3, -3.2, -2.1, -1, \ldots$ 0.1, 1.2, 2.3, 3.4

Chapter 5 ■ Skills Practice 1–7, 9, 10, 14–17. See pp. A38–A39.

Lesson 5-1 Identify whether each graph represents a function. Explain. If the graph does represent a function, is the function linear?

1. 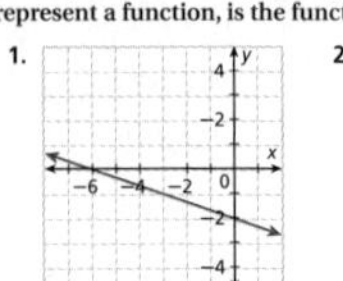
2. 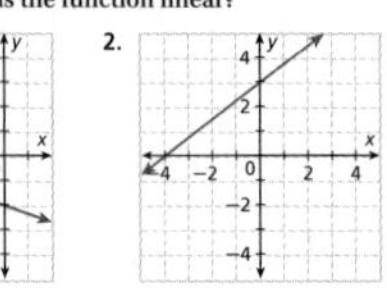
3. 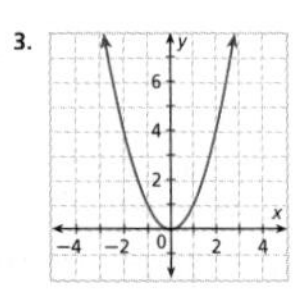

Tell whether the given ordered pairs satisfy a linear function. Explain.

4.

x	−4	−2	0	2	4
y	7	6	5	4	3

5.

x	2	5	8	11	14
y	12	8	7	3	3

Tell whether each equation is linear. If so, write the equation in standard form and give the values of *A*, *B*, and *C*.

6. $y = 8 - 3x$ 7. $\frac{x}{3} = 4 - 2y$ 8. $-3 + xy = 2$ **no** 9. $4x = -3 - 3y$

Lesson 5-2 Find the *x*- and *y*-intercepts.

10. $-4x = 2y - 1$ 11. $x - y = 3$ **x-int.: 3; y-int.: −3** 12. $2x - 3y = 12$ **x-int.: 6; y-int.: −4** 13. $2.5x + 2.5y = 5$ **x-int.: 2; y-int.: 2**

Use intercepts to graph the line described by each equation.

14. $15 = -3x - 5y$ 15. $4y = 2x + 8$ 16. $y = 6 - 3x$ 17. $-2y = x + 2$

Lesson 5-3 Find the slope of each line.

18. 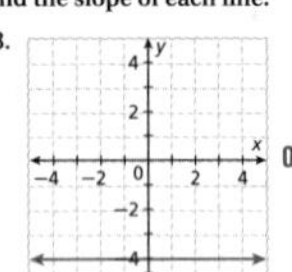 **0**

19. 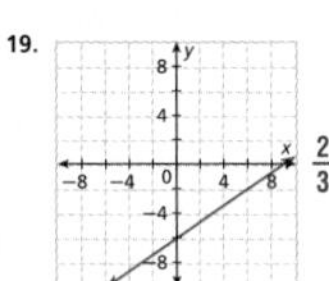 $\mathbf{\frac{2}{3}}$

Lesson 5-4 Find the slope of the line that contains each pair of points.

20. $(-1, 2)$ and $(-4, 8)$ **−2** 21. $(2, 6)$ and $(0, 1)$ $\mathbf{\frac{5}{2}}$ 22. $(-2, 3)$ and $(4, 0)$ $\mathbf{-\frac{1}{2}}$

Find the slope of the line described by each equation.

23. $2y = 42 - 6x$ **−3** 24. $3x + 4y = 12$ $\mathbf{-\frac{3}{4}}$ 25. $3x = 15 + 5y$ $\mathbf{\frac{3}{5}}$

Lesson 5-5 Find the coordinates of the midpoint of each segment.

26. $\overline{AB}$ with endpoints $A(-3, 4)$ and $B(1, 5)$ $\mathbf{\left(-1, \frac{9}{2}\right)}$

27. $\overline{CD}$ with endpoints $C(9, -8)$ and $D(9, -2)$ **(9, −5)**

Find the distance, to the nearest hundredth, between each pair of points.

28. $A(0, 6)$ and $B(4, 8)$ **4.47** 29. $J(-1, 7)$ and $K(-4, 5)$ **3.61** 30. $S(-3, -9)$ and $T(2, 3)$ **13**

Chapter 5 ■ Skills Practice 42–44. For graphs, see p. A39.

Lesson 5-6 Tell whether each equation represents a direct variation. If so, identify the constant of variation.

31. $x - 2y = 0$ **yes;** $\mathbf{\frac{1}{2}}$ 32. $x - y = 3$ **no** 33. $3y = 2x$ **yes;** $\mathbf{\frac{2}{3}}$

34. The value of *y* varies directly with *x*, and $y = 2$ when $x = -3$. Find *y* when $x = 6$. **−4**

35. The value of *y* varies directly with *x*, and $y = -3$ when $x = 9$. Find *y* when $x = 12$. **−4**

Lesson 5-7 Write the equation that describes each line in slope-intercept form.

36. slope = 2, *y*-intercept = −2 $\mathbf{y = 2x - 2}$ 37. slope = 0.25, *y*-intercept = 4 $\mathbf{y = 0.25x + 4}$

38. slope = −2, (5, 4) is on the line. 39. slope = $\frac{1}{3}$, (−8, 0) is on the line.

38. $\mathbf{y = -2x + 14}$ **39.** $\mathbf{y = \frac{1}{3}x + \frac{8}{3}}$

40. 41.

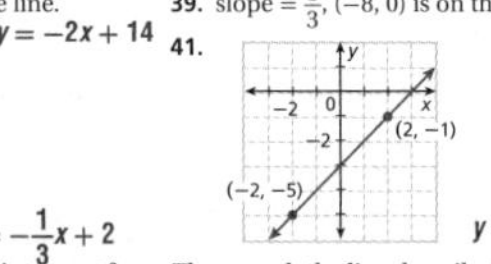

40. $\mathbf{y = -\frac{1}{3}x + 2}$ 41. $\mathbf{y = x - 3}$

Write each equation in slope-intercept form. Then graph the line described by the equation.

42. $2y = x - 3$ $\mathbf{y = \frac{1}{2}x - \frac{3}{2}}$ 43. $-3x - 2y = 1$ $\mathbf{y = -\frac{3}{2}x - \frac{1}{2}}$ 44. $2y - \frac{1}{2}x = 2$ $\mathbf{y = \frac{1}{4}x + 1}$

Lesson 5-8 Write an equation in point-slope form for the line with the given slope that contains the given point.

45. slope = 2; (0, 3) $\mathbf{y - 3 = 2(x - 0)}$ 46. slope = −1; (1, −1) $\mathbf{y + 1 = -1(x - 1)}$ 47. slope = $\frac{1}{2}$; (2, 4) $\mathbf{y - 4 = \frac{1}{2}(x - 2)}$

Write the equation that describes each line in slope-intercept form.

48. slope = 3, (−2, −5) is on the line. $\mathbf{y = 3x + 1}$ 49. (−1, 1) and (1, −2) are on the line. **49.** $\mathbf{y = -\frac{3}{2}x - \frac{1}{2}}$

50. (3, 1) and (2, −3) are on the line. $\mathbf{y = 4x - 11}$ 51. *x*-intercept = 4, *y*-intercept = −5 $\mathbf{y = \frac{5}{4}x - 5}$

Lesson 5-9 Write an equation in slope-intercept form for the line that is parallel to the given line and that passes through the given point.

52. $y = -2x + 3$; (1, 4) $\mathbf{y = -2x + 6}$ 53. $y = x - 5$; (2, −4) $\mathbf{y = x - 6}$ 54. $y = 3x$; (−1, 5) $\mathbf{y = 3x + 8}$

Write an equation in slope-intercept form for the line that is perpendicular to the given line and that passes through the given point.

55. $y = x + 1$; (3, −2) $\mathbf{y = -x + 1}$ 56. $y = -4x - 1$; (−1, 0) $\mathbf{y = \frac{1}{4}x + \frac{1}{4}}$ 57. $y = 4x + 5$; (2, −1) $\mathbf{y = -\frac{1}{4}x - \frac{1}{2}}$

Lesson 5-10 Graph $f(x)$ and $g(x)$. Then describe the transformation(s) from the graph of $f(x)$ to the graph of $g(x)$. **For graphs, see p. A39.**

58. $f(x) = x$, $g(x) = x + 2$ **trans. 2 units up** 59. $f(x) = x$, $g(x) = x - \frac{1}{2}$ **trans.** $\mathbf{\frac{1}{2}}$ **unit down**

60, 61, 63. See p. A39.

60. $f(x) = 6x + 1$, $g(x) = 2x + 1$ 61. $f(x) = 3x - 1$, $g(x) = 9x - 1$

62. $f(x) = x$, $g(x) = 2x - 1$ **rot., trans. 1 unit down** 63. $f(x) = x + 1$, $g(x) = -\frac{1}{2}x$

Chapter 6 ■ Skills Practice

Lesson 6-1 Tell whether the ordered pair is a solution of the given system.

1. $(1, 3); \begin{cases} 2x - 3y = -7 \\ -5x + 3y = 4 \end{cases}$ **yes** 2. $(-2, 2); \begin{cases} 4x + 3y = -2 \\ -2x - 2y = 2 \end{cases}$ **no** 3. $(4, -3); \begin{cases} -2x - 3y = 1 \\ x + 2y = -2 \end{cases}$ **yes**

Use the given graph to find the solution of each system.

4. $\begin{cases} y = \frac{1}{2}x - 1 \\ y = -\frac{1}{2}x + 3 \end{cases}$ **(4, 1)** 5. $\begin{cases} y = x + 1 \\ y = -x + 1 \end{cases}$ **(0, 1)**

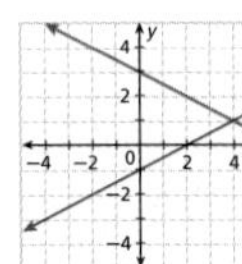

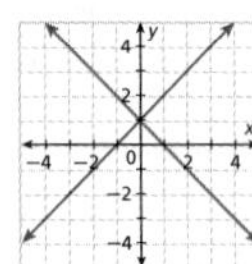

Solve each system by graphing. Check your answer.

6. $\begin{cases} y = x + 1 \\ y = -2x - 2 \end{cases}$ **(−1, 0)** 7. $\begin{cases} 3x + y = -8 \\ 3y = \frac{1}{2}x - 5 \end{cases}$ **(−2, −2)** 8. $\begin{cases} x = 2 - 2y \\ -1 = -2x - 3y \end{cases}$ **(−4, 3)**

Lesson 6-2 Solve each system by substitution.

9. $\begin{cases} y = 12 - 3x \\ y = 2x - 3 \end{cases}$ **(3, 3)** 10. $\begin{cases} 2x + y = -6 \\ -5x + y = 1 \end{cases}$ **(−1, −4)** 11. $\begin{cases} y = 11 - 3x \\ -2x + y = 1 \end{cases}$ **(2, 5)**

12. $\begin{cases} 2x + 3y = 2 \\ -\frac{1}{2}x + 2y = -6 \end{cases}$ **(4, −2)** 13. $\begin{cases} 3x - 2y = -3 \\ y = 7 - 4x \end{cases}$ **(1, 3)** 14. $\begin{cases} 4y - 2x = -2 \\ x + 3y = -4 \end{cases}$ **(−1, −1)**

Two angles whose measures have a sum of 90° are called complementary angles. For Exercises 15–17, *x* and *y* represent the measures of complementary angles. Use this information and the equation given in each exercise to find the measure of each angle.

15. $y = 9x - 10$ **x = 10°; y = 80°** 16. $y - 4x = 15$ **x = 15°; y = 75°** 17. $y = 2x + 15$ **x = 25°; y = 65°**

Lesson 6-3 Solve each system by elimination.

18. $\begin{cases} x - 3y = -1 \\ -x + 2y = -2 \end{cases}$ **(8, 3)** 19. $\begin{cases} -3x - y = 1 \\ 5x + y = -5 \end{cases}$ **(−2, 5)** 20. $\begin{cases} -x - 3y = -1 \\ 3x + 3y = 9 \end{cases}$ **(4, −1)**

21. $\begin{cases} 3x - 2y = 2 \\ 3x + y = 8 \end{cases}$ **(2, 2)** 22. $\begin{cases} 5x - 2y = -15 \\ 2x - 2y = -12 \end{cases}$ **(−1, 5)** 23. $\begin{cases} -4x - 2y = -4 \\ -4x + 3y = -24 \end{cases}$ **(3, −4)**

24. $\begin{cases} -3x - 3y = 3 \\ 2x + y = -4 \end{cases}$ **(−3, 2)** 25. $\begin{cases} 4x - 3y = -1 \\ 2x - 2y = -4 \end{cases}$ **(5, 7)** 26. $\begin{cases} 3x + 6y = 0 \\ 7x + 4y = 20 \end{cases}$ **(4, −2)**

Chapter 6 ■ Skills Practice

Lesson 6-4 Solve each system of linear equations.

27. $\begin{cases} y = 2x + 4 \\ -2x + y = 6 \end{cases}$ **no sol.** 28. $\begin{cases} -y = 3 - 5x \\ y - 5x = 6 \end{cases}$ **no sol.** 29. $\begin{cases} y + 2 = 3x \\ 3x - y = -1 \end{cases}$ **no sol.**

30. $\begin{cases} 2y = 6 - 6x \\ 3y + 9x = 9 \end{cases}$ **inf. many solutions** 31. $\begin{cases} y - 1 = -3x \\ 12x + 4y = 4 \end{cases}$ **inf. many solutions** 32. $\begin{cases} 4x - 2y = 4 \\ 3y = 6(x - 1) \end{cases}$ **inf. many solutions**

Classify each system. Give the number of solutions.

33. $\begin{cases} 2y = 2(4x - 3) \\ y - 1 = 4x \end{cases}$ **incons.; no sol.** 34. $\begin{cases} 3y + 6x = 9 \\ 2(y - 3) = -4x \end{cases}$ **34. cons., dep.; inf. many solutions** 35. $\begin{cases} 3x - 13 = 2y \\ -3y = 2x \end{cases}$ **cons., ind.; one sol.**

Lesson 6-5 Tell whether the ordered pair is a solution of the given inequality.

36. $(3, 6); y > 2x + 4$ **no** 37. $(-2, -8); y \le 3x - 2$ **yes** 38. $(-3, 3); y \ge -2x + 5$ **no**

Graph the solutions of each linear inequality. **39–46. See p. A39.**

39. $y > 2x$ 40. $y \le -3x + 2$ 41. $y \ge 2x - 1$ 42. $-y < -x + 4$

43. $y \ge -2x + 4$ 44. $y > -x - 3$ 45. $y < \frac{1}{2}x + 1\frac{1}{2}$ 46. $y \le 4x - (-1)$

Write an inequality to represent each graph.

47. 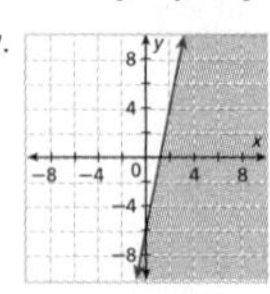 $\mathbf{y \le 5x - 6}$

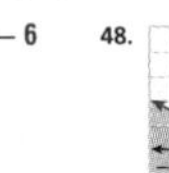

48. 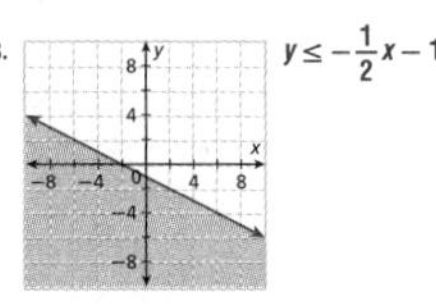 $\mathbf{y \le -\frac{1}{2}x - 1}$

Lesson 6-6 Tell whether the ordered pair is a solution of the given system.

49. $(2, 5); \begin{cases} y > 3x - 3 \\ y \ge x + 1 \end{cases}$ **yes** 50. $(3, 9); \begin{cases} y > -3x - 2 \\ y < 2x + 3 \end{cases}$ **no** 51. $(2, 3); \begin{cases} y > 2x \\ y \le x - 3 \end{cases}$ **no**

Graph each system of linear inequalities. Give two ordered pairs that are solutions and two that are not solutions.

52. $\begin{cases} x + 4y < 2 \\ 2y > 3x + 8 \end{cases}$ 53. $\begin{cases} y \le 6 - 2x \\ x - 2y < -2 \end{cases}$ 54. $\begin{cases} 2x - 2 > -3y \\ -x + 3y \ge -10 \end{cases}$

Graph each system of linear inequalities. Describe the solutions.

55. $\begin{cases} y > 2x + 1 \\ y < 2x - 2 \end{cases}$ 56. $\begin{cases} y < 3x - 1 \\ y > 3x - 4 \end{cases}$ 57. $\begin{cases} y \ge -x + 2 \\ y \ge -x + 5 \end{cases}$

58. $\begin{cases} y \ge 2x - 3 \\ y \ge 2x + 3 \end{cases}$ 59. $\begin{cases} y > -4x - 2 \\ y \le -4x - 5 \end{cases}$ 60. $\begin{cases} y \ge -2x + 1 \\ y < -2x + 6 \end{cases}$

52–60. See pp. A39–A40.

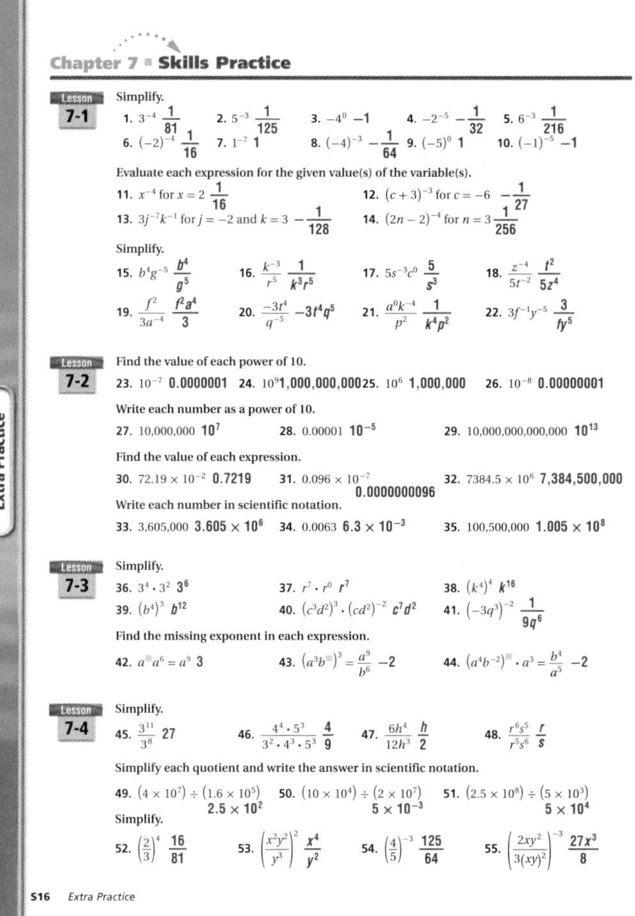

Chapter 7 ■ Skills Practice

Lesson 7-1

Simplify.

1. 3^{-4} $\frac{1}{81}$ 2. 5^{-3} $\frac{1}{125}$ 3. -4^0 -1 4. -2^{-5} $-\frac{1}{32}$ 5. 6^{-3} $\frac{1}{216}$
6. $(-2)^{-4}$ $\frac{1}{16}$ 7. 1^{-7} 1 8. $(-4)^{-3}$ $-\frac{1}{64}$ 9. $(-5)^0$ 1 10. $(-1)^{-5}$ -1

Evaluate each expression for the given value(s) of the variable(s).

11. x^{-4} for $x = 2$ $\frac{1}{16}$ 12. $(c+3)^{-3}$ for $c = -6$ $-\frac{1}{27}$
13. $3j^{-7}k^{-1}$ for $j = -2$ and $k = 3$ $-\frac{1}{128}$ 14. $(2n-2)^{-4}$ for $n = 3$ $\frac{1}{256}$

Simplify.

15. b^4g^{-5} $\frac{b^4}{g^5}$ 16. $\frac{k^{-3}}{r^5}$ $\frac{1}{k^3r^5}$ 17. $5s^{-3}c^0$ $\frac{5}{s^3}$ 18. $\frac{z^{-4}}{5t^{-2}}$ $\frac{t^2}{5z^4}$
19. $\frac{f^2}{3a^{-4}}$ $\frac{f^2a^4}{3}$ 20. $\frac{-3t^4}{q^{-5}}$ $-3t^4q^5$ 21. $\frac{a^0k^{-4}}{p^2}$ $\frac{1}{k^4p^2}$ 22. $3f^{-1}y^{-5}$ $\frac{3}{fy^5}$

Lesson 7-2

Find the value of each power of 10.

23. 10^{-7} **0.0000001** 24. 10^9 **1,000,000,000** 25. 10^6 **1,000,000** 26. 10^{-8} **0.00000001**

Write each number as a power of 10.

27. 10,000,000 10^7 28. 0.00001 10^{-5} 29. 10,000,000,000,000 10^{13}

Find the value of each expression.

30. 72.19×10^{-2} **0.7219** 31. 0.096×10^{-7} **0.0000000096** 32. 7384.5×10^6 **7,384,500,000**

Write each number in scientific notation.

33. 3,605,000 3.605×10^6 34. 0.0063 6.3×10^{-3} 35. 100,500,000 1.005×10^8

Lesson 7-3

Simplify.

36. $3^4 \cdot 3^2$ 3^6 37. $r^7 \cdot r^0$ r^7 38. $(k^4)^4$ k^{16}
39. $(b^4)^3$ b^{12} 40. $(c^3d^2)^3 \cdot (cd^2)^{-2}$ c^7d^2 41. $(-3q^3)^{-2}$ $\frac{1}{9q^6}$

Find the missing exponent in each expression.

42. $a^{■}a^6 = a^9$ **3** 43. $(a^3b^{■})^3 = \frac{a^9}{b^6}$ **−2** 44. $(a^4b^{-2})^{■} \cdot a^3 = \frac{b^4}{a^5}$ **−2**

Lesson 7-4

Simplify.

45. $\frac{3^{11}}{3^8}$ 27 46. $\frac{4^4 \cdot 5^3}{3^2 \cdot 4^3 \cdot 5^3}$ $\frac{4}{9}$ 47. $\frac{6h^4}{12h^3}$ $\frac{h}{2}$ 48. $\frac{r^6s^5}{r^5s^6}$ $\frac{r}{s}$

Simplify each quotient and write the answer in scientific notation.

49. $(4 \times 10^7) \div (1.6 \times 10^5)$ 2.5×10^2 50. $(10 \times 10^4) \div (2 \times 10^7)$ 5×10^{-3} 51. $(2.5 \times 10^8) \div (5 \times 10^3)$ 5×10^4

Simplify.

52. $\left(\frac{2}{3}\right)^4$ $\frac{16}{81}$ 53. $\left(\frac{x^2y^2}{y^3}\right)^2$ $\frac{x^4}{y^2}$ 54. $\left(\frac{4}{5}\right)^{-3}$ $\frac{125}{64}$ 55. $\left(\frac{2xy^2}{3(xy)^2}\right)^{-3}$ $\frac{27x^3}{8}$

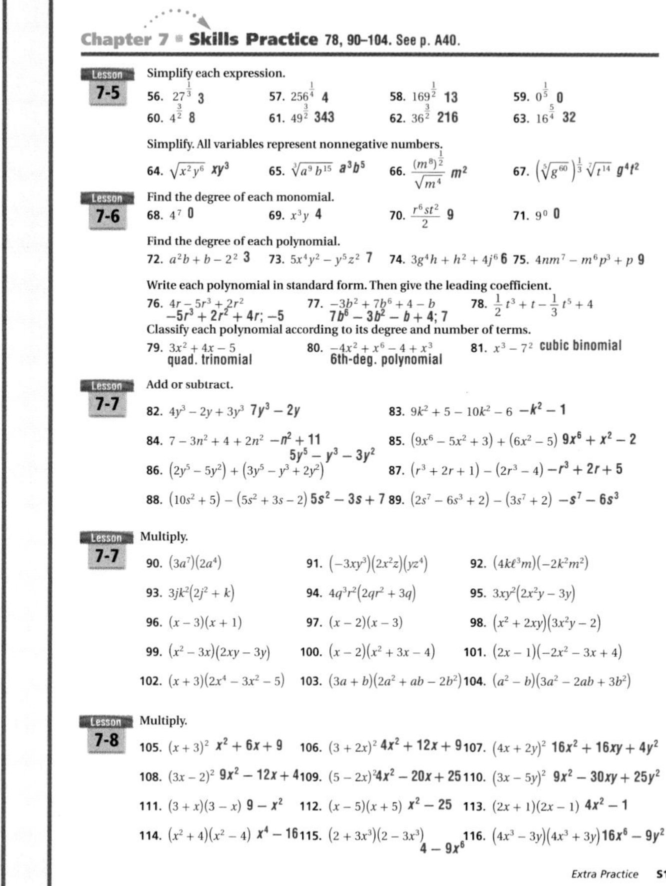

Chapter 7 ■ Skills Practice 78, 90–104. See p. A40.

Lesson 7-5

Simplify each expression.

56. $27^{\frac{1}{3}}$ **3** 57. $256^{\frac{1}{4}}$ **4** 58. $169^{\frac{1}{2}}$ **13** 59. $0^{\frac{1}{5}}$ **0**
60. $4^{\frac{3}{2}}$ **8** 61. $49^{\frac{3}{2}}$ **343** 62. $36^{\frac{3}{2}}$ **216** 63. $16^{\frac{5}{4}}$ **32**

Simplify. All variables represent nonnegative numbers.

64. $\sqrt{x^2y^6}$ xy^3 65. $\sqrt[3]{a^9b^{15}}$ a^3b^5 66. $\frac{(m^8)^{\frac{1}{2}}}{\sqrt{m^4}}$ m^2 67. $\left(\sqrt[5]{g^{60}}\right)^{\frac{1}{3}}\sqrt[7]{t^{14}}$ g^4t^2

Lesson 7-6

Find the degree of each monomial.

68. 4^7 **0** 69. x^3y **4** 70. $\frac{r^6st^2}{2}$ **9** 71. 9^0 **0**

Find the degree of each polynomial.

72. $a^2b + b - 2^2$ **3** 73. $5x^4y^2 - y^5z^2$ **7** 74. $3g^4h + h^2 + 4j^6$ **6** 75. $4nm^7 - m^6p^3 + p$ **9**

Write each polynomial in standard form. Then give the leading coefficient.

76. $4r - 5r^3 + 2r^2$ $-5r^3 + 2r^2 + 4r; -5$ 77. $-3b^2 + 7b^6 + 4 - b$ $7b^6 - 3b^2 - b + 4; 7$ 78. $\frac{1}{2}t^3 + t - \frac{1}{3}t^5 + 4$

Classify each polynomial according to its degree and number of terms.

79. $3x^2 + 4x - 5$ **quad. trinomial** 80. $-4x^2 + x^6 - 4 + x^3$ **6th-deg. polynomial** 81. $x^3 - 7^2$ **cubic binomial**

Lesson 7-7

Add or subtract.

82. $4y^3 - 2y + 3y^3$ $7y^3 - 2y$ 83. $9k^2 + 5 - 10k^2 - 6$ $-k^2 - 1$
84. $7 - 3n^2 + 4 + 2n^2$ $-n^2 + 11$ 85. $(9x^6 - 5x^2 + 3) + (6x^2 - 5)$ $9x^6 + x^2 - 2$
86. $(2y^5 - 5y^2) + (3y^5 - y^3 + 2y^2)$ $5y^5 - y^3 - 3y^2$ 87. $(r^3 + 2r + 1) - (2r^3 - 4)$ $-r^3 + 2r + 5$
88. $(10s^2 + 5) - (5s^2 + 3s - 2)$ $5s^2 - 3s + 7$ 89. $(2s^7 - 6s^3 + 2) - (3s^7 + 2)$ $-s^7 - 6s^3$

Lesson 7-7

Multiply.

90. $(3a^7)(2a^4)$ 91. $(-3xy^3)(2x^2z)(yz^4)$ 92. $(4k\ell^3m)(-2k^2m^2)$
93. $3jk^2(2j^2 + k)$ 94. $4q^3r^2(2qr^2 + 3q)$ 95. $3xy^2(2x^2y - 3y)$
96. $(x-3)(x+1)$ 97. $(x-2)(x-3)$ 98. $(x^2 + 2xy)(3x^2y - 2)$
99. $(x^2 - 3x)(2xy - 3y)$ 100. $(x-2)(x^2 + 3x - 4)$ 101. $(2x-1)(-2x^2 - 3x + 4)$
102. $(x+3)(2x^4 - 3x^2 - 5)$ 103. $(3a+b)(2a^2 + ab - 2b^2)$ 104. $(a^2 - b)(3a^2 - 2ab + 3b^2)$

Lesson 7-8

Multiply.

105. $(x+3)^2$ $x^2 + 6x + 9$ 106. $(3+2x)^2$ $4x^2 + 12x + 9$ 107. $(4x+2y)^2$ $16x^2 + 16xy + 4y^2$
108. $(3x-2)^2$ $9x^2 - 12x + 4$ 109. $(5-2x)^2$ $4x^2 - 20x + 25$ 110. $(3x-5y)^2$ $9x^2 - 30xy + 25y^2$
111. $(3+x)(3-x)$ $9 - x^2$ 112. $(x-5)(x+5)$ $x^2 - 25$ 113. $(2x+1)(2x-1)$ $4x^2 - 1$
114. $(x^2+4)(x^2-4)$ $x^4 - 16$ 115. $(2+3x^3)(2-3x^3)$ $4 - 9x^6$ 116. $(4x^3 - 3y)(4x^3 + 3y)$ $16x^6 - 9y^2$

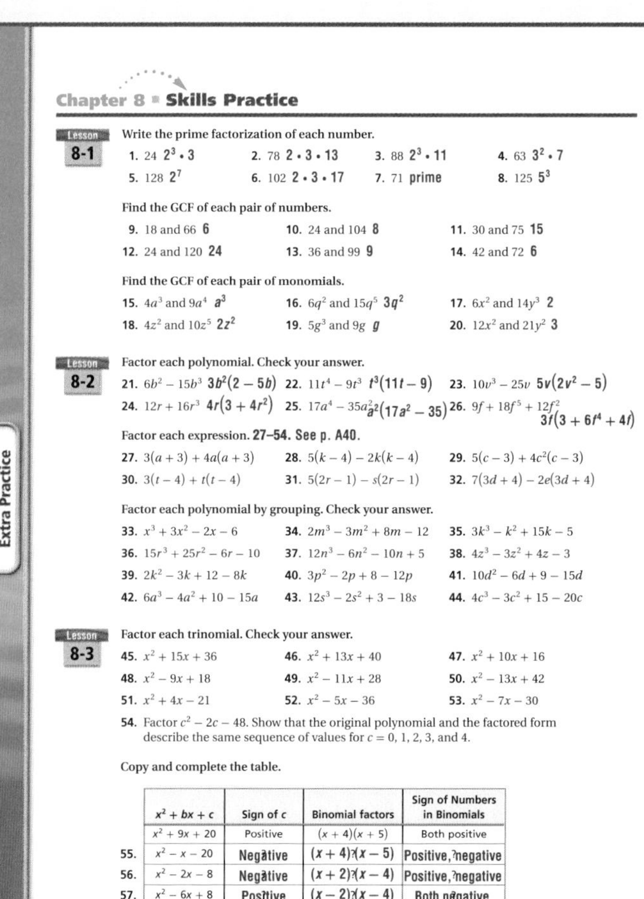

Chapter 8 ■ Skills Practice

Lesson 8-1

Write the prime factorization of each number.

1. 24 $2^3 \cdot 3$ 2. 78 $2 \cdot 3 \cdot 13$ 3. 88 $2^3 \cdot 11$ 4. 63 $3^2 \cdot 7$
5. 128 2^7 6. 102 $2 \cdot 3 \cdot 17$ 7. 71 **prime** 8. 125 5^3

Find the GCF of each pair of numbers.

9. 18 and 66 **6** 10. 24 and 104 **8** 11. 30 and 75 **15**
12. 24 and 120 **24** 13. 36 and 99 **9** 14. 42 and 72 **6**

Find the GCF of each pair of monomials.

15. $4a^3$ and $9a^4$ a^3 16. $6q^2$ and $15q^5$ $3q^2$ 17. $6x^2$ and $14y^3$ **2**
18. $4z^2$ and $10z^5$ $2z^2$ 19. $5g^3$ and $9g$ g 20. $12x^2$ and $21y^2$ **3**

Lesson 8-2

Factor each polynomial. Check your answer.

21. $6b^2 - 15b^3$ $3b^2(2 - 5b)$ 22. $11t^4 - 9t^3$ $t^3(11t - 9)$ 23. $10v^3 - 25v$ $5v(2v^2 - 5)$
24. $12r + 16r^3$ $4r(3 + 4r^2)$ 25. $17a^4 - 35a^2$ $a^2(17a^2 - 35)$ 26. $9f + 18f^5 + 12f^2$ $3f(3 + 6f^4 + 4f)$

Factor each expression. 27–54. See p. A40.

27. $3(a+3) + 4a(a+3)$ 28. $5(k-4) - 2k(k-4)$ 29. $5(c-3) + 4c^2(c-3)$
30. $3(t-4) + t(t-4)$ 31. $5(2r-1) - s(2r-1)$ 32. $7(3d+4) - 2e(3d+4)$

Factor each polynomial by grouping. Check your answer.

33. $x^3 + 3x^2 - 2x - 6$ 34. $2m^3 - 3m^2 + 8m - 12$ 35. $3k^3 - k^2 + 15k - 5$
36. $15r^3 + 25r^2 - 6r - 10$ 37. $12n^3 - 6n^2 - 10n + 5$ 38. $4z^3 - 3z^2 + 4z - 3$
39. $2k^2 - 3k + 12 - 8k$ 40. $3p^2 - 2p + 8 - 12p$ 41. $10d^2 - 6d + 9 - 15d$
42. $6a^3 - 4a^2 + 10 - 15a$ 43. $12s^3 - 2s^2 + 3 - 18s$ 44. $4c^3 - 3c^2 + 15 - 20c$

Lesson 8-3

Factor each trinomial. Check your answer.

45. $x^2 + 15x + 36$ 46. $x^2 + 13x + 40$ 47. $x^2 + 10x + 16$
48. $x^2 - 9x + 18$ 49. $x^2 - 11x + 28$ 50. $x^2 - 13x + 42$
51. $x^2 + 4x - 21$ 52. $x^2 - 5x - 36$ 53. $x^2 - 7x - 30$

54. Factor $c^2 - 2c - 48$. Show that the original polynomial and the factored form describe the same sequence of values for $c = 0, 1, 2, 3,$ and 4.

Copy and complete the table.

	$x^2 + bx + c$	Sign of c	Binomial factors	Sign of Numbers in Binomials
	$x^2 + 9x + 20$	Positive	$(x+4)(x+5)$	Both positive
55.	$x^2 - x - 20$	**Negative**	$(x+4)(x-5)$	**Positive, negative**
56.	$x^2 - 2x - 8$	**Negative**	$(x+2)(x-4)$	**Positive, negative**
57.	$x^2 - 6x + 8$	**Positive**	$(x-2)(x-4)$	**Both negative**

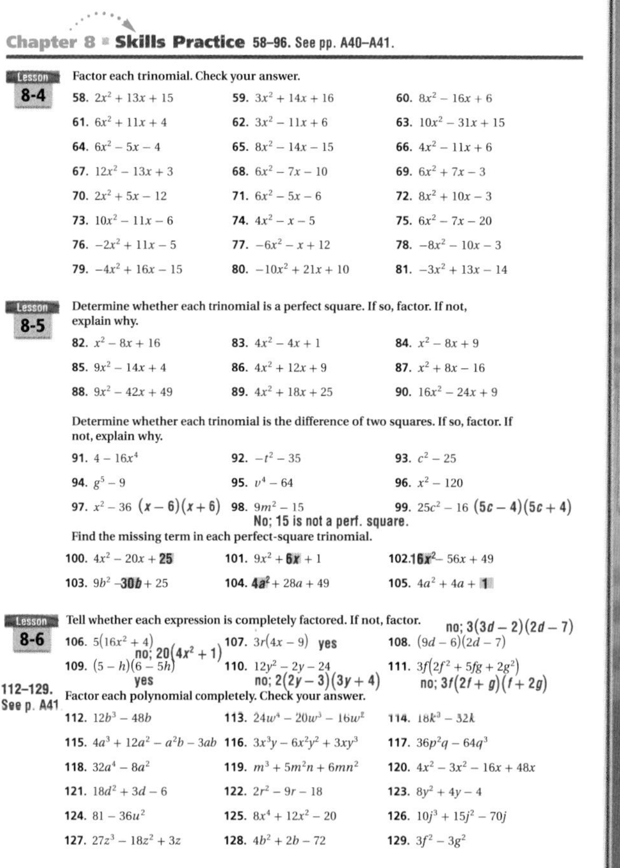

Chapter 8 ■ Skills Practice 58–96. See pp. A40–A41.

Lesson 8-4

Factor each trinomial. Check your answer.

58. $2x^2 + 13x + 15$ 59. $3x^2 + 14x + 16$ 60. $8x^2 - 16x + 6$
61. $6x^2 + 11x + 4$ 62. $3x^2 - 11x + 6$ 63. $10x^2 - 31x + 15$
64. $6x^2 - 5x - 4$ 65. $8x^2 - 14x - 15$ 66. $4x^2 - 11x + 6$
67. $12x^2 - 13x + 3$ 68. $6x^2 - 7x - 10$ 69. $6x^2 + 7x - 3$
70. $2x^2 + 5x - 12$ 71. $6x^2 - 5x - 6$ 72. $8x^2 + 10x - 3$
73. $10x^2 - 11x - 6$ 74. $4x^2 - x - 5$ 75. $6x^2 - 7x - 20$
76. $-2x^2 + 11x - 5$ 77. $-6x^2 - x + 12$ 78. $-8x^2 - 10x - 3$
79. $-4x^2 + 16x - 15$ 80. $-10x^2 + 21x + 10$ 81. $-3x^2 + 13x - 14$

Lesson 8-5

Determine whether each trinomial is a perfect square. If so, factor. If not, explain why.

82. $x^2 - 8x + 16$ 83. $4x^2 - 4x + 1$ 84. $x^2 - 8x + 9$
85. $9x^2 - 14x + 4$ 86. $4x^2 + 12x + 9$ 87. $x^2 + 8x - 16$
88. $9x^2 - 42x + 49$ 89. $4x^2 + 18x + 25$ 90. $16x^2 - 24x + 9$

Determine whether each trinomial is the difference of two squares. If so, factor. If not, explain why.

91. $4 - 16x^4$ 92. $-t^2 - 35$ 93. $c^2 - 25$
94. $g^5 - 9$ 95. $v^4 - 64$ 96. $x^2 - 120$
97. $x^2 - 36$ $(x-6)(x+6)$ 98. $9m^2 - 15$ **No; 15 is not a perf. square.** 99. $25c^2 - 16$ $(5c-4)(5c+4)$

Find the missing term in each perfect-square trinomial.

100. $4x^2 - 20x +$ **25** 101. $9x^2 +$ **6x** $+ 1$ 102. **16x²** $- 56x + 49$
103. $9b^2$ **−30b** $+ 25$ 104. **4a²** $+ 28a + 49$ 105. $4a^2 + 4a +$ **1**

Lesson 8-6

Tell whether each expression is completely factored. If not, factor.

106. $5(16x^2 + 4)$ **no; $20(4x^2 + 1)$** 107. $3r(4x - 9)$ **yes** 108. $(9d - 6)(2d - 7)$ **no; $3(3d - 2)(2d - 7)$**
109. $(5 - h)(6 - 5h)$ **yes** 110. $12y^2 - 2y - 24$ **no; $2(2y - 3)(3y + 4)$** 111. $3f(2f^2 + 5fg + 2g^2)$ **no; $3f(2f + g)(f + 2g)$**

Factor each polynomial completely. Check your answer. 112–129. See p. A41

112. $12b^3 - 48b$ 113. $24w^4 - 20w^3 - 16w^2$ 114. $18k^3 - 32k$
115. $4a^3 + 12a^2 - a^2b - 3ab$ 116. $3x^3y - 6x^2y^2 + 3xy^3$ 117. $36p^2q - 64q^3$
118. $32a^4 - 8a^2$ 119. $m^3 + 5m^2n + 6mn^2$ 120. $4x^2 - 3x^2 - 16x + 48x$
121. $18d^2 + 3d - 6$ 122. $2r^2 - 9r - 18$ 123. $8y^2 + 4y - 4$
124. $81 - 36u^2$ 125. $8x^4 + 12x^2 - 20$ 126. $10j^3 + 15j^2 - 70j$
127. $27z^3 - 18z^2 + 3z$ 128. $4b^2 + 2b - 72$ 129. $3f^2 - 3g^2$

Chapter 9 ■ Skills Practice 1–3. See p. A41.

Lesson 9-1 Tell whether each function is quadratic. Explain.

1. $y + 4x^2 = 2x - 3$ 2. $4x - y = 3$ 3. $3x^2 - 4 = y + x$

4.

x	−6	−4	−2	0	2
y	−5	−6	−4	2	11

No; the second differences are not constant.

5.

x	0	1	2	3	4
y	−5	−5	−3	1	7

Yes; the second differences are constant.

Tell whether the graph of each quadratic function opens upward or downward. Then use a table of values to graph each function. **For graphs, see p. A41.**

6. $y = -3x^2$ **downward** 7. $y = \frac{2}{3}x^2$ **upward** 8. $y = x^2 + 2$ **upward** 9. $y = -4x^2 + 2x$ **downward**

Identify the vertex of each parabola. Then find the domain and range.

10. **$(1, -3)$; D: all real numbers; R: $y \geq -3$**

11. **$(-2, 2)$; D: all real numbers; R: $y \leq 2$**

12. **$(4, 8)$; D: all real numbers; R: $y \leq 8$**

Lesson 9-2 Find the zeros of each quadratic function and the axis of symmetry of each parabola from the graph.

13. **zeros: −4 and 2; axis of symmetry: $x = -1$**

14. **zeros: 0 and 4; axis of symmetry: $x = 2$**

15. **zeros: none; axis of symmetry: $x = 1$**

Find the vertex.

16. $y = 3x^2 - 6x + 2$ **$(1, -1)$** 17. $y = -2x^2 + 8x - 3$ **$(2, 5)$** 18. $y = x^2 + 2x - 4$ **$(-1, -5)$**

Lesson 9-3 Graph each quadratic function. **19–24. See p. A41.**

19. $y = x^2 - 4x + 1$ 20. $y = -x^2 - x + 4$ 21. $y = 3x^2 - 3x + 1$

22. $y - 2 = 2x^2$ 23. $y + 3x^2 = 3x - 1$ 24. $y - 4 = x^2 + 2x$

Lesson 9-4 Order the functions from narrowest to widest.

25. $f(x) = 2x^2, g(x) = -4x^2, h(x) = -x^2$ **$g(x), f(x), h(x)$**

26. $f(x) = 3x^2, g(x) = \frac{1}{2}x^2, h(x) = -2x^2$ **$f(x), h(x), g(x)$**

27. $f(x) = 4x^2, g(x) = x^2, h(x) = -\frac{1}{4}x^2$ **$f(x), g(x), h(x)$**

28. $f(x) = 2x^2, g(x) = 5x^2, h(x) = -3x^2$ **$g(x), h(x), f(x)$**

Compare the graph of each function with the graph of $f(x) = x^2$.

29. $g(x) = 2x^2 - 2$ 30. $g(x) = -\frac{1}{2}x^2$ 31. $g(x) = -3x^2 + 1$

29–31. See p. A41.

Chapter 9 ■ Skills Practice

Lesson 9-5 Solve each quadratic equation by graphing the related function.

32. $x^2 - x - 2 = 0$ **−1, 2** 33. $x^2 - 2x + 8 = 0$ **no real solutions** 34. $2x^2 + 4x - 6 = 0$ **−3, 1**

35. $2x^2 + 9x = -4$ **$-\frac{1}{2}$, −4** 36. $2x^2 + 3 = 0$ **no real solutions** 37. $2x^2 - 2x - 12 = 0$ **−2, 3**

38. $3x^2 = -3x + 6$ **−2, 1** 39. $x^2 = 4$ **−2, 2** 40. $2x^2 + 6x - 20 = 0$ **−5, 2**

41. $-3x^2 - 2 = 0$ **no real solutions** 42. $x^2 = -2x + 8$ **−4, 2** 43. $x^2 - 2x = 15$ **−3, 5**

Lesson 9-6 Use the Zero Product Property to solve each equation. Check your answer.

44. $(x + 3)(x - 2) = 0$ **−3, 2** 45. $(x - 4)(x + 2) = 0$ **−2, 4** 46. $(x)(x - 4) = 0$ **0, 4**

47. $(2x + 6)(x - 2) = 0$ **−3, 2** 48. $(3x - 1)(x + 3) = 0$ **−3, $\frac{1}{3}$** 49. $(x)(2x - 4) = 0$ **0, 2**

Solve each quadratic equation by factoring. Check your answer.

50. $x^2 + 5x + 6 = 0$ **−3, −2** 51. $x^2 - 3x - 4 = 0$ **−1, 4** 52. $x^2 + x - 12 = 0$ **−4, 3**

53. $x^2 + x - 6 = 0$ **−3, 2** 54. $x^2 - 6x + 5 = 0$ **1, 5** 55. $x^2 + 4x - 12 = 0$ **−6, 2**

56. $x^2 = 6x - 9$ **3** 57. $2x^2 + 4x = 6$ **−3, 1** 58. $x^2 + 2x = -1$ **−1**

59. $3x^2 = 3x + 6$ **−1, 2** 60. $x^2 = x + 12$ **−3, 4** 61. $4x^2 + 8x + 4 = 0$ **−1**

Lesson 9-7 Solve using square roots. Check your answer.

62. $x^2 = 169$ **±13** 63. $x^2 = 121$ **±11** 64. $x^2 = 289$ **±17**

65. $x^2 = -64$ **no real solutions** 66. $x^2 = 81$ **±9** 67. $x^2 = -441$ **no real solutions**

68. $4x^2 - 196 = 0$ **±7** 69. $0 = 3x^2 - 48$ **±4** 70. $24x^2 + 96 = 0$ **no real solutions**

71. $10x^2 - 75 = 15$ **±3** 72. $0 = 4x^2 + 144$ **no real solutions** 73. $5x^2 - 105 = 20$ **±5**

Solve. Round to the nearest hundredth.

74. $4x^2 = 160$ **±6.32** 75. $0 = 3x^2 - 66$ **±4.69** 76. $250 - 5x^2 = 0$ **±7.07**

77. $0 = 9x^2 - 72$ **±2.83** 78. $48 - 2x^2 = 42$ **±1.73** 79. $6x^2 = 78$ **±3.61**

Lesson 9-8 Complete the square to form a perfect-square trinomial.

80. $x^2 - 8x +$ **16** 81. $x^2 + x +$ **$\frac{1}{4}$** 82. $x^2 + 10x +$ **25**

83. $x^2 - 5x +$ **$\frac{25}{4}$** 84. $x^2 + 6x +$ **9** 85. $x^2 - 7x +$ **$\frac{49}{4}$**

Solve by completing the square.

86. $x^2 + 6x = 91$ **−13, 7** 87. $x^2 + 10x = -16$ **−8, −2** 88. $x^2 - 4x = 12$ **−2, 6**

89. $x^2 - 8x = -12$ **2, 6** 90. $x^2 - 12x = -35$ **5, 7** 91. $-x^2 - 6x = 5$ **−5, −1**

92. $-x^2 - 4x + 77 = 0$ **−11, 7** 93. $-x^2 = 10x + 9$ **−9, −1** 94. $-x^2 + 63 = -2x$ **−7, 9**

Lesson 9-9 Solve using the quadratic formula. **98–100. See p. A41.**

95. $x^2 + 3x - 4 = 0$ **−4, 1** 96. $x^2 - 2x - 8 = 0$ **−2, 4** 97. $x^2 + 2x - 3 = 0$ **−3, 1**

98. $x^2 - x - 10 = 0$ 99. $2x^2 - x - 4 = 0$ 100. $2x^2 + 3x - 3 = 0$

Find the number of real solutions of each equation using the discriminant.

101. $x^2 + 4x + 1 = 0$ **2** 102. $2x^2 - 3x + 2 = 0$ **0** 103. $x^2 - 5x + 2 = 0$ **2**

104. $2x^2 - 4x + 2 = 0$ **1** 105. $x^2 + 2x - 5 = 0$ **2** 106. $2x^2 - 2x - 3 = 0$ **2**

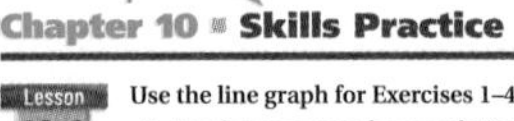

Chapter 10 ■ Skills Practice

Lesson 10-1 Use the line graph for Exercises 1–4.

1. In what year was the population the greatest? **2004**
2. Estimate the population in 2005. **19,000**
3. During which one-year period did the population increase by the greatest amount? **2003 to 2004**
4. Estimate the amount by which the population decreased from 2005 to 2006. **3,000**

Population of Midville

Use the circle graph for Exercises 5–7.

5. Which candidate received the fewest votes? **Barnes**
6. Which two candidates received approximately the same number of votes? **Jackson, Yang**
7. A total of 400 students voted in the election. How many votes did Velez receive? **152**

Voting For Student-Body President

Lesson 10-2 The daily high temperatures in degrees Celsius during a two-week period in Madison, Wisconsin, are given at right.

High Temperatures (°C)						
22	25	28	33	29	24	19
19	18	25	32	30	32	25

8–11. See p. A41.

8. Use the data to make a stem-and-leaf plot.
9. Use the data to make a frequency table with intervals.
10. Use the frequency table from Exercise 9 to make a histogram for the data.
11. Use the data to make a cumulative frequency table.

Lesson 10-3 Find the mean, median, mode, and range of each data set.

12. 42, 45, 48, 45 **mean: 45; median: 45; mode: 45; range: 6**
13. 66, 68, 68, 62, 61, 68, 65, 60 **mean: 64.75; median: 65.5; mode: 68; range: 8**

Identify the outlier in each data set, and determine how the outlier affects the mean, median, mode, and range of the data.

14. 4, 8, 15, 8, 71, 7, 6 15. 36, 7, 50, 40, 38, 48, 40

Use the data to make a box-and-whisker plot.

16. 7, 8, 10, 2, 5, 1, 10, 8, 5, 5 17. 54, 64, 50, 48, 53, 55, 57

Lesson 10-4

18. The graph shows the ages of people who listen to a radio program.
    a. Explain why the graph is misleading.
    b. What might someone believe because of the graph?
    c. Who might want to use this graph? Explain.

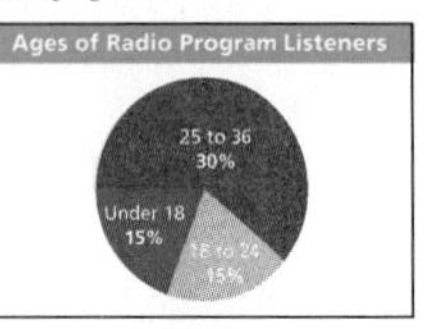

19. A researcher surveys people at the Elmwood library about the number of hours they spend reading each day. Explain why the following statement is misleading: "People in Elmwood read for an average of 1.5 hours per day."

14–19. See p. A41.

Chapter 10 ■ Skills Practice

Lesson 10-5

20. Identify the sample space and the outcome shown for the spinner at right. **Sample space: {blue, green, yellow}; outcome shown: yellow**

Write *impossible, unlikely, as likely as not, likely,* or *certain* to describe each event.

21. Two people sitting next to each other on a bus have the same birthday. **unlikely**
22. Dylan rolls a number greater than 1 on a standard number cube. **likely**

An experiment consists of randomly choosing a fruit snack from a box. Use the results in the table to find the experimental probability of each event.

Outcome	Frequency
Cherry	8
Peach	6
Blueberry	6

23. choosing a blueberry fruit snack **$\frac{3}{10}$**
24. choosing a cherry fruit snack **$\frac{2}{5}$**
25. not choosing a cherry fruit snack **$\frac{3}{5}$**

Lesson 10-6 Find the theoretical probability of each outcome.

26. rolling an even number on a number cube **$\frac{1}{2}$**
27. tossing two coins and both landing tails up **$\frac{1}{4}$**
28. randomly choosing a prime number from a bag that contains ten slips of paper numbered 1 through 10 **$\frac{2}{5}$**
29. The probability of choosing a green marble from a bag is $\frac{3}{7}$. What is the probability of not choosing a green marble? **$\frac{4}{7}$**
30. The odds against winning a game are 8:3. What is the probability of winning the game? **$\frac{3}{11}$**

Lesson 10-7 Tell whether each set of events is independent or dependent. Explain your answer.

31. You pick a bottle from a basket containing chilled drinks, and then your friend chooses a bottle. **31, 32. See p. A41.**
32. You roll a 6 on a number cube and you toss a coin that lands heads up.
33. A number cube is rolled three times. What is the probability of rolling three numbers greater than 4? **$\frac{1}{27}$**
34. An experiment consists of randomly selecting a marble from a bag, replacing it, and then selecting another marble. The bag contains 3 blue marbles, 2 orange marbles, and 5 yellow marbles. What is the probability of selecting a blue marble and then a yellow marble? **$\frac{3}{20}$**
35. Madeleine has 3 nickels and 5 quarters in her pocket. She randomly chooses one coin and does not replace it. Then she randomly chooses another coin. What is the probability that she chooses two quarters? **$\frac{5}{14}$**

Lesson 10-8 For Exercises 36 and 37, tell whether each situation involves combinations or permutations. Then give the number of possible outcomes.

36. How many different ways can three photographs be arranged in a row on a wall? **permutations; 6**
37. How many different smoothies can be made by blending two of the following fruits: oranges, bananas, strawberries, and peaches? **combinations; 6**
38. There are 6 entrants in a livestock competition at a county fair. How many different ways can the first-place, second-place, and third-place ribbons be awarded? **120**
39. An amusement park has 7 roller coasters. How many different ways can Jacinto choose 4 different roller coasters to ride? **35**

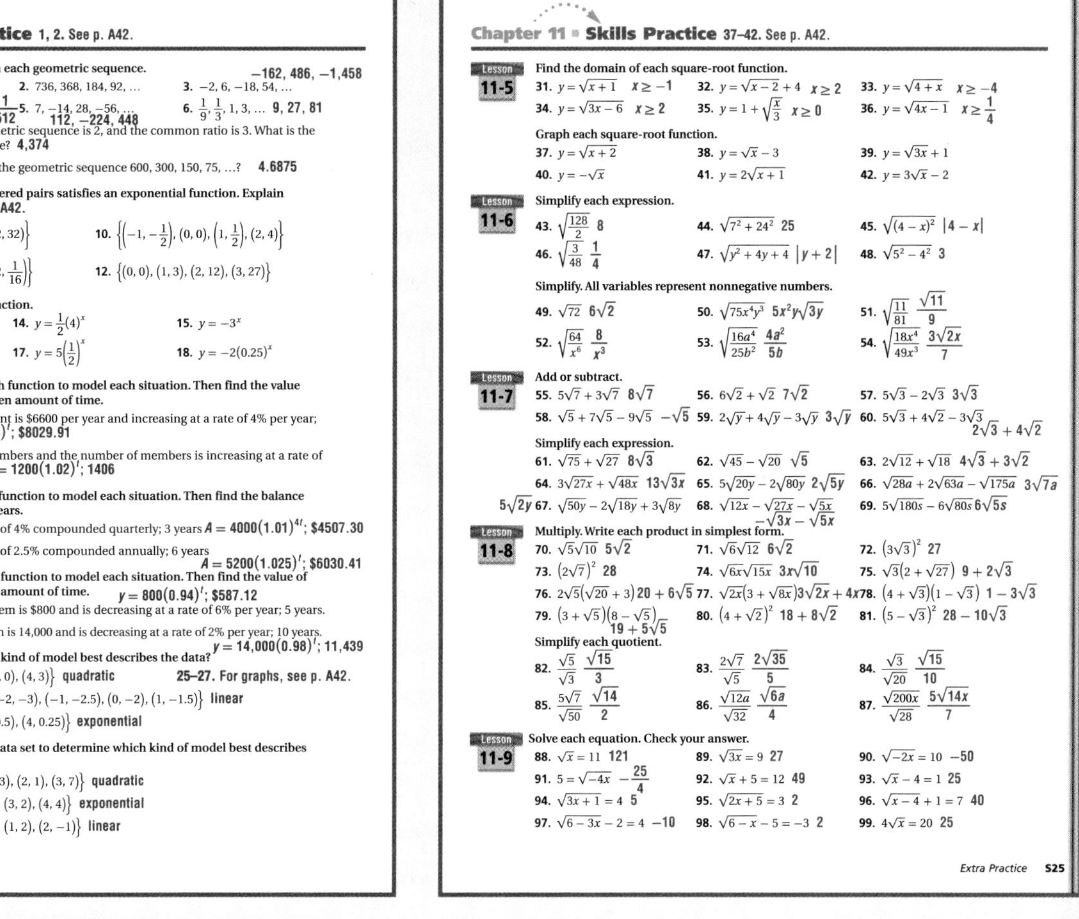

Chapter 11 ■ Skills Practice 1, 2. See p. A42.

Lesson 11-1 Find the next three terms in each geometric sequence.

1. 1, 5, 25, 125 ... 2. 736, 368, 184, 92, ... 3. −2, 6, −18, 54, ... **−162, 486, −1,458**

4. $8, 2, \frac{1}{2}, \frac{1}{8}, \ldots$ $\mathbf{\frac{1}{32}, \frac{1}{128}, \frac{1}{512}}$ 5. 7, −14, 28, −56, ... **112, −224, 448** 6. $\frac{1}{9}, \frac{1}{3}, 1, 3, \ldots$ **9, 27, 81**

7. The first term of a geometric sequence is 2, and the common ratio is 3. What is the 8th term of the sequence? **4,374**

8. What is the 8th term of the geometric sequence 600, 300, 150, 75, ...? **4.6875**

Lesson 11-2 Tell whether each set of ordered pairs satisfies an exponential function. Explain your answer. **9–18. See p. A42.**

9. $\left\{\left(-1, \frac{1}{2}\right), (0, 2), (1, 8), (2, 32)\right\}$ 10. $\left\{\left(-1, -\frac{1}{2}\right), (0, 0), \left(1, \frac{1}{2}\right), (2, 4)\right\}$

11. $\left\{(-1, 4), (0, 1), \left(1, \frac{1}{4}\right), \left(2, \frac{1}{16}\right)\right\}$ 12. $\{(0, 0), (1, 3), (2, 12), (3, 27)\}$

Graph each exponential function.

13. $y = 3(2)^x$ 14. $y = \frac{1}{2}(4)^x$ 15. $y = -3^x$

16. $y = -\frac{1}{2}(2)^x$ 17. $y = 5\left(\frac{1}{2}\right)^x$ 18. $y = -2(0.25)^x$

Lesson 11-3 Write an exponential growth function to model each situation. Then find the value of the function after the given amount of time.

19. The rent for an apartment is \$6600 per year and increasing at a rate of 4% per year; 5 years. $\mathbf{y = 6600(1.04)^t}$; **\$8029.91**

20. A museum has 1200 members and the number of members is increasing at a rate of 2% per year; 8 years. $\mathbf{y = 1200(1.02)^t}$; **1406**

Write a compound interest function to model each situation. Then find the balance after the given number of years.

21. \$4000 invested at a rate of 4% compounded quarterly; 3 years $\mathbf{A = 4000(1.01)^{4t}}$; **\$4507.30**

22. \$5200 invested at a rate of 2.5% compounded annually; 6 years $\mathbf{A = 5200(1.025)^t}$; **\$6030.41**

Write an exponential decay function to model each situation. Then find the value of the function after the given amount of time.

23. The cost of a stereo system is \$800 and is decreasing at a rate of 6% per year; 5 years. $\mathbf{y = 800(0.94)^t}$; **\$587.12**

24. The population of a town is 14,000 and is decreasing at a rate of 2% per year; 10 years. $\mathbf{y = 14{,}000(0.98)^t}$; **11,439**

Lesson 11-4 Graph each data set. Which kind of model best describes the data? **25–27. For graphs, see p. A42.**

25. $\{(0, 3), (1, 0), (2, -1), (3, 0), (4, 3)\}$ **quadratic**

26. $\{(-4, -4), (-3, -3.5), (-2, -3), (-1, -2.5), (0, -2), (1, -1.5)\}$ **linear**

27. $\{(0, 4), (1, 2), (2, 1), (3, 0.5), (4, 0.25)\}$ **exponential**

Look for a pattern in each data set to determine which kind of model best describes the data.

28. $\{(-1, -5), (0, -5), (1, -3), (2, 1), (3, 7)\}$ **quadratic**

29. $\{(0, 0.25), (1, 0.5), (2, 1), (3, 2), (4, 4)\}$ **exponential**

30. $\{(-2, 11), (-1, 8), (0, 5), (1, 2), (2, -1)\}$ **linear**

S24 *Extra Practice*

Chapter 11 ■ Skills Practice 37–42. See p. A42.

Lesson 11-5 Find the domain of each square-root function.

31. $y = \sqrt{x+1}$ $\mathbf{x \ge -1}$ 32. $y = \sqrt{x-2} + 4$ $\mathbf{x \ge 2}$ 33. $y = \sqrt{4+x}$ $\mathbf{x \ge -4}$

34. $y = \sqrt{3x-6}$ $\mathbf{x \ge 2}$ 35. $y = 1 + \sqrt{\frac{x}{3}}$ $\mathbf{x \ge 0}$ 36. $y = \sqrt{4x-1}$ $\mathbf{x \ge \frac{1}{4}}$

Graph each square-root function.

37. $y = \sqrt{x+2}$ 38. $y = \sqrt{x} - 3$ 39. $y = \sqrt{3x} + 1$

40. $y = -\sqrt{x}$ 41. $y = 2\sqrt{x+1}$ 42. $y = 3\sqrt{x} - 2$

Lesson 11-6 Simplify each expression.

43. $\sqrt{\frac{128}{2}}$ **8** 44. $\sqrt{7^2 + 24^2}$ **25** 45. $\sqrt{(4-x)^2}$ $\mathbf{|4-x|}$

46. $\sqrt{\frac{3}{48}}$ $\mathbf{\frac{1}{4}}$ 47. $\sqrt{y^2 + 4y + 4}$ $\mathbf{|y+2|}$ 48. $\sqrt{5^2 - 4^2}$ **3**

Simplify. All variables represent nonnegative numbers.

49. $\sqrt{72}$ $\mathbf{6\sqrt{2}}$ 50. $\sqrt{75x^4y^3}$ $\mathbf{5x^2y\sqrt{3y}}$ 51. $\sqrt{\frac{11}{81}}$ $\mathbf{\frac{\sqrt{11}}{9}}$

52. $\sqrt{\frac{64}{x^6}}$ $\mathbf{\frac{8}{x^3}}$ 53. $\sqrt{\frac{16a^4}{25b^2}}$ $\mathbf{\frac{4a^2}{5b}}$ 54. $\sqrt{\frac{18x^4}{49x^3}}$ $\mathbf{\frac{3\sqrt{2x}}{7}}$

Lesson 11-7 Add or subtract.

55. $5\sqrt{7} + 3\sqrt{7}$ $\mathbf{8\sqrt{7}}$ 56. $6\sqrt{2} + \sqrt{2}$ $\mathbf{7\sqrt{2}}$ 57. $5\sqrt{3} - 2\sqrt{3}$ $\mathbf{3\sqrt{3}}$

58. $\sqrt{5} + 7\sqrt{5} - 9\sqrt{5}$ $\mathbf{-\sqrt{5}}$ 59. $2\sqrt{y} + 4\sqrt{y} - 3\sqrt{y}$ $\mathbf{3\sqrt{y}}$ 60. $5\sqrt{3} + 4\sqrt{2} - 3\sqrt{3}$ $\mathbf{2\sqrt{3} + 4\sqrt{2}}$

Simplify each expression.

61. $\sqrt{75} + \sqrt{27}$ $\mathbf{8\sqrt{3}}$ 62. $\sqrt{45} - \sqrt{20}$ $\mathbf{\sqrt{5}}$ 63. $2\sqrt{12} + \sqrt{18}$ $\mathbf{4\sqrt{3} + 3\sqrt{2}}$

64. $3\sqrt{27x} + \sqrt{48x}$ $\mathbf{13\sqrt{3x}}$ 65. $5\sqrt{20y} - 2\sqrt{80y}$ $\mathbf{2\sqrt{5y}}$ 66. $\sqrt{28a} + 2\sqrt{63a} - \sqrt{175a}$ $\mathbf{3\sqrt{7a}}$

67. $\sqrt{50y} - 2\sqrt{18y} + 3\sqrt{8y}$ $\mathbf{5\sqrt{2y}}$ 68. $\sqrt{12x} - \sqrt{27x} - \sqrt{5x}$ $\mathbf{-\sqrt{3x} - \sqrt{5x}}$ 69. $5\sqrt{180s} - 6\sqrt{80s}$ $\mathbf{6\sqrt{5s}}$

Lesson 11-8 Multiply. Write each product in simplest form.

70. $\sqrt{5}\sqrt{10}$ $\mathbf{5\sqrt{2}}$ 71. $\sqrt{6}\sqrt{12}$ $\mathbf{6\sqrt{2}}$ 72. $\left(3\sqrt{3}\right)^2$ **27**

73. $\left(2\sqrt{7}\right)^2$ **28** 74. $\sqrt{6x}\sqrt{15x}$ $\mathbf{3x\sqrt{10}}$ 75. $\sqrt{3}\left(2 + \sqrt{27}\right)$ $\mathbf{9 + 2\sqrt{3}}$

76. $2\sqrt{5}\left(\sqrt{20} + 3\right)$ $\mathbf{20 + 6\sqrt{5}}$ 77. $\sqrt{2x}\left(3 + \sqrt{8x}\right)$ $\mathbf{3\sqrt{2x} + 4x}$ 78. $\left(4 + \sqrt{3}\right)\left(1 - \sqrt{3}\right)$ $\mathbf{1 - 3\sqrt{3}}$

79. $\left(3 + \sqrt{5}\right)\left(8 - \sqrt{5}\right)$ $\mathbf{19 + 5\sqrt{5}}$ 80. $\left(4 + \sqrt{2}\right)^2$ $\mathbf{18 + 8\sqrt{2}}$ 81. $\left(5 - \sqrt{3}\right)^2$ $\mathbf{28 - 10\sqrt{3}}$

Simplify each quotient.

82. $\frac{\sqrt{5}}{\sqrt{3}}$ $\mathbf{\frac{\sqrt{15}}{3}}$ 83. $\frac{2\sqrt{7}}{\sqrt{5}}$ $\mathbf{\frac{2\sqrt{35}}{5}}$ 84. $\frac{\sqrt{3}}{\sqrt{20}}$ $\mathbf{\frac{\sqrt{15}}{10}}$

85. $\frac{5\sqrt{7}}{\sqrt{50}}$ $\mathbf{\frac{\sqrt{14}}{2}}$ 86. $\frac{\sqrt{12a}}{\sqrt{32}}$ $\mathbf{\frac{\sqrt{6a}}{4}}$ 87. $\frac{\sqrt{200x}}{\sqrt{28}}$ $\mathbf{\frac{5\sqrt{14x}}{7}}$

Lesson 11-9 Solve each equation. Check your answer.

88. $\sqrt{x} = 11$ **121** 89. $\sqrt{3x} = 9$ **27** 90. $\sqrt{-2x} = 10$ **−50**

91. $5 = \sqrt{-4x}$ $\mathbf{-\frac{25}{4}}$ 92. $\sqrt{x} + 5 = 12$ **49** 93. $\sqrt{x} - 4 = 1$ **25**

94. $\sqrt{3x+1} = 4$ **5** 95. $\sqrt{2x+5} = 3$ **2** 96. $\sqrt{x-4} + 1 = 7$ **40**

97. $\sqrt{6-3x} - 2 = 4$ **−10** 98. $\sqrt{6-x} - 5 = -3$ **2** 99. $4\sqrt{x} = 20$ **25**

Extra Practice S25

Chapter 12 ■ Skills Practice

Lesson 12-1 Tell whether each relationship is an inverse variation. Explain.

1.

x	y
4	8
8	16
16	32
32	64

No; xy is not constant.

2.

x	y
2	6
3	4
6	2
12	1

Yes; xy is constant.

3.

x	y
−1	24
2	−12
4	−6
8	−3

Yes; xy is constant.

4–6. See p. A42. 4. $3xy = 10$ 5. $y - x = 6$ 6. $6xy = -1$

7, 8. For graphs, see p. A42.

7. Write and graph the inverse variation in which $y = 4$ when $x = 3$. $\mathbf{y = \frac{12}{x}}$

8. Write and graph the inverse variation in which $y = \frac{1}{2}$ when $x = 6$. $\mathbf{y = \frac{3}{x}}$

9. Let $x_1 = 6$, $y_1 = 8$, and $x_2 = 12$. Let y vary inversely as x. Find y_2. **4**

10. Let $x_1 = -4$, $y_1 = -2$, and $y_2 = 16$. Let y vary inversely as x. Find x_2. $\mathbf{-\frac{1}{2}}$

Lesson 12-2 Identify the excluded values for each rational function.

11. $y = \frac{16}{x}$ **0** 12. $y = \frac{1}{x-1}$ **1** 13. $y = -\frac{3}{x+5}$ **−5** 14. $y = \frac{20}{x+20}$ **−20**

Identify the asymptotes.

15. $y = \frac{2}{x-4}$ $\mathbf{x = 4, y = 0}$ 16. $y = \frac{8}{x+5}$ $\mathbf{x = -5, y = 0}$ 17. $y = \frac{7}{3x-2} - 6$ $\mathbf{x = \frac{2}{3}, y = -6}$ 18. $y = \frac{3}{2x-2} + 4$ $\mathbf{x = 1, y = 4}$

Graph each function. **19–26. See pp. A42–A43.**

19. $y = \frac{1}{x+3}$ 20. $y = \frac{1}{x-2}$ 21. $y = \frac{1}{x} + 4$ 22. $y = \frac{3}{x-2}$

23. $y = \frac{1}{x-3} + 2$ 24. $y = \frac{1}{x-5} - 6$ 25. $y = \frac{1}{x+2} + 5$ 26. $y = \frac{1}{x+5} + 1$

Lesson 12-3 Find the excluded value(s) of each rational expression.

27. $\frac{3}{7x}$ **0** 28. $\frac{-2}{x^2 - x}$ **0, 1** 29. $\frac{6}{x^2 + x - 12}$ **−4, 3** 30. $\frac{p+1}{p^2 + 4p - 5}$ **−5, 1**

Simplify each rational expression, if possible. Identify excluded values.

31. $\frac{4m^2}{12m}$ $\mathbf{\frac{m}{3}; m \ne 0}$ 32. $\frac{7x^5}{28x}$ $\mathbf{\frac{x^4}{4}; x \ne 0}$ 33. $\frac{4x^2 - 8x}{x-2}$ $\mathbf{4x; x \ne 2}$ 34. $\frac{2y}{y-1}$ $\mathbf{\frac{2y}{y-1}; y \ne 1}$

35. $\frac{5x^3 + 20x^2}{x+4}$ $\mathbf{5x^2; x \ne -4}$ 36. $\frac{a+1}{a-2}$ $\mathbf{\frac{a+1}{a-2}; a \ne 2}$ 37. $\frac{3y^3 + 3y}{y^2 + 1}$ **3y; no excl.** 38. $\frac{x^3 + 4x}{x^2 + 4}$ **x; no excl.**

Simplify each rational expression, if possible.

39. $\frac{b+2}{b^2 + 5b + 6}$ $\mathbf{\frac{1}{b+3}}$ 40. $\frac{x-3}{x^2 - 6x + 9}$ $\mathbf{\frac{1}{x-3}}$ 41. $\frac{y^2 - 4y - 5}{y^2 - 2y - 3}$ $\mathbf{\frac{y-5}{y-3}}$ 42. $\frac{(m+2)^2}{m^2 - 6m - 16}$ $\mathbf{\frac{m+2}{m-8}}$

43. $\frac{x^2 - 9}{x^2 + x - 12}$ $\mathbf{\frac{x+3}{x+4}}$ 44. $\frac{2-m}{3m^2 - 6m}$ $\mathbf{-\frac{1}{3m}}$ 45. $\frac{x-4}{12x^2 - 3x^3}$ $\mathbf{-\frac{1}{3x^2}}$ 46. $\frac{6-3x}{x^2 - 6x + 8}$ $\mathbf{-\frac{3}{x-4}}$

S26 *Extra Practice*

Chapter 12 ■ Skills Practice

Lesson 12-4 Multiply. Simplify your answer.

47. $\frac{4a^3}{b^3} \cdot \frac{ab}{6a^2}$ $\mathbf{\frac{2a^2}{3b^2}}$ 48. $\frac{6x^3y}{4y^4} \cdot \frac{8x^2yz^2}{3xz^5}$ $\mathbf{\frac{4x^4}{y^2z^3}}$ 49. $\frac{x-3}{2} \cdot \frac{8}{4x-12}$ **1**

50. $\frac{x-2}{x-5} \cdot \frac{2x-10}{3}$ $\mathbf{\frac{2(x-2)}{3}}$ 51. $\frac{a^2b^3}{6a^3c} \cdot \frac{9b^2}{12b^5c^2}$ $\mathbf{\frac{1}{8ac^3}}$ 52. $\frac{3x}{2x+4} \cdot \frac{3x+6}{9}$ $\mathbf{\frac{x}{2}}$

54–61. See p. A43.

53. $\frac{1}{2x+4}\left(x^2 - 2x - 8\right)$ $\mathbf{\frac{x-4}{2}}$ 54. $\frac{3x}{4x-20}\left(x^2 + x - 30\right)$ 55. $\frac{2y}{3y+15}\left(y^2 + 10y + 25\right)$

56. $\frac{4r^3 + 8r}{r^3} \cdot \frac{r}{3r^2 + 6}$ 57. $\frac{x^2 + x}{x^2 - x - 6} \cdot \frac{x-3}{6x^2 + 6x}$ 58. $\frac{a^2 - 3a - 10}{a^2 - a - 6} \cdot \frac{a^2 - 2a - 3}{a-5}$

59. $\frac{4b^2 + 4}{b-1} \cdot \frac{b^2 - 1}{8b^2 + 8}$ 60. $\frac{pq + 2q}{pq + 1} \cdot \frac{3pq + 3}{pq^2 + 2q^2}$ 61. $\frac{r^2 + 3r + 2}{4r + 4} \cdot \frac{2r + 6}{r^2 - 2r - 8}$

Divide. Simplify your answer.

62. $\frac{3x^2y^3}{x^3z^2} \div \frac{6y^4}{x^2z^5}$ $\mathbf{\frac{xz^3}{2y}}$ 63. $\frac{x^2 + 4x + 3}{3x^3 + 9x^2} \div \left(x^2 - 1\right)$ $\mathbf{\frac{1}{3x^2(x-1)}}$ 64. $\frac{p-1}{p^2 + 4p - 5} \div \frac{p^2 - 2p}{p^2 + 3p - 10}$ $\mathbf{\frac{1}{p}}$

Lesson 12-5 Add. Simplify your answer.

65. $\frac{3x}{4x^3} + \frac{5x}{4x^3}$ $\mathbf{\frac{2}{x^2}}$ 66. $\frac{x^2 + 1}{x-1} + \frac{1-3x}{x-1}$ $\mathbf{x - 2}$ 67. $\frac{2x^2}{x^2 - 2x - 3} + \frac{2x}{x^2 - 2x - 3}$ $\mathbf{\frac{2x}{x-3}}$

Subtract. Simplify your answer.

68. $\frac{5}{6y^4} - \frac{2}{6y^4}$ $\mathbf{\frac{1}{2y^4}}$ 69. $\frac{5a^2 + 1}{a^2 - a - 6} - \frac{15a + 1}{a^2 - a - 6}$ $\mathbf{\frac{5a}{a+2}}$ 70. $\frac{m^2 + 2m}{m^2 - 9} - \frac{m + 12}{m^2 - 9}$ $\mathbf{\frac{m+4}{m+3}}$

Find the LCM of the given expressions.

71. $8x^5y^8, 6x^4y^9$ $\mathbf{24x^5y^9}$ 72. $x^2 - 4, x^2 + 7x + 10$ $\mathbf{(x+2)(x-2)(x+5)}$ 73. $d^2 - 2d - 3, d^2 + d - 12$ $\mathbf{(d+1)(d-3)(d+4)}$

Add or subtract. Simplify your answer.

74. $\frac{5}{y^2} - \frac{3}{4y^2}$ $\mathbf{\frac{17}{4y^2}}$ 75. $\frac{5}{x^2 - x - 6} + \frac{1}{x+2}$ $\mathbf{\frac{1}{x-3}}$ 76. $\frac{3x}{x-2} - \frac{x}{2-x}$ $\mathbf{\frac{4x}{x-2}}$

Lesson 12-6 Divide. **77–79. See p. A43.**

77. $\left(12y^5 - 16y^2 + 4y\right) \div 4y^2$ 78. $\left(6m^4 - 18m + 3\right) \div 6m^2$ 79. $\left(16x^4 + 20x^3 - 4x\right) \div -4x^3$

80. $\frac{b^2 - 4b - 5}{b+1}$ $\mathbf{b - 5}$ 81. $\frac{2x^2 + 9x + 4}{x+4}$ $\mathbf{2x + 1}$ 82. $\frac{6a^2 - 13a - 5}{3a + 1}$ $\mathbf{2a - 5}$

Divide using long division.

83. $\left(a^2 - 5a - 6\right) \div (a + 1)$ $\mathbf{a - 6}$ 84. $\left(2x^2 + 10x + 8\right) \div (x + 4)$ $\mathbf{2x + 2}$ 85. $\left(3y^2 - 11y + 10\right) \div (y - 2)$ $\mathbf{3y - 5}$

86. $\left(3x^2 - 2x - 7\right) \div (x - 2)$ 87. $\left(2x^2 + 2x - 9\right) \div (x + 3)$ 88. $\left(5x^3 + 2x^2 - 4\right) \div (x - 2)$

Lesson 12-7 Solve. Check your answer. **86–88. See p. A43.**

89. $\frac{5}{x+1} = \frac{4}{x-1}$ **9** 90. $\frac{4}{t} = \frac{10}{t+9}$ **6** 91. $\frac{8}{m} = \frac{6}{m+1}$ **−4**

92. $\frac{4}{a-2} = \frac{8}{a+1}$ **5** 93. $\frac{3}{2y+4} = \frac{1}{y}$ **4** 94. $\frac{5}{4w-2} = \frac{6}{5w-2}$ **−2**

95. $\frac{1}{2} + \frac{3}{2m} = -\frac{1}{m^2}$ **−1, −2** 96. $\frac{x}{2} + \frac{3}{2} = \frac{2}{x}$ **−4, 1** 97. $1 - \frac{3}{a} = \frac{10}{a^2}$ **−2, 5**

Solve. Identify any extraneous solutions.

98. $\frac{3}{x+4} = \frac{x-5}{x+4}$ **8; −4 is ext.** 99. $\frac{2}{x} = \frac{x+2}{x^2 - 4}$ **4; −2 is ext.** 100. $\frac{4x}{x-4} - 7 = \frac{16}{x-4}$ **no sol.; 4 is ext.**

Extra Practice S27

Extra Practice

Chapter 1 ■ Applications Practice

Biology **Use the following information for Exercises 1 and 2.**

In general, skin cells in the human body contain 46 chromosomes. *(Lesson 1-1)*

1. Write an expression for the number of chromosomes in c skin cells. **46c**
2. Find the number of chromosomes in 8, 15, and 50 skin cells. **368; 690; 2300**
3. On a winter day in Fairbanks, Alaska, the temperature dropped from 12 °F to −16 °F. How many degrees did the temperature drop? *(Lesson 1-2)* **28 degrees**
4. **Geography** The elevation of the Dead Sea in Jordan is −411 meters. The greatest elevation on Earth is Mt. Everest, at 8850 meters. What is the difference in elevation between these two locations? *(Lesson 1-2)* **9261 m**
5. Jeremy is raising money for his school by selling magazine subscriptions. Each subscription costs $16.75. During the first week, he sells 12 subscriptions. How much money does he raise? *(Lesson 1-3)* **$201**
6. As a service charge, Nadine's checking account is adjusted by −$3 each month. What is the total amount of the adjustment over the course of one year? *(Lesson 1-3)* **−$36**
7. To go from one figure to the next in the sequence of figures, each square is split into four smaller squares. How many squares will be in Figure 5? *(Lesson 1-4)* **1024**

Figure 0 Figure 1 Figure 2

8. When you fold a sheet of paper in half and then open it, the crease creates 2 regions. Folding the paper in half 2 times creates 4 regions. How many regions do you create when you fold a sheet of paper in half 5 times? *(Lesson 1-4)* **32**
9. Dan began his stamp collection with just 5 stamps in the first year. Every year thereafter, his collection grew 5 times as large as the year before. How many stamps were in Dan's collection after 4 years? *(Lesson 1-4)* **625**
10. An art museum exhibits a square painting that has an area of 75 square feet. Find its side length to the nearest tenth. *(Lesson 1-5)* **8.7 ft**
11. **Travel** The base of the Washington Monument in Washington, D.C., is a square with an area of 336 yards. Find the length of one side of the monument's base to the nearest tenth. *(Lesson 1-5)* **18.3 yd**
12. The toll to cross a bridge is $2 for cars, $5 for trucks, and $10 for buses. The total amount of money collected can be found using the expression $2C + 5T + 10B$. Use the table to find the total amount of money collected between 10 A.M. and 11 A.M. *(Lesson 1-6)* **$338**

Bridge Tolls, 10 A.M. to 11 A.M.

Type of Vehicle	Number
Car C	104
Truck T	20
Bus B	3

13. The expression $\frac{5}{9}(F - 32)$ converts a temperature F in degrees Fahrenheit to a temperature in degrees Celsius. Convert 77 °F to degrees Celsius. *(Lesson 1-6)* **25 °C**

Use the following information for Exercises 14 and 15.

An airplane has 12 rows of seats in first class and 35 rows of seats in coach. Each row has the same number of seats. *(Lesson 1-7)*

14. The total number of seats in the plane is $12x + 35x$, where x is the number of seats in a row. Simplify the expression. **47x**
15. Find the total number of seats given that the plane has 6 seats per row. **282**

Use the following information for Exercises 16 and 17.

A sales representative earns $680 per week plus a $40 commission for each sale. *(Lesson 1-8)*

16. Write a rule for the sales representative's weekly earnings. $y = 680 + 40x$
17. Write ordered pairs for the representative's weekly earnings for 5, 8, and 10 sales. **(5, 880); (8, 1000); (15, 1080)**

Chapter 2 ■ Applications Practice

1. **Economics** In 2004, the average price of an ounce of gold was $47 more than the average price in 2003. The 2004 price was $410. Write and solve an equation to find the average price of an ounce of gold in 2003. *(Lesson 2-1)* $x + 47 = 410$; **$363**
2. During a renovation, 36 seats were removed from a theater. The theater now seats 580 people. Write and solve an equation to find the number of seats in the theater before the renovation. *(Lesson 2-1)* $x - 36 = 580$; **616**
3. A case of juice drinks contains 12 bottles and costs $18. Write and solve an equation to find the cost of each drink. *(Lesson 2-2)* $12x = 18$; **$1.50**
4. **Astronomy** Objects weigh about 3 times as much on Earth as they do on Mars. A rock weighs 42 lb on Mars. Write and solve an equation to find the rock's weight on Earth. *(Lesson 2-2)* $42 = \frac{1}{3}x$; **126 lb**
5. The county fair's admission fee is $8 and each ride costs $2.50. Sonia spent a total of $25.50. How many rides did she go on? *(Lesson 2-3)* **7**
6. At the beginning of a block party, the temperature was 84°. During the party, the temperature dropped 3° every hour. At the end of the party, the temperature was 66°. How long was the party? *(Lesson 2-3)* **6 hours**
7. **Consumer Economics** A health insurance policy costs $700 per year, plus $15 for each visit to the doctor's office. A different plan costs $560 per year, but each office visit is $50. Find the number of office visits for which the two plans have the same total cost. *(Lesson 2-4)* **4**
8. **Geometry** The formula $A = \frac{1}{2}bh$ gives the area A of a triangle with base b and height h. *(Lesson 2-5)*
   a. Solve $A = \frac{1}{2}bh$ for h. $h = \frac{2A}{b}$
   b. Find the height of a triangle with an area of 30 square feet and a base of 6 feet. **10 ft**
9. Charles is hanging a poster on his wall. He wants the top of the poster to be 84 inches from the floor but would be happy for it to be 3 inches higher or lower. Write and solve an absolute-value equation to find the maximum and minimum acceptable heights. *(Lesson 2-6)* $|x - 84| = 3$; **87 in.; 81 in.**
10. The ratio of students to adults on a school trip is 9:2. There are 6 adults on the trip. How many students are there? *(Lesson 2-7)* **27**
11. A cheetah can reach speeds of up to 103 feet per second. Use dimensional analysis to convert the cheetah's speed to miles per hour. Round to the nearest tenth. *(Lesson 2-7)* **70.2 mi/h**
12. Write and solve a proportion to find the height of the flagpole. *(Lesson 2-8)* $\frac{5.4}{8.1} = \frac{x}{27}$; **18 ft**

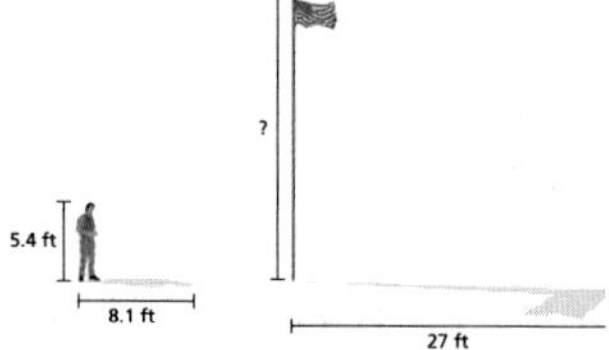

13. Paul has 8 jazz CDs. The jazz CDs are 5% of his collection. How many CDs does Paul have? *(Lesson 2-9)* **160**
14. Miguel earns an annual salary of $38,000 plus a 3.5% commission on sales. His sales for one year were $90,000. Find his total salary for the year. *(Lesson 2-10)* **$41,150**
15. How long would it take $3600 to earn simple interest of $450 at an annual interest rate of 5%? *(Lesson 2-10)* **2.5 years**
16. A store sells swimsuits at a 30% discount. What is the final price of a swimsuit that originally sold for $28? *(Lesson 2-11)* **$19.60**
17. Mei sells jam at a farmer's market for $4.20 per jar. Each jar costs Mei $3 to make. What is the markup as a percent? *(Lesson 2-11)* **40%**

Chapter 3 ■ Applications Practice 1–4, 11, 12. See p. A43.

1. At a food-processing factory, each box of cereal must weigh at least 15 ounces. Define a variable and write an inequality for the acceptable weights of the cereal boxes. Graph the solutions. *(Lesson 3-1)*
2. In order to qualify for a discounted entry fee at a museum, a visitor must be less than 13 years old. Define a variable and write an inequality for the ages that qualify for the discounted entry fee. Graph the solutions. *(Lesson 3-1)*
3. A restaurant can seat no more than 102 customers at one time. There are already 96 customers in the restaurant. Write and solve an inequality to find out how many additional customers could be seated in the restaurant. *(Lesson 3-2)*
4. **Meteorology** A hurricane is a tropical storm with a wind speed of at least 74 mi/h. A meteorologist is tracking a storm whose current wind speed is 63 mi/h. Write and solve an inequality to find out how much greater the wind speed must be in order for this storm to be considered a hurricane. *(Lesson 3-2)*

Hobbies **Use the following information for Exercises 5–7.**

When setting up an aquarium, it is recommended that you have no more than one inch of fish per gallon of water. For example, in a 30-gallon tank, the total length of the fish should be at most 30 inches. *(Lesson 3-3)*

Freshwater Fish

Name	Length (in.)
Red tail catfish	3.5
Blue gourami	1.5

5. Write an inequality to show the possible numbers of blue gourami you can put in a 10-gallon aquarium. $1.5x \leq 10$
6. Find the possible numbers of blue gourami you can put in a 10-gallon aquarium. **0, 1, 2, 3, 4, 5, or 6**
7. Find the possible numbers of red tail catfish you can put in a 20-gallon aquarium. **0, 1, 2, 3, 4, or 5**
8. The admission fee at an amusement park is $12, and each ride costs $3.50. The park also offers an all-day pass with unlimited rides for $33. For what numbers of rides is it cheaper to buy the all-day pass? *(Lesson 3-4)* **greater than 6 rides**
9. The table shows the cost of Internet access at two different cafes. For how many hours of access is the cost at Cyber Station less than the cost at Web World? *(Lesson 3-5)* **greater than 16 hours**

Internet Access

Cafe	Cost
Cyber Station	$12 one-time membership fee $1.50 per hour
Web World	No membership fee $2.25 per hour

10. Larissa is considering two summer jobs. A job at the mall pays $400 per week plus $15 for every hour of overtime. A job at the movie theater pays $360 per week plus $20 for every hour of overtime. How many hours of overtime would Larissa have to work in order for the job at the movie theater to pay a higher salary than the job at the mall? *(Lesson 3-5)* **greater than 8 hours**
11. **Health** For maximum safety, it is recommended that food be stored at a temperature between 34 °F and 40 °F inclusive. Write a compound inequality to show the temperatures that are within the recommended range. Graph the solutions. *(Lesson 3-6)*
12. **Physics** Color is determined by the wavelength of light. Wavelengths are measured in nanometers (nm). Our eyes see the color green when light has a wavelength between 492 nm and 577 nm inclusive. Write a compound inequality to show the wavelengths that produce green light. Graph the solutions. *(Lesson 3-6)*
13. Allison ran a mile in 8 minutes. She wants to run a second mile within 0.75 minute of her time for the first mile. Write and solve an absolute-value inequality to find the range of acceptable times for the second mile. *(Lesson 3-7)* $|x - 8| < 0.75$; $7.25 < x < 8.75$

Chapter 4 ■ Applications Practice 1–4, 7–8. See p. A43.

1. Donnell drove on the highway at a constant speed and then slowed down as she approached her exit. Sketch a graph to show the speed of Donnell's car over time. Tell whether the graph is continuous or discrete. *(Lesson 4-1)*
2. Lori is buying mineral water for a party. The bottles are available in six-packs. Sketch a graph showing the number of bottles Lori will have if she buys 1, 2, 3, 4, or 5 six-packs. Tell whether the graph is continuous or discrete. *(Lesson 4-1)*
3. **Health** To exercise effectively, it is important to know your maximum heart rate. You can calculate your maximum heart rate in beats per minute by subtracting your age from 220. *(Lesson 4-2)*
   a. Express the age x and the maximum heart rate y as a relation in table form by showing the maximum heart rate for people who are 20, 30, 35, and 40 years old.
   b. Is this relation a function? Explain.
4. **Sports** The table shows the number of games won by four baseball teams and the number of home runs each team hit. Is this relation a function? Explain. *(Lesson 4-2)*

Season Statistics

Wins	Home Runs
95	185
93	133
80	140
93	167

5. Michael uses 5.5 cups of flour for each loaf of bread that he bakes. He plans to bake a maximum of 4 loaves. Write a function to describe the number of cups of flour used. Find a reasonable domain and range for the function. *(Lesson 4-3)* $f(x) = 5.5x$; D: {0, 1, 2, 3, 4}; R: {0, 5.5, 11, 16.5, 22}
6. A gym offers the following special rate. New members pay a $425 initiation fee and then pay $90 per year for 1, 2, or 3 years. Write a function to describe the situation. Find a reasonable domain and range for the function. *(Lesson 4-3)* $f(x) = 425 + 90x$; D: {1, 2, 3}; R: {$515, $605, $695}
7. The function $y = 3.5x$ describes the number of miles y that the average turtle can walk in x hours. Graph the function. Use the graph to estimate how many miles a turtle can walk in 4.5 hours. *(Lesson 4-4)*
8. **Earth Science** The Kangerdlugssuaq glacier in Greenland is flowing into the sea at the rate of 1.6 meters per hour. The function $y = 1.6x$ describes the number of meters y that flow into the sea in x hours. Graph the function. Use the graph to estimate the number of meters that flow into the sea in 8 hours. *(Lesson 4-4)*
9. The scatter plot shows a relationship between the number of lemonades sold in a day and the day's high temperature. Based on this relationship, predict the number of lemonades that will be sold on a day when the high temperature is 96 °F. *(Lesson 4-5)* **48**

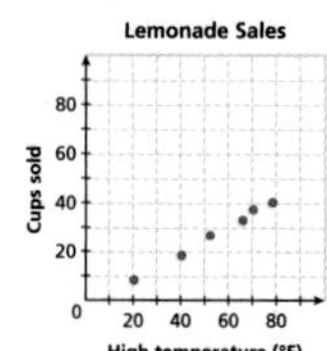

10. In month 1 the Elmwood Public Library had 85 Spanish books in its collection. Each month, the librarian plans to order 8 new Spanish books. How many Spanish books will the library have in month 15? *(Lesson 4-6)* **197**
11. Nikki purchases a card that she can use to ride the bus in her town. Each time she rides the bus $1.50 is deducted from the value of the card. After her first ride, there is $43.50 left on the card. How much money will be left on the card after Nikki has taken 12 bus rides? *(Lesson 4-6)* **$27**

Chapter 5 ■ Applications Practice 1–4, 7, 8b, 10, 11. See pp. A43–A44.

1. Jennifer is having prints made of her photographs. Each print costs \$1.50. The function $f(x) = 1.50x$ gives the total cost of the x prints. Graph this function and give its domain and range. *(Lesson 5-1)*

2. The Chang family lives 400 miles from Denver. They drive to Denver at a constant speed of 50 mi/h. The function $f(x) = 400 - 50x$ gives their distance in miles from Denver after x hours. *(Lesson 5-2)*
   a. Graph this function and find the intercepts.
   b. What does each intercept represent?

3. **History** The table shows the number of nations in the United Nations in different years. Find the rate of change for each time interval. During which time interval did the U.N. grow at the greatest rate? *(Lesson 5-3)*

Year	1945	1950	1960	1975
Number of Nations	51	60	99	144

4. The graph shows the temperature of an oven at different times. Find the slope of the line. Then tell what the slope represents. *(Lesson 5-4)*

Oven Temperature

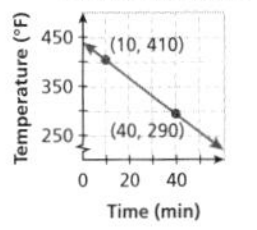

Temperature (°F): 250, 350, 450; Time (min): 0, 20, 40; points (10, 410), (40, 290)

5. A straight highway connects the towns of Dale and Winslow. On a map, the coordinates of Dale are (5, 16), and the coordinates of Winslow are (9, 24). A rest area is located on the highway at the midpoint between the towns. What are the map coordinates of the rest area? *(Lesson 5-5)* **(7, 20)**

6. On a map, a campground is at (3, 5), and a fishing area is at (8, 4). Each unit on the map represents 0.1 mile. To the nearest tenth of a mile, what is the distance between the campground and the fishing area? *(Lesson 5-5)* **0.5 mi**

7. **Sports** Competitive race-walkers move at a speed of about 9 miles per hour. Write a direct variation equation for the distance y that a race-walker will cover in x hours. Then graph. *(Lesson 5-6)*

8. A bicycle rental costs \$10 plus \$1.50 per hour. The cost as a function of the number of hours is shown in the graph. *(Lesson 5-7)*

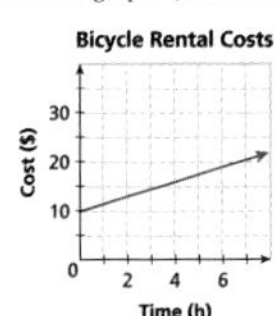

   a. Write an equation that represents the cost as a function of the number of hours. **$y = 1.5x + 10$**
   b. Identify the slope and y-intercept and describe their meaning.
   c. Find the cost of renting a bike for 6 hours. **\$19**

9. A hot-air balloon is moving at a constant rate. Its altitude is a linear function of time, as shown in the table. Write an equation in slope-intercept form that represents this function. Then find the balloon's altitude after 25 minutes. *(Lesson 5-8)* **$y = -5x + 250$; 125 m**

Balloon's Altitude	
Time (min)	Altitude (m)
0	250
7	215
12	190

10. **Geometry** Show that the points $A(2, 3)$, $B(3, 1)$, $C(-1, -1)$, and $D(-2, 1)$ are the vertices of a rectangle. *(Lesson 5-9)*

11. A phone plan for international calls costs \$12.50 per month plus \$0.04 per minute. The monthly cost for x minutes of calls is given by the function $f(x) = 0.04x + 12.50$. How will the graph change if the phone company raises the monthly fee to \$14.50? if the cost per minute is raised to \$0.05? *(Lesson 5-10)*

Chapter 6 ■ Applications Practice 4, 9–14. See p. A44.

1. Net Sounds, an online music store, charges \$12 per CD plus \$3 for shipping and handling. Web Discs charges \$10 per CD plus \$9 for shipping and handling. For how many CDs will the cost be the same? What will that cost be? *(Lesson 6-1)* **3; \$39**

2. At Rocco's Restaurant, a large pizza costs \$12 plus \$1.25 for each additional topping. At Pizza Palace, a large pizza costs \$15 plus \$0.75 for each additional topping. For how many toppings will the cost be the same? What will that cost be? *(Lesson 6-1)* **6; \$19.50**

Use the following information for Exercises 3 and 4.

The coach of a baseball team is deciding between two companies that manufacture team jerseys. One company charges a \$60 setup fee and \$25 per jersey. The other company charges a \$200 setup fee and \$15 per jersey. *(Lesson 6-2)*

3. For how many jerseys will the cost at the two companies be the same? What will that cost be? **14; \$410**

4. The coach is planning to purchase 20 jerseys. Which company is the better option? Why?

5. **Geometry** The length of a rectangle is 5 inches greater than the width. The sum of the length and width is 41 inches. Find the length and width of the rectangle. *(Lesson 6-2)* **23 in.; 18 in.**

6. At a movie theater, tickets cost \$9.50 for adults and \$6.50 for children. A group of 7 moviegoers pays a total of \$54.50. How many adults and how many children are in the group? *(Lesson 6-3)* **3 adults, 4 children**

7. **Business** A grocer is buying large quantities of fruit to resell at his store. He purchases apples at \$0.50 per pound and pears at \$0.75 per pound. The grocer spends a total of \$17.25 for 27 pounds of fruit. How many pounds of each fruit does he buy? *(Lesson 6-3)* **12 lb of apples; 15 lb of pears**

8. Bricks are available in two sizes. Large bricks weigh 9 pounds, and small bricks weigh 4.5 pounds. A bricklayer has 14 bricks that weigh a total of 90 pounds. How many of each type of brick are there? *(Lesson 6-3)* **6 large, 8 small**

9. **Sports** The table shows the time it took two runners to complete the Boston Marathon in several different years. If the patterns continue, will Shanna ever complete the marathon in the same number of minutes as Maria? Explain. *(Lesson 6-4)*

Marathon Times (min)				
	2003	2004	2005	2006
Shanna	190	182	174	166
Maria	175	167	159	151

10. Jordan leaves his house and rides his bike at 10 mi/h. After he goes 4 miles, his brother Tim leaves the house and rides in the same direction at 12 mi/h. If their rates stay the same, will Tim ever catch up to Jordan? Explain. *(Lesson 6-4)*

11. Charmaine is buying almonds and cashews for a reception. She wants to spend no more than \$18. Almonds cost \$4 per pound, and cashews cost \$5 per pound. Write a linear inequality to describe the situation. Graph the solutions. Then give two combinations of nuts that Charmaine could buy. *(Lesson 6-5)*

12. Luis is buying T-shirts to give out at a school fund-raiser. He must spend less than \$100 for the shirts. Child shirts cost \$5 each, and adult shirts cost \$8 each. Write a linear inequality to describe the situation. Graph the solutions. Then give two combinations of shirts that Luis could buy. *(Lesson 6-5)*

13. Nicholas is buying treats for his dog. Beef cubes cost \$3 per pound, and liver cubes cost \$2 per pound. He wants to buy at least 2 pounds of each type of treat, and he wants to spend no more than \$14. Graph all possible combinations of the treats that Nicholas could buy. List two possible combinations. *(Lesson 6-6)*

14. **Geometry** The perimeter of a rectangle is at most 20 inches. The length and the width are each at least 3 inches. Graph all possible combinations of lengths and widths that result in such a rectangle. List two possible combinations. *(Lesson 6-6)*

Chapter 7 ■ Applications Practice

1. The eye of a bee is about 10^{-3} m in diameter. Simplify this expression. *(Lesson 7-1)* **0.001 m**

2. A typical stroboscopic camera has a shutter speed of 10^{-6} seconds. Simplify this expression. *(Lesson 7-1)* **0.000001 s**

3. **Space Exploration** During a mission that took place in August, 2005, the Space Shuttle *Discovery* traveled a total distance of 9.3×10^6 km. The Space Shuttle's velocity was 28,000 km/h. *(Lesson 7-2)*
   a. Write the total distance that the Space Shuttle traveled in standard form. **9,300,000 km**
   b. Write the Space Shuttle's velocity in scientific notation. **2.8×10^4 km/h**

4. There are approximately 10,000,000 grains in a pound of salt. Write this number in scientific notation. *(Lesson 7-2)* **1×10^7**

5. A high-speed centrifuge spins at a speed of 2×10^4 rotations per minute. How many rotations does it make in one hour? Write your answer in scientific notation. *(Lesson 7-3)* **1.2×10^6**

6. **Astronomy** Earth travels approximately 5.8×10^8 miles as it makes one orbit of the Sun. How far does Earth travel in 50 years? (*Note:* One year is one orbit of the Sun.) Write your answer in scientific notation. *(Lesson 7-3)* **2.9×10^{10} mi**

7. **Geography** In 2005, the population of Indonesia was 2.4×10^8. This was 8 times the population of Afghanistan. What was the population of Afghanistan in 2005? Write your answer in standard form. *(Lesson 7-4)* **30,000,000**

8. The Golden Gate Bridge weighs about 1.8×10^9 lb. The Eiffel Tower weighs about 2.25×10^7 lb. How many times heavier is the Golden Gate Bridge than the Eiffel Tower? Write your answer in standard form. *(Lesson 7-4)* **80**

9. Carl has 4 identical cubes lined up in a row and wants to find the total length of the cubes. He knows that the volume of one cube is 343 in³. Use the formula $s = V^{\frac{1}{3}}$ to find the length of one cube. What is the length of the row of cubes? *(Lesson 7-5)* **28 in.**

10. A rock is thrown off a 220-foot cliff with an initial velocity of 50 feet per second. The height of the rock above the ground is given by the polynomial $-16t^2 - 50t + 220$, where t is the time in seconds after the rock has been thrown. What is the height of the rock above the ground after 2 seconds? *(Lesson 7-6)* **56 ft**

11. The sum of the first n natural numbers is given by the polynomial $\frac{1}{2}n^2 + \frac{1}{2}n$. Use this polynomial to find the sum of the first 9 natural numbers. *(Lesson 7-6)* **45**

12. **Biology** The population of insects in a meadow depends on the temperature. A biologist models the population of insect A with the polynomial $0.02x^2 + 0.5x + 8$ and the population of insect B with the polynomial $0.04x^2 - 0.2x + 12$, where x represents the temperature in degrees Fahrenheit. *(Lesson 7-7)* **$0.06x^2 + 0.3x + 20$**
   a. Write a polynomial that represents the total population of both insects.
   b. Write a polynomial that represents the difference of the populations of insect B and insect A. **$0.02x^2 - 0.7x + 4$**

13. **Geometry** The length of the rectangle shown is 1 inch longer than 3 times the width.
   a. Write a polynomial that represents the area of the rectangle. **$3x^2 + x$**
   b. Find the area of the rectangle when the width is 4 inches. *(Lesson 7-8)* **52 in²**

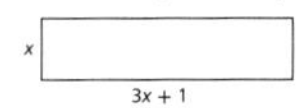

14. A cabinet maker starts with a square piece of wood and then cuts a square hole from its center as shown. Write a polynomial that represents the area of the remaining piece of wood. *(Lesson 7-9)* **$6x + 27$**

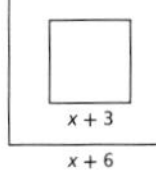

Chapter 8 ■ Applications Practice

1. Ms. Andrews's class has 12 boys and 18 girls. For a class picture, the students will stand in rows on a set of steps. Each row must have the same number of students, and each row will contain only boys or girls. How many rows will there be if Ms. Andrews puts the maximum number of students in each row? *(Lesson 8-1)* **5**

2. A museum director is planning an exhibit of Native American baskets. There are 40 baskets from North America and 32 baskets from South America. The baskets will be displayed on shelves so that each shelf has the same number of baskets. Baskets from North and South America will not be placed together on the same shelf. How many shelves will be needed if each shelf holds the maximum number of baskets? *(Lesson 8-1)* **9**

3. The area of a rectangular painting is $(3x^2 + 5x)$ ft². Factor this polynomial to find possible expressions for the dimensions of the painting. *(Lesson 8-2)* **x ft, $(3x + 5)$ ft**

4. **Geometry** The surface area of a cylinder with radius r and height h is given by the expression $2\pi r^2 + 2\pi rh$. Factor this expression. *(Lesson 8-2)* **$2\pi r(r + h)$**

5. The area of a rectangular classroom in square feet is given by $x^2 + 9x + 18$. The width of the classroom is $(x + 3)$ ft. What is the length of the classroom? *(Lesson 8-3)* **$(x + 6)$ ft**

Gardening Use the following information for Exercises 6 and 7.

A rectangular flower bed has a width of $(x + 4)$ ft. The bed will be enlarged by increasing the length, as shown. *(Lesson 8-3)*

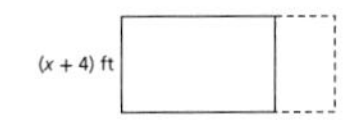

6. The original flower bed has an area of $(x^2 + 9x + 20)$ ft². What is its length? **$(x + 5)$ ft**

7. The enlarged flower bed will have an area of $(x^2 + 12x + 32)$ ft². What will be the new length of the flower bed? **$(x + 8)$ ft**

8. A rectangular poster has an area of $(6x^2 + 19x + 15)$ in². The width of the poster is $(2x + 3)$ in. What is the length of the poster? *(Lesson 8-4)* **$(3x + 5)$ in.**

9. **Physics** The height of an object thrown upward with a velocity of 38 feet per second from an initial height of 5 feet can be modeled by the polynomial $-16t^2 + 38t + 5$, where t is the time in seconds. Factor this expression. Then use the factored expression to find the object's height after $\frac{1}{2}$ second. *(Lesson 8-4)* **$-1(8t + 1)(2t - 5)$; 20 ft**

10. A rectangular pool has an area of $(9x^2 + 30x + 25)$ ft². The dimensions of the pool are of the form $ax + b$, where a and b are whole numbers. Find an expression for the perimeter of the pool. Then find the perimeter when $x = 5$. *(Lesson 8-5)* **$12x + 20$; 80**

11. **Geometry** The area of a square is $9x^2 - 24x + 16$. Find the length of each side of the square. Is it possible for x to equal 1 in this situation? Why or why not? *(Lesson 8-5)* **11. See p. A44.**

Architecture Use the following information for Exercises 12–14.

An architect is designing a rectangular hotel room. A balcony that is 5 feet wide runs along the length of the room, as shown in the figure. *(Lesson 8-6)*

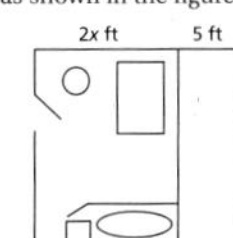

12. The area of the room, including the balcony, is $(4x^2 + 12x + 5)$ ft². Tell whether the polynomial is fully factored. Explain. **No; it can be factored as $(2x + 5)(2x + 1)$.**

13. Find the length and width of the room (including the balcony). **$(2x + 5)$ ft; $(2x + 1)$ ft**

14. How long is the balcony when $x = 9$? **19 ft**

Chapter 9 ■ Applications Practice

1. The table shows the height of a ball at various times after being thrown into the air. Tell whether the function is quadratic. Explain. *(Lesson 9-1)* **Yes; the second differences are constant.**

Time (s)	0	0.5	1	1.5	2
Height (ft)	4	20	28	28	20

2. The height of the curved roof of a camping tent can be modeled by $f(x) = -0.5x^2 + 3x$, where x is the width in feet. Find the height of the tent at its tallest point. *(Lesson 9-2)* **4.5 ft**

3. **Engineering** A small bridge passes over a stream. The height in feet of the bridge's curved arch support can be modeled by $f(x) = -0.25x^2 + 2x + 1.5$, where the x-axis represents the level of the water. Find the greatest height of the arch support. *(Lesson 9-2)* **5.5 ft**

4. **Sports** The height in meters of a football that is kicked from the ground is approximated by $f(x) = -5x^2 + 20x$, where x is the time in seconds after the ball is kicked. Find the ball's maximum height and the time it takes the ball to reach this height. Then find how long the ball is in the air. *(Lesson 9-3)* **20 m; 2 s; 4 s**

5. **Physics** Two golf balls are dropped, one from a height of 400 feet and the other from a height of 576 feet. *(Lesson 9-4)* **5. See p. A44.**
   a. Compare the graphs that show the time it takes each golf ball to reach the ground.
   b. Use the graphs to tell when each golf ball reaches the ground.

6. A model rocket is launched into the air with an initial velocity of 144 feet per second. The quadratic function $y = -16x^2 + 144x$ models the height of the rocket after x seconds. How long is the rocket in the air? *(Lesson 9-5)* **9 s**

7. A gymnast jumps on a trampoline. The quadratic function $y = -16x^2 + 24x$ models her height in feet above the trampoline after x seconds. How long is the gymnast in the air? *(Lesson 9-5)* **1.5 s**

8. A child standing on a rock tosses a ball into the air. The height of the ball above the ground is modeled by $h = -16t^2 + 28t + 8$, where h is the height in feet and t is the time in seconds. Find the time it takes the ball to reach the ground. *(Lesson 9-6)* **2 s**

9. A fireworks rocket is launched from the edge of a rooftop. The height of the rocket above the ground is modeled by $h = -16t^2 + 40t + 24$, where h is the height in feet and t is the time in seconds. Find the time it takes the rocket to hit the ground. *(Lesson 9-6)* **3 s**

10. **Geometry** The base of the triangle in the figure is five times the height. The area of the triangle is 400 in². Find the height of the triangle to the nearest tenth. *(Lesson 9-7)* **12.6 in.**

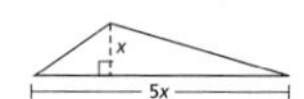

11. The length of a rectangular swimming pool is 8 feet greater than the width. The pool has an area of 240 ft². Find the length and width of the pool. *(Lesson 9-8)* **20 ft; 12 ft**

12. **Geometry** One base of a trapezoid is 4 ft longer than the other base. The height of the trapezoid is equal to the shorter base. The trapezoid's area is 80 ft². Find the height. $\left(Hint: A = \frac{1}{2}h(b_1 + b_2)\right)$ *(Lesson 9-8)* **8 ft**

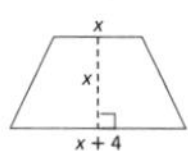

13. A referee tosses a coin into the air at the start of a football game to decide which team will get the ball. The height of the coin above the ground is modeled by $h = -16t^2 + 12t + 4$, where h is the height in feet and t is the time in seconds after the coin is tossed. Will the coin reach a height of 8 feet? Use the discriminant to explain your answer. *(Lesson 9-9)* **13. See p. A44.**

Chapter 10 ■ Applications Practice **7–9. See p. A44.**

Geography Use the following information for Exercises 1–3.

The bar graph shows the areas of the Great Lakes. *(Lesson 10-1)*

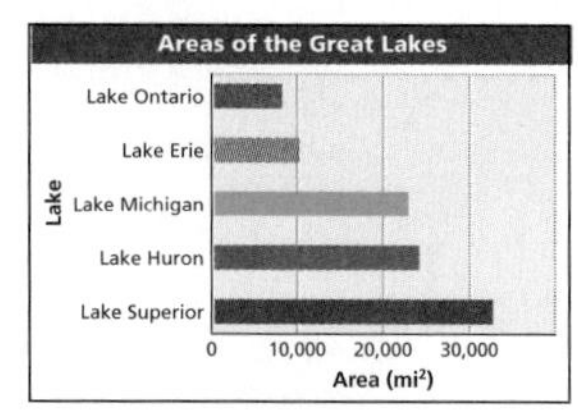

1. Estimate the difference in the areas between the lake with the greatest area and the lake with the least area. **25,000 mi²**
2. Estimate the total area of the five lakes. **94,000 mi²**
3. Approximately what percent of the total area is Lake Superior? **about 33%**
4. The scores of 18 students on a Spanish exam are given below. Use the data to make a stem-and-leaf plot. *(Lesson 10-2)* **See p. A44.**

Exam Scores								
65	94	92	75	71	83	77	73	91
82	63	79	80	77	99	76	80	88

5. The numbers of customers who visited a hair salon each day are given below. Use the data to make a frequency table with intervals. *(Lesson 10-2)* **See p. A44.**

Number of Customers Per Day						
32	35	29	44	41	25	35
40	41	32	33	28	33	34

Sports Use the following information for Exercises 6 and 7.

The numbers of points scored by a college football team in 11 games are given below. *(Lesson 10-3)*

10 17 17 14 21 7 10 14 17 17 21

6. Find the mean, median, mode, and range of the data set. **mean: 15; median: 17; mode: 17; range: 14**
7. Use the data to make a box-and-whisker plot.
8. The weekly salaries of five employees at a restaurant are \$450, \$500, \$460, \$980, and \$520. Explain why the following statement is misleading: "The average salary is \$582." *(Lesson 10-4)*
9. The graph shows the sales figures for three sales representatives. Explain why the graph is misleading. What might someone believe because of the graph? *(Lesson 10-4)*

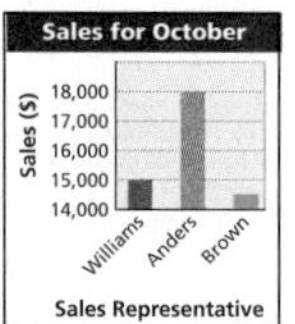

10. A manager inspects 120 stereos that were built at a factory. She finds that 6 are defective. What is the experimental probability that a stereo chosen at random will be defective? *(Lesson 10-5)* **0.05 or 5%**

Travel Use the following information for Exercises 11–13.

A row of an airplane has 2 window seats, 3 middle seats, and 4 aisle seats. You are randomly assigned a seat in the row. *(Lesson 10-6)*

11. Find the probability that you are assigned a window seat. $\frac{2}{9}$
12. Find the odds in favor of being assigned a window seat. **2:7**
13. Find the probability that you are not assigned a middle seat. $\frac{2}{3}$
14. A class consists of 19 boys and 16 girls. The teacher selects one student at random to be the class president and then selects a different student to be vice president. What is the probability that both students are girls? *(Lesson 10-7)* $\frac{24}{119}$

Chapter 11 ■ Applications Practice **5. See p. A44.**

1. Scientists who are developing a vaccine track the number of new infections of a disease each year. The values in the table form a geometric sequence. To the nearest whole number, how many new infections will there be in the 6th year? *(Lesson 11-1)* **2848**

Year	Number of New Infections
1	12,000
2	9000
3	6750

2. **Finance** For a savings account that earns 5% interest each year, the function $f(x) = 2000(1.05)^x$ gives the value of a \$2000 investment after x years. *(Lesson 11-2)*
   a. Find the investment's value after 5 years. **\$2552.56**
   b. Approximately how many years will it take for the investment to be worth \$3100? **9**

3. **Chemistry** Cesium-137 has a half-life of 30 years. Find the amount left from a 200-gram sample after 150 years. *(Lesson 11-3)* **6.25 grams**

4. The cost of tuition at a dance school is \$300 a year and is increasing at a rate of 3% a year. Write an exponential growth function to model the situation and find the cost of tuition after 4 years. *(Lesson 11-3)* $y = 300(1.03)^t$**; \$337.65**

5. Use the data in the table to describe how the price of the company's stock is changing. Then write a function that models the data. Use your function to predict the price of the company's stock after 7 years. *(Lesson 11-4)*

Stock Prices				
Year	0	1	2	3
Price (\$)	10.00	11.00	12.20	13.31

6. Use the data in the table to describe the rate at which Susan reads. Then write a function that models the data. Use your function to predict the number of pages Susan will read in 6 hours. *(Lesson 11-4)* **Susan reads 48 pages per hour; $y = 48x$; 288**

Total Number of Pages Read				
Time (h)	1	2	3	4
Pages	48	96	144	192

7. The function $f(x) = \sqrt{1.44x}$ gives the approximate distance in miles to the horizon as observed by a person whose eye level is x feet above the ground. Jamal stands on a tower so that his eyes are 180 ft above the ground. What is the distance to the horizon? Round your answer to the nearest tenth. *(Lesson 11-5)* **16.1 mi**

8. **Geometry** Given the surface area, S, of a sphere, the formula $r = \sqrt{\frac{S}{4\pi}}$ can be used to find the sphere's radius. What is the radius of a sphere with a surface area of 100 m²? Use 3.14 for π. Round your answer to the nearest hundredth of a meter. *(Lesson 11-5)* **2.82 m**

9. **Cooking** A chef has a square baking pan with sides 8 inches long. She wants to know if an 11-inch fish can fit in the pan. Find the length of the diagonal of the pan. Give the answer as a radical expression in simplest form. Then estimate the length to the nearest tenth of an inch. Tell whether the fish will fit in the pan. *(Lesson 11-6)* $8\sqrt{2}$ **in.** $\approx$ **11.3 in.; yes**

10. Alicia wants to put a fence around the irregular garden plot shown. Find the perimeter of the plot. Give your answer as a radical expression in simplest form. *(Lesson 11-7)* $11\sqrt{3}$ **m**

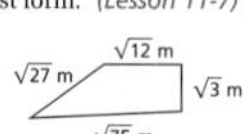

11. **Physics** The velocity of an object in meters per second is given by $\frac{\sqrt{2}\sqrt{E}}{\sqrt{m}}$, where E is kinetic energy in Joules and m is mass in kilograms. What is the velocity of an object that has 40 Joules of kinetic energy and a mass of 10 kilograms? Give the answer as a radical expression in simplest form. Then estimate the velocity to the nearest tenth. *(Lesson 11-8)* $2\sqrt{2}$ **m/s** $\approx$ **2.8 m/s**

12. A rectangular window has an area of 40 ft². The window is 8 feet long and its height is $\sqrt{x+2}$ ft. What is the value of x? What is the height of the window? *(Lesson 11-9)* $x = 23$**; 5 ft**

Chapter 12 ■ Applications Practice **1, 3, 4. See p. A44.**

1. The inverse variation $xy = 200$ relates the number of words per minute x at which a person types to the number of minutes y that it takes to type a 200-word paragraph. Determine a reasonable domain and range and then graph this inverse variation. Use the graph to estimate how many minutes it would take to type the paragraph at a rate of 60 words per minute. *(Lesson 12-1)*

2. **Business** The owner of a deli finds that the number of sandwiches sold in one day varies inversely as the price of the sandwiches. When the price is \$4.50, the deli sells 60 sandwiches. How many sandwiches can the owner expect to sell when the price is \$3.60? *(Lesson 12-1)* **75**

3. A gardener has \$30 in his budget to buy packets of seeds. He receives 3 free packets of seeds with his order. The number of packets y he can buy is $y = \frac{30}{x} + 3$, where x is the price per packet. Describe the reasonable domain and range values. Then graph the function. *(Lesson 12-2)*

4. Ashley wants to save \$1000 for a trip to Europe. She puts aside x dollars per month, and her grandmother contributes \$10 per month. The number of months y it will take to save \$1000 is $y = \frac{1000}{x + 10}$. Describe the reasonable domain and range values. Then graph the function. *(Lesson 12-2)*

5. **Geometry** Find the ratio of the area of a circle to the circumference of the circle. (*Hint:* For a circle, $A = \pi r^2$ and $C = 2\pi r$). For what radius is this ratio equal to 1? *(Lesson 12-3)* $\frac{r}{2}$**;** $r = 2$

6. **Geometry** For a cylinder with radius r and height h, the volume is $V = \pi r^2 h$, and the surface area is $S = 2\pi r^2 + 2\pi rh$. What is the ratio of the volume to the surface area for a cylinder? What is this ratio when $r = h = 1$? *(Lesson 12-3)* $\frac{rh}{2(r+h)}$**;** $\frac{1}{4}$

7. A committee consists of five more women than men. The chairperson randomly chooses one person to serve as secretary and a different person to serve as treasurer. Write and simplify an expression that represents the probability that both people who are chosen are men. What is the probability of choosing two men if there are 6 men on the committee? *(Lesson 12-4)* **7. See p. A44.**

8. **Transportation** A delivery truck makes a delivery to a town 150 miles away traveling r miles per hour. On the return trip, the delivery truck travels 20% faster. Write and simplify an expression for the truck's round-trip delivery time in terms of r. Then find the round-trip delivery time if the truck travels 55 mi/h on its way to the delivery. *(Lesson 12-5)* **8.** $\frac{275}{r}$**; 5 h**

9. **Recreation** Jordan is hiking 2 miles to a vista point at the top of a hill and then back to his campsite at the base of the hill. His downhill rate is 3 times his uphill rate, r. Write and simplify an expression in terms of r for the time that the round-trip hike will take. Then find how long the hike will take if Jordan's uphill rate is 2 mi/h. *(Lesson 12-5)* $\frac{8}{3r}$**;** $1\frac{1}{3}$ **h**

10. **Geometry** The volume of a rectangular prism is the area of the base times the height. A rectangular prism has a volume given by $(2x^2 + 7x + 5)$ cm³ and a height given by $(x + 1)$ cm. What is the area of the base of the rectangular prism? *(Lesson 12-6)* $2x + 5$

11. Tanya can deliver newspapers to all of the houses on her route in 1 hour. Her brother, Nick, can deliver newspapers along the same route in 2 hours. How long will it take to deliver the newspapers if they work together? *(Lesson 12-7)* $\frac{2}{3}$ **h or 40 min**

12. **Agriculture** Grains are harvested using a combine. A farm has two combines—one that can harvest the wheat field in 9 hours and another that can harvest the wheat field in 11 hours. How long will it take to harvest the wheat field using both combines? *(Lesson 12-7)* $4\frac{19}{20}$ **h or 4 h 57 min**

Problem-Solving Handbook

Problem Solving Handbook

Draw a Diagram

You can draw a diagram to help you visualize what the words of a problem are describing.

Problem Solving Strategies

Draw a Diagram	Make a Table
Make a Model	Solve a Simpler Problem
Guess and Test	Use Logical Reasoning
Work Backward	Use a Venn Diagram
Find a Pattern	Make an Organized List

EXAMPLE

A gardener wants to plant a 2.5-foot-wide border of flowers around a rectangular herb garden. The herb garden is 12 feet long and 7.5 feet wide. What is the area of the border?

1 Understand the Problem

You need to find the area of the garden's border. You are given the garden's dimensions and the width of the border.

2 Make a Plan

Draw and label a diagram of the herb garden with the surrounding border. Find the dimensions of the outer rectangle. Then find the area of the inner rectangle and subtract to find the area of the border.

3 Solve

length of outer rectangle: 2.5 ft + 12 ft + 2.5 ft = 17 ft
width of outer rectangle: 2.5 ft + 7.5 ft + 2.5 ft = 12.5 ft

Find the area of each rectangle:

area of outer rectangle: 17 ft × 12.5 ft = 212.5 ft²
area of inner rectangle: 12 ft × 7.5 ft = 90 ft²

Subtract:

area of border: 212.5 ft² − 90 ft² = 122.5 ft²

2.5 ft, 12 ft, 2.5 ft, 2.5 ft, 7.5 ft, 2.5 ft

4 Look Back

To check your answer, solve the problem in a different way. Divide the border into four parts and find the area of each part. Then add the areas.

17 ft × 2.5 ft = 42.5 ft²   7.5 ft × 2.5 ft = 18.75 ft²

17 ft × 2.5 ft = 42.5 ft²   7.5 ft × 2.5 ft = 18.75 ft²

42.5 ft² + 42.5 ft² + 18.75 ft² + 18.75 ft² + = 122.5 ft²

17 ft, 2.5 ft, 2.5 ft, 7.5 ft

PRACTICE

1. A circular fish pond is surrounded by a circular border of stones that is 18 inches wide. The fish pond is 4 feet in diameter. What is the area of the border? (Use 3.14 for π.) **25.905 ft²**
2. Thirty-two teams are in the first round of a softball tournament. A team is eliminated as soon as it loses a game. How many games need to be played to determine the winner? (*Hint:* Use a tree diagram.) **31 games**

Make a Model

You can make a model, or representation of the objects in a problem, to help you solve it.

Problem Solving Strategies

Draw a Diagram	Make a Table
Make a Model	Solve a Simpler Problem
Guess and Test	Use Logical Reasoning
Work Backward	Use a Venn Diagram
Find a Pattern	Make an Organized List

EXAMPLE

Mr. Duncan is using blue and white square tiles to create a pattern on his kitchen wall. The entire design will have 8 rows with 15 tiles in each row. The bottom row alternates colors starting with blue, and the row above that alternates colors starting with white. He will continue this alternating pattern so that the same two colors are never next to each other. How many of each color tile does Mr. Duncan need to complete the entire design?

1 Understand the Problem

You need to find how many of each color tile are needed. You know the number of rows and the number of tiles in each row. The colors alternate so that the same two colors are never next to each other.

2 Make a Plan

Use blocks (preferably blue and white, but any two colors would work) to make a model of the first two rows. Count how many of each color you use. Then multiply to find how many of each color would be used in the entire design.

3 Solve

Create the bottom row. Start with a blue block and alternate colors across the row until you have used 15 blocks.

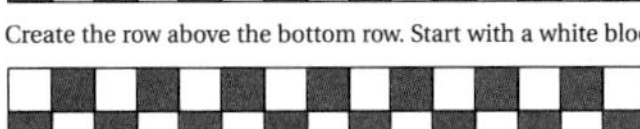

Create the row above the bottom row. Start with a white block.

You could build all 8 rows and just count the number of each color, but each group of two rows will be the same, so this way is quicker.

There will be a total of 8 rows: 4 that start with blue and 4 that start with white. Count how many of each color are used above and multiply each number by 4.

blue: 15 × 4 = 60
white: 15 × 4 = 60

Mr. Duncan needs 60 blue tiles and 60 white tiles.

4 Look Back

The grid is 15 units by 8 units, so there are 15 × 8 = 120 squares in the grid. Add the number of blue and white tiles to see if the sum is 120: 60 + 60 = 120.

PRACTICE **36 blue tiles, 24 green tiles, 60 white tiles**

1. Mr. Duncan decides to tile another area of his kitchen wall. This design will have 12 rows with 10 tiles in each row. The bottom row will repeat this pattern: blue, white, blue, blue, white. The row above the bottom row will repeat this pattern: white, green, white, white, green. He will use these two patterns for each of the remaining rows so that the first colors of each row always alternate. How many of each color tile will Mr. Duncan need?

Guess and Test

The guess and test strategy can be used when you cannot think of another way to solve the problem. Begin by making a reasonable guess, and then test it to see whether your guess is correct. If not, adjust the guess accordingly and test again. Keep guessing and testing until you correctly solve the problem.

Problem Solving Strategies

Draw a Diagram	Make a Table
Make a Model	Solve a Simpler Problem
Guess and Test	Use Logical Reasoning
Work Backward	Use a Venn Diagram
Find a Pattern	Make an Organized List

EXAMPLE

The manager of a college computer lab purchased 24 printers at a total cost of $3120. Some of the printers were laser, and some were ink jet. The laser printers cost $250 each, and the ink jet printers cost $70 each. How many of each type of printer did the manager purchase?

1 Understand the Problem

You know the cost of each type of printer and the total number of printers. You need to find the number of each type of printer purchased.

2 Make a Plan

Make reasonable first guesses for each type of printer. The sum must be 24. Then multiply each guess by the cost of each printer. Find the total and compare it to $3120. Adjust the guess as needed and continue until you find the solution.

3 Solve

Use a table to organize your guesses.

	Laser Printers	Ink Jet Printers	Total Priners	Total Cost	
1st guess	12	12	24	12($250) + 12($70) $3000 + $840 = $3840	*Too high—try fewer laser printers.*
2nd guess	6	18	24	6($250) + 18($70) $1500 + $1260 = $2760	*Too low—try more laser printers.*
3rd guess	8	16	24	8($250) + 16($70) $2000 + $1120 = $3120	*Correct!*

The manager purchased 8 laser printers and 16 ink jet printers.

4 Look Back

The total spent is $3120, and the total number of printers is 24. The solution is correct.

PRACTICE

1. All 350 seats were sold for a concert in the park. Adult tickets cost $15, and child tickets cost $5. Ticket sales totaled $4350. How many of each type of ticket were sold? **260 adult tickets and 90 child tickets**
2. Jane is 3 times as old as Theo. Luke is 5 years older than Theo. Zoe is 8 years younger than twice Theo's age, and Cassie is 6 years younger than Theo. The sum of their ages is 71. How old is each person? **Jane is 30, Theo is 10, Luke is 15, Zoe is 12, and Cassie is 4.**

Work Backward

You can work backward to solve a problem when you know the ending value and are asked to find the initial value.

Problem Solving Strategies

Draw a Diagram	Make a Table
Make a Model	Solve a Simpler Problem
Guess and Test	Use Logical Reasoning
Work Backward	Use a Venn Diagram
Find a Pattern	Make an Organized List

EXAMPLE

Lee Ann is taking a vacation in Paris, France. Her flight arrived in Paris at 9:35 A.M. on Tuesday. The plane left New York City and flew for 7 hours and 55 minutes to Nice, France, where there was a layover of 1 hour 12 minutes. From Nice the plane flew 1 hour and 25 minutes to Paris. Paris time is 6 hours ahead of New York City time. What time did the plane leave New York City?

1 Understand the Problem

You are asked to find the time that the plane left New York City. You know when the flight arrived in Paris, the length of the stops that were made along the way, and the time difference between New York City and Paris.

2 Make a Plan

Work backward from the time the plane arrived in Paris, using inverse operations. Then apply the time difference between the two cities.

3 Solve

Subtract the length of time it took to fly from Nice to Paris from the time Lee Ann arrived in Paris.
9:35 A.M. − 1 hour 25 minutes = 8:10 A.M.

Subtract the length of the layover in Nice.
8:10 A.M. − 1 hour 12 minutes = 6:58 A.M.

Subtract the length of the flight from New York to Nice.
6:58 A.M. − 7 hours 55 minutes = 11:03 P.M. Monday

Since Paris time is ahead of New York time, subtract the time difference.
11:03 P.M., Monday − 6 hours = 5:03 P.M. Monday

Lee Ann's flight left New York City on Monday at 5:03 P.M.

4 Look Back

Work forward to check your answer.
5:03 P.M. Monday + 6 h + 7 h 55 min + 1 h 12 min + 1 h 25 min
= 5:03 P.M. Monday + 16 h 32 min
= 9:35 A.M. Tuesday
This matches the information given in the problem.

PRACTICE

1. A bus arrives in Dallas, Texas, at 10:59 A.M. on Friday. The bus left Atlanta, Georgia, and took 12 hours and 15 minutes to arrive in Shreveport, Louisiana, where there was a 45-minute layover. From Shreveport it took 4 hours and 29 minutes to get to Dallas. Dallas time is 1 hour behind Atlanta time. What time did the bus leave Atlanta? **6:30 P.M. on Thursday**
2. Carolina bought a DVD player that was on sale for 90% of the original price. The total amount she paid was $135.72, which included a sales tax of $5.22. What was the original price of the DVD player? **$145.00**

Find a Pattern

If a problem involves a sequence of numbers or figures, it is often necessary to find a pattern to solve the problem.

Problem Solving Strategies

Draw a Diagram	Make a Table
Make a Model	Solve a Simpler Problem
Guess and Test	Use Logical Reasoning
Work Backward	Use a Venn Diagram
Find a Pattern	Make an Organized List

EXAMPLE

Darian created the following sequence of stars:

How many stars will be in the 6th figure?

1 Understand the Problem

You need to find the number of stars in the 6th figure. You can find the number in the first four figures by counting.

2 Make a Plan

Count the number of stars in each of the first four figures. Use the information to find a pattern and determine a general rule.

3 Solve

Look for a pattern between the position of each figure in the sequence and the number of stars in that figure.

Position	1	2	3	4
Stars	2	6	12	20

The number of stars is the square of the position number plus the position number. This rule written algebraically is $n^2 + n$.

Evaluate the expression for $n = 6$: $n^2 + n$

$6^2 + 6 = 36 + 6 = 42$

There will be 42 stars in the 6th figure.

4 Look Back

Look for another pattern. The number of stars in each position increases by 4, then by 6, then by 8. That is, the amount of increase always increases by 2. So the number of stars in the 5th position will be 20 + 10, or 30, and the number of stars in the 6th position will be 30 + 12, or 42.

PRACTICE

1. The first three figures of a pattern are shown. How many circles will be in the 10th figure? 37

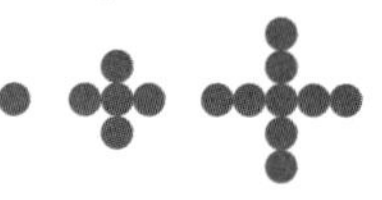

2. Lily drew the first four figures of a pattern. How many squares will be in the 7th figure? 14

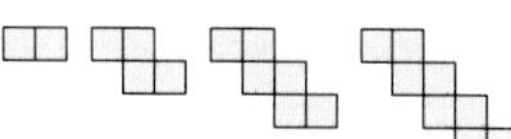

Make a Table

You can make a table to solve problems because the rows and columns can help you arrange information. Sometimes this also allows you to discover relationships that might otherwise be hard to notice.

Problem Solving Strategies

Draw a Diagram	Make a Table
Make a Model	Solve a Simpler Problem
Guess and Test	Use Logical Reasoning
Work Backward	Use a Venn Diagram
Find a Pattern	Make an Organized List

EXAMPLE

A scientist begins a culture with 500 bacteria. The number of bacteria triples every 30 minutes. How many bacteria are in the culture after $2\frac{1}{2}$ hours?

1 Understand the Problem

You are asked to find the number of bacteria in the culture after $2\frac{1}{2}$ hours. You know the initial number of bacteria, and you know that the population triples every half hour.

2 Make a Plan

Make a table with rows for time and number of bacteria. Start with the initial number in the culture. Increase the time in 30-minute increments and triple the number of bacteria with each increase. Keep extending the table until the time is $2\frac{1}{2}$ hours (150 minutes).

3 Solve

Time (min)	0	30	60	90	120	150
Bacteria	500	1500	4500	13,500	40,500	121,500

There are 121,500 bacteria in the culture after $2\frac{1}{2}$ hours.

4 Look Back

Check your answer by solving a simpler problem. The number of bacteria in the culture triples five times (150 min ÷ 30 min = 5). Start with 5 instead of 500 and triple the number five times.

$5 \times 3 = 15$

$15 \times 3 = 45$

$45 \times 3 = 135$

$135 \times 3 = 405$

$405 \times 3 = 1215$

Multiply by 100 to find the total if you had started with 500; $1215 \times 100 = 121,500$

PRACTICE

1. A dietician's report states that a 125-pound woman needs to eat about 1750 Calories a day to maintain her weight. It also states that a 132-pound woman needs 1848 Calories and a 139-pound woman needs 1946 Calories a day. Based on these values, how many Calories does a 160-pound woman need to eat each day to maintain her weight? 2240 Calories
2. Simon opened a savings account with an initial deposit of $200. At the end of each year, the account earns 4% interest. If he does not deposit or withdraw any additional money, what would his balance be at the end of 6 years? $253.06

Solve a Simpler Problem

Sometimes a problem contains numbers that make it seem difficult to solve. You can solve a simpler problem by rewriting the numbers so they are easier to compute.

Problem Solving Strategies

Draw a Diagram	Make a Table
Make a Model	Solve a Simpler Problem
Guess and Test	Use Logical Reasoning
Work Backward	Use a Venn Diagram
Find a Pattern	Make an Organized List

EXAMPLE

During a skating competition, Jules skated around the track 35 times. One lap is 0.9 mile. If Jules finished in 1 hour 30 minutes, what was his average speed?

1 Understand the Problem

You are asked to find Jules's average speed for 35 laps. You know the distance of each lap and the amount of time it took him to finish the competition.

2 Make a Plan

Solve a simpler problem by using easier numbers to do the computations.

3 Solve

Find the total distance skated.

$35(0.9)$ *There were 35 laps that measured 0.9 mile.*

$35(1 - 0.1)$ *Write 0.9 as 1 − 0.1*

$35(1) - 3.5(0.1)$ *Use the Distributive Property.*

$35 - 3.5$

31.5

Use the distance formula to find the average speed.

$d = rt$

$31.5 = r \times 1.5$ *1 hour 30 minutes = 1.5 hours*

$\frac{31.5}{1.5} = r$ *Solve for r.*

$\frac{315}{15} = r$ *Multiply the numerator and denominator by 10 to eliminate the decimals.*

$\frac{1}{15}(315) = r$

$\frac{1}{15}(300 + 15) = r$ *Write 315 as 300 + 15.*

$\frac{1}{15}(300) + \frac{1}{15}(15) = r$ *Use the Distributive Property.*

$20 + 1 = r$

$21 = r$

Jules skated at an average speed of 21 miles per hour.

4 Look Back

Each lap is a little less than 1 mile, so 35 laps is a little less than 35 miles. Round this distance to 30 miles and use $d = rt$ to find the rate when the time is 1.5 hours: 30 mi = (1.5 h)$r \longrightarrow r$ = 20 mi/h. This is close to 21 mi/h.

PRACTICE

1. Diana swam 24 laps in the pool today. One lap is 200 feet. She swam at an average rate of 4 feet per second. How many minutes did Diana swim? 20 min

Use Logical Reasoning

Use logical reasoning to solve problems when you are given several facts and can use common sense to find a missing fact.

Problem Solving Strategies

Draw a Diagram	Make a Table
Make a Model	Solve a Simpler Problem
Guess and Test	Use Logical Reasoning
Work Backward	Use a Venn Diagram
Find a Pattern	Make an Organized List

EXAMPLE 1

Five players on a baseball team wear the numbers 2, 12, 15, 34, and 42. Their positions are pitcher, catcher, first base, left field, and center field. The pitcher's number is less than the left fielder's number. The center fielder's number is greater than 25, and the left fielder wears an even number. The catcher wears number 34. What is the pitcher's number?

1 Understand the Problem

You want to find the jersey number of the pitcher. You know there are five positions and five jersey numbers. Some information about who wears which number is given.

2 Make a Plan

Organize the information in a table. Start with the fact that the catcher wears number 34 and use logical reasoning to determine the numbers of the other positions.

3 Solve

The catcher wears number 34. No other player wears 34, and the catcher wears no other number. Enter *Y's* and *N's* in the chart as shown.

The center fielder's number is greater than 25, so he must wear number 42. The left fielder cannot wear number 15 (because it is odd), and he cannot have the least number (the pitcher's number is less than his). The left fielder must wear 12.

The pitcher's number is less than 12 (the left fielder's), so he must wear number 2.

	2	12	15	34	42
Pitcher	Y	N	N	N	N
Catcher	N	N	N	Y	N
First Base	N	N	Y	N	N
Left Fielder	N	Y	N	N	N
Center Fielder	N	N	N	N	Y

Y = yes; N = no

Once you enter Y in a cell, enter N in the remaining cells for the row and the column that include it.

The pitcher wears number 2.

4 Look Back

Complete the chart if needed. Read the problem while looking at the chart to make sure there are no contradictions.

PRACTICE

1. Rose, Jill, Gaby, and Chloe bowled the scores 110, 125, 144, and 150. Jill did not bowl the 110. The person who bowled the 150 is Rose's sister and Jill's aunt. Chloe bowled the 125. What score did Jill bowl? 144

Use a Venn Diagram

You can use a Venn diagram to display relationships among sets of numbers. Circles are used to represent the individual sets.

Problem Solving Strategies

Draw a Diagram	Make a Table
Make a Model	Solve a Simpler Problem
Guess and Test	Use Logical Reasoning
Work Backward	**Use a Venn Diagram**
Find a Pattern	Make an Organized List

EXAMPLE

At a local supermarket, 194 people were given samples of two brands of orange juice. Their opinions were as follows: 120 people liked brand A, 101 people liked brand B, and 15 people did not like either brand. How many people liked only brand A?

1 Understand the Problem

The total number of people was 194, and 15 of them did not like either brand. The statement "120 people liked brand A" means some of the 120 people liked *only* brand A and some liked brand A *and* brand B. The statement "101 people liked brand B" means some of the 101 people liked *only* brand B and some liked brand A *and* brand B.

2 Make a Plan

Use a Venn diagram to show the relationship among the groups of people.

3 Solve

Draw and label two intersecting circles to show the sets of people who liked brand A and brand B. Write 15 in the area labeled "Neither."

Brand A
Both
Brand B
Neither: 15

Out of 194 people, 15 liked neither brand. Subtract 15 from 194 to find how many people liked at least one brand: $194 - 15 = 179$.

Add the number of people who liked brand A to the number of people who liked brand B: $120 + 101 = 221$. You know there are only 179 people who liked at least one brand, so subtract 179 from 221: $221 - 179 = 42$. This means 42 people were counted twice, and that 42 people liked both brands. Write 42 in the area labeled both.

Brand A
78
Both
42
Brand B
59
Neither: 15

Out of 120 people who liked brand A, 42 also liked brand B. Subtract 42 from 120 to find the number of people who liked only brand A: $120 - 42 = 78$.

So 78 people liked only brand A.

4 Look Back

Find the number of people who liked brand B only: $101 - 42 = 59$. Add all the numbers in the Venn diagram. The sum of the number who liked only brand A, the number who liked only brand B, the number who liked both brands, and the number who liked neither brand should be the total number of people surveyed: $78 + 59 + 42 + 15 = 194$.

PRACTICE

In a group of 138 people, 55 own a cat, 27 own a cat and a dog, and 42 own neither pet.

1. How many people own only a cat? 28
2. How many people own a dog? 68

Make an Organized List

If a problem asks you to find all the possible ways in which something can happen, you can make an organized list to keep track of the outcomes.

Problem Solving Strategies

Draw a Diagram	Make a Table
Make a Model	Solve a Simpler Problem
Guess and Test	Use Logical Reasoning
Work Backward	Use a Venn Diagram
Find a Pattern	**Make an Organized List**

EXAMPLE

A fair coin is tossed 4 times. What is the probability that it lands heads up at least 3 times?

1 Understand the Problem

You need to find the probability that a coin tossed 4 times lands heads up 3 or 4 times.

2 Make a Plan

The formula for probability is:

$$\text{probability} = \frac{\text{number of favorable outcomes}}{\text{total number of outcomes}}$$

The total number of outcomes is the number of items in the list. The number of favorable outcomes is the number of times the coin lands heads up 3 or 4 times.

Make an organized list of the coin tosses to find the total number of outcomes.

3 Solve

Start with heads for all 4 tosses, then heads for the first 3 tosses, then heads for the first 2 tosses, and then heads for the first toss. Repeat the pattern for tails.

HHHH	HTHH	TTTT	THTT
HHHT	HTHT	TTTH	THTH
HHTH	HTTH	TTHT	THHT
HHTT	HTTT	TTHH	THHH

There are 16 total outcomes.

There are 5 favorable outcomes.

The probability that the coin lands heads up 3 or 4 times is $\frac{5}{16}$.

4 Look Back

Double-check that each combination is listed and that no combination is written more than once. You can also use the Fundamental Counting Principle to check the total number of outcomes. For each of the 4 coin tosses, there are 2 possible outcomes, so the total number of outcomes is $2 \times 2 \times 2 \times 2 = 16$.

PRACTICE

1. A beagle, a fox terrier, an Afghan hound, and a golden retriever are competing in the finals of a dog show. How many ways can the dogs finish in first, second, and third place? 24
2. Two number cubes are rolled. What is the probability that the sum of the numbers rolled is an odd number? $\frac{1}{2}$

Selected Answers

Selected Answers

Chapter 1

1-1

Check It Out! 1a. 4 decreased by *n*; *n* less than 4 **1b.** the quotient of *t* and 5; *t* divided by 5 **1c.** the sum of 9 and *q*; *q* added to 9 **1d.** the product of 3 and *h*; 3 times *h* **2a.** $65t$ **2b.** $m + 5$ **2c.** $32d$ **3a.** 6 **3b.** 7 **3c.** 3 **4. a.** $63s$, **b.** 756 bottles; 1575 bottles; 3150 bottles

Exercises 1. variable **3.** the quotient of *f* and 3; *f* divided by 3 **5.** 9 decreased by *y*; *y* less than 9 **7.** the sum of *t* and 12; *t* increased by 12 **9.** *x* decreased by 3; the difference of *x* and 3 **11.** $w + 4$ **13.** 12 **15.** 6 **17.** the product of 5 and *p*; 5 groups of *p* **19.** the sum of 3 and *x*; 3 increased by *x* **21.** negative 3 times *s*; the product of negative 3 and *s* **23.** 14 decreased by *t*; the difference of 14 and *t* **25.** $t + 20$ **27.** 1 **29.** 2 **31a.** $h - 40$, **b.** 0; 4; 8; 12 **33.** $2x$ **35.** $y + 10$ **37.** $9ut$; 9 in²; 72 in²; 81 in²; 99 in² **39.** 13; 14; 15; 16 **41.** 6; 10; 13; 15 **43a.** $47.84 + m$; **b.** $58.53 - s$ **45.** $x + 7$; 19; 21 **47.** $x + 3$; 15; 17 **49.** F **51.** 36 **53.** 1 **55.** 45° **57.** 90° **59.** $\frac{1}{2}$ **61.** 1 **63.** Multiply the previous term by 3; 729, 2187, 6561.

1-2

Check It Out! 1a. 4 **1b.** −10 **1c.** 1.5 **2a.** −12 **2b.** −35.8 **2c.** −16 **3a.** −8 **3b.** 4 **3c.** −2 **4.** 13,018 ft

Exercises 1. opposite **3.** −8.5 **5.** $9\frac{1}{4}$ **7.** 1 **9.** $\frac{9}{16}$ **11.** −4.1 **13.** $1\frac{1}{10}$ **15.** 4 **17.** $-11\frac{3}{4}$ **19.** −30 **21.** 14 **23.** −10 **25.** 13.4 **27.** 23 °F **29.** 0.75 **31.** $-12\frac{2}{5}$ **33.** −12 **35.** 37 **37.** 0 **39.** $\frac{1}{10}$ **41.** > **43.** > **45.** < **47.** 11,331 ft **49.** never **51.** A **55.** F **57.** −9 **59.** 2 **61.** Subtract 4; −2, −6, −10 **63.** 12,660.5 ft **65.** $0.\overline{2}$ **67.** $0.\overline{36}$ **69.** 720°

1-3

Check It Out! 1a. −7 **1b.** 44 **1c.** −42 **2a.** $\frac{1}{12}$ **2b.** $-\frac{1}{4}$ **2c.** $-\frac{1}{2}$ **3a.** 0 **3b.** undefined **3c.** 0 **4.** 7.875 mi

Exercises 3. −121 **5.** 7 **7.** 2 **9.** undefined **11.** 0 **13.** about \$210,000,000 **15.** −32 **17.** $\frac{9}{10}$ **19.** −3 **21.** 0 **23.** 0 **25.** −15 °F **27.** −4 **29.** −62 **31.** 18.75 **33.** 1 **35.** −12 **37.** $\frac{3}{8}$ **39.** negative **41.** negative **43.** positive **45.** undefined **47.** 1 **49.** $\frac{1}{2}$ **51.** $-\frac{1}{5}$ **53.** $\frac{9}{8}$ **55.** 15 h per semester **57.** < **59.** > **61.** = **63a.** positive **b.** negative **c.** The product of two negative numbers is positive. The product of that positive number and a negative number is negative. **d.** no **65.** $75\left(\frac{1}{15}\right)$ **67.** $-121\left(\frac{1}{11}\right)$ **69.** never **73.** C **75.** 16 quarter notes **77.** $\frac{25}{49}$ **79.** 5 **81.** 1 **83.** $-\frac{27}{64}$ **85.** Multiply by −2; −16, 32, −64. **87.** The numbers are alternating positive and negative multiples of 5; 30, −35, 40. **89.** \$85 **91.** 1510 in² **93.** < **95.** =

1-4

Check It Out! 1a. 2^2 **1b.** x^3 **2a.** −125 **2b.** −36 **2c.** $\frac{27}{64}$ **3a.** 8^2 **3b.** $(-3)^3$ **4.** $2^8 = 256$

Exercises 1. the number of times to use the base as a factor **3.** 2^3 **5.** 49 **7.** −32 **9.** 9^2 **11.** $(-4)^3$ **13.** 3^4 **15.** $3^5 = 243$ **17.** 3^3 **19.** 27 **21.** −16 **23.** 7^2 **25.** $(-2)^3$ **27.** 4^3 **29.** $2^4 = 16$ **31.** < **33.** = **35.** = **37.** > **39.** 8 **41.** −64 **43.** −1 **45.** $\frac{1}{27}$ **47a.** 36 in² **b.** 9 in² **c.** 27 in² **49.** 6^2 **51.** $(-1)^4$ **53.** $\left(\frac{1}{3}\right)^3$ **55.** between 8000 cm³ and 15,625 cm³ **57.** 2 **59.** 4 **61.** 2 **63.** 4 **65a.** 100, 1000, 10,000 **b.** The exponent is the same as the number of zeros in the answer. **67.** C **69.** B **71.** 64 **73.** 65,536 **75a.** 4 · 4; 4 · 4 · 4 **b.** 4 · 4 · 4 · 4 · 4 = 4^5 **c.** 2 + 3 = 5; the sum of the exponents in 4^2 and 4^3 is the exponent in the product 4^5. **77.** 5 **79.** 5 minus *x*; *x* less than 5

81. *c* divided by *d*; the quotient of *c* and *d* **83.** $\frac{5}{2}$ **85.** 280

1-5

Check It Out! 1a. 2 **1b.** −5 **1c.** 3 **2a.** $\frac{2}{3}$ **2b.** $\frac{1}{2}$ **2c.** $-\frac{2}{7}$ **3.** 3.0 ft **4a.** rational number, repeating decimal **4b.** rational number, terminating decimal, integer **4c.** irrational number **4d.** natural number, whole number, integer, rational number, terminating decimal

Exercises 3. −15 **5.** 5 **7.** −3 **9.** −4 **11.** $\frac{2}{3}$ **13.** $\frac{3}{8}$ **15.** $\frac{1}{4}$ **17.** $-\frac{1}{5}$ **19.** rational number, terminating decimal, integer **21.** irrational number **23.** 11 **25.** −10 **31.** 4.1 cm **33.** rational number, terminating decimal, integer, whole number, natural number **35.** irrational number **37.** > **39.** < **41.** 45; rational number, terminating decimal, integer, whole number, natural number **43.** 34.625; rational number, terminating decimal **45.** always **47.** always **51.** 18 **53.** A **55.** D **57.** 0.9 **59.** −0.1 **61.** 4 **63.** 65 **65a.** no **67.** $\frac{1}{2}$ **69.** $-\frac{3}{16}$ **71.** −3.5 **73.** $-\frac{8}{125}$ **75.** 64

1-6

Check It Out! 1a. 48 **1b.** 2.6 **1c.** 2 **2a.** 15 **2b.** 3 **3a.** 1 **3b.** −3 **3c.** 21 **4.** 6.2(9.4 + 8) **5.** 400

Exercises 3. 15 **5.** −9 **7.** 14 **9.** 1 **11.** 14 **13.** 92 **15.** 1.5 **17.** −3 **19.** −22 **21.** 12(−2 + 6) **23.** 188.4 ft² **25.** 19 **27.** −15 **29.** 3 **31.** −5 **33.** 24 **35.** 17 **37.** −9 **39.** 17 **41.** −7 **43.** 0 **45.** $\frac{1}{4}$ **47.** 1 **49.** 6 **51.** $3 - \frac{2}{5}$ **53.** $8 - |3 \cdot 5|$ **55a.** 55 **b.** 498 **c.** 250 **d.** 10 **e.** 30 **f.** 70 **57.** $2[9 + (-x)]$ **59.** $\frac{\sqrt{7}}{3 \cdot 10}$ **63.** $3 \cdot 5 - 6 \cdot 2 = 3$ **69.** H **71.** −3 **73.** 6 **77.** 20 **79.** acute **81.** 100 **83.** −11 **85.** 8 **87.** $\frac{6}{7}$

1-7

Check It Out! 1a. 21 **1b.** 560 **1c.** 28 **2a.** 9(50) + 9(2) = 468 **2b.** 12(100) − 12(2) = 1176

2c. 7(30) + 7(4) = 238 **3a.** $100p$ **3b.** $-28.5t$ **3c.** $3m^2 + m^3$ **4a.** $6x - 15$ **4b.** $3a - 16x$

Exercises 1. Associative Property of Addition **3.** 24 **5.** 56 **7.** 118,000 **9.** 304 **11.** 456 **13.** 763 **15.** $20x$ **17.** $-9r$ **19.** $7.9x$ **21.** $9a - 31$ **23.** $7x - 3x^2$ **25.** $2a + 2$ **39.** $-3x - 14$ **43.** $13y - 10$ **45a.** Amy: 98:21; Julie: 81:12; Mardi: 83:39; Sabine: 63:47 **b.** Sabine, Julie, Mardi, Amy **47.** Commutative Property of Addition **49.** Distributive Property **51.** Distributive Property **53.** $6p + 9$ **57a.** equal **b.** 96π cm² **c.** $2(16\pi) + 96\pi = 128\pi$ cm² **59.** J **61.** $12x + 116$ **63.** $-3b - 7$ **65a.** Commutative Property of Addition **b.** Associative Property of Addition **c.** Distributive Property **d.** Rule for subtraction **67.** 36 ft² **69.** 64 **71.** $-\frac{1}{8}$ **73.** 3 **75.** −2

1-8

Check It Out!

1a. **1b.** **1c.** (graph with points T(−2, 6), S(0, 2), R(2, −3))

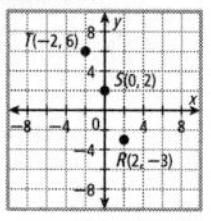

2a. none **2b.** I **2c.** III **2d.** II **3.** $y = 10 + 20x$; (1, 30), (2, 50), (3, 70), (4, 90) **4a.** (−4, −6), (−2, −5), (0, −4), (2, −3), (4, −2); line **4b.** (−3, 30), (−1, 6), (0, 3), (1, 6), (3, 30); U shape **4c.** (0, 2), (1, 1), (2, 0), (3, 1), (4, 2); V shape

Exercises 7. none **9.** none **11.** I **13.** (−2, 0), (−1, 1), (0, 2), (1, 3), (2, 4); line **15.** (−2, −4), (−1, −2), (0, 0), (1, −2), (2, −4); V shape **21.** none **23.** none **25.** II **27.** $y = 500 + 0.10x$; (500, 550), (3000, 800), (5000, 1000), (7500, 1250) **29.** (−2, −4), (−1, −1), (0, 0), (1, −1), (2, −4); U shape **31.** (−2, 7), (−1, 4), (0, 3), (1, 4), (2, 7); U shape **33.** triangle **35.** rectangle **37a.** $c = 2.90f$ **b.** *f* is input; *c* is output.

c.

f	*c*
1	2.90
2	5.80
3	8.70
4	11.60
5	14.50
6	17.40
7	20.30
8	23.20

d. 7 yards **39.** $y = \frac{1}{2}x + (-3)$; (−4,−5), (−2, −4), (0, −3), (2, −2), (4, −1); line **41a.** $y = 50 + 1.5x$ **b.** (100, 200); (150, 275); (200, 350); (250, 425); (300, 500) **43.** line **45.** line **51.** G **53.** H **57.** (−4, 4) **59.** The points make a horizontal line at *y* = 6. **61.** (−4, 5); 42 square units **63.** cylinder **65.** pentagon **67.** irrational **69.** rational, terminating decimal, integer **71.** $x^2 + 3x$

Study Guide: Review

1. constant **2.** whole numbers **3.** coefficient **4.** origin **5.** $1.99g$ **6.** $t + 3$ **7.** 5 **8.** 5 **9.** 6 **10.** $150 \div m$; 30; 25; 15 **11.** −14 **12.** −4.6 **13.** $4\frac{1}{2}$ **14.** −1 **15.** −24 **16.** 14.3 **17.** 2231 ft **18.** 90 **19.** 0 **20.** −15.2 **21.** −8 **22.** 0 **23.** undefined **24.** 9 **25.** $-\frac{2}{3}$ **26.** $\frac{15}{2}$ **27.** 3,650,000 steps **28.** 64 **29.** −27 **30.** 81 **31.** −25 **32.** $\frac{8}{27}$ **33.** $\frac{16}{25}$ **34.** 2^4 **35.** $(-10)^3$ **36.** $(-8)^2$ **37.** 12^1 **38.** 729 in³ **39.** 6 **40.** 4 **41.** −7 **42.** −12 **43.** $\frac{5}{6}$ **44.** $\frac{1}{3}$ **45.** rational number, terminating decimal, integer, whole number, natural number **46.** rational number, terminating decimal, integer, whole number **47.** rational number, terminating decimal, integer **48.** rational number, terminating decimal **49.** irrational number **50.** rational number, repeating decimal **51.** 3.6 ft **52.** 23 **53.** 8 **54.** 6 **55.** $\frac{1}{6}$ **56.** −18 **57.** 0 **58.** 62 **59.** 10 **60.** 8 **61.** 10 **62.** 8 + 7(−2) **63.** $\frac{12}{8+3}$ **64.** $4\sqrt{20 - x}$ **65.** 168 ft **66.** 40 **67.** 270 **68.** 13(100) + 13(3) = 1339 **69.** 18(100) − 18(1) = 1782 **70.** $4x$ **71.** $7y^2$ **72.** $4x + 24$ **73.** $2x^2 + 2$ **74.** $-4y + 3y^2$ **75.** $8y - a$ **76.** \$9

77–80. (graph with points B(−1, 4), C(0, 8), A(2, 3), D(5, −3))

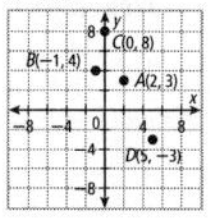

81. I **82.** IV **83.** I **84.** II **85.** III **86.** IV **87.** $y = p + \frac{1}{20}p$; (\$2, \$2.10); (\$15, \$15.75); (\$30, \$31.50); (\$40, \$42.00) **88.** (−4, 4), $\left(-1, \frac{1}{4}\right)$, (0, 0), $\left(1, \frac{1}{4}\right)$, (4, 4); U shape

Chapter 2

2-1

Check It Out! 1a. 8.8 **1b.** 0 **1c.** 25 **2a.** $\frac{1}{2}$ **2b.** −10 **2c.** 8 **3a.** 9.3 **3b.** 2 **3c.** 44 **4.** 35 years old

Exercises 3. 21 **5.** 16.3 **7.** $\frac{1}{2}$ **9.** 0 **11.** 2.3 **13.** 1.2 **15.** 32 **17.** 3.7 **19.** $\frac{17}{6}$ **21.** 9 **23.** 17 **25.** $\frac{4}{7}$ **27.** 10.5 **29.** 9 **31.** 0 **33.** −17 **35.** −3100 **37.** −0.5 **39.** 0.05 **41.** 15 **43.** 1545 **45.** 30 **47.** $\frac{1}{4}$ **49.** $a + 500 = 4732$; \$4232 **51.** $x - 10 = 12$; $x = 22$ **53.** $x + 8 = 16$; $x = 8$ **55.** $5 + x = 6$; $x = 1$ **57.** $x - 4 = 9$; $x = 13$ **59.** $m + 560 = 1680$; \$1120 **61.** $63 + x = 90$; $x = 27$ **63.** $x + 15 = 90$; $x = 75$ **65.** $h - 47 = 28$; 75 **69.** J **71.** $-\frac{12}{5}$ **73.** $-\frac{13}{12}$ **75.** 10 **77.** 90 **79.** 9 **81.** 72 **83.** 6 ft **85.** −80 **87.** −3

2-2

Check It Out! 1a. 50 **1b.** −39 **1c.** 56 **2a.** 4 **2b.** −20 **2c.** 5 **3a.** $-\frac{5}{4}$ **3b.** 1 **3c.** 612 **4.** 15,000 ft

Exercises 1. 32 **3.** 14 **5.** 19 **7.** 7 **9.** 5 **11.** 2.5 **13.** 14 **15.** −9 **17.** $\frac{1}{8}$ **19.** $16c = 192$; \$12 **21.** 24 **23.** −36 **25.** −150 **27.** 55 **29.** −3 **31.** 1 **33.** 13 **35.** 0.3 **37.** 2 **39.** −16 **41.** −3.5 **43.** −2 **45.** $\frac{7}{10}s = 392$; \$560 **49.** $4s = 84$; 21 in. **51.** $4s = 16.4$; 4.1 cm **53.** $-3x = 12$; $x = -4$ **55.** $\frac{x}{3} = -8$; $x = -24$ **57.** 6.25*h* = 50; 8 h **59.** 0.05*m* = 13.80; 276 min **61.** −2 **63.** 0; 8*y* = 0; 0 **65a.** number of data values **c.** 185,300 acres **67.** 7 **69.** 605 **71.** $\frac{3}{16}$ **73.** 5.7 **75.** $\frac{2}{3}g = 2$; 3 g **77.** D **79.** B

81a. $6c = 4.80$ **b.** $c = \$0.80$ **83.** 2 **85.** 9 **87.** 2 **89.** −20 **91.** −132 **93.** Multiply both sides by *a*. **95.** 12 **97.** 25 **99.** 6 years old **101.** 6 **103.** 16

2-3

Check It Out! 1a. 1 **1b.** 6 **1c.** 0 **2a.** $\frac{55}{4}$ **2b.** $\frac{1}{2}$ **2c.** 15 **3a.** $-\frac{5}{6}$ **3b.** 5 **3c.** 8 **4.** \$60 **5.** −42

Exercises 1. 2 **3.** −18 **5.** 2 **7.** 66 **9.** $\frac{5}{4}$ **11.** −12 **13.** 16 **15.** −3.2 **17.** 4 **19.** 15 passes **21.** 4 **23.** −4 **25.** 4 **27.** 5 **29.** −9 **31.** $\frac{1}{4}$ **33.** 1 **35.** 3 **37.** $\frac{28}{5}$ **39.** 3 **41.** 8 **43.** 7 **45.** $-\frac{1}{2}$ **47.** $x = 40$ **49.** $x = 35$ **51.** $8 - 3n = 2$; $n = 2$ **53a.** $1963 - 5s = 1863$; $s = 20$ **53b.** 3 **55.** 8 **57.** 4.5 **59.** −10 **61.** 10 **63.** $5k - 70 = 60$; 26 in. **65.** Stan: 36; Mark: 37; Wayne: 38 **67a.** 45,000; 112,500; 225,000; 337,500; $225n$ **67b.** $c = 225n$ **71.** H **73.** 27 **75.** $6\frac{1}{5}$ **77.** 14.5 **79.** −6 **81.** irrational **83.** repeating decimal, rational **85.** 8(60) + 8(1) = 488 **87.** 11(20) + 11(8) = 308 **89.** 13 **91.** −18

2-4

Check It Out! 1a. −2 **1b.** 2 **2a.** 4 **2b.** −2 **3a.** no solution **3b.** all real numbers **4.** 10 years old

Exercises 3. 1 **5.** 40 **7.** $-\frac{2}{3}$ **9.** 3 **11.** no solution **13.** all real numbers **15.** 6 **17.** 6 **19.** 2.85 **21.** 10 **23.** 6 **25.** 14 **27.** $\frac{3}{4}$ **29.** −4 **31.** no solution **33a.** 15 weeks **33b.** 180 lb **35.** $x - 30 = 14 - 3x$; $x = 11$ **37.** −4 **39.** 7 **41.** −3 **43.** 2 **45.** 1 **47.** $-\frac{7}{5}$ **49.** 4 **51.** no solution **53.** 9 **59.** F **61.** H **63.** 2 **65.** no solution **67.** −20 **69.** 6, 7, 8 **71.** \$1.68 **73.** $3y$ cm **75.** −63 **77.** 4 **79.** 2 **81.** −125 **83.** 15 **85.** 3

2-5

Check It Out! 1. about 1.46 h **2.** $i = f + gt$ **3a.** $t = \frac{5 - b}{2}$ **3b.** $V = \frac{m}{D}$

Exercises 3. $w = \frac{V}{\ell h}$ **5.** $m = 4n + 8$ **7.** $a = \frac{10}{b + c}$ **9.** $I = A - P$ **11.** $x = \frac{k + 5}{y}$ **13.** $\frac{x - 2}{3} = y$ **15.** $x = 5(a + g)$ **17.** $x = \frac{y - b}{m}$ **19.** $T = \frac{PV}{nR}$ **21.** $T = M + R$ **23.** $b = \frac{c - 2a}{2}$ **25.** $r = 7 - ax$ **27.** $x = \frac{5 - 4y}{3}$ **31.** $a = \frac{t - g}{-0.0035}$ **35.** C **37.** D **39.** $a = \frac{5}{2}\left(c + \frac{3}{4}b\right)$ **41.** $d = 500\left(t - \frac{1}{2}\right)$ **43.** $s = \frac{v^2 - u^2}{2a}$ **45.** 120 s **47.** 12 **49.** −6 **51.** 20 **53.** 12

2-6

Check It Out! 1a. −7, 7 **1b.** −5.5, 10.5 **2a.** no solutions **2b.** 4 **3.** $|x - 134| = 0.18$; minimum height: 133.82 m; maximum height: 134.18 m

Exercises 1. −6, 6 **3.** −2, 2 **5.** $-3, \frac{1}{2}$ **7.** no solutions **9.** no solutions **11.** 2.8 **13.** $|x - 207| = 2$; mile markers 205 and 209 **15.** −9, 13 ft **17.** −2, 2 **19.** 18.8, 65.28 **21.** $-\frac{14}{3}$, 4 **23.** 0 **25.** 0 **27.** $\frac{2}{3}$ **29.** $|x - 5| = 0.001$; 4.999 mm; 5.001 mm **31.** $|x - 7| = 2$; 5, 9 **33.** $|x - 1500| = 75$; 1575 bricks; 1425 bricks **35.** $|x| = 3$ **37.** $|x - 2| = 3$ **39.** sometimes **41.** always **43a.** $|t - 24| = 5$ **43b.** 19; 29 **43c.** yes **43d.** The measurements are correct to within 5 mi/h. **47.** C **49.** B **51.** Division Property of Equality; Subtraction Property of Equality; Division Property of Equality **53.** $1\frac{3}{4}$ ft **55.** $-8\frac{1}{3}$ **57.** −1.4 **59.** $T = S - R$ **61.** $w = xz - 3$ **63.** $N = 6M - S$

2-7

Check It Out! 1. 12 **2.** \$7.50/h **3.** 20.5 ft/s **4a.** −20 **4b.** 5.75 **5.** 6 in.

Exercises 1. The ratios are equivalent. **3.** 682 trillion **5.** 18,749 lb/cow **7.** 0.075 page/min **9.** 18 mi/gal **11.** $\frac{3}{5}$ **13.** 39 **15.** 6.5 **17.** 23 **19.** $\frac{3}{5} = \frac{h}{4.9}$; 2.94 m **21.** 72 **23.** \$403.90/oz **25.** 2498.4 km/h **27.** 10 **29.** −1 **31.** 13 **33.** 1.2 **35.** $\frac{1}{9}$ **37.** 45 **39.** \$84 **43.** 1.625 **45.** 3 **47.** $-\frac{2}{7}$ **49.** $\frac{11}{3}$ **51.** 3 **53.** 24 **55.** −120 **59.** A **61.** D **63.** 40°; 50° **65.** 0.0006722 people/m² **67.** −27 **69.** $-\frac{1}{32}$ **71.** 10^2 **73.** −5 **75.** 8 **77.** $V = \frac{nRT}{P}$

2-8

Check It Out! 1. 2.8 in. **2a.** $\frac{150}{x} = \frac{45}{195}$; 650 cm **2b.** $\frac{5.5}{x} = \frac{3.5}{28}$; 44 ft **3.** The ratio of the perimeters is equal to the ratio of the corresponding sides.

Exercises 3. 10 ft **7.** 7 in. **11.** 480 ft² **13.** 4 **15.** 2.8 ft **17.** 4 cm **21.** $\frac{1.5}{x} = \frac{4.5}{36}$; 12 m **23.** k^2 **25.** G **27.** $w = 4$; $x = 7.5$; $y = 8$ **29.** 16.6 cm **31.** −12 **33.** −46 **35.** (−2, 4); (−1, 1); (0, 0); (1, 1); (2, 4) **37.** (−2, −7); (−1, −4); (0, −1); (1, 2); (2, 5) **39.** 32 **41.** 3.5

2-9

Check It Out! 1a. 12 **1b.** 16.8 **1c.** 1.44 **2a.** 20% **2b.** 300% **3a.** 75 **3b.** 320 **4.** 10 karats

Exercises 3. 21 **5.** 5.6 **7.** 80% **9.** 12.5% **11.** 175 **13.** 36 **15.** 48 **17.** 2.5 **19.** 25% **21.** 50% **23.** 40 **25.** 511.1 **27.** 100 mg **29.** 2% **31.** 8% **33.** 64% **35.** 85% **37.** 85% **39.** 0.52; $\frac{13}{25}$ **41.** 90.0; $\frac{90}{100}$ **43.** 1.12; $\frac{28}{25}$ **45.** 0.06; $\frac{3}{50}$ **47.** 0.006; $\frac{3}{500}$ **49.** 0.5 is greater than $\frac{1}{2}$% because $\frac{1}{2}$% = 0.005. **51.** 0.001, 1%, $\frac{1}{10}$, 11%, 1.1 **53.** 0.49, $\frac{5}{9}$, $\frac{4}{5}$, 82%, 0.94 **55a.** 40% **b.** action **c.** 3% **d.** 36.9% **57.** box 1: 200; 100; 50 box 2: 12; 24; 148; 96 box 3: 25; 50; 100; 200 **59a.** $\frac{x}{90} = \frac{40}{100}$; \$36 **b.** \$54 **61.** F **63.** G **65.** 17.2% **67.** 88.5 **71.** 120 **73.** 160 **75.** 6 in. **77.** 3

2-10

Check It Out! 1. \$462.80 **2a.** \$270 **2b.** \$7650 **3a.** about \$3.30 **3b.** about \$5.60

Exercises 3. \$41,775 **5.** $4\frac{1}{2}$ yr **7.** about \$6.45 **9.** \$462.50 **11.** \$266.75 **13.** 5 yr **15.** about \$30 **17.** \$50,400 **19.** 2 yr **21.** \$2.89 **25.** A **27.** D **29.** 900 **31.** \$47.17 **33.** \$93 **35.** > **37.** > **39.** 12, 2 **41.** 2, $\frac{14}{3}$ **43.** 50% **45.** 80

2-11

Check It Out! 1a. 45% decrease **1b.** 20% increase **1c.** 43.75% increase **2a.** 90 **2b.** 6 **3a.** \$88 **3b.** 20% **4a.** \$15.30 **4b.** 130%

Exercises 3. 20% decrease **5.** 12.5% increase **7.** 20% decrease **9.** 61.8 **11.** 8 **13.** 70% **15.** 90% **17.** 25% decrease **19.** 400% increase

21. 30% increase **23.** 15% decrease **25.** 20% increase **27.** $8\frac{1}{3}$% decrease **29.** 252 **31.** 7.6 **33.** 15% **35.** 650% **37.** 50% **41.** 18 **43.** 200% increase **45.** 20 **47.** 60 **49.** 25% decrease **51a.** 60% **b.** $\frac{60}{100} = \frac{18}{x}$; $x = \$30$ **53.** H **55.** G **57.** 200 **59.** 625 **61.** 64 fl oz **63.** \$9.43 **65.** 80°; 170° **67.** 60°; 150° **69.** −20 **71.** 57 **73.** 36 **75.** −100 **77.** about \$4.20

Study Guide: Review

1. literal equation **2.** ratio **3.** 36 **4.** −2 **5.** −21 **6.** 18 **7.** $\frac{9}{8}$ **8.** $\frac{7}{3}$ **9.** $27 + s = 108$; 81 **10.** 7 **11.** $-\frac{10}{3}$ **12.** −90 **13.** 13 **14.** 0 **15.** −2 **16.** 17.5 **17.** −5 **18.** 40 **19.** −3 **20.** $-\frac{1}{2}$ **21.** 15 **22.** 18 **23.** 1 **24.** 41; 123°; 57° **25.** −2 **26.** −2 **27.** 1 **28.** $-\frac{2}{3}$ **29.** no solution **30.** all real numbers **31.** 9 **32.** $n = \frac{360}{c}$ **33.** $a = \frac{25}{\pi} - \ell$ **34.** 3.7 gal **35.** $x = 15, -27$ **36.** $y = 7, 3$ **37.** $y = 9, -9$ **38.** $x = 17.4, -6.6$ **39.** $g = -4, -8$ **40.** $x = \frac{5}{7}, -\frac{5}{7}$ **41.** $|x - 55| = 5$; minimum speed: 50 mi/h; maximum speed: 60 mi/h **42.** $3\frac{1}{3}$c **43.** 1080 m/h **44.** 0.85 mi/min **45.** 1.6 **46.** 54 **47.** 5 **48.** −3 **49.** 2.5 cm **50.** 16 ft **51.** The ratio of the areas is the square of the ratio of the radii. **52.** 5.29 **53.** 3105 **54.** 66.7% **55.** 400% **56.** 133.3 **57.** 240 **58.** 80% **59.** \$48,500 **60.** \$9000 **61.** about \$5.60 **62.** about \$2.20 **63.** 37% increase **64.** 33% decrease **65.** 91 **66.** 127.5 **67.** \$3.75; \$6.25 **68.** 37.5%

Chapter 3

3-1

Check It Out! 1. all real numbers greater than 4 **2a.** (number line 2 to 4) **2b.** (number line −3 to 3) **2c.** (number line −6 to 0) **3.** $x < 2.5$ **4.** d = amount employee can earn per hour; $d \geq 8.25$ (number line 0 to 12, 8.25)

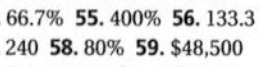

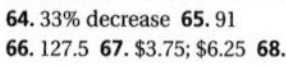

Exercises 1. A solution of an inequality makes the inequality true when substituted for the variable. **3.** all real numbers greater than −3 **5.** all real numbers greater than or equal to 3 **11.** $b > -8\frac{1}{2}$ **13.** $d < -7$ **15.** $f \leq 14$ **17.** $r < 140$ where *r* is positive **19.** all real numbers less than 2 **21.** all real numbers less than or equal to 12 **27.** $v < -11$ **29.** $x > -3.3$ **31.** $z \geq 9$ **33.** y = years of experience; $y \geq 5$ **35.** *h* is less than −5. **37.** *r* is greater than or equal to −2. **39.** $p \leq 17$ **41.** $f > 0$ **43.** p = profits; $p < 10{,}000$ **45.** e = elevation; $e \leq 5000$ **51.** D **53.** C **59.** D **61.** C **65.** < **71.** 10 **73.** 7 **75.** $3x + 3$ **77.** $g = 2b$; 16 **79.** $b = 9$ **81.** no solutions

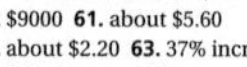

3-2

Check It Out! 1a. $s \leq 9$ (number line 0 to 12) **1b.** $t < 5\frac{1}{2}$ (number line 4 to 6) **1c.** $q < 11$ (number line 9 to 13) **2.** $11 + m \leq 15$; $m \leq 4$ where *m* is nonnegative; Sarah can consume 4 mg or less without exceeding the RDA. **3.** $250 + p > 282$; $p > 32$; Josh needs to bench press more than 32 additional pounds to break the school record.

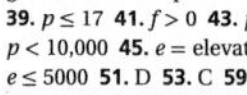

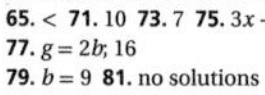

Exercises 1. $p > 6$ **3.** $x \leq -15$ **5.** $102 + t \leq 104$; $t \leq 2$ where *t* is nonnegative **7.** $a \geq 5$ **9.** $x < 15$ **11.** $1400 + 243 + w \leq 2000$; $w \leq 357$ where *w* is nonnegative **13.** $x - 10 > 32$; $x > 42$ **15.** $r - 13 \leq 15$; $r \leq 28$ **17.** $q > 51$ **19.** $p \leq 0.8$ **21.** $c > -202$ **23.** $x \geq 0$ **25.** $21 + d \leq 30$; $d \leq 9$ where *d* is nonnegative **27.** $x < 3$; B **29.** $x \leq 3$; D **31.** $p \leq 40{,}421$ where *p* is nonnegative **35. a.** 411 + 411 = 882 miles **b.** $822 + m \leq 1000$ **c.** $m \leq 178$, but *m* cannot be negative. **37.** F **39.** J **41.** $r \leq 5\frac{1}{10}$ **43.** sometimes **45.** always **47.** $y = 3 - \frac{2}{3}x$ **49.** $a = \frac{c - 2}{b}$ **51.** $k = 2s - 11$ **53.** $x = 10$ **55.** $x \geq -1$

3-3

Check It Out! 1a. $k > 6$ (number line 0 to 12) **1b.** $q \leq -10$ (number line −18 to −10) **1c.** $g > 36$ (number line 34 to 38) **2a.** $x \geq -10$ (number line −10 to −2) **2b.** $h > -17$ (number line −19 to −15) **3.** 0, 1, 2, 3, 4, 5, 6, 7, 8, 9, 10, 11, or 12 servings

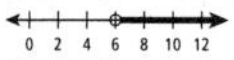

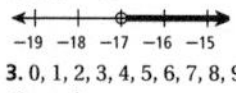

Exercises 1. $b > 9$ **3.** $d > 18$ **5.** $m \leq 1$ **7.** $s > -2$ **9.** $x > 5$ **11.** $n > -0.4$ **13.** $d > -3$ **15.** $t > -72$ **17.** 0, 1, 2, 3, 4, 5, or 6 nights **19.** $j \leq 12$ **21.** $d < 7$ **23.** $h \leq \frac{8}{5}$ **25.** $c \leq -12$ **27.** $b \geq \frac{1}{10}$ **29.** $b \leq -16$ **31.** $r < -\frac{3}{2}$ **33.** $y < 2$ **35.** $t > 4$ **37.** $z < -11$ **39.** $k \leq -7$ **41.** $p \geq -12$ **43.** $x > -3$ **45.** $x < 20$ **47.** $p \leq -6$ **49.** $b < 2$ **51.** $7x \geq 21$; $x \geq 3$ **53.** $-\frac{4}{5}b \leq -16$; $b \geq 20$ **57.** C **59.** A **67.** B **71.** $g \leq -\frac{14}{5}$ **73.** $m > \frac{4}{15}$ **75.** $x = 5$ **79.** 2^3 **81.** \$1.89/gal **83.** 35 words/min **85.** $t < 1$

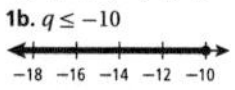

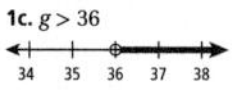

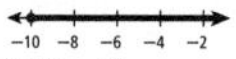

3-4

Check It Out! 1a. $x \leq -6$ (number line −8 to 0) **1b.** $x < -11$ (number line −13 to −9) **1c.** $n \leq -10$ (number line −12 to −8) **2a.** $m > 10$ (number line 8 to 12) **2b.** $x > -4$ (number line −6 to 0) **2c.** $x > 2\frac{1}{3}$ (number line 0 to 4)

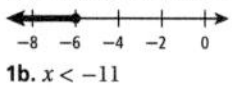

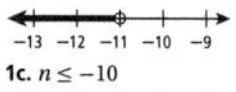

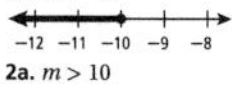

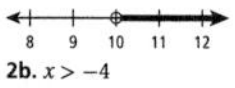

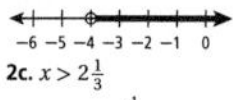

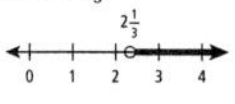

3. $\frac{95+x}{2} \ge 90$; $95 + x \ge 180$; $x \ge 85$; Jim's score must be at least 85.

Exercises **1.** $m > 6$ **3.** $x \le -2$ **5.** $x > -16$ **7.** $x \ge -9$ **9.** $x > -\frac{1}{2}$ **11.** $x \le 19$ **13.** $x > 1$ **15.** sales of more than $9000 **17.** $x \le 1$ **19.** $w < -2$ **21.** $x < -6$ **23.** $f < -4.5$ **25.** $w > 0$ **27.** $v > \frac{2}{3}$ **29.** $x > -5$ **31.** $x < -2$ **33.** $a \ge 11$ **35.** $x > 3$ **37.** starting at 29 min **39.** $x \le 2$ **41.** $x < 4$ **43.** $x < -6$ **45.** $r < 8$ **47.** $x < 7$ **49.** $p \ge 18$ **51.** $\frac{1}{2}x + 9 < 33$; $x < 48$ **53.** $4(x + 12) \le 16$; $x \le -8$ **55.** B **57.** A **59.** 24 months or more **61a.**

Number	Process	Cost
1	$350 + 3$	353
2	$350 + 3(2)$	356
3	$350 + 3(3)$	359
10	$350 + 3(10)$	380
n	$350 + 3n$	$350 + 3n$

b. $c = 350 + 3n$ **c.** $350 + 3n \le 500$; $n \le 50$; 50 CDs or fewer **65.** G **67.** 59 **69.** $x > 5$ **71.** $x > 0$ **73.** $x \ge 0$ **75.** $-3x > 0$ **77.** 7 **79.** $\frac{2}{3}$ **81.** -9 **83.** $25 + 2m = 10 + 2.5m$; $m = 30$ **85.** $a \ge 6$

3-5

Check It Out! **1a.** $x \le -2$

1b. $t < -1$

2. more than 160 flyers **3a.** $r \le 2$

3b. $x < 3$

4a. no solutions **4b.** all real numbers

Exercises **1.** $x < 3$ **3.** $x < 2$ **5.** $c < -2$ **7.** at least 34 pizzas **9.** $p < -17$ **11.** $x > 3$ **13.** $t < 6.8$ **15.** no solutions **17.** all real numbers **19.** no solutions **21.** $y > -2$ **23.** $b \ge -7$ **25.** $m > 5$ **27.** $x \ge 2$ **29.** $w \ge 6$ **31.** $r \ge -4$ **33.** no solutions **35.** all real numbers **37.** all real numbers **39.** $t < -7$ **41.** $x > 3$ **43.** $x < 2$ **45.** $x > -2$

47. $x \le -6$ **49.** 27 s **51a.** $400 + 4.50n$ **b.** $12n$ **c.** $400 + 4.50n < 12n$; $n > 53\frac{1}{3}$; 54 CDs or more **53.** $5x - 10 < 6x - 8$; $x > -2$ **55.** $\frac{3}{4}x \ge x - 5$; $x \le 20$ **59.** x can never be greater than itself plus 1. **61.** D **63.** A **67.** $x < -3$ **69.** $w \ge -1\frac{6}{7}$ **73.** 26 in. **75.** y = years; $y \ge 14$

3-6

Check It Out! **1.** $1.0 < c < 3.0$

2a. $1 < x < 5$

2b. $-3 \le n < 2$

3a. $r < 10$ OR $r > 14$

3b. $x \ge 3$ OR $x < -1$

4a. $-9 < y < -2$

4b. $x \le -13$ OR $x \ge 2$

Exercises **1.** intersection **3.** $-5 < x < 5$ **5.** $0 < x < 3$ **7.** $x < -8$ OR $x > 4$ **9.** $n < 1$ OR $n > 4$ **11.** $-5 \le a \le -3$ **13.** $c < 1$ OR $c \ge 9$ **15.** $16 \le k \le 50$ **17.** $3 \le n \le 6$ **19.** $2 < x < 6$ **21.** $x < 0$ OR $x > 3$ **23.** $x < -3$ OR $x > 2$ **25.** $q < 0$ OR $q \ge 2$ **27.** $-2 < s < 1$ **29a.** $225 + 80n$ gives the cost of the studio and technicians; the band will spend between $200 and $550. **b.** $-0.3125 \le n \le 4.0625$; n cannot be a negative number **c.** $155 **31.** $1 \le x \le 2$ **33.** $-10 \le x \le 10$ **35.** $t < 0$ OR $t > 100$ **37.** $-2 < x < 5$ **39.** $a < 0$ OR $a > 1$ **41.** $n < 2$ OR $n > 5$ **43.** $7 \le m \le 60$ **47.** D **49.** B **51.** $0.5 < c < 3$ **53.** $s \le 6$ OR $s \ge 9$ **55.** $-1 \le x \le 3$ **57.** $4x - 5$ **59.** $3a + 3$ **61.** $(-2, 3)$, $(-1, 0)$, $(0, -1)$, $(1, 0)$, $(2, 3)$; U-shaped **63.** $m < 2$ **65.** $x \le -2$

3-7

Check It Out! **1a.** $-3 \le x \le 3$

1b. $-15 \le x \le 9$

2a. $x \le -2$ OR $x \ge 2$

2b. $x \le -6$ OR $x \ge 1$

3. $|p - 125| \le 75$; $50 \le p \le 200$

4a. all real numbers **4b.** no solutions

Exercises **1.** $-3 \le x \le 3$ **3.** $-2 < x < 2$ **5.** $4 < x < 6$ **7.** $x < -22$ OR $x > 22$ **9.** $x \le -4$ OR $x \ge 4$ **11.** $x \le 1$ OR $x \ge 5$ **13.** $|x - 55| \le 25$; $30 \le x \le 80$ **15.** no solutions **17.** all real numbers **19.** no solutions **21.** $2 < x < 4$ **23.** $-3 < x < 3$ **25.** $-6 < x < 0$ **27.** $x \le -10$ OR $x \ge 10$ **29.** $x \le -10$ OR $x \ge 6$ **31.** $x < -1$ OR $x > 2$ **33.** no solutions **35.** all real numbers **37.** no solutions **39.** always **41.** sometimes **43.** $|x - 2| \le 3$; $-1 \le x \le 5$ **45.** $|a| \le 2$ **47.** $|c| \ge 6\frac{1}{2}$ **49a.** 10,010 Hz **49b.** $|x - 10{,}010| \le 9990$ **51.** $|n - 23| > 12$ **53.** $k \le 1$; the inequality is equivalent to $|x| < k - 1$, and this has no solutions when the expression on the right side is less than or equal to 0 (i.e., when $k - 1 \le 0$ or $k \le 1$). **55.** B **57.** B **61.** $1\frac{1}{2}$ **63.** $2\frac{1}{2}$ **65.** all real numbers less than 2 **67.** all real numbers greater than or equal to -6 **69.** $0 < x < 4$ **71.** $x < 1$ OR $x > 4$

Study Guide: Review

1. inequality **2.** union **3.** compound inequality **4.** intersection **5.** solution of an inequality

6.

7.

8.

9.

10.

11.

12. $a < 2$ **13.** $k \ge -3.5$ **14.** $q < -10$ **15.** t = temperature; $t \ge 72$ **16.** s = students; $s \le 12$ where s is a natural number **17.** m = minutes; $m < 30$ where m is nonnegative **18.** $t < 7$ **19.** $k \le 2$ **20.** $m > -5$ **21.** $x \ge 4.5$ **22.** $w < 9.5$ **23.** $a < 5$ **24.** $h < 1$ **25.** $v < -2$ **26.** 5.5 mi or more **27.** $18 or less **28.** $a \le 5$ **29.** $t > -3$ **30.** $p > 8$ **31.** $x \le -25$ **32.** $n > 6$ **33.** $g < -12$ **34.** $k > -7$ **35.** $r < -9$ **36.** $h < -3$ **37.** $g < 2.5$ **38.** 0, 1, 2, 3, 4, 5, 6, 7 **39.** at least 334 lanyards **40.** $x < 5$ **41.** $t \ge 6$ **42.** $m > -11$ **43.** $x < -1$ **44.** $h > -3$ **45.** $x > 1\frac{1}{2}$ **46.** $b \le 10$ **47.** $y > 3\frac{1}{2}$ **48.** $n > -15$ **49.** 0, 1, 2, 3, 4, 5, 6, 7, 8, 9, 10, 11, 12, or 13 **50.** $m < -1$ **51.** $y \ge -2$ **52.** $c < -3$ **53.** $q \le -4$ **54.** $x > 2$ **55.** $t < 3$ **56.** no solutions **57.** all real numbers **58.** $p > -\frac{1}{2}$ **59.** all real numbers **60.** $k > 2$ **61.** no solutions **62.** $8.75 > m$ **63.** $-10 < t < 4$ **64.** $-6 < k \le 7$ **65.** $r > 7$ OR $r < -2$ **66.** no solutions **67.** $-2 < p \le 5$ **68.** all real numbers **69.** $68 \le t \le 84$ **70.** $102 \le n \le 183.6$ **71.** $-22 \le x \le 22$ **72.** $x < -12$ OR $x > 4$ **73.** $-4 \le x \le 4$ **74.** $-18 < x < 0$ **75.** $x \le -3$ OR $x \ge 3$ **76.** $-3 < x < 3$ **77.** $x < -13.9$ OR $x > 13.9$ **78.** $-12.5 < x < 2.1$ **79.** $x \le 5$ OR $x \ge 9$ **80.** $x \le -4$ OR $x \ge 4$ **81.** no solutions **82.** $-16.8 \le x \le 5.8$ **83.** $|d - 72| \le 4$; $68 \le d \le 76$

Chapter 4

4-1

Check It Out! **1.** C **2a.** discrete;

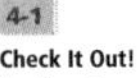

2b. continuous;

3. Possible answer: When the number of students reaches a certain point, the number of pizzas bought increases.

Exercises **1.** continuous **3.** B **5.** C **11.** A **13.** continuous **19.** The point of intersection represents the time of day when you will be the same distance from the base of the mountain on both the hike up and the hike down. **23.** C **27.** C **29.** -8 **31.** $\frac{1}{9}$ **33.** $(-2, 5)$, $(-1, 3)$, $(0, 1)$, $(1, -1)$, $(2, -3)$; line **35.** $(-2, 6)$, $(-1, 3)$, $(0, 2)$, $(1, 3)$, $(2, 6)$; U-shape **37.** $n - 5 = -2$; 3

4-2

Check It Out! **1.**

x	y
1	3
2	4
3	5

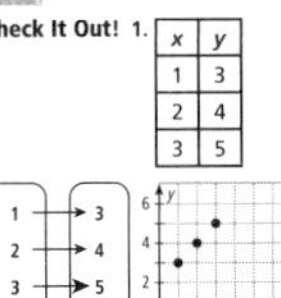

2a. D: {6, 5, 2, 1}; R: {−4, −1, 0} **2b.** D: {1, 4, 8}; R: {1, 4} **3a.** D: {−6, −4, 1, 8}; R: {1, 2, 9}; yes; each domain value is paired with exactly one range value. **3b.** D: {2, 3, 4}; R: {−5, −4, −3}; no; the domain value 2 is paired with both −5 and −4.

Exercises

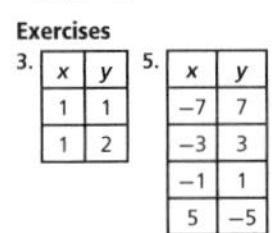

3.

x	y
1	1
1	2

5.

x	y
−7	7
−3	3
−1	1
5	−5

7. D: {−5, 0, 2, 5}; R: {−20, −8, 0, 7} **9.** D: {2, 3, 5, 6, 8}; R: {4, 9, 25, 36, 81} **11.** D: {1}; R: {−2, 0, 3, 8}; no **13.** D: {−2, −1, 0, 1, 2}; R: {1}; yes

15.

x	y
−2	−4
−1	−1
0	0
1	−1
2	−4

17. D: {3}; R: $1 \le y \le 5$ **19.** D: $-2 \le x \le 2$; R: $0 \le y \le 2$; yes **21.** yes **23.** yes **25.** yes **27.** no **29a.** D: $0 \le t \le 5$; R: $0 \le v \le 750$ **b.** yes **c.** (2, 300); (3.5, 525) **33.** G **35a.** {(−3, 5), (−1, 7), (0, 9), (1, 11), (3, 13)} **b.** D: {−3, −1, 0, 1, 3}; R: {5, 7, 9, 11, 13} **c.** yes **37.** all real numbers **39.** 27 cm **41.** $x \ge 19$

4-3

Check It Out! **1.** $y = 3x$ **2a.** independent: time; dependent: cost **2b.** independent: pounds; dependent: cost **3a.** independent: pounds; dependent: cost; $f(x) = 1.69x$ **3b.** independent: people; dependent: cost; $f(x) = 6 + 29.99x$ **4a.** 1; −7 **4b.** −5; 101 **5.** $f(x) = 500x$; D: {0, 1, 2, 3}; R: {0, 500, 1000, 1500}

Exercises **1.** dependent **3.** $y = x - 2$ **5.** independent: size of bottle; dependent: cost of water **7.** independent: hours; dependent: cost; $f(h) = 75h$ **9.** 2; 9 **11.** −1; −15 **13.** $y = -2x$ **15.** independent: size of lawn; dependent: cost **17.** independent: days late; dependent: total cost; $f(x) = 3.99 + 0.99x$ **19.** independent: gallons of gas; dependent: miles; $f(x) = 28x$ **21.** 7; 10 **23.** $f(n) = 2n + 5$; D: {1, 2, 3, 4}; R: {$7, $9, $11, $13}

25.

z	1	2	3	4
$g(z)$	−3	−1	1	3

27. $f(-6.89) \approx -16$; $f(1.01) \approx 8$; $f(4.67) \approx 20$ **33.** D **35.** 3.5 **37.** 44.1 m **39.** $y = -3$ **41.** $x = 2$ **43.** D: $x \ge 0$; R: all real numbers; no

4-4

Check It Out! **1a.**

1b.

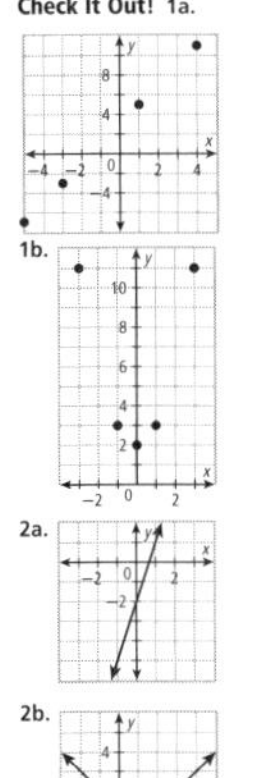

2a.

2b.

3. $x = 3$ **4.** Possible answer: about 32.5 mi

Average Speed of Lava Flow

Exercises

1.

3.

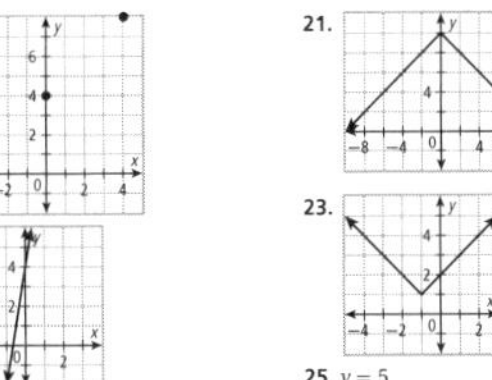

5.

7.

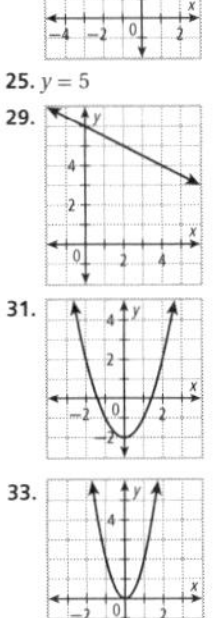

9.

11. $y = -1$

13.

15.

17.

19.

21.

23.

25. $y = 5$

29.

31.

33.

35.

37. $x = 1$ **39.** $y = -8$ **41.** yes; yes **43.** no; yes **45.** no; yes; yes **47.** yes; no; yes **55a.** $v = 10{,}000 - 1500h$ **b.** 8500 gal

c.

Time (h)	Volume (gal)
0	10,000
1	8,500
2	7,000
3	5,500
4	4,000

59. J **61.** J **63.** $y = 4x + 64$ **65.** 2^3 **67.** $p < -4$ **69.** $b \ge 20$ **71.** −3; 7

4-5

Check It Out!

1.

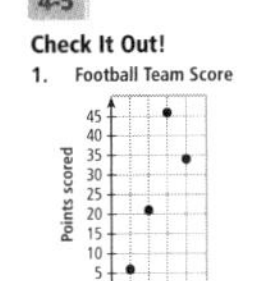

2. positive **3a.** No correlation; the temperature in Houston has nothing to do with the number of cars sold in Boston. **3b.** Positive; as the number of family members increases, more food is needed, so the grocery bill increases too. **3c.** Negative; as the number of times you sharpen your pencil increases, the length of the pencil decreases. **4.** Graph A; it cannot be graph B because graph B shows negative minutes; it cannot be graph C because graph C shows the temperature of the pie increasing, a positive correlation. **5.** about 75 rolls

Exercises **3.** no **5.** positive **7.** negative **9.** positive **11.** A **15.** positive **17.** positive **19.** A **23.** positive **25.** B

27a.

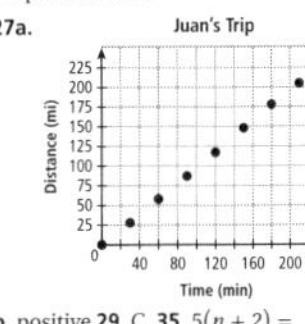

b. positive **29.** C **35.** $5(n + 2) = 2n - 8$; $n = -6$ **37.** no solution

39.

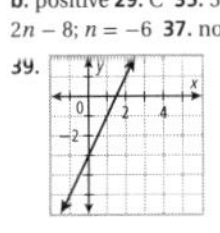

41.

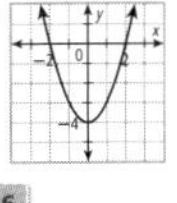

4-6

Check It Out! **1a.** yes; $\frac{1}{2}$; $\frac{5}{4}$, $\frac{7}{4}$, $\frac{9}{4}$ **1b.** no **2a.** −343 **2b.** 19.6 **3.** 750 lb

Exercises **1.** common difference **3.** yes; −0.7; −0.7, −1.4, −2.1 **5.** no **7.** −53 **9.** no **11.** yes; −9; −58, −67, −76 **13.** 5.9 **15.** 9500 mi **17.** $\frac{1}{4}$ **19.** −2.2 **21.** 0.07 **23.** $-\frac{3}{8}$, $-\frac{1}{2}$, $-\frac{5}{8}$, $-\frac{3}{4}$ **25.** −0.2, −0.7, −1.2, −1.7 **27.** −0.3, −0.1, 0.1, 0.3 **29.** 22 **31.** 122 **33b.** $9, $11, $13, $15; $a_n = 2n + 7$ **c.** $37 **d.** no **35.** −104.5 **37.** $\frac{20}{3}$ **39a.** $a_n = 6 + 3(n - 1)$ **b.** 48 **c.** $7800 **d.** $a_n = 7 + 3(n - 1)$; $8200

41a.

Time Interval	Mile Marker
1	520
2	509
3	498
4	487
5	476
6	465

b. $a_n = 520 + (n - 1)(-11)$ **c.** number of miles per interval **d.** 421 **43.** F **45.** 173 and 182; 20th and 21st terms **47a.** session 16; yes **b.** Thursday **49.** 20 **51.** $t < -2$ OR $t > 2$ **53.** negative

Study Guide: Review

1. domain **2.** negative correlation **3.** term **4.** continuous

5. continuous

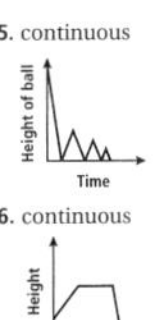

6. continuous

7. Possible answer: A family buys a fish tank and some fish. After two weeks, they buy some more fish. After two more weeks, they buy more fish. **8.** Possible answer: A monkey swings from a high branch to a lower branch. He climbs along the branch. Then he jumps to a higher branch and takes a nap.

9.

x	−1	0	2
y	0	1	1

10.

x	−2	−1	2	3
y	−1	1	3	4

11. D: {−4, −2, 0, 2}; R: {−1, 1, 3, 5} **12.** D: {−2, −1, 0, 1, 2}; R: {−1, 0} **13.** D: {0, 1, 4}; R: {−2, −1, 0, 1, 2} **14.** D: $-4 \le x \le 3$; R: $-3 \le y \le 5$ **15.** D: {−5, −3, −1, 1}; R: {−3, −2, −1, 0}; yes **16.** D: {−4, −2, 0, 2}; R: {−2, 1}; yes **17.** D: {1, 2, 3 ,4}; R: {−1, 0, 1, 2, 3}; no **18.** {(1, 5.00), (2, 6.50), (3, 8.00), (4, 9.50), (5, 11.00)}; yes **19.** yes **20.** y is 7 less than x; $y = x - 7$. **21.** y is 9 times x; $y = 9x$. **22.** independent: number of cakes; dependent: cost; $f(c) = 6c$ **23.** independent: number of CDs Raul will buy; dependent: number of CDs Tim will buy; $g(n) = 2n$ **24.** 14 **25.** −11 **26.** 6; −1

27.

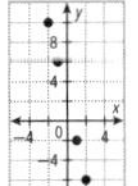

28.

29.

30.

31.

32.

33. Possible answer: $44
34. negative 35. Possible answer: 33 36. yes; −6; −4, −10, −16
37. no 38. no 39. yes; 2.5; 2, 4.5, 7
40. 105 41. −62 42. 20 43. $408
44. −15.5 °C

Chapter 5

5-1

Check It Out! **1a.** Yes; each domain value is paired with exactly one range value; yes **1b.** Yes; each domain value is paired with exactly one range value; yes **1c.** No; each domain value is not paired with exactly one range value.
2. Yes; a constant change of +2 in x corresponds to a constant change of −1 in y.

3a. yes

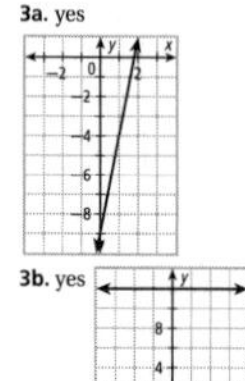

3b. yes

3c. no

4.

Rental Payment

D: {0, 1, 2, 3, ...}
R: {$10, $13, $16, $19, ...}

Exercises **1.** No; it is not in the form $Ax + By = C$. **3.** yes; yes **5.** yes **7.** yes **9.** yes **11.** no **15.** yes; no **17.** yes; no **19.** yes **23.** no **27.** yes; yes **29.** yes; yes **31.** yes; $-4x + y = 2$; $A = -4$; $B = 1$; $C = 2$ **33.** no **35.** yes; $x = 7$; $A = 1$; $B = 0$; $C = 7$ **37.** yes; $3x - y = 1$; $A = 3$; $B = -1$; $C = 1$ **39.** yes; $5x - 2y = -3$; $A = 5$, $B = -2$, $C = -3$ **41.** no **55.** no **57.** C **63.** not linear **65.** −1 **67.** $\frac{1}{9}$ **69.** 2 **71.** 9

5-2

Check It Out! **1a.** x-intercept: −2; y-intercept: 3 **1b.** x-intercept: −10; y-intercept: 6 **1c.** x-intercept: 4; y-intercept: 8
2a.

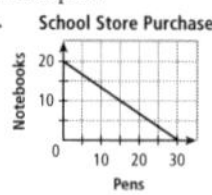

x-intercept: 30; y-intercept: 20
2b. x-intercept: number of pens that can be purchased if no notebooks are purchased; y-intercept: number of notebooks that can be purchased if no pens are purchased

3a.

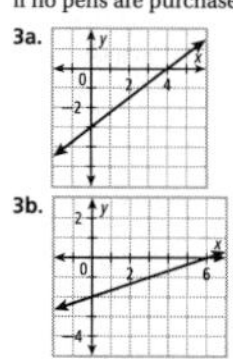

3b.

Exercises **1.** y-intercept
3. x-intercept: 2; y-intercept: −4
5. x-intercept: 2; y-intercept: −1
7. x-intercept: 2; y-intercept: 8
13. x-intercept: −1; y-intercept: 3
15. x-intercept: −4; y-intercept: 2
17. x-intercept: −4; y-intercept: 2
19. x-intercept: 2; y-intercept: 8
21. x-intercept: $\frac{1}{8}$; y-intercept: −1
35. A **37.** B **41.** F **47.** x-intercept: 950; y-intercept: −55 **49.** $c > 4$
51. $m \geq -6$ **53.** yes

5-3

Check It Out! **1.** day 1 to day 6: −53; day 6 to day 16: −7.5; day 16 to day 22: 0; day 22 to day 30: −4.375; from day 1 to day 6
2.

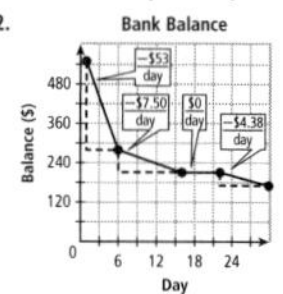

3. $-\frac{2}{5}$ **4a.** undefined **4b.** 0
5a. undefined **5b.** positive

Exercises **1.** constant **5.** $-\frac{3}{4}$
7. undefined **9.** undefined
11. positive **15.** 1 **17.** 0
19. positive **23.** $\frac{17}{18}$ **29.** C **31.** G
35. −2 **37.** D: {3}; R: {4, 2, 0, −2}; no **39.** x-intercept: 3; y-intercept: 6
41. x-intercept: $\frac{1}{4}$; y-intercept: $\frac{1}{2}$

5-4

Check It Out! **1a.** $m = 0$ **1b.** $m = 3$ **1c.** $m = 2$ **2a.** $m = \frac{1}{2}$ **2b.** $m = -3$ **2c.** $m = 2$ **2d.** $m = -\frac{3}{2}$ **3.** $m = \frac{1}{2}$; the height of the plant is increasing at a rate of 1 cm every 2 days.
4. $m = -\frac{2}{3}$

Exercises **1.** 1 **3.** $-\frac{1}{2}$ **5.** 10 **7.** $\frac{1}{540}$
9. $-\frac{5}{9}$ **11.** −4 **13.** undefined
15. $-\frac{3}{4}$ **17.** $-\frac{9}{5000}$ **19.** $-\frac{13}{5}$
23a. Car 1; 20 mi/h **b.** The speed and the slope are both equal to the distance divided by time. **c.** 20 mi/h **25a.** $y = 220 - x$ **27.** G **29.** $-\frac{b}{a}$
31. $\frac{3}{2} - y$ **33.** $x = \frac{1}{2}$ **35.** $x = -3$
37. $x = 0$ **39.** $-11 < x < -5$
41. $x \leq -7$ OR $x \geq 7$ **43.** $x \leq -8$ OR $x \geq 6$ **45.** yes

5-5

Check It Out! **1.** $\left(\frac{3}{2}, 0\right)$ **2.** (4, 3) **3.** 6.71 **4.** 17.7 mi

Exercises **3.** $\left(1\frac{1}{2}, -4\right)$ **5.** (3, 3)
7. 5.39 **9.** 10.82 **11.** (−2, −3)
13. (17, −23) **15.** (2, −8) **17.** 8.94
19. 9.22 **21.** 6.1 mi **25.** 13.42
27. 14.32 **29a.** 7.2 **b.** (0, −2) **c.** 23
31. $\overline{CD}$, $\overline{EF}$, $\overline{AB}$ **35.** B **37.** D
39. 12.5 square units **41.** ±8
43. 26 **45.** $x > -2$ **47.** $z > -4$
49. $\frac{1}{4}$

5-6

Check It Out! **1a.** no **1b.** yes; $-\frac{3}{4}$ **1c.** yes; −3 **2a.** No; possible answer: the value of $\frac{y}{x}$ is not the same for each ordered pair. **2b.** Yes; possible answer: the value of $\frac{y}{x}$ is the same for each ordered pair.
2c. No; possible answer: the value of $\frac{y}{x}$ is not the same for each ordered pair. **3.** 90
4. $y = 4x$

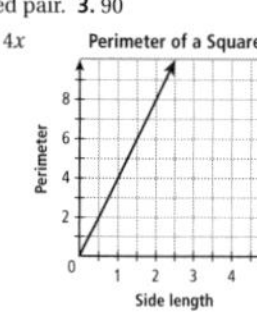

Exercises **1.** direct variation
3. yes; −4 **5.** no **7.** 18 **9.** $y = 7x$
11. yes; $\frac{1}{4}$ **13.** yes **15.** −16
17. $y = 2.50x$ **19.** no **21.** $y = -3x$

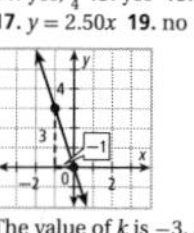

The value of k is −3, and the graph shows that the slope of the line is −3.
25. $y = 2x$

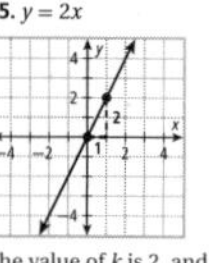

The value of k is 2, and the graph shows that the slope of the line is 2.
29. $k = -\frac{2}{9}x$

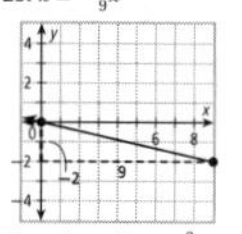

The value of k is $-\frac{2}{9}$, and the graph shows that the slope of the line is $-\frac{2}{9}$.
33. $y = -6x$

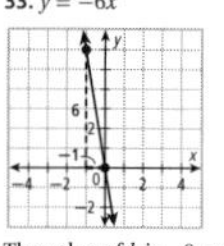

The value of k is −6, and the graph shows that the slope of the line is −6. **41.** C **43.** B **47.** $p = 7 - 4q$
49. $x = \frac{4 - 2y}{y}$ **51.** $y = -2x$ **53.** −4
55. $\frac{1}{2}$

5-7

Check It Out!
1a.

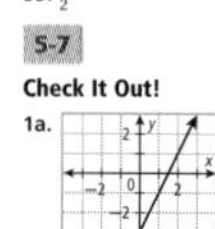

1b.

2a. $y = -12x - \frac{1}{2}$ **2b.** $y = x$
2c. $y = 8x - 25$
3a. $y = \frac{2}{3}x$

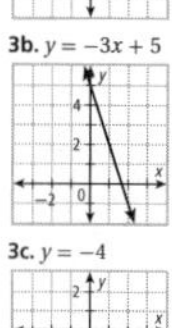

3b. $y = -3x + 5$

3c. $y = -4$

4a. $y = 18x + 200$ **4b.** slope: 18; cost per person; y-intercept: 200; fee **4c.** $3800

Exercises
1.

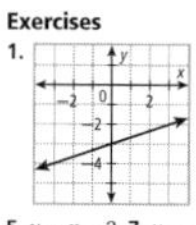

5. $y = x - 2$ **7.** $y = -3$
9. $y = -2x - 1$ **11.** $y = 3x - 1$
13a. $y = 18x + 10$ **b.** slope: 18; Helen's speed; y-intercept: 10; distance she has already biked
c. 46 mi

15.

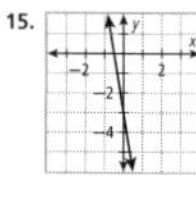

17.

19. $y = 5x - 9$ **21.** $y = -\frac{1}{2}x + 7$
23. $y = \frac{1}{2}x + 4$ **25.** $y = -2x + 8$
29. possible **31.** impossible
33. C **37.** B **39.** B **41.** $y = \frac{1}{3}x - 3$
43. −6 **45.** h = hours; $h \leq 2$ where h is nonnegative **47.** $n \leq 8$
49. $t < -3$

5-8

Check It Out!
1a. $y - 1 = 2\left(x - \frac{1}{2}\right)$
1b. $y + 4 = 0(x - 3)$
2a.

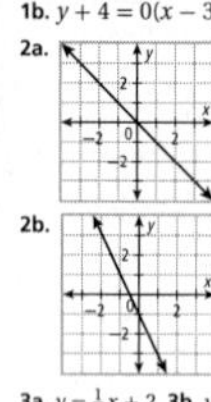

2b.

3a. $y = \frac{1}{3}x + 2$ **3b.** $y = 6x - 8$
4. x-intercept: −3; y-intercept: 9
5. $y = 2.25x + 6$; $53.25

Exercises **1.** $y + 6 = \frac{1}{5}(x - 2)$
3. $y + 7 = 0(x - 3)$ **7.** $y = -\frac{1}{3}x + 7$
9. $y = -x$ **11.** $y = -\frac{1}{2}x + 4$
13. x-intercept: 3; y-intercept: −3
15. x-intercept: −1; y-intercept: 3
17. $y - 5 = \frac{2}{9}(x + 1)$ **19.** $y - 8 = 8(x - 1)$ **23.** $y = -\frac{2}{7}x + 1$ **25.** $y = -6x + 57$ **27.** $y = -\frac{11}{2}x + 18$
29. $y = 2x - 6$ **31.** x-intercept: 1; y-intercept: −2 **33.** x-intercept: −6; y-intercept: 9 **35.** $y = -\frac{1}{500}x + 212$; 200 °F **41.** never **43a.** $y - 11 = 2.5(x - 2)$ **b.** 6 in. **c.** $16\frac{5}{8}$ in.
47. $y = -8$; $x = 4$ **49.** A **53a.** (0, 12) and (6, 8) **b.** $y = -\frac{2}{3}x + 12$
c. 18 min **55.** H **57.** $y = -3x + \frac{11}{4}$
59. $-6 \leq x \leq -1$ **63.** $y = -2x + 8$

5-9

Check It Out! **1a.** $y = 2x + 2$ and $y = 2x + 1$ **1b.** $y = 3x$ and $y - 1 = 3(x + 2)$ **2.** slope of $\overline{AB} = 0$; slope of $\overline{BC} = \frac{5}{3}$; slope of $\overline{CD} = 0$; slope of $\overline{AD} = \frac{5}{3}$; $\overline{AB}$ is parallel to $\overline{CD}$ because they have the same slope. $\overline{AD}$ is parallel to $\overline{BC}$ because they have the same slope. Since opposite sides are parallel, $ABCD$ is a parallelogram. **3.** $y = -4$ and $x = 3$; $y - 6 = 5(x + 4)$ and $y = -\frac{1}{5}x + 2$
4. slope of $\overline{PQ} = 2$; slope of $\overline{QR} = -1$; slope of $\overline{PR} = -\frac{1}{2}$; $\overline{PQ}$ is perpendicular to $\overline{PR}$ because the product of their slopes is −1. Since PQR contains a right angle, PQR is a right triangle. **5a.** $y = \frac{4}{5}x + 3$
5b. $y = -\frac{1}{5}x + 2$

Exercises **1.** parallel **3.** $y = \frac{3}{4}x - 1$ and $y - 3 = \frac{3}{4}(x - 5)$ **5.** $y = \frac{2}{3}x - 4$ and $y = -\frac{3}{2}x + 2$; $y = -1$ and $x = 3$
9. $x = 7$ and $x = -9$; $y = -\frac{5}{6}x + 8$ and $y = -\frac{5}{6}x - 4$ **11.** $y = -3x + 2$ and $3x + y = 27$; $y = \frac{1}{2}x - 1$ and $-x + 2y = 17$ **13.** $y = 6x$ and $y = -\frac{1}{6}x$; $y = \frac{1}{6}x$ and $y = -6x$ **15.** $x - 6y = 15$ and $y = -6x - 8$; $y = 3x - 2$ and $3y = -x - 11$ **17.** $y = -\frac{6}{7}x$ **19.** neither
21. parallel **23.** $y = \frac{1}{2}x - 5$
25. $y = 2x + 5$ **27.** $y = 3x + 13$
29. $y = -x + 5$ **31.** $y = 4x - 23$
33. $y = -\frac{3}{4}x$ **35.** $y = -x + 1$
37. $y = \frac{2}{5}x - \frac{31}{5}$ **39.** $y = -\frac{1}{5}x - \frac{11}{5}$
41. $y = -\frac{1}{2}x - \frac{1}{2}$ **43.** $y = \frac{1}{2}x + 6$
45. $y = x - 3$ **47.** $y = -4$ **51a.** $y = 50x$ **b.** $y = 50x + 30$ **53.** H **57.** $-\frac{1}{5}$
59. $94 + t > 112$; $t > 18$ **63.** $y = \frac{2}{3}x - 5$
65. $y = -\frac{1}{2}x - \frac{1}{2}$ **67.** $y = 3$

5-10

Check It Out!
1.

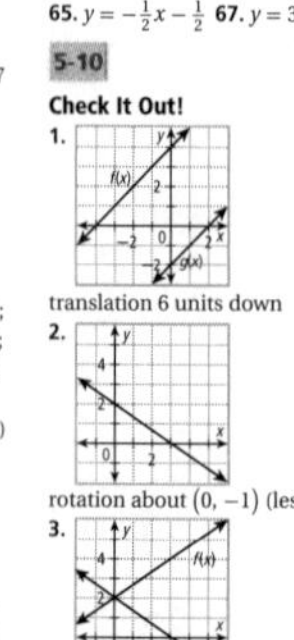

translation 6 units down
2.

rotation about (0, −1) (less steep)
3.

$g(x) = -\frac{2}{3}x + 2$
4.

reflection across y-axis and translation 2 units up **5.** The graph will be rotated about (0, 175) and become less steep; the graph will be translated 5 units up.

Exercises **1.** translation
3.

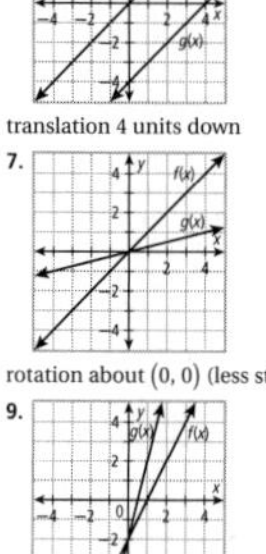

translation 4 units down
7.

rotation about (0, 0) (less steep)
9.

rotation about (0, −2) (steeper)
13.

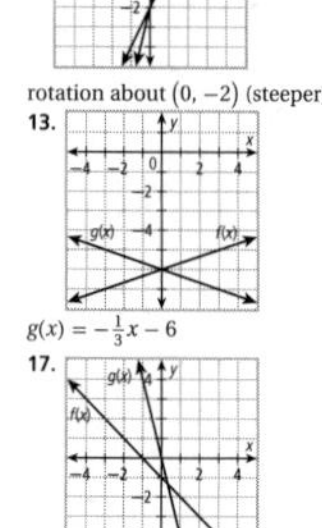

$g(x) = -\frac{1}{3}x - 6$
17.

rotation about (0, 0) (steeper) and translation 1 unit up

23.

rotation about (0, 2) (less steep)
27.

rotation about (0, 0) (steeper) and translation 5 units down
31. rotation about (0, 0) (steeper)

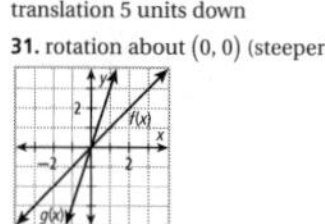

They have different slopes and the same y-intercept.
37.

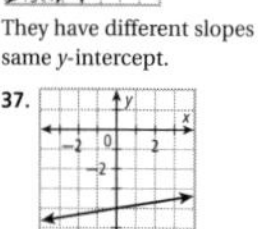

$g(x) = \frac{1}{6}x - 4$ **39.** translation 9 units down **41.** rotation about (0, 0) (steeper) **43.** rotation about (0, 0) (steeper) **45a.** $300 **b.** 20%
c. Commission changes to 25%. Base pay changes to $400. **49.** D
53. $15x$ **55.** positive **57.** negative
59. $y = -\frac{3}{5}x$ and $y + 1 = -\frac{3}{5}(x - 2)$
61. $x = 4$ and $y = -3$; $2y + x = 6$ and $y = 2x + 3$

Study Guide: Review

1. translation; rotation; reflection
2. y-intercept **3.** slope; y-intercept
4. No; a constant change of +2 in x corresponds to different changes in y. **5.** Yes; a constant change of +1 in x corresponds to a constant change of +2 in y.
6. Yes; a constant change of +1 in x corresponds to a constant change of −2 in y. **7.** No; a constant change of −1 in y corresponds to different changes in x. **8.** $5x + y = 1$; $A = 5$; $B = 1$; $C = 1$
9. $x + 6y = -2$; $A = 1$; $B = 6$; $C = -2$ **10.** $7x - 4y = 0$; $A = 7$; $B = -4$; $C = 0$ **11.** $y = 9$; $A = 0$; $B = 1$; $C = 9$
12.

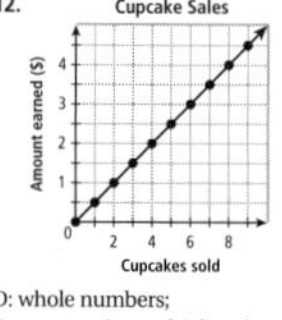

D: whole numbers;
R: nonnegative multiples of 0.5
13. x-intercept: 2; y-intercept: −4
14. x-intercept: 5; y-intercept: 6
15. x-intercept: 3; y-intercept: −9
16. x-intercept: $-\frac{1}{2}$; y-intercept: 1
17. x-intercept: −18; y-intercept: 3
18. x-intercept: $\frac{1}{3}$; y-intercept: $-\frac{1}{4}$
19.

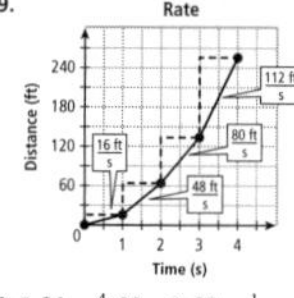

20. 5 **21.** $-\frac{4}{3}$ **22.** −3 **23.** $-\frac{1}{2}$
24. 3 **25.** 7 **26.** 4 **27.** −5 **28.** −1
29. 1 **30.** 2 **31.** undefined **32.** 0
33. (15, 15) **34.** $\left(-\frac{1}{2}, -9\right)$ **35.** 7.81 units **36.** 15.65 units **37.** 2.2 mi
38. yes; −6 **39.** yes; 1 **40.** no
41. yes; $-\frac{1}{2}$ **42.** −12
43. $y = 8x$

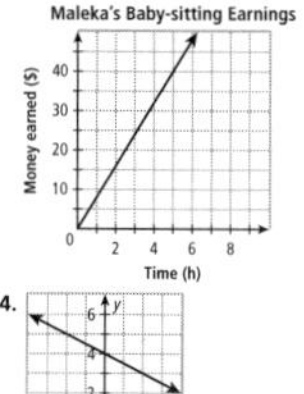

44.

45.

46. $y = \frac{1}{3}x + 5$ **47.** $y = 4x - 9$
48.

49.

50. $y = 2x + 1$ **51.** $y = -5x - 26$
52. $y = 2x + 2$ **53.** $y = 2x + 8$
54. $y = -\frac{1}{3}x$ and $y = -\frac{1}{3}x - 6$
55. $y - 2 = -4(x - 1)$ and $y = -4x - 2$ **56.** $y - 1 = -5(x - 6)$ and $y = \frac{1}{5}x + 2$ **57.** $y - 2 = 3(x + 1)$ and $y = -\frac{1}{3}x$ **58.** $y = 2x = 3$
59.

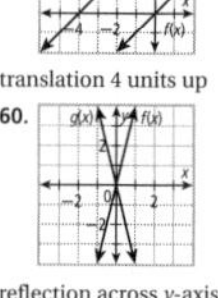

translation 4 units up
60.

reflection across y-axis
61.

reflection across y-axis
62. translation 2 units up; rotation about (0, 3) (steeper)

Chapter 6

6-1

Check It Out! **1a.** yes **1b.** no **2a.** $(-2, 3)$ **2b.** $(3, -2)$ **3.** 5 movies; $25

Exercises **1.** an ordered pair that satisfies both equations **3.** yes **5.** $(2, 1)$ **7.** $(-4, 7)$ **9.** no **11.** yes **13.** $(3, 3)$ **15.** $(3, -1)$

17a. $\begin{cases} y = 2x \\ y = 16 + 0.50x \end{cases}$

b. Carnation Sales

It represents how many carnations need to be sold to break even.
c. No, because the solution is not a whole number of carnations; 11 carnations. **19.** $(-2.4, -9.3)$ **21.** $(0.3, -0.3)$ **23.** 45 white; 120 pink **25.** 8 yr **29.** C **31.** month 11; 400 **33.** 42 **35.** 2.2 **37.** numbers less than 5 **39.** numbers greater than 6 **41.** $c \leq -9$

6-2

Check It Out! **1a.** $(-2, 1)$ **1b.** $(0, 2)$ **1c.** $(3, -10)$ **2.** $(-1, 6)$ **3.** 10 months; $860; the first option; the first option is cheaper for the first 9 months; the second option is cheaper after 10 months.

Exercises **1.** $(9, 35)$ **3.** $(3, 8)$ **5.** $(-3, -9)$ **7a.** 3 months; $136 **b.** Green Lawn **9.** $(-4, 2)$ **11.** $(-1, 2)$ **13.** $(1, 5)$ **15.** $(3, -2)$ **17.** 6 months; $360; the second option **19.** $(2, -2)$ **21.** $(8, 6)$ **23.** $(-9, -14.8)$ **25.** 12 nickels; 8 dimes

27. $\begin{cases} x + y = 1000 \\ 0.05x + 0.06y = 58 \end{cases}$; $200 at 5%; $800 at 6%

29. $x = 60°$; $y = 30°$ **35.** Possible estimate: $(1.75, -2.5)$; $(1.8, -2.4)$ **37.** F **39.** $r = 5$; $s = -2$; $t = 4$ **41.** $a = 9$; $b = 5$; $c = 0$ **45.** x-intercept: 2; y-intercept: -6 **47.** x-intercept: 8; y-intercept: 10 **49.** yes

6-3

Check It Out! **1.** $(-2, 4)$ **2.** $(4, 1)$ **3a.** $(2, 0)$ **3b.** $(3, 4)$ **4.** 9 lilies; 4 tulips

Exercises **1.** $(-4, 1)$ **3.** $(-2, -4)$ **5.** $(-6, 30)$ **7.** $(3, 2)$ **9.** $(4, -3)$ **11.** $(-1, -2)$ **13.** $(1, 5)$ **15.** $\left(6, -\frac{1}{2}\right)$ **17.** $(-1, 2)$ **19.** $(-1, 2)$

21. $\begin{cases} \ell - w = 2 \\ 2\ell + 2w = 40 \end{cases}$; length: 11 units; width: 9 units

25. $(3, 3)$ **27.** $\left(\frac{46}{7}, \frac{8}{7}\right)$ **29.** $\left(\frac{15}{7}, \frac{9}{7}\right)$

31a. $\begin{cases} 3A + 2B = 16 \\ 2A + 3B = 14 \end{cases}$ **b.** $A = 4$; $B = 2$

c. Buying the first package will save $8; buying the second package will save $7. **33.** A **35a.** s = number of student tickets; n = number of nonstudent tickets;
$\begin{cases} s + n = 358 \\ 1.50s + 3.25n = 752.25 \end{cases}$
b. $s = 235$; $n = 123$; 235 student tickets, 123 nonstudent tickets **37.** $x = 4$; $y = -1$; $z = 10$

39. $\begin{cases} x + y = 5 \\ 3(10x + y) = 42 \end{cases}$; $x = 1$; $y = 4$; the number is 14.
41. $y = 3x$ **43.** yes; $\frac{1}{2}$ **45.** no **47.** $(4, 9)$

6-4

Check It Out! **1.** Possible answer: Substitute $-2x + 5$ for y in the second equation: $2x + (-2x + 5) = 1$; $5 = 1$ ✗ **2.** Possible answer: Substitute $x - 3$ for y in the second equation: $x - (x - 3) - 3 = 0$; $3 - 3 = 0$; $0 = 0$ ✓ **3a.** consistent, dependent; infinitely many solutions **3b.** consistent, independent; one solution **3c.** inconsistent; no solution **4.** Yes; the graphs of the two equations have different slopes so they intersect.

Exercises **1.** consistent **3.** Possible answer: Substitute $-3x + 2$ for y in the first equation: $3x + (-3x + 2) = 6$; $2 = 6$ ✗ **5.** Possible answer: Substitute $-x + 3$ for y in the second equation: $x + (-x + 3) - 3 = 0$; $0 = 0$ ✓ **7.** Possible answer: Add the two equations:

$$\begin{aligned} -7x + y &= -2 \\ +7x - y &= 2 \\ 0 + 0 &= 0 \\ 0 &= 0\ ✓ \end{aligned}$$

9. inconsistent; no solutions **11.** yes **13.** Possible answer: Substitute $-x - 1$ for y in the first equation: $x + (-x - 1) = 3$; $-1 = 3$ ✗ **15.** Possible answer: Compare slopes and intercepts. $-6 + y = 2x \rightarrow y = 2x - 6$; $y = 2x - 36$; the lines have the same slope and different y-intercepts. Therefore the lines are parallel. **17.** Possible answer: Substitute $x - 2$ for y in the second equation: $x - (x - 2) - 2 = 0$; $2 - 2 = 0$; $0 = 0$ ✓ **19.** Possible answer: Compare slopes and intercepts. $-9x - 3y = -18 \rightarrow y = -3x + 6$; $3x + y = 6 \rightarrow y = -3x + 6$; the lines have the same slope and the same y-intercepts. Therefore the graphs are one line. **21.** consistent, independent; one solution **23.** Yes; the graphs of the two equations have different slopes, so they intersect. **27.** They will always have the same number; both started with 2 and add 4 every year. **29.** The graph will be 2 parallel lines. **31.** A **33.** D **35.** $p = q$; $p \neq q$ **37.** 11 km **39.** no **41.** $d = -1\frac{1}{2}$; $-6, -7\frac{1}{2}, -9$ **43.** $(-2, -4)$

6-5

Check It Out! **1a.** no **1b.** yes

2a. **2b.**

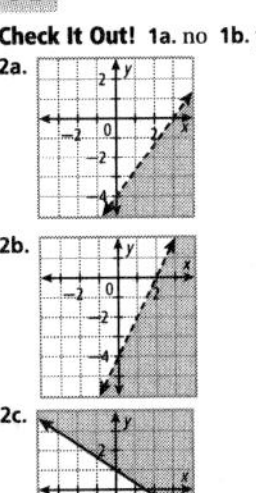

2c.

3a. $2.5b + 2g \leq 6$

3b. Olive Combinations

3c. Possible answer: (1 lb black, 1 lb green), (0.5 lb black, 2 lb green) **4a.** $y < -x$ **4b.** $y \geq -2x - 3$

Exercises **3.** yes

5.

7.

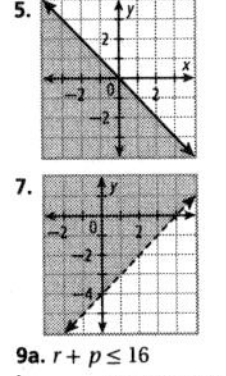

9a. $r + p \leq 16$

b. Punch Combinations

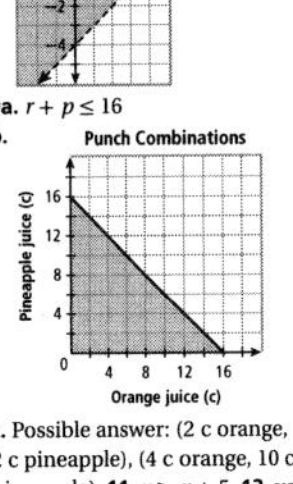

c. Possible answer: (2 c orange, 2 c pineapple), (4 c orange, 10 c pineapple) **11.** $y \geq x + 5$ **13.** yes

15.

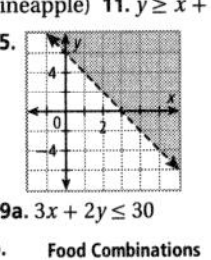

19a. $3x + 2y \leq 30$

b. Food Combinations

c. Possible answer: (3 lb hamburger, 2 lb hot dogs), (5 lb hamburger, 6 lb hot dogs) **21.** $y \leq -\frac{1}{5}x + 3$

23.

25.

29.

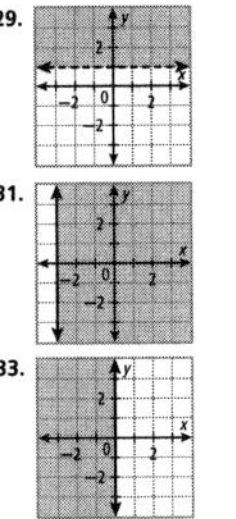

31.

33.

35.

37. $7a + 4s \geq 280$ **41.** A **43.** B **45.** C

47.

49. $y \geq \frac{1}{2}x + 3$ **51.** yes **53.** yes **55.** $y = \frac{3}{4}x + \frac{7}{4}$ **57.** $y = 3x + 1$ **59.** $y = -\frac{1}{2}x + \frac{1}{2}$ **61.** $(-2, 15)$ **63.** $(2, 5)$ **65.** $(12, 3)$

6-6

Check It Out! **1a.** yes **1b.** no

2a.

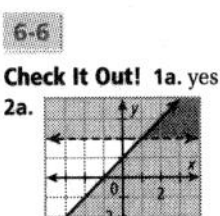

Possible answer: solutions: $(3, 3)$, $(4, 4)$; not solutions: $(-3, 1)$, $(-1, -4)$

2b.

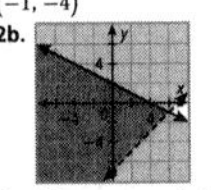

Possible answer: solutions: $(0, 0)$, $(3, -2)$; not solutions: $(4, 4)$, $(1, -6)$

3a.

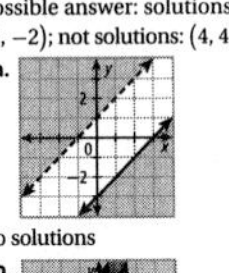

no solutions

3b.

all points between and on the parallel lines

3c.

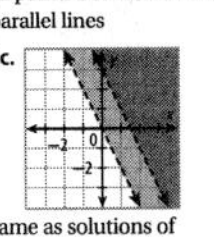

same as solutions of $y > -2x + 3$

4. Cheese Combinations

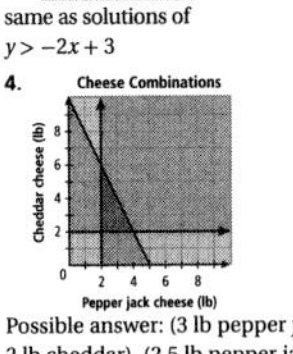

Possible answer: (3 lb pepper jack, 2 lb cheddar), (2.5 lb pepper jack, 4 lb cheddar)

Exercises **1.** all **3.** yes

5.

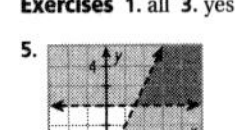

Possible answer: solutions: $(3, 3)$, $(4, 3)$; not solutions: $(0, 0)$, $(2, 1)$

7.

Possible answer: solutions: $(0, 4)$, $(1, 4)$; not solutions: $(2, -1)$, $(3, 1)$

9.

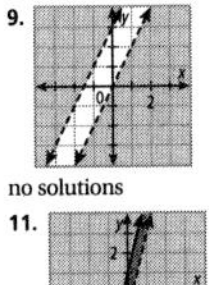

no solutions

11.

all points between the parallel lines and on the solid line

13.

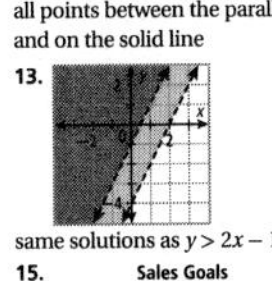

same solutions as $y > 2x - 1$

15. Sales Goals

Possible answer: (6 lemonade, 13 cupcakes), (10 lemonade, 10 cupcakes) **17.** yes

19.

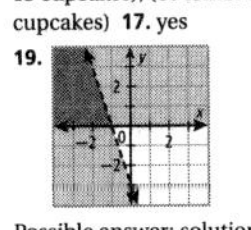

Possible answer: solutions: $(-2, 0)$, $(-3, 1)$; not solutions: $(0, 0)$, $(1, 4)$

21.

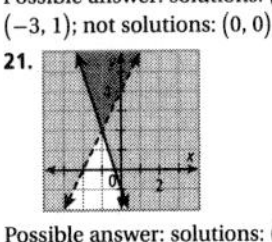

Possible answer: solutions: $(-1, 3)$, $(0, 5)$; not solutions: $(0, 0)$, $(1, 4)$

23.

no solutions

25.

All points are solutions.

27.

same solutions as $y > 2$

29. Linda's Work Hours

Possible answer: (0 h at pharmacy, 9 h babysitting), (8.5 h at pharmacy, 10 h babysitting)

31.

33.

35. $\begin{cases} y > x + 1 \\ y < x + 3 \end{cases}$

37. $\begin{cases} y < 2 \\ x \geq -2 \end{cases}$

39. Student B **45.** G **47.** about 12 square units

49.

51. 25 cm^2 **53.** 12.5 cm^2 **55.** no **57.** yes

Study Guide: Review

1. independent system **2.** system of linear equations **3.** solution of a system of linear inequalities **4.** inconsistent system **5.** independent system **6.** no **7.** yes **8.** yes **9.** no **10.** $(-1, -1)$ **11.** $(3, 4)$ **12.** 8 h; $10 **13.** $(-9, -6)$ **14.** $\left(\frac{1}{2}, -2\right)$ **15.** $(-1, 6)$ **16.** $(4, -5)$ **17.** $(-5, 2)$ **18.** $(6, 6)$ **19.** 10 h; $1350; Motor Works **20.** $(-1, 3)$ **21.** $(5, -3)$ **22.** $(11, 1)$ **23.** $(0, 3)$ **24.** $(-2, 8)$ **25.** $(3, -5)$ **26.** $(4, -6)$ **27.** $(2, 2)$ **28.** no solution **29.** infinitely many solutions **30.** $(-2, -4)$ **31.** infinitely many solutions **32.** infinitely many solutions **33.** $(-1, -3)$ **34.** no **35.** consistent, independent; one solution **36.** inconsistent; no solution **37.** consistent, dependent; infinitely many solutions **38.** inconsistent; no solution **39.** consistent, independent; one solution **40.** consistent, dependent; infinitely many solutions **41.** inconsistent; no solution **42.** no **43.** yes **44.** yes **45.** no

46.

47.

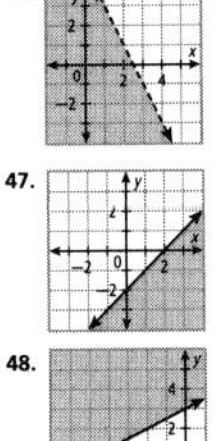

48.

49.

50.

51.

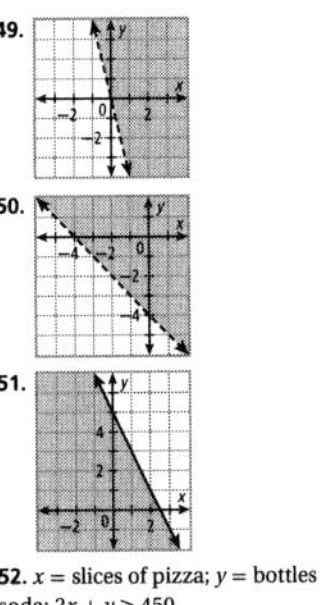

52. x = slices of pizza; y = bottles of soda; $2x + y \geq 450$

Fundraising Needs

Possible answer: $(200, 50)$, $(150, 150)$ **53.** no **54.** yes

55.

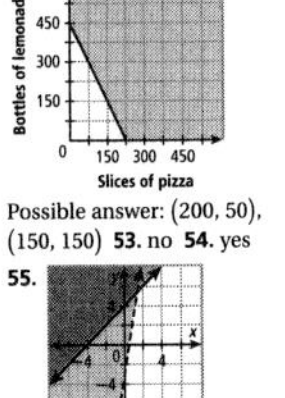

Possible answer: solutions: $(-6, 6)$, $(-10, 0)$; not solutions: $(0, 0)$, $(4, -4)$

56.

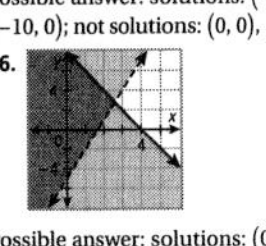

Possible answer: solutions: $(0, 0)$, $(-5, 0)$; not solutions: $(8, 0)$, $(3, -3)$

57.

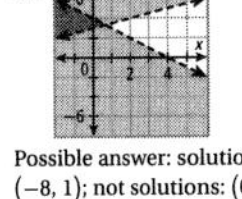

Possible answer: solutions: $(-6, 2)$, $(-8, 1)$; not solutions: $(0, 0)$, $(4, 1)$

58.

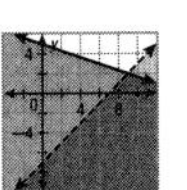

Possible answer: solutions: $(8, -8)$, $(9, 0)$; not solutions: $(0, 0)$, $(0, -4)$

59.

60.

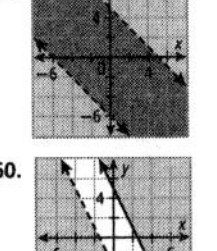

Chapter 7

7-1

Check It Out! **1.** $\frac{1}{125}$ m **2a.** $\frac{1}{10,000}$ **2b.** $\frac{1}{16}$ **2c.** $-\frac{1}{32}$ **2d.** $-\frac{1}{32}$ **3a.** $\frac{1}{64}$ **3b.** 2 **4a.** $\frac{2}{m^3}$ **4b.** $\frac{1}{7r^3}$ **4c.** g^4h^6

Exercises **1.** $\frac{1}{10,000,000}$ m **3.** 1 **5.** $\frac{1}{27}$ **7.** $-\frac{1}{512}$ **9.** 1 **11.** $\frac{1}{16}$ **13.** $\frac{1}{256}$ **15.** $-\frac{1}{32}$ **17.** $\frac{3}{k^4}$ **19.** $x^{10}d^3$ **21.** $\frac{g^6}{f^4}$ **23.** $\frac{p^7}{q}$ **25.** 1 **27.** $\frac{1}{81}$ **29.** $-\frac{1}{36}$ **31.** 1 **33.** $-\frac{1}{3}$ **35.** 4 **37.** $\frac{1}{256}$ **39.** 1 **41.** $\frac{1}{144}$ **43.** $\frac{1}{k^4}$ **45.** $\frac{b^3}{2}$ **47.** $-\frac{5}{x^3}$ **49.** $\frac{2g^{10}}{7}$ **51.** s^5t^{12} **53.** 1 **55.** $\frac{1}{q^2}$ **57.** $\frac{h^3}{6m^2k}$ **59.** $\frac{1}{16}$ **61.** $-\frac{1}{6}$ **63.** 3 **65.** 3 **67.** $\frac{a^3}{b^2}$ **69.** $\frac{w^2}{y}$ **71.** $-\frac{5}{y^6}$ **73.** $2a^3b$ **75.** $\frac{1}{3x^8y^{12}}$ **79.** never **81.** sometimes **83.** sometimes **87.** 81 **89.** 1 **91.** -3 **93.** -1 **95.** D **97.** A **103.** -2 **105.** 4 **107.** 28 **111.** $y = \frac{1}{3}x + 5$ **113.** $y = -4x + 9$

7-2

Check It Out! **1a.** 0.01 **1b.** 100,000 **1c.** 10,000,000,000 **2a.** 10^8 **2b.** 10^{-4} **2c.** 10^{-1} **3a.** 85,340,000 **3b.** 0.00163 **4a.** 1.43×10^5 km **4b.** 13,000 m/s **5.** 2×10^{-12}, 4×10^{-3}, 5.2×10^{-3}, 3×10^{14}, 4.5×10^{14}, 4.5×10^{30}

Exercises **3.** 0.00001 **5.** 100,000,000 **7.** 10^{-6} **9.** 650,300,000 **11.** 0.092 **13.** 5.85×10^{-3}, 2.5×10^{-1}, 8.5×10^{-1}, 3.6×10^8, 8.5×10^8 **15.** 0.000000001 **17.** 100,000,000,000,000 **19.** 10^6 **21.** 92,000 **23.** 0.00042 **25.** 10,000,000,000,000 **27.** 1.23×10^{-3}, 1.32×10^{-3}, 3.12×10^{-3}, 2.13×10^{-1}, 2.13×10^1, 3.12×10^2 **29.** 2.7×10^7 **31.** 2.35×10^5 **33.** 6×10^{-7} **35.** 4.12×10^{-2} **37.** yes **39.** no; 2.5×10^2 **41.** yes **43.** yes **47.** 10^{-3} **51.** F **55.** Let m = number of minutes; $m \geq 45$ **59.** $(-2, 1)$ **61.** $\frac{1}{16}$ **63.** $\frac{3}{125}$

7-3

Check It Out! **1a.** 7^{12} **1b.** 3×5^{10} **1c.** $\frac{m^5}{n^4}$ **1d.** $\frac{1}{x^7}$ **2.** 6.696×10^8 mi **3a.** 3^{20} **3b.** 1 **3c.** a^{18} **4a.** $64p^3$ **4b.** $25t^4$ **4c.** $\frac{1}{y^4}$

Exercises **1.** 2^5 **3.** n^8 **5.** 7.5×10^8 mi **7.** y^{32} **9.** $\frac{1}{3^4}$, or $\frac{1}{81}$ **11.** x^7y^{13} **13.** $36k^2$ **15.** $-8x^{15}$ **17.** b^{10} **19.** 6^8 **21.** $\frac{x}{y^3}$ **23.** 2^9, or 512 **25.** $\frac{1}{x^2}$ **27.** $\frac{a^{12}}{b^5}$ **29.** $27x^3$ **31.** $p^{28}q^{14}$ **33.** $-256x^{12}$ **35.** 6 **37.** 3 **39.** 8 **41.** $2x^3$ **43.** $2m^{10}n^6$ **45.** $108x^{13}$ **47.** $125x^6$ **49.** $3a^6$ **51.** 10^3, or 1000 **57.** $\frac{a^7}{b^5}$ **59.** $15m^{12}n^9$ **61.** $9s^2t^7$ **63.** t^7 **67.** yes **69.** $17k^2$ **71.** $6x^4$ **73.** $15a^2b^3$ **75a.** 6×10^{-7} m **b.** 3×10^8 m/s **c.** Associative and Commutative Properties of Multiplication **77.** $(6ab)^2$ **79.** $\left(\frac{1}{2kmn}\right)^2$ **81.** H **83.** F **85.** 3^{2x} **87.** $x + 1$ **89.** x^{3y+3z} **91.** x^{x^2} **93.** $x = 4$ **95.** $x = 4$ **97.** 1.728×10^{-6} **99.** 15 **101.** no **103.** 7,800,000 **105.** 98.3

7-4

Check It Out! **1a.** $\frac{n^3}{m^5}$ **1b.** $\frac{1}{y^3}$ **1c.** $\frac{n^3}{m^5}$ **1d.** $\frac{3}{16}$ **2.** 1.1×10^{-2} **3.** $12,800 **4a.** $\frac{2^6}{3^4}$, or $\frac{64}{81}$ **4b.** $\frac{a^5b^{20}}{c^{10}d^{15}}$ **4c.** $\frac{a^3}{b^3}$ **5a.** $\frac{9^3}{4^3}$, or $\frac{729}{64}$ **5b.** $\frac{b^8c^{12}}{16a^4}$ **5c.** $\frac{t}{s^4}$

Exercises **1.** 25 **3.** 3 **5.** 7×10^2 **7.** 1 **9.** $\frac{4}{25}$ **11.** $\frac{1}{a^6b^4}$ **13.** $\frac{16}{9}$ **15.** $\frac{2b^2}{3a^2}$ **17.** 27 **19.** x^5 **21.** 5×10^{-7} **23.** 7×10^{-3} **25.** 2×10^{27} kg **27.** $\frac{a^{12}}{b^6}$ **29.** $\frac{y^3}{x^6}$ **31.** $\frac{y^{25}}{x^{10}}$ **33.** $\frac{196}{9x^2}$ **35.** $2d^2$ **37.** $\frac{3x^5}{4}$ **39.** $\frac{c^4}{a^4}$ **41.** $\frac{25}{p^2}$ **43.** $\frac{1}{100}$ **45.** -1

47. 2000: 3×10; 1995: 2.84×10; 1990: 2.65×10^1 51. 3 53. 3; 4 55. B 57. A 59. 3 61. m; $(-n)$; m; $-n$; Definition of negative exponent; a^n 63. 1 65. 12 67. $x = -\frac{1}{2}$ 69. 1 71. $-125x^{12}$

7-5

Check It Out! 1a. 3 1b. 15 2a. 8 2b. 1 2c. 81 3. 1944 4a. xy^3 4b. xy

Exercises 1. 5 3. 4 5. 3 7. 6 9. 5 11. 10 13. 4 15. 32 17. 125 19. 256 21. 0 23. x^2y 25. x^3y^3 27. a^2 29. 1 31. 10 33. 8 35. 2 37. 2 39. 14 41. 8 43. 8 45. 64 47. 1000 49. 243 51. $2g$ 53. $2m$ 55. $3x^2$ 57. ab^4 59. a^8b 61. 1 63. 0 65. 625 67. 3 69. $\frac{2}{3}$ 71. $\frac{1}{4}$ 73. $\frac{4}{9}$ 75. $\frac{8}{343}$ 77. $\frac{1}{27}$ 79. $\frac{16}{625}$ 81. 1.86 in. 83. $n^{\frac{2}{3}}$ will be less than n because $\frac{2}{3} < 1$. $n^{\frac{3}{2}}$ will be greater than n because $\frac{3}{2} > 1$. 85a. 10 in. 85b. The distance doubles (20 in.). 87. B 89. C 91. a 93. x^3 95. 3 97. 36π cm²; both volume and surface area are described by 36π (although the units are different). 99. -1 101. $n < 3$ 103. $y \le -2$ 105. D: $\{-2, -1, -0, 1\}$; R: $\{0, 1, 2, 3\}$; yes; each domain value is paired with exactly one range value. 107. D: $1 \le x \le 4$; R: $2 \le y \le 4$; yes; each domain value is paired with exactly one range value.

7-6

Check It Out! 1a. 3 1b. 1 1c. 3 2a. 1 2b. 5 3a. $x^5 + 9x^3 - 4x^2 + 16$; 1 3b. $-3y^8 + 18y^5 + 14y$; -3 4a. cubic polynomial 4b. constant monomial 4c. 8th degree trinomial 5. 1606 ft

Exercises 1. d 3. a 5. 3 7. 0 9. 8 11. 3 13. 4 15. $-8a^9 + 9a^8$; -8 17. $3x^2 + 2x - 1$; 3 19. $5c^4 + 5c^3 + 3c^2 - 4$; 5 21. linear binomial 23. quartic polynomial 25. quartic trinomial 27. 4 29. 6 31. 7 33. 1 35. 4 37. 2 39. 3 41. $4.9t^3 - 4t^2 + t + 2.5$; 4.9 43. $x^{10} + x^7 - x^5 + x^3 - x$; 1 45. $5x^3 + 3x^2 + 5x - 4$; 5 47. $-d^3 + 3d^2 + 4d + 5$; -1 49. $-x^5 - x^3 + 4x^2 + 1$; -1 51. linear monomial 53. quadratic trinomial 55. quartic trinomial 57. quadratic monomial 59. always 61. never 63a. 58.5 in³ b. 66 in³ c. 0 d. yes 65. -48; 0; 3270 75. A is incorrect 77. J 79a. 58 cm; 65 cm b. 50.310 cm 81. $90 - m$ 83. inconsistent; no solutions 85. consistent and independent; one solution 87. $\frac{x^2}{y^3}$ 89. $\frac{p^4}{16}$

7-7

Check It Out! 1a. $5s^2 + s$ 1b. $20z^4 - 6$ 1c. $x^8 + 6y^8$ 1d. b^3c^2 2. $12a^3 + 15a^2 - 16a$ 3. $-2x^2 - x$ 4. $-0.05x^2 + 46x - 3200$

Exercises 1. $-3a^2 + 9a$ 3. $0.26r^4 + 0.32r^3$ 5. $3b^3c$ 7. $23n^3 + 3n + 15$ 9. $9x^2 - x - 6$ 11. $4c^4 + 8c + 6$ 13. $-3r + 11$ 15. $8a^2 + 5a + 9$ 17. $12n^2 + 6n - 3m$ 19. $d^5 + 1$ 21. $5x$ 23. $2x^3 - 5$ 25. $10t^2 + t$ 27. $x^5 + x^4$ 29. $-2t^3 + 8t^2$ 31. $-6m^3 + 2m^2 + 5m + 3$ 33. $4w^2 + 6w + 4$ 35. $t - 5$ 37. $2n - 2$ 39. $6x^2 - x - 1$ 41. $-u^3 + 3u^2 + 3u + 6$ 43. $x = \frac{3}{2}$, or 1.5 45. B is incorrect. 47. $3x + 6$ 49. $6x + 14$ 51. $2x^2 + x - 5$ 55. G 57. $3x^2 - 2$ 69. b^{11} 71. $9x^{12}$

7-8

Check It Out! 1a. $18x^5$ 1b. $10r^2t^4$ 1c. $4x^5y^5z^7$ 2a. $8x^2 + 2x + 6$ 2b. $15a^3b + 3ab^2$ 2c. $5r^3s^2 - 15r^2s^3$ 3a. $a^2 - a - 12$ 3b. $x^2 - 6x + 9$ 3c. $2a^2 + 7ab^2 - 4b^4$ 4a. $x^3 - x^2 - 6x + 18$ 4b. $3x^3 - 4x^2 + 11x + 10$ 5a. $x^2 - 4x$ 5b. 12 m²

Exercises 1. $14x^6$ 3. $3r^3s^5t^5$ 5. $21x^7y^3$ 7. $4x^2 + 8x + 4$ 9. $6a^5b^2 + 2a^4b^3$ 11. $10x^3y^4 - 5x^2y^2$ 13. $x^2 - x - 2$ 15. $x^2 - 4x + 4$ 17. $4a^4 - 2ab - 12a^3b^3 + 6b^3$ 19. $x^3 + 3x^2 - 7x + 15$ 21. $-6x^4 + 12x^3 + 4x^2 - 18x + 20$ 23. $x^3 - 4x^2 - 4x - 5$ 25a. $2x^2 - 3x$ b. 20 in² 27. $-12r^5s^5$ 29. $10a^4$ 31. $-6a^5b^6$ 33. $-12a^7b^7c^8$ 35. $9x^2 + 54s$ 37. $27x^3 - 12x^2$ 39. $10x^3t^3 - 15s^2t^5$ 41. $-10x^3 + 15x^2 + 5x$ 43. $-14x^6y^3 + 7x^5y^4$ 45. $x^2 + 8x + 16$ 47. $5x^2 + 13x - 6$ 49. $10x^2 - x - 2$ 51. $7x^2 - 52x - 32$ 53. $x^3 - x^2 - x + 10$ 55. $-10x^4 + 2x^3 + 20x^2 - 19x + 3$ 57. $8x^5 - 12x^3 - 2x^4 + 17x^2 - 21$ 59. $x^3 - 3x - 2$ 61. $-x^3 + 3x^2 - 3x + 1$ 63. $16x^2 - 48x + 36$ 65a. 3; 2; $10x^5 + 5x^3$; 5 b. 2; 2; $x^4 - x^3 + 2x^2 - 2x$; 4 c. 1; 3; $x^4 - 5x^3 + 6x^2 + x - 3$; 4 d. $m + n$ 67. $12x^2 + 12x + 3$ 69a. $2x^2$ b. 800 m² 71. $2x^2 - 7x - 30$ 73. $8x^2 - 16xy + 6y^2$ 75. $6x^2 - 9x - 6$ 77. $x^3 + 3x^2$ 79. $2x^3 - 7x^2 - 10x + 24$ 81. $8p^3 - 36p^2q + 54pq^2 - 27q^3$ 87. C 89. D 91. $-x^2 - 6$ 93. a. $x^2 - 1$ b. $8x + 16$ 95. $x^3 + 3x^2 + 2x$ 97. $a = 2$ 99. 3.61 101. 9.49

7-9

Check It Out! 1a. $x^2 + 12x + 36$ 1b. $25a^2 + 10ab + b^2$ 1c. $1 + 2c^3 + c^6$ 2a. $x^2 - 14x + 49$ 2b. $9b^2 - 12bc + 4c^2$ 2c. $a^4 - 8a^2 + 16$ 3a. $x^2 - 64$ 3b. $9 - 4y^4$ 3c. $81 - r^2$ 4. 25

Exercises 3. $4 + 4x + x^2$ 5. $4x^2 + 24x + 36$ 7. $4a^2 + 28ab + 49b^2$ 9. $x^2 - 4x + 4$ 11. $64 - 16x + x^2$ 13. $49a^2 - 28ab + 4b^2$ 15. $x^2 - 36$ 17. $4x^4 - 9$ 19. $4x^2 - 25y^2$ 21. $x^2 + 6x + 9$ 23. $x^4 + 2x^2y^2 + y^4$ 25. $4 + 12x + 9x^2$ 27. $s^4 - 14s^2 + 49$ 29. $a^2 - 16a + 64$ 31. $9x^2 - 24x + 16$ 33. $a^2 - 100$ 35. $49x^2 - 9$ 37. $25a^4 - 81$ 39. $\pi x^2 + 8\pi x + 16\pi$ 41. $x^2 + 2xy + y^2$ 43. $x^4 - 16$ 45. $x^4 - 8x^2 + 16$ 47. $1 + 2x + x^2$ 49. $x^6 - 2a^3x^3 + a^6$ 51. $36a^2 - 25b^2$ 53. 4; 4 55. 25; 25 57. 9; 9 59. -5; -5 61. 840 65. 1, 4, 9, 16, 25, 36, 49, 64, 81, 100 67. B 69. D 71. $x^3 + 4x^2 - 16x - 64$ 73. $b = \pm 2\sqrt{c}$ 75. 13 cm

Study Guide: Review

1. cubic 2. standard form of a polynomial 3. monomial 4. trinomial 5. scientific notation 6. $\frac{1}{32}$ in. 7. 1 8. 1 9. $\frac{1}{125}$ 10. $\frac{1}{10{,}000}$, or 0.0001 11. $\frac{1}{16}$ 12. $\frac{1}{36}$ 13. $\frac{27}{4}$ 14. $\frac{1}{m^7}$ 15. b 16. $-\frac{1}{2x^3y}$ 17. $2b^6c^4$ 18. $\frac{3a^2}{4c^2}$ 19. $\frac{s^2}{qr^2}$ 20. 10,000,000 21. 0.00001 22. 10^2 23. 10^{-11} 24. 325,000 25. 1800 26. 0.17 27. 0.000299 28. 5.8×10^{-7}, 6.3×10^{-3}, 2.2×10^2, 1.2×10^4 29. $38,500,000,000 30. 5^9 31. $2^3 \cdot 3^4$ 32. b^{10} 33. r^5 34. x^{12} 35. 1 36. $\frac{1}{2^3}$, or $\frac{1}{8}$ 37. $\frac{1}{5^4}$, or $\frac{1}{625}$

38. $\frac{1}{16b^6}$ 39. $g^{12}h^8$ 40. x^4y^2 41. $-x^4y^2$ 42. x^6y^{15} 43. j^6k^9 44. $\frac{1}{5}$ 45. m^8n^{30} 46. 8×10^{11} 47. 9×10^7 48. 1×10^{10} 49. 2.8×10^{15} 50. 6×10^1 51. 1.8×10^{-8} 52. 3.55×10^7 53. 64 54. m^5 55. $\frac{7}{32}$ 56. $6b$ 57. t^3v^4 58. 16 59. 5×10^1 60. 2.5×10^7 61. 9 62. 7 63. 16 64. 8 65. z^2 66. $5x^2$ 67. x^4y^3 68. m^2n^4 69. 0 70. 3 71. 6 72. 1 73. $3n^2 + 2n - 4$; 3 74. $-a^6 - a^4 + 3a^3 + 2a$; -1 75. linear binomial 76. quintic monomial 77. quartic trinomial 78. constant monomial 79. $-4t + 3$ 80. $-6x^6 - x^5$ 81. $3h^3 - 3h^2 + 5$ 82. $2m^2 - 5m - 1$ 83. $p^2 + 5p + 8$ 84. $-7z^2 - z + 10$ 85. $3g^2 + 2g + 4$ 86. $-x^2 + 4x + 8$ 87. $8r^2$ 88. $6a^6b$ 89. $18x^3y^2$ 90. $3s^6t^{14}$ 91. $2x^2 - 8x + 12$ 92. $-3a^2b^2 + 6a^3b^2 - 15a^2b$ 93. $a^2 - 3a - 18$ 94. $b^2 - 6b - 27$ 95. $x^2 - 12x + 20$ 96. $t^2 - 1$ 97. $8q^2 + 34q + 30$ 98. $20g^2 - 37g + 8$ 99. $p^2 - 8p + 16$ 100. $x^2 + 24x + 144$ 101. $m^2 + 12m + 36$ 102. $9c^2 + 42c + 49$ 103. $4r^2 - 4r + 1$ 104. $9a^2 - 6ab + b^2$ 105. $4n^2 - 20n + 25$ 106. $h^2 - 26h + 169$ 107. $x^2 - 1$ 108. $z^2 - 225$ 109. $c^4 - d^2$ 110. $9k^4 - 49$

Chapter 8

8-1

Check It Out! 1a. $2^3 \cdot 5$ 1b. $3 \cdot 11$ 1c. 7^2 1d. 19 2a. 4 2b. 5 3a. $9g^2$ 3b. 1 3c. 1 4. 7

Exercises 3. $3^2 \cdot 2^2$ 5. $3^3 \cdot 2$ 7. 7 (prime) 9. $3 \cdot 5^2$ 11. 7 13. x^2 15. 1 17. $2 \cdot 3^2$ 19. $2^2 \cdot 3$ 21. 17 23. 7^2 25. 9 27. 10 29. $9s$ 31. 5 33. $4x^2$ 35. $2n$ 39. 15 rows 41. 8 and 20; 4 43. 63 and 105; 21 45. 54 and 72; 18 47. 36; 2; 9; 3 49. 105; 5; 7 51. 2; 2; 27; 3 53. 24; 2; 6; 3 55. 2; 2; 10, 5 57. D 61. $9y$ 63. $2p^2r$ 65. $4a^2b^3$ 69. 3.12 h 71. ≈ 0.10 mi/yr 73. 40 75. $3x^2 + 14x - 3$

8-2

Check It Out! 1a. $b(5 + 9b^2)$ 1b. cannot be factored 1c. $-y^2(18y + 7)$ 1d. $2x^2(4x^2 + 2x - 1)$ 2. $2x$ cm; $(x + 2)$ cm 3a. $(4s - 5)(s + 6)$ 3b. $(7x + 1)(2x + 3)$ 3c. cannot be factored 3d. $(5x - 2)^2$ 4a. $(2b^2 + 3)(3b + 4)$ 4b. $(4r + 1)(r^2 + 6)$ 5a. $(5x^2 - 4)(3 - 2x)$ 5b. $(8 + x)(y - 1)$

Exercises 1. $5a(3 - a)$ 3. $7(-5x + 6)$ 5. $2h(6h^3 + 4h - 3)$ 7. $m(9m + 1)$ 9. $3(12f + 6f^2 + 1)$ 11. $16t(-t + 20)$ 13. $(2b + 5)(b + 3)$ 15. $(x^2 + 2)(x + 4)$ 17. $(2b^2 + 5)(2b - 3)$ 19. $(7r^2 + 6)(r - 5)$ 21. $2(r - 2)(r - 3)$ 23. $(7q - 2)(2q - 3)$ 25. $(2m^2 - 3)(m - 3)$ 27. $9y(y + 5)$ 29. $x^2(-14x^2 + 5)$ 31. $-d^2(4d^2 - d + 3)$ 33. $7c(3c + 2)$ 35. $-5g^2(g + 3)$ 37. cannot be factored 39. $(6y + 1)(y - 7)$ 41. $(-3 + 4b)(b + 2)$ 43. $(2a^2 + 3)(a - 4)$ 45. $(6x^2 + 1)(x + 3)$ 47. $(n^2 + 5)(n - 2)$ 49. $(2m^2 - 3)(m - 1)$ 51. $(2f^2 - 5)(3f - 4)$ 53. $(b^2 - 2)(b + 4)$ 55. $3v$ 57. $2k$ 59. 2; binomial; $x(x + 5)$ 61. 3; trinomial; $a^2(a^2 + a + 1)$ 63a. $100x^3$; $200x^2$; $400x$ b. $100x^3 + 200x^2 + 400x + 800$ c. $100(x^2 + 4)(x + 2)$; $1603.12 67. The sum of opposite binomials is 0. 69a. Commutative Property of Addition b. Associative Property of Addition c. Distributive Property d. Distributive Property 71. D 73. C 75. $-9ab(8ab + 5)$ 77. $(a + c)(b + d)$ 79. $(x^2 + 3)(x - 4)$ 81. 11 83. 5

8-3

Check It Out! 1a. $(x + 4)(x + 6)$ 1b. $(x + 4)(x + 3)$ 2a. $(x + 6)(x + 2)$ 2b. $(x - 6)(x + 1)$ 2c. $(x + 6)(x + 7)$ 2d. $(x - 8)(x - 5)$ 3a. $(x + 5)(x - 3)$ 3b. $(x - 4)(x - 2)$ 3c. $(x - 10)(x + 2)$

4.

n	$n^2 - 7n + 10$
0	$0^2 - 7(0) + 10 = 10$
1	$1^2 - 7(1) + 10 = 4$
2	$2^2 - 7(2) + 10 = 0$
3	$3^2 - 7(3) + 10 = -2$
4	$4^2 - 7(4) + 10 = -2$

n	$(n - 5)(n - 2)$
0	$(0 - 5)(0 - 2) = 10$
1	$(1 - 5)(1 - 2) = 4$
2	$(2 - 5)(2 - 2) = 0$
3	$(3 - 5)(3 - 2) = -2$
4	$(4 - 5)(4 - 2) = -2$

Exercises 1. $(x + 4)(x + 9)$ 3. $(x + 4)(x + 10)$ 5. $(x + 2)(x + 8)$ 7. $(x - 1)(x - 6)$ 9. $(x - 3)(x - 8)$ 11. $(x + 9)(x - 3)$ 13. $(x - 2)(x + 1)$ 15. $(x - 9)(x + 5)$ 17. $(x + 3)(x + 10)$ 19. $(x + 4)(x + 12)$ 21. $(x + 2)(x + 14)$ 23. $(x - 1)(x - 5)$ 25. $(x - 4)(x - 8)$ 27. $(x + 7)(x - 3)$ 29. $(x - 13)(x + 1)$ 31. $(x - 7)(x + 5)$ 33. C 35. D 37. They are inverse operations. 39. $(x - 2)(x - 9)$ 41. $(x + 1)(x + 9)$ 43. $(x + 6)(x + 7)$ 45. $(x + 2)(x + 9)$ 47. $(x - 3)(x + 8)$ 49. $(x - 5)(x + 9)$ 51. approximately 1.5 55. $x^2 + 6x + 8$; $(x + 4)(x + 2)$ 57. Positive; −, −; Both negative 59. Negative; +, −; Positive; Negative 61a. $d = t^2$ b. $d = 4t$ c. $t(t - 4)$ 63. true 65. false 67. 4 69. 4 71a. $(x + 10)$ ft b. $\ell = (x + 14)$ ft; $w = (x + 6)$ ft c. $A = (x^2 + 20x + 84)$ ft² 73. D 75. C 77. $(x^2 + 9)(x^2 + 9)$ 79. $(d^2 + 21)(d^2 + 1)$ 81. $(de - 5)(de + 4)$ 83. 16; 11; 29 85a. $(x + 7)$ ft b. $(4x + 26)$ ft c. $92.00 d. $36.96 e. $128.96 87. x^5 89. t^{12} 91. $(x + 2)(x^2 + 5)$ 93. $(p - 2)(2p^3 + 7)$

8-4

Check It Out! 1a. $(3x + 1)(2x + 3)$ 1b. $(3x + 4)(x - 2)$ 2a. $(2x + 5)(3x + 1)$ 2b. $(3x - 4)(3x - 1)$ 2c. $(3x + 4)(x + 3)$ 3a. $(3x - 1)(2x + 3)$ 3b. $(4n + 3)(n - 1)$ 4a. $-1(2x + 3)(3x + 4)$ 4b. $-1(3x + 2)(x + 5)$

Exercises 1. $(2x + 5)(x + 2)$ 3. $(5x - 3)(x + 2)$ 5. $(3x + 4)(x - 6)$ 7. $(x + 2)(5x + 1)$ 9. $(4x - 5)(x - 1)$ 11. $(5x + 4)(x + 1)$ 13. $(2a - 1)(2a + 5)$ 15. $(2x - 3)(x + 2)$ 17. $(10x + 1)(x - 1)$ 19. $(2x + 3)(4 - x)$

21. $-1(5x + 3)(x - 2)$ 23. $-1(2x - 1)(2x + 5)$ 25. $(3x + 2)(3x + 1)$ 27. $(n + 2)(3n + 2)$ 29. $(4c - 5)(c - 3)$ 31. $(2x + 5)(4x + 1)$ 33. $(5x - 6)(x + 3)$ 35. $(10n - 7)(n - 1)$ 37. $(7x + 1)(x + 2)$ 39. $(3x - 4)(x - 5)$ 41. $(x - 7)(4x - 3)$ 43. $(4y - 1)(3y + 5)$ 45. $(2x - 1)(2x + 3)$ 47. $(3x + 5)(x - 3)$ 49. $-1(2x - 3)(2x + 5)$ 51. $-1(3x - 2)(x + 1)$ 53. $2x^2 - 5x + 2$; $(x - 2)(2x - 1)$ 55. $(9n + 8)(n + 1)$ 57. $(2x - 1)(2x - 5)$ 59. $(3x + 8)(x + 2)$ 61. $(3x + 4)(2x - 3)$ 63. $(2x - 3)(2x - 3)$ 65. $(2x + 3)(3x + 2)$ 69a. $-16t^2 + 20t + 6$ b. $-2(4t + 1)(2t - 3)$ c. 10 ft 71. D 73. B 77. B 79. A 81. $(2x + 1)(2x + 1)$ 83. $(9x + 1)(9x + 1)$ 85. $(5x + 2)(5x + 2)$ 87. -7; -5; 5; 7 89. -6; 6 95. $(x + 1)(x - 9)$

8-5

Check It Out! 1a. yes; $(x + 2)^2$ 1b. yes; $(x - 7)^2$ 1c. no; $-6x \neq 2(3x)(2)$ 2. $4(3x + 1)$ m; 40 m 3a. yes; $(1 - 2x)(1 + 2x)$ 3b. yes; $(p^4 + 7q^3)(p^4 - 7q^3)$ 3c. No; $4y^5$ is not a perfect square.

Exercises 1. yes; $(x - 2)^2$ 3. yes; $(3x - 2)^2$ 5. yes; $(x - 3)^2$ 7. $4(x + 12)$; 88 yd 9. yes; $(s + 4)(s - 4)$ 11. yes; $(2x^2 + 3y)(2x^2 - 3y)$ 13. yes; $x^3 + 3x^3 - 3$ 15. No; the last term must be positive. 17. no; $10x \neq 2(5x)(2)$ 19. yes; $(4x - 5)^2$ 21. yes; $(1 + 2x)(1 - 2x)$ 23. No; $4x$ and $9y$ are not perfect squares. 25. yes; $(9 - 10x^2)(9 + 10x^2)$ 27. 49 29. $4y^2$ 31. $(10x + 9y)(10x - 9y)$; difference of 2 squares 33. $(2r^3 + 5s^3)(2r^3 - 5s^3)$; difference of 2 squares 35. $(x^7 + 12)(x^7 - 12)$; difference of 2 squares 39. $c = 32$ 41a. $5z - 4$ b. $20z - 16$ c. 11; 44; 121 43a. 0; 0; 100; 100; 0 b. 16; 16; 36; 36; -24 c. 25; 25; 25; 25; -25 d. 36; 36; 16; 16; -24 e. 100; 100; 0; 0; 0 45. $a - b$; $a + b$ 47. C 49. 1 51a. $a = 2$; $b = v + 2$ b. $[2 + (v + 2)][2 - (v + 2)] = (v + 4)(-v) = -v^2 - 4v$ 53. $a = 3y$; $b = y$; $(3y - 4)(9y^2 + 12y + 16)$ 55. D: {5, 4, 3, 2}; R: {2, 1, 0, −1}; yes 57. D: {2}; R: {−8, −2, 4, 10}; no 59. $6a^3 + 14a^2 - 10a$ 61. $t^2 - 8t + 16$ 63. 8

8-6

Check It Out! 1a. yes 1b. no; $4(x + 1)^2$ 2a. $4x(x + 2)^2$ 2b. $2y(x - y)(x + y)$ 3a. $(3x + 4)(x + 1)$ 3b. $2p^3(p + 6)(p - 1)$ 3c. $3q^4(3q + 4)(q + 2)$ 3d. $2(x^4 + 9)$

Exercises 1. yes 3. yes 5. no; $4(2p^2 + 1)(2p^2 - 1)$ 7. $3x^3(x + 2)(x - 2)$ 9. $2p(2q + 1)^2$ 11. $mn(n^2 + m)(n^2 - m)$ 13. $3x^2(2x - 3)(x + 1)$ 15. $(p^3 + 1)(p^2 + 3)$ 17. unfactorable 19. no; $2xy(y^2 - 4y + 5)$ 21. no; $3n^2(n + 5)(n - 5)$ 23. yes 25. $-4x(x - 3)^2$ 27. $5(d - 3)(d - 9)$ 29. $2x(7x + 5y)(7x - 5y)$ 31. unfactorable 33. $(p^2 + 4)(p + 2)(p - 2)$ 35. $(k^2 + 3)(2k + 3)$ 37. $x^2 + 12x + 36 = (x + 6)^2$ 39. $s^2 - 16s + 28 = (s - 2)(s - 14)$ 41. $b^2 - 49 = (b + 7)(b - 7)$ 45. $(3x - 1)(x + 7)$ 47. $(3x + y - 3)(3x - y - 7)$ 53. 8 55. C 57. C 59a. $V = 8p[\pi(3p + 1)^2]$ b. $r = (3p + 1)$ cm c. $h = 8$ cm; $V = 128\pi$ cm³ 61. $h^2(h^4 + 1)(h^2 + 1)$ 63. $x^{n+3}(x^2 + x + 1)$ 65. $-2n$ 67. $12.3r$ 69. $\frac{23}{2} = \frac{x}{3}$; 34.5 cm 71. $(2x - 1)(2x + 3)$

Study Guide: Review

1. prime factorization 2. greatest common factor 3. $2^2 \cdot 3$ 4. $2^2 \cdot 5$ 5. 2^5 6. prime 7. $2^3 \cdot 5$ 8. 2^6 9. $2 \cdot 3 \cdot 11$ 10. $2 \cdot 3 \cdot 19$ 11. 5 12. 12 13. 1 14. 27 15. 4 16. 3 17. $2x$ 18. $9b^2$ 19. $25r$ 20. 6 boxes; 13 rows 21. $5x(1 - 3x^2)$ 22. $16(-b + 2)$ 23. $-7(2v + 3)$ 24. $4(a^2 - 3a - 2)$ 25. $5g(g^2 - 3)(g^2 + 1)$ 26. $10(4p^2 - p + 3)$ 27. $(6x + 5)$ ft by x ft 28. $(2x + 9)(x - 4)$ 29. $(t - 6)(3t + 5)$ 30. $(5 - 3n)(6 - n)$ 31. $(b + 2)(b + 4)$ 32. $(x^2 + 7)(x - 3)$ 33. $(n^2 + 1)(n - 4)$ 34. $(2b + 5)(3b - 4)$ 35. $(2h^2 - 7)(h + 7)$ 36. $(3t + 1)(t + 6)$ 37. $(5m^2 - 1)(2m + 3)$ 38. $(4p - 3)(2p^2 + 1)$ 39. $-1(r - 5)(r - 2)$ 40. $(b^2 - 5)(b - 3)$ 41. $(t + 4)(-t^2 + 6)$ 42. $-1(3h - 1)(h - 4)$ 43. $-1(d - 1)^2$ 44. $(2 - b)(5b - 6)$ 45. $(t + 1)(5 - t)$ 46. $(2b^2 + 5)(4 - b)$ 47. $-1(3r - 1)(r - 1)$ 48. left rectangle: $2x^2 + 3x$; right rectangle: $8x + 12$; combined: $2x^2 + 8x + 3x + 12$; $(2x + 3)(x + 4)$ 49. $(x + 1)(x + 5)$ 50. $(x + 2)(x + 4)$ 51. $(x + 3)(x + 5)$ 52. $(x - 6)(x - 2)$ 53. $(x + 5)^2$ 54. $(x - 2)(x - 11)$ 55. $(x + 4)(x + 20)$ 56. $(x - 6)(x - 20)$ 57. $(x + 12)(x - 7)$ 58. $(x + 3)(x - 8)$ 59. $(x + 4)(x - 7)$ 60. $(x - 1)(x + 5)$ 61. $(x + 3)(x - 2)$ 62. $(x + 5)(x - 4)$ 63. $(x - 8)(x + 6)$ 64. $(x - 9)(x + 4)$ 65. $(x - 12)(x + 6)$ 66. $(x - 10)(x + 7)$ 67. $(x + 20)(x - 6)$ 68. $(x + 7)(x - 1)$ 69. $(y + 3)$ m 70. $(2x + 1)(x + 5)$ 71. $(3x + 7)(x + 1)$ 72. $(2x - 1)(x - 1)$ 73. $(3x + 2)(x + 2)$ 74. $(5x + 3)(x + 5)$ 75. $(2x - 3)(3x - 5)$ 76. $(4x + 5)(x + 2)$ 77. $(3x + 4)(x + 2)$ 78. $(7x - 2)(x - 5)$ 79. $(3x + 2)(3x + 4)$ 80. $(2x + 1)(x - 1)$ 81. $(3x + 1)(x - 4)$ 82. $(2x - 1)(x - 5)$ 83. $(7x + 2)(x - 3)$ 84. $(5x + 1)(x - 2)$ 85. $-1(2x - 1)(3x + 2)$ 86. $(6x + 5)(x - 1)$ 87. $(3x - 2)(2x + 7)$ 88. $-1(2x + 1)(2x - 5)$ 89. $-1(2x - 3)(5x + 2)$ 90. $12x^2 - 11x - 5$; $(4x - 5)(3x + 1)$

91. yes; $(x + 6)^2$ 92. no; $5x \neq 2(x)(5)$ 93. no; $-2x \neq 2(2x)(1)$ 94. yes; $(3x + 2)^2$ 95. no; $8x \neq 2(4x)(2)$ 96. yes; $(x + 7)^2$ 97. yes; $(10x - 9)(10x + 9)$ 98. No; 2 is not a perfect square. 99. No; 5 and 10 are not perfect squares. 100. yes; $(-12 + x^3)(-12 - x^3)$ 101. no; terms must be subtracted 102. yes; $(10p - 5q)(10p + 5q)$ 103. $(x - 5)(x + 5)$; difference of 2 squares 104. $(x + 10)^2$; perfect-square trinomial 105. $(j - k^2)(j + k^2)$; difference of 2 squares 106. $(3x - 7)^2$; perfect-square trinomial 107. $(9x + 8)^2$; perfect-square trinomial 108. $(4b^2 - 11c^3)(4b^2 + 11c^3)$; difference of 2 squares 109. no; $2(2x + 3)(x + 1)$ 110. yes 111. no; $(b^2 + 9)(b - 3)(b + 3)$ 112. yes 113. $4(x - 4)(x + 4)$ 114. $3b^3(b - 4)(b + 2)$ 115. $a^2b^3(a - b)(a + b)$ 116. $t^4(t^8 + 1)(t^4 + 1)(t^2 + 1)(t + 1)(t - 1)$ 117. $5(x + 3)(x + 1)$ 118. $2x^2(x - 5)(x + 5)$ 119. $2(s + 4)(t + 4)$ 120. $5m(5m + 2)(m - 4)$ 121. $4x(4x^2 + 1)(2x - 3)$ 122. $6s^2t(s + t^2)$ 123. $2(m + 3)(m - 3)(5m + 2)$

Chapter 9

9-1

Check It Out! 1a. Yes; the second differences are constant. 1b. Yes; the function can be written in the form $y = ax^2 + bx + c$.

2a.

2b.

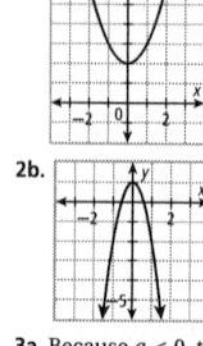

3a. Because $a < 0$, the parabola opens downward. 3b. Because $a > 0$, the parabola opens upward. 4a. vertex: $(-2, 5)$; maximum: 5 4b. vertex: $(3, -1)$; minimum: -1 5a. D: all real numbers; R: $y \ge 4$ 5b. D: all real numbers; R: $y \le 3$

Exercises 1. minimum 3. yes 5. no

7.

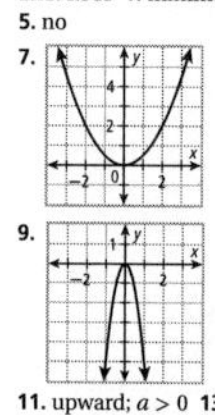

9.

11. upward; $a > 0$ 13. upward; $a > 0$ 15. downward; $a < 0$ 17. $(-3, -4)$; minimum: -4 19. D: all real numbers; R: $y \le 4$ 21. D: all real numbers; R: $y \ge -4$ 23. yes 25. yes 31. upward; $a > 0$ 33. vertex: $(0, -5)$; minimum: -5 35. D: all real numbers; R: $y \le 0$ 37. D: all real numbers; R: $y \ge -2$ 39. never 41. always 43. sometimes 45. no 47. yes 49. yes 53. quadratic 55. quadratic 57. neither 59. linear 61b. $t \ge 0$ c. 16 ft d. 2 s 65. C 67. yes 71. $(-2)^4$ 73. $42\frac{3}{4}$ mi

9-2

Check It Out! 1a. no zeros 1b. 3 2a. $x = -3$ 2b. $x = 1$ 3. $x = -\frac{1}{4}$ 4. $(2, -14)$ 5. 7 ft

Exercises 3. -1 5. no zeros 7. $x = 2$ 9. $x = -2$ 11. $x = -\frac{3}{4}$ 13. $(1, 8)$ 15. $(-2, -2)$ 17. $(-2, -9)$ 19. no zeros 21. -8, -2 23. $x = 6$ 25. $x = -\frac{1}{2}$ 27. $x = 5$ 29. $(-3.5, -12.25)$ 31. $(-2, 5)$ 33. $(1, 4.5)$ 35. $x = 0$. 37. 0 39. 2 41. B 43. 2 45. 25 ft; 100 ft 47. $y = -2x + 3$ 49. $y = -4x + 2$ 51. yes

9-3

Check It Out!

1a.

1b.

2. maximum height: 16 ft at 0.5 s; time it takes to reach the pool: 1.5 s

Exercises 1.

3.

5.

7. maximum height: 144 ft at 3 s; time in the air: 6 s

9.

11.

13.

15. $x = 4$; $(4, -16)$ 17. $x = 0$; $(0, 4)$ 19. $x = -\frac{1}{2}$; $\left(-\frac{1}{2}, -\frac{15}{4}\right)$ 21. vertex: $(0, 0)$; axis of symmetry: $x = 0$ 23. vertex: $(3, -5)$; axis of symmetry: $x = 3$ 25. vertex: $(0, -4)$; axis of symmetry: $x = 0$ 27b. D: $0 \le x \le 3.16$; R: $0 \le y \le 50$ c. about 3.16 s 31. 12 cm/s 35a. $h(t) = -16t^2 + 45t + 50$ b. approximately $(1.4, 81.6)$ 37. A 39. D 41. -1 43. x-intercept: 3; y-intercept: 6

45. no x-intercept; y-intercept: 3 **47.** $(3, -1)$ **49.** $(-1, -16)$ **51.** $(-1, 4)$

9-4

Check It Out! 1a. $f(x), g(x)$ **1b.** $g(x), f(x), h(x)$ **2a.** same width, same axis of symmetry, opens upward, translated 4 units down **2b.** narrower, same axis of symmetry, opens upward, translated 9 units up **2c.** wider, same axis of symmetry, opens upward, translated 2 units up **3a.** The graph of the ball that is dropped from a height of 100 ft is a vertical translation of the graph of the ball that is dropped from a height of 16 ft. The y-intercept of the graph of the ball that is dropped from 100 ft is 84 units higher. **3b.** The ball that is dropped from 16 ft reaches the ground in 1 s. The ball that is dropped from 100 ft reaches the ground in 2.5 s.

Exercises 1. $f(x), g(x)$ **3.** $h(x), g(x), f(x)$ **5.** same width, same axis of symmetry, opens upward, translated 6 units up **7.** wider, same axis of symmetry, opens upward, same vertex **9a.** $h_1(t) = -16t^2 + 16$, $h_2(t) = -16t^2 + 256$; the graph of h_2 is a vertical translation of the graph of h_1. The y-intercept of h_2 is 240 units higher. **b.** The baseball that is dropped from 256 ft reaches the ground in 4 s. The baseball that is dropped from 16 ft reaches the ground in 1 s. **11.** $f(x), g(x)$ **13.** $f(x), h(x), g(x)$ **19.** always **21.** never **25.** $f(x) = 3x^2 - 6$ **29.** B **31.** A **39.** D **41.** 0 **43a.** $f(x) = x^2 - 7$ **b.** $f(x) = -x^2 + 2$ **c.** $f(x) = \frac{1}{2}x^2 + 1$ **45.** no correlation

9-5

Check It Out! 1a. $x = -4$ **1b.** no real solutions **1c.** $x = -2$ or $x = 2$ **2.** 2 s

Exercises 1. zeros, x-intercepts **3.** $-4, 4$ **5.** 6 **7.** $-2, 4$ **9.** -1 **11.** no real solutions **13.** no real solutions **15.** $x = -4$ or $x = 4$ **17.** $x = \frac{1}{2}$ or $x = 5$ **19.** $x = -3$ **21.** no real solutions **23.** no real solutions **25.** always **27.** always **29.** never **31a.** 4 s **b.** 10 ft **33.** 1.4 s **35.** $-1, 1$ **41.** C **45.** no real solutions **47.** $x \approx -1.6$ or $x \approx 0.86$ **49.** $y - 4 = -3(x + 2)$ **51.** 27 **53.** x^{11} **55.** a^3b^3 **57.** $\frac{27b^2}{8a^6}$

9-6

Check It Out! 1a. $0, -4$ **1b.** $-4, 3$ **2a.** 3 **2b.** $1, -5$ **2c.** $-\frac{5}{3}$ **2d.** $\frac{1}{3}, 1$ **3.** 1.5 s

Exercises 1. $-2, 8$ **3.** $-7, -9$ **5.** $-11, 0$ **7.** $-6, 2$ **9.** $2, 3$ **11.** $-8, -2$ **13.** 4 **15.** 6 **17.** $-2, -\frac{3}{2}$ **19.** 1 s **21.** $-4, -7$ **23.** $0, 9$ **25.** $-\frac{1}{2}, \frac{1}{3}$ **27.** $-2, 4$ **29.** $-\frac{1}{3}, 1$ **31.** -2 **33.** 1 **35.** 1 **37.** 1 **39.** B **41.** 6 m **43.** 6 s **45.** no **47a.** 3 s **b.** 64 ft **c.** yes **49.** F **51.** $-5, -1$ **53.** $\frac{1}{2}, -3$ **55.** $-2, 5$ **57.** $-1, 0$ **59.** $x^2 - x - 12$ **61.** $x^2 - 4x - 12 = 48$; $x = 10$ **63.** -8 **65.** 2 **67.** $(-9, -16)$ **69.** ± 7 **71.** $3, 5$

9-7

Check It Out! 1a. ± 11 **1b.** 0 **1c.** no real solutions **2a.** no real solutions **2b.** $9, 1$ **3a.** ± 9.49 **3b.** ± 5.66 **3c.** no real solutions **4.** 45 ft

Exercises 1. ± 15 **3.** no real solutions **5.** no real solutions **7.** ± 5 **9.** no real solutions **11.** $11, -5$ **13.** ± 5.20 **15.** ± 4.47 **17.** ± 13 **19.** no real solutions **21.** no real solutions **23.** $\pm\frac{2}{9}$ **25.** $\pm\frac{5}{8}$ **27.** $\pm\frac{13}{7}$ **29.** ± 4.69 **31.** ± 10.20 **33.** ± 7.07 **35.** 6.1 s **37.** $t = \sqrt{\frac{2d}{a}}$ **39.** $a = -6$ and $b = -3$ or $a = 6$ and $b = 3$ **41.** about 4.2 ft by 8.4 ft **43.** A **45.** sometimes **47a.** $a > 0$ **b.** $a = 0$ **c.** $a < 0$ **49.** no; $x = \pm\sqrt{\frac{1}{2}}$, irrational **51.** yes; $x = \pm\frac{1}{2}$, rational **55.** H **57.** $\pm\frac{1}{4}$ **59.** $\pm\frac{8}{11}$ **61.** 13 **63.** $2, 4$ **65.** $-2, 7$

9-8

Check It Out! 1a. 36 **1b.** $\frac{25}{4}$ **1c.** 16 **2a.** $-9, -1$ **2b.** $4 \pm \sqrt{21}$ **3a.** $-\frac{1}{3}, 2$ **3b.** no real solutions **4.** 16.4 ft by 24.4 ft

Exercises 3. 4 **5.** $-5, -1$ **7.** $-6, 5$ **9.** $1, 9$ **11.** $\frac{-5 \pm 3\sqrt{5}}{2}$ **13.** no real solutions **15.** $4 \pm \sqrt{10}$ **17.** 7.2 m; 11.2 m **19.** 1 **21.** $-2, 12$ **23.** $-13, -2$ **25.** $-6, 8$ **27.** $-2, 3$ **29.** $\frac{-1 \pm \sqrt{5}}{2}$ **31.** $\frac{-15 \pm \sqrt{105}}{2}$ **33.** 4 in. **35.** $1 \pm \sqrt{7}$ **37.** $-3, \frac{1}{2}$ **39.** $-10, 2$ **41.** 81 **43.** $\frac{49}{4}$ **45.** 9 **47a.** $(10 + 2x)(24 + 2x) = 640$ **b.** 3 ft **51.** $-6 \pm \sqrt{26}$ **53.** -6 **55.** no real solutions **57.** no real solutions **61a.** $-16t^2 + 64t + 32 = 0$ **b.** 4 **c.** 4.4 s **63.** B **65.** B **67.** $-\frac{3}{2}, \frac{2}{3}$ **69.** $-\frac{2}{3} - \frac{\sqrt{7}}{3}, -\frac{2}{3} + \frac{\sqrt{7}}{3}$ **71.** $0, -\frac{b}{a}$ **77.** $x^2 - 8x + 16$ **79.** $t^2 - 8t + 16$ **81.** $64b^4 - 4$ **83.** ± 1 **85.** ± 4 **87.** ± 15 **89.** ± 1.55 **91.** ± 5.10 **93.** ± 1.48

9-9

Check It Out! 1a. $2, -\frac{1}{3}$ **1b.** $2, -\frac{1}{5}$ **2.** $\frac{8 - \sqrt{56}}{4} \approx 0.13$, $\frac{8 + \sqrt{56}}{4} \approx 3.87$ **3a.** 0 **3b.** 1 **3c.** 2 **4.** No; for the equation $45 = -16t^2 + 20t + 0$, the discriminant is negative, so the weight will not ring the bell. **5a.** $-2, -5$ **5b.** $-2, 7$ **5c.** $\frac{-4 - \sqrt{184}}{4} \approx -4.39$, $\frac{-4 + \sqrt{184}}{4} \approx 2.39$

Exercises 1. no **3.** $\frac{1}{2}, 3$ **5.** $-4, -10$ **7.** $-\frac{1}{2}, \frac{3}{2}$ **9.** $\frac{-6 - \sqrt{24}}{2} \approx -5.45$, $\frac{-6 - \sqrt{24}}{2} \approx -0.55$ **11.** $\frac{-1 - \sqrt{61}}{6} \approx 1.14$, $\frac{-1 + \sqrt{61}}{6} \approx -1.47$ **13.** $\frac{-1 - \sqrt{41}}{4} \approx -1.85$, $\frac{-1 + \sqrt{41}}{4} \approx 1.35$ **15.** 1 **17.** 0 **19.** 2 **21.** 0 **23.** yes **25.** -3 **27.** $-\frac{1}{2}$ **29.** $-3, \frac{3}{2}$ **31.** $1, 9$ **33.** $\frac{4 - \sqrt{12}}{2} \approx 0.27$, $\frac{4 + \sqrt{12}}{2} \approx 3.73$ **35.** $\frac{-7 - \sqrt{17}}{4} \approx 2.78$, $\frac{-7 + \sqrt{17}}{4} \approx -0.72$ **37.** 2 **39.** no **41.** $-5, 3$ **43.** no real solutions **45.** 2 solutions; $-2, \frac{1}{4}$ **47.** 1 solution; $\frac{2}{3}$ **49.** 2 x-intercepts; $\frac{7}{2}, -3$ **51.** 1 x-intercept; 5 **57.** A **59a.** 1 **b.** -1 **c.** -1 **d.** -1 **63.** $-10, 4$ **65.** $(r^3 + t)(s^2 + 5)$ **67.** $(n^4 - 2)(n - 6)$ **69.** $f(x), g(x)$

Study Guide: Review

1. vertex **2.** minimum; maximum **3.** zero of a function **4.** discriminant **5.** completing the square **6.** Yes; it is in standard form. **7.** No; $a = 0$ **8.** Yes; it is in standard form. **9.** No; a quadratic function does not have a power of x greater than 2.

10. **11.** **12.** **13.**

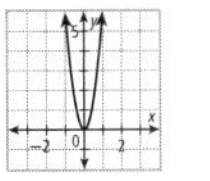

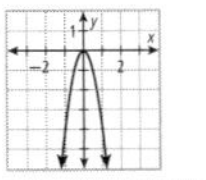

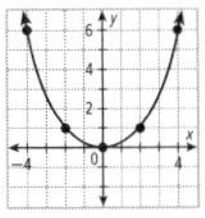

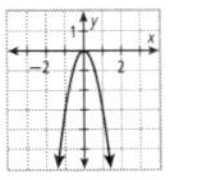

14. upward **15.** downward **16.** $(-2, -4)$; minimum: -4 **17.** -5 and 2 **18.** -1 and 2 **19.** $x = 6$; $(6, 4)$ **20.** $x = -1$; $(-1, -18)$

21. **22.**

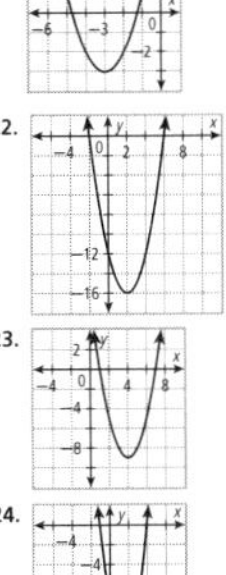

23. **24.** **25.** **26.**

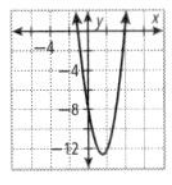

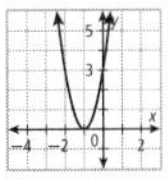

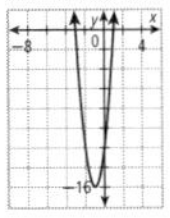

27. Water Fountain

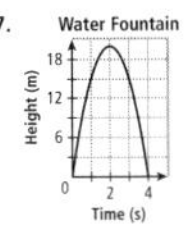

In 2 seconds, the water reaches its maximum height of 20 meters. It takes a total of 4 seconds for the water to reach the ground. **28.** $g(x), f(x)$ **29.** The graphs have the same width. **30.** $h(x), f(x), g(x)$ **31.** same width, same axis of symmetry, opens upward, vertex translated 5 units up **32.** narrower, same axis of symmetry, opens upward, vertex translated 1 unit down **33.** narrower, same axis of symmetry, opens upward, vertex translated 3 units up **34.** $x = -3$ or $x = -1$ **35.** $x = -3$ **36.** no real solutions **37.** $x = 1$ or $x = 5$ **38.** $x = 4$ **39.** $x = 1$ or $x = -1$ **40.** no real solutions **41.** $x = -5$ or $x = -1$ **42.** $x = -7$ or $x = -2$ **43.** $x = -3$ or $x = 5$ **44.** $x = -1$ or $x = 2$ **45.** $x = -5$ **46.** $x = 4.5$ **47.** $x^2 + 2x = 48$; 6 ft **48.** $x = -8$ or $x = 8$ **49.** $x = -12$ or $x = 12$ **50.** no real solutions **51.** $x = 0$ **52.** $x = -5$ or $x = 5$ **53.** $x = -\frac{5}{2}$ or $x = \frac{5}{2}$ **54.** 4 ft **55.** $x = -8$ or $x = 6$ **56.** $x = -7$ or $x = 3$ **57.** $x = 1$ or $x = 5$ **58.** $x = 5 \pm \sqrt{5}$ **59.** 16 ft by 12 ft **60.** $x = -1$ or $x = 6$ **61.** $x = -\frac{1}{2}$ or $x = 5$ **62.** $x = 1$ **63.** $x = \frac{6 \pm \sqrt{8}}{2}$ **64.** 1 **65.** 0 **66.** 2 **67.** 2

Chapter 10

10-1

Check It Out! 1a. bread **1b.** cheese and mayonnaise **2.** 2001, 2002, and 2005; about 13,000 **3.** about 18 °F **4.** Prices increased from January through July or August, and then prices decreased through November. **5.** 31.25% **6.**

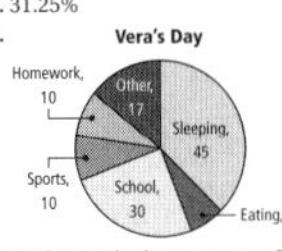

A circle graph shows parts of a whole.

Exercises 1. one part of a whole **3.** 82 animals **5.** $15 **7.** Prices at stadium A are greater than prices at stadium B. **9.** between weeks 4 and 5 **11.** 18% **13.** purple **15.** blue and green **17.** 225,000 **19.** Friday **21.** 3.5 times **23.** games 3, 4, and 5 **25.** Stock Y changed the most between April and July of 2004. **27.** $8\frac{1}{3}\%$ **31.** double line **33.** circle **35a.** Greece; about 40% **b.** United States; about 15% **37.** D **41.** 19 girls **43.** D: {−3, −1, 0, 1, 3}; R: {0, 1, 3}; yes **47.** quadratic binomial

10-2

Check It Out!

1. Temperature (°C)

Stem	Leaves
0	7
1	9
2	2 3 6 7 9
3	0 1 1 2 4 5 6 6

Key: 1|9 means 19

2.

Interval	Frequency
4–6	5
7–9	4
10–12	4
13–15	2

3. Vacation

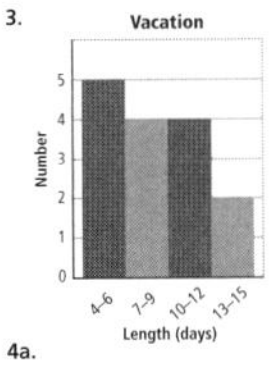

4a.

Interval	Frequency	Cumulative Frequency
28–31	2	2
32–35	7	9
36–39	5	14
40–43	3	17

4b. 9

Exercises 1. stem-and-leaf plot

3.

Austin	Stem	New York
9 9 9	1	
4 3 2 1	2	
6 5 3 2 0	3	1 3 3 3 6 6 7 9
	4	1 1 2 2

5.

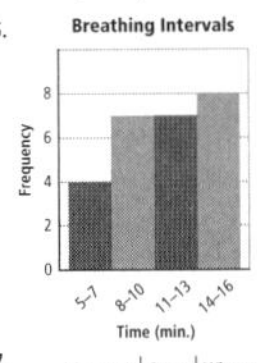

7.

Summer	Stem	Winter
	0	4 9 9
	1	1 2 3 4 9 9
9 7 7 6 5 5 3 3 2 2	2	1 7
	3	0 3 5
	4	
9 7 4 3	5	

Key: |2|1 means 21; 7|2| means 27

9.

Interval	Frequency
2.0–2.4	2
2.5–2.9	7
3.0–3.4	5
3.5–3.9	3

11a.

Interval	Frequency	Cumulative Frequency
36–38	4	4
39–41	6	10
42–44	5	15
45–47	1	16

b. 10

15a.

Interval	Frequency
160–169.9	2
170–179.9	4
180–189.9	3
190–199.9	1
200–209.9	2
210–219.9	1

19. G **21.** 8; 8; 41; 66 **23.** −2.3 **25.** 0.5 in. **27.** books

10-3

Check It Out! 1. mean: 14 lb; median: 14 lb; modes: 12 lb and 16 lb; range: 4 lb **2.** 3; the outlier decreases the mean by 3.7 and increases the range by 18. It has no effect on the median and mode. **3a.** mode: 7 **3b.** Median: 81; the median is greater than either the mean or the mode. **4.**

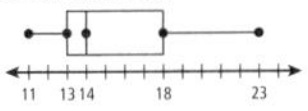

5a. The data set for 2000; the distance between the points for the least and greatest values is less for 2000 than for 2007. **5b.** about $40 million

Exercises 3. mean: 31.5; median: 33.5; mode: 44; range: 32 **5.** mean: 78.25; median: 78; mode: 78; range: 15 **7.** 13; the outlier decreases the mean by 11.15 and the median by 4. It increases the range by 51 and has no effect on the mode. **9.** Median: 83; the median is greater than the mean, and there is no mode. **13.** Simon; about 3000 points **15.** mean: 2.5; median: 2.5; modes: 2 and 3; range: 3 **17.** mean: 60; median: 60; mode: 60; range: 5 **19.** 23; the outlier increases the mean by 3, the median by 2.5, and the range by 15. It has no effect on the mode. **21.** Mean: 153; the mean is greater than the median, and there is no mode. **25.** Sneaks R Us; the middle half of the data doesn't vary as much at Sneaks R Us as at Jump N Run. **27.** mean: 5.5; median: 5.5; mode: none; range: 9 **29.** mean: 3.5; median: 3.4; mode: none; range: 5.3 **31.** mean: 24.4; median: 25; modes: 23 and 25; range: 3 **33.** mean: $15\frac{5}{6}$; median: $12\frac{1}{2}$; mode: none; range: 35 **37.** sometimes **39.** always **41.** Median; the mean is affected by the outlier of 1218, and there is no mode. **43.** Median or mode; the store wants their prices to seem low, and the median and mode are both $2.80 less than the mean. **49.** Mean: $32,000; median: $25,000; median; the outlier of $78,000 increases the mean significantly. **51.** 96 **53.** increase the mean; decrease the mean **55.** G **57.** The mean decreases by 6.6 lb. **61.** 32; typing speed is 32 words per minute. **63.** 2 **65.** 5 **67.** length: 5 yd; width: 3 yd

10-4

Check It Out! 1. Possible answer: company D; the fertilizer from company D appears to be more effective than the other fertilizers. **2.** Possible answer: taxi drivers; the drivers could justify charging higher rates by using this graph, which seems to show that gas prices have increased dramatically. **3.** Possible answer: Smith; Smith might want to show that he or she got many more votes than Atkins or Napier. **4.** The sample size is much too small.

Exercises 3a. The vertical scale does not start at 0, and the categories on the horizontal scale are not at equal time intervals. **b.** Possible answer: Tourism is decreasing rapidly. **5.** The sample size is too small. **7a.** The vertical scale does not start at 0. **b.** Possible answer: Single men pay significantly more than single women.

9a. The sectors of the graph do not add to 100%. **b.** Possible answer: Nearly half of the state's spending was for welfare. **15.** B **19.** $w \le 1500$ **21.** $b \le 20$ **23.** $t \ge -4$

10-5

Check It Out! 1. sample space: {1, 2, 3, 4, 5, 6}; outcome shown: 3 **2.** certain **3a.** $\frac{7}{20}$ **3b.** $\frac{13}{20}$ **4a.** 99.8% **4b.** 34,930

Exercises 3. sample space: {blue, red, yellow, green}; outcome shown: red **5.** impossible **7.** unlikely **9.** $\frac{3}{5}$ **11a.** 30% **b.** 54 **13.** sample space: {blue, red, yellow}; outcome shown: blue **15.** as likely as not **17.** likely **19.** $\frac{6}{25}$ **21a.** 5% **b.** 21 **27.** about 1%; about 57 **29.** B **31.** B **33.** as likely as not **35.** unlikely **37a.** 7 **b.** 8 **39.** $14 **41.** reflected across the x-axis **43.** mean: 6; median: 5; mode: 5

10-6

Check It Out! 1a. 50% **1b.** $33\frac{1}{3}\%$ **2.** 0.4 **3.** $\frac{1}{25}$

Exercises 1. complement **3.** 25% **5.** $\frac{1}{2}$ **7.** $\frac{2}{3}$ **9.** $\frac{9}{10}$ **11.** 1:12 **13.** $\frac{1}{4}$ **15.** 50% **17.** $\frac{5}{9}$ **19.** 70% **21.** $\frac{9}{10}$ **23.** $\frac{1}{5}$ **25.** $\frac{4}{5}$ **27.** 4:1 **31.** $\frac{1}{2}$ **35.** D **37.** B **41.** $(4x - 3)(x - 1)$ **43.** $\frac{1}{10}$ **45.** $\frac{13}{20}$

10-7

Check It Out! 1a. Independent; the result of rolling the number cube the first time does not affect the result of the second roll. **1b.** Dependent; choosing the first student leaves fewer students to choose from the second time. **2.** $\frac{1}{4}$ **3.** $\frac{8}{87}$

Exercises 1. dependent **3.** independent **5.** independent **7.** $\frac{1}{8}$ **9.** $\frac{1}{6}$ **11.** $\frac{1}{16}$ **13.** $\frac{4}{7}$ **15.** dependent **17.** $\frac{1}{8}$ **19.** $\frac{1}{12}$ **21.** $\frac{2}{9}$ **23a.** $\frac{27}{64}$ **b.** $\frac{1}{64}$ **25.** dependent **27.** independent **29a.** $\frac{3}{20}$ **b.** $\frac{1}{6}$ **c.** $\frac{9}{100}$ **d.** $\frac{1}{15}$ **31.** $\frac{2}{15}$ **35.** D **37.** A **39.** 72.9% **41.** 80% **43.** 48% **45.** 24 **47.** wider **49.** $\frac{3}{5}$ **51.** $\frac{5}{26}$

10-8

Check It Out! 1. 15,600 **2a.** permutation; 6 **2b.** combination; 6 **3.** 362,880 **4.** 792

Exercises 1. combination **3.** 8 **5.** combination; 6 **7.** 20,160 **9.** 35 **11.** 15,504 **13.** 441,000 **15.** combination; 10 **17.** 120 **19.** 133,784,560 **21.** $_nP_r$ **25a.** $\frac{1}{308{,}915{,}776}$ **b.** about 85,810 h **27.** J **29.** 260,130 **31.** 168 **33a.** 28 **b.** 28 **37.** $5x + 5$ **39.** independent: minutes; dependent: volume of water in tub; $f(x) = 15x$ **41.** independent: hours; dependent: total fee; $f(x) = 300 + 80x$

Study Guide: Review

1. outcome **2.** interquartile range **3.** independent events **4.** 2003 **5.** 14 more boys

6.

Stem	Leaves
0	1 7 9
1	2 4 8 9
2	2 2 4 8

Key: 1|2 means 12

7.

Comedy Camp		Days and Days
2	6	
	7	
3 1	8	0 2
	9	
4 4 2	10	3 5 9
	11	
6 2 0	12	8
	13	2 5 9

Key: |12|8 means 128; 4|10| means 104

8.

Gas Tank Capacities		
Capacity	Tally	Frequency
10–14	𝍸 I	6
15–19	𝍸 𝍸	10
20–24	III	3
25–29	III	3

9. Gas Tank Capacities

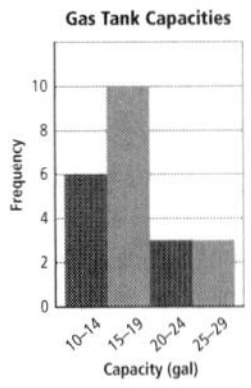

10. mean: 14; median: 12; mode: 12; range: 28 **11.** Median; the mean is higher than 4 of the 5 prices; the mode is the lowest price.

12.

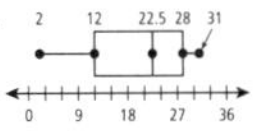

13. The scale on the vertical axis is too large. This makes the slopes of the segments less steep. **14.** Someone might believe that the price has been relatively stable when in fact it has doubled. **15.** 99.5% **16.** 24,875 **17.** 250 **18.** $\frac{1}{2}$ **19.** $\frac{1}{4}$ **20.** $\frac{5}{8}$ **21.** independent **22.** independent **23.** dependent **24.** $\frac{2048}{9555}$ **25.** 0 **26.** $\frac{256}{2401}$ **27.** 60 **28.** permutation; 604,800 **29.** combination; 220 **30.** combination; 1365

Chapter 11

11-1

Check It Out! 1a. 80, −160, 320 **1b.** 216, 162, 121.5 **2.** 7.8125 **3.** $1342.18

Exercises 3. 25, 12.5, 6.25 **5.** 1,000,000,000 **7.** 4 **9.** 162, 243, 364.5 **11.** 2058; 14,406; 100,842 **13.** $\frac{5}{32}, \frac{5}{128}, \frac{5}{512}$ **15.** 0.0000000001, or 1×10^{-10} **17.** 80; 160 **19.** $\frac{1}{3}$ **21.** $\frac{1}{7}$; $\frac{1}{49}$ **23.** 6; −48 **25.** 4913 **27.** yes; $\frac{1}{3}$ **29.** no **31.** no **33a.** 1.28 cm **b.** 40.96 cm **35.** −2, −8, −32, −128 **37.** 2, 4, 8, 16 **39.** 12, 3, $\frac{3}{4}$, $\frac{3}{16}$ **43a.** $3993; $4392.30 **b.** 1.1 **c.** $2727.27 **45.** J **47.** x^4, x^5, x^6 **49.** $1, y, y^2$ **51.** −400 **53.** the 7th term **55.** $b > 10$ **57.** $c < -\frac{1}{3}$ **61.** $f(x) = x^2 + 4$

11-2

Check It Out! **1.** 3.375 in. **2a.** no **2b.** yes

3a. **3b.** **4a.** **4b.** **5a.** **5b.**

6. after about 13 yr

Exercises **1.** no **3.** no **17.** about 2023 **19.** 289 ft **21.** yes **23.** no **35.** $y = 4.8(2)^x$ **41.** −0.125 **43a.** \$2000 **b.** 8% **c.** \$2938.66 **45.** C **45.** C **47.** D **49.** 3 **51.** The value of a is the y-intercept. **53.** 25 **55.** $9x^2$

11-3

Check It Out! **1.** $y = 1200(1.08)^t$; \$1904.25 **2a.** $A = 1200(1.00875)^{4t}$; \$1379.49 **2b.** $A = 4000(1.0025)^{12t}$; \$5083.47 **3.** $y = 48{,}000(0.97)^t$; 38,783 **4a.** 1.5625 mg **4b.** 0.78125 g

Exercises **1.** exponential growth **3.** $y = 300(1.08)^t$; 441 **5.** $A = 4200(1.007)^{4t}$; \$4965.43 **7.** $y = 10(0.84)^t$; 4.98 mg **9.** 5.5 g **11.** $y = 1600(1.03)^t$; 2150 **13.** $A = 30(1.078)^t$; 47 members **15.** $A = 7000(1.0075)^{4t}$; \$9438.44 **17.** $A = 12{,}000(1.026)^t$; \$17,635.66 **19.** $y = 58(0.9)^t$; \$24.97 **21.** growth; 61% **23.** decay; $33\frac{1}{3}$% **25.** growth; 10% **27.** growth; 25% **29.** $y = 58{,}000{,}000(1.001)^t$; 58,174,174 **31.** $y = 8200(0.98)^t$; \$7118.63 **33.** $y = 970(1.012)^t$; 1030 **35.** B **37.** 18 yr **39.** A; B **45.** D **47.** D **49.** about 20 yr **51.** 100 min, or 1 h 40 min **53.** \$225,344 **55.** 16 ft

11-4

Check It Out!

1a.

exponential

1b.

quadratic

2. quadratic **3.** The oven temperature decreases by 50 °F every 10 min; $y = -5x + 375$; 75 °F

Exercises **1.** exponential **3.** linear **5.** exponential **7.** Grapes cost \$1.79/lb; $y = 1.79x$; \$10.74 **11.** linear **13.** exponential **15.** $\ell = 6k$; linear **17.** linear **19.** $y = 0.2(4)^x$ **21.** linear **27.** C **29.** C **33.** $\frac{145}{8}$ **35.** 5, −5 **37.** $\frac{9}{4}, -\frac{9}{4}$

11-5

Check It Out! **1a.** 40 ft/s **1b.** 30.98 ft/s **2a.** $x \geq \frac{1}{2}$ **2b.** $x \geq \frac{5}{3}$

3a.

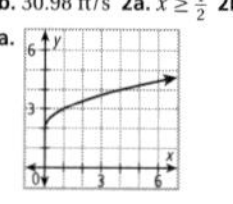

3b.

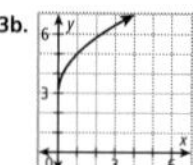

Exercises **1.** There is no variable under the square-root sign. **3.** $x \geq -6$ **5.** $x \geq 0$ **7.** $x \geq -3$ **15.** 49.96 mi/h **17.** $x \geq 0$ **19.** $x \leq \frac{3}{2}$ **21.** $x \geq -\frac{5}{3}$ **23.** $x \geq 40$ **25.** $x \geq 9$ **27.** $x \geq -\frac{2}{3}$ **37.** 3.61 units **39.** Mercury: 4214 m/s; Venus: 10,361 m/s; Earth: 11,200 m/s; Mars: 5016 m/s **45.** A **47.** C **49.** $x \leq -5$ OR $x \geq 5$ **51.** $x \leq -4$ OR $x \geq \frac{3}{2}$ **53.** D: $x \leq 3$; R: $y \leq 4$ **57a.** 2 and 4 **b.** 3, 1 **59.** $y = -\frac{1}{2}x + 2$ **61.** $9x^2 - 6x + 1$ **63.** $a^2 - 2ab^2c + b^4c^2$ **65.** $9r^2 - 4s^2$ **67.** $A = 42{,}000(1.0125)^{4t}$; \$48,751.69

11-6

Check It Out! **1a.** 8 **1b.** 7 **1c.** 13 **1d.** $|3 - x|$ **2a.** $8\sqrt{2}$ **2b.** $xy\sqrt{x}$ **2c.** $4a\sqrt{3b}$ **3a.** $\frac{2}{3}$ **3b.** $\frac{6}{x^2}$ **3c.** $\frac{y^3}{2}$ **4a.** $\frac{2\sqrt{5}}{7}$ **4b.** $\frac{z^2\sqrt{z}}{5y}$ **4c.** $\frac{p^3}{q^5}$ **5.** $60\sqrt{2}$ ft; 84.9 ft

Exercises **1.** $3x - 6$ **3.** 7 **5.** $6\sqrt{5}$ **7.** $18\sqrt{2}$ **9.** $4x^2y\sqrt{2y}$ **11.** $\frac{\sqrt{17}}{5}$ **13.** $\frac{\sqrt{6}}{7}$ **15.** $\frac{\sqrt{x}}{3}$ **17.** $\frac{6\sqrt{3}}{7}$ **19.** $\frac{16\sqrt{2}}{9}$ **21.** $\frac{5x\sqrt{2}}{13}$ **23.** $5\sqrt{41}$ mi; 32 mi **25.** 20 **27.** 9 **29.** $|x + 1|$ **31.** $|x - 3|$ **33.** $20\sqrt{10}$ **35.** $8rs\sqrt{5}$ **37.** $\frac{3\sqrt{5}}{2}$ **39.** $\frac{\sqrt{14}}{3}$ **41.** $\frac{x\sqrt{x}}{y^3}$ **43.** $\frac{8s\sqrt{3}}{7}$ **45.** $-20\sqrt{3}$ **47.** $15x\sqrt{7}$ **49.** x **51.** $\frac{x^3\sqrt{x}}{3}$ **53.** $\sqrt{36}$; 6 **55.** $\sqrt{50}$; $5\sqrt{2}$ **57.** $\sqrt{3}$ **59.** $\sqrt{20}$; $2\sqrt{5}$ **67.** C **69.** C **71.** $x\sqrt{x + 1}$ **73a.** $|x|$ **b.** x^2 **c.** $|x^3|$ **d.** x^4 **e.** $|x^5|$ **f.** x^n; $|x^n|$ **75.** no **77.** exponential

11-7

Check It Out! **1a.** $-\sqrt{7}$ **1b.** $3\sqrt{3}$ **1c.** $8\sqrt{n}$ **1d.** $\sqrt{2s} + 8\sqrt{5s}$ **2a.** $5\sqrt{6}$ **2b.** $12\sqrt{3} - 3\sqrt{2}$ **2c.** $5\sqrt{3y}$ **3.** $10\sqrt{b}$ in.

Exercises **3.** $10\sqrt{5}$ **5.** $3\sqrt{7} + 5\sqrt{2}$ **7.** $5\sqrt{6a} + 6\sqrt{5a}$ **9.** $13\sqrt{3}$ **11.** $-\sqrt{5x}$ **13.** $8\sqrt{2t} - 4\sqrt{3t}$ **15.** $6\sqrt{3}$ **17.** $-3\sqrt{11}$ **19.** $-4\sqrt{n}$ **21.** $7\sqrt{7}$ **23.** $12\sqrt{2}$ **25.** $3\sqrt{7x} - 12\sqrt{3x}$ **27.** $3\sqrt{5j}$

29. $2\sqrt{3m}$ **31.** $12\sqrt{7}$ **33.** 0 **35.** $7\sqrt{3}$ **37.** $7\sqrt{2}$ **41.** $2\sqrt{3} + 5\sqrt{5} + 5$ **43.** $8\sqrt{7x} - \sqrt{70x}$ **45.** $35\sqrt{5k}$ **47.** $5\sqrt{3} + 5\sqrt{5}$ **51.** 9 **53.** 18 **55.** $36x^2$ **57.** $16\sqrt{3}$ in.; $8\sqrt{3}$ in.; $24\sqrt{3}$ in. **59.** B **61.** A **63.** $\sqrt{x}(x + 2)$ **65.** 0 **67.** $(x + 2)\sqrt{x - 1}$ **69.** $3\sqrt{x + 1} - x\sqrt{x + 2}$ **73.** $\frac{1}{12}$ **75.** $x \geq -3$

11-8

Check It Out! **1a.** $5\sqrt{2}$ **1b.** 63 **1c.** $2m\sqrt{7}$ **2a.** $4\sqrt{3} - 3\sqrt{6}$ **2b.** $5\sqrt{2} + 4\sqrt{15}$ **2c.** $7\sqrt{k} - 5\sqrt{7k}$ **2d.** $150 - 20\sqrt{5}$ **3a.** $21 + 5\sqrt{3}$ **3b.** $83 + 18\sqrt{2}$ **3c.** $11 - 6\sqrt{2}$ **3d.** $17 - \sqrt{3}$ **4a.** $\frac{\sqrt{65}}{5}$ **4b.** $\frac{\sqrt{21a}}{6}$ **4c.** $\frac{8\sqrt{35}}{7}$

Exercises **1.** $\sqrt{6}$ **3.** 125 **5.** $3\sqrt{30a}$ **7.** $2\sqrt{6} + \sqrt{42}$ **9.** $\sqrt{35} - \sqrt{21}$ **11.** $5\sqrt{3y} + 4\sqrt{5y}$ **13.** $12 + 7\sqrt{2}$ **15.** $-5 - 2\sqrt{3}$ **17.** $81 - 30\sqrt{2}$ **19.** $\frac{\sqrt{26}}{2}$ **21.** $\frac{\sqrt{33}}{18}$ **23.** $\frac{2\sqrt{7}}{7}$ **25.** $\frac{\sqrt{5x}}{5x}$ **27.** $3\sqrt{10}$ **29.** 8 **31.** $6d\sqrt{7}$ **33.** $4\sqrt{5} - 5\sqrt{2}$ **35.** $2\sqrt{3} - 2\sqrt{5}$ **37.** $3\sqrt{f} + 12\sqrt{3f}$ **39.** $75 + 19\sqrt{15}$ **41.** $10 - \sqrt{2}$ **43.** $67 + 16\sqrt{3}$ **45.** $\frac{5\sqrt{6}}{2}$ **47.** $\frac{\sqrt{3x}}{x}$ **49.** $\frac{7\sqrt{2x}}{2}$ **51.** $2\sqrt{y}$ **53.** 180 in² **55.** $(6\sqrt{10} - 2\sqrt{5})$cm² **57.** $\sqrt{30}$ **59.** $-5 - 2\sqrt{3}$ **61.** $3\sqrt{2}$ **63.** $134\sqrt{3} + 96$ **65.** $x - 2\sqrt{xy} + y$ **67.** $3 + 2\sqrt{3x} + x$ **69.** $\frac{\pi\sqrt{6}}{4}$ s ≈ 1.9 s **71.** 269.5 ft² **75.** B **77.** D **79.** $-4\sqrt{3} + 4\sqrt{5}$ **81.** $-5 - 2\sqrt{6}$ **83.** $2 - \sqrt{3}$ **85.** $2\sqrt{6} + 2\sqrt{5}$ **87.** translation 4 units down **89.** $(x - 3)(x + 10)$ **91.** $(x + 4)(x - 4)$ **93.** $2(x^2 + 3)(x^2 - 3)$ **95.** $6\sqrt{10}$ **97.** $\frac{7x}{8y^2}$

11-9

Check It Out! **1a.** 36 **1b.** 3 **1c.** $\frac{1}{3}$ **2a.** 9 **2b.** 18 **2c.** 3 **3a.** 121 **3b.** 64 **3c.** 100 **4a.** 2 **4b.** $\frac{11}{2}$ **5a.** no solution **5b.** no solution **5c.** 4 **6.** 8; 3 cm

Exercises **1.** No; it does not contain a variable under the radical sign. **3.** −8 **5.** −144 **7.** 27 **9.** 50 **11.** −2 **13.** 9 **15.** 64 **17.** 16 **19.** 16 **21.** $\frac{4}{9}$ **23.** 100 **25.** 5 **27.** 13 **29.** 6 **31.** 2 **33.** no solution **35.** 4 **37.** 2 **39.** no solution **41.** 48 **43.** −25 **45.** 71 **47.** −8 **49.** 36 **51.** −16 **53.** 8 **55.** 9 **57.** 2 **59.** −5 **61.** 5 **63.** 1 **65.** 1 **67.** $x = 144$; 12 in. **69.** $\sqrt{x} - 3 = 4$; 49 **71.** $x = \sqrt{x + 6}$; 3 **73.** 3 in. by 1 in. **75a.** 54.88 joules **b.** 0 joules **77.** 1690 ft **79.** $x = 25$; $y = 16$ **81.** sometimes **87.** A **89.** C **91.** A **93.** 1, 2 **95.** 2 **97.** 0 **101.** 51.2 mi **103.** 10,000

Study Guide: Review

1. square-root function **2.** exponential decay **3.** common ratio **4.** exponential function **5.** 81, 243, 729 **6.** 48, −96, 192 **7.** 5, 2.5, 1.25 **8.** −256, −1024, −4096 **9.** 7,812,500 **10.** 19,131,876 **11.** yes **12.** no

13.

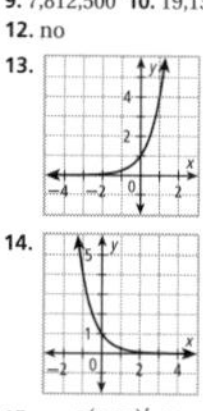

14.

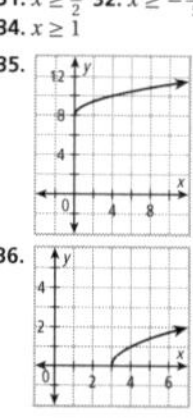

15. $y = 9(1.15)^t$; 24 **16.** $y = 24{,}500(0.96)^t$; 3182 **17.** quadratic **18.** linear **19.** exponential **20.** exponential **21.** quadratic **22.** linear **23.** $y = 1.5x$; 15 h **24.** 4.74 cm **25.** $x \geq 0$ **26.** $x \geq -4$ **27.** $x \geq 0$ **28.** $x \geq -2$ **29.** $x \geq \frac{4}{3}$ **30.** $x \geq -3$ **31.** $x \geq \frac{7}{2}$ **32.** $x \geq -\frac{18}{5}$ **33.** $x \geq \frac{3}{4}$ **34.** $x \geq 1$

35. **36.** **37.** **38.**

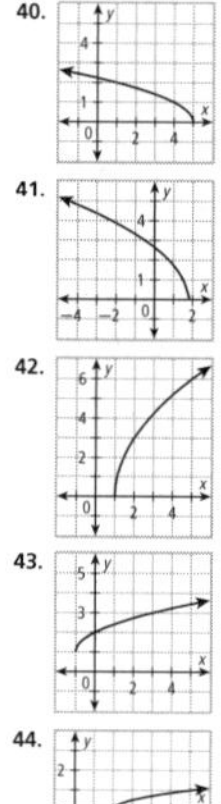

39. **40.** **41.** **42.** **43.** **44.**

45. 11 **46.** n^2 **47.** $x + 3$ **48.** 5 **49.** $6d$ **50.** $y^3\sqrt{x}$ **51.** $2\sqrt{3}$ **52.** $4b^2\sqrt{2ab}$ **53.** $\frac{\sqrt{5}}{2}$ **54.** $\frac{t}{10}$ **55.** $\frac{2}{3}$ **56.** $\frac{4p^2\sqrt{2}}{7}$ **57.** $\frac{t^4\sqrt{t}}{s}$ **58.** $\frac{2b^3\sqrt{2}}{5}$ **59.** $9\sqrt{7}$ **60.** $3\sqrt{3}$ **61.** $3\sqrt{2} + 2\sqrt{3}$ **62.** $\sqrt{5t}$ **63.** $2\sqrt{2}$ **64.** $2\sqrt{3} + 2\sqrt{5}$

65. $-2\sqrt{5x}$ **66.** $10\sqrt{6}$ **67.** $\sqrt{14}$ **68.** $3\sqrt{2}$ **69.** $6\sqrt{7x}$ **70.** 150 **71.** $4\sqrt{2} - 4$ **72.** $71 + 16\sqrt{7}$ **73.** $\frac{4\sqrt{5}}{5}$ **74.** $\frac{3a\sqrt{2}}{2}$ **75.** $\frac{\sqrt{3}}{3}$ **76.** $\frac{\sqrt{10n}}{2n}$ **77.** $\frac{\sqrt{6}}{2}$ **78.** $-\sqrt{3}$ **79.** 64 **80.** 8 **81.** 3 **82.** 25 **83.** −81 **84.** 100 **85.** 3 **86.** no solution **87.** $x = 4$ **88.** $x = 6$ **89.** $x = 7$ **90.** $x = \frac{19}{2}$ **91.** $x = 12$ **92.** $x = 3$ **93.** $x = 4$ **94.** $x = 5$

Chapter 12

12-1

Check It Out! **1a.** No; the product xy is not constant. **1b.** Yes; the product xy is constant. **1c.** No; the equation cannot be written in the form $y = \frac{k}{x}$. **2.** $y = \frac{5}{x}$

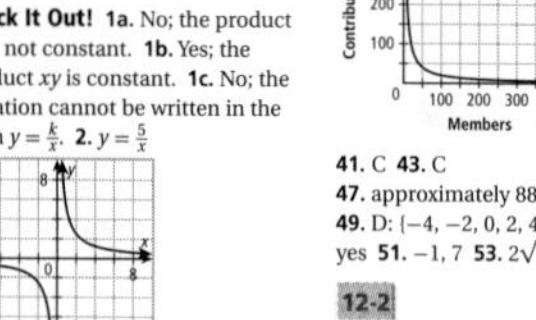

3. D: $x > 0$; R: $y > 0$; 2.5 mm³

4. 3 **5.** 80.625 lb

Exercises **3.** no **5.** yes **7.** $y = \frac{-6}{x}$

9. 4 **11.** 16 teeth **13.** yes **15.** no

17. $y = \frac{2}{x}$

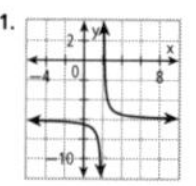

19. 2 **21.** 12 yd **23.** direct; 8 **25.** neither **27.** inverse; 12 **29.** inverse; 15 **31.** $d = \frac{10}{n}$; inverse **33.** neither **35.** $y = \frac{2000}{x}$; D: natural numbers; R: $y > 0$

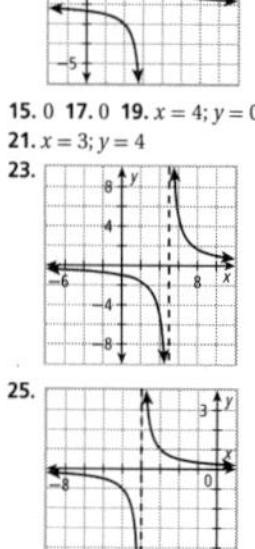

41. C **43.** C **47.** approximately 888.9 watts **49.** D: {−4, −2, 0, 2, 4}; R: {1, 3, 5}; yes **51.** −1, 7 **53.** $2\sqrt{10}$ cm

12-2

Check It Out! **1a.** 0 **1b.** 1 **1c.** −4 **2a.** $x = 5$; $y = 0$ **2b.** $x = -4$; $y = 5$ **2c.** $x = -77$; $y = -15$

3a. **3b.**

4a. D: $x > 0$; R: natural numbers > 10 **4b.**

Exercises **1.** excluded value **3.** −3 **5.** 4 **7.** $x = -5$; $y = 0$ **9.** $x = -9$; $y = -10$

11. **13.**

15. 0 **17.** 0 **19.** $x = 4$; $y = 0$ **21.** $x = 3$; $y = 4$ **23.** **25.**

27a. D: $x > 0$; R: natural numbers > 5 **b.**

29. 7 **31.** $-\frac{1}{3}$ **37.** $x = -1$; $y = 0$ **39.** $x = 2$; $y = 5$ **41.** B **43.** C **51.** D: $x > 2$ **53.** D: $x > -\frac{1}{3}$ **55.** I and III; II and IV **59.** J **61a.** yes **b.** D: all real numbers **c.** R: $0 < y \leq 1$ **d.** no **63.** $y = \frac{3}{x + 2} + 3$ **65.** −2, 3 **67.** 0.46875 cm **69.** no

12-3

Check It Out! **1a.** −5 **1b.** 0, −5 **1c.** −3, −4 **2a.** $\frac{m}{3}$; $m \neq 0$ **2b.** $6p$ **2c.** $\frac{3n}{n - 2}$; $n \neq 2$ **3a.** $\frac{1}{r + 5}$ **3b.** $\frac{b - 5}{b + 5}$ **4a.** $-\frac{3}{4 + x}$ **4b.** $-\frac{1}{x + 1}$ **4c.** $\frac{3}{x + 11}$

5. The barrel cactus with a radius of 3 inches has less of a chance to survive. Its surface-area-to-volume ratio is greater than for a cactus with a radius of 6 inches.

Exercises **3.** 0, 8 **5.** $\frac{a}{2}$; $a \neq 0$ **7.** $\frac{2}{y + 3}$; $y \neq -3$ **9.** $\frac{h}{h + 2}$; $h \neq -2$ **11.** $\frac{1}{b + 1}$ **13.** $\frac{c + 2}{c - 4}$ **15.** $\frac{j - 5}{j - 3}$ **17.** $-\frac{2}{8 + n}$ **21.** $-\frac{5}{10 + q}$ **23a.** $\frac{b_2}{b_1 + b_2}$ **b.** They will be the same: $\frac{b_2}{b_1 + b_2}$. **25.** 0 **27.** $-\frac{1}{2}$, 4 **29.** already simplified; $m \neq 4$ **31.** $\frac{t}{8}$; $t \neq 0$ **33.** $\frac{z - 1}{z + 1}$ **35.** $\frac{p - 7}{p - 5}$ **37.** $\frac{2}{x - 4}$ **39.** $-\frac{1}{b + 7}$ **43.** $\frac{p + 6}{12}$ **45.** $\frac{1}{3}$ **47.** $\frac{3w + 7}{3}$ **49.** 1 **51.** $-\frac{5 + x}{x + 2}$ **53a.** $\frac{6}{s}$ **b.** 3 **c.** 1 **57.** F **59.** sometimes **61.** sometimes **63.** $\frac{a - 3}{a + 5}$ **65.** ±14 **67.** −2, 0 **73.** −6

12-4

Check It Out! **1a.** $-\frac{9}{4}$ **1b.** $\frac{5x^2y^4}{6}$ **2.** $\frac{3m - 15}{m - 6}$ **3a.** $\frac{n + 4}{n^2 + 2n}$ **3b.** $\frac{p^2 - p - 20}{p^3 + 16p}$ **4a.** $\frac{3x - 15}{x^5}$ **4b.** $\frac{2w^6}{v^2x^3}$ **4c.** $\frac{x}{x^2 + 5x + 6}$ **5.** approximately 0.23

Exercises **1.** $\frac{6h}{5jk^2}$ **3.** $\frac{2x - 4}{3}$ **5.** $\frac{a}{6}$ **7.** $3y - 6$ **9.** $\frac{m^2 - 10m}{2}$ **11.** $a^3 + 10a^2 + 25a$ **13.** $\frac{a + 6b}{b^2}$ **15.** $\frac{1}{2}$ **17.** $\frac{2r + 28}{r - 4}$ **19.** b **21.** $\frac{1}{3x - 15}$ **23.** $-\frac{3p^8q^2}{7r^4}$ **25.** $\frac{10y + 20}{3y + 15}$ **27.** $4m^2 - 4m$ **29.** $\frac{3n^2 - 3n}{n + 8}$ **31.** 1 **33.** $-\frac{1}{2a^3}$ **35a.** $\frac{x^2}{4(4x^2 + 8x - 1)}$ **b.** $\frac{9}{236}$ **37.** b **39.** $\frac{1}{2m}$ **41.** $\frac{1}{16x}$ **43.** 1 **45a.** 64 cm **b.** 80 cm **c.** 4 **47.** H **49.** $\frac{1}{3x^2 + 9x}$ **51.** $\frac{1}{3}$ **53.** $\frac{x}{z^2}$ **55.** $\frac{1}{2a + 2}$ **57.** $m \leq 9$ **59.** $8\sqrt{3t}$ **61.** $x \neq 3$; $x = 3$ and $y = 0$ **63.** $x \neq 0$; $x = 0$ and $y = 3$ **65.** $x \neq 0$; $x = 0$ and $y = 0$

12-5

Check It Out! **1a.** 2 **1b.** $3y$ **2a.** $\frac{3}{a - 2}$ **2b.** $\frac{4b + 12}{b^2 + 3b - 4}$ **3a.** $15f^2h^2$ **3b.** $(x - 6)(x + 2)(x + 5)$ **4a.** $\frac{4d - 3}{3d^2}$ **4b.** $\frac{a + 8}{a - 2}$ **5.** $\frac{5}{24}$ h or 12.5 min

Exercises **1.** $\frac{2}{y}$ **3.** $\frac{1}{x - 4}$ **5.** $\frac{2}{a + 1}$ **7.** $6x^3y^2z$ **9.** $(y + 4)(y - 4)(y + 9)$ **11.** $\frac{x + 3}{x + 2}$ **13a.** $\frac{260}{r}$ **b.** $6\frac{1}{2}$ h **15.** $a - 1$ **17.** m **19.** $3a + 1$ **21.** $36a(3a + 1)$ **23.** $10xy^3z$ **25.** $(y + 5)(y + 2)(y + 4)$ **27.** $\frac{y + 2}{3(y - 3)}$ **29.** $\frac{19}{21z}$ **31.** $\frac{-m^2 - 6m}{4(m - 2)^2}$ **33a.** $\frac{700}{r}$ **b.** 14 h **35.** $\frac{1}{7 + c}$ **37.** $\frac{3}{2b^2}$ **39.** $\frac{x - 5}{3}$ **41.** $\frac{8x + 20}{(x + 4)(x + 2)}$ **43.** A **47.** $4x^2$; $8x^2$; $8x^3$ **49.** A **51.** D **53.** $\frac{x - 4y}{(x + y)(x - y)}$; $x \neq y$ and $x \neq -y$ **55.** $\frac{az + by + cx}{xyz}$; $x \neq 0$, $y \neq 0$, and $z \neq 0$ **61.** $\frac{1}{2}$, 4 **63.** 2; $t \neq \pm 2$ **65.** $-\frac{1}{x + 4}$; $x \neq \pm 4$

12-6

Check It Out! **1a.** $-2p + 1 - \frac{3}{p}$ **1b.** $x^2 + \frac{1}{3} - \frac{5}{2x}$ **2a.** $k + 5$ **2b.** $b - 7$ **2c.** $s + 6$ **3a.** $2y + 1$ **3b.** $a - 2$ **4a.** $3m - 5 + \frac{13}{m + 3}$ **4b.** $y + 6 + \frac{20}{y - 3}$ **5a.** $x^2 - 2x - 4 + \frac{-7}{x - 2}$ **5b.** $2p^2 - 2p + 6 + \frac{-7}{p + 1}$

Exercises **1.** $2x - \frac{1}{2}$ **3.** $7b - \frac{14}{3} + \frac{8}{b}$ **5.** $2x + 4 + \frac{3}{x}$ **7.** $2x - 3$ **9.** $2y + 5$ **11.** $x + 1$ **13.** $c + 3$ **15.** $x - 2$ **17.** $a + 2 + \frac{-1}{a + 2}$ **19.** $n + 4 + \frac{-1}{n + 4}$ **21.** $4n - 5 + \frac{-2}{2n + 1}$ **23.** $-2x^2 + 6x - 15 + \frac{35}{x + 3}$ **25.** $m + 1 + \frac{3}{m - 1}$ **27.** $4k^2 - 4k + 2 + \frac{-10}{k + 1}$ **29.** $3t + 4 - \frac{2}{t}$ **31.** $-4p + 1 + \frac{2}{p^3}$ **33.** $4t + 3$ **35.** $x - 3$ **37.** $3a - 1$ **39.** $3x + 4 + \frac{14}{x - 2}$ **41.** $3x + 1 + \frac{-2}{2x - 1}$ **43.** $2t^2 - 6t + 25 + \frac{-216}{3t + 9}$ **45.** −20 **47.** $2x - 5 + \frac{3}{x + 1}$ **51.** $0.5m + 1$ **57.** C **59.** B **61.** $3x - \frac{1}{2y} + \frac{2y}{x}$ **63.** $x + 2$ **65.** 3 m **67.** $\frac{\sqrt{15}}{15}$ **69.** $6\sqrt{5} - 5\sqrt{2}$ **71.** $4(x + 1)$ **73.** $2k^2 + 5k + 2$

12-7

Check It Out! **1a.** 2 **1b.** 1 **1c.** $-\frac{7}{6}$ **2a.** −4 **2b.** −4 **2c.** 1, 3 **3.** $22\frac{2}{9}$ min **4a.** 5; 7 is extraneous. **4b.** 1 and 5; no extraneous solutions **4c.** 4; 0 is extraneous.

Exercises **1.** rational equation **3.** −24 **5.** $-\frac{8}{3}$ **7.** $\frac{3}{2}$ **9.** $\frac{3}{5}$ **11.** $-\frac{11}{5}$ **13.** $\frac{15}{19}$ **15.** 3, $-\frac{4}{3}$ **17.** −2, 3 **19.** −1, $\frac{3}{2}$ **21.** $\frac{1}{2}$ h, or 30 min **23.** $-\frac{4}{3}$; 1 is extraneous. **25.** −2 **27.** 0 **29.** $\frac{4}{5}$ **31.** 5 **33.** $\frac{3}{2}$ **35.** −4, 3 **37.** 6 h **39.** 2; 3 is extraneous. **41.** No solution; 4 is extraneous. **43.** $\frac{240}{t}$; $t - 2$; 40 mi/h **45a.** $\frac{1}{15} = \frac{1}{24} + \frac{1}{y}$ **b.** 40 cm **c.** It will increase to 72 cm. **49.** F **53.** Eddie: 6 h; Luke 3 h; Ryan: 4 h **55.** $y = -2x$ and $y = \frac{1}{2}x + 4$ are perpendicular. **59.** 5

Study Guide: Review

1. rational expression **2.** rational function **3.** rational equation **4.** inverse variation **5.** discontinuous function **6.** Yes; the product xy is constant. **7.** No; the product xy is not constant.

8. $y = -\frac{4}{x}$ **9.** $y = \frac{1}{x}$

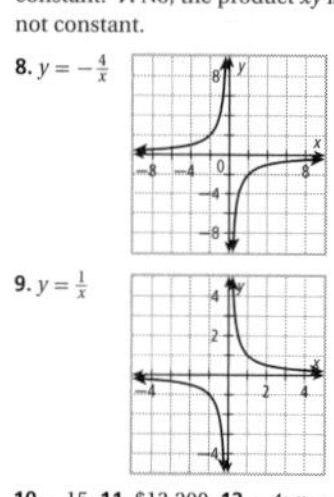

10. −15 **11.** \$13,200 **12.** −4; $x = -4$ and $y = 0$ **13.** −1; $x = -1$ and $y = 3$ **14.** −3; $x = -3$ and $y = -4$ **15.** $\frac{7}{4}$; $x = \frac{7}{4}$ and $y = 5$

16. **17.**

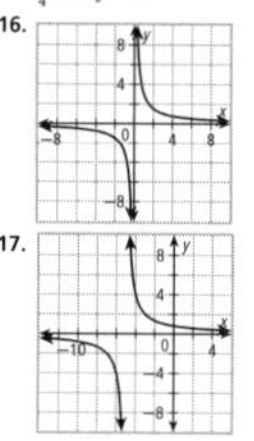

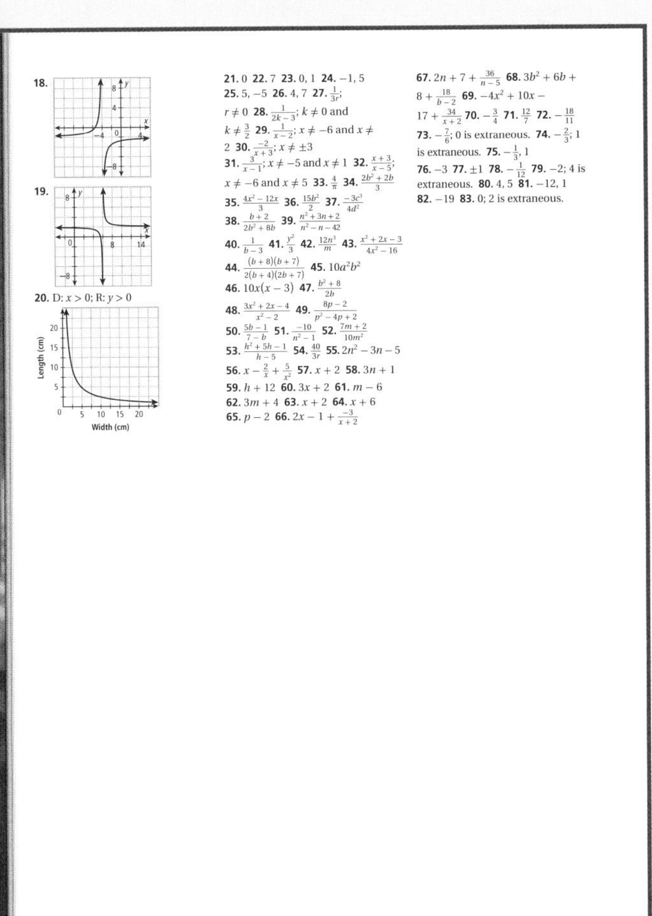

Selected Answers

18.

19.

20. D: $x > 0$; R: $y > 0$

21. 0 **22.** 7 **23.** 0, 1 **24.** $-1, 5$ **25.** $5, -5$ **26.** 4, 7 **27.** $\frac{1}{3r}$; $r \neq 0$ **28.** $\frac{1}{2k-3}$; $k \neq 0$ and $k \neq \frac{3}{2}$ **29.** $\frac{1}{x-2}$; $x \neq -6$ and $x \neq 2$ **30.** $\frac{-2}{x+3}$; $x \neq \pm 3$ **31.** $\frac{3}{x-1}$; $x \neq -5$ and $x \neq 1$ **32.** $\frac{x+3}{x-5}$; $x \neq -6$ and $x \neq 5$ **33.** $\frac{4}{\pi}$ **34.** $\frac{2b^2+2b}{3}$ **35.** $\frac{4x^2-12x}{3}$ **36.** $\frac{15b^2}{2}$ **37.** $\frac{-3c^3}{4d^2}$ **38.** $\frac{b+2}{2b^2+8b}$ **39.** $\frac{n^2+3n+2}{n^2-n-42}$ **40.** $\frac{1}{b-3}$ **41.** $\frac{y^2}{3}$ **42.** $\frac{12n^3}{m}$ **43.** $\frac{x^2+2x-3}{4x^2-16}$ **44.** $\frac{(b+8)(b+7)}{2(b+4)(2b+7)}$ **45.** $10a^2b^2$ **46.** $10x(x-3)$ **47.** $\frac{b^2+8}{2b}$ **48.** $\frac{3x^2+2x-4}{x^2-2}$ **49.** $\frac{8p-2}{p^2-4p+2}$ **50.** $\frac{5b-1}{7-b}$ **51.** $\frac{-10}{n^2-1}$ **52.** $\frac{7m+2}{10m^2}$ **53.** $\frac{h^2+5h-1}{h-5}$ **54.** $\frac{40}{3r}$ **55.** $2n^2-3n-5$ **56.** $x-\frac{2}{x}+\frac{5}{x^2}$ **57.** $x+2$ **58.** $3n+1$ **59.** $h+12$ **60.** $3x+2$ **61.** $m-6$ **62.** $3m+4$ **63.** $x+2$ **64.** $x+6$ **65.** $p-2$ **66.** $2x-1+\frac{-3}{x+2}$

67. $2n+7+\frac{36}{n-5}$ **68.** $3b^2+6b+8+\frac{18}{b-2}$ **69.** $-4x^2+10x-17+\frac{34}{x+2}$ **70.** $-\frac{3}{4}$ **71.** $\frac{12}{7}$ **72.** $-\frac{18}{11}$ **73.** $-\frac{7}{6}$; 0 is extraneous. **74.** $-\frac{2}{3}$; 1 is extraneous. **75.** $-\frac{1}{3}, 1$ **76.** -3 **77.** ± 1 **78.** $-\frac{1}{12}$ **79.** -2; 4 is extraneous. **80.** 4, 5 **81.** $-12, 1$ **82.** -19 **83.** 0; 2 is extraneous.

Selected Answers

Graphic Organizer Answers

Possible answers given.

Chapter 1

Lesson 1-1

	Words	Algebra
Addition	3 more than x	$x + 3$
Subtraction	1 less than y	$y - 1$
Multiplication	The product of 2 and n	$2n$
Division	The quotient of x and 4	$x \div 4$

Lesson 1-2

Points	Sum	Difference
A, B	Neg.	Neg.
B, A	Neg.	Pos.
C, B	Neg.	Pos.
D, A	Pos.	Pos.

Lesson 1-3

Multiplying and Dividing Numbers	
Multiplication	Division
pos • pos = pos	pos ÷ pos = pos
pos • neg = neg	pos ÷ neg = neg
neg • pos = neg	neg ÷ pos = neg
neg • neg = pos	neg ÷ neg = pos

Lesson 1-4

	Even Exponent	Odd Exponent
Positive Base	$3^2 = 9$ Positive	$3^3 = 27$ Positive
Negative Base	$(-3)^2 = 9$ Positive	$(-3)^3 = -27$ Negative

Lesson 1-5

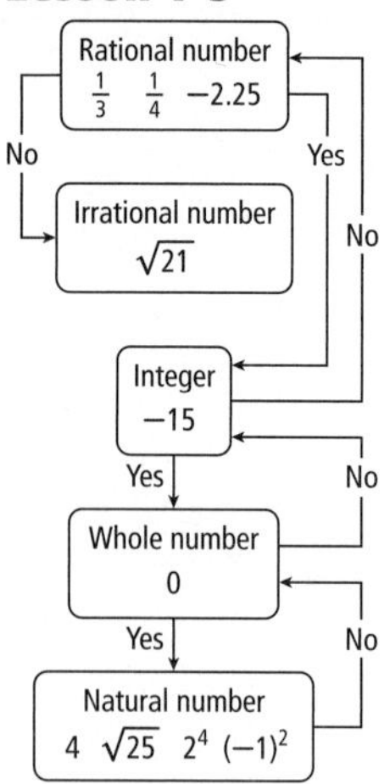

Lesson 1-6

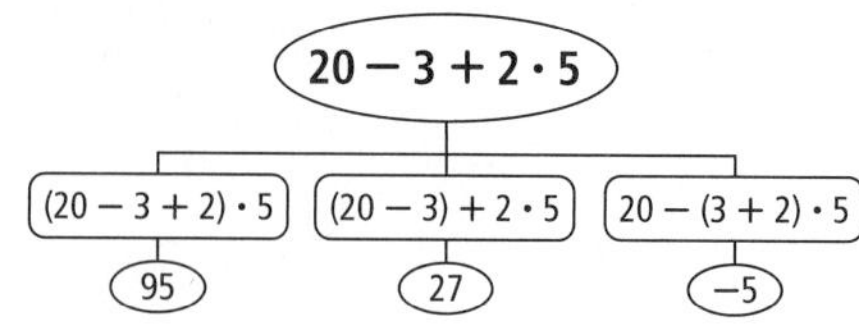

Lesson 1-7

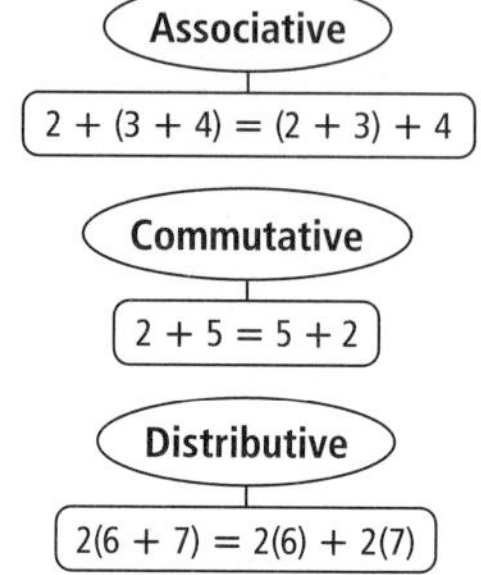

Lesson 1-8

Quadrant II x is neg. y is pos.	Quadrant I x is pos. y is pos.
x is neg. y is neg. Quadrant III	x is pos. y is neg. Quadrant IV

The Coordinate Plane

Chapter 2

Lesson 2-1

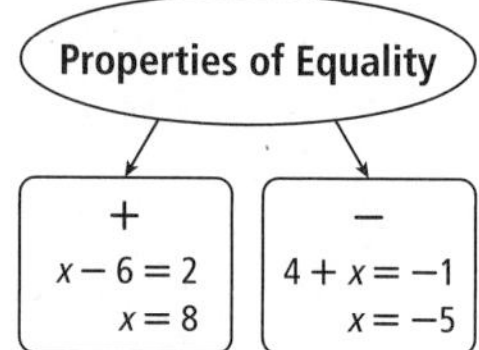

Lesson 2-2

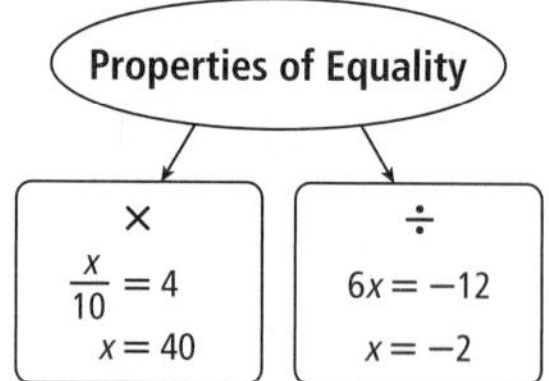

Lesson 2-3

Solving Multi-Step Equations	
$2x + 1 = 9$	$\frac{x}{3} - 2 = 1$
$2x = 8$	$\frac{x}{3} = 3$
$x = 4$	$x = 9$

Additional Answers

Lesson 2-4

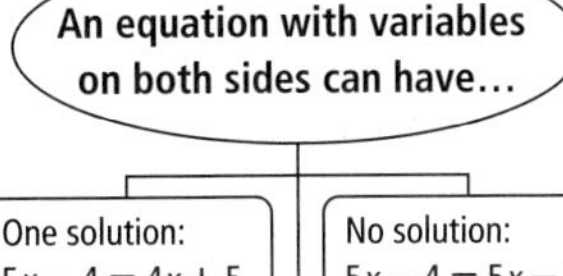

- One solution: $5x - 4 = 4x + 5$
- No solution: $5x - 4 = 5x - 3$
- Many solutions: $5x - 4 = 5x - 4$

Lesson 2-5

Common Formulas	
Subject	**Formula**
Geometry	$P = 4s$; $s = \frac{P}{4}$ (perimeter of a square is 4 times the side length)
Physical science	$F = ma$; $m = \frac{F}{a}$; $a = \frac{F}{m}$ (force equals mass times acceleration)
Earth science	$K = C + 273$; $C = K - 273$ (temperature in kelvins is Celsius temperature plus 273)

Lesson 2-6

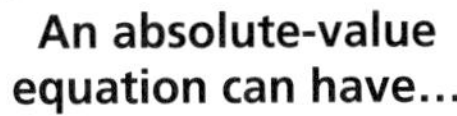

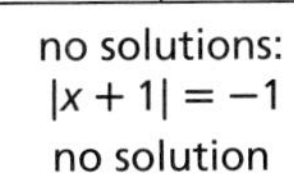

- no solutions: $|x + 1| = -1$ no solution
- one solution: $|x + 1| = 0$ -1
- two solutions: $|x + 1| = 2$ $-3, 1$

Lesson 2-7

Uses of Ratios

- Proportion: to solve for a missing quantity
- Conversion factor: to convert from one set of units to another
- Rate: to compare quantities with different units
- Scale: to make scale drawings/models or to read distances from a map
- Unit rate: to compare prices of products of different sizes

Lesson 2-8

$\triangle ABC \sim \triangle DEF$

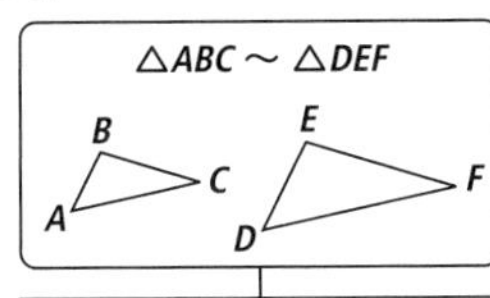

- Corresponding sides: $\overline{AB}$ corresponds to $\overline{DE}$. $\overline{BC}$ corresponds to $\overline{EF}$. $\overline{AC}$ corresponds to $\overline{DF}$.
- Corresponding angles: Angle A corresponds to angle D. Angle B corresponds to angle E. Angle C corresponds to angle F.

Lesson 2-9

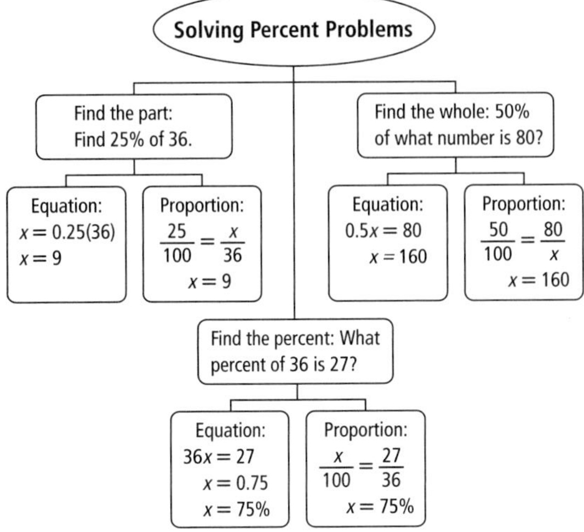

Find the percent: What percent of 36 is 27?

- Equation: $36x = 27$, $x = 0.75$, $x = 75\%$
- Proportion: $\frac{x}{100} = \frac{27}{36}$, $x = 75\%$

Lesson 2-10

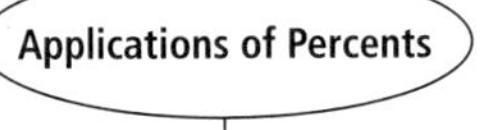

- Commission: 10% commission on sales of $1000 = $100
- Simple interest: 5% annual simple interest on $300 for 2 years = $30
- Tips: estimated 15% tip on $41.50 ≈ $6.00
- Sales tax: estimated 6.5% sales tax on $49.99 ≈ $3.00

Lesson 2-11

Percent Increase	Percent Decrease	Discount	Markup
From 40 to 50 is a 25% increase.	From 50 to 40 is a 20% decrease.	A 15% discount on an orginial price of $10.00 is $1.50, and the sale price is $8.50.	A 75% markup on a wholesale cost of $50.00 is $37.50, and the retail price is $87.50.

Chapter 3

Lesson 3-1

Inequality	Graph
$x > 1$	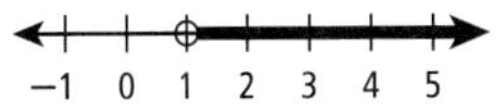 number line −1 to 5, open circle at 1, shaded right
$x \le -3$	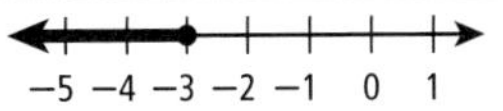 number line −5 to 1, closed circle at −3, shaded left

Lesson 3-2

Properties of Inequality

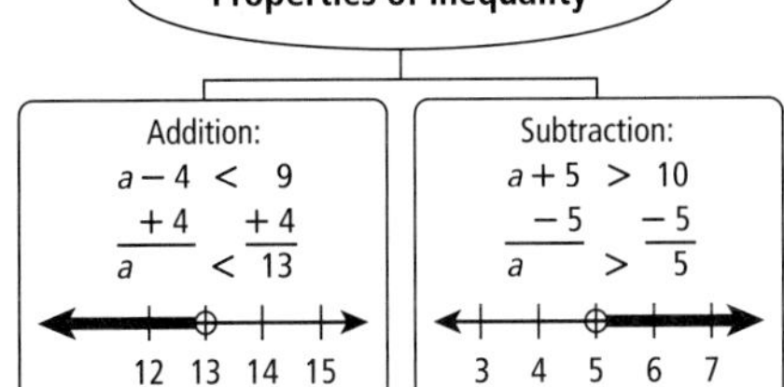

Lesson 3-3

Solving Inequalities by Using Multiplication and Division		
	By a positive number	By a negative number
Divide	$2x < 8$ $\frac{2x}{2} < \frac{8}{2}$ $x < 4$	$-3x > 9$ $\frac{-3x}{-3} < \frac{9}{-3}$ $x < -3$
Multiply	$\frac{x}{4} \leq 4$ $\frac{x}{4}(4) \leq 4(4)$ $x \leq 16$	$\frac{x}{-5} \geq 2$ $\frac{x}{-5}(-5) \leq 2(-5)$ $x \leq -10$

Lesson 3-4

Solving Multi-Step Equations and Inequalities

How are they alike? To solve multi-step equations or inequalities, follow the order of operations to simplify the expressions on both sides of the equal sign or inequality symbol, and then undo each operation.

How are they different? When solving multi-step inequalities, you must reverse the inequality symbol if you multiply or divide both sides by a negative number. There are many solutions of an inequality but usually only one solution of an equation.

Lesson 3-5

Solutions of Inequalities with Variables on Both Sides

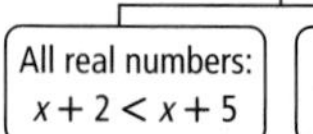

All real numbers: $x + 2 < x + 5$

No solutions: $x + 5 > x + 9$

Lesson 3-6

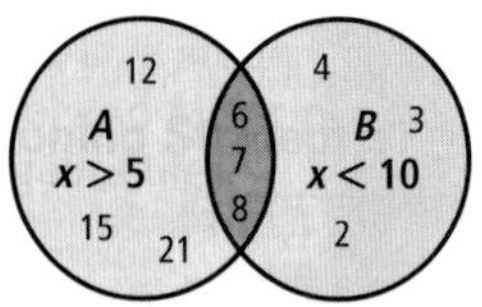

$x > 5$ AND $x < 10$	$x > 5$ OR $x < 10$
6 7 8	2 3 4 6 7 8 12 15 21

Lesson 3-7

Absolute-Value Inequalities

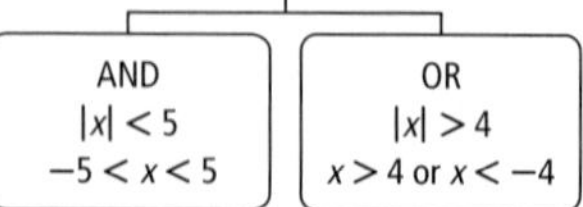

AND
$|x| < 5$
$-5 < x < 5$

OR
$|x| > 4$
$x > 4$ or $x < -4$

Chapter 4

Lesson 4-1

Key Words for Graph Segments

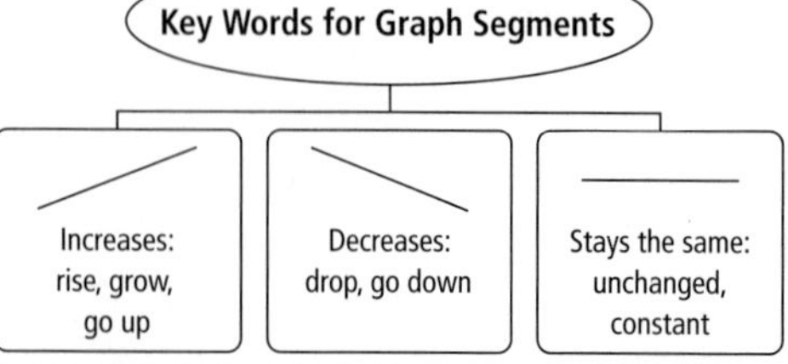

Increases: rise, grow, go up

Decreases: drop, go down

Stays the same: unchanged, constant

Lesson 4-2

A relation is ...	
a function if ... there is exactly one range element for each domain element.	not a function if ... there is more than one range element for a domain element.

Lesson 4-3

Ways to Represent Functions

Equation in function notation: $f(x) = x + 3$

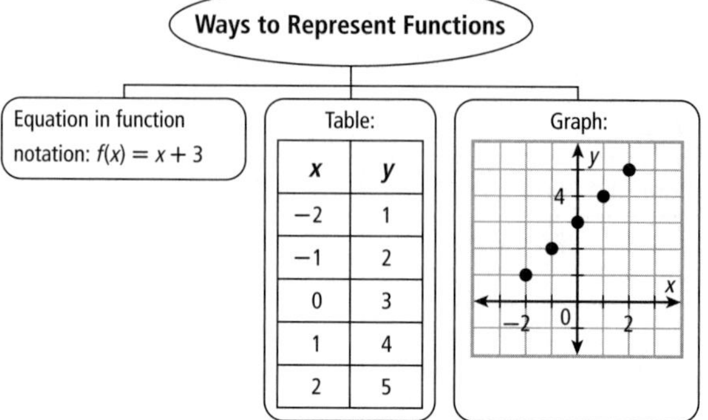

Table:

x	y
−2	1
−1	2
0	3
1	4
2	5

Graph:

Lesson 4-4

Graphing a Function

Not a real-world situation: Use a domain of all real numbers. Choose some values for *x*, and use the function to find corresponding values for *y*. Plot the points and connect them with a line or smooth curve.

Real-world situation: Use a domain that makes sense in the given situation. Choose some values for *x*, and use the function to find corresponding values for *y*. Plot the points and, if it makes sense in the situation, connect them with a line or smooth curve.

Lesson 4-5

	Graph	Example
Positive Correlation		the total price of an ice cream cone and the number of scoops
Negative Correlation		the amount of water in a watering can and the number of flowers watered
No Correlation		the number of magazines a person has and the size of the person's shoes

Lesson 4-6

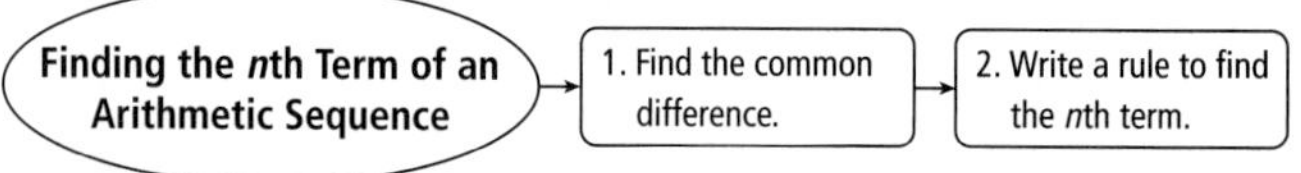

Finding the *n*th Term of an Arithmetic Sequence → 1. Find the common difference. → 2. Write a rule to find the *n*th term.

Chapter 5

Lesson 5-1

Determining Whether a Function Is Linear

- From its graph: All the points form a line.
- From its equation: It can be written in standard form, $Ax + By = C$, where A and B are not both 0. Example: $6x + 2y = -2$
- From a list of ordered pairs: A constant change in x corresponds to a constant change in y.

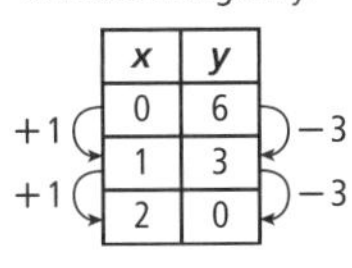

x	y
0	6
1	3
2	0

Lesson 5-2

Graphing $Ax + By = C$ Using Intercepts

1. Find the x-intercept by letting y equal 0 and solving for x.
2. Find the y-intercept by letting x equal 0 and solving for y.
3. Graph the line by plotting the points containing the intercepts and then connecting the points with a straight line.

Lesson 5-3

Slope

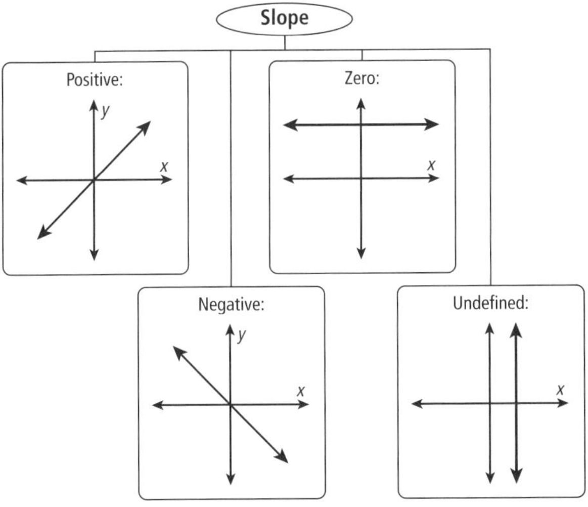

Lesson 5-4

Finding Slope

- From a graph: Begin at any point on the line. Count rise and run to another point on the line. Slope is the ratio of rise to run.
- From a table: Choose any two points from the table and substitute their coordinates into the slope formula.
- From an equation: Find the x- and y-intercepts. Substitute the points containing the intercepts into the slope formula.

Lesson 5-5

Formulas

- Midpoint Formula: $M = \left(\frac{x_1 + x_2}{2}, \frac{y_1 + y_2}{2}\right)$
- Distance Formula: $d = \sqrt{(x_2 - x_1)^2 + (y_2 - y_1)^2}$

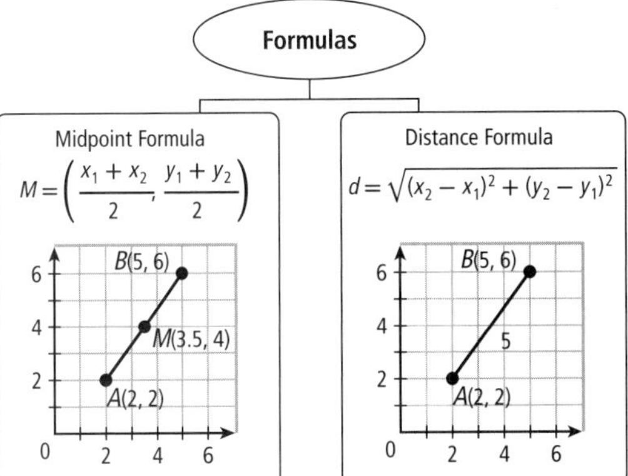

Lesson 5-6

Recognizing a Direct Variation		
From an Equation: The equation can be written in the form $y = kx$ for some nonzero value of k.	From Ordered Pairs: An equation describing the ordered pairs can be written in the form $y = kx$. Also, the ratio $\frac{y}{x}$ is constant for each ordered pair.	From a Graph: The graph is a line through (0, 0).

Lesson 5-7

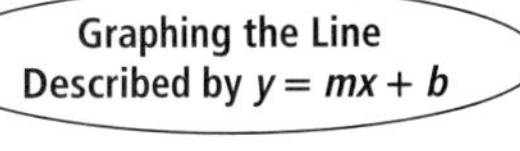

Graphing the Line Described by $y = mx + b$

1. Plot the point $(0, b)$.
2. Find a second point on the line by using the slope m to move horizontally and vertically from $(0, b)$.
3. Draw the line connecting the two points.

Lesson 5-8

Writing the Equation of a Line

- If you know two points on the line: Use the two points in the slope formula to find the slope. Then use the slope and one of the points to write the equation in point-slope form.
- If you know the slope and y-intercept: If the slope is m and the y-intercept is b, then the equation is $y = mx + b$.
- If you know the slope and a point on the line: Use the slope and the point to write the equation in point-slope form.

Lesson 5-9

- Parallel lines: same slopes
- Perpendicular lines: Product of slopes is −1.

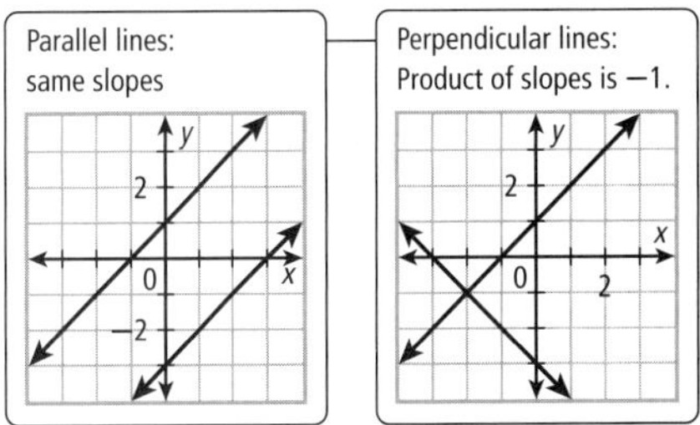

Lesson 5-10

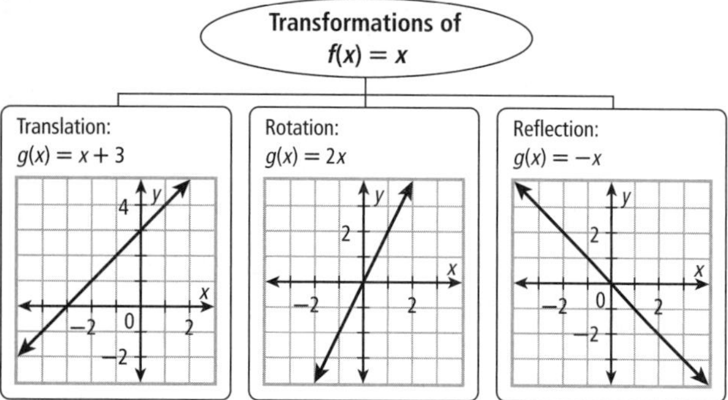

Chapter 6

Lesson 6-1

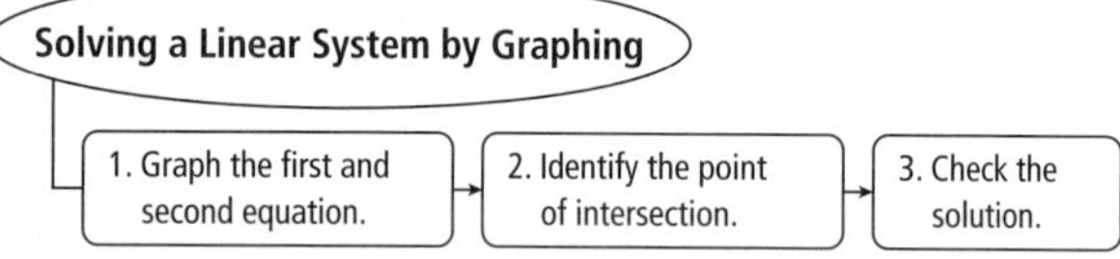

Lesson 6-2

The solution for each is (5, 3).

$\begin{cases} x + y = 8 \\ x - y = 2 \end{cases}$

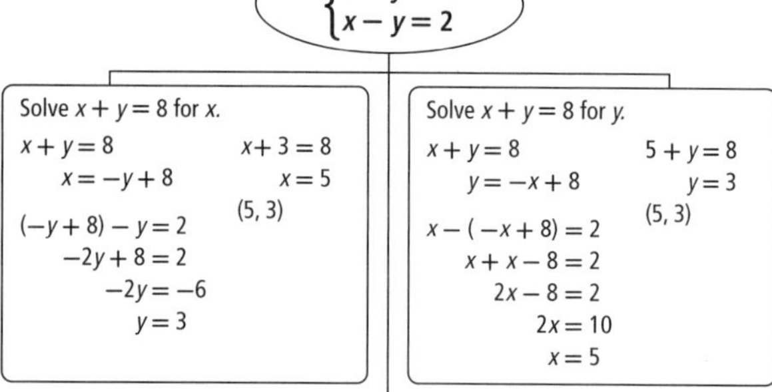

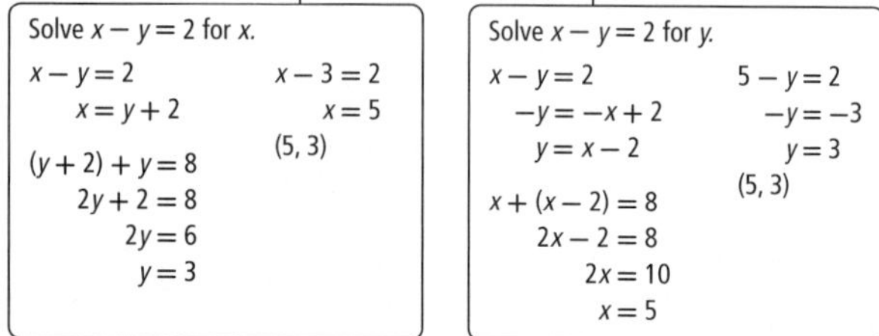

Lesson 6-3

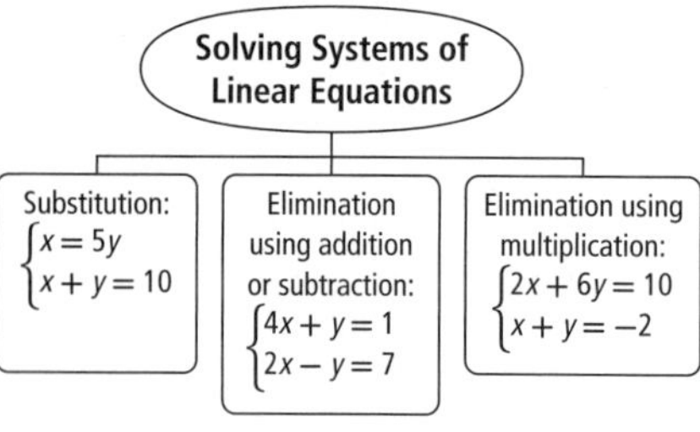

Lesson 6-4

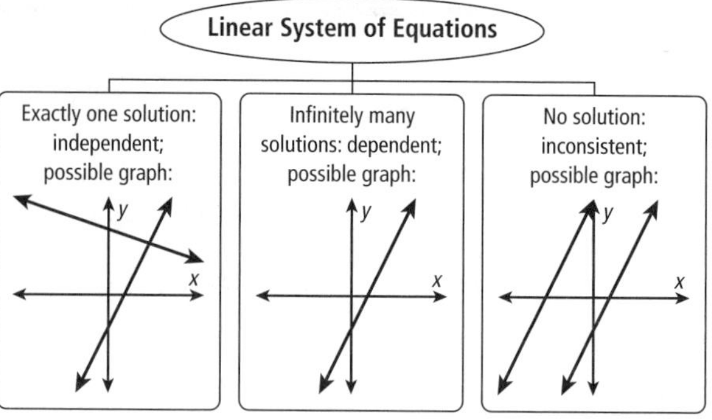

Lesson 6-5

Inequality	$y < 5x + 2$	$y > 7x - 3$	$y \leq 9x + 1$	$y \geq -3x - 2$
Symbol	$<$	$>$	$\leq$	$\geq$
Boundary Line	Dashed	Dashed	Solid	Solid
Shading	Below	Above	Below	Above

Lesson 6-6

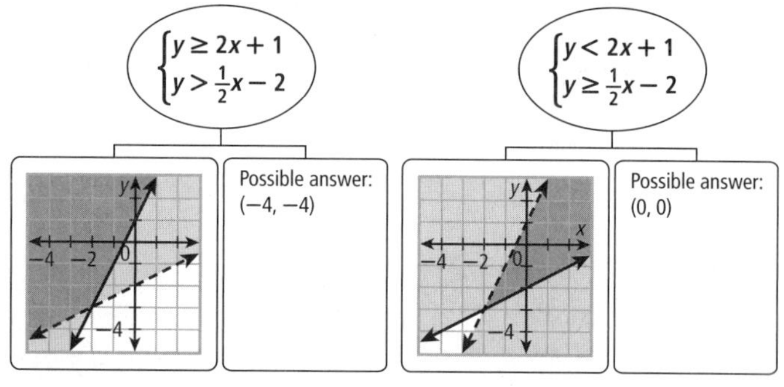

Chapter 7

Lesson 7-1

For a negative exponent in the numerator, move the power to the denominator and change the negative exponent to a positive exponent; possible answer: $2^{-3} = \frac{1}{2^3}$.

For a negative exponent in the denominator, move the power to the numerator and change the negative exponent to a positive exponent; possible answer: $\frac{4}{x^{-5}} = 4x^5$.

Lesson 7-2

Powers of 10 and Scientific Notation

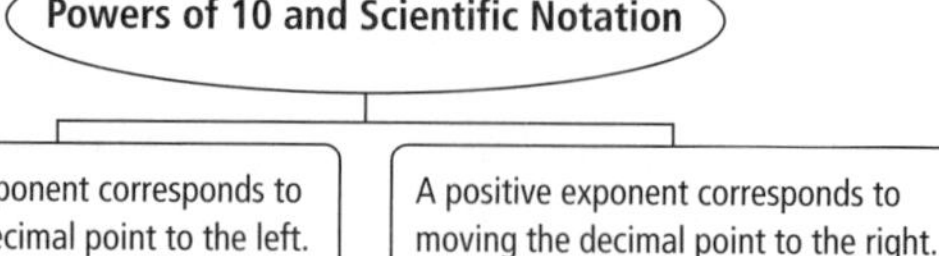

Lesson 7-3

Multiplication Properties of Exponents		
Product of Powers Property	Power of a Power Property	Power of a Product Property
$a^m a^n = a^{m+n}$ $x^2x^3 = x^5$	$(a^m)^n = a^{mn}$ $(x^2)^3 = x^6$	$(ab)^n = a^n b^n$ $(2y)^3 = 8y^3$

Lesson 7-4

If a and b are nonzero real numbers and m and n are integers, then...		
$\frac{a^m}{a^n} = a^{m-n}$ $\frac{7^5}{7^3} = 7^{5-3} = 7^2 = 49$	$\left(\frac{a}{b}\right)^n = \frac{a^n}{b^n}$ $\left(\frac{2}{3}\right)^3 = \frac{2^3}{3^3} = \frac{8}{27}$	$\left(\frac{a}{b}\right)^{-n} = \left(\frac{b}{a}\right)^n$ $\left(\frac{3}{4}\right)^{-2} = \left(\frac{4}{3}\right)^2 = \frac{4^2}{3^2} = \frac{16}{9}$

Lesson 7-5

Exponent	Definition	Numerical Example
$b^{\frac{1}{n}}$	A number raised to the power of $\frac{1}{n}$ is equal to the nth root of that number.	$36^{\frac{1}{2}} = \sqrt{36} = 6$
$b^{\frac{m}{n}}$	A number raised to the power of $\frac{m}{n}$ is equal to the nth root of that number raised to the mth power.	$36^{\frac{3}{2}} = \left(\sqrt{36}\right)^3 = 6^3 = 216$

Lesson 7-6

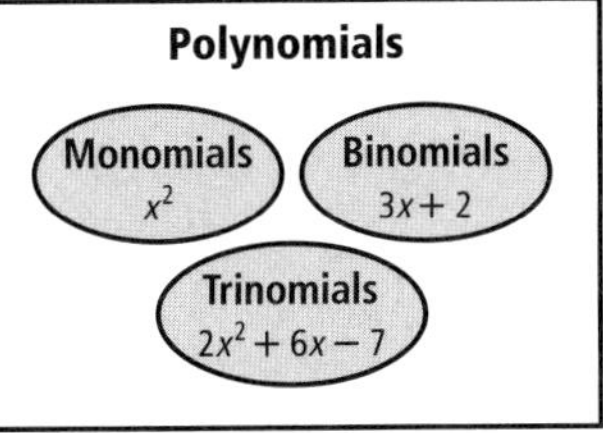

Lesson 7-7

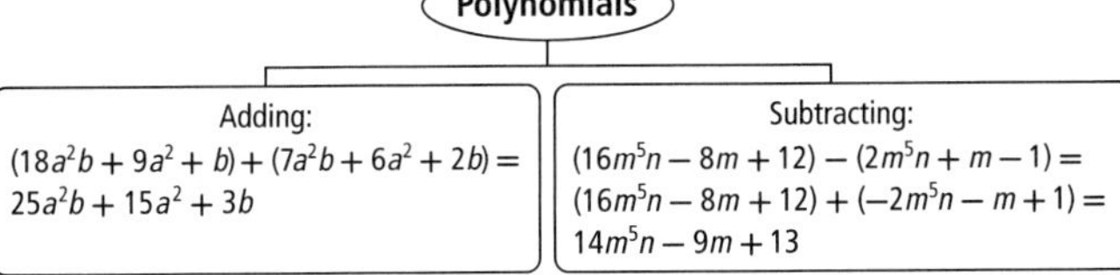

Lesson 7-8

Multiplying Polynomials

Distributive Property:
$5x(x + 2) =$
$5x^2 + 10x$

FOIL method:
$(x + 1)(x + 2) =$
$x^2 + 2x + x + 2 =$
$x^2 + 3x + 2$

Rectangle model:
$(x + 2)(x^2 + 2x + 1)$

	x^2	$+2x$	$+1$
x	x^3	$2x^2$	x
$+2$	$2x^2$	$4x$	2

$x^3 + 4x^2 + 5x + 2$

Vertical method:
$(x + 2)(x^2 + 3x + 2)$

$$\begin{array}{r} x^2 + 3x + 2 \\ \times \quad x + 2 \\ \hline 2x^2 + 6x + 4 \\ + \; x^3 + 3x^2 + 2x \\ \hline x^3 + 5x^2 + 8x + 4 \end{array}$$

Lesson 7-9

Special Products of Binomials		
Perfect-Square Trinomials		Difference of Two Squares
$(a + b)^2 = a^2 + 2ab + b^2$ $(x + 4)^2 = x^2 + 8x + 16$	$(a - b)^2 = a^2 - 2ab + b^2$ $(x - 4)^2 = x^2 - 8x + 16$	$(a + b)(a - b) = a^2 - b^2$ $(x + 4)(x - 4) = x^2 - 16$

Chapter 8

Lesson 8-1

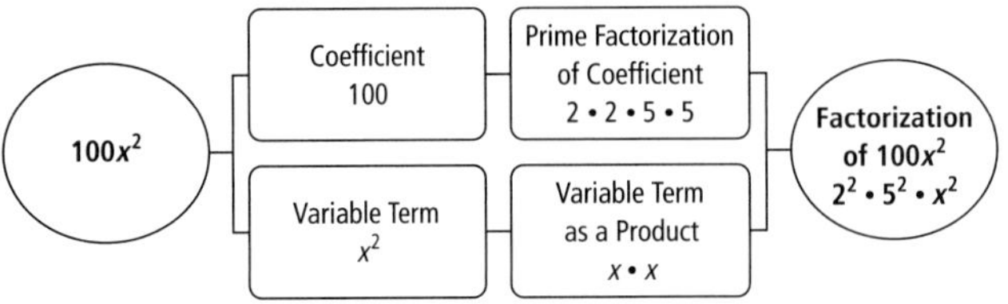

Lesson 8-2

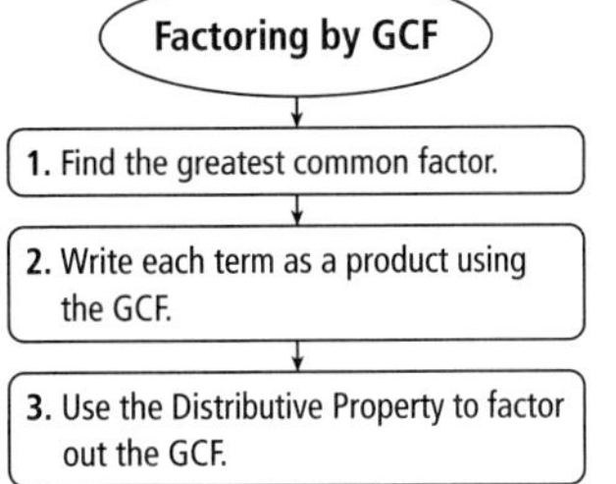

Lesson 8-3

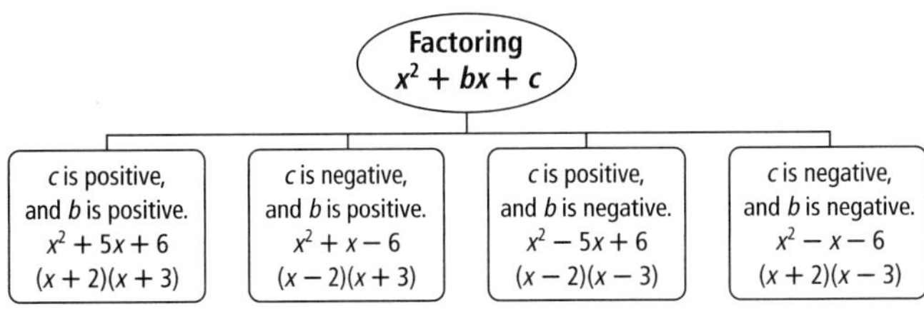

Lesson 8-4

Factoring $ax^2 + bx + c$	
$c > 0$	
$b > 0$	$b < 0$
$3x^2 + 10x + 8 = (3x + 4)(x + 2)$	$3x^2 - 10x + 8 = (3x - 4)(x - 2)$
$c < 0$	
$b < 0$	$b > 0$
$3x^2 - 10x - 8 = (3x + 2)(x - 4)$	$3x^2 + 10x - 8 = (3x - 2)(x + 4)$

Lesson 8-5

Special Product	Factored Form
Perfect-square trinomial with positive coefficient of middle term: $x^2 + 2x + 1$	$(x + 1)^2$
Perfect-square trinomial with negative coefficient of middle term: $x^2 - 2x + 1$	$(x - 1)^2$
Difference of two squares: $x^2 - 1$	$(x - 1)(x + 1)$

Lesson 8-6

Factoring Methods	
Polynomial	**Method**
1. $16x^4 - 25y^8$	A. Factoring out the GCF
2. $x^2 + 10x + 25$	B. Factoring by grouping
3. $9t^2 + 27t + 18t^4$	C. Unfactorable
4. $a^2 + 3a - 7a - 21$	D. Difference of two squares
5. $100b^2 + 81$	E. Perfect-square trinomial

Chapter 9

Lesson 9-1

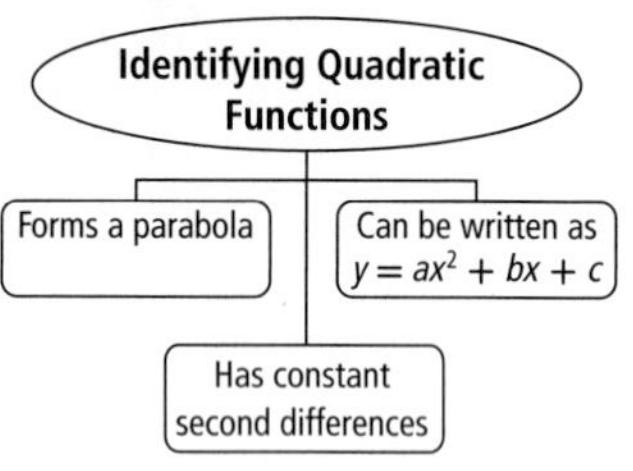

Lesson 9-2

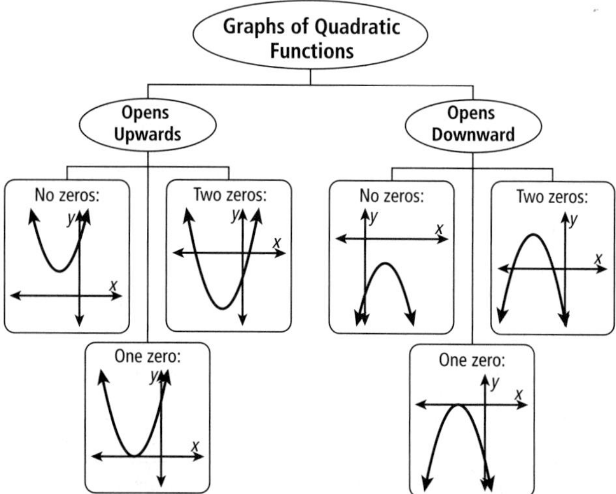

Lesson 9-3

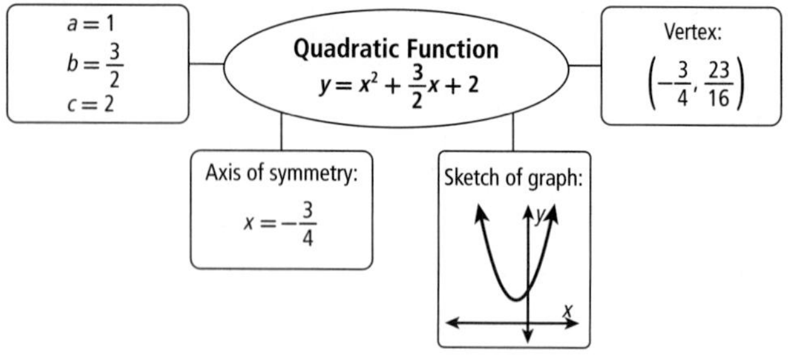

Lesson 9-4

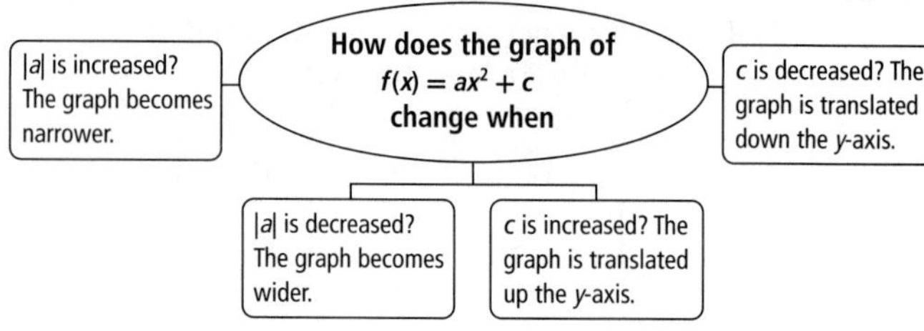

Lesson 9-5

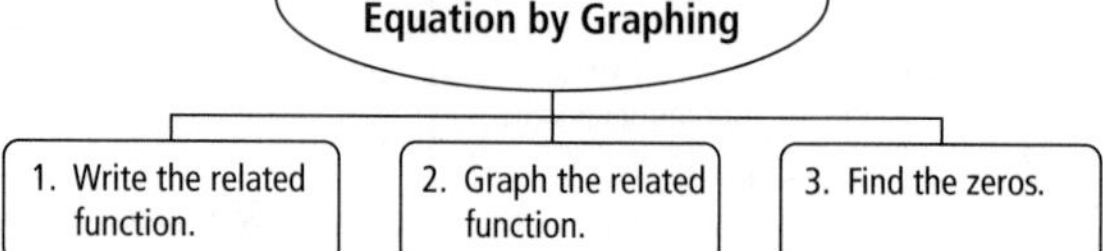

Lesson 9-6

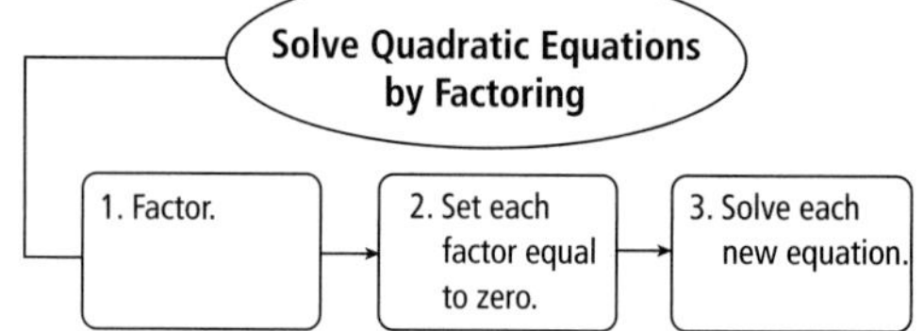

Lesson 9-7

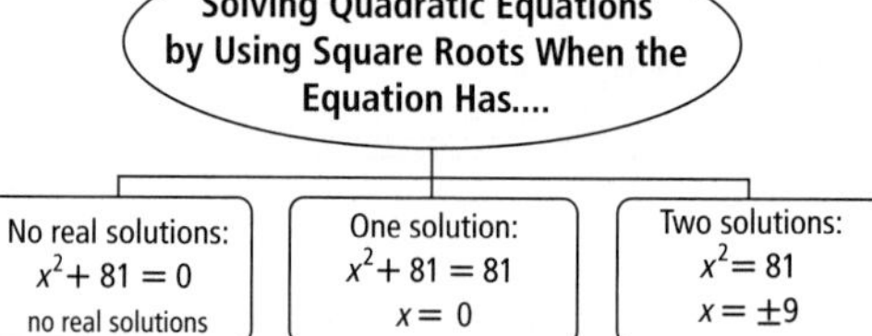

Lesson 9-8

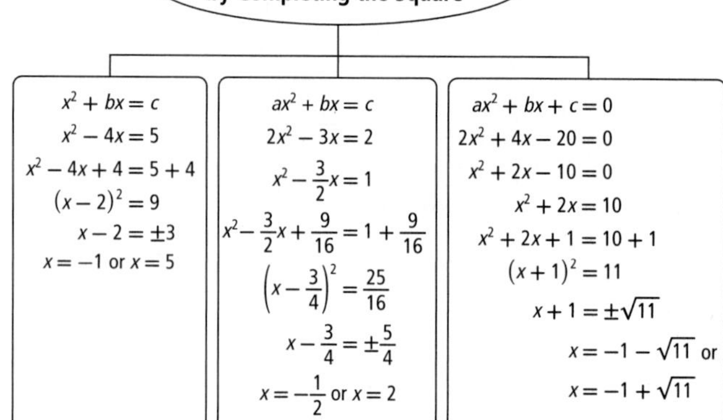

Lesson 9-9

The number of real solutions of $ax^2 + bx + c = 0$ when . . .

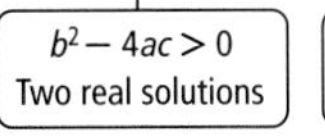

$b^2 - 4ac < 0$
No real solutions

$b^2 - 4ac = 0$
One real solution

Chapter 10

Lesson 10-1

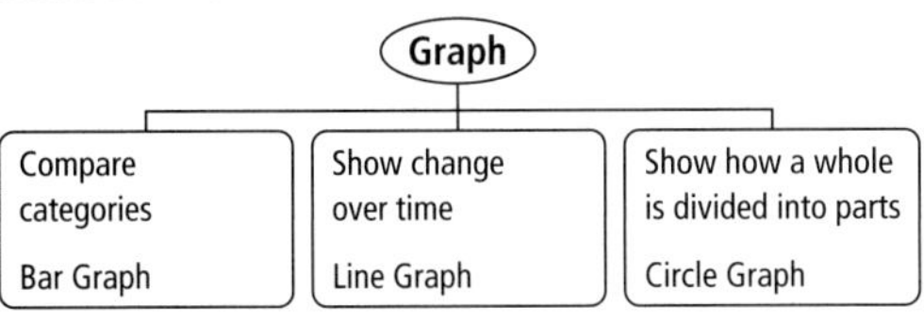

Lesson 10-2

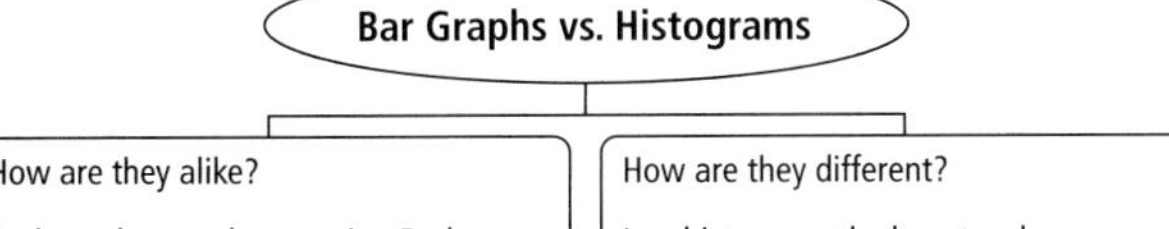

How are they alike?

Both use bars and categories. Both make it easy to compare categories.

How are they different?

In a histogram, the bars touch. A histogram shows consecutive intervals.

Lesson 10-3

Measures of Central Tendency	
Measure	**Use to Answer**
mean	What is the average?
median	What is the halfway point of the data?
mode	What is the most common value? (Can also be used to describe non-numerical data, such as favorite color.)

Lesson 10-4

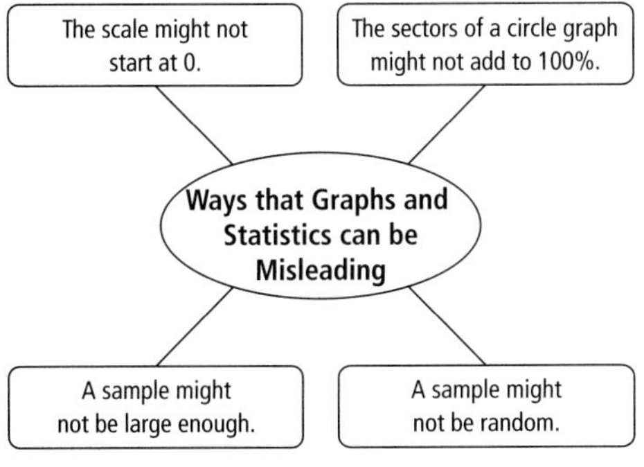

Lesson 10-5

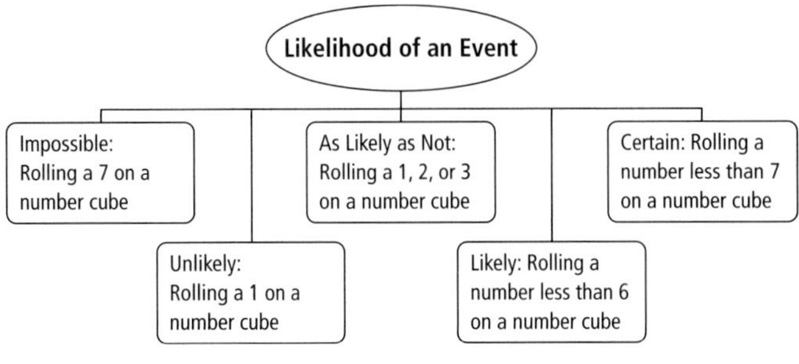

Lesson 10-6

$P(\text{black}) = \frac{1}{4}$
$P(\text{not black}) = \frac{3}{4}$
Odds in favor of black: 1:3
Odds against black: 3:1

Lesson 10-7

	Example	Probability
Dependent Events	From a bag that has three red marbles and three blue marbles	$P(A \text{ and } B) = P(A) \cdot P(B \text{ after } A)$ $= \frac{3}{6} \cdot \frac{3}{5} = \frac{9}{30} = \frac{3}{10}$
	A = choosing a red marble	
	B = choosing a blue marble	
Independent Events	A = rolling a 6 on a number cube	$P(A \text{ and } B) = P(A) \cdot P(B)$ $= \frac{1}{6} \cdot \frac{1}{6} = \frac{1}{36}$
	B = rolling a 4 on a number cube	

Lesson 10-8

	Fundamental Counting Principle	Permutation	Combination
When to use:	To find all possible outcomes when there are several items to choose from	When order matters in the arrangement of an outcome	When order does not matter in the arrangement of an outcome
Formula:	If there are m ways to choose a first item and n ways to choose a second item after the first item has been chosen, then there are $m \cdot n$ ways to choose both items.	${}_nP_r = \frac{n!}{(n-r)!}$	${}_nC_r = \frac{n!}{r!(n-r)!}$

Chapter 11

Lesson 11-1

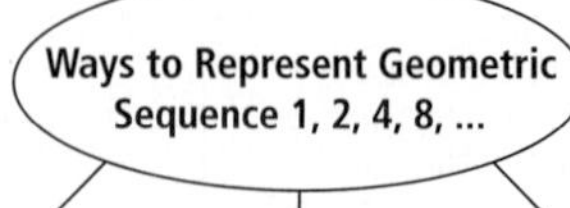

Ways to Represent Geometric Sequence 1, 2, 4, 8, ...

Table

Position	Term
1	1
2	2
3	4
4	8

Formula

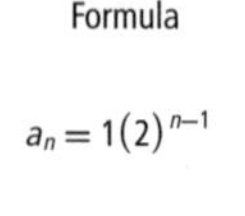

$a_n = 1(2)^{n-1}$

Words

Start with 1 and multiply each term by 2 to get the next term.

Lesson 11-2

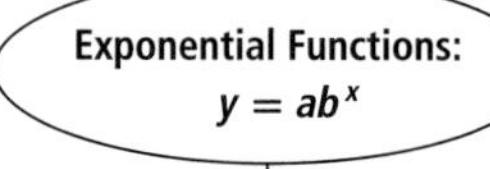

Exponential Functions: $y = ab^x$

$a > 0, b > 1$: $y = 3(2)^x$

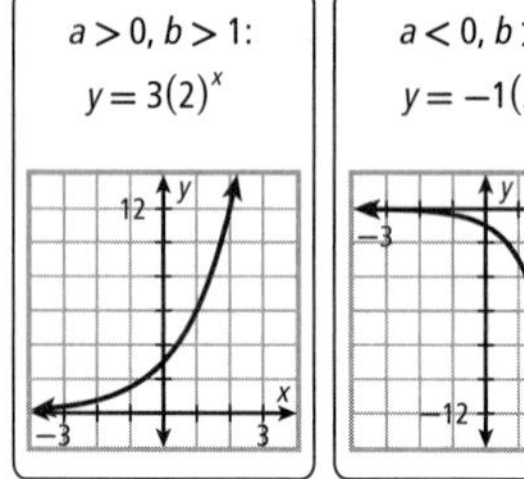

$a < 0, b > 1$: $y = -1(3)^x$

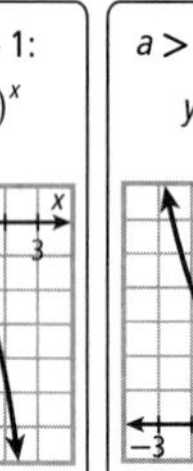

$a > 0, 0 < b < 1$: $y = 2\left(\frac{1}{2}\right)^x$

$a < 0, 0 < b < 1$: $y = -2\left(\frac{1}{3}\right)^x$

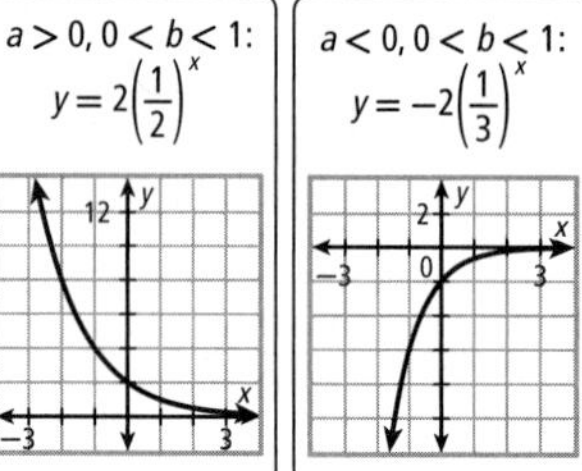

Lesson 11-3

Exponential Growth vs. Exponential Decay

How are they alike?
Both are exponential functions, have a domain of all real numbers, have a range of all real numbers greater than 0, and represent a change in quantity by the same rate over time.

How are they different?
One increases over time and the other decreases over time, in one you add the rate to 1 and in the other you subtract the rate from 1.

Lesson 11-4

Modeling Data

Linear: Points lie on a line; for a constant change in x, the first differences are constant.

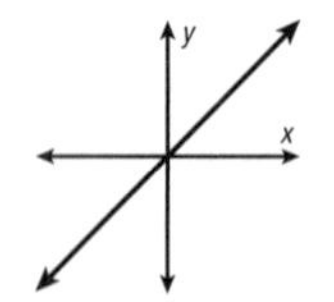

Exponential: Smooth curve that extends infinitely either up to the right, up to the left, down to the right, or down to the left; for a constant change in x, there is a constant ratio.

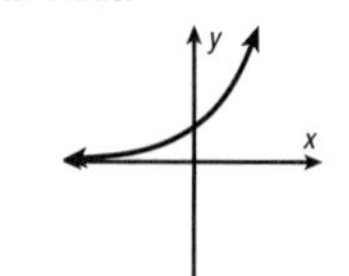

Quadratic: Points lie on a parabola and are symmetric with a vertical line through the vertex; for a constant change in x, the second differences are constant.

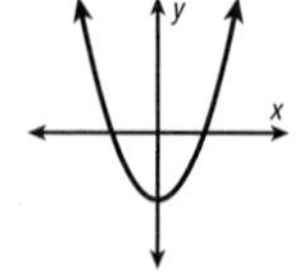

Lesson 11-5

Square-Root Functions

$y = \sqrt{x}$; $x \geq 0$

$y = \sqrt{x} + 5$; $x \geq 0$

$y = \sqrt{x + 5}$; $x \geq -5$

$y = \sqrt{5x}$; $x \geq 0$

Lesson 11-6

	Product Property of Square Roots	Quotient Property of Square Roots
Words	If $a \geq 0$ and $b \geq 0$, then $\sqrt{ab} = \sqrt{a}\sqrt{b}$.	If $a \geq 0$ and $b > 0$, then $\sqrt{\frac{a}{b}} = \frac{\sqrt{a}}{\sqrt{b}}$.
Example	$\sqrt{4 \cdot 16} = \sqrt{4}\sqrt{16} = 2 \cdot 4 = 8$	$\sqrt{\frac{49}{81}} = \frac{\sqrt{49}}{\sqrt{81}} = \frac{7}{9}$

Lesson 11-7

Like Radicals

Definition:
Radical expressions that have the same radicand and the same index

Examples:
$\sqrt{7}$ and $2\sqrt{7}$
$2\sqrt{x}$ and $-7\sqrt{x}$

Nonexamples:
$\sqrt{2}$ and $\sqrt{3}$
$\sqrt{10x}$ and $\sqrt{100x}$

Lesson 11-8

Multiplying Radical Expressions

Multiplying two square roots:

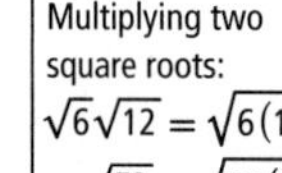

$\sqrt{6}\sqrt{12} = \sqrt{6(12)}$
$= \sqrt{72} = \sqrt{36(2)}$
$= 6\sqrt{2}$

Using the Distributive Property:
$\sqrt{2}(\sqrt{5} - \sqrt{2})$
$= \sqrt{2}\sqrt{5} - \sqrt{2}\sqrt{2}$
$= \sqrt{10} - 2$

Using FOIL:
$(2 + \sqrt{3})(4 - \sqrt{3})$
$= 8 - 2\sqrt{3} + 4\sqrt{3} - 3$
$= 5 + 2\sqrt{3}$

Lesson 11-9

Solving Radical Equations

1. $4\sqrt{x+2} = 12$
2. $\sqrt{x+2} = 3$
3. $x + 2 = 9$
4. $x = 7$

Chapter 12

Lesson 12-1

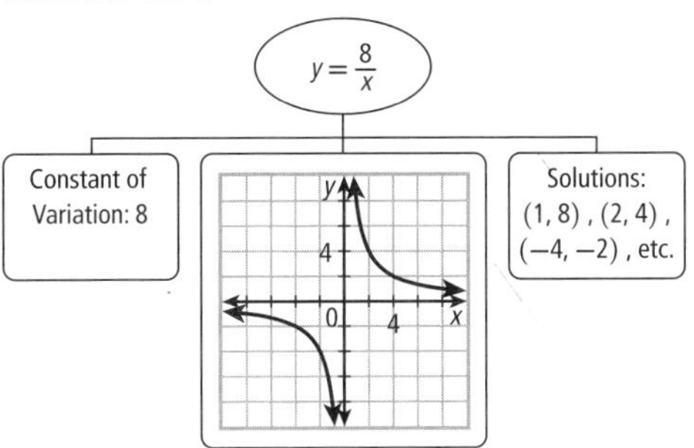

Lesson 12-2

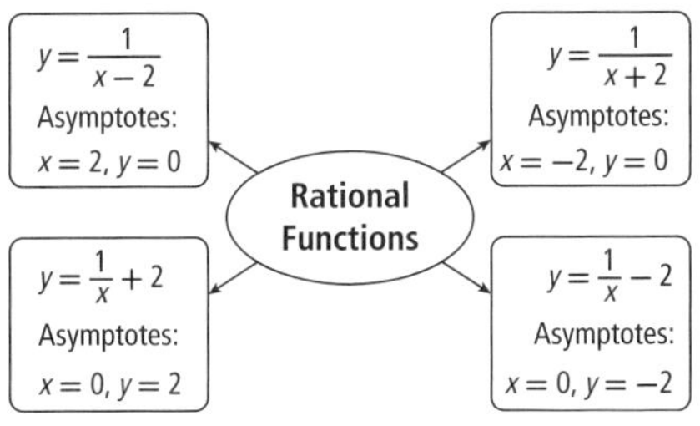

Lesson 12-3

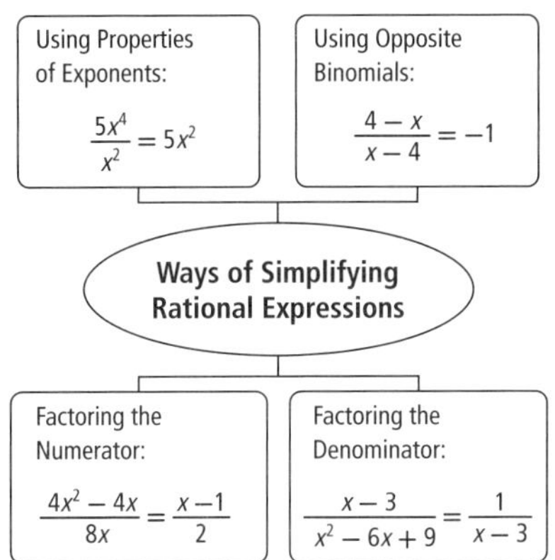

Lesson 12-4

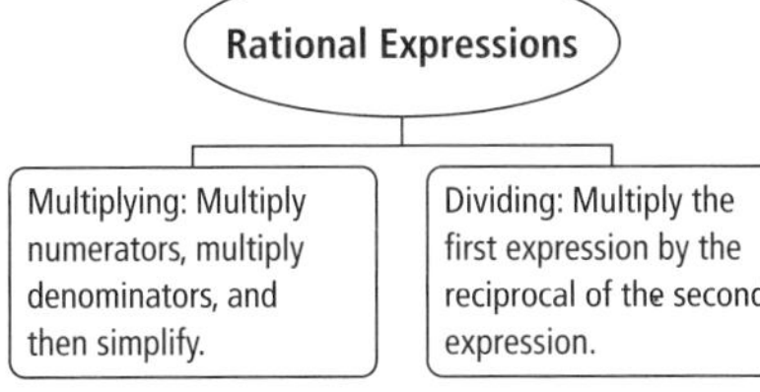

Lesson 12-5

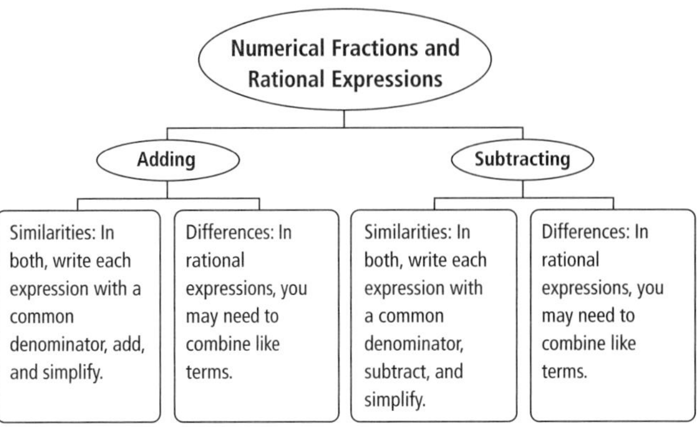

Lesson 12-6

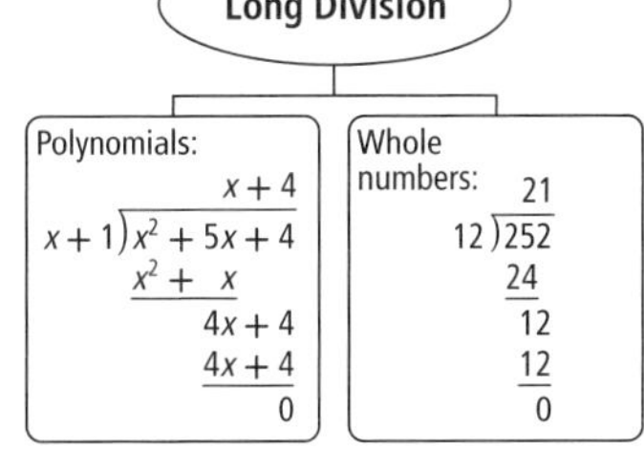

Lesson 12-7

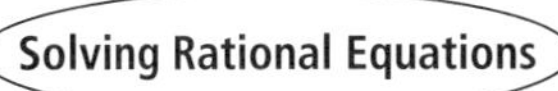

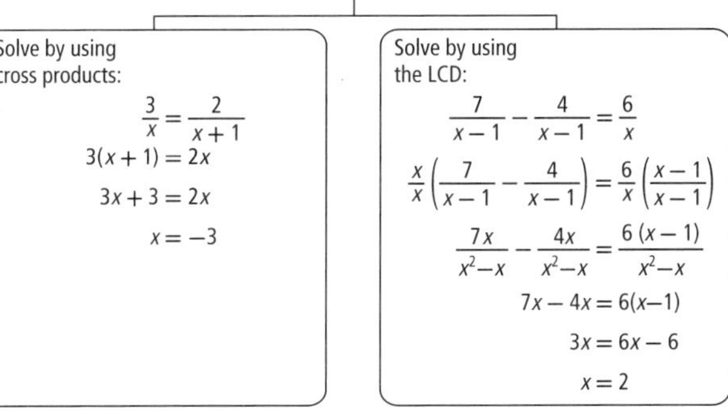

Additional Answers

Additional Answers

Chapter 1

1-1 *Exercises*

17–24. Possible answers given.

17. the product of 5 and p; 5 groups of p

18. 4 decreased by y; the difference of 4 and y

19. the sum of 3 and x; 3 increased by x

20. the product of 3 and y; 3 times y

21. negative 3 times s; the product of negative 3 and s

22. the quotient of r and 5; one-fifth r

23. 14 decreased by t; the difference of 14 and t

24. the sum of x and 0.5; x increased by 0.5

33. $2x$; possible answer: Jim has twice as many aunts as Carly, who has x aunts.

34. $17 - b$; possible answer: Sarah started with 17 apples, but lost b of them.

35. $y + 10$; possible answer: April had y CDs and then got 10 more.

1-3 *Exercises*

68–70. Possible answers given.

68. The quotient of a negative number and a positive number is always negative.

69. The product of a negative number and a positive number is always negative.

70. If $c > 0$, then $4c > c$. If $c = 0$, then $4c = c$. If $c < 0$, then $4c < c$.

1A *Multi-Step Test Prep*

1.

Depth (ft)	Pressure (psi)
0	14.7
33	29.4
66	44.1
99	58.8
132	73.5

132 ft; continue the table until the pressure reaches 73.5 psi and then find the depth in that row of the table.

1-7 *Exercises*

20. $5(x + 3) - 7x$; $5(x) + 5(3) - 7x$ (Dist. Prop.); $5x + 15 - 7x$ (Multiply.); $15 + 5x - 7x$ (Comm. Prop. of Add.); $15 - 2x$ (Combine like terms.)

21. $9(a - 3) - 4$; $9(a) - 9(3) - 4$ (Dist. Prop.); $9a - 27 - 4$ (Multiply.); $9a - 31$ (Combine like terms.)

22. $5x^2 - 2(x - 3x^2)$; $5x^2 - 2(x) + 2(3x^2)$ (Dist. Prop.); $5x^2 - 2x + 6x^2$ (Multiply.); $5x^2 + 6x^2 - 2x$ (Comm. Prop. of Add.); $11x^2 - 2x$ (Combine like terms.)

23. $6x - x - 3x^2 + 2x$; $6x - x + 2x - 3x^2$ (Comm. Prop. of Add.); $7x - 3x^2$ (Combine like terms.)

24. $12x + 8x + t - 7x$; $12x + 8x - 7x + t$ (Comm. Prop. of Add.); $13x + t$ (Combine like terms.)

25. $4a - 2(a - 1)$; $4a - 2(a) + 2(1)$ (Dist. Prop.); $4a - 2a + 2$ (Multiply.); $2a + 2$ (Combine like terms.)

38. $4(y + 6) + 9$; $4y + 24 + 9$ (Dist. Prop.); $4y + 33$ (Combine like terms.)

39. $-7(x + 2) + 4x$; $-7x - 14 + 4x$ (Dist. Prop.); $-7x + 4x - 14$ (Comm. Prop. of Add.); $-3x - 14$ (Combine like terms.)

40. $3x + 2 - 2x - 1$; $3x - 2x + 2 - 1$ (Comm. Prop. of Add.); $x + 1$ (Combine like terms.)

41. $5x - 3x + 3x^2 + 9x$; $5x - 3x + 9x + 3x^2$ (Comm. Prop. of Add.); $11x + 3x^2$ (Combine like terms.)

42. $8x + 2x - 3y - 9x$; $8x + 2x - 9x - 3y$ (Comm. Prop. of Add.); $x - 3y$ (Combine like terms.)

43. $7y - 3 + 6y - 7$; $7y + 6y - 3 - 7$ (Comm. Prop. of Add.); $13y - 10$ (Combine like terms.)

1-8 *Exercises*

13.

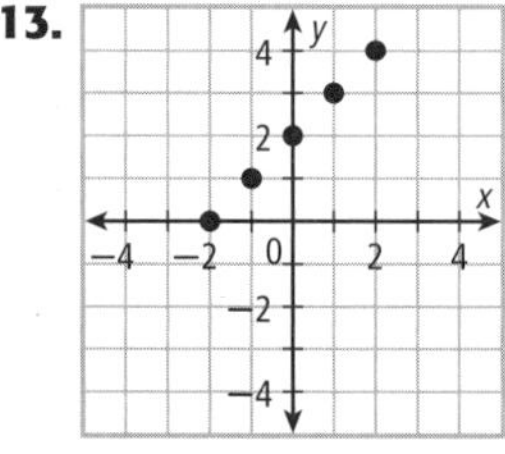

14.

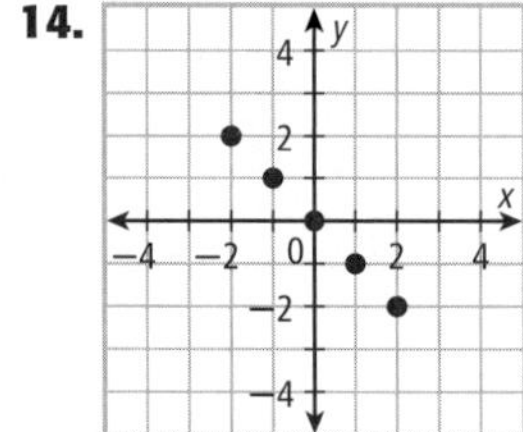

15.

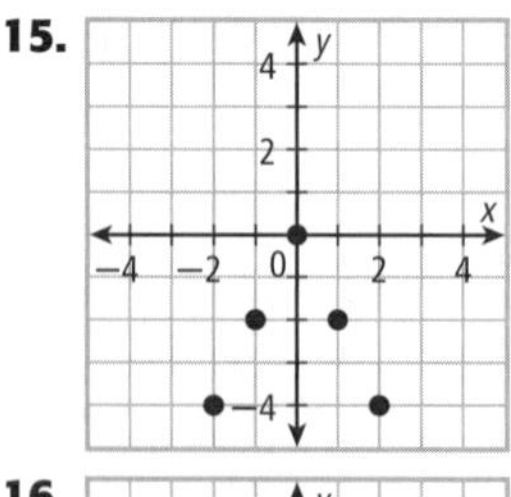

16.

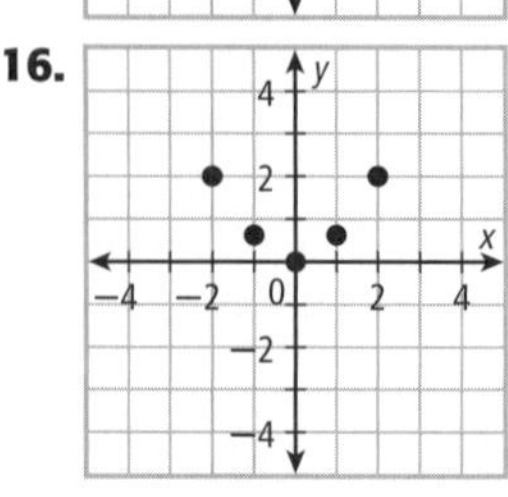

28.

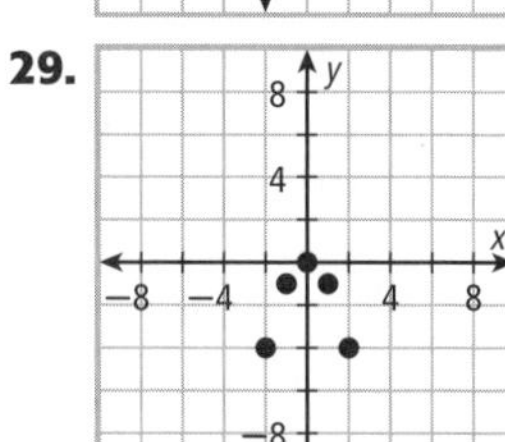

29.

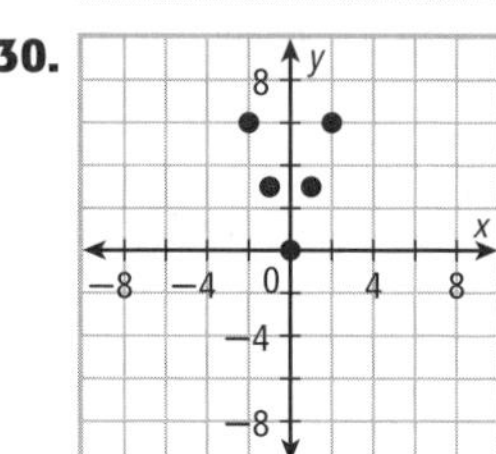

30.

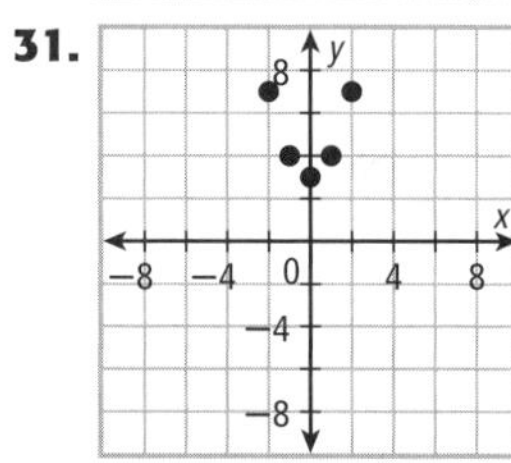

31.

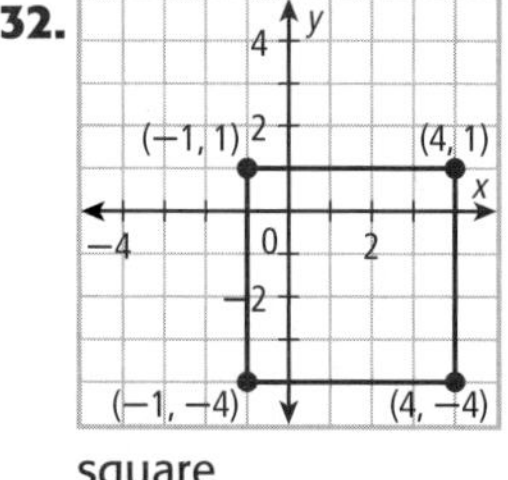

32.

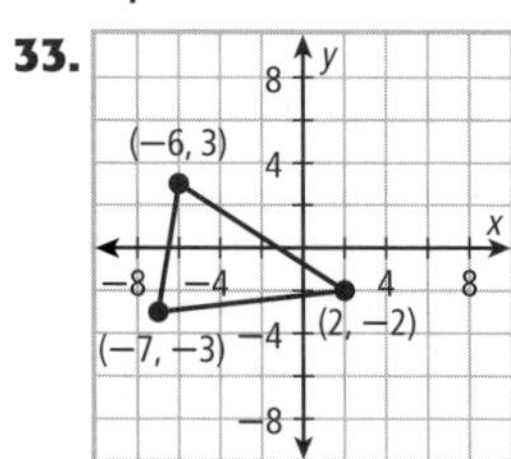

square

33.

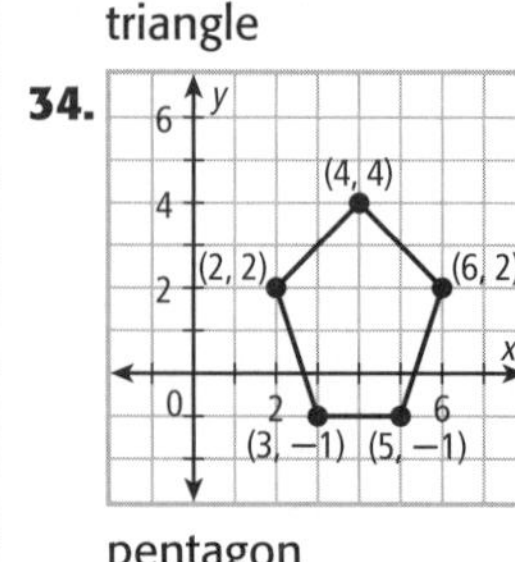

triangle

34.

pentagon

35. 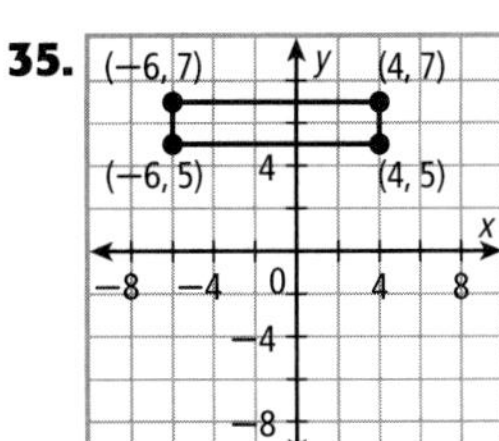

rectangle

38. 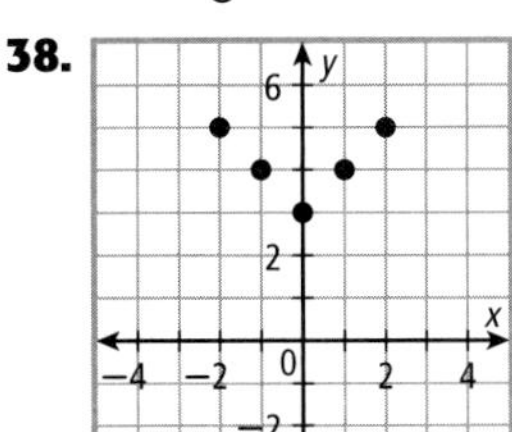

39. 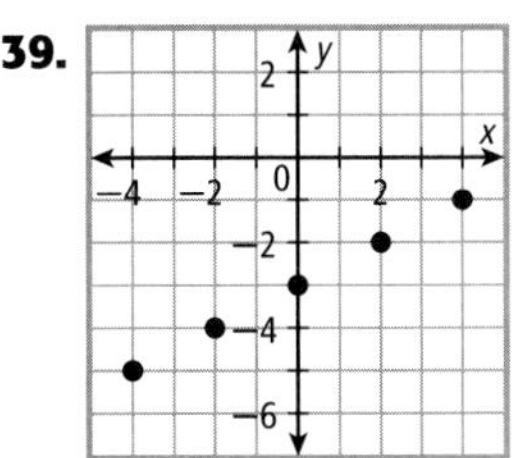

40. 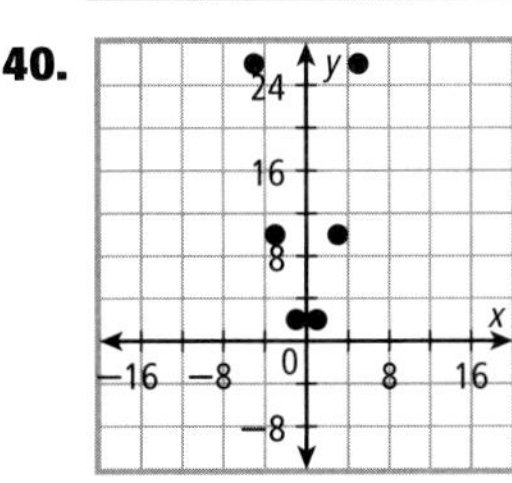

42. 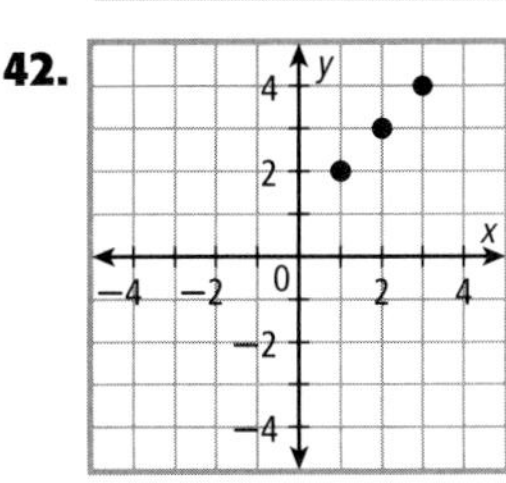

43. 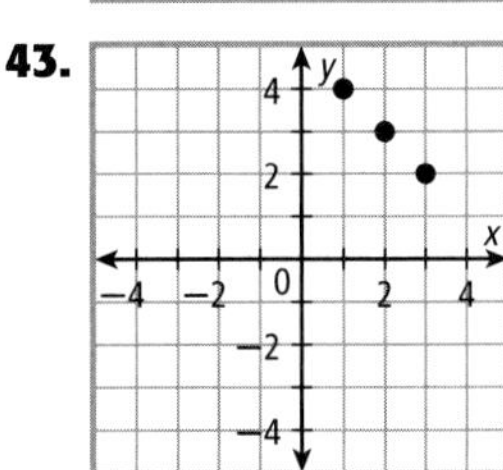

44. 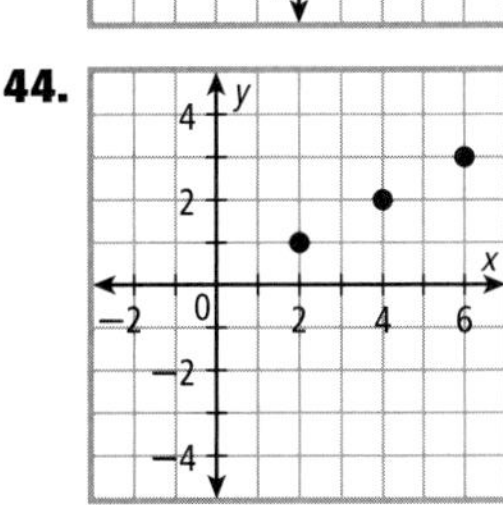

45. 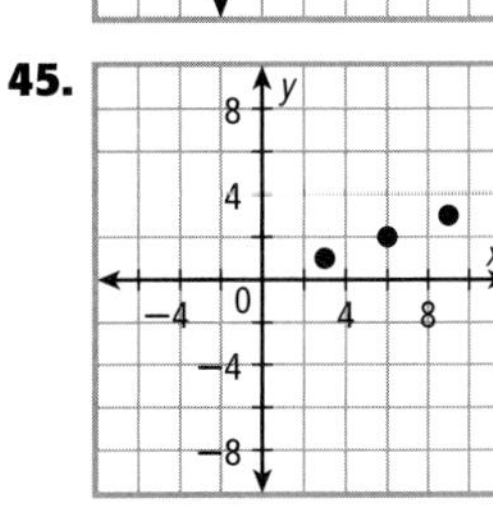

49. 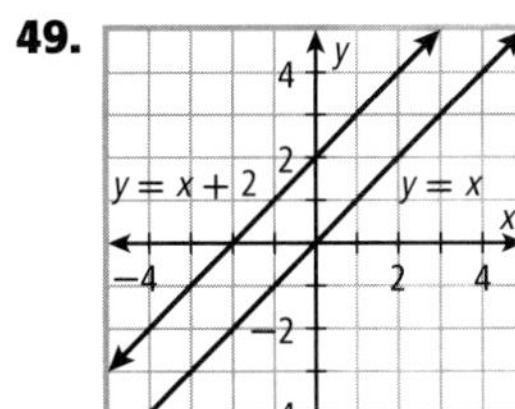

54–57. 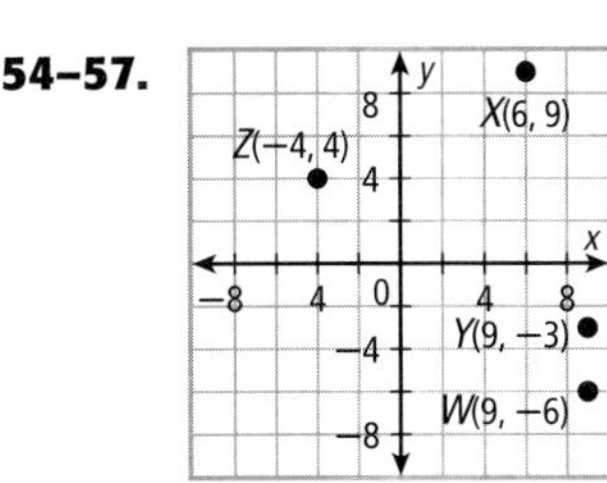

1B *Multi-Step Test Prep*

5. Lori can buy 25 stickers, or 5 packages.

Packages	Cost ($)
1	6
2	12
3	18
4	24
5	30

Stickers	Cost ($)
5	6.00
10	12.00
15	18.00
20	24.00
25	30.00

1B *Ready to Go On?*

20. $3(x + 2) - 3x$; $3x + 3(2) - 3x$ (Dist. Prop.); $3x + 6 - 3x$ (Multiply.); $6 + 3x - 3x$ (Comm. Prop. of Add.); $6 + (3x - 3x)$ (Assoc. Prop. of Add.); $6 + 0$ (Combine like terms.); 6 (Combine like terms.)

21. $x - 6x^2 + 3x + 4x^2$; $x + 3x - 6x^2 + 4x^2$ (Comm. Prop. of Add.); $(x + 3x) + (-6x^2 + 4x^2)$ (Assoc. Prop. of Add.); $4x - 2x^2$ (Combine like terms.)

22. $-2[3x + 2y + 4x - 5y]$; $-2(3x) - 2(2y) - 2(4x) - 2(-5y)$ (Dist. Prop.); $-6x + (-4y) + (-8x) + 10y$ (Multiply.); $-6x - 4y - 8x + 10y$ (Def. of Subtraction); $-6x - 8x - 4y + 10y$ (Comm. Prop. of Add.); $(-6x - 8x) + (-4y + 10y)$ (Assoc. Prop. of Add.); $-14x + 6y$ (Combine like terms.)

23–25. 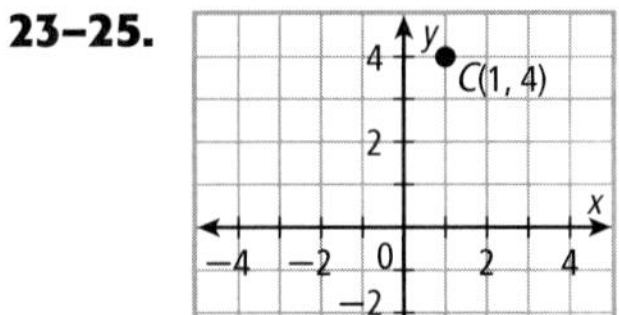

32. (−2, 5), (−1, 2), (0, 1), (1, 2), (2, 5)

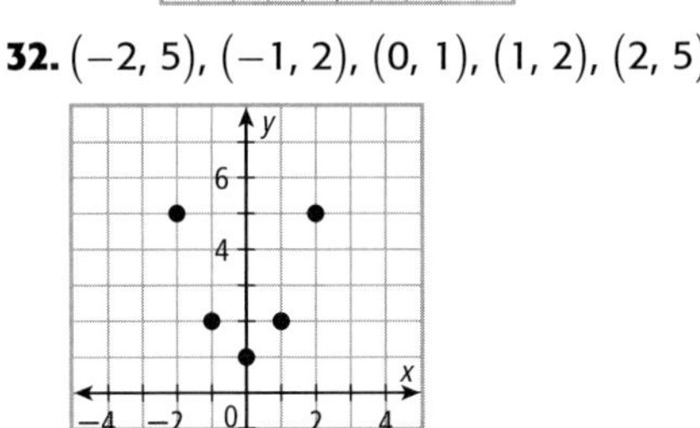

33. (−2, −3), (−1, −2), (0, −1), (1, 0), (2, 1)

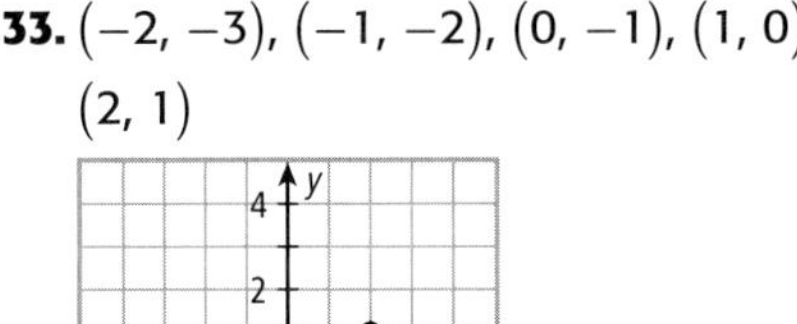

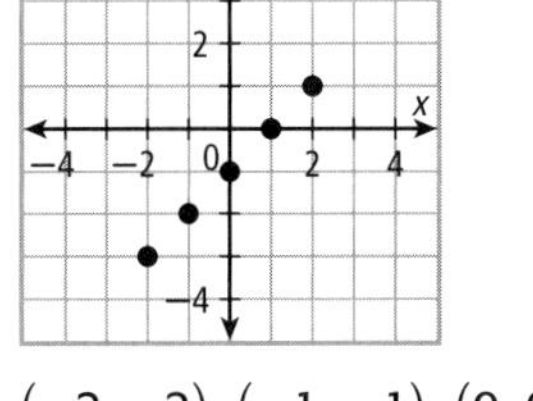

34. (−2, −2), (−1, −1), (0, 0), (1, −1), (2, −2)

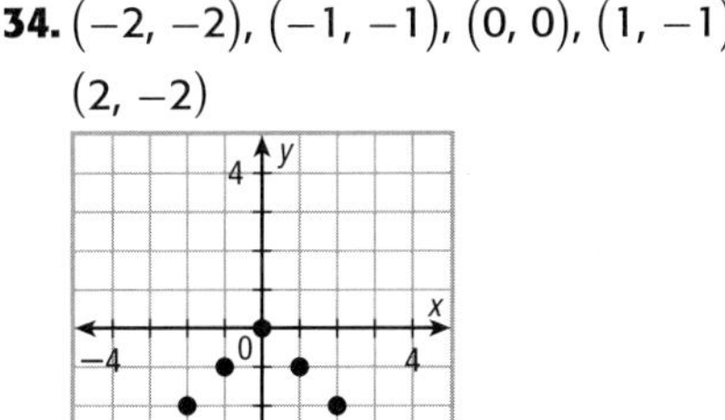

35. (−2, −3), (−1, 0), (0, 3), (1, 6), (2, 9)

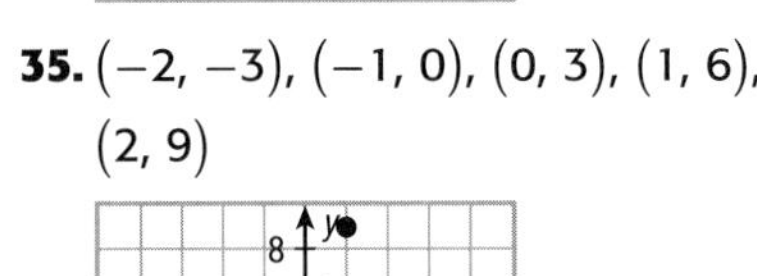

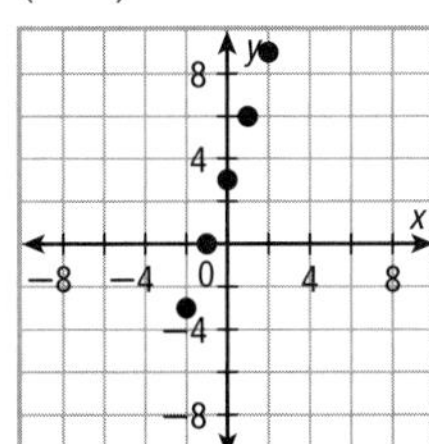

Chapter 2

2-1 *Exercises*

64a. Possible answer: the fire should cover twice as much area in 2 days as it does in 1, so multiply 2 by 1000 and the answer is 2000.

2-5 *Exercises*

34c.

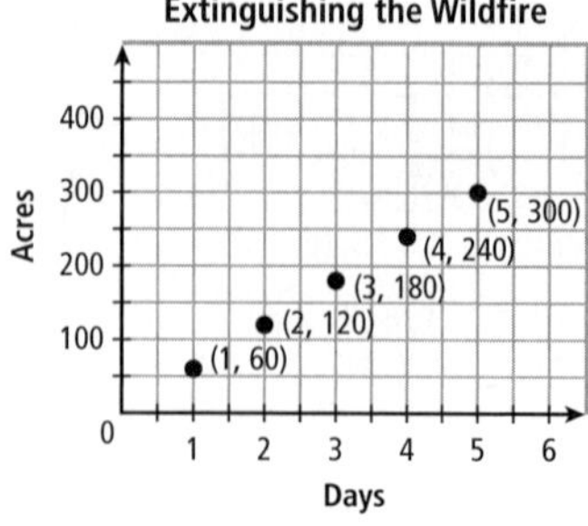

2-7 *Check It Out!*

3. Possible answer: the cyclist travels about 60 mi in 4 h, or 15 mi/h. There are about 5000 ft in 1 mi, so this speed is equivalent to 15(5000) = 75,000 ft/h. There are about 4000 s in 1 h, so this is equivalent to $\frac{75{,}000}{4000} \approx 20$ ft/s. So 20.5 ft/s is reasonable.

Chapter 3

3-2 *Exercises*

34. Both inequalities have all numbers greater than 1 as solutions; $x + 2 \geq 3$ also includes 1. The graph of $x + 2 > 3$ has an empty circle at 1, but the graph of $x + 2 \geq 3$ has a solid circle at 1.

35a. 411 + 411 = 822 miles

b. $822 + m \leq 1000$

c. $m \leq 178$, where m is nonnegative

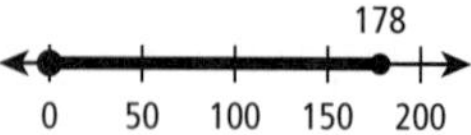

3-3 *Exercises*

27. $b \geq \frac{1}{10}$

0 $\frac{1}{10}$ $\frac{2}{10}$ $\frac{3}{10}$ $\frac{4}{10}$

28. $p < -2.5$

−4 −3.5 −3 −2.5 −2

29. $b \leq -16$

−32 −24 −16 −8 0

30. $a < -9$

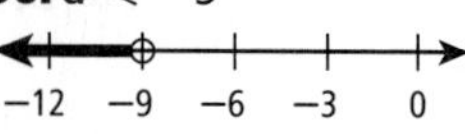

31. $r < -\frac{3}{2}$

−2 $-\frac{3}{2}$ −1 $-\frac{1}{2}$ 0

32. $p < -0.1$

−0.4 −0.3 −0.2 −0.1 0

33. $y < 2$

−3 −2 −1 0 1 2 3

34. $f > -30$

−40 −30 −20 −10 0

35. $t > 4$

0 1 2 3 4 5 6

36. $w \leq -2.4$

−2.8 −2.6 −2.4 −2.2 −2

37. $z < -11$

−13 −12 −11 −10 −9

38. $f < -3$

−6 −5 −4 −3 −2 −1 0

39. $k \leq -7$

−9 −8 −7 −6 −5

40. $b > 3.5$

3 3.5 4 4.5 5

41. $p \geq -12$

−16 −12 −8 −4 0

43. $x > -3$

−6 −5 −4 −3 −2 −1 0

44. $t \leq 8$

0 2 4 6 8 10 12

45. $x < 20$

0 10 20 30 40

46. $p \geq -30$

−40 −30 −20 −10 0

47. $p \leq -6$

−8 −6 −4 −2 0

48. $t > -\frac{1}{6}$

$-\frac{4}{6}$ $-\frac{3}{6}$ $-\frac{2}{6}$ $-\frac{1}{6}$ 0

49. $b < 2$

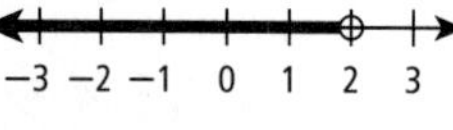

50. $r < 60$

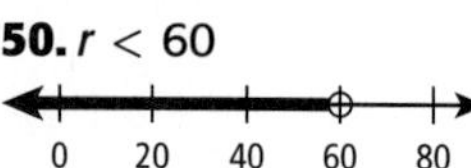

51.

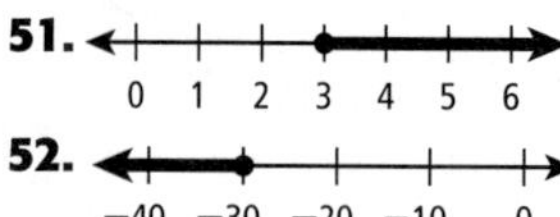

52.

−40 −30 −20 −10 0

53.

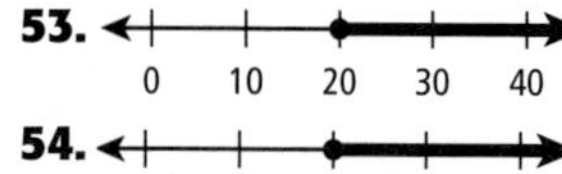

54.

0 20 40 60 80

3A *Ready To Go On?*

1. all real numbers greater than −2

2. all real numbers less than or equal to 8

3. all real numbers greater than or equal to 3

4. all real numbers greater than 1

12. $t \geq 5$ where t is a natural number

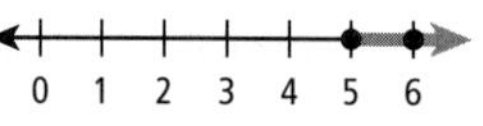

13. $a < 13$ where a is positive

0 5 10 13 15

14. $m \leq 250$ where m is nonnegative

0 50 150 250

15. $k \leq 2$

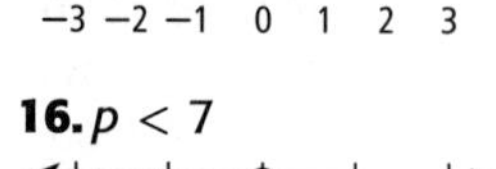

16. $p < 7$

5 6 7 8 9

17. $r \geq -4$

−6 −5 −4 −3 −2 −1 0

18. $p < -3$

−6 −5 −4 −3 −2 −1 0

21.

−3 −2 −1 0 1 2 3

22.

−12 −9 −6 −3 0

23.

0 8 16 24 32

24.

−2 $-1\frac{1}{2}$ −1 $-\frac{1}{2}$ 0

3-4 *Exercises*

16. $r > 4$

0 1 2 3 4 5 6

17. $x \leq 1$

−3 −2 −1 0 1 2 3

18. $w > 9$

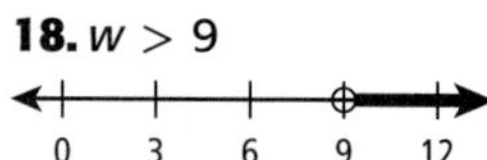

19. $w < -2$

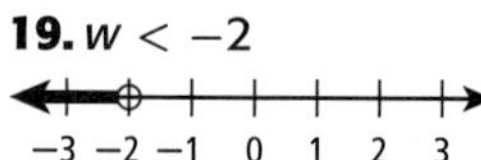

20. $v \leq 12$

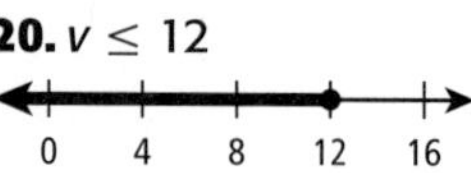

21. $x < -6$

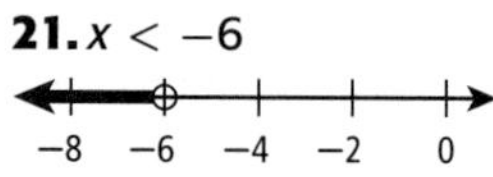

22. $z \geq 9$

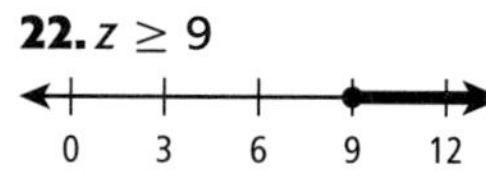

23. $f < -4.5$

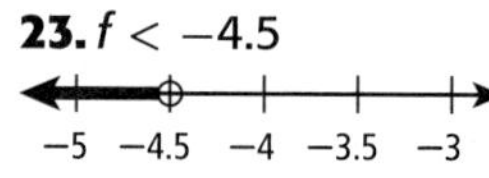

24. $n \geq 6$

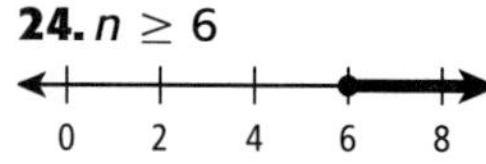

25. $w > 0$

−3 −2 −1 0 1 2 3

26. $p > -5$

−6 −5 −4 −3 −2 −1 0

27. $v > \frac{2}{3}$

0 $\frac{1}{3}$ $\frac{2}{3}$ 1

28. $x > -9$

−12 −9 −6 −3 0

29. $x > -5$

−6 −5 −4 −3 −2 −1 0

30. $h \geq 17$

15 16 17 18 19

31. $x < -2$

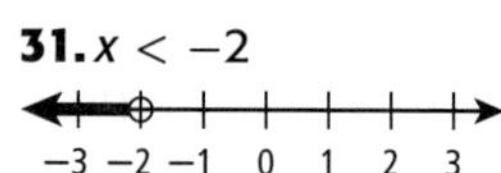

32. $x < -8$

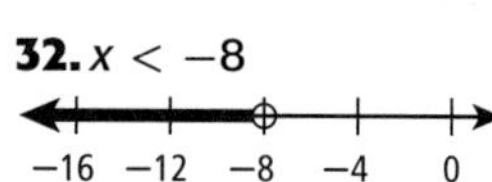

33. $a \geq 11$

9 10 11 12 13

34. $x < 19$

17 18 19 20 21

35. $x > 3$

0 1 2 3 4 5 6

36. $q \leq 16$

0 8 16 24 32

38. $x > 1$

−3 −2 −1 0 1 2 3

39. $x \leq 2$

−3 −2 −1 0 1 2 3

40. $x > 18$

16 17 18 19 20

41. $x < 4$

0 1 2 3 4 5 6

42. $x < 0$

−3 −2 −1 0 1 2 3

43. $x < -6$

−8 −6 −4 −2 0

44. $m \leq -\frac{1}{8}$

$-\frac{1}{2}$ $-\frac{3}{8}$ $-\frac{1}{4}$ $-\frac{1}{8}$ 0

45. $r < 8$

0 4 8 12 16

46. $n \leq 1.8$

1.8

0 0.5 1 1.5 2

47. $x < 7$

5 6 7 8 9

48. $n > 3.5$

2 2.5 3 3.5 4

49. $p \geq 18$

0 6 12 18 24 30

68.

0 1 2 3 4 5 6

69.

0 1 2 3 4 5 6

70.

−3 −2 −1 0 1 2 3

71.

−3 −2 −1 0 1 2 3

72.

73.

−3 −2 −1 0 1 2 3

74.

0

75.

−3 −2 −1 0 1 2 3

76.

−3 −2 −1 0 1 2 3

84.

−6 −5 −4 −3 −2 −1 0

85.

0 2 4 6 8

86.

0 1 2 3 4 5 6

3-6 *Exercises*

7.

−8 −6 −4 −2 0 2 4

8.

0 1 2 3 4 5 6

9.

0 1 2 3 4 5 6

10.

0 1 2 3 4 5 6

15.

16

0 10 20 30 40 50

16.

−3 −2 −1 0 1 2 3

17.

0 1 2 3 4 5 6

18.

0 1 2 3 4 5 6

19.

0 1 2 3 4 5 6

20.

−4 −3 −2 −1 0 1 2

21.

−6 −3 0 3 6

22.

0 1 2 3 4 5 6

23.

−3 −2 −1 0 1 2 3

60. (−2, 6), (−1, 4), (0, 2), (1 0), (2, −2)

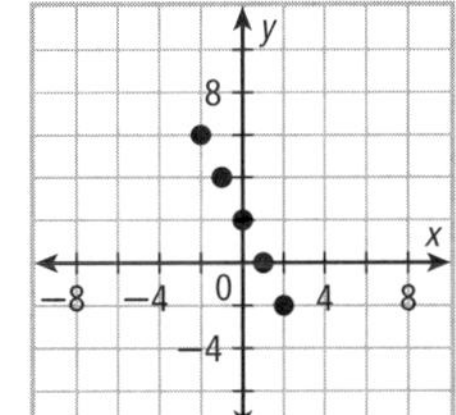

61. (−2, 3), (−1, 0,) (0, −1), (1, 0), (2, 3)

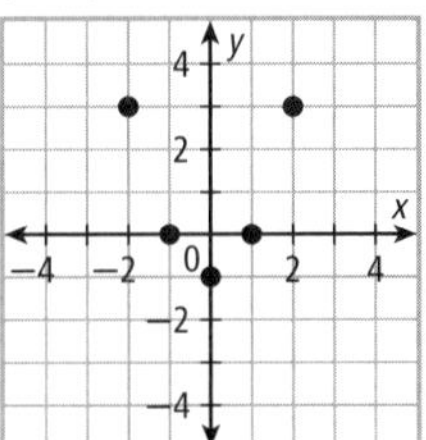

62. (−2, 2), (−1, −1), (0, −2), (1, −1), (2, 2)

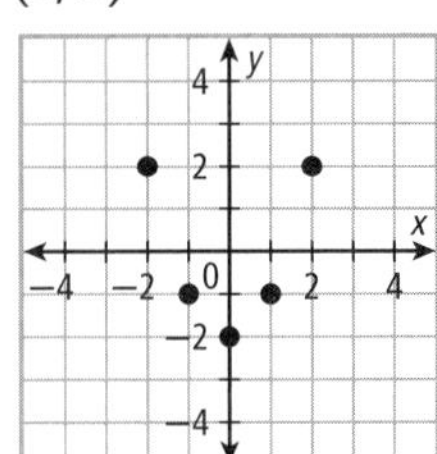

63. $m < 2$

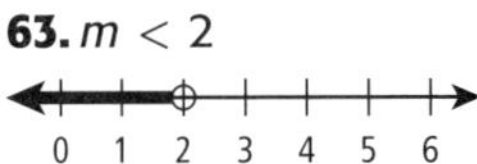

64. $x > -1$

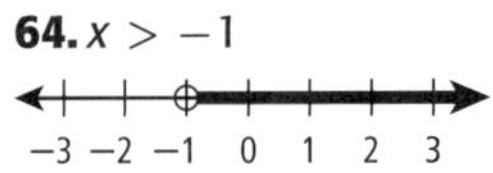

65. $x \leq -2$

−6 −5 −4 −3 −2 −1 0

3-7 *Exercises*

20. $-4 \leq x \leq 4$

−5 −4 −3 −2 −1 0 1 2 3 4 5

21. $2 < x < 4$

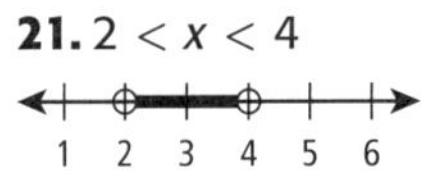

22. $-3 \leq x \leq 7$

−3 −2 −1 0 1 2 3 4 5 6 7

23. $-3 < x < 3$

−5 −4 −3 −2 −1 0 1 2 3 4 5

24. $0 \leq x \leq 4.8$

4.8

0 1 2 3 4 5

25. $-6 < x < 0$

−8 −6 −4 −2 0 2

26. $x < -1$ OR $x > 3$

−5 −4 −3 −2 −1 0 1 2 3 4 5

27. $x \leq -10$ OR $x \geq 10$

−20 −10 0 10 20

Additional Answers

28. $x < -1$ OR $x > 9$

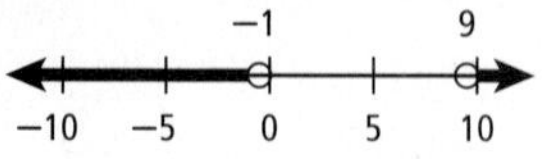

−1 9
−10 −5 0 5 10

29. $x \leq -10$ OR $x \geq 6$

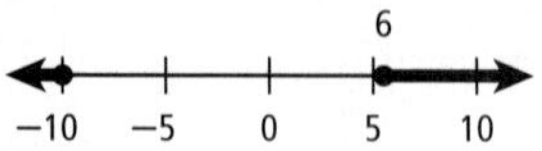

6
−10 −5 0 5 10

30. $x < 3$ OR $x > 5$

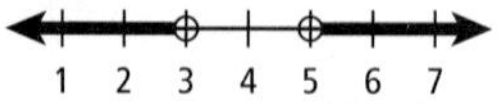

1 2 3 4 5 6 7

31. $x < -1$ OR $x > 2$

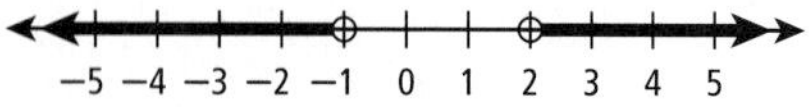

−5 −4 −3 −2 −1 0 1 2 3 4 5

32. $|x - 175| \leq 12$; $163 \leq x \leq 187$

163 187
160 165 170 175 180 185 190

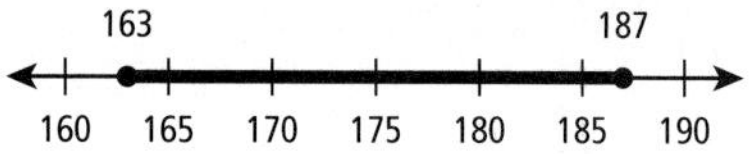

53. $k \leq 1$; the inequality is equivalent to $|x| < k - 1$, and this has no solutions when the expression on the right side is less than or equal to 0 (i.e., when $k - 1 \leq 0$ or $k \leq 1$).

54. The difference between a number and −6 must be less than 5; $|x - (-6)| < 5$; $|x + 6| < 5$

65. all real numbers less than 2

66. all real numbers less than 7

67. all real numbers greater than or equal to −6

68. all real numbers less than or equal to −7

69. $0 < x < 4$

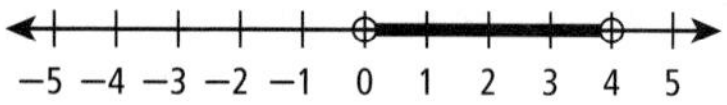

−5 −4 −3 −2 −1 0 1 2 3 4 5

70. $-2 \leq x \leq 4$

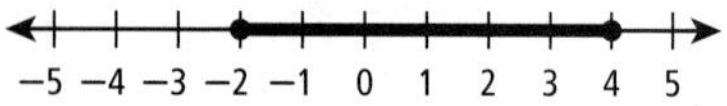

−5 −4 −3 −2 −1 0 1 2 3 4 5

71. $x < 1$ OR $x > 4$

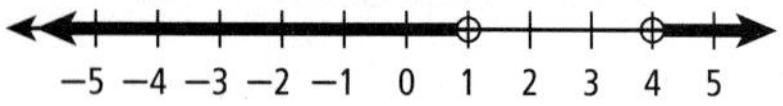

−5 −4 −3 −2 −1 0 1 2 3 4 5

72. $x \leq -1$ OR $x \geq 2$

−5 −4 −3 −2 −1 0 1 2 3 4 5

3B *Ready To Go On?*

1. 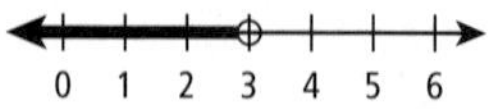 0 1 2 3 4 5 6

2. 0 1 2 3 4 5 6

3. −3 −2 −1 0 1 2 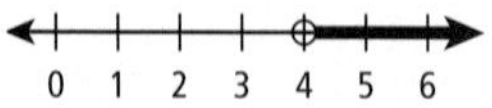 3

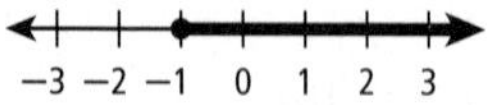

9. 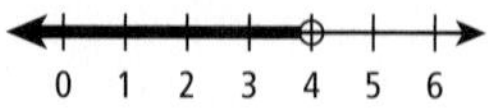 0 1 2 3 4 5 6

10. 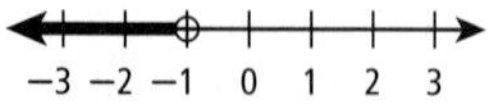 −3 −2 −1 0 1 2 3

11. 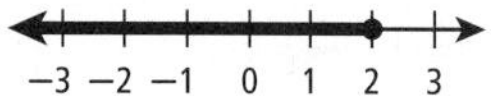 −3 −2 −1 0 1 2 3

17.  −5
−6 −4 −2 0 2 4 6

18. 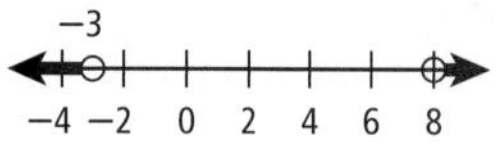 −3
−4 −2 0 2 4 6 8

20.  −3 −2 −1 0 1 2 3

22. $-3 \leq x \leq 3$

−3 3

23. $-28 < x < 14$

−28 14

24. $x \leq -7$ OR $x \geq 7$

−7 7

29.  88 132

Chapter 4

Are You Ready?

6–13.

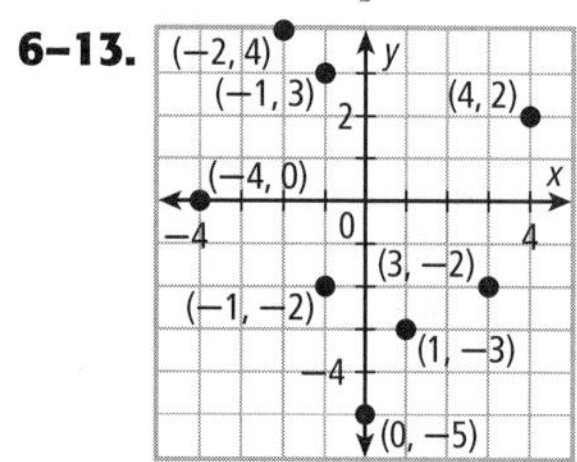

14. (−2, 3), (−1, 1), (0, −1), (1, −3), (2, −5)

15. (−2, −1), (−1, 0), (0, 1), (1, 2), (2, 3)

16. (−2, −4), (−1, −1), (0, 0), (1, −1), (2, −4)

17. $(-2, 1)$, $\left(-1, \frac{3}{2}\right)$, $(0, 2)$, $\left(1, \frac{5}{2}\right)$, $(2, 3)$

18. (−2, 1), (−1, 0), (0, 1), (1, 4), (2, 9)

19. (−2, 9), (−1, 4), (0, 1), (1, 0), (2, 1)

4-1 *Exercises*

19. The point of intersection represents the time of day when you will be the same distance from the base of the mountain on both the hike up and the hike down.

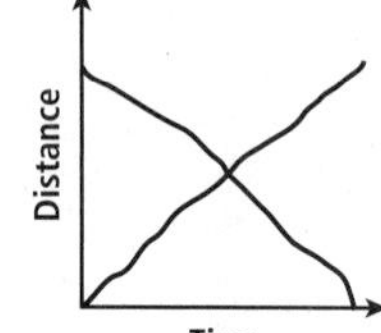

20. Both graphs would start from the origin and then rise. The graph for the brick would increase rapidly and then drop suddenly to zero. The graph for the rolled ball would increase less rapidly and then slowly drop to zero.

21. Possible answer: The number of eggs in stock in a grocery store on different days could be represented by a discrete graph. The depth of a scuba diver during a dive could be represented by a continuous graph.

22a.

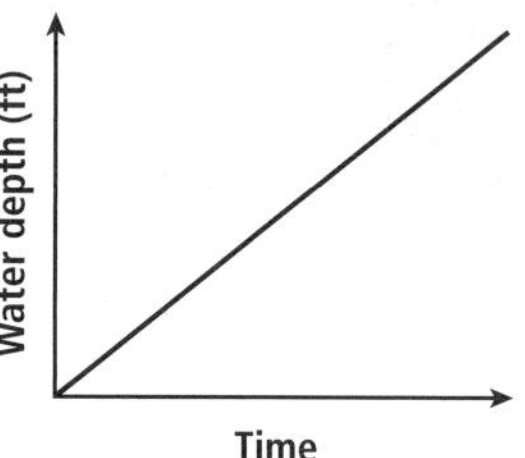

22b.

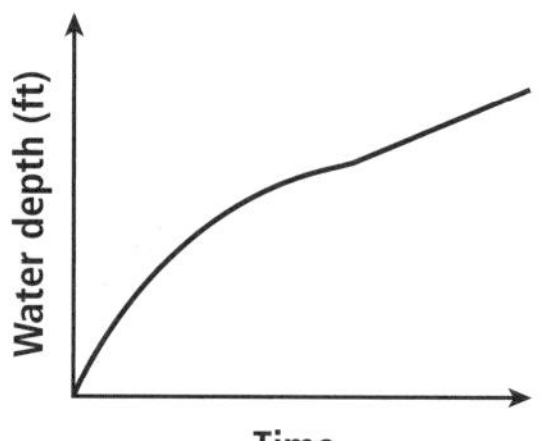

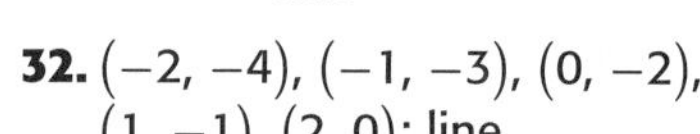

32. (−2, −4), (−1, −3), (0, −2), (1, −1), (2, 0); line

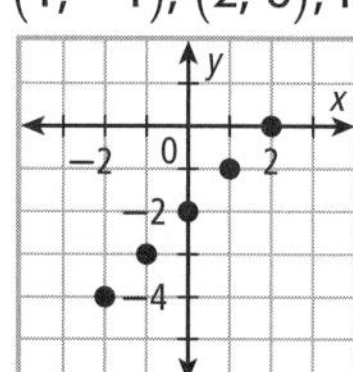

33. (−2, 5), (−1, 3), (0, 1), (1, −1), (2, −3); line

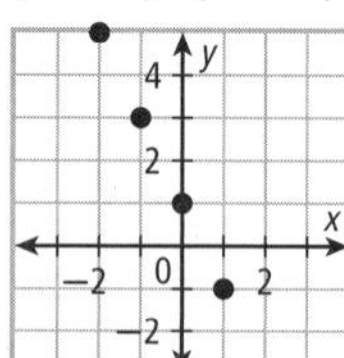

34. (−2, 3), (−1, 2), (0, 1), (1, 0), (2, 1); V-shape

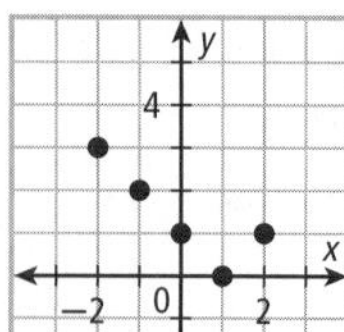

Additional Answers

35. (−2, 6), (−1, 3), (0, 2), (1, 3), (2, 6); U-shape

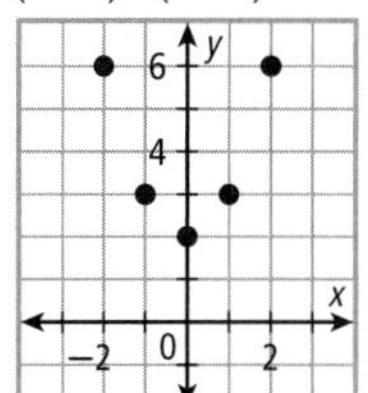

4-2 *Exercises*

3.

x	y
1	1
1	2

1 → 1
1 → 2

4.

x	y
−1	1
−2	$\frac{1}{2}$
−3	$\frac{1}{3}$
−4	$\frac{1}{4}$

−1 → 1
−2 → $\frac{1}{2}$
−3 → $\frac{1}{3}$
−4 → $\frac{1}{4}$

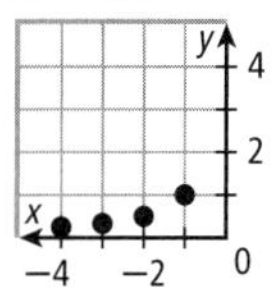

5.

x	y
−7	7
−3	3
−1	1
5	−5

−1 → 1
−3 → 3
5 → −5
−7 → 7

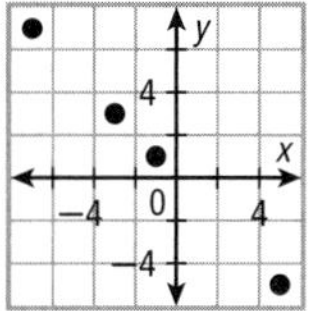

6.

x	y
0	0
2	−4
2	−2

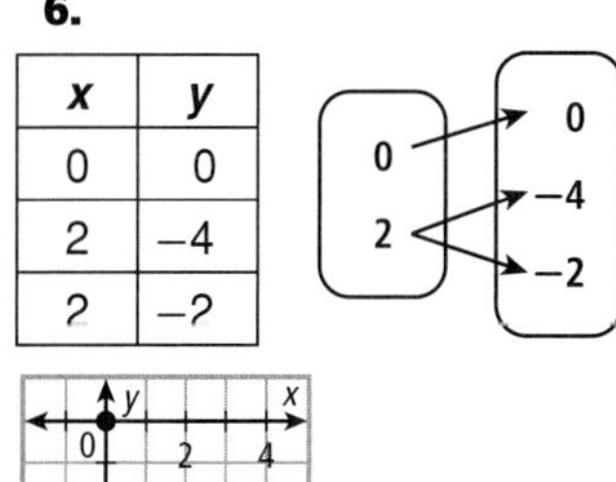

26a. {(60, 360), (120, 720), (180, 1080), (240, 1440), (300, 1800)}

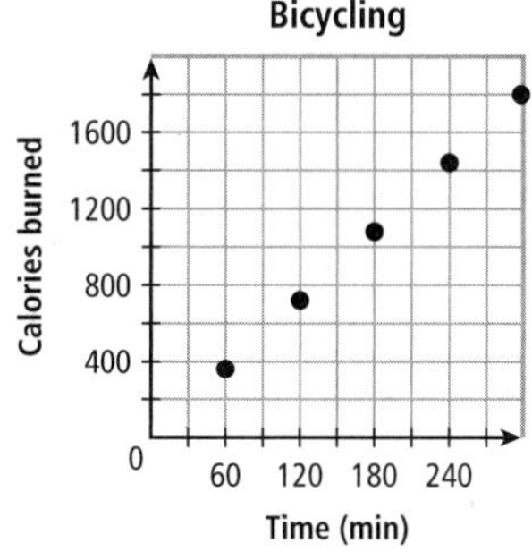

b. D: {60, 120, 180, 240, 300}; R: {360, 720, 1080, 1440, 1800}

c. Yes; each domain value is paired with exactly one range value.

4-4 *Exercises*

1.

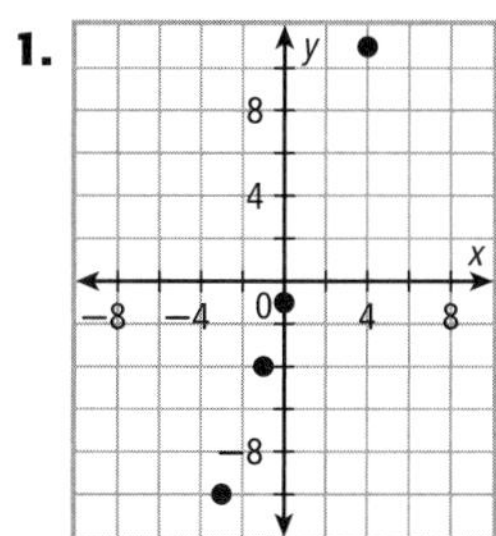

2.

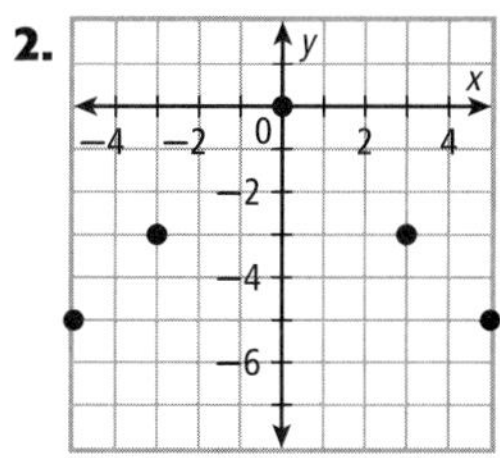

3.

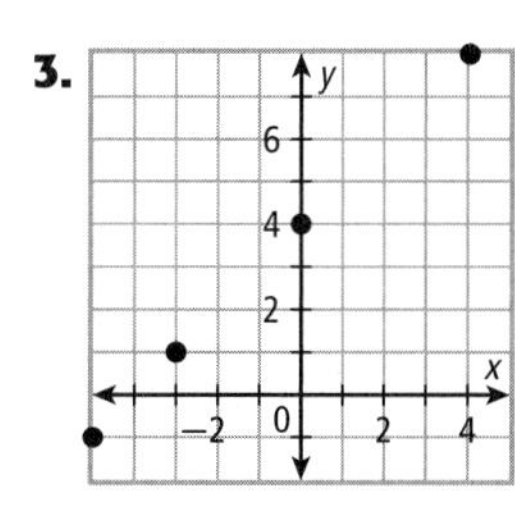

4.

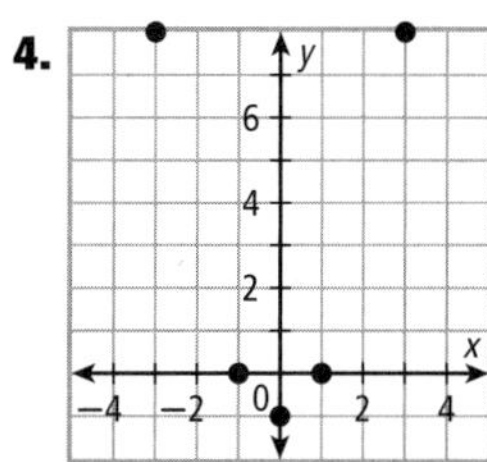

5.

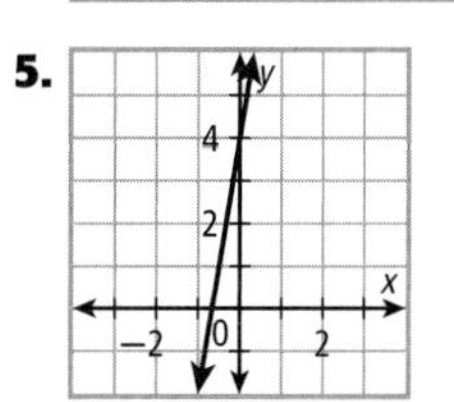

6.

7.

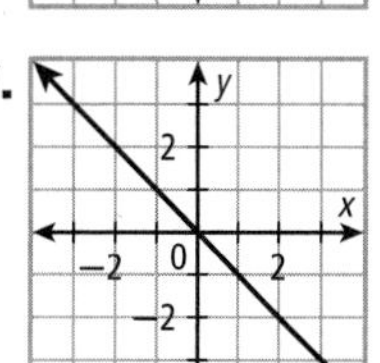

8.

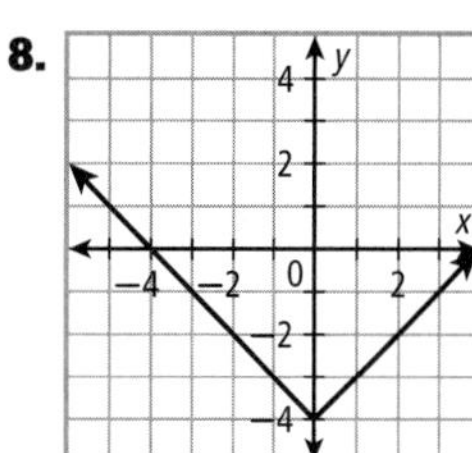

9.

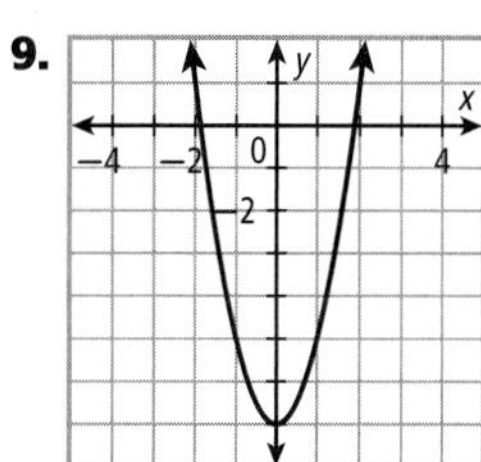

10.

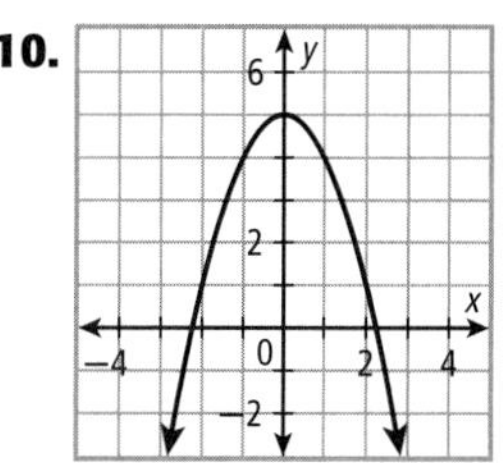

12. about 10.5 in.

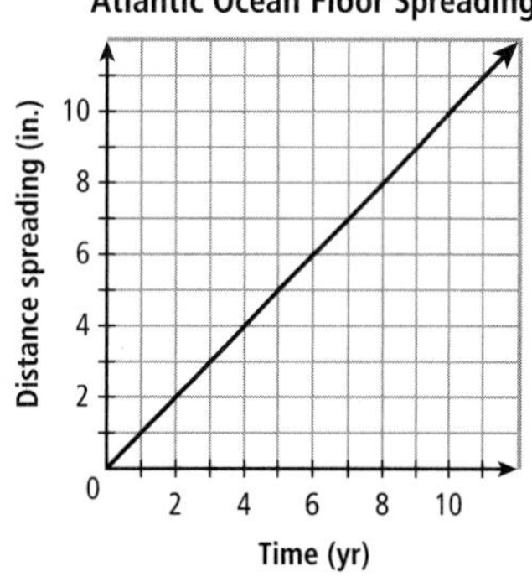

13.

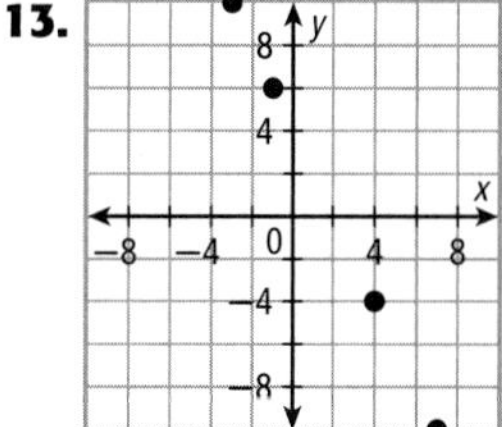

14.

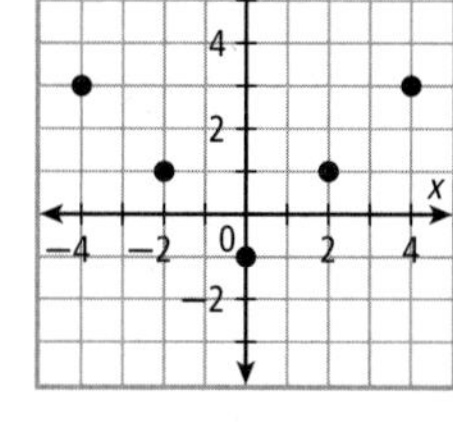

15.

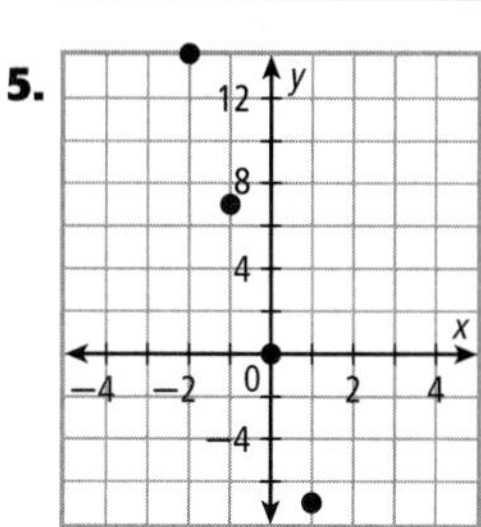

16.

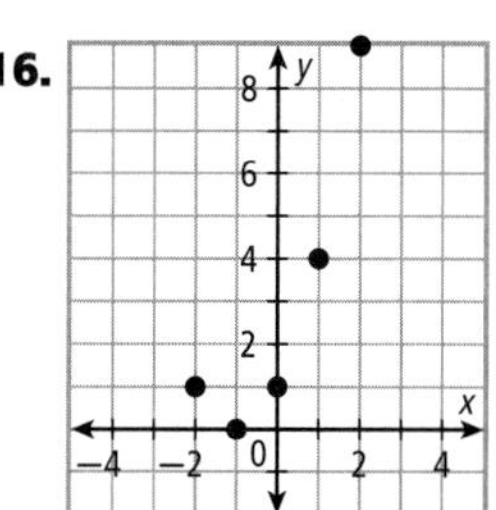

17.

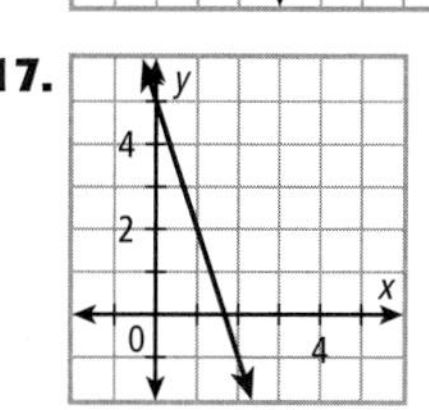

18.

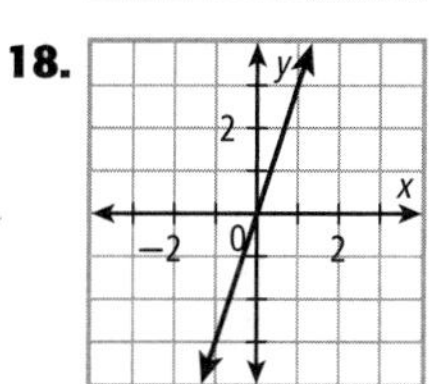

19.

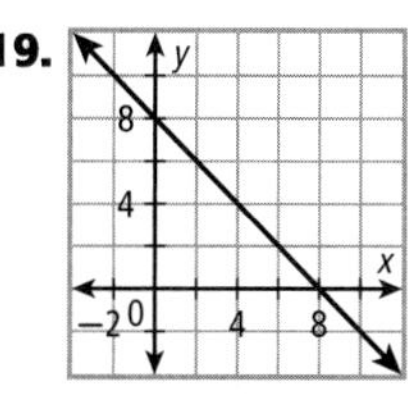

20.

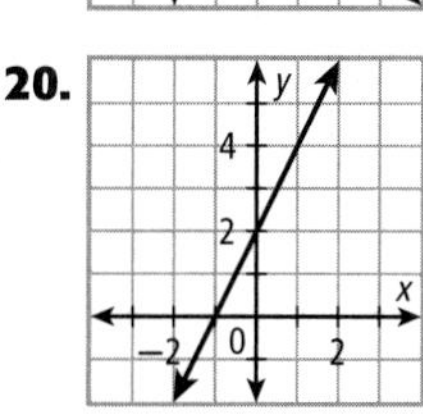

21.

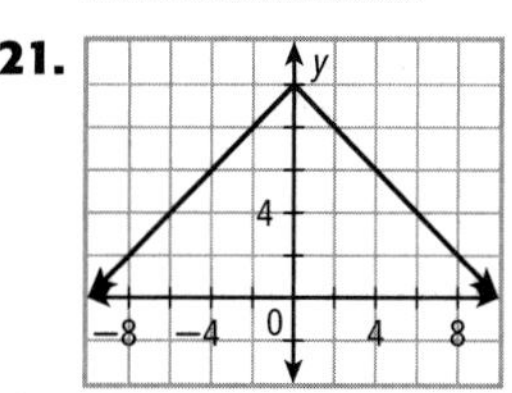

22. 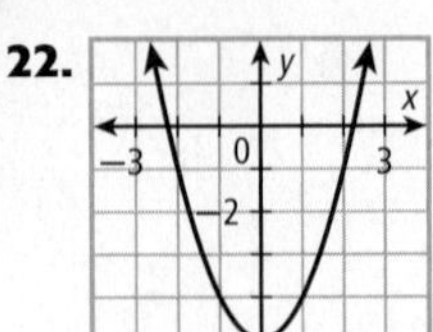

23. 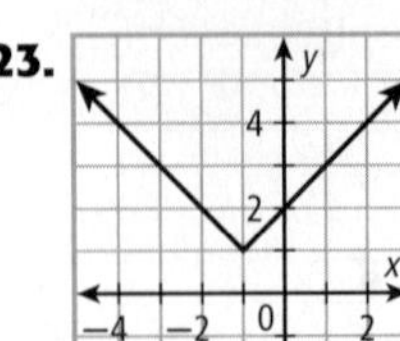

24. 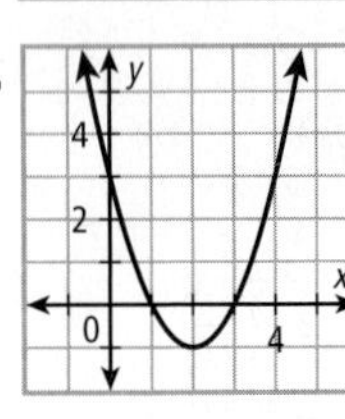

28. 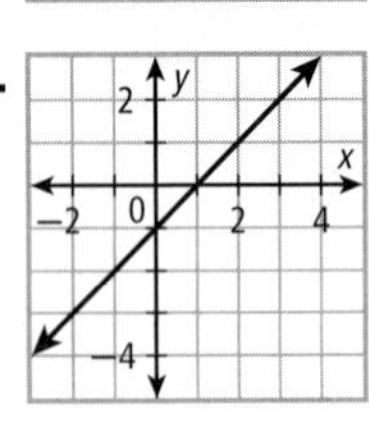

29. 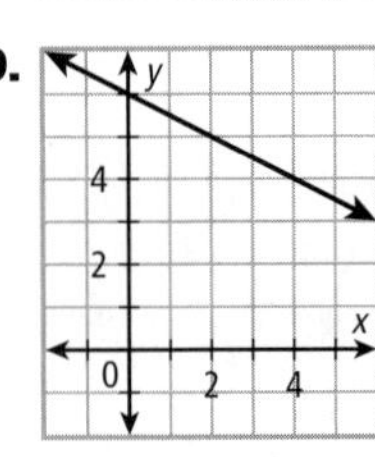

30. 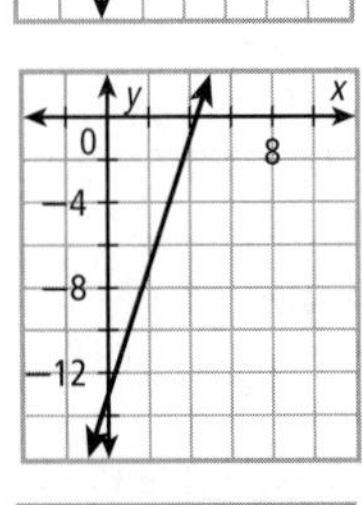

31. 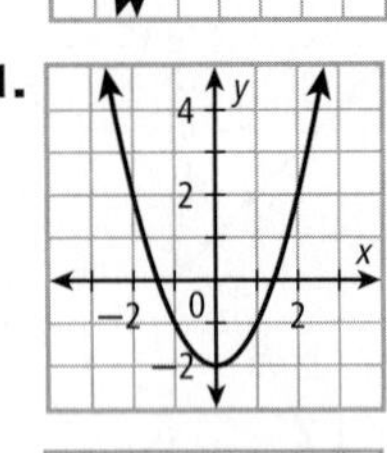

32. 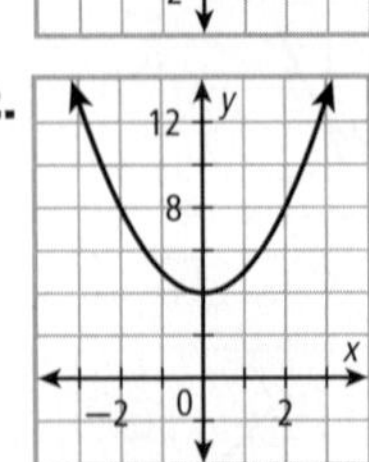

33. 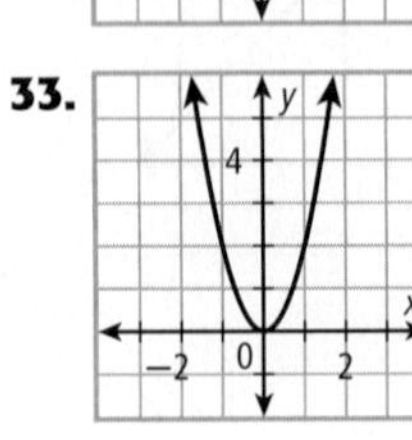

34. 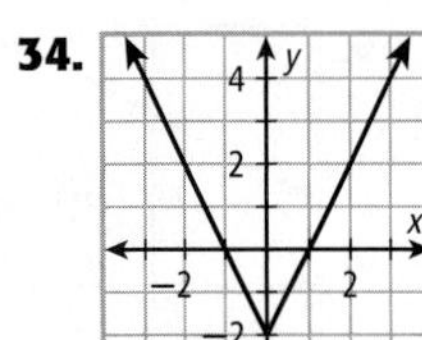

35. 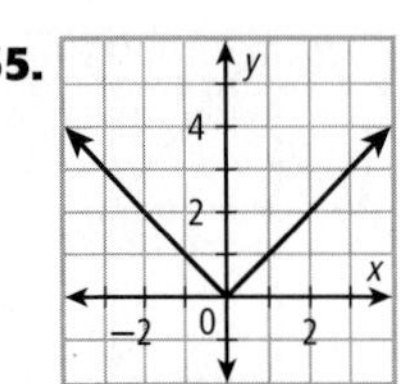

36. 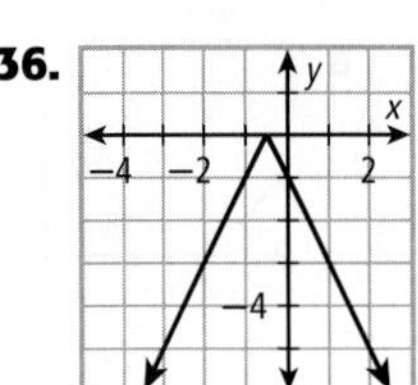

55a. $v = 10{,}000 - 1500h$

b. 8500 gal

c.

Time (h)	Volume (gal)
0	10,000
1	8,500
2	7,000
3	5,500
4	4,000

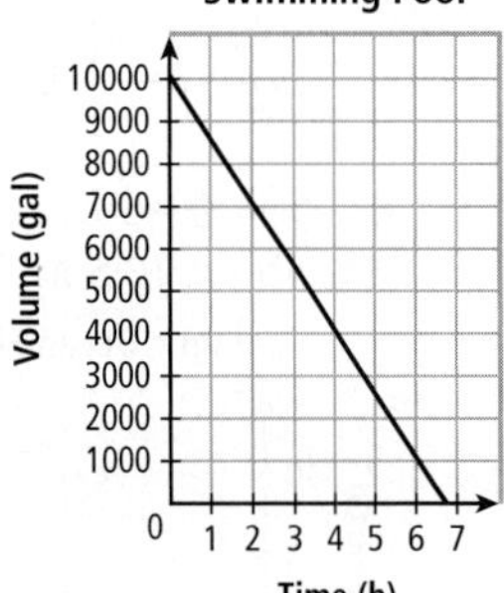

4A *Ready to Go On?*

3. 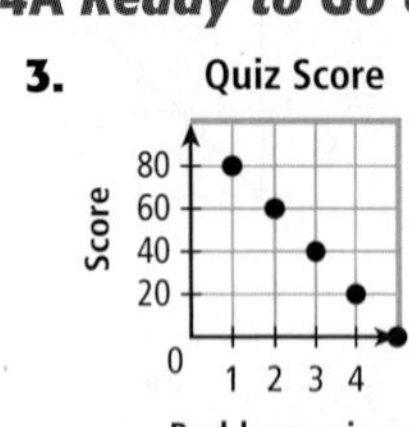

5. D: {−2, 0, 2}; R: {3}; yes; each element in the domain is assigned to exactly 1 element in the range.

6. D: $\{-4 \le x \le 2\}$; R: $\{0 \le y \le 4\}$; yes; each element in the domain is assigned to exactly one element in the range.

13. 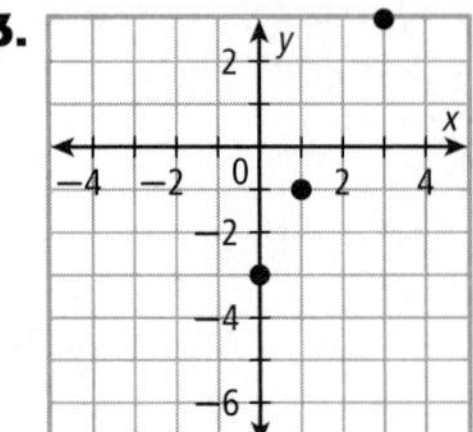

14. 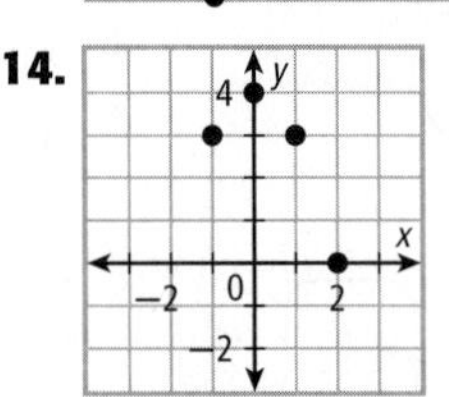

15. 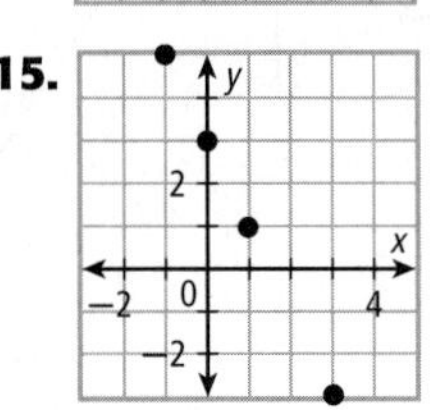

16. 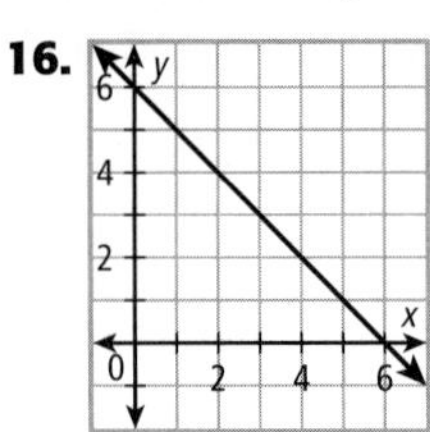

17. 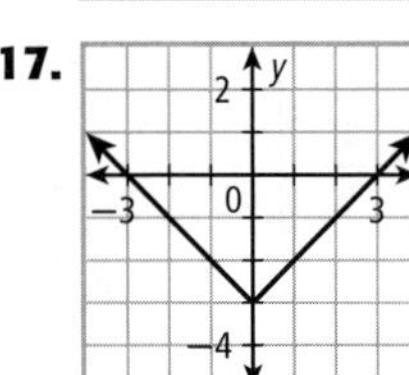

18. 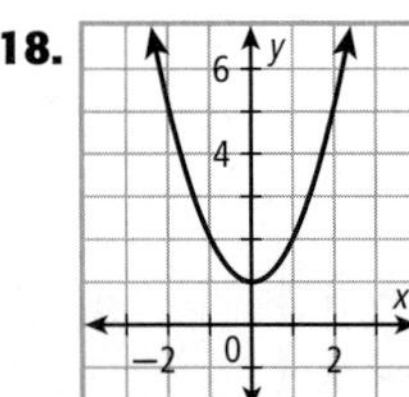

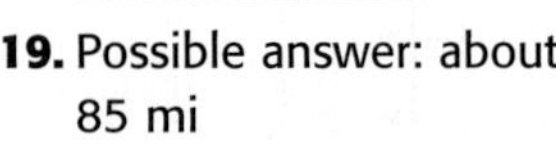
19. Possible answer: about 85 mi

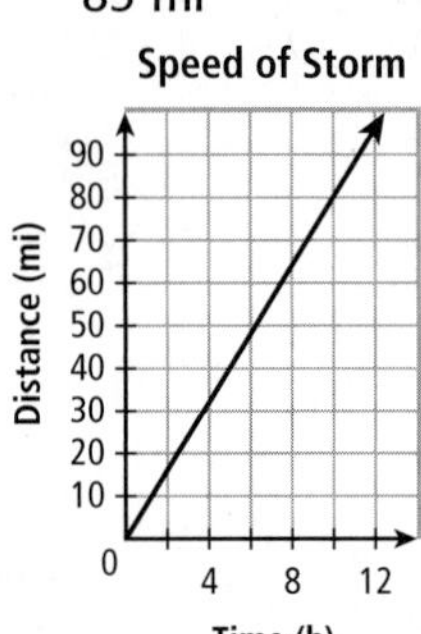

4-5 Technology Lab

1.

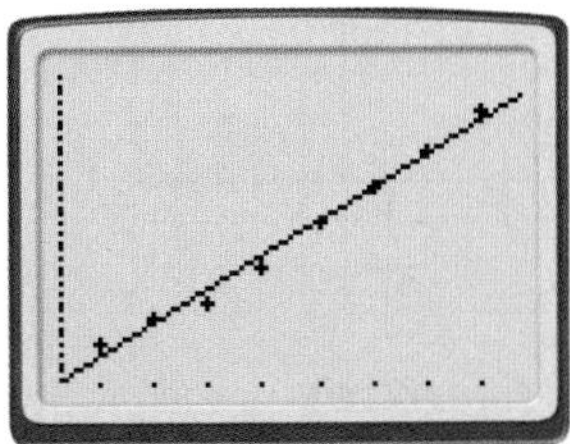

Chapter 4 Test

16.

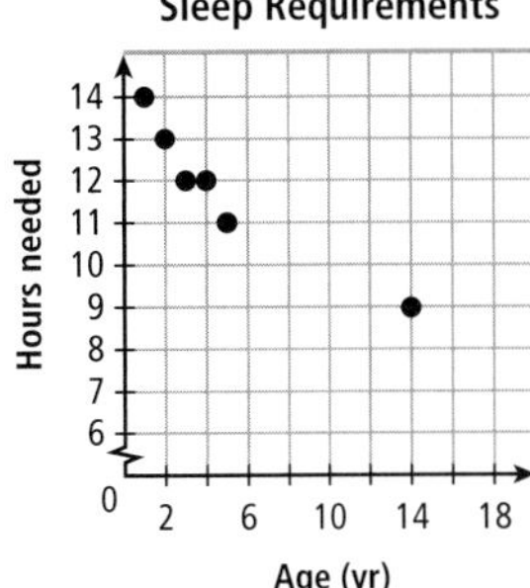

Chapter 5

Are You Ready?

5–12.

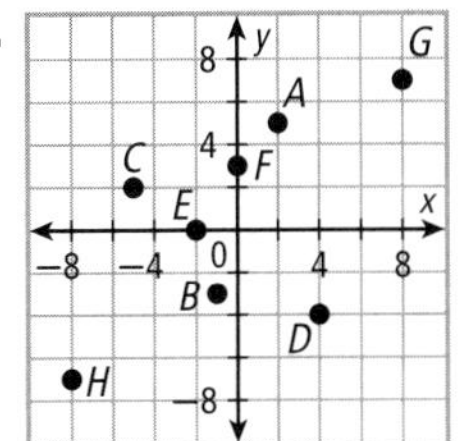

Reading and Writing Math

1.

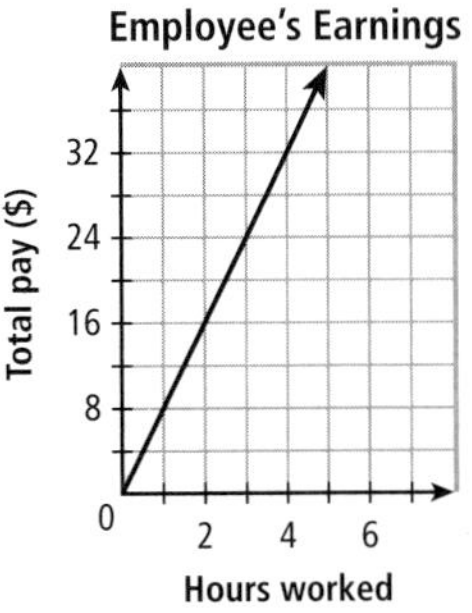

Hours Worked	Total Pay ($)
0	0
1	8
2	16
3	24
4	32
5	40

The table shows some ordered-pair solutions to the equation. The graph is a visual representation of all ordered-pair solutions to the equation, including those in the table.

2. Possible answer: An equation is useful when you need a rule to calculate how much money you make for working certain hours. A table is useful if you need a list of pay amounts for various amounts of time worked. A graph is useful to see the relationship between hours worked and total pay.

5-1 Exercises

8. A constant change of −3 in x corresponds to different changes in y.

9.

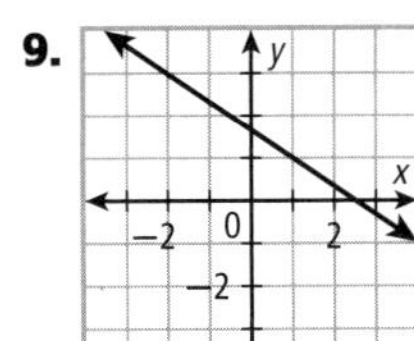

10.

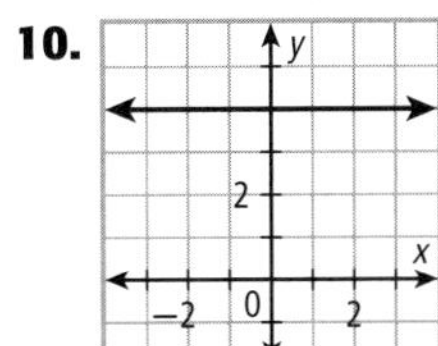

12.

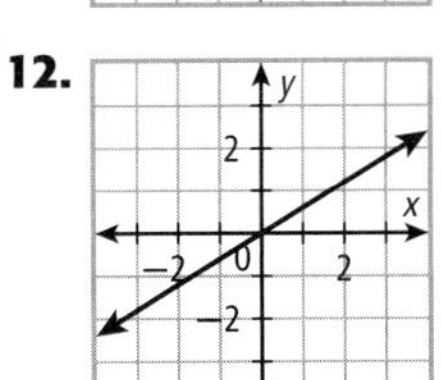

13.

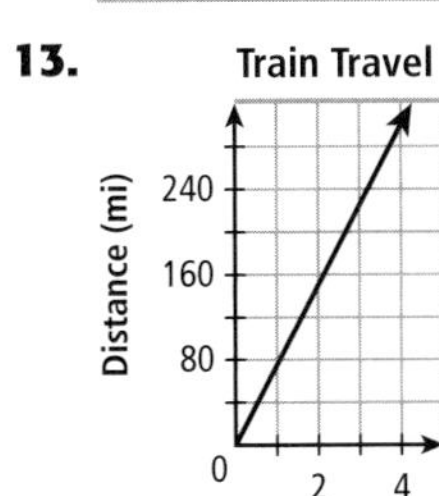

D: $x \geq 0$; R: $y \geq 0$

14.

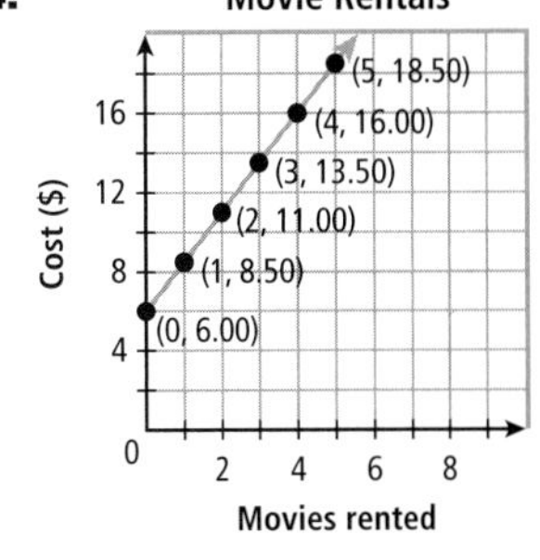

D: {0, 1, 2, 3, …}

R: {\$6.00, \$8.50, \$11.00, \$13.50, …}

15. Each domain value is paired with exactly one range value.

16. Each domain value is paired with exactly one range value.

17. Each domain value is paired with exactly one range value.

18. A constant change of +3 in x corresponds to different changes in y.

19. A constant change of +1 in x corresponds to a constant change of +1 in y.

20. A constant change of −3 in x corresponds to a constant change of −2 in y.

42.

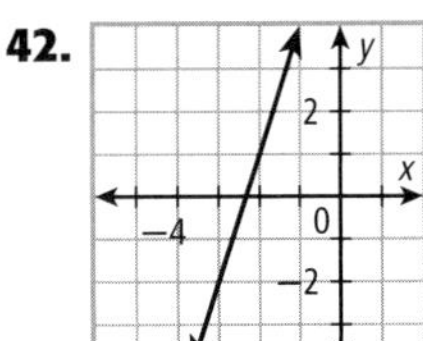

43.

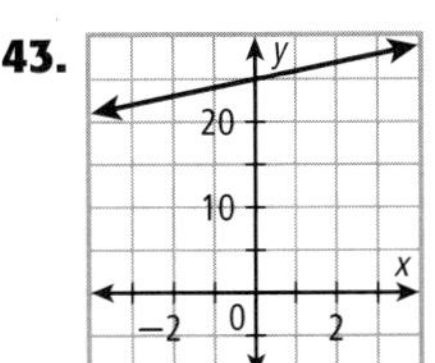

44.

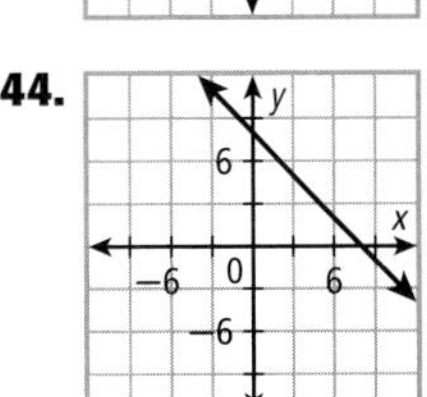

45.

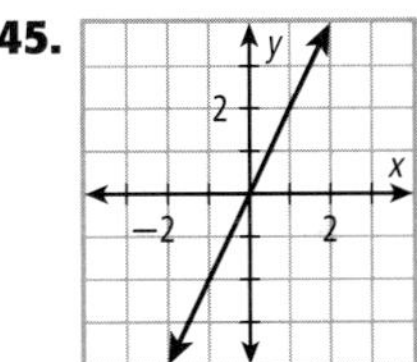

46.

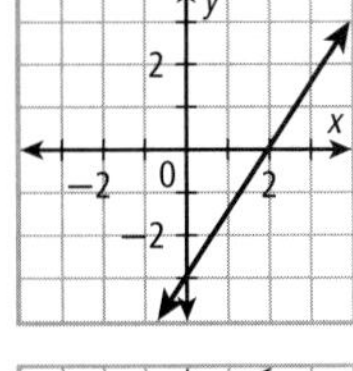

47.

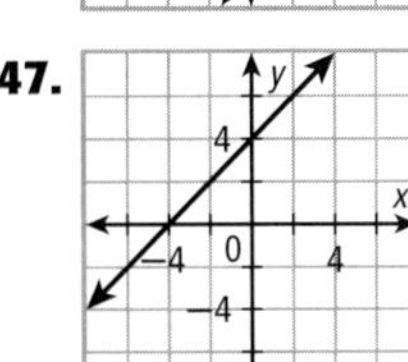

48.

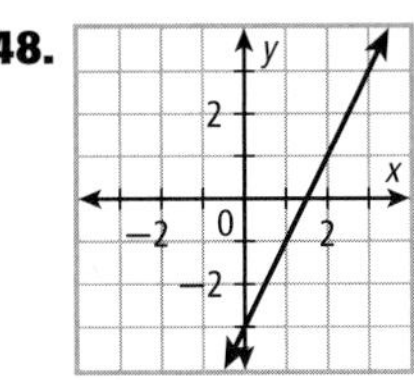

49.

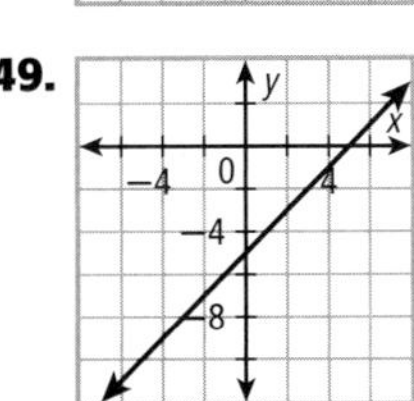

51b.

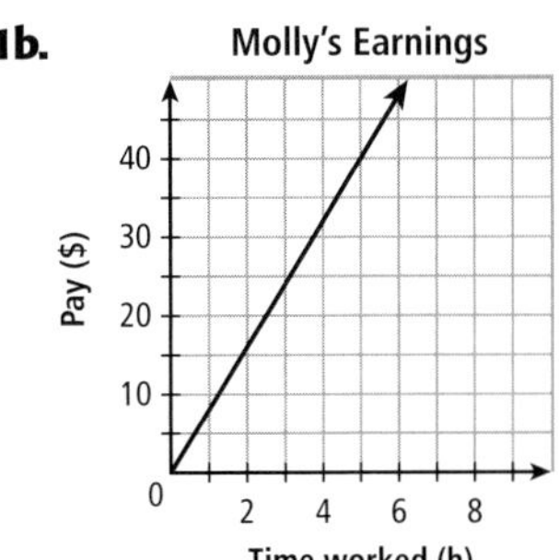

D: $x \geq 0$; R: $y \geq 0$

52. Possible answer:

x	$y = 2x - 1$
−2	−5
−1	−3
0	−1
1	1
2	3

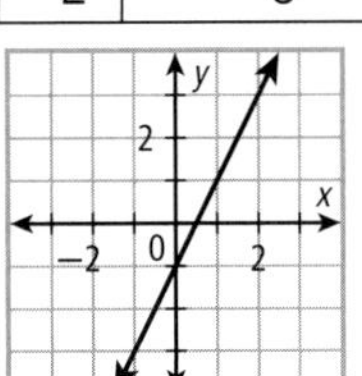

The table gives some ordered pairs (x, y) that satisfy the equation $y = 2x - 1$. The graph is a representation of all ordered pairs (x, y) that satisfy $y = 2x - 1$.

53. Possible answer: The value in cents of x dimes is $y = 10x$. Since you can have only a whole number of dimes, the domain and range are restricted to whole numbers.

54a. Possible answer: Each constant change in time (+3 minutes) corresponds with a constant change in calories (+27 Calories).

b.

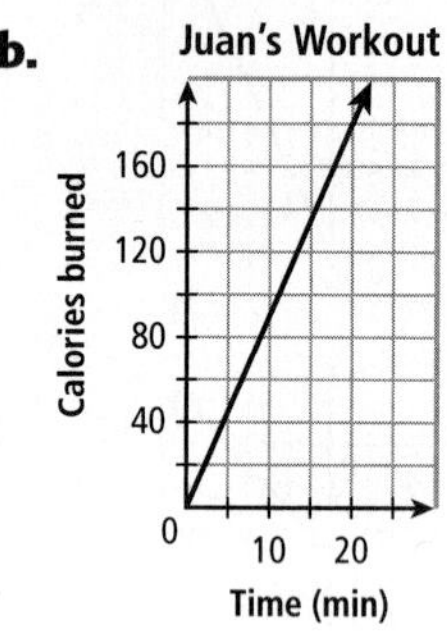

5-2 *Exercises*

9.

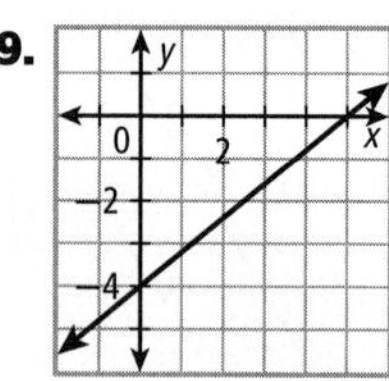

10.

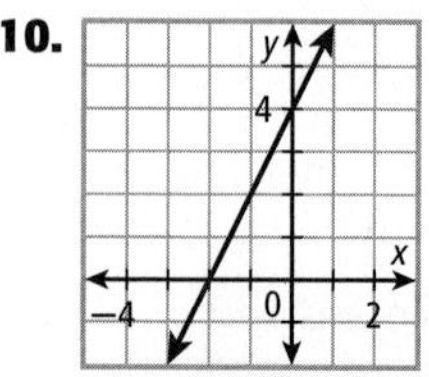

11.

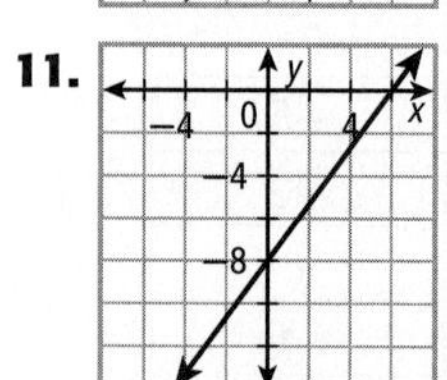

12.

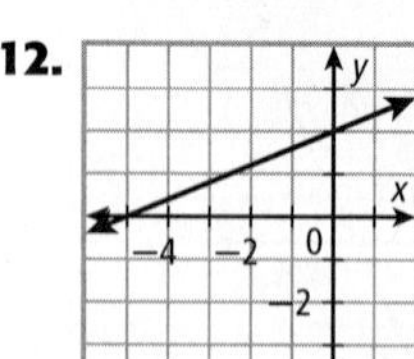

22a.

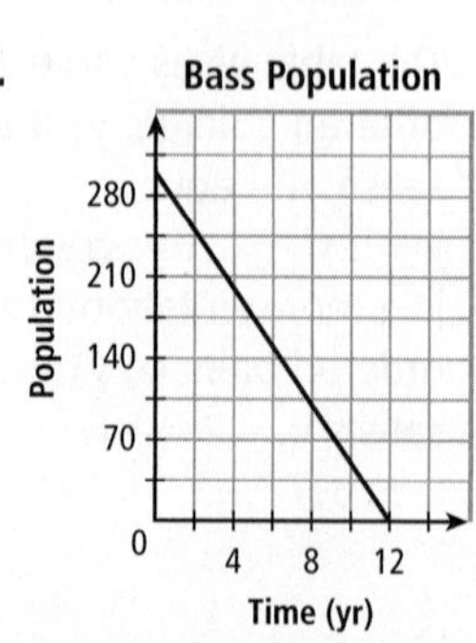

b. x-int.: time when bass pop. is 0; y-int.: number of bass originally put in lake

23a.

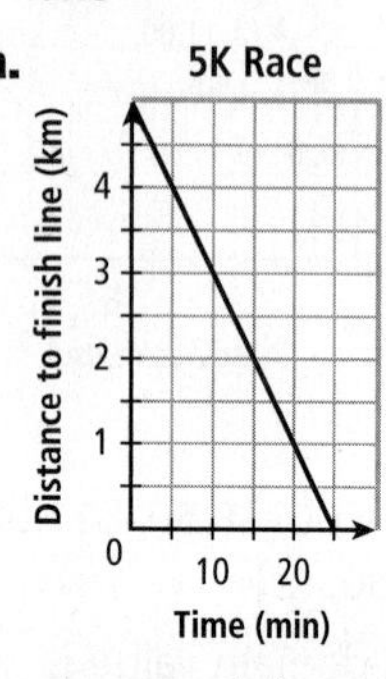

b. x-int.: total time to run race (when dist. to finish line is 0); y-int.: total length of race (when time is 0)

28.

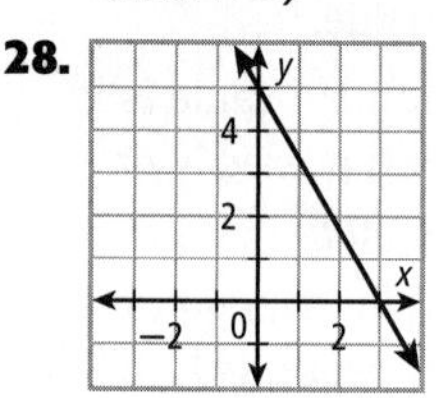

29.

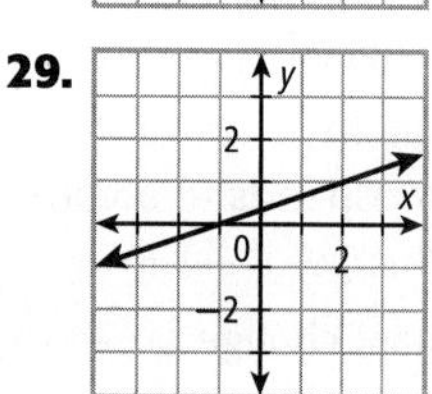

31b. The x-intercept represents the year 2400 and the y-intercept represents 7.5 million acres.

32a.

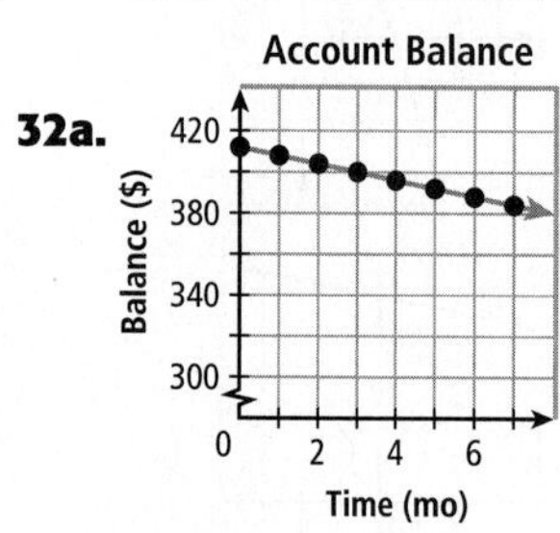

D: {0, 1, 2, 3, ...};
R: {\$412, \$408, \$404, \$400, ...}

33a.

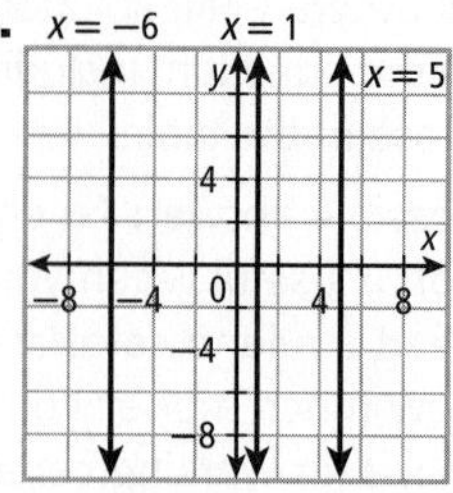

$x = -6$: x-int.: −6, no y-int.; $x = 1$: x-int.: 1, no y-int.; $x = 5$: x-int.: 5, no y-int.

b.

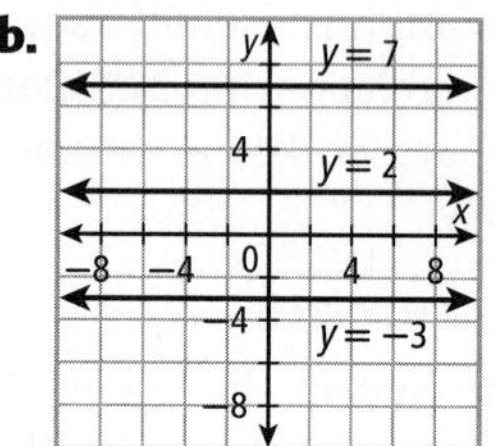

$y = -3$: no x-int., y-int.: −3;
$y = 2$: no x-int., y-int.: 2;
$y = 7$: no x-int., y-int.: 7

5-4 *Exercises*

38. $-11 < x < 11$

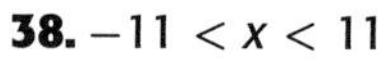

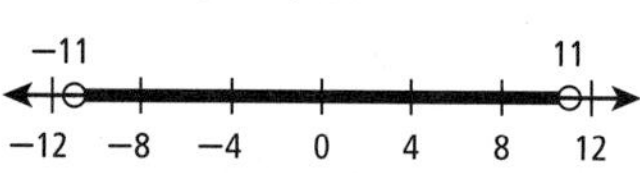

39. $-11 < x < -5$

40. $-4 \le x \le 4$

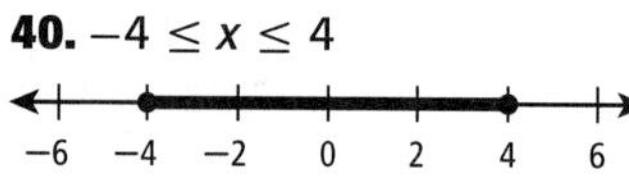

41. $x \le -7$ OR $x \ge 7$

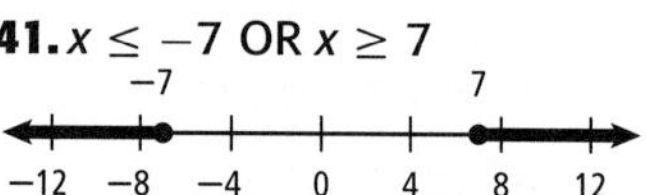

42. $x < -4$ OR $x > 16$

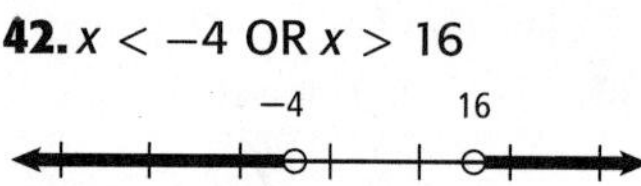

43. $x \le -8$ OR $x \ge 6$

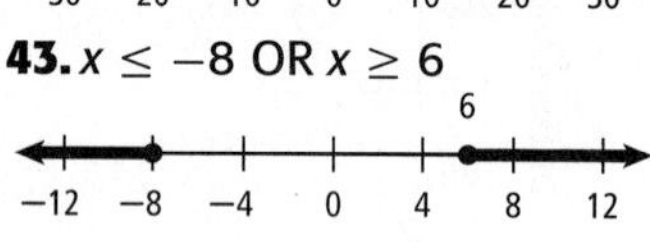

46.

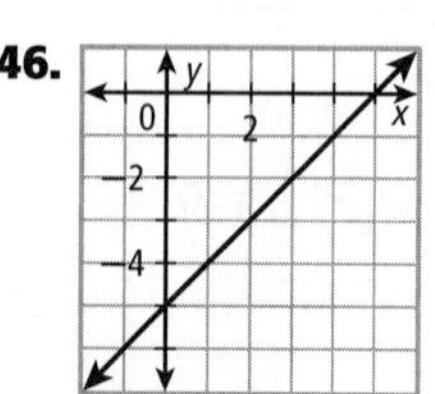

47.

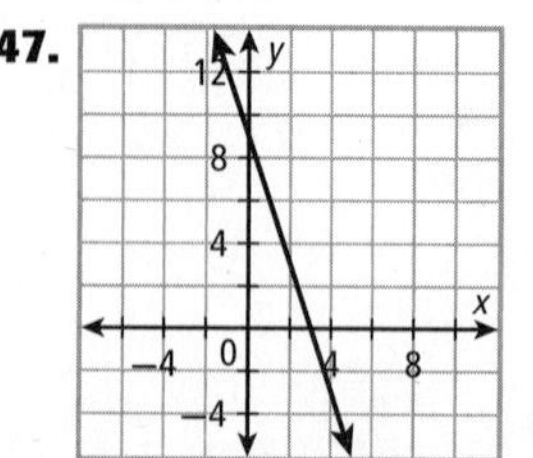

48.

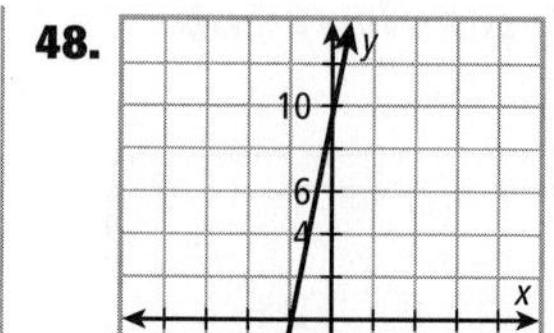

5-5 *Exercises*

32. Yes; possible answer: Rebecca used the expression $\frac{x_2 - x_1}{2} + x_1$. Rewriting with a common denominator and adding yields $\frac{x_2 + x_1}{2}$. Rewriting using the Commutative Property of Addition yields $\frac{x_1 + x_2}{2}$, which is the same expression used in the Midpoint Formula.

5-6 *Exercises*

22. $y = \frac{1}{4}x$

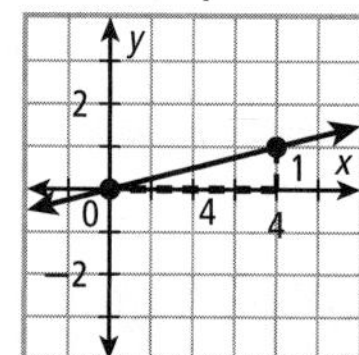

$k = \frac{1}{4}$; graph shows slope $= \frac{1}{4}$

23. $y = 4x$

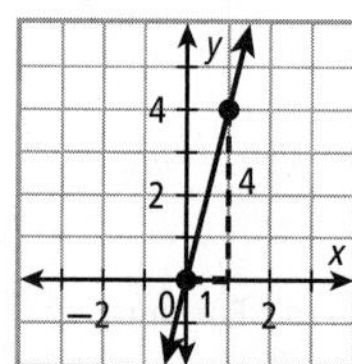

$k = 4$; graph shows slope = 4

24. $y = 3x$

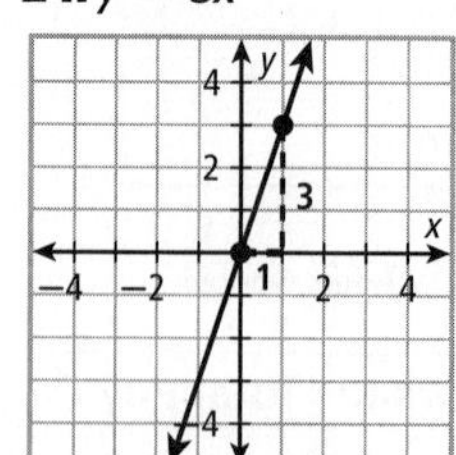

$k = 3$; graph shows slope = 3

25. $y = 2x$

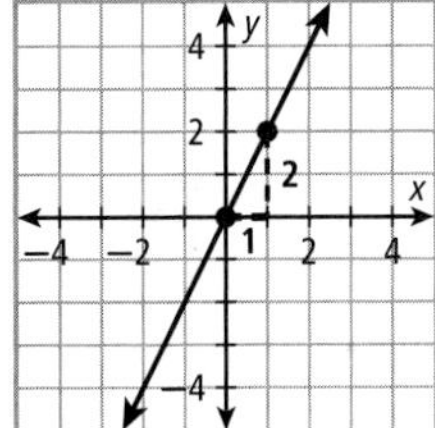

$k = 2$; graph shows slope $= 2$

26. $y = -8x$

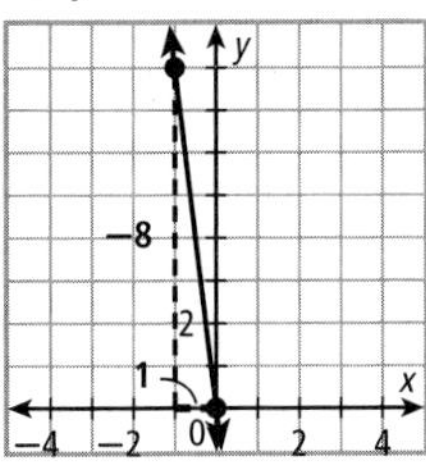

$k = -8$; graph shows slope $= -8$

27. $y = 7x$

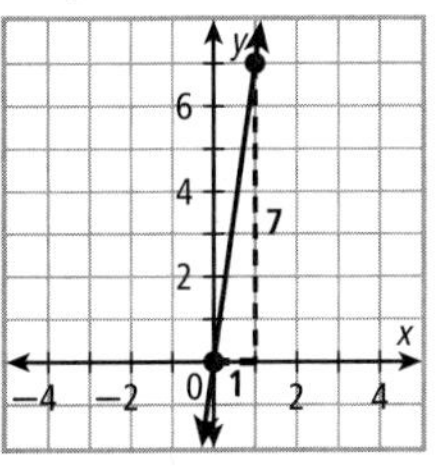

$k = 7$; graph shows slope $= 7$

28. $y = -\frac{9}{2}x$

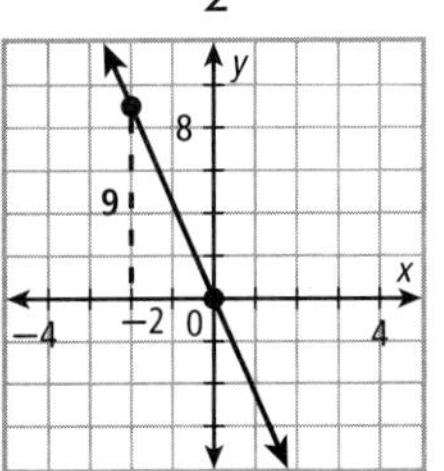

$k = -\frac{9}{2}$; graph shows slope $= -\frac{9}{2}$

29. $y = -\frac{2}{9}x$

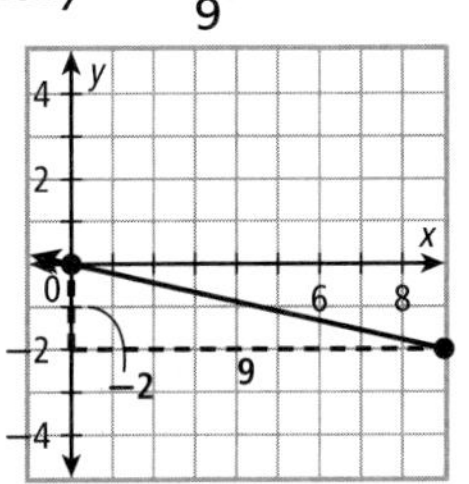

$k = -\frac{2}{9}$; graph shows slope $= -\frac{2}{9}$

30. $y = \frac{3}{2}x$

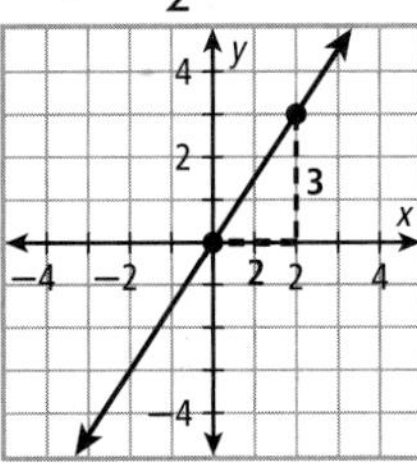

$k = \frac{3}{2}$; graph shows slope $= \frac{3}{2}$

31. $y = \frac{4}{3}x$

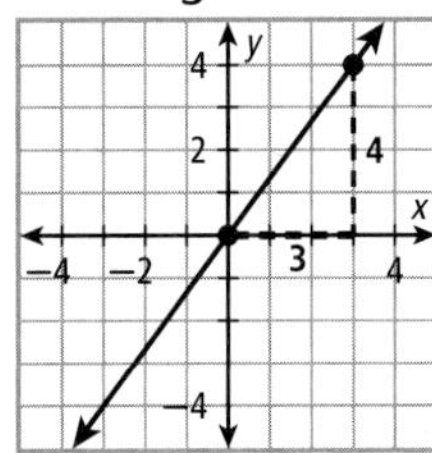

$k = \frac{4}{3}$; graph shows slope $= \frac{4}{3}$

32. $y = \frac{1}{5}x$

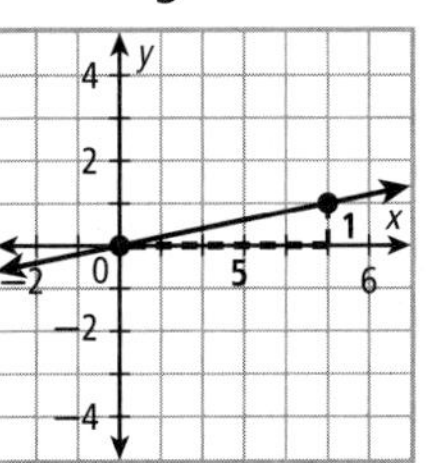

$k = \frac{1}{5}$; graph shows slope $= \frac{1}{5}$

33. $y = -6x$

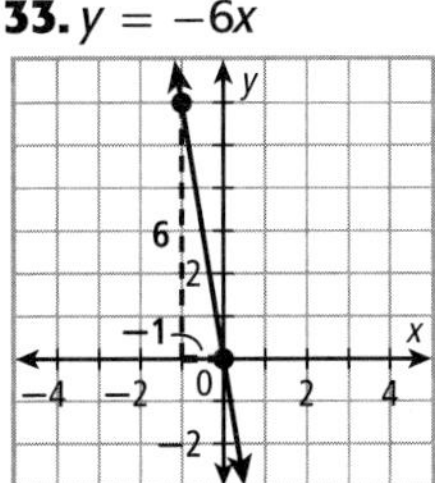

$k = -6$; graph shows slope $= -6$

34. $y = -\frac{1}{2}x$

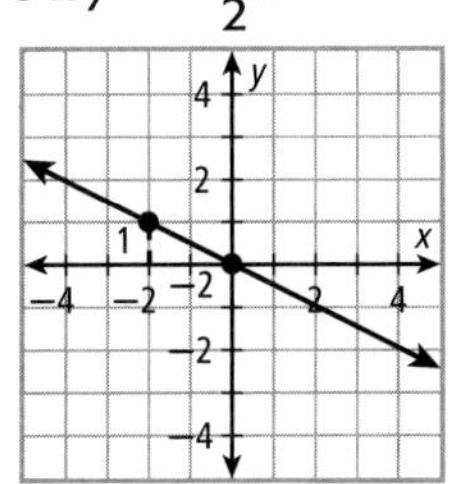

$k = \frac{1}{2}$; graph shows slope $= \frac{1}{2}$

35. $y = \frac{2}{7}x$

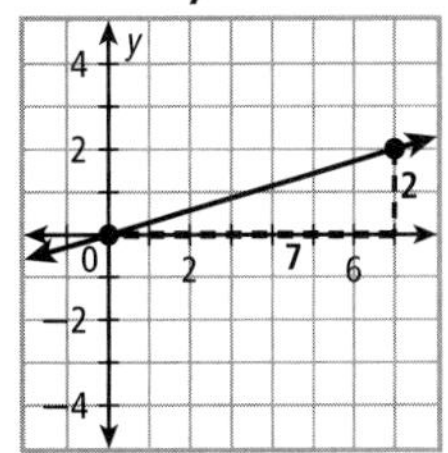

$k = \frac{2}{7}$; graph shows slope $= \frac{2}{7}$

37b.

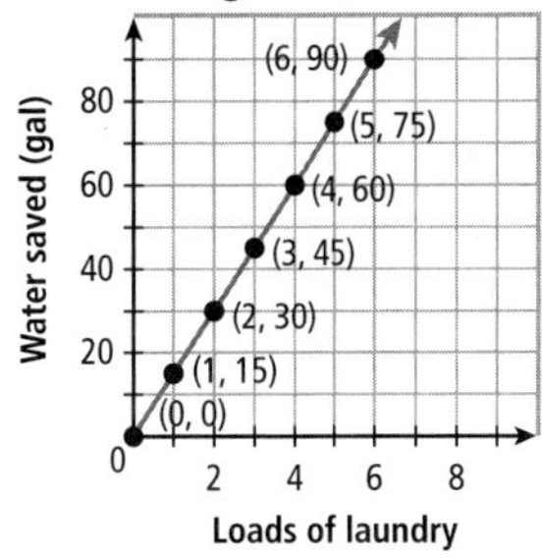

No; Mischa cannot wash a fraction of a load, so only pts. whose x-coord. is a whole number make sense.

38. Yes; since $\frac{y}{x}$ is the same for all ord. pairs, $2x$ must correspond to $2y$.

5A *Multi-Step Test Prep*

1.

Age (yr)	Maximum Heart Rate (beats/min)
13	205.95
14	205.1
15	204.25
16	203.4
17	202.55
18	201.7

2. x-int.: ≈ 255.29; y-int.: 217; slope: -0.85

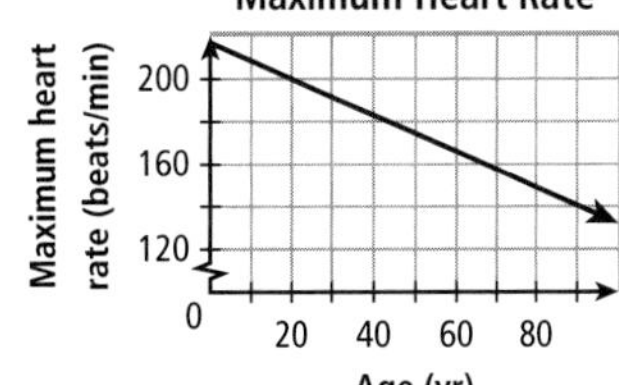

3. x-int.: the (hypothetical) age at which someone's max. heart rate would be 0 beats/min; y-int.: max. heart rate of someone who is 0 years old

4. slope: how much the max. heart rate decreases for each year that someone ages; because as age increases, max. heart rate decreases

5. The absolute value of the slope is less, so the line is less steep. The y-intercept is less, so the line crosses the y-axis at a lower point.

7. min.:
$m = 0.7(217 - 0.85a)$
$= 151.9 - 0.595a$

max.:
$m = 0.8(217 - 0.85a)$
$= 173.6 - 0.68a$

5A *Ready to Go On?*

5.

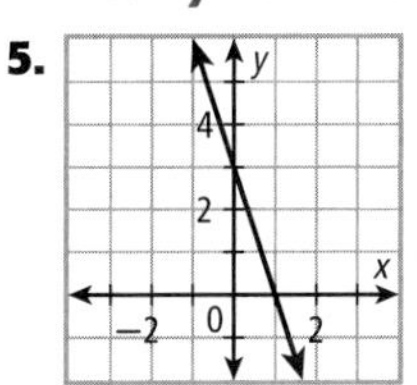

6.

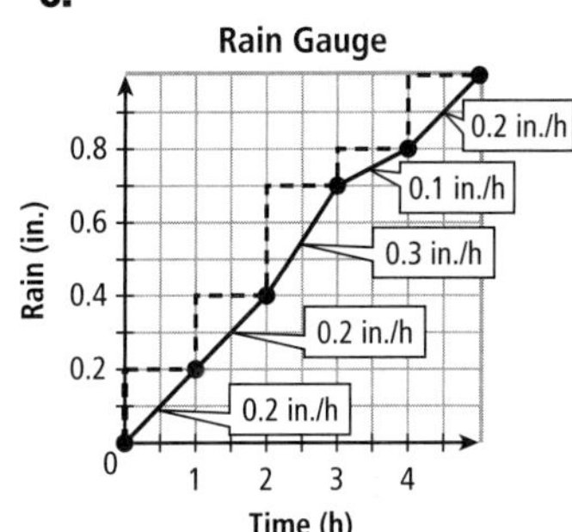

5-7 *Exercises*

2.

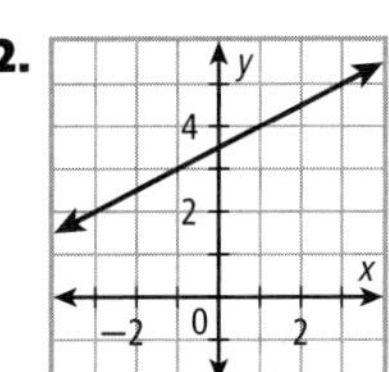

3.

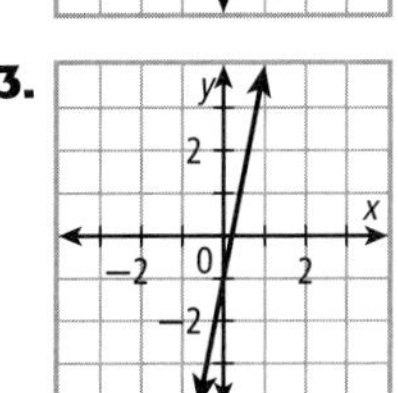

4.

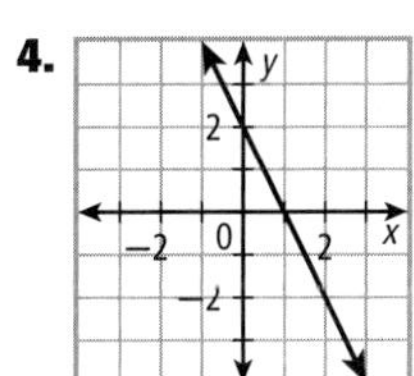

10.

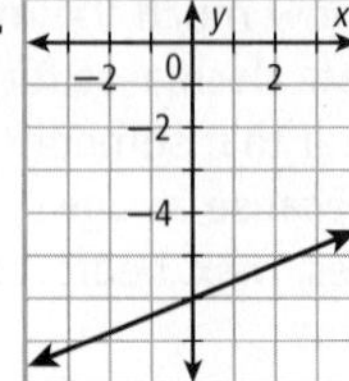

11.

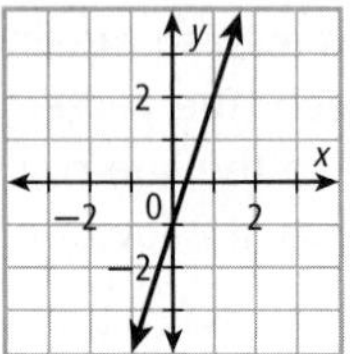

12.

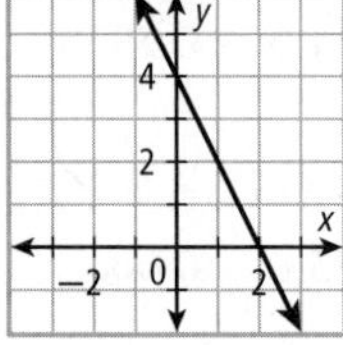

14.

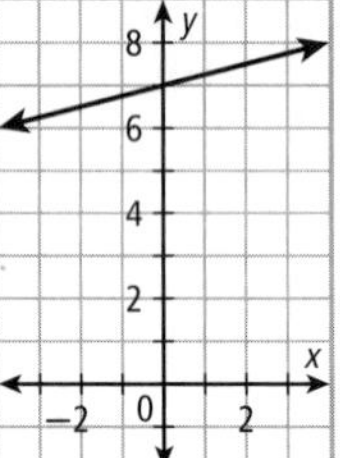

15.

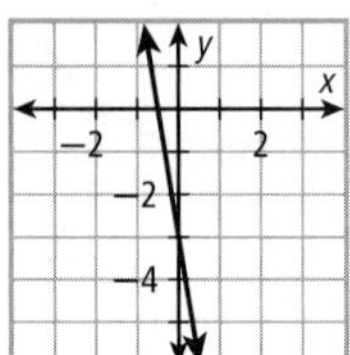

16.

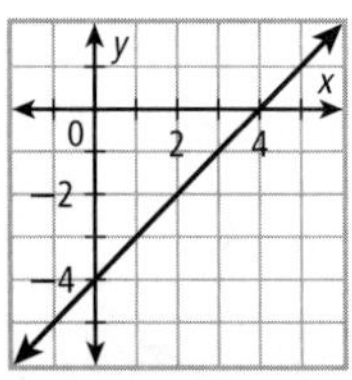

17.

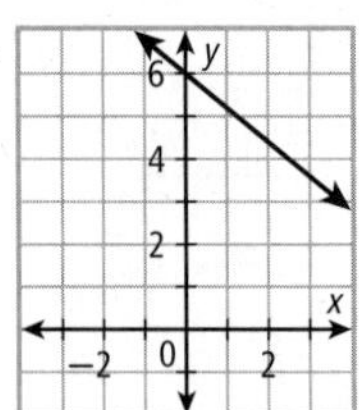

23. $y = \frac{1}{2}x + 4$

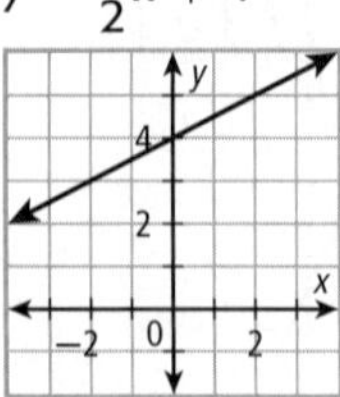

24. $y = -\frac{2}{3}x + 2$

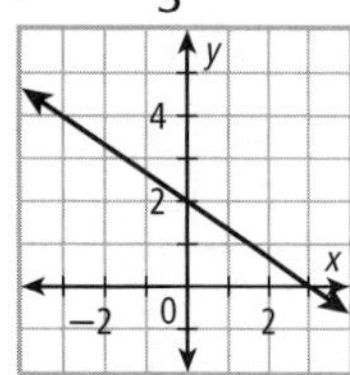

25. $y = -2x + 8$

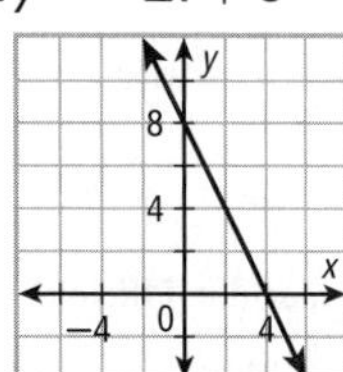

27a.

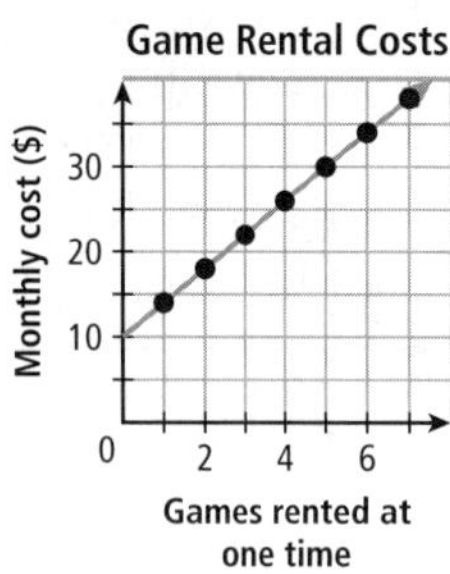

5-8 *Exercises*

59.

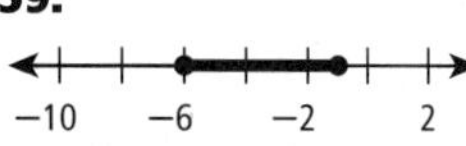

60.

−3 −2 −1 0 1 2 3

61.

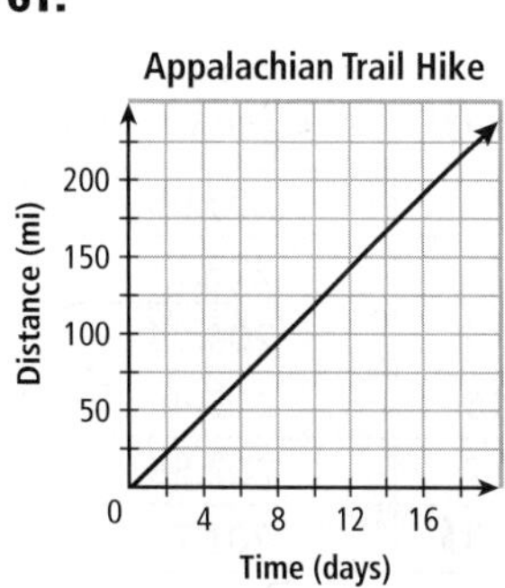

Possible answer: 216 mi

5-9 *Exercises*

55. If the line containing *A* and *B* has the same slope as the line containing *B* and *C*, then either $\overleftrightarrow{AB}$ is par. to $\overleftrightarrow{BC}$ or they are the same line. They cannot be par. because they both contain *B*. Therefore they must be the same line.

60.

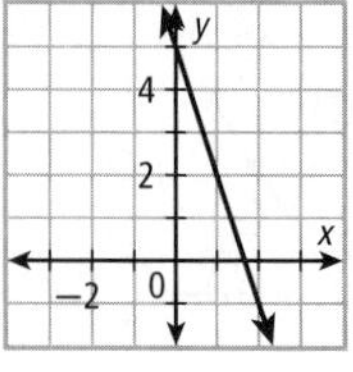

61.

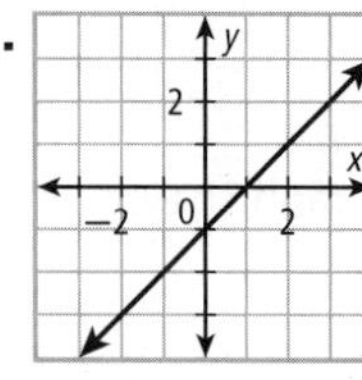

62.

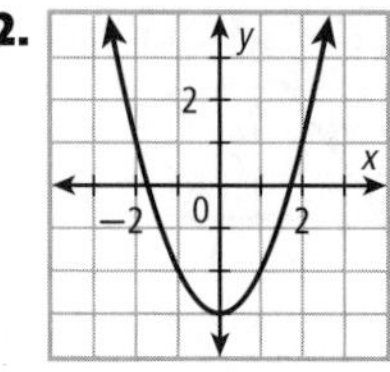

5-10 *Exercises*

9.

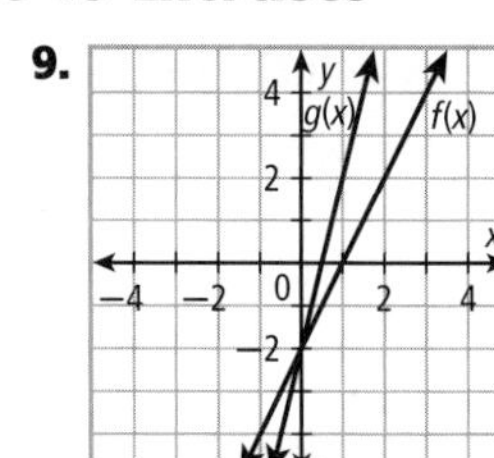

rot. about (0, −2) (steeper)

10.

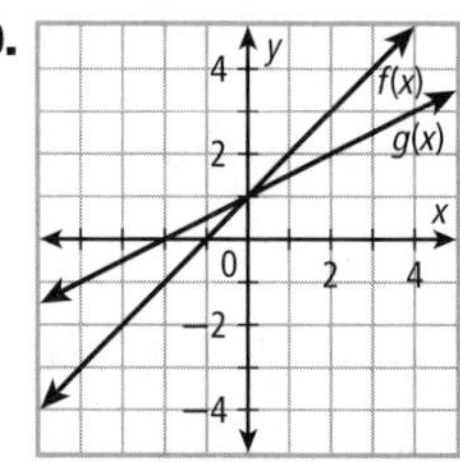

rot. about (0, 1) (less steep)

11.

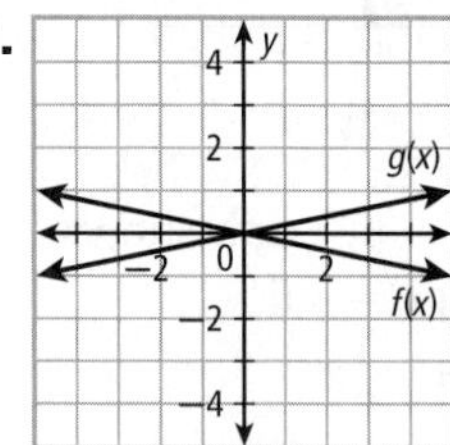

12.

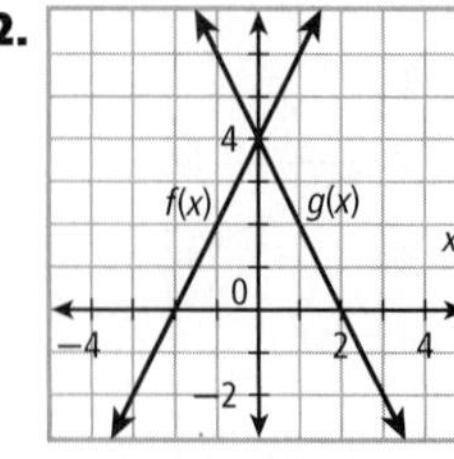

13.

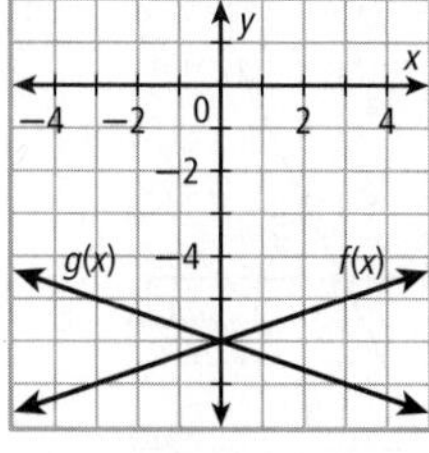

14.

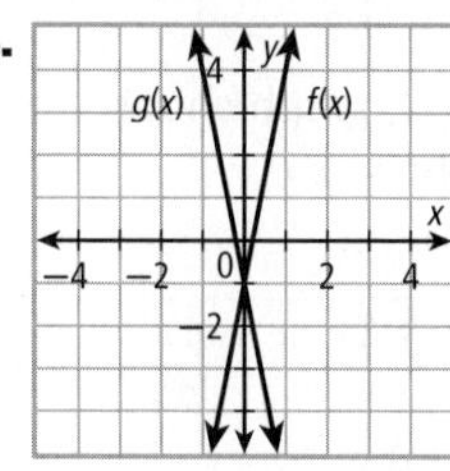

15.

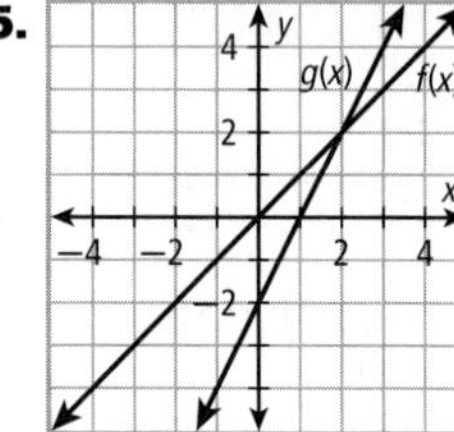

rot. about (0, 0) (steeper) and trans. 2 units down

16.

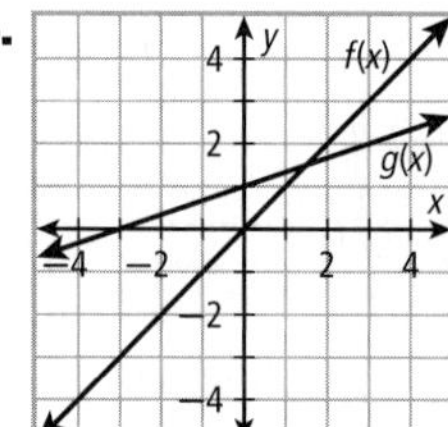

rot. about (0, 0) (less steep) and trans. 1 unit up

17.

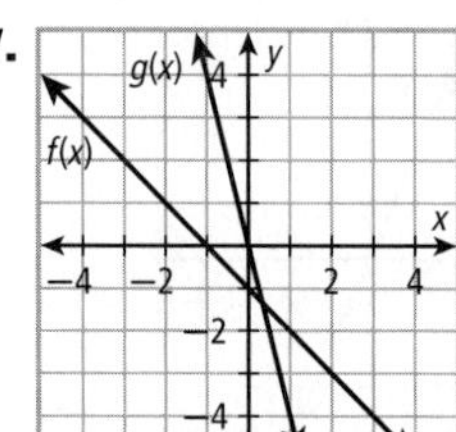

rot. about (0, 0) (steeper) and trans. 1 unit up

18.

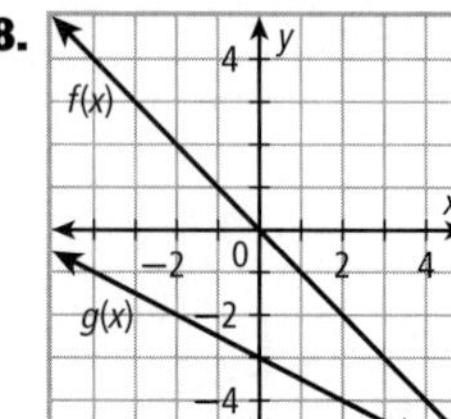

rot. about (0, 0) (less steep) and trans. 3 units down

19. translated 25 units up; rotated about (0, 25) (less steep)

20. 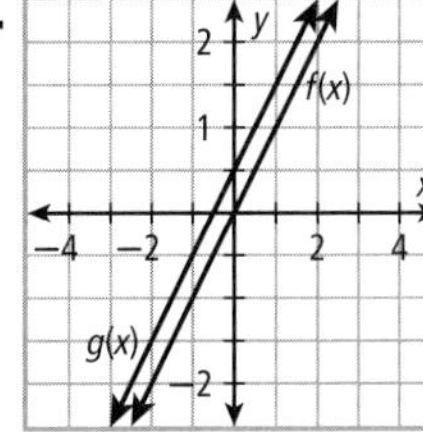

trans. $\frac{1}{2}$ unit up

21. 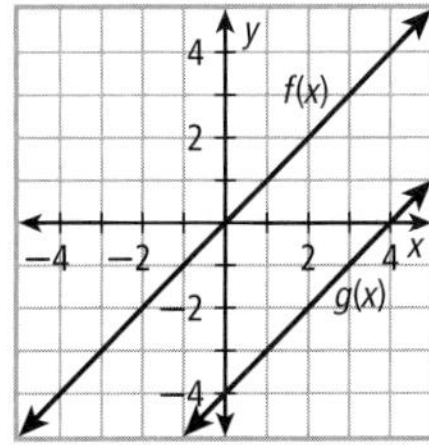

trans. 4 units down

22. 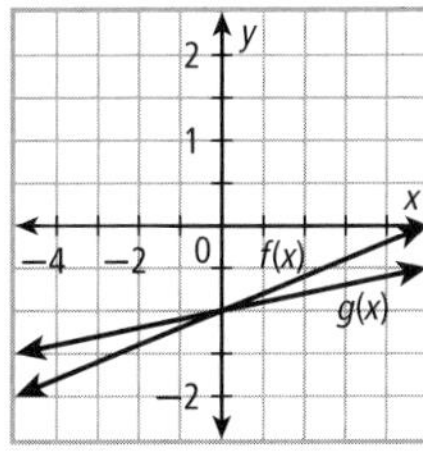

rot. about (0, −1) (less steep)

23. 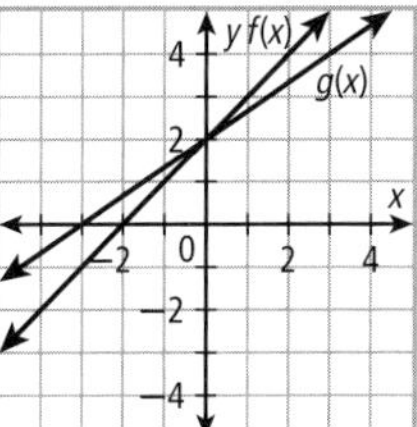

rot. about (0, 2) (less steep)

24. 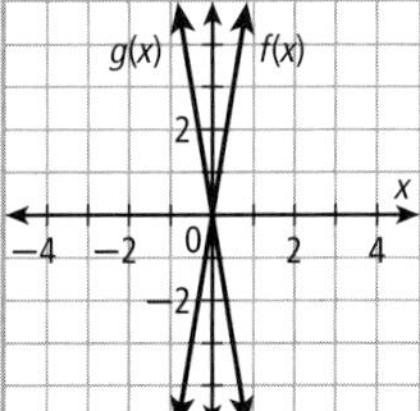

25. 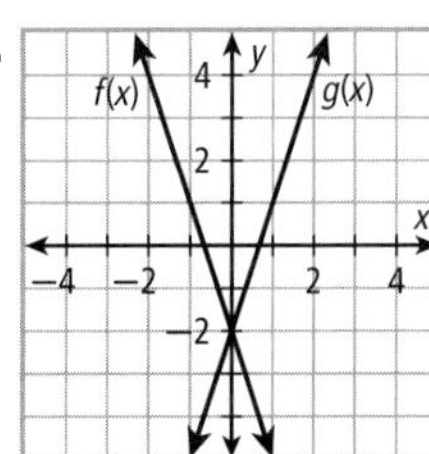

26. 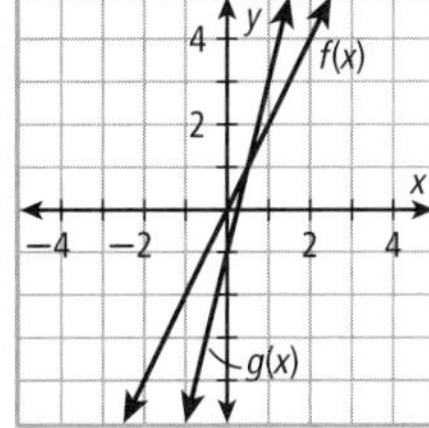

rot. about (0, 0) (steeper) and trans. 1 unit down

27. 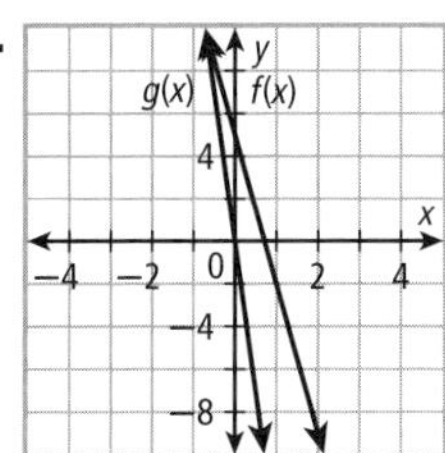

rot. about (0, 0) (steeper) and trans. 5 units down

32. rot. about (0, 0) (less steep)

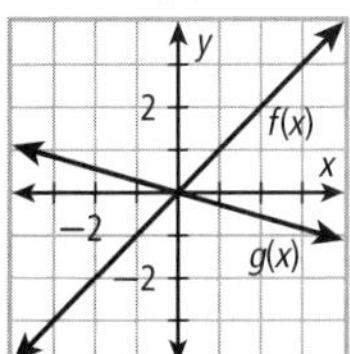

diff. slopes; same *y*-int.

33. rot. about (0, 0) (steeper) and trans. 3 units down

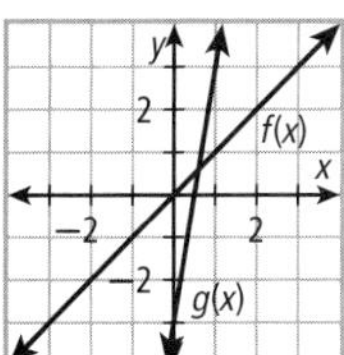

diff. slopes, diff. *y*-intercepts.

34. rot. about (0, 0) (steeper) and trans. 1 unit up

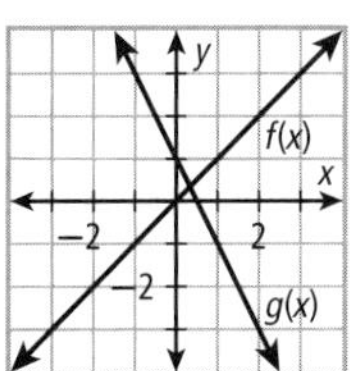

diff. slopes, diff. *y*-intercepts.

35. Possible answer:

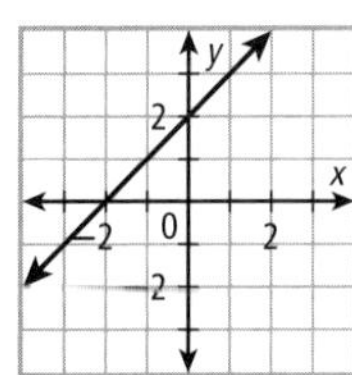

(Answers may vary depending on the point of rotation used.)

36. 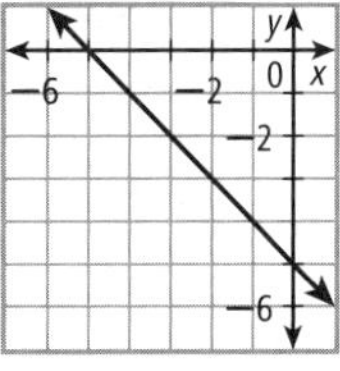

37. 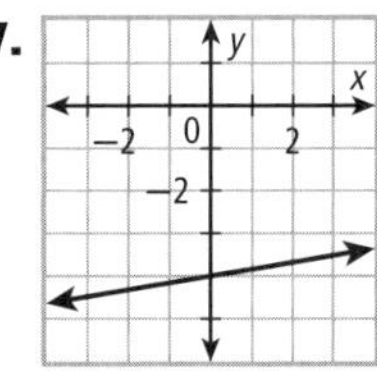

38a. 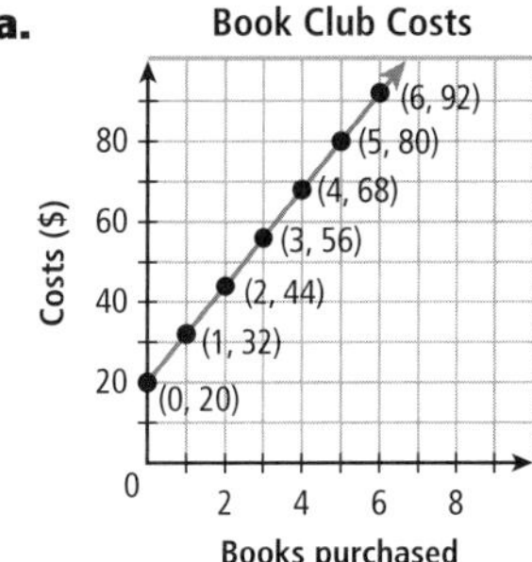

38b. 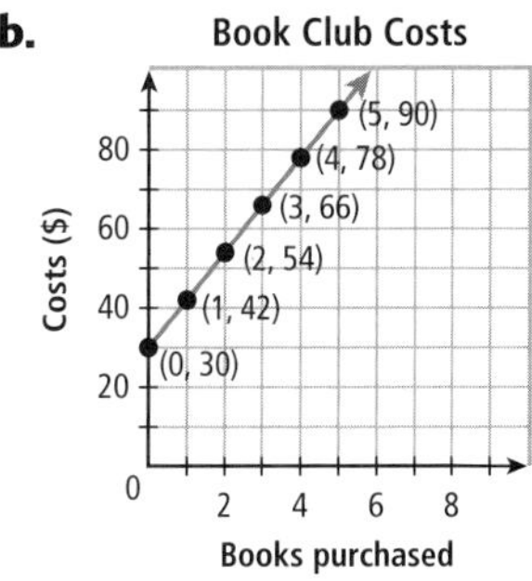

c. The graph in part **a** is translated 10 units up to get the graph in part **b.**

39. trans. 9 units down

40. ref. across *y*-axis; rot. about (0, 0)

41. rot. about (0, 0) (steeper)

42. rot. about (0, 1) (less steep), and trans. 1 unit up

43. rot. about (0, 0) (steeper)

44. rot. about (0, 0) (less steep)

47. Possible answer: A reflection across the *y*-axis multiplies the *x*-coordinate of each ordered pair by −1. For example, when $f(x) = x$ is reflected across the *y*-axis, the *x*-coordinate changes to $-x$. (i.e., $(1, 0) \to (-1, 0)$)

48a. $y = 3x$

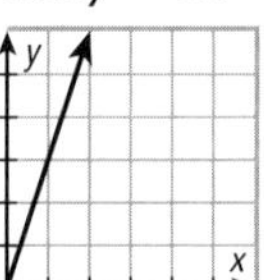

b. Possible answer: Jen is walking from the stadium to the softball field, and the stadium is 100 ft closer to the field than the school is.

c. the dist. from the school when the walk begins

51. 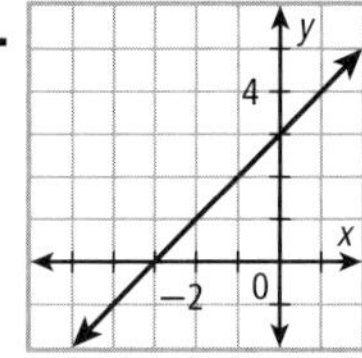

58. $y = -2x + 3$ and $y = -2x - 4$

59. $y = -\frac{3}{5}x$ and $y + 1 = -\frac{3}{5}(x - 2)$

60. $3x - 5y = 5$ and $5x + 3y = -21$; $5y = -2x - 15$ and $y = \frac{5}{2}x - 2$

61. $x = 4$ and $y = -3$; $2y + x = 6$ and $y = 2x + 3$

5B *Ready to Go On?*

1. 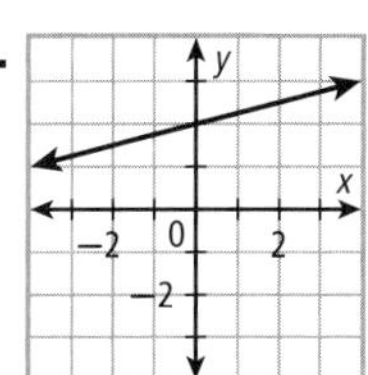

2. 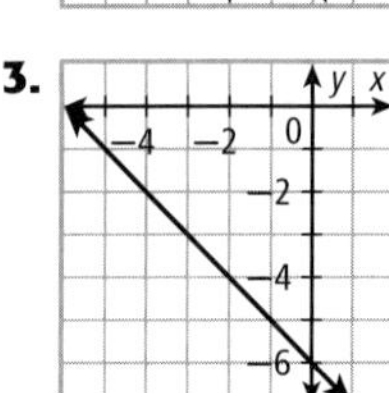

3.

Additional Answers

4.

5.

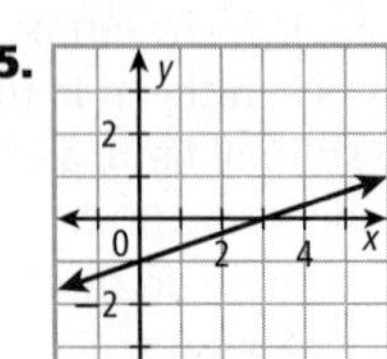

6.

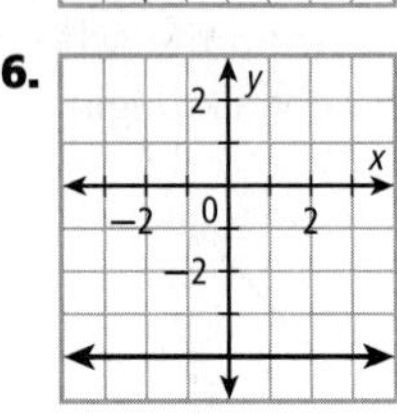

8.

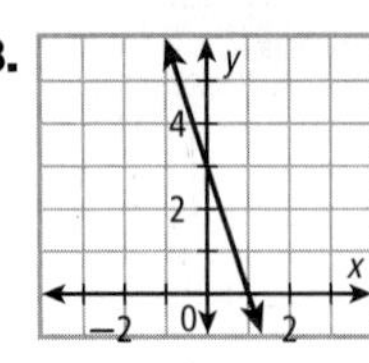

9.

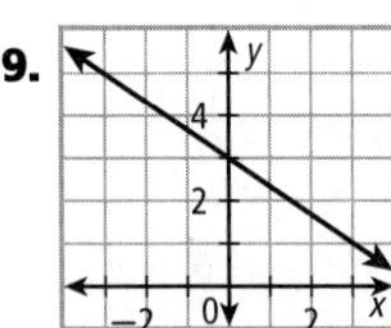

10.

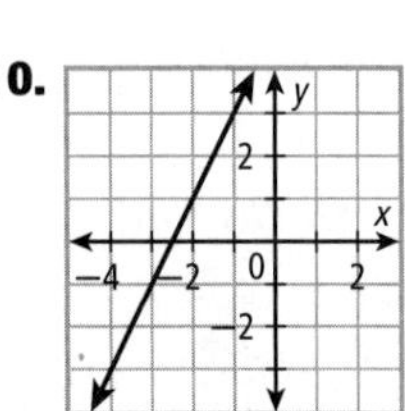

16. $y = -4x - 1$ and $y = \frac{1}{4}x$

17. $y = -\frac{3}{4}x$ and $y = \frac{4}{3}x$; $y = 4$ and $x = 3$

20.

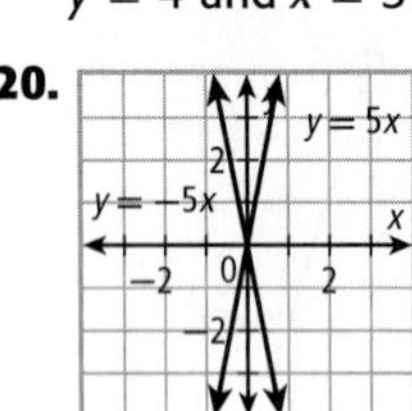

21.

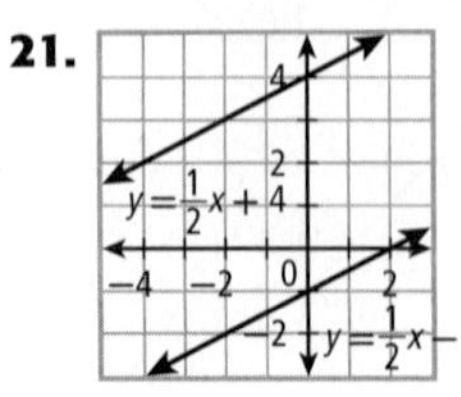

Extension *Exercises*

2. axis of symmetry: $x = -3$; vertex: $(-3, 0)$; x-int.: -3; y-int.: 3; D: all real numbers; R: $y \geq 0$; left slope: -1; right slope: 1; minimum: 0

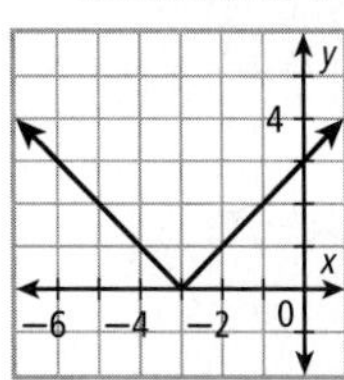

3. axis of symmetry: $x = 0$; vertex: $(0, 0)$; x-int.: 0; y-int.: 0; D: all real numbers; R: $y \geq 0$; left slope: $-\frac{1}{2}$; right slope: $\frac{1}{2}$; minimum: 0

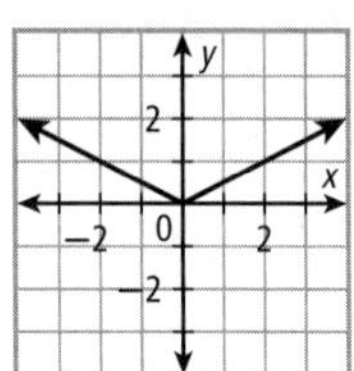

4. axis of symmetry: $x = 3$; vertex: $(3, 0)$; x-int.: 3; y-int.: 3; D: all real numbers; R: $y \geq 0$; left slope: -1; right slope: 1; minimum: 0

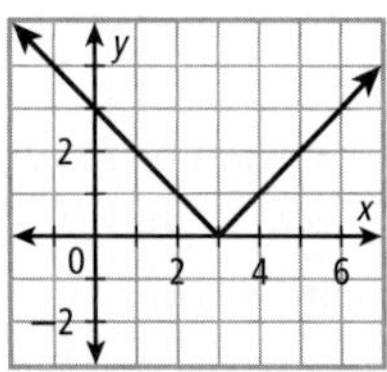

Chapter 5 Test

18. rot. about (0, 0) (less steep)

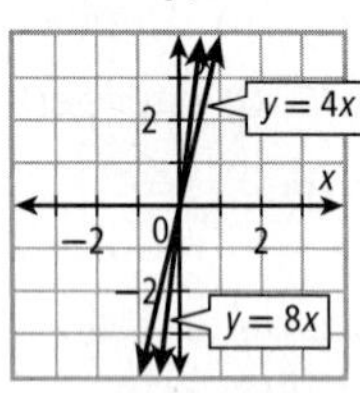

19. trans. 3 units down

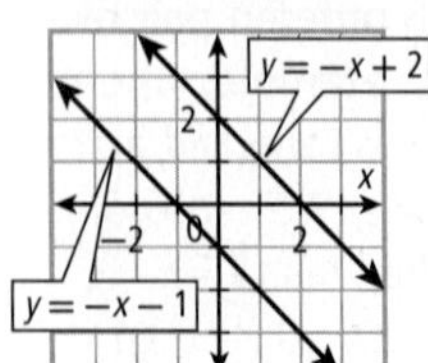

20. rot. about (0, 0) (steeper) and trans. 1 unit down

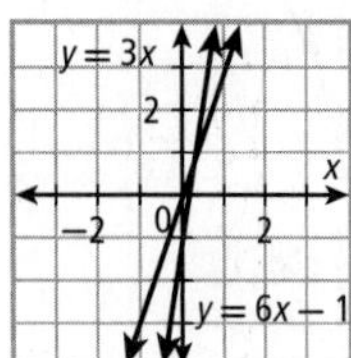

Chapter 6

Are You Ready?

6.

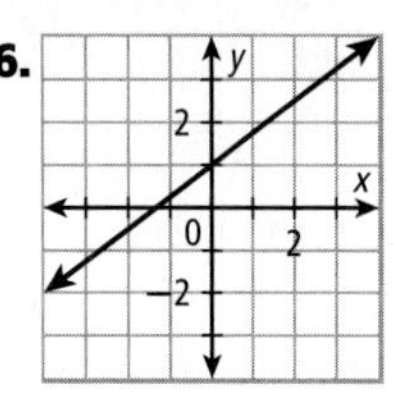

7.

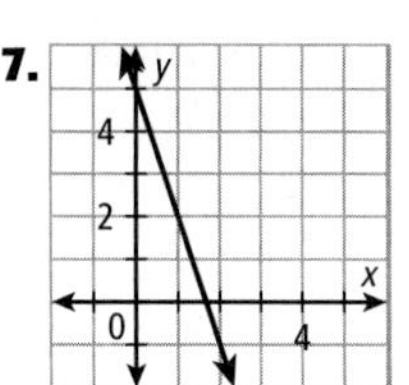

8.

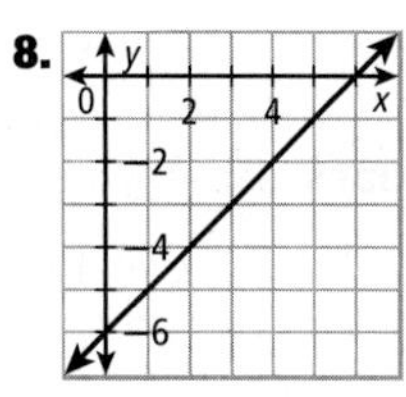

9.

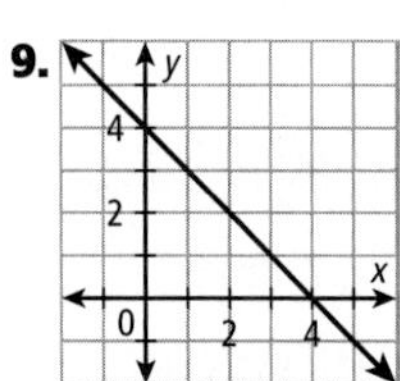

10.

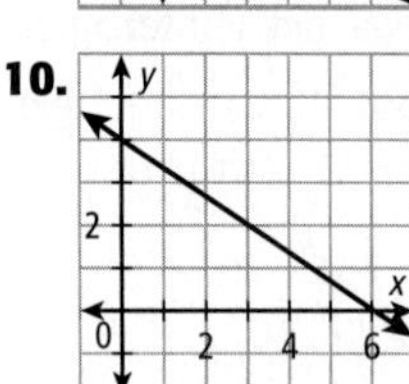

11.

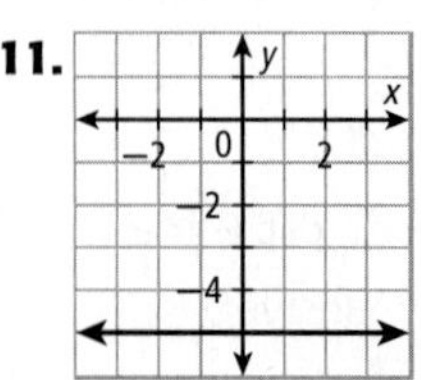

30.

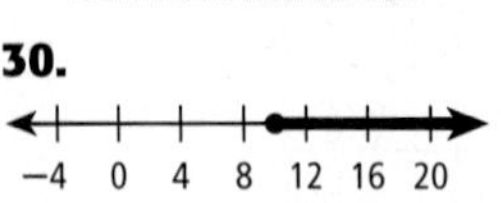

31.

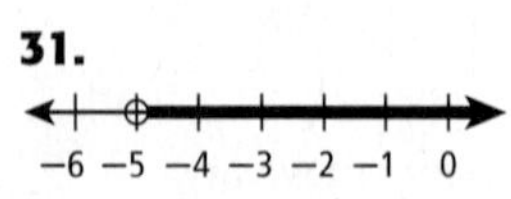

32.

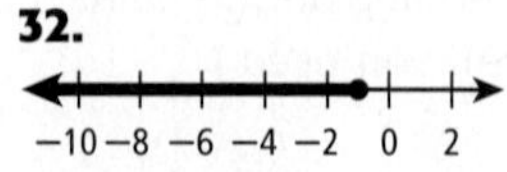

33.

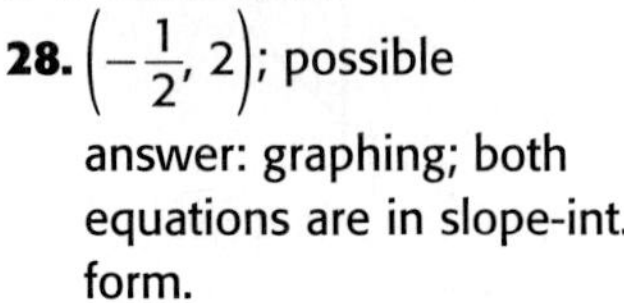

6-1 *Exercises*

18b.

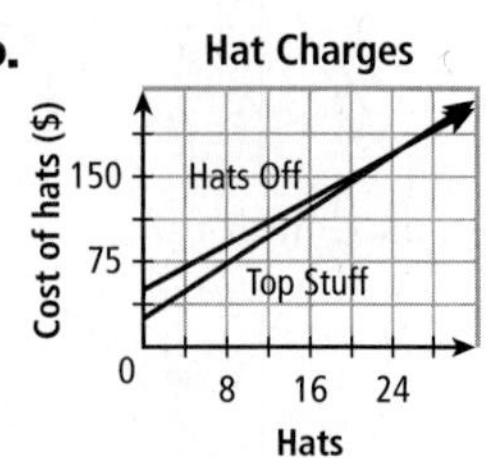

6-3 *Exercises*

28. $\left(-\frac{1}{2}, 2\right)$; possible answer: graphing; both equations are in slope-int. form.

29. $\left(\frac{15}{7}, \frac{9}{7}\right)$; possible answer: elimination; when the first equation is multiplied by -2 the x-coefficients are opposites.

6-4 *Exercises*

12. Possible answer: Substitute $2x - 2$ for y in the second equation.

$-2x + (2x - 2) = 1$
$-2 = 1$ ✗

13. Possible answer: Substitute $-x - 1$ for y in the first equation.

$x + (-x - 1) = 3$
$-1 = 3$ ✗

14. Possible answer: Substitute $-\frac{1}{2}x - 4$ for y in the first equation.

$x + 2\left(-\frac{1}{2}x - 4\right) = -4$
$x + (-x) - 8 = -4$
$-8 = -4$ ✗

15. Possible answer: Compare slopes and intercepts.

$-6 + y = 2x \rightarrow y = 2x - 6$
$y = 2x - 36$

The lines have the same slope and different y-intercepts. Therefore the lines are parallel.

16. Possible answer: Substitute $-2x + 3$ for y in the second equation.

$2x + (-2x + 3) - 3 = 0$
$0 = 0$ ✓

17. Possible answer: Substitute $x - 2$ for y in the second equation.

$x - (x - 2) - 2 = 0$

$2 - 2 = 0$

$0 = 0$ ✓

18. Possible answer: Substitute $-x - 4$ for y in the first equation.

$x + (-x - 4) = -4$

$-4 = -4$ ✓

19. Possible answer: Compare slopes and intercepts.

$-9x - 3y = -18 \rightarrow y = -3x + 6$

$3x + y = 6 \rightarrow y = -3x + 6$

The lines have the same slope and the same y-intercept. Therefore the graphs are one line.

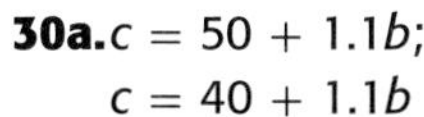

30a. $c = 50 + 1.1b$; $c = 40 + 1.1b$

b. Never; the slope, or cost of the buttons, is the same, and the initial costs, or y-intercepts, are different.

c. For the same price, the y-intercept would have to be changed to 40. Possible answers: The y-intercept may be lowered to a value less than 40, or the slope may be changed to a value less than 1.1.

6-5 *Exercises*

5.

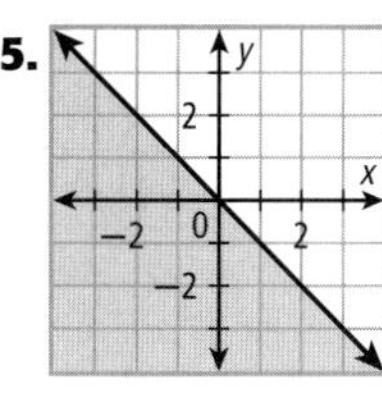

6.

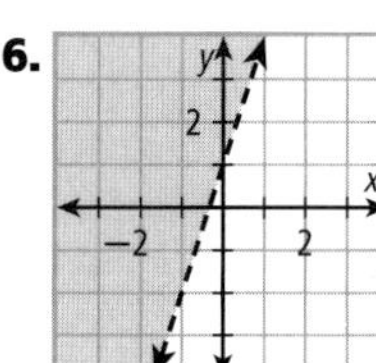

7.

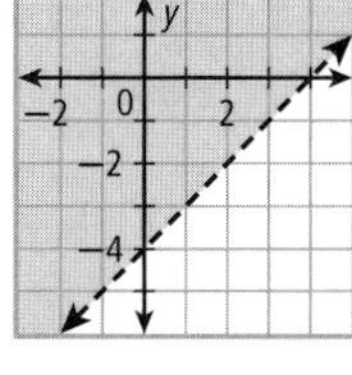

8.

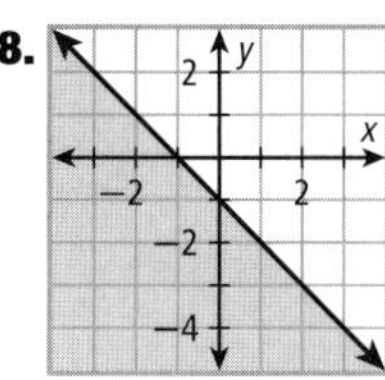

15.

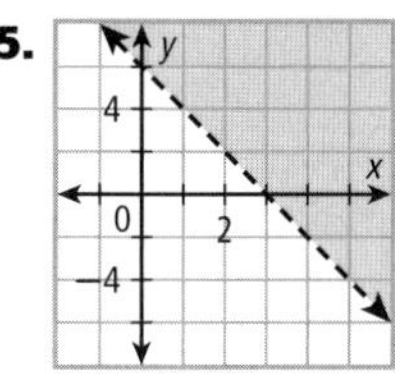

16.

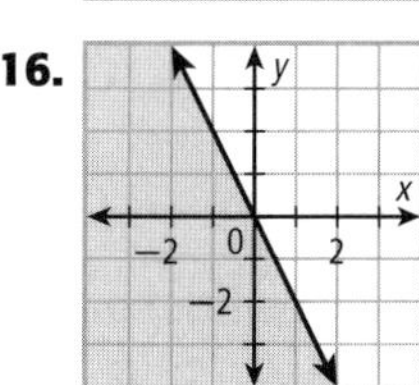

17.

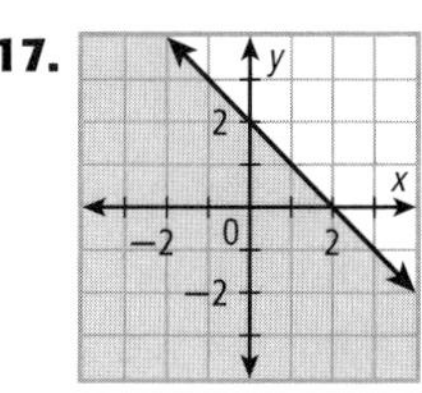

18.

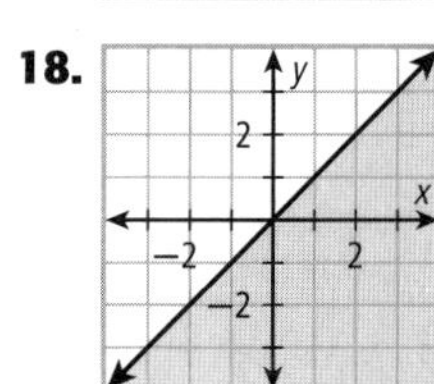

19a. $3x + 2y \leq 30$

b. Food Combinations

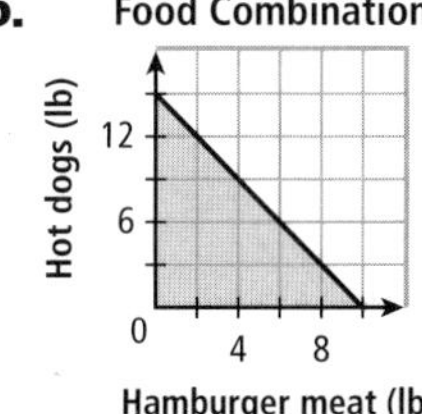

c. Possible answer: (3 lb hamburger, 2 lb hot dogs), (5 lb hamburger, 6 lb hot dogs)

27b. Possible answer: (length: 3 yd, width: 1 yd), (length: 1 yd, width: 6 yd), (length: 6 yd, width: 2 yd)

Rectangular Garden

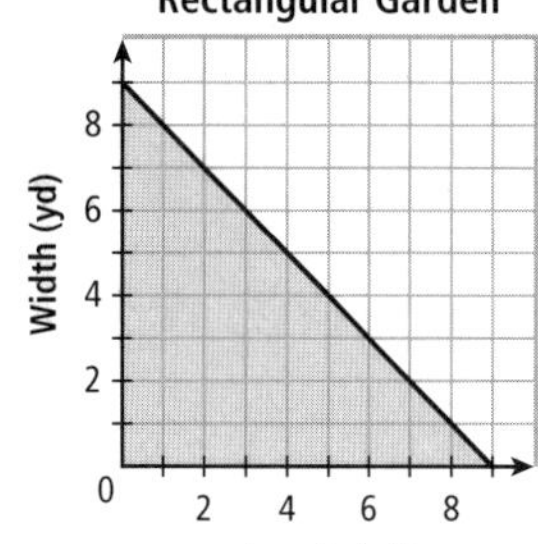

28. $15x + 11y \leq 77$; possible answer: (2, 2.5); you cannot buy half a fish.

Fish Combinations

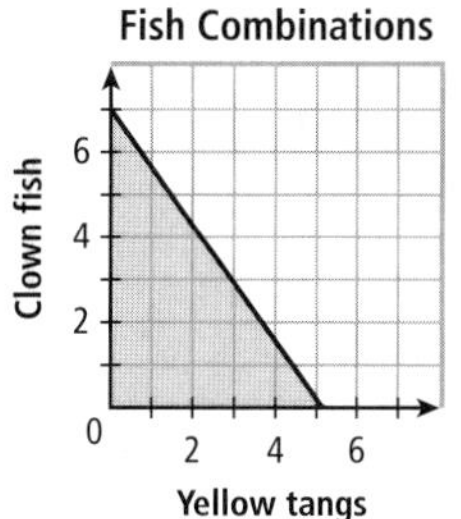

29.

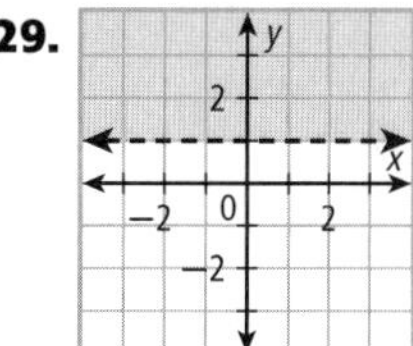

30.

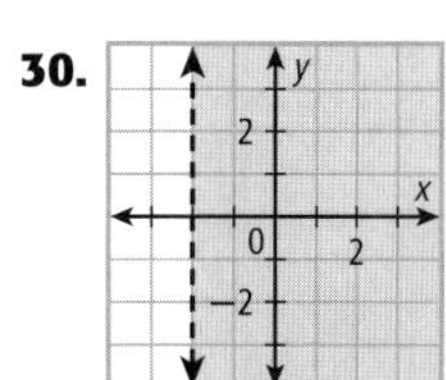

31.

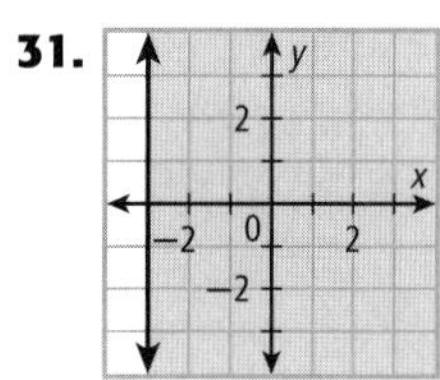

32.

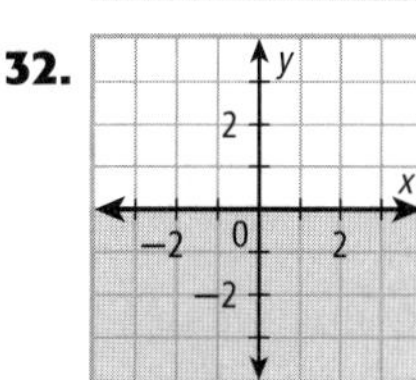

33.

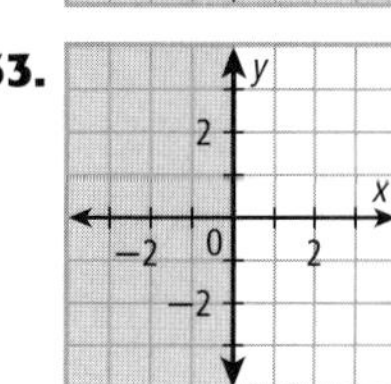

34.

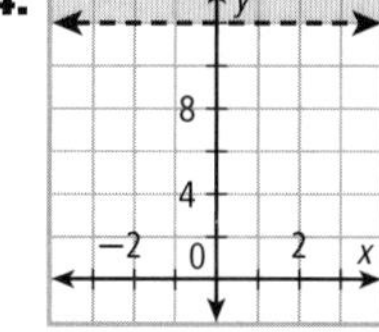

35.

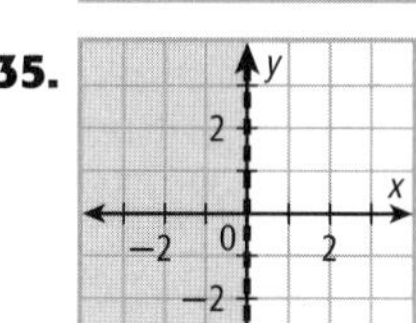

36.

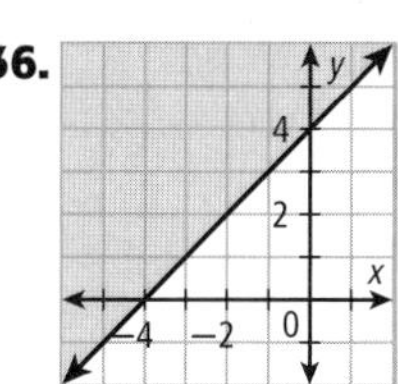

37. $7a + 4s \geq 280$; possible answer: (40, 10), (40, 20), (20, 100)

Tickets Sold

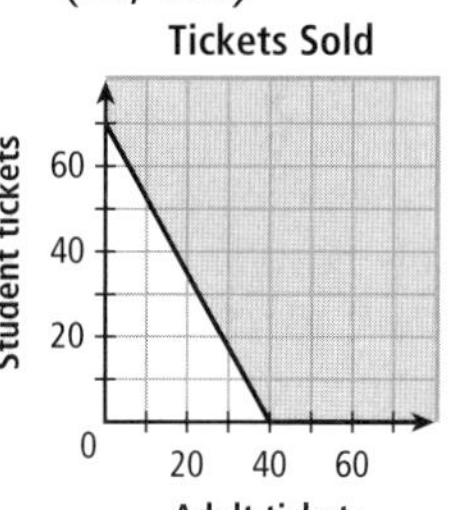

40b.

Teddy Bear Combinations

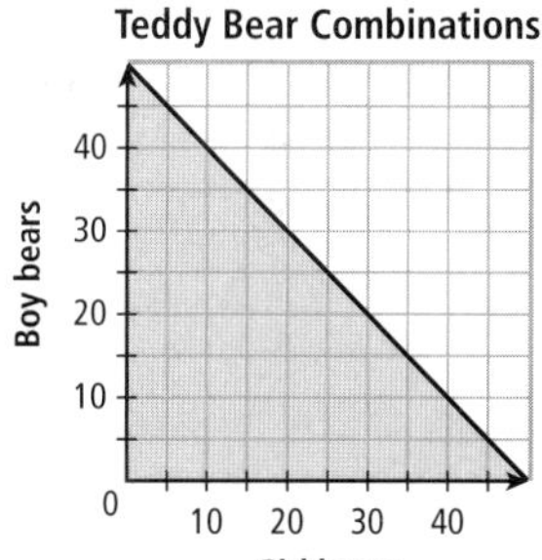

6-6 *Exercises*

5.

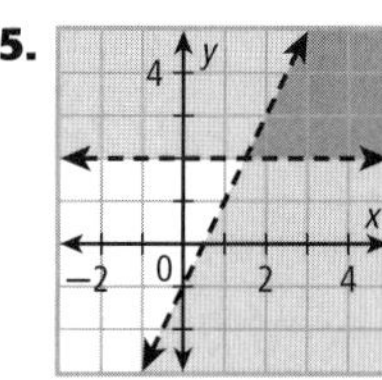

Possible answer: solutions: (3, 3), (4, 3); not solutions: (0, 0), (2, 1)

6. 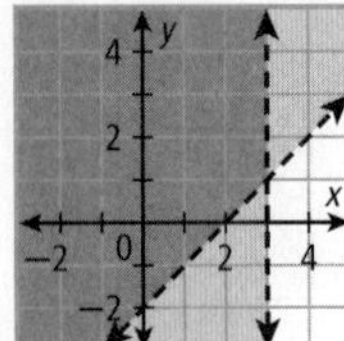

Possible answer: solutions: (0, 0), (1, 1); not solutions: (2, −1), (3, 1)

7. 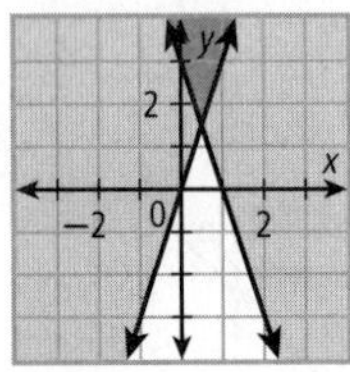

Possible answer: solutions: (0, 4), (1, 4); not solutions: (2, −1), (3, 1)

8. 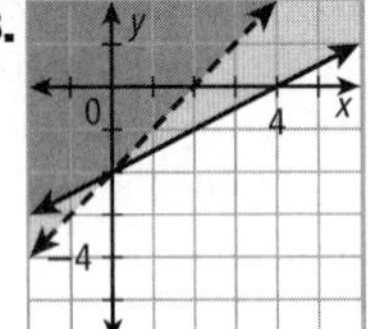

Possible answer: solutions: (0, 0), (1, 1); not solutions: (3, 0), (−3, −4)

9. 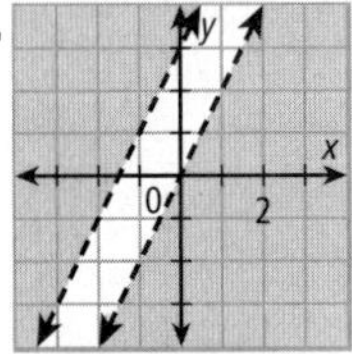

no solutions

10. 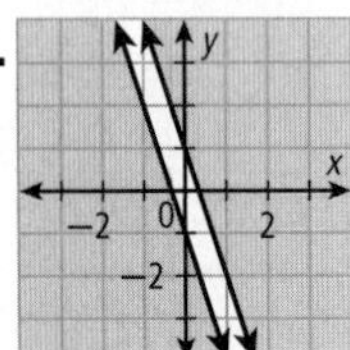

no solutions

11. 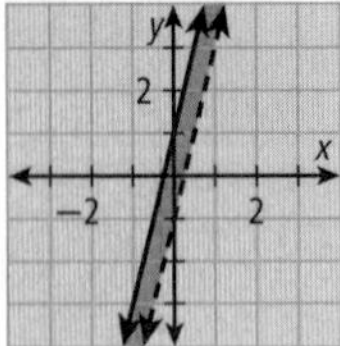

all pts. between the par. lines and on the solid line

12. 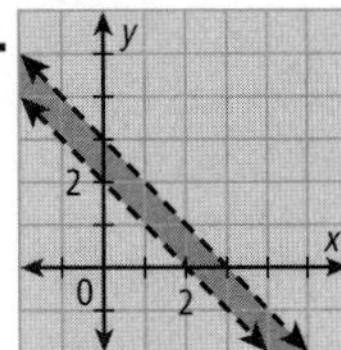

all pts. between the par. lines

13. 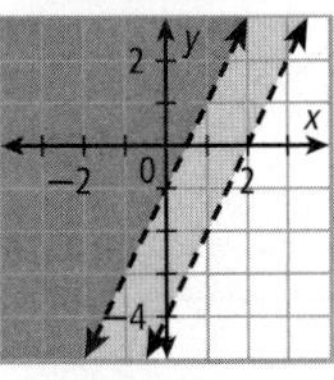

same solutions as $y > 2x - 1$

14. 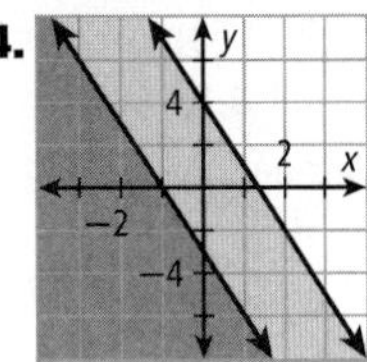

same solutions as $y \leq -3x - 3$

19. 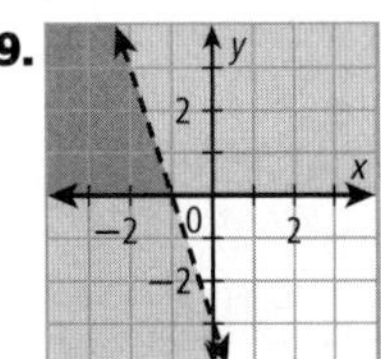

Possible answer: solutions: (−2, 0), (−3, 1); not solutions: (0, 0), (1, 4)

20. 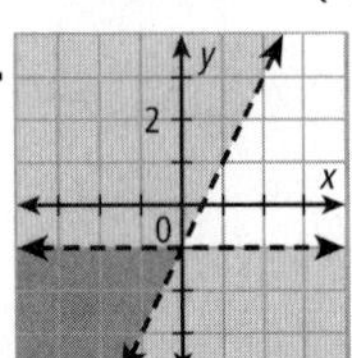

Possible answer: solutions: (−2, −2), (−3, −2); not solutions: (0, 0), (1, −4)

21. 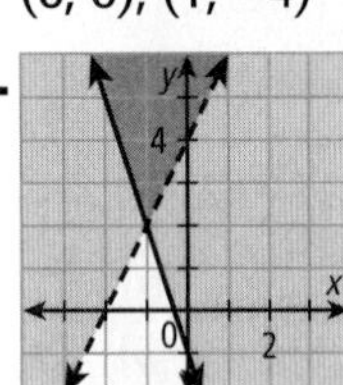

Possible answer: solutions: (−1, 3), (0, 5); not solutions: (0, 0), (1, 4)

22. 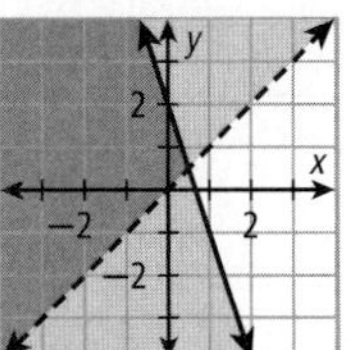

Possible answer: solutions: (−2, 0), (−3, 1); not solutions: (0, 0), (1, 4)

23. 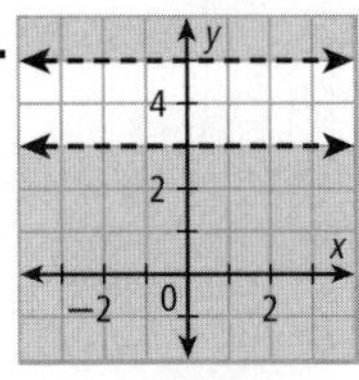

no solutions

24. 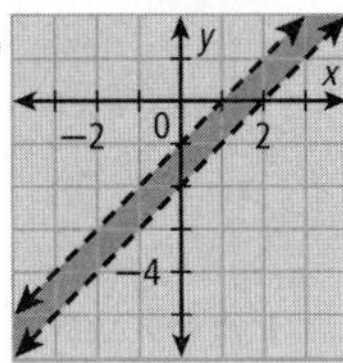

all pts. between the par. lines

25. 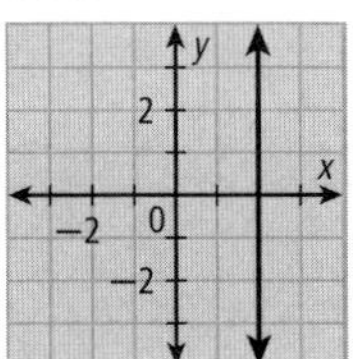

All pts. are solutions.

26. 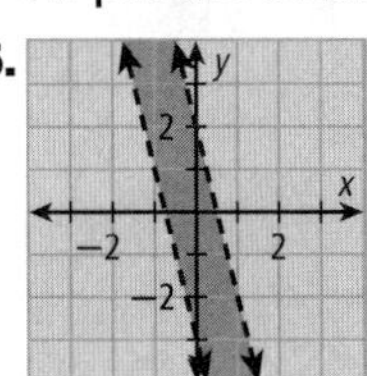

all pts. between the par. lines

27. 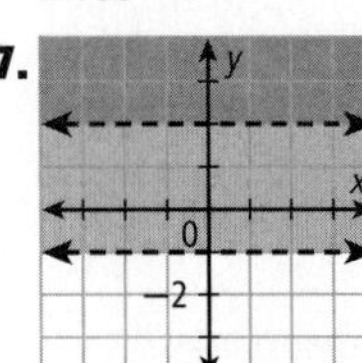

same solutions as $y > 2$

28. 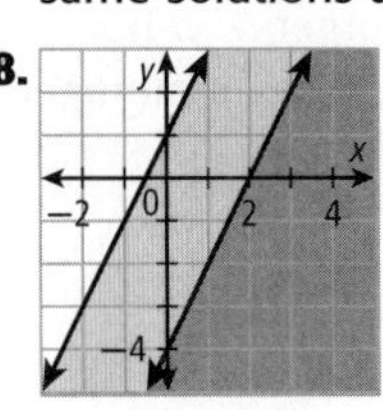

same solutions as $y \leq 2x - 4$

30. 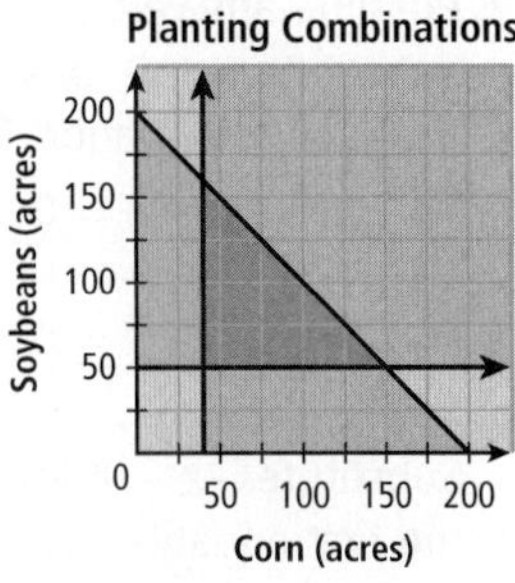

Reasonable solutions are positive rational numbers; possible answer: (60, 80), (100, 60)

31. 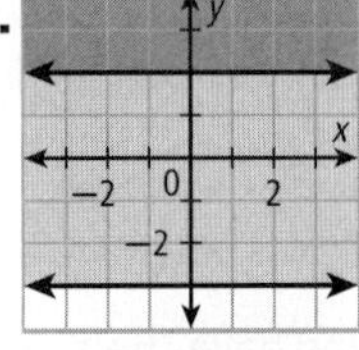

32. 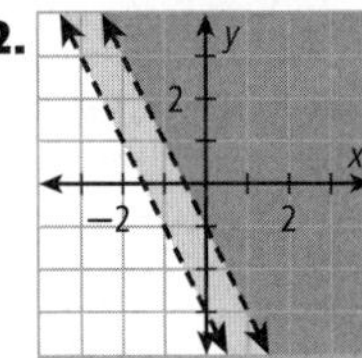

33. 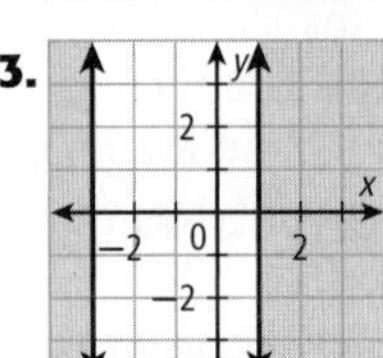

34. 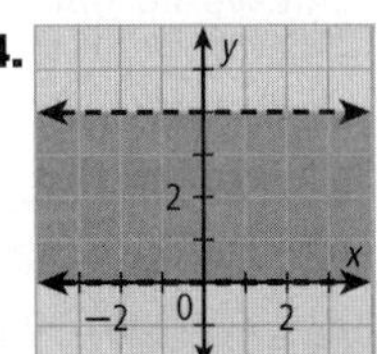

38. 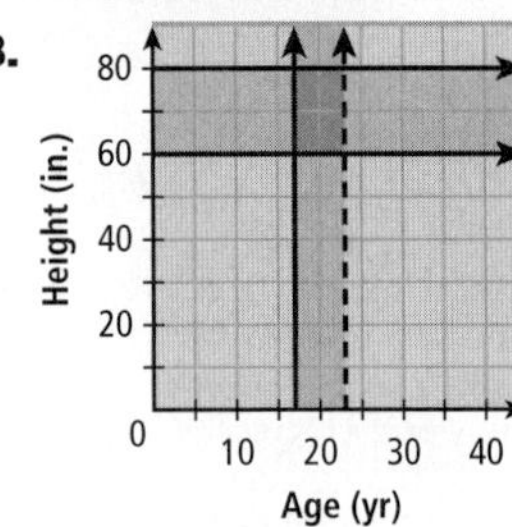

Possible answer: (20, 70), (19, 75), (18, 69)

40. 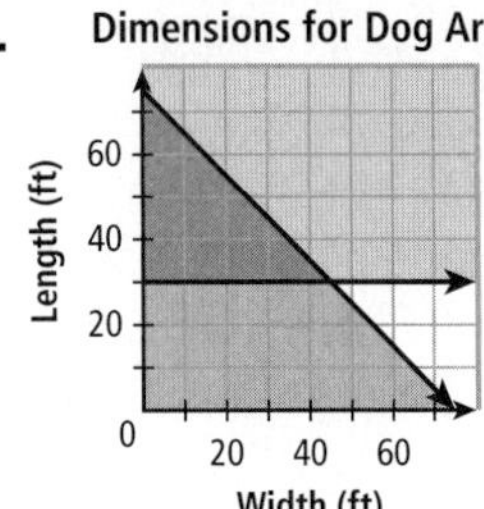

41. Yes; the solutions of the system $\begin{cases} y \geq x + 4 \\ y \leq x + 4 \end{cases}$ are represented by all the ordered pairs on the line $y = x + 4$.

42a. $x + y \leq 40$

b. $15x + 12y \geq 540$

c. Teddy Bear Combinations

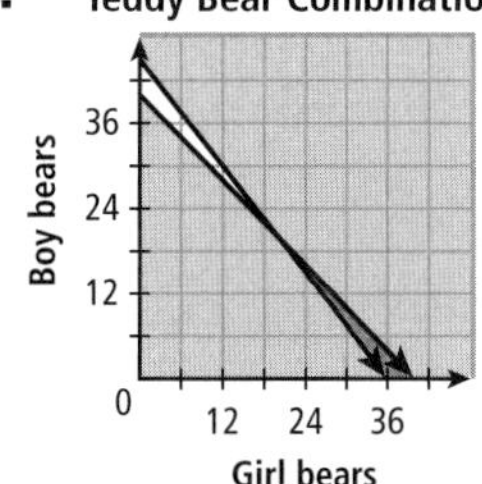

6-6 *Technology Lab*

1–3. Possible answers given.

1. (0, 0), (1, −1)

2. (0, 0), (1, 0)

3. (0, 0), (−2, 2)

4. no solution

6B *Multi-Step Test Prep*

2. Teddy Bear Combinations

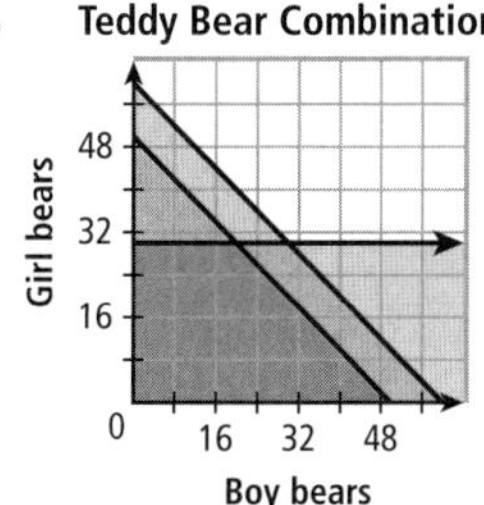

6B *Ready to Go On?*

4.

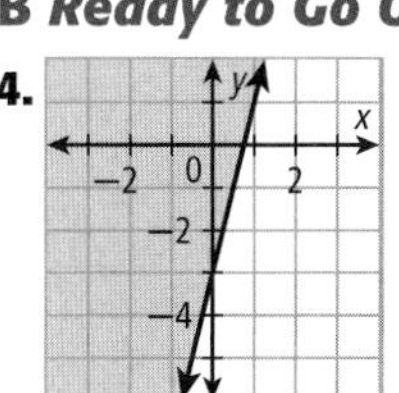

5.

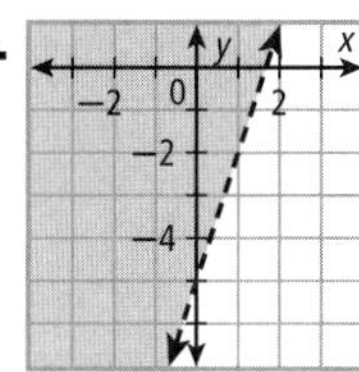

6.

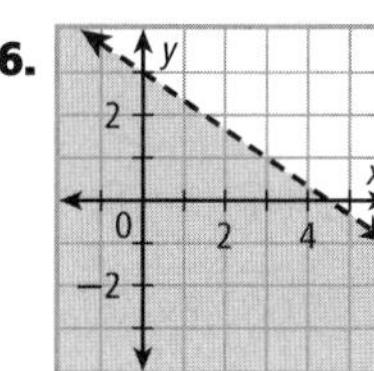

7.

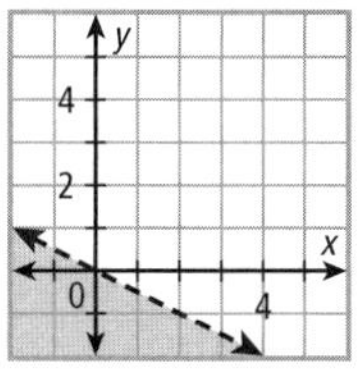

8. $30x + 15y \leq 150$

Possible Clothing Combinations

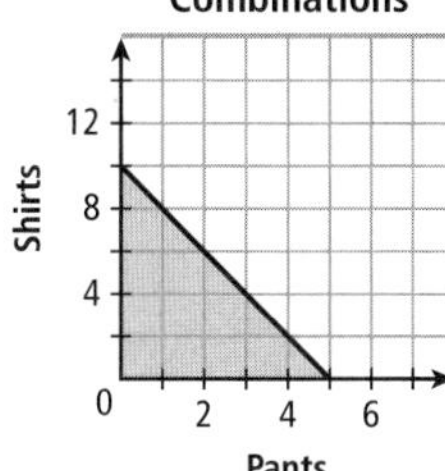

Possible answer: (4, 2), (3, 2), (2, 6)

15. Possible answer: solutions: (0, 0), (2, 2); not solutions: (−6, 0), (−4, 4)

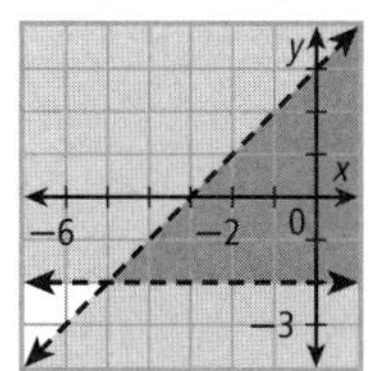

16. Possible answer: solutions: (2, 0), (2, −2); not solutions: (6, 0), (−4, 0)

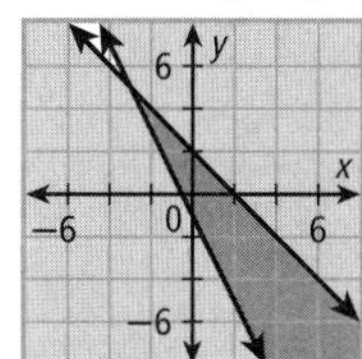

17. Possible answer: solutions: (−6, 6), (−5, 0); not solutions: (2, 0), (4, 8)

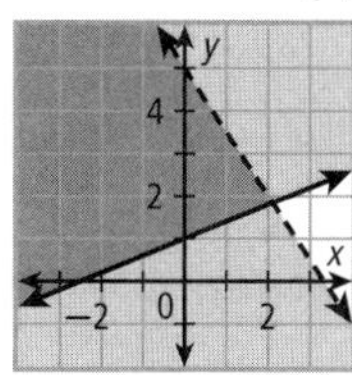

21. Let x = pounds of mangos, and y = pounds of apples.

$\begin{cases} x \leq 45 \\ y \leq 50 \\ 4x + 3y \geq 300 \end{cases}$;

possible answer: (45, 40), (42, 50)

Fruit Combinations

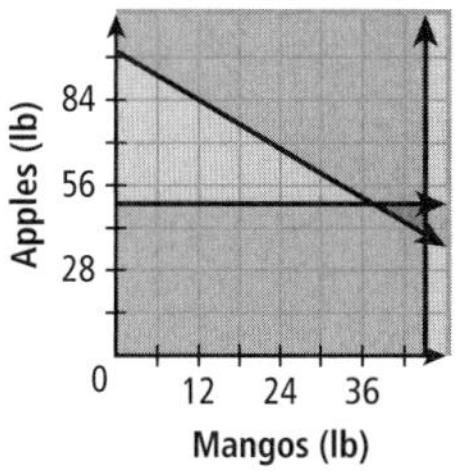

Chapter 7

7-2 *Exercises*

55.

56.

57.

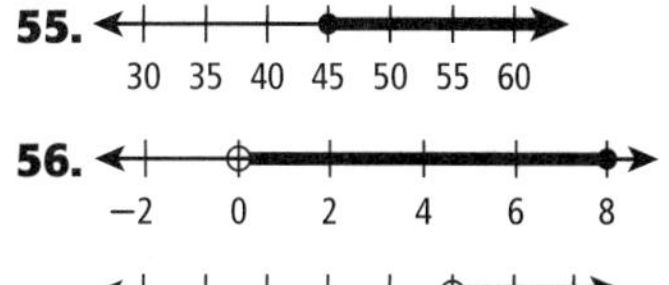

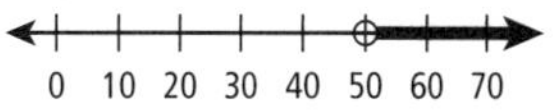

7-7 *Exercises*

66.

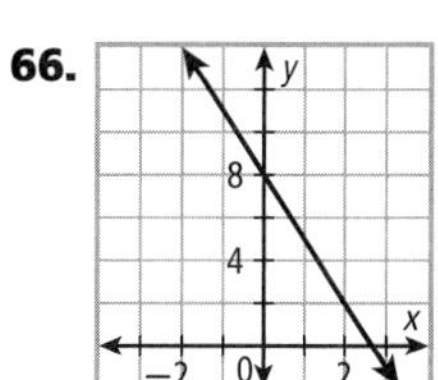

67.

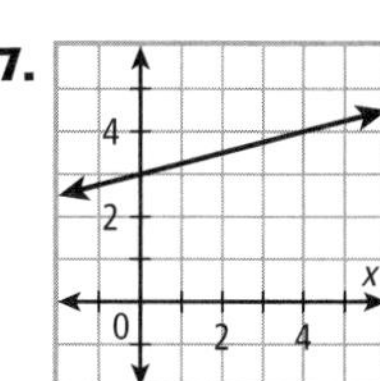

68.

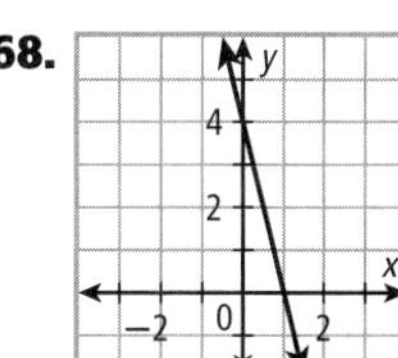

7-8 *Exercises*

49. $10x^2 - x - 2$

50. $x^2 - 3x + 2$

51. $7x^2 - 52x - 32$

52. $6x^2 + 35x + 49$

53. $x^3 - x^2 - x + 10$

54. $2x^3 - 3x^2 - 14x + 15$

55. $-10x^4 + 2x^3 + 20x^2 - 19x + 3$

56. $x^3 - 8x^2 + 21x - 18$

57. $8x^5 - 2x^4 - 12x^3 + 17x^2 - 21$

58. $x^3 - 12x^2 + 48x - 64$

59. $x^3 - 3x - 2$

60. $12x^4 + 60x^3 - 2x^2 - 2x + 40$

61. $-x^3 + 3x^2 - 3x + 1$

102.

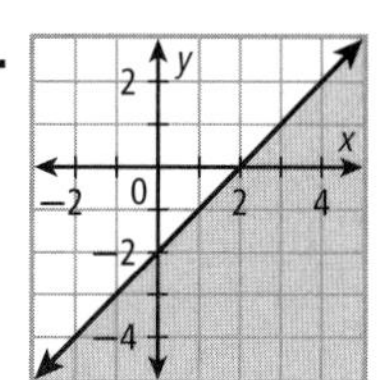

103.

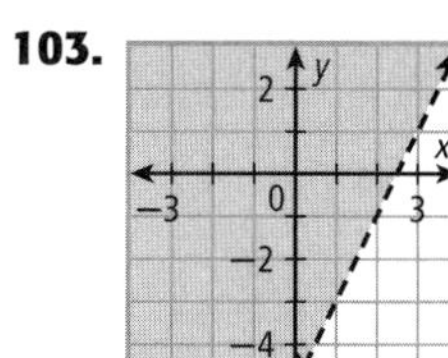

104.

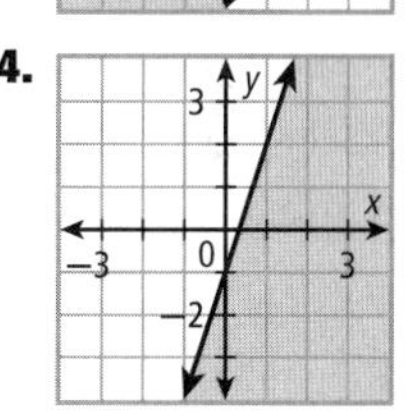

7B *Ready To Go On?*

7. cubic trinomial

8. quadratic monomial

9. quartic polynomial

10. quadratic trinomial

11. 7th-degree polynomial

12. quartic polynomial

14. $10m^3 + 11m^2 + 3m$

15. $12t^2 + 2t - 6$

16. $12d^6 + 2d^4 - 3d^2 + 1$

17. $6y^3 + 2y^2 - 3y$

18. $2n^2 - 8n$

19. $5b^3 + b^2 - 4b - 10$

21. $10h^8$

22. $-6s^9t^7$

23. $10a^4b + 6a^3b^2$

24. $9k^2 + 30k + 25$

25. $8x^5 + 2x^3y + 12x^2y + 3y^2$

26. $9p^4 + 21p^3 - 23p^2 - 15p$

28. $d^2 + 18d + 81$

29. $4t^2 + 12t + 9$

30. $4x^2 + 20xy + 25y^2$

31. $m^2 - 8m + 16$

32. $a^2 - 2ab + b^2$

33. $9w^2 - 6w + 1$

34. $c^2 - 4$

35. $25r^2 - 36$

Chapter 8

8-3 *Exercises*

16.

n	$n^2 + 6n - 7$	$(n+7)(n-1)$
0	$0^2 + 6(0) - 7 = -7$	$(0 + 7)(0 - 1) = -7$
1	$1^2 + 6(1) - 7 = 0$	$(1 + 7)(1 - 1) = 0$
2	$2^2 + 6(2) - 7 = 9$	$(2 + 7)(2 - 1) = 9$
3	$3^2 + 6(3) - 7 = 20$	$(3 + 7)(3 - 1) = 20$
4	$4^2 + 6(4) - 7 = 33$	$(4 + 7)(4 - 1) = 33$

22. $(x + 3)(x + 12)$

23. $(x - 1)(x - 5)$

24. $(x - 3)(x - 6)$

25. $(x - 4)(x - 8)$

26. $(x + 4)(x - 3)$

27. $(x + 7)(x - 3)$

28. $(x + 12)(x - 3)$

29. $(x - 13)(x + 1)$

30. $(x - 12)(x + 2)$

31. $(x - 7)(x + 5)$

32.

n	$n^2 - 12n - 45$	$(n - 15)(n + 3)$
0	$0^2 - 12(0) - 45 = -45$	$(0 - 15)(0 + 3) = -45$
1	$1^2 - 12(1) - 45 = -56$	$(1 - 15)(1 + 3) = -56$
2	$2^2 - 12(2) - 45 = -65$	$(2 - 15)(2 + 3) = -65$
3	$3^2 - 12(3) - 45 = -72$	$(3 - 15)(3 + 3) = -72$
4	$4^2 - 12(4) - 45 = -77$	$(4 - 15)(4 + 3) = -77$

38. $(x + 5)(x - 4)$

39. $(x - 2)(x - 9)$

40. $(x + 3)(x - 7)$

41. $(x + 1)(x + 9)$

42. $(x - 4)(x - 8)$

43. $(x + 6)(x + 7)$

44. $(x - 4)(x - 3)$

45. $(x + 2)(x + 9)$

46. $(x + 3)(x - 9)$

47. $(x - 3)(x + 8)$

48. $(x - 3)(x - 7)$

49. $(x - 5)(x + 9)$

50.

n	$n^2 + 11n + 28$	$(n + 4)(n + 7)$
0	$0^2 + 11(0) + 28 = 28$	$(0 + 4)(0 + 7) = 28$
1	$1^2 + 11(1) + 28 = 40$	$(1 + 4)(1 + 7) = 40$
2	$2^2 + 11(2) + 28 = 54$	$(2 + 4)(2 + 7) = 54$
3	$3^2 + 11(3) + 28 = 70$	$(3 + 4)(3 + 7) = 70$
4	$4^2 + 11(4) + 28 = 88$	$(4 + 4)(4 + 7) = 88$

8-4 *Exercises*

13. $(2a - 1)(2a + 5)$

14. $(3x - 1)(5x + 3)$

15. $(2x - 3)(x + 2)$

16. $(3n + 2)(2n - 5)$

17. $(10x + 1)(x - 1)$

18. $(x + 1)(7x - 10)$

19. $-1(2x + 3)(x - 4)$

20. $-1(2n - 1)(2n + 9)$

21. $-1(5x + 3)(x - 2)$

22. $-1(x - 2)(6x - 1)$

23. $-1(2x - 1)(2x + 5)$

24. $-1(5x + 9)(x - 2)$

25. $(3x + 2)(3x + 1)$

26. $(2x + 5)(x + 1)$

27. $(n + 2)(3n + 2)$

28. $(10d + 7)(d + 1)$

29. $(4c - 5)(c - 3)$

30. $2(3x + 1)(x + 2)$

31. $(2x + 5)(4x + 1)$

32. $(3x - 2)(2x - 3)$

33. $(5x - 6)(x + 3)$

34. $(2x + 7)(3x + 1)$

35. $(10n - 7)(n - 1)$

36. $(3x + 2)(x + 3)$

37. $(7x + 1)(x + 2)$

38. $(3n + 1)(n + 1)$

39. $(3x - 4)(x - 5)$

40. $(3x + 4)(2x + 1)$

41. $(x - 7)(4x - 3)$

42. $(5x + 3)\ (2x + 5)$

43. $(4y - 1)\ (3y + 5)$

44. $(3x - 2)(x + 4)$

45. $(2x - 1)(2x + 3)$

46. $(2n + 1)\ (n - 4)$

47. $(3x + 5)(x - 3)$

48. $(n + 1)(3n - 4)$

49. $-1(2x - 3)(2x + 5)$

50. $-1(x - 4)(3x - 4)$

51. $-1(3x - 2)(x + 1)$

52. $12x^2 + 27x + 6;\ 3(4x + 1)(x + 2)$

53. $2x^2 - 5x + 2;\ (x - 2)(2x - 1)$

54. $5x^2 + 31x - 28;\ (x + 7)(5x - 4)$

55. $(9n + 8)(n + 1)$

56. $(2x + 1)(x - 4)$

57. $(2x - 1)(2x - 5)$

58. unfactorable

59. $(3x + 8)(x + 2)$

60. $-1(3x - 1)(x + 4)$

61. $(3x + 4)(2x - 3)$

62. $(5a + 3)(2a + 1)$

63. $(2x - 3)(2x - 3)$

8-4 *Technology Lab*

5. $(x - 5)(x + 1)$

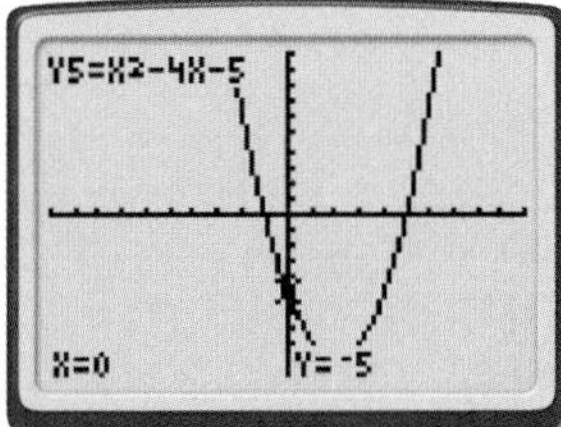

6. $(3x - 2)(x + 6)$

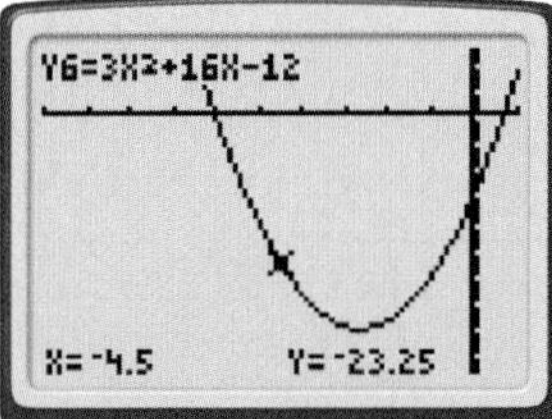

8A *Ready To Go On?*

21. $(n + 4)(n + 5)$

22. $(d - 7)(d + 1)$

23. $(x - 4)(x - 2)$

24. $(y + 10)(y - 3)$

25. $(k - 5)(k - 1)$

26. $(c - 4)(c - 6)$

27.

n	$n^2 + 3n - 4$	$(n + 4)(n - 1)$
0	$0^2 + 3(0) - 4 = -4$	$(0 + 4)(0 - 1) = -4$
1	$1^2 + 3(1) - 4 = 0$	$(1 + 4)(1 - 1) = 0$
2	$2^2 + 3(2) - 4 = 6$	$(2 + 4)(2 - 1) = 6$
3	$3^2 + 3(3) - 4 = 14$	$(3 + 4)(3 - 1) = 14$
4	$4^2 + 3(4) - 4 = 24$	$(4 + 4)(4 - 1) = 24$

28. $(2x + 1)(x + 5)$

29. $(3n + 7)(n + 3)$

30. $(5y + 3)(y - 2)$

31. $2(g - 1)(2g - 3)$

32. $6(p - 4)(p + 1)$

33. $(4d - 3)(3d + 4)$

8-5 *Exercises*

36. They are similar in that the first and last terms of each are perfect squares. They are different in that a perfect-square trinomial has 3 terms and a difference of 2 squares has 2 terms.

37. Multiply a binomial by itself. Choose 2 perfect squares, find 2 times the product of their square roots, and then write these 3 expressions as a sum.

8B *Ready To Go On?*

4. no; $-4x \neq 2(\sqrt{2}x)(2)$

5. yes; $(3x - 2)^2$

6. No; the last term must be positive.

8. yes; $(x - 11)(x + 11)$

9. No; 20 is not a perfect square.

10. yes; $(1 - 3y^2)(1 + 3y^2)$

11. yes; $(5m + 2m^3)(5m - 2m^3) = m^2(5 + 2m^2)(5 - 2m^2)$

12. No; terms must be subtracted.

13. $(r^2 - t)(r^2 + t)$

21. $3x(x - 2)^2$

22. $4m(2m + 1)(2m - 1)$

23. $5xy(x + 3)(x - 3)$

24. unfactorable

25. $3(c + 7)(c - 3)$

26. $x(x + 3)(x - 3)(x^2 + 9)$

27. $(\ell^2 - 36)$; $(\ell + 6)(\ell - 6)$

28. $a^2 - 8a + 16$; $(a - 4)^2$

29. $2v^2 + 2v - 12$; $2(v^2 + v - 6)$; $2(v + 3)(v - 2)$

30. $3h^3 + 3h^2 - 6h$; $3h(h^2 + h - 2)$; $3h(h + 2)(h - 1)$

31. $(9x)(8x) - (8y)(4y)$; $8(9x^2 - 4y^2)$; $8(3x - 2y)(3x + 2y)$

Chapter 9

Are You Ready?

5.

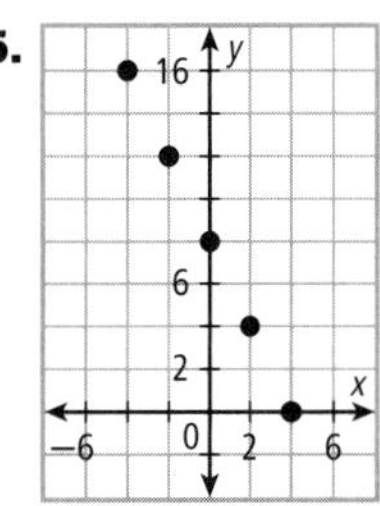

6.

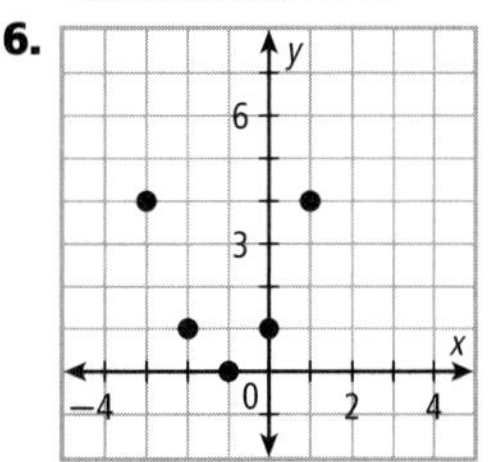

7.

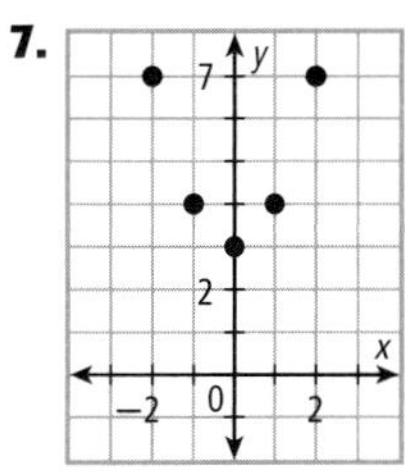

Additional Answers

8.

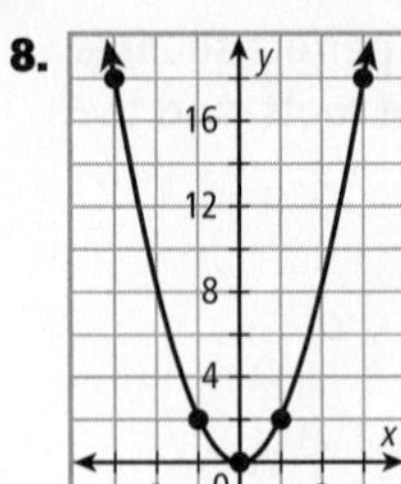

Reading and Writing Math

3–5. Possible answers given.

3. Relate it to the word *vary*, which means "differ" or "change"; a quantity that can change.

4. Lines that are exactly the same; the word *coincident* is related to the word *coincidence*, which refers to the occurrence of events at the same time.

5. By itself; the word *isolated* is related to the word *isolation*, which means "the state of being alone."

9-3 *Exercises*

21.

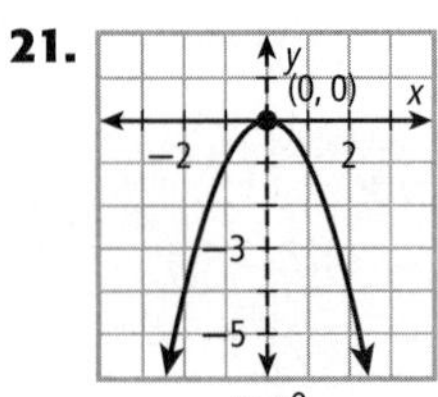

22.

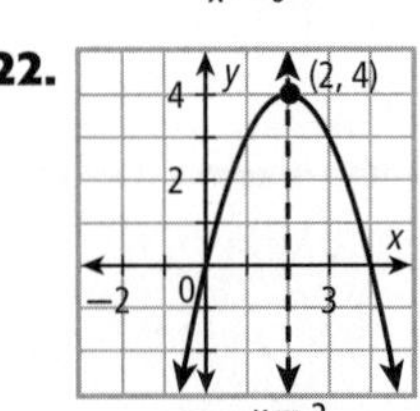

23.

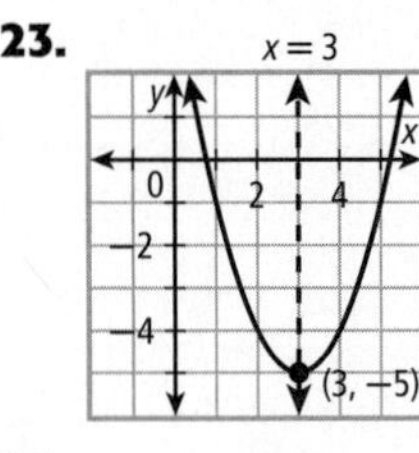

24.

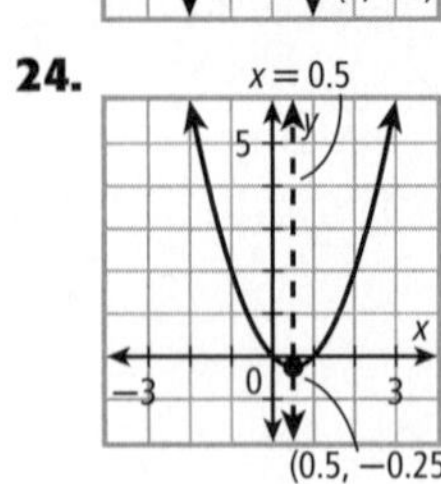

25.

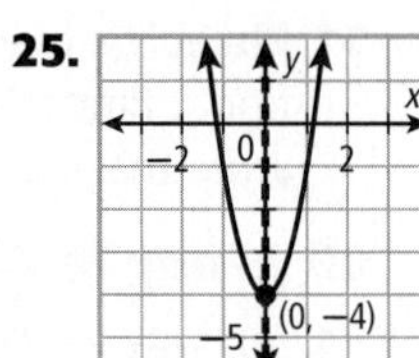

26.

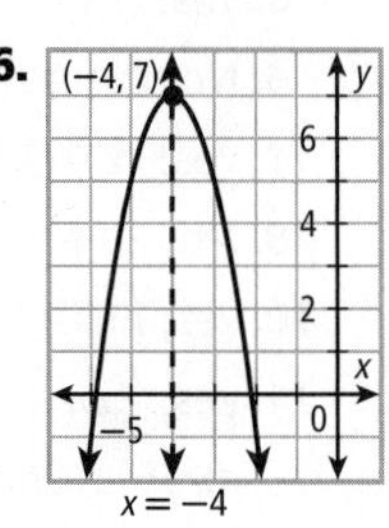

27a.

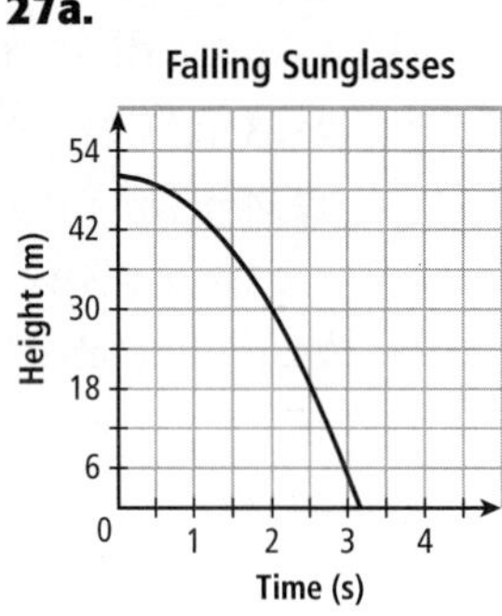

35c.

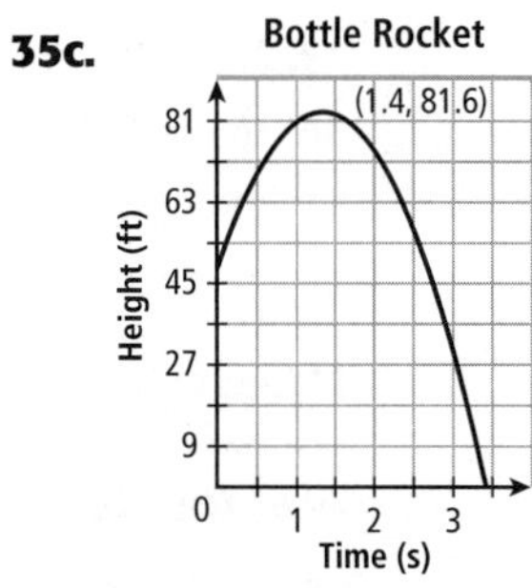

d. The vertex represents the time, 1.4 s, that the water bottle rocket has spent in the air when it reaches its highest point, 81.6 ft.

9A *Multi-Step Test Prep*

2.

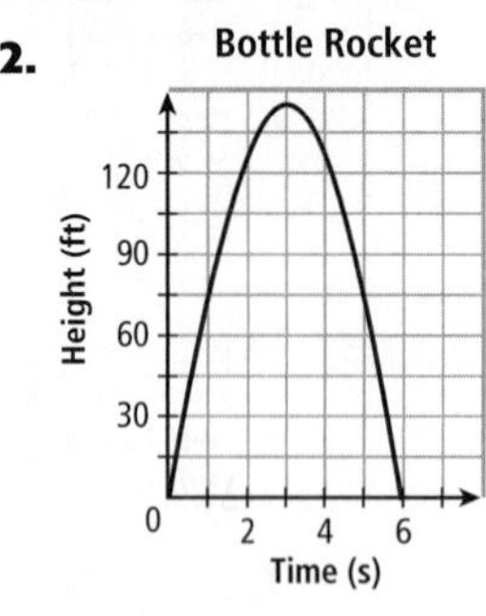

9A *Ready To Go On?*

7.

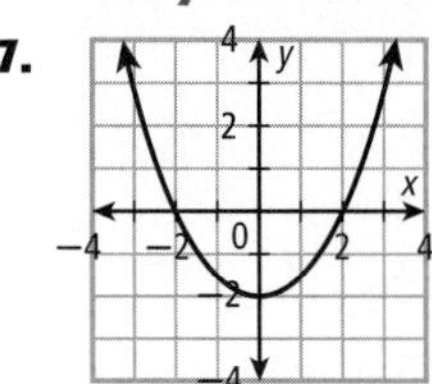

D: all real numbers R: $y \geq -2$

15.

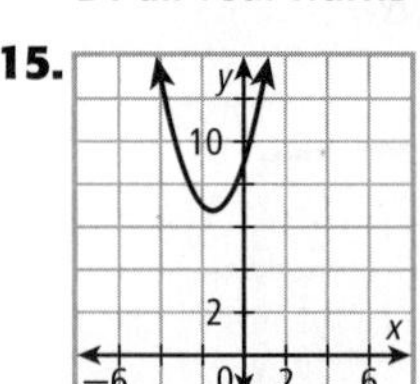

16.

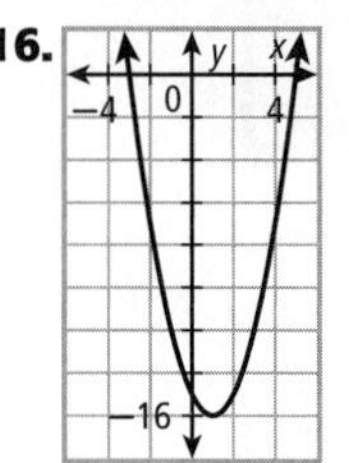

17.

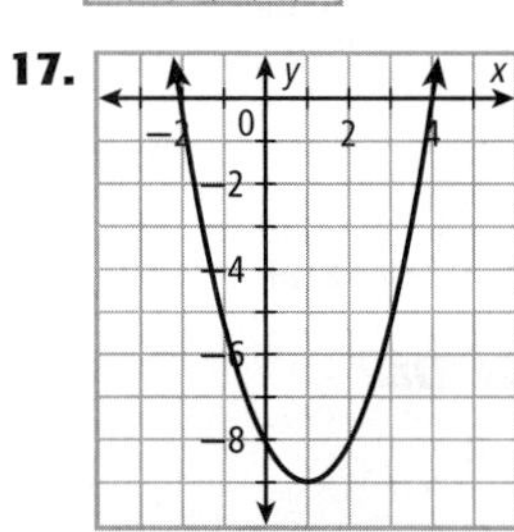

18.

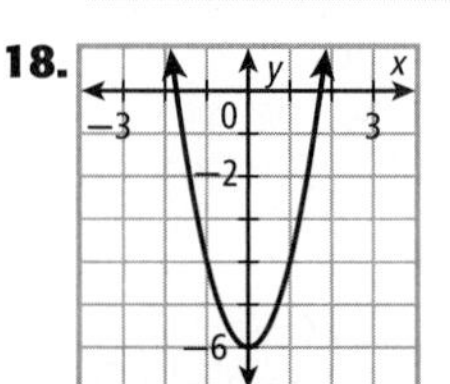

19.

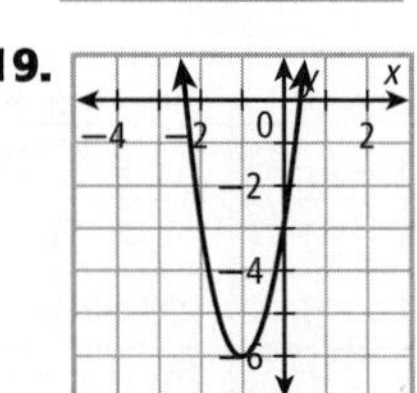

20.

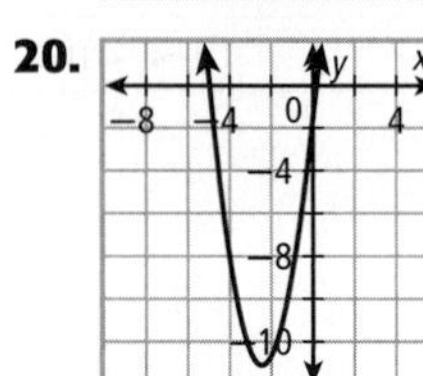

21. The graph of $g(x)$ is the same width, has the same axis of symmetry, also opens upward, and its vertex is translated 2 units down to $(0, -2)$.

22. The graph of $g(x)$ is wider, has the same axis of symmetry, also opens upward, and its vertex is the same.

23. The graph of $g(x)$ is narrower, has the same axis of symmetry, also opens upward, and its vertex is translated 3 units up to $(0, 3)$.

24. The graph of $g(x)$ has the same width, has the same axis of symmetry, opens downward, and its vertex is translated 4 units down to $(0, -4)$.

9-7 *Exercises*

53. $x^2 + 4 = 0$ is equivalent to $x^2 = -4$, which has no real solutions. $x^2 - 4 = 0$ is equivalent to $x^2 = 4$, which has two solutions (± 2).

Chapter 10

10-1 *Lesson Quiz*

1. Lamar Place and Candlerun

2. week 1

3. circle graph; to compare each type of cake to all cake orders

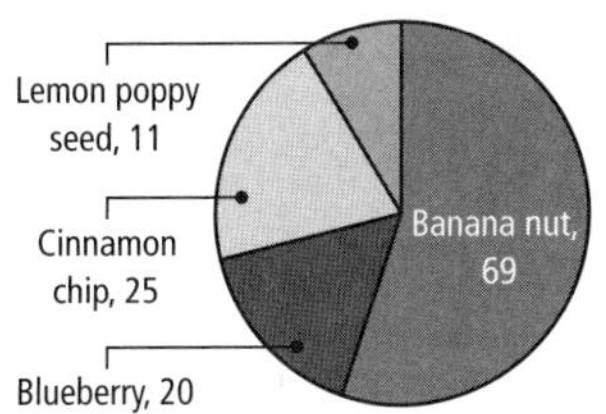

10-2 *Check It Out!*

4a.

Interval	Frequency	Cumulative Frequency
28–31	2	2
32–35	7	9
36–39	5	14
40–43	3	17

10-2 *Exercises*

4.

Interval	Frequency
19–22	4
23–26	6
27–30	5
31–34	3

5.

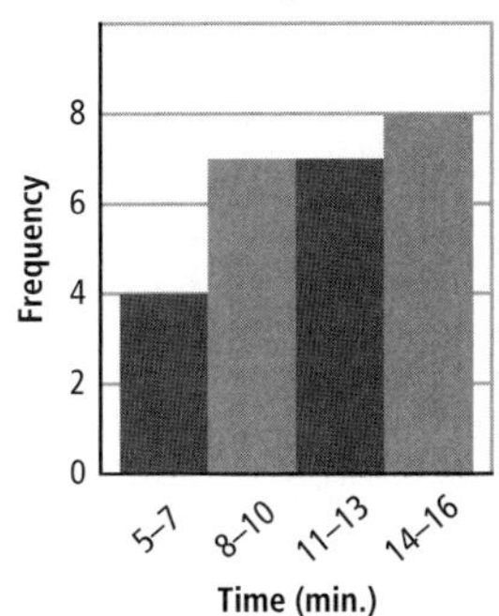

6a.

Interval	Frequency	Cumulative Frequency
750–790	1	1
700–740	2	3
650–690	2	5
600–640	3	8
550–590	2	10
500–540	5	15

7.

Summer		Winter
	0	4 9 9
	1	1 2 3 4 9 9
9 7 7 6 5 5 3 3 2 2	2	1 7
	3	0 3 5
	4	
9 7 4 3	5	

Key: 2|1 means 21
7|2 means 27

13a.

Stem	Leaves
5	9
6	0 8
7	0 2 2 5 7
8	1 4 4 8

Key: 5|9 means 59

b.

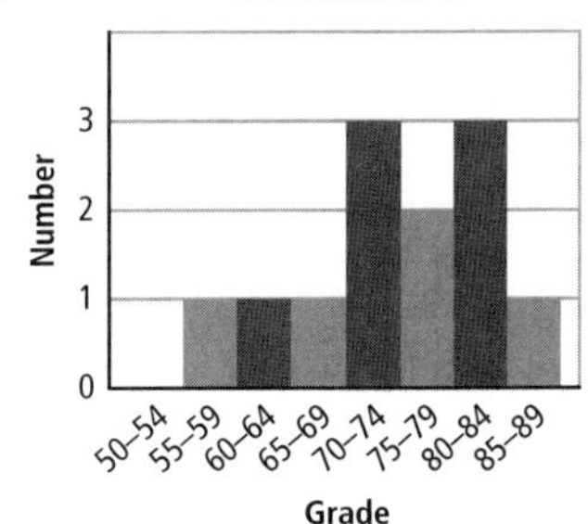

c.

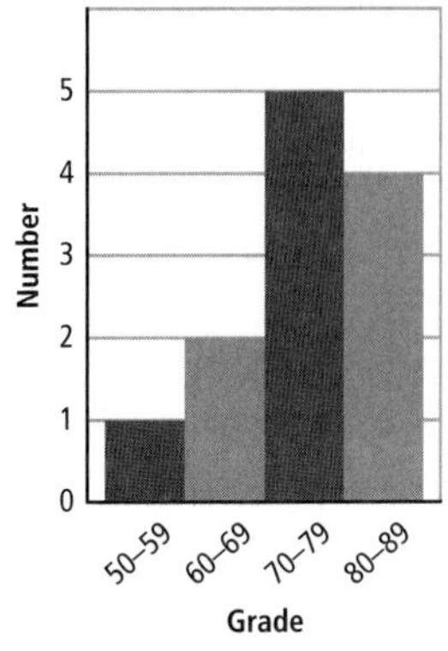

d.

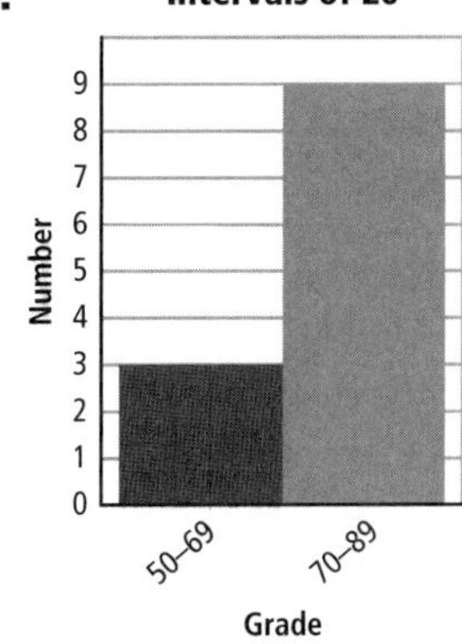

e. As the size of the interval increases, the number of bars decreases.

f. The histogram that uses intervals of 20; it makes Damien's grades look highest because the bar for 70–89 is much taller than the bar for 50–69.

10-3 *Exercises*

4. mean: 19.75; median: 21; modes: 10, 20, and 25; range: 16

5. mean: 78.25; median: 78; mode: 78; range: 15

6. 96; the outlier increases the mean by 16.5, the median by 1.5, and the range by 79. It has no effect on the mode.

7. 13; the outlier decreases the mean by 11.15 and the median by 4. It increases the range by 51 and has no effect on the mode.

8. median: 83; the mean is lower than all but one of the scores because of the outlier. There is no mode.

10.

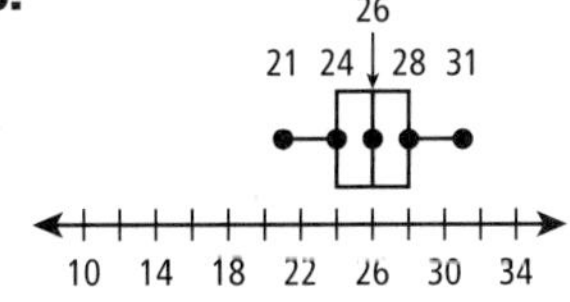

Additional Answers

11.

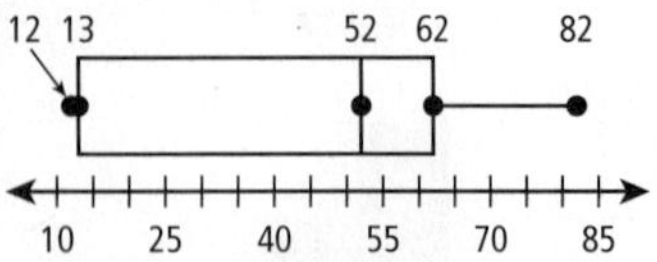

12 13 52 62 82

10 25 40 55 70 85

12. Simon; the vertical line in the box for Simon is farther to the right than the vertical line in the box for Natasha.

14. mean: 79.5; median: 82; mode: none; range: 28

15. mean: 2.5; median: 2.5; modes: 2 and 3; range: 3

16. mean: 26.875; median: 28; modes: 19, 31, and 34; range: 15

17. mean: 60; median: 60; mode: 60; range: 5

18. 8; the outlier decreases the mean by 6.5 and the median by 2.5. It increases the range by 21 and has no effect on the mode.

19. 23; the outlier increases the mean by 3, the median by 2.5, and the range by 15. It has no effect on the mode.

22.

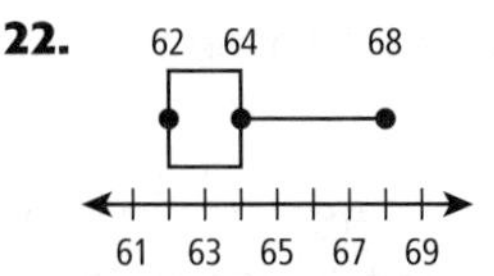

23.

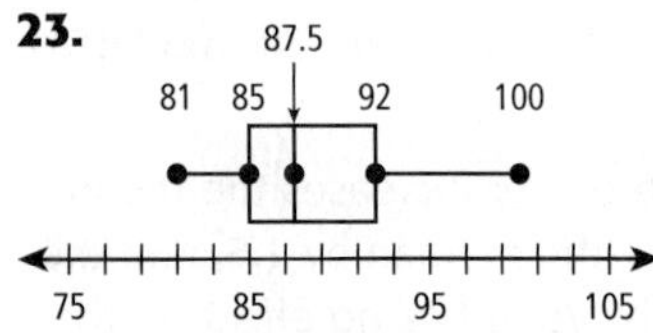

10-3 *Lesson Quiz*

4.

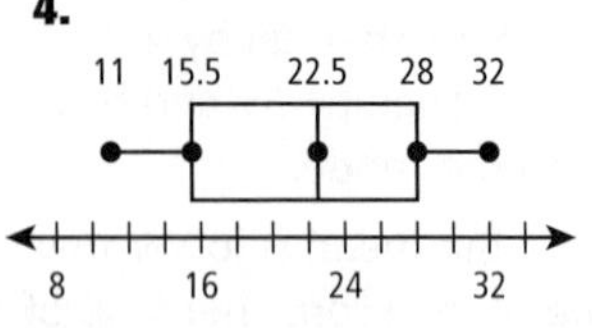

10-4 *Additional Examples*

Example 1

A. The scale on the vertical axis exaggerates the percent of satisfied customers.

B. Someone might believe that brand B has a much greater percentage of satisfied customers.

Example 2

A. The intervals on the vertical axis are not equal.

B. Someone might believe that the amount of rainfall fell dramatically from 1997 to 1999.

Example 3

A. The sectors do not add to 100%.

B. Someone might believe that the county spends most of its money on road maintenance.

Example 4

Although 3 is the mean number of pets per household, 4 of the 5 results are less than 3. In this case, the median of the data, 2, is a better measure.

10-4 *Exercises*

17a. The first question asks whether 2 people can have the same fingerprint. The second question asks whether someone could have made a mistake.

b. The fingerprint had to belong to Dr. Arenson.

c. Someone who wants to prove that the fingerprint belongs to Dr. Arenson.

d. The fingerprint might not belong to Dr. Arenson.

e. Someone who wants to prove that the fingerprint does not belong to Dr. Arenson.

22.

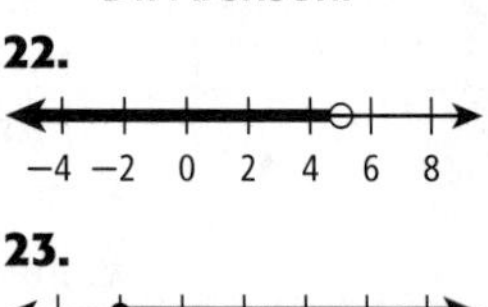

23.

−6 −4 −2 0 2 4 6

24.

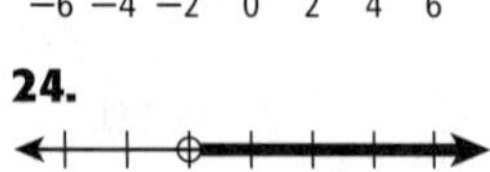

25.

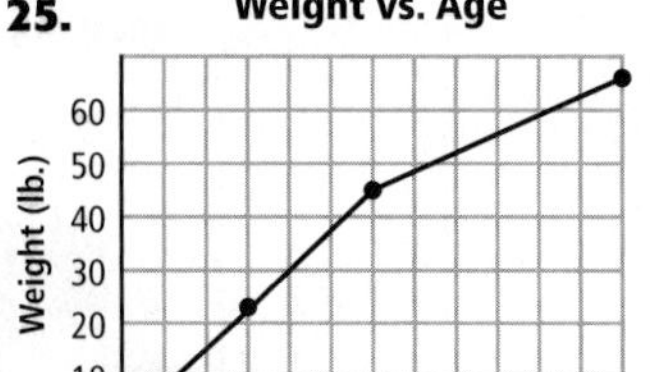

A line graph shows the change in weight over time.

10-4 *Lesson Quiz*

1. The scale exaggerates the differences among the sitting fees; someone might believe that studio Z charges much less than its competitors.

2. The vertical axis does not start at 0 which makes it appear that the number of members varied greatly from month to month; the number of members did not vary much throughout the year.

3. The sectors do not add to 100%.

4. Only 5 people were asked whether they liked to snow ski. The sample is too small.

10A *Ready To Go On?*

4.

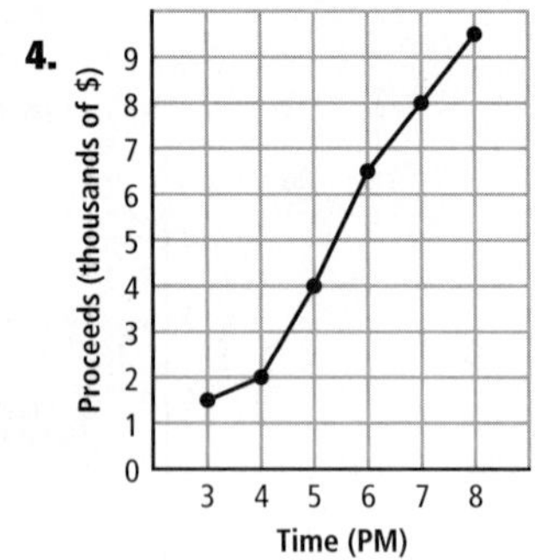

A line graph shows change over time.

5.

Stem	Leaves
2	2 4 6 6 7 8
3	0 2 3
4	1

Key: 2|7 means $27,000

6a.

Last 12 Parties	
Number of People	Frequency
15–17	6
18–20	5
21–23	0
24–26	1

b.

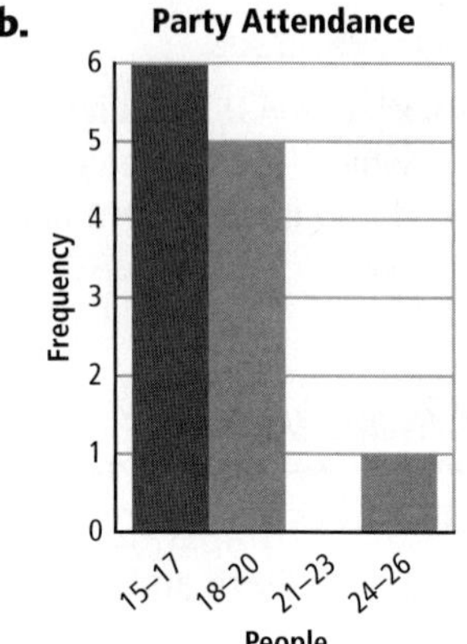

7c. Median or mode; the mean is lower than most of the temperatures because 1 day had a high of only 38 °F.

8.

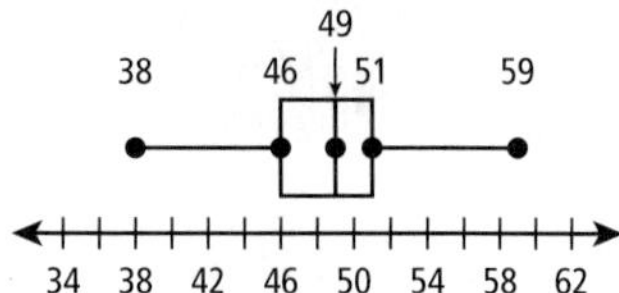

9. The vertical axis begins at 80. This might make someone believe that the value of the stock has decreased dramatically. Another company might want to devalue this company's stock.

10. The survey did not address a random sample. Because the survey was online, those who responded were probably already somewhat comfortable using technology.

10-7 *Exercises*

5. Independent; your order does not affect what your friend orders.

6. Dependent; the appointments that were already scheduled affect the appointment times available to you.

Chapter 10 Test

7. mean: ≈ 14.3; median: 13.5; mode: 14; range: 36

8.

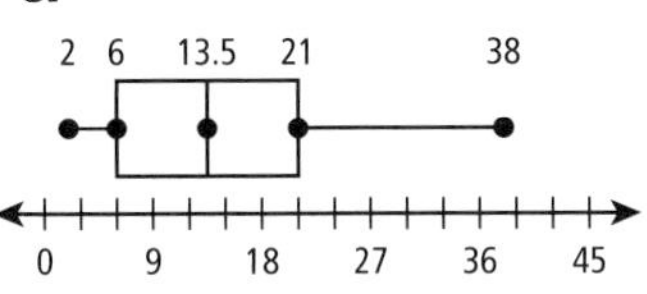

11. The total of the percentages is only 20%.

12. Someone might believe that most of the money raised goes to charitable causes.

13. The managers of the charity might be able to get more people to contribute under the invalid assumption that most of their money is going to charitable causes.

Chapter 11

Are You Ready?

14.

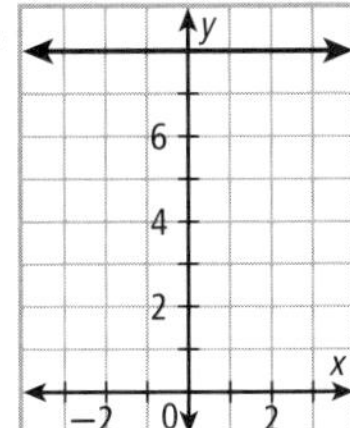

15.

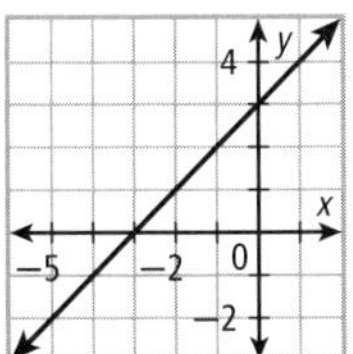

16.

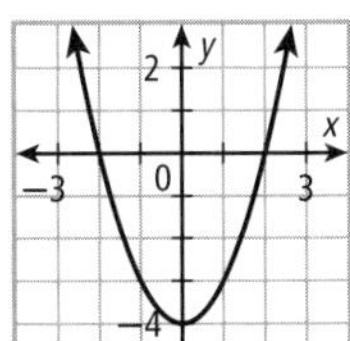

17.

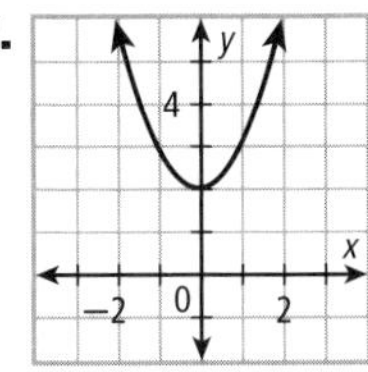

11-1 *Exercises*

41a. Stage 0:

Stage 1:

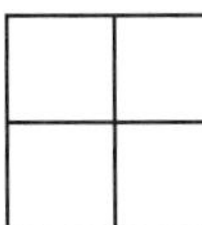

Stage 2:

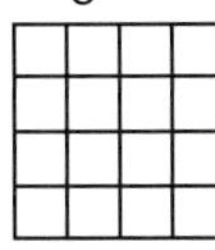

Stage 3:

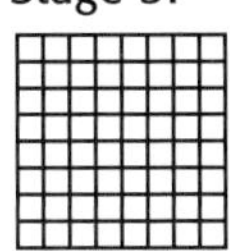

b.

Stage	Squares
0	1
1	4
2	16
3	64

54. Susanna assumed the sequence was geometric with $r = 2$. She used the formula to find $a_8 = 128$. Paul noticed a pattern of "add 1, add 2, and so on." He continued this pattern by adding 3, adding 4, etc., until he got the 8th term of 29. Both could be considered correct because it was not specified what type of sequence was given.

58.

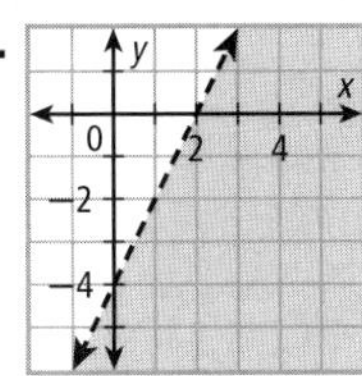

59.

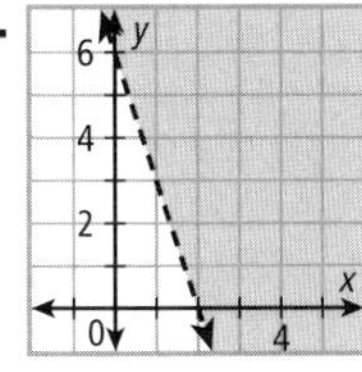

60.

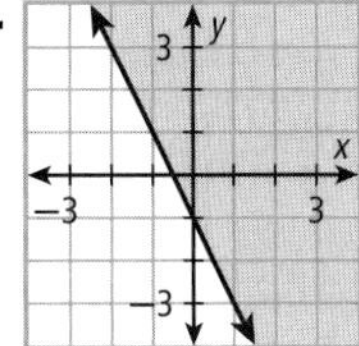

Lesson 11-2

6.

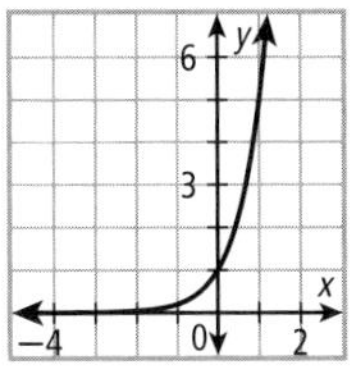

7.

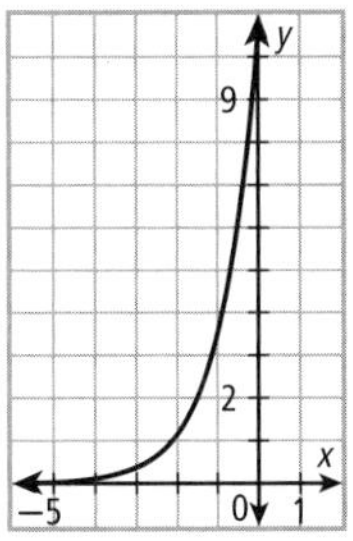

8.

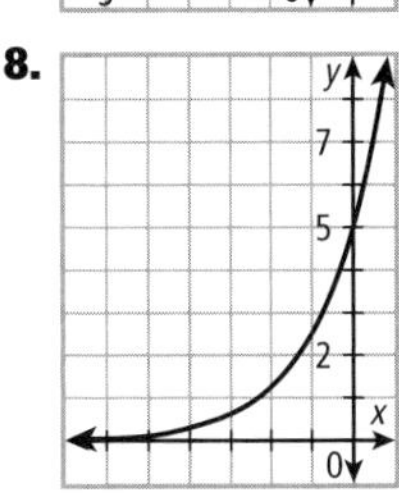

9.

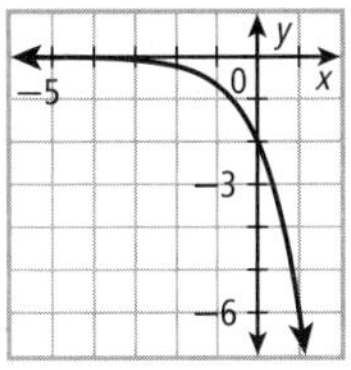

10.

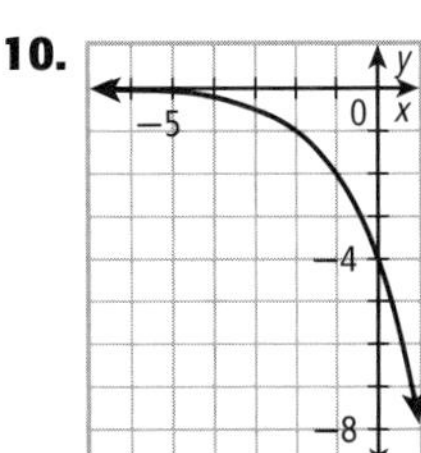

11.

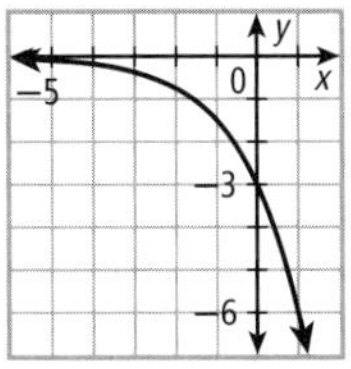

12.

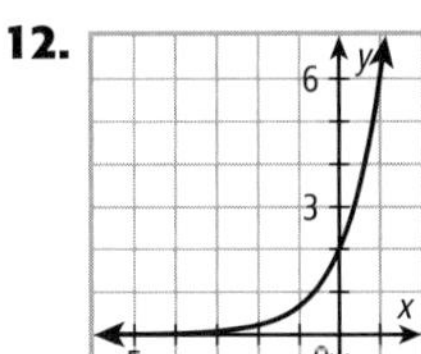

13.

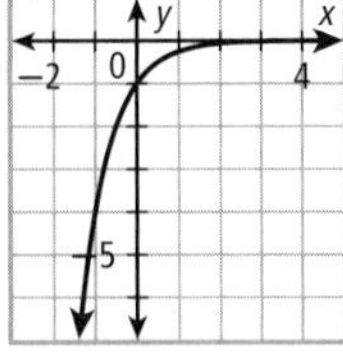

14.

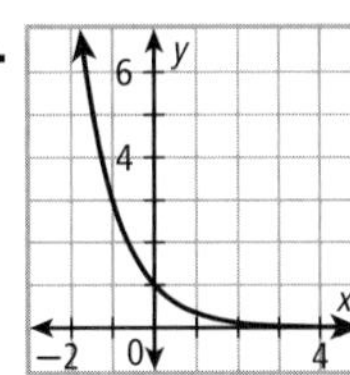

15.

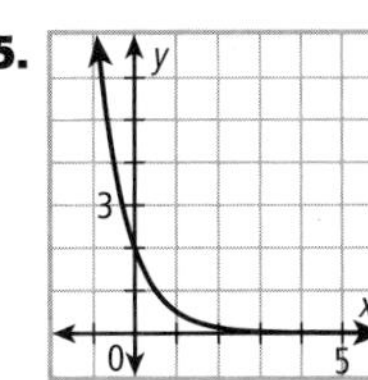

16.

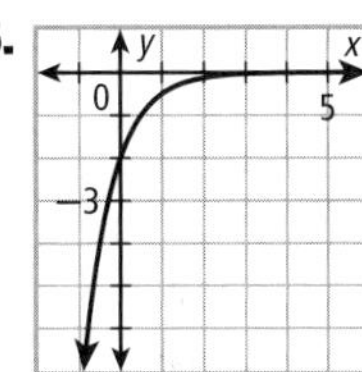

21. As the x-values change by a constant amount, the y-values are multiplied by a constant amount.

22. As the x-values change by a constant amount, the y-values are not multiplied by a constant amount.

23. As the x-values change by a constant amount, the y-values are not multiplied by a constant amount.

24. As the x-values change by a constant amount, the y-values are multiplied by a constant amount.

29.

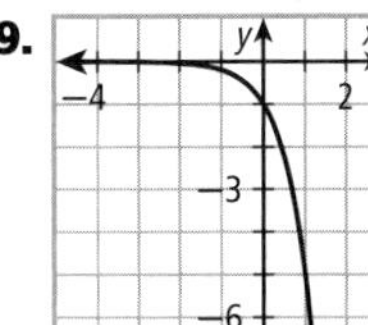

30.

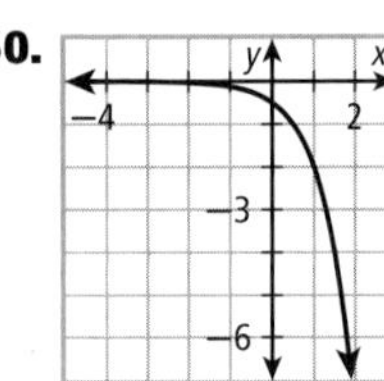

31.

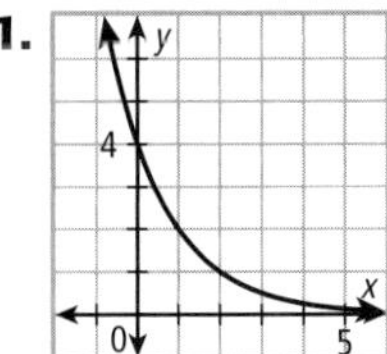

32.

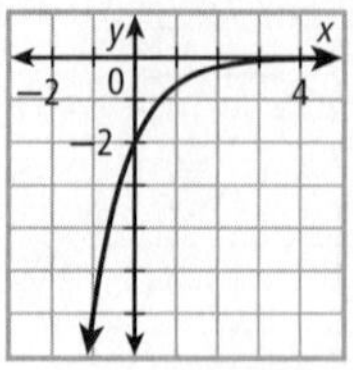

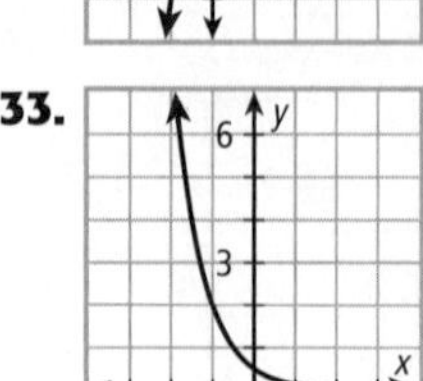

33.

38.

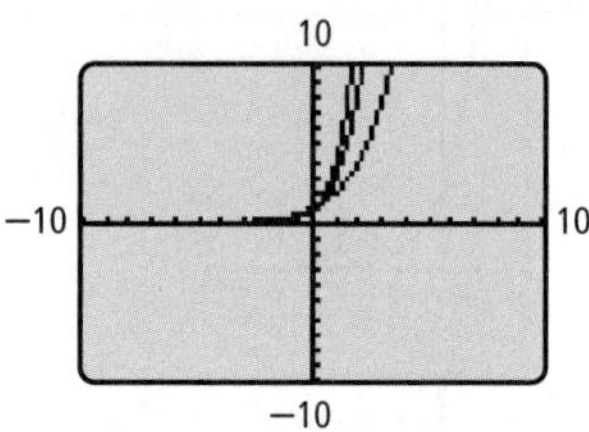

Possible answer: The graphs have the same basic shape and the same y-intercept; each graph is steeper than the one before it.

39.

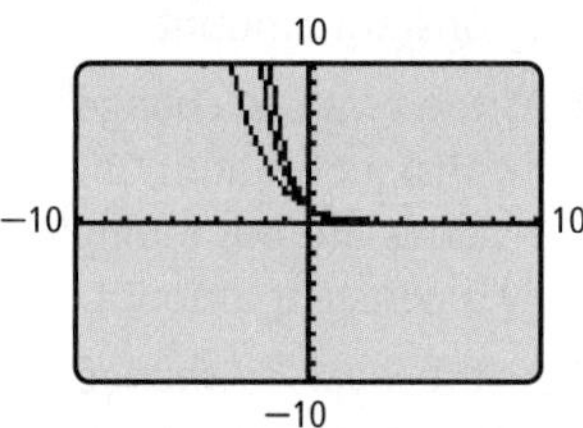

Possible answer: The graphs have the same basic shape and the same y-intercept; each graph is steeper than the one before it.

11A *Multi-Step Test Prep*

2.

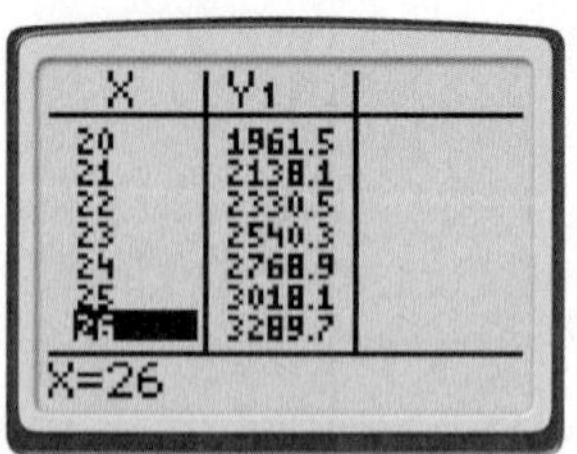

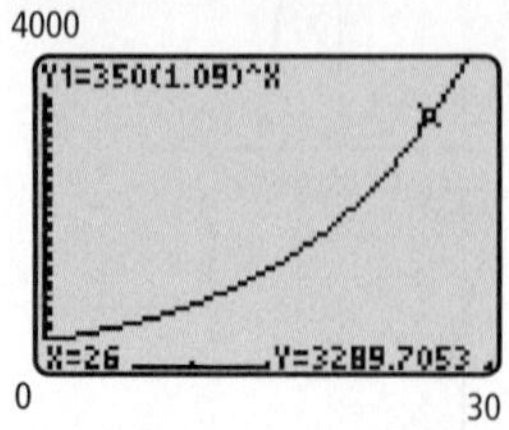

4000

Y1=350(1.09)^X

X=26 Y=3289.7053

0 30

4.

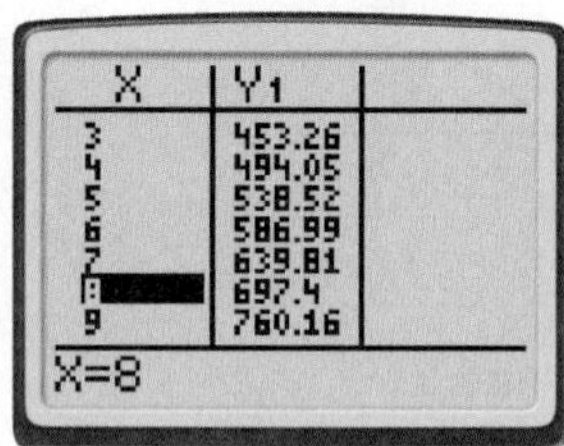

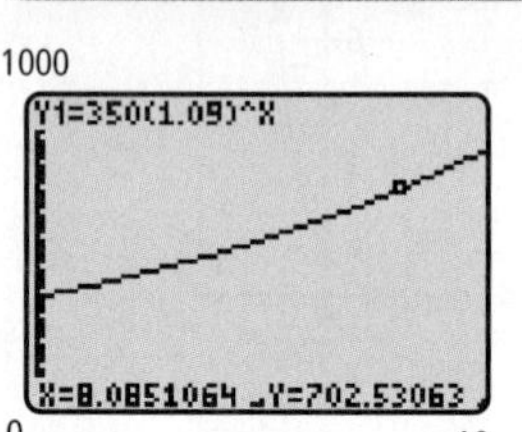

5.

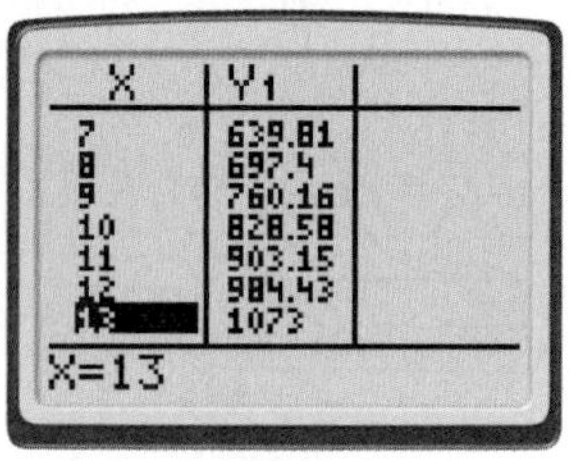

X Y1
7 639.81
8 697.4
9 760.16
10 828.58
11 903.15
12 984.43
13 1073
X=13

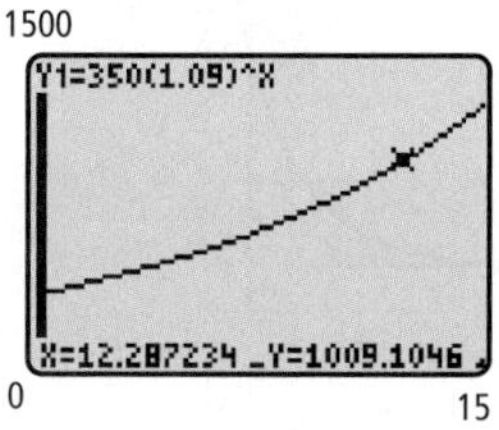

1500

Y1=350(1.09)^X

X=12.287234 Y=1009.1046

0 15

11A *Ready To Go On?*

7.

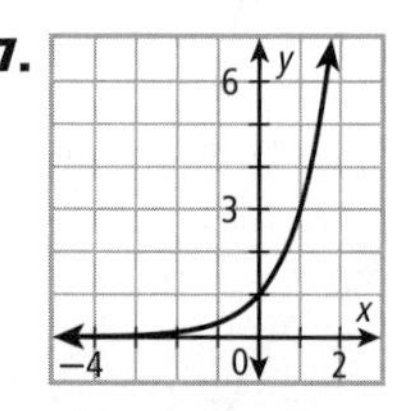

8.

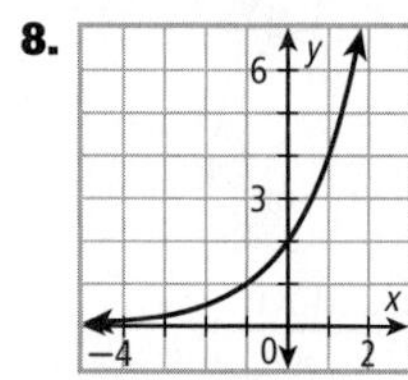

9.

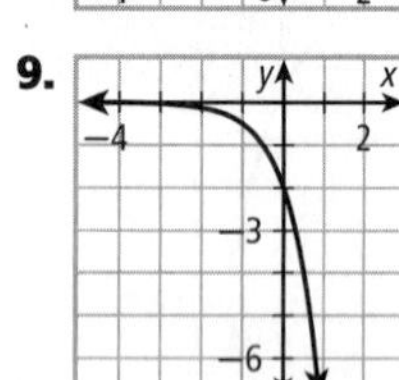

10.

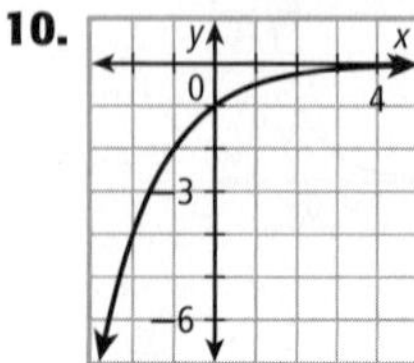

12. $y = 30{,}000(1.03)^t$; \$40,317.49

13. $y = 2000(1.00375)^{12t}$; \$2288.50

14. $y = 1200(0.8)^t$; \$491.52

16.

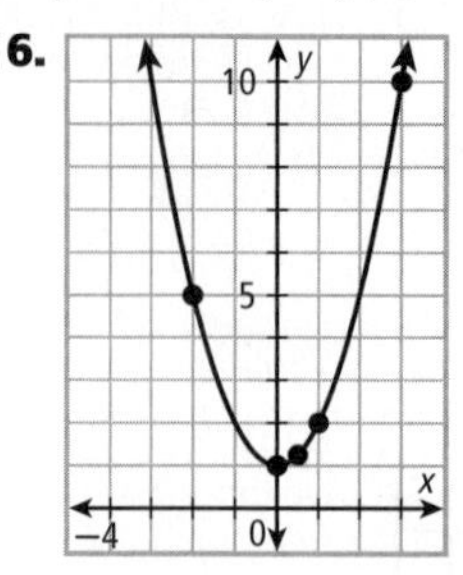

17.

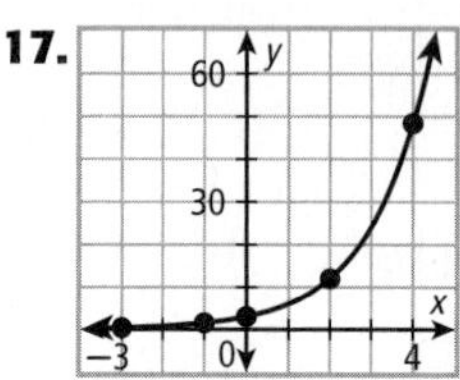

11-5 *Exercises*

28.

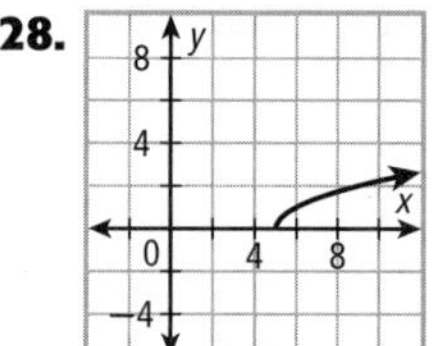

29.

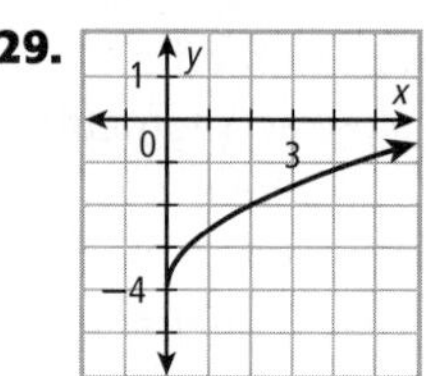

30.

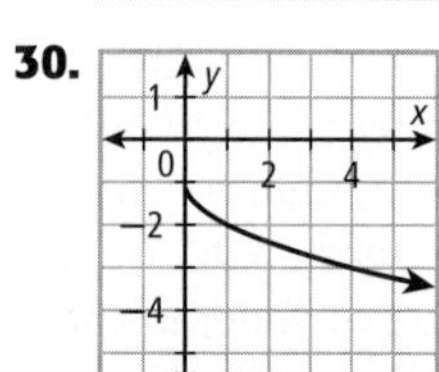

31.

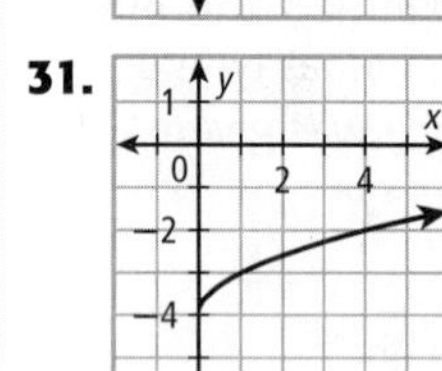

32.

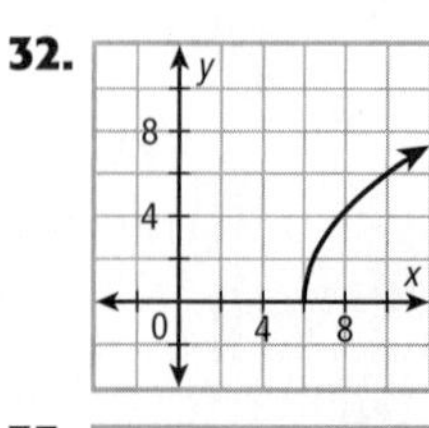

33.

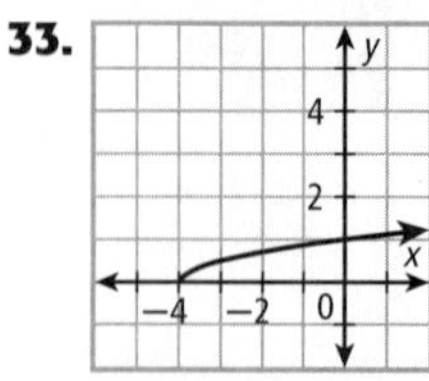

38.

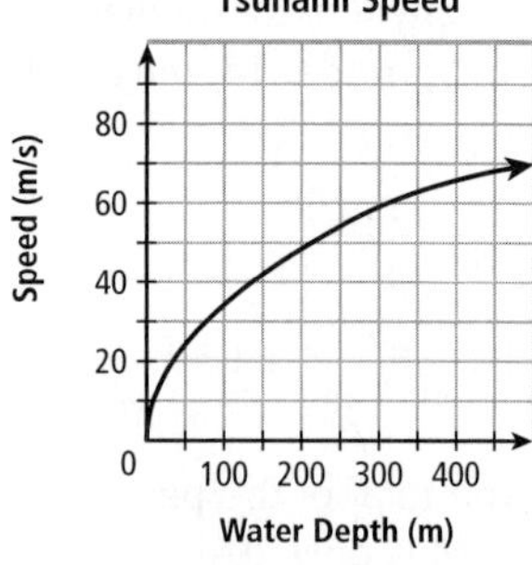

44c. No; 9.93 seconds is too fast for the ride to make one complete swing back and forth. The formula is for a pendulum that is under the influence of gravity only. This is not true for the ride.

58.

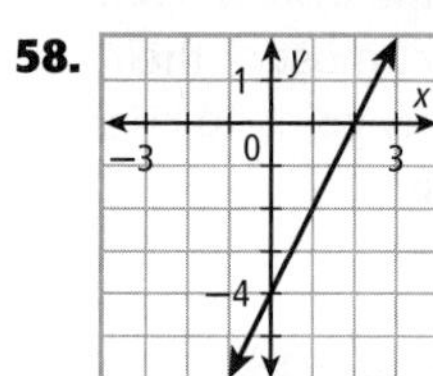

59.

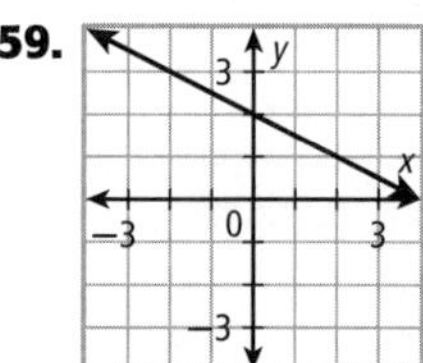

60.

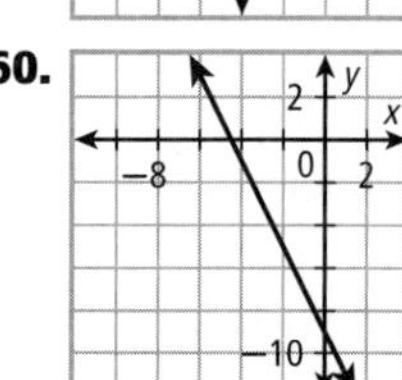

11-5 *Technology Lab*

3. The graph of $f(x) = \sqrt{x+1} + 4$ will be translated 1 unit left and 4 units up from the graph of $f(x) = \sqrt{x}$.

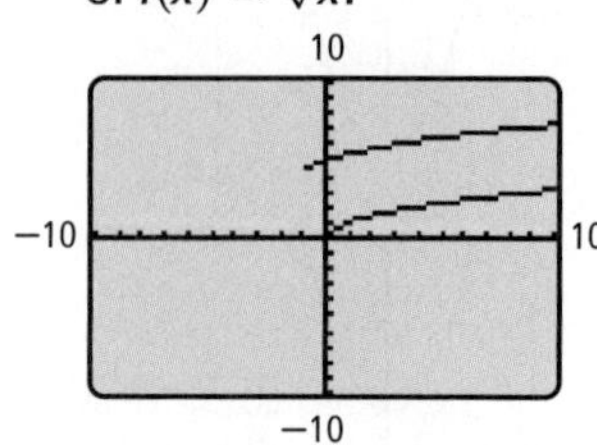

4. The graph of $f(x) = 2\sqrt{x}$ will have a steeper curve.

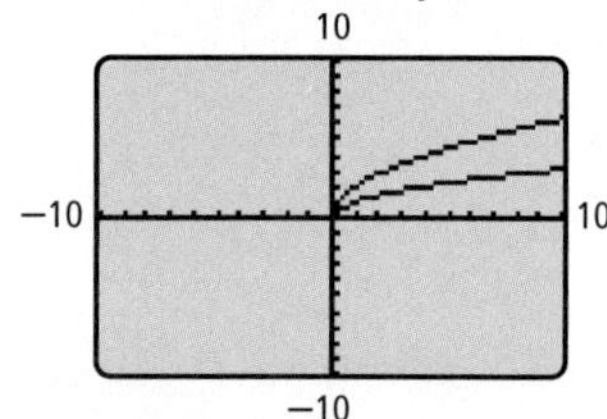

11-9 *Exercises*

105.

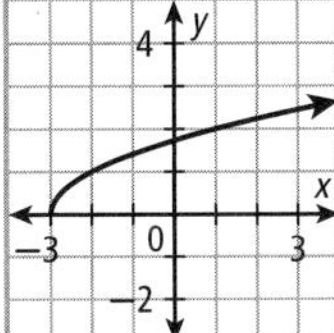

106.

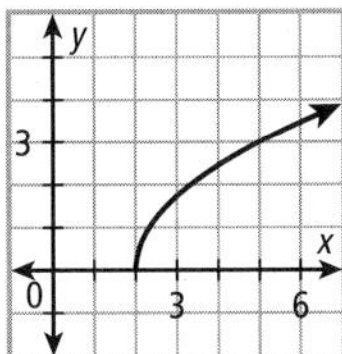

107.

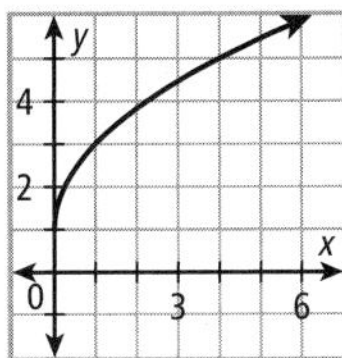

11B *Ready To Go On?*

5.

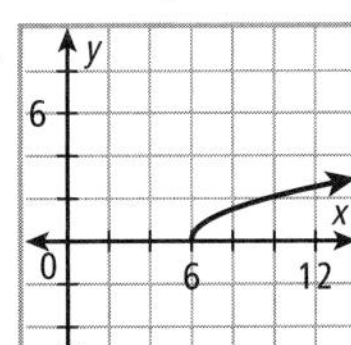

6.

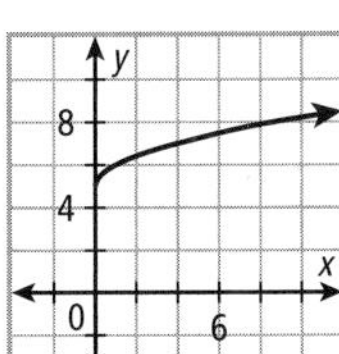

7.

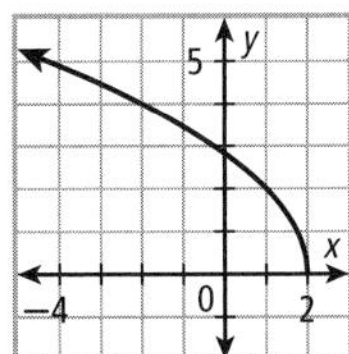

Chapter 12

12-2 *Exercises*

10.

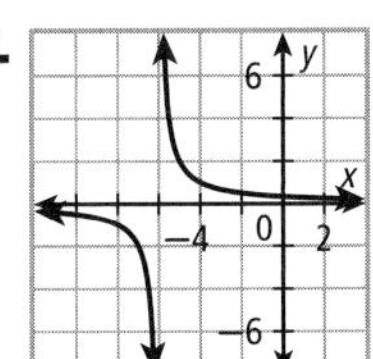

11.

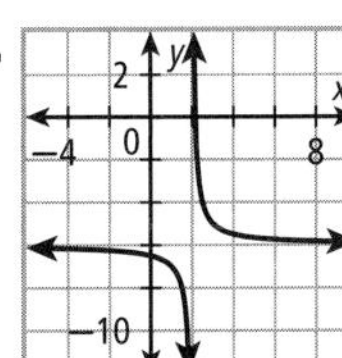

12.

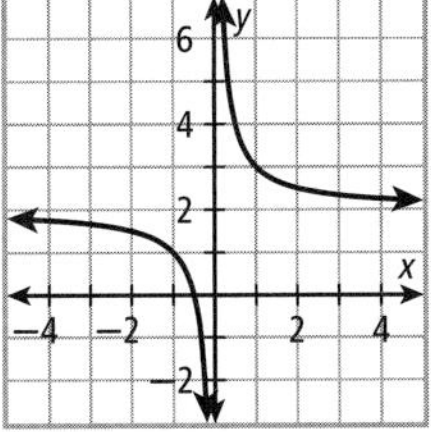

13.

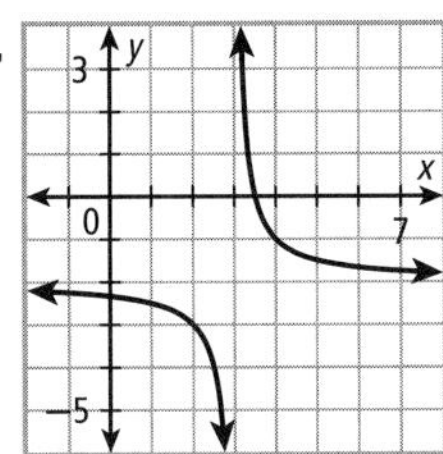

23.

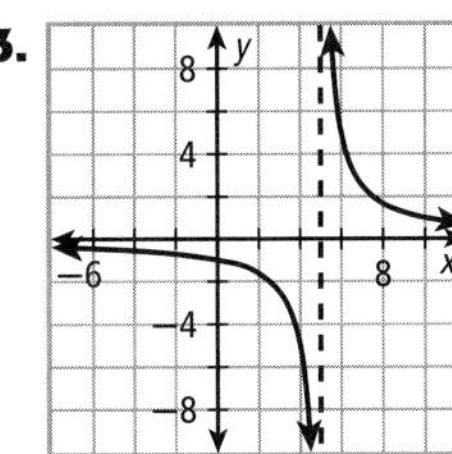

24.

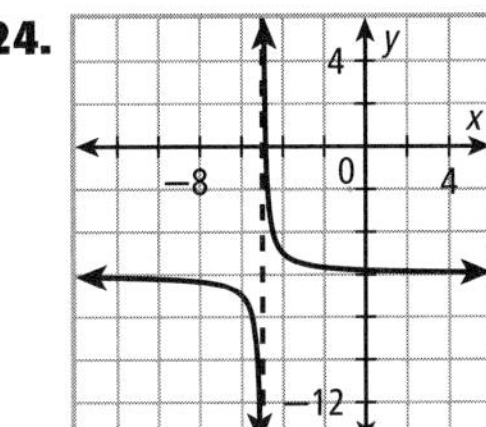

25.

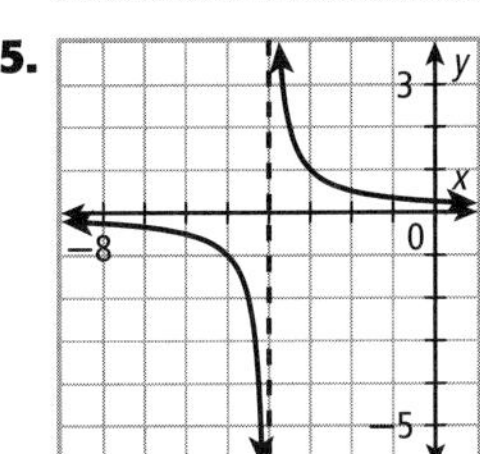

26.

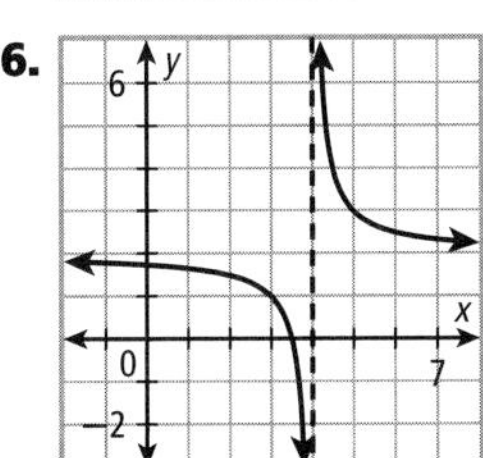

27b.

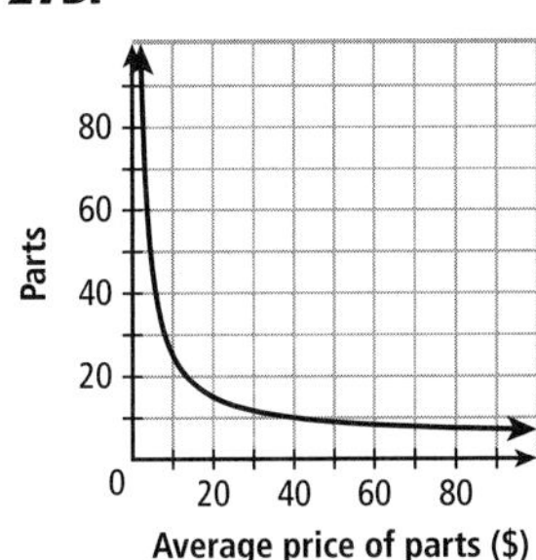

32.

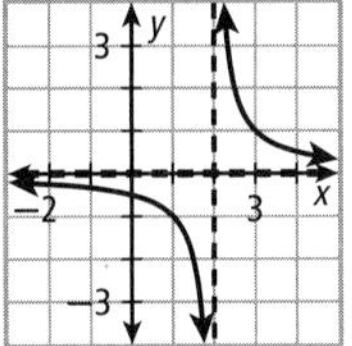

33.

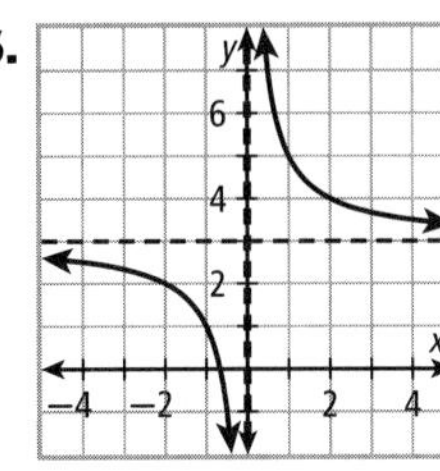

34.

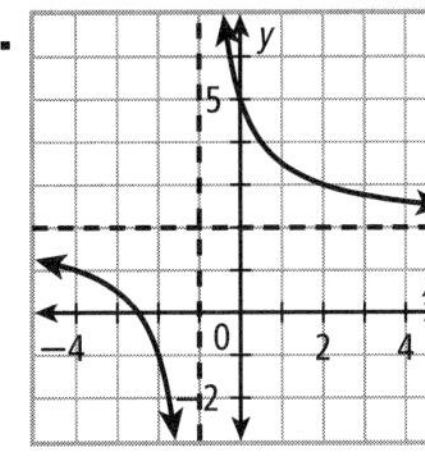

35.

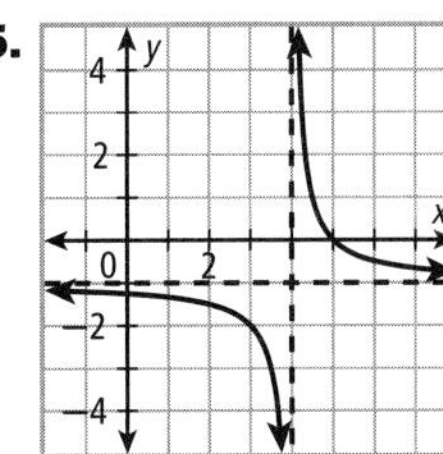

36. approx. 1.67 lumens

45. D: $x > 15$; R: $y \geq 0$

46a.

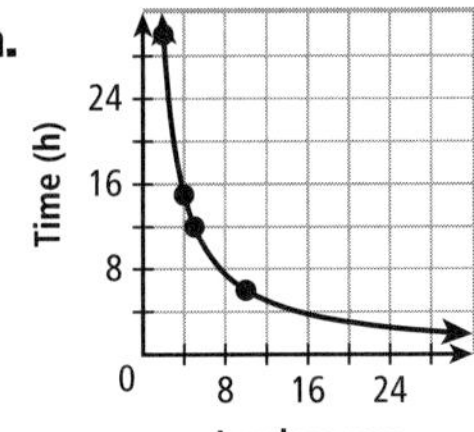

56c.

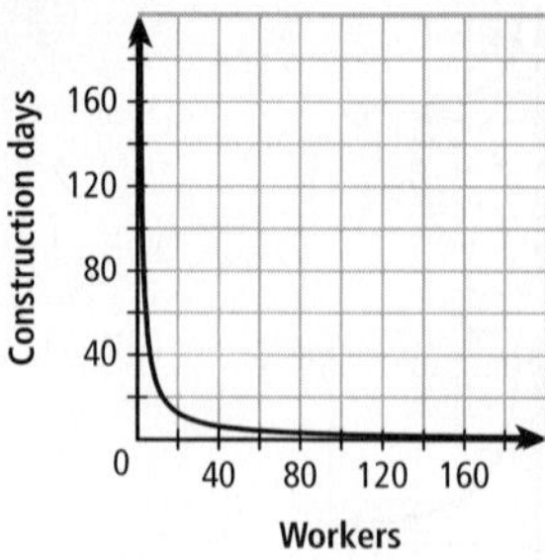

57. The graph of $y = -\frac{k}{x}$ is the reflection of the graph of $y = \frac{k}{x}$ across the x-axis.

a.

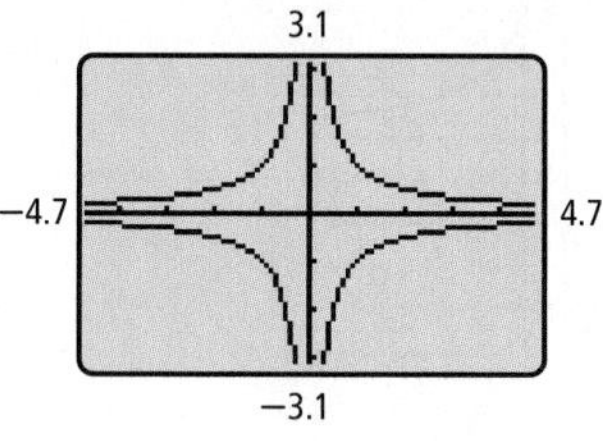

b.

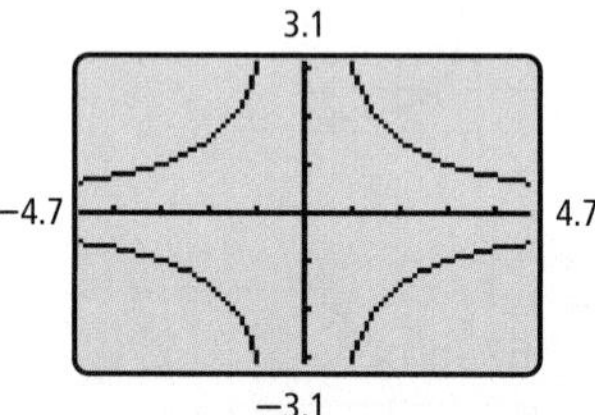

c.

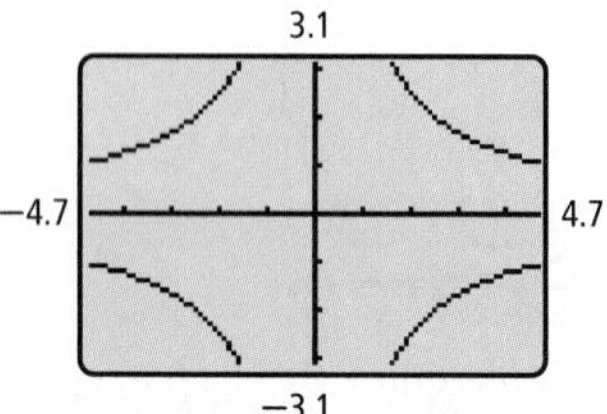

60.

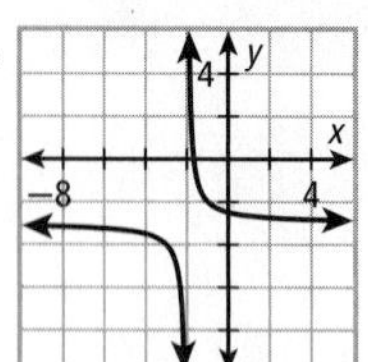

61.

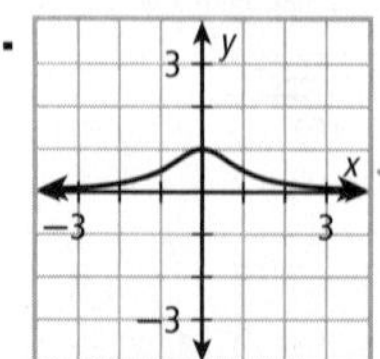

12A *Ready To Go On?*

5. constant product

6. cannot be written in the form $y = \frac{k}{x}$

7.

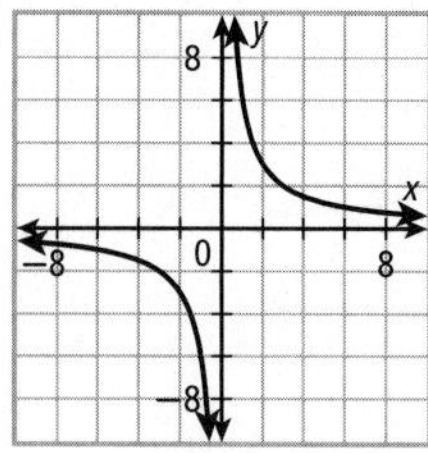

8.

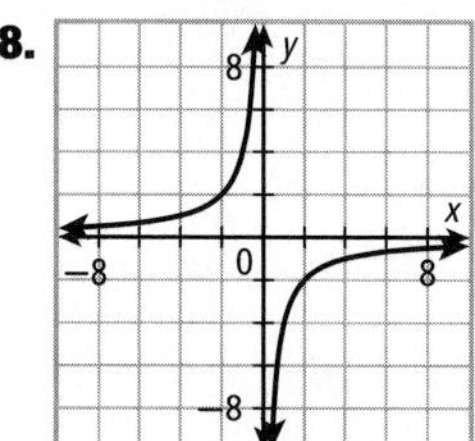

10. $x \neq 0$; $x = 0$ and $y = 0$

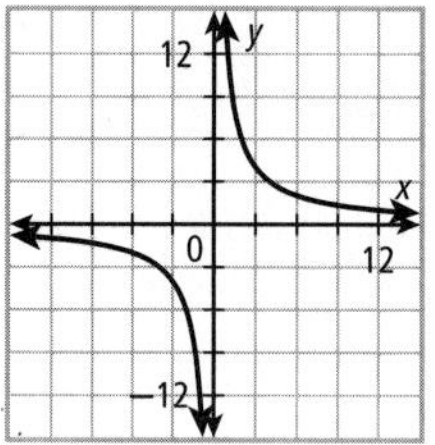

11. $x \neq -2$; $x = -2$ and $y = 0$

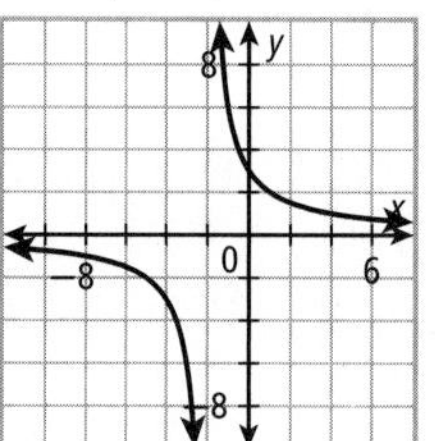

12. $x \neq 1$; $x = 1$ and $y = 0$

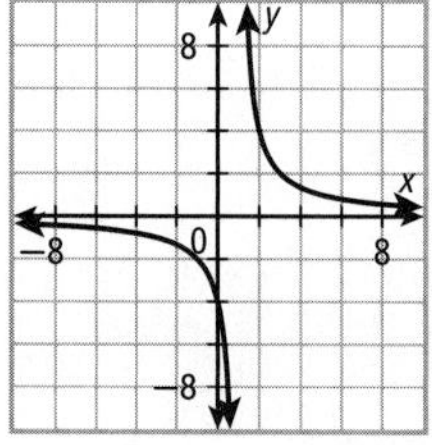

13. $x \neq -1$; $x = -1$ and $y = -3$

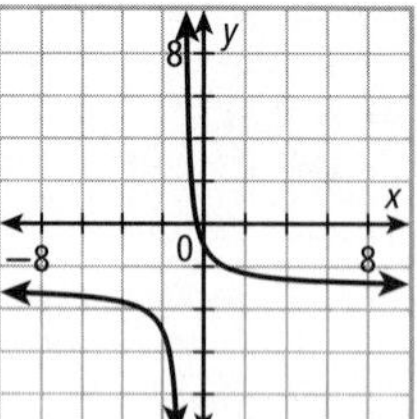

14.

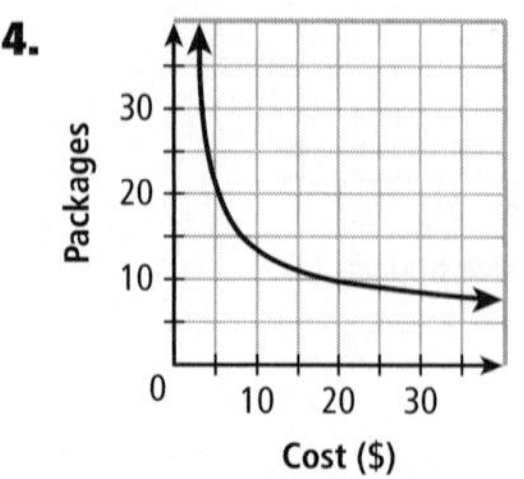

12B *Multi-Step Test Prep*

2.

x	y
0	0
2	−2.5
4	−6.667
6	−15
8	−40
10	Undefined
12	60
14	35
16	26.667

3.

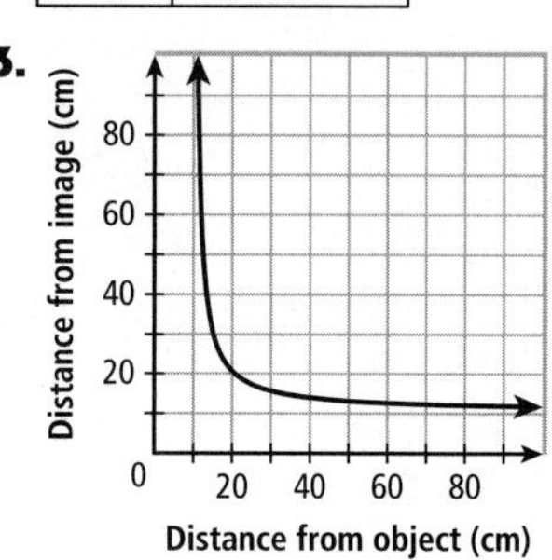

Extra Practice Skills

Chapter 1

1–4. Possible answers given.

1. 8 more than x; the sum of x and 8

2. 6 times y; the product of 6 and y

3. the difference of g and 4; 4 less than g

4. the quotient of 12 and h; 12 divided by h

44. $-1 \cdot (-1) \cdot (-1) \cdot (-1) \cdot (-1)$; -1

74. $12(100 + 8) = 1296$

75. $7(100 - 11) = 623$

76. $11(30 + 3) = 363$

80.

	Procedure	Justification
1.	$6(p - 2) + 3p$	
2.	$6(p) + 6(-2) + 3p$	Dist. Prop.
3.	$6p + (-12) + 3p$	Multiply.
4.	$6p + 3p + (-12)$	Comm. Prop. of Add.
5.	$(6p + 3p) + (-12)$	Assoc. Prop. of Add.
6.	$9p - 12$	Combine like terms.

81.

	Procedure	Justification
1.	$8q - 3 + 5q(2 + q)$	
2.	$8q - 3 + 5q(2) + 5q(q)$	Dist. Prop.
3.	$8q - 3 + 10q + 5q^2$	Multiply.
4.	$8q + 10q + 5q^2 - 3$	Comm. Prop. of Add.
5.	$(8q + 10q) + 5q^2 - 3$	Assoc. Prop. of Add.
6.	$18q + 5q^2 - 3$	Combine like terms.

82.

	Procedure	Justification
1.	$-4 + 3r - 7(2s - r)$	
2.	$-4 + 3r - 7(2s) - 7(-r)$	Dist. Prop.
3.	$-4 + 3r - 14s + 7r$	Multiply.
4.	$3r + 7r - 14s - 4$	Comm. Prop. of Add.
5.	$(3r + 7r) - 14s - 4$	Assoc. Prop. of Add.
6.	$10r - 14s - 4$	Combine like terms.

83–86.

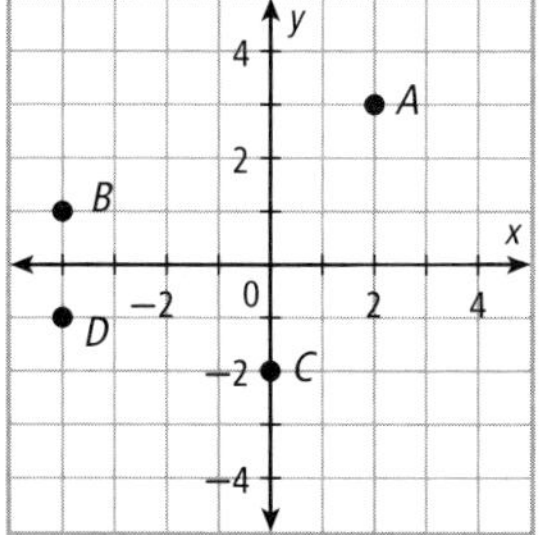

93.

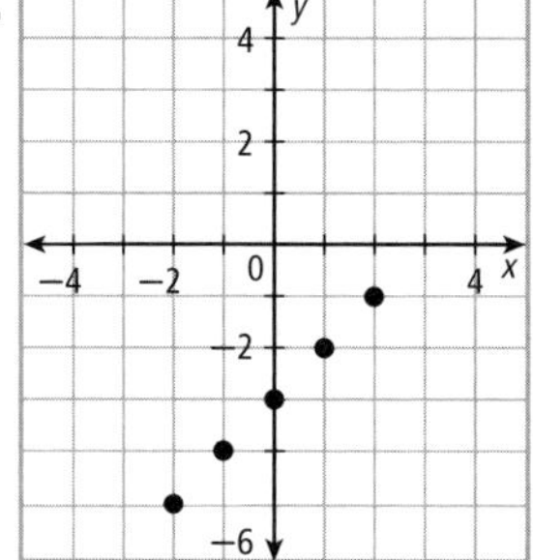

$(-2, -5), (-1, -4), (0, -3), (1, -2), (2, -1)$; line

94.

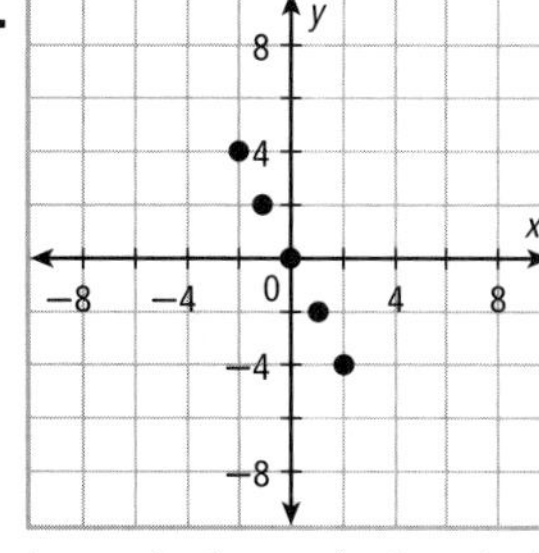

$(-2, 4), (-1, 2), (0, 0), (1, -2), (2, -4)$; line

95.

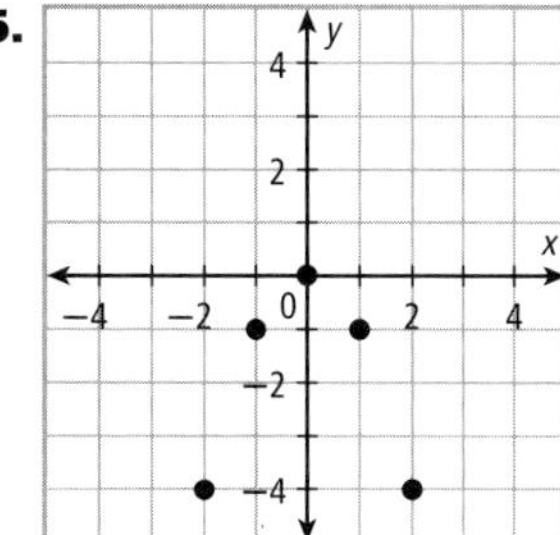

$(-2, -4), (-1, -1), (0, 0), (1, -1), (2, -4)$; U shape

96.

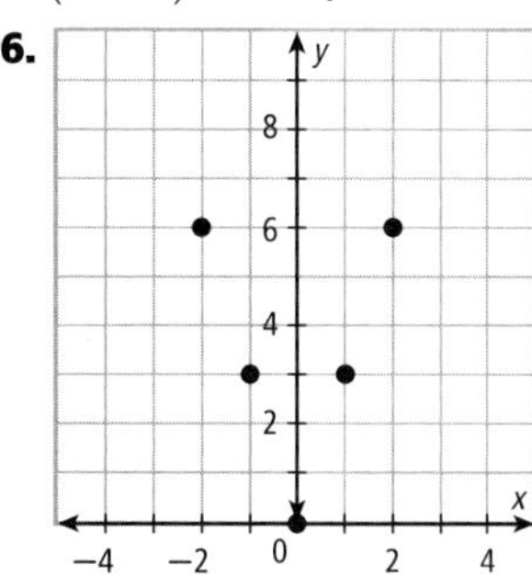

$(-2, 6), (-1, 3), (0, 0), (1, 3), (2, 6)$; V shape

97.

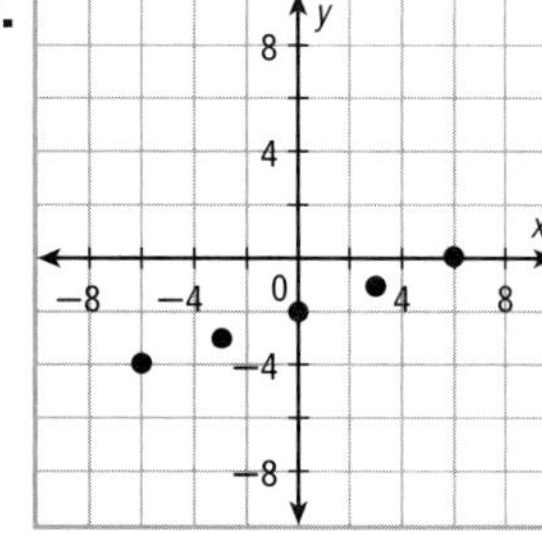

$y = \frac{1}{3}x + (-2)$; $(-6, -4), (-3, -3), (0, -2), (3, -1), (6, 0)$; line

98.

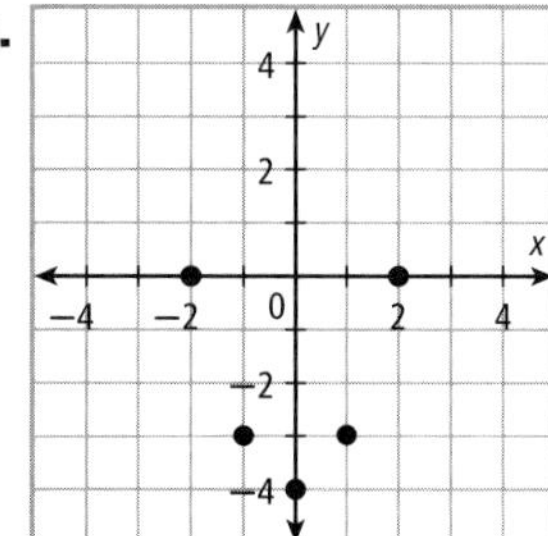

$y = x^2 - 4$; $(-2, 0), (-1, -3), (0, -4), (1, -3), (2, 0)$; U shape

Chapter 2

32. $\frac{1}{2}x + 3 = 17 - 3x$; $x = 4$

33. $2(x - 4) = x - 5$; $x = 3$

Chapter 3

1. all real numbers less than -5

2. all real numbers greater than or equal to 11

3. all real numbers greater than 9

4. all real numbers less than or equal to $\frac{3}{4}$

5. 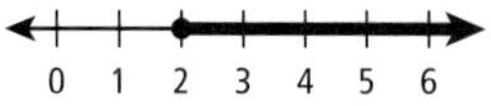 0 1 2 3 4 5 6

19. 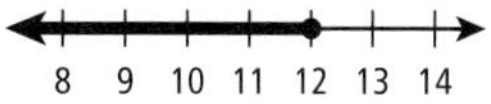 8 9 10 11 12 13 14

20.  −16 −15 −14 −13 −12 −11 −10

21.  0 1 2 3 4 5 6

22. 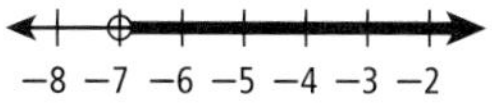 −8 −7 −6 −5 −4 −3 −2

30. 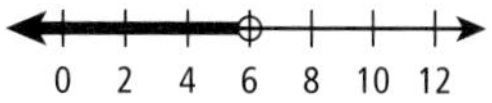 0 2 4 6 8 10 12

31. 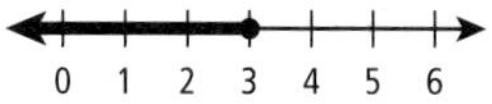 0 1 2 3 4 5 6

32. 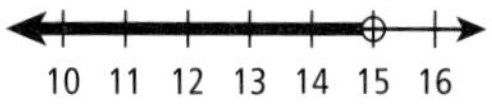 10 11 12 13 14 15 16

33. 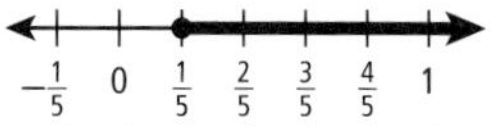 $-\frac{1}{5}$ 0 $\frac{1}{5}$ $\frac{2}{5}$ $\frac{3}{5}$ $\frac{4}{5}$ 1

34. 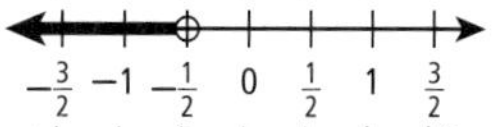 $-\frac{3}{2}$ −1 $-\frac{1}{2}$ 0 $\frac{1}{2}$ 1 $\frac{3}{2}$

35. 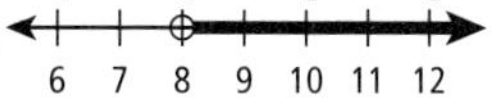 6 7 8 9 10 11 12

36. 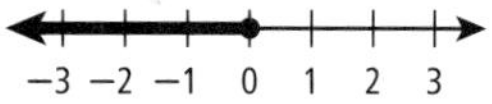 −3 −2 −1 0 1 2 3

37.  0 2 4 6 8 10 12

38. 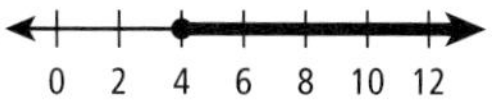 0 2 4 6 8 10 12

39. 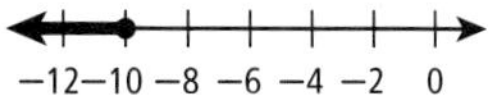 −12 −10 −8 −6 −4 −2 0

40. 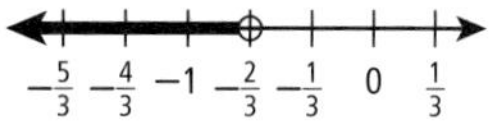 $-\frac{5}{3}$ $-\frac{4}{3}$ −1 $-\frac{2}{3}$ $-\frac{1}{3}$ 0 $\frac{1}{3}$

41. 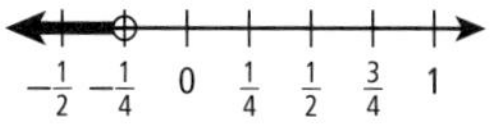 $-\frac{1}{2}$ $-\frac{1}{4}$ 0 $\frac{1}{4}$ $\frac{1}{2}$ $\frac{3}{4}$ 1

42. 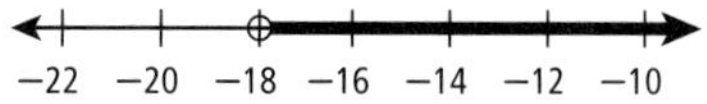 −22 −20 −18 −16 −14 −12 −10

43. 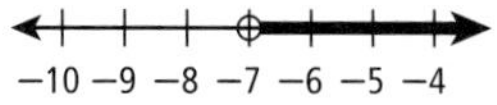 −10 −9 −8 −7 −6 −5 −4

44. 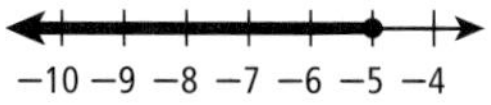 −10 −9 −8 −7 −6 −5 −4

45. 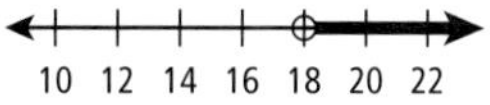 10 12 14 16 18 20 22

46. 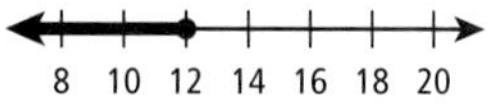 8 10 12 14 16 18 20

47. 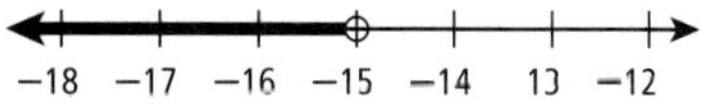 −18 −17 −16 −15 −14 13 −12

48. 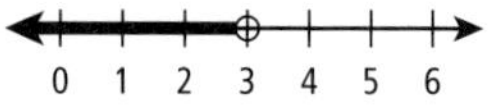 0 1 2 3 4 5 6

49. 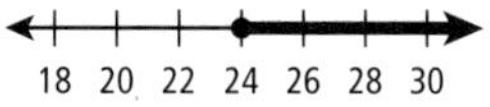 18 20 22 24 26 28 30

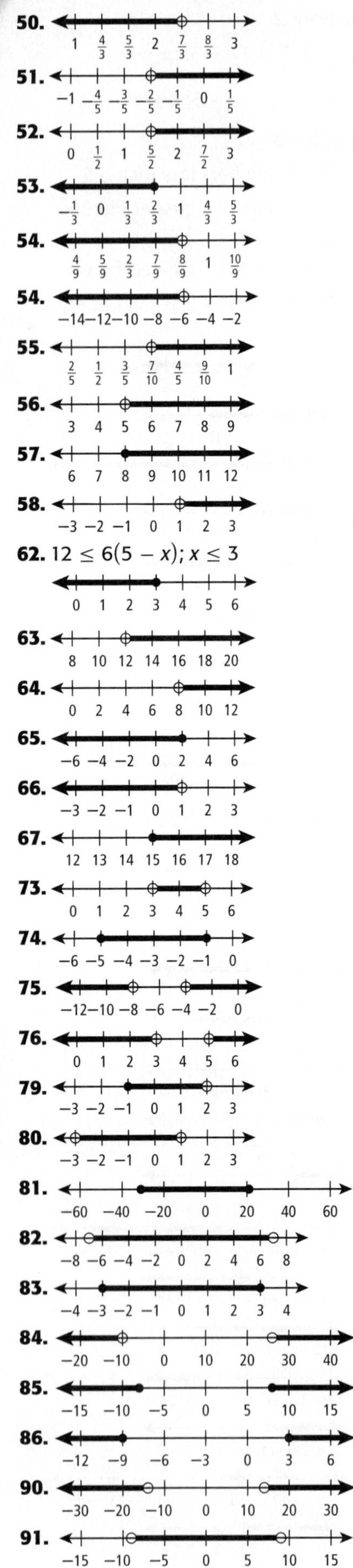

Chapter 4

4.

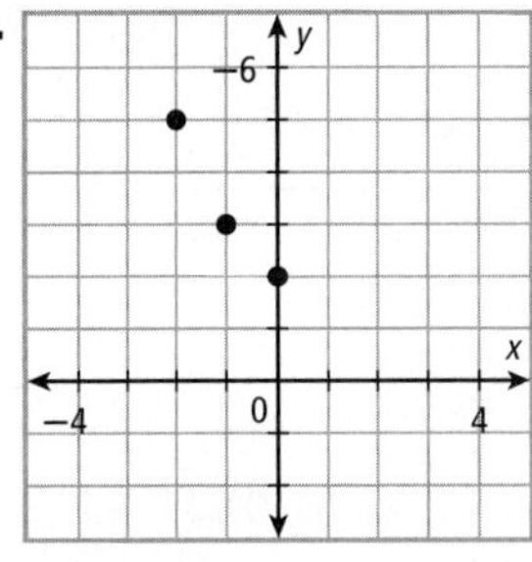

x	y
0	2
−1	3
−2	5

5.

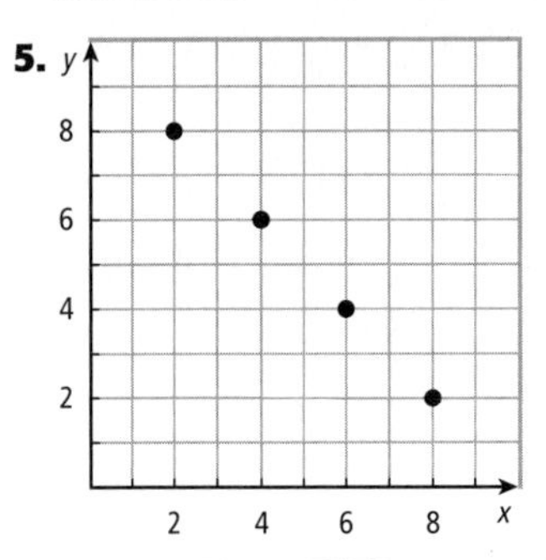

x	y
2	8
4	6
6	4
8	2

6. D: {−1, 3, 2, 5}; R: {−3, 0, 2, 4}; yes; each domain value is paired with exactly one range value.

7. D: {0, 5}; R: {−3, 1, 2, 4}; no; each domain value does not have exactly one range value.

9. D: $\{4 \le x \le 8\}$; R: $\{2 \le y \le 8\}$; yes; each domain value is paired with exactly one range value.

11. *y* is *x* squared; $y = x^2$

19.

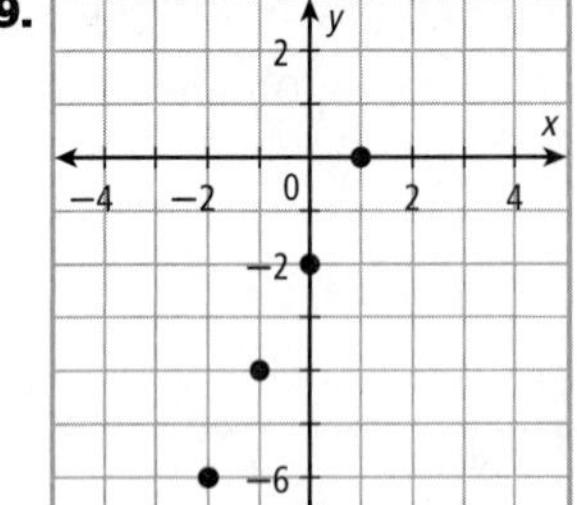

20.

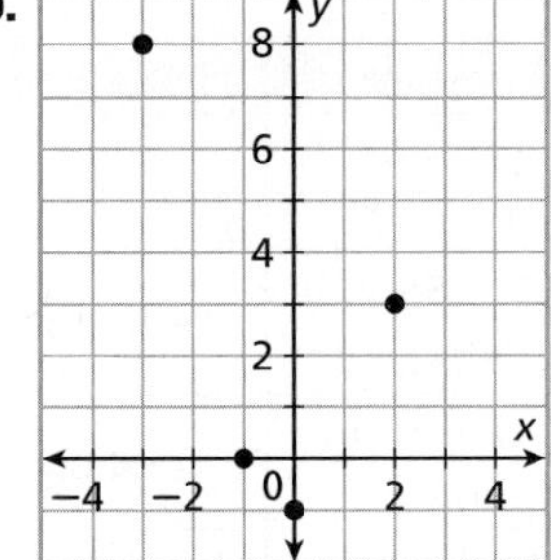

21.

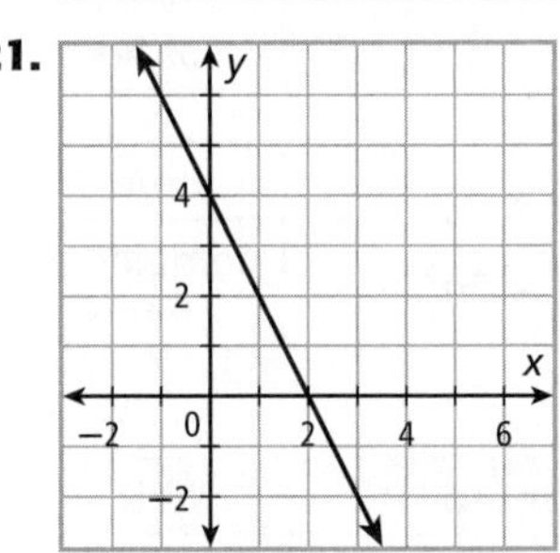

22.

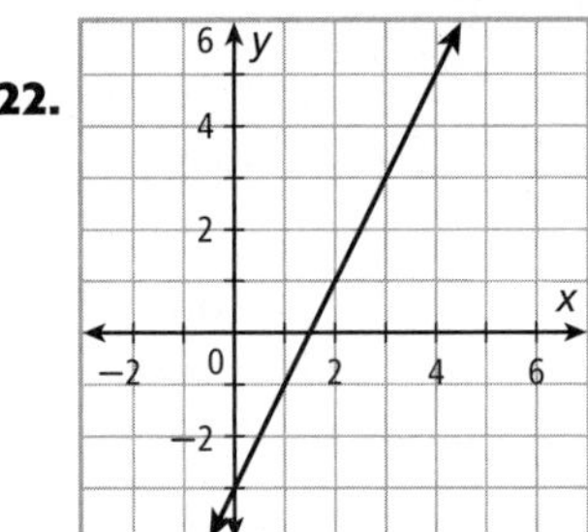

23.

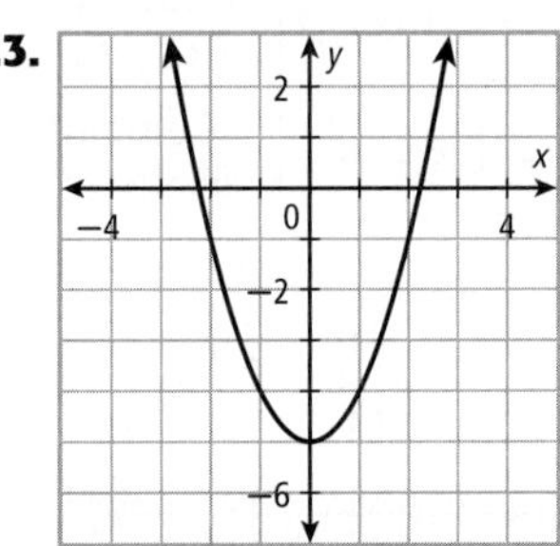

32. As the number of chess pieces captured increases, the number of pieces still on the board decreases.

33. A person's height has nothing to do with the color of his or her eyes.

34. There is probably no correlation between the data sets, and graph B shows no correlation.

35. There is a negative correlation between the data sets, and graph A shows a negative correlation.

Chapter 5

1. Yes; each domain value is paired with exactly one range value; yes

2. Yes; each domain value is paired with exactly one range value; yes

3. Yes; each domain value is paired with exactly one range value; no

4. Yes; a constant change of +2 in x corresponds to a constant change of -1 in y.

5. No; a constant change of +3 in x corresponds to different changes in y.

6. yes; $3x + y = 8$; $A = 3$; $B = 1$; $C = 8$

7. yes; $\frac{1}{3}x + 2y = 4$; $A = \frac{1}{3}$; $B = 2$; $C = 4$

9. yes; $4x + 3y = -3$; $A = 4$; $B = 3$; $C = -3$

10. x-int.: $\frac{1}{4}$; y-int.: $\frac{1}{2}$

14.
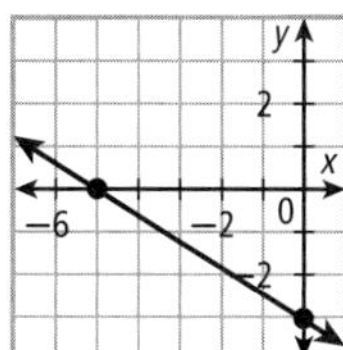

15.
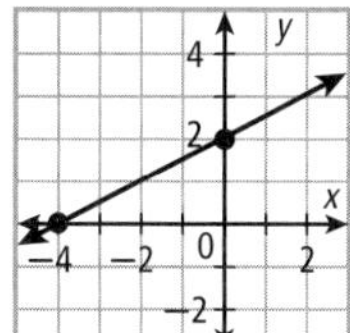

16.
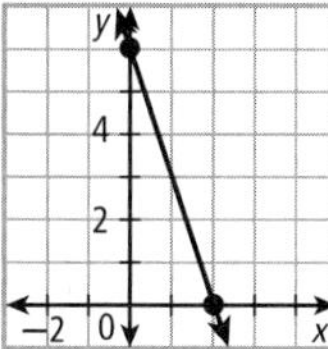

17.
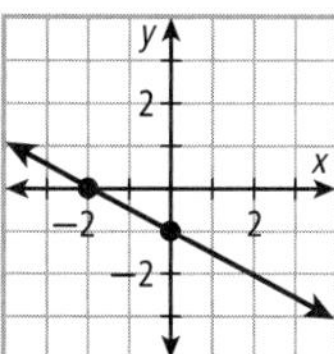

42.
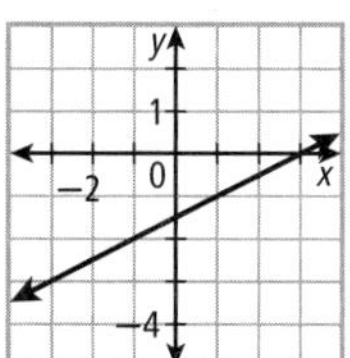

43.
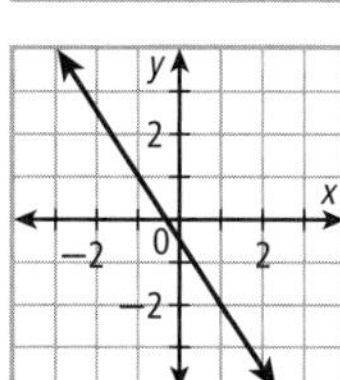

44.
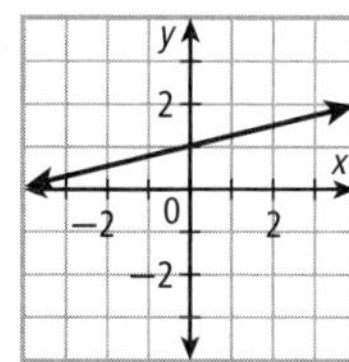

58.
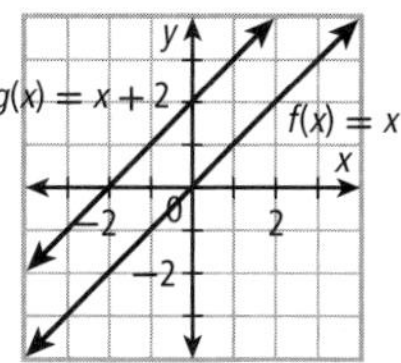

59.
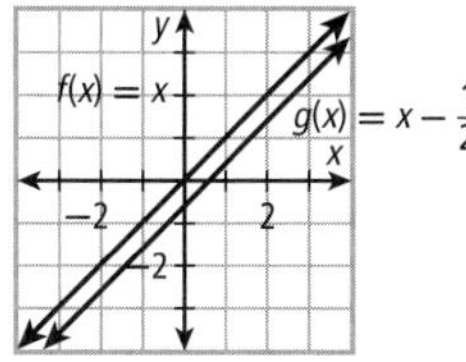

60.
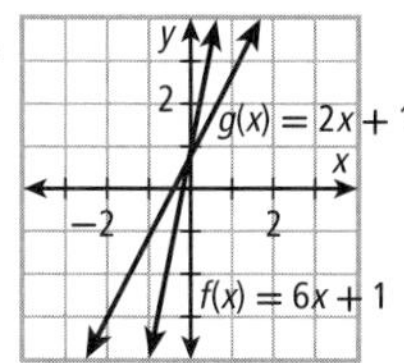

rot. about $(0, 1)$ (less steep)

61.
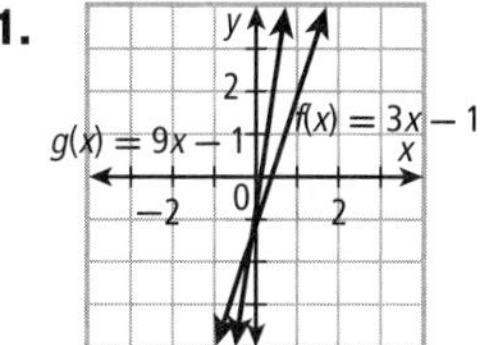

rot. about $(0, -1)$

62.
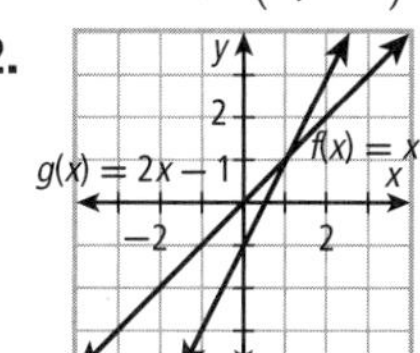

63.
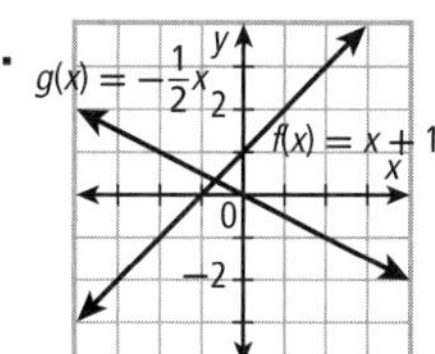

rot. and trans. 1 unit down

Chapter 6

39.
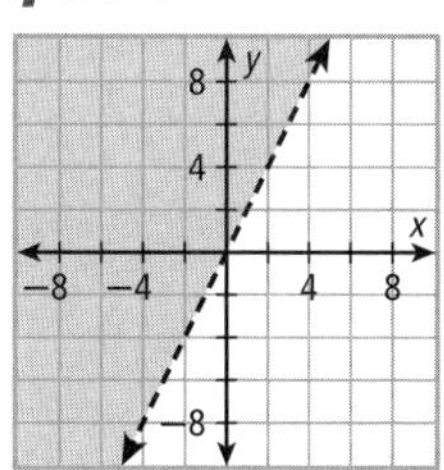

40.
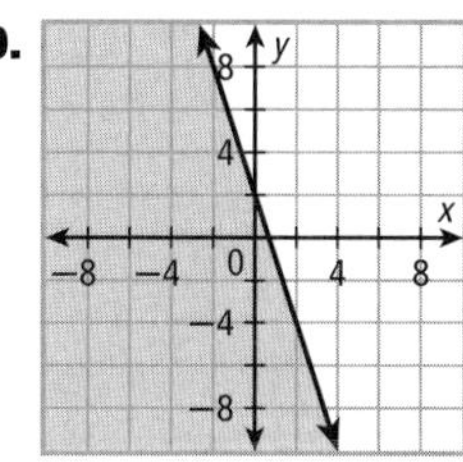

41.
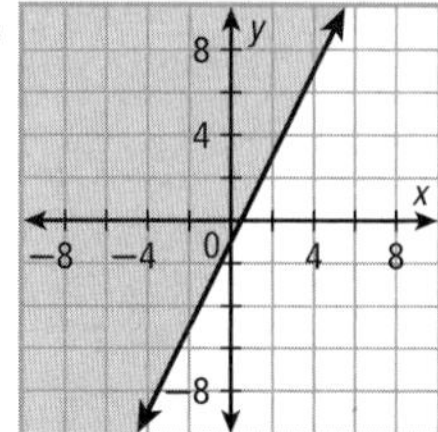

42.
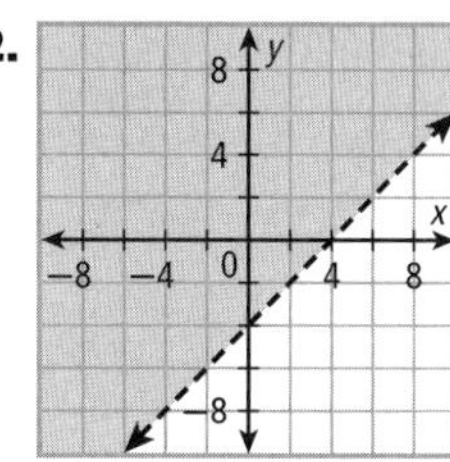

43.
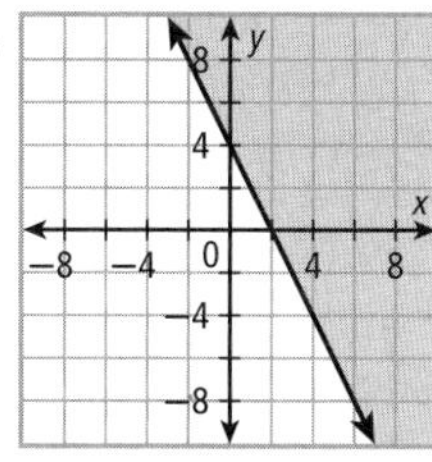

44.
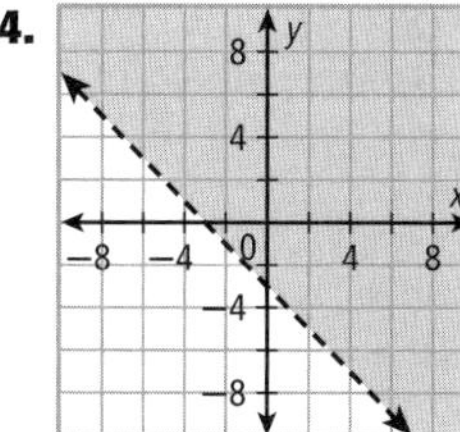

45.
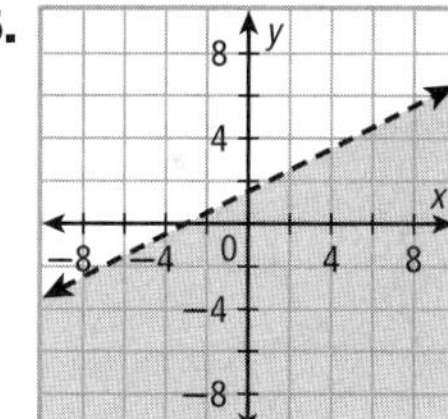

46.
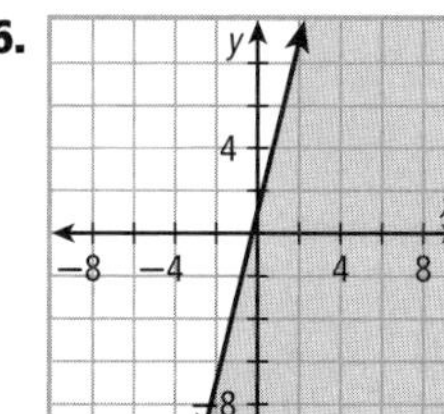

52.
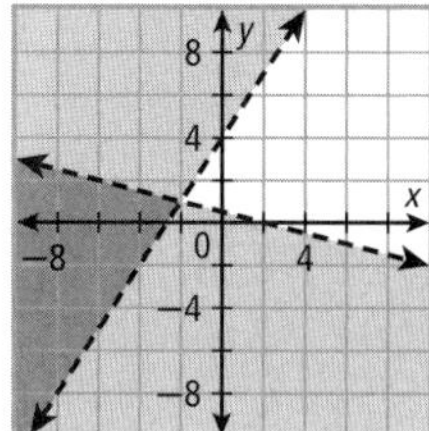

Possible answer: solutions: $(-10, 0)$ and $(-12, 1)$; not solutions: $(0, 0)$ and $(6, -2)$

53.

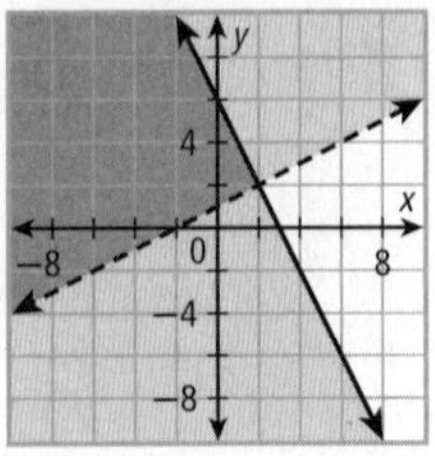

Possible answer: solutions: (–2, 6) and (0, 2); not solutions: (8, 0) and (0, 8)

54. 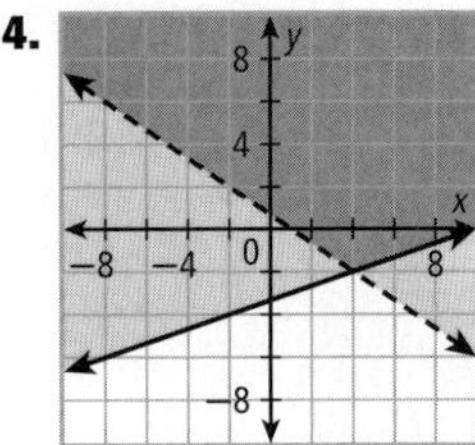

Possible answer: solutions: (4, 0) and (2, 2); not solutions: (–2, 0) and (6, –6)

55. 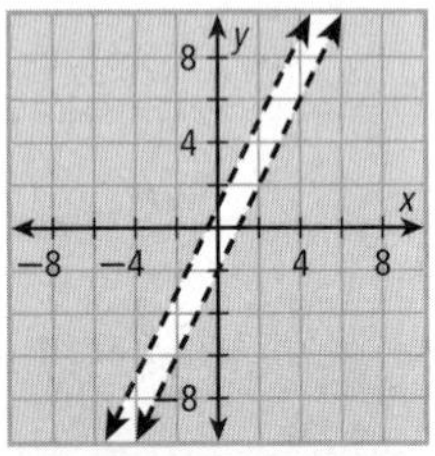 no solution

56. 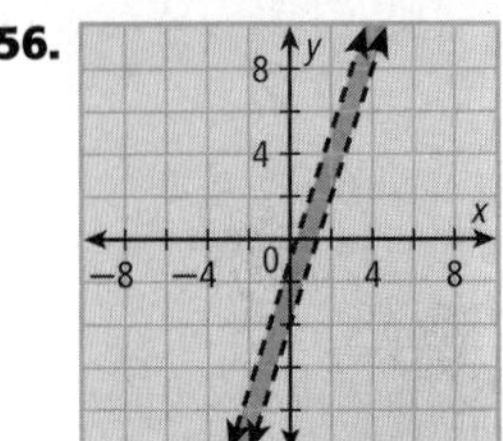

all pts. between the par. lines

57. 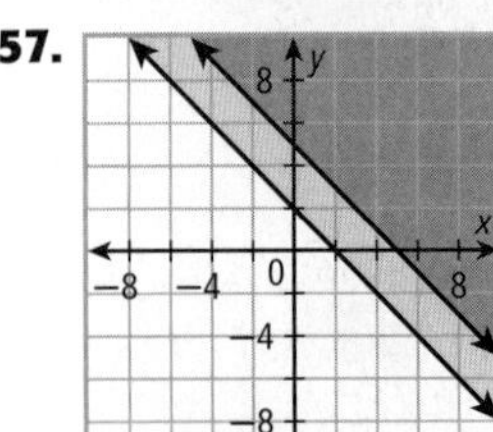

same as solutions of $y \geq -x + 5$

58. 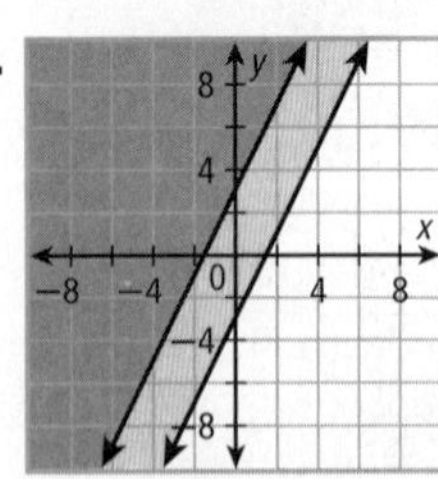

same as solutions of $y \geq 2x + 3$

59. 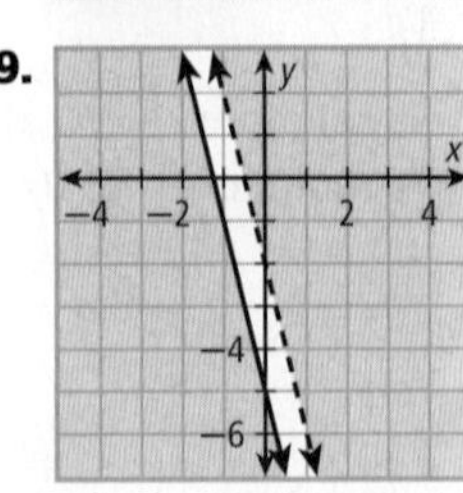

no solutions

60. 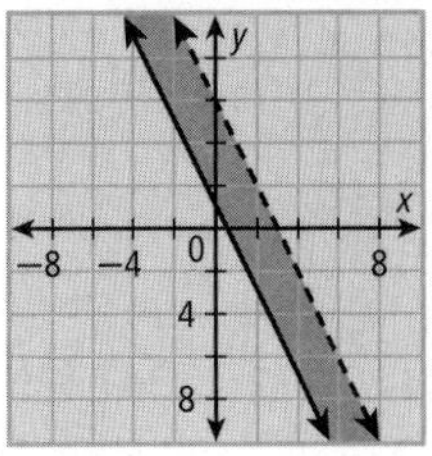 all pts. between the par. lines and on the solid line

Chapter 7

78. $-\frac{1}{3}t^5 + \frac{1}{2}t^3 + t + 4; -\frac{1}{3}$

90. $6a^{11}$

91. $-6x^3y^4z^5$

92. $-8k^3\ell^3m^3$

93. $6j^3k^2 + 3jk^3$

94. $8q^4r^4 + 12q^4r^2$

95. $6x^3y^3 - 9xy^3$

96. $x^2 - 2x - 3$

97. $x^2 - 5x + 6$

98. $3x^4y + 6x^3y^2 - 2x^2 - 4xy$

99. $2x^3y - 9x^2y + 9xy$

100. $x^3 + x^2 - 10x + 8$

101. $-4x^3 - 4x^2 + 11x - 4$

102. $2x^5 + 6x^4 - 3x^3 - 9x^2 - 5x - 15$

103. $6a^3 + 5a^2b - 5ab^2 - 2b^3$

104. $3a^4 - 2a^3b + 3a^2b^2 - 3a^2b + 2ab^2 - 3b^3$

Chapter 8

27. $(3 + 4a)(a + 3)$

28. $(5 - 2k)(k - 4)$

29. $(5 + 4c^2)(c - 3)$

30. $(3 + t)(t - 4)$

31. $(5 - s)(2r - 1)$

32. $(7 - 2e)(3d + 4)$

33. $(x + 3)(x^2 - 2)$

34. $(2m - 3)(m^2 + 4)$

35. $(3k - 1)(k^2 + 5)$

36. $(3r + 5)(5r^2 - 2)$

37. $(2n - 1)(6n^2 - 5)$

38. $(4z - 3)(z^2 + 1)$

39. $(2k - 3)(k - 4)$

40. $(3p - 2)(p - 4)$

41. $(5d - 3)(2d - 3)$

42. $(3a - 2)(2a^2 - 5)$

43. $(6s - 1)(2s^2 - 3)$

44. $(4c - 3)(c^2 - 5)$

45. $(x + 3)(x + 12)$

46. $(x + 5)(x + 8)$

47. $(x + 2)(x + 8)$

48. $(x - 3)(x - 6)$

49. $(x - 4)(x - 7)$

50. $(x - 6)(x - 7)$

51. $(x - 3)(x + 7)$

52. $(x + 4)(x - 9)$

53. $(x + 3)(x - 10)$

54.

c	$c^2 - 2c - 48$	$(c - 8)(c + 6)$
0	–48	–48
1	–49	–49
2	–48	–48
3	–45	–45
4	–40	–40

58. $(2x + 3)(x + 5)$

59. $(x + 2)(3x + 8)$

60. $(4x - 2)(2x - 3)$

61. $(2x + 1)(3x + 4)$

62. $(3x - 2)(x - 3)$

63. $(5x - 3)(2x - 5)$

64. $(3x - 4)(2x + 1)$

65. $(4x + 3)(2x - 5)$

66. $(x - 2)(4x - 3)$

67. $(3x - 1)(4x - 3)$

68. $(6x + 5)(x - 2)$

69. $(2x + 3)(3x - 1)$

70. $(2x - 3)(x + 4)$

71. $(3x + 2)(2x - 3)$

72. $(4x - 1)(2x + 3)$

73. $(5x + 2)(2x - 3)$

74. $(4x - 5)(x + 1)$

75. $(3x + 4)(2x - 5)$

76. $-1(2x - 1)(x - 5)$

77. $-1(3x - 4)(2x + 3)$

78. $-1(4x + 3)(2x + 1)$

79. $-1(2x - 5)(2x - 3)$

80. $-1(5x + 2)(2x - 5)$

81. $-1(3x - 7)(x - 2)$

82. $(x - 4)^2$

83. $(2x - 1)^2$

84. no; $-8x \neq 2(x \cdot 3)$

85. no; $-14x \neq 2(3x \cdot 2)$

86. $(2x + 3)^2$

87. No; –16 is not a perfect square.

88. $(3x - 7)^2$

89. no; $18x \neq 2(2x \cdot 5)$

90. $(4x - 3)^2$

91. $(2 - 4x^2)(2 + 4x^2)$

92. No; 35 is not a perfect square.

93. $(c - 5)(c + 5)$

94. No; g^5 is not a perfect square.

95. $(v^2 - 8)(v^2 + 8)$

96. No; 120 is not a perfect square.

112. $12b(b - 2)(b + 2)$

113. $4w^2(3w - 4)(2w + 1)$

114. $2k(3k + 4)(3k - 4)$

115. $a(4a - b)(a + 3)$

116. $3xy(x - y)^2$

117. $4q(3p - 4q)(3p + 4q)$

118. $8a^2(2a - 1)(2a + 1)$

119. $m(m + 2n)(m + 3n)$

120. $x(x + 32)$

121. $3(2d - 1)(3d + 2)$

122. $(2r + 3)(r - 6)$

123. $4(2y - 1)(y + 1)$

124. $9(3 - 2u)(3 + 2u)$

125. $4(2x^2 + 5)(x + 1)(x - 1)$

126. $5j(2j + 7)(j - 2)$

127. $3z(3z - 1)^2$

128. $2(2b + 9)(b - 4)$

129. $3(f + g)(f - g)$

Chapter 9

1. Yes; the function can be written in the form $y = ax^2 + bx + c$.

2. No; $a = 0$.

3. Yes; the function can be written in the form $y = ax^2 + bx + c$.

6.

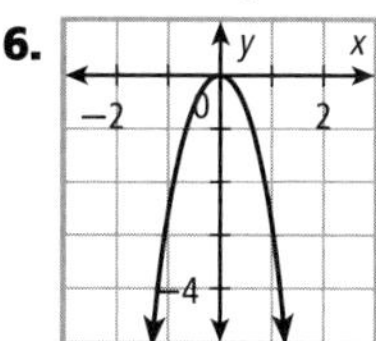

7.

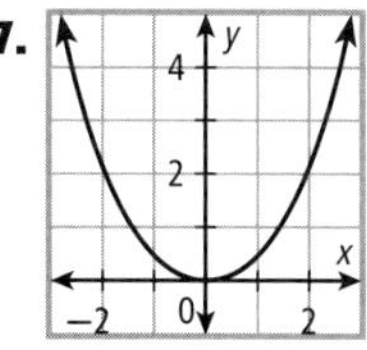

8.

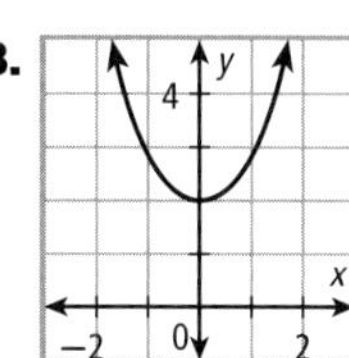

9.

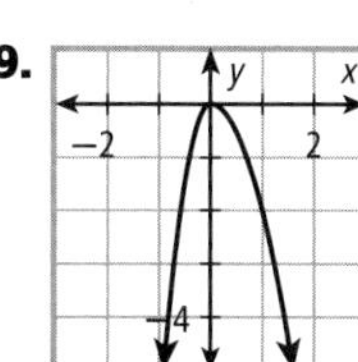

19.

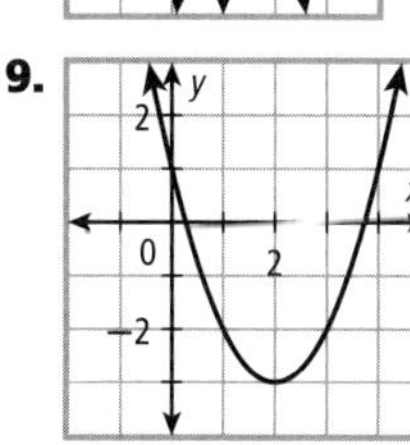

20.

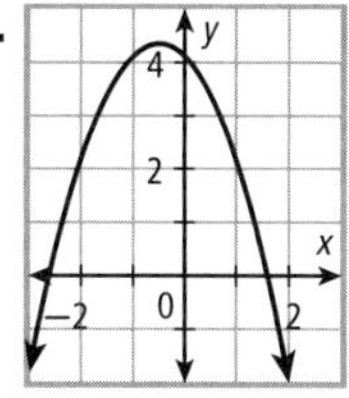

21.

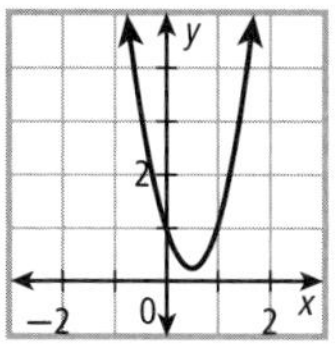

22.

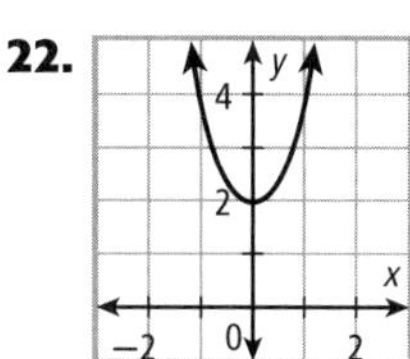

23.

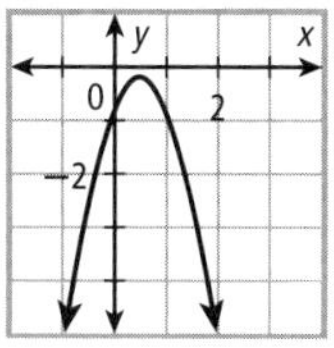

24.

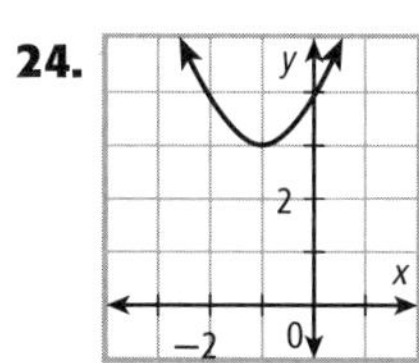

29. narrower; same axis of symmetry; both open upward; vertex of $g(x)$ is translated down 2 units

30. wider; same axis of symmetry; $g(x)$ opens downward; same vertex

31. narrower; same axis of symmetry, $g(x)$ opens downward; vertex of $g(x)$ is translated up 1 unit

98. $x \approx -2.70$ or $x \approx 3.70$

99. $x \approx -1.19$ or $x \approx 1.69$

100. $x \approx -2.19$ or $x \approx 0.69$

Chapter 10

8.

Stem	Leaves
1	8 9 9
2	2 4 5 5 5 8 9
3	0 2 2 3

Key: 1|8 means 18

9.

High Temperatures	
Temperature (°C)	Frequency
18–21	3
22–25	5
26–29	2
30–33	4

10.

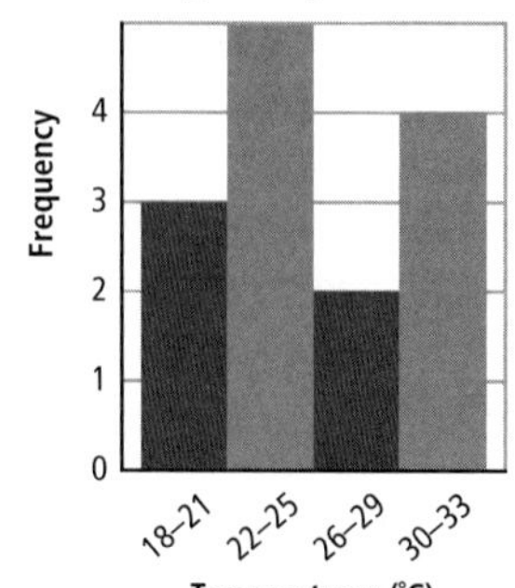

11.

High Temperatures		
Temperature (°C)	Frequency	Cumulative Frequency
18–21	3	3
22–25	5	8
26–29	2	10
30–33	4	14

14. 71; increases mean by 9, median by 0.5, and range by 56; no effect on mode

15. 7; decreases mean by 5 and range by 29; no effect on median and mode.

16.

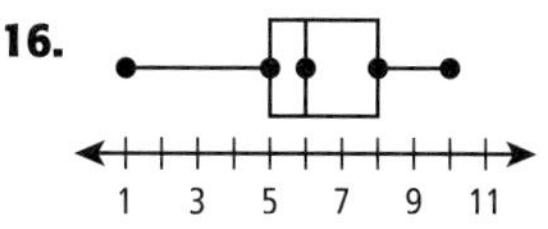

17.

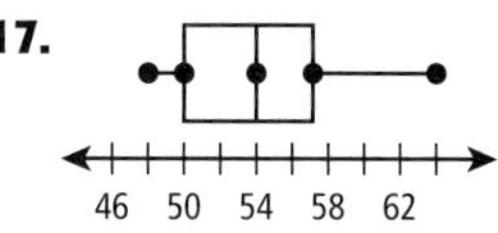

18a. The sectors do not add to 100%.

b. Most listeners are between the ages of 25 and 36.

c. Possible answer: A person selling advertising time at the station might want to use the graph to convince advertisers that most listeners are between the ages of 25 and 36.

19. The sample is biased because people at the library are likely to spend more time reading than other people in the town.

31. Dep.; after you pick a bottle, there are fewer bottles in the basket.

32. Ind.; the result of rolling the number cube does not affect the result of tossing the coin.

Chapter 11

1. 625; 3,125; 15,625

2. 46, 23, 11.5

9. Yes; as the x-values increase by a constant amount, the y-values are multiplied by a constant amount.

10. No; as the x-values increase by a constant amount, the y-values are not multiplied by a constant amount.

11. Yes; as the x-values increase by a constant amount, the y-values are multiplied by a constant amount.

12. No; as the x-values increase by a constant amount, the y-values are not multiplied by a constant amount.

13. 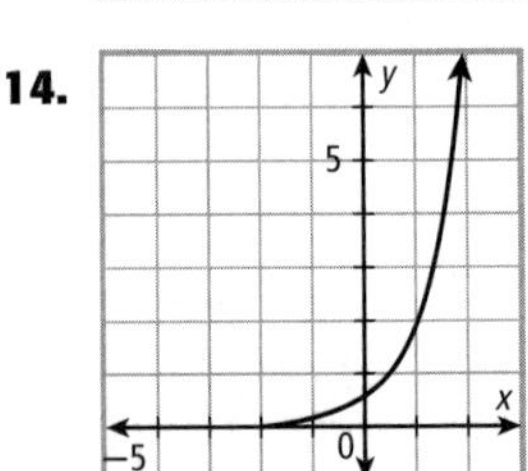

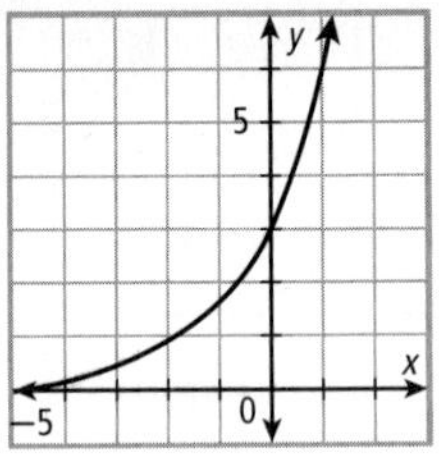

14. 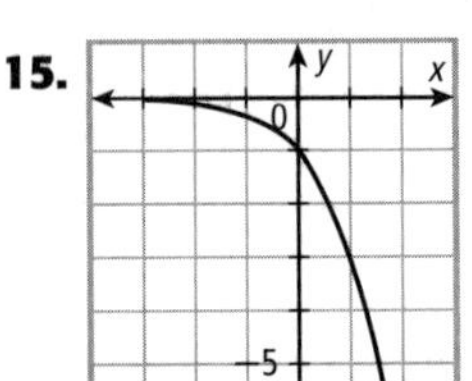

15. 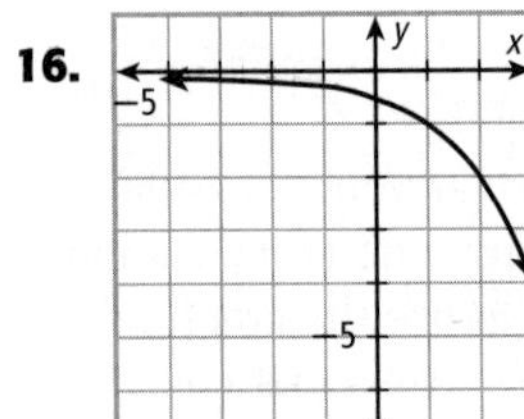

16. 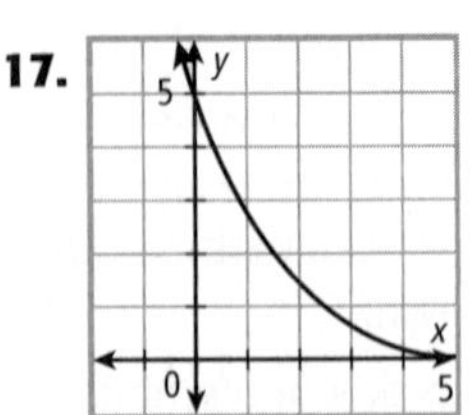

17. 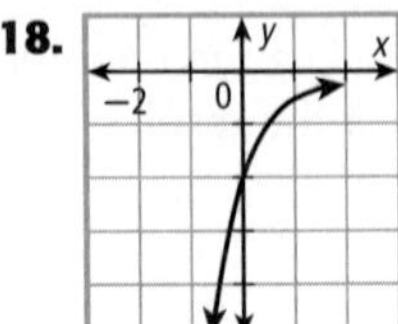

18.

25. 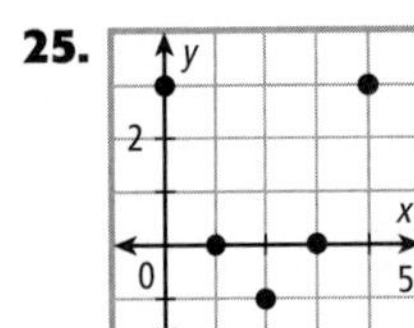

26. 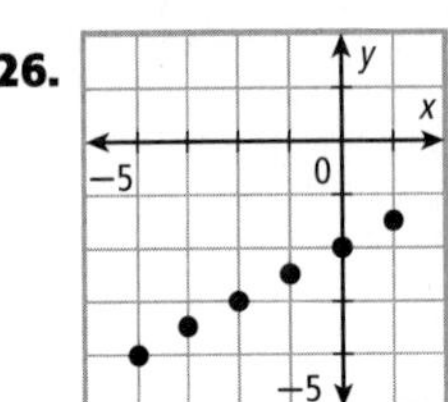

27. 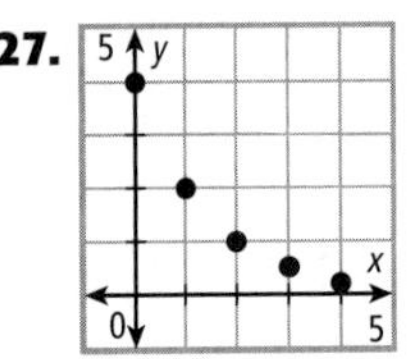

37. 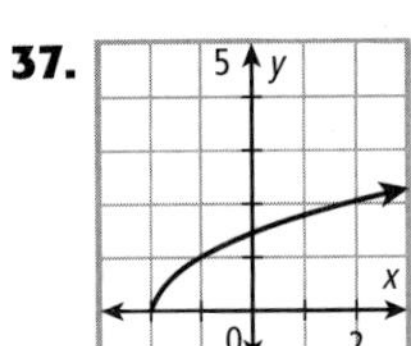

38. 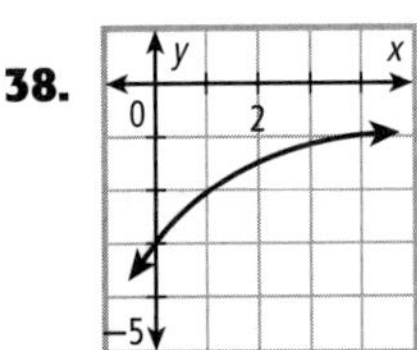

39. 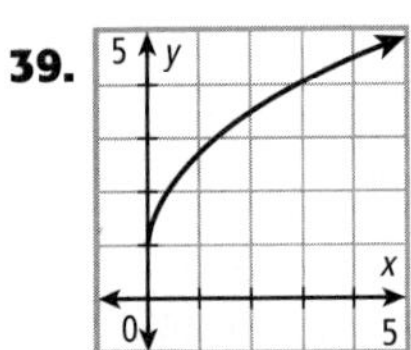

40. 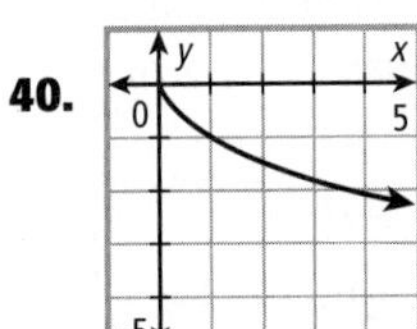

41. 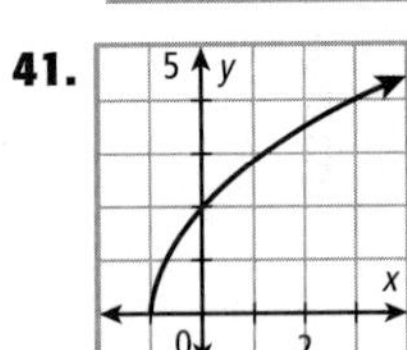

42. 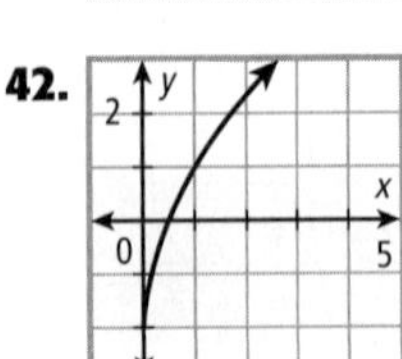

Chapter 12

4. yes; $xy = \frac{10}{3}$

5. No; the product xy is not constant.

6. yes; $xy = -\frac{1}{6}$

7. 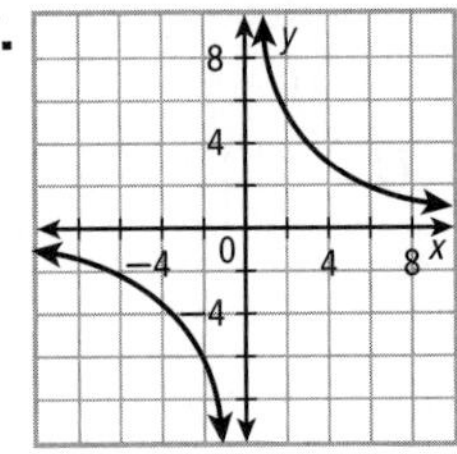

8. 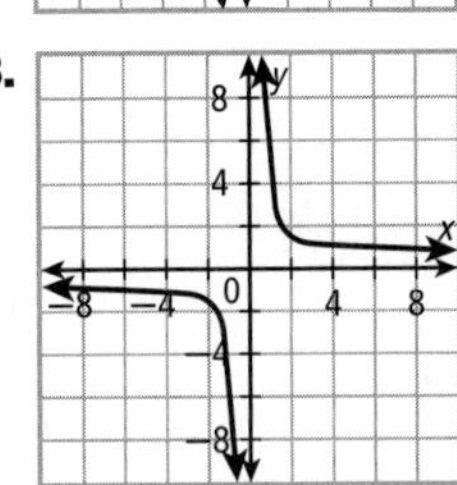

19. 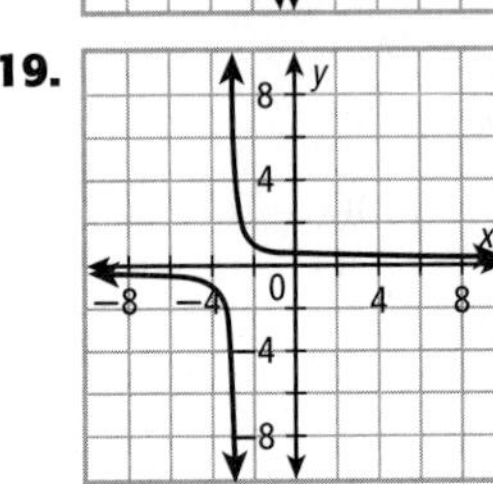

20. 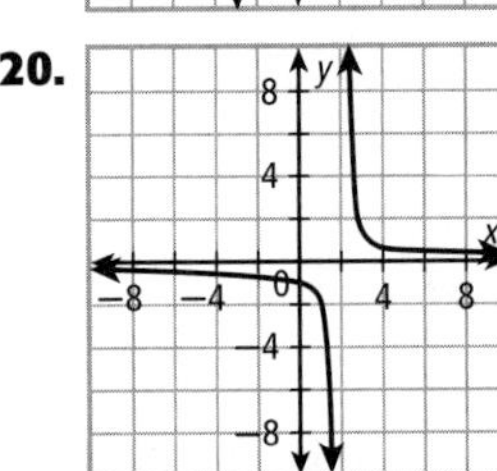

21. 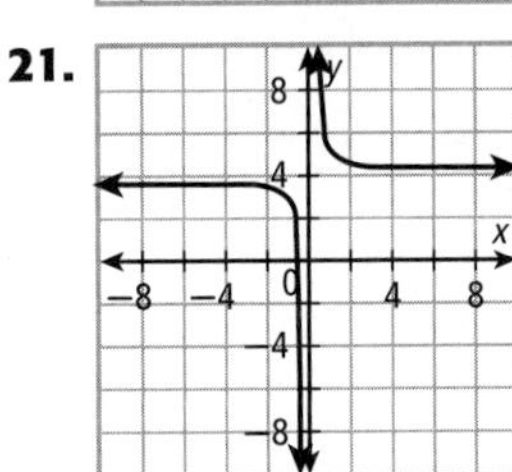

22. 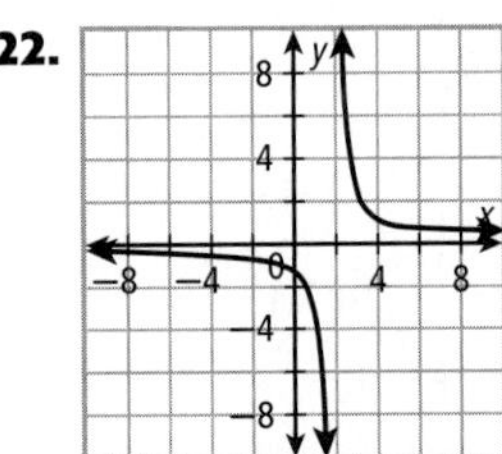

23. 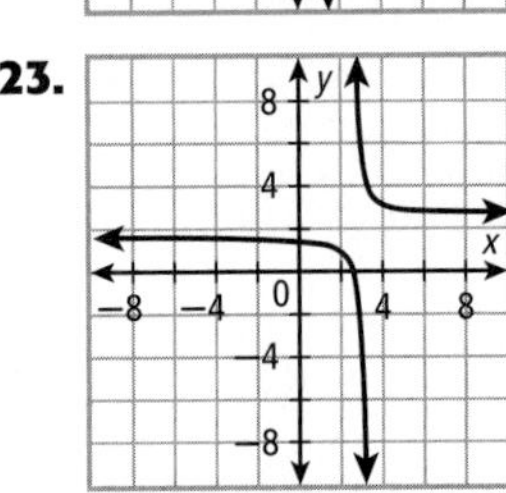

24. 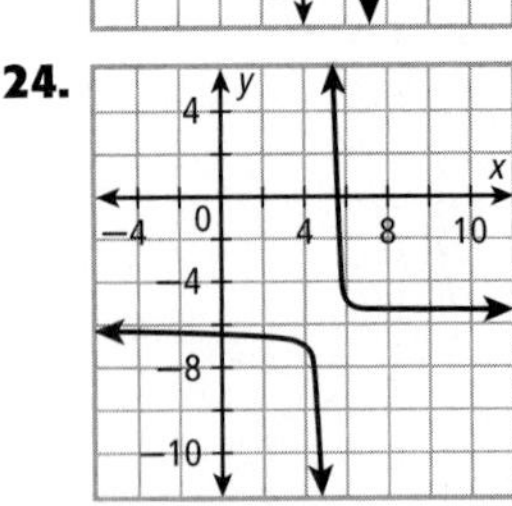

25. 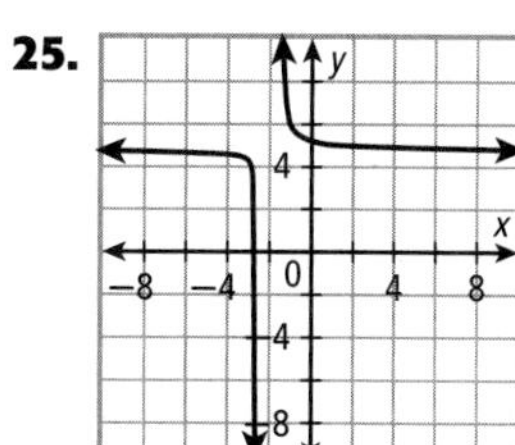

26. 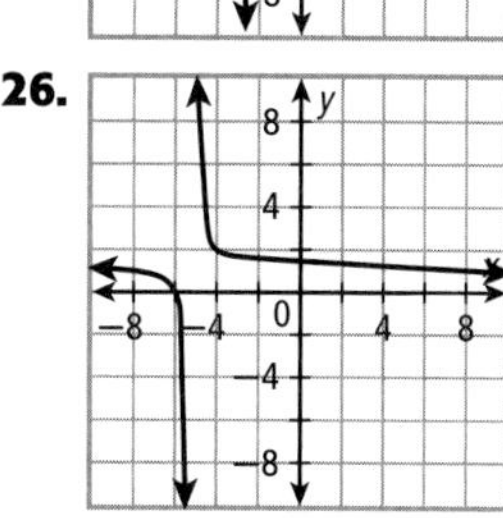

54. $\frac{3x(x + 6)}{4}$

55. $\frac{2y(y + 5)}{3}$

56. $\frac{4}{3r}$

57. $\frac{1}{6(x + 2)}$

58. $a + 1$

59. $\frac{b + 1}{2}$

60. $\frac{3}{q}$

61. $\frac{r + 3}{2(r - 4)}$

77. $3y^3 - 4 + \frac{1}{y}$

78. $m^2 - \frac{3}{m} + \frac{1}{2m^2}$

79. $-4x - 5 + \frac{1}{x^2}$

86. $3x + 4 + \frac{1}{x - 2}$

87. $2x - 4 + \frac{3}{x + 3}$

88. $5x^2 + 12x + 24 + \frac{44}{x - 2}$

Extra Practice Applications

Chapter 3

1. Let x represent the weight of a box in ounces; $x \geq 15$.

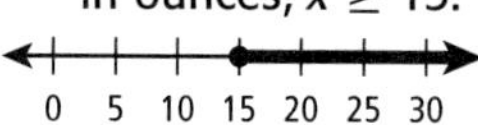

2. Let x be the age of a visitor to the museum; $x < 13$ where x is nonneg.

3. $96 + x \leq 102$; 0, 1, 2, 3, 4, 5, or 6 additional customers

4. $63 + x \geq 74$; at least 11 mi/h greater

11. $34 \leq x \leq 40$

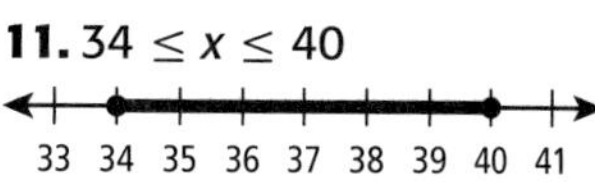

12. $492 \leq x \leq 577$

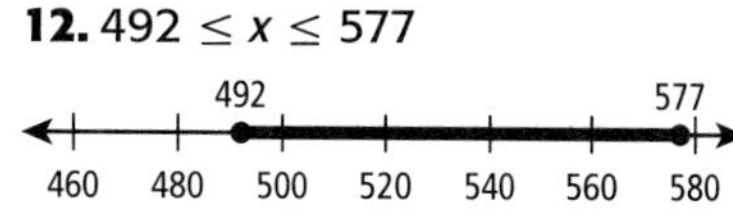

Chapter 4

1. continuous

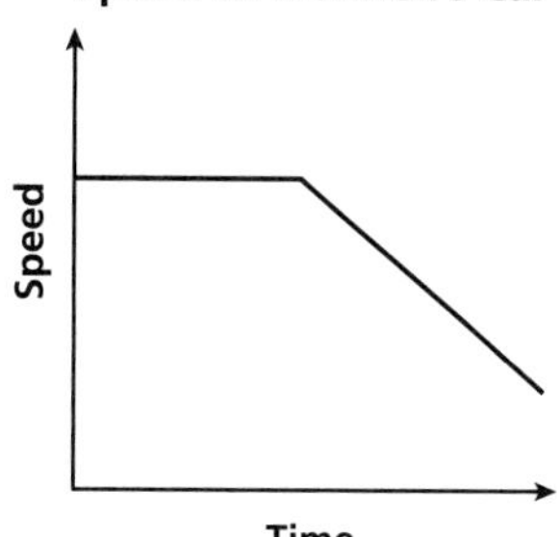

2. discrete

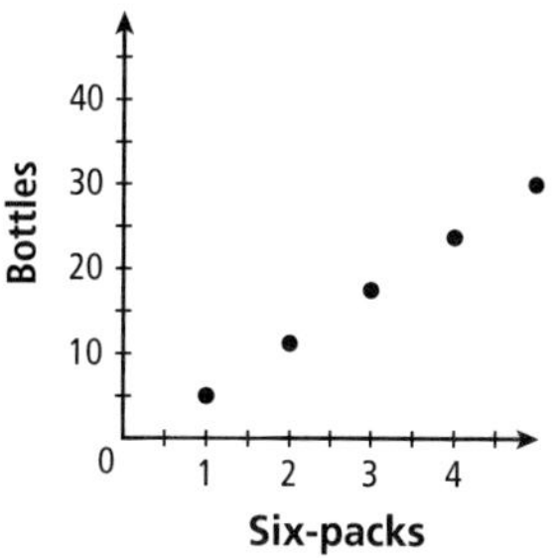

3a.

x	y
20	200
30	190
35	185
40	180

b. Yes; each domain value is paired with exactly one range value.

4. No; one of the domain values (93) is paired with more than one range value.

7. 15.75 mi

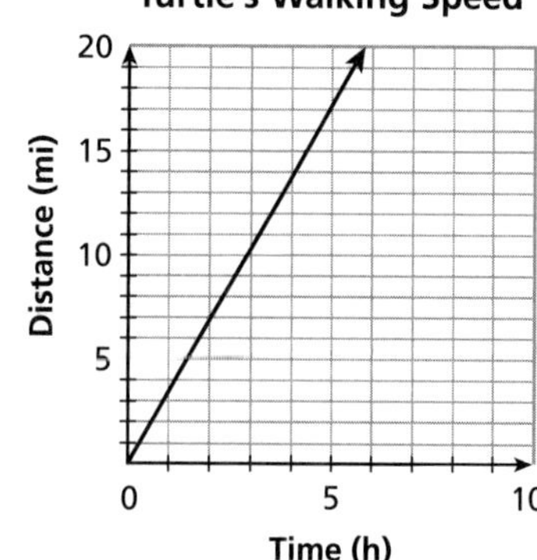

8. 12.8 m

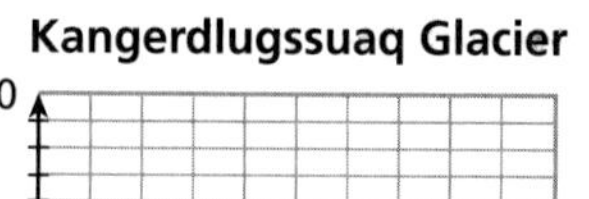

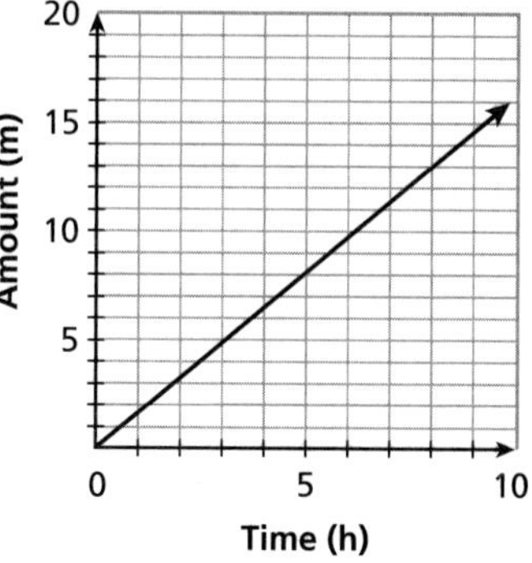

Chapter 5

1. D: {0, 1, 2, 3, ...}; R: {\$0, \$1.50, \$3.00, \$4.50, ...}

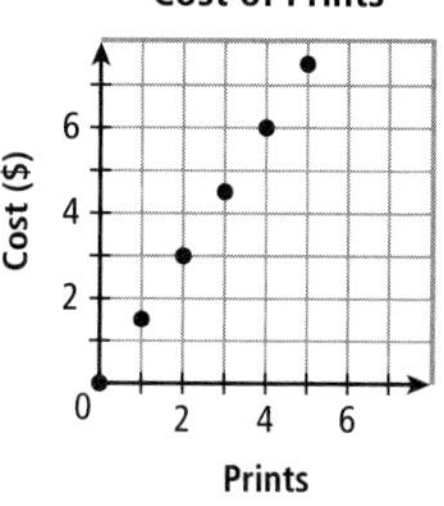

2a. 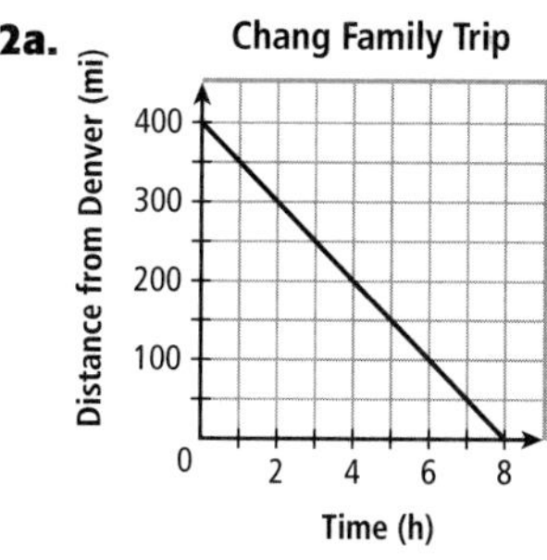

b. y-int.: 400; starting distance from Denver. x-int.: 8; time required to reach Denver (8 hours)

3. 1945 to 1950: 1.8 nations/yr; 1950 to 1960: 3.9 nations/yr; 1960 to 1975: 3 nations/yr; from 1950 to 1960

4. -4; the oven cools at a rate of 4 °F per minute.

7. $y = 9x$

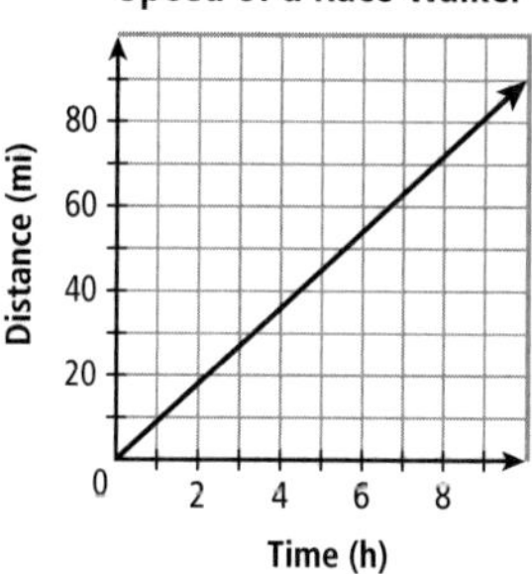

8b. y-int.: 10; initial rental fee; slope: 1.5; cost per mile.

10. slope of $\overline{AB}$ = slope of $\overline{DC} = -2$; slope of $\overline{AD}$ = slope of $\overline{BC} = \frac{1}{2}$. Therefore, $\overline{AB}$ and $\overline{BC}$ are perp., $\overline{BC}$ and $\overline{DC}$ are perp., $\overline{DC}$ and $\overline{AD}$ are perp., and $\overline{AD}$ and $\overline{AB}$ are perp., the figure has four right angles and is a rectangle.

11. trans. 2 units up; rot. about (0, 12.50)(steeper)

Chapter 6

4. The company with the \$200 setup fee is cheaper if more than 14 jerseys are purchased.

9. No; the graphs are two parallel lines.

10. Yes; the graphs have different slopes, so they intersect.

11. $4x + 5y \leq 18$, where x is the number of pounds of almonds and y is the number of pounds of cashews. Possible combinations: (2, 2), (3, 1)

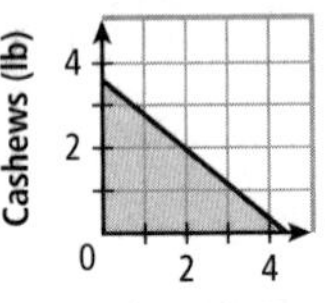

12. $5x + 8y < 100$, where x is the number of child shirts and y is the number of adult shirts. Possible combinations: (16, 2), (8, 6)

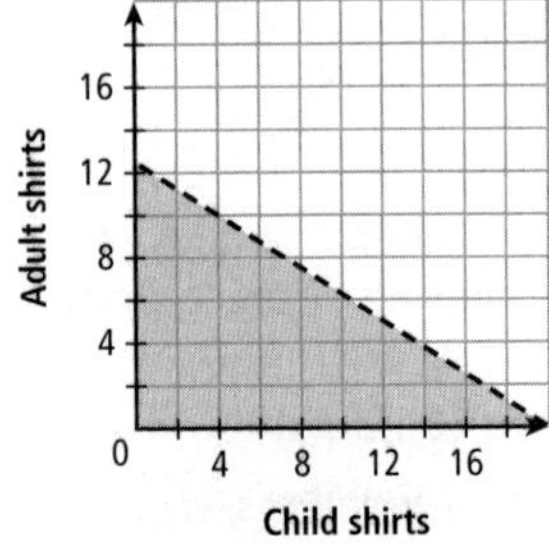

13. Possible combinations: 3 lb beef, 2 lb liver; 2 lb beef, 3 lb liver

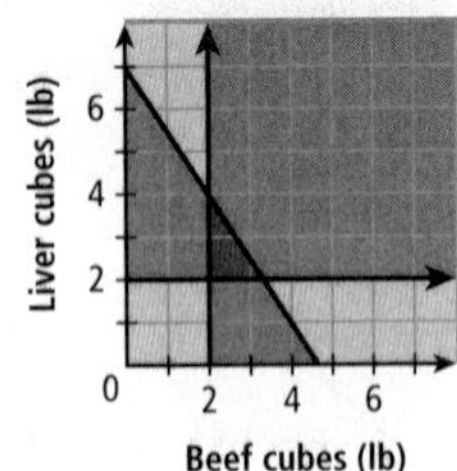

14. Possible combinations: length: 5 in., width: 5 in.; length: 6 in., width: 4 in.

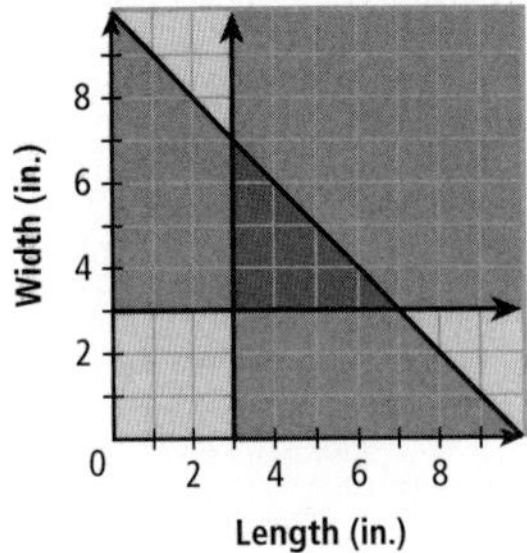

Chapter 8

11. $3x - 4$; no; the lengths of the sides cannot be negative.

Chapter 9

5a. The graph for the ball that was dropped from 576 ft is a vertical translation 176 units up of the graph for the ball that was dropped from 400 ft.

b. 5 s from 400 ft; 6 s from 576 ft

13. No; the discriminant is negative.

Chapter 10

4.

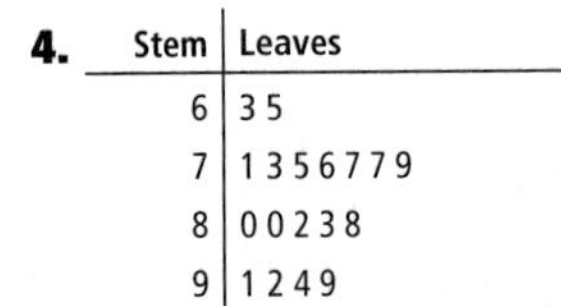

Stem	Leaves
6	3 5
7	1 3 5 6 7 7 9
8	0 0 2 3 8
9	1 2 4 9

Key: 6|5 means 65

5.

Customers Per Day	
Customers	**Frequency**
25–29	3
30–34	5
35–39	2
40–44	4

7.

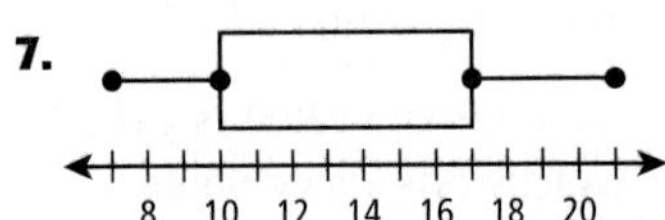

8. The mean is \$582, but 4 of the 5 employees make less than this amount.

9. The scale on the vertical axis does not begin at 0; Anders's sales were three times those of Williams's.

Chapter 11

5. The stock price increases by 10% per year; $y = 10(1.1)^x$; \$19.49

Chapter 12

1. D: $0 < x < 200$; R: $1 < y < 200$; about 3 min

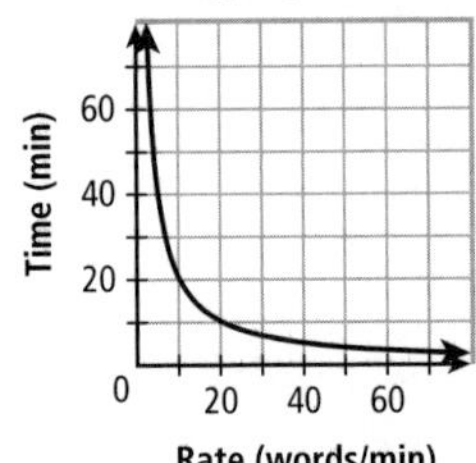

3. D: $x > 0$; R: whole numbers $y > 3$

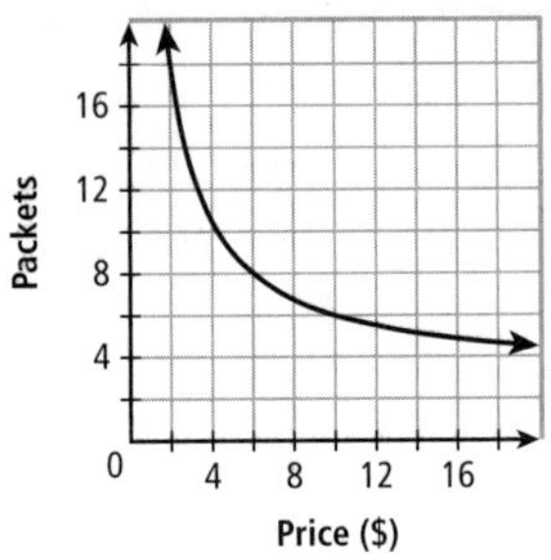

4. D: $x \geq 0$; R: $0 < y \leq 100$

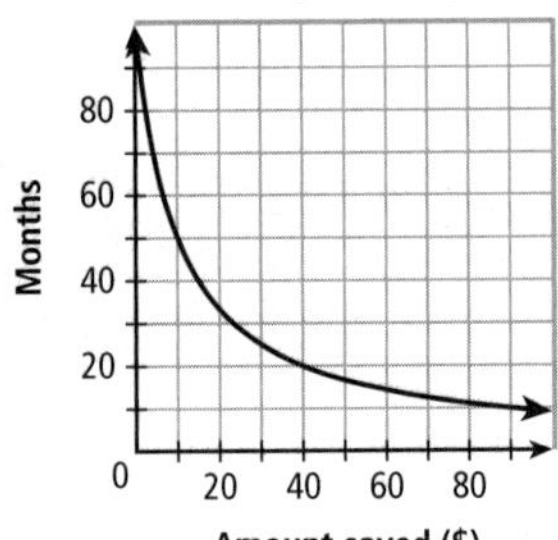

7. $\frac{x(x-1)}{2(2x+5)(x+2)}$, where x is the number of men; $\frac{15}{136}$

Glossary/Glosario

ENGLISH	SPANISH	EXAMPLES
absolute value (p. 14) The absolute value of x is the distance from zero to x on a number line, denoted $\lvert x \rvert$. $\lvert x \rvert = \begin{cases} x & \text{if } x \geq 0 \\ -x & \text{if } x < 0 \end{cases}$	**valor absoluto** El valor absoluto de x es la distancia de cero a x en una recta numérica, y se expresa $\lvert x \rvert$. $\lvert x \rvert = \begin{cases} x & \text{si } x \geq 0 \\ -x & \text{si } x < 0 \end{cases}$	$\lvert 3 \rvert = 3$ $\lvert -3 \rvert = 3$
absolute-value equation (p. 112) An equation that contains absolute-value expressions.	**ecuación de valor absoluto** Ecuación que contiene expresiones de valor absoluto.	$\lvert x + 4 \rvert = 7$
absolute-value function (p. 378) A function whose rule contains absolute-value expressions.	**función de valor absoluto** Función cuya regla contiene expresiones de valor absoluto.	$y = \lvert x + 4 \rvert$
absolute-value inequality (p. 212) An inequality that contains absolute-value expressions.	**desigualdad de valor absoluto** Desigualdad que contiene expresiones de valor absoluto.	$\lvert x + 4 \rvert > 7$
acute angle An angle that measures greater than 0° and less than 90°.	**ángulo agudo** Ángulo que mide más de 0° y menos de 90°.	
acute triangle A triangle with three acute angles.	**triángulo acutángulo** Triángulo con tres ángulos agudos.	
Addition Property of Equality (p. 79) For real numbers a, b, and c, if $a = b$, then $a + c = b + c$.	**Propiedad de igualdad de la suma** Dados los números reales a, b y c, si $a = b$, entonces $a + c = b + c$.	$\begin{aligned} x - 6 &= 8 \\ +6 \quad &\;\; +6 \\ \hline x \quad &= 14 \end{aligned}$
Addition Property of Inequality (p. 176) For real numbers a, b, and c, if $a < b$, then $a + c < b + c$. Also holds true for $>$, $\leq$, $\geq$, and $\neq$.	**Propiedad de desigualdad de la suma** Dados los números reales a, b y c, si $a < b$, entonces $a + c < b + c$. Es válido también para $>$, $\leq$, $\geq$ y $\neq$.	$\begin{aligned} x - 6 &< 8 \\ +6 \quad &\;\; +6 \\ \hline x \quad &< 14 \end{aligned}$
additive inverse (p. 15) The opposite of a number. Two numbers are additive inverses if their sum is zero.	**inverso aditivo** El opuesto de un número. Dos números son inversos aditivos si su suma es cero.	The additive inverse of 5 is −5. The additive inverse of −5 is 5.
algebraic expression (p. 6) An expression that contains at least one variable.	**expresión algebraica** Expresión que contiene por lo menos una variable.	$2x + 3y$ $4x$
algebraic order of operations *See* order of operations.	**orden algebraico de las operaciones** *Ver* orden de las operaciones.	

Glossary/Glosario **G1**

ENGLISH	SPANISH	EXAMPLES
AND (p. 204) A logical operator representing the intersection of two sets.	**Y** Operador lógico que representa la intersección de dos conjuntos.	$A = \{2, 3, 4, 5\}$ $B = \{1, 3, 5, 7\}$ The set of values that are in A AND B is $A \cap B = \{3, 5\}$.
angle A figure formed by two rays with a common endpoint.	**ángulo** Figura formada por dos rayos con un extremo común.	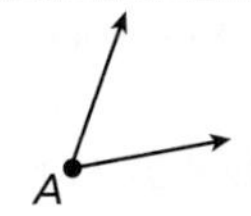
area The number of nonoverlapping unit squares of a given size that will exactly cover the interior of a plane figure.	**área** Cantidad de cuadrados unitarios de un determinado tamaño no superpuestos que cubren exactamente el interior de una figura plana.	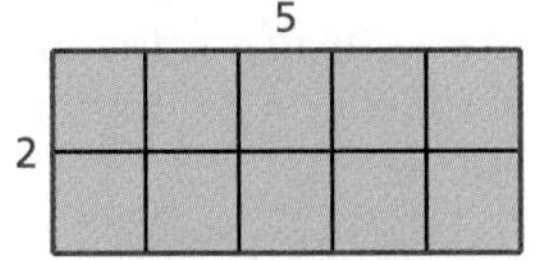 The area is 10 square units.
arithmetic sequence (p. 276) A sequence whose successive terms differ by the same nonzero number d, called the *common difference.*	**sucesión aritmética** Sucesión cuyos términos sucesivos difieren en el mismo número distinto de cero d, denominado *diferencia común.*	4, 7, 10, 13, 16, ... +3 +3 +3 +3 $d = 3$
Associative Property of Addition (p. 46) For all numbers a, b, and c, $(a + b) + c = a + (b + c)$.	**Propiedad asociativa de la suma** Dados tres números cualesquiera a, b y c, $(a + b) + c = a + (b + c)$.	$(5 + 3) + 7 = 5 + (3 + 7)$
Associative Property of Multiplication (p. 46) For all numbers a, b, and c, $(a \cdot b) \cdot c = a \cdot (b \cdot c)$.	**Propiedad asociativa de la multiplicación** Dados tres números cualesquiera a, b y c, $(a \cdot b) \cdot c = a \cdot (b \cdot c)$.	$(5 \cdot 3) \cdot 7 = 5 \cdot (3 \cdot 7)$
asymptote (p. 878) A line that a graph gets closer to as the value of a variable becomes extremely large or small.	**asíntota** Línea recta a la cual se aproxima una gráfica a medida que el valor de una variable se hace sumamente grande o pequeño.	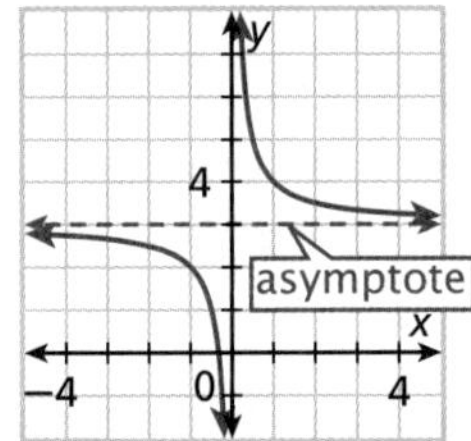
average *See* mean.	**promedio** *Ver* media.	
axis of a coordinate plane (p. 54) One of two perpendicular number lines, called the x-axis and the y-axis, used to define the location of a point in a coordinate plane.	**eje de un plano cartesiano** Una de las dos rectas numéricas perpendiculares, denominadas eje x y eje y, utilizadas para definir la ubicación de un punto en un plano cartesiano.	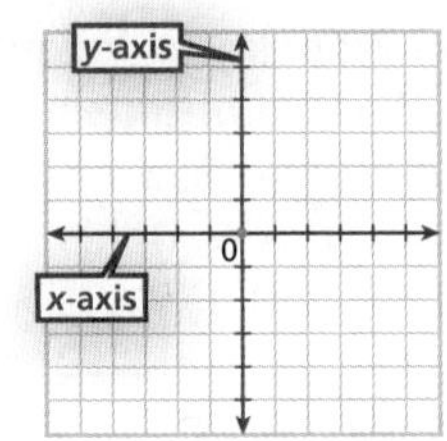
axis of symmetry (p. 378, p. 620) A line that divides a plane figure or a graph into two congruent reflected halves.	**eje de simetría** Línea que divide una figura plana o una gráfica en dos mitades reflejadas congruentes.	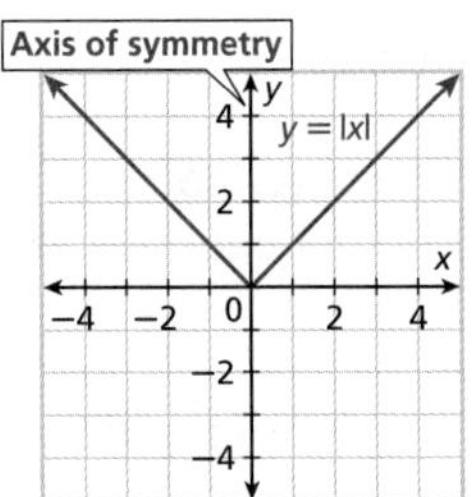

Glossary/Glosario

G2 Glossary/Glosario

B

ENGLISH	SPANISH	EXAMPLES

back-to-back stem-and-leaf plot (p. 709) A graph used to organize and compare two sets of data so that the frequencies can be compared. *See also* stem-and-leaf plot.

diagrama doble de tallo y hojas Gráfica utilizada para organizar y comparar dos conjuntos de datos para poder comparar las frecuencias. *Ver también* diagrama de tallo y hojas.

Data set A: 9, 12, 14, 16, 23, 27
Data set B: 6, 8, 10, 13, 15, 16, 21

Set A		Set B
9	0	6 8
6 4 2	1	0 3 5 6
7 3	2	1

Key: |2|1 means 21
7|2| means 27

---

bar graph (p. 700) A graph that uses vertical or horizontal bars to display data.

gráfica de barras Gráfica con barras horizontales o verticales para mostrar datos.

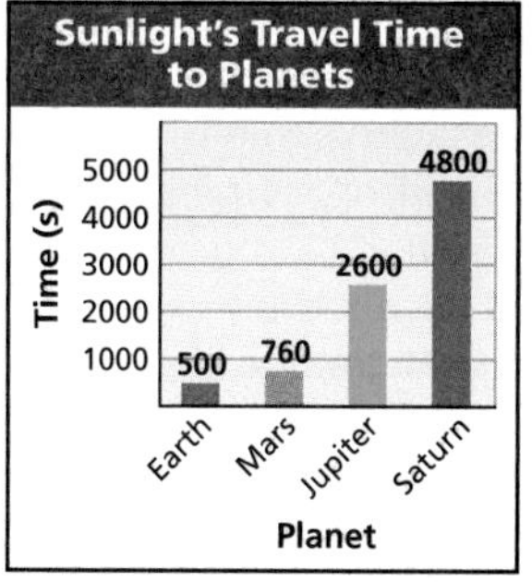

---

base of a power (p. 26) The number in a power that is used as a factor.

base de una potencia Número de una potencia que se utiliza como factor.

$3^4 = 3 \cdot 3 \cdot 3 \cdot 3 = 81$
3 is the base.

---

base of an exponential function (p. 796) The value of b in a function of the form $f(x) = ab^x$, where a and b are real numbers with $a \neq 0$, $b > 0$, and $b \neq 1$.

base de una función exponencial Valor de b en una función del tipo $f(x) = ab^x$, donde a y b son números reales con $a \neq 0$, $b > 0$ y $b \neq 1$.

In the function $f(x) = 5(2)^x$, the base is 2.

---

biased sample (p. 733) A sample that does not fairly represent the population.

muestra no representativa Muestra que no representa adecuadamente una población.

To find out about the exercise habits of average Americans, a fitness magazine surveyed its readers about how often they exercise. The population is all Americans and the sample is readers of the fitness magazine. This sample will likely be biased because readers of fitness magazines may exercise more often than other people do.

---

binomial (p. 497) A polynomial with two terms.

binomio Polinomio con dos términos.

$x + y$
$2a^2 + 3$
$4m^3n^2 + 6mn^4$

---

boundary line (p. 428) A line that divides a coordinate plane into two half-planes.

línea de límite Línea que divide un plano cartesiano en dos semiplanos.

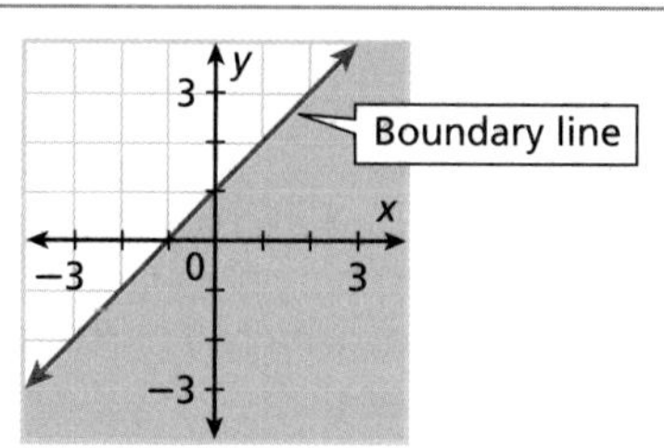

Glossary/Glosario **G3**

ENGLISH	SPANISH	EXAMPLES
box-and-whisker plot (p. 718) A method of showing how data are distributed by using the median, quartiles, and minimum and maximum values; also called a *box plot.*	**gráfica de mediana y rango** Método para mostrar la distribución de datos utilizando la mediana, los cuartiles y los valores mínimo y máximo; también llamado *gráfica de caja.*	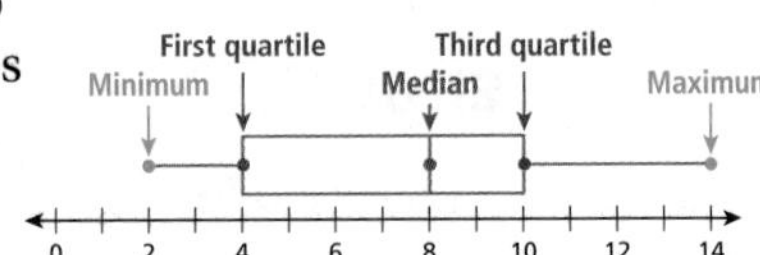

C

ENGLISH	SPANISH	EXAMPLES
Cartesian coordinate system *See* coordinate plane.	**sistema de coordenadas cartesianas** *Ver* plano cartesiano.	
center of a circle The point inside a circle that is the same distance from every point on the circle.	**centro de un círculo** Punto dentro de un círculo que se encuentra a la misma distancia de todos los puntos del círculo.	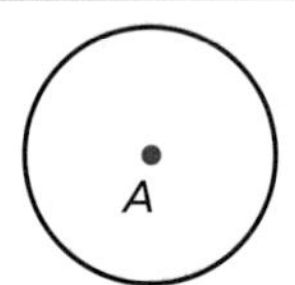
central angle of a circle An angle whose vertex is the center of a circle.	**ángulo central de un círculo** Ángulo cuyo vértice es el centro de un círculo.	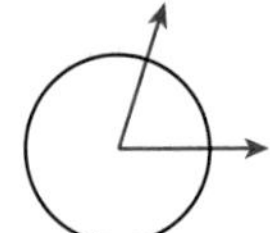
circle The set of points in a plane that are a fixed distance from a given point called the center of the circle.	**círculo** Conjunto de puntos en un plano que se encuentran a una distancia fija de un punto determinado denominado centro del círculo.	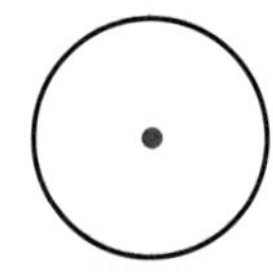
circle graph (p. 702) A way to display data by using a circle divided into non-overlapping sectors.	**gráfica circular** Forma de mostrar datos mediante un círculo dividido en sectores no superpuestos.	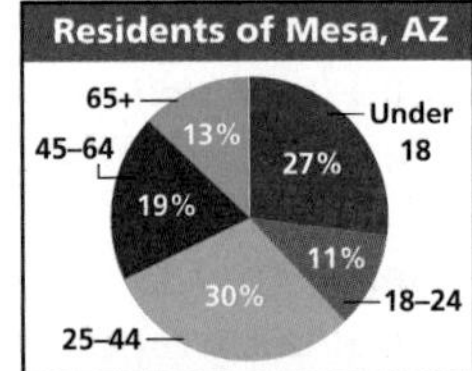
circumference The distance around a circle.	**circunferencia** Distancia alrededor de un círculo.	
coefficient (p. 48) A number that is multiplied by a variable.	**coeficiente** Número que se multiplica por una variable.	In the expression $2x + 3y$, 2 is the coefficient of x and 3 is the coefficient of y.
combination (p. 761) A selection of a group of objects in which order is *not* important. The number of combinations of r objects chosen from a group of n objects is denoted $_nC_r$.	**combinación** Selección de un grupo de objetos en la cual el orden *no* es importante. El número de combinaciones de r objetos elegidos de un grupo de n objetos se expresa así: $_nC_r$.	For objects A, B, C, and D, there are 6 different combinations of 2 objects. AB, AC, AD, BC, BD, CD
commission (p. 139) Money paid to a person or company for making a sale, usually a percent of the sale amount.	**comisión** Dinero que se paga a una persona o empresa por realizar una venta; generalmente se trata de un porcentaje del total de la venta.	

G4 Glossary/Glosario

ENGLISH	SPANISH	EXAMPLES
common difference (p. 276) In an arithmetic sequence, the nonzero constant difference of any term and the previous term.	**diferencia común** En una sucesión aritmética, diferencia constante distinta de cero entre cualquier término y el término anterior.	In the arithmetic sequence 3, 5, 7, 9, 11, ..., the common difference is 2.
common factor (p. 545) A factor that is common to all terms of an expression or to two or more expressions.	**factor común** Factor que es común a todos los términos de una expresión o a dos o más expresiones.	Expression: $4x^2 + 16x^3 - 8x$ Common factor: $4x$ Expressions: 12 and 18 Common factors: 2, 3, and 6
common ratio (p. 790) In a geometric sequence, the constant ratio of any term and the previous term.	**razón común** En una sucesión geométrica, la razón constante entre cualquier término y el término anterior.	In the geometric sequence 32, 16, 8, 4, 2, . . ., the common ratio is $\frac{1}{2}$.
Commutative Property of Addition (p. 46) For any two numbers a and b, $a + b = b + a$.	**Propiedad conmutativa de la suma** Dados dos números cualesquiera a y b, $a + b = b + a$.	$3 + 4 = 4 + 3 = 7$
Commutative Property of Multiplication (p. 46) For any two numbers a and b, $a \cdot b = b \cdot a$.	**Propiedad conmutativa de la multiplicación** Dados dos números cualesquiera a y b, $a \cdot b = b \cdot a$.	$3 \cdot 4 = 4 \cdot 3 = 12$
complement of an event (p. 745) The set of all outcomes that are not the event.	**complemento de un suceso** Todos los resultados que no están en el suceso.	In the experiment of rolling a number cube, the complement of rolling a 3 is rolling a 1, 2, 4, 5, or 6.
complementary angles Two angles whose measures have a sum of 90°.	**ángulos complementarios** Dos ángulos cuyas medidas suman 90°.	37° B 53° A
completing the square (p. 663) A process used to form a perfect-square trinomial. To complete the square of $x^2 + bx$, add $\left(\frac{b}{2}\right)^2$.	**completar el cuadrado** Proceso utilizado para formar un trinomio cuadrado perfecto. Para completar el cuadrado de $x^2 + bx$, hay que sumar $\left(\frac{b}{2}\right)^2$.	$x^2 + 6x + \blacksquare$ Add $\left(\frac{6}{2}\right)^2 = 9$. $x^2 + 6x + 9$
complex fraction (p. 904) A fraction that contains one or more fractions in the numerator, the denominator, or both.	**fracción compleja** Fracción que contiene una o más fracciones en el numerador, en el denominador, o en ambos.	$\dfrac{\frac{1}{2}}{1 + \frac{2}{3}}$
composite figure (p. 83) A plane figure made up of triangles, rectangles, trapezoids, circles, and other simple shapes, or a three-dimensional figure made up of prisms, cones, pyramids, cylinders, and other simple three-dimensional figures.	**figura compuesta** Figura plana compuesta por triángulos, rectángulos, trapecios, círculos y otras figuras simples, o figura tridimensional compuesta por prismas, conos, pirámides, cilindros y otras figuras tridimensionales simples.	

Glossary/Glosario

Glossary/Glosario G5

ENGLISH	SPANISH	EXAMPLES
compound event (p. 761) An event made up of two or more simple events.	**suceso compuesto** Suceso formado por dos o más sucesos simples.	In the experiment of tossing a coin and rolling a number cube, the event of the coin landing heads and the number cube landing on 3.
compound inequality (p. 204) Two inequalities that are combined into one statement by the word *and* or *or*.	**desigualdad compuesta** Dos desigualdades unidas en un enunciado por la palabra *y* u *o*.	$x \geq 2$ AND $x < 7$ (also written $2 \leq x < 7$) 0 2 4 6 8 $x < 2$ OR $x > 6$ 0 2 4 6 8
compound interest (p. 860) Interest earned or paid on both the principal and previously earned interest. The formula for compound interest is $A = P\left(1 + \frac{r}{n}\right)^{nt}$, where A is the final amount, P is the principal, r is the interest rate expressed as a decimal, n is the number of times interest is compounded, and t is the time.	**interés compuesto** Intereses ganados o pagados sobre el capital y los intereses ya devengados. La fórmula de interés compuesto es $A = P\left(1 + \frac{r}{n}\right)^{nt}$, donde A es la cantidad final, P es el capital, r es la tasa de interés expresada como un decimal, n es la cantidad de veces que se capitaliza el interés y t es el tiempo.	If \$100 is put into an account with an interest rate of 5% compounded monthly, then after 2 years, the account will have $100\left(1 + \frac{0.05}{12}\right)^{12 \cdot 2} = \$110.49$.
compound statement (p. 203) Two statements that are connected by the word *and* or *or*.	**enunciado compuesto** Dos enunciados unidos por la palabra *y* u *o*.	The sky is blue and the grass is green. I will drive to school or I will take the bus.
cone (p. 894) A three-dimensional figure with a circular base and a curved surface that connects the base to a point called the vertex.	**cono** Figura tridimensional con una base circular y una superficie lateral curva que conecta la base con un punto denominado vértice.	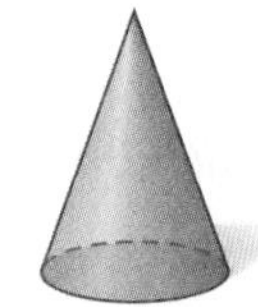
congruent Having the same size and shape, denoted by $\cong$.	**congruente** Que tiene el mismo tamaño y la misma forma, expresado por $\cong$.	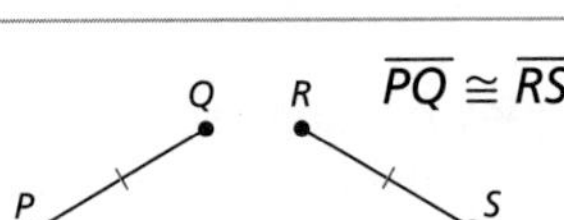 $\overline{PQ} \cong \overline{RS}$
conjugate of an irrational number (p. 845) The conjugate of a number in the form $a + \sqrt{b}$ is $a - \sqrt{b}$.	**conjugado de un número irracional** El conjugado de un número en la forma $a + \sqrt{b}$ es $a - \sqrt{b}$.	The conjugate of $1 + \sqrt{2}$ is $1 - \sqrt{2}$.
consistent system (p. 420) A system of equations or inequalities that has at least one solution.	**sistema consistente** Sistema de ecuaciones o desigualdades que tiene por lo menos una solución.	$\begin{cases} x + y = 6 \\ x - y = 4 \end{cases}$ solution: (5, 1)
constant (p. 6) A value that does not change.	**constante** Valor que no cambia.	3, 0, π

G6 Glossary/Glosario

ENGLISH	SPANISH	EXAMPLES
constant of variation (p. 336) The constant k in direct and inverse variation equations.	**constante de variación** La constante k en ecuaciones de variación directa e inversa.	$y = 5x$ ↑ constant of variation
continuous graph (p. 235) A graph made up of connected lines or curves.	**gráfica continua** Gráfica compuesta por líneas rectas o curvas conectadas.	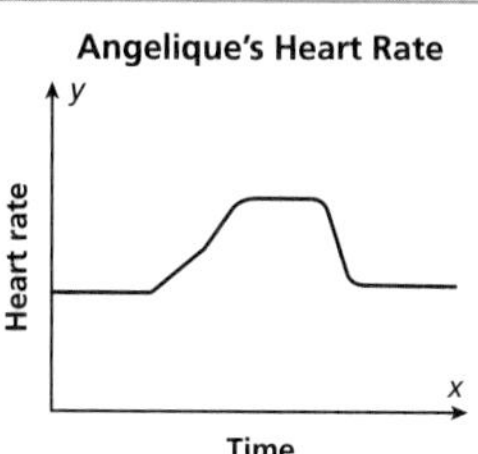
convenience sample (p. 733) A sample based on members of the population that are readily available.	**muestra de conveniencia** Una muestra basada en miembros de la población que están fácilmente disponibles.	A reporter surveys people he personally knows.
conversion factor (p. 121) The ratio of two equal quantities, each measured in different units.	**factor de conversión** Razón entre dos cantidades iguales, cada una medida en unidades diferentes.	$\frac{12 \text{ inches}}{1 \text{ foot}}$
coordinate (p. 54) A number used to identify the location of a point. On a number line, one coordinate is used. On a coordinate plane, two coordinates are used, called the x-coordinate and the y-coordinate.	**coordenada** Número utilizado para identificar la ubicación de un punto. En una recta numérica se utiliza una coordenada. En un plano cartesiano se utilizan dos coordenadas, denominadas coordenada x y coordenada y.	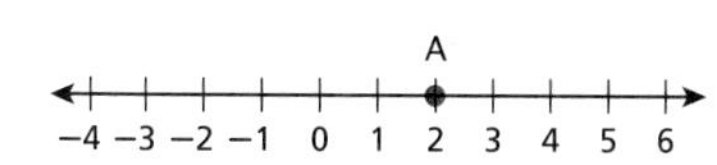 The coordinate of A is 2. 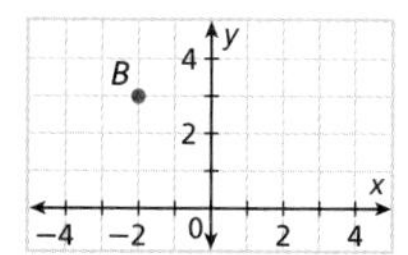 The coordinates of B are $(-2, 3)$.
coordinate plane (p. 54) A plane that is divided into four regions by a horizontal line called the x-axis and a vertical line called the y-axis.	**plano cartesiano** Plano dividido en cuatro regiones por una línea horizontal denominada eje x y una línea vertical denominada eje y.	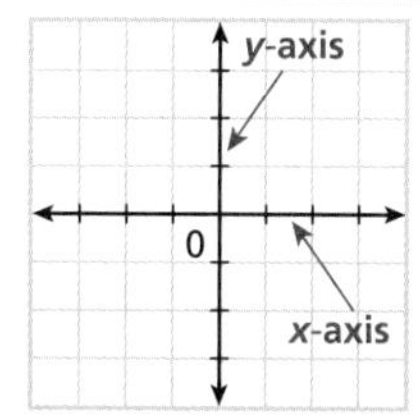
correlation (p. 266) A measure of the strength and direction of the relationship between two variables or data sets.	**correlación** Medida de la fuerza y dirección de la relación entre dos variables o conjuntos de datos.	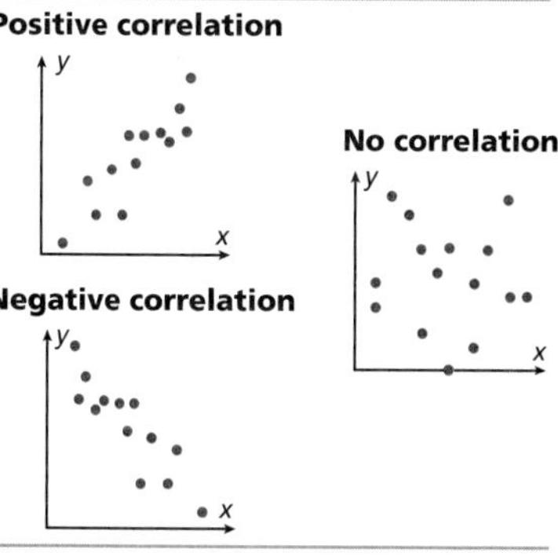
corresponding angles of polygons (p. 127) Angles in the same relative position in polygons with an equal number of angles.	**ángulos correspondientes de los polígonos** Ángulos que se ubican en la misma posición relativa en polígonos que tienen el mismo número de ángulos.	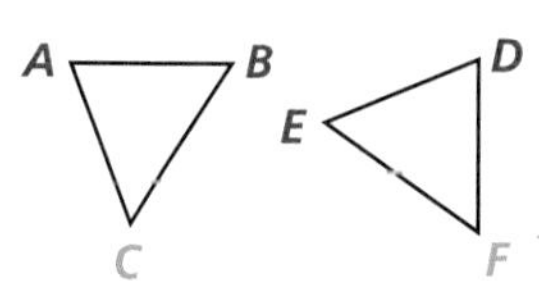 $\angle A$ and $\angle D$ are corresponding angles.

Glossary/Glosario G7

ENGLISH	SPANISH	EXAMPLES
corresponding sides of polygons (p. 127) Sides in the same relative position in polygons with an equal number of sides.	**lados correspondientes de los polígonos** Lados que se ubican en la misma posición relativa en polígonos que tienen el mismo número de lados.	A B C E D F $\overline{AB}$ and $\overline{DE}$ are corresponding sides.
cosine (p. 928) In a right triangle, the cosine of angle A is the ratio of the length of the leg adjacent to angle A to the length of the hypotenuse.	**coseno** En un triángulo rectángulo, el coseno del ángulo A es la razón entre la longitud del cateto adyacente al ángulo A y la longitud de la hipotenusa.	hypotenuse A adjacent $\cos A = \frac{\text{adjacent}}{\text{hypotenuse}}$
cross products (p. 121) In the statement $\frac{a}{b} = \frac{c}{d}$, bc and ad are the cross products.	**productos cruzados** En el enunciado $\frac{a}{b} = \frac{c}{d}$, bc y ad son productos cruzados.	$\frac{1}{2} = \frac{3}{6}$ Cross products: $2 \cdot 3 = 6$ and $1 \cdot 6 = 6$
Cross Product Property (p. 121) For any real numbers a, b, c, and d, where $b \neq 0$ and $d \neq 0$, if $\frac{a}{b} = \frac{c}{d}$, then $ad = bc$.	**Propiedad de productos cruzados** Dados los números reales a, b, c y d, donde $b \neq 0$ y $d \neq 0$, si $\frac{a}{b} = \frac{c}{d}$, entonces $ad = bc$.	If $\frac{4}{6} = \frac{10}{x}$, then $4x = 60$, so $x = 15$.
cube A prism with six square faces.	**cubo** Prisma con seis caras cuadradas.	
cube in numeration (p. 26) The third power of a number.	**cubo en numeración** Tercera potencia de un número.	8 is the cube of 2.
cube root (p. 32) A number, written as $\sqrt[3]{x}$, whose cube is x.	**raíz cúbica** Número, expresado como $\sqrt[3]{x}$, cuyo cubo es x.	$\sqrt[3]{64} = 4$, because $4^3 = 64$; 4 is the cube root of 64.
cubic equation (p. 681) An equation that can be written in the form $ax^3 + bx^2 + cx + d = 0$, where a, b, c, and d are real numbers and $a \neq 0$.	**ecuación cúbica** Ecuación que se puede expresar como $ax^3 + bx^2 + cx + d = 0$, donde a, b, c, y d son números reales y $a \neq 0$.	$4x^3 + x^2 - 3x - 1 = 0$
cubic function (p. 680) A function that can be written in the form $f(x) = ax^3 + bx^2 + cx + d$, where a, b, c, and d are real numbers and $a \neq 0$.	**función cúbica** Función que se puede expresar como $f(x) = ax^3 + bx^2 + cx + d$, donde a, b, c, y d son números reales y $a \neq 0$.	$f(x) = x^3 + 2x^2 - 6x + 8$
cubic polynomial (p. 497) A polynomial of degree 3.	**polinomio cúbico** Polinomio de grado 3.	$x^3 + 4x^2 - 6x + 2$
cumulative frequency (p. 711) The frequency of all data values that are less than or equal to a given value.	**frecuencia acumulativa** Frecuencia de todos los valores de los datos que son menores que o iguales a un valor dado.	For the data set 2, 2, 3, 5, 5, 6, 7, 7, 8, 8, 8, 9, the cumulative frequency table is shown below.

Data	Frequency	Cumulative Frequency
2	2	2
3	1	3
5	2	5
6	1	6
7	2	8
8	3	11
9	1	12

G8 *Glossary/Glosario*

ENGLISH	SPANISH	EXAMPLES
cylinder (p. 894) A three-dimensional figure with two parallel congruent circular bases and a curved surface that connects the bases.	**cilindro** Figura tridimensional con dos bases circulares congruentes paralelas y una superficie lateral curva que conecta las bases.	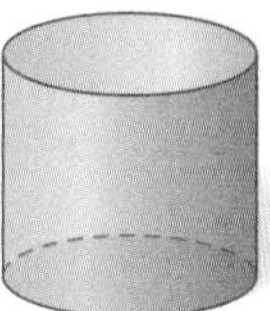

D

ENGLISH	SPANISH	EXAMPLES
data Information gathered from a survey or experiment.	**datos** Información reunida en una encuesta o experimento.	
degree measure of an angle A unit of angle measure; one degree is $\frac{1}{360}$ of a circle.	**medida en grados de un ángulo** Unidad de medida de los ángulos; un grado es $\frac{1}{360}$ de un círculo.	
degree of a monomial (p. 496) The sum of the exponents of the variables in the monomial.	**grado de un monomio** Suma de los exponentes de las variables del monomio.	$4x^2y^5z^3$ Degree: $2 + 5 + 3 = 10$ $5 = 5x^0$ Degree: 0
degree of a polynomial (p. 496) The degree of the term of the polynomial with the greatest degree.	**grado de un polinomio** Grado del término del polinomio con el grado máximo.	$3x^2y^2 + 4xy^5 - 12x^3y^2$ Degree 4 Degree 6 Degree 5 Degree 6
dependent events (p. 750) Events for which the occurrence or nonoccurrence of one event affects the probability of the other event.	**sucesos dependientes** Dos sucesos son dependientes si el hecho de que uno de ellos ocurra o no afecta la probabilidad del otro suceso.	From a bag containing 3 red marbles and 2 blue marbles, draw a red marble, and then draw a blue marble without replacing the first marble.
dependent system (p. 421) A system of equations that has infinitely many solutions.	**sistema dependiente** Sistema de ecuaciones que tiene infinitamente muchas soluciones.	$\begin{cases} x + y = 2 \\ 2x + 2y = 4 \end{cases}$
dependent variable (p. 250) The output of a function; a variable whose value depends on the value of the input, or independent variable.	**variable dependiente** Salida de una función; variable cuyo valor depende del valor de la entrada, o variable independiente.	For $y = 2x + 1$, y is the dependent variable. input: x output: y
diameter A segment that has endpoints on the circle and that passes through the center of the circle; also the length of that segment.	**diámetro** Segmento que atraviesa el centro de un círculo y cuyos extremos están sobre la circunferencia; longitud de dicho segmento.	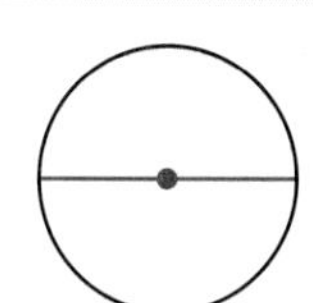
difference of two cubes (p. 584) A polynomial of the form $a^3 - b^3$, which may be written as the product $(a - b)(a^2 + ab + b^2)$.	**diferencia de dos cubos** Polinomio del tipo $a^3 - b^3$, que se puede expresar como el producto $(a - b)(a^2 + ab + b^2)$.	$x^3 - 8 = (x - 2)(x^2 + 2x + 4)$
difference of two squares (p. 523) A polynomial of thc form $a^2 - b^2$, which may be written as the product $(a + b)(a - b)$.	**diferencia de dos cuadrados** Polinomio del tipo $a^2 - b^2$, que se puede expresar como el producto $(a + b)(a - b)$.	$x^2 - 4 = (x + 2)(x - 2)$

Glossary/Glosario

Glossary/Glosario G9

ENGLISH	SPANISH	EXAMPLES
dimensional analysis (p. 121) A process that uses rates to convert measurements from one unit to another.	**análisis dimensional** Un proceso que utiliza tasas para convertir medidas de unidad a otra.	$12 \text{ pt} \cdot \frac{1 \text{ qt}}{2 \text{ pt}} = 6 \text{ qt}$
direct variation (p. 336) A linear relationship between two variables, x and y, that can be written in the form $y = kx$, where k is a nonzero constant.	**variación directa** Relación lineal entre dos variables, x e y, que puede expresarse en la forma $y = kx$, donde k es una constante distinta de cero.	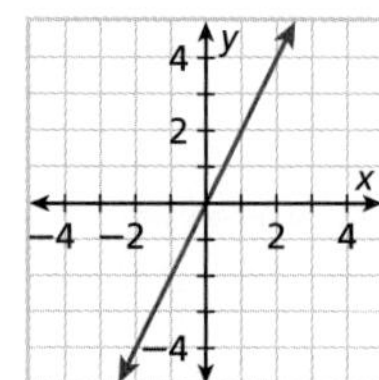 $y = 2x$
discontinuous function (p. 878) A function whose graph has one or more jumps, breaks, or holes.	**función discontinua** Función cuya gráfica tiene uno o más saltos, interrupciones u hoyos.	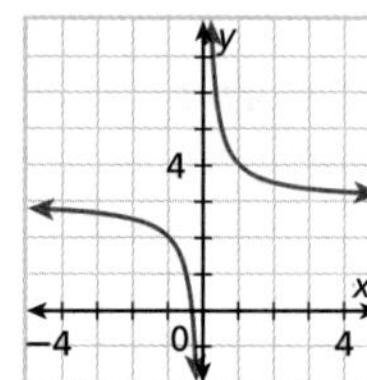
discount (p. 145) An amount by which an original price is reduced.	**descuento** Cantidad por la que se reduce un precio original.	
discrete graph (p. 235) A graph made up of unconnected points.	**gráfica discreta** Gráfica compuesta de puntos no conectados.	 
discriminant (p. 672) The discriminant of the quadratic equation $ax^2 + bx + c = 0$ is $b^2 - 4ac$.	**discriminante** El discriminante de la ecuación cuadrática $ax^2 + bx + c = 0$ es $b^2 - 4ac$.	The discriminant of $2x^2 - 5x - 3 = 0$ is $(-5)^2 - 4(2)(-3)$ or 49.
Distance Formula (p. 331) In a coordinate plane, the distance from (x_1, y_1) to (x_2, y_2) is $d = \sqrt{(x_2 - x_1)^2 + (y_2 - y_1)^2}$.	**Fórmula de distancia** En un plano cartesiano, la distancia desde (x_1, y_1) hasta (x_2, y_2) es $d = \sqrt{(x_2 - x_1)^2 + (y_2 - y_1)^2}$.	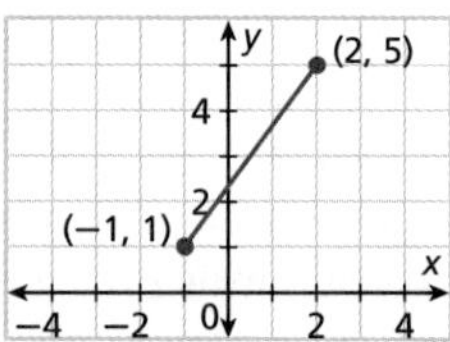 The distance from $(2, 5)$ to $(-1, 1)$ is $d = \sqrt{(-1 - 2)^2 + (1 - 5)^2}$ $= \sqrt{(-3)^2 + (-4)^2}$ $= \sqrt{9 + 16} = \sqrt{25} = 5$.
Distributive Property (p. 47) For all real numbers a, b, and c, $a(b + c) = ab + ac$, and $(b + c)a = ba + ca$.	**Propiedad distributiva** Dados los números reales a, b y c, $a(b + c) = ab + ac$, y $(b + c)a = ba + ca$.	$3(4 + 5) = 3 \cdot 4 + 3 \cdot 5$ $(4 + 5)3 = 4 \cdot 3 + 5 \cdot 3$
Division Property of Equality (p. 86) For real numbers a, b, and c, where $c \neq 0$, if $a = b$, then $\frac{a}{c} = \frac{b}{c}$.	**Propiedad de igualdad de la división** Dados los números reales a, b y c, donde $c \neq 0$, si $a = b$, entonces $\frac{a}{c} = \frac{b}{c}$.	$4x = 12$ $\frac{4x}{4} = \frac{12}{4}$ $x = 3$

Glossary/Glosario

G10 Glossary/Glosario

ENGLISH	SPANISH	EXAMPLES
Division Property of Inequality (p. 182, p. 183) If both sides of an inequality are divided by the same positive quantity, the new inequality will have the same solution set. If both sides of an inequality are divided by the same negative quantity, the new inequality will have the same solution set if the inequality symbol is reversed.	**Propiedad de desigualdad de la división** Cuando ambos lados de una desigualdad se dividen entre el mismo número positivo, la nueva desigualdad tiene el mismo conjunto solución. Cuando ambos lados de una desigualdad se dividen entra el mismo número negativo, la nueva desigualdad tiene el mismo conjunto solución si se invierte el símbolo de desigualdad.	$4x \geq 12$ $\frac{4x}{4} \geq \frac{12}{4}$ $x \geq 3$ $-4x \geq 12$ $\frac{-4x}{-4} \leq \frac{12}{-4}$ $x \leq -3$
domain (p. 240) The set of all first coordinates (or x-values) of a relation or function.	**dominio** Conjunto de todos los valores de la primera coordenada (o valores de x) de una función o relación.	The domain of the function $\{(-5, 3), (-3, -2), (-1, -1), (1, 0)\}$ is $\{-5, -3, -1, 1\}$.

E

ENGLISH	SPANISH	EXAMPLES
element Each member in a set or matrix. *See also* entry.	**elemento** Cada miembro en un conjunto o matriz. *Ver también* entrada.	
elimination method (p. 411) A method used to solve systems of equations in which one variable is eliminated by adding or subtracting two equations of the system.	**eliminación** Método utilizado para resolver sistemas de ecuaciones por el cual se elimina una variable sumando o restando dos ecuaciones del sistema.	
empty set (p. 102) A set with no elements.	**conjunto vacío** Conjunto sin elementos.	The solution set of $\|x\| < 0$ is the empty set, { }, or ∅.
entry (p. 770) Each value in a matrix; also called an element.	**entrada** Cada valor de una matriz, también denominado elemento.	3 is the entry in the first row and second column of $A = \begin{bmatrix} 2 & 3 \\ 0 & 1 \end{bmatrix}$, denoted a_{12}.
equally likely outcomes (p. 744) Outcomes are equally likely if they have the same probability of occurring. If an experiment has n equally likely outcomes, then the probability of each outcome is $\frac{1}{n}$.	**resultados igualmente probables** Los resultados son igualmente probables si tienen la misma probabilidad de ocurrir. Si un experimento tiene n resultados igualmente probables, entonces la probabilidad de cada resultado es $\frac{1}{n}$.	If a fair coin is tossed, then $P(\text{heads}) = P(\text{tails}) = \frac{1}{2}$. So the outcome "heads" and the outcome "tails" are equally likely.
equation (p. 77) A mathematical statement that two expressions are equivalent.	**ecuación** Enunciado matemático que indica que dos expresiones son equivalentes.	$x + 4 = 7$ $2 + 3 = 6 - 1$ $(x - 1)^2 + (y + 2)^2 = 4$
equilateral triangle A triangle with three congruent sides.	**triángulo equilátero** Triángulo con tres lados congruentes.	
equivalent ratios (p. 120) Ratios that name the same comparison.	**razones equivalentes** Razones que expresan la misma comparación.	$\frac{1}{2}$ and $\frac{2}{4}$ are equivalent ratios.

Glossary/Glosario **G11**

ENGLISH	SPANISH	EXAMPLES
evaluate (p. 7) To find the value of an algebraic expression by substituting a number for each variable and simplifying by using the order of operations.	**evaluar** Calcular el valor de una expresión algebraica sustituyendo cada variable por un número y simplificando mediante el orden de las operaciones.	Evaluate $2x + 7$ for $x = 3$. $2x + 7$ $2(3) + 7$ $6 + 7$ 13
event (p. 737) An outcome or set of outcomes of an experiment.	**suceso** Resultado o conjunto de resultados en un experimento.	In the experiment of rolling a number cube, the event "an odd number" consists of the outcomes 1, 3, and 5.
excluded values (p. 878) Values of x for which a function or expression is not defined.	**valores excluidos** Valores de x para los cuales no está definida una función o expresión.	The excluded values of $\frac{(x + 2)}{(x - 1)(x + 4)}$ are $x = 1$ and $x = -4$, which would make the denominator equal to 0.
experiment (p. 737) An operation, process, or activity in which outcomes can be used to estimate probability.	**experimento** Una operación, proceso o actividad en la que se usan los resultados para estimar una probabilidad.	Tossing a coin 10 times and noting the number of heads
experimental probability (p. 738) The ratio of the number of times an event occurs to the number of trials, or times, that an activity is performed.	**probabilidad experimental** Razón entre la cantidad de veces que ocurre un suceso y la cantidad de pruebas, o veces, que se realiza una actividad.	Kendra attempted 27 free throws and made 16 of them. The experimental probability that she will make her next free throw is $P(\text{free throw}) = \frac{\text{number made}}{\text{number attempted}} = \frac{16}{27} \approx 0.59$.
exponent (p. 26) The number that indicates how many times the base in a power is used as a factor.	**exponente** Número que indica la cantidad de veces que la base de una potencia se utiliza como factor.	$3^4 = 3 \cdot 3 \cdot 3 \cdot 3 = 81$ 4 is the exponent.
exponential decay (p. 807) An exponential function of the form $f(x) = ab^x$ in which $0 < b < 1$. If r is the rate of decay, then the function can be written $y = a(1 - r)^t$, where a is the initial amount and t is the time.	**decremento exponencial** Función exponencial del tipo $f(x) = ab^x$ en la cual $0 < b < 1$. Si r es la tasa decremental, entonces la función se puede expresar como $y = a(1 - r)^t$, donde a es la cantidad inicial y t es el tiempo.	$f(x) = 3\left(\frac{1}{2}\right)^x$
exponential expression An algebraic expression in which the variable is in an exponent with a fixed number as the base.	**expresión exponencial** Expresión algebraica en la que la variable está en un exponente y que tiene un número fijo como base.	2^{x+1}
exponential function (p. 796) A function of the form $f(x) = ab^x$, where a and b are real numbers with $a \neq 0$, $b > 0$, and $b \neq 1$.	**función exponencial** Función del tipo $f(x) = ab^x$, donde a y b son números reales con $a \neq 0$, $b > 0$ y $b \neq 1$.	$f(x) = 3 \cdot 4^x$

G12 *Glossary/Glosario*

ENGLISH	SPANISH	EXAMPLES
exponential growth (p. 805) An exponential function of the form $f(x) = ab^x$ in which $b > 1$. If r is the rate of growth, then the function can be written $y = a(1 + r)^t$, where a is the initial amount and t is the time.	**crecimiento exponencial** Función exponencial del tipo $f(x) = ab^x$ en la que $b > 1$. Si r es la tasa de crecimiento, entonces la función se puede expresar como $y = a(1 + r)^t$, donde a es la cantidad inicial y t es el tiempo.	$f(x) = 2^x$ 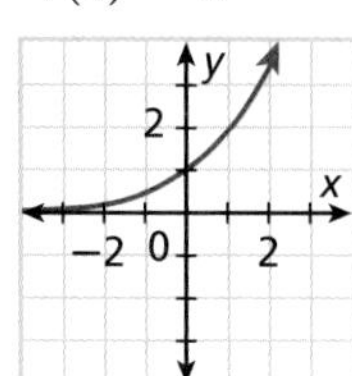
expression (p. 6) A mathematical phrase that contains operations, numbers, and/or variables.	**expresión** Frase matemática que contiene operaciones, números y/o variables.	$6x + 1$
extraneous solution (p. 848) A solution of a derived equation that is not a solution of the original equation.	**solución extraña** Solución de una ecuación derivada que no es una solución de la ecuación original.	To solve $\sqrt{x} = -2$, square both sides; $x = 4$. ***Check*** $\sqrt{4} = -2$ is false; so 4 is an extraneous solution.

F

ENGLISH	SPANISH	EXAMPLES
factor (p. 544) A number or expression that is multiplied by another number or expression to get a product. *See also* factoring.	**factor** Número o expresión que se multiplica por otro número o expresión para obtener un producto. *Ver también* factoreo.	$12 = 3 \cdot 4$ 3 and 4 are factors of 12. $x^2 - 1 = (x - 1)(x + 1)$ $(x - 1)$ and $(x + 1)$ are factors of $x^2 - 1$.
factorial (p. 762) If n is a positive integer, then n factorial, written $n!$, is $n \cdot (n - 1) \cdot (n - 2) \cdot \ldots \cdot 2 \cdot 1$. The factorial of 0 is defined to be 1.	**factorial** Si n es un entero positivo, entonces el factorial de n, expresado como $n!$, es $n \cdot (n - 1) \cdot (n - 2) \cdot \ldots \cdot 2 \cdot 1$. Por definición, el factorial de 0 será 1.	$7! = 7 \cdot 6 \cdot 5 \cdot 4 \cdot 3 \cdot 2 \cdot 1$ $= 5040$
factoring (p. 544) The process of writing a number or algebraic expression as a product.	**factorización** Proceso por el que se expresa un número o expresión algebraica como un producto.	$x^2 - 4x - 21 = (x - 7)(x + 3)$
fair (p. 744) When all outcomes of an experiment are equally likely.	**justo** Cuando todos los resultados de un experimento son igualmente probables.	When tossing a fair coin, heads and tails are equally likely. Each has a probability of $\frac{1}{2}$.
family of functions (p. 369) A set of functions whose graphs have basic characteristics in common. Functions in the same family are transformations of their parent function.	**familia de funciones** Conjunto de funciones cuyas gráficas tienen características básicas en común. Las funciones de la misma familia son transformaciones de su función madre.	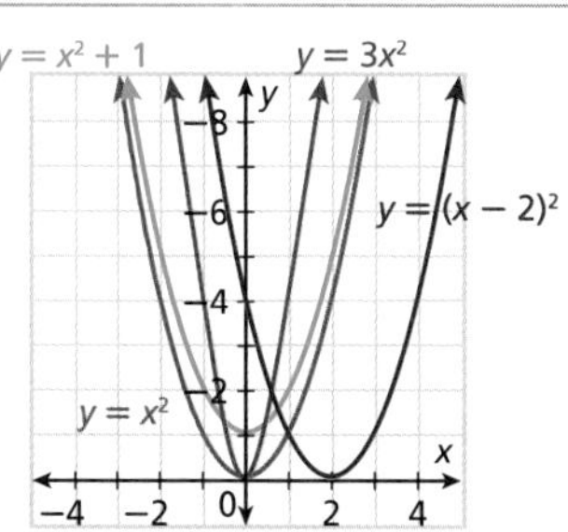

Glossary/Glosario **G13**

ENGLISH	SPANISH	EXAMPLES

first differences (p. 610) The differences between y-values of a function for evenly spaced x-values.

primeras diferencias Diferencias entre los valores de y de una función para valores de x espaciados uniformemente.

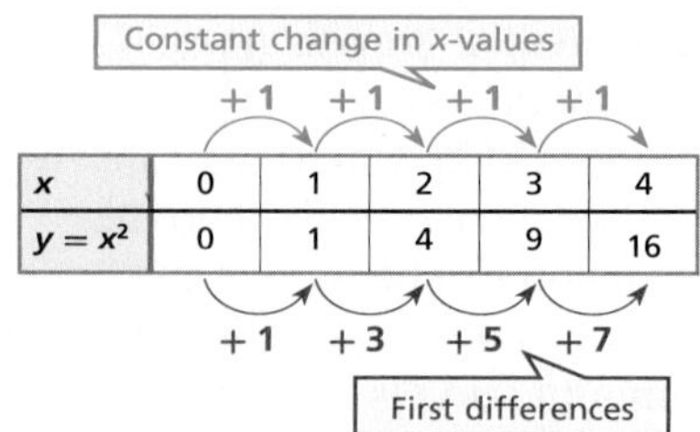

---

first quartile (p. 718) The median of the lower half of a data set, denoted Q_1. Also called *lower quartile.*

primer cuartil Mediana de la mitad inferior de un conjunto de datos, expresada como Q_1. También se llama *cuartil inferior*.

Lower half: 18, (23), 28, Upper half: 29, 36, 42
First quartile

FOIL (p. 513) A mnemonic (memory) device for a method of multiplying two binomials:

Multiply the **First** terms.
Multiply the **Outer** terms.
Multiply the **Inner** terms.
Multiply the **Last** terms.

FOIL Regla mnemotécnica para recordar el método de multiplicación de dos binomios:

Multiplicar los términos **Primeros** (***First***).
Multiplicar los términos **Externos** (***Outer***).
Multiplicar los términos **Internos** (***Inner***).
Multiplicar los términos **Últimos** (***Last***).

F L I O

$(x + 2)(x - 3) = x^2 - 3x + 2x - 6$
$= x^2 - x - 6$

---

formula (p. 107) A literal equation that states a rule for a relationship among quantities.

fórmula Ecuación literal que establece una regla para una relación entre cantidades.

$A = \pi r^2$

---

fractional exponent *See* rational exponent.

exponente fraccionario *Ver* exponente racional.

---

frequency (p. 710) The number of times the value appears in the data set.

frecuencia Cantidad de veces que aparece el valor en un conjunto de datos.

In the data set 5, 6, 6, 7, 8, 9, the data value 6 has a frequency of 2.

---

frequency table (p. 710) A table that lists the number of times, or frequency, that each data value occurs.

tabla de frecuencia Tabla que enumera la cantidad de veces que ocurre cada valor de datos, o la frecuencia.

Data set: 1, 1, 2, 2, 3, 4, 5, 5, 5, 6, 6, 6, 6
Frequency table:

Data	Frequency
1	2
2	2
3	1
4	1
5	3
6	4

---

function (p. 241) A relation in which every domain value is paired with exactly one range value.

función Relación en la que a cada valor de dominio corresponde exactamente un valor de rango.

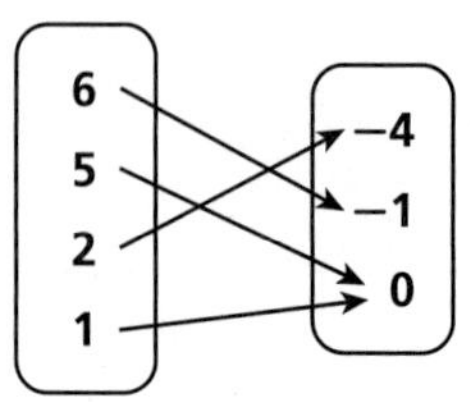

G14 Glossary/Glosario

ENGLISH | SPANISH | EXAMPLES

function notation (p. 250) If x is the independent variable and y is the dependent variable, then the function notation for y is $f(x)$, read "f of x," where f names the function.

notación de función Si x es la variable independiente e y es la variable dependiente, entonces la notación de función para y es $f(x)$, que se lee "f de x," donde f nombra la función.

equation: $y = 2x$
function notation: $f(x) = 2x$

---

function rule (p. 250) An algebraic expression that defines a function.

regla de función Expresión algebraica que define una función.

$f(x) = \underline{2x^2 + 3x - 7}$
↑
function rule

Fundamental Counting Principle (p. 760) If one event has m possible outcomes and a second event has n possible outcomes after the first event has occurred, then there are mn total possible outcomes for the two events.

Principio fundamental de conteo Si un suceso tiene m resultados posibles y otro suceso tiene n resultados posibles después de ocurrido el primer suceso, entonces hay mn resultados posibles en total para los dos sucesos.

If there are 4 colors of shirts, 3 colors of pants, and 2 colors of shoes, then there are $4 \cdot 3 \cdot 2 = 24$ possible outfits.

G

geometric sequence (p. 790) A sequence in which the ratio of successive terms is a constant r, called the common ratio, where $r \neq 0$ and $r \neq 1$.

sucesión geométrica Sucesión en la que la razón de los términos sucesivos es una constante r, denominada razón común, donde $r \neq 0$ y $r \neq 1$.

1, 2, 4, 8, 16, ...
$\cdot 2 \quad \cdot 2 \quad \cdot 2 \quad \cdot 2$ $r = 2$

---

graph of a function (p. 256) The set of points in a coordinate plane with coordinates (x, y), where x is in the domain of the function f and $y = f(x)$.

gráfica de una función Conjunto de los puntos de un plano cartesiano con coordenadas (x, y), donde x está en el dominio de la función f e $y = f(x)$.

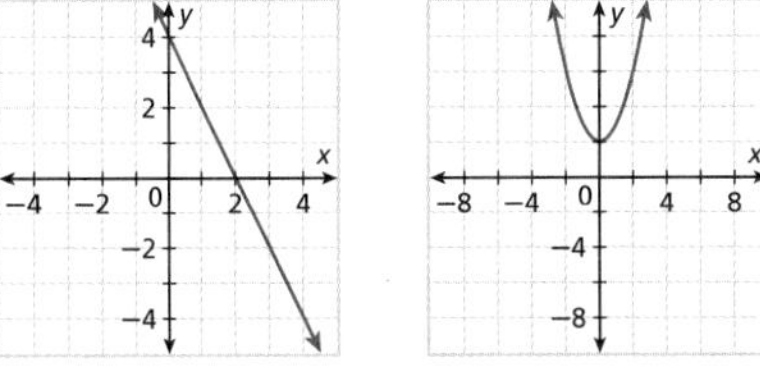

---

graph of a system of linear inequalities (p. 435) The region in a coordinate plane consisting of points whose coordinates are solutions to all of the inequalities in the system.

gráfica de un sistema de desigualdades lineales Región de un plano cartesiano que consta de puntos cuyas coordenadas son soluciones de todas las desigualdades del sistema.

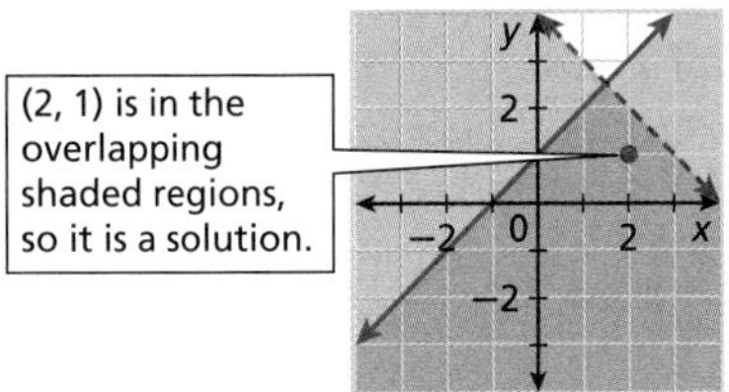

---

graph of an inequality in one variable (p. 171) The set of points on a number line that are solutions of the inequality.

gráfica de una desigualdad en una variable Conjunto de los puntos de una recta numérica que representan soluciones de la desigualdad.

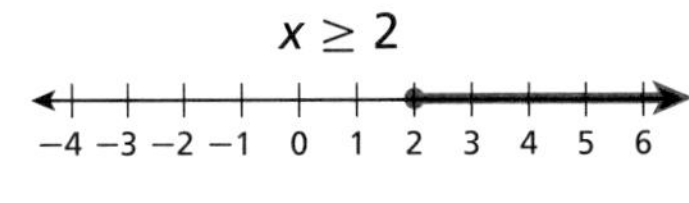

---

graph of an inequality in two variables (p. 428) The set of points in a coordinate plane whose coordinates (x, y) are solutions of the inequality.

gráfica de una desigualdad en dos variables Conjunto de los puntos de un plano cartesiano cuyas coordenadas (x, y) son soluciones de la desigualdad.

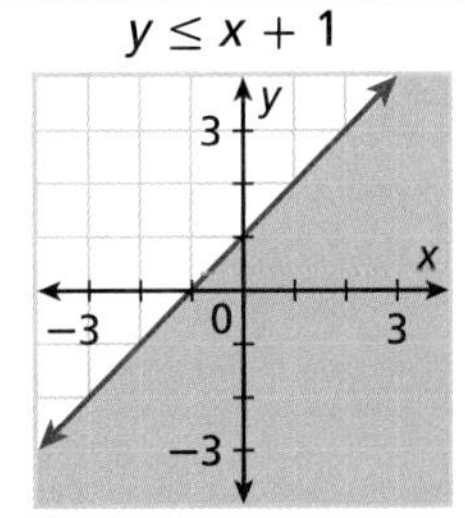

Glossary/Glosario **G15**

ENGLISH	SPANISH	EXAMPLES
graph of an ordered pair (p. 54) For the ordered pair (x, y), the point in a coordinate plane that is a horizontal distance of x units from the origin and a vertical distance of y units from the origin.	**gráfica de un par ordenado** Dado el par ordenado (x, y), punto en un plano cartesiano que está a una distancia horizontal de x unidades desde el origen y a una distancia vertical de y unidades desde el origen.	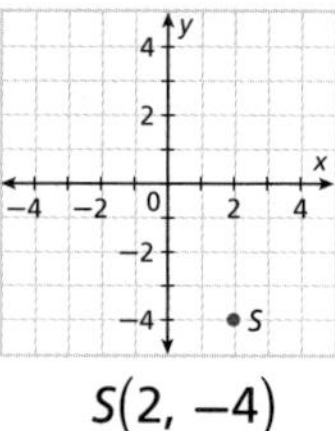 $S(2, -4)$
greatest common factor (monomials) (GCF) (p. 575) The product of the greatest integer and the greatest power of each variable that divide evenly into each monomial.	**máximo común divisor (monomios) (MCD)** Producto del entero mayor y la potencia mayor de cada variable que divide exactamente cada monomio.	The GCF of $4x^3y$ and $6x^2y$ is $2x^2y$.
greatest common factor (numbers) (GCF) The largest common factor of two or more given numbers.	**máximo común divisor (números) (MCD)** El mayor de los factores comunes compartidos por dos o más números dados.	The GCF of 27 and 45 is 9.
grouping symbols (p. 40) Symbols such as parentheses ( ), brackets [ ], and braces { } that separate part of an expression. A fraction bar, absolute-value symbols, and radical symbols may also be used as grouping symbols.	**símbolos de agrupación** Símbolos tales como paréntesis ( ), corchetes [ ] y llaves { } que separan parte de una expresión. La barra de fracciones, los símbolos de valor absoluto y los símbolos de radical también se pueden utilizar como símbolos de agrupación.	$6 + \{3 - [(4 - 3) + 2] + 1\} - 5$ $6 + \{3 - [1 + 2] + 1\} - 5$ $6 + \{3 - 3 + 1\} - 5$ $6 + 1 - 5$ 2

H

half-life (p. 807) The half-life of a substance is the time it takes for one-half of the substance to decay into another substance.	**vida media** La vida media de una sustancia es el tiempo que tarda la mitad de la sustancia en desintegrarse y transformarse en otra sustancia.	Carbon-14 has a half-life of 5730 years, so 5 g of an initial amount of 10 g will remain after 5730 years.
half-plane (p. 428) The part of the coordinate plane on one side of a line, which may include the line.	**semiplano** La parte del plano cartesiano de un lado de una línea, que puede incluir la línea.	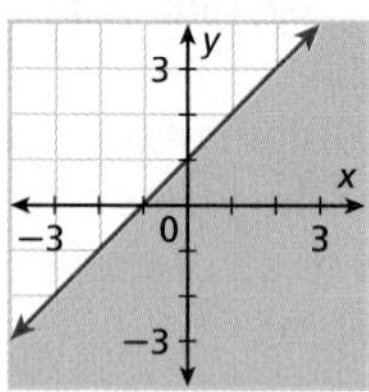
Heron's Formula (p. 834) A triangle with side lengths a, b, and c has area $A = \sqrt{s(s-a)(s-b)(s-c)}$, where s is one-half the perimeter, or $s = \frac{1}{2}(a + b + c)$.	**fórmula de Herón** Un triángulo con longitudes de lado a, b y c tiene un área $A = \sqrt{s(s-a)(s-b)(s-c)}$, donde s es la mitad del perímetro ó $s = \frac{1}{2}(a + b + c)$.	

G16 *Glossary/Glosario*

ENGLISH	SPANISH	EXAMPLES
histogram (p. 710) A bar graph used to display data grouped in intervals.	**histograma** Gráfica de barras utilizada para mostrar datos agrupados en intervalos de clases.	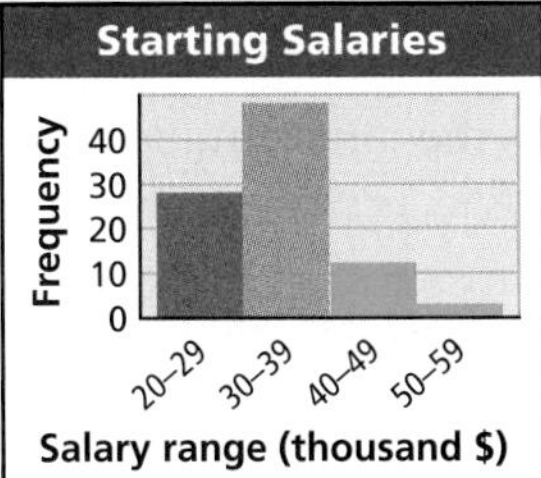
horizontal line (p. 316) A line described by the equation $y = b$, where b is the y-intercept.	**línea horizontal** Línea descrita por la ecuación $y = b$, donde b es la intersección con el eje y.	$y = 4$ 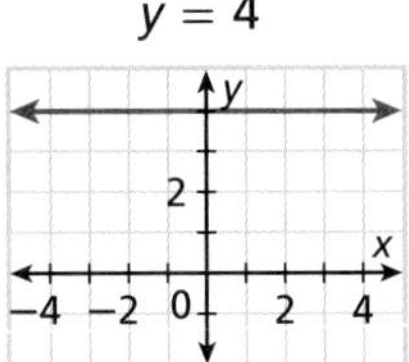
hypotenuse The side opposite the right angle in a right triangle.	**hipotenusa** Lado opuesto al ángulo recto de un triángulo rectángulo.	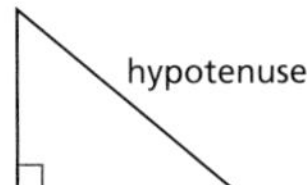

I

ENGLISH	SPANISH	EXAMPLES
identity (p. 101) An equation that is true for all values of the variables.	**identidad** Ecuación verdadera para todos los valores de las variables.	$3 = 3$ $2(x - 1) = 2x - 2$
inclusive events (p. 758) Events that have one or more outcomes in common.	**sucesos inclusivos** Sucesos que tienen uno o más resultados en común.	In the experiment of rolling a number cube, rolling an even number and rolling a number less than 3 are inclusive events because both contain the outcome 2.
inconsistent system (p. 420) A system of equations or inequalities that has no solution.	**sistema inconsistente** Sistema de ecuaciones o desigualdades que no tiene solución.	$\begin{cases} x + y = 0 \\ x + y = 1 \end{cases}$
independent events (p. 750) Events for which the occurrence or nonoccurrence of one event does not affect the probability of the other event.	**sucesos independientes** Dos sucesos son independientes si el hecho de que se produzca o no uno de ellos no afecta la probabilidad del otro suceso.	From a bag containing 3 red marbles and 2 blue marbles, draw a red marble, replace it, and then draw a blue marble.
independent system (p. 421) A system of equations that has exactly one solution.	**sistema independiente** Sistema de ecuaciones que tiene sólo una solución.	$\begin{cases} x + y = 7 \\ x - y = 1 \end{cases}$ Solution: $(4, 3)$
independent variable (p. 250) The input of a function; a variable whose value determines the value of the output, or dependent variable.	**variable independiente** Entrada de una función; variable cuyo valor determina el valor de la salida, o variable dependiente.	For $y = 2x + 1$, x is the independent variable.

Glossary/Glosario **G17**

ENGLISH	SPANISH	EXAMPLES
index (p. 488) In the radical $\sqrt[n]{x}$, which represents the *n*th root of *x*, *n* is the index. In the radical $\sqrt{x}$, the index is understood to be 2.	**índice** En el radical $\sqrt[n]{x}$, que representa la enésima raíz de *x*, *n* es el índice. En el radical $\sqrt{x}$, se da por sentado que el índice es 2.	The radical $\sqrt[3]{8}$ has an index of 3.
indirect measurement (p. 128) A method of measurement that uses formulas, similar figures, and/or proportions.	**medición indirecta** Método de medición en el que se usan fórmulas, figuras semejantes y/o proporciones.	
inequality (p. 170) A statement that compares two expressions by using one of the following signs: $<, >, \leq, \geq$, or $\neq$.	**desigualdad** Enunciado que compara dos expresiones utilizando uno de los siguientes signos: $<, >, \leq, \geq$, o $\neq$.	$x \geq 2$ −4 −3 −2 −1 0 1 2 3 4 5 6
input (p. 55) A value that is substituted for the independent variable in a relation or function.	**entrada** Valor que sustituye a la variable independiente en una relación o función.	For the function $f(x) = x + 5$, the input 3 produces an output of 8.
input-output table A table that displays input values of a function or expression together with the corresponding outputs.	**tabla de entrada y salida** Tabla que muestra los valores de entrada de una función o expresión junto con las correspondientes salidas.	Input: *x* 1, 2, 3, 4 Output: *y* 4, 7, 10, 13
integer (p. 34) A member of the set of whole numbers and their opposites.	**entero** Miembro del conjunto de números cabales y sus opuestos.	…, −3, −2, −1, 0, 1, 2, 3, …
intercept *See x*-intercept and *y*-intercept.	**intersección** *Ver* intersección con el eje *x* e intersección con el eje *y*.	
interest (p. 139) The amount of money charged for borrowing money or the amount of money earned when saving or investing money. *See also* compound interest, simple interest.	**interés** Cantidad de dinero que se cobra por prestar dinero o cantidad de dinero que se gana cuando se ahorra o invierte dinero. *Ver también* interés compuesto, interés simple.	
interquartile range (IQR) (p. 718) The difference of the third (upper) and first (lower) quartiles in a data set, representing the middle half of the data.	**rango entre cuartiles** Diferencia entre el tercer cuartil (superior) y el primer cuartil (inferior) de un conjunto de datos, que representa la mitad central de los datos.	Lower half: 18, (23), 28, Upper half: 29, (36), 42 First quartile Third quartile Interquartile range: 36 − 23 = 13
intersection (p. 205) The intersection of two sets is the set of all elements that are common to both sets, denoted by $\cap$.	**intersección de conjuntos** La intersección de dos conjuntos es el conjunto de todos los elementos que son comunes a ambos conjuntos, expresado por $\cap$.	$A = \{1, 2, 3, 4\}$ $B = \{1, 3, 5, 7, 9\}$ $A \cap B = \{1, 3\}$
inverse operations Operations that undo each other.	**operaciones inversas** Operaciones que se anulan entre sí.	Addition and subtraction of the same quantity are inverse operations: $5 + 3 = 8, 8 - 3 = 5$ Multiplication and division by the same quantity are inverse operations: $2 \cdot 3 = 6, 6 \div 3 = 2$

G18 *Glossary/Glosario*

ENGLISH	SPANISH	EXAMPLES
inverse variation (p. 871) A relationship between two variables, x and y, that can be written in the form $y = \frac{k}{x}$, where k is a nonzero constant and $x \neq 0$.	**variación inversa** Relación entre dos variables, x e y, que puede expresarse en la forma $y = \frac{k}{x}$, donde k es una constante distinta de cero y $x \neq 0$.	$y = \frac{8}{x}$ 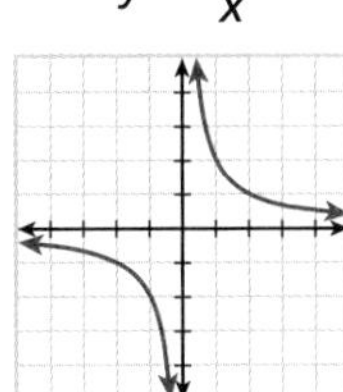
irrational number (p. 34) A real number that cannot be expressed as the ratio of two integers.	**número irracional** Número real que no se puede expresar como una razón de enteros.	$\sqrt{2}, \pi, e$
isolate the variable (p. 77) To isolate a variable in an equation, use inverse operations on both sides until the variable appears by itself on one side of the equation and does not appear on the other side.	**despejar la variable** Para despejar la variable de una ecuación, utiliza operaciones inversas en ambos lados hasta que la variable aparezca sola en uno de los lados de la ecuación y no aparezca en el otro lado.	$10 = 6 - 2x$ $\underline{-6 \quad -6}$ $4 = -2x$ $\frac{4}{-2} = \frac{-2x}{-2}$ $-2 = x$
isosceles triangle A triangle with at least two congruent sides.	**triángulo isósceles** Triángulo que tiene al menos dos lados congruentes.	

L

ENGLISH	SPANISH	EXAMPLES
leading coefficient (p. 497) The coefficient of the first term of a polynomial in standard form.	**coeficiente principal** Coeficiente del primer término de un polinomio en forma estándar.	$3x^2 + 7x - 2$ Leading coefficient: 3
least common denominator (LCD) (p. 907) The least common multiple of the denominators of two or more given fractions or rational expressions.	**mínimo común denominador (MCD)** Mínimo común múltiplo de los denominadores de dos o más fracciones dadas o expresionnes racionales.	The LCD of $\frac{3}{4}$ and $\frac{5}{6}$ is 12.
least common multiple (monomials) (LCM) (p. 906) The product of the smallest positive number and the lowest power of each variable that divide evenly into each monomial.	**mínimo común múltiplo (monomios) (MCM)** El producto del número positivo más pequeño y la menor potencia de cada variable que divide exactamente cada monomio.	The LCM of $6x^2$ and $4x$ is $12x^2$.
least common multiple (numbers) (LCM) The smallest whole number, other than zero, that is a multiple of two or more given numbers.	**mínimo común múltiplo (números) (MCM)** El menor de los números cabales, distinto de cero, que es múltiplo de dos o más números dados.	The LCM of 10 and 18 is 90.
leg of a right triangle One of the two sides of a right triangle that form the right angle.	**cateto de un triángulo rectángulo** Uno de los dos lados de un triángulo rectángulo que forman el ángulo recto.	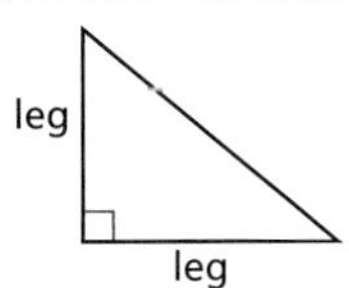

Glossary/Glosario **G19**

ENGLISH	SPANISH	EXAMPLES
like radicals (p. 835) Radical terms having the same radicand and index.	**radicales semejantes** Términos radicales que tienen el mismo radicando e índice.	$3\sqrt{2x}$ and $\sqrt{2x}$
like terms (p. 47) Terms with the same variables raised to the same exponents.	**términos semejantes** Términos con las mismas variables elevadas a los mismos exponentes.	$3a^3b^2$ and $7a^3b^2$
line A straight path that has no thickness and extends forever.	**línea** Un trazo recto que no tiene grosor y se extiende infinitamente.	ℓ
line graph (p. 701) A graph that uses line segments to show how data changes.	**gráfica lineal** Gráfica que se vale de segmentos de recta para mostrar cambios en los datos.	Marlon's Video Game Scores Score: 0, 400, 800, 1200 Game number: 1, 2, 3, 4, 5, 6
linear equation in one variable An equation that can be written in the form $ax = b$ where a and b are constants and $a \neq 0$.	**ecuación lineal en una variable** Ecuación que puede expresarse en la forma $ax = b$ donde a y b son constantes y $a \neq 0$.	$x + 1 = 7$
linear equation in two variables (p. 302) An equation that can be written in the form $Ax + By = C$ where A, B, and C are constants and A and B are not both 0.	**ecuación lineal en dos variables** Ecuación que puede expresarse en la forma $Ax + By = C$ donde A, B y C son constantes y A y B no son ambas 0.	$2x + 3y = 6$
linear function (p. 300) A function that can be written in the form $y = mx + b$, where x is the independent variable and m and b are real numbers. Its graph is a line.	**función lineal** Función que puede expresarse en la forma $y = mx + b$, donde x es la variable independiente y m y b son números reales. Su gráfica es una línea.	$y = x - 1$ y: 4, 2, −4 x: −4, −2, 0, 2, 4
linear inequality in one variable An inequality that can be written in one of the following forms: $ax < b$, $ax > b$, $ax \leq b$, $ax \geq b$, or $ax \neq b$, where a and b are constants and $a \neq 0$.	**desigualdad lineal en una variable** Desigualdad que puede expresarse de una de las siguientes formas: $ax < b$, $ax > b$, $ax \leq b$, $ax \geq b$ o $ax \neq b$, donde a y b son constantes y $a \neq 0$.	$3x - 5 \leq 2(x + 4)$
linear inequality in two variables (p. 428) An inequality that can be written in one of the following forms: $Ax + By < C$, $Ax + By > C$, $Ax + By \leq C$, $Ax + By \geq C$, or $Ax + By \neq C$, where A, B, and C are constants and A and B are not both 0.	**desigualdad lineal en dos variables** Desigualdad que puede expresarse de una de las siguientes formas: $Ax + By < C$, $Ax + By > C$, $Ax + By \leq C$, $Ax + By \geq C$ o $Ax + By \neq C$, donde A, B y C son constantes y A y B no son ambas 0.	$2x + 3y > 6$

G20 *Glossary/Glosario*

ENGLISH	SPANISH	EXAMPLES
literal equation (p. 108) An equation that contains two or more variables.	**ecuación literal** Ecuación que contiene dos o más variables.	$d = rt$ $A = \frac{1}{2}h(b_1 + b_2)$
lower quartile *See* first quartile.	**cuartil inferior** *Ver* primer cuartil.	

M

ENGLISH	SPANISH	EXAMPLES
mapping diagram (p. 240) A diagram that shows the relationship of elements in the domain to elements in the range of a relation or function.	**diagrama de correspondencia** Diagrama que muestra la relación entre los elementos del dominio y los elementos del rango de una función.	Mapping Diagram Domain: 2 → Range: A, B, C
markup (p. 145) The amount by which a wholesale cost is increased.	**margen de ganancia** Cantidad que se agrega a un costo mayorista.	
matrix (p. 770) A rectangular array of numbers.	**matriz** Arreglo rectangular de números.	$\begin{bmatrix} 1 & 0 & 3 \\ -2 & 2 & -5 \\ 7 & -6 & 3 \end{bmatrix}$
maximum of a function (p. 380, p. 612) The *y*-value of the highest point on the graph of the function.	**máximo de una función** Valor de *y* del punto más alto en la gráfica de la función.	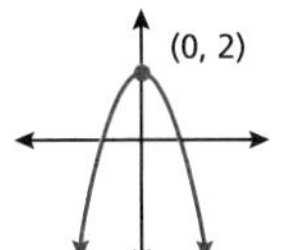 The maximum of the function is 2.
mean (p. 716) The sum of all the values in a data set divided by the number of data values. Also called the *average*.	**media** Suma de todos los valores de un conjunto de datos dividida entre el número de valores de datos. También llamada *promedio*.	Data set: 4, 6, 7, 8, 10 Mean: $\frac{4 + 6 + 7 + 8 + 10}{5} = \frac{35}{5} = 7$
measure of an angle Angles are measured in degrees. A degree is $\frac{1}{360}$ of a complete circle.	**medida de un ángulo** Los ángulos se miden en grados. Un grado es $\frac{1}{360}$ de un círculo completo.	*M* 26.8°
measure of central tendency (p. 716) A measure that describes the center of a data set.	**medida de tendencia dominante** Medida que describe el centro de un conjunto de datos.	mean, median, or mode
median (p. 716) For an ordered data set with an odd number of values, the median is the middle value. For an ordered data set with an even number of values, the median is the average of the two middle values.	**mediana** Dado un conjunto de datos ordenado con un número impar de valores, la mediana es el valor medio. Dado un conjunto de datos con un número par de valores, la mediana es el promedio de los dos valores medios.	8, 9, (9), 12, 15 Median: 9 4, 6, (7, 10), 10, 12 Median: $\frac{7 + 10}{2} = 8.5$
midpoint (p. 330) The point that divides a segment into two congruent segments.	**punto medio** Punto que divide un segmento en dos segmentos congruentes.	*A* *B* *C* Point *B* is the midpoint of $\overline{AC}$.

Glossary/Glosario **G21**

ENGLISH	SPANISH	EXAMPLES
minimum of a function (p. 380, p. 612) The *y*-value of the lowest point on the graph of the function.	**mínimo de una función** Valor de *y* del punto más bajo en la gráfica de la función.	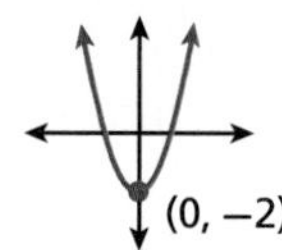 The minimum of the function is −2.
mode (p. 716) The value or values that occur most frequently in a data set; if all values occur with the same frequency, the data set is said to have no mode.	**moda** El valor o los valores que se presentan con mayor frecuencia en un conjunto de datos. Si todos los valores se presentan con la misma frecuencia, se dice que el conjunto de datos no tiene moda.	Data set: 3, 6, 8, 8, 10 Mode: 8 Data set: 2, 5, 5, 7, 7 Modes: 5 and 7 Data set: 2, 3, 6, 9, 11 No mode
monomial (p. 496) A number or a product of numbers and variables with whole-number exponents, or a polynomial with one term.	**monomio** Número o producto de números y variables con exponentes de números cabales, o polinomio con un término.	$3x^2y^4$
Multiplication Property of Equality (p. 86) If *a*, *b*, and *c* are real numbers and $a = b$, then $ac = bc$.	**Propiedad de igualdad de la multiplicación** Si *a*, *b* y *c* son números reales y $a = b$, entonces $ac = bc$.	$\frac{1}{3}x = 7$ $(3)\left(\frac{1}{3}x\right) = (3)(7)$ $x = 21$
Multiplication Property of Inequality (p. 182, p. 183) If both sides of an inequality are multiplied by the same positive quantity, the new inequality will have the same solution set. If both sides of an inequality are multiplied by the same negative quantity, the new inequality will have the same solution set if the inequality symbol is reversed.	**Propiedad de desigualdad de la multiplicación** Si ambos lados de una desigualdad se multiplican por el mismo número positivo, la nueva desigualdad tendrá el mismo conjunto solución. Si ambos lados de una desigualdad se multiplican por el mismo número negativo, la nueva desigualdad tendrá el mismo conjunto solución si se invierte el símbolo de desigualdad.	$\frac{1}{3}x > 7$ $(3)\left(\frac{1}{3}x\right) > (3)(7)$ $x > 21$ $-x \le 2$ $(-1)(-x) \ge (-1)(2)$ $x \ge -2$
multiplicative inverse (p. 21) The reciprocal of the number.	**inverso multiplicativo** Recíproco de un número.	The multiplicative inverse of 5 is $\frac{1}{5}$.
mutually exclusive events (p. 758) Two events are mutually exclusive if they cannot both occur in the same trial of an experiment.	**sucesos mutuamente excluyentes** Dos sucesos son mutuamente excluyentes si ambos no pueden ocurrir en la misma prueba de un experimento.	In the experiment of rolling a number cube, rolling a 3 and rolling an even number are mutually exclusive events.

ENGLISH	SPANISH	EXAMPLES
natural number (p. 34) A counting number.	**número natural** Número que se utiliza para contar.	1, 2, 3, 4, 5, 6, …
negative correlation (p. 267) Two data sets have a negative correlation if one set of data values increases as the other set decreases.	**correlación negativa** Dos conjuntos de datos tienen una correlación negativa si un conjunto de valores de datos aumenta a medida que el otro conjunto disminuye.	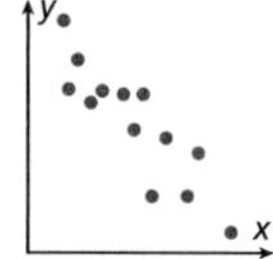

G22 Glossary/Glosario

ENGLISH	SPANISH	EXAMPLES
negative exponent (p. 460) For any nonzero real number x and any integer n, $x^{-n} = \frac{1}{x^n}$.	**exponente negativo** Para cualquier número real distinto de cero x y cualquier entero n, $x^{-n} = \frac{1}{x^n}$.	$x^{-2} = \frac{1}{x^2}$; $3^{-2} = \frac{1}{3^2}$
negative number A number that is less than zero. Negative numbers lie to the left of zero on a number line.	**número negativo** Número menor que cero. Los números negativos se ubican a la izquierda del cero en una recta numérica.	−2 is a negative number. −4 −3 −2 −1 0 1 2 3 4
negative square root (p. 32) The opposite of the principal square root of a number a, written as $-\sqrt{a}$.	**raíz cuadrada negativa** Opuesto de la raíz cuadrada principal de un número a, que se expresa como $-\sqrt{a}$.	The negative square root of 9 is $-\sqrt{9} = -3$.
net (p. 894) A diagram of the faces of a three-dimensional figure arranged in such a way that the diagram can be folded to form the three-dimensional figure.	**plantilla** Diagrama de las caras de una figura tridimensional que se puede plegar para formar la figura tridimensional.	10 m 6 m 10 m 6 m
no correlation (p. 267) Two data sets have no correlation if there is no relationship between the sets of values.	**sin correlación** Dos conjuntos de datos no tienen correlación si no existe una relación entre los conjuntos de valores.	y x
***n*th root** (p. 488) The nth root of a number a, written as $\sqrt[n]{a}$ or $a^{\frac{1}{n}}$, is a number that is equal to a when it is raised to the nth power.	**enésima raíz** La enésima raíz de un número a, que se escribe $\sqrt[n]{a}$ o $a^{\frac{1}{n}}$, es un número igual a a cuando se eleva a la enésima potencia.	$\sqrt[5]{32} = 2$, because $2^5 = 32$.
number line (p. 14) A line used to represent the real numbers.	**recta numérica** Línea utilizada para representar los números reales.	−4 −3 −2 −1 0 1 2 3 4 5 6
numerical expression (p. 6) An expression that contains only numbers and/or operations.	**expresión numérica** Expresión que contiene únicamente números y operaciones.	$2 \cdot 3 + (4 - 6)$

O

ENGLISH	SPANISH	EXAMPLES
obtuse angle An angle that measures greater than 90° and less than 180°.	**ángulo obtuso** Ángulo que mide más de 90° y menos de 180°.	
obtuse triangle A triangle with one obtuse angle.	**triángulo obtusángulo** Triángulo con un ángulo obtuso.	
odds (p. 746) A comparison of favorable and unfavorable outcomes. The odds in favor of an event are the ratio of the number of favorable outcomes to the number of unfavorable outcomes. The odds against an event are the ratio of the number of unfavorable outcomes to the number of favorable outcomes.	**probabilidades a favor y en contra** Comparación de los resultados favorables y desfavorables. Las probabilidades a favor de un suceso son la razón entre la cantidad de resultados favorables y la cantidad de resultados desfavorables. Las probabilidades en contra de un suceso son la razón entre la cantidad de resultados desfavorables y la cantidad de resultados favorables.	The odds in favor of rolling a 3 on a number cube are 1:5. The odds against rolling a 3 on a number cube are 5:1.

Glossary/Glosario

Glossary/Glosario G23

ENGLISH	SPANISH	EXAMPLES
opposite (p. 15) The opposite of a number a, denoted $-a$, is the number that is the same distance from zero as a, on the opposite side of the number line. The sum of opposites is 0.	**opuesto** El opuesto de un número a, expresado $-a$, es el número que se encuentra a la misma distancia de cero que a, del lado opuesto de la recta numérica. La suma de los opuestos es 0.	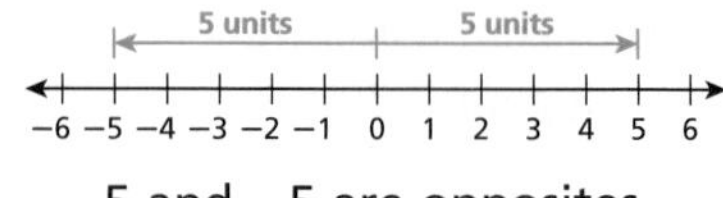 5 and −5 are opposites.
opposite reciprocal (p. 364) The opposite of the reciprocal of a number. The opposite reciprocal of any nonzero number a is $-\frac{1}{a}$.	**recíproco opuesto** Opuesto del recíproco de un número. El recíproco opuesto de a es $-\frac{1}{a}$.	The opposite reciprocal of $\frac{2}{3}$ is $-\frac{3}{2}$.
OR (p. 204) A logical operator representing the union of two sets.	**O** Operador lógico que representa la unión de dos conjuntos.	$A = \{2, 3, 4, 5\}$ $B = \{1, 3, 5, 7\}$ The set of values that are in A OR B is $A \cup B = \{1, 2, 3, 4, 5, 7\}$.
order of operations (p. 40) A process for evaluating expressions: First, perform operations in parentheses or other grouping symbols. Second, simplify powers and roots. Third, perform all multiplication and division from left to right. Fourth, perform all addition and subtraction from left to right.	**orden de las operaciones** Regla para evaluar las expresiones: Primero, realizar las operaciones entre paréntesis u otros símbolos de agrupación. Segundo, simplificar las potencias y las raíces. Tercero, realizar todas las multiplicaciones y divisiones de izquierda a derecha. Cuarto, realizar todas las sumas y restas de izquierda a derecha.	$2 + 3^2 - (7 + 5) \div 4 \cdot 3$ $2 + 3^2 - 12 \div 4 \cdot 3$ Add inside parentheses. $2 + 9 - 12 \div 4 \cdot 3$ Simplify the power. $2 + 9 - 3 \cdot 3$ Divide. $2 + 9 - 9$ Multiply. $11 - 9$ Add. 2 Subtract.
ordered pair (p. 54) A pair of numbers (x, y) that can be used to locate a point on a coordinate plane. The first number x indicates the distance to the left or right of the origin, and the second number y indicates the distance above or below the origin.	**par ordenado** Par de números (x, y) que se pueden utilizar para ubicar un punto en un plano cartesiano. El primer número, x, indica la distancia a la izquierda o derecha del origen y el segundo número, y, indica la distancia hacia arriba o hacia abajo del origen.	The ordered pair $(-2, 3)$ can be used to locate B.
origin (p. 54) The intersection of the x- and y-axes in a coordinate plane. The coordinates of the origin are $(0, 0)$.	**origen** Intersección de los ejes x e y en un plano cartesiano. Las coordenadas de origen son $(0, 0)$.	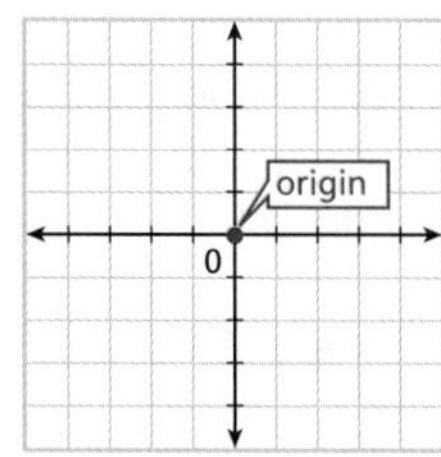
outcome (p. 737) A possible result of a probability experiment.	**resultado** Resultado posible de un experimento de probabilidad.	In the experiment of rolling a number cube, the possible outcomes are 1, 2, 3, 4, 5, and 6.
outlier (p. 716) A data value that is far removed from the rest of the data.	**valor extremo** Valor de datos que está muy alejado del resto de los datos.	
output (p. 55) The result of substituting a value for a variable in a function.	**salida** Resultado de la sustitución de una variable por un valor en una función.	For the function $f(x) = x^2 + 1$, the input 3 produces an output of 10.

G24 *Glossary/Glosario*

ENGLISH	SPANISH	EXAMPLES
P		
parabola (p. 611) The shape of the graph of a quadratic function.	**parábola** Forma de la gráfica de una función cuadrática.	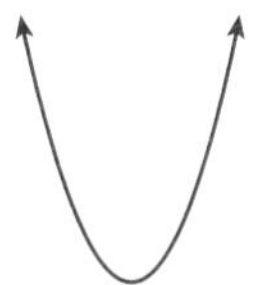
parallel lines (p. 361) Lines in the same plane that do not intersect.	**líneas paralelas** Líneas en el mismo plano que no se cruzan.	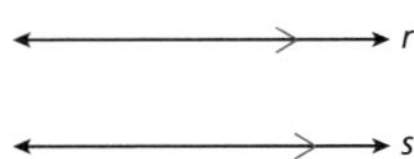
parallelogram A quadrilateral with two pairs of parallel sides.	**paralelogramo** Cuadrilátero con dos pares de lados paralelos.	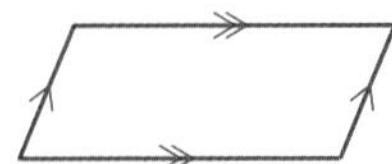
parent function (p. 369) The simplest function with the defining characteristics of the family. Functions in the same family are transformations of their parent function.	**función madre** La función más básica que tiene las características distintivas de una familia. Las funciones de la misma familia son transformaciones de su función madre.	$f(x) = x^2$ is the parent function for $g(x) = x^2 + 4$ and $h(x) = (5x + 2)^2 - 3$.
Pascal's triangle (p. 590) A triangular arrangement of numbers in which every row starts and ends with 1 and each other number is the sum of the two numbers above it.	**triángulo de Pascal** Arreglo triangular de números en el cual cada fila comienza y termina con 1 y los demás números son la suma de los dos valores que están arriba de cada uno.	1 1 1 1 2 1 1 3 3 1 1 4 6 4 1
percent (p. 133) A ratio that compares a number to 100.	**porcentaje** Razón que compara un número con 100.	$\frac{17}{100} = 17\%$
percent change (p. 144) An increase or decrease given as a percent of the original amount. *See also* percent decrease, percent increase.	**porcentaje de cambio** Incremento o disminución dada como un porcentaje de la cantidad original. *Ver también* porcentaje de disminución, porcentaje de incremento.	
percent decrease (p. 144) A decrease given as a percent of the original amount.	**porcentaje de disminución** Disminución dada como un porcentaje de la cantidad original.	If an item that costs \$8.00 is marked down to \$6.00, the amount of the decrease is \$2.00, so the percent decrease is $\frac{2.00}{8.00} = 0.25 = 25\%$.
percent increase (p. 144) An increase given as a percent of the original amount.	**porcentaje de incremento** Incremento dado como un porcentaje de la cantidad original.	If an item's wholesale cost of \$8.00 is marked up to \$12.00, the amount of the increase is \$4.00, so the percent increase is $\frac{4.00}{8.00} = 0.5 = 50\%$.
perfect square (p. 32) A number whose positive square root is a whole number.	**cuadrado perfecto** Número cuya raíz cuadrada positiva es un número cabal.	36 is a perfect square because $\sqrt{36} = 6$.

Glossary/Glosario **G25**

ENGLISH	SPANISH	EXAMPLES
perfect-square trinomial (p. 521) A trinomial whose factored form is the square of a binomial. A perfect-square trinomial has the form $a^2 - 2ab + b^2 = (a - b)^2$ or $a^2 + 2ab + b^2 = (a + b)^2$.	**trinomio cuadrado perfecto** Trinomio cuya forma factorizada es el cuadrado de un binomio. Un trinomio cuadrado perfecto tiene la forma $a^2 - 2ab + b^2 = (a - b)^2$ o $a^2 + 2ab + b^2 = (a + b)^2$.	$x^2 + 6x + 9$ is a perfect-square trinomial, because $x^2 + 6x + 9 = (x + 3)^2$.
perimeter (p. 52) The sum of the side lengths of a closed plane figure.	**perímetro** Suma de las longitudes de los lados de una figura plana cerrada.	18 ft 6 ft Perimeter = 18 + 6 + 18 + 6 = 48 ft
permutation (p. 761) An arrangement of a group of objects in which order is important.	**permutación** Arreglo de un grupo de objetos en el cual el orden es importante.	For objects *A*, *B*, *C*, and *D*, there are 12 different permutations of 2 objects. *AB, AC, AD, BC, BD, CD* *BA, CA, DA, CB, DB, DC*
perpendicular Intersecting to form 90° angles.	**perpendicular** Que se cruza para formar ángulos de 90°.	*n* *m*
perpendicular lines (p. 363) Lines that intersect at 90° angles.	**líneas perpendiculares** Líneas que se cruzan en ángulos de 90°.	*n* *m*
plane A flat surface that has no thickness and extends forever.	**plano** Una superficie plana que no tiene grosor y se extiende infinitamente.	
point A location that has no size.	**punto** Ubicación exacta que no tiene ningún tamaño.	***P*** • point *P*
point-slope form (p. 351) The point-slope form of a linear equation is $y - y_1 = m(x - x_1)$, where m is the slope and (x_1, y_1) is a point on the line.	**forma de punto y pendiente** La forma de punto y pendiente de una ecuación lineal es $y - y_1 = m(x - x_1)$, donde m es la pendiente y (x_1, y_1) es un punto en la línea.	$y - 3 = 2(x - 3)$
polygon (p. 52) A closed plane figure formed by three or more segments such that each segment intersects exactly two other segments only at their endpoints and no two segments with a common endpoint are collinear.	**polígono** Figura plana cerrada formada por tres o más segmentos tal que cada segmento se cruza únicamente con otros dos segmentos sólo en sus extremos y ningún segmento con un extremo común a otro es colineal con éste.	
polynomial (p. 496) A monomial or a sum or difference of monomials.	**polinomio** Monomio o suma o diferencia de monomios.	$2x^2 + 3xy - 7y^2$

G26 *Glossary/Glosario*

ENGLISH	SPANISH	EXAMPLES
polynomial long division (p. 914) A method of dividing one polynomial by another.	**división larga polinomial** Método por el que se divide un polinomio entre otro.	$x + 2\overline{)\,x^2 + 3x + 5}$ quotient $x + 1$; $-(x^2 + 2x)$; $x + 5$; $-(x + 2)$; 3 $\frac{x^2 + 3x + 5}{x + 2} = x + 1 + \frac{3}{x + 2}$
population (p. 732) The entire group of objects or individuals considered for a survey.	**población** Grupo completo de objetos o individuos que se desea estudiar.	In a survey about the study habits of high school students, the population is all high school students.
positive correlation (p. 267) Two data sets have a positive correlation if both sets of data values increase.	**correlación positiva** Dos conjuntos de datos tienen correlación positiva si los valores de ambos conjuntos de datos aumentan.	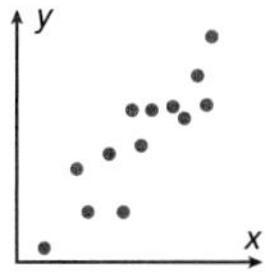 (scatter plot with axes x, y)
positive number A number greater than zero.	**número positivo** Número mayor que cero.	2 is a positive number. 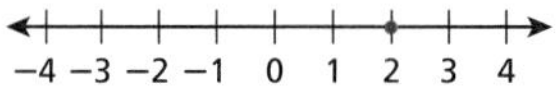 −4 −3 −2 −1 0 1 2 3 4
positive square root (p. 32) The positive square root of a number, indicated by the radical sign.	**raíz cuadrada positiva** Raíz cuadrada positiva de un número, expresada por el signo de radical.	The positive square root of 36 is $\sqrt{36} = 6$.
power (p. 26) An expression written with a base and an exponent or the value of such an expression.	**potencia** Expresión escrita con una base y un exponente o el valor de dicha expresión.	$2^3 = 8$, so 8 is the third power of 2.
Power of a Power Property (p. 476) If a is any nonzero real number and m and n are integers, then $(a^m)^n = a^{mn}$.	**Propiedad de la potencia de una potencia** Dado un número real a distinto de cero y los números enteros m y n, entonces $(a^m)^n = a^{mn}$.	$(6^7)^4 = 6^{7 \cdot 4}$ $= 6^{28}$
Power of a Product Property (p. 477) If a and b are any nonzero real numbers and n is any integer, then $(ab)^n = a^n b^n$.	**Propiedad de la potencia de un producto** Dados los números reales a y b distintos de cero y un número entero n, entonces $(ab)^n = a^n b^n$.	$(2 \cdot 4)^3 = 2^3 \cdot 4^3$ $= 8 \cdot 64$ $= 512$
Power of a Quotient Property (p. 483, p. 484) If a and b are any nonzero real numbers and n is an integer, then $\left(\frac{a}{b}\right)^n = \frac{a^n}{b^n}$.	**Propiedad de la potencia de un cociente** Dados los números reales a y b distintos de cero y un número entero n, entonces $\left(\frac{a}{b}\right)^n = \frac{a^n}{b^n}$.	$\left(\frac{3}{5}\right)^4 = \frac{3}{5} \cdot \frac{3}{5} \cdot \frac{3}{5} \cdot \frac{3}{5}$ $= \frac{3 \cdot 3 \cdot 3 \cdot 3}{5 \cdot 5 \cdot 5 \cdot 5}$ $= \frac{3^4}{5^4}$
prediction (p. 739) An estimate or guess about something that has not yet happened.	**predicción** Estimación o suposición sobre algo que todavía no ha sucedido.	
prime factorization (p. 544) A representation of a number or a polynomial as a product of primes.	**factorización prima** Representación de un número o de un polinomio como producto de números primos.	The prime factorization of 60 is $2 \cdot 2 \cdot 3 \cdot 5$.

Glossary/Glosario G27

ENGLISH	SPANISH	EXAMPLES
prime number (p. 544) A whole number greater than 1 that has exactly two positive factors, itself and 1.	**número primo** Número cabal mayor que 1 que es divisible únicamente entre sí mismo y entre 1.	5 is prime because its only positive factors are 5 and 1.
principal (p. 139) An amount of money borrowed or invested.	**capital** Cantidad de dinero que se pide prestado o se invierte.	
prism (p. 894) A polyhedron formed by two parallel congruent polygonal bases connected by faces that are parallelograms.	**prisma** Poliedro formado por dos bases poligonales congruentes y paralelas conectadas por caras laterales que son paralelogramos.	
probability (p. 737) A number from 0 to 1 (or 0% to 100%) that is the measure of how likely an event is to occur.	**probabilidad** Número entre 0 y 1 (o entre 0% y 100%) que describe cuán probable es que ocurra un suceso.	A bag contains 3 red marbles and 4 blue marbles. The probability of randomly choosing a red marble is $\frac{3}{7}$.
Product of Powers Property (p. 474) If a is any nonzero real number and m and n are integers, then $a^m \cdot a^n = a^{m+n}$.	**Propiedad del producto de potencias** Dado un número real a distinto de cero y los números enteros m y n, entonces $a^m \cdot a^n = a^{m+n}$.	$6^7 \cdot 6^4 = 6^{7+4}$ $= 6^{11}$
Product Property of Square Roots (p. 830) For $a \geq 0$ and $b \geq 0$, $\sqrt{ab} = \sqrt{a} \cdot \sqrt{b}$.	**Propiedad del producto de raíces cuadradas** Dados $a \geq 0$ y $b \geq 0$, $\sqrt{ab} = \sqrt{a} \cdot \sqrt{b}$.	$\sqrt{9 \cdot 25} = \sqrt{9} \cdot \sqrt{25}$ $= 3 \cdot 5 = 15$
proportion (p. 120) A statement that two ratios are equal; $\frac{a}{b} = \frac{c}{d}$.	**proporción** Ecuación que establece que dos razones son iguales; $\frac{a}{b} = \frac{c}{d}$.	$\frac{2}{3} = \frac{4}{6}$
pyramid (p. 894) A polyhedron formed by a polygonal base and triangular lateral faces that meet at a common vertex.	**pirámide** Poliedro formado por una base poligonal y caras laterales triangulares que se encuentran en un vértice común.	
Pythagorean Theorem If a right triangle has legs of lengths a and b and a hypotenuse of length c, then $a^2 + b^2 = c^2$.	**Teorema de Pitágoras** Dado un triángulo rectángulo con catetos de longitudes a y b y una hipotenusa de longitud c, entonces $a^2 + b^2 = c^2$.	13 cm 5 cm 12 cm $5^2 + 12^2 = 13^2$ $25 + 144 = 169$
Pythagorean triple (p. 539) A set of three positive integers a, b, and c such that $a^2 + b^2 = c^2$.	**Tripleta de Pitágoras** Conjunto de tres enteros positivos a, b y c tal que $a^2 + b^2 = c^2$.	The numbers 3, 4, and 5 form a Pythagorean triple because $3^2 + 4^2 = 5^2$.

Q

quadrant (p. 54) One of the four regions into which the x- and y-axes divide the coordinate plane.	**cuadrante** Una de las cuatro regiones en las que los ejes x e y dividen el plano cartesiano.	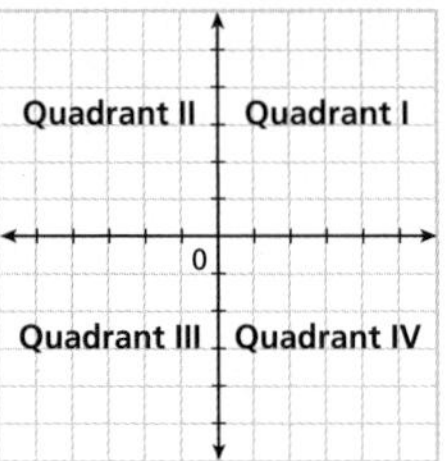

G28 Glossary/Glosario

ENGLISH	SPANISH	EXAMPLES
quadratic equation (p. 642) An equation that can be written in the form $ax^2 + bx + c = 0$, where a, b, and c are real numbers and $a \neq 0$.	**ecuación cuadrática** Ecuación que se puede expresar como $ax^2 + bx + c = 0$, donde a, b y c son números reales y $a \neq 0$.	$x^2 + 3x - 4 = 0$ $x^2 - 9 = 0$
Quadratic Formula (p. 670) The formula $x = \frac{-b \pm \sqrt{b^2 - 4ac}}{2a}$, which gives solutions, or roots, of equations in the form $ax^2 + bx + c = 0$, where $a \neq 0$.	**fórmula cuadrática** La fórmula $x = \frac{-b \pm \sqrt{b^2 - 4ac}}{2a}$, que da soluciones, o raíces, para las ecuaciones del tipo $ax^2 + bx + c = 0$, donde $a \neq 0$.	The solutions of $2x^2 - 5x - 3 = 0$ are given by $x = \frac{-(-5) \pm \sqrt{(-5)^2 - 4(2)(-3)}}{2(2)}$ $= \frac{5 \pm \sqrt{25 + 24}}{4} = \frac{5 \pm 7}{4}$ $x = 3$ or $x = -\frac{1}{2}$
quadratic function (p. 610) A function that can be written in the form $f(x) = ax^2 + bx + c$, where a, b, and c are real numbers and $a \neq 0$.	**función cuadrática** Función que se puede expresar como $f(x) = ax^2 + bx + c$, donde a, b y c son números reales y $a \neq 0$.	$f(x) = x^2 - 6x + 8$
quadratic polynomial (p. 497) A polynomial of degree 2.	**polinomio cuadrático** Polinomio de grado 2.	$x^2 - 6x + 8$
quartile The median of the upper or lower half of a data set. *See also* first quartile, third quartile.	**cuartil** La mediana de la mitad superior o inferior de un conjunto de datos. *Ver también* primer cuartil, tercer cuartil.	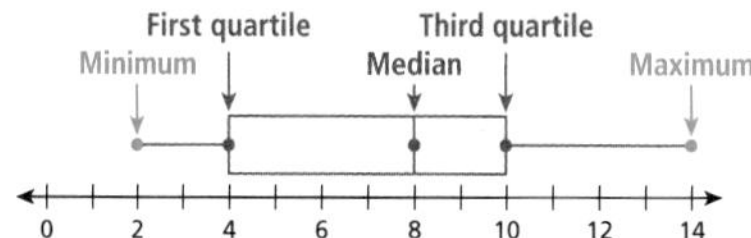
Quotient of Powers Property (p. 481) If a is a nonzero real number and m and n are integers, then $\frac{a^m}{a^n} = a^{m-n}$.	**Propiedad del cociente de potencias** Dado un número real a distinto de cero y los números enteros m y n, entonces $\frac{a^m}{a^n} = a^{m-n}$.	$\frac{6^7}{6^4} = 6^{7-4} = 6^3$
Quotient Property of Square Roots (p. 830) For $a \geq 0$ and $b > 0$, $\sqrt{\frac{a}{b}} = \frac{\sqrt{a}}{\sqrt{b}}$.	**Propiedad del cociente de raíces cuadradas** Dados $a \geq 0$ y $b > 0$, $\sqrt{\frac{a}{b}} = \frac{\sqrt{a}}{\sqrt{b}}$.	$\sqrt{\frac{9}{25}} = \frac{\sqrt{9}}{\sqrt{25}} = \frac{3}{5}$

R

ENGLISH	SPANISH	EXAMPLES
radical equation (p. 846) An equation that contains a variable within a radical.	**ecuación radical** Ecuación que contiene una variable dentro de un radical.	$\sqrt{x + 3} + 4 = 7$
radical expression (p. 829) An expression that contains a radical sign.	**expresión radical** Expresión que contiene un signo de radical.	$\sqrt{x + 3} + 4$
radical symbol (p. 32) The symbol $\sqrt{}$ used to denote a root. The symbol is used alone to indicate a square root or with an index, $\sqrt[n]{}$, to indicate the nth root.	**símbolo de radical** Símbolo $\sqrt{}$ que se utiliza para expresar una raíz. Puede utilizarse solo para indicar una raíz cuadrada, o con un índice, $\sqrt[n]{}$, para indicar la enésima raíz.	$\sqrt{36} = 6$ $\sqrt[3]{27} = 3$

Glossary/Glosario **G29**

ENGLISH	SPANISH	EXAMPLES
radicand (p. 829) The expression under a radical sign.	**radicando** Número o expresión debajo del signo de radical.	Expression: $\sqrt{x+3}$ Radicand: $x + 3$
radius A segment whose endpoints are the center of a circle and a point on the circle; the distance from the center of a circle to any point on the circle.	**radio** Segmento cuyos extremos son el centro de un círculo y un punto de la circunferencia; distancia desde el centro de un círculo hasta cualquier punto de la circunferencia.	Radius
random sample (p. 727) A sample selected from a population so that each member of the population has an equal chance of being selected.	**muestra aleatoria** Muestra seleccionada de una población tal que cada miembro de ésta tenga igual probabilidad de ser seleccionada.	Mr. Hansen chose a random sample of the class by writing each student's name on a slip of paper, mixing up the slips, and drawing five slips without looking.
range of a data set (p. 716) The difference of the greatest and least values in the data set.	**rango de un conjunto de datos** La diferencia del mayor y menor valor en un conjunto de datos.	The data set {3, 3, 5, 7, 8, 10, 11, 11, 12} has a range of $12 - 3 = 9$.
range of a function or relation (p. 240) The set of all second coordinates (or y-values) of a function or relation.	**rango de una función o relación** Conjunto de todos los valores de la segunda coordenada (o valores de y) de una función o relación.	The range of the function {(−5, 3), (−3, −2), (−1, −1), (1, 0)} is {−2, −1, 0, 3}.
rate (p. 120) A ratio that compares two quantities measured in different units.	**tasa** Razón que compara dos cantidades medidas en diferentes unidades.	$\frac{55 \text{ miles}}{1 \text{ hour}} = 55 \text{ mi/h}$
rate of change (p. 314) A ratio that compares the amount of change in a dependent variable to the amount of change in an independent variable.	**tasa de cambio** Razón que compara la cantidad de cambio de la variable dependiente con la cantidad de cambio de la variable independiente.	The cost of mailing a letter increased from 22 cents in 1985 to 25 cents in 1988. During this period, the rate of change was $\frac{\text{change in cost}}{\text{change in year}} = \frac{25 - 22}{1988 - 1985} = \frac{3}{3}$ $= 1$ cent per year.
ratio (p. 120) A comparison of two quantities by division.	**razón** Comparación de dos cantidades mediante una división.	$\frac{1}{2}$ or 1:2
rational equation (p. 920) An equation that contains one or more rational expressions.	**ecuación racional** Ecuación que contiene una o más expresiones racionales.	$\frac{x+2}{x^2+3x-1} = 6$
rational exponent (p. 489) An exponent that can be expressed as $\frac{m}{n}$ such that if m and n are integers, then $b^{\frac{m}{n}} = \sqrt[n]{b^m} = \left(\sqrt[n]{b}\right)^m$.	**exponente racional** Exponente que se puede expresar como $\frac{m}{n}$ tal que si m y n son números enteros, entonces $b^{\frac{m}{n}} = \sqrt[n]{b^m} = \left(\sqrt[n]{b}\right)^m$.	$64^{\frac{1}{6}} = \sqrt[6]{64}$
rational expression (p. 886) An algebraic expression whose numerator and denominator are polynomials and whose denominator has a degree ≥ 1.	**expresión racional** Expresión algebraica cuyo numerador y denominador son polinomios y cuyo denominador tiene un grado ≥ 1.	$\frac{x+2}{x^2+3x-1}$

G30 *Glossary/Glosario*

ENGLISH | **SPANISH** | **EXAMPLES**

rational function (p. 878) A function whose rule can be written as a rational expression.

función racional Función cuya regla se puede expresar como una expresión racional.

$$f(x) = \frac{x + 2}{x^2 + 3x - 1}$$

---

rational number (p. 34) A number that can be written in the form $\frac{a}{b}$, where a and b are integers and $b \neq 0$.

número racional Número que se puede expresar como $\frac{a}{b}$, donde a y b son números enteros y $b \neq 0$.

$3, 1.75, 0.\overline{3}, -\frac{2}{3}, 0$

---

rationalizing the denominator (p. 842) A method of rewriting a fraction by multiplying by another fraction that is equivalent to 1 in order to remove radical terms from the denominator.

racionalizar el denominador Método que consiste en escribir nuevamente una fracción multiplicándola por otra fracción equivalente a 1 a fin de eliminar los términos radicales del denominador.

$$\frac{1}{\sqrt{2}} \cdot \frac{\sqrt{2}}{\sqrt{2}} = \frac{\sqrt{2}}{2}$$

---

ray A part of a line that starts at an endpoint and extends forever in one direction.

rayo Parte de una recta que comienza en un extremo y se extiende infinitamente en una dirección.

---

real number (p. 34) A rational or irrational number. Every point on the number line represents a real number.

número real Número racional o irracional. Cada punto de la recta numérica representa un número real.

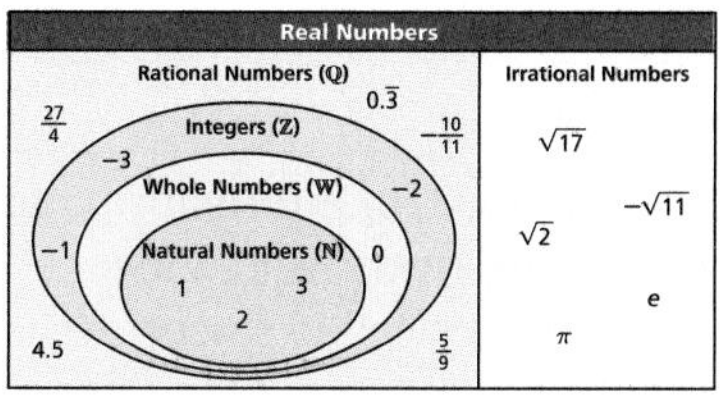

---

reciprocal (p. 21) For a real number $a \neq 0$, the reciprocal of a is $\frac{1}{a}$. The product of reciprocals is 1.

recíproco Dado el número real $a \neq 0$, el recíproco de a es $\frac{1}{a}$. El producto de los recíprocos es 1.

Number	Reciprocal
2	$\frac{1}{2}$
1	1
−1	−1
0	No reciprocal

---

rectangle A quadrilateral with four right angles.

rectángulo Cuadrilátero con cuatro ángulos rectos.

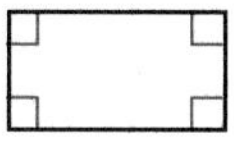

---

rectangular prism (p. 894) A prism whose bases are rectangles.

prisma rectangular Prisma cuyas bases son rectángulos.

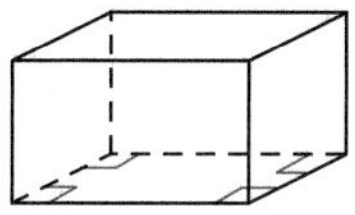

---

rectangular pyramid (p. 894) A pyramid whose base is a rectangle.

pirámide rectangular Pirámide cuya base es un rectángulo.

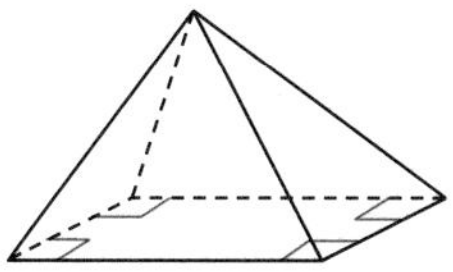

---

reflection (p. 371) A transformation that reflects, or "flips," a graph or figure across a line, called the line of reflection.

reflexión Transformación en la que una gráfica o figura se refleja o se invierte sobre una línea, denominada la línea de reflexión.

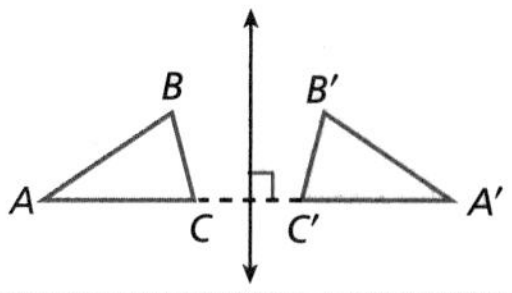

---

regular polygon A polygon that is both equilateral and equiangular.

polígono regular Polígono equilátero de ángulos iguales.

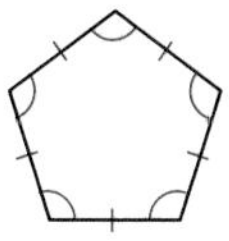

Glossary/Glosario

Glossary/Glosario **G31**

ENGLISH	SPANISH	EXAMPLES
relation (p. 240) A set of ordered pairs.	**relación** Conjunto de pares ordenados.	$\{(0, 5), (0, 4), (2, 3), (4, 0)\}$
repeating decimal (p. 34) A rational number in decimal form that has a nonzero block of one or more digits that repeat continuously.	**decimal periódico** Número racional en forma decimal que tiene un bloque de uno o más dígitos que se repite continuamente.	$1.\overline{3}, 0.\overline{6}, 2.\overline{14}, 6.77\overline{3}$
replacement set (p. 8) A set of numbers that can be substituted for a variable.	**conjunto de reemplazo** Conjunto de números que pueden sustituir una variable.	
rhombus A quadrilateral with four congruent sides.	**rombo** Cuadrilátero con cuatro lados congruentes.	
right angle An angle that measures 90°.	**ángulo recto** Ángulo que mide 90°.	
rise (p. 315) The difference in the *y*-values of two points on a line.	**distancia vertical** Diferencia entre los valores de *y* de dos puntos de una línea.	For the points $(3, -1)$ and $(6, 5)$, the rise is $5 - (-1) = 6$.
rotation (p. 370) A transformation that rotates or turns a figure about a point called the center of rotation.	**rotación** Transformación que rota o gira una figura sobre un punto llamado centro de rotación.	F′ E′ G′ D′ G F D E
run (p. 315) The difference in the *x*-values of two points on a line.	**distancia horizontal** Diferencia entre los valores de *x* de dos puntos de una línea.	For the points $(3, -1)$ and $(6, 5)$, the run is $6 - 3 = 3$.

S

ENGLISH	SPANISH	EXAMPLES
sales tax (p. 140) A percent of the cost of an item that is charged by governments to raise money.	**impuesto sobre la venta** Porcentaje del costo de un artículo que cobran los gobiernos para recaudar dinero.	
sample (p. 732) A part of the population.	**muestra** Una parte de la población.	In a survey about the study habits of high school students, a sample is a survey of 100 students.
sample space (p. 737) The set of all possible outcomes of a probability experiment.	**espacio muestral** Conjunto de todos los resultados posibles de un experimento de probabilidad.	In the experiment of rolling a number cube, the sample space is $\{1, 2, 3, 4, 5, 6\}$.
scalar (p. 771) A number that is multiplied by a matrix.	**escalar** Número que se multiplica por una matriz.	$3\begin{bmatrix}1 & -2\\ 2 & 3\end{bmatrix} = \begin{bmatrix}3 & -6\\ 6 & 9\end{bmatrix}$ (3 = scalar)
scale (p. 122) The ratio between two corresponding measurements.	**escala** Razón entre dos medidas correspondientes.	1 cm:5 mi

G32 Glossary/Glosario

ENGLISH | **SPANISH** | **EXAMPLES**

scale drawing (p. 122) A drawing that uses a scale to represent an object as smaller or larger than the actual object.

dibujo a escala Dibujo que utiliza una escala para representar un objeto como más pequeño o más grande que el objeto original.

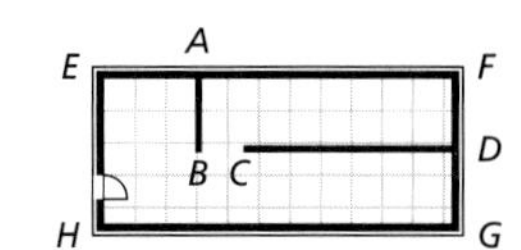

A blueprint is an example of a scale drawing.

---

scale factor (p. 129) The multiplier used on each dimension to change one figure into a similar figure.

factor de escala El multiplicador utilizado en cada dimensión para transformar una figura en una figura semejante.

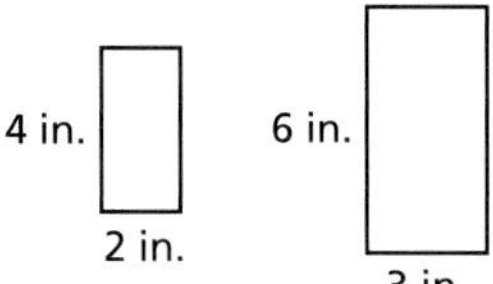

Scale factor: $\frac{3}{2} = 1.5$

---

scale model (p. 122) A three-dimensional model that uses a scale to represent an object as smaller or larger than the actual object.

modelo a escala Modelo tridimensional que utiliza una escala para representar un objeto como más pequeño o más grande que el objeto real.

---

scalene triangle A triangle with no congruent sides.

triángulo escaleno Triángulo sin lados congruentes.

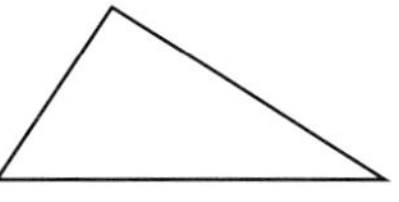

---

scatter plot (p. 266) A graph with points plotted to show a possible relationship between two sets of data.

diagrama de dispersión Gráfica con puntos que se usa para demostrar una relación posible entre dos conjuntos de datos.

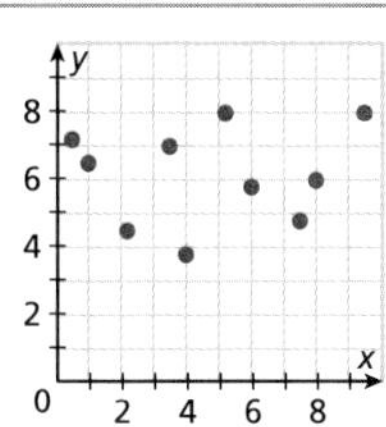

---

scientific notation (p. 467) A method of writing very large or very small numbers, by using powers of 10, in the form $m \times 10^n$, where $1 \leq m < 10$ and n is an integer.

notación científica Método que consiste en escribir números muy grandes o muy pequeños utilizando potencias de 10 del tipo $m \times 10^n$, donde $1 \leq m < 10$ y n es un número entero.

$12{,}560{,}000{,}000{,}000 = 1.256 \times 10^{13}$

$0.0000075 = 7.5 \times 10^{-6}$

---

second differences (p. 610) Differences between first differences of a function.

segundas diferencias Diferencias entre las primeras diferencias de una función.

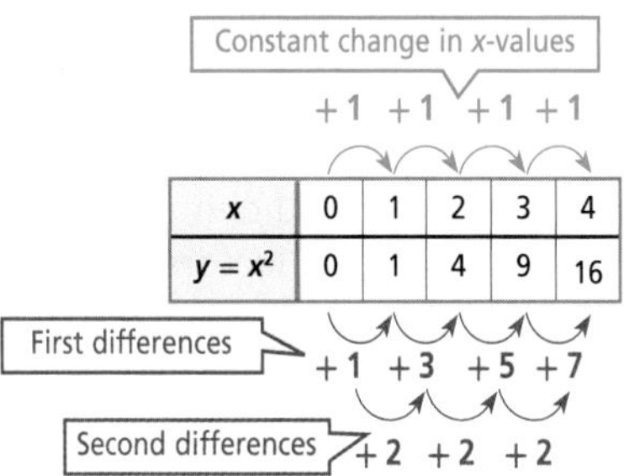

---

sequence (p. 276) A list of numbers that often form a pattern.

sucesión Lista de números que generalmente forman un patrón.

1, 2, 4, 8, 16, ...

---

set-builder notation (p. 170) A notation for a set that uses a rule to describe the properties of the elements of the set.

notación de conjuntos Notación para un conjunto que se vale de una regla para describir las propiedades de los elementos del conjunto.

$\{x | x > 3\}$ is read "The set of all x such that x is greater than 3."

Glossary/Glosario **G33**

ENGLISH | **SPANISH** | **EXAMPLES**

similar (p. 127) Two figures are similar if they have the same shape but not necessarily the same size.

semejantes Dos figuras con la misma forma pero no necesariamente del mismo tamaño.

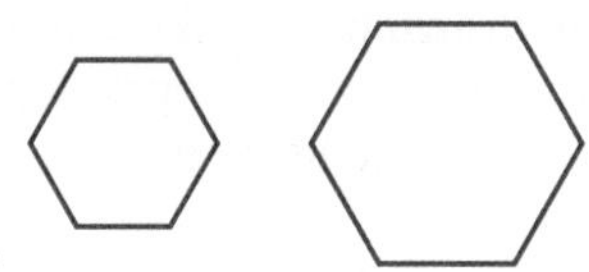

---

similarity statement (p. 127) A statement that indicates that two polygons are similar by listing the vertices in the order of correspondence.

enunciado de semejanza Enunciado que indica que dos polígonos son semejantes enumerando los vértices en orden de correspondencia.

quadrilateral $ABCD \sim$ quadrilateral $EFGH$

---

simple event (p. 761) An event consisting of only one outcome.

suceso simple Suceso que tiene sólo un resultado.

In the experiment of rolling a number cube, the event consisting of the outcome 3 is a simple event.

---

simple interest (p. 139) A fixed percent of the principal. For principal P, interest rate r, and time t in years, the simple interest is $I = Prt$.

interés simple Porcentaje fijo del capital. Dado el capital P, la tasa de interés r y el tiempo t expresado en años, el interés simple es $I = Prt$.

If \$100 is put into an account with a simple interest rate of 5%, then after 2 years, the account will have earned $I = 100 \cdot 0.05 \cdot 2 = \$10$ in interest.

---

simplest form of a square root expression (p. 829) A square root expression is in simplest form if it meets the following criteria:

1. No perfect squares are in the radicand.
2. No fractions are in the radicand.
3. No square roots appear in the denominator of a fraction.

See also rationalizing the denominator.

forma simplificada de una expresión de raíz cuadrada Una expresión de raíz cuadrada está en forma simplificada si reúne los siguientes requisitos:

1. No hay cuadrados perfectos en el radicando.
2. No hay fracciones en el radicando.
3. No aparecen raíces cuadradas en el denominador de una fracción.

Ver también racionalizar el denominador.

Not Simplest Form	Simplest Form
$\sqrt{180}$	$6\sqrt{5}$
$\sqrt{216a^2b^2}$	$6ab\sqrt{6}$
$\frac{\sqrt{7}}{\sqrt{2}}$	$\frac{\sqrt{14}}{2}$

---

simplest form of a rational expression (p. 887) A rational expression is in simplest form if the numerator and denominator have no common factors.

forma simplificada de una expresión racional Una expresión racional está en forma simplificada cuando el numerador y el denominador no tienen factores comunes.

$$\frac{x^2 - 1}{x^2 + x - 2} = \frac{(x - 1)(x + 1)}{(x - 1)(x + 2)} = \frac{x + 1}{x + 2}$$

Simplest form

G34 Glossary/Glosario

ENGLISH	SPANISH	EXAMPLES

simplest form of an exponential expression (p. 474) An exponential expression is in simplest form if it meets the following criteria:

1. There are no negative exponents.
2. The same base does not appear more than once in a product or quotient.
3. No powers, products, or quotients are raised to powers.
4. Numerical coefficients in a quotient do not have any common factor other than 1.

forma simplificada de una expresión exponencial Una expresión exponencial está en forma simplificada si reúne los siguientes requisitos:

1. No hay exponentes negativos.
2. La misma base no aparece más de una vez en un producto o cociente.
3. No se elevan a potencias productos, cocientes ni potencias.
4. Los coeficientes numéricos en un cociente no tienen ningún factor común que no sea 1.

Not Simplest Form	Simplest Form
$7^8 \cdot 7^4$	7^{12}
$(x^2)^{-4} \cdot x^5$	$\frac{1}{x^3}$
$\frac{a^5b^9}{(ab)^4}$	ab^5

simplify (p. 40) To perform all indicated operations.

simplificar Realizar todas las operaciones indicadas.

$13 - 20 + 8$
$-7 + 8$
1

simulation (p. 736) A model of an experiment, often one that would be too difficult or time-consuming to actually perform.

simulación Modelo de un experimento; generalmente se recurre a la simulación cuando realizar dicho experimento sería demasiado difícil o llevaría mucho tiempo.

sine (p. 928) In a right triangle, the ratio of the length of the leg opposite $\angle A$ to the length of the hypotenuse.

seno En un triángulo rectángulo, razón entre la longitud del cateto opuesto a $\angle A$ y la longitud de la hipotenusa.

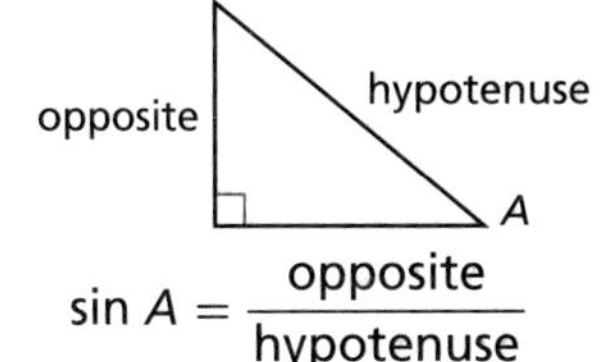

$$\sin A = \frac{\text{opposite}}{\text{hypotenuse}}$$

slope (p. 315) A measure of the steepness of a line. If (x_1, y_1) and (x_2, y_2) are any two points on the line, the slope of the line, known as m, is represented by the equation $m = \frac{y_2 - y_1}{x_2 - x_1}$.

pendiente Medida de la inclinación de una línea. Dados dos puntos (x_1, y_1) y (x_2, y_2) en una línea, la pendiente de la línea, denominada m, se representa con la ecuación $m = \frac{y_2 - y_1}{x_2 - x_1}$.

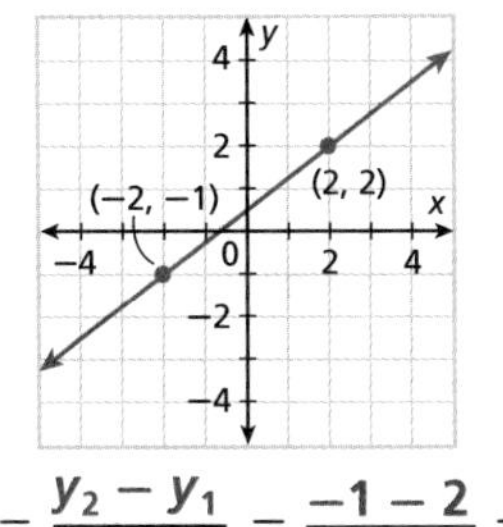

$$m = \frac{y_2 - y_1}{x_2 - x_1} = \frac{-1 - 2}{-2 - 2} = \frac{3}{4}$$

slope-intercept form (p. 345) The slope-intercept form of a linear equation is $y = mx + b$, where m is the slope and b is the y-intercept.

forma de pendiente-intersección La forma de pendiente-intersección de una ecuación lineal es $y = mx + b$, donde m es la pendiente y b es la intersección con el eje y.

$y = -2x + 4$
The slope is -2.
The y-intercept is 4.

solution of a linear equation in two variables An ordered pair or ordered pairs that make the equation true.

solución de una ecuación lineal en dos variables Un par ordenado o pares ordenados que hacen que la ecuación sea verdadera.

(4, 2) is a solution of $x + y = 6$.

Glossary/Glosario **G35**

ENGLISH	SPANISH	EXAMPLES
solution of a linear inequality in two variables (p. 428) An ordered pair or ordered pairs that make the inequality true.	**solución de una desigualdad lineal en dos variables** Un par ordenado o pares ordenados que hacen que la desigualdad sea verdadera.	(3, 1) is a solution of $x + y < 6$.
solution of a system of linear equations (p. 397) Any ordered pair that satisfies all the equations in a system.	**solución de un sistema de ecuaciones lineales** Cualquier par ordenado que resuelva todas las ecuaciones de un sistema.	$\begin{cases} x + y = -1 \\ -x + y = -3 \end{cases}$ Solution: $(1, -2)$
solution of a system of linear inequalities (p. 435) Any ordered pair that satisfies all the inequalities in a system.	**solución de un sistema de desigualdades lineales** Cualquier par ordenado que resuelva todas las desigualdades de un sistema.	$\begin{cases} y \leq x + 1 \\ y < -x + 4 \end{cases}$ (2, 1) is in the overlapping shaded regions, so it is a solution.
solution of an equation in one variable (p. 77) A value or values that make the equation true.	**solución de una ecuación en una variable** Valor o valores que hacen que la ecuación sea verdadera.	Equation: $x + 2 = 6$ Solution: $x = 4$
solution of an inequality in one variable (p. 170) A value or values that make the inequality true.	**solución de una desigualdad en una variable** Valor o valores que hacen que la desigualdad sea verdadera.	Inequality: $x + 2 < 6$ Solution: $x < 4$
solution set (p. 77) The set of values that make a statement true.	**conjunto solución** Conjunto de valores que hacen verdadero un enunciado.	Inequality: $x + 3 \geq 5$ Solution set: $\{x \mid x \geq 2\}$ −4 −3 −2 −1 0 1 2 3 4 5 6
square A quadrilateral with four congruent sides and four right angles.	**cuadrado** Cuadrilátero con cuatro lados congruentes y cuatro ángulos rectos.	
square in numeration (p. 26) The second power of a number.	**cuadrado en numeración** La segunda potencia de un número.	16 is the square of 4.
square root (p. 32) A number that is multiplied by itself to form a product is called a square root of that product.	**raíz cuadrada** El número que se multiplica por sí mismo para formar un producto se denomina la raíz cuadrada de ese producto.	$\sqrt{16} = 4$, because $4^2 = 4 \cdot 4 = 16$.
square-root function (p. 822) A function whose rule contains a variable under a square-root sign.	**función de raíz cuadrada** Función cuya regla contiene una variable bajo un signo de raíz cuadrada.	$y = \sqrt{3x} - 5$
standard form of a linear equation (p. 302) $Ax + By = C$, where A, B, and C are real numbers and A and B are not both 0.	**forma estándar de una ecuación lineal** $Ax + By = C$, donde A, B y C son números reales y A y B no son ambos cero.	$2x + 3y = 6$

G36 Glossary/Glosario

ENGLISH	SPANISH	EXAMPLES
standard form of a polynomial (p. 497) A polynomial in one variable is written in standard form when the terms are in order from greatest degree to least degree.	**forma estándar de un polinomio** Un polinomio de una variable se expresa en forma estándar cuando los términos se ordenan de mayor a menor grado.	$4x^5 - 2x^4 + x^2 - x + 1$
standard form of a quadratic equation (p. 642) $ax^2 + bx + c = 0$, where a, b, and c are real numbers and $a \neq 0$.	**forma estándar de una ecuación cuadrática** $ax^2 + bx + c = 0$, donde a, b y c son números reales y $a \neq 0$.	$2x^2 + 3x - 1 = 0$
stem-and-leaf plot (p. 709) A graph used to organize and display data by dividing each data value into two parts, a stem and a leaf.	**diagrama de tallo y hojas** Gráfica utilizada para organizar y mostrar datos dividiendo cada valor de datos en dos partes, un tallo y una hoja.	Stem | Leaves 3 | 2 3 4 4 7 9 4 | 0 1 5 7 7 7 8 5 | 1 2 2 3 *Key: 3|2 means 3.2*
stratified random sample (p. 732) A sample in which a population is divided into distinct groups and members are selected at random from each group.	**muestra aleatoria estratificada** Muestra en la que la población está dividida en grupos diferenciados y los miembros de cada grupo se seleccionan al azar.	Ms. Carter chose a stratified random sample of her school's student population by randomly selecting 30 students from each grade level.
substitution method (p. 404) A method used to solve systems of equations by solving an equation for one variable and substituting the resulting expression into the other equation(s).	**sustitución** Método utilizado para resolver sistemas de ecuaciones resolviendo una ecuación para una variable y sustituyendo la expresión resultante en las demás ecuaciones.	
Subtraction Property of Equality (p. 79) If a, b, and c are real numbers and $a = b$, then $a - c = b - c$.	**Propiedad de igualdad de la resta** Si a, b y c son números reales y $a = b$, entonces $a - c = b - c$.	$x + 6 = 8$ $\underline{\quad -6 \quad -6}$ $x \quad = 2$
Subtraction Property of Inequality (p. 176) For real numbers a, b, and c, if $a < b$, then $a - c < b - c$. Also holds true for $>$, $\leq$, $\geq$, and $\neq$.	**Propiedad de desigualdad de la resta** Dados los números reales a, b y c, si $a < b$, entonces $a - c < b - c$. Es válido también para $>$, $\leq$, $\geq$ y $\neq$.	$x + 6 < 8$ $\underline{\quad -6 \quad -6}$ $x \quad < 2$
supplementary angles Two angles whose measures have a sum of 180°.	**ángulos suplementarios** Dos ángulos cuyas medidas suman 180°.	30° 150°
surface area (p. 520) The total area of all faces and curved surfaces of a three-dimensional figure.	**área total** Área total de todas las caras y superficies curvas de una figura tridimensional.	12 cm 6 cm 8 cm Surface area $= 2(8)(12) + 2(8)(6) + 2(12)(6)$ $= 432 \text{ cm}^2$

Glossary/Glosario **G37**

ENGLISH	SPANISH	EXAMPLES
system of linear equations (p. 397) A system of equations in which all of the equations are linear.	**sistema de ecuaciones lineales** Sistema de ecuaciones en el que todas las ecuaciones son lineales.	$\begin{cases} 2x + 3y = -1 \\ x - 3y = 4 \end{cases}$
system of linear inequalities (p. 435) A system of inequalities in which all of the inequalities are linear.	**sistema de desigualdades lineales** Sistema de desigualdades en el que todas las desigualdades son lineales.	$\begin{cases} 2x + 3y > -1 \\ x - 3y \leq 4 \end{cases}$
systematic random sample (p. 732) A sample based on selecting one member of the population at random and then selecting other members by using a pattern.	**muestra sistemática** Muestra en la que se elige a un miembro de la población al azar y luego se elige a otros miembros mediante un patrón.	Mr. Martin chose a systematic random sample of customers visiting a store by selecting one customer at random and then selecting every tenth customer after that.

T

ENGLISH	SPANISH	EXAMPLES
tangent (p. 928) In a right triangle, the ratio of the length of the leg opposite $\angle A$ to the length of the leg adjacent to $\angle A$.	tangente En un triángulo rectángulo, razón entre la longitud del cateto opuesto a $\angle A$ y la longitud del cateto adyacente a $\angle A$.	opposite adjacent A $\tan A = \frac{\text{opposite}}{\text{adjacent}}$
term of an expression (p. 47) The parts of the expression that are added or subtracted.	**término de una expresión** Parte de una expresión que debe sumarse o restarse.	$3x^2 + 6x - 8$ Term Term Term
term of a sequence (p. 276) An element or number in the sequence.	**término de una sucesión** Elemento o número de una sucesión.	5 is the third term in the sequence 1, 3, 5, 7, ...
terminating decimal (p. 34) A decimal that ends, or terminates.	**decimal finito** Decimal con un número determinados de posiciones decimales.	1.5, 2.75, 4.0
theoretical probability (p. 744) The ratio of the number of equally likely outcomes in an event to the total number of possible outcomes.	**probabilidad teórica** Razón entre el número de resultados igualmente probables de un suceso y el número total de resultados posibles.	In the experiment of rolling a number cube, the theoretical probability of rolling an odd number is $\frac{3}{6} = \frac{1}{2}$.
third quartile (p. 718) The median of the upper half of a data set. Also called *upper quartile*.	**tercer cuartil** La mediana de la mitad superior de un conjunto de datos. También se llama *cuartil superior*.	Lower half Upper half 18, 23, 28, 29, (36), 42 Third quartile
tip (p. 140) An amount of money added to a bill for service; usually a percent of the bill.	**propina** Cantidad que se agrega a una factura por servicios; generalmente, un porcentaje de la factura.	
transformation (p. 369) A change in the position, size, or shape of a figure or graph.	**transformación** Cambio en la posición, tamaño o forma de una figura o gráfica.	Preimage B A C Image B′ A′ C′ $\triangle ABC \rightarrow \triangle A'B'C'$

G38 Glossary/Glosario

ENGLISH	SPANISH	EXAMPLES
translation (p. 369) A transformation that shifts or slides every point of a figure or graph the same distance in the same direction.	**traslación** Transformación en la que todos los puntos de una figura o gráfica se mueven la misma distancia en la misma dirección.	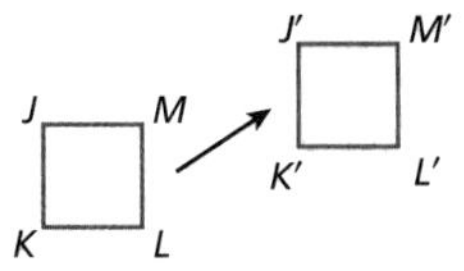 J, M, K, L; J′, M′, K′, L′
trapezoid A quadrilateral with exactly one pair of parallel sides.	**trapecio** Cuadrilátero con sólo un par de lados paralelos.	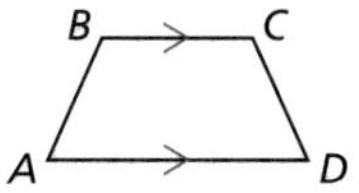 B, C, A, D
tree diagram (p. 760) A branching diagram that shows all possible combinations or outcomes of an experiment.	**diagrama de árbol** Diagrama con ramificaciones que muestra todas las combinaciones o resultados posibles de un experimento.	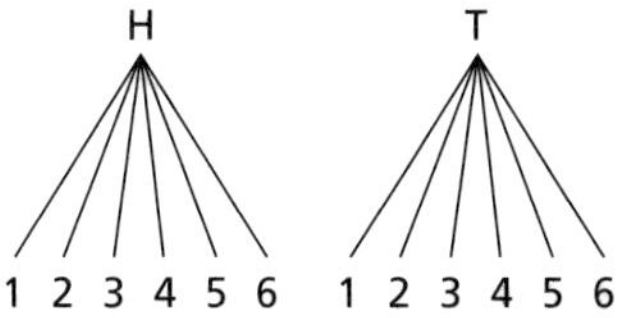 H: 1 2 3 4 5 6; T: 1 2 3 4 5 6 The tree diagram shows the possible outcomes when tossing a coin and rolling a number cube.
trend line (p. 269) A line on a scatter plot that helps show the correlation between data sets more clearly.	**línea de tendencia** Línea en un diagrama de dispersión que sirve para mostrar la correlación entre conjuntos de datos más claramente.	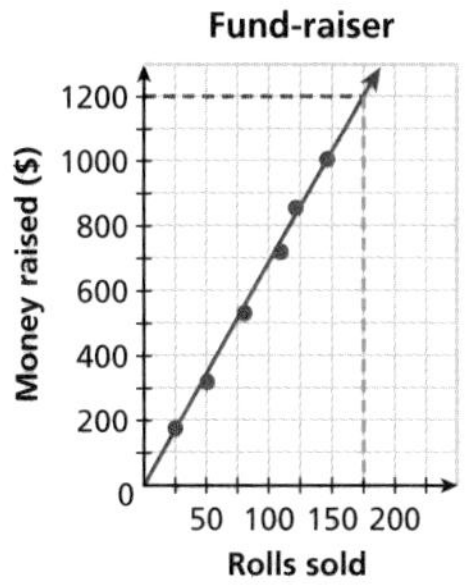 Fund-raiser; Money raised ($): 0, 200, 400, 600, 800, 1000, 1200; Rolls sold: 50, 100, 150, 200
trial (p. 737) Each repetition or observation of an experiment.	**prueba** Una sola repetición u observación de un experimento.	In the experiment of rolling a number cube, each roll is one trial.
triangle A three-sided polygon.	**triángulo** Polígono de tres lados.	
triangular prism (p. 894) A prism whose bases are triangles.	**prisma triangular** Prisma cuyas bases son triángulos.	Bases
triangular pyramid (p. 894) A pyramid whose base is a triangle.	**pirámide triangular** Pirámide cuya base es un triángulo.	
trigonometric ratio (p. 928) Ratio of the lengths of two sides of a right triangle.	**razón trigonométrica** Razón entre dos lados de un triángulo rectángulo.	A, B, C; a, b, c $\sin A = \frac{a}{c}$, $\cos A = \frac{b}{c}$, $\tan A = \frac{a}{b}$
trinomial (p. 497) A polynomial with three terms.	**trinomio** Polinomio con tres términos.	$4x^2 + 3xy - 5y^2$

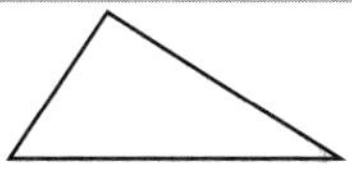

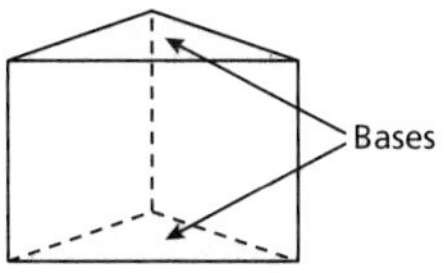

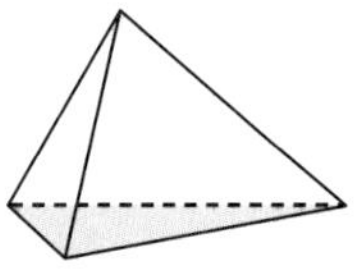

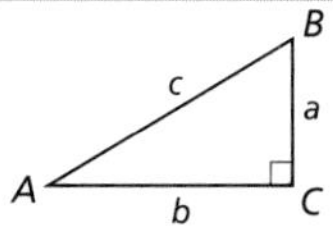

Glossary/Glosario **G39**

ENGLISH	SPANISH	EXAMPLES
U		
union (p. 206) The union of two sets is the set of all elements that are in either set, denoted by ∪.	**unión** La unión de dos conjuntos es el conjunto de todos los elementos que se encuentran en ambos conjuntos, expresado por ∪.	$A = \{1, 2, 3, 4\}$ $B = \{1, 3, 5, 7, 9\}$ $A \cup B = \{1, 2, 3, 4, 5, 7, 9\}$
unit rate (p. 120) A rate in which the second quantity in the comparison is one unit.	**tasa unitaria** Tasa en la que la segunda cantidad de la comparación es una unidad.	$\frac{30\text{ mi}}{1\text{ h}} = 30\text{ mi/h}$
unlike radicals (p. 835) Radicals with a different quantity under the radical.	**radicales distintos** Radicales con cantidades diferentes debajo del signo de radical.	$2\sqrt{2}$ and $2\sqrt{3}$
unlike terms Terms with different variables or the same variables raised to different powers.	**términos distintos** Términos con variables diferentes o las mismas variables elevadas a potencias diferentes.	$4xy^2$ and $6x^2y$
upper quartile *See* third quartile.	**cuartil superior** *Ver* tercer cuartil.	

value of a function (p. 251) The result of replacing the independent variable with a number and simplifying.	**valor de una función** Resultado de reemplazar la variable independiente por un número y luego simplificar.	The value of the function $f(x) = x + 1$ for $x = 3$ is 4.
value of a variable (p. 7) A number used to replace a variable to make an equation true.	**valor de una variable** Número utilizado para reemplazar una variable y hacer que una ecuación sea verdadera.	In the equation $x + 1 = 4$, the value of x is 3.
value of an expression (p. 7) The result of replacing the variables in an expression with numbers and simplifying.	**valor de una expresión** Resultado de reemplazar las variables de una expresión por un número y luego simplificar.	The value of the expression $x + 1$ for $x = 3$ is 4.
variable (p. 6) A symbol used to represent a quantity that can change.	**variable** Símbolo utilizado para representar una cantidad que puede cambiar.	In the expression $2x + 3$, x is the variable.
Venn diagram A diagram used to show relationships between sets.	**diagrama de Venn** Diagrama utilizado para mostrar la relación entre conjuntos.	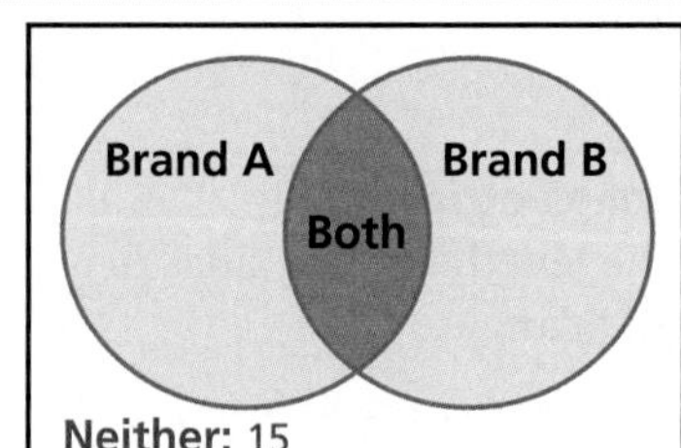
vertex of a parabola (p. 612) The highest or lowest point on the parabola.	**vértice de una parábola** Punto más alto o más bajo de una parábola.	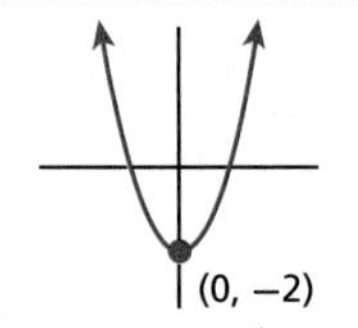 The vertex is $(0, -2)$.

G40 Glossary/Glosario

ENGLISH	SPANISH	EXAMPLES
vertex of an absolute-value graph (p. 378) The point on the axis of symmetry of the graph.	**vértice de una gráfica de valor absoluto** Punto en el eje de simetría de la gráfica.	
vertical angles The nonadjacent angles formed by two intersecting lines.	**ángulos opuestos por el vértice** Ángulos no adyacentes formados por dos líneas que se cruzan.	$\angle 1$ and $\angle 3$ are vertical angles. $\angle 2$ and $\angle 4$ are vertical angles.
vertical line (p. 316) A line whose equation is $x = a$, where a is the x-intercept.	**línea vertical** Línea cuya ecuación es $x = a$, donde a es la intersección con el eje x.	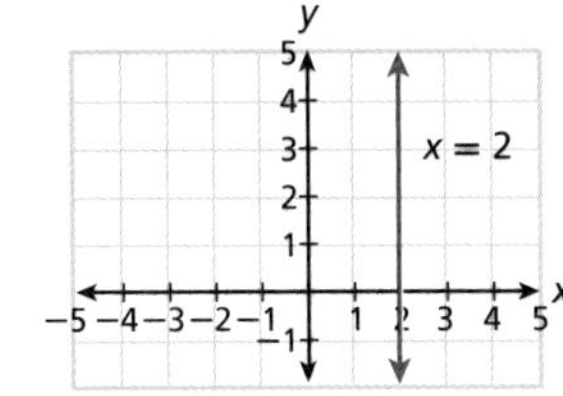
vertical-line test (p. 247) A test used to determine whether a relation is a function. If any vertical line crosses the graph of a relation more than once, the relation is not a function.	**prueba de la línea vertical** Prueba utilizada para determinar si una relación es una función. Si una línea vertical corta la gráfica de una relación más de una vez, la relación no es una función.	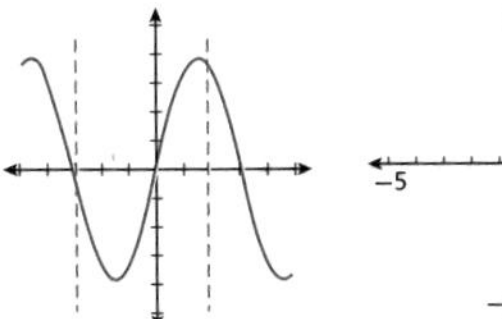 Function 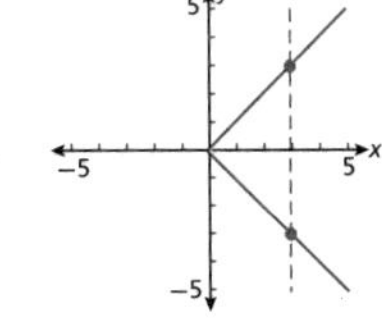 Not a function
volume (p. 520) The number of nonoverlapping unit cubes of a given size that will exactly fill the interior of a three-dimensional figure.	**volumen** Cantidad de cubos unitarios no superpuestos de un determinado tamaño que llenan exactamente el interior de una figura tridimensional.	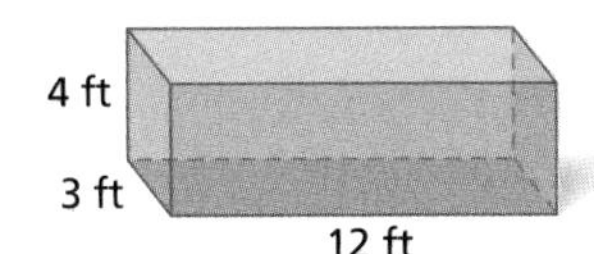 Volume $= (3)(4)(12) = 144$ ft^3
voluntary response sample (p. 733) A sample in which members choose to be in the sample.	**muestra de respuesta voluntaria** Una muestra en la que los miembros eligen participar.	A store provides survey cards for customers who wish to fill them out.

whole number (p. 34) A member of the set of natural numbers and zero.	**número cabal** Miembro del conjunto de los números naturales y cero.	0, 1, 2, 3, 4, 5, …

***x*-axis** (p. 54) The horizontal axis in a coordinate plane.	**eje *x*** Eje horizontal en un plano cartesiano.	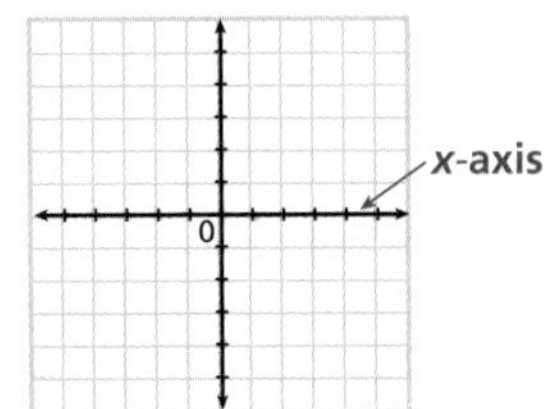

Glossary/Glosario **G41**

ENGLISH	SPANISH	EXAMPLES
x-coordinate (p. 54) The first number in an ordered pair, which indicates the horizontal distance of a point from the origin on the coordinate plane.	**coordenada x** Primer número de un par ordenado, que indica la distancia horizontal de un punto desde el origen en un plano cartesiano.	
x-intercept (p. 307) The x-coordinate(s) of the point(s) where a graph intersects the x-axis.	**intersección con el eje x** Coordenada(s) x de uno o más puntos donde una gráfica corta el eje x.	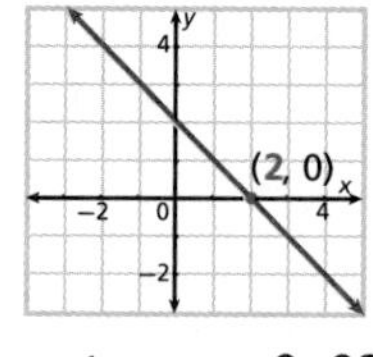 xt 0 02e

ENGLISH	SPANISH	EXAMPLES
y-axis (p. 54) The vertical axis in a coordinate plane.	**eje y** Eje vertical en un plano cartesiano.	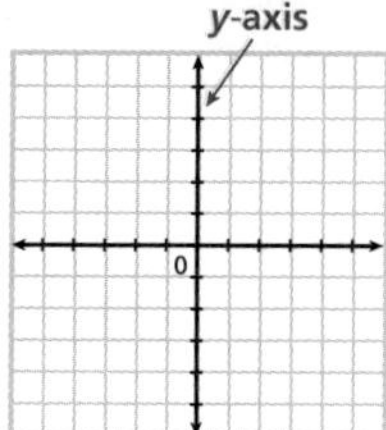
y-coordinate (p. 54) The second number in an ordered pair, which indicates the vertical distance of a point from the origin on the coordinate plane.	**coordenada y** Segundo número de un par ordenado, que indica la distancia vertical de un punto desde el origen en un plano cartesiano.	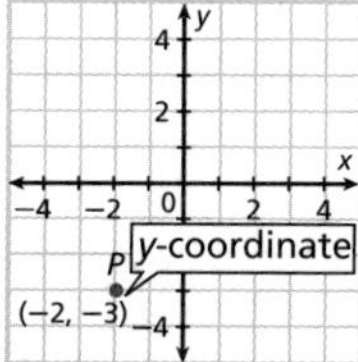
y-intercept (p. 307) The y-coordinate(s) of the point(s) where a graph intersects the y-axis.	**intersección con el eje y** Coordenada(s) y de uno o más puntos donde una gráfica corta el eje y.	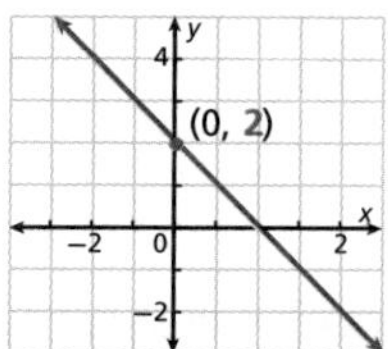 The y-intercept is 2.

ENGLISH	SPANISH	EXAMPLES
zero exponent (p. 460) For any nonzero real number x, $x^0 = 1$.	**exponente cero** Dado un número real distinto de cero x, $x^0 = 1$.	$5^0 = 1$
zero of a function (p. 619) For the function f, any number x such that $f(x) = 0$.	**cero de una función** Dada la función f, todo número x tal que $f(x) = 0$.	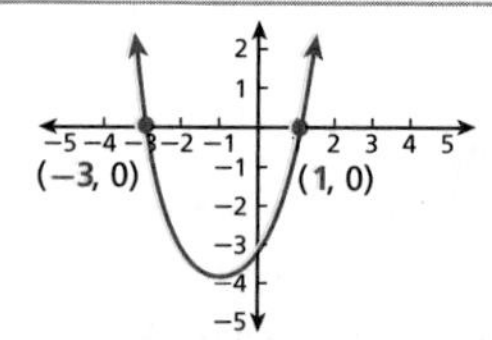 The zeros are −3 and 1.
Zero Product Property (p. 650) For real numbers p and q, if $pq = 0$, then $p = 0$ or $q = 0$.	**Propiedad del producto cero** Dados los números reales p y q, si $pq = 0$, entonces $p = 0$ o $q = 0$.	If $(x - 1)(x + 2) = 0$, then $x - 1 = 0$ or $x + 2 = 0$, so $x = 1$ or $x = -2$.

G42 Glossary/Glosario

Index

A

F

G

Q

R

T

U

Credits

Abbreviations used: (t) top, (c) center, (b) bottom, (l) left, (r) right, (bkgd) background

Photo

All images HRW Photo unless otherwise noted.

Master Icons—teens, authors (all), Sam Dudgeon/HRW.

Front Matter: Page vii (r), AP Photo/Tim Ockenden; viii (l), Sam Dudgeon/HRW; ix (r), © David McGlynn/Taxi/Getty Images; x (l), © Dennis Hallinan/Alamy Photos; xi (r), Glenn James/NBAE/Getty Images; xii (l), © Charles Gupton/CORBIS; xiii (r), © Hugh Sitton/Getty Images; xiv (l), © James Randklev/CORBIS; xv (r), Frans Lanting/Minden Pictures; xvi (l), Mike Hill/SuperStock; xvi (l) age fotostock/Superstock; xvii (r), © Robert Daly/Stone/Getty Images; xviii (tc), © Jose Luis Pelaez, Inc./CORBIS; xviii (cr), image100/Alamy; xviii (bc), © Comstock Images; xxii Victoria Smith/HRW Photo; xix (tc), Digital Vision/gettyimages; xix (cl), © PHOTOTAKE Inc./Alamy; xix (c), © Gensaku Izumiya/Sebun Photo/Getty Images; xix (cr), AP Photo/Fabio Muzzi.

Chapter Zero: Page Z26 (t), Victoria Smith/HRW.

Chapter One: Page 6 (tr), © Ray Roberts/Alamy Photos; 6 (sky), PhotoDisc/Getty Images; 8 (tc), Sam Dudgeon/HRW; 8 (tr), © Thinkstock; 10 (bl), AP Photo/NASA Haughton-Mars Project 2001, Pascal Lee; 10 (tl), © Royalty Free/CORBIS; 14 (tr), © Paul A. Souders/CORBIS; 18 (c), John Sullivan/Ribbit Photography; 18 (bl), © Royalty Free/CORBIS; 20 (tr), © Craig Aurness/CORBIS; 20 (tc), Derek & Garry Walker/Adams/PictureQuest; 22 (cr), © Dave G. Houser/CORBIS; 24 (cl), © M. Timothy O'Keefe/Alamy; 24 (bl), © Royalty Free/CORBIS; 26 (tr), © Ted Horowitz/CORBIS; 29 (br), Michael Abbey/Photo Researchers, Inc.; 30 (cl), ©2007 The Josef and Anni Albers Foundation/Artist Rights Society (ARS), New York/The Newark Museum/Art Resource, NY; 30 (bl), © Royalty Free/CORBIS; 30 (cr), PhotoDisc/Getty Images; 32 (tr), ON-PAGE CREDIT; 33 (tr), © Craig Tuttle/CORBIS; 36 (bl), © Royalty Free/CORBIS; 37 (tr), Stephanie Friedman/HRW; 38 (tl), © Royalty Free/CORBIS; 38 (cr), © Federico Cabello/SuperStock; 40 (tr), AP Photo/Mark Lennihan; 42 (cr), AP/Wide World Photos; 44 (cl), © Lucy Nicholson/Reuters/Corbis; 44 (bl), PhotoDisc/gettyimages; 46 (tr), © Sergio Moraes/Reuters/Corbis; 47 (tl), © BananaStock Ltd.; 50 (bl), PhotoDisc/gettyimages; 58 (tl), PhotoDisc/gettyimages; 58 (cl), © Stapleton Collection/CORBIS; 60 (tl), PhotoDisc/gettyimages; 60 (tr), Sam Dudgeon/HRW.

Chapter Two: Page 72–73 (all), AP Photo/Tim Ockenden; 75 (cr), Sam Dudgeon/HRW; 77 (tr), © Duomo/CORBIS; 78 (bl), RubberBall/Alamy; 79 (tl), Sam Dudgeon/HRW; 81 (tl), Dante Fenolio/Photo Researchers, Inc.; 81 (bl), © Image Ideas, Inc.; 84 (tr), © Lester Lefkowitz/CORBIS; 88 (cl), © Bettmann/CORBIS; 89 (tl), © Image Ideas, Inc.; 89 (cr), PhotoDisc/gettyimages; 92 (tr), © Tom Stewart/CORBIS; 94 (cr), © Tom Stewart/CORBIS; 97 (tl), © Robert W. Kelley/Time Life Pictures/Getty Images; 97 (cr), © Corel; 97 (bl), © Image Ideas, Inc.; 100 (tc), © Ingram Publishing; 104 (bl), © Image Ideas, Inc.; 105 (tl), © Royalty-Free/CORBIS; 106 (bl), Rob Melnychuk/gettyimages; 107 (tr), © Ezra Shaw/Getty Images; 110 (bl), © Image Ideas, Inc.; 110 (cr), Aflo Foto Agency/Alamy; 111 (cr), Pixar Animation Studios/ZUMA Press; 112 (tl), © Image Ideas, Inc.; 112 (cr), FRANCIS SPECKER/NewsCom; 115 (cl), Shedd Aquarium/Lines Jr./SeaPics.com; 118 (tr), Linda Owen; 119 (cl), © Duomo/CORBIS; 119 (bl), PhotoDisc/gettyimages; 121 (tr), Robert Harding Picture Library Ltd/Alamy; 125 (bl), PhotoDisc/gettyimages; 127 (tr), Spencer Platt/Getty Images/NewsCom; 129 (cr), Sam Dudgeon/HRW; 131 (bl), PhotoDisc/gettyimages; 136 (cl), Jessica Hill/AP/Wide World Photos; 136 (bl), PhotoDisc/gettyimages; 138 (tr), Terry Warner/www.cartoonstock.com; 142 (tr), © Rubberball Productions; 142 (bl), PhotoDisc/gettyimages; 146 (tl), PhotoDisc/gettyimages; 146 (cr), Sam Dudgeon/HRW; 146 (bl, br), © COMSTOCK, Inc.; 151 (cr), David Guttenfelder/AP/Wide World Photos; 162 (cr, b), Dan Suzio/Photo Researchers, Inc.; 163 (cr), Victoria Smith/HRW; 163 (tc), AP Photo/Charles Rex Arbogast; 163 (br), Allen Blake Sheldon/Animals Animals/Earth Scenes.

Chapter Three: Page 164–165 (all), Sam Dudgeon/HRW; 168 (tr), © Charles Crust; 169 (bl), Digital Vision/gettyimages; 172 (bl), © Creatas; 174 (tr), © Mingasson/Getty/HRW; 174 (cellphone), ©Mingasson/Getty/HRW; 175 (bc, br), © Mingasson/Getty/HRW; 178 (tl), Buzz Orr/The Gazette/AP/Wide World Photos; 178 (cr), PhotoDisc/gettyimages; 178 (bl), © Creatas; 180 (tr), on-page credit; 182 (cl), Sam Dudgeon/HRW; 184 (cl), © Reuters/CORBIS; 184 (bl), © Creatas; 186 (br), Scott Vallance/VIP Photographic/HRW; 187 (tl), © Creatas; 188 (tr), © Peter Beck/CORBIS; 190 (tr), Paul Sakuma/AP/Wide World Photos; 192 (bl), © Brand X Pictures; 194 (tr), © Ariel Skelley/CORBIS; 198 (cl), Brad Mitchell/Alamy; 198 (bl), © Brand X Pictures; 200 (bl), © Jose Luis Pelaez, Inc./CORBIS; 202 (tr), © Michele Westmorland/CORBIS; 202 (br), Sam Dudgeon/HRW; 207 (tl), © Brand X Pictures; 207 (cl), Richard Megna/Fundamental Photographs; 210 (tl), © Brand X Pictures; 210 (br), Peter Beavis/Taxi/Getty Images; 210 (cr, bl), PhotoDisc/Getty Images.

Chapter Four: Page 226–227 (all), © David McGlynn/Taxi/Getty Images; 230 (tr), © Royalty-Free/CORBIS; 234 (cl), © Bettmann/CORBIS; 234 (bl), Sam Dudgeon/HRW; 235 (bc, bl), Sam Dudgeon/HRW; 236 (tr), Aflo Foto Agency; 238 (cl), © Comstock Images/Alamy Photos; 241 (tl), Sam Dudgeon/HRW; 245 (tr), RubberBall/Alamy; 250 (tl), © Bettmann/CORBIS; 250 (bl), Sam Dudgeon/HRW; 257 (bl), Sam Dudgeon/HRW; 260 (br), Big Cheese Photo/Alamy Photos; 260 (tl), Sam Dudgeon/HRW; 262 (tr), David Welling/Animals Animals; 267 (bl), Roy Toft; 268 (bl), comstock.com; 272 (tr), © COMSTOCK, Inc.; 276 (tl), Digital Vision/gettyimages; 276 (bl), comstock.com; 278 (tl), comstock.com; 278 (bl), AP Photo/Daniel Hulshizer; 290 (tr), © Dennis Cox/WorldViews, All Rights Reserved.; 291 (br), Ed Reschke/Peter Arnold, Inc./Alamy; 291 (bl), © Randy M. Ury/CORBIS; 291 (tc), Sam Dudgeon/HRW.

Chapter Five: Page 292–293 (all), © Dennis Hallinan/Alamy Photos; 296 (tr), © Aldo Torelli/Getty Images; 301 (bl), Victoria Smith/HRW; 304 (tl), © LWA-Dann Tardif/CORBIS; 304 (cr), © Buddy Mays/CORBIS; 307 (tl), © John and Lisa Merrill/CORBIS; 308 (tl), Victoria Smith/HRW; 310 (c), © elaineitalia/Alamy; (b), © imageZebra/Alamy; 315 (bl), © Dave G. Houser/CORBIS; 316 (tl), Victoria Smith/HRW; 320 (tr), © Patrick Eden/Alamy Photos; 325 (tl), © Patrick Eden/Alamy Photos; 326 (tr), © Royalty-Free/Corbis; 328 (bl), Genevieve Vallee/Alamy; 330 (cl), Courtesy NASA/JPL-Caltech; 330 (bl), Victoria Smith/HRW; 332 (tl), Victoria Smith/HRW; 332 (br), © Rick Gomez/CORBIS; 332 (tr), © age fotostock/SuperStock; 339 (bl), © Brand X Pictures; 341 (tr), © Pixtal/SuperStock; 346 (tl), Jake Norton; 346 (bl), © Brand X Pictures; 347 (bl), image100/Alamy; 349 (tr), © Owen Franken/CORBIS; 354 (bl), © Brand X Pictures; 357 (tr), © Jim Cummins/CORBIS; 360 (c), Victoria Smith/HRW; 362 (bl), © Brand X Pictures; 362 (cl), AP Photo/Ted S. Warren; 364 (tl), © Brand X Pictures; 364 (b), © Tim Pannell/CORBIS; 364 (tr), Andy Christiansen/HRW.

Chapter Six: Page 378–379 (all), Glenn James/NBAE/Getty Images; 383 (tr), © Kwame Zikomo/SuperStock; 386 (bl), Victoria Smith/HRW; 387 (tl), © Lee Snider/Photo Images/CORBIS; 388 (bl), © R. Holz/CORBIS; 390 (tr), Cartoon copyrighted by Mark Parisi, printed with permission.; 392 (bl), © Michael Pole/SuperStock; 395 (bl), Victoria Smith/HRW; 397 (tr), Photofusion Picture Library/Alamy; 400 (tl), Victoria Smith/HRW; 402 (cl), © UNICOVER CORPORATION 1986; 402 (bl), Victoria Smith/HRW; 410 (cl), David R. Frazier Photolibrary, Inc./Alamy; 410 (bl), Victoria Smith/HRW; 412 (tl), Victoria Smith/HRW; 412 (cr), David Madison © 2005; 412 (b), © Les Stone/CORBIS; 414 (tr), © Susan Werner/Getty Images; 419 (tl), Max Gibbs/photolibrary.com; 419 (bl), Nathan Kaey/HRW; 419 (cl), PhotoDisc Blue/Getty Images; 421 (tr), © Justin Pumfrey/Taxi/Getty Images; 425 (cl), © Reuters/CORBIS; 425 (bl), Nathan Kaey/HRW; 428 (all), Nathan Kaey/HRW; 440 (bl), © Bob Krist/CORBIS; 440 (tr), © Tom Till; 441 (b), Hope Ryden/National Geographic Image Collection; 441 (tr), Image Source/Alamy.

Chapter Seven: Page 442–423 (all), © Charles Gupton/CORBIS; 446 (tr), Advertising Archive; 449 (cr), B. G. Thomson/Photo Researchers, Inc.; 450 (cl), © PHOTOTAKE Inc./Alamy; 452 (tr), Arscimed/Photo Researchers, Inc.; 454 (tr), Courtesy NASA/JPL-Caltech; 455 (br), © Mediscan/Corbis; 456 (tl), Cern/Photo Researchers, Inc.; 460 (tr), D. Parker/Photo Researchers, Inc.; 461 (bl), © Brand X Pictures; 462 (bl), © BananaStock Ltd.; 474 (br), Robert Flusic/PhotoDisc/Getty Images; 476 (tr), © Jeff Hunter/Getty Images; 480 (tl), © Don Johnston/Stone/Getty Images; 480 (bl), © Comstock, Inc.; 484 (tr), www.cartoonstock.com; 487 (frame), ©1998 Image Farm Inc.; 487 (girls), Artville/Getty Images; 488 (bl), © Comstock, Inc.; 492 (tr), © Pat and Chuck Blackley; 496 (cr), Royalty-Free/Corbis; 498 (cl), PHILIPPE DESMAZES/AFP/Getty Images; 498 (tl), © Comstock, Inc.; 501 (tr), Juniors Bildarchiv/Alamy; 506 (tr), Molly Eckler–puzzle, photo by Victoria Smith/HRW; 506 (bl), © Ruggero Vanni/CORBIS; 507 (tl), © Comstock, Inc.; 508 (tl), © Comstock, Inc.; 508 (tr), SuperStock; 508 (b), Ryan McVay/PhotoDisc/Getty Images.

Chapter Eight: Page 520–521 (all), © Hugh Sitton/Getty Images; 523 Sam Dudgeon/HRW; 527 (tr), Sam Dudgeon/HRW; 527 (b), Brian Hagiwara/FoodPix; 528 (tr), Photo by Jolesch Photography. © 2004 Drum Corps International. All rights reserved.; 528 (tl), Photo by Jolesch Photography. © 2004 Drum Corps International. All rights reserved.; 529 (t), © Royalty-Free/Corbis; 531 (tr), PhotoDisc/Getty Images; 532 (br, bc), Victoria Smith/HRW; 535 (tr), Tony Freeman/Photoedit; 536 (bl), © Royalty-Free/Corbis; 537 (cr), Sam Dudgeon/HRW; 540 (tr), Travel-Shots/Alamy; 545 (cl), Composition 17, 1919 (oil on canvas) by Doesburg, Theo van (1883–1931) © Haags Gemeentemuseum, The Hague, Netherlands/The Bridgeman Art Library Nationality/copyright status: Dutch/out of copyright; 547 (bl), Janine Wiedel Photolibrary/Alamy; 548 (tr), AP Photo/Peter Cosgrove; 551 (tl), © Stockbyte; 553 (bl), © Royalty-Free/Corbis; 556 (tl), © Royalty-Free/Corbis; 556 (br), © Peter

Photo

All Teacher-to-Teacher photos courtesy of the teachers.

Chapter One TE wrap: Page 2 (tl), Photodisc; (cl), HRW Photo

Chapter Two TE wrap: Page 70 (tl), Victoria Smith/HRW, 70 (cl), Photo-objects/Fotosearch

Chapter Three TE wrap: Page 148 (tl), Rick Davis/Darkhouse and Fun Enthusiast, 148 (cl), Comstock/Fotosearch

Chapter Four TE wrap: Page 230 (tl), Andy Christiansen/HRW, 230 (cl), www.Fotosearch.com/Photodisc

Chapter Five TE wrap: Page 300 (tl), Transtock Inc./Alamy, 300 (cl), Creatas/Punchstock.com

Chapter Six TE wrap: Page 390 (tl), HRW Photo, 390 (cl), Comstock

Chapter Seven TE wrap: Page 464 (tl), ©Hemera Technologies/Alamy Photos, 464 (cl), Comstock/HRW Photo

Chapter Eight TE wrap: Page 533 (cl), (tl), Fotosearch

Chapter Nine TE wrap: Page 604 (cl), ©Royalty-Free/CORBIS, 604 (tr), ©Photodisc/gettyimages

Chapter Ten TE wrap: Page 668 (tl), HRW Photo, 668 (cl), David Young Wolf/Photoedit

Chapter Eleven TE wrap: Page 766 (tl), ©photolibrary.com/Index Stock Imagery, Inc., 766 (cl), Victoria Smith/HRW Photo

Chapter Twelve TE wrap: Page 844 (tl), ©Brian Hagiwara/Brand X Pictures/Getty Images, 844 (cl), M. C. Escher's Wooden Ball with Fish © 2005 The M.C. Escher Company-Holland. All rights reserved. www.mcescher.com

Adams/Getty Images; 558 (tr), © Lee Snider/Photo Images/CORBIS; 559 (cr), © Yann Arthus-Bertrand/CORBIS; 563 (tl), © Stockbyte; 566 (tr), © Robbie Jack/CORBIS; 570 (tl), © Stockbyte; 570 (cl), Sheila Terry/Science Photo Library/Photo Researchers, Inc.; 572 (tl), © Stockbyte; 572 (br), David Young Wolff/Photoedit; 584 (tr), Eric Horan; 584 (br), Eric Horan; 584 (bl), PhotoDisc/Getty Images; 585 (tc), Courtesy Mike Brown/University of South Carolina; 585 (br), Mike Brown/University of South Carolina, University Publications; 585 (cr), John Sanford/Science Photo Library/Photo Researchers, Inc.

Chapter Nine: Page 586–587 (all), © James Randklev/CORBIS; 590 (tr), Aflo Foto Agency; 596 (bl), Sam Dudgeon/HRW; 599 (tr), Gary Crabbe/Alamy; 604 (bl), © Gensaku Izumiya/Sebun Photo/Getty Images; 605 (tl), Sam Dudgeon/HRW; 606 (tr), © Michael S. Yamashita/CORBIS; 610 (tl), AP Photo/Fabio Muzzi; 610 (bl), Sam Dudgeon/HRW; 613 (tr), © Craig Tuttle/CORBIS; 618 (bl), Sam Dudgeon/HRW; 620 (all), Sam Dudgeon/HRW; 622 (tr), © MedioImages/SuperStock; 624 (tr), © Digital Vision; 626 (cl), © Theo Allofs/CORBIS; 626 (bl), PhotoDisc/Getty Images; 626 (bc), © COMSTOCK, Inc.; 630 (tr), Dynamic Graphics Group/IT Stock Free/Alamy; 634 (cr), imagebroker/Alamy; 634 (bl), PhotoDisc/Getty Images; 634 (bc), © COMSTOCK, Inc.; 636 (t), © Gerald French/CORBIS; 640 (cl), Loren Winters/Visuals Unlimited; 640 (bl), PhotoDisc/Getty Images; 640 (bc), © COMSTOCK, Inc.; 645 (tr), The Garden Picture Library/Alamy; 650 (bl), PhotoDisc/Getty Images; 650 (bl), © COMSTOCK, Inc.; 652 (tr), © Powerstock/SuperStock; 656 (bl), Comstock Images/Alamy; 659 (tl), PhotoDisc/Getty Images; 659 (tc), © COMSTOCK, Inc.; 660 (tl), PhotoDisc/Getty Images; 660 (tc), © COMSTOCK, Inc.; 660 (tr), Stuart Franklin/Getty Images; 660 (b), Robert Laberge/Getty Images.

Chapter Ten: Page 672–673 (all), Frans Lanting/Minden Pictures; 678 (tr), Victoria Smith/HRW; 680 (all), Sam Dudgeon/HRW; 687 (tr), © Tom Stewart/CORBIS; 691 (cl), © Reuters/CORBIS; 694 (tr), AP Photo/Dave Martin; 696 (tr), Victoria Smith/HRW; 698 (cr), © Michael Prince/CORBIS; 707 (tl), © Bettmann/CORBIS; 710 (cr), Stuart Franklin/Getty Images; 710 (bl), Stuart Franklin/Getty Images; 712 (tr), Sam Dudgeon/HRW; 713 (tl), Sam Dudgeon/HRW; 713 (tc), United States Mint image; 713 (tc), United States Mint image; 713 (tr), Sam Dudgeon/HRW; 713 (c), United States Mint image; 713 (c), United States Mint image; 713 (bc, br), Sam Dudgeon/HRW; 716 (tl, tc), Sam Dudgeon/HRW; 716 (penny), PhotoDisc/Getty Images; 716 (dime), PhotoDisc/Getty Images; 716 (nickel), PhotoDisc/Getty Images; 716 (bl), PhotoDisc/Getty Images; 716 (bc), Sam Dudgeon/HRW; 716 (br), Victoria Smith/HRW; 717 (bl), Sam Dudgeon/HRW; 718 (cr), © European Communities; 720 (tr), © Warren Faidley/Weatherstock; 721 (bl), Aflo Foto Agency/Alamy; 722 (cr), Victoria Smith/HRW; 724 (bl), Sam Dudgeon/HRW; 727 (tl), David Young-Wolff/Alamy; 728 (tl), Peter Van Steen/HRW; 728 (bl, bc), Victoria Smith/HRW; 729 (tr), Victoria Smith/HRW; 730 (cr), Sam Dudgeon/HRW; 731 (bl), © Jose Luis Pelaez, Inc./CORBIS; 732 (tl), Sam Dudgeon/HRW; 735 (all), Sam Dudgeon/HRW; 736 (all), Sam Dudgeon/HRW; 741 (cr), Sam Dudgeon/HRW; 741 (cl), © Underwood & Underwood/CORBIS; 742 (tl), Sam Dudgeon/HRW; 743 (tr), Foodcollection.com/Alamy; 743 (bl), © Comstock Images; 744 (tl), Sam Dudgeon/HRW; 744 (b), © Handout/Hasbro/Ray Stubblebine/Reuters/CORBIS; 749 (cl), Courtesy of Blue Sky Studios/ZUMA Press; 760 (cr), Blair Seitz; 761 (br), AP Photo/John Heller; 761 (tr, bl), Tom Pawlesh.

Chapter Eleven: Page 762–763 (all), © age fotostock/Superstock; 766 (tr), Randy Lincks/Masterfile; 777 (tl), Lucidio Studio, Inc./Alamy; 781 (tr), © Wendy Stone/CORBIS; 786 (cr), Tom Goskar/Wessex Archaeology Ltd.; 789 (tr), © Stan Liu/Icon SMI/ZUMA Press; 791 (tr), Stephen Dalton/Photo Researchers, Inc.; 792 (cl), age fotostock; 796 (c), Laimute Druskis/Stock Boston/IPN; 796 (bc), © D. Hurst/Alamy; 796 (br), © Brian Hagiwara/Brand X Pictures/Alamy; 798 (tr), NASA; 802 (tl), AP Photo/Andy Eames; 802 (bl), © Brand X Pictures; 805 (tr), Steve Gottlieb/PictureQuest; 809 (bl), © Brand X Pictures; 814 (bl), © Brand X Pictures; 816 (tr), ON-PAGE CREDIT; 820 (tl), © Richard Cummins/SuperStock; 820 (bl), © Brand X Pictures; 827 (bl), AP Photo/Gregory Smith; 828 (bl), © Brand X Pictures; 830 (cr), Walker/PictureQuest; 830 (tl), © Brand X Pictures; 830 (bc), AP Photo/Anna Branthwaite.

Chapter Twelve: Page 846–847 (all), © Robert Daly/Stone/Getty Images; 849 Sam Dudgeon/HRW; 851 (tr), © RubberBall/Alamy; 853 (tl), MedioImages/Alamy; 856 (tl), AP Photo/Robert F. Bukaty; 856 (bl), PhotoDisc/Getty Images; 858 (tr), © Steve Hamblin/Alamy; 864 (bl), PhotoDisc/Getty Images; 866 (tr), Gerald C. Kelley/Photo Researchers, Inc.; 868 (bl), © Paul Barton/CORBIS; 869 (tl), © SuperStock; 871 (cl), AP Photo/Lou Krasky; 871 (bl), PhotoDisc/Getty Images; 876 (tl), PhotoDisc/Getty Images; 876 (br), AP Photo/Tyler Morning Telegraph, Tom Worner; 876 (sky), PhotoDisc/Getty Images; 878 (tr), © Stock Connection Distribution / Alamy; 885 (tr), Philippe Blondel/Photo Researchers, Inc.; 890 (tl), Photo Researchers, Inc.; 893 (tc), AP Photo/Dolores Ochoa; 893 (tr), © Nigel Francis/Robert Harding/Alamy Photos; 898 (cl), AP Photo /NASA, Nick Galante, PMRF; 900 (tr), © Tom Stewart/CORBIS; 904 (br), ON-PAGE CREDIT; 906 (b), © Dynamic Graphics Group/i2i/Alamy; 906 (movie screen), © Ralph Nelson/Imagine Entertainment/ZUMA/CORBIS; 920 (tr), Sam Dudgeon/HRW; 920 (bl), © David Bergman/Corbis; 920 (bc), AP Photo/Al Behrman; 921 (br), Bicycle Museum of America/New Bremen, Ohio/www.bicyclemuseum.com; 921 (tc), Courtesy of the Bicycle Museum of America.

Student Handbook: S2 (tl), PhotoDisc/Getty Images; S3 (br), Sam Dudgeon/HRW.

Symbols

Relation Symbols

Symbol	Meaning
$<$	is less than
$>$	is greater than
$\leq$	is less than or equal to
$\geq$	is greater than or equal to
$\neq$	is not equal to
$\approx$	is approximately equal to
$\cong$	is congruent to
$\sim$	is similar to

Real Numbers

Symbol	Meaning
$\mathbb{R}$	the set of real numbers
$\mathbb{Q}$	the set of rational numbers
$\mathbb{Z}$	the set of integers
$\mathbb{W}$	the set of whole numbers
$\mathbb{N}$	the set of natural numbers

Geometry

Symbol	Meaning
$\angle ABC$	angle ABC
$m\angle ABC$	the measure of angle ABC
$\triangle ABC$	triangle ABC
$\overline{AB}$	segment AB

Other

Symbol	Meaning
$\pm$	plus or minus
$\lvert -4 \rvert$	the absolute value of -4
$\{$	system
π	pi; $\pi \approx 3.14$ or $\pi \approx \frac{22}{7}$
$\varnothing$	empty set
$f(x)$	function notation; f of x
a_n	the nth term of a sequence
$n!$	n factorial
$P(\text{event})$	the probability of an event

Table of Measures

METRIC

Length

1 kilometer (km) = 1000 meters (m)
1 meter = 100 centimeters (cm)
1 centimeter = 10 millimeters (mm)

Capacity and Volume

1 liter (L) = 1000 milliliters (mL)

Mass

1 kilogram (kg) = 1000 grams (g)
1 gram = 1000 milligrams (mg)

CUSTOMARY

Length

1 mile (mi) = 1760 yards (yd)
1 yard = 3 feet (ft)
1 foot = 12 inches (in.)

Capacity and Volume

1 gallon (gal) = 4 quarts (qt)
1 quart = 2 pints (pt)
1 pint = 2 cups (c)
1 cup = 8 fluid ounces (fl oz)

Weight

1 ton = 2000 pounds (lb)
1 pound = 16 ounces (oz)

TIME

1 year (yr) = 365 days (d)
1 year = 12 months (mo)
1 year = 52 weeks (wk)
1 week = 7 days
1 day = 24 hours (h)
1 hour = 60 minutes (min)
1 minute = 60 seconds (s)